THE
DIRECTORY
OF
CORPORATE
AND
FOUNDATION
GIVERS

Selected Titles Published by The Taft Group

Inside Japanese Support: Descriptive Profiles and Other Information on Japanese Corporate Giving and Foundation Giving Programs

Provides detailed information on corporate and foundation giving in the United States and Japan. Includes a how-to essay on the proper way to approach Japanese sources for funding; an historical essay prepared and translated into English for the first time by the Foundation Library Center of Japan covering Japanese foundations and grantmaking; detailed profiles of major Japanese foundations and their grantmaking activities; and detailed profiles of contributions programs administered by major U.S. subsidiaries and affiliates of Japanese companies (indexed nine ways to speed access to information).

Directory of International Corporate Giving in America and Abroad

The most comprehensive source on the philanthrophic interests of foreign-owned U.S. companies and U.S. multinational giving internationally. Includes information on more than 500 companies, providing contact information, priorities, application procedures, and types and levels of both cash and in-kind support. Extensive indexes make the data easily accessible: Headquarters State, Operating Location, Grant Type, Nonmonetary Support Type, Recipient Type, Officers and Directors, Major Products/Industry, Recent Grants by State, and Foreign Parent Company Name and Country. U.S. companies are also indexed by foreign operating location and company name.

Taft Corporate Giving Directory

Provides detailed profiles of 1,000 of the largest and most important corporate charitable giving programs in the United States. Profiles describe funders, priorities, geographic preferences, background information on the decision-makers in the company and the giving programs, application procedures, nonmonetary or in-kind support, and recent grants. Eleven indexes help identify prospects: Companies by Headquarters State, Operating Location, Location of Grant Recipient, Grant Type, Nonmonetary Support, and Recipient Type; and Individuals by Name, Place of Birth, Alma Mater, Corporate Affiliation, and Nonprofit Affiliation.

Directory of Corporate and Foundation Givers

Profiles 8,000 leading funders in America, including private foundations, corporate foundations, and corporate direct giving programs. Includes contact information, program descriptions, officers and directors (including biographical information), grant types, application information, and the top ten foundation grants. Nine indexes connect you with prospective funders: Headquarters State, Operating Location, Grant Type, Nonmonetary Support Type, Recipient Type, Major Products/Industry, Officers and Directors, Grant Recipients by State, and a master index to companies and foundations.

Taft Foundation Reporter

Provides comprehensive profiles and analyses of 1,000 leading private foundations in the United States. Entries examine foundations' giving philosophies, changes in programs, history of donors, geographic preferences, application procedures, detailed biographical data on officers and trustees, typical recipients of support, and recently awarded grants. Nine indexes help target prospective funding sources: Foundations by State, Location of Grant Recipient, Grant Type, and Recipient Type; and Officers and Directors by Name, Place of Birth, Alma Mater, Corporate Affiliation, and Nonprofit Affiliation.

Corporate Giving Watch

A 16-page monthly newsletter dedicated to corporate funders and fund raisers. Helps keep subscribers aware of trends in corporate philanthropy, new corporate funding opportunities, program changes, and direct giving programs. Each issue features *Corporate Giving Profiles*, reporting the most current information available on major corporate philanthropies.

Foundation Giving Watch

A 16-page monthly newsletter devoted to private foundations and fund raisers. Keeps subscribers abreast of trends in foundation philanthropy, new funding opportunities, and program changes. Each issue contains *Foundation Updates*, featuring the most current information available on leading private philanthropic institutions and their giving policies.

ISSN:1054-108X

THE
DIRECTORY
OF
CORPORATE
AND
FOUNDATION
GIVERS
1994

A National Listing of the 8,000 Major Funding
Sources for Nonprofits

Volume 2:
P-Z
INDEXES

Katherine E. Jankowski,
Editor

The
TAFT
Group

WASHINGTON, D.C. • DETROIT • LONDON

Katherine E. Jankowski, *Editor*

Bernard Jankowski, *Production Editor*

Forrest C. Fisanich, *Editorial Assistant*

Christopher Evans, Leneta A. Hoover, Penny Rogers, *Data Entry*

Bonnie Cox, *Production/Technical Coordinator*

Mark W. Scott, *Senior Editor*

Robert J. Elster, *Publisher*

Directory of Corporate and Foundation Givers , 1994

Printed in the United States of America

ISSN: 1054-108X
ISBN: 0-930807-73-1   Collective Set
       0-930807-74-X   Volume 1
       0-930807-75-8   Volume 2

The Taft Group is the nation's leading publisher of reference, how-to, and professional information for nonprofit organizations and institutions. For further information or a catalog, contact:

The Taft Group, 12300 Twinbrook Parkway, Suite 520, Rockville, MD 20852

(800) 877-TAFT (Sales)   (301) 816-0210 (Editorial Office)

I(T)P™

The trademark **ITP** is used under license.

Contents

Volume 1

Volume 2

About This Edition

The third edition of *Directory of Corporate and Foundation Givers (CFG)* provides detailed descriptive profiles of approximately 8,000 philanthropic programs in the United States — programs associated with private foundations, corporate foundations, and corporate direct givers. *CFG* allows grant seekers and others to have quick and convenient access to data on the major U.S. funding organizations. *CFG* is the most current, most authoritative, most accessible, most detailed, and most comprehensive funding directory available.

CFG includes current data on more than 4,350 of the top private foundations, those with assets of at least $1.8 million or records of $250,000 in grants paid. The listed foundations operate in all 50 states, maintaining during the most recent reporting periods combined assets of more than $130 billion. Conveniently interfiled with these major foundation funders in *CFG's* single alphabetic sequence are more than 1,700 corporate foundations, together with more than 1,900 hard-to-pinpoint corporate direct givers. As an added benefit, *CFG* includes "brief entries" on several hundred corporate direct givers that have verified evidence of direct giving, but have declined for various reasons (corporate policy, insufficient information, etc.) to release details on their programs. *CFG* will make every effort to include more information on these direct givers in future editions as information becomes available.

The foundations and corporations profiled in *CFG* collectively gave more than **$9.0 billion** in cash contributions and the estimated value of nonmonetary support to nonprofit organizations during their most recent reporting period. New to this edition of *CFG* are 577 profiles, 217 of which are affiliated with corporations. The new foundations have assets of at least $2 million. Ninety-six have assets greater than $5 million; 40 have assets greater than $10 million; and 18 have assets greater than $30 million. The contributions programs are headquartered in 44 states and made contributions in all 50 states and internationally.

UNIQUE FEATURES MAKE *CFG* THE ONE-STOP SOURCE FOR GRANT SEEKERS

CFG contains several unique features not found in other directories of its scope — details invaluable to researchers compiling complete profiles of prospective funders. These features include the following:

Biographical Data: Biographical data on foundation officers, directors, and trustees and corporate officers provide essential background information for uncovering links and relationships between foundations and corporations and your organization's board of directors and constituency. The 1994 edition of *CFG* contains more than 5,100 new names and more than 35,000 total names. As available, biographies include the name and title of the officer or director, place and year of birth, alma mater and year of graduation, current employment, corporate affiliations, nonprofit affiliations, and philanthropic affiliations. All program officers are listed alphabetically in the Index to Officers and Directors.

Recent Grants: The recent grants section lists the top 10 grants disbursed. These top 10 grants take much of the guessing out of your prospect research, listing the actual organizations receiving major support. The grant listings include the grant amount, recipient's name, and city and state location (when provided by the source materials). *CFG* contains more than 45,000 recipients and indexes these organizations in the Index to Grant Recipients by State.

Historical Data: More than 85 percent of the foundations profiled list assets and giving figures for three years' giving; 30 percent contain contributions figures for 1993, the most recent figures available. By tracking the increases or decreases in the level of contributions and assets, philanthropic programs can be rated according to financial potential and giving trends.

Comprehensive Scope and Arrangement: Major foundation and corporate givers in America are profiled in *one* two-volume directory, organized in an easy-to-use alphabetical series. The programs listed are the most active foundations and corporations making grants today. Profiles contain the detailed information you need to evaluate your chances for funding, as well as the next step to take to approach the potential donor.

CFG profiles contain such details as who to contact, priorities, officers and directors, biographical information, how to apply, restrictions on giving, and the top 10 grants awarded. Corporate giving profiles also contain the most current financial information available, corporate officers, and major products/industry information.

Nine Easy-to-Use Indexes: Nine indexes speed access to needed information. The one piece of advice heard time and again from funders and successful fund raisers is "Do your homework." Use the indexes to target and refine your prospect research, find the best potential donors, and uncover relationships you never knew existed. The invaluable Index to Grant Recipients by State is unavailable in other directories of this scope. This unique index lists more than 45,000 grant recipients in *CFG* by state location. Each listing includes, as available, the grant recipient's name and location, size of grant, and donor. All indexes are described in more detail below.

CONTENT AND ARRANGEMENT

Volume 1 of *CFG* contains profiles in alphabetical sequence A to O. Volume 2 contains profiles in alphabetical sequence P to Z and the nine indexes. Profiles are arranged alphabetically by name. Foundations named after family members are listed alphabetically by family name, with the last name listed first. For example, the "Walter and Josephine Ford Fund" appears alphabetically in the F's, listed as the "Ford Fund, Walter and Josephine." The "Morris Goldseker Foundation of Maryland" appears alphabetically in the G's, listed as the "Goldseker Foundation of Maryland, Morris." Corporation names and corporate foundation names follow the same convention. For the user's convenience, the top of each left-hand page in the Profiles section contains the name of the first profile listed on that page. Right-hand pages are headed by the name of the last profile listed on that page.

Entries are as detailed as permitted by the information available. Contents of a profile include the foundation name or sponsoring company name and corporate foundation name, if applicable; corporate financial and major products data; contact information; giving histories; donor(s) to the foundation; typical recipients; grant types; nonmonetary support types; geographic distributions; operating locations; corporate and philanthropic program officers and directors; grants analysis; and recent grants. (See the User's Guide on page xi for detailed descriptions of the elements of a profile.)

METHOD OF COMPILATION

Entries contained in *Corporate and Foundation Givers 1994* were compiled from dozens of sources. Foundation profiles are based on the most recent Form 990 available, as well as major foundations' annual reports, guidelines, and questionnaire responses. Corporate direct giving programs are based on information provided by the companies, press releases, telephone interviews, standard business publications such as *Standard & Poors* and *Ward's Business Directory,* and data uncovered in extensive surveys of publications in the field. All corporate direct giving contacts were verified by phone within the past year.

INDEXES

Nine indexes allow researchers to locate quickly information presented in the profiles. Indexes include the following:

Index to Corporations and Foundations by Headquarters State. The headquarters state index lists alphabetically corporations and foundations by their primary location. For foundations, this information is taken from the contact information. For corporations, this information is taken from the headquarters city and state section of the profile. Because corporations and foundations primarily support organizations with geographic proximity, this index is the first stop toward locating potential donors.

Index to Corporations and Foundations by Operating Location. The operating location index provides a comprehensive listing of corporations and foundations headquartered or operating in your state. For foundations, this information is taken from the contact information. For corporations, this information is take from the headquarters city and state section of a profile and from the list of operating locations located under the contributions summary section. A company is far more likely to award grants in cities and states where it operates than in places where it doesn't have a direct presence. This pattern reflects the general corporate preference to support causes that benefit employees, stockholders, and other corporate constituencies.

Index to Corporations and Foundations by Grant Type. The grant type index lists profiles by types of financial support generally offered. Grant types include the following standard categories: award, capital, challenge, conference/seminar, department, emergency, employee matching gifts, endowment, fellowship, general support, loan, matching gifts, multiyear/continuing support, operating expenses, professorship, project, research, scholarship, and seed money. This information is taken from the grant types section of the profile found under the Contributions Summary.

Index to Corporations and Foundations by Nonmonetary Support Type. This index lists grant makers that assist nonprofit organizations in ways other than providing cash. Nonmonetary support types include the following categories: cause-related marketing and promotion, donated equipment, donated products, in-kind services, loaned employees, loaned executives, and workplace solicitation. This information is taken from the nonmonetary support types section of the profile found under the Contributions Summary.

Corporations and foundations increasingly respond favorably to creative and innovative requests for support that allow them to provide expertise, facilities, human resources, and products to leverage cash contributions. Information on corporate nonmonetary support is unique to Taft products. *CFG* contains the most extensive index available of companies interested in this growing area of corporate philanthropy, based exclusively on information provided by the companies listed.

Index to Corporations and Foundations by Recipient Type. This index lists profiles by the types of nonprofit organizations or programs they currently support or have a history of funding. This information is based on analysis of foundation Form 990s and information provided by the corporations and foundations profiled. The recipient type index helps you qualify your prospect research along philanthropic program interests. A comprehensive list of recipient types is found on page xiv.

Index to Corporations by Major Products/Industry. A company's field of business or marketing orientation often influences its charitable objectives. This index can help identify a corporation with a special interest in your cause due to the nature of its business. Banks, for instance, may be interested in economic development; insurance companies, in medical cost-control initiatives; and food processing companies, in promoting nutrition. The data in this index is taken from the major/products industry section contained in the background financial information at the top of corporate profiles. A comprehensive list of major products/industry is found on page xvi.

Index to Officers and Directors. Foundation and corporate officers, trustees, directors, and managers are arranged in alphabetical order followed by the name of the foundation. If a person appears twice in the directory, his or her name also appears twice in the index. Use this index to uncover individual relationships with foundations and corporations, people who may be able to assist your funding success.

Index to Grant Recipients by State. This unique index lists the thousands of grant recipients in *CFG* by state location when that information was provided by the foundation or corporate giver. Each listing includes, as available, the recipient's name and location, size of grant, and donor. Use this index to uncover foundations and corporations making contributions in your state, as well as the organizations supported.

Master Index to Corporations and Foundations. This index is an alphabetical arrangement of all corporations, foundations, and corporate foundations profiled in the directory, followed by the page number on which their profiles appear.

AVAILABLE IN ELECTRONIC FORMATS

Corporate and Foundation Givers 1994 is available for licensing on magnetic tape or diskette in a fielded format. Either the complete database or a custom selection of entries may be ordered. The database is available for internal data processing and nonpublishing purposes only. For information, call 800-877-TAFT.

COMMENTS AND SUGGESTIONS ARE WELCOME

We have taken care to make the *Directory of Corporate and Foundation Givers 1994* as complete and accurate as possible. Users of this directory can make important contributions to future editions by notifying the staff of programs that are not included or by providing additional information for programs currently referenced. Comments or suggestions to improve the usefulness, format, and coverage of *CFG* are always welcome. Although every effort is made to maintain accuracy, errors may occasionally occur; we will be grateful if these are called to our attention. Please contact:

Editor
Directory of Corporate and Foundation Givers
The Taft Group
12300 Twinbrook Parkway, Suite 520
Rockville, MD 20852
(301) 816-0210

User's Guide

The *Directory of Corporate and Foundation Givers 1994* helps fund raisers by collecting and providing accurate and detailed information on approximately 8,000 major corporate and foundation givers in a convenient two-volume set. Having quick access to this information is vital in today's increasingly competitive fund-raising environment. The information provided in entries is based on responses to questionnaire and telephone inquiries, research of IRS Form 990s, and careful examination of guidelines and annual reports provided by the companies profiled. Entries are as detailed as permitted by the information available.

Sample Entry

The two entries featured on page xii illustrate the standard elements of information typically provided in a profile. There are two types of profiles in *CFG*: private foundation profiles and corporate profiles. Corporate profiles contain such additional information as sponsoring company information and corporate officers. Numbered items in the sample are explained in the corresponding numbered paragraphs below and on page xiii. Please note that the profiles have been condensed for the purpose of illustration.

1. **PROFILE NAME.** Entries are arranged in a single alphabetic order by the sponsoring company or foundation name. Company-sponsored foundation names follow company names when applicable. (The index citations always refer to the company name.) Please note that a company may give directly, through a foundation, or both. If no foundation exists, the company is a direct giver.

2. **SPONSORING COMPANY INFORMATION.** As reported in 1993 issues of *Fortune* magazine (Time, Inc., New York, NY), *Standard & Poors Register of Corporations 1993* (McGraw-Hill, New York, NY), and *Ward's Business Directory of U.S. Private and Public Companies 1993* (Gale Research Inc., Detroit, MI). If the sponsoring company is a subsidiary of or affiliated with another company, this information is listed under Parent Company. Sales, profits, *Fortune* rank, number of employees, headquarters city and state, and SIC classification give a capsule look at the financial health, primary operating location, and business interests of the profiled company. Corporate giving levels are closely tied to a company's sales and profits: the more profitable a company, the greater its philanthropic potential. Many companies base their giving on a percentage of pretax profits, typically 0.5% to 2.5%, but occasionally as high as 5%. *Fortune* rank is a classic indicator of how a company compares to its peers. The number of employees also provides a quick measure of a company's size, and corporate programs are always interested in seeing charitable contributions affect the largest number of corporate employees. *Fortune* rank, as well as company sales, profits, and number of employees are given for 1992, where available. Headquarters information is indexed in the Index to Corporations and Foundations by Headquarters State. Lastly, a company's field of business or marketing orientation often influences its charitable objectives. The SIC classifications help identify corporations with a special interest in a particular activity due to the nature of their business. This information is indexed in the Index to Corporations by Major Products/Industry.

3. **CONTACT.** Respondents are asked to provide the name of the person responsible for responding to inquiries for information on corporate contributions, as well as their title, organization name, mailing address, city, state, zip code, and telephone number. If there is more than one contact, they appear in a note field immediately after the telephone number.

4. **FINANCIAL SUMMARY.** This category offers a brief picture of a foundation's financial status and giving potential based on the most current reporting periods. When specific figures for contributions were not available, annual giving ranges were often provided by corporate and foundation officers. Financial information includes recent giving, assets, and gifts received. This section ends with a foundation's EIN, Employer Identification Number, the unique nine-digit number assigned to philanthropic institutions by the Internal Revenue Service. Use the EIN to locate foundation Form 990s, keep track of name changes, and locate foundations registered in states different from current mailing addresses.

Private Foundation Profile

1 Abrons Foundation, Louis and Anne

3 CONTACT
Richard Abrons
President
Louis and Anne Abrons Foundation
c/o First Manhattan Company
437 Madison Ave.
New York, NY 10022
(212) 756-3376

4 FINANCIAL SUMMARY
Recent Giving: $3,500,000 (1993 est.); $3,667,000 (1992 approx.); $3,105,710 (1991)
Assets: $36,000,000 (1993 est.); $36,751,813 (1991); $34,158,696 (1990); $35,545,852 (1989)
EIN: 13-6061329

5 CONTRIBUTIONS SUMMARY
Donor(s): The foundation was established in 1950 by the late Louis and Anne Abrons.
Typical Recipients: • *Arts & Humanities:* arts funds, libraries, literary arts, museums/galleries, music, opera, performing arts, public broadcasting • *Civic & Public Affairs:* environmental affairs
Grant Types: general support
Geographic Distribution: New York, NY, metropolitan area

6 GIVING OFFICERS
Alix Abrons: dir
Richard Abrons: pres, dir

Edward Aranow: treas, secy *B* New York NY 1909 *ED* Columbia Univ AB 1929; Columbia Univ JD 1932 *CURR EMPL* off coun: Botein Hays Sklar & Hertzberg *NONPR AFFIL* mem: Am Bar Assn, Fed Bar Assn, NY Bar Assn, NY City Bar Assn, NY County Lawyers Assn; mem bd visitors: Columbia Law Sch
Judith Aranow: dir
Rita Aranow: vp, dir
Vicki Klein: dir

7 APPLICATION INFORMATION
Initial Approach: Restrictions on Giving: The foundation reports that it only makes contributions to preselected charitable organizations and does not accept unsolicited proposals for funds.

8 OTHER THINGS TO KNOW
The foundation estimates for 1993 the number of grants will be 190, and the highest grant will be $350,000.

9 GRANTS ANALYSIS
Number of Grants: 145
Highest Grant: $710,000
Typical Range: $1,000 to $25,000
Disclosure Period: 1991
Note: Recent grants are derived from a 1991 Form 990.

10 RECENT GRANTS
710,000 United Jewish Appeal Federation, New York, NY
265,550 Henry Street Settlement, New York, NY
200,000 Council on the Environment of New York City, New York, NY
150,000 New York City Opera, New York, NY
122,000 Wilberforce University, Wilberforce, OH

Corporate Profile

1 Allegheny Ludlum Corp. / Allegheny Ludlum Foundation

2 Sales: $1.03 billion
Employees: 5,400
Headquarters: Pittsburgh, PA
SIC Major Group: Primary Metal Industries

3 CONTACT
Jon D. Walton
Vice President-General Counsel, Contributions Chairman
Allegheny Ludlum Corp.
1000 Six PPG Pl.
Pittsburgh, PA 15222
(412) 394-2836

4 FINANCIAL SUMMARY
Recent Giving: $630,000 (1993 est.); $1,070,490 (1992); $1,163,365 (1991)
Assets: $2,604,342 (1992); $2,963,170 (1990)
Fiscal Note: Above figures for foundation only. Company has small direct giving program, which disbursed $435,748 in 1992.
EIN: 25-6228755

5 CONTRIBUTIONS SUMMARY
Typical Recipients: • *Arts & Humanities:* arts festivals, dance, history/historic preservation, libraries, music, opera, public broadcasting, theater
Grant Types: employee matching gifts and general support
Geographic Distribution: near operating locations only, with emphasis on the Pittsburgh, PA, area
Operating Locations: CT (Wallingford), PA (Pittsburgh)

6 CORP. OFFICERS
Robert P. Bozzone: *B* Glens Falls NY 1933 *ED* Rensselaer Polytech Inst BS 1955 *CURR EMPL* pres, ceo, dir: Allegheny Ludlum Corp *CORP AFFIL* dir: DQE, Duquesne Light Co
Richard P. Simmons: *B* 1931 *ED* MA Inst Tech 1953 *CURR EMPL* chmn, ceo, dir: Allegheny Ludlum Corp

GIVING OFFICERS
Jon D. Walton: trust *B* Clairton PA 1942 *ED* Purdue Univ BS 1964; Valparaiso Univ JD 1969 *CURR EMPL* vp gen coun, secy: Allegheny Ludlum Corp

7 APPLICATION INFORMATION
Initial Approach: *Initial Contact:* brief letter or proposal *Include Information On:* history of organization, amount requested, purpose for which funds are sought, and proof of tax-exempt status *When to Submit:* any time
Restrictions on Giving: Foundation does not make contributions to individuals or private foundations.

8 OTHER THINGS TO KNOW
Contributions are limited to operating communities.

9 GRANTS ANALYSIS
Number of Grants: 102
Highest Grant: $343,592
Typical Range: $500 to $15,000
Disclosure Period: 1992

10 RECENT GRANTS
346,792 United Way of Southwestern Pennsylvania, Pittsburgh, PA
52,500 WQED MacNeil/Lehrer Newshour, Pittsburgh, PA
50,000 The Carnegie, Pittsburgh, PA

5. **CONTRIBUTIONS SUMMARY.** This section contains current and background information on corporate and foundation giving programs. The original donors to private foundations are listed first. This is followed by a listing of typical recipients. The recipients are based on analysis of the most recent Form 990 available and information provided by the organizations. In many cases where direct givers do not provide detailed information on recipient types, we include information on percentage giving by category as reported by the company.

   The grant types section lists types of financial support generally offered by the profiled organization, using the following standard categories: award, capital, challenge, conference/seminar, department, emergency, employee matching gifts, endowment, fellowship, general support, loan, matching gifts, multiyear/continuing support, operating expenses, professorship, project, research, scholarship, and seed money.

   Information on nonmonetary support types also is provided, using the following categories: cause-related marketing and promotion, donated equipment, donated products, in-kind services, loaned employees, loaned executives, and workplace solicitation.

   You will find comprehensive lists of companies and foundations by type in the Index to Corporations and Foundations by Grant Type, the Index to Corporations and Foundations by Nonmonetary Support Type, and the Index to Corporations and Foundations by Recipient Type.

   Information on the geographic preference for contributions is included in the geographic distribution section. Geographic preferences for funding described here are obtained from the foundations and corporations or by tracking patterns of contributions made over a period of several years. Some programs are national or international in scope. Others adhere to strict rules limiting support to specific cities, counties, or states. Corporations generally limit contributions to their headquarters and operating communities. Knowing the geographic limitations placed on grants is a key element to successful fund raising.

   For corporations, we have included data on operating locations. This information will help you locate potential donors within your community affiliated with organized giving programs headquartered elsewhere. Operating locations are indexed by state in the Index to Corporations and Foundations by Operating Location.

6. **CORPORATE OFFICERS/GIVING OFFICERS.** Provides the names, titles, and biographical information on the principle corporate officers and foundation/giving program officers, directors, and trustees. Biographical information includes date and place of birth, education, current employment, corporate affiliations, nonprofit affiliations, and philanthropic affiliations. A comprehensive list of corporate and contributions program officers is provided in the Index to Officers and Directors.

7. **APPLICATION INFORMATION.** Describes application requirements, including initial request procedures, what to include in a proposal, and the best time to submit a request. The restrictions on giving section includes activities, programs, or organizations not supported or ineligible for support by the program profiled.

8. **OTHER THINGS TO KNOW.** Reports additional procedures, recent history, or policies that could affect your prospecting efforts not covered elsewhere in the profile. Also contains information on publications available from the contributions program.

9. **GRANTS ANALYSIS.** Lists several giving-related statistics based on most recent year for which figures are available: number of grants, highest grant, typical grant size, and disclosure period.

10. **RECENT GRANTS.** Lists the top 10 grants given by the program in the most recent reporting year. Grants are listed in descending order by amount. When the information is available, the dollar amount, recipient name, recipient location, and a brief description are provided. All grants listed with an identified state are cross-referenced in the Index to Grant Recipients by State.

Nonprofit Recipient Categories

Categories	Recipient Organization Types
Arts & Humanities	arts appreciation, arts associations, arts centers, arts festivals, arts funds, arts institutes, cinema, community arts, dance, ethnic arts, history/historic preservation, libraries, literary arts, museums/galleries, music, opera, performing arts, public broadcasting, theater, visual arts
Civic & Public Affairs	better government, business/free enterprise, civil rights, consumer affairs, economic development, economics, environmental affairs, ethnic/minority organizations, First Amendment issues, housing, international affairs, law & justice, municipalities, national security, nonprofit management, philanthropic organizations, professional/trade associations, public policy, rural affairs, safety, urban/community affairs, women's affairs, zoos/botanical gardens
Education	agricultural education, arts education, business education, career/vocational education, colleges & universities, community/junior colleges, continuing education, economic education, education administration, education associations, education funds, elementary education, engineering education, faculty development, health & physical education, international exchange, international studies, journalism education, legal education, liberal arts education, literacy, medical education, minority education, preschool education, private education (precollege), public education (precollege), religious education, science/technology education, social sciences education, special education, student aid
Health	emergency/ambulance services, geriatric health, health care cost containment, health funds, health organizations, hospices, hospitals, medical rehabilitation, medical research, medical training, mental health, nursing services, nutrition/health maintenance, outpatient health care, pediatric health, public health, single disease health associations
International	foreign education institutions, international development/relief, international health care, international organizations
Religion	churches, missionary activities, religious organizations, synagogues
Science	observatories/planetariums, science exhibits/fairs, scientific institutes, scientific organizations
Social Services	aged, animal protection, child welfare, community centers, community service organizations, counseling, day care, delinquency & crime, disabled, domestic violence, drugs & alcohol, emergency relief, employment/job training, family planning, family services, food/clothing distribution, homes, legal aid, recreation & athletics, refugee assistance, religious welfare, shelters/homelessness, united funds, volunteer services, youth organizations

Recipient Organization Types

aged .... See Social Services
agricultural education ....See Education
animal protection .... See Social Services
arts appreciation .... See Arts and Humanities
arts associations .... See Arts and Humanities
arts centers .... See Arts and Humanities
arts education ....See Education
arts festivals .... See Arts and Humanities
arts funds .... See Arts and Humanities
arts institutes .... See Arts and Humanities
better government .... See Civic and Public Affairs
business education ....See Education
business/free enterprise .... See Civic and Public Affairs
career/vocational education ....See Education
child welfare .... See Social Services
churches .... See Religion
cinema .... See Arts and Humanities
civil rights .... See Civic and Public Affairs
colleges and universities ....See Education
community and junior colleges ....See Education
community arts .... See Arts and Humanities
community centers .... See Social Services
community service organizations .... See Social Services
consumer affairs .... See Civic and Public Affairs
continuing education ....See Education
counseling .... See Social Services
dance .... See Arts and Humanities
day care .... See Social Services
delinquency and crime .... See Social Services
disabled .... See Social Services
domestic violence .... See Social Services
drugs and alcohol .... See Social Services
economic development .... See Civic and Public Affairs
economic education ....See Education
economics .... See Civic and Public Affairs
education associations ....See Education
education funds ....See Education
educational administration ....See Education
elementary education ....See Education
emergency relief .... See Social Services
emergency/ambulance services ....See Health
employment/job training .... See Social Services
engineering education ....See Education
environmental affairs .... See Civic and Public Affairs
ethnic arts .... See Arts and Humanities
ethnic/minority organizations ..... See Civic and Public Affairs
faculty development ....See Education
family planning .... See Social Services
family services .... See Social Services
First Amendment issues .... See Civic and Public Affairs
food/clothing distribution .... See Social Services
foreign education institutions ....See International
geriatric health ....See Health
health and physical education ....See Education
health funds ....See Health
health organizations ....See Health
health-care cost containment ....See Health
history/historic preservation ...... See Arts and Humanities
homes .... See Social Services
hospices ....See Health
hospitals ....See Health
housing .... See Civic and Public Affairs
international affairs .... See Civic and Public Affairs
international development/relief .... See International

international exchange .... See Education
international health care .... See International
international organizations .... See International
international studies .... See Education
journalism education .... See Education
law and justice .... See Civic and Public Affairs
legal aid ....See Social Services
legal education .... See Education
liberal arts education .... See Education
libraries .... See Arts and Humanities
literacy .... See Education
literary arts .... See Arts and Humanities
medical education .... See Education
medical rehabilitation ....See Health
medical research .... See Health
medical training ....See Health
mental health .... See Health
minority education .... See Education
missionary activities ....See Religion
municipalities .... See Civic and Public Affairs
museums/galleries .... See Arts and Humanities
music .... See Arts and Humanities
national security .... See Civic and Public Affairs
nonprofit management .... See Civic and Public Affairs
nursing services .... See Health
nutrition/health maintenance .... See Health
observatories/planetariums ....See Science
opera .... See Arts and Humanities
outpatient health care .... See Health
pediatric health .... See Health
performing arts .... See Arts and Humanities
philanthropic organizations .... See Civic and Public Affairs
preschool education .... See Education
private education (precollege) .... See Education
professional/trade associations .... See Civic and Public Affairs
public broadcasting .... See Arts and Humanities
public education (precollege) .... See Education
public health .... See Health
public policy .... See Civic and Public Affairs
recreation and athletics ....See Social Services
refugee assistance ....See Social Services
religious education .... See Education
religious organizations .... See Religion
religious welfare ....See Social Services
rural affairs .... See Civic and Public Affairs
safety .... See Civic and Public Affairs
science exhibits/fairs ....See Science
science/technology education .... See Education
scientific institutes ....See Science
scientific organizations ....See Science
shelters/homelessness ....See Social Services
single-disease health associations .... See Health
social sciences education .... See Education
special education .... See Education
student aid .... See Education
synagogues .... See Religion
theater .... See Arts and Humanities
united funds ....See Social Services
urban/community affairs .... See Civic and Public Affairs
visual arts .... See Arts and Humanities
volunteer services ....See Social Services
women's affairs .... See Civic and Public Affairs
youth organizations ....See Social Services
zoos/botanical gardens .... See Civic and Public Affairs

Taft Major Products/Industry Categories

Agricultural Production—Crops (SIC 01)

Agricultural Production —Livestock (SIC 02)

Agricultural Services (SIC 07)

Amusement & Recreation Services (SIC 79)

Apparel & Accessory Stores (SIC 56)

Apparel & Other Textile Products (SIC 23)

Automobile Repair, Services & Parking (SIC 75)

Automotive Dealers & Service Stations (SIC 55)

Building Material & Garden Supplies (SIC 52)

Business Services (SIC 73)

Chemicals & Allied Products (SIC 28)

Coal Mining (SIC 12)

Communications (SIC 48)

Depository Institutions (SIC 60)

Eating & Drinking Places (SIC 58)

Educational Services (SIC 82)

Electric, Gas & Sanitary Services (SIC 49)

Electronic & Other Electrical Equipment (SIC 36)

Engineering & Management Services (SIC 87)

Fabricated Metal Products (SIC 34)

Fishing, Hunting & Trapping (SIC 09)

Food & Kindred Products (SIC 20)

Food Stores (SIC 54)

Forestry (SIC 08)

Furniture & Fixtures (SIC 25)

Furniture & Homefurnishings Stores (SIC 57)

General Building Contractors (SIC 15)

General Merchandise Stores (SIC 53)

Health Services (SIC 80)

Heavy Construction Except Building
  Construction (SIC 16)

Holding & Other Investment Offices (SIC 67)

Hotels & Other Lodging Places (SIC 70)

Industrial Machinery & Equipment (SIC 35)

Instruments & Related Products (SIC 38)

Insurance Agents, Brokers & Service (SIC 64)

Insurance Carriers (SIC 63)

Legal Services (SIC 81)

Local and Interurban Passenger Transit (SIC 41)

Lumber and Wood Products (SIC 24)

Metal Mining (SIC 10)

Miscellaneous Manufacturing Industries (SIC 39)

Miscellaneous Retail (SIC 59)

Nonclassifiable Establishments (SIC 99)

Oil & Gas Extraction (SIC 13)

Paper & Allied Products (SIC 26)

Personal Services (SIC 72)

Petroleum & Coal Products (SIC 29)

Pipelines Except Natural Gas (SIC 46)

Primary Metal Industries (SIC 33)

Printing & Publishing (SIC 27)

Railroad Transportation (SIC 40)

Real Estate (SIC 65)

Rubber & Miscellaneous Plastics Products
  (SIC 30)

Security & Commodity Brokers (SIC 62)

Services Not Elsewhere Classified (SIC 89)

Social Services (SIC 83)

Special Trade Contractors (SIC 17)

Stone, Clay & Glass Products (SIC 32)

Textile Mill Products (SIC 22)

Tobacco Products (SIC 21)

Transportation by Air (SIC 45)

Transportation Equipment (SIC 37)

Transportation Services (SIC 47)

Trucking & Warehousing (SIC 42)

U.S. Postal Service (SIC 43)

Water Transportation (SIC 44)

Wholesale Trade—Durable Goods (SIC 50)

Wholesale Trade—Nondurable Goods (SIC 51)

List of Abbreviations

&	And	comptr	comptroller	govt	government
		Conf	Conference	grad	graduate
AA	Associate of Arts	Confed	Confederation	hon	honorable, honorary
AB	Arts, Bachelor of	Cong	Congress	Hosp	Hospital
acct	accountant	Consult	Consultant, Consulting	Hwy	Highway
admin	administration,	contr	controller		
	administrative, administrator	coo	chief operating officer	Inc	Incorporated
adv	advisor, advisory	Coop	Cooperating, Cooperative,	Indus	Industrial, Industries,
AFB	Air Force Base		Cooperation		Industry
Aff	Affairs	Corp	Corporate, Corporation	Ins	Insurance
affil	affiliation	Counc	Council	Inst	Institute, Institution
AG	Aktiengesellschaft	couns	counsel, counseling,	Intl	International
Am	America, American		counselor		
AM	Arts, Master of	CPA	Certified Public Accountant	JD	Juris Doctor
Apt	Apartment	Ct	Court	Jr	Junior
APO	Army Post Office	Ctr	Center, Centre		
archt	architect	curr	current	Legis	Legislation, Legislative,
Assn	Association	cust	customer		Legislator
Assoc(s)	Associate(s), Associated			LLB	Laws, Bachelor of
asst	assistant	DB	Divinity, Bachelor of	LLD	Laws, Doctor of
atty	attorney	del	delegate	Ln	Lane
Ave	Avenue	Dem	Democrat	LP	Limited Partnership
		dep	deputy	Ltd	Limited
b	born	Dept	Department		
BA	Bachelor of Arts	Devel	Development	MA	Master of Arts
BBA	Bachelor of Business	dir	director	MBA	Master of Business
	Administration	Distr	Distributor, Distribution,		Administration
bd	board		Distributing	Med	Medical
BD	Bachelor of Divinity	Div	Division	mem	member
BE	Bachelor of Engineering	don	donor	Meml	Memorial
BFT	Bachelor of Foreign Trade	Dr	Doctor	Metro	Metropolitan
Bldg	Building	Dr	Drive	Mfg	Manufacturing
Blvd	Boulevard			Mfr	Manufacturer
Bros	Brothers	E	East	Mgmt	Management
BS	Bachelor of Science	Econ	Economic, Economics	mgr	manager
BSChE	Bachelor of Science in	Ed	Education, Educational,	misc	miscellaneous
	Chemical Engineering		Educated	Mktg	Marketing
BSME	Bachelor of Science in	EIN	Employer Identification	Mng	Managing
	Mechanical Engineering		Number	MS	Master of Science
Bur	Bureau	empl	employment	Mt	Mount
Bus	Business	Engg	Engineering	Mus	Museum
		engr	engineer		
c/o	care of	exec	executive	N	North
CC	Country Club	Expy	Expressway	NAACP	National Association for the
ceo	chief executive officer				Advancement of Colored
cfo	chief financial officer	f/b/o	for the benefit of		People
Chap	Chapter	Fdn	Foundation	N. Ap.	Not Applicable
Chem	Chemical, Chemist,	fdr	founder	N. Av.	Not Available
	Chemistry	Fed	Federal, Federation,	Natl	National
chmn	chairman		Federated	NE	North East
chp	chairperson	Fin	Finance, Financial	No	Number
chwm	chairwoman	Fl	Floor	nonpr	nonprofit
Co	Company	FPO	Fleet Post Office	NW	North West
Coll	College	Ft	Fort		
comm	committee	Fwy	Freeway	off	office, officer
commn	commission			oper	operating, operations
commnr	commissioner	GC	Golf Club	Org	Organization
Commun	Communication(s),	gen	general		
	Community	gov	governing, governor	pers	personnel

PhB	Philosophy, Bachelor of	**ret**	retired	**Tech**	Technological, Technical, Technology
PhD	Philosophy, Doctor of	**RFD**	Rural Free Delivery		
phil	philanthropic	**Rm**	Room	**Tel & Tel**	Telephone and Telegraph
Pk	Park	**RR**	railroad	**Terr**	Terrace
Pke	Pike	**RR**	Rural Route	**Tpke**	Turnpike
Pkwy	Parkway	**Rte**	Route	**treas**	treasurer
Pl	Place	**RY**	Railway	**trust**	trustee
Plz	Plaza				
PO	Post Office	**S**	South	**Un**	United
Polytech	Polytechnic, Polytechnical	**SB**	Science, Bachelor of	**Univ**	University
pres	president	**Sch**	School	**US**	United States
prin	principal	**SE**	South East	**u/w/o**	under the will of
prof	professor	**secy**	secretary		
Prov	Province, Provincial	**sen**	senator	**vchmn**	vice chairman
Ptnr	Partner	**SM**	Science, Master of	**vp**	vice president
pub(s)	publication(s)	**Soc**	Society		
pub	public	**Sq**	Square	**W**	West
publ(s)	published, publisher, publishing	**Sr**	Senior		
		SR	Star/State Route	**YC**	Yacht Club
Pvt	Private	**St**	Saint, State, Street	**YMCA**	Young Men's Christian Association
		Sta	Station		
Rd	Road	**Ste**	Sainte, Suite	**YMHA**	Young Men's Hebrew Association
RD	Rural Delivery	**Sub(s)**	Subsidiary(ies)		
rehab	rehabilitation	**supt**	superintendent	**YWCA**	Young Women's Christian Association
rel	religious, religion	**supvr**	supervisor		
rels	relations	**Svc(s)**	Service(s)	**YWHA**	Young Women's Hebrew Association
rep	representative	**SW**	South West		
Repbl	Republican	**Sys**	System(s)		
Res	Research, Researcher				

Profiles
P-Z

PACCAR / PACCAR Foundation

Sales: $2.76 billion
Employees: 10,163
Headquarters: Bellevue, WA
SIC Major Group: Automotive
Dealers & Service Stations,
Industrial Machinery &
Equipment, Transportation
Equipment, and Wholesale
Trade—Durable Goods

CONTACT

H. Dennis Sather
Vice President & Treasurer
PACCAR Fdn.
PO Box 1518
Bellevue, WA 98009
(206) 455-7400

FINANCIAL SUMMARY

Recent Giving: $1,857,318
(1991); $4,964,874 (1990);
$1,603,151 (1989)
Assets: $9,043,652 (1991);
$2,906,200 (1990); $4,885,569
(1988)
Fiscal Note: All contributions
are made through the foundation.
EIN: 91-6030638

CONTRIBUTIONS SUMMARY

Typical Recipients: • *Arts &
Humanities:* arts funds, his-
tory/historic preservation, mu-
seums/galleries, music, opera,
performing arts, theater, visual
arts • *Civic & Public Affairs:*
business/free enterprise,
economics, international affairs, law & justice, municipalities, public policy, safety,
urban & community affairs
• *Education:* arts education,
business education, colleges &
universities, economic education, education associations,
education funds, engineering
education, minority education,
private education (precollege),
science/technology education
• *Health:* health organizations,
hospitals, pediatric health
• *Science:* scientific institutes,
scientific organizations • *Social Services:* child welfare,
employment/job training,
united funds, youth organizations
Grant Types: capital, department, employee matching gifts,
and general support
Note: Foundation supports a relatively small number of capital and endowment needs each
year.

Nonmonetary Support Types:
loaned employees and workplace solicitation
Note: Workplace solicitation is
for United Way only.
Geographic Distribution:
near headquarters and operating locations only
Operating Locations: CA
(Newark), OH (Chillicothe),
OK (Broken Arrow), TN (Madison), TX (Denton), WA (Bellevue, Burlington, Kirkland, Ren-
ton, Seattle)

CORP. OFFICERS

Joseph M. Dunn: *B* Toledo
OH 1926 *ED* OH St Univ 1949
CURR EMPL pres, dir: PAC-
CAR
Charles McGee Pigott: *B* Seat-
tle WA 1929 *ED* Stanford Univ
BS 1951 *CURR EMPL* chmn,
ceo, dir: PACCAR *CORP
AFFIL* chmn: PACCAR Fin
Corp, Trico Indus; dir: Birming-
ham Steel Co, Boeing Co,
Chevron Corp, Citibank, Citi-
corp, Seattle Times *NONPR
AFFIL* hon vp: Natl Boy
Scouts Am; mem: Bus Counc

GIVING OFFICERS

Richard P. Cooley: dir *B* Dal-
las TX 1923 *ED* Yale Univ
1944 *CORP AFFIL* chmn exec
comm: Seafirst Natl Bank; dir:
PACCAR, Un Airlines
John Maurice Fluke, Jr.: dir
B 1942 *CURR EMPL* chmn,
dir: John Fluke Mfg Co *CORP
AFFIL* dir: PACCAR, US Bank
WA *NONPR AFFIL* chmn,
mem: Greater Seattle Chamber
Commerce; mem, dir: Am Elec-
tronics Assn, Natl Assn Mfrs,
WA Bus Roundtable; mem
engg adv bd: Stanford Univ;
mem engg visiting comm: Univ
WA
Harold J. Haynes: dir *B* Ft
Worth TX 1925 *ED* TX A&M
Univ 1947 *CURR EMPL* sr
coun: Bechtel Group *CORP
AFFIL* dir: Boeing Co, Carter
Hawley Hale Stores, Citicorp,
Hewlett-Packard Co, PACCAR
NONPR AFFIL dir: Stanford
Res Inst Intl
G. Glen Morie: secy *B* Wood-
bury NJ 1942 *ED* Bowdoin
Coll 1964; Univ PA 1967
CURR EMPL vp, gen coun,
secy: PACCAR *NONPR AFFIL*
mem: Am Bar Assn, Am Corp
Couns Assn, Am Soc Corp
Secys
James Calvin Pigott: dir *B* Se-
attle WA 1936 *ED* Stanford
Univ BCE 1959; Harvard Univ
Grad Sch Bus MBA 1963

CURR EMPL pres: Pigott En-
terprises *CORP AFFIL* dir:
Americold Corp, Northern Life
Ins Co, PACCAR; pres: Mgmt
Reports & Svcs; pres, dir: Nor-
cliffe Co; vchmn: EK Williams
& Co *NONPR AFFIL* chmn,
trust: Seattle Univ
John W. Pitts: dir *B* Ashcroft
Canada 1926 *ED* McGill Univ
1949; Harvard Univ 1951
CURR EMPL chmn, pres:
Mgmt Representatives & Svc
CORP AFFIL dir: AEL Micro-
tel Ltd BC, Microtel Pacific
Res Ltd, PACCAR, Roy Fund
Ltd, Sugar Refinery Ltd BC,
Telephone Co Ltd
James H. Wiborg: dir *B* Seat-
tle WA 1924 *ED* Univ WA BA
1946 *CORP AFFIL* chmn, chief
strategist: VWR Corp; dir:
GENSCO Inc, Momentum Dis-
tribution, Northern Life Ins Co,
PACCAR, Penwest Ltd,
Seafirst Corp, Seattle First
Natl Bank, Westin Hotel Co
NONPR AFFIL trust: Univ
Puget Sound
Thornton Arnold Wilson: dir
B Sikeston MO 1921 *ED* IA St
Univ 1943; MA Inst Tech 1953
CURR EMPL chmn emeritus:
Boeing Co *CORP AFFIL* dir:
Hewlett Packard, PACCAR, Se-
attle First Natl Bank, USX
Corp, Weyerhaeuser Co
NONPR AFFIL bd govs: Aero-
space Indus Assn Am, IA St
Univ Fdn; fellow: AM Inst
Aeronautics & Astronautics;
mem: NAE; trust: Seattle Univ

APPLICATION INFORMATION

Initial Approach: *Initial Contact:* proposal *Include Information On:* evidence of 501(c)(3)
status, description of goals and
programs, background data on
key personnel, amount re-
quested, clear description of
program to be funded *When to
Submit:* any time; decisions
made quarterly
Restrictions on Giving: Foundation does not support individual dinners or special events,
fraternal organizations, goodwill advertising, political or
lobbying groups, or religious
organizations for sectarian purposes.

GRANTS ANALYSIS

Total Grants: $1,857,318
Number of Grants: 99
Highest Grant: $353,388
Typical Range: $1,000 to
$10,000
Disclosure Period: 1991

Note: Figure for average grant
excludes foundation's highest
grant of $353,388. Recent
grants are derived from a 1991
Form 990.

RECENT GRANTS

353,388 United Way of
King County, Seat-
tle, WA
166,666 St. James Cathe-
dral Grade School,
Seattle, WA
100,000 Corporate Council
for the Arts, Seat-
tle, WA
100,000 Overlake Hospital
Foundation, Belle-
vue, WA
70,000 Independent Col-
leges of Washing-
ton, Seattle, WA
69,520 United Way of Den-
ton County, Den-
ton, TX
61,434 Employee Educa-
tional Matching
Gifts
53,570 United Way of
Nashville and Mid-
dle Tennessee,
Nashville, TN
53,130 United Fund of
Ross County/Chilli-
cothe, Chillicothe,
OH
50,000 Stanford Univer-
sity, Stanford, CA

Pacific Coca-Cola Bottling Co.

Sales: $90.4 million
Employees: 600
Parent Company: Coca-Cola
Enterprises, Inc.
Headquarters: Bellevue, WA
SIC Major Group: Food &
Kindred Products

CONTACT

Tom Radcliffe
Branch Manager
Pacific Coca-Cola Bottling Co.
PO Box C93346
Bellevue, WA 98009-3346
(206) 455-2000

CONTRIBUTIONS SUMMARY

Operating Locations: WA
(Bellevue)

CORP. OFFICERS

R. Barksdale Collins: *CURR
EMPL* pres: Pacific Coca-Cola
Bottling Co

Pacific Enterprises

Sales: $5.23 billion
Employees: 40,538
Headquarters: Los Angeles, CA
SIC Major Group: Electric, Gas
& Sanitary Services, Holding
& Other Investment Offices,
Miscellaneous Retail, and Oil
& Gas Extraction

CONTACT

Carolyn Williams
Public Affairs Manager
Pacific Enterprises
555 West Fifth St., ML25F0
Los Angeles, CA 90013
(213) 244-2555

FINANCIAL SUMMARY

Recent Giving: $421,625
(1993); $1,336,578 (1992);
$1,339,000 (1991)
Fiscal Note: 1992 figure does
not include a $1,100,000 con-
tribution to the United Way.
Company reported in 1993 that
contributions budget was being
significantly cut back, but figures were unavailable.

CONTRIBUTIONS SUMMARY

Company reports 44% of contributions support health and
welfare; 23% support each education and civic and public affairs; and 9% to the arts. Company also supports a Volunteer
Incentive Program, which
provides two $100 grants to em-
ployees who give 8 hours of
their time to nonprofit organizations.

Typical Recipients: • *Arts &
Humanities:* arts associations,
arts centers, arts festivals, arts
funds, cinema, community arts,
dance, ethnic arts, history/his-
toric preservation, libraries,
museums/galleries, music, performing arts, public broadcasting, theater, visual arts • *Civic
& Public Affairs:* better government, public policy • *Education:* arts education, business
education, colleges & universities
Grant Types: capital, challenge, general support, matching, operating expenses, and
project
Nonmonetary Support Types:
in-kind services
Geographic Distribution: in
headquarters and operating
communities
Operating Locations: CA
(City of Commerce, El Se-
gundo, Los Angeles), OR

(Eugene), TX (Dallas), WA (Seattle)

CORP. OFFICERS

James R. Ukropina: *B* Fresno
CA 1937 *ED* Stanford Univ
1959; Univ Southern CA Law
Sch 1965 *CURR EMPL* chmn,
ceo, dir: Pacific Enterprises
CORP AFFIL dir: CA
Economic Devel Corp, KCET,
Lockheed Corp, Pacific Mu-
tual, Security Pacific Corp
Willis B. Wood: *B* Kansas City
MO 1934 *ED* Univ Tulsa 1957
CURR EMPL pres, ceo, dir:
Pacific Enterprises *CORP
AFFIL* dir: Great Western Fin
Corp *NONPR AFFIL* mem: Am
Gas Assn, Pacific Coast Gas
Assn, Pacific Energy Assn, Soc
Petroleum Engrs; trust: Harvey
Mudd Coll, Southwest Mus

APPLICATION INFORMATION

Initial Approach: applications
not being accepted through
1995
Restrictions on Giving: Does
not support individuals, religious organizations for sectarian
purposes, or political or lobbying groups.

GRANTS ANALYSIS

Typical Range: $2,500 to
$5,000

Pacific Gas & Electric Co.

Revenue: $10.38 billion
Employees: 26,600
Headquarters: San Francisco, CA
SIC Major Group: Electric, Gas
& Sanitary Services

CONTACT

Christine M. Riley
Administrator, Corporate
   Contributions
Pacific Gas & Electric Co.
   Community Relations
   Department
B28A
PO Box 770000
San Francisco, CA 94177
(415) 973-4951

FINANCIAL SUMMARY

Recent Giving: $8,300,000
(1993 est.); $7,400,000 (1992
approx.); $6,207,000 (1991)
Fiscal Note: Company gives directly.

CONTRIBUTIONS SUMMARY

Typical Recipients: • *Arts &
Humanities:* arts centers,

dance, ethnic arts, muse-
ums/galleries, music, opera,
performing arts, theater • *Civic
& Public Affairs:* economic development, environmental affairs, ethnic/minority organizations, urban & community
affairs, women's affairs • *Education:* career/vocational education, colleges & universities,
engineering education, minority education, science/technol-
ogy education • *Social Services:* employment/job training,
shelters/homelessness, united
funds, youth organizations
Grant Types: capital, general
support, and project
Note: Company contributes to
civic functions.
Nonmonetary Support Types:
in-kind services and loaned employees
Note: In 1992, company gave
$100,000 in nonmonetary sup-
port. This is not included in
above total. Contact for such
support is Public Affairs Repre-
sentative- Community Projects.
Geographic Distribution: in
company's service area (northern and central California); contact regional office in your area
for alternative source of funding
Operating Locations: CA
(Fresno, Oakland, Sacramento,
San Francisco, San Jose, Santa
Rosa)

CORP. OFFICERS

Richard A. Clarke: *B* San
Francisco CA 1930 *ED* Univ
CA Berkeley AB 1952; Univ
CA Berkeley JD 1955 *CURR
EMPL* chmn, ceo, dir: Pacific
Gas & Electric Co *CORP
AFFIL* dir: Potlatch Corp
NONPR AFFIL dir: CA Bus
Roundtable, CA Chamber Com-
merce, Edison Electric Inst, In-
dependent Colls Northern CA,
Invest-in-America; mem: CA
Bar Assn, Pacific Coast Elec-
tric Assn, Pacific Coast Gas
Assn
Tom Long: *B* Charleston WV
1932 *CURR EMPL* comptr:
Pacific Gas & Electric Co
CORP AFFIL chmn: Triquint
Semiconductor; dir: Planar
Sys; pres: Tektronix Devel Co;
vp, gen mgr tech group: Tek-
tronix *NONPR AFFIL* mem:
Inst Electrical & Electronics
Engrs, Soc Motion Pictures &
Television Engrs
Stanley T. Skinner: *B* Ft
Smith AR 1937 *ED* San Diego
St Coll BA 1960; Univ CA Ber-
keley MA 1961; Univ CA Ber-

keley JD 1964 *CURR EMPL*
pres, coo, dir: Pacific Gas &
Electric Co *CORP AFFIL* dir:
Alberta Natural Gas Co, Al-
berta & Southern Gas Co, Natu-
ral Gas Corp CA, Pacific Gas
Transmission Co *NONPR
AFFIL* dir: CA Econ Devel
Corp, San Francisco Chamber
Commerce, Un Way Bay Area;
mem: Bankers Club San Fran-
cisco, CA Bar Assn, Fin Offs
Northern CA, Pacific Coast
Electric Assn, Pacific Coast
Gas Assn; mem, dir: CA Cham-
ber Commerce; trust: Golden
Gate Univ
Barbara Coull Williams:
CURR EMPL vp (human re-
sources): Pacific Gas & Elec-
tric Co

GIVING OFFICERS

Christine Riley: *CURR EMPL*
admin (corp contributions):
Pacific Gas & Electric Co

APPLICATION INFORMATION

Initial Approach: *Initial Contact:* brief letter or proposal *Include Information On:* organization's name, address, phone
number, and person to contact;
brief description and history,
accomplishments, and goals;
area and number of people
served; how organization or
proposed project fits into company's charitable priorities;
amount requested and purpose
for which grant will be used;
copy of 501(c)(3) document; financial statement; current operating budget summary or outline of expected project costs;
current and anticipated funding
sources; list of governing board
members and chief manage-
ment officers; and involvement
of volunteers, including PG&E
employees *When to Submit:*
any time; first three quarters of
the year strongly recommended
Restrictions on Giving:
PG&E does not make contributions to individuals; for tickets
for contests, raffles, or other
prize-oriented activities; to
churches, synagogues, or other
religious groups unless for activities that benefit the overall
community and do not support
any religious doctrine; to fraternal organizations; to political
or lobbying groups; to advertising campaigns, other than public or service advertising; or to
reduce debts or past operating
deficits, or liquidate an organization.

Company does not respond to requests that are not in writing.

OTHER THINGS TO KNOW
Contributions usually made on year-to-year basis, with pledges generally not to exceed 2 years.

GRANTS ANALYSIS
Total Grants: $7,400,000*
Number of Grants: 264*
Typical Range: $2,500 to $20,000
Disclosure Period: 1992
Note: Figures for total grants and number of grants are approximate.

Pacific Mutual Life Insurance Co. / Pacific Mutual Charitable Foundation
Assets: $11.54 billion
Employees: 4,160
Headquarters: Newport Beach, CA

CONTACT
Robert G. Haskell
President
Pacific Mutual Fdn.
700 Newport Center Dr.
Newport Beach, CA 92660
(714) 640-3787

FINANCIAL SUMMARY
Recent Giving: $900,000 (1993 est.); $816,574 (1992); $702,949 (1991)
Assets: $8,561,930 (1991); $7,776,513 (1990); $7,801,058 (1989)
Fiscal Note: Company gives through foundation (about 80%) and directly (about 20%).
EIN: 95-3433806

CONTRIBUTIONS SUMMARY
Typical Recipients: • *Arts & Humanities:* arts centers, arts festivals, arts funds, dance, ethnic arts, libraries, museums/galleries, music, opera, performing arts, public broadcasting, theater • *Civic & Public Affairs:* better government, civil rights, consumer affairs, economic development, economics, environmental affairs, housing, law & justice, municipalities, nonprofit management, public policy, safety, urban & community affairs, women's affairs, zoos/botanical gardens • *Education:* business education, career/vocational education, colleges & universities, economic education, education funds, health & physical education, medical education, minority education, public education (precollege), student aid • *Health:* geriatric health, health care cost containment, health organizations, hospices, hospitals, medical training, mental health, nutrition & health maintenance, outpatient health care delivery, pediatric health, public health, single-disease health associations • *Social Services:* aged, child welfare, community service organizations, counseling, delinquency & crime, disabled, drugs & alcohol, emergency relief, employment/job training, family planning, family services, food/clothing distribution, homes, legal aid, shelters/homelessness, united funds, volunteer services, youth organizations
Grant Types: capital, employee matching gifts, fellowship, general support, project, research, and scholarship
Nonmonetary Support Types: donated equipment and in-kind services
Note: Nonmonetary support is provided by the company. Estimated value of support is $158,958 in 1992. It is not included in above giving figures.
Geographic Distribution: primarily to local organizations in areas with large concentrations of company employees; some state and national funding
Operating Locations: CA (Fountain Valley, Newport Beach)

CORP. OFFICERS
Harry G. Bubb: *B* Trinidad CO 1924 *ED* Stanford Univ BA 1946; Stanford Univ MBA 1949 *CURR EMPL* chmn emeritus, dir: Pacific Mutual Life Ins Co *CORP AFFIL* dir: Pacific Consulting Corp, Pacific Investment Mgmt Co *NONPR AFFIL* dir: CA Chamber Commerce, CA Econ Devel Corp, Los Angeles Chamber Commerce, Orange County Bus Comm Arts, Un Way Orange County; mem: CA Med Assn; mem adv bd: Town Hall Orange County; trust: Newport Harbor Art Mus, US Academy Decathlon
William D. Cvengros: *CURR EMPL* vchmn, chief invest off: Pacific Mutual Life Ins Co

Walter B. Gerken: *B* New York NY 1922 *ED* Wesleyan Univ BA 1948; Syracuse Univ MPA 1958 *CURR EMPL* chmn exec comm, dir: Pacific Mutual Life Ins Co *CORP AFFIL* dir: Carter Hawley Hale Stores, Mgmt Compensation Group, Southern CA Edison Co, Times Mirror Co, Whittaker Corp *NONPR AFFIL* Nature Conservancy CA; chmn bd overseers: Univ CA (Irvine); dir: Automobile Club Southern CA, CA Econ Devel Corp, Hoag Presbyterian Hosp, James Irvine Fdn; mem bd overseers: RAND/Univ CA Los Angeles Ctr Study Soviet Behavior; trust: CA Roundtable, Occidental Coll, Un Way Los Angeles, Wesleyan Univ
Thomas C. Sutton: *B* Atlanta GA 1942 *ED* Univ Toronto BS 1965; Harvard Univ 1982 *CURR EMPL* chmn, ceo, dir: Pacific Mutual Life Ins Co *NONPR AFFIL* fellow: Soc Actuaries; mem: Am Academy Actuaries, Pacific States Actuarial Club, Univ CA Affiliates Advisory Bd, Univ CA Irvine Sch Mgmt; trust: South Coast Repertory

GIVING OFFICERS
Harry G. Bubb: dir *CURR EMPL* chmn emeritus, dir: Pacific Mutual Life Ins Co (see above)
Edward R. Byrd: cfo
William D. Cvengros: dir *CURR EMPL* vchmn, chief invest off: Pacific Mutual Life Ins Co (see above)
Walter B. Gerken: dir *CURR EMPL* chmn exec comm, dir: Pacific Mutual Life Ins Co (see above)
Brenda K. Hardwig: asst secy
Robert G. Haskell: pres, dir
Patricia A. Kosky: vp *CURR EMPL* community rels mgr: Pacific Mutual Life Ins Co
Michael T. McLaughlin: gen coun
Audrey L. Milfs: secy *CURR EMPL* asst vp, secy: Pacific Mutual Life Ins Co
Marilee Roller: cfo
Thomas C. Sutton: chmn *CURR EMPL* chmn, ceo, dir: Pacific Mutual Life Ins Co (see above)

APPLICATION INFORMATION
Initial Approach: *Initial Contact:* letter or proposal *Include Information On:* proof of tax-exempt status; description of the organization and project, including needs, objectives, and evaluative criteria; budget for project, including personnel and operating costs, list of other contributors and levels of funding, and amount requested; current budget for organization, including specific sources of revenue and any contingency funds; description of volunteer support; and list of board of directors and advisory board members *When to Submit:* by September 15
Restrictions on Giving: Foundation does not support individuals; political parties, candidates, or partisan political organizations; professional associations; veterans and labor organizations, fraternal organizations, athletic clubs, or social clubs; religious organizations for sectarian or denominational purposes; or operating expenses for member agencies of United Way, except under special circumstances.

OTHER THINGS TO KNOW
Generally prefers to make annual grants. Organizations may reapply annually, but grants typically are made to one organization for no more than three consecutive years.

Grants for annual operating expenses typically range from $500 to $2,000. Most capital grants range from $10,000 to $25,000 over a two- to five-year period.

The foundation reports that each year it selects two or more areas of special fovus (e.g. AIDS, homelessness, Hispanic needs) and makes major grants in that focus area. Grants are usually made later in the calendar year after the foundation has done considerable research.

Publications: community involvement report

GRANTS ANALYSIS
Total Grants: $702,949
Number of Grants: 91*
Highest Grant: $238,669
Typical Range: $500 to $5,000
Disclosure Period: 1991
Note: Number of grants and average grant figures exclude matching gifts. Recent grants are derived from a 1991 Form 990.

RECENT GRANTS

268,170	United Way of Orange County
30,000	Serving People in Need
23,700	Interval House
23,700	Women's Transitional Living Center
20,000	Independent Colleges of Southern California, Los Angeles, CA
17,500	Newport-Harbor Art Museum, Newport Beach, CA
15,000	Newport Beach Public Library, Newport Beach, CA
14,500	UCI Foundation
13,100	Human Options
10,000	Orange County Trauma Society

Pacific Telesis Group / Pacific Telesis Foundation

Revenue: $4.59 billion
Employees: 61,346
Headquarters: San Francisco, CA
SIC Major Group:
Communications and Holding & Other Investment Offices

CONTACT

Jere A. Jacobs
President
Pacific Telesis Fdn.
130 Kearny St.
Rm. 3309
San Francisco, CA 94108
(415) 394-3693
Note: Alternate contacts are Mary Leslie, Susan Diekman, and Lee Davis, executive directors.

FINANCIAL SUMMARY

Recent Giving: $8,157,311 (1993 est.); $7,987,570 (1992); $7,522,528 (1991 approx.)

Assets: $68,750,973 (1992); $68,600,272 (1991); $62,460,587 (1990)

Fiscal Note: Above represents foundation contributions only. Company also has a direct giving program with a budget of $2,442,000 administered by Molly Hopp, director of consumer affairs. Pacific Telesis Group and its operating companies Pacific Bell and Nevada Bell also make direct contributions, not included above.

EIN: 94-2905832

CONTRIBUTIONS SUMMARY

Typical Recipients: • *Arts & Humanities:* arts appreciation, community arts, dance, ethnic arts, libraries, museums/galleries, music, opera, performing arts, theater, visual arts • *Civic & Public Affairs:* ethnic/minority organizations, housing, law & justice, nonprofit management, urban & community affairs, women's affairs • *Education:* arts education, business education, colleges & universities, community & junior colleges, economic education, elementary education, engineering education, faculty development, literacy, minority education, preschool education, public education (precollege), science/technology education, student aid • *Social Services:* aged, child welfare, day care, disabled, drugs & alcohol, homes, shelters/homelessness, united funds, volunteer services, youth organizations

Grant Types: employee matching gifts, project, and scholarship

Geographic Distribution: only to regional and local organizations operating within service areas or communities in which significant numbers of employees live

Operating Locations: CA (Bakersfield, Fresno, Los Angeles, Oakland, Orange, Riverside, Sacramento, Salinas, San Diego, San Francisco, San Jose, San Ramon, Santa Rosa), NV (Reno)

CORP. OFFICERS

Sam L. Ginn: *B* St Claire AL 1937 *ED* Auburn Univ BS 1959; Stanford Univ Sch Bus Admin 1968 *CURR EMPL* chmn, ceo, dir, pres: Pacific Telesis Group *CORP AFFIL* dir: First Interstate Bancorp *NONPR AFFIL* trust: Mills Coll

GIVING OFFICERS

Lydell L. Christensen: treas, dir *B* Walnut IA 1934 *ED* Univ NE BS 1959; Pace Coll *CURR EMPL* exec vp, cfo: Pacific Telesis Group *CORP AFFIL* dir: NV Bell, Pacific Bell Directory, PacTel Fin, PacTel Intl, PacTel RE Ins Co; pres, dir: PacTel Capital Funding, PacTel Capital Resources; vp, treas, dir: Pacific Bell *NONPR AFFIL* dir: Danish Immigrant Mus; mem: CA Utilities Fin Offs, Fin Execs Inst, Fin Offs Northern CA, NY Stock Exchange Pension Mgrs Adv Comm

Lee Davis: exec dir

Susan Diekman: exec dir *ED* Stanford Univ BA 1966; Stanford Univ ME 1967

Sam L. Ginn: chmn, dir *CURR EMPL* chmn, ceo, dir, pres: Pacific Telesis Group (see above)

Nancy Ishirashi: mem bd

Jere A. Jacobs: pres, dir

Mary Leslie: exec dir *ED* San Francisco St Univ BA 1969; Golden Gate Univ

James R. Moberg: dir *CURR EMPL* exec vp (human resources): Pacific Telesis Group

Richard W. Odgers: secy, dir *B* Detroit MI 1936 *ED* Univ MI AB 1959; Univ MI JD 1961 *CURR EMPL* exec vp, gen coun, secy: Pacific Telesis Group *CORP AFFIL* exec vp, secy: Pacific Bell *NONPR AFFIL* fellow: Am Bar Fdn, Am Coll Trial Lawyers, Am Judicature Soc; mem: Am Bar Assn, Am Law Inst, San Francisco Bar Assn

Mike Rodriguez: mem bd

Richard R. Roll: vp, dir

APPLICATION INFORMATION

Initial Approach: *Initial Contact:* organizations that serve California and are statewide or national in scope, send proposal outline to foundation; Bay area, central area, northern area, and southern area of California and Nevada organizations, send outline to appropriate area manager of Pacific Bell or Nevada Bell *Include Information On:* description of the organization's purpose and scope, including short-term and long-range objectives; evidence of how request fits foundation guidelines; standards to evaluate success of program; current total budget for organization; budget for specific project; brief statement explaining why company should provide support and how support would be recognized; copy of 501(c)(3) tax-exempt status; list of corporate and foundation funders and funding levels; evidence of strategies to develop earned income and avoid overdependence on any single source of contributed income *When to Submit:* any time *Note:* Addresses of appropriate regional contacts are available from company.

Restrictions on Giving:

Foundation does not make grants to the following organizations and/or causes: organizations without 501(c)(3) status; organizations that discriminate by race, creed, color, sex, sexual preference, age, or national origin; private foundations; "flow-through" organizations; organizations supported by the United Way; individual primary and secondary schools or school districts; capital projects; endowment funds; religious organizations for sectarian purposes; veterans groups or labor organizations when serving only their own members; individuals; general operating purposes; medical clinics or medical research; emergency funds or guarantees; special occasion or goodwill advertising; sports programs or events; political or lobbying activities; or in the form of products or services or cause-related marketing.

OTHER THINGS TO KNOW

Grants are determined on a zero-based budgeting process, which requires annual evaluation of both previously funded projects and new grant requests. Foundation grants should not be construed as establishing a precedent for further support. Foundation may request post-grant reports from organizations receiving contributions. Foundation prefers to make one-time grants, although in special circumstances grants may span up to three years. Foundation gives preference to organizations with active, diverse boards, effective leadership, and continuity of efficient administration.

GRANTS ANALYSIS

Total Grants: $7,987,570
Number of Grants: 309
Highest Grant: $1,150,843
Typical Range: $15,000 to $25,000
Disclosure Period: 1992
Note: Average grant figure provided by the company. Recent grants are derived from a 1992 grants list.

RECENT GRANTS

1,150,843	United Way of the Bay Area, CA
873,030	United Way of Los Angeles, Los Angeles, CA

231,525 United Way of Orange County, CA
211,961 United Way of San Diego County, San Diego, CA
200,000 United Way of the Bay Area, CA
192,137 United Way of Sacramento Area, Sacramento, CA
166,767 United Way of Santa Clara County, CA
.152,900 Citizens' Scholarship Foundation of America
150,000 California State University, Chico Foundation, Chico, CA
110,176 California State University, Chico Foundation, Chico, CA

Pacific Western Foundation

CONTACT
Charles F. Bannan
President
Pacific Western Fdn.
8344 East Florence, Ste. E
Downey, CA 90240
(213) 869-1524

FINANCIAL SUMMARY
Recent Giving: $236,000 (fiscal 1991); $215,790 (fiscal 1990); $234,450 (fiscal 1989)
Assets: $3,746,096 (fiscal year ending November 30, 1991); $3,459,544 (fiscal 1990); $3,563,426 (fiscal 1989)
EIN: 95-6097360

CONTRIBUTIONS SUMMARY
Donor(s): Western Gear Corp.
Typical Recipients: • *Education:* colleges & universities, religious education • *Health:* hospitals, medical research • *Religion:* churches, religious organizations • *Social Services:* community service organizations, religious welfare, youth organizations
Grant Types: general support
Geographic Distribution: focus on CA

GIVING OFFICERS
Charles F. Bannan: pres
M. Patricia Cruden: secy
Joseph T. Nally: vp
Elmer L. Stone: treas

APPLICATION INFORMATION
Initial Approach: Contributes only to preselected organizations.

GRANTS ANALYSIS
Number of Grants: 30
Highest Grant: $87,000
Typical Range: $500 to $10,000
Disclosure Period: fiscal year ending November 30, 1991

RECENT GRANTS
87,000 Santa Clara University, Santa Clara, CA
60,700 Mount St. Mary's College
10,000 Catholic Charities, Los Angeles, CA
10,000 Dominion College, Los Angeles, CA
10,000 Loyola Marymount University, Los Angeles, CA
10,000 Marycrest Manor, Los Angeles, CA
10,000 Salk Institute for Biological Studies, San Diego, CA
10,000 Sisters of Nazareth, Los Angeles, CA
5,000 St. Francis Medical Center, Los Angeles, CA
4,000 Junior Achievement, Los Angeles, CA

PacifiCorp / PacifiCorp Foundation

Revenue: $3.91 billion
Employees: 12,783
Headquarters: Portland, OR
SIC Major Group: Coal Mining, Communications, Electric, Gas & Sanitary Services, and Metal Mining

CONTACT
Ernest Bloch II
Executive Director
PacifiCorp Fdn.
700 NE Multnomah
Ste. 1600
Portland, OR 97232
(503) 731-6676
Note: Applicants may also contact the following PacifiCorp subsidiaries and divisions directly: NERCO, Inc., 111 SW Columbia, Portland, OR 97201, (503) 796-6600; Pacific Power & Light, 920 SW 6th Ave., Portland, OR 97204, (503) 243-1122; Pacific Telecom,

805 Broadway, Box 9901, Vancouver, WA 98669, (206) 696-0983.

FINANCIAL SUMMARY
Recent Giving: $2,808,053 (1991); $2,500,000 (1990 approx.); $2,250,000 (1989)
Assets: $5,174,316 (1991); $1,279,303 (1989); $3,000,000 (1988)
Fiscal Note: PacifiCorp Foundation began making most contributions on behalf of the company and its subsidiaries in 1989. Previously, all contributions were made directly by each subsidiary, with Pacific Power & Light giving on behalf of the holding company. For more information see "Other Things You Should Know."
EIN: 94-3089826

CONTRIBUTIONS SUMMARY
Typical Recipients: • *Arts & Humanities:* arts associations, history/historic preservation, museums/galleries, music, opera, performing arts, theater • *Civic & Public Affairs:* economic development, economics, environmental affairs, housing, professional & trade associations, urban & community affairs • *Education:* arts education, colleges & universities, education funds, science/technology education • *Health:* hospitals • *Social Services:* child welfare, community centers, community service organizations, recreation & athletics, united funds, youth organizations
Grant Types: capital and project
Nonmonetary Support Types: donated equipment and loaned executives
Note: No estimate is available for value of nonmonetary support, and it is not included above.
Geographic Distribution: primarily Oregon; also in Alaska, Northern California, Nevada, Montana, Utah, Washington, and Wyoming
Operating Locations: AK (Anchorage, Bethel, Fairbanks), AZ (Phoenix), CA (Chatsworth), MN (Minneapolis, Rushford), MO (St. Louis), MT (Billings), NY (New York), OR (Beaverton, Hillsboro, Portland, Salem, Wilsonville), UT (Salt Lake City), VA

(McLean), WA (Vancouver), WV

CORP. OFFICERS
Don Calvin Frisbee: *B* San Francisco CA 1923 *ED* Pomona Coll BA 1947; Harvard Univ MBA 1949 *CURR EMPL* chmn: PacifiCorp *CORP AFFIL* dir: First Interstate Bancorp, First Interstate Bank OR, Precision Castparts Corp, Standard Ins Co, Weyerhaeuser Co *NONPR AFFIL* cabinet mem: Boy Scouts Am; chmn bd trusts: Reed Coll; fdr: Am Leadership Forum OR Chap; mem: Intl Adv Comm, Japan-Western US Assn; mem exec comm: OR Partnership Intl Ed; trust: Greater Portland Trust Higher Ed, High Desert Mus, OR Indian Coll Fdn, Safari Game Search Fdn; dir: OR Bus Counc; pres: OR Commun Fdn; trust: Comm Econ Devel, Whitman Coll
Alfred M. Gleason: *B* Sheridan KS 1930 *CURR EMPL* pres, ceo, dir: PacifiCorp *CORP AFFIL* dir: Blount, Comdial Corp, Equitec Fin Group, Flight Dynamics, Tektronix; pres: Pacific Telecom Inc

GIVING OFFICERS
Ted Berns: dir
Ernest Bloch II: exec dir
David F. Bolender: mem (contributions comm) *B* Hamburg NY 1932 *ED* CO Sch Mines 1954 *CURR EMPL* pres, dir: Pacific Power & Light Co *CORP AFFIL* dir: UT Power & Light Co
Candice Brewer: mem (contributions comm)
Gerard K. Drummond: chmn *B* New York NY 1937 *ED* Cornell Univ BS 1959; Cornell Univ LLB 1963 *CURR EMPL* exec vp, dir: PacifiCorp *CORP AFFIL* chmn bd dirs: NERCO; dir: Pacific Telecom, Willamette Indus Inc *NONPR AFFIL* chmn, dir: OR Investment Counc; dir: Am Mining Congress, OR Shakespeare Festival Assn; mem: Am Bar Assn, OR Bar Assn, Providence Hosp; mem adv counc: Cornell Univ Law Sch; pres, dir: OR Symphony; trust: Reed Coll; mem: OR Counc
William Jacob Glasgow: dir *B* Portland OR 1946 *CURR EMPL* chmn, ceo, pres: Pacificorp Fin Svcs Inc *CORP AFFIL* dir: NERCO; sr vp: Pacificorp *NONPR AFFIL* mem: Am Bar Assn, Harvard

Law Sch Alumni Assn, OR Bar Assn, Portland Chamber Commerce; trust: OR Art Inst, OR Grad Inst Science Tech

Lawrence Heiner: dir

Paul Lorezini: mem (contributions comm)

William W. Lyons: chmn (contributions comm)

David Mead: mem (contributions comm)

Robert William Moench: dir *B* Albany OR 1927 *CURR EMPL* pres: Pacific Power & Light Co

Sally Alene Nofziger: secy *B* San Francisco CA 1936 *CURR EMPL* secy, vp: PacifiCorp

William Peressinni: mem (contributions comm) *B* Great Falls MT 1956 *CURR EMPL* sr vp, cfo: Pacificorp Fin Svcs *NONPR AFFIL* mem: Am Assn Equipment Lessors, Fin Execs Inst, Univ IL Varsity Assn

Verl Topham: dir *B* Paragonah UT 1934 *CURR EMPL* pres, ceo, dir: UT Power & Light Co *NONPR AFFIL* dir: Am Red Cross; mem: Am Bar Assn, Salt Lake City Chamber Commerce, Salt Lake County Bar, UT Fin & Accounting Forum, UT St Bar Assn

Brian Wirkkala: mem (contributions comm) *B* Astoria OR 1941 *CURR EMPL* vp, treas: Pacific Telecomm *CORP AFFIL* treas: Pacific Telecomm Cable; vp, treas: Cascade Autovon Co, Cencom Inc, Eagle Telecomm, Eagle Valley Commun, Gem St Utilities Corp, Northwestern Tel Sys, Pacific Telecomm Construction, Pacific Telecomm Svc Co, Peninsula Telecomm, PTI Harbor Bay, PTI Transponders, RT/FTC Communs, TelCom Construction Co, Telephone Utilites E OR, Telephone Utilities AK, Telephone Utilities OR, Telephone Utilities WA; vp, treas, asst secy: Peninsula Telecomm Sales & Svcs

APPLICATION INFORMATION

Initial Approach: *Initial Contact:* brief letter or proposal to foundation, contact person for appropriate subsidiary, or local manager *Include Information On:* description of the organization, amount requested, purpose for which funds are sought, recently audited financial statement, and proof of tax-exempt status *When to Submit:* any time

Restrictions on Giving: Grants are not made to individuals or to religious organizations for religious purposes.

OTHER THINGS TO KNOW

In the future, direct giving by the company will go only to organizations that are ineligible for grants under foundation guidelines.

Subsidiaries and divisions of PacifiCorp that contribute to the PacifiCorp Foundation include Pacific Power & Light Co., Pacific Telecom, NERCO, and PacifiCorp Financial Services. Another contributor is Utah Power & Light Co., which became a division of PacifiCorp as a result of a merger effective January 9, 1989.

GRANTS ANALYSIS

Total Grants: $2,808,053

Number of Grants: 649

Highest Grant: $126,424

Typical Range: $1,000 to $50,000

Disclosure Period: 1991

Note: Recent grants are derived from a 1991 Form 990.

RECENT GRANTS

126,424 United Way of the Great Salt Lake Area, Salt Lake City, UT

100,000 City of Salt Lake, Salt Lake City, UT

70,125 United Way of the Columbia-Willamette, Portland, OR

70,000 Oregon Museum of Science and Industry

52,500 United Way of the Columbia-Willamette, Portland, OR

52,500 United Way of the Columbia-Willamette, Portland, OR

52,500 United Way of the Columbia-Willamette, Portland, OR

52,500 United Way of the Columbia-Willamette, Portland, OR

50,000 City of Salt Lake, Salt Lake City, UT

46,000 Oregon Independent College Foundation, Portland, OR

Packaging Corporation of America

Sales: $1.55 billion
Employees: 10,275
Parent Company: Tenneco Inc.
Headquarters: Evanston, IL
SIC Major Group: Fabricated Metal Products, Lumber & Wood Products, Paper & Allied Products, and Rubber & Miscellaneous Plastics Products

CONTACT

Warren Hazelton
Director, Corporate Relations
Packaging Corporation of America
1603 Orrington Ave.
Evanston, IL 60201
(708) 492-6968

FINANCIAL SUMMARY

Fiscal Note: Company gives directly. Annual Giving Range: $250,00 to $500,000

CONTRIBUTIONS SUMMARY

Typical Recipients: • *Arts & Humanities:* community arts, general, libraries, museums/galleries, public broadcasting • *Civic & Public Affairs:* general, municipalities • *Education:* arts education, business education, career/vocational education, colleges & universities, economic education, elementary education, engineering education, general, minority education, public education (precollege), science/technology education, special education • *Health:* emergency/ambulance services, general, hospices, hospitals, nursing services, single-disease health associations • *Social Services:* community service organizations, emergency relief, food/clothing distribution, general, recreation & athletics, shelters/homelessness, united funds, youth organizations

Grant Types: award, employee matching gifts, general support, and scholarship

Nonmonetary Support Types: donated products

Geographic Distribution: in headquarters and operating communities

Operating Locations: IL (Evanston)

Note: Packaging Corp. of America operates in 100 field locations.

CORP. OFFICERS

Robert Fuqua: *CURR EMPL* vp, cfo: Packaging Corp Am

Monte Haymon: *CURR EMPL* ceo, pres: Packaging Corp Am

GIVING OFFICERS

Warren Hazelton: *CURR EMPL* dir corp rels: Packaging Corp Am

APPLICATION INFORMATION

Initial Approach: *Initial Contact:* brief letter of inquiry* *Include Information On:* a description of organization, amount requested, purpose of funds sought, recently audited financial statement, and proof of tax-exempt status *When to Submit:* any time *Note:* No phone calls will be accepted, and local requests must be made through local operating facilities.

Restrictions on Giving: The company does not support individuals, religious organizations for sectarian purposes, or political or lobbying groups.

GRANTS ANALYSIS

Typical Range: $500 to $2,500

RECENT GRANTS

Adopt-a-School, Omaha, NE
Clarke School for the Deaf, Northampton, MA
Golden Apple Foundation, Chicago, IL
Holy Cross Hospital, Salt Lake City, UT
Junior Achievement, Chicago, IL
Keep America Beautiful
Manistee County Youth Center, Filer City, MI
Milwaukee Public Museum, Milwaukee, WI
Valdosta State College, Valdosta, GA

Packard Foundation, David and Lucile

CONTACT

Colburn S. Wilbur
Executive Director
David and Lucile Packard Foundation
300 Second St., Ste. 200
Los Altos, CA 94022
(415) 948-7658

FINANCIAL SUMMARY

Recent Giving: $75,700,000 (1993 est.); $45,000,000 (1992 approx.); $32,834,909 (1991)

Assets: $1,100,000,000 (1992 approx.); $681,317,000 (1991); $227,512,098 (1990); $245,887,758 (1989)
Gifts Received: $285,000,000 (1992 approx.); $407,232,000 (1991); $15,281,396 (1990); $126,789,104 (1989)
Fiscal Note: In 1988, the foundation received stock and cash contributions valued at $12,216,011 from David Packard and the David and Lucile Packard Foundation Lead Trust I and II. The foundation is to receive annual contributions from Hewlett-Packard common stock valued at $3,282,000 through 1997, and $1,7 44,000 in 1998 through 2003. In 1991, cash contributions from David Packard amounted to $5,585,000, and $11,999,890 in 1990.
EIN: 94-2278431

CONTRIBUTIONS SUMMARY

Donor(s): The David and Lucile Packard Foundation was established in 1964. The foundation's donors are David Packard, the foundation's president, and his late wife, Lucile Salter Packard. The couple's four children, David Woodley Packard, Nancy Ann Packard Burnett, Susan Packard Orr, and Julie Elizabeth Packard, all serve on their parents' foundation.
David Packard and William Hewlett founded Hewlett-Packard Company in 1938. The company became a major manufacturer of test and measurement instruments and microcomputers. Mr. Packard also served as U.S. Secretary of Defense between 1969 and 1971.
Typical Recipients: • *Arts & Humanities:* arts associations, cinema, community arts, dance, history/historic preservation, libraries, literary arts, museums/galleries, music, opera, performing arts, theater • *Civic & Public Affairs:* environmental affairs, housing, municipalities, philanthropic organizations, public policy, women's affairs, zoos/botanical gardens • *Education:* arts education, colleges & universities, education associations, elementary education, science/technology education • *Health:* health organizations, hospitals, nursing services, pediatric health, public health • *International:* international organizations

• *Science:* scientific organizations • *Social Services:* child welfare, community service organizations, counseling, day care, disabled, employment/job training, family planning, family services, food/clothing distribution, homes, religious welfare, youth organizations
Grant Types: capital, department, general support, project, research, and seed money
Geographic Distribution: primarily San Mateo, Santa Clara, Santa Cruz and Monterey Counties, CA; some grants in the county of Pueblo, CO; national funding for child health, science and engineering fellowships, and support for science instruction in Black colleges; funding for conservation and population studies in the U.S., Mexico, and Columbia

GIVING OFFICERS

Nancy Packard Burnett: trust
Robin Chandler Duke: trust
Robert J. Glaser, MD: trust *B* St Louis MO 1918 *ED* Harvard Univ SB 1940; Harvard Univ MD 1943 *CORP AFFIL* dir: Affymax, Alza Corp, CA Water Svc Co, First Boston Inc, Hewlett-Packard Co, Nellcor *NONPR AFFIL* consult prof: Stanford Univ; editor: Pharos; fellow: Am Academy Arts Sciences, Am Assn Advancement Science; mem: Am Clinical Climatological Assn, Am Federation Clinical Res, Am Soc Clinical Investigation, Am Soc Experimental Pathology, Assn Am Med Colls, Assn Am Physicians, Central Soc Clinical Res, Inst Medicine, Natl Academy Sciences, Natl Inst Allergy Infectious Disease, Western Assn Physicians; trust: Washington Univ *PHIL AFFIL* dir: Commonwealth Fund
Dean O. Morton: trust *B* 1932 *ED* KS St Univ BE 1954; Harvard Univ MBA 1960 *CURR EMPL* exec vp, coo, dir: Hewlett-Packard Co *CORP AFFIL* dir: Saga Corp, Street Investment Corp
Susan Packard Orr: vp, trust *NONPR AFFIL* trust: Monterey Bay Aquarium Fdn, Wolf Trap Fdn Performing Arts
David Packard: pres, chmn *B* Pueblo CO 1912 *ED* Stanford Univ BA 1934; Stanford Univ MEE 1939 *CURR EMPL* chmn bd: Hewlett-Packard Co *CORP AFFIL* dir: Boeing Co, Genentech *NONPR AFFIL* dir emeritus: Wolf Trap Fdn; fellow:

Inst Electrical Electronics Engrs; hon lifetime mem: Instrument Soc Am; mem: Alpha Delta Phi, Am Enterprise Inst, Am Ordnance Assn, Bus Counc, Bus Roundtable, CA Chamber Commerce, Natl Academy Engg, Phi Beta Kappa, Pres Counc Advs Science Tech, Sigma Xi, Tau Beta Pi, Wilson Counc; mem bd overseers: Hoover Inst; trust: Herbert Hoover Fdn, Ronald Reagan Presidential Fdn; vchmn, trust: CA Nature Conservancy; mem: Fdn Study Presidential & Congressional Terms *PHIL AFFIL* mem adv counc: Hitachi Foundation; mem bd govs: Henry M Jackson Foundation
David Woodley Packard: vp, trust *CURR EMPL* pres, chmn: Ibycus Corp
Julie Elizabeth Packard: trust *CURR EMPL* exec dir: Monterey Bay Aquarium
Frank Roberts: trust
Edwin E. Van Bronkhurst: treas, trust
Colburn S. Wilbur: exec dir
Barbara Wright: secy, trust

APPLICATION INFORMATION

Initial Approach:
Written proposals should be sent to the foundation's executive director.

Proposals should include a cover letter from the executive director or board chair indicating that the proposal has the support of the agency's board. General information should include the name, address, and telephone number of the organization; its background and purpose; list of people and constituent groups served; names and affiliations of directors and trustees; and a copy of the IRS determination letter of tax-exempt status. Financial information should include the prior year's financial statements (preferably audited), sources of the organization's funds (both public and private), budget for the years in which the program will take place, detailed project budget, other sources of support, and the amount requested from the foundation. Program information should include objective and description, evidence of need and value, geographic area served, an outline of program's phases, evaluative methods, and personnel

involved and their qualifications.
Proposals are considered at the foundation's quarterly board meetings. The application deadlines for consideration at these meetings are December 15, March 15, June 15, and September 15.
The foundation's board meets in March, June, September, and December.
Restrictions on Giving: Religious programs are not supported.

OTHER THINGS TO KNOW

The foundation is affiliated with the Monterey Bay Aquarium Research Institute, the Stanford Theater Foundation, and the Packard Humanities Institute. The foundation provides other services such as managment assistance, and loans for land purchase and low-income housing.
Publications: annual report and quarterly journal, *The Future of Children*

GRANTS ANALYSIS

Total Grants: $32,834,909
Number of Grants: 294
Highest Grant: $8,500,000
Typical Range: $5,000 to $100,000
Disclosure Period: 1991
Note: Average grant figure excludes the two highest grants totaling $9,500,000. Recent grants are derived from a 1991 annual report.

RECENT GRANTS

8,500,000 Monterey Bay Aquarium Research Institute, Pacific Grove, CA — operating expenses and capital projects
1,000,000 Community Foundation of Santa Clara County, San Jose, CA — leadership gift for the Silicon Valley Arts Fund campaign
880,000 Stanford Theater Foundation, Palt Alto, CA — construction, painting, architectural, and legal costs of the Stanford Theater
500,000 California Institute of Technology, Pasadena, CA — to micromachine integrated microdevices
500,000 Columbia University, New York,

NY — to study quasar clustering at very large distances

500,000 Harvard University, Cambridge, MA — to apply elliptic curves to dense packing of spheres

500,000 Massachusetts Institute of Technology, Cambridge, MA — to study the electronic properties of nanometer-sized crystallites

500,000 New York University, New York, NY — to study how bulk properties of matter arise from microscopic laws of nature

500,000 North Carolina State University, Raleigh, NC — to research selective cleavage of nucleic acids

500,000 Pennsylvania State University, University Park, PA — to investigate the dynamics of icefields and glaciers

Packard Humanities Institute

CONTACT
Packard Humanities Institute
300 Second Street, Suite 201
Los Altos, CA 94022-3621

FINANCIAL SUMMARY
Recent Giving: $30,000 (1990)
Assets: $5,115,010 (1990)

CONTRIBUTIONS SUMMARY
Typical Recipients: • *Education:* colleges & universities
Grant Types: general support

GRANTS ANALYSIS
Total Grants: $30,000
Number of Grants: 1
Highest Grant: $30,000
Disclosure Period: 1990

RECENT GRANTS
30,000 Thesaurus Linguae Graecae, University of California at Irvine, Irvine, CA

Packer Foundation, Horace B.

CONTACT
Donald Gill
President
Horace B. Packer Fdn.
PO Box 35
Wellsboro, PA 16901
(717) 724-2884

FINANCIAL SUMMARY
Recent Giving: $111,634 (1991); $142,620 (1990); $96,464 (1989)
Assets: $1,736,562 (1991); $1,619,483 (1990); $1,661,312 (1989)
Gifts Received: $15,000 (1991)
EIN: 23-6390932

CONTRIBUTIONS SUMMARY
Donor(s): the late Horace B. Packer
Typical Recipients: • *Arts & Humanities:* libraries • *Civic & Public Affairs:* municipalities, urban & community affairs • *Education:* colleges & universities, science/technology education • *Health:* health organizations, hospitals • *Social Services:* aged, community service organizations, recreation & athletics, united funds, youth organizations
Grant Types: general support and scholarship
Geographic Distribution: limited to Tioga County, PA

GIVING OFFICERS
Carl Carson: trust
Donald Gill: vp
Harold Hershberger, Jr.: trust
John D. Lewis: trust
Rev. George Lineker: secy
William Nichols: trust
Charles G. Webb: pres

APPLICATION INFORMATION
Initial Approach: Application form required. There are no deadlines.

GRANTS ANALYSIS
Number of Grants: 25
Highest Grant: $11,500
Typical Range: $1,500 to $5,000
Disclosure Period: 1991

RECENT GRANTS
11,500 Borough of Wellsboro, Wellsboro, PA
11,500 Green Home, Wellsboro, PA
6,500 Soldiers and Sailors Memorial Hospital, Philadelphia, PA
5,800 Liberty VFW, Wellsboro, PA
5,495 Mansfield Library, Mansfield, PA
5,000 Blossburg Borough, Blossburg, PA
5,000 Borough of Westfield, Westfield, PA
5,000 Pennsylvania College of Technology, Philadelphia, PA
5,000 Williamson Band Parents Organization, Williamson, PA
4,000 Green Free Library, Wellsboro, PA

Paddington Corp.
Sales: $300.0 million
Employees: 165
Headquarters: Fort Lee, NJ
SIC Major Group: Wholesale Trade—Nondurable Goods

CONTACT
Joseph McKenna
Senior Vice President, Public Relations
Paddington Corp.
One Parker Plz.
Ft. Lee, NJ 07024
(201) 592-5700

CONTRIBUTIONS SUMMARY
Operating Locations: NJ (Fort Lee)

CORP. OFFICERS
G. William Seawright: *CURR EMPL* pres, ceo: Paddington Corp

GIVING OFFICERS
Joseph McKenna: *CURR EMPL* sr vp (pub rels): Paddington Corp

Padnos Iron & Metal Co., Louis / Louis & Helen Padnos Foundation
Sales: $76.0 million
Employees: 250
Headquarters: Holland, MI
SIC Major Group: Primary Metal Industries and Wholesale Trade—Durable Goods

CONTACT
Jeffery Padner
President
Louis Padnos Iron & Metal Co.
PO Box 1979
Holland, MI 49422
(616) 396-6521

FINANCIAL SUMMARY
Fiscal Note: Annual Giving Range: less than $100,000
EIN: 38-6053081

CONTRIBUTIONS SUMMARY
Typical Recipients: • *Arts & Humanities:* general • *Civic & Public Affairs:* general • *Education:* career/vocational education, colleges & universities, elementary education, engineering education, general, public education (precollege) • *Health:* general, hospices • *Religion:* general, synagogues • *Social Services:* child welfare, community service organizations, family services, general, youth organizations
Grant Types: capital, challenge, employee matching gifts, project, and scholarship
Geographic Distribution: in headquarters and operating communities
Operating Locations: MI (Holland)

CORP. OFFICERS
Jeffrey Padnos: *B* Holland MI 1948 *ED* Harvard Univ 1970-1974 *CURR EMPL* pres: Louis Padnos Iron & Metal Co
Seymour K. Padnos: *CURR EMPL* chmn, ceo: Louis Padnos Iron & Metal Co
Seymour K. Padnos: *B* Grand Rapids MI 1920 *ED* Hope Coll 1942 *CURR EMPL* chmn: Louis Padnos Iron & Metal Co *CORP AFFIL* dir: Brown Scrap Corp; pres: IXL Machine Shop, Malatawa Bay Dock & Terminal Co *NONPR AFFIL* pres, dir: Inst Scrap Recycling Indus

APPLICATION INFORMATION
Restrictions on Giving: Does not support individuals, religious organizations for sectarian purposes, political or lobbying groups, or organizations outside operating areas.

OTHER THINGS TO KNOW
Company is an original donor to the Louis & Helen Padnos Foundation.

GRANTS ANALYSIS
Number of Grants: 40
Highest Grant: $250,000
Typical Range: $1,000 to $2,500
Disclosure Period: fiscal year ending May 31, 1990

RECENT GRANTS
250,000 City of Holland Historic Depot, Holland, MI
60,000 Jewish Community Fund, Grand Rapids, MI
10,000 New Israel Fund, New York, NY
7,000 Children's Hospital of Michigan, Detroit, MI
5,000 Grand Rapids Public Museum, Grand Rapids, MI
5,000 World Union for Progressive Judaism, New York, NY
2,500 Grand Rapids Symphony Orchestra, Grand Rapids, MI
2,500 Holland Area Arts Council, Holland, MI
2,000 Evergreen Commons, Grand Rapids, MI
2,000 Planned Parenthood, Grand Rapids, MI

Page Belting Co. / Page Belting Co. Foundation
Sales: $3.0 million
Employees: 65
Headquarters: Concord, NH
SIC Major Group: Apparel & Other Textile Products, Chemicals & Allied Products, Leather & Leather Products, and Textile Mill Products

CONTACT
Charles Cohn
Vice President
Page Belting Co. Foundation
Commercial St.
Concord, NH 03301
(603) 225-5523

FINANCIAL SUMMARY
Recent Giving: $2,050 (1991); $2,200 (1990); $2,250 (1989)
Assets: $34,713 (1991); $32,826 (1990); $42,998 (1989)
EIN: 02-6012763

CONTRIBUTIONS SUMMARY
Typical Recipients: • *Arts & Humanities:* history/historic preservation, public broadcast-

ing • *Education:* private education (precollege) • *Social Services:* community service organizations, recreation & athletics, united funds
Grant Types: general support
Geographic Distribution: focus on Concord, NH
Operating Locations: NH (Concord)

CORP. OFFICERS
O. Conrad Trulson: *CURR EMPL* ceo, pres: Page Belting Co
John F. Weeks, Jr.: *CURR EMPL* chmn: Page Belting Co

GIVING OFFICERS
Charles E. Cohn: vp, dir
O. Conrad Trulson: pres, dir *CURR EMPL* ceo, pres: Page Belting Co (see above)

APPLICATION INFORMATION
Initial Approach: Send brief letter describing program. There are no deadlines.

GRANTS ANALYSIS
Number of Grants: 3
Highest Grant: $1,700
Typical Range: $100 to $1,700
Disclosure Period: 1991

RECENT GRANTS
1,700 United Way, Concord, NH
250 St. Paul's School, Concord, NH
100 Channel 11, Manchester, NH

Page Foundation, George B.

CONTACT
John R. Erickson
Trustee
George B. Page Fdn.
PO Drawer 1299
Santa Barbara, CA 93102
(805) 963-1841

FINANCIAL SUMMARY
Recent Giving: $83,311 (1991); $86,640 (1990); $77,784 (1989)
Assets: $2,133,787 (1991); $1,707,649 (1990); $1,794,120 (1989)
EIN: 95-6121985

CONTRIBUTIONS SUMMARY
Donor(s): Mission Linen Companies, Montecito Mfg. Co.
Typical Recipients: • *Arts & Humanities:* history/historic preservation, public broadcast-

ing • *Civic & Public Affairs:* environmental affairs, zoos/botanical gardens
• *Health:* medical research, single-disease health associations
• *Social Services:* child welfare, community service organizations, counseling, disabled, family services, food/clothing distribution, recreation & athletics, united funds, youth organizations
Grant Types: emergency, general support, multiyear/continuing support, operating expenses, and project

GIVING OFFICERS
John R. Erickson: trust
Antnony Gunterman: trust
Wayne Kees: trust
Henry W. Logan: trust
George B. Page: trust
Harold Scoilin: trust
Louis Simon: trust

APPLICATION INFORMATION
Initial Approach: Application form required. Deadline is October 30.
Restrictions on Giving: Does not support individuals.

GRANTS ANALYSIS
Number of Grants: 24
Highest Grant: $7,500
Typical Range: $1,500 to $5,000
Disclosure Period: 1991

RECENT GRANTS
7,500 Cal Farley's Boys Ranch, Santa Barbara, CA
5,000 Boy Scouts of America, Santa Barbara, CA
5,000 Cancer Foundation of Santa Barbara, Santa Barbara, CA
5,000 Family Service Agency, Santa Barbara, CA
5,000 Goleta Valley Youth Sports Association, Santa Barbara, CA
5,000 Salvation Army, Santa Barbara, CA
5,000 Santa Barbara Meals on Wheels, Santa Barbara, CA
5,000 Santa Barbara Special Olympics, Santa Barbara, CA
3,700 Good Work, Santa Barbara, CA
3,700 Santa Barbara Zoological Gardens, Santa Barbara, CA

PaineWebber / PaineWebber Foundation
Revenue: $3.16 billion
Employees: 12,900
Headquarters: New York, NY
SIC Major Group: Holding & Other Investment Offices and Security & Commodity Brokers

CONTACT
Monika Dillon
Trustee
PaineWebber Fdn.
1285 Avenue of the Americas
New York, NY 10019
(212) 713-4545

FINANCIAL SUMMARY
Recent Giving: $260,250 (1991); $207,000 (1990); $182,500 (1989)
Assets: $8,486,634 (1991); $5,456,677 (1990); $5,439,416 (1989)
Gifts Received: $1,873,040 (1991); $350,000 (1989)
Fiscal Note: In 1991, contributions were received from Painewebber Capital.
EIN: 04-6032804

CONTRIBUTIONS SUMMARY
Typical Recipients: • *Arts & Humanities:* libraries, museums/galleries • *Civic & Public Affairs:* environmental affairs • *Education:* colleges & universities, education associations
• *Health:* medical research, single-disease health associations
• *Religion:* religious organizations • *Social Services:* child welfare, food/clothing distribution
Grant Types: research
Operating Locations: MA (Boston), MD (Columbia), NY (New York), TX (Houston)

CORP. OFFICERS
Donald Baird Marron: *B* Goshen NY 1934 *ED* City Univ NY Bernard M. Baruch Coll 1951 *CURR EMPL* chmn, ceo: PaineWebber *NONPR AFFIL* mem: Securities Indus Assn; pres: Mus Modern Art

GIVING OFFICERS
Monika Dillon: trust
Paul Guenther: trust *B* New York NY 1940 *ED* Fordham Univ 1962; Columbia Univ 1964 *CURR EMPL* pres, dir: PaineWebber *CORP AFFIL* dir: Globalome Plus Fund, PaineWebber Group,

PaineWebber Mutual Funds, PaineWebber Trust Co

APPLICATION INFORMATION
Initial Approach: Send brief letter of inquiry on organization's letterhead. Deadline is December 1.

GRANTS ANALYSIS
Number of Grants: 50
Highest Grant: $25,000
Typical Range: $1,500 to $10,000
Disclosure Period: 1991

RECENT GRANTS
25,000 Governors Committee on Scholastic Achievement, New York, NY

25,000 Memorial Sloan-Kettering Cancer Center, New York, NY

25,000 New York Public Library, New York, NY

11,500 Fordham University, New York, NY

10,000 Children's Health Fund, New York, NY

10,000 Environmental Defense Fund, New York, NY

10,000 Frost Valley, New York, NY

10,000 God's Love We Deliver, New York, NY

10,000 National Gallery of Art, Washington, DC

10,000 Yorkville Community Pantry, Yorkville, NY

Paley Foundation, Goldie

CONTACT
Alex Satinsky
Trustee
Goldie Paley Fdn.
2000 Market St., 10th Fl.
Philadelphia, PA 19103-3293

FINANCIAL SUMMARY
Recent Giving: $1,425,091 (fiscal 1991); $100,000 (fiscal 1990); $25,000 (fiscal 1989)
Assets: $398,559 (fiscal year ending October 31, 1991); $1,649,263 (fiscal 1990); $1,999,477 (fiscal 1989)
EIN: 23-6392054

CONTRIBUTIONS SUMMARY
Donor(s): the late Goldie Paley

Typical Recipients: • *Arts & Humanities:* arts institutes, museums/galleries
Grant Types: general support
Geographic Distribution: limited to Philadelphia, PA

GIVING OFFICERS
Patrick S. Gallagher: trust
William S. Paley: trust *B* Chicago IL 1901 *ED* Univ PA BS 1922; Adelphi Univ LLD 1957; Bates Coll LLD 1963; Univ PA LLD 1968; Columbia Univ LLD 1975; Brown Univ LLD 1975; Pratt Inst LLD 1977; Dartmouth Coll LLD 1979; Ithaca Coll LHD 1978; Univ Southern CA LHD 1985; Rutgers Univ LHD 1986; Long Island Univ LHD 1987 *CURR EMPL* chmn: CBS *CORP AFFIL* co-chmn: Intl Herald Tribune; fdr, dir: Genetics Inst, Thinking Machines Corp *NONPR AFFIL* dir: W. Averell Harriman Inst Advanced Study Soviet Union; fdr, chmn: Mus Broadcasting; life trust: Columbia Univ, Federation Jewish Philanthropies NY; mem: Academy Political Sciences, Counc Foreign Rels, France Am Soc, Natl Inst Social Sciences, Royal Soc Arts; trust: Mus Modern Art
Alex Satinsky: trust

APPLICATION INFORMATION
Initial Approach: Contributes only to preselected organizations. Applications not accepted.
Restrictions on Giving: Does not support individuals.

GRANTS ANALYSIS
Number of Grants: 2
Highest Grant: $1,325,091
Typical Range: $100,000 to $1,325,091
Disclosure Period: fiscal year ending October 31, 1991

RECENT GRANTS
1,325,091 Museum of Television and Radio, New York, NY

100,000 Moore College of Art and Design, Philadelphia, PA

Paley Foundation, William S.

CONTACT
Patrick S. Gallagher
Executive Director
William S. Paley Foundation
1 East 53rd St., Ste. 1400
New York, NY 10022
(212) 888-2520

FINANCIAL SUMMARY
Recent Giving: $1,456,250 (1991); $3,620,150 (1990); $755,150 (1989)
Assets: $65,172,135 (1991); $66,444,188 (1990); $19,599,451 (1989)
Gifts Received: $474,139 (1991); $47,615,299 (1990); $755,150 (1989)
Fiscal Note: In 1991, the foundation received $474,139 from the estate of William S. Paley.
EIN: 13-6085929

CONTRIBUTIONS SUMMARY
Donor(s): The foundation was established in 1936 by the late William S. Paley (1901-1990), the founder and former chairman of CBS. He bequeathed more than $40 million to the foundation from his estimated personal fortune of $460 million.

Mr. Paley, a native of Chicago, began his college education at the University of Chicago but earned his bachelor's of science degree form the University of Pennsylvania in 1922. He also received honorary PhDs from Ithaca College, University of Southern California, Adelphi University, Bates College, University of Pennsylvania, Brown University, Pratt Institute, Dartmouth College, and Columbia University, where he served as a trustee from 1950 to 1973.

Mr. Paley lived in New York City, home to two of his favorite charities, the Museum of Broadcasting, which he founded in 1976, and the Museum of Modern Art, where he served as chairman from 1972 to 1985. In his will, he left his valuable private art collection to the museum.

Mr. Paley, divorced from his first wife, married Barbara (Babe) Cushing in 1947. Barbara Paley died in 1978. Jeffrey Hearst and Hillary Hearst Byers were his two children from his first marriage to the

former Dorothy Hart Hearst. He has two stepchildren by his second marriage, Amanda Ross and Stanley Mortimer, III, and two children, Kate C. Paley and William C. Paley, who currently serve as officers of the foundation.

Typical Recipients: • *Arts & Humanities:* arts associations, dance, libraries, museums/galleries • *Civic & Public Affairs:* professional & trade associations, public policy, zoos/botanical gardens • *Education:* colleges & universities, international studies, literacy, medical education • *Health:* hospices, hospitals • *International:* foreign educational institutions • *Religion:* religious organizations • *Social Services:* youth organizations
Grant Types: general support, multiyear/continuing support, professorship, and scholarship
Geographic Distribution: focus on New York, NY

GIVING OFFICERS
Patrick S. Gallagher: exec dir
George Joseph Gillespie III: dir *B* New York NY 1930 *ED* Georgetown Univ AB 1952; Harvard Univ LLB 1955 *CURR EMPL* ptnr: Cravath Swaine & Moore *CORP AFFIL* dir: Fund Am, Washington Post Co *NONPR AFFIL* dir, chmn emeritus: Natl Multiple Sclerosis Soc; mem: Am Bar Assn, NY Bar Assn, NY City Bar Assn; pres: Boys Club Madison Square; secy: Mus Broadcasting; trust, treas: Hoover Inst
Sidney W. Harl: vp, treas, dir
Henry Alfred Kissinger: chmn, dir *B* Fuerth Germany 1923 *ED* Harvard Univ AB 1950; Harvard Univ MA 1952; Harvard Univ PhD 1954 *CURR EMPL* fdr, chmn: Kissinger Assocs *CORP AFFIL* mem intl adv comm: Chase Bank *NONPR AFFIL* mem: Am Academy Arts & Sciences, Am Political Science Assn, Counc Foreign Rels, Phi Beta Kappa; trust: Metro Mus Art
Arthur L. Liman: dir *B* New York NY 1932 *ED* Harvard Univ AB 1954; Yale Univ LLB 1957 *CURR EMPL* ptnr: Paul Weiss Rifkind Wharton & Garrison *CORP AFFIL* dir: Continental Grain Co, Equitable Life Assurance Soc US *NONPR AFFIL* chmn: Mayors Comm Appointments; dir: Harvard Univ; fellow: Am Bar Fdn, Am Coll Trial Lawyers; mem: Am

Bar Assn, Lawyers Comm Civil Rights Under Bd Overseers Harvard Univ, NY Bar Assn; mem exec comm: Bar Assn City NY
John S. Minary: vp, dir
Daniel L. Mosley: sec
Kate C. Paley: dir
Phillip A. Raspe: asst treas

APPLICATION INFORMATION
Initial Approach:
Proposals should be made in writing.
The foundation reports that no particular application form is required, but full financial information should be disclosed. There are no deadlines for forwarding proposals.
Restrictions on Giving: The foundation does not make grants to individuals.

GRANTS ANALYSIS
Total Grants: $1,456,250
Number of Grants: 5
Highest Grant: $1,216,250
Typical Range: $5,000 to $60,000
Disclosure Period: 1991
Note: The average grant figure excludes a single grant of $1,216,250. Recent grants are derived from a 1991 Form 990.

RECENT GRANTS
1,216,250 Museum of Television and Radio, New York, NY — general program
150,000 Greenpark Foundation, New York, NY — Paley Park
50,000 Congregation Emanu-El in the City of New York, New York, NY — general program
30,000 New York Public Library, New York, NY — general program
10,000 Citizens Committee for New York City, New York, NY — general program

Palin Foundation

CONTACT
John F. Philips
Vice President
Palin Fdn.
7200 Falls of the Neuse
Raleigh, NC 27615
(919) 676-0676

FINANCIAL SUMMARY
Recent Giving: $584,625 (1991); $614,640 (1990); $755,201 (1989)
Assets: $8,032,464 (1991); $7,669,787 (1990); $8,040,660 (1989)
EIN: 56-1490228

CONTRIBUTIONS SUMMARY
Donor(s): Clifton L. Benson, Jr.
Typical Recipients: • *Arts & Humanities:* history/historic preservation, museums/galleries, public broadcasting • *Education:* colleges & universities, health & physical education, public education (precollege) • *Health:* hospices, single-disease health associations • *Religion:* churches, religious organizations • *Social Services:* child welfare, recreation & athletics, united funds, youth organizations
Grant Types: capital and general support

GIVING OFFICERS
Clifton L. Benson, Jr.: pres
Clifton L. Benson III: treas
Margaret P. Benson: secy
John F. Philips: vp

APPLICATION INFORMATION
Initial Approach: Applications should include the organization name, address, and telephone number; name of chief officer; list of officers responsible for grant expenditure; detailed explanation or proposed use of grant, including dollar amount for each separate purpose, and expected time of expenditure; organization income statement and balance sheet for the five most recent fiscal years; and how and by whom organization officers and directors are selected. There are no deadlines.

GRANTS ANALYSIS
Number of Grants: 48
Highest Grant: $100,000
Typical Range: $500 to $16,000

Disclosure Period: 1991

RECENT GRANTS
100,000 Meredith College, Raleigh, NC
100,000 Poe Center for Health Education, Raleigh, NC
85,000 Fellowship of Christian Athletes, Raleigh, NC
63,975 Bayleaf Church, Raleigh, NC
50,000 Hale High School, Raleigh, NC
35,000 Bayleaf Baptist Church, Raleigh, NC — building fund
35,000 Wake Forest University, Winston-Salem, NC — athletic department
16,666 Tammy Lynn Center, Raleigh, NC — building fund
12,000 Wake Forest University, Winston-Salem, NC — general fund
10,000 Presbyterian Homes, Cary, NC

Palisades Educational Foundation

CONTACT
Ralph F. Anthony
President
Palisades Educational Fdn.
665 Fifth Avenue, 2nd Fl.
New York, NY 10022
(212) 688-5151

FINANCIAL SUMMARY
Recent Giving: $280,000 (1991); $391,000 (1990); $336,000 (1989)
Assets: $4,970,706 (1991); $4,640,154 (1990); $4,850,550 (1989)
EIN: 51-6015053

CONTRIBUTIONS SUMMARY
Donor(s): Prentice-Hall
Typical Recipients: • *Arts & Humanities:* libraries • *Education:* business education, colleges & universities, community & junior colleges, education associations, student aid • *Health:* hospitals, medical research, single-disease health associations • *Social Services:* child welfare, homes, recreation & athletics, youth organizations
Grant Types: multiyear/continuing support, operating expenses, and scholarship

Geographic Distribution: focus on areas of company operations, with emphasis on northern NJ, NY, and southern CT

GIVING OFFICERS
Frederick W. Anthony: secy
Ralph F. Anthony: pres, dir
Gerald J. Dunworth, Jr.: treas
Colin Gunn: trust
Donald A. Schaefer: vp, dir

APPLICATION INFORMATION
Initial Approach: Send brief letter of inquiry describing program or project. There are no deadlines.

Restrictions on Giving: Does not support individuals or provide loans.

GRANTS ANALYSIS
Number of Grants: 29
Highest Grant: $90,000
Typical Range: $1,000 to $10,000

Disclosure Period: 1991

RECENT GRANTS
90,000 University of Bridgeport, Bridgeport, CT
80,000 Developmental Learning Systems Foundation, Caldwell, NJ
25,000 Covenant House, New York, NY
20,000 American Leprosy Missions, Elmwood Park, NJ
20,000 Johns Hopkins Medical Center, Baltimore, MD
20,000 Johns Hopkins Medical Center, Baltimore, MD — Richard Starr Ross Fund
20,000 Johns Hopkins Medical Center School of Advanced Studies, Baltimore, MD
15,000 New York University, New York, NY — Gerstenberg Chair
15,000 University of Cape Town Fund, New York, NY
12,500 Caldwell College, Caldwell, NJ — scholarship Program

Palisano Foundation, Vincent and Harriet

CONTACT
Charles J. Palisano
Trustee
Vincent and Harriet Palisano
Fdn.
PO Box 538
Orchard Park, NY 14127

FINANCIAL SUMMARY
Recent Giving: $191,482 (fiscal 1992); $165,886 (fiscal 1991); $155,888 (fiscal 1989)
Assets: $4,198,138 (fiscal year ending May 31, 1992); $4,079,846 (fiscal 1991); $3,971,776 (fiscal 1990)
EIN: 16-6052186

CONTRIBUTIONS SUMMARY
Donor(s): the late Vincent H. Palisano, the late Harriet A. Paisano
Typical Recipients: • *Arts & Humanities:* libraries, public broadcasting • *Education:* colleges & universities, private education (precollege), special education • *Religion:* churches, religious organizations
Grant Types: scholarship
Geographic Distribution: focus on the Buffalo, NY, ar

GIVING OFFICERS
James G. Hurley: trust
Charles J. Palisano: trust
Joseph S. Palisano: trust

APPLICATION INFORMATION
Initial Approach: Send brief letter of inquiry describing program or project. There are no deadlines.

GRANTS ANALYSIS
Number of Grants: 31
Highest Grant: $50,000
Typical Range: $1,500 to $5,000
Disclosure Period: fiscal year ending May 31, 1992

RECENT GRANTS
50,000 Canisius College, Buffalo, NY
20,000 Trocaire College, Buffalo, NY — computers
19,625 Hilbert College, Buffalo, NY — computers
12,000 Daemon College, Buffalo, NY — library equipment
12,000 Medaille College, Buffalo, NY
10,000 Retirement Fund for Religious, Buffalo, NY
10,000 St. Anthony of Padua Church, Buffalo, NY
10,000 St. Mary's School for the Deaf, Buffalo, NY — computers
6,000 Canisius College, Buffalo, NY
3,500 D'Youville College, Buffalo, NY

Pall Corp.
Sales: $656.9 million
Employees: 6,400
Headquarters: East Hills, NY
SIC Major Group: Industrial Machinery & Equipment, Instruments & Related Products, and Transportation Equipment

CONTACT
Eric Krasnoff
Group Vice President
Pall Corp.
2200 Northern Blvd.
East Hills, NY 11548
(516) 484-5400

CONTRIBUTIONS SUMMARY
Operating Locations: CA (City of Industry), CT (Putnam), FL (New Port Richey, Ocala, Pinellas Park), NY (Cortland, East Hills, Glen Cove, Happauge), PR (Fajardo)

CORP. OFFICERS
Maurice G. Hardy: *B* Bristol England 1930 *ED* Merchant Ventures Engring Coll 1949 *CURR EMPL* pres, ceo, dir: Pall Corp

Abraham Kransoff: *CURR EMPL* chmn, dir: Pall Corp

Palm Beach Co.
Sales: $79.0 million
Employees: 2,500
Parent Company: Crystal Brands
Headquarters: Cincinnati, OH
SIC Major Group: Apparel & Other Textile Products

CONTACT
Lori Breiner-Wyllie
Director, Human Resources
Palm Beach Co.
400 Pke. St.
Cincinnati, OH 45202
(513) 241-4260

CONTRIBUTIONS SUMMARY
Nonmonetary Support Types: donated products, loaned employees, and loaned executives
Operating Locations: OH (Cincinnati)

CORP. OFFICERS
Ed Kaminow: *CURR EMPL* pres, ceo: Palm Beach Co

Palmer-Fry Memorial Trust, Lily

CONTACT
Diane Bookmiller
Lily Palmer-Fry Memorial Trust
c/o Connecticut Bank and Trust Co., N.A.
240 Greenwich Ave.
Hartford, CT 06830
(203) 629-4051

FINANCIAL SUMMARY
Recent Giving: $212,000 (1990); $220,200 (1988)
Assets: $3,995,205 (1990); $3,604,311 (1988)
EIN: 06-6033612

CONTRIBUTIONS SUMMARY
Donor(s): the late William Henry Fry
Typical Recipients: • *Civic & Public Affairs:* environmental affairs, zoos/botanical gardens • *Religion:* religious organizations • *Social Services:* child welfare, community service organizations, counseling, disabled, recreation & athletics, shelters/homelessness, united funds, youth organizations
Grant Types: general support and operating expenses
Geographic Distribution: focus on CT, NY, and NJ

GIVING OFFICERS
Caroline M. Fry: trust
Evelyn Fry Peterson: trust

APPLICATION INFORMATION
Initial Approach: Send cover letter and full proposal. Deadline is February 1.

GRANTS ANALYSIS
Number of Grants: 57
Highest Grant: $15,000
Typical Range: $1,000 to $7,500
Disclosure Period: 1990

RECENT GRANTS
15,000 Fresh Air Fund, New York, NY
8,000 Police Athletic League, New York, NY
8,000 YMCA, New York, NY
7,500 Camp Shelter Island, New York, NY
6,500 Camp Washington, New York, NY
6,000 Camp Sloane, New York, NY
6,000 Children's Aid Society, New York, NY
6,000 Goddard-Riverside Community Center, New York, NY
6,000 Lighthouse, New York, NY
6,000 YWCA, Brooklyn, NY

Palmer Fund, Francis Asbury

CONTACT
Frederick Carter
Francis Asbury Palmer Fund
c/o U.S. Trust Co. of New York
114 West 47th St.
New York, NY 10036
(212) 852-1000

FINANCIAL SUMMARY
Recent Giving: $165,000 (fiscal 1992); $350,000 (fiscal 1990); $150,000 (fiscal 1988)
Assets: $4,037,796 (fiscal year ending April 30, 1992); $3,598,201 (fiscal 1991); $3,181,987 (fiscal 1990)
EIN: 13-6400635

CONTRIBUTIONS SUMMARY
Donor(s): the late Francis Asbury Palmer
Typical Recipients: • *Education:* colleges & universities, religious education • *Religion:* churches, missionary activities, religious organizations • *Social Services:* child welfare, community service organizations, delinquency & crime, recreation & athletics
Grant Types: general support

GIVING OFFICERS
Frederic D. Carter, Jr.: pres

William A. Chisolm: trust
E. Gayle McGuigan, Jr.: trust
William H. Sword: trust

APPLICATION INFORMATION
Initial Approach: Contributes only to preselected organizations.

Restrictions on Giving: Does not support individuals.

GRANTS ANALYSIS
Number of Grants: 13
Highest Grant: $13,000
Typical Range: $9,000 to $13,000
Disclosure Period: fiscal year ending April 30, 1992

RECENT GRANTS
13,000 Defiance College, Defiance, OH
13,000 Elon College, Elon, NC
13,000 General Theological Seminary, New York, NY
13,000 Hartford Seminary, Hartford, CT
13,000 Harvard University Divinity School, Cambridge, MA
13,000 Houghton College, Houghton, NY
13,000 Princeton Theological Seminary, Princeton, NJ
13,000 Union Theological Seminary
13,000 Vanderbilt University Divinity School, Nashville, TN
13,000 Yale University, New Haven, CT

Palmer Fund, Frank Loomis

CONTACT
Mildred E. Devine
Vice President
Frank Loomis Palmer Fund
c/o Connecticut National Bank
250 Captain's Walk
New London, CT 06320
(203) 447-6133

FINANCIAL SUMMARY
Recent Giving: $991,466 (fiscal 1991); $745,118 (fiscal 1990); $774,739 (fiscal 1989)
Assets: $15,489,786 (fiscal year ending July 31, 1991); $14,490,952 (fiscal 1990); $13,980,570 (fiscal 1989)
EIN: 06-6026043

CONTRIBUTIONS SUMMARY
Donor(s): The foundation was established in 1936 by the late Virginia Palmer.
Typical Recipients: • *Arts & Humanities:* arts centers, arts festivals, history/historic preservation, museums/galleries, music, theater • *Civic & Public Affairs:* municipalities, professional & trade associations • *Education:* colleges & universities, literacy • *Health:* hospitals • *Religion:* churches • *Science:* scientific organizations • *Social Services:* child welfare, community service organizations, drugs & alcohol, emergency relief, family planning, family services, food/clothing distribution, recreation & athletics, youth organizations
Grant Types: capital, conference/seminar, matching, project, research, scholarship, and seed money
Geographic Distribution: limited to New London, CT

GIVING OFFICERS
Connecticut National Bank trust

APPLICATION INFORMATION
Initial Approach:
Initial contact should be by telephone to request an application and guidelines.
Proposal should include a completed application form, an audited financial statement for the most recent year or a treasurer's report, and a project budget (for organizations in the formative stages); an IRS tax-exempt letter dated after 1969; and a proposed operating budget for the period of time in which the desired grant will be used. For organizations that are new or unfamiliar to the foundation, a brief organizational background is required. Please see guidelines for additional requirements for churches and municipalities.
Completed applications including all required supporting data for grants must be submitted by May 15 and November 15 of each year. If these dates fall on a Saturday or Sunday, the deadline is not extended. Applications postmarked on the day of the deadline are accepted.
Restrictions on Giving:
Grants will be limited to activities conducted or organizations located in New London. Special consideration may be given to grantees whose programs offer the possibility of matching grants. Grants are not made to individuals, for endowments, for deficit financing, or for reimbursement for items purchased prior to grant request.

OTHER THINGS TO KNOW
Publications: informational brochure including application guidelines

GRANTS ANALYSIS
Total Grants: $991,466
Number of Grants: 66
Highest Grant: $70,000
Typical Range: $1,000 to $20,000
Disclosure Period: fiscal year ending July 31, 1991
Note: Recent grants are derived from a fiscal 1991 grants list.

RECENT GRANTS
70,000 Garde Arts Center, New London, CT — arts education project
55,000 Garde Arts Center, New London, CT — outreach program
55,000 Thames Science Center, New London, CT — project robotacts
50,000 Thames Science Center, New London, CT — implement project magnet
37,500 Lawrence and Memorial Hospital, New London, CT
37,500 Lawrence and Memorial Hospital, New London, CT
37,500 Lawrence and Memorial Hospital, New London, CT
30,000 Mitchell College, New London, CT
29,600 Williams School, New London, CT — scholarships
28,613 Center A Drop In Community, New London, CT

Pamida, Inc. / Pamida Foundation
Sales: $638.1 million
Employees: 6,300
Parent Company: Pamida Holdings Corp.
Headquarters: Omaha, NE
SIC Major Group: General Merchandise Stores

CONTACT
Richard W. Ramm
Executive Vice President and Chief Executive Officer
Pamida Fdn.
PO Box 3856
Omaha, NE 68103-0856
(402) 339-2400

FINANCIAL SUMMARY
Recent Giving: $59,546 (fiscal 1991); $70,575 (fiscal 1989)
Assets: $271,395 (fiscal year ending January 31, 1991); $258,080 (fiscal 1989)
Gifts Received: $50,000 (fiscal 1991); $30,000 (fiscal 1989)
Fiscal Note: In 1991, contributions were received from Pamida.
EIN: 47-0656225

CONTRIBUTIONS SUMMARY
Typical Recipients: • *Arts & Humanities:* arts funds, general, libraries, museums/galleries • *Civic & Public Affairs:* general • *Education:* colleges & universities, general, private education (precollege) • *Health:* general, health funds • *Social Services:* general, recreation & athletics
Grant Types: challenge, conference/seminar, emergency, endowment, and general support
Geographic Distribution: in headquarters and operating communities
Operating Locations: IA, IL, KS, MI, MN, MO, MT, ND, NE, SD, WI, WY

CORP. OFFICERS
C. Clayton Burkstrand: *B* Kimball MN 1934 *ED* Univ MN *CURR EMPL* chmn, ceo: Pamida
Frank Schlosser: *B* Peoria IL 1941 *CURR EMPL* pres, coo: Pamida

GIVING OFFICERS
Karen Montague: vp
Richard W. Ramm: pres, treas *B* Omaha NE 1949 *ED* Univ NE 1972 *CURR EMPL* exec vp, cfo: Pamida *NONPR AFFIL*

mem: Am Inst CPAs, Natl Assn
Accts
Frank Washburn: vp
Byron Wolff: vp

APPLICATION INFORMATION

Initial Approach: Send a brief letter of inquiry including a description of organization, amount requested, purpose of funds sought, and proof of tax-exempt status. There are no deadlines.
Restrictions on Giving: Does not support individuals, religious organizations for sectarian purposes, political or lobbying groups, or organizations outside operating areas.

GRANTS ANALYSIS

Number of Grants: 46
Highest Grant: $10,000
Typical Range: $500 to $5,000
Disclosure Period: fiscal year ending January 31, 1991

RECENT GRANTS

10,000 Brownell-Talbot School, Omaha, NE
10,000 Creighton University, Omaha, NE
2,000 OPS Special Olympics, Omaha, NE
2,000 University of Nebraska at Omaha, Omaha, NE — Maverick Club — athletic fund
2,000 US National Ski Hall of Fame and Museum, Ishpeming, MI — building fund
1,000 Carlton Amateur Hockey Association, Carlton, MN — purchase equipment
1,000 Cloquet Community Memorial Hospital Foundation, Cloquet, MN — replace hospital equipment
1,000 Donna Reed Foundation for the Performing Arts, Denison, IA — general scholarship funding
1,000 Horizons Unlimited of Palo Alto County, Emmetsburg, IA — to purchase furnishing for two new group homes
100 Friends of Clintonville Library, Clintonville, WI — to help furnish new library with shelves and furniture

Pan-American Life Insurance Co.

Premiums: $377.19 million
Employees: 1,324
Headquarters: New Orleans, LA
SIC Major Group: Insurance Carriers

CONTACT

Eileen Lumar-Johnson
Manager, Public Relations
Pan-American Life Insurance Co.
Pan-American Life Center
New Orleans, LA 70130
(504) 566-3753

FINANCIAL SUMMARY

Recent Giving: $250,000 (1993 est.); $250,000 (1992)
Fiscal Note: Company gives directly.

CONTRIBUTIONS SUMMARY

Typical Recipients: • *Arts & Humanities:* museums/galleries, public broadcasting • *Civic & Public Affairs:* better government, business/free enterprise, economic development • *Education:* business education, colleges & universities, general • *Health:* general, medical rehabilitation, medical research, mental health • *Religion:* churches • *Social Services:* community service organizations, general, shelters/homelessness, volunteer services, youth organizations
Grant Types: award, capital, challenge, conference/seminar, employee matching gifts, general support, multiyear/continuing support, research, and scholarship
Nonmonetary Support Types: donated equipment, loaned employees, and loaned executives
Geographic Distribution: primarily headquarters area
Operating Locations: LA (New Orleans)

CORP. OFFICERS

G. Frank Purvis, Jr.: *B* Rayville LA 1914 *ED* Kemper Military Sch & Coll AA 1932; LA St Univ LLB 1935 *CURR EMPL* chmn, dir: Pan-Am Life Ins Co *CORP AFFIL* chmn, dir: Intl Reinsurance Co; dir: First Natl Bank Commerce, Pan-American de Colombia Compania de Seguros de Vi Da SA; pres, dir: Compania de Seguros Panamericana SA; dir: First Commerce Corp *NONPR AFFIL* chmn: Bus Task Force Ed, SS Huebner Fdn Ins Ed;

chmn, bd govs: Intl Ins Seminars; dir: Bus Govt Res, Council Better LA, Family Svc Soc New Orleans, New Orleans Philharmonic Symphony Soc, Summer Pop Concerts; mem: Am Bar Assn, Am Judicature Soc, Assn Life Ins Counc, Chamber Commerce Greater New Orleans Area, Health Ins Assn Am, Intl Trade Admin, LA Bar Assn, LA Independent Coll Fund, LA Law Inst, New Orleans Assn Life Underwriters; mem adv bd: Baptist Hosp, Salvation Army; mem bd commnrs: Port New Orleans; pres: YMCA New Orleans
John K. Roberts, Jr.: *B* Omaha NE 1936 *ED* Univ IA BA 1959 *CURR EMPL* pres, ceo, dir: Pan-Am Life Ins Co *CORP AFFIL* dir: Whitney Holding Corp, Whitney Natl Bank New Orleans *NONPR AFFIL* dir: Childrens Hosp, Un Way Greater New Orleans Area, YMCA; fellow: Soc Actuaries; mem: Am Academy Actuaries, Am Counc Life Ins, Health Ins Assn Am, Life Off Mgmt Assn

GIVING OFFICERS

Eileen Lumar-Johnson: *CURR EMPL* mgr pub rels: Pan-Am Life Ins Co

APPLICATION INFORMATION

Initial Approach: *Initial Contact:* brief letter of inquiry *Include Information On:* a description of organization, amount requested, purpose of funds sought, and proof of tax-exempt status *When to Submit:* any time
Restrictions on Giving: Does not support individuals or organizations outside operating areas.

GRANTS ANALYSIS

Typical Range: $50 to $1,000

Pangburn Foundation

CONTACT

Robert Lansford
Pangburn Fdn.
PO Box 2050
Ft. Worth, TX 76113
(817) 884-4151

FINANCIAL SUMMARY

Recent Giving: $351,000 (fiscal 1992); $277,050 (fiscal 1991); $236,500 (fiscal 1990)

Assets: $5,188,211 (fiscal year ending March 31, 1992); $5,199,722 (fiscal 1991); $5,105,115 (fiscal 1990)
EIN: 75-6042630

CONTRIBUTIONS SUMMARY

Typical Recipients: • *Arts & Humanities:* arts associations, community arts, dance, music, opera, public broadcasting • *Civic & Public Affairs:* zoos/botanical gardens • *Social Services:* family services, youth organizations
Grant Types: general support
Geographic Distribution: limited to the Fort Worth, TX, area

GIVING OFFICERS

Team Bank: trust

APPLICATION INFORMATION

Initial Approach: Send brief letter of inquiry and full proposal. Deadline is September 30.
Restrictions on Giving: Does not support individuals.

GRANTS ANALYSIS

Number of Grants: 22
Highest Grant: $50,000
Typical Range: $1,000 to $10,000
Disclosure Period: fiscal year ending March 31, 1992

RECENT GRANTS

50,000 Fort Worth Ballet Association, Ft. Worth, TX
50,000 Fort Worth Ballet Association, Ft. Worth, TX
50,000 Fort Worth Symphony Orchestra Association, Ft. Worth, TX
30,000 Fort Worth Zoological Association, Ft. Worth, TX
25,000 First Texas Council of Camp Fire, Ft. Worth, TX
16,000 Texas Christian University, Ft. Worth, TX
15,000 Fort Worth Opera Association, Ft. Worth, TX
15,000 KERA, Dallas, TX
15,000 North Texas Public Broadcasting, Dallas, TX
12,000 Fort Worth Symphony Orchestra Association, Ft. Worth, TX

Panhandle Eastern Corp.

Revenue: $2.44 billion
Employees: 5,121
Headquarters: Houston, TX
SIC Major Group: Coal Mining, Electric, Gas & Sanitary Services, Holding & Other Investment Offices, and Oil & Gas Extraction

CONTACT

Marla Bernard
Manager, Community Relations
Panhandle Eastern Corp.
5400 Westheimer Ct.
Houston, TX 77056-5310
(713) 627-4078

FINANCIAL SUMMARY

Recent Giving: $2,200,000 (1993 est.); $2,355,629 (1992); $1,800,000 (1991 est.)
Fiscal Note: All contributions are made directly by the company and its subsidiaries. In 1990, giving by subsidiaries totaled $80,000.

CONTRIBUTIONS SUMMARY

Typical Recipients: • *Arts & Humanities:* arts associations, arts centers, libraries, museums/galleries, music, opera, performing arts • *Civic & Public Affairs:* economics, urban & community affairs, zoos/botanical gardens • *Education:* business education, career/vocational education, colleges & universities, economic education, education funds, elementary education, engineering education, minority education, private education (precollege), public education (precollege), science/technology education • *Health:* hospitals, medical research • *Social Services:* aged, child welfare, community service organizations, drugs & alcohol, employment/job training, recreation & athletics, shelters/homelessness, united funds, volunteer services
Grant Types: capital, employee matching gifts, endowment, fellowship, general support, professorship, and research
Note: Company matches dollar-for-dollar employee gifts to education, arts and culture, hospitals, and health-related research.
Nonmonetary Support Types: donated equipment, in-kind services, loaned employees, and loaned executives

Note: In 1992, nonmonetary giving was valued at $150,000 and is not included in the above giving total. In 1990, nonmonetary giving was valued at $60,000 and is not included in the above giving total.
Geographic Distribution: primarily in Houston metropolitan area
Operating Locations: DC, MA (Boston), NY (New York), TX (Houston)

CORP. OFFICERS

Dennis Ralph Hendrix: *B* Selmer TN 1940 *ED* Univ TN BS 1962; GA St Univ MBA 1965 *CORP AFFIL* chmn, pres, ceo: TX Eastern Corp; dir: First City Bancorp TX; pres, ceo, chmn, dir: Panhandle Eastern Corp *NONPR AFFIL* dir: Am Petroleum Inst, DePelchin Childrens Ctr, Greater Houston Partnership, Harris Co Childrens Protective Svcs Fund, Natl Jr Achievement, Natl Ocean Indus Assn, TX Med Ctr, TX South Coast Un Way, Univ TN Devel Counc; mem: Interstate Natural Gas Assn Am, Natl Petroleum Counc, TX Dept Corrections; mem adv bd bus sch: GA St Univ; mem, dir: Am Gas Assn, Counc Higher Ed, Natl Assn Mfrs; trust: Brescia Coll

GIVING OFFICERS

Marla Barnard: *CURR EMPL* mgr (community rels): Panhandle Eastern Corp

APPLICATION INFORMATION

Initial Approach: *Initial Contact:* brief letter or proposal *Include Information On:* organization's goals and purpose, project and purpose for which funds are being requested, proposed budget for the project, any benefits the company will receive as a contributor, a list of board of directors, a financial statement and/or annual report, a list of other organizations contributing, and any other pertinent or helpful information *When to Submit:* October 1

OTHER THINGS TO KNOW

Texas Eastern Corporation and its giving program were acquired by Panhandle Eastern Corporation in 1989. Texas

Eastern is now a subsidiary of Panhandle Eastern.

GRANTS ANALYSIS

Total Grants: $2,355,629*
Typical Range: $1,000 to $10,000
Disclosure Period: 1992
Note: Total grants figure includes $300,000 in employee matching gifts and $150,000 donated from individual field locations.

Pannill Scholarship Foundation, William Letcher

CONTACT

William Letcher Pannill Scholarship Fdn.
PO Box 5151
Martinsville, VA 24115

FINANCIAL SUMMARY

Recent Giving: $183,873 (fiscal 1992); $190,444 (fiscal 1991); $186,479 (fiscal 1990)
Assets: $1,996,840 (fiscal year ending February 28, 1992); $2,053,368 (fiscal 1991); $2,073,473 (fiscal 1990)
EIN: 52-1375635

CONTRIBUTIONS SUMMARY

Grant Types: scholarship
Geographic Distribution: focus on VA, NC, FL and AL

GIVING OFFICERS

Frank M. Lacey, Jr.: pres
Lucy C. Martix: off
William L. Pannill: treas
James C. Smith, Jr.: vp
Lucy C. Wilson: secy

APPLICATION INFORMATION

Initial Approach: Applicants must have worked for Pannill or its predecessor for three or more years. There are no deadlines.

OTHER THINGS TO KNOW

Provides educational grants to children of Pannill employees.
Disclosure Period: fiscal year ending February 28, 1992

Pantasote Polymers

Revenue: $15.0 million
Employees: 47
Parent Company: Newsote
Headquarters: Passaic, NJ
SIC Major Group: Chemicals & Allied Products, Paper & Allied Products, and Rubber & Miscellaneous Plastics Products

CONTACT

Jeffrey Podell
President
Pantasote, Inc.
26 Jefferson St.
Passaic, NJ 07055
(201) 777-8500

CONTRIBUTIONS SUMMARY

Operating Locations: NJ (Passaic)

CORP. OFFICERS

Jeffrey Podell: *CURR EMPL* pres: Pantasote
Harry A. Russell: *B* Czech Republic 1919 *ED* Columbia Coll 1943 *CURR EMPL* vchmn: Pantasote
Henry W. Wyman: *B* Aussig Czech Republic 1919 *ED* Columbia Univ 1943; NY Univ 1944 *CURR EMPL* chmn: Pantasote *CORP AFFIL* dir: Europaische HO Canfield Co Gmbh, Industria Ossidi Sinterizzati; pres: Ilpra Srl Viale dell'Industria *NONPR AFFIL* mem: Am Arbitration Assn; pres: Panwy Fdn
Ralph M. Wyman: *B* Usti Czech Republic 1926 *ED* NY Univ 1945 *CURR EMPL* vchmn: Pantasote *CORP AFFIL* chmn: Eagle Capital Mgmt; managing ptnr: Eagle Mgmt Co, Un Eagle Mgmt Co; pres, dir: Elbe, Veritas; ptnr: Unitas Co *NONPR AFFIL* pres: Panwy Fdn

Pappas Charitable Foundation, Bessie

CONTACT

Betsy Pappas
Director of Development
Bessie Pappas Charitable Fdn.
PO Box 318
Belmont, MA 02178
(617) 862-2851

FINANCIAL SUMMARY

Recent Giving: $162,500 (1991); $128,500 (1989); $125,074 (1988)

Assets: $3,733,697 (1991); $3,164,641 (1989); $2,857,177 (1988)
EIN: 22-2540702

CONTRIBUTIONS SUMMARY
Donor(s): Thomas Anthony Pappas
Typical Recipients: • *Arts & Humanities:* community arts, museums/galleries, music, performing arts, theater • *Civic & Public Affairs:* municipalities • *Education:* minority education, private education (precollege), special education • *Health:* health organizations, hospitals, pediatric health, single-disease health associations • *Social Services:* disabled
Grant Types: general support
Geographic Distribution: focus on MA

GIVING OFFICERS
Betsy Z. Pappas: clerk, dir devel
Charles A. Pappas: pres, treas, dir
Helen K. Pappas: vp, dir
Sophia Pappas: trust
Donald J. Young: dir

APPLICATION INFORMATION
Initial Approach: Send brief letter describing program. Deadline is October 1.
Restrictions on Giving: Does not support individuals.

OTHER THINGS TO KNOW
Publications: Application Guidelines

GRANTS ANALYSIS
Number of Grants: 31
Highest Grant: $20,000
Typical Range: $1,000 to $6,000
Disclosure Period: 1991

RECENT GRANTS
20,000 Massachusetts Eye and Ear Infirmary, Boston, MA
20,000 Town of Belmont, Belmont, MA
10,000 American Hellenic Educational Center, Portland, OR
10,000 Combined Jewish Philanthropies, Boston, MA
7,500 Bridge, Boston, MA
7,000 Boston Aid to the Blind, Boston, MA
6,000 Boston Symphony Orchestra, Boston, MA

5,000 Clarke School for the Deaf, Northampton, MA
5,000 Museum of Science, Boston, MA
5,000 Odwin Learning Center, Dorchester, MA

Pappas Charitable Foundation, Thomas Anthony

CONTACT
Betsy Pappas
Thomas Anthony Pappas Charitable Fdn.
PO Box 463
Belmont, MA 02178-0463
(617) 862-2802

FINANCIAL SUMMARY
Recent Giving: $701,000 (1991); $722,500 (1990); $740,750 (1989)
Assets: $19,599,727 (1991); $18,089,636 (1990); $17,804,417 (1989)
EIN: 51-0153284

CONTRIBUTIONS SUMMARY
Donor(s): The foundation was incorporated in 1975 by the late Thomas Anthony Pappas.
Typical Recipients: • *Arts & Humanities:* arts centers, dance • *Civic & Public Affairs:* economic development, law & justice, philanthropic organizations, professional & trade associations, zoos/botanical gardens • *Education:* colleges & universities, medical education, private education (precollege), science/technology education • *Health:* hospitals, pediatric health, single-disease health associations • *Religion:* churches, religious organizations • *Social Services:* disabled, emergency relief, recreation & athletics, youth organizations
Grant Types: capital, endowment, fellowship, multi-year/continuing support, research, and scholarship
Geographic Distribution: focus on Massachusetts

GIVING OFFICERS
Betsy Z. Pappas: clerk, dir
Charles A. Pappas: pres, dir
Helen K. Pappas: vp, dir
Sophia Pappas: asst clerk
Donald J. Young: dir

APPLICATION INFORMATION
Initial Approach:
The foundation requests applications be made in writing. Applications should include the name, address, telephone number, and individual to contact; the purpose of the organization; the amount requested; the organization's other sources of support; a detailed description of the project and the use of the funds requested; and an IRS current exemption status and a copy of the latest determination letter.
The deadline for submitting proposals is September 30.
Restrictions on Giving: The foundation reports no private foundations will be considered without complete expenditure control. The foundation does not make grants to individuals.

OTHER THINGS TO KNOW
Publications: program policy statement and application guidelines

GRANTS ANALYSIS
Total Grants: $701,000
Number of Grants: 48
Highest Grant: $100,000
Typical Range: $1,000 to $15,000
Disclosure Period: 1991
Note: Average grant figure does not include the highest grant of $100,000. Recent grants are derived from a 1991 grants list.

RECENT GRANTS
100,000 Children's Hospital, Boston, MA
75,000 Massachusetts General Hospital, Boston, MA
65,000 Massachusetts General Hospital, Boston, MA
50,000 Harvard Dental School, Cambridge, MA
50,000 Kravis Center for the Performing Arts, West Palm Beach, FL
50,000 Mount Auburn Hospital, Cambridge, MA
50,000 Tufts University, Medford, MA
25,000 Boston University, Boston, MA
25,000 Massachusetts General Hospital, Boston, MA

25,000 Massachusetts Institute of Technology, Boston, MA

Paramount Communications Inc. / Paramount Communications Foundation

Sales: $4.26 billion
Employees: 12,900
Headquarters: New York, NY
SIC Major Group: Business Services, Communications, Motion Pictures, and Printing & Publishing

CONTACT
Paramount Communications Fdn.
15 Columbus Circle
New York, NY 10023
(212) 373-8000
Note: Company does not list a contact person.

FINANCIAL SUMMARY
Recent Giving: $1,242,485 (fiscal 1991); $2,300,000 (fiscal 1990 approx.); $2,500,000 (fiscal 1989 approx.)
Assets: $174,860 (fiscal year ending October 31, 1991); $170,731 (fiscal 1990); $163,778 (fiscal 1988)
Fiscal Note: Company gives only through the foundation. During 1990, the foundation was not accepting new grant requests (see "Their Priorities" section below).
EIN: 13-6089816

CONTRIBUTIONS SUMMARY
Typical Recipients: • *Arts & Humanities:* arts associations, arts centers, arts institutes, cinema, dance, history/historic preservation, museums/galleries, opera, public broadcasting, theater • *Civic & Public Affairs:* better government, business/free enterprise, civil rights, economic development, economics, environmental affairs, international affairs, professional & trade associations, public policy, women's affairs, zoos/botanical gardens • *Education:* business education, career/vocational education, colleges & universities, economic education, education administration, education associations, education funds, elementary education, literacy, medical education, minority education, private education (precollege),

student aid • *Health:* hospices, mental health, nursing services, single-disease health associations • *Social Services:* aged, child welfare, recreation & athletics, united funds

Grant Types: employee matching gifts

Geographic Distribution: primarily in corporate operating locations

Operating Locations: CA (Los Angeles), CT (Norwalk, Waterford), MA (Needham Heights), NJ (Englewood Cliffs, Paramus), NY (New Hyde Park, New York), OH (Cleveland, Independence)

CORP. OFFICERS

Martin S. Davis: *B* New York NY 1927 *ED* NY Univ; City Univ NY *CURR EMPL* chmn, ceo, dir: Paramount Communs *NONPR AFFIL* co chrmn steering comm: Barbara Bush Fdn Family Literacy; dir: Natl Multiple Sclerosis Soc; trust: Carnegie Hall, Comm Econ Devel, Econ Club, Fordham Univ, John Jay Coll Criminal Justice, NY Univ Med Ctr

GIVING OFFICERS

Susan H. Morrisroe: secy

Raymond M. Nowak: treas *B* Yonkers NY 1952 *ED* Univ Hartford 1974 *CURR EMPL* vp (accounting & systems): Paramount Communs *CORP AFFIL* exec vp, cfo: Madison Square Garden *NONPR AFFIL* mem: Am Inst CPAs, Fin Execs Inst, Inst Mgmt Accts, Natl Assn Accts

Donald Oresman: trust *B* New York NY 1925 *ED* Oberlin Coll 1946; Columbia Univ Law Sch 1957 *CURR EMPL* exec vp, secy, coun, mem exec comm, dir: Paramount Communs *CORP AFFIL* dir: Assocs Corp North Am, Assocs First Capital Corp, Northamerican Watch Corp

Samuel J. Silberman: chmn *CURR EMPL* dir: Paramount Communs

APPLICATION INFORMATION

Initial Approach: *Initial Contact:* unsolicited proposals and proposals from external sources are not considered

Restrictions on Giving: Generally does not support political or lobbying groups, religious organizations for sectarian purposes, or individuals.

OTHER THINGS TO KNOW

Company and foundation changed name from Gulf+Western in 1989.

Foundation does not consider unsolicited proposals or proposals from external sources.

GRANTS ANALYSIS

Total Grants: $1,242,485*

Number of Grants: 894

Highest Grant: $196,335

Typical Range: $1,000 to $10,000

Disclosure Period: fiscal year ending October 31, 1991

Note: Total grants figure includes $279,885 in matching gifts. Average grant figure excludes two grants for $196,335 and $100,000. Recent grants are derived from a fiscal 1991 Form 990.

RECENT GRANTS

196,335 United Way — various chapters
100,000 Lincoln Center Consolidated Corporate Fund
50,000 Academy Foundation, Beverly Hills, CA
50,000 Ronald Reagan Presidential Foundation, Washington, DC
49,390 National Merit Scholarship Corporation, Evanston, IL
42,000 Carnegie Hall, New York, NY — capital campaign
31,000 Permanent Charities Committee of Entertainment Industries, Studio City, CA
25,000 American Diabetes Association, Manchester, NH
25,000 Children's Rescue Fund, Kisco, NY
25,000 Operation Welcome Home-NYC, New York, NY

Pardee Construction Co.

Sales: $330.0 million
Employees: 400
Parent Company: Weyerhaeuser Co.
Headquarters: Los Angeles, CA
SIC Major Group: General Building Contractors

CONTACT

Donna Sanders
Administration
Pardee Construction Co.
10880 Wilshire Blvd., Ste. 1400
Los Angeles, CA 90024
(310) 475-3525

CONTRIBUTIONS SUMMARY

Operating Locations: CA (Los Angeles)

CORP. OFFICERS

David Landon: *CURR EMPL* pres: Pardee Construction Co

Pardee Foundation, Elsa U.

CONTACT

Lucille M. Dougherty
Staff Assistant
Elsa U. Pardee Foundation
Box 1866
Midland, MI 48641-1866
(517) 832-3691

FINANCIAL SUMMARY

Recent Giving: $3,012,259 (1992); $2,940,971 (1991); $3,277,281 (1990)
Assets: $64,904,155 (1992); $62,145,099 (1991); $55,734,695 (1990)
EIN: 38-6065799

CONTRIBUTIONS SUMMARY

Donor(s): Mrs. Elsa U. Pardee established the foundation in 1944 through a bequest of 8,000 shares of Dow Chemical Company stock, then valued at about $1 million, for the fight against cancer. Since then, the value of the stock has risen considerably. Mrs. Pardee, who was the wife of James T. Pardee, a chairman of Dow Chemical Co., died of cancer in 1944. The will also established a trust for the use and benefit of the Starr Commonwealth for Boys.

Typical Recipients: • *Health:* hospitals, medical research

Grant Types: project, research, and seed money

Geographic Distribution: national; no geographic restrictions

GIVING OFFICERS

Gail E. Allen: pres
W. James Allen: asst treas, asst secy
Carl Allan Gerstacker: vp, treas *B* Cleveland OH 1916 *ED* Univ MI BS 1938; Central MI

Coll Ed LLD 1957 *CURR EMPL* dir: Dundee Cement Co *CORP AFFIL* dir: Chemical Fin Corp, Eaton Corp, K mart Corp, Sara Lee Corp *NONPR AFFIL* mem: Japan-US Friendship Comm, Mfg Chemists Assn; mem adv bd: New Perspective Fund; trust: Albion Coll, Rockefeller Univ Counc

Lisa J. Gerstacker: trust
James A. Kendall: secy
Richard J. Kociba, PhD: trust, chmn med comm
Michael S. Leahy, MD: trust, mem med comm
Patrick J. Oriel: trust
Alan W. Ott: trust
Norman C. Rumple: asst treas
William D. Schuette: trust *B* Midland MI 1953 *ED* Georgetown Univ BSFS 1976; Univ San Francisco JD 1979 *NONPR AFFIL* mem: Midland Chamber Commerce, Midland Hosp Assn, Natl Rifle Assn

APPLICATION INFORMATION

Initial Approach:
Applications, available from the foundation upon written request, must accompany proposals.

Applications should include an enlarged title and description of the project; itemized budget (including other sources of funding); approval from institute where project is conducted; approval of local institutional review committee and a copy of consent (if human subjects are involved); recent reprints or other material that will complete the proposal; amount requested; duration of project; name of person to whom checks should be made payable; and the original proposal with six copies.

Applications may be sent any time during the year.

The board of trustees meets periodically to review applications.

Restrictions on Giving: The foundation does not give grants to individuals, and generally does not give to building funds, for equipment (except for specific projects), to fellowships, or for fund-raising campaigns.

OTHER THINGS TO KNOW

The foundation does not directly administer the programs which it supports. Yearly progress reports and a financial accounting of expenditures from the grantee are required.

The foundation reports that its has a goal of investing about 75% of its grant funds in research and the other 25% in patient assistance programs through Pardee treatment funds. The foundation also reports that as other projects are concluded it welcomes innovative, small-scale, short-term projects which may be difficult to fund elsewhere until some interesting results are obtained.

Publications: annual report

GRANTS ANALYSIS

Total Grants: $3,012,256
Number of Grants: 36
Highest Grant: $355,000
Typical Range: $25,000 to $150,000
Disclosure Period: 1992
Note: Recent grants are derived from a 1992 annual report.

RECENT GRANTS

355,000 Mid Michigan Alliance, Clare, MI — to assist in the control and cure of cancer through the program of the Cancer Treatment Committee of Clare, Gladwin, and Bay County

216,634 Health Research, Buffalo, NY — Roswell Park Memorial Institute — for the study of parameters that induce T-cell-mediated recognition of mammary adenocarcinomas by syngeneic C3Hf/He Mice; for the study of metastasis genes in ovarian carcinoma; for the study of endogenous retroviral sequ

200,000 Pardee Cancer Treatment Association of Greater Brazosport, Brazosport, TX — for a program supporting the cure and control of cancer

200,000 Pardee Cancer Treatment Fund of Midland, Midland, MI — to assist in the control and cure of cancer through the program of the Cancer Treatment Committee

167,083 Ohio State University, Columbus, OH — for the

study of type I and type II interleukin 1 (IL-1) receptors; for the study of topographic vaccine against HTLV-I infection; for the study of dietary fat as a promotor of mammary tumorigenesis in MMTV/v-Ha-ras transgenic mice

130,000 New York University, New York, NY — for the development of a vaccine to human malignant melanoma

126,907 University of California, CA — for the study of a mouse model of cancer and cyclin D1/bcl-1

120,000 John Muir Foundation — for a chemotherapy program for cancer patients in Contra Costa County, CA

104,292 Michigan Cancer Foundation, Detroit, MI — for the study of an immortal line of normal, human breast epithelial cells

102,443 University of Texas, TX — for study of marker potential of transforming growth factor alpha in breast and colon carcinomas; for study of vascular targeting: a new approach to the therapy of solid tumors

---

Parexel International Corp.

Sales: $42.0 million
Employees: 550
Headquarters: Cambridge, MA
SIC Major Group: Engineering & Management Services

CONTACT

Bob Hill
Finance Manager, N. American Operations
Parexel International Corp.
1 Alewife Pl.
Cambridge, MA 02140
(617) 487-9900

CONTRIBUTIONS SUMMARY

Operating Locations: MA (Cambridge)

CORP. OFFICERS

Josef H. VonRickenbach: *CURR EMPL* pres, treas: Parexel Intl Corp

RECENT GRANTS

George Washington University, Washington, DC

Parisian Inc.

Sales: $430.0 million
Employees: 5,000
Headquarters: Birmingham, AL
SIC Major Group: Apparel & Accessory Stores and Furniture & Homefurnishings Stores

CONTACT

Howard Koch
Director, Corporate Communications
Parisian Stores-Alabama
750 Lakeshore Pkwy.
Birmingham, AL 35211
(205) 940-4000

CONTRIBUTIONS SUMMARY

Nonmonetary Support Types: donated products and loaned executives
Operating Locations: AL (Birmingham)

CORP. OFFICERS

Donald E. Hess: *CURR EMPL* pres, ceo: Parisian Stores-AL
Emil C. Hess: *CURR EMPL* chmn: Parisian Stores-AL

Park Bank / Park Banks Foundation

Employees: 115
Headquarters: Milwaukee, WI

CONTACT

Cynthia K. Rutkowski
Secretary
Park Banks Foundation
7540 West Capitol Drive
Milwaukee, WI 53216
(414) 466-1940

FINANCIAL SUMMARY

Recent Giving: $92,035 (fiscal 1991); $94,727 (fiscal 1989)
Assets: $538,443 (fiscal year ending November 30, 1991); $512,177 (fiscal 1989)
Gifts Received: $125,000 (fiscal 1991); $119,000 (fiscal 1989)
Fiscal Note: In fiscal 1991, contributions were received from Park Bank.
EIN: 39-1365837

CONTRIBUTIONS SUMMARY

Typical Recipients: • *Arts & Humanities:* arts funds, performing arts • *Civic & Public Affairs:* housing, municipalities • *Education:* medical education • *Health:* hospitals • *Social Services:* child welfare, united funds
Grant Types: general support
Geographic Distribution: giving primarily in Milwaukee, WI
Operating Locations: WI (Milwaukee)

GIVING OFFICERS

Lorraine A. Kelly: dir
Michael J. Kelly: dir
P. Michael Mahoney: dir
Cynthia K. Rutkowski: secy
James W. Wright: vp, treas

APPLICATION INFORMATION

Initial Approach: Send a brief letter of inquiry and a full proposal. There are no deadlines.

GRANTS ANALYSIS

Number of Grants: 97
Highest Grant: $17,000
Typical Range: $500 to $1,000
Disclosure Period: fiscal year ending November 30, 1991

RECENT GRANTS

17,000 United Way, Milwaukee, WI

5,000 Medical College of Wisconsin, Milwaukee, WI

5,000 Milwaukee Redevelopment Corporation, Milwaukee, WI

3,500 United Performing Arts Fund, Milwaukee, WI

3,000 Columbia Hospital, Milwaukee, WI

3,000 Penfield Children's Center, Milwaukee, WI

2,500 Center for Blind and Visually Impaired Children, Milwaukee, WI

2,000 Harambee School Development Corporation, Milwaukee, WI

2,000 Medical College of Wisconsin, Milwaukee, WI

2,000 Neighborhood Housing Services, Milwaukee, WI

Park Communications Inc.

Revenue: $149.2 million
Employees: 2,370
Headquarters: Ithaca, NY
SIC Major Group:
  Communications, Instruments
  & Related Products, and
  Printing & Publishing

CONTACT

Jack Clairborne
Vice President & Assistant to
  Chairman
Park Communications Inc.
Ter. Hill, PO Box 550
Ithaca, NY 14851
(607) 272-9020
Note: Roy H. Park, chairman
  and chief executive officer, is
  another contact person at the
  same address.

CONTRIBUTIONS SUMMARY

Operating Locations: NY (Ithaca)

CORP. OFFICERS

Roy Hampton Park: *B* Dobson NC 1910 *ED* NC St Univ BS 1931; Keuka Coll LHD 1967 *CURR EMPL* chmn, ceo: Park Communs *CORP AFFIL* dir: Raymond Corp *NONPR AFFIL* chmn: NC St Univ Devel Counc; chmn bd trust: Ithaca Coll; dir: Sales Execs Club; mem: Agricultural Rels Counc, Am Agricultural Editors, Antique Automobile Club Am, Friends Ithaca Coll, Les Amis D'Escoffier Soc, Natl Press Club, NC Assn Broadcasters, NC St Univ Alumni Assn, Pub Rels Soc Am, VA Assn Broadcasters
Wright M. Thomas: *CURR EMPL* pres, coo, treas, dir: Park Communs

Park National Bank / Park National Corporation Foundation

Assets: $550.0 million
Employees: 342
Parent Company: Park National
  Corp.
Headquarters: Newark, OH
SIC Major Group: Depository
  Institutions

CONTACT

Stuart N. Parsons
Secretary & Treasurer
Park National Corporation Fdn.
c/o Park National Bank, P.O Box
  850
Newark, OH 43058-0850
(614) 349-8451

FINANCIAL SUMMARY

Recent Giving: $68,500 (1990)
Assets: $1,181,484 (1989)
EIN: 31-6429406

CONTRIBUTIONS SUMMARY

Typical Recipients: • *Arts & Humanities:* community arts, community arts, history/historic preservation, performing arts, theater • *Education:* colleges & universities, education funds • *Health:* hospitals • *Social Services:* community service organizations, united funds
Grant Types: general support
Geographic Distribution: focus on OH
Operating Locations: OH (Newark)

CORP. OFFICERS

John W. Alford: *B* Baltimore MD 1912 *ED* DePauw Univ AB 1935; Denison Univ DHL 1988 *CURR EMPL* chmn exec comm: Park Natl Corp *CORP AFFIL* chmn: Park Natl Bank; dir: Consolidated Computer Center, Contour Holdings, WE Schrider Co, Stocker & Sitler Oil Co *NONPR AFFIL* hon trust: Dawes Arboretum; life trust: Denison Univ; mem: Am Bankers Assn, Am Legion, Newark Chamber Commerce, OH Bankers Assn, OH Chamber Commerce; mem adv bd: Salvation Army; trust: Methodist Theological Sch OH
William T. McConnell: *B* Zanesville OH 1933 *ED* Denison Univ 1955; Northwestern Univ Bus A 1959 *CURR EMPL* chmn: Park Natl Corp

GIVING OFFICERS

William T. McConnell: pres, dir *CURR EMPL* chmn: Park Natl Corp (see above)
Stuart N. Parsons: secy, treas, dir *B* Johnstown OH 1942 *ED* OH St Univ 1964-1969 *CURR EMPL* vp, trust off: Park Natl Corp

APPLICATION INFORMATION

Initial Approach: Send a brief letter of inquiry, including a description of organization, amount requested, purpose of funds sought, and proof of tax-exempt status. Foundation generally supports preselected organizations.
Restrictions on Giving: Does not support individuals, political or lobbying groups, or organizations outside operating areas.

GRANTS ANALYSIS

Number of Grants: 21
Highest Grant: $34,000
Typical Range: $1,000 to $6,000
Disclosure Period: 1990

RECENT GRANTS

34,000	United Way, Newark, OH
6,000	Ohio State University, Columbus, OH
5,000	Newark Catholic Foundation, Newark, OH
5,000	Richland Carousel Park, Mansfield, OH
4,000	Ohio Dominican College, Columbus, OH
3,000	Weathervane Playhouse, Newark, OH
2,500	Licking Memorial Hospital, Newark, OH
2,000	Ohio Business Week Foundation, Columbus, OH
1,000	Ashland College, Ashland, OH
1,000	Friends of Cornell School, Johnstown, OH

Park-Ohio Industries Inc.

Sales: $115.4 million
Employees: 1,160
Headquarters: Cleveland, OH
SIC Major Group: Chemicals &
  Allied Products, Industrial
  Machinery & Equipment,
  Rubber & Miscellaneous
  Plastics Products, and Stone,
  Clay & Glass Products

CONTACT

Nancy Milen
Office Manager
Park-Ohio Industries Inc.
20600 Chagrin Blvd.
Cleveland, OH 44122-5364
(216) 991-9700

FINANCIAL SUMMARY

Fiscal Note: Annual Giving
Range: less than $100,000

CONTRIBUTIONS SUMMARY

Company reports 85% of contributions support the United Way; 10% to health and welfare; and 5% to the arts.
Typical Recipients: • *Arts & Humanities:* general • *Social Services:* general, united funds
Grant Types: general support
Operating Locations: AL (Boaz), IL (Peotone), MI (Escanaba), OH (Cleveland, Mansfield), PA (East Butler)

CORP. OFFICERS

Edward F. Crawford: *CURR EMPL* chmn, pres, ceo: Park-OH Indus
Richard Smedley Sheetz: *B* Philadelphia PA 1924 *ED* Bucknell Univ BS Engring 1946; Harvard Univ MBA 1955 *CORP AFFIL* dir: Cedar Fair Mgmt Co, Cleveland-Cliffs Inc, Cleveland-Cliffs Iron Co

APPLICATION INFORMATION

Initial Approach: Send brief letter of inquiry. There are no deadlines.

OTHER THINGS TO KNOW

Does not provide nonmonetary support.

Parke-Davis Group

Employees: 2,500
Parent Company:
  Warner-Lambert Co.
Headquarters: Morris Plains, NJ
SIC Major Group: Chemicals &
  Allied Products

CONTACT

Evelyn Self
Director, Community Affairs
Parke-Davis Group
201 Tabor Rd.
Morris Plains, NJ 07950
(201) 540-2243

FINANCIAL SUMMARY

Recent Giving: $9,200,000
(1992 approx.); $9,200,000
(1991)
Fiscal Note: Company gives directly.

CONTRIBUTIONS SUMMARY

Typical Recipients: • *Arts & Humanities:* museums/galleries, music • *Education:* colleges & universities, community & junior colleges, medical education, minority education, science/technology education

• *Health:* hospitals, medical research • *Social Services:* disabled, domestic violence, emergency relief, shelters/homelessness, volunteer services, youth organizations

Grant Types: employee matching gifts, general support, project, and research

Nonmonetary Support Types: donated equipment, donated products, and in-kind services

Geographic Distribution: principally near operating locations and to national organizations

Operating Locations: NJ (Morris Plains)

CORP. OFFICERS
Joseph E. Smith: *CURR EMPL* pres: Parke-Davis Group

GIVING OFFICERS
Evelyn Self: *CURR EMPL* dir commun aff: Parke-Davis Group

APPLICATION INFORMATION
Initial Approach: *Initial Contact:* brief letter of inquiry and a full proposal *Include Information On:* a description of organization, amount requested, purpose of funds sought, recently audited financial statement, proof of tax-exempt status, and board make-up *When to Submit:* any time **Restrictions on Giving:** Does not support individuals, religious organizations for sectarian purposes, political or lobbying groups, or organizations outside operating areas.

GRANTS ANALYSIS
Typical Range: $2,500 to $5,000

Parker Brothers and Company Inc.
Sales: $150.0 million
Employees: 125
Headquarters: Beverly, MA
SIC Major Group: Miscellaneous Manufacturing Industries

CONTACT
Parker Brothers
50 Dunham Road
Beverly, MA 01915
(508) 927-7650

CONTRIBUTIONS SUMMARY
Operating Locations: MA (Beverly)

CORP. OFFICERS
Briscoe K. Parker, Jr.: *CURR EMPL* pres, ceo: Parker Brothers

OTHER THINGS TO KNOW
All charitable contributions are handled by Hasbro, Inc. (see separate entry).

Parker Drilling Co. / Parker Foundation, Robert L.
Sales: $112.8 million
Employees: 1,695
Headquarters: Tulsa, OK
SIC Major Group: Industrial Machinery & Equipment and Oil & Gas Extraction

CONTACT
Susan Cashon
Accountant
Robert L. Parker Fdn.
Parker Bldg., Eight East Third St.
Tulsa, OK 74103
(918) 631-1331

FINANCIAL SUMMARY
Recent Giving: $147,319 (1992); $181,700 (1991); $125,155 (1990)
Assets: $144,404 (1991); $308,656 (1990); $405,420 (1989)
Gifts Received: $300,000 (1989)
Fiscal Note: In 1989, contributions were received from Robert L. Parker.
EIN: 51-0153008

CONTRIBUTIONS SUMMARY
Typical Recipients: • *Arts & Humanities:* community arts, dance, museums/galleries • *Civic & Public Affairs:* zoos/botanical gardens • *Education:* colleges & universities • *Health:* medical research, single-disease health associations • *Religion:* churches, religious organizations • *Social Services:* community service organizations, shelters/homelessness, united funds, youth organizations

Grant Types: general support
Geographic Distribution: focus on OK
Operating Locations: OK (Tulsa)

CORP. OFFICERS
Robert L. Parker, Jr.: *B* Midland TX 1948 *ED* Univ TX

1971; Univ TX 1972 *CURR EMPL* pres, coo: Parker Drilling Co
Robert L. Parker, Sr.: *CURR EMPL* chmn, ceo: Parker Drilling Co

GIVING OFFICERS
Jack E. Short: trust

APPLICATION INFORMATION
Initial Approach: Contributes only to preselected organizations.

GRANTS ANALYSIS
Number of Grants: 27
Highest Grant: $90,000
Typical Range: $250 to $1,000
Disclosure Period: 1992

RECENT GRANTS
90,000 First United Methodist Church, Tulsa, OK
61,000 First United Methodist Church, Tulsa, OK
10,900 First United Methodist Church, Tulsa, OK
10,000 United Way, Tulsa, OK
1,000 Culver Educational Foundation, Culver, IN
1,000 First United Methodist Church, Cisco, TX
1,000 Mission Society for United Methodists, Decatur, GA
600 National Multiple Sclerosis Society, Tulsa, OK
500 Cowboy Artists of America Museum, Kerrville, TX
500 Mayo Foundation for Medical Research, Rochester, MN

Parker Foundation

CONTACT
Robbin C. Powell
Assistant Secretary
Parker Fdn.
1200 Prospect St., Ste. 575
La Jolla, CA 92037
(619) 456-3038

FINANCIAL SUMMARY
Recent Giving: $746,885 (fiscal 1991); $792,728 (fiscal 1990); $693,250 (fiscal 1989)
Assets: $14,334,070 (fiscal year ending September 30, 1991); $12,403,978 (fiscal 1990); $13,256,818 (fiscal 1989)

Gifts Received: $225,000 (fiscal 1991)
Fiscal Note: In 1991, contributions were received from the Carol Larsen Trust.
EIN: 51-0141231

CONTRIBUTIONS SUMMARY
Donor(s): the late Gerald T. Parker and Inez Grant Parker
Typical Recipients: • *Arts & Humanities:* arts institutes, community arts, history/historic preservation, libraries, museums/galleries, opera, theater • *Civic & Public Affairs:* zoos/botanical gardens • *Education:* colleges & universities, public education (precollege) • *Health:* hospitals, medical research, mental health, single-disease health associations • *Social Services:* child welfare, disabled, family planning, family services, youth organizations

Grant Types: capital, emergency, general support, multi-year/continuing support, operating expenses, project, research, and seed money

Geographic Distribution: limited to San Diego County, CA

GIVING OFFICERS
William E. Beamer: secy, treas, dir
John F. Borchers: dir
Roy M. Drew: dir
Judy McDonald: dir
Kenneth R. Rearwin: pres, dir
V. Dewitt Shuck: vp, dir

APPLICATION INFORMATION
Initial Approach: Contributes only to preselected organizations.
Restrictions on Giving: Does not support individuals or provide scholarships or loans.

OTHER THINGS TO KNOW
Publications: Annual Report, Informational Brochure (including Application Guidelines)

GRANTS ANALYSIS
Number of Grants: 58
Highest Grant: $100,000
Typical Range: $2,000 to $5,000
Disclosure Period: fiscal year ending September 30, 1991

RECENT GRANTS
100,000 Old Globe Theatre, San Diego, CA

100,000 San Diego Museum of Art, San Diego, CA

90,000 San Diego Symphony Orchestra, San Diego, CA

50,000 Sharp Hospital Foundation, San Diego, CA

40,000 San Diego Historical Society, San Diego, CA

35,000 Planned Parenthood Federation of America, San Diego, CA

30,000 San Diego Museum of Man, San Diego, CA

28,000 San Diego Aerospace Museum, San Diego, CA

15,600 La Jolla Stage Company, La Jolla, CA

12,500 San Diego City Schools, San Diego, CA

Parker Foundation, Theodore Edson

CONTACT
Andrew Bailey
Secretary, Treasurer
Theodore Edson Parker Fdn.
230 Congress St.
Boston, MA 02110
(617) 426-7172

FINANCIAL SUMMARY
Recent Giving: $490,400 (1991); $426,200 (1989)
Assets: $13,455,728 (1991); $11,037,695 (1989)
EIN: 04-6036092

CONTRIBUTIONS SUMMARY
Donor(s): the late Theodore Edson Parker
Typical Recipients: • *Arts & Humanities:* arts associations, community arts, community arts, theater • *Civic & Public Affairs:* housing, law & justice, rural affairs • *Education:* community & junior colleges • *Health:* hospitals, mental health • *Social Services:* child welfare, homes, shelters/homelessness, united funds, youth organizations
Grant Types: capital and project
Geographic Distribution: limited to the greater Boston and Lowell, MA, area

GIVING OFFICERS
Andrew C. Bailey: secy, treas, trust *B* Waltham MA 1921 *ED*

Amherst Coll AB 1944; Cornell Univ LLB 1948 *CURR EMPL* atty: Powers & Hall *NONPR AFFIL* mem: Am Bar Assn, Boston Bar Assn
Karen H. Carpenter: trust
Edward L. Emerson: trust
Newell Flather: pres, trust
Thomas E. Leggat: trust
Ala H. Reid: adm

APPLICATION INFORMATION
Initial Approach: Telephone foundation or send brief letter of inquiry. There are no deadlines.
Restrictions on Giving: Does not support individuals.

OTHER THINGS TO KNOW
Publications: Application Guidelines

GRANTS ANALYSIS
Number of Grants: 26
Highest Grant: $40,000
Typical Range: $5,000 to $30,000
Disclosure Period: 1991

RECENT GRANTS
40,000 Lowell Plan, Lowell, MA

35,000 Merrimack Repertory Theatre, Merrimack, MA

35,000 YWCA, Lowell, MA

30,000 Coalition for a Better Acre, Merrimack, MA

30,000 United Way, Merrimack, MA

30,000 University of Lowell Research Foundation, Lowell, MA

25,000 Boys and Girls Club, Boston, MA

25,000 Cambodian Mutual Assistance Association, Lowell, MA

25,000 Merrimack Valley Housing Partnership, Merrimack, MA

25,000 Middlesex Community College, Middlesex, MA

Parker-Hannifin Corp. / Parker-Hannifin Foundation

Sales: $2.38 billion
Employees: 27,000
Headquarters: Cleveland, OH
SIC Major Group: Industrial Machinery & Equipment

CONTACT
Joseph D. Whiteman
Vice President, Secretary & General Counsel
Parker-Hannifin Fdn.
17325 Euclid Ave.
Cleveland, OH 44112
(216) 531-3000

FINANCIAL SUMMARY
Recent Giving: $1,435,000 (fiscal 1993 est.); $1,650,182 (fiscal 1992); $1,312,353 (fiscal 1991)
Assets: $13,241 (fiscal 1992); $36,601 (fiscal 1991); $1,748 (fiscal 1990)
Fiscal Note: All giving is through the foundation. There are no standing assets. The average monthly value of assets, given in 1991, is $73,311.
EIN: 34-6555686

CONTRIBUTIONS SUMMARY
Typical Recipients: • *Arts & Humanities:* arts centers, history/historic preservation, libraries, museums/galleries, music, opera, theater • *Civic & Public Affairs:* economic development, urban & community affairs, zoos/botanical gardens • *Education:* business education, colleges & universities, community & junior colleges, education funds, engineering education, minority education • *Health:* health funds, health organizations, hospitals, medical research, mental health • *Social Services:* community centers, drugs & alcohol, united funds, youth organizations
Grant Types: capital, employee matching gifts, general support, and scholarship
Note: Scholarships are awarded through the "Merit Scholarship Program."
Geographic Distribution: nationally
Operating Locations: AL (Huntsville, Jacksonville), AZ (Tolleson), CA (City of Industry, Culver City, Irvine, Modesto, Moorpark, Santa Fe Springs), CO, FL (St. Augustine), GA (Atlanta), IL (Broadview, Des Plaines, Northbrook), IN (Lebanon), KS, KY (Lexington), MA (Lexington, Sharon, Waltham), ME (Gray, Portland), MI (Holt, Otsego, Oxford, Plymouth, Richland, Troy), MN (Eden Prairie, Minneapolis), MS (Batesville, Madison), NY (Brooklyn, Clyde, Lyons), OH (Akron, Avon, Cincinnati, Cleveland,

Columbus, Dayton, Eastlake, Eaton, Elyria, Kent, Lewisburg, Metamora, Ravenna, St. Mary's, Wadsworth, Waverly, Wickliffe), OR (Portland), SC (Spartanburg), UT (Salt Lake City), WI (Grantsburg)

CORP. OFFICERS
Richard Bertea: *CURR EMPL* chmn exec comm, dir: Parker-Hannifin Corp
Duane E. Collins: *CURR EMPL* pres, ceo, dir: Parker-Hannifin Corp
Patrick Streeter Parker: *B* Cleveland OH 1929 *ED* Williams Coll BA 1951; Harvard Univ MBA 1953 *CURR EMPL* chmn: Parker-Hannifin Corp *NONPR AFFIL* trust: Case Western Reserve Univ, Woodruff Fdn
Dennis W. Sullivan: *B* Chicago IL 1938 *ED* Purdue Univ 1960; Case Western Reserve Univ 1969 *CURR EMPL* exec vp, coo: Parker-Hannifin Corp *CORP AFFIL* dir: Ferro Corp, Soc Natl Bank

GIVING OFFICERS
Duane E. Collins: vp, trust *CURR EMPL* pres, ceo, dir: Parker-Hannifin Corp (see above)
Patrick Streeter Parker: pres, trust *CURR EMPL* chmn: Parker-Hannifin Corp (see above)
Joseph David Whiteman: secy, trust *B* Sioux Falls SD 1933 *ED* Univ MI BA 1955; Univ MI JD 1960 *CURR EMPL* vp, secy, gen coun: Parker-Hannifin Corp *NONPR AFFIL* dir: Great Lakes Theatre Festival, Judson Retirement Commun, St Lukes Hosp; mem: Am Bar Assn, Beta Theta Pi, Phi Delta Phi

APPLICATION INFORMATION
Initial Approach: *Initial Contact:* brief letter or proposal *Include Information On:* description of the organization, amount requested, purpose for which funds are sought, recently audited financial statement, proof of tax-exempt status *When to Submit:* any time

GRANTS ANALYSIS
Total Grants: $1,435,000*
Number of Grants: 270*
Highest Grant: $100,000
Typical Range: $100 to $2,500
Disclosure Period: fiscal year ending June 30, 1993

Note: Figures are estimates for fiscal 1993. Recent grants are derived from a fiscal 1992 Form 990. Assets are for fiscal 1992.

RECENT GRANTS

- 350,000 United Way/Corporate, Cleveland, OH
- 40,000 Cleveland, Initiative for Education (CIE), Cleveland, OH
- 30,000 Cleveland Tomorrow, Cleveland, OH
- 28,910 National Merit Scholarship Program, Cleveland, OH
- 28,572 John Carroll University, Cleveland, OH — capital fund
- 25,000 Cleveland State University-Advanced Manufacturing Center, Cleveland, OH
- 25,000 University of California/Irvine Graduate Fellowship, Irvine, CA
- 25,000 University School/Huntington Valley, Cleveland, OH
- 24,000 Atlantic Foundation, Cleveland, OH
- 24,000 United Way/Orange County, Irvine, CA

Parker, Jr. Foundation, William A.

CONTACT
William A. Parker, Jr. Foundation
P.O. Box 4655
Atlanta, GA 30302-4655
(404) 588-8449

FINANCIAL SUMMARY
Recent Giving: $56,500 (fiscal 1991); $88,001 (fiscal 1990)
Assets: $2,075,914 (fiscal year ending June 30, 1991); $1,903,188 (fiscal 1990)

CONTRIBUTIONS SUMMARY
Typical Recipients: • *Arts & Humanities:* history/historic preservation • *Education:* colleges & universities • *Health:* hospitals, medical research • *Religion:* churches • *Social Services:* community service organizations
Grant Types: general support and research

GRANTS ANALYSIS
Total Grants: $56,500
Number of Grants: 12
Highest Grant: $12,500
Typical Range: $1,000 to $12,500
Disclosure Period: fiscal year ending June 30, 1991

RECENT GRANTS
- 12,500 Emory University, Atlanta, GA
- 10,000 Westminster Schools, Atlanta, GA
- 10,000 Westminster Schools, Atlanta, GA
- 6,000 Aspen Foundation, Aspen, CO
- 5,000 Atlanta Historical Society, Atlanta, GA
- 5,000 Emory University/Crawford Long Hospital, Atlanta, GA
- 3,000 Emory-Egleston Children's Research Center, Atlanta, GA
- 1,000 Peachtree Presbyterian Church, Atlanta, GA
- 1,000 Salvation Army, Atlanta, GA
- 1,000 Shortoff Miss Baptist Church, Atlanta, GA

Parker Pen USA Ltd.

Sales: $84.0 million
Employees: 600
Headquarters: Janesville, WI
SIC Major Group: Miscellaneous Manufacturing Industries

CONTACT
Vickey Hearing
Public Relations
Parker Pen USA Ltd.
PO Box 5100
Janesville, WI 53547
(608) 755-7000

CONTRIBUTIONS SUMMARY
Operating Locations: WI (Janesville)

CORP. OFFICERS
Peter Bentley: *B* Jersey City NJ 1915 *ED* Princeton Univ BA 1938; Yale Univ LLB 1941 *CURR EMPL* ptnr: Bentley Mosher & Babson *CORP AFFIL* pres: Parker Pen USA Ltd *NONPR AFFIL* dir: Royal Soc Medicine Fdn; mem: Am Bar Assn, CT Bar Assn, Soc Cutaneous Biology & Medicine, Stamford Bar Assn
Shane Dolohanty: *CURR EMPL* cfo: Parker Pen USA Ltd

Parman Foundation, Robert A.

CONTACT
John L. Hessel
Trustee
Robert A. Parman Fdn.
1419 W. Reno
Oklahoma City, OK 73102

FINANCIAL SUMMARY
Recent Giving: $311,150 (fiscal 1991); $318,650 (fiscal 1990); $388,650 (fiscal 1989)
Assets: $5,354,620 (fiscal year ending August 31, 1991); $4,613,598 (fiscal 1989); $4,548,227 (fiscal 1988)
Gifts Received: $470,395 (fiscal 1991)
EIN: 73-6098053

CONTRIBUTIONS SUMMARY
Donor(s): the late Robert A. Parman
Typical Recipients: • *Education:* colleges & universities, education associations • *Health:* hospitals, medical research • *Social Services:* community service organizations, family services, shelters/homelessness, united funds, youth organizations
Grant Types: general support
Geographic Distribution: focus on OK

GIVING OFFICERS
John L. Hessel: trust
Jerry M. Thomason: trust
Rev. J. Clyde Wheeler: trust

APPLICATION INFORMATION
Initial Approach: Send brief letter of inquiry describing program or project. There are no deadlines.
Restrictions on Giving: Does not support individuals.

GRANTS ANALYSIS
Number of Grants: 14
Highest Grant: $50,000
Typical Range: $10,000 to $25,000
Disclosure Period: fiscal year ending August 31, 1991

RECENT GRANTS

- 50,000 Oklahoma City University, Oklahoma City, OK
- 50,000 Oklahoma State University, Stillwater, OK
- 50,000 Phillips University, Enid, OK
- 50,000 Southern Nazarene University, Bethany, OK
- 25,000 Salvation Army, Oklahoma City, OK
- 25,000 Work Activity Center, Moore, OK
- 15,000 Oklahoma Medical Research Foundation, Oklahoma City, OK
- 12,000 Rainbow Fleet, Oklahoma City, OK
- 10,000 Ark Interfaith Family Shelter, Midwest City, OK
- 10,000 Central State University, Edmond, OK

Parnes Foundation, E. H.

Headquarters: Brooklyn, NY

CONTACT
Herschel Parnes
Manager
E. H. Parnes Fdn.
1606 49th St.
Brooklyn, NY 11204

FINANCIAL SUMMARY
Recent Giving: $223,606 (fiscal 1990); $117,230 (fiscal 1989)
Assets: $4,960,741 (fiscal 1989)
EIN: 23-7237932

CONTRIBUTIONS SUMMARY
Typical Recipients: • *Education:* religious education • *Religion:* religious organizations, synagogues • *Social Services:* community service organizations
Grant Types: general support
Operating Locations: NY (Brooklyn)

GIVING OFFICERS
Emanuel Panes: mgr
Herschel Parnes: mgr

APPLICATION INFORMATION
Initial Approach: Contributes only to preselected organizations.

GRANTS ANALYSIS
Number of Grants: 28

Highest Grant: $95,000
Typical Range: $500 to $10,000
Disclosure Period: fiscal year ending June 30, 1991

RECENT GRANTS

95,000 Agudath Israel of America
20,000 Beth Midrash Govoha, Lakewood, NJ
20,000 Merkey Lehinuch Torani
16,200 American Friends of Yeshiva Rashbi
10,000 Amshinov Jerusalem
10,000 BMG of Israel
10,000 Sinai Academy
8,600 Yesh Ohr Somoyach
3,600 Migdal Ohr
2,600 Kollel Zechion Menachem

Parshelsky Foundation, Moses L.

CONTACT
Tony B. Berk
Trustee
Moses L. Parshelsky Fdn.
26 Court St.
Brooklyn, NY 11242
(718) 875-8883

FINANCIAL SUMMARY
Recent Giving: $278,350 (1991); $288,350 (1990); $293,850 (1989)
Assets: $5,581,088 (1991); $5,300,360 (1990); $5,576,012 (1989)
EIN: 11-1848260

CONTRIBUTIONS SUMMARY
Donor(s): Moses L. Parshelsky
Typical Recipients: • *Arts & Humanities:* arts institutes, dance, museums/galleries, performing arts • *Civic & Public Affairs:* philanthropic organizations • *Health:* geriatric health, hospitals, medical research, single-disease health associations • *Religion:* religious organizations • *Social Services:* aged, community centers, community service organizations, disabled, family planning, food/clothing distribution, recreation & athletics, youth organizations
Grant Types: general support
Geographic Distribution: focus on Brooklyn and Queens, NY

GIVING OFFICERS
Tony B. Berk: trust
Josephine B. Krinsky: trust
Robert Daniel Krinsky: trust *B* Brooklyn NY 1937 *ED* Antioch Coll BA 1957 *CURR EMPL* pres: Segal (Martin E) Co *CORP AFFIL* pres: Segal (Martin E) Co *NONPR AFFIL* corporator: Columbia Univ Sch Social Work; mem: Am Academy Actuaries, Assn Private Pension Welfare Plans, Natl Dance Inst, Soc Actuaries; trust: Antioch Univ

APPLICATION INFORMATION
Initial Approach: Send brief letter of inquiry describing program or project. Deadline is May 31.
Restrictions on Giving: Does not support individuals.

GRANTS ANALYSIS
Number of Grants: 55
Highest Grant: $61,000
Typical Range: $1,000 to $5,000
Disclosure Period: 1991

RECENT GRANTS
61,000 American Lung Association, Brooklyn, NY — education program vs tuberculosis spread in Brooklyn
30,000 Brookdale Hospital and Medical Center, Brooklyn, NY
27,500 Metropolitan Jewish Geriatric Center, Brooklyn, NY
25,000 Kingsbrook Jewish Medical Center, Brooklyn, NY
17,500 VISIONS/Services for the Blind and Visually Impaired, New York, NY
11,000 Jewish Braille Institute of America, New York, NY
10,000 Camp Vacamas Association, New York, NY
10,000 Kingsbrook Jewish Medical Center, Brooklyn, NY
10,000 New York Philanthropic League, New York, NY

Parsons and Whittemore Inc.

Sales: $710.0 million
Employees: 2,000
Headquarters: Rye Brook, NY
SIC Major Group: Paper & Allied Products

CONTACT
Arthur Schwartz
President
Parsons & Whittemore
4 International Dr.
Rye Brook, NY 10573
(914) 937-9009

CONTRIBUTIONS SUMMARY
Operating Locations: NY (Rye Brook)

CORP. OFFICERS
Carl Clement Landegger: *B* Vienna Austria 1930 *ED* Georgetown Univ BS 1951 *CURR EMPL* chmn, dir: Black Clawson Co *CORP AFFIL* chmn: AL River Pulp Co, Parsons & Whittemore Enterprises, St Anne Nackawic Pulp & Paper Co; dir: Downingtown Mfg Co *NONPR AFFIL* dir: Georgetown Univ; trust: NY Historical Soc

George Francis Landegger: *B* 1938 *CURR EMPL* ceo: Parsons & Whittemore Enterprises

Arthur Schwartz: *CURR EMPL* pres: Parsons & Whittemore

Parsons Corp.

Revenue: $1.0 billion
Employees: 8,500
Parent Company: Ralph M. Parsons Co.
Headquarters: Pasadena, CA
SIC Major Group: Electric, Gas & Sanitary Services, Engineering & Management Services, and Heavy Construction Except Building Construction

CONTACT
Dorn Winner
Vice President & Director, Corp. Rels.
Parsons Corp.
100 West Walnut St.
Pasadena, CA 91124
(818) 440-2000
Note: Ms. Winner also is chairman of the contributions committee.

CONTRIBUTIONS SUMMARY
Nonmonetary Support Types: cause-related marketing & promotion, in-kind services, loaned employees, and loaned executives
Operating Locations: CA (Pasadena), DC (Washington), IL (Evanston), MA (Boston), NY (New York), TN (Memphis), TX (Houston)

CORP. OFFICERS
Ray W. Judson: *B* Cleveland OH 1926 *ED* Univ WA 1951 *CURR EMPL* pres: Parsons Corp
Leonard J. Pieroni: *B* Chicago IL 1939 *ED* Univ Notre Dame 1960; Northwestern Univ 1961 *CURR EMPL* chmn, ceo, dir: Parsons Corp

Parsons Foundation, Ralph M.

CONTACT
Christine Sisley
Executive Director
Ralph M. Parsons Foundation
1055 Wilshire Blvd., Ste. 1701
Los Angeles, CA 90017
(213) 482-3185

FINANCIAL SUMMARY
Recent Giving: $9,000,000 (1993 est.); $9,303,793 (1992); $5,773,922 (1991)
Assets: $190,000,000 (1992); $178,028,340 (1991); $152,967,622 (1990)
EIN: 95-6085895

CONTRIBUTIONS SUMMARY
Donor(s): The foundation was established in 1961 by Ralph M. Parsons (1896-1974). Despite his modest beginnings as the son of a Long Island fisherman, Mr. Parsons established and led one of the world's largest engineering and construction firms, Parsons Corporation. He was a pioneer in

missile and space launch facilities and nuclear plants.

In 1961, Mr. Parsons established a modest foundation. Upon his death in 1974, the grant-making organization received a bequest from his estate valued at approximately $154 million. This foundation is managed independently of the Parsons Corporation.

Typical Recipients: • *Arts & Humanities:* arts centers, cinema, history/historic preservation, museums/galleries, music, public broadcasting, theater • *Civic & Public Affairs:* environmental affairs, nonprofit management, philanthropic organizations, professional & trade associations, public policy, urban & community affairs • *Education:* arts education, colleges & universities, economic education, education associations, elementary education, engineering education, minority education, public education (precollege), science/technology education, special education, student aid • *Health:* health organizations, hospitals, medical research, outpatient health care delivery, pediatric health • *Social Services:* aged, child welfare, community centers, day care, delinquency & crime, disabled, domestic violence, emergency relief, employment/job training, family planning, food/clothing distribution, recreation & athletics, refugee assistance, shelters/homelessness, youth organizations

Grant Types: capital, challenge, fellowship, general support, project, scholarship, and seed money

Geographic Distribution: primarily Los Angeles County, CA, with the exception of higher education grants distributed to a few select national institutions in engineering education

GIVING OFFICERS

Ira J. Blanco: dir

Albert A. Dorskind: vp, cfo, dir *B* New York NY 1922 *ED* Cornell Univ 1943; Cornell Univ LLB 1948 *CURR EMPL* chmn: MCA Devel Co *CORP AFFIL* dir: Environmental Indus, Sinclair Paint Co

Robert F. Erburu: dir *B* Ventura CA 1930 *ED* Univ Southern CA BA 1952; Harvard Univ LLB 1955 *CURR EMPL* chmn, ceo, dir: Times Mirror Co

CORP AFFIL dir: Tejon Ranch Co; dir, dep chmn: Fed Reserve Bank San Francisco *NONPR AFFIL* dir: Am Newspaper Publs Assn; mem: Bus Counc, Bus Roundtable; mem bd dirs: Counc Foreign Rels, Los Angeles Festival; mem trust counc: Natl Gallery Art; trust: Art Collections & Botanical Gardens, Brookings Inst, Huntington Art Gallery, Huntington Library, Tomas Rivera Ctr

Alex Palmer Haley: dir *B* Ithaca NY 1921 *ED* Elizabeth City Teachers Coll NC 1937-1939; Simpson Coll LittD 1970 *NONPR AFFIL* mem: Authors Guild, Soc Magazine Writers *PHIL AFFIL* fdr, pres: Kinte Foundation

Leroy B. Houghton: vp

Joseph G. Hurley: pres, dir *CURR EMPL* pres: Hurley Grassini & Wrinkle

Edgar R. Jackson: vp, dir

Everett B. Laybourne: vp, dir *B* Springfield OH 1911 *ED* OH St Univ BA 1932; Harvard Univ JD 1935 *CURR EMPL* sr ptnr: Macdonald Halsted & Laybourne *CORP AFFIL* chmn bd: WAIF; dir: Brouse-Whited Packaging Co, Coldwater Investment Co, McBain Instruments, Pacific Energy Corp, Viking Indus; trust: Brite-Lite Corp *NONPR AFFIL* mem: Big Ten Univs Club Southern CA, Los Angeles County Bar Assn, Roscomare Valley Assn, Selden Soc, World Affs Counc

Christine Sisley: secy, exec dir

APPLICATION INFORMATION

Initial Approach:

Applicants should submit a preliminary letter outlining the nature of the project for which funding is sought, the amount requested, and justification for such a request. The applicant may also phone and speak to the foundation staff to discuss proposal ideas.

The preliminary letter should include brief information on the applying organization and proof of tax-exempt status.

The staff submits applications to the board of directors six times each year, in alternate months beginning in January. For the sake of fairness, applications are considered in chronological order. Due to the large number of proposals which the foundation receives, applicants should be prepared

for a period of delay leading up to a final decision.

The foundation's staff makes an initial screening of the application and a decision is made within two months on whether the applicant is qualified. The foundation does not encourage communications with its directors. If the decision is affirmative, more detailed information may be requested and a date set for a meeting or on-site visit.

Restrictions on Giving: The foundation considers providing challenge funds to launch new programs which could become self-sustaining, or to secure equipment and material which will substantially extend and improve existing services. When applicable, the foundation prefers to support programs that are innovative, or introduce new ideas, encourage inventiveness, and develop more productive methods.

OTHER THINGS TO KNOW

Publications: annual report

GRANTS ANALYSIS

Total Grants: $9,303,793

Number of Grants: 142

Typical Range: $10,000 to $50,000 and $100,000 to $250,000

Disclosure Period: 1992

Note: Highest grant figure was not available. Recent grants are derived from a 1991 annual report.

RECENT GRANTS

1,000,000 University of Southern California, Los Angeles, CA — for the construction of the Ralph M. Parsons Auditorium

500,000 Massachusetts Institute of Technology, Cambridge, MA — for the Ralph M. Parsons Graduate Fellowships

333,000 California Institute of Technology, Pasadena, CA — for a biological research study, How the Gene Regulatory System Transforms an Egg into an Embryo

250,000 Music Center of Los Angeles County, Los Angeles, CA — for the activities of the Education Division

200,000 Los Angeles Educational Partnership, Los Angeles, CA — to support and expand PLUS, a program geared toward the reform of mathematics instruction

200,000 Public Counsel, Los Angeles, CA — capital campaign to purchase and refurbish a new site to house the agency

189,000 Loyola Marymount University, Los Angeles, CA — to renovate and equip the Werts Electronics Laboratory

150,000 Art Center College of Design, Pasadena, CA — to name the Ralph M. Parsons Foundation Computer-Aided Industrial Design Center as part of a capital building expansion of the South Wing

150,000 University of Michigan, Ann Arbor, MI — for graduate fellowships in the Environmental and Water Resources Engineering Department

113,422 Don Bosco Technical Institute, Rosemead, CA — to purchase equipment for the chemistry and biology laboratories

---

Parsons - W.D. Charities, Vera Davis

CONTACT

Jay Skelton
President
Vera Davis Parsons - W.D. Charities
5050 Edgewood Court
Jacksonville, FL 32254
(904) 783-5490

FINANCIAL SUMMARY

Recent Giving: $1,219,825 (1990); $908,050 (1989); $942,483 (1988)

Assets: $24,409,162 (1990); $24,981,572 (1989); $17,214,200 (1988)

EIN: 59-6180346

CONTRIBUTIONS SUMMARY

Donor(s): The foundation was established in 1967 by Vera Davis Parsons.

Typical Recipients: • *Civic & Public Affairs:* philanthropic organizations • *Education:* agricultural education, colleges & universities, elementary education, minority education, religious education • *Health:* health funds, health organizations, hospitals, pediatric health, public health • *Religion:* churches, religious organizations • *Social Services:* child welfare, community centers, food/clothing distribution, homes, recreation & athletics, religious welfare, shelters/homelessness, united funds, youth organizations

Grant Types: general support and research

Geographic Distribution: nationally

GIVING OFFICERS

G. P. Bishop, Jr.: secy, asst treas

Robert D. Davis: vp, dir *B* 1931 *ED* Univ FL 1953; Univ FL 1953 *CURR EMPL* chmn: DDI *CORP AFFIL* dir: Am Heritage Life Ins Co, Am Heritage Life Investment, CPI Acquisition, First Union Corp, Winn-Dixie Stores; vchmn, dir: Winn-Dixie Stores *PHIL AFFIL* vp: M Austin Davis WD Family Charities

H. D. Francis: vp, asst secy

R. J. Head: dir

H. J. Skelton: pres, dir, asst treas

Charles M. Thompson: dir

APPLICATION INFORMATION

Initial Approach: Restrictions on Giving: The foundation supports preselected organizations and does not accept unsolicited requests for funds. The foundation does not make grants to individuals.

GRANTS ANALYSIS

Total Grants: $1,219,825
Number of Grants: 185
Highest Grant: $530,337
Typical Range: $1,000 to $5,000
Disclosure Period: 1990
Note: Average grant figure does not include the highest grant of $530,377. Recent grants are derived from a 1990 grants list.

RECENT GRANTS

530,337 Mayo Foundation, Rochester, MN
227,287 Jacksonville University, Jacksonville, FL
30,000 Boy Scouts of America, High Point, NC
10,000 City Rescue Mission, Jacksonville, FL
10,000 Heritage Foundation, Washington, DC
6,500 United Negro College Fund, Jacksonville, FL
5,000 Benedict College, Columbia, SC
5,000 Cardinal Hill Hospital, Lexington, KY
5,000 Frontline Outreach
5,000 Independent College Fund, Fort Worth, TX

Parthenon Sportswear / Parthenon Sportwear Foundation

Headquarters: Edison, NJ

CONTACT

Isadore Shamah
Director
Parthenon Sportswear
95 Ethel Road
Edison, NJ 08817
(908) 248-9440

FINANCIAL SUMMARY

Recent Giving: $36,200 (fiscal 1992); $60,250 (fiscal 1990)
Assets: $711,535 (fiscal year ending February 28, 1992); $585,659 (fiscal 1990)
Gifts Received: $33,000 (fiscal 1992); $59,000 (fiscal 1990)
Fiscal Note: In fiscal 1992, contributions were received from Isadore Shamah (11,000), Isaac Shamah ($11,000), and Harold Shamah ($11,000).
EIN: 22-2366563

CONTRIBUTIONS SUMMARY

Typical Recipients: • *Civic & Public Affairs:* ethnic/minority organizations • *Health:* hospitals • *Religion:* religious organizations, synagogues

Grant Types: general support
Operating Locations: NJ (Edison)

CORP. OFFICERS

Isadore Shama: *CURR EMPL* pres: Parthenon Sportwear

GIVING OFFICERS

Morris Abraham: secy
Soloman Dayan: vp
Alan Menaged: pres
Alan Shamah: treas
Isadore Shamah: dir

APPLICATION INFORMATION

Initial Approach: The foundation supports preselected organizations and does not accept unsolicited requests for funds.

GRANTS ANALYSIS

Number of Grants: 4
Highest Grant: $17,000
Typical Range: $3,000 to $10,200
Disclosure Period: fiscal year ending February 28, 1992

RECENT GRANTS

15,000 Ohr Torah Institutions of Israel, New York, NY
15,000 United Jewish Appeal Federation of Jewish Philanthropies, New York, NY
12,000 Mount Sinai Hospital and Medical Center, New York, NY
10,000 Sephardic Bikur Holim, Brooklyn, NY
2,000 Maimonides Medical Center, Brooklyn, NY

Parvin Foundation, Albert

CONTACT

Albert O. Parvin
Vice President
Albert Parvin Fdn.
10880 Wilshire Blvd., Ste. 2006
Los Angeles, CA 90024
(310) 475-5676

FINANCIAL SUMMARY

Recent Giving: $397,800 (1991); $440,525 (1990); $449,975 (1989)
Assets: $6,039,642 (1991); $5,670,657 (1990); $5,895,961 (1989)
EIN: 95-2158989

CONTRIBUTIONS SUMMARY

Donor(s): Albert O. Parvin

Typical Recipients: • *Civic & Public Affairs:* ethnic/minority organizations, public policy • *Education:* colleges & universities • *Health:* health organizations, medical research • *Religion:* religious organizations • *Social Services:* community service organizations

Grant Types: endowment and general support

GIVING OFFICERS

Henry Jaffe: dir
Albert B. Parvin: vp, dir
Phyllis Parvin: secy, dir
Stanley Parvin: dir
Bernard Silbert: dir
Robert L. Spencer: pres, dir

APPLICATION INFORMATION

Initial Approach: Send brief letter of inquiry describing program. There are no deadlines.

GRANTS ANALYSIS

Number of Grants: 23
Highest Grant: $200,000
Typical Range: $500 to $5,000
Disclosure Period: 1991

RECENT GRANTS

200,000 City of Hope, Los Angeles, CA
73,000 Princeton University, Princeton, NJ
60,000 University of California Los Angeles Kennamer Foundation, Los Angeles, CA
50,000 University of Hawaii, Honolulu, HI
5,000 Georgetown University, Washington, DC
1,500 United Jewish Appeal Federation of Jewish Philanthropies, Los Angeles, CA
1,000 Jules Stein Eye Institute, Los Angeles, CA
1,000 One Voice, Los Angeles, CA
1,000 Save-A-Heart Foundation, Los Angeles, CA
1,000 UNICEF, Los Angeles, CA

Pasadena Area Residential Aid

CONTACT
Linda M. Moore
Assistant Secretary
Pasadena Area Residential Aid
PO Box 984
Pasadena, CA 91102
(213) 681-1331

FINANCIAL SUMMARY
Recent Giving: $2,635,885 (fiscal 1992); $2,841,196 (fiscal 1991); $3,230,861 (fiscal 1990)
Assets: $2,676,808 (fiscal year ending July 31, 1992); $2,208,446 (fiscal 1991); $2,097,247 (fiscal 1990)
Gifts Received: $3,032,485 (fiscal 1992); $2,862,125 (fiscal 1991)
EIN: 95-2048774

CONTRIBUTIONS SUMMARY
Typical Recipients: • *Arts & Humanities:* arts centers, community arts, history/historic preservation, museums/galleries • *Civic & Public Affairs:* civil rights, environmental affairs, municipalities, zoos/botanical gardens • *Education:* colleges & universities, private education (precollege), science/technology education • *Health:* health organizations, hospitals, medical research, pediatric health, single-disease health associations • *Religion:* churches • *Social Services:* child welfare, community centers, community service organizations, drugs & alcohol, family planning, homes, united funds, youth organizations
Grant Types: general support

GIVING OFFICERS
James N. Gamble: treas, dir
Thayer S. Holbrook: dir
Robert R. Huffman: pres
Mary W. Johnson: dir
Thomas S. Jones III: secy, dir
Sue A. Mellado: asst secy
Robert F. Niven: dir
Lee Gilmour Paul: dir *B* Denver CO 1907 *ED* Bowdoin Coll AB 1929; Harvard Univ LLB 1932 *CURR EMPL* ptnr: Paul Hastings Janofsky & Walker *CORP AFFIL* ptnr: Paul Hastings Janofsky & Walker *NONPR AFFIL* mem: Los Angeles County Bar Assn; pres: Los Angeles Boys Club Fdn; trust: Pasadena Humane Soc, Pasadena Pub Library

Frances K. Sherwood: asst secy
Philip V. Swan: dir
Trude C. Taylor: dir
Jack D. Whitehead: dir

APPLICATION INFORMATION
Initial Approach: Contributions only to preselected organizations.

GRANTS ANALYSIS
Number of Grants: 1,159
Highest Grant: $313,200
Typical Range: $250 to $5,000
Disclosure Period: fiscal year ending July 31, 1992

RECENT GRANTS
313,200	Williams College, Williamstown, MA
286,000	Vajradhatu
80,000	Camp Manito-Wish, Boulder Junction, WI
73,798	All Saints Church
63,375	California Institute of Technology, Pasadena, CA
55,190	Scripps College, Claremont, CA
50,000	Abortion Rights Mobilization
50,000	Town of Jackson
38,272	La Canada Presbyterian Church
36,022	Westridge School

Patagonia
Sales: $120.0 million
Employees: 300
Parent Company: Lost Arrow Inc.
Headquarters: Ventura, CA
SIC Major Group: Miscellaneous Retail

CONTACT
Libby Ellis
Grants Director
Patagonia Enviromental Grant Program
259 W Santa Clara St.
Ventura, CA 93001
(805) 643-8616

FINANCIAL SUMMARY
Recent Giving: $510,000 (fiscal 1993 est.); $700,000 (fiscal 1992 approx.); $450,000 (fiscal 1991)
Fiscal Note: Company gives directly. Its annual giving range is $500,000 to $1,000,000 and is administered by Libby Ellis, grants director. See "Other Things You Should Know" for more details.

CONTRIBUTIONS SUMMARY
Typical Recipients: • *Civic & Public Affairs:* environmental affairs
Grant Types: employee matching gifts and general support
Nonmonetary Support Types: donated equipment, donated products, in-kind services, loaned employees, and loaned executives
Note: Company estimates nonmonetary support for 1992 as ranging between $400,000 and $500,000, and it is not included in giving figures above.
Geographic Distribution: no geographic restrictions; also supports international organizations
Operating Locations: CA (Ventura)

CORP. OFFICERS
Kristine McDivitt: *CURR EMPL* ceo: Patagonia
Pat O'Donnell: *CURR EMPL* ceo: Patagonia

GIVING OFFICERS
Libby Ellis: grants dir

APPLICATION INFORMATION
Initial Approach: *Initial Contact:* letter of inquiry requesting grant guidelines
Restrictions on Giving: Does not fund scientific research or radio, television, or video direct environmental education efforts. Also does not support dinners or special events, fraternal organizations, religious organizations for sectarian purposes, or member agencies of united funds.

OTHER THINGS TO KNOW
Company donates 10% of pretax profits within an annual 1% of sales pledged to preserving and restoring the natural environment.
Publications: grant guidelines

GRANTS ANALYSIS
Total Grants: $510,000
Number of Grants: 125
Typical Range: $1,000 to $3,000
Disclosure Period: fiscal year ending April 31, 1993
Note: Recent grants are derived from a 1991 grants list.

RECENT GRANTS
Association of Forest Service Employees For Environmental Ethics
East Fork Preservation Council
Inland Empire Public Lands Council, Spokane, WA
Lighthawk, Santa Fe, NM
Steelhead Society of British Columbia

Patrick Industries Inc.
Sales: $143.0 million
Employees: 800
Headquarters: Elkhart, IN
SIC Major Group: Fabricated Metal Products, Lumber & Wood Products, and Wholesale Trade—Durable Goods

CONTACT
Keith Kankel
Secretary & Treasurer
Patrick Industries
PO Box 638
Elkhart, IN 46515
(219) 294-7511

FINANCIAL SUMMARY
Fiscal Note: Annual Giving Range: less than $100,000

CONTRIBUTIONS SUMMARY
Typical Recipients: • *Arts & Humanities:* general • *Civic & Public Affairs:* general • *Education:* general • *Health:* general • *Social Services:* general
Grant Types: general support
Geographic Distribution: primarily headquarters area
Operating Locations: IN (Elkhart)

CORP. OFFICERS
David D. Lung: *B* Wolf Lake IN 1947 *ED* Western MI Univ 1970 *CURR EMPL* pres, coo: Patrick Indus
Mervin D. Lung: *B* Elkhart IN 1928 *ED* Univ NE 1954 *CURR EMPL* chmn, ceo: Patrick Indus *CORP AFFIL* dir: ILC/Patrick Metals; owner: Mervin Lung Bldg Co, Ramada Inn South Bend IN, Village Square Apartments; pres, dir: Gano Plywood

APPLICATION INFORMATION
Initial Approach: Send brief letter of inquiry. There are no deadlines.

Patrina Foundation

CONTACT

Lorinda De Roulet
Patrina Foundation
667 Madison Avenue, 18th Floor
New York, NY 10021-8029

FINANCIAL SUMMARY

Assets: $4,488,722 (1990)
Gifts Received: $4,500,000 (1990)
Fiscal Note: 1990 contribution received from Lorinda P. De Roulet.
EIN: 11-3035018
Disclosure Period: 1990

Patterson and Clara Guthrie Patterson Trust, Robert Leet

CONTACT

Peter B. Guenther
Vice President
Robert Leet Patterson and Clara Guthrie Patterson Trust
One Landmark Sq.
Stamford, CT 06904-1454
(203) 358-6124

FINANCIAL SUMMARY

Recent Giving: $543,460 (fiscal 1992); $549,961 (fiscal 1991); $535,601 (fiscal 1990)
Assets: $10,134,808 (fiscal year ending January 31, 1992); $11,003,777 (fiscal 1991); $10,646,187 (fiscal 1990)
EIN: 06-6236358

CONTRIBUTIONS SUMMARY

Donor(s): Robert Patterson Trust No. 2, the late Robert Leet Patterson, Clara Guthrie Patterson
Typical Recipients: • *Education:* colleges & universities, medical education • *Health:* hospitals, medical research, single-disease health associations
Grant Types: professorship, project, research, and seed money
Geographic Distribution: focus on CT

GIVING OFFICERS

John H. McBride: trust

APPLICATION INFORMATION

Initial Approach: Send letter requesting application form. Deadline is May 1 for June meeting and November 1 for December meeting.

Restrictions on Giving: Does not support individuals.

OTHER THINGS TO KNOW

Publications: Informational Brochure (including application guidelines)

GRANTS ANALYSIS

Number of Grants: 5
Highest Grant: $150,000
Typical Range: $50,000 to $100,000
Disclosure Period: fiscal year ending January 31, 1992

RECENT GRANTS

150,000 University of Connecticut Health Center, Storrs, CT
132,860 Deborah Hospital, Brown Mills, NJ
104,167 Columbia University, New York, NY
85,783 Yale-New Haven Hospital, New Haven, CT
70,650 Yale University, New Haven, CT

Patterson-Barclay Memorial Foundation

CONTACT

Lee Barclay Patterson Allen
Trustee
Patterson-Barclay Memorial Fdn.
1020 Spring St., N.W.
Atlanta, GA 30309
(404) 876-1022

FINANCIAL SUMMARY

Recent Giving: $327,984 (1991); $271,584 (1990); $279,572 (1989)
Assets: $8,229,899 (1991); $7,200,898 (1990); $6,280,466 (1989)
EIN: 58-0904580

CONTRIBUTIONS SUMMARY

Donor(s): Frederick W. Patterson
Typical Recipients: • *Arts & Humanities:* history/historic preservation, libraries, museums/galleries, music • *Education:* colleges & universities, private education (precollege) • *Health:* health organizations, hospices • *Religion:* churches, religious organizations • *Social Services:* community service organizations, united funds, youth organizations
Grant Types: general support

Geographic Distribution: focus on the Atlanta, GA, metropolitan area

GIVING OFFICERS

Jack W. Allen: trust
Patterson Allen: trust
Ross Arnold: trust
Mrs. Lee Barclay: trust
Robert F. Bryan: trust

APPLICATION INFORMATION

Initial Approach: The foundation reports it only makes contributions to preselected charitable organizations.
Restrictions on Giving: Does not support individuals.

GRANTS ANALYSIS

Number of Grants: 90
Highest Grant: $20,000
Typical Range: $1,000 to $5,000
Disclosure Period: 1991

RECENT GRANTS

20,000 Hospice South, Atlanta, GA
17,191 Atlanta Baptist Church, Atlanta, GA
15,000 Red Cross, Atlanta, GA
10,000 Mount Bethal Methodist Church, Atlanta, GA
10,000 Shorter College, Rome, GA
8,000 Sons of American Revolution, Atlanta, GA
7,000 Atlantic Historical Society, Atlanta, GA
7,000 Breakthru House, Atlanta, GA
5,000 Atlanta Baptist Association, Atlanta, GA
5,000 Seminary Extension, Atlanta, GA

Patterson Charitable Fund, W. I.

CONTACT

Robert B. Shust
Trustee
W. I. Patterson Charitable Fund
407 Oliver Bldg.
Pittsburgh, PA 15222
(412) 281-5580

FINANCIAL SUMMARY

Recent Giving: $123,178 (fiscal 1991); $124,424 (fiscal 1990); $115,921 (fiscal 1989)
Assets: $3,084,868 (fiscal year ending July 31, 1991);

$2,811,980 (fiscal 1990); $2,770,587 (fiscal 1989)
EIN: 25-6028639

CONTRIBUTIONS SUMMARY

Donor(s): the late W. I. Patterson
Typical Recipients: • *Arts & Humanities:* public broadcasting • *Education:* colleges & universities, legal education • *Health:* hospitals, medical research, single-disease health associations • *Social Services:* child welfare, community service organizations, disabled, food/clothing distribution, homes, shelters/homelessness, united funds, youth organizations
Grant Types: capital, emergency, general support, multi-year/continuing support, operating expenses, and research
Geographic Distribution: focus on Allegheny County, PA

GIVING OFFICERS

Martin L. Moore, Jr.: trust
Robert B. Shust: trust
Lester K. Wolf: trust

APPLICATION INFORMATION

Initial Approach: Send brief letter describing program. Deadline is June 30.
Restrictions on Giving: Does not support individuals.

GRANTS ANALYSIS

Number of Grants: 40
Highest Grant: $5,000
Typical Range: $1,000 to $5,000
Disclosure Period: fiscal year ending July 31, 1991

RECENT GRANTS

5,000 Salvation Army, Pittsburgh, PA
5,000 Washington and Jefferson College, Washington, PA
4,393 Society for the Preservation of the Duquesne Heights Incline, Pittsburgh, PA
3,000 Alzheimer's Disease and Related Disorders Association, Pittsburgh, PA
3,000 Cancer Support Network, Pittsburgh, PA — therapeutic programs for survivors
2,500 Association for Retarded Citizens Allegheny Foundation, Pittsburgh, PA

2,500 Gateway Rehabilitation Center, Aliquippa, PA — addictive diseases treatment

2,500 Spina Bifida Association of Western Pennsylvania, Pittsburgh, PA — camp program

2,500 Three Rivers Center for Independent Living, Pittsburgh, PA — renovation

2,000 Rehabilitation Institute of Pittsburgh, Pittsburgh, PA — handicapped children

Paul and C. Michael Paul Foundation, Josephine Bay

CONTACT
Frederick Bay
President and Executive Director
Josephine Bay Paul and C. Michael Paul Fdn.
PO Box 20218
West Finance Sta.
New York, NY 10025
(212) 932-0408

FINANCIAL SUMMARY
Recent Giving: $137,350 (1991); $184,334 (1990); $116,533 (1989)
Assets: $10,325,744 (1991); $2,563,383 (1990); $2,961,581 (1989)
EIN: 13-1991717

CONTRIBUTIONS SUMMARY
Donor(s): Josephine Bay Paul
Typical Recipients: • *Arts & Humanities:* arts festivals, arts institutes, history/historic preservation, music, performing arts • *Civic & Public Affairs:* women's affairs • *Education:* agricultural education • *Religion:* churches
Grant Types: general support, multiyear/continuing support, operating expenses, project, and seed money

GIVING OFFICERS
Frederick Bay: pres, exec dir
Daniel A. Demarest: secy, dir *B* Plainfield NJ 1924 *ED* Harvard Univ AB 1948; Harvard Univ LLB 1951 *NONPR AFFIL* mem: NY City Bar Assn, Phi Beta Kappa
Hans A. Ege: dir, treas
Synnova B. Hayes: dir, chmn

APPLICATION INFORMATION
Initial Approach: Send brief letter of inquiry describing program. There are no deadlines.

OTHER THINGS TO KNOW
Publications: 990- PF

GRANTS ANALYSIS
Number of Grants: 36
Highest Grant: $30,000
Typical Range: $250 to $5,000
Disclosure Period: 1991

RECENT GRANTS
30,000 Governor's Commission on Women, New York, NY

19,500 Norwegian Seamens Church, New York, NY

10,000 St. Lukes Orchestra, New York, NY

7,500 School of Living, New York, NY

7,000 American Composers Orchestra, New York, NY

5,664 Farm School, New York, NY

5,566 Revels, New York, NY

5,000 Barge Music, New York, NY

5,000 VITA, New York, NY

4,000 Seniors Resource Center, New York, NY

Pauley Foundation, Edwin W.

CONTACT
William R. Pagen
Trustees
Edwin W. Pauley Fdn.
10900 Wilshire Blvd., Ste. 521
Los Angeles, CA 90024
(213) 518-7377

FINANCIAL SUMMARY
Recent Giving: $93,000 (fiscal 1989); $265,300 (fiscal 1988)
Assets: $6,213,601 (fiscal year ending November 30, 1989); $6,850,140 (fiscal 1988)
EIN: 95-6039872

CONTRIBUTIONS SUMMARY
Donor(s): the late Edwin W. Pauley, Barbara Pauley Pagen
Typical Recipients: • *Arts & Humanities:* museums/galleries • *Education:* colleges & universities, science/technology education • *Health:* medical research, single-disease health associations

Grant Types: capital, general support, multiyear/continuing support, and scholarship
Geographic Distribution: focus on CA

GIVING OFFICERS
Barbara Pauley Pagen: trust
William Roland Pagen: trust *B* Los Angeles CA 1921 *ED* Univ CA Los Angeles 1946 *CURR EMPL* vchmn, dir: Hondo Oil & Gas Co *CORP AFFIL* vchmn, dir: Hondo Oil & Gas Co *NONPR AFFIL* mem: Am Petroleum Inst

APPLICATION INFORMATION
Initial Approach: Send brief letter of inquiry describing program or project. There are no deadlines.

GRANTS ANALYSIS
Number of Grants: 5
Highest Grant: $63,000
Disclosure Period: fiscal year ending November 30, 1989

RECENT GRANTS
63,000 University of Hawaii at Manoa, Manoa, HI

15,000 Cystic Fibrosis Foundation, Los Angeles, CA

5,000 California Museum Associates, Los Angeles, CA

5,000 John Tracy Clinic, Los Angeles, CA

5,000 University of California, Berkeley, CA

Paulstan

CONTACT
Pauline Myers
Trustee
Paulstan
PO Box 921
Cuyahoga Falls, OH 44223
(216) 928-3284

FINANCIAL SUMMARY
Recent Giving: $1,131,447 (1991); $286,600 (1990); $56,355 (1989)
Assets: $623,923 (1991); $1,494,894 (1990); $701,554 (1989)
Gifts Received: $128,610 (1991); $28,966 (1989); $35,800 (1988)
Fiscal Note: 1991 gift received from Scott D. Myers ($8,500), and Pauli ne Myers ($120,110).
EIN: 34-1462129

CONTRIBUTIONS SUMMARY
Donor(s): Stanley Myers, Pauline Myers
Typical Recipients: • *Civic & Public Affairs:* urban & community affairs • *Education:* religious education • *Religion:* missionary activities, religious organizations • *Social Services:* community service organizations
Grant Types: general support

GIVING OFFICERS
Seth Meyers: vp
Dana Myers: treas
David N. Myers: treas *B* 1900 *ED* Dyke Coll MBA 1922; Cleveland St Univ LHD 1981 *CORP AFFIL* chmn: Hastings Pavement Co *NONPR AFFIL* founder: Albert Einstein Coll Medicine, Hebrew Univ Jerusalem; hon life trust: ARC; life trust: Mt Sinai Hosp; mem: Am Ordnance Assn, Assn Asphalt Technologists, ASTM, Mus Art, Mus Natural History; mem intl adv counc: World Jewish Congress; pres emeritus: Menorah Home Aged
Pauline Myers: pres
Scott Myers: vp
Scott Myers: vp (see above)

APPLICATION INFORMATION
Initial Approach: The foundation reports it only makes contributions to preselected charitable organizations.
Restrictions on Giving: Does not support individuals.

GRANTS ANALYSIS
Highest Grant: $236,000
Typical Range: $10,000 to $100,000
Disclosure Period: 1991
Note: Incomplete grants list provided for 1991.

RECENT GRANTS
236,000 Jesus Film Project, San Bernardino, CA

154,500 CMA Headquarters, Colorado Springs, CO

141,000 RZIM, Norcross, GA

125,000 Walk through the Bible, Atlanta, GA

100,000 Bible Institute, Columbus, OH

62,500 CVCA, Cuyahoga Falls, OH

61,200 Campus Crusade for Christ, San Bernardino, CA

51,000 CHCS, Cuyahoga Falls, OH

25,000 Haggai Institute, Atlanta, GA

25,000 Slavic Gospel Association, Wheaton, IL

Paulucci Family Foundation

CONTACT
Jeno Paulucci
Paulucci Family Fdn.
201 W. First St.
Sanford, FL 32771
(407) 321-7004

FINANCIAL SUMMARY
Recent Giving: $80,492 (1991); $68,695 (1990); $60,093 (1989)
Assets: $2,312,261 (1991); $2,108,684 (1990); $2,081,826 (1989)
EIN: 41-6054004

CONTRIBUTIONS SUMMARY
Donor(s): Jeno F. Paulucci
Typical Recipients: • *Arts & Humanities:* arts festivals, ethnic arts • *Civic & Public Affairs:* ethnic/minority organizations • *Education:* colleges & universities, religious education • *Health:* hospitals, medical research, single-disease health associations • *Religion:* churches, religious organizations • *Social Services:* child welfare, community service organizations, united funds, youth organizations
Grant Types: general support
Geographic Distribution: focus on MN and FL

GIVING OFFICERS
Larry W. Nelson-Heathrow: dir, treas
Gina J. Paulucci: trust
Lois M. Paulucci: dir, vp
Luigino Francisco Paulucci: dir, pres *B* Aurora MN 1918 *ED* Hibbing Jr Coll; Franklin Pierce Coll HHD 1970 *CURR EMPL* chmn, dir: Paulucci Intl Ltd *CORP AFFIL* chmn: Hottys, Pasta Lovers, Paulucci Estates, Paulucci SpA, Shopper Express Corp; chmn, dir: Central Produce Equipment, JFP & Assoc, JFP-Gray Process Ltd, Jeno F Paulucci Enterprises; fdr, chmn: Dine at Home Corp; fdr, consultant: Jenos; fdr, pres: Hemo Inc; pres: Chop Chop Corp, Etor Realty Co *NONPR AFFIL* adv bd: Natl Frozen Food Assn; chmn, fdr: Italian Am Fdn; dir: Childrens

Home Soc; fdr, developer: City Future; fdr, pres: Northeast MN Org Econ Ed; mem: Govs Bus Adv Counc, US Off Emergency Planning; mem natl counc: USO; trust: MO Valley Coll
Michael J. Paulucci: dir, vp

APPLICATION INFORMATION
Initial Approach: Send brief letter describing program. Deadline is October 1.
Restrictions on Giving: Does not support individuals.

GRANTS ANALYSIS
Number of Grants: 17
Highest Grant: $25,000
Typical Range: $200 to $1,000
Disclosure Period: 1991

RECENT GRANTS
25,000 Catholic University, Washington, DC

12,500 United Jewish Appeal Federation of Jewish Philanthropies, St. Paul, MN

5,300 National Italian-American Foundation, Washington, DC

5,000 Pine Manor College, Chestnut Hill, MA

1,800 National Italian-American Foundation, Washington, DC

1,100 National Italian-American Foundation, Washington, DC

1,000 National Italian-American Foundation, Washington, DC

830 National Italian-American Foundation, Washington, DC

500 Glen Avon Presbyterian Church, Duluth, MN

373 National Italian-American Foundation, Washington, DC

Pax Christi Foundation

CONTACT
Pax Christi Fdn.
c/o Hutterer and Krenn
7900 Xerxes Avenue, South, Ste. 928
Minneapolis, MN 55431
(612) 831-8585

FINANCIAL SUMMARY
Recent Giving: $190,000 (fiscal 1991); $92,000 (fiscal 1990); $24,000 (fiscal 1989)
Assets: $7,844,447 (fiscal year ending June 30, 1991); $5,243,585 (fiscal 1990); $2,554,454 (fiscal 1989)
Gifts Received: $2,161,650 (fiscal 1991); $2,558,175 (fiscal 1990); $1,485,000 (fiscal 1989)
Fiscal Note: In 1991, contributions were received from Dem-Con Landfill, Inc. ($2,150,000) and Joseph C. and Jeanne M. Pahl ($11,650).
EIN: 36-3550495

CONTRIBUTIONS SUMMARY
Typical Recipients: • *Civic & Public Affairs:* housing, urban & community affairs • *Health:* single-disease health associations • *Religion:* religious organizations • *Social Services:* child welfare, community service organizations, food/clothing distribution, homes, shelters/homelessness
Grant Types: general support and operating expenses
Geographic Distribution: focus on St. Paul, MN

GIVING OFFICERS
Vincent K. Hutterer: cfo

APPLICATION INFORMATION
Initial Approach: Contributes only to preselected organizations.
Restrictions on Giving: Does not support individuals.

GRANTS ANALYSIS
Number of Grants: 11
Highest Grant: $25,000
Typical Range: $10,000 to $25,000
Disclosure Period: fiscal year ending June 30, 1991

RECENT GRANTS
25,000 Habitat for Humanity, Minneapolis, MN

25,000 Minneapolis/St. Paul Family Housing Fund, Minneapolis, MN

25,000 Minnesota Indian Women's Resource Center, Minneapolis, MN — shelter

25,000 Sharing and Caring Hands, Minneapolis, MN — feeding and clothing

25,000 Westminster Corporation, St. Paul, MN

15,000 St. Joseph Home for Children, Minneapolis, MN — shelter for abused children

10,000 Graw House of Minneapolis, Minneapolis, MN — residence for AIDS patients

10,000 Northside Residents Redevelopment Council, Minneapolis, MN — social help

10,000 Project for Pride in Living, Minneapolis, MN — shelter

10,000 Selby Area Community Development Corporation, St. Paul, MN

Paxton Co., Frank
Sales: $110.0 million
Employees: 630
Parent Company: Jeld-Wen Inc.
Headquarters: Kansas City, MO
SIC Major Group: Real Estate, Wholesale Trade—Durable Goods, and Wholesale Trade—Nondurable Goods

CONTACT
Roger Davis
President
Frank Paxton Co.
6311 St. John Ave.
Kansas City, MO 64123
(816) 483-3007

FINANCIAL SUMMARY
Fiscal Note: Annual Giving Range: less than $100,000

CONTRIBUTIONS SUMMARY
Company reports 80% of contributions support education; 10% to civic and public affairs; 5% to the arts; and 5% to health and welfare.
Typical Recipients: • *Arts & Humanities:* general • *Civic & Public Affairs:* general • *Education:* general • *Social Services:* general
Grant Types: general support

Nonmonetary Support Types: donated equipment and donated products

Operating Locations: AR (Sherwood), CO (Denver), IA (Des Moines), IL (Chicago), KY (Louisville), LA (New Orleans), MO (Kansas City), NM (Albuquerque), OH (Cincinnati), OK (Oklahoma City, Tulsa), TX (Austin, Carrollton, Ft. Worth), VA (Roanoke)

CORP. OFFICERS

Roger Davis: *CURR EMPL* ceo, pres: Frank Paxton Co

Frank Paxton, Jr.: *CURR EMPL* chmn: Frank Paxton Co

Craig Ramsey: *B* Meade KS 1951 *ED* Univ KS 1973 *CURR EMPL* cfo: Frank Paxton Co *NONPR AFFIL* mem: Am Inst CPAs, Fin Execs Inst

APPLICATION INFORMATION

Initial Approach: Send brief letter of inquiry. There are no deadlines.

Pay 'N Save Inc.

Employees: 900
Parent Company: Pacific Enterprises
Parent Sales: $100.0 million
Headquarters: Littlefield, TX
SIC Major Group: Food Stores, Miscellaneous Retail, and Wholesale Trade—Durable Goods

CONTACT

Ed Cooney
Senior Vice President, Human Resources
Pay 'N Save Inc.
PO Box 832
Littlefield, TX 79339
(806) 385-3366
Note: Kris Calvin, chief financial officer, also is a contact.

CONTRIBUTIONS SUMMARY

Operating Locations: TX (Littlefield)

CORP. OFFICERS

J. M. Jacobson: *CURR EMPL* pres, ceo: Pay N Save

William Zimmerman: *CURR ... chmn: Pay N Save*

Payless Cashways Inc.

Sales: $2.38 billion
Employees: 17,475
Headquarters: Kansas City, MO
SIC Major Group: Building Materials & Garden Supplies

CONTACT

Brenda Nolte
Public Affairs Officer
Payless Cashways Inc.
PO Box 419466
Kansas City, MO 64141
(816) 234-6183

CONTRIBUTIONS SUMMARY

Operating Locations: MA (Somerville), MN (St. Paul), MO (Kansas City)

CORP. OFFICERS

Larry P. Kunz: *CURR EMPL* pres, coo, dir: Payless Cashways
David Stanley: *B* Kansas City MO 1935 *ED* Univ WI; Columbia Univ *CURR EMPL* chmn, ceo, dir: Payless Cashways *CORP AFFIL* dir: Commerce Bank Kansas City, Digi Intl, Piper Jaffay & Hopwood, Western Auto Supply Co

PayLess Drug Stores

Sales: $1.82 billion
Employees: 16,000
Parent Company: K Mart Corp.
Headquarters: Wilsonville, OR
SIC Major Group: General Merchandise Stores and Miscellaneous Retail

CONTACT

Kathy Sherman
Community Relations Coordinator
PayLess Drug Stores
9275 SW Peyton Ln.
Wilsonville, OR 97070
(503) 682-4100

FINANCIAL SUMMARY

Fiscal Note: Company gives directly. Annual Giving Range: $1 million+

CONTRIBUTIONS SUMMARY

Typical Recipients: • *Arts & Humanities:* general • *Civic & Public Affairs:* general, public policy • *Education:* general • *Health:* general • *Social Services:* child welfare, general, youth organizations
Grant Types: general support

Geographic Distribution: in headquarters and operating communities
Operating Locations: OR (Wilsonville)

CORP. OFFICERS

Tim R. McAlear: *CURR EMPL* pres, ceo: PayLess Drug Stores

GIVING OFFICERS

Kathy Sherman: *CURR EMPL* commun rels coordinator: PayLess Drug Stores

APPLICATION INFORMATION

Initial Approach: *Initial Contact:* call or write for a copy of the contribution request form; the form must be completed and accompany any written inquiry or proposal *Include Information On:* information requested includes a description of organization, amount requested, purpose of funds sought, proof of tax-exempt status, and time frame for completing project *When to Submit:* requests must be received six to eight weeks before funds are needed

Restrictions on Giving: Does not support individuals, religious organizations for sectarian purposes, political or lobbying groups, or organizations outside operating areas.

Payne Foundation, Frank E. and Seba B.

CONTACT

M. Catherine Ryan
Second Vice President
Frank E. Payne and Seba B. Payne Foundation
c/o Continental Illinois National Bank & Trust Company
of Chicago
231 South LaSalle St.
Chicago, IL 60697
(312) 828-1785

FINANCIAL SUMMARY

Recent Giving: $3,182,840 (fiscal 1991); $2,615,477 (fiscal 1990); $2,488,820 (fiscal 1989)
Assets: $72,330,527 (fiscal year ending June 30, 1991); $68,604,520 (fiscal 1990); $63,688,219 (fiscal 1989)
EIN: 23-7435471

CONTRIBUTIONS SUMMARY

Donor(s): The Frank E. Payne and Seba B. Payne Foundation was established in 1962 by Seba B. Payne, the widow of Frank E. Payne.

Typical Recipients: • *Arts & Humanities:* history/historic preservation, libraries, museums/galleries, public broadcasting, theater • *Education:* colleges & universities, education associations, minority education, private education (precollege), student aid • *Health:* hospitals • *Religion:* churches, religious organizations • *Social Services:* aged, child welfare, community service organizations, food/clothing distribution, homes, shelters/homelessness, youth organizations
Grant Types: capital, general support, operating expenses, and project
Geographic Distribution: principally Chicago, IL, and Bethlehem, PA, areas

GIVING OFFICERS

Susan Hurd Cummings: trust
George A. Hurd: trust
Priscilla Payne Hurd: trust
Charles M. Nisen: trust *B* Milwaukee WI 1913 *ED* Univ MI AB 1934; Univ MI LLB 1935 *CURR EMPL* atty, ptnr: Nisen & Elliott *NONPR AFFIL* mem: Am Bar Assn, Fed Bar Assn
M. Catherine Ryan: bank rep, contact person *CURR EMPL* second vp: Continental IL Natl Bank & Trust Co

APPLICATION INFORMATION

Initial Approach:
Requests should be submitted in writing.
Requests should include the name, address and a brief history of the organization; a list of its officers and directors; purpose for which funds are requested; evidence of need for the proposed project; most recent financial statements, including sources of funds and information on fund-raising activities and costs; estimate of time and funds required to complete project; and proof of tax-exempt status.
There are no set deadlines for submitting requests.
The foundation board generally meets in May and December.
Restrictions on Giving:
Grants are not made to individuals.

OTHER THINGS TO KNOW

Continental Illinois National Bank and Trust Company serves as corporate trustee for the foundation.
Publications: instructions to applicants

GRANTS ANALYSIS

Total Grants: $3,182,840
Number of Grants: 44
Highest Grant: $1,000,000
Typical Range: $5,000 to $60,000
Disclosure Period: fiscal year ending June 30, 1991
Note: Figure for average grant excludes a single grant for $1 million. Recent grants are derived from a fiscal 1991 grants list.

RECENT GRANTS

1,200,000	Moravian College, Bethlehem, PA
400,000	WLVT/Channel 39, Bethlehem, PA
350,000	Madeira School, Greenway, VA
100,000	Meals on Wheels, Bethlehem, PA
100,000	Southeast Neighborhood Center, Bethlehem, PA
100,000	St. Lukes Hospital, Bethlehem, PA
100,000	Wiley House, Bethlehem, PA
75,000	Diocese of Bethlehem, Bethlehem, PA
56,040	National Merit Scholarship Corporation, Evanston, IL
50,000	Diocese of Bethlehem, Bethlehem, PA

Peabody Charitable Fund, Amelia

CONTACT

Harry Rice
Trustee
Amelia Peabody Charitable Fund
201 Devenshire St.
Boston, MA 02110
(617) 451-6177

FINANCIAL SUMMARY

Recent Giving: $4,281,273 (1991); $4,476,460 (1990); $3,701,276 (1989)
Assets: $91,811,028 (1991); $90,383,525 (1990); $94,025,515 (1989)
Gifts Received: $4,960,188 (1991); $10,846,654 (1988)
Fiscal Note: In 1988, the fund received a contribution of $10,846,654 from the estate of Amelia Peabody. In 1991, the fund received $2,503,885 from the estate of Amelia Peabody and $2,456,303 from the Frank E. Peabody Trust.
EIN: 23-7364949

CONTRIBUTIONS SUMMARY

Donor(s): The Amelia Peabody Charitable Fund was established in 1942 in Massachusetts. In 1985, the fund absorbed a share of the assets of the Eaton Foundation, also based in Massachusetts.
Typical Recipients: • *Arts & Humanities:* music, opera • *Civic & Public Affairs:* environmental affairs, housing, law & justice, urban & community affairs • *Education:* arts education, colleges & universities, community & junior colleges, education associations, literacy, private education (precollege) • *Health:* health organizations, hospitals, medical research, mental health, nursing services, outpatient health care delivery, single-disease health associations • *Social Services:* family services, food/clothing distribution, shelters/homelessness, youth organizations
Grant Types: capital, matching, and operating expenses
Geographic Distribution: usually New England and largely greater Boston area

GIVING OFFICERS

Ms. Jo Anne Borek: off
Richard Leahy: trust
Harry F. Rice: trust
Patricia E. Rice: trust

APPLICATION INFORMATION

Initial Approach:
Applicants should submit a short proposal letter.
The letter should explain the nature of the nonprofit operation, and must include a copy of the IRS exemption letter. Include figures indicating the amount of the budget spent on overhead and the amount for programs, along with financial statements for the last fiscal year. Also, proposals should identify applications pending with other foundations and any commitments resulting.
There are no application deadlines.
The officers meet as necessary to review proposals. In general, the meetings take place in April, July, October, and December. Requests for funding are considered only once, but applicants may reapply after two years. The trustees do not grant interviews or make site visits except when they consider it necessary.
Restrictions on Giving: No grants are given to individuals. Multi-year grants are not made. Also, the foundation does not make loans, nor does it make grants to support fund-raising efforts or for the purpose of producing any type of film. "Grants are usually not made to religious organizations, organizations that are supported by or have access to public funds, nonprofits that carry out their programs outside the United States, or political action groups." Proposals of nonprofits under the exemption of another umbrella organization will not be considered.

GRANTS ANALYSIS

Total Grants: $4,281,273
Number of Grants: 166
Highest Grant: $1,000,000
Typical Range: $1,000 to $5,000 and $10,000 to $50,000
Disclosure Period: 1991
Note: Average grant figure excludes the largest grant of $1,000,000. Recent grants are derived from a 1991 Form 990.

RECENT GRANTS

1,000,000	Deaconess Hospital
300,000	Boston Biomedical Research Institute, Boston, MA — for Research Department
300,000	Massachusetts Eye and Ear Infirmary, Boston, MA
200,000	Northeastern University, Boston, MA
150,000	Thayer Academy, Braintree, MA
100,000	Cape Ann Historical Association, Glouchester, MA
100,000	Dover Church
100,000	Manomet Bird Observatory, Manomet, MA
100,000	Museum of American Textile History
100,000	Plimoth Plantation, Plymouth, MA

Peabody Foundation

CONTACT

William V. Tripp, III
President
Peabody Fdn.
c/o Sherburne, Powers, and Needham
One Beacon St.
Boston, MA 02108

FINANCIAL SUMMARY

Recent Giving: $442,814 (fiscal 1990); $359,371 (fiscal 1988); $488,493 (fiscal 1987)
Assets: $9,567,484 (fiscal year ending September 30, 1990); $8,424,856 (fiscal 1988); $9,378,635 (fiscal 1987)
Gifts Received: $527,167 (fiscal 1990); $5,813 (fiscal 1988); $28,214 (fiscal 1987)
EIN: 04-2104767

CONTRIBUTIONS SUMMARY

Typical Recipients: • *Education:* special education • *Health:* hospitals, medical research, pediatric health, single-disease health associations • *Social Services:* disabled
Grant Types: general support
Geographic Distribution: focus on the Boston, MA, area

GIVING OFFICERS

Harry C. Barr: trust
Dorothy A. Brown: trust
Mrs. Paul F. Burdon: trust
J. Charles Carlson: trust
Edwin F. Cave: trust
Mrs. John L. Damon: trust
Paul W. Hagenburger, MD: trust
Mrs. Francis B. Haydock: trust
John H. Hewitt: trust
Sally D. Hurlbut: trust
Andrew G. Jessiman, MD: trust
Norman C. Nicholson, Jr.: vp, treas, trust
Mrs. Stephen D. Paine: trust
Mrs. W. Nicholas Thorndike: trust
William V. Tripp III: pres, trust

APPLICATION INFORMATION

Initial Approach: Contributes only to preselected organizations.

GRANTS ANALYSIS

Number of Grants: 11
Highest Grant: $152,500
Typical Range: $5,000 to $44,644

Disclosure Period: fiscal year ending September 30, 1990

RECENT GRANTS

152,500 Children's Hospital Medical Center, Boston, MA

90,000 Brigham and Womens Hospital, Boston, MA

44,644 Massachusetts General Hospital, Boston, MA

35,000 Joint Program in Neonatology, Boston, MA

30,670 Tufts University School of Dental Medicine, Medford, MA

30,000 N.E. Medical Center, Boston, MA

16,000 Cotting School for Handicapped Children, Boston, MA

15,000 Hearing Dog Program, Boston, MA

14,000 Agassiz Village, Waltham, MA

10,000 Massachusetts Health Research Institute, Boston, MA

Peabody Foundation, Amelia

CONTACT
Bayard Waring
Trustee
Amelia Peabody Fdn.
30 Western Ave.
Gloucester, MA 01966
(508) 283-0643

FINANCIAL SUMMARY
Recent Giving: $4,791,100 (1991); $4,825,043 (1989); $5,075,843 (1988)
Assets: $105,538,039 (1991); $93,722,163 (1989); $84,467,058 (1988)
Gifts Received: $4,960,188 (1991)
Fiscal Note: In 1991, contributions were received from the estate of Amelia Peabody ($2,503,885) and the Frank E. Peabody Trust ($2,456,302).
EIN: 04-6036558

CONTRIBUTIONS SUMMARY
Donor(s): The foundation was established in 1942 by the late Amelia Peabody. In 1985, the foundation absorbed a share of the assets of the Eaton Foundation.
Typical Recipients: • *Arts & Humanities:* arts centers, community arts, dance, museums/galleries, music, opera, performing arts, theater • *Civic & Public Affairs:* consumer affairs, environmental affairs, public policy, women's affairs, zoos/botanical gardens • *Education:* colleges & universities, private education (precollege), science/technology education, special education • *Health:* hospitals, mental health, nursing services, pediatric health, public health, single-disease health associations • *Religion:* churches • *Science:* scientific institutes, scientific organizations • *Social Services:* child welfare, community centers, community service organizations, disabled, family services, food/clothing distribution, homes, shelters/homelessness, united funds, youth organizations
Grant Types: general support
Geographic Distribution: focus on Massachusetts

GIVING OFFICERS
G. Dana Bill: trust *B* Boston MA 1926 *ED* Tufts Univ 1947; Rutgers Univ Stonier Sch Banking 1968 *CURR EMPL* pres, dir: Malden Trust Co *NONPR AFFIL* pres: Malden High Sch Scholarship
James Draper St. Clair: trust *B* Akron OH 1920 *ED* Univ IL AB 1941; Harvard Univ LLB 1947; Gettysburg Coll LLD 1975; New England Sch Law LLD 1975 *CURR EMPL* sr ptnr: Hale & Dorr *NONPR AFFIL* dir: Boston Opera Assn, Met Boston; mem: Am Bar Assn, Am Coll Trial Lawyers, Am Law Inst, Boston Bar Assn, New England Law Inst, Practicing Law Inst; pres: Horizons Youth; trust, dir: Walker Home Children
Margaret N. St. Clair: trust
Bayard D. Waring: trust
Lloyd B. Waring: trust
P. Waring: trust

APPLICATION INFORMATION
Initial Approach:
The foundation has no formal application forms. A letter of request may be sent directly to the foundation.
The letter of request should set forth the amount requested and the purposes for which funds are to be used. An original and five copies of the request should be submitted to the foundation.
Letters of request are accepted throughout the year.

The foundation's trustees meet quarterly in November, February, May, and August.

Restrictions on Giving:
Grants may not be used to support projects outside the state of Massachusetts. Grants are not made to individuals, or for endowment funds, scholarships, fellowships, or loans.

OTHER THINGS TO KNOW

Publications: annual report

GRANTS ANALYSIS

Total Grants: $4,791,100

Number of Grants: 103

Highest Grant: $1,500,000

Typical Range: $20,000 to $50,000

Disclosure Period: 1991

Note: Recent grants are derived from a 1991 grants list.

RECENT GRANTS

1,500,000 Joslin Diabetes Center, Boston, MA

500,000 Boston Ballet, Boston, MA

300,000 Clarke School for the Deaf, Northampton, MA

100,000 Appalachian Mountain Club, Boston, MA

100,000 Children's Hospital, Boston, MA

100,000 Wang Center for the Performing Arts, Boston, MA

86,000 Lahey Clinic Foundation, Burlington, MA

75,000 Huntington Theatre, Boston, MA

50,000 Beth Israel Medical Center, New York, NY

50,000 Cambridge College, Cambridge, MA

Peabody Holding Company Inc.

Sales: $1.8 billion
Employees: 9,500
Headquarters: St. Louis, MO
SIC Major Group: Chemicals & Allied Products, Coal Mining, Holding & Other Investment Offices, and Wholesale Trade—Durable Goods

CONTACT
John E. Lushefski
Vice President, Finance & Administration
Peabody Holding Company Inc.
PO Box 373
St. Louis, MO 63166
(314) 342-3400

CONTRIBUTIONS SUMMARY
Operating Locations: MO (St. Louis)

CORP. OFFICERS
I. F. Engelhardt: *CURR EMPL* ceo, pres: Peabody Holding Co
Gordon R. Parker: *CURR EMPL* chmn: Peabody Holding Co

Pearce Foundation, Dr. M. Lee

CONTACT
A. B. Wiener
Secretary-Treasurer
Dr. M. Lee Pearce Fdn.
11880 Bird Rd., Ste. 101
Miami, FL 33175
(305) 477-0222

FINANCIAL SUMMARY
Recent Giving: $365,500 (1990); $225,000 (1989); $226,250 (1988)
Assets: $6,049,267 (1990); $6,026,093 (1989); $5,159,618 (1988)
EIN: 59-2424272

CONTRIBUTIONS SUMMARY
Donor(s): M. Lee Pearce
Typical Recipients: • *Arts & Humanities:* history/historic preservation, opera, public broadcasting • *Education:* colleges & universities • *Health:* medical research, public health • *Religion:* religious organizations • *Social Services:* community service organizations, united funds
Grant Types: general support and research
Geographic Distribution: focus on FL, with emphasis on Miami

GIVING OFFICERS
Robert L. Achor: vp, dir
Marc H. Bivins: vp, dir
John Philip Mudd: vp, dir *B* Washington DC 1932 *ED* Georgetown Univ BSS 1954; Georgetown Univ JD 1956 *CURR EMPL* pres: Tropical Devel Corp *CORP AFFIL* legal coordinator: Amerifirst Bank

Miami; pres: Tropical Devel Corp *NONPR AFFIL* dir: Lasalle High Sch Miami; mem: Am Bar Assn, CA Bar Assn, DC Bar Assn, FL Bar Assn, MD Bar Assn

M. Lee Pearce, MD: pres, dir
Nora Lodge Pearce: vp, dir
A. B. Wiener: vp, secy, treas, dir

APPLICATION INFORMATION

Initial Approach: Contributes only to preselected organizations.

GRANTS ANALYSIS
Number of Grants: 9
Highest Grant: $300,000
Typical Range: $2,000 to $25,000
Disclosure Period: 1990

RECENT GRANTS
300,000 University of Miami, Coral Gables, FL
25,000 Boston University Health Policy Institute, Boston, MA
11,000 Hahnemann University, Philadelphia, PA — for grants
10,000 Florida Trust/Bonnet House, Miami, FL — historic preservation
10,000 Metropolitan Opera Association, New York, NY
5,000 Greater Miami Hebrew Academy, Miami, FL
2,000 Alton Ochsner Foundation, Baton Rouge, LA — medical research
1,500 Channel 2-WPBT
1,000 Western Carolina University Speech and Hearing, Cullowhee, NC

Pearle Vision
Sales: $850.0 million
Employees: 8,000
Parent Company: Grandmet USA Inc.
Headquarters: Dallas, TX
SIC Major Group: Instruments & Related Products and Miscellaneous Retail

CONTACT
Karen O'Neal
Public Relations Coordinator
Pearle Vision
2534 Royal Ln.
Dallas, TX 75229
(214) 277-5000

CONTRIBUTIONS SUMMARY
Priorities include the United Way of Metropolitan Dallas, Greater Dallas Chamber of Commerce, Adopt-A-School Program, and activities supported by the Pearle Vision Foundation (a nonprofit organization).
Grant Types: matching
Operating Locations: TX (Dallas)

CORP. OFFICERS
R. Howard Stanworth: *CURR EMPL* pres, ceo: Pearle

APPLICATION INFORMATION
Initial Approach: Send brief letter of inquiry, including a description of the organization, amount requested, purpose of funds sought, recently audited financial statements, and proof of tax-exempt status. There are no deadlines.

OTHER THINGS TO KNOW
Company acquired by Grand Metropolitan Inc.

Pearlstone Foundation, Peggy Meyerhoff

CONTACT
Richard I. Pearlstone
Vice President
Peggy Meyerhoff Pearlstone Fdn.
Village of Cross Keys, Village Sq. II, Ste. 212
Baltimore, MD 21210
(410) 532-2263

FINANCIAL SUMMARY
Recent Giving: $136,309 (fiscal 1992); $105,250 (fiscal 1991); $158,436 (fiscal 1990)
Assets: $4,606,448 (fiscal year ending February 28, 1992); $3,958,861 (fiscal 1991); $3,861,046 (fiscal 1990)
EIN: 52-1035731

CONTRIBUTIONS SUMMARY
Donor(s): the late Peggy Meyerhoff Pearlstone

Typical Recipients: • *Arts & Humanities:* arts centers, community arts, dance, music, performing arts, public broadcasting, theater • *Education:* education associations, education funds, private education (precollege) • *Health:* hospitals, medical research, pediatric health, single-disease health associations • *Social Services:* domestic violence, domestic violence, family services, food/clothing distribution, youth organizations
Grant Types: capital, emergency, endowment, multi-year/continuing support, project, and scholarship
Geographic Distribution: focus on Baltimore, MD

GIVING OFFICERS
Ellen P. Leary: asst secy, treas
Esther S. Pearlstone: pres
Richard L. Pearlstone: vp, secy, treas

APPLICATION INFORMATION
Initial Approach: Send brief letter of inquiry describing program or project. There are no deadlines.
Restrictions on Giving: Does not support individuals.

GRANTS ANALYSIS
Number of Grants: 31
Highest Grant: $30,000
Typical Range: $1,000 to $5,000
Disclosure Period: fiscal year ending February 28, 1992

RECENT GRANTS
30,000 New Directions Education Fund, St. Louis, MO
20,000 Maryland Food Committee, Baltimore, MD
16,667 Girl Scouts of America, Baltimore, MD
10,000 Center Stage, Baltimore, MD
6,642 Sexual Assault Recovery Center, Baltimore, MD
6,000 Beit Issie Shapiro Foundation, New York, NY
5,000 Bais Yaakou School for Girls, Baltimore, MD
5,000 Mayors Advisor Committee, Baltimore, MD
3,500 Next Ice Age, Baltimore, MD
2,500 Downtown Dance Company, Baltimore, MD

Pearson Foundation, E. M.

CONTACT
E. M. Pearson Foundation
4471 Foothill Trail
Vadnais Heights, MN
55127-6002

FINANCIAL SUMMARY
Recent Giving: $255,000 (1990)
Assets: $8,222,512 (1990)
Gifts Received: $1,850,090 (1990)
Fiscal Note: 1990 contribution in the form of 53,240 shares of Deluxe Corporation common stock received from Mathilda E. Pearson.

CONTRIBUTIONS SUMMARY
Typical Recipients: • *Arts & Humanities:* museums/galleries, public broadcasting • *Education:* colleges & universities • *Religion:* churches • *Social Services:* emergency relief, youth organizations
Grant Types: general support

GRANTS ANALYSIS
Total Grants: $255,000
Number of Grants: 42
Highest Grant: $32,000
Typical Range: $8,000 to $32,000
Disclosure Period: 1990

RECENT GRANTS
32,000 Jehovah Evangelical Lutheran Church, St. Paul, MN
12,500 Twin Cities Public Television, St. Paul, MN
10,000 Children's Home Society of Minnesota, St. Paul, MN
10,000 Concordia College, St. Paul, MN
10,000 Indianhead Council Boy Scouts of America, St. Paul, MN
10,000 Red Cross, St. Paul, MN — St. Paul area
8,000 Luther Haven Nursing Home, Montevideo, MN
8,000 Science Museum of Minnesota, St. Paul, MN
8,000 Wilderness Fellowship, Frederic, WI

Pechiney Corp.

Sales: $6.5 billion
Employees: 27,000
Headquarters: Greenwich, CT
SIC Major Group: Holding &
  Other Investment Offices,
  Primary Metal Industries, and
  Wholesale Trade—Durable
  Goods

CONTACT

Ilse A. Minkenberg
Manager, Public Relations
Pechiney Corp.
475 Steamboat Rd.
Greenwich, CT 06836-1960
(203) 661-4600

CONTRIBUTIONS SUMMARY

The contributions program is
highly decentralized. The corporate headquarters sponsors
national organizations and
some local giving, while operating plants contribute in their
communities and states. Contact Ilse Minkenberg, manager,
public relations, at Pechiney
Corp., concerning headquarters' gifts to national and local
organizations. Contributions by
Pechiney Trading International,
SA, and Pechiney World Trade
(USA) Inc., both of Greenwich,
CT, are handled by Pechiney
Corp. The operating locations
of Howmet Corp., Pechiney's
primary subsidiary, should be
contacted for information on
local giving programs.

Operating Locations: CT, IN,
MI, NJ, NV, TX, VA

CORP. OFFICERS

Jean-Francois Faivre: *CURR
EMPL* exec vp, cfo: Pechiney
Corp

Michel A. Simonnard: *B*
Amiens France 1933 *ED* Ecole
Polytech 1956; MA Inst Tech
1959 *CURR EMPL* chmn, pres,
ceo: Pechiney Corp *CORP
AFFIL* exec vp: Pechiney SA
(France)

GIVING OFFICERS

Ilse A. Minkenberg: *CURR
EMPL* mgr (pub rels):
Pechiney Corp

APPLICATION INFORMATION

Initial Approach: Submit a letter to the appropriate location
(see program description
above).

Peck Foundation, Milton and Lillian

CONTACT

Irving Lowe
Vice President
Milton and Lillian Peck Fdn.
4729 East Clearwater Pkwy.
Paradise Valley, AZ 85253
(602) 948-2454

FINANCIAL SUMMARY

Recent Giving: $361,738
(1990); $200,000 (1989);
$200,000 (1988)
Assets: $6,273,658 (1990);
$3,436,632 (1989); $2,980,302
(1988)
Gifts Received: $2,746,126
(1990)
EIN: 39-6051782

CONTRIBUTIONS SUMMARY

Donor(s): Peck Meat Packing
Corp., Emmber Brands, Inc.,
Gibbon Packing, Inc., MooBat-
tue
Typical Recipients: • *Civic &
Public Affairs:* zoos/botanical
gardens • *Religion:* religious organizations • *Social Services:*
community service organizations
Grant Types: general support
Geographic Distribution:
focus on Milwaukee, WI

GIVING OFFICERS

Irving Lowe: vp, secy
Miriam Lowe: trust
Bernard Peck: dir, pres, treas
Miriam Peck: trust

APPLICATION INFORMATION

Initial Approach: The foundation reports it only makes contributions to preselected charitable organizations. The
foundation does not accept applications.
Restrictions on Giving: Does
not support individuals.

GRANTS ANALYSIS

Number of Grants: 3
Highest Grant: $161,738
Typical Range: $100,000 to
$161,738
Disclosure Period: 1990

RECENT GRANTS

161,738 Congregation
Emanu-El, Milwau-
kee, WI
100,000 Milwaukee Jewish
Federation, Mil-
waukee, WI
100,000 Zoological Society
of Milwaukee

County, Milwau-
kee, WI

Peck/Jones Construction Corp.

Sales: $200.0 million
Employees: 375
Headquarters: Los Angeles, CA
SIC Major Group: General
  Building Contractors and
  Heavy Construction Except
  Building Construction

CONTACT

Gregg Jones
President
Peck/Jones Construction Corp.
10866 Wilshire Blvd.
Los Angeles, CA 90024
(310) 470-1885

CONTRIBUTIONS SUMMARY

Operating Locations: CA (Los
Angeles)

CORP. OFFICERS

Jerve Jones: *CURR EMPL*
pres, ceo: CL Peck Contractor

Clair Peck: *B* Los Angeles CA
1920 *ED* Stanford Univ 1942
CURR EMPL chmn, coo: CL
Peck Contractor *CORP AFFIL*
dir: AMCAP Fund, Farmers Ins
Group, Investment Co Am;
trust: Mead Housing Trust &
Devel Corp

Victor H. Siegel: *CURR EMPL*
exec vp, secy, cfo: CL Peck
Contractor

Peerless Insurance Co.

Assets: $210.0 million
Employees: 900
Parent Company: Nationale
  Nederlanden U.S. Property &
  Casualty Holdings, Inc.
Headquarters: Keene, NH
SIC Major Group: Insurance
  Carriers

CONTACT

Gwen Greeley
Manager, Communications
Peerless Insurance Co.
62 Maple Ave.
Keene, NH 03431
(603) 352-3221

FINANCIAL SUMMARY

Recent Giving: $76,000
(1990); $76,000 (1989);
$67,500 (1988)

CONTRIBUTIONS SUMMARY

Support is given to health and
human services (50% of contributions), education (25%),
civic affairs (25%), and occasionally to arts and humanities.
Typical Recipients: • *Education:* colleges & universities
• *Health:* single-disease health
associations • *Social Services:*
community service organizations, religious welfare, united
funds, youth organizations
Grant Types: general support
Nonmonetary Support Types:
loaned employees and loaned
executives
Geographic Distribution: in
the New England area
Operating Locations: CO,
DC, GA, IN, NH, NY

CORP. OFFICERS

Roger Jean: *CURR EMPL*
pres, coo: Peerless Co
Albert Kober: *CURR EMPL*
ceo: Peerless Ins Co

GIVING OFFICERS

Gwen Greeley: *CURR EMPL*
commun mgr: Peerless Ins Co

APPLICATION INFORMATION

Initial Approach: Send a letter
any time.

Peery Foundation

Former Foundation Name:
  Richard T. Peery Foundation

CONTACT

Richard T. Peery
President
Peery Fdn.
2560 Mission College Blvd.
Ste. 101
Santa Clara, CA 94050
(408) 980-0130

FINANCIAL SUMMARY

Recent Giving: $280,904 (fis-
cal 1991); $377,665 (fiscal
1990); $209,550 (fiscal 1989)
Assets: $14,241,184 (fiscal
year ending September 30,
1991); $13,388,506 (fiscal
1990); $10,977,950 (fiscal
1989)
Gifts Received: $1,166,391
(fiscal 1990); $3,479,004 (fis-
cal 1989); $135,275 (fiscal
1988)
Fiscal Note: In 1990, contributions were received from Richard T. Peery.
EIN: 94-2460894

CONTRIBUTIONS SUMMARY

Donor(s): The foundation was established in 1977 by Richard T. Peery.

Typical Recipients: • *Arts & Humanities:* history/historic preservation, performing arts • *Civic & Public Affairs:* philanthropic organizations, zoos/botanical gardens • *Education:* arts education, public education (precollege), student aid • *Religion:* churches • *Social Services:* aged, disabled, family services, youth organizations

Grant Types: multiyear/continuing support and project

Geographic Distribution: focus on California

GIVING OFFICERS

John Arrillaga: dir *B* 1938 *ED* Stanford Univ

Dennis Peery: treas

Mildred D. Peery: vp

Richard Taylor Peery: pres *B* 1940 *ED* Stanford Univ *CURR EMPL* co-owner: Peery-Arrillaga

Boyd C. Smith: dir

APPLICATION INFORMATION

Initial Approach: Restrictions on Giving: The foundation supports preselected organizations and does not accept unsolicited requests for funds. The foundation does not make grants to individuals.

GRANTS ANALYSIS

Total Grants: $280,904
Number of Grants: 33
Highest Grant: $187,500
Typical Range: $500 to $10,000
Disclosure Period: fiscal year ending September 30, 1991
Note: Average grant figure does not include the highest grant of $187,500. Recent grants are derived from a fiscal 1991 grants list.

RECENT GRANTS

187,500   Church of Latter Day Saints, Salt Lake City, UT
15,100   Performing Group for Youth, Los Altos, CA
13,560   Church of Latter Day Saints, Palo Alto, CA
10,000   Church of Latter Day Saints, Rio de Janeiro, Brazil
10,000   Pinewood High School, Los Altos, CA
10,000   Snow College Scholarship, Ephriam, UT
10,000   YMCA, Palo Alto, CA
3,000   Liahona Club, Walnut Creek, CA
2,000   Boy Scouts of America, San Mateo, CA
2,000   Palo Alto High School, Palo Alto, CA

Pegasus Gold Corp.

Parent Company: Pegasus Gold, Inc.
Parent Sales: $156.2 million
Parent Employees: 630
Headquarters: Spokane, WA
SIC Major Group: Metal Mining

CONTACT

Susan Schenk
Investor Relations
Pegasus Gold Corp.
No. 9 Post St., Ste. 400
Spokane, WA 99201
(509) 624-4653

CONTRIBUTIONS SUMMARY

Operating Locations: WA (Spokane)

CORP. OFFICERS

John L. Azlant: *CURR EMPL* vp, cfo: Pegasus Gold Corp
Lyle F. Beaudoin: *CURR EMPL* vp bus devel: Pegasus Gold Corp
John M. Wilson: *CURR EMPL* pres, ceo: Pegasus Gold Corp

GIVING OFFICERS

Susan Schenk: *CURR EMPL* investor rels: Pegasus Gold Corp

RECENT GRANTS

Marquette University, Milwaukee, WI

Peierls Foundation

CONTACT

E. J. Peierls
President
Peierls Fdn.
73 South Holman Way
Golden, CO 80401

FINANCIAL SUMMARY

Recent Giving: $227,800 (fiscal 1991); $232,500 (fiscal 1990); $205,200 (fiscal 1989)
Assets: $5,214,973 (fiscal year ending October 31, 1991); $3,687,206 (fiscal 1990); $4,600,905 (fiscal 1989)
Gifts Received: $20,000 (fiscal 1991)
Fiscal Note: In 1991, contributions were received from E.J. Peierls.
EIN: 13-6082503

CONTRIBUTIONS SUMMARY

Donor(s): the late Edgar S. Peierls

Typical Recipients: • *Civic & Public Affairs:* environmental affairs • *Education:* business education, colleges & universities, education funds, minority education, student aid • *Health:* medical research • *International:* international development/relief • *Religion:* religious organizations • *Social Services:* community service organizations, disabled, family planning, youth organizations

Grant Types: research
Geographic Distribution: focus on NY

GIVING OFFICERS

Brian Eliot Peierls: vp, treas
E. J. Peierls: pres
Ethel Peierls: secy

APPLICATION INFORMATION

Initial Approach: Contributes only to preselected organizations.
Restrictions on Giving: Does not support individuals.

GRANTS ANALYSIS

Number of Grants: 32
Highest Grant: $33,000
Typical Range: $2,700 to $18,700
Disclosure Period: fiscal year ending October 31, 1991

RECENT GRANTS

33,000   CARE, Chicago, IL
18,000   National Hispanic Scholarship Fund
17,000   Planned Parenthood Federation of America
15,000   Nature Conservancy
10,700   International Rescue Committee, New York, NY
10,200   United Negro College Fund
8,900   Stanford Graduate School of Business, Stanford, CA
8,900   Yale University, New Haven, CT
8,200   University of California, Berkeley, CA
7,100   Arthritis Foundation, NJ

Pella Corp. / Pella Rolscreen Foundation

Sales: $400.0 million
Employees: 2,500
Headquarters: Pella, IA
SIC Major Group: Lumber & Wood Products and Stone, Clay & Glass Products

CONTACT

William J. Anderson
Administrator
Pella Rolscreen Fdn.
102 Main St.
Pella, IA 50219
(515) 628-1000

FINANCIAL SUMMARY

Recent Giving: $870,000 (1993 est.); $913,358 (1992); $999,201 (1991)
Assets: $10,772,981 (1992); $9,967,682 (1991); $9,967,682 (1990)
Fiscal Note: All contributions are made through the foundation.
EIN: 23-7043881

CONTRIBUTIONS SUMMARY

Typical Recipients: • *Arts & Humanities:* history/historic preservation, libraries, museums/galleries, public broadcasting, theater • *Civic & Public Affairs:* environmental affairs • *Education:* colleges & universities, private education (precollege), public education (precollege), science/technology education, student aid • *Health:* hospitals • *Social Services:* community centers, community service organizations, family services, recreation & athletics, united funds, volunteer services, youth organizations

Grant Types: capital and employee matching gifts
Geographic Distribution: almost exclusively in Iowa, with emphasis on Marion, Mahaska, and Carroll counties
Operating Locations: IA (Pella)

CORP. OFFICERS

James Wayne Bevis: *B* Quincy FL 1934 *ED* Univ FL BS 1959 *CURR EMPL* pres, ceo, dir:

Pella Corp *CORP AFFIL* dir: IA Electric Indus Inc, IES Indus
Mary Joan Kuyper Farver: *B* 1919 *ED* Grinnell Coll BA 1941 *CURR EMPL* chmn, dir: Pella Rolscreen Corp *NONPR AFFIL* mem bd: IA Coll Fdn; mem exec comm, dir: Central Coll; mem bd: IA Pub Television Fdn

GIVING OFFICERS
William J. Anderson: adm, asst sec *B* Fort Dodge IA 1946 *CURR EMPL* secy, treas: Rolscreen Co
James Wayne Bevis: trust *CURR EMPL* pres, ceo, dir: Pella Corp (see above)
Mary Joan Kuyper Farver: trust *CURR EMPL* chmn, dir: Pella Rolscreen Corp (see above)

APPLICATION INFORMATION
Initial Approach: *Initial Contact:* full proposal (two copies) *Include Information On:* description of the organization, statement of need, amount requested, purpose for which funds are sought, project budget, recently audited financial statement, and proof of tax-exempt status *When to Submit:* any time; board meets quarterly **Restrictions on Giving:** Grants are not made to individuals, except under scholarship programs. Product donations are not made.

GRANTS ANALYSIS
Total Grants: $913,358
Number of Grants: 180*
Highest Grant: $167,000
Typical Range: $500 to $10,000
Disclosure Period: 1992
Note: Number of grants and average grant figures exclude $224,493 in matching gifts. Recent grants are derived from a 1990 Form 990.

RECENT GRANTS
167,167 Central College, Pella, IA
100,000 Municipal Golf Course-City of Pella, Pella, IA
 31,582 Iowa Natural Heritage Foundation, Des Moines, IA
 25,000 Pella Opera House Commission, Pella, IA
 20,000 Pella Christian Grade School, Pella, IA
 20,000 Pella Community Hospital, Pella, IA

20,000 University of Iowa Foundation, Iowa City, IA
15,000 Iowa College Foundation, Des Moines, IA
13,550 New Hope Village, Carroll, IA
12,500 Iowa Games, Ames, IA

Pellegrino-Realmuto Charitable Foundation

CONTACT
Joseph P. Pellegrino
Secretary, Director
Pellegrino-Realmuto Charitable Fdn.
101 Federal St., Ste. 1900
Boston, MA 02110
(617) 482-7288

FINANCIAL SUMMARY
Recent Giving: $408,780 (1991); $457,295 (1989); $99,825 (1988)
Assets: $1,819,643 (1991); $1,801,005 (1989); $1,971,865 (1988)
EIN: 04-6112614

CONTRIBUTIONS SUMMARY
Typical Recipients: • *Arts & Humanities:* museums/galleries • *Education:* colleges & universities, education funds • *Health:* hospitals • *Religion:* churches • *Social Services:* community service organizations, homes, youth organizations
Grant Types: general support

GIVING OFFICERS
Joseph Pellegrino: dir, treas
Joseph P. Pellegrino: dir, secy
Mae Realmuto: pres, dir
Mae Realmuto: pres, dir (see above)

GRANTS ANALYSIS
Number of Grants: 39
Highest Grant: $165,059
Typical Range: $200 to $10,000
Disclosure Period: 1991

RECENT GRANTS
165,059 Harvard University, Cambridge, MA
 84,941 Harvard College, Cambridge, MA
 25,000 MFA Boston, Boston, MA
 16,500 Concord Museum, Concord, MA

15,000 American Foundation, Fairfield, CT
15,000 Museum of Fine Arts, Boston, MA
10,000 Harvard College Fund, Cambridge, MA
10,000 Pike School, Andover, MA
10,000 SPNEA Boston, Boston, MA
10,000 Tufts University, Medford, MA

PemCo. Corp. / PemCo. Foundation

Sales: $9.5 million
Employees: 79
Headquarters: Bluefield, VA
SIC Major Group: Electronic & Other Electrical Equipment, Engineering & Management Services, Heavy Construction Except Building Construction, and Wholesale Trade—Durable Goods

CONTACT
Stanley O. McNaughton
Secretary & Treasurer
PemCo. Foundation
325 Eastlake Ave. E
Seattle, WA 98109
(206) 628-4027

FINANCIAL SUMMARY
Recent Giving: $567,241 (fiscal 1992); $461,927 (fiscal 1991); $386,065 (fiscal 1990)
Assets: $499,449 (fiscal year ending June 30, 1992); $173,058 (fiscal 1991); $159,186 (fiscal 1990)
Gifts Received: $884,890 (fiscal 1992); $466,900 (fiscal 1991); $144,600 (fiscal 1990)
Fiscal Note: Contributes through foundation only. In 1992, contributions were received from the Washington School Employees Credit Union ($121,982), Evergreen Bank ($40,000), PEMCO Corporation ($22,000), PEMCO Life Insurance Company ($40,000), Teacher's Foundation ($50,000), and the PEMCO Mutual Insurance Company.
EIN: 91-6072723

CONTRIBUTIONS SUMMARY
Typical Recipients: • *Education:* colleges & universities • *Health:* hospitals • *Social Services:* united funds, youth organizations
Grant Types: general support

Geographic Distribution: focus on Washington state
Operating Locations: WA (Seattle)

CORP. OFFICERS
D. M. Huber: *CURR EMPL* chmn: PemCo Corp
W. L. Sowers: *CURR EMPL* pres: PemCo Corp

GIVING OFFICERS
Sandra Kurack: vp, trust
Stanley O. McNaughton: secy, treas, trust
Astrid I. Merlino: pres, trust

APPLICATION INFORMATION
Initial Approach: *Initial Contact:* brief letter *Include Information On:* for scholarships, letter from school principal stating academic qualifications* *When to Submit:* any time *Note:* Prior period transcripts are required before current funds can be released.
Restrictions on Giving: Scholarships restricted to state of Washington residents at time of acceptance.

GRANTS ANALYSIS
Total Grants: $567,241
Number of Grants: 137*
Highest Grant: $50,000
Typical Range: $1,000 to $10,000
Disclosure Period: fiscal year ending June 30, 1992
Note: Number of grants and average grant figures do not include scholarships to individuals totaling $103,000. Recent grants are derived from a fiscal 1992 grants list.

RECENT GRANTS
50,000 Camp Brotherhood, Seattle, WA
30,250 United Way, Seattle, WA
15,000 Catholic Community Services, Seattle, WA
15,000 Independent Colleges of Washington, Seattle, WA
15,000 Junior Achievement, Mercer Island, WA
12,500 Boy Scouts of America, Everett, WA
10,915 Campfire of Snohomish County, Everett, WA
10,000 Boys and Girls Club, Everett, WA
10,000 Clymer Museum of Western Art, Ellensburg, WA

10,000 Kennedy High School, Seattle, WA

Pendergast-Weyer Foundation

CONTACT

Beverly B. Pendergast
President
Pendergast-Weyer Fdn.
c/o Grant Selection Committee
3434 West Coleman Rd.
Kansas City, MO 64111
(816) 561-6340

FINANCIAL SUMMARY

Recent Giving: $137,500 (fiscal 1991); $235,400 (fiscal 1990); $150,000 (fiscal 1989)
Assets: $4,109,289 (fiscal year ending June 30, 1991); $3,857,611 (fiscal 1990); $3,855,358 (fiscal 1989)
Gifts Received: $25 (fiscal 1990)
EIN: 43-1070676

CONTRIBUTIONS SUMMARY

Donor(s): the late Mary Louise Weyer Pendergast, Thomas J. Pendergast, Jr.
Typical Recipients: • *Education:* colleges & universities, private education (precollege), religious education • *Religion:* religious organizations • *Social Services:* child welfare, counseling
Grant Types: emergency, general support, multiyear/continuing support, operating expenses, and project
Geographic Distribution: limited to towns or cities in MO with populations under 100,000.

GIVING OFFICERS

Beverly Brayman: dir
Kenneth Burnett: dir
Dorothy Reed Hickok: dir
Beverly B. Pendergast: pres, dir
Thomas J. Pendergast, Jr.: chmn, secy, treas, dir
Joey Holter Straube: dir

APPLICATION INFORMATION

Initial Approach: Applications may be obtained by writing to the foundation's grant selection committee. There are no deadlines. The foundation does not permit its grants to be used for seed money or matching purposes, nor does it make grants to any individuals,

priests, bishops, chanceries, or school or church foundations.
Restrictions on Giving: Does not support clergymen, chanceries, or church foundations.

OTHER THINGS TO KNOW

Publications: Application Guidelines

GRANTS ANALYSIS

Number of Grants: 9
Highest Grant: $95,000
Typical Range: $250 to $5,000
Disclosure Period: fiscal year ending June 30, 1991

RECENT GRANTS

95,000 Stephens College, Columbia, MO — continuation and expansion of computer training for Catholic teachers
30,000 Stephens College, Columbia, MO — continuation of performing arts grants
5,000 Augustinian Recollect Monastery St. Cloud, West Orange, NJ
3,700 Most Precious Blood School, LeMay, MO — national telecommunications networking of computer lab to databases
2,300 Notre Dame High School, Cape Girardeum, MO
500 All Saints School, St. Peters, MO — use of facility for 8 computer courses
500 Immaculate Conception School, Jefferson City, MO — use of facility for eight computer training courses
250 Bishop Hogan High School, Kansas City, MO — use of facility for four computer training courses
250 Notre Dame High School, Cape Girardeum, MO

Pendleton Construction Corp. / Pendleton Construction Corp. Foundation

Sales: $12.5 million
Employees: 200
Headquarters: Wytheville, VA

CONTACT

William N. Pendleton
Director
Pendleton Construction Corp. Foundation
P.O. Box 549
Wytheville, VA 24382
(703) 228-8601

FINANCIAL SUMMARY

Recent Giving: $100 (1991); $68,131 (1989)
Assets: $71,754 (1991); $68,131 (1989)
EIN: 54-0846282

CONTRIBUTIONS SUMMARY

Typical Recipients: • *Civic & Public Affairs:* general • *Social Services:* united funds, youth organizations
Grant Types: general support
Operating Locations: VA (Wytheville)

CORP. OFFICERS

E. Pendleton: *CURR EMPL* cfo: Pendleton Construction Corp
Edmund Pendleton: *CURR EMPL* pres, treas: Pendleton Construction Corp

GIVING OFFICERS

Edmund Pendleton, Jr.: dir
William N. Pendleton: dir

APPLICATION INFORMATION

Initial Approach: Submit a brief letter of inquiry. There are no deadlines.

GRANTS ANALYSIS

Number of Grants: 2
Disclosure Period: 1991
Note: In 1991, contributions were of equal amounts.

RECENT GRANTS

50 Corporation for Jefferson's Poplar Forest
50 Second Presbyterian Church

Pendleton Memorial Fund, William L. and Ruth T.

CONTACT

Mark Tomlinson
Trust
William L. and Ruth T. Pendleton Memorial Fund
c/o Citibank (Arizona)
PO Box 1095
Phoenix, AZ 85001
(602) 530-1540

FINANCIAL SUMMARY

Recent Giving: $293,830 (1991); $261,421 (1990); $224,878 (1989)
Assets: $3,701,446 (1991); $3,157,808 (1990); $3,076,423 (1989)
EIN: 74-2475483

CONTRIBUTIONS SUMMARY

Typical Recipients: • *Arts & Humanities:* community arts, music • *Health:* medical research, single-disease health associations • *Religion:* churches, religious organizations • *Social Services:* community service organizations, homes, religious welfare, united funds, youth organizations
Grant Types: multiyear/continuing support and project
Geographic Distribution: focus on Phoenix, AZ

GIVING OFFICERS

Robert Burt: comm mem
Mildred May: comm mem
Janet Wilson: comm mem

APPLICATION INFORMATION

Initial Approach: Application form required. Deadline is September 30
Restrictions on Giving: Does not support individuals.

GRANTS ANALYSIS

Number of Grants: 12
Highest Grant: $44,926
Typical Range: $15,000 to $20,000
Disclosure Period: 1991

RECENT GRANTS

44,926 Christian Care Center, Phoenix, AZ
40,000 American Diabetes Association, Phoenix, AZ
37,500 Arizona Rainbow Girls Foundation, Phoenix, AZ

28,600 First Christian Church Guiding Light School, Phoenix, AZ

28,381 Alzheimer's Disease and Related Disorders Association, Phoenix, AZ

25,000 Arizona Cactus Girl Scouts, Phoenix, AZ

25,000 Arizona Rainbow Girls Foundation, Phoenix, AZ

21,322 Christian Care Management, Phoenix, AZ

19,700 Phoenix Symphony Guild, Phoenix, AZ

10,000 House of Refuge, Phoenix, AZ

Penguin USA Inc.

Sales: $400.0 million
Employees: 1,200
Parent Company: Pearson Inc.
Headquarters: New York, NY
SIC Major Group: Printing & Publishing

CONTACT
Shelley Sadler
Director, Human Resources
Penguin USA Inc.
375 Hudson St.
New York, NY 10014
(212) 366-2000

CONTRIBUTIONS SUMMARY
Operating Locations: NY (New York)

CORP. OFFICERS
Peter Mayer: *CURR EMPL* chmn: Penguin USA
John Moore: *CURR EMPL* pres, coo: Penguin USA

GIVING OFFICERS
Shelley Sadler: *CURR EMPL* dir (human resources): Penguin USA

APPLICATION INFORMATION
Initial Approach: Send letter of inquiry describing the organization and project, amount requested, and how funds will be used.

Penn Central Corp.

Sales: $2.1 billion
Employees: 19,500
Headquarters: Cincinnati, OH
SIC Major Group: Engineering & Management Services, Fabricated Metal Products, Industrial Machinery &

Equipment, and Insurance Agents, Brokers & Service

CONTACT
Karen Y. Grant
Matching Grant Coordinator
Penn Central Corp.
One East 4th St.
Cincinnati, OH 45202
(513) 579-6678

CONTRIBUTIONS SUMMARY
Company provides employee matching gifts only.
Grant Types: matching
Operating Locations: CA (Redding, Santa Monica, Van Nuys), CO (Westminster), CT (Danbury, Greenwich), FL (Clearwater, Ft. Walton Beach, Melbourne), MD (Silver Spring), NJ (South Plainfield), OH (Cincinnati), OK (Ardmore), RI (Pawtucket), TX (Longview, Waco), VA (Vienna)

CORP. OFFICERS
Carl H. Lindner III: *CURR EMPL* pres, coo: Penn Central Corp

Penn Foundation, William

CONTACT
Bernard C. Watson
President and Chief Executive Officer
William Penn Foundation
1630 Locust St.
Philadelphia, PA 19103
(215) 732-5114

FINANCIAL SUMMARY
Recent Giving: $35,764,000 (1993 est.); $35,781,048 (1992); $30,549,447 (1991)
Assets: $625,000,000 (1992 approx.); $551,000,000 (1991); $494,000,000 (1990 approx.)
Gifts Received: $11,739,000 (1992); $11,570,000 (1991); $11,391,666 (1990 approx.)
EIN: 23-1503488

CONTRIBUTIONS SUMMARY
Donor(s): The William Penn Foundation was established in 1945 by Otto Haas (1872-1960) and his wife, Phoebe. Mr. Haas immigrated to the United States from Germany at the turn of the century. He helped develop and market an innovative leather tanning process which proved to be highly popular in the United States and later in South America. He

built a career based on his expertise in industrial chemicals. His wife, Phoebe Waterman Haas, was born in North Dakota, educated at Vassar, and was an astronomer. In 1945, Otto and Phoebe Haas established the Phoebe Waterman Foundation. Reflecting the founders' postwar concerns, grants were used to fund European relief, provide scholarships for fatherless children, and support medical and educational institutions. When Otto Haas died in 1960, the foundation received the bulk of his estate. Mrs. Haas continued adding funds to the foundation until her death in 1967. In 1970, the name of the foundation was changed to the Haas Community Foundation. In 1974, it was renamed the William Penn Foundation, reflecting its close ties to Philadelphia.

Typical Recipients: • *Arts & Humanities:* arts associations, arts centers, arts festivals, arts institutes, community arts, dance, ethnic arts, history/historic preservation, libraries, literary arts, museums/galleries, music, opera, performing arts, public broadcasting, theater, visual arts • *Civic & Public Affairs:* environmental affairs, ethnic/minority organizations, housing, urban & community affairs, zoos/botanical gardens • *Education:* arts education, career/vocational education, colleges & universities, community & junior colleges, elementary education, engineering education, liberal arts education, minority education, preschool education, public education (precollege), science/technology education • *Health:* geriatric health, health organizations, pediatric health, public health • *Social Services:* aged, child welfare, community centers, community service organizations, counseling, day care, employment/job training, family planning, family services, homes, recreation & athletics, united funds, volunteer services, youth organizations

Grant Types: capital, multiyear/continuing support, and project

Geographic Distribution: mostly restricted to regional giving; some national and international giving

GIVING OFFICERS
Ernesta D. Ballard: dir *PHIL AFFIL* dir: Philadelphia Foundation
Harry E. Cerino: vp programs
Ida K. Chen: dir
Gloria Twine Chisum: dir
Fran M. Coopersmith: vp fin, treas
Graham S. Finney: dir
Carole F. Haas: dir
Chara C. Haas: dir
David W. Haas: chmn, dir
Frederick R. Haas: dir
Janet F. Haas: vchmn, dir
John Charles Haas: dir *B* Haverford PA 1918 *ED* Amherst Coll AB 1940; MA Inst Tech MSCE 1942 *NONPR AFFIL* mem: Am Chemical Soc, Am Inst Chemical Engrs *PHIL AFFIL* don, trust: John C & Chara C Haas Charitable Trust
John O. Haas: dir
Nancy B. Haas: dir
Thomas W. Haas: dir
Philip C. Herr II: dir
Roland H. Johnson: secy, sr program off
Stephanie Naidoff: dir
Edmund B. Spaeth, Jr.: dir *B* WA 1920 *ED* Harvard Univ BA 1942; Harvard Univ LLB 1948 *CURR EMPL* coun: Pepper Hamilton & Scheetz *NONPR AFFIL* dir: Ctr Professionalism, Curtis Inst Music, Diagnostic Rehabilitation Ctr, Pub Intl Law Ctr Philadelphia; fellow: Am Bar Assn; mem: Am Bar Fdn, Am Judicature Soc, Am Law Inst, Am PA, Order Coif, PA Bar Assn, Phi Beta Kappa, Philadelphia Bar Assn; sr fellow: Univ PA Law Sch; trust: Bryn Mawr Coll, Lewis M Stevens Conf Trust
Anita Arrow Summers: dir *B* New York NY 1925 *ED* Hunter Coll BA 1945; Univ Chicago MA 1947 *CORP AFFIL* bd dir, chmn audit comm: Meridian Bancorp *NONPR AFFIL* mem: Am Econ Assn, Assn Pub Policy & Mgmt; res policy counc, mem subcommittee ed governance: Comm Econ Devel New York City
Bernard C. Watson, PhD: pres, ceo, dir *ED* IN Univ BA 1951; Univ IL M Ed 1955; Univ Chicago PhD 1967; Harvard Univ 1968 *CORP AFFIL* dir: Comcast Cablevision Philadelphia, Comcast Inc, Fidelcor, Fidelity Bank, First Fidelity Bancorp, Keystone Ins Co *NONPR AFFIL* coun: Econ Devel Counc, Natl Inst Ed, NY

City Joint Ctr Political Studies, US Civil Rights Comm, US Off Ed; dir: Keystone AAA Club, Philadelphia Contributionship; mem: Am Academy Political Social Science, Am Philosophy Soc, Ctr for Study Dem Insts, William T. Grant Fdn Commn Work Family & Citizenship, Kappa Delta Pi, Phi Delta Kappa; secy, dir: NJ Academy Aquatic Svcs; sr vchmn, bd trusts, bd dirs: Greater Philadelphia Partnership; sr vchmn, trust: Natl Urban League; vchmn: PA Counc Arts; vchmn, dir: PA Convention Ctr Authority; mem comm grad sch ed bd overseers: Fed Judiciary Nominating Comm, Harvard Coll

APPLICATION INFORMATION

Initial Approach:
Applications will not be considered unless submitted in writing. Visits to the foundation and contacts with members of the board or staff are strongly discouraged. A single copy of a proposal, in writing, is sufficient.

The proposal should include a one-page summary outline; information about the agency making the request; description of the proposed project; complete financial information; copy of the IRS determination letter of tax-exempt status; list of officers and directors of the organization making the application; copy of the most recent annual report; and a copy, audited if available, of the most recent financial statement. There are no formal deadlines for funding requests.

All proposals are reviewed by the foundation staff to determine whether they fall within its areas of interest and current funding priorities. Those meeting the criteria are then subject to further study and investigation; some may then be submitted to the board of directors for consideration.

Restrictions on Giving: No grants are made to institutions which unfairly discriminate on the basis of race, creed, or sex. No grants are made to individuals or to support sectarian religious activities; or for scholarships, fellowships, or travel; lobbying or legislative activities; programs concerned with a particular disease; addiction treatment; recreational pro-

grams; or films. The foundation does not make loans or provide funds to be redistributed at an organization's discretion.

OTHER THINGS TO KNOW

Publications: annual report, grant application procedures

GRANTS ANALYSIS

Total Grants: $35,781,048
Number of Grants: 216
Highest Grant: $3,000,000
Typical Range: $10,000 to $200,000
Disclosure Period: 1992
Note: Average grant figure excludes a $3,000,000 grant. Recent grants are derived from a 1992 annual report.

RECENT GRANTS

3,000,000 Philadelphia Ranger Corps, Philadelphia, PA — a three-year grant to continue the Philadelphia Ranger Corps program

2,723,000 Beech Corporation, Philadelphia, PA — to support the non-business activities of the Cecil B. Moore Avenue Business Association

2,535,750 Sassafras Corporation, Philadelphia, PA — a three-year grant for operating costs of the Arts Bank on South Broad Street

1,200,558 Temple University, Philadelphia, PA — a four-year grant for an infant mortality reduction program in high-risk neighborhoods

1,000,000 Philadelphia Foundation, Philadelphia, PA — to help establish a community development corporation support program to increase affordable housing

1,000,000 Philadelphia Orchestra Association, Philadelphia, PA — a three-year grant toward a new concert hall

422,000 University of the Arts, Philadelphia, PA — for the installation of security gates on the Arts Bank Theater

415,766 United Way of Southeastern Pennsylvania, Philadel-

phia, PA — for the 1992 campaign

351,664 Greater Philadelphia Federation of Settlements, Philadelphia, PA

302,061 Pennsylvania Horticultural Society, Philadelphia, PA — a four-year grant for an urban tree planting project

Penn Industrial Chemical Corp. / Penn Industrial Chemical Corp. Clairton High School Fund

Headquarters: Pittsburgh, PA

CONTACT

Joan Mayo
Vice President
Penn Industrial Chemical Corp.
Integra Trust Co.
300 Fourth Ave.
Pittsburgh, PA 15278
(412) 355-4810

FINANCIAL SUMMARY

Recent Giving: $13,000 (1990); $10,750 (1989)

Assets: $427,150 (1989)

EIN: 25-6032785

CONTRIBUTIONS SUMMARY

Grant Types: scholarship

Operating Locations: PA (Pittsburgh)

APPLICATION INFORMATION

Initial Approach: Send a brief letter of inquiry.

Restrictions on Giving: Does not support political or lobbying groups, or organizations outside operating areas.

OTHER THINGS TO KNOW

Provides higher education scholarships for graduates of Clairton High School in Clairton, PA.

GRANTS ANALYSIS

Typical Range: $1,000 to $2,500

Penn Mutual Life Insurance Co.

Assets: $6.08 billion
Employees: 2,000
Headquarters: Philadelphia, PA
SIC Major Group: Insurance Carriers

CONTACT

Katherine Grady
Director, Corporate Communications
Penn Mutual Life Insurance Co.
Independence Sq.
Philadelphia, PA 19172
(215) 956-8000

CONTRIBUTIONS SUMMARY

Nonmonetary Support Types: donated products and loaned executives
Operating Locations: PA (Bryn Mawr, Philadelphia)

CORP. OFFICERS

Thomas E. Stiles: *CURR EMPL* cfo: Penn Mutual Life Ins

John E. Tait: *B* Moline IL 1932 *ED* Univ IL *CURR EMPL* chmn, pres, ceo, dir: Penn Mutual Life Ins Co *CORP AFFIL* dir: Indepro, Janney Montgomery Scott *NONPR AFFIL* dir: Am Counc Life Ins, Ins Federation PA, Mortgage Bankers Assn, Mutual Life Ins Tax Comm

Penn Savings Bank, a division of Sovereign Bank Bank of Princeton, a division of Sovereign Bank / Sovereign Bank Foundation

Assets: $1.8 billion
Employees: 303
Headquarters: Wyomissing, PA
SIC Major Group: Depository Institutions

CONTACT

Gail Dawson-White
Administrator
Sovereign Savings Bank Fdn.
1130 Berkshire Blvd.
Wyomissing, PA 19610
(215) 320-8504

FINANCIAL SUMMARY

Recent Giving: $46,673 (1991); $43,051 (1990)

Assets: $100 (1991); $1,773 (1990)
Gifts Received: $45,000 (1991); $44,825 (1990)
Fiscal Note: In 1991, contributions were received from Penn Savings Bank.
EIN: 23-2548113

CONTRIBUTIONS SUMMARY
Typical Recipients: • *Arts & Humanities:* community arts, ethnic arts • *Civic & Public Affairs:* civil rights, law & justice, rural affairs, urban & community affairs, women's affairs • *Health:* hospitals • *Social Services:* community service organizations, domestic violence, emergency relief, family planning, food/clothing distribution, shelters/homelessness, united funds, volunteer services, youth organizations
Grant Types: capital, general support, project, and seed money
Nonmonetary Support Types: cause-related marketing & promotion, donated products, and in-kind services
Geographic Distribution: primarily in the Lancaster and Reading, PA, area, and Mercer County, New Jersey
Operating Locations: PA (Wyomissing)

CORP. OFFICERS
Jay S. Sidhu: *CURR EMPL*
pres, ceo: Penn Savings Bank

GIVING OFFICERS
Gail Dawson-White: mgr
James N. Esbenshade: dir
Richard E. Mohn: dir
Joni S. Naugle: treas, secy
Jay S. Sidhu: dir *CURR EMPL*
pres, ceo: Penn Savings Bank
(see above)
Lawrence M. Thompson: pres
Theodore Ziaylek, Jr.: dir

APPLICATION INFORMATION
Initial Approach: Submit a proposal, including a brief description of the organization, needs of project, population served, proof of tax-exempt status, and list of directors. There are no deadlines.
Restrictions on Giving: Does not support individuals, religious organizations for sectarian purposes, political or lobbying groups, or organizations outside operating areas.

GRANTS ANALYSIS
Number of Grants: 64

Highest Grant: $7,500
Typical Range: $100 to $1,000
Disclosure Period: 1991

RECENT GRANTS
7,500	Scenic River Days '89, Reading, PA
5,200	United Way, Reading, PA
3,000	United Way, Lancaster, PA
2,500	Caron Foundation Capital Fund Campaign, Wernersville, PA
1,500	Lancaster Public Library, Lancaster, PA
1,500	Lancaster Summer Arts Festival, Lancaster, PA
1,500	Pennsylvania State University, University Park, PA
1,000	Berks Teen Talk Line, Reading, PA
1,000	Neighborhood Housing Services, Reading, PA
1,000	Rainbow House AIDS Hospice, Shillington, PA

Penn Traffic Co.
Sales: $2.73 billion
Employees: 23,186
Parent Company: Miller Tabak Hirsch & Co.
Headquarters: Johnstown, PA
SIC Major Group: Food Stores

CONTACT
John Stewart
Controller
Penn Traffic Co.
319 Washington St.
Johnstown, PA 15901
(814) 536-9900

CONTRIBUTIONS SUMMARY
Operating Locations: PA (Johnstown)

CORP. OFFICERS
Gary D. Hirsch: *CURR EMPL*
chmn: Penn Traffic Co
Claude J. Incaudo: *CURR EMPL* pres, ceo: Penn Traffic Co
John M. Kriak: *CURR EMPL* vp, cfo: Penn Traffic Co

Pennbank
Headquarters: Erie, PA

CONTACT
Thomas Doolin
President
Pennbank
801 State St.
Erie, PA 16501
(814) 871-1822

CONTRIBUTIONS SUMMARY
Grant Types: matching
Operating Locations: PA (Erie)

CORP. OFFICERS
Thomas Doolin: *CURR EMPL*
pres: Pennbank

Penney Foundation, James C.

CONTACT
Anne L. Romasco
Managing Director
James C. Penney Fdn.
1633 Broadway, 39th Fl.
New York, NY 10019
(212) 830-7490

FINANCIAL SUMMARY
Recent Giving: $412,000 (1991); $499,608 (1990); $460,513 (1989)
Assets: $6,714,933 (1991); $5,381,495 (1990); $5,714,894 (1989)
Gifts Received: $170,135 (1991)
EIN: 13-6114301

CONTRIBUTIONS SUMMARY
Donor(s): the late James C. Penney, Caroline A. Penney
Typical Recipients: • *Civic & Public Affairs:* environmental affairs, housing, municipalities, public policy, urban & community affairs • *Education:* colleges & universities, education funds • *Social Services:* animal protection, child welfare, community service organizations, counseling, family planning, food/clothing distribution, homes, shelters/homelessness, youth organizations
Grant Types: operating expenses, project, and seed money
Geographic Distribution: limited to the Northeast

GIVING OFFICERS
Andrew Walzer Bisset: secy, dir *B* New London CT 1919 *ED* Lafayette Coll AB 1941; Yale

Univ LLB 1948 *CURR EMPL* of coun: LeBoeuf Lamb et al *CORP AFFIL* of coun: Le-Boeuf Lamb et al; ptnr: Bisset Atkins & Saunders
Mary Wagley Copp: dir
Anne Paxton Wagley Gow: dir
Carol P. Guyer: pres, dir
Shelly D. Guyer: dir
Alissa C. Keny-Guyer: dir
Caroline A. Penney: dir
James F. Wagley: dir
Mary Frances Wagley: vp, treas, dir

APPLICATION INFORMATION
Initial Approach: Application form required. There are no deadlines.
Restrictions on Giving: Does not support individuals or provide funds for capital improvements, endowments, or scholarships.

OTHER THINGS TO KNOW
Publications: Multi-year Report

GRANTS ANALYSIS
Number of Grants: 27
Highest Grant: $50,000
Typical Range: $10,000 to $20,000
Disclosure Period: 1991

RECENT GRANTS
50,000	YWCA, New York, NY
20,000	Environmental Defense Fund, New York, NY
20,000	Federation of Appalachian Housing Enterprises, Berea, KY
20,000	Henry Street Settlement, New York, NY
20,000	Inform, New York, NY
20,000	National Fish and Wildlife Foundation, Washington, DC
20,000	Natural Resources Defense Council, New York, NY
20,000	Planned Parenthood Federation of America, New York, NY
20,000	South Bronx 2000 Local Development, Bronx, NY
15,000	Pratt Institute Center for Community and Environmental Development, Brooklyn, NY

Pennington Foundation, Irene W. and C. B.

CONTACT
C. B. Pennington
Trustee
Irene W. and C. B. Pennington
Fdn.
c/o Robert R. Casey
PO Box 1267
Baton Rouge, LA 70821
(504) 383-3412

FINANCIAL SUMMARY
Recent Giving: $550,100
(1990); $803,183 (1989);
$205,126 (1988)
Assets: $23,511,577 (1990);
$16,572,182 (1989);
$10,143,671 (1988)
Gifts Received: $6,000,000
(1990); $6,100,000 (1989);
$6,000,000 (1988)
Fiscal Note: 1990 contribution
from C. B. and Irene W. Pennington.
EIN: 72-0938097

CONTRIBUTIONS SUMMARY
Donor(s): The foundation was
established in 1982 by C. B.
Pennington amd Irene W. Pennington.
Typical Recipients: • *Civic & Public Affairs:* environmental
affairs, women's affairs • *Education:* private education (precollege), religious education
• *Health:* hospitals, medical research • *Religion:* churches
• *Social Services:* community
centers, community service organizations, food/clothing distribution, homes, shelters/homelessness, united funds, youth
organizations
Grant Types: general support
Geographic Distribution:
Baton Rouge, LA

GIVING OFFICERS
R. R. Casey: trust
Claude Bernard Pennington:
trust *B* Chunky MS 1900
CURR EMPL pres: Pennco Oil
Irene W. Pennington: trust
W. W. Williams: trust

APPLICATION INFORMATION
Initial Approach: Restrictions on Giving: The foundation supports preselected organizations and does not
accept unsolicited requests for
funds. The foundation does not
make grants to individuals.

GRANTS ANALYSIS
Total Grants: $550,100
Number of Grants: 17
Highest Grant: $400,000
Typical Range: $1,000 to
$10,000
Disclosure Period: 1990
Note: Average grant figure
does not include the highest
grant of $400,000. Recent
grants are derived from a 1990
grants list.

RECENT GRANTS
400,000   Boy Scouts of America, Baton Rouge, LA
50,000   YMCA, Baton Rouge, LA
30,000   Silliman Institute, Clinton, LA
30,000   St. Aloysius School, Baton Rouge, LA
5,000   Boy Scouts of America, Baton Rouge, LA
5,000   Catholic High School, Baton Rouge, LA
5,000   St. James Episcopal Church, Baton Rouge, LA
5,000   Woman's Club, Baton Rouge, LA
3,000   Audubon Girl Scout Council, Baton Rouge, LA
2,000   First Baptist Church of Baton Rouge, Baton Rouge, LA

Pennsylvania Dutch Co. / Pennsylvania Dutch Co. Foundation

Sales: $18.0 million
Headquarters: Mount Holly Springs, PA

CONTACT
Lincoln A. Worrell
Secretary and Manager
Pennsylvania Dutch Co.
366 Belvedere Street
Carlisle, PA 17013
(717) 486-3496

FINANCIAL SUMMARY
Recent Giving: $50,800 (fiscal
1991); $32,297 (fiscal 1990)
Assets: $69,040 (fiscal year
ending October 31, 1991);
$1,709 (fiscal 1990)
Gifts Received: $116,229 (fiscal 1991); $21,742 (fiscal 1990)
Fiscal Note: In fiscal 1992,
contributions were received
from the Pennsylvania Dutch
Co., Inc.

EIN: 23-2022526

CONTRIBUTIONS SUMMARY
Typical Recipients: • *Arts & Humanities:* libraries • *Education:* education associations,
education funds, public education (precollege) • *Health:* hospitals • *Religion:* churches • *Social Services:* youth
organizations
Grant Types: general support
Geographic Distribution: giving primarily in PA
Operating Locations: PA
(Mount Holly Springs)

CORP. OFFICERS
Jonas E. Warrell: *CURR EMPL* chmn: Pennsylvania
Dutch Co
Lincoln A. Warrell: *CURR EMPL* pres: Pennsylvania
Dutch Co

GIVING OFFICERS
Jonas E. Warrell: chmn
Lincoln A. Warrell: secy
CURR EMPL pres: Pennsylvania Dutch Co (see above)

APPLICATION INFORMATION
Initial Approach: Applications not accepted. The foundation reports it supports preselected organizations.

GRANTS ANALYSIS
Number of Grants: 36
Highest Grant: $5,000
Typical Range: $100 to $1,000
Disclosure Period: fiscal year
ending October 31, 1991

RECENT GRANTS
5,000   Trinity High School, Shiremanstown, PA — development fund
5,000   York Hospital Building Fund, York, PA
5,000   YWCA, Carlisle, PA
3,000   Pennsylvania State University, University Park, PA — college of engineering fund
3,000   St. Patrick's Catholic Church, Carlisle, PA — building fund
2,800   Americanism Education Network, Hagerstown, IN — educational materials
2,800   YMCA, Carlisle, PA
2,250   Brian Bex Report, Hagerstown, IN —

books for Freedom library
2,000   Americanism Foundation, Appleton, WI — educational materials
2,000   Americanism Foundation, Appleton, WI — educational materials

Pennsylvania General Insurance Co.

Premiums: $138.0 million
Headquarters: Philadelphia, PA
SIC Major Group: Insurance Carriers

CONTACT
Walter Farman
Chief Executive Officer
Pennsylvania General Insurance Co.
436 Walnut St.
Philadelphia, PA 19105
(215) 625-1000

FINANCIAL SUMMARY
Recent Giving: $500,000
(1992 approx.)
Fiscal Note: Company gives directly.

CONTRIBUTIONS SUMMARY
Typical Recipients: • *Arts & Humanities:* dance, museums/galleries, music • *Civic & Public Affairs:* business/free enterprise, civil rights, economic
development, urban & community affairs • *Education:* education associations, minority education • *Social Services:* united
funds
Grant Types: general support
Geographic Distribution:
Philadelphia, PA
Operating Locations: OR, PA
(Philadelphia)

CORP. OFFICERS
Walter E. Farman: *CURR EMPL* chmn, ceo, dir: PA Gen
Ins Co

GIVING OFFICERS
Walter E. Farman: *CURR EMPL* chmn, ceo, dir: PA Gen
Ins Co (see above)

APPLICATION INFORMATION
Initial Approach: *Initial Contact:* brief letter of inquiry *Include Information On:* description of the organization,
amount requested, and the purpose for which funds are

sought *When to Submit:* any time
Restrictions on Giving: Does not support for-profit organizations.

GRANTS ANALYSIS
Typical Range: $250 to $1,000

Pennsylvania Knitted Outerwear Manufacturing Association / Penn Knitted Outerwear Foundation
Headquarters: Philadelphia, PA

CONTACT
Joseph Fisher
Vice President
Penn Knitted Outerwear Foundation
1117 Land Title Bldg.
Philadelphia, PA 19110
(215) 561-2990
Note: Edward B. Shils, secretary to the trustees, is another contact.

FINANCIAL SUMMARY
Recent Giving: $11,750 (1991); $7,550 (1990); $8,001 (1989)
Assets: $49,899 (1991); $63,715 (1990); $61,163 (1989)
EIN: 23-6296951

CONTRIBUTIONS SUMMARY
Typical Recipients: • *Education:* colleges & universities, community & junior colleges, medical education, private education (precollege) • *Health:* single-disease health associations • *Religion:* religious organizations
Grant Types: general support
Geographic Distribution: focus on the northeast U.S.
Operating Locations: PA (Philadelphia)

CORP. OFFICERS
Thomas Cahill: *B* Philadelphia PA 1935 *ED* La Salle Coll 1957; St Josephs Coll *CURR EMPL* pres: Pennsylvania Knitted Outerwear Mfg Assn

GIVING OFFICERS
Albert A. Cohen: chmn, trust

APPLICATION INFORMATION
Initial Approach: Send brief letter describing program. There are no deadlines.

GRANTS ANALYSIS
Number of Grants: 16
Highest Grant: $2,300
Typical Range: $100 to $600
Disclosure Period: 1991

RECENT GRANTS
2,300 University of Pennsylvania, Philadelphia, PA
1,850 University of Pittsburgh, Pittsburgh, PA
1,300 Philadelphia College of Textiles and Sciences, Philadelphia, PA
1,000 Friends of Als, Philadelphia, PA
900 Philadelphia College of Pharmacy, Philadelphia, PA
800 Akiba Hebrew Hearing, Philadelphia, PA
800 Tenek University, Philadelphia, PA
600 Delandre Community College, Delandre, PA
600 West Chester University, West Chester, PA
400 Jewish Memorial Fund, Philadelphia, PA

Pennsylvania Power & Light
Revenue: $2.56 billion
Employees: 8,144
Headquarters: Allentown, PA
SIC Major Group: Electric, Gas & Sanitary Services

CONTACT
Marjorie H. Lauer
Manager, Board Services
Pennsylvania Power & Light
Two N Ninth St.
Allentown, PA 18101
(215) 774-5151

FINANCIAL SUMMARY
Fiscal Note: Annual Giving Range: $750,000 to $1,000,000

CONTRIBUTIONS SUMMARY
Typical Recipients: • *Arts & Humanities:* general • *Civic & Public Affairs:* general • *Education:* general • *Health:* general • *Social Services:* general
Grant Types: employee matching gifts and general support
Geographic Distribution: locally in service areas
Operating Locations: PA (Allentown, Edensburg, Harrisburg, Hazleton, Lancaster, Montoursville, Scranton)

CORP. OFFICERS
William F. Hecht: *CURR EMPL* chmn, pres, ceo: PA Power & Light Co
Francis A. Long: *CURR EMPL* exec vp, coo: PA Power & Light Co
Charles E. Russoli: *CURR EMPL* exec vp, cfo: PA Power & Light Co

APPLICATION INFORMATION
Initial Approach: *Initial Contact:* brief letter of inquiry and full proposal *Include Information On:* description of the organization, amount requested, purpose of funds sought, audited financial statement, and proof of tax-exempt status *When to Submit:* any time
Restrictions on Giving: Does not support individuals, religious organizations for sectarian purposes, or political or lobbying groups.

OTHER THINGS TO KNOW
Matches employees gifts to eligible, accredited educational institutions. Minimum gift matched is $25; maximum gift matched is $1,000 per employee per year.
Company reports that their corporate giving program is fairly static giving only to local and to traditional community programs with no targeted areas of interest.

GRANTS ANALYSIS
Disclosure Period: 1993
Note: Annual Giving Range: $750,000 to $1,000,000. Recent grants are derived from a 1993 grant list.

RECENT GRANTS
25,000 Pennsylvania State University, Harrisburg, PA — for the purchase of electric-powered van to be used in solar energy research

---

Pennzoil Co.
Sales: $2.74 billion
Employees: 6,500
Headquarters: Houston, TX
SIC Major Group: Holding & Other Investment Offices, Nonmetallic Minerals Except Fuels, Oil & Gas Extraction, and Petroleum & Coal Products

CONTACT
H. M. (Mickey) Gentry
Coordinator, Contributions
Pennzoil Co.
PO Box 2967
Houston, TX 77252
(713) 546-8538

FINANCIAL SUMMARY
Recent Giving: $3,000,000 (1992 approx.); $3,000,000 (1991 approx.); $2,500,000 (1990)
Fiscal Note: Company gives directly.

CONTRIBUTIONS SUMMARY
Typical Recipients: • *Arts & Humanities:* arts associations, arts centers, arts festivals, community arts, dance, history/historic preservation, libraries, museums/galleries, music, opera, performing arts, public broadcasting, theater • *Civic & Public Affairs:* public policy, safety, urban & community affairs, zoos/botanical gardens • *Education:* business education, colleges & universities, engineering education, science/technology education, student aid • *Health:* emergency/ambulance services, health organizations, hospices, hospitals, medical rehabilitation, medical research, pediatric health, single-disease health associations • *Social Services:* child welfare, community service organizations, delinquency & crime, disabled, drugs & alcohol, emergency relief, shelters/homelessness, united funds, youth organizations
Grant Types: employee matching gifts, general support, and research
Geographic Distribution: primary consideration given at local level to communities in which company has plants, warehouses, or refineries; rarely gives to national or international organizations
Operating Locations: LA (Shreveport), PA (Bradford, Butler, Oil City, Pittsburgh), TX (Houston)

CORP. OFFICERS
John Hugh Liedtke: *B* Tulsa OK 1922 *ED* Amherst Coll BA 1942; Harvard Univ 1943; Univ TX LLB 1947 *CURR EMPL* chmn, ceo: Pennzoil Co *NONPR AFFIL* counc overseers: Jesse H Jones Grad Sch Admin Rice Univ; dir: Am

Petroleum Inst, Houston Chamber Commerce, Independent Petroleum Assn Am, Natl Petroleum Counc, Natl Petroleum Refiners Assn, Penn Grade Assn, TX Mid-Continent Oil Gas Assn; mem: Beta Theta Pi, Phi Alpha Delta; trust: Baylor Coll Medicine, Kincaid Sch, US Naval Academy Fdn **James Leonard Pate:** *B* Mt Sterling IL 1935 *ED* Monmouth Coll BA 1963; Univ IN MBA 1965 *CURR EMPL* pres, ceo, dir: Pennzoil Co *CORP AFFIL* asst secy: Dept Commerce DC; chief economist: BFGoodrich; dir: Jiffy Lube Intl; special adv: White House; sr economist: Fed Reserve Bank Cleveland; sr vp fin: Pennzoil Co *NONPR AFFIL* bd govs: Rice Univ; dir: Am Petroleum Inst, Natl Petroleum Counc; fellow: Royal Econ Soc; mem: Am Econ Assn, Natl Assn Bus Economists, Pi Gamma Mu, Senate Monmouth Coll, Soc Social Political Scientists **James W. Shaddix:** *B* Lubbock TX 1946 *CURR EMPL* gen couns: Pennzoil Co

GIVING OFFICERS

David P. Alderson: mem (contributions comm) *B* Wilmington DE 1949 *CURR EMPL* sr vp (fin), treas: Pennzoil Co **John Davis:** mem (contributions comm) **H. M. Gentry:** *CURR EMPL* coordinator (community rels & contributions): Pennzoil Co **Thomas Hamilton:** mem (contributions comm) **Terry Hemeyer:** chmn *B* Cleveland OH 1938 *CURR EMPL* group vp (admin): Pennzoil Co *NONPR AFFIL* assoc chmn: Am Cancer Soc South TX; dir: KUHT-TV; mem: Disabled Vets Assn, Retired Offs Assn **Mark A. Malinski:** mem (contributions comm) *B* Chicago IL 1955 *CURR EMPL* group vp, contr: Pennzoil Co **James W. Shaddix:** mem (contributions comm) *CURR EMPL* gen couns: Pennzoil Co (see above)

APPLICATION INFORMATION

Initial Approach: *Initial Contact:* brief letter; no phone calls *Include Information On:* description of the organization, amount requested, purpose for which funds are sought, re-

cently audited financial statement, copy of 501(c)(3) statement *When to Submit:* before Fall, when budget is completed; proposals received after the budgeting process are not likely to be considered until the following year **Restrictions on Giving:** Company generally does not support strictly sectarian or denominational religious activities, secondary schools, veterans or fraternal organizations, individual testimonial dinners, donations that are not tax-deductible, charitable advertising, or donations of products.

GRANTS ANALYSIS

Total Grants: $3,000,000
Disclosure Period: 1991

Penske Corp.

Sales: $2.3 billion
Employees: 9,500
Headquarters: Detroit, MI
SIC Major Group: Automobile Repair, Services & Parking, Automotive Dealers & Service Stations, and Industrial Machinery & Equipment

CONTACT

Richard T. Peters
Penske Corp.
13400 West Outer Dr.
Detroit, MI 48239
(313) 592-7379

CONTRIBUTIONS SUMMARY

Operating Locations: MI (Detroit)

CORP. OFFICERS

Roger S. Penske: *B* Shaker Heights OH 1937 *CURR EMPL* chmn, pres, ceo, coo, dir: Penske Corp *CORP AFFIL* chmn, dir: Longo D Inc, Penske Truck Leasing Corp; co-fdr, dir: Championship Auto Racing Teams; dir: Am Express Co, Conner Peripherals, Shearson Lehman Hutton Holdings; pres, dir: Penske Transportation *NONPR AFFIL* dir: Truck Rental Leasing Fdn; mem: Automotive Safety Fdn; mem exec comm: Highway Users Federation

Pentair

Sales: $1.23 billion
Employees: 8,400
Headquarters: St. Paul, MN
SIC Major Group: Electronic & Other Electrical Equipment, Fabricated Metal Products, Industrial Machinery & Equipment, and Paper & Allied Products

CONTACT

Jeanne Benson
Contributions Program Administrator
Pentair, Inc.
1500 County Road, B2 West
St. Paul, MN 55113
(612) 636-7920

FINANCIAL SUMMARY

Fiscal Note: Company gives directly. Annual Giving Range: $500,000 to $900,000

CONTRIBUTIONS SUMMARY

Typical Recipients: • *Arts & Humanities:* general • *Civic & Public Affairs:* general • *Education:* general • *Health:* general • *Social Services:* general
Grant Types: capital, employee matching gifts, endowment, general support, and matching
Nonmonetary Support Types: donated equipment, donated products, loaned employees, and loaned executives
Geographic Distribution: headquarters and operating locations
Operating Locations: MN (St. Paul)

CORP. OFFICERS

Winslow H. Buxton: *CURR EMPL* pres, coo: Pentair
D. Eugene Nugent: *CURR EMPL* chmn, ceo, dir: Pentair

GIVING OFFICERS

Jeanne Benson: *CURR EMPL* contributions program admin: Pentair

APPLICATION INFORMATION

Initial Approach: *Initial Contact:* brief letter of inquiry *Include Information On:* description of the organization, amount requested, purpose of funds sought, audited financial statement, and proof of tax-exempt status *When to Submit:* any time
Restrictions on Giving: Does not support individuals, political or lobbying groups, or relig-

ious organizations for sectarian purposes.

GRANTS ANALYSIS

Typical Range: $1,000 to $3,000

Penzance Foundation

CONTACT

John M. Emery
Vice President
Penzance Foundation
237 Park Avenue, 21st Fl.
New York, NY 10017
(212) 551-3559

FINANCIAL SUMMARY

Recent Giving: $2,383,955 (fiscal 1992); $2,777,710 (fiscal 1991); $2,648,190 (fiscal 1990)
Assets: $50,724,378 (fiscal year ending April 30, 1992); $49,021,324 (fiscal 1991); $46,473,907 (fiscal 1990)
EIN: 13-3081557

CONTRIBUTIONS SUMMARY

Donor(s): The foundation was established in 1981 by Edna McConnell Clark (d. 1982). Mrs. Clark was the daughter of David Hall McConnell (d. 1937), founder of the cosmetics company, Avon Products. Two of her sons, Hays Clark and James McConnell Clark, are officers of the foundation. Mrs. Clark and her husband, W. Van Clark (d.1976), also established the Edna McConnell Clark Foundation in 1950. The foundation, which focuses on social service programs for the disadvantaged, had assets of over $430 million in fiscal 1991 and giving of almost $20 million.
Typical Recipients: • *Education:* arts education, colleges & universities, elementary education, private education (precollege), science/technology education • *Health:* health organizations, hospitals, medical research • *International:* international development/relief • *Religion:* churches • *Social Services:* child welfare, family planning, shelters/homelessness, youth organizations
Grant Types: general support
Geographic Distribution: primarily New York and Massachusetts

GIVING OFFICERS

Hays Clark: trust *B* 1919 *ED* Cornell Univ BS 1941 *NONPR AFFIL* dir: Boy Scouts Am; gov: NY Hosp

James McConnell Clark: vp, trust, treas *ED* Cornell Univ BS 1944 *NONPR AFFIL* dir: Assocs Cape Cod; pres: NY City Mission Soc; trust: Lincoln Ctr Inst, Marine Biological Lab (Woods Hole MA), Presbyterian Hosp City NY; trust, mem exec comm: Woods Hole Oceanographic Inst

John M. Emery: vp, trust, secy *B* Ann Arbor MI *ED* Princeton Univ BA 1953; Harvard Univ LLB 1958 *CURR EMPL* ptnr: Breed Abbott & Morgan *CORP AFFIL* dir: Champion Products Inc

David F. Kroenlein: asst secy

APPLICATION INFORMATION

Initial Approach: Restrictions on Giving: The foundation reports that it only makes contributions to preselected charitable organizations and does not accept unsolicited applications for funds.

GRANTS ANALYSIS

Total Grants: $2,383,955
Number of Grants: 28
Highest Grant: $700,000
Typical Range: $1,000 to $5,000 and $100,000 to $500,000
Disclosure Period: fiscal year ending April 30, 1992
Note: Recent grants are derived from a fiscal 1992 Form 990.

RECENT GRANTS

700,000	New York Hospital Cornell Medical Center Fund, New York, NY
500,000	National Academy of Sciences, Washington, DC
500,000	Presbyterian Hospital in the City of New York, New York, NY
300,000	Thompson Island Outward Bound, Boston, MA
100,000	CARE, New York, NY
50,000	Sea Education Association, Woods Hole, MA
45,000	Allen Community Outreach Center, Washington, DC
40,000	Thompson Island Outward Bound, Boston, MA
25,000	Planned Parenthood of Connecticut, New Haven, CT
17,385	Thompson Island Outward Bound, Boston, MA

People's Bank

Assets: $5.69 billion
Employees: 2,300
Headquarters: Bridgeport, CT
SIC Major Group: Depository Institutions

CONTACT

Lisa M. McGuire
Assistant Vice President, Government & Community Relations
People's Bank
850 Main St.
Bridgeport, CT 06604
(203) 338-7243

FINANCIAL SUMMARY

Recent Giving: $662,000 (1993 est.)
Fiscal Note: Company makes direct contributions.

CONTRIBUTIONS SUMMARY

Typical Recipients: • *Arts & Humanities:* arts festivals, community arts, dance, general, museums/galleries, music, performing arts, public broadcasting, theater • *Civic & Public Affairs:* economic development, general, housing • *Education:* colleges & universities, elementary education, general, preschool education, public education (precollege), social sciences education • *Social Services:* counseling, day care, employment/job training, food/clothing distribution, general, homes, shelters/homelessness, united funds, volunteer services, youth organizations
Grant Types: award, capital, employee matching gifts, loan, and multiyear/continuing support
Nonmonetary Support Types: cause-related marketing & promotion, donated equipment, in-kind services, loaned employees, and loaned executives
Geographic Distribution: primarily at headquarters and operating locations
Operating Locations: CT (Bridgeport)

CORP. OFFICERS

David E.A. Carson: *B* Birkenhead England 1934 *ED* Univ MI 1955 *CURR EMPL* ceo, pres: Peoples Bank

GIVING OFFICERS

Lisa M. McGuire: *CURR EMPL* asst vp govt & commun rels: Peoples Bank

APPLICATION INFORMATION

Initial Approach: *Initial Contact:* brief letter of inquiry and full proposal *Include Information On:* a description of organization, amount requested, purpose of funds sought, recently audited financial statement, and proof of tax-exempt status *When to Submit:* any time
Restrictions on Giving: Does not support individuals, religious organizations for sectarian purposes, or political or lobbying groups.

GRANTS ANALYSIS

Typical Range: $1,000 to $2,500

RECENT GRANTS

Barnum Festival, Bridgeport, CT
Bridgeport Economic Development Corporation, Bridgeport, CT
Bridgeport Public Education Fund, Bridgeport, CT
Bushnell Memorial Hall, Hartford, CT
Connecticut Business for Education Coalition, Danbury, CT
Connecticut Public Television, Hartford, CT
New Haven Symphony, New Haven, CT
Regional Plan Association, New York, NY
The Barnum Museum, Bridgeport, CT
United Way, CT

Peoples Drug Stores Inc.

Sales: $900.0 million
Employees: 8,000
Parent Company: Melville Corp. CVS
Headquarters: Woonsocket, RI
SIC Major Group: Miscellaneous Retail

CONTACT

David Roegge
Charitable Contributions Committee
Peoples Drug Stores/CVS
1 CVS Dr.
Woonsocket, RI 02895
800-444-1140

CONTRIBUTIONS SUMMARY

Nonmonetary Support Types: donated equipment and donated products
Operating Locations: IN (Indianapolis), RI (Woonsocket)

CORP. OFFICERS

David R. Bloom: *CURR EMPL* chmn, ceo: Peoples Drug Stores/CVS
David H. Eisenberg: *B* Washington DC 1936 *ED* Univ MD 1959 *CURR EMPL* pres, coo: Peoples Drug Stores/CVS

Peoples Energy Corp.

Revenue: $1.1 billion
Employees: 3,428
Headquarters: Chicago, IL
SIC Major Group: Electric, Gas & Sanitary Services, Holding & Other Investment Offices, and Miscellaneous Manufacturing Industries

CONTACT

Kenneth L. Gogins
Manager, Corporate Contributions
Peoples Energy Corp.
122 South Michigan Avenue, Rm. 1125
Chicago, IL 60603
(312) 431-4000

FINANCIAL SUMMARY

Recent Giving: $950,000 (1993 est.); $949,018 (1992)

CONTRIBUTIONS SUMMARY

Typical Recipients: • *Arts & Humanities:* arts associations, arts institutes, dance, ethnic arts, history/historic preservation, libraries, museums/galleries, opera, performing arts, public broadcasting, theater • *Civic & Public Affairs:* better government, civil rights, consumer affairs, economic development, economics, housing, law & justice, professional & trade associations, urban & community affairs, women's affairs, zoos/botanical gardens • *Education:* colleges & universities, community & junior colleges,

elementary education, literacy, private education (precollege), public education (precollege) • *Health:* health organizations, hospitals • *Science:* observatories & planetariums • *Social Services:* aged, child welfare, community centers, community service organizations, employment/job training, family services, homes, shelters/homelessness, united funds, volunteer services, youth organizations
Grant Types: capital, employee matching gifts, general support, and multiyear/continuing support
Nonmonetary Support Types: loaned executives
Geographic Distribution: company service area
Operating Locations: IL (Chicago, Waukegan)

CORP. OFFICERS

J. Bruce Hasch: *CURR EMPL* pres, coo: Peoples Energy Corp
Richard E. Terry: *B* Green Bay WI 1937 *ED* St Norbert Coll BA 1959; Univ WI LLB 1964 *CURR EMPL* chmn, ceo: Peoples Energy Corp *CORP AFFIL* dir: Amsted Indus, Harris Bankcorp, Harris Trust & Savings, North Shore Gas Co, Peoples Gas Light & Coke Co *NONPR AFFIL* dir: Big Shoulders, Chicago Mus Science & Indus, IL Counc Econ Ed, Inst Gas Tech; mem: Am Gas Assn, Chicago Area Central Comm, Chicago Chamber Commerce, Midwest Gas Assn; mem bus adv counc: Chicago Urban League; trust: St Norbert Coll, Xavier Univ

GIVING OFFICERS

Kenneth L. Gogins: *CURR EMPL* mgr corp commun: Peoples Energy Corp

APPLICATION INFORMATION

Initial Approach: *Initial Contact:* brief letter and proposal *Include Information On:* name, full mailing address, and telephone number of organization; background and purpose of the organization; type of request (operating or capital); geographical area served; sources of income; most recent financial statement (preferably audited); current budget and list of programs; proof of tax-exempt status; names of officers and directors; and number of professional, clerical, and volunteer

staff members *When to Submit:* any time
Restrictions on Giving: Contributions will not be made to individuals; organizations not eligible for tax-deductible support; organizations that discriminate by race, color, creed, or national origin; political organizations or campaigns; organizations whose prime purpose is to influence legislation; religious organizations for purely sectarian purposes; agencies or institutions owned and operated by local, state, or federal governments; trips or tours; or special occasion or goodwill advertising.

OTHER THINGS TO KNOW

Publications: contribution guidelines

Peoples Heritage Savings Bank

Assets: $2.1 billion
Employees: 395
Parent Company: Peoples Heritage Financial Group, Inc.
Headquarters: Portland, ME
SIC Major Group: Depository Institutions

CONTACT

Leslie McKenney
Advertising Coordinator
Peoples Heritage Savings Bank
1 Portland Sq.
Portland, ME 04101
(207) 761-8500

CONTRIBUTIONS SUMMARY

Operating Locations: ME (Portland)

CORP. OFFICERS

Robert A. Marden, Sr.: *CURR EMPL* chmn: Peoples Heritage Savings Bank
Pamela P. Plumb: *CURR EMPL* vchmn: Peoples Heritage Bank
William J. Ryan: *CURR EMPL* pres, ceo: Peoples Heritage Savings Bank

---

Pep Boys

Sales: $1.0 billion
Employees: 11,965
Headquarters: Philadelphia, PA
SIC Major Group: Automobile Repair, Services & Parking and Automotive Dealers & Service Stations

CONTACT

Dee Dalton
Administrative Assistant
Strauss Fdn.
3111 Allegheny Ave.
Philadelphia, PA 19132
(215) 229-9000

FINANCIAL SUMMARY

EIN: 23-6219939

CONTRIBUTIONS SUMMARY

Operating Locations: PA (Philadelphia)

CORP. OFFICERS

Mitchell Liebovitz: *CURR EMPL* ceo, pres: Pep Boys

OTHER THINGS TO KNOW

Company is a donor to the Strauss Foundation.

Pepper Cos.

Sales: $500.0 million
Employees: 900
Headquarters: Chicago, IL
SIC Major Group: General Building Contractors

CONTACT

Stanley Pepper
President
Pepper Cos.
643 North Orleans
Chicago, IL 60610
(312) 266-4703

CONTRIBUTIONS SUMMARY

Operating Locations: IL (Chicago)

CORP. OFFICERS

Geoffry Knudson: *CURR EMPL* pres: Pepper Cos
Thomas M. O' Leary: *CURR EMPL* cfo: Pepper Cos
Richard S. Pepper: *CURR EMPL* chmn, ceo: Pepper Cos

Pepperidge Farm, Inc.

Sales: $597.0 million
Employees: 4,800
Parent Company: Campbell Soup Co.
Headquarters: Norwalk, CT
SIC Major Group: Food & Kindred Products

CONTACT

Ann W. Davin
Manager, Corporate Communications
Pepperidge Farm, Inc.
595 Westport Ave.
Norwalk, CT 06851
(203) 846-7000

FINANCIAL SUMMARY

Fiscal Note: Company does not disclose contributions figures.

CONTRIBUTIONS SUMMARY

Company reports that 30% of funds support education; 30% support health and human services; 20% support arts and humanities; and 20% support civic and public affairs.
Geographic Distribution: grants are awarded in headquarters and operating communities
Operating Locations: CT (Norwalk)

CORP. OFFICERS

Charles V. McCarthy: *CURR EMPL* pres: Pepperidge Farm
Richard A. Shea: *CURR EMPL* pres: Pepperidge Farms

APPLICATION INFORMATION

Initial Approach: Send a brief letter of inquiry, including a description of organization, amount requested, and purpose of funds sought.
Restrictions on Giving: Does not support organizations outside operating areas.

GRANTS ANALYSIS

Typical Range: $10 to $1,000

Peppers Foundation, Ann

CONTACT

Jack H. Alexander
Ann Peppers Fdn.
PO Box 50146
Pasadena, CA 91115
(818) 449-0793

FINANCIAL SUMMARY

Recent Giving: $372,700 (1991); $359,200 (1990); $381,636 (1989)
Assets: $6,836,817 (1991); $5,698,658 (1990); $6,378,529 (1989)
EIN: 95-2114455

CONTRIBUTIONS SUMMARY

Donor(s): the late Ann Peppers

Typical Recipients: • *Arts & Humanities:* arts centers, music • *Civic & Public Affairs:* housing • *Education:* colleges & universities, education funds, public education (precollege), science/technology education • *Religion:* churches • *Social Services:* child welfare, disabled, family services, shelters/homelessness, youth organizations

Grant Types: conference/seminar, project, and scholarship

Geographic Distribution: limited to the Los Angeles, CA, metropolitan area

GIVING OFFICERS

Jack H. Alexander: secy
A. L. Burford, Jr.: secy, dir
W. Paul Colwell: pres, dir
Giles S. Hall: off
Howard O. Wilson: treas, dir

APPLICATION INFORMATION

Initial Approach: Send brief letter of inquiry describing program or project. There are no deadlines.

Restrictions on Giving: Does not support individuals.

GRANTS ANALYSIS

Number of Grants: 72
Highest Grant: $25,000
Typical Range: $1,000 to $10,000
Disclosure Period: 1991

RECENT GRANTS

25,000 Braille Institute of America, Los Angeles, CA
20,000 California Institute of Technology Industrial Relations Center, Pasadena, CA
20,000 Kare Youth League, Los Angeles, CA
17,500 Pepperdine University, Malibu, CA
15,000 California Institute of Technology, Pasadena, CA
15,000 California Institute of Technology, Pasadena, CA — Science and Engineering Scholarships
10,000 Pasadena Housing Alliance, Pasadena, CA
10,000 Polytechnic School, Los Angeles, CA
10,000 University of La Verne, La Verne, CA

10,000 Walden School, Los Angeles, CA

Pepsi-Cola Bottling Co. of Charlotte / Pepsi-Cola of Charlotte Foundation

Sales: $70.0 million
Employees: 330
Headquarters: Charlotte, NC
SIC Major Group: Food & Kindred Products

CONTACT

Dale Halton
President
Pepsi-Cola of Charlotte Foundation
PO Box 241167
Charlotte, NC 28224
(704) 523-6761

FINANCIAL SUMMARY

Recent Giving: $100,000 (1993 est.); $151,683 (1991); $88,310 (1990)

Assets: $365,071 (1991); $487,855 (1990); $402,145 (1989)

Gifts Received: $150,000 (1990); $300,000 (1989)

EIN: 56-1591985

CONTRIBUTIONS SUMMARY

Typical Recipients: • *Arts & Humanities:* arts associations, arts centers, arts festivals, arts funds, community arts, dance, history/historic preservation, libraries, museums/galleries, music, performing arts, performing arts, public broadcasting • *Civic & Public Affairs:* better government, housing, women's affairs • *Education:* colleges & universities, colleges & universities, community & junior colleges, international studies, preschool education • *Health:* hospices, single-disease health associations • *Science:* scientific institutes • *Social Services:* aged, child welfare, community service organizations, day care, drugs & alcohol, family planning, food/clothing distribution, shelters/homelessness, united funds, youth organizations

Grant Types: endowment, general support, and scholarship

Nonmonetary Support Types: donated products

Geographic Distribution: in headquarters and operating communities

Operating Locations: NC (Cabarrus County, Charlotte, Cleveland County, Gaston County, Lincoln County, Mecklenburg County, Stanly County, Union County)

CORP. OFFICERS

Dale Halton: *CURR EMPL* chmn, pres, ceo: Pepsi-Cola Bottling Co Charlotte

GIVING OFFICERS

Dale Halton: pres, dir *CURR EMPL* chmn, pres, ceo: Pepsi-Cola Bottling Co Charlotte (see above)
Phil Halton: vp, treas, dir
Darrell Holland: secy, dir

APPLICATION INFORMATION

Initial Approach: Send brief letter including a description of the organization, amount requested, purpose of funds sought, audited financial statement, and proof of tax-exempt status. There are no deadlines.

Restrictions on Giving: Does not support political or lobbying groups.

GRANTS ANALYSIS

Number of Grants: 48
Highest Grant: $27,500
Typical Range: $500 to $5,000
Disclosure Period: 1991

RECENT GRANTS

27,500 Charlotte Symphony, Charlotte, NC
25,000 North Carolina Performing Arts Center, Charlotte, NC
15,000 Science Museums of Charlotte, Charlotte, NC
11,000 To Life, Charlotte, NC
10,000 Children's Miracle Network, Charlotte, NC
10,000 University of North Carolina at Chapel Hill, Chapel Hill, NC
7,000 University of North Carolina at Chapel Hill, Chapel Hill, NC
4,000 University of North Carolina at Chapel Hill, Chapel Hill, NC
3,750 United Way, Charlotte, NC
2,900 Wing Haven Foundation, Charlotte, NC

PepsiCo / PepsiCo Foundation

Sales: $22.08 billion
Employees: 308,000
Headquarters: Purchase, NY
SIC Major Group: Eating & Drinking Places, Food & Kindred Products, and Wholesale Trade—Nondurable Goods

CONTACT

Jacqueline R. Millan
Manager, Corporate Contributions
PepsiCo Fdn.
700 Anderson Hill Rd.
Purchase, NY 10577
(914) 253-3153

FINANCIAL SUMMARY

Recent Giving: $19,500,000 (1991); $16,000,000 (1990); $16,054,000 (1989)

Assets: $19,139,846 (1991); $12,989,130 (1989)

Fiscal Note: Above figures represent combined foundation contributions and company direct giving. In 1990, foundation contributed $7.0 million. PepsiCo's subsidiaries run their own contributions programs (see "Other Things You Should Know" below).

EIN: 13-6163174

CONTRIBUTIONS SUMMARY

Typical Recipients: • *Arts & Humanities:* performing arts • *Civic & Public Affairs:* urban & community affairs • *Education:* colleges & universities, education associations • *Health:* health organizations • *Social Services:* community service organizations

Grant Types: employee matching gifts, general support, and project

Note: All grants are initiated by employees volunteering in nonprofit organizations.

Nonmonetary Support Types: donated products

Note: No estimate is available for value of nonmonetary support, and it is not included above.

Geographic Distribution: near corporate operating locations

Operating Locations: CA (Irvine), KS (Wichita), KY (Louisville), NY (Purchase, Somers), TX (Plano)

CORP. OFFICERS

D. Wayne Calloway: *B* Elkin NC 1935 *ED* Wake Forest Univ BBA 1959 *CURR EMPL* chmn, ceo: PepsiCo *CORP AFFIL* dir: Citicorp, Exxon Corp, Gen Electric Co *NONPR AFFIL* chmn, bd of trusts: Wake Forest Univ

Donald M. Kendall: *B* Sequim WA 1921 *ED* Western KY St Coll *CURR EMPL* chmn exec comm, dir, pres, ceo: PepsiCo *CORP AFFIL* dir: ARCO, Atlantic Richfield, Investors Diversified Svcs Mutual Fund Group, Lorimar-Telepictures Corp, NOVA Pharmaceutical Corp, Pan Am World Airways *NONPR AFFIL* chmn exec comm: US-USSR Trade Econ Counc; mem: Chamber Commerce US, Emergency Comm Am Trade, Intl Chamber Commerce

GIVING OFFICERS

Donald M. Kendall: chmn *CURR EMPL* chmn exec comm, dir, pres, ceo: PepsiCo (see above)

APPLICATION INFORMATION

Initial Approach: *Initial Contact:* brief letter or proposal *When to Submit:* any time *Note:* Guidelines are available. **Restrictions on Giving:** The foundation does not provide grants to individuals.

OTHER THINGS TO KNOW

PepsiCo is the parent company of a number of operating divisions, at the following addresses: Frito-Lay, Inc., 7701 Legacy Drive, Plano, TX 75024; Pizza Hut, Inc., 9111 East Douglas, Wichita, KS 67207; Taco Bell Corp., 17901 Von Karman, Irvine, CA 92714; Pepsi-Cola Co., Somers, NY 10589; and Kentucky Fried Chicken, 1441 Gardiner Lane, Louisville, KY 40213. Contributions activity is handled at each division based on their own needs.

GRANTS ANALYSIS

Total Grants: $19,500,000*
Number of Grants: 277
Highest Grant: $850,630
Typical Range: $1,000 to $30,000
Disclosure Period: 1991
Note: Contributions figure includes foundation and direct giving. Recent grants are de-

rived from a 1991 foundation Form 990.

RECENT GRANTS

850,630	National Merit Scholarship Corporation, Evanston, IL
347,207	United Way of Metropolitan Dallas, Dallas, TX
284,354	United Way of Westchester, White Plains, NY
200,000	Arizona State University, Tempe, AZ
200,000	Babson College, Wellesley, MA
200,000	Manhattanville College, Purchase, NY
200,000	New College Foundation, Sarasota, FL
200,000	Purchase College Foundation, Purchase, NY
200,000	United Negro College Fund, New York, NY
200,000	University of Virginia, Charlottesville, VA

Perdue Farms / Perdue Foundation, Arthur W.

Sales: $1.02 billion
Employees: 12,500
Headquarters: Salisbury, MD
SIC Major Group: Food & Kindred Products

CONTACT

Christine Whaley
Public Relations Coordinator
Perdue Farms
PO Box 1537
Salisbury, MD 21801
(301) 543-3000

FINANCIAL SUMMARY

EIN: 52-6054332

CONTRIBUTIONS SUMMARY

Operating Locations: MD (Salisbury)

CORP. OFFICERS

Pelham Lawrence V: *CURR EMPL* pres: Perdue Farms

Franklin Parsons Perdue: *B* Salisbury MD 1920 *ED* Salisbury St Coll 1937-1939 *CURR EMPL* chmn, dir: Perdue Farms *NONPR AFFIL* regent: Univ MD

Peridot Chemicals (NJ)

Sales: $5.0 million
Employees: 30
Parent Company: Peridot Holdings, Inc.
Headquarters: Wayne, NJ
SIC Major Group: Chemicals & Allied Products

CONTACT

Ellen Burke
Human Resources
Peridot Chemicals (NJ)
1680 Rte. 23N
Wayne, NJ 07470
(201) 696-9000

CONTRIBUTIONS SUMMARY

Operating Locations: NJ (Wayne)

CORP. OFFICERS

Peter J. Fass: *CURR EMPL* co-chmn: Peridot Chemicals (NJ)

L. John Polite, Jr.: *B* McKeesport PA 1921 *ED* Williams Coll 1942 *CURR EMPL* chmn, ceo: Peridot Chemicals (NJ) *CORP AFFIL* chmn: Orsynex, Pioneer Pharmaceutical Indus, Racon; chmn, ceo, pres, coo: Essex Chemical Corp; dir: Quixote Corp, Ravch Indus, RMI-TX, Witco Corp *NONPR AFFIL* dir: Chemical Mfrs Assn

Irwin S. Zonus: *CURR EMPL* pres, coo: Peridot Chemicals (NJ)

Perina Corp / Newberg Scholarship Trust, Gust K.

Sales: $800.0 million
Employees: 4,000
Headquarters: Chicago, IL
SIC Major Group: General Building Contractors and Heavy Construction Except Building Construction

CONTACT

Gust K. Newberg Construction Co. Scholarship Foundation
2040 N Ashland Ave.
Chicago, IL :0614
(312) 489-1400
Note: Address scholarship requests to the selection committees in the following school districts; City of Iron Mountain, Breitung Township,

Norway-Vulcan Area, North Dickinson County.

FINANCIAL SUMMARY

Recent Giving: $92,400 (fiscal 1992); $94,233 (fiscal 1990)
Assets: $930,217 (fiscal year ending June 30, 1992); $903,534 (fiscal 1990)
EIN: 38-6372554

CONTRIBUTIONS SUMMARY

Grant Types: scholarship
Geographic Distribution: focus on MI
Operating Locations: MI (Iron Mountain)

CORP. OFFICERS

Francis W. Durocher: *CURR EMPL* chmn, pres, treas: Gust K Newberg Construction Co

APPLICATION INFORMATION

Initial Approach: Request application form. There are no deadlines.

OTHER THINGS TO KNOW

Provides scholarships to individuals for higher education.
Disclosure Period: fiscal year ending June 30, 1992

Perini Corp. / Perini Memorial Foundation

Revenue: $991.9 million
Employees: 4,300
Headquarters: Framingham, MA
SIC Major Group: General Building Contractors, Heavy Construction Except Building Construction, and Real Estate

CONTACT

Bart W. Perini
Treasurer
Perini Memorial Fdn.
73 Mount Wayte Ave.
Framingham, MA 01701
(617) 875-6171
Note: Scholarship application address is c/o Perini Foundations Selection Committee, P.O. Box 31, Framingham, MA 01701.

FINANCIAL SUMMARY

Recent Giving: $151,433 (1991); $212,678 (1990); $235,480 (1989)
Assets: $2,288,505 (1991); $2,123,353 (1990); $5,802,170 (1989)

Gifts Received: $75,000 (1991); $105,000 (1990); $50,000 (1989)

Fiscal Note: In 1991, contributions were received from the Perini Corp.

EIN: 04-6118587

CONTRIBUTIONS SUMMARY

Typical Recipients: • *Arts & Humanities:* music, public broadcasting • *Civic & Public Affairs:* economics, international affairs • *Education:* business education, colleges & universities, minority education, private education (precollege) • *Health:* hospitals, single-disease health associations • *Religion:* religious organizations • *Social Services:* community service organizations, drugs & alcohol, united funds, youth organizations

Grant Types: general support and scholarship

Geographic Distribution: primarily in MA

Operating Locations: AZ (Phoenix), CA (Marysville, San Francisco), MA (Framingham), MI (Southfield), NY (Hastings-on-Hudson)

CORP. OFFICERS

David B. Perini: *B* Framingham MA 1937 *ED* Coll Holy Cross 1959; Boston Coll Law Sch 1962 *CURR EMPL* chmn, pres, ceo, dir: Perini Corp *CORP AFFIL* chmn: Perini Investment Properties Inc; dir: Dennison Mfg Co, New England Telephone Co, State Street Boston Corp *NONPR AFFIL* mem: Am Bar Assn, Soc Am Military Engrs

Joseph R. Perini: *B* Framingham MA 1930 *ED* VA Polytech Inst 1952; Univ HI 1955 *CURR EMPL* vchmn, sr vp, dir: Perini Corp *CORP AFFIL* pres: Perini Intl Corp *NONPR AFFIL* mem: Am Road Transportation Builders Assn, Am Soc Civil Engrs, Am Soc Military Engrs, Construction Indus MA

GIVING OFFICERS

Bart W. Perini: treas *CURR EMPL* vp, dir: Perini Investment Properties *CORP AFFIL* dir: Perini Corp; vp, dir: Perini Investment Properties

Charles B. Perini: vp

David B. Perini: pres *CURR EMPL* chmn, pres, ceo, dir: Perini Corp (see above)

APPLICATION INFORMATION

Initial Approach: The Perini Memorial Foundation will not be accepting any new requests for donations for the next three or four years.

Restrictions on Giving: Does not support individuals (except employee-related scholarships), research, matching gifts, or loans.

GRANTS ANALYSIS

Number of Grants: 44
Highest Grant: $25,000
Typical Range: $1,000 to $5,000
Disclosure Period: 1991

RECENT GRANTS

25,000 Dana Farber Cancer Institute, Boston, MA
10,000 Holy Cross College, Worcester, MA
7,500 Framingham Union College, Framingham, MA
5,000 American Ireland Fund, Pittsburgh, PA
5,000 Boston Against Drugs, Boston, MA
5,000 Corps of Engineers Historical Foundation, Ft. Belvoir, VA
5,000 Devereux Foundation, Devon, PA
5,000 Massachusetts General Hospital, Boston, MA
5,000 Milton Academy, Milton, MA
5,000 United Negro College Fund, Boston, MA

Perini Foundation, Joseph

Headquarters: Framingham, MA

CONTACT

Joan Lynch
Administrative Assistant
Perini Corp.
73 Mt. Wayte Ave.
Framingham, MA 01701
(508) 875-6171

FINANCIAL SUMMARY

Recent Giving: $441,869 (1989)
Assets: $10,593,742 (1989)
Gifts Received: $150,000 (1989)
Fiscal Note: In 1989, contributions were received from Perini Corp.
EIN: 04-6118587

CONTRIBUTIONS SUMMARY

Typical Recipients: • *Education:* colleges & universities, education funds, student aid • *Health:* hospices, medical research, single-disease health associations • *Religion:* churches, religious organizations • *Social Services:* aged, community service organizations, counseling, disabled, family services, homes, united funds, youth organizations

Grant Types: general support and scholarship

GIVING OFFICERS

Bart W. Perini: treas *CURR EMPL* vp, dir: Perini Investment Properties *CORP AFFIL* dir: Perini Corp; vp, dir: Perini Investment Properties

Charles B. Perini: vp

David B. Perini: pres *B* Framingham MA 1937 *ED* Coll Holy Cross 1959; Boston Coll Law Sch 1962 *CURR EMPL* chmn, pres, ceo, dir: Perini Corp *CORP AFFIL* chmn: Perini Investment Properties Inc; dir: Dennison Mfg Co, New England Telephone Co, State Street Boston Corp *NONPR AFFIL* mem: Am Bar Assn, Soc Am Military Engrs

David B. Perini: pres *CURR EMPL* chmn, pres, ceo, dir: Perini Corp (see above)

APPLICATION INFORMATION

Initial Approach: Send brief letter describing program. There are no deadlines.

GRANTS ANALYSIS

Number of Grants: 110
Highest Grant: $29,500
Typical Range: $500 to $5,000
Disclosure Period: 1989

RECENT GRANTS

29,500 Perini Memorial Foundation Scholarship Program
25,000 Dana Farber Cancer Institute, Boston, MA
15,000 Holy Cross College, Worcester, MA
15,000 Third Century Campaign, Boston, MA
7,500 Framingham Union Hospital Pledge, Framingham, MA
5,000 Boy Scouts of America, Framingham, MA
5,000 Mass General Hospital, Boston, MA
5,000 United Way, Framingham, MA
4,300 Boy Scouts of America, Boston, MA
3,933 Boston Center for Independent Living, Boston, MA

Perkin-Elmer Corp.

Sales: $874.4 million
Employees: 6,355
Headquarters: Norwalk, CT
SIC Major Group: Industrial Machinery & Equipment and Instruments & Related Products

CONTACT

Zelda Jacobs
Secretary, Corporate Contributions Comm.
Perkin-Elmer Corp.
761 Main Ave.
Norwalk, CT 06859
(203) 762-1000

CONTRIBUTIONS SUMMARY

Company reports 42% of contributions support health and welfare; 38% to education; 12% to civic and public affairs; and 8% to the arts. Company also participates in the Norwalk Adopt-A-School Program.

Typical Recipients: • *Arts & Humanities:* community arts, libraries, museums/galleries, performing arts, public broadcasting • *Civic & Public Affairs:* economic development, economics, environmental affairs, ethnic/minority organizations, housing, law & justice, urban & community affairs, women's affairs, zoos/botanical gardens • *Education:* business education, colleges & universities, community & junior colleges, continuing education, economic education, education associations, education funds, faculty development, literacy, minority education, private education (precollege), public education (precollege), science/technology education • *Health:* health organizations, hospices, hospitals, medical rehabilitation, medical research, mental health, nursing services, nutrition & health maintenance, public health • *Science:* scientific institutes, scientific organizations • *Social Services:* aged, child welfare, child welfare, community centers, community centers, community service organizations, community service organizations, counseling, counseling, day care, day care, delinquency & crime, delinquency & crime, disabled, disabled, domestic violence, domestic violence, drugs & alcohol, drugs & alcohol, emergency relief, emergency relief, employment/job training, employment/job training, family services, family services, food/clothing distribution, food/clothing distribution, homes, homes, legal aid, legal aid, recreation & athletics, recreation & athletics, shelters/homelessness, shelters/homelessness, united funds, united funds, volunteer services, volunteer services, youth organizations

Grant Types: capital, challenge, conference/seminar, emergency, fellowship, general support, loan, matching, multiyear/continuing support, operating expenses, professorship, project, research, scholarship, and seed money

Nonmonetary Support Types: donated equipment and donated products

Operating Locations: CA (Pomona), CT (Norwalk), MN (Eden Prairie), NY (Westbury)

CORP. OFFICERS

Gaynor N. Kelley: *B* New Canaan CT 1931 *ED* Delehanty Institute 1952 *CURR EMPL* chmn, pres, ceo, coo, dir: Perkin-Elmer Corp *CORP AFFIL* dir: Clark Equipment Co, Gateway Bank-Norwalk, Hercules

APPLICATION INFORMATION

Initial Approach: Send brief letter of inquiry, and a full proposal including a description of the organization, amount requested, purpose of funds sought, recently audited financial statements, and proof of tax-exempt status. There are no dealines.

Restrictions on Giving: Does not support individuals, religious organizations for sectarian purposes, or political or lobbying groups.

GRANTS ANALYSIS

Typical Range: $250 to $1,000

Perkin Fund

CONTACT

Richard S. Perkin
Trustee
Perkin Fund
c/o Morris and McVeigh
767 Third Ave.
New York, NY 10017
(203) 966-1920

FINANCIAL SUMMARY

Recent Giving: $642,700 (1991); $516,000 (1990); $468,000 (1989)

Assets: $15,580,052 (1991); $11,321,034 (1990); $11,920,927 (1989)

EIN: 13-6222498

CONTRIBUTIONS SUMMARY

Donor(s): the late Richard S. Perkin

Typical Recipients: • *Arts & Humanities:* music • *Civic & Public Affairs:* zoos/botanical gardens • *Education:* colleges & universities, medical education • *Health:* health organizations, hospitals, medical research, single-disease health associations • *Science:* observatories & planetariums • *Social Services:* youth organizations

Grant Types: general support

GIVING OFFICERS

James Gilbert Baker: trust *B* Louisville KY 1914 *ED* Univ Louisville AB 1935; Harvard Univ AM 1936; Harvard Univ PhD 1942 *CORP AFFIL* consultant: Polaroid Corp *NONPR AFFIL* mem: Am Academy Arts Sciences, Am Astronautical Soc, Am Optical Soc, Am Philosophical Soc, Natl Academy Engring, Natl Academy Sciences; research fellow: Harvard Observatory

Winnifred P. Gray: trust

John T. Perkin: trust

Mrs. Richard S. Perkin: chmn, trust

Richard T. Perkin: trust

Robert S. Perkin: trust

Roderic MacDonald Scott: trust *B* Sandusky OH 1916 *ED* Case Sch Applied Science BS 1938; Harvard Univ MA 1939; Harvard Univ PhD 1945 *CURR EMPL* consultant: Perkin-Elmer Corp *CORP AFFIL* consultant: Perkin-Elmer Corp *NONPR AFFIL* mem: Optical Soc Am

APPLICATION INFORMATION

Initial Approach: Contributes only to preselected organizations.

Restrictions on Giving: Does not support individuals.

GRANTS ANALYSIS

Number of Grants: 27

Highest Grant: $100,000

Typical Range: $10,000 to $25,000

Disclosure Period: 1991

RECENT GRANTS

100,000 Rockefeller University, New York, NY

50,000 New England Conservatory of Music, Boston, MA

50,000 New York Zoological Society, New York, NY

50,000 Society of Memorial Sloan-Kettering Cancer Center, New York, NY

40,000 Harvard University, Cambridge, MA — Smithsonian Center Astrophysics

35,000 Nantucket Maria Mitchell Association, Nantucket, MA

25,000 Astronomical Society of Pacific

25,000 Bridgeport Hospital Foundation, Bridgeport, CT

25,000 Columbia University College of Physicians and Surgeons, New York, NY

25,000 Louisville Astronomical Society, Louisville, KY

Perkins Charitable Foundation

CONTACT

Marilyn Best
Secretary, Treasurer
Perkins Charitable Fdn.
1030 Hanna Bldg.
1422 Euclid Ave.
Cleveland, OH 44115
(216) 621-0465

FINANCIAL SUMMARY

Recent Giving: $450,200 (1991); $419,100 (1990 approx.); $358,600 (1989)

Assets: $11,967,102 (1991); $9,291,930 (1990); $9,315,900 (1989)

EIN: 34-6549753

CONTRIBUTIONS SUMMARY

Donor(s): members of the Perkins family

Typical Recipients: • *Arts & Humanities:* history/historic preservation, museums/galleries • *Civic & Public Affairs:* environmental affairs, zoos/botanical gardens • *Education:* colleges & universities, medical education, private education (precollege) • *Health:* hospitals, medical training, nursing services • *Religion:* churches • *Social Services:* child welfare, community service organizations, family planning, family services, united funds, youth organizations

Grant Types: general support

Geographic Distribution: focus on OH

GIVING OFFICERS

Marilyn Best: secy, treas

George Oliva III: trust

Jacob B. Perkins: trust

Leigh H. Perkins: trust *CORP AFFIL* dir: Standard Products Co

Sallie P. Sullivan: trust

APPLICATION INFORMATION

Initial Approach: Contributes only to preselected organizations.

Restrictions on Giving: Does not support individuals.

GRANTS ANALYSIS

Number of Grants: 46

Highest Grant: $74,000

Typical Range: $1,000 to $5,000

Disclosure Period: 1991

RECENT GRANTS

74,000 Nature Conservancy, Winter Park, FL

50,000 Miss Hall's School, Pittsfield, MA

40,000 University Hospitals of Cleveland, Cleveland, OH

31,000 Madeira School, Greenway, VA

22,400 Williams College, Williamstown, MA

22,000 Frances Payne Bolton School of Nursing, Cleveland, OH

17,000 Cleveland Scholarship Programs, Cleveland, OH

16,000 Heather Hill, Chardon, OH
15,600 Asheville School, Asheville, NC
15,000 Health Hill Hospital, Cleveland, OH

Perkins Foundation, B. F. & Rose H.

CONTACT
B. F. & Rose H. Perkins Fdn.
PO Box 1064
Sheridan, WY 82801
(307) 674-8871

FINANCIAL SUMMARY
Recent Giving: $64,066 (1991); $64,626 (1990); $50,087 (1989)

Assets: $6,686,968 (1991); $6,219,797 (1990); $6,386,017 (1989)

Gifts Received: $380 (1991)

Fiscal Note: In 1991, contributions were received from Butkay Memorial.

EIN: 83-0138740

CONTRIBUTIONS SUMMARY
Donor(s): Benjamin F. Perkins

Grant Types: loan and scholarship

Geographic Distribution: focus on residents of Sheridan County, WY

GIVING OFFICERS
Donald R. Carrol: trust

Victor Garber: trust

Walter J. Pilch: trust

William D. Redle: trust

APPLICATION INFORMATION
Initial Approach: Application form required. Deadline is June 1 for fall registration; first of each month for other educational grants and for medical grants. Board meets second Monday of each month.

OTHER THINGS TO KNOW
Provides medical and educational assistance to graduates of Sheridan County High School.

Disclosure Period: 1991

Perkins Foundation, Edwin E.

CONTACT
Jane Williams
Edwin E. Perkins Fdn.
c/o First National Bank of Chicago
One First National Plaza, Ste. 0484
Chicago, IL 60670-0111
(312) 732-5586

FINANCIAL SUMMARY
Recent Giving: $120,000 (fiscal 1991); $140,000 (fiscal 1990)

Assets: $2,299,916 (fiscal year ending January 31, 1991); $2,261,625 (fiscal 1990); $2,039,312 (fiscal 1989)

EIN: 36-6090223

CONTRIBUTIONS SUMMARY
Donor(s): the late Edwin E. Perkins

Typical Recipients: • *Arts & Humanities:* arts institutes • *Education:* colleges & universities • *Health:* health organizations, hospitals, medical research • *Religion:* religious organizations • *Social Services:* child welfare, community centers, community service organizations

Grant Types: general support

GIVING OFFICERS
First National Bank of Chicago: trust

APPLICATION INFORMATION
Initial Approach: Send brief letter describing program. There are no deadlines.

GRANTS ANALYSIS
Number of Grants: 7
Highest Grant: $30,000
Typical Range: $5,000 to $20,000
Disclosure Period: fiscal year ending January 31, 1991

RECENT GRANTS
30,000 University of Minnesota Compass Institute, St. Paul, MN
20,000 Art Institute of Chicago, Chicago, IL
20,000 Chicago Institute for Neurosurgery/Research, Chicago, IL
20,000 General Medical Foundation, Park Ridge, IL

20,000 John Howard Association, Chicago, IL
5,000 National Stuttering Project, San Francisco, CA
5,000 Tuesday's Child, Chicago, IL

Perkins Foundation, Joe and Lois

CONTACT
Joe and Lois Perkins Fdn.
1212 City National Bldg.
PO Box 360
Wichita Falls, TX 76307
(817) 723-7163

FINANCIAL SUMMARY
Recent Giving: $312,011 (1991); $255,853 (1990); $74,756 (1989)

Assets: $14,539,727 (1991); $12,451,122 (1990); $11,794,248 (1989)

EIN: 75-6012450

CONTRIBUTIONS SUMMARY
Donor(s): the late J. J. Perkins

Typical Recipients: • *Arts & Humanities:* museums/galleries • *Education:* colleges & universities • *Religion:* churches, religious organizations • *Social Services:* child welfare, community service organizations, homes, united funds, youth organizations

Grant Types: capital and operating expenses

Geographic Distribution: focus on TX

GIVING OFFICERS
Glynn D. Huff: secy, treas

Charles N. Prothro: vp, dir

Charles V. Prothro: dir

Elizabeth P. Prothro: pres, dir

James E. Prothro: dir

Joe N. Prothro: dir

Mark H. Prothro: vp, dir

Herbert B. Story: dir

Kathryn Prothro Yeager: dir

APPLICATION INFORMATION
Initial Approach: Contributes only to preselected organizations.

GRANTS ANALYSIS
Number of Grants: 23
Highest Grant: $50,600
Typical Range: $225 to $13,650
Disclosure Period: 1991

RECENT GRANTS
50,600 Sundry-School and Churches, Wichita Falls, TX
41,725 Girls Club, Wichita Falls, TX
30,500 Dallas Museum of Art, Dallas, TX
25,000 First Step of Wichita Falls, Wichita Falls, TX
13,650 University of Texas Century Club, Austin, TX
11,500 Southwestern University, Georgetown, TX
7,720 Midwestern State University, Wichita Falls, TX
5,000 Boy Scouts of America, Wichita Falls, TX
5,000 Interfaith Ministries, Wichita Falls, TX
4,350 Sweetbriar College, Sweet Briar, VA

Perkins Memorial Foundation, George W.

CONTACT
George W. Perkins Memorial Fdn.
660 Madison Ave.
New York, NY 10021

FINANCIAL SUMMARY
Recent Giving: $515,500 (1991); $440,500 (1990); $447,000 (1989)

Assets: $13,337,606 (1991); $9,953,574 (1990); $9,957,735 (1989)

EIN: 13-6085859

CONTRIBUTIONS SUMMARY
Donor(s): Mrs. George W. Perkins

Typical Recipients: • *Arts & Humanities:* history/historic preservation • *Civic & Public Affairs:* environmental affairs, municipalities, zoos/botanical gardens • *Education:* arts education, colleges & universities, education funds, private education (precollege), religious education • *Health:* hospitals, medical research • *Social Services:* family planning, united funds, youth organizations

Grant Types: general support

GIVING OFFICERS
Anne P. Cabot: secy

George W. Perkins, Jr.: vp

Linn M. Perkins: pres
Penelope P. Wilson: vp

APPLICATION INFORMATION

Initial Approach: Contributes only to preselected organizations.

GRANTS ANALYSIS

Number of Grants: 55
Highest Grant: $50,000
Typical Range: $5,000 to $10,000
Disclosure Period: 1991
Note: Incomplete grants list provided in 1991.

RECENT GRANTS

25,000 Moore College of Art and Design, Philadelphia, PA

Perkins Memorial Fund, James J. and Marie Richardson

CONTACT

James J. and Marie Richardson Perkins Memorial Fund
c/o NCNB
P.O. Box 1807
Greenville, NC 27835-1807
(919) 758-4116

FINANCIAL SUMMARY

Recent Giving: $406,197 (fiscal 1991); $431,531 (fiscal 1990)
Assets: $8,211,158 (fiscal year ending September 30, 1991); $7,246,430 (fiscal 1990)

CONTRIBUTIONS SUMMARY

Typical Recipients: • *Arts & Humanities:* museums/galleries • *Education:* colleges & universities • *Health:* hospitals • *Religion:* churches • *Social Services:* aged, recreation & athletics
Grant Types: general support

GRANTS ANALYSIS

Total Grants: $406,197
Number of Grants: 35
Highest Grant: $44,565
Typical Range: $12,000 to $44,565
Disclosure Period: fiscal year ending September 30, 1991

RECENT GRANTS

44,565 Pitt County Memorial Hospital Foundation
44,565 Salvation Army
44,565 St. Paul's Episcopal Church
25,000 Greenville Museum of Art
25,000 Greenville-Pitt County Boys and Girls Club
23,013 Pitt County Council on Aging
15,000 Greenville Community Life Center
12,600 PCMH Pastoral Services
12,500 Mediation Center of Pitt County
12,000 Greenville Babe Ruth League

Perkins-Prothro Foundation

CONTACT

Charles Prothro
President
Perkins-Prothro Fdn.
PO Box 360
Wichita Falls, TX 76307
(817) 723-7163

FINANCIAL SUMMARY

Recent Giving: $661,876 (fiscal 1991); $500 (fiscal 1990); $255,102 (fiscal 1989)
Assets: $13,560,402 (fiscal year ending June 30, 1991); $11,425,138 (fiscal 1990); $9,526,628 (fiscal 1989)
Gifts Received: $582,170 (fiscal 1991)
Fiscal Note: Above figures are for fiscal year ending June 30, 1991. In 1991 the foundation shifted from a fiscal year to a calendar year. There were no distributions between July 1 and December 31, 1991. In 1991, the foundation changed from a fiscal year ending June 30 to a calendar year ending December 31. Assets for 1991 are as of December 31, 1991. Contributions received in 1991 include gifts to the foundation by Charles N. and Elizabeth P. Prothro for fiscal year ending June 30, 1991, and calendar year 1991.
EIN: 75-1247407

CONTRIBUTIONS SUMMARY

Donor(s): The foundation was established in 1967 by Charles N. Prothro, Elizabeth P. Prothro, and the late Lois Perkins.
Typical Recipients: • *Education:* colleges & universities • *Health:* health care cost containment, hospices • *Religion:* churches • *Social Services:* counseling, religious welfare
Grant Types: general support
Geographic Distribution: focus on Texas

GIVING OFFICERS

Glynn D. Huff: secy
Charles N. Prothro: pres, trust
Elizabeth P. Prothro: vp, trust
Joe N. Prothro: vp, trust
Mark H. Prothro: treas, trust
Kathryn Prothro Yeager: vp, trust

APPLICATION INFORMATION

Initial Approach: Restrictions on Giving: The foundation supports preselected organizations and does not accept unsolicited requests for funds. The foundation does not make grants to individuals.

GRANTS ANALYSIS

Total Grants: $661,876*
Number of Grants: 11
Highest Grant: $394,450
Typical Range: $1,000 to $30,000
Disclosure Period: fiscal year ending June 30, 1991
Note: Grants analysis is based on the foundation's grantmaking for fiscal year ending June 30, 1991. In 1991, the foundation changed to a calendar year accounting period. No grants were paid in the six-month period July 1 through December 31, 1991. The average grant figure does not include a grant of $394,450. Recent grants are derived from a fiscal 1991 grants list.

RECENT GRANTS

394,450 University of Texas at Austin, Austin, TX
100,000 Midwestern State University, Wichita Falls, TX
100,000 Wichita Falls Hospice Trust, Wichita Falls, TX
25,000 National Wildflower Research Center, Austin, TX
25,000 North Texas Rehabilitation Center, Wichita Falls, TX
5,000 Letot Center Capital Camp, Dallas, TX
5,000 Methodist Mission Home of San Antonio, San Antonio, TX
5,000 Pastoral Counseling Center, Wichita Falls, TX
1,000 Wichita Falls District, First United Methodist Church, Wichita Falls, TX
926 First United Methodist Church, Wichita Falls, TX

Perley Fund, Victor E.

CONTACT

Joseph J. Famularo
Trustee
Victor E. Perley Fund
1 Irving Park Pl., No. 28C
New York, NY 10003

FINANCIAL SUMMARY

Recent Giving: $110,100 (1991); $237,000 (1990); $103,130 (1989)
Assets: $3,743,025 (1991); $3,246,656 (1990); $3,368,730 (1989)
EIN: 13-6219298

CONTRIBUTIONS SUMMARY

Typical Recipients: • *Civic & Public Affairs:* urban & community affairs • *Education:* education associations, education funds • *Religion:* churches • *Social Services:* child welfare, community centers, counseling, homes, shelters/homelessness, youth organizations
Grant Types: general support and operating expenses
Geographic Distribution: focus on New York, NY

GIVING OFFICERS

Rabbi Irving Block: trust
H. Daniel Carpenter: trust
Joseph J. Famularo: trust
Barry McCarthy: trust
Rev. Albert Neibacher: trust

APPLICATION INFORMATION

Initial Approach: Send brief letter describing program. There are no deadlines.

GRANTS ANALYSIS

Number of Grants: 12
Highest Grant: $20,000
Typical Range: $3,000 to $20,000
Disclosure Period: 1991

RECENT GRANTS

20,000 Greenwich House, New York, NY
20,000 Hartley House, New York, NY
20,000 Hudson Guild, New York, NY
20,000 Lincoln Square Neighborhood, New York, NY

7,500 Boys Brotherhood, New York, NY
7,500 Educational Alliance, New York, NY
5,000 St. Timothy/St. Matthews, New York, NY
5,000 Stanley Issacs Neighborhood, New York, NY
2,000 Rena Cod, New York, NY
2,000 Seneca Neighborhood Center, Seneca, NY

Permian Corp.

Sales: $2.8 billion
Employees: 1,300
Parent Company: Asland Oil, Inc.
Headquarters: Houston, TX
SIC Major Group: Pipelines Except Natural Gas and Wholesale Trade—Nondurable Goods

CONTACT
Jack Blanton, Sr.
Chairman of Houston Endowment
Permian Corp.
700 Louisiana, Ste. 3920
Houston, TX 77002
(713) 236-1500

CONTRIBUTIONS SUMMARY
Operating Locations: TX (Houston)

CORP. OFFICERS
Jim Pasman: *CURR EMPL* chmn: Permian Corp
Gaylon H. Simmons: *CURR EMPL* pres: Permian Corp

OTHER THINGS TO KNOW
Company is an original donor to the Scurlock Foundation.

Perot Foundation

CONTACT
Margaret B. Perot
Vice President
Perot Fdn.
12377 Merit Dr., Ste. 1700
Dallas, TX 75251
(214) 788-3068

FINANCIAL SUMMARY
Recent Giving: $4,069,481 (1991); $1,422,875 (1990); $2,656,600 (1989)
Assets: $63,646,979 (1991); $64,413,225 (1990); $60,866,444 (1989)
EIN: 75-6093258

CONTRIBUTIONS SUMMARY
Donor(s): The foundation was established in 1969 by H. Ross Perot.
Typical Recipients: • *Arts & Humanities:* museums/galleries, music, opera • *Civic & Public Affairs:* philanthropic organizations • *Education:* arts education, colleges & universities, education associations, medical education, private education (precollege), public education (precollege) • *Health:* health organizations, single-disease health associations • *Religion:* churches • *Social Services:* community service organizations, food/clothing distribution, recreation & athletics, united funds, volunteer services, youth organizations
Grant Types: general support
Geographic Distribution: focus on Texas; emphasis on Dallas

GIVING OFFICERS
Sally Bell: secy, dir
Suzanne P. McGee: dir
H. Ross Perot, Jr.: trust
Margaret B. Perot: vp, dir
Mike Poss: treas, dir
John T. Walter, Jr.: trust

APPLICATION INFORMATION
Initial Approach:
The foundation has no printed annual reports, guidelines, or grant applications. A letter of request is sufficient.
Letters of request should include the purpose of the organization and the proposed use for the requested funds.
There are no deadlines for submitting proposals.

GRANTS ANALYSIS
Total Grants: $4,069,481
Number of Grants: 115
Highest Grant: $343,750
Typical Range: $500 to $40,000
Disclosure Period: 1991
Note: Recent grants are derived from a 1991 grants list.

RECENT GRANTS
343,750 University of Texas Southwestern Medical Center at Dallas, Dallas, TX — medical research
325,000 University of Texas Southwestern Medical Center at Dallas, Dallas, TX — medical research
325,000 University of Texas Southwestern Medical Center at Dallas, Dallas, TX — medical research
287,500 University of Texas Southwestern Medical Center at Dallas, Dallas, TX — medical research
250,000 Salvation Army School for Officers Training, Atlanta, GA — officers training
244,850 Neighbors United for Quality Education, Dallas, TX — establish pilot program for teacher training and early childhood education
192,000 University of Texas Southwestern Medical Center at Dallas, Dallas, TX — medical research
192,000 University of Texas Southwestern Medical Center at Dallas, Dallas, TX — medical research
192,000 University of Texas Southwestern Medical Center at Dallas, Dallas, TX — medical research
143,875 University of Texas Southwestern Medical Center at Dallas, Dallas, TX — medical research

Perpetual Benevolent Fund

CONTACT
Majorie Kelley
Perpetual Benevolent Fund
c/o BayBank Middlesex
PO Box 3422
Burlington, MA 01803
(617) 273-1700

FINANCIAL SUMMARY
Recent Giving: $86,076 (1991); $22,595 (1990); $93,025 (1989)

Assets: $2,581,118 (1991); $2,182,582 (1990); $2,036,086 (1989)

EIN: 23-7011723

CONTRIBUTIONS SUMMARY
Typical Recipients: • *Education:* colleges & universities, religious education • *Social Services:* child welfare, community service organizations, united funds, youth organizations
Grant Types: general support

GIVING OFFICERS
Baybank: trust

APPLICATION INFORMATION
Initial Approach: Request application form. There are no deadlines.

OTHER THINGS TO KNOW
In previous years supported youth organizations and community funds. No grants list was provided for 1990.

GRANTS ANALYSIS
Number of Grants: 80
Highest Grant: $5,000
Typical Range: $100 to $1,000
Disclosure Period: 1991

RECENT GRANTS
5,000 Newton Court Program, Newton, MA
3,000 Hanscom Base Operation Concern
1,800 Aquinas Junior College, Grand Rapids, MI
1,000 Aquinas College, Grand Rapids, MI
1,000 Aquinas College, Grand Rapids, MI
1,000 Aquinas College, Grand Rapids, MI
1,000 Aquinas Junior College, Grand Rapids, MI
1,000 Aquinas Junior College, Grand Rapids, MI
1,000 Children's Vacation House
1,000 Girls Club, Waltham, MA

Perpetual Trust for Charitable Giving

CONTACT
Perpetual Trust for Charitable Giving
c/o New Bank of New England
28 State Street
Boston, MA 02109

FINANCIAL SUMMARY
Recent Giving: $178,197 (1990)
Assets: $9,319,741 (1990)

EIN: 04-6026301

CONTRIBUTIONS SUMMARY
Geographic Distribution: giving primarily in Massachusetts

APPLICATION INFORMATION
Initial Approach: Contributes only to preselected organizations. Applications not accepted.
Restrictions on Giving: Does not provide grants to individuals.

GRANTS ANALYSIS
Disclosure Period: 1990
Note: No grants list was provided for 1990.

Perry Drug Stores / Perry Drug Stores Charitable Foundation
Sales: $640.8 million
Employees: 5,000
Headquarters: Pontiac, MI
SIC Major Group: Miscellaneous Retail

CONTACT
Jack A. Robinson
Trustee
Perry Drug Stores
5400 Perry Dr.
Pontiac, MI 48343
(313) 334-1300

FINANCIAL SUMMARY
Recent Giving: $43,796 (fiscal 1991); $50,438 (fiscal 1990)
Assets: $6,776 (fiscal year ending October 31, 1991)
Gifts Received: $50,000 (fiscal 1991)
Fiscal Note: In 1991, contributions were received from Perry Drug Stores.
EIN: 38-2386022

CONTRIBUTIONS SUMMARY
Typical Recipients: • *Arts & Humanities:* arts associations, community arts, music • *Civic & Public Affairs:* ethnic/minority organizations, general, zoos/botanical gardens • *Education:* colleges & universities, general • *Health:* general • *Social Services:* united funds
Grant Types: general support and matching
Nonmonetary Support Types: donated products
Geographic Distribution: primarily MI

Operating Locations: MI (Pontiac)

CORP. OFFICERS
Jack A. Robinson: *B* Detroit MI 1930 *ED* Wayne St Univ 1952 *CURR EMPL* ceo, chmn: Perry Drug Stores

Jerry S. Stone: *CURR EMPL* cfo: Perry Drug Stores

GIVING OFFICERS
Patricia A. Ambrose: trust

Berl Falbaum: trust

Jack A. Robinson: trust *CURR EMPL* ceo, chmn: Perry Drug Stores (see above)

Jerry S. Stone: trust *CURR EMPL* cfo: Perry Drug Stores (see above)

APPLICATION INFORMATION
Initial Approach: Send letter of inquiry. There are no deadlines.

GRANTS ANALYSIS
Number of Grants: 127
Highest Grant: $12,000
Typical Range: $25 to $500
Disclosure Period: fiscal year ending October 31, 1991

RECENT GRANTS
12,000	Detroit Symphony Orchestra, Detroit, MI
4,000	Detroit Symphony Orchestra, Detroit, MI
3,315	United Way, Detroit, MI
2,000	Detroit Zoological Society, Detroit, MI
2,000	Jewish National Fund, Detroit, MI
2,000	National Conference of Christians and Jews, Detroit, MI
1,500	Concerned Citizens for the Arts in Michigan, Detroit, MI
1,500	Concerned Citizens for the Arts in Michigan, Detroit, MI
1,000	Michigan Thanksgiving Day Parade Foundation, Detroit, MI
1,000	University of Michigan, Ann Arbor, MI

Perry-Griffin Foundation

CONTACT
Edward D. Lupton
Manager
Perry-Griffin Fdn.
PO Box 82
Oriental, NC 28571
(919) 249-0227

FINANCIAL SUMMARY
Recent Giving: $500 (fiscal 1992); $500 (fiscal 1991); $500 (fiscal 1988)
Assets: $1,388,293 (fiscal year ending August 31, 1992); $2,010,277 (fiscal 1991); $1,500,617 (fiscal 1988)
EIN: 56-0860864

CONTRIBUTIONS SUMMARY
Typical Recipients: • *Religion:* churches
Geographic Distribution: limited to Pamlico and Jones counties, NC

GIVING OFFICERS
Ned Delamar: dir

Ned Delamar II: dir

Lurley Hines: dir

Edward D. Lupton: mgr

Julia B. Whitty: secy

APPLICATION INFORMATION
Initial Approach: Application form required. There are no deadlines.

GRANTS ANALYSIS
Number of Grants: 2
Highest Grant: $250
Disclosure Period: fiscal year ending August 31, 1992

RECENT GRANTS
250	Bayboro Baptist Church, Bayboro, NC
250	Bayboro Methodist, Bayboro, NC

Persis Corp. / Persis Hawaii Foundation
Sales: $85.0 million
Employees: 650
Headquarters: Honolulu, HI
SIC Major Group: Printing & Publishing and Real Estate

CONTACT
Kenneth Uemura
Treasurer
Persis Hawaii Fdn.
605 Kapiolani Blvd.
Honolulu, HI 96813
(808) 525-8050

FINANCIAL SUMMARY
Recent Giving: $443,884 (1991); $436,798 (1990); $138,420 (1989)
Assets: $234 (1991); $46,618 (1990); $12,333 (1989)
Gifts Received: $395,000 (1991); $470,000 (1990); $159,500 (1989)
Fiscal Note: Contributes through foundation only. In 1991, contributions were received from the Persis Corporation.
EIN: 99-0255225

CONTRIBUTIONS SUMMARY
Typical Recipients: • *Arts & Humanities:* arts appreciation, arts associations, arts institutes, general, history/historic preservation, museums/galleries, music, performing arts, public broadcasting, theater, visual arts • *Civic & Public Affairs:* environmental affairs, first amendment issues, general • *Education:* arts education, colleges & universities, elementary education, general, private education (precollege), public education (precollege) • *Health:* general, health organizations, hospitals, medical rehabilitation, pediatric health • *Social Services:* child welfare, community service organizations, drugs & alcohol, family services, general, united funds, volunteer services, youth organizations
Grant Types: capital
Geographic Distribution: in headquarters and operating communities
Operating Locations: HI (Honolulu), TN (Knoxville, Marysville), WA (Bellevue, Kent, Port Angeles)

CORP. OFFICERS
Philip T. Gialanella: *B* Binghamton NY 1930 *ED* Harper Coll BA 1952; State Univ NY MA 1955 *CURR EMPL* exec vp, coo, dir: Persis Corp *CORP AFFIL* coo: Southeast Mags; dir: Capital Investment HI, Persis Corp, Waterhouse Properties; exec vp, publ: Honolulu Advertiser; pres: Persis Media; vp, coo: Knoxville Journal,

Northwest Media; vp, dir: ASA
Properties, HI Newspaper
Agency *NONPR AFFIL* bd
govs: Pacific Asian Aff Counc;
dir: Aloha Un Way, Boy Scouts
Am Aloha Counc, HI Theatre
Ctr, Honolulu Boy Choir, Hono-
lulu Symphony, YMCA; mem:
Am Newspaper Publs Assn, AP
Assn AZ, AP Assn CA, AP
Assn HI, AP Assn NV, HI Pubs
Assn, Japan-HI Econ Counc;
vp: HI Newspaper Agency Fdn;
vp, dir: Bay Area Steuart,
Shiny Rock Mining Corp
David Twigg-Smith: *CURR
EMPL* vchmn, secy, dir: Persis
Corp

Thurston Twigg-Smith: *B*
Honolulu HI 1921 *ED* Yale
Univ 1942 *CURR EMPL* pres,
ceo, dir: Honolulu Advertiser
CORP AFFIL chmn: Asa Prop-
erties HI, Shiny Rock Mining
Corp; dir: Am Fin Svcs, Am
Savings Bank, First Fed Am,
Hawaiian Electric Co, Hawai-
ian Electric Indus; pres, dir,
ceo: Persis Corp *NONPR
AFFIL* mem: Honolulu Cham-
ber Commerce; trust: Contem-
porary Mus, Contemporary
Mus HI, Honolulu Academy
Arts, Mus Contemporary Art,
Mus Contemporary Art Los An-
geles, Old Sturbridge, Phi-
latelic Fdn NY, Punahou Sch,
Skowhegan Sch, Skowhegan
Sch, Yale Art Gallery, Yale Art
Gallery

GIVING OFFICERS
David Twigg-Smith: vp *CURR
EMPL* vchmn, secy, dir: Persis
Corp (see above)
Thurston Twigg-Smith: pres
CURR EMPL pres, ceo, dir:
Honolulu Advertiser (see
above)
Kenneth Uemura: treas *B*
Honolulu HI 1948 *ED* Univ HI
CURR EMPL treas, comptr:
Persis Corp *CORP AFFIL* vp,
secy, dir: PH Corp *NONPR
AFFIL* asst treas: Contempo-
rary Mus; mem: Inst Newspa-
per Fin Execs, Natl Assn Corp
Treas

APPLICATION
INFORMATION
Initial Approach: *Initial Contact:* brief letter *Include Information On:* description of expected use of grant *When to
Submit:* any time

GRANTS ANALYSIS
Total Grants: $443,884
Number of Grants: 74
Highest Grant: $50,000

Typical Range: $500 to $5,000
Disclosure Period: 1991
Note: Recent grants are derived
from a 1991 grants list.

RECENT GRANTS
50,000 Bishop Museum,
Honolulu, HI
50,000 Museum of Con-
temporary Art, Los
Angeles, CA
38,500 United Way, Hono-
lulu, HI
25,000 Punahou School,
Honolulu, HI
20,000 Pacific Northwest
Ballet, Seattle, WA
15,000 Hawaii Maritime
Center, Honolulu,
HI
10,000 Bishop Museum
Support Council,
Honolulu, HI
10,000 Boys and Girls
Club, Honolulu, HI
10,000 Hawaii Plantation
Village, Honolulu,
HI
10,000 Hawaii Preparatory
Academy, Ka-
muela, HI

Pesch Family
Foundation

CONTACT
Pesch Family Fdn.
c/o Richman, Grossman and
Friedman
55 East Jackson, Ste. 2000
Chicago, IL 60604

FINANCIAL SUMMARY
Recent Giving: $295,719 (fis-
cal 1989); $1,049,032 (fiscal
1988)
Assets: $1,835,091 (fiscal year
ending March 31, 1989);
$1,988,493 (fiscal 1988)
EIN: 36-3348055

CONTRIBUTIONS
SUMMARY
Donor(s): Leroy A. Pesch
Typical Recipients: • *Arts &
Humanities:* community arts
• *Social Services:* child wel-
fare, domestic violence, youth
organizations
Grant Types: general support
Geographic Distribution:
focus on IL

GIVING OFFICERS
Erika G. Eddy: exec dir
Christopher Kniefel: dir
Linda Kniefel: dir
Alida Pesch: dir
Brian Pesch: secy, dir
Christopher Pesch: dir
Daniel Pesch: dir
Ellen Pesch: dir

Gerri Pesch: dir
Leroy Allen Pesch: pres, treas,
dir *B* Mt Pleasant IA 1931 *ED*
WA Univ MD 1956 *CURR
EMPL* chmn: Health Res Corp
CORP AFFIL chmn, ceo: Pesch
Health Group; owner, dir: Re-
public Health Corp *NONPR
AFFIL* Alpha Omega Alpha,
Sigma Xi; dir: Joffrey Ballet;
mem: Am Assn Advancement
Science, Am Assn Study Liver
Diseases, Am Federation Clini-
cal Res, Am Soc Biological
Chemists; mem adv comm:
Congressional Awards; mem
exec bd: Auditorium Theatre
Counc

APPLICATION
INFORMATION
Initial Approach: Contributes
only to preselected organizations.
Restrictions on Giving: Does
not support individuals.

GRANTS ANALYSIS
Number of Grants: 9
Highest Grant: $266,568
Typical Range: $1,000 to
$12,000
Disclosure Period: fiscal year
ending March 31, 1989

RECENT GRANTS
266,568 National Commit-
tee for the Preven-
tion of Child
Abuse, Chicago, IL
12,000 Family Builders of
Adoption, Chicago,
IL
9,900 Clement and Jessie
Stone Foundation,
Chicago, IL
5,000 Anti-Defamation
League, New York,
NY
1,000 Rainbows for the
Children, Chicago,
IL
500 Pot of Gold Golf
Classic, Chicago,
IL
202 Winifred Ward
Scholarship
Plaque, Chicago, IL
30 National Society of
Fund Raising Ex-
ecutives, Chicago,
IL

Pet / Pet Inc.
Community
Support
Foundation

Sales: $1.88 billion
Employees: 8,636
Headquarters: St. Louis, MO
SIC Major Group: Food &
Kindred Products

CONTACT
Richard Mittelbusher
President
Pet Inc. Community Support Fdn.
400 S Fourth St.
St. Louis, MO 63102
(314) 622-7700

FINANCIAL SUMMARY
Recent Giving: $667,000
(1993 est.); $663,000 (1992);
$613,000 (1991)
Assets: $99,647 (1991);
$283,118 (1989); $369,462
(1986)
Gifts Received: $442,200
(1989)
Fiscal Note: Figures include
both corporate and foundation
giving. Foundation giving in
1992 was $324,000; in 1991,
$322,000; and in 1989,
$472,000.
EIN: 43-6046149

CONTRIBUTIONS
SUMMARY
Typical Recipients: • *Arts &
Humanities:* arts associations,
music • *Civic & Public Affairs:*
business/free enterprise,
economic development • *Education:* business education, ca-
reer/vocational education, colleges & universities • *Social
Services:* child welfare, community service organizations, family planning, homes, shel-
ters/homelessness, united
funds, youth organizations
Grant Types: capital and general support
Nonmonetary Support Types:
donated products
Note: Nonmonetary support is
provided by the company and
was estimated at $728,000 in
1991. This figure is excluded
from above total giving figures.
Geographic Distribution: operating locations; primarily St.
Louis, MO
Operating Locations: GA (Atlanta, Lithonia, Rome), ID
(Buhl), IL (Chicago), MD (Fed-
eralsburg), ME (Portland), MO
(Hannibal, Kansas City, St.
Louis), NJ (Vineland), OK
(Chickasha), PA (Allentown,

Chambersburg, Erie, North East, Philadelphia), TN (Greeneville), TX (Anthony), WI (Popar)

CORP. OFFICERS
Anthony C. Knizel: *CURR EMPL* vp, contr, asst treas: Pet
Miles L. Marsh: *CURR EMPL* chmn, ceo, près: Pet
Richard L. Mittelbusher: *CURR EMPL* sr vp: Pet
Patrick G. Wesley: *CURR EMPL* treas, asst secy: Pet

GIVING OFFICERS
Anthony C. Knizel: vp, treas *CURR EMPL* vp, contr, asst treas: Pet (see above)
Miles L. Marsh: trust *CURR EMPL* chmn, ceo, pres: Pet (see above)
Richard L. Mittelbusher: pres *CURR EMPL* sr vp: Pet (see above)
Phyllis P. Vogt: secy
Patrick G. Wesley: asst treas, asst secy *CURR EMPL* treas, asst secy: Pet (see above)
James A. Westcott: vp

APPLICATION INFORMATION
Initial Approach: *Initial Contact:* brief letter and proposal *Include Information On:* description of the organization and its objectives, list of organization's board of directors and their affiliation, amount requested, purpose of program for which funds are sought, program's objectives, evaluation method of program, method of increasing community awareness and support for program, recently audited financial statement, and proof of tax-exempt status *When to Submit:* any time
Restrictions on Giving: Excluded from consideration are national health foundations; hospitals; medical research; sport programs; religious organizations for non-secterian purposes; fraternal organizations; individual schools, except for matching gifts; and individuals.
Pet does not donate to national fundraising or to communities outside of operating locations.

OTHER THINGS TO KNOW
In April 1991, Pet, Inc., became an independent public company when it spun off from the Whitman Corp., which was formerly known as IC Industries, Inc.

The foundation publishes a corporate contributions informational brochure.
Pet, Inc. also supports nonprofits through an employee volunteer grant program for organizations where Pet employees are active volunteers, and matching gift program.

GRANTS ANALYSIS
Total Grants: $613,000
Number of Grants: 18*
Highest Grant: $95,000*
Typical Range: $1,000 to $25,000*
Disclosure Period: 1991
Note: The figures for number of grants, average grant, highest grant, and typical grant range are for the foundation only. Recent grants are derived from a 1991 Form 990.

RECENT GRANTS
95,000 United Way of Greater St. Louis, St. Louis, MO
50,000 Salvation Army, St. Louis, MO
25,000 St. Louis Science Center Foundation, St. Louis, MO
10,000 Annie Malone Children's Home, St. Louis, MO
7,500 Boy Scouts of America, St. Louis Area Council, St. Louis, MO
7,000 YMCA of Greater St. Louis, St. Louis, MO
5,000 Junior Achievement of Mississippi Valley, St. Louis, MO
5,000 Mark Twain Home Foundation, St. Louis, MO
5,000 National Future Homemakers of America Foundation, Reston, VA
5,000 Philadelphia High School Academics, St. Louis, MO

Peterloon Foundation

CONTACT
Paul George Sittenfeld
Trustee
Peterloon Fdn.
580 Walnut St.
Cincinnati, OH 45202
(513) 579-5886

FINANCIAL SUMMARY
Recent Giving: $62,590 (fiscal 1991); $45,500 (fiscal 1990); $50,750 (fiscal 1989)
Assets: $4,622,537 (fiscal year ending November 30, 1991); $4,354,875 (fiscal 1990); $3,976,675 (fiscal 1989)
EIN: 31-6037801

CONTRIBUTIONS SUMMARY
Donor(s): the late John J. Emery
Typical Recipients: • *Arts & Humanities:* arts associations, arts centers, arts funds, arts institutes, community arts, public broadcasting • *Civic & Public Affairs:* zoos/botanical gardens • *Education:* private education (precollege) • *Religion:* religious organizations • *Social Services:* community service organizations, disabled, food/clothing distribution, legal aid, united funds, youth organizations
Grant Types: general support
Geographic Distribution: focus on the metropolitan Cincinnati, OH, area

GIVING OFFICERS
Henry H. Chatfield: off
Ethan Emery: trust
Irene E. Goodale: trust
Frank T. Hamilton: trust
Melissa Emery Lanier: vp
Paul George Sittenfeld: trust
Lela Emery Steele: pres, treas

APPLICATION INFORMATION
Initial Approach: Send brief letter describing program. There are no deadlines.

GRANTS ANALYSIS
Number of Grants: 22
Highest Grant: $8,500
Typical Range: $1,000 to $5,000
Disclosure Period: fiscal year ending November 30, 1991

RECENT GRANTS
8,500 Fine Arts Fund, Cincinnati, OH

8,000 United Way, Cincinnati, OH
5,000 Cincinnati Association for the Blind, Cincinnati, OH
5,000 Legal Aid Society, Cincinnati, OH
5,000 Seven Hills School, Cincinnati, OH
3,500 Work and Rehabilitation Centers, Cincinnati, OH
2,840 Lower Price Hill Schools, Cincinnati, OH
2,500 Boy Scouts of America, Cincinnati, OH
2,500 Freestore/Foodbank, Cincinnati, OH
2,500 WCET, Cincinnati, OH

Peters Foundation, Charles F.

CONTACT
J. Charles Peterson
Administrator
Charles F. Peters Fdn.
2008 Duquesne Ave.
McKeesport, PA 15132

FINANCIAL SUMMARY
Recent Giving: $125,772 (1991); $111,650 (1990); $165,530 (1989)
Assets: $2,324,564 (1991); $2,085,315 (1990); $2,107,580 (1989)
EIN: 25-6070765

CONTRIBUTIONS SUMMARY
Donor(s): Charles F. Peters
Typical Recipients: • *Education:* colleges & universities • *Health:* hospitals • *Religion:* churches, religious organizations • *Social Services:* community service organizations, united funds, youth organizations
Grant Types: general support
Geographic Distribution: limited to the McKeesport, PA, area

GIVING OFFICERS
Integra Bank/North: trust
William H. Balter: off

APPLICATION INFORMATION
Initial Approach: Send brief letter describing program. There are no deadlines.
Restrictions on Giving: Does not support individuals.

GRANTS ANALYSIS
Disclosure Period: 1991
Note: 1991 grants list not provided.

RECENT GRANTS
        5,000 McKeesport Hospital, McKeesport, PA
        5,000 Pennsylvania State University, University Park, PA
        4,000 Salvation Army, McKeesport, PA
        3,000 Community Alliance Church, Elizabeth, PA
        3,000 First United Methodist Church, Duquesne, PA
        3,000 Temple B'nai Israel, McKeesport, PA
        3,000 YMCA, McKeesport, PA
        2,000 Christian and Missionary Alliance Church, McKeesport, PA
        2,000 Christy Park United Methodist, McKeesport, PA
        2,000 Concordia Evangelical Lutheran Church, McKeesport, PA

Peters Foundation, Leon S.

CONTACT
Leon S. Peters Fdn.
4148 East Clinton Ave.
Fresno, CA 93703-2520

FINANCIAL SUMMARY
Recent Giving: $504,800 (fiscal 1991); $311,200 (fiscal 1990); $485,600 (fiscal 1989)
Assets: $10,901,138 (fiscal year ending November 30, 1991); $9,913,788 (fiscal 1990); $10,438,526 (fiscal 1989)
EIN: 94-6064669

CONTRIBUTIONS SUMMARY
Donor(s): the late Leon S. Peters
Typical Recipients: • *Arts & Humanities:* museums/galleries • *Education:* colleges & universities, education funds • *Health:* hospitals, mental health, pediatric health, single-disease health associations • *Religion:* churches, religious organizations • *Social Services:* community service organizations, disabled, emergency relief, food/clothing distribution, shelters/homelessness, youth organizations
Grant Types: capital, operating expenses, and scholarship
Geographic Distribution: focus on Fresno, CA

GIVING OFFICERS
Craig Apregan: dir
George Apregan: dir
Alice A. Peters: pres, secy, treas, dir
Darrell Peters: dir
Kenneth Peters: dir
Pete P. Peters: vp, dir
Ronald Peters: dir

APPLICATION INFORMATION
Initial Approach: Contributes only to preselected organizations.
Restrictions on Giving: Does not support individuals.

GRANTS ANALYSIS
Number of Grants: 71
Highest Grant: $50,000
Typical Range: $2,000 to $20,000
Disclosure Period: fiscal year ending November 30, 1991

RECENT GRANTS
       50,000 California Armenian Home, Fresno, CA
       35,200 California State University, Fresno, CA
       32,000 Western Diocese Religious Camp, Fresno, CA
       28,000 State Center Community College District, Fresno, CA
       27,000 Fresno Metropolitan Museum, Fresno, CA
       20,000 Fresno Pacific College, Fresno, CA
       20,000 Fresno Zoological Society, Fresno, CA
       18,000 KVPR Valley Public Radio, Fresno, CA
       15,000 Fresno Rescue Mission, Fresno, CA
       15,000 Poverello House, Fresno, CA

Peters Foundation, R. D. and Linda

CONTACT
Richard Hugo
Director
R. D. and Linda Peters Fdn.
c/o Bank One Wisconsin Trust Co., N.A.
PO Box 1308
Milwaukee, WI 53202
(414) 765-2800

FINANCIAL SUMMARY
Recent Giving: $381,924 (1990); $543,548 (1989); $481,000 (1988)
Assets: $5,068,758 (1990); $4,904,481 (1989); $3,003,736 (1988)
EIN: 39-6097994

CONTRIBUTIONS SUMMARY
Donor(s): the late R. D. Peters
Typical Recipients: • *Civic & Public Affairs:* environmental affairs • *Education:* colleges & universities, medical education, public education (precollege), science/technology education • *Religion:* churches • *Social Services:* aged, homes
Grant Types: general support, research, and scholarship
Geographic Distribution: focus on the Brillion, WI, area

GIVING OFFICERS
John S. Best: dir
John P. Bosch: dir
Harold Wolf: dir

APPLICATION INFORMATION
Initial Approach: Send cover letter and full proposal. There are no deadlines. Board meets quarterly.

GRANTS ANALYSIS
Number of Grants: 11
Highest Grant: $107,925
Typical Range: $3,000 to $15,000
Disclosure Period: 1990

RECENT GRANTS
      107,925 Brillion High School, Brillion, WI
      100,000 Milwaukee School of Engineering, Milwaukee, WI
       70,000 City of Brillion, Brillion, WI
       30,000 Brillion Housing Authority, Brillion, WI
       20,000 Northland College, Ashland, WI
       18,000 State of Wisconsin, Madison, WI
       15,000 St. Marys Catholic Church, Brillion, WI
       11,000 Trinity Evangelical Lutheran Church, Brillion, WI
        4,000 St. Bartholomew Lutheran Church, Brillion, WI
        3,000 Faith United Methodist Church, Brillion, WI

Petersen Foundation, Esper A.

CONTACT
Esper A. Petersen, Jr.
Director
Esper A. Petersen Fdn.
1300 Skokie Hwy.
Gurnee, IL 60031
(708) 336-0900

FINANCIAL SUMMARY
Recent Giving: $270,515 (1990); $253,605 (1989); $235,840 (1988)
Assets: $6,107,213 (1990); $6,067,059 (1989); $5,492,863 (1988)
EIN: 36-6125570

CONTRIBUTIONS SUMMARY
Donor(s): the late Esper A. Petersen
Typical Recipients: • *Arts & Humanities:* history/historic preservation, opera • *Civic & Public Affairs:* public policy • *Education:* colleges & universities • *Health:* health organizations, hospitals, medical research, single-disease health associations • *Religion:* churches • *Social Services:* aged, child welfare, disabled, youth organizations
Grant Types: capital, general support, and research
Geographic Distribution: focus on IL and CA

GIVING OFFICERS
Daniel H. Foster: dir
Stephen A. Malato: dir
Ann Petersen Pam: dir
Esper A. Petersen, Jr.: dir

APPLICATION INFORMATION
Initial Approach: Send letter requesting application form. Deadline is January 1.

OTHER THINGS TO KNOW
Publications: Application Guidelines

GRANTS ANALYSIS
Number of Grants: 44
Highest Grant: $44,200
Typical Range: $1,000 to $5,000
Disclosure Period: 1990

RECENT GRANTS
44,200 Los Angeles Music Center Opera, Los Angeles, CA
25,000 Faith Lutheran Church, Lake Forest, IL
20,000 Northwest Suburban Aid for the Retarded, Des Plaines, IL
17,380 YMCA, Waukegan, IL
10,000 Business and Professional People for the Public Interest, Chicago, IL
10,000 Misericordia Heart of Mercy, Chicago, IL
10,000 National Taxpayers Union Foundation, Washington, DC
10,000 University of Santa Barbara, Santa Barbara, CA
9,000 Cedars-Sinai Medical Center, Los Angeles, CA
5,500 Cedars-Sinai Medical Center, Los Angeles, CA

Peterson Builders
Sales: $65.0 million
Employees: 900
Headquarters: Sturgeon Bay, WI
SIC Major Group:
Transportation Equipment

CONTACT
Chuck St. Pierre
Vice President, Human Resources
Peterson Builders
101 Pennsylvania St., Box 650
Sturgeon Bay, WI 54235
(414) 743-5574

CONTRIBUTIONS SUMMARY
Operating Locations: WI (Sturgeon Bay)

CORP. OFFICERS
Larry Maples: *CURR EMPL* cfo: Peterson Builders
Ellsworth Lorin Peterson: *B* Sturgeon Bay WI 1924 *ED* US Merchant Marine Academy 1946 *CURR EMPL* pres: Peterson Builders *CORP AFFIL* chmn: Bank Sturgeon Bay; pres, dir: Peterson Interests *NONPR AFFIL* dir: Shipbuilders Counc Am; mem: Am Soc Naval Engrs, Natl Security Industrial Assn, Soc Naval Architects & Marine Engrs

OTHER THINGS TO KNOW
Company is an original donor to the Fred J. Peterson Foundation.

Peterson & Co. Consulting / Peterson & Co. Charitable Foundation
Headquarters: Detroit, MI
SIC Major Group:
Nonclassifiable Establishments

CONTACT
Patricia Ann Mullaney
Office Manager
Peterson & Co. Charitable Fdn.
One Woodward Avenue, Ste. 310
Detroit, MI 48226
(313) 963-6200

FINANCIAL SUMMARY
EIN: 36-3355443

CONTRIBUTIONS SUMMARY
Grant Types: matching
Operating Locations: MI (Detroit)

Peterson Foundation, Fred J.

CONTACT
Marsha L. Kerley
Secretary-Treasurer
Fred J. Peterson Fdn.
101 Pennsylvania St.
Sturgeon Bay, WI 54235
(414) 743-5574

FINANCIAL SUMMARY
Recent Giving: $150,000 (fiscal 1991); $159,450 (fiscal 1990); $208,640 (fiscal 1989)
Assets: $3,189,726 (fiscal year ending September 30, 1991); $2,661,861 (fiscal 1990); $2,912,637 (fiscal 1989)
Gifts Received: $75,000 (fiscal 1991)
EIN: 39-6075901

CONTRIBUTIONS SUMMARY
Donor(s): Peterson Builders, Inc., Fred J. Peterson, the late Irene Peterson, Ellsworth L. Peterson
Typical Recipients: • *Arts & Humanities:* public broadcasting • *Civic & Public Affairs:* economic development, municipalities, professional & trade associations, urban & community affairs • *Education:* education funds, education funds, private education (precollege), student aid • *Health:* hospitals • *Social Services:* community service organizations, recreation & athletics, united funds, youth organizations
Grant Types: capital, general support, multiyear/continuing support, and project
Geographic Distribution: focus on Door County, WI

GIVING OFFICERS
Marsha L. Kerley: secy, treas, dir
Ellsworth L. Peterson: pres, dir
Fred J. Peterson: trust
Fred J. Peterson II: vp, dir

APPLICATION INFORMATION
Initial Approach: All scholarship decisions made by Rotary International or individual colleges. Deadline is September 1.
Restrictions on Giving: Does not support individuals.

GRANTS ANALYSIS
Number of Grants: 31
Highest Grant: $100,000
Typical Range: $50 to $7,000
Disclosure Period: fiscal year ending September 30, 1991

RECENT GRANTS
100,000 Door County Memorial Hospital Foundation, WI
5,000 115 Club, WI
5,000 NWTC Foundation, WI
4,000 St. Peter and Paul School, WI — computer fund
4,000 Wisconsin Public Broadcasting, Milwaukee, WI
3,100 Sturgeon Bay Rotary Club, Sturgeon Bay, WI
3,000 Gibraltar School AODA, WI
3,000 Rotary Scholarship, WI
3,000 Wisconsin Foundation of Independent Colleges, Milwaukee, WI
3,000 YMCA, Milwaukee, WI

Peterson Memorial Fund, Chris and Mary L.

CONTACT
Paul T. Akre
Assistant Vice Presicent/Trust Officer
Chris and Mary L. Peterson Memorial Fund
U.S. National Bank of Oregon
PO Box 3168
Portland, OR 97208

FINANCIAL SUMMARY
Recent Giving: $805,610 (fiscal 1992); $583,247 (fiscal 1991)
Assets: $11,799,103 (fiscal year ending June 30, 1992); $10,994,785 (fiscal 1991)
Gifts Received: $1,191,918 (fiscal 1991)
EIN: 93-6226027

CONTRIBUTIONS SUMMARY
Typical Recipients: • *Health:* hospitals, nursing services
Grant Types: general support

GRANTS ANALYSIS
Number of Grants: 1
Highest Grant: $805,610
Disclosure Period: fiscal year ending June 30, 1992

RECENT GRANTS
583,247 Good Samaritan Foundation, Portland, OR — net income from this trust is to be paid quarterly to be used to support the hospital's nursing education program and for acquisition of medical equipment

Petrie Trust, Lorene M.

CONTACT
Doug McIntyre
Vice President and Manager
Lorene M. Petrie Trust
c/o Security Pacific Bank
  Washington, Tax Services
  Dept.
PO Box 136
Yakima, WA 98907
(509) 575-6720

FINANCIAL SUMMARY
Recent Giving: $107,556 (fiscal 1992); $372,733 (fiscal 1991); $156,612 (fiscal 1990)
Assets: $2,416,360 (fiscal year ending July 31, 1992); $2,220,405 (fiscal 1991); $2,408,921 (fiscal 1990)
EIN: 91-6256555

CONTRIBUTIONS SUMMARY
Donor(s): the late Lorene Petrie

Typical Recipients: • *Arts & Humanities:* arts associations, community arts, libraries, museums/galleries, public broadcasting, theater • *Civic & Public Affairs:* environmental affairs, municipalities • *Education:* colleges & universities, education administration • *Health:* hospitals
Grant Types: general support
Geographic Distribution: limited to Yakima and Kittitas counties, WA

GIVING OFFICERS
Security Pacific Bank, Washington: trust

APPLICATION INFORMATION
Initial Approach: Send brief letter describing program. There are no deadlines.

GRANTS ANALYSIS
Number of Grants: 7
Highest Grant: $100,000
Typical Range: $7,508 to $50,000
Disclosure Period: fiscal year ending July 31, 1992

RECENT GRANTS
100,000 St. Elizabeth Medical Center, WA
75,000 Clymer Museum, WA
50,000 Heritage College, Toppenish, WA
22,225 Children Activity Museum, WA
15,000 Central Washington University, Ellensburg, WA
7,508 Laughing Horse Summer Theater, WA
3,000 Cowiche Canyon Conservancy, WA

Petroleum Marketers
Sales: $150.0 million
Employees: 650
Headquarters: Roanoke, VA
SIC Major Group: Automotive Dealers & Service Stations, Miscellaneous Retail, and Wholesale Trade—Nondurable Goods

CONTACT
Scott Blankenship
President (Whiting Oil Subsidiary)
Petroleum Marketers
PO Box 12203
Roanoke, VA 24023
(703) 362-4900

CONTRIBUTIONS SUMMARY
Operating Locations: VA (Roanoke)

CORP. OFFICERS
Scott Blankenship: *CURR EMPL* chmn, secy, treas: Petroleum Marketers
T. M. Phelps: *CURR EMPL* pres, ceo: Petroleum Marketers

Petrolite Corp.
Sales: $323.5 million
Employees: 2,000
Headquarters: St. Louis, MO
SIC Major Group: Chemicals & Allied Products and Industrial Machinery & Equipment

CONTACT
Lori Johnson
Assistant to Director of Human Resources
Petrolite Corp.
369 Marshall Ave.
St. Louis, MO 63119
(314) 961-3500

CONTRIBUTIONS SUMMARY
Operating Locations: MO (St. Louis)

CORP. OFFICERS
William E. Nasser: *B* Shreveport LA 1939 *ED* Univ Notre Dame 1961; Univ OK 1964 *CURR EMPL* chmn, pres, ceo: Petrolite Corp *CORP AFFIL*

dir: Luzzatto & Figlio; managing dir, dir: Toyo-Petrolite Co Ltd

Petteys Memorial Foundation, Jack

CONTACT
Judy Gunnon
Jack Petteys Memorial Fdn.
PO Box 324
Brush, CO 80723
(303) 842-5101

FINANCIAL SUMMARY
Recent Giving: $158,522 (1991); $143,441 (1990); $133,815 (1989)
Assets: $3,661,364 (1991); $2,837,404 (1990); $3,052,733 (1989)
EIN: 84-6036239

CONTRIBUTIONS SUMMARY
Typical Recipients: • *Arts & Humanities:* libraries, public broadcasting • *Civic & Public Affairs:* municipalities • *Education:* colleges & universities, community & junior colleges, student aid • *Health:* health organizations, hospitals • *Social Services:* community service organizations
Grant Types: general support and scholarship
Geographic Distribution: limited to northeastern CO

GIVING OFFICERS
Farmers State Bank: trust
Robert Hansen: trust
Robert A. Perteys: trust

APPLICATION INFORMATION
Initial Approach: Send brief letter describing program. Deadline is December 1.

GRANTS ANALYSIS
Number of Grants: 39
Highest Grant: $21,000
Typical Range: $500 to $5,000
Disclosure Period: 1991

RECENT GRANTS
21,000 Colorado State University, Ft. Collins, CO
17,500 East Morgan County Hospital District, Brush, CO
10,986 University of Colorado, Boulder, CO
10,380 Northeastern Junior College, Sterling, CO
10,000 City of Brush, Brush, CO
10,000 East Morgan County Hospital Foundation, Brush, CO
9,056 Northeastern Junior College, Sterling, CO — scholarship
6,000 St. Olaf College, Northfield, MN — scholarship
5,000 Limon Memorial Library, Limon, CO
5,000 Sterling Regional Medical Center Foundation, Sterling, CO

Pettus Crowe Foundation
Headquarters: New York, NY

CONTACT
Irene Crowe
President
Pettus Crowe Fdn.
1616 P. St. NW
Ste. 100
Washington, DC 20036
(202) 328-5186

FINANCIAL SUMMARY
Recent Giving: $62,500 (1991); $72,582 (1990); $54,731 (1989)
Assets: $2,370,841 (1991); $2,117,833 (1990); $2,073,572 (1989)
Gifts Received: $885 (1991)
EIN: 23-7025310

CONTRIBUTIONS SUMMARY
Typical Recipients: • *Arts & Humanities:* libraries • *Civic & Public Affairs:* civil rights, ethnic/minority organizations, law & justice, women's affairs • *Health:* health organizations, single-disease health associations • *Religion:* religious organizations • *Social Services:* community service organizations
Grant Types: general support

APPLICATION INFORMATION
Initial Approach: Contributes only to preselected organizations.

GRANTS ANALYSIS
Number of Grants: 15
Highest Grant: $20,000
Typical Range: $1,000 to $5,000
Disclosure Period: 1991

RECENT GRANTS

20,000 Hastings Center, New York, NY

10,000 Women's Health Network, New York, NY

5,000 D.C. Women's Council on AIDS, New York, NY

5,000 Institute of Biomedical Ethics, New York, NY

5,000 Naral Foundation, Chicago, IL

5,000 New York University Network East-West Women, New York, NY

2,500 Funders Concerned About AIDS, New York, NY

2,500 National Women's Law Center, New York, NY

2,000 Norman Williams Public Library, New York, NY

1,000 National Gay and Lesbian Task Force, New York, NY

Pettus, Jr. Foundation, James T.

CONTACT
James A. Finch III
Trustee
James T. Pettus, Jr. Fdn.
7701 Forsyth, Ste. 1200
Clayton, MO 63105
(314) 725-9055

FINANCIAL SUMMARY
Recent Giving: $123,500 (1990); $100,500 (1989)
Assets: $2,466,572 (1990); $2,410,195 (1989)
Gifts Received: $100,000 (1989)
EIN: 43-6029569

CONTRIBUTIONS SUMMARY
Typical Recipients: • *Civic & Public Affairs:* housing • *Education:* career/vocational education, literacy • *Health:* single-disease health associations • *Social Services:* community service organizations, family planning, united funds, youth organizations
Grant Types: general support
Geographic Distribution: focus on HI

GIVING OFFICERS
James A. Finch III: trust
Betty Pettus: trust

James T. Pettus, Jr.: trust

APPLICATION INFORMATION
Initial Approach: Send brief letter of inquiry describing program. There are no deadlines.

GRANTS ANALYSIS
Number of Grants: 45
Highest Grant: $10,000
Typical Range: $500 to $5,000
Disclosure Period: 1990

RECENT GRANTS

10,000 Skyway Farm

8,000 United Way, Honolulu, HI

5,000 Alice Peck Day Memorial Hospital, Hanover, NH

5,000 Hospice, Honolulu, HI

5,000 Logos High School, St. Louis, MO

5,000 Paraquad, St. Louis, MO

4,500 J.V.L. Housing, St. Louis, MO

4,000 Edgewood Children's Center, St. Louis, MO

4,000 Planned Parenthood, St. Louis, MO

3,500 Planned Parenthood, Honolulu, HI

Pew Charitable Trusts

CONTACT
Deidra A. Lyngard
Communications Manager
Pew Charitable Trusts
One Commerce Sq.
2005 Market St., Ste. 1700
Philadelphia, PA 19103-7017
(215) 575-9050
Note: The foundation urges people to send letters of inquiry directly to the responsible program staff member in each area of interest if possible.

FINANCIAL SUMMARY
Recent Giving: $177,000,000 (1993 est.); $192,332,600 (1992); $143,054,300 (1991)
Assets: $3,300,000,000 (1992 est.); $3,388,048,594 (1991); $3,076,680,137 (1990)
EIN: 23-6299309

CONTRIBUTIONS SUMMARY
Donor(s): The Pew Charitable Trusts is the collective name for the seven individual charitable trusts established by the four sons and daughters of Joseph N. Pew, the founder of the Sun Oil Company. The first of the trusts, the Pew Memorial Trust, was founded in 1948. Smaller trusts were subsequently established to fund the Pews' personal philanthropic interests. Those included within the Pew Charitable Trusts are the Pew Memorial Trust; J. Howard Pew Freedom Trust; Mabel Pew Myrin Trust; J. N. Pew, Jr., Charitable Trust; Medical Trust; Mary Anderson Trust; and Knollbrook Trust. Because there is overlap in the areas that the seven trusts support, they share a single set of guidelines to establish eligibility for funding. Grant funds are allocated from the individual trusts based on their funding priorities.

John Howard Pew, the second son of Joseph N. Pew, was born in 1882 in Bradford, PA. Following graduation from Grove City College in 1900, and after taking several advanced courses at Massachusetts Institute of Technology, he joined the Sun Oil Company. He and his brother, Joseph N. Pew, Jr., assumed control of the company in 1912 after their father's death. His personal trust, established in 1957, supports organizations and institutions embodying the values of hard work, Christian values, free enterprise, and access to opportunity for all individuals. He also assisted numerous organizations dedicated to improving the quality of life in Philadelphia. J. Howard Pew died in 1971.

Mary Ethel Pew, the third child of Joseph N. Pew, was born in 1884 in Pittsburgh, PA. After graduating from Bryn Mawr College in 1906, she remained in Philadelphia where the Pew family relocated from Pittsburgh. Following her mother's death from cancer, Mary Ethel Pew devoted her resources to the support of cancer research and health care both as a volunteer and a board member for various institutions. She became particularly interested in Philadelphia's Lankenau Hospital and Institute for Cancer Research. She also funded various Philadelphia cultural, educational, and social service organizations. The Medical Trust was established in 1979 through her will.

Joseph Newton Pew, Jr., the youngest son of Joseph N. Pew, was born in 1886 in Pittsburgh, PA. After graduating with a degree in mechanical engineering from Cornell University in 1908, he worked briefly in the administrative offices of Sun Oil before leaving to learn the business from the ground up as an oilman in Illinois and as a roadlayer in South America. In 1912, upon his father's death, he became a vice president of the company. During his years at Sun, Mr. Pew focused his energies on designing new methods and products for the company. His contributions to educational and charitable institutions reflected his belief in free political expression, equal opportunity, and the free market system. The J. N. Pew, Jr., Charitable Trust was established from his estate following his death in 1963.

Mabel Pew Myrin, the youngest daughter of Joseph N. Pew, was born in 1889 in Pittsburgh, PA. Married in 1919, she and her husband, H. Alarik W. Myrin, moved to Argentina where they managed ranch property and developed mineral resources. After returning to the United States in the 1930s, they dedicated themselves to improving educational methods, aiding the handicapped, and preserving soil fertility. Mrs. Myrin strongly supported both the Waldorf educational method which takes a holistic approach to teaching, and the Camphill movement which applies Waldorf methods to the care and education of the handicapped. She also served as a trustee or board member for many institutions. The Mabel Pew Myrin Trust was established in 1957 to improve the human condition through support to the arts, education, health, and human services. She died in 1972.

Typical Recipients: • *Arts & Humanities:* arts festivals, dance, ethnic arts, history/historic preservation, museums/galleries, music, opera, performing arts, theater, visual arts • *Civic & Public Affairs:* business/free enterprise, economic development, environmental affairs, first amendment issues, housing, national security, public policy, urban & community affairs • *Education:* arts education, career/vocational education, colleges & universities, education associations, elementary education, faculty development, liberal arts education, literacy, medical education, minority education, religious education • *Health:* geriatric health, health care cost containment, mental health, nutrition & health maintenance, outpatient health care delivery, pediatric health, public health • *Religion:* religious organizations • *Social Services:* aged, child welfare, community service organizations, disabled, domestic violence, drugs & alcohol, employment/job training, family planning, family services, refugee assistance, shelters/homelessness, volunteer services, youth organizations

Grant Types: challenge, general support, operating expenses, project, research, and seed money

Geographic Distribution: nationally, with a special commitment to Philadelphia, PA; some international giving

GIVING OFFICERS

Susan Catherwood: dir
Robert G. Dunlop: dir *B* Boston MA 1909 *ED* Univ PA Wharton Sch BS 1931 *CORP AFFIL* dir: Glenmede Trust Co, Sun Co *NONPR AFFIL* mem: Beta Gamma Sigma, Sigma Phi Epsilon; trust: Univ PA
Thomas W. Langfitt, MD: pres, dir *CORP AFFIL* ceo: Glenmede Trust Co; dir: NY Life Ins Co, Smith Kline Beecham Corp, Sun Co; mem med adv comm: Gen Motors Corp *NONPR AFFIL* fellow: Royal Coll Surgeons; mem: Am Philosophical Soc, Inst Medicine, Natl Academy Sciences, Soc Neural Surgeons
Robert Emmett McDonald: dir *B* Red Wing MN 1915 *ED* Univ MN BBA; Univ MN BEE 1940 *NONPR AFFIL* Eta Nappa Nu, Tau Beta Pi
J. Howard Pew II: dir
Joseph N. Pew IV, MD: dir
Robert Anderson Pew: dir *B* Philadelphia PA 1936 *ED* Princeton Univ 1954-1956; Temple Univ BS 1959; MA Inst Tech MS Mgmt 1970 *CURR EMPL* pres: Helios Capital Corp *CORP AFFIL* dir: Glenmede Corp, Glenmede Trust Co, Sun Co Inc *NONPR AFFIL*

hon mem: Am Hosp Assn; mem, trust, chmn: Aircraft Owners Pilots Assn; trust: Temple Univ; trust, vchmn: Bryn Mawr Coll, Childrens Hosp Fdn Philadelphia
William Chase Richardson, PhD: dir *B* Passaic NJ 1940 *ED* Trinity Coll BA 1962; Univ Chicago MBA 1964; Univ Chicago PhD 1971 *NONPR AFFIL* fellow: Am Pub Health Assn; mem: Inst Medicine, Natl Academy Sciences; pres: Johns Hopkins Univ
Rebecca W. Rimel: exec dir

APPLICATION INFORMATION

Initial Approach:
Initially, a brief letter of inquiry summarizing the proposal is suggested. If the proposal falls within funding priorities and guidelines of the Trusts, an application package will be provided with further instructions.
The inquiry should summarize the project for which the potential applicant is requesting support. This should fit within guidelines for funding. Letters should include a description of the organization, nature of work and a brief history of achievements, especially as they relate to issue to be addressed; a statement of the problem you plan to address and an explanation of how it will be addressed; brief description of anticipated achievements or outcomes; description of time frame of proposed activities; estimated costs for the project or activity; and what is being requested from the Trusts. Full proposals are not encouraged without an initial contact with the staff.
Most applications may be submitted throughout the year. In culture, proposals for programs in museums and the visual arts are due by February 1 for review in June; for theater, by May 1, for review in September; for dance, by August 1, for review in December; and for music, by December 1, for review in April.
Grants are awarded in June, September, and December. As of 1993, board meetings will be held in March, June, September, and December. Applicants are asked to call the Culture program for deadline changes. New requests from previously funded organizations will be re-

viewed only after the grant period for any previous award has expired, and contract conditions have been met. Organizations whose proposals are declined must wait a minimum of twelve months before resubmitting. Occasionally the Trusts may invite an organization to submit a proposal or to participate in a trust-initiated program. An organization's application or participation in such a program will have no bearing on any subsequent request. Staff members may contact an applicant for additional information or to arrange for a meeting or site visit.

Restrictions on Giving:
Prospective applicants are encouraged to request a copy of the trusts' annual program guidelines and procedures pamphlet that provides detailed information on areas of interest to the Trusts, as well as funding restrictions.
In general, the Trusts do not provide funding for capital funds, endowments, debt reduction, general operations, library acquisitions, or individuals.

OTHER THINGS TO KNOW

The Glenmede Trust Company manages the funds and serves as trustee. In 1986, it reorganized the seven trusts into one division for purposes of grant making and administration. Although the Trusts have an interdisciplinary grants fund for propsals that fit within the guidelines of two or more programs, this status is determined by program officers at the Trusts. Applicants should apply to the program their proposal most fits.
The Trusts report that they offer occasional seminars and workshops on how to apply for grants to special programs and communications assistance to selected grantees.

Publications: annual report, guidelines and procedures, history of the Trusts, general information brochure

GRANTS ANALYSIS
Total Grants: $192,332,600*
Number of Grants: 576
Highest Grant: $7,820,000
Typical Range: $50,000* to $250,000
Disclosure Period: 1992
Note: Total grants figure includes $26,500,000 in one-time

special projects. Figure for typical range is supplied by the Trusts. The grants figures listed above are based on 1992 grants approved. Recent grants are derived from a 1992 grants list.

RECENT GRANTS
7,820,000 Philadelphia Schools Collaborative, Philadelphia, PA

6,540,000 Center for Assessment and Policy Development, Bala Cynwyd, PA

5,500,000 University of Pittsburgh, Pittsburgh, PA

4,608,500 Trustees of University of California, San Francisco, San Francisco, CA — for the Pew Health Professions Commission

3,800,000 Foundation for the Mid-South, Jackson, MS — in support of the Delta Workforce Alliance

3,500,000 Aspen Institute, Queenstown, MD — for the Pew Global Stewardship Initiative

2,800,000 Foundation for the Mid-South, Jackson, MS — in support of the Delta Enterprise Corporation

2,635,000 Philadelphia Historic Preservation Corporation, Philadelphia, PA — in support of a technical assistance and regrant program for historic house museums located in the five-county region of Southeastern Pennsylvania

2,500,000 Children's Hospital Foundation, Philadelphia, PA

2,400,000 PATHS/PRISM, Philadelphia Partnership for Education, Philadelphia, PA

Pfaffinger Foundation

CONTACT
James C. Kelly
President
Pfaffinger Foundation
Times Mirror Sq.
Los Angeles, CA 90053
(213) 237-5743

FINANCIAL SUMMARY
Recent Giving: $2,350,000
(1992 approx.); $2,286,625
(1991); $2,410,724 (1990)
Assets: $59,000,000 (1992
est.); $55,982,228 (1991);
$50,184,012 (1990);
$57,574,204 (1989)
Gifts Received: $75,000 (1992
est.); $229,402 (1991); $41,223
(1990); $1,226 (1988)
Fiscal Note: In 1990, the foundation received $37,245 from
the estate of Lee Swan and
$3,978 from the estate of Ellis
Blades.
EIN: 95-1661675

CONTRIBUTIONS SUMMARY
Donor(s): The Pfaffinger Foun-
dation was established in 1936,
with funds donated by the late
Frank Pfaffinger.
Typical Recipients: • *Civic &
Public Affairs:* consumer af-
fairs • *Education:* colleges &
universities • *Health:* hospitals
• *Social Services:* recreation &
athletics, united funds
Grant Types: general support
Geographic Distribution:
Southern California only

GIVING OFFICERS
Jim Chamberlain: treas
Robert F. Erburu: trust *B* Ven-
tura CA 1930 *ED* Univ South-
ern CA BA 1952; Harvard Univ
LLB 1955 *CURR EMPL* chmn,
ceo, dir: Times Mirror Co
CORP AFFIL dir: Tejon Ranch
Co; dir, dep chmn: Fed Reserve
Bank San Francisco *NONPR
AFFIL* dir: Am Newspaper
Publs Assn; mem: Bus Counc,
Bus Roundtable; mem bd dirs:
Counc Foreign Rels, Los Ange-
les Festival; mem trust counc:
Natl Gallery Art; trust: Art Col-
lections & Botanical Gardens,
Brookings Inst, Huntington Art
Gallery, Huntington Library,
Tomas Rivera Ctr
EuGene L. Falk: dir *B* Smith
Center KS 1943 *ED* Univ CO
Boulder BS 1967; Rochester
Inst Tech MBA 1971 *CURR
EMPL* exec vp admin: Los An-

geles Times *CORP AFFIL* dir:
Greater Philadelphia First
Corp, Metro Sunday Magazine
NONPR AFFIL dir: Philadel-
phia Chamber Commerce;
mem: Am Newspaper Publs
Assn, Pacific Area Newspapers
Pubs Assn, RIT Newspapers
Adv Counc; mem bd mgrs:
Ketchum Downtown YMCA;
mem natl adv counc: Gene
Autry Western Heritage Mus;
dir: Am Music Theater, Police
Athletic League (Philadelphia)
James C. Kelly: pres
William A. Niese: secy, dir
CURR EMPL vp, gen coun:
Los Angeles Times
Charles Robert Redmond:
chmn, dir *B* New Brunswick
NJ 1926 *ED* Rutgers Univ
1950; Univ Southern CA MBA
1960 *CURR EMPL* exec vp:
Times Mirror Co
Richard T. Schlosberg III: dir
CURR EMPL group vp newspa-
per: Times Mirror Co
Donald Franklin Wright: dir
B St Paul MN 1934 *ED* Univ
MN BME 1957; Univ MN
MBA 1958 *CURR EMPL* sr vp:
Times Mirror Co *NONPR
AFFIL* dir: Assocs CA Inst
Tech, CA Newspaper Publs
Assn, Univ MN Fdn; dir, mem:
Univ MN Alumni Club; mem
exec comm: Claremont Grad
Sch Univ Ctr; vchmn: Boy
Scouts Am Los Angeles Area
Counc

APPLICATION INFORMATION
Initial Approach:
Applicants should submit a letter and proposal.
The letter and proposal should
describe the project for which
funds are sought.
Proposals should be submitted
on or before October 1. The
board meets annually in December.
Restrictions on Giving: No
grants are given to individuals
other than persons employed or
formerly employed by the
Times Mirror Company.

GRANTS ANALYSIS
Total Grants: $193,000*
Number of Grants: 9*
Highest Grant: $80,000
Typical Range: $5,000 to
$36,000
Disclosure Period: 1991
Note: Above analysis is based
on contributions to organiza-
tions. In addition, the founda-
tion gave $2,093,625 in grants
to an undisclosed number of in-

dividuals. The total contributions for 1991 stood at
$2,286,625. Recent grants are
derived from a 1991 Form 990.

RECENT GRANTS
80,000	Los Angeles Times Summer Camp Fund, Los Angeles, CA
36,000	Independent Colleges of Southern California, Los Angeles, CA
36,000	United Way of Los Angeles County, Los Angeles, CA
15,000	Consumer Credit Counselors of Los Angeles, Los Angeles, CA
8,000	United Way of Orange County, Irvine, CA
5,000	Beyond Shelter
5,000	California Home for the Deaf, CA
5,000	Senior Care Network
3,000	Consumer Credit Counselors of Orange County, Irvine, CA

Pfeiffer Research Foundation, Gustavus and Louise

CONTACT
George R. Pfeiffer
Secretary
Gustavus and Louise Pfeiffer
Research Fdn.
300 East State St., Ste. 450
Redlands, CA 92373-0361
(714) 792-6269

FINANCIAL SUMMARY
Recent Giving: $753,355
(1991); $700,329 (1990);
$705,603 (1989)
Assets: $15,375,054 (1991);
$13,123,211 (1990);
$13,939,358 (1989)
EIN: 13-6086299

CONTRIBUTIONS SUMMARY
Donor(s): the late Gustavus A.
Pfeiffer
Typical Recipients: • *Education:* colleges & universities,
medical education, minority
education, science/technology
education • *Health:* medical research, single-disease health associations
Grant Types: general support
and research

GIVING OFFICERS
Lise P. Chapman: dir
H. Robert Herold II: vp, dir
Matthew G. Herold, Jr.: pres,
dir
Patricia Herold Nagle: dir
George R. Pfeiffer: secy,
treas, dir
Paul H. Pfeiffer, MD: dir
Robert H. Pfeiffer: dir
Milton Curtiss Rose: dir *B*
Cleveland OH 1904 *ED* Wil-
liams Coll AB 1927; Harvard
Univ LLB 1930 *CURR EMPL*
ptnr: Mudge Rose Guthrie &
Alexander *NONPR AFFIL* bd
overseers emeritus: Simons
Rock; dir: Royal Soc Medicine
Fdn; life trust: Pfeiffer Coll;
mem: Am Bar Assn, NY Bar
Assn, NY City Bar Assn, NY
County Lawyers Assn; trust:
Shaker Commun

APPLICATION INFORMATION
Initial Approach: Send brief
letter of inquiry describing program or project.
Restrictions on Giving: Does
not support individuals or provide loans.

OTHER THINGS TO KNOW
Publications: Biennial Report
(including application guidelines)

GRANTS ANALYSIS
Number of Grants: 24
Highest Grant: $50,000
Typical Range: $20,000 to
$40,000
Disclosure Period: 1991

RECENT GRANTS
50,000	College of Ozarks, Clarksville, AR
50,000	Stanford University School of Medicine, Stanford, CA
48,378	Corielle Institute for Medical Research
45,000	Instituto di Ricerche Farmacologiche "Mario Negri"
45,000	Johns Hopkins University School of Medicine, Baltimore, MD
40,000	California Institute of Technology, Pasadena, CA
40,000	Harvard University School of Medicine, Cambridge, MA
40,000	Jefferson Medical College, Philadelphia, PA

36,901 Pennsylvania State University, University Park, PA

35,685 University of Arizona College of Pharmacy, Tucson, AZ

Pfister and Vogel Tanning Co. / Pfister and Vogel Tanning Co. Foundation

Employees: 550
Parent Company: U.S. Leather Holdings
Headquarters: Milwaukee, WI
SIC Major Group: Leather & Leather Products

CONTACT

John H. Hendee
Committee Member
Pfister-Vogel Tanning Co. Foundation
1531 North Water St.
Milwaukee, WI 53202
(414) 765-5077

FINANCIAL SUMMARY

Recent Giving: $17,825 (1990); $13,600 (1989)
Assets: $284,250 (1990); $270,908 (1989)
EIN: 39-6036556

CONTRIBUTIONS SUMMARY

Typical Recipients: • *Arts & Humanities:* music, performing arts, theater • *Health:* medical research, single-disease health associations • *Social Services:* community service organizations, shelters/homelessness
Grant Types: general support
Geographic Distribution: focus on WI
Operating Locations: WI (Milwaukee)

CORP. OFFICERS

Martin Ray Berberian: *CURR EMPL* coo: Pfister & Vogel Tanning Co

GIVING OFFICERS

First Wisconsin Trust Company: trust
John H. Hendee: comm mem
Anthony M. Rood, Jr.: comm mem
Daniel J. Yakel: comm mem

APPLICATION INFORMATION

Initial Approach: Send brief letter describing program. There are no deadlines.

GRANTS ANALYSIS

Number of Grants: 8
Highest Grant: $3,200
Typical Range: $500 to $1,000
Disclosure Period: 1990

RECENT GRANTS

3,200 Wisconsin Conservatory of Music, Milwaukee, WI

2,000 Planned Parenthood, Milwaukee, WI

2,000 Wisconsin Heritages, Milwaukee, WI

1,000 Arthritis Foundation, Milwaukee, WI

1,000 Make-A-Wish Foundation, Milwaukee, WI

1,000 Milwaukee Rescue Mission, Milwaukee, WI

1,000 Seton Health Care Foundation, Milwaukee, WI

1,000 United Performing Arts Fund, Milwaukee, WI

Pfizer / Pfizer Foundation

Sales: $7.2 billion
Employees: 40,700
Headquarters: New York, NY
SIC Major Group: Chemicals & Allied Products, Food & Kindred Products, Lumber & Wood Products, and Nonmetallic Minerals Except Fuels

CONTACT

Linda B. Gornitsky
Director, Corporate Support Programs
Pfizer Inc
235 East 42nd St.
New York, NY 10017-5755
(212) 573-5936

FINANCIAL SUMMARY

Recent Giving: $17,500,000 (1993 est.); $22,739,960 (1992); $9,922,058 (1991)
Assets: $5,000,000 (1992 approx.); $3,589,470 (1990); $2,986,631 (1989)
Fiscal Note: Figures include total contributions. Company gives directly (about 90%) and through the foundation (about 10%). Company's charitable giving is decentralized. Each division responsible for its respective contributions budget.
EIN: 13-6083839

CONTRIBUTIONS SUMMARY

Typical Recipients: • *Arts & Humanities:* arts associations, arts centers, arts funds, dance, history/historic preservation, libraries, museums/galleries, music, opera, performing arts, public broadcasting, theater • *Civic & Public Affairs:* better government, business/free enterprise, civil rights, economic development, economics, environmental affairs, international affairs, law & justice, professional & trade associations, public policy, safety, urban & community affairs, women's affairs, zoos/botanical gardens • *Education:* business education, career/vocational education, colleges & universities, community & junior colleges, economic education, education associations, education funds, engineering education, faculty development, legal education, literacy, medical education, minority education, private education (precollege), public education (precollege), science/technology education • *Health:* emergency/ambulance services, geriatric health, health organizations, hospices, hospitals, medical rehabilitation, medical research, mental health, outpatient health care delivery, single-disease health associations • *International:* foreign educational institutions, international development/relief, international organizations • *Social Services:* aged, child welfare, community centers, community service organizations, counseling, delinquency & crime, disabled, drugs & alcohol, emergency relief, employment/job training, family services, legal aid, recreation & athletics, shelters/homelessness, united funds, volunteer services, youth organizations

Grant Types: capital, employee matching gifts, general support, multiyear/continuing support, operating expenses, professorship, project, research, and scholarship

Nonmonetary Support Types: donated equipment, donated products, in-kind services, loaned employees, loaned executives, and workplace solicitation

Note: Value of donated products was estimated at $9,351,860 in 1992; $317,378

in 1990; and $400,866 in 1989. This support is included in the giving totals above. Nonmonetary contributions include donations of medicine and equipment in emergencies and disaster aid. See "Other Things You Should Know" for more details.

Geographic Distribution: nationally and in communities where Pfizer and its subsidiaries operate; some emphasis on New York City
Operating Locations: CO (Boulder), CT (Groton), IN (Terre Haute), MN (Minnetonka), NJ (Rutherford), NY (New York)
Note: Also operates major facilities worldwide in the United Kingdom, France, Germany, Japan, Brazil, India, Ireland, Mexico, Argentina, Spain, and South Korea, and Puerto Rico.

CORP. OFFICERS

Edward Cushing Bessey: *B* Portland ME 1934 *ED* Dartmouth Coll AB; Dartmouth Coll MBA *CURR EMPL* dir, vchmn: Pfizer Inc *NONPR AFFIL* bd dir: Un Way Tri-St, USO Metro NY; mem natl adv comm: Agency Health Care Policy Res; mem: Counc Intl Ed Exchange, Johns Hopkins Univ
Ann M. Hardwick: *CURR EMPL* mgr (corp support programs): Pfizer Inc
Henry A. McKinnell: *CURR EMPL* cfo, exec vp: Pfizer Inc
William C. Steere, Jr.: *B* Ann Arbor MI 1936 *ED* Univ CA Santa Barbara; Stanford Univ *CURR EMPL* chmn, ceo, chmn exec comm, dir: Pfizer Inc *CORP AFFIL* dir: CT Mutual, Texaco *NONPR AFFIL* mem: Am Soc Corp Execs, Pharmaceutical Mfrs Assn, US Counc for Intl Bus Bus Counc (dir); mem exec comm: Natl Assn Retail Druggists; trust: NY Botanical Garden

GIVING OFFICERS

Terence Joseph Gallagher: secy *B* New York NY 1934 *ED* Manhattan Coll 1955; Harvard Univ JD 1958 *CURR EMPL* vp, asst gen couns: Pfizer Inc *CORP AFFIL* secy, dir: Adforce, Quigley Co, Composite Metal Products *NONPR AFFIL* dir: Am Soc Corp Secys, Calvary Hosp Fund; mem: Am Bar Assn; secy, dir: Pfizer Fdn Inc
James R. Gardner: vp *B* Wellsville NY 1944 *CURR*

EMPL sr dir corp strategic planning: Pfizer Inc *NONPR AFFIL* chmn: Natl Eagle Scout Assn New York City; colonel: USAR; dir: Boy Scouts Am Greater NY Counc; head: US Army USAR Political & Military Aff Div; mem: N Am Soc Corp Planning, Phi Kappa Phi, Planning Forum; mem adv counc: Princeton Univ Ctr Intl Studies; mem, dir: West Point Soc NY; mem faculty: US Army Command Gen Staff Coll
Kevin Keating: treas
Robert A. Wilson: pres

APPLICATION INFORMATION

Initial Approach: *Initial Contact:* brief letter or proposal *Include Information On:* description of the organization; amount requested; purpose for which funds are sought; recently audited financial statement or annual report; list of board members, trustees, and officers; other corporate supporters; proof of tax-exempt status *When to Submit:* any time; contributions committee meets regularly to consider proposals

Restrictions on Giving: Does not support individuals; veterans, political, fraternal, labor, or sectarian religious organizations; antibusiness organizations; private foundations; organizations located outside the United States; organizations not tax-exempt; organizations related to business interests of Pfizer Inc.; or independent agencies that duplicate work of United Way member agencies. Both the company and the foundation only consider applicants meeting requirements of Internal Revenue Code Section 501(c)(3); foundation requires that applicants also meet requirements of Section 509(a)(1), (2), or (3).

OTHER THINGS TO KNOW

Generally, the company sponsors local organizations in company operating communities while the foundation concentrates its efforts primarily on programs of national and international scope.
Gives special consideration to programs for which employees volunteer.
Corporate contributions committee refers appropriate re-

quests to the foundation for consideration.
Disaster aid generally dispensed through established international relief organizations. Contact operating divisions for information on nonmonetary support.

GRANTS ANALYSIS

Total Grants: $1,422,250*
Number of Grants: 164
Highest Grant: $150,000
Typical Range: $1,000 to $10,000
Disclosure Period: 1992
Note: Total grants figure is for the foundation only. Recent grants are derived from a 1992 grants list.

RECENT GRANTS

150,000 Pharmaceutical Manufacturers Association Foundation, Washington, DC
50,000 Boys and Girls Clubs, New York, NY
50,000 Lincoln Center for the Performing Arts, New York, NY
50,000 New York Botanical Garden, Bronx, NY — capital campaign
50,000 YMCA of Greater New York, New York, NY — capital campaign
30,000 Institute of Medicine/National Academy of Sciences, Washington, DC
30,000 New York Philharmonic, NY
25,000 Center on Addiction and Substance Abuse
25,000 Central Park Conservancy, New York, NY — special project
25,000 National Museum of the American Indian

Pforzheimer Foundation, Carl and Lily

CONTACT
Carl H. Pforzheimer, Jr.
President
Carl and Lily Pforzhiemer Foundation
650 Madison Avenue, 23rd Fl.
New York, NY 10022
(212) 223-6500

FINANCIAL SUMMARY
Recent Giving: $2,800,719 (1991); $1,552,259 (1990); $1,096,701 (1989)
Assets: $37,766,466 (1991); $33,591,915 (1990); $34,485,649 (1989)
EIN: 13-5624374

CONTRIBUTIONS SUMMARY
Donor(s): The foundation was established in 1942 by Carl H. Pforzheimer. His son Carl H. Pforzheimer, Jr., is the current president of the foundation and is also an investment banker with Carl H. Pforzheimer & Company located in New York. Mr. Pforzheimer served a banking apprenticeship in Europe before returning to the United States to work at Carl H. Pforzheimer & Company in 1934. He was a decorated soldier during World War II earning honors in France and the United States.
He married the former Carol Jerome Koehler in 1931. The couple has two children, Nancy Aronson and Carl Howard Pforzheimer III. Many members of the family serve as officers or directors of the foundation
Typical Recipients: • *Arts & Humanities:* arts associations, arts centers, arts institutes, community arts, dance, history/historic preservation, libraries, museums/galleries, opera, theater • *Civic & Public Affairs:* professional & trade associations, public policy, urban & community affairs • *Education:* colleges & universities, education associations, literacy • *Health:* hospitals, nursing services • *Social Services:* child welfare
Grant Types: general support
Geographic Distribution: focus on New York, NY

GIVING OFFICERS
Nancy P. Aronson: dir

Richard Watrous Couper: dir *B* Binghamton NY 1922 *ED* Hamilton Coll AB 1944; Harvard Univ AM 1948 *CORP AFFIL* dir: Security Mutual Life Ins Co *NONPR AFFIL* charter trust: Hamilton Coll; mem: Am Historical Assn, NY St Historical Assn, Org Am Historians, Phi Beta Kappa; pres emeritus: NY City Pub Library, Woodrow Wilson Natl Fellowship Fdn; trust: Episcopal Divinity Sch, Equitable Trust, Hudson River Trust
Anthony L. Ferranti: comptr
George L.K. Frelinghuysen: asst treas, dir
Mary Kitabjian: asst secy
Gloria La Rosa: asst secy
Carl A. Pforzheimer: dir
Carl H. Pforzheimer III: vp, treas, dir
Carl Howard Pforzheimer, Jr.: pres, dir *B* New York NY 1907 *ED* Harvard Univ AB 1928; Harvard Univ MBA 1930; Pace Univ DCS 1959; Capital Univ HHD 1969 *CURR EMPL* sr ptnr: Pforzheimer & Co (Carl H) *CORP AFFIL* pres, dir: Petroleum & Trading Corp *NONPR AFFIL* counc mem: Rockefeller Univ; hon dir: Harvard Univ Alumni Assn; hon fellow: Signet Soc; hon lifetime dir: Natl Civic League; hon trust: Boys Club NY, Horace Mann Sch, Mt Sinai Med Ctr; mem: Am Assn Commun Jr Colls, NY Chamber Commerce; mem emeritus: NY St Bd Regents; treas: Citizens Forum Self Govt; dir: Central Park South, Natl Academy Sch Execs
Carol K. Pforzheimer: dir
Martin Franklin Richman: secy *B* Newark NJ 1930 *ED* St Lawrence Univ BA 1950; Harvard Univ LLB 1953 *CURR EMPL* mem firm: Lord Day & Lord Barrett Smith *NONPR AFFIL* fellow: Am Bar Fdn, NY Bar Fdn; mem: Am Bar Assn, Am Law Inst, Fed Bar Assn, NY City Bar Assn, NY County Lawyers Assn, NY St Bar Assn; vchmn, trust: St Lawrence Univ
Alison A. Sherman: dir

APPLICATION INFORMATION
Initial Approach:
Send full outline of the project. There is no formal application form, but proposals should include financial information. There are no deadlines for submitting proposals.

The board meets quarterly in April, June, October, and December. Notification usually occurs following the meeting. **Restrictions on Giving:** The foundation does not make grants to individuals or for bricks and mortar projects.

GRANTS ANALYSIS

Total Grants: $2,800,719
Number of Grants: 45
Highest Grant: $310,000
Typical Range: $20,000 to $60,000
Disclosure Period: 1991
Note: Average grant figure excludes two grants of $304,000 and $310,000. Recent grants are derived from a 1991 Form 990.

RECENT GRANTS

310,000 Pace University, New York, NY
304,000 Mount Sinai Medical Center, New York, NY
150,000 City College-CUNY, New York, NY
150,000 Harvard University, Cambridge, MA
135,000 Pierpont Morgan Library, New York, NY
125,000 Wilberforce University, Wilberforce, OH
100,000 Bank Street College of Education, New York, NY
100,000 Institute of Public Administration, New York, NY
100,000 New York Experimental Glass Workshop, New York, NY
100,000 Rockefeller University, New York, NY

Pfriem Foundation, Norma F.

CONTACT

Vincent A. Griffith, Jr.
Norma F. Pfriem Foundation
961 Main Street
Bridgeport, CT 06604-4314

FINANCIAL SUMMARY

Recent Giving: $155,416 (1990)
Assets: $2,828,121 (1990)
Gifts Received: $500,000 (1990)
Fiscal Note: 1990 contribution received from Norma F. Pfriem.

CONTRIBUTIONS SUMMARY

Typical Recipients: • *Education:* colleges & universities • *Health:* hospitals • *Social Services:* youth organizations

GIVING OFFICERS

Vincent A. Griffith, Jr.: contact person

GRANTS ANALYSIS

Total Grants: $155,416
Number of Grants: 7
Highest Grant: $32,000
Typical Range: $10,000 to $32,000
Disclosure Period: 1990

RECENT GRANTS

32,000 St. Vincent's Medical Center Foundation, CT
30,500 Bridgeport Hospital Foundation, Bridgeport, CT
23,400 Newington Children's Hospital
20,000 Boy's and Girl's Club of Bridgeport, Bridgeport, CT — purchase van
20,000 Kennedy Center — purchase van
19,516 Goodwill Industries of Western Connecticut, CT — purchase of van
10,000 Fairfield University School of Nursing, Fairfield, CT

PGL Building Products

Sales: $250.0 million
Employees: 1,500
Headquarters: Auburn, WA
SIC Major Group: Wholesale Trade—Durable Goods

CONTACT

Dean Sabey
Branch Executive
PGL Building Products
PO Box 1049
Auburn, WA 98071
(206) 941-2600

CONTRIBUTIONS SUMMARY

Operating Locations: WA (Auburn)

CORP. OFFICERS

Jim Ben Edens: *CURR EMPL* pres: PGL Building Products

Phelps, Inc. / Phelps Foundation, Hensel

Sales: $500.0 million
Employees: 2,200
Headquarters: Greeley, CO
SIC Major Group: General Building Contractors and Heavy Construction Except Building Construction

CONTACT

Eric Wilson
Director
Phelps, Inc.
PO Box 0
420 Sixth Ave.
Greeley, CO 80632
(303) 352-6565

FINANCIAL SUMMARY

Recent Giving: $172,746 (fiscal 1992); $91,969 (fiscal 1989)
Assets: $375,714 (fiscal year ending May 31, 1992); $416,805 (fiscal 1989)
Gifts Received: $100,000 (fiscal 1992); $200,000 (fiscal 1989)
Fiscal Note: In fiscal 1992, contributions were received from Hensel Phelps Construction Company.
EIN: 84-0715416

CONTRIBUTIONS SUMMARY

Typical Recipients: • *Arts & Humanities:* museums/galleries • *Education:* colleges & universities, community & junior colleges, education associations • *Health:* hospitals • *Social Services:* community centers, community service organizations, united funds, volunteer services, youth organizations
Grant Types: general support
Nonmonetary Support Types: in-kind services, loaned employees, and loaned executives
Geographic Distribution: focus on CO
Operating Locations: CO (Greeley)

CORP. OFFICERS

Jerry L. Morgensen: *B* Lubbock TX 1942 *ED* TX Tech Univ 1965 *CURR EMPL* pres: Phelps

GIVING OFFICERS

Harold Evans: vp
Jerry Morgenstern: pres
Bob Ruyle: secy

APPLICATION INFORMATION

Initial Approach: Send brief letter describing program. There are no deadlines.

GRANTS ANALYSIS

Number of Grants: 54
Highest Grant: $25,000
Typical Range: $1,000 to $5,000
Disclosure Period: fiscal year ending May 31, 1992

RECENT GRANTS

25,000 University of Colorado Foundation, Boulder, CO
20,000 North Colorado Medical Center Foundation, Greeley, CO
15,000 Volunteers of America, Seattle, WA
10,428 University of Colorado, Boulder, CO
10,000 Colorado State University Foundation, Ft. Collins, CO
9,600 University of Northern Colorado, Greeley, CO
6,229 Aims Community College, Greeley, CO
5,000 American Airlines C.R. Smith Museum, Dallas, TX
4,800 Ouachita Baptist University, Arkadelphia, AR
4,216 University of Central Arkansas, Conway, AK

Phelps Dodge Corp. / Phelps Dodge Foundation

Sales: $2.59 billion
Employees: 10,000
Headquarters: Phoenix, AZ
SIC Major Group: Chemicals & Allied Products, Fabricated Metal Products, Metal Mining, and Primary Metal Industries

CONTACT

William C. Tubman
President
Phelps Dodge Fdn.
2600 N Central Ave.
Phoenix, AZ 85004
(602) 234-8100

FINANCIAL SUMMARY

Recent Giving: $1,239,405 (1993 est.); $1,235,913 (1992); $1,055,694 (1991)
Assets: $12,847,910 (1992); $11,844,695 (1991); $2,827,400 (1990)

Fiscal Note: Above figures are for the foundation only. Company also offers direct gifts. Contact for this support is Nicholas S. Balach, Vice President. Estimated value of this support was $1,525,000 in 1992.
EIN: 13-6077350

CONTRIBUTIONS SUMMARY

Typical Recipients: • *Arts & Humanities:* arts centers, arts funds, community arts, dance, history/historic preservation, libraries, museums/galleries, music, opera, public broadcasting, theater • *Civic & Public Affairs:* business/free enterprise, civil rights, economic development, economics, environmental affairs, international affairs, law & justice, public policy, safety, urban & community affairs • *Education:* business education, colleges & universities, community & junior colleges, economic education, education associations, education funds, health & physical education, international exchange, medical education, minority education, science/technology education, student aid • *Health:* health funds, health organizations, hospitals, medical training, pediatric health • *International:* international development/relief, international health care, international organizations • *Social Services:* community service organizations, family planning, recreation & athletics, religious welfare, united funds, youth organizations
Grant Types: capital, employee matching gifts, general support, multiyear/continuing support, research, and scholarship
Nonmonetary Support Types: donated products and in-kind services
Note: Nonmonetary support is provided by the company; estimated value of support is not available.
Geographic Distribution: where company maintains corporate facilities
Operating Locations: AZ (Ajo, Morenci, Phoenix), CA (Santa Fe Springs), CO (Lakewood), CT (Norwich), FL (Coral Gables), GA (Atlanta), IN (Fort Wayne), KY (Henderson), MN, MS (Starkville), NJ (Bayway, Marlboro), NM (Hurley, McKinley County, Tyrone), NY (New York), TX (El

Paso), WA (Stevens County), WY (Fremont County)

CORP. OFFICERS
Douglas Cain Yearely: *B* Oak Park IL 1936 *ED* Cornell Univ BS 1958; Harvard Univ 1968 *CURR EMPL* chmn, pres, ceo, dir: Phelps Dodge Corp *CORP AFFIL* dir: Lockheed Corp, South Peru Copper Co, Valley Natl Bank, Valley Natl Corp; pres: Phelps Dodge Indus *NONPR AFFIL* chmn: Copper Devel Assn; dir: Am Grad Sch Intl Mgmt, Phoenix Symphony; mem: AZ Econ Counc, Bus Roundtable, Conf Bd; mem, dir: Intl Copper Res Assn, NAM, Natl Electrical Mfrs Assn; vchmn: Am Mining Congress

GIVING OFFICERS
Cleveland Earl Dodge, Jr.: dir *B* New York NY 1922 *ED* Princeton Univ BSME 1943 *CURR EMPL* pres, dir: Dodge Machine Co Intl Dodge *CORP AFFIL* dir: Banded Hub Corp, Centennial Ins Co, Cleeland Corp, Display Sys, Key Bank NA, Phelps Dodge Corp; trust: Atlantic Mutual Ins Co *NONPR AFFIL* mem: Princeton Engg Assn, Princeton Rowing Assn; trust: Bennington Mus, Springfield Coll, Thousand Island Shipyard Mus, YMCA Retirement Fund
Frank J. Longto: vp, treas *B* Kingston NY 1940 *CURR EMPL* vp, treas: Phelps Dodge Corp
Mark R. Mollison: asst treas
George Barber Munroe: dir *B* Joliet IL 1922 *ED* Dartmouth Coll AB 1943; Harvard Univ LLB 1949; Oxford Univ BA 1951; Oxford Univ MA 1956 *CURR EMPL* dir: NY Life Ins Co *CORP AFFIL* chmn (fin comm), dir: Phelps Dodge Corp; dir: AMAX, Hanover Corp, Hanover Trust Co, Manville Corp, NY Times Co, Santa Fe Pacific Corp *NONPR AFFIL* assoc: Am Inst Mining Metallurgical Engrs; dir: Academy Political Sciences; mem: Am Bar Assn, Counc Foreign Rels, Minings & Metallurgical Soc Am; trust: Dartmouth Coll; trust, chmn fin comm: Metro Mus Art; vchmn, dir: NY Intl Festival Arts
Mary K. Sterling: secy *CURR EMPL* shareholder rel off: Phelps Dodge Corp
William C. Tubman: pres *B* New York NY 1932 *CURR*

EMPL vp, secy: Phelps Dodge Corp *NONPR AFFIL* dir: St Joseph Hosp Fdn; mem: Am Bar Assn, NY St Bar Assn; mem scholarship adv counc: Univ AZ; trust: Phoenix Art Mus
Douglas Cain Yearely: dir *CURR EMPL* chmn, pres, ceo, dir: Phelps Dodge Corp (see above)

APPLICATION INFORMATION
Initial Approach: *Initial Contact:* brief letter *Include Information On:* description of the organization, amount requested, purpose for which funds are sought, recently audited financial statement, and proof of tax-exempt status *When to Submit:* July through September
Restrictions on Giving: Does not support private shareholders, individuals, political or lobbying groups, dinners or special events, or goodwill advertising.

OTHER THINGS TO KNOW
Company matches employee contributions to accredited colleges and universities, including junior colleges; privately financed, nonprofit accredited secondary schools; voluntary hospitals; museums; performing arts organizations; botanical gardens; public broadcasting services; or zoological societies.
Publications: *A Tradition of Giving*

GRANTS ANALYSIS
Total Grants: $1,235,913*
Number of Grants: 140*
Highest Grant: $64,000*
Typical Range: $1,000 to $10,000
Disclosure Period: 1992
Note: Financial information is for the foundation only. Recent grants are derived from a 1992 Form 990.

RECENT GRANTS
64,000 University of Arizona, Tucson, AZ
38,000 Arizona State University, Tempe, AZ
37,220 National Merit Scholarship Corporation: Phelps Dodge Scholarships, Phoenix, AZ
35,000 Montana Tech Foundation, Butte, MT

30,000 Colorado School of Mines, Golden, CO
30,000 Phoenix Zoo
25,000 Arizona Opera Company, Phoenix, AZ
25,000 Arizona Theatre Company, Phoenix, AZ
25,000 Ballet Arizona, Phoenix, AZ
25,000 Heard Museum, Phoenix, AZ

PHH Corp. / PHH Foundation
Former Foundation Name: PHH Group Foundation
Sales: $1.93 billion
Employees: 4,600
Headquarters: Hunt Valley, MD
SIC Major Group: Automobile Repair, Services & Parking, Local & Interurban Passenger Transit, Transportation Services, and Trucking & Warehousing

CONTACT
Pilar M. Page
Manager
PHH Fdn.
PO Box 22613-HD
Baltimore, MD 21203
(410) 771-2733

FINANCIAL SUMMARY
Recent Giving: $356,918 (fiscal 1992); $382,500 (fiscal 1991); $444,828 (fiscal 1990)
Assets: $242,285 (fiscal year ending April 30, 1991); $319,469 (fiscal 1990); $391,566 (fiscal 1989)
Gifts Received: $289,900 (fiscal 1991); $356,000 (fiscal 1990); $251,013 (fiscal 1989)
Fiscal Note: Contributes through foundation only.
EIN: 52-6040911

CONTRIBUTIONS SUMMARY
Typical Recipients: • *Arts & Humanities:* community arts, general, libraries, museums/galleries, music, opera, performing arts, theater • *Civic & Public Affairs:* economics, general, municipalities, philanthropic organizations, professional & trade associations, safety, urban & community affairs, zoos/botanical gardens • *Education:* business education, colleges & universities, education funds, general, literacy, literacy, minority education, preschool education, private education (precollege), public

education (precollege), student aid • *Health:* emergency/ambulance services, general, health organizations, hospitals, medical research, outpatient health care delivery, pediatric health • *Religion:* religious organizations • *Science:* scientific institutes • *Social Services:* community service organizations, drugs & alcohol, emergency relief, food/clothing distribution, general, shelters/homelessness, united funds, youth organizations

Grant Types: award, capital, employee matching gifts, general support, and project

Nonmonetary Support Types: cause-related marketing & promotion

Geographic Distribution: limited to community where corporation headquarters is located; Baltimore, MD

Operating Locations: CT (Wilton), IL (Chicago), MD (Hunt Valley), NJ (Cherry HIll), TX (Ft. Worth)

CORP. OFFICERS

Robert Dietrich Kunisch: *B* Norwalk CT 1941 *ED* NY Univ 1963 *CURR EMPL* chmn, pres, ceo, dir: PHH Corp *CORP AFFIL* dir: Alex Brown & Sons, Greater Baltimore Co, Mercantile Bankshares Corp, Preston Corp; trust: Johns Hopkins Health Sys, Johns Hopkins Hospital; dir: Blue Cross & Blue Shield MD, Dome Corp, MEGA Inc, Mercantile-Safe Deposite & Trust *NONPR AFFIL* mem: Un Way Central MD; trust: Johns Hopkins Univ

Roy A. Meierhenry: *B* Norfolk NE 1938 *ED* Univ NE 1960; Creighton Univ 1966 *CURR EMPL* sr vp, cfo: PHH Corp *CORP AFFIL* dir: Dome Corp *NONPR AFFIL* dir: Greater Baltimore Med Ctr; mem: Fin Execs Inst

GIVING OFFICERS

Eugene Arbaugh: pres, dir *B* Manchester MI 1938 *ED* Western MD Coll 1960; Univ MD 1966 *CURR EMPL* sr vp, secy, chief mktg off: PHH Corp

Robert Dietrich Kunisch: chmn, dir *CURR EMPL* chmn, pres, ceo, dir: PHH Corp (see above)

R. W. Mitchell: treas

Pilar M. Page: mgr

D. C. Startzel: asst treas

Samuel H. Wright: secy *B* Baltimore MD 1946 *ED* Union Coll 1968; Univ MD 1972

CURR EMPL vp, gen couns: PHH Corp

APPLICATION INFORMATION

Initial Approach: *Initial Contact:* write for application form and guidelines* *Include Information On:* name, affiliation, address, and phone number of organization; how long organization has existed and geographic area served; list of principal staff and board members; list of board members employed by organization and whether the board has authorized request; list of current sources of other income, including percentages for the last three years; indication of amounts and percentages of total income spent on program services, fund-raising, administrative, and general; and copy of IRS tax exemption ruling or determination letter, current financial statement, and recent audit by a certified public accountant* *When to Submit:* any time *Note:* Requests for less than $1,000 may be submitted on the foundation's short application form. Proposals for funds in excess of $1,000 should be submitted on a PHH Foundation Form or on the applicant's organization letterhead. Responses on application form for requests for more than $1,000 must be in numeric sequence as listed above.

Restrictions on Giving: The foundation does not support organizations with major support from government funding, individuals, political activities and organizations, goodwill or journal advertisements or products, or dinners or related social activities. Grants are made only to organizations having tax-exempt status under Section 501(c)(3) of the IRS code.

OTHER THINGS TO KNOW

Publications: policy statement

GRANTS ANALYSIS

Total Grants: $356,918

Number of Grants: 36*

Highest Grant: $90,000

Typical Range: $1,000 to $10,000

Disclosure Period: fiscal year ending April 30, 1991

Note: Number of grants and average grant figures do not include $44,868 in matching gifts to education institutions. Re-

cent grants are derived from a fiscal 1991 grants list.

RECENT GRANTS

90,000	United Way, Baltimore, MD
40,000	College Bound Foundation, Baltimore, MD
25,000	Baltimore Symphony Orchestra, Baltimore, MD
25,000	Johns Hopkins University, Baltimore, MD
12,500	National Aquarium, Baltimore, MD
10,000	American Red Cross, Baltimore, MD
10,000	Eastern Economic Association, Trenton, NJ
10,000	GBMC Foundation, Baltimore, MD
10,000	Kenedy Institute, Baltimore, MD
7,000	Baltimore Symphony Orchestra, Baltimore, MD

Phibro Energy

Sales: $256.0 million
Employees: 2,149
Parent Company: Salomon Inc
Headquarters: Greenwich, CT
SIC Major Group: Oil & Gas Extraction, Petroleum & Coal Products, and Wholesale Trade—Nondurable Goods

---

CONTACT

Bob Chandiss
Director, Human Resources
Phibro Energy
600 Steamboat Rd.
Greenwich, CT 06830
(203) 221-5800

CONTRIBUTIONS SUMMARY

Operating Locations: CT (Greenwich)

CORP. OFFICERS

Robert Lavinia: *CURR EMPL* pres: Phibro Refining

Philadelphia Electric Co.

Revenue: $3.96 billion
Employees: 9,769
Headquarters: Philadelphia, PA
SIC Major Group: Electric, Gas & Sanitary Services

CONTACT

Linda Roth
Manager, Corporate Contributions
Philadelphia Electric Co.
2301 Market St.
Philadelphia, PA 19101
(215) 841-4124

FINANCIAL SUMMARY

Recent Giving: $3,200,000 (1993 est.); $2,800,000 (1992)

Fiscal Note: Company gives directly.

CONTRIBUTIONS SUMMARY

Typical Recipients: • *Arts & Humanities:* arts funds, dance, ethnic arts, libraries, music, opera • *Civic & Public Affairs:* consumer affairs, environmental affairs, housing, law & justice, urban & community affairs • *Education:* business education, colleges & universities, community & junior colleges, education funds, general, public education (precollege) • *Health:* hospitals • *Social Services:* child welfare, united funds

Grant Types: capital and operating expenses

Nonmonetary Support Types: donated equipment, in-kind services, loaned employees, and loaned executives

Note: Estimated value of nonmonetary support is not available; it is included in above total giving figures.

Geographic Distribution: in Bucks, Chester, Montgomery, Deleware, and York counties in Pennsylvania

Operating Locations: PA

CORP. OFFICERS

Corbin A. McNeill, Jr.: *B* Santa Fe NM 1939 *ED* US Naval Academy BS 1962; Naval Nuclear Power Sch; Univ CA Berkeley 1975; Syracuse Univ 1983 *CURR EMPL* pres, coo, dir: Philadelphia Electric Co *NONPR AFFIL* dir: Am Gas Assn, Am Nuclear Energy Counc, Nuclear Utility Mgmt Resources Counc; mem: Am Nuclear Soc

Joseph F. Paquette, Jr.: *B* Norwood MS 1934 *ED* Yale Univ BS 1956 *CURR EMPL* chmn, ceo: Philadelphia Electric Co *CORP AFFIL* vchmn, cfo: Consumers Power Co

GIVING OFFICERS

Linda Roth: *CURR EMPL* mgr (corp contributions): Philadelphia Electric Co

APPLICATION INFORMATION

Initial Approach: *Initial Contact:* brief letter *Include Information On:* description of the organization, amount requested, list of organizations board of directors, and copy of 501(c)(3) letter of determination *When to Submit:* any time

GRANTS ANALYSIS

Total Grants: $2,800,000
Disclosure Period: 1991

Philadelphia Industries / Farber Foundation

Sales: $225.0 million
Employees: 1,600
Headquarters: Philadelphia, PA
SIC Major Group: Fabricated Metal Products, Miscellaneous Retail, Paper & Allied Products, and Printing & Publishing

CONTACT

Jack Farber
President
Farber Foundation
1401 Walnut St.
Philadelphia, PA 19102
(215) 569-9900

FINANCIAL SUMMARY

Recent Giving: $142,575 (1991); $132,840 (1990); $228,307 (1989)
Assets: $3,211,255 (1991); $2,658,162 (1990); $2,904,326 (1989)
Gifts Received: $100,000 (1990); $100,000 (1989)
Fiscal Note: In 1990, contributions were received from Philadelphia Industries.
EIN: 23-6254221

CONTRIBUTIONS SUMMARY

Typical Recipients: • *Arts & Humanities:* community arts, dance, music • *Civic & Public Affairs:* civil rights • *Education:* colleges & universities • *Health:* hospitals • *Religion:* religious organizations • *Social Services:* community service organizations, united funds, youth organizations
Grant Types: general support
Geographic Distribution: focus on PA

Operating Locations: PA (Philadelphia)

CORP. OFFICERS

Jack Farber: *CURR EMPL* pres: Philadelphia Indus

GIVING OFFICERS

James G. Baxter: vp, treas, dir *B* Audubon NJ 1948 *ED* Lehigh Univ 1970 *CURR EMPL* vp (fin): CSS Indus *CORP AFFIL* Philadelphia Indus

Stephen V. Dubin: vp, secy, dir *B* Brooklyn NY 1938 *ED* City Univ NY 1961; Boston Univ 1961 *CURR EMPL* vp, secy, gen couns: CSS Indus *CORP AFFIL* vp, secy: Philadelphia Indus

Jack Farber: pres, dir *CURR EMPL* pres: Philadelphia Indus (see above)

APPLICATION INFORMATION

Initial Approach: Contributes only to preselected organizations.

GRANTS ANALYSIS

Number of Grants: 31
Highest Grant: $40,000
Typical Range: $100 to $1,000
Disclosure Period: 1991

RECENT GRANTS

40,000 Federation of Allied Jewish Agencies, Philadelphia, PA
31,000 American Jewish Committee, New York, NY
12,500 Center for American Jewish History/Temple University, Melrose Park, PA
10,000 Franklin Institute, Philadelphia, PA
8,500 Eagles Fly for Leukemia, Bala-Cynwyd, PA
5,000 Committee of Seventy, Philadelphia, PA
5,000 United Way, Philadelphia, PA
2,500 Magee Rehabilitation Hospital, Philadelphia, PA
1,600 Music Group, Philadelphia, PA
1,500 Urban Affairs Partnership, Philadelphia, PA

Philibosian Foundation, Stephen

CONTACT

Joyce P. Stein
Trustee
Stephen Philibosian Fdn.
46-930 West El Dorado Dr.
Indian Wells, CA 92210-8649
(619) 568-3920

FINANCIAL SUMMARY

Recent Giving: $528,460 (1991); $445,542 (1990); $582,452 (1989)
Assets: $7,588,217 (1991); $6,825,212 (1990); $8,199,356 (1989)
EIN: 23-7029751

CONTRIBUTIONS SUMMARY

Donor(s): Armenian Missionary Association of America
Typical Recipients: • *Arts & Humanities:* arts funds, arts institutes, libraries, museums/galleries, music • *Civic & Public Affairs:* ethnic/minority organizations • *Education:* arts education, private education (precollege) • *Health:* hospitals • *Religion:* churches, missionary activities, religious organizations • *Social Services:* child welfare, community service organizations, youth organizations
Grant Types: capital, endowment, multiyear/continuing support, and scholarship
Geographic Distribution: focus on CA

GIVING OFFICERS

Nazar Daghlian: trust
Mrs. Richard Danelian: trust
Stephanie Landes: trust
Albert Momjian: trust
Joyce Stein: trust

APPLICATION INFORMATION

Initial Approach: The foundation reports it only makes contributions to preselected charitable organizations.
Restrictions on Giving: Does not support individuals or provide loans.

GRANTS ANALYSIS

Number of Grants: 124
Highest Grant: $147,000
Typical Range: $500 to $5,000
Disclosure Period: 1991

RECENT GRANTS

147,000 Children Incorporated, Richmond, VA
99,000 Armenian Missionary Association, Paramus, NJ
45,500 Armenian Assembly, Washington, DC
20,000 Ararat Home, Los Angeles, CA
14,670 Brandywine Museum, Chadds Ford, PA
13,500 St. Margaret's Church, Palm Desert, CA
11,000 Community Church of Palm Springs, Palm Springs, CA
6,270 Palm Springs Friends of Philharmonic, Palm Springs, CA
6,100 Music Center United Fund, Los Angeles, CA
6,000 Cal Summer School for Arts, Northridge, CA

Philip Morris Cos.

Sales: $59.1 billion
Employees: 161,000
Headquarters: New York, NY
SIC Major Group: Food & Kindred Products, Nondepository Institutions, Real Estate, and Tobacco Products

CONTACT

Anne Dowling
Director, Corporate Contributions
Philip Morris Cos.
120 Park Ave.
New York, NY 10017
(212) 880-3366
Note: For information on international contributions contact Renee Staley, Specialist Public Relations and International Corporate Contributions Manager, at 914-335-1052.

FINANCIAL SUMMARY

Recent Giving: $60,500,000 (1993 est.); $55,000,000 (1992); $55,000,000 (1991)
Fiscal Note: Company gives directly. Above totals represent giving of all Philip Morris Cos., including subsidiaries—Philip Morris International, Philip Morris USA, Miller Brewing Co., Mission Viejo Co. and Kraft General Foods Co. See "Other Things You Should Know" for more de-

tails. Also gives limited funding through other departments which is not included above.

CONTRIBUTIONS SUMMARY

Typical Recipients: • *Arts & Humanities:* arts appreciation, arts associations, arts centers, arts institutes, community arts, dance, ethnic arts, museums/galleries, music, performing arts, visual arts • *Civic & Public Affairs:* civil rights, consumer affairs, economic development, environmental affairs, housing, philanthropic organizations, public policy, women's affairs, zoos/botanical gardens • *Education:* arts education, business education, colleges & universities, community & junior colleges, education associations, education funds, engineering education, literacy, medical education, minority education • *Health:* nutrition & health maintenance • *Social Services:* aged, community service organizations, disabled, emergency relief, employment/job training, food/clothing distribution, legal aid, shelters/homelessness

Grant Types: employee matching gifts, general support, and project

Nonmonetary Support Types: cause-related marketing & promotion, donated equipment, donated products, and in-kind services

Note: Nonmonetary donations are distributed through local plant committees. Company estimates value of nonmonetary support at conservatively 30% of cash contributions. Nonmonetary support estimate not listed in total giving figure.

Geographic Distribution: primarily in plant communities; some national organizations

Operating Locations: CA (Irwindale, Marina del Rey, Mission Viejo, Modesto, Montebello, Orange, Santa Ana), CO (Boulder, Highland Ranch), CT (Bethel, Wallingord, West Haven), FL (Ft. Myers, Orlando), GA (Albany, Moultrie), IA (Davenport, Liberty, Sigourney, West Liberty), IL (Deerfield, Glenview, Northbrook, Schiller Park, Woodstock), IN (Evansville), KY (Louisville), MA (Ludlow), MD (Baltimore), MN (Duluth), NC (Concord, Eden, Reidsville), NH (Bow), NJ (Neshanic, Ridgefield, Rockaway), NY (Auburn,

Bay Shore, Fulton, Lindenhurst, Long Island, Long Island City, New York, Tarrytown, White Plains), OH (Cleveland, Troy, Youngstown), OR (Portland), PA (Colmar, Philadelphia), SC (Newberry), TN (Memphis), TX (Ft. Worth, Temple), VA (Lynchburgh, Richmond), WA (Kent), WI (Chippewa Falls, Madison, Medford, Milwaukee, Waterloo, West Bend, Weyawwega) Note: Operates in 170 territories and countries; has foreign regional headquarters in Switzerland, Hong Kong, Australia, and Canada. List also includes all of Kraft General Foods locations.

CORP. OFFICERS

Geoffrey C. Bible: *B* Canberra Australia 1937 *CURR EMPL* pres, chief auditor off: Kraft Gen Foods

Michael Arnold Miles: *B* Chicago IL 1939 *ED* Northwestern Univ BS 1961 *CURR EMPL* chmn, ceo: Philip Morris Cos *CORP AFFIL* chmn, ceo: Kraft Foodservice; dir: Capital Holding Co, Sears Roebuck & Co, Citizens Fidelity Corp *NONPR AFFIL* dir: Counc Foreign Rels, Jr Achievement Chicago, Lyric Opera Chicago, Natl Multiple Sclerosis Soc; mem adv counc: Northwestern Univ JJ Kellogg Grad Sch Mgmt

William Murray: *CURR EMPL* pres, coo: Philip Morris Cos *NONPR AFFIL* dir: Intl Tennis Hall Fame; trust: Ailey (Alvin) Am Dance Theater, Am Mus Natural History, Polytech Univ

Hans George Storr: *B* Ritschweiler Germany 1931 *ED* Univ WI 1964 *CURR EMPL* exec vp, cfo: Philip Morris Cos *CORP AFFIL* pres, ceo: Philip Morris Credit Corp *NONPR AFFIL* mem: Am Inst CPAs, Inst Mgmt Accts, Natl Assn Accts

GIVING OFFICERS

Mark L. Bodden: mgr (corp contributions)

Anne T. Dowling: dir (corp contributions)

APPLICATION INFORMATION

Initial Approach: *Initial Contact:* letter or proposal; local or regional requests should be forwarded to the nearest Philip Morris operating company *Include Information On:* purpose of organization and activities,

description of needs to be addressed, plans for implementation and evaluation, management techniques, sources of income, population served, proof of tax-exempt status, copy of recent annual report, current total budget figures, list of board of directors, list of other corporate support; for gift renewals, include a progress report *When to Submit:* first half of calendar year, preferably the beginning of February or May *Note:* Application procedures are general grants only. Application which fall under the company's Focus Giving priorities need additional information. Refer to Philip Morris's Corporate Contributions Policy and Guidelines for further information.

Restrictions on Giving: Philip Morris does not support religious organizations or churches; fraternal groups; political parties, lobbying groups, or candidates for public office; public or commercial radio and television projects; youth-related organizations; member agencies of united funds; or religious organizations for sectarian purposes.

Company also does not give grants to individuals; to organizations for the underwriting of productions, fund-raising galas, benefits, or dinners; or to organizations which discriminate on the basis of race, creed, gender, sexual preference, or national origin.

Philip Morris generally does not support capital, building fund drives, or research for specific diseases, or disease-prevention.

In cases where monies go to nonprofit programs in foreign countries, funding must be through a U.S.-based 501(c)(3) organization.

OTHER THINGS TO KNOW

Philip Morris acquired General Foods Corp. and General Foods Fund in 1985 and Kraft and the Kraft Foundation in 1988. The two companies and their giving programs were merged to form Kraft General Foods in 1989. In 1992, Philip Morris consolidated and unified all subsidiaries giving procedures and priorities, including Kraft General Foods which used to run separate giving program. The Philip Morris name has also been

added to the Kraft General Foods Foundation and the foundation is now only used sparingly.

The company also sponsors employee matching gifts to a variety of organizations and scholarships to children of employees.

National organizations should contact Ms. Anne Dowling, Director, Corporate Contributions, at headquarters. Operating companies will accept proposals in their headquarters communitities and key operating locations for regional, or local, organizations. Listed below are the locations and contacts for Philip Morris's operating companies.

Kraft General Foods, Director, Corporate Contributions, 3 Lakes Drive, Northfield, IL 60093-2758.

Miller Brewing Company, Community Relations Representative, 3939 West Highland Blvd., Milwaukee, WI 53201.

Mission Viejo Company, Manager, Corporate Affairs, 26137 La Paz Road, Mission Viejo, CA 92691.

Philip Morris International, Corporate Affairs, 800 Westchester Ave., Rye Brook, NY 10573-1301.

Philip Morris USA, Manager, Public Affairs, 120 Park Ave., New York, NY 10017.

Publications: *Corporate Contributions Policy and Guidelines; Corporate Contributions AIDS Giving Guidelines*

GRANTS ANALYSIS

Total Grants: $55,000,000

Typical Range: $2,500 to $10,000

Disclosure Period: 1992

Philippe Foundation

CONTACT

Merton Holman
Vice President
Philippe Fdn.
122 East 42nd St.
New York, NY 10168
(212) 687-3290
Note: Alan Philippe is another contact name at the same address.

FINANCIAL SUMMARY

Recent Giving: $255,426 (1991); $232,889 (1990); $198,515 (1989)

Assets: $3,535,534 (1991); $3,146,835 (1990); $3,266,991 (1989)
Gifts Received: $70,205 (1991); $51,203 (1990); $104,039 (1989)
Fiscal Note: In 1991, contributions were received from European American Economic Corp. ($35,000), Beatrice Philippe ($20,000), and Anne Marie Philippe ($11,582).
EIN: 13-6087157

CONTRIBUTIONS SUMMARY

Donor(s): Pierre Philippe
Grant Types: endowment and research

GIVING OFFICERS

Helen P. Grenier: trust
Morton Holman: dir, vp, secy, treas
Marie-Josette Larrieu: trust
Irving London: trust
Alain Philippe: trust
Anne Philippe: trust
Anne Marie Philippe: dir, vp
Beatrice Philippe: dir, pres

APPLICATION INFORMATION

Initial Approach: Send brief letter of inquiry describing program. There are no deadlines.

OTHER THINGS TO KNOW

Provides grants for advanced study and scientific research.
Disclosure Period: 1991

Philips Foundation, Jesse

Headquarters: Dayton, OH

CONTACT

Jesse Philips
President
Jesse Philips Fdn.
One Citizens Federal Centre, Ste. 1300
Dayton, OH 45402
(513) 496-1300

FINANCIAL SUMMARY

Recent Giving: $1,445,420 (fiscal 1992); $1,285,207 (fiscal 1990); $2,419,319 (fiscal 1989)
Assets: $18,478,230 (fiscal year ending February 28, 1992); $15,410,256 (fiscal 1990); $14,705,556 (fiscal 1989)
Gifts Received: $267,910 (fiscal 1992); $206,683 (fiscal 1990); $1,688,185 (fiscal 1989)

Fiscal Note: In fiscal 1992, contributions were received from Tomkins Corp. Foundation and John W. Berry.
EIN: 31-6023380

CONTRIBUTIONS SUMMARY

Donor(s): The foundation was incorporated in 1960 by Jesse Philips, Philips Industries, Inc., and subsidiaries.
Typical Recipients: • *Arts & Humanities:* arts associations, arts centers, arts funds, community arts, dance, museums/galleries, music, performing arts, theater • *Civic & Public Affairs:* better government, business/free enterprise, environmental affairs, municipalities, nonprofit management, philanthropic organizations, zoos/botanical gardens • *Education:* arts education, colleges & universities, education funds, student aid • *Health:* hospitals, medical research, public health, single-disease health associations • *International:* international organizations • *Religion:* religious organizations • *Social Services:* animal protection, community centers, employment/job training, family planning, recreation & athletics, religious welfare, shelters/homelessness, youth organizations
Grant Types: general support and scholarship
Geographic Distribution: focus on Montgomery County, OH

GIVING OFFICERS

Thomas Craig Haas: treas, dir *B* Dayton OH 1943 *ED* OH Univ 1966 *CURR EMPL* treas: Philips Indus *CORP AFFIL* treas: Philips Indus
David T. Jeanmougin: vp *B* Cincinnati OH 1940 *ED* Xavier Univ 1962
Jesse Philips: pres *B* New York NY 1914 *ED* Oberlin Coll AB 1937; Harvard Univ MBA 1939 *CORP AFFIL* former chmn, chmn special comm: Philips Indus *NONPR AFFIL* assoc chmn: Dayton Commun Chest; chmn: Dayton Fdn IN Colls, Dayton Jewish Commun Devel Counc; dir: Dayton Better Bus Bur, Dayton Jr Achievement, Dayton Salvation Army, Good Samaritan Hosp, Jewish Commun Counc, Miami Valley Boy Scouts Am; mem: Joint Distribution Comm, Natl Retail Dry Goods Assn; mem, dir:

Dayton Chamber Commerce, Dayton Retail Merchants Assn; mem exec comm: Pres Counc Youth Exchange, Sister Cities Intl; trust: Arthritis Fdn, Dayton Opera Co, Oberlin Coll, OH Fdn IN Colls, Sinclair Coll Fdn, Univ Dayton, Wright St Univ Fdn
Caryl Phillips: vp, trust
Milton Roisman: vp, trust
Edwin L. Ryan, Jr.: secy, trust *CURR EMPL* secy, corp couns: Philips Indus

APPLICATION INFORMATION

Initial Approach:
The foundation reports that the preliminary selection process requires the submission of written applications on forms prescribed by or acceptable to the selection committee. Applicants should contact the foundation for formal application procedures.
The deadline for submitting proposals is May 1.
Restrictions on Giving: The foundation's primary giving interests include the arts, education, and medicine.

GRANTS ANALYSIS

Total Grants: $1,445,420
Number of Grants: 190
Highest Grant: $265,000
Typical Range: $500 to $10,000
Disclosure Period: fiscal year ending February 28, 1992
Note: Recent grants are derived from a fiscal 1992 grants list.

RECENT GRANTS

265,000 Dayton Museum of Natural History, Dayton, OH
140,000 Jewish Federation of Greater Dayton, Dayton, OH
102,000 Dayton Boys and Girls Club, Dayton, OH
100,000 Hillsdale College, Hillsdale, MI
80,000 Sisters Cities International
50,000 Dayton Foundation, Dayton, OH
25,000 California International Sailing Association, Irvine, CA
25,000 California International Sailing Association, Irvine, CA
25,000 Mayo Clinic, Rochester, MN
25,000 Miami Valley Health Foundation, Miami, FL

Phillipps Foundation

CONTACT

Phillipps Fdn.
c/o Security Pacffic National Bank
PO Box 100
Rancho Mirage, CA 92270

FINANCIAL SUMMARY

Recent Giving: $117,900 (1990); $155,200 (1989); $71,400 (1987)
Assets: $1,978,773 (1989); $1,806,309 (1987)
EIN: 95-6042761

CONTRIBUTIONS SUMMARY

Donor(s): the late Philip M. Virtue
Typical Recipients: • *Arts & Humanities:* history/historic preservation, opera • *Civic & Public Affairs:* economics, international affairs, public policy, urban & community affairs • *Education:* colleges & universities, economic education, education associations • *Religion:* churches, religious organizations
Grant Types: general support

GIVING OFFICERS

Donald Breese: cfo
Lauren W. Breese: secy
Tecla M. Virtue: pres

APPLICATION INFORMATION

Initial Approach: Contributes only to preselected organizations.
Restrictions on Giving: Does not support individuals.

GRANTS ANALYSIS

Number of Grants: 12
Highest Grant: $30,400
Typical Range: $3,000 to $10,000
Disclosure Period: 1990

RECENT GRANTS

30,400 First Church of Christ, Scientist
29,000 Northwood Institute, Midland, MI
15,000 Hillsdale College, Hillsdale, MI
9,500 National Education Program
8,000 International Lincoln Foundation, Idyllwild, CA
7,500 Americanism Foundation, St. Louis, MO
4,500 Chamber Opera Society of Desert

4,000 Christian Science Society
3,500 America's Future, New Rochelle, NY
3,500 Foundation for Economic Education, New York, NY

Phillips Charitable Trust, Dr. and Mrs. Arthur William

CONTACT
William J. McFate
Trustee
Dr. and Mrs. Arthur William Phillips Charitable Trust
229 Elm St., P. O. Box 316
Oil City, PA 16301
(814) 676-2736

FINANCIAL SUMMARY
Recent Giving: $409,000 (fiscal 1991); $631,579 (fiscal 1990); $433,350 (fiscal 1989)
Assets: $9,826,223 (fiscal year ending September 30, 1991); $9,621,852 (fiscal 1990); $9,546,346 (fiscal 1989)
EIN: 25-6201015

CONTRIBUTIONS SUMMARY
Donor(s): the late Arthur William Phillips
Typical Recipients: • *Civic & Public Affairs:* urban & community affairs • *Education:* colleges & universities, education associations, education funds • *Health:* health organizations, hospitals, pediatric health, single-disease health associations • *Religion:* churches • *Social Services:* child welfare, youth organizations
Grant Types: project
Geographic Distribution: focus on northwestern PA

GIVING OFFICERS
William E. Breene: trust
Hugh R. Gilmore, Jr.: trust
William J. McFate: trust

APPLICATION INFORMATION
Initial Approach: Send cover letter and full proposal (three copies). There are no deadlines.

GRANTS ANALYSIS
Number of Grants: 17
Highest Grant: $100,000
Typical Range: $5,000 to $20,000
Disclosure Period: fiscal year ending September 30, 1991

RECENT GRANTS
100,000 Clarion University Foundation, Clarion, PA
50,000 Allegheny College, Meadville, PA
50,000 Grove City College, Grove City, PA
50,000 YMCA, Franklin, PA
25,000 Allegheny Mountain Health Systems, Oil City, PA
25,000 Decision House, Oil City, PA
25,000 United Community Independence Programs, PA
10,000 American Cancer Society, New York, NY
10,000 American Heart Association, Philadelphia, PA
10,000 Foxview Manor, PA

Phillips Family Foundation, Jay and Rose

CONTACT
Patricia Cummings
Executive Director
Jay and Rose Phillips Family Foundation
2345 Kennedy St., NE
Minneapolis, MN 55413
(612) 331-6230

FINANCIAL SUMMARY
Recent Giving: $3,937,002 (1993 est.); $3,545,533 (1992 approx.); $3,152,410 (1990)
Assets: $97,700,000 (1993 est.); $77,694,329 (1992 approx.); $65,905,527 (1990); $70,909,724 (1989)
Gifts Received: $230,000 (1992); $229,966 (1991); $461,724 (1988)
Fiscal Note: The foundation received a gift of $972,355 from Jay Phillips and Rose Phillips in 1987; $461,724 from Carol Lincoln Van Trees, Suzan Levin, Dean Benson Phillips, and Tyler Jay Phillips in 1988; $229,966 from Carol Lincoln Van Tress and Suzan Levin in 1990; and $230,000 from Jay Phillips and Rose Phillips in 1992.
EIN: 41-6019578

CONTRIBUTIONS SUMMARY
Donor(s): The Phillips Foundation was incorporated in 1944, with funds donated by Jay Phillips and members of the Phillips family. The family business, Ed Phillips and Sons, wholesale liquor distributors, is located in Minneapolis, where the Phillips family resides.
Typical Recipients: • *Arts & Humanities:* arts associations, arts centers, history/historic preservation, libraries, museums/galleries, music, public broadcasting • *Civic & Public Affairs:* civil rights, economic development, housing, philanthropic organizations, public policy, urban & community affairs, women's affairs • *Education:* colleges & universities, education associations, education funds, medical education, religious education, student aid • *Health:* health organizations, hospitals, medical research, single-disease health associations • *Religion:* religious organizations, synagogues • *Social Services:* aged, child welfare, community centers, community service organizations, counseling, disabled, homes, recreation & athletics, religious welfare, shelters/homelessness, united funds, volunteer services, youth organizations
Grant Types: capital, general support, professorship, research, and scholarship
Geographic Distribution: primarily metropolitan Minneapolis/St. Paul, MN

GIVING OFFICERS
Erik Bernstein: trust
Paula P. Bernstein: trust
William Bernstein: trust
Thomas P. Cook: secy, trust
Jack I. Levin: trust
John Levin: trust
Suzan Levin: trust
Jeanne Phillips: trust
Morton B. Phillips: don, co-chmn
Pauline Phillips: trust
Rose Phillips: don, co-chmn
Neil I. Sell: asst secy

APPLICATION INFORMATION
Initial Approach:
Formal applications are not required. A brief typewritten letter with adequate documentation is acceptable.
The letter should include a brief description of the organization, amount requested, an outline of the purpose for which a grant is sought, a definition of the project, and the specific goals the project is designed to meet. Proposals should also include an explanation of how request addresses the foundation's funding priorities; a description of population served including geographical area(s) served, number of persons served, ages, income level(s), and special needs of individuals served; evidence of need for organization or project; evidence of organization's capacity to manage program or project including staff qualifications and experience; and method of evaluating effectiveness and success of program(s) or project. Other information which should be included is: itemized project budget; donor's list showing corporate and foundation support during the past 12 months; proof of tax-exempt status; copy of IRS Form 990 with schedule A; list of the board of directors, officers, and their affiliations; and a copy of the most recent audited financial statements. If nonprofit is requesting funds for a special or capital project, the following must also be submitted: a board-approved special project or capital project budget; total amount and sources of funds received or committed; and list of proposals pending with other funding sources.
Applications are accepted throughout the year.
The foundation will send confirmation of application receipt. The trustee meets approximately every three months and completed applications are reviewed in the order in which they are received. The foundation reports that the review process usually takes about three to four months.
Restrictions on Giving: The foundation will not make grants to organizations operating for profit, political campaigns or lobbying efforts to influence legislation, endowment campaigns, or individuals. The foundation requests that all initial inquiries from prospective applicants be by mail, not by telephone or by personal visits to the foundation office.

OTHER THINGS TO KNOW
The foundation was formerly called Phillips Foundation.
Publications: application brochure

GRANTS ANALYSIS
Total Grants: $3,545,533

Number of Grants: 325
Highest Grant: $200,000
Typical Range: $1,000 to
$25,000
Disclosure Period: 1992
Note: Recent grants are de-
rived from a 1992 grants list.

RECENT GRANTS

200,000 Mayo Clinic, Rochester, MN
200,000 Minneapolis Fed-
eration for Jewish
Service, Minneapo-
lis, MN
200,000 University of Minnesota, Minneapo-
lis, MN
150,000 Adath Jeshurun
Synagogue, Min-
neapolis, MN —
building fund
125,000 Beth Israel at Shalom Park, Denver,
CO — building
fund
100,000 Adath Jeshurun
Congregation, Min-
neapolis, MN
100,000 Anti-Defamation
League, New York,
NY
100,000 Boys and Girls
Club, Minneapolis,
MN
100,000 Brandeis Univer-
sity, Waltham, MA
100,000 Phillips Eye Institute, Minneapolis,
MN

Phillips Family Foundation, L. E.

CONTACT
Eileen Cohen
Director
L. E. Phillips Family Foundation
c/o National Presto Industries
3925 North Hastings Way
Eau Claire, WI 54703
(715) 839-2139

FINANCIAL SUMMARY
Recent Giving: $2,166,573
(fiscal 1992); $1,987,391 (fis-
cal 1991); $1,733,326 (fiscal
1990)
Assets: $52,771,528 (fiscal
year ending February 29,
1992); $47,054,224 (fiscal
1991); $41,116,907 (fiscal
1990)
Gifts Received: $127,201 (fis-
cal 1992); $127,201 (fiscal
1991); $1,026,759 (fiscal 1990)
Fiscal Note: In fiscal 1990, the
foundation received $899,558
from the Boy Scout Camp
Trust under the will of L. E.
Phillips and $127,201 from the
Edith Phillips 1983 Charitable

Trust. In fiscal 1992, the foundation received $127,201 from
the Edith Phillips 1983 Charitable Trust.
EIN: 39-6046126

CONTRIBUTIONS SUMMARY
Donor(s): Lewis E. Phillips established the L. E. Phillips
Charities in Wisconsin in 1943.
The foundation's name re-
cently was changed to the L. E.
Phillips Family Foundation.
Mr. Phillips was president and
director of the manufacturing
business of Ed Phillips and
Sons Company. He was head of
National Presto Industries, formerly named the National Pres-
sure Cooker Company, for over
25 years. The foundation is
administered primarily by members of the Phillips family, including Lewis E. Phillip's son-
in-law, Melvin Samuel Cohen,
who is the current chairman of
National Presto Industries.
Typical Recipients: • *Arts &
Humanities:* libraries • *Civic &
Public Affairs:* philanthropic organizations, public policy,
safety • *Education:* career/voca-
tional education, colleges &
universities • *Health:* hospitals
• *Religion:* synagogues • *Social
Services:* recreation & athletics, united funds, youth organizations
Grant Types: capital, general
support, operating expenses, research, and scholarship
Geographic Distribution: primarily northwestern Wisconsin, with emphasis on Eau
Claire and Chippewa counties

GIVING OFFICERS
James F. Bartl: secy, dir *B* St.
Paul MN 1940 *ED* St Thomas
Coll 1962; Marquette Univ
Law 1965 *CURR EMPL* secy,
coun, dir industrial rels: Natl
Presto Indus *NONPR AFFIL*
mem: Am Soc Corp Secys
Eileen Phillips Cohen: dir
PHIL AFFIL secy, treas: Cohen
(Melvin S) Foundation; trust:
Presto Foundation
Maryjo R. Cohen: vp, treas,
dir *CURR EMPL* pres, coo, cfo,
dir: Presto Indus *PHIL AFFIL*
vp: Melvin S Cohen Foundation
Melvin S. Cohen: pres, dir *B*
Minneapolis MN 1918 *ED*
Univ MN BS 1939; Univ MN
JD 1941 *CURR EMPL* chmn,
ceo: Natl Presto Indus *CORP
AFFIL* chmn: Gaurdian Svc Se-
curity Sys, Johnson Printing,
Lawrence Motors, Presto Mfg

Co, Red Wing Truck Rental,
Un Truck Leasing, World Aero-
space Corp; pres: Canton Sales
& Storage, Century Leasing &
Liquidating, Natl Defense
Corp, Presto Export; pres, dir:
Jackson Sales Storage Co, Mas-
ter Corp, Presto Intl, Presto
Parts & Svc; vp, dir: Natl Auto-
matic Pipeline Operators;
vp,dir: Natl Pipeline Co; dir:
First Natl Bank Eau Claire WI
PHIL AFFIL chmn, pres:
Presto Foundation; pres: Cohen
(Melvin S) Foundation
Melvin S. Cohen: pres, dir
CURR EMPL chmn, ceo: Natl
Presto Indus (see above)
Allen D. Hanson: asst secy,
asst treas *B* 1936 *CURR EMPL*
ceo, pres: Harvest States Coop-
erative
Edith Phillips: vp, dir

APPLICATION INFORMATION
Initial Approach:
The foundation has no formal
application requirements or procedures. Applicants should
send a letter of inquiry.
The letter should describe the
organization and project for
which funds are sought, and include a budget.
There are no application deadlines, although the foundation
prefers to receive inquiries before the end of the fiscal year.
Restrictions on Giving: The
foundation does not make
grants to individuals.

GRANTS ANALYSIS
Total Grants: $2,166,573
Number of Grants: 70
Highest Grant: $1,935,000
Typical Range: $500 to
$15,000
Disclosure Period: fiscal year
ending February 29, 1992
Note: The average grant figure
excludes one grant of
$1,935,000. Recent grants are
derived from a fiscal 1992
Form 990.

RECENT GRANTS
1,935,000 Melvin S. Cohen
Trust F/B/O, Eau
Claire, WI — trust
principal for the
benefit of Minnea-
polis Federation
for Jewish Service
32,500 University of Wis-
consin Eau Claire
Foundation, Eau
Claire, WI — visit-
ing professorship
24,260 L. E. Phillips Me-
morial Public Li-
brary, Eau Claire,

WI — building re-
modeling
20,000 L. E. Phillips Boy
Scout Camp Trust,
Eau Claire, WI —
trust capital for
benefit of boy
scout camp
17,500 University of Wis-
consin Eau Claire
Foundation, Eau
Claire, WI — in-
ternship program
15,000 United Way of Eau
Claire, Eau Claire,
WI — operating
funds
10,000 Eau Claire Fire Department, Eau
Claire, WI —
water safety and
rescue program
10,000 Mayo Foundation,
Rochester, MN —
medical school
scholarships
10,000 Wisconsin Vietnam
Veterans' Memo-
rial Project,
Neillsville, WI —
Vietnam memorial
construction
8,500 St. Joseph's Hospi-
tal, Chippewa
Falls, WI — win-
dow replacement

Phillips Foundation, A. P.

CONTACT
M. W. Wells, Jr.
President
A. P. Phillips Fdn.
PO Box 3628
Orlando, FL 32802
(407) 422-8250

FINANCIAL SUMMARY
Recent Giving: $70,370 (fiscal
1990); $138,750 (fiscal 1989);
$125,250 (fiscal 1988)
Assets: $2,663,834 (fiscal year
ending June 30, 1990);
$2,463,366 (fiscal 1989);
$2,362,890 (fiscal 1988)
EIN: 59-6165157

CONTRIBUTIONS SUMMARY
Typical Recipients: • *Arts &
Humanities:* community arts,
music • *Education:* colleges &
universities, community & junior colleges • *Health:* hospitals
• *Religion:* churches • *Science:*
observatories & planetariums
• *Social Services:* aged, community service organizations,
food/clothing distribution,
united funds, youth organizations
Grant Types: general support

Geographic Distribution: focus on central FL

GIVING OFFICERS

J.W. Jordan: secy
L.A. Wells: trust
M.W. Wells, Jr.: off

APPLICATION INFORMATION

Initial Approach: Send brief letter describing program. There are no deadlines.

GRANTS ANALYSIS

Number of Grants: 15
Highest Grant: $20,000
Typical Range: $100 to $5,000
Disclosure Period: fiscal year ending June 30, 1990

RECENT GRANTS

20,000 University of Florida, Gainesville, FL
10,000 Orlando Science Center, Orlando, FL
6,000 St. Luke's Episcopal Church, Orlando, FL
5,000 Boys and Girls Club of Central Florida, Orlando, FL
5,000 Edgewood Ranch Foundation, Orlando, FL
5,000 Florida Symphony Orchestra, Orlando, FL
5,000 Valencia Community College, Valencia, FL
5,000 YMCA, Orlando, FL
3,750 Gator Boosters, Gainesville, FL
2,500 Meals on Wheels, Orlando, FL

Phillips Foundation, Dr. P.

CONTACT

J. A. Hinson
President
Dr. P. Phillips Fdn.
60 West Robinson St.
Orlando, FL 32801
(407) 422-6105

FINANCIAL SUMMARY

Recent Giving: $752,934 (fiscal 1991); $851,147 (fiscal 1990); $195,538 (fiscal 1989)
Assets: $24,403,455 (fiscal year ending May 31, 1991); $24,403,455 (fiscal 1990); $21,717,786 (fiscal 1989)
Gifts Received: $2,659 (fiscal 1991); $2,182 (fiscal 1989)
EIN: 59-6135403

CONTRIBUTIONS SUMMARY

Donor(s): The foundation was incorporated in 1953 by the late Della Phillips and the late Howard Phillips.
Typical Recipients: • *Arts & Humanities:* arts centers, arts festivals, arts funds, community arts, history/historic preservation, museums/galleries, music, performing arts, theater • *Civic & Public Affairs:* law & justice, municipalities, philanthropic organizations • *Education:* colleges & universities, economic education, education funds, elementary education, public education (precollege) • *Health:* health funds, hospices, hospitals, medical research, nursing services, single-disease health associations • *Religion:* churches, missionary activities, religious organizations • *Science:* science exhibits & fairs, scientific institutes • *Social Services:* child welfare, community service organizations, counseling, employment/job training, family services, food/clothing distribution, homes, recreation & athletics, religious welfare, shelters/homelessness, youth organizations
Grant Types: capital, matching, operating expenses, and project
Geographic Distribution: focus on Orange County, FL

GIVING OFFICERS

H. L. Burnett: asst secy, asst treas
Richard Fletcher, Jr.: mem
J. A. Hinson: pres, chmn, dir
Ben Houston: dir
Frank M. Hubbard: mem
H. E. Johnson: dir
Thomas T. Ross: dir
R. A. Simon: exec vp, dir
Joseph Wittenstein: mem

APPLICATION INFORMATION

Initial Approach:
The foundation requests applicants submit a letter of inquiry no longer than three pages. The proposal should outline the organization's accomplishments, the objectives of the grant and whom it would benefit, the amount requested in relation to the total need, a specific outline of how the foundation's funds would be used, and the proposed method to evaluate the program's success. Attachments to the proposal should include a list of officers and directors, an annual report, a copy of the current budget and IRS letter confirming that the organization is tax-exempt under section 501(c)(3). Deadlines for submitting proposals are 30 days prior to meetings held in January, April, July, and October.
Restrictions on Giving: No grants are made to individuals or for endowment funds.

OTHER THINGS TO KNOW

Publications: application guidelines

GRANTS ANALYSIS

Total Grants: $752,934
Number of Grants: 59
Highest Grant: $125,000
Typical Range: $1,000 to $12,000
Disclosure Period: fiscal year ending May 31, 1991
Note: Average grant figure does not include the highest grant of $125,000. Recent grants are derived from a fiscal 1991 grants list.

RECENT GRANTS

125,000 Ivanhoe Foundation, Orlando, FL
100,000 Central Florida Children's Fund, Orlando, FL
100,000 United Arts of Central Florida, Orlando, FL
53,100 Orlando Science Center, Orlando, FL
51,000 Orlando Museum of Art, Orlando, FL
37,650 Orange County Public Schools, Orlando, FL
30,000 Russell Home for Atypical Children, Orlando, FL
26,340 Central Florida Young Men's Christian Association, Orlando, FL
25,050 Junior Achievement of Orange County, Orlando, FL
25,000 Life Concepts, Apopka, FL

Phillips Foundation, Ellis L.

CONTACT

Patricia A. Cate
Executive Director
Ellis L. Phillips Fdn.
13 Dartmouth College Hwy.
Lyme, NH 03768
(603) 795-2790

FINANCIAL SUMMARY

Recent Giving: $253,825 (fiscal 1991); $298,005 (fiscal 1990); $255,550 (fiscal 1989)
Assets: $5,248,241 (fiscal year ending June 30, 1991); $5,201,054 (fiscal 1990); $5,121,557 (fiscal 1989)
EIN: 13-5677691

CONTRIBUTIONS SUMMARY

Donor(s): the late Ellis L. Phillips
Typical Recipients: • *Arts & Humanities:* arts festivals, community arts, music • *Civic & Public Affairs:* environmental affairs, public policy • *Education:* colleges & universities, religious education • *Health:* health funds • *Religion:* churches, churches • *Social Services:* child welfare, family planning
Grant Types: conference/seminar, endowment, general support, multiyear/continuing support, and seed money
Geographic Distribution: focus on northern New England

GIVING OFFICERS

Patricia A. Cate: exec dir
David L. Grumman: dir
George E. McCully: dir
John W. Oelsner: dir
Walter C. Paine: dir
Ellis L. Phillips III: vp, dir
Ellis L. Phillips, Jr.: pres, dir
B New York NY 1921 *ED* Princeton Univ AB 1942; Columbia Univ LLB 1948; Keuka Coll LLD 1956 *CORP AFFIL* dir: Grumman Corp
Marion G. Phillips: dir
George C. Thompson: treas, dir
Elise Phillips Watts: secy, dir

APPLICATION INFORMATION

Initial Approach: Send brief letter of inquiry describing program or project.
Restrictions on Giving: Does not support individuals or provide funds for scholarships.

OTHER THINGS TO KNOW
Publications: Annual Report (including application guidelines)

GRANTS ANALYSIS
Number of Grants: 37
Highest Grant: $26,025
Typical Range: $4,000 to $10,000
Disclosure Period: fiscal year ending June 30, 1991

RECENT GRANTS
26,025 Trinity College of Vermont, Burlington, VT — Small School Institute
25,000 Cornell University, Ithaca, NY — renovation
25,000 New England Conservatory of Music, Boston, MA
15,000 Montshire Museum of Science, Norwich, VT — preschool science center
15,000 New Hampshire Humanities Council, Concord, NH — financial management
12,500 New England Historic Genealogical Society, Boston, MA
10,000 Family Place, White River Junction, VT — start up costs
10,000 Lebanon College, Lebanon, NH — endowment campaign
8,000 New Hampshire Community Loan Fund, Concord, NH
7,500 Thoreau Society, Concord, MA — institutional development

Phillips Foundation, Waite and Genevieve

CONTACT
Waite and Genevieve Phillips Fdn.
PO Box 5726
Santa Fe, NM 87502

FINANCIAL SUMMARY
Recent Giving: $454,837 (fiscal 1992); $468,000 (fiscal 1991); $614,000 (fiscal 1990)
Assets: $11,916,299 (fiscal year ending May 31, 1992); $11,040,322 (fiscal 1991); $10,311,691 (fiscal 1990)

EIN: 85-0335071

CONTRIBUTIONS SUMMARY
Donor(s): Waite and Genevieve Phillips Trust
Typical Recipients: • *Arts & Humanities:* history/historic preservation, museums/galleries, public broadcasting • *Civic & Public Affairs:* zoos/botanical gardens • *Education:* colleges & universities, private education (precollege) • *Health:* hospitals, single-disease health associations • *Social Services:* disabled, shelters/homelessness, united funds, youth organizations
Grant Types: general support
Geographic Distribution: focus on NM

GIVING OFFICERS
Elliott W. Phillips: pres, dir
John Phillips: vp, dir
Virginia Phillips: secy, treas, dir
Julie Puckett: vp, dir

APPLICATION INFORMATION
Initial Approach: Contributes only to preselected organizations.

GRANTS ANALYSIS
Number of Grants: 37
Highest Grant: $176,800
Typical Range: $1,000 to $10,000
Disclosure Period: fiscal year ending May 31, 1992

RECENT GRANTS
176,800 Philbrook Museum of Art, Tulsa, OK
51,637 Philmont Scout Ranch, Cimarron, NM
35,000 St. Andrews Day School, Amarillo, TX
25,000 New Mexico Museum of Natural History Foundation, Albuquerque, NM
20,000 Presbyterian Health Care Foundation, Albuquerque, NM
15,500 Harrington Discovery Center, Amarillo, TX
10,000 Building Life Skills, Kansas City, KS
10,000 M.D. Anderson Hospital and Tumor Center, Houston, TX
10,000 New Mexico Tech Presidents Club, Socorro, NM
10,000 Seymour Hospital Foundation, Seymour, TX

Phillips Petroleum Co. / Phillips Petroleum Foundation
Sales: $11.93 billion
Employees: 22,400
Headquarters: Bartlesville, OK
SIC Major Group: Oil & Gas Extraction and Petroleum & Coal Products

CONTACT
John C. West
Executive Manager
Phillips Petroleum Fdn.
Phillips Bldg., 16th Fl.
Bartlesville, OK 74004
(918) 661-9072

FINANCIAL SUMMARY
Recent Giving: $8,500,000 (1992); $5,805,020 (1991); $4,538,556 (1990)
Assets: $958,671 (1991); $857,065 (1990)
Fiscal Note: Company gives through foundation only.
EIN: 23-7326611

CONTRIBUTIONS SUMMARY
Typical Recipients: • *Arts & Humanities:* arts associations, arts centers, arts funds, cinema, community arts, dance, history/historic preservation, museums/galleries, music, opera, performing arts, public broadcasting, theater • *Civic & Public Affairs:* business/free enterprise, civil rights, economic development, economics, environmental affairs, international affairs, law & justice, municipalities, professional & trade associations, public policy, safety, urban & community affairs • *Education:* agricultural education, business education, colleges & universities, community & junior colleges, economic education, education associations, education funds, elementary education, engineering education, faculty development, health & physical education, international exchange, international studies, literacy, minority education, science/technology education, special education, student aid • *Health:* health organizations, hospitals, medical rehabilitation, medical research, mental health, nutrition & health maintenance, outpatient health care delivery, pediatric health • *International:* international development/relief, international organizations • *Science:* scientific institutes, scientific organizations • *Social Services:* aged, child welfare, community service organizations, disabled, domestic violence, drugs & alcohol, emergency relief, employment/job training, food/clothing distribution, legal aid, recreation & athletics, united funds, youth organizations
Grant Types: department, employee matching gifts, fellowship, general support, professorship, project, research, and scholarship
Nonmonetary Support Types: donated equipment
Note: Estimated value of nonmonetary support is unavailable and is not included in above figures.
Geographic Distribution: nationally, with emphasis on corporate operating locations
Operating Locations: AK (Kenai), AZ, CO (Henderson), NM (Crownpoint), OK (Bartlesville), PR, SC (Greenville), TX (Dallas, Houston, Richardson), WA (Kennewick)

CORP. OFFICERS
W. W. Allen: *CURR EMPL* pres, coo, dir: Phillips Petroleum Co
T.L. Sandridge: *B* Memphis TN 1936 *CURR EMPL* vp (intl div): Phillips Petroleum Co
C. J. Pete Silas: *B* Miami FL 1932 *ED* GA Inst Tech BSChE 1954 *CURR EMPL* chmn, ceo, dir, mem exec comm: Phillips Petroleum Co *CORP AFFIL* dir: First Natl Bank Bartlesville, First Natl Bank Tulsa *NONPR AFFIL* adv bd: GA Inst Tech, Inst Gas Tech; dir: Am Petroleum Inst, Boys Clubs Am, Bus-Indus Political Action Comm, Ethics Resource Ctr, Jr Achievement Stamford CT, Med Res Fdn Oklahoma City, OK Fdn Excellence, OK Res Fdn, Regional Med Div Fdn Bartlesville; mem: Am Counc Ed, Bartlesville Area Chamber Commerce, British N Am Comm, Bus Higher Ed Forum, Conf Bd, Counc Foreign Rels, Phi Delta Theta, US Chamber Commerce; mem chmn counc: OK Green Country; mem pro-

jects comm: Bluestem Regional Med Devel Fdn; trust: Frank Phillips Fdn, GA Tech Fdn, Univ Tulsa

GIVING OFFICERS
D. L. Cone: asst secy
W. F. Dausset: pres, dir
L. F. Francis: asst gen tax off
Charles B. Friley: vp, dir
J. W. Middleton: asst comptr
Stanley R. Mueller: dir
John C. West: exec mgr *B* Clayton MO 1908 *ED* Yale Univ 1930 *CORP AFFIL* dir: Am Bank Note Co
J. Bryan Whitworth: vp, dir *B* Baton Rouge LA 1938 *ED* Univ AL BS 1961; Univ AL JD 1964 *CURR EMPL* vp: Phillips Petroleum Co *CORP AFFIL* dir: First Bancshares, First Natl Bank *NONPR AFFIL* dir: Salk Inst Biotech Indus Assn; mem: Bartlesville Area Chamber Commerce, NY Bar Assn, OK Bar Assn; mem policy devel comm: Am Petroleum Inst
J. G. Wilson: comptr

APPLICATION INFORMATION
Initial Approach: *Initial Contact:* brief summary of proposal; if proposal meets criteria and availability of funds, more complete information may be requested *Include Information On:* full proposal includes proof of tax-exempt status; clear statement of goals, objectives, activities, and geographic scope, particularly as it relates to Phillips; names and affiliations of officers, trustees, or board of directors, including whether anyone is an employee, retiree, or board member of Phillips or its subsidiaries; number and total compensation of paid employees; number of volunteers; sources of current income; list of other corporations, foundations, or government agencies from which funding currently requested; copy of most recent 990; list of organizations and foundations contributing to organization during previous 12 months; brief description of project for which funding is requested and how long funds will be needed; description of what grant is expected to accomplish, how program is administered, and how it will be evaluated; and program budget, geographical scope, and special funding costs, if any *When to Submit:* any time

Restrictions on Giving: Foundation generally does not support individuals; sectarian or denominational/religious organizations or institutions, other than universities and colleges already receiving aid through taxation; specific disease-oriented organizations; national organizations where support can be made locally; political candidates or organizations; veterans or service clubs, except for community-wide programs; trips, tours, tickets, or banquets; endowment and bricks and mortar.

GRANTS ANALYSIS
Total Grants: $5,805,020
Number of Grants: 578*
Highest Grant: $90,250*
Typical Range: $1,000 to $20,000
Disclosure Period: 1991
Note: Number of grants, average grant, and highest grant figures exclude approximately 650 matching gifts totaling $1,573,314. Recent grants are derived from a 1991 Form 990.

RECENT GRANTS
90,250 Oklahoma State University Foundation, Stillwater, OK
83,800 University of Oklahoma Foundation, Norman, OK
78,050 Tamu Development Foundation, College Station, TX
77,695 Oklahoma Baptist University, Shawnee, OK
75,000 Oklahoma Educational Television, Oklahoma City, OK
66,100 University of Tulsa Foundation, Tulsa, OK
63,148 University of Oklahoma Foundation, Norman, OK
58,000 Kansas University Endowment Association, Lawrence, KS
56,500 Colorado School of Mines, Golden, CO
55,500 University of Arkansas Foundation, Fayetteville, AR

Phillips Trust, Edwin

CONTACT
Sandra Sheiber
Trust Administrator
Edwin Phillips Trust
PO Box 75
Newton Highlands, MA 02161
(617) 353-2200

FINANCIAL SUMMARY
Recent Giving: $256,543 (1991); $178,703 (1989); $365,966 (1988)
Assets: $6,757,063 (1990); $6,864,995 (1989); $5,416,417 (1988)
EIN: 04-6025549

CONTRIBUTIONS SUMMARY
Donor(s): the late Edwin Phillips
Typical Recipients: • *Education:* public education (precollege) • *Social Services:* disabled
Grant Types: general support and operating expenses
Geographic Distribution: focus on Plymouth County, MA

GIVING OFFICERS
Robert E. Galvin: trust
Richard A. Hall: trust
Francis C. Rogerson, Jr.: trust
Janice C. Tingley: trust
Margaret G. Trocki: trust

APPLICATION INFORMATION
Initial Approach: Send brief letter of inquiry describing program. There are no deadlines.
Restrictions on Giving: Does not support individuals.

GRANTS ANALYSIS
Number of Grants: 23
Highest Grant: $70,000
Typical Range: $1,500 to $17,000
Disclosure Period: 1991

RECENT GRANTS
70,000 Retarded Citizens, Marshfield, MA
69,300 Retarded Citizens, Marshfield, MA
20,460 Responsibility, Marshfield, MA
7,820 Marshfield Public Schools, Marshfield, MA

Phillips-Van Heusen Corp. / Phillips-Van Heusen Foundation

Sales: $904.1 million
Employees: 12,400
Headquarters: New York, NY
SIC Major Group: Apparel & Accessory Stores, Apparel & Other Textile Products, Leather & Leather Products, and Wholesale Trade—Nondurable Goods

CONTACT
Lawrence S. Phillips
President
Phillips-Van Heusen Fdn.
1290 Avenue of the Americas
New York, NY 10104
(212) 541-5200

FINANCIAL SUMMARY
Recent Giving: $358,777 (1991); $364,850 (1990); $322,030 (1989)
Assets: $1,518,356 (1991); $1,968,347 (1990); $1,968,347 (1989)
Gifts Received: $25,750 (1991); $23,000 (1990); $118,500 (1989)
Fiscal Note: Contributes through foundation only. In 1991, contributions were received from the Phillips-Van Heusen Corporation.
EIN: 23-7104639

CONTRIBUTIONS SUMMARY
Typical Recipients: • *Civic & Public Affairs:* civil rights, international affairs • *Education:* education funds, religious education • *Health:* health organizations, hospitals, medical research • *International:* international development/relief, international organizations • *Religion:* religious organizations • *Social Services:* community service organizations, united funds
Grant Types: general support
Geographic Distribution: focus on New York
Operating Locations: ME (Falmouth), NJ (Piscataway), NY (New York), PA (Philadelphia)
Note: List includes division locations.

CORP. OFFICERS
Bruce J. Klatsky: *B* New York NY 1948 *ED* Case Western Reserve Univ BS 1970; Georgetown Univ 1971 *CURR EMPL*

pres, coo, dir: Phillips-Van Heusen Corp

Lawrence S. Phillips: *B* New York NY 1927 *ED* Princeton Univ 1948 *CURR EMPL* chmn, ceo, dir: Phillips-Van Heusen Corp *CORP AFFIL* chmn, ceo, dir: Phillips-Van Heusen Corp *NONPR AFFIL* dir: Fashion Inst Tech; mem: Am Apparel Mfrs Assn

GIVING OFFICERS
Pamela N. Hootkin: secy *B* New York NY 1947 *ED* State Univ NY BA 1968; Boston Univ MA 1970 *CURR EMPL* vp, secy, treas: Phillips-Van Heusen Corp *CORP AFFIL* vp, secy, treas: Phillips-Van Heusen Corp *NONPR AFFIL* mem: Fin Womens Assn NY
Bruce J. Klatsky: pres *CURR EMPL* pres, coo, dir: Phillips-Van Heusen Corp (see above)
Lawrence S. Phillips: chmn *CURR EMPL* chmn, ceo, dir: Phillips-Van Heusen Corp (see above)
Irwin W. Winter: vp, treas *CURR EMPL* vp, cfo, dir: Phillips-Van Heusen Corp

APPLICATION INFORMATION
Initial Approach: *Initial Contact:* brief letter *Include Information On:* description of program *When to Submit:* any time

GRANTS ANALYSIS
Total Grants: $358,777
Number of Grants: 67
Highest Grant: $100,000
Typical Range: $1,000 to $5,000
Disclosure Period: 1991
Note: Recent grants are derived from a 1991 grants list.

RECENT GRANTS
100,000 American Jewish World Service, New York, NY
25,000 Sy Symm School of Business, New York, NY
20,000 Fashion Institute of Technology, New York, NY
10,000 Business Executives for National Security, New York, NY
10,000 Carnegie Council on Ethics, New York, NY
10,000 Carnegie Council on Ethics, New York, NY
10,000 Carnegie Hall Society, New York, NY
10,000 Congressional Human Rights Foundation, New York, NY
10,000 Museum of Television and Radio, New York, NY
10,000 New Israel Fund, New York, NY

Phipps Foundation, Howard

CONTACT
A Power, Jr.
Howard Phipps Fdn.
c/o Bessemer Trust Co.
630 Fifth Ave.
New York, NY 10111

FINANCIAL SUMMARY
Recent Giving: $1,656,500 (fiscal 1991); $2,292,805 (fiscal 1990); $1,059,500 (fiscal 1988)
Assets: $6,633,254 (fiscal year ending June 30, 1991); $6,527,862 (fiscal 1990); $5,927,759 (fiscal 1988)
Gifts Received: $1,528,545 (fiscal 1991); $1,528,545 (fiscal 1990)
Fiscal Note: In 1991, contributions were received from Harriett Phipps Charitable Trust.
EIN: 22-6095226

CONTRIBUTIONS SUMMARY
Donor(s): the late Harriet Phipps
Typical Recipients: • *Arts & Humanities:* history/historic preservation, libraries, museums/galleries • *Civic & Public Affairs:* environmental affairs, zoos/botanical gardens • *Education:* colleges & universities, private education (precollege) • *Religion:* churches • *Social Services:* animal protection, family planning, youth organizations
Grant Types: general support
Geographic Distribution: focus on New York, NY

GIVING OFFICERS
Howard Phipps, Jr.: trust *B* 1934 *ED* Harvard Univ AB 1955 *CORP AFFIL* dir: Bessemer Group, Bessemer Securities Corp, Bessemer Trust Co *NONPR AFFIL* pres: NY Zoological Soc; trust: Frick Collection, Lincoln Ctr Chamber Music Soc, Pierpont Morgan Library
Anne Phipps Sidamon-Eristoff: trust *B* New York NY

1932 *ED* Bryn Mawr Coll BA 1954 *NONPR AFFIL* dir: Am Mus Natural History, Greenacre Fdn, Highland Falls Pub Library, Mus Hudson Highlands; dir-at-large: Black Rock Forest Consortium; dir, secy: US Conservation Fdn, World Wildlife Fund

APPLICATION INFORMATION
Initial Approach: Send brief letter of inquiry describing program or project. There are no deadlines.

GRANTS ANALYSIS
Number of Grants: 25
Highest Grant: $450,000
Typical Range: $5,000 to $25,000
Disclosure Period: fiscal year ending June 30, 1991

RECENT GRANTS
450,000 American Museum of Natural History, New York, NY
450,000 New York Zoological Society, New York, NY
100,000 Phillips Academy, Andover, MA
100,000 World Wildlife Fund, Washington, DC
50,000 Environmental Defense Fund, New York, NY
50,000 Girl Scouts of America, New York, NY
50,000 Harvard University Library, Cambridge, MA
50,000 Old Westbury Gardens, Old Westbury, NY
50,000 Pierpont Morgan Library, New York, NY
50,000 Rockefeller University, New York, NY

Phipps Foundation, William H.

CONTACT
Hugh F. Gwin
Secretary
William H. Phipps Fdn.
PO Box 106
Hudson, WI 54016
(715) 386-9510

FINANCIAL SUMMARY
Recent Giving: $594,075 (fiscal 1991); $1,102,350 (fiscal 1989)

Assets: $11,755,705 (fiscal year ending April 30, 1991); $11,425,320 (fiscal 1989)
Gifts Received: $3,000 (fiscal 1991); $3,500 (fiscal 1989)
Fiscal Note: In 1991, contributions were received from Arnold Investment.
EIN: 39-6043312

CONTRIBUTIONS SUMMARY
Donor(s): the late Helen Clark Phipps, the late Stephen C. Phipps
Typical Recipients: • *Arts & Humanities:* arts centers, history/historic preservation • *Civic & Public Affairs:* municipalities • *Education:* public education (precollege), student aid • *Health:* hospitals • *Social Services:* community service organizations, domestic violence, recreation & athletics, youth organizations
Grant Types: capital, general support, and scholarship
Geographic Distribution: limited to the St. Croix River Valley of WI and MN

GIVING OFFICERS
Gordon Benjamin Anderson: dir *B* Minneapolis MN 1927 *ED* Univ MN *CURR EMPL* pres: Gordys *CORP AFFIL* pres: Gordy's Inc
Marie B. Blakeman: dir
Hugh G. Bryce: pres, dir
Hugh F. Gwin: secy, treas, dir
Frederick E. Nagel: vp, dir

APPLICATION INFORMATION
Initial Approach: Send cover letter and full proposal. There are no deadlines. Decisions are made within three months.
Restrictions on Giving: Does not support individuals.

GRANTS ANALYSIS
Number of Grants: 15
Highest Grant: $133,000
Typical Range: $5,000 to $17,000
Disclosure Period: fiscal year ending April 30, 1991

RECENT GRANTS
133,000 Phipps Center for the Arts, Hudson, WI
105,000 Courage Center, Folden Valley, MN
100,000 Boy Scouts of America, St. Paul, MN
100,000 Hudson Memorial Medical Center, Hudson, WI — construction on clinic

80,000 Girl Scouts of America, St. Paul, MN

17,000 Hudson Senior High School, Hudson, WI — scholarships

13,000 Community Action, Hudson, WI

10,000 Family Service of St. Croix Area, Stillwater, MN — building campaign

9,075 Junior Achievement, Minneapolis, MN

7,500 Camp St. Croix, Hudson, WI — lodge remodeling

PHM Corp.

Revenue: $1.21 billion
Employees: 2,486
Headquarters: Bloomfield Hills, MI
SIC Major Group: Depository Institutions, General Building Contractors, Holding & Other Investment Offices, and Security & Commodity Brokers

CONTACT

William J. Pulte
Chairman
PHM Corp.
33 Bloomfield Hills Pkwy.
Ste. 200
Bloomfield Hills, MI 48304
(313) 647-2750

CONTRIBUTIONS SUMMARY

Operating Locations: MI (Bloomfield Hills)

CORP. OFFICERS

Robert K. Burgess: *B* Brantrord Ontario Canada 1944 *CURR EMPL* pres: PHM Corp *CORP AFFIL* pres: Pulte Home Corp

Phoenix Home Life Mutual Insurance Co.

Assets: $10.43 billion
Employees: 4,135
Headquarters: Enfield, CT
SIC Major Group: Insurance Carriers

CONTACT

Debbie McCants
Phoenix Home Life Mutual Insurance Co.
One American Row
Hartford, CT 06115
(203) 275-5000

FINANCIAL SUMMARY

Recent Giving: $864,315 (1993 est.); $600,615 (1992)
Fiscal Note: Figure includes matching gifts and federated drives. The company gives directly.

CONTRIBUTIONS SUMMARY

Typical Recipients: • *Civic & Public Affairs:* economic development, housing • *Education:* general • *Health:* general • *Social Services:* employment/job training, united funds
Grant Types: employee matching gifts and general support
Nonmonetary Support Types: cause-related marketing & promotion
Note: Estimated value of nonmonetary support is not available. Contact for nonmonetary support is Jodi Ward, Public Affairs Assistant.
Geographic Distribution: near operating locations
Operating Locations: CT (Enfield, Hartford), MA (Greenfield), NY (Albany)

CORP. OFFICERS

John Gummere: *B* Mount Holly NJ 1928 *ED* Yale Univ BA 1948 *CURR EMPL* chmn, ceo: Phoenix Home Life Mutual Ins Co *CORP AFFIL* dir: CT Natl Bank, Health Ins Assn Am, Phoenix Equity Planning Corp, Phoenix Investment Couns Inc; pres, dir: Phoenix Am Life Ins Co, PM Holdings Inc, PML Intl *NONPR AFFIL* bd dirs: Fellow Soc Actuaries, Hartford Grad Ctr, Inst Living, Jr Achievement, Old St House; dir: Greater Hartford Chamber Commerce; mem: Sigma Xi; mem bd dirs: Med Information Bur

GIVING OFFICERS

Maura Melley: *CURR EMPL* vp (pub affairs): Phoenix Mutual Life Ins Co

APPLICATION INFORMATION

Initial Approach: *Initial Contact:* written request *Include Information On:* description of agency and its objects; amount requested; budget for upcoming year; description of other support received, including notation of support received from the United Way or any government entities; account of staff size, including qualifications; statement of organization's board and its composition; copy of most recent annual report; and proof of tax-exempt status *When to Submit:* before September 15

OTHER THINGS TO KNOW

Phoenix Mutual Life Insurance Co. has merged with Phoenix Home Life Mutual Insurance Co.

Publications: guidelines

GRANTS ANALYSIS

Total Grants: $600,615
Disclosure Period: 1992

Phoenix Resource Cos.

Sales: $14.7 million
Employees: 21
Headquarters: Bartlesville, OK
SIC Major Group: Oil & Gas Extraction

CONTACT

Debbie Banghim
Cash Manager
Pheonix Resources Company, Inc.
PO Box 3272
Bartlesville, OK 74005
(918) 847-2531

FINANCIAL SUMMARY

Fiscal Note: Annual Giving Range: less than $100,000

CONTRIBUTIONS SUMMARY

Typical Recipients: • *Arts & Humanities:* general • *Civic & Public Affairs:* general • *Education:* general • *Health:* general • *Social Services:* general
Grant Types: general support
Geographic Distribution: primarily headquarters area
Operating Locations: OK (Bartlesville)

CORP. OFFICERS

George D. Lawrence, Jr.: *B* Eatonton GA 1950 *ED* Univ GA 1972-1975 *CURR EMPL* pres, ceo: Pheonix Resources Cos

APPLICATION INFORMATION

Initial Approach: Send brief letter of inquiry. There are no deadlines.

Physicians Mutual Insurance / Physicians Mutual Insurance Co. Foundation

Assets: $504.6 million
Employees: 1,000
Headquarters: Omaha, NE
SIC Major Group: Insurance Carriers

CONTACT

Stewart Crosbie
Secretary
Physicians Mutual Insurance Co. Foundation
2600 Dodge St.
Omaha, NE 68131
(402) 633-1000

FINANCIAL SUMMARY

Recent Giving: $157,331 (1991); $105,915 (1990); $96,903 (1989)
Assets: $589,719 (1991); $697,194 (1990); $729,718 (1989)
EIN: 36-3424068

CONTRIBUTIONS SUMMARY

Typical Recipients: • *Arts & Humanities:* community arts, performing arts, theater • *Civic & Public Affairs:* economic development, municipalities • *Education:* colleges & universities, private education (precollege) • *Health:* medical research, pediatric health, single-disease health associations • *Religion:* religious organizations • *Social Services:* community service organizations, religious welfare, united funds, youth organizations
Grant Types: general support
Geographic Distribution: focus on NE
Operating Locations: NE (Omaha)

CORP. OFFICERS

Arnold W. Lempka, MD: *CURR EMPL* chmn: Physicians Mutual Ins
Robert A. Reed: *CURR EMPL* ceo, pres: Physicians Mutual Ins

GIVING OFFICERS

Bill R. Benson: vp, dir

Jerome J. Coon: treas, dir
Robert A. Reed: pres, dir
CURR EMPL ceo, pres: Physicians Mutual Ins (see above)

APPLICATION INFORMATION
Initial Approach: Request application form. There are no deadlines.

GRANTS ANALYSIS
Number of Grants: 73
Highest Grant: $31,400
Typical Range: $100 to $2,000
Disclosure Period: 1991

RECENT GRANTS
31,400 United Way, Omaha, NE
5,000 United Catholic Social Services, Omaha, NE
2,500 United Cerebral Palsy Association, Omaha, NE
1,000 River City Roundup, Omaha, NE
1,000 Roncalli High School, Omaha, NE
1,000 Siena Francis House, Omaha, NE
900 Salvation Army, Omaha, NE
900 YMCA, Omaha, NE
750 Shakespeare on the Green, Omaha, NE
625 United Way, Omaha, NE

Piankova Foundation, Tatiana

CONTACT
Peter F. DeGaetano
Secretary
Tatiana Piankova Fdn.
36 East 81st St.
New York, NY 10021

FINANCIAL SUMMARY
Recent Giving: $118,700 (fiscal 1991); $109,700 (fiscal 1990); $99,915 (fiscal 1989)
Assets: $2,604,319 (fiscal year ending July 31, 1991); $2,605,773 (fiscal 1990); $2,509,166 (fiscal 1989)
EIN: 13-3142090

CONTRIBUTIONS SUMMARY
Donor(s): Susan Polachek
Typical Recipients: • *Arts & Humanities:* arts institutes, community arts, dance, opera • *Health:* health organizations, hospices, medical research • *So-*

cial Services: aged, counseling, youth organizations
Grant Types: general support

GIVING OFFICERS
Mildred C. Brinn: dir, vp, treas
Peter F. DeGaetano: dir, secy
Peter F. DeGaetano: secy, dir

APPLICATION INFORMATION
Initial Approach: Contributes only to preselected organizations.
Restrictions on Giving: Does not support individuals.

GRANTS ANALYSIS
Number of Grants: 33
Highest Grant: $25,000
Typical Range: $100 to $6,000
Disclosure Period: fiscal year ending July 31, 1991

RECENT GRANTS
25,000 Ballet Theatre Foundation, New York, NY
16,000 Skowhegan School of Painting and Sculpture, New York, NY
10,000 Lacoste School of the Arts in France
6,500 Metropolitan Opera Association, New York, NY
5,000 Cornell University Medical Center Cardiovascular Center, New York, NY
5,000 National Academy of Design
5,000 New York Hospital-Cornell Medical Center, New York, NY
5,000 St. Bartholomews Church, New York, NY
5,000 U.S.O. of Metropolitan New York, New York, NY
5,000 Youth Counseling League, New York, NY

Pic 'N' Save Corp.
Sales: $529.1 million
Employees: 5,700
Headquarters: Dominguez, CA
SIC Major Group: General Merchandise Stores

CONTACT
Pic 'N' Save Corp.
2430 East Del Amo Blvd.
Dominguez, CA 90220-6306
(310) 537-9220

CONTRIBUTIONS SUMMARY
Operating Locations: CA (Dominguez)

CORP. OFFICERS
Leonard Setzer: *CURR EMPL* pres: Pic N Save Superstores

Pick Charitable Trust, Melitta S.

CONTACT
H. J. McComas
Trustee
Melitta S. Pick Charitable Trust
c/o Foley and Lardner
777 East Wisconsin Avenue, Ste. 3800
Milwaukee, WI 53202
(414) 289-3528

FINANCIAL SUMMARY
Recent Giving: $555,500 (fiscal 1990); $518,000 (fiscal 1987)
Assets: $14,217,595 (fiscal year ending January 31, 1990); $12,884,869 (fiscal 1987)
EIN: 23-7243490

CONTRIBUTIONS SUMMARY
Donor(s): the late Melitta S. Pick
Typical Recipients: • *Arts & Humanities:* arts funds, arts institutes, museums/galleries, music, performing arts • *Education:* colleges & universities • *Social Services:* child welfare, community centers, community service organizations, united funds, youth organizations
Grant Types: general support
Geographic Distribution: focus on southeastern WI

GIVING OFFICERS
Harrold J. McComas: trust
Joan M. Pick: trust

APPLICATION INFORMATION
Initial Approach: Send brief letter of inquiry describing program or project. There are no deadlines.
Restrictions on Giving: Does not support individuals.

GRANTS ANALYSIS
Number of Grants: 46

Highest Grant: $58,000
Typical Range: $1,000 to $10,000
Disclosure Period: fiscal year ending January 31, 1990

RECENT GRANTS
58,000 West Bend Memorial Foundation, West Bend, WI
50,000 Milwaukee Art Museum, Milwaukee, WI
50,000 United Performing Arts Fund, Milwaukee, WI
50,000 West Bend Memorial Foundation, West Bend, WI
45,000 West Bend Memorial Foundation, West Bend, WI
43,000 West Bend Memorial Foundation, West Bend, WI
25,000 Milwaukee Institute of Art and Design, Milwaukee, WI
10,000 College of Wooster, Wooster, OH
5,000 Salvation Army, Milwaukee, WI
2,000 Milwaukee Protestant Home, Milwaukee, WI

Pick, Jr. Fund, Albert

CONTACT
Nadine Van Sant
Executive Director
Albert Pick, Jr. Fund
30 North Michigan Avenue, Ste. 819
Chicago, IL 60602
(312) 236-1192

FINANCIAL SUMMARY
Recent Giving: $721,448 (1990); $1,981,989 (1989)
Assets: $14,336,635 (1990); $13,739,000 (1989)
Gifts Received: $1,445,216 (1990); $1,247,789 (1989)
EIN: 36-6071402

CONTRIBUTIONS SUMMARY
Donor(s): The foundation was incorporated in 1947 by the late Albert Pick, Jr.
Typical Recipients: • *Arts & Humanities:* arts associations, arts festivals, dance, museums/galleries, music, opera, public broadcasting • *Civic & Public Affairs:* economic development, ethnic/minority organizations • *Education:* colleges

& universities, education associations, minority education, public education (precollege), science/technology education • *Health:* hospitals, pediatric health, public health, single-disease health associations • *Science:* scientific organizations • *Social Services:* community service organizations, day care, employment/job training, family services, homes, united funds, youth organizations
Grant Types: capital, general support, multiyear/continuing support, and project
Geographic Distribution: focus on Chicago, IL

GIVING OFFICERS

Ralph I. Lewy: treas, dir *B* Leiwen Germany 1931 *ED* Roosevelt Univ BS 1953 *CURR EMPL* pres: Ralph Lewy Ltd *NONPR AFFIL* mem: Am Inst CPAs; trust: Emanuel Congregation

Nadine Van Sant: secy, dir

APPLICATION INFORMATION

Initial Approach:
The foundation requests applications be made in writing. Proposals should be as brief as possible and include the following: a history of the organization, a description of current programs, a description of the proposed project, and the intended use of the funds requested; proof of tax-exempt status from the IRS and a ruling that the organization is publicly supported under section 509(a) of the IRS code; the names, affiliations, and addresses of governing board members, officers, and staff; a current financial statement, preferably audited; the projected annual budgets for the organization and the project; a list of principal sources of income; and a description of the geographic area served.
The deadlines for submitting proposals are February 1, April 1, July 1, and October 1. Proposals from cultural organizations should be submitted by the July 1 deadline.
The board meets in March or April, June, September, and December.

Restrictions on Giving: The foundation will not consider proposals from organizations whose fiscal year ends on the same month as the board meeting's review of that request.

Grants are not made to religious organizations or for political purposes. The foundation does not support hospitals, local chapters of single-disease associations, umbrella organizations, building or endowment funds, deficit financing, longterm projects, advertising, scholarships, fundraising, or fraternal, veterans, labor, or athletic groups.

OTHER THINGS TO KNOW

Publications: program policy statement and application guidelines

GRANTS ANALYSIS

Total Grants: $721,448
Number of Grants: 180
Highest Grant: $41,666
Typical Range: $1,500 to $10,000
Disclosure Period: 1990
Note: Recent grants are derived from a 1990 grants list.

RECENT GRANTS

41,666 LaRabida Children's Hospital and Research Center, Chicago, IL
25,000 WTTW/Channel 11, Chicago, IL
24,334 United Charities of Chicago, Chicago, IL
15,000 Ravinia Festival Association, Chicago, IL
11,000 Jewish United Fund, Chicago, IL
10,000 Associated Colleges of Illinois, Chicago, IL
10,000 Chicago Board of Education, Chicago, IL
10,000 Chicago Commons Association, Chicago, IL
10,000 Children's Memorial Hospital, Chicago, IL
10,000 Illinois Mathematics and Science Academy, Chicago, IL

Picker International

Sales: $700.0 million
Employees: 6,000
Headquarters: Highland Heights, OH
SIC Major Group: Electronic & Other Electrical Equipment and Instruments & Related Products

CONTACT

Charles Woods
Vice President, Human Resources
Picker International
595 Miner Rd.
Highland Heights, OH 44143
(216) 473-3000

CONTRIBUTIONS SUMMARY

The company has no set giving priorities. In the area of arts and humanities, grants go to museums, music, and performing arts. The company supports civic and public affairs organizations working in the areas of business/free enterprise, civil rights, and public policy. Other areas of support include colleges and universities, hospitals, single-disease health associations, the United Way, and youth organizations.

Typical Recipients: • *Arts & Humanities:* museums/galleries, music, performing arts • *Civic & Public Affairs:* business/free enterprise, civil rights, public policy • *Education:* colleges & universities • *Health:* hospitals, single-disease health associations • *Social Services:* united funds, youth organizations

Geographic Distribution: principally near operating locations

Operating Locations: IL, NY, OH, PA, TX, VA

CORP. OFFICERS

Malcom Bates: *CURR EMPL* chmn: Picker Intl

K. K. Bhasin: *CURR EMPL* cfo: Picker Intl

Cary J. Nolan: *CURR EMPL* pres, ceo: Picker Intl

GIVING OFFICERS

Charles Wood: *CURR EMPL* vp (human resources): Picker Intl

APPLICATION INFORMATION

Initial Approach: Submit a letter any time. Include a description of the organization, amount requested, purpose for which funds are sought, recently audited financial statement, and proof of tax-exempt status.

Restrictions on Giving: Does not provide nonmonetary support.

Pickering Industries

Sales: $8.5 million
Employees: 45
Headquarters: Tacoma, WA
SIC Major Group: Furniture & Fixtures, Lumber & Wood Products, Water Transportation, and Wholesale Trade—Durable Goods

CONTACT

Gordon Pickering
President
Pickering Industries
2102 East D St.
Tacoma, WA 98421
(206) 572-9212

CONTRIBUTIONS SUMMARY

Operating Locations: WA (Tacoma)

CORP. OFFICERS

Gordon Pickering: *CURR EMPL* pres: Pickering Indus

RECENT GRANTS

Washington State University Foundation, Pullman, WA

Pickett and Hatcher Educational Fund

CONTACT

Robert E. Bennett
Executive Vice President
Pickett and Hatcher Educational Fund
PO Box 8169
Columbus, GA 31994
(706) 327-6586

FINANCIAL SUMMARY

Recent Giving: $1,607,078 (fiscal 1992); $1,443,732 (fiscal 1991); $1,282,762 (fiscal 1990)
Assets: $18,834,205 (fiscal year ending September 30, 1992); $17,947,935 (fiscal 1991); $15,966,572 (fiscal 1990)
EIN: 58-0566216

CONTRIBUTIONS SUMMARY

Donor(s): The foundation was incorporated in 1938 by the late Claude A. Hatcher.

Typical Recipients: • *Education:* colleges & universities, liberal arts education, student aid
Grant Types: loan
Geographic Distribution: focus on southeastern United States

GIVING OFFICERS
Robert E. Bennett: exec vp, trust
Donna Hand: trust
William B. Hardegree: trust
William K. Hatcher: pres, trust
Alice V. Haywood: secy
James W. Key: trust
William T. Miller: trust
Kenneth R. Owens: vp
F. Kenneth Scott: asst vp
C. Alex Sears, Jr.: vchmn, treas, trust

APPLICATION INFORMATION
Initial Approach:
Applicants should call the foundation or send a letter requesting application an form.
The deadline is May 15 for the school year starting in the fall; for other periods during the year, two months prior to beginning of session in which money will be used.
The board meets in May and November. Decisions are made within two months.
Restrictions on Giving: The foundation does not support students planning to enter medicine, law, the ministry, or vocational education. Grants are made solely for the purpose of educational loans. Student loans for college do not exceed $12,000 per individual.

OTHER THINGS TO KNOW
Publications: informational brochure including application guidelines

GRANTS ANALYSIS
Total Grants: $1,607,078*
Disclosure Period: fiscal year ending September 30, 1992
Note: The fiscal 1992 grants list consisted of scholarships paid to more than 600 individuals.

Pickford Foundation, Mary

CONTACT
Edward C. Stotsenberg
President
Mary Pickford Fdn.
9171 Wilshire Blvd., Ste. 512
Beverly Hills, CA 90210
(213) 273-2770

FINANCIAL SUMMARY
Recent Giving: $634,900 (fiscal 1991); $592,780 (fiscal 1990); $608,220 (fiscal 1989)

Assets: $9,447,724 (fiscal year ending May 31, 1991); $8,984,047 (fiscal 1990); $9,151,627 (fiscal 1989)
EIN: 95-6093487

CONTRIBUTIONS SUMMARY
Donor(s): the late Mary Pickford Rogers
Typical Recipients: • *Arts & Humanities:* cinema, history/historic preservation, libraries, museums/galleries, music, public broadcasting, theater • *Education:* colleges & universities • *Health:* hospitals, medical research, pediatric health, single-disease health associations • *Social Services:* aged, disabled, homes, shelters/homelessness, youth organizations
Grant Types: endowment, general support, and scholarship
Geographic Distribution: focus on CA

GIVING OFFICERS
Sull Lawrence: secy, dir
Charles B. Rogers: treas, dir
Edward G. Stotsenberg: pres, ceo, dir

APPLICATION INFORMATION
Initial Approach: Send brief letter of inquiry describing program or project. There are no deadlines.
Restrictions on Giving: Does not support individuals.

GRANTS ANALYSIS
Number of Grants: 111
Highest Grant: $55,000
Typical Range: $1,000 to $10,000
Disclosure Period: fiscal year ending May 31, 1991

RECENT GRANTS
55,000 University of Southern California Davis School of Gerontology, Los Angeles, CA
50,000 Gene Autry Museum, Los Angeles, CA
50,000 Library of Congress, Washington, DC
50,000 Motion Picture Country Home, Woodland Hills, CA
35,000 Jewish Home for the Aging, Reseda, CA
25,000 Claremont McKenna College, Claremont, CA

25,000 L.A. Philharmonic Young Musician Institute, Los Angeles, CA
20,000 Academy of Motion Picture Arts, Beverly Hills, CA
20,000 Gish Film Theatre, Bowling Green, OH
10,000 University of California Los Angeles Film and Television Archives, Los Angeles, CA

Picower Foundation, Jeffrey M. and Barbara

CONTACT
Jeffrey M. and Barbara Picower Fdn.
2000 South Ocean Boulevard
Five Sloans Curve
Palm Beach, FL 33480
(407) 585-5098

FINANCIAL SUMMARY
Recent Giving: $191,852 (1990)
Assets: $15,616,872 (1990)
Gifts Received: $12,015,000 (1990)
Fiscal Note: In fiscal 1990, contributions were received from Jeffrey M. Picower.
EIN: 13-6927043

CONTRIBUTIONS SUMMARY
Donor(s): Jeffrey M. Picower
Typical Recipients: • *Arts & Humanities:* dance • *Education:* arts education, colleges & universities, private education (precollege) • *Health:* pediatric health, single-disease health associations • *Religion:* religious organizations
Grant Types: general support

GIVING OFFICERS
Barbara Picower: trust
Jeffrey M. Picower: trust

APPLICATION INFORMATION
Initial Approach: Contributes only to preselected organizations. Applications not accepted.
Restrictions on Giving: Does not provide grants to individuals.

GRANTS ANALYSIS
Number of Grants: 57
Highest Grant: $25,000

Typical Range: $1,000 to $50,000
Disclosure Period: 1990

RECENT GRANTS
25,000 United Jewish Appeal Federation of Jewish Philanthropies, New York, NY
15,000 Nightingale Bamford School, New York, NY
15,000 Prep for Prep, New York, NY
10,000 American Ballet Theater, New York, NY
10,000 Juvenile Diabetes Foundation, Port Washington, NY
10,000 New York City Ballet, New York, NY
10,000 Nightingale Bamford School, New York, NY
10,000 Pennsylvania State University, University Park, PA
10,000 Prep for Prep, New York, NY
5,000 Memorial Sloan-Kettering Cancer Center, New York, NY

Piedmont Health Care Foundation

CONTACT
Schaefer Kendrick
Dean
Piedmont Health Care Fdn.
PO Box 2585
Greenville, PA 29602
(803) 242-5133

FINANCIAL SUMMARY
Recent Giving: $123,701 (1991); $133,483 (1990); $127,072 (1989)
Assets: $2,816,532 (1991); $2,229,723 (1990); $2,281,341 (1989)
EIN: 57-0782523

CONTRIBUTIONS SUMMARY
Typical Recipients: • *Civic & Public Affairs:* environmental affairs, women's affairs • *Education:* colleges & universities • *Health:* health organizations, hospitals, medical research, single-disease health associations • *Science:* scientific institutes • *Social Services:* child welfare, community service organizations, domestic violence, family planning, family services, youth organizations
Grant Types: general support

Piedmont Natural Gas Co., Inc. *Directory of Corporate and Foundation Givers, 1994*

Geographic Distribution: limited to the Piedmont and Greenville, SC, areas

GIVING OFFICERS
Leonard Byrne: dir, chmn
Thomas A. Devenny: mem
David Evans: dir, secy
Rob Hamby: dir, treas
Schaefer B. Kendrick: mgr
J. Lacy McLean: mem
Ann Quattlebaum: mem
John J. Schroeder: mem
Jim Tate: mem
Leigh Earle Walker: mem
Grady Wyatt: dir, vchmn

APPLICATION INFORMATION
Initial Approach: Application form required. Deadline is August 15.

GRANTS ANALYSIS
Number of Grants: 10
Highest Grant: $22,000
Typical Range: $5,000 to $15,000
Disclosure Period: 1991

RECENT GRANTS
22,000 Greenville Technical College, Greenville, PA
22,000 Speech Hearing and Learning Center, Greenville, PA
20,000 A Child's Haven, Greenville, PA
20,000 Roper Mountain Science Center Association, Greenville, PA
10,525 Greenville Council for the Prevention of Teenage Pregnancy, Greenville, PA
8,000 YMCA, Greenville, PA
7,946 American Red Cross, Greenville, PA
5,430 St. Francis Women's Hospital, Greenville, PA
5,000 United Ministries, Greenville, PA
2,800 Family Counseling Center of Greenville, Greenville, PA

Piedmont Natural Gas Co., Inc.
Assets: $665.9 million
Employees: 1,911
Headquarters: Charlotte, NC
SIC Major Group: Electric, Gas & Sanitary Services and

Furniture & Homefurnishings Stores

CONTACT
Ralph Stewart
Vice President, Human Resources
Piedmont Natural Gas Co., Inc.
PO Box 33068
Charlotte, NC 28233
(704) 364-3120

CONTRIBUTIONS SUMMARY
Operating Locations: NC (Charlotte), TX (Houston)

CORP. OFFICERS
John H. Maxheim: *B* Clinton IA 1934 *ED* IA St Univ 1958 *CURR EMPL* chmn, pres, ceo, dir: Piedmont Natural Gas Co *CORP AFFIL* dir: University Res Park, Wachovia Bank & Trust Co; pres, ceo, dir: Piedmont Exploration Co, PNG Energy Co *NONPR AFFIL* chmn: Southern Gas Assn; mem, dir: Am Gas Assn

Pieper Electric / Pieperpower Foundation
Headquarters: Milwaukee, WI

CONTACT
Julius Pieper
President
Pieper Electric
5070 North 35th Street
Milwaukee, WI 53209-5302
(414) 462-7700

FINANCIAL SUMMARY
Recent Giving: $85,323 (1990); $78,785 (1989)
Assets: $674 (1989)
Gifts Received: $81,500 (1990); $74,300 (1989)
Fiscal Note: In 1990, contributions were received from Pieper Electric, Inc.
EIN: 39-6124770

CONTRIBUTIONS SUMMARY
Typical Recipients: • *Arts & Humanities:* history/historic preservation, performing arts • *Civic & Public Affairs:* urban & community affairs, zoos/botanical gardens • *Education:* public education (precollege) • *Social Services:* food/clothing distribution, united funds
Grant Types: general support
Geographic Distribution: giving primarily in Milwaukee, WI

Operating Locations: WI (Milwaukee)

GIVING OFFICERS
Julius Pieper: pres

APPLICATION INFORMATION
Initial Approach: Submit a brief letter of inquiry.

GRANTS ANALYSIS
Number of Grants: 308
Highest Grant: $10,000
Typical Range: $100 to $1,000
Disclosure Period: 1990

RECENT GRANTS
10,000 Electrical Contracting Foundation
6,000 United Way, Milwaukee, WI
5,900 N.W. Side Community Development Loan
5,000 Hunger Task Force of Milwaukee, Milwaukee, WI
2,500 United Performing Arts Fund, Milwaukee, WI
2,100 United Way
1,671 Kopy Print — Milwaukee Public Schools
1,500 United Way, AL
1,000 Historical Sites Foundation
1,000 Zoological Society

Pier 1 Imports, Inc.
Sales: $586.7 million
Employees: 7,787
Headquarters: Fort Worth, TX
SIC Major Group: Building Materials & Garden Supplies, Furniture & Homefurnishings Stores, Miscellaneous Retail, and Wholesale Trade—Nondurable Goods

CONTACT
Mitchell Weatherly
Senior Vice President, Human Resources
Pier 1 Imports, Inc.
PO Box 961020
Ft. Worth, TX 76161-0020
(817) 878-8000

CONTRIBUTIONS SUMMARY
Operating Locations: TX (Fort Worth)

CORP. OFFICERS
Marvin Girouard: *CURR EMPL* pres, coo, dir: Pier 1 Imports
Clark A. Johnson: *CURR EMPL* chmn, ceo, dir: Pier 1 Imports

Charles R. Scott: *CURR EMPL* vchmn: Pier 1 Imports

Pierce Charitable Trust, Harold Whitworth

CONTACT
Elizabeth D. Nichols
Trustee
Harold Whitworth Pierce Charitable Trust
c/o Nichols and Pratt
50 Congress St.
Boston, MA 02109
(617) 523-6800

FINANCIAL SUMMARY
Recent Giving: $37,000 (fiscal 1991); $591,720 (fiscal 1990); $641,728 (fiscal 1989)
Assets: $13,210,564 (fiscal year ending November 30, 1991); $10,201,986 (fiscal 1990); $10,536,622 (fiscal 1989)
EIN: 04-6019896

CONTRIBUTIONS SUMMARY
Donor(s): the late Harold Whitworth Pierce
Typical Recipients: • *Arts & Humanities:* museums/galleries, music • *Civic & Public Affairs:* environmental affairs • *Education:* colleges & universities, education associations, education funds, minority education, science/technology education, student aid • *Health:* health organizations, hospitals, medical research • *Religion:* churches • *Science:* scientific institutes • *Social Services:* family planning, youth organizations
Grant Types: general support
Geographic Distribution: focus on MA

GIVING OFFICERS
James R. Nichols: trust
Harold I. Pratt: trust

APPLICATION INFORMATION
Initial Approach: Send brief letter of inquiry describing program or project. Deadlines are April 1 and October 1. Board meets in May and November.

GRANTS ANALYSIS
Highest Grant: $154,295
Typical Range: $10,000 to $40,000
Disclosure Period: fiscal year ending November 30, 1991

2130

RECENT GRANTS

154,295 Milton Hospital, Milton, MA

100,000 Museum of Science, Boston, MA

40,000 New England Conservatory of Music, Boston, MA

25,000 Appalachian Mountain Club, Boston, MA

25,000 Trustees of Reservations, Beverly, MA

20,000 WGBH Educational Foundation, Boston, MA

15,000 Boston Biomedical Research Institute, Boston, MA

15,000 United Negro College Fund, Boston, MA

13,000 A Better Chance, Boston, MA

10,940 Boston Area Educators for Social Responsibility, Boston, MA

Piggly Wiggly Southern / Piggly Wiggly Southern Foundation

Sales: $660.0 million
Employees: 6,000
Parent Company: Bruno's Inc.
Headquarters: Vidalia, GA
SIC Major Group: Food Stores

CONTACT

James A. Bolonda
Chairman
Piggly Wiggly Southern Foundation
PO Box 569
Vidalia, GA 30474
(912) 537-9871

FINANCIAL SUMMARY

Recent Giving: $32,605 (1989)
EIN: 58-6035162

CONTRIBUTIONS SUMMARY

Operating Locations: GA (Vidalia)

CORP. OFFICERS

Bill White: *CURR EMPL* pres: Piggly Wiggly Southern

GIVING OFFICERS

Dent L. Temples: secy, dir

GRANTS ANALYSIS

Disclosure Period: 1990
Note: No grants were provided in 1990.

Pilgrim Foundation

CONTACT

Sherry Yuskaitis
Executive Director
Pilgrim Fdn.
PO Box 3400
Brockton, MA 02403

FINANCIAL SUMMARY

Recent Giving: $109,302 (1990); $122,264 (1989); $54,471 (1988)
Assets: $2,592,659 (1990); $2,551,163 (1989); $2,564,778 (1988)
EIN: 04-2104834

CONTRIBUTIONS SUMMARY

Donor(s): the late Edgar B. Davis
Grant Types: scholarship
Geographic Distribution: limited to Brockton, MA

GIVING OFFICERS

Charles M Alter: trust, treas
Richard L. Drew: trust, secy
Arthur Ford: trust
Gerald Kelleher: trust, pres
Alice Lamond: trust
George Thomas: trust
Kenneth Turner: trust

APPLICATION INFORMATION

Initial Approach: Application form required. Deadline is April 1 for graduating high school students; May 1 for returning college students.

OTHER THINGS TO KNOW

Provides aid to needy families, camperships, memberships in character-building organizations, and scholarships for higher education.

Pilgrim Industries

Headquarters: Folcroft, PA

CONTACT

Vincent Dezzi
Accountant
Pilgrim Industries
710 Henderson Blvd.
Folcroft, PA 19032
(215) 534-8800

CONTRIBUTIONS SUMMARY

Operating Locations: PA (Folcroft)

Pilgrim's Pride Corp.

Sales: $786.7 million
Employees: 10,341
Headquarters: Pittsburg, TX
SIC Major Group: Agricultural Production— Livestock and Food & Kindred Products

CONTACT

Lonnie A. Pilgrim
Chief Operating Officer
Pilgrim's Pride Corp.
PO Box 93
Pittsburg, TX 75686
(903) 856-7901

CONTRIBUTIONS SUMMARY

Operating Locations: TX (Pittsburg)

CORP. OFFICERS

Bob Hendrix: *CURR EMPL* pres: Pilgrims Pride Corp
Lonnie Alfred Pilgram: *B* Pine TX 1928 *CURR EMPL* fdr, chmn, ceo, dir: Pilgrims Pride Corp
Bill Voss: *CURR EMPL* coo: Pilgrims Pride Corp

Pillsbury Co. / Grand Metropolitan Food Sector Foundation

Sales: $3.75 billion
Employees: 68,000
Parent Company: Grand Metropolitan PLC
Headquarters: Minneapolis, MN
SIC Major Group: Food & Kindred Products and Wholesale Trade—Nondurable Goods

CONTACT

Rebecca Erdahl
Executive Director
Grand Metroplitan Food Sector Fdn.
200 South Sixth St.
MS 37X5
Minneapolis, MN 55402
(612) 330-7230

FINANCIAL SUMMARY

Recent Giving: $8,000,000 (fiscal 1993 est.); $8,000,000 (fiscal 1992 approx.); $8,000,000 (fiscal 1991 approx.)
Assets: $9,113,704 (fiscal 1991); $12,182,892 (fiscal 1989)
Fiscal Note: Company gives through foundation and directly through corporate headquarters, major plants, and subsidiaries.
EIN: 41-6021373

CONTRIBUTIONS SUMMARY

Typical Recipients: • *Arts & Humanities:* community arts • *Civic & Public Affairs:* economic development • *Education:* business education, career/vocational education, elementary education, minority education, preschool education • *Health:* nutrition & health maintenance • *Social Services:* delinquency & crime, employment/job training
Grant Types: general support and project
Nonmonetary Support Types: cause-related marketing & promotion, donated equipment, and donated products
Note: Nonmonetary support was valued at $10.0 million in 1991, principally in food products donated to the Second Harvest Network of food banks. This support is not included in above total. The company also sponsors two employee volunteer programs: REACH, for current, and Golden Ambassadors, for retirees.
Geographic Distribution: near major company operating facilities
Operating Locations: MN (Minneapolis)

CORP. OFFICERS

Ian Alexander Martin: *B* Dundee Scotland 1935 *ED* St Andrews Univ Un Kingdom *CURR EMPL* ceo, mng dir, coo: Grand Metro PLC *CORP AFFIL* chmn, pres, ceo: Pillsbury Co *NONPR AFFIL* mem: British Inst Mgmt

GIVING OFFICERS

J. Howard Chandler: vp *CURR EMPL* sr exec vp, chief accounting off: Pillsbury Co
Rebecca Erdahl: *CURR EMPL* exec dir: Pillsbury Co
Raymond R. Krause: dir *B* Chicago IL 1951 *ED* Georgetown Univ 1978 *CURR EMPL* vp (govt rels): Grandmet *CORP AFFIL* chmn: Grandmet Commun Job Training Ctr *NONPR AFFIL* mem: Grandmet Food Sector Fdn, Natl Assn Mfrs, Natl Pub Aff Steering Comm, Natl Pub Affs Steering Comm; trust: Natl Child Labor Comm

Ian Alexander Martin: pres *CURR EMPL* ceo, mng dir, coo: Grand Metro PLC (see above)

John A. Powers: dir *B* New York NY 1926 *ED* St Peters Coll BA 1950 *CURR EMPL* chmn, dir: Heublein *CORP AFFIL* dir: CT Natl Bank, Hartford Natl Corp, Hartford Steam Boiler Inspection & Ins Co *NONPR AFFIL* dep chmn: Intl Distillers Vinters Ltd; mem: CT Bus & Indus Assn; mem bus adv counc: Skidmore Coll; regent: Univ Harvard; trust: Hartford Grad Ctr

APPLICATION INFORMATION

Initial Approach: *Initial Contact:* typewritten proposal *Include Information On:* amount requested; date by which funds are needed; time line of project; definition of project, including explanation of community need and specific goals and objectives of project, with identification of specific activities or methods to reach goals, and plan of evaluation; project budget and list of sources of financial support both committed and pending; brief description of the organization's history and statement of its purpose and objectives; proof of tax-exempt status; copy of most recently audited financial statements; budget for current operating year; donors' list showing corporate and foundation support during past 12 months; list of board of directors, officers, and their affiliations; copy of IRS Form 990 *When to Submit:* before end of quarter
Restrictions on Giving: Does not support dinners or special events, fraternal organizations, political or lobbying groups, goodwill advertising, religious organizations for sectarian purposes, individuals, endowment campaigns, travel expenses, health organizations, sponsorship requests, or organizations operating for profit.
Generally does not support capital campaigns.

OTHER THINGS TO KNOW

Grand Metropolitan subsidiaries include Burger King, Haagen-Dazs, Pearle Inc., and Heublein, which separately provide direct giving to nonprofit organizations.

In 1992, Grand Metropolitan plc launched a multimillion-dollar initiative in the United States, KAPOW/Kids and the Power of Work. The program, conducted by GrandMet employees, introduces children to the responsibilities and satisfactions of work through educational packets, discussions, and visits to GrandMet plants and corporate offices. GrandMet spent over $1 million on the program in its first year and is committed to continuing the program for another four years. Program activites target second, fourth, and sixth grade students in one public school in 10 GrandMet communities. The program is not open to application; however, the company is developing information packets for other schools and companies to use to replicate the program. For more information, contact Susan Enright, Program Manager, Grand Metropolitan Inc., 712 Fifth Ave., Ste. 4600, New York, NY 10019, (212) 554-9200.

GRANTS ANALYSIS

Total Grants: $8,000,000*
Disclosure Period: fiscal year ending September 30, 1992
Note: Fiscal information reflects cash contributions only. Total grants is an approximate figure. Foundation assets are from 1991. Recent grants are derived from a fiscal 1991 Form 990.

RECENT GRANTS

430,000 United Way of Minneapolis, Minneapolis, MN
106,669 University of Minnesota Foundation, Minneapolis, MN
102,609 National Child Labor Committee, New York, NY
100,000 Guthrie Theatre, Minneapolis, MN
85,000 Project for Pride in Living, Minneapolis, MN
72,200 Citizens Scholarship Foundation of America, St. Peter, MN
67,500 Minnesota Orchestral Association, Minneapolis, MN
65,000 Minneapolis Institute of Arts, Minneapolis, MN
62,500 Minnesota Private College Fund, St. Paul, MN

50,000 Dartmouth College, Hanover, NH

Pillsbury Foundation

CONTACT

Joyce S. Pillsbury
President
Pillsbury Fdn.
6 Oakleigh Ln.
St. Louis, MO 63124
(314) 535-7659

FINANCIAL SUMMARY

Recent Giving: $932,630 (1990); $400,101 (1989); $820,191 (1986)
Assets: $18,563,677 (1990); $19,518,055 (1989); $16,044,673 (1986)
Gifts Received: $1,440 (1990); $13,090 (1989); $84,500 (1986)
EIN: 43-6030335

CONTRIBUTIONS SUMMARY

Donor(s): The foundation was incorporated in 1944 by the late Edwin S. Pillsbury and the late Harriette Brown Pillsbury.
Typical Recipients: • *Arts & Humanities:* music, performing arts, public broadcasting • *Civic & Public Affairs:* law & justice, philanthropic organizations • *Education:* colleges & universities, education funds, minority education, private education (precollege), public education (precollege), religious education • *Health:* medical research, single-disease health associations • *International:* international development/relief • *Religion:* churches, religious organizations • *Social Services:* child welfare, community centers, community service organizations, counseling, family services, food/clothing distribution, homes, religious welfare, shelters/homelessness, youth organizations
Grant Types: general support
Geographic Distribution: nationally, with a focus on St. Louis, MO

GIVING OFFICERS

Joyce S. Pillsbury: pres
William E. Pillsbury: secy, treas
Linda Pillsbury Roos: vp

APPLICATION INFORMATION

Initial Approach:
The foundation has no formal grant application procedure or application form.

The foundation has no deadline for submitting proposals.
Restrictions on Giving: The foundation does not support dinners or special events, fraternal organizations, political or lobbying groups, goodwill advertising, religious organizations for sectarian purposes, individuals, endowment campaigns, travel expenses, health organizations, or organizations operating for a profit.

GRANTS ANALYSIS

Total Grants: $932,630
Number of Grants: 68
Highest Grant: $340,859
Typical Range: $500 to $10,000
Disclosure Period: 1990
Note: Average grant figure does not include the highest grant of $340,859. Recent grants are derived from a 1990 grants list.

RECENT GRANTS

340,859 William Jewell College, Liberty, MO
97,500 Stephens College, Columbia, MO
77,000 Third Baptist Church, St. Louis, MO
71,500 American Baptist Assembly, Green Lake, WI
61,100 Christian Civic Foundation, St. Louis, MO
42,500 Missouri Baptist Children's Home, St. Louis, MO
27,600 National Right to Work Legal Defense Foundation, Springfield, VA
25,860 Christian Counselors, St. Louis, MO
19,500 LOGOS School, St. Louis, MO
17,430 North Side Team Ministry, St. Louis, MO

Pilot Trust

CONTACT

David M. Knotts
Executive Director
Pilot Trust
c/o United Bank of Boulder
PO Box 299
Boulder, CO 80306
(303) 442-0351

FINANCIAL SUMMARY

Recent Giving: $174,620 (1991); $230,318 (1990); $234,664 (1989)

Assets: $3,811,127 (1991); $3,663,254 (1990); $3,380,255 (1989)
EIN: 84-6030136

CONTRIBUTIONS SUMMARY
Donor(s): the late Roger Calvert
Typical Recipients: • *Civic & Public Affairs:* environmental affairs • *Education:* faculty development, public education (precollege) • *Social Services:* child welfare, community service organizations, youth organizations
Grant Types: general support and operating expenses
Geographic Distribution: focus on Boulder County, CO

GIVING OFFICERS
Dan Calvert: trust
Richard Meekley: trust
Lawrence M. Wood: trust

APPLICATION INFORMATION
Initial Approach: Contributes only to preselected organizations. There are no deadlines.

GRANTS ANALYSIS
Number of Grants: 1
Highest Grant: $174,620
Disclosure Period: 1991

RECENT GRANTS
174,620 Cal-Wood, Boulder, CO

Pincus Family Fund

CONTACT
Pincus Family Fund
466 Lexington Ave.
New York, NY 10017

FINANCIAL SUMMARY
Recent Giving: $1,049,365 (1991); $884,000 (1990); $566,100 (1989)
Assets: $3,727,372 (1991); $2,834,662 (1990); $3,761,898 (1989)
Gifts Received: $1,075,639 (1991); $89,625 (1990); $500,000 (1989)
Fiscal Note: 1991 contributions received in 5,000 shares of Humana, Inc. ($209,375) and 28,000 shares of United Healthcare Corp. ($866,264).
EIN: 13-6089184

CONTRIBUTIONS SUMMARY
Donor(s): Lionel I. Pincus
Typical Recipients: • *Arts & Humanities:* dance, performing arts, theater • *Civic & Public Affairs:* civil rights, environmental affairs, ethnic/minority organizations, ethnic/minority organizations, public policy, women's affairs • *Education:* business education, colleges & universities, private education (precollege) • *Health:* hospitals, single-disease health associations • *International:* foreign educational institutions • *Religion:* religious organizations • *Social Services:* community service organizations
Grant Types: general support
Geographic Distribution: focus on NY

GIVING OFFICERS
Edwin Gustafson, Jr.: secy, treas
Lionel I. Pincus: don, pres, treas *B* Philadelphia PA 1931 *ED* Univ PA BA 1953; Columbia Univ MBA 1956 *CURR EMPL* chmn, ceo: EM Warburg Pincus & Co *CORP AFFIL* bd dirs: Christians Intl; dir: Commun Newspapers, Journal Co, Mattel, NH Acquisition Corp *NONPR AFFIL* mem: Counc Foreign Rels; mem adv counc: Columbia Univ Grad Sch Bus; trust: Citizens Budget Commn, Columbia Univ, Montefiore Hosp Med Ctr, Sch Am Ballet
Suzanne Pincus: vp

APPLICATION INFORMATION
Initial Approach: Contributes only to preselected organizations.
Restrictions on Giving: Does not support individuals.

GRANTS ANALYSIS
Number of Grants: 29
Highest Grant: $400,000
Typical Range: $10,000 to $25,000
Disclosure Period: 1991

RECENT GRANTS
400,000 Columbia University, New York, NY
100,000 Montefiore Medical Center, New York, NY
100,000 School of American Ballet, New York, NY
75,000 Dover Fund, New York, NY
50,000 American Diabetes Association, New York, NY
50,000 New York University, New York, NY
30,000 United Jewish Appeal Federation of Jewish Philanthropies, New York, NY
25,000 Columbia Grammar and Prep School, New York, NY
25,000 Grand Canyon Trust, Washington, DC
25,000 University of Pennsylvania, Philadelphia, PA

Pine Tree Foundation

CONTACT
A. Morris Williams, Jr.
Director
Pine Tree Fdn.
120 Righters Mill Rd.
Gladwyne, PA 19035

FINANCIAL SUMMARY
Recent Giving: $215,000 (fiscal 1991); $195,000 (fiscal 1990); $47,000 (fiscal 1988)
Assets: $4,083,969 (fiscal year ending July 31, 1991); $3,950,020 (fiscal 1990); $1,840,094 (fiscal 1988)
Gifts Received: $763,305 (fiscal 1990); $923,460 (fiscal 1988)
EIN: 22-2751187

CONTRIBUTIONS SUMMARY
Donor(s): A. Morris Williams, Jr., Ruth W. Williams
Typical Recipients: • *Education:* education funds, religious education • *Social Services:* community service organizations, food/clothing distribution, shelters/homelessness
Grant Types: general support

GIVING OFFICERS
A. Morris Williams, Jr.: dir, pres
Ruth W. Williams: dir, secy, treas

APPLICATION INFORMATION
Initial Approach: Send brief letter describing program. There are no deadlines.

GRANTS ANALYSIS
Number of Grants: 4
Highest Grant: $100,000
Typical Range: $15,000 to $50,000
Disclosure Period: fiscal year ending July 31, 1991

RECENT GRANTS
100,000 Philadelphia Scholars Fund, Philadelphia, PA
50,000 CARE, Philadelphia, PA
50,000 Salvation Army, Philadelphia, PA
15,000 Community Women Foundation Project, Philadelphia, PA

Pines Bridge Foundation

CONTACT
Elaine Weiler
Trustee
Pines Bridge Foundation
1114 Avenue of the Americas
Suite 3400
New York, NY 10036-0000
(212) 869-9700

FINANCIAL SUMMARY
Recent Giving: $250,600 (1990); $263,950 (1989)
Assets: $1,959,375 (1990); $1,260,032 (1989)
Gifts Received: $600,000 (1989)
EIN: 13-6872045

CONTRIBUTIONS SUMMARY
Donor(s): the donor is Alan G. Weiler, a trustee of the foundation
Typical Recipients: • *Arts & Humanities:* arts centers, dance, museums/galleries, music, opera, performing arts, public broadcasting, theater • *Civic & Public Affairs:* civil rights, environmental affairs, philanthropic organizations, public policy, urban & community affairs, zoos/botanical gardens • *Education:* arts education, colleges & universities, education funds, legal education, medical education • *Health:* medical research, single-disease health associations • *International:* international organizations • *Social Services:* child welfare, community service organizations, disabled, employment/job training, shelters/homelessness
Grant Types: general support and research
Geographic Distribution: broad purposes, with emphasis on education, the arts, and civic affairs

GIVING OFFICERS
Alan G. Weiler: don, trust

Elaine Weiler: trust

APPLICATION INFORMATION

Initial Approach: The foundation reports that it does not accept unsolicited applications for funds.

GRANTS ANALYSIS

Number of Grants: 37
Highest Grant: $50,000
Typical Range: $2,000 to $25,000
Disclosure Period: 1990
Note: Incomplete grants list provided in 1990.

RECENT GRANTS

50,000 University of Pennsylvania, Philadelphia, PA
25,000 Columbia Law School, New York, NY
25,000 New Israel Fund, New York, NY
16,500 Harvard School of Public Health, Boston, MA
12,500 New Israel Fund, New York, NY
12,500 Yale Comprehensive Cancer Center, New Haven, CT
10,000 Friends of Carnegie Hall, New York, NY
5,000 Brandeis University, Waltham, MA
2,500 Opera Orchestra of New York, New York, NY
2,000 Alvin Ailey Dance Theatre, New York, NY

Pinewood Foundation

CONTACT

Celeste G. Bartos
President and Director
Pinewood Foundation
3 Manhattenville Rd.
Purchase, NY 10577-2110
(914) 696-9000

FINANCIAL SUMMARY

Recent Giving: $1,253,507 (fiscal 1991); $907,817 (fiscal 1990); $572,925 (fiscal 1989)
Assets: $11,607,000 (fiscal year ending September 30, 1991); $10,050,346 (fiscal 1990); $11,368,465 (fiscal 1989)
EIN: 13-6101581

CONTRIBUTIONS SUMMARY

Donor(s): The foundation was established in 1956 by Celeste G. Bartos, its president and director. It was originally called the Celeste and Armand Bartos Foundation.
Typical Recipients: • *Arts & Humanities:* museums/galleries, music, opera, public broadcasting, visual arts • *Civic & Public Affairs:* environmental affairs, philanthropic organizations • *Health:* hospitals • *International:* foreign educational institutions • *Social Services:* family planning
Grant Types: general support
Geographic Distribution: primarily New York, NY

GIVING OFFICERS

Adam Bartos: dir
Armand P. Bartos: vp, dir *PHIL AFFIL* vp, dir: DS and RH GottesmanFoundation
Celeste G. Bartos: don, pres, dir *PHIL AFFIL* dir: DS and RH GottesmanFoundation
Benjamin Glowatz: treas *PHIL AFFIL* treas: Gottesman (D S and R H) Foundation; vp, treas: Wachenheim (Sue and Edgar) Foundation
Irwin Markow: asst treas
Peter C. Siegfried: secy
Edgar Wachenheim III: vp *PHIL AFFIL* don, pres: Wachenheim (Sue and Edgar) Foundation; vp: Gottesman (D S and R H) Foundation

APPLICATION INFORMATION

Initial Approach: Restrictions on Giving: The foundation reports that it only makes contributions to preselected organizations and does not accept unsolicited proposals for funds.

GRANTS ANALYSIS

Total Grants: $1,253,507
Number of Grants: 64
Highest Grant: $195,000
Typical Range: $1,000 to $20,000
Disclosure Period: fiscal year ending September 30, 1991
Note: The average grant figure excludes a grant for $195,000. Recent grants are derived from a fiscal 1991 Form 990.

RECENT GRANTS

195,000 Bryant Park Restoration Corporation, New York, NY
133,333 New York Hospital-Cornell Medical Center, New York,
NY — Division of Endocrinology and Metabolism
62,500 Museum of Modern Art, New York, NY
50,000 Commonweal, Bolinas, CA
50,000 Daniel Clark Foundation, Brattleboro, VT
50,000 Massachusetts Institute of Technology, Cambridge, MA
50,000 New York Hospital-Cornell Medical Center, New York, NY — Department of Plastic Surgery
50,000 Planned Parenthood of New York City, New York, NY
45,344 New York Hospital-Cornell Medical Center, New York, NY — Clinical Research Fellowship Program
35,000 International Film Seminars, New York, NY — Museum of Modern Art

Pineywoods Foundation

CONTACT

Bob Bowman
Secretary
Pineywoods Fdn.
PO Box 3659
Lufkin, TX 75903
(409) 634-7444

FINANCIAL SUMMARY

Recent Giving: $95,737 (1991); $98,756 (1990); $60,250 (1989)
Assets: $2,108,813 (1991); $1,942,387 (1990); $1,909,801 (1989)
EIN: 75-1922533

CONTRIBUTIONS SUMMARY

Donor(s): The Southland Foundation
Typical Recipients: • *Arts & Humanities:* community arts, community arts, theater • *Civic & Public Affairs:* environmental affairs, law & justice, municipalities, urban & community affairs • *Education:* education associations • *Health:* health organizations, hospitals • *Social Services:* aged, community service organizations, drugs & alcohol, united funds, youth organizations

Grant Types: capital, general support, project, and seed money
Geographic Distribution: focus on TX

GIVING OFFICERS

John Firth Anderson: trust, chmn B Saginaw MI 1928 *ED* MI St Univ BA 1949; Univ IL MS 1950 *CURR EMPL* exec presbyter: Presbytery Santa Barbara *NONPR AFFIL* charter mem: Freedom Read Fdn; mem: Am Library Assn, AZ Assn County Librarians, AZ China Counc, AZ Library Assn, CA Library Assn, Southwestern Library Assn
Bob Bowman: trust, secy
George Henderson: trust, treas B Hurtsboro AL 1932 *ED* Wayne St Univ BA 1957; Wayne St Univ MA 1959; Wayne St Univ PhD 1965 *NONPR AFFIL* mem: Am Assn Higher Ed, Am Assn Univ Profs, Am Sociological Assn, Assn Black Sociologists, Assn Supervision Curriculum Devel, Inter-Univ Seminar Armed Forces Soc, Intl Soc Law Enforcement Criminal Justice Instructors, Natl Assn Human Rights Workers; prof sociology: Univ OK
Jack McMullen, Jr.: trust
E. G. Pittman: trust
Claude Smithhart: trust

APPLICATION INFORMATION

Initial Approach: Application form required. There are no deadlines.
Restrictions on Giving: Does not support individuals.

OTHER THINGS TO KNOW

Publications: Application Guidelines

GRANTS ANALYSIS

Number of Grants: 17
Highest Grant: $20,000
Typical Range: $1,000 to $5,000
Disclosure Period: 1991

RECENT GRANTS

20,000 Pinecrest Retirement, Lufkin, TX
10,000 Stewart Blood Center, Lufkin, TX
7,500 City of Lufkin, Lufkin, TX
7,500 City of Lufkin, Lufkin, TX
7,500 City of Lufkin, Lufkin, TX

6,000 Angelina Chamber
Foundation,
Lufkin, TX
5,000 Angelina Beautiful
Clean, Lufkin, TX
5,000 ANRA, Lufkin, TX
5,000 Cherokee Civic
Theatre, Rusk, TX
3,500 Hospice of Lufkin,
Lufkin, TX

Pinkerton Foundation

CONTACT
Joan Colello
Executive Director
Pinkerton Foundation
725 Park Ave.
New York, NY 10021
(212) 772-6110

FINANCIAL SUMMARY
Recent Giving: $1,774,402
(1992); $1,354,581 (1991);
$1,345,855 (1990)
Assets: $40,112,174 (1991);
$31,782,151 (1990);
$38,327,550 (1989)
EIN: 13-6206624

CONTRIBUTIONS SUMMARY
Donor(s): The Pinkerton Foundation was established in 1966 by the late Robert Allan Pinkerton (1904-1967). Mr. Pinkerton served as the chairman and chief executive officer of Pinkerton's Inc. for more than 35 years. He was the great-grandson of Allan Pinkerton, a Scottish immigrant, who had founded in 1850 what would become the oldest and largest security company in the world. The company was sold in 1983, and today there is no connection between the foundation and Pinkerton's Inc.
Typical Recipients: • *Arts & Humanities:* arts centers • *Civic & Public Affairs:* municipalities, nonprofit management, professional & trade associations, urban & community affairs • *Education:* arts education, business education, colleges & universities, education associations, education funds, elementary education, literacy, private education (precollege), public education (precollege), special education, student aid • *Health:* public health • *Social Services:* community centers, community service organizations, disabled, domestic violence, family services, relig-

ious welfare, volunteer services, youth organizations
Grant Types: project and seed money
Geographic Distribution: focus on New York, NY

GIVING OFFICERS
Edward J. Bednarz: chmn, trust
Joan Colello: secy, exec dir, trust
Eugene E. Fey: treas, trust
George Joseph Gillespie III: pres, trust *B* New York NY 1930 *ED* Georgetown Univ AB 1952; Harvard Univ LLB 1955 *CURR EMPL* ptnr: Cravath Swaine & Moore *CORP AFFIL* dir: Fund Am, Washington Post Co *NONPR AFFIL* dir, chmn emeritus: Natl Multiple Sclerosis Soc; mem: Am Bar Assn, NY Bar Assn, NY City Bar Assn; pres: Boys Club Madison Square; secy: Mus Broadcasting; trust, treas: Hoover Inst
Michael Stewart Joyce: trust *B* Cleveland OH 1942 *ED* Cleveland St Univ BA 1967; Walden Univ PhD 1974 *CORP AFFIL* dir: WH Brady Co *NONPR AFFIL* chmn: Philanthropic Roundtable; mem: Cardinals Comm Laity, Eastern Regional Selection Panel White House Fellowships, Mt Pelerin Soc, Sovereign Military Order Malta; mem edv bd: US Information Agency Ed Exchange; mem exec comm: Pres Private Sector Study Cost Control Grace Comm; secy: Inst Ed Affs; trust: Fdn Cultural Review *PHIL AFFIL* mem selection comm: Claire Booth Luce Fund
Michael Stewart Joyce: trust (see above)
Daniel L. Mosley: trust
Thomas Joseph Sweeney, Jr.: trust *ED* Univ KS BS 1956; Harvard Univ MBA 1961 *CURR EMPL* coun: Decker Hubbard & Welden *CORP AFFIL* chmn inst trust & investment comm: Morgan Guaranty Trust Co NY; dir: Engelhard Hanovia, W R Kenan Fund *NONPR AFFIL* mem: NY St Bar Assn

APPLICATION INFORMATION
Initial Approach:
Applicants should write a brief letter of inquiry that does not exceed two pages prior to a formal proposal or application for a grant.

The letter should describe the grantee organization, the proposed project and its goals, an estimated budget, IRS 501(c)(3) status, and the name and qualifications of the person directing the project. For research or demonstration projects, the program description should also include the possibilities for practical application of the project's findings. The board meets in May and December. Letters of inquiry are welcome throughout the year.
The foundation will request other material or arrange meetings as appropriate after reviewing the initial letter.
Restrictions on Giving:
Grants are awarded only to nonprofit, public organizations that are tax-exempt under IRS 501(c)(3). The foundation does not make grants to individuals, give loans or emergency assistance, nor does it support medical research or the direct provision of health care or religious education. It generally does not make grants to support conferences, publications, or media. Proposals for building renovations or other capital projects are not considered unless they are integrally related to the foundation's program objectives or are an outgrowth of one of its grantee's programs.

OTHER THINGS TO KNOW
Publications: guidelines for grant seekers

GRANTS ANALYSIS
Total Grants: $1,774,402
Number of Grants: 73
Highest Grant: $100,000
Typical Range: $20,000 to $50,000
Disclosure Period: 1992
Note: Recent grants are derived from a 1991 Form 990.

RECENT GRANTS
100,000 Madison Square Boys and Girls Club, New York, NY — for Flatbush clubhouse
50,000 YWCA of the City of New York, New York, NY — Young Fathers Program
44,074 New York University Para-Educator Center for Young Adults, New York, NY

40,000 Citizens Committee for New York City, New York, NY — demonstration program to reduce youth involvement in drug trafficking
40,000 Nativity Mission Center, New York, NY — general support and scholarships
40,000 Vocational Foundation, New York, NY — job training program for high-risk youth
30,000 Brooklyn Childrens' Museum, Brooklyn, NY — support after-school and community programs
30,000 Forest Hills Community House, Forest Hills, NY — to support teen outreach program
30,000 Good Shepherd Services, New York, NY — an alternative high school program
30,000 Mount St. Ursula Speech Center, Bronx, NY — educational remediation

Pinkerton Tobacco Co.
Sales: $56.0 million
Employees: 500
Headquarters: Owensboro, KY
SIC Major Group: Tobacco Products

CONTACT
Betty Taylor
Office Administrator
Pinkerton Tobacco Co.
PO Box 11588
Richmond, VA 23230
(502) 685-7281

CONTRIBUTIONS SUMMARY
Company provides employee matching gifts only.
Grant Types: matching
Operating Locations: KY (Owensboro)

CORP. OFFICERS
Tom Guinan: *CURR EMPL* pres: Pinkerton Tobacco Co
Robert B. Seidensticker: *B* New York NY 1929 *ED* Univ MD 1955 *CURR EMPL* ceo: Pinkerton Tobacco Co *CORP AFFIL* chmn: Am Candy Mfg Co, Bunte Candies Corp; dir:

Pioneer Concrete of America Inc.

Sovron Regional Bank NA *NONPR AFFIL* dir: Carpenter Ctr for Performing Arts, Tobacco Merchants Assn US; mem exec comm, dir: Tobacco Inst

Pioneer Concrete of America Inc.

Sales: $100.0 million
Employees: 1,000
Headquarters: Houston, TX
SIC Major Group: Stone, Clay & Glass Products

CONTACT
Gwyen Stine
Concrete Sales
Pioneer Concrete of America Inc.
800 Gessner, Ste. 1100
Houston, TX 77024
(713) 468-6868

CONTRIBUTIONS SUMMARY
Operating Locations: TX (Houston)

CORP. OFFICERS
Ron Mattingley: *CURR EMPL* ceo, pres: Pioneer Concrete Am

Pioneer Electronics (USA) Inc.

Employees: 700
Headquarters: Long Beach, CA
SIC Major Group: Electronic & Other Electrical Equipment and Wholesale Trade—Durable Goods

CONTACT
Ron Stone
Contributions Committee
Pioneer Electronics (USA), Inc.
2265 East 220th St.
Long Beach, CA 90810
(213) 835-6177

FINANCIAL SUMMARY
Fiscal Note: Giving Range: $25,000 to $50,000 annually

CONTRIBUTIONS SUMMARY
Each year top management chooses areas of concern to be the focus of contributions. In 1991, areas of concern were terminally ill children and education. Without exception, gifts take one of two forms: a $100 cash grant or a $150 product donation. In June 1992, Pioneer Electronics donated $600,000 to Rebuild L.A., the nonprofit group spearheading the redevelopment of Los Ange-

les following riots earlier in the year. The contribution was earmarked for a new program to teach electronics to inner-city youth, for internships for high school students at Pioneer's U.S. headquarters in Long Beach, and for educational programs to be developed by Rebuild L.A. Of the total, $500,000 will go toward creation of the Pioneer Academy of Electronics, a joint effort by the company; the Maxine Waters Employment Preparation Center, a publicly financed job training agency; the Los Angeles Unified School District; the city's Board of Education; and Rebuild L.A. Beginning in September 1992, the academy planned to offer 30 high school students in South Central Los Angeles a two-year training program in electronics servicing and repair. Besides classroom instruction, the students were assigned volunteer "mentors" from Pioneer and were given the opportunity for paid summer internships at the company. The remaining $100,000 was donated to Rebuild L.A. Pioneer also plans to provide six-month paid internships to local high school students.
Typical Recipients: • *Education:* public education (precollege) • *Health:* hospitals, pediatric health, single-disease health associations • *Social Services:* disabled, family services, youth organizations
Grant Types: general support
Nonmonetary Support Types: donated products
Geographic Distribution: in states with at least one Pioneer employee

CORP. OFFICERS
Ronald N. Stone: *CURR EMPL* cfo: Pioneer Electronics (USA)
Shoichi Yamada: *CURR EMPL* pres, ceo: Pioneer Electronics (USA)

GIVING OFFICERS
Ronald N. Stone: *CURR EMPL* cfo: Pioneer Electronics (USA) (see above)

APPLICATION INFORMATION
Initial Approach: Send a letter any time, including an explanation of how the current area of concern is being served. Also

include proof of tax-exempt status.
Restrictions on Giving: At a minimum, three criteria must be successfully met for a gift proposal to be considered: the program or organization must fall within that year's area of concern; there must be at least one Pioneer employee in the state where the benefit falls; and the organization must be tax-exempt.
Company does not support individuals or lobbying groups.

OTHER THINGS TO KNOW
Written applications are accepted at any time, but proposals received toward the end of the fiscal year may be denied for lack of funds. April 1 marks the beginning for the new fiscal year.

GRANTS ANALYSIS
Typical Range: $10 to $100

RECENT GRANTS
600,000 Rebuild L.A., Los Angeles, CA

Pioneer Fund

CONTACT
Harry F. Weyher
President
Pioneer Fund
299 Park Ave.
New York, NY 10171
(212) 207-1800

FINANCIAL SUMMARY
Recent Giving: $797,213 (1989)
Assets: $6,057,000 (1989)
EIN: 51-0242968

CONTRIBUTIONS SUMMARY
Typical Recipients: • *Civic & Public Affairs:* public policy • *Education:* colleges & universities, medical education • *Health:* medical research, medical research, single-disease health associations
Grant Types: general support and research

GIVING OFFICERS
William D. Miller: dir
Marion A. Parrott: dir
Randolph L. Speight: dir
John B. Trevor, Jr.: treas, dir
Harry F. Weyher: pres, dir *ED* Harvard Univ LLB 1949 *CURR EMPL* ptnr: Olwine Connelly Chase ODonnell Weyher *CORP AFFIL* ptnr: Olwine Connelly

Chase O'Donnell Weyher
NONPR AFFIL mem: Am Bar Assn, NY Bar Assn, NY City Bar Assn

APPLICATION INFORMATION
Initial Approach: Send brief letter of inquiry describing program or project. There are no deadlines.
Restrictions on Giving: Does not support individuals.

GRANTS ANALYSIS
Number of Grants: 15
Highest Grant: $105,000
Typical Range: $3,000 to $50,000
Disclosure Period: 1989

RECENT GRANTS
105,000 University of Minnesota, Minneapolis, MN
100,000 Atlas Economic Research Foundation, Fairfax, VA
100,000 Institute for the Study of Educational Differences, Orinda, CA
100,000 University of Delaware, Newark, DE
90,000 Johns Hopkins University, Baltimore, MD
50,063 University of Western Ontario, London, Canada
50,000 Federation for American Immigration Reform, Washington, DC
48,500 Institute for the Study of Man, Washington, DC
42,250 University of Pennsylvania, Philadelphia, PA
35,000 Coalition for Freedom, Raleigh, NC

Pioneer Fund

CONTACT
Pioneer Fund
1801 California St., Ste. 4500
Denver, CO 80202

FINANCIAL SUMMARY
Recent Giving: $338,600 (1991); $53,200 (1990); $4,600 (1989)
Assets: $11,185,416 (1991); $9,763,411 (1990); $7,726,003 (1989)
Gifts Received: $590,267 (1991); $1,101,013 (1990); $546,007 (1989)
Fiscal Note: In 1991, contributions were received from Helen M. McLoraine (Denver) in the

form of municipal bonds and a cash contribution.
EIN: 36-6108943

CONTRIBUTIONS SUMMARY
Donor(s): Helen M. McLoraine
Typical Recipients: • *Arts & Humanities:* libraries • *Education:* colleges & universities • *Health:* nursing services • *Religion:* religious organizations • *Social Services:* disabled, religious welfare, united funds, youth organizations
Grant Types: general support
Geographic Distribution: focus on Denver, CO

GIVING OFFICERS
Robert Anderson: secy
Robert T. Birdsong: vp
Helen M. McLoraine: pres, treas

APPLICATION INFORMATION
Initial Approach: Contributes only to preselected organizations. There are no deadlines or restrictions.

GRANTS ANALYSIS
Number of Grants: 9
Highest Grant: $300,000
Typical Range: $100 to $5,000
Disclosure Period: 1991

RECENT GRANTS
300,000 University of Chicago, Chicago, IL
11,000 Girls Incorporated, Denver, CO
10,000 Hadley School for the Blind, Winnetka, IL
10,000 United Way, Denver, CO
5,000 Salk Institute for Biological Studies, San Diego, CA
1,000 Boy Scouts of America, Denver, CO
1,000 Lutheran General Foundation, Park Ridge, IL
500 Boys and Girls Club, Denver, CO
100 Visiting Nurse Association of Chicago, Chicago, IL

Pioneer Group
Revenue: $80.9 million
Employees: 62
Headquarters: Boston, MA
SIC Major Group: Depository Institutions, Holding & Other Investment Offices, and Security & Commodity Brokers

CONTACT
Robert Nicoson
Director, Personnel
Pioneer Group
60 State St., 17th Fl.
Boston, MA 02109
(617) 742-7825

FINANCIAL SUMMARY
Fiscal Note: Annual Giving Range: less than $100,000

CONTRIBUTIONS SUMMARY
Company provides employee matching gifts only to education, health and human services, and the arts.
Grant Types: matching
Operating Locations: MA (Boston)

CORP. OFFICERS
John F. Cogan, Jr.: *B* Boston MA 1926 *ED* Harvard Coll 1949; Harvard Univ Law Sch 1952 *CURR EMPL* pres: Pioneer Group *CORP AFFIL* chmn: Hale & Dorr, ICI Mutual Ins Co, Teberebie Goldfields Ltd; dir: Pioneer Capital Corp, Scandia Trading Co Inc; pres, dir: Pioneer Bond Fund Inc, Pioneer Fund Inc, Pioneer II Inc, Pioneer Three Inc, Pioneering Mgmt Corp *NONPR AFFIL* mem: Am Bar Assn, Intl Bar Assn; mem exec comm, gov: Investment Co Inst
William H. Keough: *B* Framingham MA 1937 *ED* Boston Coll 1959; Northeastern Univ 1967 *CURR EMPL* sr vp, cfo: Pioneer Group *NONPR AFFIL* mem: Am Mgmt Assn, Fin Execs Inst, Investment Co Inst

APPLICATION INFORMATION
Restrictions on Giving: Does not support religious organizations for sectarian purposes or political or lobbying groups.

Pioneer Hi-Bred International
Revenue: $1.1 billion
Employees: 4,601
Headquarters: Des Moines, IA
SIC Major Group: Business Services, Industrial Machinery & Equipment, Real Estate, and Wholesale Trade—Nondurable Goods

CONTACT
Judy Turvey
Director, Community Relations
Pioneer Hi-Bred International, Inc.
4445 Corporate Dr., Ste. 200
West Des Moines, IA 50265
(515) 222-6874

FINANCIAL SUMMARY
Recent Giving: $4,900,000 (1993 est.); $4,300,000 (1992 approx.); $4,800,000 (1991)
Fiscal Note: Company gives directly and through the community relations department, which had a budget of $434,000 in 1992 that is not included in the above giving figures. Company has not named a replacement for Lu Jean Cole, former director of community relations and contact for giving program.

CONTRIBUTIONS SUMMARY
Typical Recipients: • *Arts & Humanities:* community arts, dance, opera, performing arts • *Civic & Public Affairs:* economic development, international affairs, rural affairs • *Education:* agricultural education, colleges & universities, science/technology education, student aid • *Social Services:* aged, child welfare, employment/job training, united funds
Grant Types: general support and project
Nonmonetary Support Types: in-kind services
Note: Nonmonetary support is provided by the company and estimated value was $85,000 in 1993. This figure is included in the total contributions figure above.
Geographic Distribution: near headquarters, operating locations
Operating Locations: AR (Marion), AZ (Yuma), CA (Fresno, Kerman, Woodland), FL (Ft. Meyers, Homestead), GA (Tifton), HI (Kekaha), IA (Algona, Cedar Rapids, Des Moines, Durant, Dysart, Hedrick, Johnston, Marengo, Marion, Mount Pleasant, Reinbeck, Renwick, Toledo, Waterloo), ID (Nampa), IL (Good Hope, Leroy, Litchfield, Shelbyville, St. Joseph), IN (Flora, Princeton, Rushville, Tipton, Windfall, Worthington), KS (Garden City, Hutchinson), MD (Carrollton, Marshall), MI (Alma, Constantine), MS (Greenville), NC (Laurenburg,

Winterville), ND (Drayton, Grand Forks, Hillsboro, Wahpeton), NE (Doniphan, North Platte, York), OH (Bowling Green, Grand Rapids, Napoleon), PA (New Holland, Quarryville), SC (St. Matthews), SD (Huron), TN (Union City), TX (Plainview, Taft, Vernon, Weslaco), WA (Connell), WI (Arlington, Eau Claire, Janesville)

CORP. OFFICERS
Thomas N. Urban: *B* Des Moines IA 1934 *CURR EMPL* chmn, pres, dir, ceo: Pioneer Hi-Bred Intl *CORP AFFIL* dir: Bankers Trust Co, Equitable IA Cos, Holly Farms Corp, Weitz Corp

GIVING OFFICERS
Jerry Chicoine: *B* San Bernardino CA 1942 *CURR EMPL* sr vp, cfo: Pioneer Hi-Bred Intl *CORP AFFIL* dir: Central Life Acquisition Co, Edge Techs, HMO IA
Charles S. Johnson: *CURR EMPL* exec vp: NAO Operations *CORP AFFIL* dir: First Interstate Bank
Mary McBride: *CURR EMPL* vp mktg: Pioneer Hi-Bred Intl
Edward T. Shonsey: *CURR EMPL* sr vp intl oper: Pioneer Hi-Bred Intl

APPLICATION INFORMATION
Initial Approach: *Initial Contact:* brief letter *Include Information On:* history of organization; statement of purpose of project and how it will address a current need and solve a problem; cost and specific amount requested; other funding sources and indication of community involvement; program leaders; time needed to complete project; means of evaluating program's effectiveness; and proof of tax-exempt status *When to Submit:* any time
Restrictions on Giving: Company does not support emergency funding, athletic activities, individuals, health associations that do not provide direct services, political organizations, or religious organizations that promote a particular doctrine.

OTHER THINGS TO KNOW
Started an international giving program in 1990. Contributions are made to U.S.-based non-

profit organizations with an international focus and to international organizations by foreign subsidiaries.

GRANTS ANALYSIS
Total Grants: $4,300,000*
Number of Grants: 506*
Typical Range: $2,500 to $10,000
Disclosure Period: 1992
Note: Total grants, number of grants, and average grant figures are approximate. Recent grants are derived from a 1992 grant list.

RECENT GRANTS
1,500,000 Iowa State University Foundation, IA — for Partnership for Prominence Campaign to create an endowed professorship in the Agronomy Department

Pioneer Trust Bank, NA / Pioneer Trust Bank, NA, Foundation
Employees: 50
Headquarters: Salem, OR
SIC Major Group: Depository Institutions

CONTACT
Michael S. Compton
Vice President & Trust Officer
Pioneer Trust Bank, NA
PO Box 2305
Salem, OR 97308
(503) 363-3136

FINANCIAL SUMMARY
Recent Giving: $24,475 (1992 approx.); $19,950 (1991); $17,000 (1990)
Assets: $478,646 (1991); $351,993 (1989)
Gifts Received: $86,012 (1991)
Fiscal Note: In 1991, contributions were received from Pioneer Trust Bank Corporation.
EIN: 93-0881673

CONTRIBUTIONS SUMMARY
Typical Recipients: • *Arts & Humanities:* general, museums/galleries, public broadcasting • *Civic & Public Affairs:*

general, urban & community affairs • *Education:* general • *Health:* general, health organizations • *Religion:* missionary activities • *Social Services:* child welfare, general, united funds, youth organizations

Grant Types: challenge, emergency, general support, operating expenses, project, research, and seed money

Geographic Distribution: focus on OR

Operating Locations: OR (Salem)

GIVING OFFICERS
Pioneer Trust Bank, N.A.: trust

APPLICATION INFORMATION
Initial Approach: Send a full proposal including a description of organization, amount requested, purpose of funds sought, and proof of tax-exempt status. Deadline is September 15.

Restrictions on Giving: Does not support individuals, political or lobbying groups, or organizations outside operating areas.

GRANTS ANALYSIS
Number of Grants: 33
Highest Grant: $2,500
Typical Range: $500 to $1,000
Disclosure Period: 1991

RECENT GRANTS
2,500 YWCA, Salem, OR
1,500 United Way, Salem, OR
1,200 Assistance League of Salem, Salem, OR
1,000 Friends of Pioneer Cemetery, Salem, OR
1,000 Gilbert House Children Museum, Salem, OR
1,000 Mid Valley Children's Guild, Salem, OR
1,000 Oregon Public Broadcasting, Portland, OR
1,000 St. Francis Conference, Salem, OR
1,000 Union Gospel Mission, Salem, OR
500 American Red Cross, Salem, OR

Piper Foundation

CONTACT
Henry Ebeling
Secretary
Piper Fdn.
222 1/2 East Main St.
Lock Haven, PA 17745
(717) 769-6147

FINANCIAL SUMMARY
Recent Giving: $72,500 (fiscal 1991)
Assets: $1,306,937 (fiscal year ending September 30, 1991)
EIN: 24-0863140

CONTRIBUTIONS SUMMARY
Typical Recipients: • *Arts & Humanities:* libraries, libraries, theater • *Education:* student aid • *Health:* nursing services • *Social Services:* family planning, united funds
Grant Types: general support, operating expenses, and scholarship

GIVING OFFICERS
Henry Ebeling: secy

APPLICATION INFORMATION
Initial Approach: Send brief letter of inquiry. There are no deadlines.

GRANTS ANALYSIS
Number of Grants: 14
Highest Grant: $20,000
Typical Range: $2,000 to $5,000
Disclosure Period: fiscal year ending September 30, 1991

RECENT GRANTS
20,000 UTE Distribution Corporation, Roosevelt, UT — operating expenses
10,000 Clinton County United Way, Lock Haven, PA — current operating expenses
10,000 Lock Haven UMCA, Lock Haven, PA — operating expenses
5,000 Annie Haalenbake Ross Library, Lock Haven, PA — operating expenses
5,000 Lock Haven University Foundation, Lock Haven, PA— presidential scholarships
4,000 Family Planning Clinic of Lock Haven, Lock

Haven, CT — operating expenses
4,000 Millbrook Playhouse, Mill Hall, PA— operating expenses
3,000 Clinton County Historical Society, Lock Haven, PA — aviation museum
2,500 Community Nursing Service of Clinton County, Lock Haven, PA — community nursing service for needy persons requiring home health care
1,000 Salvation Army, Lock Haven, PA

Piper Foundation, Minnie Stevens

CONTACT
Michael J. Balint
Executive Director
Minnie Stevens Piper Fdn.
GPM South Tower, Ste. 200
800 NW Loop 410
San Antonio, TX 78216-5699
(512) 524-8494

FINANCIAL SUMMARY
Recent Giving: $257,594 (1990); $310,600 (1989); $30,000 (1988)
Assets: $19,706,366 (1990); $19,490,850 (1989); $16,966,715 (1988)
EIN: 74-1292695

CONTRIBUTIONS SUMMARY
Donor(s): The foundation was incorporated in 1950 by the late Randall G. Piper and the late Minnie Stevens Piper.
Typical Recipients: • *Arts & Humanities:* arts centers, arts funds, community arts, libraries, music, performing arts, public broadcasting • *Civic & Public Affairs:* philanthropic organizations • *Education:* colleges & universities, education funds, international studies, legal education, literacy, public education (precollege), religious education, student aid • *Religion:* churches • *Science:* science exhibits & fairs • *Social Services:* youth organizations
Grant Types: fellowship and scholarship
Geographic Distribution: focus on Texas

GIVING OFFICERS
Michael J. Balint: exec dir

Leatrice F. Cleveland: dir
Martin R. Harris: dir
Carlos Otero: asst dir
Frank Slavik: dir
J. Burleson Smith: dir
Bruce Thomas: dir
John H. Wilson II: dir

APPLICATION INFORMATION
Initial Approach:
The foundation has no formal grant application procedure or application form.
Applications should be submitted by February 1 and July 1. The board meets twice annually.
Restrictions on Giving:
Grants are made to organizations having a nonprofit status as stated by the IRS. The foundation reports no grants are given to organizations which discriminate on the grounds of race, color, creed, or sex, or to building or endowment funds.

OTHER THINGS TO KNOW
Publications: application guidelines, program policy statement, newsletter, and occasional reports

GRANTS ANALYSIS
Total Grants: $257,594
Number of Grants: 35
Highest Grant: $182,500
Typical Range: $500 to $2,500
Disclosure Period: 1990
Note: Average grant figure does not include the highest grant of $182,500. Recent grants are derived from a 1990 grants list.

RECENT GRANTS
182,500 Piper Scholars Program, San Antonio, TX
25,000 Piper Professors Program, San Antonio, TX
2,500 College of Saint Thomas More, Fort Worth, TX
2,500 Converse Area Public Library, Converse, TX
2,500 First Presbyterian Church, San Antonio, TX
2,500 James Dick Foundation for the Performing Arts, Roundtop, TX
2,500 KLRN TV 9, San Antonio, TX
2,500 Presidential Scholars Program, Washington, DC
2,500 San Antonio Symphony, San Antonio, TX
2,500 Southwestern Law Enforcement Institute, Richardson, TX

Piper Jaffray Cos.
Revenue: $267.83 million
Employees: 2,114
Parent Company: Piper Jaffray
Headquarters: Minneapolis, MN
SIC Major Group: Security & Commodity Brokers

CONTACT
Marina Lyon
Community Affairs
Piper Jaffray Cos.
222 S Ninth St.
Minneapolis, MN 55402
(612) 342-6082
Note: Brenda Cich and Jan Hennings are also contacts for the contributions program.

FINANCIAL SUMMARY
Recent Giving: $3,000,000 (1993 est.); $3,070,000 (1992); $1,538,000 (1991)
Fiscal Note: Company gives directly. Each of the company's branch managers is responsible for giving in community. Budget is determined on a branch by branch basis and is included in the giving figures above.

CONTRIBUTIONS SUMMARY
Typical Recipients: • *Arts & Humanities:* arts centers, arts festivals, music, theater • *Civic & Public Affairs:* general • *Education:* business education, colleges & universities, elementary education • *Social Services:* child welfare, emergency relief, family services, food/clothing distribution, general, united funds, youth organizations
Grant Types: employee matching gifts, general support, and project
Geographic Distribution: near headquarters and branch locations; also to national organizations
Operating Locations: MN (Minneapolis)
Note: Company has over 65 branch offices, most of which are in the western U.S.

CORP. OFFICERS
William H. Ellis: *CURR EMPL* pres, coo, dir: Piper Jaffray Cos
Charles N. Hayssen: *CURR EMPL* cfo: Piper Jaffray Cos
Addison Lewis Piper: *B* Minneapolis MN 1946 *ED* Williams Coll BA 1968; Stanford Univ MBA 1972 *CURR EMPL* chmn, ceo, dir: Piper Jaffray Cos *NONPR AFFIL* dir: Guthrie Theater, Minneapolis Abbott NW Hosp, MN Bus Partnership, MN Pub Radio, Stanford Bus Sch Assn, Washburn Child Guidance Ctr; dir, mem exec comm: Minneapolis Downtown Counc; mem: Securities Indus Assn

GIVING OFFICERS
Karen M. Bohn: chmn corp contributions *B* Grand Forks ND 1953 *ED* Univ ND 1975 *CURR EMPL* mng dir admin: Piper Jaffray Cos

APPLICATION INFORMATION
Initial Approach: *Initial Contact:* for Minneapolis-St. Paul organizations or national organizations, send brief letter of inquiry *Include Information On:* description of the organization, amount requested, purpose of funds sought, recently audited financial statement, and proof of tax-exempt status *When to Submit:* any time *Note:* For organizations near branch offices, contact local branch manager for further details.
Restrictions on Giving: The company does not support individuals, campaigns for elimination of diseases, basic or applied research, religious organizations for sectarian purposes, or political or lobbying groups.
Also not funded are travel expenses, teams or events, tickets, or benefits.

OTHER THINGS TO KNOW
Company reports that it donates over 5% of pretax earnings to charitable organizations.
Publications: community involvment report

GRANTS ANALYSIS
Total Grants: $3,070,000
Typical Range: $1,000 to $2,500*
Disclosure Period: 1992

Note: Typical grants range is for headquarters area. Typical grants range for branch locations is $50 to $250. Recent grants are derived from a 1992 annual report.

RECENT GRANTS
African American Film Festival, MN
Big Brothers and Sisters of Minneapolis, MN
Bismarck State College, ND
Bloomington Fine Arts Council/Anne Frank Exhibit, Bloomington, MN
Boy Scouts of America-Viking Council
Camphill Village Minnesota, MN
Carondelet Health Care Foundation, MN
Children's Museum, MN
Children's Wonderscope Museum
Columbus Hospital Gift of Life

Pirelli Armstrong Tire Corp. / Pirelli Armstrong Foundation
Sales: $750.0 million
Employees: 3,500
Headquarters: New Haven, CT
SIC Major Group: Chemicals & Allied Products and Rubber & Miscellaneous Plastics Products

CONTACT
Pat Hennessy
Executive Director
Pirelli Armstrong Foundation
500 Sargent Dr., PO Box 2001
New Haven, CT 06536-0201
(203) 784-2200

FINANCIAL SUMMARY
Recent Giving: $32,117 (1990); $140,828 (1989)
Assets: $4,927 (1989)
Gifts Received: $27,200 (1990)
EIN: 06-1263699

CONTRIBUTIONS SUMMARY
Typical Recipients: • *Social Services:* community service organizations, united funds
Grant Types: general support and matching
Geographic Distribution: headquarters and operating locations
Operating Locations: AR, CA, CT, IA, NC, TN

CORP. OFFICERS
William J. Dunn: *CURR EMPL* cfo, vp (fin): Pirelli Armstrong Tire Corp

Paul C. James: *CURR EMPL*
vchmn: Pirelli Armstrong Tire
Corp
G. Morchio: *CURR EMPL*
pres: Pirelli Armstrong Tire
Corp

GIVING OFFICERS

Pat Hennessy: exec dir *CURR
EMPL* exec dir: Pirelli Armstrong Tire Corp

APPLICATION
INFORMATION

Initial Approach: Foundation
supports preselected organizations and does not accept unsolicited requests for funds.

Pitney Bowes

Sales: $3.46 billion
Employees: 29,421
Headquarters: Stamford, CT
SIC Major Group: Industrial
Machinery & Equipment,
Paper & Allied Products,
Printing & Publishing, and
Rubber & Miscellaneous
Plastics Products

CONTACT

Mary M. McCaskey
Secretary, Corporate
Contributions Committee
Pitney Bowes Inc.
World Headquarters
Stamford, CT 06926-0700
(203) 351-7751

FINANCIAL SUMMARY

Recent Giving: $2,000,000
(1991 est.); $1,900,000 (1990);
$1,900,000 (1989)
Assets: $6,000,000 (1990)
Fiscal Note: Company gives directly.

CONTRIBUTIONS
SUMMARY

Typical Recipients: • *Arts &
Humanities:* arts centers, community arts • *Civic & Public Affairs:* civil rights, ethnic/minor-
ity organizations, housing,
urban & community affairs,
women's affairs • *Education:*
colleges & universities, education funds, elementary education, literacy, minority education, science/technology
education • *Health:* hospitals
• *Social Services:* community
service organizations, day care,
employment/job training, shel-
ters/homelessness, united funds
Grant Types: capital, em-
ployee matching gifts, and general support
Nonmonetary Support Types:
loaned executives

Note: Contributions to the
United Way.
Geographic Distribution:
near headquarters and operat-
ing locations only
Operating Locations: CT
(Danbury, Norwalk, Shelton,
Stamford, Stratford), NE
(Omaha), OH (Dayton)

CORP. OFFICERS

George Burton Harvey: *B*
New Haven CT 1931 *ED* Univ
PA BS 1954 *CURR EMPL*
chmn, pres, ceo: Pitney Bowes
CORP AFFIL dir: CBT Corp,
McGraw Hill, Northeast Utili-
ties, Norton Co *NONPR AFFIL*
dir: Bus Equipment Mfrs Assn,
CT Bus Indus Assn, New
Neighborhoods, Southwestern
Area Commerce & Indus Assn,
St Joseph Hosp; trust: CT Coll,
King Sch

GIVING OFFICERS

Mary M. McCaskey: secy corporate contributions comm

APPLICATION
INFORMATION

Initial Approach: *Initial Contact:* proposal to headquarters
Include Information On: brief
history of organization, including its objectives; amount requested, amount requested
from other corporations, and
total amount required; purpose
for which funds are sought, including discussion of the need
that is to be addressed and
what other agencies are addressing that need; description
of program and proposed outcome; recently audited financial statement; proof of tax-exempt status *When to Submit:*
any time *Note:* Corporate contributions administered at headquarters. Each branch, operating unit, and subsidiary has
smaller budget (primarily for
United Way and local community projects).
Restrictions on Giving: Does
not purchase tickets or advertising space or support conference attendance, dinners or
other special events, travel expenses, fraternal organizations,
individuals, political or lobbying groups, or religious organizations for sectarian purposes.
Pitney Bowes does not make
product donations.

GRANTS ANALYSIS

Total Grants: $1,900,000*
Number of Grants: 2,526*
Highest Grant: $539,400

Typical Range: $2,500 to
$5,000
Disclosure Period: 1990
Note: Number of grants and average grant figures include
matching gifts. Total grants figure is approximate. Recent
grants are derived from a 1990
grants list.

Piton Foundation

CONTACT

Phyllis Buchele
Grants Administrator
Piton Foundation
511 16th St., Ste. 700
Denver, CO 80202
(303) 825-6246

FINANCIAL SUMMARY

Recent Giving: $217,000 (fis-
cal 1992 approx.); $564,390
(fiscal 1991); $1,107,282 (fis-
cal 1990)
Assets: $3,000,000 (fiscal
1992 est.); $3,610,036 (fiscal
year ending November 30,
1991); $3,792,613 (fiscal
1990); $4,084,033 (fiscal 1989)
Gifts Received: $1,000,000
(fiscal 1992 est.); $1,217,059
(fiscal 1991); $1,491,827 (fis-
cal 1990); $2,880,550 (fiscal
1989)
Fiscal Note: In fiscal 1990, the
foundation received $930,778
from the Nancy Gary Chil-
dren's Trust, $443,850 from the
Rockefeller Foundation,
$67,199 from the Colorado
Trust, and $50,000 from 8
South, 54 East, Inc.
EIN: 84-0719486

CONTRIBUTIONS
SUMMARY

Donor(s): Samuel Gary, and
his wife, Nancy, founded the
Piton Foundation in 1976. Mr.
Gary is president and chairman
of the foundation; his wife is a
director and board member.
Typical Recipients: • *Civic &
Public Affairs:* business/free enterprise, economic development, environmental affairs,
housing, municipalities, nonprofit management, philanthropic organizations, public
policy, urban & community affairs, women's affairs • *Education:* career/vocational education, colleges & universities,
public education (precollege)
• *Religion:* churches • *Social
Services:* united funds, youth
organizations
Grant Types: loan

Geographic Distribution: Denver, CO

GIVING OFFICERS

James E. Bye: bd mem *B* Thief
River Falls MN 1930 *ED* Univ
MN BBA 1951; Harvard Univ
LLB 1956 *CURR EMPL* ptnr:
Holme Roberts & Owen
NONPR AFFIL fellow: Am Bar
Fdn; mem: Am Bar Assn, Am
Coll Tax Counc, CO Bar Assn,
Denver Bar Assn, Denver Es-
tate Planning Counc, Greater
Denver Tax Couns Assn; trust:
Regis Coll, Two Percent Club,
Univ CO Fdn; chmn: Alexis de
Tocqueville Soc Metro Denver,
Metro Denver GIVES; trust:
Loretto Heights Coll
Mary Gittings Cronin: exec
dir
Kate Gary: dir, bd mem
Nancy Gary: dir, bd mem
Samuel Gary: chmn, pres
Ronald W. Williams: dir, bd
mem

APPLICATION
INFORMATION

Initial Approach:
Note: Piton's grant program
will support the foundation's
operating activities in its five
program areas of Improving
Public Education, Revitalizing
Neighborhoods, Promoting
Economic Opportunities,
Strengthening Families, and
Promoting Effective Citizen Involvement. Therefore, the foundation will no longer consider
unsolicited proposals but will
invite organizations to participate in projects that supplement its operating activities.

OTHER THINGS TO
KNOW

Publications: annual report

GRANTS ANALYSIS

Total Grants: $564,390 (ap-
prox.)
Number of Grants: 64*
Highest Grant: $50,000
Typical Range: $2,000 to
$25,000
Disclosure Period: fiscal year
ending November 30, 1991
Note: Above figures exclude
minor grants for employee community service programs, small
non-grant donations in support
of special events, loans, and
the Gary Williams Employee
Fund grants. The total giving
figure including these programs is $634,832. Sample
grants are derived from a 1990
grants list.

RECENT GRANTS

50,000 Brothers Redevelopment, Denver, CO

50,000 Hope Communities, Denver, CO

40,000 Denver Emergency Housing Coalition, Denver, CO

35,000 Uptown Partnership, Denver, CO

30,000 Colorado Housing Assistance Corporation, Denver, CO — payment on general operations

30,000 Hope Communities, Denver, CO — redevelopment

30,000 Northeast Denver Housing Center, Denver, CO

27,000 Denver Civic Ventures, Denver, CO — support the work of other office

25,000 Denver Public Schools, Denver, CO — after school study hall

25,000 University of Denver, Denver, CO — Keystone Project

Pitt-Des Moines Inc. / Pittsburgh-Des Moines Inc. Charitable Trust

Revenue: $392.5 million
Employees: 2,285
Headquarters: Pittsburgh, PA
SIC Major Group: Fabricated Metal Products, General Building Contractors, Special Trade Contractors, and Wholesale Trade—Durable Goods

CONTACT

W. R. Jackson
Trustee
Pitt-Des Moines Inc.
3400 Grand Ave.
Pittsburgh, PA 15225-1582
(412) 331-3000

FINANCIAL SUMMARY

Recent Giving: $84,340 (1991); $50,945 (1989)
Assets: $1,174,722 (1991); $1,100,697 (1989)
EIN: 25-6032139

CONTRIBUTIONS SUMMARY

Typical Recipients: • *Arts & Humanities:* community arts, opera • *Civic & Public Affairs:* civil rights, economics, environmental affairs, public policy, urban & community affairs • *Education:* colleges & universities, education associations, minority education • *International:* international organizations • *Social Services:* community service organizations, emergency relief, united funds, youth organizations
Grant Types: general support
Geographic Distribution: focus on PA
Operating Locations: PA (Pittsburgh)

CORP. OFFICERS

P. O. Elbert: *CURR EMPL* chmn: Pittsburgh-Des Moines Corp
W. W. McKee: *CURR EMPL* pres, ceo: Pittsburgh-Des Moines Corp

GIVING OFFICERS

R. A. Byers: trust
W. R. Jackson: trust
J. H. Long: trust

APPLICATION INFORMATION

Initial Approach: Send brief letter describing program. There are no deadlines.

GRANTS ANALYSIS

Number of Grants: 51
Highest Grant: $25,000
Typical Range: $250 to $2,500
Disclosure Period: 1991

RECENT GRANTS

25,000 Hurricane Allen St. Lucia Rebuilding Fund, New York, NY

8,000 United Way, Des Moines, IA

6,000 United Way, Pittsburgh, PA

5,000 Allegheny Trails Council, Pittsburgh, PA

4,000 Carnegie Institute Second Century Fund, Pittsburgh, PA

3,000 LaRoche College, Pittsburgh, PA

2,500 Foundation for Independent Colleges of Pennsylvania, Mechanicsburg, PA

2,500 United Way, Wausau, WI

2,000 Heritage Foundation, Washington, DC

2,000 National Right to Work Legal Defense Fund, Springfield, VA

Pitts Foundation, William H. and Lula E.

CONTACT

Clare R. Ranney
Secretary
William H. and Lula E. Pitts Fdn.
c/o Trust Company Bank
PO Box 4655
Atlanta, GA 30302
(404) 588-8449

FINANCIAL SUMMARY

Recent Giving: $677,725 (1991); $573,725 (1989); $540,725 (1988)
Assets: $23,744,512 (1990); $20,817,323 (1989); $13,889,650 (1988)
Gifts Received: $50,000 (1990)
Fiscal Note: In 1990, contributions were received from Margaret A. Pitts.
EIN: 58-6026047

CONTRIBUTIONS SUMMARY

Donor(s): The foundation was established in 1941 by Margaret A. Pitts and the late William I. H. Pitts.
Typical Recipients: • *Civic & Public Affairs:* economic development • *Education:* colleges & universities, private education (precollege), religious education • *Religion:* churches, religious organizations • *Social Services:* aged, community service organizations, homes, religious welfare
Grant Types: capital, general support, and multiyear/continuing support
Geographic Distribution: limited to Georgia

GIVING OFFICERS

John Harris Boman, Jr.: bd mem *B* Anniston AL 1910 *ED* Marquette Univ AB 1930; Univ MI JD 1933 *CURR EMPL* secy, dir: Jackson Packing Co *NONPR AFFIL* gen couns: Boy Scouts Am; mem: Am Bar Fdn, Am Law Inst, Atlanta Bar Assn, GA Bar Assn, Lawyers Club Atlanta, St Bar GA
Bishop William Ragsdale Cannon: chmn *B* Chattanooga TN 1916 *ED* Univ GA AB 1937; Yale Univ BD 1940; Yale Univ PhD 1942; Asbury Coll DD 1950; Temple Univ LLD 1955; Emory Univ LHD 1962 *NONPR AFFIL* co-chmn: Conversations Methodists & Roman Catholics Intl Level; hon pres, chmn exec comm: World Methodist Counc; mem: Oxford Inst Wesleyan Studies; trust: Asbury Coll, La Grange Coll; vchmn, trust: Emory Univ
Carroll Payne Jones: bd mem
Thomas O. Marshall, Jr.: bd mem *B* Americus GA 1920 *ED* US Naval Academy BS 1941; Univ GA JD 1948 *NONPR AFFIL* mem: Am Bar Assn, Am Judicature Soc, Am Legion, Atlanta Bar Assn, GA Bar Assn, Judicial Coll GA, Natl Judicial Coll, Veterans Foreign Wars; trust: Andrew Coll, Southern GA Methodist Home Aged
Walter Young Murphy: bd mem *B* Chester SC 1930 *ED* Emory Univ AB 1950; Candler Sch Theology MDiv 1953 *NONPR AFFIL* dir: Un Way La Grange; mem: GA St Scholarship Commn, La Grange Chamber Commerce, Natl Assn Schs Colls & Univs Un Methodist Church; trust: West GA Med Ctr
Margaret A. Pitts: mgr
Clare Ranney: secy
Robert Strickland: bd mem *B* Atlanta GA 1927 *ED* Davidson Coll BS 1948; Atlanta Law Sch LLB 1953 *CURR EMPL* chmn, ceo, dir: SunTrust Banks *CORP AFFIL* chmn, dir: Trust Co Bank; dir: GA Power Co, GA US Corp, Investment Ctr, Life Ins Co GA, Oxford Indus, Trust Co Mortgage *NONPR AFFIL* chmn bd trusts: Emory Univ; dir Fulton County unit: Am Cancer Soc; mem: Assn Reserve City Bankers, Atlanta Arts Alliance, Atlanta Chamber Commerce, GA Bankers Assn; mem exec comm: Central Atlanta Progress Assn; trust emeritus: Westminster Schs; vp, dir: Piedmont Hosp
Kirrk Treible: bd mem

APPLICATION INFORMATION

Initial Approach:
The foundation requests applications be made in writing. The foundation has no deadline for submitting proposals.
Restrictions on Giving: The foundation does not make grants to individuals, or for loans, endowment funds, research, scholarships, fellowships, or matching gifts.

GRANTS ANALYSIS

Total Grants: $677,725
Number of Grants: 38
Highest Grant: $47,000

Typical Range: $5,000 to
$20,000
Disclosure Period: 1990
Note: Recent grants are derived
from a 1990 grants list.

RECENT GRANTS
47,000 Andrew College,
Cuthbert, GA
47,000 LaGrange College,
LaGrange, GA
40,000 Andrew College,
Cuthbert, GA
40,000 Emory University,
Atlanta, GA
40,000 LaGrange College,
LaGrange, GA
33,000 Andrew College,
Cuthbert, GA
33,000 LaGrange College,
LaGrange, GA
30,000 LaGrange College,
LaGrange, GA
30,000 South Georgia
Methodist Home
for the Aging,
Americus, GA
30,000 South Georgia
Methodist Home
for the Aging,
Americus, GA

Pittsburgh Child Guidance Foundation

CONTACT
Brigitte Alexander
Executive Director
Pittsburgh Child Guidance Fdn.
580 South Aiken Ave.
Pittsburgh, PA 15232-1502
(412) 683-7243

FINANCIAL SUMMARY
Recent Giving: $143,543
(1991); $173,075 (1990);
$215,379 (1989)
Assets: $3,873,287 (1991);
$3,543,551 (1990); $3,555,735
(1989)
Gifts Received: $500 (1991)
EIN: 25-0965465

CONTRIBUTIONS SUMMARY
Typical Recipients: • *Arts & Humanities:* libraries • *Education:* literacy • *Religion:* religious organizations • *Social Services:* child welfare, community service organizations, drugs & alcohol, family planning, family services, recreation & athletics, united funds, youth organizations
Grant Types: project and research
Geographic Distribution: limited to western PA, northern WV, and eastern OH

GIVING OFFICERS
Brigitte Alexander: exec dir
Rose M. Alvin: off
Mark B. Aronson: off
Alan A. Axelson: treas
Irvin Chamovitz, M.D.: trust
Joseph T. Christy: off
Joseph Daugerdas: trust
Judith M. Davenport: trust, secy
Mona N. Generett: trust
Munro J. Grant: trust, pres
David B. Hartmann, M.D.: trust
John D. Houston II: trust, vp
Janet F. Kreiger: trust
Ann P. Leibrick: off
Don A. Linzer: trust
A. Thomas McLamore: trust
Evelyn L. Murrin: off
Regis Murrin: trust
Marie Ford Reilly: trust
Karen VanderVen: off

APPLICATION INFORMATION
Initial Approach: Contact foundation before submitting a proposal. Deadlines are March 1, June 1, and November 1.
Restrictions on Giving: Does not support individuals.

OTHER THINGS TO KNOW
Publications: Informational Brochure (including Application Guidelines), Application Guidelines, Informational Brochure, grants list

GRANTS ANALYSIS
Number of Grants: 16
Highest Grant: $50,328
Typical Range: $3,000 to $7,500
Disclosure Period: 1991

RECENT GRANTS
50,328 Three Rivers Rowing Association, Pittsburgh, PA — to support the third year of a year-around Youth Rowing Program for children ages 10 to 16 from inner-city neighborhoods
36,250 Action-Housing, Pittsburgh, PA
7,500 D.T. Watson Rehabilitation Services, Sewickley, PA
7,500 Easter Seal Society, Pittsburgh, PA — to support children who have severely impaired siblings and to train staff to conduct support groups for these children
7,500 Youth Opportunities Unlimited, Pittsburgh, PA
5,100 Crisis Addition Recovery and Education Center, Washington, PA
5,000 East End Cooperative Ministry, Pittsburgh, PA — to support the Life Learning Curriculum in a summer day camp program for children ages 5 to 16 in the East End of Pittsburgh
4,965 Renaissance Center, Pittsburgh, PA — to evaluate a new program whose purpose is to develop parenting skills in mentally ill parents of young children
4,300 Progress for Female Offenders, Pittsburgh, PA — to provide individual play therapy for selected preschool children whose mothers are in the custody of County Prison Board
3,000 Three Rivers Adoption Council, Pittsburgh, PA — to provide counseling and support services to foster and adoptive families in crisis

Pittsburgh & Midway Coal Mining Co.
Sales: $350.0 million
Employees: 1,500
Headquarters: Englewood, CO
SIC Major Group: Coal Mining

CONTACT
Fred Neuer
Public Affairs
Pittsburgh & Midway Coal Mining Co.
PO Box 6518
Englewood, CO 80155-6518
(303) 930-3600

CONTRIBUTIONS SUMMARY
Operating Locations: CO (Englewood)

CORP. OFFICERS
Barry G. McGrath: *CURR EMPL* pres: Pittsburgh & Midway Coal Mining Co

Pittsburgh National Bank / Pittsburgh National Bank Foundation
Assets: $51.37 billion
Employees: 17,809
Parent Company: PNC Financial Corp.
Headquarters: Pittsburgh, PA
SIC Major Group: Depository Institutions

CONTACT
D. Paul Beard
Secretary, Distribution Committee
Pittsburgh National Bank Fdn.
5th Ave. & Wood St.
Pittsburgh, PA 15222
(412) 762-4222

FINANCIAL SUMMARY
Recent Giving: $2,006,260 (1992 approx.); $2,026,162 (1991); $1,908,588 (1990)
Assets: $5,744,355 (1991); $5,386,895 (1990); $5,047,875 (1988)
Fiscal Note: Giving is through the foundation only.
EIN: 25-1202255

CONTRIBUTIONS SUMMARY
Typical Recipients: • *Arts & Humanities:* arts associations, arts centers, arts festivals, community arts, history/historic preservation, libraries, literary arts, museums/galleries, music, opera, performing arts, public broadcasting, theater • *Civic & Public Affairs:* business/free enterprise, economic development, ethnic/minority organizations, housing, philanthropic organizations, professional & trade associations, safety, urban & community affairs, zoos/botanical gardens • *Education:* colleges & universities, education associations, education funds, literacy, private education (precollege) • *Health:* hospices, hospitals, medical rehabilitation, single-disease health associations • *Social Services:* aged, child welfare, community centers, community service organizations, delinquency & crime, disabled, domestic violence, employment/job training, food/clothing distribution, legal aid, recreation & athletics, shelters/homelessness, united funds, youth organizations

Grant Types: capital, employee matching gifts, general support, and multiyear/continuing support
Geographic Distribution: metropolitan Pittsburgh; surrounding communities of Allegheny County
Operating Locations: PA (Blairsville, California, Cannonsburg, Charleroi, Connellsville, Elizabeth, Homestead, Indiana, McDonald, McKees Rocks, Pittsburgh, Sewickley, Somerset, Springdale, Washington)
Note: Operates in 114 locations in southwestern Pennsylvania.

CORP. OFFICERS
Joe Robert Irwin: *B* Madison WI 1936 *ED* Univ WI BS 1958 *CURR EMPL* pres, dir: Pittsburgh Natl Bank *CORP AFFIL* chmn: PNC Intl Investment Corp; chmn, ceo: PNC Intl Bank; dir: Dinamo, Girls Hope *NONPR AFFIL* dir: Blue Cross Western PA, Civic Light Opera; instructor: Bankers Assn Sch Fin Mgmt; lecturer: Univ WI Madison; mem: Greater Pittsburgh Chamber Commerce; mem exec comm: PA Economy League; dir: Ruffed Grouse Soc Club; treas: Pittsburgh Sportsmens Luncheon Club
James Edward Rohr: *B* Cleveland OH 1948 *ED* Univ Notre Dame BA 1970; OH St Univ MBA 1972 *CURR EMPL* chmn, ceo, dir: Pittsburgh Natl Bank *CORP AFFIL* dir: Allegheny Ludlum Corp, Davison Sand & Gravel, Pvt Export Funding Corp, SHERCORP; pres: PNC Fin Corp *NONPR AFFIL* adv bd: Salvation Army; dir: Am Cancer Soc Greater Pittsburgh Unit, Shadyside Hosp, St Vincent Coll, Un Way; mem: Am Bankers Assn, Robert Morris Assocs

GIVING OFFICERS
D. Paul Beard: treas *CURR EMPL* sr vp (control div): Pittsburgh Natl Bank
Joe Robert Irwin: pres *CURR EMPL* pres, dir: Pittsburgh Natl Bank (see above)
Edward Vincent Randall, Jr.: chmn distribution comm *B* Waterbury CT 1932 *ED* Brown Univ 1956 *CURR EMPL* exec vp: Pittsburgh Natl Bank *CORP AFFIL* dir: PNC Natl Bank *NONPR AFFIL* chmn: Am Mgmt Assn, Pittsburgh

Partnership Neighborhood Devel
William Strome: secy

APPLICATION INFORMATION
Initial Approach: *Initial Contact:* brief letter or proposal *Include Information On:* description of the organization, amount requested, purpose for which funds are sought, recently audited financial statement, proof of tax-exempt status, list of officers and directors *When to Submit:* any time, except July
Restrictions on Giving: Foundation does not award scholarships or make grants to individuals.

GRANTS ANALYSIS
Total Grants: $2,026,162
Number of Grants: 348
Highest Grant: $550,000
Typical Range: $500 to $5,000
Disclosure Period: 1991
Note: Figure for average grant does not include the two highest grants of $120,000 and $550,000. Recent grants are derived from a 1991 Form 990.

RECENT GRANTS
550,000 United Way of Southwestern Pennsylvania, Pittsburgh, PA
120,000 University of Pittsburgh, Pittsburgh, PA
94,750 The Carnegie, Pittsburgh, PA
60,000 Carnegie-Mellon University, Pittsburgh, PA
60,000 Penn's Southwest Association, Pittsburgh, PA
50,000 Duquesne University, Pittsburgh, PA
50,000 Pittsburgh Partnership for Neighborhood Development, Pittsburgh, PA
40,000 Pittsburgh Opera, Pittsburgh, PA
30,000 Allegheny Conference on Community Development, Pittsburgh, PA
30,000 Pennsylvania State University, University Park, PA

Pittston Co.
Sales: $1.92 billion
Employees: 20,100
Headquarters: Stamford, CT
SIC Major Group: Business Services, Coal Mining,

Transportation by Air, and Transportation Services

CONTACT
Frank Lennon
V.P., Administration and Human Resources
Pittston Co.
100 First Stamford Pl.
PO Box 120070
Stamford, CT 06912
(203) 978-5200

CONTRIBUTIONS SUMMARY
Operating Locations: CA (Irvine), CT (Darien, Greenwich, Stamford), KY (Stone), TX (Carrollton), VA (Abingdon, Jewell Ridge, Lebanon), WV (Beckley, Lyburn)

CORP. OFFICERS
William J. Byrne, Jr.: *CURR EMPL* pres: Pittston Co
Paul W. Douglas: *B* Springfield MA 1926 *ED* Princeton Univ 1948 *CURR EMPL* chmn, ceo, dir: Pittston Co *CORP AFFIL* dir: NY Life Ins, Phelps Dodge, Philip Morris; trust: US Trust Co NY
David L. Marshall: *CURR EMPL* vchmn, cfo: Pittston Co

Pittulloch Foundation

CONTACT
Pittulloch Fdn.
250 East Ponce De Leon Avenue, Ste. 501
Decatur, GA 30031

FINANCIAL SUMMARY
Recent Giving: $400,800 (1991); $295,050 (1990); $118,750 (1989)
Assets: $11,151,081 (1991); $7,019,542 (1990); $6,755,553 (1989)
Gifts Received: $482,217 (1991); $641,733 (1990); $544,912 (1989)
Fiscal Note: In 1991, contributions were received from The Pattillo Split-Interest Trust ($287,217), Rockdale Industries, Inc. ($90,000), and Stone Mountain Industrial Park, Inc. ($105,000).
EIN: 58-1651352

CONTRIBUTIONS SUMMARY
Donor(s): Stone Mountain Industrial Park, Inc., Pattillo Split Interest Trust
Typical Recipients: • *Arts & Humanities:* community arts,

history/historic preservation, museums/galleries, music • *Civic & Public Affairs:* zoos/botanical gardens • *Education:* colleges & universities, religious education • *Social Services:* youth organizations
Grant Types: general support
Geographic Distribution: focus on Atlanta, GA

GIVING OFFICERS
John Walter Drake: secy
Warren Yancey Jobe: dir *B* Burlington NC 1940 *ED* Univ NC 1963 *CURR EMPL* exec vp, cfo, dir: GA Power Co *CORP AFFIL* dir: Piedmont-Forrest Corp, S Electric Generating Co; dir, mem exec com: Oglethorpe Univ, YMCA of Metro Atlanta; treas: Southeastern Electric Exchange *NONPR AFFIL* mem: Am Inst CPAs, Atlanta Chamber Commerce, Fin Execs Inst, GA Soc CPAs, NC CPA Soc, Soc Intl Bus Fellows; mem adv bd: GA S Univ Sch Bus, N Arts Ctr; mem funding bd: Success by Six; trust: Dekalb Counc on Econ Ed
Elizabeth M. Pattillo: dir
H. G. Pattillo: chmn, dir
Lynn L. Pattillo: pres, treas, dir
Robert A. Pattillo: dir
George L. Simpson: vchmn, dir

APPLICATION INFORMATION
Initial Approach: Contributes only to preselected organizations.
Restrictions on Giving: Does not support individuals.

GRANTS ANALYSIS
Number of Grants: 35
Highest Grant: $80,000
Typical Range: $1,000 to $6,000
Disclosure Period: 1991

RECENT GRANTS
80,000 Emory University, Atlanta, GA
70,000 Berry College, Rome, GA
26,000 Berry College, Rome, GA
25,000 Georgia State University, Atlanta, GA
25,000 Leadership Georgia, Atlanta, GA
15,000 Fernbank Museum of Natural History, Atlanta, GA
10,000 Boys and Girls Club, Dekalb, GA
10,000 State Botanical Garden of Georgia, Atlanta, GA

5,000 Foundation of Wesley Woods, Atlanta, GA
5,000 Georgetown University, Washington, DC

Pittway Corp. / Pittway Corp. Charitable Foundation

Sales: $568.3 million
Employees: 4,500
Headquarters: Chicago, IL
SIC Major Group: Electronic & Other Electrical Equipment, Fabricated Metal Products, Printing & Publishing, and Wholesale Trade—Durable Goods

CONTACT
King Harris
Vice President, Director
Pittway Corp. Charitable Fdn.
200 S Wacker St., Ste. 700
Chicago, IL 60606
(312) 831-1070

FINANCIAL SUMMARY
Recent Giving: $1,000,000 (fiscal 1993 est.); $1,152,655 (fiscal 1992); $1,198,290 (fiscal 1991)
Assets: $5,625,000 (fiscal year ending February 28, 1992); $5,253,586 (fiscal 1990)
Fiscal Note: Figures are for foundation, the company's principal philanthropic vehicle. Modest contribution budgets are also administered by subsidiaries. 1991 figure includes both matching and direct giving.
EIN: 36-6149938

CONTRIBUTIONS SUMMARY
Typical Recipients: • *Arts & Humanities:* arts associations, arts centers, arts institutes, history/historic preservation, museums/galleries, music, opera, performing arts, theater, visual arts • *Civic & Public Affairs:* better government, civil rights, economic development, ethnic/minority organizations, housing, international affairs, law & justice, philanthropic organizations, professional & trade associations, public policy, safety, urban & community affairs, women's affairs, zoos/botanical gardens • *Education:* arts education, business education, colleges & universities, economic education, edu-

cation associations, education funds, elementary education, international studies, literacy, medical education, minority education, private education (precollege), science/technology education, social sciences education, student aid • *Health:* health funds, hospices, hospitals, medical research, mental health, nursing services, pediatric health, single-disease health associations • *Science:* observatories & planetariums, scientific organizations • *Social Services:* child welfare, community service organizations, drugs & alcohol, family planning, family services, food/clothing distribution, religious welfare, united funds, youth organizations
Grant Types: employee matching gifts and general support
Geographic Distribution: emphasis on communities near company's manufacturing sites
Operating Locations: CT (Stamford), FL (Clearwater, Davie, Dunedin, Wesley Chapel), IL (Chicago, St. Charles), NY (New York, Syosset), OH (Cleveland), WI (Mukwonago)

CORP. OFFICERS
Leo A. Guthart: *B* New York NY 1937 *ED* Harvard Univ 1958; Harvard Univ MBA 1960 *CURR EMPL* vchmn, dir: Pittway Corp *CORP AFFIL* dir: Standard Shares
Irving Brooks Harris: *B* St Paul MN 1910 *ED* Yale Univ AB 1931 *CURR EMPL* chmn exec comm, dir: Pittway Corp *CORP AFFIL* chmn: Acorn Fund, William Harris Investors, Harris Realty; dir: Tera Pharmaceuticals Indus; pres: William Harris & Co, Standard Shares *NONPR AFFIL* chmn advisory bd: IL Dept Children & Family Svcs; chmn emeritus: Erickson Inst, Family Focus; co-fdr: Ounce Prevention Fund; hon chmn: Chicago Pediatric Soc; trust: Am Jewish Comm, Ed Television Assn, IL Competitive Access & Reimbursement Equity, Natl Ctr Clinical Infant Programs, Univ Chicago; vchmn: Govs Task Force Future Mental Health IL
King William Harris: *B* 1943 *ED* Harvard Univ BA 1965; Harvard Univ MBA 1969 *CURR EMPL* pres, ceo, dir: Pittway Corp *CORP AFFIL* dir: Standard Shares

Richard Neison Harris: *B* St Paul MN 1915 *ED* Yale Univ AB 1936 *CURR EMPL* chmn, dir: Pittway Corp *CORP AFFIL* chmn, dir: Standard Shares

GIVING OFFICERS
Eugene Barnett: dir
Sidney Barrows: dir
Paul Richard Gauvreau: treas *B* Chicago IL 1939 *ED* Loyola Univ 1961; Univ Chicago 1976 *CURR EMPL* vp fin, treas: Pittway Corp *CORP AFFIL* dir: Penton Learning Sys; pres, ceo: Pittway Real Estate; pres, dir: Pittway Leasing Co; treas: Curtin & Pease, Domestic Intl Sales Corp; treas, dir: BRK Electronics, Indus Publ Co, Power Publ Co; vp, treas: Pittway Corp Canada Ltd; vp, treas, dir: Family Gard, Penton Publ Co
Irving Brooks Harris: chmn, dir *CURR EMPL* chmn exec comm, dir: Pittway Corp (see above)
King William Harris: vp, dir *CURR EMPL* pres, ceo, dir: Pittway Corp (see above)
Richard Neison Harris: pres, dir *CURR EMPL* chmn, dir: Pittway Corp (see above)
William W. Harris: dir *CORP AFFIL* dir: Pittway Corp
Joseph Sclafani: secy

APPLICATION INFORMATION
Initial Approach: *Initial Contact:* brief letter or proposal *Include Information On:* description of the organization, amount requested, purpose for which funds are sought, recently audited financial statement, and proof of tax-exempt status *When to Submit:* any time
Restrictions on Giving: The foundation does not support individuals or organizations located outside the United States.

OTHER THINGS TO KNOW
In 1992, company restructured its business groups. It sold its First Alert/BRK security products business and its Barr contract packaging business. It also announced plans to spin off its Seaquist Group and to combine it with the Pfeiffer Group. Pittway Corp. Also purchased MicroLite, a lighting control business, and two magazines, *Food Management* and *Show Dailies*.

GRANTS ANALYSIS
Total Grants: $1,152,655
Number of Grants: 143*
Highest Grant: $250,000
Typical Range: $500 to $10,000
Disclosure Period: fiscal year ending February 28, 1992
Note: Number of grants and average grant excludes 405 matching grants totaling $161,372. Recent grants are derived from a fiscal 1991 Form 990.

RECENT GRANTS
325,000 Ounce of Prevention Fund, Chicago, IL
77,100 Family Focus, Chicago, IL
50,000 Ounce of Prevention Of Florida, FL
45,000 United Way Services, Cleveland, OH
39,500 University of Chicago, Chicago, IL
27,600 DePauw University, Greencastle, IN
25,000 National Center for Clinical Infant Program, Washington, DC
25,000 National Public Radio, Washington, DC
22,550 Chicago United, Chicago, IL
17,000 French American Foundation, New York, NY

Pitzman Fund

CONTACT
Roy T. Blair
Pitzman Fund
c/o Boatmen's Trust Co. of St. Louis
100 North Broadway
PO Box 14737
St. Louis, MO 63178
(314) 466-3416

FINANCIAL SUMMARY
Recent Giving: $110,626 (fiscal 1991); $54,500 (fiscal 1990); $105,500 (fiscal 1989)
Assets: $2,437,440 (fiscal year ending September 30, 1991); $2,045,505 (fiscal 1990); $2,305,296 (fiscal 1989)
EIN: 43-6023901

CONTRIBUTIONS SUMMARY
Donor(s): the late Frederick Pitzman
Typical Recipients: • *Civic & Public Affairs:* zoos/botanical gardens • *Education:* colleges & universities, private educa-

tion (precollege) • *Health:* health organizations, hospitals, mental health, pediatric health • *Religion:* churches • *Science:* scientific institutes • *Social Services:* community service organizations, counseling, disabled, drugs & alcohol, family planning, family services, united funds, youth organizations

Grant Types: general support and multiyear/continuing support

Geographic Distribution: focus on St. Louis, MO

GIVING OFFICERS

Pauline S. Eades: trust

Robert H. McRoberts: trust

APPLICATION INFORMATION

Initial Approach: Send brief letter describing program. There are no deadlines.

GRANTS ANALYSIS

Number of Grants: 65

Highest Grant: $10,000

Typical Range: $500 to $6,000

Disclosure Period: fiscal year ending September 30, 1991

RECENT GRANTS

- 10,000 Board of Trustees of Missouri Botanical Garden, St. Louis, MO
- 6,000 National Council on Alcoholism, St. Louis, MO
- 5,000 Planned Parenthood Federation of America, St. Louis, MO
- 3,000 Central Presbyterian Church, St. Louis, MO
- 2,000 Mental Health Association, St. Louis, MO
- 2,000 New City Schools, St. Louis, MO
- 2,000 Soulard Association for Family Services, St. Louis, MO
- 2,000 Soulard Association for Family Services, St. Louis, MO
- 2,000 St. Louis Science Center, St. Louis, MO
- 2,000 St. Louis Society for Crippled Children, St. Louis, MO

Pizza Hut

Sales: $2.94 billion
Employees: 130,000
Parent Company: Pepsico Inc.
Headquarters: Wichita, KS
SIC Major Group: Eating & Drinking Places and Holding & Other Investment Offices

CONTACT

Eunice Ellis
National Director
Pizza Hut
PO Box 428
Wichita, KS 67201-0428
(316) 681-9000

CONTRIBUTIONS SUMMARY

Operating Locations: KS (Wichita)

CORP. OFFICERS

Steve S. Reinemund: *CURR EMPL* ceo, pres: Pizza Hut

PK Lumber Co.

Parent Company: ERB Lumber Co.
Headquarters: Birmingham, MI
SIC Major Group: Building Materials & Garden Supplies and Lumber & Wood Products

CONTACT

PK Lumber Co.
375 South Eton
Birmingham, MI 48009
(313) 644-5300

CONTRIBUTIONS SUMMARY

Operating Locations: MI (Birmingham)

Note: company has retail operations throughout Ohio

OTHER THINGS TO KNOW

Company is an original donor to the Kuntz Foundation.

Placid Oil Co.

Sales: $140.0 million
Employees: 335
Headquarters: Dallas, TX
SIC Major Group: Oil & Gas Extraction and Petroleum & Coal Products

CONTACT

R.M. Adkins
Director, Human Resources
Placid Oil Co.
3800 Thanksgiving Tower
Dallas, TX 75201
(214) 880-1000

CONTRIBUTIONS SUMMARY

Operating Locations: TX (Dallas)

CORP. OFFICERS

Walter Fraker: *CURR EMPL* pres: Placid Oil Co

Plankenhorn Foundation, Harry

CONTACT

Abram M. Snyder
Trustee, Director
Harry Plankenhorn Fdn.
R.D. 2
Cogan Station, PA 17728

FINANCIAL SUMMARY

Recent Giving: $236,507 (1991); $214,459 (1990); $211,944 (1989)
Assets: $3,917,271 (1991); $3,529,176 (1990); $3,891,184 (1989)
Gifts Received: $300 (1991)
Fiscal Note: In 1991, contributions were received from Ruth Askoy ($100), and Mike Sanders ($200).
EIN: 24-6023579

CONTRIBUTIONS SUMMARY

Donor(s): the late Harry Plankenhorn
Typical Recipients: • *Health:* mental health, single-disease health associations • *Religion:* churches • *Social Services:* child welfare, community service organizations, counseling, disabled, emergency relief, family services, united funds, youth organizations
Grant Types: general support
Geographic Distribution: focus on Lycoming County, PA

GIVING OFFICERS

John H. Archer: off
Grove W. Deming: trust
Rev. Bruce Druckenmiller: trust
Barbara Ertel: trust
Fred A. Foulkrod: trust
A. William Gehron: off
Charles F. Greevy III: dir, vp
Phillip D. Paterson, Jr.: asst secy
W. Herbert Poff III: trust

Dean F. Rabert: off
Carl H. Sump: dir, secy
Abram M. Synder: dir, treas
Lucinda A. Wagner: trust
Eleanor W. Whiting: trust

APPLICATION INFORMATION

Initial Approach: Send brief letter describing program. There are no deadlines.

GRANTS ANALYSIS

Number of Grants: 29
Highest Grant: $80,000
Typical Range: $1,000 to $5,000
Disclosure Period: 1991

RECENT GRANTS

- 80,000 Lycoming County Association for the Blind, Lycoming, PA
- 55,000 Emergency Aid, PA
- 22,500 American Rescue Workers, Philadelphia, PA
- 22,500 Salvation Army, PA
- 10,000 Family Life Institute, PA
- 10,000 YMCA, Williamsport, PA
- 5,000 Camp Kiwanis for Underprivileged Children, Philadelphia, PA
- 5,000 Salvation Army, PA
- 3,000 Eleanor Bower Agency, PA
- 3,000 Multiple Sclerosis Society, New York, NY

Planning Research Corp.

Revenue: $684.0 million
Employees: 7,200
Parent Company: Black and Decker Corp.
Headquarters: McLean, VA
SIC Major Group: Business Services

CONTACT

Karen Vahouny
Director, Communications
Planning Research Corp.
1500 PRC Dr.
McLean, VA 22102
(703) 556-1049

FINANCIAL SUMMARY

Fiscal Note: Company does not disclose contributions figures.

CONTRIBUTIONS SUMMARY

Operating Locations: VA (McLean)

CORP. OFFICERS
Wayne Shelton: *B* Minneapolis MN 1932 *ED* Univ MN 1954-1956 *CURR EMPL* chmn, pres, ceo: Planning Res Corp *CORP AFFIL* vp: Emhart Corp

GRANTS ANALYSIS
Typical Range: $50 to $1,000

Plant Memorial Fund, Henry B.

CONTACT
Edward B. Sullivan
Henry B. Plant Memorial Fund
c/o U.S. Trust Co. of New York
114 West 47th St.
New York, NY 10036-1532

FINANCIAL SUMMARY
Recent Giving: $275,000 (1991); $277,000 (1990); $250,040 (1989)
Assets: $6,746,382 (1991); $5,591,913 (1990); $6,381,979 (1989)
EIN: 13-6077327

CONTRIBUTIONS SUMMARY
Donor(s): Amy P. Statter
Typical Recipients: • *Arts & Humanities:* museums/galleries • *Civic & Public Affairs:* environmental affairs • *Education:* colleges & universities, private education (precollege) • *Health:* health organizations, hospitals • *Religion:* churches • *Social Services:* community service organizations, family services
Grant Types: general support
Geographic Distribution: focus on NY

GIVING OFFICERS
Mrs. J. Philip Lee: pres
Phyllis S. Oxman: vp

APPLICATION INFORMATION
Initial Approach: Send brief letter of inquiry describing program or project. There are no deadlines.

GRANTS ANALYSIS
Number of Grants: 67
Highest Grant: $50,000
Typical Range: $250 to $5,000
Disclosure Period: 1991

RECENT GRANTS
50,000 St. George's School
20,000 Friends Academy, North Dartmouth, MA
10,000 Mystic Museum, Mystic, CT

10,000 New Bedford Whaling Museum, New Bedford, MA
10,000 Sea Education Association, Woods Hole, MA
7,500 Christ Church, Greenwich, CT
5,000 African Team Ministries, Sierra Madre, CA
5,000 Chewonki Foundation, Wiscasset, ME
5,000 Family Dynamics, New York, NY
5,000 Planned Parenthood Federation of America, New York, NY

Plante & Moran, CPAs

Revenue: $48.7 million
Employees: 300
Headquarters: Southfield, MI
SIC Major Group: Engineering & Management Services

CONTACT
William J. Bufe
Personnel Partner
Plante & Moran, CPAs
27400 Norhtwestern Highway,
PO Box 307
Southfield, MI 48037
(313) 352-2500

CONTRIBUTIONS SUMMARY
Company sponsors employee matching gift program; also supports community organizations.

Typical Recipients: • *Arts & Humanities:* general • *Civic & Public Affairs:* general • *Education:* general • *Health:* general • *Social Services:* general

Grant Types: matching

Geographic Distribution: primarily headquarters area

Operating Locations: MI (Southfield)

CORP. OFFICERS
Douglas Brady: *CURR EMPL* cfo: Plante & Moran CPAs

Edward M. Parks: *CURR EMPL* ptnr: Plante & Moran

APPLICATION INFORMATION
Initial Approach: Send brief letter of inquiry. There are no deadlines.

Plantronics, Inc.

Sales: $180.0 million
Employees: 1,100
Headquarters: Santa Cruz, CA
SIC Major Group: Electronic & Other Electrical Equipment

CONTACT
Debbie Meretith
Human Resources Specialist
Plantronics, Inc.
PO Box 1802
Santa Cruz, CA 95061-1802
(408) 426-5858

FINANCIAL SUMMARY
Fiscal Note: Annual Giving Range: less than $100,000

CONTRIBUTIONS SUMMARY
Cash program is small, targeting community organizations. Also matches employee gifts and provides in-kind support.
Typical Recipients: • *Arts & Humanities:* general • *Civic & Public Affairs:* general • *Education:* general • *Health:* general • *Social Services:* youth organizations
Grant Types: general support and matching
Nonmonetary Support Types: donated equipment, in-kind services, and loaned executives
Geographic Distribution: headquarters area
Operating Locations: CA (Santa Cruz)

CORP. OFFICERS
Robert Cecil: *CURR EMPL* pres, ceo: Plantronics
Lawrence W. Ward, Jr.: *CURR EMPL* cfo: Plantronics

APPLICATION INFORMATION
Initial Approach: Send letter including need and budget information.

Plaster Foundation, Robert W.

CONTACT
Robert W. Plaster Fdn.
PO Box 129
Lebanon, MO 65536

FINANCIAL SUMMARY
Recent Giving: $525,000 (fiscal 1991); $281,000 (fiscal 1990); $452,500 (fiscal 1989)
Assets: $2,950,550 (fiscal year ending November 30, 1991); $2,786,175 (fiscal 1990); $2,837,220 (fiscal 1989)

EIN: 43-1369856

CONTRIBUTIONS SUMMARY
Donor(s): Robert W. Plaster
Typical Recipients: • *Arts & Humanities:* history/historic preservation • *Civic & Public Affairs:* environmental affairs • *Education:* colleges & universities, education associations, private education (precollege) • *Religion:* churches, religious organizations
Grant Types: general support
Geographic Distribution: focus on MO

GIVING OFFICERS
Dolly Frances: trust
Lynn C. Hoover: trust
Robert W. Plaster: pres, treas
Stephen R. Plaster: vp, secy
Tammy Plaster: trust
Cheryl I. Schaefer: trust

APPLICATION INFORMATION
Initial Approach: Contributes only to preselected organizations.

Restrictions on Giving: Does not support individuals.

GRANTS ANALYSIS
Number of Grants: 3
Highest Grant: $500,000
Typical Range: $10,000 to $15,000
Disclosure Period: fiscal year ending November 30, 1991

RECENT GRANTS
500,000 Southwest Missouri State University Foundation, MO
15,000 Southwest Baptist University, Boliver, MO
10,000 Crowder College Foundation, Neosho, MO

Plastics Engineering Co.

Sales: $50.0 million
Employees: 400
Headquarters: Sheboygan, WI
SIC Major Group: Chemicals & Allied Products and Rubber & Miscellaneous Plastics Products

CONTACT

Frank Brotz
Donations and Office Manager
Plastics Engineering Co.
PO Box 758
Sheboygan, WI 53082-0758
(414) 458-2121

CONTRIBUTIONS SUMMARY

Operating Locations: WI (Sheboygan)

CORP. OFFICERS

R. T. Brotz: *CURR EMPL* pres: Plastics Engring Co

OTHER THINGS TO KNOW

Company is an original donor to the Frank G. Brotz Family Foundation.

Playboy Enterprises, Inc. / Playboy Foundation

Revenue: $174.0 million
Employees: 619
Headquarters: Chicago, IL
SIC Major Group:
Communications, Holding & Other Investment Offices, Motion Pictures, and Printing & Publishing

CONTACT

Cleo Wilson
Executive Director
Playboy Fdn.
680 North Lakeshore Dr.
Chicago, IL 60611
(312) 751-8000

FINANCIAL SUMMARY

Recent Giving: $410,000 (1993 est.); $305,000 (1992); $308,000 (1991)
Fiscal Note: Contributes through foundation only.

CONTRIBUTIONS SUMMARY

Typical Recipients: • *Arts & Humanities:* cinema, community arts, ethnic arts, public broadcasting • *Civic & Public Affairs:* civil rights, first amendment issues, law & justice, national security, philanthropic organizations, professional & trade associations, public policy, women's affairs • *Education:* journalism education • *Health:* hospices, medical research, public health, single-disease health associations • *Social Services:* aged, child welfare, community centers, community service organizations, delinquency & crime, disabled, domestic violence, employment/job training, family planning, legal aid, refugee assistance, shelters/homelessness, youth organizations
Nonmonetary Support Types: donated equipment
Note: Estimated yearly value of nonmonetary support is $200,000. This is not included in the total contributions figure.
Geographic Distribution: nationally
Operating Locations: CA (Los Angeles), IL (Chicago), NY (New York)

CORP. OFFICERS

Christie A. Hefner: *B* Chicago IL 1952 *ED* Brandeis Univ 1974 *CURR EMPL* chmn, ceo: Playboy Enterprises *NONPR AFFIL* dir: Am Civil Liberties Union IL Chapter, Magazine Publs Assn; mem: Brandeis Natl Womens Comm, Chicago Network, Comm 2000, Democratic Natl Comm Fin Counc, Goodman Theatre, Voters Choice, Young Pres Org
Hugh M. Hefner: *B* Chicago IL 1926 *ED* Univ IL BS 1949 *CURR EMPL* chmn emeritus: Playboy Enterprises *CORP AFFIL* dir: Playboy Clubs Intl; publ, editor-in-chief: Playboy Magazine

GIVING OFFICERS

Christie A. Hefner: dir *CURR EMPL* chmn, ceo: Playboy Enterprises (see above)
Burton Joseph: chmn, dir *ED* City Univ NY Brooklyn Coll
Cleo A. Wilson: exec dir

APPLICATION INFORMATION

Initial Approach: *Initial Contact:* brief letter of inquiry *Include Information On:* description of the organization, amount requested, purpose of funds sought, audited financial statement, and proof of tax-exempt status *When to Submit:* any time
Restrictions on Giving: Does not support individuals, religious organizations for sectarian purposes, scholarships, or political or lobbying groups.

OTHER THINGS TO KNOW

Also provides printing and design services, and public service advertising space in *Playboy* magazine.

Publications: foundation annual report

GRANTS ANALYSIS

Typical Range: $5,000 to $10,000
Disclosure Period: 1993
Note: No grants list provided for 1993.

Plitt Southern Theatres / Plitt Southern Theatres, Inc., Employees Fund

Headquarters: Los Angeles, CA

CONTACT

Joe S. Jackson
President
Plitt Southern Theatres, Inc., Employees Fund
1801 Century Park East, Ste. 1225
Los Angeles, CA 90067
(310) 553-5307

FINANCIAL SUMMARY

Recent Giving: $687,794 (1991); $620,284 (1990); $938,752 (1989)
Assets: $6,873,850 (1991); $6,519,598 (1990); $7,121,687 (1989)
Fiscal Note: Contributes through fund only.
EIN: 75-6037855

CONTRIBUTIONS SUMMARY

Typical Recipients: • *Arts & Humanities:* arts associations, cinema, music • *Civic & Public Affairs:* law & justice • *Education:* colleges & universities, science/technology education • *Health:* health organizations, hospitals, single-disease health associations • *International:* international organizations • *Social Services:* child welfare, youth organizations
Grant Types: general support, loan, and research
Geographic Distribution: nationally, with emphasis on California
Operating Locations: CA (Los Angeles)

CORP. OFFICERS

Roy Henry Aaron: *B* Los Angeles CA 1929 *ED* Univ CA Berkeley BA 1951; Univ Southern CA LLB 1956 *CURR EMPL* pres, ceo, dir: Showscan Film Corp *CORP AFFIL* pres, ceo, dir: Showscan Film Corp; pres, coo, dir: Plitt Entertainment Group *NONPR AFFIL* dir: Beverly Hills Bar Assn, Fdn Motion Picture Pioneers, Legion Lex, Univ CA Los Angeles Fdn, Univ Southern CA Law Alumni Assn, Women Lawyers Los Angeles

GIVING OFFICERS

Roy Henry Aaron: trust *CURR EMPL* pres, ceo, dir: Showscan Film Corp (see above)
W. R. Curtis: vp, secy, treas, trust
Raymond C. Fox: trust *B* New York NY 1930 *ED* Villanova Univ 1952; NY Univ 1957 *CURR EMPL* sr vp, dir: Plitt Entertainment Group *CORP AFFIL* sr vp, dir: Plitt Entertainment Group; sr vp, secy, dir: Showscan Film Corp
Joe S. Jackson: pres, trust
Henry G. Plitt: trust

APPLICATION INFORMATION

Initial Approach: *Note:* The foundation supports preselected organizations and does not accept unsolicited requests for funds.

GRANTS ANALYSIS

Total Grants: $687,794
Number of Grants: 31*
Highest Grant: $40,000
Typical Range: $2,000 to $11,000
Disclosure Period: 1991
Note: Number of grants and average grant figures do not include grants to individuals totaling $393,043. Recent grants are derived from a 1991 grants list.

RECENT GRANTS

40,000 Bar-Ilan University, New York, NY
30,000 Shaare Zeddek, Los Angeles, CA
25,000 Dallas Summer Musicals, Dallas, TX
25,000 Israel Defense Fund, Los Angeles, CA
25,000 St. Jude's Hospital Foundation, Los Angeles, CA
25,000 Variety Club International, Los Angeles, CA
22,000 American Film Institute, Los Angeles, CA
11,000 Foundation of Motion Pictures Pioneers, Los Angeles, CA
10,000 Share, Los Angeles, CA

10,000 Stop Cancer, Los Angeles, CA

Plough Foundation

CONTACT
Noris R. Haynes, Jr.
Executive Director and Trustee
Plough Foundation
6077 Primacy Pkwy., Ste. 230
Memphis, TN 38119
(901) 761-9180

FINANCIAL SUMMARY
Recent Giving: $4,400,000 (1993 est.); $2,601,387 (1992); $3,809,000 (1991)
Assets: $89,000,000 (1991); $75,235,012 (1990); $74,684,084 (1989)
Gifts Received: $825,000 (1991 est.); $575,000 (1990); $800,238 (1989)
Fiscal Note: Contributions have been made by Plough family members Patricia R. Burnham and Jocelyn P. Rudner.
EIN: 23-7175983

CONTRIBUTIONS SUMMARY
Donor(s): The Plough Foundation was established in 1960, with funds donated by the late Abe Plough. In 1920, Abe Plough bought the St. Joseph Company of Chattanooga, TN, best known as the manufacturer of children's aspirin. He eventually bought twenty-seven companies. A 1971 merger with the Schering pharmaceutical company resulted in the formation of the Schering-Plough Corporation.
Typical Recipients: • *Arts & Humanities:* museums/galleries, music • *Civic & Public Affairs:* economic development • *Education:* arts education, colleges & universities, elementary education, medical education, preschool education, public education (precollege) • *Health:* outpatient health care delivery • *Religion:* religious organizations • *Social Services:* child welfare, community service organizations, food/clothing distribution, religious welfare, shelters/homelessness, united funds, youth organizations
Grant Types: capital, challenge, department, endowment, fellowship, general support, project, and seed money
Geographic Distribution: primarily in Shelby County and Memphis, TN

GIVING OFFICERS
Hallam Boyd, Jr.: trust
Patricia R. Burnham: trust
Eugene J. Callahan: trust
Sharon R. Eisenberg: trust
Diane R. Goldstein: trust
Noris R. Haynes, Jr.: exec dir, trust
Cecil C. Humphreys: trust
Jocelyn P. Rudner: trust
Steven Wishnia: trust

APPLICATION INFORMATION
Initial Approach:
Proposals should be sent to the executive director. Application forms are required and are available upon request. Proposals should include information about the purpose of request, planned use of funds, background of requesting organization, references, status as to tax exemption, budgets, financial statements, and other similar data.
Proposals must be received by the 15th day of the month preceding board meetings. The foundation's board meets February, May, August, and November.
Restrictions on Giving: The foundation generally does not fund annual operating costs, private schools, or individuals.

OTHER THINGS TO KNOW
National Bank of Commerce is listed as the corporate trustee for the foundation. Many grants carry a stipulation that other contributed amounts must be obtained by the organization as matching funds.

GRANTS ANALYSIS
Total Grants: $2,601,387
Number of Grants: 74
Highest Grant: $250,000
Typical Range: $10,000 to $60,000
Disclosure Period: 1992
Note: Recent grants are derived from a 1992 grants list.

RECENT GRANTS
250,000 Memphis Jewish Federation, Memphis, TN
250,000 Memphis Jewish Home, Memphis, TN — formerly B'nai B'rith
250,000 United Way
250,000 United Way — 1992 challenge
250,000 United Way — 1992 gift

100,000 Memphis Jewish Community Center, Memphis, TN
62,500 Memphis Orchestral Society, Memphis, TN
55,000 Rhodes College, Memphis, TN
51,000 Community Foundation for Grant Information Center
50,000 Dixon Gallery, Memphis, TN

Plumsock Fund

CONTACT
John G. Rauch, Jr.
Secretary-Treasurer
Plumsock Fund
9292 North Meridian St., Ste. 312
Indianapolis, IN 46260
(317) 846-8115

FINANCIAL SUMMARY
Recent Giving: $1,300,154 (1991); $825,467 (1990); $416,453 (1989)
Assets: $6,072,206 (1991); $5,429,225 (1990); $4,960,891 (1989)
Gifts Received: $1,330,000 (1991); $1,021,300 (1990); $378,700 (1989)
Fiscal Note: In 1991, contributions were received from Sarah L. Lutz ($1,310,000), and Christopher H. Lutz ($20,000).
EIN: 35-6014719

CONTRIBUTIONS SUMMARY
Donor(s): the late Evelyn L. Lutz, Herbert B. Lutz, Sarah L. Lutz
Typical Recipients: • *Arts & Humanities:* arts centers, dance, history/historic preservation, theater • *Civic & Public Affairs:* environmental affairs, ethnic/minority organizations • *Education:* colleges & universities, journalism education • *International:* international organizations • *Religion:* churches • *Social Services:* united funds, youth organizations
Grant Types: endowment, general support, and scholarship

GIVING OFFICERS
Kenneth Chapman: dir
Edwin Fancher: pres
Marianne H. Hughes: asst secy
Christopher H. Lutz: dir
Sarah L. Lutz: dir
John G. Rauch, Jr.: secy, treas
William T. Rauch: asst treas
Daniel A. Wolf: vp

APPLICATION INFORMATION
Initial Approach: Send brief letter of inquiry describing program or project. There are no deadlines.
Restrictions on Giving: Does not support individuals or provide scholarships or fellowships.

GRANTS ANALYSIS
Number of Grants: 114
Highest Grant: $182,000
Typical Range: $500 to $15,000
Disclosure Period: 1991

RECENT GRANTS
182,000 Center for Regional Meso-American Investigations, Antigua, Guatemala
75,000 Cape Ann Historical Association, Gloucester, MA
70,000 University of Texas Press, Austin, TX
48,000 Oglala Lakota College, Kyle, SD
46,000 University of California, Berkeley, CA
45,000 New York Studio School of Drawing, Painting and Sculpture, New York, NY
45,000 Pine Manor College, Chestnut Hill, MA
40,350 House of Seven Gables, Salem, MA
36,500 Curbstone Press, Willimantic, CT
35,000 Night Kitchen/A National Children's Theater, New York, NY

Pluta Family Foundation

CONTACT
Pluta Family Fdn.
3385 Brighton Henriette Town Line Rd.
Rochester, NY 14623

FINANCIAL SUMMARY
Recent Giving: $117,647 (1990); $251,300 (1989); $270,000 (1987)
Assets: $4,316,420 (1989); $3,574,193 (1987)
EIN: 51-0176213

CONTRIBUTIONS SUMMARY
Donor(s): James Pluta, Helen Pluta, Peter Pluta, Mrs. Peter

Pluta, General Circuits, Inc., Pluta Manufacturing Corp.

Typical Recipients: • *Health:* hospitals

Grant Types: scholarship

Geographic Distribution: limited to Monroe County, NY

GIVING OFFICERS

Andrew Pluta: dir

John Pluta: dir

Peter Pluta: pres, dir

APPLICATION INFORMATION

Initial Approach: Contributes only to preselected organizations.

GRANTS ANALYSIS

Number of Grants: 2

Highest Grant: $150,000

Typical Range: $100,000 to $150,000

Disclosure Period: 1989

Note: No grants list was provided for 1990.

RECENT GRANTS

150,000 Genesee Hospital, Rochester, NY

100,000 Strong Memorial Hospital, Rochester, NY

Ply-Gem Industries, Inc.

Sales: $561.5 million
Employees: 3,400
Headquarters: New York, NY
SIC Major Group: Industrial Machinery & Equipment, Lumber & Wood Products, Paper & Allied Products, and Wholesale Trade—Durable Goods

---

CONTACT

Jeffrey Silverman
Chairman
Ply-Gem Industries, Inc.
777 3rd Avenue, 30th Fl.
New York, NY 10017-1301
(212) 832-1550

CONTRIBUTIONS SUMMARY

Operating Locations: NY (New York)

CORP. OFFICERS

Jeffrey S. Silverman: *CURR EMPL* chmn, pres, ceo, dir: Ply-Gem Indus

---

Plym Foundation

CONTACT

Murray C. Campbell
Plym Fdn.
223 N. 4th St.
Niles, MI 49120
(616) 683-8300

FINANCIAL SUMMARY

Recent Giving: $288,305 (fiscal 1991); $392,637 (fiscal 1990); $392,637 (fiscal 1989)

Assets: $3,685,723 (fiscal year ending September 30, 1991); $3,444,411 (fiscal 1990); $3,444,411 (fiscal 1989)

EIN: 38-6069680

CONTRIBUTIONS SUMMARY

Donor(s): Mrs. Francis J. Plym

Typical Recipients: • *Arts & Humanities:* music • *Civic & Public Affairs:* environmental affairs • *Education:* colleges & universities, education funds, private education (precollege), student aid • *Health:* medical research • *Religion:* churches • *Social Services:* community service organizations, family services, united funds, youth organizations

Grant Types: scholarship

Geographic Distribution: focus on MI

GIVING OFFICERS

Sarah P. Campbell: dir

Rosemary Donnelly: secy

Andrew J. Plym: dir

J. Eric Plym: vp

Lawrence John Plym: pres, dir *B* Kansas City MO 1906 *ED* Univ IL 1928; Babson Inst Fin 1929 *CURR EMPL* pres: Plym Co *CORP AFFIL* dir: Niles Broadcasting Co; pres: Plym Co *NONPR AFFIL* trust: Lake Forest Academy

APPLICATION INFORMATION

Initial Approach: Send brief letter of inquiry and full proposal. There are no deadlines.

GRANTS ANALYSIS

Number of Grants: 11

Highest Grant: $50,000

Typical Range: $1,000 to $10,000

Disclosure Period: fiscal year ending September 30, 1991

RECENT GRANTS

50,000 St. Edwards College, Detroit, MI

20,000 Augustana College, Rock Island, IL

10,000 Talbot Farms

9,005 Georgetown University, Washington, DC

5,000 Lake Forest Academy, Pasadena, CA

5,000 Lynchburg College, Lynchburg, VA

5,000 Niles Y Family Center, Niles, MI

1,000 First Presbyterian Church

1,000 Mayo Foundation for Medical Research, Rochester, MN

1,000 United Way

PMA Industries / PMA Foundation

Headquarters: Philadelphia, PA

CONTACT

Douglas M. Moe
Trustee
PMA Industries
925 Chestnut Street
Philadelphia, PA 19107
(215) 629-5412

FINANCIAL SUMMARY

Recent Giving: $285,643 (1991); $219,779 (1989)

Assets: $222,078 (1991); $249,814 (1989)

Gifts Received: $450,000 (1989)

EIN: 23-2159233

CONTRIBUTIONS SUMMARY

Typical Recipients: • *Arts & Humanities:* theater • *Civic & Public Affairs:* municipalities, philanthropic organizations • *Education:* colleges & universities, legal education • *Health:* single-disease health associations • *Social Services:* child welfare

Grant Types: employee matching gifts and general support

Geographic Distribution: giving primarily in PA

Operating Locations: PA (Philadelphia)

CORP. OFFICERS

Frederick W. Anton: *CURR EMPL* chmn: PMA Indus

William Lostus: *CURR EMPL* pres: PMA Indus

GIVING OFFICERS

Frederick W. Anton III: trust

David L. Johnson: trust

Douglas M. Moe: trust

APPLICATION INFORMATION

Initial Approach: The foundation supports preselected organizations and does not accept unsolicited requests for funds.

GRANTS ANALYSIS

Number of Grants: 65

Highest Grant: $25,000

Typical Range: $50 to $1,000

Disclosure Period: 1991

Note: Figures for 1991 do not include matching gifts.

RECENT GRANTS

25,000 Commonwealth Foundation, Harrisburg, PA

15,000 Eagles Fly for Leukemia, Bala Cynwyd, PA

7,500 Pennsylvania Free Enterprise Week, Erie, PA

6,000 Villanova University School of Law, Villanova, PA

5,000 Arden Theatre

5,000 Central Philadelphia Development Corporation, Philadelphia, PA

5,000 Tylenol Kids, Media, PA

5,000 Welcome Home Fund, Philadelphia, PA

2,500 Pennsylvania State University, University Park, PA

PMC Inc.

Sales: $975.0 million
Employees: 4,250
Headquarters: Sun Valley, CA
SIC Major Group: Chemicals & Allied Products and Rubber & Miscellaneous Plastics Products

---

CONTACT

Judy Markel
Administrative Assistant
PMC Inc.
PO Box 1367
Sun Valley, CA 91353
(818) 896-1101

CONTRIBUTIONS SUMMARY

Operating Locations: CA (Sun Valley)

CORP. OFFICERS

Thian C. Cheong: *CURR EMPL* cfo: PMC

PMI Food Equipment Group Inc.

Sales: $1.01 billion
Employees: 10,000
Parent Company: Premark International
Headquarters: Troy, OH
SIC Major Group: Industrial Machinery & Equipment

CONTACT

PMI Food Equipment Group
World Headquarters
Troy, OH 45374
(513) 332-3333

FINANCIAL SUMMARY

Fiscal Note: Annual Giving Range: less than $100,000

CONTRIBUTIONS SUMMARY

Support goes to local education (50%), health and human service (20%), arts (15%), and civic (15%) organizations.
Typical Recipients: • *Arts & Humanities:* general • *Civic & Public Affairs:* general • *Education:* general • *Health:* general • *Social Services:* general
Grant Types: general support
Geographic Distribution: headquarters and operating locations
Operating Locations: OH (Troy)

CORP. OFFICERS

Joseph Deering: *CURR EMPL* pres: PMI Food Equipment Group

APPLICATION INFORMATION

Initial Approach: Send brief letter of inquiry, including a description of the organization, amount requested, purpose of funds sought, audited financial statement, and proof of tax-exempt status. There are no deadlines.
Restrictions on Giving: Does not support individuals, religious organizations for sectarian purposes, or political or lobbying groups.

PNC Bank

Former Foundation Name: Citizens Fidelity Foundation
Employees: 2,300
Parent Company: PNC Bank Kentucky
Headquarters: Pittsburgh, PA
SIC Major Group: Depository Institutions

CONTACT

Traci Orman
Vice President, Community Relations
PNC Bank
Citizens Plz.
Louisville, KY 40296
(502) 581-2016

FINANCIAL SUMMARY

Recent Giving: $930,000 (fiscal 1993 est.); $2,149,280 (fiscal 1992); $900,000 (fiscal 1991 approx.)
Fiscal Note: Figure for 1992 represents corporate direct sponsorship programs only. Figures for prior years include giving by Citizens Fidelity Foundation, which dissolved in 1991. See "Other Things You Should Know" for more details. 1992 figure includes $485,148 in employee gifts and $1,664,132 in corporate gifts.
EIN: 31-0999030

CONTRIBUTIONS SUMMARY

Typical Recipients: • *Arts & Humanities:* arts centers, arts funds, museums/galleries • *Civic & Public Affairs:* economic development, urban & community affairs • *Education:* minority education, public education (precollege)
Grant Types: project
Nonmonetary Support Types: loaned employees
Note: Dollar value of nonmonetary support is not available. Nonmonetary support is voluntarism. Contact for this support is Sabina Rice, Special Events Officer.
Geographic Distribution: near operating locations only
Operating Locations: KY (Louisville)

CORP. OFFICERS

Michael N. Harreld: *B* Louisville KY 1944 *CURR EMPL* pres, ceo: PNC Bank
Daniel C. Ulmer, Jr.: *CURR EMPL* chmn: PNC Bank *CORP AFFIL* dir: Citizens Fidelity Corp

GIVING OFFICERS

Traci Orman: *CURR EMPL* vp (commun rels): PNC Bank

APPLICATION INFORMATION

Initial Approach: *Initial Contact:* brief letter requesting application form *Include Information On:* description of the organization; amount requested; period covered; program for which funding is requested; when, where, and how services are delivered; target group served or to be served; plan for measuring results; whether receive funding from umbrella organizations; budget information; personnel information; proof of tax-exempt status; audited financial statements; list of board of directors; list of officers and compensation; descriptive literature *When to Submit:* committee meets every other month
Restrictions on Giving: Company does not give to political candidates or causes, individuals, or goodwill advertising.

OTHER THINGS TO KNOW

The Citizens Fidelity Foundation was dissolved in late 1991 as part of the changes that ensued after Citizens Fidelity Bank & Trust Co. was acquired by PNC Financial Corp. The company now gives directly, but has substantially changed its philanthropic role from one of cash grantmaking to one of corporate sponsorship. The bank's giving programs now generally involve marketing-related efforts in which the giver lends assistance to nonprofits in the local Louisville area by promoting distribution of materials, tickets to events, and the like, rather than cash grants.
The company has changed names from Citizens Fidelity Bank & Trust Co. to PNC Bank. In 1993, the company reported that the future of a foundation was unclear at this time.
Publications: *PNC Bank Community Involvement Report*

GRANTS ANALYSIS

Total Grants: $2,149,280
Number of Grants: 300*
Highest Grant: $331,263
Typical Range: $1,000 to $10,000
Disclosure Period: fiscal year ending October 31, 1992

Note: Number of grants is approximate. Average grant figure excludes a $331,263 grant. Recent grants are derived from a 1992 annual report.

RECENT GRANTS

Actors Theatre, Louisville, KY
American Heart Association
American Heart Association, Louisville, KY
Black Achievers Program, Louisville, KY
City of Hope, Louisville, KY
Clark County Humane Association
Clark County Public Library, Lexington, KY
Class Act
Council for the Aging and the Aged
Court Appointed Special Advocates

PNC Bank

Assets: $51.37 billion
Employees: 3,642
Parent Company: PNC Bank Corp.
Headquarters: Philadelphia, PA
SIC Major Group: Depository Institutions

CONTACT

Pat Beachamp
Public Affairs Officer
PNC Bank
100 South Broad
PO Box 7648
Philadelphia, PA 19101
(215) 585-5000

FINANCIAL SUMMARY

Fiscal Note: Company gives directly. Annual Giving Range: $1 million+

CONTRIBUTIONS SUMMARY

Typical Recipients: • *Arts & Humanities:* general • *Civic & Public Affairs:* general • *Education:* general • *Social Services:* general
Grant Types: general support
Nonmonetary Support Types: donated equipment, donated products, and in-kind services
Operating Locations: PA (Philadelphia, Pittsburgh)

CORP. OFFICERS

Paul L. Audet: *CURR EMPL* cfo: Provident Natl Bank
Richard L. Smoot: *CURR EMPL* pres, ceo: Provident Natl Bank

GIVING OFFICERS
Pat Beachamp: *CURR EMPL*
pub aff off: PNC Bank

APPLICATION INFORMATION
Initial Approach: *Initial Contact:* brief letter of inquiry
When to Submit: any time

Pogo Producing Co.
Sales: $124.4 million
Employees: 98
Headquarters: Houston, TX
SIC Major Group: Oil & Gas Extraction

CONTACT
John McCoy
Vice President & Chief Admin. Officer
Pogo Producing Co.
PO Box 61289
Houston, TX 77208
(713) 651-4319

CONTRIBUTIONS SUMMARY
Grant Types: matching
Operating Locations: TX (Houston)

CORP. OFFICERS
William C. Liedtke, Jr.:
CURR EMPL chmn, pres, ceo, dir: Pogo Producing Co
D. Stephen Slack: *CURR EMPL* sr vp, cfo: Pogo Producing Co
Paul G. Van Wagenen: *CURR EMPL* chmn, pres, ceo: Pogo Producing Co

Poindexter Foundation

CONTACT
Roy W. James, Jr.
Secretary-Treasurer
Poindexter Fdn.
PO Box 1692
Shreveport, LA 71165
(318) 226-1040

FINANCIAL SUMMARY
Recent Giving: $79,500 (fiscal 1990); $75,500 (fiscal 1988)
Assets: $1,845,882 (fiscal year ending November 30, 1990); $1,552,757 (fiscal 1988)
EIN: 72-6019174

CONTRIBUTIONS SUMMARY
Donor(s): R. D. Poindexter, Superior Iron Works and Supply Co., Inc.

Typical Recipients: • *Arts & Humanities:* community arts, music • *Education:* colleges & universities, private education (precollege) • *Health:* medical research • *Social Services:* community service organizations
Grant Types: capital and general support
Geographic Distribution: focus on IA

GIVING OFFICERS
Roy W. James, Jr.: secy-treas
R.D. Poindexter: pres
John M. Shuey: vp

APPLICATION INFORMATION
Initial Approach: Send brief letter describing program. There are no deadlines.

GRANTS ANALYSIS
Number of Grants: 45
Highest Grant: $13,500
Typical Range: $500 to $5,000
Disclosure Period: fiscal year ending November 30, 1990

RECENT GRANTS
13,500 Biomedical Research Foundation, Shreveport, LA
10,000 Centenary College, Shreveport, LA — building fund
6,000 Shreveport Symphony Orchestra, Shreveport, LA
5,000 Shreveport Symphony Orchestra, Shreveport, LA
3,500 Teen Challenge, Shreveport, LA
2,500 Centenary College Choir, Shreveport, LA
2,500 Christian Service Program, Shreveport, LA
2,500 Holy Angels School, Shreveport, LA
2,500 Louisiana Council on Economic Education, Baton Rouge, LA
2,500 Louisiana State University Foundation, Baton Rouge, LA

Poinsettia Foundation, Paul and Magdalena Ecke

CONTACT
Paul Ecke, Jr.
Director
Paul and Magdalena Ecke Poinsettia Fdn.
PO Box 607
Encinitas, CA 92024
(213) 931-1277

FINANCIAL SUMMARY
Recent Giving: $215,884 (fiscal 1992); $214,108 (fiscal 1990); $218,643 (fiscal 1989)
Assets: $2,533,303 (fiscal year ending May 31, 1992); $2,509,879 (fiscal 1990); $2,523,055 (fiscal 1989)
Gifts Received: $25 (fiscal 1992)
EIN: 95-3758658

CONTRIBUTIONS SUMMARY
Donor(s): the late Magdalena Ecke
Typical Recipients: • *Arts & Humanities:* theater • *Civic & Public Affairs:* environmental affairs, zoos/botanical gardens • *Education:* colleges & universities, private education (precollege) • *Health:* hospitals • *Social Services:* community centers, community service organizations, united funds, youth organizations
Grant Types: general support

GIVING OFFICERS
Paul Ecke III: trust
Paul Ecke, Jr.: dir, vp
Barbara Ecke Winter: dir, secy

APPLICATION INFORMATION
Initial Approach: Send brief letter describing program. There are no deadlines.

GRANTS ANALYSIS
Number of Grants: 39
Highest Grant: $44,000
Typical Range: $500 to $5,000
Disclosure Period: fiscal year ending May 31, 1992

RECENT GRANTS
44,000 Pennsylvania State University, University Park, PA
32,000 Michigan State University, East Lansing, MI
25,000 Scripps Memorial Hospital Foundation, La Jolla, CA
19,000 Old Globe Theatre, San Diego, CA
17,000 University of Florida, Gainesville, FL
15,650 American Floral Endowment, Edwardsville, IL
12,000 YMCA, Encinitas, CA
10,000 United Way, San Diego, CA
4,500 National PFA Foundation, Madison, WI
3,500 Coming Together Foundation, Escondido, CA

Polaris Industries, LP
Sales: $297.7 million
Employees: 1,400
Headquarters: Minneapolis, MN
SIC Major Group: Transportation Equipment and Wholesale Trade—Durable Goods

CONTACT
Rita Gossling
Administrative Assistant
Polaris Industries, LP
1225 N. Hwy. 169
Minneapolis, MN 55441
(612) 542-0500

CONTRIBUTIONS SUMMARY
Operating Locations: MN (Minneapolis)

CORP. OFFICERS
Kenneth Larson: *B* Mower County MN 1940 *ED* Univ MN 1964; Univ MN 1978 *CURR EMPL* pres: Polaris Indus LP
Robert S. Moe: *CURR EMPL* vchmn, cfo, treas: Polaris Indus LP
W. Hall Wendel, Jr.: *CURR EMPL* chmn, ceo: Polaris Indus LP

RECENT GRANTS
Walker Art Center, Minneapolis, MN

Polaroid Corp. / Polaroid Foundation
Sales: $2.16 billion
Employees: 13,622
Headquarters: Cambridge, MA
SIC Major Group: Instruments & Related Products

CONTACT
Donna Furlong
Associate Director
Polaroid Fdn.
750 Main St., 2nd Fl.
Cambridge, MA 02139
(617) 577-3470
Note: Contact person listed above also handles noncash requests.

FINANCIAL SUMMARY
Recent Giving: $2,550,000 (1993 est.); $2,450,000 (1992 approx.); $2,295,000 (1991)
Assets: $1,032,137 (1991); $30,656 (1989)
Fiscal Note: Total giving figures above are for foundation only. Company also makes divisional grants to various nonprofits. In 1992, this support totaled $869,000.
EIN: 23-7152261

CONTRIBUTIONS SUMMARY
Typical Recipients: • *Arts & Humanities:* arts associations, arts centers, arts funds, community arts, dance, museums/galleries, music, opera, performing arts, theater, visual arts • *Civic & Public Affairs:* civil rights, environmental affairs, housing, law & justice, nonprofit management, urban & community affairs, women's affairs • *Education:* arts education, business education, career/vocational education, colleges & universities, continuing education, elementary education, engineering education, literacy, medical education, minority education, preschool education, private education (precollege), public education (precollege), science/technology education, special education • *Health:* hospices, hospitals, mental health, nursing services, outpatient health care delivery
Grant Types: capital, employee matching gifts, general support, operating expenses, project, and seed money
Nonmonetary Support Types: donated products
Note: In 1992, company gave $50,000 in nonmonetary support, which is included in the figures above. In 1993, the company estimates nonmonetary support at the same level.
Geographic Distribution: primarily greater Boston and New Bedford, MA area; small number of grants awarded in areas where distribution centers are

located; considers funding outside of Massachusetts in areas of minority higher education and photographic acquisition and exhibition; donates products nationwide
Operating Locations: CA (San Diego), GA (Atlanta), IL, MA (Boston, Cambridge), NJ (Paramus)

CORP. OFFICERS
Israel MacAllister Booth: *B* Atlanta GA 1931 *ED* Cornell Univ BME 1955; Cornell Univ MBA 1958 *CURR EMPL* pres, co-chief exec off, dir: Polaroid Corp *CORP AFFIL* dir: Western Digital Corp

GIVING OFFICERS
Israel MacAllister Booth: trust *CURR EMPL* pres, co-chief exec off, dir: Polaroid Corp (see above)
Sheldon A. Buckler: trust *B* New York NY 1931 *ED* NY Univ BA 1951; Columbia Univ PhD 1954 *CURR EMPL* vchmn bd: Polaroid Corp *CORP AFFIL* dir: Lord Corp; trust: Commonwealth Energy Sys *NONPR AFFIL* bd mgrs: MA Eye Ear Infirmary; mem: Am Chem Soc, Phi Beta Kappa; mem adv bd: Am Repertory Theatre
Richard Ford DeLima: trust *B* New York NY 1930 *ED* Amherst Coll 1951; Harvard Univ Law Sch 1955 *CURR EMPL* vp, sec, gen couns: Polaroid Corp
Milton S. Dietz: trust *B* New York NY 1931 *ED* MA Inst Tech BS 1952; MA Inst Tech MS 1954 *CURR EMPL* sr vp (strategic planning & corp devel): Polaroid Corp *NONPR AFFIL* mem: Counc Planning Execs, Pi Tau Sigma, Sigma Xi, Tau Beta Pi
Donna Furlong: assoc dir
Owen James Gaffney: trust *B* Lynn MA 1935 *ED* Boston Coll 1957; Suffolk Univ Sch Law 1966 *CURR EMPL* group vp (human resources): Polaroid Corp *CORP AFFIL* dir: Natl Micronetics
Jill Healy: sr admin
Peter Otto Kliem: trust *B* Berlin Germany 1938 *ED* Bates Coll BS 1960; Northeastern Univ MS 1965 *CURR EMPL* sr vp, dir res & engg: Polaroid Corp *CORP AFFIL* dir: PBDS Inc *NONPR AFFIL* mem: Am Chem Soc, Indus Res Inst, Natl Academy Sciences, Soc Photographic Scientists Engrs

Ralph M. Norwood: treas *B* Rochester NH 1943 *CURR EMPL* vp: Polaroid Corp *NONPR AFFIL* mem: Am Inst CPAs
William J. O'Neill, Jr.: pres *CURR EMPL* group vp (consumer photography): Polaroid Corp
Joseph Oldfield: trust *CURR EMPL* vp (worldwide mfg opers), dir: Polaroid Corp *NONPR AFFIL* dir: Natl Assn Mfrs
Marcia Schiff: exec dir, secy, mem oper comm

APPLICATION INFORMATION
Initial Approach: *Initial Contact:* grant application, letter, or proposal on organization letterhead *Include Information On:* completed grant application together with brief history of program, population served, outline of project for which support is requested, annual budget for project or for overall program if general support requested, proof of tax-exempt status, and most recently audited financial statement *When to Submit:* any time
Restrictions on Giving: The foundation does not make more than one grant to a recipient in any calendar year, or make contributions commitments beyond the current funding year; does not make contributions in the form of purchasing advertisements; and does not make grants to individuals. Also does not support political or lobbying groups, religious organizations for sectarian purposes, or dinners or special events, does not fund research.

OTHER THINGS TO KNOW
The foundation occasionally provides short-term, no-interest loans.
The foundation also makes limited donations of photographic materials. Requests for such support must be on organization letterhead, provide a statement justifying the organization's ability to qualify under Polaroid Foundation guidelines, along with an overview of how photography will be integrated into the program. No budget or statement from the accounting department is required. The organization must work with a low-income or poverty-level population, with the

mentally or physically handicapped, or with the retarded. Requests should be directed to Jill Healy, Product Donation Program, Polaroid Foundation, 750 Main St., 2nd Fl., Cambridge, MA, 02139.
A list of committee members may be obtained from the foundation.
Skills Bank is a company-sponsored employee volunteer program. It is run through the community relations office. For information, contact Verna Brookins.

GRANTS ANALYSIS
Total Grants: $2,450,000
Number of Grants: 370*
Highest Grant: $359,000
Typical Range: $100 to $10,000
Disclosure Period: 1992
Note: Fiscal information for foundation only. Number of grants and average grant figures exclude matching gifts. Foundation had no assets in 1992. Figure for assets is from 1991. Recent grants are derived from a 1991 Form 990.

RECENT GRANTS
380,000 United Way of Eastern New England — general support
45,000 Associated Grantmakers of Summer Programs for Youth, Boston, MA
25,000 Massachusetts General Hospital, Boston, MA — capital campaign
25,000 Museum of the National Center of Afro-American Artists — photographic acquisition and exhibition program
20,000 Boston Education Development Foundation, Boston Public Schools, Boston, MA — integraged learning lab
18,663 American College Testing, Iowa City, IA — scholarships for Children of Polaroid employees
15,000 Brandeis University-Saul G. Cohen Fund for Research In Chemistry, Waltham, MA — capital campaign
15,000 Local Initiatives Support Corporation, Boston, MA — general support

15,000 Photographic Resource Center, Boston, MA — exhibition program

15,000 University of Massachusetts Foundation, MA — urban scholars program

Polinger Foundation, Howard and Geraldine

CONTACT
Howard Polinger
President, Director
Howard and Geraldine Polinger Fdn.
5530 Wisconsin Avenue, Ste. 1000
Chevy Chase, MD 20815
(301) 657-3600

FINANCIAL SUMMARY
Recent Giving: $91,750 (fiscal 1991); $85,000 (fiscal 1990); $68,500 (fiscal 1987)
Assets: $1,934,302 (fiscal year ending June 30, 1991); $1,880,017 (fiscal 1990); $1,758,161 (fiscal 1987)
EIN: 52-6078041

CONTRIBUTIONS SUMMARY
Donor(s): Howard Polinger, Geraldine Polinger
Typical Recipients: • *Arts & Humanities:* community arts, music, public broadcasting • *Civic & Public Affairs:* civil rights, ethnic/minority organizations • *Education:* colleges & universities • *Religion:* religious organizations, synagogues • *Social Services:* aged, community centers, community service organizations
Grant Types: general support
Geographic Distribution: focus on the Washington, DC, area.

GIVING OFFICERS
Jan Polinger Forsgren: dir, vp
Arnold Polinger: dir, vp
David Polinger: dir, treas
Geraldine Polinger: dir, secy
Howard Polinger: dir, pres
Lorre Beth Polinger: dir, vp

APPLICATION INFORMATION
Initial Approach: Send brief letter describing program. There are no deadlines.
Restrictions on Giving: Does not support individuals.

GRANTS ANALYSIS
Number of Grants: 36
Highest Grant: $10,250
Typical Range: $500 to $8,000
Disclosure Period: fiscal year ending June 30, 1991

RECENT GRANTS
10,250 Temple Sinai, Washington, DC

8,000 Goucher College, Towson, MD

8,000 Jewish Community Center, Rockville, MD

7,000 Anti-Defamation League of B'nai B'rith, Washington, DC

7,000 Hebrew Home of Greater Washington, Rockville, MD

6,000 Jewish Social Services Agency, Rockville, MD

5,500 Jewish Council for the Aging, Rockville, MD

4,000 University Community Concerts, College Park, MD

2,500 Washington Opera, Washington, DC

2,500 WETA, Washington, DC

Polinsky-Rivkin Family Foundation

CONTACT
Jessie W. Polinsky
President
Polinsky-Rivkin Family Fdn.
836 Prospect, Ste. 202
La Jolla, CA 92037

FINANCIAL SUMMARY
Recent Giving: $727,000 (1989)
Assets: $4,107,726 (1989)
EIN: 95-4355247

CONTRIBUTIONS SUMMARY
Typical Recipients: • *Arts & Humanities:* libraries, public broadcasting • *Health:* hospitals • *Religion:* religious organizations • *Social Services:* child welfare, family planning, youth organizations
Grant Types: general support
Geographic Distribution: focus on CA

GIVING OFFICERS
Jessie W. Polinsky: pres
Arthur L. Rivkin: vp
Jeannie P. Rivkin: secy, treas

APPLICATION INFORMATION
Initial Approach: Send brief letter of inquiry describing program or project. There are no deadlines.

GRANTS ANALYSIS
Number of Grants: 12
Highest Grant: $500,000
Typical Range: $1,000 to $100,000
Disclosure Period: 1989

RECENT GRANTS
500,000 Sharp Hospital, San Diego, CA

100,000 Old Globe Theatre, Los Angeles, CA

50,000 Jerusalem Foundation, New York, NY

45,000 Storefront, Los Angeles, CA

5,000 Boys and Girls Club, Los Angeles, CA

5,000 Flo Riford Library of La Jolla, La Jolla, CA

5,000 Golda Meir Association, New York, NY

5,000 KPBS, San Diego, CA

5,000 Linda Vista Library, Linda Vista, CA

5,000 Planned Parenthood, Los Angeles, CA

Polk & Co., R.L.
Sales: $296.0 million
Employees: 7,000
Headquarters: Detroit, MI
SIC Major Group: Business Services, Miscellaneous Manufacturing Industries, Printing & Publishing, and Trucking & Warehousing

CONTACT
Ann Hoerle
Internal Auditor
R.L. Polk & Co.
1155 Brewery Park Blvd.
Detroit, MI 48207
(313) 393-0880

CONTRIBUTIONS SUMMARY
Operating Locations: MI (Detroit)

CORP. OFFICERS
John M. O'Hara: *B* Torrington CT 1929 *ED* Rutgers Univ 1962 *CURR EMPL* chmn, pres, ceo: RL Polk & Co *CORP AFFIL* dir: Standard Fed Bank
W. Ronald Pfeffer: *CURR EMPL* sr vp, cfo: Polk & Co

Polk Foundation

CONTACT
Ronald W. Wertz
Executive Director
Polk Fdn.
2000 Grant Bldg.
Pittsburgh, PA 15219
(412) 338-3464

FINANCIAL SUMMARY
Recent Giving: $163,000 (1991); $133,000 (1990); $133,000 (1989)
Assets: $3,731,737 (1991); $3,332,504 (1990); $3,492,340 (1989)
EIN: 25-1113733

CONTRIBUTIONS SUMMARY
Donor(s): the late Patricia Hillman Miller
Typical Recipients: • *Arts & Humanities:* museums/galleries • *Education:* special education • *Health:* hospitals, pediatric health
Grant Types: capital and seed money
Geographic Distribution: limited to Pittsburgh and southwestern PA

GIVING OFFICERS
H. Vaughan Baxter III: off
Patricia M. Duggan: dir
C.G. Grefenstette: dir
Henry Lea Hillman: pres, dir *B* Pittsburgh PA 1918 *ED* Princeton Univ AB 1941 *CURR EMPL* chmn: Hillman Co *CORP AFFIL* dir: Stuart Medical *NONPR AFFIL* mem: Bus Counc; mem exec comm emeritus: Allegheny Conf Commun Devel; trust: Carnegie Inst
Hugh D. Joyce: asst secy
David H. Ross: asst treas
Lawrence M. Wagner: treas *CURR EMPL* pres, dir: Hillman Coal & Coke Co *CORP AFFIL* vp, treas, dir: Hillman Mfg Co
Lawrence M. Wagner: treas
Ronald W. Wertz: exec dir

APPLICATION INFORMATION
Initial Approach: Send brief letter describing program. There are no deadlines.
Restrictions on Giving: Does not support individuals.

GRANTS ANALYSIS
Number of Grants: 3
Highest Grant: $100,000
Typical Range: $3,000 to $60,000
Disclosure Period: 1991

RECENT GRANTS

100,000 Allegheny Valley School, Coraopolis, PA

60,000 Allegheny Valley School, Coraopolis, PA

3,000 Southern Alleghenies Museum of Art, Loretto, PA

Pollock Company Foundation, William B.

CONTACT

William B. Pollock Company Fdn.
c/o Bank One, Youngstown, N.A.
6 Federal Plz. West
Youngstown, OH 44503
(216) 742-6731

FINANCIAL SUMMARY

Recent Giving: $76,025 (1991); $77,850 (1990); $73,500 (1989)
Assets: $2,079,366 (1991); $1,847,284 (1990); $1,869,797 (1989)
EIN: 34-6514078

CONTRIBUTIONS SUMMARY

Typical Recipients: • *Arts & Humanities:* community arts, history/historic preservation, music • *Civic & Public Affairs:* economic development • *Education:* colleges & universities, education associations • *Health:* health organizations • *Social Services:* community service organizations, family planning, united funds, youth organizations
Grant Types: general support
Geographic Distribution: focus on the Youngstown, OH, area

GIVING OFFICERS

Bank One of Youngstown, N.A.: trust

APPLICATION INFORMATION

Initial Approach: Send brief letter describing program. There are no deadlines.

GRANTS ANALYSIS

Number of Grants: 21
Highest Grant: $13,000
Typical Range: $1,000 to $3,000
Disclosure Period: 1991

RECENT GRANTS

13,000 Youngstown State University, Youngstown, OH

12,750 Youngstown Foundation Support Fund, Youngstown, OH

10,000 Mahoning Valley Economic Development Council, Youngstown, OH

10,000 Planned Parenthood Federation of America, Youngstown, OH

5,000 Mill Creek Park, Youngstown, OH

3,000 American National Red Cross, Youngstown, OH

3,000 Newman Center, Youngstown, OH

3,000 Ohio Foundation of Independent Colleges, Columbus, OH

3,000 United Way, Youngstown, OH

2,500 Goodwill Industries, Youngstown, OH

Pollock-Krasner Foundation

CONTACT

Linda Selvin
Grants Manager
Pollock-Krasner Fdn.
725 Park Ave.
New York, NY 10021
(212) 517-5400

FINANCIAL SUMMARY

Recent Giving: $1,669,165 (fiscal 1991); $2,159,901 (fiscal 1990); $1,376,346 (fiscal 1989)
Assets: $40,888,438 (fiscal year ending June 30, 1991); $37,544,201 (fiscal 1990); $32,410,745 (fiscal 1989)
Gifts Received: $1,931,447 (fiscal 1990)
EIN: 13-3255693

CONTRIBUTIONS SUMMARY

Donor(s): The foundation was established in 1984 by the late Lee Krasner.
Typical Recipients: • *Arts & Humanities:* visual arts
Geographic Distribution: national

GIVING OFFICERS

Charles Cabe Bergman: exec vp *B* Boston MA 1933 *ED* Harvard Univ AB 1954 *CORP AFFIL* sr assoc: Jeffcoat

Schoen & Morell *NONPR AFFIL* bd advs: Fund Arts & Culture Central & Eastern Europe; chmn: Intl Counc Am Field Svc Intercultural Programs; dir: Brandeis Univ, Brandeis Univ Creative Arts Award Comm, Circle Repertory, City Harvest, Millay Colony Arts; mem adv bd: Natl Mus Women Arts; mem bd advs: Creative Artists Network; panelist: NY St Counc Arts Visual Arts Program; special adv: Pres Commn Mental Retardation; trust: Lenox Sch

Gerald Dickler: chmn, dir *B* New York NY 1912 *ED* Columbia Univ AB 1931; Columbia Univ LLB 1933 *CORP AFFIL* dir: Capital Cities/ABC

Eugene Victor Thaw: pres, dir

APPLICATION INFORMATION

Initial Approach:

Artists interested in applying for funds should write to the foundation for an application form and information on the application procedure.

Completed applications should include a cover letter stating the specific purpose (professional, personal, and/or medical) for which funding is requested and in what amount; no more than 10 slides of the applicant's most current work, properly labeled as indicated (original works of art will not be accepted); and a self-addressed return postcard

The foundation accepts applications throughout the year.

The foundation's officers and directors are advised in the selection process by a Committee of Selection comprised of recognized authorities in the fields of the foundation's concern. If further information is required after the completed application has been received, the artist will be contacted directly by the staff. Further information, including financial data, may be requested at any time during the review process.

Restrictions on Giving: The foundation does not accept applications from commercial artists, photographers, video artists, film-makers, craft-makers, or any artist whose work primarily falls into these categories. It does not make grants to organizations, students, or for academic study.

OTHER THINGS TO KNOW

Publications: annual report and informational brochure including application guidelines.

GRANTS ANALYSIS

Total Grants: $1,669,165*
Typical Range: $2,000 to $10,000
Disclosure Period: fiscal year ending June 30, 1991
Note: The 1991 grants lists consists of scholarships paid to individuals.

Pollybill Foundation

CONTACT

Paul F. Meissner
Director
Pollybill Fdn.
735 North Water St., Ste. 1328
Milwaukee, WI 53202
(414) 273-4390

FINANCIAL SUMMARY

Recent Giving: $673,200 (1990); $569,500 (1989); $400,000 (1987)
Assets: $516,816 (1990); $1,150,312 (1989); $799,089 (1987)
Gifts Received: $675,000 (1990); $570,508 (1989); $421,300 (1987)
Fiscal Note: In 1990, contributions were received from Polly H. Van Dyke.
EIN: 39-6078550

CONTRIBUTIONS SUMMARY

Donor(s): William D. Van Dyke, Polly H. Van Dyke
Typical Recipients: • *Arts & Humanities:* arts institutes, community arts, museums/galleries, music, performing arts, theater • *Civic & Public Affairs:* environmental affairs • *Education:* colleges & universities • *Health:* hospitals, medical research, nursing services, single-disease health associations • *Social Services:* child welfare, family planning, family services, united funds, youth organizations
Grant Types: capital and general support
Geographic Distribution: focus on WI, especially Milwaukee

GIVING OFFICERS

Leonard G. Campbell, Jr.: dir
Paul F. Meissner: dir
Polly H. Van Dyke: pres, dir

William Duncan Van Dyke
III: secy *B* Milwaukee WI
1931 *ED* Princeton Univ AB
1954; Stanford Univ MBA
1956 *CURR EMPL* sr vp, dir:
Smith Barney Harris Upham &
Co *CORP AFFIL* dir: Intl Fla-
vors & Fragrances, Mountain
Oil & Gas Co; sr vp, dir: Smith
Barney Harris Upham & Co
NONPR AFFIL dir: Milwaukee
Symphony Orchestra; mem bd
regents: Milwaukee Sch En-
gring

APPLICATION INFORMATION
Initial Approach: Contributes
only to preselected organizations.

GRANTS ANALYSIS
Number of Grants: 24
Highest Grant: $150,000
Typical Range: $1,000 to
$10,000
Disclosure Period: 1990

RECENT GRANTS
150,000 Milwaukee Sym-
phony Orchestra,
Milwaukee, WI
100,000 Carroll College Art
Building, Wauke-
sha, WI
100,000 Columbia Hospital,
Milwaukee, WI
100,000 Greenwich Teen
Center, Greenwich,
CT
50,000 Milwaukee Insti-
tute of Art and
Design, Milwau-
kee, WI
25,000 Friends of the Mu-
seum, Milwaukee,
WI
25,000 Nashotah House
Campaign, De-
lafield, WI — Vi-
sion in Action
25,000 Planned Parent-
hood, Milwaukee,
WI
15,000 Blood Center of
Southwestern Wis-
consin, Milwaukee,
WI
12,500 Riveredge Nature
Center, Milwau-
kee, WI

Polychrome Corp.
Sales: $300.0 million
Employees: 2,000
Headquarters: Fort Lee, NJ
SIC Major Group: Instruments &
Related Products, Printing &
Publishing, and Rubber &
Miscellaneous Plastics Products

CONTACT
Nicholas J. Profeta
Vice President, Corporate
Secretary & Member,
Contributions Committee
Polychrome Corp.
222 Bridge Plz. South
Ft. Lee, NJ 07024
(201) 346-8800

CONTRIBUTIONS SUMMARY
Company gives to headquarters
community. At time of publication, contributions budget had
been frozen. Company reported
contributions would probably
resume in early 1993. Has supported local colleges and universities, museums and galleries, hospitals, and United
Ways. Also supports other programs that might benefit the
local community; chosen recipients depend on requests and
needs of the community.
Typical Recipients: • *Arts &
Humanities:* arts associations,
museums/galleries • *Education:* colleges & universities
• *Health:* hospitals • *Social
Services:* united funds
Grant Types: general support
and scholarship
Nonmonetary Support Types:
donated equipment and loaned
employees
Geographic Distribution:
headquarters community

CORP. OFFICERS
Melvin Ettinger: *CURR
EMPL* pres, ceo: Polychrome
Corp

GIVING OFFICERS
Nicholas J. Profeta: *CURR
EMPL* vp, corp secy, mem con-
tributions comm: Polychrome
Corp

APPLICATION INFORMATION
Initial Approach: Send a brief
letter or proposal, including a
description of the organization,
amount requested, purpose for
which funds are sought, recently audited financial statement, and proof of tax-exempt
status. It is best to apply in October and November. Contributions committee meets annually to decide the yearly budget.
Restrictions on Giving: Company does not support dinners
or special events, fraternal organizations, goodwill advertising, member agencies of united
funds, or political or lobbying
groups.

Poncin Scholarship Fund
CONTACT
Rod Johnson
Vice President
Poncin Scholarship Fund
c/o Seattle-First National Bank,
Charitable Trusts
PO Box 3586
Seattle, WA 98124
(206) 358-3388

FINANCIAL SUMMARY
Recent Giving: $138,746
(1991); $85,700 (1990);
$19,500 (1989)
Assets: $4,218,188 (1991);
$3,382,766 (1990); $3,545,486
(1989)
EIN: 91-6069573

CONTRIBUTIONS SUMMARY
Donor(s): the late Cora May
Poncin
Typical Recipients: • *Health:*
medical research
Grant Types: research
Geographic Distribution: lim-
ited to the state of WA

GIVING OFFICERS
Seattle First National Bank:
trust

APPLICATION INFORMATION
Initial Approach: Application
must be approved by head of
applicant's institution. There
are no deadlines.

OTHER THINGS TO KNOW
Provides grants for medical re-
search.
Disclosure Period: 1991

Ponderosa, Inc.
Revenue: $490.3 million
Employees: 26,000
Headquarters: Dayton, OH
SIC Major Group: Eating &
Drinking Places and Holding
& Other Investment Offices

CONTACT
Margaret Nelson
Communications Manager
Ponderosa, Inc.
PO Box 578
Dayton, OH 45401
(513) 454-2400

FINANCIAL SUMMARY
Fiscal Note: Annual Giving
Range: $100,000 to $250,000

CONTRIBUTIONS SUMMARY
Support goes to local educa-
tion, health and human service,
arts, and civic organizations.
Typical Recipients: • *Arts &
Humanities:* general • *Civic &
Public Affairs:* general • *Educa-
tion:* general • *Health:* general
• *Social Services:* general
Grant Types: general support
Nonmonetary Support Types:
donated equipment, donated
products, and in-kind services
Geographic Distribution: pri-
marily headquarters area
Operating Locations: OH
(Dayton)

CORP. OFFICERS
Gerald S. Office, Jr.: *B* Day-
ton OH 1941 *ED* Univ MI
1963; OH St Univ 1967 *CURR
EMPL* chmn, pres: Ponderosa
CORP AFFIL dir: Bank One
Dayton NA, Chemlawn Corp

APPLICATION INFORMATION
Initial Approach: Send brief
letter of inquiry. There are no
deadlines.

Pool Energy Services Co.
Sales: $225.3 million
Employees: 4,708
Headquarters: Houston, TX
SIC Major Group: Oil & Gas
Extraction and Wholesale
Trade—Durable Goods

CONTACT
Tracy Taylor
Communications Coordinator
Pool Energy Services Co.
PO Box 4271
Houston, TX 77210
(713) 954-3000

CONTRIBUTIONS SUMMARY
Operating Locations: TX
(Houston)

CORP. OFFICERS
J. T. Jongebloed: *CURR
EMPL* pres: Pool Co

Poole Equipment Co., Gregory
Sales: $84.0 million
Employees: 354
Headquarters: Raleigh, NC
SIC Major Group: Wholesale
Trade—Durable Goods

CONTACT
Sandi Jacobs
Marketing Manager
Gregory Poole Equipment Co.
PO Box 469
Raleigh, NC 27602
(919) 828-0641

CONTRIBUTIONS SUMMARY
Company provides employee matching gifts only.
Grant Types: matching
Operating Locations: NC (Raleigh)

CORP. OFFICERS
James G. Poole, Jr.: *CURR EMPL* ceo, chmn: Gregory Poole Equipment Co

---

Poole & Kent Co. / Poole and Kent Foundation
Headquarters: Baltimore, MD

CONTACT
Raymond C. Jung
Director-President
Poole & Kent Co.
4530 Hollins Ferry Road
Baltimore, MD 21227
(410) 247-2200

FINANCIAL SUMMARY
Recent Giving: $18,838 (1990); $20,100 (1989)
Assets: $100,261 (1990); $65,547 (1989)
Gifts Received: $50,000 (1990); $50,000 (1989)
Fiscal Note: In 1990, contributions were received from Monumental Investment Corporation.
EIN: 52-1471763

CONTRIBUTIONS SUMMARY
Typical Recipients: • *Education:* colleges & universities, education funds, science/technology education • *Religion:* religious organizations • *Social Services:* united funds
Grant Types: general support
Geographic Distribution: giving limited to Baltimore, MD
Operating Locations: MD (Baltimore)

CORP. OFFICERS
Raymond C. Jung: *CURR EMPL* vp, secy-treas: Poole & Kent Co
William A. Touchard: *CURR EMPL* pres: Poole & Kent Co

GIVING OFFICERS
Milton W. Crawford, Jr.: vp, secy

Raymond C. Jung: pres *CURR EMPL* vp, secy-treas: Poole & Kent Co (see above)
Edward G. Smith: vp, treas

APPLICATION INFORMATION
Initial Approach: The foundation supports preselected organizations and does not accept unsolicited requests for funds.

GRANTS ANALYSIS
Number of Grants: 7
Highest Grant: $5,000
Typical Range: $500 to $5,000
Disclosure Period: 1990

RECENT GRANTS
5,000 University of Maryland, College Park, MD
5,000 University of Maryland Foundation, College Park, MD
5,000 University of Maryland Foundation, College Park, MD
2,000 American Heart Association, Baltimore, MD
838 Baptist Book Store, Ft. Lauderdale, FL
500 Maryland Academy of Sciences, Baltimore, MD
500 United Way, Baltimore, MD

Poorvu Foundation, William and Lia

CONTACT
William Poorvu
Trustee
William and Lia Poorvu Fdn.
PO Box 380828
Cambridge, MA 02238
(617) 576-1010

FINANCIAL SUMMARY
Recent Giving: $114,000 (1991); $90,000 (1990); $79,250 (1989)
Assets: $2,256,126 (1991); $2,137,576 (1990); $1,763,741 (1989)
Gifts Received: $50,000 (1991); $50,000 (1989); $100,000 (1988)
Fiscal Note: In 1991, contributions were received from William Poorvu.
EIN: 04-2651199

CONTRIBUTIONS SUMMARY
Donor(s): William I. Poorvu
Typical Recipients: • *Arts & Humanities:* community arts, history/historic preservation, museums/galleries, music • *Civic & Public Affairs:* law & justice • *Education:* arts education, business education, colleges & universities • *Health:* hospitals, medical research, mental health, pediatric health, single-disease health associations • *Social Services:* child welfare, community service organizations
Grant Types: general support
Geographic Distribution: focus on MA

GIVING OFFICERS
Lia G. Poorvu: trust
William J. Poorvu: trust

APPLICATION INFORMATION
Initial Approach: Send brief letter describing program. There are no deadlines.

GRANTS ANALYSIS
Number of Grants: 25
Highest Grant: $50,000
Typical Range: $500 to $1,000
Disclosure Period: 1991

RECENT GRANTS
50,000 Yale University, New Haven, CT
10,000 Longy School of Music, Cambridge, MA
5,000 Cambridge Institute for Law and Justice, Cambridge, MA
5,000 Olympus High School, Cambridge, MA
3,000 Banchetto Musicals, Cambridge, MA
2,500 Facing History and Ourselves, Boston, MA
2,500 Institute Mental Health Initiatives, Cambridge, MA
1,500 Longy School of Music, Cambridge, MA
1,000 Action for Children's TV, Cambridge, MA
1,000 American Associates of Ben Gurion University, New York, NY

Pope Family Foundation, Blanche & Edker

CONTACT
Blanche & Edker Pope Family Fdn.
635 San Elijo Street
San Diego, CA 92106

FINANCIAL SUMMARY
Recent Giving: $0 (1990)
Assets: $4,380,310 (1990)
Gifts Received: $4,380,800 (1990)
EIN: 33-0404901

CONTRIBUTIONS SUMMARY
Donor(s): donors are Edker and Blance Pope

GIVING OFFICERS
Merlin L. Kastler: secy
Blanche Pope: pres
Edker III Pope: vp
Richard W. Starr: cfo
Disclosure Period: 1990

Pope Foundation

CONTACT
Anthony Pope
Vice President
Pope Foundation
211 West 56th St., Ste. 5-E
New York, NY 10019
(212) 765-4156

FINANCIAL SUMMARY
Recent Giving: $1,083,227 (1991); $1,177,500 (1990); $1,184,200 (1989)
Assets: $27,589,715 (1991); $26,009,864 (1990); $27,806,565 (1989)
EIN: 13-6096193

CONTRIBUTIONS SUMMARY
Donor(s): The foundation was established in New York in 1947 by the late Generoso Pope. Generoso Pope operated the oldest continuously published daily Italian-language newspaper in the United States, *Il Progresso Italio-Americano*. Founded in 1881, the newspaper is a record of milestones in Italian-American immigrant history and a reflection of the Italian immigrant's presence in America. Mr. Pope ran the newspaper from 1930 to 1950, when the paper had its greatest influence.
Typical Recipients: • *Civic & Public Affairs:* ethnic/minority

organizations • *Education:* colleges & universities, medical education, minority education, private education (precollege), student aid • *Health:* hospitals, medical rehabilitation, medical research • *Religion:* churches, religious organizations • *Social Services:* child welfare, food/clothing distribution, recreation & athletics
Grant Types: general support, research, and scholarship
Geographic Distribution: primarily metropolitan New York City; limited support elsewhere

GIVING OFFICERS
Anthony Pope: vp, secy, dir, don son
Catherine Pope: pres, dir, don wife
Fortune Pope: vp, treas, dir, don son

APPLICATION INFORMATION
Initial Approach:
A letter should be sent to the foundation.
The foundation has no formal application requirements or procedures. The letter should include a description of the project and organization for which funds are being sought. If further information is needed, the foundation will contact the applicant.
There are no deadlines for submitting proposals.
Applications are reviewed, and applicants are notified of the decision as soon as possible.
Restrictions on Giving: No grants are given to individuals. The foundation will fund only tax-exempt organizations.

GRANTS ANALYSIS
Total Grants: $1,083,227
Number of Grants: 57
Highest Grant: $195,000
Typical Range: $1,000 to $40,000
Disclosure Period: 1991
Note: The average grant figure excludes two grants totaling $347,500. Recent grants are derived from a 1991 Form 990.

RECENT GRANTS
195,000 New York University Medical Center, New York, NY
152,500 Providence Rest Foundation, Bronx, NY
55,000 United Hospital
50,000 Fairfield University, Fairfield, CT
50,000 Fordham University, Bronx, NY
41,700 Sisters of St. John the Baptist
40,000 Hospital for Special Surgery, New York, NY
30,000 H. E. John Cardinal O'Connor
25,000 Fairliegh Dickinson University, Rutherford, NJ
25,000 Gold Star Education

Pope Foundation, Lois B.

CONTACT
Paul J. Collins
Lois B. Pope Foundation
204 South Ocean Boulevard
Manalapan, FL 33462-3312

FINANCIAL SUMMARY
Recent Giving: $439,902 (1990)
Assets: $2,372,606 (1990)
Gifts Received: $2,005,235 (1990)
EIN: 13-3542769

CONTRIBUTIONS SUMMARY
Typical Recipients: • *Civic & Public Affairs:* professional & trade associations • *Education:* colleges & universities • *Health:* hospitals • *Religion:* synagogues
Grant Types: general support and project

GIVING OFFICERS
Anastasia M. Berrodin: vp, dir
Frank Berrodin: treas, dir
Robert C. Miller: secy
Lois B. Pope: pres, dir

GRANTS ANALYSIS
Total Grants: $439,902
Typical Range: $8,166 to $25,000
Disclosure Period: 1990

RECENT GRANTS
283,573 College of Boca Raton, FL
25,000 University Of Miami, Miami, FL
25,000 University of Pennsylvania, PA
22,500 Association of Collegiate Schools of Architecture
10,000 Bobover Yeshiva Bnei Zion
10,000 Providence Rest
8,167 College of Boca Raton, FL — Love Tree Project
8,166 Good Samaritan Hospital — Love Tree Project
8,166 Hospice of Palm Beach, Palm Beach, FL — Love Tree Project
8,166 Jackson Memorial Hospital — Love Tree Project

Pope & Talbot, Inc.
Sales: $502.3 million
Employees: 3,000
Headquarters: Portland, OR
SIC Major Group: Lumber & Wood Products and Paper & Allied Products

CONTACT
Dick Moffitt
Manager, Human Resources
Pope & Talbot, Inc.
PO Box 8171
Portland, OR 97207
(503) 228-9161

CONTRIBUTIONS SUMMARY
Grant Types: matching
Nonmonetary Support Types: donated products
Operating Locations: OR (Portland)

CORP. OFFICERS
Peter T. Pope: *CURR EMPL* chmn, pres, ceo, dir: Pope & Talbot

Porsche Cars North America, Inc. / Porsche Foundation
Sales: $250.0 million
Employees: 250
Headquarters: Reno, NV
SIC Major Group: Holding & Other Investment Offices and Wholesale Trade—Durable Goods

CONTACT
Ed Triolo
Vice President, Marketing & Comm.
Porsche Cars North America, Inc.
100 W. Liberty St., PO Box 30911
Reno, NV 89501
(702) 348-3000

FINANCIAL SUMMARY
Recent Giving: $126,094 (1991); $142,909 (1990); $82,399 (1989)
Assets: $166,652 (1991); $280,674 (1990); $396,634 (1989)
EIN: 94-3024854

CONTRIBUTIONS SUMMARY
Typical Recipients: • *Arts & Humanities:* arts associations, museums/galleries, opera, public broadcasting • *Civic & Public Affairs:* urban & community affairs • *Education:* colleges & universities • *Health:* pediatric health, single-disease health associations • *Social Services:* community service organizations, youth organizations
Geographic Distribution: only in Reno, NV, and Charleston, SC
Operating Locations: NV, SC

CORP. OFFICERS
Frederick J. Schwab: *CURR EMPL* pres, ceo: Porsche Cars N Am

GIVING OFFICERS
Luke Baer: secy
Ross Dupper: asst treas
Frederick J. Schwab: treas *CURR EMPL* pres, ceo: Porsche Cars N Am (see above)

APPLICATION INFORMATION
Initial Approach: Applications must be in writing and include a copy of IRS determination letter.
Restrictions on Giving: Porsche Cars North America is a subsidiary of Porsche Enterprises Inc., a subsidiary of Porsche AG.

GRANTS ANALYSIS
Number of Grants: 22
Highest Grant: $26,565
Typical Range: $500 to $10,000
Disclosure Period: 1991

RECENT GRANTS
26,565 Art Center College of Design, Pasadena, CA
23,647 KNPB/Channel 5
20,000 Washoe Medical Foundation, Washoe, NV
10,000 Reno Philharmonic, Reno, NV
10,000 Washoe Medical Foundation, Washoe, NV
5,438 United Way
5,000 National Judicial College, Reno, NV
5,000 Nevada Self Help Foundation, Reno, NV
4,446 KUNR
2,500 Reno/Tahoe Organizing Committee, Reno, NV

Portec, Inc.

Sales: $65.0 million
Employees: 499
Headquarters: Oak Brook, IL
SIC Major Group: Electronic &
Other Electrical Equipment,
Fabricated Metal Products,
Industrial Machinery &
Equipment, and Transportation
Equipment

CONTACT

Carrie Guski
Administrator
Portec, Inc.
122 West 22nd St.
Ste. 100
Oak Brook, IL 60521
(708) 573-4600

FINANCIAL SUMMARY

Recent Giving: $4,000 (1993
est.)

CONTRIBUTIONS SUMMARY

Company contributes 100% of
funds to social services.

Typical Recipients: • *Social
Services:* domestic violence,
food/clothing distribution, shel-
ters/homelessness

Geographic Distribution: primarily headquarters area

Operating Locations: IL (Oak
Brook)

CORP. OFFICERS

Albert Fried, Jr.: *B* New York
NY 1930 *ED* Cornell Univ BA
1952; Cornell Univ MBA 1953
CURR EMPL chmn: Portec
CORP AFFIL managing ptnr:
Albert Fried & Co; mem: NY
Stock Exchange *NONPR
AFFIL* chmn: Centurion Fdn;
pres: Fried Fdn

Michael T. Yonker: *CURR
EMPL* pres, ceo: Portec

APPLICATION INFORMATION

Initial Approach: Company
does accept applications; company makes annual selection.

Restrictions on Giving: Does
not support individuals, religious organizations for sectarian
purposes, political or lobbying
groups, or organizations outside operating areas.

GRANTS ANALYSIS

Typical Range: $2,500 to
$5,000

RECENT GRANTS

Hesed House, Aurora, IL
Salvation Army, Villa Park, IL

Porter Foundation, Mrs. Cheever

CONTACT

Alton E. Peters
Director
Mrs. Cheever Porter Fdn.
c/o Kelley, Drye and Warren
101 Park Ave.
New York, NY 10178

FINANCIAL SUMMARY

Recent Giving: $209,900 (fis-
cal 1991); $324,700 (fiscal
1990); $208,750 (fiscal 1989)
Assets: $2,856,957 (fiscal year
ending June 30, 1990);
$2,761,789 (fiscal 1989)
EIN: 13-6093181

CONTRIBUTIONS SUMMARY

Typical Recipients: • *Arts &
Humanities:* arts centers
• *Civic & Public Affairs:* municipalities, urban & community affairs • *Education:* colleges & universities, medical
education • *Social Services:*
animal protection, community
service organizations, disabled
Grant Types: general support

GIVING OFFICERS

Alton E. Peters: trust
Edgar Scott, Jr.: trust
Clifford E. Starkins: trust

APPLICATION INFORMATION

Initial Approach: Send brief
letter describing program.
There are no deadlines.

GRANTS ANALYSIS

Number of Grants: 42
Highest Grant: $55,000
Typical Range: $200 to $5,000
Disclosure Period: fiscal year
ending June 30, 1990

RECENT GRANTS

55,000 Tufts University,
Medford, MA
14,000 Huntington Town-
wide Fund, Hunt-
ington, NY
10,000 Cornell University
Veterinary School,
Ithaca, NY
10,000 University of Pennsylvania, Philadel-
phia, PA
5,000 Animal Medical
Center, New York,
NY
5,000 Goodwill Industries

5,000 New York Infir-
mary, New York,
NY
5,000 Phillips Exeter
Academy, Exeter,
NH
5,000 Society for the Prevention of Cruelty
to Animals
5,000 Youth Services

Porter Paint Co. / Porter Paint Foundation

Sales: $108.5 million
Employees: 1,000
Headquarters: Louisville, KY

CONTACT

W.R. Niblock
President
Porter Paint Foundation
400 South 13th Street
Louisville, KY 40203-1714
(502) 588-9206

FINANCIAL SUMMARY

Recent Giving: $8,500 (1990);
$10,000 (1989)
Assets: $159,591 (1990);
$163,150 (1989)
EIN: 61-1094575

CONTRIBUTIONS SUMMARY

Typical Recipients: • *Educa-
tion:* education associations,
education funds, general
Grant Types: general support
Geographic Distribution: giv-
ing primarily in KY
Operating Locations: KY
(Louisville)

CORP. OFFICERS

Robert E. Champagne: *CURR
EMPL* pres, ceo: Porter Paint
Co

GIVING OFFICERS

Robert E. Champagne: dir
CURR EMPL pres, ceo: Porter
Paint Co (see above)
W.R. Niblock: pres
R.B. York: secy-treas

APPLICATION INFORMATION

Initial Approach: Submit a
brief letter of inquiry. There
are no deadlines.

GRANTS ANALYSIS

Number of Grants: 2
Highest Grant: $6,000
Disclosure Period: 1990

RECENT GRANTS

6,000 Clarksville River-
front Foundation,
Clarksville, IN

2,500 Kentucky Educa-
tional Foundation,
Lexington, KY

Porter Testamentary Trust, James Hyde

CONTACT

Deanna O. Neely
Asst. V.P. and Trust Officer
James Hyde Porter Testamentary
Trust
c/o Trust Co. Bank of Middle
Georgia, N.A.
PO Box 4248
Macon, GA 31208
(912) 741-2265

FINANCIAL SUMMARY

Recent Giving: $192,020
(1990); $137,075 (1989)
Assets: $3,900,792 (1990);
$3,347,734 (1989)
EIN: 58-6034882

CONTRIBUTIONS SUMMARY

Donor(s): the late James Hyde
Porter
Typical Recipients: • *Arts &
Humanities:* arts institutes, his-
tory/historic preservation, mu-
seums/galleries, music • *Education:* arts education, colleges &
universities, medical education, private education (precollege) • *Social Services:* disabled, shelters/homelessness,
united funds
Grant Types: capital and general support
Geographic Distribution: limited to Bibb and Newton counties, GA

GIVING OFFICERS

Rodney Browne: mgr
Emory Greene: mgr
Rev. Lee Holiday: mgr
Kathy Kalish: mgr
Lee Robinson: mgr
Donald G. Stephenson: mgr

APPLICATION INFORMATION

Initial Approach: Application
form required. Approach foundation initially by telephone.
Deadline is April 20.

OTHER THINGS TO KNOW

Publications: Application
Guidelines

GRANTS ANALYSIS

Number of Grants: 31
Highest Grant: $30,000

Typical Range: $4,000 to
$10,000
Disclosure Period: 1990

RECENT GRANTS

30,000 Corporation of
Mercer University,
Macon, GA — com-
plete tissue culture
room

25,000 Macon Rescue Mis-
sion, Macon, GA —
purchase kitchen
equipment and
renovate elevator

18,000 Wesleyan College,
Macon, GA

10,000 Georgia Industrial
Home, Atlanta, GA
— renovation of
cottage and school
classroom equip-
ment

10,000 Macon Arts Alli-
ance, Macon, GA
— Bibb Institute
for Arts in Educa-
tion

8,000 Children's Hospi-
tal/Medcen Founda-
tion, Macon, GA —
purchase critical
care beds

8,000 Harriett Tubman
Museum and Cul-
tural Museum,
Macon, GA

7,500 Macon Outreach
Ministry, Macon,
GA

5,000 Boys Club of
Macon, Macon, GA

4,600 American Red
Cross, Macon, GA

Portland Food
Products Co.

Sales: $300.0 million
Employees: 1,500
Headquarters: Portland, OR
SIC Major Group: Chemicals &
Allied Products and Food &
Kindred Products

CONTACT
Richard Bertelotti
Vice President, Communications
Portland Food Products Co.
5320 Southwest Macadam Ave.
Portland, OR 97201
(503) 228-8188

CONTRIBUTIONS
SUMMARY
Typical Recipients: • *Arts &
Humanities:* museums/galleries
• *Science:* science exhibits &
fairs
Grant Types: general support
Operating Locations: OR
(Portland)

CORP. OFFICERS
Jeffrey Grimm: *CURR EMPL*
cfo: Portland Food Products Co
James G. Reynolds: *B* Chi-
cago IL 1943 *ED* Denison Univ
1965; Univ Chicago 1968
CURR EMPL chmn, pres, ceo:
Portland Food Products Co
CORP AFFIL chmn: Charlotte
Charles, Gray & Co, PFP Spe-
cialty Foods; dir: Solus Sys,
US Bakery

RECENT GRANTS
25,000 Oregon Museum of
Science and Indus-
try, Portland, OR

Portland General
Electric Co.

Sales: $759.84 million
Employees: 3,134
Parent Company: Portland
General Corp.
Headquarters: Portland, OR
SIC Major Group: Electric, Gas
& Sanitary Services

CONTACT
Christine H. Crossland
Community Resources Specialist
Portland General Electric Co.
121 Southwest Salmon St.
Portland, OR 97204
(503) 464-7614

FINANCIAL SUMMARY
Recent Giving: $625,000
(1993 est.); $678,000 (1992 ap-
prox.); $750,000 (1991 approx.)
Fiscal Note: Company gives
all funds directly. Besides the
Community Resources Department, other departments within
company makes limited giving.
Contact Gregg Kantor, Manager, Community Develop-
ment, or George Wyatt, Manager Goverment Affairs for
information. Budget for their
support is $196,800 and is not
included above.

CONTRIBUTIONS
SUMMARY
Typical Recipients: • *Arts &
Humanities:* arts festivals, arts
institutes, dance, ethnic arts,
music, opera, performing arts,
public broadcasting • *Civic &
Public Affairs:* consumer affairs, economic development,
environmental affairs, housing,
professional & trade associations, urban & community affairs • *Education:* business education, career/vocational
education, colleges & universities, community & junior colleges, continuing education,

education funds, science/tech-
nology education, student aid
• *Health:* public health
• *Science:* science exhibits &
fairs, scientific organizations
• *Social Services:* aged, child
welfare, community centers,
community service organizations, delinquency & crime, disabled, drugs & alcohol, emergency relief, food/clothing
distribution, shelters/homeless-
ness, united funds, volunteer
services, youth organizations
Grant Types: capital, general
support, multiyear/continuing
support, project, and scholarship
Nonmonetary Support Types:
donated equipment, donated
products, in-kind services, and
loaned executives
Note: Nonmonetary support in
1992 was $20,000. In 1991, the
value was $50,000. This sup-
port is not included in above
figures. Company also donates
the use of its facilities.
Geographic Distribution: Oregon; with emphasis on service
area
Operating Locations: OR
(Beaverton, Gresham,
Hillsboro, Oregon City, Portland, Salem, Sandy, Woodburn)

CORP. OFFICERS
Ken L. Harrison: *B* Bakers-
field CA 1942 *ED* OR St Univ
BS 1964; OR St Univ MA 1966
CURR EMPL chmn, pres, ceo,
dir: Portland Gen Electric Co
CORP AFFIL chmn, ceo, dir:
Portland Gen Corp; dir:
Sprouse Reitz

GIVING OFFICERS
Kathy Carlson: *CURR EMPL*
mgr community resources:
Portland Gen Electric Co
Christine H. Crossland:
CURR EMPL community re-
sources specialist: Portland
Gen Electric Co
Fred D. Miller: vp pub aff

APPLICATION
INFORMATION
Initial Approach: *Initial Contact:* letter or proposal *Include
Information On:* description of
the organization, amount requested, project budget, purpose for which funds are
sought, recently audited financial statement, proof of tax-exempt status *When to Submit:*
any time *Note:* Budget for following year is set in late fall.
Applicants should request PGE
contributions request form.

Restrictions on Giving: Does
not support individuals, fraternal or political groups, religious organizations for sectarian
purposes, or goodwill advertising.

GRANTS ANALYSIS
Total Grants: $678,000*
Number of Grants: 470*
Highest Grant: $10,000
Typical Range: $500 to $5,000
Disclosure Period: 1992
Note: Figures for total grants,
number of grants, and average
grant are approximate. Recent
grants are derived from a 1992
grants list.

RECENT GRANTS
78,600 Oregon Inde-
pendent College
Foundation, Port-
land, OR

10,000 Oregon Shake-
speare Festival, OR

5,000 Black United
Fund, Portland, OR

5,000 Columbia Pacific
Council of Boy
Scouts

5,000 Equity Foundation

5,000 Marylhurst College

5,000 Middle Oregon His-
torical Society, OR

5,000 Oregon Symphony
Association, OR

5,000 Oregon Trail Foun-
dation, OR

5,000 Portland State Uni-
versity Foundation,
OR

Portsmouth General
Hospital
Foundation

CONTACT
Portsmouth General Hospital
Foundation
P.O. Box 1053
Portsmouth, VA 23705-1053

FINANCIAL SUMMARY
Recent Giving: $405,157 (fis-
cal 1991)
Assets: $10,374,693 (fiscal
year ending June 30, 1991)
EIN: 54-1463392

GIVING OFFICERS
Maury W. Cooke: pres
Alan E. Gollihue: exec dir
Ernest F. Hardee: vp
C. Edward Russell, Jr.: secy
Gordon E. Saffold, Jr.: treas

GRANTS ANALYSIS
Total Grants: $405,157
Number of Grants: 31
Highest Grant: $52,695

Disclosure Period: fiscal year ending June 30, 1991

Posey Trust, Addison

CONTACT
Addison Posey Trust
c/o Wells Fargo Bank, P.O. Box 63954
San Francisco, CA 94163

FINANCIAL SUMMARY
Recent Giving: $699,591 (1990)
Assets: $5,612,084 (1990)
Gifts Received: $154,447 (1990)
EIN: 94-6612930

CONTRIBUTIONS SUMMARY
Typical Recipients: • *Social Services:* disabled, religious welfare

GRANTS ANALYSIS
Highest Grant: $664,612
Disclosure Period: 1990
Note: Incomplete grants list provided in 1990.

RECENT GRANTS
664,612 Salvation Army, San Francisco, CA
34,979 Guide Dogs for the Blind, San Rafael, CA

Posnack Family Foundation of Hollywood

CONTACT
Posnack Family Fdn of Hollywood
c/o Barnett Banks Trust Co., N.A.
PO Box 40200
Jacksonville, FL 32203-0200

FINANCIAL SUMMARY
Recent Giving: $387,150 (fiscal 1992); $653,300 (fiscal 1991); $438,850 (fiscal 1990)
Assets: $7,032,733 (fiscal year ending January 31, 1992); $6,554,305 (fiscal 1991); $6,361,344 (fiscal 1990)
Gifts Received: $261,087 (fiscal 1991); $1,049,351 (fiscal 1990); $1,477 (fiscal 1989)
EIN: 59-2484512

CONTRIBUTIONS SUMMARY
Typical Recipients: • *Civic & Public Affairs:* ethnic/minority organizations • *Education:* colleges & universities, education associations, private education (precollege) • *Health:* hospices • *International:* international organizations • *Religion:* religious organizations, synagogues • *Social Services:* community centers, disabled
Grant Types: general support

GRANTS ANALYSIS
Number of Grants: 24
Highest Grant: $60,000
Typical Range: $10,000 to $40,000
Disclosure Period: fiscal year ending January 31, 1992

RECENT GRANTS
60,000 American Associates of Ben Gurion University, New York, NY — agricultural research project
50,000 Bar-Ilan University, New York, NY
45,000 American Society for Technion, New York, NY
31,000 David Posnack Hebrew Day School
25,000 Brandeis University, Waltham, MA
25,000 Or-David Outreach
24,000 Alyn-American Society for Handicapped
18,000 PEF Israel Endowment Fund, New York, NY
10,000 American Committee for Shaare Zedek Hospital, New York, NY

Post Foundation of D.C., Marjorie Merriweather

CONTACT
Nancy Young Duncan
Treasurer
Marjorie Merriweather Post Foundation of D.C.
4155 Linnean Avenue, N.W.
Washington, DC 20008
(202) 686-8500
Note: The foundation has suspended its giving program for 1993.

FINANCIAL SUMMARY
Recent Giving: $13,000 (1991); $1,123,746 (1990)
Assets: $82,000,000 (1992 est.); $95,998,646 (1991); $81,769,135 (1990); $69,310,504 (1988)
Gifts Received: $1,733 (1991); $5,000 (1988)

Fiscal Note: In 1988, the foundation received a gift of $5,000 from the mother of Mrs. Frank A. Thomas Jr. of Charleston, WV.
EIN: 52-6080752

CONTRIBUTIONS SUMMARY
Donor(s): Marjorie Merriweather Post (1887-1973) was the only child of C.W. Post, who developed and marketed the cereal foods Post Toasties, Postum, and Grape Nuts.

Marjorie Post was married four times — to Edward B. Close (1905-1919), E.F. Hutton (1920-1935), Joseph E. Davies (1935-1955), and Herbert A. May (1958-1964). Following her divorce from May, she resumed her name of Marjorie Merriweather Post.

Through her own business talents, Marjorie Post led in the formation, in the 1930s, of the General Foods Corporation, the largest food company in the United States.

In 1967, she began the foundation with a donation of several million dollars. When she died in 1973, her New York estate was left to New York State, her Florida estate to the U.S. government, and the Washington, DC, estate, Hillwood, to the Smithsonian Institution. Eventually, Hillwood was turned over to the foundation, which continues to support its operation as a public museum.

The museum reportedly houses the most comprehensive collection of nineteenth-century Russian decorative art outside the Soviet Union. In 1983, the foundation opened a Native-American artifacts building displaying Mrs. Post's collection of Native-American art.

Typical Recipients: • *Arts & Humanities:* arts centers, community arts, dance, ethnic arts, history/historic preservation, museums/galleries, music, opera, performing arts, public broadcasting • *Civic & Public Affairs:* environmental affairs, public policy • *Education:* colleges & universities • *Health:* hospitals, single-disease health associations • *Religion:* churches • *Social Services:* aged, child welfare, community centers, family planning, food/clothing distribution, recreation & athletics, religious welfare, youth organizations

Grant Types: capital, conference/seminar, department, endowment, general support, operating expenses, project, and scholarship
Geographic Distribution: national, with emphasis on the Washington, DC, metropolitan area

GIVING OFFICERS
Melissa Cantacuzne: dir
Ellen MacNeille Charles: pres
David P. Close: secy, dir *CURR EMPL* ptnr: Dahlgren & Close *NONPR AFFIL* mem: Am Bar Assn, Assn Bar City NY, Assn Trial Lawyers Am, DC Bar Assn, Inter-Am Bar Assn, World Assn Lawyers World Peace Through Law; mem adv counc: Natl Capital Area Boy Scouts Am; pres, dir: Intl Humanities
Nina Rumbough Craig: dir
Antal Post de Bekessy: dir
Nancy Young Duncan: treas
Raymond P. Hunter: dir
Mary Draper Janney: dir
Dina Merrill Hartley: vp, dir, don daughter *B* New York *NONPR AFFIL* dir: Am Music Dramatic Academy, Joslin Diabetes Fdn, Juvenile Diabetes Fdn, NY Comm Olympic Ski Team; vp: NY City Mission Soc
Adelaide C. Riggs: dir, pres emeritus
Stanley H. Rumbough: dir
John A. Sargent: dir
Henry Strong: dir

APPLICATION INFORMATION
Initial Approach:
Prospective applicants should send a letter of inquiry to the foundation. No specific application form is required.
All applications must be submitted in writing by October 1 in order to be considered at the December board meeting.
Restrictions on Giving:
Grants are awarded only to organizations qualifying under IRS section 501(c)(3) and which are not private foundations as described in section 509(A). Grants are not made to individuals.

OTHER THINGS TO KNOW
Publications: application guidelines

GRANTS ANALYSIS
Total Grants: $13,000
Number of Grants: 1
Highest Grant: $13,000

Typical Range: $5,000* to
$30,000
Disclosure Period: 1991
Note: Figures for typical grant
are for 1990. Recent grants are
derived from a 1991 Form 990.

RECENT GRANTS

13,000 Fine Arts Museum
of San Francisco,
San Francisco, CA
— to conserve/re-
store painting

Potlatch Corp. / Potlatch Foundation for Higher Education/Potlatch Foundation II

Sales: $1.33 billion
Employees: 7,127
Headquarters: San Francisco, CA
SIC Major Group: Lumber &
Wood Products and Paper &
Allied Products

CONTACT
Joyce Laboure
Corporate Programs
  Administrator
Potlatch Corp.
PO Box 193591
San Francisco, CA 94119
(510) 947-4725

FINANCIAL SUMMARY
Recent Giving: $1,373,000
(1992 approx.); $1,602,000
(1991); $848,342 (1990)
Assets: $2,810,403 (1990);
$142,391 (1988)
Fiscal Note: Company gives
mainly through foundations.
Above figures represent combined giving of both foundations. Individual operating locations have limited giving
budgets. However, they make
their own decisions regarding
nonmonetary support.
EIN: 82-6005250

CONTRIBUTIONS SUMMARY
Typical Recipients: • *Arts &
Humanities:* dance, muse-
ums/galleries, music, opera,
performing arts • *Civic & Public Affairs:* economic development, environmental affairs
• *Education:* colleges & universities, education associations,
literacy • *Health:* hospitals
• *Social Services:* child welfare, united funds, youth organizations

Grant Types: employee match-
ing gifts, fellowship, general
support, and scholarship
Geographic Distribution: al-
most exclusively near operat-
ing facilities in the rural areas
of Arkansas, Idaho, and Minne-
sota
Operating Locations: AR
(McGehee, Prescott, Stuttgart,
Warren), CA (San Francisco,
Walnut Creek), ID (Lewiston,
Pierce, Post Falls, St. Maries),
MN (Brainerd, Cloquet, Cook,
Grand Rapids)
Note: Company gives very lim-
ited support to organizations in
San Francisco where other cor-
porate funding is plentiful.

CORP. OFFICERS
Richard Blaine Madden: *B*
Short Hills NJ 1929 *ED* Prince-
ton Univ BS 1951; Univ MI JD
1956; NY Univ MBA 1959
CURR EMPL chmn, pres, ceo,
dir: Potlatch Corp *CORP
AFFIL* dir: Consolidated
Freightways, Pacific Gas &
Electric Co, URS Corp *NONPR
AFFIL* bd govs exec comm:
San Francisco Symphony; dir:
Am Paper Inst, Natl Park Fdn,
San Francisco Opera Assn,
Smith-Kettlewell Eye Res Inst;
mem: Bus-Higher Ed Forum,
MI Bar Assn, NY Bar Assn;
mem exec comm: Bay Area
Counc; trust: Fine Arts Mus
San Francisco; trust exec
comm: Am Enterprise Inst

GIVING OFFICERS
A. L. Alford, Jr.: trust
Jack A. Buell: trust
Richard N. Congreve: trust
CURR EMPL group vp (pulp,
paperboard & packaging): Pot-
latch Corp
Brian W. Davis: secy, asst
treas *CURR EMPL* dir: Pot-
latch Corp
Ralph M. Davisson: trust
CURR EMPL vp, gen couns:
Potlatch Corp
Barbara M. Failing: trust
John B. Frazer, Jr.: trust
Robert W. Gamble: trust
Jack L. Hogan, DDS: trust
Sally J. Ihne: trust
George Frederick Jewett, Jr.:
vp *B* Spokane WA 1927 *ED*
Dartmouth Coll BA 1950; Har-
vard Univ MBA 1952 *CURR
EMPL* vchmn, dir: Potlatch
Corp *NONPR AFFIL* chmn:
Pacific Presbyterian Med Fdn;
dir: Carnegie Inst, San Fran-
cisco Ballet Assn; trust: Asia
Fdn, Natl Gallery Art

George E. Pfautsch: trust
CURR EMPL sr vp (fin), cfo:
Potlatch Corp *NONPR AFFIL*
dir: Med Svcs Bur ID
Sandra T. Powell: treas, asst
secy *CURR EMPL* treas: Pot-
latch Corp *NONPR AFFIL*
mem: AM Inst CPAs, Am Soc
Corp Secys, ID Soc CPAs, ID
State Bd Accountancy, Natl
Assn Corp Treas
John M. Richards: pres *B*
1939 *CURR EMPL* pres, coo:
Potlatch Corp *NONPR AFFIL*
pres: Potlatch Fdn For Higher
Ed
L. Pendelton Siegel: trust
CURR EMPL sr vp (fin), treas,
cfo: Potlatch Corp
Hubert D. Travaille: pres *B*
Bangkok Thailand 1939 *CURR
EMPL* vp (pub affs): Potlatch
Corp

APPLICATION INFORMATION
Initial Approach: *Initial Contact:* for Foundation for Higher
Education, request application
form between October 1 and
December 15; for Foundation
II, call *Include Information
On:* for Foundation for Higher
Education, include application,
high school transcript, ACT or
SAT results, confidential report
from principal or counselor at
current school, and two confidential letters of reference; for
Foundation II, foundation will
ask for needed information
When to Submit: for Foundation for Higher Education, February 15; for Foundation II,
any time, proposals submitted
by June will be considered for
following year's grants *Note:*
For scholarship applications,
write Potlatch Foundation for
Higher Education, PO Box
193591, San Francisco, CA
94119-3591.
Restrictions on Giving: Foundations will not consider scholarship applicants not residing
within 30 miles of a company
operating site.
Grants are not made to organizations serving only a specific
group of people.

GRANTS ANALYSIS
Total Grants: $1,602,000*
Number of Grants: 400*
Highest Grant: $500,000*
Typical Range: $1,000 to
$5,000
Disclosure Period: 1991
Note: Total grants figure in-
cludes $59,700 in Dollars for
Doers grants, $80,758 in match-

ing gifts to education, and a single grant of $325,000 from Pot-
latch Foundation II to Potlatch
Foundation for Higher Education. Number of grants, average grant, and highest grant
from 1991. Assets are from
1990. Recent grants are derived from a 1991 Form 990.

RECENT GRANTS
500,000 American Enter-
prise Institute,
Washington, DC —
145,000 Potlatch Founda-
tion for Higher
Education — PFHE
140,000 Potlatch Founda-
tion for Higher
Education — PFHE
65,000 American Enter-
prise Institute,
Washington, DC —
general
45,000 United Way-Twin
County, Lewiston,
ID — general
40,000 Lewis-Clark State
College 21st, Le-
wiston, ID — target
35,500 McGehee Public
School System —
general
30,000 Cloquet Commu-
nity Memorial Hos-
pital Foundation,
Cloquet, MN — tar-
get
27,000 HIPPY-McGehee
School District,
McGehee, AR —
target
25,000 College of St.
Scholastica, Clo-
quet, MN — target

Potomac Edison Co.
Sales: $1.25 billion
Employees: 1,042
Parent Company: Allegheny
Power System Inc.
Headquarters: Hagerstown, MD
SIC Major Group: Electric, Gas
& Sanitary Services

CONTACT
Sue Tuckwell
Personnel
Potomac Edison Co.
10435 Downsville Pke.
Hagerstown, MD 21740
(301) 790-3400

CONTRIBUTIONS SUMMARY
Operating Locations: MD
(Hagerstown)

CORP. OFFICERS
Klaus Bergman: *B* Nurnberg
Germany 1931 *ED* Columbia
Coll 1953; Columbia Univ Law
Sch 1955 *CURR EMPL* chmn,

ceo: Allegheny Power Sys
CORP AFFIL chmn, ceo:
Monongahela Power Co, Potomac Edison Co, Potomac Edison Co, West PA Power Co;
dir: OH Valley Electric Co;
pres, ceo: Allegheny Power
Svc Corp
Alan J. Noia: *CURR EMPL*
pres: Potomac Edison Co

Potomac Electric Power Co.

Revenue: $1.41 billion
Employees: 5,100
Headquarters: Washington, DC
SIC Major Group: Electric, Gas
& Sanitary Services

CONTACT
William Torgerson
Chairman, Contributions
  Committee
Potomac Electric Power Co.
1900 Pennsylvania Ave., NW,
  Rm 841
Washington, DC 20068
(202) 872-2365
Note: Alternative contact is Ann
  Monahan, (202) 872-3488.

FINANCIAL SUMMARY
Recent Giving: $1,700,000
(1992 approx.); $1,773,000
(1991); $1,700,000 (1990)
Fiscal Note: Company gives directly.

CONTRIBUTIONS SUMMARY
Typical Recipients: • *Arts &
Humanities:* arts associations,
arts centers, dance, history/his-
toric preservation, libraries,
museums/galleries, music,
opera, performing arts, public
broadcasting, theater • *Civic &
Public Affairs:* business/free enterprise, civil rights, environmental affairs, municipalities,
urban & community affairs,
women's affairs • *Education:*
colleges & universities, education associations, education
funds, literacy, minority education, public education (precollege), science/technology education, student aid • *Health:*
health organizations, hospices,
hospitals, medical research, pediatric health, single-disease
health associations • *International:* international organizations • *Religion:* churches, religious organizations • *Social
Services:* aged, animal protection, child welfare, community
service organizations, disabled,
drugs & alcohol, employ-

ment/job training, family services, food/clothing distribution,
recreation & athletics, shel-
ters/homelessness, united
funds, youth organizations
Grant Types: capital and project
Note: Does not fund general operating funds.
Geographic Distribution:
Washington, DC, area
Operating Locations: DC, MD

CORP. OFFICERS
Edward Franklin Mitchell: *B*
Harrisonburg VA 1931 *ED*
Univ VA 1956; George Wash-
ington Univ 1960 *CURR EMPL*
pres, ceo, dir: Potomac Electric
Power Co *CORP AFFIL* dir:
Acacia Mutual Life Ins Co,
Roggs Natl Bank, Suburban
Bank *NONPR AFFIL* bd dirs:
Natl Rehabilitation Hosp; bd
dirs DC Chapter: ARC; mem
adv counc: Univ MD Energy
Coll; mem, dir: MD Chamber
Commerce
William Reid Thompson: *B*
Durham NC 1924 *ED* Univ NC
BS 1945; Harvard Univ LLB
1949 *CURR EMPL* chmn, dir:
Potomac Electric Power Co
CORP AFFIL dir: Acacia Mu-
tual Life Ins Co, Geico Corp,
Riggs Natl Corp *NONPR
AFFIL* chmn: Fed City Counc;
dir: Natl Symphony Orchestra
Assn; mem: Am Bar Assn,
Assn Edison Illuminating Cos,
Bus Counc, Bus Roundtable,
Delta Kappa Epsilon, Edison
Electric Inst, Phi Beta Kappa,
Southeastern Electric Ex-
change; mem exec comm: WA
Bd Trade

GIVING OFFICERS
William Torgerson: *B* Annapolis MD 1944 *CURR EMPL* vp,
gen couns: Potomac Electric
Power Co

APPLICATION INFORMATION
Initial Approach: *Initial Contact:* letter or proposal *Include
Information On:* description of
the organization, amount requested, purpose for which
funds are sought, recently
audited financial statement,
proof of tax-exempt status
When to Submit: any time
Restrictions on Giving: Funds
organization only in company's
service territory. Does not fund
organizations outside of the
metropolitan Washington,
D.C., area.

GRANTS ANALYSIS
Total Grants: $1,700,000
Disclosure Period: 1990

Pott Foundation, Herman T. and Phenie R.

CONTACT
John P. Fetcher
Executive Director
Herman T. and Phenie R. Pott
  Fdn.
1034 South Brentwood, Ste. 1480
St. Louis, MO 63117
(314) 725-8477

FINANCIAL SUMMARY
Recent Giving: $690,900
(1990); $683,000 (1989)
Assets: $13,742,758 (1990);
$13,614,314 (1989)
EIN: 43-6041541

CONTRIBUTIONS SUMMARY
Donor(s): The foundation was
established in 1963.
Typical Recipients: • *Arts &
Humanities:* history/historic
preservation, libraries, muse-
ums/galleries, opera • *Civic &
Public Affairs:* environmental
affairs, philanthropic organizations, zoos/botanical gardens
• *Education:* colleges & universities, education funds,
science/technology education
• *Health:* health organizations,
hospitals, medical research,
mental health • *Religion:*
churches, religious organizations • *Social Services:* child
welfare, community service organizations, domestic violence,
family planning, family services, food/clothing distribution,
homes, shelters/homelessness,
united funds, youth organizations
Grant Types: multiyear/con-
tinuing support and operating
expenses
Geographic Distribution:
focus on Missouri, with an emphasis on St. Louis

GIVING OFFICERS
James Collins: mem adv comm
Roy Collins: mem adv comm
Richard Pugh Conerly: mem
adv comm *B* Jackson AL 1924
ED Univ MO BJ 1948; Harvard
Univ LLB 1952 *CORP AFFIL*
chmn: Orion Capital
John P. Fechter: mem adv
comm
Mary Greco: mem adv comm

William Grant Guerri: mem
adv comm *B* Higbee MO 1921
ED Central Methodist Coll AB
1943; Columbia Univ LLB
1946 *CURR EMPL* ptnr:
Thompson & Mitchell *CORP
AFFIL* ptnr: Thompson &
Mitchell *NONPR AFFIL* cura-
tor: Central Methodist Coll;
dir: St Louis Heart Assn, Un
Way Greater St Louis; fellow:
Fellows Am Bar; mem: Am Bar
Assn, Am Judicature Soc, Met
St Louis, MO Bar, NY City Bar
Assn
James Murphy: mem adv
comm
Phenie Pott: mem adv comm

APPLICATION INFORMATION
Initial Approach:
The foundation requests applications be made in writing.
The foundation has no deadline
for submitting proposals.
Restrictions on Giving:
Grants are made only to organizations exempt under section
501(c)(3) of the IRS code. The
foundation does not make
grants to individuals.

GRANTS ANALYSIS
Total Grants: $690,900
Number of Grants: 123
Highest Grant: $40,000
Typical Range: $500 to
$12,000
Disclosure Period: 1990
Note: Recent grants are derived
from a 1990 grants list.

RECENT GRANTS
40,000 St. Louis Mercan-
  tile Library Asso-
  ciation, St. Louis,
  MO
30,000 Grace Hill Settle-
  ment House, St.
  Louis, MO
30,000 Missouri Girls
  Town Foundation,
  Kingdom City, MO
30,000 Salvation Army
  Hope Center, St.
  Louis, MO
30,000 St. Louis Mercan-
  tile Library Asso-
  ciation, St. Louis,
  MO
30,000 Washington Univer-
  sity, St. Louis, MO
30,000 Washington Univer-
  sity, St. Louis, MO
25,000 Missouri Botanical
  Garden, St. Louis,
  MO
25,000 Whitfield School
  for Scholarships,
  St. Louis, MO
22,000 United Way of
  Greater St. Louis,
  St. Louis, MO

Pott Foundation, Robert and Elaine

CONTACT
Gordon Maynard
Trust Officer
Robert and Elaine Pott Fdn.
c/o Citizens National Bank
20 N.W. Third St.
Evansville, IN 47708

FINANCIAL SUMMARY
Recent Giving: $190,000 (fiscal 1991); $190,000 (fiscal 1990); $185,000 (fiscal 1989)
Assets: $3,378,752 (fiscal year ending March 31, 1991); $3,093,810 (fiscal 1990); $2,858,122 (fiscal 1989)
EIN: 35-6290997

CONTRIBUTIONS SUMMARY
Typical Recipients: • *Education:* colleges & universities, science/technology education
Grant Types: scholarship
Geographic Distribution: focus on IN and WI

APPLICATION INFORMATION
Initial Approach: Send brief letter describing program. Deadline is April 30.

GRANTS ANALYSIS
Number of Grants: 6
Highest Grant: $100,000
Typical Range: 9,000 to 18,000
Disclosure Period: fiscal year ending March 31, 1991

RECENT GRANTS
100,000 University of Evansville, Evansville, IN
35,000 University of Southern Indiana, Evansville, IN
15,000 Purdue University, West Lafayette, IN
15,000 Rose-Hulman Institute, Terre Haute, IN
15,000 University of Notre Dame, Notre Dame, IN
10,000 University of Wisconsin, Madison, WI

Potter Foundation, Justin and Valere

CONTACT
Justin P. Wilson
Chairman and Trustee
Justin and Valere Potter Foundation
c/o Waller, Lansden, Dortch and Davis
511 Union St., Ste. 2100
Nashville, TN 37219
(615) 244-6380
Note: Another contact is Lois Squires, trust officer, NationsBank, One NationsBank Plaza M-7, Nashville, TN 37239-1697, (615) 749-3336.

FINANCIAL SUMMARY
Recent Giving: $977,500 (1991); $1,177,000 (1990); $877,000 (1989)
Assets: $25,898,867 (1991); $21,563,402 (1990); $21,492,713 (1989)
EIN: 62-6033081

CONTRIBUTIONS SUMMARY
Donor(s): The Justin and Valere Potter Foundation was established in Tennessee in 1951 by the late Justin Potter and his wife, Valere Blair Potter. Mr. Potter, a financier and industrialist, founded the Nashville Coal Company and was chairman of the Virginia-Carolina Chemical Corporation. He also served as president of the Chemical Securities Company, chairman of the Cherokee Insurance Company, and director of Commerce Union Bank. The foundation holds a significant portion of Mobil Oil Corporation stock.
Typical Recipients: • *Arts & Humanities:* history/historic preservation, libraries, museums/galleries, music • *Education:* colleges & universities, medical education, student aid • *Social Services:* family services, religious welfare, youth organizations
Grant Types: capital, general support, operating expenses, and scholarship
Geographic Distribution: focus on metropolitan Nashville, TN

GIVING OFFICERS
Albert Menefee, Jr.: trust
Justin P. Wilson: chmn, trust *B* Oakland CA 1945 *ED* Univ Florence; Stanford Univ BA

1967; Vanderbilt Univ JD 1970; NY Univ LLM 1974 *CURR EMPL* atty: Waller Lansden Dortch Davis *NONPR AFFIL* mem: Am Bar Assn, Nashville Bar Assn, NY City Bar Assn, TN Bar Assn

APPLICATION INFORMATION
Initial Approach:
Applicants should send a letter to the foundation.
The letter should include a description of the organization, with proof of tax-exempt status. There are no specific deadlines for submitting proposals. Applications may be submitted any time.
Notification is sent within two months of receipt of proposal.
Restrictions on Giving: No grants are given to individuals.

OTHER THINGS TO KNOW
NationsBank is the corporate trustee for the foundation.

GRANTS ANALYSIS
Total Grants: $977,500
Number of Grants: 29
Highest Grant: $245,000
Typical Range: $10,000 to $50,000
Disclosure Period: 1991
Note: The average grant figure excludes the highest grant. Recent grants are derived from a 1991 Form 990.

RECENT GRANTS
245,000 Vanderbilt University School of Medicine, Nashville, TN — for Justin Potter Merit Scholarship
100,000 Cumberland Museum, Nashville, TN
100,000 Dominican Campus
50,000 Montgomery Bell Academy, Montgomery, AL
40,000 Traveller's Rest Historic House Museum, Nashville, TN
35,000 David Lipscomb College, Nashville, TN
35,000 Vanderbilt T V Archives, Nashville, TN
35,000 YCAP (YMCA), McKendree, TN
30,000 Meharry Medical Center, Nashville, TN
25,000 Blair School of Music for Youth

Symphony, Nashville, TN

Potts and Sibley Foundation

CONTACT
Robert W. Bechtel
Trustee
Potts and Sibley Fdn.
10 Cambridge Court
Midland, TX 79705
(915) 694-1032

FINANCIAL SUMMARY
Recent Giving: $67,000 (fiscal 1992); $67,000 (fiscal 1991); $109,515 (fiscal 1990)
Assets: $2,435,384 (fiscal year ending July 31, 1992); $2,139,865 (fiscal 1991); $2,026,608 (fiscal 1990)
EIN: 75-6081070

CONTRIBUTIONS SUMMARY
Donor(s): Effie Potts Sibley Irrevocable Trust
Typical Recipients: • *Arts & Humanities:* community arts, museums/galleries, music • *Civic & Public Affairs:* environmental affairs, zoos/botanical gardens • *Education:* colleges & universities • *Health:* hospitals • *Religion:* churches
Grant Types: general support
Geographic Distribution: focus on TX

GIVING OFFICERS
Robert W. Bechtel: dir
Maurice Randolph Bullock: trust *B* Colorado City TX 1913 *ED* Univ TX LLB 1936 *NONPR AFFIL* fellow: Am Bar Fdn, Am Coll Trust Estate Counc, TX Bar Fdn; mem: Am Bar Assn, Am Judicature Soc, Ft Stockton Historical Soc, Midland County Bar Assn, Pecos County Chamber Commerce, Permian Basin Petroleum Assn, Southwestern Legal Fdn, Trans-Pecos Bar Assn, TX Bar Assn, TX Trial Lawyers Assn, West TX Chamber Commerce; mem exec comm: TX Law Enforcement Fdn
D. J. Sibley, Jr.: dir

APPLICATION INFORMATION
Initial Approach: Application form required. There are no deadlines.

GRANTS ANALYSIS
Number of Grants: 28

Highest Grant: $5,000
Typical Range: $1,000 to $5,000
Disclosure Period: fiscal year ending July 31, 1992

RECENT GRANTS

5,000	Austin Symphony, Austin, TX
5,000	Midland-Odessa Symphony and Chorale, Midland, TX
5,000	Permian Basin Petroleum Museum, Midland, TX
5,000	University of Texas at Austin, Austin, TX
4,000	University of Texas at Dallas, Dallas, TX
3,000	First United Methodist Church, Ft. Stockton, TX
3,000	Seton Fund (Hospital), Austin, TX
3,000	Sibley Environmental Learning Center, Midland, TX
3,000	Sul Ross State University, Alpine, TX
3,000	Texas Nature Conservancy, San Antonio, TX

Potts Memorial Foundation

CONTACT
Charles E. Inman
Secretary
Potts Memorial Fdn.
PO Box 1015
Hudson, NY 12534
(518) 828-3365

FINANCIAL SUMMARY
Recent Giving: $172,371 (1991); $174,328 (1990); $121,511 (1989)
Assets: $2,923,522 (1991); $2,757,089 (1990); $2,764,853 (1989)
EIN: 14-1347714

CONTRIBUTIONS SUMMARY
Typical Recipients: • *Education:* colleges & universities, medical education, science/technology education • *Health:* health organizations, hospices, hospitals, medical research, single-disease health associations • *International:* international organizations • *Social Services:* aged, homes
Grant Types: capital, endowment, project, research, and scholarship

GIVING OFFICERS
Stanley Bardwell, M.D.: trust
James M. Blake, M.D.: trust, vp
Gerald D. Dorman, M.D.: trust
Charles E. Inman: trust, secy
Frank C. Maxon, Jr.: trust
J. Warren Van Deusen: trust, treas
Carl G. Whitbeck, M.D.: trust, pres

APPLICATION INFORMATION
Initial Approach: Contributes only to preselected organizations.
Restrictions on Giving: Does not support individuals or provide funds for endowments or matching gifts.

GRANTS ANALYSIS
Number of Grants: 10
Highest Grant: $74,800
Typical Range: $2,000 to $12,000
Disclosure Period: 1991

RECENT GRANTS

74,800	Columbia Greene Medical Center
38,003	Albany Medical College, Albany, NY
26,743	Alden/March Medical College
12,075	University of Southern California School of Medicine, Los Angeles, CA
10,350	University of Southern Colorado, Pueblo, CO
5,300	Penobscot Respiratory, PA
2,000	Haitian and Caribbean Foundation
1,650	John F. Kennedy Medical Center
850	Hudson Valley Community College
600	Columbia-Greene Vo-Tec Center

Pottstown Mercury / Pottstown Mercury Foundation

Employees: 180
Parent Company: Goodson Newspaper Group
Headquarters: Pottstown, PA
SIC Major Group: Printing & Publishing

CONTACT
Joseph M. Zlomek
Trustee
Pottstown Mercury Foundation
24 North Hanover St.
Pottstown, PA 19464
(215) 323-3000

FINANCIAL SUMMARY
Recent Giving: $700 (1991); $5,650 (1990); $14,800 (1989)
Assets: $90,999 (1991); $90,014 (1990); $90,024 (1989)
Gifts Received: $1,700 (1991); $5,650 (1990); $14,300 (1989)
Fiscal Note: In 1991, contributions were received from Peerless Publications.
EIN: 23-6256419

CONTRIBUTIONS SUMMARY
Typical Recipients: • *Arts & Humanities:* music • *Civic & Public Affairs:* urban & community affairs • *Health:* medical research, single-disease health associations • *Religion:* synagogues • *Social Services:* community service organizations, united funds, youth organizations
Grant Types: general support
Geographic Distribution: focus on Pottstown, PA
Operating Locations: PA (Pottstown)

CORP. OFFICERS
Nancy March: *CURR EMPL* editor: Pottstown Mercury
Joseph M. Zlomek: *CURR EMPL* publ: Pottstown Mercury

GIVING OFFICERS
Barry Hopwood: trust

APPLICATION INFORMATION
Initial Approach: Send brief letter describing program. There are no deadlines.

GRANTS ANALYSIS
Number of Grants: 2
Highest Grant: $600
Typical Range: $100 to $600
Disclosure Period: 1991

RECENT GRANTS

600	Pottstown Symphony Orchestra Association, Pottstown, PA
100	Fourth of July Homecoming Committee, Pottstown, PA

Powell Co., William / Powell Co. Foundation, William

Sales: $41.3 million
Employees: 500
Headquarters: Cincinnati, OH
SIC Major Group: Fabricated Metal Products

CONTACT
V. Anderson Coombe
Trustee
William Powell Co. Foundation
2535 Spring Grove Ave.
Cincinnati, OH 45214
(513) 852-2000

FINANCIAL SUMMARY
Recent Giving: $17,350 (1991); $17,350 (1990); $13,600 (1989)
Assets: $217,418 (1991); $311,696 (1990); $306,461 (1989)
EIN: 31-6043487

CONTRIBUTIONS SUMMARY
Typical Recipients: • *Arts & Humanities:* arts funds, history/historic preservation • *Civic & Public Affairs:* environmental affairs, zoos/botanical gardens • *Education:* colleges & universities, education funds • *Social Services:* child welfare, community service organizations, united funds, youth organizations
Grant Types: general support
Geographic Distribution: focus on Cincinnati, OH
Operating Locations: OH (Cincinnati)

CORP. OFFICERS
Vachael Anderson Coombe: *B* Cincinnati OH 1926 *ED* Yale Univ BE 1948 *CURR EMPL* chmn, dir: William Powell Co *CORP AFFIL* dir: Eagle-Picher Indus, Lodge & Shipley Co, Star Bank, Union Central Life Ins Co
D. Randy Cowart: *CURR EMPL* pres: William Powell Co

GIVING OFFICERS
Vachael Anderson Coombe: trust *CURR EMPL* chmn, dir: William Powell Co (see above)
R. S. Dunham: trust

APPLICATION INFORMATION
Initial Approach: Contributes only to preselected organizations.

GRANTS ANALYSIS
Number of Grants: 11
Highest Grant: $15,000
Typical Range: $100 to $1,000
Disclosure Period: 1991

RECENT GRANTS
　15,000 United Appeal, Cincinnati, OH
　7,500 United Appeal, Cincinnati, OH
　5,750 Cincinnati Fine Arts Fund, Cincinnati, OH
　2,750 Cincinnati Fine Arts Fund, Cincinnati, OH
　2,500 Zoological Society, Cincinnati, OH
　2,500 Zoological Society, Cincinnati, OH
　1,250 Texas Children's Hospital, Houston, TX
　1,000 University of Cincinnati, Cincinnati, OH
　1,000 Xavier University, Cincinnati, OH
　　750 Zoological Society, Cincinnati, OH

Powell Family Foundation

CONTACT
Marjorie P. Allen
President
Powell Family Foundation
PO Box 7270
Overland Park, KS 66207
(913) 344-3471

FINANCIAL SUMMARY
Recent Giving: $2,320,687 (1990); $2,520,174 (1989); $1,964,507 (1988)
Assets: $51,492,121 (1990); $52,451,162 (1989); $56,154,381 (1988)
Gifts Received: $175 (1990); $1,935 (1989)
EIN: 23-7023968

CONTRIBUTIONS SUMMARY
Donor(s): The Powell Foundation was established in 1969 by George E. Powell, former chairman of the Yellow Freight System of Delaware. The foundation gives preference to projects in the the Kansas City area where Mr. Powell lived. In keeping with Mr. Powell's beliefs, the foundation continues to support organizations that enrich the family, religious values, community involvement, and youth organizations.

The foundation gives priority to the funding of Christian Science programs and to activities and programs for youth. The foundation's trustees are members of the Powell family.
Typical Recipients: • *Arts & Humanities:* arts centers, dance, history/historic preservation, museums/galleries, performing arts, theater • *Civic & Public Affairs:* law & justice, nonprofit management, philanthropic organizations, safety, urban & community affairs, zoos/botanical gardens • *Education:* agricultural education, business education, colleges & universities, education associations, education funds, faculty development, minority education, private education (precollege), public education (precollege), special education, student aid • *Religion:* churches, religious organizations • *Social Services:* child welfare, community centers, community service organizations, family services, food/clothing distribution, recreation & athletics, religious welfare, youth organizations
Grant Types: capital, challenge, general support, operating expenses, project, and scholarship
Geographic Distribution: focus on metropolitan Kansas City, MO

GIVING OFFICERS
Marjorie Powell Allen: pres, trust, don daughter
Marilyn P. Mcleod: vp, secy, trust, don daughter
George Everett Powell, Jr.: dir *B* Kansas City MO 1926 *ED* Northwestern Univ 1946 *CURR EMPL* chmn, dir: Yellow Corp *CORP AFFIL* dir: Butler Mfg Co, First Natl Charter Corp *NONPR AFFIL* assoc trust: Nelson Atkins Mus Art; bd govs: Kansas City Art Inst; dir: Kansas City Symphony; mem: Kansas City Chamber Commerce, Northwestern Univ Bus Adv Comm Trans Ctr; trust, mem exec comm: Mid-West Res Inst
George Everett Powell III: treas *B* Kansas City MO 1948 *ED* IN Univ BSBA *CURR EMPL* pres, ceo, dir: Yellow Corp *NONPR AFFIL* bd govs: Regular Common Carrier Conf; chmn: Public Television 19, Inc; mem: Young Pres Org; trust: Midwest Res Inst
Nicholas A. Powell: dir

APPLICATION INFORMATION
Initial Approach:
The foundation does not use formal application forms. Application for a grant should be made by letter.
The presentation should be no more than five pages and should include a description of the project, the proposed budget, objectives of the program, other sources of funds, current trustees or board members, most recent audited financial statement, and a copy of the IRS letter certifying tax-exempt status.
Applications must be received at least 30 days before a meeting of the board of trustees. The board of trustees usually meets in January, April, July, and October.
Restrictions on Giving: The foundation does not make grants to individuals, or for building programs, endowments, or projects outside the United States.

OTHER THINGS TO KNOW
The foundation is incorporated in Missouri, but maintains its office in Kansas.
The foundation reports that in 1991 about 58% of grants were for less than $5,000.
Publications: annual report

GRANTS ANALYSIS
Total Grants: $2,320,687
Number of Grants: 150
Highest Grant: $150,000
Typical Range: $1,000 to $10,000 and $25,000 to $100,000
Disclosure Period: 1990
Note: The figure for average grant excludes 17 grants totaling $990,444 to the Powell Gardens. Recent grants are derived from a 1990 Form 990.

RECENT GRANTS
　150,000 Powell Gardens, Kingsville, MO — Perennial Garden
　100,000 Powell Gardens, Kingsville, MO — Perennial Garden
　90,000 Principle Foundation, Kansas City, MO — operations
　75,000 Pembroke Hill School, Kansas City, MO — scholarships
　72,700 Powell Gardens, Kingsville, MO — operating
　68,000 Powell Gardens, Kingsville, MO — operating
　67,400 Powell Gardens, Kingsville, MO — operating
　65,400 Powell Gardens, Kingsville, MO — operating
　64,500 Powell Gardens, Kingsville, MO — operating
　62,000 Boy Scouts of America — Scout Service Center

Powell Foundation, Charles Lee

CONTACT
Herbert Kunzel
Chairman and Director
Charles Lee Powell Foundation
7742 Herschel Avenue, Ste. A
La Jolla, CA 92037
(619) 459-3699

FINANCIAL SUMMARY
Recent Giving: $3,537,028 (1991); $2,955,000 (1990); $2,637,400 (1989)
Assets: $42,386,541 (1991); $35,903,664 (1990); $37,063,063 (1989)
EIN: 23-7064397

CONTRIBUTIONS SUMMARY
Donor(s): The foundation was established in 1954 by the late Charles Lee Powell.
Typical Recipients: • *Education:* colleges & universities, engineering education, science/technology education
Grant Types: general support, project, and research
Geographic Distribution: California

GIVING OFFICERS
Hugh C. Carter: dir
Lawrence W. Cox: treas, dir
James L. Focht: dir
Herbert Kunzel: chmn, dir
William D. McElroy: dir *B* Rogers TX 1917 *ED* Stanford Univ BA 1939; Reed Coll MA 1941; Princeton Univ PhD 1943 *NONPR AFFIL* mem: Am Academy Arts Sciences, Am Assn Advancement Science, Am Chemical Soc, Am Inst Biological Sciences, Am Philosophical Soc, Am Soc Bacteriologists, Am Soc Biological Chemists, Kappa Sigma, Natl Academy Sciences, Sigma Xi, Soc Gen Physiology, Soc Naturalists, Soc Zoologists; prof: Univ CA

Patricia C. McInnis: corp secy
Charles W. Rees, Jr.: dir

APPLICATION INFORMATION

Initial Approach: Restrictions on Giving: The foundation reports that it only makes contributions to preselected charitable organizations and does not accept unsolicited proposals for funds.

GRANTS ANALYSIS

Total Grants: $3,537,028
Number of Grants: 4
Highest Grant: $1,160,778
Typical Range: $608,750 to $1,160,778
Disclosure Period: 1991
Note: Recent grants are derived from a 1991 Form 990.

RECENT GRANTS

1,160,778 University of California at San Diego, San Diego, CA
908,750 Stanford University, Stanford, CA
858,750 University of Southern California, Los Angeles, CA
608,750 California Institute of Technology, Pasadena, CA

Powers Foundation

CONTACT

C. Cody White, Jr.
President
Powers Fdn.
PO Box 1607
Shreveport, LA 71165
(318) 221-0151

FINANCIAL SUMMARY

Recent Giving: $157,245 (fiscal 1991); $169,500 (fiscal 1990); $151,770 (fiscal 1987)
Assets: $3,345,974 (fiscal year ending July 31, 1991); $3,070,748 (fiscal 1990); $2,911,582 (fiscal 1987)
EIN: 75-6080974

CONTRIBUTIONS SUMMARY

Donor(s): the late Gussie N. Power
Typical Recipients: • *Arts & Humanities:* music • *Education:* colleges & universities, education funds • *Health:* medical research • *Religion:* religious organizations • *Social Services:* aged, homes, volunteer services, youth organizations

Grant Types: general support
Geographic Distribution: limited to Shreveport and Bossier County, LA

GIVING OFFICERS

C. Cody White, Jr.: pres
Sara Margaret White: vp

APPLICATION INFORMATION

Initial Approach: Send brief letter of inquiry describing program. There are no deadlines.

GRANTS ANALYSIS

Number of Grants: 13
Highest Grant: $30,000
Typical Range: $2,000 to $10,000
Disclosure Period: fiscal year ending July 31, 1991

RECENT GRANTS

30,000 Biomedical Research Foundation, Shreveport, LA
28,000 Boy Scouts of America, Shreveport, LA
25,000 Glen Retirement System, Shreveport, LA
25,000 Shreveport Symphony, Shreveport, LA
10,000 YMCA, Shreveport, LA
8,000 Volunteers of America, Shreveport, LA
7,500 Louisiana State University, Baton Rouge, LA
7,500 Shreveport Chamber Foundation for Educational Research, Shreveport, LA
4,745 Youth Enrichment Program, Shreveport, LA
3,500 Rutherford House, Shreveport, LA

Powers Higher Educational Fund, Edward W. and Alice R.

CONTACT

Edward W. and Alice R. Powers Higher Educational Fund
P.O. Box 450
Youngstown, OH 44501-0450

FINANCIAL SUMMARY

Recent Giving: $350,000 (fiscal 1991)
Assets: $9,033,174 (fiscal year ending January 31, 1991)
Gifts Received: $1,014,730 (fiscal 1991)

EIN: 34-6900472

CONTRIBUTIONS SUMMARY

Typical Recipients: • *Education:* colleges & universities
Grant Types: general support

GIVING OFFICERS

Mary A. Grace: advisory com
Alex Murphy: advisory com
Brian J. Wolf: advisory com

GRANTS ANALYSIS

Total Grants: $350,000
Number of Grants: 7
Highest Grant: $50,000
Disclosure Period: fiscal year ending January 31, 1991

RECENT GRANTS

50,000 Bethany College, Bethany, WV
50,000 College of Wooster, Wooster, OH
50,000 Lake Erie College, Painesville, OH
50,000 Mount Union College, Alliance, OH
50,000 Thiel College, Grenville, PA
50,000 Westminster College, New Wilmington, PA
50,000 Youngstown State University, Youngstown, OH

Poynter Fund

CONTACT

Catherine Heron
Secretary
Poynter Fund
490 First Ave. South
St. Petersburg, FL 33731
(813) 893-8111

FINANCIAL SUMMARY

Recent Giving: $1,192,350 (fiscal 1990); $139,499 (fiscal 1989); $163,000 (fiscal 1988)
Assets: $1,742,085 (fiscal year ending November 30, 1990); $2,867,020 (fiscal 1989); $2,597,925 (fiscal 1988)
EIN: 59-6142547

CONTRIBUTIONS SUMMARY

Donor(s): the late Henrietta M. Poynter, the late Nelson Poynter
Typical Recipients: • *Arts & Humanities:* museums/galleries • *Education:* colleges & universities, journalism education
Grant Types: endowment, general support, and scholarship

GIVING OFFICERS

Andrew E. Barnes: dir, pres
Catherine Heron: secy
John H. O'Hearn: dir, vp
Robert T. Pittman: trust
Marion K. Poynter: trust
George Rahdert: trust

APPLICATION INFORMATION

Initial Approach: Send brief letter describing program. There are no deadlines.

GRANTS ANALYSIS

Number of Grants: 5
Highest Grant: $1,000,000
Typical Range: $20,000 to $40,000
Disclosure Period: fiscal year ending November 30, 1990

RECENT GRANTS

1,000,000 Duke University, Durham, NC
40,000 American Political Science Association, Washington, DC — sponsor participation in APSA"s Congressional Fellowship Program
25,000 Eckerd College, St. Petersburg, FL
20,000 Yale University, New Haven, CT — provide seminars in modern journalism
1,000 St. Petersburg Museum of Fine Arts, St. Petersburg, FL

PPG Industries / PPG Industries Foundation

Sales: $5.85 billion
Employees: 33,700
Headquarters: Pittsburgh, PA
SIC Major Group: Chemicals & Allied Products, Electronic & Other Electrical Equipment, and Stone, Clay & Glass Products

CONTACT

Roslyn Rosenblatt
Executive Director
PPG Industries Fdn.
One PPG Pl.
Pittsburgh, PA 15272
(412) 434-2962

FINANCIAL SUMMARY

Recent Giving: $4,000,000 (1993 est.); $4,000,000 (1992 approx.); $4,422,862 (1991)
Assets: $8,244,556 (1991); $11,922,096 (1990); $10,051,501 (1989)

Fiscal Note: Above represents foundation only. Company also has limited direct giving, principally to Pittsburgh charities, under the Pennsylvania Neighborhood Assistance Act. These gifts totaled $55,000 in 1991.
EIN: 25-6037790

CONTRIBUTIONS SUMMARY

Typical Recipients: • *Arts & Humanities:* arts associations, arts festivals, community arts, dance, history/historic preservation, libraries, literary arts, museums/galleries, music, opera, performing arts, public broadcasting • *Civic & Public Affairs:* business/free enterprise, civil rights, economic development, economics, environmental affairs, ethnic/minority organizations, housing, international affairs, law & justice, municipalities, public policy, safety, urban & community affairs, women's affairs • *Education:* business education, colleges & universities, economic education, education associations, engineering education, minority education, private education (precollege), public education (precollege), science/technology education, student aid • *Health:* health care cost containment, health organizations, hospitals, medical rehabilitation, mental health, single-disease health associations • *Science:* observatories & planetariums, science exhibits & fairs, scientific institutes, scientific organizations • *Social Services:* aged, child welfare, community centers, community service organizations, day care, disabled, employment/job training, food/clothing distribution, homes, united funds, volunteer services, youth organizations
Grant Types: capital, department, employee matching gifts, general support, operating expenses, project, research, and scholarship
Geographic Distribution: nationally, with emphasis on corporate operating locations; special interest in Pittsburgh, PA, area
Operating Locations: AL (Huntsville), CA (Fresno, Torrance), DE (Dover), GA (East Point), IL (Gurnee, Mount Zion), IN (Evansville, Kokomo), KS (Kansas City), LA (Lake Charles), MD (Baltimore, Cumberland), MI (De-

troit), MO (Crystal City), NC (Lexington, Shelby), OH (Barberton, Chillicothe, Circleville, Cleveland, Crestline, Delaware), PA (Carlisle, Creighton, Ford City, Greensburg, Meadville, Pittsburgh, Springdale, Stockertown, Tipton), TX (LaPorte, Wichita Falls), WA (Chehalis), WI (Oak Creek), WV (New Martinsville)
Note: Also operates in Canada, Europe, China, and Japan.

CORP. OFFICERS

Vincent Anthony Sarni: *B* Bayonne NJ 1928 *ED* Univ RI BS 1949; NY Univ 1951; Harvard Univ 1973 *CURR EMPL* chmn, ceo, dir: PPG Indus *CORP AFFIL* dir: Asahi-Penn Chem Ltd (Tokyo), Brockway Inc, Hershey Foods Corp, Honeywell, Pittsburgh Baseball Assocs, PNC Fin Corp, PPG Canada *NONPR AFFIL* chmn: Allegheny Conf Commun Devel, Natl Org Disability, Pittsburgh Opera Soc; chmn, ceo: Inst Training Handicapped Advanced Tech; dir: Allegheny Gen Hosp, River City Band; mem: Bus Higher Ed Forum, Bus Roundtable, Chem Mfrs Assn, Soc Chem Indus; mem bus adv counc: Univ RI; trust: Carnegie-Mellon Univ, Juniata Coll, Univ RI Fdn

GIVING OFFICERS

Donald W. Bogus: mem screening comm
Stanley C. DeGreve: mem screening comm
Garry A. Goudy: mem screening comm
Raymond W. LeBoeuf: vp, dir *B* Chicago IL 1946 *ED* Northwestern Univ 1967; Univ IL 1970 *CURR EMPL* vp (fin): PPG Indus
H. Kennedy Linge: mem screening comm
Roslyn Rosenblatt: exec dir
Joseph E. Rowe: vp, dir *B* Highland Park MI 1927 *CURR EMPL* vp, chief scientist: PPG Indus *NONPR AFFIL* bd govs: IL Inst Tech Res Inst; chmn: Univ IL Coalition Advancement Indus Tech; fellow: Am Assoc Advancement Science, Inst Electrical & Electronics Engrs; mem: Am Mgmt Assoc, Am Physical Soc, Am Soc Engg Ed, Eta Kappa Nu, Natl Academy Engg, Phi Kappa Phi, Sigma Xi, Tau Beta Pi; mem indus adv bd: Univ IL

Vincent Anthony Sarni: chmn, dir *CURR EMPL* chmn, ceo, dir: PPG Indus (see above)
William V. Warnick: mem screening comm

APPLICATION INFORMATION

Initial Approach: *Initial Contact:* one- to two-page letter to foundation if organizations are located in Pittsburgh area or are national in scope; organizations serving communities where PPG facilities are located should direct inquiries to local PPG agent *Include Information On:* brief outline of purpose of organization, population it serves, how requested funds will be used *When to Submit:* by September 1 for funding the next year
Restrictions on Giving: No grant applications for less than $100 will be considered. Foundation does not support operating funds of United Way agencies; political activities or organizations; individuals; advertising in benefit publications; direct student scholarships; sectarian groups for religious purposes; telephone solicitations; special events; or fraternal organizations.

OTHER THINGS TO KNOW

To ensure sensitivity to local needs in PPG plant communities, foundation has developed a local agent system. Approximately 40 company managers, most of whom live in PPG plant communities, have been designated as local agents for the foundation. Once a year agents recommend a budget for contributions in their communities to a screening committee for presentation to the foundation board.

GRANTS ANALYSIS

Total Grants: $3,619,887*
Number of Grants: 809
Highest Grant: $440,000
Typical Range: $1,000 to $10,000
Disclosure Period: 1991
Note: Total grants figures excludes $802,975 in matching gifts. Total giving for the year is $4,422,862. Recent grants are derived from a 1991 annual report.

RECENT GRANTS

440,000 United Way, Southwestern Pennsylva-

nia, Southwestern Pennsylvania, PA
280,630 National Merit Scholarship Corporation, Evanston, IL
100,000 Carnegie Science Center, Pittsburgh, PA
100,000 University of Pittsburgh, Third Century Campaign, Pittsburgh, PA
60,000 Greater Pittsburgh Guild for the Blind Low Vision Clinic, Pittsburgh, PA
50,000 Allegheny Health Services, Mobile Mammogram Unit, Pittsburgh, PA
50,000 Pittsburgh Opera, Pittsburgh, PA — Artistic Development Fund
50,000 United Way, Southwestern Louisiana, LA
35,000 Penn's Southwest Association, PA
34,000 United Way, Huntsville, AL

PQ Corp. / PQ Corp. Foundation

Sales: $200.0 million
Employees: 1,300
Headquarters: Valley Forge, PA
SIC Major Group: Chemicals & Allied Products and Stone, Clay & Glass Products

CONTACT

Dale J. Shimer
President
PQ Corp. Foundation
Valley Forge Executive Mall, Bldg. 11
Valley Forge, PA 19482
(215) 293-7200
Note: Contact address for the PQ Matching Gifts Plan is Administrator, P.O. Box 840, Valley Forge, PA, 19482-0840.

FINANCIAL SUMMARY

Assets: $10,000 (1990)
EIN: 23-2302993

CONTRIBUTIONS SUMMARY

Typical Recipients: • *Science:* scientific institutes
Grant Types: general support
Geographic Distribution: focus on PA
Operating Locations: MA (Ashland), NJ (Parsippany), PA (Valley Forge)

CORP. OFFICERS

George P. Keeley: *CURR EMPL* chmn: PQ Corp

Richard W. Kelso: *CURR EMPL* pres, ceo: PQ Corp

GIVING OFFICERS

Michael R. Imbriani: treas, dir *B* Brooklyn NY 1943 *ED* City Univ NY 1968; City Univ NY MBA 1972 *CURR EMPL* vp, treas, cfo: PQ Corp *CORP AFFIL* dir: Captain-PG Ltd, Farrokh-PG Ltd, PQ Export Co, PQP (Columbia), Sidesa (Mexico), Sooner Specialty Chemicals

James D. McDonald: dir

Ernest G. Posner: secy, dir *B* Nashville TN 1937 *ED* Vanderbilt Univ 1959; Am Univ 1967 *CURR EMPL* vp, secy, gen couns: PQ Corp *NONPR AFFIL* mem: Am Bar Assn, Am Corp Counc Assn, Licensing Execs Soc

John M. Reed: dir

Dale J. Shimer: pres, dir *B* Wanamaker IN 1935 *ED* IN Univ 1954 *CURR EMPL* exec vp, dir: PQ Corp

APPLICATION INFORMATION

Initial Approach: Send brief letter describing program. There are no deadlines.

GRANTS ANALYSIS

Number of Grants: 1
Disclosure Period: 1990

RECENT GRANTS

10,000   Franklin Institute, Philadelphia, PA — to support scientific work of institute

Prairie Foundation

CONTACT

Barbara T. Fasken
President
Prairie Fdn.
100 Larkspur Landing Circle, Ste. 116
Larkspur, CA 94939
(415) 461-2922

FINANCIAL SUMMARY

Recent Giving: $163,200 (1991); $254,746 (1990); $185,900 (1989)
Assets: $2,091,123 (1991); $2,109,005 (1990); $2,196,233 (1989)
EIN: 75-6012458

CONTRIBUTIONS SUMMARY

Donor(s): David Fasken Special Trust

Typical Recipients: • *Arts & Humanities:* community arts, opera • *Civic & Public Affairs:* environmental affairs, zoos/botanical gardens • *Education:* private education (precollege) • *Health:* hospitals • *Religion:* religious organizations • *Social Services:* animal protection, community service organizations, disabled, homes, united funds, youth organizations
Grant Types: general support
Geographic Distribution: focus on the San Francisco, CA, area

GIVING OFFICERS

Louis A. Bartha: secy, treas
Richard S. Brooks: dir, bp
Barbara T. Fasken: dir, pres

APPLICATION INFORMATION

Initial Approach: There are no deadlines.

GRANTS ANALYSIS

Number of Grants: 14
Highest Grant: $100,000
Typical Range: $500 to $10,000
Disclosure Period: 1991

RECENT GRANTS

100,000   Marin General Hospital, San Rafael, CA
25,000   United Way, Midland, TX
15,000   Boys Club of America, San Francisco, CA
10,000   Trinity School, Midland, TX
5,000   Baykeeper, San Francisco, CA
5,000   Environmental Defense Fund, New York, NY
500   Commonwealth Club, San Francisco, CA
500   Guide Dogs for the Blind, San Rafael, CA
500   Hospital De Familia, San Francisco, CA
500   Marin Humane Society, Novato, CA

Prange Co., H. C. / Prange Co. Fund, H. C.

Sales: $470.0 million
Employees: 5,600
Headquarters: Green Bay, WI
SIC Major Group: Apparel & Accessory Stores, General

Merchandise Stores, and Miscellaneous Retail

CONTACT

Charles Prange
Treasurer
H.C. Prange Co. Fund
301 N. Washington St.
Green Bay, WI 54301
(414) 436-5135

FINANCIAL SUMMARY

Recent Giving: $107,725 (fiscal 1991); $122,750 (fiscal 1990)
Assets: $81,240 (fiscal year ending January 31, 1991); $108,603 (fiscal 1990)
Gifts Received: $27,650 (fiscal 1991); $103,000 (fiscal 1989)
Fiscal Note: Fiscal 1992 Contribution received from H.C. Prange Company.
EIN: 39-6048083

CONTRIBUTIONS SUMMARY

Typical Recipients: • *Arts & Humanities:* arts centers, performing arts, theater • *Health:* hospitals • *Social Services:* community service organizations, united funds, youth organizations
Grant Types: general support
Geographic Distribution: focus on WI
Operating Locations: WI (Green Bay)

CORP. OFFICERS

Gerald Donnelly: *CURR EMPL* chmn, ceo: HC Prange Co
Robert J. Pfeil: *CURR EMPL* sr vp, cfo: HC Prange Co

GIVING OFFICERS

John M. Sieracke: secy, treas, dir

APPLICATION INFORMATION

Initial Approach: Send brief letter describing program. There are no deadlines.

GRANTS ANALYSIS

Number of Grants: 10
Highest Grant: $25,000
Typical Range: $100 to $5,000
Disclosure Period: fiscal year ending January 31, 1991

RECENT GRANTS

25,000   Center of Performing Arts, Green Bay, WI
22,500   YMCA, Green Bay, WI
20,000   St. Elizabeth Hospital, Elizabeth, NJ

15,000   Camp Evergreen, Sheboygan, WI
8,225   Madison Art Center, Madison, WI
8,000   Other Half Video
4,000   Trees for Tomorrow, Eagle River, WI
3,000   Community Core Group
1,000   Care a Van
1,000   Wisconsin Rapids Chamber of Commerce, Wisconsin Rapids, WI

Pratt & Lambert, Inc.

Sales: $238.9 million
Employees: 1,578
Headquarters: Buffalo, NY
SIC Major Group: Chemicals & Allied Products

CONTACT

Ellie Bradford
Administrative Asst. to the President
Pratt & Lambert, Inc.
PO Box 22
Buffalo, NY 14240
(716) 873-6000

CONTRIBUTIONS SUMMARY

Nonmonetary Support Types: in-kind services and workplace solicitation
Operating Locations: NY (Buffalo)

CORP. OFFICERS

Joseph J. Castiglia: *B* North Collins NY 1934 *ED* Canisius Coll 1955 *CURR EMPL* pres, ceo: Pratt & Lambert *CORP AFFIL* dir: Fed Reserve Bank NY, Pierce & Stevens Chemical Corp, Sevenson Environmental, Southern Coatings, Un Paint Co, Vision Group Funds *NONPR AFFIL* mem: Am Inst CPAs, Natl Assn Accts

Raymond D. Stevens, Jr.: *B* Buffalo NY 1927 *ED* Univ PA 1951 *CURR EMPL* chmn: Pratt & Lambert *CORP AFFIL* dir: First Empire St Corp, Mfrs & Traders Trust Co, Niagara Share Corp

Pratt Memorial Fund

Former Foundation Name: Arthur P. Pratt and Jeanette Gladys Pratt Memorial Fund

CONTACT

Pratt Memorial Fund
c/o Union Bank
530 "B" St.
San Diego, CA 92112
(619) 230-4633

FINANCIAL SUMMARY

Recent Giving: $190,730 (fiscal 1992); $198,775 (fiscal 1991); $172,358 (fiscal 1990)
Assets: $3,305,887 (fiscal year ending April 30, 1992); $3,224,483 (fiscal 1991); $3,087,724 (fiscal 1990)
EIN: 95-6464737

CONTRIBUTIONS SUMMARY

Donor(s): the late Jeanette Gladys Pratt
Typical Recipients: • *Arts & Humanities:* community arts, history/historic preservation, museums/galleries, performing arts, theater • *Health:* hospices, hospitals, medical research, single-disease health associations • *Social Services:* aged, community service organizations, shelters/homelessness, united funds, youth organizations
Grant Types: capital, emergency, general support, multi-year/continuing support, operating expenses, and research
Geographic Distribution: limited to San Diego County, CA

GIVING OFFICERS

Union Bank (California): trust

APPLICATION INFORMATION

Initial Approach: Send brief letter describing program. There are no deadlines.
Restrictions on Giving: Does not support individuals or provide scholarships or fellowships.

GRANTS ANALYSIS

Number of Grants: 52
Highest Grant: $30,000
Typical Range: $1,000 to $5,000
Disclosure Period: fiscal year ending April 30, 1992

RECENT GRANTS

30,000 Sharp Hospital Foundation, San Diego, CA
12,500 La Jolla Cancer Research Foundation, La Jolla, CA
7,500 Senior Adult Services, San Diego, CA
5,100 Salk Institute for Biological Studies, San Diego, CA
5,000 Boy Scouts of America, San Diego, CA
5,000 International Aerospace Hall of Fame, San Diego, CA
5,000 Linda Vista Health Care Center, Linda Vista, CA
5,000 Mercy Hospital Foundation of San Diego, San Diego, CA
5,000 San Diego Opera, San Diego, CA
5,000 St. Paul's Manor Health Care Center, San Diego, CA

Precision Castparts Corp.

Sales: $538.3 million
Employees: 7,339
Headquarters: Portland, OR
SIC Major Group: Primary Metal Industries and Transportation Equipment

CONTACT

Roy Marvin
Vice President, Administration
Precision Castparts Corp.
4600 South East Harney Dr.
Portland, OR 97206
(503) 777-3881

CONTRIBUTIONS SUMMARY

Operating Locations: OR (Portland)

CORP. OFFICERS

Edward H. Cooley: *B* Philadelphia PA 1922 *ED* Swarthmore Coll 1943; Harvard Univ MBA 1974 *CURR EMPL* chmn, ceo: Precision Castparts Corp
William C. McCormick: *CURR EMPL* pres, ceo: Precision Castparts Corp

RECENT GRANTS

100,000 Oregon Museum of Science and Industry, Portland, OR

Precision Rubber Products / Precision Rubber Products Foundation

Headquarters: Lebannon, TN

CONTACT

Anita Huddleston
President
Precision Rubber Products Foundation
Hartman Dr.
Lebannon, TN 37087-8401

FINANCIAL SUMMARY

Recent Giving: $17,300 (1991); $23,458 (1989)
Assets: $572,996 (1992); $526,222 (1989)
EIN: 31-0503347

CONTRIBUTIONS SUMMARY

Typical Recipients: • *Education:* colleges & universities • *Health:* hospitals • *Social Services:* child welfare, community service organizations, youth organizations
Operating Locations: TN (Lebannon)

CORP. OFFICERS

J. Carroll: *CURR EMPL* ceo: Precision Rubber Products

GIVING OFFICERS

Gordon G. Carroll: bd mem
Howard G. Gillette: bd mem
Anita Huddleston: pres, dir
Lynn Winfree: secy, dir

APPLICATION INFORMATION

Initial Approach: Send brief letter describing program. There are no deadlines.

Preferred Risk Mutual Insurance Co.

Assets: $320.3 million
Employees: 920
Parent Company: Preferred Risk Mutual Insurance Group
Headquarters: West Des Moines, IA
SIC Major Group: Insurance Carriers

CONTACT

Phil Vanderah
Treasurer
Preferred Risk Mutual Insurance Co.
1111 Ashworth Rd.
West Des Moines, IA 50265
(515) 225-5298

FINANCIAL SUMMARY

Fiscal Note: Annual Giving Range: less than $100,000

CONTRIBUTIONS SUMMARY

Company reports 95% of contributions support health and human services, and 5% support education. Company also provides a large contribution to the United Way.

Typical Recipients: • *Education:* colleges & universities • *Health:* general • *Social Services:* drugs & alcohol, general, united funds
Grant Types: matching
Geographic Distribution: primarily IA
Operating Locations: IA (West Des Moines)

CORP. OFFICERS

Bernard Mercer: *CURR EMPL* chmn: Preferred Risk Mutual Ins Co
Robert M. Plunk: *B* Bethel Springs TN 1932 *ED* Memphis St Univ 1962; Western St Univ 1973 *CURR EMPL* pres, ceo: Preferred Risk Mutual Ins Co *CORP AFFIL* dir: Midwest Mutual, Preferred Risk Life, Sports World *NONPR AFFIL* bd govs: Natl Assn Independent Insurers; founding dir: Mothers Against Drunk Driving; mem: Am Bar Assn

APPLICATION INFORMATION

Initial Approach: Send brief letter of inquiry, including a description of the organization, amount requested, purpose of funds sought, recently audited financial statements, and proof of tax-exempt status.
Restrictions on Giving: Does not support individuals, religious organizations for sectarian purposes or political or lobbying groups.

Preformed Line Products Co.

Sales: $108.0 million
Employees: 1,000
Headquarters: Mayfield Village, OH
SIC Major Group: Electronic & Other Electrical Equipment, Instruments & Related Products, and Rubber & Miscellaneous Plastics Products

CONTACT
Robert L. Weber
Personnel Manager
Preformed Line Products Co.
660 Beta Dr.
Mayfield Village, OH 44143
(216) 461-5200

CONTRIBUTIONS SUMMARY
Company provides employee matching gifts only.
Grant Types: matching
Operating Locations: OH (Mayfield Village)

CORP. OFFICERS
Jon R. Ruhlman: *B* Cleveland OH 1927 *ED* Purdue Univ 1949; Univ CO 1950 *CURR EMPL* pres, dir: Preformed Line Products Co *CORP AFFIL* pres: Dynaflite Corp, GT Sails Inc, Sailing Inc

Premark International
Sales: $2.95 billion
Employees: 25,000
Headquarters: Deerfield, IL
SIC Major Group: Chemicals & Allied Products, Electronic & Other Electrical Equipment, Industrial Machinery & Equipment, and Rubber & Miscellaneous Plastics Products

CONTACT
Robert Hoaglund
Vice President, Control Info Systems
Premark International, Inc.
1717 Deerfield Rd.
Deerfield, IL 60015
(708) 405-6000
Note: An alternative contact is Isabell Goosen at (708) 405-6218.

FINANCIAL SUMMARY
Fiscal Note: Figures for giving are unavailable.

CONTRIBUTIONS SUMMARY
Grant Types: general support
Nonmonetary Support Types: donated equipment and donated products
Note: Figures for nonmonetary support are unavailable. Contact for nonmonetary support is Robert Matha, Director, Public Relations.

CORP. OFFICERS
Warren L. Batts: *B* Norfolk VA 1932 *CURR EMPL* chmn, ceo, dir: Premark Intl

James M. Ringter: *CURR EMPL* pres, coo: Premark Intl

GIVING OFFICERS
Robert W. Hoaglund: vp (control & information sys) *CURR EMPL* vp (control & information sys): Premark Intl

Premier Bank / Premier Foundation
Former Foundation Name: First National Bank Foundation
Parent Company: Premier Bancorp
Assets: $3.85 billion
Parent Employees: 2,731
Headquarters: Shreveport, LA
SIC Major Group: Depository Institutions and Holding & Other Investment Offices

CONTACT
Robin Branim
Trust Officer
c/o Premier Bank N.A.
PO Box 21116
Shreveport, LA 71154
(318) 226-2211

FINANCIAL SUMMARY
Recent Giving: $161,185 (fiscal 1990); $193,014 (fiscal 1988)
Assets: $593,678 (fiscal 1989); $664,410 (fiscal 1988)
Gifts Received: $61,581 (fiscal 1990); $75,000 (fiscal 1988)
Fiscal Note: For the year ending in 1990, contributions were received from Premier Bancorp.
EIN: 72-6022876

CONTRIBUTIONS SUMMARY
Typical Recipients: • *Arts & Humanities:* arts associations, music, opera, theater • *Civic & Public Affairs:* business/free enterprise • *Education:* business education, colleges & universities • *Health:* medical research • *Religion:* religious organizations • *Social Services:* community service organizations, drugs & alcohol, homes, united funds, youth organizations
Grant Types: general support
Geographic Distribution: primarily in Shreveport, LA
Operating Locations: LA (Baton Rouge, Houma, Lake Charles, Monroe, New Orleans, Shreveport)

CORP. OFFICERS
James G. Boyer: *CURR EMPL* chmn, pres, dir: Premier Bank

GIVING OFFICERS
James Blewett: treas, dir
Jerry D. Boughton: pres, dir
Mary Fain: secy, dir
Don Updegraff: vp, dir

APPLICATION INFORMATION
Initial Approach: There is no specific application form, but a copy of the organization's exemption letter should be included. There are no deadlines.

GRANTS ANALYSIS
Number of Grants: 41
Highest Grant: $15,000
Typical Range: $500 to $1,000
Disclosure Period: fiscal year ending June 30, 1990

RECENT GRANTS
15,000 Shreveport Symphony Orchestra, Shreveport, LA
12,500 Shreveport Chamber Foundation, Shreveport, LA
10,000 Neighborhood Housing Services, Shreveport, LA
7,500 Shreveport Regional Arts, Shreveport, LA
6,900 Junior Achievement, Shreveport, LA
5,000 Biomedical Research Foundation, Shreveport, LA
5,000 Junior League of Shreveport, Shreveport, LA
5,000 Shreveport Little Theatre, Shreveport, LA
5,000 Shreveport Opera, Shreveport, LA

Premier Bank Lafayette
Parent Company: Premier Bancorp
Parent Sales: $3.85 billion
Parent Employees: 2,731
Headquarters: Lafayette, LA
SIC Major Group: Depository Institutions and Holding & Other Investment Offices

CONTACT
Rae Robinson
Vice President, Marketing Director
Premier Bank
PO Box 3248
Lafayette, LA 70502
(318) 236-7000

FINANCIAL SUMMARY
Fiscal Note: Annual Giving Range: less than $100,000

CONTRIBUTIONS SUMMARY
Geographic Distribution: in headquarters and operating communities
Operating Locations: LA (Lafayette)

Premier Bank of South Louisiana
Parent Company: Premier Bancorp
Parent Sales: $3.85 billion
Parent Employees: 2,731
Headquarters: Houma, LA
SIC Major Group: Depository Institutions and Holding & Other Investment Offices

CONTACT
Chris Stanley
Account Executive
Premier Bank of South Louisiana
720 East Main St.
Houma, LA 70360
(504) 876-7800

CONTRIBUTIONS SUMMARY
Operating Locations: LA (Houma)

Premier Dental Products Co. / Julius & Ray Charlestein Foundation
Sales: $20.3 million
Employees: 175
Headquarters: Norristown, PA
SIC Major Group: Instruments & Related Products and Wholesale Trade—Durable Goods

CONTACT
Morton Charlestein
President
Julius & Ray Charlestein Foundation
1710 Romano Dr.
Norristown, PA 19401
(215) 277-3800

FINANCIAL SUMMARY
Recent Giving: $317,955 (fiscal 1991); $287,099 (fiscal 1990)
Assets: $3,318,018 (fiscal year ending June 30, 1991); $3,134,192 (fiscal 1990)
Gifts Received: $300,000 (fiscal 1991); $300,000 (fiscal 1990)
Fiscal Note: Contributes through foundation only. In

1991, contributions were received from Premier Dental Products.
EIN: 23-2310090

CONTRIBUTIONS SUMMARY

Typical Recipients: • *Arts & Humanities:* history/historic preservation, museums/galleries • *Education:* private education (precollege), religious education • *Religion:* religious organizations, synagogues • *Science:* scientific institutes • *Social Services:* community service organizations
Grant Types: general support
Geographic Distribution: national, with emphasis on Pennsylvania
Operating Locations: PA (Norristown)

CORP. OFFICERS

Gary M. Charlestein: *B* Philadelphia PA 1944 *ED* Univ PA 1966; Jewish Theological Seminary Am 1972 *CURR EMPL* ceo: Premier Dental Products Co *CORP AFFIL* dir: Espe Premier (Canada), Espe Premier Sales Co, Premier Med
Morton Charlestein: *CURR EMPL* chmn: Premier Dental Products Co
Jerrold A. Frezel: *CURR EMPL* pres, secy: Premier Dental Products Co

GIVING OFFICERS

Gary M. Charlestein: secy, treas, dir *CURR EMPL* ceo: Premier Dental Products Co (see above)
Morton Charlestein: pres, dir *CURR EMPL* chmn: Premier Dental Products Co (see above)
Jerrold A. Frezel: vp *CURR EMPL* pres, secy: Premier Dental Products Co (see above)

APPLICATION INFORMATION

Initial Approach: *Note:* The foundation supports preselected organizations and does not accept unsolicited requests for funds.

GRANTS ANALYSIS

Total Grants: $317,955
Number of Grants: 80
Highest Grant: $85,000
Typical Range: $100 to $5,000
Disclosure Period: fiscal year ending June 30, 1991
Note: Recent grants are derived from a fiscal 1991 grants list.

RECENT GRANTS

85,000	Federation Allied Jewish Appeal, Philadelphia, PA
66,000	Federation of Jewish Agencies, Philadelphia, PA — FJA Operation Exodus
40,000	Mogan David Association Armdi, Philadelphia, PA
13,000	Akiba Hebrew Academy, Philadelphia, PA
10,000	US Holocaust Memorial Museum, Washington, DC
5,000	Congregation Or Shalom, Philadelphia, PA
4,000	Jewish National Fund, Philadelphia, PA
2,850	Har Zion, Philadelphia, PA
2,000	Albert Einstein Foundation, Philadelphia, PA
2,000	Har Zion Yom Kippur Mr M, Philadelphia, PA

Premier Industrial Corp. / Premier Industrial Foundation

Sales: $637.13 million
Employees: 3,300
Headquarters: Cleveland, OH
SIC Major Group: Chemicals & Allied Products, Fabricated Metal Products, Industrial Machinery & Equipment, and Petroleum & Coal Products

CONTACT

Virginia Levi
Associate Director
Premier Industrial Fdn.
4500 Euclid Ave.
Cleveland, OH 44103
(216) 391-8300

FINANCIAL SUMMARY

Recent Giving: $1,675,378 (1991); $1,573,748 (1990); $540,983 (1989)
Assets: $3,893,060 (1991); $4,261,677 (1990); $5,921,808 (1989)
Fiscal Note: Above figures reflect contributions by foundation, which handles all major giving.
EIN: 34-6522448

CONTRIBUTIONS SUMMARY

Typical Recipients: • *Arts & Humanities:* arts associations, arts centers, dance, history/historic preservation, libraries, museums/galleries, music, opera, public broadcasting, theater • *Civic & Public Affairs:* economic development, ethnic/minority organizations, philanthropic organizations, professional & trade associations, safety, urban & community affairs, women's affairs, zoos/botanical gardens • *Education:* business education, colleges & universities, education administration, education associations, education funds, science/technology education • *Health:* health organizations, hospices, public health • *Social Services:* community service organizations, emergency relief, food/clothing distribution, homes, recreation & athletics, united funds, volunteer services, youth organizations
Grant Types: capital, general support, project, and scholarship
Geographic Distribution: primarily northeast Ohio with emphasis on Cleveland, and United Way organizations in ten cities where company divisions operate
Operating Locations: NY (Bohemia), OH (Cleveland, Wooster)

CORP. OFFICERS

John Charles Colman: *B* Cleveland OH 1927 *ED* Cornell Univ 1949; Harvard Univ 1951 *CURR EMPL* dir: Premier Indus Corp *CORP AFFIL* dir: Act II Jewelry Inc, Balmorhea Ranches Inc, DBA Sys Inc, Duplex Products Inc, Orion Capital Corp, Security Ins Co, Sesame Sys Ltd, Stein Health Svcs Inc
Bruce W. Johnson: *CURR EMPL* pres, dir: Premier Indus Corp
Jack N. Mandel: *B* Austria 1911 *ED* Fenn Coll 1930-1933 *CURR EMPL* chmn fin comm, dir: Premier Indus Corp *NONPR AFFIL* hon trust: Hebrew Univ; life trust: Cleveland Jewish Welfare Fdn, South Broward Jewish Fed; mem exec comm: Natl Conf Christians Jews; pres: Montefiore Home Aged; pres adv bd: Barry Univ; trust: FL Soc Blind, Tel Aviv Univ Mus Diaspora, Wood Hosp
Joseph C. Mandel: *B* 1913 *CURR EMPL* chmn exec comm, dir: Premier Indus Corp
Morton Leon Mandel: *B* Cleveland OH 1921 *ED* Case Western Reserve Univ 1940-1942; Pomona Coll 1943 *CURR EMPL* chmn, ceo, dir: Premier Indus Corp *CORP AFFIL* chmn: D-A Lubricant Co *NONPR AFFIL* fdr: Clean Land OH, Cleveland Project MOVE, Cleveland Tomorrow; fdr, hon pres: Mid-Town Corridor, World Confederation Jewish Commun Ctrs; hon pres: Natl Jewish Welfare Bd; life trust: Counc Jewish Feds, Jewish Commun Ctrs Cleveland, Jewish Commun Fed, Un Way Cleveland; trust: Case Western Reserve Univ, Cleveland Mus Art, Ctr Social Policy Studies, Un Way Am; trust emeritus: Mt Sinai Hosp Cleveland
Philip Stuart Sims: *B* Cleveland OH 1927 *ED* Case Western Reserve Univ 1956 *CURR EMPL* vchmn, treas: Premier Indus Corp *CORP AFFIL* exec vp, treas: Premier Indus Corp

GIVING OFFICERS

John Charles Colman: trust *CURR EMPL* dir: Premier Indus Corp (see above)
Joseph C. Mandel: trust *CURR EMPL* chmn exec comm, dir: Premier Indus Corp (see above)
Morton Leon Mandel: trust *CURR EMPL* chmn, ceo, dir: Premier Indus Corp (see above)

APPLICATION INFORMATION

Initial Approach: *Initial Contact:* brief letter or proposal; no formal application form is used *Include Information On:* description of project and justification for grant; amount and term requested; pertinent financial information; IRS exemption status, including copy of exemption letter; if available, appraisal of the requesting organization by a standard-setting organization *When to Submit:* any time

GRANTS ANALYSIS

Total Grants: $1,675,378
Number of Grants: 99
Highest Grant: $750,000
Typical Range: $500 to $10,000
Disclosure Period: 1991
Note: Fiscal information reflects foundation contributions only. Average grant figure excludes a $750,000 grant. Recent grants are derived from a 1991 Form 990.

RECENT GRANTS

- 750,000 Jewish Community Federation, Cleveland, OH
- 225,213 United Way Services
- 125,000 Neighborhood Progress, Cleveland, OH
- 116,099 Case Western Reserve University, Cleveland, OH
- 83,333 Montifiore Home, Cleveland Heights, OH
- 50,000 American Red Cross
- 50,000 Cleveland Initiative for Education, Cleveland, OH
- 36,770 Midtown Corridor
- 25,000 Cleveland Playhouse, Cleveland, OH
- 18,250 Cleanland, Ohio, Cleveland, OH

Prentice Foundation, Abra

CONTACT
Abra Prentice Fdn.
c/o Alta Enterprises
401 E. Illinois, Ste. 601
Chicago, IL 60611

FINANCIAL SUMMARY
Recent Giving: $340,000 (fiscal 1991); $336,000 (fiscal 1990); $356,000 (fiscal 1989)
Assets: $4,864,787 (fiscal year ending June 30, 1991); $4,616,241 (fiscal 1990); $4,260,652 (fiscal 1989)
Gifts Received: $2,909 (fiscal 1991)
Fiscal Note: In 1991, contributions were received from Abra Prentice Wilkin.
EIN: 36-3092281

CONTRIBUTIONS SUMMARY
Donor(s): Abra Prentice Wilkin
Typical Recipients: • *Arts & Humanities:* history/historic preservation • *Civic & Public Affairs:* zoos/botanical gardens • *Education:* colleges & universities, medical education, private education (precollege) • *Religion:* churches
Grant Types: endowment, multiyear/continuing support, and professorship

GIVING OFFICERS
Roy M. Adams: dir *B* Wilmington DE 1940 *ED* Univ DE BA 1962; IL Inst Tech JD 1969; Northwestern Univ LLM 1976

CORP AFFIL ptnr: Schiff Hardin & Waite *NONPR AFFIL* adjunct prof: Northwestern Univ; fellow: Am Coll Probate Couns, Intl Academy Estate Trust Law
William G. Demas: secy, treas, dir
Abra Prentice Wilkin: chmn, pres, dir *B* 1942 *ED* Northwestern Univ *CORP AFFIL* trust: Northwestern Meml Hosp
Jere Scott Zenko: dir

APPLICATION INFORMATION
Initial Approach: Contributes only to preselected organizations.
Restrictions on Giving: Does not support individuals.

GRANTS ANALYSIS
Number of Grants: 7
Highest Grant: $250,000
Typical Range: $10,000 to $30,000
Disclosure Period: fiscal year ending June 30, 1991

RECENT GRANTS
- 250,000 Ethel Walker School, Simsbury, CT
- 30,000 Northwestern Medical School, Chicago, IL
- 20,000 Lincoln Park Zoological Society, Chicago, IL
- 10,000 Center of Chicago Historical Society, Chicago, IL
- 10,000 Chicago Park District, Chicago, IL
- 10,000 Norman Rockwell Museum, Stockbridge, MA
- 10,000 St. Chrysostom Church, Chicago, IL

Prentis Family Foundation, Meyer and Anna

CONTACT
Ralph Kliber
Agent
Meyer and Anna Prentis Family Fdn.
1700 Guardian Bldg.
Detroit, MI 48226
(313) 398-8415

FINANCIAL SUMMARY
Recent Giving: $195,805 (1991); $213,003 (1990); $265,500 (1989)

Assets: $4,321,869 (1991); $4,559,423 (1990); $4,974,584 (1989)
EIN: 38-6090332

CONTRIBUTIONS SUMMARY
Donor(s): members of the Prentis family
Typical Recipients: • *Arts & Humanities:* arts centers, community arts, opera • *Civic & Public Affairs:* ethnic/minority organizations • *Education:* colleges & universities, private education (precollege) • *Health:* health organizations, hospitals, medical research, single-disease health associations • *Religion:* religious organizations, synagogues • *Social Services:* community service organizations
Grant Types: general support
Geographic Distribution: focus on MI

GIVING OFFICERS
Denise L. Brown: vp, trust
Barbara P. Frenkel: pres, trust
Dale P. Frenkel: secy, trust
Marvin A. Frenkel: treas, trust
Ronald E. P. Frenkel, MD: vp, trust
Tom P. Frenkel: trust
Cindy Frenkel Kanter: trust
Nelson P. Lande: trust

APPLICATION INFORMATION
Initial Approach: Send brief letter of inquiry describing program. There are no deadlines.
Restrictions on Giving: Does not support individuals.

GRANTS ANALYSIS
Number of Grants: 49
Highest Grant: $60,000
Typical Range: $500 to $4,000
Disclosure Period: 1991

RECENT GRANTS
- 60,000 Federation of Allied Jewish Appeal, Detroit, MI
- 50,000 M.L. Prentis Comprehensive Cancer Center of Metropolitan Detroit, Detroit, MI
- 10,000 Temple Beth-El, Birmingham, MI
- 5,000 Detroit Country Day School, Birmingham, MI
- 5,000 Michigan Opera Theatre, Detroit, MI
- 5,000 Yeshiva Gedolah Ateres Mordechi, Oak Park, MI

- 4,000 Beaumont Hospital, Royal Oak, MI
- 4,000 Martin Memorial Hospital, Stuart, FL
- 3,800 National Conference of Christians and Jews, Detroit, MI
- 3,000 Southern Poverty Law Center, Montgomery, AL

Prentiss Foundation, Elisabeth Severance

CONTACT
Richard E. Beeman
Secretary
Elisabeth Severance Prentiss Foundation
c/o National City Bank
PO Box 5756
Cleveland, OH 44101
(216) 575-2761

FINANCIAL SUMMARY
Recent Giving: $2,291,891 (1991); $2,211,327 (1990); $2,144,270 (1989)
Assets: $60,605,453 (1991); $48,643,267 (1990); $46,144,698 (1989)
Gifts Received: $1,394 (1991 est.); $1,394 (1990); $5,032 (1989)
EIN: 34-6512433

CONTRIBUTIONS SUMMARY
Donor(s): The Elisabeth Severance Prentiss Foundation was established in 1939 and became active following the death of Mrs. Prentiss in 1944. Her father, Louis H. Severance, was an associate of John D. Rockefeller in the Standard Oil Co. Mrs. Prentiss's main interests throughout her life were medicine and health. She provided major gifts to St. Luke's Hospital Association in Cleveland and provided in her will that St. Luke's receive half of the net income received annually from her contribution to the foundation.
Typical Recipients: • *Education:* medical education • *Health:* health care cost containment, health organizations, hospitals, medical research, medical training, outpatient health care delivery, pediatric health, single-disease health associations • *Social Services:* aged, disabled, drugs & alcohol, family planning, homes

Grant Types: capital, challenge, professorship, and research

Geographic Distribution: greater Cleveland, OH, area

GIVING OFFICERS

Quentin Alexander: pres, mgr *B* Cleveland Heights OH 1919 *ED* Univ PA BS 1941; Case Western Reserve Univ JD 1945 *CURR EMPL* atty, ptnr: Arter Hadden *NONPR AFFIL* mem: Am Bar Assn, Cleveland Bar Assn, OH Bar Assn; secy: Univ Hosps Cleveland

Richard E. Beeman: secy *B* Lima OH 1945 *ED* Yale Univ 1967; Univ PA JD 1971 *CURR EMPL* exec vp: Natl City Bank (Trust Group) *CORP AFFIL* chmn: Natl City Trust Co; dir: First Kentucky Trust Co, NC Investments; sr vp: Natl City Corp *NONPR AFFIL* mem: Counc Foreign Rels, Yale Alumni Assn; pres: Town Hall Cleveland; trust: Cleveland Counc World Affs; section co-chmn: Un Way Cleveland; trust: Cleveland Play House

Harry J. Bolwell: mgr *B* Bloomfield NJ 1925 *ED* Univ VT BS 1949; Stevens Inst Tech MS 1952 *CURR EMPL* chmn, ceo: Midland-Ross Corp *CORP AFFIL* dir: Cleveland Cliffs Inc, Cleveland-Cliffs Iron Co, Combustion Engring Co, Leaseway Transportation Corp, Natl City Corp, Provident Life Accident Ins Co *NONPR AFFIL* mem: Cleveland Chamber Commerce, OH Chamber Commerce; trust: Boys Club Cleveland, Cleveland Counc World Affs, Cleveland Scholarship Program, Laurel Sch Girls, Natl Conf Christians Jews *PHIL AFFIL* trust: Cleveland-Cliffs Foundation, Midland-Ross Foundation

William J. DeLancey: mgr *B* Chicago IL 1916 *ED* Univ MI BA 1938; Univ MI JD 1940 *CORP AFFIL* dir: Standard Oil Co OH *NONPR AFFIL* vchmn: Univ Hosps

J. Robert Killpack: mgr *B* Persia IA 1922 *ED* Miami Univ BS 1946 *CURR EMPL* chmn, ceo, dir: Natl City Corp *CORP AFFIL* dir: LDL Corp, Natl City Corp, Sherwin-Williams Co, Weatherhead Indus *NONPR AFFIL* mem: Am Inst CPAs, Fin Execs Inst

William A. Mattie: mgr *B* Mt. Horeb WI

APPLICATION INFORMATION

Initial Approach:
The foundation has no set form of application. Contact should be made by letter or proposal. Sufficient information should be included to describe completely the merits of a project and to provide full details regarding its budget and the funding requested.

Applications should be submitted prior to the meetings of the board of managers in June and December. Deadlines for their receipt are May 15 and November 15 of each year.

All grants must be approved by "...the board of managers of the foundation which is composed of five public-spirited citizens selected as provided for in the Trust Agreement and serving without compensation."

Restrictions on Giving: As a matter of policy, the foundation does not provide grants to national fund-raising organizations or to individuals for scholarships, grants-in-aid, or other personal purposes. Surveys, assessments, studies, or planning activities are generally not supported. The foundation strongly favors grant requests for specific projects over those for general operating support, and also favors organizations in the private sector over those which are primarily government supported.

OTHER THINGS TO KNOW
The terms of the foundation agreement provide that other interested persons may add funds to the trust. Such gifts may bear the name of the donor or may be added to general funds. In 1965, under the terms of a living trust agreement established by the late Mrs. Kate W. Miller with National City Bank, Trustee, "The Luther L. and Kate W. Miller Fund" was created. At the end of 1991, the foundation held $6,070,653 in this fund.

National City Bank serves as corporate trustee for the foundation. The maximum term of a grant commitment is five years.

Publications: annual report

GRANTS ANALYSIS
Total Grants: $2,291,891
Number of Grants: 23
Highest Grant: $1,050,629

Typical Range: $5,000 to $100,000
Disclosure Period: 1991
Note: The average grant figure excludes the highest grant of $1,050,629. Recent grants are derived from a 1991 grants list.

RECENT GRANTS
1,050,630	St. Luke Hospital Association, Cleveland, OH
390,708	University Hospitals of Cleveland, Cleveland, OH
250,000	Case Western Reserve University, Department of Medicine, Cleveland, OH
250,000	Cleveland Clinic Foundation, Cleveland, OH
50,000	Case Western Reserve University, Cleveland, OH
30,000	St. Luke Hospital, Cleveland, OH
25,000	Association for Retarded Citizens
25,000	Case Western Reserve University School of Medicine, University Hospitals of Cleveland, Cleveland, OH
20,000	American Red Cross of the Greater Cleveland Area, Cleveland, OH
20,000	Central School of Practical Nursing, Cleveland, OH

Presley Cos.
Revenue: $52.0 million
Employees: 250
Headquarters: Newport Beach, CA
SIC Major Group: General Building Contractors, Oil & Gas Extraction, and Real Estate

CONTACT
Wade Cable
President
Presley Cos.
PO Box 6110
Newport Beach, CA 92658
(714) 640-6400

CONTRIBUTIONS SUMMARY
Operating Locations: CA (Newport Beach)

CORP. OFFICERS
Wade Cable: *CURR EMPL* pres: Presley Cos
David Siegel: *CURR EMPL* sr vp, cfo: Presley Cos

Presser Foundation

CONTACT
Gregory D'Angelo
Presser Fdn.
Institutional Services
Bryn Mawr, PA 19010
(215) 786-7624

FINANCIAL SUMMARY
Recent Giving: $1,203,153 (fiscal 1991); $485,814 (fiscal 1990); $925,205 (fiscal 1989)
Assets: $12,079,364 (fiscal year ending June 30, 1991); $10,870,717 (fiscal 1990); $10,726,977 (fiscal 1989)
EIN: 23-2164013

CONTRIBUTIONS SUMMARY
Donor(s): the late Theodore Presser
Grant Types: capital, conference/seminar, emergency, fellowship, project, scholarship, and seed money

GIVING OFFICERS
Boyd T. Barnard: trust
Robert Capanna: trust
William M. Davison IV: trust
Morris Duane: trust *B* Philadelphia PA 1901 *ED* Harvard Univ AB 1923; Stetson Univ LLB 1927; Stetson Univ LLD 1965; Bucknell Univ LLD 1967; La Salle Coll LLD 1970; Drexel Univ LLD 1976; Womens Med Coll PA LHD 1967; Beaver Coll LittD 1969 *NONPR AFFIL* mem: Am Bar Assn, Am Lawn Tennis Assn, Am Philosophical Soc, Juristic Soc, PA Bar Assn, Philadelphia Bar Assn
Raymond S. Green: trust *B* Torrington CT 1915 *NONPR AFFIL* mem: Am Forestry Assn, Musical Fund Soc; trust: Valley Forge Military Academy Fdn
Edwin F. Heidakka: trust
Thomas M. Hyndman, Jr.: vp, trust *B* Philadelphia PA 1924 *ED* Williams Coll 1947; Univ PA 1950 *CURR EMPL* ptnr: Duane Morris & Hechsher *CORP AFFIL* dir: Penn Engring & Mfg Corp, Rochester & Pittsburgh Coal Co; ptnr: Duane Morris & Hechsher *NONPR AFFIL* mem: Am Bar Assn
Helen Laird: trust
Bruce Montgomery: secy, trust
Charles F. Nagel: treas, trust
Edith A. Reinhardt: trust
Felix Compton Robb: trust *B* Birmingham AL 1914 *ED* Bir-

mingham-Southern Coll AB 1936; Vanderbilt Univ MA 1939; Harvard Univ EdD 1952; Wesleyan Univ DPed 1968; Mercer Univ LLD 1968
NONPR AFFIL dir: Atlanta Partnership Bus Ed; exec dir emeritus: Southern Assn Colls Schs; mem: Am Soc Assn Execs; trust, chmn academic affairs comm: Eckerd Coll; trust, chmn fin comm: Un Methodist Childrens Home
Michael Stairs: trust
Henderson Supplee III: pres, trust
James D. Winsor III: trust
Philip W. Young: trust

APPLICATION INFORMATION
Initial Approach: Application forms available for scholarships and for financial aid to needy music teachers. There are no deadlines.

OTHER THINGS TO KNOW
Provides scholarships to colleges and universities for undergraduate students of music. Also provides emergency aid to needy music teachers.

Preston Trucking Co., Inc.
Revenue: $414.1 million
Employees: 7,480
Headquarters: Preston, MD
SIC Major Group: Trucking & Warehousing

CONTACT
Lynda George
Director, Public Affairs
Preston Corp.
151 Easton Blvd.
Preston, MD 21655
(410) 673-7151

CONTRIBUTIONS SUMMARY
Operating Locations: MD (Preston)

CORP. OFFICERS
Billy G. Terrel: *CURR EMPL* pres: Preston Trucking Co

Preston Trust, Evelyn W.

CONTACT
Evelyn W. Preston Trust
c/o Connecticut Bank and Trust Co., N.A.
PO Box 3334
Hartford, CT 06103
(203) 244-5000

FINANCIAL SUMMARY
Recent Giving: $121,983 (1990); $130,060 (1989); $106,071 (1988)
Assets: $2,231,252 (1990); $2,385,106 (1989); $2,160,147 (1988)
EIN: 06-0747389

CONTRIBUTIONS SUMMARY
Donor(s): the late Mary Yale Bettis, the late Evelyn Preston
Typical Recipients: • *Arts & Humanities:* community arts, music, performing arts • *Civic & Public Affairs:* municipalities, urban & community affairs, zoos/botanical gardens • *Social Services:* community centers, community service organizations, united funds, youth organizations
Grant Types: general support
Geographic Distribution: limited to Hartford, CT

APPLICATION INFORMATION
Initial Approach: Contributes only to preselected organizations.

OTHER THINGS TO KNOW
Publications: Application Guidelines

GRANTS ANALYSIS
Number of Grants: 73
Highest Grant: $6,334
Typical Range: $1,000 to $6,000
Disclosure Period: 1990

RECENT GRANTS
6,334 Garden Area Neighborhood Council, Hartford, CT
6,333 Garden Area Neighborhood Council, Hartford, CT
6,333 Garden Area Neighborhood Council, Hartford, CT
5,334 Hartford Symphony, Hartford, CT
5,333 Real Art Ways, Hartford, CT

5,000 Artist Collective, Hartford, CT
4,000 Guakia
4,000 International Performing Arts Festival
4,000 International Performing Arts Festival
3,000 Connecticut Chamber Symphony, Glastonbury, CT

Preuss Foundation

CONTACT
Peter G. Preuss
President
Preuss Fdn.
201 Lomas-Sante Fe Dr., Ste. 340
Solana Beach, CA 92075
(619) 481-4406

FINANCIAL SUMMARY
Recent Giving: $402,820 (1991); $414,872 (1990); $965,500 (1989)
Assets: $187,478 (1991); $444,234 (1990); $992,179 (1989)
Gifts Received: $314,703 (1991); $202,474 (1990); $1,058,711 (1989)
EIN: 33-0085513

CONTRIBUTIONS SUMMARY
Donor(s): Peter G. Preuss
Typical Recipients: • *Education:* colleges & universities, science/technology education • *Health:* health organizations, hospitals, medical research, single-disease health associations • *International:* international organizations
Grant Types: research

GIVING OFFICERS
Howard F. Cox: dir
Stephen A. Hurwitz: dir
Peggy L. Preuss: secy
Peter G. Preuss: pres

APPLICATION INFORMATION
Initial Approach: Contributes only to preselected organizations.

OTHER THINGS TO KNOW
Publications: Annual Report

GRANTS ANALYSIS
Number of Grants: 17
Highest Grant: $83,333
Typical Range: $2,500 to $30,000
Disclosure Period: 1991

RECENT GRANTS
83,333 University of California, San Francisco, CA
37,500 Duke University Medical Center, Durham, NC
30,000 Duke University, Durham, NC
27,500 University of California Regents, San Francisco, CA
27,500 University of California San Diego, San Diego, CA
25,000 Medizinsche Hachschule Hanover
22,500 Johns Hopkins Oncology Center, Baltimore, MD
22,500 Johns Hopkins Oncology Center, Baltimore, MD
21,840 Ludwig Institute
12,000 American Association of Neurological Surgeons

Preyer Fund, Mary Norris

CONTACT
Fredrick Preyer
Trustee
Mary Norris Preyer Fund
PO Box 20124
Greensboro, NC 27420
(919) 274-5471

FINANCIAL SUMMARY
Recent Giving: $151,000 (fiscal 1992); $216,500 (fiscal 1991); $273,996 (fiscal 1990)
Assets: $3,039,277 (fiscal year ending June 30, 1992); $2,832,903 (fiscal 1991); $2,931,085 (fiscal 1990)
EIN: 56-6068167

CONTRIBUTIONS SUMMARY
Donor(s): members of the Preyer Family
Typical Recipients: • *Arts & Humanities:* arts funds, community arts, music • *Civic & Public Affairs:* civil rights, environmental affairs, ethnic/minority organizations • *Education:* colleges & universities • *Health:* health organizations, hospitals, single-disease health associations • *Religion:* religious organizations
Grant Types: general support and seed money
Geographic Distribution: focus on NC

GIVING OFFICERS
Ellen P. Davis: trust

Mary Norris Preyer Oglesby: trust

Fred L. Preyer: trust

Jill Preyer: trust

Kelly Anne Preyer: trust

Lunsford Richardson Preyer: trust *B* Greensboro NC 1919 *ED* Princeton Univ AB 1941; Harvard Univ LLB 1949 *CORP AFFIL* dir: Piedmont Mgmt Co; off, dir: Vanguard Cellular Sys *NONPR AFFIL* hon mem: Natl Boy Scout Counc; mem: Am Bar Assn, NC Bar Assn

Norris W. Preyer: trust

Norris W. Preyer, Jr.: trust

Robert Otto Preyer: trust *B* Greensboro NC 1922 *ED* Princeton Univ AB 1945; Columbia Univ MA 1948; Columbia Univ PhD 1954 *CORP AFFIL* dir: Auto Veyer Corp, Boston Blacksides, Piedmont Fin Co, Richardson Corp *NONPR AFFIL* bd overseers: Tufts Univ; chmn: Brandeis Univ Faculty Senate, MA Civil Liberties Fund; dir: Brandeis Univ Univ Studies Program, Earl Warren Legal Training Program; mem: ACLU, MLA, NAACP; prof emeritus, chmn: Brandeis Univ Dept English & Am Lit

William Yost Preyer, Jr.: trust

APPLICATION INFORMATION

Initial Approach: Send cover letter and full proposal. There are no deadlines.

GRANTS ANALYSIS

Number of Grants: 38
Highest Grant: $10,000
Typical Range: $500 to $10,000
Disclosure Period: fiscal year ending June 30, 1992

RECENT GRANTS

10,000 NAACP, Greensboro, NC
10,000 Wake County AIDS Service Agency, Greensboro, NC
7,500 Uplift, Greensboro, NC
5,000 Crisis Assistance Ministry, Wilson, NC
5,000 Greensboro Urban Ministry, Greensboro, NC
5,000 Hudson River Sloop Clearwater, Greensboro, NC
5,000 Natural Science Center of Greensboro, Greensboro, NC
5,000 North Carolina Institute of Political Leadership, Greensboro, NC
5,000 Oglethorpe University, Atlanta, GA
5,000 Prison Fellowship USA, Greensboro, NC

Price Associates, T. Rowe / Price Associates Foundation, T. Rowe

Sales: $205.0 million
Employees: 1,538
Headquarters: Baltimore, MD
SIC Major Group: Security & Commodity Brokers

CONTACT

Brenda K. Ashworth
Administrator
T. Rowe Price Associates Fdn.
100 E Pratt St., 9th Fl.
Baltimore, MD 21202
(301) 547-2100

FINANCIAL SUMMARY

Recent Giving: $621,000 (1993 est.); $703,790 (1992); $575,000 (1991)
Assets: $1,733,442 (1991); $3,678,663 (1990); $3,372,525 (1989)
Gifts Received: $50,000 (1990); $600,000 (1989)
Fiscal Note: Above figures are for the foundation only. Company reports that it gives primarily through the foundation. In 1990, contributions were received from T. Rowe Price Associates.
EIN: 52-1231953

CONTRIBUTIONS SUMMARY

Typical Recipients: • *Arts & Humanities:* arts festivals, arts funds, arts institutes, community arts, history/historic preservation, libraries, museums/galleries, music, opera, public broadcasting, theater • *Civic & Public Affairs:* environmental affairs, public policy, urban & community affairs, zoos/botanical gardens • *Education:* arts education, business education, colleges & universities, elementary education, literacy, minority education, private education (precollege), public education (precollege) • *Health:* health organizations, hospitals, pediatric health, single-disease health associations

• *Religion:* churches, religious organizations • *Social Services:* child welfare, community service organizations, disabled, family services, food/clothing distribution, recreation & athletics, shelters/homelessness, united funds, youth organizations
Grant Types: capital, employee matching gifts, and general support
Nonmonetary Support Types: donated equipment and workplace solicitation
Note: T. Rowe Price Associates only offers nonmonetary support to the United Way. Estimated value of nonmonetary support is not available.
Geographic Distribution: focus on headquarters and operating locations
Operating Locations: MD (Baltimore)

CORP. OFFICERS

Thomas R. Broadus, Jr.: *CURR EMPL* managing dir: Price (T Rowe) Assocs
George J. Collins: *B* West Haven CT 1940 *ED* VA Military Inst 1962; Am Univ Sch Bus Admin 1970 *CURR EMPL* pres, ceo, dir: Price (T Rowe) Assocs
Carter O. Hoffman: *CURR EMPL* managing dir: Price (T Rowe) Assocs
Henry H. Hopkins: *CURR EMPL* managing dir: Price (T Rowe) Assocs
Edward Joseph Mathias: *CURR EMPL* managing dir: T Rowe Price Assocs *CORP AFFIL* chmn: New Frontiers Ltd Ptnrship, T Rowe Price New Horizons Fund, T Rowe Price Threshold Funds Ltd Ptnrship, Small Cap/Value Fund, Strategic Ptnrs Ltd Ptnrship *NONPR AFFIL* bd overseers: Univ PA Sch Arts & Sciences; mem natl adv bd: Am Univ
James Sellers Riepe: *B* Bryn Mawr PA 1943 *ED* Univ PA 1965; Univ PA 1967 *CURR EMPL* mng dir: Price (T Rowe) Assocs *CORP AFFIL* chmn: Price (T Rowe) Growth & Income Fund, Price (T Rowe) Trust Co; dir: Monumental Ins Group, Rorer Group; pres: Price (T Rowe) Investment Svcs, Price (T Rowe) Svcs *NONPR AFFIL* mem: Univ PA Gen Alumni Soc; trust: Baltimore Mus Art
George A. Roche: *B* Rochester NY 1941 *ED* Georgetown Univ

1963; Harvard Univ Sch Bus Admin 1966 *CURR EMPL* mng dir, cfo, vp: Price (T Rowe) Assocs *CORP AFFIL* dir: BRP Inc; pres, dir: T Rowe Price New Era Fund *NONPR AFFIL* dir: Enoch Pratt Free Library
Charles H. Salisbury, Jr.: *CURR EMPL* managing dir: Price (T Rowe) Assocs
M. David Testa: *CURR EMPL* managing dir: Price (T Rowe) Assocs

GIVING OFFICERS

Brenda K. Ashworth: adm
Thomas R. Broadus, Jr.: vp *CURR EMPL* managing dir: Price (T Rowe) Assocs (see above)
Patricia O. Goodyear: secy
Carter O. Hoffman: vp, treas *CURR EMPL* managing dir: Price (T Rowe) Assocs (see above)
Albert C. Hubbard, Jr.: chmn, pres

APPLICATION INFORMATION

Initial Approach: *Initial Contact:* brief letter or proposal *Include Information On:* description of program, list of organization's board members, annual report, statement of need *When to Submit:* any time
Restrictions on Giving: Company does not support individuals, religious organizations for sectarian purposes, or political or lobbying groups.

GRANTS ANALYSIS

Total Grants: $703,790
Number of Grants: 294
Highest Grant: $150,000
Typical Range: $500 to $3,000
Disclosure Period: 1992
Note: Assets figure is for 1991. Average grant figure provided by the company. Recent grants are derived from a 1990 Form 990.

RECENT GRANTS

70,000 United Way, Baltimore, MD
56,125 Center Stage, Baltimore, MD
29,425 Peabody Institute, Baltimore, MD
23,015 St. Paul School, Brooklandville, MD
15,125 Baltimore Symphony Orchestra, Baltimore, MD
14,245 Walters Art Gallery, Baltimore, MD
12,850 Stanford University Graduate

School of Business, Stanford, CA
12,625 Baltimore Zoo, Baltimore, MD
12,000 Independent College Fund of Maryland, Baltimore, MD
12,000 National Aquarium in Baltimore, Baltimore, MD

Price Company

Sales: $6.59 billion
Employees: 19,000
Headquarters: San Diego, CA
SIC Major Group: Wholesale Trade—Durable Goods and Wholesale Trade—Nondurable Goods

CONTACT
Sherrie Cousineau
Administrative Assistant
Price Company
PO Box 85466
San Diego, CA 92186-5466
(619) 581-4600

CONTRIBUTIONS SUMMARY
Operating Locations: CA (National City, San Diego, Santee)

CORP. OFFICERS
Robert J. Hunt: *CURR EMPL* exec vp, cfo: Price Co
Robert E. Price: *CURR EMPL* chmn, pres, ceo, dir: Price Co

Price Educational Foundation, Herschel C.

CONTACT
E. JoAnn Price
Trustee
Herschel C. Price Educational Fdn.
PO Box 179
Huntington, WV 25706
(304) 529-3852

FINANCIAL SUMMARY
Recent Giving: $139,150 (fiscal 1992); $134,700 (fiscal 1991); $135,550 (fiscal 1990)
Assets: $3,416,684 (fiscal year ending April 30, 1992); $3,275,061 (fiscal 1991); $2,977,170 (fiscal 1990)
EIN: 55-6076719

CONTRIBUTIONS SUMMARY
Donor(s): Herschel C. Price Foundation
Grant Types: scholarship

Geographic Distribution: focus on WV

GIVING OFFICERS
Chandos H. Peak: trust
JoAnn Price: trust

APPLICATION INFORMATION
Initial Approach: Application form required. Submit application from January to March or August to September; deadlines April 1 and October 1

OTHER THINGS TO KNOW
Provides higher education scholarships to undergraduates residing in WV or attending WV colleges.
Disclosure Period: fiscal year ending April 30, 1992

Price Foundation, Louis and Harold

CONTACT
Harold Price
Chairman
Louis and Harold Price Foundation
654 Madison Avenue, Ste. 2005
New York, NY 10021
(212) 753-0240
Note: Applicants may also contact Mrs. Rosemary Guidone, Executive Vice President, at the above address.

FINANCIAL SUMMARY
Recent Giving: $1,536,184 (1992); $1,450,661 (1991); $1,934,589 (1990)
Assets: $69,000,000 (1992 approx.); $39,316,165 (1990); $42,589,346 (1989)
EIN: 13-6121358

CONTRIBUTIONS SUMMARY
Donor(s): The Louis and Harold Price Foundation was established in 1951 by the late Louis Price and Harold Price.
Typical Recipients: • *Arts & Humanities:* arts associations, libraries • *Civic & Public Affairs:* civil rights, environmental affairs, ethnic/minority organizations, first amendment issues, housing, law & justice, philanthropic organizations • *Education:* business education, colleges & universities, religious education • *Health:* hospitals, medical rehabilitation, medical research, mental health, single-disease health associations • *International:* inter-

national development/relief, international organizations • *Religion:* churches, synagogues • *Social Services:* aged, animal protection, child welfare, community centers, counseling, emergency relief, food/clothing distribution, religious welfare, united funds, youth organizations
Grant Types: endowment, operating expenses, project, and scholarship
Geographic Distribution: primarily in metropolitan New York and Los Angeles; also in Israel

GIVING OFFICERS
Gloria W. Appel: trust
George Asch: trust
David Gerstein: trust
Rosemary Guidone: exec vp, asst treas, asst secy, trust
Harold Price: chmn, treas, trust
Pauline Price: vp, secy, trust
Linda Vitti: trust

APPLICATION INFORMATION
Initial Approach:
Prospective applicants should send a letter of inquiry or one copy of a full proposal to the foundation.
Applicants may submit proposals any time; there are no deadlines for requests.
The board generally meets in February, May, and as required. Final notification takes place in one to three months. Receipt of proposals is acknowledged, and the foundation grants interviews with applicants when deemed necessary.
Restrictions on Giving: The foundation does not give grants to individuals or for building funds.

GRANTS ANALYSIS
Total Grants: $1,536,184
Number of Grants: 126
Highest Grant: $1,011,300
Typical Range: $100 to $1,000 and $10,000 to $37,000
Disclosure Period: 1992
Note: The average grant figure excludes two large grants totaling $1,151,300. Recent grants are derived from a 1992 grants list.

RECENT GRANTS
1,011,300 Price Institute for Entrepreneurial Studies, New York, NY

140,000 Israel Emergency Fund, Beverly Hills, CA
100,000 Sara Lee Foundation, Chicago, IL
35,000 United Jewish Fund (State of Israel Bonds), Miami, FL
30,000 United Jewish Fund, Los Angeles, CA
25,000 Cedars-Sinai Medical Center, Los Angeles, CA — State of Israel Bonds
20,000 Medical Development for Israel, New York, NY
15,000 Mount Sinai Medical Center, New York, NY
13,300 Lenox Hill Hospital, New York, NY
12,800 Hadassah, New York, NY

Price Foundation, Lucien B. and Katherine E.

CONTACT
Francis V. Krukowaki
President
Lucien B. and Katherine E. Price Fdn.
896 Main St.
Manchester, CT 06040
(203) 643-4129

FINANCIAL SUMMARY
Recent Giving: $124,300 (1991); $116,050 (1990); $112,300 (1989)
Assets: $3,243,082 (1991); $2,806,372 (1990); $2,946,458 (1989)
EIN: 06-6068868

CONTRIBUTIONS SUMMARY
Typical Recipients: • *Education:* colleges & universities, private education (precollege), religious education • *Health:* hospitals • *Religion:* churches, religious organizations • *Social Services:* community service organizations
Grant Types: general support

GIVING OFFICERS
Morgan P. Ames: treas
Rt. Rev. Msgr. John A. Brown: vp
Most Rev. Joseph L. Federal: trust
Edward P. Flanagan: secy
Rev. Francis Krukowski: trust
Rt. Rev. Msgr. Edward J. Reardon: pres

APPLICATION INFORMATION

Initial Approach: Send brief letter describing program. There are no deadlines.

GRANTS ANALYSIS

Number of Grants: 30
Highest Grant: $18,000
Typical Range: $1,000 to $2,500
Disclosure Period: 1991

RECENT GRANTS

18,000 St. James School, Manchester, CT
17,000 Judge Memorial High School, Salt Lake City, UT
15,000 Diocese of Sale Lake City, Salt Lake City, UT
10,000 Notre Dame School, Price, UT
8,000 Catholic Evangelization Committee, Salt Lake City, UT
8,000 St. James School, Manchester, CT — library fund
5,000 Manchester Memorial Hospital, Manchester, CT
5,000 St. James Retirement Fund, Manchester, CT
3,000 Catholic Negro-American Mission
3,000 Sisters of St. Joseph, West Hartford, CT

Price Waterhouse-U.S. / Price Waterhouse Foundation

Sales: $1.3 billion
Employees: 13,000
Headquarters: New York, NY
SIC Major Group: Engineering & Management Services

CONTACT

Larry P. Scott
Executive Director
Price Waterhouse Fdn.
1251 Avenue of the Americas
New York, NY 10020
(212) 819-5000

FINANCIAL SUMMARY

Recent Giving: $1,800,000 (1992 approx.); $1,800,000 (1991 approx.); $1,800,000 (1990 approx.)
Assets: $22,258 (1991)
Fiscal Note: Company gives primarily through the foundation. Value of direct giving is not available. Contact human resources department in each office or operating location for information on direct gifts.
EIN: 13-6119208

CONTRIBUTIONS SUMMARY

Typical Recipients: • *Education:* business education, colleges & universities, education associations
Grant Types: department, employee matching gifts, fellowship, professorship, research, and scholarship
Geographic Distribution: nationally
Operating Locations: NY (New York)
Note: Corporate headquarters in New York City; local offices maintained in various cities nationwide

CORP. OFFICERS

James E. Daley: *CURR EMPL* co-chmn, opers ptnr: Price Waterhouse-US
Harold Haddock, Jr.: *B* Newark NJ 1932 *ED* Union Coll AA 1957; Rutgers Univ BS 1959 *CURR EMPL* natl dir (fin): Price Waterhouse-US *NONPR AFFIL* dir: Rockefeller Ctr; fellow: NJ Soc CPAs; mem: Am Inst CPAs, Fin Execs Inst, FL Inst CPAs, Greater Tampa Chamber Commerce; pres, dir: Westshore Alliance
Shaun O'Malley: *CURR EMPL* chmn, sr ptnr: Price Waterhouse-US
Dominic Tarantino: *CURR EMPL* co-chmn, mng ptnr: Price Waterhouse-US

GIVING OFFICERS

Robert Brown: dir
Thomas Frankland: dir
Richard Kearns: vp *CURR EMPL* dir human resources: Price Waterhouse
Maureen P. Kingston: secy
Robert Mulshine: dir
W. D. Pugh: dir
Larry P. Scott: exec dir
Arthur Siegel: dir
Norman Walker: pres

APPLICATION INFORMATION

Initial Approach: *Initial Contact:* brief letter or proposal to nearest local practice office *Include Information On:* description of the organization, amount requested, purpose for which funds are sought, proof of tax-exempt status *When to Submit:* any time

---

Restrictions on Giving: All giving is restricted to educational activities.
Foundation does not support individuals directly and does not give outside the United States and its possessions.

GRANTS ANALYSIS

Total Grants: $1,800,000*
Typical Range: $5,000 to $20,000
Disclosure Period: 1992
Note: Total grants figure is approximate. Assets are for 1991.

Prickett Fund, Lynn R. and Karl E.

CONTACT

Dora Head
Account Administrator
Lynn R. and Karl E. Prickett Fund
PO Box 20124
Greensboro, NC 27420
(919) 274-5471

FINANCIAL SUMMARY

Recent Giving: $882,415 (fiscal 1992); $790,250 (fiscal 1991); $573,500 (fiscal 1990)
Assets: $20,260,140 (fiscal year ending June 30, 1992); $18,978,769 (fiscal 1991); $18,778,774 (fiscal 1990)
Gifts Received: $561,831 (fiscal 1991); $5,073,411 (fiscal 1990); $291,170 (fiscal 1989)
Fiscal Note: In 1991, contributions were received from the estate of Lynn R. Prickett.
EIN: 56-6064788

CONTRIBUTIONS SUMMARY

Donor(s): The foundation was established in 1964 by the late Lynn R. Prickett.
Typical Recipients: • *Arts & Humanities:* music • *Civic & Public Affairs:* environmental affairs, ethnic/minority organizations, international affairs, philanthropic organizations, urban & community affairs, zoos/botanical gardens • *Education:* colleges & universities, education funds, private education (precollege) • *Health:* single-disease health associations • *Social Services:* animal protection, drugs & alcohol, family planning, united funds, youth organizations
Grant Types: general support
Geographic Distribution: national

GIVING OFFICERS

Charles S. Chapin: trust
Chester F. Chapin: trust
Samuel C. Chapin: trust
C. W. Cheek: trust
Lynn C. Gunzenhauser: trust
Lisa B. Prochnow: trust

APPLICATION INFORMATION

Initial Approach:

The foundation requests applicants submit a written proposal with a copy of an IRS exemption letter.

The foundation has no deadline for submitting proposals.

GRANTS ANALYSIS

Total Grants: $882,415
Number of Grants: 53
Highest Grant: $70,000
Typical Range: $1,500 to $20,000
Disclosure Period: fiscal year ending June 30, 1992
Note: Recent grants are derived from a fiscal 1992 grants list.

RECENT GRANTS

70,000 American Civil Liberties Union Foundation of Northern California, San Francisco, CA
70,000 Foundation of Greater Greensboro, Greensboro, NC
47,825 Cousteau Society, VA
47,825 Environmental Defense Fund, Washington, DC
47,825 Worldwatch Institute, Washington, DC
40,000 Center for Individual Recovery Services, Fortuna, CA
29,000 C.I.S.P.E.S. Education Fund, Washington, DC
29,000 Neighbor to Neighbor Education Fund, San Francisco, CA
29,000 US-El Salvador Institute for Democratic Development, San Francisco, CA
25,000 Wake Forest University, Winston-Salem, NC

Priddy Foundation

CONTACT
Berneice Leath
Executive Director
Priddy Fdn.
807 8th St., Ste. 600
Wichita Falls, TX 76301
(817) 723-2127

FINANCIAL SUMMARY
Recent Giving: $282,100 (fiscal 1991); $265,000 (fiscal 1990); $250,083 (fiscal 1989)
Assets: $6,325,193 (fiscal year ending November 30, 1991); $5,782,259 (fiscal 1990); $5,730,969 (fiscal 1989)
Gifts Received: $7,500 (fiscal 1991); $735,738 (fiscal 1989)
EIN: 75-6029882

CONTRIBUTIONS SUMMARY
Donor(s): the late Ashley H. Priddy, Robert T. Priddy, the late Swannanoa H. Priddy, the late Walter M. Priddy
Typical Recipients: • *Arts & Humanities:* arts centers, community arts, history/historic preservation, libraries • *Civic & Public Affairs:* urban & community affairs • *Health:* health organizations, hospitals • *Religion:* churches • *Social Services:* aged, child welfare, community service organizations, food/clothing distribution, shelters/homelessness, united funds, volunteer services, youth organizations
Grant Types: operating expenses and project
Geographic Distribution: focus on northern TX, with emphasis on Wichita Falls

GIVING OFFICERS
John Raymond Clymer, Jr.: dir
Charles B. Kreutz: dir
Berneice R. Leath: secy, treas, exec dir
Leslie Priddy Moffitt: dir
Patricia M. Morgan: dir
Charles Horne Priddy: vp, dir *B* Wichita Falls KS 1937 *ED* Univ TX 1946; Harvard Univ 1948 *CURR EMPL* chmn: Magnatex Corp *CORP AFFIL* chmn: Magnatex Corp
Hervey Amsler Priddy: dir
Robert T. Priddy: pres, dir
Ruby N. Priddy: dir

APPLICATION INFORMATION
Initial Approach: Request application from foundation.

Deadlines are April 1 and September 15. Board meets in May and November.
Restrictions on Giving: Does not support individuals.

OTHER THINGS TO KNOW
Publications: Program policy statement, Application Guidelines

GRANTS ANALYSIS
Number of Grants: 23
Highest Grant: $165,000
Typical Range: $1,000 to $5,000
Disclosure Period: fiscal year ending November 30, 1991

RECENT GRANTS
165,000	Communities Foundation of Texas, Dallas, TX
50,000	First Step of Wichita Falls, Wichita Falls, TX
7,000	Capital Area Food Bank, Austin, TX — vehicle purchase
6,250	Midwestern State University, Wichita Falls, TX
5,000	Camp Fire Council of North Texas, Wichita Falls, TX
5,000	Senior Citizens Service of North Texas, Wichita Falls, TX
5,000	Texas State Historical Association, Austin, TX
5,000	Volunteer Service Council for Wichita Falls State Hospital, Wichita Falls, TX
5,000	White House Endowment Fund, Washington, DC
2,500	Big Spring State Hospital Volunteer Advisory Council, Big Spring, TX

Primark Corp.
Revenue: $153.0 million
Employees: 2,950
Headquarters: McLean, VA
SIC Major Group: Business Services, Holding & Other Investment Offices, Nondepository Institutions, and Transportation by Air

CONTACT
Linda Livingston
Office Manager
Primark Corp.
8251 Greensboro Dr., Ste. 700
McLean, VA 22102
(703) 790-7600

FINANCIAL SUMMARY
Fiscal Note: Annual Giving Range: less than $100,000

CONTRIBUTIONS SUMMARY
Typical Recipients: • *Arts & Humanities:* general • *Civic & Public Affairs:* general • *Education:* general • *Health:* general • *Social Services:* general
Grant Types: general support
Geographic Distribution: primarily headquarters area
Operating Locations: VA (McLean)

CORP. OFFICERS
S. H. Curran: *CURR EMPL* sr vp, treas, cfo: Primark Corp
Joseph Edward Kasputys: *B* Jamaica NY 1936 *ED* City Univ NY Brooklyn Coll 1959; Harvard Univ MBA 1967 *CURR EMPL* chmn, pres, ceo, dir: Primark Corp *CORP AFFIL* dir: Lifeline Sys Inc *NONPR AFFIL* dir: Coun for Excellence in Govt; mem: Assn Corp Growth, Comm Econ Devel, Natl Assn Bus Economists, Natl Economists Club, Phi Beta Kappa

APPLICATION INFORMATION
Initial Approach: Send brief letter of inquiry. There are no deadlines.

Prime Computer, Inc.
Parent Company: ComputerVision Corp.
Revenue: $1.21 billion
Parent Employees: 5,900
Headquarters: Bedford, MA
SIC Major Group: Business Services and Industrial Machinery & Equipment

CONTACT
Sue Carens
Secretary
Prime Computer, Inc.
100 Crosby Dr.
Bedford, MA 01730
(508) 620-2800

FINANCIAL SUMMARY
Fiscal Note: Annual Giving Range: $100,000 to $250,000

CONTRIBUTIONS SUMMARY
Support goes to local education, health and human service, arts, and civic organizations.
Typical Recipients: • *Arts & Humanities:* general • *Civic & Public Affairs:* general • *Education:* general • *Health:* general
Grant Types: general support
Nonmonetary Support Types: donated equipment
Operating Locations: CA (Huntington Beach), MA (Bedford, Natick)

CORP. OFFICERS
Russell E. Plantizer: *CURR EMPL* chmn: Prime Computer
John J. Shields: *B* Worcester MA 1938 *ED* Harvard Univ Sch Bus Admin 1971; Worcester Polytech Inst *CURR EMPL* pres, ceo: Prime Computer *CORP AFFIL* sr vp: Digital Equipment Corp

Primerica Corp. / Primerica Foundation
Revenue: $5.12 billion
Employees: 15,844
Headquarters: New York, NY
SIC Major Group: Business Services, Insurance Carriers, Nondepository Institutions, and Real Estate

CONTACT
Dee Topol
President
Primerica Fdn.
65 E 55th St.
New York, NY 10022
(212) 891-8884
Note: An alternative contact is Ms. Patricia R. Byrne, Coordinator. Additionally, nonprofits can directly contact headquarters or branch offices of any Primerica subsidiary company.

FINANCIAL SUMMARY
Recent Giving: $5,000,000 (1993 est.); $3,602,494 (1992); $2,134,119 (1991)
Assets: $2,600,906 (1991); $2,500,000 (1990); $2,512,456 (1988)
Fiscal Note: The 1992 total giving figure includes $3,087,415 in gifts from the foundation and $515,079 directly from the corporation.
EIN: 13-6161154

CONTRIBUTIONS SUMMARY

Typical Recipients: • *Arts & Humanities:* arts associations, arts centers, community arts, museums/galleries, music, opera, performing arts, theater, visual arts • *Civic & Public Affairs:* economic development, housing • *Education:* preschool education, public education (precollege) • *Social Services:* community centers, day care, employment/job training, shelters/homelessness, youth organizations

Grant Types: general support and project

Nonmonetary Support Types: in-kind services and workplace solicitation

Note: Nonmonetary support for 1990 was $500,000.

Geographic Distribution: near headquarters and operating locations only

Operating Locations: DE (Wilmington), GA (Duluth), MD (Baltimore), NY (New York), TX (Fort Worth, Houston)

Note: Primerica Corp. has branch offices throughout the U.S. Its main business subsidiaries include: Smith Barney, Harris Upham & Co.; Primerica Financial Services; Commerical Credit Co.; American Capital Management & Research; RCM; Transport Life Insurance Co.; Primerica Bank; and Gulf Insurance Co.

CORP. OFFICERS

James Dimon: *B* NY 1956 *ED* Tuft Univ 1978; Harvard Univ Sch Bus Admin 1982 *CURR EMPL* pres, cfo, dir: Primerica Corp *CORP AFFIL* exec vp, cfo: Commercial Credit Co

Robert I. Lipp: *CURR EMPL* vchmn, dir: Primerica Corp

Sanford I. Weill: *B* Brooklyn NY 1933 *ED* Cornell Univ BA 1955 *CURR EMPL* chmn, ceo, dir: Primerica Corp *CORP AFFIL* chmn, pres, ceo: Comml Credit Co; dir: Am Central Mgmt & Res Inc, IDS Mutual Funds Group *NONPR AFFIL* chmn: Carnegie Hall, New York City Temporary Commn Early Childhood & Child Care Programs; dir: Baltimore Symphony Orchestra; fdr: Academy Fin; mem: Bus Roundtable, NY Soc Security Analysts; mem bd overseers: Cornell Med Coll; mem bus comm: Mus Modern Art; mem

joint bd: NY Hosp; vchmn adv counc: Johnson Grad Sch Mgmt

Frank Gustave Zarb: *B* Brooklyn NY 1935 *ED* Hofstra Univ 1957; Hofstra Univ 1961 *CURR EMPL* chmn, pres, ceo, dir: Smith Barney Harris Upham & Co *CORP AFFIL* dir: Am Stock Exchange, BMD Holdings, Securities Investor Protection Corp; mem: NY Stock Exchange; vchmn, dir: Primerica Corp *NONPR AFFIL* mem: Am Soc Pub Admin, Counc Foreign Rels, Natl Counc US-China Trade, Securities Indus Assn; trust: Gerald R Ford Fdn, Hofstra Univ

GIVING OFFICERS

Patricia Byrne: coordinator

James Dimon: trust *CURR EMPL* pres, cfo, dir: Primerica Corp (see above)

Mary Barnes Jenkins: asst sec

Robert I. Lipp: vp, treas, trust *CURR EMPL* vchmn, dir: Primerica Corp (see above)

Charles O. Prince III: sec, trust *CURR EMPL* sr vp, sec, gen counc: Primerica Corp

Dee Topol: pres, trust

Sanford I. Weill: chmn *CURR EMPL* chmn, ceo, dir: Primerica Corp (see above)

Frank Gustave Zarb: vp, trust *CURR EMPL* chmn, pres, ceo, dir: Smith Barney Harris Upham & Co (see above)

APPLICATION INFORMATION

Initial Approach: *Initial Contact:* one- or two-page preliminary proposal and a one-page line item budget for the proposed project *Include Information On:* description of nature and purpose of organization; description of project to be funded (include objectives, target groups, needs, activities, and timespan); copy of IRS tax-exempt letter; recent financial information; list of organization's governing board; description of staff; and proof that organization and services are not discriminatory in any way *When to Submit:* any time

Restrictions on Giving: The foundation does not support individuals; political organizations; religious bodies; labor organizations; agencies whose sole purpose is social or recreational; and professional, marketing or trade organizations. The following activities are not eligible for support: courtesy advertising; special events;

books, magazines, or articles in professional journals; or fundraising activities such as benefits, charitable dinners or sporting events.

The foundation does not support capital or endowment fund drives, except under special circumstances with a waiver from the foundation's board of directors, nor general operating funds for member agencies of United Way in areas where Primerica or its affiliates give to those united fund drives.

OTHER THINGS TO KNOW

In 1989, the Primerica Foundation revised its grant making and was restructured to include the Smith Barney and Commercial Credit Foundations. The combined foundation now concentrates its grant making on behalf of the Primerica Corporation and its individual business units in three areas: general grants, local contributions, and volunteer incentive program (See "Their Priorities").

GRANTS ANALYSIS

Total Grants: $3,602,494*

Number of Grants: 874

Highest Grant: $300,000

Typical Range: $1,000 to $20,000

Disclosure Period: 1992

Note: The total grants figure includes approximately $202,754 given from the employee volunteer fund. The figure for the foundation assets is from 1991. Recent grants are derived from a 1992 annual report.

RECENT GRANTS

300,000	Carnegie Hall, New York, NY
100,000	University of Pennsylvania, Wharton School of Business, Philadelphia, PA
50,000	Center on Addiction and Substance Abuse, New York, NY
50,000	Children of Alcoholics Foundation, New York, NY
50,000	Families and Work Institute, New York, NY
42,500	Fund for Public Schools, Brooklyn, NY
40,000	Child Care Action Campaign, New York, NY
40,000	Children's Defense Fund, Washington, DC
40,000	City of New York Department of Cultural Affairs, New York, NY
37,000	Child Care, Inc., New York, NY

Primerica Financial Services

Headquarters: Duluth, GA
SIC Major Group: Security & Commodity Brokers

CONTACT

Sheila Lenz
Manager, Corporate Relations
Primerica Financial Services
3100 Breckenbridge Bouldevard
Duluth, GA 30199
(404) 381-1000

CONTRIBUTIONS SUMMARY

Operating Locations: GA (Duluth)

PriMerit F.S.B.

Assets: $2.35 billion
Employees: 716
Parent Company: Southwest Gas Corp.
Headquarters: Las Vegas, NV
SIC Major Group: Depository Institutions and Nondepository Institutions

CONTACT

Delores Nielsen
Assistant to the Chariman
Southwest Gas Corp.
PO Box 98510
Las Vegas, NV 89193-8510
(702) 876-7299

FINANCIAL SUMMARY

Fiscal Note: Annual Giving Range: Company does not disclose contributions figures.

CONTRIBUTIONS SUMMARY

Support goes to local education, human service, arts, and civic organizations.

Typical Recipients: • *Arts & Humanities:* general • *Civic & Public Affairs:* general • *Education:* general • *Health:* general • *Social Services:* general

Nonmonetary Support Types: donated equipment, loaned employees, and loaned executives

Geographic Distribution: headquarters and operating locations

Operating Locations: NV (Boulder City, Carson City, Gardnerville, Henderson, Las Vegas, Reno, Sparks)

CORP. OFFICERS

Kenny C. Guinn: *B* 1936 *ED* Fresno Univ MA; UT St Univ PhD *CURR EMPL* chmn, ceo: PriMerit Bank *CORP AFFIL* chmn, ceo: Southwest Gas Corp; chmn, ceo, dir: Southwest Gas Corp

David H. Rogers: *CURR EMPL* pres, coo: PriMerit Bank

Kevin J. Sullivan: *CURR EMPL* exec vp, cfo: PriMerit FSB

APPLICATION INFORMATION

Initial Approach: Send brief letter of inquiry, including a description of the organization, amount requested, purpose of funds sought, audited financial statement, and proof of tax-exempt status. There are no deadlines.

Prince Corp. / Prince Foundation

Sales: $150.0 million
Employees: 2,000
Headquarters: Holland, MI
SIC Major Group: Apparel & Other Textile Products

CONTACT

Egdar D. Prince
President
Prince Fdn.
1057 South Shore Dr.
Holland, MI 49423
(616) 392-5151

FINANCIAL SUMMARY

Recent Giving: $4,497,415 (fiscal 1992); $2,900,225 (fiscal 1991); $4,223,343 (fiscal 1989)

Assets: $26,130,020 (fiscal year ending June 30, 1992); $24,371,106 (fiscal 1991); $18,445,039 (fiscal 1989)

Gifts Received: $2,180,000 (fiscal 1992); $6,883,297 (fiscal 1991); $6,860,000 (fiscal 1989)

Fiscal Note: In fiscal 1992, contributions were received from Prince Holding Corp. ($1,480,000), Prince Machine Corp.($50,000), Prince Corp.($250,000), and Edgar & Elsa Prince ($400,000).

EIN: 38-2190330

CONTRIBUTIONS SUMMARY

Typical Recipients: • *Arts & Humanities:* community arts • *Civic & Public Affairs:* women's affairs • *Education:* colleges & universities • *Health:* medical research, single-disease health associations • *Religion:* churches, religious organizations • *Social Services:* aged, child welfare, family planning, family services, homes, united funds, youth organizations

Grant Types: general support and operating expenses

Geographic Distribution: focus on MI

GIVING OFFICERS

Hannes Meyers, Jr.: treas, trust

Edgar D. Prince: pres, trust

Elsa D. Prince: vp, secy, trust

APPLICATION INFORMATION

Initial Approach: The foundation reports it only makes contributions to preselected charitable organizations.

GRANTS ANALYSIS

Number of Grants: 39

Highest Grant: $2,510,000

Typical Range: $1,000 to $25,000

Disclosure Period: fiscal year ending June 30, 1992

RECENT GRANTS

2,510,000	Willow Creek Church, Arlington Heights, IL
250,000	Rest Haven of Chicago, Chicago, IL
200,000	Gospel Films, Muskegon, MI
156,000	Summit Ministries, Manitou Springs, CO
150,000	O.A.R., Holland, MI
135,000	Prison Fellowship Ministries, Washington, DC
56,000	Holland Christian, Holland, MI
53,000	Michigan Family Forum, Lansing, MI
50,000	In Touch Ministries, College Park, GA
50,000	National Family Foundation, Tempe, AZ

Prince Manufacturing, Inc.

Sales: $90.0 million
Employees: 250
Parent Company: Prince Holdings
Headquarters: Lawrenceville, NJ
SIC Major Group: Miscellaneous Manufacturing Industries

CONTACT

Gail Brisini
Personnel Administrator
Prince Manufacturing, Inc.
3 Princess Rd.
Lawrenceville, NJ 08648
(609) 896-2500

CONTRIBUTIONS SUMMARY

Typical Recipients: • *Arts & Humanities:* arts associations • *Civic & Public Affairs:* urban & community affairs • *Education:* colleges & universities, private education (precollege) • *Religion:* religious organizations • *Social Services:* family services

Grant Types: general support

Operating Locations: NJ (Lawrenceville)

CORP. OFFICERS

John M. Sullivan: *B* Stamford CT 1935 *ED* NY Univ 1959 *CURR EMPL* pres, ceo: Prince Mfg

RECENT GRANTS

500,500	Focus on the Family, Arcadia, CA
500,000	Family Research Council, Los Angeles, CA
200,000	Gospel Films, Muskegon, MI
200,000	Hope College, Holland, MI
100,700	Holland Christian, Holland, MI
100,000	Holland Community Foundation, Holland, MI
100,000	Rest Haven, Holland, MI
75,000	Holland Area Arts Council, Holland, MI
75,000	Michigan Family Forum, Lansing, MI
50,000	Eton Academy, Birmingham, MI

Prince Trust, Abbie Norman

CONTACT

Abbie Norman Prince Trust
Ten South Wacker Dr., Ste. 2575
Chicago, IL 60606
(312) 454-9130

FINANCIAL SUMMARY

Recent Giving: $601,500 (1990); $776,500 (1989); $3,623,507 (1988)

Assets: $10,404,955 (1990); $11,238,698 (1989); $9,629,783 (1988)

EIN: 36-2411865

CONTRIBUTIONS SUMMARY

Typical Recipients: • *Arts & Humanities:* dance, history/historic preservation, libraries, literary arts, museums/galleries, music • *Civic & Public Affairs:* environmental affairs, urban & community affairs • *Education:* colleges & universities, private education (precollege) • *Social Services:* child welfare, community service organizations, united funds, youth organizations

Grant Types: capital, general support, multiyear/continuing support, project, research, and seed money

Geographic Distribution: limited to Chicago, IL, and RI

GIVING OFFICERS

Frederick Henry Prince: trust
William Norman Wood Prince: off

APPLICATION INFORMATION

Initial Approach: Send cover letter and full proposal. There are no deadlines. Board meets bimonthly.

Restrictions on Giving: Does not support individuals.

GRANTS ANALYSIS

Number of Grants: 36
Highest Grant: $143,000
Typical Range: $2,500 to $20,000
Disclosure Period: 1990

RECENT GRANTS

143,000	Rehabilitation Institute, Chicago, IL
30,000	Corcoran Gallery of Art, Washington, DC
30,000	Maderia School, Greenway, VA

30,000 National Gallery of Art, Washington, DC

25,000 Center for Community Change, Washington, DC

25,000 National Center for the Study of Wilson's Disease, Bronx, NY

25,000 Piedmont Environmental Council, Warrenton, VA

25,000 St. Patrick's Episcopal Day School, Washington, DC

22,000 Boy Scouts of America, Phoenix, AZ

20,000 Manna Community Development Corporation, Washington, DC

Principal Financial Group / Principal Financial Group Foundation

Sales: $6.49 billion
Employees: 12,500
Headquarters: Des Moines, IA
SIC Major Group: Insurance Carriers and Nondepository Institutions

CONTACT

Debra J. Jensen
Assistant Director, Corporate Relations
The Principal Financial Group
711 High St.
Des Moines, IA 50392-0150
(515) 247-5209

FINANCIAL SUMMARY

Recent Giving: $3,839,083 (1993 est.); $3,169,146 (1992); $2,600,000 (1991 approx.)
Assets: $22,523,917 (1990); $23,702,709 (1989); $23,400,000 (1988)
Fiscal Note: Company gives directly and through the foundation. Above figures represent total contributions, including those donated by the foundation. Totals include matching gifts.
EIN: 42-1312301

CONTRIBUTIONS SUMMARY

Typical Recipients: • *Arts & Humanities:* community arts, dance, music, opera, performing arts, public broadcasting, theater • *Civic & Public Affairs:* civil rights, consumer affairs, economic development, environmental affairs, eth-

nic/minority organizations, housing, urban & community affairs, women's affairs • *Education:* business education, career/vocational education, colleges & universities, community & junior colleges, literacy, minority education, preschool education, science/technology education • *Health:* health care cost containment, health organizations, medical research, single-disease health associations • *Social Services:* aged, day care, disabled, drugs & alcohol, employment/job training, family services, food/clothing distribution, shelters/homelessness, volunteer services, youth organizations
Grant Types: capital, employee matching gifts, general support, multiyear/continuing support, and project
Note: Employee matching gifts are given to higher education and United Way only.
Nonmonetary Support Types: donated equipment, in-kind services, and loaned employees
Note: Nonmonetary support is provided by the company to local organizations only. The value of this support is not available nor is it included in the above figures.
Geographic Distribution: primarily in Iowa; occasional consideration to national request
Operating Locations: IA (Des Moines)
Note: The Principal Financial Group and its subsidiaries operate in all 50 states.

CORP. OFFICERS

David Drury: *CURR EMPL* pres, ceo: Prin Fin Group
Thomas J. Graf: *CURR EMPL* vp: Prin Fin Group
G. David Hurd: *B* Chicago IL 1929 *ED* MI St Univ BA 1951 *CURR EMPL* chmn, ceo, dir: Prin Fin Group *CORP AFFIL* chmn: Prin Mgmt, Princor Investment Mgmt; chmn, ceo: Prin Holding Co; dir: Eppler, Guerin & Turner, Invista Capital Mgmt, Prin Casualty Ins Co, Prin Intl, Prin Mutual Life Ins Co, Princor Fin Svcs Corp, Princor Mgmt Corp, Younkers *NONPR AFFIL* dir: Drake Univ; mem: Assn Pvt Pension Welfare Plans, Employee Benefit Res Inst; mem, dir: Des Moines Chamber Commerce
Theodore Murtaugh Hutchison: *B* Iowa City IA 1932 *ED* Univ IA BA 1954;

Univ IA JD 1956; Univ MI LLM 1958 *CURR EMPL* exec vp (Corp Svc): Prin Fin Group *CORP AFFIL* dir: Prin Mutual Life Ins Co *NONPR AFFIL* dir: Grand View Coll, Hawley Fdn, IA Law Sch Fdn; mem: Am Bar Assn, Assn Life Ins Counc, Continuing Legal Ed, IA Bar Assn, IA Natural Heritage Fdn, IA Supreme Court Comm, Polk County Bar Assn

GIVING OFFICERS

Thomas J. Graf: chmn *CURR EMPL* vp: Prin Fin Group (see above)
Debra Jensen: secy *CURR EMPL* community rels mgr: Prin Fin Group

APPLICATION INFORMATION

Initial Approach: *Initial Contact:* letter and proposal *Include Information On:* itemized budget including contributions received and anticipated, expenses, other sources of funding, most recent IRS Form 990, and audited financial statement; description of the organization, including goals, geographic scope, number of paid employees and volunteers, and total salary expense; names and affiliations of officers and directors associated with organization and project; frequency of board meetings; amount requested; proof of tax-exempt status; local groups should also include evidence of approval by the Appeals Review Board of the Greater Des Moines Chamber of Commerce *When to Submit:* at least six to eight weeks in advance of monthly meetings *Note:* Applicants may be asked to meet with members of the contributions committee.
Restrictions on Giving: Does not support athletic, fraternal, social, veterans, or international organizations; conference, seminar, or festival participation; individuals, endowments, political parties or causes, trade or professional organizations, or sectarian religious organizations; goodwill advertising; capital fund drives for hospitals or health care facilities; grantmaking bodies (except for United Way and independent college funds); private foundations; or operating expenses of programs receiving United Way support.

As a general rule, the foundation gives no more than 10% of a recipient's total goal.

OTHER THINGS TO KNOW

Grant renewals are not automatic, and the foundation expects an annual report from all grant recipients.
Name changed from Principal Foundation.
Undertook re-evaluation of priorities and procedures during 1992.

GRANTS ANALYSIS

Total Grants: $2,600,000
Number of Grants: 182*
Highest Grant: $500,000*
Typical Range: $10,000 to $20,000
Disclosure Period: 1991
Note: Number of grants, average grant, highest grant, and foundation assets are for 1990. Highest grant was to United Way of Central Iowa. Recent grants are derived from a 1990 Form 990.

RECENT GRANTS

500,000 United Way of Central Iowa, Des Moines, IA

200,000 Drake University, Des Moines, IA

120,000 Fine Foundation, Des Moines, IA

100,000 Insure, Washington, DC

50,000 Homes of Oakridge, Des Moines, IA

50,000 Iowa College Foundation, Des Moines, IA

47,500 Iowa Children's and Family Services, Des Moines, IA

40,000 Civil Center of Greater Des Moines, Des Moines, IA

35,000 Des Moines Symphony, Des Moines, IA

35,000 Drake University, Des Moines, IA

Printpack, Inc.

Sales: $275.0 million
Employees: 2,000
Headquarters: Atlanta, GA
SIC Major Group: Paper & Allied Products

CONTACT
Mike Himbridge
Vice President
Printpack, Inc.
PO Box 43687
Atlanta, GA 30378
(404) 691-5830

CONTRIBUTIONS SUMMARY
Operating Locations: GA (Atlanta)

CORP. OFFICERS
Dennis M. Love: *CURR EMPL*
pres: Printpack

OTHER THINGS TO KNOW
Company is an original donor to the Gay & Erskine Love Foundation.

Pritchard Charitable Trust, William E. and Maude S.

CONTACT
Michael Spiegel
William E. and Maude S.
  Pritchard Charitable Trust
c/o Chase Manhattan Bank,
  N.A., Tax Services Div.
1211 Avenue of the Americas
New York, NY 10036
(212) 789-5325

FINANCIAL SUMMARY
Recent Giving: $106,500
(1991); $645,500 (1990);
$600,000 (1988)
Assets: $12,994,957 (1991);
$10,883,285 (1990);
$11,128,624 (1989)
Gifts Received: $3,032 (1990);
$790,359 (1989); $131,086
(1988)
EIN: 13-6824965

GIVING OFFICERS
**Chase Manhattan Bank,
N.A.:** trust
Edward J. Cunnigle: trust

APPLICATION INFORMATION
Initial Approach: Send a summary of academic qualifications. There are no deadlines.

GRANTS ANALYSIS
Number of Grants: 14
Highest Grant: $62,500
Typical Range: $1,000 to
$10,000
Disclosure Period: 1991

RECENT GRANTS
62,500 Portledge School

10,000 Human Resources
        Center
10,000 St. Mark's Episcopal Church
10,000 State University of
        New York Research Foundation,
        NY
2,000   Buttonwood Foundation
2,000   Society of St.
        Johnland
2,000   St. Charles Hospital and Rehabilitation Center
2,000   YMCA
1,000   Meals on Wheels
1,000   Visiting Nurse Association of Oyster
        Bay, Oyster Bay,
        NY

Pritzker Foundation

CONTACT
Jay Pritzker
President
Pritzker Foundation
200 West Madison St., 38th Fl.
Chicago, IL 60606
(312) 750-8400

FINANCIAL SUMMARY
Recent Giving: $10,018,144
(1990); $4,502,546 (1989);
$430,990 (1988)
Assets: $51,182,590 (1990);
$55,495,905 (1989);
$29,001,645 (1988)
Gifts Received: $1,913,271
(1990); $26,878,295 (1989);
$5,495,055 (1988)
Fiscal Note: The foundation receives continuing support from various members of the Pritzker family, PPC Trusts Nos. 1-7, Allen Turner, and Rockwood & Co. Additional companies in 1989: Ecodyne Corp., Marmon Keystone, Trans Union Credit and Cerro Copper Products.
EIN: 36-6058062

CONTRIBUTIONS SUMMARY
Donor(s): The Pritzker Foundation was established in 1944. It was originally funded, and continues to be funded, by various members of the Pritzker family. In 1902, Nicholas J. Pritzker, a Russian immigrant, established the law firm Pritzker & Pritzker. His sons, Abram N. Pritzker and Jack N. Pritzker, also lawyers, were involved in real estate development and the acquisition of numerous companies. The family's principal holdings include the privately owned Hyatt Corporation and the private holding company, Marmon Group. They also hold interests in the Conwood Corporation, and Trans Union Corporation.
Typical Recipients: • *Arts & Humanities:* arts associations, arts festivals, arts institutes, community arts, dance, history/historic preservation, libraries, literary arts, museums/galleries, music, opera, public broadcasting, theater • *Civic & Public Affairs:* better government, business/free enterprise, civil rights, environmental affairs, ethnic/minority organizations, housing, philanthropic organizations, urban & community affairs, women's affairs, zoos/botanical gardens • *Education:* arts education, career/vocational education, colleges & universities, education administration, education funds, international studies, medical education, private education (precollege), special education, student aid • *Health:* health organizations, hospitals, medical research, public health, single-disease health associations • *International:* international health care • *Religion:* churches, missionary activities, religious organizations, synagogues • *Social Services:* aged, animal protection, child welfare, community service organizations, counseling, disabled, domestic violence, drugs & alcohol, emergency relief, employment/job training, family planning, family services, recreation & athletics, united funds, volunteer services, youth organizations
Grant Types: award, capital, department, general support, and research
Geographic Distribution: almost exclusively the Chicago, IL, metropolitan area

GIVING OFFICERS
Daniel F. Pritzker: vp, dir
James N. Pritzker: don, vp, dir
Jay Arthur Pritzker: don, pres, dir *B* Chicago IL 1922 *ED* Northwestern Univ BSc 1941; Northwestern Univ JD 1947 *CURR EMPL* ptnr: Pritzker & Pritzker *CORP AFFIL* chmn: Hyatt Corp, Marmon Group; dir: Dalfort Corp; ptnr: Chicago Mill & Lumber Co, MICA Lumber Corp *NONPR AFFIL* life trust: Univ Chicago; mem: Am Bar Assn, Chicago Bar Assn
John A. Pritzker: vp, dir

Nicholas J. Pritzker: don, vp, secy, dir *B* 1946 *ED* Lake Forest Coll BA *CURR EMPL* pres: Hyatt Devel Corp *CORP AFFIL* dir: Hyatt Corp; ptnr: Pritzker & Pritzker *NONPR AFFIL* dir: Goodman Theatre; trust: Chicago Architects Fdn
Penny F. Pritzker: vp, asst secy, dir
Robert Alan Pritzker: chmn, vp, dir *B* Chicago IL 1926 *ED* IL Inst Tech BS 1946; Univ IL *CURR EMPL* ceo, pres, dir: Marmon Group *CORP AFFIL* ceo: Leasametric Inc; ceo, pres, dir: Marmon Corp; dir: Cerro Copper Products Co, Dalfort Corp, Hyatt Corp, S&W Berisford PLC, Southern Peru Copper Corp; dir, pres: Union Tank Car Co; pres, ceo, dir: Marmon Indus Corp; pres, dir: Colson Group, Marmon Holdings, Marmon Indus *NONPR AFFIL* chmn: Field Mus Natural History; chmn, trust: IL Inst Tech; mem: Natl Academy Engring; trust: Rush-Presbyterian-St Lukes Med Ctr; trust, chmn: Chicago Symphony Orchestra
Thomas Jay Pritzker: don, vp, treas, asst secy, dir *B* Chicago IL 1950 *ED* Claremont Mens Coll BA 1971; Univ Chicago MBA 1972; Univ Chicago JD 1976 *CURR EMPL* pres: Hyatt Corp *CORP AFFIL* chmn: Health Care Compare Corp; dir: Dalfort Corp; ptnr: Pritzker & Pritzker *NONPR AFFIL* chmn: Indo-US Subcomm; mem: Am Bar Assn, Chicago Bar Assn, IL Bar Assn; trust: Art Inst Chicago
Simon Zunamon: asst treas

APPLICATION INFORMATION
Initial Approach: Restrictions on Giving: The foundation reports no specific grant-making procedures. Grants are given to a variety of preselected organizations determined by the funds manager.

GRANTS ANALYSIS
Total Grants: $10,018,114
Number of Grants: 230
Highest Grant: $7,600,000
Typical Range: $100 to $1,000 and $10,000 to $100,000
Disclosure Period: 1990
Note: The average grant figure excludes a $7,600,000 grant to the Pritzker Family Philanthropic Fund. Recent grants are derived from a 1990 grants list.

RECENT GRANTS

7,600,000 Pritzker Family
Philanthropic
Fund, Chicago, IL
500,000 Jewish United
Fund, Chicago, IL
— bond contribu-
tion
382,000 Hyatt Foundation,
Chicago, IL — Pri-
vate Foundation
200,000 Northwestern Uni-
versity School of
Law, Evanston, IL
200,000 Shedd Aquarium,
Chicago, IL
100,000 Jewish United
Fund, Chicago, IL
100,000 Lincoln Park Zo-
ological Society,
Chicago, IL
88,300 National Strategy
Forum, Chicago, IL
67,125 Museum of Con-
temporary Art, Chi-
cago, IL
51,100 Wendy Will Case
Cancer Fund, Chi-
cago, IL

Pro-line Corp.

Sales: $34.0 million
Employees: 275
Headquarters: Dallas, TX
SIC Major Group: Chemicals &
Allied Products and Wholesale
Trade—Nondurable Goods

CONTACT

Elaine McNeely
Assistant to the President
Pro-line Corp.
2121 Panoramic Circle
Dallas, TX 75212
(214) 631-4247

CONTRIBUTIONS
SUMMARY

Operating Locations: TX
(Dallas)

CORP. OFFICERS

Comer J. Cottrell: *B* Mobile
AL 1931 *ED* Univ Detroit 1952
CURR EMPL chmn, pres, ceo:
Pro-line Corp *CORP AFFIL*
chmn: CAC III Investments;
dir: Dallas Fin Corp, TX Commerce Bank-Dallas, Western
Pacific Indus *NONPR AFFIL*
chmn: Dallas Family Hosp;
vchmn: Bishop Coll

RECENT GRANTS

Save the Children, New York,
NY

Procter & Gamble Co. / Procter & Gamble Fund

Sales: $29.89 billion
Employees: 80,350
Headquarters: Cincinnati, OH
SIC Major Group: Chemicals &
Allied Products, Food &
Kindred Products, and Paper &
Allied Products

CONTACT

Robert R. Fitzpatrick, Jr.
Vice President & Secretary
The Procter & Gamble Fund
PO Box 599
Cincinnati, OH 45201
(513) 945-8486

FINANCIAL SUMMARY

Recent Giving: $37,870,443
(fiscal 1992); $32,000,000 (fis-
cal 1991); $36,000,000 (fiscal
1990)
Fiscal Note: Above figures include foundation and direct giving. Foundation giving totaled
$17,530,144 in 1992;
$16,300,000 in 1991; and
$15,443,200 in 1990. Interna-
tional contributions totaled
$4,141,298 in 1992.
EIN: 31-6019594

CONTRIBUTIONS
SUMMARY

Typical Recipients: • *Arts &
Humanities:* arts associations,
arts centers, history/historic
preservation, museums/galler-
ies, music, opera, theater
• *Civic & Public Affairs:* busi-
ness/free enterprise, economic
development, economics, environmental affairs, housing, public policy, safety, urban & community affairs, zoos/botanical
gardens • *Education:* colleges
& universities, economic education, minority education, public education (precollege), student aid • *Health:* health
organizations • *Social Services:* child welfare, community
service organizations, united
funds, youth organizations
Grant Types: capital, employee matching gifts, and general support
Nonmonetary Support Types:
donated products and loaned
executives
Note: Company provided
$5,250,000 in nonmonetary sup-
port in 1991, which is included

in total giving figure above.
Company also donates some
land. Nonmonetary support is
administered by Second Har-
vest. Contact is Robert Fitzpa-
trick, Jr. at address above.
Geographic Distribution:
communities where Procter &
Gamble maintains facilities
Operating Locations: AZ
(Phoenix), CA (Hayward, Mod-
esto, Oxnard, Sacramento,
South San Francisco), GA (Al-
bany, Augusta), IA (Iowa City),
KS (Kansas City), KY (Lexing-
ton), LA (Alexandria, New Or-
leans), MA (Quincy), MD (Bal-
timore), MO (Cape Girardeau,
Kansas City, St. Louis), NC
(Greensboro, Greenville), NJ
(Phillipsburg), NY (New York,
Norwich), OH (Cincinnati,
Lima), PA (Allentown, Hat-
boro, Mehoopany), SC (Green-
ville), TN (Jackson, Memphis),
TX (Corsicana, Levelland,
Sherman), WI (Green Bay)
Note: Also operates in Puerto
Rico, Latin America, India,
Pacific Rim, and Taiwan.

CORP. OFFICERS

Edwin L. Artzt: *B* New York
NY 1930 *ED* Univ OR *BJ* 1951
CURR EMPL chmn, dir: Proc-
ter & Gamble Co *CORP AFFIL*
dir: GTE Corp, Teradyne; pres:
Procter & Gamble Intl *NONPR
AFFIL* mem: Natl Foreign
Trade Counc; mem adv counc:
Conf Bd Europe; mem exec
comm US counc: Intl Chamber
Commerce; vp: Am Chamber
Commerce Belgium

GIVING OFFICERS

Richard A. Bachhuber, Jr.:
vp, trust
Stona James Fitch: vp, trust *B*
Wetumka OK 1931 *ED* Univ
OK BA 1955 *CURR EMPL* vp
(mfg): Procter & Gamble Co
NONPR AFFIL adv counc:
Univ OK Sch Bus Admin;
chmn bd dirs: Childrens Fam-
ily House; trust: Cincinnati
Playhouse Park
Robert R. Fitzpatrick, Jr.:
vp, secy
R. M. Neago: asst secy
Eric G. Nelson: vp, trust
Robert Louis Wehling: pres,
trust *B* Chicago IL 1938 *CURR
EMPL* vp: Procter & Gamble
Co *NONPR AFFIL* campaign
dir: Advertising Counc; dir:
Just Say No Intl; mem: Assn
Natl Advertisers, Phi Beta
Kappa; mem allocations comm:
Fine Arts Fund; mem ed task

force: Bus Roundtable; trust:
Un Way Cincinnati

APPLICATION
INFORMATION

Initial Approach: *Initial Contact:* brief letter or proposal *Include Information On:* description of the organization,
amount requested, purpose for
which funds are sought, recently audited financial statement, proof of tax-exempt
status *When to Submit:* any time
Restrictions on Giving: Fund
does not support individuals,
goodwill advertising, dinners
or special events, fraternal or
political organizations, religious organizations for sectarian
purposes, or endowments.

OTHER THINGS TO
KNOW

Company also specializes in
disposable diapers, cellulose
pulp, chemicals, shortenings,
oils, cake mixes, peanut butter,
potato chips, coffee, tea, animal feed, and personal care products.

GRANTS ANALYSIS

Total Grants: $37,870,443
Number of Grants: 299*
Highest Grant: $3,142,400
Typical Range: $500 to
$50,000 and $75,000 to
$250,000
Disclosure Period: fiscal year
ending June 30, 1992
Note: Figure for number of
grants excludes "aggregates,"
grants less than $500 awarded
to a number of recipients in the
same field. Average grant figure excludes aggregates and
the six highest grants totaling
$5,745,800. Recent grants are
derived from a fiscal 1992 annual report.

RECENT GRANTS

3,142,400 United Way
715,000 Cincinnati-Ohio
Arts Center, Cincin-
nati, OH
585,400 Cincinnati Educa-
tional Initiatives,
Cincinnati, OH
465,000 Advertising Coun-
cil, New York, NY
— Education Re-
form Project
438,000 Special Olympics
400,000 Cincinnati Art Museum, Cincinnati,
OH
277,500 Fine Arts Fund,
Cincinnati, OH
255,500 Caring Program for
Kids
249,900 Just Say No

246,600 Liga-Con Cancer

Procter & Gamble Cosmetic & Fragrance Products / Procter & Gamble/Noxell Foundation

Former Foundation Name:
Noxell Foundation
Employees: 2,069
Parent Company: Procter & Gamble
Parent Sales: $29.89 billion
Headquarters: Hunt Valley, MD
SIC Major Group: Chemicals & Allied Products

CONTACT

Catherine Warburton
P&G/Noxell Fdn.
11050 York Rd.
Hunt Valley, MD 21030
(410) 785-7300

FINANCIAL SUMMARY

Recent Giving: $980,000 (1993 est.); $980,000 (1992); $1,349,400 (1991)
Assets: $1,609,442 (1991); $1,970,914 (1990); $3,255,195 (1989)
Fiscal Note: All contributions are made through the foundation.
EIN: 52-6041435

CONTRIBUTIONS SUMMARY

Typical Recipients: • *Arts & Humanities:* arts centers, arts festivals, dance, history/historic preservation, libraries, museums/galleries, music, opera, public broadcasting, theater, visual arts • *Civic & Public Affairs:* civil rights, economic development, environmental affairs, ethnic/minority organizations, housing, international affairs, law & justice, philanthropic organizations, professional & trade associations, urban & community affairs, zoos/botanical gardens • *Education:* arts education, business education, career/vocational education, colleges & universities, economic education, education associations, education funds, health & physical education, medical education, minority education, religious education, science/technology education • *Health:* health organizations, hospitals, medical rehabilitation, mental health, nursing services, outpatient health care delivery, public health, single-disease health associations • *Religion:* churches • *Science:* scientific institutes • *Social Services:* aged, child welfare, community service organizations, disabled, domestic violence, drugs & alcohol, food/clothing distribution, recreation & athletics, religious welfare, shelters/homelessness, united funds, youth organizations

Grant Types: capital, challenge, employee matching gifts, endowment, general support, research, and scholarship

Geographic Distribution: emphasis on Baltimore, MD, metropolitan area; some support to national organizations

Operating Locations: MD (Baltimore, Cockeysville, Hunt Valley)

CORP. OFFICERS

William Robert McCartin: *B* Baltimore MD 1928 *ED* Johns Hopkins Univ 1954 *CURR EMPL* treas: Noxell Corp *CORP AFFIL* secy, treas, dir: Drumcar

GIVING OFFICERS

Carroll A. Bodie: vp *CURR EMPL* vp, gen coun, secy: Noxell Corp

George Lloyd Bunting, Jr.: vp *B* Baltimore MD 1940 *ED* Loyola Coll BS 1962; Columbia Univ MBA 1964 *CORP AFFIL* chmn, ceo: Noxzema (Toronto); dir: AS Abell, Chesapeake & Potomac Telephone Co MD, MNC Fin Corp, Noxell Corp (UK), USF&G Cos *NONPR AFFIL* dir: Cosmetic Toiletry & Fragrance Assn

Robert M. Jakobe: treas

John A. Saxton: pres

APPLICATION INFORMATION

Initial Approach: *Initial Contact:* brief letter or proposal *Include Information On:* description of the organization, amount requested, purpose for which funds are sought, recently audited financial statement, current budget, list of officers and directors, proof of 501(c)(3) status *When to Submit:* any time; board meets quarterly

OTHER THINGS TO KNOW

Company changed name from Noxell Corp. to Procter & Gamble Cosmetic & Fragrance Products because of recent ownership change.

GRANTS ANALYSIS

Total Grants: $1,349,400
Number of Grants: 119
Highest Grant: $215,000
Typical Range: $1,000 to $10,000
Disclosure Period: 1991
Note: Average grant figure excludes grants of $215,000; $161,760; and three $100,000 grants. Recent grants are derived from a 1991 Form 990.

RECENT GRANTS

215,000 Center Stage, Baltimore, MD
161,760 United Way of Central Maryland, Baltimore, MD
100,000 Baltimore Opera Company, Baltimore, MD
100,000 CollegeBound Foundation, Baltimore, MD
100,000 University of Maryland, College Park, MD
85,500 Maryland Institute, College of Art, Baltimore, MD
50,000 YMCA of Greater Baltimore, Baltimore, MD
45,000 Cosmetic, Toiletry and Fragrance Association, Washington, DC
35,000 Villa Julie College, Stevenson, MD
27,500 Baltimore Zoological Society, Baltimore, MD

Proctor Trust, Mortimer R.

CONTACT

Green Mountain Bank Trust Department
80 West St.
Rutland, VT 05701
(802) 775-2525

FINANCIAL SUMMARY

Recent Giving: $201,968 (1991); $126,008 (1990); $108,573 (1989)
Assets: $2,797,987 (1991); $2,602,513 (1990); $2,634,499 (1989)
EIN: 03-6020099

CONTRIBUTIONS SUMMARY

Typical Recipients: • *Arts & Humanities:* libraries • *Civic & Public Affairs:* municipalities, urban & community affairs • *Education:* elementary education, international studies, public education (precollege), religious education • *Religion:* churches, religious organizations • *Social Services:* community service organizations, youth organizations
Grant Types: emergency, operating expenses, and project
Geographic Distribution: limited to Proctor, VT

APPLICATION INFORMATION

Initial Approach: Send brief letter of inquiry describing program. There are no deadlines.

OTHER THINGS TO KNOW

Publications: Annual Report

GRANTS ANALYSIS

Number of Grants: 12
Highest Grant: $47,251
Typical Range: $1,000 to $10,000
Disclosure Period: 1991

RECENT GRANTS

47,251 Proctor Elementary School Playground, Proctor, VT
39,839 Town of Proctor, Proctor, VT
37,460 Proctor Elementary School, Proctor, VT
34,511 Proctor School System, Proctor, VT
10,353 St. Dominic's Catholic Church, Proctor, VT
8,982 Proctor School System Youth League, Proctor, VT
8,000 Putland Central Supervisory Union, Proctor, VT
6,108 Union Church of Proctor, Proctor, VT
5,128 Proctor Free Library, Proctor, VT
3,700 St. Paul Lutheran Church, Proctor, VT

Producers Livestock Marketing Association

Sales: $53.0 million
Employees: 100
Headquarters: North Salt Lake, UT
SIC Major Group: Wholesale Trade—Nondurable Goods

CONTACT
Clair Okelberry
General Manager
Producers Livestock Marketing, Inc.
170 West Center
North Salt Lake, UT 84054
(801) 292-2424

FINANCIAL SUMMARY
Fiscal Note: Annual Giving Range: less than $100,000

CONTRIBUTIONS SUMMARY
Typical Recipients: • *Arts & Humanities:* general • *Civic & Public Affairs:* general • *Education:* general • *Health:* general • *Social Services:* general
Grant Types: general support
Nonmonetary Support Types: in-kind services and loaned employees
Geographic Distribution: primarily headquarters area
Operating Locations: UT (North Salt Lake)

CORP. OFFICERS
Mike Urrutia: *CURR EMPL* pres: Producers Livestock Mktg

APPLICATION INFORMATION
Initial Approach: Send brief letter of inquiry. There are no deadlines.

Progressive Corp.

Revenue: $1.73 billion
Employees: 5,591
Headquarters: Cleveland, OH
SIC Major Group: Holding & Other Investment Offices and Insurance Carriers

CONTACT
Betty J. Powers
Executive Assistant
Progressive Corp.
Box 5070
Cleveland, OH 44101
(216) 464-8000
Note: In 1993, the company has decided to give only to the United Way. This policy will be reviewed in late 1993 or early 1994.

FINANCIAL SUMMARY
Recent Giving: $454,000 (1992); $708,000 (1991); $780,000 (1990)
Fiscal Note: Company gives directly.

CONTRIBUTIONS SUMMARY
Typical Recipients: • *Social Services:* united funds
Grant Types: project
Geographic Distribution: near headquarters and operating locations only
Operating Locations: CA (Richmond, Sacramento), CO (Colorado Springs), FL (Tampa), OH (Cleveland), TX (Austin), VA (Richmond)

CORP. OFFICERS
Peter Benjamin Lewis: *B* Cleveland OH 1933 *ED* Princeton Univ AB 1955 *CURR EMPL* chmn, pres, ceo, dir: Progressive Corp *CORP AFFIL* chmn, ceo: Mayfield Corp, Progressive Am Life Ins Co, Progressive Casualty Life Ins Co, Progressive Specialty Life Ins Co; chmn, pres, ceo: Progressive Mutual Life Ins Co *NONPR AFFIL* mem: Chief Exec Offs Assn, World Bus Counc; mem, pres cleveland chap: Soc Chartered Property Casualty Underwriters; trust: Cleveland Ctr Contemporary Art, Greater Cleveland Growth Assn, Hillcrest Hosp

GIVING OFFICERS
Betty J. Powers: *CURR EMPL* exec asst: Progressive Corp

APPLICATION INFORMATION
Initial Approach: *Initial Contact:* letter *Include Information On:* complete description of proposed project; complete budget for proposed project, including other sources of funding, amount requested, and organization's ability to leverage additional funds; plans for project evaluation; names and qualifications of individuals who will administer project; time frame; concise history of organization, its goals, and objectives; most recently audited financial statement; proof of tax-exempt status; list of board of directors or trustees; list of other contributors to organization *When to Submit:* any time

Restrictions on Giving:
In 1993, the company is restricting its giving to the United Way. This policy will be reviewed late in 1993 or early 1994 to decide whether to continue only giving to the United Way.
Grants are made only to organizations that have been designated tax-exempt by the Internal Revenue Service.
Does not award grants to individuals, religious organizations for sectarian purposes, fraternal organizations, or goodwill advertising.

OTHER THINGS TO KNOW
Prefers to fund special projects, as opposed to operating, benefit, capital, or endowment support.

GRANTS ANALYSIS
Total Grants: $454,000
Number of Grants: 3
Highest Grant: $448,000
Disclosure Period: 1992
Note: Average grant and typical grant figures do not apply to the grant analysis becasue of the limited number of grants. Recent grants are derived from a 1989 grants list.

RECENT GRANTS
200,000	Cleveland Initiative for Education, Cleveland, OH
50,000	Great Lakes Theater Festival, Cleveland, OH
25,000	Cleveland Center for Contemporary Art, Cleveland, OH
9,000	WCPN
6,000	Van Evert Dance Company

Promus Cos.

Sales: $1.0 billion
Employees: 22,400
Headquarters: Memphis, TN
SIC Major Group: Amusement & Recreation Services and Hotels & Other Lodging Places

CONTACT
Mary Jane Fuller
Director, Community Relations
The Promus Cos.
1023 Cherry Rd.
Memphis, TN 38117
(901) 762-8823
Note: Ms. Fuller is contact person for grant requests in the Memphis, Tennessee area. Requests originating in Nevada or New Jersey should be directed to Community Relations for Harrah's at 702-786-3232; requests in Texas should be directed to Embassy Suites, Inc. at 214-556-1133.

FINANCIAL SUMMARY
Recent Giving: $1,400,000 (1991 approx.); $1,200,000 (1990); $2,200,000 (1989)
Fiscal Note: All contributions are made directly by the corporation.

CONTRIBUTIONS SUMMARY
Typical Recipients: • *Arts & Humanities:* arts funds, museums/galleries, music, opera, public broadcasting, theater • *Civic & Public Affairs:* economic development, economics, environmental affairs, urban & community affairs • *Education:* colleges & universities, community & junior colleges, minority education, science/technology education • *Social Services:* united funds
Grant Types: capital, challenge, employee matching gifts, endowment, general support, project, scholarship, and seed money
Nonmonetary Support Types: donated equipment, donated products, in-kind services, loaned employees, loaned executives, and workplace solicitation
Note: Estimated value of nonmonetary support is not available and is not included in contributions figures above.
Geographic Distribution: near headquarters and operating locations only
Operating Locations: NJ (Atlantic City), NV (Las Vegas, Reno), TN (Memphis), TX (Irving)

CORP. OFFICERS
Charles Albert Ledsinger, Jr.: *B* Memphis TN 1950 *CURR EMPL* sr vp, cfo: Promus Cos *CORP AFFIL* dir: Friendly Ice Cream Corp, Perkins Family Restaurants LP, Perkins Mgmt Co, TN Restaurant Co *NONPR AFFIL* dir: Memphis Concert Ballet, Memphis Devel Fdn
Michael David Rose: *B* Akron OH 1942 *ED* Univ Cincinnati BBA 1963; Harvard Univ LLB 1966 *CURR EMPL* chmn, ceo, dir: Promus Cos *CORP AFFIL* dir: Ashland Oil, First TN Natl

Corp, Gen Mills *NONPR AFFIL* dir: Memphis Arts Counc; fellow advance mgmt program: Harvard Univ Grad Sch Bus Admin; hon chmn bd trust: Jr Achievement; mem: Am Hotel Motel Assn, Conf Bd, Future Memphis, Jobs Skills Task Force, OH Bar Assn, Svc Indus Counc US Chamber Commerce, Young Pres Org; mem bd advs: Univ Cincinnati

Philip G. Satre: *B* Palo Alto CA 1949 *ED* Stanford Univ BA 1971; Univ CA Davis JD 1975; MA Inst Tech 1982 *CURR EMPL* pres, coo: Promus Cos *CORP AFFIL* ceo, pres: Harrahs Hotels & Casinos *NONPR AFFIL* mem: Am Bar Assn, CA Bar Assn, NV Bar Assn, Order Coif, Phi Kappa Phi, Stanford Alumni Assn, Young Pres Org

GIVING OFFICERS

Mary Jane Fuller: *CURR EMPL* dir (community rels): Promus Cos

Ben C. Peternell: sr vp (human resources) *B* Fort Wayne IN 1945 *ED* Hanover Coll BA 1968; IN Univ MBA 1970 *CURR EMPL* sr vp (human resources): Promus Cos *NONPR AFFIL* active: Germantown TN Youth Soccer Club; chmn, dir: WKNO Pub Radio-TV; mem: Conf Personnel Offs; mem comm on 21st century: Rhodes Coll

APPLICATION INFORMATION

Initial Approach: *Initial Contact:* brief letter *Include Information On:* description of the organization, amount requested, purpose for which funds are sought, recently audited financial statement, proof of tax-exempt status *When to Submit:* any time

Restrictions on Giving: Does not support dinners or special events, religious or veterans organizations, individuals, health agencies, or member agencies of United Way.

OTHER THINGS TO KNOW

Company sold its Holiday Inns, Inc. subsidiary in 1990 and changed its name from Holiday Corp. to The Promus Cos. Reduction in total contributions for 1990 reflects reduction in company size.

Promus Cos. includes Hampton Inn, Embassy Suites, Harrah's, and Homewood Suites.

Subsidiaries of Promus Cos. handle grant requests for the areas in which they are located.

Employees and executives are active volunteers in community groups including Junior Achievement, Chamber of Commerce, Visitors Bureau, Memphis Arts Council, Leadership Memphis, Christian Brothers College, WKNO, and the Private Industry Council.

GRANTS ANALYSIS

Total Grants: $1,200,000
Typical Range: $10,000 to $15,000
Disclosure Period: 1990

Property Capital Trust

Assets: $215.7 million
Employees: 25
Headquarters: Boston, MA
SIC Major Group: Holding & Other Investment Offices

CONTACT

Anthony Fox
Senior Vice President
Property Capital Trust
One Post Office Sq., Ste. 2100
Boston, MA 02109
(617) 451-2400

CONTRIBUTIONS SUMMARY

Operating Locations: MA (Boston)

CORP. OFFICERS

John A. Cervieri, Jr.: *B* Suffern NY 1931 *ED* Columbia Univ 1951; Harvard Univ MBA 1959 *CURR EMPL* mgr trustee, ceo: Property Capital Trust *CORP AFFIL* chmn, ceo: Americana Hotels & Realty Corp; dir: BayBank Boston NA, BayBanks

Robert M. Melzer: *CURR EMPL* pres, coo: Property Capital Trust

Propp Sons Fund, Morris and Anna

CONTACT

Morris and Anna Propp Sons Fund
405 Park Avenue, Ste. 1103
New York, NY 10022

FINANCIAL SUMMARY

Recent Giving: $207,958 (1991); $193,384 (1990); $167,954 (1989)
Assets: $5,069,646 (1991); $4,231,442 (1990); $4,411,723 (1989)
Gifts Received: $25,556 (1991); $19,577 (1990); $28,420 (1989)
Fiscal Note: In 1991, contributions were received from M.J. Propp.
EIN: 13-6099110

CONTRIBUTIONS SUMMARY

Donor(s): members of the Propp family
Typical Recipients: • *Arts & Humanities:* museums/galleries • *Civic & Public Affairs:* ethnic/minority organizations • *Education:* colleges & universities, private education (precollege), religious education • *Health:* health organizations, hospitals, medical research, single-disease health associations • *International:* international organizations • *Religion:* religious organizations, synagogues • *Social Services:* community service organizations, united funds
Grant Types: general support
Geographic Distribution: focus on New York, NY

GIVING OFFICERS

Ephraim Propp: dir
M. J. Propp: dir
Seymour Propp: dir

APPLICATION INFORMATION

Initial Approach: Contributes only to preselected organizations.
Restrictions on Giving: Does not support individuals.

GRANTS ANALYSIS

Number of Grants: 105
Highest Grant: $77,000
Typical Range: $100 to $5,000
Disclosure Period: 1991

RECENT GRANTS

  77,000 United Jewish Appeal Federation of

                Jewish Philanthropies, New York, NY
15,000 Jewish Center Torah Society, New York, NY
10,000 Rabbi Isaac Elchanan Theological Seminary, New York, NY
 9,300 Westchester Day School, Westchester, NY
 9,000 Keren Menachem, New York, NY
 8,000 Yeshiva University, New York, NY
 6,000 American Committee for Shaare Zedek Hospital, New York, NY
 4,000 American Friends of Israel Museum, New York, NY
 3,800 Appeal of Conscience Foundation, New York, NY
 3,500 CHAMAH, New York, NY

Prospect Hill Foundation

CONTACT

Constance Eiseman
Executive Director
Prospect Hill Foundation
420 Lexington Avenue, Ste. 3020
New York, NY 10170
(212) 370-1144

FINANCIAL SUMMARY

Recent Giving: $2,094,000 (fiscal 1993 est.); $1,768,785 (fiscal 1992); $1,641,015 (fiscal 1991)
Assets: $43,000,000 (fiscal 1993 est.); $40,521,740 (fiscal year ending June 30, 1991); $39,069,397 (fiscal 1990); $34,145,781 (fiscal 1988)
Gifts Received: $208,638 (fiscal 1991); $1,567,487 (fiscal 1987); $1,461,911 (fiscal 1986)
Fiscal Note: In 1987, contributions derived from trusts established by Carrie Sperry Beinecke, Frederick W. Beinecke and William S. Beinecke. In 1989, the foundation changed its fiscal year from a calendar year to one ending June 30.
EIN: 13-6075567

CONTRIBUTIONS SUMMARY

Donor(s): The Prospect Hill Foundation was established in 1960. William S. Beinecke, the foundation's donor and president, was chairman of Sperry & Hutchinson Company of New York City. In 1983, the

foundation merged with the Frederick W. Beinecke Fund, which was established by his parents, Frederick and Carrie Sperry Beinecke.
Typical Recipients: • *Arts & Humanities:* museums/galleries, music • *Civic & Public Affairs:* environmental affairs, international affairs, national security, public policy, zoos/botanical gardens • *Education:* colleges & universities, student aid • *International:* international organizations • *Social Services:* family planning
Grant Types: capital, challenge, department, general support, matching, project, and scholarship
Geographic Distribution: broad geographic distribution, with emphasis on New York

GIVING OFFICERS
Robert Barletta: treas
Elizabeth G. Beinecke: vp, dir
Frederick W. Beinecke: dir *B* Stamford CT 1943 *ED* Yale Univ BA 1966; Univ VA JD 1972 *CURR EMPL* pres, dir: Antaeus Enterprises *CORP AFFIL* dir: Catalina Mktg Corp, Long Lake Energy Corp, Nature Food Ctrs, Rehab Clinics *NONPR AFFIL* mem: Assn Bar City New York; trust: NY Zoological Soc, Phillips Academy, Trudeau Inst; dir: Outward Bound; vp, dir: NY City Ballet
John B. Beinecke: vp, dir
William S. Beinecke: don, pres, dir *B* New York NY 1914 *ED* Yale Univ BA 1936; Columbia Univ LLB 1940 *CURR EMPL* co-fdr: Casey Beinecke & Chase *CORP AFFIL* dir: Antaeus Enterprises *NONPR AFFIL* chmn: Hudson River Fdn Scientific Environmental Res; mem: Counc Foreign Rels; mem bd mgrs: NY Botanical Garden
Constance Eiseman: exec dir, secy
Frances Beinecke Elston: dir
Nettie Foskett: adm
Sarah Beinecke Richardson: dir

APPLICATION INFORMATION
Initial Approach: Letters of request (no more than three pages) should be submitted to the foundation (in duplicate) in accordance with requirements listed in the Grants and Guidelines brochure.

Letters should summarize the organization's history and goals; project for which funding is sought; contribution of the project to other work in the field or to the organization's own development; and include the organization's total budget and staff size; project budget; and a list of the organization's board of directors. If the foundation is interested in the proposal, more information will be requested.
Grant requests may be submitted any time. The foundation's directors meet three or four times a year.
All material is reviewed by the executive director and one or more board members. Response generally is provided within four weeks. Whenever possible, applicants will be visited by a representative of the foundation before it finally acts on a proposal.
Restrictions on Giving: The foundation does not consider grants for individuals, scholarly research, or sectarian religious activities. It favors project support over general support requests. Proposals from arts, cultural, and educational institutions should be upon invitation only. The foundation requires a final narrative and financial report from each application.

OTHER THINGS TO KNOW
Publications: grants and guidelines brochure (should be requested before letter of request is submitted)

GRANTS ANALYSIS
Total Grants: $1,641,015*
Number of Grants: 90
Highest Grant: $300,000
Typical Range: $10,000 to $25,000
Disclosure Period: fiscal year ending June 30, 1991
Note: Above figures exclude matching gifts totaling $115,300. Total giving is $1,756,315. Average grant figure excludes a grant of $300,000. Recent grants are derived from a fiscal 1991 Form 990.

RECENT GRANTS
320,000 Columbia University in the City of New York/School of Law, New York, NY — a new professorship in inter-

national environmental law
85,000 New York Philharmonic, New York, NY — capital campaign; general support
50,000 American Museum of Natural History, New York, NY — the restoration of murals
50,000 New York Zoological Society, New York, NY — to endow the Crisis Fund for Vanishing Wildlife
45,000 Lincoln Center Theater, New York, NY — the capital campaign; continued general support
40,000 Planned Parenthood of New York City, New York, NY — toward pregnancy prevention services and public education
40,000 Save the Bay, Providence, RI — general support
34,000 Phillips Academy, Andover, MA — capital campaign to renovate George Washington Hall
30,000 International Women's Health Coalition, New York, NY — for reproductive health activities in Latin America
30,000 Natural Resources Defense Council, New York, NY — revise the legal framework for United States nuclear non-proliferation policy; to strengthen the 1972 Clean Water Act

---

Protherapy of America
Employees: 200
Headquarters: Bloomfield Hills, MI

CONTACT
Theresa Bozonik
Director of Human Resources
Protherapy of America
PO Box 809
Bloomfield Hills, MI 48303
(313) 646-1150

CONTRIBUTIONS SUMMARY
Company makes personal grants/loans to physical/occupational therapy students.
Typical Recipients: • *Education:* student aid
Grant Types: scholarship
Operating Locations: MI (Bloomfield Hills)

APPLICATION INFORMATION
Initial Approach: Description of program and verification of standing in program.
Restrictions on Giving: Does not support religious organizations for sectarian purposes, or political or lobbying groups.

GRANTS ANALYSIS
Typical Range: $5,000 to $10,000

Prouty Foundation, Olive Higgins

CONTACT
John M. Dolan
Vice President
Olive Higgins Prouty Fdn.
c/o Bank of New England, N.A.
28 State St.
Boston, MA 02109
(617) 573-6415

FINANCIAL SUMMARY
Recent Giving: $111,000 (1990); $104,000 (1989); $94,000 (1988)
Assets: $1,890,479 (1990); $1,736,793 (1989); $1,707,691 (1988)
EIN: 04-6046475

CONTRIBUTIONS SUMMARY
Donor(s): Olive Higgins Prouty
Typical Recipients: • *Arts & Humanities:* museums/galleries, performing arts • *Education:* agricultural education, colleges & universities, education associations • *Health:* hospitals, single-disease health associations • *Social Services:* family services, youth organizations
Grant Types: capital, general support, and operating expenses

Geographic Distribution:
focus on the Greater Worcester,
MA, area

GIVING OFFICERS
Thomas P. Jalkut: trust
Lewis I. Prouty: treas
Richard Prouty: trust, pres
Jane Prouty Smith: trust, vp
William M. Smith III: trust

**APPLICATION
INFORMATION**
Initial Approach: Send brief
letter describing program.
Deadline is September 30.
Restrictions on Giving: Does
not support individuals.

**OTHER THINGS TO
KNOW**
Publications: Application
Guidelines

GRANTS ANALYSIS
Number of Grants: 29
Highest Grant: $5,000
Typical Range: $2,000 to
$4,000
Disclosure Period: 1990

RECENT GRANTS
5,000 Girls Club, Worcester, MA
5,000 Mechanics Hall, Worcester, MA
5,000 Mount Auburn Hospital, Worcester, MA
5,000 Worcester Center for Performing, Worcester, MA
4,000 Family to Family, Worcester, MA
3,000 British American Education Foundation, Worcester, MA
3,000 Cambridge Center for Adult Education, Cambridge, MA
3,000 Farm School, Worcester, MA
3,000 Parkinsons Disease Foundation, Worcester, MA
2,000 Milton Academy, Worcester, MA

Providence Energy Corp.

Assets: $16.0 billion
Employees: 5000
Headquarters: Providence, RI
SIC Major Group: Electric, Gas
& Sanitary Services, Holding
& Other Investment Offices,
and Real Estate

CONTACT
Jeffrey G. McCall
Assistant to the President
Providential Life & Accident
Insurance Company
100 Weybosset St.
Providence, RI 02903
(401) 272-1947

FINANCIAL SUMMARY
Fiscal Note: Annual Giving
Range: $1,000,000 to
$5,000,000

**CONTRIBUTIONS
SUMMARY**
Company supports education,
minority affairs, the arts, and
communioty organizations.
Typical Recipients: • *Arts &
Humanities:* arts appreciation,
arts associations, arts festivals,
general, libraries, museums/galleries, music, opera, performing arts, visual arts • *Civic &
Public Affairs:* civil rights,
economic development, environmental affairs, ethnic/minority organizations, general, housing, urban & community affairs
• *Education:* colleges & universities, community & junior colleges, economic education, general, health & physical
education, liberal arts education, private education (precollege), public education (precollege), science/technology
education • *Health:* general
• *Social Services:* community
service organizations, drugs &
alcohol, food/clothing distribution, general, shelters/homelessness, united funds, youth organizations
Grant Types: capital, employee matching gifts, general
support, and operating expenses
Nonmonetary Support Types:
donated equipment, in-kind
services, loaned executives,
and workplace solicitation
Operating Locations: MA
(North Attleboro), RI (Providence)

CORP. OFFICERS
James H. Dodge: *CURR
EMPL* ceo, pres: Providence
Energy Corp

**APPLICATION
INFORMATION**
Initial Approach: Send letter
of inquiry including a description of organization, amount requested, purpose of funds
sought, and proof of tax-exempt status.

Providence Journal Company / Providence Journal Charitable Foundation

Sales: $262.0 million
Employees: 3,700
Headquarters: Providence, RI
SIC Major Group:
Communications and Printing
& Publishing

CONTACT
Lincoln Pratt
Corporate Director, Community
Relations
Providence Journal Co.
75 Fountain St.
Providence, RI 02902
(401) 277-7514

FINANCIAL SUMMARY
Recent Giving: $800,000
(1992 approx.); $619,849
(1991 approx.); $710,000
(1990)
Assets: $2,778,898 (1991);
$2,195,100 (1988)
Fiscal Note: Company gives
through foundation only.
EIN: 05-6015372

**CONTRIBUTIONS
SUMMARY**
Typical Recipients: • *Arts &
Humanities:* arts appreciation,
arts centers, history/historic
preservation, libraries, museums/galleries, music, performing arts • *Civic & Public Affairs:* economic development,
environmental affairs, ethnic/minority organizations,
housing, professional & trade
associations, women's affairs
• *Education:* arts education, career/vocational education, colleges & universities, public
education (precollege)
• *Health:* health organizations,
hospices, hospitals, single-disease health associations • *Social Services:* aged, child welfare, community centers, drugs
& alcohol, family planning,
united funds, youth organizations
Grant Types: capital, general
support, multiyear/continuing
support, scholarship, and seed
money
Nonmonetary Support Types:
donated equipment and in-kind
services
Note: Company gives about
$10,000 annually in nonmonetary gifts. This figure is not included in the above totals.

Geographic Distribution:
throughout Rhode Island and
nearby Massachusetts
Operating Locations: RI
(Providence)

CORP. OFFICERS
Stephen Hamblett: *B* Nashua
NH 1934 *ED* Harvard Coll
1957 *CURR EMPL* chmn, ceo:
Providence Journal Co

GIVING OFFICERS
Stephen Hamblett: trust
CURR EMPL chmn, ceo: Providence Journal Co (see above)
Lincoln Pratt: trust *CURR
EMPL* corp dir (community
rels): Providence Journal Co

**APPLICATION
INFORMATION**
Initial Approach: *Initial Contact:* brief letter or proposal *Include Information On:* mission
statement, amount requested,
other sources of funding, proof
of tax-exempt status, recent financial statements, list of
board of directors *When to Submit:* any time

GRANTS ANALYSIS
Total Grants: $619,849
Number of Grants: 74
Highest Grant: $191,000
Typical Range: $1,000 to
$10,000
Disclosure Period: 1991
Note: Recent grants are derived
from a 1991 Form 990.

RECENT GRANTS
191,000 United Way of Southeastern New England
40,000 Miriam Hospital
30,000 International Institute of Rhode Island, Providence, RI
25,000 Community Preparatory School
25,000 Rhode Island School of Design, Providence, RI
20,000 University of Rhode Island, Kingston, RI
13,333 Central Congregational Church
13,333 St. Michael's Church
12,500 Providence Education Fund, Providence, RI
11,000 Rhode Island Anti-Drug Coalition, RI

Provident Life & Accident Insurance Co.

Assets: $10.02 billion
Employees: 5,315
Headquarters: Chattanooga, TN
SIC Major Group: Insurance Carriers

CONTACT

Jeffrey G. McCall
Assistant to the President
Provident Life & Accident
 Insurance Co.
One Fountain Sq.
Chattanooga, TN 37402
(615) 755-1947

FINANCIAL SUMMARY

Fiscal Note: Company gives directly. Annual Giving Range: $1 million to $2 million

CONTRIBUTIONS SUMMARY

Typical Recipients: • *Arts & Humanities:* arts appreciation, arts associations, arts festivals, libraries, museums/galleries, music, opera, performing arts, visual arts • *Civic & Public Affairs:* civil rights, economic development, environmental affairs, housing, urban & community affairs • *Education:* colleges & universities, community & junior colleges, economic education, health & physical education, liberal arts education, private education (precollege), public education (precollege), science/technology education • *Social Services:* community service organizations, drugs & alcohol, food/clothing distribution, shelters/homelessness, united funds, youth organizations
Grant Types: capital, employee matching gifts, general support, and operating expenses
Nonmonetary Support Types: donated equipment, in-kind services, loaned executives, and workplace solicitation
Geographic Distribution: headquarters and operating locations
Operating Locations: TN (Chattanooga)

CORP. OFFICERS

Thomas C. Hardy: *CURR EMPL* exec vp, coo: Provident Life & Accident Ins Co
Winston W. Walker: *B* Traverse City MI 1943 *ED* Tulane Univ 1965; Univ GA 1969 *CURR EMPL* ceo, pres: Provi-

dent Life & Accident Ins Co
CORP AFFIL dir: Am Natl Bank, Provident Natl Assurance Co

GIVING OFFICERS

Jeffrey G. McCall: *CURR EMPL* asst to pres: Provident Life & Accident Ins Co

APPLICATION INFORMATION

Initial Approach: *Initial Contact:* brief letter of inquiry *Include Information On:* description of the organization, amount requested, purpose of funds sought, audited financial statement, and proof of tax-exempt status *When to Submit:* apply by early fall for the next year
Restrictions on Giving: Does not support individuals or operating funds for colleges/universities.

Provident Mutual Life Insurance Co. of Philadelphia

Assets: $3.4 billion
Employees: 800
Headquarters: Philadelphia, PA
SIC Major Group: Insurance Carriers

CONTACT

Keith Brant
Director, Corporate
 Communications
Provident Mutual Life Insurance
 Co. of Philadelphia
1600 Market St.
Philadelphia, PA 19103
(215) 636-5000

FINANCIAL SUMMARY

Fiscal Note: Company gives directly only. Annual Giving Range: $500,000 to $1 million

CONTRIBUTIONS SUMMARY

Typical Recipients: • *Arts & Humanities:* general • *Civic & Public Affairs:* general • *Education:* general • *Health:* general • *Social Services:* general
Grant Types: matching
Nonmonetary Support Types: in-kind services
Note: In-kind services are in the form of printing services performed for nonprofit groups. Nonmonetary support does not exceed $10,000 yearly and is included in total contribution figures.

Geographic Distribution: giving limited to the greater Philadelphia region
Operating Locations: DE (Wilmington), PA (Philadelphia)

CORP. OFFICERS

Lester J. Rowell, Jr.: *B* Cleveland OH 1932 *ED* Penn St Univ BA 1955 *CURR EMPL* chmn, pres, ceo: Provident Mutual Life Ins Co of Philadelphia *CORP AFFIL* dir: Continental Am Life Ins Co, Provident Mutual Life & Annuity Co Am, Sigma Am Corp, Delfi Am Corp, USO Philadelphia, WA Square Life Ins Co *NONPR AFFIL* dir: Paoli Meml Hosp, Philadelphia Drama Guild; mem: Agency Offs Round Table, Greater Philadelphia Chamber Commerce, Life Ins Mktg & Res Assn; vchmn major accts: Un Way Southeastern PA; mem: Natl Assn Life Underwriters

GIVING OFFICERS

Keith Brant: *CURR EMPL* dir corp commun: Provident Mutual Life Ins Co Philadelphia

APPLICATION INFORMATION

Initial Approach: *Initial Contact:* brief letter of inquiry *Include Information On:* a description of organization, amount requested, purpose of funds sought, recently audited financial statement, and proof of tax-exempt status *When to Submit:* any time

---

Provigo Corp. Inc.

Headquarters: San Rafael, CA
SIC Major Group: Holding & Other Investment Offices and Wholesale Trade—Nondurable Goods

CONTACT

Raleigh Jardine
Director, Operations
Provigo Corp.
33 San Pablo Ave.
San Rafael, CA 94903
(415) 472-5860

FINANCIAL SUMMARY

Fiscal Note: Annual Giving Range: less than $100,000

CONTRIBUTIONS SUMMARY

Social services are the highest priority, with united funds receiving the most support.

Youth organizations and community centers also are supported. Civic and public affairs, education, and health receive frequent contributions. Civic contributions go to better government, business and free enterprise, urban and community affairs, safety organizations, and municipalities. Education contributions support colleges and universities and public education (precollege); health contributions support hospitals and substance abuse programs. Libraries also are of interest.
Typical Recipients: • *Arts & Humanities:* libraries • *Civic & Public Affairs:* better government, business/free enterprise, municipalities, safety, urban & community affairs • *Education:* colleges & universities, public education (precollege) • *Health:* hospitals • *Social Services:* community centers, drugs & alcohol, united funds, youth organizations
Grant Types: capital and general support
Nonmonetary Support Types: donated products
Geographic Distribution: near headquarters and operating locations only
Operating Locations: CA, VA

CORP. OFFICERS

Claude A. Savard: *CURR EMPL* pres, coo: Provigo Corp

GIVING OFFICERS

Raleigh Jardine: *CURR EMPL* dir (oper): Provigo Corp

APPLICATION INFORMATION

Initial Approach: Initial contact may be by phone call or letter. Letter should include a description of the organization, amount requested, and purpose for which funds are sought. Applications are accepted at any time.
Restrictions on Giving: Company does not contribute to fraternal organizations, individuals, political or lobbying groups, or religious organizations for sectarian purposes.

Prudential-Bache Securities / Prudential Securities Foundation

Sales: $180.0 million
Employees: 13,000
Parent Company:
Prudential-Securities Group
Headquarters: New York, NY
SIC Major Group: Security & Commodity Brokers

CONTACT
Elizabeth Longley
Vice President, Corporate Affairs
Prudential Securities Foundation
199 Water St., 33th Fl.
New York, NY 10292
(212) 214-4884
Note: An alternate contact is Bruno Bissetta at 100 Gold St., New York, NY 10292.

FINANCIAL SUMMARY
Recent Giving: $645,948 (fiscal 1992); $446,190 (fiscal 1991); $522,030 (fiscal 1990)
Assets: $36,867 (fiscal year ending January 31, 1992); $31,786 (fiscal 1990); $36,630 (fiscal 1989)
Gifts Received: $530,000 (fiscal 1989)
Fiscal Note: Company gives primarily through the foundation.
EIN: 13-6193023

CONTRIBUTIONS SUMMARY
Typical Recipients: • *Arts & Humanities:* libraries, museums/galleries, music, performing arts, theater • *Civic & Public Affairs:* business/free enterprise, civil rights, environmental affairs, housing, law & justice, zoos/botanical gardens • *Education:* colleges & universities, education associations, literacy • *Health:* health organizations, hospitals, mental health, single-disease health associations • *International:* international organizations • *Religion:* churches, religious organizations, synagogues • *Social Services:* aged, community service organizations, disabled, shelters/homelessness, united funds, youth organizations
Grant Types: emergency and general support
Geographic Distribution: focus on New York

Operating Locations: IL (Chicago), MA (Boston), NJ (Newark), NY (New York)

CORP. OFFICERS
George L. Ball: *B* Evanston IL *ED* Brown Univ BA *CURR EMPL* couns, product devel: J&W Seligman & Co *NONPR AFFIL* bd overseers: Duke Comprehensive Cancer Ctr; dir: Paper Mill Playhouse; mem: Presidential Adv Counc Pvt Sector Initiative, Securities Indus Assn; mem bus comm: Metro Mus Art; trust: Brown Univ, Joint Counc Econ Ed, Natl Symphony Orchestra; vchmn bd trusts: South St Seaport Mus
James T. Barton: *CURR EMPL* pres: Prudential-Bache Securities Inc
Bruno George Bissetta: *B* New York NY 1934 *ED* NY Univ 1956 *CURR EMPL* first vp: Prudential-Bache Securities Inc *CORP AFFIL* first vp: Prudential-Bache Securities Inc *NONPR AFFIL* mem: Am Inst CPAs, Natl Assn Accts
Arthur H. Burton, Jr.: *B* Philadelphia PA 1934 *ED* Princeton Univ AB *CURR EMPL* vchmn: Prudential-Bache Securities Inc *CORP AFFIL* dir: Options Clearing Corp *NONPR AFFIL* dir: Un Way Minneapolis; mem: Ins Fed PA, Minneapolis Chamber Commerce, PA Economy League; mem exec comm: Ins Fed MN
Leland B. Paton: *B* Worcester MA 1943 *CURR EMPL* group pres capital mkts, mem exec comm: Prudential-Bache Securities Inc *CORP AFFIL* mem: NY Stock Exchange *NONPR AFFIL* mem: Am Mktg Assn, Securities Indus Assn

GIVING OFFICERS
Bruno George Bissetta: vp, treas *CURR EMPL* first vp: Prudential-Bache Securities Inc (see above)
Lisa J. Finnell: asst secy
Alan D. Hogan: vp
Howard A. Knight: pres *B* Providence RI 1942 *ED* Williams Coll BA 1963; Yale Univ JD 1966 *CURR EMPL* chmn, ceo, pres: Avalon Corp *CORP AFFIL* dir: Paringa Mining & Exploration Co, Saugatuck Capital Corp *NONPR AFFIL* mem: Am Assn Petroleum Geologists, Am Bar Assn, Petroleum Soc NY, Soc Petroleum Engrs

Elizabeth Longley: vp corp affairs
Nathalie P. Maio: vp, secy
Loren Schechter: vp

APPLICATION INFORMATION
Initial Approach: *Initial Contact:* brief letter describing program *When to Submit:* any time

GRANTS ANALYSIS
Total Grants: $645,948
Number of Grants: 92
Highest Grant: $200,000
Typical Range: $500 to $5,000
Disclosure Period: fiscal year ending January 31, 1992
Note: Recent grants are derived from a fiscal 1992 Form 990.

RECENT GRANTS
200,000	United Way of Tri State, New York, NY
92,000	United Way of Tri State, New York, NY
35,000	New York City Partnership, New York, NY
20,000	Brown University, Boston, MA
20,000	New York Infirmary Beekman Downtown Hospital, New York, NY
19,287	National Merit Scholarship
17,029	New York Public Library, New York, NY
17,028	New York Public Library, New York, NY
15,000	Cardinal's Committee of the Laity, New York, NY
11,250	South Street Seaport Museum, New York, NY

Prudential Insurance Co. of America / Prudential Foundation

Assets: $154.77 billion
Employees: 101,600
Headquarters: Newark, NJ
SIC Major Group: Insurance Carriers

CONTACT
Deborah J. Gingher
Secretary and Vice President
Prudential Fdn.
Prudential Plz.
751 Broad St.
15th Fl.
Newark, NJ 07102-3777
(201) 802-7354

FINANCIAL SUMMARY
Recent Giving: $16,811,550 (1993 est.); $15,708,212 (1992); $15,718,412 (1991)
Assets: $125,703,000 (1992); $124,174,000 (1991); $96,224,000 (1990)
Fiscal Note: Above figures are for foundation only. These figures include $2,453,271 in matching gifts to education and $3,062,000 in grants to United Ways; in addition, grants through the Prudential Community Champions program totaled $512,500. Direct giving totaled $327,000 in 1992.
EIN: 22-2175290

CONTRIBUTIONS SUMMARY
Typical Recipients: • *Arts & Humanities:* arts associations, arts centers, arts funds, arts institutes, community arts, history/historic preservation, museums/galleries, music, opera, performing arts, public broadcasting • *Civic & Public Affairs:* business/free enterprise, civil rights, consumer affairs, economic development, economics, environmental affairs, ethnic/minority organizations, law & justice, nonprofit management, public policy, safety, urban & community affairs, women's affairs • *Education:* arts education, business education, career/vocational education, colleges & universities, community & junior colleges, continuing education, economic education, education administration, education associations, education funds, elementary education, faculty development, health & physical education, literacy, medical education, minority education, private education (precollege), public education (precollege), special education • *Health:* emergency/ambulance services, geriatric health, health care cost containment, health organizations, hospitals, medical rehabilitation, medical training, mental health, outpatient health care delivery • *Social Services:* aged, child welfare, community

centers, community service organizations, counseling, delinquency & crime, disabled, drugs & alcohol, emergency relief, employment/job training, family planning, family services, food/clothing distribution, homes, legal aid, recreation & athletics, shelters/homelessness, united funds, volunteer services, youth organizations **Grant Types:** award, challenge, conference/seminar, department, emergency, employee matching gifts, fellowship, general support, operating expenses, project, scholarship, and seed money **Nonmonetary Support Types:** donated equipment, in-kind services, loaned employees, and loaned executives Note: Nonmonetary support was valued at $327,000 in 1992 and $5,300,000 in 1991. This support is not included in above figures. Requests for nonmonetary support should be addressed to William E. Brooks, Vice President, Community Initiatives Division. **Geographic Distribution:** near operating locations, with special emphasis on New Jersey and the city of Newark; also nationally **Operating Locations:** AR (Little Rock), AZ (Phoenix, Scottsdale), CA (Fresno, Irvin, Los Angeles, Pleasanton, Sacramento, Sunnyvale, Van Gury, Westlake Village, Woodland Hills), DC, FL (Coral Gables, Deerfield Beach, Fort Lauderdale, Jacksonville, Maitland, Orlando, Tampa Bay), GA (Atlanta), IL (Chicago, Des Plaines, Downers Grove), IN (Indianapolis), LA (Monroe, New Orleans), MA (Boston), MI (Southfield), MN (Minneapolis), MO (Creve Coere), MS (Greenville), NC (Charlotte), NE (Kearny, Omaha), NJ (Chatham, Holmdel, Iselin, Newark, Parsippany, Pleasantville), NY (New York), OH (Cincinnati, Columbus, Mansfield), OK (Oklahoma City, Tulsa), PA (Fort Washington, Horsham, Philadelphia), TN (Memphis, Nashville), TX (Austin, Bellaire, Dallas, Houston, San Antonio), VA (Richmond), WA (Tri Cities), WY (Casper)

CORP. OFFICERS

Garnett Lee Keith, Jr.: *B* Atlanta GA 1935 *ED* GA Inst Tech BS 1957; Harvard Univ

MBA 1962 *CURR EMPL* vchmn (investments), dir: Prudential Ins Co Am *CORP AFFIL* dir: AEA Investors, Inland Steel Indus, Supervalu Stores *NONPR AFFIL* mem: Inst Chartered Fin Analysts; trust, mem bd pensions: Un Presbyterian Church USA **Robert Cushing Winters:** *B* Hartford CT 1931 *ED* Yale Univ BA 1953; Boston Univ 1963 *CURR EMPL* chmn, ceo, dir: Prudential Ins Co Am *CORP AFFIL* dir: AlliedSignal; pres: Pruco Inc *NONPR AFFIL* chmn: Greater Newark Chamber Commerce; dir: Regional Plan Assn; fellow, dir: Soc Actuaries; mem: Am Academy Actuaries, Am Counc Life Ins, Bus Counc, Bus Roundtable, Life Off Mgmt Assn, NJ Chamber Commerce, Partnership NJ, Sigma Xi

GIVING OFFICERS

Peter Bushyeager: program off health & human svcs **Lisle C. Carter:** trust *CORP AFFIL* dir: Prudential Ins Co Am *NONPR AFFIL* sr vp, gen coun: Un Way Am **Carolyne K. Davis:** trust **James Robert Gillen:** trust *B* New York NY 1937 *ED* Harvard Univ BA 1959; Harvard Univ LLD 1965 *CURR EMPL* sr vp, gen coun: Prudential Ins Co Am *NONPR AFFIL* mem: Am Bar Assn, Assn Life Ins Counc, NJ Bar Assn **Deborah J. Gingher:** vp, secy **Peter B. Goldberg:** pres **Barbara Halaburda:** program off (ed) **Jon E. Hanson:** trust **Karen Heid:** program off Focus on Children **Joanne Brown Lee:** treas **Dorothy K. Light:** chmn *B* Alden IA 1937 *ED* Univ IA 1959; Univ IA 1961 *CURR EMPL* vp, secy: Prudential Ins Co Am *CORP AFFIL* dir: NJ Resources **Eugene Michael O'Hara:** sr vp, comptr *B* Newark NJ 1937 *ED* Rutgers Univ BS 1962; Community Coll NY *CURR EMPL* sr vp, comptr: Prudential Ins Co Am *NONPR AFFIL* mem: Fin Execs Inst, Life Off Mgmt Assn **Paul Gerard O'Leary:** vp *B* Boston MA 1935 *ED* Harvard Univ AB 1956; Univ PA MBA 1958 *CURR EMPL* vp (portfolio mgmt): Prudential Investment Corp *NONPR AFFIL* mem: Am Nuclear Insurers,

Assn Ins & Fin Analysts, Ins Inst Highway Safety, Inst Chartered Fin Analysts, NY Soc Security Analysts **Donald E. Procknow:** trust *B* Madison SD 1923 *ED* Univ WI BSEE 1947 *CORP AFFIL* dir: CPC Corp, Ingersoll-Rand Co, JP Morgan & Co, Morgan Guaranty Trust Co, Prudential Ins Co Am *NONPR AFFIL* mem: Tau Beta Pi; trust: Drew Univ **Mary Puryear:** program off (culture & arts) **Don Treloar:** program off (bus & civic affairs) **Robert Cushing Winters:** trust *CURR EMPL* chmn, ceo, dir: Prudential Ins Co Am (see above) **Edward Donald Zinbarg:** trust *B* New York NY 1934 *ED* City Univ NY 1954; NY Univ PhD 1959 *CURR EMPL* exec vp (Pru Investment Corp): Prudential Ins Co Am *NONPR AFFIL* mem: An Fin Assn, NY Soc Security Analysts; mem invest comm: Un Way Essex & W Hudson NJ; trust: Trenton St Coll

APPLICATION INFORMATION

Initial Approach: *Initial Contact:* letter or brief abstract regarding funding proposal *Include Information On:* proof of tax-exempt status; latest audited financial statement and Form 990; description of the organization and geographic scope; type, amount, and duration of request; description, expected results, evaluative criteria, budget, and geographical scope of project; names and affiliations of board members, compensation, and number of meetings held; number, compensation, and qualifications of employees and volunteers; itemized budget; breakdown of current sources of income and list of other sources being approached; and statement that periodic reports will be furnished *When to Submit:* any time; board meets in April, August, and December *Note:* Every proposal will receive a response. Organizations may call or write to clarify the status of a proposal only after six weeks have passed since its submission.

Restrictions on Giving: In general, grants are not made to veterans, labor, religious, political, fraternal, or external athletic groups, except when pro-

gram benefits or provides services to the community at large; individuals; organizations that do not have 501(c)(3) status; general operating support for single-disease health organizations; goodwill advertising; or grant-making organizations other than the United Way.

OTHER THINGS TO KNOW

Over the next several years, the foundation plans to shift its emphasis; top priority categories will receive increased funding. In particular, greater emphasis will be on stabilization of health care costs and focus on children. Also, special attention will be paid to organizations in New Jersey, especially Newark, and the four regional headquarters cities of Philadelphia, PA; Jacksonville, FL; Minneapolis, MN; and Los Angeles, CA.

GRANTS ANALYSIS

Total Grants: $15,708,212*
Number of Grants: 780*
Highest Grant: $333,000
Typical Range: $1,000 to $20,000
Disclosure Period: 1992
Note: Fiscal information for foundation only. Number of grants and average grant figures exclude matching gifts to education totaling $2,453,271; contributions to United Ways totaling $3,062,000; and grants through the Prudential Champions Awards Program totaling $512,500. Recent grants are derived from a 1992 annual report.

RECENT GRANTS

333,000 University of Southern California Ethel Percy Andrus Gerontology Center, CA — establish a university chair in gerontology

200,000 Partnership for New Jersey, Early Childhood Facilities Fund, Brunswick, NJ — create a financial intermediary to expand and improve childcare facilities

175,000 Center on Budget and Policy Priorities, Washington, DC — improve coordination among federal programs for children

165,000 Life Underwriter
Training Council
(LUTC), Bethesda,
MD — insurance
education

133,000 Independent College Fund of New
Jersey, Summit, NJ
— general support
and urban initiative
program

130,000 New Jersey Performing Arts Center at Newark Corporation, Newark,
NJ — new arts center construction

125,000 Commission on
Presidential Debates, Washington,
DC — educational
programs and
preparation for
1992 debates

125,000 Recruiting New
Teachers, Cambridge, MA — nationwide minority
teacher recruiting
initiative

105,000 Center on Addiction and Substance
Abuse at Columbia
University, New
York, NY — drug-abuse prevention
efforts for Newark
youth

105,000 New Community
Corporation, Newark, NJ — provide
summer employment for Newark
youth and fund a
publication describing the organization's 25-year history

PSI Energy / PSI Foundation

Assets: $2.09 billion
Employees: 4,143
Parent Company: PSI Resources
Headquarters: Plainfield, IN
SIC Major Group: Electric, Gas & Sanitary Services

CONTACT
Connie Carter
PSI Energy
251 N. Illinios St.
Ste. 1400
Indianapolis, IN 46204
(317) 488-3532
Note: The toll free number for the foundation is 800-428-4337. The foundation may be contacted for general information and an application form. However, applicants are requested to submit their application to the district office closest to them for review and endorsement. A complete list of district offices is available in the foundation's grant application packet.

FINANCIAL SUMMARY
Recent Giving: $1,300,000 (1993 approx.); $1,114,530 (1991)
Fiscal Note: Contributes through foundation only.

CONTRIBUTIONS SUMMARY
Typical Recipients: • *Arts & Humanities:* community arts, general, performing arts • *Civic & Public Affairs:* economic development, environmental affairs, general, urban & community affairs • *Education:* colleges & universities, elementary education, faculty development, general, public education (precollege) • *Health:* general • *Social Services:* general, united funds, youth organizations
Grant Types: conference/seminar, project, scholarship, and seed money
Nonmonetary Support Types: cause-related marketing & promotion, donated equipment, in-kind services, and workplace solicitation
Geographic Distribution: company service area, comprised of 69 counties in Indiana
Operating Locations: IN (Attica, Aurora, Bedford, Bloomington, Brazil, Carmel, Clarksville, Clinton, Columbus, Connersville, Corydon, Danville, Franklin, Greencastle, Greensburg, Greenwood, Huntington, Indianapolis, Kokomo, Lafayette, Madison, Martinsville, New Castle, Noblesville, North Manchester, Princeton, Rochester, Seymour, Shelbyville, Sullivan, Terre Haute, Vincennes, Wabash)

CORP. OFFICERS
J. Wayne Leonard: *CURR EMPL* vp, cfo: PSI Energy
James E. Rogers, Jr.: *CURR EMPL* chmn, pres, ceo: PSI Energy

GIVING OFFICERS
Connie Carter: mgr

APPLICATION INFORMATION
Initial Approach: *Initial Contact:* phone call to request application guidelines and grant application form* *Include Information On:* grant application form requests the following information: organization name, address, phone number, and federal tax identification number; name and title of contact person; a brief description of the organization's mission, goals, and objectives; and project information, including name, date of project, total project cost, dollar amount requested, number of people project benefits, county within which project is located, additional counties benefiting from project, project description, and a list of PSI employees involved in the project and a description of their roles; attachments requested include a copy of 501(c)(3) tax exemption letter; a copy of organization's current budget and the project budget, showing all project revenues and expenses; the names and addresses of the organization's board of directors; and other supplementary material that describe the organization *When to Submit:* January 1, April 1, July 1, and October 1 *Note:* Applicants are encouraged to call the foundation to discuss their proposals prior to submission. The phone number is 1-800-428-4337, extension 3532, or, in the Indianapolis area, (317) 488-3532. Applicants are requested to submit their grant application to the district office closest to them for review and endorsement by the district manager. Managers and employees are involved in the decision-making process, and the foundation reports it is important for the PSI district manager in applicant's service area to be knowledgeable about its project. A complete list of district offices and phone numbers is available in the foundation's grant application guidelines.
Restrictions on Giving: The foundation does not fund advertising; post-event funding; projects/organizations benefiting an individual or a few persons; or veterans, labor, religious, politcal, external athletic, or fraternal groups. Generally, gifts for athletic programs and facilities are beyond the scope of foundation's program.

OTHER THINGS TO KNOW
Company is looking for partnerships between the company and organizations that enhance the future of Indiana communities. Grants are for specific projects or designated programs. Grants are made on a one-year basis. Re-application is necessary for consideration of a grant renewal. Special consideration is given to programs with a statewide scope that benefit citizens in company's service area. Some organizations receiving grants from the PSI Foundation will be offered the added benefit of an energy audit of their facilities at PSI's expense. The audit provides the organization with recommendations to save on energy costs.

GRANTS ANALYSIS
Total Grants: $1,114,530
Number of Grants: 408
Highest Grant: $54,375
Typical Range: $200 to $5,000
Disclosure Period: 1991
Note: Recent grants are derived from a 1991 grants list.

RECENT GRANTS
54,375 United Way, Indianapolis, IN
51,600 Indiana Manufacturers Association Alliance, Indianapolis, IN
39,075 Indiana Repertory Theatre, Indianapolis, IN
35,000 Indianapolis Symphony Orchestra, Indianapolis, IN
25,000 Hoosier Alliance Against Drugs, Indianapolis, IN
25,000 Indiana Sports Corporation, Indianapolis, IN
24,350 Salvation Army, Indianapolis, IN
23,585 Indiana University Foundation, Bloomington, IN
22,050 Butler University, Butler, IN
21,000 Connor Prairie Foundation

Psychists

CONTACT
Psychists
72 Cummings Point Rd.
Stamford, CT 06902

FINANCIAL SUMMARY
Recent Giving: $106,650 (fiscal 1990); $117,000 (fiscal 1989)
Assets: $3,143,156 (fiscal year ending August 31, 1990); $3,150,610 (fiscal 1989)

EIN: 13-1869530

CONTRIBUTIONS SUMMARY

Donor(s): the late Richard L. Parish, American Flange and Manufacturing Co.

Typical Recipients: • *Education:* colleges & universities, private education (precollege) • *Health:* hospitals, medical research, nursing services, single-disease health associations

Grant Types: general support and research

GIVING OFFICERS

David L. McKissock: vp, secy

Richard L. Parish, Jr.: pres, treas

APPLICATION INFORMATION

Initial Approach: Contributes only to preselected organizations.

GRANTS ANALYSIS

Number of Grants: 39

Highest Grant: $50,000

Typical Range: $1,000 to $2,000

Disclosure Period: fiscal year ending August 31, 1990

RECENT GRANTS

50,000 St. Vincents Hospital, New Haven, CT

2,600 Foxcroft School, Middleburg, VA

2,600 Occidental College, Los Angeles, CA

2,000 Central DuPage Hospital, Seattle, WA

2,000 Elizabeth General Medical Center Foundation, Elizabeth, NJ

2,000 Greenwich Hospital Association, Greenwich, CT

2,000 Memorial Sloan-Kettering Cancer Center, New York, NY

2,000 Mental Health Association of Greater Chicago, Chicago, IL

2,000 Mental Health Association of Union County, New Haven, CT

2,000 Skidmore College, Saratoga Springs, NY

Public Service Co. of Colorado

Sales: $1.73 billion
Employees: 6,500
Headquarters: Denver, CO
SIC Major Group: Electric, Gas & Sanitary Services

CONTACT

Tom Currigan
Director, External Affairs
Public Service Co. of Colorado
PO Box 840
Denver, CO 80201-0840
(303) 294-2407
Note: For additional contact information see "Other Things You Should Know."

FINANCIAL SUMMARY

Recent Giving: $1,269,562 (1993); $1,011,449 (1992); $1,377,815 (1991)
Fiscal Note: Company gives directly only. Separate contribution budgets are managed by each of 9 regional divisions. This support is not included in above figures.

CONTRIBUTIONS SUMMARY

Typical Recipients: • *Arts & Humanities:* arts associations, arts centers, arts festivals, community arts, dance, ethnic arts, history/historic preservation, museums/galleries, music, opera, performing arts, public broadcasting • *Civic & Public Affairs:* economic development, environmental affairs, women's affairs, zoos/botanical gardens • *Education:* business education, colleges & universities, economic education, minority education, science/technology education • *Health:* pediatric health • *Social Services:* aged, child welfare, community service organizations, family services, united funds, volunteer services, youth organizations

Grant Types: employee matching gifts, general support, and project

Nonmonetary Support Types: donated equipment and in-kind services

Note: Above figures include nonmonetary support, valued at approximately $75,000 annually. Also provides technical support.

Geographic Distribution: primarily Colorado, with emphasis on Denver

Operating Locations: CO (Alamosa, Boulder, Brush, Den-

ver, Evergreen, Ft. Collins, Greeley, Leadville, Pueblo, Silverthorne, Sterling), WY (Cheyenne)

CORP. OFFICERS

Delwin D. Hock: *B* Colorado Springs CO 1935 *ED* Univ CO BS 1956 *CURR EMPL* chmn, pres, ceo, dir: Pub Svc Co CO *CORP AFFIL* chmn: Banncock Ctr Corp, Cheyenne Light Fuel & Power Co, Fuel Resources Devel Co, PS CO Credit Corp, PSR Investments *NONPR AFFIL* chmn: Greater Denver Chamber Commerce, Western Gas Supply Co; dir: Assn Edison Illuminating Cos, CO Alliance Bus, Greater Denver Corp, INROADS, Natl Natural Gas Vehicle Coalition, Nuclear Mgmt Resources Counc, Transit Construction Authority; mem: Am Gas Assn, Am Inst CPAs, CO Forum, CO Soc, Edison Electric Inst, Western Energy Supply Transmission Assocs, Western Regional Counc

GIVING OFFICERS

Tom Currigan: *CURR EMPL* dir external aff: Pub Svc Co CO

APPLICATION INFORMATION

Initial Approach: *Initial Contact:* letter of application and an executive summary of the program (not to exceed two pages) *Include Information On:* legal name and address; summary of organization with date started, history, mission, names of board of directors and staff, and complete budget; overview of program/project request, with mission, targeted population, unique aspects, evaluation strategies, anticipated results; amount and purpose of grant request, program/ project, budget, and time line; copy of letter designating tax-exempt status; most recent audit report; list of other corporate and foundation support for both program and project *When to Submit:* any time

Restrictions on Giving: Does not make grants for general operating funds, capital campaigns, or endowments. Does not give to individuals or political parties nor does it provide free gas, electricity, or heat. United Way contributions are provided through annual corporate and employee fund-raising drive.

OTHER THINGS TO KNOW

Giving program underwent reorganization in mid-1991. Tom Currigan is a temporary contact person until various positions are filled.

Letters of application should be sent to Ms. Melinda Reed, Associate Program Officer for Corporate Contributions.

Grant applications for $5,000 or more are reviewed quarterly. Submit application by April in order to be considered for next year's budget.

GRANTS ANALYSIS

Total Grants: $1,377,815

Typical Range: $1,000 to $10,000

Disclosure Period: 1991

Note: Recent grants are derived from a 1991 grants list.

RECENT GRANTS

Adams County Historical Society, Brighton, CO
Arvada Hockey, Arvada, CO
Auraria Foundation, Denver, CO
Boy Scouts of America, Boulder, CO — Troop 457
Breckenridge Music Institute, Breckenridge, CO
Breckenridge Outdoor Education Center, Breckenridge, CO
Cheyenne Artist Guild, Cheyenne, WY
Colorado Ballet, Denver, CO
Colorado Easter Seal Society, Lakewood, CO
Colorado Outward Bound School, Denver, CO

Public Service Co. of New Mexico / PNM Foundation

Assets: $2.34 billion
Employees: 3,150
Headquarters: Albuquerque, NM
SIC Major Group: Electric, Gas & Sanitary Services

CONTACT

Shandra Manning
Community Relations Coordinator
Public Service Co. if New Mexico
Alvarado Sq.
Albuquerque, NM 87158
(505) 848-2700

FINANCIAL SUMMARY

Recent Giving: $130,371 (1991); $100,280 (1989); $66,690 (1988)

Assets: $4,283,576 (1991); $3,865,425 (1989); $3,358,563 (1988)
Gifts Received: $91,806 (1988)
EIN: 85-0309005

CONTRIBUTIONS SUMMARY

Typical Recipients: • *Arts & Humanities:* museums/galleries • *Civic & Public Affairs:* business/free enterprise, ethnic/minority organizations • *Education:* colleges & universities, faculty development, public education (precollege) • *Health:* hospitals • *Social Services:* day care, youth organizations
Grant Types: capital, challenge, endowment, matching, project, and seed money
Geographic Distribution: primarily in NM
Operating Locations: NM (Albuquerque)

CORP. OFFICERS

John Tryon Ackerman: *B* Cleveland OH 1941 *ED* Univ NM 1968; NM St Univ 1971 *CURR EMPL* chmn, pres, ceo: Pub Svc Co NM *CORP AFFIL* dir: First Interstate Bank, Paragon Resources *NONPR AFFIL* mem: Am Mgmt Assn, Natl Soc Professional Engrs
W. M. Eglinton: *CURR EMPL* exec vp, coo, dir: Pub Svc Co of New Mexico

GIVING OFFICERS

John Tryon Ackerman: dir *CURR EMPL* chmn, pres, ceo: Pub Svc Co NM (see above)
William Eglinton: dir
James B. Mulcock: pres, dir *CURR EMPL* sr vp, secy: Pub Svc Co NM *CORP AFFIL* sr vp, secy: Pub Svc Co NM
Joellyn Murphy: vp, dir *CURR EMPL* vp: Pub Svc Co NM *CORP AFFIL* vp: Pub Svc Co NM
John Von Rusten: secy, treas, dir

APPLICATION INFORMATION

Initial Approach: Application form required; board meeds quarterly. Deadline for Distinguished Educator Award Program is April 30, 1991. Board meets quarterly.

OTHER THINGS TO KNOW

Publications: Informational Brochure

GRANTS ANALYSIS

Number of Grants: 10
Highest Grant: $15,000
Typical Range: $2,000 to $11,000
Disclosure Period: 1991
Note: Number, size, and range of grant figures do not include majority of contributions: matching gifts and distinguished educator awards.

RECENT GRANTS

15,000 Casa Esperanza, Albuquerque, NM
11,400 Youth Development, Albuquerque, NM
10,000 Albuquerque Museum Foundation, Albuquerque, NM
10,000 Santa Fe Partners in Education, Santa Fe, NM
9,000 New Mexico Highlands University Foundation, NM
5,100 University of New Mexico Foundation, Albuquerque, NM
5,000 Eastern New Mexico University, Portales, NM
5,000 International Space Hall of Fame Foundation
5,000 La Compania de Teatro de Albuquerque, Albuquerque, NM
5,000 Western New Mexico University, Silver City, NM

Public Service Co. of Oklahoma

Sales: $604.0 million
Employees: 1,976
Parent Company: Central & South West Corp.
Headquarters: Tulsa, OK
SIC Major Group: Electric, Gas & Sanitary Services

CONTACT

Carole Hicks
Manager, Community Development
Public Service Co. of Oklahoma
PO Box 201
Tulsa, OK 74102
(918) 599-2033

FINANCIAL SUMMARY

Recent Giving: $500,000 (1992); $500,000 (1991); $500,000 (1990)
Fiscal Note: Company gives directly.

CONTRIBUTIONS SUMMARY

Typical Recipients: • *Arts & Humanities:* general • *Civic & Public Affairs:* general • *Education:* general • *Health:* general • *Social Services:* general
Nonmonetary Support Types: donated equipment, in-kind services, loaned employees, loaned executives, and workplace solicitation
Geographic Distribution: giving is limited to southeastern and southwestern Oklahoma
Operating Locations: OK (Tulsa), WY (Sheridan)

CORP. OFFICERS

Robert L. Zemanek: *CURR EMPL* pres, ceo: Publ Svc OK

GIVING OFFICERS

Carole Hicks: *CURR EMPL* mgr commun devel: Publ Svc Co OK

APPLICATION INFORMATION

Initial Approach: *Initial Contact:* brief letter of inquiry *Include Information On:* description of the organization, amount requested, purpose of funds sought, recently audited financial statements, and proof of tax-exempt status *When to Submit:* proposals should be received at least 30 days in advance of need
Restrictions on Giving: Does not support individuals, religious organizations for sectarian purposes, political or lobbying groups, controversial organizations or membership-only or discriminatory groups.

GRANTS ANALYSIS

Typical Range: $1,000 to $2,500

Public Service Electric & Gas Co.

Parent Company: Public Service Enterprise Group
Revenue: $5.35 billion
Parent Employees: 13,185
Headquarters: Newark, NJ
SIC Major Group: Electric, Gas & Sanitary Services

CONTACT

Maria B. Pinho
General Manager, Corporate Contributions
Public Service Electric and Gas Co.
80 Park Plz.
PO Box 570
Newark, NJ 07101
(201) 430-8660

FINANCIAL SUMMARY

Recent Giving: $3,100,000 (1993 est.); $2,870,000 (1992); $2,760,000 (1991)
Fiscal Note: Company gives directly.

CONTRIBUTIONS SUMMARY

Typical Recipients: • *Arts & Humanities:* arts centers, arts funds, history/historic preservation, libraries, museums/galleries, performing arts, public broadcasting, theater • *Civic & Public Affairs:* economic development, environmental affairs, ethnic/minority organizations, housing, law & justice, professional & trade associations, public policy, safety, urban & community affairs, women's affairs • *Education:* business education, career/vocational education, colleges & universities, community & junior colleges, elementary education, engineering education, minority education, private education (precollege), public education (precollege), science/technology education • *Health:* emergency/ambulance services, hospitals • *Science:* science exhibits & fairs, scientific institutes • *Social Services:* aged, child welfare, community service organizations, counseling, delinquency & crime, disabled, drugs & alcohol, employment/job training, food/clothing distribution, recreation & athletics, united funds, youth organizations
Grant Types: capital, challenge, employee matching gifts, general support, project, scholarship, and seed money
Nonmonetary Support Types: donated equipment, donated products, in-kind services, and loaned executives
Note: Value of nonmonetary support is unavailable and is not included in above figures.
Geographic Distribution: primarily in service area; education grants awarded nationally
Operating Locations: NJ (Camden, Elizabeth, Jersey

City, New Brunswick, Newark, Paramus, Paterson, Ridgewood, Trenton)
Note: Also operates in the Virgin Islands.

CORP. OFFICERS
E. James Ferland: *B* Boston MA 1942 *ED* Univ ME BSME 1964; Univ New Haven MBA 1979; Harvard Univ Sch Bus Admin *CURR EMPL* chmn, pres, ceo: Enterprise Group *CORP AFFIL* chmn, ceo: Pub Svc Electric & Gas Co; chmn, pres, ceo, dir: CT Yankee Co, ME Yankee Co, VT Yankee Co; dir: Commun Energy Alternatives Inc, Energy Devel Corp, Energy Pipeline Corp, Energy Terminal Svcs Corp, First Fidelity Bancorp, Gasdel Pipeline Sys Inc, Hartford Steam Boiler Inspection & Ins Co, Mutual Benefit Life Ins Co, Pub Svc Resources Corp *NONPR AFFIL* dir: Am Nuclear Energy Counc, Electric Power Res Inst, Mulberry Street Urban Renewal Corp

APPLICATION INFORMATION
Initial Approach: *Initial Contact:* letter accompanied by full proposal *Include Information On:* description of the organization and project, budget, and proof of tax-exempt status *When to Submit:* any time
Restrictions on Giving: Does not support individuals, member agencies of united funds, political or lobbying groups, or religious organizations for sectarian purposes.

OTHER THINGS TO KNOW
Publications: corporate responsiblity report

GRANTS ANALYSIS
Total Grants: $2,870,000*
Highest Grant: $326,000
Typical Range: $1,000 to $5,000
Disclosure Period: 1992
Note: Total grants figure is approximate.

Public Welfare Foundation

CONTACT
Larry Kressley
Executive Director
Public Welfare Foundation
2600 Virginia Avenue, NW, Ste. 505
Washington, DC 20037-1977
(202) 965-1800

FINANCIAL SUMMARY
Recent Giving: $17,500,000 (fiscal 1993 est.); $17,432,200 (fiscal 1992); $16,750,568 (fiscal 1991)
Assets: $259,097,945 (fiscal year ending October 31, 1992); $250,284,699 (fiscal 1991); $244,146,780 (fiscal 1990)
EIN: 54-0597601

CONTRIBUTIONS SUMMARY
Donor(s): The Public Welfare Foundation was founded in 1947 by Charles Edward Marsh, an Ohio newspaperman. Mr. Marsh believed that newspapers were semi-public utilities which contributed to the improvement of society. This philosophy, coupled with a strong humanitarian instinct, inspired him to use the income from some of the newspapers he owned to establish a foundation.
Typical Recipients: • *Civic & Public Affairs:* environmental affairs, housing, law & justice, rural affairs, urban & community affairs • *Health:* geriatric health, health organizations, hospices, outpatient health care delivery, pediatric health, public health, single-disease health associations • *International:* international health care • *Social Services:* aged, child welfare, community service organizations, delinquency & crime, domestic violence, employment/job training, family planning, homes, legal aid, refugee assistance, shelters/homelessness
Grant Types: general support, operating expenses, project, and seed money
Geographic Distribution: international and national

GIVING OFFICERS
Ms. Linda J. Campbell: secy, asst treas
Antoinette M. Haskell: dir
Robert H. Haskell: dir
Veronica T. Keating: treas, dir

Claudia Haines Marsh: dir emeritus
Robert R. Nathan: dir *B* Dayton OH 1908 *ED* Univ PA BS 1931; Univ PA MA 1933; Georgetown Univ LLB 1938 *CURR EMPL* chmn: Robert R Nathan Assocs *CORP AFFIL* consultant: DC Natl Bank; dir: Josam Mfg Co *NONPR AFFIL* hon chmn: Natl Consumers League; mem: Counc Foreign Rels, Soc Intl Devel; mem econ policy counc: Un Nations Assn
Myrtis H. Powell: dir
Thomas J. Scanlon: vp, dir
Thomas W. Scoville: dir
Jerome W. D. Stokes: dir
C. Elizabeth Warner: dir
C. Elizabeth Warner: dir
Donald T. Warner: chmn, dir
Murat Willis Williams: dir *B* Richmond VA 1914 *ED* Univ VA AB 1935; Oxford Univ BA 1938; Oxford Univ MA 1943 *NONPR AFFIL* adv: WA Off Latin Am; dir: Pub Welfare Fdn; mem: AM Comm East-West Accord, Delta Psi, Intl Inst Strategic Studies, Phi Beta Kappa, Univ VA Soc Fellows

APPLICATION INFORMATION
Initial Approach:
Applicants should send a proposal to the foundation.
A cover letter (maximum of two pages) should include the name, address, and telephone number of the applicant organization; contact person; description and purpose of organization; tax-exempt status; amount requested; total annual budget; period of time for which grant is requested; purpose of grant; other sources of income including amounts; and the date submitted. Proposals should be no more than ten pages in length, and should include the organization's history; needs and problem statement; goals and objectives; plan of action; past year's accomplishments; method of evaluation; long-term plans for continuation of program, including future financing; and project budget. Also include descriptions of the structure and administration of the organization; its budget and financial statements of the past year; letters of recommendation; other sources and amounts of funding; and the name and telephone number of the foundation staff member who investigated the program.

Requests for grants may be submitted at any time and are reviewed by the screening committee on a daily basis.
The foundation requests that all proposals be written in English and applicants not submit letters of inquiry or request preliminary meetings. Within one month of receiving the proposal, the foundation will notify the applicant whther the proposal has been accepted for consideration. It generally takes three to four months for the foundation to notify the applicant if it has approved the proposal. Funds should be sought for the following operating year in most cases. Decisions are made by the board of directors which meets regularly during the year.
Restrictions on Giving: The foundation generally does not fund conferences, endowments, foreign study, graduate work, individuals, publications, research projects, scholarships, seminars, and workshops. On a project-by-project basis, the foundation will maintain flexibility in these areas.

OTHER THINGS TO KNOW
Each year over half of the grantees are first-time recipients.
Publications: annual report; application guidelines (Spanish translation available)

GRANTS ANALYSIS
Total Grants: $17,322,200*
Number of Grants: 417*
Highest Grant: $250,000
Typical Range: $10,000 to $50,000
Disclosure Period: fiscal year ending October 31, 1992
Note: The total grants and number of grants figures exclude 26 trustee-initiated grants totaling $110,000. Total giving is $17,432,200. Recent grants are derived from a fiscal 1992 annual report.

RECENT GRANTS
250,000 Friends of the Earth, Washington, DC
250,000 Natural Resources Defense Council, New York, NY
250,000 Southern Center for Human Rights, Atlanta, GA
200,000 Environmental Defense Fund, New York, NY

200,000 Families USA Foundation, Washington, DC
150,000 Center on Budget and Policy Priorities, Washington, DC
150,000 Food Research and Action Center, Washington, DC
150,000 For Love of Children, Washington, DC
150,000 Sarah's Circle, Washington, DC
125,000 Geneva B. Scruggs Community Health Care Center, Buffalo, NY

Publicker Industries, Inc.

Sales: $93.6 million
Employees: 950
Headquarters: Old Greenwich, CT
SIC Major Group: Chemicals & Allied Products, Electronic & Other Electrical Equipment, Textile Mill Products, and Wholesale Trade—Durable Goods

CONTACT
Jim Weis
Chief Financial Officer
Publicker Industries, Inc.
1445 East Putnam Ave.
Old Greenwich, CT 06870
(203) 637-4500

CONTRIBUTIONS SUMMARY
Operating Locations: CT (Old Greenwich)

CORP. OFFICERS
David L. Herman: *CURR EMPL* pres, ceo, dir: Publicker Indus
James J. Weis: *CURR EMPL* vp, cfo: Publicker Indus

Publix Supermarkets / Jenkins Foundation

Sales: $6.1 billion
Employees: 68,000
Headquarters: Lakeland, FL
SIC Major Group: Food Stores

CONTACT
Barbara Jenkins
President
Publix Supermarkets
PO Box 407
Lakeland, FL 33802
(813) 688-1188

CONTRIBUTIONS SUMMARY
Nonmonetary Support Types: cause-related marketing & promotion, donated equipment, donated products, and in-kind services
Operating Locations: FL (Lakeland)

CORP. OFFICERS
Mark C. Hollis: *ED* Stetson Univ; MI St Univ *CURR EMPL* pres: Publix Supermarkets

Puett Foundation, Nelson

CONTACT
Nelson Puett Fdn.
PO Box 9038
Austin, TX 78766
(512) 453-6611

FINANCIAL SUMMARY
Recent Giving: $263,830 (fiscal 1992); $454,386 (fiscal 1991); $138,410 (fiscal 1990)
Assets: $5,073,173 (fiscal year ending February 28, 1992); $4,545,782 (fiscal 1991); $4,094,970 (fiscal 1990)
Gifts Received: $355,000 (fiscal 1992); $347,865 (fiscal 1991); $335,000 (fiscal 1990)
Fiscal Note: In 1992, contributions were received from Nelson Puett ($300,000) and Nelson Puett Mortgage Co. ($55,000).
EIN: 74-6062365

CONTRIBUTIONS SUMMARY
Donor(s): Nelson Puett, Nelson Puett Mortgage Co.
Typical Recipients: • *Civic & Public Affairs:* housing, public policy, zoos/botanical gardens • *Education:* education funds, public education (precollege) • *Health:* medical research • *Religion:* churches • *Social Services:* community service organizations, homes
Grant Types: capital, fellowship, general support, loan, project, research, and scholarship
Geographic Distribution: focus on TX

GIVING OFFICERS
Robert C. Osborne: secy, treas
Nelson Puett: pres
Ruth B. Puett: vp

APPLICATION INFORMATION
Initial Approach: Information on scholarships available from individual high schools.
Restrictions on Giving: Does not support individuals.

OTHER THINGS TO KNOW
Provides higher education scholarships for local high school graduates.
Publications: Program policy statement, financial statement

GRANTS ANALYSIS
Number of Grants: 76
Highest Grant: $55,955
Typical Range: $100 to $1,000
Disclosure Period: fiscal year ending February 28, 1992

RECENT GRANTS
55,955 Project Homes, TX
52,250 Project Homes, TX
42,750 Project Homes, TX
35,150 Project Homes, TX
21,780 Project Homes, TX
5,000 Council for National Policy, TX
5,000 Council for National Policy, TX
5,000 Mayo Foundation for Medical Research, Rochester, MN
3,500 Austin Independent School District, Austin, TX
3,400 Austin Independent School District, Austin, TX

Puget Sound National Bank

Assets: $3.1 billion
Employees: 2,100
Parent Company: Puget Sound Bancorp.
Headquarters: Tacoma, WA
SIC Major Group: Depository Institutions

CONTACT
Katie Weiss
Assistant Vice President & Manager
Puget Sound National Bank
1119 Pacific Avenue, PO Box 11500, MS-8300
Tacoma, WA 98411
(206) 593-3600

CONTRIBUTIONS SUMMARY
Operating Locations: WA (Tacoma)

CORP. OFFICERS
William W. Phillip: *CURR EMPL* chmn, ceo: Puget Sound Natl Bank
Don G. Vandenheuvel: *CURR EMPL* Puget Sound Natl Bank
Don G. Vandenheuvel: *CURR EMPL* pres, cfo: Puget Sound Natl Bank

Puget Sound Power & Light Co.

Sales: $1.02 billion
Employees: 2,665
Headquarters: Bellevue, WA
SIC Major Group: Electric, Gas & Sanitary Services

CONTACT
Beverley DuFort
Manager, Corporate Contributions, Volunteerism
Puget Sound Power & Light Co.
Consumer Affairs Dept., OBC-09N
PO Box 97034
Bellevue, WA 98009-9734
(206) 462-3799

FINANCIAL SUMMARY
Recent Giving: $655,000 (1991 approx.); $596,000 (1990 approx.); 567,000 (1989)
Fiscal Note: Company gives directly. See "Other Things You Should Know" for more details.

CONTRIBUTIONS SUMMARY
Typical Recipients: • *Arts & Humanities:* arts associations, arts centers, arts funds, arts institutes, dance, museums/galleries, music, theater • *Civic & Public Affairs:* better government, economic development, environmental affairs, law & justice • *Education:* business education, colleges & universities • *Health:* mental health, single-disease health associations • *Social Services:* aged, disabled, united funds, volunteer services

Grant Types: employee matching gifts, operating expenses, and project

Nonmonetary Support Types: in-kind services, loaned employees, and loaned executives

Note: Estimate of value for nonmonetary support is unavailable.

Geographic Distribution: primarily in Washington State

Operating Locations: WA (Bellevue, Bellingham, Bremerton, Olympia)

CORP. OFFICERS

John W. Ellis: *B* Seattle WA 1928 *ED* Univ WA BS 1952; Univ WA JD 1953 *CURR EMPL* chmn: Puget Sound Power Light Co *CORP AFFIL* dir: Powertech Labs Inc, SAFECO Corp, UTILX Corp, Washington Mutual Savings Bank *NONPR AFFIL* chmn: Seattle Regional Panel White House Fellows; dir: Overlake Hosp, Seattle Sailing Fdn, Seattle Science Fdn, Un Way King County; dir, mem exec comm: Seattle/King County Econ Devel Counc; mem: Am Bar Assn, Assn Edison Illuminating Cos, Edison Electric Inst, King County Bar Assn, Natl Assn Electric Cos, Phi Delta Phi, Phi Gamma Delta, Seattle Chamber Commerce, WA Bar Assn; mem adv bd: Univ WA Sch Bus Admin, WA St Econ Partnership; pres: Un for WA; trust: Seattle Univ

Richard R. Sonstelie: *B* Ottawa Canada 1945 *ED* US Military Academy 1966; Harvard Univ 1974 *CURR EMPL* pres, cfo, dir: Puget Sound Power & Light Co *CORP AFFIL* dir: First Interstate Bank WA *NONPR AFFIL* active: Vietnam Veterans Leadership Program; bd advs: Resource Ctr Handicapped; chmn, trust: Bellvue Comm Coll; civilian aide: Secy Army; dir: Jr Achievement Greater Puget Sound, Seattle Science Ctr; mem: Edison Electric Inst, Seattle Chamber Commerce, West Point Soc Puget Sound

GIVING OFFICERS

Gene Andrews: mem contributions comm

Beverly DuFort: mgr corp contributions volunteerism

James W. Eldridge: mem contributios comm *CURR EMPL* contr: Puget Sound Power Light Co

William J. Finnegan: mem contributions comm *CURR EMPL* vp (engring): Puget Sound Power Light Co

Neil Lawrence McReynolds: mem contributions comm *B* Seattle WA 1934 *ED* Univ WA BA 1956 *CURR EMPL* sr vp (corp relations): Puget Sound Power Light Co *CORP AFFIL* dir: Continental Savings Bank *NONPR AFFIL* dir: Corp Counc Arts, Fred Hutchinson Cancer Res Ctr, Independent Colls WA, Seattle-King County Econ Devel Counc; dir, mem: Greater Seattle Chamber Commerce; mem: Norhtwest Electric Light Power Assn, Pub Rels Soc Am, Sigma Delta Chi

Russel E. Olson: mem contributions comm *B* Seattle WA 1931 *ED* Univ WA BA 1959; Univ WA exec devel 1968; Pacific Lutheran Univ MBA 1982 *CURR EMPL* vp (fin), treas: Puget Sound Power Light Co *CORP AFFIL* dir: Interwest Savings Bank *NONPR AFFIL* elder: Overlake Christian Church; mem: Electric League Pacific Northwest, Fin Execs Inst, Northwest Electric Light Power Assn, Providence Fdn; mem fid bd visitors: Pacific Lutheran Univ

APPLICATION INFORMATION

Initial Approach: *Initial Contact:* request guidelines and information form, then apply in writing to Corporate Contributions Committee, Puget Sound Power & Light Co., PO Box 97034 OBC-9N, Bellvue, WA 98009-9734 *Include Information On:* description of the organization, amount requested, purpose for which funds are sought, recently audited financial statement, proof of tax-exempt status *When to Submit:* any time; budgeting begins in September

Restrictions on Giving: Company will not make grants supporting contests, raffles, or other prize-oriented activities; individuals or "team" projects, mass mailings and form letters, organizations that discriminate for any reason including race, color, religion, creed, age, sex, or national origin; special occasion goodwill advertising; churches and other religious organizations unless activities benefit the overall community and does not support any specific religious doctrine; organiza-

tions that IRS rulings would render ineligible for tax-deductible contributions; political organizations, campaigns of candidates for public office support of ballot issues or organizations whose prime purpose is to influence legislation; fraternal or labor organizations; requests that are not in writing; the general funds of tax-supported educational institutions; organizations that are themselves strictly grant-making bodies; trips or tours; endowment funds; individuals; or national organizations.

OTHER THINGS TO KNOW

Company declined to verify giving.

Publications: *A Tradition of Caring: Puget Power's Community Service Report*

GRANTS ANALYSIS

Total Grants: $655,000*

Typical Range: $1,000 to $10,000

Disclosure Period: 1991

Note: Total grants figure is estimated. Recent grants are derived from a 1991 "Community Service Report."

RECENT GRANTS

Boy Scouts of America, Mount Baker Area Council

Challenge Series — annual program of downhill gravity-car races for disabled children

Eastside YMCA Earth Corps

Fish Fest — outing for handicapped children at company trout-rearing ponds

Gatekeeper Program — customer-contact employees are trained to recognize and respond to signs that a vulnerable older person may be in trouble

Goodwill Games, Seattle, WA — a multicultural athletic competition

Junior Achievement, Seattle, WA

Radio Help Program, Bellevue, WA — makes Puget Power vehicles a ready resource from which to make emergency calls for help

Salvation Army, St. Louis, MO — help eligible customers in need pay their energy bills during difficult times

Seattle Symphony, Seattle, WA

Pukall Lumber / Pukall Lumber Foundation

Headquarters: Woodruff, WI

CONTACT

Roger Pukall
President
Pukall Lumber Foundation
AV 10894 Highway 70 East
Woodruff, WI 54568
(715) 356-3252

FINANCIAL SUMMARY

Recent Giving: $22,764 (fiscal 1990)

Assets: $317,619 (fiscal year ending June 30, 1990)

Gifts Received: $15,000 (fiscal 1990)

Fiscal Note: In fiscal 1990, contributions were received from the Pukall Lumber Co.

EIN: 23-7396586

CONTRIBUTIONS SUMMARY

Typical Recipients: • *Arts & Humanities:* performing arts • *Civic & Public Affairs:* municipalities, safety • *Education:* colleges & universities • *Health:* hospitals, medical rehabilitation • *Religion:* churches

Grant Types: general support

Geographic Distribution: giving limited to north central WI

Operating Locations: WI (Woodruff)

CORP. OFFICERS

Robert L. Pukall: *CURR EMPL* pres: Pukall Lumber

GIVING OFFICERS

Mary Pukall: dir

Roger L. Pukall: dir

Debra Pukall-Christiansen: dir

APPLICATION INFORMATION

Initial Approach: Applicants should submit a brief history of organization and description of its mission; detailed description of project and amount of funding requested; and copy of IRS determination letter; There are no deadlines.

Restrictions on Giving: The foundation does not make grants to individuals.

GRANTS ANALYSIS

Number of Grants: 31

Highest Grant: $7,500

Typical Range: $100 to $1,000

Disclosure Period: fiscal year ending June 30, 1990

RECENT GRANTS

7,500	Howard Young Medical Center, Woodruff, WI
2,500	Calvary Lutheran Church, Minocqua, WI
1,500	Town of Arbor Vitae, Arbor Vitae, WI
1,000	Arbor Vitae Voluntary Fire Department, Arbor Vitae, WI
1,000	Community Church, Boulder Junction, WI
1,000	Northland College, Ashland, WI
1,000	Rehabilitation Center Lakeland Council, Woodruff, WI
1,000	Wausau Area Performing Arts Foundation, Wausau, WI
564	Ducks Unlimited, Minocqua, WI
500	Trinity Lutheran Church, Minocqua, WI

Pulitzer Publishing Co. / Pulitzer Publishing Co. Foundation

Sales: $393.37 million
Employees: 2,900
Headquarters: St. Louis, MO
SIC Major Group:
  Communications and Printing & Publishing

CONTACT

Ronald H. Ridgway
Secretary & Treasurer
Pulitzer Publishing Co. Fdn.
900 N Tucker Blvd.
St. Louis, MO 63101
(314) 340-8000

FINANCIAL SUMMARY

Recent Giving: $559,433 (1991); $500,000 (1990 approx.); $805,526 (1989)
Assets: $742,411 (1991); $772,079 (1989); $733,528 (1988)
Fiscal Note: Company gives through the foundation only.
EIN: 43-6052854

CONTRIBUTIONS SUMMARY

Typical Recipients: • *Arts & Humanities:* arts appreciation, arts associations, arts funds, arts institutes, dance, history/historic preservation, libraries, museums/galleries, music, opera, public broadcasting, theater, visual arts • *Civic & Public Affairs:* business/free enterprise, civil rights, economic development, environmental affairs, first amendment issues, international affairs, professional & trade associations • *Education:* business education, colleges & universities, education funds, international exchange, journalism education, legal education, medical education, minority education, private education (precollege), science/technology education, student aid • *Health:* hospices, hospitals, mental health, pediatric health, single-disease health associations • *Religion:* churches, religious organizations • *Social Services:* aged, child welfare, community service organizations, emergency relief, employment/job training, family planning, family services, food/clothing distribution, homes, religious welfare, united funds, youth organizations
Grant Types: capital, endowment, general support, project, and scholarship
Geographic Distribution: primarily in St. Louis, MO, metropolitan area
Operating Locations: AZ (Phoenix, Tucson), IN (Fort Wayne), MO (St. Louis), NC (Winston-Salem), NE (Omaha), NM (Albuquerque), PA (Lancaster), SC (Greenville)

CORP. OFFICERS

Joseph Pulitzer, Jr.: *B* St Louis MO 1913 *ED* Harvard Univ AB 1936 *CURR EMPL* chmn, dir: Pulitzer Publ Co *CORP AFFIL* mem intl adv bd: Sing Tao Newspapers Ltd *NONPR AFFIL* mem: Am Newspaper Publs Assn, Am Soc Newspaper Editors, Assn Harvard Alumni; mem exec comm: St Louis Symphony Soc
Michael Edgar Pulitzer: *B* St Louis MO 1930 *ED* Harvard Univ AB 1951; Harvard Univ LLB 1954 *CURR EMPL* pres, ceo, dir: Pulitzer Publ Co *CORP AFFIL* pres, ceo, dir: Lerner Newspaper, Pulitzer Community Newspapers; pres, ceo, publ, editor, dir: Star Publ Co; vchmn, dir: KETV, KKLT-FM, KOAT, KTAR-AM, WDSU, WGAL, WLKY, WXII, WYFF *NONPR AFFIL* trust: St Louis Univ

GIVING OFFICERS

David Lipman: dir *B* Springfield MO 1931 *ED* Univ MO *CURR EMPL* managing editor: St. Louis Post Dispatch *CORP AFFIL* vp, dir: Pulitzer Productions *NONPR AFFIL* chmn: Intl Am Press Assn, Press Club St Louis; chmn bd advs: Univ MO Sch Journalism Natl Alumni Assn; dir: Mid-Am Press Inst, New Directions News; mem: Am Soc Newspaper Editors, Assoc Press Mng Editors Assn, Football Writers Assn Am, Kappa Tau Alpha, MO Editors & Publs Assn, Omicron Delta Kappa, Sigma Delta Chi; vchmn, mem: MO Soc Newspaper Editors
Michael Edgar Pulitzer: vchmn, pres, dir *CURR EMPL* pres, ceo, dir: Pulitzer Publ Co (see above)
Joseph Pulitzer IV: dir
Ronald H. Ridgway: secy, treas, dir *CURR EMPL* vp (fin), treas, dir: St Louis Post Dispatch *CORP AFFIL* Pulitzer Publ Co
Nicholas G. Tenniman IV: dir *CURR EMPL* vp (newspaper opers): Pulitzer Publ Co
William Franklin Woo: dir *B* Shanghai People's Republic of China 1936 *ED* Univ KS BA 1960 *CURR EMPL* editor: St Louis Post Dispatch

APPLICATION INFORMATION

Initial Approach: *Initial Contact:* brief letter or proposal *Include Information On:* description of the organization, amount requested, purpose for which funds are sought, recently audited financial statement, proof of tax-exempt status *When to Submit:* any time

OTHER THINGS TO KNOW

Foundation receives contributions from KETV Television, Omaha, NE; KOAT Television, Albuquerque, NM; Phoenix Broadcasting Co., AZ; Pulitzer Broadcasting Co., St. Louis, MO; Pulitzer Publishing Co., St. Louis, MO; Star Publishing Co., Tucson, AZ; WGAL Television, Lancaster, PA; WPTA Television, Fort Wayne, IN; WXII Television, Winston-Salem, NC; and WYFF Television, Greenville, SC.

GRANTS ANALYSIS

Total Grants: $559,433
Number of Grants: 90

Highest Grant: $90,500
Typical Range: $2,000 to $20,000
Disclosure Period: 1991
Note: Recent grants are derived from a 1991 Form 990.

RECENT GRANTS

90,500	United Way of Greater St. Louis, St. Louis, MO
50,000	Columbia University, New York, NY
50,000	St. Louis Art Museum, St. Louis, MO
50,000	St. Louis Symphony Society, St. Louis, MO
50,000	St. Louis Symphony Society, St. Louis, MO
20,000	Museum of Broadcasting, New York, NY
20,000	Pennsylvania State University, University Park, PA
20,000	University of Arizona, Tucson, AZ
16,000	University of Missouri, Columbia, MO
15,000	Arts and Education Fund, St. Louis, MO

Pullman Educational Foundation, George M.

CONTACT

John H. Munger
Executive Director
George M. Pullman Educational Fdn.
5020 South Lake Shore Dr., Ste. 307
Chicago, IL 60615
(312) 363-6191

FINANCIAL SUMMARY

Recent Giving: $623,700 (fiscal 1991); $603,868 (fiscal 1990); $595,500 (fiscal 1989)
Assets: $16,730,062 (fiscal year ending July 31, 1991); $15,980,835 (fiscal 1990); $15,289,894 (fiscal 1989)
EIN: 36-2216171

CONTRIBUTIONS SUMMARY

Donor(s): The foundation was incorporated in 1949 by the late George Mortimer Pullman and the late Harriet Sanger Pullman.
Typical Recipients: • *Education:* student aid

Grant Types: scholarship
Geographic Distribution: limited to Cook County, IL

GIVING OFFICERS
Robert W. Bennett: dir
Edward McCormick Blair, Jr.: treas
Edward McCormick Blair: dir *B* Chicago IL 1915 *ED* Yale Univ BA 1938; Harvard Univ MBA 1940 *CURR EMPL* sr ptnr: William Blair & Co *CORP AFFIL* dir: Phoenix Svcs *NONPR AFFIL* chmn bd trusts: Coll Atlantic; life trust: Univ Chicago
Robert C. McCormack: dir *B* New York NY 1939 *ED* Univ NC AB; Univ Chicago MBA *CURR EMPL* asst sec navy fin mgmt: US Dept Defense
Phillip Lowden Miller: pres
Warren Pullman Miller: dir
Mary Nissenson: dir
Harry Maynard Oliver, Jr.: secy *B* Kansas City MO 1921 *ED* Williams Coll BA 1943
Rev. Sam A. Portaro, Jr.: dir
George A. Ranney, Jr.: vp, dir
William Julius Wilson: dir *B* Derry Township PA 1935 *ED* Wilberforce Univ BA 1958; Bowling Green St Univ MA 1961; WA St Univ PhD 1966 *NONPR AFFIL* chmn dept sociology, prof: Univ Chicago; dir: Ctr Advanced Study Behavioral Sciences, Ctr Natl Policy; dir, mem: Chicago Urban League; fellow: Am Academy Arts & Sciences, Am Assn Advancement Science; mem: Am Philosophical Soc, Am Sociological Assn, Intl Sociological Assn, Lucy Flower Univ, Soc Study Social Problems, Sociological Res Assn; mem adv bd: Environmental Devel Pub Policy, Social Science Book Club; mem natl bd dirs: Inst Res Poverty, Randolph Inst (A Philip); trust: Spelman Coll

APPLICATION INFORMATION
Initial Approach:
Applicants must contact the foundation for a formal application.
The deadline for freshmen is January 1; upper classmen, May 1; vocational technical students, April 11; renewal college students, June 1.
The board meets quarterly.
Restrictions on Giving: The foundation makes grants to residents of Cook County, IL or to children and grandchildren of a graduate of Pullman Free School of Manual Training.

OTHER THINGS TO KNOW
Publications: biennial report and informational brochure

GRANTS ANALYSIS
Total Grants: $623,700*
Typical Range: $500 to $5,000
Disclosure Period: fiscal year ending July 31, 1991
Note: The 1991 grants list consists of scholarships paid to individuals.

Puterbaugh Foundation

CONTACT
Don C. Phelps
Managing Trustee
Puterbaugh Fdn.
PO Box 729
McAlester, OK 74502
(918) 426-1591

FINANCIAL SUMMARY
Recent Giving: $229,403 (1991); $255,176 (1990); $249,856 (1989)
Assets: $7,489,479 (1991); $6,886,607 (1990); $6,783,056 (1989)
EIN: 73-6092193

CONTRIBUTIONS SUMMARY
Donor(s): the late Jay Garfield Puterbaugh, the late Leela Oliver Puterbaugh
Typical Recipients: • *Civic & Public Affairs:* economic development • *Education:* colleges & universities • *Health:* hospitals, medical research • *Social Services:* child welfare, community service organizations, drugs & alcohol, family planning, family services, homes, united funds, youth organizations
Grant Types: capital, endowment, general support, professorship, project, and scholarship
Geographic Distribution: focus on OK

GIVING OFFICERS
Frank G. Edwards: trust
Don C. Phelps: managing trust
Norris J. Welker: trust

APPLICATION INFORMATION
Initial Approach: Send brief letter of inquiry describing program or project. Deadline is January 15 for payment in December.
Restrictions on Giving: Does not support individuals.

OTHER THINGS TO KNOW
Publications: Financial Statement

GRANTS ANALYSIS
Number of Grants: 36
Highest Grant: $50,000
Typical Range: $300 to $3,000
Disclosure Period: 1991

RECENT GRANTS
50,000　Oklahoma State University Foundation, Stillwater, OK
40,000　University of Oklahoma Foundation, Norman, OK
25,000　Boys Club of America, McAlester, OK
25,000　Eastern Oklahoma State College, Burton, OK
15,000　McAlester Economic Development Authority, McAlester, OK
10,000　Baptist Medical Center, McAlester, OK
10,000　Goodland Presbyterian Children's Home, McAlester, OK
8,132　United Way, McAlester, OK
6,000　Pittsburgh County Youth Shelter, Pittsburgh, OK — deprived children support
5,000　McAlester Alcoholism Council, McAlester, OK

Putnam Foundation

CONTACT
David F. Putnam
Trustee
Putnam Fdn.
150 Congress St.
Keene, NH 03431
(603) 352-1130

FINANCIAL SUMMARY
Recent Giving: $287,090 (fiscal 1991); $253,150 (fiscal 1990); $200,063 (fiscal 1989)
Assets: $4,484,729 (fiscal year ending October 31, 1991); $4,108,670 (fiscal 1990); $4,244,037 (fiscal 1989)
Gifts Received: $4,989 (fiscal 1991); $19,643 (fiscal 1990)
Fiscal Note: In 1991, contributions were received from David F. Putnam.
EIN: 02-6011388

CONTRIBUTIONS SUMMARY
Donor(s): David F. Putnam
Typical Recipients: • *Arts & Humanities:* community arts, history/historic preservation, music, public broadcasting • *Civic & Public Affairs:* environmental affairs, philanthropic organizations • *Education:* arts education, colleges & universities, education funds • *Health:* health organizations, hospitals • *Religion:* religious organizations • *Social Services:* community service organizations, united funds
Grant Types: capital and general support
Geographic Distribution: limited to NH

GIVING OFFICERS
David F. Putnam: dir
James A. Putnam: dir *CURR EMPL* vp, dir: Markem Corp *CORP AFFIL* vp, dir: Markem Corp
Rosamund P. Putnam: dir

APPLICATION INFORMATION
Initial Approach: Contributes only to preselected organizations.

GRANTS ANALYSIS
Number of Grants: 53
Highest Grant: $50,000
Typical Range: $1,000 to $10,000
Disclosure Period: fiscal year ending October 31, 1991

RECENT GRANTS
50,000　MacDowell Colony, Keene, NH
50,000　MacDowell Colony, Keene, NH
15,000　Channel 11, Manchester, NH
11,290　New England Colleges Fund, Keene, NH
10,000　American Red Cross, Keene, NH
10,000　Cedarcrest Construction Campaign, Keene, NH
10,000　Dartmouth-Hitchcock Medical Center, Hanover, NH
10,000　Keene Public Library, Keene, NH
10,000　Monadnock Music, Monadnock, NH — Lend an Ear Program
10,000　Plymouth State College Cultural Arts Center, Plymouth, MA

Putnam Prize Fund for the Promotion of Scholarship, William Lowell

CONTACT
George Putnam
Trustee
William Lowell Putnam Prize Fund for the Promotion of Scholarship
One Post Office Sq.
Boston, MA 02109
(617) 292-1402

FINANCIAL SUMMARY
Recent Giving: $177,000 (1991); $134,750 (1990); $146,750 (1989)
Assets: $6,616,672 (1991); $5,129,926 (1990); $4,882,052 (1989)
EIN: 04-6130905

CONTRIBUTIONS SUMMARY
Donor(s): the late Elizabeth Putman

GIVING OFFICERS
George Putnam III: trust

APPLICATION INFORMATION
Initial Approach: Applicants must apply through their schools.

OTHER THINGS TO KNOW
Conducts a mathematics contest that awards prizes for higher education.

GRANTS ANALYSIS
Number of Grants: 2
Highest Grant: $160,000
Typical Range: $17,000 to $160,000
Disclosure Period: 1991

Pyramid Foundation

CONTACT
Pyramid Fdn.
PO Box 13225
Tampa, FL 33681-3225

FINANCIAL SUMMARY
Recent Giving: $189,690 (1991); $190,530 (1990); $172,854 (1989)
Assets: $2,042,859 (1991); $2,061,519 (1990); $2,103,393 (1989)
EIN: 13-6083997

CONTRIBUTIONS SUMMARY
Typical Recipients: • *Arts & Humanities:* arts centers, community arts, museums/galleries, opera, performing arts • *Education:* religious education • *Health:* hospitals, medical research, pediatric health, single-disease health associations • *Religion:* religious organizations • *Social Services:* aged, community service organizations, disabled, united funds, youth organizations
Grant Types: general support
Geographic Distribution: focus on NY

GIVING OFFICERS
Donald B. Cohen: vp
Michael Cohen: treas

APPLICATION INFORMATION
Initial Approach: Contributes only to preselected organizations.
Restrictions on Giving: Does not support individuals.

GRANTS ANALYSIS
Number of Grants: 39
Highest Grant: $100,000
Typical Range: $500 to $5,000
Disclosure Period: 1991

RECENT GRANTS
100,000 Long Island Jewish Medical Center, New Hyde Park, NY
10,000 St. George Greek Orthodox Church
7,000 Metropolitan Opera, New York, NY
5,000 American Foundation for AIDS Research, New York, NY
5,000 Jewish Theological Seminary, New York, NY
5,000 St. John's Hospital, Santa Monica, CA
5,000 Tampa Bay Performing Arts Center, Tampa, FL
5,000 Tampa Museum of Art, Tampa, FL
5,000 United Jewish Appeal Federation of Jewish Philanthropies, New York, NY
5,000 YMCA, Westchester, NY

Pyramid Technology Corp.
Sales: $227.9 million
Employees: 1,193
Headquarters: Mountain View, CA
SIC Major Group: Business Services and Industrial Machinery & Equipment

CONTACT
Gary Valenzuela
Vice President
Pyramid Technology Corp.
3860 North First St.
San Jose, CA 95134
(415) 965-7200

CONTRIBUTIONS SUMMARY
Typical Recipients: • *Education:* colleges & universities, engineering education
Grant Types: general support
Nonmonetary Support Types: donated equipment
Operating Locations: CA (Mountain View)

CORP. OFFICERS
Richard H. Lussier: *CURR EMPL* chmn, pres, ceo: Pyramid Techs Corp
Kent L. Robertson: *CURR EMPL* sr vp, cfo: Pyramid Technology Corp

RECENT GRANTS
376,950 College of Engineering — donated computer equipment

Qantas Airways Ltd.
Headquarters: San Francisco, CA
SIC Major Group: Transportation by Air

CONTACT
Earnest Beyl
Public Relations Officer
Qantas Airways Ltd.
560 Pine St.
San Francisco, CA 94108
(415) 956-4703

CONTRIBUTIONS SUMMARY
Small program giving away tickets to select nonprofit organizations in Los Angeles and San Francisco gateway cities.
Operating Locations: CA (San Francisco)

CORP. OFFICERS
W. L. Dix: *CURR EMPL* chmn: Qantas Airways Ltd

G. E. Howling: *CURR EMPL* sr vp (America): Qantas Airways Ltd

GIVING OFFICERS
Earnest Beyl: *CURR EMPL* publ rels off: Qantas Airways Ltd

Quabaug Corp. / Quabaug Corp. Charitable Foundation
Sales: $30.0 million
Employees: 300
Headquarters: North Brookfield, MA
SIC Major Group: Rubber & Miscellaneous Plastics Products

CONTACT
John E. Hodgson
Trustee
Quabaug Corp. Charitable Foundation
18 School St.
North Brookfield, MA 01535-1926
(508) 867-7731

FINANCIAL SUMMARY
Recent Giving: $41,450 (1991); $50,350 (1990); $45,700 (1989)
Assets: $695,647 (1991); $683,800 (1990); $678,583 (1989)
EIN: 51-0179366

CONTRIBUTIONS SUMMARY
Typical Recipients: • *Education:* colleges & universities, religious education, science/technology education • *Health:* emergency/ambulance services, hospitals • *Religion:* churches, religious organizations • *Social Services:* disabled, united funds, youth organizations
Grant Types: general support
Geographic Distribution: focus on Worcester, MA
Operating Locations: MA (North Brookfield)

CORP. OFFICERS
Allan S. Dunkerly: *CURR EMPL* pres: Quabaug Corp
Herbert M. Varnum: *CURR EMPL* chmn: Quabaug Corp

GIVING OFFICERS
John E. Hodgson: trust
Herbert M. Varnum: trust *CURR EMPL* chmn: Quabaug Corp (see above)
Jean S. Varnum: trust

APPLICATION INFORMATION

Initial Approach: Send brief letter describing program. There are no deadlines.

GRANTS ANALYSIS

Number of Grants: 67
Highest Grant: $3,000
Typical Range: $500 to $1,000
Disclosure Period: 1991

RECENT GRANTS

3,000　First Congregational Church, Paxton, MA
1,500　Christ Memorial Church, North Brookfield, MA
1,500　First Congregational Church, North Brookfield, MA
1,500　St. Joseph Church, North Brookfield, MA
1,000　Anna Maria College, Paxton, MA
1,000　Junior Achievement, Worcester, MA
1,000　North Brookfield Ambulance Squad, North Brookfield, MA
1,000　Two/Ten National Foundation Charity Trust, Boston, MA
1,000　Worcester County Horticultural Society, Worcester, MA
1,000　Worcester Polytechnic Institute, Worcester, MA

Quad City Osteopathic Foundation

CONTACT

Eugene Holst
President
Quad City Osteopathic Fdn.
c/o ERA Associates
6236 North Brady St.
Davenport, IA 52806
(319) 386-5204

FINANCIAL SUMMARY

Recent Giving: $237,144 (fiscal 1990); $221,414 (fiscal 1989)
Assets: $4,401,532 (fiscal year ending November 30, 1990); $4,239,060 (fiscal 1989)
Gifts Received: $8,125 (fiscal 1989)
EIN: 42-0666090

CONTRIBUTIONS SUMMARY

Geographic Distribution: focus on IA and IL

GIVING OFFICERS

Dennis D. Boekhoff: dir
Gregory Garvin: dir
Karen Griggs: dir
Margo Hancock: dir
Cal Harnsen: treas, dir
Eugene R. Holst: pres, dir
Lydia Jordan-Fellner: dir
James D. King: secy, dir
Michael Roeder: chmn, dir
David W. Seitz: vchmn, dir

APPLICATION INFORMATION

Initial Approach: Send brief letter of inquiry describing program or project There are no deadlines.

OTHER THINGS TO KNOW

Awards scholarships for research and education in osteopathy.
Publications: Newsletter, Annual Report

Quaker Chemical Corp. / Quaker Chemical Foundation

Sales: $200.0 million
Employees: 936
Headquarters: Conshohocken, PA
SIC Major Group: Chemicals & Allied Products, Industrial Machinery & Equipment, Lumber & Wood Products, and Petroleum & Coal Products

CONTACT

Karen Miller
Secretary to the Foundation
Quaker Chemical Corp.
Elm and Lee Streets
Conshohocken, PA 19428
(215) 832-4119

FINANCIAL SUMMARY

Recent Giving: $390,000 (fiscal 1993 est.); $426,183 (fiscal 1992); $392,797 (fiscal 1991)
Assets: $298,991 (fiscal year ending June 30, 1992); $313,547 (fiscal 1991); $319,737 (fiscal 1990)
Gifts Received: $402,000 (fiscal 1992); $378,000 (fiscal 1991); $360,000 (fiscal 1990)
Fiscal Note: Contributes through foundation only. In fiscal 1992, contributions were received from the Quaker Chemical Corporation.

EIN: 23-6245803

CONTRIBUTIONS SUMMARY

Typical Recipients: • *Arts & Humanities:* community arts, history/historic preservation, museums/galleries, performing arts • *Civic & Public Affairs:* environmental affairs, zoos/botanical gardens • *Education:* colleges & universities, private education (precollege) • *Health:* health organizations, hospitals, medical research, nutrition & health maintenance, single-disease health associations • *Social Services:* child welfare, community service organizations, disabled, homes, recreation & athletics, united funds, youth organizations
Grant Types: general support
Nonmonetary Support Types: loaned employees and loaned executives
Geographic Distribution: primarily in operating areas
Operating Locations: CA (Placentia, Pomona, South El Monte), DE (Wilmington), GA (Savannah), MI (Detroit), OK (Sepulpa), PA (Conshohocken, King of Prussia, Philadelphia), TX (Conroe, Fort Worth)

CORP. OFFICERS

Peter A. Benoliel: *B* Philadelphia PA 1932 *ED* Princeton Univ 1953; Univ PA 1958 *CURR EMPL* chmn, ceo: Quaker Chem Corp *CORP AFFIL* dep chmn: Fed Reserve Bank Philadelphia; dir: Bell Telephone Co PA
Sigismundus W. Lubsen: *CURR EMPL* pres, coo: Quaker Chem Corp

GIVING OFFICERS

Katherine N. Coughenour: trust
Edwin J. Delattre: trust *CORP AFFIL* dir: Quaker Chem Corp
Alan J. Keyser: trust
Karen Miller: secy
Karl Henry Spaeth: chmn, trust *B* Philadelphia PA 1929 *ED* Haverford Coll AB 1951; Harvard Univ JD 1958 *CURR EMPL* vp, secy: Quaker Chem Corp *CORP AFFIL* secy: AC Products, Gen Chemicals, Multi-Chem Products, Quaker Petro Chemicals Co, Quaker Sealants & Coatings Co, Selby Battersby Co; secy, dir: Quaker Chem Corp-DE *NONPR AFFIL* bd overseers: Univ PA; dir: Chestnut Hill Academy, Opera Co Philadelphia; mem: Am Soc

Corp Secys, Comm 70, Montgomery Bar Assn, PA Bar Assn, Philadelphia Comm Foreign Rels, Philadelphia Comm Foreign Rels
J. Everett Wick: trust
Jane Williams: trust

APPLICATION INFORMATION

Initial Approach: *Initial Contact:* request guidelines from foundation *When to Submit:* application must be received no later than April 20
Restrictions on Giving: Distributions limited to geographic locations where the corporation has operations in the United States.

GRANTS ANALYSIS

Total Grants: $426,183
Number of Grants: 175*
Highest Grant: $7,000
Typical Range: $400 to $2,500
Disclosure Period: fiscal year ending June 30, 1992
Note: Number of grants and average grant figures do not include matching gifts totaling $109,660 or scholarships to individuals totaling $92,820. Recent grants are derived from a fiscal 1992 grants list.

RECENT GRANTS

7,000　Philadelphia Museum of Art, Philadelphia, PA
4,500　Stanford University, Stanford, CA
4,000　Cornell University, Ithaca, NY
4,000　Franklin Institute, Philadelphia, PA
4,000　International House of Philadelphia, Philadelphia, PA
4,000　Michigan State University, East Lansing, MI
4,000　Millersville University, Millersville, PA
4,000　Montgomery Health Foundation, Norristown, PA
4,000　Philadelphia Orchestra, Philadelphia, PA — children's concerts
4,000　Rosemont College, Rosemont, PA

Quaker Hill Foundation

CONTACT
E. S. Sheldon
Quaker Hill Fdn.
c/o King, King and Goldsack
450 Somerset St.
Plainfield, NJ 07060
(201) 756-7806

FINANCIAL SUMMARY
Recent Giving: $129,205
(1991); $128,351 (1990);
$129,106 (1989)
Assets: $2,666,336 (1991);
$2,361,027 (1990); $2,482,563
(1989)
EIN: 13-6088786

CONTRIBUTIONS SUMMARY
Donor(s): Edith S. Stevens, the
late John P. Stevens, Jr.
Typical Recipients: • *Arts &
Humanities:* community arts, li-
braries, music • *Civic & Public
Affairs:* environmental affairs
• *Education:* private education
(precollege) • *Health:* hospi-
tals, nursing services • *Social
Services:* child welfare, coun-
seling, day care, family plan-
ning
Grant Types: general support

GIVING OFFICERS
Phebe S. Miner: trust
Edith S. Sheldon: trust
Edith Stevens: off
John P. Stevens III: trust

APPLICATION INFORMATION
Initial Approach: Contributes
only to preselected organizations.
Restrictions on Giving: Does
not support individuals.

GRANTS ANALYSIS
Number of Grants: 13
Highest Grant: $30,000
Typical Range: $2,000 to
$10,000
Disclosure Period: 1991
Note: 1991 figures do not in-
clude $31,360 in matching
grants.

RECENT GRANTS
30,000 St. Ignatius Loyola
Day Nursery, New
York, NY
15,000 Minnesota Chorale,
Minneapolis, MN
10,000 Museum for Ameri-
can Textile His-
tory, North An-
dover, MA

10,000 Visiting Nurses Association, Andover,
MA
5,000 BAND, Langhorne,
PA
5,000 Moses Brown
School, Provi-
dence, RI
5,000 Voyage House,
Philadelphia, PA
4,630 A Safe Place, Portsmouth, NH
4,000 Manchester Public
Library, Manches-
ter, MA
3,015 Center for Respon-
sible Funding,
Philadelphia, PA

Quaker Oats Co. / Quaker Oats Foundation
Sales: $5.58 billion
Employees: 28,200
Headquarters: Chicago, IL
SIC Major Group: Apparel &
Accessory Stores, Food &
Kindred Products, Food Stores,
and Miscellaneous
Manufacturing Industries

CONTACT
Charles E. Curry
Assistant Secretary
Quaker Oats Fdn.
321 N Clark St.
Ste. 27-5
Chicago, IL 60610
(312) 222-7377
Note: Organizations located in
communities where Quaker has
a facility should contact the
local management to review
the impact of their group on
the community. This initial
contact should be followed by
a formal request directed to the
manager of that operating unit.
Organizations not located in a
Quaker community should
send grant proposals to the
contact above.

FINANCIAL SUMMARY
Recent Giving: $2,197,317
(fiscal 1991); $3,030,317 (fis-
cal 1990); $2,842,774 (fiscal
1989)
Assets: $3,465,434 (fiscal year
ending June 30, 1991);
$4,763,364 (fiscal 1989)
Fiscal Note: Above figures represent foundation giving only.
In addition to foundation giving, company makes direct contributions. Corporate and division contributions and
nonmonetary giving totaled
$8,100,000 in 1990.
EIN: 36-6084548

CONTRIBUTIONS SUMMARY
Typical Recipients: • *Arts &
Humanities:* arts associations,
arts centers, arts festivals, arts
funds, arts institutes, community arts, dance, ethnic arts, his-
tory/historic preservation, libraries, literary arts,
museums/galleries, music,
opera, performing arts, public
broadcasting, theater • *Civic &
Public Affairs:* business/free enterprise, civil rights, economic
development, economics, eth-
nic/minority organizations,
housing, municipalities, professional & trade associations,
public policy, safety, urban &
community affairs, women's affairs, zoos/botanical gardens
• *Education:* agricultural education, business education, ca-
reer/vocational education, colleges & universities,
community & junior colleges,
economic education, education
associations, education funds,
elementary education, engineering education, legal education,
medical education, minority
education, preschool education,
private education (precollege),
public education (precollege),
science/technology education,
student aid • *Health:* health
care cost containment, health
organizations, hospices, hospitals, medical rehabilitation,
medical research, mental
health, nutrition & health maintenance, single-disease health
associations • *Science:* scientific organizations • *Social
Services:* aged, child welfare,
community service organizations, counseling, day care, disabled, domestic violence, drugs
& alcohol, emergency relief,
employment/job training, family planning, family services,
food/clothing distribution,
homes, legal aid, recreation &
athletics, refugee assistance,
shelters/homelessness, united
funds, youth organizations
Grant Types: capital, challenge, employee matching
gifts, fellowship, general support, multiyear/continuing support, project, scholarship, and
seed money
Nonmonetary Support Types:
donated equipment, donated
products, in-kind services, and
loaned executives
Note: Direct giving and nonmonetary support was estimated at $8,100,000 in 1990.
In 1989, nonmonetary support

was valued at $5,500,000.
Most nonmonetary support is
provided to Second Harvest
and several other food bank af-
filiates that distribute food products to the needy.
Geographic Distribution: principally near operating locations
and to national organizations
Operating Locations: CA
(Oakland, Redwood City, San
Leandro), FL (De Land, Kissim-
mee), IA (Cedar Rapids), IL
(Barrington, Bridgeview, Chi-
cago, Danville, Kankakee,
Pekin), IN (Indianapolis), KS
(Lawrence, Manhattan,
Topeka), KY (Louisville, Mur-
ray), MI (Battle Creek), MO
(St. Joseph), NC (Asheville),
NY (Macedon), PA (Boyer-
town, Mountaintop, Shireman-
stown), TN (Jackson, New-
port), TX (Dallas, Houston,
Marshall), VT (Putney), WA
(Seattle)
Note: Also operates in Canada,
Mexico, and Europe.

CORP. OFFICERS
William D. Smithburg: *B* Chi-
cago IL 1938 *ED* DePaul Univ
BS 1959; Northwestern Univ
Sch Bus Admin MBA 1960
CURR EMPL chmn, ceo, dir:
Quaker Oats Co *CORP AFFIL*
dir: Abbott Laboratories, Corn-
ing Glass Works, Northern
Trust Co, Northern Trust Corp,
Prime Capital Corp *NONPR
AFFIL* dir: Grocery Mfrs Assn

GIVING OFFICERS
Frank Carlucci: dir
Weston R. Christopherson:
dir *B* Walum ND 1925 *ED*
Univ ND BS 1949; Univ ND
JD 1951 *CURR EMPL* chmn,
ceo: Northern Trust Corp
CORP AFFIL dir: Ameritech,
Aurrera, Borg-Warner Corp,
GATX Corp, IL Bell Telephone
Co, SA Mexico City *NONPR
AFFIL* mem: Bus Counc, Chi-
cago Comm, Chicago Un,
Metro Chicago Un Way/Cru-
sade Mercy, Northwestern Univ
Assocs; trust: Univ Chicago
Janet Cooper: treas
Charles E. Curry: asst secy
William Jesse Kennedy III:
dir *B* Durham NC 1922 *ED* VA
St Coll 1942; NY Univ Sch Bus
Admin 1948 *CURR EMPL*
chmn, pres, ceo: NC Mutual
Life Ins Co *CORP AFFIL*
chmn: UNC Ventures; dir: In-
vestors Title Co, Jones Group,
Mobil Corp, Pfizer Inc, Quaker
Oats Co; vchmn, dir: Mechan-
ics & Farmers Bank *NONPR*

AFFIL chmn adv counc: Un Students Aid Funds; dir: Durham Tech Commun Coll Fdn, John Avery Boys Club, NC Citizens Assn, Res Triangle Fdn; mem bd visitors: NC Central Univ; southeast regional adv counc: Boy Scouts Am; trust: Conf Bd, NC Soc Fin Analyst
Bernard Krimm: secy
Luther C. McKinney: vp, dir *B* Dallas Center IA 1931 *ED* IA St Univ 1953; Univ IL Sch Law LLB 1959 *CURR EMPL* sr vp (law corp affairs), secy, dir: Quaker Oats Co *NONPR AFFIL* mem: Am Bar Assn
Donald Edward Meads: dir *B* Salem MA 1920 *ED* Dartmouth Coll 1942; Harvard Univ Sch Bus Admin 1947 *CURR EMPL* chmn, pres: Carver Assocs *CORP AFFIL* dir: CIGNA Corp, Perdue Farms, Philadelphia First Group, Quaker Oats Co *NONPR AFFIL* chmn: Valley Forge Military Academy & Coll; dir: Independence Hall Assn, World Aff Counc Philadelphia; hon dir: Marine Corps Scholarship Fdn; trust: Thomas Jefferson Univ
Gertrude Geraldine Michelson: dir *B* Jamestown NY 1925 *ED* PA St Univ BA 1945; Columbia Univ LLB 1947 *CURR EMPL* sr vp, dir, mem exec comm: RH Macy & Co *CORP AFFIL* dir: Chubb Corp, Discount Corp, Gen Electric Co, Goodyear Tire & Rubber Co, Harper & Row, Irving Bank Corp, Irving Trust Co, Quaker Oats Co, Stanley Works; gov: Am Stock Exchange; trust, dir: Rand Corp *NONPR AFFIL* chmn, bd trust: Columbia Univ; dir: Am Arbitration Assn, Better Bus Bur Metro NY, Helena Rubinstein Fdn, Markle Fdn, Work Am Inst; mem: NY City Chamber Commerce, Women's Forum; mem adv counc: Catalyst, Columbia Univ Grad Sch Bus; trust: Interracial Counc Bus Opportunity, Spelman Coll
William D. Smithburg: pres, chmn, dir *CURR EMPL* chmn, ceo, dir: Quaker Oats Co (see above)
William Lee Weiss: dir *B* Big Run PA 1929 *ED* PA St Univ BS 1951 *CURR EMPL* chmn, ceo: Ameritech Corp *CORP AFFIL* dir: Abbott Laboratories, Continental Bank Corp, Continental IL Natl Bank & Trust Co, Quaker Oats Co, USG Corp; pres, dir: Bell Telephone Group *NONPR AFFIL*

bd govs, mem: Bus Counc; chmn: Information Indus Counc, Mus Science & Indus; dir: Chicago Counc Foreign Rels; mem: Bus Comm Arts, Bus Roundtable, Phi Delta Theta, Tau Beta Pi, Un Way Am, Western Soc Engrs; mem adv counc: Northwestern Univ Kellogg Sch Bus; mem natl adv bd: IL Math Science Academy; trust, mem comm econ devel: Lyric Opera Chicago

APPLICATION INFORMATION

Initial Approach: *Initial Contact:* brief letter or proposal *Include Information On:* name, address, and telephone number of organization; representative to whom all correspondence should be addressed; description of the organization, including purpose, and geographical area and population served; amount requested; purpose for which funds are sought; description of the organization's current activities and project goals, as well as plans for meeting those goals; description of the organization's relationship to the community and objectives of the foundation; recently audited financial statement; proof of tax-exempt status; list of board of directors, including financial and volunteer support *When to Submit:* any time
Restrictions on Giving: Foundation does not make grants to religious organizations, individuals, elected officials, political or lobbying groups, or for advertising.

OTHER THINGS TO KNOW

Foundation support has been guided by a matched concept of giving, which relies on participation from local operating units. By focusing support in Quaker communities, foundation provides managers they need to address concerns at the local level.
List of contributions advisory committee members is available from the foundation.

GRANTS ANALYSIS

Total Grants: $2,197,317
Number of Grants: 368
Highest Grant: $200,000
Typical Range: $500 to $5,000
Disclosure Period: fiscal year ending June 30, 1991

Note: Figure for average grant excludes the two highest grants totaling $164,247 and $200,000. Recent grants are derived from a fiscal 1991 Form 990.

RECENT GRANTS

200,000	Metropolitan Chicago United Way/Crusade of Mercy, Chicago, IL
164,247	Maricopa County Treasurer, Phoenix, AZ
80,413	National Merit Scholarship Corporation, Chicago, IL
60,000	United Way of Buffalo and Erie County, Buffalo, NY
58,000	United Way of East Central Iowa, Cedar Rapids, IA
33,025	St. Joseph Greater United Way, St. Joseph, MO
33,000	Corporate Community Schools of America, Chicago, IL
30,000	United Negro College Fund, Chicago, IL
30,000	University of Buffalo Foundation, Buffalo, NY
25,000	National Lakotak Center, Evanston, IL

Quaker State Corp.

Sales: $813.6 million
Employees: 4,525
Headquarters: Oil City, PA
SIC Major Group: Coal Mining, Petroleum & Coal Products, Wholesale Trade—Durable Goods, and Wholesale Trade—Nondurable Goods

CONTACT
Joyce A. McFadden
Assistant Corporate Secretary
Quaker State Corp.
255 Elm St., PO Box 989
Oil City, PA 16301
(814) 676-7676

FINANCIAL SUMMARY
Fiscal Note: Annual Giving Range: $100,000 to $250,000

CONTRIBUTIONS SUMMARY
Support goes to local education, health and human service, arts, and civic organizations.
Typical Recipients: • *Arts & Humanities:* general • *Civic & Public Affairs:* general • *Educa-*

tion: general • *Health:* general • *Social Services:* general
Grant Types: general support and matching
Geographic Distribution: primarily headquarters area
Operating Locations: PA (Oil City)

CORP. OFFICERS
C. A. Conrad: *CURR EMPL* pres, coo: Quaker State Corp
Jack W. Corn: *CURR EMPL* chmn, ceo: Quaker St Corp

APPLICATION INFORMATION
Initial Approach: Send brief letter of inquiry. There are no deadlines.

Quality Inn International

Revenue: $76.0 million
Employees: 1,100
Parent Company: Manor Care Inc.
Headquarters: Silver Spring, MD
SIC Major Group: Hotels & Other Lodging Places

CONTACT
Robert C. Hazard, Jr.
Chairman & Chief Executive Officer
Quality Inn International
10750 Columbia Pke.
Silver Spring, MD 20901
(301) 593-5600

CONTRIBUTIONS SUMMARY
Operating Locations: MD (Silver Spring)

CORP. OFFICERS
Robert C. Hazard, Jr.: *CURR EMPL* pres, ceo: Quality Inns Intl
Gerald W. Pettit: *CURR EMPL* coo: Quality Inns Intl

Quality Metal Finishing Foundation

CONTACT
R. Earl Pierson
Secretary/Treasurer
Quality Metal Finishing Fdn.
4th and Walnut St.s
Byron, IL 61010
(815) 234-2711

FINANCIAL SUMMARY
Recent Giving: $32,250 (fiscal 1991)

Assets: $65,519 (fiscal year ending September 30, 1991)
Gifts Received: $25,000 (fiscal 1991)
Fiscal Note: In fiscal year 1991, contributions were received from the Quality Metal Finishing Co.
EIN: 36-2604285

CONTRIBUTIONS SUMMARY
Typical Recipients: • *Civic & Public Affairs:* municipalities • *Education:* education associations, private education (precollege) • *Health:* hospitals • *Social Services:* united funds, youth organizations
Grant Types: general support

GIVING OFFICERS
R. Earl Pierson: secy, treas

APPLICATION INFORMATION
Initial Approach: Send brief letter of inquiry. There are no deadlines.

GRANTS ANALYSIS
Number of Grants: 46
Highest Grant: $4,000
Typical Range: $100 to $1,000
Disclosure Period: fiscal year ending September 30, 1991

RECENT GRANTS
4,000 Crusader Central Clinic
3,000 Byron Education Association
2,500 St. Anthony Medical Center
2,500 United Way
2,000 Village of Progress
1,500 Rockford Memorial Development Fund, Rockford, IL
1,500 Swedish American Medical Foundation
1,000 Blackhawk Area Council 660
1,000 Boylan Central Catholic High School
1,000 Outward Bound, New York, NY

Quanex Corp. / Quanex Foundation
Sales: $588.9 million
Employees: 2,603
Headquarters: Houston, TX
SIC Major Group: Primary Metal Industries

CONTACT
Paul Kraft
Manager, Corporate Affairs
Quanex Fdn.
1900 West Loop South, Ste. 1500
Houston, TX 77027
(713) 961-4600

FINANCIAL SUMMARY
Recent Giving: $130,557 (1991); $109,977 (1990); $112,399 (1989)
Assets: $2,323,244 (1991); $2,026,040 (1990); $2,086,609 (1989)
EIN: 36-6065490

CONTRIBUTIONS SUMMARY
Typical Recipients: • *Civic & Public Affairs:* municipalities, rural affairs, safety, urban & community affairs • *Education:* agricultural education, education funds • *Health:* emergency/ambulance services, medical research, single-disease health associations • *Social Services:* community service organizations, shelters/homelessness, united funds, youth organizations
Grant Types: general support
Geographic Distribution: focus on TX
Operating Locations: AR (Fort Smith), IN (Griffith, Hammond, Huntington), MI (Jackson, South Lyon), NV (Verdi), TX (Bellville, Houston, Rosenberg)
Note: List includes division and plant locations.

CORP. OFFICERS
Carl E. Pfeiffer: *CURR EMPL* chmn: Quanex Corp
Robert C. Snyder: *CURR EMPL* pres, ceo, coo: Quanex Corp

GIVING OFFICERS
J. K. Peery: vp, dir
W.M. Rose: dir, vp
Robert C. Snyder: pres, dir *CURR EMPL* pres, ceo, coo: Quanex Corp (see above)

APPLICATION INFORMATION
Initial Approach: Send brief letter describing program. Deadline is October 31.

GRANTS ANALYSIS
Number of Grants: 104
Highest Grant: $20,000
Typical Range: $100 to $1,000
Disclosure Period: 1991

RECENT GRANTS
20,000 Houston Livestock Show and Rodeo, Houston, TX
11,050 United Way, Griffith, IN
9,327 United Way, Houston, TX
8,000 Houston Livestock Show and Rodeo, Houston, TX
6,420 National Merit Scholarship, Evanston, IL
5,000 South Lyon Fire Department, South Lyon, MI
3,800 United Way, Jackson, MI
3,700 Fort Bend County Fair Association, Rosenberg, TX
3,000 ABET, Boca Raton, FL
3,000 United Way, Reno, NV

Quantum Chemical Corp.
Sales: $1.12 billion
Employees: 11,000
Headquarters: New York, NY
SIC Major Group: Chemicals & Allied Products and Wholesale Trade—Nondurable Goods

CONTACT
Arden Melick
Director, Corporate Communications
Quantum Chemical Corp.
99 Park Ave.
New York, NY 10016
(212) 551-0438
Note: Company prefers not to receive faxed requests.

FINANCIAL SUMMARY
Recent Giving: $850,000 (1992 approx.); $850,000 (1991); $850,000 (1990)
Fiscal Note: Company gives directly.

CONTRIBUTIONS SUMMARY
Typical Recipients: • *Arts & Humanities:* libraries, museums/galleries, music • *Civic & Public Affairs:* law & justice, safety • *Education:* colleges & universities, elementary education, private education (precollege) • *Health:* emergency/ambulance services, hospitals • *Social Services:* drugs & alcohol
Grant Types: capital, employee matching gifts, general support, research, and scholarship

Nonmonetary Support Types: donated equipment
Note: In 1991, company provided $30,000 in nonmonetary support. This is not included in above total.
Geographic Distribution: generally near headquarters and operating locations
Operating Locations: CA, CT, DE, FL, IA, IL, KS, KY, LA, MA, MD, ME, MN, MO, MS, NC, ND, NH, RI, SC, TN, TX, VA, VT, WA, WI, WV
Note: Also operates in Brazil. Rarely makes international grants.

CORP. OFFICERS
John Hoyt Stookey: *B* New York NY 1930 *ED* Amherst Coll 1952; Columbia Univ 1955 *CURR EMPL* chmn, ceo, pres, dir: Quantum Chem Corp *CORP AFFIL* chmn, treas: Petrolane; dir: Rexham Corp, Riegel Textile Corp *NONPR AFFIL* fdr, pres: Berkshire Boys Choir; mem: Alpha Pi Mu, Counc Foreign Rels, Delta Kappa Epsilon; mem adv bd: Grosvenor Neighborhood House; mem bd dirs: Assn Better NY; trust: Bio-Energy Counc, Boston Symphony Orchestra, Coll Human Svcs, Counc Ams

GIVING OFFICERS
Arden Melick: *CURR EMPL* dir (corp communications): Quantum Chem Corp

APPLICATION INFORMATION
Initial Approach: *Initial Contact:* letter of intention and organizational fact sheet *Include Information On:* description of the organization, amount requested, purpose for which funds are sought, recently audited financial statement, proof of tax-exempt status *When to Submit:* late summer or early fall

OTHER THINGS TO KNOW
In general, successful proposals are sponsored by senior management or employee groups.

GRANTS ANALYSIS
Total Grants: $850,000
Typical Range: $1,000 to $5,000
Disclosure Period: 1991

Quebecor Printing (USA) Inc.

Sales: $845.0 million
Employees: 6,300
Headquarters: St. Paul, MN
SIC Major Group: Printing & Publishing

CONTACT

Sheila Bergman
Director, Human Resources Services
Quebecor Printing (USA) Inc.
1999 Shepard Rd.
St. Paul, MN 55116
(612) 690-7200

CONTRIBUTIONS SUMMARY

Operating Locations: MN (St. Paul)

CORP. OFFICERS

John T. Collins: *CURR EMPL* ceo, pres: Quebecor Printing (USA)

Quest for Truth Foundation

CONTACT

DeLancey B. Lewis
Secretary
Quest for Truth Fdn.
221 First Ave. West, Ste. 405
Seattle, WA 98119-4224
(206) 284-4424

FINANCIAL SUMMARY

Recent Giving: $212,863 (fiscal 1991); $214,000 (fiscal 1989); $100,000 (fiscal 1988)
Assets: $5,225,496 (fiscal year ending September 30, 1991); $5,163,656 (fiscal 1989); $4,193,082 (fiscal 1988)
EIN: 91-1190760

CONTRIBUTIONS SUMMARY

Typical Recipients: • *Education:* colleges & universities • *Health:* health organizations
Grant Types: research

GIVING OFFICERS

Ellen S. Davies: pres, dir
Bradley F. Henke: vp, dir
Delancey B. Lewis: secy, treas, dir
Paul Kenneth Scripps: vp, dir *CORP AFFIL* dir: EW Scripps Co

APPLICATION INFORMATION

Initial Approach: Application form required. There are no deadlines. Decisions are made within two months.

GRANTS ANALYSIS

Number of Grants: 7
Highest Grant: $60,000
Typical Range: $10,000 to $50,000
Disclosure Period: fiscal year ending September 30, 1991

RECENT GRANTS

60,000 Fred Hutchinson Cancer Research Center, Seattle, WA — support the publication of the Scientific Report and other papers as may benefit from the Scientific Community and inform the General Public of research in process at the Center

50,000 Pacific Northwest Research Foundation, Seattle, WA — to support a study of the impact of pollution of Puget Sound

39,800 Utah State University, Logan, UT — research and support for the publication of book entitled "Yellowstone: Ecological Malpractice."

33,063 University of Washington, Seattle, WA — to support the research project "Our Changing Atmosphere"

10,000 Dental Health Foundation, San Rafael, CA — to support the dissemination to the general public of information regarding Dental Health obtained by analysis, study and research

10,000 San Diego Historical Society, San Diego, CA — to support the research and publication of "San Diego History"

10,000 Utah State University, Logan, UT — to support the "Festival of the American West"

Questar Corp.

Sales: $632.3 million
Employees: 2,610
Headquarters: Salt Lake City, UT
SIC Major Group: Electric, Gas & Sanitary Services and Oil & Gas Extraction

CONTACT

Janice W. Bates
Director, Community Affairs
Questar Corp.
180 East First South St.
PO Box 11150
Salt Lake City, UT 84147
(801) 534-5435

FINANCIAL SUMMARY

Recent Giving: $550,000 (1993 est.); $500,000 (1992); $402,000 (1991)
Fiscal Note: Company gives directly.

CONTRIBUTIONS SUMMARY

Typical Recipients: • *Arts & Humanities:* arts festivals, dance, general, history/historic preservation, museums/galleries, music, opera, performing arts, theater • *Civic & Public Affairs:* better government, business/free enterprise, economic development, environmental affairs, general, nonprofit management, philanthropic organizations, professional & trade associations, zoos/botanical gardens • *Education:* business education, career/vocational education, colleges & universities, community & junior colleges, economic education, engineering education, general • *Health:* general, health organizations, hospitals, medical rehabilitation, single-disease health associations • *Science:* science exhibits & fairs • *Social Services:* child welfare, community service organizations, day care, disabled, drugs & alcohol, food/clothing distribution, general, legal aid, shelters/homelessness, united funds, volunteer services, youth organizations
Grant Types: capital, emergency, general support, multi-year/continuing support, project, and scholarship
Nonmonetary Support Types: donated equipment, donated products, in-kind services, loaned employees, and loaned executives
Geographic Distribution: all of Utah, most of Wyoming, and limited amounts in Colorado and Oklahoma
Operating Locations: UT (Salt Lake City)

CORP. OFFICERS

Don Cash: *B* Shamrock TX 1942 *CURR EMPL* chmn, pres, ceo, dir: Questar Corp *CORP AFFIL* ceo, pres: Universal Resources Corp, Wexpro Co; chmn, pres, ceo: Celsius Energy Co

GIVING OFFICERS

Janice W. Bates: *CURR EMPL* dir commun aff: Questar Corp

APPLICATION INFORMATION

Initial Approach: *Initial Contact:* brief letter of inquiry *Include Information On:* description of the organization, amount requested, purpose of funds sought, recently audited financial statements, board of directors list (including salaries), and proof of tax-exempt status *When to Submit:* any time
Restrictions on Giving: Does not support individuals, religious organizations for sectarian purposes, or fraternal organizations. Will not support national health organizations unless it can be determined that funds will remain in the company's service area.

GRANTS ANALYSIS

Typical Range: $1,000 to $2,500

Quincy Newspapers / Oakley-Lindsay Foundation of Quincy Newspapers & Quincy Broadcasting Co.

Sales: $43.8 million
Employees: 400
Headquarters: Quincy, IL
SIC Major Group: Communications and Printing & Publishing

CONTACT
Thomas A. Oakley
President
Oakley-Lindsay Foundation of
 Quincy Newspapers & Quincy
 Broadcasting Co.
130 South Fifth St.
Quincy, IL 62301-3916
(217) 223-5100

FINANCIAL SUMMARY
Recent Giving: $56,035
(1990); $64,287 (1989)
Assets: $772,480 (1990);
$670,268 (1989)
Gifts Received: $90,574
(1990); $101,260 (1989)
EIN: 23-7025198

CONTRIBUTIONS SUMMARY
Typical Recipients: • *Arts & Humanities:* arts funds, community arts, history/historic preservation • *Education:* colleges & universities, education funds, private education (precollege) • *Health:* hospitals • *Social Services:* community service organizations, recreation & athletics, united funds, youth organizations
Grant Types: general support
Geographic Distribution: focus on IL
Operating Locations: IL (Quincy)

CORP. OFFICERS
Thomas A. Oakley: *CURR EMPL* pres: Quincy Newspapers

GIVING OFFICERS
Joseph Bonansinga: vp, dir
James W. Collins: dir
Joseph I. Conover: dir
Don E. Fuller: dir
Richard P. Herbst: dir
Arthur O. Lindsay: dir
Donald Lindsay: dir
F. M. Lindsay, Jr.: vp, dir
Allen M. Oakley: dir
David Oakley: dir
Peter A. Oakley: secy, dir
Thomas A. Oakley: pres, dir
CURR EMPL pres: Quincy Newspapers (see above)
Gregory J. Ptacin: dir
Clark L. Widerman: dir

APPLICATION INFORMATION
Initial Approach: Send brief letter describing program. There are no deadlines.

GRANTS ANALYSIS
Number of Grants: 26
Highest Grant: $10,000
Typical Range: $1,000 to $5,000

Disclosure Period: 1990

RECENT GRANTS
10,000 Quincy Park District, Quincy, IL — riverfront development
5,000 Newton Memorial Hospital, Newton, NJ
5,000 Quincy College Music Department, Quincy, IL — equipment
5,000 St. Mary Hospital, Quincy, IL — communication system
3,952 Quincy Community Little Theatre and Designees, Quincy, IL
2,500 Mayo Foundation, Rochester, MN — medical education and research
2,500 Siouxland Community Soup Kitchen, Sioux City, IA
2,500 Sunset Home, Quincy, IL — elderly transportation
2,000 Illinois State Historical Society, Springfield, IL
2,000 Project Future, South Bend, IN — economic development

Quinlan Foundation, Elizabeth C.

CONTACT
Richard A. Klein
President
Elizabeth C. Quinlan Fdn.
1205 Foshay Tower
Minneapolis, MN 55402
(612) 333-8084

FINANCIAL SUMMARY
Recent Giving: $81,760
(1989); $127,625 (1988)
Assets: $2,413,752 (1989);
$2,150,135 (1988)
EIN: 41-0706125

CONTRIBUTIONS SUMMARY
Donor(s): the late Elizabeth C. Quinlan
Typical Recipients: • *Arts & Humanities:* community arts, museums/galleries, public broadcasting • *Education:* colleges & universities, education funds, private education (precollege), religious education • *Religion:* churches, religious organizations • *Social Services:* community service organiza-

tions, united funds, youth organizations
Grant Types: emergency, endowment, general support, multiyear/continuing support, operating expenses, project, research, scholarship, and seed money
Geographic Distribution: limited to MN

GIVING OFFICERS
Lucia L. Crane: vp
Eileen L. Grundman: trust
Anne L. Klein: trust
Richard A. Klein: pres, treas
Mary Elizabeth Lahiff: secy
Eugene P. McCahill: trust

APPLICATION INFORMATION
Initial Approach: Send brief letter describing program. Deadline is September 1.
Restrictions on Giving: Does not support individuals.;

OTHER THINGS TO KNOW
Publications: Annual Report (includes Application Guidelines).

GRANTS ANALYSIS
Number of Grants: 44
Highest Grant: $20,000
Typical Range: $1,000 to $5,000
Disclosure Period: 1989

RECENT GRANTS
20,000 College of St. Thomas, St. Paul, MN
10,000 St. Olaf Catholic Church, Minneapolis, MN
10,000 St. Paul Seminary, St. Paul, MN
6,000 Minnesota Private College Fund, St. Paul, MN
6,000 United Way, Minneapolis, MN
5,000 Academy of Holy Angels, Richfield, MN
3,000 Cenacle, Wayzata, MN
1,000 Archdiocesan AIDS Ministry Program, Minneapolis, MN
1,000 Catholic Charities, Minneapolis, MN
1,000 Minnesota Public Radio, St. Paul, MN

Quivey-Bay State Foundation

CONTACT
Ted Cannon
Secretary-Treasurer
Quivey-Bay State Fdn.
1515 East 20th St.
Scottsbluff, NE 69361
(308) 635-7701

FINANCIAL SUMMARY
Recent Giving: $147,932 (fiscal 1990); $129,932 (fiscal 1989); $133,232 (fiscal 1988)
Assets: $2,359,916 (fiscal year ending January 31, 1990); $2,194,684 (fiscal 1989); $2,039,899 (fiscal 1988)
EIN: 47-6024159

CONTRIBUTIONS SUMMARY
Donor(s): M. S. Oulvey, Mrs. M. S. Quivey
Typical Recipients: • *Arts & Humanities:* arts centers, history/historic preservation • *Civic & Public Affairs:* zoos/botanical gardens • *Education:* education funds • *Religion:* churches, religious organizations • *Social Services:* animal protection, community centers, community service organizations, recreation & athletics, united funds
Grant Types: general support
Geographic Distribution: focus on NE

GIVING OFFICERS
Ted Cannon: secy, treas
Earl R. Cherry: pres

APPLICATION INFORMATION
Initial Approach: Send brief letter of inquiry describing program. There are no deadlines.
Restrictions on Giving: Does not support individuals or provide funds for endowments.

GRANTS ANALYSIS
Number of Grants: 56
Highest Grant: $15,000
Typical Range: $1,000 to $10,000
Disclosure Period: fiscal year ending January 31, 1990

RECENT GRANTS
15,000 Boy Scouts of America, Lincoln, NE
15,000 YMCA, Lincoln, NE
10,000 Camp Fire Girls, Lincoln, NE

10,000 Chadron State Foundation, Lincoln, NE
10,000 Nebraska Community College Scholarship Fund, Lincoln, NE
10,000 Nebraska General Hospital, Lincoln, NE
10,000 Nebraska Independent College Foundation, Lincoln, NE
5,132 Federated Churches, New York, NE
3,500 United Way, Lincoln, NE
3,000 Riverside Zoological Society, Lincoln, NE

R. F. Foundation

CONTACT
H. Blair White
President
R. F. Fdn.
One First National Plaza, Rm. 4700
Chicago, IL 60603
(815) 758-3461

FINANCIAL SUMMARY
Recent Giving: $270,000 (1990); $220,000 (1989); $200,000 (1988)
Assets: $6,113,384 (1990); $6,340,347 (1989); $5,198,848 (1988)
EIN: 36-6069098

CONTRIBUTIONS SUMMARY
Donor(s): Thomas H. Roberts, Thomas H. Roberts, Jr., Eleanor T. Roberts, Mary R. Roberts
Typical Recipients: • *Education:* colleges & universities, minority education • *Health:* health organizations, hospitals • *Religion:* religious organizations • *Social Services:* aged, child welfare, community service organizations, shelters/homelessness, united funds
Grant Types: emergency, multiyear/continuing support, and operating expenses
Geographic Distribution: limited to the Chicago and DeKalb County, IL, area

GIVING OFFICERS
Charles C. Roberts: secy, treas, dir
Mary Eleanor Roberts: vp, dir
Thomas H. Roberts, Jr.: treas *B* DeKalb IL 1924 *ED* IA St Univ 1949; Harvard Univ 1955

CORP AFFIL dir: DeKalb Energy Co, DeKalb Genetics Corp, IMCERA Group
H. Blair White: pres, dir *B* Burlington IA 1927 *ED* Univ IA BA 1950; Univ IA JD 1951; Univ IA BA 1950; Univ IA JD 1951 *CURR EMPL* ptnr: Sidley & Austin *CORP AFFIL* dir: Bankmont Fin Corp, DeKalb Energy Co, DeKalb Energy Corp, DeKalb Genetics Co, DeKalb Genetics Corp, RR Donnelley & Sons Co, RR Donnelley & Sons Co, Kimberly-Clark Corp; ptnr: Sidley & Austin *NONPR AFFIL* dir: Auxiliary Cook County Hosp, Childrens Meml Hosp Chicago, Childrens Memorial Hosp, Rush-Presbyterian-St Lukes Med Ctr, Rush-Presbyterian-St Lukes Med Ctr; mem: Am Bar Assn, Am Bar Assn, Am Coll Trial Lawyers, Am Coll Trial Lawyers, Chicago Bar Assn, Chicago Bar Assn, IL Bar Assn, IL Bar Assn, 7th Fed Circuit Bar Assn

APPLICATION INFORMATION
Initial Approach: Send cover letter and full proposal. There are no deadlines.
Restrictions on Giving: Does not support individuals or provide scholarships or loans.

GRANTS ANALYSIS
Number of Grants: 34
Highest Grant: $55,000
Typical Range: $1,000 to $15,000
Disclosure Period: 1990

RECENT GRANTS
55,000 United Way
50,000 Rockford College, Rockford, IL — pledge
20,000 United Way
20,000 United Way
15,000 VAC
14,000 Growing Place
10,000 Children's Memorial Hospital, Chicago, IL
10,000 National Captioning Institute, Falls Church, VA
10,000 VAC — Meals on Wheels (Kitchen)
8,000 University of Illinois, Urbana, IL — fellowship program

R. L. Stowe Mills Inc.

Sales: $80.0 million
Employees: 1,200
Headquarters: Belmont, NC
SIC Major Group: Textile Mill Products

CONTACT
Gene Thompson
Director, Industrial Relations
R. L. Stowe Mills Inc.
PO Box 351
Belmont, NC 28012
(704) 825-5314

CONTRIBUTIONS SUMMARY
Operating Locations: NC (Belmont, McAdenville)

CORP. OFFICERS
J.M. Carstarphen: *CURR EMPL* vchmn, ceo, treas: Stowe Mills
Daniel J. Stowe: *CURR EMPL* chmn, pres: Stowe Mills

OTHER THINGS TO KNOW
Company is an original donor to the Robert Lee Stowe, Jr., Foundation.

R. P. Foundation

CONTACT
Robert O. Peterson
Chief Executive Officer
R. P. Fdn.
833 Pearl St.
La Jolla, CA 92037
(619) 224-4808

FINANCIAL SUMMARY
Recent Giving: $96,304 (fiscal 1991); $126,000 (fiscal 1990); $192,500 (fiscal 1989)
Assets: $6,148,116 (fiscal year ending November 30, 1991); $6,202,650 (fiscal 1990); $5,015,782 (fiscal 1989)
EIN: 95-2536736

CONTRIBUTIONS SUMMARY
Donor(s): Robert O. Peterson
Typical Recipients: • *Arts & Humanities:* arts festivals, community arts, history/historic preservation, public broadcasting • *Civic & Public Affairs:* municipalities, philanthropic organizations • *Education:* colleges & universities • *Religion:* religious organizations • *Science:* scientific institutes • *Social Services:* community

service organizations, youth organizations
Grant Types: emergency and general support
Geographic Distribution: focus on CA and NY

GIVING OFFICERS
Karren Baldwin: secy
John J. McCloskey: secy, dir
Maureen F. O'Connor: cfo, dir *B* San Diego CA 1946 *ED* San Diego St Univ B 1970
Robert O. Peterson: ceo, dir

APPLICATION INFORMATION
Initial Approach: Send brief letter of inquiry describing program or project. There are no deadlines.

GRANTS ANALYSIS
Number of Grants: 11
Highest Grant: $25,000
Typical Range: $1,000 to $10,000
Disclosure Period: fiscal year ending November 30, 1991

RECENT GRANTS
25,000 San Diego Youth Symphony, San Diego, CA
25,000 St. Vincent de Paul, San Diego, CA
23,000 KPBS, San Diego, CA
15,196 University of California, La Jolla, CA
10,000 Our Lady of Sacred Heart School, San Diego, CA
10,000 University of California Regents, La Jolla, CA
8,000 Hoover Foundation, Stanford, CA
2,500 Mendocino Music Festival, Mendocino, CA
1,000 Mendocino Community Library, Mendocino, CA
1,000 Project Concern International, San Diego, CA

R&B Tool Co. / Redies Foundation, Edward F.

Sales: $37.0 million
Employees: 230
Headquarters: Saline, MI
SIC Major Group: Industrial Machinery & Equipment

CONTACT

Geoff Crosbie
Controller
R&B Tool Co.
118 East Michigan Ave.
Saline, MI 48176
(313) 429-9421

FINANCIAL SUMMARY

Recent Giving: $86,500 (1991); $84,000 (1990); $46,500 (1989)
Assets: $2,629,958 (1991); $2,147,790 (1990); $1,843,192 (1989)
Gifts Received: $200,000 (1991); $250,000 (1990); $500,000 (1989)
EIN: 38-2391326

CONTRIBUTIONS SUMMARY

Typical Recipients: • *Arts & Humanities:* libraries • *Civic & Public Affairs:* municipalities • *Health:* emergency/ambulance services, health organizations, hospitals • *Social Services:* aged, community service organizations, homes, united funds, youth organizations
Grant Types: general support
Geographic Distribution: focus on MI
Operating Locations: MI (Saline)

CORP. OFFICERS

Robert D. Redies: *CURR EMPL* chmn: R&B Tool Co

GIVING OFFICERS

James D. Buhr: trust
Wilbur K. Pierpont: trust
Robert D. Redies: trust *CURR EMPL* chmn: R&B Tool Co (see above)
Milton E. Stemen: trust *CURR EMPL* pres: R&B Tool Co

APPLICATION INFORMATION

Initial Approach: Send a brief letter of inquiry and a full proposal. Include a description of organization, amount requested, purpose of funds sought, recently audited financial statement, and proof of tax-exempt status. Deadline is February 1, 1992.

GRANTS ANALYSIS

Number of Grants: 12
Highest Grant: $50,000
Typical Range: $1,000 to $5,000
Disclosure Period: 1991

RECENT GRANTS

50,000 City of Saline, Saline, MI

10,000 Saline Community Hospital, Saline, MI
5,000 Mill Pond Manor
5,000 Saline Library, Saline, MI
4,000 Glacier Hills Nursing Center
3,000 Washtenaw Community College, Ann Arbor, MI
2,000 Camp DeSales
2,000 Foundation for Saline Area Schools, Saline, MI
2,000 Houghton Memorial Scholarship
1,500 Boy Scouts of America

Rabb Charitable Foundation, Sidney and Esther

CONTACT

Carol R. Goldberg
Trustee
Sidney and Esther Rabb Charitable Fdn.
c/o Boston Safe Deposit & Trust Co.
One Boston Pl.
Boston, MA 02108
(617) 722-7347

FINANCIAL SUMMARY

Recent Giving: $249,697 (1991); $102,652 (1990); $101,500 (1989)
Assets: $3,779,503 (1991); $3,501,254 (1990); $3,364,828 (1989)
EIN: 04-6039595

CONTRIBUTIONS SUMMARY

Donor(s): the late Sidney R. Rabb
Typical Recipients: • *Arts & Humanities:* museums/galleries, music • *Education:* colleges & universities • *Health:* hospitals • *Religion:* synagogues • *Social Services:* family planning
Grant Types: general support
Geographic Distribution: focus on MA, with emphasis on Boston

GIVING OFFICERS

Helene R. Cahners-Kaplan: trust
Carol Rabb Goldberg: trust *B* Newton MA 1931 *ED* Tufts

Univ BA 1955; Harvard Univ Sch Bus Admin 1969 *CURR EMPL* pres: AVCAR Group *CORP AFFIL* dir: Aicorp, Gillette Co, Lotus Devel Corp; trust: Putnam Fund Group *NONPR AFFIL* bd overseers: WGBH Ed Fdn; bd regents: Higher Ed Comm; bd visitors: Boston Univ Med Sch; dir: Greater Boston Arts Fund, Harvard Univ Bus Sch Alumni Assn, John F Kennedy Library Fdn; mem: Babson Coll Fdn; mem bus adv counc: Carnegie-Mellon Univ; mem natl counc adv comm: Tufts Univ Ctr Pub Svc

APPLICATION INFORMATION

Initial Approach: Send brief letter of inquiry describing program or project. There are no deadlines.

GRANTS ANALYSIS

Number of Grants: 21
Highest Grant: $19,667
Typical Range: $1,000 to $10,000
Disclosure Period: 1991

RECENT GRANTS

19,667 Combined Jewish Philanthropies, Boston, MA
14,485 Beth Israel Hospital, Boston, MA
12,500 Boston Symphony Orchestra, Boston, MA
10,000 Combined Jewish Philanthropies, Boston, MA
10,000 Falmouth Jewish Congregation, East Falmouth, MA
5,000 Children's Medical Center, Boston, MA
5,000 Harvard University Medical School, Boston, MA
4,000 Facing History and Ourselves National Foundation, Brookline, MA
4,000 New England Conservatory of Music, Boston, MA
4,000 Temple Israel, Boston, MA

Rabb Charitable Trust, Sidney R.

CONTACT

Helene Cahners-Kaplan
Trustee
Sidney R. Rabb Charitable Trust
c/o Boston Safe Deposit and Trust Company
One Boston Pl.
Boston, MA 02108
(617) 722-3533

FINANCIAL SUMMARY

Recent Giving: $293,714 (fiscal 1991); $76,750 (fiscal 1990); $24,330 (fiscal 1988)
Assets: $6,430,556 (fiscal year ending August 31, 1990); $6,464,629 (fiscal 1988)
EIN: 22-2754563

CONTRIBUTIONS SUMMARY

Donor(s): Esther V. Rabb
Typical Recipients: • *Arts & Humanities:* community arts, museums/galleries, music • *Civic & Public Affairs:* philanthropic organizations • *Education:* colleges & universities, medical education • *Health:* hospitals, pediatric health • *Religion:* religious organizations, synagogues • *Social Services:* aged, child welfare, family planning, united funds, youth organizations
Grant Types: capital
Geographic Distribution: Focus on MA

GIVING OFFICERS

Helene R. Cahners-Kaplan: trust
Andrew James Casner: trust *B* Chicago IL 1907 *ED* Univ IL AB 1930; Univ IL LLB 1929; Columbia Univ JSD 1941; Harvard Univ LLD 1969 *CORP AFFIL* chmn law editorial bd: Little Brown & Co Inc *NONPR AFFIL* mem: Am Bar Assn, Am Law Inst, Boston Bar Assn, MA Bar Assn; prof: Harvard Univ
Carol Rabb Goldberg: trust *B* Newton MA 1931 *ED* Tufts Univ BA 1955; Harvard Univ Sch Bus Admin 1969 *CURR EMPL* pres: AVCAR Group *CORP AFFIL* dir: Aicorp, Gillette Co, Lotus Devel Corp; trust: Putnam Fund Group *NONPR AFFIL* bd overseers: WGBH Ed Fdn; bd regents: Higher Ed Comm; bd visitors: Boston Univ Med Sch; dir: Greater Boston Arts Fund, Harvard Univ Bus Sch Alumni

Assn, John F Kennedy Library Fdn; mem: Babson Coll Fdn; mem bus adv counc: Carnegie-Mellon Univ; mem natl counc adv comm: Tufts Univ Ctr Pub Svc

Esther V. Rabb: trust

APPLICATION INFORMATION

Initial Approach: Send full proposal. Deadline is June 30. Board meets in August.
Restrictions on Giving: Does not support individuals.

GRANTS ANALYSIS

Number of Grants: 12
Highest Grant: $68,253
Typical Range: $1,000 to $12,500
Disclosure Period: fiscal year ending August 31, 1990

RECENT GRANTS

68,253 Combined Jewish Philanthropies, Boston, MA
50,000 Northeastern University, Boston, MA
25,000 Northeastern University, Boston, MA
19,667 Combined Jewish Philanthropies, Boston, MA
14,485 Beth Israel Hospital, Boston, MA
12,500 Boston Symphony Orchestra, Boston, MA
12,500 Boston Symphony Orchestra, Boston, MA
10,000 McLean Hospital, Belmont, MA
6,667 Hebrew Rehabilitation Center for the Aged, Boston, MA
5,000 Harvard Medical School, Cambridge, MA

Rabb Foundation, Harry W.

CONTACT

Richard A. Zarlengo
Secretary-Treasurer
Harry W. Rabb Fdn.
6242 South Elmira Circle
Englewood, CO 80111
(303) 773-3918

FINANCIAL SUMMARY

Recent Giving: $131,410 (fiscal 1991); $112,770 (fiscal 1990); $120,160 (fiscal 1989)
Assets: $2,014,162 (fiscal year ending June 30, 1991); $1,980,827 (fiscal 1990); $1,952,988 (fiscal 1989)
EIN: 23-7236149

CONTRIBUTIONS SUMMARY

Typical Recipients: • *Arts & Humanities:* community arts, opera, public broadcasting • *Religion:* religious organizations • *Social Services:* aged, homes, united funds, youth organizations

Grant Types: general support

Geographic Distribution: focus on Denver, CO

GIVING OFFICERS

Myles Dolan: trust, vp

Jacob B. Kaufman: trust, pres

Richard A. Zarlengo: trust, secy, treas

APPLICATION INFORMATION

Initial Approach: Send brief letter describing program. There are no deadlines.

GRANTS ANALYSIS

Number of Grants: 75
Highest Grant: $24,000
Typical Range: $500 to $5,000
Disclosure Period: fiscal year ending June 30, 1991

RECENT GRANTS

24,000 Allied Jewish Federation, Denver, CO
6,000 Mount St. Vincent Home, Denver, CO
5,350 Hospice, Denver, CO
5,000 Hospice, Lakewood, CO
5,000 Hospice, Denver, CO
5,000 Pearl St. Temple Emanuel Foundation, Denver, CO
3,000 American Parkinson's Disease Association, New York, NY
2,650 Opera Colorado, Denver, CO
2,250 Sacred Heart House, Denver, CO
2,200 Rose Foundation, Denver, CO

Racal-Milgo

Employees: 2,900
Headquarters: Sunrise, FL
SIC Major Group: Electronic & Other Electrical Equipment

CONTACT

Linda Huett
Manager, Employee Relations
Racal-Milgo
1601 North Harrison Pkwy.
Sunrise, FL 33323
(305) 846-1601

CONTRIBUTIONS SUMMARY

Nonmonetary Support Types: donated equipment and donated products

Operating Locations: FL (Sunrise)

CORP. OFFICERS

Edward Bleckner, Jr.: *B* Pompano FL 1933 *ED* Univ FL 1954 *CURR EMPL* chmn, ceo: Racal-Milgo

James K. Norman: *CURR EMPL* pres: Racal-Milgo

Racetrac Petroleum

Sales: $676.0 million
Employees: 2,000
Headquarters: Atlanta, GA
SIC Major Group: Automotive Dealers & Service Stations and Wholesale Trade—Nondurable Goods

CONTACT

Sue Jackson
Personnel Director
Racetrac Petroleum
PO Box 105035
Atlanta, GA 30348
(404) 431-7600

CONTRIBUTIONS SUMMARY

Operating Locations: GA (Atlanta)

CORP. OFFICERS

Carl Bolch, Jr.: *B* St Louis MO 1943 *ED* Univ PA 1964; Duke Univ 1967 *CURR EMPL* chmn, ceo: Racetrac Petroleum *NONPR AFFIL* mem: Am Bar Assn; pres: Soc Independent Gasoline Marketers Am

Max V. Lenker: *CURR EMPL* pres: Racetrac Petroleum

Rachal Foundation, Ed

CONTACT

Curtis Robert
President
Ed Rachal Fdn.
104 E. Rice
Falfurrias, TX 78355

FINANCIAL SUMMARY

Recent Giving: $625,210 (1992); $670,200 (1990); $578,594 (1987)
Assets: $16,519,071 (1992); $12,040,550 (1990); $12,472,902 (1987)
EIN: 74-1116595

CONTRIBUTIONS SUMMARY

Typical Recipients: • *Arts & Humanities:* libraries • *Education:* colleges & universities, education funds • *Health:* emergency/ambulance services, medical research, single-disease health associations • *Religion:* churches • *Social Services:* drugs & alcohol, emergency relief
Grant Types: general support
Geographic Distribution: focus on TX

GIVING OFFICERS

Adelfa B. Maldonado: secy
Curtis D. Robert: pres
Curtis D. Robert, Jr.: vp, secy

APPLICATION INFORMATION

Initial Approach: Send brief letter of inquiry describing program or project. There are no deadlines.

GRANTS ANALYSIS

Number of Grants: 13
Highest Grant: $150,000
Typical Range: $5,000 to $25,000
Disclosure Period: 1992
Note: 08/31

RECENT GRANTS

150,000 Texas A&I University, Kingsville, TX
140,000 New Covenant Church, Falfurrias, TX
60,000 South Texas Alcohol and Drug Rehabilitation Center, Alice, TX
50,000 Brooks County Area Volunteer Emergency Response Team, Falfurrias, TX

50,000 First United Methodist Church, Falfurrias, TX

50,000 Rural South Texas Development Corporation, Falfurrias, TX

40,000 Brooks County Independent School District, Falfurrias, TX

37,000 Sacred Heart Catholic Church, Falfurrias, TX

35,000 City of Falfurrias, Falfurrias, TX

5,935 Brooks County Hospital Recreational Community Fund, Falfurrias, TX

Radiator Specialty Co. / Blumenthal Foundation

Former Foundation Name: Blumenthal Foundation for Charity, Religion and Education
Sales: $130.0 million
Employees: 800
Headquarters: Charlotte, NC
SIC Major Group: Chemicals & Allied Products, Fabricated Metal Products, and Rubber & Miscellaneous Plastics Products

CONTACT
Philip Blumenthal
Trustee
Blumenthal Foundation
PO Box 34689
Charlotte, NC 28234
(704) 377-6555
Note: The telephone number is for the Radiator Specialty Company, 1900 Wilkinson Boulevard, Charlotte, NC, 28208, where the foundation office is located.

FINANCIAL SUMMARY
Recent Giving: $1,054,572 (fiscal 1993); $1,001,374 (fiscal 1992); $969,237 (fiscal 1991)
Assets: $21,195,856 (fiscal year ending April 30, 1992); $20,962,744 (fiscal 1991); $20,177,461 (fiscal 1990)
Gifts Received: $84,339 (fiscal 1992); $88,417 (fiscal 1991); $68,593 (fiscal 1990)
Fiscal Note: In fiscal 1992, contributions were received from the Radiator Specialty Company.
EIN: 56-0793667

CONTRIBUTIONS SUMMARY
Typical Recipients: • *Civic & Public Affairs:* environmental affairs • *Education:* colleges & universities, community & junior colleges, religious education • *Health:* mental health, single-disease health associations • *Religion:* religious organizations, synagogues • *Social Services:* child welfare, family planning, youth organizations
Grant Types: capital, conference/seminar, endowment, operating expenses, project, and seed money
Geographic Distribution: near headquarters only with a focus on North Carolina, especially on the Charlotte area
Operating Locations: NC (Charlotte)

CORP. OFFICERS
Alan Blumenthal: *CURR EMPL* pres: Radiator Specialty Co
Herman Blumenthal: *B* Savannah GA 1915 *ED* Univ NC *CURR EMPL* chmn, ceo: Radiator Specialty Co *CORP AFFIL* dir: NCNB Corp

GIVING OFFICERS
Alan Blumenthal: trust *CURR EMPL* pres: Radiator Specialty Co (see above)
Anita Blumenthal: trust
Herman Blumenthal: chmn, trust *CURR EMPL* chmn, ceo: Radiator Specialty Co (see above)
Philip Blumenthal: trust
Samuel Blumenthal, PhD: trust

APPLICATION INFORMATION
Initial Contact: Applicants should send one copy of a brief letter proposal.
Include Information On: The proposal should be signed by an authorized official of the petitioning organization and the first paragraph should contain the amount and purpose of the request. The proposal should also include the following: a concise description of the project; what the project hopes to accomplish; total project cost and its duration; funds currently committed or pledged to the project and from what sources; other prospective funding sources; an evaluation plan and, if needed, how future funding will be obtained; phone number where a contact person for the project may be reached during normal business hours; and the name to whom the check is to be made payable. In addition, materials should be attached to the proposal including the following: a line-item budget for the proposed project, if applicable, and a budget for the organization's total operations including expected income and expenditure; a list of the governing board of the petitioning organization; and a copy of the IRS tax-exempt determination letter, except in the cases of governmental agencies and churches.
Deadlines: There are no deadlines for submitting proposals.
Review Process: The foundation's board of trustees meets quarterly to consider grant applications.
Note: No grants are made to individuals for any purpose.

OTHER THINGS TO KNOW
Publications: procedures and requirements for submitting grant proposals

GRANTS ANALYSIS
Total Grants: $1,001,374
Number of Grants: 192
Highest Grant: $125,500
Typical Range: $1,000 to $10,000
Disclosure Period: fiscal year ending April 30, 1992
Note: Average grant figure excludes two grants totaling $225,500. Recent grants are derived from a fiscal 1992 Form 990.

RECENT GRANTS
125,500 Charlotte Jewish Federation, Charlotte, NC

100,000 Blumenthal Jewish Home, Clemmons, NC

75,000 Wildacres Retreat, Little Switzerland, NC

64,000 Temple Beth El V'Shalom, Charlotte, NC

51,500 Jewish Federation, Charlotte, NC

35,000 CAJE-Carolina Agency for Jewish Education, Charlotte, NC

31,000 University of North Carolina at Charlotte, Charlotte, NC

27,175 Queens College, Charlotte, NC

26,100 Arts and Science Council, Charlotte, NC

22,500 Sierra Club Foundation, San Francisco, CA

Radin Foundation

CONTACT
H. Marcus Radin
President
Radin Fdn.
444 West Shaw Ave.
Fresno, CA 93704
(209) 226-5711

FINANCIAL SUMMARY
Recent Giving: $273,661 (1991); $305,085 (1990); $277,500 (1989)
Assets: $6,792,151 (1991); $6,157,891 (1990); $5,962,781 (1989)
EIN: 23-7155525

CONTRIBUTIONS SUMMARY
Donor(s): the late Leta H. Radin
Typical Recipients: • *Arts & Humanities:* arts associations, community arts, museums/galleries, music, opera, public broadcasting • *Civic & Public Affairs:* zoos/botanical gardens • *Education:* colleges & universities • *Health:* hospitals, pediatric health, single-disease health associations • *Religion:* synagogues • *Social Services:* community service organizations, family services
Grant Types: general support
Geographic Distribution: focus on Fresno, CA

GIVING OFFICERS
Larry A. Meyer: secy, treas, dir
H. Marcus Radin: pres, dir
Bruce Rosenblatt: vp, dir

APPLICATION INFORMATION
Initial Approach: Send cover letter and full proposal. There are no deadlines.
Restrictions on Giving: Does not support individuals.

GRANTS ANALYSIS
Number of Grants: 24
Highest Grant: $59,000
Typical Range: $1,000 to $10,000
Disclosure Period: 1991

RECENT GRANTS
59,000 St. Agnes Medical Center, Fresno, CA

55,000 Fresno Community Hospital, Fresno, CA

45,000 California State University Fresno Foundation, Fresno, CA

35,611 Vally Children's Hospital, Fresno, CA

10,300 San Joquain College, Fresno, CA

10,000 KMTF Channel 18, Fresno, CA

5,000 Fresno Arts Center and Museum, Fresno, CA

5,000 Fresno Metropolitan Museum, Fresno, CA

5,000 Fresno Philharmonic Orchestra, Fresno, CA

5,000 Fresno Zoological Society, Fresno, CA

Ragan Charitable Foundation, Carolyn King

CONTACT
Charles Buchholz
Carolyn King Ragan Charitable Fdn.
c/o First National Bank of Atlanta
PO Box 4148
Atlanta, GA 30302
(404) 332-6586

FINANCIAL SUMMARY
Recent Giving: $214,000 (fiscal 1990); $141,000 (fiscal 1989)
Assets: $3,264,958 (fiscal year ending September 30, 1990); $2,495,374 (fiscal 1989)
EIN: 58-6138950

CONTRIBUTIONS SUMMARY
Donor(s): the late Carolyn King Ragan
Typical Recipients: • *Education:* religious education • *Religion:* churches, missionary activities, religious organizations
Grant Types: general support
Geographic Distribution: limited to GA (except for two specific out-of-state beneficiaries).

APPLICATION INFORMATION
Initial Approach: Send brief letter of inquiry describing program. There are no deadlines.
Restrictions on Giving: Does not support individuals.

GRANTS ANALYSIS
Number of Grants: 9
Highest Grant: $35,000
Typical Range: $7,000 to $35,000
Disclosure Period: fiscal year ending September 30, 1990

RECENT GRANTS
35,000 Second Ponce De Leon Baptist Church, Atlanta, GA

35,000 Southern Baptist Theological Seminary, Louisville, KY

32,500 Second Ponce De Leon Baptist Church, Atlanta, GA

32,500 Southern Baptist Theological Seminary, Louisville, KY

25,000 Atlanta Baptist Association for the Clark Howell-Techwood Baptist Center, Atlanta, GA

20,000 Brewton-Parker College, Mount Vernon, GA

14,000 Siloam Baptist Church, Marion, AL

13,000 Siloam Baptist Church, Marion, AL

7,000 Georgia Baptist Children's Home and Family Ministries, Palmetto, GA

Ragen, Jr. Memorial Fund Trust No. 1, James M.

CONTACT
James M. Ragen, Jr. Memorial Fund Trust No. 1
30 North Michigan Ave.
Chicago, IL 60602-3402

FINANCIAL SUMMARY
Recent Giving: $144,000 (1990); $132,400 (1989); $180,000 (1987)
Assets: $2,328,161 (1990); $2,343,037 (1989); $2,249,055 (1987)
EIN: 23-7444822

CONTRIBUTIONS SUMMARY
Typical Recipients: • *Education:* colleges & universities, private education (precollege) • *Health:* hospitals • *Religion:* churches, missionary activities, religious organizations • *Social Services:* child welfare, community service organizations, disabled, united funds, youth organizations
Grant Types: general support

GIVING OFFICERS
Mary Lou Murphy: mem
Francis W. Ragen: mem
Robert E. Ragen: mem
Virginia E. Ragen: mem
Patricia Schaefer: mem

APPLICATION INFORMATION
Initial Approach: Send brief letter of inquiry describing program. There are no deadlines.

GRANTS ANALYSIS
Number of Grants: 24
Highest Grant: $21,000
Typical Range: $1,000 to $10,000
Disclosure Period: 1990

RECENT GRANTS
21,000 Americraft School, Palatka, FL

18,000 University of Washington, Seattle, WA

16,000 St. Patricks Church, Miami, FL

13,500 Carmel High School for Boys, Mundelein, IL

12,000 Guide Dog Foundation for the Blind, Smithtown, NY

10,000 St. Annes Maternity Home, Los Angeles, CA

5,000 Children's Club Assistance League, Los Angeles, CA

5,000 Good Shepherd Center, Los Angeles, CA

5,000 St. Brendans Church, Los Angeles, CA

3,000 Good Samaritan Hospital, Los Angeles, CA

Rahr Malting Co. / Rahr Foundation

Sales: $31.0 million
Employees: 150
Headquarters: Manitowoc, WI
SIC Major Group: Food & Kindred Products

CONTACT
JoAnn Weyenberg
Manager
Rahr Foundation
605 E. Washington St.
Manitowoc, WI 54220
(414) 682-6571
Note: Corporation address is 567 Grain Exchange, Minneapolis, MN 55415; Tel.: (612) 332-5161

FINANCIAL SUMMARY
Recent Giving: $115,951 (1990); $167,774 (1989)
Assets: $3,301,367 (1990); $3,377,722 (1989)
EIN: 39-6046046

CONTRIBUTIONS SUMMARY
Typical Recipients: • *Arts & Humanities:* community arts • *Civic & Public Affairs:* environmental affairs • *Education:* colleges & universities, education funds • *Health:* hospitals, medical research • *Social Services:* community service organizations, disabled, domestic violence, united funds
Grant Types: general support
Geographic Distribution: focus on WI
Operating Locations: WI (Manitowoc)

CORP. OFFICERS
John Alsip III: *CURR EMPL* pres, coo: Rahr Malting Co
T. C. Haffenreffer, Jr.: *CURR EMPL* vchmn: Rahr Malting Co
Guido R. Rahr, Jr.: *B* Milwaukee WI 1928 *ED* Dartmouth Coll 1951 *CURR EMPL* chmn, ceo: Rahr Malting Co

GIVING OFFICERS
George D. Gackle: secy, treas, dir *B* Kulm ND 1925 *ED* Univ ND 1949 *CURR EMPL* dir: Rahr Malting Co *CORP AFFIL* vp, dir: Lakeside Machine Shop
Jack D. Gage: dir
Frederick W. Rahr: vp, dir
Guido R. Rahr, Jr.: pres, dir *CURR EMPL* chmn, ceo: Rahr Malting Co (see above)

APPLICATION INFORMATION
Initial Approach: Send brief letter describing program. There are no deadlines.

GRANTS ANALYSIS
Number of Grants: 78
Highest Grant: $50,573
Typical Range: $100 to $6,000
Disclosure Period: 1990

RECENT GRANTS
50,573 Rahr Foundation Scholarship Fund, Manitowoc, WI

12,500 Minnesota Private College Fund, St. Paul, MN

11,000 Domestic Violence Center, Manitowoc, MN

7,000 United Way, Min-
neapolis, MN
6,600 Rahr Memorial
School Forest
5,000 Bascom Palmer
Eye Institute,
Miami, FL
5,000 Conservation Inter-
national, Washing-
ton, DC
5,000 Hospitality House,
Minneapolis, MN
5,000 Minnesota Opera,
St. Paul, MN
4,500 Wisconsin Founda-
tion of Independent
Colleges, Milwau-
kee, WI

Rainwater Charitable Foundation

CONTACT
Joseph Autem
Treasurer
Rainwater Charitable Foundation
777 Main Street, Suite 2700
Fort Worth, TX 76102

FINANCIAL SUMMARY
Recent Giving: $0 (1990)
Assets: $2,067,240 (1990)
Gifts Received: $2,067,240
(1990)
EIN: 75-2356333

CONTRIBUTIONS SUMMARY
Donor(s): donors are Mr. and
Mrs. Richard Rainwater

GIVING OFFICERS
Joseph W. Autem: treas
Gerald W. Haddock: dir
Karen E. Rainwater: secy
Richard E. Rainwater: pres
Disclosure Period: 1990

Raker Foundation, M. E.

CONTACT
John E. Hogan
President
M. E. Raker Fdn.
3242 Mallard Cove Ln.
Ft. Wayne, IN 46804
(219) 436-2182

FINANCIAL SUMMARY
Recent Giving: $303,076 (fis-
cal 1991); $243,110 (fiscal
1990); $269,048 (fiscal 1989)
Assets: $6,643,510 (fiscal year
ending June 30, 1991);
$6,517,054 (fiscal 1990);
$6,392,330 (fiscal 1989)
EIN: 31-1040474

CONTRIBUTIONS SUMMARY
Donor(s): the late M. E. Raker
Typical Recipients: • *Civic &
Public Affairs:* environmental
affairs • *Education:* colleges &
universities, private education
(precollege), religious education • *Health:* hospitals • *Religion:* churches, religious organizations • *Social Services:* aged,
community service organizations, youth organizations
Grant Types: general support

GIVING OFFICERS
John E. Hogan: pres
John N. Pichon, Jr.: dir
Stephen J. Williams: dir

APPLICATION INFORMATION
Initial Approach: Application
form required. There are no
deadlines.
Restrictions on Giving: Does
not support individuals.

GRANTS ANALYSIS
Number of Grants: 43
Highest Grant: $49,837
Typical Range: $1,000 to
$10,000
Disclosure Period: fiscal year
ending June 30, 1991

RECENT GRANTS
49,837 Indiana University,
Ft. Wayne, IN
15,000 Indiana-Purdue
University Founda-
tion, Ft. Wayne, IN
15,000 Project Renew, Ft.
Wayne, IN — com-
puter needs
15,000 Turnstone, Ft.
Wayne, IN —
equipment
12,500 Lutheran Hospital
Foundation, Ft.
Wayne, IN
10,000 Allen County Coun-
cil on Aging, Ft.
Wayne, IN — trans-
portation program
10,000 Association Re-
tarded Citizens of
Allen County, Ft.
Wayne, IN —
group home im-
provements
10,000 Bishop Luers High
School, Ft. Wayne,
IN — academic
success program
10,000 Bishop Luers High
School, Ft. Wayne,
IN — scholarships
7,500 Boy Scouts of
America, Ft.
Wayne, IN

Raleigh Linen Service/National Distributing Co. / Davis Foundation, Inc.

Sales: $470.0 million
Employees: 1,650
Headquarters: Atlanta, GA
SIC Major Group: Wholesale
Trade—Nondurable Goods

CONTACT
Alfred A. Davis
President
Davis Foundation, Inc.
One National Dr.
Atlanta, GA 30336
(404) 696-9440

FINANCIAL SUMMARY
Recent Giving: $2,507,326
(fiscal 1992); $834,613 (fiscal
1991); $1,249,550 (fiscal 1990)
Assets: $101,972 (fiscal year
ending July 31, 1992);
$492,631 (fiscal 1991);
$135,025 (fiscal 1990)
Gifts Received: $2,100,000
(fiscal 1992); $1,260,000 (fis-
cal 1991); $1,294,100 (fiscal
1990)
Fiscal Note: Contributes
through foundation only. In fiscal 1992, contributions were received from Alfred A. Davis
($1,200,000), National Distrib-
uting Co. ($900,000), and in-
vestments ($80,424).
EIN: 58-6035088

CONTRIBUTIONS SUMMARY
Typical Recipients: • *Arts &
Humanities:* community arts,
museums/galleries • *Civic &
Public Affairs:* ethnic/minority
organizations • *Education:* colleges & universities, medical
education, religious education
• *International:* international
organizations • *Religion:* religious organizations • *Social
Services:* community centers,
community service organizations
Grant Types: endowment and
general support
Geographic Distribution: nationally, with an emphasis on
Atlanta, GA
Operating Locations: GA (Atlanta)

CORP. OFFICERS
Michael C. Carlos: *B* Atlanta
GA 1927 *ED* GA St Univ
CURR EMPL pres, ceo: Natl
Distributing Co

GIVING OFFICERS
Alfred A. Davis: pres *CURR
EMPL* chmn: Natl Distributing
Co
Jay M. Davis: vp

APPLICATION INFORMATION
Initial Approach: *Initial Contact:* letter *Include Information
On:* as much information and
details as possible *When to Submit:* any time

GRANTS ANALYSIS
Total Grants: $2,507,326
Number of Grants: 46
Highest Grant: $545,000
Typical Range: $1,000 to
$50,000
Disclosure Period: fiscal year
ending July 31, 1992
Note: Average grant figure
does not include the two larg-
est grants totaling $957,000.
Recent grants are derived from
a fiscal 1992 grants list.

RECENT GRANTS
545,000 Atlanta Jewish Federation, Atlanta,
GA
412,000 High Museum of
Art, Atlanta, GA
350,000 Alfred A. Davis Research Center, At-
lanta, GA
310,600 American Friends
of Hebrew Univer-
sity, New York, NY
200,000 Cedars-Sinai Hospital, Atlanta, GA
200,000 Friends of Israel
Diaspora Museum
75,000 Health Champions,
Atlanta, GA
50,000 Atlanta Ballet, Atlanta, GA
50,000 Atlanta Jewish
Community Center,
Atlanta, GA
50,000 Center for Surgical
Anatomy, Atlanta,
GA

Rales and Ruth Rales Foundation, Norman R.

CONTACT
Norman R. Rales and Ruth Rales
Fdn.
4000 North Federal Hwy., No.
204
Boca Raton, FL 33431

FINANCIAL SUMMARY
Recent Giving: $210,380 (fis-
cal 1990); $81,292 (fiscal
1989); $60,472 (fiscal 1988)

Assets: $4,248,822 (fiscal year ending November 30, 1990); $3,780,511 (fiscal 1989); $2,360,682 (fiscal 1988)
Gifts Received: $105,960 (fiscal 1989); $88,300 (fiscal 1988)
Fiscal Note: In 1989, contributions were received from Norman R. Rales.
EIN: 59-6874589

CONTRIBUTIONS SUMMARY
Donor(s): Norman R. Rales
Typical Recipients: • *Arts & Humanities:* arts festivals • *Civic & Public Affairs:* ethnic/minority organizations • *Education:* private education (precollege) • *Health:* hospitals, medical research, single-disease health associations • *Religion:* churches, religious organizations, synagogues • *Social Services:* community service organizations
Grant Types: general support
Geographic Distribution: focus on NY and FL

GIVING OFFICERS
Morris Edelstein: trust
Norman R. Rales: trust
Ruth Rales: trust

APPLICATION INFORMATION
Initial Approach: Contributes only to preselected organizations. Applications not accepted.

GRANTS ANALYSIS
Number of Grants: 15
Highest Grant: $175,250
Typical Range: $100 to $5,000
Disclosure Period: fiscal year ending November 30, 1990

RECENT GRANTS
175,250 South Palm Beach County Jewish Federation, Boca Raton, FL
6,000 Betty Ford Foundation, Rancho Mirage, CA
5,000 Boca Raton Community Hospital, Boca Raton, FL
5,000 Jewish Association Residential Care, Boca Raton, FL
5,000 United Way, Delray Beach, FL
2,580 Washington Hebrew Congregation, Washington, DC
2,500 A.T. Medical Research Foundation, Los Angeles, CA
2,500 Hospital for Sick Children, Washington, DC
2,000 Institute of Aerobics Research, Dallas, TX
1,050 Lupus Foundation of America, New York, NY

Raley's
Sales: $1.05 billion
Employees: 8,500
Headquarters: Sacramento, CA
SIC Major Group: Food Stores and Miscellaneous Retail

CONTACT
Joyce Teel
Director, Community & Employee Relations
Raley's
PO Box 15618
Sacramento, CA 95852
(916) 373-3333

FINANCIAL SUMMARY
Fiscal Note: Annual Giving Range: $100,000 to $250,000

CONTRIBUTIONS SUMMARY
Support goes to local education, health and human service, arts, and civic organizations.
Typical Recipients: • *Arts & Humanities:* general • *Civic & Public Affairs:* general • *Education:* general • *Health:* general • *Social Services:* general
Grant Types: general support
Nonmonetary Support Types: cause-related marketing & promotion, donated products, in-kind services, and workplace solicitation
Geographic Distribution: primarily headquarters area
Operating Locations: CA (Sacramento)

CORP. OFFICERS
Charles L. Collings: *B* Wewoka OK 1925 *ED* Univ TX *CURR EMPL* pres: Raleys *CORP AFFIL* secy, dir: Ins Buyers
Thomas P. Raley: *B* Lead Hill AR 1902 *CURR EMPL* chmn: Raleys *CORP AFFIL* pres, dir: Ins Buyers Corp, Raleys NV
Keith F. Tronson: *CURR EMPL* cfo: Raleys

APPLICATION INFORMATION
Initial Approach: Send brief letter of inquiry. There are no deadlines.

Ralston Purina Co. / Ralston Purina Trust Fund
Sales: $7.76 billion
Employees: 56,127
Headquarters: St. Louis, MO
SIC Major Group: Electronic & Other Electrical Equipment and Food & Kindred Products

CONTACT
Fred H. Perabo
Secretary, Board of Control
Ralston Purina Trust Fund
Checkerboard Sq.
St. Louis, MO 63164
(314) 982-3234

FINANCIAL SUMMARY
Recent Giving: $2,080,225 (fiscal 1991); $2,300,000 (fiscal 1990 approx.); $2,285,200 (fiscal 1989)
Assets: $17,027,154 (fiscal year ending August 31, 1991); $15,696,740 (fiscal 1989); $15,320,640 (fiscal 1988)
Fiscal Note: Above figures include trust fund contributions only. Company direct contributions total about $2.0 million annually.
EIN: 43-1209652

CONTRIBUTIONS SUMMARY
Typical Recipients: • *Arts & Humanities:* arts associations, arts centers, history/historic preservation, libraries, museums/galleries, music, performing arts, public broadcasting • *Civic & Public Affairs:* business/free enterprise, civil rights, environmental affairs, international affairs, professional & trade associations, public policy, urban & community affairs • *Education:* arts education, career/vocational education, colleges & universities, education funds, medical education, minority education, private education (precollege), science/technology education • *Health:* health care cost containment, hospitals, medical research, nursing services, pediatric health • *Religion:* religious organizations • *Science:* scientific institutes • *Social Services:* aged, child welfare, community service organizations, delinquency & crime, disabled, drugs & alcohol, employment/job training, family planning, food/clothing distribution, homes, recreation & athletics, religious welfare, shelters/homelessness, united funds, volunteer services, youth organizations
Grant Types: capital, endowment, general support, and project
Nonmonetary Support Types: cause-related marketing & promotion, donated equipment, donated products, in-kind services, loaned employees, loaned executives, and workplace solicitation
Note: Value of nonmonetary is not available and is not included in above figures.
Geographic Distribution: primarily St. Louis and company plant locations
Operating Locations: CA (Los Angeles, San Diego), CO (Denver), CT, IA (Davenport), KY (Louisville), MN (Minneapolis), MO (St. Louis), NY, OH (Cincinnati, Zanesville), TN (Memphis)

CORP. OFFICERS
Paul Harold Hatfield: *B* Topeka KS 1936 *ED* KS St Univ 1959 *CURR EMPL* pres (protein technologies intl): Ralston Purina Co *NONPR AFFIL* dir: Japan-Am Soc, US/Yugoslavia Trade Econ Counc; mem: US/USSR Trade Econ Counc
W. H. Lacey: *B* 1940 *CURR EMPL* pres (grocery products group), vp: Ralston Purina Co
W. P. McGinness: *CURR EMPL* pres (branded foods group): Ralston Purina Co
William Paul Stiritz: *B* Jasper AR 1934 *ED* Northwestern Univ BS 1959; St Louis Univ MA 1968 *CURR EMPL* chmn, ceo, pres, dir: Ralston Purina Co *CORP AFFIL* dir: Angelica Corp, Ball Corp, Boatmens Bancshares, Centerre Bancorp, Gen Am Life Ins Co, SC Johnson & Son, May Dept Stores Co *NONPR AFFIL* dir: Grocery Mfrs Am, WA Univ

GIVING OFFICERS
R. E. Bell: mem (bd control)
John H. Morris, Jr.: mem (bd control) *B* Pittsburgh PA 1942 *ED* WV Univ 1964; Case Western Reserve Univ 1983 *CURR EMPL* vp (corp strategic planning): Ralston Purina Co *CORP AFFIL* exec vp, dir: RPM
James Morton Neville: mem (bd control) *B* Minneapolis MN 1939 *ED* Univ MN BA 1961; Univ MN LLB 1964 *CURR EMPL* vp, secy, gen coun: Ral-

ston Purina Co *NONPR AFFIL*
mem: Am Bar Assn, Am Corp
Counc Assn, Am Soc Corp
Secys, Hennepin County Bar
Assn, MD Bar Assn, MN Bar
Assn, Phi Delta Phi, Psi Upsilon, St Louis Bar Assn, Univ
MN Law Alumni Assn, US Supreme Court Bar Assn
Fred H. Perabo: secy (bd control) *CURR EMPL* dir (employee rels & community affairs): Ralston Purina Co
E. D. Richards: mem (bd control)
C. S. Sommer: mem (bd control)

APPLICATION INFORMATION
Initial Approach: *Initial Contact:* brief letter or proposal *Include Information On:* clear
statement of the problem/need,
accomplishments by a particular date, background on organization and staff that administer
grant, general plan for post-
grant evaluation, proof of
501(c)(3) status, amount requested, detailed program
budget, copy of most recent financial statement, letter from
board chairman or chief administrative officer endorsing proposal *When to Submit:* any time
Restrictions on Giving: The
fund does not support organizations unable to produce
501(c)(3) tax determination letters; individuals for other than
educational purposes; religious
or politically partisan causes;
projects that require funding
outside the United States or its
possessions; loans or investment funds; veterans or fraternal organizations, unless they
furnish services to the general
public; tickets for dinners,
benefits, exhibits, conferences,
sports events, or other short-
term activities; advertisements;
underwriting of deficits or
postevent funding; or research
that is not action-oriented.

OTHER THINGS TO KNOW
Preference is given to projects
that offer a maximum multi-
plier effect, a good basis for
replication, and a prevention
component.

GRANTS ANALYSIS
Total Grants: $2,080,225
Number of Grants: 55
Highest Grant: $500,000
Typical Range: $5,000 to
$40,000

Disclosure Period: fiscal year
ending August 31, 1991
Note: Figure for average grant
excludes foundation's largest
grant of $500,000. Recent
grants are derived from a fiscal
1991 Form 990.

RECENT GRANTS
500,000 Washington Univer-
sity, St. Louis, MO
200,000 St. Louis Science
Center, St. Louis,
MO
195,000 United Way of
Greater St. Louis,
St. Louis, MO
195,000 United Way of
Greater St. Louis,
St. Louis, MO
195,000 United Way of
Greater St. Louis,
St. Louis, MO
180,000 United Way of
Greater St. Louis,
St. Louis, MO
125,000 American Youth
Foundation, St.
Louis, MO
60,000 KETC Channel
Nine, St. Louis,
MO
46,225 National Merit
Scholarship Corpo-
ration, Evanston, IL
40,000 Arts and Education
Council of Greater
St. Louis, St.
Louis, MO

Ramapo Trust

CONTACT
Stephen L. Schwartz
Trustee
Ramapo Trust
126 East 56th St., Tenth Fl.
New York, NY 10022
(212) 308-7355

FINANCIAL SUMMARY
Recent Giving: $2,286,732
(fiscal 1991); $3,402,722 (fis-
cal 1990); $3,127,159 (fiscal
1989)
Assets: $27,151,878 (fiscal
year ending June 30, 1991);
$25,681,216 (fiscal 1990);
$36,203,832 (fiscal 1989)
Gifts Received: $135,000 (fis-
cal 1988); $135,000 (fiscal
1987)
Fiscal Note: The trust received
gifts in fiscal 1987 and fiscal
1988 from the Ramapo Charitable Lead Trust.

EIN: 13-6594279

CONTRIBUTIONS SUMMARY
Donor(s): The Ramapo Trust
was established in 1973, with
Henry L. Schwartz as donor.
Typical Recipients: • *Civic &
Public Affairs:* philanthropic organizations, public policy
• *Education:* colleges & universities, medical education
• *Health:* geriatric health,
health organizations, hospitals,
outpatient health care delivery
• *Social Services:* aged, community centers, community service organizations, family services, youth organizations
Grant Types: matching, project, research, and seed money
Geographic Distribution: no
geographic restrictions

GIVING OFFICERS
Arthur Norman Field: trust *B*
New York NY 1935 *ED* City
Univ NY BBA 1955; Harvard
Univ LLB 1958 *CURR EMPL*
ptnr: Shearman & Sterling
CORP AFFIL chmn bd: West-
ern ME Radio; dir: Sunset Re-
alty Corp, Trizec Stamford,
North Central Oil Corp; mem
bd dirs: Wave Hill *NONPR
AFFIL* dir: Brookdale Fdn; fel-
low: Am Bar Fdn, NY Bar Fdn;
mem: Am Bar Assn, Am Law
Inst, NY Bar Assn, NY City
Bar Assn, NY County Lawyers
Assn; mem bd dirs: Washing-
ton Square Legal Svcs
Karen Hart: trust
Harold Resnick: trust *B* New
York NY
Danylle Rudin: compliance off
Andrew Schreier: trust
William Schreier: trust
Stephen L. Schwartz: trust *B*
New York NY 1948 *ED*
Carnegie Inst Tech BFA
NONPR AFFIL mem: Am Soc
Composers Authors & Publs,
Dramatists Guild, Natl Acad-
emy Recording Arts & Sciences
Rebecca Shaffer: trust
Mary Ann Van Clief: trust
PHIL AFFIL vp, secy-treas:
Brookdale Foundation

APPLICATION INFORMATION
Initial Approach:
The trust has no formal application guidelines for proposals. A
concept letter should be sent before making a proposal.
If the trust is interested in an
applicant's concept letter, it
will request a proposal. At that
time, it will define what mate-

rial should be included in the
proposal.
Restrictions on Giving: The
trust does not fund capital improvements, individuals, operating budgets, the media, or the
arts. All applicants must have
IRS 501(c)(3) or equivalent
status.

OTHER THINGS TO KNOW
The trust is affiliated with the
Brookdale and Glendale Foun-
dations, both located in New
York.

GRANTS ANALYSIS
Total Grants: $2,286,731
Number of Grants: 58
Highest Grant: $350,000
Typical Range: $10,000 to
$60,000
Disclosure Period: fiscal year
ending June 30, 1991
Note: Recent grants are derived
from a 1991 grants list.

RECENT GRANTS
350,000 Hunter Col-
lege/Brookdale
Center on Aging,
New York, NY
255,000 Yeshiva University,
New York, NY
178,369 Mount Sinai Medi-
cal Center, New
York, NY
120,000 Harvard University
Medical School,
Boston, MA
114,960 St.
Luke's/Roosevelt
Hospital, New
York, NY
93,821 Memorial Sloan-
Kettering Cancer
Center, New York,
NY
86,058 Rockefeller University, New York, NY
85,000 Johns Hopkins Uni-
versity, Baltimore,
MD
71,012 Visions Services,
New York, NY
67,935 University of Ari-
zona, Tucson, AZ

Ramlose Foundation, George A.

CONTACT
David L. Taylor
Secretary
George A. Ramlose Fdn.
c/o Adams and Blinn
43 Thorndike St.
Cambridge, MA 02141
(617) 577-9700

FINANCIAL SUMMARY
Recent Giving: $78,220 (fiscal 1992); $25,000 (fiscal 1991); $75,000 (fiscal 1990)
Assets: $1,867,921 (fiscal year ending April 30, 1992); $1,709,648 (fiscal 1991); $1,709,648 (fiscal 1990)
EIN: 04-6048231

CONTRIBUTIONS SUMMARY
Donor(s): the late George Ramlose
Typical Recipients: • *Arts & Humanities:* community arts, music, performing arts • *Education:* arts education, colleges & universities • *Health:* health organizations, medical research, nursing services, single-disease health associations • *Social Services:* community service organizations, counseling, youth organizations
Grant Types: general support, operating expenses, project, and research

GIVING OFFICERS
Ernest F. Boyce: trust
James P. Fisher: dir, vp
John A. Logan: dir, vp
Lloyd W. Moseley: dir, pres
A. Leavitt Taylor: dir, treas
David L. Taylor: dir, secy
Kenneth Wilson: dir, vp

APPLICATION INFORMATION
Initial Approach: Contributes only to preselected organizations.

GRANTS ANALYSIS
Number of Grants: 34
Highest Grant: $7,500
Typical Range: $500 to $1,000
Disclosure Period: fiscal year ending April 30, 1992

RECENT GRANTS
7,500 Charleston Symphony Orchestra, Charleston, SC
5,000 Alzheimer's Disease and Related Disorders Association, Grand Rapids, MI
5,000 American Music Scholarship Association, Cincinnati, OH
5,000 Burnham Walker Center, Fitchburg, MA
5,000 Harvard University, Cambridge, MA
5,000 Porter Hills Presbyterian Village, Grand Rapids, MI
5,000 Visiting Nurses Association, Dedham, MA
3,500 Cumberland College, Williamsburg, KY
3,000 Cotting School, Lexington, MA
3,000 Habitat for Humanity, Pingah Forest, NC

Ranco, Inc.
Sales: $200.0 million
Employees: 4,700
Parent Company: Siebe
Headquarters: Dublin, OH
SIC Major Group: Fabricated Metal Products, Industrial Machinery & Equipment, Instruments & Related Products, and Transportation Equipment

CONTACT
Teri Collins
Treasurer
Ranco, Inc.
PO Box 248
Dublin, OH 43017
(614) 873-9200

FINANCIAL SUMMARY
Fiscal Note: Annual Giving Range: less than $100,000

CONTRIBUTIONS SUMMARY
Typical Recipients: • *Arts & Humanities:* general • *Civic & Public Affairs:* general • *Education:* general • *Health:* general • *Social Services:* general
Grant Types: general support
Geographic Distribution: primarily headquarters area
Operating Locations: OH (Dublin)

CORP. OFFICERS
Bob Smialek: *CURR EMPL* pres: Ranco
E. Barrie Stephens: *CURR EMPL* chmn, ceo: Ranco *CORP AFFIL* ceo: Barber-Colman Co, Siebe North; chmn, ceo: Robertshaw Controls Co

APPLICATION INFORMATION
Initial Approach: Send brief letter of inquiry. There are no deadlines.

Rand McNally and Co. / Rand McNally Foundation
Sales: $430.0 million
Employees: 3,800
Headquarters: Skokie, IL
SIC Major Group: Printing & Publishing

CONTACT
Andrew McNally, III
President & CEO
Rand McNally Foundation
Post Office Box 7600
Chicago, IL 60680
(708) 673-9100

FINANCIAL SUMMARY
Recent Giving: $191,795 (1989); $77,665 (1988)
Assets: $968,190 (1989); $1,001,000 (1988)
Gifts Received: $250,050 (1989)
Fiscal Note: In 1989, contributions were received from Rand McNally Co.
EIN: 36-3514596

CONTRIBUTIONS SUMMARY
Operating Locations: IL (Skokie)

CORP. OFFICERS
John S. Bakalar: *B* Lynn MA 1948 *ED* Univ PA 1970; Stanford Univ 1973 *CURR EMPL* exec vp, cro: Rand McNally & Co *CORP AFFIL* dir: Transitron
Andrew McNally IV: *B* New York NY 1939 *ED* Univ NC 1963 *CURR EMPL* pres: Rand McNally & Co

GIVING OFFICERS
John S. Bakalar: exec vp, dir *CURR EMPL* exec vp, cro: Rand McNally & Co (see above)
Thomas F. Carroll: asst secy
Andrew McNally III: chmn *B* Chicago IL 1909 *ED* Yale Univ 1931
Andrew McNally IV: dir *CURR EMPL* pres: Rand McNally & Co (see above)
Martin J. Rosinski: treas, asst secy, dir *B* Hammond IN 1938 *ED* St Josephs Coll 1960 *CURR EMPL* corp contr: Rand McNally & Co *NONPR AFFIL* mem: Natl Assn Accts
Richard G. Sander: secy

APPLICATION INFORMATION
Initial Approach: Send brief letter describing program. There are no deadlines.
Disclosure Period: 1989

Rand-Whitney Packaging-Delmar Corp.
Sales: $22.0 million
Employees: 175
Parent Company: Rand-Whitney Container Corp.
Headquarters: Leominster, MA
SIC Major Group: Paper & Allied Products

CONTACT
Fernand Larue
Director of Human Resources
Rand-Whitney Packaging-Delmar Corp.
248 Industrial Rd.
Leominster, MA 01453
(508) 537-1701

CONTRIBUTIONS SUMMARY
Operating Locations: MA (Leominster)

CORP. OFFICERS
Robert Crafton: *CURR EMPL* pres: Rand-Whitney Packaging - Delmar Corp

OTHER THINGS TO KNOW
Company is an original donor to the Jacob & Frances Hiatt Foundation.

Randa

CONTACT
Randa
c/o Rist Alabama Bank Trust Department
8 Commerce St.
Montgomery, AL 36134
(205) 832-8200

FINANCIAL SUMMARY
Recent Giving: $295,900 (1991); $183,350 (1990); $120,850 (1989)
Assets: $8,954,636 (1991); $5,380,571 (1990); $4,607,748 (1989)
EIN: 63-6048966

CONTRIBUTIONS SUMMARY
Donor(s): Adolf Weil, Jr., Robert S. Weil
Typical Recipients: • *Arts & Humanities:* arts institutes, community arts, museums/galleries • *Civic & Public Affairs:* zoos/botanical gardens • *Education:* colleges & universities • *Social Services:* aged, child welfare, community service organizations, food/clothing distribution, homes, united funds, youth organizations
Grant Types: general support

GIVING OFFICERS
First Alabama Bank: fiscal agent
M.J. Rothschild: off
Adolf Weil, Jr.: trust

APPLICATION INFORMATION
Initial Approach: Contributes only to preselected organizations.

GRANTS ANALYSIS
Number of Grants: 74
Highest Grant: $34,500
Typical Range: $200 to $5,000
Disclosure Period: 1991

RECENT GRANTS
- 34,500 Montgomery Zoo, Montgomery, AL
- 30,000 Southern Research Institute, Montgomery, AL
- 26,000 Eye Research Foundation, Montgomery, AL
- 26,000 Montgomery Symphony Orchestra, Montgomery, AL
- 25,500 Montgomery Area Food Bank, Montgomery, AL
- 25,000 United Way, Montgomery, AL
- 15,000 Nelson Gallery Foundation, Kansas City, MO
- 11,000 United Way, Montgomery, AL
- 10,000 Dartmouth College, Hanover, NH
- 10,000 University of Alabama at Birmingham, Birmingham, AL

Randleigh Foundation Trust

CONTACT
Thomas S. Kenan III
Trust
Randleigh Fdn Trust
P.O. Box 2729
Chapel Hill, NC 27514
(919) 968-0618

FINANCIAL SUMMARY
Recent Giving: $262,000 (fiscal 1992); $252,506 (fiscal 1991)
Assets: $5,432,504 (fiscal year ending March 31, 1992); $5,672,782 (fiscal 1991)
EIN: 13-6207897

CONTRIBUTIONS SUMMARY
Donor(s): the late William R. Kenan, Jr.
Typical Recipients: • *Arts & Humanities:* arts associations, dance • *Education:* colleges & universities, elementary education, private education (precollege), special education • *Social Services:* animal protection
Grant Types: general support

GIVING OFFICERS
Frank H. Kenan: trust
James G. Kenan: trust
James G. Kenan III: trust
Owen G. Kenan: trust
Thomas S. Kenan III: trust
Garrett Kirk, Jr.: trust

APPLICATION INFORMATION
Initial Approach: Contributes only to preselected organizations. Applications not accepted.
Restrictions on Giving: Does not provide grants to individuals.

GRANTS ANALYSIS
Number of Grants: 30
Highest Grant: $30,000
Typical Range: $1,000 to $30,000
Disclosure Period: fiscal year ending March 31, 1992

RECENT GRANTS
- 30,000 Duke School for Children, Durham, NC
- 28,000 Duplin County Board of Education
- 25,000 Lexington School for the Deaf Foundation, Jackson Heights, NY
- 25,000 Nightingale Bamford School, New York, NY
- 20,000 Brown University Drama Department, Providence, RI
- 20,000 Shakertown at Pleasant Hill Kentucky, Pleasant Hill, KY
- 15,000 North Carolina Veterinary Medical Foundation, NC
- 11,500 University of North Carolina Charlotte, Charlotte, NC
- 10,000 American Ballet Theater, New York, NY
- 10,000 University of Kentucky, Lexington, KY — humanities book endowment

Randolph Foundation
Former Foundation Name: H. Smith Richardson Charitable Trust

CONTACT
H. Smith Richardson, Jr.
Chairman
Randolph Foundation
200 East 94th St.
Ste. 1615
New York, NY 10128
(212) 996-1853
Note: Another address is c/o Piedmont Financial Company, P.O. Box 20124, Greensboro, NC 27420, (919) 274-5471.

FINANCIAL SUMMARY
Recent Giving: $2,000,000 (fiscal 1993 est.); $1,800,000 (fiscal 1992 approx.); $2,592,190 (fiscal 1991)
Assets: $42,000,000 (fiscal 1993 est.); $40,000,000 (fiscal 1992 est.); $41,335,935 (fiscal year ending June 30, 1991); $42,344,648 (fiscal 1990); $295,440,854 (fiscal 1989)
Gifts Received: $50,000 (fiscal 1991)
Fiscal Note: In fiscal 1991, the foundation received $50,000 from an anonymous donor.
EIN: 23-7245123

CONTRIBUTIONS SUMMARY
Donor(s): The foundation was established by the late H. Smith Richardson, Sr. (d. 1972), in 1976. His father, Lunsford Richardson of North Carolina, founded in 1905 Vicks Chemical Company, which manufactured Vicks Vaporub. H. Smith Richardson, Sr., built Richardson -Merrill, Inc. In 1981, the company was sold to Dow Chemical Company for $80 million. The family then founded Richardson-Vicks, Inc., a manufacturer of consumer products that makes Clearasil and Nyquil. The company merged with Proctor & Gamble in 1985. Today, the family owns a large part of the Piedmont Mangement Company headquartered in New York.
Typical Recipients: • *Civic & Public Affairs:* better government, economics, international affairs, law & justice, public policy, urban & community affairs • *Education:* colleges & universities, public education (precollege) • *Social Services:* community service organizations
Grant Types: project
Geographic Distribution: throughout the United States only

GIVING OFFICERS
Heather S. Richardson: trust
Henry Smith Richardson, Jr.: trust *B* Greensboro NC 1920 *ED* Yale Univ B A 1942 *CORP AFFIL* dir: Piedmont Mgmt Co, Richardson-Vicks
Peter L. Richardson: trust *B* 1954 *CORP AFFIL* dir: Piedmont Mgmt Co, Richardson Corp *PHIL AFFIL* trust: Grace Jones Richardson Trust
Robert Randolph Richardson: trust *B* Greensboro NC 1926 *CURR EMPL* chmn: Piedmont Mgmt Co *CORP AFFIL* dir: Richardson Corp, Richardson-Vicks *PHIL AFFIL* trust: H Smith Richardson Charitable Trust
Stuart Smith Richardson: trust *B* 1947 *CURR EMPL* chmn, dir: Richardson-Vicks *CORP AFFIL* chmn: Vanguard Cellular Sys; dir: Piedmont Mgmt Co; vchmn, dir: Richardson Corp *PHIL AFFIL* trust: Grace Jones Richardson Trust

APPLICATION INFORMATION
Initial Approach:
Applicants should send a letter proposal.
The letter of application should include the following: a brief overview statement outlining the purpose, scope and desirability of the project; a brief de-

scription of the applicant organization including the credentials of the key personnel and financials for the organization; detailed schedules of work, timetables, budget, and goals for the project; evidence that the proposed or similar project has not been earlier and adequately carried out by this or another organization or individual; a description of the audience for which the project is intended; and, copies of the IRS tax-determination status as a 501(c)(3) or equivalent organization.

There are no deadlines for submitting proposals.

Grants are normally approved quarterly; hovvever, the foundation maintains no specific review periods.

Restrictions on Giving: The foundation reports that it originates many of its grant commitments. It does not make grants to individuals. Also, at the present time, the foundation normally does not favorably respond to deficit funding of previously established operations, operating support, "brick and mortar" building projects, programs related to the arts, historic restoration projects, research in the physical sciences or the medical field, and nondomestic proposals.

OTHER THINGS TO KNOW
Publications: proposal guidelines

GRANTS ANALYSIS
Total Grants: $2,592,190
Number of Grants: 34
Highest Grant: $240,000
Typical Range: $20,000 to $100,000
Disclosure Period: fiscal year ending June 30, 1991
Note: Recent grants are derived from a fiscal 1991 Form 990.

RECENT GRANTS
150,000 Institute on Religion and Democracy, Washington, DC
150,000 Ohio State University, Columbus, OH
125,000 Freedom House, New York, NY
125,000 Institute for Contemporary Studies, San Francisco, CA
125,000 Washington Strategy Seminar, Arlington, VA

100,000 Vanderbilt University, Nashville, TN
89,000 Northgate Parkinson Fund, New York, NY
78,000 American Enterprise Institute, Washington, DC
75,000 Atlantic Legal Foundation, New York, NY
74,693 Rutgers University, New Brunswick, NJ

Random House Inc.
Sales: $170.0 million
Employees: 1,500
Parent Company: Newhouse Publications Corp.
Headquarters: New York, NY
SIC Major Group: Printing & Publishing

CONTACT
Alexander MacGregor
Vice President, Administration
Random House Inc.
201 East 50th St.
New York, NY 10022
(212) 751-2600

CONTRIBUTIONS SUMMARY
Operating Locations: NY (New York)

CORP. OFFICERS
Alberto Vitale: *CURR EMPL* chmn, pres, ceo: Random House

Rangeley Educational Trust
CONTACT
Paul I. Turner
Vice President
Rangeley Educational Trust
c/o Crestar Bank, N.A.
PO Box 4911
Martinsville, VA 24115
(703) 632-6361

FINANCIAL SUMMARY
Recent Giving: $191,823 (fiscal 1991); $94,662 (fiscal 1990); $194,924 (fiscal 1989)
Assets: $2,026,270 (fiscal year ending October 31, 1991); $1,806,992 (fiscal 1990); $1,756,098 (fiscal 1989)
EIN: 54-6077906

CONTRIBUTIONS SUMMARY
Grant Types: loan
Geographic Distribution: limited to the city of Martinsville and Henry County, VA

GIVING OFFICERS
Crestar Bank: trust

APPLICATION INFORMATION
Initial Approach: Interviews usually required. Application form required. Deadline is May 1.

OTHER THINGS TO KNOW
Provides scholarship loans for higher education.
Disclosure Period: fiscal year ending October 31, 1991

Rankin and Elizabeth Forbes Rankin Trust, William
CONTACT
William Rankin and Elizabeth Forbes Rankin Trust
c/o The Chase Manhattan Bank, N.A., Tax Serv. Div.
1211 Avenue of the Americas, 36th Fl.
New York, NY 10036
(212) 789-5027

FINANCIAL SUMMARY
Recent Giving: $211,968 (1991); $218,088 (1990); $208,770 (1989)
Assets: $6,648,204 (1991); $5,539,461 (1990); $5,881,133 (1989)
EIN: 13-6584984

CONTRIBUTIONS SUMMARY
Typical Recipients: • *Health:* health organizations, medical research, single-disease health associations • *Social Services:* community service organizations, disabled, youth organizations
Grant Types: general support

APPLICATION INFORMATION
Initial Approach: Send brief letter of inquiry describing program or project. There are no deadlines.

GRANTS ANALYSIS
Highest Grant: $5,212
Disclosure Period: 1991

RECENT GRANTS
5,212 American Cancer Society, New York, NY
5,212 American Heart Association, New York, NY

5,212 American Red Cross, New York, NY
5,212 Associated Blind, New York, NY
5,212 Salvation Army, New York, NY
4,754 American Cancer Society, New York, NY
4,754 American Heart Association, New York, NY
4,754 American Red Cross, New York, NY
4,754 Associated Blind, New York, NY
4,754 Salvation Army, New York, NY

Ranney Foundation, P. K.
CONTACT
Phillip A. Ranney
Secretary
P. K. Ranney Fdn.
1525 National City Bank Bldg.
Cleveland, OH 44114
(216) 696-4200

FINANCIAL SUMMARY
Recent Giving: $259,000 (1991); $200,000 (1990); $250,000 (1989)
Assets: $5,771,422 (1991); $5,314,453 (1990); $5,354,914 (1989)
EIN: 23-7343201

CONTRIBUTIONS SUMMARY
Typical Recipients: • *Arts & Humanities:* history/historic preservation, museums/galleries • *Civic & Public Affairs:* municipalities • *Education:* colleges & universities, education funds, health & physical education • *Health:* emergency/ambulance services, health organizations, hospitals • *Social Services:* community service organizations
Grant Types: endowment, general support, multiyear/continuing support, and research
Geographic Distribution: focus on OH

GIVING OFFICERS
Robert K. Bissell: vp
Peter K. Ranney: pres, treas
Phillip A. Ranney: secy

APPLICATION INFORMATION
Initial Approach: Send cover letter and full proposal. There are no deadlines.

GRANTS ANALYSIS
Number of Grants: 16
Highest Grant: $60,000
Typical Range: $5,000 to $10,000
Disclosure Period: 1991

RECENT GRANTS
- 60,000 Eliza Jennings Group, Cleveland, OH
- 50,000 Cleveland Foundation, Cleveland, OH
- 25,000 Cleveland Museum of Natural History, Cleveland, OH
- 20,000 University of Hawaii Foundation, Honolulu, HI
- 20,000 University School, Shaker Heights, OH
- 15,000 Salvation Army, Cleveland, OH
- 10,000 Cleveland Clinic Foundation, Cleveland, OH
- 10,000 Cleveland Health Education Museum, Cleveland, OH
- 10,000 Mad River Valley Ambulance Service, Mad River, OH
- 10,000 Oceanic Institute, OH

Ransburg Corp.
Sales: $320.0 million
Employees: 2,500
Parent Company: Illinois Tool Works Inc.
Headquarters: Indianapolis, IN
SIC Major Group: Electronic & Other Electrical Equipment, Fabricated Metal Products, Industrial Machinery & Equipment, and Instruments & Related Products

CONTACT
Duane Rohlfing
Vice President, Public Relations
Ransburg Corp.
3939 West 56th St.
Indianapolis, IN 46208
(317) 298-5000

FINANCIAL SUMMARY
Fiscal Note: Annual Giving Range: $100,000 to $250,000

CONTRIBUTIONS SUMMARY
Support goes to local education, health and human service, arts, and civic organizations.
Typical Recipients: • *Arts & Humanities:* general • *Civic & Public Affairs:* general • *Education:* general • *Health:* general • *Social Services:* general
Grant Types: general support

Geographic Distribution: company operating locations
Operating Locations: IN (Indianapolis), OH (Akron, Toledo), PA (Hatfield), PR (Naguabo)

CORP. OFFICERS
Charles H. Moore, Jr.: *B* Coatsville PA 1929 *ED* Cornell Univ 1952 *CURR EMPL* pres: Ransburg Corp *CORP AFFIL* dir: Fundamental Mgmt Corp, IN Natl Bank, Turner Corp

APPLICATION INFORMATION
Initial Approach: Send letter of inquiry.

Ransom Fidelity Company

CONTACT
R. E. Olds Anderson
President
Ransom Fidelity Company
702 Michigan National Tower
Lansing, MI 48933
(517) 482-1538

FINANCIAL SUMMARY
Recent Giving: $126,852 (1991); $125,300 (1990); $125,500 (1989)
Assets: $4,025,347 (1991); $3,277,385 (1990); $3,037,766 (1989)
EIN: 38-1485403

CONTRIBUTIONS SUMMARY
Donor(s): the late Ransom E. Olds
Typical Recipients: • *Civic & Public Affairs:* environmental affairs, zoos/botanical gardens • *Education:* colleges & universities • *Health:* health organizations, hospitals • *Religion:* churches, religious organizations • *Social Services:* animal protection, community service organizations, united funds, youth organizations
Grant Types: general support
Geographic Distribution: focus on MI

GIVING OFFICERS
R.E. Olds Anderson: pres

APPLICATION INFORMATION
Initial Approach: Application form required. There are no deadlines.
Restrictions on Giving: Does not support individuals.

GRANTS ANALYSIS
Number of Grants: 31
Highest Grant: $14,400
Typical Range: $1,000 to $5,000
Disclosure Period: 1991

RECENT GRANTS
- 14,400 Nature Way Association, Lansing, MI
- 10,000 Highfields, Onodaga, MI — new building
- 10,000 Hillsdale college, Hillsdale, MI — ultracentrifuge
- 10,000 Salvation Army, Lansing, MI
- 8,500 Capital Area Humane Society, Lansing, MI
- 7,500 American Red Cross, Lansing, MI
- 5,050 Hospice of Michigan, Lansing, MI
- 5,000 All Saints Episcopal Church, East Lansing, MI — renovations and operations
- 5,000 Michigan State University Mildred Erickson Fellowship, East Lansing, MI — reactivate students
- 5,000 St. Lawrence Hospital and Health Care Services, Lansing, MI — for renovation

Raper Foundation, Tom

CONTACT
Tom Raper Fdn.
PO Box 1365
Richmond, IN 47375

FINANCIAL SUMMARY
Recent Giving: $91,609 (fiscal 1990); $72,421 (fiscal 1989); $63,819 (fiscal 1988)
Assets: $1,890,055 (fiscal year ending November 30, 1990); $1,658,128 (fiscal 1989); $1,263,491 (fiscal 1988)
Gifts Received: $200,000 (fiscal 1990); $267,548 (fiscal 1989); $177,480 (fiscal 1988)
Fiscal Note: In 1990, contributions were received from Thomas R. Raper.
EIN: 31-0999060

CONTRIBUTIONS SUMMARY
Donor(s): Thomas R. Raper

GIVING OFFICERS
Sally Fares: trust

Mildred Raper: trust
Ray J. Raper: vp, secy, dir
Suzanne D. Raper: trust
Thomas R. Raper: pres, dir
Carolyn Runzer: trust

APPLICATION INFORMATION
Initial Approach: Application form required. There are no deadlines.

OTHER THINGS TO KNOW
Provides grants to individuals for travel and study related to Christian ministries.

Rapp Foundation, Robert Glenn

CONTACT
Robert Glenn Rapp Fdn.
2301 N.W. 39th Expressway, Ste. 300
Oklahoma City, OK 73112
(405) 525-8331

FINANCIAL SUMMARY
Recent Giving: $65,800 (1991); $21,500 (1990); $10,300 (1989)
Assets: $7,609,129 (1991); $4,742,819 (1990); $6,247,681 (1989)
EIN: 73-0616840

CONTRIBUTIONS SUMMARY
Donor(s): the late Florence B. Clark
Typical Recipients: • *Education:* colleges & universities, medical education, private education (precollege), religious education • *Health:* hospices, hospitals, medical research • *Religion:* religious organizations • *Social Services:* disabled, united funds
Grant Types: capital and general support
Geographic Distribution: focus on Oklahoma City, OK

GIVING OFFICERS
Jilene Boghetich: trust
Stanley B. Catlett: trust
Merry Knowles: trust
James H. Milligan: trust
Lois Darlene Milligan: trust
Margaret L. Milligan: trust
Michael Milligan: trust

APPLICATION INFORMATION
Initial Approach: Send brief letter of inquiry describing program or project. Deadline is October 1.

Restrictions on Giving: Does not support individuals.

GRANTS ANALYSIS
Number of Grants: 21
Highest Grant: $12,500
Typical Range: $1,000 to $5,000
Disclosure Period: 1991

RECENT GRANTS
12,500 Salk Institute for Biological Studies, San Diego, CA
5,000 Heritage Hall School, Oklahoma City, OK — books and supplies
5,000 Jane Brooks School for Deaf, Chickasha, OK — dormitory mortgage
5,000 Mount St. Mary School, Oklahoma City, OK — endowment funding
4,000 Bishop McGuiness High School, Oklahoma City, OK — new wing
4,000 Oklahoma Christian College, Oklahoma City, OK — equipment for laboratories
4,000 Oklahoma Medical Research, Oklahoma City, OK — library
3,800 St. Gregory's College, Shawnee, OK — satellite dish and video camera recorder
3,000 Mercy Hospice, Oklahoma City, OK — staff training
3,000 Oklahoma Medical Research, Oklahoma City, OK — Fleming Scholars program

Raskin Foundation, Hirsch and Braine

CONTACT
William W. Prager, Jr.
Vice President
Hirsch and Braine Raskin Fdn.
270 Madison Avenue, Rm. 1201
New York, NY 10016

FINANCIAL SUMMARY
Recent Giving: $108,000 (fiscal 1992); $134,600 (fiscal 1991); $104,600 (fiscal 1990)
Assets: $2,259,560 (fiscal year ending February 28, 1992); $2,215,245 (fiscal 1991); $2,202,893 (fiscal 1990)
EIN: 13-6085867

CONTRIBUTIONS SUMMARY
Donor(s): the late Hirsch Raskin, the late Braine Raskin
Typical Recipients: • *Civic & Public Affairs:* ethnic/minority organizations, women's affairs • *Education:* colleges & universities, minority education • *Health:* hospitals • *Religion:* religious organizations, synagogues • *Science:* scientific institutes • *Social Services:* community service organizations, youth organizations
Grant Types: general support and scholarship
Geographic Distribution: focus on New York, NY

GIVING OFFICERS
William W. Prager, Jr.: dir, vp
William W. Prager, Sr.: dir, secy
Rose Raskin: dir, pres

APPLICATION INFORMATION
Initial Approach: Send brief letter of inquiry describing program. There are no deadlines.

GRANTS ANALYSIS
Number of Grants: 9
Highest Grant: $40,000
Typical Range: $2,000 to $5,000
Disclosure Period: fiscal year ending February 28, 1992

RECENT GRANTS
40,000 American Committee for the Weizmann Institute, New York, NY
38,000 United Jewish Appeal Federation of Jewish Philanthropies, Washington, DC
5,500 American Friends of Hebrew University, New York, NY
5,000 Hadassah Hospital, New York, NY
5,000 New Israel Fund, New York, NY
5,000 Project Interchange, New York, NY
5,000 US Holocaust Memorial Museum, Washington, DC
2,500 Congregation Ha Avas Achim, New York, NY
2,000 YMCA, New York, NY

Raskob Foundation, Bill

CONTACT
Patricia M. Garey
1st Vice President
Bill Raskob Fdn.
PO Box 4019
Wilmington, DE 19807
(302) 655-4440

FINANCIAL SUMMARY
Recent Giving: $194,950 (1991); $137,850 (1990); $174,600 (1989)
Assets: $3,204,683 (1991); $2,890,942 (1990); $2,973,087 (1989)
EIN: 51-0110185

CONTRIBUTIONS SUMMARY
Donor(s): the late John J. Raskob, the late Helena S. Raskob Corcoran
Grant Types: loan

GIVING OFFICERS
Nina B. Bennett: trust
Theodore H. Bremekamp III: trust
Patsy R. Bremer: trust
William S. Bremer: trust
Gerard S. Garey: dir, secy
Patricia M. Garey: dir, vp
Sister Pat Geuting: trust
Alexandra M. Kupis: asst treas
Jakob T. Raskob: trust
William F. Raskob III: trust
Edward H. Robinson: dir, pres
Kathleen D. Smith: dir, treas
J. Michael Stanton, Jr.: trust

APPLICATION INFORMATION
Initial Approach: The foundation strongly suggests all applicants first apply for government loans or grants. Currently, no applications accepted from incoming students on any level, foreign students, or American students studying abroad.

OTHER THINGS TO KNOW
Provides loans to individuals for higher education.
Publications: Application Guidelines

Raskob Foundation for Catholic Activities

CONTACT
Gerard S. Garey
President
Raskob Foundation for Catholic Activities
Kennett Pke. and Montchanin Rd.
PO Box 4019
Wilmington, DE 19807
(302) 655-4440

FINANCIAL SUMMARY
Recent Giving: $3,838,369 (1992); $3,614,120 (1991); $3,550,315 (1990)
Assets: $92,893,000 (1992); $93,739,776 (1991); $82,620,335 (1990)
Gifts Received: $1,100 (1991)
EIN: 51-0070060

CONTRIBUTIONS SUMMARY
Donor(s): The Raskob Foundation was established in 1945 by John J. Raskob and his wife, Helena S. Raskob. Mr. Raskob (d. 1950) was vice president of DuPont, chairman of the board of General Motors, and one of the builders of the Empire State Building. The foundation that he established is unusual in that it is a membership corporation, with the membership made up primarily of Raskob family members. There are over 90 members.
Typical Recipients: • *Education:* colleges & universities, community & junior colleges, faculty development, private education (precollege), religious education, special education • *Health:* health organizations, hospices, hospitals • *International:* foreign educational institutions, international development/relief, international health care, international organizations • *Religion:* churches, missionary activities, religious organizations • *Social Services:* aged, child welfare, community service organizations, counseling, day care, disabled, domestic violence, drugs & alcohol, employment/job training, family planning, family services, food/clothing distribution, homes, legal aid, recreation & athletics, refugee assistance, religious welfare, shelters/homelessness, volun-

teer services, youth organizations

Grant Types: capital, general support, project, and seed money

Geographic Distribution: national and international

GIVING OFFICERS

Ann R. Borden: trust-at-large

Ron P. Brown: southeast area trust

Helen R. Doordan: trust-at-large, mem communicating & coordinating & other comms *PHIL AFFIL* dir: Raskob (Bill) Foundation

Michael G. Duffy: 2nd vp

Gerard S. Garey: pres, ceo, ex-officio trust, mem communicating & coordinating

Anthony W. Raskob: chmn bd trusts, mem communicating & coordinating & other comms

B. Russell Raskob: corp secy

Jakob T. Raskob: southwest area trust, mem communicating & coordinating comm

William F. Raskob III: treas, trust, mem communicating & coordinating & other comms *PHIL AFFIL* dir: Raskob (Bill) Foundation

Dana P. Robinson: trust-at-large

Edward H. Robinson: first vp

Kerry A. Robinson: northeast area trust

APPLICATION INFORMATION

Initial Approach:

The foundation should be contacted by letter to determine eligibilty and obtain an application form and guidelines.

A full application requires a completed original application form; narrative summary of the proposal (not to exceed five pages); detailed budget of the proposed project; copy of the latest annual auditor's report or financial statement, listing actual income, assets, and expenditures; and a letter from the Ordinary of the Diocese (where the project will take place) commenting on the proposed project.

Applications for the spring board of trustees' meeting must be received between December 8th and February 8th. Applications for the fall meeting must be received between June 8th and August 8th. Applicants are urged to submit applications as early as possible during these time periods.

The board of trustees meets twice a year, in the spring and fall. Applications are considered on their merits. Need and the good to be accomplished are prime considerations. It is the board's policy to stretch its funds to help as many different Catholic activities as it can. Most grants are, therefore, under $12,000.

Restrictions on Giving: The foundation only accepts applications from Roman Catholic tax-exempt organizations listed in the *Official Catholic Directory* published by P.J. Kenedy & Sons, New York. The foundation does not accept applications for debt reduction, scholarly research leading to a degree, continuing subsidies, or for after-the-fact funding. It makes no grants to individuals or for tuition, scholarships, fellowships, or endowments. As a general rule, capital campaigns and construction projects have a low priority.

OTHER THINGS TO KNOW

The foundation has a particular interest in projects in which self-help and local support are demonstrated.

Publications: biennial report

GRANTS ANALYSIS

Total Grants: $3,838,369

Number of Grants: 630

Highest Grant: $50,000

Typical Range: $1,000 to $12,000

Disclosure Period: 1992

Note: Recent grants are derived from a 1991 Form 990.

RECENT GRANTS

100,000 Our Lady of Solace Parish, Syracuse, NY — repair roof of parish school

100,000 Pennsylvania Catholic Conference, Harrisburg, PA — research/publicity to raise awareness of value and quality of Catholic education and parental choice in education

70,000 Catholic Relief Services, Baltimore, MD — to assist refugee Kurds in Mid-East to aid Bangledesh cyclone victims

50,000 Diocese of Wilmington, Wilmington, DE — consultant

fees/salaries/operating costs of a development/endowment campaign for Diocesan elementary and secondary schools

50,000 Fr. Martin's Ashley, Havre de Grace, MD — construct/furnish a medical wing in new building of inpatient treatment center for alcoholics/chemically-addicted

45,000 Salpointe Catholic High School, Tucson, AZ — toward capital campaign

30,000 National Black Catholic Congress, Baltimore, MD — work shops for training clergy, African Ministries Program, lay leaders

25,000 Funding and Donors Interested in Catholic Activities, Washington, DC — 1991 membership dues and program expenses

25,000 Paulist Productions, Pacific Palisades, CA — toward production costs on a film on Dorothy Day

25,000 Saints Peter and Paul Parish, Easton, MD — toward construction of a modular, 8-classroom building for the high school

Rasmussen Foundation

CONTACT

Rasmussen Foundation
2360 Shasta Way
Simi Valley, CA 93065-1800

FINANCIAL SUMMARY

Recent Giving: $39,230 (1990)

Assets: $2,147,190 (1990)

Gifts Received: $594,150 (1990)

EIN: 77-0166925

CONTRIBUTIONS SUMMARY

Typical Recipients: • *Arts & Humanities:* ethnic arts, muse-

ums/galleries, public broadcasting • *Education:* colleges & universities • *Health:* health organizations, single-disease health associations • *Social Services:* community service organizations, youth organizations

Grant Types: general support and research

GIVING OFFICERS

Dean Rasmussen: pres

Larry Rasmussen: vp

Vicki Rasmussen: cfo

APPLICATION INFORMATION

Initial Approach: The foundation reports it only makes contributions to preselected organizations and does not accept unsolicited requests for funds.

GRANTS ANALYSIS

Total Grants: $39,230

Highest Grant: $10,900

Typical Range: $1,000 to $10,900

Disclosure Period: 1990

RECENT GRANTS

10,900 Henry Mayo Newhall Memorial Health Foundation, Valencia, CA

10,000 Boy and Girls Scout of Santa Clarita Valley, Newhall, CA

5,000 Simon Wiesenthal Center, Los Angeles, CA

2,500 American Red Cross, Los Angeles Chapter, Valencia, CA

2,500 Craft and Folk Arts Museum, Long Beach, CA

2,500 KCET, Public Television, Los Angeles, CA

1,800 College of the Canyon Foundation, Valencia, CA

1,000 Assistance Guild of S. Clarita, Newhall, CA

1,000 Dystonia Medical Research Foundation, Beverly Hills, CA

1,000 St. Labre Indian School, Ashland, MT

Ratner Foundation, Milton M.

CONTACT
Charles R. McDonald
V.P. and Secretary
Milton M. Ratner Fdn.
17515 West Nine Mile Rd., Ste. 875
Southfield, MI 48075
(313) 424-9373

FINANCIAL SUMMARY
Recent Giving: $209,300 (fiscal 1990); $218,300 (fiscal 1989); $190,500 (fiscal 1988)
Assets: $5,668,196 (fiscal 1990); $5,548,520 (fiscal 1989); $5,016,032 (fiscal 1988)
EIN: 38-6160330

CONTRIBUTIONS SUMMARY
Donor(s): Milton M. Ratner Trust
Typical Recipients: • *Arts & Humanities:* libraries, music • *Civic & Public Affairs:* municipalities • *Education:* colleges & universities, education funds, private education (precollege), religious education • *Health:* hospitals, medical research, pediatric health, single-disease health associations • *Religion:* religious organizations • *Social Services:* recreation & athletics, united funds, volunteer services
Grant Types: capital, endowment, general support, project, research, and scholarship
Geographic Distribution: focus on MI and GA

GIVING OFFICERS
Mary Jo Ratner Corley: pres, trust
J. Beverly Langford: treas, trust
Charles R. McDonald: vp, secy, trust

APPLICATION INFORMATION
Initial Approach: Send brief letter describing program. Deadline is September 15.
Restrictions on Giving: Does not support individuals.

GRANTS ANALYSIS
Number of Grants: 42
Highest Grant: $40,000
Typical Range: $1,000 to $10,000
Disclosure Period: fiscal year ending August 31, 1991

RECENT GRANTS
40,000 Emory University, Atlanta, GA
10,000 Berry College, Rome, GA
10,000 Calhoun High School, Calhoun, GA
10,000 Children's Hospital Medical Center, Detroit, MI
10,000 Cumberland College, Williamsburg, KY
10,000 Shorter College, Rome, GA
10,000 Temple Beth-El, Dalton, GA
10,000 Union College of Kentucky, Barbourville, KY
10,000 United Way, Calhoun, GA
 8,000 Jewish Welfare Federation, New Haven, CT

Ratshesky Foundation, A. C.

CONTACT
Cecily Morse
A. C. Ratshesky Fdn.
38 Concord Ave.
Cambridge, MA 02138
(617) 547-4590

FINANCIAL SUMMARY
Recent Giving: $196,000 (1991); $141,000 (1989); $164,800 (1988)
Assets: $5,495,290 (1991); $3,408,299 (1989); $3,070,577 (1988)
Gifts Received: $522,771 (1991)
Fiscal Note: In 1991, contributions were received from estate of Hetty Koffenburgh.
EIN: 04-6017426

CONTRIBUTIONS SUMMARY
Donor(s): the late A. C. Ratshesky, and family
Typical Recipients: • *Arts & Humanities:* dance, music • *Civic & Public Affairs:* civil rights, ethnic/minority organizations, law & justice, philanthropic organizations, public policy, urban & community affairs • *Health:* hospitals, pediatric health, public health • *Religion:* religious organizations • *Social Services:* child welfare, community service organizations, counseling, family planning, united funds, youth organizations
Grant Types: capital, emergency, general support, operating expenses, project, and scholarship
Geographic Distribution: focus on the greater Boston, MA, area

GIVING OFFICERS
Roberta Morse Levy: trust
Edith Morse Milender: trust
Alan R. Morse, Jr.: trust, treas
Eric Robert Morse: trust, secy
John Morse, Jr.: trust, vp
Theresa Morse: trust, pres
Timothy Morse: trust

APPLICATION INFORMATION
Initial Approach: Application form required. There are no deadlines.

OTHER THINGS TO KNOW
Publications: Biennial report, Application Guidelines

GRANTS ANALYSIS
Number of Grants: 91
Highest Grant: $10,000
Typical Range: $1,000 to $2,000
Disclosure Period: 1991

RECENT GRANTS
10,000 AGM Summer Camp, Boston, MA
10,000 AGM Summer Fund, Boston, MA
 5,000 Planned Parenthood Federation of America, Cambridge, MA
 4,000 United South End Settlement Houses, Boston, MA
 3,500 New England Conservatory of Music, Boston, MA
 3,000 Associated Grantmakers of Massachusetts, Boston, MA
 3,000 Boston Ballet Company, Boston, MA
 3,000 Dimock Community Health Center, Dimock, MA
 3,000 La Alianza Hispana, Boston, MA
 2,500 Wang Center, Boston, MA

Rauch Foundation

CONTACT
Allen Greenblah
Rauch Fdn.
225 West 34th St.
New York, NY 10001

FINANCIAL SUMMARY
Recent Giving: $374,040 (fiscal 1991); $880,480 (fiscal 1990); $648,700 (fiscal 1989)
Assets: $15,473,353 (fiscal year ending November 30, 1991); $13,434,795 (fiscal 1990); $13,520,530 (fiscal 1989)
Gifts Received: $514,500 (fiscal 1991); $100,216 (fiscal 1990); $678,043 (fiscal 1989)
EIN: 11-2001717

CONTRIBUTIONS SUMMARY
Donor(s): Philip J. Rauch, Louis Rauch
Typical Recipients: • *Arts & Humanities:* museums/galleries, music • *Education:* colleges & universities, private education (precollege) • *Health:* hospitals, medical research • *Religion:* churches • *Social Services:* aged, child welfare, family services, homes, youth organizations
Grant Types: conference/seminar, project, research, and seed money
Geographic Distribution: focus on east coast states between Boston, MA, and Washington, DC

GIVING OFFICERS
Nancy R. Douzinas: vp, dir
Gerald I. Lustig: vp, dir
Louis Rauch: pres, dir
Philip J. Rauch: vp

APPLICATION INFORMATION
Initial Approach: Contributes only to preselected organizations.
Restrictions on Giving: Does not support individuals or provide deficit financing, loans, or scholarships.

GRANTS ANALYSIS
Highest Grant: $20,000
Disclosure Period: fiscal year ending November 30, 1991
Note: 1991 grants list not provided.

RECENT GRANTS
20,000 Wells College, Aurora, NY

11,000 St. Christopher Ottilie
6,540 Wartburg Lutheran Services, Dubuque, IA
5,000 Smith College, Northampton, MA
3,000 Brevard Music Center, Brevard, NC
3,000 Brookville Reformed Church, Brookville, NY
3,000 Friends Academy
2,000 Baptist Home of Brooklyn, Brooklyn, NY
2,000 Experiment in International Living
2,000 I.N.N.

Ravenswood Aluminum Corp.

Sales: $240.0 million
Employees: 1,350
Headquarters: Ravenswood, WV
SIC Major Group: Primary Metal Industries

CONTACT
Carol Crow
Administrative Assistant
Ravenswood Aluminum Corp.
PO Box 98
Ravenswood, WV 26164
(304) 273-6000

CONTRIBUTIONS SUMMARY
Operating Locations: WV (Ravenswood)

CORP. OFFICERS
R. Emmett Boyle: *CURR EMPL* chmn, pres, ceo: Ormet Corp. *CORP AFFIL* pres, ceo: Ormet Corp
Bob Holliday: *CURR EMPL* cfo: Ravenswood Aluminum Corp
Donald W. Worlledge: *CURR EMPL* pres, coo: Ravenswood Aluminum Corp

Ray Foundation

CONTACT
Shirley Bradenburg
Ray Fdn.
1111 Third Avenue, Ste. 2770
Seattle, WA 98101
(206) 292-9101

FINANCIAL SUMMARY
Recent Giving: $467,234 (fiscal 1992); $410,867 (fiscal 1991); $70,431 (fiscal 1990)
Assets: $12,436,969 (fiscal year ending June 30, 1992);

$11,682,559 (fiscal 1991); $11,300,087 (fiscal 1990)
EIN: 81-0288819

CONTRIBUTIONS SUMMARY
Donor(s): James C. Ray, the late Joan L. Ray
Typical Recipients: • *Arts & Humanities:* history/historic preservation, museums/galleries, music • *Education:* colleges & universities, community & junior colleges, private education (precollege) • *Health:* mental health • *Social Services:* child welfare, community service organizations, drugs & alcohol, youth organizations
Grant Types: capital, emergency, general support, multiyear/continuing support, operating expenses, project, research, and seed money
Geographic Distribution: focus on AZ, OR, and WA

GIVING OFFICERS
Shirley C. Brandenburg: secy, treas
John S. Darrell: dir
Dennis O. Dugan: dir
James C. Ray: pres, dir
June M. Ray: dir

APPLICATION INFORMATION
Initial Approach: Send brief letter of inquiry and full proposal. Deadlines are September 15 and April 15. Board meets in November and June. Decisions are made immediately following board meetings.
Restrictions on Giving: Does not support individuals.

OTHER THINGS TO KNOW
Publications: Application Guidelines

GRANTS ANALYSIS
Number of Grants: 19
Highest Grant: $125,000
Typical Range: $5,000 to $15,000
Disclosure Period: fiscal year ending June 30, 1992

RECENT GRANTS
125,000 EAA Aviation Foundation, Oshkosh, WI
100,000 Monticello, Charlottesville, VA
100,000 St. Anne's Belfield School, Charlottesville, VA
30,000 EAA Aviation Foundation, Oshkosh, WI

18,000 Roosevelt School District 66, Phoenix, AZ
15,000 Children's Trust Foundation, Seattle, WA
15,000 Phoenix Symphony, Phoenix, AZ
10,000 Buffalo Bill Historical Center, Cody, WY
10,000 EAA Aviation Foundation, Oshkosh, WI
10,000 Seattle Central Community College Foundation, Seattle, WA

Raychem Corp.

Sales: $1.29 billion
Employees: 11,415
Headquarters: Menlo Park, CA
SIC Major Group: Primary Metal Industries

CONTACT
Michal Mendelsohn
Community Relations
Raychem Corp.
300 Constitution Dr.
Mail-Stop 111-8708
Menlo Park, CA 94025
(415) 361-4355

FINANCIAL SUMMARY
Fiscal Note: Company gives directly. Annual Giving Range: $250,000 to $500,000

CONTRIBUTIONS SUMMARY
Typical Recipients: • *Civic & Public Affairs:* general • *Education:* general
Grant Types: award
Nonmonetary Support Types: donated equipment, donated products, in-kind services, and loaned employees
Geographic Distribution: in headquarters and operating communities
Operating Locations: CA (Menlo Park, San Jose, Santa Clara), TN (Oak Ridge)

CORP. OFFICERS
Paul M. Cook: *B* Ridgewood NJ 1924 *ED* MA Inst Tech 1947 *CURR EMPL* chmn: Raychem Corp *CORP AFFIL* dir: Catalytica Assocs, Chem Fabrics Corp, SRI Intl
Michael T. Everett: *B* Nashua NH 1949 *ED* Dartmouth Coll BA 1971; Univ PA JD 1974 *CURR EMPL* vp, chief legal off, sec: Raychem Corp
Robert J. Saldich: *B* New York NY 1933 *ED* Rice Univ

BSChE; Harvard Univ MBA *CURR EMPL* pres, ceo: Raychem Corp *CORP AFFIL* pres: Raynet Corp *NONPR AFFIL* mem: CA Roundtable, San Francisco Comm Foreign Rels

GIVING OFFICERS
Michal Mendelsohn: *CURR EMPL* commun rels: Raychem Corp

APPLICATION INFORMATION
Initial Approach: *Initial Contact:* brief letter of inquiry *Include Information On:* a description of organization and amount requested

Raymark Corp.

Sales: $27.1 million
Employees: 358
Headquarters: Manheim, PA
SIC Major Group: Holding & Other Investment Offices, Industrial Machinery & Equipment, Textile Mill Products, and Transportation Equipment

CONTACT
Elaine Gantz
Employee Relations
Raymark Corp.
123 East Stiegel St.
Manheim, PA 17545
(717) 665-2211

CONTRIBUTIONS SUMMARY
Operating Locations: PA (Manheim)

CORP. OFFICERS
Bradley C. Smith: *CURR EMPL* pres: Raymark Corp

Raymond Corp. / Raymond Foundation

Sales: $140.7 million
Employees: 1,137
Headquarters: Binghamton, NY
SIC Major Group: Industrial Machinery & Equipment

CONTACT
Terri Brant
Assistant Executive Secretary
Raymond Corp.
45 Lewis St.
Binghamton, NY 13901
(607) 771-8098

FINANCIAL SUMMARY
Recent Giving: $34,000
(1990); $120,374 (1989);
$54,503 (1988)
Assets: $1,349,530 (1990);
$1,424,461 (1989); $2,561,104
(1988)
Gifts Received: $34,650
(1990); $55,000 (1989);
$41,000 (1988)
Fiscal Note: In 1989, contributions were received from the
Raymond Corporation.
EIN: 16-6047847

CONTRIBUTIONS SUMMARY
Typical Recipients: • *Arts & Humanities:* history/historic
preservation, public broadcasting • *Civic & Public Affairs:*
public policy, rural affairs
• *Education:* business education, colleges & universities,
education associations, literacy
• *Health:* health organizations,
single-disease health associations • *Social Services:* community service organizations, recreation & athletics, united
funds, volunteer services,
youth organizations
Grant Types: capital, matching, and project
Geographic Distribution: limited to areas of company operations in NY and CA
Operating Locations: NY
(Binghamton), VI (St. Thomas)

CORP. OFFICERS
Ross K. Colquhoun: *CURR EMPL* pres, ceo, dir: Raymond
Corp
George G. Raymond, Jr.: *B*
Brooklyn NY 1921 *ED* Cornell
Univ 1942 *CURR EMPL* chmn,
dir: Raymond Corp *CORP AFFIL* chmn: Raymond Indus
Equipment Ltd; dir: GN
Johnston Equipment Co Ltd,
Natl Bank & Trust Co of Norwich NY, Rath & Strong, Security Mutual Life Ins Co, Tier
Parts Warehousing

GIVING OFFICERS
James F. Barton: chmn
Terri Brant: asst exec secy
Robert T. Cline: trust *B* Binghamton NY 1941 *ED* Cornell
Univ 1964; State Univ NY

1967 *CURR EMPL* vp (org &
planning): Crowley Foods
Robert C. Eldred: trust
Patrick J. McManus: treas
Jean C. Raymond: trust
Stephen S. Raymond: vchmn
George G. Raymond III: exec
secy
George G. Raymond, Jr.: trust
John Riley: trust
David E. Sonn: trust
Jeanette L. Williamson: trust
Lee J. Wolf: trust *B* Allenton
WI 1915 *ED* WI St Coll 1940;
Marquette Univ 1947 *CURR EMPL* dir: Raymond Corp
Madeleine R. Young: trust

APPLICATION INFORMATION
Initial Approach: Send detailed request; other sources of
funding; federal tax-exempt determination letter; and annual
budget, annual report, and project budget. There are no deadlines. Board meets March,
June, September, and December.
Restrictions on Giving: Does
not support individuals, endowment funds, or operating budgets. Does not make loans.

OTHER THINGS TO KNOW
Publications: Application
Guidelines

GRANTS ANALYSIS
Number of Grants: 5
Highest Grant: $17,500
Typical Range: $2,500 to
$17,500
Disclosure Period: 1990

RECENT GRANTS
17,500 Greene-PTA Playground
5,000 Alfred University,
Alfred, NY
5,000 Lourdes Hospital,
Binghamton, NY
4,000 Triangle Fire Department
2,500 Greene Historical
Society

Raymond Educational Foundation

CONTACT
Elden D. Bills
President
Raymond Educational Fdn.
PO Box 1423
Flagstaff, AZ 86002
(602) 779-6263

FINANCIAL SUMMARY
Recent Giving: $135,000 (fiscal 1992); $166,600 (fiscal
1991); $144,400 (fiscal 1990)
Assets: $2,553,458 (fiscal year
ending April 30, 1992);
$2,419,981 (fiscal 1991);
$2,261,516 (fiscal 1990)
EIN: 86-6050920

CONTRIBUTIONS SUMMARY
Donor(s): the late R. O. Raymond
Typical Recipients: • *Arts & Humanities:* community arts,
history/historic preservation,
music • *Education:* arts education, colleges & universities,
education associations, education funds, medical education,
student aid • *Health:* hospices
• *Science:* observatories &
planetariums • *Social Services:*
community service organizations
Grant Types: capital, multiyear/continuing support, and
scholarship
Geographic Distribution: limited to Coconino County, AZ

GIVING OFFICERS
Catherine Adel: trust
Valeen T. Aery: trust
Eldon Bills: dir, evp
Platt C. Cline: trust
Robert E. Gaylord: secy
Henry L. Giclas: dir, pres
Wilfred Killip: trust
Joyce Leamon: trust
John Stilley: dir, treas
Ralph Wheeler: trust

APPLICATION INFORMATION
Initial Approach: Send brief
letter of inquiry describing program. There are no deadlines.

OTHER THINGS TO KNOW
Publications: Program Policy
Statement

GRANTS ANALYSIS
Number of Grants: 11
Highest Grant: $100,600

Typical Range: $1,000 to
$10,000
Disclosure Period: fiscal year
ending April 30, 1992

RECENT GRANTS
100,600 North Arizona University, Flagstaff,
AZ
10,000 Flagstaff Symphony, Flagstaff,
AZ
4,000 Northern Arizona
University, Flagstaff, AZ
4,000 Northland Hospice,
Flagstaff, AZ
3,500 Lowell Observatory, Flagstaff, AZ
3,500 Pioneer Historical
Society, Flagstaff,
AZ
3,500 Sunshine Rescue
Mission, Flagstaff,
AZ — aid to poor
2,400 Northern Arizona
University, Flagstaff, AZ — music
camp
1,500 Flagstaff Unified
School, Flagstaff,
AZ
1,000 Flagstaff Festival
of Arts, Flagstaff,
AZ

Rayovac Corp.
Sales: $402.0 million
Employees: 2,500
Headquarters: Madison, WI
SIC Major Group: Electronic &
Other Electrical Equipment

CONTACT
Jolene Woodlee
Public Affairs Administrator
Rayovac Corp.
601 Rayovac Dr.
PO Box 44960
Madison, WI 53744-4960
(608) 275-3340

CONTRIBUTIONS SUMMARY
Operating Locations: WI
(Madison)

CORP. OFFICERS
Judith D. Pyle: *CURR EMPL*
vchmn: Rayovac Corp
Thomas F. Pyle: *B* Philadelphia PA 1941 *ED* LaSalle Coll
1962; Univ WI 1963 *CURR EMPL* chmn, pres, ceo: Rayovac Corp *CORP AFFIL* dir:
First WI Natl Bank Madison,
Johnson Worldwide Assocs, Kewaunee Scientific Corp
Marvin Siegert: *CURR EMPL*
vp, cfo: Rayovac Corp

Raytheon Co.

Sales: $9.06 billion
Employees: 63,400
Headquarters: Lexington, MA
SIC Major Group: Heavy Construction Except Building Construction, Instruments & Related Products, Oil & Gas Extraction, and Printing & Publishing

CONTACT
Janet Taylor
Administrator, Corporate Contributions
Raytheon Company
141 Spring St.
Lexington, MA 02173
(617) 862-6600

FINANCIAL SUMMARY
Recent Giving: $5,750,000 (1993 est.); $5,000,000 (1992 approx.); $5,750,000 (1990 approx.)
Fiscal Note: All contributions are made directly by the company.
EIN: 04-6052788

CONTRIBUTIONS SUMMARY
Typical Recipients: • *Arts & Humanities:* museums/galleries • *Civic & Public Affairs:* environmental affairs, nonprofit management, urban & community affairs • *Education:* colleges & universities, engineering education, minority education, science/technology education • *Health:* geriatric health, health care cost containment, public health • *Social Services:* community service organizations, disabled, united funds, youth organizations
Grant Types: capital, challenge, and project
Nonmonetary Support Types: donated products
Note: Estimated nonmonetary suppor is not available but is included in the figures above (See "Other Things You Shoul Know" for details). For information, contact Janet Taylor.
Geographic Distribution: operating locations, especially eastern New England
Operating Locations: AL (Huntsville), CA (Goleta, Mountain View), MA (Andover, Bedford, Billerica, Burlington, Lexington, Lowell, Marlboro, Northboro, Quincy, Sudbury, Tewksbury, Waltham, Wayland), NH (Hudson, Manchester), NM (White Sands), RI (Portsmouth), TN (Bristol)

CORP. OFFICERS
Max Emil Bleck: *B* Buffalo NY 1927 *ED* Rensselaer Polytec Inst BS 1949; Univ Buffalo 1950-1951 *CURR EMPL* pres, dir: Raytheon Co *CORP AFFIL* chmn, ceo, dir: Beech Aircraft Corp
Dennis J. Picard: *CURR EMPL* chmn, ceo, pres, dir: Raytheon Co

GIVING OFFICERS
Janet C. Taylor: *CURR EMPL* mgr, corp contributions: Raytheon Co

APPLICATION INFORMATION
Initial Approach: *Initial Contact:* cover letter and written proposal (five pages or less) *Include Information On:* brief background description of the organization's origins and current programs; description of request, need, and specific objectives to be addressed, implementation plan, and relevance of request to company's corporate contributions program; specific amount requested, time period to be covered, and list of other confirmed or expected sources of support; description of geographic area and population groups to be served; copy of IRS letter indicating 501(c)(3) tax-exemption; current operating budget, budget for requested project, and list of current corporate and foundation grants; list of the board of directors and their affiliations *When to Submit:* March 31, June 30, and September 30 *Note:* Telephone inquiries about a proposal's eligibility or status are not encouraged and personal interviews are not always possible. Follow-up contact for additional information is made by Raytheon representatives as needed.
Restrictions on Giving: Generally does not support individuals; religious, fraternal, political, athletic, or veterans organizations; disease-specific organizations; independent elementary and secondary schools; organizations whose activities are primarily international; United Way affiliates for operating support; basic research projects; organizations serving limited numbers of clients or requests for sponsorship of local groups or individuals to participate in regional or national competitions or events;

productions for public television or radio; private foundations; or organizations whose applications have been denied within the past 12 months.

OTHER THINGS TO KNOW
Multiple-year grants are considered for capital purposes or for efforts to address a program or management component within a defined timetable so that assessment of quality and progress can be made.
Range of one-year grants is $1,000 to $10,000; typical size is $5,000. Multiyear commitments paid over three to five years range from $10,000 to $250,000.
Requests for product donations of kitchen and laundry appliances and marine electronics are considered in lieu of, or as a supplement to, cash grants. These items may be requested on a one-time basis to meet specific programmatic needs or to be used for fund-raising purposes.

GRANTS ANALYSIS
Total Grants: $5,000,000
Typical Range: $1,000 to $10,000
Disclosure Period: 1992
Note: Recent grants are derived from a 1992 grants list.

RECENT GRANTS
Adaptive Environments, Boston, MA — broad educational and awareness campaign called the "Community Access Initiative"
Associated Grantmakers of Massachusetts, MA — "Summer Funding"
Boston's University Hospital, Boston, MA — "The Elders Living at Home Program"
Bristol Regional Rehabilitation Center, Bristol, TN
Children's Hospital, Boston, MA
Community School of Music and Arts, Mountain View, CA
Discovery Museums, Acton, MA
Museum of Afro-American History, Boston, MA
Red Acre Farm Hearing Dog Center, Stow, MA
Santa Barbara Industry Education Council, Santa Barbara, CA — "Adopt-A-School"

Raytheon Engineers & Constructors

Sales: $610.0 million
Employees: 6,000
Parent Company: Raytheon Co.
Headquarters: Philadelphia, PA
SIC Major Group: Engineering & Management Services and General Building Contractors

CONTACT
John Renouf
Vice President, Human Resources
Raytheon Engineers & Constructors
PO Box 8223
Philadelphia, PA 19101
(215) 422-4400

FINANCIAL SUMMARY
Fiscal Note: Company does not disclose contributions figures.

CONTRIBUTIONS SUMMARY
Company sponsors employee matching gift program; also supports community organizations.
Typical Recipients: • *Arts & Humanities:* general • *Civic & Public Affairs:* general • *Education:* general • *Health:* general • *Social Services:* general
Grant Types: matching
Geographic Distribution: primarily headquarters area
Operating Locations: CO (Denver), FL (Tampa), IL (Chicago), MA (Boston), PA (Philadelphia)

CORP. OFFICERS
Charles Q. Miller: *CURR EMPL* pres, ceo, dir: Un Engineers & Constructors Intl
George W. Sarney: *CURR EMPL* chmn, dir: Un Engineers & Constructors Intl

APPLICATION INFORMATION
Initial Approach: Send brief letter of inquiry. There are no deadlines.

RB&W Corp.

Sales: $164.2 million
Employees: 1,100
Headquarters: Mentor, OH
SIC Major Group: Fabricated Metal Products, Industrial Machinery & Equipment, and Wholesale Trade—Durable Goods

CONTACT

Kent Holcumb
Vice President, Human Resources
RB&W Corp.
5970 Heisley Rd.
Mentor, OH 44060
(216) 357-1200

FINANCIAL SUMMARY

Fiscal Note: Annual Giving Range: less than $100,000

CONTRIBUTIONS SUMMARY

Support goes to local education, human service, arts, and civic organizations. Company reports 50% goes to health and human services; 20% each to the arts and civic affairs; and 10% to education.
Typical Recipients: • *Arts & Humanities:* general • *Civic & Public Affairs:* general • *Education:* general • *Social Services:* general
Nonmonetary Support Types: donated equipment and donated products
Geographic Distribution: headquarters and operating locations including Rock Falls, IL; Chicago, IL; Kent, OH; Corapolis, PA; and Dayton, OH
Operating Locations: IL (Chicago, Rock Falls), OH (Dayton, Kent, Mentor), PA (Corapolis)

CORP. OFFICERS

Ronald C. Drabik: *CURR EMPL* vp, cfo: RB&W Corp
John J. Lohrman: *B* Ellsworth IA 1920 *ED* Creighton Univ 1941; Univ PA 1949 *CURR EMPL* chmn, ceo, dir: RB&W Corp *CORP AFFIL* dir: Bank One Cleveland NA, GArco Machinery, Lamson & Sessions Canada Ltd, Thomas William Lench Holdings Ltd

APPLICATION INFORMATION

Initial Approach: Send brief letter of inquiry, including a description of the organization, amount requested, purpose of funds sought, audited financial statement, and proof of tax-exempt status. There are no deadlines.
Restrictions on Giving: Does not support individuals or political or lobbying groups.

Read Foundation, Charles L.

CONTACT

Rodger H. Herrigel
Secretary
Charles L. Read Fdn.
374 Millburn Ave.
Millburn, NJ 07841
(201) 379-5850

FINANCIAL SUMMARY

Recent Giving: $149,150 (1991); $171,500 (1990); $150,750 (1989)
Assets: $2,984,734 (1991); $2,712,312 (1990); $2,840,417 (1989)
EIN: 22-6053510

CONTRIBUTIONS SUMMARY

Donor(s): Charles L. Read
Typical Recipients: • *Arts & Humanities:* libraries • *Education:* colleges & universities, education funds • *Health:* hospitals, medical research, mental health • *Social Services:* child welfare, community service organizations, day care, shelters/homelessness, united funds, youth organizations
Grant Types: general support
Geographic Distribution: focus on NJ and NY

GIVING OFFICERS

Richard Eisenberg: vp
Saul Eisenberg: treas
Fred Herrigel III: pres
Rodger Herrigel: secy

APPLICATION INFORMATION

Initial Approach: Send brief letter of inquiry describing program. There are no deadlines.

GRANTS ANALYSIS

Number of Grants: 89
Highest Grant: $23,000
Typical Range: $500 to $1,500
Disclosure Period: 1991

RECENT GRANTS

23,000 Trust and Agency Fund Hancock Central School, Hancock, NY
11,500 Louise Adelia Read Memorial Library, Hancock, NY
10,000 Drew University, Madison, NJ
6,000 Southside Hospital, Bayshore, NY
5,000 Church of the Good Shepherd
5,000 Overlook Hospital Foundation, Summit, NJ
3,000 Bi-Cultural Day School, Stamford, CT
3,000 Episcopal Ministries of Bergen Hill, Jersey City, NJ
3,000 Lutheran Home for the Aging, Smithtown, NY
3,000 National Jewish Hospital/Research Center

Reade Industrial Fund

CONTACT

Ruth E. Forbes
Reade Industrial Fund
111 West Monroe St.
Chicago, IL 60603
(312) 461-2603

FINANCIAL SUMMARY

Recent Giving: $147,772 (1990); $146,048 (1989); $161,939 (1988)
Assets: $3,674,242 (1990); $2,627,101 (1989); $2,360,980 (1988)
EIN: 36-6048673

CONTRIBUTIONS SUMMARY

Donor(s): the late Edith M. Reade
Geographic Distribution: limited to IL residents, particularly to Chicago and its surrounding area

APPLICATION INFORMATION

Initial Approach: Application form required. There are no deadlines.

GRANTS ANALYSIS

Disclosure Period: 1990
Note: Provides grants to individuals only.

Reader's Digest Association / Reader's Digest Foundation

Sales: $2.66 billion
Employees: 7,400
Headquarters: Pleasantville, NY
SIC Major Group: Printing & Publishing

CONTACT

J. Edward Hall
President
Reader's Digest Fdn.
Pleasantville, NY 10570
(914) 241-5370

FINANCIAL SUMMARY

Recent Giving: $2,825,000 (1992 approx.); $1,938,502 (1991); $2,563,414 (1990)
Assets: $25,306,032 (1991); $20,887,772 (1990); $21,275,691 (1989)
Fiscal Note: Company also gives directly. Figures for direct giving are not available and are not included in the totals listed above.
EIN: 13-6120380

CONTRIBUTIONS SUMMARY

Typical Recipients: • *Education:* colleges & universities, journalism education, literacy
Grant Types: employee matching gifts, project, and scholarship
Geographic Distribution: nationally
Operating Locations: NY (New York, Pleasantville)

CORP. OFFICERS

George V. Grune: *B* White Plains NY 1929 *ED* Duke Univ BA 1952; Univ FL 1955-1956 *CURR EMPL* chmn, pres, ceo, coo: Readers Digest Assn *CORP AFFIL* dir: Assoc Dry Goods, Avon Products, Chem Bank, Chem NY Corp, CPC Intl, GTE Corp, Sterling Drug *NONPR AFFIL* dir: Boys Club Am; mem bd overseers, bd mgrs: Counc Conservators NY Pub Library, Counc Fin Aid Ed, Counc Foreign Rels, Inst France, Meml Sloan Kettering Cancer Ctr; mem conf bd, dir: Metro Opera Assn; mem policy comm: Bus Roundtable; trust: Duke Univ, Metro Mus Art, NY Zoological Soc, Rollins Coll Roy E Crummer Grad Sch Bus

GIVING OFFICERS

Mary Graniero: secy
Joseph M. Grecky: dir *B*
Pottsville PA 1939 *ED* Rutgers
Univ 1961 *CURR EMPL* vp
(human resources): Readers Di-
gest
George V. Grune: chmn, dir
CURR EMPL chmn, pres, ceo,
coo: Readers Digest Assn (see
above)
J. Edward Hall: pres, dir
Carole Margaret Howard: dir
B Halifax Canada 1945 *ED*
Univ CA 1967; Pace Univ 1978
CURR EMPL vp, dir pub rels
& commun policy: Readers Di-
gest Assn
Ross Jones: treas *B* New York
NY 1942 *CURR EMPL* vp,
treas: Readers Digest Assn
CORP AFFIL dir: CML Group
Inc, 59 Wall Street Fund, N Am
Reinsurance Co, NYC
Barbara J. Morgan: dir
CURR EMPL editor-in-chief
(condensed books): Readers Di-
gest Assn
John A. Pope, Jr.: dir *CURR
EMPL* vp editor-in-chief (gen-
eral books): Readers Digest
Assn
Kenneth Y. Tomlinson: dir *B*
Mt Airy NC 1944 *ED* Ran-
dolph-Macon Coll 1966 *CURR
EMPL* editor in chief: Readers
Digest
William Totten: dir

APPLICATION INFORMATION

Initial Approach: *Initial Contact:* brief letter *Include Information On:* description of project and the sponsoring
organization; description of
need, target group, and timetable; explanation of why funding would solve a problem and
meet a need; current itemized
budget for project and organization; total project cost, other
funding sources, and total requested from foundation; and
evidence of tax-exempt status
and latest IRS Form 990 *When
to Submit:* by January 15 to be
considered for second half of
year, by April 15 for educational grants for an academic
year beginning in September,
by September 15 to be considered for the following calendar
year
Restrictions on Giving: The
foundation does not support individuals or religious, veterans,
fraternal, political, environmental, or cultural organizations.
Grants are not made for dinners, audiovisual productions,

legislative or lobbying purposes, or to nontax-exempt organizations.
The foundation generally does
not support capital or endowment campaigns, medical research, health-related activities, international charities,
local chapters of national organizations, conferences, publications, or annual operating
costs.

OTHER THINGS TO KNOW

The foundation prefers to support direct service projects
rather than grants for general
support or to intermediary funding agencies.
Funding is generally one-time,
and exceptions generally are
limited to a maximum of three
consecutive years.
The foundation seeks to support those organizations that
demonstrate responsible management and that provide
timely reports to the directors
of the foundation on the dispo-
sition of funds and program results.

GRANTS ANALYSIS

Total Grants: $1,938,502
Number of Grants: 68*
Highest Grant: $50,000
Typical Range: $10,000 to
50,000
Disclosure Period: 1991
Note: Number of grants figure
excludes college scholarships
for employees' children, matching grants, and grants to organizations where employees are
volunteers. Recent grants are
derived from a 1991 Form 990.

RECENT GRANTS

50,000 Literacy Volunteers
of Westchester
County, Elmsford,
NY
50,000 Westchester Educa-
tion Coalition,
White Plains, NY
35,000 Literacy Volunteers
of New York City,
New York, NY
35,000 Local Education Initiatives, White
Plains, NY
35,000 Sister Cities International, Alexan-
dria, VA
30,000 National Press
Foundation, Wash-
ington, DC
30,000 White Plains
School District,
White Plains, NY

25,800 United Negro Col-
lege Fund, New
York, NY
25,000 Clay County Board
of Education,
Celina, TN
25,000 Direct Marketing
Foundation, New
York, NY

Reading & Bates Corp.

Revenue: $126.8 million
Employees: 1,500
Headquarters: Houston, TX
SIC Major Group: Electric, Gas
& Sanitary Services and Oil &
Gas Extraction

CONTACT

Janet Smith
Human Resources Analyst
Reading & Bates Corp.
901 Thread Needle St.
200 Easton
Houston, TX 77079
(713) 496-5000

FINANCIAL SUMMARY

Fiscal Note: Annual Giving
Range: $100,000 to $250,000

CONTRIBUTIONS SUMMARY

Support goes to local education, health and human service,
arts, and civic organizations.

Typical Recipients: • *Arts &
Humanities:* general • *Civic &
Public Affairs:* general • *Educa-
tion:* general • *Health:* general
• *Social Services:* general

Grant Types: general support

Nonmonetary Support Types:
donated equipment, loaned employees, and loaned executives

Geographic Distribution: primarily headquarters area

Operating Locations: TX
(Houston)

CORP. OFFICERS

J. T. Angel: *CURR EMPL* pres,
coo: Reading & Bates Corp

P. B. Lloyd: *CURR EMPL*
chmn, ceo: Reading & Bates
Corp

T. W. Nagel: *CURR EMPL* cfo:
Reading & Bates Corp

APPLICATION INFORMATION

Initial Approach: Send brief
letter of inquiry. There are no
deadlines.

Reasoner, Davis & Fox

Headquarters: Washington, DC

CONTACT

Philip J. Sweeney
Assistant Secretary
Bloedorn Fdn.
888 17th St., NW, Ste. 800
Washington, DC 20006
(202) 463-8282

CONTRIBUTIONS SUMMARY

Typical Recipients: • *Arts &
Humanities:* general • *Civic &
Public Affairs:* general • *Educa-
tion:* general • *Health:* general
• *Social Services:* general

Grant Types: capital, general
support, and professorship

Geographic Distribution:
only in headquarters area

Operating Locations: DC
(Washington)

APPLICATION INFORMATION

Initial Approach: Send a brief
letter of inquiry and a full proposal.

Restrictions on Giving: Does
not support individuals, religious organizations for sectarian
purposes, political or lobbying
groups, or organizations outside operating areas.

OTHER THINGS TO KNOW

Company is an original donor
to Bloedorn Foundation.

Rebsamen Companies, Inc. / Rebsamen Fund

Sales: $33.0 million
Employees: 440
Headquarters: Little Rock, AR
SIC Major Group: Insurance
Agents, Brokers & Service,
Miscellaneous Retail, Printing
& Publishing, and Wholesale
Trade—Durable Goods

CONTACT

Pat Lavender
Secretary
Rebsamen Fund
PO Box 3198
Little Rock, AR 72203
(501) 661-4800

FINANCIAL SUMMARY

Recent Giving: $151,317 (fis-
cal 1989); $126,130 (fiscal
1988)

Assets: $1,253,940 (fiscal year ending November 30, 1989); $1,118,354 (fiscal 1988)
Gifts Received: $171,875 (fiscal 1989)
Fiscal Note: In 1989, substantial contributions were from Rebsamen Companies, Inc.
EIN: 71-6053911

CONTRIBUTIONS SUMMARY
Typical Recipients: • *Arts & Humanities:* arts centers, community arts, public broadcasting • *Education:* colleges & universities, education funds, student aid • *Health:* medical research • *Religion:* religious organizations • *Social Services:* united funds, youth organizations
Grant Types: general support and scholarship
Geographic Distribution: primarily in AR
Operating Locations: AR (Little Rock)

CORP. OFFICERS
Sam C. Sowell: *B* Searcy AR 1933 *ED* Washington Univ 1957 *CURR EMPL* pres, dir: Rebsamen Co *CORP AFFIL* chmn: International Graphics Indus; dir: First Commercial Bank

GIVING OFFICERS
Patricia Lavender: secy/treas
H. Maurice Mitchell: vp
Sam C. Sowell: vp *CURR EMPL* pres, dir: Rebsamen Co (see above)
Kenneth Pat Wilson: pres

APPLICATION INFORMATION
Initial Approach: There is no particular form in which applications should be submitted. There are no deadlines.

GRANTS ANALYSIS
Number of Grants: 87
Highest Grant: $28,000
Typical Range: $200 to $2,000
Disclosure Period: fiscal year ending November 30, 1989

RECENT GRANTS
28,000 United Way, Little Rock, AR
6,000 Arkansas Arts Center, Little Rock, AR
5,000 Arkansas Center for Eye Research, Little Rock, AR
5,000 Baptist Medical System Support Center, Little Rock, AR — Nursing School
5,000 Boy Scouts of America, Little Rock, AR
5,000 Boy Scouts of America, Little Rock, AR
5,000 Independent Colleges of Arkansas, Little Rock, AR
5,000 Little Rock Boys Club, Little Rock, AR
5,000 Wildwood, Latham, NY
5,000 Winrock International Institute for Agriculture, Morrilton, AR — for goat breeding, nutrition, management, farming development

Reckitt & Colman
Sales: $570.0 million
Employees: 3,500
Parent Company: Reckitt & Colman
Headquarters: Wayne, NJ
SIC Major Group: Chemicals & Allied Products, Food & Kindred Products, and Holding & Other Investment Offices

CONTACT
Airwick Industries Inc.
1655 Valley Rd.
Wayne, NJ 07470
(201) 633-6700

CONTRIBUTIONS SUMMARY
Operating Locations: NJ (Wayne)

CORP. OFFICERS
Andrew Scott: *CURR EMPL* vp, cfo: Reckitt & Colman
Michael Turrell: *CURR EMPL* pres: Reckitt & Colman

Recognition Equipment
Sales: $155.2 million
Employees: 1,368
Headquarters: Dallas, TX
SIC Major Group: Business Services and Industrial Machinery & Equipment

CONTACT
Peggy Wisner
Chairman, Contributions Committee
Recognition Equipment
PO Box 660204
Dallas, TX 75266-0204
(214) 579-6000

FINANCIAL SUMMARY
Recent Giving: $50,000 (1993 est.)

CONTRIBUTIONS SUMMARY
Company contributes 60% of funds to health and human services; 25% to arts and humanities; and 15% to education.
Typical Recipients: • *Arts & Humanities:* arts centers, arts festivals, arts institutes, community arts, ethnic arts, history/historic preservation, museums/galleries, music, opera, performing arts, theater • *Civic & Public Affairs:* nonprofit management, safety, zoos/botanical gardens • *Education:* colleges & universities, community & junior colleges, faculty development • *Health:* emergency/ambulance services, geriatric health, health organizations, hospitals, medical research, pediatric health, public health, single-disease health associations • *Science:* scientific institutes • *Social Services:* aged, animal protection, community centers, day care, domestic violence, drugs & alcohol, food/clothing distribution, homes, shelters/homelessness, united funds, volunteer services, youth organizations
Grant Types: award
Nonmonetary Support Types: donated equipment and donated products
Geographic Distribution: Grants are awarded in headquarters and operating communities.
Operating Locations: TX (Dallas)

CORP. OFFICERS
Gilbert H. Lamphere: *CURR EMPL* chmn: Recognition Equipment
Robert Vanourek: *CURR EMPL* co-ceo: Recognition Equipment

APPLICATION INFORMATION
Initial Approach: Send a full proposal, including a description of organization, amount requested, purpose of funds

sought, recently audited financial statement, and proof of tax-exempt status.
Restrictions on Giving: Does not support individuals, religious organizations for sectarian purposes, and political or lobbying groups.

GRANTS ANALYSIS
Typical Range: $10 to $1,000

RECENT GRANTS
Baylor Medical Center, Dallas, TX
Dallas Museum of Natural History, Dallas, TX
Dallas Symphony, Dallas, TX
Irving Medical Center, Irving, TX
Irving Opera, Irving, TX
Irving Symphony, Irving, TX
Irving YMCA, Irving, TX
North Texas Leukemia Society, Dallas, TX
Society for the Prevention of Cruelty to Animals, Dallas, TX
United Way, Dallas, TX

Red Devil / Red Devil Foundation
Employees: 400
Headquarters: Union, NJ

CONTACT
Jane T. Lee
Trustee
Red Devil Foundation
2400 Vauxhall Road
Union, NJ 07083-5035
(908) 688-6900

FINANCIAL SUMMARY
Recent Giving: $10,643 (fiscal 1991); $26,979 (fiscal 1989)
Assets: $8,688 (fiscal year ending November 30, 1991); $18,101 (fiscal 1989)
Gifts Received: $10,000 (fiscal 1991); $10,000 (fiscal 1989)
EIN: 22-6063889

CONTRIBUTIONS SUMMARY
Typical Recipients: • *Arts & Humanities:* theater • *Education:* colleges & universities, student aid • *Health:* hospitals • *Social Services:* recreation & athletics, youth organizations
Grant Types: general support and scholarship
Geographic Distribution: giving primarily in NJ
Operating Locations: NJ (Union)

CORP. OFFICERS
Donald Hall: *CURR EMPL* pres: Red Devil

George L. Lee: *CURR EMPL* chmn: Red Devil

GIVING OFFICERS

George L. Lee, Jr.: trust
Jane T. Lee: mgr
John L. Lee: trust

APPLICATION INFORMATION

Initial Approach: Personnel Department informs employees. There are no deadlines.

GRANTS ANALYSIS

Number of Grants: 71
Highest Grant: $722
Typical Range: $50 to $100
Disclosure Period: fiscal year ending November 30, 1991

RECENT GRANTS

722 Papermill Play-
    house
600 Muhlenberg Col-
    lege, Muhlenberg,
    PA — scholarships
600 Rutgers University,
    Rutgers, NJ —
    scholarships
600 Rutgers University,
    Rutgers, NJ —
    scholarships
600 Rutgers University,
    Rutgers, NJ —
    scholarships
600 Rutgers University,
    Rutgers, NJ —
    scholarships
600 Somerset Medical
    Center, Somerset,
    NJ
500 Gladstone Eques-
    trian Association
500 YMCA
350 USET

Red Food Stores, Inc.

Sales: $750.0 million
Employees: 6,000
Parent Company: Pramer, Inc.
Headquarters: Chattanooga, TN
SIC Major Group: Food Stores

CONTACT

Jim Bowen
Personnel
Red Food Stores, Inc.
PO Box 22008
Chattanooga, TN 37422
(615) 892-8029

CONTRIBUTIONS SUMMARY

Operating Locations: TN
(Chattanooga)

CORP. OFFICERS

James Bolonda: *CURR EMPL* pres, ceo: Red Food Stores

Red Wing Shoe Co. / Red Wing Shoe Co. Foundation

Sales: $86.0 million
Employees: 1,200
Headquarters: Red Wing, MN
SIC Major Group: Leather & Leather Products

CONTACT

Joseph P. Goggin
Secretary, Treasurer
Red Wing Shoe Co. Fdn.
314 Main St.
Red Wing, MN 55066
(612) 388-8211

FINANCIAL SUMMARY

Recent Giving: $340,837 (1991); $297,010 (1990); $300,000 (1987 est.)
Assets: $486,386 (1991); $411,921 (1990); $516,744 (1985)
Gifts Received: $300,000 (1991); $300,000 (1990)
Fiscal Note: Contributes through foundation only. In 1991, contributions were received from the Red Wing Shoe Company.
EIN: 41-6020177

CONTRIBUTIONS SUMMARY

Typical Recipients: • *Arts & Humanities:* arts centers, history/historic preservation, music, performing arts, public broadcasting, theater • *Civic & Public Affairs:* business/free enterprise, economic development, environmental affairs, law & justice, nonprofit management • *Education:* business education, colleges & universities, economic education, education associations, education funds, public education (precollege), social sciences education • *Health:* single-disease health associations • *Social Services:* disabled, recreation & athletics, united funds, youth organizations

Grant Types: capital and general support

Nonmonetary Support Types: donated products

Geographic Distribution: limited to Minnesota, primarily Red Wing, Minneapolis, and St. Paul

Operating Locations: MN (Red Wing)

CORP. OFFICERS

William G. Sweasy: *CURR EMPL* chmn, pres: Red Wing Shoe Co

GIVING OFFICERS

Joseph P. Goggin: secy, treas *CURR EMPL* vp; cfo: Red Wing Shoe Co

William G. Sweasy: pres *CURR EMPL* chmn, pres: Red Wing Shoe Co (see above)

William J. Sweasy: vp

APPLICATION INFORMATION

Initial Approach: *Initial Contact:* brief letter *Include Information On:* description of the organization's activities or projects, copy of tax exemption certificate *When to Submit:* any time

Restrictions on Giving: The foundation does not make grants to individuals.

GRANTS ANALYSIS

Total Grants: $340,837

Number of Grants: 38

Highest Grant: $170,000

Typical Range: $500 to $5,000

Disclosure Period: 1991

Note: Recent grants are derived from a 1991 grants list.

RECENT GRANTS

170,000 Red Wing School
        District 256, Envi-
        ronmental Learn-
        ing Center, Red
        Wing, MN
 50,000 Goodhue County
        Historical Society,
        Red Wing, MN
 34,600 T.B. Sheldon Audi-
        torium, Red Wing,
        MN
 11,500 United Way, Red
        Wing, MN
 10,000 Red Wing Arts As-
        sociation, Red
        Wing, MN
  8,400 YMCA, Red Wing,
        MN
  7,000 KTCA, St. Paul,
        MN
  6,500 Minnesota Private
        College Fund, Min-
        neapolis, MN
  5,000 American Museum
        of Wildlife, Red
        Wing, MN
  4,000 Science Museum,
        St. Paul, MN

Redfield Foundation, Nell J.

CONTACT

Gerald C. Smith
Director
Nell J. Redfield Fdn.
PO Box 61
Reno, NV 89504
(702) 323-1373

FINANCIAL SUMMARY

Recent Giving: $370,577 (1990); $362,660 (1989); $373,193 (1988)
Assets: $6,259,446 (1990); $5,281,872 (1989); $3,968,049 (1988)
EIN: 23-7399910

CONTRIBUTIONS SUMMARY

Typical Recipients: • *Education:* colleges & universities, community & junior colleges • *Health:* hospitals, medical research, pediatric health • *Social Services:* aged, animal protection, child welfare, community service organizations, disabled, domestic violence, food/clothing distribution, recreation & athletics, shelters/homelessness, united funds, youth organizations

Grant Types: capital and scholarship

Geographic Distribution: focus on Reno, NV

GIVING OFFICERS

Iris G. Brewerton: dir
Betty Alyce Jones: dir
Helen Jeane Jones: dir
Gerald C. Smith: dir
Kenneth G. Walker: dir

APPLICATION INFORMATION

Initial Approach: Send letter requesting application form. Deadline is January 15 through June 1.

GRANTS ANALYSIS

Number of Grants: 37
Highest Grant: $50,000
Typical Range: $1,000 to $10,000
Disclosure Period: 1990

RECENT GRANTS

50,000 University of Ne-
       vada, Reno, NV —
       construct experi-
       mental theater
31,397 Children's Cabinet,
       Reno, NV — bed-
       room equipment
       for shelter

25,000 Northern Nevada Center for Independent Living, Reno, NV — therapy

25,000 St. Marys Regional Medical Center, Reno, NV — cardiac monitors

23,350 University of Nevada Department of Speech Pathology, Reno, NV — equipment

19,600 YWCA, Reno, NV

13,000 Special Recreation Services, Reno, NV — camp program

10,000 Food Bank of Northern Nevada, Sparks, NV

10,000 St. Vincents Emergency Services, Reno, NV — food

Redlands Federal Bank

Employees: 350
Headquarters: Redlands, CA
SIC Major Group: Depository Institutions

CONTACT
Carol A. Snodgress
Senior Vice President
Redlands Federal Bank
PO Box 3260
Redlands, CA 92373
(714) 793-2391
Note: Telephone extension is 212.

FINANCIAL SUMMARY
Fiscal Note: Company does not disclose contributions figures.

CONTRIBUTIONS SUMMARY
Company supports local education, human service, arts, and civic organizations.
Typical Recipients: • *Education:* general • *Social Services:* general
Grant Types: matching
Geographic Distribution: primarily in CA
Operating Locations: CA (Redlands)

APPLICATION INFORMATION
Initial Approach: Send brief letter of inquiry, including a description of the organization, amount requested, purpose of funds sought, recently audited financial statements, and proof of tax-exempt status. There are no deadlines.

GRANTS ANALYSIS
Typical Range: $1,000 to $2,500

Redman Foundation

CONTACT
Karen Baxter
Executive Director
Redman Fdn.
7215 Skillman No. 310, Ste. 287
Dallas, TX 75231

FINANCIAL SUMMARY
Recent Giving: $423,500 (1991); $253,464 (1990); $227,930 (1989)
Assets: $5,951,082 (1991); $5,610,568 (1990); $5,572,205 (1989)
EIN: 38-6045047

CONTRIBUTIONS SUMMARY
Donor(s): the late Harold F. Redman, the late Clara M. Redman
Typical Recipients: • *Arts & Humanities:* public broadcasting • *Civic & Public Affairs:* housing • *Education:* colleges & universities, community & junior colleges, medical education • *Religion:* churches • *Social Services:* child welfare, community centers, community service organizations, family services, food/clothing distribution
Grant Types: capital, endowment, operating expenses, and scholarship
Geographic Distribution: focus on TX

GIVING OFFICERS
Karen Baxter: exec dir
William E. Collins: trust
Mrs. James Redman: trust

APPLICATION INFORMATION
Initial Approach: Send brief letter of inquiry describing prorgam. There are no deadlines.
Restrictions on Giving: Does not support individuals.

OTHER THINGS TO KNOW
Publications: Application Guidelines

GRANTS ANALYSIS
Number of Grants: 52
Highest Grant: $33,000
Typical Range: $3,000 to $10,000
Disclosure Period: 1991

RECENT GRANTS
33,000 University of Texas at Dallas, Dallas, TX

25,000 Dallas Foundation, Dallas, TX

22,000 University of Texas Southwestern Medical School, Dallas, TX

20,000 Methodist Bread Basket, Dallas, TX

17,000 Wesley Rankin Community Center, Dallas, TX

16,000 Center for Housing Resources, Dallas, TX

16,000 Shelter Ministries, Dallas, TX

14,000 Child Care Partnership, Dallas, TX

13,500 Trinity River Mission, Dallas, TX

10,000 Common Ground, Dallas, TX

Redman Industries

Sales: $375.0 million
Employees: 4,000
Parent Company: Redman Holding Corp.
Headquarters: Dallas, TX
SIC Major Group: Building Materials & Garden Supplies, Fabricated Metal Products, Lumber & Wood Products, and Primary Metal Industries

CONTACT
Carolyn Miller
Personnel Assistant
Redman Industries
2550 Walnut Hill Ln.
Dallas, TX 75229
(214) 353-3600

CONTRIBUTIONS SUMMARY
Operating Locations: TX (Dallas)

CORP. OFFICERS
Jim Callier: *CURR EMPL* chmn, pres: Redman Indus
Fergus Walker: *CURR EMPL* exec vp, cfo: Redman Indus

OTHER THINGS TO KNOW
Company is an original donor to the Redman Foundation.

Reebok International Ltd. / Reebok Foundation

Sales: $3.06 billion
Employees: 4,500
Headquarters: Stoughton, MA
SIC Major Group: Transportation Equipment and Wholesale Trade—Nondurable Goods

CONTACT
Reebok Fdn.
100 Technology Ctr. Dr.
Stoughton, MA 02072
(617) 341-7946
Note: The foundation prefers to be contacted in writing. The foundation does not list a contact person.

FINANCIAL SUMMARY
Recent Giving: $3,000,000 (1993); $2,700,000 (1992); $2,000,000 (1991)
Assets: $5,000,000 (1992 est.); $2,439,600 (1990); $2,439,600 (1988)
Fiscal Note: Company gives through the foundation and directly. In 1988 the foundation and company gave $23 million for Human Rights work.
EIN: 22-2709235

CONTRIBUTIONS SUMMARY
Grant Types: employee matching gifts and project
Nonmonetary Support Types: donated products
Note: Product donations are only considered for those organizations that are recipients of cash grants or by programs that are enhanced by the volunteer participation of Reebok employees.
Geographic Distribution: primarily in Massachusetts; nationally; and internationally through Human Rights Awards
Operating Locations: MA (Marlborough, Stoughton), OR (Portland)

CORP. OFFICERS
Paul R. Duncan: *B* Selmer TN 1940 *ED* Dartmouth Coll 1962; Dartmouth Coll Amos Tuck Sch Bus Admin 1963 *CURR EMPL* cfo, exec vp, dir: Reebok Intl Ltd *CORP AFFIL* dir: BGS Sys, Cabletron Sys
Paul Fireman: *B* Cambridge MA 1944 *ED* Boston Univ *CURR EMPL* chmn, pres, ceo, coo: Reebok Intl Ltd *CORP AFFIL* dir: Abiomed

GIVING OFFICERS
Sharon Cohen: exec dir, trust
Paul R. Duncan: cfo, trust
CURR EMPL cfo, exec vp, dir:
Reebok Intl Ltd (see above)

APPLICATION INFORMATION
Initial Approach: *Initial Contact:* request and submission of "Summary Request Form" from the foundation, which the director evaluates to decide if a full proposal is desired. If so, the foundation will request that a full proposal be completed and submitted by mail. *Include Information On:* if full proposal requested, include the following: application form and cover letter; specific projects and goals with timetable for achievement; history and background of organization; methods of self-evaluation; income and expense budget; financial statements for recent year; proof of tax-exempt status; list of key staff and board of directors; any additional materials *When to Submit:* any time
Restrictions on Giving: Contributions are awarded to organizations which provide equal access to funding and equal opportunity, and do not discriminate based on race, religion or sex. The Foundation does not support: individuals, political organizations, advertising/program books, dinner table sponsorship, fraternal organizations, or medical research.
The foundation stresses that it only supports 501(c)3 organizations.

OTHER THINGS TO KNOW
Foundation conducts evaluations of supported programs and projects.
Publications: summary request form

GRANTS ANALYSIS
Total Grants: $2,700,000
Disclosure Period: 1992
Note: Recent grants are derived from a 1991 foundation Form 990. The company also gives directly and those recipients are not represented.

RECENT GRANTS
250,000 Northeastern University, Boston, MA
166,166 City Year, Boston, MA

142,500 Combined Jewish Philanthropies, New York, NY
125,000 Trans Africa, Washington, DC
80,000 National Urban League, New York, NY
51,500 Impact II, Boston, MA
50,000 Carter Center for Human Rights, Atlanta, GA
50,000 Celebration of Black Cinema
50,000 NAACP
50,000 United Way

Reed Foundation

CONTACT
J. Sinclair Armstrong
Secretary
Reed Foundation
444 Madison Avenue, Ste. 2901
New York, NY 10022-6902
(212) 223-1330

FINANCIAL SUMMARY
Recent Giving: $552,464 (1991); $867,303 (1990); $1,151,803 (1989)
Assets: $10,242,542 (1991); $9,842,686 (1990); $12,035,694 (1989)
EIN: 13-1990017

CONTRIBUTIONS SUMMARY
Donor(s): Founded by the late Samuel Rubin, the Reed Foundation operated as a private foundation for 35 years under the name of the Samuel Rubin Foundation. In December 1985, the foundation made arrangements to distribute half of its assets to a separate, unaffiliated foundation. The name of the original foundation was then changed to the Reed Foundation.
Samuel Rubin (1901-1978) was founder of the Spanish Trading Corporation and Faberge Perfumes. He was a founder of the New York University Bellevue Medical Center; chairman of the advisory board of Fordham Hospital; president of the American-Israel Cultural Foundation and the American Symphony Orchestra; and a trustee of the New York Medical Center, Sydenham Hospital, and the Spoleto Festival.
Typical Recipients: • *Arts & Humanities:* arts centers, arts festivals, community arts, music, theater • *Civic & Public Affairs:* better government,

civil rights, philanthropic organizations • *Education:* colleges & universities, international exchange, legal education • *Health:* medical research • *Social Services:* community service organizations, legal aid
Grant Types: general support and project
Geographic Distribution: broad geographic distribution; emphasis on the State of New York

GIVING OFFICERS
James Sinclair Armstrong: secy, asst treas *B* New York NY 1915 *ED* Harvard Univ AB 1938; Harvard Univ JD 1941 *CURR EMPL* atty: Whitman & Ransom *NONPR AFFIL* chmn: Comm Oppose Sale St Bartholomews Church, English Speaking Union US, Natl Inst Social Sciences; dir: Laymens Club; mem: Am Bar Assn, Am Law Inst, Am Soc Venerable Order St John Jerusalem, Co Adventurers, Harvard Law Sch Assn, Horticulture Soc NY, Hugenot Soc Am, Navy League US, NY City Bar Assn, NY Historical Soc, NY Soc Library, Pilgrims US, Practicing Law Inst, Soc Colonial Wars, St Nicholas Soc NY; mem, chmn standing comm: St Andrews Soc St NY; trust emeritus: Gunnery Sch; vchmn intl counc: English Speaking Union Commonwealth; vestryman: L'Eglise Frangaise du St Esprit
Jane Gregory Rubin: treas
Reed Rubin: pres

APPLICATION INFORMATION
Initial Approach:
Applicants should send a letter of request, describing the project to be funded. If the project is of interest to the board of directors, a proposal will be requested.
Proposals should give a detailed description of the project, including its administration, operation, budget, and other sources of funding. Also required are copies of the most recent 990 Form and tax-exempt status letter from the IRS. There are no deadlines for application. The board meets on a flexible schedule approximately once every two months. The board of directors is capable of acting quickly on proposals, and applicants can expect immediate acknowledgement

of receipt and a decision within two months.
Restrictions on Giving: No grants are given to individuals.

GRANTS ANALYSIS
Total Grants: $552,464
Number of Grants: 32
Highest Grant: $216,000
Typical Range: $1,000 to $25,000
Disclosure Period: 1991
Note: Recent grants are derived from a 1991 Form 990.

RECENT GRANTS
216,000 Research Institute for the Study of Man, New York, NY
66,664 University of Virginia School of Law, Charlottesville, VA
25,000 Community Services Society, New York, NY
25,000 Poets House
25,000 Under One Roof
22,500 Lincoln Center for the Performing Arts, New York, NY
20,000 American Trust for Oxford University, New York, NY
15,000 Preservation League of New York State, Albany, NY
15,000 Volunteer Lawyers for the Arts, New York, NY
10,000 Intar

Reed Foundation

CONTACT
David W. Reed
Reed Foundation
P.O. Box 67
Gilbertsville, KY 42044-0067

FINANCIAL SUMMARY
Assets: $9,250,000 (1990)
Gifts Received: $9,250,000 (1990)
EIN: 61-1189284

GIVING OFFICERS
David W. Reed: trust
Disclosure Period: 1990

Reed Foundation, Philip D.

CONTACT
Patricia Anderson
Secretary
Philip D. Reed Fdn.
570 Lexington Avenue, Rm. 923
New York, NY 10022
(212) 836-3330

FINANCIAL SUMMARY
Recent Giving: $2,181,000 (fiscal 1992); $1,405,500 (fiscal 1991); $1,542,500 (fiscal 1990)
Assets: $7,340,918 (fiscal year ending June 30, 1992); $7,852,853 (fiscal 1991); $8,553,033 (fiscal 1990)
Gifts Received: $772,500 (fiscal 1992); $64,312 (fiscal 1991)
Fiscal Note: In fiscal 1992, contributions were received from Phillip D. Reed.
EIN: 13-6098916

CONTRIBUTIONS SUMMARY
Donor(s): the late Philip D. Reed
Typical Recipients: • *Arts & Humanities:* history/historic preservation, museums/galleries, public broadcasting • *Civic & Public Affairs:* environmental affairs, international affairs • *Education:* colleges & universities, education associations, faculty development, international studies, legal education, student aid • *Health:* hospitals • *Religion:* churches • *Social Services:* community service organizations, family planning, family services, united funds, youth organizations
Grant Types: general support
Geographic Distribution: focus on NY

GIVING OFFICERS
Patricia Anderson: secy, dir
Philip D. Reed: chmn, pres
Harold Abraham Segall: vp, treas, dir *B* New York NY 1918 *ED* Cornell Univ BA 1938; Yale Univ LLB 1941 *CURR EMPL* ptnr: Gilbert Segall & Young *CORP AFFIL* ptnr: Gilbert Segall & Young *NONPR AFFIL* mem: Am Bar Assn, Jewish Commun Ctr NY, NY City Bar Assn
Kathryn R. Smith: trust

APPLICATION INFORMATION
Initial Approach: Send brief letter of inquiry describing program or project. There are no deadlines.
Restrictions on Giving: Does not support individuals.

GRANTS ANALYSIS
Number of Grants: 29
Highest Grant: $500,000
Typical Range: $15,000 to $50,000
Disclosure Period: fiscal year ending June 30, 1992

RECENT GRANTS
500,000 University of California, Davis, CA
308,500 Council on Foreign Relations, New York, NY — Philip D. Reed Senior Fellowship in Science and Technology
250,000 Eisenhower Exchange Fellowships, Philadelphia, PA — Philip D. Reed Fellowship
200,000 Woodrow Wilson National Fellowship Foundation, Princeton, NJ — program in public policy and international affairs
150,000 Medical Center at Princeton, Princeton, NJ — capital fund
125,000 Smithsonian Institution, Washington, DC — environmental research center education building
100,000 Teach for America, New York, NY — general support
60,000 Smithsonian Institution, Washington, DC — new opportunities in animal health sciences fellowships
50,000 Nature Conservancy, San Francisco, CA
50,000 Planned Parenthood Federation of America, New York, NY

Reed Publishing USA
Revenue: $818.0 million
Employees: 4,100
Headquarters: Newton, MA
SIC Major Group: Business Services, Holding & Other Investment Offices, and Printing & Publishing

CONTACT
Robert Krakoff
Chairman
Reed Publishing USA
275 Washington St.
Newton, MA 02158
(617) 964-3030

CONTRIBUTIONS SUMMARY
Operating Locations: CT, MA, NY

CORP. OFFICERS
Robert Krakoff: *CURR EMPL* chmn, ceo: Reed Publ USA
Timothy O'Brien: *CURR EMPL* cfo: Reed Publ USA

Reedman Car-Truck World Center / Reedman FCS Foundation
Sales: $165.0 million
Employees: 700
Headquarters: Langhorne, PA
SIC Major Group: Automobile Repair, Services & Parking and Automotive Dealers & Service Stations

CONTACT
Elizabeth DeYoung
Manager
Reedman FCS Foundation
US Route One
c/o Reedman Corp.
Langhorne, PA 19047-9801
(215) 757-4961

FINANCIAL SUMMARY
Recent Giving: $7,415 (1990); $10,650 (1989)
Assets: $269,268 (1990); $206,400 (1989)
EIN: 22-2463892

CONTRIBUTIONS SUMMARY
Typical Recipients: • *Civic & Public Affairs:* environmental affairs • *Education:* colleges & universities • *Health:* hospitals, medical research, single-disease health associations • *Social Services:* community service organizations
Grant Types: general support
Geographic Distribution: focus on PA
Operating Locations: PA (Langhorne)

CORP. OFFICERS
Ralph Reedman, Jr.: *CURR EMPL* pres: Reedman Chevrolet

GIVING OFFICERS
Herbert Reedman: dir
Ralph Reedman: off
Stanley Reedman: dir
Thomas Reedman: dir

APPLICATION INFORMATION
Initial Approach: Send brief letter describing program. There are no deadlines.

GRANTS ANALYSIS
Number of Grants: 10
Highest Grant: $2,000
Typical Range: $130 to $2,000
Disclosure Period: 1990

RECENT GRANTS
2,000 Lehigh University, Bethlehem, PA
2,000 St. Marys Hospital
1,100 Jefferson Medical Center
1,000 Iacocca Foundation
155 American Cancer Society
155 Fox Chase Cancer Center, Philadelphia, PA
145 Zoological Society
135 Washington Crossing Scholarship Foundation, Washington Crossing, PA
130 National Glaucoma Research
130 National Wildlife Federation, Washington, DC

Reell Precision Manufacturing
Sales: $8.0 million
Employees: 100
Headquarters: St. Paul, MN
SIC Major Group: Industrial Machinery & Equipment

CONTACT
Lee Johnson
Chief Executive Officer
Reell Precision Manufacturing
1259 Wolters Blvd.
St. Paul, MN 55110
(612) 484-2447

CONTRIBUTIONS SUMMARY
Operating Locations: MN (St. Paul)

CORP. OFFICERS
Robert Wahlstedt: *CURR EMPL* pres: Reell Precision Mfg

Reeves Foundation

CONTACT
Don A. Ulrich
Executive Director
Reeves Fdn.
PO Box 441
Dover, OH 44622
(216) 364-4660

FINANCIAL SUMMARY
Recent Giving: $731,493
(1991); $918,929 (1990);
$570,499 (1989)
Assets: $15,833,464 (1991);
$13,860,033 (1990);
$13,862,615 (1989)
EIN: 34-6575477

CONTRIBUTIONS SUMMARY
Donor(s): The foundation was established in 1966 by the late Margaret J. Reeves, the late Helen F. Reeves, and the late Samuel J. Reeves.
Typical Recipients: • *Arts & Humanities:* history/historic preservation • *Civic & Public Affairs:* urban & community affairs • *Education:* colleges & universities, education funds, public education (precollege) • *Religion:* churches • *Social Services:* shelters/homelessness, united funds
Grant Types: capital, matching, operating expenses, and project
Geographic Distribution: focus on Tuscarawas County, OH

GIVING OFFICERS
W. E. Lieser: treas, trust
Thomas J. Patton: trust
Ronald L. Pissocra: trust
Margaret H. Reeves: pres, trust
Thomas R. Scheffer: vp, trust
Don A. Ulrich: exec dir
Jeffry Wagner: trust
W. E. Zimmerman: exec vp

APPLICATION INFORMATION
Initial Approach:
Applications should be in writing and include a concise outline of the amount and purpose of the funds.
The foundation has no deadline for submitting proposals.
The board meets bimonthly.
Restrictions on Giving: The foundation reports grants are made for charitable and educational purposes, with emphasis on capital expenditures rather than operating budgets. No grants are made to individuals, or for annual campaigns, seed money, emergency funds, deficit financing, land acquisition, renovation projects, endowment funds, fellowships, special projects, publications, conferences, or loans.

GRANTS ANALYSIS
Total Grants: $731,493
Number of Grants: 14
Highest Grant: $400,000
Typical Range: $5,000 to $30,000
Disclosure Period: 1991
Note: Average grant figure does not include the highest grant of $400,000. Recent grants are derived from a 1991 grants list.

RECENT GRANTS
400,000 Moravian College, Bethlehem, PA
108,484 North Canton Medical Foundation, North Canton, OH
50,000 Dover Historical Society, Dover, OH
28,565 Tuscampus-Kent State University, New Philadelphia, OH
27,745 Dover City Schools, Dover, OH
26,857 New Philadelphia Fire Department, New Philadelphia, OH
25,000 Tuscampus City Council of Churches, New Philadelphia, OH
18,462 New Philadelphia Quaker Club, New Philadelphia, OH
14,762 Self-Help Center, New Philadelphia, OH
10,000 Ohio Foundation of Independent Colleges, Columbus, OH

Reflection Riding

CONTACT
J. Nelson Irvine
Director
Reflection Riding
1000 Tallan Bldg., Two Union Sq.
Chattanooga, TN 37402
(615) 821-9582

FINANCIAL SUMMARY
Recent Giving: $217,205
(1989); $169,060 (1988)
Assets: $2,419,977 (1991);
$2,098,909 (1990); $2,386,470 (1989)
Gifts Received: $26,444
(1991); $89,030 (1990);
$60,694 (1989)
EIN: 62-0570240

CONTRIBUTIONS SUMMARY
Typical Recipients: • *Civic & Public Affairs:* zoos/botanical gardens
Grant Types: operating expenses
Geographic Distribution: focus on TN

GIVING OFFICERS
Mrs. Oscar Brock: dir
Michael R. Campbell: dir
William Crutchfield, Jr.: dir
David Hopkins, Jr.: vp, secy, dir
John Huckaba: dir
J. Nelson Irvine: dir
Mrs. James B. Irvine, Jr.: dir
Carolyn King: dir
H. Grant Law, Jr.: pres, dir
Mrs. John M. Martin: dir
Jack McDonald: dir
Mrs. John R. H. McDonald: dir
Mrs. E. L. Mitchell, Jr.: dir
Z. Cartter Patten III: dir
Mrs. William D. Pettway, Jr.: dir
Fred Robinson: dir
Kelley L. Vaughn: dir
Mrs. John K. Woodworth: vp, treas, dir
Mrs. James O. B. Wright: dir

OTHER THINGS TO KNOW
The foundation does not make contributions, grants, gifts, or loans, nor does it accept unsolicited applications for such. The foundation's principal charitable activity is the operation and maintenance of a modified arboretum which is open to the public.
Disclosure Period: 1991

Reflector Hardware Corp.
Sales: $62.0 million
Employees: 1,000
Headquarters: Melrose Park, IL
SIC Major Group: Furniture & Fixtures

CONTACT
Linda Lazzaro
Personnel Director
Reflector Hardware Corp.
1400 North 25th Ave.
Melrose Park, IL 60160
(708) 345-2500

CONTRIBUTIONS SUMMARY
Operating Locations: IL (Melrose Park)

CORP. OFFICERS
Al R. Umans: B New York NY 1927 ED Univ Rochester CURR EMPL pres, treas: Reflector Hardware Corp CORP AFFIL chmn, pres: Garcy Corp; dir: Medhab, Monroe Commun; pres, dir: Kathi Broadcasting, Sharon Broadcasting; pres, treas, dir: Spacemaster Corp; vchmn, dir: USW Corp; vp, dir: Goer Mfg Co NONPR AFFIL trust: Mt Sinai Hosp Med Ctr

Regenstein Foundation

CONTACT
Joseph Regenstein, Jr.
President
Regenstein Foundation
8600 West Bryn Mawr Avenue, Ste. 705N
Chicago, IL 60631
(312) 693-6464

FINANCIAL SUMMARY
Recent Giving: $2,432,244
(1990); $4,973,172 (1989);
$3,560,812 (1988)
Assets: $85,667,771 (1990);
$82,473,918 (1989);
$75,162,304 (1988)
EIN: 36-3152531

CONTRIBUTIONS SUMMARY
Donor(s): The foundation was established in 1950, with the late Joseph and Helen Regenstein as donors.
Typical Recipients: • *Arts & Humanities:* arts institutes, history/historic preservation, libraries, museums/galleries, music, opera • *Civic & Public Affairs:* philanthropic organizations, public policy, zoos/botanical gardens • *Education:* colleges & universities, private education (precollege) • *Health:* hospitals, medical rehabilitation, nursing services • *Social Services:* child welfare, community service organizations, disabled, family plan-

ning, food/clothing distribution, homes, religious welfare, united funds, youth organizations

Grant Types: capital, endowment, general support, loan, multiyear/continuing support, and project

Geographic Distribution: Illinois, primarily the metropolitan Chicago area

GIVING OFFICERS
Ramona D. Baiocchi: asst secy
Anita Bury: asst secy
John Eggum: secy, treas, dir *B* Chicago IL 1913 *ED* Walton Sch Commerce *CORP AFFIL* dir: Arvey Corp
Betty R. Hartman: vp, dir
Robert A. Mecca: vp, dir
Joseph Regenstein, Jr.: pres, dir *B* Chicago IL 1923 *ED* Brown Univ 1945 *CURR EMPL* chmn: Arvey Corp
Randall A. Watkins: contr, asst treas

APPLICATION INFORMATION
Initial Approach:
Brief requests in letter form should be addressed to the foundation's president. Requests should include a cover letter, signed or approved by the organization's chief executive, summarizing the request, and describing the organization, proposed use of funds, desired results, and other sources of funds; one copy of the proposal; copy of the IRS determination letter of tax-exempt status; recently audited financial statement; budget statement for the current and subsequent year; and the amount requested. Additional information often is requested by the foundation. There are no deadlines for submitting proposals.
Restrictions on Giving: The foundation reports that most grants are made on the initiative of the foundation's trustees; only a very small percentage of applicants can expect to obtain funds. Because long-range pledges often make income unavailable for substantial periods of time, it is suggested that applicants needing immediate help apply to individuals or businesses in a position to make immediate grants. The foundation does not make grants to individuals. The foundation does not conduct personal interviews with

an applicant except upon the foundation's initiative.

OTHER THINGS TO KNOW
Publications: general information letter

GRANTS ANALYSIS
Total Grants: $2,432,244
Number of Grants: 37
Highest Grant: $600,000
Typical Range: $1,000 to $25,000 and $40,000 to $100,000
Disclosure Period: 1990
Note: The average grant figure excludes a $600,000 grant. Recent grants are derived from a 1990 grants list.

RECENT GRANTS
  600,000 Field Museum of Natural History, Chicago, IL
  500,000 Art Institute of Chicago, Chicago, IL
  330,000 Lambs Farm, Libertyville, IL
  250,000 John G. Shedd Aquarium, Chicago, IL
  250,000 Newberry Library, Chicago, IL
   75,000 Orchestral Association, Chicago, IL
   75,000 WTTW Chicago, Chicago, IL
   66,323 Rosary College, River Forest, IL
   50,000 Chicago Historical Society, Chicago, IL
   50,000 Lyric Opera of Chicago, Chicago, IL

Regis Corp. / Regis Foundation
Revenue: $307.7 million
Employees: 14,000
Headquarters: Minneapolis, MN
SIC Major Group: Business Services, Personal Services, and Wholesale Trade—Durable Goods

CONTACT
Myron Kunin
President
Regis Fdn.
7201 Metro Blvd.
Minneapolis, MN 55439
(612) 947-7777

FINANCIAL SUMMARY
Recent Giving: $610,848 (fiscal 1991); $446,448 (fiscal 1990); $919,563 (fiscal 1989)
Gifts Received: $610,848 (fiscal 1991); $446,583 (fiscal 1990); $919,822 (fiscal 1989)

Fiscal Note: Above figures are for the foundation only. 1990 contribution received from Regis Corp.
EIN: 41-1410790

CONTRIBUTIONS SUMMARY
Typical Recipients: • *Arts & Humanities:* arts associations, arts centers, museums/galleries, music, theater • *Education:* business education, colleges & universities, education administration • *Health:* pediatric health • *Religion:* religious organizations, synagogues • *Social Services:* community service organizations, united funds, youth organizations
Grant Types: general support and scholarship
Note: Scholarship program is administered by the Minneapolis Board of Education.
Geographic Distribution: primarily Minneapolis, MN
Operating Locations: MN (Minneapolis)

CORP. OFFICERS
Myron Kunin: *CURR EMPL* chmn, pres, ceo: Regis Corp

GIVING OFFICERS
Frank Evangelist: secy *CURR EMPL* sr vp (fin), secy, dir: Regis Corp
Bert Gross: asst secy
Jack Holewa: vp
Myron Kunin: pres *CURR EMPL* chmn, pres, ceo: Regis Corp (see above)

APPLICATION INFORMATION
Initial Approach: *Initial Contact:* brief letter of inquiry *Include Information On:* description of the organization, amount request, and purpose for which funds are sought *When to Submit:* any time
Note: Applications for scholarships are available at Minneapolis public high schools.

GRANTS ANALYSIS
Total Grants: $610,848
Number of Grants: 11
Highest Grant: $357,000
Typical Range: $5,000 to $72,000
Disclosure Period: fiscal year ending June 30, 1991
Note: Average grant figure excludes the highest grant of $357,000. Recent grants are derived from a fiscal 1991 Form 990.

RECENT GRANTS
357,000 Minneapolis Federation of Jewish Services, Minneapolis, MN
130,000 Minneapolis Board of Education, Minneapolis, MN
 72,000 Walker Art Center, Minneapolis, MN
 21,500 Guthrie Theater, Minneapolis, MN
  8,548 University of Minnesota, Minneapolis, MN
  7,000 U.S. Holocaust Memorial Museum, Washington, DC
  6,000 United Way, Minneapolis, MN
  5,200 Temple Israel, Minneapolis, MN
  2,500 Minnesota Orchestral Association, Minneapolis, MN
  1,000 St. Cloud State University, St. Cloud, MN

REI-Recreational Equipment, Inc.
Sales: $311.6 million
Employees: 3,000
Headquarters: Kent, WA
SIC Major Group: Miscellaneous Retail and Wholesale Trade—Durable Goods

CONTACT
Christopher M. Doyle
Public Relations Coordinator
Recreational Equipment, Inc.
6750 S 228th St.
Kent, WA 98032
(206) 395-5957

FINANCIAL SUMMARY
Recent Giving: $519,368 (1993 est.); $429,374 (1992); $402,621 (1991)
Fiscal Note: Company makes contributions directly.

CONTRIBUTIONS SUMMARY
Typical Recipients: • *Civic & Public Affairs:* environmental affairs • *Social Services:* community service organizations, recreation & athletics
Grant Types: award, endowment, and scholarship
Nonmonetary Support Types: donated equipment and donated products
Geographic Distribution: operating locations
Operating Locations: AK (Anchorage), AZ (Tempe), CA (Berkeley, Carson, Citrus

Heights, Cupertino, Northridge, San Carlos, San Diego, San Dimas, Santa Ana), CO (Denver, Westminister), GA (Atlanta), IL (Niles), MA (Reading), MD (College Park), MN (Bloomington, Roseville), NC (Cary), NM (Albuquerque), NY (New Rochelle), OR (Eugene, Portland, Tigard), PA (Conshohocken), TX (Austin), UT (Salt Lake City), VA (Bailey's Crossroads), WA (Bellevue, Federal Way, Kent, Lynnwood, Seattle, Spokane)

CORP. OFFICERS

Wally Smith: *CURR EMPL* pres, ceo: REI-Recreational Equipment

GIVING OFFICERS

Christopher M. Doyle: *CURR EMPL* pub rels coordinator: REI-Recreational Equipment

APPLICATION INFORMATION

Initial Approach: *Initial Contact:* call and request guidelines before applying *Include Information On:* for Corporate Contributions Program, submit written request no longer than two pages, with description of program's goals, objectives, action plans, estimated number of people to benefit from project, plans to acknowledge REI's support, project budget, fact sheet, background information on oganization, special brochures or pamphlets if available, contact name and telephone number, completed Hold Harmless Agreement attached to application procedures, copy of general liability certificate, if organization has received REI assistance in the past, submit to Christopher Doyle, REI Public Affairs, P.O. Box 1938, Sumner, WA 98390-0800; for Enviromental Committee funding, include the formal application with a description of the organization not to exceed four pages, and project budget, submit to Judy Patrick, Public Affairs Secretary, REI, P.O. Box 1938, Sumner, WA 98390-0800; for Trails Advocacy Grants, submit a simple, concise proposal with clear statement of goals, objectives, action plans, evaluation procedures, a budget, and background information on organization to Kathleen Beamer, Public Affairs Director, REI, P.O. Box 1938, Sumner, WA

98390-0800. *When to Submit:* any time

OTHER THINGS TO KNOW

REI works to protect the outdoors for recreation by contributing to organizations protecting rivers, trails, wildlands, and social programs directly related to outdoor recreation. Programs that do not qualify for grants may still be eligible for discounts on quality outdoor gear and clothing. Groups in need may contact REI's Commercial Sales Department at 1-800-258-4567.

REI stores organize and fund an annual service project, relying on volunteer commitment to perform local conservation-oriented work. Efforts are wide-reaching, from cleaning up Seattle's Lake Union by kayak, to building trail sections along San Francisco's Bay Area Ridge Trail. In 1991 and 1992, REI stores coordinated projects involving 4,757 volunteers who donated 24,282 hours to local conservation activities.

Other community involvement activities include free education clinics and demo days to inform and assist members and customers with outdoor pursuits, providing informational publications and brochures, and dedicating retail space for environmental centers for information and learning centers for conservation and environmental issues.

Publications: *REI-Recreational Equipment, Inc. Corporate Contributions Program Guidelines*

GRANTS ANALYSIS

Total Grants: $429,374
Disclosure Period: 1992

Reich & Tang L.P.

Revenue: $53.5 million
Employees: 124
Headquarters: New York, NY
SIC Major Group: Security & Commodity Brokers

CONTACT

Richard DeSanctis
Controller
Reich & Tang L.P.
100 Park Avenue, 28th Fl.
New York, NY 10017
(212) 370-1110

CONTRIBUTIONS SUMMARY

Operating Locations: NY (New York)

CORP. OFFICERS

Robert F. Hoerle: *CURR EMPL* chmn: Reich & Tang LP
Oscar L. Tang: *CURR EMPL* pres, ceo: Reich & Tang

OTHER THINGS TO KNOW

Company is an original donor to the Tang Fund.

Reicher Foundation, Anne & Harry J.

CONTACT

Hermia Gould
Secretary-Treasurer
Anne & Harry J. Reicher Fdn.
1173-A Second Avenue, Box 363
New York, NY 10021
(212) 599-0500

FINANCIAL SUMMARY

Recent Giving: $1,040,000 (1991); $205,500 (1990); $792,763 (1989)
Assets: $5,249,827 (1991); $4,200,441 (1990); $4,623,739 (1989)
Gifts Received: $1,764,509 (1991)
Fiscal Note: In 1991, contributions were received from Harry J. Reicher Trust ($1,439,510) and Estate of Sydell Markelson ($275,000).
EIN: 13-6115086

CONTRIBUTIONS SUMMARY

Typical Recipients: • *Health:* geriatric health, hospitals, medical research, pediatric health, single-disease health associations • *Religion:* religious organizations, synagogues • *Social Services:* community service organizations
Grant Types: general support
Geographic Distribution: focus on the greater New York, NY, metropolitan area

GIVING OFFICERS

Rabbi Bulfour Brickner: vp
Hermia Gould: secy, treas
Harold Lamberg: pres

Leonard Zalkin: vp

APPLICATION INFORMATION

Initial Approach: The foundation reports it only makes contributions to preselected charitable organizations.
Restrictions on Giving: Does not support individuals.

GRANTS ANALYSIS

Number of Grants: 40
Highest Grant: $600,000
Typical Range: $1,000 to $5,000
Disclosure Period: 1991

RECENT GRANTS

600,000 Hospital for Joint Diseases and Medical Center, New York, NY
100,000 Settlement Housing Fund, New York, NY
75,000 St. Luke's-Roosevelt Hospital Center, New York, NY
50,000 Stephen Wise Free Synagogue, New York, NY
25,000 Beth Israel Hospice, New York, NY
25,000 Halom House, Cincinnati, OH
15,000 World Union For Progressive Judaism, Ithaca, NY
10,000 Citizens Committee for Children of New York City, New York, NY
10,000 Hebrew Union College Jewish Institute of Religion, Cincinnati, OH
10,000 Karen Horney Clinic, New York, NY

Reichhold Chemicals, Inc.

Sales: $765.59 million
Employees: 3,958
Headquarters: Research Triangle Park, NC
SIC Major Group: Chemicals & Allied Products, Rubber & Miscellaneous Plastics Products, and Wholesale Trade—Nondurable Goods

CONTACT

Richard W. Fisher
Senior Vice President, Human
  Resources
Reichhold Chemicals, Inc.
PO Box 13582
Research Triangle Park, NC
  27709
(919) 990-7500

CONTRIBUTIONS SUMMARY

Company primarily provides
support for employee matching
gifts. Company tries to divide
contributions evenly between
arts, education, and health and
human services. Prefers to support organizations that directly
affect company's employee
base. Plants throughout the
United States have discretionary spending budgets; large
grants are approved by corporate headquarters.
Typical Recipients: • *Arts &
Humanities:* arts funds, libraries, museums/galleries, music,
performing arts • *Education:*
business education, colleges &
universities, economic education, public education (precollege) • *Health:* health organizations, hospitals, single-disease
health associations • *Social
Services:* community service organizations, united funds,
youth organizations
Grant Types: employee matching gifts, general support, and
project
Geographic Distribution: primarily headquarters area

CORP. OFFICERS

Thomas Mitchell: *CURR
EMPL* pres, ceo: Reichhold
Chemicals

GIVING OFFICERS

Richard W. Fisher: *CURR
EMPL* sr vp (human resources): Reichhold Chemicals

APPLICATION INFORMATION

Initial Approach: Send letter
of inquiry including a description of the organization, need
addressed, and amount requested. Plants can be contacted directly. Other subsidiaries of Dainippon administer
independent programs.

Reidler Foundation

CONTACT

Diana L. James
Secretary-Treasurer
Reidler Fdn.
c/o Hazleton National Bank
Broad and Laurel Sts.
Hazleton, PA 18201
(717) 459-4251

FINANCIAL SUMMARY

Recent Giving: $200,000 (fiscal 1991); $185,000 (fiscal
1990); $180,000 (fiscal 1989)
Assets: $5,362,193 (fiscal year
ending October 31, 1991);
$4,732,926 (fiscal 1990);
$4,785,320 (fiscal 1989)
Gifts Received: $28,219 (fiscal 1991); $25,313 (fiscal
1989); $24,558 (fiscal 1988)
Fiscal Note: In 1991, contributions were received from
Howard D. and Ann B. Fegan.
EIN: 24-6022888

CONTRIBUTIONS SUMMARY

Donor(s): John W. Reidler
Typical Recipients: • *Arts &
Humanities:* libraries, music
• *Civic & Public Affairs:*
zoos/botanical gardens • *Education:* colleges & universities,
education funds • *Health:* hospitals • *International:* international organizations • *Religion:*
churches • *Social Services:*
aged, community service organizations, family planning,
united funds, youth organizations
Grant Types: general support
Geographic Distribution:
focus on the Ashland and
Hazleton, PA, areas

GIVING OFFICERS

Ann B. Fegan: vp
Howard D. Fegan: dir
Eugene C. Fish: dir
Robert K. Gicking: vp *B*
Hazleton PA 1931 *ED* Lafayette Coll 1952 *CURR EMPL*
pres, dir: Hazleton Natl Bank
CORP AFFIL pres: First Valley
Corp; pres, dir: Hazleton Natl
Bank
Carl J. Reidler: dir
Paul G. Reidler: pres

APPLICATION INFORMATION

Initial Approach: Send brief
letter of inquiry describing program or project. There are no
deadlines.
Restrictions on Giving: Does
not support individuals.

GRANTS ANALYSIS

Number of Grants: 77
Highest Grant: $20,000
Typical Range: $500 to
$10,000
Disclosure Period: fiscal year
ending October 31, 1991

RECENT GRANTS

20,000   Ashlands Trusts
Helping Hand, Ashland, PA
20,000   Trinity Lutheran
Church, PA
10,000   Susquehanna University, Selinsgrove, PA
6,500   Lehigh University,
Bethlehem, PA
5,000   Geisinger Foundation, Danville, PA
5,000   Lutheran Welfare
Center, PA — dental care unit
5,000   Planned Parenthood Federation of
America, PA
4,000   MMI, PA
3,000   Hazleton Area Public Library, Hazleton, PA
3,000   Heifer Project International, Little
Rock, AR

Reilly Industries / Reilly Foundation

Sales: $120.0 million
Employees: 800
Headquarters: Indianapolis, IN
SIC Major Group: Chemicals &
  Allied Products and Petroleum
  & Coal Products

CONTACT

Lorraine D. Schroeder
Trustee
Reilly Fdn.
1510 Market Sq. Center
151 North Delaware St.
Indianapolis, IN 46204
(317) 248-6468

FINANCIAL SUMMARY

Recent Giving: $452,136
(1991); $473,054 (1990);
$273,794 (1989)
Assets: $586,854 (1991);
$654,172 (1990); $679,424
(1989)
Gifts Received: $350,000
(1991); $350,000 (1990);
$250,000 (1989)
Fiscal Note: Contributes
through foundation only. In
1991, contributions were received from Reilly Industries.
EIN: 35-2061750

CONTRIBUTIONS SUMMARY

Typical Recipients: • *Arts &
Humanities:* museums/galleries, music • *Education:* colleges & universities, education
funds, student aid • *Health:*
hospitals • *Social Services:*
aged, community service organizations, food/clothing distribution, shelters/homelessness, united funds, youth
organizations
Grant Types: general support
and scholarship
Geographic Distribution: limited to areas of company operations
Operating Locations: IN (Indianapolis)

CORP. OFFICERS

Robert D. McNeeley: *CURR
EMPL* pres, dir: Reilly Indus
Thomas E. Reilly, Jr.: *CURR
EMPL* chmn, pres, dir: Reilly
Indus *CORP AFFIL* dir: INB
Natl Bank

GIVING OFFICERS

Rolla E. McAdams: trust
CURR EMPL vchmn, dir:
Reilly Indus
Elizabeth C. Reilly: trust
Thomas E. Reilly, Jr.: trust
CURR EMPL chmn, pres, dir:
Reilly Indus (see above)
Lorraine D. Schroeder: trust
Clarke L. Wilhelm: trust

APPLICATION INFORMATION

Initial Approach: *Initial Contact:* brief letter *Include Information On:* after first grants
are awarded, receipts and grade
reports are required for scholarship grants *When to Submit:*
any time
Restrictions on Giving: Scholarship awards are limited to
children of qualified employees.

GRANTS ANALYSIS

Total Grants: $452,136
Number of Grants: 94*
Highest Grant: $43,200
Typical Range: $500 to
$10,000
Disclosure Period: 1991
Note: Number of grants and average grant figures do not include scholarships to individuals totaling $18,546 or
matching gifts totaling $8,475.
Recent grants are derived from
a 1991 grants list.

RECENT GRANTS

43,200   United Way, Indianapolis, IN

25,000 Associated Colleges of Indiana, Indianapolis, IN
25,000 Hanover College, Hanover, IN
25,000 Indianapolis Symphony Orchestra, Indianapolis, IN
25,000 Indianapolis Symphony Orchestra, Indianapolis, IN
25,000 Indianapolis Zoological Society, Indianapolis, IN
24,000 Junior Achievement, Indianapolis, IN
20,000 Children's Museum, Indianapolis, IN
17,000 Ruth Lilly Center for Health, Indianapolis, IN
16,000 Butler University, Butler, IN

Reily & Co., William B. / Reily Foundation

Sales: $100.0 million
Employees: 1,200
Headquarters: New Orleans, LA
SIC Major Group: Food & Kindred Products, Miscellaneous Retail, and Wholesale Trade—Nondurable Goods

CONTACT

H. Eustis Reily
President
Reily Fdn.
640 Magazine St.
New Orleans, LA 70130
(504) 524-6131

FINANCIAL SUMMARY

Recent Giving: $664,178 (1990); $617,265 (1989)
Assets: $6,093,069 (1990); $5,131,176 (1989)
Gifts Received: $1,200,000 (1990); $1,100,000 (1989)
Fiscal Note: Contributes through foundation only. In 1990, contributions were received from the William B. Reily Company.
EIN: 72-6029179

CONTRIBUTIONS SUMMARY

Typical Recipients: • *Arts & Humanities:* arts associations, arts centers, history/historic preservation • *Civic & Public Affairs:* better government, environmental affairs, housing, municipalities, safety, urban & community affairs • *Education:* colleges & universities, educa-

tion associations, education funds, minority education, religious education • *Health:* health organizations, single-disease health associations • *Religion:* churches, religious organizations • *Science:* scientific organizations • *Social Services:* community service organizations, day care, disabled, family planning, family services, food/clothing distribution, religious welfare, youth organizations
Grant Types: capital and general support
Geographic Distribution: focus on Louisiana
Operating Locations: LA (New Orleans)

CORP. OFFICERS

William Boatner Reily III: *CURR EMPL* pres, dir: William B Reily & Co

GIVING OFFICERS

Joan Coulter: secy, treas
H. Eustis Reily: pres, dir *CURR EMPL* secy, dir: William B Reily & Co
Robert D. Reily: vp, dir *CURR EMPL* vp, dir: William B Reily & Co
William Boatner Reily III: dir *CURR EMPL* pres, dir: William B Reily & Co (see above)

APPLICATION INFORMATION

Initial Approach: *Initial Contact:* send a full proposal *Include Information On:* description of the organization, amount requested, purpose of funds sought, recently audited financial statement, and proof of tax-exempt status. *When to Submit:* any time
Restrictions on Giving: Does not support individuals, religious organizations for sectarian purposes, political or lobbying groups, or organizations outside operating areas.

GRANTS ANALYSIS

Total Grants: $664,178
Number of Grants: 67
Highest Grant: $62,500
Typical Range: $250 to $6,500
Disclosure Period: 1990
Note: Recent grants are derived from a 1990 grants list.

RECENT GRANTS

62,500 Greater New Orleans Regional Foundation, New Orleans, LA

51,000 Junior Achievement, New Orleans, LA
51,000 Touro Infirmary, New Orleans, LA
51,000 Xavier University, New Orleans, LA
50,000 Metairie Park Country Day, New Orleans, LA
50,000 Metropolitan Arts, New Orleans, LA
50,000 Tulane University, New Orleans, LA
25,000 Planned Parenthood, New Orleans, LA
20,000 Parkway Partners, New Orleans, LA
20,000 Society for Coalition of Equity Education, New Orleans, LA

Reinberger Foundation

CONTACT

Robert N. Reinberger
Co-Director
Reinberger Foundation
27600 Chagrin Blvd.
Cleveland, OH 44122
(216) 292-2790

FINANCIAL SUMMARY

Recent Giving: $1,985,817 (1991); $2,062,500 (1990); $1,872,920 (1989)
Assets: $55,650,454 (1991); $47,136,548 (1990); $49,818,395 (1989)
Gifts Received: $4,836,859 (1988)
EIN: 34-6574879

CONTRIBUTIONS SUMMARY

Donor(s): The Reinberger Foundation was established in 1968 by Clarence T. Reinberger, a Cleveland businessman who developed the Automotive Parts Company and later became the chairman of Genuine Parts. Following Mr. Reinberger's death in 1968, the foundation received half of its current assets. The remainder of its assets were acquired following the death of Mr. Reinberger's wife, Louise. The Reinbergers had no children; the foundation is directed by two of Mr. Reinberger's nephews.
Typical Recipients: • *Arts & Humanities:* arts associations, arts centers, arts festivals, arts institutes, history/historic preservation, libraries, museums/galleries, music, opera,

public broadcasting, theater • *Civic & Public Affairs:* nonprofit management, philanthropic organizations, zoos/botanical gardens • *Education:* arts education, colleges & universities, education funds, medical education • *Health:* health organizations • *Religion:* churches • *Social Services:* community centers, family planning, youth organizations
Grant Types: capital, challenge, department, endowment, and general support
Geographic Distribution: primarily Cleveland and Columbus, OH

GIVING OFFICERS

Richard Heer Oman: secy *B* Columbus OH 1926 *ED* OH St Univ BA 1948; OH St Univ JD 1951 *CURR EMPL* ptnr: Porter Wright Morris Arthur *NONPR AFFIL* fellow: OH St Bar Fdn; mem: Am Bar Assn, Am Coll Probate Couns, Am Coll Trust & Estate Couns, Columbus Bar Assn, OH St Bar Assn *PHIL AFFIL* trust: Patton (Mary Louise) Foundation
Robert N. Reinberger: co-dir, trust
William C. Reinberger: co-dir, trust

APPLICATION INFORMATION

Initial Approach:
There are no application forms or guidelines. Applicants should submit one copy of a full proposal.
Written applications should include a clear statement of purpose and a copy of the organization's exemption letter from the IRS. The foundation will request further information on proposals of interest.
There are no deadlines for proposals.
The board of directors meets in March, June, September, and December. The review process takes about six months. The board acknowledges the receipt of an application and may require an interview.
Restrictions on Giving: No grants are made to individuals.

GRANTS ANALYSIS

Total Grants: $1,985,817
Number of Grants: 54
Highest Grant: $100,000
Typical Range: $5,000 to $50,000
Disclosure Period: 1991

Note: Average grant figures excludes a $100,000 grant. Recent grants are derived from a 1991 Form 990.

RECENT GRANTS

100,000 Cleveland Clinic Foundation, Cleveland, OH

100,000 Cleveland Opera, Cleveland, OH

100,000 Columbus Academy, Columbus, OH

100,000 Trilogy Fund of the Columbus Foundation, Columbus, OH

90,000 Cleveland Ballet, Cleveland, OH

75,000 Musical Arts Association, Cleveland, OH

70,000 Cleveland Institute of Art, Cleveland, OH

70,000 Judson Retirement Community, Cleveland, OH

66,667 Salvation Army, Cleveland, OH

66,000 Cleveland Museum of Natural History, Cleveland, OH

Reinghardt Foundation, Albert

CONTACT
Gordon M. Dougherty
Trustee
Albert Reinghardt Foundation
1140 San Antonio Dr.
Long Beach, CA 90807
(310) 424-1621

FINANCIAL SUMMARY
Recent Giving: $807,070 (fiscal 1992); $331,000 (fiscal 1991)
Assets: $2,162,455 (fiscal year ending June 30, 1991)
EIN: 33-6049527

GIVING OFFICERS
William H. Clemo: trust
Gordon M. Dougherty: trust

APPLICATION INFORMATION
Initial Approach: The foundation reports no specific application guidelines. Send a brief letter of inquiry, including statement of purpose, amount requested, and proof of tax-exempt status.

GRANTS ANALYSIS
Total Grants: $331,000
Number of Grants: 11
Highest Grant: $100,000

Disclosure Period: fiscal year ending June 30, 1991

Reinhart Institutional Foods / Reinhart Family Foundation, D.B.
Sales: $190.0 million
Employees: 500
Headquarters: La Crosse, WI
SIC Major Group: Wholesale Trade—Durable Goods and Wholesale Trade—Nondurable Goods

CONTACT
Nancy Hengel
Manager
D. B. Reinhart Family Fdn.
636 L. Hauser Rd.
Onalaska, WI 54650
(608) 782-4999

FINANCIAL SUMMARY
Recent Giving: $347,064 (fiscal 1991); $228,744 (fiscal 1990)
Assets: $5,708,299 (fiscal year ending August 31, 1991); $5,426,790 (fiscal 1990)
Gifts Received: $50,000 (fiscal 1991); $5,050,000 (fiscal 1990)
Fiscal Note: Contributes through foundation only. In 1991, contributions were received from Reinhart Institutional Foods.
EIN: 39-1564353

CONTRIBUTIONS SUMMARY
Typical Recipients: • *Arts & Humanities:* history/historic preservation • *Education:* colleges & universities, private education (precollege) • *Health:* hospitals, medical research, single-disease health associations • *Religion:* churches, religious organizations • *Social Services:* community centers, united funds, youth organizations
Grant Types: general support
Geographic Distribution: focus on Wisconsin
Operating Locations: WI (La Crosse, Onalaska)

CORP. OFFICERS
DeWayne B. Reinhart: *B* 1920 *ED* Superior St Teachers Coll *CURR EMPL* pres: Reinhart Institutional Foods *CORP AFFIL* pres: Reinhart Food Svc

GIVING OFFICERS
Gerald E. Connolly: trust *B* Boston MA 1943 *ED* Coll Holy Cross BS 1965; Univ VA JD 1972 *CURR EMPL* ptnr: Quarles & Brady *CORP AFFIL* dir: Alpha Cellulose Corp, Hatco Corp, Infratol Mfg Corp, Sunlite Plastics; secy: Hometown; secy, dir: Reinhart Real Estate Group, Reinhart Retail Group; vp, secy, dir: Reinhart Institutional Foods *NONPR AFFIL* mem: Am Bar Assn

Nancy Hengel: mgr

DeWayne B. Reinhart: trust *CURR EMPL* pres: Reinhart Institutional Foods (see above)

Marjorie A. Reinhart: trust

APPLICATION INFORMATION
Initial Approach: *Initial Contact:* brief letter *When to Submit:* any time

GRANTS ANALYSIS
Total Grants: $347,064
Number of Grants: 78
Highest Grant: $35,000
Typical Range: $500 to $5,000
Disclosure Period: fiscal year ending August 31, 1991
Note: Recent grants are derived from a fiscal 1991 grants list.

RECENT GRANTS

35,000 Viterbo College, La Crosse, WI

25,000 Blessed Sacrament Endowment Fund, La Crosse, WI

25,000 Children's Hospital Foundation, Milwaukee, WI

25,000 Department of Ophthalmology, Madison, WI

25,000 Diocese of La Crosse, La Crosse, WI

25,000 University of Wisconsin, Superior, WI

20,000 Horatio Alger Association, Garden Grove, CA

17,500 City of Shell Lake, Shell Lake, WI — Arrasmith Library

15,000 Arthritis Foundation of Wisconsin, West Allis, WI

15,000 St. Francis Foundation, La Crosse, WI

Reinhold Foundation, Paul E. and Ida Klare

CONTACT
June R. Myers
Chairman
Paul E. and Ida Klare Reinhold Fdn.
112 West Adams St., No. 1725
Jacksonville, FL 32202-3859
(904) 354-2359

FINANCIAL SUMMARY
Recent Giving: $149,381 (1990); $240,386 (1989)
Assets: $3,683,927 (1989)
EIN: 59-6140495

CONTRIBUTIONS SUMMARY
Donor(s): the late Paul E. Reinhold
Typical Recipients: • *Arts & Humanities:* museums/galleries • *Education:* colleges & universities, private education (precollege) • *Health:* hospitals, single-disease health associations • *Religion:* churches, religious organizations • *Social Services:* community service organizations, religious welfare, youth organizations
Grant Types: capital, general support, and project
Geographic Distribution: focus on FL

GIVING OFFICERS
Thomas E. Camp III: trust
Leah B. Giebeig: secy
Ralph H. Martin: trust
June R. Myers: chmn, treas

APPLICATION INFORMATION
Initial Approach: Send letter requesting application form. Deadlines are April 30 and September 30.
Restrictions on Giving: Does not support individuals.

OTHER THINGS TO KNOW
Publications: Annual Report

GRANTS ANALYSIS
Number of Grants: 28
Highest Grant: $25,000
Typical Range: $1,000 to $10,000
Disclosure Period: 1990

RECENT GRANTS

25,000 Lutheran Social Services, Jacksonville, FL

20,000 Hillyer House, Florida Christian

Care Centers, Jacksonville, FL

11,000 Living with Loss, Jacksonville, FL

10,000 Alzheimer's Disease and Related Disorders Association, Jacksonville, FL

10,000 American Horse Trials, Annapolis, MD

10,000 St. Lukes Hospital, Jacksonville, FL

8,041 University of Florida, Gainesville, FL

5,000 Children's Haven of Clay County, Orange Park, FL

5,000 Episcopal High School, Jacksonville, FL

5,000 Newberry College, Newberry, SC

Reisman Charitable Trust, George C. and Evelyn R.

CONTACT
David Andelman
Trustee
George C. and Evelyn R.
 Reisman Charitable Trust
c/o Lourie and Cutler
60 State St.
Boston, MA 02109
(617) 742-6720

FINANCIAL SUMMARY
Recent Giving: $439,545 (1990); $609,638 (1989); $507,858 (1988)
Assets: $9,410,936 (1990); $9,032,809 (1989); $8,825,764 (1988)
EIN: 04-2743096

CONTRIBUTIONS SUMMARY
Donor(s): George C. Reisman, Apparel Retail Corp.
Typical Recipients: • *Civic & Public Affairs:* philanthropic organizations, women's affairs • *Education:* private education (precollege) • *Health:* hospitals, single-disease health associations • *Religion:* religious organizations • *Social Services:* disabled, united funds
Grant Types: general support

GIVING OFFICERS
David Andelman: trust
Evelyn R. Reisman: trust
Mrs. George C. Reisman: trust *CURR EMPL* chmn, pres, treas, ceo: Apparel Retail Corp
Howard Reisman: trust
Robert Reisman: trust

David Rothstein: trust

APPLICATION INFORMATION
Initial Approach: Send brief letter of inquiry describing program or project. There are no deadlines.

GRANTS ANALYSIS
Number of Grants: 35
Highest Grant: $350,000
Typical Range: $100 to $1,000
Disclosure Period: 1990

RECENT GRANTS
350,000 Combined Jewish Philanthropies, Boston, MA

50,000 Beth Israel Hospital, Boston, MA

10,000 Beth Israel Hospital Vascular Research Fund, Boston, MA

10,000 United Way, Boston, MA

2,500 Beth Israel Hospital, Boston, MA

1,000 Beth Israel Hospital, Boston, MA

1,000 Friends of Dana Farber Cancer Institute, Boston, MA

1,000 Hebrew Rehabilitation Center for the Aged, Roslindale, MA

1,000 Recuperative Center Committee, Boston, MA

1,000 Recuperative Center Committee, Boston, MA

Reiss Coal Co., C. / Reiss Coal Co. Scholarship Fund Trust, C.

Sales: $90.0 million
Employees: 21
Parent Company: Koch Carbon Co.
Headquarters: Sheboygan, WI
SIC Major Group: Miscellaneous Retail and Wholesale Trade—Durable Goods

CONTACT
Russell J. Schulz
President
C. Reiss Coal Co. Scholarship Fund Trust
PO Box 0663
Sheboygan, WI 53082-0328
(414) 457-4411

FINANCIAL SUMMARY
Recent Giving: $1,000 (1991); $5,000 (1990); $3,500 (1989)

Assets: 0 (1991); $958 (1990); $2,046 (1989)
Gifts Received: $4,002 (1990); $4,000 (1989)
EIN: 39-6038890

CONTRIBUTIONS SUMMARY
Grant Types: scholarship
Geographic Distribution: focus on WI and IL
Operating Locations: WI (Sheboygan)

CORP. OFFICERS
William Reiss, Jr.: *CURR EMPL* pres: C. Reiss Coal Co

GIVING OFFICERS
Ron Dales: secy, dir
David Rauwerdink: pres, dir
William Reiss, Jr.: treas, dir *CURR EMPL* pres: C. Reiss Coal Co (see above)

APPLICATION INFORMATION
Initial Approach: Request application form. There are no deadlines.

OTHER THINGS TO KNOW
Provides scholarships to individuals for higher education.
Disclosure Period: 1991

Relations Foundation

Headquarters: Skokie, IL

CONTACT
Janet Madrigal
President
Relations Fdn.
7450 North McCormick Blvd.
Skokie, IL 60076
(312) 446-4211

FINANCIAL SUMMARY
Recent Giving: $489,302 (1989); $352,389 (1988)
Assets: $3,430,723 (1989); $3,200,014 (1988)
Gifts Received: $600,000 (1989); $420,000 (1988)
Fiscal Note: In 1989, contributions were received from Fel-Pro Inc. and Fel-Pro Realty.
EIN: 23-7032294

CONTRIBUTIONS SUMMARY
Donor(s): Fel-Pro Inc.
Typical Recipients: • *Arts & Humanities:* music • *Civic & Public Affairs:* urban & community affairs, women's affairs • *Education:* colleges & universities, education associations,

religious education • *Health:* medical research, single-disease health associations • *International:* international development/relief, international organizations • *Social Services:* child welfare, employment/job training, family planning, food/clothing distribution, religious welfare, united funds, youth organizations
Grant Types: general support and operating expenses
Geographic Distribution: primarily in the Chicago, IL, area

GIVING OFFICERS
Barbara Kessler: secy, dir
Dennis L. Kessler: vp, dir *CURR EMPL* pres, dir: Fel-Pro
Joseph Radov: pres, dir
Sylvia M. Radov: vp, dir
Carol Weinberg: vp, dir
Daniel C. Weinberg: vp, dir
David Weinberg: treas, dir *CURR EMPL* co-chmn: Fel-Pro

APPLICATION INFORMATION
Initial Approach: Send brief letter and proposal. There are no deadlines. Board meets in April, July, and November.
Restrictions on Giving: Does not support endowments or provide loans. Organizations must be educational, religious, or charitable as defined under IRS Section 170(c).

OTHER THINGS TO KNOW
Publications: Application Guidelines

GRANTS ANALYSIS
Number of Grants: 152
Highest Grant: $88,000
Typical Range: $1,000 to $3,000
Disclosure Period: 1989

RECENT GRANTS
88,000 Jewish United Fund, Chicago, IL

58,439 Urban Gateways, Chicago, IL

50,000 New Israel Fund, New York, NY

33,914 Community Youth Creative Learning Experience (CYCLE), Chicago, IL

22,000 Dystonia, Chicago, IL

10,000 Les Turner ALS Foundation, Skokie, IL

10,000 Spertus College of Judaica, Chicago, IL

6,000 Greater Chicago
Food Depository,
Chicago, IL
6,000 Ounce of Preven-
tion Fund, Chi-
cago, IL
5,000 Chicago Action for
Soviet Jewry, High-
land Park, IL

Reliable Life Insurance Co.

Sales: $420.2 million
Employees: 1,200
Headquarters: Webster Groves,
MO
SIC Major Group: Insurance
Carriers

CONTACT
Bradley H. Sinclair
Vice President, Corporate
Services
Reliable Life Insurance Co.
231 West Lockwood Ave.
Webster Groves, MO 63119
(314) 968-6714
Note: Telephone extension is
314.

FINANCIAL SUMMARY
Recent Giving: $130,000
(1993 est.)

CONTRIBUTIONS SUMMARY
Company reports 35% of contributions support education;
25% each to civic affairs and
health and human services; and
15% to the arts. Company promotes voluntarism through the
Boy Scouts, blood drives with
the American Red Cross and recycling activites where money
is donated to chosen charities.
Typical Recipients: • *Arts &
Humanities:* arts appreciation,
arts associations, arts centers,
arts funds, arts institutes, community arts, dance, general,
music, opera, performing arts
• *Civic & Public Affairs:*
economic development, environmental affairs, ethnic/minor-
ity organizations, general, philanthropic organizations, urban
& community affairs • *Education:* arts education, colleges &
universities, continuing education, education funds, elementary education, general, minority education, preschool
education, student aid
• *Health:* general, health funds,
health organizations, nutrition
& health maintenance, single-
disease health associations • *Social Services:* child welfare,
community service organiza-

tions, day care, disabled, drugs
& alcohol, food/clothing dis-
tribution, general, homes, shel-
ters/homelessness, youth or-
ganizations
Grant Types: employee match-
ing gifts and scholarship
Nonmonetary Support Types:
donated equipment
Geographic Distribution: pri-
marily in MO, but also in
seven other states where com-
pany does business.
Operating Locations: AR (El
Dorado, Jonesboro, Little
Rock, Texarkana), KS (Kansas
City), MO (Webster Groves),
TX (Austin, Beaumont,
Brownsville, Corpus Christi,
Dallas, Fort Worth, Harlingen,
Houston, Longview, Lubbock,
McAllen, Midland, San Anto-
nio, Sherman, Tyler, Waco)

CORP. OFFICERS
Bernal T. Chomeau: *B* St.
Louis MO 1931 *ED* Southeast
MO St Coll 1954; Univ WI
1956 *CURR EMPL* chmn, ceo:
Reliable Life Ins Co
Douglas D. Chomeau: *B* St.
Louis MO 1937 *ED* Carleton
Coll 1958 *CURR EMPL* pres:
Reliable Life Ins Co

APPLICATION INFORMATION
Initial Approach: Send a brief
letter of inquiry and a full proposal. Include a description of
organization, amount re-
quested, purpose of funds
sought, recently audited financial statement, and proof of tax-
exempt status. There are no
deadlines.
Restrictions on Giving: Does
not support individuals, religious organizations for sectarian
purposes, political or lobbying
groups, or organizations outside operating areas.

GRANTS ANALYSIS
Typical Range: $1,000 to
$2,500

RECENT GRANTS
AFRAS, St. Louis, MO
Aunts and Uncles, St. Louis,
MO
Christmas In April, Harlingen,
TX
Even Start Program, St. Louis,
MO
INSURE for Hurricane An-
drew, FL
Missouri Colleges, Inc., MO
Muny Grantors Fund, St.
Louis, MO

Urban League of St. Louis, St.
Louis, MO
Webster Groves Day Care, St.
Louis, MO
Webster University, St. Louis,
MO

Reliance Electric Co. / Reliance Electric Co. Charitable, Scientific & Educational Trust

Sales: $1.53 billion
Employees: 14,200
Headquarters: Cleveland, OH
SIC Major Group: Electronic &
Other Electrical Equipment
and Industrial Machinery &
Equipment

CONTACT
Edward R. Towns
Secretary
Reliance Electric Co. Charitable,
Scientific & Educational Trust
6065 Parkland Blvd.
Cleveland, OH 44124
(216) 266-5826

FINANCIAL SUMMARY
Recent Giving: $800,000
(1993 est.); $833,295 (1992);
$878,600 (1991)
Assets: $120,000 (1991);
$154,694 (1989)
Fiscal Note: All contributions
are made through the founda-
tion.
EIN: 34-6505329

CONTRIBUTIONS SUMMARY
Typical Recipients: • *Arts &
Humanities:* arts associations,
arts institutes, dance, his-
tory/historic preservation, mu-
seums/galleries, music, performing arts, theater • *Civic &
Public Affairs:* business/free enterprise, civil rights, economic
development, public policy,
urban & community affairs
• *Education:* arts education,
business education, colleges &
universities, continuing education, engineering education, minority education, public education (precollege),
science/technology education
• *Health:* health care cost containment, health organizations,
hospitals, single-disease health
associations • *Social Services:*
aged, child welfare, community centers, community service organizations, disabled, domestic violence, drugs &

alcohol, family planning,
united funds, volunteer services, youth organizations
Grant Types: capital, em-
ployee matching gifts, general
support, multiyear/continuing
support, and scholarship
Geographic Distribution: operating locations, emphasis on
Cleveland, OH; U.S.-based nonprofit organizations with an international focus
Operating Locations: CT (Collinsville), GA (Athens, Gainesville, Toccoa), IL (Chicago),
IN (Columbus, Madison,
Mishawaka), MN (North
Mankato), NC (Asheville,
King's Mountain), OH (Ashtabula, Cleveland, Lorain), SC
(Greenville, St. Stephen), TN
(Rogersville), TX (Bedford)

CORP. OFFICERS
John C. Morley: *B* Saginaw
MI 1931 *ED* Yale Univ BA
1954; Univ MI MBA 1958
CURR EMPL pres, ceo, dir: Re-
liance Electric Co

GIVING OFFICERS
Edward R. Towns: secy
CURR EMPL secy: Reliance
Electric Co

APPLICATION INFORMATION
Initial Approach: *Initial Contact:* brief letter or proposal *Include Information On:* description of the organization,
amount requested, purpose for
which funds are sought, recently audited financial statement, IRS determination letter
When to Submit: any time
Restrictions on Giving: Does
not give to dinners or special
events, fraternal organizations,
goodwill advertising, individuals, member agencies of united
funds, or political or lobbying
groups.

GRANTS ANALYSIS
Total Grants: $833,295*
Number of Grants: 600*
Typical Range: $500 to $5,000
Disclosure Period: 1992
Note: Fiscal information is ap-
proximate. Foundation assets
are for 1991. Recent grants are
derived from a 1991 Form 990.

RECENT GRANTS
60,000 Case Western Re-
serve University,
Cleveland, OH
30,000 Case Western Re-
serve University,
Cleveland, OH

28,750 United Way of Greater Cleveland, Cleveland, OH
28,750 United Way of Greater Cleveland, Cleveland, OH
28,750 United Way of Greater Cleveland, Cleveland, OH
25,000 Athens Area Technical Institute, Athens, OH
22,000 Greenville Habitat for Humanity, Greenville, SC
15,000 Clemson University, Clemson, SC
15,000 Clemson University, Clemson, SC
13,750 United Way of Northeast Georgia, Athens, GA

Reliance Group Holdings, Inc.

Assets: $11.25 billion
Employees: 9,500
Headquarters: New York, NY
SIC Major Group: Engineering & Management Services, Holding & Other Investment Offices, and Insurance Carriers

CONTACT

Brian Martin
Vice President, Communications
Reliance Group Holdings, Inc.
55 East 52nd St.
New York, NY 10055
(212) 909-1100

FINANCIAL SUMMARY

Fiscal Note: Annual Giving Range: $100,000 to $250,000

CONTRIBUTIONS SUMMARY

Support goes to local education, health and human service, arts, and civic organizations.
Typical Recipients: • *Arts & Humanities:* general • *Civic & Public Affairs:* general • *Education:* general • *Health:* general • *Social Services:* general
Grant Types: general support
Geographic Distribution: primarily headquarters area
Operating Locations: NY (New York)

CORP. OFFICERS

Robert M. Steinberg: *B* Brooklyn NY 1942 *ED* NC St Univ 1964 *CURR EMPL* chmn, ceo: Reliance Group Holdings *CORP AFFIL* chmn, ceo: Reliance Ins Co; dir: Frank B Hall & Co, Telemundo Group, Zenith Natl Ins Corp

Saul Philip Steinberg: *B* Brooklyn NY 1939 *ED* Univ PA BS 1959 *CURR EMPL* fdr, chmn, ceo: Reliance Group Holdings *CORP AFFIL* chmn exec & fin comm: Reliance Ins Cos; dir: Days Inn, Flying Tiger Line, Frank B Hall & Co, Symbol Technologies, Telemundo, Tiger Intl, Zenith Natl Ins Corp

APPLICATION INFORMATION

Initial Approach: Send brief letter of inquiry. There are no deadlines.

Reliance Insurance Cos.

Assets: $4.2 billion
Employees: 5,500
Parent Company: Reliance Fianancial Services Corp.
Headquarters: Philadelphia, PA
SIC Major Group: Insurance Carriers

CONTACT

Richard Earl
Vice President
Reliance Insurance Cos.
4 Penn Center Plz.
Philadelphia, PA 19103
(215) 864-4671

CONTRIBUTIONS SUMMARY

Company sponsors employee matching gift program; also supports community organizations.
Typical Recipients: • *Arts & Humanities:* general • *Civic & Public Affairs:* general • *Education:* general • *Health:* general • *Social Services:* general
Grant Types: matching
Geographic Distribution: primarily headquarters area
Operating Locations: CA (Encino, San Francisco), NY (Bohemia, Briarcliff Manor), PA (Philadelphia)

CORP. OFFICERS

Dean W. Case: *B* Detroit MI 1936 *ED* Univ MI *CURR EMPL* pres, coo, dir: Reliance Ins Co *CORP AFFIL* dir: Agena Corp, First WI Natl Bank Madison, Reliance Fin Svcs, Reliance Group Holdings; pres, ceo: Gen Casualty Cos *NONPR AFFIL* dir: Natl Assn Independent Insurers
Robert M. Steinberg: *B* Brooklyn NY 1942 *ED* NC St Univ 1964 *CURR EMPL* chmn,

ceo: Reliance Group Holdings *CORP AFFIL* chmn, ceo: Reliance Ins Co; dir: Frank B Hall & Co, Telemundo Group, Zenith Natl Ins Corp
Saul Philip Steinberg: *B* Brooklyn NY 1939 *ED* Univ PA BS 1959 *CURR EMPL* fdr, chmn, ceo: Reliance Group Holdings *CORP AFFIL* chmn exec & fin comm: Reliance Ins Cos; dir: Days Inn, Flying Tiger Line, Frank B Hall & Co, Symbol Technologies, Telemundo, Tiger Intl, Zenith Natl Ins Corp

APPLICATION INFORMATION

Initial Approach: Send brief letter of inquiry. There are no deadlines.

Remmele Engineering, Inc.

Sales: $60.0 million
Employees: 430
Headquarters: St. Paul, MN
SIC Major Group: Industrial Machinery & Equipment

CONTACT

Connie Pheifer
Credit Collection Supervisor
Remmele Engineering, Inc.
1211 Pierce Butler Rte.
St. Paul, MN 55104
(612) 645-3451

CONTRIBUTIONS SUMMARY

Operating Locations: MN (St. Paul)

CORP. OFFICERS

Paul Foster: *CURR EMPL* cfo: Remmele Engring
Tom Moore: *CURR EMPL* pres: Remmele Engring
William J. Saul: *CURR EMPL* chmn: Remmele Engring

Rennebohm Foundation, Oscar

CONTACT

John L. Sonderegger
Secretary
Oscar Rennebohm Fdn.
PO Box 5187
Madison, WI 53719
(608) 274-1030

FINANCIAL SUMMARY

Recent Giving: $1,264,400 (1990); $1,202,999 (1989); $789,350 (1987)

Assets: $24,755,202 (1990); $24,985,261 (1989); $19,614,943 (1987)
EIN: 39-6039252

CONTRIBUTIONS SUMMARY

Donor(s): The foundation was incorporated in 1949 by the late Oscar Rennebohm.
Typical Recipients: • *Arts & Humanities:* arts centers, history/historic preservation • *Civic & Public Affairs:* housing, municipalities, public policy, zoos/botanical gardens • *Education:* colleges & universities, education funds • *Health:* health organizations, hospitals, medical rehabilitation • *Social Services:* child welfare, community service organizations, disabled, family services, food/clothing distribution, shelters/homelessness, united funds, volunteer services, youth organizations
Grant Types: capital, general support, and research
Geographic Distribution: limited to Madison, WI

GIVING OFFICERS

Patrick E. Coyle: dir
Frederick W. Jensen: dir
Dennis G. Maki: dir *B* River Falls WI 1940 *ED* Univ WI BS; Univ WI MS; Univ WI MD *NONPR AFFIL* attending physician: Univ WI Ctr Trauma & Life Support; fellow: Am Coll Physicians, Infectious Diseases Soc Am, Soc Critical Care Medicine, Surgical Infection Soc; hosp epidemiologist: Univ WI Hosp & Clinic; mem: Am Dental Assn, Am Federation Clinical Res, Am Soc Microbiology; mem, pres: Soc Hosp Epidemiologists Am; sr assoc editor: Infection Control & Hosp Epidemiology
Mary F. Rennebohm: vp, dir
Steven Skolaski: pres, treas, dir
John L. Sonderegger: secy, dir
Leona A. Sonderegger: asst secy, dir
William H. Young: dir
Lenor Zeeh: dir

APPLICATION INFORMATION

Initial Approach:
The foundation has no formal grant application procedure or application form.
The foundation has no deadline for submitting proposals.
Restrictions on Giving: The foundation makes grants to

charitable, educational, scientific, or religious organizations.

GRANTS ANALYSIS
Total Grants: $1,264,400
Number of Grants: 16
Highest Grant: $470,000
Typical Range: $24,000 to $75,000
Disclosure Period: 1990
Note: Average grant figure does not include the highest grant of $470,000. Recent grants are derived from a 1990 grants list.

RECENT GRANTS
470,000 Edgewood College, Madison, WI
359,500 University of Wisconsin Foundation, Madison, WI
100,000 Easter Seal Society of Wisconsin, Madison, WI
75,000 City of Madison Parks Division, Madison, WI
64,500 Wisconsin Taxpayer Alliance, Madison, WI
50,000 Family Services, Madison, WI
50,000 Oakwood Village, Madison, WI
26,000 Meriter Hospital, Madison, WI
25,000 Attic Angels Association, Madison, WI
25,000 Family Enhancement, Madison, WI

Renner Foundation

CONTACT
Robert R. Renner
President
Renner Fdn.
1146 Hanna Bldg.
Cleveland, OH 44114
(216) 623-0909

FINANCIAL SUMMARY
Recent Giving: $122,800 (fiscal 1992); $130,000 (fiscal 1991); $124,000 (fiscal 1989)
Assets: $2,902,052 (fiscal year ending May 31, 1991); $2,620,065 (fiscal 1989); $2,371,707 (fiscal 1988)
Gifts Received: $2,140 (fiscal 1991)
EIN: 34-0684303

CONTRIBUTIONS SUMMARY
Donor(s): the late R. Richard Renner, M.D.
Typical Recipients: • *Education:* colleges & universities
Grant Types: general support

GIVING OFFICERS
Lillian M. Kozan: secy
David F. Percy: trust
Frank E. Percy: trust
Ruth A. Percy: trust
Daniel S. Renner: trust
Jane Renner: trust
Jennie S. Renner: trust
John W. Renner: vp, trust
Richard R. Renner: treas, trust
Robert R. Renner: pres, trust
Carlton B. Schnell: trust
Gary L. Slapnicker: exec dir

APPLICATION INFORMATION
Initial Approach: The foundation reports it only makes contributions to preselected charitable organizations.
Restrictions on Giving: Does not support individuals.

GRANTS ANALYSIS
Number of Grants: 1
Highest Grant: $122,800
Disclosure Period: fiscal year ending May 31, 1991

RECENT GRANTS
122,800 Bethany College, Bethany, WV

Rennie Scholarship Fund, Waldo E.

CONTACT
Yvonne Baca
Waldo E. Rennie Scholarship Fund
c/o First Interstate Bank of Denver, N.A.
PO Box 5825
Denver, CO 80217
(303) 293-5923

FINANCIAL SUMMARY
Recent Giving: $113,587 (fiscal 1991); $98,753 (fiscal 1990); $180,853 (fiscal 1989)
Assets: $2,002,542 (fiscal year ending September 30, 1991); $1,830,534 (fiscal 1990); $1,825,942 (fiscal 1989)
EIN: 84-6138107

CONTRIBUTIONS SUMMARY
Grant Types: scholarship
Geographic Distribution: focus on CO

GIVING OFFICERS
First Interstate Bank of Denver: trust

APPLICATION INFORMATION
Initial Approach: Send brief letter describing situation. There are no deadlines.

OTHER THINGS TO KNOW
Provides scholarships to individuals for higher education.

Replogle Foundation, Luther I.

CONTACT
Gwenn Gebhard
Luther I. Replogle Fdn.
726 Fifth St. N.E.
Washington, DC 20012

FINANCIAL SUMMARY
Recent Giving: $274,990 (1990); $316,940 (1989); $237,733 (1988)
Assets: $7,704,070 (1990); $7,587,853 (1989); $7,276,399 (1988)
EIN: 36-6141697

CONTRIBUTIONS SUMMARY
Typical Recipients: • *Arts & Humanities:* arts institutes, museums/galleries, music, theater • *Education:* colleges & universities, religious education • *Health:* hospitals • *International:* foreign educational institutions • *Religion:* churches, religious organizations • *Social Services:* child welfare, community service organizations, family planning, youth organizations
Grant Types: general support
Geographic Distribution: focus on Chicago, IL

GIVING OFFICERS
Elizabeth R. Dickie: pres, treas
James D. Hinchliff: vp
William Otto Petersen: secy
B Chicago IL 1926 *ED* Harvard Univ AB 1949; Harvard Univ LLB 1952 *CURR EMPL* ptnr: Vedder Price Kaufman & Kamholz *CORP AFFIL* ptnr: Vedder Price Kaufman & Kamholz *NONPR AFFIL* dir: Chicago Youth Ctrs, Taylor Inst; mem: Am Bar Assn, Chicago Bar Assn, IL Bar Assn; vchmn, mem exec bd: Auditorium Theatre Counc

APPLICATION INFORMATION
Initial Approach: Send brief letter of inquiry describing program or project. There are no deadlines.

GRANTS ANALYSIS
Number of Grants: 87
Highest Grant: $61,000
Typical Range: $500 to $6,000
Disclosure Period: 1990

RECENT GRANTS
61,000 American School of Classical Studies in Athens, New York, NY
25,000 Holy Family Lutheran Church School, Chicago, IL
20,000 First Presbyterian Church of Chicago, Chicago, IL
20,000 Lorene Replogle Counseling Center, Chicago, IL
20,000 McCormick Theological Seminary, Chicago, IL
17,600 American Academy in Rome, New York, NY
8,000 Merit Music Program, Chicago, IL
7,500 Hellenic Foundation, Chicago, IL
6,000 H.O.M.E., Chicago, IL
5,600 University of Chicago, Chicago, IL

Republic Automotive Parts, Inc.

Sales: $80.2 million
Employees: 691
Headquarters: Brentwood, TN
SIC Major Group: Automotive Dealers & Service Stations and Wholesale Trade—Durable Goods

CONTACT
Hal Pruett
Director, Employee Relations
Republic Automotive Parts, Inc.
PO Box 2088
Brentwood, TN 37024
(615) 373-2050

FINANCIAL SUMMARY
Fiscal Note: Annual Giving Range: less than $100,000

CONTRIBUTIONS SUMMARY
Typical Recipients: • *Arts & Humanities:* general • *Civic & Public Affairs:* general • *Educa-*

tion: general • *Health:* general • *Social Services:* general
Grant Types: general support
Geographic Distribution: primarily headquarters area
Operating Locations: TN (Brentwood)

CORP. OFFICERS
Edgar R. Berner: *CURR EMPL* chmn: Republic Automotive Parts
Donald B. Hauk: *B* Oak Ridge TN 1944 *ED* Univ TX 1966; TX Christian Univ 1969 *CURR EMPL* exec vp, cfo: Republic Automotive Parts
Keith M. Thompson: *CURR EMPL* pres, ceo: Republic Automotive Parts

APPLICATION INFORMATION
Initial Approach: Send brief letter of inquiry. There are no deadlines.

Republic Engineered Steels
Sales: $670.0 million
Employees: 5,000
Headquarters: Massillon, OH
SIC Major Group: Primary Metal Industries

CONTACT
Harold Kelly
Vice President, Law & Public Affairs
Republic Engineered Steels
410 Oberlin Rd. Southwest
Massillon, OH 44647
(216) 837-6000

CONTRIBUTIONS SUMMARY
Operating Locations: OH (Massillon)

CORP. OFFICERS
Russell Maier: *CURR EMPL* pres, ceo: Republic Engineered Steels
James B. Riley: *CURR EMPL* cfo: Republic Engineered Steels

Republic Financial Services, Inc.
Sales: $1.01 billion
Employees: 1,060
Parent Company: Winterthur Swiss Insurance Co.
Headquarters: Dallas, TX
SIC Major Group: Holding & Other Investment Offices and Insurance Carriers

CONTACT
Lori Moore
Director of Corporate Communications
Republic Financial Services, Inc.
PO Box 660560
Dallas, TX 75266
(214) 559-1222

CONTRIBUTIONS SUMMARY
Operating Locations: TX (Dallas)

CORP. OFFICERS
William R. Miller: *CURR EMPL* chmn: Republic Fin Svcs
Harry W. Wilcott: *CURR EMPL* pres, ceo: Republic Fin Svcs

Republic New York Corp.
Assets: $37.14 billion
Employees: 18,000
Headquarters: New York, NY
SIC Major Group: Holding & Other Investment Offices

CONTACT
J. Phillip Burgess
Vice President, Director of Corporate Communications
Republic New York Corp.
452 Fifth Ave.
New York, NY 10018
(212) 525-6597

FINANCIAL SUMMARY
Recent Giving: $1,000,000 (1991 approx.); $1,000,000 (1990 approx.); $1,000,000 (1989 approx.)
Fiscal Note: All contributions are made directly by the company.

CONTRIBUTIONS SUMMARY
Typical Recipients: • *Arts & Humanities:* dance, libraries, museums/galleries, music, opera, performing arts, public broadcasting, theater • *Civic & Public Affairs:* economic development, ethnic/minority organizations, housing, public policy, zoos/botanical gardens • *Education:* career/vocational education, colleges & universities, faculty development, minority education, religious education • *Social Services:* aged, community service organizations, disabled, drugs & alcohol, employment/job training, food/clothing distribution, shelters/homelessness, youth organizations

Grant Types: employee matching gifts, general support, multiyear/continuing support, and project
Nonmonetary Support Types: donated equipment and in-kind services
Note: No estimate is available for value of nonmonetary support, and it is not included above.
Geographic Distribution: principally in the New York metropolitan area
Operating Locations: CA (Beverly Hills, Los Angeles), FL (Miami), NY (New York, New York), TX (Corpus Christi)

CORP. OFFICERS
Cyril S. Dwek: *B* Kobe Japan 1936 *ED* Univ PA Wharton Sch BS 1958 *CURR EMPL* vchmn, dir: Republic NY Corp *CORP AFFIL* vchmn, dir, exec vp: Republic Natl Bank NY *NONPR AFFIL* bd adv: Brazilian Inst Bus Programs, Pace Univ; mem, vp: Brazilian Am Chamber Commerce
Ernest Ginsberg: *B* Syracuse NY 1931 *ED* Syracuse Univ BA 1953; Syracuse Univ JD 1955; Georgetown Univ LLM 1963 *CURR EMPL* vchmn, gen coun, dir: Republic NY Corp *CORP AFFIL* dir: Colonial Savings & Loan, Manhattan Savings Bank, Safra Bank NA; vchmn: Republic Natl Bank NY *NONPR AFFIL* mem: Am Bar Assn, NY Bar Assn, NY St Bankers Assn, Phi Delta Phi, Phi Sigma Delta; vchmn: Roundabout Theatre Co
Jeffrey Craig Keil: *B* West Orange NJ 1943 *ED* Univ PA 1965; Harvard Univ MBA 1968 *CURR EMPL* pres, dir: Republic NY Corp *CORP AFFIL* chmn: Safra Bank NA; vchmn, dir: Republic Natl Bank NY
John A. Pancetti: *CURR EMPL* vchmn, dir: Republic NY Corp
Vito S. Portea: *CURR EMPL* vchmn: Republic NY Corp
Dov C. Schlein: *B* Haifa Israel 1947 *ED* City Univ NY 1970 *CURR EMPL* pres, coo, dir: Republic Natl Bank NY *CORP AFFIL* pres, coo, dir: Republic Natl Bank NY *NONPR AFFIL* mem: Am Inst CPAs, Comex NY
Walter Weiner: *B* Brooklyn NY 1930 *ED* Univ MI BA 1952; Univ MI JD 1953 *CURR EMPL* chmn, ceo, dir: Republic NY Corp *CORP AFFIL* chmn, ceo: Republic Natl Bank NY;

dir: Big V Supermarkets, Manhattan Savings Bank, Republic Bank Corp, Safra Republic Holdings *NONPR AFFIL* bd visitors: Univ MI Law Sch; mem: Am Bankers Assn, Am Bar Assn, Assn Bar City NY, NY Bar Assn, NY Holocaust Meml Commn; treas, dir: Bryant Park Restoration Corp, Intl Sephardic Ed Fdn; trust: Guild Hall

GIVING OFFICERS
J. Phillip Burgess: vp, dir corp comm *CURR EMPL* vp: Republic NY Corp
James LoGatto: mem contributions comm *CURR EMPL* sr vp: Republic Natl Bank NY
Joseph Rhatigan: *CURR EMPL* vp: Republic Natl Bank NY
Phyllis Rosenblum: 1st vp *CURR EMPL* first vp: Republic Natl Bank NY

APPLICATION INFORMATION
Initial Approach: *Initial Contact:* letter *Include Information On:* background and budget of organization, range of support sought, purpose of contribution, list of board/organization officers, proof of tax-exempt status *When to Submit:* any time
Restrictions on Giving: Program does not support political or lobbying groups or veterans organizations.

GRANTS ANALYSIS
Total Grants: $1,000,000
Typical Range: $100 to $2,000
Disclosure Period: 1991

Research Corporation

CONTACT
Brian H. Andreen
Vice President
Research Corporation
101 North Wilmot Rd., Ste. 250
Tucson, AZ 85711-3332
(602) 571-1111

FINANCIAL SUMMARY
Recent Giving: $3,494,403 (1991); $2,715,675 (1990); $3,491,812 (1989)
Assets: $90,289,218 (1991); $81,577,531 (1990); $82,658,024 (1989)
Gifts Received: $629,500 (1991); $428,000 (1990); $394,500 (1989)
EIN: 13-1963407

CONTRIBUTIONS SUMMARY

Donor(s): Research Corrporation was founded in 1912, with the late Frederick Gardner Cottrell as a donor. Dr. Cottrell, a noted scientist, inventor, and philanthropist, established the foundation for the advancement of science and technology with the assistance of the Secretary of the Smithsonian Institution, Charles Doolittle Walcott. The Research Corporation, which was one of the first U.S. foundations, was the only one wholly devoted to science.

Dr. Cottrell, born in Oakland, CA, in 1877, received a bachelor's degree from the University of California in 1896. He taught high school chemistry, before pursuing advanced degrees from the University of Berlin in 1901 and the University of Leipzig in 1902. Dr. Cottrell then returned to America to teach at the University of California.

While an instructor at the University of California, he invented the Cottrell Electrical Precipitator. The devise, which is still in use today, became the primary means for controlling industrial air pollution and the basis for his fortune.

In 1912, after taking a job with the U.S. Bureau of Mines, he established Research Corporation with the enormous profits from his invention. Dr. Cottrell believed that science should be the principal beneficiary for his invention and wanted the foundation to provide means for scientific investigation and research by contributing funds to the Smithsonian Insitution and other institutions. For the foundation's board, he recruited men prominent in academe and industry, including Mr. Walcott, as the foundation's first president.

Over the past 80 years, the Research Corporation has contributed well over $100 million to research projects proposed by young academic scientists. More than 20 of whom later won Nobel Prizes. A number of other prominent academic inventors have followed Dr. Cottrell's example and have contributed inventions to the corporation for the furthering of academic science. It has nearly 20,000 patents and licenses.

Dr. Cottrell married Jessie May in 1904. The couple had two children both of whom died while infants. Dr. Cottrell died in 1948.

Typical Recipients: • *Education:* colleges & universities
Grant Types: research
Geographic Distribution: nationally

GIVING OFFICERS

Brian Andreen: vp
Stuart B. Crampton: dir *B* New York NY 1936 *ED* Williams Coll BA 1958; Oxford Univ Worcester Coll BA 1960; Harvard Univ PhD 1964; Oxford Univ Worcester Coll MA 1965 *NONPR AFFIL* mem: Am Assn Physics Teachers, Sigma Phi, Sigma Xi; prof: Williams Coll
Helen Day: secy *CURR EMPL* secy: Res Corp
Michael P. Doyle: dir *NONPR AFFIL* prof: Trinity Univ
Robert Michael Gavin, Jr.: dir *B* Coatesville PA 1940 *ED* St Johns Univ BA 1962; IA St Univ PhD 1966 *CORP AFFIL* dir: AMEV Funds *NONPR AFFIL* mem: Am Chemical Soc; prest: Macalester Coll; trust: MN Science Mus
Suzanne D. Jaffe: treas, dir *CURR EMPL* managing dir: Angelo Gordon & Co
John William Johnstone, Jr.: dir *B* Brooklyn NY 1932 *ED* Hartwick Coll BA 1954; Harvard Univ MBA 1970 *CURR EMPL* chmn, pres, ceo, dir: Olin Corp *CORP AFFIL* dir: Am Brands, HL Fin Group, Home Life Ins Co *NONPR AFFIL* dir: Am Productivity Ctr, Chem Mfrs Assn, Soap Detergent Assn, Southwestern Area Commerce & Indus Assn; mem: Am Mgmt Assn, Soc Chem Indus; trust: Hartwick Coll
John Paul Schaefer: pres, ceo, dir *B* New York NY 1928 *ED* Polytech Inst BS 1955; Univ IL PhD 1958 *CURR EMPL* pres: Res Corp *CORP AFFIL* dir: Natl Starch & Chemical Corp, Olin Corp; mem adv bd: Great Am First Savings Bank; dir: Tucson Airport Authority *NONPR AFFIL* mem: Am Assn Advancement Science, Am Chemical Soc, AZ Academy, Natl Audubon Soc, Nature Conservancy, Newcomen Soc North Am, Phi Kappa Phi, Phi Lambda Upsilon, Sigma Ki, Tucson Audobon Soc

Joan Selverstone Valentine: dir *NONPR AFFIL* prof: Univ CA Los Angeles
Geoffrey King Walters: dir *B* Baton Rouge LA 1931 *ED* Rice Univ BA 1953; Duke Univ PhD 1956 *NONPR AFFIL* mem: Am Geophysical Union; prof: Rice Univ
Laurel Lynn Wilkening: dir *B* Richland WA 1944 *ED* Reed Coll BA 1966; Univ CA San Diego PhD 1970 *NONPR AFFIL* chmn: Natl Space Counc, Space Policy Adv Bd; mem: Am Assn Advancement Science, Am Astronomical Soc, Am Geophysical Union, Intl Astronomical Union, Meteoritical Soc, Phi Beta Kappa; prof, provost: Univ WA Seattle

APPLICATION INFORMATION

Initial Approach:
Applicants should submit a precise preliminary letter.
The letter should describe the nature of the project, the significance of the problem, and the schedule and plan of procedure. A breakdown of the financial needs, along with a synopsis of sources of funding, including Research Corporation, should be provided. A brief vita or description of the credentials and background of the principal investigator for the project will also be helpful. There are target dates for specific programs at the foundation, such as the Cottrell College Science Awards, Partners in Science, and Research Opportunity Awards. Contact the foundation for specifics.
After internal evaluation, formal applications will be invited from those inquiries that are of further interest.
Restrictions on Giving: Cottrell College Science Awards encourage research with undergraduates and are open to faculty in non-PhD granting departments of astronomy, chemistry, and physics. Partners in Science awards are made to colleges and universities to support collaborative summer research between a high school science teacher and a science faculty mentor. Research Opportunity Awards target tenured science faculty aimed at re-establishing research programs. It is restricted to PhD granting departments of astronomy, chemistry, and physics, and the first step is a nomi-

nation by the department chair. Guidelines for specific programs are available from the foundation.
Occasionally, proposals may be considered for novel research projects that are unlikely to receive support from more traditional sources. Requests for funding that might be obtained from other more appropriate sources, to supplement already substantial funding or to simply extend mature projects, are not encouraged.

OTHER THINGS TO KNOW

Publications: annual report, application form, application guidelines, newsletter, program brochures

GRANTS ANALYSIS

Total Grants: $3,494,403*
Number of Grants: 151
Highest Grant: $510,000
Typical Range: $10,000 to $30,000
Disclosure Period: 1991
Note: Total grants figure includes grants approved for future payment. Recent grants are derived from a 1992 partial list of grants approved.

RECENT GRANTS

68,000 Hendrix College, Conway, AZ — introducing scientific enquiry into the high school

56,121 Northern Arizona University, Flagstaff, AZ — National Undergraduate Research Observatory

36,500 Dickinson College, Carlisle, PA — alpha, beta-dehydropeptides as building blocks for efficient peptide modification

35,830 Colby College, Waterville, ME — dynamics of excited molecules in external fields

35,000 Moorhead State University, Moorhead, MN — boron based polymers and ceramic precursors via the coupling of borane clusters with diborylalkanes

34,600 Furman University, Greenville, SC — new approaches to macromolecule/ligand binding analysis using capillary electrophoresis

33,500 Kalamazoo College, Kalamazoo, MI — heavy-atom effect on reactions of imidogen with small hydrocarbons in cryogenic rare gas matrices

33,100 Hamilton College, Clinton, NY — state distributions and energy transfer in ligands ejected by photolysis of organometallic compounds

33,000 Alma College, Alma, MI

32,984 University of South Dakota, Vermillion, SD — lanthanide to ligand energy transfer in a molecular beam

Research-Cottrell Inc.

Sales: $225.9 million
Employees: 800
Parent Company: Air & Water Technologies Corp.
Headquarters: Somerville, NJ
SIC Major Group: Engineering & Management Services and Instruments & Related Products

CONTACT

Harvey Goldman
Executive Vice President
Research-Cottrell Inc.
PO Box 1500
Somerville, NJ 08876
(908) 685-4529

CONTRIBUTIONS SUMMARY

Company sponsors employee matching gift program; also supports community organizations.

Typical Recipients: • *Arts & Humanities:* general • *Civic & Public Affairs:* general • *Education:* general • *Health:* general • *Social Services:* general

Grant Types: matching

Geographic Distribution: primarily headquarters area

Operating Locations: CA (Irvine), CO (Denver), IL (Chicago), NC (Sharpsburg), NJ (Somerville)

CORP. OFFICERS

Donald Deieso: *CURR EMPL* pres, ceo: Research-Cottrell

APPLICATION INFORMATION

Initial Approach: Send brief letter of inquiry. There are no deadlines.

Research Institute of America

Sales: $44.0 million
Employees: 550
Parent Company: Thomson Professional Publishing Co.
Headquarters: New York, NY
SIC Major Group: Engineering & Management Services and Printing & Publishing

CONTACT

Bob Romeao
Controller
Research Institute of America
910 Sylvan Ave.
Inglewood, NJ 07632
(201) 569-4000

CONTRIBUTIONS SUMMARY

Company provides employee matching gifts only.
Grant Types: matching
Operating Locations: NY (New York)

CORP. OFFICERS

Louis Lucarell: *CURR EMPL* pres, ceo: Res Inst Am

Resnick Foundation, Jack and Pearl

CONTACT

Pearl Resnick
President and Treasurer
Jack and Pearl Resnick Foundation
c/o Jack Resnick & Sons
110 East 59th Street
New York, NY 10022-1304
(212) 421-1300

FINANCIAL SUMMARY

Recent Giving: $1,617,332 (fiscal 1991); $795,707 (fiscal 1990)
Assets: $1,871,943 (fiscal year ending March 31, 1991); $444,752 (fiscal 1990)
Gifts Received: $3,000,000 (fiscal 1991); $1,230,707 (fiscal 1990)
Fiscal Note: In fiscal 1990, the foundation received $1,230,707 from Jack Resnick.
EIN: 13-3579145

CONTRIBUTIONS SUMMARY

Donor(s): the donor is Jack Resnick

Typical Recipients: • *Arts & Humanities:* music • *Civic & Public Affairs:* business/free enterprise • *Education:* colleges & universities, religious education • *Health:* hospitals • *International:* foreign educational institutions • *Religion:* religious organizations, synagogues • *Social Services:* homes, religious welfare, united funds

Grant Types: general support

GIVING OFFICERS

Burton P. Resnick: vp, secy, dir
Pearl Resnick: pres, treas, dir
Steven J. Rotter: asst secy, dir

GRANTS ANALYSIS

Total Grants: $1,617,332
Number of Grants: 12
Highest Grant: $1,140,000
Typical Range: $25,000 to $100,000
Disclosure Period: fiscal year ending March 31, 1991

RECENT GRANTS

1,140,000 Yeshiva University, New York, NY
141,666 United Jewish Appeal, FL
100,000 United Jewish Appeal, NY
91,666 Jewish Federation of Palm Beach County, Palm Beach, FL
75,000 Theological Seminary of America
63,000 Hebrew Home, Riverdale
25,000 Bar-Ilan University, NY
25,000 Clal National Jewis Center
25,000 Simon Wiesenthal Center, Los Angeles, CA
25,000 U.S. Holocaust Memorial Council

Restaurant Associates, Inc.

Sales: $250.0 million
Employees: 6,500
Parent Company: Restaurant Association Corp.
Headquarters: New York, NY
SIC Major Group: Eating & Drinking Places

CONTACT

Max Pine
President & Chief Executive Officer
Restaurant Associates, Inc.
120 West 45 St., 16th Fl.
New York, NY 10036
(212) 789-8100

CONTRIBUTIONS SUMMARY

Nonmonetary Support Types: donated equipment and donated products
Operating Locations: NY (New York)

CORP. OFFICERS

Martin Brody: *B* Newark NJ 1921 *ED* MI St Univ 1943 *CURR EMPL* vchmn: Restaurant Associates *CORP AFFIL* dir: Jaclyn, WA Natl NY
Max Pine: *B* Cincinnati OH 1934 *ED* Northwestern Univ 1956; Harvard Univ MBA 1958 *CURR EMPL* pres, ceo: Restaurant Associates
Hiroshi Tanaka: *CURR EMPL* chmn: Restaurant Assocs Corp

Retirement Research Foundation

CONTACT

Marilyn Hennessy
Executive Vice President
Retirement Research Foundation
8765 West Higgins Rd., 401
Chicago, IL 60631
(312) 714-8080

FINANCIAL SUMMARY

Recent Giving: $6,000,000 (1993 est.); $5,626,564 (1992); $6,631,301 (1991)
Assets: $135,000,000 (1992 est.); $134,398,165 (1991); $115,079,417 (1990)
EIN: 36-2429540

CONTRIBUTIONS SUMMARY

Donor(s): "The Retirement Research Foundation was established by John D. MacArthur, a Chicago resident and businessman, in 1950. Upon Mr. MacArthur's death in 1978, the foundation was the recipient of major assets and began active grant making in 1979. MacArthur also established the John D. and Catherine T. MacArthur Foundation. However, each foundation is separate and totally independent of the other."

Typical Recipients: • *Civic & Public Affairs:* ethnic/minority organizations, housing, non-profit management, professional & trade associations, public policy • *Education:* community & junior colleges, continuing education • *Health:* geriatric health, health care cost containment, health organizations, hospitals, medical research, mental health, nursing services, outpatient health care delivery • *Social Services:* aged, community centers, community service organizations, disabled, employment/job training, food/clothing distribution, homes, shelters/homelessness, volunteer services
Grant Types: challenge, multi-year/continuing support, project, research, and seed money
Geographic Distribution: no geographic restrictions, with exception of direct service development projects

GIVING OFFICERS
Floyd A. Caldini: treas
Duane Chapman: trust
Robert P. Ewing: trust, secy *B* Kirksville MO 1925 *ED* Northeast MO St Univ BS 1948 *CORP AFFIL* consultant, dir: ICH Corp; dir: Bankers Multiple Line Ins Co, Citizens Bank & Trust Co, Constitution Life Ins Co, Marquette Natl Life Ins Co, Prepaid Legal Svcs, Union Bankers Ins Co *NONPR AFFIL* mem: Health Ins Assn Am, Intl Assn Health Underwriters, Natl Assn Life Underwriters
Marilyn Hennessy: exec vp, exec dir
Brian F. Hofland, PhD: vp, program off
Edward J. Kelly: chmn bd, trust *B* Des Moines IA 1911 *ED* IA St Univ BA 1934; IA St Univ JD 1936 *CURR EMPL* atty, ptnr: Whitfield Musgrave Selvy Kelly & Eddy *NONPR AFFIL* mem: Am Bar Assn, Des Moines Chamber Commerce, IA Bar Assn, Intl Assn Ins Counc, Polk County Bar Assn; mem bd dirs: Defense Res Inst, Northwest Commun Hosp, Polk County Legal Aid Soc; pres: Des Moines Health Ctr, Des Moines Soc Crippled Children Adults, IA Defense Counc Assn
Sister Stella Louise: trust *CURR EMPL* pres: St Mary Nazareth Hosp
Nathaniel P. McParland, MD: trust
Marvin Meyerson: trust

Joe L. Parkin: pres, trust
John F. Santos: trust
Ruth Ann Watkins: trust

APPLICATION INFORMATION
Initial Approach:
The foundation does not have a standard application form. Applications must be submitted in writing.
Applications should include a two- to three-page summary of the project, its significance, and its cost. In addition, proposals should address specific project objectives, and give a detailed description of methods. A timetable and line item budget, including other sources of funds and a budget justification, should be included. If relevant, plans for continued support should be described. Curricula vitae, not to exceed five pages, should be included for project directors and key staff. Information on the applicant organization should include its history, accomplishments, financial reports, annual reports, and specific qualifications for the proposed project. A copy of the applicant's tax-exempt status under Section 501(c)(3), and of classification as "not a private foundation" under Section 509(a) of the Internal Revenue Code, must be included. All applications must be signed by the chief executive officer of the applicant organization and submitted in triplicate.
Research proposals should describe the experimental design, procedures to be used to accomplish the objectives, sequence of the investigation, kinds of data to be obtained, and the means by which data will be analyzed and interpreted. Model projects and service proposals should describe the project design, target group, change to be effected, resources and method of delivery, sequence of activities planned to meet project objectives, and methods and criteria to be used to evaluate the outcome of the project.
Education and training proposals should describe the target group; educational needs to be met; content, methods, sequence, and location of educational experiences; and the methods and criteria which will be used to evaluate the educational program.

Deadlines for receipt of applications are February 1, May 1, and August 1.
Decisions are usually made four months after the deadline dates. The foundation is particularly interested in innovative projects which develop and demonstrate new approaches to the problems of the aged and which have the potential for regional or national impact. Funding of service development projects is limited to the seven Midwestern states (Illinois, Indiana, Iowa, Kentucky, Michigan, Missouri, Wisconsin) and Florida. When projects of equal significance are being considered, priority will be given to organizations serving the Chicago metropolitan area.
Restrictions on Giving: The foundation does not provide support for construction of facilities; general operating expenses of established organizations; endowment or developmental campaigns; scholarships; loans; grants to individuals; projects outside the United States; dissertation research; production of films or videos; or conferences, publications, and travel, unless they are components of foundation-funded projects. Generally, support of projects beyond a three-year period will not be provided.

OTHER THINGS TO KNOW
Publications: program guidelines and application procedures, two-year report, 10-year retrospective report

GRANTS ANALYSIS
Total Grants: $5,626,564
Number of Grants: 176
Highest Grant: $350,000
Typical Range: $20,000 to $125,000
Disclosure Period: 1992
Note: Recent grants are derived from a 1992 grants list.

RECENT GRANTS
350,000 Center City Limited Partnership, Chicago, IL — to provide bridge financing for low-income senior housing in Elgin

278,201 University of Minnesota, St. Paul, MN — to test effectiveness and applicability of struc-

tural process for assessing the values and preferences of older long term care clients

271,550 Center for Elderly Suicide Prevention and Grief Related Services, San Francisco, CA — to evaluate the effectiveness and efficiency of three intervention techniques in the prevention of suicide in older adults

225,000 Park Ridge Center, Chicago, IL — to establish a Fellowship in Ethics, Values and The Meaning of Aging

200,000 St. Joseph's Home for the Elderly, Palatine, IL — to continue renovation

150,000 Chinese American Service League, Chicago, IL — to develop a senior services department to provide social services, counseling and outreach to homebound Chinese elderly

135,650 United Charities of Chicago, Chicago, IL — to develop the elder Mentors Project which will link senior adults with youth at risk of delinquent behavior

135,010 University of Illinois, Ubrana-Champaign, Champaign, IL — a program to provide supportive services and assistance with housing modification for senior homeowners in metropolitan Chicago area

135,000 Shepherd's Centers of America, Kansas City, MO — to continue development of Shepherd's Centers nationwide

128,847 Coalition of Limited Speaking Elderly, Chicago, IL — to support and expand the Coaliton's consortium of community-based ethnic agencies serving the elderly

Reviva Labs

Headquarters: Haddonfield, NJ
SIC Major Group: Food &
Kindred Products

CONTACT

Stephen Strassler
President
Reviva Labs
705 Hopkins Rd.
Haddonfield, NJ 08033
(609) 428-3885

CONTRIBUTIONS SUMMARY

Company provides at least
1.2% of pre-tax earnings to
charity.
Operating Locations: NJ (Haddonfield)

CORP. OFFICERS

Stephen Strassler: *CURR EMPL* pres: Reviva Labs

Revlon / Revlon Foundation

Employees: 38,100
Parent Company: Revlon Group
Parent Sales: $1.61 billion
Headquarters: New York, NY
SIC Major Group: Chemicals &
Allied Products and Health
Services

CONTACT

Phyllis Orta
Director, Community Relations
Revlon Fdn.
625 Madison Ave.
New York, NY 10153
(212) 572-5000

FINANCIAL SUMMARY

Recent Giving: $2,966,193
(1991); $1,709,962 (1990);
$5,090,921 (1989)
Assets: $1,267,342 (1991);
$1,686,295 (1990); $198,251
(1989)
Fiscal Note: Company gives
primarily through foundation.
EIN: 13-6126130

CONTRIBUTIONS SUMMARY

Typical Recipients: • *Arts & Humanities:* arts centers, museums/galleries, music • *Civic & Public Affairs:* ethnic/minority organizations, urban & community affairs • *Education:* colleges & universities, education funds, minority education, private education (precollege), religious education, science/technology education • *Health:* hospitals, single-disease health associations • *Religion:* relig-

ious organizations • *Social Services:* community service organizations, shelters/homelessness, united funds
Grant Types: employee matching gifts, general support, and project
Geographic Distribution: nationally and locally where company has operating divisions
Operating Locations: CA (La Jolla, Sunnyvale), CT (Stamford), FL (Jacksonville, Miami Lakes), MS, NJ (Edison), NY (New York, Tarrytown), OK (Muskogee), TN (Knoxville), VA (Springfield)
Note: Also operates in Caparra, Puerto Rico.

CORP. OFFICERS

Howard Gittis: *B* Philadelphia PA 1934 *ED* Univ PA 1955; Univ PA Sch Law 1958 *CURR EMPL* vchmn, dir: MacAndrews & Forbes Group *CORP AFFIL* dir: Andrews Group, Harron Commun Corp, PNC Fin Corp, Provident Natl Bank; vchmn: Revlon
Ronald Owen Perelman: *B* Greensboro NC 1943 *ED* Univ PA BA 1964; Univ PA Wharton Sch MBA 1966 *CURR EMPL* chmn, ceo, dir: Revlon *CORP AFFIL* chmn: Natl Health Labs, Technicolor; chmn bd: Andrews Group; chmn, ceo, dir: MacAndrews & Forbes Holdings; dir: Four Star Intl; pres, chmn bd: First Gibraltar Holdings *NONPR AFFIL* trust: NY Univ
Bruce Slovin: *B* New York NY 1935 *ED* Cornell Univ 1957; Harvard Univ Law Sch JD 1960 *CURR EMPL* pres, dir: Revlon *CORP AFFIL* dir: Andrews Group, Cantel Indus, Continental Health Affiliates, Four Star Intl, Gulf Resources & Chem Corp, Moore Med Corp, Oak Hill Sportswear Corp, Stendig Indus; pres, coo, dir: Revlon Group; pres, dir: MacAndrews & Forbes Group, MacAndrews & Forbes Holdings

GIVING OFFICERS

Nancy T. Gardiner: exec vp
Richard E. Halperin: pres, dir *B* New York NY 1954 *ED* Boston Univ 1976; New England Sch Law JD 1979 *CURR EMPL* sr vp: MacAndrews & Forbes Group *CORP AFFIL* exec vp, special counc to chmn: Revlon Group
Wade Hampton Nichols III: vp, secy *B* Bronxville NY 1942

ED Yale Univ B A 1964; Columbia Univ LLB 1967 *CURR EMPL* sr vp, gen couns: Revlon *CORP AFFIL* vp: MacAndrews & Forbes Holdings *NONPR AFFIL* mem: Am Bar Assn, Am Soc Corp Secys
Phyllis Orta: mgr
H. Lenore Van Reed: asst secy

APPLICATION INFORMATION

Initial Approach: *Initial Contact:* brief letter or proposal *Include Information On:* description of the organization, amount requested, purpose for which funds are sought, recently audited financial statement, proof of tax-exempt status *When to Submit:* any time

OTHER THINGS TO KNOW

The Revlon Foundation only makes grants to preselected organizations and does not take unsolicited requests.

GRANTS ANALYSIS

Total Grants: $2,966,193
Number of Grants: 29
Highest Grant: $1,200,000
Typical Range: $10,000 to $50,000
Disclosure Period: 1991
Note: Recent grants are derived from a 1991 Form 990.

RECENT GRANTS

1,200,000	United Jewish Appeal, New York, NY
800,000	University of California Los Angeles School of Medicine, Los Angeles, CA
215,000	Machne Israel, Brooklyn, NY
100,000	Nightingale Bamford School, New York, NY
100,000	Ronald Reagan Presidential Foundation and Library, Washington, DC
90,000	Carnegie Hall, New York, NY
54,000	Lubavitch Center, Brooklyn, NY
50,000	John F. Kennedy Medical Center, Edison, NJ
50,000	Operation Welcome Home, New York, NY
50,000	Teamwork Foundation, New York, NY

Revson Foundation, Charles H.

CONTACT

Eli N. Evans
President
Charles H. Revson Foundation
444 Madison Avenue, 30th Fl.
New York, NY 10022
(212) 935-3340

FINANCIAL SUMMARY

Recent Giving: $7,179,774
(1991); $5,773,428 (1990);
$7,383,731 (1989)
Assets: $96,141,192 (1990);
$105,601,687 (1989);
$82,158,200 (1988)
Gifts Received: $112,991
(1990); $4,719,029 (1989);
$230,973 (1987)
EIN: 13-6126105

CONTRIBUTIONS SUMMARY

Donor(s): Charles H. Revson founded Revlon in 1932 and built the company into a major international corporation. During his life, Mr. Revson donated over $10 million in charitable contributions through the Charles H. Revson Foundation, which he incorporated in 1956. On his death in 1975, the foundation received a bequest from his estate.
The board of directors is given broad latitude to guide the foundation's course of charitable giving. Currently, the directors are following a giving policy based upon Mr. Revson's own philanthropic interests. Grants under this policy were first made in 1978.
Typical Recipients: • *Arts & Humanities:* dance, ethnic arts • *Civic & Public Affairs:* better government, housing, philanthropic organizations, public policy, urban & community affairs, women's affairs • *Education:* legal education, science/technology education • *Health:* medical training • *International:* foreign educational institutions • *Social Services:* legal aid, youth organizations
Grant Types: conference/seminar, fellowship, and research
Geographic Distribution: emphasis on New York City, with some national giving

GIVING OFFICERS

Adrian W. DeWind: dir *B* Chicago IL 1913 *ED* Grinnell Coll AB 1934; Sorbonne 1932-33;

Harvard Univ LLB 1937; City Univ NY LLD 1976 *CURR EMPL* atty, ptnr: Paul Weiss Rifkind Wharton & Garrison *NONPR AFFIL* chmn, dir: Natural Resources Defense Counc; dir: Comm Modern Courts, Lawyers Comm Civil Rights Under Law, Lawyers Comm Intl Human Rights, Natl Comm Against Discrimination Housing; dir, mem exec comm: Legal Defense Fund; fellow: Am Bar Fdn, NY Bar Fdn; mem: Am Bar Assn, Am Law Inst, Fed Bar Counc, NY City Bar Assn, St Bar Assn; mem bd visitors: Coll NY; trust: New Sch Social Res

Eli N. Evans: pres

Lisa Goldberg: vp

Beatrix Ann Hamburg, MD: dir *B* Jacksonville FL 1923 *ED* Vassar Coll AB 1944; Yale Univ MD 1948 *NONPR AFFIL* mem: Academy Res Behavioral Medicine, Am Assn Advancement Science, Am Pub Health Assn, Inst Medicine Natl Academy Sciences, NY Academy Medicine, Soc Adolescent Medicine, Soc Professional Child Psychiatry, Soc Study Social Biology; mem comm behavior & soc: Govenors Task Force Life Law, Natl Academy Sciences, Pub Health Counc St NY; mem, fellow: Am Academy Child Psychiatry; prof psychiatry & pediatrics: Mt Sinai Sch Medicine

Matina Horner: chmn *B* Boston MA 1939 *ED* Bryn Mawr Coll AB 1961; Univ MI MS 1963; Univ MI PhD 1968; Dickinson Coll LLD 1973 *CORP AFFIL* dir: Boston Edison Co, Fed Reserve Bank Boston, Liberty Mutual Life Ins Co, Time; exec vp: TIAA-CREF NY City *NONPR AFFIL* dir: Beth Israel Hosp, Womens Res Ed Inst; mem: Assn Am Colls, Counc Foreign Rels, Natl Inst Social Sciences, Natl Org Women, Phi Beta Kappa, Phi Delta Kappa, Phi Kappa Phi; mem adv comm: Womens Leadership Conf Natl Security; mem exec comm: New England Colls Fund; pres emerita: Radcliffe Coll; trust: Comm Econ Devel, Inst Health Professions, MA Gen Hosp, Twentieth Century Fund; trust, pres: Fund City NY; dir: Counc Fin Aid Ed; mem adv counc: Natl Science Fdn; mem exec comm: Counc Competitiveness; trust: Am Coll Greece, MA Eye Ear

Infirmary *PHIL AFFIL* trust: Twentieth Century Fund
Joshua Lederberg: dir *B* Montclair NJ 1925 *ED* Columbia Univ BA 1944; Yale Univ PhD 1947 *CORP AFFIL* dir: Celanese Corp, Cetus Corp, JD Wolfensohn, Procter & Gamble Co; mem: US Dept Energy *NONPR AFFIL* dir: Am Type Culture Coll, Bulletin Atomic Scientists, Chemical Indus Inst Toxicology, Inst Scientific Information; fellow: Am Academy Arts Sciences, Am Assn Advancement Science, Am Philosophical Soc, NY Academy Medicine; mem: Natl Academy Sciences, Royal Soc London, Sackler Fdn, US Defense Science Bd; mem study sections: Natl Inst Health, Natl Science Fdn; pres: Rockefeller Univ *PHIL AFFIL* trust: Conservation Foundation
Arthur Levitt, Jr.: dir *B* Brooklyn NY 1931 *ED* Williams Coll BA 1952 *CURR EMPL* chmn: Levitt Media Co *CORP AFFIL* chmn: Levitt Media Co, NY City Econ Devel Corp; dir: Baker & Tayloy Distr, FDM Holdings, First Empire St Corp, NY Daily News, Shared Med Sys Corp; trust: East NY Savings Bank *NONPR AFFIL* chmn: Am Bus Counc, Task Force Future Devel W Side Manhattan; mem: Am Bus Conf, Equitable Life Assurance Soc US, NY St Counc Arts; trust: Williams Coll *PHIL AFFIL* dir: Dole Foundation
Matthew Nimetz: dir *CURR EMPL* ptnr: Paul, Weiss, Rifkind, Wharton & Garrison *NONPR AFFIL* chmn: UN Devel Corp, World Resources Inst; dir: Counc US & Haly; mem: Assn Bar City NY, Counc Foreign Rels, NY St Adv Counc St Productivity; trust: Williams Coll
Charles H. Revson, Jr.: dir

APPLICATION INFORMATION
Initial Approach:
Applicants should send a letter to the foundation.
The letter should include a description of the proposed project and the purpose and activities of the applicant organization. It also should include background information on the project, objectives of the project, and methods to be used in accomplishing them; qualifications and responsibili-

ties of the principal staff members; budget, amount, duration and specific purposes of requested grant; plans for evaluation and future funding; other sources of support; tax-exempt status; financial statements; and a list of board of directors with their affiliations.
Applications may be submitted any time.
The board meets in April, June, October, and December.
Restrictions on Giving: Support is not given for local health appeals, individuals, building or endowment funds, general support, or matching gifts. No loans are made.

OTHER THINGS TO KNOW
Publications: biennial report

GRANTS ANALYSIS
Total Grants: $7,179,744
Number of Grants: 95
Highest Grant: $1,000,000
Typical Range: $15,000 to $100,000
Disclosure Period: 1991
Note: Figure for average grant excludes a single grant for $1,000,000. Recent grants are derived from a 1991 grants list.

RECENT GRANTS
1,000,000 Israel Academy of Sciences, Jerusalem, Israel — to support the Basic Research Fund
350,000 New School for Social Research, New York, NY — support of a New York City Environmental Simulation Center
300,000 Jewish Media Fund, New York, NY — to support further development, testing, and distribution of the Jewish Heritage Video Collection
275,000 New York University, New York, NY — support of the Urban Research Center
250,000 Jewish Media Fund, New York, NY — for the second phase of development of Jewish Heritage Video Collection
238,000 Columbia University, New York, NY — support of the Charles H. Revson Fellows Program

220,000 New York University School of Law, New York, NY — to support 50 internships in public interest law
220,000 Women's Law and Public Policy Fellowship Program, Washington, DC — to support Fellowship Program
183,000 Legal Aid Society, New York, NY — to continue support of the Homeless Family Rights Project
150,000 Waterford Institute, Provo, UT — support of a model program to introduce Waterford Institute's integrated instructional computer system to the New York City public schools

Rexene Products Co.
Sales: $449.7 million
Employees: 1,283
Headquarters: Dallas, TX
SIC Major Group: Chemicals & Allied Products, Holding & Other Investment Offices, and Petroleum & Coal Products

CONTACT
Neil Deuroy
Director, Communications & Pub. Affairs
Rexene Products Co.
5005 LBJ Fwy., Occidental Tower
Dallas, TX 75244
(214) 450-9000

CONTRIBUTIONS SUMMARY
Operating Locations: TX (Dallas)

CORP. OFFICERS
Herm Rosenman: *CURR EMPL* vchmn, cfo: Rexene Products Co
Andrew J. Smith: *CURR EMPL* ceo, pres: Rexene Products Co

Rexham Inc. / Rexham Corp. Foundation

Sales: $600.0 million
Employees: 4,000
Headquarters: Charlotte, NC
SIC Major Group: Fabricated Metal Products, Holding & Other Investment Offices, Paper & Allied Products, and Rubber & Miscellaneous Plastics Products

CONTACT

Peggy Harrington
Paralegal
Rexham Corp. Fdn.
7315 Pineville-Matthews Rd.
Charlotte, NC 28226
(704) 551-1500

FINANCIAL SUMMARY

Recent Giving: $103,378 (1990); $128,274 (1989); $114,000 (1988)
Assets: $9,493 (1990); $13,127 (1989)
Gifts Received: $100,000 (1990)
Fiscal Note: Figures do not include contributions by subsidiaries.
EIN: 13-6165669

CONTRIBUTIONS SUMMARY

Typical Recipients: • *Arts & Humanities:* performing arts • *Education:* colleges & universities • *Health:* pediatric health, single-disease health associations • *Social Services:* child welfare, united funds, youth organizations
Grant Types: capital, challenge, endowment, general support, matching, and scholarship
Geographic Distribution: only in operating communities
Operating Locations: CT, MA, NC, OH, SC

CORP. OFFICERS

Eric Priestly: *CURR EMPL* pres, ceo: Rexham

GIVING OFFICERS

Joseph P. Keniry: vp, treas
Keith F. Kennedy: pres, secy, dir *B* New London CT 1925 *ED* Yale Coll 1949; Harvard Univ 1953 *CURR EMPL* sr vp, secy, couns, dir: Rexham

APPLICATION INFORMATION

Initial Approach: Submit a brief letter or proposal at any time, including a description of the organization, amount requested, purpose, financial statement, and proof of tax-exempt status.
Restrictions on Giving: Contributions ae limited to communities in which Rexham Corp. and its subsidiaries operate. Rexham does not support dinners or special events, fraternal organizations, goodwill advertising, individuals, political or lobbying groups, or religious organizations for sectarian purposes.

GRANTS ANALYSIS

Highest Grant: $30,842
Typical Range: $25 to $1,000
Disclosure Period: 1990

RECENT GRANTS

30,842 United Way, Charlotte, NC
10,000 Johnson C. Smith University, Charlotte, NC
5,000 CPCC Foundation, Raleigh, NC
5,000 Discovery Place Capital Campaign, Charlotte, NC
5,000 Puerto Rico Disaster Relief Telethon, Washington, DC
5,000 Puerto Rico USA Foundation, Washington, DC
3,500 Boy Scouts of America, Raleigh, NC
3,000 Amethyst Foundation, Charlotte, NC
3,000 YMCA, Charlotte, NC
2,000 Mercy Fund, Charlotte, NC

Reynolds Charitable Trust, Kate B.

CONTACT

E. Ray Cope
Executive Director
Kate B. Reynolds Charitable Trust
2422 Reynolda Rd.
Winston-Salem, NC 27106-4606
(919) 723-1456

FINANCIAL SUMMARY

Recent Giving: $12,800,000 (fiscal 1993 est.); $16,668,855 (fiscal 1992); $13,536,677 (fiscal 1991)
Assets: $304,000,000 (fiscal 1993 est.); $302,963,585 (fiscal year ending August 31, 1992); $289,949,928 (fiscal 1991); $249,973,101 (fiscal 1990)
EIN: 56-6036515

CONTRIBUTIONS SUMMARY

Donor(s): The Kate B. Reynolds Charitable Trust was created in 1947 under the will of Mrs. William N. Reynolds of Winston-Salem. She designated that one-fourth of the income from the trust be used for the poor and needy in Winston-Salem and Forsyth County and that three-fourths of the income be used for charity patients in North Carolina hospitals. In 1971, the trustees sought a broader interpretation of the Health Care Divsion of the trust because of social and economic changes that had occurred in the state. By action of the court, the trustees were authorized to provide health care or assistance if a substantial benefit would be derived by needy persons, even though some benefit might be derived by others.
Typical Recipients: • *Education:* community & junior colleges, medical education, special education • *Health:* geriatric health, health organizations, hospices, hospitals, mental health, pediatric health, public health, single-disease health associations • *Social Services:* aged, child welfare, domestic violence, homes
Grant Types: capital, challenge, general support, operating expenses, project, and seed money
Geographic Distribution: health care grants are limited to North Carolina; poor and needy grants are limited to Winston-Salem, NC, and Forsyth County, NC

GIVING OFFICERS

E. Ray Cope: exec dir, dir (poor & needy div)
Joan N. Danieley: program off (health care div)
W. Vance Frye: dir (health care div)
Karen Yoak Lewis: off mgr, secy
Sara C. Smith: program off (poor & needy div)

APPLICATION INFORMATION

Initial Approach: Organizations seeking grants should call for an application. Grant applications should contain a description of funding arrangements, including a budget for the entire project, the total cost, and the amount sought from the trust. Applications to other funding sources should be noted. In the case of continuing projects, plans for future funding and evidence of the feasibility of such funding should be given. Also, a copy of the IRS letter confirming current 501(c)(3) status should be included.

Applications to the Health Care Division are due by close of business on March 15 and September 15, or the first business day thereafter if the deadline falls on a holiday or weekend. The advisory board meets in May and November to evaluate the proposals and make grant recommendations to the trustee. Applications to the Poor and Needy Division are due by close of business on the first business day of January, May, and August. The proposals are considered by the advisory board in February, June, and September, and recommendations are made to the trustee. Shortly after consideration by the advisory boards, all organizations that properly complete applications are notified of the trustee's decision.
Restrictions on Giving: Grants are not made to individuals, to private foundations, or for medical research.

OTHER THINGS TO KNOW

Wachovia Bank of North Carolina, N.A., serves as the corporate trustee of the trust.
Publications: annual report, grant applications (including guidelines) for each division

GRANTS ANALYSIS

Total Grants: $16,668,855
Number of Grants: 144
Highest Grant: $1,127,671
Typical Range: $20,000 to $200,000
Disclosure Period: fiscal year ending August 31, 1992
Note: Average grant figure excludes a $1,127,671 grant. Recent grants are derived from a 1992 annual report.

RECENT GRANTS

1,127,671 Wilkes Regional Medical Center, North Wilkesboro, NC — to develop integrated primary health care services for the county
922,400 Cape Fear Community College, Wilmington, NC — to

887,479 Governor's Institute on Alcohol and Substance Abuse, Research Triangle Park, NC — comprehensive curriculum on alcohol and other drugs at each of the four medical schools

540,000 Family Services — facility purchase and renovations to house the Headstart and Special Enrichment programs

500,000 Special Children's School — to build a specially designed facility

473,402 Wayne Memorial Hospital, Goldsboro, NC — to establish an intermediate care nursery

368,578 University of North Carolina-Chapel Hill, Chapel Hill, NC — to initiate a B.S.N. program

326,443 North Carolina Foundation for Alternative Health Programs, Raleigh, NC — to develop prepaid managed mental health services for children

320,000 County of Hoke, Raeford, NC — to establish a community-based primary health care center

310,000 Step One — startup operating expenses for an intensive outpatient program

Reynolds Foundation, Christopher

CONTACT

Jack Clareman
Executive Director
Christopher Reynolds Fdn.
121 East 61st St.
New York, NY 10021
(212) 838-2920

FINANCIAL SUMMARY

Recent Giving: $1,388,882 (fiscal 1992); $1,311,060 (fiscal 1991); $1,387,762 (fiscal 1990)

Assets: $21,467,248 (fiscal year ending January 31, 1992);

establish additional allied health services

$21,801,154 (fiscal 1991); $22,270,056 (fiscal 1990)

EIN: 13-6129401

CONTRIBUTIONS SUMMARY

Donor(s): The foundation was incorporated in 1952 by the late Libby Holman Reynolds.

Typical Recipients: • *Civic & Public Affairs:* international affairs, philanthropic organizations, public policy • *Education:* colleges & universities, international studies, social sciences education • *International:* international development/relief • *Religion:* religious organizations • *Social Services:* child welfare, disabled, employment/job training, refugee assistance, volunteer services

Grant Types: conference/seminar, multiyear/continuing support, project, and research

Geographic Distribution: focus on U.S. organizations providing humanitarian aid to Indochina (Vietnam, Laos, and Cambodia) and promoting reconciliation with these countries

GIVING OFFICERS

John R. Boettiger: dir
Jack Clareman: secy, treas, dir
Suzanne Derrer: dir
Michael Kahn: pres, dir
Andrea Panaritis: exec dir

APPLICATION INFORMATION

Initial Approach:

The foundation does not use a formal grant application form.

Proposals should include specific objectives, detailed estimated budgets, qualifications of the organizations and individuals involved, and proof of tax-exempt status from the IRS. Six copies of the application are required.

Restrictions on Giving: The foundation does not make grants for building funds, medical research, educational or religious institutions (except in relation to research on subjects that fall within the scope of the foundation's current interests), or general operating or overhead expenses (except for newly organized entities whose objectives fall within the areas of the foundation's current interests).

OTHER THINGS TO KNOW

Publications: multiyear report including application guidelines

GRANTS ANALYSIS

Total Grants: $1,388,882
Number of Grants: 59
Highest Grant: $127,250
Typical Range: $5,000 to $50,000
Disclosure Period: fiscal year ending January 31, 1992

Note: Recent grants are derived from a fiscal 1992 grants list.

RECENT GRANTS

127,250 Harvard Institute of International Development, Cambridge, MA

82,893 Institute of International Education, Houston, TX

80,000 Harvard Institute of International Development, Cambridge, MA

78,666 American Friends Service Committee, Philadelphia, PA

62,500 American Council of Learned Societies, New York, NY

62,500 Aspen Institute, Washington, DC

61,868 Harvard Institute of International Development, Cambridge, MA

61,867 Harvard Institute of International Development, Cambridge, MA

52,200 Mennonite Central Committee, Elkhart, IN

49,000 Mennonite Central Committee, Elkhart, IN

Reynolds Foundation, Donald W.

CONTACT

E.H. Patterson
Director
Donald W. Reynolds Foundation
PO Box 17017
Ft. Smith, AR 72917
(501) 785-7810
Note: The foundation can be reached directly at 920 Rogers Ave., Fort Smith, AR 72901.

The foundation does not list a contact person.

FINANCIAL SUMMARY

Recent Giving: $391,378 (fiscal 1991); $7,393,461 (fiscal 1990); $226,112 (fiscal 1988)

Assets: $6,910,825 (fiscal year ending June 30, 1991); $6,844,572 (fiscal 1990); $12,661,693 (fiscal 1988)

Gifts Received: $6,000,000 (fiscal 1988)

EIN: 71-6053383

CONTRIBUTIONS SUMMARY

Donor(s): The foundation was established in 1954 by Donald W. Reynolds, who owns Donrey Media Group that includes more than 50 daily newspapers, radio and television stations, and billboard and cable operations. In 1977, Mr. Reynolds signed over all his stock and assets to the foundation to assure continuity for the company. The foundation stands to inherit a business which Forbes magazine has estimated to be worth $950 million.

Mr. Reynolds graduated from the University of Missouri School of Journalism in 1927. He purchased his first newspaper in 1940 in Oklahoma. He lives in Las Vegas. Mr. Reynolds, 85, has three children and has been married three times. His children are not involved with the foundation.

Typical Recipients: • *Arts & Humanities:* arts associations, arts centers, community arts, libraries, museums/galleries, music • *Civic & Public Affairs:* business/free enterprise, economic development, environmental affairs, first amendment issues, municipalities, professional & trade associations, women's affairs • *Education:* business education, colleges & universities, education associations, education funds, literacy, student aid • *Health:* health funds, health organizations, single-disease health associations • *Social Services:* child welfare, community service organizations, counseling, family services, recreation & athletics, united funds, youth organizations

Grant Types: capital, endowment, general support, and scholarship

Geographic Distribution: focus on the Midwest

GIVING OFFICERS

Don R. Buris: dir
Bob G. Bush: dir
Robert Staples Howard: dir *B* Wheaton MN 1924 *ED* Univ MN *CURR EMPL* pres: Howard Publs *CORP AFFIL* chmn: Howtek, Presstek
George O. Kleier: asst treas
E. H. Patterson: treas, dir *CURR EMPL* exec vp, cfo: Donrey Inc
Ross Pendergraft: asst treas
Donald E. Pray: secy
Donald Worthington Reynolds: don *B* Ft. Worth TX 1906 *ED* Univ MO BJ 1927 *CURR EMPL* chmn, ceo, dir: Donrey Inc *CORP AFFIL* dir: Thomas Edison Inns; owner, pres, ceo: KBRS Springdale, KEXO Grand Junction, KOCM-FM Newport Beach, KOLO Reno; pres, ceo: Donrey Cablevision, Donrey Outdoor Advertising; publ: Aberdeen Daily World, Auburn Daily Times, Bartlesville Examiner-Enterprise, Blackwell Journal-Tribune, Booneville Democrat, Borger News Herald, Chickasha Express, Chico Enterprise Record, Cleburne Times Review, Daily Report, Durant Daily Democrat, Ely Times & Carson City Appeal, Frederick Daily Leader, Gainesville Daily Register, Guthrie Daily Leader, Guymon Daily Herald, Henryetta Freelance, HI Tribune-Herald Hilo, Holdenville News, Jacksonville Progress, Kailua-Kona West HI Today, Kilgore News Herald, Las Vegas Review-Journal, Lompoc Record, Moberly Monitor-Index, Northwest AR Morning News, Okmulgee Times, Oskaloosa Herald, Pauls Valley Daily Democrat, Pawhuska Daily Journal-Capital, Picayune Item, Pomona Progress-Bulletin, Poplarville Democrat, Red Bluff Daily News, Redlands Daily Facts, Sherman Democrat, Southwest Times Record, Springdale News, Vallejo Times-Herald, Washington Times-Herald, Weatherford Democrat, Wewoka Daily Times *NONPR AFFIL* mem: Am Legion, Am Soc Newspaper Editors, Natl Assn Radio TV Broadcasters, Pi Kappa Alpha, Sigma Delta Chi, Southern Newspaper Publs Assn
Fred Wesley Smith: pres, dir *B* Arkoma OK 1934 *ED* AR Polytech Coll *CURR EMPL* pres: Donrey Media Group

CORP AFFIL dir: First Interstate Bank NV; pres: Donrey Media Group *NONPR AFFIL* mem exec bd: Univ Ozarks; mem exec bd (Las Vegas): Boy Scouts Am; trust: Univ NV Las Vegas Fdn, Univ Ozarks

APPLICATION INFORMATION

Initial Approach:
There are no application forms. Requests for grants should be submitted in writing on the letterhead of the applying organization and signed by the chief executive officer or other authorized person.

Proposals should include the goals, purpose, and significance of the project, qualifications of persons responsible for carrying out the project, list of organization's officers, and a copy of the IRS tax-determination letter. Requests should contain financial plans including the amount of the grant requested and total funds needed for the project, a list of other donors and their contributions to the project, a list of challenge grants, a budget for the proposed project, fuunding source after the foundation's grant expires, applicant's most recent income and expense statement and balance statement, and organization's operating budget for the coming year. Deadlines are March 15, June 15, September 15, and December 15.

The board meets quarterly.

Restrictions on Giving: The foundation does not make grants to individuals and generally does not make ongoing committments though a large gift may be spread out over more than one fiscal year.

OTHER THINGS TO KNOW

Publications: application guidelines

GRANTS ANALYSIS

Total Grants: $391,378
Number of Grants: 142
Highest Grant: $100,250
Typical Range: $1,000 to $10,000
Disclosure Period: fiscal year ending June 30, 1991
Note: Recent grants are derived from a fiscal 1991 Form 990. Average grant figure excludes highest grant of $100,250.

RECENT GRANTS

6,989,261 University of Missouri, Columbia, MO

31,250 Oklahoma State University Endowment Fund, Stillwater, OK

30,000 Meadows School, Las Vegas, NV

20,000 American Newspapers Publishers Association Foundation

20,000 Bartlesville Public Library, Bartlesville, OK

20,000 Boys Town USA, NV

12,000 Old Ft. Museum, Ft. Smith, AR

10,000 Arkansas State University Foundation, Jonesboro, AR

10,000 Baylor University, Waco, TX

10,000 Brigham Young University, Salt Lake City, UT

Reynolds Foundation, Edgar

CONTACT
Fred M. Glade, Jr.
Chairman
Edgar Reynolds Fdn.
204 North Walnut St.
Grand Island, NE 68801
(308) 384-0957

FINANCIAL SUMMARY
Recent Giving: $170,950 (1990); $225,450 (1989); $138,189 (1987)
Assets: $4,362,741 (1990); $4,262,690 (1989); $3,772,082 (1987)
EIN: 47-0589941

CONTRIBUTIONS SUMMARY
Donor(s): the late Edgar Reynolds
Typical Recipients: • *Civic & Public Affairs:* philanthropic organizations • *Education:* colleges & universities • *Health:* hospitals • *Social Services:* child welfare, recreation & athletics, united funds, youth organizations
Grant Types: capital, research, and scholarship
Geographic Distribution: focus on NE

GIVING OFFICERS
Fred M. Glade, Jr.: chmn, dir
Robert Mattke: dir
Frances Reynolds: secy, treas, dir

Harlan Speer: dir

APPLICATION INFORMATION
Initial Approach: Application form required. There are no deadlines.

OTHER THINGS TO KNOW
Publications: Application Guidelines

GRANTS ANALYSIS
Number of Grants: 3
Highest Grant: $166,700
Typical Range: $2,000 to $2,250
Disclosure Period: 1990

RECENT GRANTS
166,700 College Park Grand Island Foundation, Grand Island, NE

2,250 Central Nebraska Goodwill, Grand Island, NE

2,000 University of Nebraska Foundation, Lincoln, NE

Reynolds Foundation, Eleanor T.

CONTACT
Alethia P. Haynes
Trustee
Eleanor T. Reynolds Fdn.
PO Box 156
Bristol, TN 37621

FINANCIAL SUMMARY
Recent Giving: $142,626 (1989); $62,199 (1988)
Assets: $1,940,168 (1989); $1,924,883 (1988)
Gifts Received: $1,831,803 (1988)
EIN: 62-1342279

CONTRIBUTIONS SUMMARY
Donor(s): the late Eleanor T. Reynolds
Typical Recipients: • *Social Services:* community service organizations, disabled, youth organizations
Grant Types: general support

GIVING OFFICERS
Alethia P. Haynes: trust
David Bruce Haynes: trust
David S. Haynes: trust

APPLICATION INFORMATION

Initial Approach: Contributes only to preselected organizations.

GRANTS ANALYSIS

Number of Grants: 5
Highest Grant: $108,129
Typical Range: $7,500 to $15,500
Disclosure Period: 1989

RECENT GRANTS

108,129 Summer Camp "A Leg Up" Program, Tucson, AZ — for handicapped children conducted by Therapeutic Riding Center for the Handicapped

15,500 Virginia Intermont College, Richmond, VA — handicapped program

10,000 Jericho Shrine Temple — crippled children program

7,500 National Junior Tennis League, Norristown, PA

1,497 Phillip Adcock School Scholarship

Reynolds Foundation, J. B.

CONTACT

Walter E. Bixby
Vice President
J. B. Reynolds Fdn.
3520 Broadway, PO Box 139
Kansas City, MO 64111
(816) 753-7000

FINANCIAL SUMMARY

Recent Giving: $493,544 (1990); $448,970 (1989); $407,300 (1987)
Assets: $10,304,646 (1990); $9,841,890 (1989); $8,726,399 (1987)
EIN: 44-6014359

CONTRIBUTIONS SUMMARY

Donor(s): Walter Edwin Bixby, Sr., the late Pearl G. Reynolds
Typical Recipients: • *Arts & Humanities:* community arts, museums/galleries, music, opera, performing arts • *Education:* colleges & universities • *Health:* health organizations, hospitals, medical research, single-disease health associations • *Social Services:* child welfare, community service organi-

zations, united funds, youth organizations
Grant Types: capital, conference/seminar, emergency, general support, multiyear/continuing support, research, and seed money
Geographic Distribution: focus on a 150-mile radius of Kansas City, MO

GIVING OFFICERS

Joseph Reynolds Bixby: pres, trust
Kathryn Bixby: trust
Walter Edwin Bixby: vp, treas, trust *B* Kansas City MO 1932 *ED* Univ MO BS 1953 *CURR EMPL* vchmn: KS City Life Ins Co *CORP AFFIL* dir: Sunset Life Ins Co; vchmn: KS City Life Ins Co *NONPR AFFIL* dir: Boy Scouts Am, Kansas City Art Inst, Kansas City Chamber Commerce, Kansas City Lyric Opera, Kansas City Symphony; mem: Am Counc Life Ins; trust: Columbia Coll
Richard L. Finn: secy
Ann Bixby Oxler: trust

APPLICATION INFORMATION

Initial Approach: Contributes only to preselected organizations.
Restrictions on Giving: Does not support individuals.

GRANTS ANALYSIS

Number of Grants: 96
Highest Grant: $30,000
Typical Range: $125 to $5,000
Disclosure Period: 1990

RECENT GRANTS

30,000 Kansas City Art Institute, Kansas City, MO

27,500 Barstow School, Kansas City, MO

25,000 Channel 19, Kansas City, MO

25,000 Rockhurst College, Kansas City, MO

25,000 University of Missouri Arthritis Center, Columbia, MO

20,000 Research Medical Center, Kansas City, MO

15,000 Boy Scouts of America, Kansas City, MO

12,000 Avila College, Kansas City, MO

10,000 Columbia College, Columbia, MO

10,000 Westport '89 Committee, Westport, CT

Reynolds Foundation, Richard S.

CONTACT

David P. Reynolds
President
Richard S. Reynolds Foundation
6601 West Broad St.
Richmond, VA 23230
(804) 281-4801

FINANCIAL SUMMARY

Recent Giving: $1,829,711 (fiscal 1992); $1,663,300 (fiscal 1991); $1,166,270 (fiscal 1990)
Assets: $38,352,215 (fiscal year ending June 30, 1992); $36,627,365 (fiscal 1991); $36,014,400 (fiscal 1990)
Gifts Received: $62,290 (fiscal 1992); $64,877 (fiscal 1991); $68,613 (fiscal 1990)
Fiscal Note: In fiscal 1991, the foundation received $64,877 from David P. Reynolds under trust agreement dated December 30, 1960. In fiscal 1992, the foundation received $62,290 from David P. Reynolds.
EIN: 54-6037003

CONTRIBUTIONS SUMMARY

Donor(s): The foundation was established in 1965 by the late Julia L. Reynolds.
Typical Recipients: • *Arts & Humanities:* arts associations, dance, history/historic preservation, museums/galleries, music, opera, theater • *Civic & Public Affairs:* environmental affairs, professional & trade associations, zoos/botanical gardens • *Education:* business education, colleges & universities, education associations, education funds, medical education, private education (precollege), special education, student aid • *Health:* health funds, hospitals, medical research • *Religion:* churches, religious organizations • *Social Services:* aged, child welfare, disabled, employment/job training, recreation & athletics
Grant Types: capital, conference/seminar, endowment, general support, multiyear/continuing support, operating expenses, project, research, and scholarship
Geographic Distribution: focus on Richmond, VA

GIVING OFFICERS

Mrs. Glenn R. Martin: vp, dir
David Parham Reynolds: pres, dir *B* Bristol TN 1915 *CURR EMPL* chmn emeritus, dir: Reynolds Metals Co *CORP AFFIL* chmn, dir: Eskimo Pie Corp *NONPR AFFIL* dir: Richmond Symphony; hon mem: AIA; mem: Aluminum Assn, Bus Comm Arts, Primary Aluminum Inst; trust emeritus: Lawrenceville Sch, Univ Richmond
Richard Samuel Reynolds III: secy, dir *B* New York NY 1934 *ED* Princeton Univ 1956 *CURR EMPL* managing dir: Reynolds Trusts
William Gray Reynolds, Jr.: treas, dir *B* New York NY 1939 *ED* Univ PA BA 1962; Univ VA 1965 *CURR EMPL* vp (govt rels & pub affairs): Reynolds Metals Co *CORP AFFIL* dir: Central Fidelity Bank NA, Eskimo Pie Corp

APPLICATION INFORMATION

Initial Approach: Applicants should send a brief letter with the outline of the proposal.
Proposals should include verification of applicant's tax-exempt status by the IRS.
There are no deadlines.

GRANTS ANALYSIS

Total Grants: $1,829,711
Number of Grants: 26
Highest Grant: $400,000
Typical Range: $5,000 to $50,000
Disclosure Period: fiscal year ending June 30, 1992
Note: Recent grants are derived from a fiscal 1992 grants list. Average grant figure excludes two high grants of $400,000 each.

RECENT GRANTS

220,000 Virginia Tech Foundation, Blacksburg, VA — for renovations at the continuing education center and Reynolds Homestead

200,000 Medical College of Virginia, Richmond, VA — for chair of neurosurgery

200,000 University of Pennsylvania, Philadelphia, PA — Wharton School scholarship fund

200,000 Virginia Museum Foundation, Richmond, VA — endowment for decorative arts

150,000 Mountain Retreat Association, Montreat, NC — for lodge addition at the Presbyterian conference center

100,000 Collegiate Schools, Richmond, VA — for capital campaign

100,000 Medical College of Virginia, Richmond, VA — for neurosurgery research lab support

100,000 St. Mary's Health Care Foundation, Richmond, VA — for Bon Secours Health Center campaign

50,000 Elk Hill Farm, Goochland, VA — for swimming pool

40,000 Richmond Children's Museum, Richmond, VA — for operating expenses

Reynolds Foundation, Z. Smith

CONTACT
Thomas W. Lambeth
Executive Director
Z. Smith Reynolds Foundation
101 Reynolda Village
Winston-Salem, NC 27106-5199
(919) 725-7541

FINANCIAL SUMMARY
Recent Giving: $9,327,731 (1993 est.); $8,880,330 (1992); $16,018,073 (1991)
Assets: $251,000,000 (1993 est.); $249,779,668 (1992); $245,536,253 (1991); $213,501,354 (1990)
Gifts Received: $11,000,000 (1993 est.); $10,513,034 (1992); $11,028,863 (1991); $12,431,158 (1990)
Fiscal Note: The foundation has received contributions from the Zachary Smith Reynolds Trust and the W. N. Reynolds Trust. Asset figures listed above are for these two trusts which directly feed the foundation.
EIN: 58-6038145

CONTRIBUTIONS SUMMARY
Donor(s): The Z. Smith Reynolds Foundation was established in 1936 by members of

the Reynolds family. It was chartered by Richard J. Reynolds and his sisters, Mary Reynolds Babcock and Nancy Susan Reynolds. The original assets of the foundation were siblings' shares of an inheritance from their brother, Zachary Smith Reynolds, son of Richard Joshua Reynolds, founder of the tobacco company which bears his name. Later, their uncle, William N. Reynolds (also of R. J. Reynolds Tobacco Company), left most of his estate to the foundation. All four donors served as original trustees, and their descendants comprise about half of the board of trustees.

Typical Recipients: • *Arts & Humanities:* public broadcasting • *Civic & Public Affairs:* better government, business/free enterprise, civil rights, economic development, environmental affairs, ethnic/minority organizations, first amendment issues, housing, law & justice, rural affairs, urban & community affairs, women's affairs • *Education:* community & junior colleges, education funds, elementary education, literacy, minority education, preschool education, public education (precollege) • *Social Services:* child welfare, day care, delinquency & crime, domestic violence, drugs & alcohol, employment/job training, family planning, family services, legal aid
Grant Types: conference/seminar, general support, operating expenses, project, and seed money
Geographic Distribution: only in North Carolina

GIVING OFFICERS
Smith Bagley: trust *PHIL AFFIL* pres, dir: Sapelo Island Foundation
Josephine D. Clement: trust
Daniel G. Clodfelter: trust *ED* Univ NC *CURR EMPL* atty: Moore Van Allen & Allen
Joseph G. Gordon: treas, trust
Hubert Humphrey: trust *B* Charlotte NC 1928 *ED* Wake Forest Univ BA 1948; Univ NC JD 1951 *CURR EMPL* atty: Brooks Pierce McLendon Humphrey & Leonard *NONPR AFFIL* mem: Am Bar Assn, Am Coll Trial Lawyers, Am Law Inst, NC Bar Assn; trust: Wake Forest Univ
Joseph E. Kilpatrick: asst dir

Thomas W. Lambeth: exec dir, secy, asst treas
Valeria L. Lee: program off
Katharine Babcock Mountcastle: trust *B* Philadelphia PA 1931 *ED* Sweet Briar Coll BA 1952 *NONPR AFFIL* dir: Friends Earth, NY Womens Fdn, People Am Way, Rural Advancement Fund, World Policy Inst; trust: Sapelo Island Res Fdn
Mary Mountcastle: pres, trust
Stephen L. Neal: trust *B* Winston-Salem NC 1934 *ED* Univ CA Santa Barbara; Univ HI BA 1963 *NONPR AFFIL* chmn US Congress: Subcomm Domestic Monetary Policy; mem US Congress: Comm Banking Fin Urban Affs, Comm Govt Opers
Jane S. Patterson: trust *CURR EMPL* vp: ITT
Martha Pridgen: asst secy, dir admin
Sherwood Hubbard Smith, Jr.: trust *B* Jacksonville FL 1934 *ED* Univ NC AB 1956; Univ NC JD 1960 *CURR EMPL* chmn, ceo, dir: Carolina Power & Light Co *CORP AFFIL* dir: Durham Corp, Durham Life Ins Co, Edison Electric Inst, First Wachovia Corp, Hackney Bros Body Co, Wachovia Corp; mem: Edison Illuminating Cos; dir: Southeastern Electric Exchange *NONPR AFFIL* chmn: Nuclear Power Oversight Comm; chmn bd trust: Rex Hosp; dir: Inst Nuclear Power Opers; mem: Am Nuclear Soc, Bus Counc, Bus Roundtable, Electric Power Res Inst, Greater Raleigh Chamber Commerce, Kenan Inst Pvt Enterprise, NC Counc Mgmt & Devel, Phi Beta Kappa, Pres Counc Intl Youth Exchange, US Chamber Commerce, US World Energy Conf; pres, dir: Bus Fdn NC; trust: Comm Econ Devel; vchmn: Morehead Scholarship Comm Univ NC, US Counc Energy Awareness; vchmn, mem: Microelectronics Ctr NC
Zachary Taylor Smith II: vp, trust *B* Mount Airy NC 1923 *ED* Univ NC AB 1947 *NONPR AFFIL* dir: Univ NC Arts Sciences Fdn; mem: Citizens Planning Counc, Winston-Salem Chamber Commerce; mem adv counc hosp: Duke Univ; mem co-fdrs club: Univ NC Med Sch; mem natl dev counc: Univ NC; mem Reynolds Scholarship Comm, trust: Wake Forest Univ; vchmn, dir: Friends Greensboro Library;

dir: Leadership Winston-Salem; mem adv counc: Univ NC Carolina Challenge; mem bd visitors: Duke Univ Inst Pub Affs *PHIL AFFIL* dir: Med Fdn; mem bd visitors: Devotion Fdn
Lloyd P. Tate, Jr.: trust

APPLICATION INFORMATION
Initial Approach:
Applicants are asked to contact the foundation by phone or via a brief introductory letter.
A three-page application form, available from the foundation, must be submitted in addition to a proposal. The proposal should be limited to three single-spaced typed pages. Only one unbound copy must be submitted. The proposal should contain a concise description of the project; total funds needed; a list of other funding sources; demonstrated need for the project; a list of the project's objectives and how they are to be accomplished; description of the organization; and a list of board members, with a brief explanation of how they are elected. Include the standards by which evaluation of the project is to be measured. If the organization is not new, a list of previous achievements should be included in a separate report. Supplemental information may be included at the discretion of the applicant organization. Attach a one-page, line-item budget for fiscal year of funding request, and if funds are requested for a specific project, include a one-page, line-item budget for the project, as well as anticipated income and expenditures. Non-governmental agencies must also include a copy of the organization's 501(c)(3) tax exemption certification.
The board of trustees meets twice a year to consider applications. The meeting dates are the third Friday in May, for which the deadline is February 1, and the third Friday in November, for which the deadline is August 1. Proposals postmarked or hand-delivered after the deadline date will not be accepted under any circumstances.
Restrictions on Giving: The foundation is limited by its charter to making grants in North Carolina. Organizations which operate both within and

outside North Carolina may be eligible for consideration only for programs operated exclusively in North Carolina. The foundation does not make grants to individuals. Scholarships are provided, but only through predesignated institutions.

OTHER THINGS TO KNOW

The foundation was established by the same family that established two other North Carolina foundations: Mary Reynolds Babcock Foundation, and Kate B. Reynolds Charitable Trusts. The foundation is separate from the other two foundations.

The foundation sponsors conferences, seminars, and workshops.

Publications: annual report

GRANTS ANALYSIS

Total Grants: $8,880,330
Number of Grants: 247
Highest Grant: $1,000,000
Typical Range: $20,000 to $60,000
Disclosure Period: 1992
Note: Recent grants are derived from a 1992 grants list.

RECENT GRANTS

225,000 Environmental Defense Fund of North Carolina, Raleigh, NC — to support the ongoing work in three major program areas: air quality, toxics and solid waste, and water quality wetlands

155,000 North Carolina Institute of Justice, Raleigh, NC — operational support for the North Carolina Center on Crime and Punishment to work for criminal justice reform and crime prevention

150,000 Gateway Community Development Corporation, Henderson, NC — operating support for three years

150,000 Reynolda House, Winston-Salem, NC — general operational support for three years for the Museum of American Art

150,000 Rocky Mount/Edgecombe Community

Development Corporation, Rocky Mount, NC — operational support for three years to develop and maintain key core staff positions

150,000 Southern Environmental Law Center, Charlottesville, NC — operational support for the North Carolina office of the Law Center

150,000 Tanglewood Park Foundation, Clemmons, NC — to develop a new winter light show to help the Park achieve economic self-sufficiency

125,000 North Carolina Association of Community Development Corporations, Raleigh, NC — operational support for two years to assist the Association in better serving member Community Development Corporations and to stablize its operations

125,000 Public School Forum of North Carolina, Raleigh, NC — general operational support to continue the Forum's role as a change agent and consensus builder around education policy and practices in North Carolina

125,000 University of North Carolina, Greensboro, NC — for support of the Katharine Smith Reynolds Scholarships for 1992-93

Reynolds Metals Co. / Reynolds Metals Co. Foundation

Sales: $5.62 billion
Employees: 30,600
Headquarters: Richmond, VA
SIC Major Group: Metal Mining, Primary Metal Industries, Rubber & Miscellaneous Plastics

Products, and Wholesale Trade—Durable Goods

CONTACT

Janice M. Bailey
Assistant to the General Manager
Reynolds Metals Co. Fdn.
PO Box 27003
Richmond, VA 23261-7003
(804) 281-2222

FINANCIAL SUMMARY

Recent Giving: $800,000 (1993 est.); $1,000,000 (1992 approx.); $858,014 (1991)
Assets: $10,327,455 (1991); $8,236,951 (1990); $5,834,137 (1989)
Fiscal Note: All contributions are made through the foundation.
EIN: 54-1084698

CONTRIBUTIONS SUMMARY

Typical Recipients: • *Arts & Humanities:* arts associations, arts centers, museums/galleries, music, performing arts, public broadcasting, theater • *Civic & Public Affairs:* economics, environmental affairs, ethnic/minority organizations, housing, philanthropic organizations, professional & trade associations, public policy, safety, urban & community affairs, zoos/botanical gardens • *Education:* career/vocational education, colleges & universities, community & junior colleges, economic education, education associations, education funds, elementary education, minority education, private education (precollege), public education (precollege), science/technology education • *Health:* hospitals, medical rehabilitation, medical research, pediatric health, single-disease health associations • *Social Services:* child welfare, community service organizations, disabled, domestic violence, drugs & alcohol, food/clothing distribution, recreation & athletics, united funds, youth organizations
Grant Types: capital, employee matching gifts, general support, and project
Nonmonetary Support Types: donated equipment
Note: The company donates equipment and scrap metal. Amount of nonmonetary support is unavailable and is not included in the above figures.
Geographic Distribution: limited to communities where com-

pany has major operating facilities
Operating Locations: AL (Sheffield), CT (Stratford), DE (Wilmington), HI (Ewa Beach), IL (McCook), KY (Louisville), MO (Kansas City), NY (Syracuse), OR (Troutdale), RI (Providence), TX (El Campo, Malakoff), VA (Bristol, Grottoes, Richmond)
Note: Also operates internationally in Australia, Europe, Central and South America, Bermuda, Canada, Jamaica, and the Philippines.

CORP. OFFICERS

Richard G. Holder: *B* Paris TN *ED* Vanderbilt Univ 1953 *CURR EMPL* chmn, ceo, dir: Reynolds Metals Co *CORP AFFIL* dir: NationsBank VA NA
Henry S. Savedge, Jr.: *B* Dendron VA 1933 *ED* Univ Richmond 1955 *CURR EMPL* exec vp, cfo: Reynolds Metals Co

GIVING OFFICERS

Janice M. Bailey: adm
Yale M. Brandt: dir *B* 1930 *CURR EMPL* exec vp (fabricating opers): Reynolds Metals Co
Donald T. Cowles: vp, gen couns, secy, dir *CURR EMPL* vp, gen couns, secy: Reynolds Metals Co
Donna C. Dabney: asst secy
Carol L. Dillon: asst secy
Richard G. Holder: dir *CURR EMPL* chmn, ceo, dir: Reynolds Metals Co (see above)
Douglas M. Jerrold: vp
D. Michael Jones: asst secy *CURR EMPL* pres: West One Bancorp
John Rudolph McGill: vp, dir *B* Paterson NJ 1936 *ED* Syracuse Univ 1957; Syracuse Univ 1967 *CURR EMPL* vp (human resources): Reynolds Metals Co
Randolph Nicklas Reynolds: dir *B* Louisville KY 1941 *ED* Bellarmine Coll BA 1966; Univ Louisville 1968 *CURR EMPL* pres, ceo, dir: Reynolds Intl *CORP AFFIL* dir: Dominion Bancshares, Dominion Natl Bank Richmond, Eskimo Pie Corp; vp, dir: Reynolds Metals Co *NONPR AFFIL* bd sponsors: Coll William & Mary; dir: Bellarmine Coll, YMCA Richmond
William Gray Reynolds, Jr.: dir *B* New York NY 1939 *ED* Univ PA BA 1962; Univ VA 1965 *CURR EMPL* vp (govt rels & pub affairs): Reynolds Metals Co *CORP AFFIL* dir:

Central Fidelity Bank NA, Eskimo Pie Corp
D. Brickford Rider: pres
Henry S. Savedge, Jr.: dir *CURR EMPL* exec vp, cfo: Reynolds Metals Co (see above)
Julian Howard Taylor: vp, treas, dir *B* Emporia KS 1943 *CURR EMPL* vp, treas: Reynolds Metals Co *NONPR AFFIL* mem: Natl Assn Corp Treas

APPLICATION INFORMATION

Initial Approach: *Initial Contact:* proposal *Include Information On:* organization's purpose, description of program and goals for current year, IRS determination letter, current budget information showing income and expenditures, list of board of directors, use for requested funds, history of achievement *When to Submit:* no later than September 1 *Note:* For grant requests of $5,000 or more, a grant application form (R-3-2), available from the foundation, must be submitted with accompanying information.
Restrictions on Giving: Foundation generally does not support causes and organizations outside designated geographical areas served by foundation; religious organizations for sectarian purposes; veterans, fraternal, or similar organizations, unless contribution will benefit entire community; conferences, trips, or tours; operating expenses of member agencies of united funds; advertising, tickets, or tables for benefits; public or private preschool and primary educational institutions; duplicated funds during the same year; or organizations acting as fundraising agents for others (excluding United Way). Foundation will make no contributions to political or lobbying groups or to individuals.

OTHER THINGS TO KNOW

Publications: policies and guidelines

GRANTS ANALYSIS

Total Grants: $858,014
Number of Grants: 229
Highest Grant: $80,000
Typical Range: $250 to $5,000
Disclosure Period: 1991
Note: Recent grants are derived from a 1991 Form 990.

RECENT GRANTS

80,000 United Way of Greater Richmond, Richmond, VA
60,000 College of William and Mary, Williamsburg, VA
31,000 Metropolitan United Way, Louisville, KY
25,000 National Chamber Foundation, Washington, DC
25,000 United Way/Crusade of Mercy, Chicago, IL
25,000 Virginia Polytechnic Institute and State University, Blacksburg, VA
21,000 Virginia Foundation of Independent Colleges, Richmond, VA
20,416 Virginia Commonwealth University, Richmond, VA
15,000 United Way of Shoals, Florence, AL
14,000 Keep America Beautiful, Stamford, CT

Reynolds & Reynolds Co. / Reynolds & Reynolds Company Foundation

Sales: $647.5 million
Employees: 4,700
Headquarters: Dayton, OH
SIC Major Group: Business Services, Educational Services, Industrial Machinery & Equipment, and Printing & Publishing

CONTACT

Susan Webster
Administrator
Reynolds & Reynolds Co.
PO Box 2608
Dayton, OH 45401
(513) 449-4490

FINANCIAL SUMMARY

Recent Giving: $500,000 (fiscal 1992 approx.); $592,000 (fiscal 1991); $831,165 (fiscal 1990)
Assets: $45,177 (fiscal year ending September 30, 1990); $11,281 (fiscal 1989)
Gifts Received: $865,000 (fiscal 1990); $215,000 (fiscal 1989)
Fiscal Note: Contributes through foundation only. In 1990, contributions were received from Reynolds & Reynolds Company.
EIN: 31-1168299

CONTRIBUTIONS SUMMARY

Typical Recipients: • *Arts & Humanities:* arts centers, arts funds, arts institutes, community arts, dance, music, opera, performing arts, public broadcasting, theater • *Civic & Public Affairs:* economic development, philanthropic organizations • *Education:* education funds, literacy, public education (precollege)
Grant Types: general support and project
Nonmonetary Support Types: donated equipment, in-kind services, and loaned executives
Geographic Distribution: focus on Ohio
Operating Locations: CA (San Diego), IL (Elk Grove), IN (Lebanon), OH (Dayton), OK (Oklahoma City)

CORP. OFFICERS

David R. Holmes: *B* Salt Lake City UT 1940 *ED* Stanford Univ BA 1963; Northwestern Univ MBA 1965 *CURR EMPL* chmn, pres, ceo: Reynolds & Reynolds Co *CORP AFFIL* dir: Bank One Dayton *NONPR AFFIL* mem: Am Mgmt Assn, Dayton Chamber Commerce, Dayton Philharmonic Orchestra Assn
Dale L. Medford: *B* Dayton OH 1950 *ED* Miami Univ (OH) 1972 *CURR EMPL* vp, cfo: Reynolds & Reynolds Co *NONPR AFFIL* mem: Am Inst CPAs, Fin Execs Inst, Natl Investor Rels Inst

GIVING OFFICERS

Janet Brewer: trust
Peter A. Granson: trust
John R. Martin: trust
Ken Sutter: trust
Tom Suttmiller: trust
Susan Webster: admin

APPLICATION INFORMATION

Initial Approach: *Initial Contact:* brief letter requesting application form; telephone inquiries will be advised to submit proposals in writing *Include Information On:* grant application will outline the mission or purpose of the organization; statement of need and a description of how the proposed program will meet that need; population served; amount requested and how it will be used; any other sources of funding and amounts; plans for permanent financial support, plans for evaluating and reporting results, and the name of the contact person, along with their address and phone number* *Note:* The following information should be attached to the application: a copy of the organization's 501(c)(3) tax exemption letter from the IRS and a 509(a)(1) letter is established prior to 1975, the organization's most recent year-end financial statement. a copy of the organization's current operating budget, current sources of income, the names and occupations of the board of trustees and officers, and the organization's annual report or other relevant publications.
Restrictions on Giving: Foundation does not contribute to organizations without tax-exempt status; sectarian organizations having an exclusively religious purpose; individuals; political parties, offices, or candidates; fraternal or veteran's organizations; primary or secondary schools (except for occasional special projects); organizations which cannot provide adequate accounting records or procedures; courtesy advertising; tax-supported colleges and universities for operating purposes (except for occasional special projects); funding for deficits or debt retirement; or endowments.
Organizations receiving funds through the United Way generally are not considered for additional gifts towards operations, programs, or capital campaigns. In general, organizations repeating a request in the same fiscal year will not be considered for additional funding. An approved grant does not necessarily indicate that continued support will automatically be available the following year. Grant requests must be resubmitted annually unless otherwise stipulated.

OTHER THINGS TO KNOW

Publications: foundation guidelines and application form

GRANTS ANALYSIS

Total Grants: $831,165
Number of Grants: 64
Highest Grant: $253,750

Typical Range: $1,000 to $11,000

Disclosure Period: fiscal year ending September 30, 1990

Note: Recent grants are derived from a fiscal 1990 grants list.

RECENT GRANTS

253,750 United Way, Dayton, OH

100,000 Arts Center Foundation, Dayton, OH

100,000 University of Dayton, Dayton, OH

80,000 Dayton Museum of Natural History, Dayton, OH

35,000 IBFI Foundation, Dayton, OH

27,000 Dayton Art Institute, Dayton, OH

25,000 Hospice of Dayton, Dayton, OH

20,000 Dayton Foundation, Dayton, OH — New Futures Fund

17,500 Arts Dayton, Dayton, OH

15,000 Arts Dayton, Dayton, OH

RGK Foundation

CONTACT

Gregory A. Kozmetsky
President
RGK Foundation
2815 San Gabriel
Austin, TX 78705-3596
(512) 474-9298

FINANCIAL SUMMARY

Recent Giving: $2,000,000 (1993 est.); $2,071,082 (1992); $914,033 (1991)

Assets: $40,000,000 (1993 est.); $38,000,000 (1992 est.); $37,519,990 (1991); $32,758,152 (1990)

Gifts Received: $1,000,000 (1993 est.); $1,897,575 (1992); $1,436,022 (1991); $984,344 (1990)

Fiscal Note: In 1990, the foundation received $947,250 worth of stock from George and Ronya Kozmetsky who also donated $1,577 in cash. Other donors included the Bechtel Corporation, $15,000, Andersen Consulting, $10,000, University of Texas, $8,867, and University of Kentucky, $1,000. In 1991, the foundation received $1,324,375 worth of stock from Gregory and Ronya Kozmetsky. Other donors included Southwestern Bell,

$102,000; NCRO Corporation, $5,000; and MCC, $4,000. EIN: 74-6077587

CONTRIBUTIONS SUMMARY

Donor(s): The RGK Foundation was established in 1966 by Dr. George Kozmetsky and his wife. Dr. Kozmetsky currently sits on the board of several corporations including Teledyne, Inc., which he co-founded in 1960.

Dr. Kozmetsky, a son of Russian immigrants, was born in Seattle, WA, in 1917. He taught at Harvard University and Carnegie-Mellon University before he started his business career in Los Angeles with Hughes Aricraft Company (1952-54), then Litton Company (1954-59). He left Teledyne in 1966 when he took the positon of dean of the college and graduate school of business at the University of Texas at Austin. He stayed there for 16 years until 1982 when he went on to head the school's Institute for Constructive Capitalism.

Currently, Dr. Kozmetsky serves on the RGK Foundation as its donor and trustee. His wife, Ronya, and his two children Gregory Allen Kozmetsky and Nadya Anne Kozmetsky Scott, also serve on the foundation.

Typical Recipients: • *Education:* business education, colleges & universities, literacy, medical education, science/technology education • *Health:* health organizations, single-disease health associations • *International:* foreign educational institutions

Grant Types: conference/seminar, research, and scholarship

Geographic Distribution: nationally, with emphasis on Texas, particularly Austin; also to international organizations

GIVING OFFICERS

Patricia Ann Hayes: trust *B* Binghamton NY 1944 *ED* Coll St Rose BA; Georgetown Univ PhD *CURR EMPL* pres: St Edwards Univ *NONPR AFFIL* dir: KLRU-Pub TV, TX Chamber Commerce; mem: Assn TX Colls & Univs, Independent Colls & Univs TX, Natl Comm Migrant Ed, Seton Fin Counc, Southern Assn Colls & Schs

Charles Edwin Hurwitz: trust *B* Kilgore TX 1940 *ED* Univ

OK BA 1962 *CURR EMPL* chmn, pres, ceo: Federated Devel Co *CORP AFFIL* chmn: Fed Reinsurance Corp, Pacific Lumber Co; chmn, ceo: Maxxam Group, Maxxam Inc; dir: Horizon Corp, Kaiser Aluminum & Chemical Corp, KaiserTech Ltd, MCO Resources

Cynthia Kozmetsky: trust

George Kozmetsky: trust *B* Seattle WA 1917 *ED* Univ WA BA 1938; Harvard Univ MBA 1947; Harvard Univ DCS 1957 *CURR EMPL* chmn: Inst Constructive Capitalism Univ TX *CORP AFFIL* dir: Dell Computer Corp, Hydril Co, KMS Indus, La Quinta Motor Inns, PaineWebber Devel Corp, Scientific & Engring Software Indus, Teledyne *NONPR AFFIL* chmn, mem: Inst Mgmt Science; dir: Univ TX; mem: Am Inst CPAs, Am Soc Oceanography, Assn Advancement Med Instrumentation, British Interplanetary Soc

Gregory Kozmetsky: don, pres, treas, trust

Ronya Kozmetsky: chmn, secy, trust

Nadya Kozmetsky Scott: vp, trust

APPLICATION INFORMATION

Initial Approach:
Applicants should call the foundation to request an application form.

The proposal should contain an introductory letter, a brief background of the organization, a description of the proposed project, a concise statement of the necessity for the project, an explanation of the use of the funds, the amount requested, a detailed project budget, other potential sources of funding and, for non-individual grant seekers, proof of charitable status.

There are no deadlines for submitting grant proposals.

OTHER THINGS TO KNOW

In addition to its grant-making activities, the foundation also sponsors conferences.

Publications: informational brochure (including application form and guidelines)

GRANTS ANALYSIS

Total Grants: $2,071,082
Number of Grants: 92
Highest Grant: $300,000

Typical Range: $10,000 to $30,000

Disclosure Period: 1992

Note: Recent grants are derived from a 1991 grants list.

RECENT GRANTS

100,000 St. Edward's University, Austin, TX — support for Center for Teaching Excellence

85,000 Medical University of South Carolina, Charleston, SC — support for scleroderma research

81,000 University of Texas Health Science Center at San Antonio, Department of Medicine, San Antonio, TX — support for medical research project "Antibodies to Retroviral Proteins in Autoimmunity"

37,325 University of Texas at Austin, Center for Research on Communication Technology and Society, Austin, TX — support for telecommunications forum "The Coming Intelligent Network"

30,626 Dartmouth Medical School, Hanover, NH — support for medical research project "Receptor-Mediated Induction and Suppression of Collagenase Synthesis"

30,000 Seton Fund — support for heart transplant endowment challenge

27,500 American Society for Cell Biology — support for Summer Research Fellowship Program

25,000 University of Texas MD Anderson Cancer Center — support for cancer research

20,000 Desert Research Institute, University of Nevada System — support for "The First Heinz Symposium on the Competitive Market System and The Environment"

17,424 American Lung Association — support for research project "Pulmonary Function During Exercise in Insulin Dependent Diabetes Mellitus"

Rhoades Fund, Otto L. and Hazel E.

CONTACT
Harry M. Coffman
Otto L. and Hazel E. Rhoades Fund
6106 North Landers
Chicago, IL 60646

FINANCIAL SUMMARY
Recent Giving: $157,000 (1989); $108,500 (1988)
Assets: $2,184,400 (1989); $2,002,744 (1988)
EIN: 36-2994856

CONTRIBUTIONS SUMMARY
Donor(s): Otto L. Rhoades
Typical Recipients: • *Arts & Humanities:* arts institutes, community arts, public broadcasting • *Health:* hospices, hospitals, medical research, single-disease health associations • *Religion:* churches • *Social Services:* community service organizations, disabled, food/clothing distribution, shelters/homelessness
Grant Types: general support
Geographic Distribution: focus on IL

GIVING OFFICERS
Julius Lewis: dir, secy *B Ohama NE* 1931 *ED Univ* Chicago BA 1950; Univ Chicago MA 1954; Yale Univ LLB 1957 *CURR EMPL* ptnr: Sonnenschein Carlin Nath & Rosenthal *NONPR AFFIL* dir: Recordings for Blind; mem: Am Bar Assn, Chicago Bar Assn, Legal Club Chicago; secy, dir: Alliance Francaise de Chicago
Hazel T. Rhoades: pres
H. Allan Stark: trust

APPLICATION INFORMATION
Initial Approach: Send brief letter describing program. There are no deadlines.

GRANTS ANALYSIS
Number of Grants: 14
Highest Grant: $20,000
Typical Range: $2,500 to $10,000
Disclosure Period: 1989

RECENT GRANTS
20,000 Recording for the Blind, Chicago, IL

12,000 Public Television, Chicago, IL
10,000 Art Institute of Chicago, Chicago, IL
10,000 Elgin Academy, Chicago, IL
7,500 Ada McKinley Community Services, Chicago, IL
7,500 Chicago Coalition for the Homeless, Chicago, IL
5,000 Easter Seal Society, Chicago, IL
5,000 Eye Research Foundation, Chicago, IL
5,000 Lambs, Chicago, IL
5,000 Salvation Army, Chicago, IL

Rhode Island Hospital Trust National Bank / Memorial Baptist Church Trust

Former Foundation Name: Rhode Island Hospital Trust
Assets: $2.88 billion
Employees: 1,331
Parent Company: Bank of Boston Corp.
Headquarters: Providence, RI
SIC Major Group: Depository Institutions

CONTACT
Susan Baxter
Assistant Vice President, Corporate Comm
Rhode Island Hospital Trust Corp. Giving Program
One Hospital Trust Plz.
Providence, RI 02903
(401) 278-7683

FINANCIAL SUMMARY
Recent Giving: $39,921 (1991); $53,179 (1989)
Assets: $1,095,778 (1991); $1,033,812 (1989)
EIN: 05-6004511

CONTRIBUTIONS SUMMARY
Typical Recipients: • *Religion:* churches, religious organizations
Grant Types: fellowship and general support
Geographic Distribution: focus on RI
Operating Locations: RI (Providence)

CORP. OFFICERS
Alden M. Anderson: *CURR EMPL* chmn, pres, ceo, dir: RIHT Fin Corp

Michael V. Frazier: *CURR EMPL* sr vp, cfo: Rhode Island Hospital Trust Natl Bank

APPLICATION INFORMATION
Initial Approach: Contributes only to preselected organizations.

GRANTS ANALYSIS
Number of Grants: 1
Highest Grant: $39,920
Disclosure Period: 1991

RECENT GRANTS
39,920 Memorial Baptist Church

Rhodebeck Charitable Trust

CONTACT
Hyler C. Held
Trustee
Rhodebeck Charitable Trust
c/o Turk, Marsh, Kelly & Hoare
575 Lexington Ave.
New York, NY 10022-6102
(212) 371-1660

FINANCIAL SUMMARY
Recent Giving: $823,628 (fiscal 1992); $1,678,732 (fiscal 1991); $656,212 (fiscal 1990)
Assets: $16,956,422 (fiscal year ending April 30, 1991); $15,660,388 (fiscal 1990); $14,730,637 (fiscal 1989)
EIN: 13-3413293

CONTRIBUTIONS SUMMARY
Donor(s): The foundation was established in 1987 by the late Mildred T. Rhodebeck.
Typical Recipients: • *Civic & Public Affairs:* law & justice, urban & community affairs • *Religion:* churches, religious organizations • *Social Services:* community centers, community service organizations, food/clothing distribution, homes, recreation & athletics, shelters/homelessness, youth organizations
Grant Types: general support and project
Geographic Distribution: limited to Arizona and New York, NY

GIVING OFFICERS
Hyler C. Held: trust *PHIL AFFIL* trust: Merrill (Ingram) Foundation

APPLICATION INFORMATION
Initial Approach: Restrictions on Giving: The foundation supports preselected organizations and does not accept unsolicited requests for funds. The foundation does not make grants to individuals.

GRANTS ANALYSIS
Total Grants: $1,678,732
Number of Grants: 21
Highest Grant: $1,050,000
Typical Range: $10,000 to $60,000
Disclosure Period: fiscal year ending April 30, 1991
Note: No grants list was provided for fiscal 1992. Average grant figure for fiscal 1991 does not include the highest grant of $1,050,000. Recent grants are derived from a fiscal 1991 grants list.

RECENT GRANTS
1,050,000 Fountain House, New York, NY
100,000 Community Funds, New York, NY
64,732 Partnership for the Homeless, New York, NY — employment coordinator
60,000 Grand Street Settlement, New York, NY
60,000 Lower East Side Catholic Area Conference, New York, NY — construction expenses
60,000 South Bronx 2000, Bronx, NY
50,000 Holy Apostles Soup Kitchen, New York, NY
25,000 City Harvest, New York, NY
25,000 Hunter College, Brookdale Center on Aging, New York, NY
25,000 Mental Health Law Project, New York, NY

Rhoden Charitable Foundation, Elmer C.

CONTACT
Janet E. Rhoden
President
Elmer C. Rhoden Charitable Fdn.
2200 East 147th St.
Kansas City, MO 64141
(816) 941-2290

FINANCIAL SUMMARY
Recent Giving: $218,992 (fiscal 1991); $186,792 (fiscal 1990); $223,500 (fiscal 1989)
Assets: $4,864,094 (fiscal year ending July 31, 1991); $4,608,535 (fiscal 1990); $4,270,177 (fiscal 1989)
EIN: 43-1337876

CONTRIBUTIONS SUMMARY
Typical Recipients: • *Education:* colleges & universities, social sciences education • *Health:* health organizations • *Religion:* churches, religious organizations • *Social Services:* community service organizations, youth organizations
Grant Types: capital and scholarship
Geographic Distribution: focus on KS

GIVING OFFICERS
Lois D. Lacy: secy, treas
Charles G. Randall: asst secy, asst treas
Janet E. Rhoden: pres
Marilyn A. Rhoden: vp

APPLICATION INFORMATION
Initial Approach: Contributes only to preselected organizations.

GRANTS ANALYSIS
Number of Grants: 7
Highest Grant: $159,882
Typical Range: $3,000 to $10,000
Disclosure Period: fiscal year ending July 31, 1991

RECENT GRANTS
159,882 Village Presbyterian Church, Prairie Village, KS — renovation of preschool facilities
30,200 Operation Discovery School, Kansas City, MO — replacement of playground
9,880 Village Presbyterian Church, Prairie Village, KS — radio broadcast series, 1991
6,000 Community Services League
5,000 Kansas University School of Social Welfare, Lawrence, KS — social policy conference
5,000 Wyandotte House, Kansas City, KS
3,000 Health Fair, Kansas City, MO

Rhone-Poulenc Inc.
Sales: $2.92 billion
Employees: 5,800
Headquarters: Princeton, NJ
SIC Major Group: Chemicals & Allied Products, Food & Kindred Products, and Rubber & Miscellaneous Plastics Products

CONTACT
Ron Gurozynski
Manager, Corporate Communications
Rhone-Poulenc Inc.
CN5266
Princeton, NJ 08543-5266
(908) 297-0100

FINANCIAL SUMMARY
Fiscal Note: Annual Giving Range: $100,000 to $250,000

CONTRIBUTIONS SUMMARY
Rhone-Poulenc Inc. has no set giving priorities; rather it handles requests on a case-by-case basis. Past recipients have fallen mainly in the areas of arts and and social services. Cultural support goes to dance, music, the performing arts, libraries, museums, and galleries. Social services funding includes community service and youth organizations and sports teams. Funds programs for the disabled, the elderly, and drug and alcohol rehabilitation. Also gives to education, including public (precollege) schools. Contributes to hospitals and single-disease health associations such as the American Heart Association and the Cancer Society.
Typical Recipients: • *Arts & Humanities:* dance, libraries, museums/galleries, music, performing arts • *Education:* public education (precollege) • *Health:* hospitals, single-disease health associations • *Social Services:* aged, community service organizations, disabled, drugs & alcohol, youth organizations
Grant Types: general support
Geographic Distribution: principally near operating locations and to national organizations
Operating Locations: CT, NC, NJ, OR, SC, TN, TX, WA

CORP. OFFICERS
M. S. Leo: *CURR EMPL* sr vp, chief admin off, gen couns, dir: Rhone-Poulenc
Peter Neff: *CURR EMPL* pres, ceo, coo: Rhone-Poulenc
Pierre Valla: *CURR EMPL* vp, cfo: Rhone-Poulenc

GIVING OFFICERS
Ron Gurozynski: *CURR EMPL* mgr (corp commun): Rhone-Poulenc

APPLICATION INFORMATION
Initial Approach: A letter may be submitted at any time and should include a description of the organization and the purpose for which funds are sought, along with the amount requested.
Restrictions on Giving: Does not give to religious organizations for sectarian purposes, or to civic and public affairs. Subsidiaries administer independent giving programs. Does not provide nonmonetary support.

OTHER THINGS TO KNOW
Rhone-Poulenc operates in 23 states.

Rhone-Poulenc Rorer
Sales: $3.82 billion
Employees: 23,454
Headquarters: Collegeville, PA
SIC Major Group: Chemicals & Allied Products and Holding & Other Investment Offices

CONTACT
Dianne Solomon
Corporate Contributions Administrator
Rhone-Poulenc Rorer
500 Arcola Rd.
PO Box 1200
Collegeville, PA 19426-0107
(215) 628-6000

FINANCIAL SUMMARY
Recent Giving: $2,000,000 (1992 approx.); $1,200,000 (1991 approx.); $1,200,000 (1990)
Fiscal Note: All contributions are made directly by the company. Total giving figures are approximate. Figures are for U.S. giving only.

CONTRIBUTIONS SUMMARY
Typical Recipients: • *Arts & Humanities:* arts centers, museums/galleries, music • *Civic & Public Affairs:* business/free enterprise, environmental affairs, urban & community affairs, zoos/botanical gardens • *Education:* business education, colleges & universities, medical education • *Health:* health organizations, hospitals • *Social Services:* community service organizations, united funds
Grant Types: capital, employee matching gifts, general support, project, research, and scholarship
Nonmonetary Support Types: donated equipment, donated products, in-kind services, loaned employees, loaned executives, and workplace solicitation
Note: Estimated value of nonmonetary support was $200,000 in 1991 and is not included in figures above.
Geographic Distribution: primarily in operating locations
Operating Locations: CA (San Leandro), DE (Lewes), GA (Tucker), IL (Oak Forest), PA (Collegeville, Ft. Washington)
Note: Also operates in Puerto Rico.

CORP. OFFICERS
Robert Elston Cawthorn: *B* Masham England 1935 *ED* Cambridge Univ BA 1959 *CURR EMPL* chmn, pres, ceo, dir: Rhone Poulenc Rorer *CORP AFFIL* dir: Cytogen Corp, First PA Corp, Immune Response Corp, Sun Co; dir, trust: Univ Health Realty Income Trust *NONPR AFFIL* dir, trust: Un Way Southeastern PA; mem: Greater Philadelphia Chamber Commerce, Pharmaceutical Mfrs Assn; trust: Baldwin School

GIVING OFFICERS
Dianne Solomon: contributions adm

APPLICATION INFORMATION

Initial Approach: *Initial Contact:* brief letter *Include Information On:* organization's purpose and background, proof of tax-exempt status, current financial statement, verification of company employee involvement (if applicable) *When to Submit:* any time; requests received by October 1 are more favorably considered for funding the following year

OTHER THINGS TO KNOW

Company has recently undergone a merger.

GRANTS ANALYSIS

Total Grants: $1,200,000*
Number of Grants: 150*
Typical Range: $1,000 to $10,000
Disclosure Period: 1991
Note: Figures are approximate and do not include international giving. Recent grants are derived from a 1991 grants list.

RECENT GRANTS

Avington Memorial Hospital, Avington, PA
Greater Philadelphia First Foundation, Philadelphia, PA
Hope Lodge Historical Center, Ft. Washington, PA
Junior Achievement, Stamford, CT
Metropolitan Collegiate Center, Germantown, PA
Pharmacists Against Drug Abuse, Spring House, PA
YMCA, Philadelphia, PA

Rice Charitable Foundation, Albert W.

CONTACT
Stephen Fritch
Vice President
Albert W. Rice Charitable Fdn.
c/o Shawmut Worcester County Bank, M.A., Trust Dept.
446 Main St.
Worcester, MA 01608
(508) 793-4205

FINANCIAL SUMMARY
Recent Giving: $219,333 (1991); $247,933 (1990); $243,946 (1989)
Assets: $4,036,642 (1991); $3,681,826 (1990); $3,882,420 (1989)
EIN: 04-6028085

CONTRIBUTIONS SUMMARY
Donor(s): the late Albert W. Rice
Typical Recipients: • *Arts & Humanities:* arts centers, community arts, history/historic preservation, museums/galleries, performing arts • *Civic & Public Affairs:* rural affairs • *Health:* hospices • *Religion:* churches • *Science:* scientific institutes • *Social Services:* united funds, youth organizations
Grant Types: general support
Geographic Distribution: focus on Worcester, MA

GIVING OFFICERS
Shawmut Bank, N.A.: trust

APPLICATION INFORMATION
Initial Approach: Send brief letter of inquiry describing program or project. Deadlines are April 1 and October 1.
Restrictions on Giving: Does not support individuals.

GRANTS ANALYSIS
Number of Grants: 15
Highest Grant: $40,000
Typical Range: $5,000 to $25,000
Disclosure Period: 1991

RECENT GRANTS
40,000 Worcester Historical Museum, Worcester, MA
30,000 American Antiquarian Society, Worcester, MA
25,000 Old Sturbridge Village, Sturbridge, MA
25,000 United Way, Worcester, MA
20,000 New England Science Center, Worcester, MA
20,000 Worcester Academy, Worcester, MA
12,500 YWCA, Worcester, MA
10,000 Girls Club, Worcester, MA
10,000 Worcester Horticultural Society, Worcester, MA
5,000 Mechanics Hall, Worcester, MA

Rice Family Foundation, Jacob and Sophie

CONTACT
Jacob and Sophie Rice Family Fdn.
c/o Hamilton and Co.
PO Box 6370
Vero Beach, FL 32961

FINANCIAL SUMMARY
Recent Giving: $87,500 (1990); $92,500 (1989); $107,500 (1988)
Assets: $1,996,593 (1990); $1,999,891 (1989); $1,741,326 (1988)
EIN: 13-6264756

CONTRIBUTIONS SUMMARY
Donor(s): the late Mathilde T. Rice
Typical Recipients: • *Education:* colleges & universities • *Health:* hospitals, medical research, single-disease health associations • *Religion:* churches, religious organizations • *Social Services:* disabled, homes
Grant Types: general support
Geographic Distribution: focus on NY

GIVING OFFICERS
Richard G. Keneven: trust
Edwin McMahon Singer: trust

APPLICATION INFORMATION
Initial Approach: Send brief letter describing program. There are no deadlines.

GRANTS ANALYSIS
Number of Grants: 10
Highest Grant: $25,000
Typical Range: $2,500 to $10,000
Disclosure Period: 1990

RECENT GRANTS
25,000 Cardinal's Committee for the Laity, New York, NY
20,000 Benedictine Hospital, New York, NY
10,000 Calvary Hospital, Bronx, NY
5,000 American Lung Association, New York, NY
5,000 Catholic Charities, New York, NY
5,000 Columbia College, New York, NY
5,000 St. Josephs Home for the Blind, New York, NY
5,000 St. Peters Church, New York, NY
5,000 St. Roses Home, New York, NY
2,500 Covenant House, New York, NY

Rice Foundation

CONTACT
Arthur A. Nolan, Jr.
President and Director
Rice Foundation
222 Waukegan Rd.
Glenview, IL 60025
(708) 998-6666

FINANCIAL SUMMARY
Recent Giving: $4,209,587 (1990); $3,139,750 (1989); $7,031,644 (1988)
Assets: $78,670,372 (1990); $78,593,255 (1989); $70,621,471 (1988)
Gifts Received: $1,000 (1990); $3,581,415 (1988); $23,600 (1987)
Fiscal Note: In 1988, the foundation received two contributions totaling $3,579,915 from the estate of Ada Rice, and $1,500 from James Daugherty III.
EIN: 36-6043160

CONTRIBUTIONS SUMMARY
Donor(s): The Rice Foundation was established in 1947 by the late Daniel F. Rice.
Typical Recipients: • *Arts & Humanities:* arts associations, arts institutes, dance, history/historic preservation, museums/galleries • *Civic & Public Affairs:* environmental affairs, zoos/botanical gardens • *Education:* arts education, private education (precollege), science/technology education • *Health:* geriatric health, health organizations, hospitals, single-disease health associations • *Religion:* religious organizations • *Social Services:* child welfare, community centers, family services, recreation & athletics, religious welfare, shelters/homelessness, youth organizations
Grant Types: general support
Geographic Distribution: focus on Illinois, primarily Chicago

GIVING OFFICERS
Marilynn B. Alsdorf: dir
James Daugherty, Jr.: secy, dir
Donald Graham: dir
Arthur A. Nolan, Jr.: pres, dir

Patricia Nolan: vp, treas, dir

Peter Nolan: off mgr, grants consultant

Edward Reilly: grants consultant

Betrice Sheridan: vp, dir

David P. Winchester: dir

Barbara M. J. Wood: dir

APPLICATION INFORMATION

Initial Approach:

Applications should be submitted in writing.

Applications should include a statement describing the applicant organization and its activities, the amount and purpose of the grant requested, and proof of IRS tax-exempt status.

The foundation reports no application deadlines.

Restrictions on Giving: No grants are made to individuals.

GRANTS ANALYSIS

Total Grants: $4,209,587

Number of Grants: 50

Highest Grant: $1,501,837

Typical Range: $1,000 to $25,000

Disclosure Period: 1990

Note: The average grant figure excludes four grants totaling $3,501,837. Recent grants are derived from a 1990 grants list.

RECENT GRANTS

1,501,837 Art Institute, Chicago, IL

1,000,000 Field Museum of Natural History, Chicago, IL

500,000 Chicago Historical Society, Chicago, IL

500,000 John G. Shedd Aquarium, Chicago, IL

101,000 Lincoln Park Zoological Society, Chicago, IL

100,000 Rehabilitation Institute of Chicago, Chicago, IL

50,000 University of Chicago Medical Center, Chicago, IL

40,000 Our Lady of Perpetual Help Church, IL

40,000 Peacock Camp, Lake Forest, IL

32,000 St. Ignatius College Preparatory, Chicago, IL

Rice Foundation, Ethel and Raymond F.

CONTACT
Robert B. Oyler
President
Ethel and Raymond F. Rice Fdn.
700 Massachusetts
Lawrence, KS 66044
(913) 843-0420
Note: George M. Clem, Treasurer, is another contact name at the same address.

FINANCIAL SUMMARY
Recent Giving: $322,200 (1991); $310,925 (1990); $270,300 (1989)
Assets: $7,771,898 (1991); $6,997,288 (1990); $7,152,628 (1989)
EIN: 23-7156608

CONTRIBUTIONS SUMMARY
Typical Recipients: • *Arts & Humanities:* arts centers, history/historic preservation, museums/galleries, music • *Education:* colleges & universities, education funds, medical education, student aid, student aid • *Health:* mental health, nursing services • *Religion:* churches • *Social Services:* animal protection, disabled, drugs & alcohol, recreation & athletics
Grant Types: general support and scholarship
Geographic Distribution: limited to the Lawrence, KS, area

GIVING OFFICERS
Ellis D. Bever: consultant
George M. Clem: treas
Robert B. Oyler: pres
James W. Paddock: secy

APPLICATION INFORMATION
Initial Approach: Send cover letter and full proposal. Deadline is November 15.

GRANTS ANALYSIS
Number of Grants: 98
Highest Grant: $28,000
Typical Range: $1,000 to $10,000
Disclosure Period: 1991

RECENT GRANTS
28,000 Kansas University Endowment, Lawrence, KS — Rice Scholarships

13,000 Douglas County Historical Society,

Lawrence, KS — museum support

11,000 Lawrence Arts Center, Lawrence, KS

10,000 Douglas County Visiting Nurses, Lawrence, KS

10,000 Williams Educational Fund, Lawrence, KS — scholarships

9,500 Audio Reader, University of Kansas, Lawrence, KS

8,000 Plymouth Congregational Church, Lawrence, KS

7,600 Lawrence United Fund, Lawrence, KS

7,500 Plymouth Congregational Church, Lawrence, KS

7,500 Salvation Army, Lawrence, KS

Rice Foundation, Helen Steiner

CONTACT
Eugene Ruehlmann
Trustee
Helen Steiner Rice Fdn.
221 East Fourth St., Ste. 2100
Cincinnati, OH 45201
(513) 451-4939

FINANCIAL SUMMARY
Recent Giving: $199,800 (fiscal 1992); $143,000 (fiscal 1991); $146,650 (fiscal 1990)
Assets: $5,530,024 (fiscal year ending June 30, 1992); $4,064,764 (fiscal 1991); $3,563,109 (fiscal 1990)
Gifts Received: $1,050 (fiscal 1992)
EIN: 31-0978383

CONTRIBUTIONS SUMMARY
Donor(s): the late Helen Steiner Rice

Typical Recipients: • *Arts & Humanities:* community arts, museums/galleries • *Education:* community & junior colleges, education funds, private education (precollege) • *Health:* health organizations, hospices, hospitals • *Social Services:* aged, community centers, community service organizations, disabled, youth organizations

Grant Types: emergency, general support, multiyear/continuing support, operating expenses, project, and seed money

Geographic Distribution: limited to the greater Cincinnati area and Lorain, OH

GIVING OFFICERS
Willis David Gradison, Jr.: trust *B* Cincinatti OH 1928 *ED* Yale Univ AB 1948; Harvard Univ MBA 1951; Harvard Univ DCS 1954 *CORP AFFIL* gen ptnr: Gradison (WD) & Co
Eugene P. Ruehlmann: trust
Donald E. Weston: trust *B* Cincinnati OH 1935 *ED* Bowdoin Coll 1957 *CURR EMPL* chmn: Gradison & Co *CORP AFFIL* chmn, ceo: Gradison Cash Reserves Trust, Gradison Govtome Fund, Gradison Growth Trust, Gradison US Govt Trust; dir: Gradison Leasing Co

APPLICATION INFORMATION
Initial Approach: Application form required. Deadline is July 1.
Restrictions on Giving: Does not support individuals.

OTHER THINGS TO KNOW
Publications: Annual Report (including application guidelines)

GRANTS ANALYSIS
Number of Grants: 36
Highest Grant: $20,000
Typical Range: $2,000 to $10,000
Disclosure Period: fiscal year ending June 30, 1992

RECENT GRANTS
20,000 Museum Center, Cincinnati, OH

15,000 St. Rita School for the Deaf, Cincinnati, OH

15,000 Wesley Hall, Cincinnati, OH

10,000 Hamilton County Department of Human Services, Cincinnati, OH

10,000 Jewish Vocational Services, Cincinnati, OH

10,000 Lower Price Hill Community School, Cincinnati, OH

10,000 YMCA, Cincinnati, OH

10,000 YWCA, Cincinnati, OH

5,000 Lorain County Community College Women's Link, Elyria, OH

5,000 Neighborhood House Association

of Lorain, Lorain, OH

Riceland Foods, Inc.

Sales: $320.0 million
Employees: 2,100
Headquarters: Stuttgart, AR
SIC Major Group: Food & Kindred Products

CONTACT
Bill Reede
Director Corporate Communications
Riceland Foods, Inc.
PO Box 927
Stuttgart, AR 72160
(501) 673-5500

CONTRIBUTIONS SUMMARY
Operating Locations: AR (Stuttgart)

CORP. OFFICERS
Richard E. Bell: *B* Clinton IL 1934 *ED* Univ IL 1957-1958 *CURR EMPL* pres, ceo: Riceland Foods *CORP AFFIL* dir: First Commercial Corp
Tommy Hillman: *CURR EMPL* vchmn: Riceland Foods
Stewart E. Jessup: *CURR EMPL* chmn: Riceland Foods

Rich Co., F.D. / Rich Foundation, Inc.

Revenue: $5.0 million
Employees: 25
Headquarters: Stamford, CT
SIC Major Group: Heavy Construction Except Building Construction and Real Estate

CONTACT
Rich Fdn., Inc.
One Landmark Sq.
Stamford, CT 06901
(203) 359-2900

FINANCIAL SUMMARY
Recent Giving: $5,000 (fiscal 1991); $57,783 (fiscal 1990); $490,782 (fiscal 1989)
Assets: $81 (fiscal year ending June 30, 1991); $1 (fiscal 1990); $848,304 (fiscal 1987)
Gifts Received: $5,100 (fiscal 1991); $58,600 (fiscal 1990); $491,081 (fiscal 1989)
Fiscal Note: In 1991, contributions were received from F. D. Rich Company.
EIN: 22-2544173

CONTRIBUTIONS SUMMARY
Typical Recipients: • *Arts & Humanities:* arts centers, arts festivals, museums/galleries, music, opera, public broadcasting • *Civic & Public Affairs:* better government • *Health:* hospitals • *Social Services:* child welfare, united funds, youth organizations
Grant Types: general support
Geographic Distribution: primarily in lower Stamford, CT
Operating Locations: CT (Stamford)

CORP. OFFICERS
Frank D. Rich, Jr.: *CURR EMPL* chmn, dir: FD Rich Co
Robert N. Rich: *CURR EMPL* pres, dir: FD Rich Co

GIVING OFFICERS
Joseph F. Fahey, Jr.: pres
Lawrence Gochberg: secy
Harold Spelke: treas

APPLICATION INFORMATION
Initial Approach: Applicants are urged to consult with the foundation staff in the development of their proposals. (Ms. Robin Roscillo, Assistant Secretary, 359-2900). Proposal deadline is August 15. Board meets in September for budgets commencing October 1 and ending September 30 of the following calendar year; March for supplementary budget requests.
Restrictions on Giving: Grants are made only to selected, qualified non-profit organizations. Foundation does not make contributions to organizations whose purpose involves the solicitation of propaganda or to organizations that attempt to influence legislation, the outcome of public elections, or voter registration drives. The foundation may not make contributions for any purpose other than for religious, charitable, scientific, literary, or educational purposes.

GRANTS ANALYSIS
Number of Grants: 2
Highest Grant: $5,000
Typical Range: $20 to $5,000
Disclosure Period: fiscal year ending June 30, 1991

RECENT GRANTS
5,000 Friends of Post 53
2,000 Secretary of State, Washington, DC

Rich Foundation

CONTACT
Anne Berg
Grant Consultant
Rich Foundation
10 Piedmont Center, Ste. 802
Atlanta, GA 30305
(404) 262-2266

FINANCIAL SUMMARY
Recent Giving: $867,500 (fiscal 1992); $937,300 (fiscal 1991); $738,300 (fiscal 1990)
Assets: $25,849,829 (fiscal year ending January 31, 1992); $21,215,342 (fiscal 1991); $19,547,186 (fiscal 1990)
EIN: 58-6038037

CONTRIBUTIONS SUMMARY
Donor(s): The foundation was established in 1942 in Georgia by the officers of Rich's, Inc., a chain of department stores based in Atlanta, and was funded by profits of Rich's, Inc. until 1976.
Typical Recipients: • *Arts & Humanities:* arts centers, dance, museums/galleries, opera • *Civic & Public Affairs:* philanthropic organizations, zoos/botanical gardens • *Education:* colleges & universities, literacy • *Health:* hospitals, medical research, single-disease health associations • *Social Services:* community centers, disabled, shelters/homelessness, united funds, youth organizations
Grant Types: capital and general support
Geographic Distribution: metropolitan Atlanta, GA

GIVING OFFICERS
Thomas Asher: vp, secy
David S. Baker: trust *B* Jacksonville FL 1937 *ED* Univ PA BS 1958; Harvard Univ LLB 1961 *CURR EMPL* trust: Carnegie Capital Mutual Funds *CORP AFFIL* ptnr: Powell Goldstein Frazer & Murphy *NONPR AFFIL* mem: Am Bar Assn, Am Law Inst, GA Bar Assn
Joel Goldberg: pres
Joseph Heyman: treas
Margaret S. Weiller: trust

APPLICATION INFORMATION
Initial Approach: Applicants should submit a preliminary letter to the foundation.

The letter should include an autobiographical sketch of the organization, estimate of project expenses, and list of other sources of funding.
The quarterly deadlines for submitting proposals are December 15, March 15, June 15, and September 15.

GRANTS ANALYSIS
Total Grants: $867,500
Number of Grants: 43
Highest Grant: $175,000
Typical Range: $5,500 to $25,000
Disclosure Period: fiscal year ending January 31, 1992
Note: This figure excludes the largest grant of $175,000. Recent grants are derived from a fiscal 1992 Form 990.

RECENT GRANTS
175,000 United Way of Atlanta, Atlanta, GA
75,000 Emory University, Atlanta, GA
65,000 Woodruff Arts Center, Atlanta, GA
50,000 Atlanta Historical Center, Atlanta, GA
50,000 Camp Twin Lakes
50,000 Egleston Hospital
50,000 Oglethorpe University, Atlanta, GA
25,000 American Red Cross
25,000 Tommy Nobis Center, Marietta, GA
20,000 Carl Radcliff Dance Theatre, Atlanta, GA

Rich Products Corp. / Rich Foundation

Sales: $820.0 million
Employees: 6,500
Headquarters: Buffalo, NY
SIC Major Group: Communications and Food & Kindred Products

CONTACT
David Rich
Executive Director
Rich Fdn.
1150 Niagara St.
Buffalo, NY 14240
(716) 878-8000

FINANCIAL SUMMARY
Recent Giving: $307,203 (1991); $300,842 (1990); $256,245 (1989)
Assets: $1,029,009 (1991); $815,559 (1990); $721,497 (1989)
Gifts Received: $380,000 (1991); $240,000 (1990); $280,000 (1988)

Fiscal Note: Contributes through foundation only. In 1991, contributions were received from Rich Products Corporation.
EIN: 16-6026199

CONTRIBUTIONS SUMMARY

Typical Recipients: • *Arts & Humanities:* arts associations, arts centers, history/historic preservation, museums/galleries, music • *Civic & Public Affairs:* economic development, zoos/botanical gardens • *Education:* business education, colleges & universities, legal education, student aid • *Health:* health organizations, hospitals, pediatric health • *Religion:* religious organizations • *Social Services:* community service organizations, food/clothing distribution, recreation & athletics, united funds, youth organizations
Grant Types: general support
Geographic Distribution: primarily in New York
Operating Locations: GA (St. Simons Island), NY (Buffalo), OH (Hilliard), VA (Winchester)

CORP. OFFICERS

Robert E. Rich, Jr.: *B* 1941 *ED* Univ Rochester MBA *CURR EMPL* pres: Rich Products Corp *NONPR AFFIL* vchmn, dir: Buffalo Sabres hockey Club

GIVING OFFICERS

David A. Rich: exec dir *B* Buffalo NY 1944 *ED* Bradley Univ 1970 *CURR EMPL* secy, dir: Rich Products Corp *CORP AFFIL* dir: Rich Commun Corp

APPLICATION INFORMATION

Initial Approach: *Initial Contact:* formal letter request *When to Submit:* any time

GRANTS ANALYSIS

Total Grants: $307,203
Number of Grants: 162
Highest Grant: $100,000
Typical Range: $200 to $2,000
Disclosure Period: 1991
Note: Recent grants are derived from a 1991 grants list.

RECENT GRANTS

100,000 University of Buffalo Foundation, Buffalo, NY
35,000 St. Paul's Cathedral, Buffalo, NY

25,000 Greater Buffalo Development Foundation, Buffalo, NY
20,000 Forward in Faith Campaign, Buffalo, NY
10,000 Buffalo Philharmonic Orchestra, Buffalo, NY
10,000 On With Life, Buffalo, NY
5,000 Canisius College, Buffalo, NY
4,250 United Way, Buffalo, NY
4,250 United Way, Buffalo, NY
4,250 United Way, Buffalo, NY

Richardson Benevolent Foundation, C. E.

CONTACT

Betty S. King
Secretary
C. E. Richardson Benevolent Fdn.
74 West Main St., Rm. 211
PO Box 1120
Pulaski, VA 24301
(703) 980-6628

FINANCIAL SUMMARY

Recent Giving: $136,720 (fiscal 1991); $128,845 (fiscal 1990); $132,909 (fiscal 1989)
Assets: $2,696,403 (fiscal year ending May 31, 1991); $2,965,867 (fiscal 1990); $2,841,457 (fiscal 1989)
EIN: 51-0227549

CONTRIBUTIONS SUMMARY

Typical Recipients: • *Arts & Humanities:* arts centers • *Civic & Public Affairs:* municipalities • *Education:* colleges & universities, community & junior colleges, religious education, student aid • *Social Services:* community service organizations, recreation & athletics, united funds, youth organizations
Grant Types: general support
Geographic Distribution: limited to 30 miles north and south of Interstate 81 from Lexington to Abingdon, VA

GIVING OFFICERS

Betty S. King: secy

James D. Miller: trust
Annie S. Muire: trust
James C. Turk: trust

APPLICATION INFORMATION

Initial Approach: Application form required. Deadline is September 15.
Restrictions on Giving: Does not support individuals.

OTHER THINGS TO KNOW

Publications: Application Guidelines

GRANTS ANALYSIS

Number of Grants: 46
Highest Grant: $20,000
Typical Range: $500 to $10,000
Disclosure Period: fiscal year ending May 31, 1991

RECENT GRANTS

20,000 Roanoke College, Salem, VA — fund the Richardson Bibliographic classroom
12,000 County of Pulaski, Pulaski, VA — construction of arena
10,000 New River Community College Educational Foundation, Dublin, VA — expand library
5,000 Fine Arts Center for the New River Valley, Pulaski, VA — building repairs
5,000 Radford University Foundation, Radford, VA — student scholarship assistance
5,000 Southern Seminary College, Buena Vista, VA — dormitory renovations
5,000 Virginia Foundation for Independent Colleges, Richmond, VA
5,000 YMCA, Pulaski, VA
4,000 Ferrum College, Ferrum, VA — student scholarship assistance
3,500 Joy Ranch, Hillsville, VA — vehicle to transport children

Richardson Charitable Trust, Anne S.

CONTACT

Patricia Kelly
Anne S. Richardson Charitable Trust
c/o Chemical Bank
30 Rockefeller Plz.
New York, NY 10112
(212) 621-2180

FINANCIAL SUMMARY

Recent Giving: $523,500 (fiscal 1991); $520,500 (fiscal 1990); $396,400 (fiscal 1988)
Assets: $9,196,173 (fiscal year ending July 31, 1991); $9,095,480 (fiscal 1990); $8,000,301 (fiscal 1988)
EIN: 13-6192516

CONTRIBUTIONS SUMMARY

Donor(s): the late Anne S. Richardson
Typical Recipients: • *Arts & Humanities:* history/historic preservation, libraries, museums/galleries, opera • *Civic & Public Affairs:* environmental affairs, women's affairs • *Education:* colleges & universities • *Health:* hospices, hospitals • *Social Services:* domestic violence, united funds, youth organizations
Grant Types: general support
Geographic Distribution: focus on CT and NY

GIVING OFFICERS

Chemical Bank: trust

APPLICATION INFORMATION

Initial Approach: Send brief letter of inquiry describing program or project. There are no deadlines.
Restrictions on Giving: Does not support individuals or provide endowment funds, scholarships, or loans.

GRANTS ANALYSIS

Number of Grants: 38
Highest Grant: $10,000
Typical Range: $1,000 to $10,000
Disclosure Period: fiscal year ending July 31, 1991

RECENT GRANTS

10,000 Metropolitan Opera Association, New York, NY
10,000 Mid-Manhattan Center, New York, NY

10,000 National Victim Center, Washington, DC

10,000 New York Open Center, New York, NY

10,000 Salvation Army, New York, NY

10,000 Second Mile, State College, PA

10,000 Trudeau Institute, Sarnac Lake, NY

10,000 Women in Need, New York, NY

10,000 Woodstock Theological Center, Woodstock, NY

10,000 YWCA, New York, NY

Richardson County Bank and Trust Co. / Richardson County Bank and Trust Co. Centennial Trust

Employees: 22
Headquarters: Falls City, NE

CONTACT
Janet Aitken
Head of Bookeeping
Richardson County Bank and Trust Co. Centennial Trust
1616 Harlan Street
P.O. Box 248
Falls City, NE 68355
(402) 245-2486

FINANCIAL SUMMARY
Recent Giving: $500 (fiscal 1991); $1,000 (fiscal 1990)
Assets: $10,646 (fiscal year ending September 30, 1991); $10,229 (fiscal 1990)
EIN: 47-6125243

CONTRIBUTIONS SUMMARY
Grant Types: scholarship
Geographic Distribution: giving limited to Richardson County, NE
Operating Locations: NE (Falls City)

CORP. OFFICERS
John H. Morehead: *CURR EMPL* pres: Richardson County Bank & Trust Co

APPLICATION INFORMATION
Initial Approach: Submit a brief letter of inquiry. Deadline is April 1 for fall term.

OTHER THINGS TO KNOW
Provides scholarships for graduates of Richardson County, Nebraska high schools who wish to enter a four-year college in the U.S. and who major in business or agriculture.
Disclosure Period: fiscal year ending September 30, 1991

Richardson Foundation, Frank E. and Nancy M.

CONTACT
Frank E. and Nancy M. Richardson Foundation
c/o Ursray Capital Corporation
375 Park Avenue
New York, NY 10152-0103

FINANCIAL SUMMARY
Recent Giving: $1,105,128 (fiscal 1991)
Assets: $1,979,497 (fiscal year ending March 31, 1991)
EIN: 13-3440317

CONTRIBUTIONS SUMMARY
Typical Recipients: • *Arts & Humanities:* history/historic preservation, libraries, museums/galleries, opera • *Civic & Public Affairs:* international affairs • *Education:* colleges & universities • *International:* foreign educational institutions • *Religion:* churches
Grant Types: general support

GIVING OFFICERS
Frank E. Richardson: trust
Nancy M. Richardson: trust

APPLICATION INFORMATION
Initial Approach: The foundation reports it only makes contributions to preselected organizations and does not accept unsolicited requests for funds.

GRANTS ANALYSIS
Total Grants: $1,105,128
Highest Grant: $533,169
Typical Range: $7,000 to $15,000
Disclosure Period: fiscal year ending March 31, 1991

RECENT GRANTS
533,169 Metropolitan Museum of Art, New York, NY

340,000 American Friends of Magdakeb College, Oxford, England

60,000 United Nations Association, New York, NY

15,000 Frick Art Reference Library, New York, NY

11,000 Harvard University, Cambridge, MA

10,000 Eighth Church of Christ, New York, NY

10,000 Historic Hudson Valley, Tarrytown, NY

10,000 University of Miami, Miami, FL — Marc Boniconti fund

7,250 Metropolitan Opera Guild, New York, NY

7,000 Metropolitan Opera Association, New York, NY

Richardson Foundation, Sid W.

CONTACT
Valleau Wilkie, Jr.
Executive Director
Sid W. Richardson Foundation
309 Main St.
Ft. Worth, TX 76102
(817) 336-0494

FINANCIAL SUMMARY
Recent Giving: $11,000,000 (1993); $9,144,800 (1992); $10,942,707 (1991)
Assets: $255,000,000 (1993 est.); $250,169,000 (1992); $245,920,328 (1991); $229,400,000 (1990)
EIN: 75-6015828

CONTRIBUTIONS SUMMARY
Donor(s): The foundation was established in 1947 by the late Sid W. Richardson (d. 1959) to support organizations and programs serving the people of Texas. The purpose of the foundation, as stated in the charter, is "to support any benevolent, charitable, educational, or missionary undertaking."
In 1962, the foundation acquired substantial assets from the late Mr. Richardson's estate. In 1965, income from the assets became available, and the foundation began its major grant-making program. Sid Richardson was a life-long resident of Texas, with interests in oil, cattle, and land. He also collected western art, which is on permanent exhibit in the foundation-supported Sid Richardson Collection of Western Art. "Although his interests reached beyond Texas and his personal contacts were worldwide, he retained his immediate concern for the people of his home state. For this reason, he provided in the Foundation's charter that all grants be awarded to recipients within the state of Texas."
Typical Recipients: • *Arts & Humanities:* arts associations, music • *Education:* colleges & universities, elementary education, faculty development, private education (precollege), public education (precollege) • *Health:* emergency/ambulance services, hospitals, medical research • *Social Services:* day care, disabled, food/clothing distribution, homes, united funds, youth organizations
Grant Types: general support, multiyear/continuing support, operating expenses, and research
Geographic Distribution: Texas, especially Ft. Worth area

GIVING OFFICERS
Lee Marshall Bass: vp, dir *B* Fort Worth TX 1956 *ED* Yale Univ 1979; Univ PA MBA 1982 *CORP AFFIL* div off: Drew Indus, LTV Corp, Southern Union Co *NONPR AFFIL* mem natl adv bd: Whitney Mus Am Art
Nancy Lee Bass: vp, dir
Perry R. Bass: pres, dir *B* Wichita Falls TX 1914 *ED* Yale Univ BS 1937 *CURR EMPL* pres, dir: Perry R Bass Inc *CORP AFFIL* chmn: Sid Richardson Carbon & Gas Co; dir: Bass Brothers Enterprises *NONPR AFFIL* chmn: TX Parks Wildlife Comm; mem: All Am Wildcatters, Am Assn Petroleum Geologists, Independent Petroleum Assn Am, Longhorn Counc Boy Scouts Am; mem ad hoc comm: TX Energy Natural Resources Adv Comm; mem adv comm bd visitors: Univ Cancer Fdn MD Anderson Hosp Tumor Inst; mem bd govs: Ochsner Med Fdn; mem exec comm: Am Petroleum Inst, Natl Oil Policy Comm Future Petroleum Problems, Natl Petroleum Counc, TX Mid-Continent Oil & Gas Assn
Sid Richardson Bass: vp, dir *B* Fort Worth TX 1943 *ED* Yale Univ 1965; Stanford Univ MBA 1968 *CURR EMPL* Sid R

Bass Inc *NONPR AFFIL* trust: Yale Univ
M. E. Chappell: treas
Jo Helen Rosacker: secy, assoc dir
Valleau Wilkie, Jr.: exec vp, exec dir *B* Summit NJ 1923 *ED* Yale Univ BA 1948; Harvard Univ MA 1954 *NONPR AFFIL* dir: Natl Charities Info Bur; mem: Counc Fdns, Delta Kappa Upsilon, Headmasters Assn, Northeast Assn Schs Colls; mem bd dirs: Fdn Ctr

APPLICATION INFORMATION
Initial Approach:
Applicants should send a preliminary letter briefly describing the project or program prior to filing a formal application. If the project falls within foundation guidelines, a formal proposal will be accepted.
The foundation will supply a grant application form requesting information regarding the nature of the organization, objectives, activities, personnel, need to be met, and the project. Applicants may submit any additional information and supplementary proposal in narrative form, to clarify and explain the application.
Applications must be received by March 1, June 1, or September 1 for consideration at directors meetings in the spring, summer, or fall, respectively. Foundation staff may conduct a site visit after a formal application has been accepted. Board decisions on all requests are reported by mail.
Restrictions on Giving:
Grants are limited to programs and projects in Texas. No grants are made to individuals. Organizations generally must be classified as tax-exempt under Section 501(c)(3) of the Internal Revenue Code, and as other than a private foundation, Section 509(a). Alternatively, an organization may qualify if it is classified under Section 170(c)(1) and the contribution is to be used exclusively for public purposes.

OTHER THINGS TO KNOW
Grantees receive a letter of agreement outlining the terms and conditions of the grant. The Sid Richardson Foundation is related to the Bass Foundation (Ft. Worth).
Publications: annual report

GRANTS ANALYSIS
Total Grants: $9,144,800
Number of Grants: 130
Highest Grant: $516,232
Typical Range: $5,000 to $75,000 and $100,000 to $300,000
Disclosure Period: 1992
Note: Recent grants are derived from a 1992 grants list.

RECENT GRANTS
516,232 Ft. Worth Country Day School, Ft. Worth, TX — support faculty trust
500,000 Cook-Ft. Worth Children's Medical Center, Ft. Worth, TX — provide assistance in the completion of the fifth floor of the facility
500,000 Ft. Worth Country Day School, Ft. Worth, TX — support Capital and Endowment Campaign
500,000 Harris Hospital-Methodist, Ft. Worth, TX — assist with establishment of Outpatient Surgery Center
500,000 Texas A&M University Development Foundation, College Station, TX — support International Center for Bat Research and Education
300,000 Ft. Worth Zoological Association, Ft. Worth, TX — support completion of construction of World of Primates exhibit
274,377 Ft. Worth Symphony Orchestra Association, Ft. Worth, TX — support 91-92 concert season
250,000 Child Study Center, Ft. Worth, TX — support Bright Futures Campaign to fund expansion of facilities
250,000 Texas Christian University, Ft. Worth, TX — purchase equipment for science departments
205,000 Ft. Worth Independent School District, Ft. Worth, TX — support Keystone project

Richardson Foundation, Smith

CONTACT
Peter L. Richardson
President
Smith Richardson Foundation
477 Madison Avenue, 17th Fl.
New York, NY 10022
(212) 688-3392
Note: Inquiries concerning the children and families at risk programs should be directed to the Smith Richardson Foundation, 266 Post Road East, Westport, CT, 06880, (203) 454-1068.

FINANCIAL SUMMARY
Recent Giving: $13,905,694 (1989); $8,600,916 (1988); $11,380,387 (1987)
Assets: $295,440,854 (1989); $229,848,722 (1988); $216,584,227 (1987)
EIN: 56-0611550

CONTRIBUTIONS SUMMARY
Donor(s): In 1935, the Smith Richardson Foundation was established by the late H. Smith Richardson (d. 1972) and his wife, the late Grace Jones Richardson. H. Smith Richardson's father, Lunsford Richardson, founded the Vicks Chemical Company in 1905. Under H. Smith Richardson's leadership, the company grew to become one of the world's leading over-the-counter drug companies. Throughout his life he gave generously, and maintained a direct interest in people and institutions working to improve the lives of others. Members of the Richardson family hold interests in Dow Chemical, Bristol-Meyers, Sterling Drug, and Piedmont Management Companies.
Typical Recipients: • *Arts & Humanities:* arts centers, public broadcasting • *Civic & Public Affairs:* better government, business/free enterprise, economic development, economics, international affairs, law & justice, national security, public policy • *Education:* arts education, business education, colleges & universities, economic education, international studies, legal education, social sciences education • *Social Services:* child welfare, community service organizations, domestic violence, family services, united funds

Grant Types: project and research
Geographic Distribution: primarily to national organizations; limited international giving

GIVING OFFICERS
R. Larry Coble: treas
Robert M. DeMichele: trust
Donald Kagan: mem bd govs *B* Kurshan Lithuania 1932 *ED* Brooklyn Coll AB 1954; Brown Univ MA 1955; OH St Univ PhD 1958 *CORP AFFIL* dean: Yale Col *NONPR AFFIL* mem: Am Assn Ancient Historians, Am Historical Assn, Am Philological Assn; prof history & classics: Yale Univ
Robert H. Mulreany: trust *B* Brooklyn NY 1915 *ED* NY Univ LLB 1940 *CURR EMPL* off couns: DeForest & Duer *CORP AFFIL* chmn: NJ Waste Water Treatment Trust, Un Water Resources; chmn, dir: Hackensack Water Co, Natl St Bank Elizabeth NJ, Spring Valley Water Co; dir: Constellation Bancorp; trust: Provident Loan Soc *NONPR AFFIL* mem: Am Bar Assn, Bar Assn; trust: Tuskegee Inst, Westfield YMCA; trust, pres: Overlook Hosp Fdn *PHIL AFFIL* trust: Westfield Foundation
William E. Odom: mem bd govs *B* Cookesville TN 1932 *ED* US Military Academy BS 1954; Columbia Univ MA 1962; Columbia Univ PhD 1970 *CURR EMPL* dir: Natl Security Studies Hudson Inst *CORP AFFIL* chmn: Ford Credit Canada *NONPR AFFIL* adjunct prof political science: Yale Univ; mem: Academy Political Science Congregationalist, Am Assn Advancement Slavic Studies, Am Political Science Assn, Assn US Army, Counc Foreign Rels, Intl Inst Strategic Studies
Lunsford Richardson Preyer: mem bd govs *B* Greensboro NC 1919 *ED* Princeton Univ AB 1941; Harvard Univ LLB 1949 *CORP AFFIL* dir: Piedmont Mgmt Co; off, dir: Vanguard Cellular Sys *NONPR AFFIL* hon mem: Natl Boy Scout Counc; mem: Am Bar Assn, NC Bar Assn *PHIL AFFIL* trust: Norris & Kathryn Preyer Fund; vp, dir: Foundation Greater Greensboro
Heather S. Richardson: trust, mem bd govs
Henry Smith Richardson, Jr.: chmn, trust, mem bd govs, don

son *B* Greensboro NC 1920 *ED* Yale Univ BA 1942 *CORP AFFIL* dir: Piedmont Mgmt Co, Richardson-Vicks

Lunsford Richardson, Jr.: mem bd govs *B* Greensboro NC 1924 *ED* Lehigh Univ 1946 *CURR EMPL* chmn: Richardson Corp Greensboro *CORP AFFIL* chmn: Reinsurance Corp NY; dir: Lexington Mgmt Co, Piedmont Mgmt Co

Peter L. Richardson: pres *B* 1954 *CORP AFFIL* dir: Piedmont Mgmt Co, Richardson Corp *PHIL AFFIL* trust: Grace Jones Richardson Trust

Stuart Smith Richardson: trust, mem bd govs *B* 1947 *CURR EMPL* chmn, dir: Richardson-Vicks *CORP AFFIL* chmn: Vanguard Cellular Sys; dir: Piedmont Mgmt Co; vchmn, dir: Richardson Corp *PHIL AFFIL* trust: Grace Jones Richardson Trust

Henry S. Rowen: mem bd govs *B* Boston MA 1925 *ED* MA Inst Tech BS 1949; Oxford Univ MPh 1955 *NONPR AFFIL* mem: Dept Defense, Intl Inst Strategic Studies; mem, chmn defense policy bd: World Resources Inst; sr fellow: Stanford Univ Hoover Inst; mem: Chief Naval Opers Exec Panel, Dept Defense, Organizers Group European Am Workshop (Marina del Rey)

E. William Stetson III: mem bd govs

James Quinn Wilson: mem bd govs *NONPR AFFIL* chmn: Police Fdn; dir: Inst Ed Affs, New England Electric System; fellow: Am Academy Arts Sciences; mem: Am Philosophical Soc, Am Political Science Assn, Sloan Commn Cable Commun; mem counc academic advs: Am Enterprise Inst; prof mgmt: Univ CA Los Angeles; mem: Pres Foreign Intelligence Adv Bd *PHIL AFFIL* chmn, dir: Police Foundation (DC)

APPLICATION INFORMATION

Initial Approach: Applicants should send a letter to the foundation.

Application letters should include a brief overview statement outlining the purpose, scope, and desirability of the project; brief description of the organization including credentials of the personnel administering the program; detailed schedule of the work and

budget of the project; evidence that the project has not been carried out before; and a description of the population for which the project is intended. All letters must be accompanied by copies of IRS tax-exempt determination letter. Grant requests generally are approved quarterly; however, applicants may submit grant requests any time. The board reviews and evaluates applications upon receipt.

Restrictions on Giving: The foundation does not make grants to individuals. It also does not provide funding for deficit budgets of previously established operations, projects relating to building construction, the arts, medical programs, historic restoration projects, or research in the physical sciences.

OTHER THINGS TO KNOW

Publications: annual report

GRANTS ANALYSIS

Total Grants: $13,905,694
Number of Grants: 182
Highest Grant: $2,500,000
Typical Range: $5,000 to $25,000 and $50,000 to $150,000
Disclosure Period: 1989
Note: Recent grants are derived from a 1989 grants list.

RECENT GRANTS

2,500,000 Cystic Fibrosis Foundation, Rockville, MD
1,600,000 Center for Creative Leadership, Greensboro, NC
1,000,000 Center for Creative Leadership, Greensboro, NC
500,000 Cystic Fibrosis Foundation, Rockville, MD
330,000 Yale University-Bush Center, New Haven, CT
220,000 National Center for Clinical Infant Programs, Arlington, VA
219,700 Freedom House, New York, NY
200,000 Ethics and Public Policy Center, Washington, DC
176,500 Atlas Economic Research Foundation, Fairfax, VA
153,533 University of North Carolina at Chapel Hill, Chapel Hill, NC

Richardson Fund, Grace

CONTACT

H. S. Richardson, Jr.
Trustee
Grace Richardson Fund
c/o Piedmont Financial Co.
PO Box 20124
Greensboro, NC 27420-0124
(919) 274-5471

FINANCIAL SUMMARY

Recent Giving: $90,000 (fiscal 1992); $84,729 (fiscal 1991); $84,729 (fiscal 1990)

Assets: $2,017,105 (fiscal year ending June 30, 1992); $1,901,216 (fiscal 1991); $1,901,216 (fiscal 1990)

EIN: 56-6067849

CONTRIBUTIONS SUMMARY

Typical Recipients: • *Health:* health organizations, hospitals, medical research, pediatric health, single-disease health associations • *Social Services:* child welfare

Grant Types: general support and research

GIVING OFFICERS

Henry Smith Richardson, Jr.: trust *B* Greensboro NC 1920 *ED* Yale Univ BA 1942 *CORP AFFIL* dir: Piedmont Mgmt Co, Richardson-Vicks

Robert Randolph Richardson: trust *B* Greensboro NC 1926 *CURR EMPL* chmn: Piedmont Mgmt Co *CORP AFFIL* dir: Richardson Corp, Richardson-Vicks

Grace R. Stetson: trust

APPLICATION INFORMATION

Initial Approach: Send brief letter describing program. There are no deadlines.

GRANTS ANALYSIS

Number of Grants: 2
Highest Grant: $64,000
Disclosure Period: fiscal year ending June 30, 1992

RECENT GRANTS

64,000 Children's Hospital, Denver, CO
26,000 Headwater Academy, Bozeman, MT

Richardson Fund, Mary Lynn

CONTACT

Adele Richardson Ray
Trustee
Mary Lynn Richardson Fund
PO Box 20124
Greensboro, NC 27420
(919) 274-5471

FINANCIAL SUMMARY

Recent Giving: $265,480 (1990); $242,626 (1989)

Assets: $4,463,667 (1990); $4,784,315 (1989)

EIN: 06-6025946

CONTRIBUTIONS SUMMARY

Donor(s): the late Mary Lynn Richardson

Typical Recipients: • *Education:* religious education • *Health:* health funds • *Religion:* churches, missionary activities, religious organizations • *Social Services:* aged, child welfare, disabled, family planning, family services, food/clothing distribution, shelters/homelessness, youth organizations

Grant Types: emergency, general support, and operating expenses

Geographic Distribution: gives internationally, limited to NC for domestic programs

GIVING OFFICERS

Eric R. Calhoun: trust
James F. Connolly: mgr
Betsy Boney Mead: trust
William Yost Preyer, Jr.: trust
Lisa B. Prochnow: trust
Adele Richardson Ray: trust

APPLICATION INFORMATION

Initial Approach: Send cover letter and full proposal. Deadlines are April 1 and October 1.

GRANTS ANALYSIS

Number of Grants: 34
Highest Grant: $50,750
Typical Range: $1,000 to $10,000
Disclosure Period: 1990

RECENT GRANTS

50,750 Presbyterian Church, Louisville, KY
15,000 Presbyterian School of Christian Education, Richmond, VA

14,000 Greensboro Urban Ministry, Greensboro, NC
10,000 Andean Rural Health Care, Lake Junaluska, NC
10,000 Family and Children's Service, Greensboro, NC
10,000 Greensboro Public Schools, Greensboro, NC
10,000 Lutheran Family Services, Raleigh, NC
10,000 Operation Smile International, Greensboro, NC
10,000 Presbyterian Church, Louisville, KY
10,000 Worldwide Christian Schools, Grandville, MI

Richfood Holdings / Richfood Educational Trust

Sales: $1.24 billion
Headquarters: Richmond, VA

CONTACT
A.G. Mason Dirickson
Trustee
Richfood Educational Trust
P.O. Box 26967
Richmond, VA 23261-6967
(804) 746-6489

FINANCIAL SUMMARY
Recent Giving: $6,250 (1990)
Assets: $2,515 (1990)
Gifts Received: $6,500 (1990)
EIN: 54-6050704

CONTRIBUTIONS SUMMARY
Grant Types: scholarship
Geographic Distribution: giving limited to Virginia
Operating Locations: VA (Richmond)

CORP. OFFICERS
Richard Bondareff: *CURR EMPL* chmn: Richfood Holdings
W.C. Taliaferro: *CURR EMPL* pres, ceo: Richfood Holdings

GIVING OFFICERS
A.G. Mason Dirickson: trust
Edgar E. Poore: trust
Martha B. Ward: trust

APPLICATION INFORMATION
Initial Approach: Submit a brief letter of inquiry. There are no deadlines.

OTHER THINGS TO KNOW
Provides scholarships to accredited colleges and universities for children of employees of Richfood, who wish to attain a degree and are in need of financial aid.

Richley, Inc.
Sales: $500.0 million
Employees: 2
Headquarters: Los Angeles, CA
SIC Major Group: Holding & Other Investment Offices

CONTACT
James Bond
Controller
Richley, Inc.
1200 Wilshire Blvd., Ste. 406
Los Angeles, CA 90017
(213) 481-1800

CONTRIBUTIONS SUMMARY
Operating Locations: CA (Los Angeles)

CORP. OFFICERS
Joseph C. Dunn: *CURR EMPL* secy, treas: Richley
Richard C. Dunn: *CURR EMPL* pres: Richley

RECENT GRANTS
Loyola Marymount University, Los Angeles, CA

Richmond Foundation, Frederick W.

CONTACT
Pauline Nunen
Executive Director
Frederick W. Richmond Fdn.
PO Box 33
Wantagh, NY 11793
(516) 579-3373

FINANCIAL SUMMARY
Recent Giving: $318,151 (fiscal 1991); $273,695 (fiscal 1990); $229,400 (fiscal 1989)
Assets: $3,328,769 (fiscal year ending June 30, 1991); $3,294,643 (fiscal 1990); $3,349,162 (fiscal 1989)
Gifts Received: $177,250 (fiscal 1989)
EIN: 13-6124582

CONTRIBUTIONS SUMMARY
Donor(s): Frederick W. Richmond

Typical Recipients: • *Arts & Humanities:* arts institutes, community arts, dance, museums/galleries, music, public broadcasting • *Civic & Public Affairs:* ethnic/minority organizations • *Education:* colleges & universities, education associations • *Health:* medical research, single-disease health associations • *International:* international organizations • *Social Services:* child welfare, youth organizations
Grant Types: fellowship, project, research, and seed money

GIVING OFFICERS
Barbara Bode: dir *B* Evanston IL 1940 *ED* Univ MD BA 1962 *CURR EMPL* dir: Rainbow TV Works *NONPR AFFIL* consultant: Counc Fdns; dir: Natl Comm Responsive Philanthropy, Rainbow TV Works; mem: Women Fdns
William J. Butler: secy, dir *B* Brighton MA 1924 *NONPR AFFIL* chmn adv comm: Univ Cincinnati Sch Law Inst Human Rights; dir emeritus: Intl League Human Rights, NY Civil Liberties Union; intl legal observer: Intl Human Rights Org; mem: Am Bar Assn, Am Soc Intl Law, Assn Bar City New York, Counc Foreign Rels, Inter-Am Assn Democracy Freedom, Intl Commn Jurists, Intl Law Assn; mem exec comm: League Abolish Capital Punishment; mem standing comm human rights: World Peace Through Law Ctr
Helen Fioratti: dir
Steven N. Kaufmann: dir
Pauline Nunen: exec dir
Frederick W. Richmond: dir
Timothy E. Wyman: pres, dir

APPLICATION INFORMATION
Initial Approach: Send brief letter of inquiry describing program or project. There are no deadlines.
Restrictions on Giving: Does not support individuals.

GRANTS ANALYSIS
Number of Grants: 92
Highest Grant: $72,600
Typical Range: $500 to $10,000
Disclosure Period: fiscal year ending June 30, 1991

RECENT GRANTS
72,600 Metropolitan Museum of Art, New York, NY

13,500 Tanglewood Music Center Fellowship Program
12,500 International Foundation for Art Research (IFAR)
12,500 International Foundation for Art Research (IFAR)
12,500 National Italian-American Foundation, Washington, DC
12,500 National Italian-American Foundation, Washington, DC
10,000 Academy of Arts Campaign
10,000 American Friends of Cambridge University, Arlington, VA
10,000 Norman Rockwell Campaign, Stockbridge, MA
10,000 Tanglewood Music Center

Richmond Newspapers
Sales: $120.0 million
Employees: 1,500
Parent Company: Media General
Headquarters: Richmond, VA
SIC Major Group: Printing & Publishing

CONTACT
Roger Kain
Promotions
Richmond Newspapers
PO Box 85333
Richmond, VA 23293-0001
(804) 649-6000

CONTRIBUTIONS SUMMARY
Operating Locations: VA (Richmond)

CORP. OFFICERS
J. Stewart Bryan III: *CURR EMPL* pres: Richmond Newspapers

Ricoh Corp.
Sales: $949.29 million
Employees: 3,000
Headquarters: West Caldwell, NJ
SIC Major Group: Industrial Machinery & Equipment and Instruments & Related Products

CONTACT

Emil Florio
Public Relations Manager
Ricoh Corp.
5 Dedrick Pl.
West Caldwell, NJ 07006
(201) 882-2000

FINANCIAL SUMMARY

Recent Giving: $75,000
(1992); $50,000 (1991);
$200,000 (1989)

CONTRIBUTIONS SUMMARY

Ricoh Corp. contributions have been considerably cut back. Focus for 1993 is environmental affairs, children, and inner-city minority causes. Supports community-based organizations serving people in need. In Fall 1990, Ricoh helped set up a bank of fax machines in 19 communities throughout California to enable friends and relatives of military personnel to receive messages from those participating in Desert Storm. It also helped put together a fax network for the Lost Child Network, a nationwide group of police precincts committed to the recovery of abducted children. Ricoh Corp., its parent, and its international subsidiaries committed $1.7 million to support the 1991 Olympics. The company also is building a worldwide Olympic Fax Network, which will enable the International Olympics Committee to exchange information, ultimately linking 166 countries on six continents.
Typical Recipients: • *Civic & Public Affairs:* environmental affairs, safety • *Education:* colleges & universities, elementary education • *Social Services:* child welfare
Grant Types: general support
Nonmonetary Support Types: donated products and in-kind services
Geographic Distribution: near headquarters and in areas of largest markets
Operating Locations: NJ (West Caldwell)

CORP. OFFICERS

Hisashi Kubo: *CURR EMPL* chmn: Ricoh Corp
E. L. Steenburgh: *CURR EMPL* pres, coo: Ricoh Corp

GIVING OFFICERS

Emil Florio: *CURR EMPL* publ rels mgr: Ricoh Corp

APPLICATION INFORMATION

Initial Approach: Initial letter should be submitted on letterhead at any time. Include a description of the organization, specific request, Federal identification number, and a complete outline of the project to be funded.
Restrictions on Giving: Does not support political or lobbying groups or religious organizations for sectarian purposes. Ricoh gives nonmonetary support in the form of donated copies, cameras, and facsimile machines.

GRANTS ANALYSIS

Typical Range: $10 to $1,000

Ricoh Electronics Inc.

Employees: 1,187
Headquarters: Tustin, CA
SIC Major Group: Industrial Machinery & Equipment, Instruments & Related Products, and Miscellaneous Manufacturing Industries

---

CONTACT

Kim Cunningham
Deputy Director, Public Affairs
Ricoh Electronics Inc.
1 Ricoh Sq.
1100 Valencia Ave.
Tustin, CA 92680
(714) 556-2500

CONTRIBUTIONS SUMMARY

Due to budget constraints, all funding is directed to selected business-school partnerships. Company makes both nonmonetary (equipment and in-kind services, and cameras) and cash contributions. Company also promotes voluntarism and supports employee involvement in community organizations.
Typical Recipients: • *Education:* elementary education, science/technology education
Nonmonetary Support Types: donated products and in-kind services
Operating Locations: CA (Tustin)

CORP. OFFICERS

Ryutaro Baba: *CURR EMPL* sr vp, secy: Ricoh Electronics
Katsumi Yoshida: *CURR EMPL* pres: Ricoh Electronics

GIVING OFFICERS

Phyllis Badham: *CURR EMPL* dir pub aff: Ricoh Electronics
Kim Cunnningham: *CURR EMPL* pub aff dept: Ricoh Electronics

APPLICATION INFORMATION

Initial Approach: Company does not accept accept applications for support.
Restrictions on Giving: The company does not support individuals, fraternal organizations, political or lobbying groups, or religious organizations for sectarian purposes.

RECENT GRANTS

Century High School, Santa Ana, CA
Madison Elementary School, Santa Ana, CA
Richards Middle School, Lawrenceville, GA
Tustin Unified School District, Tustin, CA
Westpark Elementary School, Irvine, CA

Rider-Pool Foundation

CONTACT

Edwin F. Meehan
Rider-Pool Fdn.
Provident National Bank
1632 Chestnut St.
Philadelphia, PA 19103
(215) 585-5491

FINANCIAL SUMMARY

Recent Giving: $309,856 (1990); $287,752 (1989); $316,096 (1988)
Assets: $5,786,254 (1990); $5,351,296 (1989); $4,956,211 (1988)
Gifts Received: $405,063 (1990)
Fiscal Note: 1990 contribution received under the will of Dorothy Rider Pool.
EIN: 23-6207356

CONTRIBUTIONS SUMMARY

Donor(s): Dorothy Rider-Pool
Typical Recipients: • *Arts & Humanities:* arts centers • *Civic & Public Affairs:* municipalities • *Education:* colleges & universities, education funds, public education (precollege) • *Social Services:* aged, animal protection, community service organizations
Grant Types: capital, emergency, endowment, fellowship, general support, project, and research
Geographic Distribution: focus on Allentown, PA

GIVING OFFICERS

Edward L. Donnely: trust
Leon C. Holt, Jr.: trust *B* Reading PA 1925 *ED* Lehigh Univ BA 1948; Univ PA LLB 1951 *CURR EMPL* vchmn, chief admin off, dir: Air Products & Chemicals *CORP AFFIL* dir: VF Corp; vchmn, chief admin off, dir: Air Products & Chemicals *NONPR AFFIL* dir: Lehigh County Un Fund; mem: Allentown Chamber Commerce, Am Bar Assn, NY City Bar Assn, Tunkhannock Creek Assn; mem adv bd: Univ PA Inst Law Econ; mem exec comm: Machinery Allied Products Inst; trust: Allentown Art Mus, Comm Econ Devel, Pool (Dorothy Rider) Health Care Trust

APPLICATION INFORMATION

Initial Approach: Send brief letter of inquiry describing program or project. There are no deadlines.

GRANTS ANALYSIS

Disclosure Period: 1991
Note: 1991 grant information not available.

RECENT GRANTS

59,401 Allentown School District, Allentown, PA — to provide funding for the mini grant program

45,000 Lehigh County Senior Citizens, PA — to provide support for the creation of a financial development office

39,714 Salisbury School District, Salisbury, PA — to provide funding for the mini grant program

25,000 Miley House, PA — to support and develop the orchard hills campus and house an acute care psychiatric facility for children

24,400 Girls Club of Allentown, Allentown, PA — to provide funding for support and personal costs and evaluation of the program

20,000 Allentown Art Museum, Allentown, PA — to provide

exhibits entitled America Worked Representing 1990

20,000 Learning Club, PA — to provide funding for underwriting the quality control element of the program

15,000 Treatment Trends, PA

10,000 Allentown College, Center Valley, PA — to provide funding for a scholars program for nursing students

10,000 Cedar Crest College, Allentown, PA — to provide funding for a pool scholars program for nursing students

Ridgefield Foundation

CONTACT
Marguerite M. Riposanu
Secretary
Ridgefield Fdn.
641 Lexington Avenue, 26th Fl.
New York, NY 10022
(212) 750-9330

FINANCIAL SUMMARY
Recent Giving: $348,150 (fiscal 1992); $412,325 (fiscal 1991); $366,150 (fiscal 1990)
Assets: $7,172,351 (fiscal year ending February 28, 1992); $6,867,336 (fiscal 1991); $6,292,474 (fiscal 1990)
EIN: 13-6093563

CONTRIBUTIONS SUMMARY
Donor(s): Henry J. Leir, Erna D. Leir, Continental Ore Corp., International Ore and Fertilizer Corp.
Typical Recipients: • *Arts & Humanities:* museums/galleries • *Civic & Public Affairs:* ethnic/minority organizations, international affairs • *Education:* colleges & universities, education funds, international studies • *Health:* hospitals • *International:* international development/relief, international health care, international organizations • *Religion:* religious organizations • *Social Services:* aged, community service organizations, youth organizations
Grant Types: general support
Geographic Distribution: focus on NY for local services; giving in the U.S. and Israel for education

GIVING OFFICERS
Alan K. Docter: dir
Arthur S. Hoffman: dir
Marcelo Leipziger: dir
Henry J. Leir: pres, dir
Louis J. Lipton: vp, dir
Jean Mayer: dir
Marguerite M. Riposanu: secy
Jerome Shelby: dir *B* New York NY 1930 *ED* NY Univ AB 1950; Harvard Univ LLB 1953 *CURR EMPL* ptnr: Cadwalader Wickersham & Taft *CORP AFFIL* dir: Marine Transport Lines; exec vp, dir: Energy Transportation Corp; ptnr: Cadwalader Wickersham & Taft *NONPR AFFIL* mem: NY City Bar Assn
Samuel Sitkoff: treas, dir

APPLICATION INFORMATION
Initial Approach: Contributes only to preselected organizations.
Restrictions on Giving: Does not support individuals or provide funds for scholarships or loans.

GRANTS ANALYSIS
Number of Grants: 72
Highest Grant: $30,000
Typical Range: $100 to $10,000
Disclosure Period: fiscal year ending February 28, 1992

RECENT GRANTS
30,000 International Fund for Education and Career Development, Los Angeles, CA

24,000 University of California, Irvine, CA

20,000 National Institute on Aging, Bethesda, MD

20,000 New York Hospital, New York, NY

12,500 Fund for Higher Education, Los Angeles, CA

10,000 American ORT Federation, New York, NY

10,000 Anti-Defamation League, New York, NY

10,000 Boys Town of Jerusalem, New York, NY

10,000 Help and Reconstruction, New York, NY

10,000 Jerusalem Foundation, New York, NY

Rieke Corp. / Rieke Corp. Foundation
Sales: $17.0 million
Employees: 300
Parent Company: TriMas Corp.
Headquarters: Auburn, IN
SIC Major Group: Fabricated Metal Products, Industrial Machinery & Equipment, and Rubber & Miscellaneous Plastics Products

CONTACT
Donald E. Kelley
Trustee
Rieke Corp. Foundation
500 West Seventh St.
Auburn, IN 46706-2289
(219) 925-3700

FINANCIAL SUMMARY
Recent Giving: $26,000 (1991); $26,000 (1990)
Assets: $618,346 (1991); $517,367 (1990)
Gifts Received: $10,000 (1991); $10,000 (1990)
Fiscal Note: In 1991, contributions were received from Rieke Corporation.
EIN: 51-0158651

CONTRIBUTIONS SUMMARY
Typical Recipients: • *Arts & Humanities:* history/historic preservation, libraries, museums/galleries • *Civic & Public Affairs:* municipalities • *Health:* geriatric health, health organizations, hospitals • *Social Services:* aged, animal protection, child welfare, community service organizations, disabled, united funds, youth organizations
Grant Types: general support
Geographic Distribution: focus on IN
Operating Locations: IN (Auburn)

CORP. OFFICERS
D. E. Kelly: *CURR EMPL* pres: Rieke Corp

GIVING OFFICERS
Donald Kelly: trust
Glenn T. Rieke: trust
Mahloh E. Rieke: trust

APPLICATION INFORMATION
Initial Approach: Send brief letter describing program. There are no deadlines.

GRANTS ANALYSIS
Number of Grants: 9
Highest Grant: $7,500

Typical Range: $1,000 to $6,000
Disclosure Period: 1991

RECENT GRANTS
7,500 United Way, Auburn, IN

6,000 DeKalb City Council on Aging, Auburn, IN

3,000 Auburn Automotive Heritage, Auburn, IN

3,000 Eckhart Public Library, Auburn, IN

2,000 DeKalb City Parent Group for Handicapped Children, Auburn, IN

2,000 DeKalb Humane Society, Auburn, IN

1,000 American Cancer Society, Auburn, IN

1,000 City of Garrett Parks, Garrett, IN

500 Big Brothers and Big Sisters, Auburn, IN

Rienzi Foundation

CONTACT
Rienzi Fdn.
2001 Kirby Dr., Ste. 714
Houston, TX 77019

FINANCIAL SUMMARY
Recent Giving: $107,950 (1991); $173,400 (1990); $94,025 (1989)
Assets: $3,878,898 (1991); $3,254,932 (1990); $3,072,900 (1989)
EIN: 74-1484331

CONTRIBUTIONS SUMMARY
Typical Recipients: • *Arts & Humanities:* community arts, museums/galleries, music, performing arts, theater • *Education:* colleges & universities, medical education • *Health:* health organizations, hospitals • *Religion:* churches, religious organizations • *Social Services:* child welfare, community service organizations, counseling, disabled, food/clothing distribution, homes, united funds, youth organizations
Grant Types: general support
Geographic Distribution: focus on Houston, TX

GIVING OFFICERS
Evangeline Ehrensberger: chief adm
Carroll S. Masterson: trust
Harris Masterson: trust
Isla C. Reckling: trust
Randa R. Roach: trust

Bert F. Winston: trust
Lynn David Winston: trust

APPLICATION INFORMATION

Initial Approach: Contributes only to preselected organizations.
Restrictions on Giving: Does not support individuals.

GRANTS ANALYSIS
Number of Grants: 64
Highest Grant: $10,250
Typical Range: $100 to $1,000
Disclosure Period: 1991

RECENT GRANTS
10,250 Holly Hall, Houston, TX
10,000 Center for the Retarded, Houston, TX
10,000 Children's Museum, Houston, TX
6,000 United Way, Houston, TX
5,000 Baylor College of Medicine, Houston, TX
5,000 Houston Symphony, Houston, TX
5,000 M.D. Anderson Hospital Park, Houston, TX
5,000 Trinity Episcopal Church, Houston, TX
3,000 End Hunger, Houston, TX
2,500 Life Flight, Houston, TX

Riggs Benevolent Fund

CONTACT
Anne Roark
Riggs Benevolent Fund
c/o Worthen Bank and Trust Co., N.A., Trust Dept.
PO Box 1681
Little Rock, AR 72203-1681
(501) 378-1248

FINANCIAL SUMMARY
Recent Giving: $269,550 (1991); $202,200 (1989); $205,500 (1988)
Assets: $4,345,756 (1991); $3,558,672 (1989); $3,132,115 (1988)
Gifts Received: $215,500 (1991); $309,261 (1989); $109,275 (1988)
Fiscal Note: In 1991, contributions were received from John A. Riggs, Jr. ($107,500), Lamar Riggs ($5,000), John A. Riggs, III ($3,000), and Riggs Tractor Co. ($100,000).
EIN: 71-6050130

CONTRIBUTIONS SUMMARY
Donor(s): members of the Riggs family, Robert G. Cress, J. A. Riggs Tractor Co.
Typical Recipients: • *Civic & Public Affairs:* municipalities, urban & community affairs • *Education:* colleges & universities, education funds, science/technology education • *Health:* hospitals, nursing services, pediatric health • *Social Services:* child welfare, community service organizations, family services, united funds, youth organizations
Grant Types: general support and scholarship
Geographic Distribution: focus on AR

GIVING OFFICERS
Robert G. Cress: trust *CURR EMPL* pres: JA Riggs Tractor Co
John A. Riggs III: trust *B* Little Rock AR 1934 *ED* Univ AR 1957 *CURR EMPL* chmn: JA Riggs Tractor Co *CORP AFFIL* dir: Worthen Natl Bank AR

APPLICATION INFORMATION
Initial Approach: Send brief letter of inquiry describing program. There are no deadlines.

GRANTS ANALYSIS
Number of Grants: 55
Highest Grant: $50,000
Typical Range: $1,000 to $5,000
Disclosure Period: 1991

RECENT GRANTS
50,000 Vera Lloyd Presbyterian Home, Little Rock, AR
48,500 United Way, Little Rock, AR
20,000 Boys Club of America, Little Rock, AR
10,000 Baptist Medical Foundation, Nursing School, Little Rock, AR
10,000 VAMS Foundation, Little Rock, AR
6,000 Center for Youth and Families, Little Rock, AR
5,000 Aerospace Education Center, Little Rock, AR
5,000 Arkansas Children's Hospital, Little Rock, AR
5,000 Arkansas Research Center, Little Rock, AR
5,000 Linden Hill School, Little Rock, AR

Riggs National Bank
Employees: 2,000
Parent Company: Riggs National Corp.
Assets: $5.07 billion
Headquarters: Washington, DC
SIC Major Group: Depository Institutions

CONTACT
Barbara Silla
Contributions Manager
Riggs National Bank
800 17th St., 4th Fl.
Washington, DC 20006
(202) 835-5486

FINANCIAL SUMMARY
Fiscal Note: Company gives directly. Annual Giving Range: $500,000 to $1 million

CONTRIBUTIONS SUMMARY
Typical Recipients: • *Arts & Humanities:* general • *Civic & Public Affairs:* general, housing, housing • *Education:* general • *Social Services:* general
Grant Types: general support
Nonmonetary Support Types: donated equipment, in-kind services, loaned employees, and loaned executives
Operating Locations: DC (Washington)

CORP. OFFICERS
Joe Lewis Allbritton: *B* D'Lo MS 1924 *ED* Baylor Univ LLB 1949; Baylor Univ JD 1969; CA Baptist Coll LHD 1973 *CURR EMPL* owner, chmn, ceo: Perpetual Corp *CORP AFFIL* chmn: Allbritton Commun Co, Allbritton News Bur, First Charleston Corp, Houston Fin Svcs Ltd, Hudson Dispatch, Jobaro Corp, KATV Television, KTUL Television, Lazy Lane Farms, Lazy Lane Stables, News Printing Co, Perfin Corp, Pierce Brothers, Pierce Natl Life Ins Co, Trenton Times Corp, Univ Bancshares, Westfield News Advertiser, WSET Inc; chmn, ceo: Riggs Natl Corp; chmn, trust: Mitre Corp; dep chmn: Riggs AP Bank Ltd; fdr: Allnewsco *NONPR AFFIL* mem: Assn Reserve City Bankers, Greater WA Bd Trade, TX Bar Assn; trust: Fed City Counc, Natl Geographic Soc

GIVING OFFICERS
Barbara Silla: *CURR EMPL* contributions mgr: Riggs Natl Bank

APPLICATION INFORMATION
Initial Approach: *Initial Contact:* brief letter of inquiry *Include Information On:* a description of organization, amount requested, purpose of funds sought, recently audited financial statement, and proof of tax-exempt status *When to Submit:* any time

Rigler-Deutsch Foundation

CONTACT
Lloyd E. Rigler-Lawrence E. Deutsch Foundation
PO Box 828
Burbank, CA 91503
(213) 878-0283
Note: Foundation is also known as the Ledler Foundation. It is located at 1800 West Magnolia Boulevard, Burbank, CA, 91506. The foundation does not list a contact person.

FINANCIAL SUMMARY
Recent Giving: $2,324,452 (1991); $2,100,466 (1990); $845,484 (1989)
Assets: $65,233,912 (1991); $57,236,488 (1990); $58,811,113 (1989)
Gifts Received: $10,553 (1989); $46,706,631 (1988)
Fiscal Note: In 1988, the foundation received $46,706,631 from the estate of Lawrence E. Deutsch.
EIN: 95-6155653

CONTRIBUTIONS SUMMARY
Donor(s): The foundation was established in 1966 by the late Lawrence E. Deutsch and Lloyd E. Rigler, the current president of the foundation.
Typical Recipients: • *Arts & Humanities:* arts centers, community arts, dance, museums/galleries, music, opera, public broadcasting, theater • *Civic & Public Affairs:* better government, civil rights, environmental affairs • *Education:* international studies, science/technology education • *Health:* medical research, single-disease health associations • *Social Services:* family planning

Grant Types: endowment and general support
Geographic Distribution: focus on Los Angeles, CA, and New York, NY

GIVING OFFICERS

Morton Masure: cfo
Donald Rigler: secy
James Rigler: vp
Lloyd E. Rigler: pres, don, dir

APPLICATION INFORMATION

Initial Approach:
Applicants should send a brief letter of inquiry, preferably limited to one page.
The letter should describe the project and its cost.
There are no deadlines.

OTHER THINGS TO KNOW

The foundation reports that it does not accept unsolicited requests for funds.

GRANTS ANALYSIS

Total Grants: $2,324,452
Number of Grants: 162
Highest Grant: $529,999
Typical Range: $1,000 to $25,000
Disclosure Period: 1991
Note: Average grant figure excludes two grants totaling $1,029,999. Recent grants are derived from a 1991 Form 990.

RECENT GRANTS

529,999 Joffrey Ballet, New York, NY
500,000 New York City Opera, New York, NY
250,000 Simon Wiesenthal Center, Los Angeles, CA
100,000 New York City Opera, New York, NY
100,000 North American Conference on Ethiopian Jewry
50,000 Carnegie Hall, New York, NY
50,000 Los Angeles Library, Los Angeles, CA — Save the Books
40,000 American Ballet Theater, New York, NY
40,000 American Technion Society
40,000 American Technion Society

Riley Foundation, Mabel Louise

CONTACT

Newell Flather
Administration
Riley Foundation
230 Congress St., Third Fl.
Boston, MA 02110
(617) 426-7172
Note: The foundation reports that Naomi Tuchmann, Administrator, and Philip Hall, Foundation Assistant, are also contacts.

FINANCIAL SUMMARY

Recent Giving: $1,600,000 (fiscal 1993 est.); $1,443,400 (fiscal 1992); $1,790,700 (fiscal 1991)
Assets: $36,852,350 (fiscal 1991); $34,741,237 (fiscal 1990); $30,298,643 (fiscal 1989)
EIN: 04-6278857

CONTRIBUTIONS SUMMARY

Donor(s): Mabel Louis Riley, the only child of Agnes Winslow Riley and Charles E. Riley, was born in Boston in 1883. Her father was president of H & B American Machine Company in Pawtucket, RI. Described as "generous and concerned for the needs of others," she supported numerous charities throughout her lifetime. Miss Riley died in 1971, and with her death provided for the charitable organizations she had supported. A portion of her wealth went to friends, families, and charities. The remainder was used to establish the Mabel Louise Riley Charitable Trust, now known as the Riley Foundation, which became active in May 1972.
Typical Recipients: • *Arts & Humanities:* arts centers, arts funds, museums/galleries, performing arts, theater • *Civic & Public Affairs:* civil rights, economic development, ethnic/minority organizations, housing, nonprofit management, urban & community affairs • *Education:* career/vocational education, colleges & universities, literacy, minority education, special education • *Social Services:* child welfare, community centers, community service organizations, counseling, day care, disabled, drugs & alcohol, employment/job training, family plan-

ning, refugee assistance, youth organizations
Grant Types: capital, challenge, project, and seed money
Geographic Distribution: primarily Boston; secondary interest in Newton and Cape Cod, MA

GIVING OFFICERS

Andrew C. Bailey: trust *B* Waltham MA 1921 *ED* Amherst Coll AB 1944; Cornell Univ LLB 1948 *CURR EMPL* atty: Powers & Hall *NONPR AFFIL* mem: Am Bar Assn, Boston Bar Assn
Douglas Danner: trust *B* Philadelphia PA 1924 *ED* Harvard Univ AB 1946; Boston Univ JD 1949 *CURR EMPL* atty: Powers & Hall *NONPR AFFIL* fellow: Am Coll Trial Lawyers; mem: Am Bar Assn, Am Soc Law Medicine, Boston Bar Assn, MA Bar Assn, MA Defense Lawyers Assn
Newell Flather: adm
Jeanne M. Hession: trust *B* Boston MA 1930 *ED* Boston Univ 1952; Suffolk Univ law 1956 *CURR EMPL* vp, assoc coun: Boston Safe Deposit & Trust Co
Robert W. Holmes, Jr.: trust *B* Fall River MA 1944 *ED* Harvard Univ BA 1967; Boston Univ JD 1970 *CURR EMPL* atty: Powers & Hall *NONPR AFFIL* mem: Am Bar Assn, Boston Bar Assn, MA Bar Assn
Naomi Tuchmann: adm

APPLICATION INFORMATION

Initial Approach:
There is no standard application form. Formal proposals may be sent to the foundation's office.
All proposals must include a brief history of the organization, its goals, achievements, indication of whom it serves, and what services it performs; list of board members and resumes and qualifications of involved staff; organization's current and anticipated operating budgets, recent audited financial statement, and complete copy of the most recent IRS 990 form; and a current copy of the IRS tax exemption letter that additionally indicates the organization's status as a public charity. The proposal should also provide a brief description of the reason for which the grant is required, including goals, specific objectives, ex-

planation of the project's compatability with other programs implemented by the organization, description of special events or approaches planned, and a timetable of these activities. Also required are the project's budget, indication of other potential sources of support, future means of support, summary of expected benefits of the project, and the proposed method of evaluation of these benefits.
Trustee meetings are held in April-May and October-November. Proposals should reach the foundation no later than February 15 and August 15. It is strongly recommended that proposals be submitted well before the deadlines.
Applicants are welcome to contact the program staff before submitting proposals. The trustees may make field visits to interesting programs and will hold meetings with those organizations selected for funding.

Restrictions on Giving:
Grants generally are not made to charitable organizations outside Massachusetts, toward deficits or regular operating budgets, for sole source of support, for activities supported by the general public, to units of government, or to individuals or organizations on behalf of individuals. Grants are not made to support personal needs, travel, research, publications, loans, scholarships, national organizations, campaigns, health organizations, scientific research, or sectarian religious purposes.

OTHER THINGS TO KNOW

Applicants who have been refused requests for funding must wait a full year prior to reapplication. Organizations that have received grants should wait two full years before reapplication.

Publications: annual report

GRANTS ANALYSIS

Total Grants: $1,443,400
Number of Grants: 44
Highest Grant: $135,000
Typical Range: $30,000 to $100,000
Disclosure Period: fiscal year ending May 31, 1992
Note: Recent grants are derived from a fiscal 1991 Form 990.

RECENT GRANTS

80,000 Dudley Street Neighborhood Initiative, Roxbury, MA — executive search, operating support

75,000 Youthbuild Boston, Boston, MA — for unemployed youth

55,000 Dudley Street Neighborhood Initiative, Roxbury, MA — operations/"visionary" contribution

53,000 Nuestra Comunidad Development Corporation, Roxbury, MA — for a community organizer and half-time secretary

50,000 Boston Foundation Human Services, Boston, MA — for the diversity initiative

50,000 Community Music Center, Boston, MA — for renovation and reconstruction

50,000 Dimock Community Health Center, Roxbury, MA — for the capital campaign

50,000 Dimock Community Health Center, Roxbury, MA — renovation of Goddard Building and construction of youth center

50,000 N.F. Conservatory, Boston, MA — handicapped access renovations for Jordan Hall

50,000 North End Union, Boston, MA — building improvement program

Riley Stoker Co.

Sales: $100.0 million
Employees: 750
Parent Company: Ashland Oil, Inc.
Headquarters: Worcester, MA
SIC Major Group: Fabricated Metal Products, Heavy Construction Except Building Construction, Industrial Machinery & Equipment, and Special Trade Contractors

CONTACT

Robert Morrow
Vice President, Government Affairs
Riley Stoker Co.
5 Neponset St.
PO Box 15040
Worcester, MA 01615-0040
(508) 852-7100

CONTRIBUTIONS SUMMARY

Operating Locations: MA (Worcester)

CORP. OFFICERS

H. K. Smith: *CURR EMPL* chmn, pres: Riley Stoker Co

OTHER THINGS TO KNOW

Company is an original donor to the Fred Harris Daniels Foundation.

Ringier-America

Sales: $625.0 million
Employees: 3,455
Headquarters: Itasca, IL
SIC Major Group: Printing & Publishing

CONTACT

Francine Overton
Senior Staff Advisor, Human Resources
Ringier-America
One Pierce Pl., Ste. 800
Itasca, IL 60143-1272
(708) 285-6000

FINANCIAL SUMMARY

Fiscal Note: Annual Giving Range: $100,000 to $150,000

CONTRIBUTIONS SUMMARY

No set giving priorities. Gives to the arts and to cultural organizations, including libraries, museums, and galleries. Funds education at the precollege (public and private), college, and university levels. In addition, funds education associations. Social services grants support child welfare, delinquency and crime programs, united funds, and youth organizations.

Typical Recipients: • *Arts & Humanities:* libraries, museums/galleries • *Education:* colleges & universities, education associations, private education (precollege), public education (precollege) • *Health:* hospitals, single-disease health associations • *Social Services:* child welfare, united funds, youth organizations

Grant Types: general support

Geographic Distribution: no geographic restrictions

Operating Locations: AR, AZ, CA, IL, KS, MS, NC, TN, WI

CORP. OFFICERS

Edward C. Nytko: *CURR EMPL* pres, ceo: Ringier Am

Francine Overton: *CURR EMPL* sr staff adv (human res): Ringier-Am

APPLICATION INFORMATION

Initial Approach: Submit a letter before September in order to receive funding for the following year. Include a description of the organization, purpose for which funds are sought, the benefits of the organization/project, and a recent annual report.

Restrictions on Giving: Does not provide nonmonetary support.

Rinker Materials Corp. / Rinker Cos. Foundation

Sales: $310.0 million
Employees: 1,875
Parent Company: CSR America, Inc.
Headquarters: West Palm Beach, FL
SIC Major Group: Fabricated Metal Products, Nonmetallic Minerals Except Fuels, and Stone, Clay & Glass Products

---

CONTACT

Frank LaPlaca
Administrator
Rinker Cos. Fdn.
1501 Belvedere Rd.
West Palm Beach, FL 33406
(407) 833-5555
Note: Foundation reports a freeze on giving to continue at least until March 1992.

FINANCIAL SUMMARY

Recent Giving: $1,367,970 (fiscal 1991); $1,341,283 (fiscal 1990); $1,238,712 (fiscal 1989)

Assets: $8,886,183 (fiscal year ending March 31, 1991); $8,171,692 (fiscal 1990)

Fiscal Note: Company gives through the foundation only.

EIN: 59-6139266

CONTRIBUTIONS SUMMARY

Typical Recipients: • *Education:* business education, colleges & universities, private education (precollege), student aid • *Health:* hospitals • *Religion:* churches • *Social Services:* child welfare, united funds, youth organizations

Grant Types: general support and scholarship

Geographic Distribution: primarily Florida, with emphasis on Dade and Palm Beach Counties

Operating Locations: FL (Miami, West Palm Beach)

CORP. OFFICERS

R. K. Barton: *CURR EMPL* chmn: Rinker Materials Corp

William L. Snyder: *B* Philadelphia PA 1935 *CURR EMPL* ceo, dir, pres: Rinker Materials Corp

GIVING OFFICERS

J. F. Jackson: trust

E. B. Jordan: trust

R. H. Kohler: trust

Frank LaPlaca: admin

W. J. Payne: vp, trust, secy

Marshall Edison Rinker, Sr.: trust *B* Cowan IN 1904 *ED* Ball St Univ *CURR EMPL* fdr, chmn: ME Rinker Sr Cos *CORP AFFIL* ceo, chmn: Rinker Realty Corp; chmn emeritus: Rinker Materials Corp; dir: FL East Coast Indus, FL East Coast Railway Co *NONPR AFFIL* mem: FL Concrete Products Assn, Natl Concrete Masonry Assn, Natl Ready Mixed Concrete Assn; trust emeritus: Stetson Univ

William L. Snyder: pres, trust *CURR EMPL* ceo, dir, pres: Rinker Materials Corp (see above)

K. H. Watson: treas, trust *CURR EMPL* pres, dir: Rinker Materials Corp

APPLICATION INFORMATION

Initial Approach: *Initial Contact:* brief letter or proposal *Include Information On:* description of the organization, amount requested, purpose for which funds are sought, recently audited financial statement, proof of tax-exempt status *When to Submit:* any time

Restrictions on Giving: Scholarships limited to residents of Florida pursuing majors in business or construction and maintaining grade point averages of at least 2.5.

GRANTS ANALYSIS
Total Grants: $1,367,970
Typical Range: $1,000 to $10,000
Disclosure Period: fiscal year ending March 31, 1991
Note: Recent grants are derived from a 1990 grants list.

RECENT GRANTS
500,000 Palm Beach Atlantic College, West Palm Beach, FL
250,000 First Baptist Church
120,000 Stetson University, De Land, FL
100,000 University of Florida, Gainesville, FL
50,000 Good Samaritan Hospital
38,900 United Way of Dade County, Miami, FL
19,050 United Way of Broward County, Ft. Lauderdale, FL
15,450 United Way of Palm Beach County, West Palm Beach, FL
15,250 Heart of Florida United Way, Orlando, FL
10,000 Florida International University, Miami, FL

Rinker, Sr. Foundation, M. E.

CONTACT
M. E. Rinker, Sr. Foundation
310 Okeechobee Boulevard
West Palm Beach, FL 33401-6432

FINANCIAL SUMMARY
Recent Giving: $2,128,000 (1991)
Assets: $51,222,159 (1991)
EIN: 65-0088775

GIVING OFFICERS
James F. Jackson, Jr.: secy
R. Hagan Kohler, Jr.: treas
David B. Rinker, Sr.: pres
John J. Rinker, Sr.: vp
Marshall E. Rinker, Sr.: vp
Marshall E. Rinker, Sr.: ceo (see above)
R. M. Strickland, Jr.: trust

APPLICATION INFORMATION
Initial Approach: The foundation reports it only makes contributions to preselected organi-

zations and does not accept unsolicited requests for funds.

GRANTS ANALYSIS
Total Grants: $2,128,000
Number of Grants: 14
Highest Grant: $800,000
Disclosure Period: 1991

Rio Grande Railroad
Revenue: $2.8 billion
Employees: 26,300
Headquarters: Denver, CO
SIC Major Group: Holding & Other Investment Offices, Railroad Transportation, and Trucking & Warehousing

CONTACT
W.J. Lovett
Personnel Administrator
Rio Grande Railroad
PO Box 5482
Denver, CO 80217
(303) 634-2547

CONTRIBUTIONS SUMMARY
Operating Locations: CO (Denver)

CORP. OFFICERS
W. J. Holtman: *CURR EMPL* chmn, pres: Rio Grande Indus

Riordan Foundation

CONTACT
Charles Hargrove
Riordan Fdn.
Trust Service Department
300 South Grand Avenue, 29th Floor
Los Angeles, CA 90071
(213) 629-4824

FINANCIAL SUMMARY
Recent Giving: $1,849,172 (fiscal 1991)
Assets: $14,101,138 (fiscal year ending November 30, 1991)
EIN: 95-3779967

CONTRIBUTIONS SUMMARY
Donor(s): Richard J. Riordan and Jill Riordan
Typical Recipients: • *Civic & Public Affairs:* environmental affairs, municipalities • *Education:* education funds, literacy • *Science:* scientific organizations • *Social Services:* united funds
Grant Types: general support

GIVING OFFICERS
Paul T. Guinn: secy

Mary O'Dell: dir
Jill Riordan: chmn
Richard J. Riordan: ceo

APPLICATION INFORMATION
Initial Approach: Contributes only to preselected organizations. Applications not accepted.
Restrictions on Giving: Does not provide grants to individuals.

GRANTS ANALYSIS
Number of Grants: 49
Highest Grant: $1,112,523
Typical Range: $1,000 to $25,000
Disclosure Period: fiscal year ending November 30, 1991

RECENT GRANTS
1,112,523 Rx for Reading, Milwaukee, WI
200,000 Pasadena Unified School District, Pasadena, CA
75,000 United Teachers Education Foundation
50,000 East Valley Organization
50,000 United Way
50,000 United Way
34,814 Archdiocesan Education Foundation
25,000 L.E.A.R.N.
25,000 Tides Foundation, San Francisco, CA
25,000 Valley Science Foundation

Rippel Foundation, Fannie E.

CONTACT
Edward W. Probert
Vice President and Secretary
Fannie E. Rippel Foundation
The Concourse at Beaver Brook
PO Box 569
Annandale, NJ 08801-0569
(908) 735-0990

FINANCIAL SUMMARY
Recent Giving: $4,345,352 (fiscal 1992); $2,855,595 (fiscal 1991); $3,687,466 (fiscal 1990)
Assets: $60,325,785 (fiscal year ending April 30, 1992); $59,367,960 (fiscal 1991); $53,819,172 (fiscal 1990)
EIN: 22-1559427

CONTRIBUTIONS SUMMARY
Donor(s): Julius S. Rippel, the foundation's donor, was born in Newark, NJ, and resided in

the area until his death in 1950. Mr. Rippel was an orphan who began working at an early age. He became wealthy as a young man, and was widely respected in his community as a banker and an investor. In his will, he provided for the establishment of the Fannie E. Rippel Foundation in memory of his wife.
Typical Recipients: • *Health:* hospitals, medical research
Grant Types: capital, general support, project, and research
Geographic Distribution: wide geographic distribution, with emphasis on New Jersey and New York; some international funding

GIVING OFFICERS
Bruce N. Bensley: trust, mem
S. Jervis Brinton, Jr.: trust, mem *B* Ardmore PA 1923 *ED* Williams Coll BA 1948; NY Univ MBA 1953; Rutgers Univ Stonier Sch Banking 1959 *NONPR AFFIL* mem bd govs: NJ St Opera; trust: Boys Club Newark, Colonial Symphony Soc, Kessler Inst Rehab, Marcus L Ward Home, Morris Mus Arts Sciences *PHIL AFFIL* treas, trust: Community Foundation New Jersey
G. Frederick Hockenjos: trust, mem
John L. Kidde: trust, mem *B* Montclair NJ 1934 *ED* Princeton Univ 1959 *CURR EMPL* pres: KDM Devel Corp *CORP AFFIL* adv: Highland Expansion Fund; dir: Asset Mgmt Advs, Australasia, Canadian Am Investment Mgmt, Celtic Trust Co, Construction Specialties Corp, Drukker Commun, FKC Intl, Futures Group, Interfin, Intl Agritech Resources, Intl Resources Group, Juniper Ptnrs, Pasco Intl, Pratt & Reed Corp, US Intl Publ Co; mem adv bd: Metalbanc, Midatlantic Natl Bank/North; pres: MacDonald Co *NONPR AFFIL* chmn bd trusts: Assist; trust: Intl Coll Cayman Island, Intl Coll Cayment Islands, Clara Maass Med Ctr, Montclair Art Mus, Open Space Inst, Pace Univ, Stevens Inst Tech; vchmn: Commun Fdn, Kimberly Academy Montclair *PHIL AFFIL* pres: Community Foundation New Jersey, Albert Payson Terhune Foundation
Janet E. Luther: treas
Edward W. Probert: vp, secy

Eric R. Rippel: pres, trust, mem *B* Morristown NJ *ED* Columbia Univ
Nancy L. Ryan: asst secy

APPLICATION INFORMATION

Initial Approach:
The foundation does not use standard application forms. A detailed letter may be sent to the foundation office.
Include details of the project, project's cost, indication that the proposed project is approved by the institution, and the signature of a senior executive in the institution. The applicant organization will be notified if additional information is required.
Applications may be submitted any time.
Fund requests are read initially by the foundation staff. If the proposal falls within the foundation's giving range, it is reviewed further by the board of trustees.
Restrictions on Giving:
Grants are not made to individuals, endowments, or challenge campaigns. Operating budgets are supported rarely.

OTHER THINGS TO KNOW

The foundation prefers to make a few larger grants, rather than many small ones.
Publications: annual report

GRANTS ANALYSIS

Total Grants: $4,345,352
Number of Grants: 26
Highest Grant: $500,000
Typical Range: $100,000 to $300,000
Disclosure Period: fiscal year ending April 30, 1992
Note: Recent grants are derived from a fiscal 1992 grants list.

RECENT GRANTS

500,000 Intersearch Institute, Annandale, NJ — toward the cost of the operations, drug development and research program expenses
250,000 Cold Spring Harbor Laboratory, Cold Spring Harbor, NY — toward the cost of purchasing certain equipment for the Laboratory's new Bio-Technology Center
250,000 Preventive Medicine Institute, New York, NY — toward the cost of equipping PMI/Strang's new clinic and of purchasing a gas chromatography/mass spectrometry machine
250,000 West Virginia University, Morgantown, WV — toward the cost of purchasing equipment for the cancer research laboratories
225,000 Rockfeller University, New York, NY — toward the cost of purchasing laboratory equipment for basic and clinical investigation in biomedical sciences
200,000 New England Deaconess Hospital, Boston, MA — toward the cost of purchasing core equipment for the hospital's Laboratory of Cancer Biology
200,000 Thomas Jefferson University, Philadelphia, PA — toward the cost of purchasing certain equipment for a new cardiology research laboratory
200,000 University of Texas M. D. Anderson Cancer Center, Houston, TX — toward the cost of a comprehensive chemoprevention research program on the study of cancers of the lung, head, neck and esophagus
192,100 Mount Sinai Medical Center, New York, NY — toward the cost of purchasing major equipment to be used in cancer research
183,235 Johns Hopkins Hospital, Baltimore, MD — toward the cost of purchasing an elutriator and cell separation and washing equipment

Risdon Corp.
Sales: $120.0 million
Employees: 1,500
Parent Company: CMB Packaging S.A.
Headquarters: Naugatuck, CT
SIC Major Group: Business Services, Fabricated Metal Products, and Rubber & Miscellaneous Plastics Products

CONTACT
Jerry Mackesy
Vice President, Industrial Relations
Risdon Corp.
One Risdon St.
Naugatuck, CT 06770
(203) 723-6100

FINANCIAL SUMMARY
Fiscal Note: Annual Giving Range: $100,000 to $250,000

CONTRIBUTIONS SUMMARY
Support goes to local education, health and human service, arts, and civic organizations.
Typical Recipients: • *Arts & Humanities:* general • *Civic & Public Affairs:* general • *Education:* general • *Health:* general • *Social Services:* general
Grant Types: general support
Nonmonetary Support Types: donated products, loaned employees, and loaned executives
Geographic Distribution: primarily headquarters area
Operating Locations: CT (Naugatuck)

CORP. OFFICERS
Paul Holderith: *CURR EMPL* pres: Risdon Corp
Howard Lomax: *CURR EMPL* cfo: Risdon Corp

APPLICATION INFORMATION
Initial Approach: Send brief letter of inquiry. There are no deadlines.

Riser Foods
Sales: $1.02 billion
Employees: 6,500
Headquarters: Bedford Heights, OH
SIC Major Group: Food Stores and Wholesale Trade—Nondurable Goods

CONTACT
Tina Milkovich
Director, Consumer Affairs
Riser Foods
5300 Richmond Rd.
Bedford Heights, OH 44146
(216) 292-7000

CONTRIBUTIONS SUMMARY
Operating Locations: OH (Bedford Heights)

CORP. OFFICERS
Anthony C. Rego: *CURR EMPL* co-chmn, co-ceo: Riser Foods

Ritchie Memorial Foundation, Charies E. and Mabel M.

CONTACT
Ronald B. Tynan
Vice President
Charies E. and Mabel M. Ritchie Memorial Fdn.
c/o First National Bank of Ohio
106 South Main St.
Akron, OH 44308
(216) 384-7311

FINANCIAL SUMMARY
Recent Giving: $227,000 (1991); $226,850 (1990); $202,576 (1989)
Assets: $5,693,813 (1991); $4,930,997 (1990); $4,977,694 (1989)
EIN: 34-6500802

CONTRIBUTIONS SUMMARY
Donor(s): the late Mabel M. Ritchie
Typical Recipients: • *Arts & Humanities:* community arts, history/historic preservation, museums/galleries, music • *Education:* colleges & universities, education funds, public education (precollege), student aid • *Health:* nursing services • *Religion:* religious organizations • *Social Services:* aged, child welfare, community centers, community service organizations, food/clothing distribution, religious welfare, united funds, youth organizations
Grant Types: capital, general support, and operating expenses
Geographic Distribution: limited to Summit County, OH

GIVING OFFICERS
First National Bank of Ohio trust

Edward F. Carter: off
Kathryn M. Hunter: off
John Doyle Ong: off *B*
Uhrichsville OH 1933 *ED* OH
St Univ BA 1954; OH St Univ
MA 1954; Harvard Univ LLB
1957 *CURR EMPL* chmn, ceo,
dir: BFGoodrich *CORP AFFIL*
dir: Ameritech Corp,
ASARCO, Cooper Indus,
Kroger Co *NONPR AFFIL* dir:
Chem Mfrs Assn, Natl Alliance
Bus; mem: Bus Counc, Bus
Roundtable, Conf Bd, OH Bar
Assn, Phi Alpha Theta, Phi
Beta Kappa, Rubber Mfrs
Assn; mem adv bd: Blossom
Music Ctr; pres bd trusts: West-
ern Reserve Academy; trust:
Case Western Reserve Univ,
Mus Arts Assn Cleveland

APPLICATION INFORMATION

Initial Approach: Send cover
letter and full proposal. Deadlines are January 1, April 1,
July 1, and October1.
Restrictions on Giving: Does
not support individuals.

GRANTS ANALYSIS

Number of Grants: 51
Highest Grant: $20,000
Typical Range: $1,000 to
$5,000
Disclosure Period: 1991

RECENT GRANTS

20,000 Lake Erie College,
        Painesville, OH —
        scholarship fund
15,000 University of
        Akron, Akron, OH
10,000 Hale Farm and Vil-
        lage, Bath, OH
10,000 National Invention
        Center, Akron, OH
8,000 Blossom Music
        Center Endow-
        ment, Cuyahoga
        Falls, OH
8,000 United Way,
        Akron, OH
6,000 Boy Scouts of
        America, Akron,
        OH
6,000 Tallmadge High
        School, Tallmadge,
        OH
5,750 Boys Hope, Cleve-
        land, OH
5,000 Catholic Service
        League of Summit
        County, Akron, OH

Rite Aid Corp.

Sales: $3.78 billion
Employees: 30,490
Headquarters: Harrisburg, PA
SIC Major Group: Automotive
    Dealers & Service Stations,

Holding & Other Investment
Offices, and Miscellaneous
Retail

CONTACT

Jolene Zelinski
Donations Coordinator
Rite Aid Corp.
PO Box 3165
Harrisburg, PA 17105
(717) 761-2633

CONTRIBUTIONS SUMMARY

Operating Locations: PA (Harrisburg)

CORP. OFFICERS

Alexander Grass: *B* Scranton
PA 1927 *ED* Univ FL LLB
1949 *CURR EMPL* chmn:
Super Rite Foods *CORP AFFIL*
chmn: Super Rite Foods; chmn,
ceo: Rite Aid Corp; dir: Hasbro
NONPR AFFIL mem: Natl
Assn Chain Drug Stores; mem
bd govs: Jewish Agency for Is-
rael; vchmn: Harrisburg Hosp
Martin Lehrman Grass: *B*
Harrisburg PA 1954 *ED* Univ
PA BA 1976; Cornell Univ
MBA 1978 *CURR EMPL*
vchmn: Super Rite Foods
CORP AFFIL pres, coo, dir:
Rite Aid Corp; vchmn: Super
Rite Foods

Rite-Hite Corp. / Rite-Hite Corp. Foundation

Sales: $130.0 million
Employees: 650
Headquarters: Milwaukee, WI
SIC Major Group: Industrial
    Machinery & Equipment,
    Miscellaneous Manufacturing
    Industries, and Wholesale
    Trade—Durable Goods

CONTACT

Arthur K. White
Rite-Hite Corp. Foundation
8900 North Arbon Dr.
Milwaukee, WI 53223-2437
(414) 355-2600

FINANCIAL SUMMARY

Recent Giving: $48,935 (1989)
Assets: $126,642 (1989)
EIN: 39-1522057

CONTRIBUTIONS SUMMARY

Typical Recipients: • *Arts &
Humanities:* arts festivals, community arts, museums/galler-
ies, performing arts, theater
• *Education:* private education
(precollege) • *Health:* medical

research, single-disease health
associations • *Social Services:*
child welfare, community service organizations, united funds,
youth organizations
Grant Types: general support
Geographic Distribution:
focus on Milwaukee, WI
Operating Locations: WI (Milwaukee)

CORP. OFFICERS

Clem Maslowski: *CURR
EMPL* cfo: Rite-Hite Corp
Michael H. White: *CURR
EMPL* chmn: Rite-Hite Corp

GIVING OFFICERS

Thomas J. Semran: secy,
treas, dir
Michael H. White: pres, dir
CURR EMPL chmn: Rite-Hite
Corp (see above)
Morgan P. White: dir

APPLICATION INFORMATION

Initial Approach: Send brief
letter including a description of
the organization, amount requested, purpose of funds
sought, audited financial statement, and proof of tax-exempt
status. There are no deadlines.

GRANTS ANALYSIS

Number of Grants: 46
Highest Grant: $14,210
Typical Range: $100 to $2,000
Disclosure Period: 1989

RECENT GRANTS

14,210 Maple Dale/Indian
        Hill School, Mil-
        waukee, WI
8,000 Milwaukee World
        Festival, Milwau-
        kee, WI
4,000 United Way, Mil-
        waukee, WI
2,000 United Performing
        Arts Fund, Milwau-
        kee, WI
1,800 Lombardi Cancer
        Society, Milwau-
        kee, WI
1,750 Friends of Schlitz
        Audubon Center,
        Bayside, WI
1,610 Greater Milwaukee
        Committee for
        Community Devel-
        opment, Milwau-
        kee, WI
1,500 Boys and Girls
        Club, Milwaukee,
        WI
1,500 Milwaukee Art Mu-
        seum, Milwaukee,
        WI
1,000 Children's Service
        Society, Milwau-
        kee, WI

Rittenhouse Foundation

CONTACT

Arthur Klein
President
Rittenhouse Fdn.
Lewis Tower Bldg., Ste. 2034
Philadelphia, PA 19102
(215) 735-3863

FINANCIAL SUMMARY

Recent Giving: $102,375
(1991); $50,472 (1990);
$106,250 (1989)
Assets: $1,873,302 (1991);
$1,837,174 (1990); $1,848,472
(1989)
EIN: 23-6005622

CONTRIBUTIONS SUMMARY

Donor(s): the late Philip Klein
Typical Recipients: • *Arts &
Humanities:* arts institutes,
community arts, libraries,
music, performing arts, theater
• *Education:* colleges & universities, community & junior colleges • *Religion:* religious organizations, synagogues
• *Social Services:* community
service organizations, united
funds, youth organizations
Grant Types: multiyear/con-
tinuing support and seed money
Geographic Distribution:
focus on the Philadelphia, PA,
area

GIVING OFFICERS

Arthur Luce Klein: pres, treas
B Carbondale PA 1916 *ED*
Univ MI BA 1939; Univ MI
MA 1940; Univ MI PhD 1948;
Sorbonne postgrad 1947 *CURR
EMPL* chmn: Spoken Arts
NONPR AFFIL dir: Boys Club
New Rochelle; mem pres adv
comm: Coll New Rochelle
Esther Klein: dir, exec. vp
Karen Mannes: secy
Michael Lehman Temin: secy
B Philadelphia PA 1933 *ED*
Yale Univ BA 1954; Univ PA
LLB 1957 *CURR EMPL* ptnr:
Wolf Block Schorr & Solis-
Cohen *NONPR AFFIL* dir: Citi-
zens Comm Pub Ed Philadel-
phia; lecturer: Univ PA Law
Sch; mem: Am Bar Assn, PA
Bar Assn, Philadelphia Bar
Assn

APPLICATION INFORMATION

Initial Approach: Send brief
letter describing program.
There are no deadlines.

Restrictions on Giving: Does not support individuals.

OTHER THINGS TO KNOW
Publications: Annual Report (including application guidelines)

GRANTS ANALYSIS
Number of Grants: 109
Highest Grant: $7,500
Typical Range: $100 to $3,500
Disclosure Period: 1991

RECENT GRANTS
7,500 Philadelphia Orchestra Association, Philadelphia, PA
5,000 Academy of Music, Philadelphia, PA
5,000 West Oak Lane Community Development Corporation, Philadelphia, PA
4,000 Free Library of Philadelphia, Philadelphia, PA
4,000 Temple Beth Zion, Philadelphia, PA
4,000 United Way, Philadelphia, PA
3,500 Walnut Street Theater, Philadelphia, PA
2,500 Jerusalem Foundation, New York, NY
1,750 Boys and Girls Club, Philadelphia, PA
1,500 Balch Institute, Philadelphia, PA

Ritter Charitable Trust, George W. & Mary F.

CONTACT
Michael D. Wilkins
George W. & Mary F. Ritter Charitable Trust
c/o Society Bank & Trust
Three Seagate
Toledo, OH 43699
(419) 259-8217

FINANCIAL SUMMARY
Recent Giving: $264,650 (fiscal 1991); $250,314 (fiscal 1990); $221,508 (fiscal 1989)
Assets: $5,166,818 (fiscal year ending November 30, 1991); $4,483,657 (fiscal 1990); $4,615,986 (fiscal 1989)
EIN: 34-6781636

CONTRIBUTIONS SUMMARY
Typical Recipients: • *Arts & Humanities:* libraries, museums/galleries • *Civic & Public Affairs:* law & justice • *Education:* colleges & universities • *Health:* hospitals, pediatric health • *Religion:* churches, religious organizations • *Social Services:* community service organizations, youth organizations
Grant Types: general support and operating expenses
Geographic Distribution: focus on the Toledo, OH, area

GIVING OFFICERS
Society Bank & Trust: trust
Larry Firestien: mem scholarship selection comm
Edgar A. Gibson: mem scholarship selection comm
James D. Harvey: mem scholarship selection comm

APPLICATION INFORMATION
Initial Approach: Send brief letter describing program. There are no deadlines.

GRANTS ANALYSIS
Number of Grants: 25
Highest Grant: $38,198
Typical Range: $5,000 to $10,000
Disclosure Period: fiscal year ending November 30, 1991

RECENT GRANTS
38,198 Toledo Hospital, Toledo, OH
35,464 Baldwin-Wallace College, Berea, OH
25,465 Ritter Library Board of Trustees, Vermillion, OH
20,134 Shriners Hospital for Crippled Children, Toledo, OH
10,186 Flower Hospital, Sycvania, OH
10,186 Ohio State Bar Association, Columbus, OH
10,186 Riverside Foundation for Riverside Hospital, Toledo, OH
10,186 YMCA, Toledo, OH
10,186 YWCA, Toledo, OH
1,993 Toledo Lodge Masons of Ohio, Toledo, OH

Ritter Foundation

CONTACT
Toby G. Ritter
Vice President
Ritter Fdn.
1776 Broadway, Ste. 1700
New York, NY 10019
(212) 757-4646

FINANCIAL SUMMARY
Recent Giving: $339,948 (fiscal 1991); $116,572 (fiscal 1990); $248,050 (fiscal 1989)
Assets: $5,413,738 (fiscal year ending November 30, 1991); $4,900,418 (fiscal 1990); $4,811,489 (fiscal 1989)
EIN: 13-6082276

CONTRIBUTIONS SUMMARY
Donor(s): Gladys Ritter Livingston, the late Irene Ritter, the late Lena Ritter, the late Louis Ritter, the late Sidney Ritter
Typical Recipients: • *Civic & Public Affairs:* civil rights, ethnic/minority organizations, philanthropic organizations • *Education:* colleges & universities, medical education • *Health:* hospitals, medical research, single-disease health associations • *Religion:* religious organizations, synagogues • *Social Services:* community service organizations, disabled, family planning, shelters/homelessness
Grant Types: general support
Geographic Distribution: focus on New York, NY

GIVING OFFICERS
Gladys Ritter Livingston: pres, trust
Alan I. Ritter: treas, trust
David Ritter: vp, trust
Toby G. Ritter: vp, secy, trust
Frances R. Weisman: off

APPLICATION INFORMATION
Initial Approach: Contributes only to preselected organizations.
Restrictions on Giving: Does not support individuals.

GRANTS ANALYSIS
Number of Grants: 125
Highest Grant: $45,400
Typical Range: $100 to $3,000
Disclosure Period: fiscal year ending November 30, 1991

RECENT GRANTS
45,400 United Jewish Appeal Federation of Jewish Philanthropies, New York, NY
44,100 I Have a Dream Foundation, New York, NY
43,060 Cornell University, Ithaca, NY
27,335 Albert Einstein College of Medicine, New York, NY
21,000 Dalton School, New York, NY
15,000 National Alliance for Research on Schizophrenia and the Depressions, Great Neck, NY
13,000 Lenox Hill Hospital, New York, NY
10,000 Larchmont Temple, New York, NY
10,000 University of Rochester, Rochester, NY
5,000 Guide Dog Foundation for the Blind, New York, NY

Ritter Foundation, May Ellen and Gerald

CONTACT
Emma A. Daniels
President
May Ellen and Gerald Ritter Fdn.
9411 Shore Rd.
Brooklyn, NY 11209
(718) 836-4080

FINANCIAL SUMMARY
Recent Giving: $255,473 (1990); $250,050 (1989); $183,735 (1988)
Assets: $7,172,713 (1990); $7,360,803 (1989); $6,928,292 (1988)
EIN: 13-6114269

CONTRIBUTIONS SUMMARY
Donor(s): the late Gerald Ritter, the late May Ellen Ritter
Typical Recipients: • *Arts & Humanities:* public broadcasting • *Education:* colleges & universities, private education (precollege) • *Health:* hospitals, medical research, single-disease health associations • *Religion:* churches, religious organizations • *Social Services:* aged, child welfare, community service organizations, disabled, emergency relief, food/clothing distribution, religious welfare, youth organizations
Grant Types: general support

GIVING OFFICERS
Emma A. Daniels: pres
Sophie Distanovich: treas
John Parker: vp

Helen Rohan: secy

APPLICATION INFORMATION

Initial Approach: Send brief letter of inquiry describing program or project. There are no deadlines.

Restrictions on Giving: Does not support individuals.

GRANTS ANALYSIS

Number of Grants: 33
Highest Grant: $111,000
Typical Range: $250 to $1,000
Disclosure Period: 1990

RECENT GRANTS

111,000 St. Vincents Hospital and Medical Center of New York, New York, NY
75,000 St. Patricks Church
33,250 St. Annes Home for the Aged, San Francisco, CA
30,000 College of Notre Dame, Belmont, CA
25,000 Catholic Charities
25,000 Catholic Charities
25,000 Father Flanagan's Boys Home, Boys Town, NE
25,000 Flowers With Care, Astoria, NY
25,000 Holy Names College, Oakland, CA
25,000 Little Sisters of the Poor

River Blindness Foundation

CONTACT

William R. Baldwin
President
River Blindness Foundation
141 Southwest Freeway
One Sugar Creek Place, Suite 6200
Sugarland, TX 77478
(713) 491-1600

FINANCIAL SUMMARY

Recent Giving: $28,898 (fiscal 1990)

Assets: $4,844,975 (fiscal year ending November 30, 1990)

Gifts Received: $4,967,701 (fiscal 1990)

Fiscal Note: In fiscal 1990, the foundation received $2,483,851 from John J. Moores and $2,483,850 from Rebecca Baas Moores.
EIN: 76-0300186

CONTRIBUTIONS SUMMARY

Donor(s): the donors are John J. Moores, the foundation's chairman, and Rebecca Baas Moores, the foundation's secretary and treasurer

Typical Recipients: • *Science:* scientific organizations

Grant Types: general support

Geographic Distribution: Bethesda, MD

GIVING OFFICERS

Rebecca Baas Moores: secy, treas
William R. Baldwin: pres
Brian O. L. Duke: med dir
Sanfra Johnson: asst to pres
John Moores: bd chmn, don
Donald T. Rice: vp

APPLICATION INFORMATION

Initial Approach: Contact foundation for an application. Applicants must enclose a copy of the filed application for a donation of the drug, Mectizan, with the Mectizan Expert Committee, which is located in Atlanta, GA.

GRANTS ANALYSIS

Total Grants: $28,898
Number of Grants: 1
Highest Grant: $28,898
Disclosure Period: fiscal year ending November 30, 1990

RECENT GRANTS

28,898 International Eye Foundation, Bethesda, MD — Kwara State Blindness Prevention Program

River Branch Foundation

CONTACT

Walter L. Woolfe
Trustee
River Branch Fdn.
1514 Nira St.
Jacksonville, FL 32207
(904) 396-5831

FINANCIAL SUMMARY

Recent Giving: $157,632 (1990); $267,164 (1989); $146,500 (1988)

Assets: $5,308,028 (1990); $5,547,774 (1989); $4,561,825 (1988)

EIN: 22-6054887

CONTRIBUTIONS SUMMARY

Donor(s): J. Seward Johnson 1951 and 1961 Charitable Trusts, the Atlantic Foundation

Typical Recipients: • *Arts & Humanities:* community arts, museums/galleries • *Education:* colleges & universities, science/technology education • *Health:* single-disease health associations • *Religion:* churches, religious organizations • *Social Services:* family planning, united funds, youth organizations

Grant Types: general support

Geographic Distribution: focus on the Jacksonville, FL, area

GIVING OFFICERS

A. M. Foote, Jr.: trust
Nathan J. Travassos: trust
Walter L. Woolfe: trust

APPLICATION INFORMATION

Initial Approach: Contributes only to preselected organizations.

Restrictions on Giving: Does not support individuals.

GRANTS ANALYSIS

Number of Grants: 10
Highest Grant: $50,000
Typical Range: $2,000 to $10,000
Disclosure Period: 1990

RECENT GRANTS

50,000 Jacksonville Art Museum, Jacksonville, FL
43,464 University of North Florida, Jacksonville, FL
25,000 Harbor Branch Foundation, Ft. Pierce, FL
25,000 Jacksonville Museum of Arts and Sciences, Jacksonville, FL
25,000 St. Marys Episcopal Church, Jacksonville, FL
21,500 Young Life, Jacksonville, FL
13,000 North East Florida Institute for Science, Jacksonville, FL
10,000 Beaks, Jacksonville, FL
10,000 Diagnostic Center, Jacksonville, FL
5,000 Hubbard House, Jacksonville, FL

River Road Charitable Corporation

CONTACT

Carolyn M. Osteen
Esq.
River Road Charitable Corporation
c/o Ropes and Gray
One International Pl.
Boston, MA 02110-2624
(617) 951-7237

FINANCIAL SUMMARY

Recent Giving: $112,281 (1991); $54,231 (1989); $40,100 (1988)

Assets: $4,462,412 (1991); $3,818,729 (1989); $3,296,922 (1988)

EIN: 04-6169258

CONTRIBUTIONS SUMMARY

Typical Recipients: • *Education:* colleges & universities, science/technology education

Grant Types: general support

GIVING OFFICERS

Francis Hardon Burr: trust *B* Nahant MA 1914 *ED* Harvard Univ AB 1935; Harvard Univ LLB 1938; Harvard Univ LLD 1982 *CURR EMPL* coun: Ropes & Gray *CORP AFFIL* dir: Harvard Mgmt Co, Raytheon Co, State St Growth Fund Inc, State St Investment Corp; of coun: Ropes & Gray *NONPR AFFIL* fellow: Harvard Coll; mem: Am Assn Advancement Science, Am Bar Assn, Am Bar Fdn, Am Law Inst, Boston Bar Assn; pres: MA Gen Hosp

William A. Coolidge: pres, trust

Catherine C. Lastavica: trust
Angelo C. Luongo: treas
Carolyn M. Osteen: clerk

APPLICATION INFORMATION

Initial Approach: Contributes only to preselected organizations.

Restrictions on Giving: Does not support individuals.

GRANTS ANALYSIS

Number of Grants: 2
Highest Grant: $87,281
Typical Range: $25,000 to $87,281
Disclosure Period: 1991

RECENT GRANTS

87,281 Massachusetts Institute of Technology, Cambridge, MA

25,000 Balliol College, Oxford, England

Rivers and Trails North East

Headquarters: The Forks, ME

CONTACT

Rivers and Trails North East
PO Box 90
The Forks, ME 04985
(207) 663-4441

CONTRIBUTIONS SUMMARY

Company provides employee matching gifts only.

Grant Types: matching

Riviana Foods

Sales: $290.0 million
Employees: 1,550
Headquarters: Houston, TX
SIC Major Group: Food & Kindred Products

CONTACT

Jack M. Nolingberg
Vice President, Employee Relations
Riviana Foods
PO Box 2636
Houston, TX 77252
(713) 529-3251

CONTRIBUTIONS SUMMARY

Company sponsors employee matching gift program; also supports community organizations.

Typical Recipients: • *Arts & Humanities:* general • *Civic & Public Affairs:* general • *Education:* general • *Health:* general • *Social Services:* general

Grant Types: matching

Geographic Distribution: primarily headquarters area

Operating Locations: TX (Houston)

CORP. OFFICERS

Frank A. Godchaux III: *B* Nashville TN 1927 *ED* St Johns Military Academy 1944; Vanderbilt Univ 1949 *CURR EMPL* chmn, dir: Riviana Foods *CORP AFFIL* dir: Chart House, First Commerce Corp New Orleans, Sysco Corp

Joseph A. Hafner, Jr.: *B* Bernardino CA 1944 *ED* Dartmouth Coll 1966-1967 *CURR*

EMPL pres, ceo, dir: Riviana Foods

APPLICATION INFORMATION

Initial Approach: Send brief letter of inquiry. There are no deadlines.

Rixson Foundation, Oscar C.

CONTACT

Thomas J. Elliott
President
Oscar C. Rixson Fdn.
307 Gregory Way
Hendersonville, NC 28739
(704) 891-5490

FINANCIAL SUMMARY

Recent Giving: $172,500 (1991); $243,896 (1990); $142,923 (1989)

Assets: $2,388,717 (1991); $2,056,174 (1990); $2,044,713 (1989)

Gifts Received: $53,767 (1991)

EIN: 13-6129767

GIVING OFFICERS

Donald Dunkerton: trust
Nathan E. Dunkerton: vp, secy, dir
Nathan E. Dunkerton: vp, secy, dir (see above)
Thomas J. Elliot: pres, dir
Thomas J. Elliot: pres, dir (see above)
Thomas J. Elliot, Jr.: mem
James M. Gilbert: mem
Joseph Giordano: mem *B* New York NY 1932 *ED* PA Military Coll BSIE 1955 *CURR EMPL* sr vp, dir, chief tech off: Fedders Corp *CORP AFFIL* pres: Nycor; sr vp: Rotorex Corp
William R. Kusche, Jr.: trust
Alan Mojonnier: dir, treas
Timothy C. Van Wyck: mem
Richard Yeskoo: mem

APPLICATION INFORMATION

Initial Approach: Send brief letter describing program. There are no deadlines.

OTHER THINGS TO KNOW

Provides grants to individuals for Christian missions.

GRANTS ANALYSIS

Number of Grants: 97
Highest Grant: $3,000
Typical Range: $500 to $1,000
Disclosure Period: 1991

Note: Does not include grants made for individual scholarships in 1991.

RECENT GRANTS

3,000 Emmaus Bible College, Dubuque, IA

2,500 Emmaus Correspondence School

1,500 International Teams, Prospect Heights, IL

1,500 Missionary Enterprises

1,000 Biblical Theological Seminary, Hatfield, PA

1,000 Christian Overcomers

1,000 Community Bible Church

1,000 Dallas Theological Seminary, Dallas, TX

1,000 Day Star University, Nairobi, Kenya

1,000 Transformation International

RJR Nabisco Inc. / RJR Nabisco Foundation

Sales: $15.73 billion
Employees: 120,334
Parent Company: Kohlberg Kravis Roberts & Co.
Headquarters: New York, NY
SIC Major Group: Food & Kindred Products, Holding & Other Investment Offices, and Tobacco Products

CONTACT

Joellen M. Shiffman
Manager, Grants and Contributions
RJR Nabisco Inc.
1455 Pennsylvania Ave., NW, Ste. 550
Washington, DC 20004
(202) 626-7270

Note: Company headquarters is in New York. Address is 1301 Avenue of the Americas, 34th Floor, New York, NY 10019, (212) 258-5600.

FINANCIAL SUMMARY

Recent Giving: $45,000,000 (1992); $35,000,000 (1991 est.); $35,000,000 (1990)

Assets: $74,710,666 (1991); $62,944,278 (1990); $61,470,682 (1989)

Fiscal Note: Company operates a highly decentralized giving program, disbursing contributions directly from headquarters, subsidiaries, and a foundation. While these programs are autonomous, totals

are included in above figures. One subsidiary, Nabisco Brands, sponsors its own foundation.

EIN: 58-1681920

CONTRIBUTIONS SUMMARY

Typical Recipients: • *Arts & Humanities:* arts associations, arts centers, community arts, dance, history/historic preservation, libraries, museums/galleries, music, performing arts • *Civic & Public Affairs:* better government, business/free enterprise, public policy, rural affairs, urban & community affairs, women's affairs • *Education:* agricultural education, arts education, business education, colleges & universities, education funds, elementary education, faculty development, minority education, public education (precollege), science/technology education, student aid • *Health:* hospitals, medical research • *Social Services:* community service organizations, united funds, youth organizations

Grant Types: capital, challenge, department, employee matching gifts, fellowship, general support, operating expenses, project, research, and scholarship

Note: Matching gifts are for arts and education only.

Nonmonetary Support Types: donated equipment, donated products, in-kind services, and workplace solicitation

Note: Estimated value of nonmonetary support was more than $4,000,000 in 1989. Noncash support consists primarily of product donations to Second Harvest food bank. Nonmonetary support is included in above total giving figures.

Geographic Distribution: near major operating facilities and to national organizations

Operating Locations: CA (San Leandro), DC, NC (Winston-Salem), NJ (East Hanover, Parsippany), NY (Bronx, New York), PR (Guaynabo), WI (Wrightstown)

Note: Listed above are major operating locations only. Company also operates throughout the United States and internationally.

GIVING OFFICERS

Roger D. Semerad: pres *B* Troy NY 1940 *ED* Union Coll BA 1962 *CURR EMPL* sr vp:

RJR Nabisco *NONPR AFFIL*
dir: Bryce Harlow Fdn, Madison Ctr Ed Aff; mem: Natl Counc Standards Testing, Secys Commn Achieving Necessary Skills; treas: New Am Schs Devel Corp
Joellen M. Shiffman: mgr, grants & contributions

APPLICATION INFORMATION

Initial Approach: *Initial Contact:* preliminary letter; for Next Century Schools Program, request an application (available in August) *Include Information On:* proposed project, including analysis of purpose, need, goals, timetable for completion, and evaluative criteria; background information on organization, including governing board and qualifications of proposed leaders; financial information, including evidence of tax-exempt status, latest audited financial statement, and budget; list of other sources of funding and plan for future support *When to Submit:* any time
Restrictions on Giving: The following generally are not eligible for grants: for-profit organizations; individuals; conferences, workshops, or tours, except as part of other funded programs; production of films, videotapes, books, and magazines; associations, athletic groups, social clubs, and similar organizations; sectarian or denominational religious groups; courtesy advertising, benefits, and raffle tickets; endowment funds; operating expenses for health and welfare organizations where such organizations are supported through federated campaigns such as the United Way or arts funds or councils; sports or marathons; or educational institutions supported by organizations such as an independent college fund or the United Negro College Fund.

GRANTS ANALYSIS

Total Grants: $8,823,702*
Number of Grants: 56
Highest Grant: $900,000
Typical Range: $20,000 to $500,000
Disclosure Period: 1991
Note: Total grants figure is for the foundation only. Average grant excludes three grants totaling $1,900,000. Recent

grants are derived from a 1991 Form 990.

RECENT GRANTS

900,000 Bowman Gray School of Medicine, Winston-Salem, NC — capital campaign
500,000 Barbara Bush Foundation for Family Literacy, Washington, DC — general support
500,000 New American Schools Development Corporation, Washington, DC — general support
383,333 Central Park Conservancy, New York, NY — program support
353,498 National Merit Scholarships, Evanston, IL — scholarship
250,000 Model High School, Bloomfield Hills, MI
250,000 Rosman Elementary, Rosmon, NC
250,000 Stanley Elementary School, Kansas City, KS
230,046 New York Public Library, Schomburg Center, New York, NY — program support
224,912 Dwight Morrow High School, Englewood, NJ

RLC Corp.
Headquarters: Wilmington, DE

CONTACT
Pat Bagley
Vice President & Treasurer
RLC Corp.
One Rollins Plaza, PO Box 1791
Wilmington, DE 19899
(302) 426-2700

CONTRIBUTIONS SUMMARY
Operating Locations: DE (Wilmington)

Roadway Services, Inc.
Revenue: $3.17 billion
Employees: 37,900
Headquarters: Akron, OH
SIC Major Group: Holding & Other Investment Offices and Trucking & Warehousing

CONTACT
Gail Fronk
Secretary to the Chairman
Roadway Services, Inc.
1077 Gorge Blvd.
Akron, OH 44310
(216) 384-8184

CONTRIBUTIONS SUMMARY
Operating Locations: CA (San Jose), OH (Akron, Worthington), PA (Coraopolis), SC (Greer)

CORP. OFFICERS
Joseph M. Clapp: *B* Greensboro NC 1936 *ED* Univ NC 1958 *CURR EMPL* chmn, pres, dir: Roadway Svcs

---

Robbins & Myers, Inc. / Robbins & Myers Foundation
Sales: $78.7 million
Employees: 593
Headquarters: Dayton, OH
SIC Major Group: Electronic & Other Electrical Equipment and Industrial Machinery & Equipment

CONTACT
Daniel Duval
President
Robbins & Myers Fdn.
1400 Kettering Tower
Dayton, OH 45423
(513) 222-2610

FINANCIAL SUMMARY
Recent Giving: $100,751 (1991); $104,500 (1990); $74,053 (1989)
Assets: $50,213 (1991); $24,734 (1990); $18,133 (1989)
Gifts Received: $104,850 (1990); $75,553 (1989)
Fiscal Note: In 1990, contributions were received from Robbins and Myers, Inc.
EIN: 31-6064597

CONTRIBUTIONS SUMMARY
Typical Recipients: • *Arts & Humanities:* community arts, dance, history/historic preservation, museums/galleries, performing arts, theater • *Civic & Public Affairs:* municipalities, urban & community affairs • *Education:* colleges & universities, education funds, student aid • *Social Services:* community centers
Grant Types: general support

Nonmonetary Support Types: donated equipment, donated products, and loaned employees
Geographic Distribution: focus on OH
Operating Locations: OH (Dayton)

CORP. OFFICERS
Daniel W. Duval: *CURR EMPL* pres, ceo: Robbins & Myers
Maynard H. Murch IV: *CURR EMPL* chmn: Robbins & Myers
George M. Walker III: *CURR EMPL* vp, cfo: Robbins & Myers

GIVING OFFICERS
Daniel W. Duval: pres, mgr *CURR EMPL* pres, ceo: Robbins & Myers (see above)
Maynard H. Murch IV: chmn *CURR EMPL* chmn: Robbins & Myers (see above)
J. M. Rigot: secy
George M. Walker III: treas *CURR EMPL* vp, cfo: Robbins & Myers (see above)

APPLICATION INFORMATION
Initial Approach: Send brief letter including a description of the organization, amount requested, and purpose of funds sought. There are no deadlines.
Restrictions on Giving: Does not support individuals, religious organizations for sectarian purposes, or political or lobbying groups.

GRANTS ANALYSIS
Number of Grants: 38
Highest Grant: $15,000
Typical Range: $1,000 to $5,000
Disclosure Period: 1991

RECENT GRANTS
15,000 Cleveland Museum of Natural History, Cleveland, OH
11,100 Clark and Champaign Counties, Springfield, OH
10,000 Clark Civic Center, Columbus, OH
7,250 National Merit Scholarship, Evanston, IL
6,000 Ohio Foundation of Independent Colleges, Columbus, OH
6,000 Rio Grande University (President's Home), Rio Grande, OH
5,000 City of Kettering, Kettering, OH

5,000 Dayton Museum of Natural History, Dayton, OH

3,000 Dayton Ballet Association, Dayton, OH

Roberts Foundation

Headquarters: San Francisco, CA

CONTACT

George R. Roberts
Vice President
Roberts Fdn.
101 California St., Ste. 4550
San Francisco, CA 94111
(415) 771-4300

FINANCIAL SUMMARY

Recent Giving: $3,549,395 (1991); $2,884,862 (1990); $1,131,414 (1989)
Assets: $15,211,750 (1991); $9,928,270 (1990); $5,501,920 (1989)
Gifts Received: $1,633,550 (1990); $400,000 (1989); $3,321,579 (1988)
Fiscal Note: In 1990, contributions were received from George R. Roberts.
EIN: 94-2967074

CONTRIBUTIONS SUMMARY

Typical Recipients: • *Arts & Humanities:* community arts, dance, museums/galleries, music, opera, public broadcasting • *Civic & Public Affairs:* environmental affairs, housing • *Education:* colleges & universities, private education (precollege) • *Religion:* religious organizations • *Social Services:* animal protection, child welfare, disabled, religious welfare, united funds, youth organizations
Grant Types: general support
Geographic Distribution: limited to CA

GIVING OFFICERS

John P. McLoughlin: vp
George Rosenberg Roberts: don, vp, secy-treas *B* Houston TX 1943 *ED* Claremont Mens Coll BA 1966; Univ CA Hastings Coll JD 1969 *CURR EMPL* ptnr: Kohlberg Kravis Roberts & Co *CORP AFFIL* beneficial owner: Conagra, Fred Meyer Inc; dir: BCI Holdings Corp, Duracell, Duracell Holdings Corp, Houdaille Indus, Lily-Tulip Inc, Malone & Hyde, Marley Co, NI Indus, Owens-Illinois, RJR Nabisco Capital Corp, RJR Nabisco Holdings Corp, RJR Nabisco

Holdings Group, Sargent Indus, Stop & Shop Cos, Stop & Shop Holdings, Stop & Shop Supermarket Holding Co, Storer Commun, Walter Indus; dir, beneficial owner: Autozone, Duracell Intl, Idex Corp, Safeway Stores, Union TX Petroleum Holdings
Leanne B. Roberts: pres, dir

APPLICATION INFORMATION

Initial Approach: Contributes only to preselected organizations.
Restrictions on Giving: Does not support individuals.

GRANTS ANALYSIS

Number of Grants: 104
Highest Grant: $300,000
Typical Range: $10,000 to $50,000
Disclosure Period: 1991

RECENT GRANTS

300,000 Culver Military Academy, Culver, IN
200,000 Dunn School, San Francisco, CA
200,000 Dunn School, San Francisco, CA
200,000 Dunn School, San Francisco, CA
200,000 Museum of Modern Art, New York, NY
150,000 Dunn School, San Francisco, CA
150,000 Fine Arts Museum of San Francisco, San Francisco, CA
100,000 San Francisco Symphony, San Francisco, CA
75,000 San Francisco SPCA, San Francisco, CA
50,000 American Academy of Achievement, Malibu, CA

Roberts Foundation, Dora

CONTACT

Rick Piersall
Vice President
Dora Roberts Fdn.
PO Box 2050
Ft. Worth, TX 76113
(817) 884-4442

FINANCIAL SUMMARY

Recent Giving: $1,593,103 (fiscal 1991); $1,529,651 (fiscal 1990); $874,294 (fiscal 1989)
Assets: $24,119,759 (fiscal year ending June 30, 1991);

$22,009,428 (fiscal 1990); $21,112,272 (fiscal 1989)
Gifts Received: $5,000 (fiscal 1991); $14,000 (fiscal 1990)
EIN: 75-6013899

CONTRIBUTIONS SUMMARY

Donor(s): The foundation was established in 1948 by the late Dora Roberts.
Typical Recipients: • *Arts & Humanities:* history/historic preservation, museums/galleries, music • *Civic & Public Affairs:* municipalities • *Education:* community & junior colleges, education funds, public education (precollege) • *Health:* hospices, hospitals, medical rehabilitation • *Religion:* churches • *Social Services:* animal protection, community centers, food/clothing distribution, homes, youth organizations
Grant Types: general support
Geographic Distribution: limited to Texas, with a focus on Big Spring

GIVING OFFICERS

Roger Canter: bd mem
Ralph W. Caton: chmn
Mrs. Horace Garrett: bd mem
Sue Garrett Partee: bd mem
J. P. Taylor: bd mem
R. H. Weaver: bd mem

APPLICATION INFORMATION

Initial Approach:
The foundation requests applications be made in writing. Proposals should include the purpose and amount of the request, a list of board members, and a copy of an IRS exemption letter.
The deadline for submitting proposals is September 30. The board meets annually in October or November. Decisions are generally made by the end of December.
Restrictions on Giving: The foundation does not make grants to individuals.

GRANTS ANALYSIS

Total Grants: $1,593,103
Number of Grants: 23
Highest Grant: $500,000
Typical Range: $5,000 to $50,000
Disclosure Period: fiscal year ending June 30, 1991
Note: Average grant figure does not include the highest grant of $500,000. Recent

grants are derived from a fiscal 1991 grants list.

RECENT GRANTS

500,000 Big Spring YMCA, Big Spring, TX
210,000 Howard County Junior College, Big Spring, TX
136,030 Dora Roberts Rehabilitation Center, Big Spring, TX
105,500 Heritage Museum of Big Spring, Big Spring, TX
100,000 St. Mary's Episcopal Church, Big Spring, TX
66,573 Big Spring YMCA, Big Spring, TX
50,000 Big Bend Regional Medical Center, Big Spring, TX
50,000 City of Big Spring, Big Spring, TX
50,000 Lubbock Methodist Hospital, Lubbock, TX
50,000 Salvation Army, Big Spring, TX

Roberts Foundation, Summerfield G.

CONTACT

David Jackson
Trustee
Summerfield G. Roberts Foundation
NCNB Texas National Bank, P.O. Box 831041
Dallas, TX 75283-1041

FINANCIAL SUMMARY

Assets: $7,678,299 (fiscal year ending June 30, 1991)
Gifts Received: $3,993,615 (fiscal 1991)
EIN: 75-232926

CONTRIBUTIONS SUMMARY

Donor(s): initial funding of foundation from assets of the estate of Summerfield G. Roberts
Typical Recipients: • *Education:* business education, engineering education • *Health:* medical research
Grant Types: general support, research, and scholarship

GIVING OFFICERS

David Jackson: co-trust
Disclosure Period: fiscal year ending March 31, 1991

Robertshaw Controls Co. / Robertshaw Controls Co. Charitable & Ed Foundation

Sales: $600.0 million
Employees: 8,500
Headquarters: Richmond, VA
SIC Major Group: Electronic & Other Electrical Equipment, Industrial Machinery & Equipment, Instruments & Related Products, and Transportation Equipment

CONTACT
Chloe Pemerton
Director, Personnel
Robertshaw Controls Co.
1701 Byrd Ave.
Richmond, VA 23230
(804) 289-4200

FINANCIAL SUMMARY
Recent Giving: $36,660 (1991)
Assets: $43,451 (1991); $13,425 (1990); $98,015 (1989)
Gifts Received: $65,000 (1991)
Fiscal Note: Annual Giving Range: $50,0000 to $100,000 In 1991, contributions were received from the Robertshaw Controls Co.
EIN: 54-6033124

CONTRIBUTIONS SUMMARY
Typical Recipients: • *Arts & Humanities:* arts associations, museums/galleries, performing arts, theater • *Civic & Public Affairs:* economic development, safety • *Education:* business education, colleges & universities, education associations, education funds, literacy • *Health:* hospitals, pediatric health, single-disease health associations • *Social Services:* child welfare, united funds, youth organizations
Grant Types: capital, endowment, general support, project, research, and scholarship
Geographic Distribution: principally near operating locations and to national organizations
Operating Locations: CA, CT, MI, NV, OH, TN, VA

CORP. OFFICERS
Leslie J. Jezuit: *CURR EMPL* pres, coo: Robertshaw Controls Co
E. Barrie Stephens: *CURR EMPL* chmn, ceo: Ranco

CORP AFFIL ceo: Barber-Colman Co, Siebe North; chmn, ceo: Robertshaw Controls Co

GIVING OFFICERS
John Kizer: vp, dir

APPLICATION INFORMATION
Initial Approach: Submit a brief letter or proposal, including a description of the organization, amount requested, purpose for which funds are sought, a recently audited financial statement, proof of tax-exempt status, and a list of other sources of income.
Restrictions on Giving: The foundation does not support causes and organizations outside designated geographical areas; religious organizations for sectarian purposes; veterans organizations, fraternal orders of clubs, neighborhood clubs or associations, private clubs, or other similar organizations, unless the contribution would benefit the entire community and have a purpose which would otherwise justify the donation; conferences, trips, or tours; operating expenses of organzations receiving United Way support; advertising, tickets, or tables for benefits; preschool, primary, or secondary education institutions, public or private; duplicating funds such as capital funds or operating funds during the same year; an organization acting as agent for (collecting money for) another, except for United Way; individuals; or political organizations, campaigns, or activities.
The foundation gives preference to organizations which efficiently address a foundation priority area, have a good reputation in the community, are well managed, provide a needed service to a wide segment of the population through sound and well-developed programs or activities, have active governing boards and competent leadership, keep fund and administrative expenses to a reasonable level, and do not duplicate services offered by other organizations.

OTHER THINGS TO KNOW
The foundation reports that 50% of giving goes to health and welfare (including United Way), 35% goes to education, and the remaining 15% is divided among youth organizations, civic affairs, and arts and culture.

GRANTS ANALYSIS
Number of Grants: 44
Highest Grant: $15,600
Typical Range: $100 to $500
Disclosure Period: 1991

RECENT GRANTS
15,600 United Way, Richmond, VA
2,360 National Merit Scholarship Corporation, Evanston, IL
1,500 Marymont Foundation, Richmond, VA
1,500 Theatre Virginia, Richmond, VA
1,000 United Way, Holland, MI
1,000 Virginia Museum Foundation, Richmond, VA
750 Virginia Special Olympics, Alexandria, VA
500 American Cancer Society, Glen Allen, VA
500 American Heart Association, Richmond, VA
500 American Lung Association, Richmond, VA

Robertson Brothers / Robertson Brothers Co. Charitable Foundation

Sales: $18.0 million
Employees: 35
Headquarters: Bloomfield Hills, MI

CONTACT
John C. Rogers
Trustee
Robertson Brothers Co. Charitable Foundation
3883 Telegraph Road
Suite 202
Bloomfield Hills, MI 48302
(313) 644-3460

FINANCIAL SUMMARY
Recent Giving: $2,550 (1991); $8,025 (1989)
Assets: $92 (1991); $511 (1989)
Gifts Received: $2,550 (1991); $8,300 (1989)
EIN: 38-2801803

CONTRIBUTIONS SUMMARY
Typical Recipients: • *Civic & Public Affairs:* housing • *Education:* colleges & universities, student aid • *Health:* single-disease health associations • *Social Services:* community service organizations, homes, united funds
Grant Types: general support and scholarship
Operating Locations: MI (Bloomfield Hills)

GIVING OFFICERS
Norman E. Heilenman: trust
David W. Robertson: trust
John C. Rogers: trust

APPLICATION INFORMATION
Initial Approach: Applicants should submit a detailed description of project and amount of funding requested; a statement of problem project will address; and a copy of IRS determination letter. There are no deadlines.

GRANTS ANALYSIS
Number of Grants: 5
Highest Grant: $1,000
Typical Range: $100 to $950
Disclosure Period: 1991

RECENT GRANTS
1,000 United Way, Ann Arbor, MI
950 Michigan State University Scholarship, East Lansing, MI
400 Guest House, Ann Arbor, MI
100 Ann Arbor Housing Bureau for Seniors, Ann Arbor, MI
100 Leukemia Society of America, Ann Arbor, MI

Robin Family Foundation, Albert A.

CONTACT
Albert A. Robin Family Fdn.
1333 North Wells St.
Chicago, IL 60610

FINANCIAL SUMMARY
Recent Giving: $444,900 (fiscal 1990); $461,437 (fiscal 1989); $414,846 (fiscal 1988)
Assets: $145,478 (fiscal year ending September 30, 1990); $150,908 (fiscal 1989); $240,469 (fiscal 1988)

Gifts Received: $433,000 (fiscal 1990); $380,000 (fiscal 1989); $370,000 (fiscal 1988)
Fiscal Note: 1990 contribution from the Robin 1986 Charitable Income Trust.
EIN: 36-3096033

CONTRIBUTIONS SUMMARY
Donor(s): Robin 1986 Charitable Income Trust
Typical Recipients: • *Arts & Humanities:* arts institutes, museums/galleries, music • *Civic & Public Affairs:* ethnic/minority organizations • *Education:* colleges & universities • *Health:* single-disease health associations • *Religion:* religious organizations • *Social Services:* community service organizations, united funds, youth organizations
Grant Types: general support
Geographic Distribution: focus on IL

GIVING OFFICERS
Linda Miller: dir
Albert A. Robin: pres
Constance Robin: dir
Richard J. Robin: secy, treas
Stephen H. Robin: vp

APPLICATION INFORMATION
Initial Approach: Contributes only to preselected organizations.
Restrictions on Giving: Does not support individuals.

GRANTS ANALYSIS
Number of Grants: 31
Highest Grant: $150,000
Typical Range: $25 to $1,000
Disclosure Period: fiscal year ending September 30, 1990

RECENT GRANTS
150,000 Art Institute of Chicago, Chicago, IL
150,000 Roosevelt University, Chicago, IL
100,000 Jewish United Fund, Chicago, IL
10,000 Palm Springs Desert Museum, Palm Springs, CA
5,600 American Jewish Committee, New York, NY
5,000 Jewish Federation, Chicago, IL
1,000 Alzheimer's Disease and Related Disorders Association, Chicago, IL
1,000 American Friends of Israel Philharmonic Orchestra, New York, NY
500 United Way, Chicago, IL
400 Palm Springs Desert Museum, Palm Springs, CA

Robinson Foundation

CONTACT
Robinson Fdn.
c/o Gifford & Dearing
700 South Flower St., Ste. 1222
Los Angeles, CA 90017
(213) 626-4481

FINANCIAL SUMMARY
Recent Giving: $132,300 (fiscal 1992); $132,939 (fiscal 1991); $98,828 (fiscal 1990)
Assets: $2,076,462 (fiscal year ending June 30, 1992); $2,105,096 (fiscal 1991); $2,018,083 (fiscal 1990)
Gifts Received: $200,000 (fiscal 1991)
Fiscal Note: In 1991, contributions were received from Laura A. Robinson.
EIN: 95-3681443

CONTRIBUTIONS SUMMARY
Donor(s): Laura Robinson
Typical Recipients: • *Arts & Humanities:* community arts, music • *Education:* colleges & universities, private education (precollege), science/technology education • *Health:* hospitals, mental health • *Religion:* churches • *Social Services:* community service organizations, recreation & athletics, united funds, volunteer services, youth organizations
Grant Types: general support
Geographic Distribution: focus on MA

GIVING OFFICERS
C. Grant Gifford: trust, chmn
Daniel E. Robinson: trust
Laura A. Robinson: trust

APPLICATION INFORMATION
Initial Approach: Application form required. There are no deadlines.
Restrictions on Giving: Does not support individuals.

GRANTS ANALYSIS
Number of Grants: 23
Highest Grant: $26,000
Typical Range: $1,000 to $10,000
Disclosure Period: fiscal year ending June 30, 1992

RECENT GRANTS
26,000 First Church of Christ, Scientist, Boston, MA
16,500 Clairbourn School, San Gabriel, CA
11,800 Troy High School, Fullerton, CA
11,100 Principia College, Elsah, IL
10,000 Titan Athletic Foundation, Fullerton, CA
5,000 Aimansor Center, South Pasadena, CA
5,000 California Institute of Technology, Pasadena, CA
5,000 Harey Mudd College, Claremont, CA
5,000 Thomas Jefferson Center, Pasadena, CA
5,000 Volunteers of America, Los Angeles, CA

Robinson Foundation

CONTACT
Gary A. Messersmith
Trustee
Robinson Fdn.
5555 San Felipe, 17th Fl.
Houston, TX 77056
(713) 627-2500

FINANCIAL SUMMARY
Recent Giving: $66,000 (1990); $75,500 (1989); $125,000 (1988)
Assets: $1,782,776 (1990); $1,686,878 (1989); $2,175,790 (1988)
EIN: 76-0231150

CONTRIBUTIONS SUMMARY
Donor(s): Jamie A. Robinson, George A. Robinson
Typical Recipients: • *Arts & Humanities:* history/historic preservation, museums/galleries • *Civic & Public Affairs:* environmental affairs, zoos/botanical gardens • *Education:* colleges & universities, private education (precollege)
Grant Types: general support, operating expenses, and research
Geographic Distribution: focus on TX

GIVING OFFICERS
Gary A. Messersmith: trust
George Anderson Robinson: pres, trust *B* 1959 *ED* TX A&M; St Thomas Univ *CURR EMPL* co-owner, dir: Robinson Interests
Jamie Abercrombie Robinson: vp, trust *B* 1957 *ED* Amherst Coll; Rice Univ *CURR EMPL* co-owner, dir: Robinson Interests

APPLICATION INFORMATION
Initial Approach: Send brief letter describing program. There are no deadlines.

GRANTS ANALYSIS
Number of Grants: 7
Highest Grant: $30,000
Typical Range: $2,500 to $18,500
Disclosure Period: 1990

RECENT GRANTS
30,000 EAA Aviation Foundation, Oshkosh, WI
18,500 Texas A & M Research Foundation, College Station, TX
5,000 Caesar Klegerg Wildlife Institute, Kingsville, TX
5,000 Foundation for the Museum of Medical Science, Houston, TX
2,500 Sunshine Kids, Houston, TX
2,500 Wildlife Conservation Fund, Columbus, OH

Robinson Foundation, J. Mack

CONTACT
J. Mack Robinson Foundation
4370 Peachtree Road, NE
Atlanta, GA 30319-3023
(404) 231-1111

FINANCIAL SUMMARY
Recent Giving: $129,000 (1990)
Assets: $2,468,688 (1990)
Gifts Received: $358,225 (1990)
EIN: 58-1758256

CONTRIBUTIONS SUMMARY
Typical Recipients: • *Arts & Humanities:* history/historic preservation, museums/galleries • *Education:* colleges & universities, private education (precollege) • *Health:* medical research
Grant Types: general support and research

GIVING OFFICERS
J. Mack Robinson: trust

APPLICATION INFORMATION
Initial Approach: The foundation reports no specific application guidelines. Send a brief letter of inquiry, including statement of purpose, amount requested, and proof of tax-exempt status.

GRANTS ANALYSIS
Total Grants: $129,000
Number of Grants: 6
Typical Range: $5,000 to $50,000
Disclosure Period: 1990

RECENT GRANTS
50,000 Atlanta Historical Society, Atlanta, GA
32,000 Brookwood School
22,000 Shepherd Spinal Center
10,000 High Museum of Art, GA
10,000 Oglethorpe University, GA
5,000 Shorter College, GA

Robinson Fund, Charles Nelson

CONTACT
Diane O. Stables
Fleet Bank, N.A.
One Constitution Plz.
Hartford, CT 06115

FINANCIAL SUMMARY
Recent Giving: $100,730 (fiscal 1992); $104,615 (fiscal 1991); $95,400 (fiscal 1990)
Assets: $2,737,127 (fiscal year ending June 30, 1992); $2,446,833 (fiscal 1991); $2,329,452 (fiscal 1990)
Gifts Received: $2,339 (fiscal 1992)
EIN: 06-6029468

CONTRIBUTIONS SUMMARY
Donor(s): the late Charles Nelson Robinson
Typical Recipients: • *Arts & Humanities:* community arts, dance, music, theater • *Social Services:* community centers, community service organizations, day care, family planning, united funds, youth organizations
Grant Types: general support
Geographic Distribution: focus on Hartford, CT

GIVING OFFICERS
Fleet Bank, N.A. (Connecticut): trust

APPLICATION INFORMATION
Initial Approach: Application form required. Deadlines are January 15, May 15, and September 15.

OTHER THINGS TO KNOW
Publications: Application Guidelines

GRANTS ANALYSIS
Number of Grants: 48
Highest Grant: $7,000
Typical Range: $500 to $5,000
Disclosure Period: fiscal year ending June 30, 1992

RECENT GRANTS
7,000 Youth Challenge of Greater Hartford, Hartford, CT
5,000 Bushnell Park Foundation, Hartford, CT
5,000 Camp Courant, Hartford, CT
5,000 Hartford Area Child Care, Hartford, CT
5,000 United Way, Hartford, CT
5,000 Youth Under Severe Stress, Hartford, CT
4,000 South Park Inn, Hartford, CT
3,500 Hartford Neighborhood Centers, Hartford, CT
3,000 Achievement Unlimited, Hartford, CT
3,000 Chrysalis Center, Hartford, CT

Robinson Fund, Maurice R.

CONTACT
Sidney P. Marland
The Maurice R. Robinson Fund, Inc.
730 Broadway
New York, NY 10003
(212) 505-3706

FINANCIAL SUMMARY
Recent Giving: $239,115 (fiscal 1992); $132,580 (fiscal 1991); $100,307 (fiscal 1990)
Assets: $7,465,214 (fiscal year ending March 31, 1992); $4,667,237 (fiscal 1991); $2,834,988 (fiscal 1990)

Gifts Received: $40,000 (fiscal 1992); $1,034,880 (fiscal 1991)
Fiscal Note: In fiscal 1992, contributions were received from Scholastic, Inc.
EIN: 13-6161094

CONTRIBUTIONS SUMMARY
Typical Recipients: • *Arts & Humanities:* libraries, museums/galleries • *Civic & Public Affairs:* civil rights, professional & trade associations, public policy • *Education:* arts education, colleges & universities, education funds, journalism education, public education (precollege) • *Religion:* churches • *Social Services:* child welfare, community service organizations, family services
Grant Types: general support

GIVING OFFICERS
Katherine Carsky: trust
Sturges F. Cary: trust
Claudia Cohl: vp, trust
Anne Devanie: secy
Sidney P. Marland, Jr.: pres, trust
Raymond A. Occhipinti: treas
Marian I. Steffens: asst secy
Barbara D. Sullivan: trust

APPLICATION INFORMATION
Initial Approach: Send brief letter of inquiry describing program. There are no deadlines.

GRANTS ANALYSIS
Number of Grants: 34
Highest Grant: $50,000
Typical Range: $1,000 to $10,000
Disclosure Period: fiscal year ending March 31, 1992

RECENT GRANTS
50,000 Graham Windham Services to Families and Children
25,000 Constitutional Rights Foundation
25,000 Council for the Advancement of Citizenship
20,000 Rutgers University, New Brunswick, NJ
20,000 Rutgers University, New Brunswick, NJ
11,500 Friends of Town of Pelham Public Library
10,415 Trinity College
10,000 Columbia University School of Journalism, New York, NY

10,000 National Council of Teachers of English
10,000 Tisch School of Fine Arts

Robinson Mountain Fund, E. O.

CONTACT
Juanita Stollings
Secretary-Treasurer
E. O. Robinson Mountain Fund
425 Holiday Rd.
Lexington, KY 40502

FINANCIAL SUMMARY
Recent Giving: $429,720 (fiscal 1991); $391,000 (fiscal 1990)
Assets: $10,455,076 (fiscal year ending June 30, 1991); $9,950,930 (fiscal 1990); $8,710,214 (fiscal 1988)
Gifts Received: $1,275 (fiscal 1990); $389,430 (fiscal 1988)
EIN: 61-0449642

CONTRIBUTIONS SUMMARY
Donor(s): the late Edward O. Robinson
Typical Recipients: • *Education:* colleges & universities • *Health:* hospitals, medical research, single-disease health associations • *Social Services:* family planning
Grant Types: general support
Geographic Distribution: focus on eastern KY

GIVING OFFICERS
Arthur C. Aumack: dir
J. C. Codell, Jr.: dir *B* Winchester KY 1919 *ED* Univ KY *CURR EMPL* pres: Whaley Corp *CORP AFFIL* dir: First Natl Bank Jackson, KY Utilities Co; pres: Whaley Corp; pres, dir: C-G-W Inc, Codell Construction Co, Codell Equipment Co; vchmn, dir: Citizens Fidelity Bank & Trust Co; vp, dir: Contractors Svc & Supply Co *NONPR AFFIL* dir: Am Road Transportation Builders Assn, Speed (JB) Art Mus; vchmn, mem exec comm, dir: Transylvania Univ
William Engle III: dir
Mary P. Fox, MD: dir
Lyman V. Ginger: pres, dir
Francis S. Hutchins: dir
N. Mitchell Meade: vp, dir
Harold H. Mullis: dir
Burl Phillips, Jr.: dir
J. Phil Smith: dir
Robert A. Sparks, Jr.: dir
Juanita Stollings: secy, treas

Vinson A. Watts: dir

APPLICATION INFORMATION

Initial Approach: Send full proposal. Board meets every four months.
Restrictions on Giving: Does not support individuals.

GRANTS ANALYSIS

Number of Grants: 38
Highest Grant: $20,000
Typical Range: $5,000 to $10,000
Disclosure Period: fiscal year ending June 30, 1991

RECENT GRANTS

20,000 Morehead State University, Morehead, KY — scholarships
20,000 Speech Clinic, Hazard, KY — speech therapy for children
20,000 Union College, Barbourville, KY — scholarships
10,000 Panco Youth Center, Oneida, KY
10,000 Pikeville College, Pikeville, KY — scholarships
8,000 Transylvania University, Lexington, KY — scholarships
5,000 Body Recall, Berea, KY — geriatric care
5,000 Federation of Appalachian Housing Enterprises, Berea, KY — home loans
5,000 God's Pantry, Lexington, KY — food distribution
5,000 Midway College, Midway, KY — scholarships

Robison Foundation, Ellis H. and Doris B.

Headquarters: Troy, NY

CONTACT

James Robison
President
Ellis H. and Doris B. Robison Fdn.
161 River St.
Troy, NY 12180
(518) 274-5941

FINANCIAL SUMMARY

Recent Giving: $183,226 (1991); $168,719 (1990); $142,104 (1989)
Assets: $5,463,315 (1991); $3,986,334 (1990); $3,854,990 (1989)

EIN: 22-2470695

CONTRIBUTIONS SUMMARY

Typical Recipients: • *Arts & Humanities:* community arts, dance, history/historic preservation, libraries, museums/galleries, music, public broadcasting • *Civic & Public Affairs:* environmental affairs • *Education:* colleges & universities, education funds, medical education • *Health:* geriatric health, health organizations, hospitals, medical research, pediatric health • *Religion:* churches • *Social Services:* community service organizations, united funds, youth organizations
Grant Types: general support and scholarship

GIVING OFFICERS

Elissa R. Prout: secy, treas
James A. Robison: pres
Richard G. Robison: vp
Barbara R. Sporck: dir

APPLICATION INFORMATION

Initial Approach: Contributes only to preselected organizations.

GRANTS ANALYSIS

Number of Grants: 47
Highest Grant: $79,469
Typical Range: $1,000 to $5,000
Disclosure Period: 1991

RECENT GRANTS

79,469 WMHT, Albany, NY
25,000 Albany College of Pharmacy, Albany, NY
16,600 Rensselaer County Historical Society, Troy, NY
15,307 Samaritan Hospital Foundation, Troy, NY
11,000 Albany Academy, Albany, NY
10,000 American Music Scholarship Association, Cincinnati, OH
8,500 St. Mary's Hospital Foundation, Troy, NY
5,200 St. John's Episcopal Church, Cincinnati, OH
5,000 Children's Hospital Medical Center, Cincinnati, OH
5,000 Church of Redeemer, Cincinnati, OH

Roblee Foundation, Joseph H. and Florence A.

CONTACT

Carol M. Duhme
President
Joseph H. and Florence A. Roblee Fdn.
c/o Boatmen's Trust Co. of St. Louis
PO Box 14737
St. Louis, MO 63178

FINANCIAL SUMMARY

Recent Giving: $478,325 (1990); $377,313 (1989); $366,725 (1988)
Assets: $10,783,827 (1990); $10,672,221 (1989); $8,877,014 (1988)
EIN: 43-6109579

CONTRIBUTIONS SUMMARY

Donor(s): the late Louise Roblee McCarthy, Florence Robes Trust
Typical Recipients: • *Arts & Humanities:* museums/galleries • *Education:* colleges & universities, community & junior colleges, religious education • *Health:* health organizations, medical research, mental health, single-disease health associations • *Social Services:* child welfare, community service organizations, family planning, family services, homes, youth organizations
Grant Types: capital, emergency, endowment, project, scholarship, and seed money
Geographic Distribution: focus on MO

GIVING OFFICERS

Carol M. Duhme: pres, trust
Warren Duhme: bd mem
Barbara Foorman: bd mem
Roblee McCarthy, Jr.: bd mem
Nancy Richardson: bd mem
Marjorie M. Robins: trust
Carol R. von Arx: bd mem

APPLICATION INFORMATION

Initial Approach: Send cover letter and full proposal (four copies). Deadlines are March 15 and September 15. Board meets in June and October. Decisions are made by July 1 and December 1.
Restrictions on Giving: Does not support individuals or provide loans.

GRANTS ANALYSIS

Number of Grants: 52
Highest Grant: $10,000
Typical Range: $1,000 to $10,000
Disclosure Period: 1990

RECENT GRANTS

10,000 Annie Malone's Children's Home, St. Louis, MO
10,000 Girls Club of St. Louis, St. Louis, MO
10,000 Kidsplace, St. Louis, MO
10,000 Operation Brightside, St. Louis, MO
10,000 YMCA, New York, NY
8,400 Consolidated Neighborhood Services, St. Louis, MO
7,500 University of Missouri, St. Louis, MO
5,000 St. Louis Effort for AIDS, St. Louis, MO
5,000 Strongly Oriented for Action, St. Louis, MO
5,000 United Nations Association, St. Louis, MO

Robson Foundation, LaNelle

CONTACT

Edward J. Robson
President
LaNelle Robson Fdn.
25612 E. J. Robson Blvd.
Sun Lakes, AZ 85248
(602) 895-9200

FINANCIAL SUMMARY

Recent Giving: $90,860 (fiscal 1992); $142,375 (fiscal 1991); $106,653 (fiscal 1990)
Assets: $1,872,949 (fiscal year ending January 31, 1992); $1,741,751 (fiscal 1991); $2,036,096 (fiscal 1990)
Gifts Received: $2,000 (fiscal 1992); $2,275 (fiscal 1991)
Fiscal Note: In 1991, contributions were received from Fennemore Craig.
EIN: 74-2461052

CONTRIBUTIONS SUMMARY

Typical Recipients: • *Arts & Humanities:* community arts,

music, performing arts • *Civic & Public Affairs:* environmental affairs • *Education:* colleges & universities • *Health:* health organizations, pediatric health, single-disease health associations • *Religion:* churches • *Social Services:* united funds, youth organizations
Grant Types: general support
Geographic Distribution: focus on AZ

GIVING OFFICERS
Lynda Estes: off
Edward J. Robson: pres, dir
Kimberly A. Robson: vp
Mark E. Robson: vp
Robert D. Robson: vp
Steven S. Robson: vp, treas, dir
Lynda Robson-Weiser: secy, dir

APPLICATION INFORMATION
Initial Approach: Send brief letter describing program. There are no deadlines.

GRANTS ANALYSIS
Number of Grants: 16
Highest Grant: $25,000
Typical Range: $500 to $3,000
Disclosure Period: fiscal year ending January 31, 1992

RECENT GRANTS
25,000 American Heart Association, Phoenix, AZ
15,000 Phoenix Performing Arts Center, Phoenix, AZ
12,500 St. Stevens Church, Sun Lakes, AZ
10,000 United Way, Phoenix, AZ
3,250 Harrington Arthritis Research Center, Phoenix, AZ
2,860 All Saints Church, Phoenix, AZ
2,500 Boys Ranch, Boy's Ranch, AZ
2,500 Goldwater Institute, Flagstaff, AZ
2,000 Life's Journey, Phoenix, AZ
2,000 University of Arizona, Tucson, AZ

Roche Relief Foundation, Edward and Ellen

CONTACT
Anne Smith Ganey
Edward and Ellen Roche Relief Fdn.
c/o U.S. Trust Co. of New York
114 West 47th St.
New York, NY 10036-1532
(212) 852-3683

FINANCIAL SUMMARY
Recent Giving: $160,650 (1991); $146,150 (1990); $179,500 (1989)
Assets: $4,831,677 (1991); $4,125,219 (1990); $4,220,850 (1989)
EIN: 13-5622067

CONTRIBUTIONS SUMMARY
Donor(s): the late Edward Roche
Typical Recipients: • *Civic & Public Affairs:* philanthropic organizations • *Education:* colleges & universities • *Religion:* religious organizations • *Social Services:* child welfare, community centers, community service organizations, counseling, disabled, domestic violence, employment/job training, religious welfare, youth organizations
Grant Types: general support, project, and seed money
Geographic Distribution: focus on NY, CT, and NJ

GIVING OFFICERS
United States Trust Company, New York: trust

APPLICATION INFORMATION
Initial Approach: Send brief letter of inquiry describing program or project. There are no deadlines.
Restrictions on Giving: Does not support individuals or provide matching gifts or loans.

OTHER THINGS TO KNOW
Publications: Program policy statement

GRANTS ANALYSIS
Number of Grants: 51
Highest Grant: $13,000
Typical Range: $1,000 to $5,000
Disclosure Period: 1991

RECENT GRANTS
13,000 New York Regional Association of Grantmakers, New York, NY
13,000 Salvation Army, New York, NY
5,000 Boys Hope, Staten Island, NY
5,000 Counseling and Human Development Center, New York, NY
5,000 Funding Partnership for People with Disabilities, Washington, DC
5,000 Hofstra University, Hempstead, NY
5,000 International Center for the Disabled, New York, NY
5,000 International Center for the Disabled, New York, NY
5,000 Seton Hall University, South Orange, NJ
5,000 Sheltering Arms Children's Service, New York, NY

Rochester Community Savings Bank
Assets: $3.96 billion
Employees: 1,815
Headquarters: Rochester, NY
SIC Major Group: Depository Institutions and Nondepository Institutions

CONTACT
Jean Van Etten
Public Relations Officer
Rochester Community Savings Bank
235 East Main St.
Rochester, NY 14604
(716) 258-3080

FINANCIAL SUMMARY
Fiscal Note: Annual Giving Range: $100,000 to $250,000

CONTRIBUTIONS SUMMARY
Company reports 52% of contributions support health and welfare, which includes the United Way; 23% to education; 13% to housing; and 12% to the arts.
Typical Recipients: • *Arts & Humanities:* general • *Civic & Public Affairs:* general, housing • *Education:* general • *Social Services:* general, united funds

Nonmonetary Support Types: in-kind services, loaned employees, loaned executives, and workplace solicitation
Operating Locations: NY (Rochester)

CORP. OFFICERS
Joseph F. Hammele: *B* Rochester NY 1929 *ED* Holy Cross Coll 1951; Univ Rochester 1961 *CURR EMPL* vchmn, dir: Rochester Community Savings Bank *CORP AFFIL* dir: Rochester Credit Center, Rochester Credit & Fin Mgmt Assn *NONPR AFFIL* mem: Natl Counc Savings Inst
Lowell C. Patric: *CURR EMPL* pres, coo, dir: Rochester Community Savings Bank
Edward J. Pettinella: *CURR EMPL* exec vp, cfo: Rochester Community Savings Bank
Leonard S. Simon: *B* Passaic NJ 1936 *ED* MA Inst Tech 1958; Columbia Univ 1963 *CURR EMPL* chmn, ceo, dir: Rochester Community Savings Bank *CORP AFFIL* dir: Fed Home Loan Bank of NY *NONPR AFFIL* dir: Natl Counc Savings Insts, Savings Bank Assn NY, Teachers Ins Annuity Assn; mem: Journal Fin Svcs Res

Rochester Gas & Electric Corp.
Revenue: $853.27 million
Employees: 2,755
Headquarters: Rochester, NY
SIC Major Group: Electric, Gas & Sanitary Services

CONTACT
John W. Edmunds
Chairman, Corporate Contributions
Rochester Gas & Electric Corp.
89 East Ave.
Rochester, NY 14649
(716) 724-8864

FINANCIAL SUMMARY
Recent Giving: $600,000 (1993 est.); $564,000 (1992); $500,000 (1991)

CONTRIBUTIONS SUMMARY
Typical Recipients: • *Arts & Humanities:* arts centers, general, museums/galleries, music, public broadcasting, theater • *Civic & Public Affairs:* better government, civil rights, consumer affairs, economic development, environmental affairs, general, safety, urban & com-

munity affairs, zoos/botanical gardens • *Education:* colleges & universities, general • *Health:* hospitals • *Social Services:* general, united funds
Grant Types: award
Nonmonetary Support Types: loaned executives
Geographic Distribution: in headquarters and operating communities
Operating Locations: NY (Rochester)

CORP. OFFICERS

Paul W. Briggs: *CURR EMPL* chmn exec & fin comm: Rochester Gas & Electric Corp
Roger W. Kober: *B* Webster NY 1933 *ED* Clarkson Coll 1955; Rochester Inst Tech 1983 *CURR EMPL* chmn, pres, ceo: Rochester Gas & Electric Corp

GIVING OFFICERS

John W. Edmunds: *CURR EMPL* chmn corp contributions: Rochester Gas & Electric Corp

APPLICATION INFORMATION

Initial Approach: *Initial Contact:* brief letter of inquiry *Include Information On:* a description of organization, amount requested, purpose of funds sought, recently audited financial statement, and proof of tax-exempt status *When to Submit:* any time
Restrictions on Giving: Does not support individuals, religious organizations for sectarian purposes, political or lobbying groups, or organizations outside operating areas.

Rochester Midland Corp.

Sales: $50.0 million
Employees: 1,200
Headquarters: Rochester, NY
SIC Major Group: Chemicals & Allied Products, Miscellaneous Manufacturing Industries, and Paper & Allied Products

CONTACT

Daniel S. Brown
Vice President, Personnel
Rochester Midland Corp.
PO Box 1515
Rochester, NY 14603
(716) 336-2220

FINANCIAL SUMMARY

Recent Giving: $26,000 (1992 approx.); $25,000 (1991)

CONTRIBUTIONS SUMMARY

Support goes to civic affairs (35%); health and human services and education (25% each); and the arts (15%). Company supports voluntarism through the United Way and blood drives.

Typical Recipients: • *Civic & Public Affairs:* better government, urban & community affairs • *Education:* colleges & universities • *Social Services:* united funds

Grant Types: capital and general support

Geographic Distribution: Primarily in New York

Operating Locations: NY (Rochester)

CORP. OFFICERS

Harlan D. Calkins: *B* Rochester NY 1932 *ED* Hamilton Coll 1954 *CURR EMPL* chmn, pres, dir: Rochester Midland Corp *CORP AFFIL* chmn: Rochester Midland; dir: Norstar Bank, Rochester Telephone Corp

APPLICATION INFORMATION

Initial Approach: Send brief letter of inquiry, including a description of the organization, amount requested, and purpose of funds sought. There are no deadlines.

Restrictions on Giving: Does not support individuals, religious organizations for sectarian purposes, or political or lobbying groups.

GRANTS ANALYSIS

Typical Range: $50 to $1,000

RECENT GRANTS

United Way, Roc, NY
United Way, Des Moines, IA
United Way, Aurora, IL
United Way, Omaha, NE
United Way, Fort Wayne, IN

Rochester & Pittsburgh Coal Co.

Sales: $311.4 million
Employees: 1,575
Headquarters: Indiana, PA
SIC Major Group: Coal Mining

CONTACT

Dave Davis
Manager, Human Resources
Rochester & Pittsburgh Coal Co.
655 Church St.
Indiana, PA 15701
(412) 349-5800

CONTRIBUTIONS SUMMARY

Operating Locations: PA (Indiana)

CORP. OFFICERS

Thomas W. Garges, Jr.: *CURR EMPL* pres, ceo: Rochester & Pittsburgh Coal Co
W. G. Kegel: *CURR EMPL* chmn: Rochester & Pittsburgh Coal Co

Rochester Telephone Corp.

Revenue: $703.22 million
Employees: 4,559
Headquarters: Rochester, NY
SIC Major Group: Communications

CONTACT

Betty J. Weiss
Public Affairs Coordinator
Rochester Telephone Corp.
180 S. Clinton Ave.
Rochester, NY 14646
(716) 777-7813

FINANCIAL SUMMARY

Recent Giving: $1,000,000 (1992 approx.); $1,000,000 (1991); $1,000,000 (1990)
Fiscal Note: Company gives directly.

CONTRIBUTIONS SUMMARY

Typical Recipients: • *Arts & Humanities:* general • *Civic & Public Affairs:* economic development, general • *Education:* colleges & universities, elementary education, general, minority education, public education (precollege), science/technology education • *Social Services:* aged, disabled, general, volunteer services
Grant Types: general support
Geographic Distribution: in company's service area
Operating Locations: AL (Atmore, Millport, Monroeville), GA (Fairmount, Statesboro), IL (Champaign, DePue, Mount Pu-

laski, Orion, Rushville), IN (Fairmont, Thornton), KS (Allen), MA (Burlington), MI (Brooklyn, Jackson, Ontonagon), MS (Rienzi), ND (Minot), NJ (Edison), NY (Buffalo, East Syracuse, Elmsford, Holcomb, Hopewell Junction, Keeseville, Latham, Monroe, New York, Poughkeepsie, Rochester), PA (Barnesville, Breezewood, Canton, Lester, New Holland, Shinglehouse), VT (Burlington), WI (Cecil, Clintonville, Medford, Mondovi, New Richmond, Viroqua)

CORP. OFFICERS

Ronald L. Bittner: *B* Bethlehem PA 1941 *ED* Muhlenberg Coll 1963; Univ Rochester 1978 *CURR EMPL* pres, ceo: Rochester Telephone Corp *CORP AFFIL* mem mgmt comm: Natl Telecommun Network

GIVING OFFICERS

Betty J. Weiss: *CURR EMPL* publ aff coordinator: Rochester Telephone Corp

APPLICATION INFORMATION

Initial Approach: *Initial Contact:* letter requesting application guidelines *Include Information On:* requirements outlined in guidelines *When to Submit:* any time

Restrictions on Giving: Does not support individuals, religious organizations for sectarian purposes, political causes or candidates, organizations that discriminate, goodwill advertising, operating expenses of organizations during the life of a capital program pledge, operating expenses of United Way-supported organizations, organizations involved in medical research or patient care (except for building campaigns), organizations outside operating territories, organizations that serve a small segment or draw support from a very limited base, or mass mailing requests not addressed to the assistant manager of community and media relations or another employee.

OTHER THINGS TO KNOW

Publications: contributions policy brochure

Rochlin Foundation, Abraham and Sonia

CONTACT
Larry Rochlin
President
Abraham and Sonia Rochlin Fdn.
275 Hill St., Ste. 250
Reno, NV 89501
(702) 827-4193

FINANCIAL SUMMARY
Recent Giving: $1,441,350 (1991); $1,396,000 (1990); $1,354,700 (1989)
Assets: $23,364,858 (1991); $21,055,543 (1990); $22,576,148 (1989)
Gifts Received: $7 (1991)
Fiscal Note: In 1991, contributions were received from estate of Sonia Rochlin.
EIN: 94-1696244

CONTRIBUTIONS SUMMARY
Donor(s): The foundation was established in 1969 by the late Abraham Rochlin and the late Sonia Rochlin.
Typical Recipients: • *Arts & Humanities:* libraries, museums/galleries, public broadcasting • *Civic & Public Affairs:* ethnic/minority organizations, philanthropic organizations • *Education:* private education (precollege) • *Health:* hospices, single-disease health associations • *International:* foreign educational institutions, international development/relief • *Religion:* synagogues • *Social Services:* aged, food/clothing distribution
Grant Types: general support
Geographic Distribution: internationally

GIVING OFFICERS
Anne R. Boschwitz: secy, treas
Franz L. Boschwitz: vp
Larry Rochlin: pres

APPLICATION INFORMATION
Initial Approach: Restrictions on Giving: The foundation supports preselected organizations and does not accept unsolicited requests for funds.

OTHER THINGS TO KNOW
Publications: annual report

GRANTS ANALYSIS
Total Grants: $1,441,350
Number of Grants: 31
Highest Grant: $425,000
Typical Range: $2,500 to $40,000
Disclosure Period: 1991
Note: Average grant figure does not include the highest grant of $425,000. Recent grants are derived from a 1991 grants list.

RECENT GRANTS
425,000 P.E.F. Israel Endowment Fund, New York, NY
250,000 Joint Distribution Committee, New York, NY
200,000 Friends of Tel Hashomer, Los Angeles, CA
100,000 American Committee for Weizmann Institute, San Francisco, CA
100,000 Jerusalem Foundation, New York, NY
75,000 American Friends of Tel Aviv University, New York, NY
50,000 American Friends of Open University of Israel, New York, NY
50,000 HIAS, New York, NY
40,000 University of Wisconsin Foundation, Madison, WI
25,000 Aleph Society, New York, NY

Rock Foundation, Milton and Shirley

CONTACT
Milton L. Rock
President
Milton and Shirley Rock Fdn.
229 South 18th St.
Philadelphia, PA 19103
(215) 790-7555

FINANCIAL SUMMARY
Recent Giving: $82,485 (fiscal 1992); $135,100 (fiscal 1991); $438,000 (fiscal 1990)
Assets: $1,873,465 (fiscal year ending August 31, 1991); $1,920,436 (fiscal 1990); $1,876,225 (fiscal 1989)
EIN: 22-2670382

CONTRIBUTIONS SUMMARY
Typical Recipients: • *Arts & Humanities:* community arts, dance, music • *Civic & Public Affairs:* law & justice • *Social Services:* community service organizations, united funds
Grant Types: general support
Geographic Distribution: focus on Philadelphia, PA

GIVING OFFICERS
Susan Rock Herzog: vp, secy
Milton L. Rock: dir, pres
Robert H. Rock: dir, vp

APPLICATION INFORMATION
Initial Approach: Contributes only to preselected organizations. Applications not accepted.

GRANTS ANALYSIS
Number of Grants: 6
Highest Grant: $105,000
Typical Range: $500 to $10,000
Disclosure Period: fiscal year ending August 31, 1991

RECENT GRANTS
105,000 Pennsylvania Ballet Association, Philadelphia, PA
10,350 Curtis Institute of Music, Philadelphia, PA
10,000 United Way, Philadelphia, PA
5,000 Philadelphia Orchestra, Philadelphia, PA
4,000 Franklin Institute, Philadelphia, PA
500 Friends of Moss Rehabilitation, Philadelphia, PA
250 Public Interest Law Center of Philadelphia, Philadelphia, PA

Rock Hill Telephone Co.

Sales: $20.0 million
Employees: 270
Headquarters: Rock Hill, SC
SIC Major Group: Communications

CONTACT
Libby Brown
Rock Hill Telephone Co.
330 East Black St.
Rock Hill, SC 29730
(803) 324-9011

CONTRIBUTIONS SUMMARY
Operating Locations: SC (Rock Hill)

CORP. OFFICERS
Frank S. Barnes, Jr.: *CURR EMPL* pres: Rock Hill Telephone Co

OTHER THINGS TO KNOW
Company is an original donor to the Hopewell Foundation.

Rockefeller Brothers Fund

CONTACT
Benjamin R. Shute, Jr.
Secretary
Rockefeller Brothers Fund
1290 Avenue of the Americas, Rm. 3450
New York, NY 10104
(212) 373-4200

FINANCIAL SUMMARY
Recent Giving: $11,042,604 (1992); $10,899,501 (1991); $8,306,904 (1990)
Assets: $285,580,344 (1992); $317,926,715 (1991); $275,262,103 (1990)
Gifts Received: $1,147,606 (1992); $37,599 (1989); $188,267 (1988)
Fiscal Note: The fund occasionally receives gifts from various Rockefeller family members. In 1988, gifts were received from David Rockefeller, Mr. and Mrs. George D. O'Neill, and the Martha Baird Rockefeller Trust. In 1989, a cash contribution was received from the Martha Baird Rockefeller Trust.
EIN: 13-1760106

CONTRIBUTIONS SUMMARY
Donor(s): The Rockefeller family's fortune stems from John Davison Rockefeller (1839-1937), founder of the Standard Oil Trust and the first billionaire in history. His five grandsons, Nelson, John, Laurance, Winthrop, and David, and his granddaughter, Abby Rockefeller Mauze, established the Rockefeller Brothers Fund in 1940. A substantial gift from their father, John D. Rockefeller, Jr. in 1951, and a bequest from his estate in 1960, constitute the fund's basic endowment.
Typical Recipients: • *Arts & Humanities:* museums/galleries • *Civic & Public Affairs:* economic development, environmental affairs, international affairs, nonprofit management, urban & community affairs • *Education:* colleges & universities, education associations, international exchange, interna-

tional studies, public education (precollege) • *International:* international organizations • *Science:* scientific organizations

Grant Types: challenge, general support, matching, multiyear/continuing support, and project

Geographic Distribution: international, national, and New York City

GIVING OFFICERS

Catharine O. Broderick: trust
Colin Goetze Campbell: pres, trust *B* New York NY 1935 *ED* Cornell Univ AB 1957; Columbia Univ JD 1960 *CORP AFFIL* corporator: Liberty Bank Savings; dir: Hartford Steam Boiler Inspection & Ins Co, Middlesex Mutual Assurance Co, Pitney Bowes, Sysco Corp, Winrock Intl Inst Agriculture Devel *NONPR AFFIL* dir: Inst Future, Middlesex Meml Hosp; mem: Counc Foreign Rels; pres: Wesleyan Univ; trust: Colonial Williamsburg Fdn, Goodspeed Opera House Fdn, Inst Architecture Urban Studies

Jonathan F. Fanton: trust
Neva R. Goodwin: trust *B* New York NY 1944 *ED* Radcliffe Coll AB 1966; Radcliffe Coll MPA 1982; Boston Univ PhD 1987 *NONPR AFFIL* exec dir: Tufts Univ Ctr Study Global Devel Change

T. George Harris: trust *B* Simpson County KY 1924 *ED* Univ KY 1964; Yale Univ BA 1949 *CURR EMPL* editor-in-chief: Jack & Jill Childrens Digest *CORP AFFIL* editor-in-chief: Psychology Today Magazine *NONPR AFFIL* bd science adv: Am Broadcasting Sys's 20-20 Program, Inst Advancement Health; dir: Am Health Fdn, Natl Volunteer Ctrs; mem: Phi Beta Kappa; mem adv comm: YMCA

Kenneth Lipper: trust *B* New York NY 1941 *ED* Columbia Univ BA; Harvard Univ JD; NY Univ LLM *CURR EMPL* chmn: Lipper & Co *CORP AFFIL* dir: EM Corp, Fiat, Neutrogena Corp *NONPR AFFIL* adjunct prof intl affairs, trust: Columbia Univ Sch Intl Pub Affs; mem: Counc Foreign Rels; trust: Am Counc Germany, Archaeological Inst Am, Yale Univ Sch Org & Mgmt

William Henry Luers: trust *B* Springfield IL 1929 *ED* Hamilton Coll AB 1951; Columbia

Univ MA 1957; Northwestern Univ 1951-52 *CORP AFFIL* dir: Discount Corp, IDEX Corp, Transco Energy Co *NONPR AFFIL* dir: Intl Res Exchanges Bd, Scudder New Europe Fund; mem: Counc Foreign Rels; pres: Metro Mus Art; trust adv counc: Appeal of Conscience Fdn

Jessica Tuchman Mathews: trust *B* New York NY 1946 *ED* Radcliffe Coll BA 1967; CA Inst Tech PhD 1973 *CURR EMPL* vp, dir (research): World Resources Inst *NONPR AFFIL* dir: Fed Am Scientists, Population Res Bur, Radcliffe Coll; distinguished fellow: Aspen Inst; mem: Counc Foreign Rels, Environmental Protection Agency Trade & Environmental Comm Natl Adv Counc Environmental Policy & Tech, Inst Intl Econs, Inter-Am Dialogue, Overseas Devel Counc, Un Nations Assn; mem adv comm: US Dept St Dept Oceans Environment Sciences, US Global Interests 1990s Am Assembly; panel mem: Am Assn Advancement Science, Natl Academy Sciences, Off Tech Assessment

Abby Milton Rockefeller O'Neill: chmn, trust *B* Oyster Bay NY 1928 *PHIL AFFIL* pres, trust: Greenacre Foundation

Richard D. Parsons: trust *B* New York NY 1948 *ED* Univ HI; Union Univ JD; Adelphi Univ LLD (hon) *CURR EMPL* chmn, ceo: Dime Savings Bank NY *CORP AFFIL* dir: Fed Natl Mortgage Assn, Philip Morris Co, Time-Warner *NONPR AFFIL* trust: Howard Univ, Metro Mus Art

Russell Alexander Phillips, Jr.: exec vp *B* Charlotte NC 1937 *ED* Duke Univ AB 1959; Yale Univ LLB 1962 *NONPR AFFIL* dir: Academy Political Sciences; mem: Counc Foreign Rels, DC Bar Assn, NC Bar Assn, Phi Beta Kappa; pres bd trusts: Lingnan Univ; trust: Intl Inst Rural Reconstruction; trust, vp: Asian Cultural Counc

David Rockefeller, Jr.: trust *B* New York NY 1941 *ED* Harvard Univ AB 1963; Harvard Univ JD 1966 *CURR EMPL* vchmn: Rockefeller Family & Assocs *NONPR AFFIL* chmn: Recruiting Young Teachers; trust: Boston Plan Excellence Pub Schs, Mus Modern Art; trust, mem: Cantata Singers; trust, overseer: Boston Sym-

phony Orchestra; trust, vchmn: Missing Half

Richard Gilder Rockefeller: trust *B* 1949 *ED* Harvard Univ 1971; Harvard Univ EdM 1973; Harvard Univ MD 1979 *CURR EMPL* physician: Clinical Faculty

Rodman Clark Rockefeller: trust *B* New York NY 1932 *ED* Dartmouth Coll BA 1954; Columbia Univ MS 1957 *CURR EMPL* chmn, dir: Pocantico Devel Assocs *CORP AFFIL* dir: Booker PLC, Booker Plc, Rockefeller Fin Svcs; chmn: Arbor Acres Farm *NONPR AFFIL* chmn: US Counc Mexico US Bus Conf Counc Am; dir: Americas Soc, New York City Phelps Meml Hosp Ctr, NY Blood Ctr, Phelps Meml Hosp Ctr, US-Mexico Cultural Exchange, US Mexico Cultural Exchange; mem: Counc Foreign Rels, NY St Rep Fin Comm; trust: Dartmouth Coll, Mus Modern Art, New Sch Social Res, Nelson A Rockefeller Ctr Social Sciences

Steven Clark Rockefeller: vchmn, trust *B* 1936 *ED* Princeton Univ AB 1958; Union Theological Seminary MDiv 1963; Columbia Univ PhD 1973 *NONPR AFFIL* comr: Natl Comm Environment; prof, adm: Middlebury Coll

Benjamin R. Shute, Jr.: secy, treas

Stephen Frederick Starr: trust *B* New York NY 1940 *ED* Yale Univ BA 1962; Cambridge Univ MA 1964; Princeton Univ PhD 1968 *NONPR AFFIL* dir: Great Lakes Colls Assn; mem: Am Assn Advancement Slavic Studies, Am Counc Ed, Am Historical Assn, Counc Foreign Rels, Greater New Orleans Regional Fdn, LA Repertory Jazz Ensemble, Trilateral Comm; pres: Oberlin Coll

APPLICATION INFORMATION

Initial Approach:
Letters of inquiry (no more than two to three pages in length) should be addressed to the fund's secretary.
Letters of inquiry should include a description of the organization and project, how it relates to the fund's program, information on principal staff members, synopsis of the budget, and the amount requested. Full proposals, when requested, should include a complete description of the or-

ganization or project, background and research leading to the development of the proposal, methods by which the project will be carried out, qualifications and experience of principal staff members, list of board members and advisors, detailed budget, copy of the organization's IRS determination letter of tax-exempt status, and a copy of the organization's most recent financial statement (preferably audited). There are no deadlines for submitting proposals.
If a project is taken up for grant consideration, the staff will ask for additional information, including a full proposal, and, usually, an interview. Proposals from former grantees will be considered only after earlier grants have been evaluated and the grantees have submitted the necessary reports of expenditures of those grants.
Restrictions on Giving: The fund does not make grants to individuals, nor does it generally support research, graduate study, or the writing of books or dissertations by individuals.

OTHER THINGS TO KNOW

When David Rockefeller retired, it marked the end of the active involvement of the founding trustees with the fund. It also marked the beginning of the Fund for Asian Projects. This new fund will be used to support projects in Asia related to the interests of the Ramon Magsaysay Award Foundation and of the Magsaysay awardees. Grants from this fund will be made by the trustees of the Rockefeller Brothers Fund with recommendations from a board of advisors made up of Magsaysay Awardees and officers of the Ramon Magsaysay Award Foundation.
Publications: annual report

GRANTS ANALYSIS
Total Grants: $11,042,604
Number of Grants: 220
Highest Grant: $540,000
Typical Range: $25,000 to $300,000
Disclosure Period: 1992
Note: Recent grants are derived from a 1992 grants list.

RECENT GRANTS
1,000,000 American Farmland Trust, Wash-

ington, DC — continued support for the membership development component of the organization's five-year capital campaign

600,000 Institute for East-west Studies, New York, NY — general budgetary support

540,000 Asian Cultural Council, New York, NY — toward general operating expenses

525,000 Worldwatch Institute, Washington, DC — general budgetary support

420,000 Community Service Society of New York, New York, NY — continued support for a project to forestall increased divestment and abandonment of low-income housing

300,000 Fund for New York City Public Education, New York, NY — continued support for a model conflict resolution and peer mediation program

265,000 New York City Partnership Foundation, New York, NY — continued support for the Community Partners Program

225,000 Center for Policy Alternatives, Washington, DC — for the center's sustainable development program

225,000 Friends of Women's World Banking, New York, NY — to establish affiliates of Women's World Banking (WWB) in Central and Eastern Europe

210,000 International Institute of Rural Reconstruction, New York, NY — to support an expansion of the institute's work in sustainable agriculture

Rockefeller Family & Associates

Headquarters: New York, NY

CONTACT
Wade Greene
Manager, Matching Gift Program
Rockefeller Family & Associates
30 Rockefeller Plz.
Rm. 5600
New York, NY 10112
(212) 649-5600

CONTRIBUTIONS SUMMARY
Company provides employee matching gifts only.
Grant Types: matching
Operating Locations: NY (New York)

Rockefeller Family Fund

CONTACT
Donald K. Ross
Director and Secretary
Rockefeller Family Fund
1290 Avenue of the Americas, Rm. 3450
New York, NY 10104
(212) 373-4252

FINANCIAL SUMMARY
Recent Giving: $1,916,000 (1993 est.); $1,763,305 (1992 approx.); $1,561,971 (1991)
Assets: $38,958,000 (1992 approx.); $36,228,747 (1991); $29,000,000 (1990)
Gifts Received: $627,978 (1992); $638,366 (1991); $525,000 (1990)
Fiscal Note: The fund reports that recent giving figures and assets figures for 1992 are approximates. Audited figures for 1992 are not yet available.
EIN: 13-6257658

CONTRIBUTIONS SUMMARY
Donor(s): The fund was established in 1967 by the Rockefeller family. Board trustees are fourth and fifth generation family members, descendants of John Davison Rockefeller (1839-1937), founder of the Standard Oil Trust and the first billionaire in history. Third generation family members, David and Laurance S. Rockefeller, are honorary trustees.
Typical Recipients: • *Civic & Public Affairs:* better government, environmental affairs,

public policy, women's affairs • *Health:* public health
Grant Types: challenge, general support, and project
Geographic Distribution: national (the fund does not generally consider projects which pertain to one city or state, unless the project could serve as a national model); the Foundation does not give international grants.

GIVING OFFICERS
Hope Aldrich: trust *B* 1938 *ED* Smith Coll *CURR EMPL* editor, publ: Santa Fe Reporter *PHIL AFFIL* pres: Millstream Fund
Nancy C. Anderson: trust
Anne Bartley: trust, vp
Clare Pierson Buden: trust, vp *B* 1956
Dana Chasin: trust *B* 1963 *ED* Yale Univ BA 1983 *CURR EMPL* atty: Kaye Scholer
Laura Spelman Rockefeller Chasin: trust *B* 1936 *NONPR AFFIL* trust: Spelman Coll
Richard M. Chasin: trust *B* Brooklyn NY 1936 *ED* Yale Univ BA 1956; Harvard Univ MD 1960 *NONPR AFFIL* Phi Beta Kappa; assoc prof clin psychiatry: Harvard Univ Med Sch; del: Intl Physicians Prevention Nuclear War; mem: Am Academy Child Psychiatry, Am Family Therapy Assn, Am Psychiatric Assn
Jon L. Hagler: mem fin comm *B* Harlingen TX 1936 *ED* TX A&M Univ BA 1958; Harvard Univ MBA 1963 *CURR EMPL* chmn: Hagler Mastrovita & Hewitt *NONPR AFFIL* mem: Boston Soc Security Analysts, Investment Tech Assn, NY Soc Security Analysts; mem investment adv comm, trust: African-Am Inst
David W. Kaiser: trust
Bevis Longstreth: chmn fin comm *B* New York NY 1934 *ED* Princeton Univ BS 1956; Harvard Univ LLM 1961 *CURR EMPL* ptnr: Debevoise & Plimpton *NONPR AFFIL* dir: Symphony Space; mem: Am Bar Assn, Am Law Inst, NY City Bar Assn
Bruce Mazlish: vp, trust *B* New York NY 1923 *ED* Columbia Univ BA 1944; Columbia Univ MA 1947; Columbia Univ PhD 1955 *NONPR AFFIL* editor: Journal Interdisciplinary History, Psychohistory Review; fellow: Am Academy Arts Sciences; prof history, chmn rhetoric: MA Inst Tech

Alida Messinger: trust *B* 1949 *PHIL AFFIL* trust: Rockefeller (John D III) Fund
Charles H. Mott: mem fin comm *B* New York NY 1931 *ED* Williams Coll 1953 *CURR EMPL* pres: John W Bristol & Co
Peter M. O'Neill: trust
Hilda Ochoa: mem fin comm *CURR EMPL* mgr: World Bank Pension Fund
Mary Louise Pierson: trust *B* 1959
David Rockefeller, Sr.: hon trust *B* New York NY 1915 *ED* Harvard Univ BS 1936; Univ Chicago PhD 1940 *CURR EMPL* chmn intl adv comm, dir: Chase Manhattan Bank *CORP AFFIL* chmn: Rockefeller Ctr Properties; chmn, dir: Rockefeller Group *NONPR AFFIL* chmn: Americas Soc; chmn exec comm: Rockefeller Univ; dir: Counc Foreign Rels; dir, hon chmn: Ctr Inter-Am Rels; life trust: Univ Chicago; mem: Intl Exec Svc Corps; mem exec comm: Downtown Lower Manhattan Assn; trust, chmn: Mus Modern Art
Diana Newell-Rowan Rockefeller: trust *ED* Chatham Coll 1966; Univ Chicago MA 1967
Laurance Spelman Rockefeller: hon trust *B* New York NY 1910 *ED* Princeton Univ BA 1932 *CORP AFFIL* chmn: Woodstock Resort Corp; dir: Readers Digest Assn *NONPR AFFIL* comr emeritus: Palisades Interstate Park Comm; hon chmn: NY Zoological Soc; hon trust: Natl Geographic Soc; trust emeritus: Princeton Univ *PHIL AFFIL* trust: Greenacre Foundation
Richard Gilder Rockefeller: pres, trust, mem fin comm *B* 1949 *ED* Harvard Univ 1971; Harvard Univ EdM 1973; Harvard Univ MD 1979 *CURR EMPL* physician: Clinical Faculty
Steven Clark Rockefeller: trust *B* 1936 *ED* Princeton Univ AB 1958; Union Theological Seminary MDiv 1963; Columbia Univ PhD 1973 *NONPR AFFIL* comr: Natl Comm Environment; prof, adm: Middlebury Coll
Wendy Gordon Rockefeller: vp, trust *ED* Princeton Univ 1979 *CURR EMPL* research assoc: Natural Resources Defense Counc *NONPR AFFIL* vchmn: Mothers & Others Pesticide Limits

Donald K. Ross: dir, secy *B* Rochester NY 1925 *ED* Yale Univ BE 1946; Harvard Univ MBA 1948 *CURR EMPL* chmn exec comm, dir: NY Life Ins Co *CORP AFFIL* dir: Consolidated Edison Co NY *NONPR AFFIL* trust: Colonial Williamsburg Fdn
Loren D. Ross: mem fin comm
Abby Rockefeller Simpson: trust *B* 1958 *PHIL AFFIL* trust, don: Greenacre Foundation
James S. Sligar: coun
Jeremy P. Waletzky: mem fin comm

APPLICATION INFORMATION
Initial Approach:
Written proposals should be sent to the foundation's director and secretary.
Proposals should include the following information: the need for the program; program objectives and plan of action; staff and organizational qualifications; list of other organizations involved in similar projects and ways the proposed project is different; amount requested; line item budget; proposed method of evaluation; organization's budget, with projected sources of income (including membership contributions, if applicable); most recent financial statement; and certificate of tax-exempt status. There are no deadlines for submitting proposals.
Acknowledgment is sent within five days of receipt of proposals; requests that fall outside of the fund's program areas are immediately declined. Proposals accepted for consideration are referred to a program officer for review, which may include a site visit or meeting. All grants are made by the board of trustees or by the executive committee acting on its behalf.
The full board meets twice a year; the executive committee usually meets three additional times. After the board makes a decision on the request, the applicant is contacted by letter. If the board approves the grant, funding usually is given within two weeks.
Restrictions on Giving: The fund reports that grants are rarely made to organizations which traditionally enjoy popular support, such as universities, museums, or hospitals. The fund does not give to aca-

demic or scholarly research (favoring, instead, entrepreneurial, action-oriented projects likely to yield tangible results), individuals, profit-making businesses, construction or restoration projects, programs dealing with international issues, or for debt reduction. The und also does not support international organizations or projects that are international in scope.

OTHER THINGS TO KNOW
Publications: annual report

GRANTS ANALYSIS
Total Grants: $1,763,305
Number of Grants: 79
Highest Grant: $45,000
Typical Range: $15,000 to $25,000
Disclosure Period: 1992
Note: Recent grants are derived from a 1991 annual report.

RECENT GRANTS
50,000 Ms. Foundation for Women, New York, NY — Reproductive Rights Coalition Fund, which provides financial support and technical assistance to reproductive rights groups
40,000 Center for the Study of Public Policy, Boston, MA — for the Military Toxics Project which investigates practices fo the Department of Defense
40,000 Environmental Support Center, Washington, DC — to strengthen state environmental groups by providing coordinated fundraising and technical assistance
35,000 Child Care Employee Project, Berkeley, CA — to help pay the salary of a development director
35,000 Southwest Research and Information Center, Albuquerque, NM — for work on issues pertaining to the Department of Energy's nuclear weapons production facilities
30,000 9 to 5, Working Women Education Fund, Cleveland,

OH — to help increase grassroots activism of working women on issues such as pregnancy and maternity benefits, sexual harassment, and family and medical leave
30,000 Center for Responsive Politics, Washington, DC — for the "Money in Politics Connection" project
30,000 Center on Budget and Policy Priorities, Washington, DC — to develop public policy initiatives on a wide range of issues affecting low-income people
30,000 Children's Defense Fund, Washington, DC — provides technical assistance to states and helps ensure that low-income children receive the full benefit of new federal child care and Head Start funds
30,000 Environmental Research Foundation, Washington, DC — for technical assistance to grassroots environmental groups

Rockefeller Foundation

CONTACT
Lynda Mullen
Secretary
Rockefeller Foundation
1133 Avenue of the Americas
New York, NY 10036
(212) 869-8500
Note: Proposals and applications may also be sent to the director of the relevant division or program. This information is located in the "Officers and Directors" section of the profile.

FINANCIAL SUMMARY
Recent Giving: $100,562,000 (1991); $94,717,353 (1990); $78,072,560 (1989)

Assets: $2,190,830,000 (1991); $1,971,970,559 (1990); $2,152,247,157 (1989)

EIN: 13-1659629

CONTRIBUTIONS SUMMARY
Donor(s): The Rockefeller Foundation was established in 1913 by John Davison Rockefeller (1839-1937), founder of the Standard Oil Trust and the first billionaire in history. J.D. Rockefeller and his partners began their first refinery in 1863. By the early 1900s, Standard Oil Company controlled more than 80 percent of the country's refinery capacity. When the company was dissolved in 1911, Rockefeller became the major stockholder in several oil companies including the predecessors of Exxon, Chevron, Amoco, and Mobil. His son, John D. Rockefeller, Jr., was the primary recipient of most of his fortune. The foundation is now independent of the Rockefeller family; however, members of the family control the smaller Rockefeller Brothers Fund, established by John D. Rockefeller, Jr., and his children.
Typical Recipients: • *Arts & Humanities:* arts associations, arts centers, arts festivals, arts institutes, cinema, community arts, dance, ethnic arts, literary arts, museums/galleries, music, performing arts, public broadcasting, theater • *Civic & Public Affairs:* civil rights, economic development, economics, environmental affairs, ethnic/minority organizations, housing, international affairs, law & justice, nonprofit management, philanthropic organizations, public policy, urban & community affairs, women's affairs • *Education:* agricultural education, arts education, colleges & universities, international exchange, literacy, medical education, minority education, science/technology education, student aid • *Health:* health organizations, medical research, medical training, pediatric health, public health • *International:* foreign educational institutions, international development/relief, international health care, international organizations • *Science:* scientific institutes, scientific organizations • *Social Services:* family planning
Grant Types: conference/seminar, fellowship, multiyear/continuing support, project, and research

Geographic Distribution: international and national

GIVING OFFICERS

Alan Alda: trust *B* New York NY 1936 *ED* Fordham Univ BS 1956 *NONPR AFFIL* mem: Dirs Guild Am, Screen Actors Guild Am, Writers Guild Am

Alberta Bean Arthurs: dir (arts & humanities) *B* Framingham MA 1932 *ED* Wellesley Coll BA 1954; Bryn Mawr Coll PhD 1972 *CORP AFFIL* dir: Culbro Corp, Techo-Serve *NONPR AFFIL* mem: Counc Foreign Rels

Al Binger: sr program off (global environment)

Joseph R. Bookmeyer: mgr fellowship off

Dr. Harold Brown, Phd: trust *B* New York NY 1927 *ED* Columbia Univ AB 1945; Columbia Univ AM 1946; Columbia Univ PhD 1949; Stevens Inst Tech Engring 1964 *CORP AFFIL* dir: AMAX, CBS, Cummins Engine Co, IBM Corp, Mattel, Philip Morris Co, Synergen; ptnr: EM Warburg Pincus & Co; dir: Polaris Steering Co *NONPR AFFIL* chmn, consultant: Foreign Policy Res Inst; dir: Counc Foreign Rels; mem: Am Academy Arts Sciences, Am Physical Soc, Natl Academy Engg, Natl Academy Sciences, Phi Beta Kappa, Sigma Xi; trust: Rand Corp

Henry G. Cisneros: trust *B* San Antonio TX 1947 *ED* TX A&M Univ BA 1969; Harvard Univ Pub Admin 1973; George Washington Univ Pub Admin 1975 *CURR EMPL* Mayor: San Antonio TX *NONPR AFFIL* chmn: Fire Police Pension Fund, Unite San Antonio; mem: Twentieth Century Fund Ed Task Force; mem bus adv comm: Trinity Univ; mem comm visual arts: TX A&M Univ; mem strategy counc: Natl Democratic Party; trust: City Pub Svc Bd, City Water Bd *PHIL AFFIL* mem: Eisenhower Foundation

Johnnetta Betsch Cole: trust *B* Jacksonville FL 1936 *ED* Fisk Univ 1953; Oberlin Coll BA 1957; Northwestern Univ MA 1959; Northwestern Univ PhD 1967 *CORP AFFIL* dir: Coca-Cola Enterprises, Nations Bank GA *NONPR AFFIL* dir: Am Counc Ed, Feminist Press; fellow: Am Anthropological Assn; mem: Assn Am Colls, Assn Black Anthropologists; mem editorial bd: The Black-

scholar; pres: Intl Womens Anthropology Conf, Spelman Coll

Margaret Rockefeller Dulany: trust *B* 1947 *ED* Harvard Univ AB 1969; Harvard Univ EdM 1973; Harvard Univ EdD 1976 *CURR EMPL* pres: Synergos Inst

John Robert Evans: chmn bd trusts *B* Toronto Canada 1929 *ED* Univ Toronto MD 1952; Oxford Univ DPhil 1955 *CURR EMPL* vp, commercial dir: Allelix (Canada) *CORP AFFIL* dir: Alcan Aluminum Ltd, Canadian Corp Mgmt, Connaught Labs, Defasco Inc, MDS Health Group, Montreal Southern Inc, Pasteur Merieux Serums & Vaccines, Royal Bank Canada, Torstar Ltd, Trimark Fin Corp *NONPR AFFIL* chmn: African Med Res Fdn; fellow: Royal Coll Physicians (London), Royal Coll Physicians Surgeons Canada, Royal Soc Canada; hon fellow: London Sch Hygiene & Tropical Medicine, Univ Coll Oxford; prof cardiology: Univ Toronto Med Sch

Sally Ferris: dir admin

Frances FitzGerald: trust *B* 1940 *ED* Radcliffe Coll 1962

Daniel P. Garcia: trust *B* Los Angeles CA 1947 *ED* Loyola Univ BBA 1970; Univ Southern CA MBA 1971; Univ CA Los Angeles JD 1974 *CURR EMPL* ptnr: Munger Tolles & Olson *NONPR AFFIL* dir: Mexican Am Legal Defense Ed Fund

James O. Gibson: dir (equal opportunity)

Peter C. Goldmark, Jr.: pres, trust *B* New York NY 1940 *ED* Harvard Univ BA 1962 *CORP AFFIL* sr vp: Times Mirror Co

Ronald E. Goldsberry: trust *CURR EMPL* gen mgr (plastic products div): Ford Motor Co

Robert W. Herdt: dir (agricultural sciences)

William David Hopper: trust *B* Ottawa Ontario Canada 1927 *ED* McGill Univ BS 1950; Cornell Univ PhD 1957 *CURR EMPL* sr vp: Haldor Topsoe *CORP AFFIL* sr vp: World Bank *NONPR AFFIL* chmn: Comm Fund Commodities, Counsultative Comm; chmn bd trusts: Intl Fertilizer Devel Ctr; dir: Acres, Inst Res on Pub Policy; fellow: Royal Agricultural Soc England; mem: Am Academy Arts Sciences, Intl Womens Health Coalition Group, World Academy Arts

Sciences; trust, chmn exec comm: Population Counc

Karen Nicholson Horn: trust *B* Los Angeles CA 1943 *ED* Pomona Coll BA 1965; Johns Hopkins Univ PhD 1971 *CURR EMPL* chmn, ceo, dir: Bank One Cleveland NA *CORP AFFIL* dir: Eli Lilly & Co, Rubbermaid, TRW *NONPR AFFIL* trust: Cleveland Clinic Fdn, Cleveland Orchestra, Cleveland Tomorrow; trust, vchmn: Case Western Reserve Univ *PHIL AFFIL* trust: Cleveland Clinic Foundation

Alice Stone Ilchman: trust *B* Cincinnati OH 1935 *ED* Mt Holyoke Coll BA 1957; Syracuse Univ MPA 1958; London Sch Econ PhD 1965 *CORP AFFIL* dir: J&W Seligman Cos, NY Telephone Co *NONPR AFFIL* chmn comm womens employment: Natl Academy Sciences; mem: Am Ditchley Fdn, Comm Econ Devel, Counc Foreign Rels, Intl Res Exchanges Bd, Natl Academy Pub Admin, Natl Org Women Legal Defense Ed Fund, Smithsonian Counc, Yonkers Emergency Fin Control Bd; mem bd adv: South Africa Corp, Univ Cape Town; pres: Sarah Lawrence Coll; trust: Experiment Intl Living; mem bd advs: NY Tel Co

Richard Hampton Jenrette: trust *B* Raleigh NC 1929 *ED* Univ NC BA 1951; Harvard Univ MBA 1957 *CURR EMPL* chmn, dir: Equitable Life Assurance Soc US *CORP AFFIL* chmn: Donaldson Lufkin & Jenrette; dir: Advanced Micro Devices, News & Observer Publ Co, Roses Stores; pres, ceo: Equitable Investment Corp; chmn, dir: Equitable Variable Life Ins Co *NONPR AFFIL* chmn: Adv Counc Historic Preservation; dir: Bus Fdn NC, Historic Hudson Valley, White House Endowment Fund; mem: Inst Chartered Fin Analysts, NY Soc Security Analysts, Securities Indus Assn; mem govs counc: Hudson Valley Greenway; trust: NY Historical Soc

Tom Johnson: trust *CURR EMPL* chmn: Los Angeles Times *PHIL AFFIL* dir: Times Mirror Foundation

Frank Karel III: vp (communications) *B* Orlando FL 1935 *ED* Univ FL BS 1961; NY Univ MBA 1983 *NONPR AFFIL* mem: Am Assn Advancement Science, Communs Network Philanthropy, Natl Assn Science Writers, Pub Rels

Soc Am *PHIL AFFIL* vp (communications): Johnson (Robert Wood) Foundation

Charles J. Lang: comptr

Robert S. Lawrence: dir (health sciences) *NONPR AFFIL* chmn: Comm Health & Human Rights; editor: Am Journal Preventive Medicine; fellow: ACP; mem: Expert Panel Preventive Svcs, Phi Beta Kappa

Arthur Levitt, Jr.: trust *B* Brooklyn NY 1931 *ED* Williams Coll BA 1952 *CURR EMPL* chmn: Levitt Media Co *CORP AFFIL* chmn: Levitt Media Co, NY City Econ Devel Corp; dir: Baker & Tayloy Distr, FDM Holdings, First Empire St Corp, NY Daily News, Shared Med Sys Corp; trust: East NY Savings Bank *NONPR AFFIL* chmn: Am Bus Counc, Task Force Future Devel W Side Manhattan; mem: Am Bus Conf, Equitable Life Assurance Soc US, NY St Counc Arts; trust: Williams Coll *PHIL AFFIL* dir: Dole Foundation

Robert Clive Maynard: trust *B* Brooklyn NY 1937 *ED* Harvard Univ 1966 *CURR EMPL* owner, editor, publ: Oakland Tribune *CORP AFFIL* dir: Assoc Press *NONPR AFFIL* adv bd: Stanford Univ Grad Sch Bus; dir: Bay Area Counc, Marcus Foster Ed Inst Ctr Law & Politics, Mills Coll, Newspaper Advertising Bur; mem: Am Newspaper Publs Assn, Coll Preparatory Sch Bd, Counc Foreign Rels, Pulitzer Prize Bd, Sigma Delta Chi, Urban Strategies Counc, US Supreme Court Historical Soc; mem natl bd govs: Media Soc Seminars; mem western region adv bd: Am Press Inst; trust: Fdn Am Communs, Pacific Sch Religion *PHIL AFFIL* trust: Foundation Am Communications

Joyce L. Moock: assoc vp

Lynda Mullen: secy

Pasquale Pesce: dir (Bellagio Study & Conf Ctr)

Kenneth Prewitt: sr vp *B* Alton IL 1936 *ED* Southern Methodist Univ BA 1958; Washington Univ MA 1959; Stanford Univ PhD 1963 *NONPR AFFIL* chmn gov bd: Intl Ctr Insect Physiology Ecology; dir: Ctr Advanced Study Behavioral Sciences, Intl Res Exchanges Bd, Washington Univ; fellow: Am Academy Arts Sciences, Am Assn Advancement Science; mem: Am

Political Science Assn, Counc Foreign Rels
Hugh B. Price: vp
Steven W. Sinding: dir (population sciences)
Alvaro Umana: trust *CURR EMPL* pres: Centro de Investigaciones Sociales Ambientales y Tecnologicas
David A. White: treas
Harry Woolf: trust *B* New York NY 1923 *ED* Univ Chicago BS 1948; Univ Chicago MA 1949; Cornell Univ PhD 1955 *CORP AFFIL* dir: Alex Brown Mutual Funds; mem bd dirs: Westmark Intl; trust, scientific adv: Cluster C Funds Merrill Lynch *NONPR AFFIL* adv counc dept comparative literature: Princeton Univ; fellow: Academy Intl d'Histoire des Sciences, Am Assn Advancement Science; mem: Am Academy Arts Sciences, Am Philosophical Soc, Counc Foreign Rels, History Science Soc, Intl Res Exchanges Bd, Phi Alpha Theta, Phi Beta Kappa, Sigma Xi; mem adv counc: John F Kennedy Inst Handicapped Children; mem adv panel: WGBH NOVA; mem bd govs: Tel-Aviv Univ; mem editorial bd: Interdisciplinary Science Reviews; research prof: Inst Advanced Study Princeton Univ; chmn, trust-at-large: Univs Res Assn; mem adv counc: Natl Science Fdn *PHIL AFFIL* mem bd dirs: Alex Brown Mutual Funds

APPLICATION INFORMATION
Initial Approach:
Grant requests and fellowship applications should be addressed to the director of the relevant program or to the foundation's secretary. To apply for a Bellagio residency or to use the conference facilities, write to the Bellagio Center Office, c/o Rockefeller Foundation, 1133 Avenue of the Americas, New York, NY 10036.
No special form is required for grant applications. They should, however, include a description of the proposed project or fellowship activity with clearly stated plans and objectives; comprehensive plan for total funding of the project during and after the proposed grant period; listing of the applicant's qualifications and accomplishments; and, if applicable, a description of the institutional setting.

There are no stated deadlines for submitting applications. The board of trustees, which meets in April, June, September, and December, sets program guidelines and financial policy and approves all appropriations. Proposals are evaluated on the following criteria: relevance of project to the foundation's programs; potential for contributing significantly to the well-being of mankind; extent of the applicant's efforts to secure funding from other sources; and the applicant's record of achievement.
Restrictions on Giving: The foundation does not give or lend money for personal aid to individuals; appraise or subsidize cures or inventions; contribute to the establishment of local hospitals, churches, schools, libraries, welfare agencies, or to their building or operating funds; finance any project involving private profit; support efforts to influence legislation; or invest in securities on a philanthropic basis. The foundation normally does not make grants for general support or endowments.

OTHER THINGS TO KNOW
Publications: annual report and brochures

GRANTS ANALYSIS
Total Grants: $100,562,000
Number of Grants: 1,013
Highest Grant: $1,239,601
Typical Range: $25,000 to $300,000
Disclosure Period: 1991
Note: Recent grants are derived from a 1991 grants list.

RECENT GRANTS
1,239,601 University of California, San Francisco, San Francisco, CA — to support program on Health of the Public
700,000 International Rice Research Institute, Manila, Philippines — research
700,000 Measuring Agricultural Constraints in Eastern and Southern Africa — for agricultural production
700,000 World Health Organization, Geneva, Switzerland — to monitor health and safety

of Norplant contraceptive method
638,000 McMaster University, Hamilton, Canada — to support Clinical Epidemiology and Training Center
600,000 Pesticide Use: Environment and Health — to study effects of agricultural pesticide use in developing countries
600,000 Rockefeller University, New York, NY — research
541,000 International Council for Research in Agroforestry, Nairobi, Kenya
500,000 International Irrigation Management Institute, Colombo, Sri Lanka — for irrigation agencies in Bangladesh
500,000 Social Science Research Council, New York, NY — for interdisciplinary research on the underclass

Rockefeller Foundation, Winthrop

CONTACT
Mahlon A. Martin
President
Winthrop Rockefeller Foundation
308 East Eighth St.
Little Rock, AR 72202
(501) 376-6854
Note: Grant requests should be directed to Dianne Williams for Civic Affairs, Freeman McKindra for Economic Development, and Jacqueline Cox-New for Education. Community Incentive grant requests should be sent to Freeman McKindra, and Program-Related Investments to Mahlon A. Martin.

FINANCIAL SUMMARY
Recent Giving: $2,764,000 (1993 est.); $2,132,223 (1992); $1,949,683 (1991)
Assets: $75,000,000 (1993 est.); $74,078,190 (1991); $56,000,000 (1990); $56,889,286 (1989)
Gifts Received: $690,000 (1993 est.); $690,000 (1992 est.); $517,500 (1987); $920,000 (1986)
Fiscal Note: In 1987, the foundation received $517,500 from

a trust under the will of Winthrop Rockefeller.
EIN: 71-0285871

CONTRIBUTIONS SUMMARY
Donor(s): The Winthrop Rockefeller Foundation is successor to the Rockwin Fund, which was established by Winthrop Rockefeller to support his charitable interests during his lifetime. Upon his death in 1973, Mr. Rockefeller bequeathed money to a charitable trust to be used for innovative purposes, and a foundation was established shortly thereafter. Winthrop Rockefeller was governor of Arkansas from 1966 to 1970 and a grandson of John D. Rockefeller. He was Arkansas's first Republican governor since reconstruction, as well as a successful cattle rancher and businessman. He was dedicated to improving educational and economic opportunities in Arkansas, and to improving relations among races.
Typical Recipients: • *Civic & Public Affairs:* economic development, ethnic/minority organizations, housing, nonprofit management, public policy, rural affairs • *Education:* colleges & universities, education administration, elementary education, literacy, minority education, public education (precollege), science/technology education
Grant Types: seed money
Geographic Distribution: primarily Arkansas

GIVING OFFICERS
James D. Berstein: dir
Willard Gatewood: dir
Joe B. Hatcher: dir *B* Ft Worth TX 1936 *ED* Wichita St Univ BA 1960; Univ KS MA 1967; Univ KS PhD 1968 *CORP AFFIL* vchmn, dir: First Commercial Bank of Little Rock *NONPR AFFIL* dir: AR Commun Fund, Ar St Counc Econ Ed, Arthritis Fdn, CARTI, Faulkner County Hospice; mem: Conway Chamber Commerce, Counc Advancement Support Ed; pres: Hendrix Coll
Leslie Lilly: dir
Mahlon A. Martin: pres
Cora D. McHenry: vchmn *NONPR AFFIL* exec dir: AR Ed Assn
Olly Neal: dir
Robert D. Pugh: chmn *CURR EMPL* chmn bd: Portland Gin Co

Andree Roaf: dir
Winthrop Paul Rockefeller:
dir *B* New York NY 1948 *ED*
TX Christian Univ 1974 *CURR
EMPL* ceo: Winrock Farms
CORP AFFIL dir: Union Natl
Bank AR; owner: Allied
Marine *NONPR AFFIL* dir:
Ducks Unltd; don: Winrock
Intl Inst Agricultural Devel;
fdr, pres, chmn: Billfish Fdn
Thomas B. Shropshire: dir
CURR EMPL consultant:
Miller Brewing Co
Kathryn Waller: dir

APPLICATION INFORMATION

Initial Approach:
Requests for support may be initiated by telephone or letter,
and directed to the lead program officer of the appropriate
priority area.
Initial requests should suc-
cinctly describe the project and
how it will address a particular
problem or goal, and give the
background of the organization, a list of personnel, budget
estimate, and amount needed.
A copy of an IRS 501(c)(3) tax-
exempt determination letter
should also be included. A formal proposal, submitted at the
request of the foundation, must
be single spaced, unbound, on
one side of white 8 1/2" x 11"
paper, and submitted in triplicate. The proposal must list the
legal name of the organization,
address, telephone number, primary contact person, and current board and staff members.
A three- to four-page narrative
must include a statement of the
problem to be addressed, description of the organization activities and constituents, goals
(with working plans and time
frames), number of people to
benefit, geographical area
served, listing of similar programs or projects (with expla-
nations of differences and cooperative efforts), anticipated
results, methods of evaluation,
and plans for continuation of
project after grant period. An
itemized budget for the project
and the organization must include amount requested for the
first year and subsequent years;
amount of funding to be obtained from other sources; and
differentiation between cash-
match and in-kind contributions. Also include amount of
funding that may be leveraged;
resume of project coordinator;
signatures of chief executive

and chairman of the board; and
an audited financial statement
(if available). Additional information may be requested. The
following information should
be included if applicable to the
project: an analysis of past or
ongoing projects that fulfill a
similar need; a clear explanation of the steps to be used to
determine the effectiveness of
the project, how it will serve as
a model for other projects, and
how the knowledge gained
from the project will be distributed so it can be used by other
groups; information about projects the organization has received grants for in the past;
and information on applications for the project the organization has made to other funding sources.
Inquiries and applications are
accepted throughout the year.
Formal proposals for a major
grant should be submitted at
least three months before the
next scheduled board meeting.
The foundation program staff
will apprise grant seekers of appropriate deadlines. Re-application deadlines for multiple-
year grants are established by
the appropriate program officer.
Program officers evaluate initial inquiries to determine
whether or not a full proposal
will be warranted. The solicitation of a formal proposal does
not guarantee a grant. The
board of directors meets in
June and December to consider
proposals for new grant projects. Preference is given to
proposals potentially serving
as a model, exhibiting a track
record of accomplishments and
effective management, present-
ing a realistic workplan and
budget, showing efforts to obtain funding from other
sources, and cooperating with
other organizations working in
the same field.
Restrictions on Giving: The
foundation generally does not
fund capital expenditures, endowments, scholarships, fellowships, annual or general fund
drives, projects with an impact
outside of Arkansas, most
types of research, travel, individuals, projects completed
prior to application, project deficits, or normal operating
costs.

OTHER THINGS TO KNOW

Grantee must use funds in accordance with proposal. The
foundation may withold payments if it is not satisfied with
a grantee's performance.
The foundation, in cooperation
with the Shorebank Corporation of Chicago, has invested
several million dollars in the
Southern Development Bancorporation to provide financial
and technical assistance
through affiliated ventures addressing rural economic development.
Publications: annual report

GRANTS ANALYSIS

Total Grants: $1,949,683
Number of Grants: 191
Highest Grant: $100,000
Typical Range: $500 to
$2,000 and $10,000 to $50,000
Disclosure Period: 1991
Note: Recent grants are de-
rived from a 1991 grants list.

RECENT GRANTS

100,000 University of Ar-
kansas Foundation,
Fayettsville, AR —
a leadership and or-
ganizational devel-
opment training
program
72,334 Philander Smith
College, Little
Rock, AR — year-
round evening pro-
gram to allow
working students
time to complete
their college de-
gree requirements
70,000 Arkansas Educa-
tion Renewal Con-
sortium, Conway,
AR — to help se-
lected Arkansas
schools address the
needs of children
in middle-grade
schools
60,000 Teach For America
— support out-
standing college
graduates to serve
as Teacher Corps
members in Arkan-
sas
51,140 Nonprofit Re-
sources, Little
Rock, AR — to in-
crease knowledge
in grassroots fund
raising
50,000 Searcy County Air-
port Commission,
Searcy, AR — sup-
port a grassroots at-
tempt to design a
local economy by

building on exist-
ing resources
49,830 Arkansas Coalition
Against Violence
to Women and Chil-
dren — for the Coa-
lition to become
self-sustaining and
organizationlly
sound
49,550 University of Ar-
kansas at Little
Rock/School of
Law, Little Rock,
AR — fellowships
for Black law
scholars
48,500 Delta Community
Development Cor-
poration, Brinkley,
AR — to address
causes and condi-
tions of economic
depression and
under- and unem-
ployment in east-
ern Arkansas
47,821 Arkansas Advo-
cates for Children
and Families, Lit-
tle Rock, AR — en-
hance organiza-
tional strength and
decrease depend-
ency on foundation
grants

Rockefeller Fund, David

CONTACT
Marnie Pillsbury
Executive Director
David Rockefeller Fund
1290 Avenue of the Americas -
Room 3450
New York, NY 10104
(212) 649-5600

FINANCIAL SUMMARY
Recent Giving: $136,625
(1990); $0 (1989)
Assets: $2,650,189 (1990);
$3,001,689 (1989)
Gifts Received: $3,000,000
(1989)
EIN: 13-3533359

CONTRIBUTIONS SUMMARY
Donor(s): the donor is David
Rockefeller, Jr., the foundation's president
Geographic Distribution: initially limited to the Seal Harbor, ME, and Pocantico, NY,
communities

GIVING OFFICERS
Colin G. Cambell, Jr.: dir
Christopher J. Kennan, Jr.:
dir
Marnie Pillsbury, Jr.: exec dir

Abby Rockefeller, Jr.: dir
David Rockefeller, Jr.: don, pres, dir
Richard E. Salomon, Jr.: secy

APPLICATION INFORMATION

Initial Approach: The fund reports that in its first few years of operation, it expects to limit its grant-making program to tax-exempt organizations which are located in the Seal Harbor, ME, and Pocantico, NY, communities. There are no deadlines for applications for funds, and no particular application form is used.

GRANTS ANALYSIS

Total Grants: $136,625
Number of Grants: 48
Highest Grant: $25,000
Disclosure Period: 1990

Rockefeller Trust, Winthrop

CONTACT

Marion Burton
Winthrop Rockefeller Trust
2230 Cottondale Ln., Ste. 6
Little Rock, AR 72202
(501) 661-9294

FINANCIAL SUMMARY

Recent Giving: $7,061,952 (fiscal 1991); $4,427,515 (fiscal 1989); $3,044,494 (fiscal 1988)
Assets: $76,506,068 (fiscal year ending June 30, 1991); $86,438,344 (fiscal 1989); $41,227,377 (fiscal 1988)
EIN: 71-6082655

CONTRIBUTIONS SUMMARY

Donor(s): The foundation was established in 1973 by the late Winthrop Rockefeller.
Typical Recipients: • *Arts & Humanities:* history/historic preservation • *Civic & Public Affairs:* economic development, economics, international affairs, philanthropic organizations • *Education:* agricultural education, colleges & universities • *International:* international development/relief • *Science:* scientific organizations
Grant Types: conference/seminar, matching, project, and seed money
Geographic Distribution: focus on Arkansas

GIVING OFFICERS

Marion Burton: trust
J. Richardson Dilworth: trust
Donal C. O'Brien, Jr.: trust
Winthrop Paul Rockefeller: trust *B* New York NY 1948 *ED* TX Christian Univ 1974 *CURR EMPL* ceo: Winrock Farms *CORP AFFIL* dir: Union Natl Bank AR; owner: Allied Marine *NONPR AFFIL* dir: Ducks Unltd; don: Winrock Intl Inst Agricultural Devel; fdr, pres, chmn: Billfish Fdn
Robert Schults: trust

APPLICATION INFORMATION

Initial Approach:
The foundation requests applications be made in writing. Applications should include full information about the organization's tax-exempt status and financial history.
The foundation has no deadline for submitting proposals.
Restrictions on Giving: The foundation does not make grants to individuals.

GRANTS ANALYSIS

Total Grants: $7,061,952
Number of Grants: 8
Highest Grant: $3,702,952
Typical Range: $50,000 to $500,000
Disclosure Period: fiscal year ending June 30, 1991
Note: Average grant figure does not include the highest grant of $3,702,952. Recent grants are derived from a fiscal 1991 grants list.

RECENT GRANTS

3,702,952 Winrock International Institute for Agricultural Development, Morrilton, AR
1,050,000 Texas Christian University Ranch Management, Fort Worth, TX
1,000,000 Colonial Williamsburg Foundation, Williamsburg, VA
690,000 Winthrop Rockefeller Foundation, Little Rock, AR
500,000 Hendrix College, Conway, AR
54,000 Arkansas Aviation Historical Society, Little Rock, AR
50,000 Worldwatch Institute, Washington, DC
15,000 University of Arkansas Foundation, Little Rock, AR

Rockfall Foundation

CONTACT

Virginia R. Rollefson
Executive Director
Rockfall Fdn.
27 Washington St.
Middletown, CT 06457
(203) 347-0340

FINANCIAL SUMMARY

Recent Giving: $11,078 (fiscal 1991); $11,400 (fiscal 1990); $86,459 (fiscal 1989)
Assets: $1,893,640 (fiscal year ending June 30, 1991); $1,864,555 (fiscal 1990); $1,747,360 (fiscal 1989)
Gifts Received: $19,623 (fiscal 1991); $4,093 (fiscal 1990)
EIN: 06-6000700

CONTRIBUTIONS SUMMARY

Typical Recipients: • *Arts & Humanities:* history/historic preservation • *Civic & Public Affairs:* environmental affairs, zoos/botanical gardens • *Education:* colleges & universities, public education (precollege)
Grant Types: general support and project
Geographic Distribution: limited to Middlesex County, CT

GIVING OFFICERS

Joan D. Mazzotta: dir, vp
John F. Reynolds III: dir, pres
Bruce H. Watrous: treas
Arthur E. Webster, Jr.: dir, secy

APPLICATION INFORMATION

Initial Approach: Application form required. Deadline is March 15.

OTHER THINGS TO KNOW

Publications: Annual Report, Application Guidelines

GRANTS ANALYSIS

Number of Grants: 6
Highest Grant: $6,078
Typical Range: $800 to $1,000
Disclosure Period: fiscal year ending June 30, 1991

RECENT GRANTS

6,078 Annual Symposium
1,000 Allyn Brook Park
1,000 University of Connecticut Extension Center Haddam, Storrs, CT
800 Haddam Kennyworth Middle Schools

Rockford Acromatics Products Co./Aircraft Gear Corp. / DAO Foundation

Sales: $53.0 million
Employees: 460
Headquarters: Rockford, IL
SIC Major Group: Industrial Machinery & Equipment and Transportation Equipment

CONTACT

Nobel Olson
Trustee
DAO Foundation
611 Beacon St.
Rockford, IL 61111
(708) 594-2100

FINANCIAL SUMMARY

Recent Giving: $60,520 (fiscal 1991); $60,239 (fiscal 1990); $57,700 (fiscal 1989)
Assets: $1,729,004 (fiscal year ending March 31, 1991); $1,649,702 (fiscal 1990); $1,528,139 (fiscal 1989)
EIN: 36-6101712

CONTRIBUTIONS SUMMARY

Typical Recipients: • *Civic & Public Affairs:* women's affairs • *Education:* colleges & universities, private education (precollege) • *Health:* health organizations, medical rehabilitation • *Social Services:* family services, youth organizations
Grant Types: general support
Geographic Distribution: primarily Rockford, IL
Operating Locations: IL (Rockford)

CORP. OFFICERS

Dean A. Olson II: *CURR EMPL* chmn: Rockford Acromatics Products Co/Aircraft Gear Corp

GIVING OFFICERS

Amy Olson: trust
Nancy N. Olson: trust
Nobel Olson: trust
Pat Olson: trust

APPLICATION INFORMATION

Initial Approach: Send letter containing brief description of need and intended use.

GRANTS ANALYSIS

Number of Grants: 32
Highest Grant: $10,200
Typical Range: $100 to $3,100

Disclosure Period: fiscal year ending March 31, 1991

RECENT GRANTS

10,200 North Central College, Naperville, IL

9,350 Keith Country Day School, Rockford, IL

6,425 Rockford Women's Club, Rockford, IL

5,300 Rock Valley College Foundation, Rockford, IL

5,000 University of Illinois College of Engineering, Champaign, IL

3,150 North Rockford Convalescent Home, Rockford, IL

3,000 Family Advocate, Rockford, IL

3,000 Northern Illinois Blood Bank, Rockford, IL

3,000 University of Illinois Foundation, Champaign, IL

2,500 New American Theatre, Rockford, IL

Rockford Products Corp. / Rockford Products Corp. Foundation

Sales: $90.0 million
Employees: 850
Headquarters: Rockford, IL
SIC Major Group: Fabricated Metal Products and Transportation Equipment

CONTACT

Dennis J. Schaer
Secretary
Rockford Products Corp. Foundation
707 Harrison Ave.
Rockford, IL 61104
(815) 397-6000

FINANCIAL SUMMARY

Recent Giving: $89,300 (1990); $78,950 (1989)
Assets: $706,747 (1990); $795,467 (1989)
EIN: 36-3407027

CONTRIBUTIONS SUMMARY

Typical Recipients: • *Arts & Humanities:* community arts, museums/galleries, performing arts, theater • *Civic & Public Affairs:* zoos/botanical gardens • *Education:* colleges & universities, public education (precollege) • *Health:* health organizations • *Social Services:* child welfare, community service organizations, united funds, youth organizations

Grant Types: general support

Geographic Distribution: focus on IL

Operating Locations: IL (Rockford)

CORP. OFFICERS

R. Ray Wood: *B* Coffeyville KS 1942 *ED* Univ WY 1966; Northern IL Univ 1974 *CURR EMPL* chmn, pres, ceo: Rockford Products Corp

GIVING OFFICERS

William Derry: dir

Michael C. Gann: secy, treas

Richard Goff: dir

Thomas Johnson: dir

David Peterson: dir

R. Ray Wood: pres, dir *CURR EMPL* chmn, pres, ceo: Rockford Products Corp (see above)

APPLICATION INFORMATION

Initial Approach: Send brief letter describing program. There are no deadlines.

GRANTS ANALYSIS

Number of Grants: 24
Highest Grant: $40,000
Typical Range: $250 to $5,000
Disclosure Period: 1990

RECENT GRANTS

40,000 United Way, Rockford, IL

5,000 Boy Scouts of America, Rockford, IL

5,000 Rockford College, Rockford, IL

5,000 YMCA, Rockford, IL

4,000 Barbara Olson School of Hope, Rockford, IL

4,000 Riverfront Museum Park, Rockford, IL

2,000 Mill, Rockford, IL

2,000 Northern Illinois Blood Bank, Rockford, IL

2,000 Salvation Army, Rockford, IL

1,500 Salvation Army, Rockford, IL

Rockwell Foundation

CONTACT

H. Campbell Stuckeman
Secretary
Rockwell Fdn.
3818 USX Tower
600 Grant St.
Pittsburgh, PA 15219
(412) 765-3990

FINANCIAL SUMMARY

Recent Giving: $440,000 (1990); $441,000 (1989)
Assets: $9,508,811 (1990); $9,186,878 (1989)
EIN: 25-6035975

CONTRIBUTIONS SUMMARY

Donor(s): the late Willard F. Rockwell and family

Typical Recipients: • *Arts & Humanities:* arts festivals, community arts, dance, music, opera, performing arts • *Civic & Public Affairs:* environmental affairs, zoos/botanical gardens • *Education:* colleges & universities • *Health:* hospitals, medical research, single-disease health associations • *Religion:* churches, religious organizations • *Social Services:* child welfare, community service organizations, united funds, youth organizations

Grant Types: capital, endowment, general support, multiyear/continuing support, operating expenses, and scholarship

Geographic Distribution: focus on PA

GIVING OFFICERS

George Peter Rockwell: secy, trust

Russell A. Rockwell: trust

Willard Frederick Rockwell, Jr.: trust *B* Boston MA 1914 *ED* PA St Univ BS 1935; PA St Univ IE 1955; Grove City Coll LLD *CORP AFFIL* dir: Astrotech Intl Corp, Lone Star Indus *NONPR AFFIL* chmn exec comm: Tax Fdn; dir: World Affs Counc; fellow: Royal Soc Arts; mem: Am Inst Industrial Engrs, Am Ordnance Assn, Am Petroleum Inst, Am Soc Mechanical Engrs, Am Water Works Assn, Conf Bd, Greater Pittsburgh Airport Advisory Bd, PA Chamber Commerce, Smithsonian Assocs, Soc Automotive Engrs; trust: Aerospace Ed Fdn, Am Enterprise Inst, Carnegie Mus Natural History,

Grove City Coll, Univ Southern CA

Herman Campbell Stuckemann: secy, trust *ED* PA St Univ BS 1937 *CURR EMPL* chmn: Precise Corp *CORP AFFIL* chmn: Precise Corp

APPLICATION INFORMATION

Initial Approach: Send brief letter of inquiry describing program or project. There are no deadlines.

Restrictions on Giving: Does not support individuals or provide loans.

GRANTS ANALYSIS

Disclosure Period: 1991
Note: 1991 grants in form of fellowships.

RECENT GRANTS

25,000 Riverview Children's Center, Oakmont, PA

25,000 St. Thomas Episcopal Church, Miami, FL

24,000 Pennsylvania State University, University Park, PA

20,000 Point Park College, Pittsburgh, PA

15,000 Regent University, Virginia Beach, VA

12,000 Civic Light Opera, Pittsburgh, PA

10,000 21st Century Space Foundation, Washington, DC

10,000 Forbes Health Foundation, Pittsburgh, PA

10,000 Pittsburgh Center for the Arts, Pittsburgh, PA

10,000 Sweetwater Art Center, Sewickley, PA

Rockwell Fund

CONTACT

Joe M. Green, Jr.
President
Rockwell Fund
910 Travis, Ste. 2310
Houston, TX 77002
(713) 659-7204

FINANCIAL SUMMARY

Recent Giving: $2,600,000 (1992 approx.); $2,672,650 (1991); $2,337,650 (1990)
Assets: $62,817,033 (1991); $55,725,822 (1990); $56,670,866 (1989)
EIN: 74-6040258

CONTRIBUTIONS SUMMARY

Donor(s): The fund was established in 1931, with members of the James M. Rockwell family, Rockwell Brothers & Company, and Rockwell Lumber Company as donors.

Typical Recipients: • *Arts & Humanities:* arts associations, dance, history/historic preservation, libraries, museums/galleries, music, opera, performing arts, public broadcasting, theater • *Civic & Public Affairs:* environmental affairs, zoos/botanical gardens • *Education:* colleges & universities, elementary education, legal education, liberal arts education, literacy, private education (precollege), religious education, special education, student aid • *Health:* health organizations, hospices, hospitals, medical rehabilitation, medical research, mental health, nursing services, single-disease health associations • *Religion:* churches, religious organizations • *Science:* science exhibits & fairs • *Social Services:* aged, animal protection, child welfare, community centers, community service organizations, counseling, delinquency & crime, disabled, drugs & alcohol, emergency relief, employment/job training, family planning, family services, food/clothing distribution, homes, shelters/homelessness, united funds, volunteer services, youth organizations

Grant Types: capital, operating expenses, project, research, and scholarship

Geographic Distribution: Texas, primarily the Houston area; limited giving out of Houston area

GIVING OFFICERS

R. Terry Bell: vp, trust
Joe M. Green, Jr.: pres, fdn mgr
Helen N. Sterling: secy, treas, trust

APPLICATION INFORMATION

Initial Approach:
Applicants should contact the foundation to request a copy of its application data sheet and guidelines.
Applications should include the name, address, and telephone number of the organization; name of contact person; number of years organization

has been in continuous operation; brief statement regarding the project; current operating budget; audited financial statement for previous year which includes fund-raising expenses and sources of income; list of board members; amount requested; whether grant will be used exclusively for public purposes; and a copy of the organization's IRS determination letter of tax-exempt status.
One month prior to each quarterly trustee meeting.

OTHER THINGS TO KNOW

Publications: application data sheet, guidelines

GRANTS ANALYSIS

Total Grants: $2,672,650
Number of Grants: 166
Highest Grant: $70,000
Typical Range: $10,000 to $30,000
Disclosure Period: 1991
Note: Recent grants are derived from a 1991 Form 990.

RECENT GRANTS

70,000 St. Agnes Academy, Houston, TX — academic scholarships
50,000 Houston-Galveston Area Food Bank, Houston, TX — construction and renovation of existing facility
50,000 New Mexico Military Institute, Roswell, NM — scholarships and centennial projects
50,000 South Texas College of Law, Houston, TX — furnishing two new conference rooms
50,000 Stella Link Redevelopment Association, Houston, TX — land acquisition and develop deteriorated neighborhood
50,000 Texas Tech University Foundation, Lubbock, TX — funding of two professorships
50,000 United Way of the Texas Gulf Coast, Houston, TX — 1991 annual campaign
40,000 Houston School for Deaf Children, Houston, TX — faculty development/psychologist

and research consultants
35,000 Hermann Eye Fund, Houston, TX — pediatric ophthalmology professorship
35,000 Rice University, Houston, TX — model science lab; faculty support; lecture series

Rockwell International Corp. / Rockwell International Corp. Trust

Sales: $10.99 billion
Employees: 79,000
Headquarters: Seal Beach, CA
SIC Major Group: Electronic & Other Electrical Equipment, Fabricated Metal Products, Industrial Machinery & Equipment, and Rubber & Miscellaneous Plastics Products

CONTACT

William R. Fitz
Rockwell International Corp. Trust
625 Liberty Ave.
Pittsburgh, PA 15222-3123
(412) 565-5803

FINANCIAL SUMMARY

Recent Giving: $11,100,000 (fiscal 1993 est.); $11,400,000 (fiscal 1992); $12,800,000 (fiscal 1991)
Assets: $13,000,000 (fiscal year ending September 30, 1992 est.); $14,016,702 (fiscal 1991); $25,652,896 (fiscal 1989)
Fiscal Note: Above figures include giving by Rockwell International Corporation Trust, Rockwell International Canadian Trust, Rockwell International Corporation United Kingdom Trust, and direct giving by Rockwell International Corporation and its wholly owned subsidiaries. In 1992, direct giving totaled $1.4 million.
EIN: 25-1072431

CONTRIBUTIONS SUMMARY

Typical Recipients: • *Arts & Humanities:* arts associations, arts centers, arts festivals, arts funds, arts institutes, community arts, dance, history/historic preservation, libraries, museums/galleries, music, opera, performing arts, public

broadcasting, theater • *Civic & Public Affairs:* business/free enterprise, civil rights, economic development, economics, environmental affairs, housing, international affairs, law & justice, national security, nonprofit management, professional & trade associations, public policy, safety, urban & community affairs, women's affairs, zoos/botanical gardens • *Education:* business education, career/vocational education, colleges & universities, community & junior colleges, continuing education, economic education, education associations, education funds, engineering education, faculty development, literacy, minority education, science/technology education, special education, student aid • *Health:* health care cost containment, health organizations, hospices, hospitals, medical rehabilitation, mental health, outpatient health care delivery, pediatric health, single-disease health associations • *Science:* science exhibits & fairs, scientific institutes, scientific organizations • *Social Services:* child welfare, community service organizations, counseling, delinquency & crime, disabled, domestic violence, drugs & alcohol, emergency relief, employment/job training, family services, legal aid, recreation & athletics, shelters/homelessness, united funds, volunteer services, youth organizations

Grant Types: capital, employee matching gifts, general support, project, and scholarship
Note: Company matches employee gifts on a one-to-one basis to colleges and accredited public and private elementary and high schools. Company will match a maximum of $10,000 per employee per year.
Nonmonetary Support Types: donated equipment
Note: No estimate is available for value of nonmonetary support, and it is not included in above figures. William R. Fitz handles nonmonetary support requests, but decisions are made at local facilities.
Geographic Distribution: primarily where company maintains facilities; nationally to education
Operating Locations: CA (Anaheim, Canoga Park, Downey, El Segundo, Los An-

geles, Santa Barbara, Seal Beach), IL (Chicago, Downers Grove), MA (Waltham), MI (Troy), OH (Highland Heights), PA (Pittsburgh), TX (Richardson), WI (Milwaukee), PR

CORP. OFFICERS

W. Michael Barnes: *CURR EMPL* vp, cfo: Rockwell Intl Corp

Donald Ray Beall: *B* Beaumont CA 1938 *ED* San Jose St Coll BS 1960; Univ Pittsburgh MBA 1961 *CURR EMPL* chmn, ceo, dir: Rockwell Intl Corp *CORP AFFIL* dir: Amoco Corp, Baker Intl Corp, First Intl Bancshares, Interfirst Corp, Times Mirror Co *NONPR AFFIL* bd overseers: Univ CA Irvine; campaign chmn (West PA): Am Diabetes Assn; dir: Dallas Counc World Affs, Un Way Allegheny County; fellow: Am Inst Aeronautics & Astronautics; mem: Armed Forces Communs Electronics Assn, Beta Gamma Sigma, Bus Counc, Bus Higher Ed Forum, Bus Roundtable, Dallas Citizens Counc, Defense Adv Comm Trade, Defense Preparedness Assn, Electronic Indus Assn, Navy League, Pres Export Counc, Sigma Alpha Epsilon, Soc Automotive Engrs, Soc Mfg Engrs, Young Pres Org; trust: Univ Pittsburgh

Kent March Black: *B* Carrollton IL 1939 *ED* Univ IL 1962 *CURR EMPL* exec vp, coo: Rockwell Intl Corp *CORP AFFIL* adv comm: Natl Security Telecommunications *NONPR AFFIL* dir: Assn Higher Ed N TX, Dallas Co Commun Coll District Fdn; mem: Aerospace Indus Assn, Natl Mgmt Assn, Naval Aviation Indus Counc; mem adv bd: Univ IL Coll Engg; mem devel bd: Univ TX Dallas; mem exec bd: Circle Ten Counc Boy Scouts Am

S. Iacobellis: *B* Fresno CA 1929 *ED* CA St Univ Fresno BSME 1952; Univ CA Los Angeles MS 1963 *CURR EMPL* exec vp, coo: Rockwell Intl Corp *NONPR AFFIL* fellow: Am Inst Aeronautics & Astronautics; mem: Soc Mfg Engrs

GIVING OFFICERS

W. Michael Barnes: mem (trust comm) *CURR EMPL* vp, cfo: Rockwell Intl Corp (see above)

Donald Ray Beall: mem (trust comm) *CURR EMPL* chmn, ceo, dir: Rockwell Intl Corp (see above)

Robert Louis Cattoi: mem (trust comm) *B* Hurley WI 1926 *ED* Univ WI BEE 1950 *CURR EMPL* sr vp (research & engring): Rockwell Intl Corp *CORP AFFIL* dir: Microelectronics & Computer Tech Corp, Software Productivity Consortium *NONPR AFFIL* mem: Eta Kappa Nu, Inst Electrical Electronics Engrs, NSPE, Phi Eta Sigma, Phi Kappa Phi, Soc Automotive Engrs, Tau Beta Pi; mem aerospace tech counc: Am Inst Architects; mem engg bd councs: Univ Southern CA

Lee H. Cramer: asst secy, mem (trust comm) *B* Pittsburgh PA 1945 *ED* PA St Univ BS 1967; Southern Methodist Univ MBA 1968 *CURR EMPL* vp, treas: Rockwell Intl Corp *CORP AFFIL* dir: First South Savings Assn

Richard S. Mau: mem (trust comm) *CURR EMPL* vp (communications): Rockwell Intl Corp

APPLICATION INFORMATION

Initial Approach: *Initial Contact:* brief letter or proposal *Include Information On:* description of the organization, amount requested, purpose for which funds are sought, recently audited financial statement, proof of tax-exempt status, list of other funding sources *When to Submit:* any time

Restrictions on Giving: Does not support individuals, fraternal organizations, political or lobbying groups, goodwill advertising, or religious organizations for sectarian purposes.

GRANTS ANALYSIS

Total Grants: $11,400,000
Number of Grants: 1,200*
Highest Grant: $500,000
Typical Range: $5,000 to $10,000
Disclosure Period: fiscal year ending September 30, 1992
Note: Number of grants excludes matching gifts. Recent grants are derived from a fiscal 1992 grants list.

RECENT GRANTS

1,900,000 United Way
400,000 Society of Automotive Engineers' VISION 200 Program, Alexandria, VA
100,000 American National Red Cross — to aid the victims of Hurricanes Andrew and Iniki
100,000 American National Red Cross — to aid the victims of Hurricanes Andrew and Iniki

---

Rodale Press

Sales: $180.0 million
Employees: 1,080
Headquarters: Emmaus, PA
SIC Major Group: Printing & Publishing

CONTACT

Jackie Hurley
Manager, Corporate Communications
Rodale Press
33 East Minor St.
Emmaus, PA 18098
(215) 967-5171

CORP. OFFICERS

Robert H. Rodale: *B* NY 1930 *ED* Lehigh Univ 1952 *CURR EMPL* chmn, dir: Rodale Press
Robert Teufel: *CURR EMPL* pres, dir: Rodale Press

RECENT GRANTS

1,000,000 Lehigh University, Bethlehem, PA — to establish and endow Robert D. Rodale Faculty Chair in Writing

---

Roddenbery Co., Inc., W.B. / Roddenbery Foundation

Sales: $50.0 million
Employees: 400
Headquarters: Cairo, GA
SIC Major Group: Food & Kindred Products

CONTACT

Juliam B. Roddenbery, Jr.
Secretary
Roddenbery Foundation
First Ave. Northeast, PO Box 60
Cairo, GA 31728-0060
(912) 377-2102

FINANCIAL SUMMARY

Recent Giving: $2,590 (1989)
Assets: $1,929 (1989)
EIN: 58-0905872

CONTRIBUTIONS SUMMARY

Typical Recipients: • *Civic & Public Affairs:* environmental affairs • *Education:* colleges & universities • *Religion:* churches
Grant Types: general support
Geographic Distribution: focus on GA
Operating Locations: GA (Cairo)

CORP. OFFICERS

Julian B. Roddenbery, Jr.: *CURR EMPL* ceo, pres: WB Roddenbery Co

GIVING OFFICERS

Julian B. Roddenbery, Jr.: secy, treas, dir *CURR EMPL* ceo, pres: WB Roddenbery Co (see above)
Julian B. Roddenbery, Sr.: chmn, dir
Ralph J. Roddenbery: vchmn, dir *B* Cairo GA 1925 *ED* Univ NC 1945-1947

APPLICATION INFORMATION

Initial Approach: Send brief letter describing program. There are no deadlines.

GRANTS ANALYSIS

Number of Grants: 3
Highest Grant: $1,690
Typical Range: $100 to $1,690
Disclosure Period: 1989

RECENT GRANTS

1,690 First Baptist Church, Cairo, GA
800 Mercer University, Macon, GA
100 Birdsong Nature Center, Thomasville, GA

Roddis Foundation, Hamilton

CONTACT

Augusta D. Roddis
Secretary, Treasurer
Hamilton Roddis Fdn.
1108 East Fourth St.
Marshfield, WI 54449

FINANCIAL SUMMARY

Recent Giving: $148,350 (1989); $143,100 (1987)
Assets: $3,631,639 (1989); $3,087,094 (1987)
EIN: 39-6077001

CONTRIBUTIONS SUMMARY

Donor(s): the late Hamilton Roddis, Augusta D. Roddis,

Catherine P. Roddis, Roddis Plywood Corp.
Typical Recipients: • *Arts & Humanities:* history/historic preservation, museums/galleries • *Civic & Public Affairs:* civil rights • *Education:* medical education • *Health:* medical research • *Religion:* churches, missionary activities, religious organizations • *Social Services:* child welfare, disabled, united funds, youth organizations
Grant Types: general support

GIVING OFFICERS
Mrs. Gordon R. Connor: vp, dir
Augusta D. Roddis: secy, treas, dir
William H. Roddis II: pres, dir

APPLICATION INFORMATION
Initial Approach: Contributes only to preselected organizations.
Restrictions on Giving: Does not support individuals.

GRANTS ANALYSIS
Number of Grants: 46
Highest Grant: $18,000
Typical Range: $500 to $2,500
Disclosure Period: 1990

RECENT GRANTS
18,000 Camp Five Museum Foundation, Laona, WI
13,750 St. Albans Episcopal Church, Marshfield, WI
12,000 Ball Pavillion, Gibsonia, PA
12,000 University of Wisconsin Foundation, Madison, WI
11,000 Mayo Foundation, Rochester, MN
10,000 Heritage Foundation, Washington, DC
10,000 Johns Hopkins University, Baltimore, MD
5,500 Living Church Foundation, Boston, MA
5,000 Wisconsin Historical Foundation, Madison, WI
4,000 Suomi College, Hancock, MI

Rodgers Foundation, Richard & Dorothy

CONTACT
Dorothy F. Rodgers
President, Treasurer
Richard & Dorothy Rodgers Fdn.
1633 Broadway, Ste. 3801
New York, NY 10022

FINANCIAL SUMMARY
Recent Giving: $575,645 (1991); $375,125 (1990); $485,065 (1989)
Assets: $2,603,514 (1991); $2,480,190 (1990); $2,330,847 (1989)
Gifts Received: $326,760 (1991); $508,205 (1990); $583,911 (1989)
Fiscal Note: In 1991, contributions were received from Dorothy F. Rodgers.
EIN: 13-6062852

CONTRIBUTIONS SUMMARY
Donor(s): the late Richard Rodgers, Dorothy F. Rodgers
Typical Recipients: • *Arts & Humanities:* arts centers, libraries, museums/galleries, music, performing arts, public broadcasting, theater • *Civic & Public Affairs:* ethnic/minority organizations • *Education:* colleges & universities, medical education • *Health:* health organizations, hospitals, medical research, pediatric health • *Religion:* religious organizations • *Social Services:* community service organizations, disabled, youth organizations
Grant Types: general support
Geographic Distribution: focus on New York, NY

GIVING OFFICERS
Lawrence C. Butterwieser: secy
Dorothy F. Rodgers: pres, treas

APPLICATION INFORMATION
Initial Approach: Contributes only to preselected organizations.
Restrictions on Giving: Does not support individuals.

GRANTS ANALYSIS
Number of Grants: 109
Highest Grant: $75,000
Typical Range: $75 to $5,000
Disclosure Period: 1991

RECENT GRANTS
75,000 United Jewish Appeal Federation of Jewish Philanthropies, New York, NY
60,000 Jewish Museum, New York, NY
35,000 Lenox Hill Hospital, New York, NY
35,000 New York Hospital Department of Social Work, New York, NY
25,000 Lincoln Center Theater, New York, NY
25,000 New York Public Library, New York, NY
25,000 University of Louisville, Louisville, KY
25,000 YMCA, New York, NY
20,000 Julliard School, New York, NY
18,000 Channel Thirteen, New York, NY

Rodgers Trust, Elizabeth Killam

CONTACT
Nathan Newbury III
Trustee
Elizabeth Killam Rodgers Trust
One International Pl.
Boston, MA 02110
(617) 439-2000

FINANCIAL SUMMARY
Recent Giving: $205,000 (fiscal 1992); $235,000 (fiscal 1991); $263,810 (fiscal 1990)
Assets: $5,279,210 (fiscal year ending April 30, 1992); $4,921,264 (fiscal 1991); $4,382,664 (fiscal 1990)
EIN: 04-6385523

CONTRIBUTIONS SUMMARY
Donor(s): the late Elizabeth Killam Rodgers
Typical Recipients: • *Arts & Humanities:* museums/galleries • *Civic & Public Affairs:* environmental affairs • *Education:* colleges & universities, education funds, science/technology education • *Health:* health funds
Grant Types: general support
Geographic Distribution: focus on MA

GIVING OFFICERS
Nathan Newbury III: trust
John Breed Newhall: trust *B* Salem MA 1932 *ED* Harvard Univ 1954; Harvard Univ 1959 *CURR EMPL* chmn: Gurney (DB) Co *CORP AFFIL* chmn: Gurney (DB) Co *NONPR AFFIL* mem: Am Bar Assn

APPLICATION INFORMATION
Initial Approach: Send brief letter of inquiry or full propsosal. There are no deadlines.

GRANTS ANALYSIS
Number of Grants: 4
Highest Grant: $100,000
Typical Range: $5,000 to $50,000
Disclosure Period: fiscal year ending April 30, 1992

RECENT GRANTS
100,000 Peabody Museum of Salem, Salem, MA
50,000 Massachusetts Institute of Technology, Cambridge, MA
50,000 South Shore Health and Education Foundation, Portland, ME
5,000 Appalachian Mountain Club, Boston, MA

Rodman Foundation

CONTACT
E. Redman Titcomb, Jr.
President
Rodman Fdn.
2100 First National Bank Bldg.
St. Paul, MN 55101
(612) 228-0935

FINANCIAL SUMMARY
Recent Giving: $149,000 (1990); $168,875 (1989); $167,550 (1988)
Assets: $1,750,523 (1990); $1,674,281 (1989); $1,562,725 (1988)
Gifts Received: $13,150 (1990); $87,500 (1989); $87,500 (1988)
Fiscal Note: In 1990, contributions were received from the F. R. and E. W. Titcomb Trust.
EIN: 23-7025570

CONTRIBUTIONS SUMMARY
Donor(s): members of the Titcomb family
Typical Recipients: • *Arts & Humanities:* community arts, history/historic preservation, museums/galleries, music, performing arts, theater • *Education:* colleges & universities, science/technology education • *Health:* hospitals, medical research • *Religion:* religious or-

ganizations • *Science:* scientific institutes, scientific organizations • *Social Services:* united funds, youth organizations

Grant Types: capital, operating expenses, and scholarship

Geographic Distribution: focus on MN

GIVING OFFICERS

Joseph S. Micallef: secy

Bruce L. Titcomb: dir

Daniel C. Titcomb: dir

E. Rodman Titcomb, Jr.: dir, pres

Edward Rodman Titcomb: dir *B* Tacoma WA 1919 *ED* Yale Univ; Univ WA *CORP AFFIL* dir: Boise Cascade Corp

Frederic W. Titcomb: dir

Julie C. Titcomb: vp, dir *B* Spokane WA 1923 *ED* Stanford Univ

APPLICATION INFORMATION

Initial Approach: Send brief letter describing program. There are no deadlines.

GRANTS ANALYSIS

Number of Grants: 31

Highest Grant: $50,000

Typical Range: $250 to $5,000

Disclosure Period: 1990

RECENT GRANTS

50,000 Hamline University, St. Paul, MN

25,000 Science Museum of Minnesota, St. Paul, MN

16,750 United Hospital Foundation, St. Paul, MN — United Nineties Campaign

10,000 University of Puget Sound, Tacoma, WA

6,600 United Way, St. Paul, MN

5,000 Freshwater Biological Research Foundation, Navarre, MN

5,000 Merriam Park Community Center, St. Paul, MN

5,000 Seattle Art Museum, Seattle, WA — Weyerhaeuser Gallery

4,500 YMCA, St. Paul, MN

2,100 Union Gospel Mission Association, St. Paul, MN

Roe Foundation

CONTACT

Thomas A. Roe
Chairman
Roe Fdn.
712 Crescent Ave.
Greenville, SC 29601
(803) 235-8955

FINANCIAL SUMMARY

Recent Giving: $567,760 (1991); $557,343 (1990); $533,480 (1989)

Assets: $10,919,717 (1991); $9,465,119 (1990); $9,904,344 (1989)

EIN: 23-7011541

CONTRIBUTIONS SUMMARY

Donor(s): Thomas A. Roe

Typical Recipients: • *Civic & Public Affairs:* better government, public policy • *Education:* education associations

Grant Types: capital, emergency, general support, multiyear/continuing support, operating expenses, and seed money

GIVING OFFICERS

Edwin J. Feulner, Jr.: vchmn, trust *B* Chicago IL 1941 *ED* Regis Coll BS 1963; Univ PA Wharton Sch MBA 1964 *CORP AFFIL* vchmn: Credit Intl Bank *NONPR AFFIL* Bohemian; chmn: Citizens Am Ed Fdn, Inst European Defense Strategic Studies; distinguished fellow: Mobilization Concepts Devel Ctr; mem: Am Econ Assn, Am Political Science Assn, Inst d'Etudes Politiques, Intl Inst Strategic Studies, Mont Pelerin Soc, Philadelphia Soc, US Strategic Inst; mem bd govs, mem exec comm: Counc Natl Policy; mem natl adv bd: Ctr Ed Res Free Enterprise, TX A&M Univ; pres: Heritage Fdn; trust: Am Counc Germany, Intercollegiate Studies Inst, Lehrman Inst, Regis Univ, St James Sch; vchmn: Aequus Inst

Roger E. Meiners: trust

Shirley W. Roe: secy, trust

Thomas Anderson Roe: chmn, treas, trust *B* Greenville SC 1927 *ED* Furman Univ BS 1948; Furman Univ LLD 1980 *NONPR AFFIL* mem: Greenville Chamber Commerce, Natl Assn Home Builders, Natl Lumber Bldg Material Dealers Assn; mem exec comm, dir: Peace Ctr Performing Arts;

trust: Free Congress Fdn, Heritage Fdn

Paul M. Weyrich: trust *ED* Univ WI AA 1962

APPLICATION INFORMATION

Initial Approach: Send brief letter of inquiry and full proposal. There are no deadlines.

OTHER THINGS TO KNOW

Publications: Program policy statement

GRANTS ANALYSIS

Number of Grants: 67

Highest Grant: $75,000

Typical Range: $1,000 to $10,000

Disclosure Period: 1991

RECENT GRANTS

75,000 Intercollegiate Studies Institute, Bryn Mawr, PA

55,000 Free Congress Foundation, Washington, DC

55,000 Heritage Foundation, Washington, DC

52,500 South Carolina Policy Council, Columbia, SC

50,000 Statenet

10,000 Capital Research Center, Washington, DC

10,000 Cascade Policy Institute

10,000 Foundation Francisco Marroquin

10,000 International Policy Forum

10,000 Leadership Institute, Springfield, VA

Roehl Foundation

CONTACT

Peter Roehl
Vice President
Roehl Fdn.
PO Box 168
Oconomowoc, WI 53066-0168
(414) 569-3000

FINANCIAL SUMMARY

Recent Giving: $103,850 (fiscal 1991); $100,376 (fiscal 1989)

Assets: $2,081,995 (fiscal year ending June 30, 1991); $2,139,822 (fiscal 1989)

Gifts Received: $9,452 (fiscal 1989)

Fiscal Note: In 1989, contributions were received from the estate of F. C. Roehl.

EIN: 39-6048089

CONTRIBUTIONS SUMMARY

Donor(s): Peter G. Roehl

Typical Recipients: • *Education:* private education (precollege) • *Health:* hospitals • *Religion:* churches, religious organizations • *Social Services:* community service organizations, homes

Grant Types: general support and research

Geographic Distribution: focus on WI

GIVING OFFICERS

Nathalia E. Christian: secy

Janet L. Roehl: trust

Ora C. Roehl: pres

Peter G. Roehl: vp, treas

APPLICATION INFORMATION

Initial Approach: Send brief letter describing program. There are no deadlines.

Restrictions on Giving: Does not support individuals.

GRANTS ANALYSIS

Number of Grants: 40

Highest Grant: $10,000

Typical Range: $100 to $6,000

Disclosure Period: fiscal year ending June 30, 1991

RECENT GRANTS

10,000 Northwestern Preparatory School, Watertown, WI

6,500 St. Matthew's Evangelical Lutheran Church, Oconomowoc, WI

6,500 St. Paul's Evangelical Lutheran Church, Lake Mills, WI

6,000 University Hospital, Boston, MA

5,000 Church of Resurrection, Hartland, WI

5,000 Church of Resurrection, Hartland, WI

5,000 Martin Luther Preparatory School, Prairie du Chien, WI

5,000 University Lake School, Hartland, WI

5,000 University Lake School Special Programs, Hartland, WI

5,000 Westby Coon Prairie Lutheran Church, Westby, WI

Rogers Charitable Trust, Florence

CONTACT
Nolan P. Clark
Administrator
Florence Rogers Charitable Trust
PO Box 36006
Fayetteville, NC 28303
(919) 484-2033

FINANCIAL SUMMARY
Recent Giving: $165,021 (fiscal 1992); $141,299 (fiscal 1991); $205,878 (fiscal 1990)
Assets: $4,213,142 (fiscal year ending March 31, 1992); $4,020,153 (fiscal 1991); $3,916,209 (fiscal 1990)
EIN: 56-6074515

CONTRIBUTIONS SUMMARY
Donor(s): the late Florence L. Rogers
Typical Recipients: • *Arts & Humanities:* community arts, history/historic preservation, museums/galleries, music, theater • *Civic & Public Affairs:* environmental affairs, safety, zoos/botanical gardens • *Education:* colleges & universities, education associations, public education (precollege), religious education • *Health:* single-disease health associations • *Religion:* churches, religious organizations • *Social Services:* aged, community service organizations, disabled, recreation & athletics, united funds, youth organizations
Grant Types: challenge, emergency, general support, operating expenses, and scholarship
Geographic Distribution: focus on Fayetteville, NC

GIVING OFFICERS
Nolan P. Clark: trust
Joann Barnette Stancil: adm
John C. Tally: trust

APPLICATION INFORMATION
Initial Approach: Send brief letter of inquiry describing program or project. There are no deadlines.

OTHER THINGS TO KNOW
Publications: Informational Brochure (including application guidelines)

GRANTS ANALYSIS
Number of Grants: 85
Highest Grant: $18,000
Typical Range: $500 to $2,500
Disclosure Period: fiscal year ending March 31, 1992

RECENT GRANTS
18,000 North Carolina Museum of History, Cape Fear, NC — Museum of Cape Fear

15,000 Fayetteville State University, Fayetteville, NC

9,300 YMCA, Fayetteville, NC

8,574 Methodist College, Fayetteville, NC — microscopes and steam scrubber washer

5,600 East Carolina University, Greenville, NC

5,000 Fayetteville Technical Community College Foundation, Fayetteville, NC

3,725 Methodist College, Fayetteville, NC — purchase of human anatomy model

3,200 City of Fayetteville Police Department, Fayetteville, NC — to support judo program

3,200 Methodist College, Fayetteville, NC — equipment in communications department

3,145 Salvation Army, Fayetteville, NC

Rogers Corp.
Sales: $182.4 million
Employees: 2,989
Headquarters: Rogers, CT
SIC Major Group: Chemicals & Allied Products, Electronic & Other Electrical Equipment, and Rubber & Miscellaneous Plastics Products

CONTACT
Karen Rhoades
Secretary to Director of Human Resources
Rogers Corp.
One Technology Dr.
Rogers, CT 06263
(203) 774-9605

CONTRIBUTIONS SUMMARY
Typical Recipients: • *Civic & Public Affairs:* philanthropic organizations, women's affairs • *Education:* colleges & universities, journalism education
Operating Locations: CT (Rogers)

CORP. OFFICERS
Norman L. Greenman: *B* New York NY 1923 *ED* MA Inst Tech 1947-1948 *CURR EMPL* prees, ceo: Rogers Corp *CORP AFFIL* dir: Moldex, Southern New England Telephone Co

Rogers Family Foundation

CONTACT
Irving E. Rogers, Jr.
Trustee
Rogers Family Fdn.
PO Box 100
Lawrence, MA 01842
(508) 685-1000

FINANCIAL SUMMARY
Recent Giving: $399,200 (1991); $348,379 (1990); $304,050 (1989)
Assets: $9,970,909 (1991); $8,864,212 (1990); $8,060,499 (1989)
Gifts Received: $139,301 (1991); $401,982 (1990); $572,472 (1989)
Fiscal Note: In 1991, contributions were received from Andover Publishing Co. ($5,000), Eagle-Tribune Publishing Co. (104,549), Rogers Investment Corp. ($2,300), Eagle-Tribune Realty Trust ($15,000), Irving E. Rogers, Jr. ($7,500), and Derry Publishing Co. ($4,952).
EIN: 04-6063152

CONTRIBUTIONS SUMMARY
Donor(s): Irving E. Rogers, Eagle-Tribune Publishing Co., Martha B. Rogers
Typical Recipients: • *Arts & Humanities:* community arts, history/historic preservation, libraries, museums/galleries, music • *Education:* colleges & universities, student aid • *Health:* hospitals • *Religion:* churches • *Social Services:* community centers, day care, disabled, united funds, youth organizations
Grant Types: general support
Geographic Distribution: limited to the greater Lawrence, MA, area

GIVING OFFICERS
Irving E. Rogers, Jr.: trust *CURR EMPL* pres, publisher, treas, gen mgr: Eagle-Tribune Publishing Co
Martha B. Rogers: trust
Richard M. Wyman: trust

APPLICATION INFORMATION
Initial Approach: Contributes only to preselected organizations.
Restrictions on Giving: Does not support individuals.

GRANTS ANALYSIS
Number of Grants: 65
Highest Grant: $31,500
Typical Range: $1,000 to $5,000
Disclosure Period: 1991

RECENT GRANTS
31,500 Merrimack Valley United Fund, Lawrence, MA

25,000 Boys Club of America, Lawrence, MA

25,000 Greater Lawrence Community Foundation, Lawrence, MA

25,000 Holy Family Hospital and Medical Center, Methuen, MA

25,000 Lahey Clinic Foundation, Burlington, MA

25,000 Lawrence General Hospital Foundation, Lawrence, MA

25,000 Merrimack College Scholarship Program, North Andover, MA

25,000 YMCA, Lawrence, MA

10,000 Boys and Girls Club, East Derry, NH

10,000 Museum of Textile History, North Andover, MA

Rogers Foundation

CONTACT
Robert M. Rogers
Director
Rogers Fdn.
PO Box 130489
Tyler, TX 75713
(214) 595-3701

FINANCIAL SUMMARY
Recent Giving: $615,100 (1991); $416,579 (1990); $426,400 (1989)
Assets: $4,403,341 (1991); $4,220,052 (1990); $4,945,103 (1989)
EIN: 75-2143064

CONTRIBUTIONS SUMMARY
Donor(s): Robert M. Rogers
Typical Recipients: • *Arts & Humanities:* community arts, museums/galleries • *Educa-*

tion: colleges & universities, elementary education, religious education • *Health:* health organizations, hospitals, medical research • *Religion:* religious organizations • *Social Services:* child welfare, community service organizations, youth organizations

Grant Types: capital, general support, and scholarship

Geographic Distribution: focus on Tyler, TX

GIVING OFFICERS

Louise H. Rogers: dir

Rebecca J. Rogers: dir

Robert McDonald Rogers: dir *B* Buckner MO 1926 *CURR EMPL* chmn, ceo: TCA Cable TV *CORP AFFIL* co-owner: Rogers Venture Enterprises; dir: TCA Cable TV

Robert McDonald Rogers: dir *CURR EMPL* chmn, ceo: TCA Cable TV (see above)

APPLICATION INFORMATION

Initial Approach: Send cover letter and full proposal. There are no deadlines.

Restrictions on Giving: Does not support individuals.

GRANTS ANALYSIS

Number of Grants: 15

Highest Grant: $350,000

Typical Range: $150 to $27,000

Disclosure Period: 1991

RECENT GRANTS

350,000	Baylor University, Waco, TX
256,300	East Texas Baptist University, Marshall, TX
1,500	PATH, Tyler, TX
1,250	Birdwell Elementary School and PTA, Tyler, TX
1,000	Salvation Army, Tyler, TX
750	Tyler Junior League, Tyler, TX
700	Tyler Museum of Art, Tyler, TX
500	American Heart Association, Tyler, TX
500	Parent Services Center, Tyler, TX
500	Tommy Paul Memorial Fund, Tyler, TX

Rogers Foundation

CONTACT
Richard W. Agee
President
Rogers Fdn.
1131 M St., Ste. A
Lincoln, NE 68508
(402) 477-3725

FINANCIAL SUMMARY
Recent Giving: $297,400 (1991); $267,900 (1990); $233,220 (1989)
Assets: $6,105,065 (1991); $5,749,773 (1990); $6,222,395 (1989)
EIN: 47-6026897

CONTRIBUTIONS SUMMARY
Donor(s): the late Richard H. Rogers

Typical Recipients: • *Arts & Humanities:* community arts, history/historic preservation, music • *Civic & Public Affairs:* municipalities, safety, urban & community affairs • *Education:* medical education • *Health:* health organizations • *Religion:* churches, religious organizations • *Social Services:* animal protection, disabled, united funds, youth organizations

Grant Types: general support
Geographic Distribution: focus on Lincoln and Lancaster County, NE

GIVING OFFICERS
Eloise R. Agee: vp, secy
Richard Agee: pres, treas
Rex Marquart: vp

APPLICATION INFORMATION
Initial Approach: Send cover letter and full proposal.
Restrictions on Giving: Does not support for religious activities, national organizations, or organizations supported by government agencies.

OTHER THINGS TO KNOW
Publications: Application Guidelines

GRANTS ANALYSIS
Number of Grants: 40
Highest Grant: $35,000
Typical Range: $2,000 to $20,220
Disclosure Period: 1991

RECENT GRANTS

35,000	University of Nebraska Press, Lincoln, NE
30,000	Madonna Foundation, Lincoln, NE
25,000	Bright Lights, Lincoln, NE
20,000	Lincoln Symphony Orchestra Association, Lincoln, NE
10,000	Capital Area Humane Society, Lincoln, NE
10,000	Sniffles, Lincoln, NE
10,000	St. John United Church of Christ, La Pointe, WI
10,000	Town of LaPointe, Wisconsin Fire Department, LaPointe, WI
10,000	YMCA, Lincoln, NE
10,000	YWCA, Lincoln, NE

Rogers Foundation, Mary Stuart

CONTACT
Cleveland J. Stockton
Vice President
Mary Stuart Rogers Fdn.
PO Box 3153
Modesto, CA 95353
(209) 523-6416

FINANCIAL SUMMARY
Recent Giving: $240,000 (1991); $205,000 (1990); $130,000 (1989)
Assets: $7,655,201 (1991); $5,579,951 (1990); $5,029,819 (1989)
Gifts Received: $559,170 (1991); $202,982 (1990); $385,839 (1989)
EIN: 77-0099519

CONTRIBUTIONS SUMMARY
Typical Recipients: • *Education:* colleges & universities • *Health:* hospitals, medical research, pediatric health, single-disease health associations • *Religion:* churches • *Social Services:* child welfare, disabled, religious welfare, shelters/homelessness, united funds, youth organizations
Grant Types: general support
Geographic Distribution: focus on CA

GIVING OFFICERS
Mary Stuart Rogers: pres, dir
Cleveland J. Stockton: vp, dir

APPLICATION INFORMATION
Initial Approach: Contributes only to preselected organizations.

GRANTS ANALYSIS
Number of Grants: 20
Highest Grant: $35,000
Typical Range: $5,000 to $15,000
Disclosure Period: 1991

RECENT GRANTS

35,000	California State University, Modesto, CA
20,000	Guide Dogs for the Blind, Los Angeles, CA
20,000	St. Vincent de Paul Society, San Francisco, CA
15,000	American Cancer Society, Modesto, CA
15,000	American Heart Association, Modesto, CA
15,000	Boy Scouts of America, Modesto, CA
15,000	Children's Hospital, Palo Alto, CA
15,000	Children's Hospital Medical Center, Los Angeles, CA
15,000	Salvation Army, Modesto, CA
10,000	American Foundation for the Blind, New York, NY

Rogow Birken Foundation

CONTACT
Rogow Birken Fdn.
c/o Cummings and Lockwood
Cityplace
Hartford, CT 06103

FINANCIAL SUMMARY
Recent Giving: $10,000 (fiscal 1992); $200,000 (fiscal 1991); $7,645 (fiscal 1990)
Assets: $2,249,189 (fiscal year ending March 31, 1991); $2,722,119 (fiscal 1990); $2,635,128 (fiscal 1989)
Gifts Received: $202,895 (fiscal 1990); $49,289 (fiscal 1989); $16,338 (fiscal 1988)
Fiscal Note: In 1990, contributions were received from Louis B. Rogow.
EIN: 06-1051591

CONTRIBUTIONS SUMMARY
Donor(s): Louis B. Rogow

Typical Recipients: • *Civic & Public Affairs:* ethnic/minority organizations • *Education:* colleges & universities
Grant Types: general support

GIVING OFFICERS
Herman H. Copelin: secy
Edward Rogin: trust
Bruce Rogow: trust
Louis B. Rogow: pres, treas

APPLICATION INFORMATION
Initial Approach: Contributes only to preselected organizations.

GRANTS ANALYSIS
Number of Grants: 1
Highest Grant: $200,000
Disclosure Period: fiscal year ending March 31, 1991

RECENT GRANTS
   200,000 American Society for Technion, New York, NY

Rohatyn Foundation, Felix and Elizabeth
Former Foundation Name: Felix G. Rohatyn Foundation

CONTACT
Felix G. Rohatyn
President
Felix and Elizabeth Rohatyn Fdn.
c/o Lazard Freres & Co.
One Rockefeller Plz.
New York, NY 10020
(212) 632-6507

FINANCIAL SUMMARY
Recent Giving: $993,905 (1991); $668,025 (1990); $515,891 (1989)
Assets: $4,421,672 (1991); $4,443,016 (1990); $4,357,588 (1989)
Gifts Received: $400,000 (1991); $412,183 (1990); $400,000 (1989)
Fiscal Note: In 1991, contributions were received from Felix G. Rohatyn.
EIN: 23-7015644

CONTRIBUTIONS SUMMARY
Donor(s): Felix G. Rohatyn
Typical Recipients: • *Arts & Humanities:* arts centers, community arts, dance, libraries, opera, public broadcasting • *Civic & Public Affairs:* urban & community affairs • *Education:* education funds, elementary education, public educa-

tion (precollege) • *Health:* hospitals, medical research, single-disease health associations • *Social Services:* community centers, community service organizations, disabled
Grant Types: general support
Geographic Distribution: focus on the New York, NY, area

GIVING OFFICERS
Vivien Stiles Duffy: dir
Melvin L. Heineman: secy, treas
Elizabeth Rohatyn: vp
Felix George Rohatyn: pres *B* Vienna Austria 1928 *ED* Middlebury Coll BS 1948 *CURR EMPL* ptnr: Lazard Freres & Co *CORP AFFIL* dir: Howmet Turbine Components Corp, MCA, Schlumberger Ltd; ptnr: Lazard Freres & Co

APPLICATION INFORMATION
Initial Approach: Send brief letter of inquiry describing program or project. There are no deadlines.
Restrictions on Giving: Does not support individuals.

GRANTS ANALYSIS
Number of Grants: 124
Highest Grant: $365,000
Typical Range: $500 to $5,000
Disclosure Period: 1991

RECENT GRANTS
   365,000 WNET Thirteen, New York, NY
   200,000 Waterford Institute, Provo, UT
    50,000 Carnegie Hall Society, New York, NY
    50,000 Fund for New York City Education, New York, NY
    50,000 New York Public Library, New York, NY
    20,000 New York Public Library, New York, NY
    20,000 Presbyterian Hospital, New York, NY
    15,000 Lenox Hill Neighborhood Association, New York, NY
    12,500 Memorial Sloan-Kettering Cancer Center, New York, NY
    10,000 Carnegie Hall Society, New York, NY

Rohlik Foundation, Sigmund and Sophie

CONTACT
Sigmund and Sophie Rohlik Fdn.
16500 North Park Dr., Apt. 1520
Southfield, MI 48075
(313) 559-1967

FINANCIAL SUMMARY
Recent Giving: $86,200 (fiscal 1992); $260,500 (fiscal 1990); $3,850 (fiscal 1989)
Assets: $2,498,811 (fiscal year ending June 30, 1992); $2,250,700 (fiscal 1990); $2,273,251 (fiscal 1989)
EIN: 38-6056443

CONTRIBUTIONS SUMMARY
Donor(s): the late Sigmund Rohlik, Sophie Rohlik
Typical Recipients: • *Arts & Humanities:* music • *Civic & Public Affairs:* environmental affairs, ethnic/minority organizations • *Education:* colleges & universities, minority education, private education (precollege), student aid • *Health:* hospitals • *Religion:* religious organizations • *Social Services:* community service organizations
Grant Types: general support

GIVING OFFICERS
Moe Baumer: dir, vp, secy
David Hertzberg: trust
Charles Levin: trust
Joseph Levin: trust
Sophie Rohlik: pres, treas

APPLICATION INFORMATION
Initial Approach: Contributes only to preselected organizations. Applications not accepted.

GRANTS ANALYSIS
Number of Grants: 17
Highest Grant: $20,000
Typical Range: $200 to $15,000
Disclosure Period: fiscal year ending June 30, 1992

RECENT GRANTS
   20,000 Bar-Ilan University, New York, NY
   15,000 Akiva Hebrew Day School, Lathrup Village, MI
   15,000 American Society for Technion, New York, NY

   15,000 Hillel Day School, Farmington Hills, MI
    5,000 American Committee for the Weizmann Institute, New York, NY
    2,500 American Committee for Shaare Zedek Hospital, New York, NY
    2,500 Fresh Air Society, West Bloomfield, MI
    2,000 Salvation Army, Southfield, MI
    1,500 Detroit Symphony Orchestra, Detroit, MI
    1,500 United Negro College Fund, Detroit, MI

Rohm and Haas Company
Sales: $2.76 billion
Employees: 14,000
Headquarters: Philadelphia, PA
SIC Major Group: Chemicals & Allied Products and Rubber & Miscellaneous Plastics Products

CONTACT
Delbert S. Payne
Manager, Corporate Social Investment
Rohm and Haas Co.
Independence Mall West
Philadelphia, PA 19105
(215) 592-2863

FINANCIAL SUMMARY
Recent Giving: $4,300,000 (1992 approx.); $4,300,000 (1991); $4,300,000 (1990)
Fiscal Note: Company gives directly.

CONTRIBUTIONS SUMMARY
Typical Recipients: • *Arts & Humanities:* arts appreciation, arts associations, arts festivals, arts funds, arts institutes, community arts, dance, ethnic arts, history/historic preservation, libraries, museums/galleries, music, opera, performing arts, public broadcasting, theater • *Civic & Public Affairs:* better government, business/free enterprise, civil rights, economic development, environmental affairs, housing, law & justice, nonprofit management, urban & community affairs, zoos/botanical gardens • *Education:* agricultural education, arts education, business education, career/vocational education, colleges & universities,

community & junior colleges, economic education, education administration, education associations, education funds, engineering education, faculty development, liberal arts education, literacy, minority education, preschool education, private education (precollege), public education (precollege), science/technology education, special education, student aid • *Health:* emergency/ambulance services, geriatric health, health care cost containment, health organizations, hospices, hospitals, medical rehabilitation, medical research, mental health, nursing services, outpatient health care delivery, pediatric health, public health • *Science:* science exhibits & fairs, scientific institutes, scientific organizations • *Social Services:* aged, child welfare, community centers, community service organizations, disabled, drugs & alcohol, emergency relief, employment/job training, family services, food/clothing distribution, homes, recreation & athletics, shelters/homelessness, united funds, volunteer services, youth organizations
Grant Types: capital, challenge, department, employee matching gifts, fellowship, general support, project, scholarship, and seed money
Nonmonetary Support Types: donated equipment, donated products, in-kind services, loaned employees, and loaned executives
Note: Nonmonetary giving totaled $140,000 in 1990. This support is not included in above figures. Company sponsored employee volunteer programs include Dollars For Doers and Volunteer Recognition Programs.
Geographic Distribution: primarily in communities where employees live and company has facilities; limited support to national organizations
Operating Locations: CA (Newark, Carson, Hayward, Irvine, La Miraoa), CT (Kensington), IL (Chicago Heights, Illiopolis, Kankakee, Lemont), KY (Louisville), MA (Marlborough), NC (Charlotte), PA (Bellefonte, Bristol, Philadelphia), TN (Knoxville), TX (Bayport, Houston)

CORP. OFFICERS
John Patrick Mulroney: *B* Philadelphia PA 1935 *ED* Univ PA BS 1957; Univ PA MS 1959 *CURR EMPL* pres, coo, dir: Rohm & Haas Co *CORP AFFIL* dir: Aluminum Co Am, Teradyne *NONPR AFFIL* mem: Academy Natural Sciences, Am Chem Soc, Am Inst Chem Engrs, Greater Philadelphia Chamber Commerce, Greater Philadelphia First Corp, Soc Chem Indus, Univ PA; pres: Opera Co NY
J. Lawrence Wilson: *B* Rosedale MS 1936 *ED* Vanderbilt Univ BSME 1958; Harvard Univ MBA 1963 *CURR EMPL* chmn, ceo, dir: Rohm & Haas Co *CORP AFFIL* dir: Shipley Co, Vanguard Group Mutual Funds; mem: Cummins Engine Co *NONPR AFFIL* chmn: Phil High School Academies; mem: Culver Ed Fdn, Pres Export Counc, Vanderbilt Univ

GIVING OFFICERS
Delbert S. Payne: mgr corp social investment

APPLICATION INFORMATION
Initial Approach: *Initial Contact:* proposal *Include Information On:* organization's name and purpose, length of service, funding sources, current objectives and priorities, proof of tax-exempt status, descriptive literature as available (project outlines, programs, brochures, etc.) *When to Submit:* any time
Restrictions on Giving: Company does not support fraternal organizations, political or lobbying groups, religious organizations for sectarian purposes, or individuals.

OTHER THINGS TO KNOW
Community activity guidelines set by corporate management; individual plants determine scope of program and specific activities.
Rohm and Haas tries to channel employees into community activities supported by company.
Contributions not awarded on basis of indefinitely continuing or unquestioned support. Even when multiyear pledges made, Rohm and Haas retains right to terminate support if appropriate.
Rohm and Haas occasionally provides seed money grants,

usually as an outright gift or in the form of a matching or challenge grant.

GRANTS ANALYSIS
Total Grants: $4,300,000*
Typical Range: $1,000 to $5,000
Disclosure Period: 1991
Note: Total grants figure is approximate.

Rohr Inc.
Sales: $1.28 billion
Employees: 9,800
Headquarters: Chula Vista, CA
SIC Major Group:
   Transportation Equipment

CONTACT
John Walsh
Director, Corporate Relations
Rohr Inc.
PO Box 878
Chula Vista, CA 91912
(619) 691-2808

FINANCIAL SUMMARY
Recent Giving: $500,000 (1993); $500,000 (1992)
Fiscal Note: Company gives directly.

CONTRIBUTIONS SUMMARY
Typical Recipients: • *Arts & Humanities:* arts associations, music, performing arts, public broadcasting, theater • *Civic & Public Affairs:* economic development, economics, environmental affairs, ethnic/minority organizations, law & justice, zoos/botanical gardens • *Education:* business education, colleges & universities, community & junior colleges, continuing education, elementary education, engineering education, minority education • *Health:* health organizations, hospices, hospitals, single-disease health associations • *Science:* science exhibits & fairs • *Social Services:* aged, community centers, community service organizations, counseling, delinquency & crime, disabled, domestic violence, drugs & alcohol, emergency relief, family planning, family services, food/clothing distribution, united funds, youth organizations
Grant Types: capital, challenge, employee matching gifts, general support, multiyear/continuing support, operating expenses, project, and scholarship

Nonmonetary Support Types: donated equipment, in-kind services, and loaned employees
Note: Contact for nonmonetary support is Patricia Johnson, Public Affairs Specialist. Estimated value of nonmonetary support in 1992 was $5,000.
Geographic Distribution: headquarters and operating locations
Operating Locations: AL (Fairhope, Foley), AR (Heber Springs, Sheridan), CA (Chula Vista, Moreno Valley, Riverside), MD (Hagerstown), TX (San Marcos), WA (Auburn)

CORP. OFFICERS
James J. Kerley: *CURR EMPL* chmn: Rohr
Robert H. Ray: *CURR EMPL* pres, ceo: Rohr

GIVING OFFICERS
John Walsh: *CURR EMPL* dir corp rels: Rohr

APPLICATION INFORMATION
Initial Approach: *Initial Contact:* brief letter of inquiry *Include Information On:* description of the organization, amount requested, purpose of funds sought, audited financial statement, and proof of tax-exempt status *When to Submit:* any time

---

Rolfs Foundation, Robert T.

CONTACT
Arthur P. Hoberg
Vice President
Robert T. Rolfs Fdn.
735 South Main St.
West Bend, WI 53095
(414) 335-1234

FINANCIAL SUMMARY
Recent Giving: $243,575 (fiscal 1990); $143,900 (fiscal 1989); $80,900 (fiscal 1988)
Assets: $4,308,225 (fiscal year ending September 30, 1990); $4,597,849 (fiscal 1989); $2,421,891 (fiscal 1988)
Gifts Received: $5,000 (fiscal 1990); $1,750,000 (fiscal 1989); $475,000 (fiscal 1988)
Fiscal Note: In 1990, contributions were received from Amity Leather Products Compnay.
EIN: 39-1390015

CONTRIBUTIONS SUMMARY

Typical Recipients: • *Arts & Humanities:* community arts, music, performing arts, theater • *Education:* engineering education, minority education, science/technology education, student aid • *Health:* hospitals • *Social Services:* community service organizations, food/clothing distribution, united funds, youth organizations

Grant Types: capital, general support, and scholarship

Geographic Distribution: focus on IN and WI

GIVING OFFICERS

Arthur P. Hoberg: vp

Robert T. Rolfs: pres *B* Milwaukee WI 1926 *ED* Univ Notre Dame 1943 *CURR EMPL* pres, dir: Amity Leather Products Co

John F. Rozek: secy, treas

APPLICATION INFORMATION

Initial Approach: Send brief letter describing program. There are no deadlines.

GRANTS ANALYSIS

Number of Grants: 22

Highest Grant: $90,000

Typical Range: $1,000 to $2,000

Disclosure Period: fiscal year ending September 30, 1990

RECENT GRANTS

90,000 YMCA, West Bend, WI

62,000 St. Joseph's Community Hospital, West Bend, WI

20,000 CARE, Chicago, IL

20,000 International Rescue Committee, New York, NY

10,000 Milwaukee Symphony Friends, Milwaukee, WI

10,000 United Negro College Fund, Milwaukee, WI

7,000 United Performing Arts Fund, Milwaukee, WI

6,000 Milwaukee School of Engineering, Milwaukee, WI

2,500 Arthritis Foundation, West Allis, WI

2,500 Full Shelf Pantry, West Bend, WI

Rolfs Foundation, Thomas J.

CONTACT

Arthur P. Hoberg
Vice President
Thomas J. Rolfs Fdn.
735 South Main St.
West Bend, WI 53095
(414) 335-1234

FINANCIAL SUMMARY

Recent Giving: $151,400 (fiscal 1990); $75,000 (fiscal 1988)

Assets: $2,662,446 (fiscal year ending September 30, 1990); $2,311,179 (fiscal 1988)

Gifts Received: $5,000 (fiscal 1990); $475,000 (fiscal 1988)

Fiscal Note: In 1990, contributions were received from Amity Leather Products Company.

EIN: 39-6043350

CONTRIBUTIONS SUMMARY

Donor(s): Amity Leather Products Co.

Typical Recipients: • *Education:* colleges & universities, education associations • *Health:* health organizations • *Religion:* missionary activities

Grant Types: scholarship

Geographic Distribution: focus on WI

GIVING OFFICERS

Arthur P. Hoberg: vp

Thomas J. Rolfs: pres *CURR EMPL* chmn, dir: Amity Leather Products Co

John F. Rozek: secy, treas

APPLICATION INFORMATION

Initial Approach: Send brief letter of inquiry describing program. There are no deadlines.

GRANTS ANALYSIS

Number of Grants: 25

Highest Grant: $50,000

Typical Range: $1,000 to $3,000

Disclosure Period: fiscal year ending September 30, 1990

RECENT GRANTS

50,000 Notre Dame University, Notre Dame, IN

15,000 Wisconsin Foundation of Independent Colleges, Milwaukee, WI

12,750 Rolfs Educational Foundation, Milwaukee, WI

12,000 Blood Center of Southeastern Wisconsin, Milwaukee, WI

10,000 Cedar Lake Home Campus, West Bend, WI

10,000 St. Vincent de Paul Society, West Bend, WI

6,000 Mount Mary College, Milwaukee, WI

4,000 Salvadorian Mission Warehouse, New Holstein, WI

3,000 Experimental Aircraft Association, Oshkosh, WI

3,000 Washington County Campus Foundation, West Bend, WI

Rollins Inc.

Revenue: $475.6 million
Employees: 8,000
Headquarters: Atlanta, GA
SIC Major Group: Agricultural Services and Business Services

CONTACT

Judy Donner
Public Relations Manager
Rollins Inc.
PO Box 647
Atlanta, GA 30301
(404) 888-2217

FINANCIAL SUMMARY

Fiscal Note: Annual Giving Range: less than $100,000

CONTRIBUTIONS SUMMARY

Company reports 30% of contributions support civic and public affairs; 30% to education; 30% to health and welfare; and 10% to other organizations.

Typical Recipients: • *Civic & Public Affairs:* general • *Education:* general • *Social Services:* general

Operating Locations: GA (Atlanta)

CORP. OFFICERS

Gary W. Rollins: *CURR EMPL* pres, coo, dir: Rollins

R. Randall Rollins: *CURR EMPL* chmn, ceo, dir: Rollins

Rollins Environmental Services, Inc.

Assets: $257.9 million
Employees: 1,233
Headquarters: Wilmington, DE
SIC Major Group: Electric, Gas & Sanitary Services

CONTACT

Eileen Gallucio
Administrator in Personnel
Rollins Environmental Services, Inc.
PO Box 2349
Wilmington, DE 19899
(302) 426-3535

CONTRIBUTIONS SUMMARY

Operating Locations: DE (Wilmington)

CORP. OFFICERS

Nicholas Pappas: *CURR EMPL* pres, coo, dir: Rollins Environmental Svcs

John William Rollins, Sr.: *B* Keith GA 1916 *CURR EMPL* fdr, chmn, ceo, dir: Rollins Environmental Svcs *CORP AFFIL* chmn: Rollins Jamaica; chmn, ceo: Rollins Truck Leasing Corp; co-fdr, dir: Rollins Inc; dir: FPA Corp, Matlack Sys, RPC Energy Svcs

Rollins Luetkemeyer Charitable Foundation

CONTACT

Robert F. Wilson
Vice President
Rollins Luetkemeyer Charitable Fdn.
600 Fairmount Ave.
Ste. 106
Towson, MD 21204
(410) 296-6363

FINANCIAL SUMMARY

Recent Giving: $427,725 (1991); $535,970 (1990); $412,150 (1989)

Assets: $11,026,630 (1991); $10,005,080 (1990); $10,073,429 (1989)

Gifts Received: $1,000,000 (1990)

Fiscal Note: In 1990, contributions were received from Mary E. Rollins.

EIN: 52-6041536

CONTRIBUTIONS SUMMARY

Typical Recipients: • *Arts & Humanities:* community arts, theater • *Civic & Public Affairs:* safety, urban & community affairs • *Education:* colleges & universities, private education (precollege) • *Health:* hospitals, medical research • *Religion:* churches • *Social Services:* food/clothing distribution, homes, united funds

Grant Types: general support

Geographic Distribution: focus on the Baltimore, MD, area

GIVING OFFICERS

Anne A. Luetkemeyer: secy, dir

John A. Luetkemeyer, Jr.: dir

John A. Luetkemeyer, Sr.: pres, dir

Mary E. Rollins: dir

Anne L. Stone: dir

James D. Stone: dir

Robert F. Wilson: vp, treas

APPLICATION INFORMATION

Initial Approach: Send brief letter of inquiry describing program or project. There are no deadlines.

Restrictions on Giving: Does not support individuals.

GRANTS ANALYSIS

Number of Grants: 103

Highest Grant: $100,000

Typical Range: $100 to $5,000

Disclosure Period: 1991

RECENT GRANTS

100,000 McDonogh School, Owings Mills, MD

50,000 Center Stage, Baltimore, MD

50,000 Collier County Community Foundation, Naples, FL

50,000 Goucher College, Baltimore, MD

30,000 Roland Park Police, Baltimore, MD

25,000 Roland Park Police, Baltimore, MD

20,000 Evergreen House Foundation, Baltimore, MD

15,000 Garrison Forest School, Garrison, MD

10,000 Foxcroft School, Middleburg, VA

10,000 Harvard College, Cambridge, MA

Rolls-Royce Inc.

Sales: $26.0 million
Employees: 400
Headquarters: Reston, VA
SIC Major Group: Industrial Machinery & Equipment and Transportation Equipment

CONTACT

Robert Stangarone
Vice President, Public Affairs
Rolls-Royce Inc.
11911 Freedom Dr.
Reston, VA 22090
(703) 834-1700

CONTRIBUTIONS SUMMARY

Operating Locations: CT, DE, OH, VA

CORP. OFFICERS

J. W. Sandford: *CURR EMPL* pres, coo: Rolls-Royce

GIVING OFFICERS

Robert Stangarone: *CURR EMPL* vp (pub affs): Rolls-Royce

Rolm Systems

Sales: $380.0 million
Employees: 2,300
Parent Company: Siemens Corp.
Headquarters: Santa Clara, CA
SIC Major Group: Electronic & Other Electrical Equipment and Industrial Machinery & Equipment

CONTACT

Tricia Webster
Community Relations Liason
Rolm Systems
4900 Old Ironsides Dr., MS 128
Santa Clara, CA 95054
(408) 492-2000

CONTRIBUTIONS SUMMARY

Grant Types: matching

Operating Locations: CA (Santa Clara)

CORP. OFFICERS

Bernd Schmidtchen: *CURR EMPL* vp, cfo: Rolm Sys

Peter Triballa: *CURR EMPL* pres: Rolm Sys

Romill Foundation

CONTACT

Andrew A. Smith, Jr.
Romill Fdn.
c/o Wilmington Trust Co.
Rodney Sq. North
Wilmington, DE 19890
(302) 651-1546

FINANCIAL SUMMARY

Recent Giving: $458,974 (1991); $517,815 (1990); $494,599 (1989)

Assets: $1,587,301 (1991); $1,537,002 (1990); $1,862,252 (1989)

Gifts Received: $157,343 (1991); $262,782 (1990); $247,886 (1989)

EIN: 13-6102069

CONTRIBUTIONS SUMMARY

Donor(s): Roger Milliken

Typical Recipients: • *Arts & Humanities:* arts associations, libraries • *Civic & Public Affairs:* environmental affairs, municipalities • *Education:* colleges & universities, education associations, private education (precollege) • *Religion:* churches • *Social Services:* child welfare, united funds, youth organizations

Grant Types: general support and scholarship

Geographic Distribution: focus on Spartanburg County, SC

GIVING OFFICERS

Lawrence Heagney: treas *CURR EMPL* secy: Milliken & Co *CORP AFFIL* secy: Milliken & Co

Gerrish Milliken, Jr.: trust *B* New York NY 1917 *ED* Yale Univ 1940 *CORP AFFIL* dir: Milliken & Co

Justine V. Milliken: trust

Minot King Milliken: trust *B* New York NY 1916 *ED* Princeton Univ 1937 *CURR EMPL* vp, treas, dir: Milliken & Co *CORP AFFIL* dir: Great Northern Nekoosa Corp, Mercantile Stores Co, Union Pacific Corp

APPLICATION INFORMATION

Initial Approach: Contributes only to preselected organizations.

GRANTS ANALYSIS

Number of Grants: 22

Highest Grant: $162,500

Typical Range: $2,500 to $20,000

Disclosure Period: 1991

RECENT GRANTS

162,500 Converse College, Spartanburg, SC

107,657 Spartanburg Day School, Spartanburg, SC

50,000 Free Congress and Education Foundation, Spartanburg, SC

25,000 Arts Council of Spartanburg, Spartanburg, SC

20,000 Leadership Institute, Springfield, VA

17,500 United Way, Spartanburg, SC

12,606 Episcopal Church of Advent, Spartanburg, SC

10,000 American Spectator Educational Foundation, Spartanburg, SC

10,000 Eastside Improvement Society, Spartanburg, SC

9,000 Wofford College, Spartanburg, SC

RosaMary Foundation

CONTACT

Louis M. Freeman
Chairman
RosaMary Foundation
PO Box 51299
New Orleans, LA 70151-1299
(504) 895-1984

FINANCIAL SUMMARY

Recent Giving: $1,373,673 (1991); $1,272,083 (1990); $1,090,507 (1989)

Assets: $33,206,575 (1991); $28,247,792 (1990); $28,718,188 (1989)

EIN: 72-6024696

CONTRIBUTIONS SUMMARY

Donor(s): The RosaMary Foundation was established in 1939, with funds donated by members of the Alfred Bird Freeman family. The foundation was named after Alfred Bird Freeman's daughters, Mrs. Rosa Keller and Mrs. Mary Ella Wisdom. Alfred Bird Freeman (1881-1957) was chairman of the Louisiana Coca-Cola Bottling Company.

Typical Recipients: • *Arts & Humanities:* arts associations, arts centers, dance, museums/galleries, music, performing arts • *Civic & Public Af-*

fairs: economic development, environmental affairs, philanthropic organizations, public policy, zoos/botanical gardens • *Education:* colleges & universities, private education (precollege) • *Health:* health organizations, hospitals • *Religion:* churches, religious organizations • *Social Services:* child welfare, community service organizations, homes, religious welfare, united funds

Grant Types: capital, challenge, endowment, general support, research, scholarship, and seed money

Geographic Distribution: New Orleans, LA

GIVING OFFICERS

Adelaide W. Benjamin: trust

Louis M. Freeman: chmn, trust *B* Chicago IL 1940 *ED* Yale Univ 1958-1960; Tulane Univ 1960-1963 *CURR EMPL* chmn: Ozone Spring Water Co *NONPR AFFIL* dir: Bur Govt Res, Counc Better LA, Covenant House, Gulf Coast Conservation Assn, Metro Area Comm, SE Counc Fdns, Tulane Univ, Un Way Greater New Orleans Area; pv: LA World Exploration; trust: Fdn MidSouth, Greater New Orleans Fdn

Richard W. Freeman, Jr.: trust

Charles Keller, Jr.: trust *PHIL AFFIL* don, chmn bd trusts: Keller Family Foundation; trust: Greater New Orleans Foundation

Rosa Freeman Keller: trust *PHIL AFFIL* don, trust: Keller Family Foundation

Betty Wisdom: trust

APPLICATION INFORMATION

Initial Approach:
Applicants should submit a letter of proposal to the chairman of the foundation. An authorized official of the petitioning organization must sign the proposal.

Proposals should include the amount and purpose of the request, a description of the project and what it hopes to accomplish, its cost, funds on hand or requested and from what sources, other sources approached for funding, and how future funding will be secured if the project is continuous. The foundation also requires operating budgets for the project and the organization, a list of the governing board, and a copy of the organization's IRS determination letter.

There are no deadlines for submitting proposals.

The trustees meet generally at six-month intervals beginning in the spring of each year to make funding decisions.

Restrictions on Giving: Primary consideration will be given to those organizations whose operations are conducted in the greater New Orleans area. Grants are not made to individuals.

GRANTS ANALYSIS

Total Grants: $1,373,673

Number of Grants: 40

Highest Grant: $200,000

Typical Range: $5,000 to $50,000

Disclosure Period: 1991

Note: Recent grants are derived from a 1991 Form 990.

RECENT GRANTS

200,000 Audubon Institute, New Orleans, LA

200,000 United Way for the Greater New Orleans Area, New Orleans, LA

150,000 New Orleans Museum of Art, New Orleans, LA

150,000 New Orleans Museum of Art, New Orleans, LA

75,000 Alton Ochsner Medical Foundation, New Orleans, LA

75,000 New Orleans Philharmonic Symphony Society, New Orleans, LA

50,000 Tulane University, New Orleans, LA

50,000 University of New Orleans, New Orleans, LA

50,000 Xavier University of Louisiana, New Orleans, LA

37,500 Touro Infirmary, New Orleans, LA

Rose Foundation, Billy

CONTACT

Terri C. Mangino
Executive Director and Assistant Secretary
Billy Rose Foundation
One Dag Hammarskjold Plaza, 47th Fl.
New York, NY 10017
(212) 349-4141

FINANCIAL SUMMARY

Recent Giving: $1,334,500 (1991); $1,528,500 (1990); $1,272,000 (1989)

Assets: $9,112,402 (1991); $8,230,938 (1990); $9,876,950 (1989)

EIN: 13-6165466

CONTRIBUTIONS SUMMARY

Donor(s): The Billy Rose Foundation was incorporated in 1958 by Billy Rose. During his lifetime, Mr. Rose's interests included theatrical production, songwriting, the stock market, real estate investments, and art collecting. His activities in the stock market accounted for much of the fortune he had amassed by the time of his death in 1966. His will provided for a bequest of more than $10 million to the foundation.

Typical Recipients: • *Arts & Humanities:* arts associations, arts centers, arts festivals, arts institutes, cinema, dance, history/historic preservation, libraries, museums/galleries, music, opera, public broadcasting, theater, visual arts • *Civic & Public Affairs:* environmental affairs, philanthropic organizations, public policy • *Education:* arts education, colleges & universities, education associations • *Health:* health organizations, hospitals, medical research, nursing services, single-disease health associations • *Religion:* religious organizations • *Social Services:* community centers, family planning, religious welfare, youth organizations

Grant Types: general support and project

Geographic Distribution: emphasis on New York City

GIVING OFFICERS

Arthur Cantor: chmn, dir *B* Boston MA 1920

James R. Cherry: vp, dir

Terri C. Mangino: exec dir, asst secy

Edward T. Walsh, Jr.: secy, asst treas

Charles Wohlstetter: pres, dir *B* 1910 *CURR EMPL* chmn, dir: Contel Corp *CORP AFFIL* dir: New Court Asset Mgmt, Tesoro Petroleum Corp; vchmn: GTE Corp *NONPR AFFIL* adjunct prof: AL Sch Bus Admin; chmn: Inst Ed Affs; chmn adv panel: Intl Cultural & Ed Exchange US Information Agency; mem: Am Enterprise Inst, Counc World Communs, French Academy Wine; mem adv counc: Rockefeller Univ; natl ambassador: Salk Inst; reg chmn: Pres Commn White House Fellowships; trust: Fdn Res Medicine & Biology, Freedoms Fdn Valley Forge; vchmn, trust: John F Kennedy Ctr Performing Arts, Natl Symphony Orchestra Assn

APPLICATION INFORMATION

Initial Approach:
Applications should be submitted in the form of a letter to the foundation.

The letter should summarize the need for support and include the amount of the request. A copy of the IRS determination letter of tax-exempt status and any recent publicity articles should also be included. There are no deadlines for submitting letters of request.

GRANTS ANALYSIS

Total Grants: $1,334,500

Number of Grants: 89

Highest Grant: $325,000

Typical Range: $2,500 to $25,000

Disclosure Period: 1991

Note: Average grant figure excludes the highest grant of $325,000. Recent grants are derived from a 1991 Form 990.

RECENT GRANTS

325,000 American Friends of The Israel Museum, New York, NY

50,000 American Enterprise Institute for Public Policy Research, Washington, DC

50,000 Carnegie Hall, New York, NY

50,000 Israel Morshet

50,000 Jerusalem Foundation, New York, NY

50,000 National Symphony Orchestra, Washington, DC

50,000 New York Philhar-
monic, New York,
NY — Young Peo-
ple's Concerts

50,000 New York Theatre,
New York, NY

40,000 Metropolitan
Opera Association,
New York, NY

25,000 American Theatre
Wing, New York,
NY

Roseburg Forest Products Co. / Ford Family Foundation

Sales: $600.0 million
Employees: 3,539
Parent Company: RLC Industries
Co.
Headquarters: Roseburg, OR
SIC Major Group: Lumber &
Wood Products and Wholesale
Trade—Durable Goods

CONTACT
Ronald C. Parker
Treasurer
Roseburg Forest Products Co.
PO Box 1088
Roseburg, OR 97470
(503) 679-3311

FINANCIAL SUMMARY
Fiscal Note: Annual Giving
Range: $1,00,000 to $5,000,000
EIN: 93-6026156

CONTRIBUTIONS SUMMARY
Typical Recipients: • *Arts &
Humanities:* arts appreciation,
arts associations, arts centers,
community arts, libraries,
music, performing arts • *Civic
& Public Affairs:* general,
safety • *Education:* career/voca-
tional education, colleges &
universities, community & junior colleges, elementary education, general, preschool education, science/technology
education • *Health:* emer-
gency/ambulance services, general, health organizations
• *Science:* general, scientific institutes • *Social Services:* aged,
child welfare, community centers, counseling, day care, domestic violence, drugs & alcohol, general, homes, recreation
& athletics, shelters/homeless-
ness, united funds, volunteer
services, youth organizations
Grant Types: award, capital,
challenge, emergency, general
support, and multiyear/continu-
ing support

Geographic Distribution: in
headquatres and operating communities
Operating Locations: CA
(Weed), OR (Roseburg)

CORP. OFFICERS
Kenneth W. Ford: *CURR
EMPL* chmn: Roseburg Forest
Products Co
William A. Whelan: *CURR
EMPL* pres: Roseburg Forest
Products Co

GIVING OFFICERS
Ronald C. Parker: treas

APPLICATION INFORMATION
Initial Approach: *Initial Contact:* send a full proposal *Include Information On:* a description of organization,
amount requested, purpose of
funds sought, and proof of tax-
exempt status *When to Submit:*
March 15 is the annual deadline for applications
Restrictions on Giving: The
Ford Family Foundation only
provides funding to charitable
organizations and does not support individuals. The majority
of their contributions goes to
organizations within Oregon
and Northern California, but
this is not a requirement to receive funding.

OTHER THINGS TO KNOW
Company is an original donor
to the Ford Family Foundation.

GRANTS ANALYSIS
Total Grants: $2,760,477
Number of Grants: 66
Highest Grant: $1,816,509
Typical Range: $1,000 to
$12,000
Disclosure Period: fiscal year
ending April 30, 1992
Note: Recent grants are de-
rived from a fiscal 1992 grants
list.

RECENT GRANTS
1,816,509 Douglas Commu-
nity Foundation

230,000 Linfield College,
McMinnville, OR
— health/PE com-
plex

150,000 OMSI, OR — new
complex

100,000 Oregon Inde-
pendent College
Foundation,
Eugene, OR

75,000 Umpqua Commu-
nity College, Rose-
burg, OR

29,000 United Way of
Douglas County,
OR

25,000 Safe Haven Home,
Roseburg, OR —
assist in meeting

25,000 Winston Training
School, Winston,
OR

20,000 Phoenix School,
Roseburg, OR —
operating funds

15,643 Umpqua Valley
Christian School,
Roseburg, OR

Rosemount, Inc.

Sales: $1.26 billion
Employees: 10,000
Parent Company: Emerson
Electric Co.
Headquarters: Eden Prairie, MN
SIC Major Group: Instruments &
Related Products

CONTACT
Susan Hilk
Corporate Contributions
Rosemount, Inc.
12001 Technology Dr.
Eden Prairie, MN 55344
(612) 941-5560

CONTRIBUTIONS SUMMARY
Operating Locations: MN
(Eden Prairie)

CORP. OFFICERS
Robert J. Bateman: *CURR
EMPL* ceo: Rosemount
John M. Berra: *CURR EMPL*
pres: Rosemount
Vernon H. Heath: *CURR
EMPL* chmn, ceo: Rosemount
Randy P. Smith: *CURR EMPL*
vp, cfo: Rosemount

RECENT GRANTS
Walker Art Center, Minneapolis,
MN

Rosen Foundation, Joseph

CONTACT
Abraham A. Rosen
President
Joseph Rosen Fdn.
PO Box 334, Lenox Hill Sta.
New York, NY 10021
(212) 249-1550

FINANCIAL SUMMARY
Recent Giving: $454,141 (fis-
cal 1992); $478,043 (fiscal
1991); $433,350 (fiscal 1990)
Assets: $13,001,328 (fiscal
year ending June 30, 1992);

$12,335,513 (fiscal 1991);
$11,643,120 (fiscal 1990)
Gifts Received: $25,000 (fis-
cal 1992); $55,000 (fiscal
1991); $368,500 (fiscal 1990)
Fiscal Note: Fiscal 1992 con-
tribution recieved from Tranel
Inc.
EIN: 13-6158412

CONTRIBUTIONS SUMMARY
Typical Recipients: • *Arts &
Humanities:* arts institutes,
community arts, museums/gal-
leries, performing arts, theater
• *Civic & Public Affairs:* environmental affairs, ethnic/minor-
ity organizations • *Education:*
colleges & universities
• *Health:* hospitals, medical research, single-disease health associations • *Religion:* religious
organizations, synagogues • *Social Services:* community centers, disabled
Grant Types: general support

GIVING OFFICERS
Irving S. Bobrow: vp, asst
treas
Abraham A. Rosen: pres, dir
Jonathan P. Rosen: vp, secy,
dir
Miriam Rosen: treas, dir

APPLICATION INFORMATION
Initial Approach: The foundation reports it only makes contributions to preselected charitable organizations.

GRANTS ANALYSIS
Number of Grants: 191
Highest Grant: $100,000
Typical Range: $100 to $1,000
Disclosure Period: fiscal year
ending June 30, 1992

RECENT GRANTS
100,000 Greater Hartford
Jewish Community
Center, Hartford,
CT

50,000 Amherst College,
Amherst, MA

32,800 Metropolitan Mu-
seum of Art, New
York, NY

30,000 American Friends
of Israel Museum,
New York, NY

17,000 Bayith Lapleitot,
New York, NY

15,000 PEF Israel Endow-
ment Fund, New
York, NY

14,000 American ORT Fed-
eration, New York,
NY

13,500 Metropolitan Opera Association, New York, NY

10,000 United Jewish Appeal Federation of Jewish Philanthropies, New York, NY

6,000 Yale University, New Haven, CT

Rosen Foundation, Michael Alan

CONTACT
Michael Alan Rosen Foundation
c/o Savitsky, Satin & Geibelson
2049 Century Park East, Suite 3700
Los Angeles, CA 90067
(310) 553-1040

FINANCIAL SUMMARY
Recent Giving: $0 (1991); $0 (1990)
Assets: $1,910,274 (1990)
Gifts Received: $350,100 (1990)
Fiscal Note: 1990 contributions received from Arlene Rosen ($250,000), and Tobi Haleen ($100,000).
EIN: 94-3024736

GIVING OFFICERS
Tobi Haleen: vp, secy
Arlene Rosen: pres, treas
Robert A. Satin: asst treas

APPLICATION INFORMATION
Initial Approach: The foundation reports no specific application guidelines. Send a brief letter of inquiry, including statement of purpose, amount requested, and proof of tax-exempt status.

GRANTS ANALYSIS
Total Grants: $0
Disclosure Period: 1990

Rosenbaum Foundation, Paul and Gabriella

CONTACT
Edith Leonian
Executive Vice President
Paul and Gabriella Rosenbaum Fdn.
1723 South Michigan
Chicago, IL 60616
(312) 987-9500

FINANCIAL SUMMARY
Recent Giving: $1,283,222 (fiscal 1990); $1,668,106 (fis-

cal 1989); $1,243,946 (fiscal 1988)
Assets: $2,047,925 (fiscal year ending September 30, 1990); $2,889,067 (fiscal 1989); $634,975 (fiscal 1988)
Gifts Received: $439,797 (fiscal 1990); $3,778,387 (fiscal 1989); $1,028,290 (fiscal 1988)
Fiscal Note: Fiscal 1990 contribution received in securities from Gabriella Rosenbaum.
EIN: 36-3204862

CONTRIBUTIONS SUMMARY
Donor(s): Gabriella Rosenbaum
Typical Recipients: • *Arts & Humanities:* arts funds, community arts • *Civic & Public Affairs:* municipalities, urban & community affairs • *Education:* colleges & universities, private education (precollege), religious education, religious education • *Religion:* religious organizations • *Social Services:* aged, child welfare, family planning, family services, family services
Grant Types: general support and project

GIVING OFFICERS
Madge Goldman: exec vp, treas
Edith Leonian: exec vp
Norman R. Liebling: secy
Gabriella Rosenbaum: chmn, vp

APPLICATION INFORMATION
Initial Approach: Send brief letter of inquiry describing program or project.

GRANTS ANALYSIS
Number of Grants: 10
Highest Grant: $343,420
Typical Range: $50,000 to $100,000
Disclosure Period: fiscal year ending September 30, 1990

RECENT GRANTS
343,420 Planned Parenthood, Chicago, IL

323,037 Council for Jewish Elderly, Evanston, IL — senior social services

175,150 Columbia College, Chicago, IL — cultural activity

123,504 City of Chicago, Chicago, IL — community activities

90,000 Stony Brook Foundation-State University of New

York, Stony Brook, NY

87,267 Spertus College of Judaica, Chicago, IL — Jewish culture and history education

79,000 Massachusetts Institute of Technology, Boston, MA — research

46,849 Drexel University, Philadelphia, PA

Rosenberg Family Foundation, William

CONTACT
Ann Rosenberg
Vice President
William Rosenberg Family Fdn.
6586 Patio Ln.
Boca Raton, FL 33433
(407) 392-2189

FINANCIAL SUMMARY
Recent Giving: $174,100 (1991); $160,250 (1990); $141,700 (1989)
Assets: $2,928,020 (1991); $2,670,645 (1990); $2,644,637 (1989)
Gifts Received: $75 (1991); $480,000 (1989)
EIN: 59-2675613

CONTRIBUTIONS SUMMARY
Donor(s): Ann Rosenberg, William Rosenberg
Typical Recipients: • *Arts & Humanities:* public broadcasting • *Education:* education administration, education associations • *Health:* hospices, medical research, single-disease health associations • *Religion:* religious organizations, synagogues • *Social Services:* child welfare, domestic violence
Grant Types: endowment, multiyear/continuing support, professorship, research, and seed money

GIVING OFFICERS
Ann Rosenberg: dir, vp, secy
William Rosenberg: pres, treas *B* Boston MA 1916 *CURR EMPL* fdr, chmn emeritus: Dunkin Donuts *CORP AFFIL* chmn exec comm, dir: Big V Supermarkets *NONPR AFFIL* trust: Intl Franchise Assn

APPLICATION INFORMATION
Initial Approach: Contributes only to preselected organizations.
Restrictions on Giving: Does not support individuals.

GRANTS ANALYSIS
Number of Grants: 24
Highest Grant: $100,000
Typical Range: $1,000 to $2,500
Disclosure Period: 1991

RECENT GRANTS
100,000 Dana Farber Cancer Institute, Boston, MA

38,600 Temple Beth-El, Boca Raton, FL

10,000 William H. Harris Foundation, Boston, MA — medical research

3,000 Diabetes Research Center of Massachusetts General Hospital, Boston, MA

2,500 National Center for Missing and Exploited Children, Arlington, VA — assist in search for missing children

2,500 WGBH Educational Foundation, Boston, MA

2,500 WPBT Communications Foundation, Miami, FL

2,000 Cardiology Research Trust of Massachusetts General Hospital, Boston, MA

2,000 Hospice by the Sea, Boca Raton, FL

1,000 Aid to Victims of Domestic Assault, Delray Beach, FL

Rosenberg Foundation

CONTACT
Kirke P. Wilson
Executive Director and Secretary
Rosenberg Foundation
47 Kearny St. Ste. 804
San Francisco, CA 94108
(415) 421-6105

FINANCIAL SUMMARY
Recent Giving: $2,000,000 (1993 est.); $1,950,615 (1992); $1,258,945 (1990)
Assets: $38,133,000 (1992 approx.); $32,976,725 (1990); $32,930,720 (1989)
EIN: 94-1186182

CONTRIBUTIONS SUMMARY

Donor(s): The Rosenberg Foundation was established in 1935 with a bequest from Max L. Rosenberg, a native Californian and head of Rosenberg Brothers and Co., a San Francisco dried fruit firm. In 1969, the foundation received an additional bequest from the estate of Mrs. Charlotte S. Mack, one of the foundation's early directors.

Typical Recipients: • *Civic & Public Affairs:* civil rights, ethnic/minority organizations, housing, law & justice, philanthropic organizations, rural affairs, urban & community affairs, women's affairs • *Education:* minority education • *Social Services:* community service organizations, legal aid

Grant Types: project

Geographic Distribution: primarily California

GIVING OFFICERS

Phyllis Cook: pres, dir

Benton W. Dial: dir

Robert F. Friedman: dir

Honorable Thelton E. Henderson: dir

Herma Hill Kay: dir *B* Orangeburg SC 1934 *ED* Southern Methodist Univ BA 1956; Univ Chicago JD 1959 *NONPR AFFIL* mem: Am Academy Arts & Sciences, Am Law Inst, Assn Am Law Schs, Bar US Supreme Court, CA Bar Assn, CA Women Lawyers, Order Coif; prof law, dean: Univ CA Berkeley; trust, dir: Equal Rights Advocates CA

Leslie L. Luttgens: treas, dir *PHIL AFFIL* dir, trust: Johnson (Walter S) Foundation

Mary S. Metz: dir *B* Rockhill SC 1937 *ED* Furman Univ BA 1958; Inst Phonetique; Sorbonne; LA St Univ PhD 1966 *CORP AFFIL* dir: Longs Drug Stores, Lucky Stores, Pacific Gas & Electric Co, Pacific Telesis, PacTel & PacBell, Union Bank *NONPR AFFIL* adv counc: Grad Sch Bus Stanford, Stanford Grad Sch Bus; assoc: Gannett Ctr Media Studies; dean extension: Univ CA; dean of extension: Univ CA; dir: World Affs Counc Northern CA; exec comm: Womens Coll Coalition; mem: Assn Independent CA Colls Univs, Bus-Higher Ed Forum, Natl Assn Independent Colls Univs, Phi Beta Kappa, Phi Kappa Phi,

Southern Conf Language Teaching, Western Coll Assn, Womens Forum West; mem ed bd: Liberal Ed, Liberal Ed; pres: Mills Coll; trust: Am Conservatory Theater; mem adv counc: SRI; mem comm leadership devel: Am Counc Ed

S. Donley Ritchey: vp, dir *B* Derry Township PA 1933 *ED* San Diego St Univ BS 1955; San Diego St Univ MS 1963 *CORP AFFIL* dir: Crocker Natl Bank, Crocker Natl Corp, Lucky Stores *NONPR AFFIL* dir: Bay Area Counc, Sloan Alumni Adv Bd, Stanford Univ, Western Assn Food Chains; dir, vchmn industrial rels: Food Mktg Inst

Norvel Smith: dir *NONPR AFFIL* assoc vice-chancellor: Univ CA Berkeley

Kirke P. Wilson: exec dir, secy

APPLICATION INFORMATION

Initial Approach:

Letters of inquiry describing the proposed project, the applying organization, and anticipated budget should be sent to the foundation. If the proposed project falls within the foundation's program priorities, a formal application will be requested.

A formal application should include a written proposal indicating the problem to be addressed; the plan of the project and its activities and goals; names and qualifications of the staff; the lasting significance of the project; anticipated goals and proposed evaluation of the project; future plans for the project; an itemized budget indicating project cost; grant amount requested; other sources of support; length of time for which support is requested and estimated future budgets; and materials describing the organization such as history, experience, a copy of IRS form indicating tax-exempt status, list of board members, and indication of the organization's status on affirmative action in reference to gender and minority groups. Applications may be submitted any time.

After a formal application has been received by the foundation, a visit and interview will be arranged. There is generally a two- to three-month waiting period before the foundation reviews an application.

Restrictions on Giving: No grants are given for scholarships, endowments, capital purposes, operating purposes, or matching gifts.

OTHER THINGS TO KNOW

Approved grants are paid in installments. Organizations receiving support are required to provide the foundation with periodic progress reports and itemized expenditure lists. The foundation expects unexpended funds to be returned.

Publications: policies and procedures brochure, and anniversary report

GRANTS ANALYSIS

Total Grants: $1,950,615*

Number of Grants: 48

Highest Grant: $104,000

Typical Range: $5,000 to $50,000

Disclosure Period: 1992

Note: Figures are based on grants authorized for 1992. Recent grants are derived from a 1992 grants list.

RECENT GRANTS

90,000 Radio Bilingue, Fresno, CA — Noticiero Latino

87,565 Immigrant Legal Resource Center, San Francisco, CA — Immigrant Children's project

85,000 Asian Pacific American Legal Center of Southern California, Los Angeles, CA — Language Rights project

85,000 Rural Community Assistance Corporation, Sacramento, CA — San Diego Farmworker Housing

75,000 Children Now, Oakland, CA — Building a Child Support System for the Twenty-first Century project

75,000 Mexican American Legal Defense and Educational Fund, Los Angeles, CA — California Language Rights program

75,000 National Housing Law Project, Berkeley, CA — Residents' Assistance project

70,000 Legal Services of Northern California, Sacramento,

CA — child support project

70,000 Los Angeles Center for Economic Survival, West Hollywood, CA — Affordable Housing Preservation project

69,000 Center for Community Advocacy, Salinas, CA — Farm Worker Housing project

Rosenberg Foundation, Alexis

CONTACT

Alexis Rosenberg Fdn.
c/o Fidelity Bank, N.A.
Broad and Walnut Sts.
Philadelphia, PA 19109
(215) 985-8361

FINANCIAL SUMMARY

Recent Giving: $81,500 (fiscal 1992); $92,500 (fiscal 1990); $66,000 (fiscal 1989)

Assets: $2,592,884 (fiscal year ending June 30, 1992); $2,238,211 (fiscal 1990); $2,057,982 (fiscal 1989)

EIN: 23-2222722

CONTRIBUTIONS SUMMARY

Donor(s): the late Alexis Rosenberg

Typical Recipients: • *Arts & Humanities:* community arts, performing arts, theater • *Education:* colleges & universities, medical education • *Health:* hospitals • *Social Services:* community service organizations, united funds, youth organizations

Grant Types: general support

Geographic Distribution: focus on PA

GIVING OFFICERS

Edward Daley: trust

Robert Kauffman Greenfield: trust, pres *B* Philadelphia PA 1915 *ED* Swarthmore Coll AB 1936; Harvard Univ LLB 1939; PA Coll Podiatric Medicine LHD 1990 *CURR EMPL* coun: Montgomery McCracken Walker & Rhoads *NONPR AFFIL* mem: Am Bar Assn, PA Bar Assn, Philadelphia Bar Assn; trust: PA Coll Podiatric Medicine

APPLICATION INFORMATION

Initial Approach: Send brief letter describing program. There are no deadlines.

Restrictions on Giving: Does not support individuals.

GRANTS ANALYSIS

Number of Grants: 23

Highest Grant: $5,000

Typical Range: $1,000 to $5,000

Disclosure Period: fiscal year ending June 30, 1992

RECENT GRANTS

5,000 Dignity Housing Youth Services, Philadelphia, PA

5,000 Easter Seal Society, Philadelphia, PA

5,000 Education for Patenting, Philadelphia, PA

5,000 Germantown Friends School, Philadelphia, PA

5,000 Philadelphia Futures, Philadelphia, PA

5,000 Philadelphia Society for Services to Children, Philadelphia, PA

5,000 St. Joseph's University, Philadelphia, PA

5,000 Supportive Child/Adult Network, Philadelphia, PA

5,000 Temple University, Philadelphia, PA

5,000 YMCA, Abington, PA

Rosenberg Foundation, Henry and Ruth Blaustein

CONTACT

Henry A. Rosenberg, Jr.
President
Henry and Ruth Blaustein Rosenberg Fdn.
Blaustein Bldg.
PO Box 238
Baltimore, MD 21203

FINANCIAL SUMMARY

Recent Giving: $1,555,012 (1990); $979,850 (1989); $841,800 (1988)

Assets: $8,102,378 (1990); $8,906,102 (1989); $7,896,510 (1988)

Gifts Received: $387,500 (1990); $337,500 (1989); $330,000 (1988)

EIN: 52-6038384

CONTRIBUTIONS SUMMARY

Donor(s): Ruth Blaustein Rosenberg, Henry A. Rosenberg, Jr.

Typical Recipients: • *Arts & Humanities:* community arts, museums/galleries, music • *Education:* colleges & universities, private education (precollege) • *Health:* health organizations, hospitals, pediatric health • *Religion:* religious organizations • *Social Services:* community service organizations

Grant Types: general support

Geographic Distribution: focus on the greater Baltimore, MD, area

GIVING OFFICERS

Judith R. Hoffberger: trust

Ruth R. Marder: trust

Henry A. Rosenberg, Jr.: pres, trust *B* Pittsburgh PA 1929 *ED* Hobart Coll BA 1952 *CURR EMPL* chmn, chmn exec comm, ceo, dir: Crown Central Petroleum Corp *CORP AFFIL* dir: Am Trading & Production Corp, Signet Banking Corp, US Fidelity & Guaranty Co; mem listed co adv comm: Am Stock Exchange *NONPR AFFIL* chmn, dir, mem exec comm: Natl Petroleum Refiners Assn; dir: Crohn's & Colitis Fdn, Goucher Coll, Johns Hopkins Hosp, McDonogh Sch, Natl Aquarium, Natl Aquarium Baltimore, Natl Flag Day Fdn, Un Way Central MD, YMCA Greater Baltimore; mem: Am Petroleum Inst, Natl Petroleum Counc, Twenty-Five Year Club Petroleum Indus; mem adv bd: William Donald Schaefer Ctr Pub Policy; mem natl exec bd: Boy Scouts Am

Ruth Blaustein Rosenberg: chmn, trust *CORP AFFIL* dir: Am Trading & Production Corp

Frank A. Strzelczyk: secy, treas

APPLICATION INFORMATION

Initial Approach: Send brief letter of inquiry describing program or project. There are no deadlines.

GRANTS ANALYSIS

Number of Grants: 102

Highest Grant: $353,500

Typical Range: $250 to $5,000

Disclosure Period: 1990

RECENT GRANTS

353,500 Associated Jewish Charities and Welfare Fund, Baltimore, MD

270,000 Baltimore Symphony Orchestra, Baltimore, MD

71,100 McDonogh School, McDonogh, MD

50,000 Baltimore Hebrew Congregation, Baltimore, MD

30,500 Bennington College Corporation, Bennington, VT

20,000 Community Foundation of the Greater Baltimore Area, Baltimore, MD

16,750 Hobart and William Smith Colleges, Geneva, NY

15,000 Concert Artists of Baltimore, Baltimore, MD

15,000 National Flag Day Foundation, Baltimore, MD

12,000 Boy Scouts of America, Baltimore, MD

Rosenberg Foundation, Sunny and Abe

CONTACT

Sonia Rosenberg
Vice President
c/o Star Industries, Inc.
345 Underhill Blvd.
Syosset, NY 11791
(718) 895-8950

FINANCIAL SUMMARY

Recent Giving: $524,550 (1991); $307,285 (1990); $386,275 (1989)

Assets: $11,058,677 (1991); $9,327,385 (1990); $9,471,043 (1989)

Gifts Received: $500,000 (1988)

EIN: 13-6210591

CONTRIBUTIONS SUMMARY

Donor(s): Abraham Rosenberg

Typical Recipients: • *Civic & Public Affairs:* environmental affairs, ethnic/minority organizations, women's affairs • *Education:* colleges & universities, education funds, medical education, private education (precollege) • *Health:* geriatric health, hospitals • *International:* international development/relief • *Religion:* religious organizations • *Social Services:* child welfare, homes

Grant Types: general support

GIVING OFFICERS

Susan Goldstein: secy, trust

Abraham Rosenberg: pres, treas

Michael Rosenberg: secy, trust

Sonia Rosenberg: vp, secy

APPLICATION INFORMATION

Initial Approach: Send brief letter of inquiry describing program or project. There are no deadlines.

GRANTS ANALYSIS

Number of Grants: 67

Highest Grant: $236,000

Typical Range: $100 to $1,000

Disclosure Period: 1991

RECENT GRANTS

236,000 United Jewish Appeal Federation of Jewish Philanthropies, New York, NY

76,000 Educational Alliance, New York, NY

30,000 Jerusalem Foundation, New York, NY

30,000 New York University Student Art Center Lounge, New York, NY

25,000 Stony Brook University Foundation, Stony Brook, NY

20,000 Dalton School, New York, NY

15,000 Baruch College, New York, NY

10,200 Women's American ORT, Palm Beach, FL

10,000 New York University Medical Center, New York, NY

5,400 Town Club Foundation, New York, NY

Rosenberg Foundation, William J. and Tina

CONTACT

Richard Chapman
William J. and Tina Rosenberg Fdn.
c/o Southeast Bank, N.A.
One S.E. Financial Center
Miami, FL 33131
(305) 375-6839

FINANCIAL SUMMARY

Recent Giving: $125,350 (fiscal 1991); $88,100 (fiscal 1990); $134,412 (fiscal 1989)

Assets: $2,876,529 (fiscal year ending April 30, 1990); $2,773,194 (fiscal 1989)
EIN: 23-7088390

CONTRIBUTIONS SUMMARY

Donor(s): the late Tina Rosenberg
Typical Recipients: • *Arts & Humanities:* arts centers, music, performing arts, theater • *Education:* community & junior colleges • *Social Services:* child welfare, counseling, family services, united funds, youth organizations
Grant Types: general support
Geographic Distribution: focus on Dade County, FL

GIVING OFFICERS

Jack G. Admire: trust

APPLICATION INFORMATION

Initial Approach: Send brief letter describing program. There are no deadlines.
Restrictions on Giving: Does not support individuals.

OTHER THINGS TO KNOW

Publications: Application Guidelines

GRANTS ANALYSIS

Number of Grants: 13
Highest Grant: $20,000
Typical Range: $1,000 to $10,000
Disclosure Period: fiscal year ending April 30, 1990

RECENT GRANTS

20,000 Museum of Science, Miami, FL
15,600 Haitian Refugee Center, Miami, FL
10,000 Coconut Grove Playhouse, Coconut Grove, FL
10,000 Encounters in Excellence, Miami, FL
10,000 Public Education Fund, Miami, FL
7,500 Florida State University, Tallahassee, FL
7,500 Local Initiatives Support Corporation, Miami, FL
5,000 Junior Orange Bowl Committee, Miami, FL
5,000 Miami Dade Community College Foundation, Miami, FL
5,000 Southern Scholarship Foundation, Tallahassee, FL

Rosenberg, Jr. Family Foundation, Louise and Claude

CONTACT

Louise and Claude Rosenberg, Jr. Family Foundation
2465 Pacific Avenue
San Francisco, CA 94115-1237
(415) 921-2465

FINANCIAL SUMMARY

Recent Giving: $680,895 (fiscal 1991); $476,100 (fiscal 1990)
Assets: $12,362,138 (fiscal year ending October 31, 1991); $7,270,253 (fiscal 1990)
Gifts Received: $2,665,169 (fiscal 1991)
EIN: 94-3031132

CONTRIBUTIONS SUMMARY

Typical Recipients: • *Arts & Humanities:* dance, music • *Civic & Public Affairs:* environmental affairs • *Education:* business education • *Health:* medical research • *Religion:* synagogues • *Social Services:* child welfare, community centers, family services, united funds
Grant Types: general support and research

GIVING OFFICERS

John P. Levin, Jr.: dir
Claude N. Rosenberg, Jr.: secy, dir
Louise J. Rosenberg: pres, dir

APPLICATION INFORMATION

Initial Approach: The foundation reports no specific application guidelines. Send a brief letter of inquiry, including statement of purpose, amount requested, and proof of tax-exempt status.

GRANTS ANALYSIS

Total Grants: $680,895
Number of Grants: 46
Highest Grant: $150,000
Typical Range: $10,000 to $100,000
Disclosure Period: fiscal year ending October 31, 1991

RECENT GRANTS

150,000 Stanford Graduate School of Business, Palo Alto, Stanford, CA
100,000 Jewish Community Center, San Francisco, CA
83,000 Jewish Community Federation, San Francisco, CA
75,000 Jewish Family and Children's Services, San Francisco, CA
73,895 Developmental Studies Center, San Ramon, CA
30,000 United Way, San Francisco, CA
25,000 Congregation Emanu-El, San Francisco, CA
25,000 Conservation International Foundation, Washington, DC
14,500 San Francisco Ballet, San Francisco, CA
10,000 San Francisco Symphony Adventures, San Francisco, CA

Rosenbloom Foundation, Ben and Esther

CONTACT

Ben Rosenbloom
Chairman
Ben and Esther Rosenbloom Fdn.
106 Old Court Rd., Ste. 302
Baltimore, MD 21208
(410) 653-0239

FINANCIAL SUMMARY

Recent Giving: $444,190 (1991); $626,818 (1990); $215,584 (1989)
Assets: $16,990,817 (1991); $2,235,234 (1990); $1,772,039 (1989)
Gifts Received: $7,525 (1991)
Fiscal Note: In 1991, contributions were received from Ben Rosenbloom.
EIN: 52-1258672

CONTRIBUTIONS SUMMARY

Donor(s): The foundation was established in 1982 by Ben Rosenbloom.
Typical Recipients: • *Arts & Humanities:* history/historic preservation, music • *Civic & Public Affairs:* ethnic/minority organizations, public policy • *Education:* business education, colleges & universities, religious education • *Health:* hospitals, single-disease health associations • *International:* foreign educational institutions • *Religion:* religious organizations, synagogues • *Social Services:* united funds
Grant Types: general support
Geographic Distribution: eastern United States, focus on Baltimore, MD

GIVING OFFICERS

Ben Rosenbloom: chmn
Esther Rosenbloom: vp
Howard Rosenbloom: pres

APPLICATION INFORMATION

Initial Approach:
The foundation requests applications be made in writing. Written proposals should include information describing the organization and the purpose for which the funds will be used.
The foundation has no deadline for submitting proposals. Applications are reviewed as they are received.
Restrictions on Giving: The foundation reports applicants are limited to corporations qualifying under section 501(c)(3) status. The foundation does not make grants to individuals.

GRANTS ANALYSIS

Total Grants: $444,190
Number of Grants: 58
Highest Grant: $210,000
Typical Range: $500 to $5,000
Disclosure Period: 1991
Note: Average grant figure does not include the highest grant of $210,000. Recent grants are derived from a 1991 grants list.

RECENT GRANTS

210,000 Associated Jewish Community Federation, Baltimore, MD
30,300 Anti-Defamation League of B'nai B'rith, New York, NY
30,000 Associated Jewish Charities, Baltimore, MD
25,000 College-Bound Foundation, Baltimore, MD
25,000 Sinai Hospital, Baltimore, MD
20,000 US Holocaust Memorial Museum, Washington, DC
17,590 Chizuk Amund Congregation, Baltimore, MD
13,000 P.E.F. Israel Endowment Fund, New York, NY
11,000 Hadassah, New York, NY

10,000 Villa Julie College, Baltimore, MD

Rosenbluth Travel Agency

Revenue: $135.0 million
Employees: 3,000
Headquarters: Philadelphia, PA
SIC Major Group:
Transportation Services

CONTACT
Patricia DiSantis
Corporate Contributions
Rosenbluth Travel Agency
1515 Walnut St.
Philadelphia, PA 19102
(215) 563-1070

CONTRIBUTIONS SUMMARY
Operating Locations: PA (Philadelphia)

CORP. OFFICERS
Eugene Block: *CURR EMPL* co-chmn: Rosenbluth Travel Agency
David Fisher: *CURR EMPL* cfo: Rosenbluth Travel Agency
Hal F. Rosenbluth: *CURR EMPL* pres, ceo: Rosenbluth Travel Agency
Harold S. Rosenbluth: *CURR EMPL* co-chmn: Rosenbluth Travel Agency

Rosenhaus Peace Foundation, Sarah and Matthew

CONTACT
Irving Rosenhaus
Managing Director
Sarah and Matthew Rosenhaus Peace Fdn.
Picatinny Rd.
Morristown, NJ 07960
(201) 267-6583

FINANCIAL SUMMARY
Recent Giving: $678,000 (fiscal 1987)
Assets: $10,516,204 (fiscal year ending July 31, 1987)
Gifts Received: $235,447 (fiscal 1987)
EIN: 13-6136983

CONTRIBUTIONS SUMMARY
Donor(s): the late Sarah Rosenhaus, the late Matthew B. Rosenhaus
Typical Recipients: • *Civic & Public Affairs:* international affairs • *Education:* religious education • *Health:* medical re-

search • *Religion:* religious organizations
Grant Types: general support
Geographic Distribution: focus on NJ and NY

GIVING OFFICERS
Robert Bobrow: treas, dir
Anetra Chester: dir
Jerome Cossman: dir
Alice Fetro: secy, dir
Harriet Grosc: dir
Albert Rosenhaus: dir
Irving R. Rosenhaus: managing dir
Lawrence Rosenhaus: dir
Gila Rosenhaus Weiner: dir

APPLICATION INFORMATION
Initial Approach: Contributes only to preselected organizations.
Restrictions on Giving: Does not support individuals.

Rosenkranz Foundation

CONTACT
Rosenkranz Foundation
650 Fifth Avenue, 27th Floor
New York, NY 10019-6108

FINANCIAL SUMMARY
Recent Giving: $197,188 (fiscal 1990)
Assets: $5,507,943 (fiscal year ending November 30, 1990)
EIN: 13-3321145

GIVING OFFICERS
Linda Rike: secy
Margaret Rosenkranz: treas, dir
Robert Rosenkranz: pres, dir

APPLICATION INFORMATION
Initial Approach: The foundation reports it only makes contributions to preselected organizations and does not accept unsolicited requests for funds.

GRANTS ANALYSIS
Total Grants: $197,188
Number of Grants: 24
Highest Grant: $140,500
Disclosure Period: fiscal year ending November 30, 1990

Rosenstiel Foundation

CONTACT
Maurice Greenbaum
Rosenstiel Fdn.
c/o Rosenman & Colin
575 Madison Aenue, 11th Fl.
New York, NY 10022
(212) 940-8837

FINANCIAL SUMMARY
Recent Giving: $589,625 (1991); $550,475 (1989); $590,075 (1988)
Assets: $14,918,523 (1991); $13,821,561 (1989); $11,937,644 (1988)
EIN: 06-6034536

CONTRIBUTIONS SUMMARY
Donor(s): The foundation was incorporated in 1950 by the late Lewis S. Rosenstiel.
Typical Recipients: • *Arts & Humanities:* arts associations, cinema, dance, museums/galleries, music, opera, performing arts, public broadcasting, theater • *Civic & Public Affairs:* ethnic/minority organizations, philanthropic organizations, zoos/botanical gardens • *Education:* arts education, colleges & universities, medical education, science/technology education • *Health:* health organizations, hospitals, medical research, public health, single-disease health associations • *Religion:* churches, religious organizations • *Science:* scientific institutes • *Social Services:* counseling, shelters/homelessness
Grant Types: general support and seed money
Geographic Distribution: eastern United States, with a focus on New York, NY

GIVING OFFICERS
Maurice C. Greenbaum: secy *B* Detroit MI 1918 *ED* Wayne St Univ BA 1938; Univ MI JD 1941; NY Univ LLM 1948 *CURR EMPL* couns: Rosenman & Colin *CORP AFFIL* dir: Entotech, Novo Nordisk Biochem, Novo Nordisk Bioindustrials, Scrambler, Wigwam *NONPR AFFIL* assoc trust: North Shore Univ Hosp; dir: World Rehab Fund
Elizabeth R. Kabler: vp
Blanka A. Rosenstiel: pres

APPLICATION INFORMATION
Initial Approach: Restrictions on Giving: The foundation supports preselected organizations and does not accept unsolicited requests for funds. The foundation does not make grants to individuals.

GRANTS ANALYSIS
Total Grants: $589,625
Number of Grants: 83
Highest Grant: $145,000
Typical Range: $1,000 to $6,000
Disclosure Period: 1991
Note: Average grant figure does not include the highest grant of $145,000. Recent grants are derived from a 1991 grants list.

RECENT GRANTS
145,000 American Institute of Polish Culture, Miami, FL
60,000 Chopin Foundation of US, Miami, FL
50,000 Brandeis University, Bigel Institute for Health Policy, Waltham, MA
32,500 New York Citizens Committee on Health Care Decisions, New York, NY
30,900 Metropolitan Museum of Art, New York, NY
25,000 Rosentiel School of Marine and Atmospheric Science, University of Miami, Miami, FL
25,000 Whitney Museum of American Art, New York, NY
20,500 Operation Smile, Norfolk, VA
20,000 American Center for Polish Culture, Stamford, CT
15,000 Coconut Grove Playhouse State Theater of Florida, Gainesville, FL

Rosenthal Foundation

CONTACT
Rosenthal Foundation
3300 First National Tower
Louisville, KY 40202-3197

FINANCIAL SUMMARY
Recent Giving: $234,340 (1990)
Assets: $4,297,845 (1990)
EIN: 61-1161776

GIVING OFFICERS

Betty M. Rosenthal: secy, treas
Warren W. Rosenthal: pres, mgr
Martin S. Weinberg: dir

APPLICATION INFORMATION

Initial Approach: The foundation reports it only makes contributions to preselected organizations and does not accept unsolicited requests for funds.

GRANTS ANALYSIS

Total Grants: $234,340
Number of Grants: 41
Highest Grant: $50,000
Disclosure Period: 1990

Rosenthal Foundation, Benjamin J.

CONTACT

Ann Smith
Benjamin J. Rosenthal Fdn.
36 South State St., Rm. 802
Chicago, IL 60603
(312) 726-6163

FINANCIAL SUMMARY

Recent Giving: $122,245 (1989); $128,250 (1987)
Assets: $3,057,480 (1989); $2,872,200 (1987)
EIN: 36-2523643

CONTRIBUTIONS SUMMARY

Donor(s): Benjamin J. Rosenthal
Typical Recipients: • *Arts & Humanities:* public broadcasting • *Civic & Public Affairs:* environmental affairs, international affairs, public policy, zoos/botanical gardens • *Education:* religious education • *Health:* health organizations, hospices • *Religion:* churches, missionary activities, religious organizations • *Social Services:* child welfare, community service organizations, homes, united funds, youth organizations
Grant Types: general support
Geographic Distribution: focus on Chicago, IL

GIVING OFFICERS

Melissa Foulke: secy
Elaine R. Moseley: vp, treas
Gladys R. Tartiere: pres

APPLICATION INFORMATION

Initial Approach: Contributes only to preselected organizations.

GRANTS ANALYSIS

Number of Grants: 290
Highest Grant: $5,400
Typical Range: $100 to $2,000
Disclosure Period: 1989

RECENT GRANTS

5,400 Chicago Youth Centers, Chicago, IL
5,000 Chicago Tribune Charities Christmas Fund, Chicago, IL
5,000 Chicago Youth Centers, Chicago, IL
5,000 Lincoln Park Zoological Society, Chicago, IL
5,000 Maram's, Chicago, IL
3,000 Johns Hopkins University School of Medicine, Baltimore, MD
2,500 United Way, Chicago, IL
2,250 Account for Prisoners of War and Missing in Action, Chicago, IL
2,000 United Charities of Chicago, Chicago, IL
2,000 YMCA, Chicago, IL

Rosenthal Foundation, Ida and William

CONTACT

Catherine C. Brawer
President
Ida and William Rosenthal Fdn.
90 Park Ave.
New York, NY 10016
(212) 953-1418

FINANCIAL SUMMARY

Recent Giving: $292,516 (fiscal 1990); $356,090 (fiscal 1989)
Assets: $4,436,316 (fiscal year ending August 31, 1990); $4,435,996 (fiscal 1989)
EIN: 13-6141274

CONTRIBUTIONS SUMMARY

Donor(s): the late Ida Rosenthal, the late William Rosenthal
Typical Recipients: • *Arts & Humanities:* dance, museums/galleries, music • *Civic & Public Affairs:* civil rights, women's affairs • *Education:* colleges & universities, education funds, legal education, minority education, private education (precollege) • *Health:* hospitals • *Social Services:* child welfare, community centers, community service organizations, youth organizations
Grant Types: project, scholarship, and seed money
Geographic Distribution: focus on NY and Hudson County, NJ; some support also in GA, FL, and WV; support for projects in the Dominican Republic through national organizations.

GIVING OFFICERS

Catherine Coleman Brawer: pres, dir *B* New York NY 1943 *ED* Sarah Lawrence Coll 1964; NY Univ 1966 *CORP AFFIL* dir: Maidenform Inc
Robert A. Brawer: vp, dir
Elizabeth J. Coleman: vp, dir
Abraham Pascal Kanner: vp *B* New York NY 1911 *ED* NY Univ 1931; Harvard Univ 1933 *CURR EMPL* sr vp: Maidenform *CORP AFFIL* sr vp: Maidenform Inc
David C. Masket: vp, treas, dir
Steven N. Masket: secy
Robert N. Stroup: dir

APPLICATION INFORMATION

Initial Approach: Send brief letter of inquiry describing program or project. There are no deadlines.
Restrictions on Giving: Does not support individuals or provide loans.

GRANTS ANALYSIS

Number of Grants: 42
Highest Grant: $100,000
Typical Range: $1,000 to $10,000
Disclosure Period: fiscal year ending August 31, 1990

RECENT GRANTS

100,000 Barnard College, New York, NY — scholarship endowment
29,600 Community Service Society of New York, New York, NY — for La Romana education project for school improvement
20,000 Montefiore Womens Center, New York, NY — support for child development specialist to establish program for children of minority women participating in the Center's AIDS-related counseling programs
12,000 Paideia School, Atlanta, GA — to institute beginning French classes in eighth grade
10,250 Boy Scouts of America, Bayonne, NJ
10,000 Ethical Culture Schools, New York, NY — Joseph A. Coleman scholarship fund and capital campaign
10,000 Institute of Fine Arts, New York University, New York, NY — fellowship for outstanding first-year student
8,230 Lenox Hill Hospital, New York, NY — in support of patient assistance and community entitlement program in department of social work
7,000 Independent Curators Incorporated, New York, NY — support of exhibition and catalogue Eternal Metaphors: New Art from Italy
5,000 Katonah Art Gallery, Katonah, NY

Rosenthal Foundation, Richard and Hinda

CONTACT

Hinda Gould Rosenthal
President
Richard and Hinda Rosenthal Fdn.
5 High Ridge Park
Stamford, CT 06905
(203) 322-9900

FINANCIAL SUMMARY

Recent Giving: $159,810 (1990); $68,271 (1989); $320,000 (1988)
Assets: $11,615,660 (1990); $11,201,937 (1989); $9,800,000 (1988)
Gifts Received: $13,406 (1990)
Fiscal Note: In 1990, contributions were received from Richard L. Rosenthal.
EIN: 13-6104817

CONTRIBUTIONS SUMMARY

Donor(s): Richard I. Rosenthal
Typical Recipients: • *Arts & Humanities:* arts centers, cinema, museums/galleries, music, public broadcasting • *Civic & Public Affairs:* civil rights, environmental affairs, ethnic/minority organizations • *Education:* colleges & universities, medical education, religious education • *Health:* hospitals, medical research, pediatric health, single-disease health associations • *Religion:* religious organizations • *Social Services:* child welfare, disabled, youth organizations
Grant Types: capital, general support, project, and research

GIVING OFFICERS

Hinda Gould Rosenthal: pres, trust
Richard L. Rosenthal, Jr.: vp, trust
Richard Laurence Rosenthal: chmn, trust *B* Winnipeg Manitoba Canada 1915 *ED* NY Univ BS 1936 *CURR EMPL* chmn, chmn exec comm: Citizens Utilities Co *CORP AFFIL* chmn, chmn exec comm: Citizens Utilities Co; dir: Executive Re Inc; pres, treas, dir: Assets Admin & Mgmt Inc; pres, treas, trust: Aldred Investment Trust *NONPR AFFIL* mem: World Bus Counc
Jamie G. R. Wolf: vp, trust

APPLICATION INFORMATION

Initial Approach: Contributes only to preselected organizations.
Restrictions on Giving: Does not support individuals.

OTHER THINGS TO KNOW

Publications: Program Policy Statement

GRANTS ANALYSIS

Number of Grants: 124
Highest Grant: $15,000
Typical Range: $25 to $5,000
Disclosure Period: 1990

RECENT GRANTS

15,000 University of California Los Angeles Children's Neurological Research, Los Angeles, CA
7,500 American Film Institute, Washington, DC
7,500 Duke University, Durham, NC
7,500 University of Chicago, Chicago, IL
7,500 University of Virginia, Charlottesville, VA
5,000 Pediatric AIDS Foundation, Los Angeles, CA
4,500 Choate Rosemary Hall, Wallingford, CT
3,658 American College of Physicians, Philadelphia, PA
3,000 Liberty Hill Foundation, Santa Monica, CA
3,000 Mount Sinai Medical Center, New York, NY

Rosenthal Foundation, Richard and Lois

CONTACT

Richard and Lois Rosenthal Fdn.
Spicer and Oppenheim
Seven World Trade Center
New York, NY 10048

FINANCIAL SUMMARY

Recent Giving: $578,200 (1989); $350,231 (1987)
Assets: $739,320 (1987)
EIN: 23-7048452

CONTRIBUTIONS SUMMARY

Donor(s): the late Richard Rosenthal
Typical Recipients: • *Religion:* religious organizations, synagogues • *Social Services:* youth organizations
Grant Types: general support
Geographic Distribution: focus on New York, NY

GIVING OFFICERS

Lois Rosenthal: vp, dir

APPLICATION INFORMATION

Initial Approach: Contributes only to preselected organizations.
Restrictions on Giving: Does not support individuals.

GRANTS ANALYSIS

Number of Grants: 2
Highest Grant: $528,200
Disclosure Period: 1989

RECENT GRANTS

528,200 Richard G. Rosenthal YM-YWHA of Northern Westchester, Pleasantville, NJ
60,000 Congregation of Sons of Israel, Briarcliff Manor, NY

Rosenthal Foundation, Samuel

CONTACT

Charlotte R. Kramer
Trustee
Samuel Rosenthal Foundation
Halle Bldg., Ste. 810
1228 Euclid Ave.
Cleveland, OH 44115-8125
(216) 523-8125

FINANCIAL SUMMARY

Recent Giving: $795,423 (fiscal 1991); $671,789 (fiscal 1990); $601,530 (fiscal 1989)
Assets: $10,583,553 (fiscal year ending March 31, 1991); $10,003,676 (fiscal 1990); $9,633,828 (fiscal 1989)
EIN: 34-6558832

CONTRIBUTIONS SUMMARY

Donor(s): Work Wear Corp., Inc.
Typical Recipients: • *Arts & Humanities:* community arts, music • *Education:* colleges & universities, medical education, religious education • *Health:* hospitals, medical research, nursing services, pediatric health • *Religion:* religious organizations, synagogues • *Social Services:* aged, community centers, community service organizations, family planning, food/clothing distribution, homes
Grant Types: general support and research
Geographic Distribution: focus on Cleveland, OH

GIVING OFFICERS

Cynthia R. Boardman: trust
Jane R. Horvitz: trust
Charlotte R. Kramer: trust
Mark R. Kramer: trust
Leighton A. Rosenthal: trust *B* Buffalo NY 1915 *ED* Univ PA *CURR EMPL* pres: Lars Aviation *CORP AFFIL* pres: Lars Aviation *NONPR AFFIL* dir: OH Motorists Assn; trust: Jewish Commun Federation Cleveland, Preservation Fdn Palm Beach

APPLICATION INFORMATION

Initial Approach: Send brief letter of inquiry describing program. There are no deadlines.
Restrictions on Giving: Does not support individuals.

OTHER THINGS TO KNOW

Publications: Application Guidelines

GRANTS ANALYSIS

Number of Grants: 72
Highest Grant: $315,000
Typical Range: $1,000 to $5,000
Disclosure Period: fiscal year ending March 31, 1991

RECENT GRANTS

315,000 Jewish Community Federation, Cleveland, OH
50,000 Children's Hospital, Boston, MA — cardiovascular surgical research
50,000 Cleveland Clinic Foundation, Cleveland, OH — medical research
50,000 Cleveland College of Jewish Studies, Cleveland, OH — teacher training in Jewish education
50,000 Montefiore Home, Cleveland Heights, OH
17,500 Harvest for Hunger, Cleveland, OH
16,667 Hathaway Brown School, Shaker Heights, OH — capital campaign
15,000 Georgetown University, Washington, DC
12,500 Fessenden School, West Newton, MA
10,000 Children's Hospital, Boston, MA — cerebral palsy clinic

Rosenthal-Statter Foundation

CONTACT

Rosenthal-Statter Foundation
766 Old Hammonds Ferry Road
Linthicum, MD 21090-2151

FINANCIAL SUMMARY

Recent Giving: $835,000 (1990)
Assets: $1,876,220 (1990)
Gifts Received: $281,138 (1990)
EIN: 52-6390308

CONTRIBUTIONS SUMMARY

Typical Recipients: • *Health:* health organizations, medical research, pediatric health, sin-

gle-disease health associations
• *Religion:* synagogues
Grant Types: general support
and research

APPLICATION INFORMATION

Initial Approach: The foundation reports no specific application guidelines. Send a brief letter of inquiry, including statement of purpose, amount requested, and proof of tax-exempt status.

GRANTS ANALYSIS

Total Grants: $835,000
Number of Grants: 12
Highest Grant: $500,000
Typical Range: $5,000 to $15,000
Disclosure Period: 1990

RECENT GRANTS

500,000 Sinai Hospital, Baltimore, MD
250,000 Baltimore Hebrew Congregation, Baltimore, MD
15,000 Sinai Hospital, Baltimore, MD
10,000 Hadassah Medical Institutions, Baltimore, MD
10,000 JFK Institute, Baltimore, MD
10,000 Mind-Brain Institute, Baltimore, MD
10,000 Mount Washington Hospital, Baltimore, MD
10,000 Save-A-Heart Foundation, Baltimore, MD
10,000 Shrine for Crippled Children, Baltimore, MD
5,000 Beth Tfiloh Congregation, Baltimore, MD

Rosenwald Family Fund, William

CONTACT

David P. Steinmann
Secretary
William Rosenwald Family Fund
122 East 42nd St., 24th Fl.
New York, NY 10168
(212) 697-2420

FINANCIAL SUMMARY

Recent Giving: $1,128,130 (1991); $509,845 (1990); $2,141,234 (1989)
Assets: $15,032,216 (1991); $14,322,579 (1990); $15,663,906 (1989)
EIN: 13-1635289

CONTRIBUTIONS SUMMARY

Donor(s): The foundation was incorporated in 1938 by William Rosenwald and family.
Typical Recipients: • *Arts & Humanities:* arts centers, theater, visual arts • *Civic & Public Affairs:* international affairs, philanthropic organizations, professional & trade associations • *Education:* colleges & universities, literacy, medical education, private education (precollege) • *Health:* hospitals • *International:* international organizations • *Religion:* churches, religious organizations • *Social Services:* child welfare, community service organizations, youth organizations
Grant Types: general support
Geographic Distribution: focus on New York

GIVING OFFICERS

Nina K. Rosenwald: vp, dir *PHIL AFFIL* chmn, pres: William & Mary Rosenwald Foundation; vp, dir: Am Philanthropic Foundation
William Rosenwald: pres, treas, dir *B* Chicago IL 1903 *ED* MA Inst Tech BS 1924 *NONPR AFFIL* chmn: 88 Pacesetters Campaign; dir, hon vp: Am Jewish Joint Distribution Comm; dir, life mem: Counc Jewish Federations; hon life trust: Mus Science & Indus Chicago; hon natl chmn: Am Jewish Comm; hon pres: Un Jewish Appeal Federation Jewish Philanthropies NY; hon trust: Tuskegee Univ; mem exec comm: Israel Ed Fund; vp: Hebrew Immigrant Aid Soc *PHIL AFFIL* life trust: Federation Jewish Philanthropies NY
Alice Rosenwald Sigelman: vp, dir *PHIL AFFIL* chmn, dir: Forest House Fund; vp: William & Mary Rosenwald Foundation; vp, dir: Am Philanthropic Foundation
David P. Steinmann: secy
Elizabeth Rosenwald Varet: vp, dir *ED* Harvard Univ AB 1965 *CORP AFFIL* dir: Am Securities Corp, Amtek, Ketema Corp *PHIL AFFIL* chmn: Am Charitable Fund; vp, dir: Am Philanthropic Foundation, William & Mary Rosenwald Foundation

APPLICATION INFORMATION

Initial Approach: Restrictions on Giving: The founda-

tion supports preselected organizations and does not accept unsolicited requests for funds. The foundation does not make grants to individuals.

GRANTS ANALYSIS

Total Grants: $1,128,130
Number of Grants: 44
Highest Grant: $814,100
Typical Range: $1,000 to $8,000
Disclosure Period: 1991
Note: Average grant figure does not include the highest grant of $814,100. Recent grants are derived from a 1991 grants list.

RECENT GRANTS

814,100 United Jewish Appeal Federation, New York, NY
166,280 Kirksville College, Kirksville, MO — Osteopathic Medicine
30,000 American Jewish Committee, New York, NY
26,800 National Book Foundation, New York, NY
20,000 New York Hospital Cornell Medical Center, New York, NY
10,000 Pan American Center, New York, NY
6,000 Ragosin Institute, New York, NY
5,000 Day School, New York, NY
5,000 Jewish Center of Hamptons, East Hampton, NY
4,000 International Center of Photography, New York, NY

Rose's Stores, Inc.

Sales: $1.42 billion
Employees: 18,000
Headquarters: Henderson, NC
SIC Major Group: Apparel & Accessory Stores, Eating & Drinking Places, General Merchandise Stores, and Miscellaneous Retail

CONTACT

George Blackburn
Vice President
Rose's Stores, Inc.
218-220 Garrett St.
PO Drawer 947
Henderson, NC 27536
(919) 430-2600

CONTRIBUTIONS SUMMARY

Operating Locations: NC (Henderson)

CORP. OFFICERS

R. Edward Anderson: *CURR EMPL* sr vp, cfo: Roses Stores
George L. Jones: *CURR EMPL* pres, ceo: Roses Stores

Ross Corp. / Ross Foundation

Employees: 250
Headquarters: Grafton, OH
SIC Major Group: Electric, Gas & Sanitary Services

CONTACT

Maureen M. Cromling
President
Ross Foundation
36790 Giles Rd.
Grafton, OH 44044-9752
(216) 748-2200

FINANCIAL SUMMARY

Recent Giving: $41,910 (fiscal 1992); $49,631 (fiscal 1991); $26,400 (fiscal 1990)
Assets: $162,749 (fiscal year ending May 31, 1990)
Gifts Received: $100,000 (fiscal 1990)
Fiscal Note: In fiscal 1992, contributions were received from the Ross Corporation.
EIN: 34-1442262

CONTRIBUTIONS SUMMARY

Typical Recipients: • *Arts & Humanities:* libraries • *Education:* general
Grant Types: award and challenge
Geographic Distribution: focus on OH
Operating Locations: OH (Grafton)

CORP. OFFICERS

Maureen M. Cromling: *CURR EMPL* chmn, pres: Ross Corp

GIVING OFFICERS

Maureen M. Cromling: pres, dir *CURR EMPL* chmn, pres: Ross Corp (see above)
William E. Cromling: trust

William E. Cromling II: trust
David L. Herzer: secy, dir
Linda Huntley: trust
Gary R. Ross: vp, dir

APPLICATION INFORMATION

Initial Approach: Send a brief letter of inquiry and a full proposal. Include a description of organization, amount requested, purpose of funds sought, recently audited financial statement, and proof of tax-exempt status.

Restrictions on Giving: Does not support individuals, religious organizations for sectarian purposes, or political or lobbying groups.

GRANTS ANALYSIS

Number of Grants: 5
Highest Grant: $11,400
Typical Range: $500 to $5,000
Disclosure Period: fiscal year ending May 31, 1990

RECENT GRANTS

11,400 Midview Local School District, Grafton, OH — challenge grant
6,500 Leadership Lorain County, Lorain, OH
5,000 Elyria Memorial Hospital, Elyria, OH — support of program
3,000 Lorain County Community College Womens Link, Elyria, OH — support
500 Learning Directory Grant, Elyria, OH — publication of 1990 Learning directory

Ross Foundation

CONTACT
Hal Ross
Vice President
Ross Fdn.
105 South Broadway, Ste. 730
Wichita, KS 67202-2009
(316) 264-4981

FINANCIAL SUMMARY
Recent Giving: $115,125 (1991); $110,275 (1990); $109,500 (1989)
Assets: $2,752,856 (1991); $2,639,708 (1990); $2,622,530 (1989)
EIN: 48-6125814

CONTRIBUTIONS SUMMARY

Donor(s): the late G. Murray Ross

Typical Recipients: • *Arts & Humanities:* arts associations, arts centers, community arts, history/historic preservation • *Education:* colleges & universities, education associations • *Religion:* churches, religious organizations • *Social Services:* child welfare, community service organizations, youth organizations

Grant Types: general support

Geographic Distribution: focus on KS

GIVING OFFICERS
Norman W. Jeter: pres
Hal Ross: vp
Susan Ross Sheets: secy, treas

APPLICATION INFORMATION
Initial Approach: Contributes only to preselected organizations.

GRANTS ANALYSIS
Number of Grants: 10
Highest Grant: $50,000
Typical Range: $250 to $3,000
Disclosure Period: 1991

RECENT GRANTS

50,000 Kansas State University, Manhattan, KS
50,000 Ottowa University, Ottowa, KS
6,025 Historic Wichita, Wichita, KS
3,000 Kansas Action for Children, Wichita, KS
3,000 Wichita Center for the Arts, Wichita, KS
1,500 FHS Endowment Association Venture Fund, Wichita, KS
750 Association for Community Arts Agencies of Kansas, Wichita, KS
400 Hays Arts Council, Hays, KS
250 Hays Community Assistance Center, Hays, KS
200 Hays Public Schools Foundation, Hays, KS

Ross Foundation

CONTACT
Ross M. Whipple
President
Ross Fdn.
PO Box 335
Arkadelphia, AR 71923
(501) 246-9881
Note: The foundation can be reached directly at 1039 Henderson Street, Arkadelphia, AR 71923.

FINANCIAL SUMMARY
Recent Giving: $349,717 (1991); $322,441 (1990); $321,046 (1989)
Assets: $21,620,101 (1991); $19,175,558 (1990); $18,276,500 (1989)
Gifts Received: $93,241 (1991)
EIN: 71-6060574

CONTRIBUTIONS SUMMARY
Donor(s): The foundation was established in 1966 by Jane Ross and the estate of the late Esther C. Ross, with approximately 18,000 acres of southern Arkansas timberland.
Typical Recipients: • *Arts & Humanities:* performing arts • *Civic & Public Affairs:* environmental affairs, municipalities • *Education:* colleges & universities, economic education, education associations, literacy, public education (precollege), science/technology education • *Health:* hospitals • *Social Services:* animal protection, emergency relief, united funds, youth organizations
Grant Types: capital, endowment, general support, matching, project, research, and seed money
Geographic Distribution: limited to Arkadelphia and Clark County, AR

GIVING OFFICERS
Peggy Clark: trust
Toney D. McMillan: trust
Robert Rhodes: trust
Jane Ross: trust mgr
Ross M. Whipple: trust dir

APPLICATION INFORMATION
Initial Approach: Potential applicants are encouraged to contact the foundation by telephone or letter and request a copy of the grant application form. Before submitting a specific request for support,

some organizations may wish to send a short letter inquiring about the foundation's possible interest for which funds are being sought.
Proof of 501(c)(3) status is required at the time of application.
Applications are accepted throughout the year.
All grant requests are reviewed and researched by the foundation's staff before presentation to the board of trustees. Further information and an interview or visit may be requested. Applicants will be notified of the board's decision following meetings held in February, May, August, and November.
Restrictions on Giving: No grants are made to individuals or for scholarships, fellowships, or loans.

OTHER THINGS TO KNOW
Publications: informational brochure and application guidelines

GRANTS ANALYSIS
Total Grants: $349,717
Number of Grants: 37
Highest Grant: $75,000
Typical Range: $1,000 to $10,000
Disclosure Period: 1991
Note: Recent grants are derived from a 1991 grants list.

RECENT GRANTS

75,000 Arkadelphia Public Schools, Arkadelphia, AR — math/science project
44,504 Dawson Educational Co-op, Little Rock, AR — minigrants
35,000 Joint Educational Consortium, Little Rock, AR — 1990-91 budget
21,550 Arkansas Game and Fish Foundation, Little Rock, AR — big timber area
20,000 Clark County, Little Rock, AR
20,000 Joint Educational Consortium, Little Rock, AR — 1991-92 budget
12,500 Henderson State University, Arkadelphia, AR — field-based study
10,000 Arkadelphia Public Schools, Arkadelphia, AR — minigrants

10,000 Arkansas Research Center, Little Rock, AR — start-up funds

10,000 Clark County, Little Rock, AR

Ross Foundation, Arthur

CONTACT
Arthur Ross
President
Arthur Ross Fdn.
c/o Yohalem, Gillman, & Co.
477 Madison Ave.
New York, NY 10022-5802
(212) 737-7311

FINANCIAL SUMMARY
Recent Giving: $1,179,487 (1989)
Assets: $6,569,532 (1989)
Gifts Received: $64,037 (1989)
EIN: 13-6121436

CONTRIBUTIONS SUMMARY
Donor(s): Arthur Ross
Typical Recipients: • *Arts & Humanities:* community arts, history/historic preservation, literary arts, museums/galleries • *Civic & Public Affairs:* environmental affairs, municipalities, zoos/botanical gardens • *Education:* colleges & universities • *Health:* hospitals • *Religion:* churches • *Social Services:* food/clothing distribution, shelters/homelessness
Grant Types: general support and scholarship
Geographic Distribution: focus on NY

GIVING OFFICERS
Tom Bernstein: dir
John Howard Dobkin: dir *B* Hartford CT 1942 *ED* Yale Univ BA 1964; NY Univ JD 1968 *NONPR AFFIL* dir: Creative Artists Network, Municipal Art Soc, Sch Am Ballet; mem: CT Bar Assn; mem adv bd: Archives Am Art; pres: Historic Hudson Valley
George Joseph Gillespie III: secy, dir *B* New York NY 1930 *ED* Georgetown Univ AB 1952; Harvard Univ LLB 1955 *CURR EMPL* ptnr: Cravath Swaine & Moore *CORP AFFIL* dir: Fund Am, Washington Post Co *NONPR AFFIL* dir, chmn emeritus: Natl Multiple Sclerosis Soc; mem: Am Bar Assn, NY Bar Assn, NY City Bar Assn; pres: Boys Club Madison

Square; secy: Mus Broadcasting; trust, treas: Hoover Inst
William Theodore Golden: dir *B* New York NY 1909 *ED* Univ PA AB 1930; Columbia Univ MA 1979 *CORP AFFIL* dir: Block Drug Co, Gen Am Investors Co, Verde Exploration Ltd *NONPR AFFIL* chmn, mem gov counc: Courant Inst Math & Sciences; chmn, trust: Am Mus Natural History; dir: Columbia Univ Grad Faculties Alumni; fellow, mem bd govs: NY Academy Sciences; fellow, treas, dir: Am Assn Advancement Science; mem: Am Academy Arts & Sciences, Am Philosophical Soc, Counc Foreign Rels, History & Science Soc, Marine Biological Lab (Woods Hole MA), Natl Academy Pub Admin; mem bd overseers: Univ PA Sch Arts & Sciences; mem bd visitors: City Univ NY Grad Ctr; mem counc: Rockefeller Univ; secy, trust: Carnegie Inst; treas, trust: Hebrew Free Loan Soc; trust: Catskill Ctr Conservation Devel, Neuroscience Res Fdn, Univ PA Press; trust emeritus: Haskins Laboratories; trust, vchmn: Barnard Coll; vchmn, trust: Am Trust British Library, Mt Sinai Sch Medicine
Arthur Ross: pres, treas, dir *B* New York NY 1910 *ED* Columbia Univ BS 1931; Univ PA Wharton Sch 1930 *CURR EMPL* vchmn: Central Natl - Gottesman *CORP AFFIL* dir: Dreyfus Corp, Lazard Special Equities Fund; vchmn: Central Natl - Gottesman *NONPR AFFIL* dir: Barnard Coll, Bryant Park Restoration Corp (NY), Central Park Commun Fund, Central Park Conservancy, NY Landmarks Conservancy; mem: Am Assn Advancement Science, Asia Soc, Counc Foreign Rels, Foreign Policy Assn, Intl Inst Strategic Studies; mem bd overseers: Univ PA Grad Sch Fine Arts; mem counc: Cooper-Hewitt Mus; trust: Am Mus Natural History; trust, vp: Spanish Inst
Clifford A. Ross: exec vp, dir
Janet C. Ross: vp, dir
Ralph M. Sussman: dir
Paul E. Taylor, Jr.: dir
William J. Vanden Heuval: dir
Edgar Wachenheim III: dir

APPLICATION INFORMATION
Initial Approach: Contributes only to preselected organizations.

OTHER THINGS TO KNOW
Publications: Annual Report

GRANTS ANALYSIS
Number of Grants: 67
Highest Grant: $234,000
Typical Range: $1,000 to $12,500
Disclosure Period: 1989

RECENT GRANTS
234,000 UNA of the USA, New York, NY

109,318 Central Park Conservancy, New York, NY

62,911 Arthur Ross Gallery of Art, New York, NY

50,000 Blair House Restoration Fund, Atlanta, GA

50,000 Cathedral of St. John the Divine, New York, NY

47,100 Municipal Arts Society, New York, NY

42,541 Asia Society, New York, NY

40,000 American Museum of Natural History, New York, NY

40,000 Boys Harbor, New York, NY

35,000 Eldridge Street Synagogue, New York, NY

Ross Foundation, Lyn & George M.

CONTACT
Lyn & George M. Ross Fdn.
c/o Goldman Sachs & Co.
85 Broad St., Tax Dept.
New York, NY 10004-2106

FINANCIAL SUMMARY
Recent Giving: $520,836 (fiscal 1992); $185,667 (fiscal 1991); $135,500 (fiscal 1990)
Assets: $5,354,210 (fiscal year ending February 28, 1992); $5,076,503 (fiscal 1991); $4,156,658 (fiscal 1990)
Gifts Received: $585,600 (fiscal 1991); $637,884 (fiscal 1990); $611,545 (fiscal 1989)
EIN: 23-2049592

CONTRIBUTIONS SUMMARY
Donor(s): George M. Ross
Typical Recipients: • *Arts & Humanities:* arts associations, history/historic preservation, museums/galleries, music • *Civic & Public Affairs:* ethnic/minority organizations • *Education:* colleges & univer-

sities • *Religion:* religious organizations, synagogues • *Social Services:* child welfare, community service organizations, united funds, youth organizations
Grant Types: general support
Geographic Distribution: focus on Philadelphia, PA

GIVING OFFICERS
George Martin Ross: trust *B* Philadelphia PA 1933 *ED* Drexel Univ BS 1955 *CURR EMPL* ptnr: Goldman Sachs & Co *CORP AFFIL* ptnr: Goldman Sachs & Co *NONPR AFFIL* chmn emeritus, mem exec comm: Philadelphia Drama Guild; dir: Academy Music Philadelphia, Natl Fdn Jewish Culture, Philadelphia Orchestra; mem: Greater Philadelphia Chamber Commerce, Urban Affs Partnership; mem natl bd govs, mem exec comm, dir Philadelphia: Am Jewish Comm; vp, mem exec comm: Federation Jewish Agencies Greater Philadelphia
Lyn M. Ross: trust

APPLICATION INFORMATION
Initial Approach: Send brief letter of inquiry describing program or project. There are no deadlines.
Restrictions on Giving: Does not support individuals.

GRANTS ANALYSIS
Number of Grants: 110
Highest Grant: $250,000
Typical Range: $500 to $7,500
Disclosure Period: fiscal year ending February 28, 1992

RECENT GRANTS
250,000 Jewish Federation, Philadelphia, PA

50,000 Drexel University, Philadelphia, PA

43,000 Pennsylvania Academy of Fine Arts, Philadelphia, PA

23,000 Main Line Reform Temple, Wynnewood, PA

20,000 National Museum of American Jewish History, Philadelphia, PA

12,000 American Jewish Committee, New York, NY

11,000 United Way, Philadelphia, PA

10,000 Philadelphia Orchestra, Philadelphia, PA

10,000 US Holocaust Memorial Museum, Washington, DC
8,500 Jewish Museum, New York, NY

Ross Foundation, Walter G.

CONTACT
Ian Jones
Walter G. Ross Fdn.
Metropolitan Sq.
655 15th St., N.W.
Washington, DC 20005
(202) 383-6396

FINANCIAL SUMMARY
Recent Giving: $330,000 (1991); $372,500 (1990); $388,000 (1989)
Assets: $7,183,240 (1991); $7,091,235 (1990); $6,933,729 (1989)
EIN: 52-6057560

CONTRIBUTIONS SUMMARY
Typical Recipients: • *Education:* colleges & universities • *Health:* health organizations, hospices, hospitals, pediatric health, single-disease health associations • *Social Services:* community service organizations, family services, homes, youth organizations
Grant Types: capital and general support
Geographic Distribution: limited to the Washington, DC, area and FL

GIVING OFFICERS
Eugene L. Bernard: trust
Gladys Bludworth: trust
Lloyd H. Elliot: chmn, trust
J. Hillman Zahn: trust

APPLICATION INFORMATION
Initial Approach: Send brief letter of inquiry describing program or project. Deadline is September 15.

OTHER THINGS TO KNOW
Publications: Application Guidelines

GRANTS ANALYSIS
Number of Grants: 13
Highest Grant: $100,000
Typical Range: $5,000 to $25,000
Disclosure Period: 1991

RECENT GRANTS
100,000 George Washington University, Washington, DC
50,000 Bascom Palmer Eye Institute, Miami, FL
25,000 Boy Scouts of America, Washington, DC
25,000 George Washington University, Washington, DC
25,000 Washington Home
20,000 Berea College, Berea, KY
15,000 Gallaudet University, Washington, DC
10,000 Easter Seal Society, FL
10,000 Hospital for Sick Children, Washington, DC
10,000 Miami Heart Institute, Miami, FL

Ross, Johnston & Kersting
Revenue: $.0 thousand
Employees: 4
Headquarters: Durham, NC
SIC Major Group: Engineering & Management Services

CONTACT
Juliette J. Clodfelter
Administrative Assistant
Ross, Johnston & Kersting
112 Swift Ave.
Durham, NC 27705
(919) 286-0721

FINANCIAL SUMMARY
Fiscal Note: Annual Giving Range: less than $100,000

CONTRIBUTIONS SUMMARY
Company provides employee matching gifts only, up to $2,500 per employee.
Grant Types: employee matching gifts
Geographic Distribution: primarily in NC
Operating Locations: NC (Durham)

CORP. OFFICERS
J. David Ross: *CURR EMPL* chmn, pres, ceo: Ross Johnston & Kersting

APPLICATION INFORMATION
Initial Approach: Send brief letter of inquiry, including a description of the organization, amount requested, purpose of funds sought, recently audited

financial statements, and proof of tax-exempt status. There are no deadlines.

Ross Laboratories
Revenue: $1.5 billion
Employees: 2,400
Parent Company: Abbott Labs
Headquarters: Columbus, OH
SIC Major Group: Chemicals & Allied Products and Food & Kindred Products

CONTACT
Bill Wade
Director, Fiscal Services
Ross Laboratories
625 Cleveland Ave.
Columbus, OH 43215
(614) 624-7677

FINANCIAL SUMMARY
Fiscal Note: Company does not disclose contributions figures.

CONTRIBUTIONS SUMMARY
Typical Recipients: • *Arts & Humanities:* general, libraries, opera, theater • *Civic & Public Affairs:* better government, civil rights, general, zoos/botanical gardens • *Education:* colleges & universities, general • *Health:* general, health organizations, hospitals • *Social Services:* aged, animal protection, child welfare, community centers, community service organizations, general, homes, shelters/homelessness, united funds, youth organizations
Grant Types: award, capital, emergency, employee matching gifts, general support, and research
Nonmonetary Support Types: donated products and in-kind services
Geographic Distribution: in headquarters and operating communities
Operating Locations: OH (Columbus)

CORP. OFFICERS
John C. Kane: *B* 1939 *ED* West Chester St Coll BS 1961 *CURR EMPL* pres: Ross Laboratories

APPLICATION INFORMATION
Initial Approach: Send a brief letter of inquiry and a full proposal. Include a description of organization, amount requested, purpose of funds

sought, and proof of tax-exempt status.
Restrictions on Giving: Does not support individuals and religious organizations for sectarian purposes.

GRANTS ANALYSIS
Typical Range: $50 to $1,000

RECENT GRANTS
George Washington University, Washington, DC

Ross Memorial Foundation, Will

CONTACT
Edmond C. Young
Treasurer
Will Ross Memorial Fdn.
c/o Bank One Wisconsin Trust Co., N.A.
PO Box 1308
Milwaukee, WI 53201
(414) 765-2842

FINANCIAL SUMMARY
Recent Giving: $340,700 (1990); $388,200 (1989)
Assets: $3,302,444 (1990); $3,478,778 (1989)
Gifts Received: $11,618 (1990); $706,354 (1989)
EIN: 39-6044673

CONTRIBUTIONS SUMMARY
Typical Recipients: • *Arts & Humanities:* arts institutes, community arts, performing arts, theater • *Civic & Public Affairs:* environmental affairs • *Education:* colleges & universities • *Religion:* religious organizations • *Social Services:* community service organizations, homes, shelters/homelessness, united funds, youth organizations
Grant Types: general support
Geographic Distribution: focus on Milwaukee, WI

GIVING OFFICERS
John D. Bryson, Jr.: vp, dir
David L. Kinnamon: secy, dir
Mary Ann LaBahn: treas, dir
Richard R. Teschner: vp, dir
Edmond C. Young: pres, dir

APPLICATION INFORMATION
Initial Approach: Send brief letter describing program. There are no deadlines.

GRANTS ANALYSIS
Number of Grants: 38
Highest Grant: $60,000

Typical Range: $500 to $8,000
Disclosure Period: 1990

RECENT GRANTS

60,000 United Way, Milwaukee, WI

50,000 UPAF, Milwaukee, WI

25,000 Medical College of Wisconsin, Milwaukee, WI

20,000 Alverno College, Milwaukee, WI

20,000 Blood Center of Southeastern Wisconsin, Milwaukee, WI

20,000 Next Door Foundation, Milwaukee, WI

20,000 Planned Parenthood, Milwaukee, WI

15,000 Second Harvesters of Wisconsin, Milwaukee, WI

10,000 Park People, Milwaukee, WI

10,000 University of Wisconsin Madison Medical School, Milwaukee, WI

Roth Family Foundation

CONTACT
Sukey Garcetti
Executive Director
Roth Family Fdn.
12021 Wilshire Blvd., Ste. 505
Los Angeles, CA 90025
(213) 471-4441

FINANCIAL SUMMARY
Recent Giving: $262,630 (fiscal 1991); $322,698 (fiscal 1990); $299,700 (fiscal 1989)
Assets: $7,427,982 (fiscal year ending October 31, 1991); $6,375,111 (fiscal 1990); $7,266,399 (fiscal 1989)
EIN: 23-7008897

CONTRIBUTIONS SUMMARY
Donor(s): Louis Roth and Co., the late Louis Roth, the late Fannie Roth, the late Marry Roth
Typical Recipients: • *Arts & Humanities:* arts funds, community arts, dance, music, public broadcasting, theater • *Civic & Public Affairs:* civil rights, public policy • *Education:* colleges

& universities, education associations • *Religion:* religious organizations • *Social Services:* child welfare, family planning, youth organizations
Grant Types: general support
Geographic Distribution: focus on CA

GIVING OFFICERS
Gilbert Garcetti: dir
Sukey Garcetti: dir
Michael Roth: dir *B* Brooklyn NY 1945 *ED* City Coll NY BS 1967; Boston Univ JD 1971; NY Univ LLM 1973 *CURR EMPL* ceo, coo: Mutual Of NY *CORP AFFIL* dir: Am Capital Mgmt & Res, Natl Benefit Life Ins Co *NONPR AFFIL* mem: Am Inst CPAs, CT Soc CPAs, Stamford Tax Assn
Patricia Roth: dir
Susan Roth: dir

APPLICATION INFORMATION
Initial Approach: Send brief letter of inquiry describing program or project. There are no deadlines.
Restrictions on Giving: Does not support individuals.

GRANTS ANALYSIS
Number of Grants: 106
Highest Grant: $25,000
Typical Range: $1,000 to $5,000
Disclosure Period: fiscal year ending October 31, 1991

RECENT GRANTS

25,000 KCET, Los Angeles, CA

10,835 KCRW, Santa Monica, CA

10,000 Reed College, Portland, OR

8,250 Planned Parenthood Federation of America, Los Angeles, CA

6,000 Music Center Unified Fund, Los Angeles, CA

5,000 Los Angeles Educational Partnership, Los Angeles, CA

5,000 Los Angeles Unified School District, Los Angeles, CA

5,000 People for the American Way, Washington, DC

5,000 Proyecto Pastoral, Los Angeles, CA

4,000 UAHC, New York, NY

Roth Foundation

CONTACT
Linda Schwartz
Trustee
Roth Fdn.
Huntington Plaza, Ste. 310
Huntington Valley, PA 19006
(215) 947-3750

FINANCIAL SUMMARY
Recent Giving: $458,123 (fiscal 1991); $93,838 (fiscal 1990); $1,729,850 (fiscal 1989)
Assets: $917,585 (fiscal year ending October 31, 1991); $1,244,824 (fiscal 1990); $1,285,380 (fiscal 1989)
Gifts Received: $30,000 (fiscal 1991); $126,763 (fiscal 1988)
EIN: 23-6271428

CONTRIBUTIONS SUMMARY
Donor(s): Edythe M. Roth, the late Abraham Roth
Typical Recipients: • *Health:* health organizations, hospitals, single-disease health associations
Grant Types: research and scholarship
Geographic Distribution: focus on PA

GIVING OFFICERS
Henry Rosenberger: trust
Edythe M. Roth: trust
Roland Roth: trust
Linda Schwartz: trust

APPLICATION INFORMATION
Initial Approach: Applicants must have completed one year in a recognized school of nursing. Scholarship awards are made directly to nursing institution on recipient's behalf. There are no deadlines.

OTHER THINGS TO KNOW
Provides scholarships for nursing education.

GRANTS ANALYSIS
Number of Grants: 8
Highest Grant: $250,000
Typical Range: $26,000 to $31,000
Disclosure Period: fiscal year ending October 31, 1991

RECENT GRANTS

250,000 Hadassah Medical Relief, New York, NY

31,800 Methodist Hospital, Philadelphia, PA

30,000 Abington Memorial Hospital, Abington, PA

30,000 Episcopal Hospital, Philadelphia, PA

30,000 Frankford Hospital, Philadelphia, PA

30,000 Northeastern Hospital of Philadelphia, Philadelphia, PA

30,000 Roxborough Memorial Hospital, Philadelphia, PA

26,323 Fox Chase Cancer Institute, Philadelphia, PA

Roth Foundation, Louis T.

CONTACT
Louis T. Roth
President
Louis T. Roth Fdn.
2225 Douglas Blvd.
Louisville, KY 40205-1903
(502) 454-3124

FINANCIAL SUMMARY
Recent Giving: $136,637 (fiscal 1992); $123,781 (fiscal 1991); $118,713 (fiscal 1990)
Assets: $2,216,973 (fiscal year ending April 30, 1992); $1,936,494 (fiscal 1991); $1,928,598 (fiscal 1990)
Gifts Received: $107,104 (fiscal 1992); $91,346 (fiscal 1991); $105,557 (fiscal 1990)
Fiscal Note: In 1992, contributions were received from Louis T. Roth.
EIN: 61-0624305

CONTRIBUTIONS SUMMARY
Donor(s): Louis T. Roth
Typical Recipients: • *Arts & Humanities:* arts funds, museums/galleries • *Civic & Public Affairs:* ethnic/minority organizations, women's affairs • *Religion:* religious organizations, synagogues • *Social Services:* community centers, community service organizations, homes, united funds, youth organizations
Grant Types: general support
Geographic Distribution: focus on Louisville, KY

GIVING OFFICERS
Bruce J. Roth: treas
David M. Roth: secy
Louis T. Roth: pres

APPLICATION INFORMATION

Initial Approach: Contributes only to preselected organizations. Applications not accepted.

GRANTS ANALYSIS

Number of Grants: 50
Highest Grant: $71,150
Typical Range: $150 to $1,600
Disclosure Period: fiscal year ending April 30, 1992

RECENT GRANTS

71,150 United Jewish Campaign, Louisville, KY
11,700 United Way, Louisville, KY
10,000 Jewish Hospital Foundation, Louisville, KY
10,000 Keneseth Israel Congregation, Louisville, KY
4,500 Keneseth Israel Congregation, Louisville, KY
4,000 Jewish Federation, Cincinnati, OH
2,800 Adath Jeshurun Congregation, Louisville, KY
2,150 Congregation Beth Ann Israel, Philadelphia, PA
1,750 Fifteen Telecommunications, Louisville, KY
1,600 Metropolitan Museum of Art, New York, NY

Rothschild Foundation, Hulda B. and Maurice L.

CONTACT
Donald A. Kress
Hulda B. and Maurice L. Rothschild Fdn.
c/o First National Bank of Chicago
One First National Plaza, Ste. 0101
Chicago, IL 60670-0111
(312) 732-6473

FINANCIAL SUMMARY
Recent Giving: $523,372 (1990); $506,387 (1989); $523,485 (1988)
Assets: $6,951,007 (1990); $7,581,644 (1989); $6,883,821 (1988)
EIN: 36-6752787

CONTRIBUTIONS SUMMARY

Donor(s): the late Hulda O. Rothschild
Typical Recipients: • *Arts & Humanities:* arts institutes, dance, museums/galleries, music • *Education:* colleges & universities • *Health:* hospitals • *Religion:* religious organizations • *Social Services:* aged, community service organizations, united funds
Grant Types: project and seed money
Geographic Distribution: focus on the Chicago, IL, metropolitan area

GIVING OFFICERS
Beatrice Cummings Mayer: trust
Robert N. Mayer: pres, trust

APPLICATION INFORMATION
Initial Approach: Contributes only to preselected organizations.
Restrictions on Giving: Does not support individuals or provide scholarships or loans.

OTHER THINGS TO KNOW
Publications: Application Guidelines

GRANTS ANALYSIS
Number of Grants: 15
Highest Grant: $128,325
Typical Range: $4,500 to $52,601
Disclosure Period: 1990

RECENT GRANTS
128,325 Michael Reese Hospital and Medical Center, Chicago, IL
102,660 Jewish Federation
51,330 Art Institute Michigan at Adams, Chicago, IL
51,330 Orchestral Association, Chicago, IL
51,330 United Way, Chicago, IL
51,330 University of Chicago, Chicago, IL
25,000 Museum of Contemporary Art, Los Angeles, CA — senior outreach
12,832 Northwestern University, Evanston, IL
12,832 University of Minnesota, Minneapolis, MN
10,000 Friends for Parks

Rotterman Trust, Helen L. and Marie F.

CONTACT
Louis T. Shulman
Trustee
Helen L. and Marie F. Rotterman Trust
900 Courthouse Plaza, S.W.
Dayton, OH 45402
(513) 228-1111

FINANCIAL SUMMARY
Recent Giving: $120,707 (fiscal 1991); $150,900 (fiscal 1990); $126,800 (fiscal 1989)
Assets: $2,681,949 (fiscal year ending July 31, 1991); $2,734,053 (fiscal 1990); $2,665,303 (fiscal 1989)
EIN: 31-6236156

CONTRIBUTIONS SUMMARY
Typical Recipients: • *Education:* colleges & universities, religious education • *Religion:* churches, missionary activities, religious organizations • *Social Services:* community service organizations
Grant Types: general support and scholarship

GIVING OFFICERS
Charles F. Collins: trust
John O. Hubler: trust
Louis T. Shulman: trust

APPLICATION INFORMATION
Initial Approach: Individual applicants should include Trinity College application and a copy of high school record and certification of Catholic church affiliation where applicable. Deadline is 4 to 6 months prior to beginning of school year for scholarships.

GRANTS ANALYSIS
Number of Grants: 7
Highest Grant: $87,000
Typical Range: $6,000 to $14,500
Disclosure Period: fiscal year ending July 31, 1991

RECENT GRANTS
87,000 Trinity College, Washington, DC
14,500 Catholic University of America, Washington, DC
14,500 Maryknoll Fathers, Maryknoll, NY
7,250 Maryknoll Sisters, Maryknoll, NY
7,250 Medical Missionary Sisters, Philadelphia, PA

Rouge Steel Co.

Sales: $680.0 million
Employees: 4,500
Parent Company: Ford Motors Co.
Headquarters: Dearborn, MI
SIC Major Group: Primary Metal Industries

CONTACT
Bill Hornberger
Employee Relations
Rouge Steel Co.
3001 Miller Rd.
Rouge Office Bldg. 2003
Dearborn, MI 48121
(313) 322-3000

CONTRIBUTIONS SUMMARY
Operating Locations: MI (Dearborn)

CORP. OFFICERS
Louis D. Camino: *CURR EMPL* pres, ceo: Rouge Steel Co
Gary Latednesse: *CURR EMPL* cfo: Rouge Steel Co

Roundy's Inc.

Sales: $2.5 billion
Employees: 5,000
Headquarters: Pewaukee, WI
SIC Major Group: Food Stores, Wholesale Trade—Durable Goods, and Wholesale Trade—Nondurable Goods

CONTACT
Dave Busch
Corporate Vice President
Roundy's Inc.
23000 Roundy Dr.
Pewaukee, WI 53072
(414) 547-7999

CONTRIBUTIONS SUMMARY
Operating Locations: WI (Pewaukee)

CORP. OFFICERS
John Dickson: *CURR EMPL* ceo, pres: Roundys
Robert D. Ranus: *CURR EMPL* vp, cfo: Roundys

Rouse Co. / Rouse Co. Foundation

Revenue: $573.5 million
Employees: 5,488
Headquarters: Columbia, MD
SIC Major Group: General
Building Contractors, Holding
& Other Investment Offices,
and Real Estate

CONTACT

Edwin A. Daniels, Jr.
Executive Director
The Rouse Co. Fdn.
10275 Little Patuxent Pkwy..
Columbia, MD 21044
(410) 992-6330

FINANCIAL SUMMARY

Recent Giving: $120,168
(1991); $159,166 (1990);
$95,000 (1989)
Assets: $2,667,304 (1991);
$2,240,860 (1990); $2,282,461
(1989)
Gifts Received: $80,825
(1991); $179,000 (1990);
$385,162 (1989)
Fiscal Note: In 1991, contributions were received from the
Rouse Company.
EIN: 52-6056273

CONTRIBUTIONS SUMMARY

Typical Recipients: • *Arts & Humanities:* arts associations, arts centers, arts funds, community arts, dance, ethnic arts, libraries, literary arts, music, performing arts, public broadcasting, theater, visual arts • *Civic & Public Affairs:* zoos/botanical gardens • *Education:* arts education, business education, colleges & universities, community & junior colleges, legal education • *Health:* hospices, hospitals • *Science:* scientific institutes • *Social Services:* aged, child welfare, domestic violence, employment/job training, food/clothing distribution, homes, shelters/homelessness, united funds, volunteer services, youth organizations
Grant Types: capital, challenge, department, endowment, general support, multiyear/continuing support, operating expenses, project, scholarship, and seed money
Nonmonetary Support Types: donated equipment and in-kind services
Geographic Distribution: primarily in the central MD area
Operating Locations: AR (Fayetteville), CA (Santa Mon-

ica), CO (Colorado Springs, Denver), CT (New Haven), DC (Washington), FL (Jacksonville, Miami, Tallahassee, Tampa), GA (Atlanta, Augusta, Decatur), IA (Ames, Cedar Falls, Keokuk, Marshalltown, Muscatine, W. Burlington), IL (Mt. Prospect), KY (Louisville), LA (Gretna, New Orleans, Shreveport), MA (Boston, Springfield), MD (Baltimore, Easton, Glen Burnie, Owings Mills, Parkville), MI (Taylor), MN (Minnetonka), MO (St. Louis), NC (Charlotte), NJ (Burlington, Cherry HIll, Paramus, Voorhees, Wayne, Woodbridge), NY (New York, Staten Island), OH (Dayton, Toledo), PA (Exton, Greensburg, Philadelphia, Plymouth Meeting), TX (Austin, Ft. Worth, Galveston, Houston, San Antonio), VA (Norfolk), WA (Seattle), WI (Milwaukee)

CORP. OFFICERS

Mathias DeVito: *B* Trenton NJ 1930 *ED* Univ MD Sch Law 1954 *CURR EMPL* chmn, pres, ceo, dir: Rouse Co *CORP AFFIL* dir: First Natl Bank MD, Trizec Corp Ltd, US Air Inc

GIVING OFFICERS

R. Harwood Beville: trust
Edwin A. Daneis, Jr.: exec dir, trust
Mathias J. Devito: pres, trust
Richard G. McCanley: secy-treas, trust

APPLICATION INFORMATION

Initial Approach: Send brief letter of inquiry. If initial review suggests that a request for funding is appropriate, such requests should include request for a specific amount of money and an explanation of its intended use; a brief description of the organization, its history and activity; the names and qualifications of the persons who will administer the grant; and a copy of most recent tax exemption statement. For a specific project or program, include goals and objectives, population to be served, schedule for implementation, and method of evaluating its effectiveness. There are no deadlines.
Restrictions on Giving: Does not support religious programs, individuals, or political advo-

cacy. Organizations must be tax-exempt under 501(c)(3).

OTHER THINGS TO KNOW

Publications: Informational Brochure (including Application Guidelines)

GRANTS ANALYSIS

Number of Grants: 8
Highest Grant: $31,000
Typical Range: $5,000 to $25,000
Disclosure Period: 1991

RECENT GRANTS

31,000	College of Notre Dame of Maryland, Baltimore, MD
20,000	Greater Baltimore Medical Center, Baltimore, MD
16,668	Union Memorial Hospital, Baltimore, MD
12,500	Our Daily Bread, Baltimore, MD
10,000	Academy of Natural Sciences, Philadelphia, PA
10,000	Alvin Ailey Dance Theatre Foundation of Maryland, Baltimore, MD
10,000	B.U.I.L.D., Baltimore, MD
10,000	Meals on Wheels, Baltimore, MD

Rowan Cos., Inc.

Sales: $272.2 million
Employees: 2,565
Headquarters: Houston, TX
SIC Major Group: Oil & Gas
Extraction and Transportation
by Air

CONTACT

E. E. Thiele
Vice President, Administration
Rowan Cos., Inc.
5450 Transco Tower
2800 Post Oak Blvd., Ste. 5450
Houston, TX 77056-6196
(713) 621-7800

CONTRIBUTIONS SUMMARY

Operating Locations: AK (Anchorage), LA (Lake Charles), TX (Houston, Odessa)

CORP. OFFICERS

C. Robert Palmer: *B* Gorman TX 1934 *ED* Southern Methodist Univ 1957; Southern Methodist Univ 1966 *CURR EMPL* chmn, pres, ceo, dir: Rowan Cos *CORP AFFIL* dir: Am Petroleum Inst; mem: Natl Petroleum Council

Rowland Foundation

CONTACT

Philip DuBois
Vice President
Rowland Foundation
PO Box 13
Cambridge, MA 02238
(617) 497-4634

FINANCIAL SUMMARY

Recent Giving: $1,618,145
(fiscal 1991); $1,959,536 (fiscal 1990); $1,336,255 (fiscal 1989)
Assets: $43,502,411 (fiscal year ending November 30, 1991); $36,484,938 (fiscal 1990); $35,829,313 (fiscal 1989)
Gifts Received: $5,335,036
(fiscal 1991)
EIN: 04-6046756

CONTRIBUTIONS SUMMARY

Donor(s): The Rowland Foundation was established by Edwin H. and Helen M. Land in 1960 as Edwin H. Land-Helen M. Land, Inc. The foundation has been operating under its present name since 1972. Edwin Land, inventor of the light polarizer and the Land camera (which introduced the one-step, self-developing film process), founded Polaroid Corporation in 1937, and has served as its chairman, president, and director of research. A major philanthropist, he founded the Rowland Institute for Science, and created a $100 million charitable trust for the Land Education Development Fund at the Massachusetts Institute of Technology.
Typical Recipients: • *Arts & Humanities:* arts associations, libraries, museums/galleries, music, public broadcasting • *Civic & Public Affairs:* environmental affairs • *Education:* arts education, colleges & universities, medical education, minority education, special education, student aid • *Health:* health organizations, hospitals, medical research, pediatric health, single-disease health associations • *Science:* scientific institutes, scientific organizations • *Social Services:* disabled, employment/job training, family planning, religious welfare, united funds
Grant Types: general support, project, research, and scholarship

Geographic Distribution: primarily New England

GIVING OFFICERS

Jennifer Land DuBois: trust, don daughter

Philip DuBois: pres, trust

Edwin Herbert Land: don, pres, trust *B* Bridgeport CT 1909 *ED* Norwich Univ; Harvard Univ *NONPR AFFIL* fellow: Am Academy Arts Sciences, Natl Academy Sciences, Photographic Soc Am, Royal Photographic Soc Great Britain, Soc Photographic Scientists & Engrs; mem: Am Optical Soc, Am Philosophical Soc, German Photographic Soc, Inst Electrical Electronics Engrs, Natl Academy Engring, NY Academy Sciences, Royal Inst Great Britain, Soc Photography Science Tech Japan; visiting prof: MA Inst Tech

Helen Maislen Land: vp, treas, trust

Julius Silver: secy *B* Philadelphia PA 1900 *ED* NY Univ BA 1922; Columbia Univ JD 1924 *CURR EMPL* sr ptnr: Silver & Solomon *CORP AFFIL* vp, chmn exec comm, dir: Polaroid Corp *NONPR AFFIL* fdr: Silver (Julius) Inst Biomedical Engring; mem: Gallatin Soc, NY City Bar Assn, NY County Lawyers Assn, Phi Beta Kappa, Phi Epsilon Pi, Zeta Beta Tau; trust emeritus: NY Univ

APPLICATION INFORMATION

Initial Approach:
Applicants should send a brief letter.
The letter should outline the nature of the request, amount needed, and background information on the history and objectives of the organization. Also include proof of IRS tax exemption.
Applications may be submitted any time; the board meets as needed.

Restrictions on Giving: No grants are made to individuals or for buildings or endowment funds.

GRANTS ANALYSIS

Total Grants: $1,618,145
Number of Grants: 43
Highest Grant: $250,000
Typical Range: $10,000 to $35,000 and $50,000 to $150,000
Disclosure Period: fiscal year ending November 30, 1991

Note: Average grant figure does not include the foundation's three highest grants totaling $481,848. Recent grants are derived from a fiscal 1991 Form 990.

RECENT GRANTS

250,000   Crotched Mountain Foundation, Greenfield, MA
189,304   Harvard University and Colleges, Cambridge, MA
147,797   Massachusetts General Hospital, Boston, MA
100,000   Kedaly Center of America, Wellesley, MA
100,000   Mount Auburn Hospital Foundation, Cambridge, MA
100,000   WGBH Public Broadcasting, Boston, MA
50,000   Tafts College, Medford, MA
50,000   Trust for New Hampshire Lands, Concord, NH
35,000   Boston Athenaeum, Boston, MA
35,000   Metropolitan Museum of Art, New York, NY

Royal Crown Cos., Inc.

Sales: $138.1 million
Employees: 250
Parent Company: Chesapeake Financial Corp.
Headquarters: Miami Beach, FL
SIC Major Group: Eating & Drinking Places and Food & Kindred Products

CONTACT

Bill Adams
Sales Promotions
Royal Crown Cos., Inc.
PO Box 414210
Miami Beach, FL 33141-0210
(305) 866-7771
Note: Local organizations should contact area bottlers.

CONTRIBUTIONS SUMMARY

Operating Locations: FL (Miami Beach)

CORP. OFFICERS

Steven Posner: *B* 1943 *ED* Univ Miami BS; Univ Miami LLD *CURR EMPL* vchmn, chmn exec comm, dir: Sharon Steel Corp *CORP AFFIL* chmn: Birdsboro Corp, NVF Co, Southeastern Pub Svc Co, Wilson Brothers; chmn, pres, ceo, dir: Evans Products Co, Mueller Brass Co; pres, dir: Securities Mgmt Corp; vchmn: Royal Crown Cos; vchmn, dir: APL Corp

Victor N. Posner: *B* Baltimore MD 1918 *CURR EMPL* chmn, ceo, pres, dir: DWG Corp *CORP AFFIL* chmn: PA Engring Corp; chmn, ceo, dir: Salem Corp; chmn, dir: Graniteville Co, Natl Propane Corp; chmn, pres, ceo, dir: APL Corp, Birdsboro Corp, NVF Co, Southeastern Pub Svc Co; chmn, pres, dir: Wilson Bros; dir: Penn Engring & Mfg Co; pres, dir: Adams Packing Assn, Blume Tree Svcs

---

Royal Group Inc. / Royal Insurance Foundation

Premiums: $1.61 billion
Employees: 6,000
Headquarters: Charlotte, NC
SIC Major Group: Holding & Other Investment Offices and Insurance Carriers

---

CONTACT

Linda Holland
Director, Foundation and Community Relations
Royal Group Inc.
9300 Arrowpoint Blvd.
Charlotte, NC 28201-1000
(704) 522-2057

FINANCIAL SUMMARY

Recent Giving: $435,000 (1992 approx.); $381,000 (1991); $353,478 (1990)
Assets: $49,435 (1990)
Gifts Received: $370,942 (1990); $353,478 (1989)
Fiscal Note: Contributes through foundation only.
EIN: 56-1658178

CONTRIBUTIONS SUMMARY

Typical Recipients: • *Arts & Humanities:* arts appreciation, arts associations, arts centers, community arts, dance, ethnic arts, general, history/historic preservation, libraries, museums/galleries, music, opera, performing arts, public broadcasting, theater, visual arts • *Civic & Public Affairs:* better government, business/free enterprise, civil rights, economic development, environmental affairs, ethnic/minority organizations, general, housing, safety • *Education:* business education, career/vocational educa-

tion, colleges & universities, continuing education, education funds, elementary education, general, literacy, minority education, preschool education, private education (precollege), public education (precollege) • *Health:* emergency/ambulance services, general, geriatric health, health funds, health organizations, hospices, hospitals • *Social Services:* aged, child welfare, community centers, community service organizations, counseling, disabled, drugs & alcohol, family services, general, homes, refugee assistance, shelters/homelessness, united funds, volunteer services, youth organizations

Grant Types: capital, employee matching gifts, general support, operating expenses, project, and scholarship

Nonmonetary Support Types: cause-related marketing & promotion, donated equipment, in-kind services, loaned employees, and workplace solicitation

Geographic Distribution: primarily in the headquarters area, but also through 30 field offices across the country

Operating Locations: CA, IL, MD, MO, NC (Charlotte), OK, SD

CORP. OFFICERS

William E. Buckley: *CURR EMPL* chmn, pres, ceo, dir: Royal Ins Co Am *CORP AFFIL* chmn, pres, ceo, coo: Royal Group

GIVING OFFICERS

Victor Daley: pres *B* Hartford CT 1943 *ED* Providence Coll 1965; Roosevelt Univ *CURR EMPL* sr vp chief admin off: Royal Ins

Linda Holland: treas *CURR EMPL* dir fdn & commun rels: Royal Group

Robert Humphreys, Jr.: dir
Arthur D. Pershetz: secy
C. Ronald Riley: dir

APPLICATION INFORMATION

Initial Approach: *Initial Contact:* write for application form *Include Information On:* completed application; statement answering the question, Why is Royal Insurance an appropriate donor?; list of current board of directors; schedule of board meetings; proof of IRS tax exemption; and current financial statement *When to Submit:* any time

Restrictions on Giving: Does not support individuals, religious organizations for sectarian purposes, political or lobbying groups, organizations outside operating areas, fraternal organizations, medical research, veterans organizations, broadcast fundraising, or endowments.

No funding may be secured through telephone solicitation or direct mail marketing. Contributions also will not be made to an organization solely because a company officer or employee is involved in fundraising efforts.

OTHER THINGS TO KNOW

The majority of contributions stay within the state of North Carolina and are decided upon at corporate headquarters. Field offices across the United States have autonomy to make smaller discretionary donations. At the headquarters, the board of directors meets quarterly to vote on all expenditures of over $2,500.

Capital funding requests are presented for consideration once per year at the annual meeting of the board of directors. Priority is given to industry-related projects.

Publications: application guidelines

GRANTS ANALYSIS

Total Grants: $352,478
Number of Grants: 10*
Highest Grant: $25,000
Typical Range: $1,000 to $5,000
Disclosure Period: 1990
Note: Number of grants and average grant figure taken from a partial grants list. Recent grants are derived from a 1990 grants list.

RECENT GRANTS

25,000 Performing Arts Center, Charlotte, NC
25,000 University of North Carolina Charlotte, Charlotte, NC
15,000 Queens College, Charlotte, NC
10,000 Discovery Place, Charlotte, NC
10,000 Spirit Square, Charlotte, NC
5,000 Bounce Back for Homeless, Charlotte, NC
5,000 Child Care Task Force, Charlotte, NC
5,000 CPCC, Charlotte, NC
5,000 YWCA, Charlotte, NC
1,000 North Carolina Education Fund, Charlotte, NC

Royal Insurance Co. of America

Premiums: $576.32 million
Parent Company: Royal Insurance
Headquarters: Aurora, IL
SIC Major Group: Insurance Carriers

CONTACT

Paul Kanshire
Territorial Administrative Manager
Royal Insurance Co. of America
495 North Commons Dr.
Aurora, IL 60504
(708) 820-2200

CONTRIBUTIONS SUMMARY

Grant Types: matching
Operating Locations: IL (Aurora)

CORP. OFFICERS

William E. Buckley: *CURR EMPL* chmn, pres, ceo, dir: Royal Ins Co Am *CORP AFFIL* chmn, pres, ceo, coo: Royal Group

Royston Manufacturing Corp. / Hopeman Memorial Fund

Headquarters: Waynesboro, VA

CONTACT

Robert Cindrick
Assistant to the President
Hopeman Memorial Fund
PO Box 1345
Waynesboro, VA 22980
(703) 949-9200

FINANCIAL SUMMARY

Fiscal Note: Annual Giving Range: $100,000 to $250,000
EIN: 54-1156930

CONTRIBUTIONS SUMMARY

Operating Locations: VA (Waynesboro)

RPM, Inc.

Sales: $500.3 million
Employees: 2,700
Headquarters: Medina, OH
SIC Major Group: Chemicals & Allied Products, Rubber & Miscellaneous Plastics Products, and Wholesale Trade—Nondurable Goods

CONTACT

Bill Roemer
Director, Operations
RPM, Inc.
PO Box 724
Medina, OH 44258
(216) 225-3192

CONTRIBUTIONS SUMMARY

Operating Locations: OH (Medina)

CORP. OFFICERS

James A. Karman: *CURR EMPL* pres: RPM

Thomas C. Sullivan: *B* Cleveland OH 1927 *ED* Miami Univ 1959 *CURR EMPL* chmn, ceo: RPM

RSR Corp.

Sales: $160.0 million
Employees: 825
Headquarters: Dallas, TX
SIC Major Group: Primary Metal Industries

CONTACT

Howard Meyers
Chairman
RSR Holding Corp.
1111 West Mockingbird Ln., Ste. 1000
Dallas, TX 75247
(214) 631-6070

CONTRIBUTIONS SUMMARY

Operating Locations: TX (Dallas)

CORP. OFFICERS

Howard M. Meyers: *CURR EMPL* chmn, pres: RSR Holding Corp

RTM / RTM Foundation

Headquarters: Atlanta, GA

CONTACT

Dennis E. Cooper
Chairman and Executive Director
RTM
5995 Barfield Road, N.E.
Atlanta, GA 30328
(404) 256-4900

FINANCIAL SUMMARY

Recent Giving: $249,950 (1990); $557,570 (1989)
Assets: $1,072 (1990); $74,532 (1989)
Gifts Received: $172,482 (1990); $553,302 (1989)
Fiscal Note: In 1990, contributions were received from RTM Enterprises, Inc.
EIN: 58-1662253

CONTRIBUTIONS SUMMARY

Typical Recipients: • *Arts & Humanities:* arts centers, music • *Education:* colleges & universities, religious education • *Health:* health funds, single-disease health associations • *Social Services:* youth organizations
Grant Types: general support
Geographic Distribution: giving primarily in Atlanta, GA
Operating Locations: GA (Atlanta)

CORP. OFFICERS

Russell V. Umphenour: *CURR EMPL* chmn, pres, ceo: RTM

GIVING OFFICERS

Dennis E. Cooper: chmn, exec dir
Russell V. Umphenour, Jr.: pres
Sharon S. Umphenour: dir
C.L. Wagner, Jr.: dir
Russell Welch: secy

APPLICATION INFORMATION

Initial Approach: The foundation supports preselected organizations and does not accept unsolicited requests for funds.
Restrictions on Giving: The foundation does not make grants to individuals.

GRANTS ANALYSIS

Number of Grants: 43
Highest Grant: $50,000
Typical Range: $500 to $2,500
Disclosure Period: 1990

RECENT GRANTS

50,000 Evangel College, Springfield, MO

30,000 Sheperd Spinal Center, Atlanta, GA

25,000 Beat Leukemia Research, Atlanta, GA — general support

20,000 Lassiter High School, Marietta, GA

12,500 Atlanta Symphony Orchestra, Atlanta, GA — general support

11,000 Big Brothers and Big Sisters, Atlanta, GA

10,000 Woodruff Arts Center, Atlanta, GA — general support

10,000 Woodruff North, Atlanta, GA

7,500 Northside Hospital Foundation, Atlanta, GA

5,000 Southern California College, Costa Mesa, CA

Ruan Foundation Trust, John

CONTACT

John Ruan
Trustee
John Ruan Fdn Trust
3200 Ruan Center
Des Moines, IA 50309
(515) 245-2555

FINANCIAL SUMMARY

Recent Giving: $1,157,458 (fiscal 1991); $191,717 (fiscal 1990); $112,665 (fiscal 1989)

Assets: $3,833,031 (fiscal year ending June 30, 1991); $5,076,067 (fiscal 1990); $3,388,592 (fiscal 1989)

Gifts Received: $240,000 (fiscal 1990); $20,000 (fiscal 1989); $199,842 (fiscal 1988)

Fiscal Note: 1990 contribution from John Ruan.

EIN: 42-6059463

CONTRIBUTIONS SUMMARY

Donor(s): John Ruan

Typical Recipients: • *Arts & Humanities:* community arts, history/historic preservation • *Civic & Public Affairs:* better government • *Education:* business education, colleges & universities • *Health:* health organizations • *Social Services:* child welfare, community service organizations, family planning, homes, recreation & ath-

letics, united funds, youth organizations

Grant Types: general support

Geographic Distribution: focus on Des Moines, IA

GIVING OFFICERS

Elizabeth J. Ruan: trust

John Ruan III: trust *B* Des Moines IA 1943 *ED* Northwestern Univ 1966 *CURR EMPL* pres: Ruan Ctr Corp *CORP AFFIL* pres: Ruan Ctr Corp

APPLICATION INFORMATION

Initial Approach: Send brief letter describing program. There are no deadlines.

GRANTS ANALYSIS

Number of Grants: 112

Highest Grant: $1,100,000

Typical Range: $50 to $5,000

Disclosure Period: fiscal year ending June 30, 1991

RECENT GRANTS

1,100,000 World Food Prize, Des Moines, IA

5,000 Richard Nixon Presidential Archives Foundation, Washington, DC

5,000 Vote America Foundation, Washington, DC

3,500 Business Education Alliance, Des Moines, IA

2,600 Variety Club of Iowa, Cedar Rapids, IA

2,500 Homes of Oakridge, Des Moines, IA

2,500 United Way, Des Moines, IA

2,500 YMCA, Des Moines, IA

1,250 Iowa College Foundation, Des Moines, IA

1,000 Planned Parenthood Federation of America, Des Moines, IA

Rubbermaid / Rubbermaid Foundation

Sales: $1.81 billion
Employees: 9,754
Headquarters: Wooster, OH
SIC Major Group: Rubber & Miscellaneous Plastics Products

CONTACT

Richard D. Gates
President
Rubbermaid Fdn.
1147 Akron Rd.
Wooster, OH 44691
(216) 264-6464

FINANCIAL SUMMARY

Recent Giving: $994,562 (1991); $1,252,689 (1990); $703,358 (1989)

Assets: $5,534,478 (1991); $5,513,711 (1989)

Fiscal Note: Above figures reflect foundation giving only. Direct contributions are very limited. Foundation figures for 1988 are not available.

EIN: 34-1533729

CONTRIBUTIONS SUMMARY

Typical Recipients: • *Arts & Humanities:* arts associations, arts centers, history/historic preservation, museums/galleries • *Civic & Public Affairs:* business/free enterprise, economic development, ethnic/minority organizations, law & justice, philanthropic organizations • *Education:* agricultural education, business education, colleges & universities, economic education, education associations, education funds, private education (precollege), public education (precollege) • *Health:* health organizations, hospitals • *Social Services:* community centers, drugs & alcohol, homes, united funds, youth organizations

Grant Types: capital and employee matching gifts

Note: Scholarships are available only for Rubbermaid employees.

Nonmonetary Support Types: donated products

Note: Company provides an unspecified amount of nonmonetary giving. Contact Chris Zaleha, secretary to Home Products Division president and general manager for information.

Geographic Distribution: primarily in communities where it has facilities

Operating Locations: NC (Statesville), OH (Wooster), VA (Winchester)

Note: Company operates at 25 to 30 locations in the United States

CORP. OFFICERS

Joseph Gerard Meehan: *B* Washington DC 1931 *CURR*

EMPL sr vp, cfo: Rubbermaid *NONPR AFFIL* dir: Wooster Area Chamber Commerce; mem: Fin Execs Inst, Kiwanis

Wolfgang R. Schmitt: *B* Koblenz Germany 1944 *CURR EMPL* co-chmn: Rubbermaid *CORP AFFIL* dir: Parker-Hannifin Corp *NONPR AFFIL* mem: Natl Housewares Mfrs Assn

GIVING OFFICERS

Richard Daniel Gates: pres *B* Trenton MO 1942 *ED* Univ MO 1964; Rollins Coll MCS 1968; Harvard Univ 1976 *CURR EMPL* sr vp: Rubbermaid *NONPR AFFIL* chmn: Wooster Growth Assn; chmn major indus capital campaign: Boy Scouts Am Camp; chmn, trust: Wayne Ctr Arts; dir: Main St Wooster; mem: All Am City Comm, Natl Assn Corp Treas, Wooster City Fin Task Force; mem parents comm: St Pauls Sch

Joseph Gerard Meehan: vp, trust *CURR EMPL* sr vp, cfo: Rubbermaid (see above)

James A. Morgan: secy, trust *B* Forest City NC 1935 *CURR EMPL* sr vp, secy, coun: Rubbermaid *NONPR AFFIL* mem: Appraisers Assn Am

Wolfgang R. Schmitt: trust *CURR EMPL* co-chmn: Rubbermaid (see above)

APPLICATION INFORMATION

Initial Approach: *Initial Contact:* letter *Include Information On:* details about project, amount requested, background of organization, IRS status *When to Submit:* any time

Restrictions on Giving: Foundation does not support individuals or organizations not tax exempt under IRS guidelines. Most grants go to organizations near Rubbermaid operating locations.

Only requests from organizations located in Wayne County and Wooster, OH, will be considered. Susidiary locations can submit requests to the foundation.

OTHER THINGS TO KNOW

Organizations that do not meet IRS guidelines for tax-exemption may be able to obtain some funds directly from Rubbermaid Inc.

GRANTS ANALYSIS
Total Grants: $944,562*
Number of Grants: 171
Highest Grant: $250,000
Typical Range: $1,000 to $10,000
Disclosure Period: 1991
Note: Figure includes matching gifts. Recent grants are derived from a 1991 Form 990.

RECENT GRANTS
250,000　Wooster Community Hospital, Wooster, OH
175,000　College of Wooster, Wooster, OH
55,000　Akron University (Polymer Center), Akron, OH
41,500　Ohio Foundation of Independent Colleges, OH
32,500　United Way of Wooster, Wooster, OH
32,500　United Way of Wooster, Wooster, OH
32,500　United Way of Wooster, Wooster, OH
32,500　United Way of Wooster, Wooster, OH
20,000　Cleveland Clinic Foundation, Cleveland, OH
20,000　Orrville Hospital Foundation

Rubenstein Charitable Foundation, Lawrence J. and Anne

CONTACT
Richard I. Kaner
Trustee
Lawrence J. and Anne Rubenstein Charitable Fdn.
Boston Harbor Trust Company
40 Rowes Wharf
Boston, MA 02110
(617) 439-6700

FINANCIAL SUMMARY
Recent Giving: $420,205 (fiscal 1992); $409,785 (fiscal 1991); $392,104 (fiscal 1990)
Assets: $11,934,444 (fiscal year ending May 31, 1992); $11,116,414 (fiscal 1991); $8,666,092 (fiscal 1990)
Gifts Received: $1,907,004 (fiscal 1991)

Fiscal Note: In 1991, contributions were received from Anne C. Rubenstein.
EIN: 04-6087371

CONTRIBUTIONS SUMMARY
Donor(s): the late Lawrence J. Rubenstein, Anne C. Rubenstein
Typical Recipients: • *Arts & Humanities:* dance, museums/galleries • *Civic & Public Affairs:* philanthropic organizations, women's affairs • *Education:* colleges & universities • *Health:* hospitals, medical research, nursing services, pediatric health • *International:* international development/relief • *Religion:* religious organizations • *Social Services:* child welfare, community centers
Grant Types: capital, emergency, endowment, general support, and project
Geographic Distribution: focus on MA

GIVING OFFICERS
Austin Cable: trust
Richard I. Kaner: trust
Frank Kopelman: trust

APPLICATION INFORMATION
Initial Approach: Contributes only to preselected organizations.

GRANTS ANALYSIS
Number of Grants: 14
Highest Grant: $142,000
Typical Range: $10,000 to $20,000
Disclosure Period: fiscal year ending May 31, 1992

RECENT GRANTS
142,000　Children's Hospital, Boston, MA
50,000　Brandeis University, Waltham, MA
43,295　Massachusetts General Hospital, Boston, MA
40,000　Jewish Community Center, Boston, MA
25,000　Carole Fund, Boston, MA
20,000　Children's Museum, Boston, MA
20,000　Jewish Community Center, Boston, MA
20,000　Visiting Nurse Association, Boston, MA — Cancer Care
12,500　Brigham and Women's Hospital, Boston, MA — Cardiac Transplant Program
12,500　Cardiac Surgical Research Fund of Brigham and Women's Hospital, Boston, MA — Cardiac Transplant Project

Rubenstein Foundation, Philip

CONTACT
Herbert Rubenstein
President
Philip Rubenstein Fdn.
400 W. Boden St.
Milwaukee, WI 53207
(414) 769-1000

FINANCIAL SUMMARY
Recent Giving: $1,632,726 (fiscal 1992); $631,632 (fiscal 1990); $680,981 (fiscal 1989)
Assets: $3,476,945 (fiscal year ending January 31, 1992); $2,721,506 (fiscal 1990); $2,736,702 (fiscal 1989)
Gifts Received: $400,000 (fiscal 1990); $215,500 (fiscal 1989); $1,300,000 (fiscal 1988)
Fiscal Note: In 1990, contributions were received from Associated Sales and Bag, Co. ($100,000) and Philip Rubenstein ($300,000).
EIN: 93-0757026

CONTRIBUTIONS SUMMARY
Donor(s): Philip Rubenstein
Typical Recipients: • *Civic & Public Affairs:* ethnic/minority organizations • *Education:* private education (precollege) • *Health:* health organizations, hospitals, medical research • *Religion:* religious organizations, synagogues • *Social Services:* community service organizations, united funds, youth organizations
Grant Types: general support and research

GIVING OFFICERS
Jeff Aronin: vp, secy, dir
Herbert Rubenstein: vp, dir

APPLICATION INFORMATION
Initial Approach: Send brief letter describing program. There are no deadlines.

GRANTS ANALYSIS
Number of Grants: 26
Highest Grant: $1,081,000
Typical Range: $100 to $5,000
Disclosure Period: fiscal year ending January 31, 1992

RECENT GRANTS
1,081,000　Milwaukee Jewish Federation, Milwaukee, WI
200,000　Milwaukee Jewish Home Foundation, Milwaukee, WI
160,000　Milwaukee Jewish Day School, Milwaukee, WI
100,000　Congregation Emanuel, Milwaukee, WI
30,000　Jewish Community Federation, Milwaukee, WI
25,000　Milwaukee Jewish Home, Milwaukee, WI
20,000　Milwaukee Jewish Community, Milwaukee, WI
5,000　Congregation Shalom, Milwaukee, WI
4,000　Milwaukee Heart Research, Milwaukee, WI
1,450　United Way, Milwaukee, WI

Rubin Family Fund, Cele H. and William B.

CONTACT
Ellen R. Gordon
President
Cele H. and William B. Rubin Family Fund
32 Monadnock Rd.
Wellesley Hills, MA 02181
(617) 235-1075

FINANCIAL SUMMARY
Recent Giving: $697,800 (1991); $576,175 (1989); $544,875 (1988)
Assets: $22,302,853 (1991); $13,999,665 (1989); $11,826,184 (1988)
Gifts Received: $575,000 (1991); $475,000 (1989); $450,000 (1988)
Fiscal Note: In 1991, contributions were received from Tootsie Roll Industries, Inc.
EIN: 11-6026235

CONTRIBUTIONS SUMMARY
Donor(s): The foundation was incorporated in 1943 by members of the Joseph Rubin family, the Sweets Co. of America, Inc., Joseph Rubin and Sons, Inc., Tootsie Roll Industries, Inc., and others.
Typical Recipients: • *Arts & Humanities:* libraries • *Civic & Public Affairs:* philanthropic or-

ganizations, women's affairs • *Education:* business education, colleges & universities, education funds, medical education • *Religion:* religious organizations • *Science:* observatories & planetariums • *Social Services:* youth organizations

Grant Types: general support

Geographic Distribution: focus on Massachusetts and New York

GIVING OFFICERS

Ellen R. Gordon: pres, dir *B* New York NY 1931 *ED* Brandeis Univ BA 1965; Vassar Coll; Harvard Univ *CURR EMPL* pres, coo, dir: Tootsie Roll Indus *CORP AFFIL* dir: CPC Intl; vp, dir: HDI Investment Corp *NONPR AFFIL* chp, pres: Comm 200 Fdn; mem: Natl Confectioners Assn; mem adv counc: Stanford Univ Grad Sch Bus; mem bd fellows: Harvard Univ Sch Med

Melvin Jay Gordon: vp, dir *B* Boston MA 1919 *ED* Harvard Univ BA 1941; Harvard Univ MBA 1943 *CURR EMPL* chmn, ceo: Tootsie Roll Indus *CORP AFFIL* pres: Lisa Gordon Inc, Wendy Gordon Inc, HDI Investment Corp, MJG *NONPR AFFIL* dir: Inst Man Science; visiting comm: Russian Res Ctr

APPLICATION INFORMATION

Initial Approach:
The foundation has no formal grant application procedure or application form.
The foundation has no deadline for submitting proposals.

GRANTS ANALYSIS

Total Grants: $697,800

Number of Grants: 31

Highest Grant: $344,000

Typical Range: $250 to $1,000

Disclosure Period: 1991

Note: Average grant figure does not include a grant for $344,000 and a grant for $325,000. Recent grants are derived from a 1991 grants list.

RECENT GRANTS

344,000 Old Colony Charitable Fund, Houston, MA

325,000 Harvard University, Cambridge, MA

5,000 Rensselaerville Institute, Rensselaerville, NY

3,500 Boston University School of Medicine, Boston, MA

2,750 Boston Women's Health Book Collective, Watertown, MA

2,500 Harvard Business School, Cambridge, MA

2,500 Harvard University, Cambridge, MA

2,500 Harvard-Radcliffe Parents Fund, Cambridge, MA

1,000 Girl Scouts of Chicago, Chicago, IL

1,000 Neve Yerushalaim, New York, NY

Rubin Foundation, Rob E. & Judith O.

CONTACT

Rob E. & Judith O. Rubin Fdn.
c/o Goldman, Sachs & Co. - Tax Dept.
85 Broad St., 30th Fl.
New York, NY 10004
(212) 902-6897

FINANCIAL SUMMARY

Recent Giving: $508,085 (fiscal 1991); $667,325 (fiscal 1990); $738,310 (fiscal 1989)

Assets: $3,163,256 (fiscal year ending August 31, 1991); $2,456,241 (fiscal 1990); $2,181,791 (fiscal 1989)

Gifts Received: $1,000,000 (fiscal 1991); $938,416 (fiscal 1990); $1,038,552 (fiscal 1989)

Fiscal Note: In 1991, contributions were received from Robert E. Rubin.

EIN: 13-3050749

CONTRIBUTIONS SUMMARY

Donor(s): Robert E. Rubin

Typical Recipients: • *Arts & Humanities:* arts funds, dance, public broadcasting, theater • *Civic & Public Affairs:* public policy • *Education:* colleges & universities • *Health:* hospitals • *Religion:* religious organizations, synagogues • *Social Services:* recreation & athletics, youth organizations

Grant Types: general support

Geographic Distribution: focus on New York, NY

GIVING OFFICERS

Judith O. Rubin: trust

Robert E. Rubin: trust *B* New York NY 1938 *ED* Harvard Univ AB 1960; London Sch Econ 1960-61; Yale Univ LLB 1964 *CURR EMPL* mem mgmt comm, ptnr, co chmn: Goldman Sachs & Co *NONPR AFFIL*

chmn: New York City Host Comm 1992 Dem Convention; dir: Ctr Natl Policy, Harvard Mgmt Co; mem: Comm Natl Elections, Govs Comm Trade Competitiveness, Govs Counc Econ & Fiscal Priorities, Mayor's Counc Econ Advs, Phi Beta Kappa, SEC Mktg Oversight & Fin Svcs Adv Comm; mem adv comm intl capitalmarkets: Fed Reserve Bank NY; mem comm univ resources: Harvard Univ; ptnr, dir: New York City Partnership; trust: Am Ballet Theatre Fdn, Carnegie Corp, Mt Sinai Med Ctr, WNET-TV/Channel 13; dir: Democrats 90s; mem investment adv counc: NYC Pension Fund; mem regulatory adv comm: NY Stock Exchange

Roy J. Zuckerberg: trust *B* New York NY 1936 *ED* Lowell Technological Inst BS 1958 *CURR EMPL* head div: Goldman Sachs & Co *NONPR AFFIL* mem bd overseers: Albert Einstein Coll Medicine; trust: Brooklyn Mus, Long Island Hearing Speech Soc, Long Island Jewish Med Ctr

APPLICATION INFORMATION

Initial Approach: Send brief letter of inquiry describing program or project. There are no deadlines.

Restrictions on Giving: Does not support individuals.

GRANTS ANALYSIS

Number of Grants: 44

Highest Grant: $100,000

Typical Range: $2,000 to $15,000

Disclosure Period: fiscal year ending August 31, 1991

RECENT GRANTS

100,000 NYBAC Convention Promotion and Services Fund, New York, NY

62,000 Playwrights Horizons, New York, NY

50,000 92nd Street YM/YWHA, New York, NY

47,060 Playwrights Horizons, New York, NY

25,000 WNET Thirteen, New York, NY

20,000 Center for National Policy, Washington, DC

13,500 Collegiate School, New York, NY

12,500 Ballet Theater Foundation, New York, NY

12,500 Boy Scouts of America, New York, NY

Rubin Foundation, Samuel

CONTACT

Cora Weiss
President
Samuel Rubin Foundation
777 United Nations Plz.
New York, NY 10017
(212) 697-8945

FINANCIAL SUMMARY

Recent Giving: $794,750 (fiscal 1991); $811,900 (fiscal 1990); $832,970 (fiscal 1989)

Assets: $11,788,594 (fiscal year ending June 30, 1991); $11,794,787 (fiscal 1990); $11,880,019 (fiscal 1989)

Gifts Received: $157,500 (fiscal 1986)

EIN: 13-6164671

CONTRIBUTIONS SUMMARY

Donor(s): The Samuel Rubin Foundation was incorporated in New York in 1949 from funds donated by the late Samuel Rubin. Mr. Rubin was the founder of Faberge. He also was a founder of the New York University Bellevue Medical Center and the American Symphony Orchestra.

Typical Recipients: • *Arts & Humanities:* arts associations, arts centers, cinema, literary arts, museums/galleries, performing arts, public broadcasting • *Civic & Public Affairs:* business/free enterprise, international affairs, national security, philanthropic organizations, public policy, safety • *Education:* career/vocational education, colleges & universities, education associations, education funds, health & physical education, legal education, science/technology education • *International:* international organizations • *Social Services:* employment/job training, homes, shelters/homelessness

Grant Types: general support and project

Geographic Distribution: national and international

GIVING OFFICERS
Charles L. Mandelstam: secy
CURR EMPL Dornbush
Mensch Mandelstam & Silverman NY City *NONPR AFFIL*
couns: N Salem NY Open Land
Fdn; mem: Assn Bar City NY,
NY St Bar Assn, Phi Beta
Kappa; mem, dir: Societe d'Exploitation Agricole Rhodienne;
trust, couns, dir: NY Sch Volunteer Program
Ralph Shikes: dir
Cora Weiss: pres
Daniel Weiss: dir
Judy Weiss: vp
Peter Weiss: treas *B* Vienna
Austria 1925 *ED* St Johns Coll
AB 1949; Yale Univ JD 1952
Tamara Weiss: dir

APPLICATION INFORMATION
Initial Approach:
The foundation has no formal
application procedures. Applicants should submit a proposal
in writing.
A proposal must describe in detail the organization and the
project. Include a budget and
tax-exempt status letter.
There are no deadlines for applying.
The board reviews applications
on a quarterly basis.

OTHER THINGS TO KNOW
Publications: program policy
statement

GRANTS ANALYSIS
Total Grants: $794,750
Number of Grants: 124
Highest Grant: $206,500
Typical Range: $1,000 to
$10,000
Disclosure Period: fiscal year
ending June 30, 1991
Note: The average grant figure
excludes high grants of
$206,500 and $50,000. Recent
grants are derived from a fiscal
1991 grants list.

RECENT GRANTS
206,500 Institute for Policy
Studies, Washington, DC
50,000 Center for Constitutional Rights, New
York, NY
30,000 SANE/FREEZE
Education Fund,
Washington, DC
25,000 Downtown Community Television
Center, New York,
NY
25,000 Hampshire College, Amherst, MA

23,000 A. J. Muste Memorial Institute, NY
15,000 Lawyers Committee on Nuclear Policy, New York, NY
15,000 Research Foundation of State University of New
York, Albany, NY
10,000 Center for International Policy, Washington, DC
10,000 Fairness and Accuracy in Reporting,
New York, NY

Rubinstein Foundation, Helena

CONTACT
Diane Moss
President
Helena Rubinstein Foundation
405 Lexington Avenue, 15th Fl.
New York, NY 10174
(212) 986-0806

FINANCIAL SUMMARY
Recent Giving: $4,000,000
(fiscal 1993 est.); $4,050,781
(fiscal 1992); $4,588,452 (fiscal 1991)
Assets: $33,177,354 (fiscal
year ending May 31, 1992);
$33,589,037 (fiscal 1991);
$36,319,413 (fiscal 1990)
EIN: 13-6102666

CONTRIBUTIONS SUMMARY
Donor(s): The foundation was
created in 1953 by businesswoman Helena Rubinstein. Ms.
Rubinstein was born in Poland
in 1871, and at the age of 20
she began her cosmetics business with one product, a face
cream. Her cosmetics empire
expanded to London in 1902,
to Paris in 1906, and to New
York in 1912. During her lifetime she accumulated significant collections of African
sculptures, modern paintings
and sculptures, Oriental and
Oceanic art, and Egyptian antiques. The foundation was a
major beneficiary of her legacy
when she died in 1965.
Typical Recipients: • *Arts &
Humanities:* dance, libraries,
museums/galleries, music, performing arts, public broadcasting, theater, visual arts • *Education:* arts education, colleges &
universities, literacy, minority
education, preschool education, science/technology education, student aid • *Health:*
health organizations, hospitals,

medical rehabilitation, medical
research, medical training,
nursing services, pediatric
health, public health, single-disease health associations • *Social Services:* child welfare,
counseling, drugs & alcohol,
employment/job training, family planning, family services,
recreation & athletics, shelters/homelessness, united
funds, youth organizations
Grant Types: fellowship, general support, multiyear/continuing support, research, and
scholarship
Geographic Distribution: primarily New York, NY; minimal
support nationally and internationally

GIVING OFFICERS
Robert S. Friedman: secy,
treas
Oscar Kolin: pres emeritus
Gertrude Geraldine Michelson: chmn *B* Jamestown NY
1925 *ED* PA St Univ BA 1945;
Columbia Univ LLB 1947
CURR EMPL sr vp, dir, mem
exec comm: RH Macy & Co
CORP AFFIL dir: Chubb Corp,
Discount Corp, Gen Electric
Co, Goodyear Tire & Rubber
Co, Harper & Row, Irving
Bank Corp, Irving Trust Co,
Quaker Oats Co, Stanley
Works; gov: Am Stock Exchange; trust, dir: Rand Corp
NONPR AFFIL chmn, bd trust:
Columbia Univ; dir: Am Arbitration Assn, Better Bus Bur
Metro NY, Helena Rubinstein
Fdn, Markle Fdn, Work Am
Inst; mem: NY City Chamber
Commerce, Women's Forum;
mem adv counc: Catalyst, Columbia Univ Grad Sch Bus;
trust: Interracial Counc Bus Opportunity, Spelman Coll
Diane Moss: pres, ceo
Robert Moss: dir
Martin Eli Segal: dir *B*
Vitebsk Union of Soviet Socialist Republics 1916 *CURR
EMPL* chmn emeritus: Martin
E Segal Co *NONPR AFFIL* adv
trustee: Am Scandinavian Fdn;
bd advisors: Library Am; bd
visitors: City Univ NY Grad
Sch & Univ Ctr; chmn: NY Intl
Festival Arts; chmn emeritus:
Lincoln Ctr Performing Arts;
dir: Am Pub Radio; founding
mem publs comm: Pub Interest; mem: Natl Bd of Young
Audiences; mem visitors
comm: Harvard Univ Sch Pub
Health; pres emeritus: Film
Soc Lincoln Ctr; trust emeritus: Inst Advanced Studies

Louis E. Slesin: dir
Suzanne Slesin: dir

APPLICATION INFORMATION
Initial Approach:
There is no application form.
Organizations seeking funding
should submit a letter rather
than make telephone inquiries.
Written proposals must outline
the project, describe goals, provide a budget, state the amount
requested, list other funding
sources, and give a succinct history of the organization.
Proposals are accepted throughout the year.
Every proposal is acknowledged by letter. Additional information may be requested if
the proposal is of interest to
the foundation. A meeting or
site visit may be arranged by
the foundation. Funding decisions are made in May and November. Grants are not renewed automatically, but are
considered on the basis of
evaluation of reports, site visits, priorities, and the availability of funds.
Restrictions on Giving:
Grants are made only to tax-exempt nonprofit organizations.
Scholarship and fellowship
grants are made directly to institutions. General operating
grants are made, but the foundation prefers to support specific
projects or programs. The foundation does not support individuals, film or video projects,
endowments, capital campaigns, loans, or emergency
funds. Funding is limited by
present and long-term commitments and fiscal constraints.

OTHER THINGS TO KNOW
Publications: annual report

GRANTS ANALYSIS
Total Grants: $4,050,871
Number of Grants: 207
Highest Grant: $300,000
Typical Range: $5,000 to
$25,000
Disclosure Period: fiscal year
ending May 31, 1992
Note: Recent grants are derived from a fiscal 1992 annual
report.

RECENT GRANTS
300,000 United States Holocaust Memorial
Museum Campaign, Washington,
DC — endowment
of The Cinema in

242,000 United Jewish Appeal-Federation of Jewish Philanthropies of New York, New York, NY — general support

200,000 WNET/Thirteen, New York, NY — year-round sponsorship of children's television programming

104,000 New York University Medical Center, Department of Obstetrics and Gynecology, New York, NY — establishment of clinic and research program for postmenopausal women

100,000 American Friends of Tel Aviv Museum of Art, New York, NY — Rov V. and Niuta Titus Endowment Fund

100,000 Columbia University, School of Law, New York, NY — establishment of the G. G. Michelson Public Interest Fellows

100,000 Duke University Medical Center, Department of Ophthalmology, Durham, NC — establishment of Helena Rubinstein Foundation Chair in Ophthalmology

100,000 Whitney Museum of American Art, New York, NY — fellowship endowment and annual fellowships

83,333 Weizmann Institute of Science, American Committee, New York, NY — Helena Rubinstein Postdoctoral Fellowship in Biomedical Sciences and Cancer Research

60,000 Children's Blood Foundation, New York, NY — AIDS research and ongoing support of clinic

the museum's Cultural and Conference Center in memory of Helena Rubinstein

Ruddick Corp. / Dickson Foundation

Revenue: $1.48 billion
Employees: 13,500
Headquarters: Charlotte, NC
SIC Major Group: Food Stores, Holding & Other Investment Offices, Printing & Publishing, and Textile Mill Products

CONTACT
Colleen Colbert
Secretary
Dickson Fdn.
2000 Two First Union Center
Charlotte, NC 28282
(704) 372-5404

FINANCIAL SUMMARY
Recent Giving: $1,086,350 (1991); $833,714 (1989)
Assets: $27,101,587 (1991); $25,965,053 (1989)
Fiscal Note: Contributes through foundation only.
EIN: 56-6022339

CONTRIBUTIONS SUMMARY
Typical Recipients: • *Arts & Humanities:* community arts, performing arts, theater • *Civic & Public Affairs:* environmental affairs, ethnic/minority organizations, philanthropic organizations, urban & community affairs • *Education:* business education, colleges & universities, community & junior colleges, medical education • *Health:* health organizations, hospices, hospitals, medical research, single-disease health associations • *Religion:* churches, religious organizations • *Social Services:* community service organizations, united funds, youth organizations
Grant Types: general support
Geographic Distribution: focus on North Carolina
Operating Locations: NC (Charlotte, Mount Holly), PA (Philadelphia)

CORP. OFFICERS
Alan Thomas Dickson: *B* Charlotte NC 1931 *ED* NC St Univ BS 1953; Harvard Univ MBA 1955 *CURR EMPL* chmn: Am & Efird Mills *CORP AFFIL* dir: Chatham Mfg Co, Harris-Teeter Super Markets, Jordan Graphics, Lance, NCNB Corp, Royal Group, Sonoco Products Co; pres, dir: Ruddick Corp *NONPR AFFIL* trust, dir: Central Piedmont Commun Coll

R. Stuart Dickson: *B* Charlotte NC 1929 *ED* Davidson Coll 1929 *CURR EMPL* chmn: Ruddick Corp *CORP AFFIL* chmn: Harris-Teeter Super Markets; dir: Am & Efird Mills, First Union Corp, Jordan Graphics, Kings Entertainment Co, PCA Intl, Ruddick Investment Co, Textron, Un Dominion Indus Ltd *NONPR AFFIL* bd visitors: Davidson Coll, Queens Coll, Univ NC Charlotte; chmn: Charlotte-Mecklenberg Hosp Authority; dir: NC Inst Medicine; mem: Charlotte Chamber Commerce, Newcomen Soc NC; trust: Arts & Science Counc, Wake Forest Univ

GIVING OFFICERS
Alan Thomas Dickson: pres *CURR EMPL* chmn: Am & Efird Mills (see above)
Colleen S. Dickson: secy, treas
R. Stuart Dickson: chmn *CURR EMPL* chmn: Ruddick Corp (see above)
Rush S. Dickson II: vp
Thomas W. Dickson: vp

APPLICATION INFORMATION
Initial Approach: *Initial Contact:* brief letter of inquiry *Include Information On:* description of the organization, amount requested, and purpose of funds *When to Submit:* any time
Restrictions on Giving: Does not support individuals. Usually does not support programs outside of North Carolina.

GRANTS ANALYSIS
Total Grants: $1,086,350
Number of Grants: 245
Highest Grant: $85,000
Typical Range: $1,000 to $10,000
Disclosure Period: 1991
Note: Recent grants are derived from a 1991 grants list.

RECENT GRANTS
85,000 McCallie School, Chattanooga, TN

50,000 Charlotte Country Day School, Charlotte, NC

50,000 North Carolina Performing Arts Center, Charlotte, NC

30,000 Culver Military Academy, Culver, IN

25,000 Lenoir Rhyne College, Hickory, NC

25,000 Queens College, Charlotte, NC

25,000 Rockefeller University, New York, NY

21,000 Duke Comprehensive Cancer Center, Duke University Medical Center, Durham, NC

20,000 Amethyst Foundation, Charlotte, NC

20,000 Central Piedmont Community College, Charlotte, NC

Rudin Foundation

CONTACT
Susan H. Rapaport
Administrator
Rudin Fdn.
345 Park Ave.
New York, NY 10154
(212) 644-8500

FINANCIAL SUMMARY
Recent Giving: $978,369 (1991); $898,838 (1990); $579,563 (1989)
Assets: $1,063,155 (1991); $894,877 (1990); $934,639 (1989)
Gifts Received: $1,134,500 (1991); $838,500 (1990); $604,400 (1989)
EIN: 13-6113064

CONTRIBUTIONS SUMMARY
Donor(s): Jack Rudin, Lewis Rudin
Typical Recipients: • *Arts & Humanities:* music • *Civic & Public Affairs:* business/free enterprise, ethnic/minority organizations, law & justice, municipalities, philanthropic organizations, urban & community affairs, zoos/botanical gardens • *Education:* colleges & universities, private education (precollege) • *Health:* health organizations, hospitals, medical research, single-disease health associations • *Religion:* religious organizations, synagogues • *Social Services:* aged, child welfare, delinquency & crime, recreation & athletics, united funds, youth organizations
Grant Types: general support
Geographic Distribution: focus on New York, NY

GIVING OFFICERS
Milton N. Hoffman: dir
David B. Levy: treas, dir
Jack Rudin: pres, dir *B* 1924 *CURR EMPL* chmn: Rudin Mgmt Co *NONPR AFFIL* head: NY City Marathon Comm; planning comm: Celebration Arts

Lewis Rudin: vp, dir *B* 1927
CURR EMPL pres: Rudin
Mgmt Co *NONPR AFFIL*
chmn: Assn Better NY
May Rudin: dir
Lewis Steinman: dir
Morton Witzling: secy, dir
Adelaide Rudin Zisson: dir

APPLICATION INFORMATION

Initial Approach: Send brief letter of inquiry describing program or project. There are no deadlines.
Restrictions on Giving: Does not support individuals.

GRANTS ANALYSIS

Number of Grants: 150
Highest Grant: $500,000
Typical Range: $1,000 to $5,000
Disclosure Period: 1991

RECENT GRANTS

500,000 United Jewish Appeal Federation of Jewish Philanthropies, New York, NY
54,000 United Cerebral Palsy Association, New York, NY
25,000 New York City Business Assistance Corporation, New York, NY
17,000 American Jewish Congress, New York, NY
13,600 New York Theatre, New York, NY
11,040 New York City Police Foundation, New York, NY
10,000 Abraham Joshua Heschel School, New York, NY
10,000 American Red Cross, New York, NY
10,000 Anti-Defamation League, New York, NY
10,000 Citizens Crime Commission of New York, New York, NY

Rudin Foundation, Louis and Rachel

CONTACT

Susan H. Rapaport
Administrator
Louis and Rachel Rudin
 Foundation
345 Park Avenue, 33rd Fl.
New York, NY 10154
(212) 644-8500

FINANCIAL SUMMARY

Recent Giving: $942,800 (fiscal 1992); $1,277,500 (fiscal 1991); $1,260,000 (fiscal 1989)
Assets: $20,707,608 (fiscal year ending July 31, 1992); $20,695,824 (fiscal 1991); $27,621,463 (fiscal 1989)
EIN: 23-7039549

CONTRIBUTIONS SUMMARY

Donor(s): The foundation was established in New York in 1968.
Typical Recipients: • *Education:* colleges & universities, medical education
Grant Types: fellowship, general support, research, and scholarship
Geographic Distribution: primarily New York

GIVING OFFICERS

Lydia Heimlich: vp, dir
Natalie Lewin: treas, dir
Susan H. Rapaport: adm
Jack Rudin: pres, dir *B* 1924
CURR EMPL chmn: Rudin
Mgmt Co *NONPR AFFIL* head:
NY City Marathon Comm; planning comm: Celebration Arts
Lewis Rudin: secy, dir *B* 1927
CURR EMPL pres: Rudin
Mgmt Co *NONPR AFFIL*
chmn: Assn Better NY
Lewis Steinman: dir

APPLICATION INFORMATION

Initial Approach:
Applicants should submit a letter of inquiry.
Letters should include a description of requesting school's educational training programs. There are no deadlines for requesting funds.
Restrictions on Giving: The foundation only makes grants to aid medical education. No capital grants are considered.

GRANTS ANALYSIS

Total Grants: $942,800
Number of Grants: 25
Highest Grant: $85,000

Typical Range: $20,000 to $60,000
Disclosure Period: fiscal year ending July 31, 1992
Note: Recent grants are derived from a fiscal 1992 Form 990.

RECENT GRANTS

85,000 Yeshiva University-Albert Einstein College of Medicine, New York, NY — medical scholarships
75,000 Columbia University College of Physicians and Surgeons, New York, NY — medical scholarships
75,000 St. Vincent's Hospital School of Nursing, New York, NY — scholarships
66,000 North General Hospital-Helen Fuld School of Nursing, New York, NY — scholarships
65,000 New York University School of Medicine, New York, NY — medical scholarships
55,000 New York University Nursing Division of the School of Education, Health, Nursing and the Arts Professions, New York, NY — scholarships
45,000 Bronx Community College Department of Nursing, Bronx, NY — scholarships
45,000 Cornell University Medical College, New York, NY — medical scholarships
41,000 Cornell University Medical College, New York, NY — scholarships for NYC residencies
40,000 Columbia University School of Nursing, New York, NY — Joint Program with MSKCC; in Graduate Oncology Scholarships to nurses in NYC hospitals

Rudin Foundation, Samuel and May

CONTACT

Susan H. Rapaport
Administrator
c/o Rudin
345 Park Ave.
New York, NY 10154
(212) 644-8500

FINANCIAL SUMMARY

Recent Giving: $7,306,700 (fiscal 1992); $5,353,544 (fiscal 1990); $6,101,200 (fiscal 1989)
Assets: $1,595,736 (fiscal year ending June 30, 1992); $3,673,427 (fiscal 1990); $2,197,910 (fiscal 1989)
Gifts Received: $6,453,898 (fiscal 1992); $5,984,540 (fiscal 1990); $5,989,540 (fiscal 1989)
Fiscal Note: In fiscal 1992, contributions were received from Samuel Rudin.
EIN: 13-2906946

CONTRIBUTIONS SUMMARY

Donor(s): the late Samuel Rudin
Typical Recipients: • *Arts & Humanities:* arts centers, arts festivals, dance, history/historic preservation, museums/galleries, music, public broadcasting, theater, visual arts • *Education:* colleges & universities • *Health:* health organizations, hospitals • *Social Services:* community service organizations, disabled, drugs & alcohol, recreation & athletics
Grant Types: general support
Geographic Distribution: focus on New York, NY

GIVING OFFICERS

Beth Rudin DeWoody: vp, dir
Madeleine Rudin Johnson: dir
Eric C. Rudin: vp, dir
Jack Rudin: pres, dir *B* 1924
CURR EMPL chmn: Rudin
Mgmt Co *NONPR AFFIL* head:
NY City Marathon Comm; planning comm: Celebration Arts
Katherine L. Rudin: dir
Lewis Rudin: exec vp, secy, treas, dir *B* 1927 *CURR EMPL*
pres: Rudin Mgmt Co *NONPR AFFIL* chmn: Assn Better NY
May Rudin: chmn, dir
William Rudin: dir

APPLICATION INFORMATION

Initial Approach: Send brief letter of inquiry describing program or project. There are no deadlines.

GRANTS ANALYSIS
Number of Grants: 138
Highest Grant: $215,000
Typical Range: $5,000 to $30,000
Disclosure Period: fiscal year ending June 30, 1992

RECENT GRANTS
215,000 Memorial Sloan-Kettering Cancer Center, New York, NY
185,000 Columbia University Harlem Hospital, New York, NY
150,000 Columbia University, New York, NY
134,000 New York International Festival of Arts, New York, NY
125,000 Lenox Hill Hospital, New York, NY
80,000 Gay Men's Health Crisis, New York, NY
75,000 Memorial Sloan-Kettering Cancer Center, New York, NY
65,000 Gay Men's Health Crisis, New York, NY
50,000 American Committee for the Tel Aviv Foundation, New York, NY
50,000 Emergency Shelter, New York, NY

Rudy, Jr. Trust, George B.

CONTACT
George B. Rudy, Jr. Trust
c/o The York Bank and Trust Co.
21 East Market St.
York, PA 17401
(717) 843-8651

FINANCIAL SUMMARY
Recent Giving: $331,323 (fiscal 1991); $248,622 (fiscal 1989); $256,223 (fiscal 1988)
Assets: $5,208,135 (fiscal year ending September 30, 1991); $4,836,626 (fiscal 1989); $4,391,591 (fiscal 1988)
EIN: 23-6708045

CONTRIBUTIONS SUMMARY
Typical Recipients: • *Education:* colleges & universities • *Health:* health organizations • *Religion:* churches • *Social Services:* child welfare, commu-

nity service organizations, youth organizations
Grant Types: operating expenses
Geographic Distribution: focus on York, PA

GIVING OFFICERS
York Bank and Trust Company: trust

APPLICATION INFORMATION
Initial Approach: Contributes only to preselected organizations.
Restrictions on Giving: Does not support individuals.

GRANTS ANALYSIS
Number of Grants: 5
Highest Grant: $66,265
Typical Range: $66,264 to $66,265
Disclosure Period: fiscal year ending September 30, 1991

RECENT GRANTS
66,265 St. Mark's Evangelical Lutheran Church, York, PA
66,265 Visiting Nurses Association, York, PA
66,265 York College of Pennsylvania, York, PA
66,264 Salvation Army, York, PA
66,264 YMCA, York, PA

Ruffin Foundation, Peter B. & Adeline W.

CONTACT
Edward G. McAnaney
President
Peter B. & Adeline W. Ruffin Fdn.
150 East 42nd St.
New York, NY 10017-5612

FINANCIAL SUMMARY
Recent Giving: $935,000 (fiscal 1990); $707,500 (fiscal 1989); $607,500 (fiscal 1988)
Assets: $12,783,711 (fiscal year ending November 30, 1990); $13,374,366 (fiscal 1989); $11,358,138 (fiscal 1988)
Gifts Received: $501,017 (fiscal 1989); $2,077,320 (fiscal 1988)
EIN: 13-6170484

CONTRIBUTIONS SUMMARY
Typical Recipients: • *Arts & Humanities:* museums/galleries • *Education:* colleges & univer-

sities, private education (precollege) • *Health:* health organizations, medical research, nursing services, single-disease health associations • *International:* international development/relief • *Religion:* religious organizations • *Social Services:* child welfare, community service organizations, shelters/homelessness, united funds, youth organizations
Grant Types: endowment and professorship

GIVING OFFICERS
Sheila Kostanecki: trust
Brian T. McAnaney: trust
Edward G. McAnaney: pres, treas, trust
Francis A. McAnaney: vp, trust
Kevin G. McAnaney: trust
Marion Simmons: secy

APPLICATION INFORMATION
Initial Approach: Contributes only to preselected organizations.

GRANTS ANALYSIS
Number of Grants: 28
Highest Grant: $400,000
Typical Range: $2,500 to $25,000
Disclosure Period: fiscal year ending November 30, 1990

RECENT GRANTS
400,000 University of Notre Dame, Notre Dame, IN
200,000 Woodberry Forest School, Woodberry Forest, VA
100,000 University of Virginia, Charlottesville, VA
25,000 St. Marys College, Notre Dame, IN
20,000 AmeriCares Foundation, New Canaan, CT
15,000 Center for Hope, Darien, CT
15,000 Covenant House, New York, NY
15,000 Salvation Army, New York, NY
15,000 United Negro College Fund, New York, NY
10,000 United Cerebral Palsy Association, Purchase, NY

Rukin Philanthropic Foundation, David and Eleanore

CONTACT
Julius Elsen
Director
David and Eleanore Rukin Philanthropic Fdn.
17 Franklin Tpke.
Mahwah, NJ 07430
(201) 529-3666

FINANCIAL SUMMARY
Recent Giving: $212,574 (1991); $245,712 (1990); $154,535 (1989)
Assets: $2,235,276 (1991); $2,039,442 (1990); $2,282,749 (1989)
EIN: 22-1715380

CONTRIBUTIONS SUMMARY
Donor(s): David Rukin, Eleanore Rukin, Barnert Rukin, Susan Eisen
Typical Recipients: • *Civic & Public Affairs:* environmental affairs, ethnic/minority organizations • *Education:* colleges & universities • *Health:* health organizations, hospitals • *International:* international organizations • *Religion:* churches, religious organizations • *Social Services:* community centers, community service organizations, youth organizations
Grant Types: general support

GIVING OFFICERS
Julius Eisen: dir
Susan Eisen: dir
Barnett Rukin: dir
Eleanore Rukin: dir

APPLICATION INFORMATION
Initial Approach: Send brief letter of inquiry describing program or project. There are no deadlines.

GRANTS ANALYSIS
Number of Grants: 123
Highest Grant: $76,000
Typical Range: $100 to $1,000
Disclosure Period: 1991

RECENT GRANTS
76,000 Jewish Federation
50,000 United Jewish Campaign, New York, NY
25,035 Brandeis University, Waltham, MA
25,000 YM-YWHA of Bergen County
5,000 Jewish Home for Rehabilitation

2,022 South Palm Beach County Jewish Federation, Palm Beach, FL
2,000 Boca Raton Community Hospital Foundation, Boca Raton, FL
1,500 Lewis Jewish Community Center, Palm Beach, FL
1,120 Florida Atlantic University, FL
1,000 Florida Atlantic University, FL

Rumbaugh Foundation, J. H. and F. H.

CONTACT
William R. Cunningham
J. H. and F. H. Rumbaugh Fdn.
First Union National Bank
PO Box 44245
Jacksonville, FL 32231-4245
(904) 361-5814

FINANCIAL SUMMARY
Recent Giving: $199,199 (fiscal 1992); $193,752 (fiscal 1991); $217,269 (fiscal 1990)
Assets: $4,252,074 (fiscal year ending March 31, 1992); $4,098,505 (fiscal 1991); $3,588,731 (fiscal 1990)
Gifts Received: $477 (fiscal 1992)
EIN: 59-6851866

CONTRIBUTIONS SUMMARY
Typical Recipients: • *Education:* colleges & universities
Grant Types: general support
Geographic Distribution: focus on PA

APPLICATION INFORMATION
Initial Approach: Contributes only to preselected organizations.
Restrictions on Giving: Does not support individuals.

GRANTS ANALYSIS
Number of Grants: 3
Highest Grant: $66,400
Typical Range: $63,399 to $63,400
Disclosure Period: fiscal year ending March 31, 1992

RECENT GRANTS
66,400 Beaver College, Glenside, PA
66,400 Mercersburg Academy, Mercersburg, PA

66,399 Lafayette College, Easton, PA

Rupp Foundation, Fran and Warren

CONTACT
Tim Smith
Fran and Warren Rupp Fdn.
40 Sturges Ave.
Mansfield, OH 44902-1912
(419) 522-2345

FINANCIAL SUMMARY
Recent Giving: $2,345,000 (1991); $263,500 (1990); $283,169 (1989)
Assets: $11,636,987 (1991); $10,229,869 (1990); $9,852,828 (1989)
Gifts Received: $210,185 (1991); $332,633 (1990); $7,080,294 (1989)
Fiscal Note: In 1991, contributions were received from Frances H. Rupp Marital Trust ($183,185), Sharon A. Rupp Charitable Lead Trust ($9,000), Suzanne R. Hartung Charitable Lead Trust ($9,000), and John W. Rupp Charitable Lead Trust ($9,000).
EIN: 34-1230690

CONTRIBUTIONS SUMMARY
Donor(s): Fran Rupp, Warren Rupp
Typical Recipients: • *Arts & Humanities:* arts funds, community arts, music, theater • *Civic & Public Affairs:* environmental affairs • *Health:* medical research • *Religion:* religious organizations • *Social Services:* community service organizations, domestic violence, shelters/homelessness, united funds, youth organizations
Grant Types: general support
Geographic Distribution: focus on Mansfield, OH

GIVING OFFICERS
Frances R. Christian: chmn
Suzanne R. Hartung: trust
Fran Rupp: off
Sheron A. Rupp: trust
Donald Smith: secy, treas
Tim S. Smith: secy, treas

APPLICATION INFORMATION
Initial Approach: Send brief letter describing program. There are no deadlines.

GRANTS ANALYSIS
Number of Grants: 24
Highest Grant: $2,100,000

Typical Range: $500 to $10,000
Disclosure Period: 1991

RECENT GRANTS
2,100,000 Renaissance Theatre, Mansfield, OH
50,000 Mansfield Symphony Society, Mansfield, OH
35,000 Wyoming Nature Conservancy, Lander, WY
20,000 Habitat for Humanity, Mansfield, OH
20,000 Nature Conservancy, Columbus, OH
20,000 Wilda, Columbus, OH
15,000 YWCA, Mansfield, OH
10,000 Boy Scouts of America, Mansfield, OH
10,000 Planned Parenthood Federation of America, Mansfield, OH
10,000 Salk Institute for Biological Studies, San Diego, CA

Russ Togs / Russ Togs Foundation
Sales: $217.1 million
Employees: 2,300
Headquarters: New York, NY
SIC Major Group: Apparel & Other Textile Products

CONTACT
Kenneth Sitomer
Trustee
Russ Togs Fdn.
1411 Broadway
New York, NY 10018
(212) 642-8500

FINANCIAL SUMMARY
Recent Giving: $47,160 (1990); $46,925 (1989); $148,060 (1988)
Assets: $5,958 (1990); $4,139 (1989); $4,605 (1988)
Gifts Received: $49,000 (1990); $46,500 (1989); $146,000 (1988)
Fiscal Note: In 1990, contributions were received from Russ Togs, Inc.
EIN: 13-6086149

CONTRIBUTIONS SUMMARY
Typical Recipients: • *Civic & Public Affairs:* women's affairs • *Health:* medical research, mental health, single-disease health associations • *International:* foreign educational institutions, international health

care • *Religion:* religious organizations • *Social Services:* aged, community centers, youth organizations
Grant Types: general support
Geographic Distribution: focus on NY
Operating Locations: NJ (Paterson), NY (Long Island City, New York), TN (Sparta)

CORP. OFFICERS
Eli L. Rousso: *B* New York NY 1920 *CURR EMPL* chmn, dir: Russ Togs *CORP AFFIL* dir: Gotham Bank (NYC)
Kenneth Sitomer: *CURR EMPL* pres, ceo: Russ Togs

GIVING OFFICERS
Eli L. Rousso: trust *CURR EMPL* chmn, dir: Russ Togs (see above)
Herman Saporta: trust
Kenneth Sitomer: trust *CURR EMPL* pres, ceo: Russ Togs (see above)

APPLICATION INFORMATION
Initial Approach: Requests for contributions require no formal application. There are no deadlines.

GRANTS ANALYSIS
Number of Grants: 32
Highest Grant: $10,000
Typical Range: $200 to $1,000
Disclosure Period: 1990

RECENT GRANTS
10,000 United Jewish Appeal Federation of Jewish Philanthropies, New York, NY
5,400 Boy Scouts of America, New York, NY
5,000 Inner-City Scholarship Fund, New York, NY
4,000 National Jewish Center for Immunology and Respiratory Medicine, Denver, CO
2,500 AIDS Foundation of Chicago, Chicago, IL
2,500 Labor Heritage Program
2,400 Heart Research Foundation, New York, NY
2,400 Sephardic Home for the Aged, Brooklyn, NY
2,000 CFDA Foundation
1,500 Boy Scouts of America, Chicago, IL

Russell Charitable Foundation, Tom

CONTACT

Leslie R. Bishop
Secretary
Tom Russell Charitable Fdn.
1315 West 22nd St., Ste. 300
Oak Brook, IL 60521
(708) 571-4600

FINANCIAL SUMMARY

Recent Giving: $455,000 (fiscal 1991); $440,000 (fiscal 1990); $450,000 (fiscal 1989)
Assets: $10,068,656 (fiscal year ending August 31, 1991); $9,522,514 (fiscal 1990); $9,405,337 (fiscal 1989)
EIN: 36-6082517

CONTRIBUTIONS SUMMARY

Donor(s): the late Thomas C. Russell, Wrap-On Co., Inc., Huron and Orleans Building Corp.
Typical Recipients: • *Arts & Humanities:* history/historic preservation, libraries • *Education:* colleges & universities • *Health:* medical research, single-disease health associations • *Religion:* churches • *Science:* scientific organizations • *Social Services:* aged, child welfare, community service organizations, shelters/homelessness, youth organizations
Grant Types: general support
Geographic Distribution: focus on the metropolitan Chicago, IL, area

GIVING OFFICERS

Leslie R. Bishop: secy, dir
Thomas A. Hearn: vp, dir
John Lindquist: dir
J. Tod Meserow: treas, dir

APPLICATION INFORMATION

Initial Approach: Send cover letter and full proposal. Grants usually made in July and August.
Restrictions on Giving: Does not support individuals.

OTHER THINGS TO KNOW

Publications: Application Guidelines

GRANTS ANALYSIS

Number of Grants: 56
Highest Grant: $20,000
Typical Range: $2,000 to $20,000

Disclosure Period: fiscal year ending August 31, 1991

RECENT GRANTS

20,000 Boys and Girls Club, Chicago, IL
20,000 Cumberland College, Williamsburg, KY
20,000 Duke Comprehensive Cancer Center, Durham, NC
20,000 HOME Communication Channel, Dublin, OH
20,000 LaGrange Memorial Treatment Pavilion, Hinsdale, IL
20,000 Senior Friends, Hartford, CT
15,000 Chicago Academy of Sciences, Chicago, IL
15,000 Chicago Metro History Fair, Chicago, IL
12,500 Young Life, Chicago, IL
12,000 Lawndale Community Church, Chicago, IL

Russell Charitable Trust, Josephine S.

CONTACT

Nancy C. Gurney
Exec. Asst.
Josephine S. Russell Charitable Trust
c/o The Central Trust Co., N.A.
PO Box 1198
Cincinnati, OH 45201-1198
(513) 651-8377

FINANCIAL SUMMARY

Recent Giving: $307,639 (fiscal 1991); $268,874 (fiscal 1990); $197,030 (fiscal 1989)
Assets: $6,186,158 (fiscal year ending June 30, 1991); $5,985,727 (fiscal 1990); $5,350,947 (fiscal 1989)
EIN: 31-6195446

CONTRIBUTIONS SUMMARY

Donor(s): the late Josephine Schell Russell
Typical Recipients: • *Arts & Humanities:* arts centers, community arts, history/historic preservation, literary arts, music, theater • *Civic & Public Affairs:* zoos/botanical gardens • *Education:* colleges & universities • *Health:* health organizations, pediatric health • *Social Services:* child welfare, community service organizations, disabled, united funds, youth organizations

Grant Types: capital, project, and seed money
Geographic Distribution: limited to the greater Cincinnati, OH, area

APPLICATION INFORMATION

Initial Approach: Send brief letter of inquiry describing program or project.
Restrictions on Giving: Does not support individuals or provide loans.

OTHER THINGS TO KNOW

Publications: Informational Brochure (including application guidelines)

GRANTS ANALYSIS

Number of Grants: 62
Highest Grant: $15,000
Typical Range: $1,000 to $10,000
Disclosure Period: fiscal year ending June 30, 1991

RECENT GRANTS

15,000 Union Terminal Trust Fund, Cincinnati, OH
10,000 Cincinnati Zoo and Botanical Garden, Cincinnati, OH
10,000 Victory Neighborhood Service — renovation
10,000 WCET, Cincinnati, OH
10,000 Womens Research and Development Center, Cincinnati, OH — school project
9,000 Comprehensive Community Child Care
7,500 Living Arrangements for the Developmentally Disabled (L.A.D.D.), Cincinnati, OH
7,500 McNicholas High School — learning disabilities
7,000 Boy Scouts of America
7,000 Children's Home of Northern Kentucky, KY

Russell Corp. / Russell Foundation

Sales: $804.6 million
Employees: 14,976
Headquarters: Alexander City, AL
SIC Major Group: Apparel & Other Textile Products and Textile Mill Products

CONTACT

Jim Nabors
Controller
Russell Corp.
Drawer 272
Alexander City, AL 35010
(205) 329-4000

CONTRIBUTIONS SUMMARY

Operating Locations: AL (Alexander City)

CORP. OFFICERS

John C. Adams: *CURR EMPL* pres, coo: Russell Corp
E. C. Gwaltney: *CURR EMPL* chmn, ceo: Russell Corp
James D. Nabors: *B* Sylacauga AL 1942 *CURR EMPL* vp, cfo, dir: Russell Corp *CORP AFFIL* dir: First Natl Bank Alexander City *NONPR AFFIL* dir: AL Sch Fine Arts; mem: Fin Execs Inst; mem bd visitors: Univ AL; trust: Judson Coll

Russell Educational Foundation, Benjamin and Roberta

CONTACT

James D. Nabors
Vice President
Benjamin and Roberta Russell Educational Fdn.
PO Box 272
Alexander City, AL 35010
(205) 329-4224

FINANCIAL SUMMARY

Recent Giving: $918,183 (1990); $908,166 (1989); $915,917 (1987)
Assets: $23,930,440 (1990); $27,629,889 (1989); $16,344,884 (1987)
EIN: 63-0393126

CONTRIBUTIONS SUMMARY

Donor(s): The foundation was established in 1944 by the late Benjamin Russell.
Typical Recipients: • *Arts & Humanities:* arts associations, libraries, public broadcasting

• *Education:* colleges & universities, community & junior colleges, education funds, science/technology education • *Health:* single-disease health associations • *Social Services:* animal protection, delinquency & crime, emergency relief, food/clothing distribution, youth organizations
Grant Types: general support and scholarship
Geographic Distribution: southeastern United States, with a focus on Alabama

GIVING OFFICERS
Roberta A. Baumgardner: trust
James W. Brown, Jr.: trust
Ann R. Caceres: trust
Julia G. Fuller: trust
Nancy R. Gwaltney: dir, pres
James D. Nabors: vp, cfo *B* Sylacauga AL 1942 *CURR EMPL* vp, cfo, dir: Russell Corp *CORP AFFIL* dir: First Natl Bank Alexander City *NONPR AFFIL* dir: AL Sch Fine Arts; mem: Fin Execs Inst; mem bd visitors: Univ AL; trust: Judson Coll
Benjamin Russell: dir, vp
Edith L. Russell: trust
Julia W. Russell: trust

APPLICATION INFORMATION
Initial Approach: Restrictions on Giving: The foundation supports preselected organizations and does not accept unsolicited requests for funds.

GRANTS ANALYSIS
Total Grants: $918,183
Number of Grants: 31
Highest Grant: $150,000
Typical Range: $3,000 to $25,000
Disclosure Period: 1990
Note: Average grant figure does not include a grant for $150,000 and a grant for $125,000. Recent grants are derived from a 1990 grants list.

RECENT GRANTS
150,000 Children's Harbor, Staten Island, NY
125,000 University of Alabama in Birmingham, Birmingham, AL
124,700 Russell Hospital, Alexander City, AL
105,000 Alexander City Board of Education, Alexander City, AL
75,000 Lyman Ward Military Academy, Camp Hill, AL
25,000 Alabama Public Television, Birmingham, AL
25,000 Alcoholism Council of Central Alabama, Birmingham, AL
25,000 ARISE, Pomona, CA
25,000 Auburn University Foundation, Auburn, AL
20,000 Medical Park Foundation, LaGrange, GA

Russell Memorial Foundation, Robert

CONTACT
Norman H. Lipoff
Trustee
Robert Russell Memorial Fdn.
c/o Greenberg, Traurig, et al.
1221 Brickell Ave.
Miami, FL 33131
(305) 579-0500

FINANCIAL SUMMARY
Recent Giving: $895,000 (fiscal 1991); $1,115,000 (fiscal 1990); $482,000 (fiscal 1989)
Assets: $16,791,175 (fiscal year ending August 31, 1991); $15,388,300 (fiscal 1990); $13,507,789 (fiscal 1989)
Gifts Received: $75,000 (fiscal 1991); $1,883,953 (fiscal 1990); $8,315,418 (fiscal 1989)
Fiscal Note: In 1991, contributions were received from the estate of Robert Russell.
EIN: 59-2486579

CONTRIBUTIONS SUMMARY
Donor(s): The foundation was established in 1984.
Typical Recipients: • *Arts & Humanities:* arts appreciation, arts funds, history/historic preservation, museums/galleries • *Civic & Public Affairs:* national security • *Education:* colleges & universities, community & junior colleges, international studies, medical education, public education (precollege), religious education • *Health:* hospitals, medical training • *International:* foreign educational institutions • *Religion:* religious organizations • *Social Services:* community centers, employment/job training, united funds
Grant Types: general support
Geographic Distribution: focus on Dade County, FL

GIVING OFFICERS
Norman H. Lipoff: trust
Simeon D. Spear: trust

APPLICATION INFORMATION
Initial Approach: Restrictions on Giving: The foundation supports preselected organizations and does not accept unsolicited requests for funds. The foundation does not make grants to individuals.

GRANTS ANALYSIS
Total Grants: $895,000
Number of Grants: 18
Highest Grant: $375,000
Typical Range: $10,000 to $35,000
Disclosure Period: fiscal year ending August 31, 1991
Note: Average grant figure does not include the highest grant of $375,000. Recent grants are derived from a fiscal 1991 grants list.

RECENT GRANTS
375,000 Greater Miami Jewish Federation, Miami, FL
125,000 Israel Education Fund
95,000 High School in Israel, Miami, FL
50,000 South Dade Jewish Community Center, FL
35,000 American Friends of Shalom Hartman Institute
25,000 Ben-Gurion University of Negev, New York, NY
25,000 Holocaust Memorial Committee
25,000 Institute for the Advancement of Education in Jaffa, Brooklyn, NY
25,000 United Way
20,000 Holocaust Documentation and Education Center, Miami, FL

Russell Trust, Josephine G.

CONTACT
Clifford E. Elias
Trustee
Josephine G. Russell Trust
70 East St.
Methuen, MA 01844
(617) 687-0151

FINANCIAL SUMMARY
Recent Giving: $284,550 (1991); $235,025 (1989); $187,725 (1988)
Assets: $5,918,340 (1991); $5,489,149 (1989); $5,045,030 (1988)
EIN: 04-2136910

CONTRIBUTIONS SUMMARY
Typical Recipients: • *Arts & Humanities:* libraries • *Civic & Public Affairs:* urban & community affairs • *Health:* hospitals, medical research, pediatric health • *Social Services:* child welfare, community service organizations, united funds, youth organizations
Grant Types: capital, emergency, general support, project, and scholarship
Geographic Distribution: limited to the greater Lawrence, MA, area

GIVING OFFICERS
Archer L. Bolton, Jr.: trust
Roger N. Bower: trust
Clifford E. Elias: trust
Marsha E. Rich: trust

APPLICATION INFORMATION
Initial Approach: Send brief letter of inquiry describing program or project. Deadline is January 31.
Restrictions on Giving: Does not support individuals.

OTHER THINGS TO KNOW
Publications: Application Guidelines

GRANTS ANALYSIS
Number of Grants: 35
Highest Grant: $66,700
Typical Range: $2,000 to $5,000
Disclosure Period: 1991

RECENT GRANTS
66,700 Lawrence General Hospital, Lawrence, MA
40,000 Holy Family Hospital, Lawrence, MA

30,000 Greater Lawrence Community Foundation, Lawrence, MA

15,000 Merrimack Valley United Fund, Lawrence, MA

10,500 Lawrence Public Library, Lawrence, MA

10,000 Big Brothers and Big Sisters, Lawrence, MA

10,000 Phillips Academy, Andover, MA

10,000 YMCA, Lawrence, MA

10,000 YWCA, Lawrence, MA

8,000 Brooks School, Lawrence, MA

Rust International Corp.

Revenue: $600.0 million
Employees: 2,100
Parent Company: Wheelabrator Technologies Inc.
Headquarters: Birmingham, AL
SIC Major Group: Engineering & Management Services and General Building Contractors

CONTACT
Marianne Morrow
Manager of Corporate Communications
Rust International Corp.
POBox 101
Birmingham, AL 35201
(205) 995-7166

CONTRIBUTIONS SUMMARY
Company provides employee matching gifts only.
Grant Types: matching
Operating Locations: AL (Birmingham), PA (Pittsburgh, Williamsport)

CORP. OFFICERS
Rodney C. Gilbert: *B* Birmingham AL 1939 *ED* Univ AL 1967 *CURR EMPL* chmn, ceo: Rust International Corp
John J. Goody: *CURR EMPL* vp, cfo: Rust Intl Corp

Rust-Oleum Corp.

Sales: $89.0 million
Employees: 442
Headquarters: Vernon Hills, IL
SIC Major Group: Chemicals & Allied Products

CONTACT
Joan Kroll
Executive Administrative Assistant
Rust-Oleum Corp.
11 Hawthorn Pkwy.
Vernon Hills, IL 60061
(708) 367-7700

CONTRIBUTIONS SUMMARY
Nonmonetary Support Types: donated products
Operating Locations: IL (Vernon Hills)

CORP. OFFICERS
Donald C. Ferguson: *CURR EMPL* pres: Rust-Oleum Corp
Leonard P. Judy: *CURR EMPL* chmn, ceo: Rust-Oleum Corp

Rutgers Community Health Foundation

CONTACT
Rutgers Community Health Foundation
One Worlds Fair Drive
Somerset, NJ 08873-1345
(201) 469-4300

FINANCIAL SUMMARY
Recent Giving: $284,025 (fiscal 1990)
Assets: $4,898,034 (fiscal year ending June 30, 1990)
EIN: 22-2847302

CONTRIBUTIONS SUMMARY
Typical Recipients: • *Health:* hospitals, nursing services, pediatric health, single-disease health associations • *Social Services:* delinquency & crime, family planning, religious welfare
Grant Types: department

GIVING OFFICERS
Francis T. Drury: chmn
Gary M. Gorran: treas
Nadine B. Shanler: secy

APPLICATION INFORMATION
Initial Approach: The foundation reports no specific application guidelines. Send a brief letter of inquiry, including statement of purpose, amount requested, and proof of tax-exempt status.

GRANTS ANALYSIS
Total Grants: $284,025
Number of Grants: 33
Highest Grant: $10,000

Disclosure Period: fiscal year ending June 30, 1990

RECENT GRANTS
10,000 Chilton Memorial Hospital
10,000 Community Nursing Services, City of Vineland, NJ
10,000 Department of Pediatrics/RUWJUSM
10,000 Eric B. Chandler Health Center
10,000 Family Planning Services of Cumberland and Gloucester, NJ
10,000 Huntington's Disease Society of America, New Jersey Chapter, NJ
10,000 New Jersey Association on Correction, NJ
10,000 Planned Parenthood of Bergen County, NJ
10,000 Providence House
10,000 St. John's Clinic/Catholic Charities

Rutledge Charity, Edward

CONTACT
John Frampton
President
Edward Rutledge Charity
PO Box 758
Chippewa Falls, WI 54729
(715) 723-6618

FINANCIAL SUMMARY
Recent Giving: $119,969 (fiscal 1990); $19,415 (fiscal 1989)
Assets: $2,905,550 (fiscal year ending May 31, 1990); $2,737,366 (fiscal 1989)
EIN: 39-0806178

CONTRIBUTIONS SUMMARY
Donor(s): the late Edward Rutledge
Grant Types: loan, operating expenses, project, and scholarship
Geographic Distribution: limited to Chippewa County, WI

GIVING OFFICERS
John Frampton: pres, dir
Gerald Naiberg: secy, treas
Richard H. Stafford: vp, dir

APPLICATION INFORMATION
Initial Approach: Application form required for scholarships. Scholarship applications must be submitted by July 1.

OTHER THINGS TO KNOW
Provides relief to the poor and scholarships to individuals for higher education.

Ryan Family Charitable Foundation

CONTACT
Kay W. Martin
Executive Secretary
Ryan Family Charitable Fdn.
3001 Gills Falls Rd.
Mt. Airy, MD 21771
(301) 795-0266

FINANCIAL SUMMARY
Recent Giving: $825,412 (fiscal 1990); $1,563,432 (fiscal 1989)
Assets: $4,050 (fiscal year ending November 30, 1990); $43,755 (fiscal 1989)
Gifts Received: $70,000 (fiscal 1990); $726,650 (fiscal 1989)
Fiscal Note: In fiscal 1990, contributions were received from James P. Ryan.
EIN: 52-1102104

CONTRIBUTIONS SUMMARY
Donor(s): James P. Ryan
Typical Recipients: • *Civic & Public Affairs:* environmental affairs, housing • *Education:* agricultural education • *Health:* hospitals • *Religion:* missionary activities, religious organizations • *Social Services:* community service organizations, family services, food/clothing distribution, recreation & athletics, youth organizations
Grant Types: general support, project, and seed money
Geographic Distribution: focus on Baltimore, MD

GIVING OFFICERS
George Kalivrentos: dir
Barbara M. Ryan: dir
Daniel M. Ryan: dir
James P. Ryan, Jr.: dir
James Patrick Ryan: vp *B* Pittsburgh PA 1932 *ED* Allegheny Coll 1954 *CURR EMPL* consultant, chmn exec comm: Ryland Group
Kathleen C. Ryan: dir
Linda M. Ryan: pres
Peter D. Ryan: dir

APPLICATION INFORMATION

Initial Approach: Send brief letter of inquiry describing program or project. There are no deadlines. The foundation board meets quarterly. Decisions are made one month after board meeting.

Restrictions on Giving: Does not support individuals or fund loans or publications.

OTHER THINGS TO KNOW

Publications: Program policy statement, application guidelines

GRANTS ANALYSIS

Number of Grants: 54
Highest Grant: $101,254
Typical Range: $50 to $10,000
Disclosure Period: fiscal year ending November 30, 1990

RECENT GRANTS

101,254　Race Track Chaplaincy of America, Long Island, NY
65,550　Accord Foundation, Bethesda, MD
50,000　Emmaus House, New York, NY
50,000　Non-Violence International, Washington, DC
50,000　Norton Hospital, Baltimore, MD
50,000　Santa Cruz Mission, Pittsburgh, PA
40,000　Maryland Horsemen's Assistance Fund, Baltimore, MD
40,000　St. Ambrose Housing Aid Center, Baltimore, MD
36,290　Carole Haven Center, Westminster, MD
30,000　Chesapeake Center, Baltimore, MD

Ryan Foundation, David Claude

CONTACT

Jerome D. Ryan
President
David Claude Ryan Fdn.
PO Box 6409
San Diego, CA 92106
(619) 291-7311, ext. 1321

FINANCIAL SUMMARY

Recent Giving: $205,278 (1989); $160,942 (1988)
Assets: $2,680,257 (1989); $2,525,638 (1988)
Gifts Received: $70,000 (1989); $80,000 (1988)

EIN: 95-6051140

CONTRIBUTIONS SUMMARY

Donor(s): Jerome D. Ryan, Gladys B. Ryan
Typical Recipients: • *Civic & Public Affairs:* zoos/botanical gardens • *Health:* emergency/ambulance services • *Religion:* churches, missionary activities, religious organizations • *Social Services:* community service organizations, food/clothing distribution, united funds, youth organizations
Grant Types: multiyear/continuing support
Geographic Distribution: focus on CA, with emphasis on San Diego

GIVING OFFICERS

Gladys B. Ryan: vp, secy, treas
Jerome D. Ryan: pres
Stephen M. Ryan: vp

APPLICATION INFORMATION

Initial Approach: Send brief letter describing program. There are no deadlines.
Restrictions on Giving: Does not support individuals.

GRANTS ANALYSIS

Number of Grants: 42
Highest Grant: $80,000
Typical Range: $1,000 to $6,000
Disclosure Period: 1989

RECENT GRANTS

80,000　Mission Aviation Fellowship, Redlands, CA
27,500　San Diego Youth for Christ, San Diego, CA
14,377　First United Methodist Church, San Diego, CA
6,000　Billy Graham Evangelistic Association, Minneapolis, MN
6,000　Salvation Army, San Diego, CA
6,000　San Diego Rescue League, San Diego, CA
6,000　Spreckles Organ Society, San Diego, CA
5,000　Westminister Woods, San Diego, CA
3,000　Food for the Hungry, San Diego, CA
3,000　Zoological Society of San Diego, San Diego, CA

Ryan Foundation, Nina M.

CONTACT

Nina M. Ryan Fdn.
Jaycox Rd.
Cold Spring, NY 10516
(914) 434-3561

FINANCIAL SUMMARY

Recent Giving: $129,834 (1991); $41,867 (1990); $62,025 (1989)
Assets: $3,033,775 (1991); $2,791,341 (1990); $2,647,099 (1989)
EIN: 13-6111038

CONTRIBUTIONS SUMMARY

Typical Recipients: • *Arts & Humanities:* arts associations, arts institutes, music • *Civic & Public Affairs:* environmental affairs, philanthropic organizations • *Education:* colleges & universities • *Health:* hospitals, medical research, single-disease health associations • *Religion:* churches, religious organizations • *Social Services:* child welfare, community service organizations, united funds, youth organizations
Grant Types: general support

GIVING OFFICERS

R.F. Bell: off
Richard O. Berner: off
Thomas Roland Berner: vp, treas
Tanya Fedoruk: secy
Olga Formissaro: off
Winifred B. Parker: pres

APPLICATION INFORMATION

Initial Approach: Contributes only to preselected organizations.
Restrictions on Giving: Does not support individuals or provide funds for scholarships.

GRANTS ANALYSIS

Number of Grants: 14
Highest Grant: $111,139
Typical Range: $200 to $5,000
Disclosure Period: 1991

RECENT GRANTS

111,139　Bauman Foundation
5,000　Harvard University, Cambridge, MA
5,000　New York Philharmonic, New York, NY
4,000　Lake Waramaug Task Force
1,500　St. Elizabeth Memorial Chapel
1,000　Newburg East Jehovas Witnesses
1,000　Trinity School
210　Metropolitan Museum of Art, New York, NY
200　New Amsterdam Singers
200　South Forty

Ryan Foundation, Patrick G. and Shirley W.

CONTACT

Patrick G. and Shirley W. Ryan Fdn.
123 North Wacker Dr., Ste. 1190
Chicago, IL 60606

FINANCIAL SUMMARY

Recent Giving: $515,903 (fiscal 1990); $504,690 (fiscal 1989); $719,575 (fiscal 1987)
Assets: $9,314 (fiscal year ending November 30, 1990); $5,193 (fiscal 1989); $338,457 (fiscal 1987)
Gifts Received: $516,500 (fiscal 1990); $505,000 (fiscal 1989); $700,100 (fiscal 1987)
Fiscal Note: In 1990, contributions were received from Patrick and Shirley Ryan.
EIN: 36-3305162

CONTRIBUTIONS SUMMARY

Donor(s): Ryan Holding Corp. of Illinois, Ryan Enterprises Corp.
Typical Recipients: • *Arts & Humanities:* history/historic preservation, music, opera, theater • *Civic & Public Affairs:* zoos/botanical gardens • *Education:* colleges & universities, education associations • *Health:* medical research, single-disease health associations • *Religion:* churches • *Social Services:* child welfare, community service organizations, youth organizations
Grant Types: general support
Geographic Distribution: focus on IL

GIVING OFFICERS

Glen E. Hess: secy, dir
Patrick G. Ryan: vp, dir *B* Milwaukee WI 1937 *ED* Northwestern Univ BS 1959 *CURR EMPL* chmn, ceo, pres: AON Corp *CORP AFFIL* chmn: Globe Life Ins, James S Kemper & Co, Pat Ryan & Assocs, Ryan Ins Co, VA Surety Co;

chmn, ceo: Combined Ins Co Am, Rollins Burdick Hunter Co; chmn, pres, ceo: Rollins Hudig Hall Group; dir: Commonwealth Edison Co, First Chicago Corp, First Natl Bank, Gould Inc, Penske Corp; pres: Dearborn Life Ins Co, Riverside Acceptance Corp; pres, dir: Abacus Life Ins, Geneva Surety Ins Co, Lincoln-Standard Life Ins Co; vchmn: Combined Life Ins Co NY; vp, dir: AMRA Svcs, Self Insurers Svc; dir: Stone Container Corp; pres, ceo: Combined Intl Corp *NONPR AFFIL* trust: Field Mus Natural History, Northwestern Univ, Rush-Presbyterian-St Lukes Med Ctr
Shirley W. Ryan: pres, dir

APPLICATION INFORMATION

Initial Approach: Contributes only to preselected organizations.

GRANTS ANALYSIS

Number of Grants: 36
Highest Grant: $100,000
Typical Range: $1,000 to $10,000
Disclosure Period: fiscal year ending November 30, 1990

RECENT GRANTS

100,000 Big Shoulders Fund, Chicago, IL
100,000 National College of Education, Evanston, IL
50,000 Lyric Opera of Chicago, Chicago, IL
30,000 WGN Neediest Children's Fund, Chicago, IL
25,000 Chicago Council on Foreign Relations, Chicago, IL
25,000 Loyola Academy, Chicago, IL
25,000 National Strategy Forum, Chicago, IL
25,000 St. Francis De Sales Church, Chicago, IL — Lake Geneva
20,000 Saints Faith, Hope, and Charity Church, Winnetka, IL
15,000 Dartmouth Parents Fund, Hanover, NH

Ryder System / Ryder System Charitable Foundation

Sales: $5.19 billion
Employees: 41,695
Headquarters: Miami, FL
SIC Major Group: Automobile Repair, Services & Parking, Insurance Carriers, Local & Interurban Passenger Transit, and Transportation Equipment

CONTACT

Ross Roadman
Executive Director
Ryder System Charitable Fdn.
3600 NW 82nd Ave.
Miami, FL 33166
(305) 593-3642

FINANCIAL SUMMARY

Recent Giving: $3,000,000 (1992 approx.); $2,124,798 (1991); $2,336,453 (1990 approx.)
Assets: $204,061 (1991); $845,025 (1989); $982,000 (1988)
Fiscal Note: Above figures include annual direct giving of approximately $400,000.
EIN: 59-2462315

CONTRIBUTIONS SUMMARY

Typical Recipients: • *Arts & Humanities:* dance, museums/galleries, music, opera, theater • *Civic & Public Affairs:* economic development, ethnic/minority organizations, housing • *Education:* business education, colleges & universities, education funds, minority education, public education (precollege) • *Social Services:* drugs & alcohol, united funds, volunteer services, youth organizations
Grant Types: challenge, employee matching gifts, general support, project, and scholarship
Nonmonetary Support Types: donated equipment, in-kind services, loaned employees, loaned executives, and workplace solicitation
Note: Estimated value of nonmonetary support is $50,000 to $75,000 annually. This amount is included in the contributions figures above.
Geographic Distribution: primarily greater Miami and Dade County, FL, and through community initiative programs in

Dallas, Atlanta, Cincinnati, St. Louis, and Los Angeles.
Operating Locations: CA (Los Angeles), FL (Miami), MI (Bloomfield Hills), NY (Buffalo), OH (Cincinnati), TX (Dallas), WI (Janesville)

CORP. OFFICERS

M. Anthony Burns: *B* Mesquite NV 1942 *ED* Brigham Young Univ 1964; Univ CA Berkeley 1965 *CURR EMPL* chmn, pres, ceo, dir: Ryder Sys *CORP AFFIL* dir: Chase Manhattan Corp, JCPenney, Pfizer Inc *NONPR AFFIL* assoc trust: Univ PA; bd govs, chmn: SE Region Un Way Am; bd overseers: Univ PA Wharton Sch Bus; dir, trust, chmn: Un Way Dade County; mem: Bus Counc, Bus Higher Ed Forum, Bus Roundtable; mem bd visitors grad sch bus: Univ NC Chapel Hill; mem natl adv counc sch mgmt: Brigham Young Univ; trust: Natl Urban League, Univ Miami
Edwin Allen Huston: *B* Dayton OH 1938 *ED* Amherst Coll 1960; Harvard Univ MBA 1962 *CURR EMPL* sr exec vp, cfo: Ryder Sys *CORP AFFIL* chmn, dir: Fed Reserve Bank Atlanta; dir: Peter Kuntz Co *NONPR AFFIL* trust: Ft Lauderdale Art Mus

GIVING OFFICERS

Wendell R. Beard: dir *CURR EMPL* vp (off chmn): Ryder Sys
M. Anthony Burns: pres, dir *CURR EMPL* chmn, pres, ceo, dir: Ryder Sys (see above)
C. Robert Campbell: dir *CURR EMPL* Ryder Sys
Dwight D. Denny: dir *CURR EMPL* exec vp, gen mgr leasing services: Ryder Sys
James B. Griffin: dir
James Michael Herron: secy, dir *B* Chicago IL 1934 *ED* Univ MO AB 1955; Northwestern Univ 1958-59; Washington Univ JD 1961; Harvard Univ 1982 *CURR EMPL* sr exec vp, gen coun: Ryder Sys *NONPR AFFIL* dir: Am Soc Corp Secys, Am Trucking Assn, Assn Bar City NY, Bar Assn Metro St Louis, Dade County Bar Assn, FL Bar Assn; mem: Am Bar Assn, MO Bar Assn; mem natl counc: Washington Univ Sch Law; pres, dir: Greater Miami Opera Assn; treas, dir: ATA Litigation Ctr
Edwin Allen Huston: vp, dir *CURR EMPL* sr exec vp, cfo: Ryder Sys (see above)

Larry S. Mulkey: dir *CURR EMPL* pres (Ryder Distribution Resources): Ryder Sys
Jeffrey John Murphy: asst secy *B* Jersey City NJ 1946 *CURR EMPL* vp, secy, asst gen couns: Ryder Sys
Geraldo R. Riordan: dir *CURR EMPL* sen vp, gen mgr consumer retail: Ryder Sys
Ross Roadman: exec dir
Gina S. Russ: asst secy
Terence L. Russell: dir
Harvey Smalheiser: vp *B* New York NY 1942 *CURR EMPL* sr vp (planning & development): Ryder Sys *NONPR AFFIL* dir, treas, chmn fin commpres: Miami City Ballet; mem: AICPAs, Am Trucking Assn, Miami Chamber Commerce, NJ Soc CPAs, NY Bar Assn, Tax Execs Inst, US Chamber Commerce
Fred Ray Stuever: asst secy *CURR EMPL* vp (legal opers): Ryder Sys

APPLICATION INFORMATION

Initial Approach: *Initial Contact:* submit one written copy of request *Include Information On:* description of project; current data on organization's financial status and management, board of directors, and scope of service to the community; why project is appropriate for company to support *When to Submit:* first half of the calendar year for funding in following fiscal year
Restrictions on Giving: Does not support organizations which discriminate by reason of sex, race, color, creed, or national origin; religious organizations or activities for the propagation of a particular religious faith or creed; political organizations, campaigns, or candidates; organizations whose primary purpose is to influence legislation; veterans or fraternal organizations; individuals; goodwill advertising; or operating expenses of member agencies of united funds.

OTHER THINGS TO KNOW

Company encourages volunteer participation of management in organizations it supports.
Ryder also specializes in repair and overhall of jet turboprop engines for airline, business aircraft, and helicopters.

GRANTS ANALYSIS

Total Grants: $1,724,798*
Number of Grants: 319*
Highest Grant: $351,329*
Typical Range: $100 to $10,000
Disclosure Period: 1991
Note: Figures are for foundation giving only. Recent grants are derived from a 1991 Form 990.

RECENT GRANTS

351,328	United Way of Dade County, Miami, FL
175,671	United Way of Dade County, Miami, FL
175,657	United Way
50,000	Florida International University, Miami, FL
50,000	Greater Miami Opera, Miami, FL
39,750	Florida A&M University, Tallahassee, FL
30,000	Institute for Educational Leadership, Washington, DC
30,000	Texas State Technical Institute, Waco, TX
25,000	Beacon Council, Boston, MA
25,000	Coconut Grove Playhouse, Coconut Grove, FL

Rykoff & Co., S.E.

Sales: $700.0 million
Employees: 2,835
Parent Company: Rykoff-Sexton Inc.
Headquarters: Los Angeles, CA
SIC Major Group: Food & Kindred Products and Wholesale Trade—Nondurable Goods

CONTACT

Jay Moore
Vice President
S.E. Rykoff & Co.
761 Terminal St.
Los Angeles, CA 90021
(213) 622-4131

CONTRIBUTIONS SUMMARY

Operating Locations: CA (Los Angeles)

CORP. OFFICERS

Chris G. Adams: *CURR EMPL* pres, coo: SE Rykoff & Co

Ryland Group

Sales: $1.44 billion
Employees: 2,800
Headquarters: Columbia, MD
SIC Major Group: General Building Contractors and Nondepository Institutions

CONTACT

Sharon Green
Marketing Assistant
Ryland Group
11000 Broken Land Pkwy.
Columbia, MD 21044
(410) 715-7222

FINANCIAL SUMMARY

Fiscal Note: Company gives directly. Annual Giving Range: $500,000 to $1 million

CONTRIBUTIONS SUMMARY

Typical Recipients: • *Health:* health organizations, hospitals, medical research, single-disease health associations • *Social Services:* general
Grant Types: general support and research
Operating Locations: MD (Baltimore, Columbia), VA (Richmond)

CORP. OFFICERS

Alan P. Hoblitzell, Jr.: *B* St Louis MO 1931 *ED* Princeton Univ BS 1953 *CURR EMPL* exec vp, cfo: Ryland Group *CORP AFFIL* ceo: MD Natl Corp; chmn, ceo, dir: MNC Fin; dir: PHH Group *NONPR AFFIL* mem: Reserve City Bankers Assn, Robert Morris Assocs; treas: Municipal Arts Soc; trust: MD Inst
Roger W. Schipke: *B* St. Louis MO *ED* Washington Univ BS; NY Univ MBA *CURR EMPL* chmn, pres, ceo: Ryland Group

GIVING OFFICERS

Sharon Green: *CURR EMPL* mktg asst: Ryland Group

APPLICATION INFORMATION

Initial Approach: *Initial Contact:* brief letter of inquiry *Include Information On:* a description of organization, amount requested, purpose of funds sought, recently audited financial statement, and proof of tax-exempt status *When to Submit:* any time
Restrictions on Giving: Contributions are made only in the areas of health and human suffering.

S.G. Foundation

CONTACT

William P. Shannahan
Vice President
S.G. Fdn.
7855 Ivanhoe Avenue, Ste. 420
La Jolla, CA 92037
(619) 454-3237

FINANCIAL SUMMARY

Recent Giving: $11,000 (1989); $115,635 (1988)
Assets: $5,566,597 (1990); $4,782,973 (1989); $3,874,603 (1988)
Gifts Received: $363,750 (1990); $14,500 (1989); $50,000 (1988)
Fiscal Note: In 1991, contributions were received from Scheduling Corporation of America ($10,000) and miscellaneous ($12,050).
EIN: 33-0048410

CONTRIBUTIONS SUMMARY

Donor(s): F. Javier Alverdo
Typical Recipients: • *Religion:* missionary activities, religious organizations • *Social Services:* drugs & alcohol
Grant Types: endowment

GIVING OFFICERS

Stuart C. Gildred: pres
William P. Shannahan: vp, secy

APPLICATION INFORMATION

Initial Approach: Send brief letter of inquiry describing program or project. There are no deadlines.

GRANTS ANALYSIS

Disclosure Period: 1990
Note: No grants were provided in 1990.

RECENT GRANTS

7,500	World Impact, Los Angeles, CA
2,500	Mercy Corps International, Portland, OR
1,000	Network Drug Free, Solvang, CA

S.T.J. Group, Inc.

Sales: $314.6 million
Employees: 4,011
Headquarters: Stamford, CT
SIC Major Group: Electronic & Other Electrical Equipment

CONTACT

Steven Meyers
Senior Vice President, Administration
Sprague Technologies, Inc.
Four Stamford Forum
Stamford, CT 06901
(203) 964-8600

CONTRIBUTIONS SUMMARY

Operating Locations: CT (Stamford)

CORP. OFFICERS

Edward F. Kosnik: *CURR EMPL* pres, ceo: Sprague Techs

Saab Cars USA, Inc.

Sales: $750.0 million
Employees: 200
Headquarters: Norcross, GA
SIC Major Group: Automotive Dealers & Service Stations and Wholesale Trade—Durable Goods

CONTACT

Tom Reis
Director, Human Resources
Saab Cars USA, Inc.
4405-A Saab Dr.
PO Box 563
Norcross, GA 30091
(404) 279-0100

CONTRIBUTIONS SUMMARY

Operating Locations: GA (Norcross)

CORP. OFFICERS

William S. Kelly: *CURR EMPL* pres, ceo: Saab Cars USA
P. Henry Mueller: *CURR EMPL* chmn: Saab Cars USA

GIVING OFFICERS

Marie Burke: *CURR EMPL* donations mgr: Saab Cars USA
Tom Reis: *CURR EMPL* dir (human resources): Saab Cars USA
Steven Rossi: *CURR EMPL* dir (pub rels): Saab Cars USA

Sacharuna Foundation

CONTACT

Sacharuna Fdn.
84 State St.
Boston, MA 02109

FINANCIAL SUMMARY

Recent Giving: $189,500 (1990); $527,377 (1989); $209,498 (1988)

Assets: $8,925,218 (1990); $11,382,621 (1989); $10,472,331 (1988)

Gifts Received: $2,000 (1989); $4,000 (1988)

EIN: 13-3264132

CONTRIBUTIONS SUMMARY

Donor(s): Lavinia Currier, Jack Robinson

Typical Recipients: • *Civic & Public Affairs:* environmental affairs, international affairs, public policy, rural affairs, urban & community affairs, zoos/botanical gardens • *International:* international development/relief, international health care, international organizations • *Religion:* churches, religious organizations

Grant Types: general support

GIVING OFFICERS

Lavinia Currier: trust

APPLICATION INFORMATION

Initial Approach: Contributes only to preselected organizations.

GRANTS ANALYSIS

Number of Grants: 12

Highest Grant: $57,500

Typical Range: $1,000 to $10,000

Disclosure Period: 1990

RECENT GRANTS

57,500 Conservation Fund, Arlington, VA

40,000 Tibet Fund, New York, NY

25,000 New England Small Farm Institute, Northhampton, MA

10,000 Project Lighthawk, Santa Fe, NM

10,000 Riverdale Center of Religion, Bronx, NY

10,000 Shechen Tennyi Vargneling, New York, NY

7,000 St. Johns Cathedral, New York, NY

5,000 Buddhist Perception of Nature

5,000 Conservation Council of Virginia, Richmond, VA

5,000 Food and Water, Denville, NJ

Sachs Electric Corp.

Revenue: $49.5 million

Employees: 700

Parent Company: Sachs Holdings, Inc.

Headquarters: Chesterfield, MD

SIC Major Group: Engineering & Management Services and Special Trade Contractors

CONTACT

Chris Butler
Personnel Director
Sachs Electric Corp.
16300 Justus Post Rd.
Chesterfield, MO 63017
(314) 532-2000

CONTRIBUTIONS SUMMARY

Operating Locations: MD (Chesterfield)

CORP. OFFICERS

Larry N. Plunkett: *B* Hannibal MO 1945 *ED* Univ MO 1969 *CURR EMPL* pres, ceo: Sachs Electric Corp *CORP AFFIL* dir: Mark Twain Bank *NONPR AFFIL* dir: Assoc General Contractors St Louis; mem: Academy Electrical Contracting; vp, mem natl exec comm: Natl Electrical Contractors Assn

Louis S. Sachs: *B* St Louis MO 1928 *ED* Washington Univ 1948 *CURR EMPL* chmn: Sachs Electric Corp *CORP AFFIL* chmn: Sachs Energy Mgmt, Sachs Holdings, Sachs Properties

OTHER THINGS TO KNOW

Company is an original donor to the Sachs Fund.

Sachs Foundation

CONTACT

Morris A. Esmiol, Jr.
President
Sachs Fdn.
90 South Cascade Avenue, Ste. 1410
Colorado Springs, CO 80903
(719) 633-2353

FINANCIAL SUMMARY

Recent Giving: $601,842 (1991); $589,455 (1990); $585,309 (1989)

Assets: $2,748,145 (1991); $2,244,428 (1990); $1,948,915 (1989)

Gifts Received: $858,894 (1990); $949,886 (1989); $843,798 (1988)

EIN: 84-0500835

CONTRIBUTIONS SUMMARY

Donor(s): the late Henry Sachs

Grant Types: scholarship

Geographic Distribution: limited to CO

GIVING OFFICERS

Stuart P. Dodge: vp, dir

Morris A. Esmiol, Jr.: pres, dir

William J. Hybl: off *B* Des Moines IA 1942 *ED* CO Coll BA 1964; Univ CO JD 1967 *CURR EMPL* pres: El Pomar Investment Co *CORP AFFIL* dir: Bankshares Co, Broadmoor Hotel, Broadmoor Mgmt Co, First Natl Bank CO Springs, KN Energy, Manitou & Pikes Peak Railway Co; exec vp, dir: Garden City Co

Marjorie Sanchez: secy, treas

Ben S. Wendelken: vp, dir *B* Colorado Springs CO 1899 *ED* CO Coll BA 1922; Univ MI JD 1925

APPLICATION INFORMATION

Initial Approach: Send letter requesting application form. Requires written application, including picture, references, and financial history.

OTHER THINGS TO KNOW

Provides graduate and undergraduate scholarships for African-American residents of CO.

Publications: Financial statement, Application Guidelines

GRANTS ANALYSIS

Disclosure Period: 1991

Note: In 1991, all contributions were made to individuals.

Sachs Fund

CONTACT

Louis S. Sachs
Trustee
Sachs Fund
400 Chesterfield Center, Ste. 600
Chesterfield, MO 63017
(314) 537-1000

FINANCIAL SUMMARY

Recent Giving: $193,500 (fiscal 1992); $147,900 (fiscal 1991); $180,275 (fiscal 1990)

Assets: $3,217,278 (fiscal year ending April 30, 1992); $2,727,000 (fiscal 1991); $2,452,004 (fiscal 1990)

Gifts Received: $50,000 (fiscal 1990); $50,000 (fiscal 1989)

EIN: 43-6032385

CONTRIBUTIONS SUMMARY

Donor(s): Samuel C. Sachs, Sachs Electric Corp.

Typical Recipients: • *Arts & Humanities:* arts institutes, community arts, music, public broadcasting • *Civic & Public Affairs:* environmental affairs, zoos/botanical gardens • *Education:* colleges & universities • *Health:* hospitals • *Religion:* religious organizations • *Science:* scientific institutes • *Social Services:* community service organizations, drugs & alcohol, united funds, youth organizations

Grant Types: general support

Geographic Distribution: focus on MO

GIVING OFFICERS

Louis S. Sachs: trust *B* St Louis MO 1928 *ED* Washington Univ 1948 *CURR EMPL* chmn, dir: Sachs Electric Co *CORP AFFIL* chmn: Sachs Properties Inc; chmn, dir: Sachs Electric Co

Mary L. Sachs: trust

Jerome W. Sandweiss: trust *CORP AFFIL* dir: Sachs Electric Co

APPLICATION INFORMATION

Initial Approach: The foundation reports it only makes contributions to preselected charitable organizations.

Restrictions on Giving: Does not support individuals.

GRANTS ANALYSIS

Number of Grants: 28

Highest Grant: $56,000

Typical Range: $500 to $5,000

Disclosure Period: fiscal year ending April 30, 1992

RECENT GRANTS

56,000 Washington University, St. Louis, MO

50,000 Jewish Federation, St. Louis, MO

13,000 United Way, St. Louis, MO

10,000 Maryville University, St. Louis, MO

10,000 Missouri Botanical Garden, St. Louis, MO

10,000 St. Louis Science Center, St. Louis, MO

6,000 St. Louis Symphony, St. Louis, MO

5,000 Crossroads Drug Abuse Program, St. Louis, MO

5,000 JCCA Campaign,
St. Louis, MO

5,000 JCCA Samp Sabra,
St. Louis, MO

Saemann Foundation, Franklin I.

CONTACT
Ray E. Plummer
Trustee
Franklin I. Saemann Fdn.
c/o Plummer and Co., CPAs
PO Box 956
Warsaw, IN 46581

FINANCIAL SUMMARY
Recent Giving: $292,248 (fiscal 1992); $291,437 (fiscal 1990); $212,000 (fiscal 1988)
Assets: $5,776,682 (fiscal year ending June 30, 1992); $5,878,366 (fiscal 1990); $6,840,258 (fiscal 1988)
Gifts Received: $412,575 (fiscal 1992)
EIN: 62-6171002

CONTRIBUTIONS SUMMARY
Donor(s): Franklin I. Saemann
Typical Recipients: • *Arts & Humanities:* community arts, public broadcasting • *Education:* colleges & universities • *Health:* single-disease health associations • *Religion:* churches • *Social Services:* child welfare, united funds, youth organizations
Grant Types: general support
Geographic Distribution: focus on IA

GIVING OFFICERS
B. Inez Feldman: trust
Duane G. Huffer: trust
Ray E. Plummer: trust
Irene L. Saemann: trust

APPLICATION INFORMATION
Initial Approach: Send brief letter of inquiry describing program or project. There are no deadlines. Board meets in June.

GRANTS ANALYSIS
Number of Grants: 10
Highest Grant: $185,000
Typical Range: $5,000 to $30,000
Disclosure Period: fiscal year ending June 30, 1992

RECENT GRANTS
185,000 Wartburg College, Waverly, IA

30,000 YMCA, Warsaw, IN

15,000 Combined Community Services, Warsaw, IN

15,000 Tri Kappa of Warsaw, Warsaw, IN

10,000 Heartline Pregnancy Care and Counseling, Warsaw, IN

10,000 Prince of Peace Lutheran Church, Warsaw, IN

9,500 Beaman Home, Warsaw, IN

5,000 American Parkinson's Disease Association, New York, NY

5,000 Kosciusko County Theatre, Warsaw, IN

3,500 Big Brothers and Big Sisters, Warsaw, IN

SAFECO Corp.
Assets: $7.35 billion
Employees: 3,878
Headquarters: Seattle, WA
SIC Major Group: Holding & Other Investment Offices, Insurance Carriers, Real Estate, and Security & Commodity Brokers

CONTACT
Jill Ryan
Community Relations Manager & Assistant Vice President
SAFECO Corp.
SAFECO Plz.
Seattle, WA 98185
(206) 545-5015

FINANCIAL SUMMARY
Recent Giving: $5,874,000 (1993 est.); $5,591,000 (1992 approx.); $4,708,000 (1991 approx.)
Fiscal Note: Company gives directly.

CONTRIBUTIONS SUMMARY
Typical Recipients: • *Arts & Humanities:* arts funds, community arts, dance, history/historic preservation, libraries, museums/galleries, opera, performing arts, public broadcasting, visual arts • *Civic & Public Affairs:* economic development, environmental affairs, ethnic/minority organizations, housing, nonprofit management, public policy, safety, urban & community affairs, zoos/botanical gardens • *Education:* arts education, business education, colleges & universities, continuing education, economic education, education associations, elementary education, literacy, minority education, private education (precollege), public education (precollege) • *Health:* health care cost containment, health organizations, mental health, nutrition & health maintenance, public health, single-disease health associations • *Social Services:* aged, community service organizations, day care, delinquency & crime, disabled, drugs & alcohol, emergency relief, employment/job training, shelters/homelessness, united funds, volunteer services, youth organizations
Grant Types: capital, challenge, employee matching gifts, general support, and operating expenses
Nonmonetary Support Types: donated equipment and in-kind services
Note: Value of nonmonetary support is not available and is not included in above figures.
Geographic Distribution: near corporate operating locations in the United States
Operating Locations: CA (Fountain Valley, Los Angeles, Pleasanton), CO (Lakewood), FL (Maitland), GA (Stone Mountain), IL (Chicago), MO (Sunset Hills), OH (Cincinnati), OR (Lake Oswego), TN (Nashville), TX (Dallas), VA (Richmond), WA (Redmond, Seattle, Spokane)

CORP. OFFICERS
Roger Harry Eigsti: *B* Vancouver WA 1942 *ED* Linfield Coll 1964 *CURR EMPL* pres, ceo, dir: SAFECO Corp *CORP AFFIL* dir: Employee Benefit Claims WI, First Natl Ins Co Am, Gen Am Corp, Gen Am Corp TX, Gen Ins Co Am, GSL Corp, SAFECO Ins Co Am, SAFECO Natl Ins Co, SAFECO Natl Life Ins, SAFECO Properties, SAFECO Surplus Lines Ins Co, WI Pension & Group Svc; chmn: SAFECO CA Tax Free Income Fund, SAFECO Equity Fund, SAFECO Growth Fund, SAFECO Income Fund, SAFECO Money Market Mutual Fund, SAFECO Municipal Bond Fund, SAFECO Tax Free Money Market Fund; dir: SAFECO Asset Mgmt Co, SAFECO Assigned Benefits Svc Co, SAFECO Investment Mgmt Corp, SAFECO Securities, SAFECO Title Ins Co; sr vp: SAFECO Ins Co IL; sr vp, dir: SAFECO Life Ins Co; vp, secy, dir: SAFECO Credit Co

GIVING OFFICERS
Robert C. Alexander: mem (contributions comm) *CURR EMPL* vp (Seattle branch): SAFECO Ins Cos
Roger Butz, M.D.: mem (contributions comm) *CURR EMPL* vp (med dir): SAFECO Life Co
Richard Campbell: mem (contributions comm) *CURR EMPL* vp (pers): SAFECO Corp
James W. Cannon: mem (contributions comm) *B* 1927 *CURR EMPL* exec vp: SAFECO Ins Co Am *CORP AFFIL* pres: Gen Ins Co Am, Safeco Ins Co Am, Safeco Lloyds Ins Co, Safeco Natl Ins Co, Safeco Surplus Lines Ins Co
Boh A. Dickey: mem (contributions comm) *B* Helena MT 1944 *ED* Univ MT 1966 *CURR EMPL* exec vp, cfo: SAFECO Corp *CORP AFFIL* chmn: SAFECO Mutual Funds
Roger Harry Eigsti: mem (contributions comm) *CURR EMPL* pres, ceo, dir: SAFECO Corp (see above)
Mary Frawley: mem (contributions comm) *CURR EMPL* asst dir claims: SAFECO Ins Cos
Gordon C. Hamilton: mem (contributions comm) *CURR EMPL* vp (pub rels): SAFECO Ins Cos
Elizabeth Jones: mem (contributions comm) *CURR EMPL* mgr (shareholder services): SAFECO Mutual Funds
Jill Ryan: chmn (contributions comm) *CURR EMPL* community rels mgr, asst vp: SAFECO Ins Cos
Richard Zunker: mem (contributions comm) *CURR EMPL* dir: SAFECO Life Co

APPLICATION INFORMATION
Initial Approach: *Initial Contact:* brief letter or proposal, no more than two pages in length, to SAFECO headquarters in Seattle or to branch office nearest the proposed project location *Include Information On:* description of the organization; amount requested; assessment of need; purpose for which funds are sought; project's scope; geographical area and people served; evaluation plans and methods; audited financial statement for the last two years; overall budget of organi-

zation, including income and expenses for last two years and year in which contribution is sought; donor's list for past 12 months; list of board of directors and their affiliations; proof of tax-exempt status *When to Submit:* any time
Restrictions on Giving: As a general rule, SAFECO does not make contributions to individuals; projects or programs operating outside the United States; national programs, endowment funds, or unrestricted operating funds for agencies that receive United Way or similar umbrella support from organizations already supported by SAFECO; religious or political groups or projects; general fundraising events; goodwill advertising; loans and investments; or fraternal organizations.

OTHER THINGS TO KNOW
Company sets aside approximately two percent of pretax income annually for contributions programs.
Company will consider requests from communities where significant numbers of SAFECO employees live and work.
Contributions are given for one year with no implied renewals.
Company may require recipients to provide an audited financial statement at year's end and periodic reports on the project.

GRANTS ANALYSIS
Total Grants: $4,708,000*
Number of Grants: 839*
Disclosure Period: 1991
Note: Number of grants and average grants figures exclude approximately 1,700 matching grants valued at $196,456. Recent grants are derived from a 1989 grants list.

RECENT GRANTS
Alzheimer's Association, Atlanta, GA
Big Brothers of Nashville, Nashville, TN
Cincinnati Youth Symphony, Cincinnati, OH
Dogs for the Deaf, Central Point, OR
Gwinnett Senior Services, Lawrenceville, GA
Hambrick Elementary School, Stone Mountain, GA
Helena Film Society, Helena, MT

Judevine Center for Autistic Children, St. Louis, MO
Make-A-Wish Foundation, Seattle, WA
Nathan Hale High School, Seattle, WA

Safeguard Scientifics Foundation

CONTACT
Gerald M. Wilk
Treasurer
Safeguard Scientifics Fdn.
435 Devon Park Dr., 800
Wayne, PA 19087
(215) 293-0600

FINANCIAL SUMMARY
Recent Giving: $75,000 (1991)
Assets: $772,688 (1991)
Gifts Received: $205,000 (1991)
Fiscal Note: In 1991, contributions were received from the Safeguard Scientifics, Inc.
EIN: 23-2571278

CONTRIBUTIONS SUMMARY
Typical Recipients: • *Arts & Humanities:* arts associations • *Civic & Public Affairs:* philanthropic organizations • *Education:* arts education, economic education • *Health:* health organizations, single-disease health associations • *Social Services:* youth organizations
Grant Types: general support

GIVING OFFICERS
Gerald M. Wilk: treas

APPLICATION INFORMATION
Initial Approach: Send brief letter of inquiry. There are no deadlines.

GRANTS ANALYSIS
Number of Grants: 11
Highest Grant: $39,000
Typical Range: $500 to $5,000
Disclosure Period: 1991

RECENT GRANTS
39,000 Franklin Institute, Philadelphia, PA
10,000 Boy Scouts of America, Philadelphia, PA
5,000 University of the Arts, Philadelphia, PA
5,000 University of the Arts, Philadelphia, PA

3,000 American Heart Association, Bridgeport, CT
1,000 Foundation at Paoli, Paoli, PA
1,000 Philadelphia OIC, Philadelphia, PA
500 Cystic Fibrosis Foundation, Philadelphia, PA
500 Moss Rehabilitation, Philadelphia, PA
500 Pennsylvania Council on Economic Education, Reading, PA

Safety-Kleen Corp.
Sales: $695.0 million
Employees: 6,500
Headquarters: Elgin, IL
SIC Major Group: Chemicals & Allied Products, Industrial Machinery & Equipment, and Petroleum & Coal Products

CONTACT
Robert Burian
Vice President, Personnel
Safety-Kleen Corp.
777 Big Timber Rd.
Elgin, IL 60123
(708) 697-8460

CONTRIBUTIONS SUMMARY
Operating Locations: IL (Elgin)

CORP. OFFICERS
Donald W. Brinckman: *B* Chicago IL 1931 *ED* Northwestern Univ 1954; Northwestern Univ 1959 *CURR EMPL* chmn, pres, ceo, coo, dir: Safety-Kleen Corp *CORP AFFIL* dir: Johnson Worldwide Assocs, Paychex *NONPR AFFIL* mem: Am Bus Conf

Safeway, Inc.
Sales: $15.15 billion
Employees: 104,900
Headquarters: Oakland, CA
SIC Major Group: Food Stores

CONTACT
Robert Bradford
Senior Vice President, Public Affairs
Safeway, Inc.
201 4th St.
Oakland, CA 94660
(510) 891-3265

FINANCIAL SUMMARY
Fiscal Note: Company gives approximately $11 million in nonmonetary support. A small

amount of monetary support is available through Mr. Bradford. Persons may also contact local store managers for cash and product donations.

CONTRIBUTIONS SUMMARY
Nonmonetary Support Types: donated products and loaned employees
Note: Most nonmonetary support consists of food and beverage donations.
Geographic Distribution: near operating locations
Operating Locations: CA (Oakland, Richmond, Walnut Creek), CO (Denver), VA (Richmond)

CORP. OFFICERS
Robert E. Bradford: *B* Roanoke VA 1931 *ED* Washington & Lee Univ 1954; Harvard Univ 1971 *CURR EMPL* sr vp (pub aff): Safeway
Steven A. Burd: *CURR EMPL* pres, coo: Safeway
Peter Alden Magowan: *B* New York NY 1942 *ED* Stanford Univ BA 1964; Oxford Univ MA 1966 *CURR EMPL* chmn, ceo, pres: Safeway *CORP AFFIL* dir: Opportunity Funding Corp, Pacific Gas & Electric Co, Vons Cos, Chrysler Corp *NONPR AFFIL* mem: Food Mktg Inst, Bus Roundtable, US Chamber Commerce

Sagamore Foundation

CONTACT
Martin S. Fox
Principal Manager
Sagamore Fdn.
570 Broad St.
Newark, NJ 07102
(201) 622-3624

FINANCIAL SUMMARY
Recent Giving: $98,925 (fiscal 1991); $224,075 (fiscal 1990); $204,626 (fiscal 1989)
Assets: $3,582,184 (fiscal year ending November 30, 1991); $3,221,180 (fiscal 1990); $2,980,262 (fiscal 1989)
EIN: 22-1825723

CONTRIBUTIONS SUMMARY
Typical Recipients: • *Civic & Public Affairs:* philanthropic organizations • *Health:* hospitals • *Religion:* religious organizations • *Social Services:* commu-

nity service organizations, united funds

Grant Types: general support and research

Geographic Distribution: focus on NJ

GIVING OFFICERS

Martin S. Fox: secy, treas
Issac Gielchinsky: vp
J. Mansoor Hussain: off
Victor Parsonnet: pres
Alexander Shapiro: vp

APPLICATION INFORMATION

Initial Approach: Contributes only to preselected organizations.

Restrictions on Giving: Does not support individuals.

GRANTS ANALYSIS

Number of Grants: 1
Highest Grant: $98,925
Disclosure Period: fiscal year ending November 30, 1991

RECENT GRANTS

98,925 Philanthropic Fund of Jewish Community Foundation, East Orange, NJ

Sage Foundation

CONTACT

Melissa Sage Booth
Chairman, President, and
Treasurer
Sage Foundation
34705 West Twelve Mile Rd.,
Ste. 355
Farmington Hills, MI 48331
(313) 963-6420

FINANCIAL SUMMARY

Recent Giving: $1,489,325 (1991); $1,954,889 (1990); $2,412,349 (1989)
Assets: $34,404,633 (1991); $28,980,185 (1990); $48,686,320 (1989)
EIN: 38-6041518

CONTRIBUTIONS SUMMARY

Donor(s): In 1954, the Sage Foundation was established by the late Charles F. Sage and his wife, the late Effa L. Sage. Upon Mr. Sage's death in 1961, the foundation received stock in Tecumseh Products Company, valued at more than $7 million, substantially boosting its level of assets.

Typical Recipients: • *Arts & Humanities:* arts associations, arts institutes, music • *Civic & Public Affairs:* municipalities,

nonprofit management, philanthropic organizations • *Education:* agricultural education, arts education, colleges & universities, legal education, public education (precollege), special education • *Health:* health organizations, hospices, hospitals, medical research, single-disease health associations • *Religion:* churches, religious organizations • *Social Services:* child welfare, family services, homes, recreation & athletics, religious welfare, youth organizations

Grant Types: capital, endowment, fellowship, general support, project, research, and scholarship

Geographic Distribution: primarily Michigan

GIVING OFFICERS

John J. Ayaub: vp, secy, trust
John H. Booth: asst secy, trust
Melissa Sage Booth: chmn, pres, treas, trust
Genevieve R. Sage: trust
James E. Van Doren: trust

APPLICATION INFORMATION

Initial Approach:
Initial contact should be in writing.
Applicants should include the amount of funds needed, intended outcome of the project or program, plans to evaluate the results, photocopy of the organization's tax-exempt determination letter, and the name of the individual who will be responsible for administering the program. General information that would aid the board of trustees in making its decision should be included.
Applicants may submit requests any time.

Restrictions on Giving: The foundation has no grant-making restrictions as to geographic area, charitable fields, or types of institutions.

GRANTS ANALYSIS

Total Grants: $1,489,325
Number of Grants: 64
Highest Grant: $450,000
Typical Range: $5,000 to $50,000
Disclosure Period: 1991
Note: Average grant figure excludes grants of $450,000 and $100,000. Recent grants are derived from a 1991 Form 990.

RECENT GRANTS

450,000 Hillsdale College, Hillsdale, MI — to

defray construction costs of the Sage Center for Cultural and Performing Arts

100,000 Hillsdale College, Hillsdale, MI — construction costs of the Sage Center for Cultural and Performing Arts

100,000 Mercy College of Detroit, Detroit, MI — to defray expenses in connection with the renovation of the Student/Conference Center

100,000 Rush-Presbyterian-St. Luke's Medical Center, Chicago, IL — defray the costs and expenses incurred by St. Luke's Fashion Show

65,000 Art Institute of Chicago, Chicago, IL — to endow the Sage Foundation Chair in Fashion Design

50,000 Boys Hope, St. Louis, MO — general, charitable and educational purposes

50,000 Camp Ability Foundation, Chicago, IL — general, charitable and educational purposes

50,000 Infant Jesus of Prague Parish, Flossmoor, IL — general, charitable, religious, and educational purposes

50,000 Regis High School, New York, NY — to establish a scholarship endowment fund

50,000 St. Joseph Health Care Foundation, Chicago, IL — general, charitable and educational purposes

Sage Foundation, Russell

CONTACT

Madeline G. Spitaleri
Secretary
Russell Sage Foundation
112 East 64th St.
New York, NY 10021
(212) 750-6000

FINANCIAL SUMMARY

Recent Giving: $2,000,000 (fiscal 1993 est.); $1,903,617

(fiscal 1992); $1,887,748 (fiscal 1991)

Assets: $115,000,000 (fiscal 1993 est.); $122,032,917 (fiscal year ending August 31, 1992); $111,088,305 (fiscal 1991); $106,246,550 (fiscal 1990)

Gifts Received: $19,171 (fiscal 1987)

Fiscal Note: 1987 contributions were derived from Women in Education Carnegie Corporation of New York and from Census Research Projects.
EIN: 13-1635303

CONTRIBUTIONS SUMMARY

Donor(s): Mrs. Margaret Olivia Sage founded the Russell Sage Foundation in 1907. It is among the oldest private foundations operating in the United States. Russell Sage (1816-1906) was an investor in railroads and other securities. He was president of the Poughkeepsie and Eastern Railway, as well as the Empire and Bay State Telegraph Company. His wife, Margaret Olivia Slocum Sage (1828-1918), was a noted philanthropist. She founded the Russell Sage College of Practical Arts in Troy, NY; acquired Marsh Island in the Gulf of Mexico for a bird sanctuary; and gave $1 million in gifts to Emma Willard Seminary and Rensselaer Polytechnic Institute. Other beneficiaries included the YMCA of New York, the American Seaman's Friend Society, Northfield Seminary, Sage Institute of Pathology, and Syracuse University.

The Sage Foundation was established to improve the social and living conditions in the nation, and helped pioneer programs dealing with society's downtrodden, the elderly, city planning, consumer credit, labor legislation, nursing, and social security. Other early areas of interest included the improvement of "hospital and prison conditions, and the development of social work as a profession." Since World War II, the exclusive interest of the foundation has been the area of social science research.

Typical Recipients: • *Civic & Public Affairs:* economics, public policy • *Education:* colleges & universities, economic education, social sciences education

Grant Types: conference/seminar and research
Geographic Distribution: national

GIVING OFFICERS
Anne Pitts Carter: trust *B* New York NY 1925 *ED* Queens Coll AB 1945; Radcliffe Coll PhD 1949 *NONPR AFFIL* chmn: Intl Input-Output Conf Organizing Comm (Switzerland Austria Japan); dir: Resources for Future; fellow: Am Assn Advancement Science, Econometric Soc; mem: Am Econ Assn, Federation Am Scientists; mem adv counc: Electric Power Res Inst; prof econ: Brandeis Univ
Joel E. Cohen: trust *B* Washington DC 1944 *ED* Harvard Univ BA 1965; Harvard Univ MA 1967; Harvard Univ MPH 1970; Harvard Univ PhD 1970; Harvard Univ DPH 1973 *NONPR AFFIL* fellow: Am Academy Arts & Sciences, Am Assn Advancement Science; mem: Am Mathematical Soc, Am Population Assn, Am Soc Naturalists, Am Statistical Assn, Cambridge Philosophical Soc, NASA Life Sciences Adv Comm, Natl Ctr Health Ed, NY Mayors Comm Science & Tech, Soc for Industrial Applied Math, Social Svc Res Counc Comm on Problems Policy; mem bd math scientists: Natl Res Counc; trust: Black Rock Forest Preserve; chmn bd: Societal Inst Math Sciences *PHIL AFFIL* mem ed adv bd: Guggenheim (John Simon) Memorial Foundation
Peggy C. Davis: trust
Phoebe C. Ellsworth: trust
Ira Katznelson: trust
James E. March: chmn, trust *B* Cleveland OH 1928 *ED* Univ WI BA 1949; Yale Univ MA 1950; Yale Univ PhD 1953 *NONPR AFFIL* mem: Academia Italiana Economia Aziendale, Am Academy Arts Sciences, Am Econ Assn, Am Political Science Assn, Am Psychological Assn, Am Sociological Assn, Natl Academy Ed, Natl Academy Sciences, Phi Beta Kappa, Royal Swedish Academy Sciences, Sigma Xi; prof mgmt, higher ed, , sociology: Stanford Univ
Howard Raiffa: trust *NONPR AFFIL* prof managerial econ: Harvard Univ Sch Bus
John Shepard Reed: trust *B* Chicago IL 1939 *ED* Washington & Jefferson Coll BA 1959;

MA Inst Tech BS 1961; MA Inst Tech MS 1965 *CURR EMPL* chmn, ceo: Citicorp & Citibank NA *CORP AFFIL* dir: Monsanto Co, Philip Morris Co, Un Techs Corp; mem bd: Rand Corp *NONPR AFFIL* chmn: Coalition Svc Indus, NY Blood Ctr, Svcs Policy Adv Comm US Trade Rep; mem bd: Ctr Advanced Study Behavioral Sciences, MA Inst Tech, Meml Sloan-Kettering Cancer Ctr, Woodrow Wilson Intl Ctr Scholars; mem policy comm: Bus Roundtable; vchmn: Bus Counc
Loren D. Ross: treas
Neil J. Smelser: trust *B* Kahoka MO 1930 *ED* Harvard Univ BA 1952; Harvard Univ PhD 1958; Oxford Univ Magdalen Coll BA 1954; Oxford Univ Magdalen Coll MA 1959; San Francisco Psychoanalytic Inst 1971 *NONPR AFFIL* assoc dir: Inst Intl Rels; mem: Am Sociological Assn, Pacific Sociological Assn; prof sociology: Univ CA Berkeley; trust: Ctr Advanced Study Behavioral Sciences
Madeline Spitalari: secy
Harold Tanner: trust *B* New York NY 1932 *CURR EMPL* pres: Tanner & Co *NONPR AFFIL* co-fdr: Volunteer Urban Consult Group; dir: Harvard Univ Bus Sch Assocs; mem: Counc Foreign Rels; trust: Cornell Univ
Marta Tienda, PhD: trust
Eric Wanner: pres, trust *ED* Amherst Coll BA; Harvard Univ PhD 1969 *NONPR AFFIL* mem: Am Assn Advancement Science, Am Psychological Assn, Cognitive Science Soc
William Julius Wilson: trust *B* Derry Township PA 1935 *ED* Wilberforce Univ BA 1958; Bowling Green St Univ MA 1961; WA St Univ PhD 1966 *NONPR AFFIL* chmn dept sociology, prof: Univ Chicago; dir: Ctr Advanced Study Behavioral Sciences, Ctr Natl Policy; dir, mem: Chicago Urban League; fellow: Am Academy Arts & Sciences, Am Assn Advancement Science; mem: Am Philosophical Soc, Am Sociological Assn, Intl Sociological Assn, Lucy Flower Univ, Soc Study Social Problems, Sociological Res Assn; mem adv bd: Environmental Devel Pub Policy, Social Science Book Club; mem natl bd dirs: Inst Res Poverty, Randolph Inst (A Philip); trust: Spelman Coll

APPLICATION INFORMATION
Initial Approach:
A preliminary letter of inquiry should be sent to the president. The preliminary letter should include a summary of project objectives, a work plan, a listing of the qualifications of those engaged in the project, and an estimated budget. The foundation will then contact the applicant to provide more detailed information.
There are no application deadlines. Organizations should receive notification approximately three months after submitting an application. Board meetings are held in October, February, and June. If proposals coincide with foundation interests, an interview may be arranged.
Restrictions on Giving: The foundation does not support capital or endowment funds, independent ongoing activities of other institutions, scholarships, annual campaigns, emergency funds, deficit financing, or operating budgets.

OTHER THINGS TO KNOW
Publications: newsletter, biennial report, and application guidelines

GRANTS ANALYSIS
Total Grants: $1,903,617
Typical Range: $5,000 to $50,000
Disclosure Period: fiscal year ending August 31, 1992
Note: The number of, average, and highest grant figures were unavailable at time of publication. Recent grants are derived from a 1990 and 1991 biennial report.

RECENT GRANTS
247,970 University of Chicago, Chicago, IL — "The Handbook of Research Synthesis"
190,290 Social Science Research Council, New York, NY — "Neighborhood and Family Influences on the Development of Poor Urban Children and Adolescents"
182,321 University of Texas at Austin, Austin, TX — "The Home Economics of Sin-

gle Parent Households"
117,000 Joint Center for Political Studies — "A Transnational Look at Poverty"
109,425 University of Chicago, Evanston, IL — "School-to-Work Transition"
105,000 Research Synthesis Advisory Committee
100,260 Northwestern University, Evanston, IL — "The Effects of Spatial and Skill Mismatches on Minority Employment"
100,000 Harvard University, Cambridge, MA — "Experiments on Distributed Choice"
99,047 National Bureau of Economic Research, Cambridge, MA — "The Intergenerational Mobility of Immigrants"
92,168 University of Chicago, Chicago, IL — "Evaluation of Government Training Programs"

Sailors' Snug Harbor of Boston

CONTACT
Stephen Little
President
Sailors' Snug Harbor of Boston
c/o TL Condon and Co.
170 Water St.
Plymouth, MA 02360
(617) 423-6688

FINANCIAL SUMMARY
Recent Giving: $208,678 (fiscal 1992); $227,500 (fiscal 1990); $221,131 (fiscal 1989)
Assets: $4,354,460 (fiscal year ending April 30, 1992); $3,815,796 (fiscal 1990); $3,783,654 (fiscal 1989)
EIN: 04-2104430

CONTRIBUTIONS SUMMARY
Typical Recipients: • *Arts & Humanities:* music • *Civic & Public Affairs:* ethnic/minority organizations • *Health:* health funds, hospitals • *Religion:* religious organizations • *Social Services:* aged, child welfare, community centers, disabled, family planning, family services
Grant Types: general support

Geographic Distribution: focus on the Boston, MA, area

GIVING OFFICERS
Richard E. Byrd: trust
Charles K. Cobb, Jr.: trust
G. Lincoln Dow, Jr.: trust
Joseph E. Eaton: trust
Charles Russell Eddy, Jr.: trust *B* Newton MA 1940 *ED* Univ PA 1963; Univ PA MBA 1968 *CURR EMPL* vp, trust off: Fiduciary Trust Co *CORP AFFIL* vp, trust off: Fiduciary Trust Co
Stephen Little: pres, trust
Robert W. Loring: trust
Francis B. Lothrop, Jr.: treas, trust
Everett Morse, Jr.: trust
John Allen Perkins: trust *B* New Bedford MA 1919 *ED* Harvard Univ AB 1940; Harvard Univ LLB 1943 *CURR EMPL* dir: Greater Boston Legal Svcs *NONPR AFFIL* dir: Greater Boston Legal Svcs; mem: Am Coll Probate Couns, Am Law Inst, Boston Bar Assn, Intl Academy Estate Trust Law, MA Bar Assn
Charles E. Rogerson II: secy, treas, trust
Thomas Rogerson: trust
G. West Saltonstall: trust
William Lawrence Saltonstall: trust *B* Newton MA 1927 *ED* Harvard Univ AB 1950; Harvard Univ MBA 1952 *CURR EMPL* ptnr, trust: Saltonstall & Co
Henry Wheeler: trust
Benjamin Williams: trust
Thomas B. Williams, Jr.: trust

APPLICATION INFORMATION
Initial Approach: Send cover letter and full proposal.
Restrictions on Giving: Does not support individuals.

GRANTS ANALYSIS
Number of Grants: 19
Highest Grant: $40,000
Typical Range: $5,000 to $10,000
Disclosure Period: fiscal year ending April 30, 1992

RECENT GRANTS
   40,000 New Bedford Child and Family Services, New Bedford, MA
   25,000 Children's Friend and Family Service Society, Boston, MA
   15,000 University Hospital, Boston, MA

   12,000 Boston Aging Concerns Young and Old United, Boston, MA
   12,000 Inquilinos Boricuas en Accion, Boston, MA
   12,000 La Alianza Hispana, Boston, MA
   10,000 Elderlink, Boston, MA
   10,000 Freedom House, Boston, MA
   10,000 Greater Boston Legal Services, Boston, MA
   10,000 Massachusetts Senior Action Council, Boston, MA

Saint Croix Foundation

CONTACT
Jeffrey T. Peterson
Saint Croix Fdn.
332 Minnesota St.
PO Box 64704
St. Paul, MN 55164
(612) 291-5114

FINANCIAL SUMMARY
Recent Giving: $344,760 (1990); $272,700 (1989)
Assets: $3,356,186 (1990); $3,323,856 (1989)
Gifts Received: $170,000 (1990)
Fiscal Note: In 1990, contributions were received from the I. Hardenbergh Charitable Annuity Trust.
EIN: 41-6011826

CONTRIBUTIONS SUMMARY
Typical Recipients: • *Arts & Humanities:* community arts, history/historic preservation, music, opera, performing arts, theater • *Education:* education funds • *Health:* health organizations, hospitals, pediatric health • *Social Services:* child welfare, community service organizations, united funds, youth organizations
Grant Types: general support

GIVING OFFICERS
Edgerton Bronson: dir, treas
Robert S. Davis: pres, dir *B* Stillwater MN 1914 *ED* Univ MN 1934 *CURR EMPL* dir: HM Smyth Co *CORP AFFIL* dir: Chicago Milwaukee Corp, SPH Hotel Corp
Gabrielle Hardenbergh: dir, secy
Quentin O. Heimerman: dir, vp

Raymond A. Reister: trust

APPLICATION INFORMATION
Initial Approach: Send brief letter describing program. There are no deadlines.

GRANTS ANALYSIS
Number of Grants: 68
Highest Grant: $25,000
Typical Range: $1,000 to $7,000
Disclosure Period: 1990

RECENT GRANTS
   25,000 Lakeview Memorial Hospital, Stillwater, MN
   25,000 Ordway Music Theater, St. Paul, MN
   20,200 United Way, St. Paul, MN
   15,000 United Hospital, St. Paul, MN
   10,000 Minnesota Historical Society, St. Paul, MN
   10,000 Minnesota Orchestral Association, Minneapolis, MN
   10,000 Rebuild Resources, Minneapolis, MN
   10,000 Resources for Child Caring, St. Paul, MN
    9,000 Minnesota Private College Fund, St. Paul, MN
    5,000 Minnesota Opera, St. Paul, MN

St. Faith's House Foundation

CONTACT
Ann D. Phillips
Chairman, Grants Committee
St. Faith's House Fdn.
16 Crest Dr.
Tarrytown, NY 10591
(914) 631-6065

FINANCIAL SUMMARY
Recent Giving: $200,000 (fiscal 1991); $199,750 (fiscal 1990); $190,000 (fiscal 1989)
Assets: $5,954,215 (fiscal year ending June 30, 1989)
Gifts Received: $487 (fiscal 1989)
EIN: 13-1740123

CONTRIBUTIONS SUMMARY
Typical Recipients: • *Civic & Public Affairs:* housing • *Education:* private education (precollege) • *Health:* hospitals, pediatric health • *Social Services:* child welfare, community serv-

ice organizations, day care, family planning, family services, youth organizations
Grant Types: emergency, multiyear/continuing support, project, and seed money
Geographic Distribution: limited to Westchester County, NY

GIVING OFFICERS
Daniel H. Childs: treas, dir
Mrs. Robert L. Huston: dir
Mrs. John C. Keenan: dir
Mrs. Robert W. Lyman: dir
Horace J. McAfee: secy, dir *B* Heflin LA 1905 *ED* Southern Methodist Univ AB 1926; Columbia Univ JD 1931 *NONPR AFFIL* mem: Am Judicature Soc, NY Bar Assn, NY City Bar Assn, NY County Lawyers Assn
Mrs. Arthur O. Mojo: dir
Robert C. Myers: dir
Ann D. Phillips: dir
Mrs. Joseph E. Rogers: dir
Mrs. William Shore: vp, dir
Mrs. J. B. Stewart: dir
Harvey J. Struthers, Jr.: dir
Mrs. Maarten van Hengel: pres, dir

APPLICATION INFORMATION
Initial Approach: Application form required. Deadlines are March 1, September 1, and December 1.
Restrictions on Giving: Does not support individuals or provide funds for operating expenses.

OTHER THINGS TO KNOW
Publications: Application Guidelines

GRANTS ANALYSIS
Number of Grants: 24
Highest Grant: $20,000
Typical Range: $2,500 to $15,000
Disclosure Period: fiscal year ending June 30, 1989

RECENT GRANTS
   20,000 Children's Village, New York, NY
   10,000 Big Brothers and Big Sisters, Yonkers, NY
   10,000 Clear View School, New York, NY
   10,000 D.R. Reed Speech Center, New York, NY
   10,000 Echo Hills, New York, NY
   10,000 Housing Action Council, New York, NY

10,000 Ossining Child
Care Center, Oss-
ining, NY
10,000 Ossining Open
Door, Ossining, NY
10,000 Phelps Pre-Natal
Clinic, NY
10,000 Yonkers Youth Con-
nection, Yonkers,
NY

Saint Gerard Foundation

CONTACT
J. B. Mooney
President
Saint Gerard Fdn.
1990 Huntington Bldg.
Cleveland, OH 44115
(216) 523-1551

FINANCIAL SUMMARY
Recent Giving: $725,065
(1991); $491,537 (1990);
$877,930 (1989)
Assets: $2,739,128 (1990);
$2,944,828 (1989); $3,010,097
(1988)
Gifts Received: $85,638
(1990); $519,476 (1989);
$616,555 (1988)
Fiscal Note: In 1991, contributions were received from Mr.
and Mrs. Brian G. Mooney
($25,000) and the Mixhael X.
Mooney Trust ($126,638).
EIN: 34-6574667

CONTRIBUTIONS SUMMARY
Donor(s): Mooney Chemicals
Typical Recipients: • *Civic & Public Affairs:* civil rights
• *Education:* colleges & univer-
sities, private education (precollege), religious education
• *Health:* health organizations,
hospitals, medical research, single-disease health associations
• *Religion:* churches, religious
organizations • *Social Services:*
community service organizations
Grant Types: general support

GIVING OFFICERS
Brian G. Mooney: trust
Elizabeth C. Mooney: vp, trust
James B. Mooney: pres, treas, trust
William E. Reichard: secy

APPLICATION INFORMATION
Initial Approach: The foundation reports it only makes contributions to preselected charitable organizations.

Restrictions on Giving: Does
not support individuals.

GRANTS ANALYSIS
Number of Grants: 141
Highest Grant: $35,000
Typical Range: $100 to $1,000
Disclosure Period: 1990

RECENT GRANTS
35,000 Family of the
Americas Founda-
tion, Mandville, LA
30,100 Providence House,
Cleveland, OH
30,000 FACT, Clearwater,
FL
27,700 St. Augustine
School, Dallas, TX
25,100 St. Michaels Acad-
emy, Austin, TX
25,000 Cleveland Central
Catholic High
School Endowment
Fund, Cleveland,
OH
25,000 Diocese of St. Pe-
tersburg Educa-
tional Appeal, St.
Petersburg, FL
25,000 Notre Dame Cathe-
dral Latin School,
Chardon, OH
25,000 Tampa Jesuit High
School, Tampa, FL
15,500 University of Dal-
las, Irving, TX

St. Giles Foundation
Former Foundation Name: The
House of St. Giles the Cripple

CONTACT
Richard T. Arkwright
President
St. Giles Fdn.
One Hanson Pl.
Brooklyn, NY 11217
(212) 338-9001

FINANCIAL SUMMARY
Recent Giving: $605,000 (fis-
cal 1991); $588,000 (fiscal
1990); $405,500 (fiscal 1988)
Assets: $16,021,314 (fiscal
year ending March 31, 1991);
$14,254,267 (fiscal 1990);
$11,303,467 (fiscal 1988)
Gifts Received: $425,632 (fis-
cal 1991); $288,074 (fiscal
1990); $71,850 (fiscal 1988)
Fiscal Note: In 1991, contributions were received from the estate of Ann B. Hallett.
EIN: 11-1630806

CONTRIBUTIONS SUMMARY
Donor(s): The foundation was
established by the James Tisdale Trust, Jesse Ridley, the

late Louis W. Arnold, and the
late Marvin Leavens.
Typical Recipients: • *Education:* colleges & universities,
medical education • *Health:*
hospitals, medical research, pediatric health • *Religion:* religious organizations • *Social
Services:* disabled
Grant Types: general support
and research
Geographic Distribution:
focus on New York

GIVING OFFICERS
Richard T. Arkwright: pres
John J. Bennett, Jr.: secy
Edward Ridley Finch, Jr.:
gen coun *B* Westhampton
Beach NY 1919 *ED* Princeton
Univ AB 1941; NY Univ JD
1947 *CURR EMPL* gen couns:
Am Intl Petroleum Corp
NONPR AFFIL fellow: Am Bar
Fdn; mem: Am Arbitration
Assn, Am Bar Assn, Am Inst
Aeronautics Astronautics, Am
Judicature Soc, Am Law Inst,
Fed Bar Assn, FL Bar Assn,
Inter-Am Bar Assn, Intl Astro-
nautical Academy, Intl Bar
Assn, Judge Advocates Assn,
NY Bar Assn, PA Bar Assn;
mem faculty adv comm: Prince-
ton Univ; pres: Crippled Chil-
drens Friendly Aid Assn, Finch
Trusts; pres, dir: NY Inst Spe-
cial Ed, St Nicholas Soc NY;
trust: Cathedral St John Divine,
St Andrews Dune Church
John H. Livingston: vp
Robert B. Mackay: trust
Samuel H. Owens: treas

APPLICATION INFORMATION
Initial Approach:
The foundation requests applicants submit a detailed written
request for funding.
The foundation has no deadline
for submitting proposals.
Restrictions on Giving: The
foundation reports there are no
restrictions; the primary interest is in children's orthopedics.

GRANTS ANALYSIS
Total Grants: $605,000
Number of Grants: 6
Highest Grant: $150,000
Typical Range: $50,000 to
$150,000
Disclosure Period: fiscal year
ending March 31, 1991
Note: Recent grants are derived
from a fiscal 1991 grants list.

RECENT GRANTS
150,000 New York Hospital
Cornell Medical

Center, New York,
NY
150,000 St. Joseph Chil-
dren's Services,
New York, NY —
equipment, sup-
plies and site prepa-
ration for the medi-
cal and dental
facilities
130,000 North Shore Uni-
versity Hospital,
Manhasset, NY —
to purchase a
Tecan Robotic Cell
Harvester and Ge-
nevision Multiscan-
ning System
100,000 Columbia Presbyterian Hospital, New
York, NY — for
the continuation of
research and study
of growth plate
50,000 Brooklyn Society
for the Prevention
of Cruelty to Chil-
dren, Brooklyn,
NY — to expand
existing group
home for girls
25,000 Pediatric Orthopaedic Society of
North America,
New York, NY —
support field of pe-
diatric orthopaedics

St. Joe Paper Co.
Sales: $582.1 million
Employees: 5,120
Headquarters: Jacksonville, FL
SIC Major Group:
Communications, Food &
Kindred Products, Paper &
Allied Products, and Railroad
Transportation

CONTACT
Massey Petty
Manager
St. Joe Paper Co.
PO Box 1380
Jacksonville, FL 32201
(904) 396-6600

CONTRIBUTIONS SUMMARY
Operating Locations: FL
(Jacksonville)

CORP. OFFICERS
Robert E. Nedley: *CURR
EMPL* pres, coo: St Joe Paper
Co

Saint Johnsbury Trucking Co.

Sales: $330.0 million
Employees: 4,500
Parent Company: Sun Carriers Inc.
Headquarters: Holliston, MA
SIC Major Group: Holding & Other Investment Offices and Trucking & Warehousing

CONTACT
Dorothy Nolan
Assistant to the President
Saint Johnsbury Trucking Co.
PO Box 6590
Holliston, MA 01746
(508) 429-5920

CONTRIBUTIONS SUMMARY
Operating Locations: MA (Holliston)

CORP. OFFICERS
William M. Clifford: *CURR EMPL* pres, ceo, dir: Saint Johnsbury Trucking Co

St. Mary's Catholic Foundation

CONTACT
Richard J. Reuscher
Trustee
St. Mary's Catholic Fdn.
1935 State St.
St. Marys, PA 15857
(814) 781-1591

FINANCIAL SUMMARY
Recent Giving: $898,589 (fiscal 1992); $416,820 (fiscal 1991); $614,290 (fiscal 1990)
Assets: $4,401,296 (fiscal year ending January 31, 1992); $4,601,439 (fiscal 1991); $4,369,089 (fiscal 1990)
Gifts Received: $473,137 (fiscal 1992); $460,813 (fiscal 1991); $706,228 (fiscal 1990)
Fiscal Note: In 1992, contributions were received from Keystone Carbon Co. ($199,900), Keystone Thermistor Corp. ($188,500), Keystone Investment Corp. ($49,900), and E B & Associates ($34,812).
EIN: 25-6036961

CONTRIBUTIONS SUMMARY
Donor(s): the late Benedict R. Reuscher, the late Alfred A. Gleixner, Richard J. Reuscher, R.B. Reuscher, E.H. Gleixner, William E. Reuscher, EB and Associates, Keystone Carbon Co.

Typical Recipients: • *Civic & Public Affairs:* urban & community affairs • *Education:* colleges & universities, private education (precollege), religious education • *Religion:* churches, religious organizations • *Social Services:* community service organizations

Grant Types: general support, multiyear/continuing support, operating expenses, research, and seed money

Geographic Distribution: focus on Erie Diocese, PA, with emphasis on the St. Mary's area

GIVING OFFICERS
E. H. Gleixner: pres, trust
C. J. Kogovsek: trust
R. B. Reuscher: trust
Richard J. Reuscher: secy, treas, trust *B* St Marys PA 1934 *ED* Univ Notre Dame 1957 *CURR EMPL* pres, dir: Keystone Carbon Co *CORP AFFIL* pres, dir: Keystone Carbon Co
William E. Reuscher: vp, trust *CURR EMPL* secy: Keystone Carbon Co *CORP AFFIL* secy: Keystone Carbon Co

APPLICATION INFORMATION
Initial Approach: The foundation reports it only makes contributions to preselected charitable organizations.
Restrictions on Giving: Does not support individuals or provide loans.

GRANTS ANALYSIS
Number of Grants: 26
Highest Grant: $248,814
Typical Range: $5,000 to $25,000
Disclosure Period: fiscal year ending January 31, 1992

RECENT GRANTS
248,814　Elk County Christian High School, St. Marys, PA
200,000　Diocese of Harrisburg, Harrisburg, PA
60,000　Elk County Christian High School, St. Marys, PA
39,500　Queen of World School, St. Marys, PA
32,300　St. Marys Parochial School, St. Marys, PA
30,000　St. Joseph Church, Mt. Jewett, PA
30,000　University of Notre Dame, Notre Dame, IN
25,000　Archdiocese of Newark, Newark, NJ
25,000　Morality in Media, New York, NY
23,950　Sacred Heart Church and School, St. Marys, PA

Saint Paul Cos.

Revenue: $4.49 billion
Employees: 10,914
Headquarters: Saint Paul, MN
SIC Major Group: Insurance Carriers

CONTACT
Mary Pickard
Community Affairs Officer
The St. Paul Companies
385 Washington St.
St. Paul, MN 55102
(612) 221-7757

FINANCIAL SUMMARY
Recent Giving: $9,700,000 (1993 est.); $9,215,966 (1992); $8,327,100 (1991)
Fiscal Note: Totals above include giving by subsidiaries, which averages $800,000 annually.

CONTRIBUTIONS SUMMARY
Typical Recipients: • *Arts & Humanities:* arts funds, arts institutes, dance, ethnic arts, literary arts, museums/galleries, music, performing arts, public broadcasting, theater • *Civic & Public Affairs:* economic development, economics, housing, nonprofit management • *Education:* career/vocational education, colleges & universities, education funds, minority education • *Health:* public health • *Social Services:* community service organizations, united funds, youth organizations

Grant Types: capital, employee matching gifts, general support, multiyear/continuing support, operating expenses, project, and seed money

Nonmonetary Support Types: donated equipment and workplace solicitation

Note: Value of nonmonetary support is not available and is not included in above totals. The company also provides printing services to nonprofits.

Geographic Distribution: primarily St. Paul and Minneapolis, MN; state of Minnesota; and communities in which company has major operations; national and international organizations have low priority

Operating Locations: CO, CT, DE, FL, HI, ID, IL, KS, LA, MA, MN, MT, ND, NE, NJ, NY, OH, OR, PA, TX, WA, WI

Note: Operates 29 service centers throughout United States. Also has operations in England.

CORP. OFFICERS
Douglas West Leatherdale: *B* Morden Canada 1936 *ED* Un Coll Canada BA 1957 *CURR EMPL* chmn, pres, ceo: St Paul Cos *CORP AFFIL* dir: Athena Assurance Co, Atwater McMillan, Carlyle Capital LP, Graham Resources, John Nuveen & Co, Natl Ins Wholesalers, Ramsey Ins, 77 Water St, St Paul Fin Group, St Paul Fire & Marine Ins Co, St Paul Fire & Marine Ins Co (UK) Ltd, St Paul Guardian Ins Co, St Paul Land Resources, St Paul Mercury Ins Co, St Paul Oil & Gas Corp, St Paul Plymouth Ctr, St Paul Properties, St Paul Real Estate IL, St Paul Risk Svcs, St Paul Surplus Lines Ins Co, Un HealthCare Corp *NONPR AFFIL* dir: Twin Cities Pub Television; mem: Fin Execs Inst, Twin Cities Soc Security Analysts

GIVING OFFICERS
Thomas McKeown: *B* Albert Lea MN 1929 *ED* St Johns Univ 1952 *CURR EMPL* exec vp, chief adm off: St Paul Cos
Polly Nyberg: *CURR EMPL* community affairs manager: St Paul Cos
Mary Pickard: *CURR EMPL* community affairs off: St Paul Cos
Sharon Tolbert-Glover: *CURR EMPL* community affairs program mgr: St Paul Cos

APPLICATION INFORMATION
Initial Approach: *Initial Contact:* completed application materials *Include Information On:* name, address, contact person, telephone number, and date of application; history and purpose of organization; three-year budget history and three-year projected budget; list of board members and affiliations; proof of tax-exemption and Minnesota Charities Registration; purpose of request (including organization's involvement in concept, needs

assessment, goals, and benefits); amount of request (including duration, additional sources of support, and amounts pledged); program budget; evaluative criteria; plans for on-going funding; evidence of co-operation with similar agencies *When to Submit:* any time (applicants seeking funds before end of calendar year should submit applications no later than September 18) *Note:* All the information listed in the applications requirements must be included for request to be considered. Organizations seeking funds for programs that have not previously received funding from The St. Paul Cos. should begin the process by submitting a one-page letter describing the new request.
Restrictions on Giving: Contribution funds will not be used for religious organizations unless seeking funds in the direct interest of the entire community; veterans, fraternal, political, or lobbying organizations; benefits or fund raisers; advertising; individuals; scholarships to individuals unless part of ongoing scholarship program of an educational institution or other nonprofit organization which selects the scholarship recipients; sectarian purposes; and generally not to organizations which are part of a United Way or other federated giving drive to which company is contributing, except to provide funding for management technical assistance, housing or education for communities of color.

OTHER THINGS TO KNOW

Subsidiaries located outside St. Paul administer their own contributions programs. These include Seaboard Surety Company (Bedminster, NJ); St. Paul Reinsurance Management Corp. (New York, NY); and Minet Holdings PLC (London, England).
Corporate contributions currently average about 2% of pre-tax operating earnings averaged over a three-year period.
Publications: community affairs report

GRANTS ANALYSIS

Total Grants: $9,215,966
Number of Grants: 271
Highest Grant: $500,000

Typical Range: $5,000 to $50,000
Disclosure Period: 1992
Note: Recent grants are derived from a 1992 annual report.

RECENT GRANTS

500,000 Family Housing Fund of Minneapolis and St. Paul, Minneapolis, MN — provide affordable rental housing for low-income families

451,270 Twin Cities Public Television-KTCA, St. Paul, MN — support for additional programs for Minnesota Century

369,825 United Way of the St. Paul Area, St. Paul, MN — operating support

333,000 Children's Museum, St. Paul, MN — capital campaign support to relocate in downtown St. Paul

300,000 Science Museum of Minnesota, St. Paul, MN — bridge fund

250,000 Minnesota Public Radio, St. Paul, MN — support for the 25th Anniversary Campaign for equipment replacement

200,000 Catholic Charities/Dorothy Day, Minneapolis, MN — renovation of Center, which serves the homeless in downtown St. Paul

200,000 St. Paul Chamber Orchestra, St. Paul, MN — endowment/bridge campaign support

188,000 United Way of the St. Paul Area, St. Paul, MN — capital campaign

153,514 United Arts, St. Paul, MN — to produce multi-cultural training tools using the arts as vehicles for both understanding and expressing diversity

St. Paul Federal Bank for Savings

Assets: $3.66 billion
Employees: 865
Parent Company: St. Paul Bancorp Inc.
Headquarters: Chicago, IL
SIC Major Group: Depository Institutions and Nondepository Institutions

CONTACT

Jo Woods
Loan Officer
St. Paul Federal Bank for Savings
6700 West North Ave.
Chicago, IL 60635
(312) 804-2459

CONTRIBUTIONS SUMMARY

Operating Locations: IL (Chicago)

CORP. OFFICERS

Patrick J. Agnew: *B* Chicago IL 1942 *ED* DePaul Univ 1966 *CURR EMPL* pres, coo: St Paul Fed Bank for Savings
Faustin A. Pipal: *CURR EMPL* vchmn: St Paul Fed Bank Savings
Joseph C. Scully: *CURR EMPL* chmn, ceo: St Paul Fed Bank for Savings

Saks Fifth Ave.

Sales: $1.4 billion
Employees: 8,000
Parent Company: Investcorp
Headquarters: New York, NY
SIC Major Group: Apparel & Accessory Stores and General Merchandise Stores

CONTACT

Helen O'Hagan
Vice President and Director of Corp. Rel
Saks Fifth Ave.
611 5th Ave.
5th floor
New York, NY 10022
(212) 940-4195

CONTRIBUTIONS SUMMARY

Nonmonetary Support Types: donated products
Operating Locations: NY (New York)

CORP. OFFICERS

Melvin Jacobs: *B* New York NY 1926 *ED* PA St Univ 1947 *CURR EMPL* chmn, ceo, dir: Saks Fifth Ave

Arthur Martinez: *CURR EMPL* vchmn, dir: Saks Fifth Ave
Philip Miller: *CURR EMPL* vchmn, dir: Saks Fifth Ave
Burton Tansky:

Salem News Publishing Co.

Sales: $9.0 million
Employees: 130
Headquarters: Salem, MA
SIC Major Group: Printing & Publishing

CONTACT

Ken Newbegin
Director, Promotion
Salem News Publishing Co.
155 Washington St.
Salem, MA 01970
(508) 744-0600

CONTRIBUTIONS SUMMARY

Operating Locations: MA (Salem)

CORP. OFFICERS

Kenneth R. Newbegin: *CURR EMPL* pres, co-publ: Salem News Publ Co
William B. Newbegin:

Salgo Charitable Trust, Nicholas M.

CONTACT

Robert A. Page
Trustee
Nicholas M. Salgo Charitable Trust
300 West Douglas, Ste. 1000
Wichita, KS 67202
(316) 261-5364

FINANCIAL SUMMARY

Recent Giving: $272,917 (fiscal 1991); $86,782 (fiscal 1990); $166,226 (fiscal 1989)
Assets: $2,335,880 (fiscal year ending November 30, 1991); $2,434,365 (fiscal 1990); $2,245,806 (fiscal 1989)
Gifts Received: $245 (fiscal 1991); $200,000 (fiscal 1990); $2,325,883 (fiscal 1989)
Fiscal Note: In 1991, contributions were received from Nicolas M. Salgo.
EIN: 48-6250539

CONTRIBUTIONS SUMMARY

Donor(s): Nicholas M. Salgo
Typical Recipients: • *Arts & Humanities:* museums/galleries • *Civic & Public Affairs:* inter-

national affairs • *Education:* colleges & universities, education funds, international exchange, international studies • *Health:* health organizations • *International:* international organizations • *Social Services:* shelters/homelessness

Grant Types: general support

GIVING OFFICERS
Robert A. Page: trust

APPLICATION INFORMATION
Initial Approach: Contributes only to preselected organizations.

GRANTS ANALYSIS
Number of Grants: 18
Highest Grant: $141,509
Typical Range: $400 to $5,000
Disclosure Period: fiscal year ending November 30, 1991

RECENT GRANTS
141,509 Salgo Trust for Education, Wichita, KS
63,544 University of Budapest, Budapest, Hungary
25,000 Salgo Trust for Education, Wichita, KS
6,000 Textile Museum, Washington, DC
5,000 Center for Strategic International Studies, Washington, DC
3,702 Salgo Trust for Education, Wichita, KS
1,500 Neighborhood Coalition for Shelter, New York, NY
1,000 American Numismatic Society, Colorado Springs, CO
1,000 American Red Cross, Washington, DC
1,000 Council of Ambassadors, Washington, DC

Salomon / Salomon Foundation

Parent Company: Salomon Inc
Revenue: $8.19 billion
Parent Employees: 8,431
Headquarters: New York, NY
SIC Major Group: Nondepository Institutions and Security & Commodity Brokers

CONTACT
Jane E. Heffner
Vice President
Salomon Inc.
7 World Trade Ctr.
New York, NY 10048
(212) 783-7434

FINANCIAL SUMMARY
Recent Giving: $3,500,000 (1993 est.); $3,600,000 (1992 approx.); $2,577,190 (1991)
Assets: $500,000 (1992); $2,216,520 (1991); $6,000,000 (1989)
Fiscal Note: All giving is through the company. See "Other Things You Should Know" for more details.
EIN: 13-3388259

CONTRIBUTIONS SUMMARY
Typical Recipients: • *Arts & Humanities:* libraries, museums/galleries, music, opera, public broadcasting, theater, visual arts • *Civic & Public Affairs:* economic development, ethnic/minority organizations, law & justice, women's affairs, zoos/botanical gardens • *Education:* arts education, business education, economic education, elementary education, literacy, minority education, public education (precollege) • *Health:* hospitals, medical research, single-disease health associations • *Social Services:* delinquency & crime, drugs & alcohol, emergency relief, employment/job training, food/clothing distribution, legal aid, recreation & athletics, youth organizations
Grant Types: employee matching gifts, general support, and operating expenses
Geographic Distribution: nationally, with emphasis on cities where company operates
Operating Locations: CA (Los Angeles, San Francisco), CT (Westport), GA (Atlanta), IL (Chicago), MA (Boston), NY (New York), TX (Dallas)

CORP. OFFICERS
Robert Edwin Denham: *CURR EMPL* chmn, ceo, dir: Salomon *NONPR AFFIL* mem: Am Bar Assn, Los Angeles County Bar Assn, St Bar CA; trust: Cathedral Corp Diocese Los Angeles, Polytech Sch Pasadena
Andrew J. Hall: *CURR EMPL* chmn, ceo: Phibro Energy Inc
Deryck C. Maughan: *B* Consett England 1947 *ED* Univ

London Kings Coll BA 1969; Stanford Univ MBA 1978 *CURR EMPL* chmn, ceo: Salomon Bros *CORP AFFIL* ceo, dir: Salomon Bros Holding Co; dir: Salomon

GIVING OFFICERS
Jane E. Heffner: vp corp contributions

APPLICATION INFORMATION
Initial Approach: *Initial Contact:* brief letter or proposal *Include Information On:* proof of tax-exempt status *When to Submit:* any time
Restrictions on Giving: Not considered for contributions are fraternal organizations, political or lobbying groups, or groups for sectarian purposes.

OTHER THINGS TO KNOW
The company responds to all funding requests addressed to either of its two main segments: Salomon Brothers and Phibro Energy.
Company, which gave about half of its giving through the Salomon Foundation, now gives entirely through direct gifts.

GRANTS ANALYSIS
Total Grants: $3,500,000
Number of Grants: 460*
Highest Grant: $100,000
Typical Range: $1,000 to $5,000
Disclosure Period: 1992
Note: Number of grants and average grant figures are approximate. Recent grants are derived from a 1991 Form 990.

RECENT GRANTS
204,030 Salomon-Robeson Scholarship Program
107,500 United Way of Tri-State, New York, NY
100,000 United Jewish Appeal-Federation of Jewish Philanthropies of New York, New York, NY
50,000 Lincoln Center for the Performing Arts, New York, NY
50,000 Stop Cancer, Los Angeles, CA
27,984 Yale University, New Haven, CT
25,897 Harvard University, Cambridge, MA
25,000 Cardinal's Committee of the Laity on

Wall Street, New York, NY
25,000 Inner-City Scholarship Fund, Cleveland, OH
21,180 Princeton University, Princeton, NJ

Salomon Foundation, Richard & Edna

CONTACT
R. M. Schleicher
Vice President
Richard & Edna Salomon Fdn.
45 Rockefeller Plz.
New York, NY 10111
(212) 903-1216

FINANCIAL SUMMARY
Recent Giving: $609,250 (1990); $584,000 (1989); $578,250 (1987)
Assets: $2,537,892 (1990); $3,014,141 (1989); $2,894,655 (1987)
EIN: 13-6163521

CONTRIBUTIONS SUMMARY
Donor(s): Richard B. Salomon
Typical Recipients: • *Arts & Humanities:* arts centers, cinema, libraries, museums/galleries • *Civic & Public Affairs:* international affairs • *Education:* colleges & universities, private education (precollege) • *Health:* health organizations, hospitals • *Social Services:* united funds
Grant Types: general support
Geographic Distribution: focus on New York, NY

GIVING OFFICERS
Merwin Lewis: secy
Edna Salomon: dir
Richard B. Salomon: pres, dir *B* New York NY 1912 *ED* Brown Univ PhB 1932; Brown Univ LLD 1972 *CORP AFFIL* managing ptnr: Riverbank Assocs *NONPR AFFIL* chancellor emeritus: Brown Univ; dir: Common Cause; trust: Lincoln Ctr Performing Arts; vchmn: NY Pub Library
Richard E. Salomon: dir
Raymond M. Schleicher: vp, treas, dir

APPLICATION INFORMATION
Initial Approach: Send brief letter of inquiry describing program or project. There are no deadlines.

Restrictions on Giving: Does not support individuals.

GRANTS ANALYSIS
Number of Grants: 39
Highest Grant: $200,000
Typical Range: $500 to $10,000
Disclosure Period: 1990

RECENT GRANTS
200,000 New York Public Library, New York, NY
65,000 Rockefeller University, New York, NY
60,000 Brown University, Providence, RI
50,000 Lincoln Center for the Performing Arts, New York, NY
45,000 Institute for East-West Security Studies, New York, NY
17,500 Bens Education Fund, Washington, DC
15,000 Museum of Modern Art, New York, NY
13,500 Planned Parenthood, New York, NY
12,500 Enterprise Foundation, Columbia, MD
10,000 Mayo Foundation, Rochester, MN

Saltonstall Charitable Foundation, Richard

CONTACT
Dudley H. Willis
Trustee
Richard Saltonstall Charitable Fdn.
50 Congress St., Rm. 800
Boston, MA 02109
(617) 227-8660

FINANCIAL SUMMARY
Recent Giving: $475,000 (1991); $439,000 (1989); $485,000 (1988)
Assets: $13,504,872 (1991); $10,005,378 (1989); $8,734,151 (1988)
EIN: 04-6078934

CONTRIBUTIONS SUMMARY
Typical Recipients: • *Arts & Humanities:* museums/galler-

ies, music, public broadcasting
• *Civic & Public Affairs:* rural affairs, women's affairs, zoos/botanical gardens
• *Health:* hospitals • *Social Services:* disabled, united funds, youth organizations

Grant Types: general support and research

Geographic Distribution: focus on MA

GIVING OFFICERS
Robert Ashton Lawrence: trust *B* Brookline MA 1926 *ED* Yale Univ 1947 *CURR EMPL* exec vp, dir: State Street Res & Mgmt Co *CORP AFFIL* exec vp, dir: State Street Res & Mgmt Co; mem exec comm, dir: Affiliated Publs; vp, dir: State St Growth Fund Inc, State St Investment Corp

Dudley H. Willis: trust

APPLICATION INFORMATION
Initial Approach: Send brief letter of inquiry describing program or project. There are no deadlines.

GRANTS ANALYSIS
Number of Grants: 26
Highest Grant: $50,000
Typical Range: $5,000 to $25,000
Disclosure Period: 1991

RECENT GRANTS
50,000 Sherborn Rural Land Foundation, Boston, MA
40,000 Brigham and Women's Hospital, Boston, MA
40,000 New England Medical Center, Boston, MA
40,000 Trustees of Reservations, Beverly, MA
40,000 United Way, Boston, MA
34,500 WGBH Educational Foundation, Boston, MA
30,000 Massachusetts 4-H Club, Boston, MA
25,000 Massachusetts General Hospital, Boston, MA
25,000 Museum of Science, Boston, MA
20,000 Boston Symphony Orchestra, Boston, MA

Saltz Foundation, Gary

CONTACT
Anita Saltz
President
Gary Saltz Fdn.
600 Madison Avenue, 20th Fl.
New York, NY 10022

FINANCIAL SUMMARY
Recent Giving: $52,000 (fiscal 1989)
Assets: $4,459,187 (fiscal year ending April 30, 1990); $3,322,538 (fiscal 1989)
Gifts Received: $2,000,000 (fiscal 1990); $500,000 (fiscal 1989)
EIN: 13-3267114

CONTRIBUTIONS SUMMARY
Donor(s): Jack Saltz, Anita Saltz
Typical Recipients: • *Education:* private education (precollege) • *Health:* medical research, single-disease health associations
Grant Types: research

GIVING OFFICERS
Anita Saltz: pres
Leonard Saltz: treas
Ronald Saltz: vp
Susan Saltz: secy

APPLICATION INFORMATION
Initial Approach: Contributes only to preselected organizations.

GRANTS ANALYSIS
Disclosure Period: fiscal year ending April 30, 1990
Note: No grants were provided in 1990.

RECENT GRANTS
35,000 Juvenile Diabetes Foundation, New York, NY
17,000 Yad Tikva, New York, NY

Salvatori Foundation, Henry

CONTACT
Henry Salvatori
President
Henry Salvatori Fdn.
1901 Ave. of the Stars, Suite 600
Los Angeles, CA 90067
(913) 346-5445

FINANCIAL SUMMARY
Recent Giving: $606,275 (fiscal 1991)
Assets: $8,406,891 (fiscal year ending June 30, 1991)
Gifts Received: $8,711,273 (fiscal 1991)
Fiscal Note: In fiscal 1991, contributions were received from Henry Salvatori.
EIN: 95-4287740

CONTRIBUTIONS SUMMARY
Donor(s): Henry Salvatori the late Gail Sarver and Sarver, Inc.
Typical Recipients: • *Arts & Humanities:* history/historic preservation • *Civic & Public Affairs:* international affairs
• *Education:* colleges & universities, social sciences education
Grant Types: conference/seminar and general support
Geographic Distribution: giving limited to Osborne County, KS

GIVING OFFICERS
Pete Bohm: bd mem
William C. Cady: bd mem
Paul S. Gregory: bd mem
Charles Kesler: dir
Edwin Meese IV: dir
Simon Ramo: dir
Simon Ramon: dir
Henry Salvatori: pres
Steve Sindscheffel: bd mem
Frederick E. Vandenberg: secy, treas
Melvin Wilcoxson: bd mem

APPLICATION INFORMATION
Initial Approach: Application form not required for scholarships. Submit one proposal. Deadline is April 1 for scholarships and December 31 for grants. Board meeting dates vary.
Restrictions on Giving: Does not provide grants to individuals.

OTHER THINGS TO KNOW
Publications: informational brochure

GRANTS ANALYSIS
Number of Grants: 6
Highest Grant: $200,000
Typical Range: $25,000 to $150,000
Disclosure Period: fiscal year ending June 30, 1991

RECENT GRANTS
200,000 Heritage Foundation, Washington, DC — espouse founding principles
175,000 Claremont Institute for Study of Statesmanship and Political Philosophy, Montclair, CA — seminar for teachers on the founding principles
150,000 Hillsdale College, Hillsdale, MI — create college chair in traditional values
31,275 Harvey Mudd College, Claremont, CA — produce audio tapes teaching children about founding fathers
25,000 Institute for World Politics, Washington, DC — teaching the founding principles
25,000 Young America's Foundation, Herndon, VA — college lecture series

Salwil Foundation

CONTACT
William L. Searle
President
Salwil Fdn.
400 Skokie Blvd., Ste. 675
Northbrook, IL 60062
(708) 291-1030

FINANCIAL SUMMARY
Recent Giving: $105,609 (1990); $102,667 (1989); $96,125 (1987)
Assets: $2,246,496 (1990); $2,181,451 (1989); $2,057,882 (1987)
EIN: 36-3377945

CONTRIBUTIONS SUMMARY
Donor(s): William L. Searle
Typical Recipients: • *Civic & Public Affairs:* environmental affairs • *Education:* colleges & universities, private education (precollege) • *Health:* hospitals, pediatric health • *Religion:* churches, religious organizations • *Social Services:* animal protection, family services, youth organizations
Grant Types: general support

GIVING OFFICERS
Marriane L. Pahle: dir
Sally B. Searle: vp, secy, treas
William Louis Searle: pres *B* Evanston IL 1928 *ED* Univ MI BA 1951; Harvard Univ MBA 1969; Univ MI BA 1951; Harvard Univ postgrad 1969 *CORP AFFIL* dir: Boulevard Bancorp, Earl-Kinship Capital Corp, MS Valley Airlines *NONPR AFFIL* dir: Chicago Symphony Orchestra Assn, Field Mus

APPLICATION INFORMATION
Initial Approach: Contributes only to preselected organizations.

GRANTS ANALYSIS
Number of Grants: 18
Highest Grant: $17,122
Typical Range: $1,000 to $11,000
Disclosure Period: 1990

RECENT GRANTS
17,122 Focus on the Family, Pomona, CA
11,122 Children's Memorial Medical Center, Chicago, IL
11,000 Lake Forest Country Day School, Lake Forest, IL
8,870 Church of Holy Spirit, Lake Forest, IL
7,000 Crown Ministries, Euclid, MN
7,000 Teen Ranch, Marlette, MI
5,625 Women's Foundation of Colorado, Denver, CO
5,000 African Wildlife Foundation, Washington, DC
5,000 Lake Forest Hospital, Lake Forest, IL
5,000 Rhino and Elephant Foundation, New York, NY

Sammons Enterprises / Sammons Foundation
Sales: $2.4 billion
Employees: 5,000
Headquarters: Dallas, TX
SIC Major Group: Communications, Holding & Other Investment Offices, Hotels & Other Lodging Places, and Insurance Carriers

CONTACT
Robert Korba
President
Sammons Enterprises
300 Crescent Court, Ste. 700
Dallas, TX 75201
(214) 855-2800

CONTRIBUTIONS SUMMARY
Operating Locations: TX (Dallas)

CORP. OFFICERS
Gale Brown: *CURR EMPL* treas: Sammons Enterprises
Robert Korba: *CURR EMPL* pres: Sammons Enterprises

Sams Foundation, Earl C.

CONTACT
Dorothy P. Tate
President
Earl C. Sams Fdn.
101 North Shoreline Dr., Ste. 602
Corpus Christi, TX 78401
(512) 888-6485

FINANCIAL SUMMARY
Recent Giving: $222,032 (1991); $483,444 (1990); $913,249 (1989)
Assets: $16,970,172 (1991); $13,398,924 (1990); $15,107,744 (1989)
EIN: 74-1463151

CONTRIBUTIONS SUMMARY
Donor(s): The foundation was incorporated in 1946 by the late Earl C. Sams.
Typical Recipients: • *Arts & Humanities:* museums/galleries, public broadcasting • *Civic & Public Affairs:* zoos/botanical gardens • *Religion:* churches • *Social Services:* drugs & alcohol, emergency relief, shelters/homelessness, youth organizations
Grant Types: capital, operating expenses, and project
Geographic Distribution: focus on south Texas

GIVING OFFICERS
Bruce Sams Hawn: dir
Ed Jensen: asst treas
Susan Ohnmacht: secy
Dorothy P. Tate: pres, dir
Royce D. Tate: dir
Susan Hawn Thames: dir

APPLICATION INFORMATION
Initial Approach: The foundation requests written proposals with adequate information for the board of directors to evaluate and make a decision.

The foundation has no deadline for submitting proposals.

The board meets semi-annually.

Restrictions on Giving: Grants are made solely to tax-exempt organizations. The foundation does not make grants to individuals.

GRANTS ANALYSIS
Total Grants: $222,032
Number of Grants: 17
Highest Grant: $76,000
Typical Range: $500 to $5,500
Disclosure Period: 1991

Note: Average grant figure does not include a grant for $76,000 and a grant for $70,000. Recent grants are derived from a 1991 grants list.

RECENT GRANTS
76,000 Valley Zoological Society, Brownsville, TX
70,000 Texas State Aquarium, Corpus Christi, TX
63,582 Passage House, Corpus Christi, TX
3,000 South Texas Emergency Corps, Corpus Christi, TX
1,600 Art Museum of South Texas, Corpus Christi, TX
1,000 Boy Scouts of America, San Antonio, TX
1,000 Church of Good Shepherd, Corpus Christi, TX
1,000 KEDT Public Television, Corpus Christi, TX
1,000 Palmer Drug Abuse Program, Corpus Christi, TX

Samsung America Inc.
Employees: 60
Headquarters: Fort Lee, NJ
SIC Major Group: Wholesale Trade—Durable Goods and Wholesale Trade—Nondurable Goods

CONTACT
B.U. Chung
President
Samsung America Inc.
105 Challenger Rd.
Ridgefield Park, NJ 07662
(201) 229-5000

CONTRIBUTIONS SUMMARY
Operating Locations: CA, FL, GA, NJ, NY

CORP. OFFICERS
B. U. Chung: *CURR EMPL*
pres: Samsung Am

GIVING OFFICERS
B. U. Chung: *CURR EMPL*
pres: Samsung Am (see above)
Young Kim: *CURR EMPL* gen mgr (gen affs div): Samsung Am

Samuels Foundation, Fan Fox and Leslie R.

CONTACT
Eva Burt
Program Assistant
Fan Fox and Leslie R. Samuels Foundation
630 Fifth Avenue, Ste. 2255
New York, NY 10111
(212) 315-2940

FINANCIAL SUMMARY
Recent Giving: $4,000,000 (fiscal 1993 est.); $3,580,021 (fiscal 1992); $4,019,615 (fiscal 1991)
Assets: $114,000,000 (fiscal 1993 est.); $111,832,513 (fiscal year ending July 31, 1992); $106,034,237 (fiscal 1991); $101,510,082 (fiscal 1990)
Gifts Received: $379,826 (fiscal 1991); $1,150,000 (fiscal 1990); $300,000 (fiscal 1989)
Fiscal Note: Each year the foundation has received bequests from the estates of Leslie R. Samuels and Fan Fox Samuels. The foundation reports that the 1993 bequest is the final one.
EIN: 13-3124818

CONTRIBUTIONS SUMMARY
Donor(s): The late Mr. and Mrs. Leslie R. Samuels established the foundation in Utah in 1959, originally calling it the Samuels-Auerbach Foundation. The foundation was reincorporated in New York in 1981.

Typical Recipients: • *Arts & Humanities:* dance, music, opera, performing arts, theater • *Health:* geriatric health, hospitals, pediatric health
Grant Types: multiyear/continuing support, project, and seed money
Geographic Distribution: New York, NY, metropolitan area

GIVING OFFICERS
Morton J. Bernstein: chmn, dir
Eva M. Burt: program asst
Marvin A. Kaufman: pres, dir
Joseph C. Mitchell: vp, treas, dir
Carlos Dupre Moseley: vp, dir *B* Laurens SC 1914 *ED* Duke Univ BA 1935; Philadelphia Conservatory Music 1941-44 *NONPR AFFIL* chmn emeritus: NY Philharmonic Symphony Soc; mem: Mu Phi Epsilon, Phi Beta Kappa, Phi Eta Sigma, Phi Kappa Lambda; trust: Converse Coll; chmn performing arts advisory comm: Asia Soc; mem: Natl Counc Arts
Muriel Nasser: secy, dir

APPLICATION INFORMATION
Initial Approach:
Letters of inquiry should be directed to the foundation's program officer. There are no application forms.
A copy of 501(c)3 letter, board of directors list, project budget, most recent financial statement, and current contributors list. Letters should briefly summarize the proposal and state the amount requested. Costly presentations are discouraged. All letters are acknowledged within two months. If a proposal is of interest, an appointment will be arranged to discuss details before it is presented to the board. The board meets in January, April, July, and October.

OTHER THINGS TO KNOW
The foundation reports that it no longer supports arts-in-education programming, community service, education, or media. The foundation also does not support individuals.
Publications: biennial report

GRANTS ANALYSIS
Total Grants: $3,580,021
Number of Grants: 155*
Highest Grant: $250,000*

Typical Range: $1,000 to $10,000 and $25,000 to $100,000
Disclosure Period: fiscal year ending July 31, 1992
Note: Figures for number of grants, average grant, and highest grant are from 1991. Recent grants are derived from a fiscal 1991 grants list.

RECENT GRANTS
250,000 New York City Opera, New York, NY — for 1991 production of "Die Soldaten"
220,000 Hospital for Joint Diseases Orthopaedic Institute, New York, NY — toward construction of the Samuels Urgent Care Center
125,000 Lincoln Center for the Performing Arts, New York, NY
110,000 Long Island Jewish Medical Center, New Hyde Park, NY — toward founding a Regional Neonatal Satellite Program
100,000 Beth Israel Medical Center, New York, NY — towards the construction, renovation and furnishing of the Samuel's Planetree Model Hospital Unit
100,000 Metropolitan Opera Association, New York, NY — for the Carlos Moseley Music Pavillion
100,000 New York Public Library, New York, NY — for an exhibition celebrating the life and work of George Balanchine
98,875 Long Island Jewish Medical Center, New Hyde Park, NY — to establish a Geriatric Assessment Team
75,000 Brooklyn Academy of Music, Brooklyn, NY — support of Opera/Music Theater 1992-1994
75,000 New York Shakespeare Festival, New York, NY — for the upcoming production of John Ford's 'Tis Pity She's a Whore

San Diego Gas & Electric
Revenue: $1.79 billion
Employees: 4,175
Headquarters: San Diego, CA
SIC Major Group: Electric, Gas & Sanitary Services, Industrial Machinery & Equipment, and Real Estate

CONTACT
Becky Obayashi
Corporate Contribution Administrator
San Diego Gas & Electric
PO Box 1831
San Diego, CA 92112
(619) 696-4299

FINANCIAL SUMMARY
Recent Giving: $1,600,000 (1993 est.); $1,800,000 (1992)
Fiscal Note: Company gives directly. Figure for 1993 does not include $18,650 distributed separately.

CONTRIBUTIONS SUMMARY
Typical Recipients: • *Arts & Humanities:* arts centers, arts festivals, arts funds, arts institutes, community arts, dance, ethnic arts, history/historic preservation, libraries, museums/galleries, music, opera, performing arts, theater, visual arts • *Civic & Public Affairs:* economic development, environmental affairs, ethnic/minority organizations, professional & trade associations, safety, zoos/botanical gardens • *Education:* arts education, business education, career/vocational education, colleges & universities, economic education, education funds, elementary education, engineering education, health & physical education, literacy, medical education, minority education, preschool education, science/technology education • *Health:* geriatric health, health organizations, hospices, hospitals, medical research, mental health, single-disease health associations • *Science:* observatories & planetariums, science exhibits & fairs, scientific organizations • *Social Services:* aged, child welfare, community centers, community service organizations, counseling, day care, delinquency & crime, disabled, drugs & alcohol, emergency relief, employment/job training, family services, food/clothing distribution, legal aid, recrea-

tion & athletics, shelters/homelessness, united funds, volunteer services, youth organizations

Grant Types: capital, conference/seminar, emergency, general support, matching, operating expenses, project, research, and scholarship

Nonmonetary Support Types: donated equipment, in-kind services, and loaned employees

Geographic Distribution: primarily at headquarters and operating locations

Operating Locations: CA (Irvine, San Diego, Santa Ana)

CORP. OFFICERS

Thomas A. Page: *B* Niagara Falls NY 1933 *ED* Purdue Univ BS 1955; Purdue Univ MS 1963 *CURR EMPL* chmn, ceo, dir: San Diego Gas & Electric Co

Jack E. Thomas: *CURR EMPL* pres: San Diego Gas & Electric Co

GIVING OFFICERS

Becky Obayashi: *CURR EMPL* corp contributions admin: San Diego Gas & Electric Co

APPLICATION INFORMATION

Initial Approach: *Initial Contact:* brief letter of inquiry *Include Information On:* description of the organization, amount requested, purpose of funds sought, recently audited financial statements, and proof of tax-exempt status *When to Submit:* any time

Restrictions on Giving: Does not support individuals, religious organizations for sectarian purposes, travel organizations, or political or lobbying groups.

GRANTS ANALYSIS

Typical Range: $1,000 to $2,500

San Diego Trust & Savings Bank

Assets: $1.8 billion
Employees: 1,700
Parent Company: San Diego Financial Corp.
Headquarters: San Diego, CA
SIC Major Group: Depository Institutions

CONTACT

Jackie Hill
Vice President of Public Relations
San Diego Trust & Savings Bank
530 Broadway, Ste. 1016
San Diego, CA 92101
(619) 557-2200

FINANCIAL SUMMARY

Recent Giving: $560,000 (1993 est.)

Fiscal Note: Company gives directly only.

CONTRIBUTIONS SUMMARY

Typical Recipients: • *Arts & Humanities:* history/historic preservation, museums/galleries • *Civic & Public Affairs:* urban & community affairs • *Education:* colleges & universities • *Health:* health organizations, hospitals, pediatric health • *Social Services:* child welfare, community service organizations, youth organizations

Grant Types: general support

Geographic Distribution: only in headquarters area

Operating Locations: CA (San Diego)

CORP. OFFICERS

Duane W. Drake: *CURR EMPL* exec vp, cfo: San Diego Trust & Savings Bank

Brian Gowland: *CURR EMPL* coo: San Diego Trust & Savings Bank

Daniel D. Herde: *CURR EMPL* ceo, pres: San Diego Trust & Savings Bank

GIVING OFFICERS

Jackie Hill: *CURR EMPL* vp pub rels: San Diego Trust & Savings Bank

APPLICATION INFORMATION

Initial Approach: *Initial Contact:* brief letter of inquiry* *Include Information On:* a description of organization, amount requested, and purpose of funds sought *When to Submit:* any time *Note:* Requests for funds must be in writing.

Restrictions on Giving: Does not support individuals, religious organizations for sectarian purposes, political or lobbying groups, or organizations outside operating areas.

RECENT GRANTS

American Heart Association, San Diego, CA
Center for Children, San Diego, CA
Childrens Hospital, San Diego, CA
Community Foundation, San Diego, CA
Museum of Art, San Diego, CA
Natural History Museum, San Diego, CA
Salvation Army, San Diego, CA
San Diego State University, San Diego, CA
University of San Diego, San Diego, CA
Youth and Community Service, San Diego, CA

San Francisco Federal Savings & Loan Association

Assets: $3.13 billion
Employees: 777
Parent Company: SFFed Corp.
Headquarters: San Francisco, CA
SIC Major Group: Depository Institutions

CONTACT

Lawrence Beller
Chief Marketing Officer
San Francisco Federal Savings & Loan Association
88 Kearny St.
San Francisco, CA 94108
(415) 955-5800

CONTRIBUTIONS SUMMARY

Operating Locations: CA (San Francisco)

CORP. OFFICERS

Roger L. Gordan: *CURR EMPL* ceo, pres: San Francisco Federal Savings & Loan Association

Paul Weinberg: *CURR EMPL* exec vp, cfo: San Francisco Fed Savings & Loan Assn

Sanders Trust, Charles

CONTACT

Charles Sanders Trust
c/o Sallonstall and Co.
50 Congress St., Ste. 800
Boston, MA 02109
(617) 227-8660

FINANCIAL SUMMARY

Recent Giving: $122,588 (1991); $138,710 (1989)

Assets: $2,875,236 (1991); $2,571,189 (1989)
EIN: 04-6022091

CONTRIBUTIONS SUMMARY

Typical Recipients: • *Education:* agricultural education • *Health:* hospitals • *Social Services:* community service organizations, family services, united funds, youth organizations

Grant Types: general support

GIVING OFFICERS

George Lewis: trust
William I. Saltonstall: trust
Dudlee H. Willis: trust

APPLICATION INFORMATION

Initial Approach: Send brief letter describing program. There are no deadlines.

GRANTS ANALYSIS

Number of Grants: 1
Highest Grant: $122,588
Disclosure Period: 1991

RECENT GRANTS

122,588 Sanders Fund, Boston, MA

Sandia National Laboratories

Sales: $1.16 billion
Employees: 8,450
Parent Company: AT&T Co.
Headquarters: Albuquerque, NM
SIC Major Group: Engineering & Management Services

CONTACT

Sandia National Laboratories
PO Box 5800
Albuquerque, NM 87185
(505) 844-5678

CONTRIBUTIONS SUMMARY

Operating Locations: NM (Albuquerque)

Sandoz Corp. / Sandoz Foundation Am

Sales: $2.5 billion
Employees: 11,500
Headquarters: New York, NY
SIC Major Group: Chemicals & Allied Products, Engineering & Management Services, Holding & Other Investment Offices, and Wholesale Trade—Nondurable Goods

CONTACT

Craig D. Burrell
Vice President, Marketing
Sandoz Corp.
608 Fifth Ave.
New York, NY 10020
(212) 307-1122

FINANCIAL SUMMARY

Recent Giving: $188,900
(1991); $37,150 (1989);
$40,914 (1988)
Assets: $5,820,161 (1991);
$5,857,221 (1989)
EIN: 13-6193034

CONTRIBUTIONS SUMMARY

Typical Recipients: • *Civic & Public Affairs:* professional & trade associations • *Education:* career/vocational education, colleges & universities, science/technology education, student aid • *Health:* health organizations, medical research
Grant Types: department, fellowship, general support, professorship, research, and scholarship
Geographic Distribution: nationally, with emphasis on operating locations
Operating Locations: CA, ID, IL, MN, NC, NJ, NY, OH

CORP. OFFICERS

Heinz Imhos: *CURR EMPL*
ceo: Sandoz Corp
Roland Loesser: *CURR EMPL*
group vp (fin), cfo: Sandoz Corp

GIVING OFFICERS

Herbert J. Brennan: secy *B* Brooklyn NY 1935 *ED* Seton Hall Univ 1956; NY Univ 1970 *CURR EMPL* vp (law), secy: Sandoz Pharmaceuticals Corp *NONPR AFFIL* mem: Am Bar Assn, Am Corp Counc Assn
Kenneth L. Brewton, Jr.: vp
Craig D. Burrell: vp *CURR EMPL* vp mktg: Sandoz Corp
Daniel C. Wagniere: pres *CURR EMPL* chmn: Sandoz Pharmaceuticals Corp

APPLICATION INFORMATION

Initial Approach: A brief, one- or two-page letter may be submitted at any time, explaining the project, the amount requested, and when funds are needed. The foundation will contact the applicant if further information is required.
Restrictions on Giving: Foundation grants generally are restricted to the areas of health and education, particularly bio-

medical research and related fields.

GRANTS ANALYSIS

Number of Grants: 15
Highest Grant: $35,000
Typical Range: $10,000 to $35,000
Disclosure Period: 1991

RECENT GRANTS

35,000 Boston University College of Communication, Boston, MA
35,000 Boston University School of Public Health, Boston, MA
35,000 University of Virginia, Charlottesville, VA — health sciences center
25,000 Council for International Organizations of Medical Sciences (CIOMS) — programs in ethics
25,000 Council for International Organizations of Medical Sciences (CIOMS) — programs in ethics
25,000 University of Medicine and Dentistry, Stratford, NJ — Environmental and Occupation Health Sciences Institute
15,000 Charles Louis Davis Foundation — registry of study materials
10,000 Nebraska Wesleyan University, Lincoln, NE — science education program
10,000 North Carolina State University, Raleigh, NC — Pulp and Paper Science Technology scholarship program
10,000 University of Notre Dame, Notre Dame, IN — scholarship fund for chemistry

Sandusky International Inc. / Sandusky International Foundation

Sales: $24.5 million
Employees: 221
Headquarters: Sandusky, OH
SIC Major Group: Industrial Machinery & Equipment

CONTACT

Richard A. Hargrave
Vice President - Finance & Administration
Sandusky International Inc.
615 West Market St., PO Box 5012
Sandusky, OH 44870-1281
(419) 626-5340

FINANCIAL SUMMARY

Recent Giving: $60,000 (1993 est.); $193,421 (1991); $155,234 (1990)
Assets: $318,643 (1991); $300,866 (1990); $242,351 (1989)
Gifts Received: $200,000 (1991); $200,000 (1990); $150,000 (1989)
Fiscal Note: In 1991, contributions were received from Sandusky International Inc.
EIN: 34-6596951

CONTRIBUTIONS SUMMARY

Typical Recipients: • *Arts & Humanities:* community arts, libraries, museums/galleries, performing arts, theater • *Civic & Public Affairs:* economic development • *Education:* colleges & universities, elementary education, private education (preccollege), public education (precccollege), science/technology education • *Social Services:* child welfare, community centers, community service organizations, united funds, youth organizations
Grant Types: capital, challenge, and general support
Geographic Distribution: focus primarily on Sandusky, OH area
Operating Locations: OH (Sandusky)

CORP. OFFICERS

Charles W. Rainger: *B* Cleveland OH 1933 *ED* Case Western Reserve Univ 1955 *CURR EMPL* pres: Sandusky Foundry & Machine Co *CORP AFFIL* chmn: Sandusky Ltd; dir: OH Edison Co, Third Natl Bank

GIVING OFFICERS

Carlos G. Alafita: trust
Richard A. Hargrave: trust
Edward A. McPhillamy: trust
Charles W. Rainger: trust *CURR EMPL* pres: Sandusky Foundry & Machine Co (see above)
Daniel A. Scott: trust

APPLICATION INFORMATION

Initial Approach: Send brief letter including a description of the organization, amount requested, purpose of funds sought, audited financial statement, and proof of tax-exempt status. There are no deadlines.
Restrictions on Giving: Does not support individuals, religious organizations for sectarian purposes, or political or lobbying groups.

GRANTS ANALYSIS

Number of Grants: 33
Highest Grant: $50,000
Typical Range: $250 to $5,000
Disclosure Period: 1991

RECENT GRANTS

50,000 Parkview Place, Sandusky, OH
25,000 Girl Scouts of America, Sandusky, OH
25,000 Norman Rockwell Museum, Stockbridge, MA
15,000 YMCA, Sandusky, OH
11,000 United Way, Sandusky, OH
10,338 Sandusky City School, Sandusky, OH — Gazebo Public Address System
10,000 Goodwill Industries, Sandusky, OH
9,000 Sandusky State Theatre, Sandusky, OH — restoration fund
5,000 Greater Erie County Marketing Group, Sandusky, OH
5,000 St. Mary's Central Catholic High School, Sandusky, OH — computer fund

Sandy Foundation, George H.

CONTACT

Chester R. MacPhee, Jr.
Trustee
George H. Sandy Fdn.
PO Box 591717
San Francisco, CA 94159
(415) 929-1129

FINANCIAL SUMMARY

Recent Giving: $652,000 (1991); $640,000 (1990); $539,000 (1989)
Assets: $13,628,530 (1991); $13,285,260 (1990); $13,351,121 (1989)

EIN: 94-6054473

CONTRIBUTIONS SUMMARY

Donor(s): the late George H. Sandy

Typical Recipients: • *Civic & Public Affairs:* philanthropic organizations • *Education:* colleges & universities, student aid • *Health:* medical research, pediatric health, single-disease health associations • *Religion:* churches, religious organizations • *Social Services:* animal protection, child welfare, disabled, drugs & alcohol, food/clothing distribution, homes, recreation & athletics, shelters/homelessness, volunteer services, youth organizations

Grant Types: multiyear/continuing support and operating expenses

Geographic Distribution: limited to the San Francisco Bay, CA, area

GIVING OFFICERS

Thomas E. Feeney: trust
Chester R. MacPhee, Jr.: trust

APPLICATION INFORMATION

Initial Approach: Send brief letter of inquiry describing program or project. There are no deadlines.

Restrictions on Giving: Does not support individuals or provide matching gifts, scholarships, or loans.

GRANTS ANALYSIS

Number of Grants: 85
Highest Grant: $45,000
Typical Range: $1,000 to $25,000
Disclosure Period: 1991

RECENT GRANTS

45,000 San Francisco SPCA, San Francisco, CA
30,000 Recreation Center for the Handicapped, San Francisco, CA
20,000 Boys and Girls Club, San Francisco, CA
20,000 St. Mary's College, Morga, CA — scholarship
20,000 University of San Francisco, San Francisco, CA
20,000 Volunteer Auxiliary of Youth Guidance, San Francisco, CA

19,000 YMCA, San Francisco, CA
16,000 DeMolay Foundation of California, Richmond, CA
15,000 College of Marin, Kentfield, CA
15,000 Guide Dogs for the Blind

Sandy Hill Foundation

CONTACT

Rose Bruttaniti
Sandy Hill Foundation
c/o Wesray Corporation
330 South Street, P.O. Box 1975
Morristown, NJ 07962-1975
(201) 540-9020

FINANCIAL SUMMARY

Recent Giving: $1,170,955 (fiscal 1990); $937,268 (fiscal 1989)
Assets: $11,591,114 (fiscal year ending July 31, 1990); $10,903,432 (fiscal 1989)
Gifts Received: $1,828,750 (fiscal 1990); $5,849,843 (fiscal 1989)
Fiscal Note: Fiscal 1990 contribution received from Frank E. Walsh, Jr.
EIN: 22-2668774

CONTRIBUTIONS SUMMARY

Donor(s): the donor is Frank E. Walsh, Jr., president and director of the foundation

Typical Recipients: • *Civic & Public Affairs:* philanthropic organizations, urban & community affairs • *Education:* colleges & universities, education associations, education funds, private education (precollege), student aid • *Health:* health organizations, hospices, hospitals, single-disease health associations • *Social Services:* child welfare, community service organizations, disabled, domestic violence, food/clothing distribution, homes, recreation & athletics, religious welfare, shelters/homelessness, united funds, youth organizations

Grant Types: capital, general support, multiyear/continuing support, operating expenses, and scholarship

Geographic Distribution: primarily New Jersey

GIVING OFFICERS

Rose Bruttaniti, Jr.: contact person

Frank E. Walsh, Jr.: don, pres, dir
Jeffrey R. Walsh, Jr.: mgr
Mary D. Walsh, Jr.: secy, dir

APPLICATION INFORMATION

Initial Approach: The foundation reports that no special forms or materials are needed for application. There are no deadlines for proposals and no restrictions on giving.

GRANTS ANALYSIS

Number of Grants: 76
Highest Grant: $210,000
Typical Range: $20,000 to $50,000
Disclosure Period: fiscal year ending July 31, 1990
Note: Incomplete grants list provided in fiscal 1990.

RECENT GRANTS

210,000 Lehigh University, Bethlehem, PA
210,000 Seton Hall University, South Orange, NJ
200,000 University of Vermont, Burlington, VT
50,000 Boys and Girls Clubs of Newark, Newark, NJ
50,000 New Community Corporation, Newark, NJ
50,000 Seton Hall Prep, West Orange, NJ
30,000 Immaculata College, Immaculata, PA
25,000 Seton Hall Pre, West Orange, NJ
25,000 University of Vermont, Burlington, VT
20,000 St. Benedicts Prep, Newark, NJ

Sang Foundation, Elsie O. and Philip D.

CONTACT

Elsie O. Sang
President
Elsie O. and Philip D. Sang Fdn.
180 East Pearson St., Apt. 5805
Chicago, IL 60611
(312) 943-4714

FINANCIAL SUMMARY

Recent Giving: $301,275 (fiscal 1991); $302,000 (fiscal 1990); $367,400 (fiscal 1989)
Assets: $2,756,264 (fiscal year ending October 31, 1990);

$2,849,082 (fiscal 1989); $2,929,481 (fiscal 1988)
EIN: 36-6214200

CONTRIBUTIONS SUMMARY

Typical Recipients: • *Arts & Humanities:* history/historic preservation, music • *Civic & Public Affairs:* ethnic/minority organizations • *Education:* colleges & universities • *Health:* hospitals, medical research • *International:* international organizations • *Religion:* religious organizations, synagogues • *Social Services:* aged, community service organizations, disabled

Grant Types: general support
Geographic Distribution: focus on Chicago, IL

GIVING OFFICERS

Bernard Sang: secy
Elsie O. Sang: pres

APPLICATION INFORMATION

Initial Approach: The foundation reports it only makes contributions to preselected charitable organizations.
Restrictions on Giving: Does not support individuals.

GRANTS ANALYSIS

Number of Grants: 37
Highest Grant: $145,000
Typical Range: $500 to $1,000
Disclosure Period: fiscal year ending October 31, 1990

RECENT GRANTS

145,000 Olin, Sang, Ruby Institute Camp, Oconomowoc, WI
75,000 Jewish United Fund, Chicago, IL
10,000 Art Institute of Chicago, Chicago, IL
10,000 Oak Park Temple, Oak Park, IL
10,000 Operation Exodus, Chicago, IL
5,000 American Association International Center-University Teaching of Jewish Civilization, New York, NY
5,000 Council for Jewish Elderly, Chicago, IL
5,000 Jewish National Fund, New York, NY
5,000 Orchestral Association, Chicago, IL
3,000 Mayo Foundation for Medical Research, Rochester, MN

Sanguinetti Foundation, Annunziata

CONTACT
Eugene I. Ranghiasci
Annunziata Sanguinetti Fdn.
c/o Wells Fargo Bank, N.A.
420 Montgomery St., 5th Fl.
San Francisco, CA 94163
(415) 396-3215

FINANCIAL SUMMARY
Recent Giving: $229,500 (fiscal 1992); $236,000 (fiscal 1991); $226,750 (fiscal 1990)
Assets: $4,089,249 (fiscal year ending September 30, 1992); $3,914,274 (fiscal 1991); $3,500,476 (fiscal 1990)
EIN: 94-6073762

CONTRIBUTIONS SUMMARY
Donor(s): the late Annunziata Sanguinetti
Typical Recipients: • *Health:* hospitals, mental health, pediatric health • *Religion:* religious organizations • *Social Services:* child welfare, community centers, disabled, homes, recreation & athletics, religious welfare, united funds, youth organizations
Grant Types: general support and project
Geographic Distribution: limited to San Francisco, CA

GIVING OFFICERS
Wells Fargo Bank, N.A.: trust

APPLICATION INFORMATION
Initial Approach: Send brief letter of inquiry describing program or project. Submit letter between July and October 31.
Restrictions on Giving: Does not support individuals or provide endowments.

OTHER THINGS TO KNOW
Publications: Application Guidelines

GRANTS ANALYSIS
Number of Grants: 44
Highest Grant: $15,000
Typical Range: $2,000 to $10,000
Disclosure Period: fiscal year ending September 30, 1992

RECENT GRANTS
15,000 Edgewood
15,000 Mount St. Joseph's Home for Girls
13,000 Easter Seal Society, San Francisco, CA
10,000 Mount St. Joseph-St. Elizabeth, San Francisco, CA
10,000 Performing Arts Workshop
10,000 St. Luke's Hospital Foundation, San Francisco, CA
10,000 St. Mary's Hospital — McAuley Neuropsychiatric Institute
10,000 St. Mary's Hospital — Sister Philipps Clinic
8,000 Community Hospice Foundation, San Francisco, CA
8,000 St. Mary's Foundation/Mcauley Neuropsychiatric Institute, San Francisco, CA

Santa Fe International Corp.

Sales: $1.0 billion
Employees: 4,400
Headquarters: Alhambra, CA
SIC Major Group: Heavy Construction Except Building Construction, Oil & Gas Extraction, and Real Estate

CONTACT
Gordon M. Anderson
President
Santa Fe International Corp.
Two Lincoln Centre
5420 LBJ Freeway, Ste. 1100
Dallas, TX 75240-2648
(214) 701-7300

FINANCIAL SUMMARY
Fiscal Note: Company gives directly. Annual Giving Range: $250,000 to $500,000

CONTRIBUTIONS SUMMARY
Typical Recipients: • *Arts & Humanities:* general • *Civic & Public Affairs:* general • *Education:* general • *Health:* general • *Social Services:* general
Operating Locations: CA (Alhambra, Live Oak), LA (Houma, Lafayette, New Orleans), OK (Oklahoma City, Tulsa), TX (Dallas, Giddings, Houston)

CORP. OFFICERS
Gordon M. Anderson: *B* Los Angeles CA 1932 *ED* Glendale Coll AA 1951; Univ Southern CA BSME 1954 *CURR EMPL* pres: Santa Fe Intl Corp *CORP AFFIL* dir: St Jude Hosp; mem: Intl Assn Oilwell Drilling Contractors *NONPR AFFIL* Young Pres Org

GIVING OFFICERS
Gordon M. Anderson: *CURR EMPL* pres: Santa Fe Intl Corp (see above)

OTHER THINGS TO KNOW
At time of publication, Santa Fe International Corporation was in the process of restructuring and relocating. The contributions program will fall under the authority of the Dallas, TX, office, which will not be in operation until after July 16, 1993. Contact current office in Alhambra, CA, for more information.

Santa Fe Pacific Corp. / Santa Fe Pacific Foundation

Revenue: $2.49 billion
Employees: 15,431
Headquarters: Schaumburg, IL
SIC Major Group: Holding & Other Investment Offices, Oil & Gas Extraction, Railroad Transportation, and Wholesale Trade—Nondurable Goods

CONTACT
Catherine A. Westphal
President
Santa Fe Pacific Fdn.
1700 E Golf Rd.
Schaumburg, IL 60173-5860
(708) 995-6000

FINANCIAL SUMMARY
Recent Giving: $1,000,000 (1993 est.); $1,227,660 (1992); $440,200 (1991)
Assets: $1,225,299 (1992); $2,113,556 (1991); $1,413,021 (1990)
Fiscal Note: Almost all contributions are made through the foundation, but individual departments occasionally make direct grants. Direct gifts are not included for 1991 or 1992 total giving figures.
EIN: 36-6051896

CONTRIBUTIONS SUMMARY
Typical Recipients: • *Arts & Humanities:* arts associations, arts centers, arts funds, arts institutes, community arts, dance, history/historic preservation, libraries, museums/galleries, music, opera, performing arts, theater • *Civic & Public Affairs:* better government, economics, environmental affairs, ethnic/minority organizations, law & justice, public policy, urban & community affairs, women's affairs • *Education:* agricultural education, business education, colleges & universities, continuing education, economic education, education associations, engineering education, health & physical education, medical education, minority education, public education (precollege), science/technology education, social sciences education, special education, student aid • *Health:* medical rehabilitation, medical training, mental health, pediatric health • *Social Services:* aged, child welfare, community service organizations, counseling, disabled, domestic violence, drugs & alcohol, emergency relief, employment/job training, food/clothing distribution, homes, legal aid, shelters/homelessness, volunteer services, youth organizations
Grant Types: capital, employee matching gifts, general support, operating expenses, and scholarship
Nonmonetary Support Types: donated equipment and in-kind services
Note: The foundation does not specify value of nonmonetary support.
Geographic Distribution: company service areas, principally the midwestern, southwestern, and western United States
Operating Locations: AZ, CA (Los Angeles, San Diego, San Francisco), CO, IL (Chicago), KS, MO (Kansas City), NM (Albuquerque), OK, TX (Dallas, Houston)

CORP. OFFICERS
Robert Duncan Krebs: *B* Sacramento CA 1942 *ED* Stanford Univ BA 1964; Harvard Univ MBA 1966 *CURR EMPL* chmn, pres, ceo: Santa Fe Southern Pacific Corp *CORP AFFIL* chmn, ceo: Atchison Topeka & Santa Fe Railway Co; dir: Catellus Devel Corp, Northern Trust Corp, Phelps Dodge Corp, Santa Fe Energy Resources, Santa Fe Indus, Santa Fe Pacific Realty Corp; pres, dir: SFELP Inc *NONPR AFFIL* mem: Assn Am RRs, Kappa Sigma, Northwestern Univ Assn, Phi Beta Kappa, Stanford

Univ Alumni Assn; trust: Glenwood Sch Boys, Lake Forest Coll, Northwestern Meml Hosp Chicago, John G Shedd Aquarium

GIVING OFFICERS
C. R. Ice: dir
Dennis R. Johnson: asst treas
Linda K. McJicker: asst secy, asst treas
Max W. Prosser: vp, secy, treas
Erben J. Schulot: asst treas
I. Toole, Jr.: dir
Catherine A. Westphal: pres, dir
R. T. Zitting: dir

APPLICATION INFORMATION
Initial Approach: *Initial Contact:* proposal with a brief cover letter *Include Information On:* description of the organization, amount requested, copy of IRS tax-exempt ruling, list of organization's officers and directors, narrative detailing organization's purpose and concerns, program objectives and methods by which they will be accomplished, outline of future funding of ongoing projects, other sources of support, recently audited financial statement, budget data *When to Submit:* any time *Note:* Major requests in excess of $20,000 are reviewed annually in the fall if received prior to September 1; proposals received later are considered in the following year.
Restrictions on Giving: In general, the foundation does not support individuals; political, religious, fraternal, or veterans organizations; hospitals; national health organizations or their local chapters; preschool, primary, or secondary schools; goodwill advertising; tax-supported schools or agencies; operating funds of organizations funded by United Way; tours, conferences, dinners, seminars, workshops, testimonials, or endowment funds; grantmaking foundations; or programs beyond stated geographic areas of interest.

OTHER THINGS TO KNOW
In April 1989, Santa Fe Southern Pacific Corporation changed its name to Santa Fe Pacific Corporation as a result of the sale of Southern Pacific Transportation Company to Rio Grande Industries in October 1988. Santa Fe Southern Pacific Foundation was renamed Santa Fe Pacific Foundation in January 1989. Organizations wishing to be considered for future funding should submit a progress report for evaluation and a proposal containing current information. The foundation matches employee gifts to eligible educational and cultural organizations. Private hospitals are also eligible for funds. Gifts are matched on a dollar-for-dollar basis from $25 to $5,000. Foundation limits funds matched to $5,000 per employee per calendar year.

GRANTS ANALYSIS
Total Grants: $1,131,359*
Number of Grants: 155*
Highest Grant: $99,803
Typical Range: $500 to $10,000
Disclosure Period: 1992
Note: Total, number of, and average grant figures exclude $96,301 in employee matching gifts. Recent grants are derived from a 1992 grants list.

RECENT GRANTS
175,805 United Way/Crusade of Mercy, Chicago, IL
100,000 United Way of Greater Topeka, Topeka, KS
99,803 National Merit Scholarship Corporation, Evanston, IL
60,000 National 4-H Educational Awards Program, Chevy Chase, MD
39,500 Future Farmers of America, Madison, WI
35,825 American Indian Science and Engineering Society, Boulder, CO
35,000 Frontier Army Museum, Ft. Leavenworth, KS
22,950 United Way of the Greater Kansas City
20,000 Kansas Independent College Fund, Topeka, KS
20,000 Lake Forest College, Lake Forest, IL

Santa Maria Foundation

CONTACT
Frank M. Vest
Santa Maria Fdn.
Charleston National Plaza, Ste. 1300
PO Box 3969
Charleston, WV 25339

FINANCIAL SUMMARY
Recent Giving: $126,434 (1990); $120,733 (1989); $106,275 (1988)
Assets: $2,374,461 (1990); $2,431,102 (1989); $2,317,577 (1988)
EIN: 13-2938749

CONTRIBUTIONS SUMMARY
Donor(s): Peter Grace, Margaret F. Grace
Typical Recipients: • *Education:* colleges & universities, religious education • *Health:* hospitals • *Religion:* religious organizations • *Social Services:* community service organizations
Grant Types: general support and operating expenses
Geographic Distribution: focus on NY

GIVING OFFICERS
James Philip Bolduc: vp *B* Danville IL 1949 *ED* Northeastern Univ BBA 1972 *CURR EMPL* vp: CT Natural Gas Corp *CORP AFFIL* dir: Affiliated Resources Corp, Hartford Steam Co *NONPR AFFIL* mem: Am Gas Assn, Am Mgmt Assn, New England Gas Assn
J. Peter Grace: pres, dir *B* Manhasset NY 1913 *ED* Yale Univ BA 1936; Yale Univ BA 1936 *CURR EMPL* chmn, dir: WR Grace & Co *CORP AFFIL* chmn: Del Taco Restaurants; chmn, dir: Chemed Corp, El Torito Restaurants; dir: Atlantic Reinsurance Co, Canonie Environ Svcs Corp, Centennial Ins Co, Creative Restaurant Mgmt, DuBois Chemicals, Grace Energy Corp, Milliken & Co, Natl Sanitary Supply Co, Office Warehouse, Omnicare, Restaurant Enterprises Group, Roto-Rooter, Stone & Webster, Universal Furniture Ltd; dir emeritus: Ingersoll-Rand Co; hon dir: Brascan Ltd; trust: Atlantic Mutual Ins Co *NONPR AFFIL* chmn: Radio Free Europe/Radio Liberty Fund; chmn counc natl trusts: Natl Jewish Ctr Immunology Respiratory Medicine Denver; chmn, dir: Americares Fdn; co-chmn: Citizens Against Govt Waste; dir: Boys Clubs Am; emeritus trust: Notre Dame Univ; mem: Counc Foreign Rels; pres, dir: Catholic Youth Org Archdiocese NY; pres, trust: Grace Inst; trust: US Counc Intl Bus
Margaret F. Grace: trust
Patrick P. Grace: dir, secy
Theresa G. Sears: trust

APPLICATION INFORMATION
Initial Approach: Contributes only to preseleced organizations.

GRANTS ANALYSIS
Number of Grants: 27
Highest Grant: $25,000
Typical Range: $400 to $5,000
Disclosure Period: 1990

RECENT GRANTS
25,000 Archdiocese of Malines, Malines, WV
20,000 Trinity College, Deerfield, IL
15,000 Starkey Hearing Foundation, Charleston, WV
12,500 Diocese of Palm Beach, Palm Beach, FL
10,000 Monastery of Bethlehem, Bethlehem, PA
7,000 Mount Desert Medical Center, Charleston, WV
5,000 Theologian-In-Residence Program, Charleston, WV
4,166 Society of the Holy Child, Charleston, WV
3,000 St. Marys Church, Charleston, WV

Sanwa Bank Ltd. New York
Headquarters: New York, NY
SIC Major Group: Depository Institutions and Holding & Other Investment Offices

CONTACT
Kathlene Davidson
Secretary to General Manager
The Sanwa Bank Ltd. New York
Park Ave. Plz.
55 East 52nd St.
24th Fl.
New York, NY 10055
(212) 339-6300

CONTRIBUTIONS SUMMARY
Company makes contributions on a case-by-case basis, primarily supporting local organizations. In 1990, gave $1.25 million to New York University, through parent company. Most contributions are coordinated with parent.

CORP. OFFICERS
Minoru Eda: *CURR EMPL* gen mgr: Sanwa Bank Ltd NY

GIVING OFFICERS
Kathlene Davidson: *CURR EMPL* secy to gen mgr: Sanwa Bank Ltd NY

Sanyo Audio Manufacturing (U.S.A.) Corp.
Sales: $21.0 million
Employees: 250
Headquarters: Milroy, PA
SIC Major Group: Electronic & Other Electrical Equipment

CONTACT
Pam Bailey
Personnel Director
Sanyo Audio Manufacturing (U.S.A.) Corp.
Fisher Park
Milroy, PA 17063
(717) 667-2101

CONTRIBUTIONS SUMMARY
Operating Locations: PA (Milroy)

CORP. OFFICERS
Takeshi Harada: *CURR EMPL* pres: Sanyo Audio Mfg (USA) Corp

Sanyo Fisher Service Corp.
Sales: $30.0 million
Employees: 270
Parent Company: Sanyo Fisher USA Corp.
Headquarters: Compton, CA
SIC Major Group: Miscellaneous Repair Services and Wholesale Trade—Durable Goods

CONTACT
Jose Balbin
Vice President
Sanyo Fisher Service Corp.
1200 West Artesia
Compton, CA 90220
(310) 537-5830

CONTRIBUTIONS SUMMARY
Operating Locations: CA (Compton)

CORP. OFFICERS
K. Tominaga: *CURR EMPL* pres: Sanyo Fisher Svc Corp

Sanyo Fisher U.S.A. Corp.
Sales: $28.0 million
Employees: 110
Headquarters: Little Ferry, NJ
SIC Major Group: Electronic & Other Electrical Equipment and Wholesale Trade—Durable Goods

CONTACT
Frank Iacobelli
Manager, Operations & Personnel
Sanyo Business Systems Corp. & Home Appliance Division
200 Riser Rd.
Little Ferry, NJ 07643
(201) 641-2333

CONTRIBUTIONS SUMMARY
Operating Locations: NJ (Little Ferry)

CORP. OFFICERS
Hiroshi Suzuki: *CURR EMPL* pres: Sanyo Bus Sys Corp & Home Appliance Division

Sanyo Manufacturing Corp.
Sales: $210.0 million
Employees: 500
Parent Company: Sanyo Fisher U.S.A. Corp.
Headquarters: Forrest City, AR
SIC Major Group: Electronic & Other Electrical Equipment and Industrial Machinery & Equipment

CONTACT
Sandra Taylor
Manager, Human Resources
Sanyo Manufacturing Corp.
3333 Sanyo Rd.
Forrest City, AR 72335
(501) 633-5030

FINANCIAL SUMMARY
Fiscal Note: Annual Giving Range: less than $100,000

CONTRIBUTIONS SUMMARY
Company reports 60% of contributions support education; and 40% to civic and public affairs.
Typical Recipients: • *Civic & Public Affairs:* general • *Education:* general
Nonmonetary Support Types: donated equipment and donated products
Operating Locations: AR (Forrest City), CA (Chatsworth)

CORP. OFFICERS
Karou Iue: *CURR EMPL* chmn, dir: Sanyo Mfg Corp
K. Matusumra: *CURR EMPL* pres, dir: Sanyo Mfg Corp

APPLICATION INFORMATION
Initial Approach: Send brief letter of inquiry. There are no deadlines.

Sapirstein-Stone-Weiss Foundation
Former Foundation Name: Jacob Sapirstein Foundation of Cleveland

CONTACT
Mary Kay Incandela
Financial Administrator
Sapirstein-Stone-Weiss Fdn.
10500 American Rd.
Cleveland, OH 44144
(216) 252-7300

FINANCIAL SUMMARY
Recent Giving: $1,314,774 (fiscal 1990); $1,143,854 (fiscal 1989); $1,620,938 (fiscal 1988)
Assets: $17,763,221 (fiscal year ending May 31, 1990); $17,533,121 (fiscal 1989); $17,070,939 (fiscal 1988)
EIN: 34-6548007

CONTRIBUTIONS SUMMARY
Donor(s): The foundation was incorporated in 1952 by the late Jacob Sapirstein.
Typical Recipients: • *Civic & Public Affairs:* philanthropic organizations • *Education:* colleges & universities, private education (precollege), religious education • *Health:* hospitals • *Religion:* religious organizations, synagogues • *Social Services:* child welfare, community centers, community service organizations, homes, united funds
Grant Types: general support
Geographic Distribution: focus on eastern United States

GIVING OFFICERS
Gary Lippe: trust
Irving I. Stone: pres *B* Cleveland OH 1909 *ED* Case Western Reserve Univ *CURR EMPL* fdr/chmn, chmn exec comm, dir: Am Greetings Corp *NONPR AFFIL* chmn: Hebrew Academy Cleveland; dir: Cleveland Inst Art, Jewish Commun Federation, Young Israel Cleveland; dir, life mem: Yeshiva Univ; trust: Simon Wiesenthal Ctr Holocaust Studies; vp: Am Assn Jewish Ed, Am Friends Boys Town Jerusalem, Bur Jewish Ed
Gary Weiss: vp, secy, trust
Jeffrey Weiss: trust
Morry Weiss: vp, treas *B* Czech Republic 1940 *ED* Wayne St Univ; Case Western Reserve Univ BS 1963 *CURR EMPL* chmn, ceo: Am Greetings Corp *CORP AFFIL* dir: Artistic Greetings, McDonald & Co, Natl City Bank, Syratech

APPLICATION INFORMATION
Initial Approach:

The foundation requests applications be made in writing.

The foundation has no deadline for submitting proposals.

Restrictions on Giving: The foundation does not make grants to individuals, or for scholarships, fellowships, or loans.

GRANTS ANALYSIS

Total Grants: $1,314,774

Number of Grants: 55

Highest Grant: $600,000

Typical Range: $1,000 to $15,000

Disclosure Period: fiscal year ending May 31, 1990

Note: Average grant figure does not include the highest grant of $600,000. Recent grants are derived from a fiscal 1990 grants list.

RECENT GRANTS

600,000 Jewish Community Federation, Cleveland, OH

357,895 Hebrew Academy of Cleveland, Cleveland, OH

73,000 Yeshiva University, New York, NY

50,000 Montefiore Medical Center, Bronx, NY

25,000 United Way, Cleveland, OH

20,000 Jewish Community Center, Cleveland, OH

20,000 Ofeg, Wickliffe, OH

12,999 Young Israel Camp Stone, Cleveland, OH

10,000 Bellefaire/Jewish Children's Bureau, Cleveland, OH

10,000 Beth Medrash Govoha of America, Brooklyn, NY

Sara Lee Corp. / Sara Lee Foundation

Sales: $13.24 billion
Employees: 128,000
Headquarters: Chicago, IL
SIC Major Group: Apparel & Other Textile Products, Food & Kindred Products, Textile Mill Products, and Tobacco Products

CONTACT
Robin Tryloff
Executive Director
Sara Lee Fdn.
Three First Natl. Plz.
Chicago, IL 60602-4260
(312) 558-8448
Note: Ms. Tryloff also is senior manager, community relations of the Sara Lee Corporation. The foundation gives only in the Chicago area. Requests for support from organizations in operating communities should be addressed directly to local divisions.

FINANCIAL SUMMARY
Recent Giving: $14,100,000 (fiscal 1993 est.); $12,800,000 (fiscal 1992 approx.); $11,703,339 (fiscal 1991)
Assets: $2,800,000 (fiscal 1990); $4,700,000 (fiscal 1989)
Fiscal Note: Above figures include worldwide cash contributions by the company and foundation. Foundation giving totaled about $5.5 million in 1992 and $5.0 million in 1991. In 1992 contributions by other company departments totaled $149,000 and in 1993 about $200,000. Contact Elynor Williams, vice president, for details.
EIN: 36-3150460

CONTRIBUTIONS SUMMARY
Typical Recipients: • *Arts & Humanities:* arts associations, arts centers, arts festivals, arts institutes, cinema, community arts, dance, ethnic arts, history/historic preservation, libraries, museums/galleries, music, opera, performing arts, theater, visual arts • *Civic & Public Affairs:* better government, civil rights, economic development, ethnic/minority organizations, housing, law & justice, philanthropic organizations, urban & community affairs, women's affairs, zoos/botanical gardens • *Education:* arts education, business education, career/vocational education, colleges & universities, international exchange, literacy, minority education • *Health:* health organizations • *International:* international organizations • *Science:* observatories & planetariums • *Social Services:* aged, child welfare, community centers, community service organizations, counseling, day care, disabled, domestic violence, drugs

& alcohol, employment/job training, family planning, family services, food/clothing distribution, homes, legal aid, refugee assistance, shelters/homelessness, united funds, volunteer services, youth organizations
Grant Types: award, employee matching gifts, general support, multiyear/continuing support, operating expenses, project, and seed money
Nonmonetary Support Types: donated equipment, donated products, in-kind services, loaned employees, loaned executives, and workplace solicitation
Note: Above figures do not include product donations, valued at $7.0 million in 1992, $5.1 million in 1991, and $2.3 million in 1989. See "Other Things You Should Know" for more details.
Geographic Distribution: Chicago metropolitan area and where divisions operate; limited support for national organizations
Operating Locations: AL (Athens, Florence, Montgomery, Scottsboro, Slocomb), AR (Clarksville, Little Rock), AZ (Glendale), CA (Hayward, LaMirada, Los Angeles, Modesto, San Diego, San Francisco, San Lorenzo), CT (Stamford), DE (Dover), FL (Miami, Pinellas Park, Tampa, Tampa), GA (Atlanta, Calhoun, Cartersville, Eastman, Eatonton, Fitzgerald, Midway, Milledgeville, Newnan, Raburn Gap, Wrightsville), IA (Des Moines, New Hampton, Storm Lake), IL (Batavia, Bensenville, Champaign, Chicago, Chicago, Elk Grove Village, Schaumburg), IN (Dubois, Indianapolis), KS (Lenexa), KY (Alexandria), LA (New Orleans), MI (Detroit, Detroit, Grand Rapids, Livonia, Traverse City, Zeeland), MN (Minneapolis), MO (Kansas City, St. Joseph, St. Louis), MS (Forest, Jackson, Olive Branch, West Point), NC (Advance, Asheboro, Asheville, Carey, Charlotte, Clayton, Dunn, Eden, Forest City, High Point, Jefferson, Kernersville, Laurel Hill, Lumberton, Maxton, Mocksville, Morganton, Mt. Airy, Rockingham, Rural Hill, Sanford, Sparta, Tarboro, Weaverville, Winston-Salem, Yadkinville), ND (Fargo), NJ (Secaucus), NM (Las Cruces),

NV (Henderson), NY (New York, Perry, Rochester), OH (Cincinnati, Columbus, Valley View), OR (Portland), PA (Douglassville, Philadelphia, Pittsburgh), SC (Barnwell, Bennettsville, Charleston, Columbia, Conway, Florence, Gaffrey, Greenville, Harsville, Marion), TN (Cordova, Lavergne, Martin, Memphis, Mountain City, Nasville, Newbern), TX (Dallas), VA (Galax, Gretna, Hillsville, Martinsville, Rocky Mount, Salem), WA (Algona, Tacoma), WI (Greenbay, Milwaukee, New London)
Note: Company also operates internationally with plants in Australia, England, the Netherlands, Canada, France, and Spain.

CORP. OFFICERS
John H. Bryan: *B* West Point MS 1936 *ED* Rhodes Coll BA; Rhodes Coll BBA 1958; MS St Univ Sch Bus Admin MBA 1960 *CURR EMPL* chmn, ceo, dir: Sara Lee Corp *CORP AFFIL* dir: Amoco Corp, First Chicago Corp, First Natl Bank Chicago *NONPR AFFIL* dir: Un Way Crusade Mercy; mem: Bus Counc, Bus Roundtable, Grocery Mfrs Assn; mem bus adv counc: Chicago Urban League; mem fine arts comm: US Dept St; mem natl corps comm: Un Negro Coll Fund; trust: Art Inst Chicago, Comm Econ Devel, Rush-Presbyterian-St Lukes Med Ctr, Univ Chicago; dir: Catalyst, Natl Womens Econ Alliance
Paul Fulton: *CURR EMPL* pres, dir: Sara Lee Corp

GIVING OFFICERS
John H. Bryan: dir *CURR EMPL* chmn, ceo, dir: Sara Lee Corp (see above)
David B. Ellis: asst treas
Merri Ex: program consultant
Paul Fulton: dir *CURR EMPL* pres, dir: Sara Lee Corp (see above)
Sonya Jackson: asst dir
Robert Lee Lauer: pres, dir *B* Crook CO 1933 *ED* Bowling Green St Univ BS 1956 *CURR EMPL* vp (corp affairs): Sara Lee Corp *NONPR AFFIL* chmn: Grocery Mfrs Am; dir: Advertising Counc, Arthur Page Soc, Chicago Equity Fund, Intl Theatre Festival Chicago, Pub Affs Counc, Second Harvest Natl Food Bank Network; mem: Bus Comm Arts

NY City, Econ Club Chicago, Pub Rels Soc Am
William Lipsman: asst secy
Gina Mullen: asst dir
Michael E. Murphy: dir *B* Winchester MA 1936 *ED* Boston Coll BS 1958; Harvard Univ Sch Bus Admin MBA 1962 *CURR EMPL* exec vp, dir: Sara Lee Corp *CORP AFFIL* corp controller, vp admin: Hanes Corp; dir: GATX Corp *NONPR AFFIL* dir: Lyric Opera Chicago, Northwestern Meml Hosp; mem: Beta Gamma Sigma, Fin Execs Inst, Hoboken Chamber Commerce, Intl Platform Assn, Miami Chamber Commerce, Quiment Scholar Alumni Group, Un Nations Assn, Winston-Salem Chamber Commerce; mem, dir: Natl Assn Mfrs; trust: Boston Coll
Gordon Harold Newman: vp, secy *B* Sioux City IA 1933 *ED* Univ IA 1955; Univ IA JD 1961 *CURR EMPL* sr vp, secy, gen coun: Sara Lee Corp *NONPR AFFIL* mem: Am Bar Assn, Am Soc Corp Secys, Chicago Bar Assn, IL Bar Assn, Northwestern Univ Assocs
Robin Tryloff: exec dir
Elynor A. Williams: dir

APPLICATION INFORMATION
Initial Approach: *Initial Contact:* brief letter or telephone call requesting annual contributions report and application; to apply to divisions, call local division for information *Include Information On:* along with application, submit most recently audited financial statement, current operating budget, annual report (or other materials summarizing programs), list of directors and their affiliations, proof of tax-exempt status, list of public and private support of $500 or more received during the most recently completed fiscal year *When to Submit:* no later than first working day of March, September, or December for consideration at quarterly meetings held during those months *Note:* Proposals must be submitted on the foundation's application form.
Restrictions on Giving: The following are not eligible for grants: capital and endowment campaigns; individuals; organizations with a limited constituency, such as fraternal or veterans groups; organizations that limit services to members of

one religious group or seek to propagate a particular belief or creed; political organizations or groups promoting one ideological view; elementary or secondary schools, either public or private; single-disease organizations; tickets to dinners and other events; goodwill advertising in yearbooks or dinner programs; or national or international organizations with limited relationship to local Sara Lee operations.

OTHER THINGS TO KNOW
Sara Lee's contributions program is decentralized. In 1992, about two-fifths of total contributions are made by the foundation, which is chiefly the philanthropic vehicle for the Chicago corporate office. The remainder was distributed by divisions, which administer their own programs, including nonmonetary giving and volunteer services.
Organizations should not submit a contribution application more than once in any 12-month period. Grants are not automatically renewed, and recipients desiring renewed support should submit a request approximately two months prior to the anniversary of their grants. A renewal request should include the organization's most recent audited financial statement, current year's operating budget, updated board of directors list, and summary of how the previous year's grant was used. An application form is not necessary for grant renewal requests. Sara Lee maintains a policy that annual contributions shall represent at least 2% of domestic pretax income.
At the corporate and division levels, company forms active partnerships with particularly effective local organizations and encourages employee involvement.

GRANTS ANALYSIS
Total Grants: $5,511,000*
Number of Grants: 306
Highest Grant: $348,000
Typical Range: $1,000 to $15,000
Disclosure Period: fiscal year ending June 27, 1992
Note: Total grant figure represents foundation giving only. Average grant figure excludes $1,300,000 in matching gifts, a

$348,000 grant, and $150,000 in foundation-administered programs. Asset figure is for 1990. Recent grants are derived from a fiscal 1992 grants list.

RECENT GRANTS
348,000 United Way/Crusade of Mercy, Chicago, IL — corporate support for the Chicago metropolitan area's 1991 campaign
135,000 Art Institute of Chicago, Chicago, IL — first payment of a two-year, $200,000 grant for The New World
135,000 Museum of Contemporary Art, Chicago, IL — first payment of a two-year, $250,000 grant to support the Museum's 25th anniversary exhibition, Art at the Armory: Occupied Territory, and for operating support
120,000 Lyric Opera of Chicago, Chicago, IL — first payment of a two-year, $200,000 grant for sponsorship of Mefistofele and for operating support
85,000 Chicago Historical Society, Chicago, IL — final payment of a two-year, $150,000 grant to sponsor the exhibit A City Comes of Age: Chicago in the 1890s, and for general operating support
75,000 Ballet Chicago, Chicago, IL — first payment of a two-year, $150,000 grant for the development of an original full-length ballet of Hansel and Gretel
75,000 Wisdom Bridge Theatre, Chicago, IL — to sponsor the presentation of The Great Gatsby
51,000 Youth Guidance, Chicago, IL — to support social services at Harper High School, Sara Lee Corporation's "adopted" school
50,000 Chicago Children's Museum, Chicago, IL — for a sponsorship of the new OAXACA Village exhibit which pre-

sented information about life in a rural Mexican town
50,000 Clark Atlanta University, Atlanta, GA — to provide scholarships for MBA students at the School of Business

Sara Lee Hosiery
Employees: 300
Parent Company: Sara Lee Corp.
Parent Sales: $13.32 billion
Headquarters: Winston-Salem, NC
SIC Major Group: Textile Mill Products

CONTACT
Larry Willard
Manager, General Accounting
Sara Lee Hosiery
5650 University Pkwy.
Winston-Salem, NC 27105
(919) 519-3893

FINANCIAL SUMMARY
Recent Giving: $350,000 (1992 approx.); $300,000 (1991)

CONTRIBUTIONS SUMMARY
Typical Recipients: • *Arts & Humanities:* arts appreciation, arts associations, arts funds, community arts, general, history/historic preservation, libraries, literary arts, museums/galleries, music, performing arts, public broadcasting, visual arts • *Civic & Public Affairs:* better government, business/free enterprise, civil rights, consumer affairs, economic development, environmental affairs, ethnic/minority organizations, general, philanthropic organizations, urban & community affairs • *Education:* business education, career/vocational education, community & junior colleges, education funds, elementary education, general, liberal arts education, literacy, minority education, preschool education, private education (precollege) • *Health:* emergency/ambulance services, general, health organizations, hospices, hospitals, public health • *Religion:* churches • *Social Services:* aged, animal protection, child welfare, community service organizations, counseling, day care, disabled, domestic violence, drugs & alcohol, emergency relief, family services,

food/clothing distribution, general, refugee assistance, shelters/homelessness, united funds, volunteer services, youth organizations
Grant Types: award, capital, emergency, employee matching gifts, fellowship, general support, operating expenses, project, and seed money
Geographic Distribution: in headquarters and operating communities
Operating Locations: AK (Clarksville), CA (Cerritos), IL (Champaign), MS (Jackson, Olive Branch), NC (Lumberton, Rockingham, Winston-Salem, Yadkinville), NM (Mesilla), NV (Henderson), SC (Bennettsville, Florence, Hartsville, Marion), VA (Salem)

CORP. OFFICERS
Robert Moore: *CURR EMPL* cfo: Sara Lee Hosiery
John Piazza: *CURR EMPL* ceo: Sara Lee Hosiery

GIVING OFFICERS
Larry Willard: *CURR EMPL* mgr gen acct: Sara Lee Hosiery

APPLICATION INFORMATION
Initial Approach: *Initial Contact:* letter of inquiry *Include Information On:* a description of organization, amount requested, purpose of funds sought, recently audited financial statement, and proof of tax-exempt status *When to Submit:* any time
Restrictions on Giving: The company does not support national or statewide United Way recipients.

GRANTS ANALYSIS
Typical Range: $50 to $5,000

Sargent Electric Co.
Revenue: $71.0 million
Employees: 800
Headquarters: Pittsburgh, PA
SIC Major Group: Special Trade Contractors

CONTACT
Frederic B. Sargent
Chief Executive Officer
Sargent Electric Co.
P. O. Box 30
Pittsburgh, PA 15230
(412) 391-0588

FINANCIAL SUMMARY
Fiscal Note: Annual Giving Range: $100,000 to $250,000

CONTRIBUTIONS SUMMARY
Support goes to local education, human service, arts, and civic organizations.
Typical Recipients: • *Arts & Humanities:* general • *Civic & Public Affairs:* general • *Education:* general • *Social Services:* general
Geographic Distribution: headquarters and operating locations
Operating Locations: PA (Pittsburgh)

CORP. OFFICERS
Peter Hannaway: *CURR EMPL* pres: Sargent Electric Co
Frederic B. Sargent: *CURR EMPL* ceo: Sargent Electric Co

APPLICATION INFORMATION
Initial Approach: Send brief letter of inquiry, including a description of the organization, amount requested, purpose of funds sought, audited financial statement, and proof of tax-exempt status. There are no deadlines.

GRANTS ANALYSIS
Typical Range: $1,000 to $2,500

Sargent Foundation, Newell B.

CONTACT
Newell B. Sargent
Trustee
Newell B. Sargent Fdn.
821 Pulliam Ave.
Worland, WY 82401

FINANCIAL SUMMARY
Recent Giving: $37,430 (fiscal 1991); $128,382 (fiscal 1990); $119,831 (fiscal 1989)
Assets: $4,016,114 (fiscal year ending October 31, 1991); $3,122,386 (fiscal 1990); $2,773,312 (fiscal 1989)
Gifts Received: $400,000 (fiscal 1991); $600,000 (fiscal 1990); $800,000 (fiscal 1989)
Fiscal Note: In 1991, contributions were received from Newell B. Sargent.
EIN: 83-0271536

CONTRIBUTIONS SUMMARY
Donor(s): Newell B. Sargent
Typical Recipients: • *Arts & Humanities:* arts festivals, community arts, music • *Civic & Public Affairs:* economic development, law & justice, municipalities, urban & community affairs • *Education:* colleges & universities, community & junior colleges • *Health:* hospitals, pediatric health • *Religion:* churches • *Social Services:* disabled, homes
Grant Types: general support and scholarship
Geographic Distribution: focus on WY, with emphasis on Worland

GIVING OFFICERS
Douglas W. Morrison: trust
Newell B. Sargent: trust
Charles W. Smith: trust

APPLICATION INFORMATION
Initial Approach: Send brief letter describing program. There are no deadlines.

GRANTS ANALYSIS
Number of Grants: 39
Highest Grant: $5,810
Typical Range: $500 to $1,000
Disclosure Period: fiscal year ending October 31, 1991

RECENT GRANTS
5,810	City of Worland, Worland, WY
5,000	Friends of Washakie County Museum, Worland, WY
2,000	Brigham Young University, Provo, UT
2,000	Casper Community College, Casper, WY
2,000	University of Wyoming, Laramie, WY
1,500	Central Wyoming Rescue Mission, Casper, WY
1,500	Northwest Community College, Powell, WY
1,500	Primary Children's Hospital, Salt Lake City, UT
1,000	Northwest Community College, Powell, WY
1,000	University of Wyoming, Laramie, WY

Sarkeys Foundation

CONTACT
Cheri D. Cartwright
Assistant Secretary and Director of Grants
Sarkeys Foundation
116 South Peters, Rm. 219
Norman, OK 73069
(405) 364-3703

FINANCIAL SUMMARY
Recent Giving: $2,500,000 (fiscal 1993 est.); $2,617,017 (fiscal 1992); $2,498,000 (fiscal 1991)
Assets: $63,000,000 (fiscal 1993 est.); $63,313,629 (fiscal year ending November 30, 1992); $58,000,000 (fiscal 1991 approx.); $49,490,520 (fiscal 1990)
EIN: 73-0736496

CONTRIBUTIONS SUMMARY
Donor(s): The foundation was established in 1962, with S. J. Sarkeys as the donor.
Typical Recipients: • *Arts & Humanities:* arts institutes, dance, libraries, museums/galleries, music, theater • *Civic & Public Affairs:* environmental affairs, housing, philanthropic organizations, zoos/botanical gardens • *Education:* agricultural education, colleges & universities, literacy, medical education, public education (precollege), student aid • *Health:* hospitals, medical rehabilitation, outpatient health care delivery, single-disease health associations • *Religion:* religious organizations • *Social Services:* child welfare, community service organizations, disabled, employment/job training, family services, food/clothing distribution, homes, youth organizations
Grant Types: capital, challenge, professorship, project, and research
Geographic Distribution: Oklahoma

GIVING OFFICERS
Richard Bell: trust
Cheri D. Cartwright: asst secy-treas, dir of grants
Richard Hefler: mgr
Jane Joyroe: vp, trust
Joseph Morris: secy, treas, trust
Robert Rennie: trust
Robert Rizley: pres, trust
Paul Sharp: trust *CURR EMPL* regents prof emeritus:

Univ OK *NONPR AFFIL* dir: Cleveland County Red Cross, Cleveland County YMCA; mem: Disciples Of Christ Church, Phi Alpha Theta, Phi Beta Kappa, Phi Delta Kappa, Phi Kappa Phi, Pi Gamma Nu
Lee Anne Wilson: trust

APPLICATION INFORMATION

Initial Approach:
Proposals sould be single-spaced, unbound, stapled, and printed on only one side of white, 8 1/2-inch by 11-inch paper.
Proposals should contain the name, address, phone number, contact person, and brief history of the organization; copy of the IRS determination letter of tax-exempt status; names of principal officers, directors, and key staff; budget for the project including amount requested as well as other sources of support, including a list of all outstanding requests for funds; and a copy of organization's most recent audit, if available, or a financial report or organizational budget. Include a three- to four-page description of the project with a description of the organization's activities; problem or need project will address; outline of project including goals, objectives, activities, and timetable; geographical area and number of people to be served by project; description of similar projects; evaluation process; source of funds in operating budget and an indication of approximately what percentage of that budget is spent on fund raising; and plans for continuing project after grant ends. Applications should be submitted by February 15 or August 15.
The trustees meet in January, April, July, and October. Grant proposals are considered at the April and October meetings. Organizations whose applications are accepted for inclusion on the agenda for the April or October meetings will be notified and required to submit additional copies of their proposals.
Restrictions on Giving: The foundation normally does not fund local programs appropriately financed within the community, or direct mail solicitations. The foundation makes no grants to individuals, nor does

it take responsibility for permanent financing of a program.

OTHER THINGS TO KNOW
Publications: guidelines for proposals brochure

GRANTS ANALYSIS
Total Grants: $2,617,017
Number of Grants: 74
Highest Grant: $400,000
Typical Range: $10,000 to $50,000
Disclosure Period: fiscal year ending November 30, 1992
Note: Recent grants are derived from a fiscal 1992 grants list.

RECENT GRANTS
250,000 University of Tulsa, Tulsa, OK
230,000 University of Oklahoma Foundation, Norman, OK
200,000 Sutton Avian Research Center
200,000 Sutton Avian Research Center
100,000 Billy Graham Evangelistic Association
100,000 St. Simeon's Episcopal Home
84,000 Phillips University, Enid, OK
83,000 Phillips University, Enid, OK
60,000 Norman Public School Foundation, Norman, OK
56,400 Will Rogers Heritage Trust

Sarofim Foundation

CONTACT
Fayez Sarofim
Trustee
Sarofim Fdn.
Two Houston Center, Ste. 2907
Houston, TX 77010
(713) 654-4484

FINANCIAL SUMMARY
Recent Giving: $225,000 (fiscal 1991); $270,000 (fiscal 1990); $258,850 (fiscal 1989)
Assets: $6,576,229 (fiscal year ending June 30, 1991); $6,079,239 (fiscal 1990); $5,261,210 (fiscal 1989)
EIN: 23-7065248

CONTRIBUTIONS SUMMARY
Donor(s): Fayez Sarofim, Louisa Stude Sarofim
Typical Recipients: • *Education:* private education (precollege) • *International:* foreign educational institutions
Grant Types: general support

Geographic Distribution: focus on Houston, TX

GIVING OFFICERS
E. Rudge Allen, Jr.: trust
Fayez Shalaby Sarofim: trust *B* Cairo Egypt 1929 *ED* Univ CA Berkeley; Harvard Univ Sch Bus Admin *CURR EMPL* fdr, pres, dir: Fayez Sarofim & Co *CORP AFFIL* dir: Argonaut Group, Callahan Mining Corp, Imperial Holly Corp, Mesa, Teledyne, Unitrin
Louisa Stude Sarofim: trust *ED* Smith Coll

APPLICATION INFORMATION
Initial Approach: Send brief letter of inquiry describing program or project. There are no deadlines.

GRANTS ANALYSIS
Number of Grants: 1
Highest Grant: $225,000
Disclosure Period: fiscal year ending June 30, 1991

RECENT GRANTS
225,000 Awty International School, Houston, TX

Saroyan Foundation, William

CONTACT
Robert Setrakian
Trustee
William Saroyan Fdn.
1905 Baker St.
San Francisco, CA 94115-2012
(415) 433-9400

FINANCIAL SUMMARY
Recent Giving: $5,017 (fiscal 1988)
Assets: $2,323,138 (fiscal year ending September 30, 1990); $2,223,751 (fiscal 1989); $2,211,310 (fiscal 1988)
EIN: 94-1657684

CONTRIBUTIONS SUMMARY
Donor(s): William Saroyan
Typical Recipients: • *Arts & Humanities:* libraries
Grant Types: general support

GIVING OFFICERS
Anthony Melchior Frank: trust *B* Berlin Germany 1931 *ED* Dartmouth Coll BA 1953; Dartmouth Coll MBA 1954 *CORP AFFIL* chmn, dir: CA Housing Fin Agency; dir: Al-

lianz Ins Co, Am Fed Home Loan Bank San Francisco; trust, treas: Blue Shield CA *NONPR AFFIL* bd overseers: Tuck Sch; chmn bd Visitors: Univ CA Los Angeles Sch Architecture & Planning; mem: Chief Execs Org, World Bus Forum; trust: Am Conservatory Theater
Harold Howard Haak: trust *B* Madison WI 1935 *ED* Univ WI BA 1957; Univ WI MA 1958; Princeton Univ PhD 1963 *NONPR AFFIL* dir: Fdn 21st Century, Fresno Econ Devel Corp; mem: Army Adv Panel ROTC Affs, NCAA Pres Comm; mem bd visitors: Air Univ; pres: CA St Univ (Fresno)
James D. Hart: trust
Cosette Saroyan: trust
Robert Setrakian: trust

APPLICATION INFORMATION
Initial Approach: Send brief letter describing program. There are no deadlines.

GRANTS ANALYSIS
Disclosure Period: fiscal year ending September 30, 1990
Note: No grants were provided in 1990.

Sasco Foundation

CONTACT
Uwe Lindner
Vice President
Sasco Fdn.
c/o Manufacturers Hanover Trust Co.
270 Park Ave.
New York, NY 10017
(212) 270-9453

FINANCIAL SUMMARY
Recent Giving: $226,375 (1991); $213,000 (1989); $239,000 (1988)
Assets: $5,318,432 (1991); $4,494,759 (1989); $4,157,181 (1988)
EIN: 13-6046567

CONTRIBUTIONS SUMMARY
Donor(s): the late Leila E. Riegel, Katherine R. Emory
Typical Recipients: • *Arts & Humanities:* history/historic preservation, libraries • *Civic & Public Affairs:* environmental affairs • *Education:* colleges & universities, private education (precollege)
• *Health:* hospitals, medical re-

search, nursing services • *Religion:* churches • *Social Services:* child welfare, community service organizations, family planning, family services, united funds, youth organizations
Grant Types: general support
Geographic Distribution: focus on NY, CT, and ME

GIVING OFFICERS
Manufacturers Hanover Trust Company: trust

APPLICATION INFORMATION
Initial Approach: Send cover letter and full proposal. Deadline is November 30.
Restrictions on Giving: Does not support individuals.

GRANTS ANALYSIS
Number of Grants: 62
Highest Grant: $20,000
Typical Range: $500 to $5,000
Disclosure Period: 1991

RECENT GRANTS
20,000 Trion School System
10,000 Buckley School, Sherman Oaks, CA
10,000 Central Park Conservancy, New York, NY
10,000 Maine Coast Heritage Trust, Northeast Harbor, ME
10,000 Planned Parenthood
5,000 Channel 13, New York, NY
5,000 Connecticut Audubon Society, Fairfield, CT
5,000 Nature Conservancy, Long Island, NY
5,000 Orbis
5,000 Trinity Parish, New York, NY

Sattler Beneficial Trust, Daniel A. and Edna J.

CONTACT
Daniel A. and Edna J. Sattler Beneficial Trust
200 East Carrillo St., Ste. 400
Santa Barbara, CA 93101
962-0011

FINANCIAL SUMMARY
Recent Giving: $120,000 (fiscal 1991); $103,000 (fiscal 1990); $159,402 (fiscal 1989)
Assets: $2,491,008 (fiscal year ending June 30, 1991);

$2,523,741 (fiscal 1990); $2,342,384 (fiscal 1989)
EIN: 23-7127370

CONTRIBUTIONS SUMMARY
Donor(s): the late Edna J. Relyea

Typical Recipients: • *Civic & Public Affairs:* philanthropic organizations • *Education:* private education (precollege) • *Health:* medical research, single-disease health associations • *Religion:* churches • *Social Services:* disabled, drugs & alcohol, homes

Grant Types: general support
Geographic Distribution: focus on the Santa Barbara, CA, area

GIVING OFFICERS
H. Clarke Gaines: trust
Robert M Jones: trust
Cecil I. Smith: trust

APPLICATION INFORMATION
Initial Approach: Contributes only to preselected organizations.
Restrictions on Giving: Does not support individuals.

GRANTS ANALYSIS
Number of Grants: 7
Highest Grant: $23,600
Typical Range: $11,800 to $23,600
Disclosure Period: fiscal year ending June 30, 1991

RECENT GRANTS
23,600 Cancer Foundation of Santa Barbara, Santa Barbara, CA
23,600 Santa Barbara Foundation, Santa Barbara, CA
23,600 St. Vincents, Santa Barbara, CA
11,800 Guide Dogs for the Blind, San Rafael, CA
11,800 Hillside House, Santa Barbara, CA
11,800 Marymount School of Santa Barbara, Santa Barbara, CA
11,800 Santa Barbara Council on Alcoholism, Santa Barbara, CA
2,000 California Province of Society of Jesus, Los Gatos, CA

Saturno Foundation

CONTACT
Eugene I. Ranghiasci
Saturno Fdn.
c/o Wells Fargo Bank, N.A.
PO Box 63954
San Francisco, CA 94163
(818) 304-3422

FINANCIAL SUMMARY
Recent Giving: $275,211 (fiscal 1991); $52,091 (fiscal 1989); $211,784 (fiscal 1988)
Assets: $6,753,098 (fiscal year ending October 31, 1991); $5,453,233 (fiscal 1989); $5,075,162 (fiscal 1988)
Gifts Received: $260,008 (fiscal 1990)
EIN: 94-6073765

CONTRIBUTIONS SUMMARY
Donor(s): the late Joseph Saturno, Victor Saturno

Typical Recipients: • *International:* international organizations • *Social Services:* child welfare, community service organizations, homes, youth organizations

Grant Types: general support and operating expenses
Geographic Distribution: focus on Italy and CA

GIVING OFFICERS
Wells Fargo Bank, N.A.: trust

APPLICATION INFORMATION
Initial Approach: Send brief letter of inquiry describing program or project. There are no deadlines.
Restrictions on Giving: Does not support individuals or provide scholarships or loans.

GRANTS ANALYSIS
Number of Grants: 6
Highest Grant: $82,563
Typical Range: $13,000 to $55,000
Disclosure Period: fiscal year ending October 31, 1991

RECENT GRANTS
82,563 Italian Red Cross, San Francisco, CA
82,563 Sierra Nevada Red Cross, Reno, NV
55,042 Italian Welfare Agency, San Francisco, CA
27,521 American Red Cross, Oakland, CA
13,761 American Red Cross, San Francisco, CA

13,761 Carina, San Francisco, CA

Saul Foundation, Joseph E. & Norma G.

CONTACT
Joseph Saul
President
Joseph E. & Norma G. Saul Fdn.
c/o Saul Partners
630 Fifth Avenue, Ste. 2518
New York, NY 10111
(212) 969-9040

FINANCIAL SUMMARY
Recent Giving: $559,600 (fiscal 1990); $230,000 (fiscal 1989); $299,500 (fiscal 1988)
Assets: $2,982,571 (fiscal year ending September 30, 1990); $3,322,554 (fiscal 1989); $3,237,978 (fiscal 1988)
EIN: 13-3254180

CONTRIBUTIONS SUMMARY
Donor(s): Joseph E. Saul

Typical Recipients: • *Arts & Humanities:* museums/galleries • *Education:* colleges & universities • *Religion:* religious organizations • *Social Services:* aged, community service organizations, homes

Grant Types: general support

GIVING OFFICERS
Lynn T. Fischer: trust
Andrew Marshall Saul: dir *B* New York NY 1946 *ED* Univ PA BS 1968 *CURR EMPL* ptnr: Saul Ptnrs *CORP AFFIL* dir: Cache Inc *NONPR AFFIL* trust: Fed Jewish Philanthropies, Long Island Jewish Hillside Med Ctr, Mt Sinai Med Ctr, Un Jewish Appeal Fed
Joseph E. Saul: pres, treas
Norma G. Saul: secy, trust
Sidney J. Silberman: trust

APPLICATION INFORMATION
Initial Approach: The foundation reports it only makes contributions to preselected charitable organizations.

GRANTS ANALYSIS
Number of Grants: 8
Highest Grant: $150,000
Typical Range: $2,500 to $55,000
Disclosure Period: fiscal year ending September 30, 1990

RECENT GRANTS

250,000 University of Pennsylvania, Philadelphia, PA
150,000 Jewish Home and Hospital for the Aged, New York, NY
100,000 Solomon R. Guggenheim Museum, New York, NY
55,000 New York City Ballet, New York, NY
2,500 North Shore University Hospital, Manhasset, NY
1,000 Anti-Defamation League, New York, NY
1,000 United States Equestrian Team, Gladstone, NJ
100 Boys Harbor, New York, NY

Saunders Charitable Foundation, Helen M.

CONTACT
Coleman H. Casey
Trustee
Helen M. Saunders Charitable Fdn.
c/o Shipman and Goodwin
One American Row
Hartford, CT 06103-2819
(203) 251-5000

FINANCIAL SUMMARY
Recent Giving: $109,954 (fiscal 1992); $122,481 (fiscal 1991); $140,675 (fiscal 1990)
Assets: $3,101,724 (fiscal year ending June 30, 1992); $2,987,605 (fiscal 1991); $2,996,938 (fiscal 1990)
EIN: 06-6284362

CONTRIBUTIONS SUMMARY
Typical Recipients: • *Arts & Humanities:* arts associations, music, performing arts, public broadcasting • *Education:* colleges & universities, education associations, education funds • *Health:* hospitals • *Religion:* churches
Grant Types: endowment and general support
Geographic Distribution: focus on CT, with emphasis on Hartford

GIVING OFFICERS
Coleman H. Casey: trust

APPLICATION INFORMATION
Initial Approach: Send brief letter describing program. There are no deadlines.
Restrictions on Giving: Does not support individuals.

OTHER THINGS TO KNOW
Publications: Application Guidelines

GRANTS ANALYSIS
Number of Grants: 62
Highest Grant: $17,000
Typical Range: $500 to $2,500
Disclosure Period: fiscal year ending June 30, 1992

RECENT GRANTS
17,000 Wadsworth Atheneum, Hartford, CT — endowment pledge
10,000 Lasell College, Newton, MA — annual giving
6,125 Lasell College, Newton, MA — challenge grant
6,000 Hartford Symphony Orchestra, Hartford, CT — Capriccio newsletter for 91-92
5,000 Hartford Hospital, Hartford, CT — for the Campaign for Hartford Hospital
4,125 University of Hartford, Hartford, CT
3,500 Greater Hartford Arts Council, Hartford, CT — annual operating gift
2,500 Connecticut Association of Independent Schools, Madison, WI
2,500 Hartford College for Women, Hartford, CT — University of Hartford Affiliation
2,500 Horace Bushnell Memorial Hall, Hartford, CT — annual fund

Saunders Foundation

CONTACT
James M. Kelly
Vice President
Saunders Fdn.
c/o First Florida Bank, Trust Dept.
PO Box 31265
Tampa, FL 33601
(813) 224-1861

FINANCIAL SUMMARY
Recent Giving: $685,079 (1991); $635,427 (1989); $499,127 (1988)
Assets: $10,212,870 (1991); $9,289,825 (1989); $9,320,741 (1988)
EIN: 59-6152326

CONTRIBUTIONS SUMMARY
Donor(s): the late William N. Saunders and Ruby Lee Saunders
Typical Recipients: • *Arts & Humanities:* arts centers, community arts, history/historic preservation, museums/galleries, performing arts, public broadcasting • *Civic & Public Affairs:* urban & community affairs, zoos/botanical gardens • *Education:* colleges & universities, education funds, medical education • *Health:* geriatric health, hospices, medical research • *Religion:* churches, religious organizations • *Social Services:* homes, united funds, youth organizations
Grant Types: capital, operating expenses, project, and scholarship
Geographic Distribution: focus on western FL

GIVING OFFICERS
Michael G. Emmanuel: secy, dir
James M. Kelly: vp, treas, dir
Herbert G. McKay: pres, dir
Solon F. O'Neal, Jr.: dir

APPLICATION INFORMATION
Initial Approach: Application form required. There are no deadlines. Board meets first Wednesday of each month.

OTHER THINGS TO KNOW
Publications: Application Guidelines

GRANTS ANALYSIS
Number of Grants: 43
Highest Grant: $100,000
Typical Range: $10,000 to $20,000
Disclosure Period: 1991

RECENT GRANTS
100,000 University of South Florida Foundation, Tampa, FL
50,000 Lowry Park Zoological Society, Tampa, FL — construction of amphitheater
50,000 Museum of Science and Industry, Tampa, FL — construction of planetarium
50,000 Tampa Bay Performing Arts Center, Tampa, FL
50,000 University of Tampa, Tampa, FL
40,000 Suncoast Ronald McDonald House, Tampa, FL
30,000 Eckerd College, St. Petersburg, FL — purchase of database
25,000 Community Foundation of Greater Tampa, Tampa, FL
25,000 Florida Orchestra, Tampa, FL
25,000 Metropolitan Ministries, Tampa, FL

Savannah Electric & Power Co.

Assets: $352.5 million
Employees: 672
Parent Company: Southern Co.
Headquarters: Savannah, GA
SIC Major Group: Electric, Gas & Sanitary Services

CONTACT
E. Olin Veale
Senior Vice President & CFO
Savannah Electric & Power Co.
PO Box 968
Savannah, GA 31402
(912) 232-7171

CONTRIBUTIONS SUMMARY
Operating Locations: GA (Savannah)

CORP. OFFICERS
Arthur M. Gignilliat, Jr.: *CURR EMPL* pres, ceo: Savannah Electric & Power Co

Savin Corp.

Sales: $312.2 million
Employees: 1,087
Headquarters: Stamford, CT
SIC Major Group:
Miscellaneous Repair Services
and Wholesale
Trade—Durable Goods

CONTACT

Rita Warford
Manager, Human Resources
Savin Corp.
Nine West Broad St.
PO Box 10270
Stamford, CT 06904-2270
(203) 967-5000

FINANCIAL SUMMARY

Fiscal Note: Annual Giving
Range: less than $100,000

CONTRIBUTIONS SUMMARY

Company reports 100% of contributions goes to the United Way.
Typical Recipients: • *Social Services:* united funds
Operating Locations: CT (Stamford)

CORP. OFFICERS

Georgio Bielli: *CURR EMPL* coo: Savin Corp
Brian L. Merriman: *CURR EMPL* pres: Savin Corp
William T. Smith: *CURR EMPL* vchmn, coo: Savin Corp
E. P. van den Boogaard: *CURR EMPL* chmn, ceo: Savin Corp

APPLICATION INFORMATION

Initial Approach: Applications not accepted; company only supports the United Way.

Sawyer Charitable Foundation

CONTACT

Carol S. Parks
Executive Director
Sawyer Charitable Fdn.
142 Berkeley St.
Boston, MA 02116
(617) 267-2414

FINANCIAL SUMMARY

Recent Giving: $232,950 (1991); $237,475 (1990); $238,630 (1989)
Assets: $5,156,492 (1991); $5,076,985 (1990); $5,092,280 (1989)

Gifts Received: $5,200 (1991); $38,400 (1990); $164,800 (1989)
Fiscal Note: In 1991, contributions were received from Brattle Company ($3,000), and First Federal Parking Corporation ($2,200).
EIN: 04-6088774

CONTRIBUTIONS SUMMARY

Donor(s): Frank Sawyer, William Sawyer, The Brattle Co. Corp., St. Botolph Holding Co., First Franklin Parking Corp.
Typical Recipients: • *Arts & Humanities:* history/historic preservation • *Health:* health organizations, hospices, hospitals, medical research, single-disease health associations • *Religion:* churches, religious organizations, synagogues • *Social Services:* child welfare, community service organizations, disabled, religious welfare, united funds
Grant Types: endowment and general support
Geographic Distribution: focus on the greater New England area

GIVING OFFICERS

Carol S. Parks: exec dir, trust
Frank Sawyer: trust
Mildred F. Sawyer: trust

APPLICATION INFORMATION

Initial Approach: Send cover letter and full proposal. Deadline is October 15.
Restrictions on Giving: Does not support individuals or provide funds for operating budgets or building projects.

GRANTS ANALYSIS

Number of Grants: 78
Highest Grant: $25,250
Typical Range: $500 to $5,000
Disclosure Period: 1991

RECENT GRANTS

25,250 Knights of Don Orione, Boston, MA
18,000 Rosie's Place, Boston, MA
15,100 Carroll Center for the Blind, Boston, MA
13,200 Salvation Army, Boston, MA
11,000 Shriners Burns Institute, Boston, MA
10,200 Cardinal Bernard Law, Boston, MA
10,000 Combined Jewish Philanthropies, Boston, MA

10,000 Little Sisters of Poor, Boston, MA
10,000 New England for Little Wanderers, Boston, MA
5,050 United Way, Boston, MA

Scaife Family Foundation

CONTACT

Joanne B. Beyer
Vice President
Scaife Family Foundation
Three Mellon Bank Center
525 William Penn Pl., Ste. 3900
Pittsburgh, PA 15219-1708
(412) 392-2900

FINANCIAL SUMMARY

Recent Giving: $5,970,950 (1991); $4,691,142 (1990); $4,081,550 (1989)
Assets: $115,858,659 (1991); $86,901,937 (1990); $77,959,456 (1989)
Gifts Received: $12,536,475 (1991); $12,505,805 (1990); $8,938,325 (1989)
Fiscal Note: The foundation receives gifts from the trust for grandchildren of Sarah Mellon Scaife.
EIN: 25-1427015

CONTRIBUTIONS SUMMARY

Donor(s): The Scaife Family Foundation was established in 1983 by the late Sarah Mellon Scaife (d. 1965) by the conditions of a trust she provided for her grandchildren. She was the sister of Richard King Mellon, daughter of Richard B. Mellon, and granddaughter of Judge Thomas Mellon, who founded the family's banking and investment fortune.
Typical Recipients: • *Arts & Humanities:* history/historic preservation, libraries • *Civic & Public Affairs:* housing, law & justice, municipalities, philanthropic organizations, public policy, safety, urban & community affairs, women's affairs • *Education:* career/vocational education, colleges & universities, economic education, education funds, literacy, medical education, science/technology education, student aid • *Health:* health funds, health organizations, hospices, hospitals, medical research, single-disease health associations • *Religion:* religious organizations • *Social Services:* child wel-

fare, community centers, counseling, disabled, drugs & alcohol, food/clothing distribution, religious welfare, shelters/homelessness, youth organizations
Grant Types: capital, conference/seminar, department, general support, operating expenses, project, and scholarship
Geographic Distribution: focuses on Pittsburgh and western Pennsylvania areas

GIVING OFFICERS

Joanne B. Beyer: vp, treas
Donald A. Collins: trust
Sanford B. Ferguson: pres
David N. Scaife: co-chmn, trust
Jennie K. Scaife: co-chmn, trust
James Mellon Walton: trust *B* Pittsburgh PA 1930 *ED* Yale Univ BA 1953; Harvard Univ MBA *CURR EMPL* vchmn: MMC Group *CORP AFFIL* dir: Gulf Corp; dir, secy: Joseph Horne Co; pres: TiberCo; vp, dir: Arctic Circle *NONPR AFFIL* corporator: Western PA Sch Blind; dir: Irish Investment Fund, One Hundred Friends Pittsburgh Art; life trust: Carnegie-Mellon Univ; life trust, pres emeritus: Carnegie Inst, Carnegie Library; mem: Cultural District Devel Comm; mem exec comm: Allegheny Conf Commun Devel; mem sponsoring comm: Penns Southwest Assn; treas: Carnegie Hero Fund Commn; trust: Presbyterian Univ Health System, Presbyterian Univ Hosp *PHIL AFFIL* treas, trust: Carnegie Hero Fund; trust: Matthew T Mellon Foundation

APPLICATION INFORMATION

Initial Approach:
Initial inquiries to the foundation should be in letter form signed by the organization's president, or authorized representative, and have the approval of the organization's board of directors.
The letter should include a concise description of the specific program for which funds are requested. Additional information must include a budget for the program and for the organization, the latest audited financial statement, annual report, list of the board of directors, and a copy of the organization's current IRS tax exemp-

tion ruling under section 501(c)(3). Additional information may be requested if needed for further evaluation. Requests may be submitted at any time, but the foundation normally considers grants in June and December.

The foundation promises that requests will be acted upon as expeditiously as possible.

Restrictions on Giving: The foundation does not make loans and will not consider grants to individuals.

OTHER THINGS TO KNOW

Publications: annual report

GRANTS ANALYSIS

Total Grants: $5,970,950
Number of Grants: 89
Highest Grant: $1,000,000
Typical Range: $30,000 to $75,000
Disclosure Period: 1991
Note: Average grant figure does not contain a grant of $1,000,000. Recent grants are derived from a 1991 Form 990.

RECENT GRANTS

1,000,000 The Carnegie, Pittsburgh, PA — second century fund

700,000 University of Pittsburgh School of Medicine, Pittsburgh, PA — renovation of Scaife Hall

300,000 Police Foundation, Washington, DC — experimental evaluation of a positive peer influence program

200,000 Extra-Mile Foundation, Pittsburgh, PA — scholarship fund for inner-city elementary schools

175,000 Mel Blount Youth Home of Washington County, Claysville, PA — capital support

150,000 Housing Opportunities, McKeesport, PA — operating support/revolving loan fund

140,000 ACTION-Housing, Pittsburgh, PA

136,000 American Council for Drug Education, Rockville, MD

135,000 Linsly School, Wheeling, WV — scholarship funds for Kanawha Valley students

127,000 Pittsburgh History and Landmarks

Foundation, Pittsburgh, PA — capital support for construction of River Plaza

Scaife Foundation, Sarah

CONTACT

Richard M. Larry
President
Sarah Scaife Foundation
Three Mellon Bank Center
525 William Penn Pl., Ste. 3900
Pittsburgh, PA 15219-1708
(412) 392-2900

FINANCIAL SUMMARY

Recent Giving: $11,206,000 (1991); $9,091,500 (1990); $8,304,000 (1989)
Assets: $224,771,296 (1991); $205,517,340 (1990); $203,133,504 (1989)
EIN: 25-1113452

CONTRIBUTIONS SUMMARY

Donor(s): The Sarah Scaife Foundation was established in 1941. The foundation's donor, the late Sarah Mellon Scaife (d. 1965), was the sister of Richard King Mellon, daughter of Richard B. Mellon, and granddaughter of Judge Thomas Mellon, who founded the family's banking and investment fortune.

Typical Recipients: • *Arts & Humanities:* public broadcasting • *Civic & Public Affairs:* economic development, economics, environmental affairs, international affairs, law & justice, national security, public policy • *Education:* colleges & universities, economic education, education associations, international studies, legal education, private education (precollege)

Grant Types: capital, conference/seminar, department, fellowship, general support, project, research, and scholarship

Geographic Distribution: national for public policy programs; Pittsburgh and Allegheny County, PA, for education, culture, health, and recreation projects

GIVING OFFICERS

Anthony John Adrian Bryan: trust *B* Saltillo Mexico 1923 *ED* Harvard Univ MBA 1947 *CURR EMPL* dir: Koppers Co *CORP AFFIL* dir: Allegheny

Intl Inc, Chrysler Corp, Fed Express Corp, Hamilton Oil Corp, IMETAL (Paris), PNC Fin Corp, Sunbeam/Oster Co *NONPR AFFIL* dir: Foreign Policy Assn; trust: Carnegie Endowment Intl Peace *PHIL AFFIL* trust: Koppers Co Foundation

Edwin J. Feulner, Jr.: trust *B* Chicago IL 1941 *ED* Regis Coll BS 1963; Univ PA Wharton Sch MBA 1964 *CORP AFFIL* vchmn: Credit Intl Bank *NONPR AFFIL* Bohemian; chmn: Citizens Am Ed Fdn, Inst European Defense Strategic Studies; distinquished fellow: Mobilization Concepts Devel Ctr; mem: Am Econ Assn, Am Political Science Assn, Inst d'Etudes Politiques, Intl Inst Strategic Studies, Mont Pelerin Soc, Philadelphia Soc, US Strategic Inst; mem bd govs, mem exec comm: Counc Natl Policy; mem natl adv bd: Ctr Ed Res Free Enterprise, TX A&M Univ; pres: Heritage Fdn; trust: Am Counc Germany, Intercollegiate Studies Inst, Lehrman Inst, Regis Univ, St James Sch; vchmn: Aequus Inst

Richard M. Larry: pres, trust
R. Daniel McMichael: secy
Allan H. Meltzer: trust *B* Boston MA 1928 *ED* Duke Univ AB 1948; Univ CA Los Angeles MA 1955; Univ CA Los Angeles PhD 1958 *CORP AFFIL* dir: Cooper Tire & Rubber Co *NONPR AFFIL* chmn: Shadow Open Mkt Comm; consultant, mem bd govs: Fed Deposit Ins Corp, Fed Reserve Sys; dir: Commonwealth Fdn, Global Econ Action Inst; hon adv: Inst Monetary Studies Bank Japan; mem: Am Econ Assn, Am Fin Assn, Philadelphia Soc, Pres Econ Policy Adv Bd, Western Econ Assn; prof: Carnegie-Mellon Grad Sch Industrial Admin, John M Olin Univ; visiting fellow: Hoover Inst; visiting scholar: Am Enterprise Inst
Richard Mellon Scaife: chmn, trust *B* Pittsburgh PA 1932 *ED* Yale Univ 1950; Univ Pittsburgh BA 1957 *CURR EMPL* owner, chmn, publ: Tribune Review Publ Co *CORP AFFIL* dir: Air Tool Parts & Svc Co, City Commun, First Boston, Parax Corp, Sierra Publ Co *NONPR AFFIL* bd regents: Pepperdine Univ; dir: Goodwill Indus, Historical Soc Western PA, Pennsylvanians Effective Govt, Pittsburgh History

Landmarks Fdn, Preservation Action; mem: Pittsburgh Zoological Park Comm; trust: Brandywine Conservancy, Carnegie Inst, Deerfield Academy; vp, dir: Western PA Hosp
Donald C. Sipp: vp (investments), treas
Barbara L. Slaney: vp, asst secy
James Mellon Walton: trust *B* Pittsburgh PA 1930 *ED* Yale Univ BA 1953; Harvard Univ MBA *CURR EMPL* vchmn: MMC Group *CORP AFFIL* dir: Gulf Corp; dir, secy: Joseph Horne Co; pres: TiberCo; vp, dir: Arctic Circle *NONPR AFFIL* corporator: Western PA Sch Blind; dir: Irish Investment Fund, One Hundred Friends Pittsburgh Art; life trust: Carnegie-Mellon Univ; life trust, pres emeritus: Carnegie Inst, Carnegie Library; mem: Cultural District Devel Comm; mem exec comm: Allegheny Conf Commun Devel; mem sponsoring comm: Penns Southwest Assn; treas: Carnegie Hero Fund Commn; trust: Presbyterian Univ Health System, Presbyterian Univ Hosp *PHIL AFFIL* treas, trust: Carnegie Hero Fund; trust: Matthew T Mellon Foundation

APPLICATION INFORMATION

Initial Approach:
Applicants should send initial inquiries in letter form signed by the chief executive officer or authorized representative. Letters should also indicate evidence of the board of directors' approval.

Include the organization's latest audited financial statement and annual report; current annual budget; list of officers and directors with their major affiliations; and a copy of a tax-exempt status letter from the IRS. Requests may be submitted any time.

The foundation board meets in February, May, September, and November to consider grant applications. Requests are acted upon as quickly as possible.

Restrictions on Giving: The foundation does not make grants to individuals or nationally organized fund-raising groups.

OTHER THINGS TO KNOW

Publications: annual report

GRANTS ANALYSIS
Total Grants: $11,206,000
Number of Grants: 122
Highest Grant: $650,000
Typical Range: $25,000 to $200,000
Disclosure Period: 1991
Note: Average grant figure excludes two grants totaling $1,020,000. Recent grants are derived from a 1991 grants list.

RECENT GRANTS
650,000 Heritage Foundation, Washington, DC

500,000 Western Pennsylvania Conservancy, Pittsburgh, PA

370,000 Institute for Foreign Policy Analysis, Cambridge, MA

353,000 Center for Strategic and International Studies, Washington, DC

325,000 Free Congress Research and Education Foundation, Washington, DC

300,000 National Association of Scholars, Princeton, NJ — general operating support

300,000 University of Virginia Law School Foundation, Charlottesville, VA — security law

250,000 Social Philosophy and Policy Foundation, Bowling Green, OH — general operating support

200,000 Brandywine Conservancy, Chadds Ford, PA

200,000 Intercollegiate Studies Institute, Bryn Mawr, PA

Scaler Foundation

CONTACT
Scaler Fdn.
2200 Post Oak Blvd., Ste. 707
Houston, TX 77056
(713) 627-2440

FINANCIAL SUMMARY
Recent Giving: $2,282,100 (1991); $1,366,900 (1990); $760,827 (1989)
Assets: $19,211,795 (1991); $11,951,656 (1990); $11,169,630 (1989)
Gifts Received: $8,781,505 (1991); $103,455 (1989); $60,380 (1987)
Fiscal Note: In 1991, contributions were received from

Georges de Menil ($82,688) and Rock Trust ($8,698,817).
EIN: 74-6036684

CONTRIBUTIONS SUMMARY
Typical Recipients: • *Arts & Humanities:* libraries, museums/galleries • *Education:* colleges & universities • *Health:* hospitals • *International:* international health care, international organizations • *Religion:* churches
Grant Types: general support, multiyear/continuing support, operating expenses, and project
Geographic Distribution: focus on the United States and France

GIVING OFFICERS
Eric Boissonnas: pres, dir
Sylvie Boissonnas: vp, dir
Elliott Amos Johnson: secy, treas, dir *B* Soldier IA 1907 *ED* Univ Chicago PhB 1928; Univ Chicago JD 1931 *CURR EMPL* ptnr: Johnson Wurzer & Tingleaf *CORP AFFIL* ptnr: Johnson Wurzer & Tingleaf *NONPR AFFIL* chmn: South TX Coll Law; mem: Am Bar Assn, Am Petroleum Inst, Houston Bar Assn, Houston Soc Fin Analysts, Petroleum Equipment Suppliers Assn, Profit Sharing Counc Am, Tax Res Assn, TX Bar Assn, TX Mfrs Assn; trust emeritus: Univ Houston Fdn

APPLICATION INFORMATION
Initial Approach: Contributes only to preselected organizations.
Restrictions on Giving: Does not support individuals or provide loans.

GRANTS ANALYSIS
Number of Grants: 12
Highest Grant: $1,586,673
Typical Range: $1,500 to $50,000
Disclosure Period: 1991

RECENT GRANTS
1,586,673 La Fondation de France, Paris, France — "ARS Gratia Vitae" project

245,000 Foundation for French Museums, New York, NY

100,000 Menil Foundation, Houston, TX

80,000 Maison des Sciences de l'Homme Public, Paris, France

80,000 University of Chicago, Chicago, IL

56,800 Presbyterian Church, Louisville, KY

52,127 French-American Foundation, New York, NY

50,000 American Library in Paris, Paris, France

15,000 French-American Foundation, New York, NY

10,000 American Hospital in Paris, Neuilly-sur-Seine, France

SCANA Corp.
Employees: 4,422
Parent Sales: $1.15 billion
Headquarters: Columbia, SC
SIC Major Group: Electric, Gas & Sanitary Services and Local & Interurban Passenger Transit

CONTACT
Joann Butler
Coordinator, Community Services
SCANA Corp.
Columbia, SC 29218
(803) 748-3000

FINANCIAL SUMMARY
Recent Giving: $1,000,000 (1992 approx.)
Fiscal Note: Company gives directly.

CONTRIBUTIONS SUMMARY
Typical Recipients: • *Arts & Humanities:* general • *Civic & Public Affairs:* general • *Education:* general • *Health:* general • *Social Services:* general
Grant Types: general support
Nonmonetary Support Types: donated equipment, loaned employees, and loaned executives
Geographic Distribution: company operating locations
Operating Locations: SC (Columbia)

CORP. OFFICERS
Lawrence M. Gressette, Jr.: *B* St Matthews SC 1932 *ED* Clemson Univ 1954 *CURR EMPL* chmn, pres, ceo: SCANA Corp
W. B. Timmerman: *CURR EMPL* cfo: SCANA Corp

GIVING OFFICERS
Joann Butler: *CURR EMPL* coordinator commun svcs: Scana Corp

APPLICATION INFORMATION
Initial Approach: *Initial Contact:* brief letter of inquiry *Include Information On:* a description of organization, amount requested, purpose of funds sought, recently audited financial statement, and proof of tax-exempt status *When to Submit:* budget is fixed by the first of the year; requests for funding are best received during the last half of the year
Restrictions on Giving: Does not support organizations without 501(c)(3) status or organizations not located within company's operating area.

Schadt Foundation

CONTACT
Charles F. Schadt, Sr.
President
Schadt Fdn.
4821 Shady Grove Rd.
Memphis, TN 38117
(901) 526-8637

FINANCIAL SUMMARY
Recent Giving: $170,500 (1989); $151,000 (1988)
Assets: $2,913,236 (1990); $3,178,664 (1989); $3,061,979 (1988)
EIN: 62-6040050

CONTRIBUTIONS SUMMARY
Donor(s): Charles F. Schadt, Sr., the late Harry E. Schadt, Sr., Harry E. Schadt, Jr.
Typical Recipients: • *Arts & Humanities:* dance, museums/galleries, public broadcasting • *Education:* colleges & universities, private education (precollege) • *Religion:* religious organizations • *Social Services:* child welfare, family planning, food/clothing distribution, united funds, youth organizations
Grant Types: general support
Geographic Distribution: limited to Shelby County, TN

GIVING OFFICERS
Charles F. Schadt, Jr.: trust
Charles F. Schadt, Sr.: trust
Harry E. Schadt, Jr.: trust
Reid Schadt: trust
Stephen C. Schadt, Sr.: dir, pres
Lynn Schadt Thomas: dir, secy

APPLICATION INFORMATION

Initial Approach: Contributes only to preselected organizations. Applications not accepted.
Restrictions on Giving: Does not support individuals.

GRANTS ANALYSIS

Number of Grants: 39
Highest Grant: $21,000
Typical Range: $500 to $8,000
Disclosure Period: 1990

RECENT GRANTS

21,000 Memphis University School, Memphis, TN
11,000 Hutchinson School, Memphis, TN
10,000 YMCA, Memphis, TN
8,000 Community Foundation of Greater Memphis, Memphis, TN
7,500 LeBonheur Children's Hospital, Memphis, TN
7,500 YMCA, Memphis, TN
6,500 Boy Scouts of America, Memphis, TN
6,000 United Way, Memphis, TN
5,000 Metropolitan Interfaith Association, Memphis, TN
5,000 WKNO-TV, Memphis, TN

Schaffer Foundation, H.

CONTACT

Herman Stall
President
H. Schaffer Fdn.
670 Franklin St.
Schenectady, NY 12305

FINANCIAL SUMMARY

Recent Giving: $490,000 (fiscal 1990); $327,000 (fiscal 1989); $3,346,500 (fiscal 1988)
Assets: $6,822,225 (fiscal year ending October 31, 1990); $6,877,744 (fiscal 1989); $6,673,396 (fiscal 1988)
EIN: 22-2325485

CONTRIBUTIONS SUMMARY

Donor(s): the late Harry M. Schaffer, Schaffer Stores Co.
Typical Recipients: • *Arts & Humanities:* public broadcasting • *Civic & Public Affairs:* ethnic/minority organizations • *Education:* colleges & univer-

sities • *Health:* hospices, hospitals • *Religion:* religious organizations, synagogues • *Social Services:* aged, community centers, community service organizations, united funds
Grant Types: general support

GIVING OFFICERS

Richard R. Bieber: secy, treas
Herman Stall: pres
Lawrence A. Wien: vp

APPLICATION INFORMATION

Initial Approach: Send brief letter of inquiry describing program or project. There are no deadlines.

GRANTS ANALYSIS

Number of Grants: 10
Highest Grant: $100,000
Typical Range: $25,000 to $75,000
Disclosure Period: fiscal year ending October 31, 1990

RECENT GRANTS

100,000 Temple Gates of Heaven, Schenectady, NY
75,000 United Way, Schenectady, NY
50,000 Senior Citizens Center of Schenectady County, Schenectady, NY
50,000 Siena College, Loundonville, NY
35,000 United Jewish Appeal Federation of Jewish Philanthropies, Latham, NY
30,000 Jewish Community Center, Schenectady, NY
25,000 Albany Medical Center Foundation, Albany, NY
25,000 Ellis Hospital Foundation, Schenectady, NY
25,000 Northeastern Association of the Blind at Albany, Albany, NY
25,000 Schenectady Museum Association, Schenectady, NY

Schaffer Foundation, Michael & Helen

CONTACT

Michael I. Schaffer
Principal Manager
Michael & Helen Schaffer Fdn.
295 Madison Ave.
New York, NY 10017
(212) 689-4321

FINANCIAL SUMMARY

Recent Giving: $586,064 (fiscal 1992); $619,326 (fiscal 1991); $326,662 (fiscal 1990)
Assets: $9,095,887 (fiscal year ending July 31, 1992); $7,855,808 (fiscal 1991); $5,811,041 (fiscal 1990)
Gifts Received: $750,000 (fiscal 1992); $2,000,000 (fiscal 1991); $502,500 (fiscal 1990)
EIN: 13-6159235

CONTRIBUTIONS SUMMARY

Donor(s): Michael I. Schaffer
Typical Recipients: • *Arts & Humanities:* public broadcasting • *Education:* colleges & universities • *Health:* health organizations, hospitals, medical research, single-disease health associations • *Religion:* religious organizations, synagogues • *Science:* scientific institutes • *Social Services:* community service organizations, youth organizations
Grant Types: general support

GIVING OFFICERS

Wendy Appel: dir, trust
Helen Schaffer: mgr
Michael J. Schaffer: mgr
Peter Schaffer: dir, trust

APPLICATION INFORMATION

Initial Approach: Contributes only to preselected organizations.

GRANTS ANALYSIS

Number of Grants: 68
Highest Grant: $51,000
Typical Range: $500 to $10,000
Disclosure Period: fiscal year ending July 31, 1992

RECENT GRANTS

51,000 New York University Medical Center, New York, NY
50,000 American Society for Technion, New York, NY

50,000 United Jewish Appeal Federation of Jewish Philanthropies, New York, NY
45,480 Educational Broadcasting, New York, NY
41,000 New Rochelle Hospital Medical Center, New Rochelle, NY
31,000 Albert Einstein College of Medicine, New York, NY
28,000 American Foundation for AIDS Research, New York, NY
25,000 Linus Pauling Institute of Science and Medicine, Palo Alto, CA
25,000 Memorial Sloan-Kettering Cancer Center, New York, NY
25,000 UNICEF, New York, NY

Schamach Foundation, Milton

CONTACT

Jack Goodman
Secretary-Treasurer
Milton Schamach Fdn.
810 Belmont Ave.
North Haledon, NJ 07508
(201) 423-9494

FINANCIAL SUMMARY

Recent Giving: $175,066 (fiscal 1992); $172,670 (fiscal 1991); $166,940 (fiscal 1990)
Assets: $2,647,247 (fiscal year ending August 31, 1992); $2,604,197 (fiscal 1991); $2,364,824 (fiscal 1990)
EIN: 23-7051147

CONTRIBUTIONS SUMMARY

Donor(s): the late Milton Schamach
Typical Recipients: • *Civic & Public Affairs:* ethnic/minority organizations • *Education:* colleges & universities • *Health:* geriatric health, health organizations, hospitals, medical research, mental health, pediatric health • *International:* foreign educational institutions • *Social Services:* aged
Grant Types: general support and research
Geographic Distribution: focus on NJ

GIVING OFFICERS

Andrew E.R. Frommelt, Jr.: trust

Alvin S. Goodman: trust *B* New York NY 1925 *ED* City Coll NY 1944; Columbia Univ MS 1948; NY Univ PhD 1966 *NONPR AFFIL* mem: Am Geophysics Union, Am Soc Engring Ed, Am Water Resources Assn, Intl Water Resources Assn, Water Pollution Control Federation; prof civil engring: Polytech Univ

Jack Goodman: secy, treas

Jay Rubenstein: trust

Gene Schamach: pres

Howard Schamach: trust

Rhoda Schamach: trust

Robert Schamach: trust

APPLICATION INFORMATION

Initial Approach: Send brief letter describing program. Deadline is May 31

Restrictions on Giving: Does not support individuals.

GRANTS ANALYSIS

Number of Grants: 29

Highest Grant: $25,400

Typical Range: $1,000 to $8,245

Disclosure Period: fiscal year ending August 31, 1992

RECENT GRANTS

25,400 Hackensack Medical Center Foundation, Hackensack, NJ

25,000 Daughters of Miriam Center for the Aged, Clifton, NJ

20,000 American Friends of Hebrew University, New York, NY

9,250 St. Joseph's Hospital and Medical Center, Paterson, NJ

8,000 Wayne General Hospital, Wayne, NJ

7,500 Deborah Hospital Foundation, Brown Mills, NJ

7,500 Pascack Valley Hospital Foundation, Westwood, NJ

7,500 Valley Hospital Foundation, Ridgewood, NJ

7,000 Columbia University, New York, NY

7,000 Wills Eye Hospital, Philadelphia, PA

Schapiro Fund, M. A.

CONTACT
M. A. Schapiro Fund
One Chase Manhattan Plz.
New York, NY 10005
(212) 425-6800

FINANCIAL SUMMARY
Recent Giving: $29,250 (1991); $6,250 (1990); $1,024,450 (1989)
Assets: $2,295,419 (1990); $2,468,157 (1989); $2,969,364 (1988)
EIN: 13-6089254

CONTRIBUTIONS SUMMARY
Donor(s): Morris A. Schapiro
Typical Recipients: • *Arts & Humanities:* arts centers, museums/galleries • *Civic & Public Affairs:* civil rights, economic development, environmental affairs, ethnic/minority organizations • *Education:* colleges & universities, minority education, social sciences education • *Health:* hospitals, medical research, single-disease health associations • *International:* international organizations • *Social Services:* religious welfare
Grant Types: general support
Geographic Distribution: focus on New York, NY

GIVING OFFICERS
Thomas J. Mirante: vp
Morris A. Schapiro: pres, dir *B* Shavly Lithuania 1903 *ED* Columbia Univ BA 1923 *CURR EMPL* pres: Schapiro (MA) & Co *CORP AFFIL* pres: Schapiro (MA) & Co *NONPR AFFIL* mem: Am Inst Mining Metallurgical Engrs, NY Soc Security Analysts Inst, Securities Indus Assn
Nathaniel Whitehorn: treas *ED* Univ PA 1931; Columbia Univ 1934 *CORP AFFIL* dir: Fish Schurman Corp

APPLICATION INFORMATION
Initial Approach: Contributes only to preselected organizations.
Restrictions on Giving: Does not support individuals.

GRANTS ANALYSIS
Number of Grants: 4
Highest Grant: $25,000
Disclosure Period: 1990

RECENT GRANTS
25,000 Moreshet Israel, New York, NY

2,500 Institute of Human Relations, New York, NY

1,250 American Friends of Israel Museum, New York, NY

500 Committee for Economic Development, New York, NY

Schautz Foundation, Walter L.

CONTACT
Madalene I. Schautz
President
Walter L. Schautz Fdn.
150 East Grove St.
Scranton, PA 18510
(717) 344-1174

FINANCIAL SUMMARY
Recent Giving: $166,008 (fiscal 1992); $124,346 (fiscal 1991); $152,194 (fiscal 1990)
Assets: $3,738,937 (fiscal year ending January 31, 1992); $3,273,839 (fiscal 1991); $3,001,941 (fiscal 1990)
Gifts Received: $10,400 (fiscal 1992)
EIN: 24-6018362

CONTRIBUTIONS SUMMARY
Donor(s): Walter I. Schautz, Madalene I. Schautz, Grove Silk Co.
Typical Recipients: • *Civic & Public Affairs:* philanthropic organizations • *Education:* colleges & universities, religious education, science/technology education • *Social Services:* child welfare, community service organizations, united funds, youth organizations
Grant Types: general support
Geographic Distribution: focus on PA

GIVING OFFICERS
Madalene I. Schautz: pres
Walter I. Schautz, Jr.: treas

APPLICATION INFORMATION
Initial Approach: Contributes only to preselected organizations.

GRANTS ANALYSIS
Number of Grants: 90
Highest Grant: $10,000
Typical Range: $500 to $4,000

Disclosure Period: fiscal year ending January 31, 1992

RECENT GRANTS
10,000 Friendship House, PA

10,000 Johnson Technical Institute, PA

7,000 Wyoming Seminary, Wyoming, PA

5,500 Salvation Army, Scranton, PA

5,200 Pennsylvania State University, University Park, PA

5,080 Boys and Girls Club, Scranton, PA

5,000 Partners of Youth, PA

4,250 United Way, Philadelphia, PA

4,000 Camphill Foundation, Bethlehem, PA

4,000 Princeton Theological Seminary, Princeton, NJ

Schecter Private Foundation, Aaron and Martha

CONTACT
Gene Glasser
Trustee
Aaron and Martha Schecter Private Fdn.
1060 North Northlake Dr.
Hollywood, FL 33019
(305) 921-6111

FINANCIAL SUMMARY
Recent Giving: $136,480 (fiscal 1992); $121,135 (fiscal 1991); $117,014 (fiscal 1990)
Assets: $2,595,850 (fiscal year ending September 30, 1992); $2,449,581 (fiscal 1991); $2,241,327 (fiscal 1990)
Gifts Received: $1,000 (fiscal 1992); $1,000 (fiscal 1991)
Fiscal Note: In fiscal 1991, contributions were received from Julie Schecter.
EIN: 59-2185762

CONTRIBUTIONS SUMMARY
Typical Recipients: • *Arts & Humanities:* community arts, performing arts, theater • *Civic & Public Affairs:* civil rights, ethnic/minority organizations, international affairs, public policy • *Education:* colleges & universities, education funds, student aid • *Religion:* religious organizations • *Social Services:* community service organizations
Grant Types: general support

GIVING OFFICERS
Gene Glasser: trust
Aaron Schecter: trust
Martha Schecter: trust

APPLICATION INFORMATION
Initial Approach: Contributes only to preselected organizations.

GRANTS ANALYSIS
Number of Grants: 93
Highest Grant: $30,000
Typical Range: $100 to $5,000
Disclosure Period: fiscal year ending September 30, 1992

RECENT GRANTS
30,000 Funding Exchange, New York, NY
10,000 A.J. Muste Memorial Institute
10,000 Haymarket Peoples Fund, Haymarket, OH
7,000 Haymarket Peoples Fund, Haymarket, OH
5,000 American Civil Liberties Union Foundation, New York, NY
5,000 Center of International Policy, Washington, DC
5,000 Fund for Open Society
5,000 Ploughshares Fund
2,500 Americans for Peace Now, New York, NY
2,500 Center for Defense Information, Washington, DC

Scheirich Co., H.J. / Scheirich Co. Foundation, H.J.
Sales: $20.0 million
Employees: 250
Headquarters: Louisville, KY
SIC Major Group: Lumber & Wood Products

CONTACT
H.J. Scheirich III
Chairman
H.J. Scheirich Co. Foundation
PO Box 37120
Louisville, KY 40233

FINANCIAL SUMMARY
Recent Giving: $19,406 (1990); $15,935 (1989)

Assets: $16,707 (1990); $516,707 (1989)
EIN: 61-6031045

CONTRIBUTIONS SUMMARY
Typical Recipients: • *Arts & Humanities:* arts funds, community arts, music, opera • *Civic & Public Affairs:* urban & community affairs • *Social Services:* community service organizations, united funds
Grant Types: general support
Geographic Distribution: focus on KY
Operating Locations: KY (Louisville)

CORP. OFFICERS
Charles A. Mays: *B* Williamstown KY 1939 *ED* Univ KY 1961 *CURR EMPL* pres: HJ Scheirich Co *CORP AFFIL* dir: Bluegrass Electronics, Citizens Fidelity Bank Oldham County
H. J. Scheirich III: *CURR EMPL* chmn: HJ Scheirich Co

GIVING OFFICERS
Catherine G. Hines: trust
Charles A. Mays: trust
Judy F. Noble: mgr, trust
H. J. Scheirich III: chmn, trust *CURR EMPL* chmn: HJ Scheirich Co (see above)

APPLICATION INFORMATION
Initial Approach: Send brief letter describing program. There are no deadlines.

GRANTS ANALYSIS
Number of Grants: 5
Highest Grant: $14,226
Typical Range: $680 to $14,226
Disclosure Period: 1990

RECENT GRANTS
14,226 Louisville Community Foundation, Louisville, KY
2,500 United Way, Louisville, KY
2,000 Salvation Army, Louisville, KY
680 Kentucky Opera, Louisville, KY

Schenck Fund, L. P.

CONTACT
Patrick Clark
Vice President
L. P. Schenck Fund
c/o Midlantic National Bank, Trust Dept.
41 Oak St.
Ridgewood, NJ 07450
(201) 652-8499

FINANCIAL SUMMARY
Recent Giving: $416,627 (fiscal 1992); $440,175 (fiscal 1991); $437,731 (fiscal 1990)
Assets: $8,466,332 (fiscal year ending August 31, 1992); $8,027,294 (fiscal 1991); $7,340,100 (fiscal 1990)
EIN: 22-6040581

CONTRIBUTIONS SUMMARY
Donor(s): the late Lillian Pitkin Schenck
Typical Recipients: • *Arts & Humanities:* community arts, libraries, music • *Education:* public education (precollege) • *Health:* hospitals, mental health • *Social Services:* child welfare, community centers, community service organizations, disabled, family planning, family services, youth organizations
Grant Types: capital, general support, operating expenses, and project
Geographic Distribution: limited to the Englewood, NJ, area

GIVING OFFICERS
Mary Lou Heath: trust
Mary P. Oenslager: trust
Elizabeth N. Thatcher: trust

APPLICATION INFORMATION
Initial Approach: Send cover letter and full proposal (three copies). Deadline is August 1.
Restrictions on Giving: Does not support individuals.

GRANTS ANALYSIS
Number of Grants: 26
Highest Grant: $125,128
Typical Range: $2,000 to $10,000
Disclosure Period: fiscal year ending August 31, 1992

RECENT GRANTS
125,128 Social Services Federation, Englewood, NJ
45,000 Youth Consultation Services, Newark, NJ
40,000 Community Center for Mental Health, Englewood, NJ
40,000 Community Center for Mental Health, Englewood, NJ
35,000 Friendship House, Hackensack, NJ
25,000 Holy Name Hospital, Teaneck, NJ
20,000 Boys and Girls Club, Clifton, NJ
20,000 Van Ost Institute for Family Living, Englewood, NJ
10,500 Planned Parenthood Federation of America, Englewood, NJ
10,000 Englewood Public Library, Englewood, NJ

Schepp Foundation, Leopold

CONTACT
Edythe Bobrow
Executive Director
Leopold Schepp Fdn.
15 East 26th St., Ste. 1900
New York, NY 10010
(212) 889-9737

FINANCIAL SUMMARY
Recent Giving: $603,800 (fiscal 1992); $605,500 (fiscal 1990); $593,900 (fiscal 1989)
Assets: $10,206,764 (fiscal year ending February 28, 1992); $10,282,465 (fiscal 1990); $10,377,488 (fiscal 1989)
Gifts Received: $10,710 (fiscal 1992)
EIN: 13-5562353

CONTRIBUTIONS SUMMARY
Donor(s): the late Leopold Schepp, the late Florence L. Schepp
Grant Types: fellowship and research

GIVING OFFICERS
William L. D. Barrett: trust
Edythe Bobrow: exec dir
Carvel H. Cartmell: trust
Kathryn Batchelber Cashman: trust
Sue Ann Dawson: trust
Clementine Z. Estes: trust
Barbara Tweed Estill: pres, trust
Elizabeth N. Gaillard: vp, trust
Charles E. Hodges: vp, trust
C. Edwin Linville: trust
Linda B. McKean: trust
Barbara McLendon: trust

Priscilla C. Perkins: trust
Benjamin Phillips: trust
Banning Repplier: trust
Samuel Thorne, Jr.: treas,
trust *ED* Boston Univ 1943
CURR EMPL mng dir: Scudder
Stevens & Clark *CORP AFFIL*
managing dir: Scudder Stevens
& Clark
George R. Walker: trust
Eugenia B. Willard: trust

APPLICATION INFORMATION
Initial Approach: Application
form required; contact foundation by telephone.

OTHER THINGS TO KNOW
Provides scholarships for pro-
fessional or vocational educa-
tion.
Publications: Application
Guidelines
Disclosure Period: fiscal year
ending February 28, 1992

Scherer Foundation, Karla

CONTACT
Karla Scherer
Chairman
Karla Scherer Foundation
400 Renaissance Center, Suite
500
Detroit, MI 48243
(313) 259-4520

FINANCIAL SUMMARY
Recent Giving: $188,548
(1989)
Assets: $4,040,352 (1989)
Gifts Received: $2,008,921
(1989)
Fiscal Note: In 1989, the foundation received $2,008,921
from Karla Scherer. During its
initial year, the foundation
made a number of small grants
to organizations outside its
main priority of women's issues and education.
EIN: 38-2877392

CONTRIBUTIONS SUMMARY
Donor(s): the donor is Karla
Scherer, the foundation's chairman
Typical Recipients: • *Arts &
Humanities:* arts institutes, libraries, museums/galleries,
music • *Civic & Public Affairs:*
environmental affairs,
women's affairs • *Education:*
arts education, colleges & universities, education associations, preschool education, pri-

vate education (precollege)
• *Health:* hospitals • *Social
Services:* child welfare, dis-
abled, youth organizations
Grant Types: general support
and scholarship
Geographic Distribution: na-
tionally

GIVING OFFICERS
David Hempstead: asst secy
Karla Scherer: chmn, don
Theodore Souris: asst secy

GRANTS ANALYSIS
Highest Grant: $100,350
Typical Range: $500 to $5,000
Disclosure Period: 1989
Note: Incomplete grants list
provided in 1989.

RECENT GRANTS
100,350 Eton Academy, MI
  6,500 Michigan Metro
        Girl Scouts, MI
  5,000 University Liggett
        School, MI
  3,800 Foundation for Stu-
        dent Communica-
        tion, NJ
  1,898 Miss Hall's
        School, MA
  1,000 Cradle Society, IL
  1,000 Detroit Institute of
        Arts, Detroit, MI
  1,000 Detroit Symphony
        Orchestra, Detroit,
        MI
  1,000 Interlochen Center
        for the Arts, MI
    500 Recording for the
        Blind, NJ

Schering Laboratories
Headquarters: Miami Lakes, FL
SIC Major Group: Chemicals &
  Allied Products

CONTACT
Karen Toomey
Manager, Human Relations
Schering Laboratories
13900 Northwest 57th Court
Miami Lakes, FL 33014
(305) 364-9100

CONTRIBUTIONS SUMMARY
Operating Locations: FL
(Miami Lakes)

Schering-Plough Corp. / Schering-Plough Foundation
Sales: $4.09 billion
Employees: 19,700
Headquarters: Madison, NJ
SIC Major Group: Chemicals &
  Allied Products

CONTACT
Rita Sacco
Assistant Secretary
Schering-Plough Fdn.
One Giralda Farms
Madison, NJ 07940-1000
(201) 822-7412
Note: Contact for information on
  direct contributions is Ms. Joan
  Henderson at (201) 822-7000.

FINANCIAL SUMMARY
Recent Giving: $3,168,669
(1991); $2,726,257 (1990);
$2,671,233 (1989)
Assets: $17,333,918 (1991);
$15,973,670 (1990);
$15,600,000 (1989)
Gifts Received: $1,500,000
(1991)
Fiscal Note: Company gives
through foundation (about
75%) and directly (about 25%).
Total giving for 1989 excludes
direct corporate contributions
of $969,000. In 1990, direct
contributions were approximately $1,000,000. See "Other
Things You Should Know" for
more details.
EIN: 22-1711047

CONTRIBUTIONS SUMMARY
Typical Recipients: • *Arts &
Humanities:* arts associations,
arts centers, arts festivals, community arts, dance, history/his-
toric preservation, libraries,
museums/galleries, music,
theater • *Civic & Public Affairs:* civil rights, nonprofit
management, philanthropic organizations, public policy
• *Education:* arts education,
business education, colleges &
universities, education associations, education funds, faculty
development, health & physical education, medical education, minority education,
science/technology education,
student aid • *Health:* hospitals,
medical research, medical training, public health, single-disease health associations • *International:* international
development/relief, international health care, international

organizations • *Social Services:* drugs & alcohol, united
funds, youth organizations
Grant Types: capital, employee matching gifts, fellowship, general support, professorship, research, scholarship, and
seed money
Nonmonetary Support Types:
donated equipment, donated
products, in-kind services, and
loaned employees
Note: Value of nonmonetary
support is unavailable. (See
"Other Things You Should
Know").
Geographic Distribution: em-
phasizes locations in which corporation has major facilities,
and national organizations
Operating Locations: AR (Lit-
tle Rock), CA (La Mirada, Palo
Alto, San Leandro), FL
(Miami, Pembroke Pines), GA
(Chamblee, Chatsworth), IL
(Alsip, Chicago, Niles), NE
(Elkhorn, Omaha), NJ (Allen-
town, Bloomfield, Carteret,
Cream Ridge, Kenilworth, La-
fayette, Madison, Maplewood,
Union), NY, PR (Hato Rey, Las
Piedres, Manati), TN (Cleve-
land, Memphis), TX (Irving)
Note: Also operates in Missis-
sauga, Ontario, Canada, and
Pointe Claire, Quebec, Canada.

CORP. OFFICERS
Donald R. Conklin: *B* Bound
Brook NJ 1936 *ED* Williams
Coll BA 1958; Rutgers Univ
MBA 1961 *CURR EMPL* pres
(pharmaceutical opers): Scher-
ing-Plough Corp *NONPR
AFFIL* dir: Mt Kemble Hosp
Richard Jay Kogan: *B* New
York NY 1941 *ED* City Univ
NY 1963; NY Univ MBA 1968
CURR EMPL pres, coo, dir:
Schering-Plough Corp *CORP
AFFIL* dir: Gen Signal Corp,
Natl Westminster Bancorp,
Rite Aid Corp *NONPR AFFIL*
chmn, trust: Food Drug Law
Inst; dir: Accts Network Am;
mem bd overseers: NY Univ
Stern Sch Bus; treas, dir: Phar-
maceutical Mfrs Assn; trust: St
Barnabas Med Ctr
Robert Peter Luciano: *B* New
York NY 1933 *ED* City Coll
NY BBA 1954; Univ MI JD
1958 *CURR EMPL* chmn, ceo,
dir: Schering-Plough Corp
CORP AFFIL dir: AlliedSignal,
Bank NY, CR Bard, Merrill
Lynch & Co, Borden *NONPR
AFFIL* dir: Natl Assn Mfrs, NJ
St Chamber Commerce, Un
Way Tri-St; mem: Am Bar
Assn, NY Bar Assn

GIVING OFFICERS

David E. Collins: trust, mem
Donald R. Conklin: trust *CURR EMPL* pres (pharmaceutical opers): Schering-Plough Corp (see above)
Hugh Alfred D'Andrade: trust *B* Metuchen NJ 1938 *ED* Rutgers Univ BA 1961; Columbia Univ LLB 1964 *CURR EMPL* exec vp (admin), dir: Schering-Plough Corp *CORP AFFIL* dir: Molecular Devices Corp *NONPR AFFIL* dir: Indus Biotechnology Assn; mem: Am Bar Assn, NJ Bar Assn; mem bd overseers: NJ Inst Tech Fdn; trust: Drew Univ
Harold Russell Hiser, Jr.: trust *B* Decatur IL 1931 *ED* Princeton Univ BSE 1953 *CURR EMPL* exec vp (fin): Schering-Plough Corp *NONPR AFFIL* trust: Patroit Group Investment Trust
Richard Jay Kogan: trust, mem *CURR EMPL* pres, coo, dir: Schering-Plough Corp (see above)
Allan Stanford Kushen: pres *B* Chicago IL 1929 *ED* Univ Miami 1952; NY Univ 1955 *CURR EMPL* sr vp (pub affairs): Schering-Plough Corp *CORP AFFIL* dir, mem adv comm: Allendale Ins Co *NONPR AFFIL* assoc law: Am Coll Legal Medicine; dir: Pub Aff Counc; mem: Am Bar Assn, FL Bar Assn, NJ Bar Assn, NY St Bar Assn, Phi Delta Phi; trust: Food & Drug Law Inst, Kean Coll, Morris Mus Arts Sciences, Newark Mus; trust, pres: Arts Counc Morris Area
Robert Peter Luciano: trust *CURR EMPL* chmn, ceo, dir: Schering-Plough Corp (see above)
Joseph S. Roth: secy
Rita Sacco: asst secy
Jack L. Wyszomierski: treas

APPLICATION INFORMATION

Initial Approach: *Initial Contact:* letter or proposal on organization letterhead *Include Information On:* specific purpose for which funding is sought, background information on requesting organization, major programs and services rendered, proof of tax-exempt status, latest audited financial statement, program budget (if application relates to specific activity); supporting material (including annual report) is desirable *When to Submit:* requests must be received before February 1 or July 1 (foundation board meets twice annually in March and October) *Note:* Requests that do not include the information above will be returned to applicants.

Restrictions on Giving: Grants are not made to individuals.

OTHER THINGS TO KNOW

Occasionally makes product donations, primarily to assist efforts of U.S. organizations working in developing countries. Surplus equipment is made available to organizations in operating communities. Foundation historically pays grants for annual support in the fourth quarter of the year. Company declined to furnish updated contributions data.

GRANTS ANALYSIS

Total Grants: $3,168,669*
Number of Grants: 572*
Highest Grant: $250,000
Typical Range: $50 to $1,000 and $5,000 to $50,000
Disclosure Period: 1991
Note: Total grants figure is for the foundation only. Number of grants and average grant include matching gifts. Recent grants are derived from a 1991 Form 990.

RECENT GRANTS

250,000 New Jersey Vietnam Veterans Memorial Committee, Trenton, NJ
100,025 Foundation of University of Medicine and Dentistry, Newark, NJ
100,000 Liberty Science Center and Hall of Technology, Jersey City, NJ
95,000 University of Michigan, College of Pharmacy, Ann Arbor, MI
69,108 Drew University, Madison, NJ
68,030 Fairleigh Dickinson University, Madison, NJ
63,307 National Merit Scholarship Corporation, Evanston, IL
62,250 Fordham University, Bronx, NY
60,000 Pharmaceutical Manufacturers Association Foundation, Washington, DC
50,150 Morristown Memorial Hospital, Morristown, NJ

Schering Trust for Arthritis Research, Margaret Harvey

CONTACT

Margaret Harvey Schering Trust for Arthritis Research
431 South 7th Street, Suite 2424
Minneapolis, MN 55415-1692
(612) 333-6896

FINANCIAL SUMMARY

Recent Giving: $75,000 (1990); $0 (1989)
Assets: $2,362,213 (1990); $1,690,823 (1989)
Gifts Received: $100,000 (1990)
EIN: 36-3616824

CONTRIBUTIONS SUMMARY

Typical Recipients: • *Health:* single-disease health associations
Grant Types: general support

APPLICATION INFORMATION

Initial Approach: The foundation reports it only makes contributions to preselected organizations and does not accept unsolicited requests for funds.

GRANTS ANALYSIS

Total Grants: $75,000
Number of Grants: 1
Highest Grant: $75,000
Disclosure Period: 1990

RECENT GRANTS

75,000 Arthritis Foundation, GA

Scherman Foundation

CONTACT

David F. Freeman
Executive Director and Treasurer
The Scherman Foundation, Inc.
315 West 57th St., Ste. 204
New York, NY 10019
(212) 489-7143

FINANCIAL SUMMARY

Recent Giving: $4,000,000 (1993 est.); $4,089,646 (1992); $3,779,685 (1991)
Assets: $70,000,000 (1993 est.); $68,643,998 (1992); $73,772,134 (1991); $62,655,200 (1990)
EIN: 13-6098464

CONTRIBUTIONS SUMMARY

Donor(s): The Scherman Foundation was established in 1941 by members of the Scherman family, including the late Harry Scherman. Mr. Scherman, who died in 1969, was one of the founders of the Book-of-the-Month Club. During his lifetime, Mr. Scherman served as a director of the National Bureau of Economic Research and as a trustee of the Mannes College of Music.

Typical Recipients: • *Arts & Humanities:* dance, libraries, literary arts, museums/galleries, music, opera, performing arts, public broadcasting, theater, visual arts • *Civic & Public Affairs:* civil rights, economic development, environmental affairs, ethnic/minority organizations, housing, law & justice, national security, nonprofit management, public policy, urban & community affairs, zoos/botanical gardens • *Education:* arts education, education associations • *International:* international development/relief, international health care • *Social Services:* aged, domestic violence, employment/job training, family planning, family services, food/clothing distribution, legal aid, shelters/homelessness, volunteer services, youth organizations
Grant Types: challenge, general support, multiyear/continuing support, operating expenses, and project
Geographic Distribution: national, with emphasis on metropolitan New York City for the arts and social welfare programs

GIVING OFFICERS

Helen Edey, MD: dir
David Forgan Freeman: exec dir, treas *B* Chicago IL 1918 *ED* Princeton Univ AB 1940; Yale Univ LLB 1947 *NONPR AFFIL* mem: Monmouth County Mental Health Bd
Axel G. Rosin: pres, dir
Katharine S. Rosin: secy, dir
Anthony M. Schulte: dir
Sandra Silverman: dir, asst secy
Karen R. Sollins: dir
Marcia T. Thompson: dir

APPLICATION INFORMATION

Initial Approach:

There are no application forms. Applicants should submit a brief letter outlining the purpose for which funds are sought.

Include a budget, recent financial statement listing sources of support, evidence of tax-exempt status, and names of members of the board of directors and of key personnel.

There are no deadlines for submitting proposals.

Applications which fall within the scope of interests of the foundation are considered and acted upon by the board at its meetings. The board meets four times a year; dates of the meetings are not fixed.

Restrictions on Giving: The foundation generally excludes from consideration all applications requesting grants for colleges, universities, professional schools, or individuals.

OTHER THINGS TO KNOW

Publications: annual report; statement of policy and procedures

GRANTS ANALYSIS

Total Grants: $4,089,646
Number of Grants: 146
Highest Grant: $130,000
Typical Range: $10,000 to $35,000
Disclosure Period: 1992
Note: Recent grants are derived from a 1991 annual report.

RECENT GRANTS

100,000 New York Public Library, New York, NY — book fund for branch libraries
100,000 New York Public Library, New York, NY — general support
80,000 Legal Aid Society, New York, NY
75,000 American Civil Liberties Union Foundation, New York, NY
75,000 American Civil Liberties Union Foundation, New York, NY — reproductive freedom project
75,000 United Jewish Appeal - Federation of Jewish Philanthropies of New York, New York, NY — Federation of Jewish Philanthropies
70,000 Natural Resources Defense Council, New York, NY
60,000 Lawyers' Committee for Civil Rights Under Law, Washington, DC — Alien Rights Law Project
55,000 Parks Council, New York, NY — Urban Conservation Corp
55,000 United Jewish Appeal - Federation of Jewish Philanthropies of New York, New York, NY — United Jewish Appeal

Schermer Charitable Trust, Frances

CONTACT

Saul Friedman
Trustee
Frances Schermer Charitable Trust
3560 Sandburg Dr.
Youngstown, OH 44515
(216) 793-3570
Note: An alternate contact is James L. Pazol, 21 Wickliffe Circle, Youngstown, OH 44515. The phone number is (216) 792-6033.

FINANCIAL SUMMARY

Recent Giving: $123,493 (fiscal 1991); $153,750 (fiscal 1990); $124,683 (fiscal 1989)
Assets: $1,987,654 (fiscal year ending June 30, 1991); $1,970,392 (fiscal 1990); $1,936,663 (fiscal 1989)
EIN: 95-6685749

CONTRIBUTIONS SUMMARY

Donor(s): the late Charles I. Schermer, Frances Schermer
Typical Recipients: • *Civic & Public Affairs:* ethnic/minority organizations • *Education:* colleges & universities • *Religion:* religious organizations, synagogues • *Social Services:* child welfare, united funds, youth organizations
Grant Types: general support
Geographic Distribution: focus on CA and OH

GIVING OFFICERS

City National Bank Trust Department: trust
Security Pacific National Bank: trust

APPLICATION INFORMATION

Initial Approach: Send brief letter describing program. There are no deadlines.
Restrictions on Giving: Does not support individuals.

GRANTS ANALYSIS

Number of Grants: 39
Highest Grant: $66,500
Typical Range: $1,000 to $10,000
Disclosure Period: fiscal year ending June 30, 1991

RECENT GRANTS

66,500 Youngstown Foundation, Youngstown, OH
15,688 Youngstown State University, Youngstown, OH
12,500 Zionist of America, Youngstown, OH
11,000 Mahoning Lodge 339 B'nai B'rith, Mahoning, OH
10,000 United Jewish Appeal Federation of Jewish Philanthropies, Youngstown, OH
7,500 Kent State University, Kent, OH
5,000 Jewish Federation, Youngstown, OH
4,137 Congregation Ohev Tzedek, Youngstown, OH
2,500 Jewish Federation, Los Angeles, CA
2,500 Kent State University, Kent, OH

Scheuer Family Foundation, S. H. and Helen R.

CONTACT

Richard J. Scheuer
President
S. H. and Helen R. Scheuer Family Foundation
104 East 40th St., Ste. 503
New York, NY 10016
(212) 573-8350

FINANCIAL SUMMARY

Recent Giving: $7,837,919 (fiscal 1991); $13,081,495 (fiscal 1990); $7,050,545 (fiscal 1989)
Assets: $25,322,478 (fiscal year ending November 30, 1991); $27,799,665 (fiscal 1990); $38,916,391 (fiscal 1989)
Gifts Received: $5,109,350 (fiscal 1991); $6,322,816 (fis-

cal 1990); $4,089,086 (fiscal 1989)
Fiscal Note: In fiscal 1988, David Cohen contributed funds in lieu of Joan Scheuer. In fiscal 1989, the foundation received contributions from the trusts and estates of Helen R. Scheuer and David J. Cohen. In fiscal 1990, the foundation received contributions from Richard J. Scheuer, vice president of the foundation.
EIN: 13-6062661

CONTRIBUTIONS SUMMARY

Donor(s): The late S. H. Scheuer, a New York investor and philanthropist, and his wife, Helen R. Scheuer, with other family members, donated funds toward the foundation's incorporation in New York in 1943. Mr. Scheuer was interested in subsidized housing for the elderly.
Typical Recipients: • *Arts & Humanities:* dance, museums/galleries, music, opera • *Civic & Public Affairs:* business/free enterprise, economic development, environmental affairs, international affairs, philanthropic organizations, public policy, urban & community affairs • *Education:* colleges & universities, private education (precollege), religious education, student aid • *Health:* geriatric health • *International:* foreign educational institutions, international organizations • *Religion:* religious organizations, synagogues • *Social Services:* aged, community service organizations, counseling, disabled, family services, recreation & athletics, religious welfare, united funds, youth organizations
Grant Types: capital, project, research, and scholarship
Geographic Distribution: primarily New York City metropolitan area and Israel

GIVING OFFICERS

Harvey Brecher: secy
Amy Scheuer Cohen: vp
Harold Cohen: treas
Eli S. Garber: asst secy, treas
Richard J. Scheuer: pres

APPLICATION INFORMATION

Initial Approach:
Applicants should send a brief letter proposal of one to three pages.

The proposal should contain the following: proof of IRS tax-exempt status; a short history of the organization and its purpose; a description of the project goal and qualifications of the staff involved; the amount of funding requested; and anticipated long- and short-term advantages of the project affecting the foundation, as well as all others who stand to benefit.

The foundation does not report any deadlines.

Restrictions on Giving: In the past, the foundation only made contributions to preselected charitable organizations. Now, however, the foundation does review unsolicited applications for funds.

GRANTS ANALYSIS

Total Grants: $7,837,919

Number of Grants: 240

Highest Grant: $1,505,000

Typical Range: $2,000 to $50,000

Disclosure Period: fiscal year ending November 30, 1991

Note: The average grant figure excludes a single grant of $1,505,000. Recent grants are derived from a fiscal 1991 Form 990.

RECENT GRANTS

1,505,000   Jewish Museum, New York, NY

663,411   United Jewish Appeal Federation of Jewish Philanthropies of New York, New York, NY

333,000   Metropolitan Jewish Geriatric Center, New York, NY

288,205   P.E.F. Israel Endowment Funds

204,000   New York University, New York, NY

200,000   Lincoln Center for the Performing Arts, New York, NY

200,000   United States Holocaust Memorial Council

157,298   Brandeis University, Waltham, MA

157,294   Jewish Association for Services for the Aged, New York, NY

155,908   Camp Isabella Freedman of Connecticut, New York, NY

Schey Foundation

CONTACT

Schey Fdn.
2167 Savannah Pkwy.
Westlake, OH 44145

FINANCIAL SUMMARY

Recent Giving: $155,555 (1991); $168,158 (1990); $119,920 (1989)

Assets: $2,770,319 (1990); $2,744,511 (1989)

EIN: 34-1502219

CONTRIBUTIONS SUMMARY

Donor(s): Ralph E. Schey, Walter A. Rajki

Typical Recipients: • *Arts & Humanities:* community arts, dance, music, opera, performing arts, theater • *Civic & Public Affairs:* zoos/botanical gardens • *Education:* colleges & universities, education funds • *Health:* hospitals, pediatric health, single-disease health associations • *Religion:* churches • *Social Services:* community service organizations, united funds, youth organizations

Grant Types: capital and general support

Geographic Distribution: focus on OH

GIVING OFFICERS

David E. Cook: trust

Lucille L. Schey: trust

Ralph E. Schey: pres, trust *B* Cleveland OH 1924 *ED* OH Univ 1948; Harvard Univ Bus A 1950 *CURR EMPL* chmn, ceo: Scott Fetzer Co

APPLICATION INFORMATION

Initial Approach: Contributes only to preselected organizations.

GRANTS ANALYSIS

Number of Grants: 28

Highest Grant: $34,219

Typical Range: $1,000 to $6,500

Disclosure Period: 1990

Note: 28 $40,562

RECENT GRANTS

34,219   Ohio University, Athens, OH

10,587   Cleveland Ballet, Cleveland, OH

6,720   United Way, Cleveland, OH

6,500   Harvard Business School Fund, Cambridge, MA

2,500   Great Lakes Theatre, Rocky River, OH

1,100   Highland Presbyterian Church, Highland, OH

1,000   American Cancer Society, Cleveland, OH

1,000   United Way, Columbus, OH

525   Cleveland Zoological, Cleveland, OH

500   Playhouse Square, Cleveland, OH

Schieffelin Residuary Trust, Sarah I.

CONTACT

A. Bostley
Sarah I. Schieffelin Residuary Trust
c/o The Bank of New York
One Wall St.
New York, NY 10015

FINANCIAL SUMMARY

Recent Giving: $299,288 (fiscal 1992); $296,949 (fiscal 1991); $261,299 (fiscal 1990)

Assets: $7,510,877 (fiscal year ending March 31, 1992); $7,008,486 (fiscal 1991); $6,388,506 (fiscal 1990)

EIN: 13-6724459

CONTRIBUTIONS SUMMARY

Donor(s): the late Sarah I. Schieffelin

Typical Recipients: • *Arts & Humanities:* arts centers, history/historic preservation, libraries, museums/galleries, opera, performing arts • *Civic & Public Affairs:* environmental affairs, zoos/botanical gardens • *Religion:* churches • *Social Services:* animal protection, child welfare, community service organizations, disabled

Grant Types: multiyear/continuing support

Geographic Distribution: focus on New York, NY

GIVING OFFICERS

Thomas Bolger Fenlon: trust *B* Long Branch NJ 1904 *ED* Georgetown Univ AB 1925; Columbia Univ LLB 1928 *CURR EMPL* ptnr: Emmet Marvin & Martin *CORP AFFIL* ptnr: Emmet Marvin & Martin *NONPR AFFIL* dir: Traphagen Sch Fashion; mem: Am Bar Assn, NY Bar Assn, NY City

Bar Assn; trust: St Catherines Church

APPLICATION INFORMATION

Initial Approach: Contributes only to preselected organizations.

Restrictions on Giving: Does not support individuals.

GRANTS ANALYSIS

Number of Grants: 31

Highest Grant: $30,000

Typical Range: $1,000 to $5,000

Disclosure Period: fiscal year ending March 31, 1992

RECENT GRANTS

30,000   National Audubon Society, New York, NY

30,000   National Wildlife Federation, New York, NY

30,000   St. Mary's Episcopal Church, New York, NY

30,000   St. Thomas Church, New York, NY

25,000   Covenant House, New York, NY

25,000   St. Mary's Episcopal Church, New York, NY

20,000   New York Public Library, New York, NY

10,000   Lincoln Center for the Performing Arts, New York, NY

10,000   Museum of Natural History, New York, NY

10,000   Nature Conservancy, New York, NY

Schieffelin & Somerset Co.

Sales: $80.0 million
Employees: 400
Headquarters: New York, NY
SIC Major Group: Wholesale Trade—Nondurable Goods

CONTACT

Richard Martonchik
Director, Human Resources
Schieffelin & Co.
2 Park Ave.
New York, NY 10016
(212) 251-8200

FINANCIAL SUMMARY

Fiscal Note: Annual Giving Range: $50,000 to $100,000

CONTRIBUTIONS SUMMARY
Schieffelin & Somerset Co. divides its giving program into three categories: industry relations, employee relations, and community relations. In industry relations, support goes to organizations supported by the alcoholic beverage industry and to programs that honor executives, other employees, or customers for their work in the industry. Employee relations contributions go to organizations in which employees are personally involved. These contributions are made only at the request of employees who demonstrate a commitment (of time or money) to the organizations. Community relations support goes to organizations or programs that enhance the immediate neighborhood of Schieffelin & Somerset's headquarters location. Within these categories, civic and public affairs, social services, arts and humanities, and education all receive support. Professional and trade associations are most frequently supported. Other contributions go to arts associations, dance, music, ethnic arts, drug and alcohol abuse programs, and minority and career and vocational education.
Typical Recipients: • *Arts & Humanities:* arts associations, dance, ethnic arts, museums/galleries, music • *Civic & Public Affairs:* professional & trade associations • *Education:* career/vocational education, minority education • *Social Services:* drugs & alcohol
Grant Types: capital, general support, and scholarship
Nonmonetary Support Types: donated products
Geographic Distribution: no geographic restrictions
Operating Locations: CA, HI, NY

CORP. OFFICERS
J. Penniston Kavanaugh: *CURR EMPL* pres, ceo: Schieffelin & Somerset Co
George Reichling: *CURR EMPL* sr vp (sales): Schieffelin & Somerset Co
Clinton Rodenberg: *CURR EMPL* sr vp (mktg): Schieffelin & Somerset Co

GIVING OFFICERS
Anne Luther: *CURR EMPL* sr vp (pub rels), chmn: Schieffelin & Somerset Co

Richard Martonchik: *CURR EMPL* dir (human resources): Schieffelin & Somerset Co

APPLICATION INFORMATION
Initial Approach: Submit a brief letter to the chairman of the contributions committee 6 to 8 months before grant is needed, preferably before September when contributions are budgeted for the following calendar year. Include a description of the organization and the specific program or function (if applicable); date and location of the event; name, address and telephone number of the organization; amount requested and the form in which it is requested; a brief description of the anticipated benefit and how it will affect Schieffelin & Somerset Co.; and proof of tax-exempt status. Evaluative criteria in the decision-making process are the relevancy of the organization's objectives, the extent to which a contribution will foster these objectives, and the moral and financial integrity of the applicant organization.
Restrictions on Giving: The company does not contribute to political parties, candidates, or partisan causes, or to religious or sectarian organizations whose services or benefits are limited to members.
The company does contribute for advertising, especially courtesy in yearbooks, souvenir publications, event programs, or for dinners and other functions.

OTHER THINGS TO KNOW
All applications are reviewed by the contributions committee. Requests for grants above $5,000 must be approved by the company president on the recommendation of the senior vice president and public relations director.
Product donations and occasional cash contributions also are made by Moet-Hennessy U.S. Corp.

Schiff Foundation

CONTACT
David T. Schiff
President
Schiff Fdn.
485 Madison Avenue, 20th Fl.
New York, NY 10022
(212) 751-3180

FINANCIAL SUMMARY
Recent Giving: $322,216 (1991); $1,056,150 (1990); $1,004,055 (1989)
Assets: $10,567,041 (1991); $8,677,284 (1990); $10,639,634 (1989)
EIN: 13-6088221

CONTRIBUTIONS SUMMARY
Donor(s): the late John M. Schiff, the late Edith B. Schiff, David T. Schiff, Peter G. Schiff
Typical Recipients: • *Arts & Humanities:* community arts, history/historic preservation, museums/galleries, music • *Civic & Public Affairs:* environmental affairs, zoos/botanical gardens • *Education:* business education, colleges & universities, private education (precollege) • *Health:* health organizations, hospitals, medical research, nursing services • *Religion:* churches • *Social Services:* child welfare, community service organizations, disabled, family planning, youth organizations
Grant Types: capital, general support, professorship, project, and research
Geographic Distribution: focus on NY

GIVING OFFICERS
Sandra Frey Davies: secy
Andrew N. Schiff: treas
David Tevele Schiff: pres, dir *B* New York NY 1936 *ED* Yale Univ BE 1958 *CURR EMPL* mng ptnr: KLS Enterprises *CORP AFFIL* managing ptnr: KLS Enterprises; vchmn: Am Crown Life Ins Co *NONPR AFFIL* dir: Am Hosp Paris Fdn; mem: Provident Loan Soc NY; mem adv bd dirs: Outward Bound; mem bd govs: Yale Univ Art Gallery; trust: Citizens Budget Comm NY, Metro Mus Art; trust Greater NY counc: Boy Scouts Am
Peter G. Schiff: vp, dir

APPLICATION INFORMATION
Initial Approach: Contributes only to preselected organizations.
Restrictions on Giving: No grants to individuals.

GRANTS ANALYSIS
Number of Grants: 153
Highest Grant: $100,000
Typical Range: $500 to $5,000
Disclosure Period: 1991

RECENT GRANTS
100,000 New York Zoological Society, New York, NY
25,000 Lake Forest College, Lake Forest, IL
10,700 Youth Counseling League, New York, NY
8,000 Boy Scouts of America, New York, NY
8,000 New York Zoological Society, New York, NY
5,000 Animal Medical Center, New York, NY
5,000 Boy Scouts of America, New York, NY
5,000 Metropolitan Museum of Art, New York, NY
5,000 Outward Bound, New York, NY
5,000 Society for the Preservation of Long Island Antiquities, NY

Schiff Foundation, Dorothy
Former Foundation Name: The Pisces Foundation

CONTACT
Adele Hall Sweet
President
Dorothy Schiff Fdn.
30 Rockefeller Plz.
New York, NY 10112
(212) 621-2146

FINANCIAL SUMMARY
Recent Giving: $401,500 (1990); $401,500 (1988); $339,460 (1987)
Assets: $8,249,840 (1990); $8,249,840 (1988); $6,625,248 (1987)
Gifts Received: $102,031 (1987)
EIN: 13-6018311

CONTRIBUTIONS SUMMARY

Donor(s): the late Dorothy Schiff, New York Post Corp.

Typical Recipients: • *Arts & Humanities:* libraries, museums/galleries, public broadcasting • *Civic & Public Affairs:* environmental affairs • *Education:* colleges & universities, minority education, social sciences education • *Health:* hospitals, medical research, single-disease health associations • *Social Services:* child welfare, community service organizations, family planning, family services, youth organizations

Grant Types: general support

Geographic Distribution: focus on NY

GIVING OFFICERS

Mortimer W. Hall: treas
Sarah-Ann Kramarsky: secy
Adele Hall Sweet: pres

APPLICATION INFORMATION

Initial Approach: Send brief letter of inquiry describing program or project. There are no deadlines.

Restrictions on Giving: Does not support individuals or provide loans.

GRANTS ANALYSIS

Number of Grants: 40
Highest Grant: $25,000
Typical Range: $70 to $5,000
Disclosure Period: 1990

RECENT GRANTS

25,000 American Foundation for AIDS Research, New York, NY

25,000 Memorial Sloan-Kettering Cancer Center, New York, NY

25,000 New York Public Library, New York, NY

25,000 New York Public Library, New York, NY — manuscript department

25,000 Roosevelt Institute, Hyde Park, NY

25,000 Woods Hole Research Center, Woods Hole, MA

10,000 Lenox Hill Hospital, New York, NY

10,000 New School for Social Research, New York, NY

10,000 Planned Parenthood Federation of America, New York, NY

10,000 Planned Parenthood Federation of America, New York, NY

Schiff Foundation, John J. and Mary R.

CONTACT

John J. and Mary R. Schiff Fdn.
PO Box 145496
Cincinnati, OH 45250-5496

FINANCIAL SUMMARY

Recent Giving: $329,888 (fiscal 1990); $274,413 (fiscal 1989)

Assets: $9,597,031 (fiscal year ending June 30, 1990); $8,572,852 (fiscal 1989)

EIN: 31-1077222

CONTRIBUTIONS SUMMARY

Donor(s): John J. Schiff, Mary R. Schiff

Typical Recipients: • *Arts & Humanities:* museums/galleries • *Education:* colleges & universities • *Health:* hospitals

Grant Types: general support

Geographic Distribution: focus on OH

GIVING OFFICERS

Susan S. Rheingold: trust
John Jefferson Schiff: chmn, don *B* Cincinnati OH 1916 *ED* OH St Univ BSc 1938 *CURR EMPL* ceo: Cincinnati Fin Corp *CORP AFFIL* chmn: CFC Investment Co; chmn exec comm, dir: Cincinnati Ins Co; dir: Cincinnati Casualty Co, Ins Federation OH *NONPR AFFIL* mem: Queen City; pres: Cincinnati Art Mus; trust: Am Inst Property Liability Underwriters; vp: Deaconess Hosp Cincinnati, Griffith Ins Fdn
Thomas R. Schiff: trust

APPLICATION INFORMATION

Initial Approach: Send brief letter of nquiry. There are no deadlines.

GRANTS ANALYSIS

Number of Grants: 8
Highest Grant: $192,888
Typical Range: $10,000 to $40,000
Disclosure Period: fiscal year ending June 30, 1990

RECENT GRANTS

192,888 Cincinnati Art Museum, Cincinnati, OH

40,000 Xavier University, Cincinnati, OH

30,000 Deaconess Hospital, Cincinnati, OH

25,000 Ohio State University, Columbus, OH

20,000 Children's Hospital, Cincinnati, OH

10,000 Contemporary Arts Center, Cincinnati, OH

10,000 Images, Images, Images, Cincinnati, OH

2,000 University of Cincinnati Foundation, Cincinnati, OH

Schiff, Hardin & Waite / Schiff, Hardin & Waite Foundation

Sales: $50.0 million
Employees: 550
Headquarters: Chicago, IL
SIC Major Group: Legal Services

CONTACT

Thomas P. Luning
President
Schiff, Hardin & Waite Foundation
233 South Wacker Dr., Ste. 7200
Chicago, IL 60606
(312) 876-1000

FINANCIAL SUMMARY

Recent Giving: $170,000 (fiscal 1993 est.); $170,000 (fiscal 1991); $198,718 (fiscal 1990)

Assets: $10,533 (fiscal year ending November 30, 1990); $25,179 (fiscal 1989)

Gifts Received: $184,072 (fiscal 1990); $384,521 (fiscal 1989)

EIN: 36-3465740

CONTRIBUTIONS SUMMARY

Typical Recipients: • *Civic & Public Affairs:* civil rights, ethnic/minority organizations, law & justice, zoos/botanical gardens • *Education:* colleges & universities, education associations • *Religion:* religious organizations • *Social Services:* legal aid, religious welfare, united funds, united funds, youth organizations

Grant Types: general support, matching, operating expenses, and scholarship

Geographic Distribution: focus on IL

Operating Locations: IL (Chicago)

CORP. OFFICERS

Thomas P. Luning:

GIVING OFFICERS

Lawrence Block: dir
Joseph P. Collins: dir
Marci Eisenstein: dir
Allan Horwich: secy, dir
Thomas P. Luning: pres (see above)
William A. Montgomery: dir
Roger Pascal: dir *B* Chicago IL 1941 *ED* Univ MI AB 1962; Harvard Univ JD 1965 *CURR EMPL* ptnr: Schiff Hardin & Waite *CORP AFFIL* ptnr: Schiff Hardin & Waite *NONPR AFFIL* dir, gen coun (IL): Am Civil Liberties Union; mem: Am Bar Assn, Chicago Counc Lawyers
Scott E. Pickens: pres, treas, dir

APPLICATION INFORMATION

Initial Approach: Send brief letter of inquiry, including a description of the organization, amount requested, purpose of funds sought, and proof of tax-exempt status. There are no deadlines.

Restrictions on Giving: Does not support individuals, religious organizations for sectarian purposes, or political or lobbying groups.

GRANTS ANALYSIS

Number of Grants: 139
Highest Grant: $47,960
Typical Range: $150 to $1,500
Disclosure Period: fiscal year ending November 30, 1990

RECENT GRANTS

47,960 Roger Baldwin Foundation, Chicago, IL

12,250 Northwestern School, Chicago, IL

12,040 Roger Baldwin Foundation, Chicago, IL

10,000 Crusade of Mercy, Chicago, IL

8,500 Legal Aid Bureau, Chicago, IL

3,500 Public Interest, Chicago, IL

1,375 Literary Council of Chicago, Chicago, IL

1,000 Chicago Zoological Society, Chicago, IL

1,000 Princeton University, Princeton, NJ

Schillig Trust, Ottilie

CONTACT
Ottilie Schillig Trust
PO Box 5307
Brandon, MS 39047

FINANCIAL SUMMARY
Recent Giving: $319,000 (fiscal 1992); $300,000 (fiscal 1991); $600,000 (fiscal 1990)
Assets: $1,215,958 (fiscal year ending June 30, 1992); $1,393,965 (fiscal 1991); $1,898,962 (fiscal 1990)
EIN: 64-0673508

CONTRIBUTIONS SUMMARY
Donor(s): the late Ottilie Schillig
Typical Recipients: • *Education:* colleges & universities, private education (precollege)
Grant Types: general support

GIVING OFFICERS
James T. Baird: trust

GRANTS ANALYSIS
Highest Grant: $250,000
Disclosure Period: fiscal year ending June 30, 1992
Note: Incomplete grants list provided in fiscal 1992.

RECENT GRANTS
250,000 University of Southern Mississippi, Hattiesburg, MS
50,000 University of Mississippi, University, MS

Schilling Motors / Schilling Foundation
Sales: $30.1 million
Employees: 100
Headquarters: Memphis, TN
SIC Major Group: Automotive Dealers & Service Stations

CONTACT
Nattie W. Schilling
Chairwoman
Schilling Foundation
PO Box 172079
Memphis, TN 38187-2079

FINANCIAL SUMMARY
Recent Giving: $184,460 (1989)
Assets: $9,384 (1989)
Gifts Received: $180,000 (1989)
EIN: 62-1185878

CONTRIBUTIONS SUMMARY
Typical Recipients: • *Arts & Humanities:* community arts, music • *Civic & Public Affairs:* zoos/botanical gardens • *Education:* colleges & universities • *Health:* hospitals, medical research, single-disease health associations • *Religion:* churches, religious organizations • *Social Services:* community service organizations, united funds, youth organizations
Grant Types: general support
Geographic Distribution: focus on TN
Operating Locations: TN (Memphis)

GIVING OFFICERS
Gary W. Curbo: dir, secy/treas
Harry L. Smith: dir, pres
Mary E. Smith: dir

APPLICATION INFORMATION
Initial Approach: Send brief letter describing program. There are no deadlines.

GRANTS ANALYSIS
Number of Grants: 88
Highest Grant: $25,428
Typical Range: $250 to $5,000
Disclosure Period: 1989

RECENT GRANTS
25,428 Idlewild Presbyterian Church, Memphis, TN
25,000 Love Worth Finding, Cordova, TN
25,000 Memphis Symphony Orchestra, Memphis, TN
20,000 St. Jude Childrens Research Hospital, Memphis, TN
5,000 Boy Scouts of America, Memphis, TN
5,000 Christ United Methodist Church, Memphis, TN
5,000 Dixon Gallery and Gardens, Memphis, TN
5,000 Fellowship of Christian Athletes, Memphis, TN
5,000 Memphis State University, Memphis, TN
3,500 Mid-America Seminary, Memphis, TN

Schimmel Foundation

CONTACT
J. H. Cohn
Schimmel Foundation
75 Eisenhower Parkway
Roseland, NJ 07068

FINANCIAL SUMMARY
Recent Giving: $3,600,050 (1990)
Assets: $4,890,248 (1990)
Gifts Received: $7,709,952 (1990)
EIN: 65-0170821

CONTRIBUTIONS SUMMARY
Donor(s): donor is Norbert Schimmel
Typical Recipients: • *Arts & Humanities:* music • *International:* international organizations • *Religion:* churches, religious organizations
Grant Types: general support

GIVING OFFICERS
Stuart Bender: trust
Alan K. Bloom: secy, trust
Stephen B. Schmimmel: trust

GRANTS ANALYSIS
Total Grants: $3,600,050
Number of Grants: 7
Highest Grant: $3,365,300
Typical Range: $250 to $18,000
Disclosure Period: 1990

RECENT GRANTS
3,365,300 Friends of the Israel Museum
150,500 Fogg Museum of Harvard University, Cambridge, MA
56,000 Gospel Crusade
18,000 Los Angeles County Museum of Art, Los Angeles, CA
5,000 American Friends of Hatoreh
5,000 Jewish Museum, New York, NY
250 United Cerebral Palsey

Schindler Elevator Corp.
Sales: $480.0 million
Employees: 6,000
Parent Company: Schindler Holding AG
Headquarters: Morristown, NJ
SIC Major Group: Industrial Machinery & Equipment

CONTACT
Schindler Elevator Corp.
PO Box 1935-ML 226
Morristown, NJ 07962-1935
(201) 984-9500

CONTRIBUTIONS SUMMARY
Operating Locations: NJ (Morristown)

CORP. OFFICERS
David J. Bauhs: *CURR EMPL* ceo: Schindler Elevator Corp
Roland W. Hess: *CURR EMPL* vp, cfo: Schindler Elevator Corp

Schiro Fund

CONTACT
Bernard Schiro
President
Schiro Fund
25 Brookside Blvd.
West Hartford, CT 06107
(203) 232-5854

FINANCIAL SUMMARY
Recent Giving: $328,105 (1991); $320,441 (1990); $324,485 (1989)
Assets: $6,665,625 (1991); $5,621,358 (1990); $6,192,767 (1989)
EIN: 06-6056977

CONTRIBUTIONS SUMMARY
Donor(s): Bernard W. Schiro, the late Beatrice Fox Auerbach
Typical Recipients: • *Arts & Humanities:* dance, libraries, opera, public broadcasting • *Civic & Public Affairs:* civil rights, ethnic/minority organizations, philanthropic organizations • *Education:* colleges & universities • *Health:* medical research, single-disease health associations • *Religion:* churches, religious organizations, synagogues • *Social Services:* community service organizations, family planning, family services, united funds, youth organizations
Grant Types: general support
Geographic Distribution: focus on CT

GIVING OFFICERS
Georgette A. Koopman: trust
Bernard Schiro: pres, trust
Dorothy A. Schiro: secy, treas, trust

APPLICATION INFORMATION
Initial Approach: Send brief letter describing program. There are no deadlines.

GRANTS ANALYSIS
Number of Grants: 290
Highest Grant: $77,600
Typical Range: $100 to $1,000
Disclosure Period: 1991

RECENT GRANTS
77,600 Hartford Foundation for Public Giving, Hartford, CT
35,300 Jewish Federation, Hartford, CT
20,000 Connecticut AIDS Consortium, Hartford, CT
20,000 Moses Stern Memorial, Hartford, CT
15,500 Farmington Valley Jewish Congregation, Simsbury, CT
11,750 United Way, Hartford, CT
10,750 Planned Parenthood Federation of America, New Haven, CT
8,500 Planned Parenthood Federation of America, New York, NY
5,100 American Red Cross, Hartford, CT
5,000 Connecticut Community Care, Wethersfield, CT

Schlegel Corp.
Sales: $180.0 million
Employees: 1,500
Parent Company: BTR Dunlop Inc.
Headquarters: Rochester, NY
SIC Major Group: Apparel & Other Textile Products, Rubber & Miscellaneous Plastics Products, and Wholesale Trade—Durable Goods

CONTACT
Roberta Quarta
President
Schlegel Corp.
1555 Jefferson Rd.
Rochester, NY 14623
(716) 427-7200

CONTRIBUTIONS SUMMARY
Operating Locations: NY (Rochester)

CORP. OFFICERS
Wayne Bowser: *CURR EMPL* pres: Schlegel Corp
M. John McManus: *CURR EMPL* vp: Schlegel Corp

Schlegel Foundation, Oscar C. and Augusta

CONTACT
Oscar C. and Augusta Schlegel Foundation
c/o M & I First National Bank
321 North Main Street
West Bend, WI 53095-3319
(414) 338-0611

FINANCIAL SUMMARY
Recent Giving: $198,500 (fiscal 1990)
Assets: $4,035,458 (fiscal year ending March 31, 1990)
EIN: 39-1586544

GIVING OFFICERS
W.D. Hausmann: secy
Marilyn L. Holmquist: asst secy
Allan C. Kieckhafer: vchmn
C.A. Nelson: chmn

APPLICATION INFORMATION
Initial Approach: The foundation reports it only makes contributions to preselected organizations and does not accept unsolicited requests for funds.

GRANTS ANALYSIS
Total Grants: $198,500
Number of Grants: 10
Highest Grant: $100,000
Disclosure Period: fiscal year ending March 31, 1990

Schlieder Educational Foundation, Edward G.

CONTACT
Blanc A. Parker
Edward G. Schlieder Educational Fdn.
431 Gravier St., Ste. 400
New Orleans, LA 70130
(504) 581-6084

FINANCIAL SUMMARY
Recent Giving: $1,013,539 (1991); $752,587 (1989); $916,492 (1988)
Assets: $21,976,826 (1991); $19,914,162 (1989); $16,179,375 (1988)
EIN: 72-0408974

CONTRIBUTIONS SUMMARY
Donor(s): The foundation was incorporated in 1945 by the late Edward G. Schlieder.

Typical Recipients: • *Education:* colleges & universities, engineering education, medical education, private education (precollege), religious education, science/technology education
Grant Types: capital, endowment, operating expenses, and research
Geographic Distribution: limited to educational institutions in Louisiana

GIVING OFFICERS
John F. Bricker: dir
Donald J. Nalty: pres, dir
Blanc A. Parker: exec consultant
Morgan L. Shaw: dir
George G. Westfeldt, Jr.: secy, treas, dir
Thomas D. Westfeldt: dir

APPLICATION INFORMATION
Initial Approach:
The foundation requests applications be made in writing, outlining the proposal.
The foundation has no deadline for submitting proposals.
Restrictions on Giving: The foundation reports grants are made to educational institutions only. No grants are made to individuals, or for loans, endowment or building funds, general purposes, scholarships, fellowships, or operating budgets.

OTHER THINGS TO KNOW
Publications: annual report

GRANTS ANALYSIS
Total Grants: $1,013,539
Number of Grants: 17
Highest Grant: $120,000
Typical Range: $20,000 to $100,000
Disclosure Period: 1991
Note: Recent grants are derived from a 1991 grants list.

RECENT GRANTS
120,000 Louisiana State University, Edward G. Schlieder Chair of Information Sciences, Baton Rouge, LA
100,000 Louisiana State University, Stanley Scott Cancer Center of Excellence, Baton Rouge, LA
100,000 Loyola University, New Orleans, LA
100,000 Tulane University, New Orleans, LA — Edward G.

Schlieder Chair in Medical Oncology
100,000 Tulane University, New Orleans, LA — James W. Wilson Jr. Center
100,000 Tulane University Department of Anesthesiology, New Orleans, LA
100,000 University of New Orleans, New Orleans, LA — Edward G. Schlieder Chair in Engineering
50,000 Centenary College of Louisiana, Shreveport, LA — Mickle Hall of Science
50,000 Louisiana State University, Pennington Biomedical Research Center, Baton Rouge, LA
35,500 Tulane University, New Orleans, LA — Edward G. Schlieder Chair in Medical Oncology

Schlinger Foundation

CONTACT
Schlinger Foundation
830 Coachman Place
Clayton, CA 94517-1527
(415) 672-2926

FINANCIAL SUMMARY
Recent Giving: $590,000 (1990); $148,500 (1989)
Assets: $14,746,118 (1990); $14,138,224 (1989)
EIN: 94-4065303

CONTRIBUTIONS SUMMARY
Typical Recipients: • *Civic & Public Affairs:* environmental affairs, zoos/botanical gardens • *Education:* medical education, science/technology education • *Health:* mental health
Grant Types: department, general support, and scholarship

APPLICATION INFORMATION
Initial Approach: The foundation reports it only makes contributions to preselected organizations and does not accept unsolicited requests for funds.

GRANTS ANALYSIS
Total Grants: $590,000
Number of Grants: 10
Highest Grant: $250,000

Typical Range: $2,000 to $50,000
Disclosure Period: 1990

RECENT GRANTS

250,000 California Academy of Sciences Department of Entomology, CA
150,000 California Institute of Technology, CA
50,000 Nature Conservancy Fund, VA
50,000 University of California College of Chemistry, CA
50,000 University of Illinois, IL
22,500 University of California Medical Center Department of Psychiatry, CA
7,500 Scripps College Scholarship Fund, CA
5,000 Columbus Zoo, Columbus, OH
3,000 Mayflower Congregational Church, CA
2,000 Yosemite Association, CA

Schlink Foundation, Albert G. and Olive H.

CONTACT
Robert A. Wiedemann
President
Albert G. and Olive H. Schlink Fdn.
401 Citizens National Bank Bldg.
Norwalk, OH 44857
(419) 668-8211

FINANCIAL SUMMARY
Recent Giving: $365,200 (1991); $274,735 (1990); $282,765 (1989)
Assets: $8,189,872 (1991); $7,151,400 (1990); $7,597,338 (1989)
EIN: 34-6574722

CONTRIBUTIONS SUMMARY
Typical Recipients: • *Education:* colleges & universities • *Health:* hospitals, medical research, single-disease health associations • *Social Services:* aged, community service organizations, disabled, food/clothing distribution, religious welfare, shelters/homelessness
Grant Types: general support and research
Geographic Distribution: focus on OH

GIVING OFFICERS
John D. Allton: treas, trust
Curtis J. Koch: trust
Charles Koppleman: off
Dorothy E. Wiedemann: vp, trust
Robert A. Wiedemann: pres, secy, trust

APPLICATION INFORMATION
Initial Approach: Send brief letter of inquiry describing program or project. There are no deadlines.
Restrictions on Giving: Does not support individuals.

GRANTS ANALYSIS
Number of Grants: 17
Highest Grant: $143,000
Typical Range: $5,000 to $10,000
Disclosure Period: 1991

RECENT GRANTS

143,000 Little Sisters of Poor
35,000 American Diabetes Association, New York, NY
32,000 Sight Center, Toledo, OH
26,000 St. Francis Rehabilitation Hospital, Green Springs, OH
25,000 Salk Institute for Biological Studies, San Diego, CA
16,000 US Power Squadron
15,000 University of Michigan, Ann Arbor, MI
11,000 Bowling Green State University, Bowling Green, OH
10,000 American Diabetes Association, New York, NY
10,000 St. Vincent Charity Hospital, Cleveland, OH

Schloss & Co., Marcus / Rexford Fund
Sales: $3.0 million
Employees: 40
Headquarters: New York, NY
SIC Major Group: Security & Commodity Brokers

CONTACT
Irwin Schloss
Principal Manager
Marcus Schloss & Co.
One Whitehall St.
New York, NY 10004
(212) 483-1500

FINANCIAL SUMMARY
Recent Giving: $156,452 (1991); $123,291 (1990); $127,423 (1989)
Assets: $1,428,281 (1991); $1,440,659 (1990); $1,455,112 (1989)
Gifts Received: $173,243 (1989); $208,014 (1988)
Fiscal Note: 1989 contribution from Marcus Schloss & Co.
EIN: 13-6222049

CONTRIBUTIONS SUMMARY
Typical Recipients: • *Arts & Humanities:* arts associations, libraries • *Civic & Public Affairs:* environmental affairs • *Education:* colleges & universities • *Health:* single-disease health associations • *Religion:* religious organizations, synagogues • *Social Services:* united funds, united funds
Geographic Distribution: focus on New York, NY
Operating Locations: NY (New York)

GIVING OFFICERS
Douglas Schloss: dir
Irwin Schloss: secy, dir
Richard Schloss: dir
Alan S. Sexter: pres
Paul J. Zuckerberg: treas, dir

APPLICATION INFORMATION
Initial Approach: Contributes only to preselected organizations. Applications not accepted.
Restrictions on Giving: Does not support individuals.

GRANTS ANALYSIS
Number of Grants: 158
Highest Grant: $15,000
Typical Range: $100 to $2,500
Disclosure Period: 1991

RECENT GRANTS

15,000 Hobart and William Smith Colleges, Geneva, NY
10,000 Hobart and William Smith Colleges, Geneva, NY
8,500 Newark Boys and Girls Club, Newark, NJ
6,000 Operation Exodus, West Nyack, NY

5,000 National Multiple Sclerosis Society, New York, NY
5,000 Usdan Center for the Performing Arts, New York, NY
3,500 American Federation of Arts, New York, NY
3,500 City Center, New York, NY
3,000 Yeshiva University, New York, NY
3,000 Yeshiva University, New York, NY

Schlumberger Ltd. / Schlumberger Foundation
Sales: $6.15 billion
Employees: 53,000
Parent Company: Schlumberger Ltd., Paris, France
Headquarters: New York, NY
SIC Major Group: Industrial Machinery & Equipment, Instruments & Related Products, and Oil & Gas Extraction

CONTACT
Arthur W. Alexander
Executive Secretary
Schlumberger Fdn.
277 Park Ave.
New York, NY 10172-0266
(212) 350-9455

FINANCIAL SUMMARY
Recent Giving: $762,101 (1991); $750,753 (1990); $674,848 (1989)
Assets: $18,833,582 (1991); $16,788,845 (1990); $15,268,828 (1989)
Fiscal Note: All contributions are made through the foundation.
EIN: 23-7033142

CONTRIBUTIONS SUMMARY
Typical Recipients: • *Arts & Humanities:* arts centers, dance, libraries, museums/galleries, public broadcasting • *Civic & Public Affairs:* economic development, environmental affairs, ethnic/minority organizations, nonprofit management, professional & trade associations • *Education:* arts education, colleges & universities, education associations, faculty development, international studies, medical education, minority education, special education, student aid • *Health:* hospitals, medical re-

search • *Social Services:* disabled, food/clothing distribution, legal aid, shelters/homelessness

Grant Types: capital, fellowship, general support, professorship, project, research, and scholarship

Geographic Distribution: nationally to education; other contributions concentrated in New York City area

Operating Locations: CA (Mountain View, Oxnard, San Jose), CT (Bridgeport), GA (Atlanta, Norcross), MI (Ann Arbor), NY (Elmsford, New York, Syosset), OR (Medford), PA (Archbold), TX (Dallas, Houston, Sugarland)

Note: Company maintains operations throughout the world.

CORP. OFFICERS

Dugald Euan Baird: *B* Aberdeen Scotland 1937 *ED* Univ Cambridge 1960 *CURR EMPL* chmn, pres, ceo, dir: Schlumberger Ltd

Roland Genin: *B* Thuilley France 1927 *ED* Arts et Metiers 1949 *CURR EMPL* vchmn, dir: Schlumberger Ltd

GIVING OFFICERS

Arthur W. Alexander: exec secy *CURR EMPL* vp, dir (pers): Schlumberger Ltd

John D. Ingram: dir

George Hiram Jewell: dir *B* Fort Worth TX 1922 *ED* Univ TX BA 1942; Univ TX LLB 1950 *CURR EMPL* Couns: Baker & Botts *CORP AFFIL* dir: Bank Southwest Houston, Pogo Producing Co, Schlumberger Ltd, Southwest Bancshares *NONPR AFFIL* fellow: Am Bar Fdn, Am Coll Tax Counc; mem: Am Bar Assn; mem adv counc: Univ TX Coll Natural Sciences; trust: TX Children's Hosp

Pierre Marcel Schlumberger: dir *B* 1943 *ED* Yale Univ BA 1963; Southern Methodist Univ LLD 1966

Roy Ray Shourd: dir *B* East St Louis IL 1927 *ED* Univ MO 1950 *CURR EMPL* exec vp (drilling & products): Schlumberger Ltd *NONPR AFFIL* mem: Am Petroleum Inst

APPLICATION INFORMATION

Initial Approach: *Initial Contact:* brief letter or proposal *Include Information On:* description of the organization, amount requested, purpose for which funds are sought, recently audited financial statement, proof of tax-exempt status *When to Submit:* any time

GRANTS ANALYSIS

Total Grants: $762,101
Number of Grants: 86
Highest Grant: $45,000
Typical Range: $1,000 to $10,000
Disclosure Period: 1991
Note: Recent grants are derived from a 1991 Form 990.

RECENT GRANTS

45,000 California Institute of Technology, Division of Earth and Planetary Sciences, Pasadena, CA

25,000 Awty International School, Houston, TX

25,000 Nature Conservancy, Arlington, VA

25,000 Oregon State University, Department of Mechanical Engineering, Corvallis, OR

25,000 University of Minnesota, Department of Civil and Mineral Engineering, Minneapolis, MN

20,000 University of California at Berkeley, Department of Geology and Geophysics, Berkeley, CA

20,000 University of Southern California, Department of Geological Sciences, Los Angeles, CA

15,000 California Institute of Technology, Pasadena, CA

15,000 Carnegie-Mellon University, Pittsburgh, PA

15,000 Museum of American Folk Art, New York, NY

Schmidlapp Trust No. 1, Jacob G.

CONTACT

Carolyn F. McCoy
Foundation Officer
Jacob G. Schmidlapp Trust Charitable Foundations Screening Committee
Fifth Third Bank, Department 00864
Cincinnati, OH 45263
(513) 579-5476

FINANCIAL SUMMARY

Recent Giving: $1,611,242 (fiscal 1991); $1,586,964 (fiscal 1990); $1,534,338 (fiscal 1989)

Assets: $30,648,995 (fiscal year ending September 30, 1990); $32,443,966 (fiscal 1989); $27,622,555 (fiscal 1988)

EIN: 31-6019680

CONTRIBUTIONS SUMMARY

Donor(s): Jacob Godfrey Schmidlapp (1849-1919), a successful Cincinnati banker and industrialist, was also a deeply committed philanthropist. In addition to establishing the Jacob G. Schmidlapp Trust, he funded the Emma Louise Schmidlapp wing of the Cincinnati Art Museum in memory of his daughter; the Rudolph Oscar Schmidlapp Fund to maintain the Cincinnati Art Museum, in memory of an infant son; and the Emilie Balke Schmidlapp dormitory at the Cincinnati College of Music, in memory of his wife. He also created the Charlotte Schmidlapp Fund in memory of another daughter killed in an automobile accident.

Unusual for its time, this fund has been providing no-interest education loans and counseling to women from the Cincinnati area since 1908. Mr. Schmidlapp funded his charitable trusts in 1908 and played an active role in deciding what each should support. He believed that experiments in grant making should be encouraged. Even if unsuccessful, the knowledge gained from one's mistakes would ensure overall progress.

Typical Recipients: • *Arts & Humanities:* arts funds, history/historic preservation, museums/galleries • *Civic & Public Affairs:* housing,

philanthropic organizations • *Education:* private education (precollege), public education (precollege), special education • *Health:* geriatric health, health funds, health organizations, hospices, hospitals, mental health, pediatric health, single-disease health associations • *Religion:* churches • *Social Services:* aged, child welfare, community centers, community service organizations, counseling, day care, disabled, drugs & alcohol, emergency relief, family planning, homes, recreation & athletics, religious welfare, shelters/homelessness, united funds, volunteer services, youth organizations

Grant Types: capital, challenge, and seed money
Geographic Distribution: greater Cincinnati area

GIVING OFFICERS

Fifth Third Bank trust

Carolyn F. McCoy: fdn off (Fifth Third Bank)

APPLICATION INFORMATION

Initial Approach:
A short letter should be sent to the foundation officer describing a proposal before submitting a completed application. The trust does not have an application form; it does provide detailed information on the desired format of a written application.

Formal applications should include name, address, and telephone number of the organization; date established; national affiliations, if any; purposes and activities of the organization and services provided; purpose and amount of requested grant; budget; list of other sources of funding; plans for permanent funding if project is a continuing one; latest balance sheet and annual operating statement, including percentages of budget received from United Way and from federal, state, or other sources; percentage of costs paid by program recipients; and date of most recent prior application to a foundation administered by the Fifth Third Bank. A document must also be provided stating that if a grant is received, a report will be made within one month of completion of the project detailing how the funds were spent. Additional material, such as pamphlets or supporting letters, should not be included.

Applications must be submitted by February 1, May 1, August 1, or November 1 in order to be considered at the next meeting. Meetings are scheduled for March, June, September, and December.

All grants are reviewed by the Charitable Foundations Screening Committee which forwards recommendations to the trust committee of the board of directors of the Fifth Third Bank. All grants must be approved by the trust committee.

Restrictions on Giving: The trust does not make grants for operating or other non-capital expenses, for sectarian religious or political purposes, for scholarships, or to other foundations or individuals.

OTHER THINGS TO KNOW

The Fifth Third Bank acts as corporate trustee for the Schmidlapp Trust as well as for several other related charities (Charlotte R. Schmidlapp Fund, Eleanor C. U. Alms Trust, Charles Moerlein Foundation, and Charles E. Schell Foundation).

Organizations receiving grants from any of the trusts are generally not eligible for additional grants during the following three years.

Publications: annual report

GRANTS ANALYSIS

Total Grants: $1,586,964
Number of Grants: 48
Highest Grant: $150,000
Typical Range: $1,000 to $50,000
Disclosure Period: fiscal year ending September 30, 1990
Note: Recent grants are derived from a fiscal 1990 Form 990.

RECENT GRANTS

150,000 St. Xavier High School, Cincinnati, OH — capital campaign
125,000 Cancer Center — computer
118,286 Children's Hospital Medical Center/W.S. Rowe Division, Cincinnati, OH
113,972 Children's Hospital Medical Center, Cincinnati, OH
100,000 Cincinnati Youth Collaboration, Cin-

cinnati, OH — start-up program
75,000 Boy Scouts, Cincinnati, OH — capital campaign
65,000 Children's Hospital Medical Center/W.S. Rowe Division, Cincinnati, OH — pediatric grant
60,000 United Way, Cincinnati, OH — contribution
50,000 Seven Hills School, Cincinnati, OH — capital campaign
50,000 St. Joseph Infant and Maternity Home, Cincinnati, OH — capital campaign

Schmidlapp Trust No. 2, Jacob G.

CONTACT
Carolyn F. McCoy
Fdn. Officer
Jacob G. Schmidlapp Trust No. 2
c/o Fifth Third Bank Dept.
00864, Trust Div.
Cincinnati, OH 45263
(513) 579-6034

FINANCIAL SUMMARY
Recent Giving: $145,147 (fiscal 1991); $145,147 (fiscal 1990); $89,442 (fiscal 1989)
Assets: $2,379,996 (fiscal year ending September 30, 1990); $2,617,861 (fiscal 1989)
EIN: 31-6020109

CONTRIBUTIONS SUMMARY
Donor(s): the late Jacob G. Schmidlapp
Typical Recipients: • *Arts & Humanities:* history/historic preservation, public broadcasting • *Education:* elementary education, private education (precollege) • *Social Services:* community service organizations, day care, united funds, youth organizations
Grant Types: capital and general support
Geographic Distribution: focus on the greater Cincinnati, OH, area

APPLICATION INFORMATION
Initial Approach: Request application form. Deadlines are February 1, May 1, August 1, and November 1.
Restrictions on Giving: Does not support individuals.

OTHER THINGS TO KNOW
Publications: Annual Report, Application Guidelines

GRANTS ANALYSIS
Number of Grants: 12
Highest Grant: $35,000
Typical Range: $3,000 to $30,000
Disclosure Period: fiscal year ending September 30, 1990

RECENT GRANTS
35,000 Dominican Community Services — renovation of daycare facility
34,750 WCET, Cincinnati, OH
15,000 Historic Southwest Ohio, Cincinnati, OH — reconstruction of Sharon Woods Village
10,000 Northern Kentucky Easter Seals, KY — hearing and air conditioning
10,000 Seton High School — renovate auditorium
10,000 United Church Homes — capital campaign
10,000 Ursuline Academy, Dallas, TX — sound system
5,000 March of Dimes
5,000 Mother of Mercy High School — for typewriters
3,500 Mariemont Players — lighting system

Schmidt Charitable Foundation, William E.

CONTACT
William E. Schmidt Charitable Fdn.
2 Larkspur
Belleville, IL 62221

FINANCIAL SUMMARY
Recent Giving: $255,000 (fiscal 1990)
Assets: $5,774,508 (fiscal year ending April 30, 1990); $4,462,691 (fiscal 1987)
EIN: 37-1098426

CONTRIBUTIONS SUMMARY
Donor(s): William E. Schmidt
Typical Recipients: • *Education:* colleges & universities • *Health:* hospitals • *Religion:* churches, religious organizations • *Social Services:* commu-

nity service organizations, disabled, family services
Grant Types: general support
Geographic Distribution: focus on IL

GIVING OFFICERS
Lucille Barton: dir
Robert Lamear: dir
John Schmidt: dir

APPLICATION INFORMATION
Initial Approach: Contributes only to preselected organizations.

GRANTS ANALYSIS
Number of Grants: 39
Highest Grant: $50,000
Typical Range: $1,000 to $10,000
Disclosure Period: fiscal year ending April 30, 1990

RECENT GRANTS
50,000 Blackburn College, Carlinville, IL
40,000 Lutheran Child and Family Services, River Forest, IL
15,000 McKendree College, Lebanon, IL
10,000 Blackburn College, Carlinville, IL
10,000 Wartburg College, Waverly, IA
5,000 Central Institute for the Deaf, St. Louis, MO
5,000 Gillespie Ministerial Alliance, Gillespie, IL
5,000 Holy Family Catholic Church, Litchfield, IL
5,000 Shriners Hospital for Crippled Children, Tampa, FL
5,000 St. Francis Hospital Foundation, Litchfield, IL

Schmidt & Sons, C. / Schmidt Foundation, Christian
Headquarters: Philadelphia, PA

CONTACT
William T. Elliot
Trustee
Christian Schmidt Foundation
127 Edward St.
Philadelphia, PA 19123-1699
(215) 928-4000

FINANCIAL SUMMARY
Assets: $4,246 (1989); $4,299 (1988)
EIN: 23-6391018

CONTRIBUTIONS SUMMARY

Grant Types: general support
Operating Locations: PA (Philadelphia)

CORP. OFFICERS

William T. Elliott: *CURR EMPL* pres: C Schmidt & Sons
William H. Pflaumer: *CURR EMPL* chmn: C Schmidt & Sons

GIVING OFFICERS

William H. Pflaumer: trust *CURR EMPL* chmn: C Schmidt & Sons (see above)

GRANTS ANALYSIS

Disclosure Period: 1990
Note: No grants were provided in 1990.

Schmitt Foundation, Arthur J.

CONTACT

John A. Donahue
Executive Director
Arthur J. Schmitt Fdn.
Two North LaSalle St.
Chicago, IL 60602
(708) 853-0231

FINANCIAL SUMMARY

Recent Giving: $1,176,450 (fiscal 1990); $1,139,425 (fiscal 1989)
Assets: $16,189,879 (fiscal year ending June 30, 1990); $15,526,204 (fiscal 1989)
EIN: 36-2217999

CONTRIBUTIONS SUMMARY

Donor(s): The foundation was incorporated in 1941 by the late Arthur J. Schmitt.
Typical Recipients: • *Arts & Humanities:* community arts, museums/galleries, music • *Civic & Public Affairs:* housing, professional & trade associations, urban & community affairs • *Education:* colleges & universities, private education (precollege), religious education • *Health:* health funds • *Religion:* religious organizations • *Social Services:* child welfare, community service organizations, day care, disabled, food/clothing distribution, homes, shelters/homelessness, youth organizations
Grant Types: endowment, fellowship, general support, and scholarship
Geographic Distribution: focus on Chicago, IL, metropolitan area

GIVING OFFICERS

Richard Charles Becker: dir *B* Chicago IL 1931 *ED* Fournier Inst Tech BS 1953; Univ IL BS 1953; Univ IL MS 1954; Univ IL 1956; Univ IL PhD 1959 *NONPR AFFIL* chmn: Associated Colls IL, Chicago Metro Higher Ed Counc, Counc West Suburban Colls, West Suburban Regional Academic Consortium; mem: Am Physical Soc, Am Physicians Soc, Natl Assn Independent Colls & Univs; off: Federation Independent IL Colls & Univs; regent: Natl Eagles Scout Assn
John J. Gearen: pres, ceo
William A. Maloney: vp, treas
Daniel E. Mayworm: dir
Patricia Shevlin: dir
Edmund Anton Stephan: secy *B* Chicago IL 1911 *ED* Univ Notre Dame AB 1933; Harvard Univ LLD 1939 *CURR EMPL* sr ptnr: Mayer Brown & Platt *CORP AFFIL* hon dir: Brunswick Corp, Marsh & McLennan Cos *NONPR AFFIL* emeritus chmn bd trusts: Univ Notre Dame; mem: Am Bar Assn, Chicago Bar Assn, IL Bar Assn
Peter J. Wrenn: dir

APPLICATION INFORMATION

Initial Approach:
The foundation requests applications be made in writing. Proposals should be submitted in triplicate and include a cover letter and a full proposal of the project for which the organization is seeking assistance.
Restrictions on Giving: The foundation does not make grants to individuals, or for capital or building funds, matching gifts, and loans.

OTHER THINGS TO KNOW

Publications: application guidelines

GRANTS ANALYSIS

Total Grants: $1,176,450
Number of Grants: 75
Highest Grant: $100,000
Typical Range: $1,000 to $20,000
Disclosure Period: fiscal year ending June 30, 1990
Note: Recent grants are derived from a fiscal 1990 grants list.

RECENT GRANTS

100,000 Big Shoulders Fund, Chicago, IL
100,000 Marquette University, Milwaukee, WI — endowment
100,000 University of Notre Dame, Notre Dame, IN — endowment
75,000 Illinois Benedictine College, Lisle, IL
75,000 Loyola University, Chicago, IL
55,000 DePaul University, Chicago, IL — scholarships
55,000 Loyola University, Chicago, IL — scholarships
55,000 Marquette University, Milwaukee, WI — scholarships
55,000 University of Notre Dame, Notre Dame, IN — scholarships
50,000 DePaul University Capital Project, Chicago, IL

Schneider Foundation Corp., Al J.

CONTACT

Al J. Schneider
President
Al J. Schneider Fdn Corp.
3720 Seventh St. Rd.
Louisville, KY 40216
(502) 448-6351

FINANCIAL SUMMARY

Recent Giving: $259,869 (fiscal 1992); $275,327 (fiscal 1991); $255,889 (fiscal 1990)
Assets: $2,478,933 (fiscal year ending February 28, 1992); $2,037,380 (fiscal 1991); $1,767,763 (fiscal 1990)
Gifts Received: $481,000 (fiscal 1992); $491,000 (fiscal 1991); $477,000 (fiscal 1989)
Fiscal Note: 1992 contribution from Al J. Schneider.
EIN: 61-0621591

CONTRIBUTIONS SUMMARY

Donor(s): Al J. Schneider
Typical Recipients: • *Arts & Humanities:* arts festivals, community arts • *Civic & Public Affairs:* rural affairs • *Education:* colleges & universities, religious education • *Health:* medical research, single-disease health associations • *Religion:* churches, religious organizations • *Social Services:* child welfare, community service organizations, homes, religious welfare, shelters/homelessness, youth organizations
Grant Types: general support

Geographic Distribution: focus on KY

GIVING OFFICERS

Robert L. Ackerson: secy, treas
Al J. Schneider: pres, trust
Thelma E. Schneider: vp

APPLICATION INFORMATION

Initial Approach: Send brief letter of inquiry describing program or project.

GRANTS ANALYSIS

Number of Grants: 96
Highest Grant: $33,200
Typical Range: $100 to $1,500
Disclosure Period: fiscal year ending February 28, 1992

RECENT GRANTS

33,200 Kentucky Fair and Exposition Center, Louisville, KY
23,300 Catholic Services Appeal, KY
15,000 St. Meinrad Archabbey, St. Meinrad, IN
15,000 Ursuline Sisters, KY
12,029 Sister Michaela, KY
10,895 Boy Scouts of America, KY
10,000 Cedar Lake Lodge, Louisville, KY
10,000 Passionist Nuns of Owensville, Owensboro, KY
8,000 Southern Baptist Theological Seminary, KY
6,000 King Solomon Baptist Church, KY

Schneider Foundation, Robert E.

CONTACT

Robert E. Schneider Fdn.
150 East Ontario St.
Chicago, IL 60611

FINANCIAL SUMMARY

Recent Giving: $120,000 (1989); $100,050 (1988)
Assets: $2,779,964 (1989); $2,389,570 (1988)
Gifts Received: $102,000 (1989); $100,050 (1988)
Fiscal Note: In 1989, contributions were received from Phyllis and Melvin Schneider.
EIN: 36-6212061

CONTRIBUTIONS SUMMARY

Donor(s): Phyllis Schneider, Melvin Schneider

Typical Recipients: • *Civic & Public Affairs:* environmental affairs • *Education:* colleges & universities • *Health:* hospitals, medical research, mental health, single-disease health associations • *Social Services:* disabled, recreation & athletics

Grant Types: general support

GIVING OFFICERS

Frederic Schneider: trust
Melvin Schneider: dir, pres
Phyllis Schneider: secy, treas
Richard Schneider: trust

APPLICATION INFORMATION

Initial Approach: Contributes only to preselected organizations.

GRANTS ANALYSIS

Number of Grants: 12
Highest Grant: $72,000
Typical Range: $50 to $5,000
Disclosure Period: 1989

RECENT GRANTS

72,000 Northwestern University, Evanston, IL

15,000 Maryville Academy, Des Plaines, IL

5,000 Northwestern University, Evanston, IL

2,500 Alliance for the Mentally Ill of Chicago, Chicago, IL

100 March of Dimes, Nashville, TN

100 Scholarship and Guidance Association, Chicago, IL

100 World Wildlife Fund, Washington, DC

50 Salvation Army, Chicago, IL

50 Special Olympics, Millwood, VA

Schneiderman Foundation, Roberta and Irwin

CONTACT

Roberta and Irwin Schneiderman Foundation
c/o Cahill, Gordon & Reindel
80 Pine Street
New York, NY 10005-1702
(212) 701-3000

FINANCIAL SUMMARY

Recent Giving: $42,500 (1990); $29,500 (1989)

Assets: $2,610,925 (1990); $1,994,149 (1989)

Gifts Received: $499,343 (1990)

EIN: 13-3422543

CONTRIBUTIONS SUMMARY

Typical Recipients: • *Arts & Humanities:* arts festivals • *Social Services:* family planning

Grant Types: general support

GIVING OFFICERS

Irwin Schneiderman: dir, pres, secy
Roberta Schneiderman: dir, vp, treas
John R. Young: dir

APPLICATION INFORMATION

Initial Approach: The foundation reports it only makes contributions to preselected organizations and does not accept unsolicited requests for funds.

GRANTS ANALYSIS

Total Grants: $42,500
Number of Grants: 5
Highest Grant: $35,000
Typical Range: $1,000 to $3,000
Disclosure Period: 1990

RECENT GRANTS

35,000 Planned Parenthood of New York City, New York, NY

3,000 New York Shakespeare Festival, New York, NY

2,500 Prep for Prep, New York, NY

1,000 Lighthouse, New York, NY

1,000 Public Education Association, New York, NY

Schnuck Markets

Sales: $1.02 billion
Employees: 14,000
Headquarters: St. Louis, MO
SIC Major Group: Food Stores

CONTACT

Schnuck Markets
11420 Lackland Rd.
PO Box 46928
St. Louis, MO 63146
(314) 994-9900

FINANCIAL SUMMARY

Fiscal Note: Company does not disclose contributions figures.

CONTRIBUTIONS SUMMARY

Geographic Distribution: in headquarters and operating communities

Operating Locations: IL, IN (Evansville), MO (Kansas City, St. Louis)

CORP. OFFICERS

Craig Schnuck: *CURR EMPL* chmn, ceo: Schnuck Markets

GRANTS ANALYSIS

Typical Range: $50 to $1,000

Schoenbaum Family Foundation

CONTACT

Rena Williams
Schoenbaum Family Foundation
P.O. Box 1793
Charleston, WV 25326
(304) 348-7093

FINANCIAL SUMMARY

Recent Giving: $327,050 (1990); $272,500 (1989)

Assets: $4,387,843 (1990); $4,333,806 (1989)

EIN: 65-0043921

CONTRIBUTIONS SUMMARY

Typical Recipients: • *Civic & Public Affairs:* environmental affairs • *Education:* colleges & universities • *International:* foreign educational institutions • *Social Services:* disabled, domestic violence, religious welfare, youth organizations

Grant Types: general support and project

APPLICATION INFORMATION

Initial Approach: The foundation reports no specific application guidelines. Send a brief letter of inquiry, including statement of purpose, amount requested, and proof of tax-exempt status.

GRANTS ANALYSIS

Total Grants: $327,050
Number of Grants: 27
Highest Grant: $175,000
Typical Range: $5,000 to $10,000
Disclosure Period: 1990

RECENT GRANTS

175,000 West Virginia University Foundation, WV

80,000 Sarasota-Manatee Jewish Federation, Sarasota, FL

10,000 Project Return Florida, FL

5,000 American Friends of the Hebrew University, CA

5,000 Boys Club of Sarasota County, Sarasota, FL

5,000 Branches Domestic Violence Shelter, WV

5,000 Greenpeace USA, DC

5,000 Life is for Everyone, FL

5,000 Mana-Sota Lighthouse for the Blind, FL

5,000 United Jewish Appeal Passage to Freedom, NY

Schoenleber Foundation

CONTACT

Peter C. Haensel
President
Schoenleber Fdn.
740 North Plankinton Avenue, Ste. 510
Milwaukee, WI 53203-2403
(414) 276-3400

FINANCIAL SUMMARY

Recent Giving: $262,649 (1990); $274,381 (1989); $32,045 (1987)

Assets: $4,322,690 (1990); $4,548,420 (1989); $3,734,529 (1987)

Gifts Received: $800 (1990); $1,200,000 (1989); $2,976,795 (1987)

EIN: 39-1049364

CONTRIBUTIONS SUMMARY

Donor(s): the late Marie and Louise Schoenleber

Typical Recipients: • *Arts & Humanities:* community arts,

history/historic preservation, theater • *Education:* colleges & universities • *Health:* hospitals, pediatric health • *Social Services:* counseling, family planning, family services
Grant Types: general support
Geographic Distribution: focus on the greater Milwaukee, WI, area

GIVING OFFICERS
Frank W. Bastian: secy, dir
Peter C. Haensel: pres, dir
Walter Schorrak: dir

APPLICATION INFORMATION
Initial Approach: Application form required. Send brief letter of inquiry and full proposal.

GRANTS ANALYSIS
Number of Grants: 16
Highest Grant: $50,000
Typical Range: $10,000 to $25,000
Disclosure Period: 1990

RECENT GRANTS
50,000 University of Wisconsin Foundation, Madison, WI — toward the endowment of the Schoenleber Scholarship Fund
25,000 Concordia University, Mequon, WI
25,000 University of Wisconsin Foundation, Madison, WI — toward the Schoenleber Freshmen Seminary Fund
22,149 Milwaukee County Historical Society, Milwaukee, WI — for funding of an assistant curator for the library
20,000 Milwaukee Career Cooperative, Milwaukee, WI — toward the start-up operating funds to assure the effective, stable establishment of the new Cooperative divisions
15,000 Milwaukee Public Library Foundation, Milwaukee, WI — for the improvements to the Humanities Library
15,000 Milwaukee School of Engineering, Milwaukee, WI — toward the endowment of a scholarship for outstanding students
10,000 Bethesda Lutheran Home, Watertown,

WI — remodeling project
10,000 Volunteer Services for the Visually Handicapped, Milwaukee, WI
10,000 Wisconsin Lutheran College, Milwaukee, WI — for the funding of five presidential scholarship annually over a period of five years

Scholastic Inc.
Sales: $422.9 million
Employees: 3,362
Parent Company: Scholastic Corp.
Headquarters: New York, NY
SIC Major Group: Business Services, Holding & Other Investment Offices, and Printing & Publishing

CONTACT
Kent Allison
Director, Professional Relations
Scholastic Inc.
8316 Pineville-Matthews Rd.
Ste. 280-1
Charlotte, NC 28226
Note: Corporate headquarters is located at 730 Broadway, New York, NY 10003.

CONTRIBUTIONS SUMMARY
Operating Locations: NY (New York)

CORP. OFFICERS
Frederic J. Bischoff: *CURR EMPL* exec vp, cfo: Scholastic
Richard Robinson: *CURR EMPL* chmn, ceo: Scholastic

OTHER THINGS TO KNOW
The North Carolina office of Scholastic Inc. handles donations of surplus paperback books to such educational projects as read-a-thons and Parents as Reading Partners.

Scholl Foundation, Dr.

CONTACT
Jack E. Scholl
Executive Director
Dr. Scholl Foundation
11 South LaSalle St., Ste. 2100
Chicago, IL 60603
(312) 782-5210

FINANCIAL SUMMARY
Recent Giving: $7,000,000 (1992 approx.); $7,363,250 (1991); $7,640,285 (1990)
Assets: $132,403,956 (1991); $112,379,265 (1990); $123,247,118 (1989)
EIN: 36-6068724

CONTRIBUTIONS SUMMARY
Donor(s): The Dr. Scholl Foundation (formerly William M. Scholl Foundation) was created in 1947 by Dr. William M. Scholl. "At 18, he enrolled in Illinois Medical College, now Loyola University, and was awarded his M.D. degree in 1904. That same year, he established Scholl, Inc., a manufacturer of orthopedic devices and footwear. He died in 1968 leaving Scholl, Inc., and the foundation in the hands of his nephews. The foundation received the bulk of his estate, and Scholl, Inc., was sold in 1979."
Typical Recipients: • *Arts & Humanities:* libraries, museums/galleries, music, opera • *Civic & Public Affairs:* better government, professional & trade associations, zoos/botanical gardens • *Education:* arts education, colleges & universities, education associations, elementary education, faculty development, legal education, medical education, minority education, private education (precollege), science/technology education, special education, student aid • *Health:* health organizations, hospitals, single-disease health associations • *International:* international health care, international organizations • *Religion:* churches, religious organizations • *Science:* scientific organizations • *Social Services:* aged, child welfare, community centers, disabled, family services, food/clothing distribution, recreation & athletics, religious welfare, shelters/homelessness, volunteer services, youth organizations

Grant Types: project
Geographic Distribution: no geographic restrictions; emphasis on Illinois

GIVING OFFICERS
George W. Alexander: asst secy-treas, dir
William T. Branham: dir
Neil Flanagin: dir *B* Chicago IL 1930 *ED* Yale Univ BA 1953; Univ MI JD 1956 *CURR EMPL* ptnr: Sidley & Austin (Chicago) *NONPR AFFIL* fellow: Am Coll Investment Counc; mem: Am Bar Assn, Chicago Bar Assn, Intl Bar Assn
William B. Jordan III: dir
Leonard J. Knirko: treas
Pamela Scholl Mahaffee: dir
Jack E. Scholl: exec dir, dir
Michael L. Scholl: dir
William H. Scholl: pres, dir
Douglas C. Witherspoon: dir

APPLICATION INFORMATION
Initial Approach:
Applicants should obtain a copy of the foundation's standard application form. The form is required along with one copy of a full proposal.
Applications must be received by May 15 to be considered for current year program.
Applications are acknowledged. The foundation notifies applicants of its decisions in November, and distribution of grants occurs in December.
Restrictions on Giving: "In general, the Foundation does not consider the following for funding: organizations not eligible for tax-deductible support; political organizations or campaigns, or groups whose prime purpose is to influence legislation; foundations that are themselves grant-making bodies; public education; grants to individuals; general endowment grants; unrestricted purpose grants; general support grants; grants for the reduction of an operating deficit or to liquidate a debt; testimonial dinners and similar benefit programs involving purchases of tables, tickets, or advertisements; or installment grants, but the Foundation gives consideration to subsequent applications pertaining to the same project."

OTHER THINGS TO KNOW
Applicants in the areas of culture, religion, social services,

and general charitable purposes must present their request in the form of a special project or program designed to achieve a desirable result. All grantees are asked to sign an agreement which requires a full report to be filed at the conclusion of the project, including a statement of the results achieved by the grant. Only one application per organization will be considered annually.
Publications: program guidelines and application procedures

GRANTS ANALYSIS
Total Grants: $7,361,000*
Number of Grants: 320
Highest Grant: $350,000
Typical Range: $10,000 to $50,000
Disclosure Period: 1991
Note: The above giving figure excludes $2,250 in scholarships. Recent grants are derived from a 1990 grants list.

RECENT GRANTS
200,000 Center for Strategic and International Studies, Washington, DC — funding to support Quadrangular Forum
150,000 Georgetown University Medical Center, Washington, DC — endow academic professorship and support pediatric project
100,000 American Bar Association, Chicago, IL — funding for conferences and workshops
100,000 Dr. Scholl College of Podiatric Medicine, Chicago, IL — funding for scholarship and museum project
100,000 Orchestral Association, Chicago, IL — funding for ensemble program outreach activities
80,000 Clearbrook Center for Handicapped, Rolling Meadows, IL — funding for electrical upgrading and security at central facility
76,000 Lincoln Park Zoological Society, Chicago, IL — funding for three programs as requested
75,000 A. C. Buehler YMCA, Palatine,

IL — partially fund capital campaign
75,000 DePaul University, Chicago, IL — establish an expendable scholarship fund
75,000 Syracuse University, Syracuse, NY — to endow the Remembrance Scholarships

Scholler Foundation

CONTACT
Frederick L. Fuges
Secretary
Scholler Fdn.
1100 One Penn Center Plz.
Philadelphia, PA 19103
(215) 568-7500

FINANCIAL SUMMARY
Recent Giving: $461,854 (1991); $456,989 (1990); $409,173 (1989)
Assets: $11,397,622 (1991); $9,993,152 (1990); $10,203,971 (1989)
EIN: 23-6245158

CONTRIBUTIONS SUMMARY
Donor(s): the late F.C. Scholler
Typical Recipients: • *Civic & Public Affairs:* environmental affairs • *Education:* colleges & universities, private education (precollege), religious education • *Health:* health organizations, hospitals, medical research, pediatric health • *Religion:* religious organizations • *Social Services:* child welfare, day care, disabled, recreation & athletics
Grant Types: general support and research
Geographic Distribution: limited to the Delaware Valley, PA

GIVING OFFICERS
Edwin C. Dreby III: trust
Frederick L. Fuges: secy, trust
E. Brooks Keffer, Jr.: trust

APPLICATION INFORMATION
Initial Approach: Send cover letter and full proposal. There are no deadlines.
Restrictions on Giving: Does not support individuals or provide loans.

GRANTS ANALYSIS
Number of Grants: 17
Highest Grant: $43,100
Typical Range: $3,400 to $25,000

Disclosure Period: 1991

RECENT GRANTS
43,100 Pennsylvania Hospital, Philadelphia, PA
39,997 Corielle Institute for Medical Research, Camden, NJ
31,705 Center in the Park, Philadelphia, PA
25,000 Fox Chase Cancer Center, Philadelphia, PA
23,500 Glaucoma Services Foundation to Prevent Blindness, Philadelphia, PA
21,000 Abington Friends School, Jenkinstown, PA — van purchase
20,000 Mercy Catholic Medical Center, Philadelphia, PA — ventilator
17,000 Children's Hospital Medical Center, Philadelphia, PA
15,091 Frankford Hospital, Philadelphia, PA
15,000 Atlantic City Day Nursery, Atlantic City, NJ

Schoonmaker J-Sewkly Valley Hospital Trust

CONTACT
Helen M. Collins
Schoonmaker J-Sewkly Valley Hospital Trust
One Mellon Bank Center
Pittsburgh, PA 15230
(412) 234-4625

FINANCIAL SUMMARY
Recent Giving: $207,000 (fiscal 1991); $61,350 (fiscal 1990); $174,982 (fiscal 1989)
Assets: $4,288,082 (fiscal year ending September 30, 1991); $3,729,862 (fiscal 1990); $3,593,609 (fiscal 1989)
EIN: 25-6016020

CONTRIBUTIONS SUMMARY
Typical Recipients: • *Civic & Public Affairs:* women's affairs • *Education:* colleges & universities • *Health:* health organizations, hospitals • *Religion:* churches • *Social Services:* community service organizations, united funds, youth organizations
Grant Types: general support
Geographic Distribution: focus on Pittsburgh, PA

GIVING OFFICERS
Mellon Bank, N.A.: trust

APPLICATION INFORMATION
Initial Approach: Send letter requesting application form. There are no deadlines.

GRANTS ANALYSIS
Number of Grants: 10
Highest Grant: $46,705
Typical Range: $9,000 to $20,000
Disclosure Period: fiscal year ending September 30, 1991

RECENT GRANTS
46,705 Princeton University, Princeton, NJ
46,705 Sewickley Valley Hospital, Sewickley, PA
46,705 United Way, Pittsburgh, PA
18,680 St. Stephens Church, Sewickley, PA
9,341 Boy Scouts of America, Pittsburgh, PA
9,341 Red Cross, Pittsburgh, PA
9,341 Shadyside Hospital, Pittsburgh, PA
8,000 United Way, Pittsburgh, PA
6,091 Kenmore Association, Pittsburgh, PA
6,091 Women's Committee- The Carnegie, Pittsburgh, PA

Schott Foundation

CONTACT
Owen Schott
CEO and Director
Schott Fdn.
1000 Parkers Lake Rd.
Wayzata, MN 55391
(612) 475-1173

FINANCIAL SUMMARY
Recent Giving: $196,042 (fiscal 1992)
Assets: $3,113,786 (fiscal year ending March 31, 1992)
EIN: 41-1392014

CONTRIBUTIONS SUMMARY
Typical Recipients: • *Arts & Humanities:* museums/galleries, public broadcasting • *Civic & Public Affairs:* environmental affairs • *Education:* colleges & universities, science/technology education • *Health:* health funds
Grant Types: general support

·

GIVING OFFICERS
Owen Schott: ceo, dir

APPLICATION INFORMATION
Initial Approach: Send brief letter of inquiry. There are no deadlines.

GRANTS ANALYSIS
Number of Grants: 32
Highest Grant: $50,000
Typical Range: $500 to $5,000
Disclosure Period: fiscal year ending March 31, 1992

RECENT GRANTS
50,000 Park Nicollet Medical Foundation, MN
25,000 Bell Museum, MN
24,000 Twin Cities Public Television, St. Paul, MN
15,000 University of Minnesota Foundation, MN
10,000 Massachusetts Institute of Technology, Cambridge, MA
10,000 Virginia Polytechnic Institute and State University, Blacksburg, VA
7,500 Wisconsin Electric Power Electronic Consortium, Milwaukee, WI
7,000 Groves Learning Center, MN
6,400 University of Minnesota, Minneapolis, MN
5,000 Nature Conservancy, MN

Schottenstein Foundation, Jerome & Saul

CONTACT
Jerome & Saul Schottenstein Fdn.
1800 Moler Rd.
Columbus, OH 43207-1698

FINANCIAL SUMMARY
Recent Giving: $1,370,225 (1991); $1,089,000 (1990); $249,000 (1989)
Assets: $235,992 (1991); $1,074,403 (1990); $1,524,489 (1989)
Gifts Received: $500,000 (1991); $500,000 (1990); $300,000 (1989)
Fiscal Note: In 1991, contributions were received from Saul Schottenstein ($250,000) and Jerome Schottenstein ($250,000).
EIN: 31-1038192

CONTRIBUTIONS SUMMARY
Donor(s): Saul Schottenstein, Jerome Schottenstein

Typical Recipients: • *Arts & Humanities:* history/historic preservation • *Education:* private education (precollege), religious education • *Health:* medical research • *Religion:* religious organizations • *Social Services:* aged, community service organizations, homes

Grant Types: capital and research

Geographic Distribution: focus on Columbus, OH

GIVING OFFICERS
Jay L. Schottenstein: treas *CURR EMPL* vchmn, exec vp, dir: Schottenstein Stores Corp *CORP AFFIL* dir: Valley Fair Corp; exec vp, dir: Schottenstein Stores Corp; vchmn, exec vp: Value City Furniture

Jerome M. Schottenstein: vp B Columbus OH 1926 *CURR EMPL* chmn, dir: Schottenstein Stores Corp *CORP AFFIL* chmn: Valley Fair Corp; chmn, dir: Schottenstein Stores Corp; pres, dir: Kroehler Furniture Mfg Co

Saul Schottenstein: pres *CURR EMPL* pres, dir: Schottenstein Stores Corp

Saul Schottenstein: pres *CURR EMPL* pres, dir: Schottenstein Stores Corp (see above)

APPLICATION INFORMATION
Initial Approach: Contributes only to preselected organizations.

GRANTS ANALYSIS
Number of Grants: 5
Highest Grant: $900,000
Disclosure Period: 1991

RECENT GRANTS
900,000 Mesorah Heritage Foundation, Brooklyn, NY
250,000 Columbus Torah School, Columbus, OH
159,375 Aish Hatorah, Columbus, OH
40,850 Columbus Jewish Home for the Aged, Columbus, OH
20,000 Harding Evans Foundation, Worthington, OH

Schottenstein Stores Corp.
Sales: $1.1 billion
Employees: 10,000
Headquarters: Columbus, OH
SIC Major Group: Furniture & Homefurnishings Stores and General Merchandise Stores

CONTACT
Herbert Minkin
Vice President, Human Resources
Schottenstein Stores Corp.
3241 Westerville Rd.
Columbus, OH 43224
(614) 471-4722

CONTRIBUTIONS SUMMARY
Operating Locations: OH (Columbus)

CORP. OFFICERS
Jay L. Schottenstein: *CURR EMPL* vchmn, exec vp, dir: Schottenstein Stores Corp *CORP AFFIL* dir: Valley Fair Corp; exec vp, dir: Schottenstein Stores Corp; vchmn, exec vp: Value City Furniture

Jerome Schottenstein: *CURR EMPL* chmn, dir: Schottenstein Stores Corp

Saul Schottenstein: *CURR EMPL* pres, dir: Schottenstein Stores Corp

Schowalter Foundation

CONTACT
Willis Harder
Trustee
Schowalter Fdn.
726 Main St.
Newton, KS 67114
(316) 283-3720

FINANCIAL SUMMARY
Recent Giving: $209,400 (1991); $220,950 (1990); $192,050 (1989)
Assets: $4,103,616 (1991); $3,954,004 (1990); $3,807,044 (1989)
EIN: 48-0623544

CONTRIBUTIONS SUMMARY
Donor(s): the late J. A. Schowalter

Typical Recipients: • *Arts & Humanities:* libraries • *Education:* colleges & universities, religious education • *Religion:* churches, missionary activities, religious organizations

Grant Types: capital, project, and scholarship

Geographic Distribution: limited to the Midwest.

GIVING OFFICERS
Howard E. Baumgartner: trust
Allen Becker: trust
Ben T. Ensz: trust
Willis Harder: trust
Howard Hershberger: trust
Elvin D. Yoder: trust

APPLICATION INFORMATION
Initial Approach: Send cover letter and full proposal. Deadlines are March 1 and September 1. Board meets in April and October.

OTHER THINGS TO KNOW
Publications: Application Guidelines

GRANTS ANALYSIS
Number of Grants: 45
Highest Grant: $15,300
Typical Range: $1,000 to $10,000
Disclosure Period: 1991

RECENT GRANTS
15,300 Goshen College, Goshen, IN
10,500 Church of God in Christ Mennonite, Moundridge, KS
10,000 Associated Mennonite Biblical Seminaries, Elkhart, IN
10,000 Bethel College, North Newton, KS
10,000 Church of God in Christ Mennonite, Moundridge, KS
10,000 General Conference Mennonite Church, Newton, KS
9,500 Mennonite Church, Elkhart, IN
7,500 Church of God in Christ Mennonite, Moundridge, KS
5,000 Mennonite Central Committee, Akron, OH
5,000 Offender/Victim Ministries, Newton, KS

Schrafft and Bertha E. Schrafft Charitable Trust, William E.

CONTACT
John M. Wood, Jr.
Trustee
William E. Schrafft and Bertha E. Schrafft Charitable Trust
One Financial Center, 26th Fl.
Boston, MA 02111
(617) 350-6100

FINANCIAL SUMMARY
Recent Giving: $798,000 (1991); $679,600 (1988)
Assets: $17,129,983 (1991); $13,423,232 (1988)
EIN: 04-6065605

CONTRIBUTIONS SUMMARY
Donor(s): The foundation was established in 1946 by the late William E. and the late Bertha E. Schrafft.
Typical Recipients: • *Arts & Humanities:* arts appreciation, arts festivals, dance, museums/galleries, music, visual arts • *Civic & Public Affairs:* philanthropic organizations, zoos/botanical gardens • *Education:* literacy, minority education, private education (precollege), science/technology education • *Health:* hospitals, pediatric health, single-disease health associations • *Science:* science exhibits & fairs • *Social Services:* employment/job training, family services, homes, united funds, youth organizations
Grant Types: endowment, general support, multiyear/continuing support, operating expenses, and scholarship
Geographic Distribution: Massachusetts, with a focus on Boston

GIVING OFFICERS
Lavinia B. Chase: trust
Karen Faulkner: exec dir
Robert H. Jewell: trust
Arthur Parker: trust
John M. Wood, Jr.: trust

APPLICATION INFORMATION
Initial Approach: The foundation requests applications be made in writing. The foundation has no deadline for submitting proposals.

The board meets six times a year. Decisions are made within two months.
Restrictions on Giving: The foundation reports grants are made only to tax-exempt organizations in existence for at least three years. No grants are made to individuals, or for matching gifts, seed money, emergency funds, deficit spending, or loans.

OTHER THINGS TO KNOW
Publications: annual report and application guidelines

GRANTS ANALYSIS
Total Grants: $798,000
Number of Grants: 88
Highest Grant: $80,000
Typical Range: $3,000 to $10,000
Disclosure Period: 1991
Note: Recent grants are derived from a 1991 grants list.

RECENT GRANTS
80,000 United Way, Boston, MA
25,000 Boston Plan ACCESS, Boston, MA
25,000 Gordon College, Hamilton, MA
25,000 Winchester Photographic Exhibit (Griffin), Winchester, MA
20,000 Boys and Girls Club, Boston, MA
20,000 Children's Hospital, Boston, MA
20,000 Family Service of Greater Boston, Boston, MA
20,000 Federated Dorchester Neighborhood Houses, Dorchester, MA
20,000 Jobs for Youth, Boston, MA
17,500 New England Colleges Fund, Boston, MA

Schramm Foundation

CONTACT
Lesley E. Kring
President
Schramm Fdn.
8528 West 10th Ave.
Lakewood, CO 80215
(303) 232-1772

FINANCIAL SUMMARY
Recent Giving: $187,255 (fiscal 1992); $192,235 (fiscal 1991); $184,750 (fiscal 1990)
Assets: $4,553,139 (fiscal year ending June 30, 1992); $4,285,340 (fiscal 1991); $4,132,383 (fiscal 1990)
EIN: 84-6032196

CONTRIBUTIONS SUMMARY
Typical Recipients: • *Arts & Humanities:* public broadcasting • *Education:* colleges & universities, education associations • *Health:* hospitals, medical research, single-disease health associations • *Religion:* churches, religious organizations • *Social Services:* day care, disabled, family planning, homes, united funds, youth organizations
Grant Types: general support and operating expenses
Geographic Distribution: limited to CO

GIVING OFFICERS
Joseph Heit: treas
Gary S. Kring: secy
Lesley E. Kring: pres
Arnold Tietze: vp

APPLICATION INFORMATION
Initial Approach: Send brief letter of inquiry describing program or project. Deadline is August 15.
Restrictions on Giving: Does not support individuals.

GRANTS ANALYSIS
Number of Grants: 37
Highest Grant: $20,000
Typical Range: $1,000 to $5,000
Disclosure Period: fiscal year ending June 30, 1992

RECENT GRANTS
20,000 AMC Cancer Research, Denver, CO
12,500 KRMA TV, Denver, CO
10,000 KRMA TV, Denver, CO
10,000 Mount Zion Lutheran Church, Denver, CO
10,000 Parkinsons Association of Rockies, Denver, CO
 9,753 Lutheran Medical Center, Wheatridge, CO
 8,815 Sewall Child Development Center, Denver, CO
 8,000 Friends of Maria Mitchell, Denver, CO
 7,500 St. Anthony Hospital, Denver, CO
 7,500 University of Colorado Foundation, Boulder, CO

Schreiber Foods, Inc. / Bush-D.D. Nusbaum Foundation, M.G.
Sales: $675.0 million
Employees: 2,300
Headquarters: Green Bay, WI
SIC Major Group: Food & Kindred Products and Industrial Machinery & Equipment

CONTACT
Robert J. Pruess
Vice President & Secretary-Treasurer
M.G. Bush-D.D. Nusbaum Foundation
425 Pine St.
PO Box 19010
Green Bay, WI 54301
(414) 437-7601

FINANCIAL SUMMARY
Recent Giving: $2,000 (1991); $5,000 (1989)
Assets: $110,215 (1991); $80,578 (1989)
Gifts Received: $10,000 (1991); $10,000 (1989)
Fiscal Note: In 1991, contributions were received from Schreiber Foods.
EIN: 39-1537768

CONTRIBUTIONS SUMMARY
Typical Recipients: • *Arts & Humanities:* history/historic preservation, performing arts, theater • *Education:* colleges & universities, medical education • *Health:* nursing services
Grant Types: general support
Geographic Distribution: focus on WI
Operating Locations: WI (Green Bay)

CORP. OFFICERS
Robert Bush: *CURR EMPL* chmn: Schreiber Foods
John C. Meng: *CURR EMPL* pres, ceo: Schreiber Foods
Dick Ward: *CURR EMPL* cfo: Schreiber Foods

GIVING OFFICERS
Robert Bush: pres, dir *CURR EMPL* chmn: Schreiber Foods (see above)
D. D. Nusbaum: dir
R. J. Preuss: vp, secy, treas, dir

APPLICATION INFORMATION
Initial Approach: Send brief letter describing program. There are no deadlines.

GRANTS ANALYSIS
Number of Grants: 2
Highest Grant: $1,000
Disclosure Period: 1991

RECENT GRANTS
1,000 St. Norbert College, De Pere, WI
1,000 University of Wisconsin, Madison, WI

Schroeder Foundation, Walter

CONTACT
William T. Gaus
Vice President and Treasurer
Walter Schroeder Foundation
1000 North Water St.
13th Fl.
Milwaukee, WI 53202
(414) 287-7177

FINANCIAL SUMMARY
Recent Giving: $600,000 (fiscal 1993 est.); $627,150 (fiscal 1992); $1,034,397 (fiscal 1991)
Assets: $6,783,674 (fiscal 1992 est.); $7,505,516 (fiscal year ending June 30, 1991); $7,801,669 (fiscal 1990); $8,490,569 (fiscal 1989)
EIN: 39-6065789

CONTRIBUTIONS SUMMARY
Donor(s): Walter Schroeder established the foundation in 1963. Mr. Schroeder was president of Chris Schroeder and Son Company, a general insurance, real estate, and mortgage loan company in Milwaukee. He was also president of several hotel companies, and was a member of several hotel and restaurant associations.
Typical Recipients: • *Arts & Humanities:* arts centers, arts festivals, arts funds, arts institutes, museums/galleries, music, performing arts, theater • *Civic & Public Affairs:* business/free enterprise, environmental affairs, zoos/botanical gardens • *Education:* arts education, colleges & universities, education funds, private education (precollege), public education (precollege) • *Health:* health organizations, hospitals, medical research, pediatric health, single-disease health as-

sociations • *Religion:* religious organizations • *Science:* scientific organizations • *Social Services:* aged, animal protection, child welfare, community centers, community service organizations, disabled, family services, homes, religious welfare, united funds, volunteer services, youth organizations
Grant Types: capital, general support, project, and research
Geographic Distribution: focus on Milwaukee County, WI

GIVING OFFICERS
William Thomas Gaus: vp, treas, dir *B* Berlin Germany 1928 *ED* Marquette Univ 1951; Marquette Univ JD 1954 *CURR EMPL* sr vp, chief trust off: Marshall & Ilsley Trust Co *NONPR AFFIL* mem: Am Bar Assn
Robert M. Hoffer: dir *B* Muncie IN 1921 *ED* Ball St Univ BS 1948; Univ MI MBA 1949 *CORP AFFIL* chmn, ceo, dir: WICOR; dir: Applied Power, Badger Meter, WI Gas Co, WICOR; trust: Northwestern Mutual Life Ins Co *NONPR AFFIL* dir: Am Gas Assn, Athletes for Youth Org, Blood Ctr Southeastern WI, Blue Coats Fdn, Columbia Health Systems, Greater Milwaukee Comm, Inst Gas Tech, Jr Achievement Southeastern WI, Med Coll WI, Metro Milwaukee Assn Commerce, YMCA; mem: Am Inst CPAs, MI Assn CPAs, Midwest Gas Assn; mem, dir: WI Utilities Assn
Ruthmarie Lawrenz: dir
John A. Puelicher: pres, dir *B* Milwaukee WI 1920 *ED* Univ WI 1943; Univ Wisconsin BA 1943; Harvard Grad Sch Bus Admin *CORP AFFIL* dir: WR Grace & Co, Great Northern Nekoosa Corp, M&I Capital Markets Group, M&I Data Services, M&I Marshall & Ilsley Bank, Modine Mfg Co, Modine Mfg Co, Mosinee Paper Corp, Sentry Ins Co, Sundstrand Corp, Sundstrand Corp, WR Grace & Co *NONPR AFFIL* trust emeritus: Marquette Univ
Marjorie Vallier: secy, dir

APPLICATION INFORMATION
Initial Approach:
Applicants should send a letter to the foundation.
There is no formal policy for applications. A letter outlining

the nature of the proposed grant is recommended.
There are no deadlines for submitting requests.
The board meets in February, May, August, and November. Final notification on decisions varies.

OTHER THINGS TO KNOW
Grants are not made to individuals.

GRANTS ANALYSIS
Total Grants: $1,034,397
Number of Grants: 76
Highest Grant: $100,000
Typical Range: $500 to $50,000
Disclosure Period: fiscal year ending June 30, 1991
Note: Average grant figure excludes two grants totaling $175,000. Recent grants are derived from a fiscal 1991 Form 990.

RECENT GRANTS
100,000 Blood Center Research Center, Milwaukee, WI — health care
75,000 Florentine Opera Company, Milwaukee, WI — cultural
60,000 Zoological Society of Milwaukee County, Milwaukee, WI — cultural
50,000 Cardinal Stritch College, Milwaukee, WI — educational
50,000 Columbia Hospital, Milwaukee, WI — health care
50,000 Medical College of Milwaukee, Milwaukee, WI — educational
50,000 Museum of Science, Economics and Technology, Milwaukee, WI — cultural
50,000 Riveredge Nature Center, Newburg, WI — educational
50,000 St. Francis Children's Activity Center, Milwaukee, WI — concern for youth
50,000 United Lutheran Program for the Aging, Milwaukee, WI — social services

Schulman Inc., A.
Sales: $736.0 million
Employees: 1,491
Headquarters: Akron, OH
SIC Major Group: Chemicals & Allied Products and Rubber & Miscellaneous Plastics Products

CONTACT
Robert Stefanko
Chairman, CFO
A. Schulman, Inc.
3550 West Market St., PO Box 1710
Akron, OH 44309
(216) 666-3751

CONTRIBUTIONS SUMMARY
Operating Locations: OH (Akron)

CORP. OFFICERS
Terry L. Haines: *CURR EMPL* pres, ceo: A Schulman

Schulman Management Corp.
Sales: $60.0 million
Employees: 120
Headquarters: White Plains, NY
SIC Major Group: Real Estate

CONTACT
Michele Palermo
Schulman Management Corp.
925 Westchester Ave.
White Plains, NY 10604
(914) 761-5562
Note: Doug Ramsay may also be used as a contact name.

CONTRIBUTIONS SUMMARY
Grant Types: matching

Schultz Foundation

CONTACT
Clifford G. Schultz II
President
Schultz Fdn.
c/o Schultz Bldg.
PO Box 1200
Jacksonville, FL 32201
(904) 354-3603

FINANCIAL SUMMARY
Recent Giving: $122,222 (1990); $89,191 (1989)
Assets: $2,423,669 (1989)
EIN: 59-1055869

CONTRIBUTIONS SUMMARY
Donor(s): the late Mae W. Schultz, the late Geneive S.

Ayers, Frederick H. Schultz, Nancy R. Schultz

Typical Recipients: • *Civic & Public Affairs:* environmental affairs, ethnic/minority organizations, public policy • *Health:* medical research, single-disease health associations • *Social Services:* community service organizations, community service organizations, homes, united funds, volunteer services, youth organizations

Grant Types: general support

Geographic Distribution: focus on Jacksonville, FL, and GA

GIVING OFFICERS

Catherine Kelly: trust

John Richard Reilly: secy, treas *B* Dubuque IA 1928 *ED* Univ Notre Dame AB 1959; Harvard Univ MBA 1964 *CURR EMPL* chmn, ceo: K-III Holdings

Clifford G. Schultz II: dir, pres

Frederick H. Schultz, Jr.: trust

John R. Schultz: trust

Nancy R. Schultz: dir, vp

APPLICATION INFORMATION

Initial Approach: Contributes only to preselected organizations.

Restrictions on Giving: Does not support individuals.

OTHER THINGS TO KNOW

Publications: Annual Report

GRANTS ANALYSIS

Number of Grants: 101

Highest Grant: $10,025

Typical Range: $25 to $1,000

Disclosure Period: 1989

RECENT GRANTS

10,025 Jacksonville Zoological Society, Jacksonville, FL

10,000 Volunteers of America, Jacksonville, FL

8,150 Museum of Science and History, Jacksonville, FL

7,500 University of North Florida Music Department, Jacksonville, FL

5,100 Jacksonville Symphony Orchestra, Jacksonville, FL

5,000 Nature Conservancy, Winter Park, FL

5,000 Paideia School, Atlanta, GA

5,000 United Way, Jacksonville, FL

5,000 Youth Leadership Jacksonville, Jacksonville, FL

4,000 Hope Haven, Jacksonville, FL

Schultz Foundation

CONTACT

George L. Schultz
President
Schultz Fdn.
825 Bloomfield Avenue, Ste. 105
Verona, NJ 07015
(201) 857-9303

FINANCIAL SUMMARY

Recent Giving: $709,734 (fiscal 1992); $623,564 (fiscal 1991); $663,558 (fiscal 1990)

Assets: $18,638,007 (fiscal year ending June 30, 1992); $18,594,720 (fiscal 1991); $17,424,664 (fiscal 1990)

Gifts Received: $7,700 (fiscal 1992)

Fiscal Note: Fiscal In 1992, contributions were received from George L. Schultz.

EIN: 22-6103387

CONTRIBUTIONS SUMMARY

Donor(s): The foundation was incorporated in 1966 by the late Mabel L. Schultz and other members of the Schultz family. In 1987, the foundation merged with The William Lightfoot Schultz Foundation which was incorporated in 1952.

Typical Recipients: • *Arts & Humanities:* arts centers, community arts, dance, history/historic preservation, music, public broadcasting, theater • *Civic & Public Affairs:* better government, environmental affairs, philanthropic organizations • *Education:* colleges & universities, medical education, minority education, private education (precollege) • *Health:* health organizations, hospices, hospitals, medical research • *Religion:* churches • *Social Services:* child welfare, family planning, united funds, youth organizations

Grant Types: capital, general support, operating expenses, project, research, scholarship, and seed money

Geographic Distribution: focus on eastern United States

GIVING OFFICERS

John Barker: trust

Margaret Schultz Bilotti: trust

Marilyn Schultz Blackwell: trust

Katharine Schultz Fieldhouse: trust

Douglas C. Rigg: trust

Elizabeth Schultz Rigg: vp, trust

Geoffrey B. Rigg: trust

George L. Schultz: pres, treas, trust

Margaret F. Schultz: secy, trust

APPLICATION INFORMATION

Initial Approach:
The foundation has no formal grant application procedure or application form.

The foundation has no deadline for submitting proposals.

Restrictions on Giving: The foundation does not support individuals, deficit financing, endowment funds, equipment, land acquisition, or loans.

GRANTS ANALYSIS

Total Grants: $709,734

Number of Grants: 42

Highest Grant: $100,000

Typical Range: $1,000 to $15,000

Disclosure Period: fiscal year ending June 30, 1992

Note: Average grant figure does not include the highest grant of $100,000. Recent grants are derived from a fiscal 1992 grants list.

RECENT GRANTS

100,000 Princeton University, Princeton, NJ — blood brain barrier research

86,512 Foundation of University of Medicine and Dentistry, Newark, NJ

62,500 Greenwich Hospital Association, Greenwich, CT — cancer center building campaign

62,082 Memorial Sloan-Kettering Cancer Center, New York, NY — for cancer research

60,000 College of Physicians and Surgeons of Columbia University, New York, NY — markers of early blood vessel injury research project

50,000 Foundation of University of Medicine and Dentistry, Newark, NJ

50,000 Planned Parenthood Federation of America, NJ — national assistance family planning

37,500 Heritage Foundation, Washington, DC — healthcare reform project

20,000 College of Physicians and Surgeons of Columbia University, New York, NY — purchase of PCR machine

20,000 North Essex Development and Action Council, Essex, MA — treatment and prevention of substance abusers

Schumann Foundation, Florence and John

CONTACT

Bill Moyers
President
Florence and John Schumann Foundation
33 Park St.
Montclair, NJ 07042
(201) 783-6660

FINANCIAL SUMMARY

Recent Giving: $5,000,000 (1993 est.); $7,196,720 (1992); $5,782,200 (1991)

Assets: $83,000,000 (1992 est.); $83,423,276 (1991); $76,873,659 (1990)

Gifts Received: $19,316,250 (1990)

Fiscal Note: In 1990, the foundation received shares of IBM stock valued at $19,316,250 from Mrs. Florence Schumann.

EIN: 22-6044214

CONTRIBUTIONS SUMMARY

Donor(s): The Florence and John Schumann Foundation was established in 1961. It was founded and endowed by gifts from Florence F. Schumann (d. 1991) and her late husband, John J. Schumann, Jr., who served on the board from 1961 until his death in 1964.

In 1988, the foundation established the Schumann Fund for New Jersey, endowing it for $20 million. The fund makes grants to Essex County groups and to organizations that address statewide problems; and the philanthropic priorities of John and Florence Schumann. The Schumann Foundation, with a remaining endowment of $50 million, now funds programs on a national level.

Typical Recipients: • *Arts & Humanities:* public broadcasting • *Civic & Public Affairs:* better government, environmental affairs, international affairs, law & justice, public policy • *Education:* colleges & universities

Grant Types: general support, project, and seed money

Geographic Distribution: national

GIVING OFFICERS

David S. Bate: secy, treas, trust

Howard Denton Brundage: trust *B* Newark NJ 1923 *ED* Dartmouth Coll BA 1944 *CURR EMPL* vp: Dresdner Smith Barney Harris Upham

Edwin Deacon Etherington: trust *B* Bayonne NJ 1924 *ED* Wesleyan Univ BA 1948; Yale Univ JD 1952 *NONPR AFFIL* chmn: Lymes Youth Svcs Bd; hon chmn: Hobe Sound Child Care Ctr; incorporator: Natl Housing Partnership; mem: Kappa Beta Phi, Order Coif, Phi Beta Kappa Assocs, Phi Delta Phi, Phi Phi Beta Kappa; pres emeritus: Wesleyan Univ; trust: Coll Wooster; hon trust: Hammonasset Sch

Caroline Schumann Mark: vp, trust

Patricia A. McCarthy: adm off

Bill Moyers: pres *CURR EMPL* exec editor: Pub Aff Television *NONPR AFFIL* fellow: Am Academy Arts & Sciences

Robert F. Schumann: chmn, trust

W. Ford Schumann: vp, trust

APPLICATION INFORMATION

Initial Approach:

There is no standard application form. Written proposals should be submitted to the president of the foundation. Include a description of the organization's objectives, activities, and leadership; and a detailed discussion of the purpose of the proposed project and plan for its accomplishment. The proposal should also include a copy of the latest financial statement, expense budget identifying sources of income, time frame and future funding plans, and evidence of IRS tax-exempt status.

Proposals should be submitted before January 15, April 15,

August 15, or October 15; in each case, six weeks prior to the board of trustees' meetings. The foundation replies as quickly as possible to requests. Some requests may be reserved for the next quarterly meeting.

Restrictions on Giving: The foundation does not encourage applications for capital campaigns, annual giving, endowment, or direct support of individuals.

OTHER THINGS TO KNOW

The foundation created the Schumann Fund for New Jersey in 1988.

Publications: annual report

GRANTS ANALYSIS

Total Grants: $7,196,720

Number of Grants: 80

Highest Grant: $1,000,000

Typical Range: $15,000 to $100,000

Disclosure Period: 1992

Note: Recent grants are derived from a 1992 grants list.

RECENT GRANTS

1,000,000 Children's Defense Fund, Washington, DC — to support the Crusade for Children/Challenge to the Community

340,426 Columbia University Graduate School of Journalism, New York, NY — to create a special training program

250,000 Arkansas Institute for Social Justice, Little Rock, AR — a four-year grant to ACORN of Brooklyn, New York

250,000 National Audubon Society, New York, NY — to support construction

220,000 Independent Production Fund, New York, NY — to support the Voices of the Electorate project

200,000 Center for Responsive Politics, Washington, DC — support

150,000 National Toxics Campaign Fund, Boston, MA — to promote grassroots organizing

150,000 New Prospect, Princeton, NJ — to improve and promote the publica-

tion The American Prospect

134,000 National Public Radio, Washington, DC — to cover costs of a full-time reporter

105,000 Center for Investigative Reporting, San Francisco, CA — to support investigation of the environmental backlash movement

---

Schumann Fund for New Jersey

CONTACT

Julie A. Keenan
Executive Director
Schumann Fund for New Jersey
33 Park St.
Montclair, NJ 07042
(201) 509-9883
Note: The foundation shares its office with the Florence and John Schumann Foundation.

FINANCIAL SUMMARY

Recent Giving: $1,108,000 (1992); $1,193,111 (1991)

Assets: $21,099,234 (1991)

EIN: 52-1556076

CONTRIBUTIONS SUMMARY

Donor(s): The foundation was established in 1988 by the Florence and John Schumann Foundation.

Typical Recipients: • *Arts & Humanities:* public broadcasting • *Civic & Public Affairs:* environmental affairs, ethnic/minority organizations, public policy • *Education:* education associations, private education (precollege) • *Social Services:* child welfare, day care, family services, food/clothing distribution, recreation & athletics, shelters/homelessness

Grant Types: multiyear/continuing support and project

Geographic Distribution: New Jersey with a focus on Essex County

GIVING OFFICERS

Aubin Z. Ames: trust

Leonard S. Coleman: vchmn, trust

Christopher J. Daggett: trust

Andrew Christian Halvorsen: trust *B* Englewood NJ 1946 *ED* Brown Univ 1968; Univ PA MBA 1972 *CURR EMPL* cfo, mem off pres: Beneficial Corp

George R. Harris: chmn, trust

Barbara H. Malcolm: trust

Alan Rosenthal: trust

Donald Malcolm Wilson: trust *B* Glen Ridge NJ 1925 *ED* Yale Univ 1948 *NONPR AFFIL* dir: Citizens Crime Comm, Ctr Analysis Pub Issues, Guggenheim Mus, Natl Corp Fund Dance, Reading Is Fundamental; mem: Counc Foreign Rels; mem adv counc: Edward R Murrow Ctr Tufts Univ

APPLICATION INFORMATION

Initial Approach:

Applicants should submit a written proposal.

The propsal should include a description in some detail of the proposed project and the plan for accomplishment. The proposal should be accompanied by a copy of the organization's latest financial statement, an expense budget which specifically identifies all sources of income, the project's time frame and future funding plans, and a copy of the organization's IRS tax-exempt determination letter. Proposals should be submitted before January 15, April 15, August 15, or October 15, which is approximately six weeks before the following board meeting.

The board meets four times a year in March, June, October, and December. The foundation indicates that action on proposals may be reserved for a later quarter, but it will reply as promptly as possible as to the status of all requests.

Restrictions on Giving: In general, the fund does not accept applications for capital campaigns, annual giving, endowment, direct support of individuals, and local programs in counties other than Essex.

OTHER THINGS TO KNOW

Publications: annual report including application guidelines

GRANTS ANALYSIS

Total Grants: $1,193,111

Number of Grants: 39*

Highest Grant: $111,000

Typical Range: $15,000 to $50,000

Disclosure Period: 1991

Note: Number of grants figure excludes trustee-initiated grants. Average grant figure excludes the fund's highest grant of $111,000, or $105,000 in trustee-initiated grants. Recent grants are derived from a 1991 annual report.

RECENT GRANTS

111,000 Woodrow Wilson School of Public and International Affairs, Council on New Jersey Affairs, Princeton, NJ — multi-year grant

80,000 Babyland Nursery, Newark, NJ — child care provider that the foundation has supported since 1971

50,000 Nature Conservancy, Arlington, VA — supports the "Campaign for the Delaware," a four-state initiative to protect the Delaware River Basin

50,000 North Ward Center, Newark, NJ — continuing support

45,000 Unified Vailsburg Services Organization, Newark, NJ — grass-roots community organization provides Meals-on-Wheels, senior citizen services, youth and day care programs, and neighborhood housing development

42,000 Chad School, Newark, NJ

40,000 Catholic Community Services, Newark, NJ — supports emergency shelters for homeless mothers and children in Newark

40,000 Education Law Center, Philadelphia, PA — supports the Equal Educational Opportunity Project which strives to achieve parity in per-pupil spending throughout New Jersey public schools

32,111 Rutgers University Foundation, Department of Biological Sciences, New Brunswick, NJ — supports efforts to restore native plant communities on capped landfills in the Meadowlands

30,000 Foundation of the University of Medicine and Dentistry of New Jersey, Newark, NJ — to train day care

providers to identify the developmental needs of preschool children

---

Schust Foundation, Clarence L. and Edith B.

CONTACT

Clarence L. and Edith B. Schust Fdn.
c/o Fort Wayne National Bank
110 West Berry St.
PO Box 110
Ft. Wayne, IN 46801
(219) 426-0555

FINANCIAL SUMMARY

Recent Giving: $314,443 (fiscal 1992); $203,447 (fiscal 1991); $177,061 (fiscal 1990)
Assets: $3,925,215 (fiscal year ending April 30, 1992); $3,771,480 (fiscal 1991); $3,437,633 (fiscal 1990)
EIN: 31-1064803

CONTRIBUTIONS SUMMARY

Typical Recipients: • *Civic & Public Affairs:* environmental affairs, professional & trade associations • *Education:* religious education • *Health:* health organizations, hospitals, medical research • *Religion:* churches, religious organizations • *Social Services:* disabled, united funds, youth organizations
Grant Types: general support
Geographic Distribution: focus on IN and IL

APPLICATION INFORMATION

Initial Approach: Send cover letter and full proposal. There are no deadlines.

GRANTS ANALYSIS

Number of Grants: 36
Highest Grant: $50,000
Typical Range: $1,000 to $10,000
Disclosure Period: fiscal year ending April 30, 1992

RECENT GRANTS

50,000 IPFW Scholarship Fund, Ft. Wayne, IN

45,310 Fort Wayne Community Foundation, Ft. Wayne, IN

25,000 Lutheran Social Services, Ft. Wayne, IN

20,619 Trinity English Lutheran Church, Ft. Wayne, IN

13,810 YMCA, Ft. Wayne, IN

13,310 Lutheran Hospital Foundation, Ft. Wayne, IN

10,310 American Red Cross, Ft. Wayne, IN

10,310 Indiana Demolay Foundation, Franklin, IN

10,310 Indiana Masonic Home Foundation, Indianapolis, IN

10,310 Parkview Foundation, Ft. Wayne, IN

Schwab & Co., Charles

Assets: $5.9 billion
Employees: 2,900
Parent Company: Charles Schwab Corp.
Headquarters: San Francisco, CA
SIC Major Group: Security & Commodity Brokers

CONTACT

Karen Ens
Coordinator, Corporate Contributions
Charles Schwab & Co.
101 Montgomery St.
San Francisco, CA 94104
(415) 627-8415

FINANCIAL SUMMARY

Recent Giving: $1,500,000 (1993)
Fiscal Note: Company gives directly.

CONTRIBUTIONS SUMMARY

Typical Recipients: • *Arts & Humanities:* arts associations, community arts, libraries, museums/galleries, music, opera, performing arts, public broadcasting • *Civic & Public Affairs:* environmental affairs, nonprofit management, philanthropic organizations, urban & community affairs, zoos/botanical gardens • *Education:* business education, economic education, public education (precollege) • *Health:* single-disease health associations • *Social Services:* animal protection, community service organizations, disabled, emergency relief, employment/job training, family services, food/clothing distribution, recreation & athletics, shelters/homelessness, united

funds, volunteer services, youth organizations
Grant Types: capital, general support, matching, multi-year/continuing support, operating expenses, project, and scholarship
Nonmonetary Support Types: in-kind services
Note: In-kind services consist of printing.
Geographic Distribution: primarily headquarters and in geographic areas where there are Schwab branch offices
Operating Locations: CA (San Francisco), NJ (Jersey City)

CORP. OFFICERS

David S. Pottruck: *B* 1948 *ED* Univ PA BA 1970; Univ PA MBA 1972 *CURR EMPL* pres, ceo, dir: Charles Schwab & Co
Charles R. Schwab: *CURR EMPL* chmn, dir: Charles Schwab & Co
Lawrence J. Stupski: *CURR EMPL* vchmn, dir: Charles Schwab & Co

GIVING OFFICERS

Karen Ens: *CURR EMPL* coordinator corp contributions: Charles Schwab & Co

APPLICATION INFORMATION

Initial Approach: *Initial Contact:* write to company requesting guidelines *Include Information On:* after receipt of guidelines, send brief letter of inquiry and full proposal, including a description of the organization, purpose of funds sought, recently audited financial statements, list of board members, list of current funding sources, and proof of tax-exempt status *When to Submit:* any time
Restrictions on Giving: Does not provide capital, challenge, or seed grants; purchase tickets to fundraisers, banquets, awards dinners, etc.; or purchase advertising in print or radio.

OTHER THINGS TO KNOW

Publications: program guidelines

GRANTS ANALYSIS

Typical Range: $1,000 to $2,500

Schwab Foundation, Charles and Helen

CONTACT

Charles and Helen Schwab
Foundation
873 jSutter Street, Suite B
San Francisco, CA 94109
(415) 771-4300

FINANCIAL SUMMARY

Recent Giving: $33,000 (fiscal
1990)
Assets: $3,474,832 (fiscal year
ending October 31, 1990)
Gifts Received: $148,750 (fiscal 1990)
EIN: 94-3053861

CONTRIBUTIONS SUMMARY

Typical Recipients: • *Arts &
Humanities:* museums/galleries, music
Grant Types: general support

GIVING OFFICERS

Lyman Casey: pres, dir
Helen Schwab: secy, treas, dir
Charles S. Schway: dir

APPLICATION INFORMATION

Initial Approach: The foundation reports it only makes contributions to preselected organizations and does not accept unsolicited requests for funds.

GRANTS ANALYSIS

Total Grants: $33,000
Number of Grants: 4
Highest Grant: $20,800
Typical Range: $500 to $20,000
Disclosure Period: fiscal year ending October 31, 1990

RECENT GRANTS

20,000 Bay Area Discovery Museum, Salsalito, CA
10,000 San Francisco Symphony, San Francisco, CA
2,500 San Francisco Symphony Volunteer, San Francisco, CA
500 Charles Armstrong School, Belmont, CA

Schwan's Sales Enterprises

Sales: $650.0 million
Employees: 5,000
Headquarters: Marshall, MN
SIC Major Group: Food &
Kindred Products

CONTACT

Rosie Goblish
Personnel
Schwan's Sales Enterprises
115 West College Dr.
Marshall, MN 56258
(507) 532-3274

CONTRIBUTIONS SUMMARY

Operating Locations: MN
(Marshall)

CORP. OFFICERS

Marvin Maynard Schwan: *B*
Marshall MN 1929 *ED* Bethany
Lutheran Coll *CURR EMPL*
pres: Schwans Sales Enterprises

Schwartz and Robert Schwartz Foundation, Bernard

CONTACT

Bernard Schwartz
President
Bernard Schwartz and Robert
Schwartz Fdn.
12th Fl., Packard Bldg.
Philadelphia, PA 19102
(215) 977-2104

FINANCIAL SUMMARY

Recent Giving: $481,135 (fiscal 1991); $315,000 (fiscal 1990); $221,150 (fiscal 1989)
Assets: $17,905,216 (fiscal year ending August 31, 1991); $13,927,030 (fiscal 1990); $10,546,406 (fiscal 1989)
Gifts Received: $2,973,141 (fiscal 1991); $3,000,000 (fiscal 1990); $5,295,000 (fiscal 1989)
Fiscal Note: 1991 contribution from Robert S. Schwartz.
EIN: 23-2267403

CONTRIBUTIONS SUMMARY

Donor(s): The foundation was established in 1983 by Robert S. Schwartz.
Typical Recipients: • *Arts &
Humanities:* museums/galleries
• *Education:* education funds
• *Health:* geriatric health • *Religion:* religious organizations, synagogues • *Social Services:* community service organizations, united funds
Grant Types: general support
Geographic Distribution:
focus on Pennsylvania, with an emphasis on Philadelphia

GIVING OFFICERS

Bernard Schwartz: pres *B*
New York NY 1923 *ED* City
Coll NY BSS; NY Univ LLB;
Harvard Univ LLM; Cambridge Univ PhD; Cambridge
Univ LLD *NONPR AFFIL* corresponding mem: Natl Academy Law & Social Sciences;
mem: Am Bar Assn

Robert S. Schwartz: treas

APPLICATION INFORMATION

Initial Approach: Restrictions on Giving: The foundation supports preselected organizations and does not accept unsolicited requests for funds. The foundation does not make grants to individuals.

GRANTS ANALYSIS

Total Grants: $481,135
Number of Grants: 19
Highest Grant: $166,935
Typical Range: $750 to $20,000
Disclosure Period: fiscal year ending August 31, 1991
Note: Average grant figure does not include the highest grant of $166,935. Recent grants are derived from a fiscal 1991 grants list.

RECENT GRANTS

166,935 Federation of Jewish Agencies of Greater Philadelphia, Philadelphia, PA
101,000 Federated Allied Jewish Appeal, Philadelphia, PA
100,000 Federated Allied Jewish Appeal, Philadelphia, PA
50,000 Institute for the Advancement of Education in Jaffa, Brooklyn, NY
20,000 Crime Prevention Association of Philadelphia, Philadelphia, PA
10,000 United Way, Philadelphia, PA
5,000 Jewish Federation of South New Jersey, NJ
2,000 Temple Adath Israel, Merion, PA
1,000 Franklin Institute, Philadelphia, PA
1,000 Philadelphia Museum of Art, Philadelphia, PA

Schwartz Foundation, Arnold A.

CONTACT

Edwin D. Kunzman
President
Arnold A. Schwartz Fdn.
c/o Kunzman, Coley, Yospin and
Bernstein
15 Mountain Blvd.
Warren, NJ 07060
(201) 757-7800

FINANCIAL SUMMARY

Recent Giving: $172,300 (fiscal 1991); $151,208 (fiscal 1990); $152,500 (fiscal 1989)
Assets: $3,977,606 (fiscal year ending November 30, 1991); $3,603,623 (fiscal 1990); $3,528,031 (fiscal 1989)
EIN: 22-6034152

CONTRIBUTIONS SUMMARY

Donor(s): the late Arnold A. Schwartz
Typical Recipients: • *Arts &
Humanities:* libraries • *Education:* private education (precollege), special education
• *Health:* health organizations, hospitals • *Social Services:*
child welfare, community service organizations, disabled, family services, youth organizations
Grant Types: general support
Geographic Distribution:
focus on northern NJ

GIVING OFFICERS

Victor DiLeo: trust
Louis Harding: vp
Edwin D. Kunzman: pres
Steven Kunzman: secy, treas
David Lackland: trust
Robert Shapiro: trust
Kenneth Trunbull: trust

APPLICATION INFORMATION

Initial Approach: Send brief letter describing program. Deadline is September 30.
Restrictions on Giving: Does not support individuals or provide funds for endowments;

GRANTS ANALYSIS

Number of Grants: 54
Highest Grant: $17,100
Typical Range: $1,000 to $5,000
Disclosure Period: fiscal year ending November 30, 1991

RECENT GRANTS

17,100	Muhlenberg Regional Medical Center, Plainfield, NJ
9,000	A.A. Schwartz Memorial Library, West Orange, NJ
7,500	Matheny School, Peapack, NJ
7,000	Mcauley School for Exceptional Children
6,500	American Red Cross, New York, NY
6,000	Edison Sheltered Workshop, Edison, NJ
6,000	YMCA
5,000	Somerset Home for Temporarily Displaced Children, Somerset, NJ
5,000	Somerset Medical Center, Somerset, NJ
5,000	Summit Speech School

Schwartz Foundation, Bernard Lee

CONTACT
Bernard Lee Schwartz Fdn.
c/o Delaware Corp. Management
1105 North Market St.
Wilmington, DE 19899

FINANCIAL SUMMARY
Recent Giving: $391,181 (fiscal 1991); $388,355 (fiscal 1990); $408,280 (fiscal 1989)
Assets: $12,710,896 (fiscal year ending September 30, 1991); $13,403,511 (fiscal 1990); $12,656,260 (fiscal 1989)
Gifts Received: $100,000 (fiscal 1991); $190,990 (fiscal 1990); $190,300 (fiscal 1989)
Fiscal Note: In 1991, contributions were received from Tilda R. Orr.
EIN: 13-6096198

CONTRIBUTIONS SUMMARY
Donor(s): the late Bernard L. Schwartz
Typical Recipients: • *Arts & Humanities:* dance, museums/galleries, visual arts • *Education:* colleges & universities, education associations • *Health:* health organizations, hospitals, medical research • *Religion:* synagogues • *Social Services:* emergency relief

Grant Types: general support and research

GIVING OFFICERS
Tilda R. Orr: secy
Donald N. Ravitch: vp
Eric A. Schwartz: dir
Michael L. Schwartz: treas, dir
Rosalyn R. Schwartz: pres, dir

APPLICATION INFORMATION
Initial Approach: Contributes only to preselected organizations.

GRANTS ANALYSIS
Number of Grants: 11
Highest Grant: $295,000
Typical Range: $1,000 to $15,000
Disclosure Period: fiscal year ending September 30, 1991

RECENT GRANTS

295,000	Bryn Mawr College, Bryn Mawr, PA
37,000	Scripps Memorial Hospital Foundation, La Jolla, CA
24,000	United World College
15,000	International Center of Philosophy
6,167	Pomfret School, Pomfret, CT
5,000	Scripps Clinic and Research Foundation, La Jolla, CA
3,500	National Dance Institute, New York, NY
1,844	University of California San Francisco Foundation, San Francisco, CA
1,000	Congregation Emanuel, New York, NY
1,000	Jewish Community Federation

Schwartz Foundation, David

CONTACT
Richard J. Schwartz
President
David Schwartz Fdn.
720 Fifth Ave.
New York, NY 10019
(212) 586-4225

FINANCIAL SUMMARY
Recent Giving: $1,346,274 (fiscal 1992); $1,486,363 (fiscal 1991); $1,660,385 (fiscal 1990)
Assets: $14,285,344 (fiscal year ending May 31, 1992); $14,139,407 (fiscal 1991); $14,455,322 (fiscal 1990)
EIN: 22-6075974

CONTRIBUTIONS SUMMARY
Donor(s): The foundation was incorporated in 1945 by Jonathan Logan, Inc., David Schwartz, and others.
Typical Recipients: • *Arts & Humanities:* arts centers, arts festivals, history/historic preservation, museums/galleries, music, opera, performing arts, theater • *Civic & Public Affairs:* environmental affairs, ethnic/minority organizations, international affairs, public policy, zoos/botanical gardens • *Education:* colleges & universities, legal education, medical education, private education (precollege), religious education • *Health:* hospitals, medical research, single-disease health associations • *Religion:* religious organizations, synagogues • *Social Services:* child welfare, community service organizations, family planning, family services, shelters/homelessness, youth organizations
Grant Types: general support
Geographic Distribution: focus on New York, NY

GIVING OFFICERS
Stephen D. Gardner: secy, dir
Irene Schwartz: dir
Richard J. Schwartz: pres, dir
Sheila Schwartz: vp, treas

APPLICATION INFORMATION
Initial Approach: Restrictions on Giving: The foundation supports preselected organizations and does not accept unsolicited requests for funds. The foundation does not make grants to individuals.

GRANTS ANALYSIS
Total Grants: $1,346,274
Number of Grants: 117
Highest Grant: $454,764
Typical Range: $500 to $25,000
Disclosure Period: fiscal year ending May 31, 1992
Note: Recent grants are derived from a fiscal 1992 grants list.

RECENT GRANTS

454,764	Cornell University, Ithaca, NY
150,000	United Jewish Appeal Federation, New York, NY
75,000	Lincoln Center for the Performing Arts, New York, NY
60,000	Brandeis University, Waltham, MA
50,000	Jerusalem Foundation, New York, NY
37,500	Smithsonian Institute/NMAA, Washington, DC
34,500	Metropolitan Museum of Art, New York, NY
30,000	Archives of American Art
30,000	Cooper Union
30,000	Historic Hudson Valley, NY

Schwartz Fund for Education and Health Research, Arnold and Marie

CONTACT
Arnold and Marie Schwartz Fund for Education and Health Research
465 Park Ave.
New York, NY 10022

FINANCIAL SUMMARY
Recent Giving: $499,725 (fiscal 1992); $502,344 (fiscal 1991); $432,340 (fiscal 1990)
Assets: $4,897,222 (fiscal year ending March 31, 1991); $6,021,241 (fiscal 1990); $5,561,943 (fiscal 1988)
EIN: 23-7115019

CONTRIBUTIONS SUMMARY
Donor(s): Arnold Schwartz Charitable Trust.
Typical Recipients: • *Arts & Humanities:* arts institutes, history/historic preservation, museums/galleries, music, opera, public broadcasting • *Civic & Public Affairs:* environmental affairs, zoos/botanical gardens • *Education:* colleges & universities, health & physical education, medical education • *Health:* hospitals • *Religion:* churches, synagogues • *Social Services:* child welfare, community service organizations, recreation & athletics, youth organizations
Grant Types: general support
Geographic Distribution: focus on the New York, NY area

GIVING OFFICERS
Sylvia Kassel: dir
Ruth Kerstein: secy, dir

Marie D. Schwartz: pres

APPLICATION INFORMATION
Initial Approach: Send brief letter of inquiry describing program or project. There are no deadlines.

GRANTS ANALYSIS
Number of Grants: 79
Highest Grant: $156,000
Typical Range: $25 to $10,000
Disclosure Period: fiscal year ending March 31, 1991
Note: No grants listed for fiscal 1992.

RECENT GRANTS
156,000 New York University, New York, NY
102,450 Arnold and Marie Schwartz College of Pharmacy and Health Sciences, Brooklyn, NY
55,000 National Trust for Historic Preservation, Washington, DC
25,000 San Antonio Museum of Art, San Antonio, TX
25,000 St. Marys Hospital Foundation, West Palm Beach, FL
10,200 Police Athletic League, New York, NY
10,000 American Council of Pharmaceutical Education, Chicago, IL
10,000 Long Island University, Brookville, NY
10,000 Queens College Foundation, Flushing, NY
10,000 United Way, Greenwich, CT

Schwob Foundation, Simon

CONTACT
Henry Schwob
President
Simon Schwob Fdn.
PO Box 1014
Columbus, GA 31902
(404) 327-4582

FINANCIAL SUMMARY
Recent Giving: $150,815 (1991); $163,550 (1990); $136,237 (1989)
Assets: $4,219,238 (1991); $3,950,261 (1990); $3,526,109 (1989)
EIN: 58-6038932

CONTRIBUTIONS SUMMARY
Donor(s): Schwob Manufacturing Co., Schwob Realty Co., Schwob Co. of Florida
Typical Recipients: • *Arts & Humanities:* community arts, libraries, museums/galleries, music, public broadcasting • *Civic & Public Affairs:* civil rights, ethnic/minority organizations • *Education:* colleges & universities, private education (precollege) • *Health:* geriatric health, hospitals • *Religion:* religious organizations, synagogues • *Social Services:* community service organizations
Grant Types: general support
Geographic Distribution: focus on GA

GIVING OFFICERS
Hannah Harrison: secy, treas
Henry Schwob: pres
Jane Beth Schwob: trust
Joyce Schwob: vp
Simone Schwob: trust

APPLICATION INFORMATION
Initial Approach: Send brief letter describing program. There are no deadlines.

GRANTS ANALYSIS
Number of Grants: 19
Highest Grant: $47,500
Typical Range: $500 to $5,000
Disclosure Period: 1991

RECENT GRANTS
47,500 Jewish Welfare Federation, Columbus, GA
31,000 Columbus College Foundation, Columbus, GA
12,000 Columbus Symphony Orchestra, Columbus, GA
11,950 Columbus Museum, Columbus, GA
11,065 Temple Israel, Columbus, GA
5,000 Bradley Center, Columbus, GA
5,000 Emory Geriatric Hospital, Atlanta, GA
5,000 John Amos Cancer Center, Columbus, GA
5,000 Pacelli High School, Columbus, GA
5,000 Patrons of Music, Columbus, GA

SCI Systems, Inc.
Sales: $1.12 billion
Employees: 9,762
Headquarters: Huntsville, AL
SIC Major Group: Electronic & Other Electrical Equipment, Industrial Machinery & Equipment, and Instruments & Related Products

CONTACT
Robert Delaurentis
Finance
SCI Systems, Inc.
PO Box 1000
Huntsville, AL 35807
(205) 882-4800

CONTRIBUTIONS SUMMARY
Operating Locations: AL (Huntsville)

CORP. OFFICERS
Olin B. King: *CURR EMPL* chmn: SCI Sys
A. Eugene Sapp, Jr.: *CURR EMPL* pres: SCI Sys

Science Applications International Corp.
Revenue: $1.2 billion
Employees: 15,000
Headquarters: San Diego, CA
SIC Major Group: Engineering & Management Services and Wholesale Trade—Durable Goods

CONTACT
Anita D. Jones
Senior Programs Administrator
Science Applications International Corp.
1710 Goodridge Dr., PO Box 1303
McLean, VA 22102
(703) 821-4300

FINANCIAL SUMMARY
Fiscal Note: Annual Giving Range: $100,000 to $250,000

CONTRIBUTIONS SUMMARY
Contributions are only made at the request of employees (Science Applications International is an employee-owned company).
Typical Recipients: • *Arts & Humanities:* arts festivals, public broadcasting • *Civic & Public Affairs:* business/free enterprise, economic development, environmental affairs, ethnic/minority organizations, national security, professional & trade associations, women's affairs • *Education:* business education, career/vocational education, colleges & universities, community & junior colleges, continuing education, education associations, engineering education, minority education, science/technology education • *Health:* health organizations, hospices • *Science:* scientific institutes, scientific organizations • *Social Services:* community service organizations, disabled, employment/job training, united funds

Grant Types: award, conference/seminar, employee matching gifts, general support, multiyear/continuing support, operating expenses, research, and scholarship

Nonmonetary Support Types: donated equipment

Geographic Distribution: Company principally gives near operating locations and to national organizations.

Operating Locations: CA (San Diego), VA (McLean)

Note: Company is also located in 70 other locations within the U.S.

CORP. OFFICERS
J. Robert Beyster: *CURR EMPL* chmn, ceo: Science Applications Intl Corp

APPLICATION INFORMATION
Initial Approach: Company gives to preselected organizations and does not solicit applications.

Restrictions on Giving: Does not give to individuals, religious organizations for sectarian purposes, and political or lobbying groups.

GRANTS ANALYSIS
Typical Range: $1,000 to $2,500

Scientific-Atlanta
Sales: $493.65 million
Employees: 3,000
Headquarters: Norcross, GA
SIC Major Group: Electronic & Other Electrical Equipment and Instruments & Related Products

CONTACT

Elinor Melton
Director, Community Affairs
Scientific-Atlanta
One Technology Pkwy.
Norcross, GA 30092
(404) 903-4607

FINANCIAL SUMMARY

Fiscal Note: Company gives directly. Annual Giving Range: $250,000 to $500,000

CONTRIBUTIONS SUMMARY

Typical Recipients: • *Arts & Humanities:* general • *Civic & Public Affairs:* general • *Education:* general • *Health:* general • *Social Services:* general

Grant Types: general support

Nonmonetary Support Types: donated equipment

Geographic Distribution: headquarters and operating locations

Operating Locations: CA (San Diego), GA (Atlanta, Norcross)

Note: Company operates seven divisions in the two operating locations.

CORP. OFFICERS

William E. Johnson: *B* St. Paul MN 1941 *ED* Yale Univ 1963; Harvard Coll 1967 *CURR EMPL* chmn, ceo, dir: Scientific-Atlanta

GIVING OFFICERS

Elinor Melton: *CURR EMPL* dir commun aff: Scientific-Atlanta

APPLICATION INFORMATION

Initial Approach: *Initial Contact:* send brief letter of inquiry *Include Information On:* description of the organization and purpose of funds sought *When to Submit:* any time

---

Scientific Brake & Equipment Co.

Sales: $10.0 million
Employees: 50
Headquarters: Saginaw, MI
SIC Major Group: Wholesale Trade—Durable Goods

CONTACT

Thomas T. Princing
President
Scientific Brake & Equipment Co.
PO Box 840
Saginaw, MI 48606
(517) 755-4411

CONTRIBUTIONS SUMMARY

Company sponsors employee matching gift program; also supports community organizations.

Typical Recipients: • *Arts & Humanities:* general • *Civic & Public Affairs:* general • *Education:* general • *Health:* general • *Social Services:* general

Grant Types: matching

Geographic Distribution: primarily headquarters area

Operating Locations: MI (Saginaw)

CORP. OFFICERS

Tom Princing: *CURR EMPL* pres: Scientific Brake & Equipment Co

APPLICATION INFORMATION

Initial Approach: Send brief letter of inquiry. There are no deadlines.

SCM Chemicals Inc.

Sales: $1.0 billion
Employees: 2,400
Parent Company: Hanson Industries, Inc
Headquarters: Baltimore, MD
SIC Major Group: Chemicals & Allied Products

CONTACT

Louis Kistner
Director, Community Relations
SCM Chemicals Inc.
7 St. Paul St., Ste. 1010
Baltimore, MD 21202
(410) 783-1073

CONTRIBUTIONS SUMMARY

Operating Locations: MD (Baltimore)

CORP. OFFICERS

Donald V. Borst: *CURR EMPL* pres: SCM Chems

Scott and Fetzer Co. / Scott and Fetzer Foundation

Sales: $890.0 million
Employees: 13,000
Parent Company: Berkshire Hathaway Inc.
Headquarters: Westlake, OH
SIC Major Group: Electronic & Other Electrical Equipment, Fabricated Metal Products, Printing & Publishing, and Wholesale Trade—Durable Goods

---

CONTACT

Edie DeSantis
Finance
Scott and Fetzer Foundation
28800 Clemens Rd.
Westlake, OH 44145
(216) 892-3000

FINANCIAL SUMMARY

Recent Giving: $257,387 (1990); $178,561 (1989)
Assets: $1,170,898 (1989)
Fiscal Note: In 1990, contributions were received from Scott and Fetzer Co.
EIN: 34-6596076

CONTRIBUTIONS SUMMARY

Typical Recipients: • *Arts & Humanities:* arts centers, community arts, libraries, music, performing arts, theater • *Civic & Public Affairs:* municipalities, urban & community affairs • *Education:* colleges & universities, education associations • *Health:* health funds, health organizations, hospitals, medical research, single-disease health associations • *Social Services:* community service organizations, united funds, youth organizations
Grant Types: general support
Geographic Distribution: focus on OH
Operating Locations: OH (Westlake)

CORP. OFFICERS

Ralph E. Schey: *B* Cleveland OH 1924 *ED* OH Univ 1948; Harvard Univ Bus A 1950 *CURR EMPL* chmn, ceo: Scott Fetzer Co
Kenneth J. Semelsberger: *B* Marsteller PA 1936 *ED* OH St Univ BB A 1970; Cleveland St Univ MBA 1972 *CURR EMPL* pres, coo: Scott & Fetzer Co *CORP AFFIL* pres: Stahl Div Scott & Fetzer Co; production mgr: Holan Corp; Sales & Con-

tracts mgr: Barth Cleve McNeil Corp

GIVING OFFICERS

C. L. Medford: secy

Ralph E. Schey: chmn *CURR EMPL* chmn, ceo: Scott Fetzer Co (see above)

Ken J. Semelsberger: pres

William W. T. Stephans: vp, treas

APPLICATION INFORMATION

Initial Approach: Send brief letter describing program. There are no deadlines.

GRANTS ANALYSIS

Number of Grants: 241
Highest Grant: $50,000
Typical Range: $25 to $1,000
Disclosure Period: 1989

RECENT GRANTS

50,000 Cleveland Clinic Foundation, Cleveland, OH
50,000 Cleveland Clinic Foundation, Cleveland, OH
25,000 Cleveland Tomorrow, Cleveland, OH
15,000 Direct Selling Educational Foundation, Washington, DC
15,000 Direct Selling Educational Foundation, Washington, DC
10,000 Cleveland Orchestra, Cleveland, OH
10,000 Playhouse Square Foundation, Cleveland, OH
10,000 Playhouse Square Foundation, Cleveland, OH
5,000 United Way, Cincinnati, OH
5,000 US Committee for UNICEF, Cleveland, OH

Scott, Foresman & Co.

Employees: 13,000
Parent Company: HarperCollins Publishers
Headquarters: Glenview, IL
SIC Major Group: Printing & Publishing

CONTACT

Stuart Cohn
Vice President, Human
  Resources
Scott, Foresman & Co.
1900 East Lake Ave.
Glenview, IL 60025
(708) 729-3000

FINANCIAL SUMMARY

Recent Giving: $300,000
(1993 est.)
Fiscal Note: Company gives directly.

CONTRIBUTIONS SUMMARY

Typical Recipients: • *Arts & Humanities:* general • *Civic & Public Affairs:* general • *Education:* general • *Social Services:* general
Grant Types: general support
Nonmonetary Support Types: donated products and workplace solicitation
Operating Locations: IL (Glenview), NY (New York)

CORP. OFFICERS

Richard E. Peterson: *B* Spokane WA 1941 *ED* Univ MO BS 1963; Univ Chicago MBA 1975 *CURR EMPL* pres, ceo, dir: Scott Foresman & Co *CORP AFFIL* dir: Canadian Publ Co, Evanston Hosp Corp *NONPR AFFIL* dir: Western Golf Assn; mem: Assn Am Publs

GIVING OFFICERS

Stuart Cohn: *CURR EMPL* vp human resources: Scott Foresman & Co

APPLICATION INFORMATION

Initial Approach: *Initial Contact:* brief letter of inquiry *Include Information On:* a description of organization, amount requested, purpose of funds sought, and proof of tax-exempt status *When to Submit:* any time
Restrictions on Giving: Does not support individuals, political or lobbying groups, or religious organizations for sectarian purposes.

Scott Foundation, Virginia Steele

CONTACT

Sandra S. Bradner
Virginia Steele Scott Fdn.
1151 Oxford Rd.
San Marino, CA 91108
(818) 405-2226

FINANCIAL SUMMARY

Recent Giving: $246,267 (fiscal 1991); $459,635 (fiscal 1990); $300,500 (fiscal 1989)
Assets: $3,218,452 (fiscal year ending June 30, 1990); $2,736,430 (fiscal 1989)
Gifts Received: $147,180 (fiscal 1990); $135,141 (fiscal 1989)
Fiscal Note: 1991 contribution recived from Grace C. Scott Trust.
EIN: 23-7365076

CONTRIBUTIONS SUMMARY

Donor(s): the late Virginia Steele Scott and Grace C. Scott
Typical Recipients: • *Arts & Humanities:* arts associations, arts centers, arts institutes, community arts, libraries, music
Grant Types: general support
Geographic Distribution: focus on Pasadena, CA

GIVING OFFICERS

Blake Reynolds Nevius: dir *B* Winona MN 1916 *ED* Antioch Coll BA 1938; Univ Chicago MA 1941; Univ Chicago PhD 1947 *CURR EMPL* mem: Modern Language Assn Am *NONPR AFFIL* mem: Modern Language Assn; prof emeritus: Univ CA Los Angeles
Charles Newton: pres, dir
Robert R. Wark: dir *ED* Harvard Univ AM 1949; Harvard Univ PhD 1952 *CURR EMPL* lecturer: CA Inst Technology *NONPR AFFIL* lecturer: CA Inst Tech; mem: Assn Art Mus Dirs, Coll Art Assn Am

APPLICATION INFORMATION

Initial Approach: Send brief letter of inquiry describing program or project. Deadline is September 30.

GRANTS ANALYSIS

Number of Grants: 8
Highest Grant: $212,267
Typical Range: $2,500 to $10,000
Disclosure Period: fiscal year ending June 30, 1990

RECENT GRANTS

212,267	Henry E. Huntington Library and Art Gallery, San Marino, CA
10,000	University of California Los Angeles Oral History Program, Los Angeles, CA
5,000	Armory Center for the Arts, CA
5,000	Pacific Asia Museum, CA
5,000	Pasadena Symphony Association, Pasadena, CA
4,000	Art Center College of Design, CA
2,500	Coleman Chamber Music Association, Los Angeles, CA
2,500	Foothill Master Chorale, Los Angeles, CA

Scott Foundation, Walter

CONTACT

Thorpe A. Hickerson
President
Walter Scott Fdn.
PO Box 1161
Wilmington, VT 05363

FINANCIAL SUMMARY

Recent Giving: $218,900 (fiscal 1991); $199,500 (fiscal 1990); $174,500 (fiscal 1989)
Assets: $4,853,296 (fiscal year ending September 30, 1991); $4,813,341 (fiscal 1990); $4,690,370 (fiscal 1989)
EIN: 13-5681161

CONTRIBUTIONS SUMMARY

Typical Recipients: • *Education:* legal education, medical education, special education • *Health:* hospitals, medical research • *Social Services:* disabled, emergency relief, recreation & athletics
Grant Types: capital, endowment, multiyear/continuing support, operating expenses, research, and seed money
Geographic Distribution: focus on the New York, NY, metropolitan area and lower CT

GIVING OFFICERS

Norman A. Hill: dir
Brett R. Nickerson: dir
Glendon A. Nickerson: dir
Jocelyn A. Nickerson: vp, exec dir
Lisa B. Nickerson: dir

Thorpe A. Nickerson: pres, secy, treas, dir

APPLICATION INFORMATION

Initial Approach: Send brief letter describing program. There are no deadlines.
Restrictions on Giving: Does not support individuals.

GRANTS ANALYSIS

Number of Grants: 36
Highest Grant: $30,000
Typical Range: $2,000 to $8,000
Disclosure Period: fiscal year ending September 30, 1991

RECENT GRANTS

30,000	Clarke School for the Deaf, Northampton, MA
30,000	Helen Hayes Hospital, New York, NY
25,000	New York Law School, New York, NY
10,000	Deafness Research Foundation, New York, NY
10,000	Lexington School for the Deaf Foundation, Jackson Heights, NY
8,000	Yale University, New Haven, CT
5,000	AGMA Emergency Relief Fund, New York, NY
5,000	Breckenridge Development Fund, Breckenridge, CO
5,000	St. Luke's-Roosevelt Hospital Center, New York, NY
5,000	Vermont Handicapped Ski and Sports Association, Brownsville, VT

Scott Foundation, William E.

CONTACT

Robert W. Decker
President
William E. Scott Fdn.
City Center Two
301 Commerce St., Ste. 2400
Ft. Worth, TX 76102
(817) 336-0361

FINANCIAL SUMMARY

Recent Giving: $463,200 (fiscal 1992); $410,650 (fiscal 1991); $568,100 (fiscal 1990)
Assets: $12,628,621 (fiscal year ending May 31, 1992); $10,838,152 (fiscal 1991); $8,851,942 (fiscal 1990)

EIN: 75-6024661

CONTRIBUTIONS SUMMARY

Donor(s): the late William E. Scott

Typical Recipients: • *Arts & Humanities:* arts associations, community arts, dance, history/historic preservation, museums/galleries • *Civic & Public Affairs:* zoos/botanical gardens • *Education:* private education (precollege) • *Health:* health organizations, medical research, single-disease health associations • *Religion:* churches • *Social Services:* community service organizations, united funds, youth organizations

Grant Types: capital, general support, and project

Geographic Distribution: limited to TX, with emphasis on the Fort Worth-Tarrant County area, and in LA, OK, and NM

GIVING OFFICERS

Robert W. Decker: dir, pres
Raymond O. Kelly III: dir, vp

APPLICATION INFORMATION

Initial Approach: Send brief letter describing program. There are no deadlines.

Restrictions on Giving: Does not support individuals.

OTHER THINGS TO KNOW

Publications: Application Guidelines

GRANTS ANALYSIS

Number of Grants: 41
Highest Grant: $100,000
Typical Range: $1,000 to $20,000
Disclosure Period: fiscal year ending May 31, 1992

RECENT GRANTS

100,000 Fort Worth Zoological Association, Ft. Worth, TX
60,000 Child Study Center, Ft. Worth, TX
35,000 Arts Council of Fort Worth and Tarrant County, Ft. Worth, TX
30,000 First Texas Council of Camp Fire, Ft. Worth, TX
25,000 Davey O'Brien Educational and Charitable Trust, Ft. Worth, TX
20,000 Fort Worth Ballet, Ft. Worth, TX

20,000 Museum of Science and History, Ft. Worth, TX
17,200 Community Foundation of Metropolitan Tarrant County, Ft. Worth, TX
15,000 Amon Carter Museum, Ft. Worth, TX
13,500 United Way, Ft. Worth, TX

Scott Foundation, William R., John G., and Emma

CONTACT

Clinton Webb
Treasurer
William R., John G., and Emma Scott Fdn.
c/o Davenport & Co.
801 East Main St.
Richmond, VA 23210
(804) 780-2035

FINANCIAL SUMMARY

Recent Giving: $274,000 (fiscal 1991); $301,250 (fiscal 1990); $253,758 (fiscal 1989)
Assets: $6,252,298 (fiscal year ending September 30, 1991); $5,493,867 (fiscal 1990); $5,886,654 (fiscal 1989)
EIN: 54-0648772

CONTRIBUTIONS SUMMARY

Donor(s): the late John G. Scott, Emma Scott Taylor

Typical Recipients: • *Civic & Public Affairs:* housing, rural affairs • *Education:* colleges & universities, private education (precollege), science/technology education • *Religion:* religious organizations • *Social Services:* aged, child welfare, community service organizations, homes, shelters/homelessness, youth organizations

Grant Types: capital and general support

Geographic Distribution: focus on VA

GIVING OFFICERS

Royal E. Cabell, Jr.: secy, trust
Rev. Don Raby Edwards: trust
Charles M. Guthridge: trust
T. Justin Moore, Jr.: vp, trust
B Richmond VA 1925 *ED*

Princeton Univ 1947; Univ VA 1950 *CURR EMPL* coun: Hunton & Williams *CORP AFFIL* coun: Hunton & Williams; dir: Central Fidelity Banks, Dominion Resources, GTE Corp, Philip Morris Cos

Edwin Palmer Munson: trust *B* Richmond VA 1935 *ED* Univ VA 1957; Univ Richmond 1980 *CURR EMPL* vp, legal coun: Computer Co *CORP AFFIL* vp, legal coun: Computer Co

Thomas W. Murrell, Jr.: pres, trust

Elizabeth Copeland Norfleet: trust

C. Cotesworth Pinckney: trust

E. Bryson Powell: trust

Clinton Webb: treas, asst to pres

APPLICATION INFORMATION

Initial Approach: Send brief letter of inquiry. Deadline is March 1 for scholarships.

GRANTS ANALYSIS

Number of Grants: 14
Highest Grant: $35,000
Typical Range: $5,000 to $20,000
Disclosure Period: fiscal year ending September 30, 1991
Note: 1991 figures do not include $24,000 in scholarships to individuals.

RECENT GRANTS

35,000 Kenmore Association, Fredericksburg, VA
30,000 Hollins College, Roanoke, VA
25,000 Shenandoah University Library, Winchester, VA
20,000 Elk Hill Farm, Goochland, VA
20,000 Metropolitan Area Resource Clearinghouse, Richmond, VA
20,000 Powhatan School, Boyce, VA
20,000 University of South, Sewanee, TN
15,000 Cross-Over Ministry, Richmond, VA
15,000 Richmond Community Senior Center, Richmond, VA
10,000 Stuart Hall School, Waynesboro, VA

Scott Fund, Olin

CONTACT

Melvin A. Dyson
President
Olin Scott Fund
PO Box 1208
Bennington, VT 05201
(802) 447-1096

FINANCIAL SUMMARY

Recent Giving: $100,000 (fiscal 1992); $75,000 (fiscal 1990); $75,000 (fiscal 1989)
Assets: $2,548,109 (fiscal year ending June 30, 1992); $2,656,306 (fiscal 1991); $2,453,647 (fiscal 1990)
EIN: 03-6005697

CONTRIBUTIONS SUMMARY

Donor(s): the late Olin Scott
Typical Recipients: • *Education:* colleges & universities, community & junior colleges
Grant Types: loan and scholarship
Geographic Distribution: limited to Bennington County, VT

GIVING OFFICERS

Robert E. Cummings, Jr.: secy
Melvin A. Dyson: pres, treas
Kelton B. Miller: vp

APPLICATION INFORMATION

Initial Approach: Application form required. There are no deadlines.

GRANTS ANALYSIS

Number of Grants: 4
Highest Grant: $50,000
Disclosure Period: fiscal year ending June 30, 1992

RECENT GRANTS

50,000 Southern Vermont College, VT
25,000 Bennington College, Bennington, VT
25,000 Community College of Vermont, VT

Scott, Jr. Charitable Foundation, Walter

CONTACT
Walter Scott, Jr.
Principal Manager
Walter Scott, Jr. Charitable Fdn.
500 Energy Plz.
409 South 17th St.
Omaha, NE 68102
(402) 341-6000

FINANCIAL SUMMARY
Recent Giving: $190,950 (1990); $101,050 (1989); $238,050 (1988)
Assets: $4,382,079 (1990); $5,545,326 (1989); $4,876,443 (1988)
EIN: 47-6038363

CONTRIBUTIONS SUMMARY
Donor(s): Walter Scott, Jr.
Typical Recipients: • *Arts & Humanities:* history/historic preservation, music, opera • *Civic & Public Affairs:* environmental affairs, zoos/botanical gardens • *Education:* colleges & universities, liberal arts education, private education (precollege) • *Religion:* churches • *Social Services:* animal protection, united funds, youth organizations
Grant Types: general support
Geographic Distribution: focus on Omaha, NE

GIVING OFFICERS
Walter Scott, Jr.: trust *B* 1931 *CURR EMPL* chmn, pres, dir: Peter Kiewit Sons *NONPR AFFIL* pres: Joslyn Art Mus

APPLICATION INFORMATION
Initial Approach: Contributes only to preselected organizations.
Restrictions on Giving: Does not support individuals.

GRANTS ANALYSIS
Number of Grants: 17
Highest Grant: $104,000
Typical Range: $500 to $10,000
Disclosure Period: 1990

RECENT GRANTS
104,000 Omaha Zoological Foundation, Omaha, NE
35,000 Countryside Community Church, Omaha, NE
15,000 Joslyn Liberal Arts Society, Omaha, NE
10,000 United Way, Omaha, NE
6,500 Brownell-Talbot School, Omaha, NE
6,000 Omaha Symphony Association, Omaha, NE
2,500 Ducks Unlimited, Long Grove, IL
2,000 Omaha Ballet, Omaha, NE
2,000 University of Nebraska Foundation, Lincoln, NE
1,500 Boys and Girls Club, Omaha, NE

Scott Paper Co. / Scott Paper Co. Foundation

Sales: $4.88 billion
Employees: 37,000
Headquarters: Philadelphia, PA
SIC Major Group: Forestry, Lumber & Wood Products, Paper & Allied Products, and Textile Mill Products

CONTACT
Frances Rizzardi
Manager, Corporate Contributions
Scott Paper Co. Fdn.
One Scott Plz.
3rd Fl.
Philadelphia, PA 19113
(215) 522-6160

FINANCIAL SUMMARY
Recent Giving: $2,690,000 (1993 est.); $2,656,366 (1992); $3,362,000 (1991)
Assets: $0 (1992); 19,192 (1991); 0 (1990)
Fiscal Note: All cash contributions are made through the foundation.
EIN: 23-6231564

CONTRIBUTIONS SUMMARY
Typical Recipients: • *Arts & Humanities:* public broadcasting, theater • *Education:* pre-school education
Grant Types: general support
Nonmonetary Support Types: cause-related marketing & promotion and donated products
Note: Value of nonmonetary support and is included in above totals.
Geographic Distribution: headquarters and operating locations only
Operating Locations: AL (Mobile), AR (Rogers), DE (Dover), KY (Bowling Green, Owensboro), MA (Boston), ME (Skowhegan, Waterville, Westbrook, Winslow), MI (Muskegon), MS (Hattiesburg), NY (Fort Edward), PA (Chester, Philadelphia), TX (San Antonio), WA (Everett), WI (Marinette, Oconto Falls, Oshkosh)

CORP. OFFICERS
Philip Edward Lippincott: *B* Camden NJ 1935 *ED* Dartmouth Coll BA 1957; MI St Univ MBA 1964 *CURR EMPL* chmn, ceo, dir: Scott Paper Co *CORP AFFIL* dir: Campbell Soup Co, Exxon Corp; trust: Penn Mutual Life Ins Co *NONPR AFFIL* bd overseers: Dartmouth Inst; dir: Bus Counc, Fox Chase Cancer Ctr, Grocery Mfrs Assn; mem: Beta Gamma Sigma, Kappa Kappa Kappa, Paper Distribution Counc, Pi Sigma Epsilon, Soc Friends; mem advertising policy comm: Assn Natl Advertisers; mem exec comm, dir: Am Paper Inst

GIVING OFFICERS
John J. Butler: trust
Thomas P. Czepiel: trust *B* Deep River CT 1932 *CURR EMPL* vp (mfg): Scott Paper Co
Philip Edward Lippincott: trust *CURR EMPL* chmn, ceo, dir: Scott Paper Co (see above)
James A. Morrill: trust
Frances Rizzardi: secy
Frances Rizzardi: mgr
Paul N. Schregel: trust *CURR EMPL* sr vp: Scott Paper Co

APPLICATION INFORMATION
Initial Approach: *Initial Contact:* request application from foundation; for programs in Scott communities, proposal should be sent to local plant manager; all other proposals should be directed to the headquarters *Include Information On:* description and general purpose of organization; 3-year budget history and current budget; amount requested; purpose for which funds are sought; project budget; recently audited financial statement; explanation of how project will be evaluated; list of board of directors; proof of tax-exempt status *When to Submit:* any time
Restrictions on Giving: Support is not guaranteed beyond one year. Grants are not made to organizations without nonprofit, tax-exempt status; veterans organizations; religious organizations; labor organizations; fraternal organizations; entertainment groups; organizations requesting good-will advertising; organizations based outside the United States; endowment funds; government agencies; national health funds; individuals; political parties or candidates; special events such as walkathons; or scholarship support other than through the foundation's McCabe Scholars Program.

OTHER THINGS TO KNOW
The foundation will support programs to help find solutions to problems of needy children in Scott communities.

Low priority areas include programs of national and international scope, long-term commitments, capital campaigns, and participation in benefit dinners.

GRANTS ANALYSIS
Total Grants: $2,656,366
Number of Grants: 293
Highest Grant: $125,000
Typical Range: $5,000 to $10,000
Disclosure Period: 1992

Note: Figure for average grant is supplied by the foundation. Recent grants are derived from a 1992 annual report.

RECENT GRANTS
242,330 United Way
242,330 United Way
Chester Education Foundation Summer Training and Employment Program, Chester, PA
Children's Museum of Maine, Portland, ME — funded the development of an exciting paper-related exhibit
Michigan Partnership for New Education, MI
Mobile County Public Schools, Mobile, AL — "Sixth Day Academic Program"
Muskegon Metropolitan Partnership for New Education, Muskegon, WI
Pennsylvania Department of Higher Education, Philadelphia, PA — "Philadelphia Parents as Teachers"
Philadelphia School District, Philadelphia, PA
School District of Marinette, Marinette, WI — Project Success

Scotty's, Inc.

Sales: $571.0 million
Employees: 7,000
Headquarters: Winter Haven, FL
SIC Major Group: Building
  Materials & Garden Supplies

CONTACT

Jerry Jargensen
Controller
Scotty's, Inc.
PO Box 939
Winter Haven, FL 33882
(813) 299-1111

FINANCIAL SUMMARY

Fiscal Note: Annual Giving
Range: less than $100,000

CONTRIBUTIONS SUMMARY

Typical Recipients: • *Arts & Humanities:* general • *Civic & Public Affairs:* general • *Education:* general • *Health:* general • *Social Services:* general
Grant Types: general support
Geographic Distribution: primarily headquarters area
Operating Locations: FL (Winter Haven)

CORP. OFFICERS

Danny Crow: *CURR EMPL* cfo: Scottys
Daryl L. Lansdale: *CURR EMPL* chmn, ceo: Scottys

APPLICATION INFORMATION

Initial Approach: Send brief letter of inquiry. There are no deadlines.

Scoular Co. / Scoular Foundation

Headquarters: Omaha, NE

CONTACT

Marshall E. Faith
President
Scoular Foundation
2027 Dodge Street
Omaha, NE 68102
(402) 342-3500

FINANCIAL SUMMARY

Recent Giving: $80,669 (1990)
Assets: $5,706 (1990)
Gifts Received: $85,000 (1990)
Fiscal Note: In 1990, contributions were received from the Scoular Company.
EIN: 36-3323189

CONTRIBUTIONS SUMMARY

Typical Recipients: • *Arts & Humanities:* museums/galleries

• *Education:* colleges & universities, education funds • *Religion:* religious organizations • *Social Services:* child welfare, recreation & athletics, youth organizations
Grant Types: general support
Geographic Distribution: giving limited to areas of company operations in NE and IA
Operating Locations: NE (Omaha)

CORP. OFFICERS

Marshall E. Faith: *CURR EMPL* pres, ceo: Scoular Co
Ronald D. Nelson: *CURR EMPL* cfo: Scoular Co

GIVING OFFICERS

Marshall E. Faith: pres *CURR EMPL* pres, ceo: Scoular Co (see above)
Duane A. Fischer: dir
Ronald D. Nelson: secy-treas *CURR EMPL* cfo: Scoular Co (see above)

APPLICATION INFORMATION

Initial Approach: Submit a brief letter of inquiry. There are no deadlines.

GRANTS ANALYSIS

Number of Grants: 48
Highest Grant: $25,000
Typical Range: $100 to $500
Disclosure Period: 1990

RECENT GRANTS

25,000 Bellevue College Foundation, Bellevue, NE
11,040 College of St. Mary, Omaha, NE
3,603 Boy Scouts of America, Omaha, NE
3,340 Ak-Sar-Ben Youth Foundation, Omaha, NE
1,000 Boys Club of America, Omaha, NE
  750 Children's Square/USA, Council Bluffs, IA
  660 Fellowship of Christian Athletes, Bellevue, NE
  500 Edmonson Youth Development, Omaha, NE
  500 Fontenelle Forect, Bellevue, NE
  500 Joslyn Art Museum, Omaha, NE

Scripps Co., E.W. / Scripps Howard Foundation

Sales: $1.26 billion
Employees: 8,000
Headquarters: Cincinnati, OH
SIC Major Group: Printing & Publishing

CONTACT

Mary Lou Marusin
Executive Director
Scripps Howard Fdn.
PO Box 5380
Cincinnati, OH 45201
(513) 977-3036

FINANCIAL SUMMARY

Recent Giving: $920,000 (1993 est.); $945,170 (1992); $788,883 (1991)
Assets: $16,835,373 (1992); $16,349,414 (1991); $12,910,070 (1990)
Fiscal Note: Above figures for foundation only. Company also makes contributions directly from corporate funds. Contact for this support is M. Denise Kupriois, Corporate Secretary. Estimate of support is not available.
EIN: 31-6025114

CONTRIBUTIONS SUMMARY

Typical Recipients: • *Civic & Public Affairs:* first amendment issues, professional & trade associations • *Education:* colleges & universities, journalism education, minority education, student aid
Grant Types: project and scholarship
Nonmonetary Support Types: donated equipment
Note: Estimate value of nonmonetary support is not available and is excluded from above total giving figures.
Geographic Distribution: nationally, with emphasis on operating locations
Operating Locations: AL (Birmingham), AZ (Phoenix), CA (Los Angeles, Redding, Sacramento, San Luis Obispo, South Gate, Thousand Oaks, Tulare, Ventura, Watsonville), CO (Denver, Longmont), DC, FL (Bonita Springs, Destin, Hollywood, Jupiter, Naples, Palm Beach, Port St. Lucie, Stuart, Tampa), GA (Rome), IN (Evansville), KY (Covington), MD (Baltimore), MI (Detroit), MO (Kansas City), NM (Albequerque), NY (New York), OH

(Cincinnati, Cleveland), OK (Tulsa), OR (Portland), PA (Pittsburgh), SC, TN (Chattanooga, Knoxville, Memphis), TX (El Paso), VA, WA (Bremerton), WV

CORP. OFFICERS

Lawrence Arthur Leser: *B* Cincinnati OH 1935 *ED* Xavier Univ 1957 *CURR EMPL* pres, ceo, dir: EW Scripps Co *CORP AFFIL* dir: Heekin Can Inc, Soc Corp, Union Central Life Ins Co; mem natl adv bd: Chem Bank *NONPR AFFIL* bd govs: Newspaper Assn Am
Charles Edward Scripps: *B* San Diego CA 1920 *ED* Coll William & Mary 1938-1940; Pomona Coll 1940-1941 *CURR EMPL* chmn, dir: EW Scripps Co *CORP AFFIL* chmn: Scripps-Howard; dir: Scripps-Howard Broadcasting Co, Star Banc Corp, Star Bank NA *NONPR AFFIL* Theta Delta Chi; bd govs: Webb Sch; dir: Commun Improvement Corp Cincinnati; mem: CAP; mem natl bd adv: Salvation Army; trust: Freedoms Fdn

GIVING OFFICERS

William Robert Burleigh: mem *B* Evansville IN 1935 *ED* Marquette Univ BS 1957 *CURR EMPL* exec vp: Scripps-Howard Newspapers *NONPR AFFIL* mem: Alpha Sigma Nu, Am Soc Newspaper Editors
John H. Burlingame: mem
D. J. Castellini: treas *CURR EMPL* vp, treas, secy, contr: Scripps (EW) Co
Judy G. Clabes: trust *B* Henderson KY 1945 *ED* Univ KY BA 1967; ID St Univ pub admin 1984 *CORP AFFIL* dir: Huntington Bank Kenton County; pres, publ: Picture this! books *NONPR AFFIL* chmn: Dinsmore Homestead Fdn; dir: KY Ctr Pub Issues, KY Ed Television Authority; fdr: First Amendment Ctr; mem: Am Soc Newspaper Editors, Natl Fed Press Women; pres: First Amendment Congress, Spiral Festival
Colleen Christner Conant: trust *B* Oklahoma City OK 1947 *CURR EMPL* mng editor: Commercial Appeal *NONPR AFFIL* mem: Assoc Press Mng Editors Assn, Scripps Howard Mng Editors Assn
Steve Crawford: trust *B* Cedar Rapids IA 1952 *ED* IA St Univ 1974 *CURR EMPL* vp: Grinnell Mutual Reinsurance Co

CORP AFFIL dir: Grinnell Select Ins Co
Charlotte Moore English: trust
David R. Huhn: mem *B* Cincinnati OH 1937
Ron Klayman: trust
Paul Frederick Knue: trust *B* Lawrenceburg IN 1947 *CURR EMPL* editor: Cincinnati Post *NONPR AFFIL* mem: Am Soc Newspaper Editors, Assoc Press Mng Editors Assn; trust: Assoc Press Soc OH
Denise Kuprionis: secy *NONPR AFFIL* mem: Am Soc Newspaper Editors
Lawrence Arthur Leser: mem *CURR EMPL* pres, ceo, dir: EW Scripps Co (see above)
Mary Lou Marusin: exec dir
Daniel Joseph Meyer: mem *B* Flint MI 1936 *ED* Purdue Univ BS 1958; IN Univ MBA 1963 *CURR EMPL* chmn, ceo, dir: Cincinnati Milacron *CORP AFFIL* dir: Hubbell, EW Scripps Co, Star Banc Corp *NONPR AFFIL* mem: Am Inst CPAs
Nicholas B. Paumgarten: mem *B* Philadelphia PA 1945 *CURR EMPL* managing dir: J P Morgan & Co *CORP AFFIL* dir: E W Scripps Co
Carole Philipps: trust
Sue Porter: trust
Albert J. Schettelkotte: pres, ceo, trust, mem *B* Cheviot OH 1927 *CURR EMPL* sr vp: Scripps Howard Broadcasting Co
Charles Edward Scripps: mem *CURR EMPL* chmn, dir: EW Scripps Co (see above)
Marilyn Joy Scripps: trust
Paul Kenneth Scripps: trust *CORP AFFIL* dir: EW Scripps Co
Robert P. Scripps, Jr.: trust *CURR EMPL* dir: EW Scripps Co
Dan Thomasson: trust *B* Shelbyville IN 1933 *CURR EMPL* editor: Scripps Howard News Svc *CORP AFFIL* vp: Scripps Howard Newspapers Cincinnati *NONPR AFFIL* mem: Am Soc Newspaper Editors, Sigma Delta Chi, White House Correspondents Assn; mem natl pub aff counc: IN Univ; pres: Raymond Clapper Fdn; trust: Franklin Coll

APPLICATION INFORMATION

Initial Approach: *Initial Contact:* special grants applicants, send brief letter or proposal; for scholarship programs, sub-

mit a letter, stating college major and career goal by December 20 to receive scholarship application *Include Information On:* for special grants: brief description of project and expected results, line-item budget, amount requested, and proof of tax-exempt status *When to Submit:* special grant proposals are reviewed as received; completed scholarship application due February 25
Restrictions on Giving: Foundation discourages requests for grants which are not related to program areas described above. Generally declines to fund public causes, public radio and television, campus newspapers, governmental studies, seminars, operating funds, capital campaigns, annual appeals, and international projects. Grants normally not made to other private foundations.
Does not support dinners or special events, fraternal organizations, good will advertising, individuals, political or lobbying groups, or religious organizations for sectarian purposes.

OTHER THINGS TO KNOW

Publications: *Scripps Howard Foundation 1992 Progress Report: Sowing the Seeds of Opportunity,* guidelines

GRANTS ANALYSIS

Total Grants: $945,170*
Number of Grants: 373*
Highest Grant: $100,000*
Typical Range: $1,000* to $3,000
Disclosure Period: 1992
Note: Figures are for the foundation only. Recent grants are derived from a 1991 Form 990.

RECENT GRANTS

100,000 Rochester Institute of Technology, Rochester, NY — fourth year of 5-year pledge/newspaper operations center
75,000 Ohio University Fund, Athens, OH — ninth year of ten-year pledge/E.W. Scripps endowment program
35,410 Indiana University Foundation, Bloomington, IN — Roy W. Howard Seminar
25,000 Rochester Institute of Technology, Rochester, NY —

Robert P. Scripps Graphic Arts Scholarship
20,000 American Press Institute, Reston, VA — support of four Ted Scripps Fellows
10,925 University of Michigan, Ann Arbor, MI — first year of six-year pledge/Environmental Journalism Fellows
10,000 Center for Workforce Preparation and Quality Education — literacy
10,000 Greater Pittsburgh Literacy Council, Pittsburgh, PA — literacy
10,000 Literacy Volunteers of New York City, New York, NY — literacy
10,000 Ohio University Foundation, Athens, OH — Midwest Newspaper Workshop for Minorities

---

Scripps Foundation, Ellen Browning

CONTACT
Douglas Dawson
Administrative Accountant
Ellen Browning Scripps Fdn.
Union Bank, Trust Dept.
PO Box 1907
La Jolla, CA 92038
(619) 230-4770

FINANCIAL SUMMARY
Recent Giving: $745,500 (fiscal 1992); $673,600 (fiscal 1991); $664,000 (fiscal 1990)
Assets: $15,370,277 (fiscal year ending June 30, 1992); $14,742,608 (fiscal 1991); $14,190,827 (fiscal 1990)
EIN: 95-1644633

CONTRIBUTIONS SUMMARY
Donor(s): The foundation was established in 1935 by late Ellen Browning Scripps and the late Robert Paine Scripps.
Typical Recipients: • *Arts & Humanities:* history/historic preservation, museums/galleries • *Civic & Public Affairs:* environmental affairs, women's affairs, zoos/botanical gardens • *Education:* colleges & universities, private education (precollege) • *Health:* hospices, hospitals, medical research • *Social*

Services: child welfare, youth organizations
Grant Types: general support
Geographic Distribution: focus on San Diego County, CA

GIVING OFFICERS
Ellen Scripps Davis: trust
Deborah Goddard: trust
Edward S. Meanley: trust
Paul Kenneth Scripps: trust *CORP AFFIL* dir: EW Scripps Co

APPLICATION INFORMATION
Initial Approach: Restrictions on Giving: The foundation supports preselected organizations and does not accept unsolicited requests for funds. The foundation does not make grants to individuals.

GRANTS ANALYSIS
Total Grants: $764,760
Number of Grants: 42
Highest Grant: $60,000
Typical Range: $1,000 to $20,000
Disclosure Period: fiscal year ending June 30, 1992
Note: Recent grants are derived from a fiscal 1992 grants list.

RECENT GRANTS
60,000 Scripps Clinic and Research Foundation, La Jolla, CA
55,000 San Diego Zoological Society, San Diego, CA
55,000 San Diego Zoological Society, San Diego, CA — San Pasqual Wild Animal Park
50,000 Bishops School, La Jolla, CA
50,000 Francis W. Parker School, San Diego, CA
50,000 Scripps College, Claremont, CA
50,000 Scripps Memorial Hospital, La Jolla, CA
30,000 Horseless Carriage Foundation, San Diego, CA
25,000 Knox College, Galesburg, IL
25,000 San Diego Historical Society, San Diego, CA

Scrivner, Inc.
Sales: $3.3 billion
Employees: 11,900
Headquarters: Oklahoma City, OK
SIC Major Group: Food Stores and Wholesale Trade—Nondurable Goods

CONTACT
Meribeth Sloan
Director, Corporate Communications
Scrivner, Inc.
5701 North Shartel
Oklahoma City, OK 73118
(405) 841-5500

FINANCIAL SUMMARY
Fiscal Note: Annual Giving Range: $100,000 to $200,000

CONTRIBUTIONS SUMMARY
Supports community organizations providing a direct service and local chapters of national organizations. Highest priority is health, supporting health funds and organizations, single-disease health associations, pediatric health, substance abuse organizations, and medical research. In education, also a high priority, support goes to colleges and universities, with emphasis on business, engineering, and elementary education. Also supports united funds, volunteer services, athletic events, and organizations serving youth and the disabled. Dance, music, community arts, and arts associations also receive support. Civic support goes to urban and community affairs, better government, business and free enterprise organizations, and professional and trade associations.
Typical Recipients: • *Arts & Humanities:* arts associations, arts centers, arts funds, community arts, dance, ethnic arts, history/historic preservation, libraries, museums/galleries, music, performing arts, public broadcasting, theater • *Civic & Public Affairs:* better government, business/free enterprise, civil rights, economic development, environmental affairs, international affairs, law & justice, municipalities, professional & trade associations, public policy, safety, urban & community affairs, women's affairs, zoos/botanical gardens • *Education:* business education, career/voca-

tional education, colleges & universities, economic education, education associations, elementary education, engineering education, international exchange, international studies, literacy, minority education, private education (precollege), public education (precollege), science/technology education, student aid • *Health:* health care cost containment, health funds, health organizations, hospitals, medical research, mental health, pediatric health, single-disease health associations • *Religion:* religious organizations • *Science:* scientific organizations • *Social Services:* aged, child welfare, community centers, community service organizations, disabled, domestic violence, drugs & alcohol, employment/job training, family services, refugee assistance, religious welfare, united funds, youth organizations
Grant Types: capital, endowment, general support, matching, and project
Nonmonetary Support Types: donated products, loaned employees, and workplace solicitation
Geographic Distribution: corporate headquarters gives in Oklahoma; operating divisions make contributions in almost every state east of the Rockies
Operating Locations: AL, IA, IL, KS, NE, NY, OK, TN, TX, WA

CORP. OFFICERS
William T. Bishop: *CURR EMPL* pres, coo, dir: Scrivner
Jerry D. Metcalf: *CURR EMPL* chmn, ceo, dir: Scrivner

GIVING OFFICERS
Meribeth Sloan: *CURR EMPL* dir (corp commun): Scrivner

APPLICATION INFORMATION
Initial Approach: Send a brief letter at any time. Include a description of the organization, amount requested, purpose for which funds are sought, a recently audited financial statement, and proof of tax-exempt status.
Restrictions on Giving: The following are not considered for charitable contributions: fraternal organizations, goodwill advertising, individuals, and religious organizations for sectarian purposes.

GRANTS ANALYSIS
Typical Range: $2,500 to $10,000

Scrivner of North Carolina Inc.
Sales: $360.0 million
Employees: 500
Parent Company: Scrivner
Headquarters: Warsaw, NC
SIC Major Group: Wholesale Trade—Nondurable Goods

CONTACT
Gayle Cavenaugh
Executive Secretary
Scrivner North Carolina Corp.
Highway 117 South
Warsaw, NC 28398
(919) 293-7821

CONTRIBUTIONS SUMMARY
Main areas of concern are civic and public affairs, education, and social services. Arts and humanities and health organizations receive minor support.
Typical Recipients: • *Arts & Humanities:* arts associations • *Civic & Public Affairs:* better government, business/free enterprise, civil rights, economic development, law & justice, professional & trade associations, safety • *Education:* colleges & universities, public education (precollege) • *Health:* hospitals • *Social Services:* youth organizations
Grant Types: general support
Nonmonetary Support Types: donated products
Geographic Distribution: only in North Carolina
Operating Locations: NC

CORP. OFFICERS
William C. Garner: *CURR EMPL* ceo: Scrivner NC

GIVING OFFICERS
Gayle Cavenaugh: *CURR EMPL* exec secy: Scrivner NC

APPLICATION INFORMATION
Initial Approach: Send a letter at any time.

Scroggins Foundation, Arthur E. and Cornelia C.

CONTACT
Stan Simpson
Treasurer
Arthur E. and Cornelia C. Scroggins Fdn.
PO Box 1112
Dodge City, KS 67801

FINANCIAL SUMMARY
Recent Giving: $56,000 (1991); $66,000 (1990); $51,800 (1989)
Assets: $1,844,550 (1991); $1,719,062 (1990); $1,623,122 (1989)
EIN: 48-0945437

CONTRIBUTIONS SUMMARY
Typical Recipients: • *Arts & Humanities:* libraries • *Education:* colleges & universities, community & junior colleges, special education • *Health:* health organizations • *Social Services:* child welfare, community service organizations, food/clothing distribution, recreation & athletics, shelters/homelessness, united funds, youth organizations
Grant Types: scholarship
Geographic Distribution: focus on the Dodge City, KS, area

GIVING OFFICERS
Frank Mapel: secy
Roderic H. Simpson: pres
Stanley D. Simpson: treas
Robert Ven John: trust
George Voss: vp

APPLICATION INFORMATION
Initial Approach: Application form required. There are no deadlines.
Restrictions on Giving: Does not support individuals.

GRANTS ANALYSIS
Number of Grants: 35
Highest Grant: $6,000
Typical Range: $500 to $1,000
Disclosure Period: 1991

RECENT GRANTS
6,000 Meals on Wheels, Dodge City, KS
4,000 City of Dodge City Parks and Recreation, Dodge City, KS

4,000 Dodge City Head Start Project, Dodge City, KS

4,000 St. Mary of Plains, Dodge City, KS

3,000 Dodge City Public Library, Dodge City, KS

3,000 Sacred Heart, Dodge City, KS

2,000 Bethel Home, Dodge City, KS

2,000 Ford County 4-H Foundations, Dodge City, KS

1,500 Dodge City Community College, Dodge City, KS — daycare center

1,500 Dodge City Community College, Dodge City, KS — nursing scholarships

SCT Yarns / SCT Foundation

Employees: 2,000
Headquarters: Chattanooga, TN

CONTACT
Belinda B. Hicks
Treasurer
SCT Yarns
1800 South Watkins Street
Chattanooga, TN 37404
(615) 622-3131

FINANCIAL SUMMARY
Recent Giving: $42,319 (fiscal 1990)
Assets: $49,447 (fiscal year ending August 31, 1990)
Gifts Received: $45,000 (fiscal 1990)
Fiscal Note: In fiscal 1990, contributions were received from SCT Yarns, Inc.
EIN: 62-0988410

CONTRIBUTIONS SUMMARY
Typical Recipients: • *Education:* education funds • *Social Services:* united funds, youth organizations
Grant Types: general support and scholarship
Geographic Distribution: giving primarily in TN and surrounding states
Operating Locations: TN (Chattanooga)

CORP. OFFICERS
Joseph W. Thatcher: *CURR EMPL* chmn: SCT Yarns
J. Don Trotter: *CURR EMPL* pres: SCT Yarns

GIVING OFFICERS
C.D. Cox: trust

Floyd w. Craig: secy
David D. Groves: chmn
C.W. Hammer: trust
Belinda B. Hicks: treas
T.J. Manson: trust
J.E. Moore: trust
J. Don Trotter: trust *CURR EMPL* pres: SCT Yarns (see above)

APPLICATION INFORMATION
Initial Approach: Awards scholarships to children of employees of SCT Yarns, who have been continuously employed by the Co. for two or more years.

GRANTS ANALYSIS
Number of Grants: 50
Highest Grant: $10,000
Typical Range: $100 to $500
Disclosure Period: fiscal year ending August 31, 1990
Note: In fiscal 1990, number of grants does not include scholarships and matching gifts.

RECENT GRANTS
10,000 Chattanooga Boys Club, Chattanooga, TN

2,000 United Way, Chattanooga, TN

1,500 United Way, Chattanooga, TN

1,500 United Way, Chattanooga, TN

1,000 Piedmont Adopt-A-School, Chattanooga, TN

1,000 Piedmont Adopt-A-School, Chattanooga, TN

500 Chattanooga Boys Club, Chattanooga, TN

500 United Way, Atlanta, GA

500 United Way, Atlanta, GA

500 United Way, Chattanooga, TN

Scurlock Foundation

CONTACT
L. L. Blanton
President
Scurlock Fdn.
700 Louisiana, Ste. 3920
Houston, TX 77002
(713) 236-1500

FINANCIAL SUMMARY
Recent Giving: $545,166 (1991); $609,300 (1990); $535,322 (1989)
Assets: $8,873,597 (1991); $7,943,049 (1990); $7,959,116 (1989)

Gifts Received: $62,708 (1991); $22,451 (1990); $28,540 (1989)
Fiscal Note: 1991 contribution recieved from Scurlock Oil Company.
EIN: 74-1488953

CONTRIBUTIONS SUMMARY
Donor(s): the late E. C. Scurlock, Scurlock Oil Co., the late D. E. Farnsworth, the late W. C. Scurlock, I. S. Blanton
Typical Recipients: • *Arts & Humanities:* arts associations, dance, history/historic preservation, libraries, museums/galleries, opera, performing arts • *Civic & Public Affairs:* women's affairs, zoos/botanical gardens • *Education:* colleges & universities, private education (precollege) • *Health:* hospitals, medical research, pediatric health, single-disease health associations • *Religion:* churches, religious organizations • *Social Services:* child welfare, community service organizations, day care, disabled, united funds, united funds, volunteer services, youth organizations
Grant Types: capital, emergency, endowment, general support, and research
Geographic Distribution: focus on TX

GIVING OFFICERS
Eddy S. Blanton: dir
Jack Sawtelle Blanton: pres, dir *B* Shreveport LA 1927 *ED* Univ TX BA 1947; Univ TX LLB 1950 *CURR EMPL* ceo, pres, dir: Eddy Refining Co *CORP AFFIL* dir: Ashland Oil, Baker Hughes, Burlington Northern, Pogo Producing Co, Southwestern Bell Corp, TX Commerce Bancshares, TX Commerce Bank NA *NONPR AFFIL* mem: Delta Kappa Epsilon, Ex-Students Assn Univ TX, Houston Chamber Commerce, Mid-Continent Oil & Gas Assn, Natl Petroleum Counc, Natl Tennis Assn, Phi Alpha Delta, Phi Delta Phi, Sam Houston Meml Assn, Sons Republic TX, TX Independent Oil Producers & Refiners, US Lawn Tennis Assn
Jack Sawtelle Blanton, Jr.: dir *B* Houston TX 1953 *ED* Univ TX 1975 *CURR EMPL* chmn: Nicklos Drilling Co *CORP AFFIL* chmn: Nicklos Drilling Co
Laura Lee Blanton: dir

Kenneth Fisher: secy, treas, dir
Ben F. Love: vp, dir *B* Paris TX 1924 *ED* Univ TX BBA 1948 *CORP AFFIL* dir: Burlington Northern, Cox Enterprises, Lilly (Eli) & Co, Mitchell Energy & Devel Corp, TX Commerce Bancshares *NONPR AFFIL* chmn counc overseers: Rice Univ Jesse H Jones Grad Sch Admin
Elizabeth B. Wareing: dir

APPLICATION INFORMATION
Initial Approach: Send brief letter describing program. There are no deadlines.
Restrictions on Giving: Does not support individuals or provide loans.

GRANTS ANALYSIS
Number of Grants: 126
Highest Grant: $50,000
Typical Range: $1,000 to $5,000
Disclosure Period: 1991

RECENT GRANTS
50,000 Texas Children's Hospital, Houston, TX

48,300 Lon Morris College, Jacksonville, TX

36,000 American Council for the Arts, Houston, TX

13,000 Neuhaus Education Center, Houston, TX

12,700 M.D. Anderson Hospital, Houston, TX

10,450 Museum of Fine Arts, Houston, TX

10,200 Children's Museum, Houston, TX

10,000 Second Baptist School Fund, Houston, TX

10,000 Southern Methodist University, Dallas, TX

10,000 United Way, Houston, TX

Scurry Foundation, D. L.

CONTACT
James Burgess
Trustee
D. L. Scurry Fdn.
P. O. Box 5026
Columbia, SC 29250
(803) 738-9021

FINANCIAL SUMMARY
Recent Giving: $188,250 (fiscal 1992); $165,525 (fiscal 1991); $168,400 (fiscal 1990)
Assets: $4,253,228 (fiscal year ending June 30, 1992); $3,948,568 (fiscal 1991); $3,912,137 (fiscal 1990)
EIN: 57-6036622

CONTRIBUTIONS SUMMARY
Donor(s): the late D. L. Scurry
Typical Recipients: • *Civic & Public Affairs:* environmental affairs • *Education:* colleges & universities, community & junior colleges, medical education • *Social Services:* animal protection, child welfare, disabled, youth organizations
Grant Types: endowment and scholarship
Geographic Distribution: limited to SC

GIVING OFFICERS
James F. Burgess: trust

APPLICATION INFORMATION
Initial Approach: Send cover letter and full proposal. There are no deadlines.
Restrictions on Giving: Does not support individuals.

GRANTS ANALYSIS
Number of Grants: 80
Highest Grant: $6,000
Typical Range: $1,000 to $3,000
Disclosure Period: fiscal year ending June 30, 1992

RECENT GRANTS
6,000 Camden Military College, Camden, NJ
5,500 North Greenville College, Greenville, SC
5,500 Rocky Bottom Camp for Blind
5,000 Anderson College
5,000 Columbia College, New York, NY
5,000 Furman University, Greenville, SC
5,000 Greenville Technical College, Greenville, SC
5,000 South Carolina Wildlife Association, Greenville, SC
4,000 Boys Home of South, Greenville, SC
4,000 Connie Maxwell Children's Home, Greenville, SC

SDB Foundation

CONTACT
Elois Veltman
Secretary
SDB Fdn.
PO Box 926
Fallbrook, CA 92028
(619) 728-4390

FINANCIAL SUMMARY
Recent Giving: $3,661,016 (fiscal 1990); $96,965 (fiscal 1989); $72,723 (fiscal 1988)
Assets: $3,547,179 (fiscal 1989); $3,491,710 (fiscal 1988)
Gifts Received: $75,000 (fiscal 1990); $20,000 (fiscal 1989); $1,500,000 (fiscal 1988)
EIN: 94-2973293

CONTRIBUTIONS SUMMARY
Donor(s): Sarah D. Barder
Typical Recipients: • *Education:* colleges & universities, private education (precollege)
Grant Types: project, scholarship, and seed money
Geographic Distribution: focus on CA, NV, AZ, and UT

GIVING OFFICERS
Sarah D. Barder: pres
John W. Duncan: treas
Elois Veltman: secy

APPLICATION INFORMATION
Initial Approach: Application form required. There are no deadlines.

OTHER THINGS TO KNOW
Publications: Informational Brochure

GRANTS ANALYSIS
Number of Grants: 12
Highest Grant: $1,650,000
Typical Range: $8,000 to $49,000
Disclosure Period: fiscal year ending July 31, 1990

RECENT GRANTS
1,650,000 Johns Hopkins University, Baltimore, MD
1,500,000 Meadows School, Las Vegas, NV
210,000 Idyllwild Arts Foundation, Idyllwild, CA
100,000 Meadows School, Las Vegas, NV
48,760 Johns Hopkins University, Baltimore, MD
45,000 Meadows School, Las Vegas, NV
43,710 Johns Hopkins University, Baltimore, MD
10,110 Temecula Union School District, Temecula, CA
9,600 St. Judes Ranch, Boulder City, NV

Sea-Land Service
Sales: $3.1 billion
Employees: 8,500
Parent Company: CSX Corp.
Headquarters: Washington, DC
SIC Major Group: Trucking & Warehousing and Water Transportation

CONTACT
Peter Finnerty
Vice President, Public Afairs
Sea-Land Service
1331 Pennsylvania Ave. N.W., Ste. 560
Washington, DC 20004
(202) 783-1117

FINANCIAL SUMMARY
Fiscal Note: Annual Giving Range: $100,000 to $250,000

CONTRIBUTIONS SUMMARY
Support goes to local education, human services, arts, and civic organizations.
Typical Recipients: • *Arts & Humanities:* general • *Civic & Public Affairs:* general • *Education:* general • *Health:* general • *Social Services:* general
Operating Locations: DC (Washington)

CORP. OFFICERS
John P. Clancey: *CURR EMPL* pres, ceo: Sea-Land Svc
John W. Snow: *B* Toledo OH 1939 *ED* Univ Toledo BA; George Washington Univ Law Sch LLB *CURR EMPL* chmn, pres, ceo, dir: CSX Corp *CORP AFFIL* chmn, dir: Sea-Land Svc; dir: Bassett Furniture Indus, Best Products Co, Columbia Gas Sys, NationsBank Corp, Textron; chmn: CSX Transportation; dir: Am Commercial Lines, CSX Hotels, CSX Realty, RF & P Corp *NONPR AFFIL* dir: VA Mus Fine Arts; mem: VA Bar Assn; dir: Am Commercial Lines

APPLICATION INFORMATION
Restrictions on Giving: Does not support religious organizations for sectarian purposes or political or lobbying groups.

OTHER THINGS TO KNOW
Sea-Land is a business unit of CSX Corp., Richmond, VA.

Seaboard Corp.
Sales: $875.9 million
Employees: 10,970
Parent Company: Seaboard Flour
Headquarters: Chestnut Hill, MA
SIC Major Group: Agricultural Services, Food & Kindred Products, Trucking & Warehousing, and Wholesale Trade—Nondurable Goods

CONTACT
Jesse Bechtold
Corporate Controller
Seaboard Corp.
200 Boylston St.
Chestnut Hill, MA 02167
(617) 332-8492

CONTRIBUTIONS SUMMARY
Operating Locations: KS (Shawnee Mission)

CORP. OFFICERS
H. H. Bresky: *CURR EMPL* pres: Seaboard Corp
Joe E. Rodriques: *CURR EMPL* exec vp, cfo: Seaboard Corp

Seabury Foundation

CONTACT
Ray Harris
Trustee
Seabury Fdn.
c/o The Northern Trust Co.
50 South LaSalle St.
Chicago, IL 60675
(312) 630-6000

FINANCIAL SUMMARY
Recent Giving: $972,038 (1990); $1,116,715 (1989); $605,700 (1988)
Assets: $17,205,039 (1990); $18,688,466 (1989); $15,773,077 (1988)

EIN: 36-6027398

CONTRIBUTIONS SUMMARY

Donor(s): The foundation was established in 1947 by the late Charles Ward Seabury and the late Louise Lovett Seabury.

Typical Recipients: • *Arts & Humanities:* libraries, museums/galleries, music, opera, public broadcasting • *Civic & Public Affairs:* ethnic/minority organizations • *Education:* colleges & universities, international exchange, public education (precollege), religious education, special education • *Health:* hospitals, medical rehabilitation, medical research, nursing services, pediatric health, single-disease health associations • *International:* foreign educational institutions, international organizations • *Social Services:* emergency relief, food/clothing distribution, homes, united funds, youth organizations

Grant Types: general support and scholarship

Geographic Distribution: focus on the greater Chicago, IL, area

GIVING OFFICERS

Clara Seabury Boone: trust
Daniel William Boone: trust
Robert S. Boone: trust
Charles B. Fisk: trust
Ray Harris: trust
Seabury J. Hibben: trust
Elizabeth Seabury Mitchell: trust
Louis Fisk Morris: trust
Charlene Brown Seabury: trust
David G. Seabury: trust

APPLICATION INFORMATION

Initial Approach:
The foundation has no formal grant application procedure or application form.
The foundation has no deadline for submitting proposals.
Restrictions on Giving: The foundation reports it has developed a schedule of qualified charitable organizations to which contributions are made on a somewhat annual basis. Grants are not made to individuals, and the foundation does not make loans.

GRANTS ANALYSIS

Total Grants: $972,038
Number of Grants: 162
Highest Grant: $50,000

Typical Range: $1,000 to $15,000

Disclosure Period: 1990

Note: Recent grants are derived from a 1990 grants list.

RECENT GRANTS

50,000 Children's Memorial Medical Center, Chicago, IL

50,000 Hadley School for the Blind, Winnetka, IL

50,000 Visiting Nurse Association, Evanston, IL

42,000 Paul Oliver Memorial Hospital, Frankfort, MI

35,000 Visiting Nurse Association, Chicago, IL

28,000 Uptown Habitat for Humanity, Chicago, IL

27,900 Friends of Colorado State Library for the Blind and Physically Handicapped, Denver, CO

25,000 Chicago Symphony Orchestra, Chicago, IL

25,000 Presbyterian Home, Evanston, IL

25,000 Rehabilitation Institute, Chicago, IL

Seafirst Corp. / Seafirst Foundation

Employees: 7,200
Parent Company: BankAmerica Corp.
Headquarters: Seattle, WA
SIC Major Group: Depository Institutions and Holding & Other Investment Offices

CONTACT

Nadine Troyer
Vice President
Seafirst Fdn.
PO Box 34661
Seattle, WA 98124-1661
(206) 358-3443

FINANCIAL SUMMARY

Recent Giving: $1,341,554 (1992); $1,377,441 (1991); $1,397,654 (1990)

Assets: $1,377,441 (1991); $1,400,000 (1989)

Fiscal Note: Company made direct contributions totaling $1,502,417 in 1992. Thiis amount is not included in the figures above.

EIN: 91-1094720

CONTRIBUTIONS SUMMARY

Typical Recipients: • *Arts & Humanities:* arts centers, community arts, dance, museums/galleries, music, opera, performing arts, theater • *Civic & Public Affairs:* housing, urban & community affairs, zoos/botanical gardens • *Education:* agricultural education, arts education, business education, career/vocational education, colleges & universities, economic education, literacy, minority education, special education • *Health:* health organizations, hospitals, outpatient health care delivery • *Social Services:* child welfare, community service organizations, disabled, employment/job training, family services, united funds, youth organizations

Grant Types: challenge, general support, project, and seed money

Nonmonetary Support Types: donated equipment, in-kind services, and loaned executives
Note: Nonmonetary support is provided by the company. Estimated value of nonmonetary support is unavailable and is not included in figures above. Contact Wanda Roraback, Assistant Vice President, for information.

Geographic Distribution: exclusively in Washington

Operating Locations: WA (Seattle)
Note: Operates 200 branches in the state of Washington.

CORP. OFFICERS

Rick Collette: *CURR EMPL* sr vp, mgr: Seafirst Corp
Jack David: *B* Seattle WA 1943 *ED* Seattle Univ 1967; Harvard Univ Sch Bus Admin *CURR EMPL* exec vp (mktg): Seafirst Corp
Luther Sherman Helms III: *B* Lubbock TX 1943 *ED* Univ AZ 1966; Santa Clara Univ 1968 *CURR EMPL* chmn, ceo: Seafirst Corp *CORP AFFIL* pres: Seattle First Natl Bank
W. Thomas Porter: *B* Corning NY 1934 *ED* Rutgers Univ BS 1954; Univ WA MBA 1959; Columbia Univ PhD 1964 *CURR EMPL* exec vp: Seafirst Corp *NONPR AFFIL* mem: Am Inst CPAs; trust: VA Mason Med Fdn
Wally Webster: *CURR EMPL* vp, mgr: Seafirst Corp

GIVING OFFICERS

Rick Collette: trust *CURR EMPL* sr vp, mgr: Seafirst Corp (see above)
Jack David: trust *CURR EMPL* exec vp (mktg): Seafirst Corp (see above)
Hal Greene: trust
Becki Johnson: trust
Diane Mackey: trust
Richard E. Odelgard: pres *B* Snohomish WA 1940 *ED* Whitman Coll 1962 *CURR EMPL* sr vp: Seattle First Natl Bank
W. Thomas Porter: trust *CURR EMPL* exec vp: Seafirst Corp (see above)
Nadine Troyer: vp, secy, trust, program dir
Wally Webster: trust *CURR EMPL* vp, mgr: Seafirst Corp (see above)
Jim Williams: treas

APPLICATION INFORMATION

Initial Approach: *Initial Contact:* request application (letter no longer than two pages) *Include Information On:* specific amount of request; how funds will be used; purpose and objectives of organization; geographical area and population served; names and qualifications of persons who will administer funds; proposed timetable for project; potential benefit to Seafirst; list of Seafirst employees involved in organization; most recent financial statement; list of current officers and directors; project budget; most recent financial statement; list of other funding sources; and proof of tax-exempt status *When to Submit:* any time, but requests received after October 1 may be carried over to January

Restrictions on Giving: Foundation generally does not support research; endowments, memorials, or operating deficits; travel expenses; political issues; individuals; fraternal organizations; production of video tapes, films, or publications; hospital operating funds and the maintenance of medical facilities; single-disease organizations; primary or secondary schools; parent-teacher associations; discriminatory organizations; national organizations, including national conventions held locally or scholarships other than Seafirst scholarship programs. Does not support churches or other religious organizations for purposes of religious advocacy.

OTHER THINGS TO KNOW

Priority given to special project support; less emphasis on capital campaigns.

Publications: *Seafirst Contributions, Guidelines for Giving*

GRANTS ANALYSIS

Total Grants: $1,341,441
Number of Grants: 64
Highest Grant: $554,910
Typical Range: $5,000 to $20,000
Disclosure Period: 1992

Note: Fiscal information for foundation only. The average grant figure excludes the highest grant of $554,910. Recent grants are derived from a 1992 grants list. Assets are for 1991.

RECENT GRANTS

554,910 United Ways of Washington, Seattle-Tacoma-Olympia, Seattle, WA
161,478 Seafirst Scholarships, Seattle, WA
75,000 Corporate Council for the Arts
40,000 Pacific Northwest Ballet, Seattle, WA
25,000 Children's Hospital Foundation, Seattle, WA
25,000 Heritage College, Seattle, WA
25,000 Pacific Science Center, Seattle, WA
21,000 Seattle Arts Stabilization Fund, Seattle, WA
20,000 Fred Hutchinson Cancer Research Center, Seattle, WA
20,000 Oregon Museum of Science and Industry, Portland, OR

Seagate Technology

Sales: $2.67 billion
Employees: 43,000
Headquarters: Scotts Valley, CA
SIC Major Group: Industrial Machinery & Equipment

CONTACT

Julie Still
Communications, Public Relations
Seagate Technology
PO Box 66360, Bldg. 1
Scotts Valley, CA 95067-0360
(408) 438-6550

CONTRIBUTIONS SUMMARY

Operating Locations: CA (Scotts Valley)

CORP. OFFICERS

David T. Mitchell: *CURR EMPL* pres, coo: Seagate Technology
Alan F. Shugart: *CURR EMPL* chmn, ceo: Seagate Technology
Donald L. Waite: *CURR EMPL* sr vp, cfo: Seagate Technology

Seagram & Sons, Joseph E. / Bronfman Foundation, Samuel

Sales: $6.35 billion
Employees: 13,151
Parent Company: Seagram Company Ltd., Montreal, Canada
Headquarters: New York, NY
SIC Major Group: Food & Kindred Products

CONTACT

Claire Cullen
Director, Corporate Philanthropy
Joseph E. Seagram & Sons, Inc.
375 Park Ave.
New York, NY 10152
(212) 572-7000

FINANCIAL SUMMARY

Recent Giving: $6,374,857 (1991); $6,252,761 (1990); $6,480,942 (1989)
Assets: $12,307,375 (1991); $20,195,364 (1989); $9,300,326 (1987)
Fiscal Note: Company and subsidiaries give through foundation only. Sales companies may give individually, but such grants must be approved by the foundation.
EIN: 13-6084708

CONTRIBUTIONS SUMMARY

Typical Recipients: • *Arts & Humanities:* arts centers, museums/galleries • *Civic & Public Affairs:* business/free enter-prise, civil rights, ethnic/minority organizations, international affairs, public policy • *Education:* business education, colleges & universities, minority education, religious education, student aid • *Health:* medical research • *International:* foreign educational institutions, international organizations • *Religion:* religious organizations • *Social Services:* drugs & alcohol, legal aid, youth organizations

Grant Types: challenge, fellowship, general support, professorship, and research

Nonmonetary Support Types: donated products

Note: Value of nonmonetary support is unavailable and is not included above.

Geographic Distribution: primarily New York City

Operating Locations: CA (Los Angeles), FL (Bradenton, Tampa), IL (Des Plaines), IN (Lawrenceburg), KY (Louisville), MD (Baltimore), NY (New York), OH (Cleveland)

CORP. OFFICERS

Edgar Miles Bronfman: *B* Montreal Quebec Canada 1929 *ED* Williams Coll 1946-1949; McGill Univ BA 1951 *CURR EMPL* chmn, ceo, dir: Joseph E Seagram & Sons *CORP AFFIL* chmn, ceo, dir: Seagram Co Ltd; dir: Clevepak Corp, EI du-Pont de Nemours & Co *NONPR AFFIL* bd delegates: Un Am Hebrew Congregation; chmn, trust: Bnai Brith Anti-Defamation League NY; dir: Am Technician Soc, Intl Exec Svc Corps, Un Negro Coll Fund, US-USSR Trade Econ Counc, Weizmann Inst; hon chmn: Fdn Jewish Philanthropies; mem bd overseers: Bnai Brith Intl Trust; mem fin comm: Natl Urban League

Edgar Miles Bronfman, Jr.: *B* Montreal Quebec Canada 1929 *CURR EMPL* pres, coo: John E Seagram & Sons

GIVING OFFICERS

Stephen Edward Banner: treas, trust *B* New York NY 1938 *ED* Yale Univ BA; Harvard Univ LLB *CURR EMPL* sr exec vp, dir: Seagram Co Ltd *NONPR AFFIL* lecturer: Practicing Law Inst; mem: Assoc Bar City NY

Samuel Bronfman II: pres, trust

Claire Cullen: secy *CURR EMPL* dir (corp philanthropy): Joseph E Seagram & Sons
William K. Friedman: trust *CURR EMPL* vp (corp aff): Joseph E Seagram & Sons
Richard Karl Goeltz: trust *B* Chicago IL 1942 *ED* Brown Univ AB 1964; Columbia Univ MBA 1966 *CURR EMPL* exec vp (fin), dir: Seagram (Joseph E) & Sons *CORP AFFIL* vp, treas, contr: Seagram Co Ltd *NONPR AFFIL* dir: New Germany Fund, Opera Orchestra NY; mem: Beat Gamma Sigma; trust: 59 Wall St Fund

APPLICATION INFORMATION

Initial Approach: *Initial Contact:* letter *Include Information On:* reason for requesting support, amount needed, proof of tax-exempt status *When to Submit:* any time *Note:* Further information will be requested if foundation is interested.

Restrictions on Giving: Does not support individuals.

GRANTS ANALYSIS

Total Grants: $6,374,857
Number of Grants: 19
Highest Grant: $1,043,752
Typical Range: $1,000 to $250,000
Disclosure Period: 1991

Note: Figure for average grant does not include foundation's four highest grants. Recent grants are derived from a 1991 Form 990.

RECENT GRANTS

1,043,752 Endowment for Research in Human Biology, Boston, MA
1,000,000 Bronfman Center for Jewish Life
1,000,000 World Jewish Congress-American Section, New York, NY
435,000 Edgar M. Bronfman Youth Fellowships in Israel
333,667 United Jewish Appeal Federation Campaign, New York, NY
288,000 Columbia University, New York, NY
264,103 East-West Forum
200,000 New York Public Library, New York, NY
150,000 United Negro College Fund, New York, NY

135,000 B'nai B'rith, New York, NY

Sealaska Corp. / Sealaska Heritage Foundation

Sales: $100.0 million
Employees: 630
Headquarters: Juneau, AK
SIC Major Group: Food & Kindred Products, Lumber & Wood Products, and Stone, Clay & Glass Products

CONTACT
Ron Williams
Shareholder Relations Coordinator
Sealaska Corp.
One Sealaska Plaza, Ste. 400
Juneau, AK 99801
(907) 586-1512

FINANCIAL SUMMARY
Recent Giving: $45,000 (1991); $60,000 (1990)

CONTRIBUTIONS SUMMARY
Typical Recipients: • *Arts & Humanities:* ethnic arts • *Civic & Public Affairs:* environmental affairs • *Education:* minority education • *Health:* health organizations • *Social Services:* aged
Grant Types: general support
Geographic Distribution: primarily AK
Operating Locations: AK (Juneau)

CORP. OFFICERS
Byron Mallott: *CURR EMPL* ceo, pres: Sealaska Corp
William Strafford: *CURR EMPL* cfo: Sealaska Corp

APPLICATION INFORMATION
Initial Approach: Send brief letter of inquiry, including a description of the organization, amount requested, purpose of funds sought, audited financial statement, and proof of tax-exempt status. There are no deadlines.
Restrictions on Giving: Does not support individuals, religious organizations for sectarian purposes, or political or lobbying groups.

Sealed Air Corp.
Sales: $435.1 million
Employees: 2,770
Headquarters: Saddle Brook, NJ
SIC Major Group: Chemicals & Allied Products, Paper & Allied Products, and Rubber & Miscellaneous Plastics Products

CONTACT
T.J. Dermott Dunphy
President
Sealed Air Corp.
Park 80 Plz. East
Saddle Brook, NJ 07662
(201) 791-7600

FINANCIAL SUMMARY
Fiscal Note: Annual Giving Range: less than $100,000

CONTRIBUTIONS SUMMARY
Support goes to local education, human service, arts, and civic organizations. Includes matching gifts.
Typical Recipients: • *Arts & Humanities:* general • *Civic & Public Affairs:* general • *Education:* general • *Health:* general • *Social Services:* general
Grant Types: matching
Operating Locations: NJ (Saddle Brook)

CORP. OFFICERS
T.J. Dermot Dunphy: *CURR EMPL* pres, ceo, dir: Sealed Air Corp

APPLICATION INFORMATION
Initial Approach: Send letter of inquiry.

Sealright Co., Inc. / Sealright Foundation, Inc.
Sales: $258.3 million
Employees: 1,746
Headquarters: Overland Park, KS
SIC Major Group: Paper & Allied Products and Rubber & Miscellaneous Plastics Products

CONTACT
Marvin W. Ozley
President
Sealright Foundation, Inc.
7601 College Blvd., Ste. 1400
Overland Park, KS 66210
(913) 344-9000

FINANCIAL SUMMARY
Recent Giving: $17,335 (1993 est.); $13,485 (1991)
Assets: $277,397 (1991)
Gifts Received: $10,000 (1991)

EIN: 15-6019087

CONTRIBUTIONS SUMMARY
Typical Recipients: • *Arts & Humanities:* community arts, general, museums/galleries, music, performing arts, theater • *Civic & Public Affairs:* business/free enterprise, general • *Education:* business education, economic education, general • *Health:* general, health organizations, hospitals, medical research, pediatric health, single-disease health associations • *Social Services:* aged, community centers, community service organizations, counseling, disabled, domestic violence, drugs & alcohol, emergency relief, general, religious welfare, shelters/homelessness, youth organizations
Grant Types: capital, employee matching gifts, general support, and research
Nonmonetary Support Types: donated equipment
Geographic Distribution: primarily KS and MO
Operating Locations: KS (Overland Park)

CORP. OFFICERS
Marvin W. Ozley: *CURR EMPL* chmn, pres, ceo: Sealright Co

APPLICATION INFORMATION
Initial Approach: Send a brief letter of inquiry and a full proposal. Include a description of organization, amount requested, purpose of funds sought, and proof of tax-exempt status.
Restrictions on Giving: Does not support individuals, or political or lobbying groups.

GRANTS ANALYSIS
Number of Grants: 33
Highest Grant: $2,000
Typical Range: $200 to $1,000
Disclosure Period: 1991

RECENT GRANTS
2,000 Midwest Ear Institute
1,200 Children's Place
1,200 Salvation Army
1,000 American Red Cross, New York, NY
1,000 Children's Mercy Hospital for Golf Classic, Kansas City, MO
750 De La Salle Education Center

600 Association for Retarded Citizens of Johnson County
500 Cystic Fibrosis Foundation
500 Youth Symphony Association, Kansas City, MO
250 Children's Center for the Visually Impaired

Sealy, Inc.
Sales: $623.9 million
Employees: 4,500
Parent Company: Sealy
Headquarters: Cleveland, OH
SIC Major Group: Furniture & Fixtures and Holding & Other Investment Offices

CONTACT
Jeffrey Claypool
Vice President, Human Resources
Sealy, Inc.
1228 Euclid Ave.
Cleveland, OH 44115
(216) 522-1310

CONTRIBUTIONS SUMMARY
Contributions suspended. Past recipients primarily local organizations.
Operating Locations: AR (Springdale), AZ (Phoenix), CA (Carson), CO (Colorado Springs), CT (Oakville), GA (Tucker), IL (Batavia), IN (Rensselaer), KS (Kansas City), MA (Randolph), MD (Baltimore), MI (Taylor), MN (St. Paul), MS (Pontotoc), NY (Albany), OH (Cleveland, Columbiana, Lockland), PA (Delano), PR (Rio Piedras), TN (Memphis), TX (Brenham, Richland Hills), VA (Bluefield)

CORP. OFFICERS
Malcolm Candlish: *CURR EMPL* chmn, pres, ceo, dir: Sealy
Douglas Schrank: *CURR EMPL* cfo: Sealy

Searle & Co., G.D. / Searle Charitable Trust
Sales: $1.49 billion
Employees: 10,000
Parent Company: Monsanto Co.
Headquarters: Skokie, IL
SIC Major Group: Chemicals & Allied Products

CONTACT

Charles L. Fry
Corporate Vice President, Public
Affairs
Searle Charitable Trust
PO Box 5110
Chicago, IL 60680
(708) 982-7000

FINANCIAL SUMMARY

Recent Giving: $500,000
(1993 est.); $800,000 (1992 approx.); $590,000 (1991 approx.)
Assets: $344,060 (1989)
Fiscal Note: Company gives
through foundation only.
EIN: 36-6785886

CONTRIBUTIONS SUMMARY

Typical Recipients: • *Arts & Humanities:* arts associations,
arts funds, arts institutes,
dance, libraries, music, opera,
performing arts, theater • *Civic & Public Affairs:* business/free
enterprise, consumer affairs,
economic development, international affairs, law & justice,
public policy, women's affairs
• *Education:* arts education, career/vocational education, colleges & universities, community & junior colleges,
continuing education,
economic education, education
associations, education funds,
public education (precollege),
science/technology education
• *Health:* health organizations,
hospitals, medical research,
nursing services, nutrition &
health maintenance, public
health, single-disease health associations • *Science:* observatories & planetariums, scientific
institutes • *Social Services:*
aged, child welfare, legal aid,
united funds, youth organizations
Grant Types: employee matching gifts and general support
Nonmonetary Support Types:
donated products
Note: Value of nonmonetary
support is not available and is
not included in the figures
above.
Geographic Distribution: nationally, with emphasis on operating communities
Operating Locations: IL (Chicago, Skokie)
Note: Also operates internationally.

CORP. OFFICERS

Sheldon Gerald Gilgore, MD:
B Philadelphia PA 1932 *ED* Villanova Univ BS 1952; Jefferson Med Coll MD 1956 *CURR*

EMPL chmn, ceo, dir: GD
Searle & Co *CORP AFFIL*
chmn, pres, ceo, dir: Searle
Laboratories *NONPR AFFIL*
dir: CT Grand Opera Co, Evanston Hosp Corp, Lyric Opera
Chicago, Natl Mus Health
Medicine Fdn, Pharmaceutical
Mfrs Assn; mem: Am Bar Assn,
Am Coll Clinical Pharmacology & Chemotherapy, Am Diabetes Assn, Am Fed Clinical
Res, NY Academy Sciences;
mem pres' counc: Meml Sloan-Kettering Cancer Ctr

GIVING OFFICERS

Peter L. Baron: dir *CURR
EMPL* vp (human resources):
Searle (GD) & Co
Robert Lee Bogomolny: dir *B*
Cleveland OH 1938 *ED* Harvard Univ AB 1960; Harvard
Univ LLB 1963 *CURR EMPL*
vp, gen coun, secy: Searle
(GD) & Co *NONPR AFFIL* dir:
Orchard Village; mem: Am Bar
Assn, Am Corp Couns Assn,
Biotechnology Devel Corp,
Food & Drug Law Inst, Greater
Cleveland Bar Assn, IL Bar
Assn, OH Bar Assn; trust: Glenkirk Fdn
Richard U. De Schutter: dir *B*
Detroit MI 1940 *ED* Univ AZ
BS 1964; Univ AZ MS 1965
CURR EMPL pres (intl opers),
adv mem bd dirs: Searle (GD)
& Co *CORP AFFIL* dir: IL Central RR; vp, mng dir: Monsanto
In Chem Co *NONPR AFFIL*
dir: Chicago Jr Achievement;
mem industrial adv bd: Univ
AZ Coll Engg
Charles L. Fry: chmn, secy *B*
Denver CO 1934 *CURR EMPL*
corp vp (pub aff): Searle (GD)
& Co *NONPR AFFIL* mem:
Natl Health Counc
Sheldon Gerald Gilgore, MD:
vchmn *CURR EMPL* chmn,
ceo, dir: GD Searle & Co (see
above)

APPLICATION INFORMATION

Initial Approach: *Initial Contact:* brief letter or proposal *Include Information On:* description of the organization,
amount requested, purpose for
which funds are sought, recently audited financial statement, proof of tax-exempt
status *When to Submit:* any time
Restrictions on Giving: No
grants awarded to individuals,
sectarian religious groups,
political organizations, or organizations supported by
United Way Crusade of Mercy.

Company does not award scholarships.

GRANTS ANALYSIS

Total Grants: $590,000*
Number of Grants: 90*
Highest Grant: $125,000*
Typical Range: $250 to $3,000
Disclosure Period: 1990
Note: Total grants figure is approximate. Number of grants
and average grant figures are
from 1989 and do not include
over $50,000 in matching gifts.
Assets are from 1989. Recent
grants are derived from a 1989
Form 990.

RECENT GRANTS

125,000   United Way Crusade of Mercy, Chicago, IL
31,500   Trustees of Tufts College, Boston, MA
31,080   Citizens Scholarship Foundation of America, St. Peter, MN — company-sponsored employee scholarships
20,000   Medicine in the Public Interest, Boston, MA
20,000   Royal College of General Practitioners Research Unit, Manchester, England — part of five-year grant to support study of the effects of hormones on postmenopausal subjects
15,000   American Council on Science and Health, New York, NY — to assist in the completion of a series of new programs
15,000   Thomas Jefferson University, Philadelphia, PA — to underwrite a rheumatology lab
12,500   Lyric Opera of Chicago, Chicago, IL
10,000   Duke University, Durham, NC
10,000   Friends of the Children's Inn at National Institute of Health, Washington, DC

Sears Family Foundation

CONTACT

David W. Swetland
Trustee
Sears Family Fdn.
907 Park Bldg.
Cleveland, OH 44114
(216) 241-6434

FINANCIAL SUMMARY

Recent Giving: $118,583
(1991); $141,183 (1990);
$141,910 (1989)
Assets: $2,458,846 (1991);
$2,293,781 (1990); $2,248,890
(1989)
Gifts Received: $48,355
(1991); $27,500 (1990)
Fiscal Note: In 1991, contributions were received from David
W. Swetland ($20,000), Polly
M. Swetland ($12,925), Ruth
Swetland Eppig ($6,693), and
David S. Swetland ($8,737).
EIN: 34-6522143

CONTRIBUTIONS SUMMARY

Donor(s): the late Anna L.
Sears, the late Lester M. Sears,
the late Ruth P. Sears, the late
Mary Ann Swetland
Typical Recipients: • *Arts & Humanities:* arts institutes,
community arts, dance, music,
theater • *Civic & Public Affairs:* environmental affairs,
zoos/botanical gardens • *Education:* arts education, colleges &
universities • *Health:* hospitals
• *Social Services:* community
service organizations, employment/job training, family planning, united funds
Grant Types: capital, emergency, general support, multiyear/continuing support, operating expenses, and research
Geographic Distribution: limited to the Cleveland, OH, area

GIVING OFFICERS

Ruth Swetland Eppig: trust
David Sears Swetland: trust
David W. Swetland: trust
Polly M. Swetland: off

APPLICATION INFORMATION

Initial Approach: Send brief
letter describing program.
There are no deadlines.
Restrictions on Giving: Does
not support individuals.

GRANTS ANALYSIS

Number of Grants: 48
Highest Grant: $50,000

Typical Range: $500 to $1,000
Disclosure Period: 1991

RECENT GRANTS

- 50,000 Vocational Guidance Services, Cleveland, OH
- 25,000 Museum of Natural History, Cleveland, OH
- 10,000 United Way, Cleveland, OH
- 8,333 Nature Conservancy, Cleveland, OH
- 7,000 Shaker Lakes Regional Nature Center, Shaker Heights, OH
- 5,000 Music School Settlement, Cleveland, OH
- 3,000 Junior League of Cleveland, Cleveland, OH
- 3,000 Planned Parenthood Federation of America, Cleveland, OH
- 3,000 Planned Parenthood Federation of America, Cleveland, OH
- 2,000 Great Lakes Theatre Festival, Cleveland, OH

Sears, Roebuck and Co. / Sears-Roebuck Foundation

Sales: $59.1 billion
Employees: 403,000
Headquarters: Chicago, IL
SIC Major Group: General Merchandise Stores, Insurance Carriers, and Miscellaneous Retail

---

CONTACT

Paula A. Banks
President & Executive Director
The Sears-Roebuck Fdn.
Sears Tower
Dept. 903 BSC 6-15
Chicago, IL 60684
(708) 286-7112
Note: Ms. Banks also is Director, Corporate Contributions, of Sears, Roebuck and Co.

FINANCIAL SUMMARY

Recent Giving: $27,646,311 (fiscal 1991); $23,381,475 (fiscal 1990); $27,246,890 (fiscal 1989)
Assets: $2,716,856 (fiscal year ending January 31, 1991); $2,546,335 (fiscal 1990)
Gifts Received: $575 (fiscal 1991)

Fiscal Note: Figures include contributions made by Sears, Roebuck and Co., the Sears-Roebuck Foundation, Sears Merchandise Group, the Allstate Foundation, Dean Witter Financial Group, and Coldwell Banker Real Estate Group (see separate entry on the Allstate Foundation). See "Other Things You Should Know."
EIN: 36-6032266

CONTRIBUTIONS SUMMARY

Typical Recipients: • *Education:* business education, career/vocational education, minority education • *Social Services:* employment/job training, united funds
Grant Types: project
Geographic Distribution: nationally
Operating Locations: CA (Irvine, Laguna Hills, Los Angeles, San Francisco), DC, DE (Wilmington), IL (Chicago, Glenview, Northbrook), MO (Kansas City), NY (New York, White Plains)

CORP. OFFICERS

Edward A. Brennan: *B* Chicago IL 1934 *ED* Marquette Univ BA 1955 *CURR EMPL* chmn, pres, ceo, dir: Sears Roebuck & Co *CORP AFFIL* chmn, ceo: Sears Merchandise Group; dir: AMR Corp, 3M Co; mem: NY Stock Exchange *NONPR AFFIL* bd govs: Un Way Am; dir: Chicago Counc Foreign Rels; mem: Bus Counc, Bus Roundtable, Chicago Mus Science Indus, Chicago Urban League, Conf Bd, Pres Export Counc; trust: De Paul Univ, Marquette Univ, Rush-Presbyterian-St Lukes Med Ctr, Savings Profit Sharing Fund Sears Employees

GIVING OFFICERS

Paula A. Banks: pres, exec dir *CURR EMPL* dir (corp contributions): Sears Roebuck & Co
Edward A. Brennan: dir *CURR EMPL* chmn, pres, ceo, dir: Sears Roebuck & Co (see above)
Jim Constantine: treas, dir
Warren F. Cooper: dir *CURR EMPL* vp (corp pers): Sears Roebuck & Co
Guy Eberhart: dir
Julie A. Hansen: secy
Peter Jerszynski: dir
Charles Moran: dir

Kenneth F. Mountcastle, Jr.: dir *B* Winston-Salem NC 1928 *ED* Univ NC 1950 *CURR EMPL* sr vp: Dean Witter Reynolds *NONPR AFFIL* bd visitors: Univ NC Chapel Hill; dir: Bus Execs Natl Security, Friends Thirteen, Giraffe Project, Inform, Mary Reynolds Babcock Fdn, NYC Fresh Air Fund; trust: Corp Fdn
Charles J. Ruder: chmn, dir *CURR EMPL* vp (corp pub affairs): Sears Roebuck & Co
Kristine Sandrick: dir
David Shute: dir *B* Crystal MI 1931 *ED* Princeton Univ BA 1953; Univ MI JD 1959 *CURR EMPL* sr vp, corp gen coun, secy: Sears Roebuck & Co *NONPR AFFIL* mem: Am Bar Assn, Am Enterprise Inst, Assn Gen Couns, Chicago Bar Assn, Econ Club Chicago, IL Bar Assn; mem adv bd: Univ CA Berkeley Natl Ctr Fin Svcs; mem adv comm corp coun ctr: Northwestern Univ Sch Law; mem planning comm: Corp Counc Inst; trust: Library Intl Rels; mem: Lawyers Comm Natl Ctr St Courts; mem adv bd: Chicago Volunteer Legal Svcs Fdn
Rita P. Wilson: dir *B* Philadelphia PA 1946 *CURR EMPL* sr vp, dir: Allstate Ins Co

APPLICATION INFORMATION

Initial Approach: *Initial Contact:* brief letter requesting a copy of the Sears, Roebuck and Co. Corporate Responsibility Report *Include Information On:* after reviewing a copy of the Sears, Roebuck and Co. Annual Program Report, proposals should include: a description of the organization, its purpose, history, and programs; description of problem organization wishes to solve; explanation of how proposed activity relates to Sears National Priorities; summary of monetary support needed and how it will be used; plan for periodic reporting and final evaluation; most recently audited financial statement and proposed budget; sources of income, including corporate donors and amounts; list of board of directors and their affiliations; copy of 501(c)(3) status statement *When to Submit:* any time *Note:* While multiyear funding commitments may be made, grant renewals are not automatic. Requests for additional support must be submit-

ted annually along with an interim report on the organization's progress.
Restrictions on Giving: Grants generally do not support individuals; political, labor, or fraternal organizations; religious organizations or endeavors; advertising in books, brochures, pamphlets, or yearbooks; or programs outside the United States. Foundation does not provide capital, endowment, or operating grants.

OTHER THINGS TO KNOW

The Foundation funds specific national programs related to the following National Priorities by category, in order of importance: Education - workforce readiness - and Health & Human Service - voluntarism. Parallel to the foundation, Sears, Roebuck and Co. corporate contributions are allocated in response to major grant requests from national organizations or for activities in the company's headquarters city, Chicago. Community programs or activities are supported by local units of Sears' four business groups: Sears Merchandise Group, Allstate Insurance Group, Dean Witter Financial Services Group, and Coldwell Banker Real Estate Group. See separate entry for more detailed information about the Allstate Foundation.
To be considered national, programs and organizations must serve a multiple-state area. During the 1990s, Sears will continue to emphasize and fully integrate education in each of its funding priorities. The goal is to serve as a catalyst to create a holistic approach to education. Funding will be used as a strategic tool to leverage opportunities for greater impact within and between the organizations supported.

GRANTS ANALYSIS

Total Grants: $2,716,856*
Number of Grants: 23
Highest Grant: $1,427,500
Typical Range: $10,000 to $100,000
Disclosure Period: fiscal year ending January 31, 1991
Note: Fiscal information for foundation only. Average grant figure does not include the largest grant of $1,427,500. Recent

grants are derived from a fiscal 1991 Form 990.

RECENT GRANTS

1,427,500	Foundation for Higher Education, Stamford, CT
225,000	Family Communication, Pittsburgh, PA
147,641	Modern Talking Picture Service, Tampa, FL
142,480	Princeton Center for Leadership Training, Princeton, NJ
130,539	Hispanic Association of Colleges and Universities, San Antonio, TX
125,000	United Negro College Fund, Chicago, IL
117,000	Joint Council on Economic Education, New York, NY
100,000	National Center-Neighborhood Enterprise, Washington, DC
66,593	University of Wisconsin, Madison, WI
50,000	Big Shoulder Fund, Chicago, IL

Seascape Senior Housing, Inc.

CONTACT
Seascape Senior Housing, Inc.
105 Cooper Street, Suite 219
Santa Cruz, CA 95060-4530
(415) 632-6712

FINANCIAL SUMMARY
Recent Giving: $0 (fiscal 1991); $0 (fiscal 1990)

Assets: $4,256,650 (fiscal year ending March 31, 1991); $4,342,098 (fiscal 1990)

EIN: 94-2911626

GIVING OFFICERS
Jennifer Davis: bd mem

Arnie Fischman: pres

Gordon Shepherd: bd mem

Richard Ulrey: bd mem

GRANTS ANALYSIS
Total Grants: $0

Disclosure Period: fiscal year ending March 31, 1991

Seasongood Good Government Foundation, Murray and Agnes

CONTACT
D. David Altman
Executive Secretary
Murray and Agnes Seasongood Good Government Fdn.
414 Walnut St., Ste. 1006
Cincinnati, OH 45202
(513) 721-2181

FINANCIAL SUMMARY
Recent Giving: $98,286 (1991); $123,204 (1990); $166,410 (1989)

Assets: $3,482,804 (1991); $2,970,596 (1990); $3,033,067 (1989)

Gifts Received: $4,350 (1991)

EIN: 31-1220827

CONTRIBUTIONS SUMMARY
Typical Recipients: • *Arts & Humanities:* museums/galleries • *Civic & Public Affairs:* better government, environmental affairs, law & justice, public policy • *Education:* colleges & universities, education associations, legal education

Grant Types: general support

Geographic Distribution: focus on Cincinnati, OH

GIVING OFFICERS
D. David Altman: exec secy

William T. Bahlman, Jr.: treas

William Baughin: secy

David D. Black: vp

William Robert Burleigh: trust *B* Evansville IN 1935 *ED* Marquette Univ BS 1957 *CURR EMPL* exec vp: Scripps-Howard Newspapers *NONPR AFFIL* mem: Alpha Sigma Nu, Am Soc Newspaper Editors

Robert W. Hilton, Jr.: trust

Jon Hoffheimer: trust

Mrs. Herbert Hoffheimer: trust

Gail Levin: trust

Nancy Minson: trust

Edward Padgett: trust

Bruce I. Petrie, Sr.: pres

Henry R. Winkler: vp

APPLICATION INFORMATION
Initial Approach: Application form required.

OTHER THINGS TO KNOW
Publications: Informational Brochure

GRANTS ANALYSIS
Number of Grants: 10

Highest Grant: $25,000

Typical Range: $2,500 to $7,500

Disclosure Period: 1991

RECENT GRANTS

25,000	Center for Mediation of Disputes, Cincinnati, OH
19,886	Cincinnati Museum Center Foundation, Cincinnati, OH
7,500	North Carolina State University, Raleigh, NC
7,000	ICMA, Washington, DC
7,000	University of Cincinnati Foundation, Cincinnati, OH
5,000	AIR, Cincinnati, OH
4,000	Izaak Walton League of America, Arlington, VA
3,000	Cincinnati Youth Collaborative, Cincinnati, OH
2,600	National Civic League, Denver, CO
2,500	American Judicature Society, Chicago, IL

Seattle Times Co.

Sales: $230.0 million
Employees: 2,500
Headquarters: Seattle, WA
SIC Major Group: Printing & Publishing

CONTACT
Frances Malone
Public Relations Manager
Seattle Times Co.
PO Box 70
Seattle, WA 98111
(206) 464-2346

CONTRIBUTIONS SUMMARY
Company does not disclose information regarding charitable contributions.

Operating Locations: WA (Seattle)

CORP. OFFICERS
Carolyn S. Kelly: *CURR EMPL* vp, cfo: Seattle Times Co

H. Mason Sizemore: *CURR EMPL* pres: Seattle Times Co

Seaver Charitable Trust, Richard C.

CONTACT
Myron E. Harpole
Trustee
Richard C. Seaver Charitable Trust
350 South Figueroa St., Ste. 270
Los Angeles, CA 90071
(213) 624-1311

FINANCIAL SUMMARY
Recent Giving: $189,000 (1991); $168,000 (1990); $164,000 (1989)

Assets: $3,372,773 (1991); $3,551,214 (1990); $3,548,232 (1989)

EIN: 95-3311102

CONTRIBUTIONS SUMMARY
Typical Recipients: • *Arts & Humanities:* arts centers, history/historic preservation, museums/galleries, music, opera • *Civic & Public Affairs:* municipalities, safety • *Education:* colleges & universities, elementary education, religious education • *Health:* hospitals • *Religion:* churches, religious organizations • *Social Services:* community service organizations, family services

Grant Types: general support

Geographic Distribution: focus on CA

GIVING OFFICERS
Myron E. Harpole: trust

APPLICATION INFORMATION
Initial Approach: Contributes only to preselected organizations.

Restrictions on Giving: Does not support individuals.

GRANTS ANALYSIS
Number of Grants: 33

Highest Grant: $53,676

Typical Range: $2,000 to $15,000

Disclosure Period: 1991

RECENT GRANTS

53,676	American Cancer Society, Topeka, KS
53,676	FMSU Endowment Association, Mays, KS
25,000	Los Angeles Music Center, Los Angeles, CA
20,000	Osborne County, Osborne, KS

15,000 City of Osborne, Osborne, KS

15,000 Harvard-Westlake School, Los Angeles, CA

12,611 USD 392, Osborne, KS

10,000 Los Angeles County Museum of Art, Los Angeles, CA

10,000 Metropolitan Opera, New York, NY

5,000 Curtis School, Los Angeles, CA

Seaver Institute

CONTACT
Richard Call
President
Seaver Institute
800 West 6th St., Ste. 1410
Los Angeles, CA 90017
(213) 688-7550

FINANCIAL SUMMARY
Recent Giving: $1,627,405 (fiscal 1993 est.); $1,765,862 (fiscal 1992); $1,640,887 (fiscal 1991)

Assets: $34,000,000 (fiscal 1993 est.); $33,892,297 (fiscal year ending June 30, 1992); $33,088,806 (fiscal 1991); $32,000,000 (fiscal 1990 approx.)

Gifts Received: $125,000 (fiscal 1993 est.); $117,700 (fiscal 1992); $47,256 (fiscal 1991); $240,000 (fiscal 1990)

Fiscal Note: The foundation receives annual funding from trusts established by Mr. Seaver.

EIN: 95-6054764

CONTRIBUTIONS SUMMARY
Donor(s): The Seaver Trust was created in 1955 by the late Frank R. Seaver. It is the recipient of annual funds under other trusts established by Mr. Seaver.

Typical Recipients: • *Arts & Humanities:* arts associations, arts funds, museums/galleries • *Education:* colleges & universities • *Health:* medical research, single-disease health associations • *Social Services:* child welfare, drugs & alcohol, recreation & athletics, youth organizations

Grant Types: project and research

Geographic Distribution: national

GIVING OFFICERS
Dr. David Alexander: dir

Richard Allen Archer: dir *B* Los Angeles CA 1927 *ED* Univ Southern CA BS 1949 *CURR EMPL* chmn: Jardine Emett & Chandler *CORP AFFIL* dir: Hydril Co, Imperial Corp Am, Jardine Ins Brokers *NONPR AFFIL* mem: Am Soc Chartered Property Casualty Underwriters, Chief Execs Org, Ins Brokers Soc Southern CA, Natl Assn Casualty Surety Execs, Natl Assn Ins Brokers, Natl Assn Surety Bond Producers, Wings Fdn, Young Pres Org

Dr. Richard W. Call: pres, ceo, dir *B* Los Angeles CA 1924 *ED* Stanford Univ 1945; Stanford Univ 1947 *NONPR AFFIL* fellow: Am Coll Physicians

Cameron Cooper: dir

Victoria Seaver Dean: dir

John F. Hall: vp, treas

Myron Harpole: asst secy, dir

Leroy Edward Hood: dir *B* Missoula MT 1938 *ED* CA Inst Tech BS 1960; Johns Hopkins Univ MD 1964; CA Inst Tech Phd 1968 *NONPR AFFIL* dir: Natl Science Fdn Science & Tech Ctr Molecular Biotechnology; mem: Am Academy Arts & Sciences, Am Assn Immunologists, Am Assn Advancement Science, Natl Academy Sciences

Raymond Jallow: dir *B* Baghdad Iraq 1933 *ED* Univ Baghdad BA 1953; Univ Southern CA MA 1956; Univ CA Los Angeles PhD 1966 *CURR EMPL* chmn: Jallow Intl Ltd *CORP AFFIL* chmn: Oxford Tech Corp; chmn, ceo: Oxford Imaging Co *NONPR AFFIL* dir: US Arab Chamber Commerce; mem: Am Mgmt Assn, Am Statistical Assn, Blue Key, Natl Assn Bus Economists; mem adv bd: CA Polytech St Univ; mem econ adv comm: Am Bankers Assn; mem monetary affairs comm US counc: Intl Chamber Commerce; mem new dimensions comm: CA Lutheran Coll

Blanche Ebert Seaver: chmn, dir

Christopher Seaver: secy, dir

Martha Seaver: dir

Richard C. Seaver: vchmn, dir *B* Los Angeles CA 1922 *ED* Pomona Coll BA 1946; Univ CA Berkeley JD 1949 *CURR EMPL* chmn: Hydril Co *CORP AFFIL* chmn: Los Angeles Branch Fed Reserve Bank San Francisco; dir: De Anza Land & Leisure Corp; vchmn, dir: Seaver Inst *NONPR AFFIL* dir: Episcopal Church Fdn, Hosp of Good Samaritan; mem: Am Bar Assn, CA Bar Assn, Los Angeles County Bar Assn; trust: Doheny Eye Inst, Episcopal Diocesan Investment Trust, Harvard Westlake Sch, Los Angeles County Mus Natural History, Pomona Coll; vp, dir: Los Angeles Music Ctr Opera Assn

APPLICATION INFORMATION
Initial Approach:
Proposals should be addressed to the president of the trust. Applicants seeking support from the trust should submit a letter of inquiry and one copy of a brief proposal. This should include a description of the project, time period needed for completion and funding, amount needed, budget, and any other pertinent information. There are no deadlines for submitting proposals.

Preliminary reviews are conducted by the president, who then sends favorable proposals to the benefactions committee for final review.

Restrictions on Giving: No grants are made to individuals.

GRANTS ANALYSIS
Total Grants: $1,765,862

Number of Grants: 23*

Highest Grant: $400,000

Typical Range: $1,000 to $100,000

Disclosure Period: fiscal year ending June 30, 1992

Note: The figures for number of grants and average grant excludes 13 grants from the "Director Designated Grants Fund" and the "President's Discretionary Fund" totaling $195,877 in fiscal 1992. Recent grants are derived from a fiscal 1992 grants list.

RECENT GRANTS
400,000 California Institute of Technology, Pasadena, CA

150,000 Doheny Eye Institute, Los Angeles, CA

150,000 Massachusetts Institute of Technology, Cambridge, MA

144,000 Institute for Advanced Study, Princeton, NJ

133,600 Juilliard School, New York, NY

100,000 Beyond Shelter, Los Angeles, CA

100,000 National Geographic, Washington, DC

100,000 Princeton University, Princeton, NJ

77,295 Johns Hopkins University/CTY, Baltimore, MD — Talent Search

65,090 Johns Hopkins University/CTY, Baltimore, MD — public policy

Seaway Food Town
Sales: $571.2 million
Employees: 4,762
Headquarters: Maumee, OH
SIC Major Group: Food Stores and Miscellaneous Retail

CONTACT
Richard Iott
President
Seaway Food Town
1020 Ford St.
Maumee, OH 43537
(419) 893-9401

FINANCIAL SUMMARY
Fiscal Note: Company makes direct contributions. Annual Giving Range: $500,000 to $1 million

CONTRIBUTIONS SUMMARY
Typical Recipients: • *Arts & Humanities:* arts appreciation, arts associations, arts centers, arts festivals, community arts, ethnic arts, libraries, museums/galleries, opera, performing arts, public broadcasting, theater, visual arts • *Civic & Public Affairs:* consumer affairs, philanthropic organizations, zoos/botanical gardens • *Education:* arts education, colleges & universities, elementary education, literacy • *Health:* geriatric health, health care cost containment, health organizations, hospitals, nursing services, nutrition & health maintenance, pediatric health • *Religion:* churches, synagogues • *Science:* science exhibits & fairs • *Social Services:* aged, child welfare, community centers, community service organizations, disabled, domestic violence, drugs & alcohol, food/clothing distribution, recreation & athletics, shelters/homelessness, youth organizations

Grant Types: award, endowment, general support, and multiyear/continuing support
Nonmonetary Support Types: cause-related marketing & promotion, donated equipment, donated products, in-kind services, and workplace solicitation
Geographic Distribution: only in headquarters area
Operating Locations: OH (Maumee)

CORP. OFFICERS
Richard B. Iott: *CURR EMPL*
pres: Seaway Food Town
Wallace D. Iott: *CURR EMPL*
chmn, ceo: Seaway Food Town

GIVING OFFICERS
Richard B. Iott: *CURR EMPL*
pres: Seaway Food Town (see above)

APPLICATION INFORMATION
Initial Approach: *Initial Contact:* brief letter of inquiry and full proposal *Include Information On:* a description of organization, amount requested, purpose of funds sought, and proof of tax-exempt status *When to Submit:* one month in advance of date funds are needed
Restrictions on Giving: Does not support individuals, political or lobbying groups, or organizations outside operating areas.

GRANTS ANALYSIS
Typical Range: $2,500 to $5,000

RECENT GRANTS
American Heart Association, Toledo, OH
Citifest, Toledo, OH
Easter Seals, Perrysburg, OH
Epilepsy Foundation, Toledo, OH
March of Dimes, Toledo, OH
National Family Service, Toledo, OH
Toledo Museum of Art, Toledo, OH
Toledo Opera, Toledo, OH
Toledo Repertoire Theatre, Toledo, OH
Toys for Tots, Perrysburg, OH

Seay Charitable Trust, Sarah M. and Charles E.

CONTACT
Charles E. Seay
Trustee
Sarah M. and Charles E. Seay Charitable Trust
300 Crescent Court, Ste. 1370
Dallas, TX 75201
(214) 855-7955

FINANCIAL SUMMARY
Recent Giving: $1,092,961 (fiscal 1991); $456,451 (fiscal 1990); $397,924 (fiscal 1989)
Assets: $2,292,042 (fiscal year ending May 31, 1991); $1,837,673 (fiscal 1990); $1,887,378 (fiscal 1989)
Gifts Received: $107,565 (fiscal 1991); $24,199 (fiscal 1990)
Fiscal Note: In 1991, contributions were received from Charles E. Seay ($54,240) and Sarah M. Seay ($53,325).
EIN: 75-1894505

CONTRIBUTIONS SUMMARY
Donor(s): Charles E. Seay, Sarah M. Seay
Typical Recipients: • *Arts & Humanities:* community arts, museums/galleries, music • *Education:* colleges & universities, private education (precollege) • *Health:* hospitals, medical research, pediatric health • *Religion:* churches • *Social Services:* child welfare, united funds, youth organizations
Grant Types: general support
Geographic Distribution: focus on TX

GIVING OFFICERS
Charles E. Seay: trust
Charles E. Seay, Jr.: trust
Sarah M. Seay: trust
Stephen M. Seay: trust

APPLICATION INFORMATION
Initial Approach: Contributes only to preselected organizations. Applications not accepted.
Restrictions on Giving: Does not support individuals.

GRANTS ANALYSIS
Number of Grants: 54
Highest Grant: $500,000
Typical Range: $500 to $5,000
Disclosure Period: fiscal year ending May 31, 1991

RECENT GRANTS
500,000 Southwestern Medical School of University of Texas at Dallas, Dallas, TX — establish two chairs in child psychiatry
300,590 Children's Medical Foundation of Texas, Dallas, TX — building fund
66,666 University of Texas at Austin, Austin, TX
35,445 Children's Presbyterian Health-Care Center, Plano, TX — ropes course, flagpoles, lighting
30,000 Dallas Museum of Art, Dallas, TX
25,000 Texas Scottish Rite Hospital, Dallas, TX
25,000 University of Texas School of Law, Austin, TX
20,700 University of Texas at Austin, Austin, TX
17,125 Highland Park Presbyterian Church Day School, Dallas, TX
10,500 Highland Park Presbyterian Church, Dallas, TX

Seay Memorial Trust, George and Effie

CONTACT
Elizabeth D. Seaman
Consultant
George and Effie Seay Memorial Trust
c/o Sovran Bank, N.A., Trust Dept.
PO Box 26903
Richmond, VA 23261
(804) 788-2963

FINANCIAL SUMMARY
Recent Giving: $128,600 (fiscal 1991); $115,065 (fiscal 1990); $111,300 (fiscal 1989)
Assets: $2,528,417 (fiscal year ending June 30, 1991); $2,384,596 (fiscal 1990); $2,197,714 (fiscal 1989)
EIN: 54-6030604

CONTRIBUTIONS SUMMARY
Donor(s): the late George J. Seay, the late Effie L. Seay
Typical Recipients: • *Arts & Humanities:* museums/galleries • *Civic & Public Affairs:* environmental affairs, municipalities • *Health:* emergency/ambulance services, health organizations, hospices, hospitals • *Religion:* religious organizations • *Social Services:* child welfare, community service organizations, family planning, united funds, youth organizations
Grant Types: capital, general support, operating expenses, and project
Geographic Distribution: limited to VA

APPLICATION INFORMATION
Initial Approach: Send brief letter describing program. Deadlines are May 1 and November 1.
Restrictions on Giving: Does not support individuals.

OTHER THINGS TO KNOW
Publications: Informational Brochure (including Application Guidelines).

GRANTS ANALYSIS
Number of Grants: 18
Highest Grant: $10,000
Typical Range: $2,000 to $5,000
Disclosure Period: fiscal year ending June 30, 1991

RECENT GRANTS
10,000 Family Resource Center, Wytheville, VA
10,000 YWCA, Richmond, VA
9,800 Literacy Council of Metro Richmond, Richmond, VA
9,600 Greater Richmond Informed Parents, Richmond, VA
8,200 Goochland Fellowship and Family Service, Goochland, VA
7,500 Travelers Aid Society, Richmond, VA
7,000 Richmond Chaplaincy Service, Richmond, VA
6,650 Friends Association for Children, Richmond, VA
6,500 Museum of the Confederacy, Richmond, VA
5,000 Family and Children's Service, Richmond, VA

Sebastian Foundation

CONTACT
James R. Sebastian
Trustee
Sebastian Fdn.
82 Ionia, N.W., Ste. 360
Grand Rapids, MI 49503
(616) 454-7661

FINANCIAL SUMMARY
Recent Giving: $337,130 (fiscal 1992); $309,850 (fiscal 1991); $297,500 (fiscal 1989)
Assets: $6,959,920 (fiscal year ending August 31, 1992); $6,833,767 (fiscal 1990); $6,151,961 (fiscal 1989)
EIN: 38-2340219

CONTRIBUTIONS SUMMARY
Donor(s): Audrey M. Sebastian, James R. Sebastian
Typical Recipients: • *Arts & Humanities:* community arts, museums/galleries • *Civic & Public Affairs:* international affairs • *Education:* colleges & universities, minority education, private education (precollege) • *Religion:* religious organizations • *Social Services:* community service organizations, homes, religious welfare, united funds, youth organizations
Grant Types: general support
Geographic Distribution: focus on the Grand Rapids and Kent County areas, MI

GIVING OFFICERS
Audrey M. Sebastian: trust
David S. Sebastian: trust
James R. Sebastian: trust
John O. Sebastian: trust

APPLICATION INFORMATION
Initial Approach: Send cover letter and full proposal. There are no deadlines.
Restrictions on Giving: Does not support individuals.

GRANTS ANALYSIS
Number of Grants: 48
Highest Grant: $50,000
Typical Range: $250 to $5,000
Disclosure Period: fiscal year ending August 31, 1992

RECENT GRANTS
50,000 United Way, Grand Rapids, MI
25,000 American Red Cross, Grand Rapids, MI
25,000 Grand Rapids Public Museum, Grand Rapids, MI
25,000 Porter Hills Presbyterian Village, Grand Rapids, MI
20,000 Albion College, Albion, MI
15,000 YWCA, Grand Rapids, MI
12,680 Gerontology Network Services, Grand Rapids, MI
11,000 YMCA, Grand Rapids, MI
10,000 Guiding Light Mission, Grand Rapids, MI
10,000 Inner City Christian Federation, Grand Rapids, MI

SECO

Revenue: $540.51 million
Employees: 4,960
Headquarters: Pittsburgh, PA
SIC Major Group: Fabricated Metal Products and Special Trade Contractors

CONTACT
Dean Zimmer
Vice President, Personnel
SECO
222 Berkeley St.
Boston, MA 02116
(617) 357-6500

CONTRIBUTIONS SUMMARY
Supports local arts, education, health, and civic groups.

Typical Recipients: • *Arts & Humanities:* general • *Civic & Public Affairs:* general • *Education:* general • *Health:* general

Geographic Distribution: primarily in operating locations in PA, MO, MA, and TX

Operating Locations: CA (Monrovia), MO (St. Louis), NC (Clinton), OK (Oklahoma City), PA (Ambridge, Green Tree, Pittsburgh, Zelienople)

Note: Five divisions of H.H. Robertson Co. can be found in operating cities.

CORP. OFFICERS
Benny J. Barbour: *CURR EMPL* pres, coo: HH Robertson Co
Jack Hatcher: *CURR EMPL* chmn, ceo, dir: HH Robertson Co

Second Foundation

CONTACT
Phillip A. Ranney
Director
Second Fdn.
1525 National City Bank Bldg.
Cleveland, OH 44114
(216) 696-4200

FINANCIAL SUMMARY
Recent Giving: $1,241,469 (1991); $1,959,770 (1989)
Assets: $29,005,678 (1991); $25,341,573 (1989)
EIN: 34-1436198

CONTRIBUTIONS SUMMARY
Donor(s): The foundation was established in 1984 by the 1525 Foundation.
Typical Recipients: • *Arts & Humanities:* libraries, museums/galleries • *Civic & Public Affairs:* municipalities, philanthropic organizations • *Education:* colleges & universities • *Health:* health funds, hospitals • *Social Services:* child welfare, domestic violence, emergency relief, youth organizations
Grant Types: endowment, general support, matching, multiyear/continuing support, operating expenses, and seed money
Geographic Distribution: focus on Cleveland, OH

GIVING OFFICERS
Phillip A. Ranney: secy, treas, dir
Hubert H. Schneider: pres, dir
Thelma G. Smith: vp, dir

APPLICATION INFORMATION
Initial Approach:
There are no formal grant application forms. Written applications should be sent to the foundation.
Written proposals should include a brief description of the organization, the purpose of the grant request, any applicable financial data, the names of other contributors to the project, and a copy of the organizations IRS tax-exempt letter.
The foundation has no deadlines for proposals.
The foundation's trustees meet frequently and will usually notify the organization one month after receipt of the proposal.
Restrictions on Giving: The foundation does not make loans and does not make grants to individuals.

GRANTS ANALYSIS
Total Grants: $1,241,469
Number of Grants: 15
Highest Grant: $447,343
Typical Range: $6,000 to $50,000
Disclosure Period: 1991
Note: Average grant figure does not include a grant for $447,343 and a grant for $254,098. Recent grants are derived from a 1991 grants list.

RECENT GRANTS
447,343 Case Western Reserve University, Cleveland, OH
254,098 Cleveland Museum of Natural History, Cleveland, OH
250,000 University of Findley, Findley, OH
95,028 Berea College, Berea, KY
50,000 American Red Cross, Cleveland, OH
50,000 University Circle, Cleveland, OH
25,000 Cleveland Recycling Center, Cleveland, OH
20,000 Achievement Center for Children, Cleveland, OH
20,000 Bellflower Center for Prevention of Child Abuse, Cleveland, OH
10,000 Metro Health Foundation, Cleveland, OH

Security Benefit Life Insurance Co. / Security Benefit Life Insurance Co. Charitable Trust

Employees: 600
Headquarters: Topeka, KS
SIC Major Group: Holding & Other Investment Offices, Insurance Carriers, Nondepository Institutions, and Security & Commodity Brokers

CONTACT
Howard R. Fricke
Trustee
Security Benefit Life Insurance
   Co. Charitable Trust
700 Harrison St.
Topeka, KS 66636
(913) 295-3000

FINANCIAL SUMMARY
Recent Giving: $320,256
(1991); $128,165 (1990);
$183,007 (1989)
Assets: $761,355 (1991);
$321,637 (1990); $876,474
(1989)
Gifts Received: $986,512
(1991)
Fiscal Note: Contributes
through foundation only. In
1991, contributions were received from Security Benefit
Life Insurance Company.
EIN: 48-6211612

**CONTRIBUTIONS
SUMMARY**
Typical Recipients: • *Arts &
Humanities:* dance, music
• *Education:* colleges & universities, economic education, education funds • *Health:* health
organizations, pediatric health,
single-disease health associations • *Social Services:* family
services, united funds, youth organizations
Grant Types: general support
and matching
Nonmonetary Support Types:
donated equipment and in-kind
services
Geographic Distribution: primarily Kansas, specifically
Topeka
Operating Locations: KS
(Topeka)

CORP. OFFICERS
J.H. Abrahams: *B* Topeka KS
1913 *ED* Univ Chicago 1935
CURR EMPL chmn, dir: Secu-
rity Benefit Life Ins Co *CORP
AFFIL* dir: Capitol Fed Sav-
ings & Loan Assn, Didde
Graphic Sys Corp
Howard Fricke: *CURR EMPL*
pres, ceo, dir: Security Benefit
Life Ins Co

GIVING OFFICERS
**Security Benefit Trust Com-
pany:** trust
Howard R. Fricke: trust

**APPLICATION
INFORMATION**
Initial Approach: *Initial Contact:* brief letter *When to Submit:* any time

GRANTS ANALYSIS
Total Grants: $320,256
Number of Grants: 109
Highest Grant: $34,000
Typical Range: $300 to $4,500
Disclosure Period: 1991
Note: Recent grants are de-
rived from a 1991 grants list.

RECENT GRANTS
34,000 United Way,
           Topeka, KS
26,000 University of Kan-
           sas, Lawrence, KS
25,000 Kansas State Uni-
           versity, Manhattan,
           KS
25,000 Menninger Founda-
           tion, Topeka, KS
11,000 Friends of the
           Topeka Zoo,
           Topeka, KS
10,000 Arts Center of
           Topeka, Topeka, KS
7,250   Washburn Univer-
           sity, Topeka, KS
6,000   Model Block Pro-
           gram, Topeka, KS
5,750   Topeka Rescue
           Mission, Topeka,
           KS
5,000   Capper Founda-
           tion, Topeka, KS

Security Capital Corp.
Sales: $2.1 million
Employees: 27
Headquarters: Houston, TX
SIC Major Group: Holding &
   Other Investment Offices,
   Insurance Agents, Brokers &
   Service, and Real Estate

CONTACT
Anita Flynn
Security Capital Corp.
111 North Loop West, Ste. 600
Houston, TX 77008
(713) 880-5497

**CONTRIBUTIONS
SUMMARY**
Operating Locations: TX
(Houston)

CORP. OFFICERS
Brian Fitzgerald: *CURR
EMPL* chmn, dir: Security
Capital Corp
A. G. Gebauer: *CURR EMPL*
pres, dir: Security Capital Corp

Security Life Insurance Co. of America
Sales: $93.0 million
Employees: 70
Parent Company: Security
   American Financial Enterprises
Headquarters: Minneapolis, MN
SIC Major Group: Insurance
   Carriers

CONTACT
Orem Robbins
Chairman
Security Life Insurance Co. of
   America
6681 Country Club Dr.
Minneapolis, MN 55427-4698
(612) 544-2121

**CONTRIBUTIONS
SUMMARY**
Operating Locations: MN
(Minneapolis)

CORP. OFFICERS
Harlan Mills: *CURR EMPL*
pres: Security Life Ins Co Am

RECENT GRANTS
Carleton College, Northfield, MN

Security Life of Denver
Assets: $1.71 billion
Employees: 445
Headquarters: Denver, CO
SIC Major Group: Insurance
   Carriers

CONTACT
Denise Wright
Administrative Assistant,
   Marketing Comm
Security Life of Denver
Security Life Center, 1290
   Broadway
Denver, CO 80203
(303) 860-1290

FINANCIAL SUMMARY
Recent Giving: $75,000
(1992); $100,000 (1991);
$100,000 (1990)

**CONTRIBUTIONS
SUMMARY**
Program supports the range of
typical contributions categories
— arts and humanities, civic
and public affairs, education,
health, and social services.
Typical Recipients: • *Arts &
Humanities:* arts appreciation,
arts associations, arts centers,
arts festivals, community arts,
dance, ethnic arts, general, his-
tory/historic preservation, li-

braries, literary arts, muse-
ums/galleries, music, opera,
performing arts, public broadcasting, theater, visual arts
• *Civic & Public Affairs:* consumer affairs, economic development, environmental affairs,
ethnic/minority organizations,
general, philanthropic organizations, public policy, urban &
community affairs, women's affairs, zoos/botanical gardens
• *Education:* arts education,
business education, colleges &
universities, economic education, education funds, elementary education, general, health
& physical education, literacy,
minority education, private education (precollege), public education (precollege) • *Health:*
general, health care cost containment, health organizations,
medical research, public health
• *Science:* scientific institutes
• *Social Services:* child welfare, community service organizations, domestic violence,
drugs & alcohol, emergency relief, family services, food/cloth-
ing distribution, general, recreation & athletics,
shelters/homelessness, united
funds, volunteer services,
youth organizations
Grant Types: award, capital,
employee matching gifts, general support, multiyear/continu-
ing support, and project
Nonmonetary Support Types:
donated equipment, in-kind
services, and workplace solicitation
Geographic Distribution: in
Colorado, with emphasis on
Denver, and in states where
there is an agent
Operating Locations: CO,
DC, GA, IN, NH

CORP. OFFICERS
Stan Benfell: *CURR EMPL*
pres: Security Life Denver
R. G. Hillard: *CURR EMPL*
ceo: Security Life Denver Ins
Co

GIVING OFFICERS
Barbara Gill: *CURR EMPL*
admin asst: Security Life Denver Ins Co
Lilly Kovacevic: *CURR EMPL*
corp commun specialist: Security Life Denver

**APPLICATION
INFORMATION**
Initial Approach: Send brief
letter of inquiry including a description of the organization,
amount requested, purpose of

funds sought, and time frame within which contribution is needed.

Restrictions on Giving: Does not support political or lobbying groups or religious organizations for sectarian purposes.

GRANTS ANALYSIS
Typical Range: $100 to $1,000

RECENT GRANTS
Channel Six, CO — Public Television
Colorado AIDS Project, CO
Denver Arts Museum, Denver, CO
Denver Association of Life Underwriters, Denver, CO
Denver Botanic Gardens, Denver, CO
Denver National Historical Society, Denver, CO
Denver Public Library, Denver, CO
Multiple Sclerosis, CO
United Way, CO
Volunteers for Outdoor Colorado, CO

Security State Bank / Security State Bank Charitable Trust
Headquarters: Great Bend, KS
SIC Major Group: Depository Institutions

CONTACT
Stephen J. Mermis
President
Security State Bank Charitable Trust
P.O. Box 909
Great Bend, KS 67530
(816) 860-7711

FINANCIAL SUMMARY
Recent Giving: $9,450 (1991); $9,911 (1990); $11,937 (1989)
Assets: $42,592 (1991); $49,418 (1990); $5,431 (1989)
EIN: 48-6109832

CONTRIBUTIONS SUMMARY
Typical Recipients: • *Arts & Humanities:* museums/galleries, music, theater • *Civic & Public Affairs:* economic development, environmental affairs, municipalities, safety • *Education:* colleges & universities, community & junior colleges • *Health:* hospitals • *Social Services:* youth organizations
Grant Types: endowment and general support

Geographic Distribution: focus on KS
Operating Locations: KS (Great Bend)

CORP. OFFICERS
Michael Moye: *CURR EMPL* pres: Security St Bank

GIVING OFFICERS
United Missouri Bank of Kansas City: trust

APPLICATION INFORMATION
Initial Approach: Send brief letter describing program. There are no deadlines.

GRANTS ANALYSIS
Number of Grants: 24
Highest Grant: $2,000
Typical Range: $100 to $500
Disclosure Period: 1991

RECENT GRANTS
2,000 Barton County Community College, Great Bend, KS
2,000 Chaflin Volunteer Fire Department, Chaflin, KS
500 Catholic Social Services, Great Bend, KS
500 Great Bend Community Theatre Building Fund, Great Bend, KS
500 Stafford County 4-H Council, St. John, KS
500 Wichita State University, Wichita, KS
400 National Youth Leadership Council, Hays, KS
350 Golden Belt Community Concert Association, Great Bend, KS
250 Kansas State University, Manhattan, KS
250 USD 428 Foundation, Great Bend, KS

Sedco Inc.
Sales: $5.5 million
Employees: 14
Headquarters: Channel View, TX
SIC Major Group: Wholesale Trade—Durable Goods

CONTACT
Paul Sonnemann
Personnel, Manager
Sedco Inc.
P. O. Box 1569
Channelview, TX 77530
(713) 457-7400

CONTRIBUTIONS SUMMARY
Operating Locations: TX (Channel View)

Sedgwick James Inc.
Employees: 5,949
Revenue: $489.15 million
Headquarters: New York, NY
SIC Major Group: Insurance Agents, Brokers & Service

CONTACT
Kelly Perry
Matching Gifts Coordinator
Sedgwick James Inc.
5350 Poplar Ave.
Memphis, TN 38119
(901) 761-1550
Note: Barbara Durson may also be used as an additional contact name.

FINANCIAL SUMMARY
Fiscal Note: Annual Giving Range: less than $100,000

CONTRIBUTIONS SUMMARY
Support goes to local education, human service, arts, and civic organizations. Company also sponsors Community Service Awards for volunteer activity. Company operates a matching gift program for employees and their spouses.
Typical Recipients: • *Arts & Humanities:* arts appreciation, arts associations, arts centers, arts festivals, arts funds, arts institutes, community arts, dance, ethnic arts, history/historic preservation, libraries, literary arts, museums/galleries, music, opera, performing arts, public broadcasting, theater, visual arts • *Civic & Public Affairs:* environmental affairs, safety, zoos/botanical gardens • *Education:* agricultural education, arts education, business education, career/vocational education, colleges & universities, community & junior colleges, continuing education, economic education, education administration, education associations, education funds, elementary education, engineering education, faculty development, health & physical educa-

tion, international exchange, international studies, journalism education, legal education, liberal arts education, literacy, medical education, minority education, preschool education, private education (precollege), public education (precollege), science/technology education, social sciences education, special education, student aid • *Science:* observatories & planetariums, scientific organizations • *Social Services:* general
Grant Types: matching
Geographic Distribution: primarily in TN
Operating Locations: TN (Memphis)

CORP. OFFICERS
Donald K. Morford: *CURR EMPL* pres: Sedgwick James

GIVING OFFICERS
Kelly Perry: *CURR EMPL* matching gifts coordinator: Sedgewick James

APPLICATION INFORMATION
Initial Approach: Send brief letter of inquiry, including a description of the organization, amount requested, purpose of funds sought, recently audited financial statements, and proof of tax-exempt status. Deadline is December 15, and all requests after the deadline will be considered the following year.
Restrictions on Giving: Does not support individuals, religious organizations for sectarian purposes (however programs sponsored by a religious organization may be eligible), fraternal organizations, veteran's organizations, unions, or political or lobbying groups.

See Foundation, Charles

CONTACT
Charles O. See
President
Charles See Fdn.
11100 N.E. 8th St., Ste. 610
Belleville, WA 98004
(206) 635-7250

FINANCIAL SUMMARY
Recent Giving: $108,800 (1991); $100,200 (1990); $78,700 (1989)

Assets: $2,183,265 (1991); $1,889,683 (1990); $1,935,852 (1989)
EIN: 95-6038358

CONTRIBUTIONS SUMMARY

Donor(s): Charles B. See
Typical Recipients: • *Arts & Humanities:* community arts, music • *Civic & Public Affairs:* ethnic/minority organizations, international affairs, zoos/botanical gardens • *Education:* colleges & universities • *Health:* hospitals, medical research, mental health, pediatric health, single-disease health associations • *Social Services:* child welfare, united funds
Grant Types: general support
Geographic Distribution: focus on CA

GIVING OFFICERS

Rhonda Logan: asst secy
Anne R. See: vp, secy, dir
Charles B. See: pres, dir
Harry A. See: dir
Richard W. See: dir

APPLICATION INFORMATION

Initial Approach: Send brief letter describing program. Deadline is November 14.
Restrictions on Giving: Does not support individuals.

GRANTS ANALYSIS

Number of Grants: 38
Highest Grant: $20,000
Typical Range: $1,000 to $2,000
Disclosure Period: 1991

RECENT GRANTS

20,000 Virginia Mason Medical Foundation, Tacoma, WA
15,000 Southern California Psychoanalytic Facility, Beverly Hills, CA
10,000 Carnegie Council on Ethics, New York, NY
5,000 Children's Garden, San Rafael, CA
4,500 Friends of Tel Aviv University, Los Angeles, CA
3,000 Inglewood Residence Services, Bothell, WA
2,500 Child Help USA, Woodland Hills, CA
2,000 Amnesty International, Washington, DC
2,000 Fred Hutchinson Cancer Research, Bellevue, WA

2,000 United Way, Seattle, WA

Seebee Trust, Frances

CONTACT

Minh Le
Trust Administrator
Frances Seebee Trust
c/o Wells Fargo Bank, N.A.
525 Market St., 17th Fl.
San Francisco, CA 94163

FINANCIAL SUMMARY

Recent Giving: $255,582 (fiscal 1992); $182,650 (fiscal 1991); $259,867 (fiscal 1990)
Assets: $2,850,446 (fiscal year ending January 31, 1992); $2,950,717 (fiscal 1991); $2,387,435 (fiscal 1990)
EIN: 95-6795278

CONTRIBUTIONS SUMMARY

Typical Recipients: • *Civic & Public Affairs:* environmental affairs, zoos/botanical gardens • *Education:* colleges & universities • *Health:* medical research, single-disease health associations • *Social Services:* animal protection
Grant Types: research
Geographic Distribution: focus on CA

GIVING OFFICERS

Wells Fargo Bank, N.A.: trust

APPLICATION INFORMATION

Initial Approach: Contributes only to preselected organizations.
Restrictions on Giving: Does not support individuals.

GRANTS ANALYSIS

Number of Grants: 20
Highest Grant: $32,791
Typical Range: $5,000 to $10,000
Disclosure Period: fiscal year ending January 31, 1992

RECENT GRANTS

32,791 Arthritis Foundation, Los Angeles, CA
32,791 University of Southern California Cancer Research Center, Los Angeles, CA
25,000 Digit Fund, San Francisco, CA
20,000 Center for Marine Conservation, Washington, DC

20,000 Fund for Animals, San Francisco, CA
15,000 Hemopet, San Francisco, CA
15,000 Pet Protection Society, San Francisco, CA
12,500 Leakey Foundation, San Francisco, CA
10,000 Animal Alliance, San Francisco, CA
10,000 Morris Animal Foundation, San Francisco, CA

Seeley Foundation

CONTACT

Hugo J. Melvoin
Trustee
Seeley Fdn.
115 South LaSalle St., Rm. 2500
Chicago, IL 60603

FINANCIAL SUMMARY

Recent Giving: $201,000 (1990); $205,000 (1989); $201,000 (1988)
Assets: $2,522,900 (1990); $2,560,421 (1989); $2,417,776 (1988)
EIN: 36-6049991

CONTRIBUTIONS SUMMARY

Donor(s): the late Halsted H. Seeley, Laurel H. Seeley
Typical Recipients: • *Arts & Humanities:* arts associations • *Civic & Public Affairs:* environmental affairs • *Health:* mental health
Grant Types: endowment and research

GIVING OFFICERS

Judith S. Fales: trust
Hugo J. Melvoin: trust
Ellen F. Roberts: trust
Dana M. Seeley: trust
Miles G. Seeley: trust
Miles P. Seeley: trust

APPLICATION INFORMATION

Initial Approach: Send brief letter of inquiry describing program. There are no deadlines.

GRANTS ANALYSIS

Number of Grants: 7
Highest Grant: $150,000
Typical Range: $2,000 to $12,000
Disclosure Period: 1990

RECENT GRANTS

150,000 Menninger Foundation, Topeka, KS — Seeley Fellows Program

30,000 Menninger Foundation, Topeka, KS — Seeley Professorship in Psychiatry
12,000 Nature Conservatory, New Haven, CT
5,000 Menninger Foundation, Topeka, KS — Voluntary Controls Department
5,000 Menninger Foundation, Topeka, KS — Voluntary Controls Department
2,000 Nature Conservatory, New Haven, CT
1,000 Society for the Arts, New Haven, CT

Seevak Family Foundation

CONTACT

Seevak Family Fdn.
c/o Goldman, Sachs and Co., Tax Dept.
85 Broad St., 30th Fl.
New York, NY 10004
(212) 902-6897

FINANCIAL SUMMARY

Recent Giving: $201,892 (fiscal 1992); $138,565 (fiscal 1991); $175,014 (fiscal 1990)
Assets: $2,354,623 (fiscal year ending March 31, 1992); $2,287,553 (fiscal 1991); $2,416,417 (fiscal 1990)
Gifts Received: $10,000 (fiscal 1990); $135,250 (fiscal 1989)
EIN: 13-3102898

CONTRIBUTIONS SUMMARY

Donor(s): Sheldon Seevak, Elinor A. Seevak
Typical Recipients: • *Arts & Humanities:* museums/galleries • *Civic & Public Affairs:* ethnic/minority organizations, women's affairs • *Education:* colleges & universities, legal education • *Health:* hospitals, medical research, single-disease health associations • *Religion:* religious organizations • *Social Services:* aged, community service organizations, family planning
Grant Types: general support

GIVING OFFICERS

Elinor A. Seevak: trust
Sheldon Seevak: trust *B* Boston MA 1929 *ED* Univ IL AB 1950; Harvard Univ JD 1953; NY Univ LLM 1961 *CURR*

EMPL ptnr: Goldman Sachs & Co *NONPR AFFIL* dir: Univ Chicago Emotionally Disturbed; dir, chmn devel comm: Alzheimers Disease Related Disorders Assn; mem: Intl Counc Shopping Ctrs, Natl Assn Corp Real Estate, Natl Assn Industrial Parks, NY Real Estate Bd, Urban Land Inst; trust: Newark Beth Israel Med Ctr

APPLICATION INFORMATION
Initial Approach: Contributes only to preselected organizations.
Restrictions on Giving: Does not support individuals.

GRANTS ANALYSIS
Number of Grants: 71
Highest Grant: $67,500
Typical Range: $100 to $1,000
Disclosure Period: fiscal year ending March 31, 1992

RECENT GRANTS
67,500 United Jewish Appeal Federation of Jewish Philanthropies, East Orange, NJ
25,000 New York University School of Social Work Building Fund, New York, NY
10,000 Alzheimer's Disease and Related Disorders Association, New York, NY
10,000 Harvard Law School Fund, Cambridge, MA
10,000 New York Women's Foundation, New York, NY
10,000 United Jewish Appeal Federation of Jewish Philanthropies, Newark, NJ
10,000 United Jewish Appeal Federation of Jewish Philanthropies, East Orange, NJ
10,000 University of Pennsylvania Trustees, Philadelphia, PA
5,000 Boston Latin School, Boston, MA
5,000 Family Services and Child Guidance Center, Orange, NJ

Sefton Foundation, J. W.

CONTACT
Thomas W. Sefton
President
J. W. Sefton Fdn.
PO Box 1871
San Diego, CA 92112

FINANCIAL SUMMARY
Recent Giving: $172,576 (1990); $165,794 (1989)
Assets: $3,945,288 (1990); $4,010,095 (1989)
EIN: 95-1513384

CONTRIBUTIONS SUMMARY
Donor(s): the late J.W. Sefton, Jr.
Typical Recipients: • *Arts & Humanities:* history/historic preservation, museums/galleries • *Civic & Public Affairs:* law & justice, municipalities, zoos/botanical gardens • *Education:* private education (precollege) • *Health:* hospitals • *Social Services:* animal protection
Grant Types: general support
Geographic Distribution: focus on San Diego, CA

GIVING OFFICERS
Gordon T. Frost: secy, trust
Gordon E. McNary: treas, trust
Donna K. Sefton: vp, trust
Thomas W. Sefton: pres, trust *B* New York NY 1917 *CURR EMPL* pres: San Diego Fin Corp *CORP AFFIL* ceo, dir: San Diego Trust & Savings Bank; pres: San Diego Fin Corp

APPLICATION INFORMATION
Initial Approach: Contributes only to preselected organizations.

GRANTS ANALYSIS
Number of Grants: 9
Highest Grant: $90,000
Typical Range: $1,000 to $6,000
Disclosure Period: 1990

RECENT GRANTS
90,000 San Diego Zoological Society, San Diego, CA — aviaries
25,000 San Diego Maritime Museum, San Diego, CA
22,650 Presidio Little League, San Diego, CA — baseball field
20,000 San Diego Police Department, San Diego, CA — firearms training
10,000 American Ornithologist's Union, San Diego, CA
3,000 Richard J. Donovan Correctional Facility, San Diego, CA — refurbishing
911 San Diego Police Department, San Diego, CA — honor awards
515 San Diego Sheriff Department, San Diego, CA — awards
500 Army and Navy Academy (San Diego), San Diego, CA — computer memory boards

Sega of America / Sega Youth Education & Health Foundation

Headquarters: Redwood City, CA
SIC Major Group: Miscellaneous Repair Services

CONTACT
Sega Youth Education & Health Foundation
130 Shoreline Dr.
Redwood City, CA 94065
(415) 508-2800
Note: The company does not list a specific contact person.

FINANCIAL SUMMARY
Recent Giving: $2,500,000 (1993 est.); $2,500,000 (1992 approx.)
Assets: $3,000,000 (1992 approx.)
Fiscal Note: Company gives primarily through the foundation.

CONTRIBUTIONS SUMMARY
Typical Recipients: • *Education:* education associations, minority education, public education (precollege), science/technology education • *Health:* pediatric health
Grant Types: general support, operating expenses, and project
Geographic Distribution: no geographic restrictions

CORP. OFFICERS
Tom Kalinske: *CURR EMPL* pres: Sega Am

GIVING OFFICERS
Trizia L. Carpenter:
Tom Kalinske: *CURR EMPL* pres: Sega Am (see above)
Dave Rosen: *CURR EMPL* cochmn: Sega Enterprises

APPLICATION INFORMATION
Initial Approach: *Initial Contact:* written inquiry for grant guidelines *Include Information On:* guidelines will provide all required information *When to Submit:* any time *Note:* Applicants should first contact the foundation in writing to request guidelines and a general information questionnaire. Applications should be sent to the trust administrator of Sega Youth Education & Health Foundation. The company requests that applicants do not contact corporate officers. Information requested in the questionnaire includes the following: name, address, and phone number of agency; mission statement; geographic area served; date agency was organized or incorporated; hours of operation; name of organization's president and executive director; current number of board members; other sources of funding for program; other sources of funding for agency; amount requested; annual operating budget; high priority services provided; brief program description; and copy of IRS letter stating 501(c)(3) status. This information must be submitted in typewritten format not to exceed two pages.
Restrictions on Giving: Does not fund general operations of specific schools.
Does not make grants to individuals or private shareholders. Also does not fund organizations where a substantial part of activities is carrying on propaganda or otherwise attempting to influence legislation.
Grants are awarded only to charitable organizations as defined by section 501(c)(3) of the IRS code.

OTHER THINGS TO KNOW
The foundation was established in March 1992 with monies from Sega of America, Redwood City, CA, and Sega Enterprises, Tokyo, Japan.
Foundation makes grants of $1,000 and up.

Sega prefers to fund innovative and effective programs that impact relatively large numbers of children, particularly those efforts being made in major urban areas. When possible, Sega will collaborate with other funding sources. Programs should demonstrate a specific need for Sega support, be well managed, and receive wide interest as evidenced by broad public and business support.

The company requested that the names of the company and foundation officers be deleted.

GRANTS ANALYSIS
Total Grants: $2,500,000*
Disclosure Period: 1993
Note: Total giving figure is approximate. Assets are for 1992. Recent grants are derived from a 1992 grants list.

RECENT GRANTS
300,000   A Better Chance, Boston, MA — minority student scholarships

300,000   Pediatric AIDS Foundation, Santa Monica, CA — "Educating Our Children" video project

250,000   George Lucas Educational Foundation, Nicasio, CA — multimedia prototype development

200,000   National Foundation for the Improvement of Education — for the Christa McAuliffe Institute for Pioneer Teachers

141,012   American Academy of Pediatrics, Chicago, IL — pediatric emergency CD-ROM development

100,000   Cal State Dominguez Hills/Challenger Learning Center, Carson, CA — space shuttle replication and science curriculum

100,000   Lucile Salter Packard Children's Hospital at Stanford, Palo Alto, CA — pediatric advice line

75,000   Mathematics, Engineering, Science Achievement (MESA) at the University of California at Berkeley, Berkeley, CA — Saturday Academy

    math and science program

64,000   Clearpool School, Brooklyn, NY — model year-round school program

50,000   Just Say No to Drugs, Oakland, CA — drug prevention and education

Segal Charitable Trust, Barnet

CONTACT
Barnet Segal Charitable Trust
PO Box S-1
Carmel, CA 93921

FINANCIAL SUMMARY
Recent Giving: $691,200 (fiscal 1992); $535,400 (fiscal 1991); $664,650 (fiscal 1990)
Assets: $13,241,549 (fiscal year ending March 31, 1992); $13,161,748 (fiscal 1991); $11,477,681 (fiscal 1990)
EIN: 77-6024786

CONTRIBUTIONS SUMMARY
Typical Recipients: • *Arts & Humanities:* community arts, libraries, music, theater • *Civic & Public Affairs:* international affairs, law & justice, municipalities • *Social Services:* aged, domestic violence, family planning, family services, food/clothing distribution, homes, youth organizations
Grant Types: general support
Geographic Distribution: focus on Monterey County, CA

GIVING OFFICERS
Herbert Berman: trust

APPLICATION INFORMATION
Initial Approach: Contributes only to preselected organizations.

GRANTS ANALYSIS
Number of Grants: 22
Highest Grant: $200,000
Typical Range: $2,000 to $50,000
Disclosure Period: fiscal year ending March 31, 1992

RECENT GRANTS
200,000   Natividad Medical Foundation, Salinas, CA — ambulatory care center building fund

100,000   City of Monterey, Monterey, CA — sports center building fund

80,000   Peninsula Outreach Welcome House, Seaside, CA — food and shelter for the homeless

50,000   Monterey Institute of International Studies, Monterey, CA — building fund

44,500   Boys and Girls Club, Seaside, CA

37,500   Family Resource Center, Seaside, CA — building fund

26,000   Carmel Music Society, Carmel, CA

24,200   Legal Services for Seniors, Pacific Grove, CA

20,000   Food Bank for Monterey County, Monterey, CA

20,000   Monterey College of Law, Monterey, CA

Segerstrom Foundation

CONTACT
Malcolm Ross
Segerstrom Fdn.
c/o C. J. Segerstrom and Sons
3315 Fairview Rd.
Costa Mesa, CA 92626

FINANCIAL SUMMARY
Recent Giving: $236,200 (1991); $310,000 (1990); $222,500 (1989)
Assets: $1,847,386 (1991); $1,793,004 (1990); $1,954,854 (1989)
EIN: 33-0269599

CONTRIBUTIONS SUMMARY
Typical Recipients: • *Arts & Humanities:* arts centers, arts institutes, community arts, dance, music, opera, performing arts, theater • *Education:* colleges & universities, medical education • *Social Services:* community service organizations, youth organizations
Grant Types: general support
Geographic Distribution: focus on CA

GIVING OFFICERS
Mark Heim: secy, cfo
Malcom Ross: pres
Harold Segerstrom, Jr.: trust, dir *B* 1927 *CURR EMPL* CJ Segerstrom & Sons
Henry T. Segerstrom: trust, dir *B* 1923 *ED* Stanford Univ *CURR EMPL* mng ptnr: CJ Segerstrom & Sons *CORP*

AFFIL dir: Safeco Corp, SCE Corp, Security Pacific Corp, Security Pacific Natl Bank *NONPR AFFIL* chmn: Orange County Performing Arts Ctr Endowment Comm; fellow: Fraternity Friends Music Ctr, Huntington Library, Polar Star Sweden, Stanford Univ, Swedish Royal Round Table; mem: Sigma Chi
Nellie Ruth Segerstrom: trust
Ted Segerstrom: trust

APPLICATION INFORMATION
Initial Approach: Send brief letter describing program. There are no deadlines.

GRANTS ANALYSIS
Number of Grants: 6
Highest Grant: $100,000
Typical Range: $10,000 to $50,000
Disclosure Period: 1991

RECENT GRANTS
100,000   Orange County Performing Arts Center, Costa Mesa, CA

50,000   Pacific Symphony, San Francisco, CA

50,000   South Coast Repertory Theater, Newport Beach, CA

25,000   Opera Pacific, Costa Mesa, CA

10,000   YWCA, Los Angeles, CA

1,200   University of California Irvine College of Medicine, Irvine, CA

Sehn Foundation

CONTACT
Sehn Fdn.
23874 Kean Ave.
Dearborn, MI 48124

FINANCIAL SUMMARY
Recent Giving: $291,356 (1991); $300,106 (1990); $337,316 (1989)
Assets: $2,963,860 (1991); $2,991,697 (1990); $3,150,491 (1989)
Gifts Received: $19,724 (1990); $141,294 (1989); $162,000 (1988)
Fiscal Note: In 1990, contributions were received from James T. Sehn.
EIN: 38-6160784

CONTRIBUTIONS SUMMARY
Donor(s): Francis J. Sehn, James T. Sehn

Typical Recipients: • *Civic & Public Affairs:* philanthropic organizations • *Education:* colleges & universities, private education (precollege) • *Health:* medical research • *Religion:* religious organizations • *Social Services:* community service organizations
Grant Types: general support
Geographic Distribution: focus on Detroit, MI

GIVING OFFICERS
Francis J. Sehn: pres

APPLICATION INFORMATION
Initial Approach: Contributes only to preselected organizations.

GRANTS ANALYSIS
Highest Grant: $250,000
Typical Range: $1,500 to $12,500
Disclosure Period: 1991

RECENT GRANTS
250,000 Papal Foundation, Philadelphia, PA
14,100 St. Hugo of the Hills Church, Bloomfield Hills, MI
12,500 Academy of Scared Heart, Detroit, MI
10,000 Catholic Services Appeal, Detroit, MI
10,000 Providence Hospital Foundation, Southfield, MI
6,000 Guest House, Detroit, MI
2,705 Greenfields School, Tucson, AZ
2,000 Northwestern University, Evanston, IL
1,780 Gateway Montessori, Detroit, MI
1,500 March of Dimes, Detroit, MI

Seibel Foundation, Abe and Annie

CONTACT
Judith T. Whelton
V.P. and Trust Officer
Abe and Annie Seibel Fdn.
c/o The United States National Bank
PO Box 179
Galveston, TX 77553
(409) 763-1151

FINANCIAL SUMMARY
Recent Giving: $2,362,462 (fiscal 1992); $1,949,655 (fiscal 1991); $1,721,425 (fiscal 1989)

Assets: $21,758,754 (fiscal year ending July 31, 1992); $19,077,627 (fiscal 1991); $17,585,368 (fiscal 1989)
EIN: 74-6035556

CONTRIBUTIONS SUMMARY
Donor(s): The foundation was established in 1960 by the late Abe Seibel and the late Annie Seibel.
Typical Recipients: • *Education:* student aid
Grant Types: loan
Geographic Distribution: limited to graduates of Texas high schools attending Texas colleges and universities

GIVING OFFICERS
Bernard Demoratsky: dir
Rabbi Martin Levy: dir
F. A. Odom: dir

APPLICATION INFORMATION
Initial Approach:
Applicants should contact the foundation for a formal application.
The fornal application requests information on the applicants choice of college, specific loan data, parental or guardian and a co-signer information, personal references, and previous educational data. The foundation requests applicants attach a photogrpah to the application, and make arrangements for a transcript to be sent to the directors. A personal interview will also be sheduled before a decision is made.
The deadline for submitting applications is February 28.
Restrictions on Giving: The foundation makes loans only to high school students in Texas wishing to attend Texas colleges. The loans are only to support four-year undergraduate degrees.

OTHER THINGS TO KNOW
Publications: application guidelines

GRANTS ANALYSIS
Total Grants: $2,547,722*
Number of Grants: 1,710
Typical Range: $1,000 to $1,500
Disclosure Period: fiscal year ending July 31, 1992
Note: The fiscal 1992 grants list consists of 1,710 scholarship awards to individuals.

Seid Foundation, Barre

CONTACT
Blooma Stark
Barre Seid Fdn.
55 East Monroe
Chicago, IL 60603
(312) 899-5502

FINANCIAL SUMMARY
Recent Giving: $669,150 (1990); $495,435 (1989); $158,600 (1987)
Assets: $5,660,511 (1990); $3,102,231 (1989); $2,360,645 (1987)
Gifts Received: $3,000,000 (1990); $850,000 (1989); $500,000 (1987)
Fiscal Note: In 1990, contributions were received from Barre Seid.
EIN: 36-3342443

CONTRIBUTIONS SUMMARY
Donor(s): Barre Seid
Typical Recipients: • *Arts & Humanities:* arts institutes, community arts, music, opera • *Civic & Public Affairs:* ethnic/minority organizations • *Education:* arts education, colleges & universities • *Religion:* religious organizations • *Social Services:* aged, child welfare, community service organizations, homes, united funds, youth organizations
Grant Types: general support
Geographic Distribution: focus on Chicago, IL

GIVING OFFICERS
Joyce B. Markle: secy
Leonard Schanfield: dir
Barre Seid: pres, treas

APPLICATION INFORMATION
Initial Approach: Send brief letter of inquiry describing program. There are no deadlines.

GRANTS ANALYSIS
Number of Grants: 41
Highest Grant: $110,000
Typical Range: $1,000 to $25,000
Disclosure Period: 1990

RECENT GRANTS
110,000 University of Chicago, Chicago, IL
100,000 Council for Jewish Elderly, Chicago, IL
100,000 Roosevelt University, Chicago, IL

50,000 Illinois Children's Home and Aid Society, Chicago, IL
50,000 Jewish United Fund, Chicago, IL
50,000 School of Art Institute, Chicago, IL
25,000 CATO Institute, Washington, DC
25,000 DePaul University School of Music, Chicago, IL
25,000 Teach for America, Chicago, IL
10,000 Shepherd House, Las Vegas, NV

Seidman Family Foundation

CONTACT
Augusta Eppinga
Trustee
Seidman Family Fdn.
99 Monroe Avenue, N.W., Ste. 800
Grand Rapids, MI 49503
(616) 453-7719

FINANCIAL SUMMARY
Recent Giving: $117,000 (1990); $111,589 (1989); $113,073 (1988)
Assets: $2,583,930 (1990); $2,501,111 (1989); $2,343,899 (1988)
EIN: 13-6098204

CONTRIBUTIONS SUMMARY
Donor(s): the late Frank E. Seidman, the late Esther I. Seidman
Typical Recipients: • *Arts & Humanities:* cinema, community arts, museums/galleries • *Civic & Public Affairs:* environmental affairs • *Education:* colleges & universities • *Health:* hospitals • *Social Services:* community service organizations, counseling, united funds, youth organizations
Grant Types: capital, endowment, general support, multiyear/continuing support, and research
Geographic Distribution: focus on MI

GIVING OFFICERS
Augusta Eppinga: trust
I. William Seidman: trust
O. Thomas Seidman: trust
Sarah B. Seidman: trust

APPLICATION INFORMATION
Initial Approach: Send brief letter of inquiry describing program. There are no deadlines.

Restrictions on Giving: Does not support individuals.

GRANTS ANALYSIS
Number of Grants: 28
Highest Grant: $50,000
Typical Range: $500 to $10,000
Disclosure Period: 1990

RECENT GRANTS
50,000 Grand Valley State University, Allendale, MI — Esther L. Seidman Chair in Management

20,000 Grand Rapids Youth Commonwealth, Grand Rapids, MI — renovation

10,000 Nantucket Cottage Hospital, Nantucket, MA — endowment fund

5,000 Corcoran Gallery of Art, Washington, DC

5,000 Grand Rapids Public Museum, Grand Rapids, MI — capital campaign

5,000 United Methodist Community House, Grand Rapids, MI

2,000 Arizona State University College of Business, Tempe, AZ

2,000 Washington Performing Arts Society, Washington, DC

2,000 Woodbury College, Montpelier, VT

1,500 Wagon Mound Public Schools, Wagon Mound, NM — art, science, and library department

Seiler Corp.
Sales: $200.0 million
Employees: 5,800
Parent Company: International Catering Corp.
Headquarters: Waltham, MA
SIC Major Group: Business Services, Eating & Drinking Places, and Engineering & Management Services

CONTACT
Laurel Lafevre
President's Office
Seiler Corp.
153 Second Ave.
Waltham, MA 02254
(617) 890-6200

CONTRIBUTIONS SUMMARY
Operating Locations: MA (Walthem)

CORP. OFFICERS
Michel Landel: *CURR EMPL* pres: Seiler Corp

RECENT GRANTS
Simmons College, Boston, MA

Selby and Marie Selby Foundation, William G.

CONTACT
Robert E. Perkins
Executive Director
William G. Selby and Marie Selby Foundation
1800 Second St., Ste. 905
Sarasota, FL 34236
(813) 957-0442

FINANCIAL SUMMARY
Recent Giving: $2,245,267 (fiscal 1992); $1,852,922 (fiscal 1991); $1,730,063 (fiscal 1990)
Assets: $59,793,521 (fiscal year ending May 31, 1992); $54,609,701 (fiscal 1991); $47,891,694 (fiscal 1990)
Gifts Received: $1,500 (fiscal 1991)
EIN: 59-6121242

CONTRIBUTIONS SUMMARY
Donor(s): The William G. Selby and Marie Selby Foundation was endowed by William G. Selby and his wife in 1955. Mr. Selby, who died in 1956, was a co-founder of the Selby Oil Company in Ohio. In addition, he was a large stockholder in Texaco, and owned extensive mineral interests in the Colorado Rocky Mountain region. The foundation is affiliated with the Beattie, Sarasota County, Paddock, and Posey Foundations, all of First Union Bank.
Typical Recipients: • *Arts & Humanities:* community arts • *Civic & Public Affairs:* municipalities • *Education:* arts education, career/vocational education, colleges & universities, community & junior colleges, education administration, minority education, preschool education, science/technology education, student aid • *Health:* mental health, single-disease health associations • *Social Services:* aged, animal protection, disabled, family services, food/clothing distribution, youth organizations
Grant Types: capital, general support, and scholarship
Geographic Distribution: Sarasota, FL, and adjoining counties

GIVING OFFICERS
C. William Curtis: mem admin comm
John Davidson: mem admin comm
S. Anthony DeDeyn: chmn, mem admin comm
William Gaar: mem admin comm
Wendel Kent: mem admin comm
Robert E. Perkins: exec dir
Charles E. Stottlemyer: mem admin comm

APPLICATION INFORMATION
Initial Approach:
Applicants should contact the administrative agent for a copy of their application procedures and application forms. Applications must include a proposal abstract, using a form available from the foundation, that provides a brief description of the proposal; its objective, time period, and total budget; amount requested; and name, telephone number, and address of person completing the application. Required documentation includes proof of IRS tax-exempt and non-private foundation status, balance sheet and income statement, project budget, names and affiliations of directors or trustees, name and qualifications of person proposed to administer the grant, and a statement that the request is executed by an authorized person. Supporting information may be submitted to describe the organization and the project. Three copies of the request must be submitted, with at least two copies of accompanying printed material. The board meets in June and December. Application deadlines are February 1 and August 1 for capital grants. The grants committee reviews proposals and notifies applicants of their decisions within five months of the deadline. The trustees evaluate applications on the basis of the proposed project's value to society, soundness of sponsoring organization, sources of other financial support, and assurance of future maintenance of the project without an undesirable financial burden to the sponsoring organization or taxpayer.
Restrictions on Giving: No grants are given to individuals, or for endowment funds, operating budgets, continuing support, annual campaigns, deficit financing, seed money, or emergency funds. It also does not support special projects, research, graduate study, publications, travel, surveys, seminars, workshops, conferences, loans, fund raising, or program advertising. The foundation generally does not give to organizations outside of Sarasota and adjoining counties, to other foundations, or to the United Way. It prefers not to support projects that are normally financed by public tax funds. The foundation usually does not make grants payable in installments in future years.

OTHER THINGS TO KNOW
A representative of First Union Bank serves as a corporate trustee for the foundation.
In order to be eligible for a Selby scholarship, a student must be a bona fide resident of Sarasota or Manatee Counties before attending college, and must attend a participating Florida college or university. A minimum grade point average of 3.0 is required. Students seeking a scholarship should write to the Florida college or university in which he or she has an interest. No scholarships are awarded by the foundation directly to individuals.
Publications: application guidelines

GRANTS ANALYSIS
Total Grants: $2,245,267
Number of Grants: 82
Highest Grant: $178,154
Typical Range: $5,000 to $50,000

Disclosure Period: fiscal year ending May 31, 1992

Note: Grants analysis includes 17 scholarship programs totaling $370,000. Recent grants are derived from a fiscal 1992 grants list.

RECENT GRANTS

333,500 Florida College General Scholarship Program

250,500 Sarasota County Public Schools Foundation, Sarasota, FL — scholarships, field trips, equipment

178,154 School Board of Sarasota County, Sarasota, FL — science fair, Selby tutorial

100,000 City of Sarasota, Sarasota, FL — development of a park

100,000 Hospice of Sarasota, Sarasota, FL — build a hospice house in Venice

100,000 Safe Place and Rape Crisis Center of Sarasota, Sarasota, FL — construction of 8-bedroom shelter

95,500 Community Mobile Meals, Sarasota, FL — purchase and renovation of new facility

77,049 Mote Marine Laboratory, Sarasota, FL — equipment and cable linkage

75,000 Florida Sheriffs Youth Ranch Foundation, Boys Ranch, FL — construction of campus residence

75,000 Manatee County Association for the Retarded, Bradenton, FL — renovation of service center

Self Foundation

CONTACT
Frank J. Wideman, Jr.
Executive Vice President
The Self Foundation
Drawer 1017
Greenwood, SC 29648
(803) 941-4036

FINANCIAL SUMMARY
Recent Giving: $1,145,882 (1992); $1,219,180 (1991); $1,111,505 (1990)

Assets: $30,000,000 (1992 est.); $29,323,216 (1991); $25,046,546 (1990)

EIN: 57-0400594

CONTRIBUTIONS SUMMARY
Donor(s): The Self Foundation was founded in 1942 by the late James C. Self. Mr. Self was the founder of Greenwood Mills in Greenwood, SC. The original purpose of the foundation was to construct a hospital for Greenwood County. This mission was realized on November 1, 1951. At the time of the hospital's dedication, Mr. Self remarked that it was, "a debt of gratitude to the community that has been good to me."

Typical Recipients: • *Arts & Humanities:* libraries, museums/galleries, theater • *Civic & Public Affairs:* nonprofit management • *Education:* arts education, colleges & universities, literacy, science/technology education • *Health:* hospitals • *Social Services:* aged, community service organizations, youth organizations

Grant Types: capital, challenge, and project

Geographic Distribution: South Carolina, with emphasis on Greenwood area

GIVING OFFICERS
William B. Allin: treas
Joseph M. Anderson: trust
Virginia S. Brennan: trust
Carroll H. Brooks: trust
Lynn W. Hodge: trust
Dr. Sally E. Self: trust
James C. Self: pres, trust *B* Greenwood SC 1919 *ED* Citadel BS 1941 *CURR EMPL* chmn exec comm, dir: Greenwood Mills Inc *CORP AFFIL* dir: Duke Power Co, Greenwood Motor Lines, SC Natl Bank; pres: Textile Investments Co *NONPR AFFIL* life mem bd trusts: Clemson Univ; mem: Am Textile Mfrs Inst, NY Cotton Exchange, SC Textile Mfrs Assn
James C. Self, Jr.: vp, trust *CURR EMPL* chmn, dir: Greenwood Mills
W. M. Self: secy, trust *CURR EMPL* pres, dir: Greenwood Mills
Paul E. Welder: trust *B* Kansas City MO 1943 *CURR EMPL* exec vp fin: Greenwood Mills
Frank J. Wideman, Jr.: exec vp

APPLICATION INFORMATION
Initial Approach:
There are no application forms. A written proposal must be submitted.

Proposals must include a description of the organization's objectives and activities, its leadership, the project for which support is sought, and an implementation plan. Applicants also must include a copy of the organization's latest budget with income sources, a copy of IRS tax-exempt determination letter, and the most recent financial statement.

Proposals must be received by March 1, June 1, September 1, or December 1. Trustees meet the third week of March, June, September, and December. Late applications are held for consideration at the next meeting.

The trustees prefer to fund those organizations that have the financial potential to sustain projects on a continuing basis after funding.

Restrictions on Giving: No grants are made to individuals or for loans. The foundation also refrains from making recurring grants.

OTHER THINGS TO KNOW
Beside making grants, the foundation also provides conferences and seminars.

Publications: annual report

GRANTS ANALYSIS
Total Grants: $1,145,882
Number of Grants: 24
Highest Grant: $300,000
Typical Range: $15,000 to $60,000
Disclosure Period: 1992
Note: Recent grants are derived from a 1992 grants list.

RECENT GRANTS

300,000 Lander University Foundation, Greenwood, SC — for establishing an electronic campus

150,000 Greenwood Methodist Home, Greenwood, SC — assist with cost of rehabilitating the Health Center

86,196 Abbeville-Greenwood Regional Library, Greenwood, SC — assist in cost of computer system

66,667 Independent Colleges and Universi-

ties of South Carolina, Columbia, SC — conduit for grant to Erskine College to assist with Campus Master Plan for computers

60,000 Family YMCA of Greenwood, Greenwood, SC — assist with cost of new facility

60,000 South Carolina Foundation of Independent Colleges, Columbia, SC — general support

59,177 South Carolina Foundation of Independent Colleges, Columbia, SC — conduit for four Virginia Turner Self Scholarships at Converse College

54,972 Tri-County Technical College, Pendleton, SC — medical laboratory technology equipment

50,000 Furman University, Greenville, SC — assist with cost of math/computer science building in honor of Dick Riley

50,000 Greenwood Genetic Center, Greenwood, SC — cost of architectural and engineering drawings and related documents re establishing a Research Institute

Semmes Foundation

CONTACT
Thomas R. Semmes
President
Semmes Fdn.
800 Navarro, Ste. 210
San Antonio, TX 78205
(512) 225-0807

FINANCIAL SUMMARY
Recent Giving: $383,868 (1991); $380,851 (1990); $337,180 (1989)

Assets: $9,447,390 (1991); $8,419,661 (1990); $6,549,402 (1989)

EIN: 74-6062264

CONTRIBUTIONS SUMMARY
Donor(s): the late Douglas R. Semmes

Typical Recipients: • *Arts & Humanities:* arts centers, arts festivals, libraries, museums/galleries, public broadcast-

ing • *Civic & Public Affairs:* national security, philanthropic organizations • *Education:* colleges & universities, public education (precollege) • *Religion:* churches • *Social Services:* community service organizations, family services, united funds, youth organizations
Grant Types: capital, conference/seminar, emergency, general support, multiyear/continuing support, operating expenses, professorship, project, research, and seed money
Geographic Distribution: focus on the San Antonio, TX, area

GIVING OFFICERS
Carol Duffell: secy, treas
John R. Hannah: dir
Lucian L. Morrison, Jr.: dir
D. R. Semmes, Jr.: dir
Julia Yates Semmes: dir
Thomas R. Semmes: pres

APPLICATION INFORMATION
Initial Approach: Send cover letter and full proposal. There are no deadlines.
Restrictions on Giving: Does not support individuals or provide loans.

GRANTS ANALYSIS
Number of Grants: 25
Highest Grant: $200,000
Typical Range: $250 to $5,000
Disclosure Period: 1991

RECENT GRANTS
200,000　McNay Art Museum, San Antonio, TX — auditorium project
50,000　Morrison Family Foundation, San Antonio, TX
50,000　Texas Military Institute, San Antonio, TX
25,000　Christ Episcopal Church, San Antonio, TX
10,000　Alamo Public Communications Council, San Antonio, TX — education project
10,000　United Way, San Antonio, TX
7,500　YMCA, San Antonio, TX
6,608　McNay Art Museum, San Antonio, TX
5,000　Baptist Children Hospital, San Antonio, TX
3,000　Boy Scouts of America, San Antonio, TX

Semple Foundation, Louise Taft

CONTACT
Dudley S. Taft
Louise Taft Semple Fdn.
1808 Cincinnati Commerce Center
600 Vine St.
Cincinnati, OH 45202
(513) 381-2838

FINANCIAL SUMMARY
Recent Giving: $483,200 (1991); $549,800 (1990); $533,450 (1989)
Assets: $14,917,389 (1991); $12,693,008 (1990); $13,296,371 (1989)
EIN: 31-0653526

CONTRIBUTIONS SUMMARY
Donor(s): The foundation was incorporated in 1941 by the late Louise Tafl Semple.
Typical Recipients: • *Arts & Humanities:* arts funds, museums/galleries, music, opera • *Education:* colleges & universities, legal education, private education (precollege), public education (precollege) • *Social Services:* child welfare, family services, united funds, youth organizations
Grant Types: capital, endowment, matching, and scholarship
Geographic Distribution: focus on the Cincinnati and Hamilton County, OH, area

GIVING OFFICERS
James R. Bridgeland, Jr.: secy, trust *CORP AFFIL* dir: First Natl Bank Cincinnati, First Natl Cincinnati Corp
Norma F. Gentzler: treas
John T. Lawrence, Jr.: trust
Mrs. John T. Lawrence, Jr.: trust
Walter L. Lingle, Jr.: trust
Dudley S. Taft: pres, trust
Mrs. Robert A. Taft II: trust
Robert A. Taft, Jr.: trust *ED* Yale Univ BA 1939; Harvard Univ LLB 1942 *CURR EMPL* couns: Taft Stettinius & Hollister *NONPR AFFIL* mem: Am Bar Assn, DC Bar Assn, OH Bar Assn

APPLICATION INFORMATION
Initial Approach: Initial contact may be a full written request for funding. The foundation does not have a specific application form.

Written request should include the name, address, and telephone number of the applying organization, as shown on the IRS tax-exempt letter; the purpose and activities of the organization; the geographic areas served by the organization; the names of the officers, board of directors (or trustees), executive director, and secretary; the amount of the grant requested (with a budget for the project) and the purpose for which it will be used; any other sources contacted for support, with the amounts requested from each; and the organization's latest balance sheet and annual operating statement.

Grant requests are accepted throughout the year.

The foundation's board of trustees considers grant proposals and makes funding decisions.

Restrictions on Giving: The foundation does not support individuals, general purposes, research, or loans.

GRANTS ANALYSIS
Total Grants: $483,200
Number of Grants: 31
Highest Grant: $60,500
Typical Range: $5,000 to $20,000
Disclosure Period: 1991
Note: Recent grants are derived from a 1991 grants list.

RECENT GRANTS
75,000　Taft School, Watertown, CT
60,500　Fine Arts Fund, Cincinnati, OH
56,400　United Way, Cincinnati, OH
30,000　Museum Center at Cincinnati Union Terminal, Cincinnati, OH
25,000　Seven Hills Neighborhood Houses, Cincinnati, OH
25,000　Seven Hills Schools, Cincinnati, OH
20,000　Saint John's Social Center, Cincinnati, OH
20,000　Saint Joseph Home, Cincinnati, OH
15,000　Cincinnati Hills Christian Academy, Cincinnati, OH
15,000　Cincinnati Opera, Cincinnati, OH

Seneca Foods Corp. / Seneca Foods Foundation
Sales: $320.9 million
Employees: 2,964
Headquarters: Pittsford, NY
SIC Major Group: Apparel & Other Textile Products, Food & Kindred Products, and Transportation by Air

CONTACT
William T. Nanovsky
Chief Financial Officer
Seneca Foods Foundation
1162 Pittsford-Victor Rd.
Pittsford, NY 14534
(716) 385-9500

FINANCIAL SUMMARY
Recent Giving: $89,017 (fiscal 1991)
Assets: $1,965,009 (fiscal year ending July 31, 1991)
Fiscal Note: Annual Giving Range:
EIN: 22-2996324

CONTRIBUTIONS SUMMARY
Typical Recipients: • *Arts & Humanities:* general • *Civic & Public Affairs:* general • *Education:* general • *Health:* general • *Social Services:* general, youth organizations
Grant Types: general support
Geographic Distribution: headquarters and operating locations
Operating Locations: MN (Rochester), NY (Marion, Pittsford)

CORP. OFFICERS
Frederick W. Leick: *B* Lakewood OH 1943 *ED* Case Western Reserve Univ 1967 *CURR EMPL* ceo, pres: Seneca Foods Corp

GIVING OFFICERS
Devra A. Bevona: treas
Kraig H. Kayser: dir *CURR EMPL* vp, cfo: Seneca Foods Corp
Frederick W. Leick: pres, ceo, dir *CURR EMPL* ceo, pres: Seneca Foods Corp (see above)
William T. Nanovsky: sr vp, cfo
Susan W. Stuart: dir
Jeffrey L. Van Riper: controller
Arthur S. Wolcott: chmn, dir

APPLICATION INFORMATION
Initial Approach: Send brief letter of inquiry, including a de-

scription of the organization, amount requested, purpose of funds sought, audited financial statement, and proof of tax-exempt status. There are no deadlines.

Restrictions on Giving: Does not support individuals, religious organizations for sectarian purposes, or political or lobbying groups.

GRANTS ANALYSIS
Number of Grants: 60
Highest Grant: $25,000
Typical Range: $50 to $1,000
Disclosure Period: fiscal year ending July 31, 1991

RECENT GRANTS
25,000 Cornell University, Ithaca, NY
21,714 United Way
5,000 Cornell University, Ithaca, NY
5,000 Keuka College, Keuka Park, NY
5,000 YMCA
4,000 Camp Good Days
3,900 Disabled Children of M.C.
3,000 Special Olympics
2,000 Al Sigl Center for Rehabilitation Agencies, Rochester, NY
2,000 University of Wisconsin, Madison, WI

Senior Citizens Foundation

CONTACT
Beth Morgan
Senior Citizens Foundation
1375 Peachtree Street, NE, Suite 450
Atlanta, GA 30309-3113
(404) 881-5950

FINANCIAL SUMMARY
Recent Giving: $565,016 (fiscal 1991); $175,243 (fiscal 1990)
Assets: $3,247,158 (fiscal year ending September 30, 1991); $3,154,140 (fiscal 1990)
EIN: 58-1797772

CONTRIBUTIONS SUMMARY
Typical Recipients: • *Social Services:* aged
Grant Types: general support

GIVING OFFICERS
James E. Arnett: chmn
Sharon Denney: vchmn
Kimsey Mckinley: treas

APPLICATION INFORMATION
Initial Approach: The foundation reports no specific application guidelines. Send a brief letter of inquiry, including statement of purpose, amount requested, and proof of tax-exempt status.

GRANTS ANALYSIS
Number of Grants: 1
Highest Grant: $565,016
Disclosure Period: fiscal year ending September 30, 1991

RECENT GRANTS
175,243 Senior Citizens Services of Metropolitan Atlanta, Atlanta, GA

Senior Services of Stamford

CONTACT
Linda Thomsen
Treasurer
Senior Services of Stamford
680 Summer St.
Stamford, CT 06901
(203) 324-6584

FINANCIAL SUMMARY
Recent Giving: $333,676 (fiscal 1992); $401,996 (fiscal 1991); $137,339 (fiscal 1990)
Assets: $9,804,117 (fiscal year ending February 28, 1992); $9,453,039 (fiscal 1991); $9,539,425 (fiscal 1990)
Gifts Received: $2,250 (fiscal 1992)
EIN: 06-0646916

CONTRIBUTIONS SUMMARY
Typical Recipients: • *Civic & Public Affairs:* housing • *Health:* geriatric health, health organizations • *Social Services:* food/clothing distribution
Geographic Distribution: limited to Stamford, CT

GIVING OFFICERS
Steven Ayres: secy
Robert J. Bromfield: treas
J. Robert Bromley: pres
Thomas C. Mayers: vp

APPLICATION INFORMATION
Initial Approach: Send brief letter describing situation. There are no deadlines.

OTHER THINGS TO KNOW
Provides grants to elderly individuals for payments for medical services.

GRANTS ANALYSIS
Number of Grants: 5
Highest Grant: $34,500
Typical Range: $2,600 to $30,000
Disclosure Period: fiscal year ending February 28, 1992

RECENT GRANTS
34,500 Senior Neighborhood Support, Stamford, CT — meal program, recreation and outreach
23,725 Meals on Wheels, Stamford, CT
23,000 Stamford Family Housing Corporation, Stamford, CT — fund inner-city senior center
5,000 Interfaith Caregivers, Stamford, CT — senior visitor program
1,000 FISH, Stamford, CT — transportation to medical appointments
924 Jewish Family Services, Stamford, CT — transportation for companions to elderly
400 Jewish Center Adult Program, Stamford, CT — scholarships for summer "camp"

Sentinel Communications Co. / Orlando Sentinel Charities Fund

Sales: $250.0 million
Employees: 1,400
Parent Company: Tribune Co.
Headquarters: Orlando, FL
SIC Major Group: Printing & Publishing

CONTACT
Nancy F. Peed
Community Relations Manager
Sentinel Communications Co.
633 North Orange Ave.
Orlando, FL 32801
(407) 420-5591

FINANCIAL SUMMARY
Recent Giving: $375,000 (1993 est.); $900,000 (1991 approx.)

Fiscal Note: Contributions for 1991 include contributions by the Orlando Sentinel Charities Fund, $200,000; Orlando Sentinel Santa Fund, $300,000; and direct corporate contributions, $400,000. Estimate for 1993 is for direct contributions.

CONTRIBUTIONS SUMMARY
Typical Recipients: • *Arts & Humanities:* arts appreciation, arts associations, arts centers, arts funds, history/historic preservation, museums/galleries, music, theater, visual arts • *Civic & Public Affairs:* environmental affairs, ethnic/minority organizations, first amendment issues, housing, urban & community affairs • *Education:* colleges & universities, community & junior colleges, continuing education, journalism education, literacy, minority education, preschool education, public education (precollege) • *Health:* health organizations, hospices, nutrition & health maintenance, pediatric health, public health • *Social Services:* aged, child welfare, community service organizations, day care, family services, food/clothing distribution, homes, shelters/homelessness, united funds, volunteer services, youth organizations
Grant Types: capital, employee matching gifts, and project
Geographic Distribution: limited to East Central Florida
Operating Locations: FL (Orlando)

CORP. OFFICERS
Harold R. Lifvendahl: *CURR EMPL* pres, publ, dir: Sentinel Communs Co

GIVING OFFICERS
Nancy F. Peed: *CURR EMPL* comm rels mgr: Sentinel Communs Co

APPLICATION INFORMATION
Initial Approach: *Initial Contact:* brief letter of inquiry *Include Information On:* a description of the organization, amount requested, purpose of funds sought, and proof of tax-exempt status *When to Submit:* any time
Restrictions on Giving: Does not support individuals, religious organizations for sectarian purposes, political or lobbying

groups, or organizations outside operating areas.

GRANTS ANALYSIS
Typical Range: $1,000 to $50,000

Sentry Insurance Co. / Sentry Life Group Foundation
Assets: $1.11 billion
Employees: 4,550
Headquarters: Stevens Point, WI
SIC Major Group: Insurance Carriers

CONTACT
Debbie Klasinski
Administrative Assistant
Sentry Insurance
1800 North Point Dr.
Stevens Point, WI 54481
(715) 346-6526

FINANCIAL SUMMARY
Recent Giving: $294,186 (1991); $330,646 (1990); $293,458 (1989)
Assets: $18,329 (1991); $23,954 (1990); $47,399 (1989)
Gifts Received: $289,000 (1991); $305,000 (1990); $167,500 (1989)
Fiscal Note: Contributes through foundation only. In 1991, contributions were received from Sentry Insurance, A Mutual Company.
EIN: 39-1037370

CONTRIBUTIONS SUMMARY
Typical Recipients: • *Arts & Humanities:* community arts, libraries • *Education:* education funds • *Health:* health organizations, hospitals, medical research, pediatric health • *Social Services:* community service organizations, recreation & athletics, united funds, youth organizations
Grant Types: general support
Geographic Distribution: nationally
Operating Locations: WI (Stevens Point)

CORP. OFFICERS
Larry C. Ballard: *B* Des Moines IA 1935 *ED* Drake Univ BS 1957 *CURR EMPL* chmn, pres, ceo: Sentry Ins *CORP AFFIL* chmn: Dairyland Ins, Middlesex Ins Co, Patriot Gen Ins Co, Sentry Aviation Svcs, Sentry Investors Life Ins Co, Sentry Svcs; chmn, ceo: Sentry Life Ins; dir: Century

Commun Corp, Competetive WI, M&I First National Bank, Sentry Equity Svcs, Sentry Investment Mgmt *NONPR AFFIL* fellow: Soc Actuaries; mem: Am Academy Actuaries; trust: Am Inst Property Liability Underwriters, Ins Inst Am

GIVING OFFICERS
William R. Beversdorf: vp
Emil Fleischauer, Jr.: secy, dir *B* Colby WI 1927 *CURR EMPL* vp, corp sec, gen counc: Sentry Ins A Mutual Co *CORP AFFIL* dir: WI Ins Alliance; vp, dir: Life Ins Co & Affiliates *NONPR AFFIL* mem: Am Bar Assn
Lillian P. Hanson: vp, exec dir, dir
Bernard C. Hlavac: dir
Debbie Klasinski: admin asst
Marion J. Krakowiecki: treas
Alfred C. Noel: pres, dir
James C. Noonan: asst secy
Carroll George Smith: dir

APPLICATION INFORMATION
Initial Approach: *Initial Contact:* brief letter *Include Information On:* description of program and amount of contribution sought *When to Submit:* any time

GRANTS ANALYSIS
Total Grants: $294,186
Number of Grants: 58*
Highest Grant: $95,000
Typical Range: $100 to $3,000
Disclosure Period: 1991
Note: Number of grants and average grant figures do not include matching gifts totaling $23,283.

RECENT GRANTS
95,000 United Way, Milwaukee, WI
50,000 University of Wisconsin Stevens Point Foundation, Madison, WI
25,000 Wisconsin Foundation of Independent Colleges, Milwaukee, WI
15,000 Cap Services, Milwaukee, WI — Family Crisis Center
7,500 Rawhide Boys Ranch, Milwaukee, WI
7,000 Boy Scouts of America, Milwaukee, WI
7,000 Woodland Girl Scout Council, Woodland, WI

5,000 Marshfield Medical Research Foundation, Milwaukee, WI
5,000 Village of Plover Library Fund, Plover, WI
3,890 University of Wisconsin Stevens Point Foundation, Madison, WI

Sequa Corp. / Sequa Foundation of Delaware
Sales: $1.87 billion
Employees: 15,700
Headquarters: New York, NY
SIC Major Group: Chemicals & Allied Products, Industrial Machinery & Equipment, Instruments & Related Products, and Transportation Equipment

CONTACT
Stuart Z. Krinsly
Senior Executive Vice President
Sequa Fdn. of Delaware
200 Park Ave.
New York, NY 10166
(212) 986-5500

FINANCIAL SUMMARY
Recent Giving: $222,760 (1990); $309,286 (1989); $344,640 (1988)
Assets: $410,263 (1990); $221,077 (1989); $443,054 (1988)
EIN: 23-7000821

CONTRIBUTIONS SUMMARY
Typical Recipients: • *Arts & Humanities:* museums/galleries • *Civic & Public Affairs:* ethnic/minority organizations, national security • *Social Services:* counseling, drugs & alcohol, youth organizations
Operating Locations: AR (Camden), CA (Gardena, Rancho Dominguez), CT (Bridgeport, East Granby), FL (Fort Walton Beach, Stuart), LA (Houma), MA (Needham), MD (Rockville), MO (St. Louis), NH (Amherst, Merrimack, Nashua), NJ (East Rutherford), NY (New York, Orangesburg), OK (Midwest City), PA (Harrisburg), SC (Chester), TX (Dallas, Groves, Hurst, San Antonio), VA (Alexandria, Gainesville)

CORP. OFFICERS
Norman E. Alexander: *B* New York NY 1914 *ED* Columbia

Univ AB 1934; Columbia Univ LLB 1936 *CURR EMPL* chmn, ceo: Sequa Corp *CORP AFFIL* chmn, dir: Ampacet Corp, Chromalloy Am Corp; dir: Atlantic Res Corp, Chock Full O'Nuts Corp, Interim Sys Corp *NONPR AFFIL* counc, trust, mem: Natl Assn Mfrs; dir, mem: Chief Execs Forum; mem: Conf Bd; trust: Rockefeller Univ
Robert E. Davis: *B* Madison IL 1931 *ED* Univ MO 1953; Washington Univ *CURR EMPL* pres, coo, dir: Sequa Corp *CORP AFFIL* dir: H&R Block, Erbamont NV, HIMONT, USF&G Corp

GIVING OFFICERS
Norman E. Alexander: pres, trust *CURR EMPL* chmn, ceo: Sequa Corp (see above)

GRANTS ANALYSIS
Highest Grant: $100,000

RECENT GRANTS
100,000 92nd Street YMHA, New York, NY
43,500 American Jewish Committee, New York, NY
10,000 Anti-Defamation League, New York, NY
10,000 Jewish Museum, New York, NY
5,000 American Jewish Committee, New York, NY
5,000 Children of Alcoholics Foundation, New York, NY
5,000 Jewish Institute for National Security Affairs, Washington, DC
5,000 Jewish Museum, New York, NY
5,000 New York Times Neediest Cases Fund, New York, NY
5,000 Salvation Army, New York, NY

Sequoia Foundation

CONTACT
Frank D. Underwood
Executive Director
Sequoia Foundation
820 A St., Ste. 345
Tacoma, WA 98402
(206) 627-1634

FINANCIAL SUMMARY
Recent Giving: $3,816,949 (fiscal 1991); $3,557,052 (fis-

cal 1990); $3,094,149 (fiscal 1989)
Assets: $18,766,633 (fiscal year ending August 31, 1991); $18,120,556 (fiscal 1990); $17,732,712 (fiscal 1989)
Gifts Received: $2,410,000 (fiscal 1991); $3,105,000 (fiscal 1990); $2,850,000 (fiscal 1989)
Fiscal Note: The foundation receives contributions from both the 1973 and 1975 Irrevocable Trusts of C. Davis Weyerhaeuser.
EIN: 91-1178052

CONTRIBUTIONS SUMMARY
Donor(s): The foundation was established in 1982 by C. Davis Weyerhaeuser, a son of the late Frederick Edward Weyerhaeuser, who was a president of Weyerhaeuser Timber Company. Born in Tacoma, WA, in 1902, and educated at Yale University, C. Davis Weyerhaeuser served as an executive with Weyerhaeuser for 25 years.
Typical Recipients: • *Civic & Public Affairs:* environmental affairs, international affairs, national security, philanthropic organizations, public policy • *Education:* colleges & universities, private education (precollege), religious education • *Health:* health organizations, hospitals • *Social Services:* child welfare, family planning, recreation & athletics, religious welfare, youth organizations
Grant Types: capital, general support, and project
Geographic Distribution: national with emphasis on the western and northwestern United States, especially Tacoma and Seattle, WA

GIVING OFFICERS
Linda P. BeMiller: program dir
James R. Hanson: mem
Nicholas C. Spika: secy
Frank D. Underwood: exec dir, mem
Annette Thayer Black Weyerhaeuser: dir, mem
Gail T. Weyerhaeuser: vp, dir, mem *NONPR AFFIL* trust: Tacoma Art Mus *PHIL AFFIL* trust: Greater Tacoma Community Foundation
William Toycen Weyerhaeuser: pres, treas, dir, mem *B* Tacoma WA 1943 *ED* Stanford Univ 1966; Fuller Grad Sch Psychology PhD 1975 *CURR EMPL* owner, chmn:

Yelm Telephone Co *CORP AFFIL* dir: Potlatch Corp *NONPR AFFIL* mem: Am Psychological Assn; vchmn: Univ Puget Sound

APPLICATION INFORMATION
Initial Approach:
Applicants may contact the foundation by submitting two copies of a typewritten summary letter, or by submitting two copies of a complete application.
A summary letter should include a statement of the project with objectives, description of the organization, project budget, amount requested, and proof of IRS tax-exempt status. Grant seekers submitting a full proposal should include a summary letter; legal name, address, and telephone number of the organization; a list of names and affiliations of the organization's board of directors and chief administrative officer; complete financial statements for the organization's most recent fiscal year and current operating budget; description of the project and objectives; description of beneficiaries of the project; substantiation of the extent of need for these benefits; project timetable; method and criteria for assessing the project's effectiveness; qualifications of key personnel; detailed expense budget; list of other possible sources of support; and, if appropriate, an explanation of how the project is to be continued after the funding period ends. The full proposal must also include copies of the most recent IRS 501(c)(3) and 509(a) status determination letters and a statement by the chief administrative officer claiming that he will take full responsibility for proper fiscal management and accounting for any grant received, that he will file timely reports, and that no part of the grant will be used to propagandize or to influence elections or legislation. Requests for funding are accepted throughout the year. The foundation staff will review requests to determine if the project falls within current guidelines. In the case of an applicant submitting a summary letter, the staff will seek additional detailed information. Action on proposals ordinarily oc-

curs between 30 and 60 days from the date a complete grant request is received.
Restrictions on Giving: The foundation gives a high priority to organizations that seek other sources of funding and that receive little or no support from public tax funds. The foundation generally will not provide funding for annual appeals; debt retirement; individuals; scholarships or fellowships; endowments; film production or the publication of books, periodicals, or monographs; local organizations; private foundations or operating foundations; propaganda; conferences, seminars, or travel of individuals or groups; or for voter registration programs.

OTHER THINGS TO KNOW
The Sequoia Foundation was the donor of the New Horizon Foundation, established in 1984.

GRANTS ANALYSIS
Total Grants: $3,816,949
Number of Grants: 46
Highest Grant: $2,692,000
Typical Range: $5,000 to $50,000
Disclosure Period: fiscal year ending August 31, 1991
Note: Average grant figure excludes a $2,692,000 grant to the New Horizon Foundation. Recent grants are derived from a fiscal 1991 grants list.

RECENT GRANTS
2,692,000 New Horizon Foundation, Seattle, WA — unrestricted grant
203,750 Conservation International Foundation, Washington, DC — program support
100,000 Woodlands Mountain Institute, Franklin, WV — program support
75,000 Nature Conservancy International, Washington, DC — program support
62,500 Food Research and Action Center, Washington, DC — program support
60,000 Fuller Graduate School of Psychology, Pasadena, CA — program support

55,000 Phillips Exeter Academy, Exeter, NH — capital needs
50,000 Pacific Lutheran University, Tacoma, WA — capital needs
50,000 World Wildlife Fund, Washington, DC — capital needs
50,000 Yosemite Institute, Sausalito, CA — capital needs

Servco Pacific / Servco Foundation
Employees: 1,400
Headquarters: Honolulu, HI

CONTACT
George J. Fukunaga
Chairman and Director
Servco Foundation
990 Fort St. Mall, Suite 500
P.O. Box 2788
Honolulu, HI 96803
(808) 521-6511

FINANCIAL SUMMARY
Recent Giving: $157,575 (fiscal 1992)
Assets: $3,217,893 (fiscal year ending June 30, 1992)
Gifts Received: $4,807 (fiscal 1992)
Fiscal Note: In fiscal 1992, contributions were received from Servco Pacific, Inc.
EIN: 99-0248256

CONTRIBUTIONS SUMMARY
Typical Recipients: • *Arts & Humanities:* museums/galleries, music • *Civic & Public Affairs:* municipalities • *Education:* business education, colleges & universities • *Health:* hospitals • *Social Services:* united funds
Grant Types: general support
Geographic Distribution: giving limited to HI
Operating Locations: HI (Honolulu)

CORP. OFFICERS
George J. Fukanaga: *CURR EMPL* chmn, ceo: Servco Pacific
Thomas I. Fukanaga: *CURR EMPL* pres, coo: Servco Pacific

GIVING OFFICERS
Patrick D. Ching: treas
Edith M. Endo: secy
Gerald K. Harbottle: vp
Jean H. Nakagawa: vp
George S. Sakurai: vp

APPLICATION INFORMATION

Initial Approach: Send brief letter of inquiry. There are no deadlines.*

Note: For scholarship requests, write for formal application.

OTHER THINGS TO KNOW

Awards scholarships for higher education to spouses and children of Servco Pacific employees.

GRANTS ANALYSIS

Number of Grants: 136
Highest Grant: $25,000
Typical Range: $500 to $1,000
Disclosure Period: fiscal year ending June 30, 1992

RECENT GRANTS

```
25,000  Japanese American
        Museum, Los Ange-
        les, CA
 7,500  American Red
        Cross, Honolulu, HI
 6,500  Pacific Institute of
        Chemical Depend-
        ency, Honolulu, HI
 5,000  University of Ha-
        waii Community
        Colleges, Hono-
        lulu, HI
 3,500  Aloha United Way,
        Honolulu, HI
 2,500  Palama Settlement,
        Honolulu, HI
 2,500  University of Ha-
        waii at Manda Col-
        lege of Business,
        Honolulu, HI
 2,125  Honolulu Sym-
        phony Orchestra,
        Honolulu, HI
 2,125  University of Wash-
        ington, Seattle, WA
 2,000  Kapiolani Medical
        Center, Honolulu,
        HI
```

Service Corp. International

Revenue: $643.2 million
Employees: 11,000
Headquarters: Houston, TX
SIC Major Group:
Nondepository Institutions, Personal Services, and Real Estate

CONTACT

Larry Moller
Manager, Human Resources
Service Corp. International
PO Box 130548
Houston, TX 77219
(713) 522-5141

CONTRIBUTIONS SUMMARY

Operating Locations: TX (Houston)

CORP. OFFICERS

L. William Heiligbrodt: *CURR EMPL* pres, coo, dir: Svc Corp Intl
Robert L. Waltrip: *CURR EMPL* chmn, ceo, dir: Svc Corp Intl

ServiceMaster Co. L.P. / ServiceMaster Foundation

Revenue: $2.1 billion
Employees: 21,000
Headquarters: Downers Grove, IL
SIC Major Group: Business Services, Chemicals & Allied Products, Engineering & Management Services, and Personal Services

CONTACT

Kay Bitts
Executive Manager
ServiceMaster Co. L.P.
2300 Warrenville Rd.
Downers Grove, IL 60515
(708) 968-8194

FINANCIAL SUMMARY

Recent Giving: $233,500 (1990)
Assets: $195,745 (1990)
Gifts Received: $219,130 (1990)
Fiscal Note: In 1990, contributions were received from ServiceMaster Foundation.
EIN: 36-3529559

CONTRIBUTIONS SUMMARY

Typical Recipients: • *Arts & Humanities:* general • *Civic & Public Affairs:* general • *Education:* general • *Health:* general • *Social Services:* general
Grant Types: general support
Nonmonetary Support Types: donated products
Geographic Distribution: headquarters area
Operating Locations: IL (Downers Grove)

CORP. OFFICERS

Kenneth N. Hansen: *CURR EMPL* vchmn: ServiceMaster Co LP
Robert F. Keith: *CURR EMPL* exec vp, cfo: ServiceMaster LP
C. William Pollard: *CURR EMPL* chmn, ceo, dir: ServiceMaster Co LP
Kenneth T. Wessner: *CURR EMPL* vchmn: ServiceMaster Co LP

APPLICATION INFORMATION

Initial Approach: Send brief letter of inquiry, including a description of the organization, amount requested, purpose of funds sought, audited financial statement, and proof of tax-exempt status. There are no deadlines.

GRANTS ANALYSIS

Number of Grants: 19
Highest Grant: $25,000
Typical Range: $2,000 to $10,000
Disclosure Period: 1990

Servico, Inc.

Revenue: $150.0 million
Employees: 4,000
Parent Company: FCD Hospitality, Inc.
Headquarters: West Palm Beach, FL
SIC Major Group: Engineering & Management Services, Holding & Other Investment Offices, and Hotels & Other Lodging Places

CONTACT

Dave Buddemeyer
Vice President of Operations
Servico, Inc.
1601 Belvedere Rd., Ste. 501
West Palm Beach, FL 33406
(407) 689-9970

CONTRIBUTIONS SUMMARY

Operating Locations: FL (West Palm Beach)

CORP. OFFICERS

David E. Hawthoren: *CURR EMPL* ceo: Servico
Vartank Tchekmeian: *CURR EMPL* pres: Servico
Thomas Walker: *CURR EMPL* chmn: Servico

Servistar Corp. / Servistar Foundation

Sales: $1.5 billion
Employees: 1,400
Headquarters: Butler, PA
SIC Major Group: Wholesale Trade—Durable Goods

CONTACT

Russ Thomas
Vice President, Personnel
Servistar Corp.
PO Box 1510
Butler, PA 16003
(412) 283-4567

FINANCIAL SUMMARY

Recent Giving: $8,000 (1993 est.); $3,000 (1992 approx.); $3,000 (1991)

CONTRIBUTIONS SUMMARY

Typical Recipients: • *Education:* career/vocational education
Grant Types: award and scholarship
Nonmonetary Support Types: cause-related marketing & promotion, donated equipment, and donated products
Geographic Distribution: in headquarters and operating communities
Operating Locations: PA (Butler)

CORP. OFFICERS

Peter G. Kelly: *CURR EMPL* chmn: Servistar Corp
Donald Smyth: *CURR EMPL* vchmn: Servistar Corp
Lawrence T. Zehfuss: *CURR EMPL* pres, ceo: Servistar Corp

APPLICATION INFORMATION

Initial Approach: Foundation does not accept applications.
Restrictions on Giving: Contributes only to dependents of Servistar employees.

GRANTS ANALYSIS

Typical Range: $1,000 to $2,500

Seton Co.

Sales: $220.0 million
Employees: 550
Headquarters: Morristown, NJ
SIC Major Group: Chemicals & Allied Products, Leather & Leather Products, and Textile Mill Products

CONTACT

Philip D. Kaltenbacher
Chairman
Seton Co.
2500 Monroe Blvd.
Morristown, NJ 07104
(201) 485-4800

CONTRIBUTIONS SUMMARY

Company sponsors employee matching gift program; also supports community organizations.

Typical Recipients: • *Arts & Humanities:* general • *Civic & Public Affairs:* general • *Education:* general • *Health:* general • *Social Services:* general

Grant Types: matching

Geographic Distribution: primarily headquarters area

Operating Locations: NJ (Morristown), OH (Canton, Toledo), PA (Frazer, Norristown, Saxton)

CORP. OFFICERS

Philip D. Kaltenbacher: *CURR EMPL* chmn, ceo, dir: Seton Co

T. Sertell: *CURR EMPL* pres, coo, dir: Seton Co

APPLICATION INFORMATION

Initial Approach: Send brief letter of inquiry. There are no deadlines.

Setzer Foundation

CONTACT

Setzer Fdn.
2555 Third St., Ste. 200
Sacramento, CA 95818

FINANCIAL SUMMARY

Recent Giving: $258,825 (fiscal 1992); $200,337 (fiscal 1991); $189,090 (fiscal 1990)

Assets: $7,164,664 (fiscal year ending March 31, 1992); $6,139,188 (fiscal 1991); $4,681,908 (fiscal 1990)

EIN: 94-6115578

CONTRIBUTIONS SUMMARY

Donor(s): members of the Setzer family

Typical Recipients: • *Arts & Humanities:* community arts, museums/galleries, opera, public broadcasting • *Civic & Public Affairs:* environmental affairs, zoos/botanical gardens • *Health:* hospitals, medical research, single-disease health associations • *Social Services:*

child welfare, recreation & athletics, youth organizations

Grant Types: general support

Geographic Distribution: focus on CA

GIVING OFFICERS

G. Cal Setzer: trust
Hardie C. Setzer: trust
Mark Setzer: trust

APPLICATION INFORMATION

Initial Approach: Contributes only to preselected organizations.

Restrictions on Giving: Does not support individuals.

GRANTS ANALYSIS

Number of Grants: 108
Highest Grant: $20,000
Typical Range: $1,000 to $3,000
Disclosure Period: fiscal year ending March 31, 1992

RECENT GRANTS

20,000 Sacramento Regional Foundation, Sacramento, CA

10,000 KVIE Public Television, Sacramento, CA

10,000 River Oak Center for Children, Sacramento, CA

10,000 Sacramento Blood Center, Sacramento, CA

10,000 Shriners Hospital, Sacramento, CA

5,000 Crocker Art Museum, Sacramento, CA

5,000 Rudolph Steiner College, Fair Oaks, CA

5,000 Sharing Place, Sacramento, CA

4,800 Eagle Lake Camp, Sacramento, CA

3,000 Society of American Foresters, Sacramento, CA

Seven Springs Foundation

CONTACT

Dorothy S. Lyddon
President
Seven Springs Fdn.
PO Box 687
Cupertino, CA 95015-0687

FINANCIAL SUMMARY

Recent Giving: $98,600 (1990); $86,600 (1989); $82,700 (1988)

Assets: $2,038,287 (1990); $2,303,637 (1989); $2,130,138 (1988)

Gifts Received: $3,559 (1990); $29,717 (1989); $2,269 (1988)

Fiscal Note: In 1990, contributions were received from Dorothy S. Lyddon.

EIN: 94-2570260

CONTRIBUTIONS SUMMARY

Typical Recipients: • *Arts & Humanities:* ethnic arts, museums/galleries • *Civic & Public Affairs:* environmental affairs, ethnic/minority organizations, public policy, urban & community affairs, women's affairs • *Science:* scientific institutes • *Social Services:* youth organizations

Grant Types: project

Geographic Distribution: focus on CA

GIVING OFFICERS

Alvin T. Levitt: dir, secy, treas
John Knight Lyddon: trust
pres Lyddon: off

APPLICATION INFORMATION

Initial Approach: Contributes only to preselected organizations. Applications not accepted.

GRANTS ANALYSIS

Number of Grants: 45
Highest Grant: $10,000
Typical Range: $500 to $1,500
Disclosure Period: 1990

RECENT GRANTS

10,000 Institute of Noetic Sciences, Sausalito, CA

10,000 Resource Renewal Institute, Sausalito, CA

10,000 WISE, San Francisco, CA

5,000 Center for Policy Development, Oakland, CA

5,000 Earth Day 1990, Stanford, CA

5,000 Peace Links, Washington, DC

4,000 Center for Investigative Reporting, San Francisco, CA

4,000 National Museum of Women in the Arts, Washington, DC

3,000 Global Fund for Women, Menlo Park, CA

2,500 Grand Canyon Trust, Washington, DC

Seventh Generation

Sales: $6.0 million
Employees: 50
Headquarters: Colchester, VT
SIC Major Group: Miscellaneous Retail and Wholesale Trade—Nondurable Goods

CONTACT

Oren Kronick
Assistant to the CEO
Seventh Generation
Colchester, VT 05446-1672
(802) 655-6777

CONTRIBUTIONS SUMMARY

Operating Locations: VT (Colchester)

CORP. OFFICERS

Jeffrey Hollender: *CURR EMPL* ceo: Seventh Generation

Sewall Foundation, Elmina

CONTACT

Elmina B. Sewall
President
Elmina Sewall Fdn.
245 Commercial St.
Portland, ME 04101

FINANCIAL SUMMARY

Recent Giving: $421,735 (fiscal 1991); $357,129 (fiscal 1990); $234,000 (fiscal 1988)

Assets: $6,622,592 (fiscal year ending September 30, 1991); $5,286,335 (fiscal 1990); $4,192,641 (fiscal 1988)

Gifts Received: $700,000 (fiscal 1991); $600,000 (fiscal 1990); $642,850 (fiscal 1988)

Fiscal Note: In 1991, contributions were received from Elmina B. Sewall.

EIN: 01-0387404

CONTRIBUTIONS SUMMARY

Donor(s): Elmina B. Sewall

Typical Recipients: • *Arts & Humanities:* history/historic preservation • *Civic & Public Affairs:* environmental affairs • *Health:* medical research, pediatric health, single-disease health associations • *Religion:* churches • *Social Services:* animal protection, community service organizations, disabled, family planning, united funds, youth organizations

Grant Types: general support

APPLICATION INFORMATION
Initial Approach: Contributes only to preselected organizations.
Restrictions on Giving: Does not support individuals.

GRANTS ANALYSIS
Number of Grants: 68
Highest Grant: $67,000
Typical Range: $1,000 to $10,000
Disclosure Period: fiscal year ending September 30, 1991

RECENT GRANTS
67,000 Animal Welfare Society
15,500 Massachusetts SPCA, Boston, MA
12,135 National Society of Colonial Dames of American in the State of Connecticut, McLean, VA
12,000 Wildlife Conservation International
12,000 World Wildlife Fund, Washington, DC
10,000 Nature Conservancy
10,000 Planned Parenthood Federation of America
10,000 Red Acre Farm Hearing Dog Center
7,500 Camp Clara Barton
7,500 Maine Coast Heritage Trust, Portland, ME

Sewell Foundation, Warren P. and Ava F.

CONTACT
R. C. Otwell
Warren P. and Ava F. Sewell Fdn.
301 Hamilton Ave.
Bremen, GA 30110

FINANCIAL SUMMARY
Recent Giving: $10,500 (fiscal 1989); $70,280 (fiscal 1988)
Assets: $4,907,174 (fiscal year ending January 31, 1989); $4,884,165 (fiscal 1988)
EIN: 58-6041342

CONTRIBUTIONS SUMMARY
Donor(s): Warren P. Sewell
Typical Recipients: • *Religion:* churches
Grant Types: capital
Geographic Distribution: focus on GA

GIVING OFFICERS
Lamar R. Plunkett: trust
Jack Worley: trust

APPLICATION INFORMATION
Initial Approach: Send brief letter of inquiry describing program or project. There are no deadlines. Board meets every two months.

Sexton Foundation

CONTACT
Yvonne Sexton
Sexton Fdn.
RR 1 Box 178
Grey Eagle, MN 56336
(612) 285-4321

FINANCIAL SUMMARY
Recent Giving: $99,000 (fiscal 1991); $91,175 (fiscal 1990); $84,500 (fiscal 1989)
Assets: $2,812,324 (fiscal year ending November 30, 1991); $2,076,473 (fiscal 1990); $2,146,963 (fiscal 1989)
Gifts Received: $200,000 (fiscal 1991)
EIN: 41-1312086

CONTRIBUTIONS SUMMARY
Typical Recipients: • *Civic & Public Affairs:* environmental affairs • *Education:* colleges & universities, religious education • *Religion:* churches, missionary activities, religious organizations • *Social Services:* community service organizations, food/clothing distribution, religious welfare, youth organizations
Grant Types: general support

APPLICATION INFORMATION
Initial Approach: Send brief letter describing program. There are no deadlines.

GRANTS ANALYSIS
Number of Grants: 20
Highest Grant: $18,000
Typical Range: $1,000 to $11,000
Disclosure Period: fiscal year ending November 30, 1991

RECENT GRANTS
18,000 College of St. Benedicts, St. Joseph, MN
10,000 Proyecto Adelanti, Dallas, TX
10,000 St. Anthony's School, Dallas, TX

7,000 Sisters of St. Marys, Harringer, TX
6,000 Denton City Clinic, Denton, TX
5,000 Archdiocesan AIDS Ministry, Minneapolis, MN
4,000 Committee of Peace, Washington, DC
3,500 St. Peter and Paul School, St. Cloud, MN
2,500 Wilderness Inquiry, Minneapolis, MN
2,000 Center for Global Education, Minneapolis, MN

Seybert Institution for Poor Boys and Girls, Adam and Maria Sarah
Former Foundation Name: Seybert Institution

CONTACT
Judith L. Bardes
Manager
Adam and Maria Sarah Seybert Institution for Poor Boys and Girls
PO Box 8228
Philadelphia, PA 19101-8228
(215) 828-8145

FINANCIAL SUMMARY
Recent Giving: $284,972 (1991); $305,390 (1990); $182,467 (1989)
Assets: $5,263,178 (1991); $4,549,375 (1990); $4,648,348 (1989)
EIN: 23-6260105

CONTRIBUTIONS SUMMARY
Donor(s): the late Henry Seybert
Typical Recipients: • *Civic & Public Affairs:* ethnic/minority organizations, women's affairs • *Education:* colleges & universities, elementary education, private education (precollege), student aid • *Health:* health funds • *Religion:* religious organizations • *Social Services:* child welfare, community service organizations, counseling, family planning, family services, food/clothing distribution, homes, youth organizations
Grant Types: emergency, research, scholarship, and seed money
Geographic Distribution: limited to Philadelphia, PA

GIVING OFFICERS
William C. Bullitt: pres, trust
Susan C. Day, MD: trust
Graham S. Finney: trust
Hon. Lois G. Forer: vp, trust
Steven R. Garfinkel: secy, treas, trust *B* Philadelphia PA 1943 *ED* Temple Univ 1966 *CURR EMPL* sr vp, comptr: CoreStates Fin Corp *CORP AFFIL* sr vp, comptr: CoreStates Fin Corp
Rev. David I. Hagan: trust
Lallie L. O'Brien: trust
Carver A. Portlock: trust

APPLICATION INFORMATION
Initial Approach: Send brief letter of inquiry describing program. There are no deadlines.
Restrictions on Giving: Does not support individuals.

OTHER THINGS TO KNOW
Publications: Application Guidelines, Annual Report

GRANTS ANALYSIS
Number of Grants: 61
Highest Grant: $28,610
Typical Range: $1,500 to $10,000
Disclosure Period: 1991

RECENT GRANTS
28,610 Germantown Academy Program, Ft. Washington, PA
16,233 Douglass Elementary School, Philadelphia, PA
16,080 Hunter Elementary School, Philadelphia, PA
10,000 Greater Philadelphia Women's Medical Fund, Philadelphia, PA
10,000 Maternity Care Coalition of Greater Philadelphia, Philadelphia, PA
10,000 Planned Parenthood Federation of America, Philadelphia, PA
8,000 St. Hugh Catholic School, Philadelphia, PA — Fine Arts Program
7,500 US Catholic Conference, Philadelphia, PA — Franciscan Residence
6,000 Philadelphia Society for Services to Children, Philadelphia, PA — Kids 'N Kin Program
5,000 Philabundance, Philadelphia, PA —

Emergency Food
Project

Seymour and Troester Foundation

CONTACT
Seymour and Troester Fdn.
21500 Harper Ave.
St. Clair Shores, MI 48080

FINANCIAL SUMMARY
Recent Giving: $145,500
(1990); $153,000 (1989);
$153,000 (1988)
Assets: $3,209,688 (1990);
$3,187,633 (1989); $3,150,866
(1988)
EIN: 38-6062647

CONTRIBUTIONS SUMMARY
Donor(s): the late Charles E.
Troester
Typical Recipients: • *Arts &
Humanities:* arts centers • *Education:* colleges & universities,
private education (precollege),
religious education • *Religion:*
churches • *Social Services:*
child welfare, community service organizations, food/cloth-
ing distribution
Grant Types: general support

GIVING OFFICERS
Kathleen Anderson: vp, secy,
trust
Marcella Lilly: trust
B. A. Seymour, Jr.: pres, treas,
trust
Mrs. B. A. Seymour, Sr.:
chmn, trust

APPLICATION INFORMATION
Initial Approach: Contributes
only to preselected organizations.
Restrictions on Giving: Does
not support individuals.

GRANTS ANALYSIS
Number of Grants: 21
Highest Grant: $50,000
Typical Range: $1,000 to
$10,000
Disclosure Period: 1990

RECENT GRANTS
50,000 Trinity College,
Deerfield, IL
16,500 Georgetown Uni-
versity, Washing-
ton, DC
10,000 Sisters, Servants of
the Immaculate
Heart of Mary, Im-
maculata, PA
10,000 University of De-
troit, Detroit, MI
10,000 University of De-
troit Jesuit High
School and Acad-
emy, Detroit, MI
5,000 Archdiocese of De-
troit, Detroit, MI
5,000 University of Day-
ton, Dayton, OH
5,000 Villanova Univer-
sity, Philadelphia,
PA
3,000 Capuchin Commu-
nity Center Soup
Kitchen, Detroit,
MI

Seymour Foundation, W. L. and Louise E.

CONTACT
W. L. and Louise E. Seymour
Fdn.
c/o Ameritrust Texas N.A.
PO Box 99016
El Paso, TX 79999-0016
(915) 747-1930

FINANCIAL SUMMARY
Recent Giving: $158,300
(1992); $162,500 (1991);
$117,200 (1990)
Assets: $4,094,930 (1992);
$3,934,164 (1991); $3,528,677
(1990)
EIN: 74-6315820

CONTRIBUTIONS SUMMARY
Donor(s): the late Louise E.
Seymour
Typical Recipients: • *Education:* colleges & universities
• *Social Services:* child welfare, day care, disabled, em-
ployment/job training, united
funds, youth organizations
Grant Types: endowment and
general support
Geographic Distribution:
focus on El Paso, TX

GIVING OFFICERS
Ameritrust Texas, N.A.: trust

APPLICATION INFORMATION
Initial Approach: Send brief
letter of inquiry describing program or project. There are no
deadlines.
Restrictions on Giving: Does
not support individuals.

GRANTS ANALYSIS
Number of Grants: 12
Highest Grant: $31,000
Typical Range: $5,000 to
$30,000

Disclosure Period: 1992
Note: 03/31/91

RECENT GRANTS
31,000 House of Cor-
nelius, El Paso, TX
30,000 Lighthouse for the
Blind, El Paso, TX
— living skills
25,150 National Center for
Employment of
Disabled, El Paso,
TX
20,000 YMCA, El Paso,
TX
15,000 Boy Scouts of
America, El Paso,
TX
10,000 CASA, El Paso,
TX — child advo-
cacy
8,000 Bridge Center for
Contemporary Art,
El Paso, TX —
learning disability
program for chil-
dren
5,000 Bridges School, El
Paso, TX — dys-
lexic program
5,000 Danforth Youth
Collaborative, Dan-
forth, TX — youth
program
5,000 El Paso Rehabilita-
tion Center, El
Paso, TX

SGS-Thomson Microelectronics Inc.

Sales: $330.0 million
Employees: 1,900
Headquarters: Carrollton, TX
SIC Major Group: Electronic &
Other Electrical Equipment

CONTACT
Bill Mack
Director, Human Resources
SGS-Thomson Microelectronics
Inc.
1310 Electronic Dr.
Carrollton, TX 75006
(214) 466-6000

CONTRIBUTIONS SUMMARY
Operating Locations: TX
(Carrollton)

CORP. OFFICERS
Daniel Queyssac: *CURR
EMPL* pres: SGS-Thomson Mi-
croelectronics

Shafer Foundation, Richard H. and Ann

CONTACT
Fannie L. Shafer
Manager
Richard H. and Ann Shafer Fdn.
8 East Long St., Rm. 400
Columbus, OH 43215
(614) 224-8111

FINANCIAL SUMMARY
Recent Giving: $87,250
(1991); $88,750 (1990);
$88,750 (1989)
Assets: $1,930,586 (1991);
$1,613,168 (1990); $1,800,029
(1989)
Gifts Received: $5,000 (1991)
Fiscal Note: In 1991, contributions were received from Central Oil Asphalt Corporation.
EIN: 31-6029095

CONTRIBUTIONS SUMMARY
Donor(s): Richard A. Shafer
the late Ohio Road Paving Co.
Typical Recipients: • *Arts &
Humanities:* public broadcasting • *Education:* colleges &
universities • *Health:* hospitals,
medical research, pediatric
health • *Religion:* churches
• *Social Services:* community
service organizations, disabled,
recreation & athletics, united
funds, youth organizations
Grant Types: general support
Geographic Distribution: limited to OH

GIVING OFFICERS
Homer W. Lee: trust
John Reese: trust
Fannie L. Shafer: trust, mgr

APPLICATION INFORMATION
Initial Approach: Send proposal. Deadline is December
10.

GRANTS ANALYSIS
Number of Grants: 30
Highest Grant: $30,000
Typical Range: $500 to $1,000
Disclosure Period: 1991

RECENT GRANTS
30,000 Ohio State Univer-
sity Development
Fund, Columbus,
OH
10,000 Children's Hospi-
tal, Columbus, OH
10,000 Otterbein College,
Columbus, OH
10,000 St. Anthonys Hospital, Columbus, OH

2,500 Central College
Presbyterian
Church, Columbus,
OH

2,500 Central Ohio Radio
Reading Service,
Columbus, OH

2,250 Pilot Dogs, Colum-
bus, OH

1,500 Friends of WOSU,
Columbus, OH

1,500 Recreation Unlim-
ited, Columbus, OH

1,000 Special Wish Foun-
dation, Columbus,
OH

Shaffer Family Charitable Trust

CONTACT
Jack M. Shaffer
Trustee
Shaffer Family Charitable Trust
Route 9, P.O. Box 45
Candy Lane and Bingen Road
Bethlehem, PA 18015
Note: The trust does not list a
telephone number.

FINANCIAL SUMMARY
Recent Giving: $68,599
(1990); $67,500 (1989)
Assets: $2,350,200 (1990);
$1,520,689 (1989)
Gifts Received: $725,000
(1990); $634,753 (1989)
Fiscal Note: In 1989, the foun-
dation received $634,753 from
members of the Shaffer family.
EIN: 23-2502319

CONTRIBUTIONS SUMMARY
Donor(s): the donors are
David and Susan Shaffer, Rose
Shaffer, Cecile Shaffer, and
Jack M. Shaffer, trustees of the
trust
Typical Recipients: • *Civic &
Public Affairs:* philanthropic organizations • *Education:* colleges & universities • *Health:*
health funds • *Religion:*
churches • *Social Services:*
emergency relief, religious welfare, united funds
Grant Types: general support
Geographic Distribution: primarily Bethlehem, PA

GIVING OFFICERS
Cecile Shaffer: don, trust
David Shaffer: don, trust
Jack M. Shaffer: don, trust
Rose Shaffer: don, trust
Susan Shaffer: don, trust

APPLICATION INFORMATION
Initial Approach: The trust reports that an organization seeking a gift may use its usual
fundraising brochure and appeal material. There are no
deadlines.

GRANTS ANALYSIS
Total Grants: $68,599
Number of Grants: 8
Highest Grant: $16,666
Typical Range: $2,500 to
$16,666
Disclosure Period: 1990

RECENT GRANTS
16,666 Jewish Federation
of Allentown

12,500 Bethlehem United
Jewis Appeal

10,000 Lehigh Valley
Easter Seals, PA

10,000 United Way

8,600 New Bethany Min-
istry

5,000 American Red
Cross

3,333 LHDC-Allied Hall

2,500 Diocese of Allen-
town

Shaklee Corp.

Sales: $627.47 million
Employees: 1,200
Parent Company: Yamanouchi
Pharmaceutical Co.
Headquarters: San Francisco, CA
SIC Major Group:
Miscellaneous Retail

CONTACT
Karin Topping
Director, Public Relations
Shaklee Corp.
444 Market St.
San Francisco, CA 94111
(415) 954-3000

FINANCIAL SUMMARY
Recent Giving: $450,000
(1993 est.); $438,000 (1992);
$427,000 (1991)
Fiscal Note: Company gives directly. Totals exclude giving by
subsidiaries.

CONTRIBUTIONS SUMMARY
Typical Recipients: • *Arts &
Humanities:* museums/galler-
ies, music, opera, performing
arts • *Civic & Public Affairs:*
better government, environmental affairs, zoos/botanical gardens • *Education:* colleges &
universities, health & physical
education • *Health:* nutrition &
health maintenance • *Social
Services:* united funds, youth
organizations
Grant Types: employee matching gifts, general support, mul-
tiyear/continuing support, project, and scholarship
Nonmonetary Support Types:
donated equipment and in-kind
services
Note: In 1993, nonmonetary
support was estimated at
$125,000. In 1992, support was
$120,000. In 1990, support was
$115,000. This suppport is ex-
cluded in total giving figures
Geographic Distribution:
areas where company employees live and to national organizations
Operating Locations: CA (La
Palma, San Francisco), IL (Bedford Park), NJ (Dayton), OK
(Norman)

CORP. OFFICERS
David M. Chamberlain: *B*
Fort Benning GA 1943 *ED*
Univ PA BS 1965; Harvard
Univ MBA 1969 *CURR EMPL*
chmn, pres, ceo: Shaklee Corp
NONPR AFFIL dir: San Fran-
cisco Boys & Girls Club, San
Francisco Opera Assn, US
Chamber Commerce, Washing-
ton CA Roundtable; pres: San
Francisco Chamber Commerce

GIVING OFFICERS
Donald Karn: *CURR EMPL*
pres (corp contributions
comm): Shaklee Canada
John Teft: *CURR EMPL* sr vp
(bus strategies): Shaklee Corp
Karin Topping: *CURR EMPL*
dir (publ rels): Shaklee Corp

APPLICATION INFORMATION
Initial Approach: *Initial Contact:* typewritten letter no
longer than two pages *Include
Information On:* description of
the organization including history, function, goals, and objectives; description and specific
objectives of current program
or project for which funds are
being requested; amount requested, specific uses for it,
and benefits expected; geographic area and persons served
by organization, program, or
project *When to Submit:* any
time, requests reviewed on a
quarterly basis; if preliminary
evaluation meets with policy
and priorities, organization
may be asked to complete formal application
Restrictions on Giving: Contributions generally not considered for individuals; research;
capital or building funds; sectarian or religious institutions
that do not serve the general
public on a nondenominational
basis; political groups; conferences or seminars; fraternal orders, veterans, or labor groups;
contests, raffles, or prize-oriented events; goodwill advertising; or organizations primarily
funded through united funds or
federated campaigns.

GRANTS ANALYSIS
Total Grants: $438,000
Typical Range: $1,000 to
$10,000
Disclosure Period: 1992

Shapell Foundation, Nathan and Lilly

CONTACT
Nathan and Lilly Shapell Fdn.
8383 Wilshire Blvd., Ste. 724
Beverly Hills, CA 90211-2470

FINANCIAL SUMMARY
Recent Giving: $177,350 (fis-
cal 1992); $371,000 (fiscal
1991); $56,350 (fiscal 1990)
Assets: $4,391,863 (fiscal year
ending May 31, 1992);
$3,830,375 (fiscal 1991);
$3,421,590 (fiscal 1990)
Gifts Received: $170,293 (fis-
cal 1992); $176,520 (fiscal
1991); $84,300 (fiscal 1990)
Fiscal Note: In fiscal 1992,
contributions were received
from Berwyn Corporation
($10,000), Shapell Industries
($57,580), Nathan Shapell
($87,040), and Leadership
Homes ($15,464).
EIN: 95-6047847

CONTRIBUTIONS SUMMARY
Donor(s): Nathan Shapell
Typical Recipients: • *Arts &
Humanities:* museums/galleries
• *Civic & Public Affairs:* eth-
nic/minority organizations
• *Education:* colleges & univer-
sities, religious education
• *Health:* hospitals • *Religion:*
religious organizations, syna-
gogues • *Social Services:* com-
munity service organizations
Grant Types: general support

GIVING OFFICERS
Howard Schwartz: asst secy
Lilly Shapell: secy, treas
Nathan Shapell: pres *B* Sos-
nowiec Poland 1922 *CURR
EMPL* chmn, ceo, dir: Shapell
Indus

APPLICATION INFORMATION

Initial Approach: Contributes only to preselected organizations.

GRANTS ANALYSIS
Number of Grants: 9
Highest Grant: $150,000
Typical Range: $1,000 to $5,000
Disclosure Period: fiscal year ending May 31, 1992

RECENT GRANTS

150,000 Bar-Ilan University, New York, NY
5,500 United Jewish Appeal Federation of Jewish Philanthropies, Los Angeles, CA
5,000 Los Angeles County Museum of Art, Los Angeles, CA
5,000 Vista Del Mar, Los Angeles, CA
4,500 Cedars-Sinai Medical Center, Los Angeles, CA
4,000 Hebrew University, Los Angeles, CA
2,250 Tel Hashomer, Los Angeles, CA
1,000 Stephen Wise Temple, Los Angeles, CA
100 Luden Center, Los Angeles, CA

Shapell Industries, Inc. / Shapell Foundation

Revenue: $95.0 million
Employees: 425
Headquarters: Beverly Hills, CA
SIC Major Group: General Building Contractors and Real Estate

CONTACT
Howard Schwartz
Administrative Asst. to the President
Shapell Industries, Inc.
8383 Wilshire Blvd., Ste. 724
Beverly Hills, CA 90211
(213) 651-4402

CONTRIBUTIONS SUMMARY
Operating Locations: CA (Beverly Hills)

CORP. OFFICERS
Nathan Shapell: *CURR EMPL* chmn, pres: Shapell Indus

Shapero Foundation, Nate S. and Ruth B.

CONTACT
Nate S. and Ruth B. Shapero Fdn.
2290 First National Bldg.
Detroit, MI 48216-1555

FINANCIAL SUMMARY
Recent Giving: $214,185 (fiscal 1992); $222,912 (fiscal 1991); $189,550 (fiscal 1990)
Assets: $2,669,368 (fiscal year ending April 30, 1992); $2,524,686 (fiscal 1991); $2,409,578 (fiscal 1990)
EIN: 38-6041567

CONTRIBUTIONS SUMMARY
Donor(s): the late Nate S. Shapero, Ray A. Shapero
Typical Recipients: • *Arts & Humanities:* arts institutes, community arts, music, performing arts • *Civic & Public Affairs:* municipalities • *Education:* colleges & universities, religious education • *Religion:* religious organizations, synagogues • *Social Services:* community service organizations, religious welfare, united funds, volunteer services, youth organizations
Grant Types: general support
Geographic Distribution: focus on MI

GIVING OFFICERS
Alan E. Schwartz: trust *B* Detroit MI 1925 *ED* Univ MI BA 1947; Harvard Univ LLB 1950 *CURR EMPL* sr mem: Honigman Miller Schwartz & Cohn *CORP AFFIL* dir: Comerica, Core Indus, Detroit Edison Co, Handleman Co, Howell Indus Inc, PHM Corp, Unisys Corp *NONPR AFFIL* dir: Detroit Econ Growth Corp, Detroit Renaissance, Jewish Welfare Fdn Detroit, Metro Affs Corp, New Detroit; trust: Commun Fdn SE MI, Harper-Grace Hosp, Interlochen Arts Academy; vp, dir: Un Fdn; vp, mem exec comm: Detroit Symphony Orchestra; advmem: Arts Comm City of Detroit; mem: MI Bar Assn; mem visitors comm bd: Harvard Univ Law Sch
Marianne S. Schwartz: trust
J.E. Shapero: treas
Ray A. Shapero: chmn
Gloria Stalla: secy

APPLICATION INFORMATION
Initial Approach: Contributes only to preselected organizations.

GRANTS ANALYSIS
Number of Grants: 38
Highest Grant: $90,000
Typical Range: $100 to $5,000
Disclosure Period: fiscal year ending April 30, 1992

RECENT GRANTS
90,000 Federation of Allied Jewish Appeal, Detroit, MI
40,160 Temple Beth-El, Detroit, MI
23,000 Detroit Symphony Orchestra, Detroit, MI
17,500 Boy Scouts of America, Detroit, MI
5,500 Archives of American Art, New York, NY
5,500 Madonna College, St. Paul, MN
5,000 United Way, Detroit, MI
4,230 Detroit Institute of Arts, Detroit, MI
2,150 Michigan Thanksgiving Day Parade Foundation, Detroit, MI
2,000 United Jewish Charities, Detroit, MI

Shapiro, Inc. / Shapiro Charitable Trust, J. B. & Maurice C.
Headquarters: Potomac, MD

CONTACT
J.B. & Maurice C. Shapiro Charitable Trust
12012 Piney Glen Ln.
Potomac, MD 20854

FINANCIAL SUMMARY
Recent Giving: $3,515,000 (fiscal 1992); $640,000 (fiscal 1991); $450,000 (fiscal 1990)
Assets: $8,393,645 (fiscal year ending July 31, 1992); $11,269,957 (fiscal 1991); $11,201,993 (fiscal 1990)
EIN: 52-6073880

CONTRIBUTIONS SUMMARY
Typical Recipients: • *Arts & Humanities:* arts centers, public broadcasting • *Civic & Public Affairs:* ethnic/minority organizations, urban & community affairs • *Health:* hospitals, pediatric health • *Religion:* religious organizations • *Social Services:* animal protection, community service organizations, food/clothing distribution, religious welfare, united funds
Grant Types: general support
Geographic Distribution: primarily in the Washington, DC, area

GIVING OFFICERS
Kathleen Carpenter Kester: trust
Leonard S. Melrod: trust
Gary Roggin: trust
Perry L. Sandler: trust

APPLICATION INFORMATION
Initial Approach: Foundation reports it contributes only to preselected organizations. Applications not accepted.

GRANTS ANALYSIS
Number of Grants: 12
Highest Grant: $3,000,000
Typical Range: $5,000 to $25,000
Disclosure Period: fiscal year ending July 31, 1992

RECENT GRANTS
3,000,000 George Washington University, Washington, DC
125,000 Hospital for Sick Children, Washington, DC
75,000 Suburban Hospital, Bethesda, MD
50,000 Jewish Social Service Agency, Rockville, MD
50,000 Luther Place N Street Village, Washington, DC
50,000 United Jewish Appeal Federation of Jewish Philanthropies, Rockville, MD
25,000 Children's Oncology Center, Washington, DC
25,000 Community for Creative Non-Violence, Washington, DC
25,000 Strathmore Hall Foundation, Rockville, MD
25,000 WETA Television, Washington, DC

Shapiro Charity Fund, Abraham

CONTACT
George Shapiro
Trustee
Abraham Shapiro Charity Fund
63 Sprague St.
Readville, MA 02136
(617) 361-1201

FINANCIAL SUMMARY
Recent Giving: $378,900 (1991); $326,000 (1990); $315,500 (1989)
Assets: $5,342,242 (1991); $5,053,137 (1990); $5,601,353 (1989)
EIN: 04-6043588

CONTRIBUTIONS SUMMARY
Donor(s): Abraham Shapiro
Typical Recipients: • *Civic & Public Affairs:* ethnic/minority organizations, philanthropic organizations • *Education:* colleges & universities • *Health:* hospitals, pediatric health, single-disease health associations • *Religion:* religious organizations • *Social Services:* united funds
Grant Types: general support
Geographic Distribution: focus on MA

GIVING OFFICERS
Arthur S. Goldberg: trust
George Shapiro: trust
Philip Shir: trust

APPLICATION INFORMATION
Initial Approach: Send brief letter of inquiry describing program or project. The foundation board meets quarterly.
Restrictions on Giving: Does not support individuals or provide loans, scholarships, or matching gifts.

GRANTS ANALYSIS
Number of Grants: 15
Highest Grant: $145,000
Typical Range: $500 to $50,000
Disclosure Period: 1991

RECENT GRANTS
145,000 Combined Jewish Philanthropies, Boston, MA
80,000 Brandeis University, Waltham, MA
50,000 American Friends of Hebrew University, New York, NY
50,000 Northeast Medical Center, Boston, MA
25,000 Children's Hospital Medical Center, Boston, MA
15,000 Handi Kids, Boston, MA
4,000 United Way, Boston, MA
2,500 Chabad House, Boston, MA
2,500 Recuperative Center, Boston, MA
1,000 Alzheimer's Disease and Related Disorders Association, Boston, MA

Shapiro Family Foundation, Soretta and Henry

CONTACT
Henry Shapiro
Trustee
Soretta and Henry Shapiro Family Fdn.
1540 North Lake Shore Dr.
Chicago, IL 60610

FINANCIAL SUMMARY
Recent Giving: $386,863 (1991); $418,515 (1990); $442,659 (1989)
Assets: $2,641,645 (1991); $2,688,237 (1990); $2,943,146 (1989)
EIN: 23-7063846

CONTRIBUTIONS SUMMARY
Donor(s): Isaac and Fannie Shapiro Memorial Foundation
Typical Recipients: • *Arts & Humanities:* arts festivals, arts institutes, community arts, music, opera • *Civic & Public Affairs:* ethnic/minority organizations, philanthropic organizations • *Education:* colleges & universities, religious education • *Health:* hospitals • *Religion:* religious organizations • *Social Services:* community service organizations, united funds, youth organizations
Grant Types: research
Geographic Distribution: focus on Chicago, IL

GIVING OFFICERS
Henry Shapiro: trust *B* Chelsea MA 1915 *ED* Northwestern Univ BS 1937 *CORP AFFIL* dir: Ft Howard Corp

APPLICATION INFORMATION
Initial Approach: Send brief letter describing program. There are no deadlines.

GRANTS ANALYSIS
Number of Grants: 308
Highest Grant: $132,000
Typical Range: $500 to $5,000
Disclosure Period: 1991

RECENT GRANTS
132,000 Jewish United Fund, Chicago, IL
50,000 Chicago Symphony, Chicago, IL
50,000 Northwestern University, Evanston, IL
10,000 Jewish Theological Seminary, New York, NY
10,000 Orchestral Association, Chicago, IL
5,000 American Friends of Hebrew University, New York, NY
5,000 American Friends of Israel Philharmonic Orchestra, Chicago, IL
5,000 Art Institute of Chicago, Chicago, IL
5,000 Lyric Opera of Chicago, Chicago, IL
5,000 University of Chicago, Chicago, IL

Shapiro Foundation, Carl and Ruth

CONTACT
Carl and Ruth Shapiro Fdn.
Two North Breakers Row
Palm Beach, FL 33480

FINANCIAL SUMMARY
Recent Giving: $699,340 (1991); $372,585 (1989); $436,750 (1988)
Assets: $6,587,050 (1991); $3,005,850 (1989); $2,274,461 (1988)
Gifts Received: $3,292,635 (1991); $400,000 (1989)
Fiscal Note: In 1991, contributions were received from Carl Shapiro.
EIN: 04-6135027

CONTRIBUTIONS SUMMARY
Typical Recipients: • *Education:* colleges & universities, private education (precollege) • *Health:* hospitals, medical research, pediatric health • *Religion:* religious organizations
Grant Types: general support

GIVING OFFICERS
Carl Shapiro: pres
Ruth Shapiro: secy

APPLICATION INFORMATION
Initial Approach: Contributes only to preselected organizations.

GRANTS ANALYSIS
Number of Grants: 43
Highest Grant: $235,000
Typical Range: $1,000 to $20,000
Disclosure Period: 1991

RECENT GRANTS
235,000 Combined Jewish Philanthropies, Boston, MA
180,000 Kravis Center for the Performing Arts, West Palm Beach, FL
104,000 Brandeis University, Waltham, MA
50,000 Combined Jewish Philanthropies, Boston, MA
25,000 Children's Medical Center, Boston, MA
20,000 Wellesley College, Wellesley, MA
15,000 Wang Center, Boston, MA
12,000 Brimmer and May School, Boston, MA
10,000 Jewish Federation, Boston, MA
10,000 Recuperative Center, Boston, MA

Shapiro Foundation, Charles and M. R.

CONTACT
Phillip B. Heller
President
Charles and M. R. Shapiro Fdn.
200 North LaSalle St.
Chicago, IL 60601
(312) 346-3100

FINANCIAL SUMMARY
Recent Giving: $1,161,349 (fiscal 1991); $1,125,430 (fiscal 1990); $958,690 (fiscal 1988)
Assets: $17,397,235 (fiscal year ending July 31, 1991); $16,727,967 (fiscal 1990); $14,789,290 (fiscal 1988)
EIN: 36-6109757

CONTRIBUTIONS SUMMARY
Donor(s): The foundation was incorporated in 1958 by the late Charles Shapiro, the late Mary Shapiro, the late Molly Shapiro, and the late Morris R. Shapiro.

Typical Recipients: • _Arts & Humanities:_ history/historic preservation, music • _Civic & Public Affairs:_ ethnic/minority organizations • _Education:_ colleges & universities, religious education • _Health:_ hospices • _International:_ foreign educational institutions • _Religion:_ religious organizations, synagogues • _Social Services:_ child welfare, disabled, emergency relief, refugee assistance, youth organizations
Grant Types: general support
Geographic Distribution: some nationally, with a focus on Chicago, IL

GIVING OFFICERS
Andrew Akos: vp
Phillip B. Heller: pres
Joseph L. Muskal: secy

APPLICATION INFORMATION
Initial Approach: Restrictions on Giving: The foundation supports preselected organizations and does not accept unsolicited requests for funds. The foundation does not make grants to individuals.

GRANTS ANALYSIS
Total Grants: $1,161,349
Number of Grants: 74
Highest Grant: $384,000
Typical Range: $1,000 to $50,000
Disclosure Period: fiscal year ending July 31, 1991
Note: Recent grants are derived from a fiscal 1991 grants list.

RECENT GRANTS
384,000 Temple Sholom, Chicago, IL
225,000 Jewish United Fund, Chicago, IL
85,000 Hebrew Union College Jewish Institute Religion, Cincinnati, OH
50,000 Chicago Chapter Magen David Adom, Chicago, IL
40,000 Association of Jewish Blind of Chicago, Chicago, IL
35,000 Hebrew Theological College, Skokie, IL
30,000 Olin Sang Ruby Union Institute, Chicago, IL
27,500 Board of Jewish Education, Chicago, IL
25,100 American Friends of Sanz Medical Center, Chicago, IL — Laniado Hospital

25,000 American Committee for Weizmann Institute, New York, NY

Shapiro Fund, Albert

CONTACT
Irving Cohen
Secretary-Treasurer
Albert Shapiro Fund
2 Hopkins Plaza, Ste. 1200
Baltimore, MD 21201
(410) 385-4099

FINANCIAL SUMMARY
Recent Giving: $229,466 (fiscal 1992); $225,681 (fiscal 1991); $169,600 (fiscal 1989)
Assets: $4,437,496 (fiscal year ending May 31, 1991); $4,290,211 (fiscal 1989); $3,332,495 (fiscal 1988)
EIN: 52-1300277

CONTRIBUTIONS SUMMARY
Typical Recipients: • _Arts & Humanities:_ museums/galleries, music, performing arts • _Civic & Public Affairs:_ ethnic/minority organizations, philanthropic organizations • _Health:_ geriatric health, hospitals • _International:_ international development/relief • _Religion:_ religious organizations • _Social Services:_ religious welfare, united funds
Grant Types: general support
Geographic Distribution: focus on Baltimore, MD, and Palm Beach, FL

GIVING OFFICERS
Irving Cohen: secy, treas
Albert Shapiro: pres _B_ Somerville MA 1913 _ED_ Univ MD BS 1934; Univ MD MD 1937
Eileen C. Shapiro: vp _ED_ Harvard Univ MBA 1981 _CURR EMPL_ pres: Hillcrest Group

APPLICATION INFORMATION
Initial Approach: Send brief letter of inquiry describing program or project. There are no deadlines.
Restrictions on Giving: Does not support individuals.

GRANTS ANALYSIS
Number of Grants: 35
Highest Grant: $110,000
Typical Range: $1,000 to $5,000
Disclosure Period: fiscal year ending May 31, 1991

RECENT GRANTS
110,000 Associated Jewish Charities and Welfare Fund, Baltimore, MD
16,666 Associated Jewish Charities and Welfare Fund, Baltimore, MD
5,000 Baltimore Hebrew Congregation, Baltimore, MD
5,000 Beth Israel Hospital, Boston, MA
5,000 Holocaust Memorial Museum, Washington, DC
5,000 St. Marys Hospital Foundation, West Palm Beach, FL
1,000 Jewish Federation of Palm Beach County, Palm Beach, FL
350 Hadassah, Palm Beach, FL
200 Jewish Guild for the Blind, Palm Beach, FL
150 Torah Institute of Baltimore, Baltimore, MD

Share Foundation

CONTACT
James Jeffrey
Manager
Share Fdn.
11901 Grandview Rd.
Grandview, MO 64030
(816) 966-2222

FINANCIAL SUMMARY
Recent Giving: $952,452 (1990); $894,990 (1989); $715,890 (1988)
Assets: $18,710,117 (1990); $18,171,910 (1989); $13,045,066 (1988)
Gifts Received: $5,425 (1990)
Fiscal Note: In 1990, contributions were received from Demi Lloyd Kiersznowski.
EIN: 43-6054985

CONTRIBUTIONS SUMMARY
Donor(s): The foundation was established in 1965 by Harry J. Lloyd and House of Lloyd, Inc.
Typical Recipients: • _Education:_ colleges & universities, private education (precollege), religious education • _Health:_ medical research, mental health, single-disease health associations • _International:_ international development/relief • _Religion:_ churches, religious organizations • _Social Services:_ child welfare, community serv-

ice organizations, counseling, family planning, food/clothing distribution, homes, recreation & athletics, religious welfare, shelters/homelessness, united funds, volunteer services, youth organizations
Grant Types: general support
Geographic Distribution: some national, with a focus on Kansas City, MO

GIVING OFFICERS
Jami Kay: dir
Demi Lloyd Kiersznowski: dir
Harry J. Lloyd: pres, treas
Patricia A. Lloyd: asst treas
Gene Rietfors: vp

APPLICATION INFORMATION
Initial Approach:
The foundation requests applications be made in writing. Written proposals should include a description of the organization, its history, and its purpose; documentation of 501(c)(3) charity status; a full review of the proposed project for which funds are requested; a summary of the program and its budget; a copy of the most recent annual report and a list of board members; and a copy of the current operating budget. The foundation has no deadline for submitting proposals.
Restrictions on Giving: The foundation reports grants are primarily given to support Christian causes. The foundation does not make grants to individuals.

GRANTS ANALYSIS
Total Grants: $952,422
Number of Grants: 157
Highest Grant: $100,000
Typical Range: $200 to $10,000
Disclosure Period: 1990
Note: Recent grants are derived from a 1990 grants list.

RECENT GRANTS
100,000 Southwest Baptist University, Bolivar, MO
90,367 I'm Third Foundation, Kansas City, MO
50,000 Life Action Ministries, Kansas City, MO
50,000 Ministry of Money, Gaithersburg, MD
39,559 I'm Friend Foundation, Kansas City, MO
38,361 Khilath Israel Synagogue, Kansas City, MO

35,000 Slavic Gospel Association, Wheaton, IL

30,690 William Jewell College, Liberty, MO

30,000 All Stars Community Outreach for Christ, Kansas City, MO

30,000 Bill Glass Evangelistic Association, Cedar Hill, TX

Share Trust, Charles Morton

CONTACT
Charles Morton Share Trust
c/o Liberty National Bank and Trust Co.
PO Box 25848, Trust Dept.
Oklahoma City, OK 73125
(405) 231-6815

FINANCIAL SUMMARY
Recent Giving: $410,560 (fiscal 1992); $306,100 (fiscal 1990); $632,560 (fiscal 1987)
Assets: $7,824,986 (fiscal year ending June 30, 1990); $7,314,609 (fiscal 1987)
EIN: 73-6090984

CONTRIBUTIONS SUMMARY
Donor(s): the late Charles Morton Share
Typical Recipients: • *Arts & Humanities:* libraries, museums/galleries • *Civic & Public Affairs:* municipalities • *Education:* colleges & universities, education funds, public education (precollege) • *Health:* hospitals, medical research • *Social Services:* community service organizations, disabled, youth organizations
Grant Types: scholarship
Geographic Distribution: focus on OK

GIVING OFFICERS
J. R. Holder: trust
C. E. Johnson: trust
Gertrude Myers: trust
B. H. Thornton: trust

APPLICATION INFORMATION
Initial Approach: Send cover letter and full proposal. There are no deadlines.
Restrictions on Giving: Does not support individuals.

GRANTS ANALYSIS
Number of Grants: 17
Highest Grant: $75,000
Typical Range: $1,500 to $5,000

Disclosure Period: fiscal year ending June 30, 1990

RECENT GRANTS
75,000 City of Alva, Alva, OK

50,000 Alva Public Schools, Alva, OK

50,000 Cherokee Strip Museum Association, Alva, OK

35,000 Woods County Commission, District 2, Alva, OK

32,000 Alva Public Schools, Alva, OK

30,000 City of Alva, Alva, OK — capital improvements

20,000 Oklahoma Pharmacy Heritage Foundation, Oklahoma City, OK

15,000 Museum of Plains, OK

14,000 City of Alva, Alva, OK

10,000 Boy Scouts of America, Alva, OK

Shared Medical Systems Corp.
Revenue: $438.7 million
Employees: 4,093
Headquarters: Malvern, PA
SIC Major Group: Business Services

CONTACT
Marilyn Marchant
Chairman
Shared Medical Systems Corp.
51 Valley Stream Pkwy.
Malvern, PA 19355
(215) 219-6300

CONTRIBUTIONS SUMMARY
Operating Locations: PA (Malvern)

CORP. OFFICERS
R. J. Macaleer: *CURR EMPL* chmn, ceo: Shared Med Sys Corp

Sharon Steel Corp. / SharonSteel Foundation
Sales: $500.0 million
Employees: 3,000
Headquarters: Farrell, PA
SIC Major Group: Coal Mining, Fabricated Metal Products, Primary Metal Industries, and Wholesale Trade—Durable Goods

CONTACT
Melvin G. Sander
Trustee
SharonSteel Fdn.
15 Roemer Blvd.
Farrell, PA 16121
(412) 983-6336

FINANCIAL SUMMARY
Recent Giving: $102,750 (1991); $177,075 (1990); $468,350 (1989)
Assets: $2,969,185 (1991); $2,928,727 (1990); $2,900,362 (1989)
EIN: 25-6063133

CONTRIBUTIONS SUMMARY
Typical Recipients: • *Arts & Humanities:* community arts, music, opera, performing arts, public broadcasting, theater • *Education:* colleges & universities • *Health:* hospitals, medical research, single-disease health associations • *Religion:* religious organizations • *Social Services:* community service organizations, recreation & athletics, united funds, youth organizations
Grant Types: general support
Geographic Distribution: focus on PA
Operating Locations: PA (Farrell)

CORP. OFFICERS
John D. Fry: *CURR EMPL* pres, coo: Sharon Steel Corp
Wolfgang Jansen: *CURR EMPL* co-chmn: Sharon Steel Corp
Walter Sieckman: *CURR EMPL* co-chmn, ceo: Sharon Steel Corp

GIVING OFFICERS
Christian L. Oberbeck: trust
Malvin G. Sander: trust

APPLICATION INFORMATION
Initial Approach: Send brief letter describing program. There are no deadlines.

GRANTS ANALYSIS
Number of Grants: 6
Highest Grant: $75,000
Typical Range: $500 to $1,000
Disclosure Period: 1991

RECENT GRANTS
75,000 WYTV/Youngstown Broadcasting Company Community Service Grant, Youngstown, OH

25,000 Buhl Farm Trust, Wheatland, PA

1,000 City of Sharon Desquicentennial, Sharon, PA

750 Junior Achievement, Farrell, PA

500 Farrell/Wheatland Little League, Farrell, PA

500 Westminster College Annual Fund, Farrell, PA

Sharp Electronics Corp.
Sales: $2.0 billion
Employees: 2,100
Headquarters: Mahwah, NJ
SIC Major Group: Electronic & Other Electrical Equipment, Industrial Machinery & Equipment, and Instruments & Related Products

CONTACT
Manfred Edelman
Vice President, Human Resources
Sharp Electronics Corp.
Sharp Plz.
Mahwah, NJ 07430
(201) 529-8200

FINANCIAL SUMMARY
Fiscal Note: Annual Giving Range: $100,000 to $200,000

CONTRIBUTIONS SUMMARY
Company reports 40% of contributions go to education; 30% to health and human services; and 30% to civic affairs. Interests include educational organizations, community organizations, and youth organizations in local operating communities.
Typical Recipients: • *Education:* colleges & universities • *Social Services:* community service organizations, united funds, youth organizations
Geographic Distribution: WGIV: headquarters and operating locations
Operating Locations: NY (Mahwah)

CORP. OFFICERS
Sueyuki Hirooka: *CURR EMPL* chmn, pres: Sharp Electronics

GIVING OFFICERS
Manfred Edelman: *CURR EMPL* vp (human resources): Sharp Electronics Corp

APPLICATION INFORMATION
Initial Approach: Initial contact may be a brief letter of in-

quiry; however, unsolicited requests are not encouraged.

Sharp Foundation

CONTACT
Sharp Fdn.
1370 Avenue of the Americas, 20th Fl.
New York, NY 10019-4602

FINANCIAL SUMMARY
Recent Giving: $1,286,026 (fiscal 1990); $641,430 (fiscal 1989)
Assets: $3,249,935 (fiscal year ending June 30, 1990); $2,462,391 (fiscal 1989)
Gifts Received: $1,463,125 (fiscal 1990); $1,039,375 (fiscal 1989)
EIN: 13-3253731

CONTRIBUTIONS SUMMARY
Donor(s): Peter J. Sharp
Typical Recipients: • *Arts & Humanities:* arts centers, dance, libraries, museums/galleries, music, opera, performing arts, public broadcasting • *Social Services:* community service organizations, disabled
Grant Types: scholarship
Geographic Distribution: focus on New York, NY

GIVING OFFICERS
Charles Herrick: treas
Peter J. Sharp: pres
Joy Weber: secy

APPLICATION INFORMATION
Initial Approach: Contributes only to preselected organizations.
Restrictions on Giving: Does not support individuals.

GRANTS ANALYSIS
Number of Grants: 22
Highest Grant: $1,077,360
Typical Range: $1,500 to $25,000
Disclosure Period: fiscal year ending June 30, 1990

RECENT GRANTS
1,077,360 Metropolitan Museum of Art, New York, NY
220,000 Lincoln Center for the Performing Arts, New York, NY
192,500 Juilliard School, New York, NY
108,000 Solomon R. Guggenheim Museum, New York, NY
58,333 Art Museum at Princeton University, Princeton, NJ
33,333 Metropolitan Opera Association, New York, NY
25,000 Quebec Labrador Foundation, Ipswich, MA
25,000 Simon's Rock of Bard College, Great Barrington, MA
15,000 International Center for the Disabled, New York, NY
10,000 Spoleto Festival USA, Charleston, SC

Sharp Foundation, Charles S. and Ruth C.

CONTACT
Ruth Collins Sharp
President
Charles S. and Ruth C. Sharp Fdn.
c/o Security Bank Bldg., No. 504
2626 Cole Ave.
Dallas, TX 75204

FINANCIAL SUMMARY
Recent Giving: $204,850 (1991); $151,700 (1990); $188,600 (1989)
Assets: $3,666,493 (1991); $3,412,401 (1990); $3,380,425 (1989)
Gifts Received: $50,965 (1989); $56,393 (1986)
EIN: 75-6045366

CONTRIBUTIONS SUMMARY
Donor(s): Charles S. Sharp, Ruth Collins Sharp
Typical Recipients: • *Arts & Humanities:* public broadcasting • *Education:* colleges & universities, medical education • *Health:* hospitals, medical research, nursing services, single-disease health associations • *Religion:* churches, religious organizations • *Social Services:* community service organizations, counseling, united funds, youth organizations
Grant Types: general support and operating expenses
Geographic Distribution: focus on Dallas, TX

GIVING OFFICERS
Margot Cryer: secy, treas, dir
Sally S. Jacobson: dir
Susan S. McAdam: dir
Charles S. Sharp, Jr.: dir

Ruth Collins Sharp: pres, dir

APPLICATION INFORMATION
Initial Approach: Contributes only to preselected organizations.

GRANTS ANALYSIS
Number of Grants: 29
Highest Grant: $50,000
Typical Range: $500 to $5,000
Disclosure Period: 1991

RECENT GRANTS
50,000 Visiting Nurses Association, Dallas, TX
31,000 Albert Schweitzer Foundation, Great Barrington, MA
27,500 Salvation Army, Dallas, TX
10,000 AIDS Arms Network, Dallas, TX
10,000 AIDS Resource Center, Dallas, TX
10,000 Baylor College of Dentistry, Dallas, TX
8,000 East Dallas Cooperative Parish, Dallas, TX
5,000 Bethphage of Dallas, Dallas, TX
5,000 Collegiate School, New York, NY

Sharp Foundation, Evelyn

CONTACT
Evelyn Sharp
President
Evelyn Sharp Fdn.
1370 Avenue of the Americas
New York, NY 10019
(212) 603-1333

FINANCIAL SUMMARY
Recent Giving: $290,577 (fiscal 1992); $244,910 (fiscal 1991); $233,000 (fiscal 1990)
Assets: $6,459,555 (fiscal year ending June 30, 1992); $5,745,936 (fiscal 1991); $5,756,911 (fiscal 1990)
EIN: 13-6119532

CONTRIBUTIONS SUMMARY
Donor(s): Evelyn Sharp, and others
Typical Recipients: • *Arts & Humanities:* dance, museums/galleries, opera, performing arts, public broadcasting, theater • *Education:* arts education • *Health:* medical research • *Social Services:* child welfare, disabled, family planning, family services, youth organizations
Grant Types: general support
Geographic Distribution: focus on NY

GIVING OFFICERS
Mary Cronson: vp, trust
Paul Cronson: vp, trust
Jeremiah Milbank, Jr.: vp, trust *B* New York NY 1920 *ED* Yale Univ BA 1942; Harvard Univ MBA 1948; Manhattan Coll LLD *CURR EMPL* pres: Cypress Woods Corp *NONPR AFFIL* chmn: Boys & Girls Clubs Am; hon pres: Intl Ctr Disabled; trust: Madison Ctr Ed Affs
Peter J. Sharp: vp, trust
Barry Tobias: treas

APPLICATION INFORMATION
Initial Approach: Send brief letter of inquiry describing program or project. There are no deadlines.

GRANTS ANALYSIS
Number of Grants: 23
Highest Grant: $50,000
Typical Range: $2,000 to $5,000
Disclosure Period: fiscal year ending June 30, 1992

RECENT GRANTS
50,000 Solomon Guggenheim Museum, New York, NY
38,077 WNET Thirteen, New York, NY
30,000 New York City Ballet, New York, NY
30,000 New York City Opera, New York, NY
21,000 Juilliard School, New York, NY
20,000 Boys and Girls Club, New York, NY
20,000 Planned Parenthood Federation of America, New York, NY
10,000 Brooklyn Academy of Music, Brooklyn, NY
8,000 National Dance Institute, New York, NY
7,000 Harlem School of Arts, New York, NY

Shatford Memorial Trust, J. D.

CONTACT
Barbara Strohmeier
J. D. Shatford Memorial Trust
c/o Chemical Bank
30 Rockefeller Plz.
New York, NY 10112
(212) 621-2148

FINANCIAL SUMMARY
Recent Giving: $175,180 (1990); $99,516 (1989); $5,598 (1988)

Assets: $4,840,981 (1990); $3,891,340 (1989); $3,208,972 (1988)

Gifts Received: $789,182 (1990); $36,626 (1989); $26,623 (1988)

Fiscal Note: In 1990, contributions were received from H.J. Stratford Trust.

EIN: 13-6029993

CONTRIBUTIONS SUMMARY
Typical Recipients: • *Education:* public education (precollege) • *Social Services:* community centers

Grant Types: scholarship

Geographic Distribution: limited to Nova Scotia, Canada

GIVING OFFICERS
Willard R. Brown: trust

APPLICATION INFORMATION
Initial Approach: Application form available for scholarship grants. There are no deadlines.

GRANTS ANALYSIS
Highest Grant: $5,000

Disclosure Period: 1990

Note: Incomplete grants list provided in 1990.

RECENT GRANTS
5,000 Black Point Community Center — for fencing and bleachers for the ball field

2,000 Mill Cove District School — for library books and shelves

2,000 Shatford Memorial School — for math program material and books

Shattuck Charitable Trust, S. F.

CONTACT
Joe McGrane
S. F. Shattuck Charitable Trust
c/o Bank One Wisconsin Trust Co., N.A.
PO Box 1308, Tax Section
Milwaukee, WI 53201
(414) 727-3281

FINANCIAL SUMMARY
Recent Giving: $101,510 (fiscal 1991); $92,000 (fiscal 1990); $71,000 (fiscal 1988)

Assets: $1,783,047 (fiscal 1988)

EIN: 39-6048820

CONTRIBUTIONS SUMMARY
Typical Recipients: • *Civic & Public Affairs:* municipalities, zoos/botanical gardens • *Education:* colleges & universities, medical education, private education (precollege), religious education • *Health:* hospitals • *Social Services:* child welfare, youth organizations

Grant Types: general support

APPLICATION INFORMATION
Initial Approach: Contributes only to preselected organizations.

GRANTS ANALYSIS
Number of Grants: 23

Highest Grant: $21,000

Typical Range: $1,000 to $5,000

Disclosure Period: fiscal year ending October 31, 1989

Note: No contribution list given for 1991.

RECENT GRANTS
21,000 YMCA, Neenah, WI

12,000 Meharry Medical College, Nashville, TN

10,000 Boys and Girls Brigade, Neenah, WI

10,000 City of Neenah, Neenah, WI — Anderson Sculpture Riverside Park

5,000 Watauga County Hospital, Boone, NC

3,000 Maryville College, Maryville, TN

3,000 Masters School, Dobbs Ferry, NY

3,000 Princeton Theological Seminary, Princeton, NJ

3,000 Scripps College, Claremont, CA

2,000 Project Hope, Millwood, VA

Shaw Charitable Trust, Mary Elizabeth Dee

CONTACT
Jack D. Lampros
Secretary
Mary Elizabeth Dee Shaw Charitable Trust
c/o First Security Bank of Utah, N.A.
PO Box 9936
Ogden, UT 84409
(801) 626-9533

FINANCIAL SUMMARY
Recent Giving: $100,000 (1990); $191,534 (1989); $85,204 (1988)

Assets: $2,613,119 (1990); $2,605,983 (1989); $2,316,680 (1988)

Gifts Received: $157,000 (1990)

EIN: 87-6116370

CONTRIBUTIONS SUMMARY
Donor(s): the late Mary Elizabeth Dee Shaw

Typical Recipients: • *Education:* colleges & universities

Grant Types: general support

Geographic Distribution: limited to UT

GIVING OFFICERS
Dean W. Hurst: comm

Donnell B. Stewart: vchmn

Elizabeth D.S. Stewart: chmn

Venna Storey: comm

C.W. Stromberg: comm

APPLICATION INFORMATION
Initial Approach: Send brief letter describing program. There are no deadlines.

Restrictions on Giving: Does not support individuals.

GRANTS ANALYSIS
Number of Grants: 1

Highest Grant: $100,000

Disclosure Period: 1990

RECENT GRANTS
100,000 Weber State College, Ogden, UT

Shaw Foundation, Arch W.

CONTACT
William W. Shaw
Trustee
Arch W. Shaw Fdn.
Thomasville Rt. Box 60-B
Birch Tree, MO 65438
(417) 764-3701

FINANCIAL SUMMARY
Recent Giving: $411,000 (1990); $420,000 (1989); $400,000 (1988)

Assets: $9,262,888 (1990); $8,408,974 (1989); $6,795,612 (1988)

EIN: 36-6055262

CONTRIBUTIONS SUMMARY
Typical Recipients: • *Arts & Humanities:* history/historic preservation, libraries, museums/galleries • *Civic & Public Affairs:* environmental affairs, zoos/botanical gardens • *Education:* colleges & universities • *Health:* hospitals • *Social Services:* community service organizations, food/clothing distribution, united funds, youth organizations

Grant Types: general support

Geographic Distribution: focus on IL

GIVING OFFICERS
Arch W. Shaw II: trust

John I. Shaw: trust

Roger D. Shaw: trust

William W. Shaw: trust

APPLICATION INFORMATION
Initial Approach: Send brief letter of inquiry describing program or project. There are no deadlines.

Restrictions on Giving: Does not support individuals.

GRANTS ANALYSIS
Number of Grants: 60

Highest Grant: $25,000

Typical Range: $1,000 to $10,000

Disclosure Period: 1990

RECENT GRANTS
25,000 Ozark Medical Center, West Plains, MO — Alzheimers building fund

25,000 Ozark Medical Center, West Plains, MO — Alzheimers building fund

15,000 Joslin Diabetes Center, Boston, MA — general fund

15,000 Northwestern Memorial Foundation, Evanston, IL — general fund

15,000 University of Missouri School of Forestry, Columbia, MO — building fund

10,000 Children's Memorial Hospital, Chicago, IL — general fund

10,000 Greater Chicago Food Depository, Chicago, IL — general fund

10,000 Holy Family Community, Chicago, IL — general fund

10,000 Hospice, Barrington, IL

10,000 Northwestern Memorial Foundation, Evanston, IL — endowment fund

Shaw Foundation, Gardiner Howland

CONTACT
Thomas Coury
Executive Director
Gardiner Howland Shaw Fdn.
95 Berkeley St.
Boston, MA 02108
(617) 451-9206

FINANCIAL SUMMARY
Recent Giving: $441,120 (fiscal 1992); $428,375 (fiscal 1991); $364,650 (fiscal 1990)
Assets: $11,988,930 (fiscal year ending April 30, 1992); $11,179,620 (fiscal 1991); $10,294,116 (fiscal 1990)
EIN: 04-6111826

CONTRIBUTIONS SUMMARY
Donor(s): the late Gardner Howland Shaw
Typical Recipients: • *Social Services:* community service organizations, counseling, delinquency & crime, employment/job training
Grant Types: emergency, multiyear/continuing support, operating expenses, and project
Geographic Distribution: limited to MA

GIVING OFFICERS
James D. Colt: trust
John Lowell: trust *B* Westwood MA 1919 *ED* Harvard Univ 1942 *CURR EMPL* ptnr:

Welch & Forbes *NONPR AFFIL* chmn: WGBH Ed Fdn
Guido R. Perera, Jr.: trust
Kenneth S. Safe, Jr.: trust

APPLICATION INFORMATION
Initial Approach: Telephone foundation or send brief letter of inquiry. Deadlines are January 2, May 1, and September 1.
Restrictions on Giving: Does not support individuals or provide funds for equipment, land acquisition, renovations, scholarships, or fellowships.

OTHER THINGS TO KNOW
Publications: Annual report (including application guidelines)

GRANTS ANALYSIS
Number of Grants: 45
Highest Grant: $27,000
Typical Range: $2,500 to $10,000
Disclosure Period: fiscal year ending April 30, 1992

RECENT GRANTS
27,000 Crime and Justice Foundation, Boston, MA — education initiative/criminal mediation

20,000 Boston Chinese: Youth Essential Service, Boston, MA — youth offenders

20,000 Dimock Community Health Center, Roxbury, MA

20,000 Project Coach, New Bedford Juvenile Offender Program, New Bedford, MA

20,000 Social Justice for Women, Boston, MA

20,000 United Way, Worcester, MA

17,500 Dorchester Youth Collaborative, Cambridge, MA — inner city youth offenders

17,500 Emerge, Cambridge, MA — counseling for male batterers

15,000 Franklin County Mediation Service, Greenfield, MA — criminal mediation

15,000 Harvard University Law School-Criminal Justice Institute, Cambridge, MA — clinical program

Shaw Foundation, Walden W. and Jean Young

CONTACT
Walden W. and Jean Young Shaw Fdn.
30 North LaSalle St., Ste. 3100
Chicago, IL 60602

FINANCIAL SUMMARY
Recent Giving: $423,000 (fiscal 1990); $414,000 (fiscal 1989); $397,000 (fiscal 1988)
Assets: $10,103,903 (fiscal year ending June 30, 1990); $8,981,565 (fiscal 1989); $8,341,508 (fiscal 1988)
Gifts Received: $563,751 (fiscal 1990); $151,796 (fiscal 1989); $283,495 (fiscal 1988)
Fiscal Note: In 1990, contributions were received from Shaw Charitable Income and Iler Remainder Trust.
EIN: 36-6162196

CONTRIBUTIONS SUMMARY
Donor(s): Walden W. Shaw, Jean Young Shaw
Typical Recipients: • *Education:* colleges & universities • *Health:* hospitals, pediatric health, single-disease health associations
Grant Types: general support

GIVING OFFICERS
Florence Iler: vp
Newell Carey Iler: dir, pres
Robert Gordon Iler: trust
Walter Roth: secy, treas

APPLICATION INFORMATION
Initial Approach: Contributes only to preselected organizations.
Restrictions on Giving: Does not support individuals.

GRANTS ANALYSIS
Highest Grant: $117,500
Disclosure Period: fiscal year ending June 30, 1990
Note: No grants list was provided for 1990.

RECENT GRANTS
117,500 Pediatric Cancer Research Foundation of Orange County, Los Angeles, CA

100,000 Children's Memorial Hospital, Chicago, IL

100,000 Hoag Memorial Hospital, Newport Beach, CA

100,000 University of Chicago, Chicago, IL

40,000 Erikson Institute, Chicago, IL

25,000 Mercy Foundation, Rosenburg, IL

Shaw Fund for Mariner's Children

CONTACT
Claire M. Tolias
Shaw Fund for Mariner's Children
64 Concord Ave.
Norwood, MA 02062

FINANCIAL SUMMARY
Recent Giving: $2,000 (1991); $8,500 (1990); $110,362 (1989)
Assets: $3,999,381 (1991); $3,314,518 (1990); $3,228,007 (1989)
Gifts Received: $150 (1991)
EIN: 04-2104861

CONTRIBUTIONS SUMMARY
Donor(s): the late Robert Gould Shaw
Grant Types: endowment, operating expenses, project, research, and scholarship
Geographic Distribution: limited to residents of MA

GIVING OFFICERS
James B. Ames: trust
Walter Amory: trust
Mrs. George B. Blake: trust
Colin A. Canham: consultant
Edward D. Cook, Jr.: trust
Ingersoll Cunningham: trust
Andrew A. Hunter: off
Mrs. Raymond I. Montminy: trust
Norman C. Nicholson, Jr.: treas
Paul H. Ockers: trust
Carolyn M. Osteen: mem
Francis G. Shaw: pres
Marguerite G. Shaw: trust
S. Parkman Shaw: trust
Thomas Whiteside: vp

APPLICATION INFORMATION
Initial Approach: Send brief letter describing situation. There are no deadlines.

OTHER THINGS TO KNOW
Provides grants to assist needy mariners and their families.
Disclosure Period: 1991

Shaw Industries

Sales: $1.75 billion
Employees: 14,700
Headquarters: Dalton, GA
SIC Major Group: Textile Mill
  Products

CONTACT

William C. Lusk
Senior Vice President, Treasurer
Shaw Industries
616 East Walnut Ave.
Dalton, GA 30720
(706) 278-3812

FINANCIAL SUMMARY

Fiscal Note: Annual Giving
Range: $250,000 to $500,000

CONTRIBUTIONS SUMMARY

Typical Recipients: • *Arts &
Humanities:* general • *Civic &
Public Affairs:* general • *Educa-
tion:* general • *Health:* general
• *Social Services:* general
Grant Types: general support
Nonmonetary Support Types:
donated equipment
Geographic Distribution:
headquarters and operating lo-
cations
Operating Locations: CA
(Santa Fe Springs), GA (Car-
tersville, Chickamauga, Dal-
ton, Eton, Lafayette, Ring-
gold), IL (Elk Grove Village),
SC (Trenton), TN (South Pitts-
burgh), TX (Dallas)

CORP. OFFICERS

George E. Shaw: *CURR
EMPL* chmn, dir: Shaw Indus
Robert E. Shaw: *CURR EMPL*
pres, ceo: Shaw Indus

GIVING OFFICERS

William C. Lusk: *CURR
EMPL* sr vp, treas: Shaw Indus

APPLICATION INFORMATION

Initial Approach: *Initial Contact:* brief letter of inquiry *Include Information On:* description of the organization,
amount requested, purpose of
funds sought, and proof of tax-
exempt status *When to Submit:*
any time

Shawmut Bank of Franklin County / Shawmut Charitable Foundation

Parent Company: Shawmut
  National Corp.
Headquarters: Greenfield, MA
SIC Major Group: Depository
  Institutions

CONTACT

Jack O'Laughlin
Manager
Shawmut Bank of Franklin
  County
324 Main St., PO Box 671
Greenfield, MA 01301
(413) 772-0221

FINANCIAL SUMMARY

Fiscal Note: Annual Giving
Range: less than $100,000
EIN: 04-6023794

CONTRIBUTIONS SUMMARY

Typical Recipients: • *Arts &
Humanities:* general • *Civic &
Public Affairs:* general • *Educa-
tion:* general • *Social Services:*
general
Grant Types: general support
Nonmonetary Support Types:
loaned employees and loaned
executives
Geographic Distribution: op-
erating communities
Operating Locations: MA
(Greenfield)

CORP. OFFICERS

Arnold G. Blackstone: *CURR
EMPL* pres, ceo: Shawmut
Bank of Franklin County

APPLICATION INFORMATION

Initial Approach: Send letter
of inquiry.

Shawmut National Corp. / Shawmut Charitable Foundation

Assets: $25.28 billion
Employees: 10,609
Headquarters: Boston, MA
SIC Major Group: Holding &
  Other Investment Offices

CONTACT

Maxine Dean
Assistant Vice President,
  Community Relations
Connecticut National Bank
777 Main St.
MSN 988
Hartford, CT 06115
(203) 728-2274
Note: Contact for organizations
in the Boston area is Dinah
Waldsmith, Shawmut Bank
Boston, One Federal Street,
Boston, MA 02211, (617)
292-3748.

FINANCIAL SUMMARY

Recent Giving: $3,000,000
(1992 approx.); $3,000,000
(1991 approx.); $3,900,000
(1990 approx.)
Assets: $45,995 (1991)
Fiscal Note: Company gives directly and through the foundation, which gave $1,938,450 in
1991.
EIN: 04-6023794

CONTRIBUTIONS SUMMARY

Typical Recipients: • *Arts &
Humanities:* arts associations,
arts centers, arts funds, arts institutes, community arts,
dance, ethnic arts, history/his-
toric preservation, libraries,
museums/galleries, music,
opera, performing arts, public
broadcasting, theater, visual
arts • *Civic & Public Affairs:*
business/free enterprise, civil
rights, consumer affairs,
economic development,
economics, environmental affairs, ethnic/minority organizations, housing, law & justice,
nonprofit management, urban
& community affairs, women's
affairs, zoos/botanical gardens
• *Education:* arts education,
business education, career/vo-
cational education, colleges &
universities, community & junior colleges, continuing education, economic education, education associations,
engineering education, health
& physical education, liberal
arts education, literacy, minority education, public education
(precollege), social sciences
education, student aid
• *Health:* health funds, health
organizations, hospices, hospitals, medical rehabilitation,
medical training, mental
health, nutrition & health maintenance, outpatient health care
delivery, pediatric health, public health • *Science:* scientific
institutes • *Social Services:*

aged, child welfare, community centers, community service organizations, counseling,
day care, delinquency & crime,
disabled, domestic violence,
drugs & alcohol, employ-
ment/job training, family planning, family services,
food/clothing distribution,
homes, recreation & athletics,
refugee assistance, shel-
ters/homelessness, united
funds, volunteer services,
youth organizations
Grant Types: capital, em-
ployee matching gifts, general
support, and operating expenses
Geographic Distribution:
throughout Massachusetts, Connecticut, and Rhode Island
Operating Locations: CT,
MA, RI

CORP. OFFICERS

Joel Barnes Alvord: *B* Man-
chester CT 1938 *ED* Dartmouth
Coll BA 1960; Dartmouth Coll
Amos Tuck Sch Bus Admin
MBA 1961 *CURR EMPL*
chmn, ceo, dir: Shawmut Natl
Corp *CORP AFFIL* chmn, ceo,
dir: CT Natl Bank; chmn, pres,
coo, dir: Hartford Natl Corp;
dir: Hartford Steam Boiler In-
spection & Ins Co *NONPR
AFFIL* dir: Inst Living; mem:
Reserve City Bankers Assn;
trust: Wadsworth Atheneum
John P. Hamill: *B* New York
NY 1940 *ED* Coll Holy Cross
AB 1961; NY Univ 1964
CURR EMPL vchmn: Shawmut
Natl Corp *CORP AFFIL* pres,
ceo, dir: Shawmut Bank
Gunnar S. Overstrom, Jr.: *B*
Buffalo NY 1942 *CURR EMPL*
pres, coo: Shawmut Natl Corp
CORP AFFIL pres, ceo: CT
Natl Bank *NONPR AFFIL*
mem: Am Bankers Assn, Am
Bankers Assn

APPLICATION INFORMATION

Initial Approach: *Initial Contact:* proposal or telephone call
to SNC affiliate bank *Include
Information On:* description of
the organization, amount requested, purpose for which
funds are sought, budget, recently audited financial statement, annual report, proof of
tax-exempt status, list of board
members, list of other supporters *When to Submit:* application deadlines vary by state
(contact local SNC affiliate
bank)
Restrictions on Giving: Does
not support individuals, na-

tional medical foundations, or political, religious, or fraternal organizations.

OTHER THINGS TO KNOW

Matching gifts program is for cultural, private secondary, public and private postsecondary educational institutions only.

Connecticut organizations may contact Ms. Maxine Dean, Assistant Vice President, public affairs, MSN351, Connecticut National Bank, 777 Main Street, Hartford, CT 06115, (203) 728-2000. Massachusetts organizations may contact Ms. Dinah Waldsmith, Shawmut Bank Boston, One Federal Street, Boston, MA 02211, (617) 292-3748. Rhode Island organizations may contact Mr. Harold Greene, assistant vice president, administration, People's Bank, 333 Central Avenue, Johnstown, RI 02919, (401) 275-1000.

GRANTS ANALYSIS

Total Grants: $1,938,450*
Number of Grants: 313*
Highest Grant: $424,733*
Typical Range: $1,000 to $10,000*
Disclosure Period: 1991
Note: Figures represent foundation giving only. Recent grants are derived from a 1991 Form 990.

RECENT GRANTS

424,733   United Way of Eastern New England, Boston, MA
80,000   United Way of Worcester, Worcester, MA
50,000   Northeastern University, Boston, MA
37,000   Children's Hospital, Boston, MA
29,800   Pioneer Valley United Way, Springfield, MA
25,000   Boston Neighborhood Housing Services/Mortgage Services Pilot Program, Boston, MA
25,000   Child Care Initiative
20,000   Boston Neighborhood Housing Service, Boston, MA
20,000   Boston Neighborhood Housing Services, Boston, MA
20,000   Massachusetts General Hospital, Boston, MA

Shawmut Needham Bank, N.A.

Headquarters: Needham, MA

CONTACT

Barbara Blais
Manager
Shawmut Needham Bank, N.A.
965 Great Plain Ave.
Needham, MA 02192
(617) 455-1600

CONTRIBUTIONS SUMMARY

Operating Locations: MA (Needham)

Shawmut Worcester County Bank, N.A. / Shawmut Charitable Foundation

Former Foundation Name: Shawmut Worcester County Bank Charitable Foundation
Employees: 728
Headquarters: Worcester, MA
SIC Major Group: Depository Institutions

CONTACT

Michael Toomey
Senior Vice President, Consumer Loans
Shawmut Worcester County Bank
446 Main St.
Worcester, MA 01608
(508) 793-4401

FINANCIAL SUMMARY

Recent Giving: $17,400 (1990); $4,000 (1989); $301,350 (1988)
Assets: $95,316 (1990); $105,407 (1989); $101,275 (1988)
Gifts Received: $200,000 (1988)
EIN: 04-2746775

CONTRIBUTIONS SUMMARY

Typical Recipients: • *Arts & Humanities:* music, theater • *Civic & Public Affairs:* environmental affairs, housing, international affairs • *Education:* business education, colleges & universities, education associations • *Health:* hospitals • *International:* international development/relief • *Social Services:* employment/job training, shelters/homelessness, united funds
Grant Types: capital and general support

Geographic Distribution: limited to agencies within the Shawmut Worcester County Bank area
Operating Locations: MA (Worcester)

CORP. OFFICERS

Christopher W. Bramley: *CURR EMPL* pres, ceo: Shawmut Worcester County Bank NA

John D. Hunt: *CURR EMPL* chmn: Shawmut Worcester County Bank NA

GIVING OFFICERS

Christopher W. Bramley: pres, dir *CURR EMPL* pres, ceo: Shawmut Worcester County Bank NA (see above)

John D. Hunt: vp, dir *CURR EMPL* chmn: Shawmut Worcester County Bank NA (see above)

John M. Lydon: secy-treas

Michael J. Toomey: dir

APPLICATION INFORMATION

Initial Approach: Send brief letter, including descriptive brochures. There are no deadlines.

GRANTS ANALYSIS

Number of Grants: 10
Highest Grant: $20,000
Disclosure Period: 1990

RECENT GRANTS

20,000   Assumption College, Worcester, MA
15,000   Shawmut Bank Caring Tree Program, Worcester, MA
10,000   Worcester Common Ground Piedmont Co-op, Worcester, MA
5,450   Massachusetts Job Training, Worcester, MA
5,000   Alternatives Unlimited, Worcester, MA
5,000   Haywood Hospital, Worcester, MA
2,500   Habitat for Humanity, Worcester, MA
2,500   Worcester Forum Theatre Ensemble, Worcester, MA
2,000   Alliance for Education, Worcester, MA
1,500   Children's Hospital League, Worcester, MA

Shaw's Supermarkets / Shaw's Market Trust

Sales: $1.14 billion
Employees: 14,000
Headquarters: East Bridgewater, MA
SIC Major Group: Business Services, Food Stores, and Holding & Other Investment Offices

CONTACT

Deborah Shaw
Client Service Administrator
Fleet Trust Co.
P.O. Box 3555
Portland, ME 04104
(207) 874-5232

FINANCIAL SUMMARY

Recent Giving: $305,138 (fiscal 1992); $338,950 (fiscal 1991); $609,305 (fiscal 1990)
Assets: $2,383,226 (fiscal year ending July 31, 1992); $1,930,873 (fiscal 1991); $1,778,784 (fiscal 1990)
Gifts Received: $150,000 (fiscal 1992)
Fiscal Note: Contributes through foundation only. In fiscal 1992, contributions were received from Shaw's Supermarkets.
EIN: 01-6008389

CONTRIBUTIONS SUMMARY

Typical Recipients: • *Arts & Humanities:* arts funds, libraries, museums/galleries, music, public broadcasting, theater • *Education:* colleges & universities • *Health:* hospitals, single-disease health associations • *Social Services:* child welfare, community service organizations, united funds, youth organizations
Grant Types: capital, challenge, and general support
Nonmonetary Support Types: donated products
Geographic Distribution: near headquarters and operating locations only, including southern Maine, southern New Hampshire, and Massachusetts
Operating Locations: MA, ME (Portland), NH, NY (Rochester), RI

CORP. OFFICERS

James Demme: *CURR EMPL* pres: Shaws Supermarkets

David B. Jenkins: *CURR EMPL* chmn, ceo: Shaws Super-markets

GIVING OFFICERS
Fleet Bank of Maine: trust

APPLICATION INFORMATION
Initial Approach: *Note:* The foundation supports prese-lected organizations and does not accept unsolicited requests for funds.
Restrictions on Giving: Does not support dinners or special events, fraternal organizations, goodwill advertising, individu-als, or political or lobbying groups.

GRANTS ANALYSIS
Total Grants: $305,138
Number of Grants: 45
Highest Grant: $79,500
Typical Range: $1,000 to $5,000
Disclosure Period: fiscal year ending July 31, 1992
Note: Recent grants are de-rived from a fiscal 1992 grants list.

RECENT GRANTS
79,500 United Way of Eastern New Eng-land, Boston, MA
35,000 United Way, Port-land, ME
25,000 YMCA, Portland, ME
20,000 South Shore Natu-ral Science Center, Boston, MA
18,000 Concord Area Trust for Commu-nity Housing, Con-cord, MA
10,000 Combined Jewish Philanthropies of Greater Boston, Boston, MA
10,000 Museum of Science, Boston, MA
8,000 Children's Mu-seum of Maine, Portland, ME
5,000 Central Maine Healthcare, Port-land, ME
5,000 Commitment to the Future, Boston, MA

Shea Co., John F. / Shea Co. Foundation, J. F.
Revenue: $100.0 million
Employees: 600
Headquarters: Walnut, CA
SIC Major Group: Heavy Construction Except Building Construction

CONTACT
Ron Lakey
Secretary
John F. Shea Co.
655 Brea Canyon Rd.
Walnut, CA 91789
(714) 594-0941

FINANCIAL SUMMARY
Recent Giving: $711,955 (1991); $160,621 (1990); $97,700 (1989)
Assets: $1,071,585 (1991); $1,605,353 (1990); $1,175,619 (1989)
Gifts Received: $35,291 (1990)
Fiscal Note: Contributes through foundation only. In 1990, contributions were re-ceived from John F. Shea Co.
EIN: 95-2554052

CONTRIBUTIONS SUMMARY
Typical Recipients: • *Arts & Humanities:* music • *Health:* hospitals, single-disease health associations • *Religion:* churches, religious organiza-tions • *Social Services:* shel-ters/homelessness, united funds
Grant Types: general support
Geographic Distribution: pri-marily California and Arizona
Operating Locations: CA (Walnut)

CORP. OFFICERS
John F. Shea: *CURR EMPL* pres: John F. Shea Company

GIVING OFFICERS
Ronald L. Lakey: secy
Edmund H. Shea: secy
John F. Shea: pres *CURR EMPL* pres: John F. Shea Com-pany (see above)
Peter O. Shea: treas

APPLICATION INFORMATION
Initial Approach: *Note:* The foundation supports prese-lected organizations and does not accept unsolicited requests for funds.
Restrictions on Giving: Does not support individuals.

GRANTS ANALYSIS
Total Grants: $711,955
Number of Grants: 41
Highest Grant: $83,336
Typical Range: $2,000 to $4,200
Disclosure Period: 1991
Note: Recent grants are de-rived from a 1991 grants list.

RECENT GRANTS
83,336 Arizona Depart-ment of Education, Phoenix, AZ
83,336 Arizona Depart-ment of Education, Phoenix, AZ
83,336 Arizona Depart-ment of Education, Phoenix, AZ
83,336 Arizona Depart-ment of Education, Phoenix, AZ
83,336 Arizona Depart-ment of Education, Phoenix, AZ
83,320 Arizona Depart-ment of Education, Phoenix, AZ
50,000 Franklin McKinley School District, CA
25,000 Franklin McKinley School District, CA
25,000 Franklin McKinley School District, CA
25,000 Franklin McKinley School District, CA

Shea Foundation

CONTACT
John F. Shea
President, Trustee
Shea Fdn.
655 Brea Canyon Rd.
Walnut, CA 91789

FINANCIAL SUMMARY
Recent Giving: $197,000 (fis-cal 1991); $165,000 (fiscal 1990); $157,900 (fiscal 1989)
Assets: $3,535,915 (fiscal year ending November 30, 1991); $3,221,289 (fiscal 1990); $3,358,824 (fiscal 1989)
EIN: 95-6027824

CONTRIBUTIONS SUMMARY
Donor(s): members of the Shea family
Typical Recipients: • *Arts & Humanities:* literary arts, muse-ums/galleries • *Education:* col-leges & universities, minority education, private education (precollege), public education (precollege) • *Health:* health or-ganizations, hospitals, medical research, single-disease health associations • *Religion:*

churches, religious organiza-tions • *Social Services:* disabled
Grant Types: scholarship
Geographic Distribution: focus on CA

GIVING OFFICERS
Ronald L. Lakey: cfo
Patricia Ann Shea Meek: vp
John F. Shea: pres, trust *CURR EMPL* pres: John F. Shea Company
James G. Shontere: secy

APPLICATION INFORMATION
Initial Approach: Send cover letter and full proposal. There are no deadlines.

GRANTS ANALYSIS
Number of Grants: 87
Highest Grant: $22,000
Typical Range: $500 to $2,000
Disclosure Period: fiscal year ending November 30, 1991

RECENT GRANTS
22,000 Americanism Foun-dation, St. Louis, MO
20,000 New Directions
13,500 Centinela Hospital, Los Angeles, CA
10,000 Jesuit School
6,000 All Hallows Insti-tute, Bronx, NY
4,000 Crittenton Center
2,500 Archbishop Ma-honey Archdiocese
2,000 American Cancer Society, New York, NY
2,000 Bishop Gooden Home
2,000 Boulder School for Student Urantia, Boulder, CO

Shea Foundation, Edmund and Mary

CONTACT
Edmund and Mary Shea Foundation
655 Brea Canyon Road
Walnut, CA 91789-3010
(714) 594-0941

FINANCIAL SUMMARY
Recent Giving: $61,383 (1990); $111,065 (1989)
Assets: $2,051,535 (1990); $2,556,667 (1989)
Gifts Received: $3,375 (1990)
EIN: 95-4107214

CONTRIBUTIONS SUMMARY
Typical Recipients: • *Arts & Humanities:* libraries • *Educa-*

tion: religious education, science/technology education • *Health:* hospitals, pediatric health • *Religion:* churches
Grant Types: general support

GRANTS ANALYSIS
Total Grants: $61,383
Number of Grants: 22
Highest Grant: $10,000
Typical Range: $2,000 to $10,000
Disclosure Period: 1990

RECENT GRANTS
10,000 Massachusetts Institute of Technology, MA
10,000 Santa Clara University, Santa Clara, CA
8,333 Jesuit School of Theology
5,000 Pasadena Public Library, Pasadena, CA
5,000 PICO
4,200 Guild of Pasadena Children's Hospital, Pasadena, CA
3,100 St. Andrew's Church
2,500 Corpus Christi Church, Corpus Christi, TX
2,500 University of California at Santa Barbara Foundation, CA
2,000 St. Andrew's School

Shea Foundation, John and Dorothy

CONTACT
John and Dorothy Shea Foundation
655 Brea Canyon Road
Walnut, CA 91789-3010
(714) 594-0941

FINANCIAL SUMMARY
Recent Giving: $1,506,937 (1990); $1,842,624 (1989)
Assets: $10,810,588 (1990); $11,794,217 (1989)
Gifts Received: $5,625 (1990)
EIN: 95-4084694

CONTRIBUTIONS SUMMARY
Typical Recipients: • *Education:* colleges & universities, private education (precollege), public education (precollege) • *Religion:* churches • *Social Services:* child welfare, shelters/homelessness
Grant Types: general support

APPLICATION INFORMATION
Initial Approach: The foundation reports it only makes contributions to preselected organizations and does not accept unsolicited requests for funds.

GRANTS ANALYSIS
Total Grants: $1,506,937
Number of Grants: 73
Highest Grant: $360,993
Typical Range: $20,000 to $200,000
Disclosure Period: 1990

RECENT GRANTS
360,993 Archdiocese of Los Angeles, Los Angeles, CA
300,000 Pasadena Unified Schools, Pasadena, CA
222,807 Archdiocese of Los Angeles, Los Angeles, CA
200,000 Pasadena School District, Pasadena, CA
193,714 Archdiocese of Los Angeles, Los Angeles, CA
50,000 New Children's Shelter Fund
23,500 St. Phillip the Apostle Church
22,100 Loyola High School
22,100 Mayfield Senior School
20,000 Georgetown University, DC

Sheadle Trust, Jasper H.

CONTACT
Jasper H. Sheadle Trust
c/o Ameritrust Co., N.A.
900 Euclid Ave.
Cleveland, OH 44101
(216) 737-3139

FINANCIAL SUMMARY
Recent Giving: $129,505 (1991); $114,850 (1989); $104,781 (1988)
Assets: $3,184,050 (1991); $2,830,741 (1989); $2,371,697 (1988)
EIN: 34-6506457

CONTRIBUTIONS SUMMARY
Donor(s): the late Jasper H. Sheadle
Geographic Distribution: limited to Cuyahoga and Mahoning counties, OH

GIVING OFFICERS
John J. Donnelly: mgr

Frank I. Harding III: mgr *B* Cleveland OH 1944 *ED* Univ MI BA 1966; Case Western Reserve Univ JD 1969 *CURR EMPL* pres, ceo trust group: AmeriTrust Co *CORP AFFIL* dir: Meteor Crater Enterprises, Miller Co; pres: Bar T Bar Fiduciary Holding Co; pres, ceo trust group: AmeriTrust Co *NONPR AFFIL* mem: Cleveland Bar Assn, Estate Planning Counc Cleveland, OH Bar Assn; trust: Childrens Aid Soc Cleveland, Cleveland Inst Art, Perkins (Hanna) Sch
Rt. Rev. James R. Moodey: mgr

APPLICATION INFORMATION
Initial Approach: Contributes only to preselected organizations.

OTHER THINGS TO KNOW
Provides financial assistance to people in need for help with housing, food, and medical expenses.
Disclosure Period: 1991

Sheafer Charitable Trust, Emma A.

CONTACT
Hildy J. Simmons
Vice President
Emma A. Sheafer Charitable Trust
c/o Morgan Guaranty Trust Co. of New York
60 Wall St.
New York, NY 10015

FINANCIAL SUMMARY
Recent Giving: $127,000 (1991); $125,475 (1989); $138,200 (1988)
Assets: $3,984,719 (1991); $3,479,611 (1989); $3,692,127 (1988)
EIN: 51-0186114

CONTRIBUTIONS SUMMARY
Donor(s): the late Emma A. Sheafer
Typical Recipients: • *Arts & Humanities:* arts associations, arts centers, community arts, dance, history/historic preservation, music, opera, theater
Grant Types: endowment, general support, multiyear/continuing support, operating expenses, project, and seed money
Geographic Distribution: limited to NY

GIVING OFFICERS
Morgan Guaranty Trust Company of New York
trust
John C. Russell: trust

APPLICATION INFORMATION
Initial Approach: Send brief letter of inquiry describing program or project. Deadlines are mid-April and mid-October.
Restrictions on Giving: Does not support individuals or provide scholarships or loans.

GRANTS ANALYSIS
Number of Grants: 15
Highest Grant: $10,000
Typical Range: $5,000 to $10,000
Disclosure Period: 1991

RECENT GRANTS
10,000 Academy of American Poets, New York, NY
10,000 Art Resources, New York, NY
10,000 Circle in the Square, New York, NY
10,000 Cunningham Dance Foundation, Chicago, IL
10,000 Deja Vu Dance Theatre, New York, NY
10,000 En Garde Arts, New York, NY
10,000 Meet the Composer, New York, NY
10,000 Orpheus Chamber Orchestra, New York, NY
10,000 Playwrights Horizons, New York, NY
10,000 Under One Roof, New York, NY

Sheaffer Inc.

Sales: $89.0 million
Employees: 1,000
Headquarters: Ft. Madison, IA
SIC Major Group: Miscellaneous Manufacturing Industries and Paper & Allied Products

CONTACT
Walter Walz
Sheaffer Pen
301 Ave. H
Ft. Madison, IA 52627
(319) 372-3300

CONTRIBUTIONS SUMMARY
Program makes at least one large capital grant a year and then gives multiple smaller

gifts to health, the arts, and social services.

Typical Recipients: • *Arts & Humanities:* arts associations, arts centers, community arts, dance, history/historic preservation, libraries, museums/galleries, music, performing arts, theater • *Education:* colleges & universities • *Health:* health care cost containment, health organizations, hospitals, mental health, single-disease health associations • *Social Services:* child welfare, community centers, community service organizations, disabled, drugs & alcohol, employment/job training, family services, united funds, youth organizations

Grant Types: capital and general support

Nonmonetary Support Types: donated products and workplace solicitation

Operating Locations: IA (Fort Madison)

CORP. OFFICERS

Ron Draper: *CURR EMPL* cfo: Sheaffer

John Goldcamp: *CURR EMPL* vp, gen mgr: Sheaffer

Michael Johnstone: *CURR EMPL* pres, ceo: Sheaffer

GIVING OFFICERS

Walter Waltz: *CURR EMPL* Sheaffer

APPLICATION INFORMATION

Initial Approach: For large grants, write letter one year in advance. Include a description of the organization, amount and purpose of funds sought, a recently audited financial statement, and proof of tax-exempt status. For smaller contributions, send a letter any time including the same information.

Shearson, Lehman & Hutton

Revenue: $12.5 billion
Employees: 34,000
Parent Company: American Express Co.
Headquarters: New York, NY
SIC Major Group: Holding & Other Investment Offices and Security & Commodity Brokers

CONTACT

Francine Kittredge
Senior Vice President & Director
Shearson, Lehman & Hutton
200 Vesey St.
New York, NY 10285
(212) 298-2000

CONTRIBUTIONS SUMMARY

Grant Types: matching
Operating Locations: NY (New York)

CORP. OFFICERS

Howard L. Clark: *CURR EMPL* chmn, ceo: Shearson Lehman & Hutton

Ronald J. Yoo: *CURR EMPL* vchmn: Shearson Lehman & Hutton

Sheily Co., J.L.
Headquarters: St. Paul, MN

CONTACT

Diane Minnick
Director, Personnel
J.L. Sheily Co.
2915 Waters Rd., Ste. 105
Eagan, MN 55121
(612) 683-0600

CONTRIBUTIONS SUMMARY

Operating Locations: MN (St. Paul)

Sheinberg Foundation, Eric P.

CONTACT

Eric P. Sheinberg Fdn.
c/o Goldman, Sachs and Co., Tax Dept.
85 Broad St., 30th Fl.
New York, NY 10004

FINANCIAL SUMMARY

Recent Giving: $157,450 (fiscal 1992); $157,700 (fiscal 1991); $144,950 (fiscal 1990)
Assets: $3,241,559 (fiscal year ending June 30, 1992); $3,144,301 (fiscal 1991); $3,373,478 (fiscal 1990)
Gifts Received: $283,941 (fiscal 1992); $300,000 (fiscal 1991); $498,984 (fiscal 1990)
Fiscal Note: In fiscal 1992, contributions were received from Eric P. Sheinberg.
EIN: 13-7004291

CONTRIBUTIONS SUMMARY

Donor(s): Eric P. Sheinberg

Typical Recipients: • *Arts & Humanities:* community arts, libraries, museums/galleries • *Civic & Public Affairs:* civil rights, environmental affairs, municipalities, zoos/botanical gardens • *Education:* private education (precollege) • *Health:* hospitals, medical research, single-disease health associations • *Social Services:* community service organizations, family services, recreation & athletics, youth organizations

Grant Types: general support
Geographic Distribution: focus on New York, NY

GIVING OFFICERS

Eric P. Sheinberg: trust
Michael Steinhardt: trust

APPLICATION INFORMATION

Initial Approach: Contributes only to preselected organizations.

Restrictions on Giving: Does not support individuals.

GRANTS ANALYSIS

Number of Grants: 66
Highest Grant: $25,000
Typical Range: $100 to $5,000
Disclosure Period: fiscal year ending June 30, 1992

RECENT GRANTS

25,000 Police Athletic League, New York, NY — capital campaign
20,000 Mt. Sinai Medical Center, New York, NY — Gus and Janet Levy Library Fund
10,000 Central Park Conservancy, New York, NY
10,000 Mt. Sinai Medical Center, New York, NY
10,000 New York Public Library, New York, NY
10,000 Police Athletic League, New York, NY
6,000 Metropolitan Museum of Art, New York, NY
5,000 American Jewish Committee, New York, NY
5,000 Human Rights Watch, New York, NY
5,000 New York Zoological Society, New York, NY

Sheldahl Inc.

Sales: $86.7 million
Employees: 1,162
Headquarters: Northfield, MN
SIC Major Group: Electronic & Other Electrical Equipment and Rubber & Miscellaneous Plastics Products

CONTACT

Bev Brumbaugh
Vice President, Human Resources
Sheldahl Inc.
PO Box 170
Northfield, MN 55057
(507) 663-8220

CONTRIBUTIONS SUMMARY

Company sponsors employee matching gift program; also supports community organizations.

Typical Recipients: • *Arts & Humanities:* general • *Civic & Public Affairs:* general • *Education:* general • *Health:* general • *Social Services:* general
Grant Types: matching
Geographic Distribution: primarily headquarters area
Operating Locations: CA (Tustin), MI (Clarkston), MN (Northfield), SD (Aberdeen)

CORP. OFFICERS

James E. Donaghy: *B* Pittsburgh PA 1934 *ED* Harvard Univ 1956; MA Inst Tech 1958 *CURR EMPL* pres, ceo, dir: Sheldahl *CORP AFFIL* dir: Datakey Inc *NONPR AFFIL* dir: Inst Electrical Interconnections Packaging; mem: Natl Assn Mfrs

James S. Womack: *CURR EMPL* chmn, dir: Sheldahl

APPLICATION INFORMATION

Initial Approach: Send brief letter of inquiry. There are no deadlines.

Shelden Fund, Elizabeth, Allan and Warren

CONTACT
W. Warren Shelden
President
Elizabeth, Allan and Warren
Shelden Fund
333 West Fort Bldg., Ste. 1870
Detroit, MI 48226
(313) 963-2356

FINANCIAL SUMMARY
Recent Giving: $208,500
(1991); $240,000 (1989)
Assets: $4,389,358 (1991);
$3,555,361 (1989)
EIN: 38-6052198

CONTRIBUTIONS SUMMARY
Donor(s): the late Elizabeth
Warren Shelden, the late Allan
Shelden III, W. Warren Shelden
Typical Recipients: • *Arts &
Humanities:* history/historic
preservation, museums/galleries, music • *Education:* medical education • *Health:* hospitals, medical research,
pediatric health • *Social Services:* community service organizations, disabled, united funds,
youth organizations
Grant Types: capital, endowment, general support, multiyear/continuing support, and research
Geographic Distribution:
focus on MI

GIVING OFFICERS
William G. Butler: trust
Robert W. Emke, Jr.: off
Tina M. Krizanic: asst secy
Virginia D. Shelden: vp, trust
W. Warren Shelden: pres, trust
William W. Shelden, Jr.:
treas, trust
Robert M. Surdam: trust *B* Albany NY 1917 *ED* Williams
Coll BA 1939 *CORP AFFIL*
dir: NBD Bancorp

APPLICATION INFORMATION
Initial Approach: Send cover
letter and full proposal. There
are no deadlines. Board meets
in December or January.
Restrictions on Giving: Does
not support individuals or provide funds for scholarships.

GRANTS ANALYSIS
Number of Grants: 26
Highest Grant: $90,000
Typical Range: $1,000 to
$10,000

Disclosure Period: 1991

RECENT GRANTS
90,000 United Way, Detroit, MI
30,000 University Liggett School, Grosse Pointe, MI — annual fund, endowment
15,000 Detroit Symphony Orchestra, Detroit, MI
12,500 Children's Hospital Medical Center, Detroit, MI
10,000 Boy Scouts of America, Detroit, MI
7,000 Salvation Army, Southfield, MI
5,000 Children's Center, Detroit, MI
5,000 Community Foundation for Southeastern Michigan, Detroit, MI
5,000 Henry Ford Hospital, Detroit, MI — community cholesterol program at Heart and Vascular Institute
5,000 Wayne State University, Detroit, MI — clinical research building

Sheldon Foundation, Ralph C.

CONTACT
Paul B. Sullivan
Executive Director
Ralph C. Sheldon Fdn.
710 Hotel Jamestown Bldg.
Jamestown, NY 14702
(716) 664-9850

FINANCIAL SUMMARY
Recent Giving: $1,345,676
(fiscal 1992); $1,483,540 (fiscal 1991); $1,426,716 (fiscal 1990)
Assets: $5,589,865 (fiscal year ending May 31, 1992);
$5,422,908 (fiscal 1991);
$5,204,298 (fiscal 1990)
Gifts Received: $1,091,032
(fiscal 1992); $1,095,925 (fiscal 1991); $1,184,720 (fiscal 1990)
Fiscal Note: In fiscal 1992,
contributions were received
from Isabella M. Sheldon Trust.
EIN: 16-6030502

CONTRIBUTIONS SUMMARY
Donor(s): Julia S. Livengood,
Isabel M. Sheldon

Typical Recipients: • *Arts &
Humanities:* community arts
• *Civic & Public Affairs:* environmental affairs, zoos/botanical gardens • *Education:* community & junior colleges
• *Health:* hospices, hospitals
• *Social Services:* child welfare, community service organizations, disabled, united funds,
youth organizations
Grant Types: capital, emergency, and general support
Geographic Distribution:
focus on southern Chautauqua
County, NY

GIVING OFFICERS
Miles L. Lasser: treas, dir
Walter L. Miller: vp, dir
J. Elizabeth Sheldon: pres, dir
Paul B. Sullivan: secy, exec dir
Barclay O. Wellman: dir
Robert G. Wright: vp, dir

APPLICATION INFORMATION
Initial Approach: Contributes
only to preselected organizations.
Restrictions on Giving: Does
not support individuals or religious organizations.

GRANTS ANALYSIS
Number of Grants: 37
Highest Grant: $250,000
Typical Range: $1,000 to
$20,000
Disclosure Period: fiscal year
ending May 31, 1992

RECENT GRANTS
250,000 WCA Hospital, Jamestown, NY
250,000 YMCA, Jamestown, NY
167,000 City of Jamestown, Jamestown, NY
140,000 Jamestown Community College, Jamestown, NY
75,000 Jamestown Audubon Society, Jamestown, NY
63,000 United Way, Jamestown, NY
55,000 Chautauqua Institution, Chautauqua, NY
54,650 Chautauqua Lake Association, Lakewood, NY
50,000 Boy Scouts of America, Falconer, NY
50,000 Lucille Ball Festival of New Comedy, Jamestown, NY

Shell Oil Co. / Shell Oil Co. Foundation

Sales: $21.7 billion
Employees: 29,437
Headquarters: Houston, TX
SIC Major Group: Chemicals &
Allied Products, Oil & Gas
Extraction, and Petroleum &
Coal Products

CONTACT
J. N. Doherty
Senior Vice President
Shell Oil Co. Fdn.
Two Shell Plz.
Box 2099
Houston, TX 77252
(713) 241-3617
Note: For international giving
contact F.M. Rabbe, Senior
Administrative Representative.

FINANCIAL SUMMARY
Recent Giving: $18,000,000
(1993 est.); $18,500,000 (1992
approx.); $21,230,000 (1991)
Assets: $7,048,255 (1992);
$7,563,736 (1991);
$10,641,679 (1990)
Fiscal Note: Total giving figures include about $2 million
in corporate and subsidiary direct giving to organizations not
usually supported by the foundation. Also made $3,000,000
in grants from other company
departments; contact W. F.
Butin, General Manager, External Affairs, for details.
EIN: 13-6066583

CONTRIBUTIONS SUMMARY
Typical Recipients: • *Arts &
Humanities:* arts festivals,
dance, history/historic preservation, libraries, museums/galleries, music, opera, performing
arts, theater • *Civic & Public
Affairs:* business/free enterprise, civil rights, economic development, economics, environmental affairs, ethnic/minority
organizations, international affairs, law & justice, public policy, safety, urban & community
affairs, women's affairs,
zoos/botanical gardens • *Education:* business education, career/vocational education, colleges & universities, economic
education, education associations, elementary education, engineering education, faculty development, international
studies, journalism education,
legal education, minority education, private education (precollege), public education (precollege), science/technology

education, student aid
• *Health:* health funds, health organizations, hospices, hospitals, medical rehabilitation, medical research, mental health, single-disease health associations • *International:* international development/relief • *Science:* science exhibits & fairs, scientific organizations • *Social Services:* aged, child welfare, community centers, community service organizations, delinquency & crime, disabled, drugs & alcohol, emergency relief, family services, food/clothing distribution, shelters/homelessness, united funds, volunteer services, youth organizations
Grant Types: capital, department, employee matching gifts, general support, operating expenses, project, and research
Note: Capital and project grants not made in the area of education. Matching gifts are for degree-granting educational institutions only.
Nonmonetary Support Types: loaned employees and loaned executives
Note: Value of nonmonetary support is not available and is not included in above figures. For details on company's non-monetary giving, contact Manager, Corporate Relations.
Geographic Distribution: nationally, with emphasis on communities where Shell employees are located
Operating Locations: AK (Anchorage), AL, CA (Anaheim, Bakersfield, Huntington Beach, Los Angeles, Martinez, San Francisco), DC, FL (Ft. Lauderdale, Tampa), IL (Chicago, Oak Brook, Wood River), IN (Indianapolis), LA (Baton Rouge, Geismar, New Orleans, Norco), MA (Boston, Fall River), MD (Baltimore), MI (Detroit, Gaylord, Kalkaska, Manistee, Traverse City), MO (St. Louis), NJ (Newark, Sewaren), NM (Hobbs), NY (New York), OH (Belpre, Cleveland, Columbus, Dayton, Marietta), TX (Dallas, Houston, Midland, Odessa), WA (Anacortes, Mount Vernon, Seattle), WV (Parkersburg)
Note: Also operates internationally.

CORP. OFFICERS

C. A. J. Herkstroter: *CURR EMPL* chmn: Shell Oil Co
S. L. Miller: *B* Kansas City MO 1945 *ED* Univ IL 1967
CURR EMPL vp (refining & mktg): Shell Oil Co
Davis Bates Richardson: *B* Fayetteville AR 1929 *ED* Univ AR BS 1951; Univ AR MS 1955; Univ AR PhD 1956 *CURR EMPL* vp: Shell Oil Co *CORP AFFIL* pres: Shell Devel Co *NONPR AFFIL* dir: Natl Assn Mfrs; dir, mem exec comm: Chem Mfrs Assn; mem: Am Assn Advancement Science, Am Chem Soc, Petroleum Club, Soc Chem Indus
Frank H. Richardson: *B* White River SD 1933 *ED* SD Sch Mines BS 1955 *CURR EMPL* pres, ceo, dir: Shell Oil Co *NONPR AFFIL* mem mgmt comm: Am Petroleum Inst
Chuck W. Wilson: *B* 1939 *ED* Univ NM 1962 *CURR EMPL* exec vp (products), dir: Shell Oil Co

GIVING OFFICERS

B. E. Bernard: dir
Philip Joseph Carroll: mem exec comm, dir *B* New Orleans LA 1937 *ED* Loyola Univ 1958; Tulane Univ 1961 *CURR EMPL* exec vp (admin): Shell Oil Co *NONPR AFFIL* adv counc: Tulane Univ Ctr Bioenvironmental Res; dir: Am Counc Capital Formation, Am Petroleum Inst, TX Med Ctr, Western States Petroleum Assn; mem: 25 Year Club Petroleum Indus; mem bd visitors: Univ IA Coll Bus Admin; mem conf bd: Counc Chief Admin Offs; trust: Comm Econ Devel, Fdn Bus Politics Econs, Harris County Childrens Protective Svcs Fund, Keystone Ctr
J. N. Doherty: sr vp, mem exec comm, dir
Norman Edward Gautier: treas *B* New Franklin MO 1939 *ED* Univ MO 1961 *CURR EMPL* treas: Shell Oil Co *NONPR AFFIL* mem: Am Inst CPAs, Am Petroleum Inst; pres Houston chapter: Fin Execs Inst
T. J. Howard: asst secy
Ronald L. Kuhns: secy
B. W. Levan: vp, dir *B* St Louis IL 1941 *ED* Southern IL Univ 1964; Univ IL 1966 *CURR EMPL* vp (human resources): Shell Oil Co
Jack Edward Little: mem exec comm, dir *B* Dallas TX 1938 *ED* TX A&M Univ 1960; TX A&M Univ 1966 *CURR EMPL* exec vp (exploration & production), dir: Shell Oil Co *CORP AFFIL* mem equity adv comm: Gen Electric Invest-

ment Corp *NONPR AFFIL* dir: Am Petroleum Inst, YMCA Greater Houston Area; dir, mem exec comm: Natl Ocean Indus Assn; mem: Mid-Continent Oil Gas Assn, Soc Petroleum Engrs; mem external adv comm: TX A&M Coll Engg; trust, mem exec comm: Un Way TX Gulf Coast
Ramon Lopez: dir *B* Tampa FL 1933 *CURR EMPL* vp mfg & tech: Shell Oil Co
Jere Paul Parrish: mem exec comm, dir *B* Lovington NM 1965 *ED* Univ TX 1965 *CURR EMPL* vp corp aff: Shell Oil Co
Frank H. Richardson: pres, chmn exec comm, dir *CURR EMPL* pres, ceo, dir: Shell Oil Co (see above)
Lane E. Sloan: vp, dir *B* Houston TX 1947 *ED* Univ CO BS 1969; Univ CO 1970; Univ Houston MS 1979 *CURR EMPL* vp (fin & info services): Shell Oil Co *NONPR AFFIL* mem: Am Petroleum Inst, Fin Execs Inst, Sigma Iota Epsilon, TX Soc CPAs
L. L. Smith: dir *B* Cleveland OH 1936 *ED* GA Inst Tech 1958 *CURR EMPL* vp (production): Shell Oil Co

APPLICATION INFORMATION

Initial Approach: *Initial Contact:* brief letter *Include Information On:* description of structure, purpose, history, and program of organization; summary of need and use for support; detailed financial data on organization (independent audit, budget, sources of income, breakdown of expenditures by program, administration, and fund raising); copies of forms 501(c)(3), 509(a), and 990; list of donors and level of support *When to Submit:* any time; contributions are planned in advance for each calendar year
Restrictions on Giving: Foundation prefers not to contribute to capital campaigns of national organizations; endowment or development funds; special requests from colleges and universities or state or area college fund-raising associations; or hospital operating expenses.
Does not support individuals, dinners or special events, fraternal organizations, goodwill advertising, political or lobbying groups, or religious organizations for sectarian purposes.

OTHER THINGS TO KNOW

Companies participating in the Shell Oil Co. Foundation include Shell Oil Co., Shell Offshore, Inc., Shell Pipe Line Corp., Shell Western E&P, Inc., Pecten Chemicals, Inc., Pecten International Co., and Pecten Middle East Services Co.
Individual employee contributions of up to $500 to colleges, universities, and private secondary schools are matched on a two for one basis. Amounts contributed in excess of $500 up to the maximum $2,500 limit will be matched on a dollar-for-dollar basis. Minimum gift matched is $25.
Publications: Pattern for Giving

GRANTS ANALYSIS

Total Grants: $18,500,000*
Number of Grants: 3,092
Highest Grant: $200,000*
Typical Range: $500 to $10,000
Disclosure Period: 1992
Note: Total grants figure includes foundation and direct giving. Recent grants are derived from a 1991 Form 990.

RECENT GRANTS

200,000 Baylor College of Medicine, Houston, TX
200,000 Texas A&M University Development Foundation-Institute of Biosciences and Technology; Corporate-GEO, College Station, TX
150,000 Rice University, Houston, TX
150,000 University of Texas at Austin, Austin, TX
130,000 Foundation for Exceptional Children, Reston, VA
100,000 Friends of the Zoo-Aquarium of the Americas, New Orleans, LA
100,000 Houston Symphony Society, Houston, TX
100,000 National Action Council for Minorities in Engineering, New York, NY
100,000 St. Luke's Episcopal Hospital, Houston, TX
87,975 Tulane University-Education Reform in Louisiana, New Orleans, LA

Shelter Mutual Insurance Co. / Shelter Insurance Foundation

Assets: $2.03 billion
Employees: 1,500
Headquarters: Columbia, MO
SIC Major Group: Insurance Carriers

CONTACT

Raymond E. Jones
Secretary & Director
Shelter Insurance Fdn.
1817 West Broadway
Columbia, MO 65218
(314) 874-4290

FINANCIAL SUMMARY

Recent Giving: $255,502 (fiscal 1991); $244,178 (fiscal 1990); $168,700 (fiscal 1989)
Assets: $1,575,225 (fiscal year ending June 30, 1991); $1,501,638 (fiscal 1990); $1,384,715 (fiscal 1989)
Gifts Received: $193,490 (fiscal 1991); $252,936 (fiscal 1990); $305,945 (fiscal 1989)
EIN: 43-1224155

CONTRIBUTIONS SUMMARY

Typical Recipients: • *Arts & Humanities:* music • *Education:* business education, colleges & universities, education associations, student aid, student aid • *Health:* medical research, single-disease health associations • *Social Services:* disabled, youth organizations
Grant Types: general support, research, and scholarship
Geographic Distribution: restricted to AR, CO, IL, IN, IA, KS, KY, LA, MS, MO, NE, OK and TN; emphasis on Columbia, MO
Operating Locations: MO (Columbia)

CORP. OFFICERS

Gustav J. Lehr: *CURR EMPL* chmn, ceo, dir: Shelter Mutual Ins Co
John W. Lenox: *CURR EMPL* vchmn, exec vp, dir: Shelter Mutual Ins Co
Robert W. Maupin: *CURR EMPL* pres, coo, dir: Shelter Mutual Ins Co

GIVING OFFICERS

Robert T. Cox: dir
J. Donald Duello: treas, dir
Raymond E. Jones: secy, dir
Howard B. Lang: dir

Gustav J. Lehr: pres, dir *CURR EMPL* chmn, ceo, dir: Shelter Mutual Ins Co (see above)
John W. Lenox: dir *CURR EMPL* vchmn, exec vp, dir: Shelter Mutual Ins Co (see above)
Jean J. Madden: dir
Robert W. Maupin: vp, dir *CURR EMPL* pres, coo, dir: Shelter Mutual Ins Co (see above)
B.R. Minnick: asst secy, dir
James A. Offutt: dir
Jack L. Petit: dir
Mark Zimmer: dir

APPLICATION INFORMATION

Initial Approach: Send letter with brief description of request. There are no deadlines.

GRANTS ANALYSIS

Number of Grants: 7
Highest Grant: $231,279
Typical Range: $500 to $3,500
Disclosure Period: fiscal year ending June 30, 1991

RECENT GRANTS

231,279 Agent Scholarship Awards, Columbia, MO
13,000 University of Missouri College of Business, Columbia, MO
3,500 Columbia College, Columbia, MO
3,500 Stephens College, Columbia, MO
1,500 Woodhaven Learning Center, Columbia, MO
500 Cancer Research Center, Columbia, MO
273 Christian Record Braille Foundation, Lincoln, NE

Shelton Cos. / Shelton Foundation

Revenue: $2.0 million
Employees: 10
Headquarters: Charlotte, NC
SIC Major Group: Real Estate

CONTACT

James E. Harris
Secretary-Treasurer
Shelton Cos.
3600 One First Union Ctr.
301 S. College St.
Charlotte, NC 28202
(704) 348-2200

FINANCIAL SUMMARY

Recent Giving: $504,833 (1990)
Assets: $1,347,639 (1990)
Gifts Received: $671,615 (1990)
Fiscal Note: Contributes through foundation only. In 1990, contributions were received from the Shelton Cos.
EIN: 58-1596729

CONTRIBUTIONS SUMMARY

Typical Recipients: • *Arts & Humanities:* arts appreciation, arts centers, history/historic preservation • *Civic & Public Affairs:* better government, environmental affairs, zoos/botanical gardens • *Education:* arts education, colleges & universities, medical education, science/technology education • *Health:* hospitals, single-disease health associations • *Religion:* churches • *Science:* scientific institutes • *Social Services:* community service organizations, family services, food/clothing distribution, homes, recreation & athletics, religious welfare, united funds, youth organizations
Grant Types: capital, general support, and multiyear/continuing support
Geographic Distribution: primarily North Carolina, with an emphasis on the Charlotte area
Operating Locations: NC (Charlotte)

CORP. OFFICERS

Charles M. Shelton: *CURR EMPL* pres: Shelton Cos

GIVING OFFICERS

James E. Harris: treas-secy
Ballard G. Norman: asst secy
Charles M. Shelton: pres *CURR EMPL* pres: Shelton Cos (see above)
R. Edwin Shelton: vp
Jack Zarrow: exec vp

APPLICATION INFORMATION

Initial Approach: *Note:* The foundation supports preselected organizations and does not accept unsolicited requests for funds.

Restrictions on Giving: Does not make grants to individuals.

GRANTS ANALYSIS

Total Grants: $504,833
Number of Grants: 27
Highest Grant: $150,000
Typical Range: $500 to $5,000
Disclosure Period: 1990
Note: Recent grants are derived from a 1990 grants list.

RECENT GRANTS

150,000 High Point College, High Point, NC
100,000 Wake Forest University, Winston-Salem, NC
60,000 Crosby
55,500 Winston-Salem State University, Winston-Salem, NC
30,000 United Way, Charlotte, NC
20,000 Friends of First Ladies
20,000 Medical Center, Charlotte, NC
10,000 Nature Science Center, Charlotte, NC
7,500 Art Council, Charlotte, NC
5,000 Bowman Gray School of Medicine

Shemanski Testamentary Trust, Tillie and Alfred

CONTACT

Don Porter
Vice President
Tillie and Alfred Shemanski Testamentary Trust
c/o Seattle First National Bank
PO Box 3586
Seattle, WA 98124
(206) 358-3388

FINANCIAL SUMMARY

Recent Giving: $311,874 (1990); $78,472 (1989); $167,042 (1988)
Assets: $3,238,041 (1990); $1,374,828 (1989); $3,139,583 (1988)
EIN: 91-6196855

CONTRIBUTIONS SUMMARY

Donor(s): Alfred Shemanski, the late Tillie Shemanski
Typical Recipients: • *Education:* colleges & universities • *Health:* hospitals, medical research, single-disease health associations • *Religion:* synagogues • *Social Services:* child

welfare, community centers, disabled, family services, united funds, youth organizations

Grant Types: general support
Geographic Distribution: focus on WA

APPLICATION INFORMATION

Initial Approach: Send brief letter of inquiry describing program or project. Deadline is November 30

GRANTS ANALYSIS

Number of Grants: 30
Highest Grant: $4,700
Typical Range: $600 to $3,000
Disclosure Period: 1990

RECENT GRANTS

4,700 United Way, Seattle, WA
3,100 Jewish Federation, Seattle, WA
3,000 Caroline Kline Galland Home, Seattle, WA
3,000 Jewish Community Center, Mercer Island, WA
2,000 Camp Brotherhood, Bellevue, WA
2,000 Youth Chaplaincy Program, Seattle, WA
1,200 American Cancer Society, Seattle, WA
1,200 Fred Hutchinson Cancer Research Center, Seattle, WA
1,200 Medical Foundation Harborview Medical Center, Seattle, WA
1,200 Multiple Sclerosis Society, Seattle, WA

Shenandoah Foundation

CONTACT

Shenandoah Fdn.
50 Fremont St., Ste. 3600
San Francisco, CA 94105
(415) 768-4946

FINANCIAL SUMMARY

Recent Giving: $118,400 (1991); $113,000 (1990); $99,150 (1989)

Assets: $2,388,237 (1991); $2,359,668 (1990); $2,301,442 (1989)

EIN: 94-1675019

CONTRIBUTIONS SUMMARY

Typical Recipients: • *Arts & Humanities:* arts centers, museums/galleries • *Education:* colleges & universities, education funds, private education (precollege) • *Health:* medical research, single-disease health associations • *Religion:* churches • *Social Services:* animal protection

Grant Types: general support
Geographic Distribution: focus on CA

GIVING OFFICERS

Elizabeth H. Bechtel: dir, vp
Stephen Davison Bechtel, Jr.: investment mgr *B* Oakland CA 1925 *ED* Purdue Univ BCE 1946; Stanford Univ MBA 1948 *CURR EMPL* chmn emeritus: Bechtel Group *CORP AFFIL* dir: IBM Corp *NONPR AFFIL* comm: Bus Roundtable; councillor: Conf Bd; dir: Am Soc French Legion Honor; mem: Am Inst Mechanical Engrs, Fellowship Engg, Labor Mgmt Group, Natl Action Counc Minorities Engg; mem adv counc: Stanford Univ Grad Sch Bus; mem bldg & grounds comm: CA Inst Tech; mem pres counc: Purdue Univ; trust: CA Inst Tech
A. Barlow Ferguson: dir, secy
Shana B. Johnstone: dir, pres
Theodore J. Van Bebber: treas

APPLICATION INFORMATION

Initial Approach: Contributes only to preselected organizations.

GRANTS ANALYSIS

Number of Grants: 35
Highest Grant: $25,000
Typical Range: $500 to $1,000
Disclosure Period: 1991

RECENT GRANTS

25,000 Head-Royce School, Oakland, CA — 2nd Century Fund
25,000 Orme School, Mayer, AZ
15,000 Georgetown University, Washington, DC
10,000 Santa Catalina School, Monterey, CA
6,600 Georgetown University, Washington, DC
6,500 Head-Royce School, Oakland, CA

5,000 Charlotte Country Day School, Charlotte, NC
3,000 ASPCA
3,000 Regional Center for the Arts
3,000 University of California Davis, Davis, CA — School of Veterinary Medicine

Shenandoah Life Insurance Co.

Sales: $131.83 million
Employees: 219
Headquarters: Roanoke, VA
SIC Major Group: Insurance Carriers

CONTACT

Genevieve Henderson
Assistant Corporate Secretary
Shenandoah Life Insurance Co.
PO Box 12847
Roanoke, VA 24029
(703) 985-4400
Note: Telephone extension is ext. 203.

FINANCIAL SUMMARY

Recent Giving: $105,000 (1993 est.); $108,392 (1992); $87,440 (1991)

Fiscal Note: Figures do not include public relations donations.

CONTRIBUTIONS SUMMARY

Company reports 27% of contributions go to the arts; 43% to civic affairs; 25% to education; 3% to health and human services; and 2% to business education and research, and economics and government. Company actively supports the United Way, YMCA, YWCA, American Red Cross, Junior Achievement, Boy Scouts, and Girl Scouts. Company provides time off from work to employees to allow them to volunteer for charitable organizations. Also sponsors a loaned employee program, works closely with a local elementary school, and promotes special events for students.

Typical Recipients: • *Arts & Humanities:* arts appreciation, arts associations, arts centers, dance, ethnic arts, history/historic preservation, libraries, literary arts, museums/galleries, music, opera, performing arts, public broadcasting, theater, visual arts • *Civic & Public Affairs:* better government, civil

rights, economic development, economics, environmental affairs, ethnic/minority organizations, professional & trade associations, safety, urban & community affairs, zoos/botanical gardens • *Education:* business education, colleges & universities, community & junior colleges, economic education, education associations, education funds, faculty development, health & physical education, medical education, minority education, special education, student aid • *Health:* emergency/ambulance services, health care cost containment, health funds, health funds, health organizations, medical research, medical training, mental health, single-disease health associations • *Science:* observatories & planetariums, science exhibits & fairs • *Social Services:* community service organizations, counseling, emergency relief, employment/job training, food/clothing distribution, recreation & athletics, shelters/homelessness, united funds, youth organizations

Grant Types: capital, emergency, employee matching gifts, general support, operating expenses, project, and scholarship

Nonmonetary Support Types: donated equipment, in-kind services, loaned employees, loaned executives, and workplace solicitation

Geographic Distribution: primarily VA

Operating Locations: VA (Roanoke)

CORP. OFFICERS

Charles D. Cox III: *CURR EMPL* vp, cfo: Shenandoah Life Ins Co
Hartley R. Gaston: *CURR EMPL* vp-info systems and svcs: Shenandoah Life Ins Co
Pearl H. Gearhart: *CURR EMPL* vp-admin: Shenandoah Life Ins Co
James E. Harshaw: *CURR EMPL* vp-group: Shenandoah Life Ins Co
Joseph E. Stephenson III: *CURR EMPL* pres, ceo, dir: Shenandoah Life Ins Co
Richard C. Wagner: *CURR EMPL* vp-indv ins svcs: Shenandoah Life Ins Co
P. Greggory Williams: *CURR EMPL* vp-investment, treas: Shenandoah Life Ins Co

APPLICATION INFORMATION

Initial Approach: Send full proposal including a description of the organization, amount requested, the purpose of the funds sought, and proof of tax exempt status. All requests must be in writing. There are no deadlines.

Restrictions on Giving: Does not support individuals, religious organizations for sectarian purposes, entertainment groups, war veterans organizations, advertising, athletic events such as golf or tennis tournaments, fund-raising endeavors of United Way agencies, or political or lobbying groups.

OTHER THINGS TO KNOW

Publications: Contributions Policy

GRANTS ANALYSIS

Note: Company reports that grant size varies.

RECENT GRANTS

American Red Cross - Roanoke Chapter, Roanoke, VA

Foundation for Roanoke Valley, Roanoke, VA

Jefferson Center Foundation, Roanoke, VA

Julian Stanley Wise Foundation, Roanoke, VA

Roanoke College Library, Salem, VA

The River Foundation, Roanoke, VA

Virginia Muesem of Transportation, Roanoke, VA

Virginia Tech Foundation, Blacksburg, VA—Tommorow's Teachers Program

Western Virginia Foundatin for Arts & Sciences, Roanoke, VA

YMCA of Roanoke Valley, Roanoke, VA

Shepherd Foundation

CONTACT

Richard B Passen
Trustee
Shepherd Foundation
69 Wesley Street
South Hackensack, NJ 07606-1597
(201) 343-5200

FINANCIAL SUMMARY

Recent Giving: $132,000 (1992); $30,000 (1990); $15,000 (1989)

Assets: $4,045,609 (1992); $2,010,061 (1990); $1,639,392 (1989)

Gifts Received: $578,700 (1992); $500,000 (1990)

EIN: 22-6460210

CONTRIBUTIONS SUMMARY

Grant Types: general support

GIVING OFFICERS

Lynn S. Bovenizer: trust
Richard B. Passen: trust
Charles V. Schaefer III: trust
Charles V. Schaefer, Jr.: trust

APPLICATION INFORMATION

Initial Approach: The foundation reports it only makes contributions to preselected organizations and does not accept unsolicited requests for funds.

GRANTS ANALYSIS

Number of Grants: 2
Highest Grant: $122,000
Disclosure Period: 1992

RECENT GRANTS

30,000 Stevens Institute of Technology, Castle Point, NJ

Sheppard Foundation, Lawrence B.

CONTACT

Paul E. Spears
President
Lawrence B. Sheppard Fdn.
c/o Hanover Shoe Farms
PO Box 339
Hanover, PA 17331
(717) 637-8931

FINANCIAL SUMMARY

Recent Giving: $176,000 (fiscal 1989); $83,000 (fiscal 1988); $81,000 (fiscal 1987)

Assets: $2,535,491 (fiscal year ending November 30, 1990); $2,543,624 (fiscal 1989); $2,302,917 (fiscal 1988)

EIN: 23-6251690

CONTRIBUTIONS SUMMARY

Donor(s): Lawrence B. Sheppard

Typical Recipients: • *Arts & Humanities:* libraries • *Education:* private education (precollege) • *Health:* health organizations, hospitals, medical research, nursing services, single-disease health associations • *Religion:* churches • *Social Services:* united funds, youth organizations

Grant Types: capital and general support

Geographic Distribution: focus on the Hanover, PA, area

GIVING OFFICERS

Charlotte S. Devan: vp
Lawrence S. Devan: trust
W. Todd Devan: trust
Betty J. Nolt: treas
Horace E. Smith: secy
Paul E. Spears: pres
Patricia S. Winder: trust

APPLICATION INFORMATION

Initial Approach: Send brief letter of inquiry describing program. Deadline is October 31.

GRANTS ANALYSIS

Number of Grants: 27
Highest Grant: $25,000
Typical Range: $1,000 to $6,000
Disclosure Period: fiscal year ending November 30, 1990

RECENT GRANTS

25,000 YMCA, Hanover, PA

20,000 Delone Catholic High School, McSherrystown, PA

12,000 Visiting Nurses Association, Hanover, PA

10,000 Clearview Terrace II, Hanover, PA

9,000 Trotting Horse Museum, Goshen, NY

8,000 American Cancer Society, Hanover, PA

8,000 Mount Olivet Cemetery Association, Hanover, PA

8,000 St. Vincent de Paul Church, Hanover, PA

7,000 American Red Cross, Hanover, PA

7,000 Hanover Area Historical Society, Hanover, PA

Sheridan Foundation, Thomas B. and Elizabeth M.

CONTACT

James I. Sinclair
President
Thomas B. and Elizabeth M. Sheridan Fdn.
Executive Plz. II, Ste. 604
11350 McCormick Rd.
Hunt Valley, MD 21031
(301) 771-0475

FINANCIAL SUMMARY

Recent Giving: $256,400 (1991); $232,400 (1990); $245,900 (1989)

Assets: $7,861,020 (1991); $6,098,752 (1990); $6,508,373 (1989)

EIN: 52-6075270

CONTRIBUTIONS SUMMARY

Donor(s): the late Thomas B. and Elizabeth M. Sheridan

Typical Recipients: • *Arts & Humanities:* history/historic preservation, museums/galleries, music • *Education:* colleges & universities, private education (precollege) • *Social Services:* child welfare, youth organizations

Grant Types: capital, emergency, endowment, general support, multiyear/continuing support, operating expenses, project, scholarship, and seed money

Geographic Distribution: focus on the greater Baltimore, MD, area

GIVING OFFICERS

L. Patrick Deering: vp, trust
J. Robert Kenealy: treas, trust
James L. Sinclair: pres, trust
John B. Sinclair: secy, trust

APPLICATION INFORMATION

Initial Approach: Send letter requesting application form. There are no deadlines. Board meets in March, June, September, and December.

Restrictions on Giving: Does not support individuals or fund loans or matching gifts.

OTHER THINGS TO KNOW
Publications: Application guidelines, program policy statement

GRANTS ANALYSIS
Number of Grants: 14
Highest Grant: $50,500
Typical Range: $3,000 to $25,000
Disclosure Period: 1991

RECENT GRANTS
50,500 Garrison Forest School, Garrison, MD
50,000 Notre Dame Preparatory School, Baltimore, MD
41,000 Baltimore Symphony Orchestra, Baltimore, MD
25,000 Maryvale Preparatory School, Brooklandville, MD
25,000 Mercy High School, Baltimore, MD
20,000 St. Frances-Charles Hall High School, Baltimore, MD
15,000 Maryland Historical Society, Baltimore, MD
10,000 Park School, Brooklandville, MD
6,000 Lehigh University, Bethlehem, PA
3,900 Loyola College, Baltimore, MD

Sherman Educational Fund

CONTACT
Reggie Laconi
Chairman, Selection Committee
Sherman Educational Fund
c/o Sullivan Peoples State Bank
32 South Court St.
Sullivan, IN 47882
(812) 268-4379

FINANCIAL SUMMARY
Recent Giving: $151,805 (1991); $173,364 (1990); $169,558 (1989)
Assets: $3,004,655 (1991); $2,889,998 (1990); $2,838,826 (1989)
EIN: 35-6020497

CONTRIBUTIONS SUMMARY
Grant Types: scholarship
Geographic Distribution: limited to IN residents

GIVING OFFICERS
Paul Asbury: comm mem

Jim Case: comm mem
Sarah J. Geitz: comm mem
Dale Knotts: comm mem
Reggie Laconi: chmn
Rick Walters: comm mem

APPLICATION INFORMATION
Initial Approach: Contact foundation for application form. Deadline is April 1.

OTHER THINGS TO KNOW
Provides scholarships to individuals for higher education.

GRANTS ANALYSIS
Disclosure Period: 1991
Note: In 1991, all contributions went to individuals.

Sherman Educational Fund, Mabel E.

CONTACT
Larry Dugan
Trust Officer
Mabel E. Sherman Educational Fund
c/o Citizens First National Bank
Storm Lake, IA 50588
(712) 732-5440

FINANCIAL SUMMARY
Recent Giving: $73,576 (fiscal 1991); $69,439 (fiscal 1990); $90,909 (fiscal 1989)
Assets: $1,973,302 (fiscal year ending June 30, 1991); $1,905,079 (fiscal 1990); $1,846,754 (fiscal 1989)
EIN: 42-6278859

CONTRIBUTIONS SUMMARY
Typical Recipients: • *Education:* colleges & universities
Grant Types: loan
Geographic Distribution: limited to IA, with preference given to residents of Ida and Cherokee counties

GIVING OFFICERS
Citizens First National Bank: trust

APPLICATION INFORMATION
Initial Approach: Loan application forms may be obtained from grantee colleges. There are no deadlines.

OTHER THINGS TO KNOW
Provides grants to Buena Vista College, Cornell College,

Morningside College, and Westmar College to finance student loans.
Publications: Annual Report

GRANTS ANALYSIS
Number of Grants: 4
Highest Grant: $23,714
Typical Range: $10,225 to $22,825
Disclosure Period: fiscal year ending June 30, 1991

RECENT GRANTS
23,714 Buena Vista College, Storm Lake, IA
22,825 Morningside College, Sioux City, IA
16,810 Cornell College, Mt. Vernon, IA
10,225 Teikyo Westmar University, LeMars, IA

Sherman Family Charitable Trust, George and Beatrice

CONTACT
George and Beatrice Sherman Family Charitable Trust
c/o Goulston and Storrs
400 Atlantic Ave.
Boston, MA 02110
(617) 574-6418

FINANCIAL SUMMARY
Recent Giving: $373,610 (fiscal 1992); $400,130 (fiscal 1991); $382,515 (fiscal 1990)
Assets: $3,624,868 (fiscal year ending June 30, 1992); $3,654,990 (fiscal 1991); $3,529,559 (fiscal 1990)
EIN: 04-6223350

CONTRIBUTIONS SUMMARY
Donor(s): the late George Sherman
Typical Recipients: • *Arts & Humanities:* museums/galleries • *Civic & Public Affairs:* ethnic/minority organizations • *Education:* colleges & universities, medical education • *Health:* hospitals, medical research • *Religion:* religious organizations, synagogues • *Social Services:* disabled
Grant Types: general support
Geographic Distribution: focus on MA

GIVING OFFICERS
Jacob Lewiton: trust
Alan W. Rottenberg: trust
Norton L. Sherman: trust

Marvin Sparrow: trust

APPLICATION INFORMATION
Initial Approach: Contributes only to preselected organizations.

GRANTS ANALYSIS
Number of Grants: 104
Highest Grant: $50,000
Typical Range: $100 to $2,500
Disclosure Period: fiscal year ending June 30, 1992

RECENT GRANTS
50,000 Brandeis University, Waltham, MA
50,000 Combined Jewish Philanthropies, Boston, MA
35,000 American Society for Technion, New York, NY
25,000 American Society for Technion, Boston, MA
25,000 Beth Israel Hospital, Boston, MA
25,000 Boston University School of Medicine, Boston, MA
25,000 Boston University School of Medicine, Boston, MA
25,000 Brandeis University, Waltham, MA
20,000 American Society for Technion, Boston, MA
10,000 Brandeis University, Waltham, MA

Sherwin-Williams Co. / Sherwin-Williams Foundation
Sales: $2.26 billion
Employees: 15,906
Headquarters: Cleveland, OH
SIC Major Group: Building Materials & Garden Supplies, Chemicals & Allied Products, and Miscellaneous Manufacturing Industries

CONTACT
Barbara Gadosik
Director, Corporate Contributions
Sherwin-Williams Fdn.
101 Prospect Ave. NW
Cleveland, OH 44115
(216) 566-2511

FINANCIAL SUMMARY
Recent Giving: $630,000 (1992 approx.); $637,653 (1991); $590,000 (1990 approx.)
Assets: $6,467,672 (1991); $6,457,478 (1989)

Fiscal Note: Company gives through foundation only.
EIN: 34-6555476

CONTRIBUTIONS SUMMARY

Typical Recipients: • *Arts & Humanities:* history/historic preservation, museums/galleries, opera, performing arts • *Civic & Public Affairs:* economic development, urban & community affairs • *Education:* business education, colleges & universities, economic education • *Social Services:* disabled, united funds, youth organizations

Grant Types: capital, employee matching gifts, and general support

Geographic Distribution: in areas of headquarters office and plant locations

Operating Locations: CA (Anaheim, Oakland), GA (Morrow), IL (Chicago, Elk Grove Village), KY (Richmond), MD (Baltimore, Crisfield), NC (Greensboro), NJ (Newark), OH (Bedford Heights, Cleveland, Deshler), TX (Garland)

CORP. OFFICERS

John Gerald Breen: *B* Cleveland OH 1934 *ED* John Carroll Univ BS 1956; Case Western Reserve Univ MBA 1961 *CURR EMPL* chmn, ceo, dir: Sherwin-Williams Co *CORP AFFIL* dir: Goodyear Tire & Rubber Co, Mead Corp, Natl City Bank, Parker-Hannifin Corp

Thomas Allen Commes: *B* Aurora IL 1942 *ED* St Thomas Coll 1964 *CURR EMPL* pres, coo, dir: Sherwin-Williams Co *CORP AFFIL* dir: Centerior Energy Corp, Soc Natl Bank

GIVING OFFICERS

John Gerald Breen: chmn, trust *CURR EMPL* chmn, ceo, dir: Sherwin-Williams Co (see above)

Thomas Allen Commes: asst secy, trust *CURR EMPL* pres, coo, dir: Sherwin-Williams Co (see above)

Barbara Gadosik: dir (corporate contributions)

Thomas Kroeger: asst secy, trust *CURR EMPL* vp (human resources): Sherwin-Williams Co

Larry Pitorak: secy, treas, trust *B* Chardon OH 1946 *CURR EMPL* sr vp (fin), treas, cfo: Sherwin-Wiliams Co

APPLICATION INFORMATION

Initial Approach: *Initial Contact:* brief letter or proposal to local Sherwin-Williams operating facility *Include Information On:* description of the organization, amount requested, purpose for which funds are sought, operating budget, list of donors and amounts recieved for past 12 months, recently audited financial statement, proof of tax-exempt status *When to Submit:* any time

Restrictions on Giving: Foundation does not support endowments, individuals, research, religious or political organizations, dinners or special events, fraternal organizations, goodwill advertising, member agencies of united funds, or elementary and secondary education.

GRANTS ANALYSIS

Total Grants: $637,653
Number of Grants: 500
Highest Grant: $154,000
Typical Range: $500 to $2,000
Disclosure Period: 1991
Note: Recent grants are derived from a 1991 Form 990.

RECENT GRANTS

159,400 United Way Services, Cleveland, OH

30,000 Cleveland Tomorrow, Cleveland, OH

25,000 John Carroll University, (School of Business), University Heights, OH

21,748 United Way/Crusade of Mercy, Chicago, IL

21,000 American Red Cross, Cleveland, OH

16,000 Cleveland Development Foundation/Inner-City School Fund, Cleveland, OH

12,500 Cleveland Museum of Natural History, Cleveland, OH

12,000 Musical Arts Association, Cleveland, OH

10,000 Case Western Reserve University, School of Medicine, Cleveland, OH

10,000 Cleveland Public Schools/Scholarship-In-Escrow-Program, Cleveland, OH

Sherwood Medical Co.

Sales: $700.0 million
Employees: 6,500
Parent Company: American Home Products Corp.
Headquarters: St. Louis, MO
SIC Major Group: Instruments & Related Products

CONTACT

Herbert Martin
Vice President, Human Resources
Sherwood Medical Co.
1915 Olive St.
St. Louis, MO 63103
(314) 621-7788

CONTRIBUTIONS SUMMARY

Operating Locations: MO (St. Louis)

CORP. OFFICERS

David A. Low: *CURR EMPL* pres: Sherwood Med Co
Jack Stafford: *CURR EMPL* chmn: Sherwood Med Co

Shiffman Foundation

CONTACT

Milton J. Miller
Shiffman Fdn.
2290 First National Bldg.
Detroit, MI 48226
(413) 586-4012

FINANCIAL SUMMARY

Recent Giving: $134,786 (fiscal 1991); $103,480 (fiscal 1990); $131,728 (fiscal 1989)
Assets: $2,035,719 (fiscal year ending September 30, 1991); $1,990,543 (fiscal 1990); $1,956,066 (fiscal 1989)
EIN: 38-1396850

CONTRIBUTIONS SUMMARY

Donor(s): Abraham Shiffman
Typical Recipients: • *Arts & Humanities:* museums/galleries • *Civic & Public Affairs:* ethnic/minority organizations, international affairs, public policy • *Education:* public education (precollege) • *Religion:* religious organizations, synagogues • *Social Services:* community service organizations, united funds, youth organizations

Grant Types: general support
Geographic Distribution: focus on Detroit, MI

GIVING OFFICERS

Beatrice Alexander: trust
Edward Allardice: trust
Bruce Gershenson: treas, trust
Lisa Kaichen: trust
Janet S. Kohn: trust, secy
Robert I. Kohn, Jr.: trust, vp
N. James Levey: trust, pres
Richard Levey: trust, vp
Lester Morris: trust
Victor Shiffman: trust

APPLICATION INFORMATION

Initial Approach: Contributes only to preselected organizations. Applications not accepted.
Restrictions on Giving: Does not support individuals.

GRANTS ANALYSIS

Number of Grants: 51
Highest Grant: $25,100
Typical Range: $100 to $5,000
Disclosure Period: fiscal year ending September 30, 1991

RECENT GRANTS

25,100 Federation of Allied Jewish Appeal, Detroit, MI

13,050 Jewish Community Federation, Cleveland, OH

12,000 Peace Development Fund, Detroit, MI

9,600 Children's Museum Friends, Detroit, MI

8,250 Congregation Shaarey Zedek, Detroit, MI

6,500 Taproot Community Education Center, Detroit, MI

5,000 Rehabilitation Institute, Detroit, MI

5,000 United Community Services, Detroit, MI

5,000 United Way, Detroit, MI

3,000 American Jewish Committee, New York, NY

Shinnick Educational Fund, William M.

CONTACT
William M. Shinnick
Educational Fund
534 Market St.
Zanesville, OH 43701
(614) 452-2273

FINANCIAL SUMMARY
Recent Giving: $212,215 (fiscal 1991); $177,683 (fiscal 1990); $179,430 (fiscal 1989)
Assets: $2,040,723 (fiscal year ending June 30, 1991); $2,818,285 (fiscal 1990); $2,676,232 (fiscal 1989)
Gifts Received: $87,910 (fiscal 1991); $84,770 (fiscal 1990); $76,995 (fiscal 1989)
EIN: 31-4394168

CONTRIBUTIONS SUMMARY
Donor(s): William M. Shinnick, Eunice Hale Buckingham.
Grant Types: loan and scholarship
Geographic Distribution: limited to Muskingum, OH

GIVING OFFICERS
William S. Barry: trust
Hazel L. Butterfield: trust, pres
Harold Gottlieb: trust
Annabelle Kinney: secy
J. Linsalm Knapp: trust
Norma Littick: trust

APPLICATION INFORMATION
Initial Approach: Request application form. Deadline is June 30.

OTHER THINGS TO KNOW
Provides educational loans and scholarships to students for higher education.

Shirk Foundation, Russell and Betty

CONTACT
James A. Shirk
Vice President
Russell and Betty Shirk Fdn.
103 North Robinson St.
Bloomington, IL 61701
(309) 827-8580

FINANCIAL SUMMARY
Recent Giving: $513,825 (1990); $280,075 (1989); $224,475 (1988)
Assets: $6,752,887 (1990); $6,180,508 (1989); $5,826,371 (1988)
Gifts Received: $492,000 (1990)
Fiscal Note: In 1990, contributions were received from Russell o. shirk ($492,000).
EIN: 23-7022709

CONTRIBUTIONS SUMMARY
Donor(s): Russell O. Shirk, James A. Shirk
Typical Recipients: • *Arts & Humanities:* arts centers • *Education:* colleges & universities, private education (precollege) • *Health:* hospitals, medical research • *Social Services:* child welfare, community service organizations, united funds, youth organizations
Grant Types: capital, operating expenses, and scholarship
Geographic Distribution: focus on IL

GIVING OFFICERS
Merrick C. Hayes: dir
B. J. Shirk: secy, treas
James A. Shirk: vp, dir
Russell O. Shirk: pres, dir

APPLICATION INFORMATION
Initial Approach: Send brief letter of inquiry describing program or project. There are no deadlines.

GRANTS ANALYSIS
Number of Grants: 24
Highest Grant: $460,000
Typical Range: $500 to $7,000
Disclosure Period: 1990

RECENT GRANTS
460,000 Illinois Wesleyan University, Bloomington, IL
10,125 Illinois State Foundation, Illinois State University, Normal, IL
10,000 Wesley United Methodist Foundation, Bloomington, IN
10,000 YMCA, Bloomington, IL
4,000 McLean County Youth Hockey, Bloomington, IL
3,000 American Red Cross, Bloomington, IL
3,000 University of Illinois, Urbana, IL
2,000 Occupational Development Center, Normal, IL
2,000 Park United Methodist Church, Bloomington, IL
1,500 Butler University, Indianapolis, IN

Shoemaker Co., R.M.
Revenue: $95.0 million
Employees: 200
Headquarters: West Conshohocken, PA
SIC Major Group: General Building Contractors and Nonmetallic Minerals Except Fuels

CONTACT
Del Wark
Vice President & Treasurer
R.M. Shoemaker Co.
One Tower Bridge PO Box 888
West Conshohocken, PA 19428
(215) 941-5500

CONTRIBUTIONS SUMMARY
Operating Locations: PA (West Conshohocken)

CORP. OFFICERS
John K. Ball: *CURR EMPL* ceo, pres: RM Shoemaker Co

Shoemaker Fund, Thomas H. and Mary Williams

CONTACT
Paul Keperlins
Assistant Vice President
Thomas H. and Mary Williams Shoemaker Fund
c/o Corestates Bank
PO Box 7558
Philadelphia, PA 19101
(215) 786-7624

FINANCIAL SUMMARY
Recent Giving: $321,000 (1990); $280,053 (1989)
Assets: $5,121,917 (1990); $5,605,906 (1989)
EIN: 23-6209783

CONTRIBUTIONS SUMMARY
Donor(s): the late Mary Williams Shoemaker, the late Thomas H. Shoemaker, Thomas H. and Mary Williams Shoemaker Trust
Typical Recipients: • *Civic & Public Affairs:* better government, international affairs, municipalities, public policy • *Education:* private education (precollege), religious education • *Religion:* religious organizations • *Social Services:* community service organizations, family services, united funds, youth organizations
Grant Types: capital, endowment, general support, multiyear/continuing support, operating expenses, scholarship, and seed money
Geographic Distribution: focus on PA

GIVING OFFICERS
William P. Camp: mgr
Alan Reeve Hunt: mgr
Barbara Sprogell Jacobson: secy, mgr
H. Mather Lippincott, Jr.: mgr
Regina Hallowell Peasley: mgr

APPLICATION INFORMATION
Initial Approach: Send cover letter and full proposal. Deadlines are April 15 and October 15.
Restrictions on Giving: Does not support individuals.

OTHER THINGS TO KNOW
Publications: Application Guidelines

GRANTS ANALYSIS
Number of Grants: 65
Highest Grant: $33,000
Typical Range: $1,000 to $8,000
Disclosure Period: 1990

RECENT GRANTS
33,000 Friends World Committee for Consultation, Philadelphia, PA
28,000 Friends General Conference, Philadelphia, PA
24,000 Pendle Hill, Philadelphia, PA
19,000 George School, Newton, MA

2445

15,000 Friends Information Center
15,000 Quaker United Nations House
13,500 Friends Journal
13,000 Jane Addams Peace Association
13,000 Westtown School, Philadelphia, PA
10,000 Quaker School at Horsham

Shoemaker Trust for Shoemaker Scholarship Fund, Ray S.

CONTACT
Ray S. Shoemaker Trust for Shoemaker Scholarship Fund
Harrisburg Community College
Cameron St.
Harrisburg, PA 17108
(717) 780-2400

FINANCIAL SUMMARY
Recent Giving: $149,785 (fiscal 1991); $120,408 (fiscal 1990); $73,023 (fiscal 1989)
Assets: $3,681,645 (fiscal year ending September 30, 1991); $3,115,968 (fiscal 1990); $2,146,923 (fiscal 1989)
Gifts Received: $4,025 (fiscal 1990); $250 (fiscal 1988)
Fiscal Note: In 1990, contributions were received from Vivian L. Pautier.
EIN: 23-6237250

CONTRIBUTIONS SUMMARY
Donor(s): Ray S. Shoemaker
Grant Types: scholarship

GIVING OFFICERS
Commonwealth National Bank: trust
Norma Gotwalt: dir
Benjamin Lowengard: dir
Joseph M. Melillo: dir
William Wood: dir

APPLICATION INFORMATION
Initial Approach: Application form required. Deadline is April 1.

OTHER THINGS TO KNOW
Funds a scholarship program for graduates of greater Harrisburg, PA, area high schools.

Shoenberg Foundation

CONTACT
William W. Ross
Secretary-Treasurer
Shoenberg Fdn.
200 North Broadway, Ste. 1475
St. Louis, MO 63102
(314) 421-2247

FINANCIAL SUMMARY
Recent Giving: $458,900 (1990); $485,200 (1989); $475,100 (1988)
Assets: $4,911,308 (1990); $4,919,572 (1989); $4,757,959 (1988)
EIN: 43-6028764

CONTRIBUTIONS SUMMARY
Donor(s): the late Sydney M. Shoenberg
Typical Recipients: • *Arts & Humanities:* history/historic preservation, museums/galleries • *Civic & Public Affairs:* environmental affairs, zoos/botanical gardens • *Health:* hospitals, medical research, pediatric health, single-disease health associations • *Religion:* religious organizations • *Social Services:* child welfare, community service organizations, disabled, family planning, youth organizations
Grant Types: capital, general support, multiyear/continuing support, and research
Geographic Distribution: focus on MO

GIVING OFFICERS
E. L. Langenberg: vp, dir
William W. Ross: secy, treas, dir
Robert H. Schoenberg: pres, dir
Sydney M. Schoenberg, Jr.: chmn, dir

APPLICATION INFORMATION
Initial Approach: Contributes only to preselected organizations.
Restrictions on Giving: Does not provide grants to individuals.

GRANTS ANALYSIS
Number of Grants: 35
Highest Grant: $121,000
Typical Range: $100 to $5,000
Disclosure Period: 1990

RECENT GRANTS
121,000 Missouri Botanical Garden, St. Louis, MO
101,500 St. Louis Art Museum, St. Louis, MO
100,000 Jewish Hospital of St. Louis, St. Louis, MO
30,000 Central Institute for the Deaf, St. Louis, MO
28,000 United Way, St. Louis, MO
25,000 Children's Hospital, St. Louis, MO
15,000 Jewish Federation of St. Louis, St. Louis, MO
10,000 Missouri Historical Society, St. Louis, MO
4,500 Arts and Education Fund Drive, St. Louis, MO
3,000 American Cancer Society, St. Louis, MO

Shoney's Inc.
Sales: $1.06 billion
Employees: 29,000
Headquarters: Nashville, TN
SIC Major Group: Eating & Drinking Places and Holding & Other Investment Offices

CONTACT
Sue Downs
Director, Corporate & Community Affairs
Shoney's Inc.
1727 Elm Hill Pke.
Nashville, TN 37210
(615) 231-2891

FINANCIAL SUMMARY
Fiscal Note: Company makes direct contributions. Annual Giving Range: $250,000 to $500,000.

CONTRIBUTIONS SUMMARY
Typical Recipients: • *Arts & Humanities:* arts festivals, arts institutes, community arts, ethnic arts, music, opera, performing arts, public broadcasting, theater • *Education:* business education, colleges & universities, community & junior colleges, education funds, elementary education, preschool education, private education (precollege), public education (precollege), student aid • *Health:* health funds, health organizations, hospitals, public health • *Religion:* churches • *Science:* science exhibits & fairs • *Social Services:* child welfare, community centers, community service organizations, counseling, day care, delinquency & crime, domestic violence, drugs & alcohol, emergency relief, employment/job training, family services, food/clothing distribution, homes, united funds, volunteer services, youth organizations
Grant Types: general support and scholarship
Nonmonetary Support Types: cause-related marketing & promotion, donated products, and in-kind services
Note: Nonmonetary support totals $85,000 annually.
Geographic Distribution: headquarters and operating locations
Operating Locations: TN (Nashville)

CORP. OFFICERS
W. Craig Barber: *CURR EMPL* cfo, vp: Shoneys
Taylor H. Henry, Jr.: *B* Mobile AL 1935 *CURR EMPL* ceo: Shoneys *CORP AFFIL* dir: Restaurant Mgmt Svcs *NONPR AFFIL* dir: TN St Univ; mem: AL Soc CPAs, Am Inst CPAs, Fin Execs Inst, TN Soc CPAs

GIVING OFFICERS
Sue Downs: *CURR EMPL* dir corp & commun aff: Shoneys

APPLICATION INFORMATION
Initial Approach: *Initial Contact:* letter of inquiry *Include Information On:* a description of organization, amount requested, purpose of funds sought, recently audited financial statement, and proof of tax-exempt status *When to Submit:* any time

OTHER THINGS TO KNOW
The company also operates Bootstraps Awards, Inc., a nonprofit scholarship program. Annual college tuition scholarships are presented to five high school seniors from Middle Tennessee. For scholarship information, contact Linda Bloodworth.

Shook Foundation, Barbara Ingalls

CONTACT
Barbara Ingalls Shook
Chairman
Barbara Ingalls Shook Fdn.
206 Hart Fell Cresent
Birmingham, AL 35223
(205) 970-0062

FINANCIAL SUMMARY
Recent Giving: $208,168 (fiscal 1991); $199,590 (fiscal 1990); $188,873 (fiscal 1989)
Assets: $5,305,552 (fiscal year ending August 31, 1991); $4,763,237 (fiscal 1990); $4,885,976 (fiscal 1989)
Gifts Received: $88,000 (fiscal 1990)
Fiscal Note: In 1990, contributions were received from Robert Ingalls Testamentary Trust.
EIN: 63-0792812

CONTRIBUTIONS SUMMARY
Typical Recipients: • *Civic & Public Affairs:* environmental affairs, zoos/botanical gardens • *Education:* colleges & universities • *Health:* hospitals, pediatric health • *Religion:* churches, religious organizations • *Social Services:* united funds
Grant Types: research
Geographic Distribution: focus on AL and CO

GIVING OFFICERS
Adele Shook Merck: trust
Barbara Ingalls Shook: chmn, treas, dir
Elesabeth Ridgely Shook: trust
Ellen Gregg Shook: trust
Robert P. Shook: pres, secy, dir
William Bew White, Jr.: trust

APPLICATION INFORMATION
Initial Approach: Send brief letter that includes proof of tax-exempt status. There are no deadlines. Decisions are made within six months.

OTHER THINGS TO KNOW
Publications: Application Form

GRANTS ANALYSIS
Number of Grants: 37
Highest Grant: $60,000
Typical Range: $100 to $6,000
Disclosure Period: fiscal year ending August 31, 1991

RECENT GRANTS
60,000 University of Alabama Birmingham Medical and Education Foundation, Birmingham, AL
40,000 University of Alabama Birmingham, Birmingham, AL — Camellia Pavilion
26,600 St. Vincent's Hospital Foundation, Birmingham, AL
25,000 Baptist Hospital Foundation, Birmingham, AL
10,100 Children's Hospital Foundation, Birmingham, AL
6,250 Aspen Foundation, Birmingham, AL
6,000 Eye Foundation Hospital, Birmingham, AL
6,000 United Way, Birmingham, AL
5,000 Episcopal Church of Advent, Birmingham, AL
5,000 Southern Research Institute, Birmingham, AL

Shoong Foundation, Milton

CONTACT
Fred Hom
Milton Shoong Fdn.
1401 Lakeshore Dr.
Oakland, CA 94612
(415) 465-0242

FINANCIAL SUMMARY
Recent Giving: $208,424 (1991); $298,837 (1990); $342,208 (1989)
Assets: $5,863,040 (1991); $5,640,561 (1990); $5,664,402 (1989)
EIN: 94-1200291

CONTRIBUTIONS SUMMARY
Donor(s): the late Joe Shoong, the late Rose Shoong, Milton W. Shoong, Betty Shoong Bird, Doris Shoong Lee, National Dollar Stores, Ltd., Richard Tam, Corinne Shoong
Typical Recipients: • *Arts & Humanities:* cinema, ethnic arts • *Civic & Public Affairs:* ethnic/minority organizations, zoos/botanical gardens • *Education:* colleges & universities, education associations • *Health:* medical research, mental health, single-disease health associations • *International:* international organizations • *Social Services:* child welfare, disabled, shelters/homelessness, youth organizations
Grant Types: capital, operating expenses, research, scholarship, and seed money
Geographic Distribution: focus on CA

GIVING OFFICERS
Howard T. Garrigan: vp, dir
Theodore K. Lee: vp, dir
Peter Mantegani: vp, dir
Charles Pius: vp, dir
Milton W. Shoong: pres, dir
Ed Sue: vp
Dwight Wright: vp, dir

APPLICATION INFORMATION
Initial Approach: Send brief letter of inquiry describing program or project. There are no deadlines.
Restrictions on Giving: Does not support individuals or provide loans.

GRANTS ANALYSIS
Number of Grants: 28
Highest Grant: $154,000
Typical Range: $250 to $2,000
Disclosure Period: 1991
Note: Above does not include individual scholarships.

RECENT GRANTS
154,000 Milton Shoong Chinese Cultural Center, Oakland, CA
12,000 American Cinema Awards Foundation, Studio City, CA — library building fund
6,000 SHARE, Beverly Hills, CA
5,500 Mt. Diablo Hospital Foundation, Concord, CA — cancer center building fund
5,250 Boys Town of Italy, San Francisco, CA — homeless children
2,500 San Francisco Zoological Society, San Francisco, CA
2,100 Medical Research Institute, San Francisco, CA
2,000 Equestrian Therapy for Handicapped Riders, Simi, CA
1,300 Girls Town of Italy, San Francisco, CA — homeless girls support
1,000 University of California Berkeley Foundation, Berkeley, CA

Shore Fund

CONTACT
Helen M. Collins
Shore Fund
c/o Mellon Bank, N.A.
P.O. Box 185
Pittsburgh, PA 15230-0185
(412) 234-4695

FINANCIAL SUMMARY
Recent Giving: $482,525 (1991); $1,769,000 (1990)
Assets: $2,411,420 (1991); $2,221,331 (1990)
Gifts Received: $241,019 (1991)
Fiscal Note: In fiscal 1991, contributions were received from the U.S. Trust.
EIN: 25-6220659

CONTRIBUTIONS SUMMARY
Donor(s): Benjamin R. Fisher and Fisher Charitable Trusts I and II
Typical Recipients: • *Civic & Public Affairs:* business/free enterprise, environmental affairs • *Education:* education funds, private education (precollege) • *Health:* hospitals, medical rehabilitation, public health
Grant Types: general support
Geographic Distribution: giving primarily in Pennsylvania

GIVING OFFICERS
Christine F. Allen: trust
Benjamin Fisher, Jr.: trust
Lillian Fisher: trust
Margaret F. McKean Walnutwood: trust

APPLICATION INFORMATION
Initial Approach: request application guidelines.

GRANTS ANALYSIS
Number of Grants: 35
Highest Grant: $200,000
Typical Range: $1,000 to $3,000
Disclosure Period: 1991

RECENT GRANTS
200,000 Children's Hospital Medical Center, Pittsburgh, PA
50,000 Conservancy, Pittsburgh, PA
50,000 Gateway Rehabilitation Center, Aliquippa, PA
50,000 Rehabilitation Institute, Pittsburgh, PA

25,000 Cancer Support Network, Pittsburgh, PA

10,000 Population/Environmental Balance, Washington, DC

5,000 Ellis School, Pittsburgh, PA

5,000 Masters School Annual Fund, Dobbs Ferry, NY

5,000 PAAR, Pittsburgh, PA

5,000 Pittsburgh Incorporated, Pittsburgh, PA

Shorenstein Foundation, Walter H. and Phyllis J.

CONTACT
Walter H. and Phyllis J. Shorenstein Fdn.
555 California St., Ste. 4900
San Francisco, CA 94104
(415) 772-7025

FINANCIAL SUMMARY
Recent Giving: $1,378,725 (1991); $700,500 (1989); $380,028 (1988)
Assets: $392,777 (1991); $81,677 (1989); $13,251 (1988)
Gifts Received: $390,430 (1991); $764,000 (1989); $310,000 (1988)
EIN: 94-6113160

CONTRIBUTIONS SUMMARY
Donor(s): Phyllis J. Shorenstein, Walter H. Shorenstein
Typical Recipients: • *Arts & Humanities:* museums/galleries, music, opera, public broadcasting • *Civic & Public Affairs:* public policy • *Education:* colleges & universities, education associations • *Health:* hospitals • *Religion:* religious organizations, synagogues • *Science:* scientific institutes • *Social Services:* united funds, youth organizations
Grant Types: general support
Geographic Distribution: focus on San Francisco, CA

GIVING OFFICERS
Iona Blampied: off
Debra Schiff: secy
Douglas W. Shorenstein: treas
Phyllis J. Shorenstein: vp
Walter H. Shorenstein: pres

APPLICATION INFORMATION
Initial Approach: Contributes only to preselected organizations.
Restrictions on Giving: Does not support individuals.

GRANTS ANALYSIS
Number of Grants: 32
Highest Grant: $261,000
Typical Range: $10,000 to $25,000
Disclosure Period: 1991

RECENT GRANTS
261,000 United Way, San Francisco, CA
200,000 United Way, San Francisco, CA
172,000 Joan Shorenstein Barone Foundation for Harvard, San Francisco, CA
105,000 United Way, San Francisco, CA
75,000 United Way, San Francisco, CA
75,000 United Way, San Francisco, CA
50,000 United Way, San Francisco, CA
35,000 United Way, San Francisco, CA
35,000 United Way, San Francisco, CA
27,500 Stanford University, Stanford, CA

Shott, Jr. Foundation, Hugh I.

CONTACT
Richard W. Wilkinson
President
Hugh I. Shott, Jr. Fdn.
c/o First National Bank of Bluefield
500 Federal St.
Bluefield, WV 24701
(304) 325-8181

FINANCIAL SUMMARY
Recent Giving: $1,110,343 (1991); $722,500 (1990); $404,500 (1989)
Assets: $23,272,138 (1991); $20,735,718 (1990); $6,531,649 (1989)
Gifts Received: $13,017,748 (1990); $910,362 (1989)
Fiscal Note: In 1990, contributions were received from estate of Jane Shott.
EIN: 55-0650833

CONTRIBUTIONS SUMMARY
Donor(s): The foundation was established in 1985 by the late Hugh I. Shott, Jr.
Typical Recipients: • *Arts & Humanities:* arts appreciation, arts associations, arts funds, community arts • *Civic & Public Affairs:* business/free enterprise, municipalities, urban & community affairs • *Education:* colleges & universities, community & junior colleges, public education (precollege) • *Social Services:* community service organizations
Grant Types: capital, general support, and matching
Geographic Distribution: focus on West Virginia

GIVING OFFICERS
First National Bank of Bluefield
trust
Scott Shott: vp
Richard W. Wilkinson: pres *ED* Univ VA 1955-1962 *CURR EMPL* pres, dir: Pocahontas Bankshares Corp *CORP AFFIL* pres, ceo, dir: First Natl Bank Bluefield

APPLICATION INFORMATION
Initial Approach:
The foundation requests applications be made in writing. The foundation has no deadline for submitting proposals. The board meets monthly.

GRANTS ANALYSIS
Total Grants: $1,110,343
Number of Grants: 11
Highest Grant: $300,000
Typical Range: $5,000 to $100,000
Disclosure Period: 1991
Note: Average grant figure does not include the highest grant of $300,000. Recent grants are derived from a 1991 grants list.

RECENT GRANTS
300,000 Bluefield State College Foundation, Bluefield, WV
290,000 Concord College Foundation, Athens, WV
205,000 Tazewell County Public School System, Tazewell, VA
149,843 City of Bluefield Sanitary Board, Bluefield, WV
100,000 West Virginia University Foundation, Morgantown, WV
25,000 New River Parkway Development Authority, Winton, WV
15,000 City of Bluefield, Bluefield, WV
12,500 Main Street Bluefield, Bluefield, WV
5,000 West Virginia Business Foundation, Charleston, WV
5,000 West Virginia Roundtable Foundation, Charleston, WV

Shreveport Publishing Corp.
Sales: $1.0 million
Employees: 5
Headquarters: Shreveport, LA
SIC Major Group: Printing & Publishing

CONTACT
Charles T. Beaird
President
Shreveport Publishing Corp.
PO Box 31110
Shreveport, LA 71130
(318) 459-3242

CONTRIBUTIONS SUMMARY
Operating Locations: LA (Shreveport)

CORP. OFFICERS
Charles T. Beaird: *CURR EMPL* pres, publ, treas: Shreveport Publ Corp

OTHER THINGS TO KNOW
Company is an original donor to the Charles T. Beaird Foundation.

Shubert Foundation

CONTACT
Lynn L. Seidler
Executive Director
Shubert Foundation
234 West 44th St.
New York, NY 10036
(212) 944-3777

FINANCIAL SUMMARY
Recent Giving: $3,558,000 (fiscal 1992); $3,554,800 (fiscal 1991); $3,065,200 (fiscal 1990)
Assets: $119,244,000 (fiscal year ending May 31, 1992); $115,449,000 (fiscal 1991); $116,445,658 (fiscal 1990)

Gifts Received: $150,000 (fiscal 1992); $162,683 (fiscal 1991); $155,063 (fiscal 1990)
Fiscal Note: The foundation receives contributions from the estate and trust of Lee Shubert under his will.
EIN: 13-6106961

CONTRIBUTIONS SUMMARY

Donor(s): The Shubert Foundation was established in 1945 as the Sam S. Shubert Foundation by Lee and Jacob J. Shubert in memory of their brother. The name was changed to the Shubert Foundation in 1971. The brothers contributed annually to the foundation. The foundation's funds were increased significantly by funds received from the estate of Lee Shubert in 1970 and from the estate of Jacob J. Shubert in 1972. The foundation is the sole shareholder of the Shubert Organization, which owns and operates the Shubert theaters. These theaters, and some associated real estate, are the principal assets of the foundation.
Typical Recipients: • *Arts & Humanities:* arts associations, dance, performing arts, theater • *Education:* arts education
Grant Types: general support
Geographic Distribution: to national organizations only

GIVING OFFICERS

Bernard B. Jacobs: pres *B* New York NY 1916 *ED* NY Univ BA 1937; Columbia Univ Law Sch JD 1940 *CURR EMPL* pres: Shubert Org *NONPR AFFIL* vp, dir: League NY Theaters Producers
John Werner Kluge: vp *B* Chemnitz Germany 1914 *ED* Columbia Univ BA 1937 *CURR EMPL* chmn, pres, dir: Metromedia *CORP AFFIL* chmn, treas: Kluge & Co, Tri-Suburban Broadcasting Corp; chmn, treas, dir: Kluge Finkelstein & Co; chmn, treas, pres: Silver City Sales Co; dir: Belding Heminway Co, Chock Full O Nuts, Just One Break Inc, Marriott-Hot Shoppes, Natl Bank MD, Waldorf Astoria Corp; mem adv counc: Mfrs Hanover Trust Co *NONPR AFFIL* bd gov: NY Coll Osteopathic Medicine; dir: Brand Names Fdn, Shubert Org; exec vp: Un Cerebral Palsy Assn; mem: Advertising Club Washington, Advertising Counc New York City, Grocery Mfrs Reps

Washington, Grocery Wheels Washington, Natl Assn Radio TV Broadcasters, Natl Food Brokers Assn, Natl Sugar Brokers Assn, Washington Bd Trade, Washington Food Brokers Assn; treas: Preventive Medicine Inst; trust: Miliken Univ Strang Clinic *PHIL AFFIL* chmn, don: Kluge Foundation
Gerald Schoenfeld: chmn
Lee J. Seidler: treas *B* Newark NJ 1935 *ED* Columbia Univ BA 1956; Columbia Univ MS 1957; Columbia Univ PhD 1965 *CORP AFFIL* dir: Safecard Svcs; gen ptnr: Bear Stearns & Co *NONPR AFFIL* dir, mem: NY St Soc CPAs; mem: Am Accounting Assn, Fin Analysts Federation, Fin Execs Inst; mem counc: Am Inst CPAs; prof accounting: NY Univ
Lynn L. Seidler: exec dir
Michael Ira Sovern: vp *B* New York NY 1931 *ED* Columbia Univ AB 1953; Columbia Univ LLB 1955 *CORP AFFIL* dir: AT&T, Chemical Bank, GNY Ins Group, Orion Pictures Corp, Shubert Org *NONPR AFFIL* Chancellor Kent prof: Columbia Univ Sch Law; fellow: Am Academy Arts Sciences; mem: Am Arbitration Assn, Am Bar Assn, Am Law Inst, Counc Foreign Rels, Natl Academy Arbitrators, NJ Bd Mediation Panel Arbitration, NY City Bar Assn, Pulitzer Prize Bd; mem bd dirs: Asian Cultural Counc, NAACP Legal Defense Ed Fund; mem panel arbitrators: Fed Mediation Conciliation Svc; pres: Columbia Univ
Irving M. Wall: secy

APPLICATION INFORMATION

Initial Approach:
All requests must be submitted on the foundation's application form.
Applicants must include audited financial statements for the most recent fiscal years and a copy of 501(c)3 tax exemption status letter. The statement should include comparative statement to the prior year. Applications are available after September 1 and must be received no later than December 1 to qualify for a grant.
The foundation uses various criteria in the evaluation of an applicant's program. Performing theater and dance organizations

are evaluated with respect to their contribution to their discipline as a whole. Larger, well-established organizations are expected to demonstrate their continued ability to develop and produce significant additions to their discipline. Smaller organizations are evaluated with respect to their size and resources. Both types of organizations are evaluated in terms of their effectiveness and efficiency in reaching audiences. Arts-related organizations are evaluated on the importance and value of their work as demonstrated by past and current performances. Financial need and responsibility are also important factors of the evaluation process. College and university drama departments are evaluated in terms of their ability to develop and educate new talent. The role that the school takes in theatrical innovation is considered. Preference is given to private universities.
Organizations improving the urban environment in which theaters operate are accorded preference. Non-arts-related organizations are sometimes allocated support, but they must possess unique attributes which demonstrate their deservedness. All grants are announced and disbursed in the spring of each year.
Restrictions on Giving: The foundation will not provide funds for audience development, direct subsidies to reduced admission price, theatrical productions for specialized audiences, brick and mortar projects, capital purposes, or to individuals.

OTHER THINGS TO KNOW

Publications: annual report

GRANTS ANALYSIS

Total Grants: $3,558,000
Number of Grants: 137
Highest Grant: $200,000
Typical Range: $5,000 to $50,000
Disclosure Period: fiscal year ending May 31, 1992
Note: Recent grants are derived from a fiscal 1992 grants list.

RECENT GRANTS

  200,000 Lincoln Center Theater, New York, NY

  200,000 New York Shakespeare Festival, New York, NY
  150,000 Mark Taper Forum, Los Angeles, CA
  120,000 Manhattan Theatre Club, New York, NY
  100,000 Columbia University, New York, NY — Presidential Scholars Program
  100,000 Long Wharf Theatre, New Haven, CT
   85,000 Actors Theatre of Louisville, Louisville, KY
   80,000 American Ballet Theatre, New York, NY
   80,000 New York City Ballet, New York, NY
   80,000 Playwrights Horizons, New York, NY

Shughart, Thomson & Kilroy, P.C. / Shughart, Thomson & Kilroy Charitable Foundation Trust

Headquarters: Kansas City, MO

CONTACT

George Leaonard
Trustee
Shughart, Thomson & Kilroy, P.C.
120 West 12th St.
Kansas City, MO 64105
(816) 421-3355

FINANCIAL SUMMARY

Recent Giving: $72,318 (1991); $66,990 (1990); $32,921 (1989)
Assets: $213,233 (1991); $248,872 (1990); $137,222 (1989)
Gifts Received: $24,363 (1991); $169,522 (1990); $27,018 (1989)
Fiscal Note: In 1991, contributions were received from Shughart, Thomson & Kilroy.
EIN: 43-1273591

CONTRIBUTIONS SUMMARY

Typical Recipients: • *Arts & Humanities:* dance, museums/galleries, music • *Civic & Public Affairs:* business/free enterprise, urban & community affairs • *Education:* colleges & universities, colleges & universities • *Health:* hospitals, single-disease health associations • *Religion:* religious organiza-

tions • *Social Services:* child welfare, youth organizations
Grant Types: endowment and general support
Geographic Distribution: primarily in the greater Kansas City, MO, area
Operating Locations: MO (Kansas City)

GIVING OFFICERS
Jack L. Campbell: trust
W. Terrence Kilroy: trust
George E. Leonard: trust

APPLICATION INFORMATION
Initial Approach: Send brief letter stating request and use of funds. There are no deadlines. Board meets monthly.

GRANTS ANALYSIS
Number of Grants: 71
Highest Grant: $15,000
Typical Range: $100 to $500
Disclosure Period: 1991

RECENT GRANTS
15,000 Kansas City Metropolitan Bar Association, Kansas City, MO
10,000 Washburn University, Topeka, KS — endowment funds
6,000 UMKC Advocacy Program, Kansas City, MO
2,100 Kansas City Friends of Alvin Ailey, Kansas City, MO
2,000 American Royal Association, Kansas City, MO
1,800 Gillis Center, Kansas City, KS — Kansas City Spirit Festival
1,550 Leukemia Society of America, Kansas City, MO
1,500 American Polled Hereford Foundation, Kansas City, MO
1,250 Friends of Chamber Music, Kansas City, MO
1,000 Kansas City Neighborhood Alliance, Kansas City, MO

Shuster Memorial Trust, Herman

CONTACT
Bernard Glassman
Herman Shuster Memorial Trust
1200 Four Penn Center Plaza
Philadelphia, PA 19103-0000
(215) 569-5571

FINANCIAL SUMMARY
Recent Giving: $500,000 (fiscal 1991); $250,000 (fiscal 1990)
Assets: $2,043,042 (fiscal year ending February 28, 1991); $2,355,470 (fiscal 1990)
EIN: 23-6875505

CONTRIBUTIONS SUMMARY
Grant Types: general support

GIVING OFFICERS
Warren Rubin: trust
Walter Shuster: trust

APPLICATION INFORMATION
Initial Approach: The foundation reports it only makes contributions to preselected organizations and does not accept unsolicited requests for funds.

GRANTS ANALYSIS
Total Grants: $500,000
Number of Grants: 2
Highest Grant: $400,000
Typical Range: $100,000 to $400,000
Disclosure Period: fiscal year ending February 28, 1991

RECENT GRANTS
400,000 State of Israel-Israel Air Force Helicopter Flight School
100,000 State of Israel-Israel Defense Services, Joint Services Command and Staff College

Shuwa Investments Corp.
Sales: $259.0 million
Employees: 250
Headquarters: Los Angeles, CA
SIC Major Group:
  Nondepository Institutions

CONTACT
Yoshio Yamashita
Vice Chairman
Shuwa Investments Corp.
801 South Grand
Ste. 600
Los Angeles, CA 90017
(213) 489-2757

FINANCIAL SUMMARY
Recent Giving: $750,000 (1990); $1,142,511 (1989); $775,925 (1988)
Fiscal Note: Annual Giving Range: $50,000 to $150,000

CONTRIBUTIONS SUMMARY
Support is made in such traditional giving categories as education, civic and public affairs, the arts, and social services.
Typical Recipients: • *Arts & Humanities:* museums/galleries • *Civic & Public Affairs:* municipalities • *Education:* student aid • *Social Services:* united funds
Grant Types: general support
Geographic Distribution: primarily in headquarters and operating locations, some national
Operating Locations: CA (Los Angeles)

CORP. OFFICERS
Takaji Kobayashi: *CURR EMPL* pres: Shuwa Investments Corp
Yoshio Yamashita: *CURR EMPL* vchmn: Shuwa Investments Corp

GIVING OFFICERS
Mary Nishina: *CURR EMPL* admin asst to vchmn: Shuwa Investments Corp

APPLICATION INFORMATION
Initial Approach: Send proposal any time, including a description of the organization and amount and purpose of funds sought
Restrictions on Giving: The New York office of Shuwa Investments makes its contributions at the behest of Tokyo. The California office has an independent program.

Shwayder Foundation, Fay
Former Foundation Name: Fay S. Carter Foundation

CONTACT
Fay Shwayder
President
Fay Shwayder Fdn.
6050 West Jewell Ave.
Lakewood, CO 80226
(303) 988-0041

FINANCIAL SUMMARY
Recent Giving: $188,570 (fiscal 1991); $224,590 (fiscal 1989)
Assets: $2,001,748 (fiscal year ending November 30, 1991); $2,860,574 (fiscal 1989)
EIN: 84-6041358

CONTRIBUTIONS SUMMARY
Donor(s): Fay Shwayder
Typical Recipients: • *Arts & Humanities:* arts institutes, community arts, dance, music, performing arts • *Civic & Public Affairs:* civil rights, ethnic/minority organizations, zoos/botanical gardens • *Education:* colleges & universities • *Health:* health organizations • *Religion:* religious organizations • *Social Services:* family planning, family services
Grant Types: general support
Geographic Distribution: focus on CO

GIVING OFFICERS
Judy Drake: trust
Sydney N. Freidman: secy, treas
Susan Hedling: trust
Fay Shwayder: dir, pres

APPLICATION INFORMATION
Initial Approach: Contributes only to preselected organizations.

GRANTS ANALYSIS
Number of Grants: 32
Highest Grant: $100,000
Typical Range: $500 to $10,000
Disclosure Period: fiscal year ending November 30, 1991

RECENT GRANTS
100,000 Federation of Allied Jewish Appeal, Denver, CO
10,000 Colorado Symphony, Denver, CO
10,000 CSM Foundation, Denver, CO
10,000 Denver Botanic Gardens, Denver, CO
10,000 National Jewish Center for Immunology and Respiratory Medicine, Denver, CO

6,000 Denver Public Library, Denver, CO

5,050 University of Denver, Denver, CO

4,000 Antioch College, Yellow Springs, OH

3,000 Planned Parenthood Federation of America, Seattle, WA

3,000 University of Colorado Foundation, Boulder, CO

SICO Foundation

CONTACT
SICO Fdn.
15 Mount Joy St.
Mt. Joy, PA 17552
(717) 653-1411

FINANCIAL SUMMARY
Recent Giving: $481,500 (fiscal 1991); $481,000 (fiscal 1990); $455,000 (fiscal 1989)
Assets: $11,204,042 (fiscal year ending May 31, 1991); $10,915,344 (fiscal 1990); $10,762,510 (fiscal 1989)
EIN: 23-6298332

CONTRIBUTIONS SUMMARY
Donor(s): the late Clarence Schock
Typical Recipients: • *Education:* colleges & universities
Grant Types: scholarship
Geographic Distribution: limited to DE and specified counties in PA and NJ

GIVING OFFICERS
Anthony Francis Ceddia: dir *B* Boston MA 1944 *ED* Northeastern Univ BS 1965; Northeastern Univ MEd 1968; Univ MA Ed D 1980 *CORP AFFIL* mem adv bd: Orrstown Bank *NONPR AFFIL* mem: Am Assn Higher Ed, Am Assn St Colls Univs, Middle Sts Assn Colls Schs; pres: Shippensburg Univ
Harrison Lueders Diehl, Jr.: dir *B* Philadelphia PA 1935 *ED* Albright Coll 1957 *CURR EMPL* treas, dir: First Mt Joy Corp *CORP AFFIL* treas, dir: First Mount Joy Corp, SICO Co
William H. Duncan: vp, dir
Franklin Roosevelt Eichler: treas, dir *B* Florin PA 1933 *ED* Elizabethtown Coll BSBA 1957 *CURR EMPL* pres, dir: Rollman Supply Co *CORP AFFIL* dir: Union Natl Mount Joy Bank; pres, dir: First Mount Joy Corp, Rollman Supply Co, SICO Co *NONPR AFFIL* mem: Natl Assn Accts

Fred S. Engle: secy, dir
Harry K. Gerlach: pres, dir
Carl R. Hallgren: dir
Joseph D. Moore: dir
Forest R. Schaffer: dir
John N. Weidman: dir

APPLICATION INFORMATION
Initial Approach: Contributes only to preselected organizations.

OTHER THINGS TO KNOW
Publications: Informational Brochure, Application Guidelines

GRANTS ANALYSIS
Number of Grants: 10
Highest Grant: $105,000
Typical Range: $12,000 to $108,500
Disclosure Period: fiscal year ending May 31, 1991

RECENT GRANTS
105,000 Millersville University, Millersville, PA
69,000 University of Delaware, Newark, DE
66,000 Shippensburg University, Shippensburg, PA
62,000 West Chester University, West Chester, PA
46,000 Kutztown University, Kutztown, PA
33,000 Delaware State College, Dover, DE
25,000 Cheyney University, Cheyney, PA
23,000 Glassboro State College, Glassboro, NJ
22,500 Stockton State College, Pomona, NJ

Siebe North Inc.
Sales: $252.0 million
Employees: 3,000
Parent Company: Siebe
Headquarters: Charleston, SC
SIC Major Group: Instruments & Related Products and Rubber & Miscellaneous Plastics Products

CONTACT
Herbert Boland
Director, Personnel
Siebe North Inc.
PO Box 70729
Charleston, SC 29415
(803) 554-0660

CONTRIBUTIONS SUMMARY
The vast majority of the company's donations are in the form of matching grants of employee gifts to United Way. Remaining contributions are made on a case-by-case, nonstructured basis to local charities.
Typical Recipients: • *Social Services:* disabled, united funds
Grant Types: general support
Geographic Distribution: principally near headquarters and operating locations
Operating Locations: CA, FL, IL, OH, PA, RI, SC (Charleston), VA, WI

CORP. OFFICERS
John W. Lynch: *CURR EMPL* pres: Siebe North

GIVING OFFICERS
Herbert Boland: *CURR EMPL* dir (personnel): Siebe North

APPLICATION INFORMATION
Initial Approach: Send letter any time, including a description of the organization, amount and purpose of funds sought, a recently audited financial statement, and proof of tax-exempt status.

Siebert Lutheran Foundation

CONTACT
Jack S. Harris
President
Siebert Lutheran Foundation
2600 North Mayfair Rd., Ste. 390
Wauwatosa, WI 53226-1392
(414) 257-2656

FINANCIAL SUMMARY
Recent Giving: $2,750,000 (1993 est.); $2,613,842 (1992); $2,317,425 (1991)
Assets: $58,000,000 (1993 est.); $57,900,000 (1992 est.); $49,720,659 (1991); $47,702,419 (1990)
Gifts Received: $20,150 (1988); $34,400 (1987)
EIN: 39-6050046

CONTRIBUTIONS SUMMARY
Donor(s): The Siebert Lutheran Foundation was established in 1952 by Albert F. Siebert (1879-1960), founder of Milwaukee Electric Tool Company. Mr. Siebert "elected to give his entire interest in his company to religious causes, using the Siebert Lutheran Foundation to accomplish this gift."
Born on October 18, 1879, in Dayton, OH, the son of a Lutheran minister, Albert F. Siebert pursued a sales career with National Cash Register, later accepting a position as sales manager of the A. H. Peterson Manufacturing Company in Milwaukee, WI. In 1924, he founded the Milwaukee Electric Tool Company, leading it to expansion and prosperity. During the Depression, the company underwent financial difficulties. Mr. Siebert, a religious man, vowed that if his company survived he would give his entire interest in the company to the church. The company prospered beyond his expectations, and the foundation materialized as a result of his vow. Before Mr. Siebert's death, he was able to witness the initial impact of the foundation on the Lutheran community. In 1976, the foundation sold its interest in Milwaukee Electric Tool Corporation to Amstar Corporation.
Typical Recipients: • *Education:* colleges & universities, continuing education, elementary education, faculty development, liberal arts education, preschool education, private education (precollege), religious education • *Health:* geriatric health, hospitals • *Religion:* churches, religious organizations • *Social Services:* aged, child welfare, day care, disabled, youth organizations
Grant Types: capital, conference/seminar, project, and seed money
Geographic Distribution: mainly Wisconsin

GIVING OFFICERS
Richard D. Barkow: secy, dir
Glen W. Buzzard: chmn, dir
Frederick H. Groth: treas, dir
Jack S. Harris: pres
John E. Koenitzer: vchmn, dir
Raymond J. Perry: dir
Armour F. Swanson: asst treas, dir

Neil A. Turnbull: dir

APPLICATION INFORMATION

Initial Approach:
The foundation suggests that applicants request detailed instructions prior to submission of a grant proposal. A personal meeting, telephone interview, or a written outline of the project is recommended before submitting a full proposal. Grant proposals must follow a dictated format and be numbered according to a four-part outline. Part one must include the full legal name of the organization or congregation, with address and telephone number; name of chief executive officer or pastor with title, business address, and telephone number; name of individual preparing the proposal, with title, business address, and telephone number; amount of funds needed; and a brief description or outline of project/program. Part two must include responses to questions outlined in the proposal instructions. Part three must be attached with the following information: a copy of IRS tax-exempt determination letter, current financial statement or audited report, program or project budget, and a copy of the minutes of the organization's governing body or the congregation's church council authorizing the grant proposal. Part four is for any attachments or other information which support the grant proposal, such as printed materials, charts, graphs, photographs, or illustrations. One copy of each will suffice. Mail the completed proposal in a large flat envelope. It should be accompanied by a brief letter describing the project/program and the amount requested.
Deadlines for grant proposals are March 15, June 15, September 15, and December 15. The board of directors schedules its meetings during the month following each deadline. If the 15th falls on a holiday or weekend, the closing date for grant proposals will be the last working day prior to the holiday or weekend.
The foundation requires that applicants follow set guidelines when submitting grant proposals. A brief transmittal letter must accompany each proposal.

This letter should be typewritten on the organization's or church's letterhead and signed by the chief executive officer or pastor. It is not necessary to include letters of recommendation or testimonials from other sources. Photographs and exhibits should be kept to a minimum. Prior to submitting proposals, authorization should be received from the applicant's governing body or from the church board or council. Grant proposals should be brief and concise. Applicants will be notified of approval or rejection of their requests. If approved, grantees may be required to sign and return a grant agreement form prior to the distribution of funds.
Restrictions on Giving:
Grants occasionally are made to provide seed money or start-up costs for a project. Grants generally are given for a one-year period. Recipients must be tax-exempt and must operate within the United States. Grants are not approved for other grant-making foundations, church camps, energy-saving projects, endowment funds, undergraduate and graduate fellowships and scholarships, purchase and maintenance of vehicles, computers or word processors, or trusts or other grant-making foundations. Grants generally are not given to churches for capital or operating expenses.

OTHER THINGS TO KNOW

Publications: application guidelines, policy guidelines

GRANTS ANALYSIS

Total Grants: $2,613,842
Number of Grants: 231
Highest Grant: $250,000
Typical Range: $2,500 to $25,000
Disclosure Period: 1992
Note: Recent grants are derived from a 1992 grants list.

RECENT GRANTS

250,000 Carthage College, Kenosha, WI — capital campaign
200,000 Concordia University, Mequon, WI — capital campaign
100,000 Next Door Foundation, Milwaukee, WI — capital project
100,000 Next Door Foundation, Milwaukee,

WI — capital project
100,000 Next Door Foundation, Milwaukee, WI — renovation of Helwig community center
100,000 United Lutheran Program for Aging, Milwaukee, WI — building needs
100,000 United Lutheran Program for Aging, Milwaukee, WI — capital improvement campaign
100,000 United Lutheran Program for Aging, Milwaukee, WI — daycare, health services and worship center
100,000 Wisconsin Lutheran College, Milwaukee, WI — construction of recreation center
75,000 Carthage College, Kenosha, WI — capital campaign

Siemens Medical Systems Inc.

Sales: $1.7 billion
Employees: 7,700
Parent Company: Siemens Corp.
Headquarters: Iselin, NJ
SIC Major Group: Instruments & Related Products

CONTACT

Peter Nebel
Vice President, Finance
Siemens Medical Corp./Siemens Medical Systems
186 Wood Avenue, South
Iselin, NJ 08830
(908) 321-3400

CONTRIBUTIONS SUMMARY

Operating Locations: CA (Concord, Sylmar), IL (Hoffman Estates, Milton), NC (Charlotte), NJ (Iselin, Piscataway), WI (Milton)

CORP. OFFICERS

Friedrich Kuhrt: *CURR EMPL* chmn, dir: Siemens Med Corp
Robert MacKinnon: *CURR EMPL* pres, ceo: Siemens Med Corp

Sierra Health Foundation

CONTACT

Len McCandliss
President
Sierra Health Foundation
2525 Natomes Park Dr., Ste. 200
Sacramento, CA 95833
(916) 922-4755

FINANCIAL SUMMARY

Recent Giving: $2,500,000 (fiscal 1993 est.); $1,174,502 (fiscal 1992); $2,413,288 (fiscal 1991)
Assets: $100,000,000 (fiscal 1993 est.); $95,794,367 (fiscal year ending June 30, 1992); $85,469,757 (fiscal 1991); $84,069,346 (fiscal 1990)
EIN: 68-0050036

CONTRIBUTIONS SUMMARY

Donor(s): The perpetual funding base for Sierra Health Foundation's philanthropic efforts was provided by Foundation Health Plan and Foundation Health Corporation, formerly known as Americare Health Corporation. Sierra Health Foundation was incorporated in 1984, in conjunction with the conversion of Foundation Health Plan (FHP) from nonprofit to for-profit status.
Typical Recipients: • *Health:* mental health, single-disease health associations
Grant Types: conference/seminar, loan, multiyear/continuing support, and project
Geographic Distribution: focus on Northern California

GIVING OFFICERS

Dorothy Beaumont: vp, cfo
Byron Demorest, MD: dir
George Deubel: dir
J. Rod Eason: chmn, dir
Albert R. Jonsen: dir *B* San Francisco CA 1931 *ED* Gonzaga Univ BA 1955; Gonzaga Univ MA 1956; Yale Univ PhD 1967 *NONPR AFFIL* mem artificial heart assessment panel: Natl Heart & Lung Inst; mem commn AIDS res: Natl Res Assn; prof, chmn dept med history & ethics: Univ WA Med Sch; mem: Am Soc Law Medicine
Leo McAllister: secy, dir
Len McCandliss: pres, dir
Robert E. Petersen: dir *B* Los Angeles CA 1926 *CURR EMPL* fdr, chmn: Petersen Publ Co *CORP AFFIL* owner: Petersen

Galleries, Petersen Productions, Scandia Restaurant *NONPR AFFIL* dir: Boys Club Am

Gordon Duane Schaber: dir *B* Ashley ND 1927 *ED* Sacramento St Coll AB 1949; Univ CA San Francisco JD 1952 *CURR EMPL* vchmn: Capitol Bank Commerce *CORP AFFIL* chmn: River City Cablevision *NONPR AFFIL* acting dean, prof: McGeorge Sch Law Univ Pacific; dir: Sacramento Regional Fdn; fellow: Am Bar Fdn; mem: Am Judicature Soc, Better Bus Bur, Comm Study Law Sch Process, Fin Aid Svcs Comm, League of Women Voters, Order of Coif, Phi Delta Phi, Sacramento Bar Assn; mem adv bd: Coll Pub Interest Law, Sacramento Bee Performing Arts Fund; mem bd advs: Pacific Legal Fdn; mem Sacramento chapter: Muscular Dystrophy Assn; mem, secy: Am Bar Assn; mem task force: Student Fin Aid Comm & Govt Rels; panelist: Sacramento Bee Secret Witness Program; vchmn: CA Ed Facilities Authority

James Schubert, MD: dir

Wendy Everett Watson: dir

APPLICATION INFORMATION

Initial Approach:
Applicants should submit a brief letter of intent of fewer than three pages.
Letters should include the name and mission of the organization seeking funds; name, address, and phone number of contact person; and proof of the organization's tax-exempt status. The letter should also include a description of the health issue to be addressed; description of the proposed project; budget; list of other funding sources; and plans for sustaining the project when a grant from the foundation expires.
After review of letters of intent, applicants will receive specific proposal instructions and deadlines.
The foundation accepts and reviews initial letters continuously. The foundation's board meets quarterly to review final funding requests.
Restrictions on Giving: The foundation does not support individuals, endowments, lobbying efforts, or projects that benefit only the members of a

private or religious group. The foundation supports recreation programs, operating budgets, deficits, clinical research, major equipment purchases, and conferences on a limited basis.

OTHER THINGS TO KNOW

Besides making grants, the foundation also supports conferences and seminars/workshops.
Publications: grants list, newsletter, application guidelines, informational brochure, fact sheet, occasional report

GRANTS ANALYSIS

Total Grants: $1,174,502
Number of Grants: 63
Highest Grant: $150,000
Typical Range: $15,000 to $75,000
Disclosure Period: fiscal year ending June 30, 1992
Note: Recent grants are derived from a fiscal 1992 partial grants list.

RECENT GRANTS

115,000 Center for Community Health and Well-Being
100,000 River Oak Center for Children, River Oak, CA
50,000 Big Valley Medical Center
41,000 Family Services of Butte and Glenn Counties, CA
37,000 Sierra Foothills AIDS Foundation, Nevada City, CA
24,500 San Joaquin AIDS Foundation, San Joaquin, CA
24,000 Stanislaus Community AIDS Project, Stanislaus, CA
23,500 Solano AIDS Tasks Force, Solano, CA
12,500 Healthy Mothers, Healthy Babies, CA
10,000 San Francisco Foundation, San Francisco, CA

Sierra Pacific Industries / Sierra Pacific Foundation

Sales: $310.0 million
Employees: 2,300
Headquarters: Redding, CA
SIC Major Group: Lumber & Wood Products

CONTACT

Myron Abrahemsen
Sierra Pacific Industries
PO Box 1341
Eureka, CA 95501
(707) 443-3111

FINANCIAL SUMMARY

Recent Giving: $139,018 (fiscal 1992); $126,940 (fiscal 1991); $106,147 (fiscal 1990)
Assets: $1,622,207 (fiscal year ending June 30, 1992); $1,633,300 (fiscal 1990); $1,576,064 (fiscal 1989)
EIN: 94-2574178

CONTRIBUTIONS SUMMARY

Typical Recipients: • *Arts & Humanities:* museums/galleries, music, public broadcasting • *Civic & Public Affairs:* business/free enterprise, safety, urban & community affairs • *Education:* student aid • *Health:* health organizations, hospices, medical research, nutrition & health maintenance, single-disease health associations • *Social Services:* child welfare, recreation & athletics, united funds, youth organizations
Grant Types: general support and scholarship
Note: Company names have the locations in their title, such as Burney Div., Quincy Div., etc.

CORP. OFFICERS

A.A. Emmerson: *CURR EMPL* pres, dir: Sierra Pacific Indus

GIVING OFFICERS

Carolyn Emmerson Dietz: treas
Ida Emmerson: pres
Richard L. Smith: vp

APPLICATION INFORMATION

Initial Approach: Applications should be submitted upon request. Application deadline is March 30.

GRANTS ANALYSIS

Number of Grants: 84
Highest Grant: $9,700
Typical Range: $200 to $500
Disclosure Period: fiscal year ending June 30, 1992
Note: Number, size, and range of grants figures exclude scholarship grants to individuals.

RECENT GRANTS

9,700 Humboldt State University, Arcata, CA
7,500 Shasta Senior Nutrition Program
5,000 Medical Research Institute
5,000 Sierra Valley District Hospital
4,316 KIXE, Los Angeles, CA
4,316 Medical Research Institute
4,000 Boy Scouts of America
2,812 Trinity County Junior Livestock
2,579 Lassen County Junior Livestock
2,400 Carter House Auction

Sierra Pacific Resources / Sierra Pacific Resources Charitable Foundation

Assets: $1.36 billion
Employees: 1,818
Headquarters: Reno, NV
SIC Major Group: Electric, Gas & Sanitary Services, Holding & Other Investment Offices, and Real Estate

CONTACT

Sierra Pacific Resources Charitable Foundation
Post Office Box 30150
Reno, NV 89520
(702) 689-3600

FINANCIAL SUMMARY

Recent Giving: $165,459 (1989)
Assets: $146,479 (1989)
Gifts Received: $310,205 (1989)
EIN: 88-0244735

CONTRIBUTIONS SUMMARY

Typical Recipients: • *Arts & Humanities:* community arts, opera • *Civic & Public Affairs:* economic development, environmental affairs, safety • *Education:* agricultural education, legal education, public education (precollege) • *Health:* hospitals, medical research, single-disease health associations • *Social Services:* community service organizations, disabled, family planning, united funds, youth organizations
Grant Types: general support

Operating Locations: NV
(Reno)

CORP. OFFICERS
Austin W. Stedham: *B* Salina
KS 1928 *ED* KS St Univ 1952
CURR EMPL chmn, pres, ceo:
Sierra Pacific Resources

GIVING OFFICERS
Stanton K. Berdrow: dir,
secy, treas
Joe L. Gremban: dir, pres
Austin W. Stedham: vp, dir
CURR EMPL chmn, pres, ceo:
Sierra Pacific Resources (see
above)

**APPLICATION
INFORMATION**
Initial Approach: Send brief
letter describing program.
There are no deadlines.

GRANTS ANALYSIS
Number of Grants: 192
Highest Grant: $8,600
Typical Range: $50 to $10,000
Disclosure Period: 1989

RECENT GRANTS
8,600 KIXE, Los Ange-
les, CA
7,550 Red Bluff Union
School District,
Los Angeles, CA
5,250 Siskiyou County
Office of Educa-
tion, Los Angeles,
CA
3,822 Planned Parent-
hood Federation of
America, Los Ange-
les, CA
3,000 Firechiefs Associa-
tion of Trinity
County, Los Ange-
les, CA
3,000 Willow Creek Fire
Department, Wil-
low Creek, CA
2,977 Trinity County Jun-
ior Livestock, Los
Angeles, CA
2,775 Arcata Little
League, Arcata, CA
2,500 Hayfork Little
League, Hayfork,
CA
2,000 Court Appointed
Advocate of Hum-
boldt, Humboldt,
CA

Sifco Industries Inc. / Sifco Foundation
Sales: $65.3 million
Employees: 577
Headquarters: Cleveland, OH
SIC Major Group: Fabricated
Metal Products

CONTACT
Charles F. Bixler
Treasurer
Sifco Foundation
970 East 64th St.
Cleveland, OH 44103
(216) 881-8600

FINANCIAL SUMMARY
Recent Giving: $94,735
(1991); $100,615 (1990);
$78,706 (1989)
Assets: $334,758 (1991);
$274,941 (1990); $218,318
(1989)
Gifts Received: $135,000
(1991); $135,000 (1990);
$90,000 (1989)
Fiscal Note: In 1991, contribu-
tions were received from
SIFCO Industries.
EIN: 34-6531019

**CONTRIBUTIONS
SUMMARY**
Typical Recipients: • *Arts &
Humanities:* libraries • *Education:* colleges & universities,
education funds, international
studies, public education (precollege), science/technology education • *Health:* health organizations • *Social Services:*
community service organizations, united funds, youth organizations
Grant Types: general support
Geographic Distribution:
focus on OH
Operating Locations: MN
(Minneapolis), OH (Cleveland,
Independence)

CORP. OFFICERS
Jeffrey P. Gotschall: *CURR
EMPL* ceo, pres: Sifco Indus
David Vincent Ragone: *B*
New York NY 1930 *ED* MA
Inst Tech SB 1951; MA Inst
Tech SM 1952; MA Inst Tech
ScD 1953 *CORP AFFIL* dir:
Augat Inc, BFGoodrich, Cabot
Corp, Cleveland-Cliffs Inc,
Sifco Inc; gen ptnr: Ampersand
Specialty Materials Ventures;
trust: MITRE Corp *NONPR
AFFIL* mem: Sigma Xi, Tau
Beta Pi; sr lecturer: MA Inst
Tech; pres: Case Western Re-
serve Univ
Charles H. Smith, Jr.: *CURR
EMPL* chmn: Sifco Indus

GIVING OFFICERS
C.F. Bixler: treas
C.M. Blair: trust
R.A. Demetter: asst secy
G.D. Gotschall: secy
Jeffrey P. Gotschall: trust
CURR EMPL ceo, pres: Sifco
Indus (see above)

R.S. Gray: trust
K. O'Donnell: vp
H.S. Richey: trust
E.J. Schmidt: trust
M.F. Scott: trust
Charles H. Smith, Jr.: pres
CURR EMPL chmn: Sifco
Indus (see above)
H.D. Smith: trust

**APPLICATION
INFORMATION**
Initial Approach: The foundation reports it makes contribution to preselected organizations and does not accept
unsolicited requests for funds.
Initial Approach: Send brief
letter describing program.
There are no deadlines.

GRANTS ANALYSIS
Number of Grants: 134
Highest Grant: $5,000
Typical Range: $100 to $1,100
Disclosure Period: 1991

RECENT GRANTS
5,000 Massachusetts Institute of Technology,
Cambridge, MA
3,200 United Way, Min-
neapolis, MN
3,000 Inner City School
Fund, Cleveland,
OH
3,000 John Carroll Uni-
versity, University
Heights, OH
2,500 Ohio Foundation of
Independent Col-
leges, Columbus,
OH
2,500 United Way, Cleve-
land, OH
2,000 Cleveland Clinic
Foundation, Cleve-
land, OH
2,000 Connecticut Col-
lege International
Center, Motzikin,
CT

Sigma-Aldrich Corp.
Sales: $589.4 million
Employees: 4,192
Headquarters: St. Louis, MO
SIC Major Group: Chemicals &
Allied Products and Fabricated
Metal Products

CONTACT
Kirk Richter
Controller
Sigma-Aldrich Corp.
3050 Spruce St.
St. Louis, MO 63103
(314) 771-5765

**CONTRIBUTIONS
SUMMARY**
Operating Locations: IL
(Highland), MO (St. Louis), NJ
(Metuchen), WI (Milwaukee)

CORP. OFFICERS
Alfred Robert Bader: *B* Vi-
enna Austria 1924 *ED* Queens
Univ BS 1945; Queens Univ
BA 1946; Queens Univ MS
1947; Harvard Univ MA 1949;
Harvard Univ PhD 1950;
Queens Univ LLD 1986 *CURR
EMPL* treas: B & K Enterprises
CORP AFFIL co-fdr: Sigma-
Aldrich Corp *NONPR AFFIL*
fellow: Royal Soc Arts; mem:
Am Chemical Soc
C. Tom Cori: *CURR EMPL*
chmn, pres, ceo, dir: Sigma-
Aldrich Corp

Signet Bank/Maryland / Signet Bank/Maryland Charitable Trust
Assets: $12.09 billion
Parent Company: Signet
Banking Corp.
Parent Employees: 4,702
Headquarters: Baltimore, MD
SIC Major Group: Depository
Institutions

CONTACT
Gail H. Sanders
Assistant Vice President, Public
Affairs
Signet Bank/Maryland
PO Box 1077
Baltimore, MD 21203
(410) 332-5878

FINANCIAL SUMMARY
Recent Giving: $673,000
(1993 est.); $673,000 (1992 ap-
prox.); $646,000 (1991 approx.)
Fiscal Note: Company gives
through the trust and directly.
Direct giving is approximately
$48,000 annually and is in-
cluded in above figures. For information, contact Gail H.
Sanders, Assistant Vice President of Public Affairs.

CONTRIBUTIONS SUMMARY

Typical Recipients: • *Arts & Humanities:* arts centers, arts festivals, history/historic preservation, libraries, museums/galleries, music, opera, performing arts, public broadcasting, theater • *Civic & Public Affairs:* business/free enterprise, economic development, environmental affairs, housing, international affairs, professional & trade associations, urban & community affairs, women's affairs • *Education:* business education, career/vocational education, colleges & universities, community & junior colleges, continuing education, economic education, education associations, elementary education, faculty development, literacy, minority education, private education (precollege), public education (precollege), special education, student aid • *Health:* health funds, hospitals, medical rehabilitation, pediatric health, single-disease health associations • *Science:* science exhibits & fairs • *Social Services:* aged, child welfare, community service organizations, day care, disabled, employment/job training, family services, homes, united funds, volunteer services, youth organizations

Grant Types: capital, challenge, endowment, general support, and multiyear/continuing support

Nonmonetary Support Types: cause-related marketing & promotion, donated equipment, loaned employees, loaned executives, and workplace solicitation

Note: Nonmonetary support is provided by the company. Estimated value for support was $21,500 for 1991. This amount is included in the figures above. Contact Diane Fitzhugh for information on nonmonetary support.

Geographic Distribution: Baltimore metropolitan area; the Maryland Eastern Shore

Note: Bank has 88 locations throughout central Maryland and on the Eastern Shore.

CORP. OFFICERS

Kenneth H. Trout: *B* Bridgeton NJ 1948 *CURR EMPL* pres, ceo: Signet Bank MD *NONPR AFFIL* dir: B & O Railroad Mus, Washington-Baltimore Regulatory Assn

GIVING OFFICERS

H. Victor Rieger, Jr.: exec vp, trust *CURR EMPL* exec vp (credit): Signet Bank/MD

Gail H. Sanders: asst vp *CURR EMPL* asst vp: Signet Bank/MD

Kenneth H. Trout: trust *CURR EMPL* pres, ceo: Signet Bank MD (see above)

APPLICATION INFORMATION

Initial Approach: *Initial Contact:* proposal *Include Information On:* description of the organization, amount requested, purpose for which funds are sought, program budget, recently audited financial statement, and proof of tax-exempt status *When to Submit:* any time *Note:* Bank does not respond to telephone solicitations.

Restrictions on Giving: Generally does not fund social functions, member agencies of United Way or Combined Health Agencies, organizations located outside of Maryland, religious organizations for religious purposes, individuals, tax-supported institutions, non-tax-exempt organizations, or organizations that actively oppose the bank on selected issues.

OTHER THINGS TO KNOW

Priority is given to special programs rather than providing support for ongoing activities. Bank also is interested in major institutional development of expansion programs for which there is a demonstrated need.

A grant in one year does not ensure future funding.

GRANTS ANALYSIS

Total Grants: $625,500
Number of Grants: 120
Highest Grant: $100,000
Typical Range: $1,000 to $10,000
Disclosure Period: 1991
Note: Above figures are for the trust only and do not include direct giving or nonmonetary support.

Sigourney Award Trust, Mary S.

CONTACT

James D. Devine
Trustee
Mary S. Sigourney Award Trust
P.O. Box 10206
Bainbridge Island, WA
 98110-0206
(206) 842-1097

FINANCIAL SUMMARY

Recent Giving: $90,000 (1991); $80,000 (1990)
Assets: $3,005,422 (1991); $2,637,585 (1990)
EIN: 77-6054596

OTHER THINGS TO KNOW

Awards grants to individuals for research in psychoanalysis.

Disclosure Period: 1991

Silicon Systems Inc.

Sales: $140.0 million
Employees: 1,800
Parent Company: TDK Corp.
Headquarters: Tustin, CA
SIC Major Group: Electronic & Other Electrical Equipment

CONTACT

John Holtrust
Vice President, Human Resources
Silicon Systems Inc.
14351 Myford Rd
Tustin, CA 92680
(714) 731-7110

CONTRIBUTIONS SUMMARY

Operating Locations: CA (Tustin)

CORP. OFFICERS

William E. Bendush: *CURR EMPL* sr vp, cfo: Silicon Sys
Alan King: *CURR EMPL* pres: Silicon Sys

RECENT GRANTS

162,500 University California, Irvine, Irvine, CA

Silver Spring Foundation

CONTACT

Silver Spring Fdn.
410 North Michigan Avenue, Rm. 590
Chicago, IL 60611

FINANCIAL SUMMARY

Recent Giving: $439,000 (1990); $432,000 (1989); $303,000 (1988)
Assets: $5,788,970 (1989); $4,829,292 (1988)
Gifts Received: $250,000 (1990); $260,000 (1989); $110,000 (1988)
Fiscal Note: In 1989, contributions were received from the Miami Corporation.
EIN: 23-6254662

CONTRIBUTIONS SUMMARY

Donor(s): Charles Deering McCormick, Miami Corp.
Typical Recipients: • *Arts & Humanities:* arts institutes, opera • *Civic & Public Affairs:* ethnic/minority organizations • *Education:* colleges & universities • *Health:* hospices, hospitals • *Social Services:* disabled, family planning
Grant Types: general support

GIVING OFFICERS

Charles Deering McCormick: trust
Charles E. Schroeder: trust *B* Chicago IL 1935 *ED* Dartmouth Coll 1957 *CURR EMPL* pres: Boulevard Bancorp *CORP AFFIL* dir: Blvd Bank North Am, Natl Blvd Bank Chicago, Natl Standard Co; pres, dir: Cutler Oil & Gas Corp, Miami Corp *NONPR AFFIL* mem: Fin Analysts Soc Chicago; trust: Northwestern Meml Hosp, Northwestern Univ

APPLICATION INFORMATION

Initial Approach: Contributes only to preselected organizations.

GRANTS ANALYSIS

Number of Grants: 22
Highest Grant: $97,000
Typical Range: $2,000 to $20,000
Disclosure Period: 1990

RECENT GRANTS

97,000 Wisconsin Historical Foundation, Madison, WI

75,000 Chicago City Day School, Chicago, IL

50,000 College of the Atlantic, Cobblestone Fund, Bar Harbor, ME

25,000 Groton School, Library Renovation Fund, Groton, MA

25,000 Lyric Opera of Chicago, Chicago, IL

20,000 Northwestern Memorial Hospital, Evanston, IL

20,000 Northwestern Memorial Hospital, Evanston, IL — Wesley Pavilion

20,000 Northwestern University, Evanston, IL

20,000 Planned Parenthood, Chicago, IL

10,000 North Avenue Day Nursery, Chicago, IL

Silverburgh Foundation, Grace, George & Judith

CONTACT
c/o Leipziger & Breskin
230 Park Avenue
New York, NY 10169

FINANCIAL SUMMARY
Recent Giving: $65,000 (fiscal 1991)
Assets: $3,101,330 (fiscal year ending August 31, 1991)
Gifts Received: $3,128,966 (fiscal 1991)
EIN: 13-3585189

CONTRIBUTIONS SUMMARY
Donor(s): substantial contributor is the estate of George Silverburgh
Typical Recipients: • *Civic & Public Affairs:* women's affairs • *Health:* pediatric health • *Social Services:* child welfare, employment/job training, religious welfare
Geographic Distribution: New York

GIVING OFFICERS
Leonard Weintraub: treas
Dori Wollen: vp
Roger C. Wollen: pres

GRANTS ANALYSIS
Total Grants: $65,000
Number of Grants: 5
Highest Grant: $25,000
Typical Range: $5,000 to $25,000

Disclosure Period: fiscal year ending August 31, 1991

RECENT GRANTS
25,000 Children's House, NY

20,000 Jobs for Youth, NY

10,000 United Jewish Appeal, NY

5,000 Make-a-Wish Foundation, NY

5,000 Women on the Job, NY

Silverman Fluxus Collection Foundation, Gilbert and Lila

CONTACT
Gilbert Silverman
President
Gilbert and Lila Silverman Fluxus Collection Foundation
24321 Mulberry Court
Southfield, MI 48034
(313) 353-9200

FINANCIAL SUMMARY
Recent Giving: $0 (1991); $0 (1990); $0 (1989)
Assets: $2,989,626 (1990); $2,947,370 (1989)
Gifts Received: $158,397 (1990); $134,458 (1989)
Fiscal Note: In 1991, contributions were received from Gilbert & Lila Silverman.
EIN: 38-2839549

CONTRIBUTIONS SUMMARY
Donor(s): the donors are Gilbert Silverman, the foundation's president, and Lila Silverman, the foundation's secretary
Typical Recipients: • *Arts & Humanities:* museums/galleries

GIVING OFFICERS
Jon Hendricks: vp
Gilbert B. Silverman: don, pres
Lila Silverman: don, secy, treas
Disclosure Period: 1990

Silverman Foundation, Marty and Dorothy

CONTACT
Lorin Silverman
Director
Marty and Dorothy Silverman Foundation
150 East 58th St., 26th Fl.
New York, NY 10155
(212) 832-9170
Note: All correspondence should be in writing.

FINANCIAL SUMMARY
Recent Giving: $4,868,150 (fiscal 1991)
Assets: $110,938,613 (fiscal year ending July 31, 1991)
Gifts Received: $2,500 (fiscal 1991); $35,007,000 (fiscal 1990); $30,717,200 (fiscal 1989)
EIN: 22-2777449

CONTRIBUTIONS SUMMARY
Donor(s): In fiscal 1991, the foundation received $2,500 from the officers: Marty Silverman, president; Carol Goldsmith, vice president; Joan Noritz, vice president; and Lorin Silverman, secretary and treasurer.
In fiscal 1990, the foundation received $35 million from CJL Investment Company of Scarsdale, NY; $5,000 from miscellaneous donors; and $2,000 from Wilbur Silverman of Miami Beach, FL.
In fiscal 1989, the foundation received $20 million from CJL Investment Company; $9,804,700 from Marty Silverman; $907,500 from North American Corporation of Sioux Falls, SD; and $5,000 in miscellaneous donations.
In fiscal 1988, the foundation received $1,190,354 from the CJL Investment Company in care of Century Equipment Leasing located in New York, NY; $40,354 from the DTC Corporation of Sioux Falls, SD; $16,074 from Marty Silverman; $15,000 from the Jodi Simon Charitable Trust located in North Woodmere, NY; and $10,000 each from Bernard Rosenberg and Frank Nevwirth.
Typical Recipients: • *Health:* hospitals • *Social Services:* aged, employment/job training
Grant Types: capital, general support, and project

Geographic Distribution: New York, NY

GIVING OFFICERS
Carol Goldsmith: vp, don, dir
Joan H. Noritz: vp, don, dir
Lorin Silverman: secy, treas, don, dir
Marty Silverman: pres, don, dir

APPLICATION INFORMATION
Initial Approach:
Applicants should send a written proposal to the foundation. Proposal should contain a description of the nature of the organization, a copy of the IRS tax-exempt determination letter, financial statements, and a list of officers and directors. There are no deadlines for submitting proposals.
The board meets usually every two or three months.

GRANTS ANALYSIS
Total Grants: $4,868,150
Number of Grants: 3*
Highest Grant: $3,000,000
Disclosure Period: fiscal year ending July 31, 1991
Note: Number of grants does not contain unspecified miscellaneous grants that amounted to $650. Average grant and typical range figures are not applicable due to restriced number of grant recipients. Recent grants are derived from a fiscal 1991 grants list.

RECENT GRANTS
3,000,000 St. Lukes-Roosevelt Hospital Center, New York, NY — warehouse building

1,862,500 United Jewish Appeal Federation, New York, NY — fund for programs for the aged

6,000 American ORT Federation, New York, NY

Silverweed Foundation

CONTACT
Silverweed Fdn.
c/o Yohalem Gillman and Co.
477 Madison Ave.
New York, NY 10022-5802
(212) 371-2100

FINANCIAL SUMMARY
Recent Giving: $385,359 (1991)

Assets: $8,231,771 (1991)
EIN: 13-3496446

CONTRIBUTIONS SUMMARY

Typical Recipients: • *Arts & Humanities:* arts festivals, community arts • *Civic & Public Affairs:* law & justice, urban & community affairs • *Education:* medical education • *Religion:* religious organizations • *Social Services:* family services
Grant Types: general support
Geographic Distribution: giving primarily in New York, NY

GIVING OFFICERS

Karen Freedman: pres
Nina P. Freedman: vp, treas
Susan K. Freedman: vp, secy

APPLICATION INFORMATION

Initial Approach: Contributes only to preselected organizations. Applications not accepted.
Restrictions on Giving: Does not provide grants to individuals.

GRANTS ANALYSIS

Number of Grants: 30
Highest Grant: $70,000
Typical Range: $1,000 to $25,000
Disclosure Period: 1991

RECENT GRANTS

70,000 Public Art Fund
50,000 Lilith Publications
50,000 United Jewish Appeal Federation of Jewish Philanthropies, New York, NY
40,000 Ackerman Institute, New York, NY
30,000 Ethical-Fieldstone Fund, New York, NY
25,000 Albert Einstein College of Medicine, New York, NY
25,000 Eldridge Street Project, New York, NY
15,000 Big Apple Circus, New York, NY
10,000 Center for Family Life, New York, NY
10,000 Paper Bag Players

Silvestri Corp.

Sales: $55.5 million
Employees: 300
Headquarters: Chicago, IL
SIC Major Group: Business Services, Electronic & Other Electrical Equipment, Stone, Clay & Glass Products, and Wholesale Trade—Nondurable Goods

CONTACT

Bettye Hogg
Vice President, Sales
Silvestri Corp.
2720 N. Paulina St.
Chicago, IL 60614
(312) 871-5200

CONTRIBUTIONS SUMMARY

Company provides educational matching gifts only.
Grant Types: matching
Operating Locations: IL (Chicago)

CORP. OFFICERS

Richard Feldstein: *CURR EMPL* chmn: Silvestri Corp
William Ripley: *CURR EMPL* pres: Silvestri Corp

APPLICATION INFORMATION

Initial Approach: Applications not accepted.

Simkins Industries, Inc.

Sales: $215.0 million
Employees: 2,000
Headquarters: New Haven, CT
SIC Major Group: Paper & Allied Products

CONTACT

Barbara Camera
Secretary
Simkins Industries, Inc.
PO Box 1870
New Haven, CT 06508
(203) 787-7171

FINANCIAL SUMMARY

Fiscal Note: Annual Giving Range: less than $100,000

CONTRIBUTIONS SUMMARY

Typical Recipients: • *Arts & Humanities:* general • *Civic & Public Affairs:* general • *Education:* general • *Health:* general • *Social Services:* general
Grant Types: general support
Geographic Distribution: primarily headquarters area
Operating Locations: CT (New Haven)

CORP. OFFICERS

James N. Galvin: *CURR EMPL* vp fin, dir: Simkins Indus
Leon J. Simkins: *CURR EMPL* chmn, pres, dir: Simkins Indus

APPLICATION INFORMATION

Initial Approach: Send brief letter of inquiry. There are no deadlines.

Simmons Family Foundation, R. P.

CONTACT

R. P. Simmons Family Fdn.
Birchmere Quaker Hollow Rd.
Sewickley, PA 15143

FINANCIAL SUMMARY

Recent Giving: $612,883 (1991); $616,033 (1990); $481,983 (1989)
Assets: $7,555,680 (1991); $5,098,224 (1990); $4,529,316 (1989)
Gifts Received: $2,017,500 (1991); $2,081,250 (1990); $1,284,375 (1989)
Fiscal Note: In 1991, contributions were received from Richard P. Simmons ($1,987,500), and Amy Simmons Sebastian ($30,000).
EIN: 25-6277068

CONTRIBUTIONS SUMMARY

Donor(s): Richard P. Simmons
Typical Recipients: • *Arts & Humanities:* arts centers, community arts, music, opera • *Education:* colleges & universities, literacy, private education (precollege), science/technology education • *Health:* health organizations, hospitals • *Social Services:* community service organizations, united funds, youth organizations
Grant Types: endowment, general support, professorship, and scholarship
Geographic Distribution: focus on PA

GIVING OFFICERS

Richard P. Simmons: trust *B* 1931 *ED* MA Inst Tech 1953 *CURR EMPL* chmn, ceo, dir: Allegheny Ludlum Corp

APPLICATION INFORMATION

Initial Approach: Contributes only to preselected organizations.
Restrictions on Giving: Does not support indivduals.

GRANTS ANALYSIS

Number of Grants: 60
Highest Grant: $25,000
Typical Range: $100 to $5,000
Disclosure Period: 1991

RECENT GRANTS

25,000 Pittsburgh Symphony Society, Pittsburgh, PA
25,000 Sewickley Academy, Sewickley, PA
25,000 United Way, Pittsburgh, PA
21,000 Pittsburgh Center for the Arts, Pittsburgh, PA
5,000 Pittsburgh Literacy Council, Pittsburgh, PA
5,000 Sewickley Valley Hospital, Sewickley, PA
5,000 Sweetwater Art Center, Sewickley, PA
3,000 Sewickley Academy, Sewickley, PA
2,500 Worchester Polytechnic Institute, Worcester, PA
1,500 Worchester Polytechnic Institute, Worcester, PA

Simon Charitable Trust, Esther

CONTACT

Leanne Workman
Administrator
Esther Simon Charitable Trust
St. David's Center, A-200
150 Radnor-Chester Rd.
St. David's, PA 19087
(215) 341-9270

FINANCIAL SUMMARY

Recent Giving: $800,000 (1992 approx.); $902,600 (1991); $704,000 (1990)
Assets: $8,655,322 (1992 est.); $8,375,322 (1991); $9,120,971 (1990); $9,141,835 (1989)
EIN: 23-6286763

CONTRIBUTIONS SUMMARY

Donor(s): Esther Annenberg Simon, daughter of Triangle Publications founder Moses L. Annenberg, and a sister of the company's chairman, Walter Annenberg, established the Esther Simon Charitable Trust in 1952 in New York. The foundation is one of nine Pennsylvania foundations established by the Annenberg family.
Typical Recipients: • *Arts & Humanities:* arts associations, dance, history/historic preservation, museums/galleries, music, theater • *Civic & Public Affairs:* environmental affairs • *Education:* arts education, colleges & universities, pre-

school education • *Health:* hospitals, pediatric health • *Religion:* churches

Grant Types: general support, project, and research

Geographic Distribution: the Northeast, principally New York

GIVING OFFICERS

Walter Hubert Annenberg: trust *B* Milwaukee WI 1908 *ED* Univ PA Wharton Sch *NONPR AFFIL* bd govs: St Josephs Coll Academy Food Mktg; bd lay trusts: Villanova Univ; fdr, pres: Annenberg Sch Communs; fellow: PA Academy Fine Arts; mem: Alliance Francaise Philadelphia, Am Newspaper Publs Assn, Am Philosophy Soc, Am Soc Newspaper Editors, Am Swedish History Fdn, Cum Laude Soc, English Speaking Union US, Friars Sr Soc, Inter-Am Press Assn, Intl Press Inst, Natl Army-Navy Mus, Natl Neiman Fund Comm, Navy League, Newcomen Soc, Phi Sigma Delta, Sigma Delta Chi; original incorporator, bd dirs, trust emeritus: Eisenhower Med Ctr; trust: Dermatology Fdn, Metro Mus Art, Natl Trust Historic Preservation, Un Fund, Un Fund Philadelphia Area, Univ PA; trust-at-large: Fdn Independent Colls; trust emeritus: Peddie Sch; trust emeritus: Philadelphia Mus Art

Mrs. Leanne M. Workman: adm

APPLICATION INFORMATION

Initial Approach: Restrictions on Giving: The foundation does not invite grant proposals nor does it give grants to individuals. Guidelines and annual reports are not available.

OTHER THINGS TO KNOW

The foundation is closely related to the Harriett Ames, Evelyn Hall, Lita Hazen, Janet Hooker, and Polly Levee Charitable Trusts.

GRANTS ANALYSIS

Total Grants: $902,600
Number of Grants: 74
Highest Grant: $100,000
Typical Range: $1,000 to $25,000
Disclosure Period: 1991
Note: Recent grants are derived from a 1991 Form 990.

RECENT GRANTS

100,000 Creative Alternatives of New York, New York, NY

63,000 Skowhegan School of Painting and Sculpture, New York, NY

55,000 John F. Kennedy Center for the Performing Arts, Washington, DC

50,000 Jewish Federation of Palm Beach County, West Palm Beach, FL

50,000 Manhattan Theatre Club, New York, NY

50,000 Mount Sinai Hospital, New York, NY

50,000 Paul Taylor Dance Foundation, New York, NY

40,000 Winston Preparatory School, New York, NY

35,000 New York Public Library Astor, Lenox and Tilden Foundation, New York, NY

25,000 Steppingstone Foundation, Boston, MA

Simon Foundation, Jennifer Jones

CONTACT

Ronald H. Dykhuizen
Jennifer Jones Simon Fdn.
411 West Colorado Blvd.
Pasadena, CA 91105
(818) 449-6840

FINANCIAL SUMMARY

Recent Giving: $240,000 (fiscal 1991); $323,200 (fiscal 1990); $294,500 (fiscal 1989)
Assets: $5,371,368 (fiscal year ending November 30, 1991); $4,743,481 (fiscal 1990); $4,376,401 (fiscal 1989)
Gifts Received: $288,562 (fiscal 1991); $332,926 (fiscal 1990); $279,981 (fiscal 1989)
Fiscal Note: In 1991, contributions were received from John E. Braun 1981 Charitable Annuity Trust ($20,000) and Norton Simon Charitable Lead Trust ($268,562).
EIN: 95-3660147

CONTRIBUTIONS SUMMARY

Donor(s): Norton Simon, Norton Simon, Inc., and its subsidiaries and predecessors, Braun 1981 Charitable Annuity Trust, Norton Simon Charitable Lead Trust
Typical Recipients: • *Arts & Humanities:* cinema • *Education:* education associations • *Health:* medical research, mental health
Grant Types: general support and research
Geographic Distribution: focus on CA

GIVING OFFICERS

Thomas E. Bryant: trust
Ronald H. Dykhuizen: asst secy, asst treas
Daniel X. Freedman: trust
Anne McKenna: trust
Michael E. Phelps: trust
Jennifer Jones Simon: chmn, pres, trust
Norton Simon: trust
Walter W. Timoshuk: vp, treas, trust, secy
Robert Walker: trust

APPLICATION INFORMATION

Initial Approach: Contributes only to preselected organizations.
Restrictions on Giving: Does not support individuals or provide loans, scholarships, or matching gifts.

GRANTS ANALYSIS

Number of Grants: 10
Highest Grant: $50,000
Typical Range: $10,000 to $50,000
Disclosure Period: fiscal year ending November 30, 1991

RECENT GRANTS

50,000 NARSAD, Great Neck, NY

50,000 University of California Regents, Los Angeles, CA

45,000 University of California Regents, Los Angeles, CA

33,000 Hereditary Disease Foundation, Santa Monica, CA

26,000 University of California Regents, Los Angeles, CA

12,500 University of California Regents, Los Angeles, CA

10,000 University of California Regents, Los Angeles, CA

10,000 University of California Regents, Los Angeles, CA

3,000 University of California Regents, Los Angeles, CA

500 Pen American Center, New York, NY

Simon Foundation, Robert Ellis

CONTACT

Robert Ellis Simon Fdn.
152 South Lasky Dr., Penthouse Ste.
Beverly Hills, CA 90212

FINANCIAL SUMMARY

Recent Giving: $185,279 (1991); $197,503 (1989); $222,674 (1987)
Assets: $4,235,082 (1991); $3,762,745 (1989); $3,251,221 (1987)
EIN: 95-6035905

CONTRIBUTIONS SUMMARY

Donor(s): the late Robert Ellis Simon
Typical Recipients: • *Health:* mental health • *Social Services:* child welfare, community service organizations, counseling, family services, united funds, youth organizations
Grant Types: project and seed money
Geographic Distribution: limited to Los Angeles County, CA

GIVING OFFICERS

Donald Simon: trust
Joan G. Willens: trust
Harold M. Williams: trust *B* Philadelphia PA 1928 *ED* Univ CA Los Angeles AB 1946; Harvard Univ LLB 1949 *NONPR AFFIL* co-chmn: Pub Commn Los Angeles Govt; mem: CA Bar Assn, Comm Econ Devel, Counc Foreign Rels; regent: Univ CA; trust: Natl Humanities Ctr

APPLICATION INFORMATION

Initial Approach: Contributes only to preselected organizations.

GRANTS ANALYSIS

Number of Grants: 5
Highest Grant: $49,800
Typical Range: $20,000 to $40,000
Disclosure Period: 1991

RECENT GRANTS

49,800 Psychiatric Clinic for Youth, Los Angeles, CA

48,700 Mental Health Association, Los Angeles, CA

45,963 California School of Professional Psychology, Los Angeles, CA

22,986 Dede Hersch Mental Health Center, Los Angeles, CA
17,830 El Nido Services, Los Angeles, CA

Simon Foundation, Sidney, Milton and Leoma

CONTACT
Joseph C. Warner
Trustee
Sidney, Milton and Leoma Simon Fdn.
2025 N.W. 29th Rd.
Boca Raton, FL 33431

FINANCIAL SUMMARY
Recent Giving: $468,500 (fiscal 1992); $445,000 (fiscal 1991); $422,000 (fiscal 1990)
Assets: $11,757,907 (fiscal year ending May 31, 1992); $11,166,216 (fiscal 1991); $10,617,672 (fiscal 1990)
EIN: 13-6175218

CONTRIBUTIONS SUMMARY
Donor(s): the late Milton Simon
Typical Recipients: • *Arts & Humanities:* performing arts, public broadcasting • *Civic & Public Affairs:* environmental affairs, ethnic/minority organizations, zoos/botanical gardens • *Health:* hospitals, medical research, single-disease health associations • *Religion:* synagogues • *Social Services:* child welfare, disabled, recreation & athletics, youth organizations
Grant Types: research

GIVING OFFICERS
Joseph C. Warner: trust
Meryl Warner: trust
Alan Wechsler: trust

APPLICATION INFORMATION
Initial Approach: Send brief letter of inquiry describing program or project. There are no deadlines.

GRANTS ANALYSIS
Number of Grants: 64
Highest Grant: $12,000
Typical Range: $5,000 to $8,000
Disclosure Period: fiscal year ending May 31, 1992

RECENT GRANTS
12,000 Beth Israel Hospital, Boston, MA
12,000 Educational Broadcasting, New York, NY
12,000 Play Schools Association, New York, NY
11,000 American Foundation for the Blind, New York, NY
11,000 American Jewish Committee, New York, NY
11,000 Hadassah Hospital Medical Organization, New York, NY
10,000 Columbia Presbyterian Medical Center, New York, NY
10,000 National Jewish Center for Immunology and Respiratory Medicine, Denver, CO
10,000 United Jewish Appeal Federation of Jewish Philanthropies, New York, NY
9,000 New York Zoological Society, New York, NY

Simon Foundation, William E. and Carol G.

CONTACT
William E. Simon
Chairman
William E. and Carol G. Simon Foundation
c/o William E. Simons & Sons
310 South St., PO Box 1913
Morristown, NJ 07962-1913
(201) 898-0293

FINANCIAL SUMMARY
Recent Giving: $1,657,373 (1991); $525,201 (1990)
Assets: $11,378,167 (1991); $10,341,399 (1990)
Gifts Received: $416,400 (1991); $40,000 (1990)
EIN: 13-6217788

CONTRIBUTIONS SUMMARY
Donor(s): The William E. and Carol G. Simon Foundation was established in the mid 1980s by William E. Simon, former secretary of the treasury under former Presidents Richard Nixon and Gerald Ford. Mr. Simon was born in 1927 in Paterson, NJ, went to Newark Academy, then Lafayette College where he graduated in 1951 with a bachelor's degree in government and law. He went right to work on Wall Street, specializing in government securities and municipal bonds. He rose to become a senior partner in Salomon Brothers, a large investment firm where his annual salary is estaimated to have been between $2 million and $3 million in 1971 and 1972.

He left Wall street in 1972 when he was appointed as the deputy secretary of the treasury under George Schultz. One year later, Mr. Simon was named the administrator of the Federal Energy Office where, as the "energy czar," he coordinated the country's energy policy during the energy crisis. He left that post to become the secretary of the treasury in 1974 where he served until 1977, when he left government service.

Before he began his government service, Mr. Simon had placed in a blind trust his assets which had declined about 60% in value. Once back in private life, Mr. Simon began to rebuild his personal wealth by establishing his own network of consultancies and corporate relationships. He combined his economic expertise with his recent government service to negotiate financial opportunities with the largest companies in the country. He joined a dozen or so blue-chip corporate and philanthropic boards including Xerox Corporation and the John M. Olin Foundation.

In 1981, Mr. Simon and Ray Chambers founded Wesray Corporation, an investment and banking firm that specialized in leveraged buyouts. The company became one of the the largest private companies in the country with sales of $1.8 billion in 1983. Today, Mr. Simon directs his own company, William E. Simon and Sons located in Morristown, NJ. His personal fortune was estimated to be approximately $300 million in 1991.

Mr. Simon's accomplishments reflect a personal philosophy of hard work and a belief in the free enterprise system. His associates have described him as a nonstop worker who can regularly put in 18-hour days. He authored two books including "A Time for Truth" an account of his Washington, DC, experiences and conservative economics, which was a bestseller for 30 weeks. He donated the proceeds to his alma mater, Lafayette College in Easton, PA. He has served on or is currently serving on the boards of more than 60 charitable organizations. He has received more than 50 awards, and he is a member of more than 20 clubs across the country.

He married the former Carol Girard in 1950. The couple has seven children: William E. Simon, Jr., John P. Simon, Mary Beth Simon Streep, Carol Leigh Simon Porges, Aimee Simon Bloom, Julie Ann Simon and Johanna Katrina Simon. The nine members of the family serve as officers or directors of the William E. and Carol Simon Foundation.

Typical Recipients: • *Arts & Humanities:* arts associations, arts funds, cinema, dance, history/historic preservation, libraries, museums/galleries, music • *Civic & Public Affairs:* better government, civil rights, ethnic/minority organizations, first amendment issues, municipalities, philanthropic organizations, professional & trade associations, public policy, safety, urban & community affairs, women's affairs • *Education:* arts education, business education, career/vocational education, colleges & universities, education associations, education funds, private education (precollege), religious education, special education • *Health:* health organizations, hospices, hospitals, nursing services, public health, single-disease health associations • *International:* international organizations • *Religion:* churches, religious organizations • *Social Services:* animal protection, child welfare, community centers, community service organizations, disabled, drugs & alcohol, family services, food/clothing distribution, homes, recreation & athletics, shelters/homelessness, united funds, youth organizations
Grant Types: capital, endowment, general support, operating expenses, and scholarship
Geographic Distribution: nationally, with emphasis on the Northeast particularly New York and New Jersey

GIVING OFFICERS
Aimee Simon Bloom: dir
Carol Leigh Simon Porges: dir
Carol G. Simon: pres, dir
J. Peter Simon: vp, secy, dir
Johanna K. Simon: dir

Julie A. Simon: dir
William E. Simon, Jr.: treas, dir
William Edward Simon: chmn, dir B Paterson NJ 1927 *ED* Lafayette Coll BA 1951 *CURR EMPL* chmn, pres: William E Simon & Sons *CORP AFFIL* chmn emeritus: Wesray Corp; co chmn: WSPG Intl Los Angeles; dir: All St Ins Co, Calvin Bullock Ltd, Johnson & Johnson, Pompano Park Realty *NONPR AFFIL* bd govs: Natl Counc Recording Blind, NY Hosp, Hugh O'Brien Youth Federation, Ronald Reagan Presidential Fdn; chmn bd trusts: US Olympic Fdn; chmn investment comm: US Air Force Academy; co chmn, dir: Endowment Comm Covenant House; dir: Am Friends Covent Gardens, Atlantic Counc US, Boys Harbor, Catholic Big Brothers, Citizens Against Govt Waste, Citizens Network Foreign Affs, Courage Fdn, Intl Fdn Ed Self Help, Kissinger Assocs, Natl Football Fdn Hall Fame, Royal Ballet, Sequoia Inst, Space Studies Inst; dir, mem budget fin comm: Gerald R Ford Fdn; hon chmn: Comm Preservation Treasury Bldg, Inst Ed Affs; hon co-chmn: Liberty Park Fdn, Natl Fitness Fdn, Suffolk County Vietnam Veterans Meml Comm, US Fitness Academy Campaign; hon trust: Adelphi Univ, Newark Boys Chorus Sch; mem: Amwell Valley Conservancy, Asia Soc, Assn NJ Rifle & Pistol, Counc Foreign Rels, Explorers Club, Friendly Sons St Patrick, Intl Comm Human Dignity, Morality Media, Order Malta, PA Soc, Pilgrims US, Villa Taverna Soc; mem adv bd: Action Inst, Catholics Committed Support Pope, Ctr Christianity Common Good, Ctr Intl Mgmt Ed Univ Dallas, John D J Moore Scholarship Fund, Pacific Security Res Inst, Private Sectors Initiative Fdn, SAIL Adventures Learning, Univ Southern CA Bus Admin, US Assn Blind Athletes, Womens Sports Fdn; mem adv bd, secy, treas: Jesse Owens Fdn; mem adv counc: Consumer Alert; mem bd overseers: Exec Counc Foreign Diplomats, Hoover Inst; mem chmn comm: Natl Counc Alcoholism & Drug Dependence; mem comm: Cardinals Comm Laity; mem counc: Templeton Coll; mem exec bd adm comm: US Olympic Comm; mem exec

comm: Bretton Woods Comm, Daytop Village; mem hon comm: Womens Econ Roundtable; mem inaugural adv bd: Gene Autry Western Heritage Mus; mem intl adv bd: Intl Ctr Disabled; mem intl councillors: Ctr Strategic Intl Studies; mem natl adv bd: Sudden Infant Death Syndrome; mem natl counc, trust: Freedom Foundation Valley Forge; mem natl steering comm: Jefferson Energy Foundation; mem organizing comm: World Cup 94; mem policy counc: Tax Fdn; mem visiting comm: St Univ NY Stony Brook Marine Sciences Res Ctr; pres: Richard Nixon Presidential Library Birthplace Fdn; prin: Counc Excellence Govt, Counc Excellence in Govt; trust: Animal Med Ctr, Boston Univ, Hillsdale Coll, Marshall (George C) Res Fdn, Natl Investors Hall Fame; trust emeritus: Lafayette Coll; trust, mem fin comm: Heritage Fdn; trust, mem investment comm, mem exec adv counc: Univ Rochester Simon Sch
Mary B. Simon Streep: dir

APPLICATION INFORMATION
Initial Approach:
The foundation has no standard application form. Proposals should be made in writing and sent to the foundation.
Grant applications require a description of the proposed project, the amount requested and a copy of the IRS determination letter stating that the organization is a tax-exempt charitable organization.
Applications may be submitted at any time.
Restrictions on Giving: The foundation does not list any restrictions or limitations on awards, such as by geographical areas, charitable fields, kinds of institutions, or other factors.

OTHER THINGS TO KNOW
In 1990, the foundation received $40,000 worth of ENSR Corporation stock from William E. Simon.

GRANTS ANALYSIS
Total Grants: $1,657,373
Number of Grants: 224
Highest Grant: $166,667
Typical Range: $500 to $5,000 and $25,000 to $100,000
Disclosure Period: 1991

Note: Recent grants are derived from a 1991 Form 990.

RECENT GRANTS

166,667	Archdiocese of New York, New York, NY
100,000	Manhattanville College, Purchase, NY
100,000	University of Rochester, Rochester, NY
100,000	University of Rochester, Rochester, NY
100,000	University of Rochester, Rochester, NY
100,000	University of Rochester, Rochester, NY
100,000	University of Rochester, Rochester, NY
100,000	University of Rochester, Rochester, NY
50,000	Asia Society, New York, NY
50,000	Morristown Memorial Health Foundation, Morristown, NJ
50,000	Union Hospital Foundation for Happiness, Union, NJ

Simon & Schuster Inc.
Sales: $1.51 billion
Employees: 9,500
Parent Company: Paramount Communications
Headquarters: New York, NY
SIC Major Group: Business Services, Motion Pictures, and Printing & Publishing

CONTACT
Kate Fischer
Senior Communications Associate
Simon & Schuster Inc.
1230 Avenue of the Americas
New York, NY 10020
(212) 698-7000

CONTRIBUTIONS SUMMARY
Operating Locations: NY (New York)

CORP. OFFICERS
Andrew Evans: *CURR EMPL* vp, cfo: Simon & Schuster
Richard E. Snyder: *CURR EMPL* ceo, pres: Simon & Schuster

Simone Foundation

CONTACT
Simone Fdn.
21001 Van Born Rd.
Taylor, MI 48180

FINANCIAL SUMMARY
Recent Giving: $582,625 (fiscal 1989); $357,725 (fiscal 1988)
Assets: $2,001,762 (fiscal year ending October 31, 1989); $2,537,444 (fiscal 1988)
EIN: 38-1799107

CONTRIBUTIONS SUMMARY
Donor(s): Alex Maroogian, Masco Corp.
Typical Recipients: • *Civic & Public Affairs:* ethnic/minority organizations • *Education:* religious education • *Religion:* churches, religious organizations • *Social Services:* community service organizations, community service organizations, family planning
Grant Types: general support

GIVING OFFICERS
Christine Simone: vp
David Simone: secy, treas
Louise Simone: pres
Mark Simone: dir

APPLICATION INFORMATION
Initial Approach: Contributes only to preselected organizations.

GRANTS ANALYSIS
Number of Grants: 19
Highest Grant: $448,563
Typical Range: $100 to $5,000
Disclosure Period: fiscal year ending October 31, 1989

RECENT GRANTS

448,563	Armenian General Benevolent Union, Saddle Brook, NJ
51,000	St. Nersess Armenian Seminary, New Rochelle, NY
28,812	St. Nersess Armenian Seminary, New Rochelle, NY
25,000	Zoryan Institute, Cambridge, MA
9,950	Armenian General Benevolent Union, Saddle Brook, NJ
5,000	Diocese of the Armenian Church of America, New York, NY
2,500	Kahil Gibran Centennial, Detroit, MI

2,500 St. Stephens Arme-
nian Church, El-
beron, NJ
2,000 American Red
Cross, New York,
NY
1,500 Film Society of
Lincoln Center,
New York, NY

Simplex Time Recorder Co.

Sales: $510.0 million
Employees: 4,000
Headquarters: Gardner, MA
SIC Major Group: Electronic &
Other Electrical Equipment,
Industrial Machinery &
Equipment, and Instruments &
Related Products

CONTACT
Richard Lepkowski
Manager, Employee Relations
Simplex Time Recorder Co.
Simplex Plz.
Gardner, MA 01441
(508) 632-2500

CONTRIBUTIONS SUMMARY
Operating Locations: MA
(Gardner)

CORP. OFFICERS
Thomas A. Curtin: *CURR
EMPL* vp, cfo: Simplex Time
Recorder Co
Edward G. Watkins: *CURR
EMPL* chmn, pres: Simplex
Time Recorder Co

Simplot Co., J.R. / Simplot Foundation, J.R.

Sales: $1.6 billion
Employees: 9,500
Headquarters: Boise, ID
SIC Major Group: Agricultural
Production— Livestock,
Chemicals & Allied Products,
and Food & Kindred Products

CONTACT
Adelia Garro Simplot
Community Relations
Coordinator
J.R. Simplot Co.
One Capital Center
999 Main St., Ste. 1300
Boise, ID 83702
(208) 336-2110

CONTRIBUTIONS SUMMARY
Geographic Distribution:
Grants are awarded in head-

quarters and operating commu-
nities.
Operating Locations: ID
(Boise)

CORP. OFFICERS
John Richard Simplot: *B*
Dubuque IA 1909 *CURR
EMPL* fdr, chmn: JR Simplot
Co *CORP AFFIL* dir: Continen-
tal Life & Accident Co, First
Security Corp, Micron Tech,
Morrison-Knudsen
Gordon C. Smith: *CURR
EMPL* pres: JR Simplot Co

APPLICATION INFORMATION
Initial Approach: Send a brief
letter of inquiry and a full proposal. Include a description of
organization, amount re-
quested, purpose of funds
sought, and proof of tax-exempt status.
Restrictions on Giving: Does
not support individuals, religious organizations for sectarian
purposes, or political or lobbying groups.

GRANTS ANALYSIS
Typical Range: $1,000 to
$2,500

Simpson Foundation

CONTACT
Simpson Fdn.
c/o First Alabama Bank
PO Box 511
Montgomery, AL 36134

FINANCIAL SUMMARY
Recent Giving: $209,968 (fis-
cal 1992); $323,500 (fiscal
1991); $282,665 (fiscal 1990)
Assets: $5,345,860 (fiscal year
ending April 30, 1992);
$5,276,928 (fiscal 1991);
$5,272,376 (fiscal 1990)
EIN: 63-0925496

CONTRIBUTIONS SUMMARY
Typical Recipients: • *Educa-
tion:* colleges & universities
Grant Types: scholarship
Geographic Distribution: lim-
ited to residents of Wilcox
County, AL

GIVING OFFICERS
Lulu E. Pamer: trust
John R. Stewart: trust

APPLICATION INFORMATION
Initial Approach: Application
form required. Applications accepted January 1 to March 31.

OTHER THINGS TO KNOW
Provides scholarships for local
area residents.

GRANTS ANALYSIS
Number of Grants: 23
Highest Grant: $40,585
Typical Range: $1,000 to
$10,250
Disclosure Period: fiscal year
ending April 30, 1992

RECENT GRANTS
40,585 Auburn University,
Auburn, AL
37,700 University of Ala-
bama, Tuscaloosa,
AL
24,550 Alabama A&M
University, Nor-
mal, AL
20,300 University of Ala-
bama, Birming-
ham, AL
17,750 Livingston Univer-
sity, Livingston, AL
13,500 Troy State Univer-
sity, Troy, GA
11,000 University of Ala-
bama, Huntsville,
AL
10,250 Auburn University
at Montgomery,
Montgomery, AL
9,500 Alabama State Uni-
versity, Montgom-
ery, AL
5,250 University of Mon-
tevallo, Mon-
tevallo, AL

Simpson Foundation

CONTACT
W. H. B. Simpson
Simpson Fdn.
PO Box 528
Greenville, SC 29602
(803) 297-3451

FINANCIAL SUMMARY
Recent Giving: $104,350
(1990); $122,265 (1989);
$64,580 (1988)
Assets: $2,801,457 (1990);
$3,963,017 (1989); $3,245,806
(1988)
Gifts Received: $1,000
(1989); $1,404 (1988)
EIN: 57-6017451

CONTRIBUTIONS SUMMARY
Donor(s): W. H. B. Simpson,
Mrs. W. H. B. Simpson.
Typical Recipients: • *Educa-
tio :* colleges & universities,
religious education • *Health:*
geriatric health, hospitals, single-disease health associations
• *Religion:* churches, religious

organizations • *Social Services:* aged, child welfare, youth
organizations
Grant Types: general support
Geographic Distribution:
focus on NC and SC

GIVING OFFICERS
Willou R. Bichel: trust
C. L. Efrid, Jr.: dir
Sarah Belk Gambrell: dir *B*
Charlotte NC 1918 *ED* Sweet
Briar Coll BA 1939; Erskine
Coll D Hum 1970 *CURR
EMPL* vp, dir: Belk Stores
NONPR AFFIL dir: Opera
Carolina, Parkinsons Disease
Fdn, Planned Parenthood,
YWCA; hon bd dir: YWCA;
hon trustee: Cancer Res Inst;
mem: Daughters Am Revolu-
tion, Fashion Group, Natl Soc
Colonial Dames; trust: Prince-
ton Theological Seminary,
Johnson C Smith Univ, Warren
Wilson Coll; trust nat bd:
YWCA
Nell M. Rice: dir
Charles W. White: dir

APPLICATION INFORMATION
Initial Approach: Send brief
letter of inquiry on letterhead
describing program or project.
Deadlines are May 1 and November 1.

GRANTS ANALYSIS
Number of Grants: 29
Highest Grant: $15,000
Typical Range: $500 to $2,000
Disclosure Period: 1990

RECENT GRANTS
15,000 Furman University,
Greenville, SC
11,000 Converse College,
Spartanburg, SC
10,000 Samaritan's Purse,
Spartanburg, SC
8,000 Cancer Research
Institute, New
York, NY
8,000 Fourth Presbyte-
rian Church, Spar-
tanburg, SC
5,500 Presbyterian Col-
lege, Clinton, SC
5,000 Spoleto Festival
USA, Charleston,
SC
4,500 Harold Jennings
Foundation, Spar-
tanburg, SC
4,000 Columbia Bible
College, Spartan-
burg, SC

Simpson Foundation

CONTACT
Robert E. Carlson
Vice President and Trust
Simpson Fdn.
c/o City Bank and Trust Co.
One Jackson Sq.
Jackson, MI 49201

FINANCIAL SUMMARY
Recent Giving: $145,550 (fiscal 1992); $144,416 (fiscal 1991); $130,124 (fiscal 1990)
Assets: $3,469,036 (fiscal year ending September 30, 1992); $3,157,227 (fiscal 1991); $2,763,460 (fiscal 1990)
EIN: 38-6054058

CONTRIBUTIONS SUMMARY
Donor(s): the late Robert J. Simpson
Typical Recipients: • *Arts & Humanities:* history/historic preservation • *Civic & Public Affairs:* municipalities, urban & community affairs • *Education:* colleges & universities, education funds, public education (precollege) • *Social Services:* community service organizations, food/clothing distribution
Grant Types: capital, emergency, endowment, and project
Geographic Distribution: limited to Hillsdale County

APPLICATION INFORMATION
Initial Approach: Send brief letter of inquiry describing program. Deadline is October 1.
Restrictions on Giving: Does not support individuals or provide funds for scholarships or fellowships.

GRANTS ANALYSIS
Number of Grants: 1
Highest Grant: $145,550
Disclosure Period: fiscal year ending September 30, 1992

RECENT GRANTS
145,550 Hillsdale County Community Foundation, Hillsdale, MI

Simpson Foundation, John M.

CONTACT
John M. Simpson Fdn.
33 North Dearborn St., Rm. 1300
Chicago, IL 60602

FINANCIAL SUMMARY
Recent Giving: $77,000 (1989); $138,050 (1988)
Assets: $2,495,912 (1989); $1,899,481 (1988)
Gifts Received: $338,427 (1989); $519,782 (1988)
EIN: 36-6071621

CONTRIBUTIONS SUMMARY
Typical Recipients: • *Arts & Humanities:* museums/galleries • *Civic & Public Affairs:* environmental affairs, zoos/botanical gardens • *Health:* hospices, hospitals • *Religion:* religious organizations • *Social Services:* community service organizations, family planning, food/clothing distribution, youth organizations
Grant Types: general support

GIVING OFFICERS
J.D. Brown: secy
P.J. Herbert: vp
treas Lang: off
W.J. McDermott: vp
Patricia S. Okieffe: trust
Howard B. Simpson: trust
Nancy T. Simpson: pres
William Simpson: trust

APPLICATION INFORMATION
Initial Approach: Contributes only to preselected organizations.

GRANTS ANALYSIS
Number of Grants: 17
Highest Grant: $14,500
Typical Range: $500 to $5,000
Disclosure Period: 1989

RECENT GRANTS
14,500 Tucson Medical Center Foundation, Tucson, AZ
10,000 Erie Health Clinic, Chicago, IL
10,000 Little Brothers of the Poor, Chicago, IL
8,000 Planned Parenthood, Honolulu, HI
8,000 West Hawaii Support Council, Honolulu, HI
5,000 Arizona Nature Conservancy, Phoenix, AZ
5,000 Palm Beach Martin County Medical Center, Palm Beach, FL
4,000 Northern Hawaii Hospice, Honolulu, HI
3,000 Institute for Human Services, Chicago, IL
2,000 Rehabilitation Institute, Chicago, IL

Simpson Industries / Simpson Industries Fund

Sales: $191.9 million
Employees: 1,471
Headquarters: Birmingham, MI
SIC Major Group:
    Transportation Equipment

CONTACT
Deborah Baluch
Simpson Industries
32100 Telegraph Rd., Ste. 120
Birmingham, MI 48025
(313) 540-6200

FINANCIAL SUMMARY
Recent Giving: $102,878 (fiscal 1992); $123,132 (fiscal 1990); $117,695 (fiscal 1989)
Assets: $252,148 (fiscal year ending March 31, 1992); $273,527 (fiscal 1990); $273,191 (fiscal 1989)
Gifts Received: $60,000 (fiscal 1992); $100,000 (fiscal 1991); $60,000 (fiscal 1989)
Fiscal Note: In 1992, contributions were received from Simpson Industries.
EIN: 38-2157102

CONTRIBUTIONS SUMMARY
Typical Recipients: • *Arts & Humanities:* arts institutes, community arts, history/historic preservation, music • *Education:* colleges & universities, community & junior colleges, health & physical education • *Health:* health organizations • *Social Services:* community service organizations, recreation & athletics, united funds, volunteer services
Grant Types: general support
Operating Locations: MI (Birmingham), OH (Troy)

CORP. OFFICERS
Robert W. Navarre: *CURR EMPL* chmn, ceo: Simpson Indus

Roy E. Parrott: *CURR EMPL* pres, coo: Simpson Indus

GIVING OFFICERS
K.E. Berman: trust
Robert W. Navarre: chmn *CURR EMPL* chmn, ceo: Simpson Indus (see above)
Roy E. Parrott: trust *CURR EMPL* pres, coo: Simpson Indus (see above)
Charles K. Winter: trust

APPLICATION INFORMATION
Initial Approach: Send brief letter describing program. There are no deadlines.

GRANTS ANALYSIS
Number of Grants: 49
Highest Grant: $27,407
Typical Range: $500 to $2,000
Disclosure Period: fiscal year ending March 31, 1992
Note: Figures for fiscal 1992 do not include matching gifts totaling $7,587.

RECENT GRANTS
27,407 United Way
25,000 Hillsdale College, Hillsdale, MI — health education and sports complex
10,000 Jackson Community College, Jackson, MI — tech training equipment
4,885 United Way
4,140 Litchfield Community Chest
1,484 United Way
1,055 United Way
1,000 Interlochen Center for the Arts, Interlochen, MI
1,000 Manufacturing Engineering Education Foundation
500 American Enterprise Institute, Washington, DC

Simpson Investment Co. / Matlock Foundation

Sales: $970.0 million
Employees: 8,400
Parent Company: Kamilche Co.
Headquarters: Seattle, WA
SIC Major Group: Holding & Other Investment Offices

CONTACT

Lin Smith
Public Affairs Assistant
Matlock Fdn.
1201 Third Ave., Ste. 4900
Seattle, WA 98101-3045
(206) 224-5196

FINANCIAL SUMMARY

Recent Giving: $800,000 (1992 approx.); $1,185,431 (1991); $2,068,567 (1990)
Assets: $188,860 (1989)
Fiscal Note: Figures above are for foundation only. An estimated $200,000 in contributions is budgeted for direct corporate giving in 1993. Contact Maureen Frisch, vice president of public affairs, for direct corporate support.
EIN: 91-6029303

CONTRIBUTIONS SUMMARY

Typical Recipients: • *Arts & Humanities:* arts associations, arts institutes, community arts, dance, history/historic preservation, libraries, museums/galleries, music, opera, performing arts, public broadcasting, theater • *Civic & Public Affairs:* business/free enterprise, economic development, environmental affairs, municipalities, public policy, safety, zoos/botanical gardens • *Education:* business education, career/vocational education, colleges & universities, community & junior colleges, continuing education, economic education, private education (precollege), public education (precollege), science/technology education • *Health:* emergency/ambulance services, hospices, hospitals, nursing services • *Religion:* churches • *Science:* science exhibits & fairs • *Social Services:* aged, child welfare, community centers, community service organizations, domestic violence, drugs & alcohol, emergency relief, employment/job training, food/clothing distribution, united funds, youth organizations
Grant Types: capital, endowment, general support, project, and seed money
Note: Contact for nonmonetary support is Maureen Frisch, vice president of public affairs.
Nonmonetary Support Types: donated products, loaned employees, and loaned executives

Note: An estimated $75,000 in nonmonetary support is budgeted for 1993. This number is not included in the figures above.

Geographic Distribution: Washington, Oregon, California, Michigan, Pennsylvania, Texas, Vermont, Iowa, New York

Operating Locations: CA (San Francisco), IA, MI (Plainwell, Vicksburg), NY (Warwick), OR (Eugene, Portland, West Linn), PA, TX, VT, WA (Seattle, Shelton, Tacoma)

Note: Operating locations reflect only major facilities; company also operates in various cities and towns in the above states.

CORP. OFFICERS

Furman Colin Moseley: *B* Spartanburg SC 1934 *ED* Elon Coll BA 1956 *CURR EMPL* pres, dir: Simpson Investment Co *CORP AFFIL* chmn: Simpson Paper Co; dir: Eaton Corp, Owens Corning Fiberglas Corp

William Garrard Reed, Jr.: *B* 1940 *ED* Harvard Univ MBA 1969 *CURR EMPL* chmn: Simpson Investment Co *CORP AFFIL* dir: Microsoft Corp, SAFECO Corp, Seafirst Corp, Seattle First Natl Bank, Simpson Paper Co, Simpson Plainwell Paper Co, WA Mutual Savings Bank

GIVING OFFICERS

Maureen Frisch: pres, dir

Furman Colin Moseley: dir *CURR EMPL* pres, dir: Simpson Investment Co (see above)

Colleen Musgrave: secy

William Garrard Reed, Jr.: dir *CURR EMPL* chmn: Simpson Investment Co (see above)

Lin Smith: pub affairs asst

APPLICATION INFORMATION

Initial Approach: *Initial Contact:* letter or telephone call requesting grant application *When to Submit:* one month before the board meetings (usually in March, July, and November)

Restrictions on Giving: Does not support individuals, fraternal or political organizations, dinners or special events, or religious organizations for sectarian purposes.

OTHER THINGS TO KNOW

Foundation is sponsored by Simpson Investment Company and its subsidiaries, which include Simpson Paper Company, Simpson Timber Company, and Pacific Western Extruded Plastics Company.

GRANTS ANALYSIS

Total Grants: $800,000*
Number of Grants: 507*
Highest Grant: $68,450*
Typical Range: $500* to $15,000
Disclosure Period: 1992
Note: Foundation assests are for 1989. Total grant figure is from 1992. Number of grants, average grant, highest grant, and typical grant figures are from 1991. Recent grants are derived from a 1989 grants list.

RECENT GRANTS

66,667	Greater Tacoma Community Foundation, Tacoma, WA — Broadway Theatre — capital
57,240	United Way of King County, Seattle, WA — operating
35,000	Protestant Espicopal Churches and Dioceses of United States, Seattle, WA — capital
35,000	Safe Streets Campaign, Tacoma, WA — capital
32,000	Children's Museum of Tacoma, Tacoma, WA — capital
30,325	Mason County Senior Activities Association, Shelton, WA — operating
27,125	United Way of Gulf Coast, Pasadena, TX — operating
26,450	United Way of Humboldt County, Eureka, CA — operating
26,050	United Way of Tacoma/Pierce County, Tacoma, WA — operating
26,000	United Way of Mason County, Shelton, WA — operating

Simpson Paper Co.

Sales: $860.0 million
Employees: 5,000
Parent Company: Simpson Investment Co.
Headquarters: San Francisco, CA
SIC Major Group: Paper & Allied Products

CONTACT

Susan Taylor
Public Affairs
Simpson Paper Co.
One Post St., Ste. 3100
San Francisco, CA 94104
(415) 391-8140

CONTRIBUTIONS SUMMARY

Typical Recipients: • *Education:* colleges & universities, religious education • *Health:* hospitals, medical research, single-disease health associations
Operating Locations: CA (San Francisco)

CORP. OFFICERS

J. J. Fannon: *CURR EMPL* pres, dir: Simpson Paper Co
Furman C. Mosely: *CURR EMPL* chmn, dir: Simpson Paper Co

Simpson PSB Foundation

CONTACT

Barclay Simpson
President
Simpson PSB Fdn.
3669 Mt. Diablo Blvd.
Lafayette, CA 94549

FINANCIAL SUMMARY

Recent Giving: $96,115 (1990)
Assets: $27,225 (1990)
Gifts Received: $100,000 (1990)
Fiscal Note: In 1990, contributions were received from the Simpson Manufacturing Co., Inc.
EIN: 68-0168017

CONTRIBUTIONS SUMMARY

Typical Recipients: • *Arts & Humanities:* libraries, museums/galleries • *Education:* arts education, business education, colleges & universities • *Social Services:* shelters/homelessness
Grant Types: general support

GIVING OFFICERS

Barclay Simpson: pres

APPLICATION INFORMATION
Initial Approach: Send brief letter of inquiry. There are no deadlines.

GRANTS ANALYSIS
Number of Grants: 23
Highest Grant: $30,000
Typical Range: $500 to $10,000
Disclosure Period: 1990

RECENT GRANTS
30,000	California College of Arts and Crafts, Los Angeles, CA
10,000	Haas School of Business
10,000	University of California Library, Berkeley, CA
10,000	University of California Library, Berkeley, CA
9,200	Regents of the University of California, Berkeley, CA
5,000	University Art Museum
4,100	St. Mary's College
2,500	Lindsay Museum
2,500	San Francisco Museum of Modern Art, San Francisco, CA
2,000	Shelter's Right Hand

Singer Company
Sales: $991.6 million
Employees: 24,000
Headquarters: Edison, NJ
SIC Major Group: Electronic & Other Electrical Equipment and Furniture & Fixtures

CONTACT
Barbara Lerro
Human Resources Manager
Singer Company
200 Metroplex, PO Box 1909
Edison, NJ 08818-1909
(908) 287-0707

CONTRIBUTIONS SUMMARY
Operating Locations: NJ (Edison)

CORP. OFFICERS
John Flaherty: *CURR EMPL*
pres: SSMC

Sinsheimer Fund, Alexandrine and Alexander L.

CONTACT
T. E. Roepe
Vice President
Alexandrine and Alexander L. Sinsheimer Fund
c/o Manufacturers Hanover Trust Co.
270 Park Ave.
New York, NY 10017
(212) 270-9111

FINANCIAL SUMMARY
Recent Giving: $354,318 (fiscal 1991); $347,696 (fiscal 1990); $351,312 (fiscal 1989)
Assets: $8,576,624 (fiscal year ending April 30, 1991); $8,061,046 (fiscal 1990); $7,516,858 (fiscal 1989)
EIN: 13-6047421

CONTRIBUTIONS SUMMARY
Donor(s): the late Alexander L. Sinsheimer, the late Alexandrine Sinsheimer
Typical Recipients: • *Education:* colleges & universities, medical education
Grant Types: general support and research
Geographic Distribution: limited to the New York, NY, metropolitan area

APPLICATION INFORMATION
Initial Approach: Application form required. Deadline is February 15.

GRANTS ANALYSIS
Number of Grants: 10
Highest Grant: $64,722
Typical Range: $20,000 to $64,722
Disclosure Period: fiscal year ending April 30, 1991

RECENT GRANTS
64,772	Columbia University, New York, NY
64,772	Cornell University Medical Center, New York, NY
64,772	New York University School of Medicine, New York, NY
40,000	Rockefeller University, New York, NY
20,000	Albert Einstein College of Medicine, New York, NY
20,000	Health Science Center State, NY
20,000	Mount Sinai School of Medicine, New York, NY
20,000	State University of New York, Albany, NY
20,000	State University of New York, Albany, NY
20,000	University of Medicine and Dentistry of New Jersey, Newark, NJ

Sioux Steel Co. / Sioux Steel Co. Foundation
Sales: $15.0 million
Employees: 150
Headquarters: Sioux Falls, SD
SIC Major Group: Industrial Machinery & Equipment

CONTACT
Max L. Rysdon
President & Treasurer
Sioux Steel Co. Foundation
196 1/2 East Sixth St.
Sioux Falls, SD 57102
(605) 336-1750

FINANCIAL SUMMARY
Recent Giving: $48,252 (1991); $87,859 (1990)
Assets: $582,780 (1991); $605,690 (1990)
EIN: 46-6012618

CONTRIBUTIONS SUMMARY
Typical Recipients: • *Education:* religious education • *Religion:* churches, religious organizations • *Social Services:* child welfare, community service organizations, recreation & athletics, united funds, youth organizations
Grant Types: general support
Geographic Distribution: focus on SD
Operating Locations: SD (Sioux Falls)

CORP. OFFICERS
P. M. Rysdon: *CURR EMPL*
pres, treas: Sioux Steel Co
K. Vander Tuig: *CURR EMPL*
cfo: Sioux Steel Co

GIVING OFFICERS
Robert W. Price: asst treas
Jimmie Rysdon: asst secy
Lorraine Rysdon: dir
Phillip M. Rysdon: vp, secy, dir

APPLICATION INFORMATION
Initial Approach: Send brief letter describing program. There are no deadlines.

GRANTS ANALYSIS
Number of Grants: 16
Highest Grant: $58,624
Typical Range: $1,000 to $5,000
Disclosure Period: 1991

RECENT GRANTS
58,624	YMCA, Sioux Falls, SD
5,700	United Way, Sioux Falls, SD
5,500	First Baptist Church, Sioux Falls, SD
5,000	Children's Inn, Sioux Falls, SD
4,000	Sioux Falls Youth Hockey, Sioux Falls, SD
3,000	North American Baptist Seminary, Sioux Falls, SD
1,000	Lutheran Social Services, Sioux Falls, SD
1,000	McCrossan Boys Ranch, Sioux Falls, SD
1,000	YMCA, Sioux Falls, SD
750	O'Gorman High School Foundation, Sioux Falls, SD

Siragusa Foundation

CONTACT
John R. Siragusa
Vice President
Siragusa Fdn.
919 North Michigan, Ste. 2701
Chicago, IL 60611
(312) 280-0833

FINANCIAL SUMMARY
Recent Giving: $403,000 (1989)
Assets: $10,200,374 (1989)
EIN: 36-3100492

CONTRIBUTIONS SUMMARY
Donor(s): Ross D. Siragusa
Typical Recipients: • *Arts & Humanities:* arts institutes, museums/galleries, opera • *Civic & Public Affairs:* zoos/botanical gardens • *Education:* colleges & universities • *Health:* hospitals, medical research, single-disease health associations • *Religion:* religious organizations • *Social Services:* child welfare, community service or-

ganizations, youth organizations

Grant Types: operating expenses, project, research, and scholarship

Geographic Distribution: focus on the Midwest, with preference to the Chicago, IL, metropolitan area

GIVING OFFICERS

Roy M. Adams: dir *B* Wilmington DE 1940 *ED* Univ DE BA 1962; IL Inst Tech JD 1969; Northwestern Univ LLM 1976 *CORP AFFIL* ptnr: Schiff Hardin & Waite *NONPR AFFIL* adjunct prof: Northwestern Univ; fellow: Am Coll Probate Couns, Intl Academy Estate Trust Law

George E. Driscoll: dir

Alisa S. Perrotte: dir

Melvyn H. Schneider: dir

John Robert Siragusa: vp, dir *B* Chicago IL 1932 *ED* Northwestern Univ 1955 *CURR EMPL* vp: Game-Time

Martha P. Siragusa: dir

Richard Donald Siragusa: dir *CURR EMPL* vp: Game-Time

Ross David Siragusa, Jr.: dir *B* Chicago IL 1930 *ED* Yale Univ 1953 *CURR EMPL* pres: Game Time *CORP AFFIL* dir: AmSouth Bank Corp, Rockwell Intl

Ross David Siragusa, Sr.: don *B* Buffalo NY 1906

Theodore M. Siragusa: dir

James B. Wilson: dir

APPLICATION INFORMATION

Initial Approach: Contributes only to preselected organizations.

Restrictions on Giving: Does not support individuals or provide loans or endowment funds.

OTHER THINGS TO KNOW

Publications: Application Guidelines

GRANTS ANALYSIS

Number of Grants: 70
Highest Grant: $35,000
Typical Range: $1,000 to $5,000
Disclosure Period: 1989

RECENT GRANTS

35,000 Children's Memorial Foundation, Chicago, IL
30,000 Northwestern Memorial Foundation, Chicago, IL
30,000 School of the Art Institute of Chicago, Chicago, IL
20,000 Villa Scalabrini, Northlake, IL
10,000 Eli Schulman Playground/Seneca Park Fund, Chicago, IL
10,000 Elmhurst College, Elmhurst, IL
10,000 Illinois Wesleyan University, Bloomington, IL
10,000 Lutheran General Foundation, Park Ridge, IL
10,000 Northwestern University School of Law, Evanston, IL
10,000 University of Chicago, Chicago, IL

SIT Investment Associates, Inc. / SIT Investment Associates Foundation

Sales: $6.0 million
Employees: 36
Headquarters: Minneapolis, MN
SIC Major Group: Security & Commodity Brokers

CONTACT

Gloria A. Westlake
Officer
SIT Investment Associates Fdn.
4600 Norwest Center
90 South 7th St.
Minneapolis, MN 55402
(612) 332-3223

FINANCIAL SUMMARY

Recent Giving: $107,130 (1990); $108,900 (1989)
Assets: $2,746,541 (1990); $2,294,950 (1989)
Gifts Received: $501,500 (1990); $723,700 (1989)
Fiscal Note: In 1990, contributions were received from SIT Investment Associates, Inc.
EIN: 41-1468021

CONTRIBUTIONS SUMMARY

Typical Recipients: • *Arts & Humanities:* arts institutes, community arts, performing arts • *Civic & Public Affairs:* housing, philanthropic organizations, women's affairs • *Education:* business education • *Health:* health organizations, hospices, single-disease health associations • *Religion:* missionary activities • *Social Services:* child welfare, community centers, community service organizations, counseling, delinquency & crime, disabled, drugs & alcohol, family services, food/clothing distribution, homes, shelters/homelessness, united funds, youth organizations

Grant Types: general support

Geographic Distribution: focus on MN

Operating Locations: MN (Minneapolis)

CORP. OFFICERS

Eugene C. Sit: *CURR EMPL* pres, ceo, treas: SIT Investment Associaties

GIVING OFFICERS

Douglas C. Jones: trust
Peter L. Mitchelson: trust
Eugene C. Sit: trust
Glorita A. Westlake: trust

APPLICATION INFORMATION

Initial Approach: Send brief letter describing program. There are no deadlines.

GRANTS ANALYSIS

Number of Grants: 75
Highest Grant: $10,000
Typical Range: $150 to $5,000
Disclosure Period: 1990

RECENT GRANTS

10,000 Minneapolis Foundation, Minneapolis, MN
10,000 United Way
7,500 Incarnation House, Minneapolis, MN
7,500 Walker Art Center, Minneapolis, MN
5,000 Greater Minneapolis Food Bank, Minneapolis, MN
5,000 Minnesota Orchestral Association, Minneapolis, MN
4,000 Loring-Nicollet-Bethlehem Community Center, Minneapolis, MN
4,000 Salvation Army
3,000 Minneapolis Institute of Arts, Minneapolis, MN
2,750 Hartford Business School, Hartford, CT

Six Flags Theme Parks Inc.

Sales: $390.0 million
Employees: 1,300
Headquarters: Arlington, TX
SIC Major Group: Amusement & Recreation Services and
Holding & Other Investment Offices

CONTACT

Larry Cochron
President
Six Flags Theme Parks Inc.
400 Interpace Pkwy., Bldg. C, 3rd Fl.
Parsippany, NJ 07054
(201) 402-8100

CONTRIBUTIONS SUMMARY

Operating Locations: NJ (Parsippany), TX (Arlington)

CORP. OFFICERS

Larry Cochran: *CURR EMPL* pres, ceo: Six Flags Theme Parks
R. Yeisley: *CURR EMPL* cfo: Six Flags Theme Parks

Sizzler International / Sizzler International Foundation

Former Foundation Name: Collins Food International Foundation
Sales: $541.65 million
Employees: 17,900
Headquarters: Los Angeles, CA

CONTACT

James A. Collins
President
Sizzler International
12655 W. Jefferson Blvd.
Los Angeles, CA 90066
(310) 827-2300

FINANCIAL SUMMARY

Recent Giving: $193,501 (fiscal 1992); $241,153 (fiscal 1990)
Assets: $137,160 (fiscal year ending March 31, 1992); $13,501 (fiscal 1990)
Gifts Received: $325,000 (fiscal 1992); $100,000 (fiscal 1990)
Fiscal Note: In fiscal 1992, contributions were received from Sizzler International, Inc.
EIN: 95-4168176

CONTRIBUTIONS SUMMARY

Typical Recipients: • *Arts & Humanities:* history/historic preservation • *Education:* colleges & universities, education funds • *Social Services:* child welfare, united funds, youth organizations

Grant Types: general support

Operating Locations: CA (Los Angeles)

CORP. OFFICERS
Richard P. Bermingham:
James A. Collins: *B* Huntington Park CA 1926 *ED* Univ CA Los Angeles BS 1950 *CURR EMPL* chmn, dir: Sizzler Intl *CORP AFFIL* chmn: Collins Foods Intl *NONPR AFFIL* bd dirs: CA Restaurant Assn; mem: Natl Restaurant Assn

GIVING OFFICERS
Richard P. Bermingham: cfo (see above)
James A. Collins: pres *CURR EMPL* chmn, dir: Sizzler Intl (see above)
Christopher R. Thomas: secy *CURR EMPL* vp fin: Sizzler Intl

APPLICATION INFORMATION
Initial Approach: The foundation supports preselected organizations and does not accept unsolicited requests for funds.

GRANTS ANALYSIS
Number of Grants: 49
Highest Grant: $42,054
Typical Range: $100 to $1,000
Disclosure Period: fiscal year ending March 31, 1992

RECENT GRANTS
42,054 United Way, Los Angeles, CA
25,000 California State Polytechnic University, Los Angeles, CA
20,000 Union Rescue Mission, Los Angeles, CA
11,000 Boy Scouts of America, Los Angeles, CA
10,025 University of California Los Angeles Foundation, Los Angeles, CA
10,000 Beynon Children's Education Trust, Los Angeles, CA
10,000 Education Foundation's Challenge Fund, Los Angeles, CA
7,600 Boy Scouts of America, Los Angeles, CA
6,000 Junior Achievement, Los Angeles, CA
5,000 California Museum Foundation, Los Angeles, CA

Sjostrom & Sons / Sjostrom & Sons Foundation
Headquarters: Rockford, IL

CONTACT
Joel Sjostrom
Director
Sjostrom & Sons Foundation
1129 Harrison Ave.
Rockford, IL 61125-0766
(815) 226-0330

FINANCIAL SUMMARY
Recent Giving: $13,200 (fiscal 1991); $6,500 (fiscal 1990)
Assets: $441,075 (fiscal year ending July 31, 1990)
Gifts Received: $85,000 (fiscal 1990)
EIN: 36-3225935

CONTRIBUTIONS SUMMARY
Typical Recipients: • *Arts & Humanities:* music • *Education:* education associations, public education (precollege) • *Health:* medical rehabilitation • *Social Services:* homes, united funds, youth organizations
Grant Types: general support
Geographic Distribution: giving limited to Rockford, IL
Operating Locations: IL (Rockford)

CORP. OFFICERS
Joel Sjostrom: *CURR EMPL* pres: Sjostrom & Sons

GIVING OFFICERS
Lyon Breen: dir
Joel Sjostrom: dir *CURR EMPL* pres: Sjostrom & Sons (see above)
Kristopher Sjostrom: dir

APPLICATION INFORMATION
Initial Approach: Send a brief letter of inquiry and a full proposal. There are no deadlines.
Restrictions on Giving: The foundation does not make grants to individuals.

GRANTS ANALYSIS
Number of Grants: 10
Highest Grant: $5,000
Typical Range: $500 to $1,000
Disclosure Period: fiscal year ending July 31, 1990

RECENT GRANTS
5,000 United Way, Rockford, IL
2,500 Rockford Public Schools Foundation, Rockford, IL
1,000 Barbara Olson School of Hope, Rockford, IL
1,000 Center for Sight and Hearing Impaired, Rockford, IL
1,000 Rosecrance Center, Rockford, IL
1,000 YMCA, Rockford, IL
500 Northwestern Illinois Special Olympics, Rockford, IL
500 P.A. Peterson Home, Rockford, IL
400 Junior Achievement, Rockford, IL
300 Kishwaukee Valley Concert Bank, Rockford, IL

Skadden, Arps, Slate, Meagher and Flom Fellowship Foundation

CONTACT
Skadden, Arps, Slate, Meagher and Flom Fellowship Foundation
919 Third Avenue
New York, NY 10022-3904
(212) 735-3000

FINANCIAL SUMMARY
Recent Giving: $1,435,437 (1990); $511,802 (1989)
Assets: $7,137,012 (1990); $6,100,095 (1989)
Gifts Received: $2,000,000 (1990)
EIN: 13-3455231

GRANTS ANALYSIS
Total Grants: $1,435,437
Disclosure Period: 1990

Skaggs Alpha Beta Co.
Headquarters: Richardson, TX
SIC Major Group: Food Stores and Miscellaneous Retail

CONTACT
Michael Miller
President
Skaggs Alpha Beta Co.
1100 Executive Dr., Ste. 100
Richardson, TX 75081
(214) 238-7231

CONTRIBUTIONS SUMMARY
Operating Locations: TX (Richardson)

CORP. OFFICERS
Michael Miller: *CURR EMPL* pres: Skaggs Alpha Beta Co

Skaggs Foundation, L. J. and Mary C.

CONTACT
Philip M. Jelley
Secretary and Foundation Manager
L. J. and Mary C. Skaggs Foundation
1221 Broadway, 21st Fl.
Oakland, CA 94612
(510) 451-3300
Note: Applicants seeking additional information about the foundation should contact David Knight, program director.

FINANCIAL SUMMARY
Recent Giving: $1,398,745 (1993); $1,558,245 (1992); $1,988,580 (1991)
Assets: $4,428,028 (1992); $6,137,979 (1991); $7,500,000 (1990 approx.)
Gifts Received: $480,000 (1992); $720,000 (1991); $920,000 (1988)
Fiscal Note: The foundation has received contributions from the L. J. Skaggs Foundation Trust.
EIN: 94-6174113

CONTRIBUTIONS SUMMARY
Donor(s): The foundation was established in 1967 by Mr. and Mrs. L. J. Skaggs to provide a funding source for small innovative projects. Grants initially were made in the area of medical research and projects related to diabetes. Following Mr. Skaggs' death in 1970 and an increase in assets due to bequests from his estate, the foundation broadened the scope of its interests.
Typical Recipients: • *Arts & Humanities:* history/historic preservation, museums/galleries, music, opera, performing arts, theater • *Civic & Public Affairs:* environmental affairs
Grant Types: project and research
Geographic Distribution: principally to national organizations; theater grants limited to Northern California

GIVING OFFICERS
Donald D. Crawford, Jr.: treas, mem bd dirs *B* Long

Beach CA 1936 *ED* Univ Southern CA 1957 *CURR EMPL* ptnr: Crawford Petroleum Co
Jayne C. Davis: vp, mem bd dirs
Philip M. Jelley: secy, fdn mgr, mem bd dirs
David Knight: program dir, asst secy
Catherine L. O'Brien: vp, mem bd dirs
Mary C. Skaggs: pres, mem bd dirs

APPLICATION INFORMATION

Initial Approach:
Applicants should submit a brief letter of intent describing the organization, and listing the amount requested, purpose for which funds are sought, income and expense information, and key personnel. The foundation staff will then determine whether or not a full proposal is appropriate. Mass-mailed, photocopied, or printed funding requests are not given serious consideration.

A full proposal should include a history and background of the organization, purpose for grant, method for achieving goals and tasks, amount requested, total budget, and an explanation of how funds will be used. Applicants also must include a listing of other committed and anticipated funding, statement illustrating the experience of personnel involved with the program, listing of the organization's board of trustees with professional affiliations, and a copy of the IRS tax-exempt status letter.

Letters of intent are accepted between January 15 and June 1 from applicants interested in being considered for the following year's funding. Full invited proposals must be received by September 1 for consideration at the November board meeting. The foundation evaluates proposals according to various criteria. Full proposals are analyzed with regard to foundation priorities and objectives; stability and integrity of the applicant organization; experience of key personnel; financial position of the applicant; whether the proposal duplicates or works in conjunction with similar projects; whether the project meets a demonstrated need; whether the project will receive continued community support; and, in the

case of cultural programs, the level of demonstrated artistic achievement of key personnel. The directors generally favor requests putting forth creative responses to broad social problems. Applicants in the performing arts are by foundation invitation only. Proposals in areas of social concerns not directly related to the foundation's primary interests will not be given strong consideration.

Restrictions on Giving: The foundation will not fund individuals, capital or annual fund drives, residence home programs, halfway houses, sectarian religious organizations, or budget deficits.

OTHER THINGS TO KNOW

The foundation expects to be informed of grants received from other sources while the proposal is being reviewed. The foundation also expects to receive informal progress reports during the length of the project. All unexpended funds given for a specific project must be returned. Applicants whose requests have been denied occasionally will be invited to resubmit applications.

Publications: annual report, grant policies and procedures

GRANTS ANALYSIS

Total Grants: $1,398,745*
Number of Grants: 73*
Highest Grant: $250,000
Typical Range: $5,000 to $25,000
Disclosure Period: 1993
Note: The above fiscal analysis excludes approximately 30 small (under $5,000) discretionary grants totaling $100,000. Recent grants are derived from a 1993 grants list.

RECENT GRANTS

250,000 San Francisco Opera, San Francisco, CA — to underwrite production of Verdi's I Vesperi Siciliani for fall 1993
75,000 Santa Fe Opera, Santa Fe, NM — general production grant for Strauss' Capriccio for 1993 season
60,000 Global Fund for Women, Menlo Park, CA — provide funds to groups that are

committed to women's wellbeing
50,000 Grace Cathedral, San Francisco, CA — completion of Meditation Garden
30,000 Colonial Williamsburg Foundation, Williamsburg, VA — preparation of an interpretive program relating to urban history in Colonial America
25,000 Mission Dolores, San Francisco, CA — restoration of historic California mission
25,000 New Mexico Community Foundation, Santa Fe, NM — to assist in developing church preservation plans
25,000 Notre Dame University, Notre Dame, IN — to support the mid-career faculty development program
25,000 Oregon Shakespeare Festival, Ashland, OR — to underwrite production of Shakespeare's Cymbeline to be presented at the 1993 Festival
25,000 The Huntington, San Marino, CA — to provide for research on development of natural gardens in England during the 18th Century

Skandia America Reinsurance Corp.

Assets: $1.4 billion
Employees: 350
Headquarters: New York, NY
SIC Major Group: Holding & Other Investment Offices, Insurance Agents, Brokers & Service, and Insurance Carriers

CONTACT

Cynthia Yonich
Assistant Secretary
Skandia America Corp.
One Liberty Plz.
New York, NY 10006
(212) 978-4700

FINANCIAL SUMMARY

Fiscal Note: Annual Giving Range: $100,000 to $250,000

CONTRIBUTIONS SUMMARY

Donations to education, primarily business oriented, accounted for 25% of support. The remainder funded health and welfare organizations. The program is fluid and has no publicly stated objectives.

Typical Recipients: • *Arts & Humanities:* museums/galleries • *Education:* business education • *Health:* single-disease health associations • *Social Services:* aged, community service organizations, drugs & alcohol

Grant Types: general support and matching

Geographic Distribution: in the New York area

Operating Locations: CA, CT, GA, IL, NY

CORP. OFFICERS

Steven J. Bensinger: *CURR EMPL* exec vp, cfo: Skandia Am Reins Corp

James F. Dowd: *CURR EMPL* pres, ceo: Skandia Am Reins Corp

Scott D. Moore: *CURR EMPL* sr vp, cfo: Skandia Am Reins Corp

GIVING OFFICERS

Cynthia Yonich: *CURR EMPL* asst secy: Skandia Am Corp

APPLICATION INFORMATION

Initial Approach: Send a proposal before September for funding the following year, including information about the organization, the amount and purpose of funds sought, and proof of tax-exempt status.

GRANTS ANALYSIS

Typical Range: $1,000 to $2,500

SKF USA, Inc.

Sales: $750.0 million
Employees: 1,866
Parent Company: SKF Aktiebologet, Gothenburg, Sweden
Headquarters: King of Prussia, PA
SIC Major Group: Industrial Machinery & Equipment and Transportation Equipment

CONTACT

John Lonati
Vice President, Administration
SKF USA, Inc.
1100 First Ave.
King of Prussia, PA 19406
(215) 962-4300

FINANCIAL SUMMARY

Fiscal Note: Annual Giving
Range: less than $100,000

CONTRIBUTIONS SUMMARY

Company reports 60% of contributions support civic and public affairs; and 40% to education.

Typical Recipients: • *Civic & Public Affairs:* general • *Education:* general

Grant Types: general support

Nonmonetary Support Types: cause-related marketing & promotion, donated equipment, and donated products

Operating Locations: GA (Atlanta, Gainesville), IN (Bremen), KY (Glasgow), NV (Reno), NY (Jamestown), OH (Youngstown), PA (Allentown, Altoona, Bethlehem, Hanover, King of Prussia, Kulpsville, Shippensburg, Wayne)

CORP. OFFICERS

Raymond B. Langton: *CURR EMPL* pres, dir: SKF USA

Charles E. Long: *CURR EMPL* chmn, dir: SKF USA

GIVING OFFICERS

John Lonati: *CURR EMPL* vp (human resources): SKF USA

APPLICATION INFORMATION

Initial Approach: Send brief letter of inquiry. There are no deadlines.

Skidmore, Owings & Merrill / Skidmore, Owings & Merrill Foundation

Revenue: $35.0 million
Employees: 350
Headquarters: Chicago, IL
SIC Major Group: Engineering & Management Services

CONTACT

Adrian Smith
Partner
Skidmore, Owings & Merrill
33 West Monroe St.
Chicago, IL 60603
(312) 554-9090

FINANCIAL SUMMARY

Recent Giving: $374,300 (fiscal 1991); $57,400 (fiscal 1989); $43,400 (fiscal 1988)
Assets: $2,537,983 (fiscal year ending August 31, 1991); $2,838,711 (fiscal 1989); $2,961,846 (fiscal 1988)
Gifts Received: $250,000 (fiscal 1991); $323,455 (fiscal 1989); $359,042 (fiscal 1988)
Fiscal Note: Contributes through foundation only. In 1991, contributions were received from Skidmore, Owings & Merrill.
EIN: 36-2969068

CONTRIBUTIONS SUMMARY

Typical Recipients: • *Education:* student aid
Grant Types: fellowship
Geographic Distribution: nationally
Operating Locations: IL (Chicago)

CORP. OFFICERS

David M. Childs: *CURR EMPL* mng ptnr, ceo: Skidmore Owings & Merrill

GIVING OFFICERS

Emilio Ambasz: dir *B* Resistencia, Chaco Argentina 1943 *CURR EMPL* pres: Emilio Ambasz & Assoc *CORP AFFIL* chief design consult: Cummins Engine Co; pres: Emilio Embasz Design Group Ltd
Edward C. Bassett: dir
Thomas H. Beeby: dir *CURR EMPL* ptnr: Hammond, Beeby & Babka *NONPR AFFIL* mem exec comm: Chicago Inst Architecture & Urbanism
David M. Childs: dir *CURR EMPL* mng ptnr, ceo: Skidmore Owings & Merrill (see above)
Henry N. Cobb: dir *B* Boston MA 1926 *ED* Harvard Univ AB 1947 *CURR EMPL* ptnr: Pei Cobb Freed & Ptnrs *NONPR AFFIL* fellow: Am Acad Arts & Sciences, Am Inst Architects; mem: Am Acad Inst Arts & Letters
Lawrence S. Doane: vchmn
H. Laurence Fuller: dir *B* Moline IL 1938 *ED* Cornell Univ BSChE 1961; DePaul Univ JD 1965 *CURR EMPL* chmn, ceo:

Amoco Corp *CORP AFFIL* dir: Abbott Labs, Chase Manhattan Bank NA, Chase Manhattan Corp *NONPR AFFIL* dir: Chicago Rehab Inst, Chicago Un; mem: Am Petroleum Inst, IL Bar Assn; trust: Northwestern Univ, Orchestral Assn
Frank O. Gehry: dir *B* Toronto Canada 1929 *CURR EMPL* prin: Frank O. Gehry & Assocs *NONPR AFFIL* fellow: Am Inst Architects; trust: Hereditary Disease Fdn
Bruce J. Graham: chmn *B* Bogota Colombia 1925 *ED* Univ PA BFA, BArch 1949 *CURR EMPL* ptnr: Graham & Graham *NONPR AFFIL* fellow: Am Inst Archts; mem: Inst Urbanism & Planning Peru, Royal Architectural Inst CAN, Royal Inst British Archts, Urban Land Inst; mem adv bd govs: Urban Land Res Fdn; pres: Chicago Inst Architecture & Urbanism; trust: Univ PA Sch Fine Arts
Michael Graves: dir *B* Indianapolis IN 1934 *CURR EMPL* pres: Michael Graves Archt *NONPR AFFIL* fellow: Am Inst Archts, Soc Fellows Am Academy Rome; mem: Am Academy Inst Arts & Letters; trust: Am Academy Rome
William Randolph Hearst III: dir *B* Washington DC 1949 *ED* Harvard Univ AB 1972 *CURR EMPL* publ: San Francisco Examiner
Howard Krane: legal counsel
Diane Legge Lohan: secy-treas
Michael A. McCarthy: dir *B* Buffalo NY 1934 *ED* Cornell Univ BArch 1957; Harvard Univ MArch 1964 *CURR EMPL* ptnr: Skidmore Owings & Merrill *NONPR AFFIL* fellow: Am Inst Archts; mem: Architectural League, Chase Manhattan Bank Art Comm, Municipal Arts Soc; mem adv counc: Cornell Univ Coll Architecture Art & Planning
Charles W. Moore: dir
Adrian Smith: contact person *CURR EMPL* ptnr: Skidmore Owings & Merrill
Robert A.A. Stern: dir
Stanley Tigerman: dir *B* Chicago IL 1930 *ED* Yale Univ BArch; Yale Univ MArch *CURR EMPL* prof architecture: Univ IL Chicago *NONPR AFFIL* fellow: Am Inst Archts

APPLICATION INFORMATION

Initial Approach: *Initial Contact:* brief letter *Include Information On:* description of the

---

purpose for the application, the use to which the grant monies would be applied if received, the amount requested, and documentation of tax-exempt status *When to Submit:* any time
Restrictions on Giving: Grants, scholarships and fellowships are principally awarded to individuals or organizations for the purpose of education, research, or publication in or directly related to the fields of architecture or architecture engineering.

GRANTS ANALYSIS

Total Grants: $374,300
Number of Grants: 1*
Highest Grant: $350,000
Disclosure Period: fiscal year ending August 31, 1991
Note: In fiscal 1991, only one nonindividual grant was awarded. Recent grants are derived from a fiscal 1991 grants list.

RECENT GRANTS

350,000 Chicago Institute for Architecture and Urbanism, Chicago, IL

Skillman Foundation

CONTACT

Leonard W. Smith
President
Skillman Foundation
333 West Fort St., Ste. 1350
Detroit, MI 48226
(313) 961-8850

FINANCIAL SUMMARY

Recent Giving: $16,000,000 (1993 est.); $14,500,000 (1992 approx.); $16,474,379 (1991)
Assets: $350,000,000 (1993 est.); $350,000,000 (1992 approx.); $357,386,436 (1991); $281,411,901 (1990); $291,785,886 (1989)
Gifts Received: $7,032,649 (1989); $499,000 (1988); $457,000 (1987)
Fiscal Note: The foundation received unrestricted, annual cash contributions from the estate of Rose P. Skillman.
EIN: 38-1675780

CONTRIBUTIONS SUMMARY

Donor(s): The Skillman Foundation is a private foundation incorporated in Detroit, MI, in 1960 by Rose P. Skillman, who was the widow of Robert Skillman (d. 1945), an early and longtime officer and director of

3M Corporation. During their lifetimes, the Skillman's philanthropic interests focused on providing asistance and care for children and young people, especially the disadvantaged living in Southeastern Michigan.

The foundation operated as a conduit for Rose Skillman's philanthropic giving until her death in 1983, after which time the assets were distributed to the foundation.

Typical Recipients: • *Arts & Humanities:* arts institutes, music, opera • *Civic & Public Affairs:* philanthropic organizations, professional & trade associations, public policy • *Education:* colleges & universities, education funds, student aid • *Social Services:* child welfare, community service organizations, counseling, drugs & alcohol, youth organizations

Grant Types: capital, endowment, general support, matching, multiyear/continuing support, project, research, scholarship, and seed money

Geographic Distribution: focus on Southeastern Michigan, principally metropolitan Detroit

GIVING OFFICERS

James A. Aliber: trust *CURR EMPL* chmn, ceo, dir: First Fed MI

Lillian Bauder: trust

William McNulty Brodhead: trust *B* Cleveland OH 1941 *ED* Wayne St Univ AB 1965; Univ MI JD 1967 *CURR EMPL* atty: Plunkett Cooney Rutt Watters Stanczyk & Pedersen

Bernadine N. Denning: trust

Walter E. Douglas: trust *CURR EMPL* pres: Avis Ford

Jean E. Gregory: vp, treas

William Ellis Hoglund: chmn bd trusts *B* Stockholm Sweden 1934 *ED* Princeton Univ AB 1956; Univ MI MBA 1958 *CURR EMPL* exec vp, cfo: Gen Motors Corp *NONPR AFFIL* mem visiting comm: Univ MI Sch Bus; trust: William Beaumont Hosp

Kari Schlachenhaufen: vp programs

Alan E. Schwartz: trust *B* Detroit MI 1925 *ED* Univ MI BA 1947; Harvard Univ LLB 1950 *CURR EMPL* sr mem: Honigman Miller Schwartz & Cohn *CORP AFFIL* dir: Comerica, Core Indus, Detroit Edison Co, Handleman Co, Howell Indus Inc, PHM Corp, Unisys Corp

NONPR AFFIL dir: Detroit Econ Growth Corp, Detroit Renaissance, Jewish Welfare Fdn Detroit, Metro Affs Corp, New Detroit; trust: Commun Fdn SE MI, Harper-Grace Hosp, Interlochen Arts Academy; vp, dir: Un Fdn; vp, mem exec comm: Detroit Symphony Orchestra; advmem: Arts Comm City of Detroit; mem: MI Bar Assn; mem visitors comm bd: Harvard Univ Law Sch

Leonard W. Smith: pres, secy, trust

Jane R. Thomas: trust

APPLICATION INFORMATION

Initial Approach:

Call or write the foundation for guidelines. In general, the foundation does not consider letters of inquiry but responds only to grant applications.

The foundation does not have a standard application form. Applications should be clear and concise and contain: a cover letter, including an authorized statement signed by organization chair and individual responsible for the program; title page, containing the name of organization, the name of the department or division administering the grant, the name of the organization's president and/or the individual responsible for the project, the organization's address and phone number, the amount of grant request, the time period for support, name of the project, the program area to which the proposal is directed; and type of support requested; and a two-page summary of proposal, summarizing essential elements of the proposal.

Full proposals should be no longer than eight pages and should contain the following: one sentence statement of purpose; need for the project and problems it addresses; goal of the project, including objectives and results to be achieved; project plan describing project history and past accomplishments, target population, number of people to be served, timeline, and a list of specific activities; description of the organization, including a short history, mission statement, and description of services; revenue plan, including list of other sources of funding; evaluation plan, including

method of evaluation, any addition questions, information sources and analysis, the individual who will conduct the evaluation; plan for continued support of the project following the conclusion of the foundation's funding; total project budget, including the foundation's portion itemized and budget narative; an audited financial statment or unaudited Form 990; list of staff, including qualifications or principal persons responsible for implementing, supervising, and evaluating the project; list of the nonprofit's board, including occupations and affiliations; copy of organization's proof of tax-exempt status; letter of support from collaborating organizations; and an organization brochure and most recent annual report.

There are no deadlines for submission of applications except for requests from arts and culture organizations. The deadline for those organizations is April 1 of each year.

The foundation's trustees review grant applications five times each year, generally in February, April, June, September, and November. The review process for applications takes three months and the foundation will notify the organization in writing when a decision has been made. Other than applications which fall outside the foundation's geographic focus or program areas, the foundation does not provide applicants with assessments of their chances for approval.

Restrictions on Giving: The foundation reports that it does not make grants which may jeopardize an organization's public charity status because the amount requested is too large in relation to the past level of public support; to organizations that had revenues of less than $100,000 for the preceding year; to new organizations; to purchase or construct facilities or building owned by units of government; for endowments, annual drives, fund-raising events, research, or deficit funding; to generic fund-raising requests; for loans; to individuals, including scholarships; and to organizations that discriminate against people because of their age, race, sex, or ethnicity. The

foundation also does not make grants for less than $10,000.

OTHER THINGS TO KNOW

The foundation asks all prosepective applicants to review its Grantmaking Policies and Procedures before submitting a proposal. The foundation discourages contact with any trustee regarding specific applications. Generally, only one grant will be made to an organization in a year.

One month after notification of grant approval, the foundation meets with nonprofits to discuss reporting requirements. The foundation requires organizations to submit period reports and information about the program, including a signed copy of award letter, six-month progress and expenditure report, final evaluation and expenditure reports, etc.

Publications: annual report, newsletter, grantmaking policies and procedures

GRANTS ANALYSIS

Total Grants: $16,474,379

Number of Grants: 129

Highest Grant: $2,503,263

Typical Range: $25,000 to $150,000

Disclosure Period: 1991

Note: Average grant figure excludes a $2,503,263 grant. Recent grants are derived from a 1992 partial grants list.

RECENT GRANTS

2,250,000 Founders Society Detroit Institute of Arts, Detroit, MI — extraordinary operating support

369,000 Lake Shore Public Schools, St. Clair Shores, MI — technical and career education academy program

300,000 Detroit Symphony Orchestra Hall, Detroit, MI — extraordinary operating support

300,000 Hunger Action Coalition, Detroit, MI — emergency assistance for food providers

286,000 School District of the City of Royal Oak, Royal Oak, MI — curriculum design and career awareness program

280,000 Caregivers, Detroit, MI — "Parents Plus"

275,000 Ennis Center for Children, Detroit, MI — general operating support

250,000 Michigan Health Care Education and Research Foundation, Detroit, MI — health insurance program for uninsured Michigan children

250,000 St. Vincent and Sarah Fisher Center, Farmington Hills, MI — emergency shelter and infant mortality program

200,000 Heat and Warmth Fund also known as Thaw Fund, Detroit, MI — emergency heating assistance for low-income households

Skinner Corp. / Skinner Foundation

Employees: 950
Headquarters: Seattle, WA
SIC Major Group: Security & Commodity Brokers

CONTACT
Sandra Fry
Director
Skinner Fdn.
1326 5th Avenue, 711
Seattle, WA 98101
(206) 623-6480

FINANCIAL SUMMARY
Recent Giving: $790,000 (fiscal 1993 est.); $1,035,243 (fiscal 1992); $830,477 (fiscal 1991)
Assets: $3,769,232 (fiscal 1991); $5,351,315 (fiscal 1990); $4,860,462 (fiscal 1989)
Fiscal Note: Company gives through foundation only.
EIN: 91-6025144

CONTRIBUTIONS SUMMARY
Typical Recipients: • *Arts & Humanities:* arts associations, arts centers, arts funds, community arts, dance, museums/galleries, music, opera, public broadcasting, theater • *Civic & Public Affairs:* economic development, environmental affairs, housing, urban & community affairs, women's affairs, zoos/botanical gardens • *Education:* arts education, business education, colleges & universities, public education (precollege), special education

• *Health:* hospices, hospitals, mental health, outpatient health care delivery, public health
• *Social Services:* aged, child welfare, community centers, community service organizations, counseling, day care, delinquency & crime, disabled, domestic violence, drugs & alcohol, emergency relief, employment/job training, family planning, family services, food/clothing distribution, shelters/homelessness, united funds, youth organizations
Grant Types: capital, employee matching gifts, and general support
Geographic Distribution: Washington, Oregon, Idaho, Alaska, and Hawaii, where Skinner Corp., NC Machinery, and Alpac Corp. maintain operating locations
Operating Locations: AK, HI, ID, OR, WA (Seattle-headquarters)

CORP. OFFICERS
Paul Skinner: *CURR EMPL* chmn, pres, ceo, dir: Skinner Corp

GIVING OFFICERS
John S. Behnke: trust
Sally Skinner Behnke: trust *CORP AFFIL* dir: WA Mutual Savings Bank
Shari Dunkelman Behnke: trust
Sandra Fry: dir
Arthur E. Nordhoff: trust
Charles G. Nordhoff: trust
Nancy Nordhoff: trust
Catherine E. Skinner: chmn, trust
David Skinner: trust *B* Seattle WA 1920 *ED* Dartmouth Coll 1942 *CURR EMPL* chmn: Skinner Corp *CORP AFFIL* chmn: Alpac Corp; dir: Boeing Co, MacDonald Detwiler & Assocs Ltd, Northern Commercial Co, Pacific Northwest Bell Telephone Co, Safeco Corp
Kathryn L. Skinner: trust

APPLICATION INFORMATION
Initial Approach: *Initial Contact:* letter, including a brief organizational description and outline of the nature of the request, to Sandra Fry, Director of the Skinner Foundation or to local branch manager of NC Machinery Co. (WA, AK) or Alpac Corp. (WA, AK, HI) *Include Information On:* if request is favorable, applicant will be asked to submit a com-

plete application form and ten copies, including detailed organizational information; purpose of request, including total required funding for program or project, amount requested, type of grant requested, number of people served, evaluative criteria, and project start and completion dates; campaign status to date, including other sources of funding; financial information; board information; volunteer information; staff information; tax-exempt status *When to Submit:* any time *Note:* Inquiries about the foundation should be sent to the Skinner Foundation. A complete list of Alpac Corp. and NC Machinery foundation committee members may be obtained by calling the foundation.

Restrictions on Giving: Funds are not awarded to individuals; dinners or special events; fraternal organizations; goodwill advertising, political or lobbying groups; organizations that discriminate on the basis of race, color, religion, creed, age, sex, or national origin; or religious organizations unless funds are to be used for a community project.

The foundation generally does not make grants for operating funds to United Way agencies or recipients of grants from the Corporate Council for the Arts.

OTHER THINGS TO KNOW
Skinner Corporation, Alpac Corporation, and NC Machinery Co. all support the Skinner Foundation.

Contributions to the foundation from each of the operating companies generally account for 5% of company's pretax earnings.

Employee volunteerism is strongly encouraged. Activities include teaching economics in junior high schools, conducting seminars on small business administration, and serving on community college advisory boards.

Foundation performs a follow-up evaluation within a year of grant approval.

In fiscal 1991, about 85% of funds went to organizations in Washington; 8% in Alaska; 2% in Oregon; 1% in Hawaii; and less than 1% in Idaho.

GRANTS ANALYSIS
Total Grants: $1,035,243
Number of Grants: 491
Highest Grant: $50,000
Typical Range: $1,000 to $10,000
Disclosure Period: fiscal year ending March 31, 1992
Note: Figure for assets is from 1991. Recent grants are derived from a fiscal 1992 grants list.

RECENT GRANTS
50,000 University of Washington, Seattle, WA — the Campaign

30,185 United Way of King County, Seattle, WA

25,000 Fred Hutchinson Cancer Research Center, Seattle, WA

21,352 United Way of King County, Seattle, WA

16,666 Seattle Zoological Society, Seattle, WA

15,000 Heritage College, Seattle, WA

15,000 Northwest School for Hearing-Impaired Children, Seattle, WA

15,000 Seattle Repertory Theatre, Seattle, WA

13,360 United Way of Anchorage, Anchorage, AK

12,500 KCTS Association, Seattle, WA

Skirball Foundation

CONTACT
Morris H. Bergreen
President
Skirball Foundation
767 Fifth Avenue, 43rd Fl.
New York, NY 10153
(212) 832-8500

FINANCIAL SUMMARY
Recent Giving: $8,259,211 (1991); $12,557,720 (1990); $2,654,640 (1989)
Assets: $28,141,467 (1990); $37,019,678 (1989); $30,496,249 (1988)
Gifts Received: $4,108,387 (1990); $2,548,070 (1989); $5,689,167 (1988)
Fiscal Note: The foundation receives contributions from the Jack H. Skirball Revocable Trust, the Jack H. Skirball Discretionary Trust, and Berkshire Hathaway, Inc.
EIN: 34-6517957

CONTRIBUTIONS SUMMARY

Donor(s): The foundation was established in Ohio in 1950 by the late Jack Skirball and his wife, Audrey Skirball Kenis. Mr. Skirball, born in Homestead, PA, grew up in Cleveland, OH, and was ordained a rabbi at Hebrew Union College in Cincinnati. After serving in the rabinate for nine years, he entered the motion picture industry. As a producer, his most famous films, "Saboteur" and "Shadow of a Doubt," were directed by Alfred Hitchcock. Mr. Skirball won three Academy Awards for short subjects during his career. He died in 1985.

Typical Recipients: • *Arts & Humanities:* arts appreciation, arts associations, ethnic arts, museums/galleries, music • *Civic & Public Affairs:* civil rights, ethnic/minority organizations, international affairs, public policy, zoos/botanical gardens • *Education:* colleges & universities • *Health:* health organizations, hospitals, medical research, single-disease health associations • *International:* international organizations • *Religion:* religious organizations • *Social Services:* family services, food/clothing distribution, legal aid, religious welfare, youth organizations
Grant Types: general support
Geographic Distribution: primarily Los Angeles, CA; New York, NY; and Cincinnati, OH

GIVING OFFICERS

Morris H. Bergreen: pres, trust
Martin Blackman: secy
Robert D. Goldfarb: vp
George Harrison Heyman, Jr.: treas *B* New York NY 1916 *ED* City Coll NY BBA 1936; NY Univ MBA 1938 *CURR EMPL* adv dir: Shearson Lehman Brothers *NONPR AFFIL* fellow pres counc: Tulane Univ; mem: Beta Gamma Sigma; trust: NY Univ
Audrey Skirball-Kenis: don, vp
Robert M. Tanenbaum: asst treas

APPLICATION INFORMATION

Initial Approach: Restrictions on Giving: The foundation reports that it primarily makes contributions to preselected charitable organizations and accepts only limited unsolicited applications for funds.

GRANTS ANALYSIS

Total Grants: $8,259,211
Number of Grants: 46
Highest Grant: $2,000,000
Typical Range: $1,000 to $10,000 and $25,000 to $200,000
Disclosure Period: 1991
Note: The average grant figure excludes four grants totaling $5,000,000. Recent grants are derived from a 1991 Form 990.

RECENT GRANTS

2,000,000	Hebrew Union College, Cincinnati, OH
1,000,000	Hebrew Union College, Cincinnati, OH
1,000,000	Hebrew Union College, Cincinnati, OH
1,000,000	Hebrew Union College, Cincinnati, OH
500,000	New York University, New York, NY
250,000	Hebrew Union College Institute of Religion, Cincinnati, OH
250,000	Jewish Museum, New York, NY
250,000	Los Angeles Music Center Opera, Los Angeles, CA
200,000	American Friends of Israel Museum, New York, NY
200,000	Greater Los Angeles Zoo Association, Los Angeles, CA

Sky Chefs, Inc.

Sales: $470.0 million
Employees: 8,200
Headquarters: Arlington, TX
SIC Major Group: Eating & Drinking Places

CONTACT

Carole Cooke
Senior Vice President, Finance
Sky Chefs, Inc.
601 Ryan Plz. Dr.
Arlington, TX 76011-4099
(817) 792-2123

CONTRIBUTIONS SUMMARY

Operating Locations: AL, AZ, FL, KS, OH, TX, WA

CORP. OFFICERS

James J. O'Neill: *CURR EMPL* pres, ceo: Sky Chefs
William S. Woodside: *CURR EMPL* chmn: Sky Chefs

GIVING OFFICERS

Carole Cooke: *CURR EMPL* sr vp (fin): Sky Chefs

Skyline Corp.

Sales: $339.1 million
Employees: 2,820
Headquarters: Elkhart, IN
SIC Major Group: Fabricated Metal Products, Lumber & Wood Products, and Transportation Equipment

CONTACT

Cary Goodrich
Administrative Assistant
Skyline Corp.
PO Box 743
Elkhart, IN 46515
(219) 294-6521

CONTRIBUTIONS SUMMARY

Operating Locations: IN (Elkhart)

CORP. OFFICERS

Arthur Julius Decio: *B* Elkhart IN 1930 *ED* DePaul Univ *CURR EMPL* chmn, ceo: Skyline Corp *CORP AFFIL* dir: Banc One IN, NIPSCO Indus, Schwarz, Exeter, Chukerman, Schwarz Paper Co *NONPR AFFIL* chmn adv counc: Un Way Elkhart; dir: Special Olympics Intl; fellow, trust: Univ Notre Dame; life mem: NAACP; life mem, vchmn adv bd: Natl Salvation Army; mem: Chicago Pres Assn, Chief Execs Org, Manufactured Housing Inst, Mobile Home Mfrs Assn; mem adv bd: Goshen Coll; vchmn, trust: Holy Cross Coll
Ronald F. Kloska: *CURR EMPL* pres: Skyline Corp

Slant/Fin Corp. / Slant/Fin Foundation

Sales: $49.4 million
Employees: 400
Headquarters: Greenvale, NY
SIC Major Group: Electronic & Other Electrical Equipment, Fabricated Metal Products, and Industrial Machinery & Equipment

CONTACT

Melvin Dubin
President
Slant/Fin Fdn.
100 Forest Dr.
Greenvale, NY 11548
(516) 484-2600

FINANCIAL SUMMARY

Recent Giving: $425,280 (fiscal 1992); $439,560 (fiscal 1991); $536,063 (fiscal 1990)
Assets: $604,421 (fiscal year ending June 30, 1992); $823,736 (fiscal 1991); $1,163,430 (fiscal 1990)
Gifts Received: $170,000 (fiscal 1992); $65,000 (fiscal 1991); $250,000 (fiscal 1990)
Fiscal Note: All contributions are made by the foundation. Contributions received from Slant/Fin Corp.
EIN: 11-2752009

CONTRIBUTIONS SUMMARY

Typical Recipients: • *Arts & Humanities:* arts associations, history/historic preservation, libraries, literary arts, museums/galleries, music, opera • *Civic & Public Affairs:* environmental affairs, ethnic/minority organizations, international affairs, law & justice, philanthropic organizations, professional & trade associations, public policy, safety, urban & community affairs, zoos/botanical gardens • *Education:* colleges & universities, education funds, medical education, minority education, religious education, science/technology education • *Health:* hospices, hospitals, medical research, outpatient health care delivery, pediatric health, single-disease health associations • *International:* foreign educational institutions, international organizations • *Religion:* religious organizations, synagogues • *Social Services:* aged, animal protection, child welfare, community centers, community service organizations, disabled, food/clothing distribution, homes, recreation & athletics, religious welfare, shelters/homelessness, united funds, youth organizations
Grant Types: general support
Geographic Distribution: nationally, with emphasis on New York
Operating Locations: NY (Greenvale)
Note: Slant/Fin Corp.'s subsidiaries are Slant/Fin Ltd. (Missis-

sauga, ON, Canada) and Slant/Fin-Hidron Ltd. (Tel-Aviv, Israel).

CORP. OFFICERS
Delcy Brooks: *CURR EMPL* secy: Slant/Fin Corp
Donald Brown: *CURR EMPL* vp, treas, dir: Slant/Fin Corp
Melvin Dubin: *B* Brooklyn NY 1923 *ED* NY Univ 1946 *CURR EMPL* pres, dir: Slant/Fin Corp *CORP AFFIL* chmn: Logimetrics; pres: Slant/Fin-Hidron Ltd

GIVING OFFICERS
Delcy Brooks: secy, dir *CURR EMPL* secy: Slant/Fin Corp (see above)
Donald Brown: treas, dir *CURR EMPL* vp, treas, dir: Slant/Fin Corp (see above)
Melvin Dubin: pres, dir *CURR EMPL* pres, dir: Slant/Fin Corp (see above)
John Svitek: vp, dir

APPLICATION INFORMATION
Restrictions on Giving: The foundation reports that it donates only to pre-selected charitable organizations and does not accept unsolicited requests for funds.

GRANTS ANALYSIS
Total Grants: $425,280
Number of Grants: 202
Highest Grant: $105,000
Typical Range: $100 to $2,500
Disclosure Period: fiscal year ending June 30, 1992
Note: Recent grants are derived from a fiscal 1992 Form 990.

RECENT GRANTS
105,000 American Technion Society, Baltimore, MD
39,445 United Jewish Appeal-Federation of Jewish Philanthropies of New York, New York, NY
25,700 Long Island Jewish Hospital, Long Island, NY
22,000 Anti-Defamation League, New York, NY
20,000 Holocaust Publications, New York, NY
15,000 American National Sick Fund Israel
15,000 Friends of the Arts
15,000 Hofstra University, Hempstead, NY
10,000 Temple Israel of Great Neck, Great Neck, NY
10,000 Washington Institute for Near East

Policy, Washington, DC

Slaughter Foundation, Charles

CONTACT
Myles A. Cane
President
Charles Slaughter Fdn.
c/o Milgrim, Thomajan and Lee
53 Wall St.
New York, NY 10005-2815
(212) 858-5342

FINANCIAL SUMMARY
Recent Giving: $115,000 (fiscal 1991); $110,000 (fiscal 1990); $105,000 (fiscal 1989)
Assets: $2,645,271 (fiscal 1991); $2,405,757 (fiscal 1990); $2,608,537 (fiscal 1989)
EIN: 13-3055995

CONTRIBUTIONS SUMMARY
Typical Recipients: • *Education:* medical education • *Health:* hospitals, medical research, single-disease health associations
Grant Types: research
Geographic Distribution: focus on New York, NY

GIVING OFFICERS
Myles A. Cane: pres
Kenneth T. Donaldson: trust
William E. Friedman: secy, treas

APPLICATION INFORMATION
Initial Approach: Contributes only to preselected organizations.
Restrictions on Giving: Does not support individuals.

OTHER THINGS TO KNOW
Publications: Financial statement

GRANTS ANALYSIS
Number of Grants: 3
Highest Grant: $65,000
Typical Range: $20,000 to $30,000
Disclosure Period: fiscal year ending October 31, 1992

RECENT GRANTS
65,000 St. Luke's-Roosevelt Hospital Center, New York, NY
30,000 St. Luke's-Roosevelt Hospital

Center, New York, NY
20,000 Columbia University College of Physicians and Surgeons, New York, NY

Slaughter, Jr. Foundation, William E.

CONTACT
William E. Slaughter, Jr. Fdn.
32949 Bingham Ln.
Birmingham, AL 48010
(313) 666-9300

FINANCIAL SUMMARY
Recent Giving: $190,865 (1989); $115,460 (1988)
Assets: $1,895,917 (1989); $1,722,255 (1988)
EIN: 38-6065616

CONTRIBUTIONS SUMMARY
Donor(s): William E. Slaughter, Jr.
Typical Recipients: • *Arts & Humanities:* community arts, opera • *Education:* colleges & universities • *Social Services:* child welfare, community centers, community service organizations, united funds, youth organizations
Grant Types: general support

GIVING OFFICERS
Charles Hida: dir, secy
GLoria Slaughter: trust
Kent C. Slaughter: trust
William E. Slaughter, Jr.: pres, treas, dir *B* Chicago IL 1908 dir, pres, treas *ED* Northwestern Univ 1928; Detroit Inst Tech 1933 *NONPR AFFIL* mem: Am Petroleum Inst, MI Chamber Commerce, Natl Assn Mfrs; trust: Boys Girls Clubs Southeastern MI
William E. Slaughter, Jr.: pres, treas, dir dir, pres, treas (see above)
William E. Slaughter IV: dir, vp

APPLICATION INFORMATION
Initial Approach: Contributes only to preselected organizations. Applications not accepted.
Restrictions on Giving: Does not support individuals.

GRANTS ANALYSIS
Number of Grants: 53
Highest Grant: $39,800

Typical Range: $1,000 to $6,000
Disclosure Period: 1989

RECENT GRANTS
39,800 Boys Clubs of Broward County, Ft. Lauderdale, FL
36,025 Boys and Girls Club, Detroit, MI
27,000 Opera Guild, Ft. Lauderdale, FL
26,250 Navy League of the United States, Oakland County, Pontiac, MI
10,000 Boys Clubs of Metro Denver, Denver, CO
6,000 Washington Legal Foundation, Washington, DC
5,200 Capuchin Community Center, Detroit, MI
5,000 Petoskey Music Boosters, Petoskey, MI
4,500 Principia Corporation, St. Louis, MO
2,500 Old Newsboys Good Fellow Fund, Detroit, MI

Slemp Foundation

CONTACT
Slemp Fdn.
c/o Star Bank, N.A., Cincinnati
PO Box 1118
Cincinnati, OH 45201
(513) 632-4585

FINANCIAL SUMMARY
Recent Giving: $614,209 (fiscal 1991); $563,820 (fiscal 1990); $177,750 (fiscal 1987)
Assets: $10,280,998 (fiscal year ending June 30, 1991); $10,141,510 (fiscal 1990); $7,618,752 (fiscal 1987)
EIN: 31-6025080

CONTRIBUTIONS SUMMARY
Donor(s): the late C. Bascom Slemp
Typical Recipients: • *Arts & Humanities:* community arts, libraries • *Civic & Public Affairs:* environmental affairs, municipalities • *Education:* career/vocational education, colleges & universities, public education (precollege) • *Social Services:* child welfare, recreation & athletics, youth organizations
Grant Types: capital, emergency, endowment, scholarship, and seed money

GIVING OFFICERS
Campbell S. Edmonds: trust
Mary Virginia Edmonds: trust
John A. Reid: trust
Nancy E. Smith: trust

APPLICATION INFORMATION
Initial Approach: Application forms provided for scholarship applicants. Deadline is October 1 for scholarships.

GRANTS ANALYSIS
Number of Grants: 38
Highest Grant: $200,000
Typical Range: $1,000 to $10,000
Disclosure Period: fiscal year ending June 30, 1991

RECENT GRANTS
200,000 Treasurer of Virginia Department of Conservation, Richmond, VA
50,000 Lee County Public School, Jonesville, VA
50,000 Powell Valley Primary School, Big Stone Gap, VA
20,000 Pro-Art Association, Wise, VA
15,000 Woodway Volunteer Fire Department, Pennington Gap, VA
10,000 Ferrum College, Ferrum, VA
10,000 Mountain Empire Community College Education Foundation, Big Stone Gap, VA
7,062 Lonesome Pine Regional Library, Wise, VA
7,000 Lee County Public School, Jonesville, VA
6,000 Virginia Coop Extension Service, Jonesville, VA

Slifka Foundation, Alan B.

CONTACT
Alan B. Slifka Fdn.
477 Madison Avenue, 8th Fl.
New York, NY 10022

FINANCIAL SUMMARY
Recent Giving: $833,470 (fiscal 1991); $627,029 (fiscal 1990); $560,945 (fiscal 1989)
Assets: $1,667,724 (fiscal year ending November 30, 1991); $2,052,148 (fiscal 1990); $1,442,142 (fiscal 1989)

Gifts Received: $325,000 (fiscal 1991); $1,128,673 (fiscal 1990); $386,000 (fiscal 1989)
Fiscal Note: In 1991, contributions were received from Alan B. Slifka.
EIN: 13-6192257

CONTRIBUTIONS SUMMARY
Donor(s): Alan B. Slifka
Typical Recipients: • *Arts & Humanities:* arts centers, community arts, performing arts, visual arts • *Civic & Public Affairs:* ethnic/minority organizations, philanthropic organizations, zoos/botanical gardens • *Education:* colleges & universities, legal education, private education (precollege) • *Religion:* churches, religious organizations, synagogues • *Social Services:* child welfare, community centers, community service organizations, disabled, recreation & athletics, united funds, youth organizations
Grant Types: general support
Geographic Distribution: focus on NY

GIVING OFFICERS
Peter Schmidt: secy
Alan B. Slifka: pres *B* New York NY 1929 *ED* Yale Univ 1951; Harvard Univ 1953 *CURR EMPL* mng ptnr: Slifka (Alan B) & Co/Halycon Partnerships *CORP AFFIL* dir: Pall Corp; managing ptnr: Slifka (Alan B) & Co/Halycon Partnerships
Virginia Slifka: vp

APPLICATION INFORMATION
Initial Approach: Contributes only to preselected organizations.

GRANTS ANALYSIS
Number of Grants: 248
Highest Grant: $100,000
Typical Range: $200 to $2,000
Disclosure Period: fiscal year ending November 30, 1991

RECENT GRANTS
100,000 Congregation B'nai Jeshurun, New York, NY
66,000 Abraham Fund, New York, NY
50,000 Big Apple Circus, New York, NY
37,200 Abraham Fund, New York, NY
33,000 United Jewish Appeal Federation of Jewish Philanthropies, New York, NY

30,000 Abraham Fund, New York, NY
25,000 Abraham Fund, New York, NY
25,000 Abraham Fund, New York, NY
25,000 United Jewish Appeal Federation of Jewish Philanthropies, New York, NY
20,000 Abraham Joshua Heschel School, New York, NY

Slifka Foundation, Joseph and Sylvia

CONTACT
Joseph Slifka
President
Joseph and Sylvia Slifka Fdn.
477 Madison Ave.
New York, NY 10022
(212) 753-5766

FINANCIAL SUMMARY
Recent Giving: $312,660 (fiscal 1991); $200,363 (fiscal 1990); $171,410 (fiscal 1989)
Assets: $3,661,002 (fiscal year ending October 31, 1991); $2,947,664 (fiscal 1990); $2,699,077 (fiscal 1989)
Gifts Received: $806,915 (fiscal 1991); $223,250 (fiscal 1990); $100,000 (fiscal 1988)
Fiscal Note: In fiscal 1991, contributions were received from Joseph and Sylvia Slifka.
EIN: 13-6106433

CONTRIBUTIONS SUMMARY
Typical Recipients: • *Arts & Humanities:* museums/galleries, public broadcasting • *Civic & Public Affairs:* ethnic/minority organizations • *Education:* colleges & universities, private education (precollege) • *Health:* hospitals, medical research • *Religion:* religious organizations, synagogues • *Social Services:* child welfare, community centers, community service organizations, youth organizations
Grant Types: general support and research

GIVING OFFICERS
Alan B. Slifka: treas *B* New York NY 1929 *ED* Yale Univ 1951; Harvard Univ 1953 *CURR EMPL* mng ptnr: Slifka (Alan B) & Co/Halycon Partnerships *CORP AFFIL* dir: Pall Corp; managing ptnr: Slifka (Alan B) & Co/Halycon Partnerships

Barbara Slifka: trust
Joseph Slifka: pres
Sylvia Slifka: vp

APPLICATION INFORMATION
Initial Approach: Send brief letter describing program. There are no deadlines.

GRANTS ANALYSIS
Number of Grants: 108
Highest Grant: $60,000
Typical Range: $500 to $5,000
Disclosure Period: fiscal year ending October 31, 1991

RECENT GRANTS
60,000 United Jewish Appeal Federation of Jewish Philanthropies, New York, NY
60,000 United Jewish Appeal Federation of Jewish Philanthropies, New York, NY
50,000 Abraham Joshua Heschel School, New York, NY
10,000 B'nai Jeshurin Temple, New York, NY
10,000 Big Apple Circus, New York, NY
10,000 Colgate University, Hamilton, NY
10,000 Michael Wolk Heart Foundation, New York, NY
5,500 Congregation Emanuel, New York, NY
5,000 Congregation Emanuel, New York, NY
5,000 Eldridge Street Project, New York, NY

Sloan Foundation, Alfred P.

CONTACT
Ralph E. Gomory
President
Alfred P. Sloan Foundation
630 Fifth Avenue, Ste. 2550
New York, NY 10111
(212) 649-1649

FINANCIAL SUMMARY
Recent Giving: $30,000,000 (1992 approx.); $28,561,076 (1991); $21,199,731 (1990)
Assets: $727,641,989 (1991); $612,221,359 (1990); $622,070,457 (1989)
Gifts Received: $243,356 (1990)
EIN: 13-1623877

CONTRIBUTIONS SUMMARY

Donor(s): Alfred Pritchard Sloan, Jr., was born in New Haven, CT, on May 23, 1875. After graduating with a degree in electrical engineering from the Massachusetts Institute of Technology in 1892, he began his career with the Hyatt Roller Bearing Company in Newark, NJ. He became president of the company at the age of 24. In 1916, the company merged with the United Motors Company, and two years later became part of the General Motors Company. Alfred Sloan was elected president in 1923; and subsequently served as chief executive officer for twenty-three years until 1946. In 1937, he was elected chairman of GM. He resigned the chairmanship in 1956, remaining honorary chairman until his death in 1966. He established the Alfred P. Sloan Foundation in 1934.

Typical Recipients: • *Arts & Humanities:* museums/galleries, public broadcasting • *Civic & Public Affairs:* economics, international affairs, national security, philanthropic organizations, professional & trade associations, public policy • *Education:* colleges & universities, economic education, education associations, engineering education, faculty development, international studies, minority education, science/technology education, social sciences education • *Science:* scientific organizations

Grant Types: conference/seminar, department, fellowship, multiyear/continuing support, project, and research

Geographic Distribution: national

GIVING OFFICERS

Lucy Wilson Benson: trust *B* New York NY 1927 *ED* Smith Coll BA 1949; Smith Coll MA 1955 *CURR EMPL* pres: Benson & Assocs *CORP AFFIL* dir: Combustion Engring Co, Commun Satellite Corp, Dreyfus Convertible Securities Fund, Dreyfus Fund, Dreyfus Liquid Assets, Dreyfus Long-Term Govt Fund, Dreyfus Third Century Fund, Dreyfus US Guaranteed Money Fund, Gen Reinsurance Corp, Grumman Corp, Science Applications Intl Corp *NONPR AFFIL* dir: Catalyst, Intl Exec Svc

Corps, Logistics Mgmt Inst; mem: Am Civil Liberties Union, Assn Am Indian Affs, Counc Foreign Rels, East African Wildlife Soc, Intl Inst Strategic Studies, Jersey Wildlife Preservation Trust Channel Islands, John F Kennedy Sch Govt, NAACP, Natl Academy Pub Admin, Trilateral Commn, Un Nations Assn, Urban League; trust: Lafayette Coll; vchmn: Citizens Network Foreign Affs

Stephen Lee Brown: trust, chmn investment comm, mem exec & audit comm *B* Providence RI 1937 *ED* Middlebury Coll AB 1958 *CURR EMPL* vchmn, pres, coo, dir: John Hancock Mutual Life Ins Co *CORP AFFIL* dir: John Hancock Freedom Securities Corp, Towle Mfg Co *NONPR AFFIL* dir: Boston Housing Partnership, Boston Police Athletic League; fellow: Soc Actuaries; mem: Am Academy Actuaries; trust: Boston Mus Science

Stewart Fred Campbell: fin vp, secy *B* St Louis MO 1931 *ED* Lehigh Univ BS 1954; NY Univ MBA 1961 *CORP AFFIL* dir: Pocono Hotels Corp *NONPR AFFIL* trust, pres: Meml Home Upper Montclair

Lloyd Charles Elam: trust *B* Little Rock AR 1928 *ED* Roosevelt Univ BS 1950; Univ WA MD 1957 *CORP AFFIL* dir: Dominion Bank Middle TN, Kraft Gen Foods, Merck & Co, Premark Intl, South Central Bell Telephone Co *NONPR AFFIL* dir: Commun Equity Econ Devel Corp; distinguished service prof psychiatry, chancellor: Meharry Med Coll; mem: Am Med Assn, Am Psychiatric Assn, Natl Med Assn

S. Parker Gilbert: trust, mem *B* New York NY 1933 *ED* Yale Univ BA 1956 *CORP AFFIL* dir: Burlington Resources, ITT Corp, Morgan Stanley Group

Ralph E. Gomory: pres, trust, mem exec & investment comms *B* Brooklyn Heights NY 1929 *ED* Williams Coll 1950; Princeton Univ 1954 *CORP AFFIL* dir: Ashland Oil, Bank NY, Lexmark Intl, Washington Post Co; sr vp (science & tech): IBM Corp; dir: IBM World Trade Asia Pacific Group *NONPR AFFIL* fellow: Am Academy Arts & Sciences, Am Philosophical Soc, Econometric Soc; mem: Counc Foreign Rels, Natl Academy En-

gring, Natl Academy Sciences, President's Counc Adv Sci & Tech; mem counc grad sch: Yale Univ; chmn visiting comm div applied sciences: Harvard Univ; trust: Princeton Univ

Howard Wesley Johnson: commission trust, chmn exec comm, mem investment comm *B* Chicago IL 1922 *ED* Central Coll BA 1943; Univ Chicago MA 1947 *CORP AFFIL* dir: Champion Intl Corp, EI du Pont de Nemours & Co, John Hancock Mutual Life Ins Co, JP Morgan & Co, Morgan Guaranty Trust Co, Fed Dept Stores *NONPR AFFIL* fellow: Am Academy Arts Sciences, Am Assn Advancement Science; hon chmn: MA Inst Tech; hon trust: Aspen Inst Humanistic Studies; mem: Am Philosophical Soc, Counc Foreign Rels, Phi Gamma Delta; mem-at-large: Boy Scouts Am; mem corp: Mus Science Boston, Woods Hole Oceanographic Inst; trust: Boston Mus Fine Arts; trust emeritus: Wellesley Coll; dir: Museo de Arte de Ponce; trust: Natl Arts Stabilization Fdn

Howard H. Kehrl: trust *B* Detroit MI 1923 *ED* IL Inst Tech BS 1944; Univ Notre Dame MSME 1948 *CORP AFFIL* dir: Dayton-Hudson Corp *NONPR AFFIL* adv counc: Univ Notre Dame Coll Engring; dir: Un Fdn Detroit; mem: Automotive Org Team, Engring Soc Detroit, MI Soc Prof Engrs, Soc Automotive Engrs; mem Sloan Chair fellows comm: MA Inst Tech

Donald Newton Langenberg: trust *B* Devil's Lake ND 1932 *ED* IA St Univ BS 1953; Univ CA Los Angeles MS 1955; Univ CA Berkeley PhD 1959 *NONPR AFFIL* chancellor: Univ MD System Adelphi; fellow: Am Assn Advancement Science, Am Assoc AdvancementS, Am Physical Soc; mem: Natl Academy Univ Res Admin, Sigma Xi; chancellor: Univ IL Chicago

Cathleen Synge Morawetz: trust, mem audit comm *B* Toronto Canada 1923 *ED* Univ Toronto BA 1945; MA Inst Tech SM 1946; NY Univ PhD 1951 *NONPR AFFIL* fellow: Am Assn Advancement Science; mem: Am Academy Arts Sciences, Am Mathematical Soc, Natl Academy Sciences, Soc Industrial Ap-

plied Math; prof, dir: Courant Inst Mathematical Sciences NY Univ

Frank D. Press: trust, mem exec comm *B* Brooklyn NY 1924 *ED* City Univ NY BS 1944; Columbia Univ MA 1946; Columbia Univ PhD 1949 *CURR EMPL* pres: Natl Academy Sciences *NONPR AFFIL* foreign mem: Academy Sciences USSR; mem: Am Academy Arts Sciences, Am Assn Univ Profs, Am Geophysics Union, Am Philosophical Soc, French Academy Sciences, Legion Honor, Natl Academy Pub Admin, Natl Academy Sciences, Natl Science Bd, Royal Soc, Seismological Soc Am, Soc Exploration Geophysicists, US Delegation Test Ban Negotiations; mem counc: Geological Soc Am; mem lunar & planetary missions bd: NASA; participant: Bilateral Science Agreement Peoples Republic China & USSR

Lewis Thompson Preston: trust, chmn audit comm *B* New York NY 1926 *ED* Harvard Univ 1951 *CURR EMPL* pres: Intl Bank Reconstruction & Devel *CORP AFFIL* bd overseers: Coll Retirement Equity Fund, Teachers Insurance & Annuity Assn; dir: Anheiser-Busch, British Petroleum, Fed Reserve Bank NY, Gen Electric Co, J P Morgan, L'Air Liquide *NONPR AFFIL* dir: Urban Fdn USA; mem: Assn Reserve City Bankers, Counc Foreign Rels; mem intl adv bd: Allianz A G

Harold Tafler Shapiro: trust, mem exec & investment comms *B* Montreal Canada 1935 *ED* McGill Univ B Commerce 1956; Princeton Univ PhD 1964 *CORP AFFIL* mem tech adv counc: Ford Motor Co; dir: Dow Chemical *NONPR AFFIL* dir: Natl Bur Econ Res; fellow: Am Academy Arts & Sciences; mem: Am Philosophy Soc, Pres Comm Advisors Science & Tech; mem adv bd: Am Bd Internal Medicine, Soc Advancement Behavioral Econs; pres: Princeton Univ; mem exec comm: Assn Am Univs; mem inst medicine: Natl Academy Sciences; sr fellow: MI Soc Fellows; trust: Interlochen Ctr for the Arts, Univ Res Assn

Arthur Louis Singer, Jr.: vp *B* Scranton PA 1929 *ED* Williams Coll AB 1950; Univ MI MBA 1952 *NONPR AFFIL* dir: Un

Neighborhood Houses NY; mem publs comm: Pub Interest; mem visiting comm: MA Inst Tech Ctr Intl Studies; mem visitors comm: New Sch Soc Res Sch Mgmt

Roger B. Smith: trust *B* Columbus OH 1925 *ED* Univ MI BBA 1947; Univ MI MBA 1949 *CORP AFFIL* dir: Citicorp, Gen Motors Corp, Intl Paper Corp, Johnson & Johnson, Pepsico *NONPR AFFIL* mem: Bus Counc

Robert M. Solow: trust

APPLICATION INFORMATION

Initial Approach:
The foundation advises applicants to send a brief letter of inquiry to determine whether a project or organization falls within funding guidelines. Letters of application should be addressed to the foundation's president.

There are no standard application forms. A letter of application should include details about the applicant and the proposed project, and information regarding the cost and duration of the work. Excluding recognized institutions of higher education, new organizations must provide tax-status information. The foundation has no deadlines for applications.

Grants of $30,000 or less are made throughout the year by foundation officers. Larger grants are approved by the trustees, who meet five times annually. The foundation screens proposals for technical feasibility and competence, social relevance, financial stability, and for their relation to the foundation's interests.

Restrictions on Giving: Foundation interests do not include primary or secondary education, religion, creative or performing arts, medical research, health care, or humanities. Grants will not be made for endowments, buildings, or equipment. Grants are rarely made for general support or for activities outside the United States. The foundation's program in public management has been terminated.

OTHER THINGS TO KNOW

Publications: annual report

GRANTS ANALYSIS

Total Grants: $28,561,076

Number of Grants: 309
Highest Grant: $1,486,125
Typical Range: $10,000 to $50,000 and $100,000 to $500,000
Disclosure Period: 1991
Note: The average grant figure excludes three grants totaling $3,486,125. Recent grants are derived from a 1991 grants list.

RECENT GRANTS

1,486,125 California, University of Berkeley, Berkeley, CA — support for three years for the Consortium on Competitiveness and Cooperation at Berkeley, Columbia, Stanford, Harvard/MIT

1,000,000 ETV Endowment of South Carolina, Spartanburg, SC — support for a six-part television series on the contribution and social impact of engineering

1,000,000 WGBH Educational Foundation, Boston, MA — support for a four-part television series on competitiveness

935,000 Stanford University, Stanford, CA — support to initiate a Center for the Study of the Computer Industry

926,814 Massachusetts Institute of Technology, Cambridge, MA — support for a program of research and education to further understand and improve U.S. industrial performance

803,950 Massachusetts Institute of Technology, Cambridge, MA — support for a new program for the study of the pharmaceutical industry

800,000 MPC Corporation, Pittsburgh, PA — partial support for the initial funding of a center for the study of the steel industry

740,000 Stanford University, Stanford, CA — partial support for Ph.D. program in manufacturing

687,000 Massachusetts Institute of Technology, Cambridge,

MA — support of a three year study of the automobile industry at MIT, through its Center for Technology, Policy and Industrial Development

624,183 Foundation for American Economics Competitiveness, Washington, DC — partial funding for the support of research on the time horizon on U.S. industrial investment for the Council of Competitiveness and the Harvard Business School

---

Slusher Charitable Foundation, Roy W.

CONTACT
Charles A. Fuller, Jr.
Foundation Manager
Roy W. Slusher Charitable Fdn.
P.O. Box 10327
Springfield, MO 65805-0327
(417) 868-4545

FINANCIAL SUMMARY
Recent Giving: $256,779 (fiscal 1992); $152,931 (fiscal 1990)
Assets: $6,236,020 (fiscal year ending February 28, 1992); $6,255,270 (fiscal 1991)
EIN: 43-6339151

CONTRIBUTIONS SUMMARY
Typical Recipients: • *Education:* student aid • *Health:* hospitals, pediatric health, single-disease health associations • *Religion:* religious organizations • *Social Services:* religious welfare, youth organizations
Grant Types: general support
Geographic Distribution: giving primarily in Missouri

GIVING OFFICERS
Charles A. Fuller, Jr.: foundation mgr

APPLICATION INFORMATION
Initial Approach: Send brief letter of inquiry. There are no deadlines.

GRANTS ANALYSIS
Number of Grants: 35
Highest Grant: $42,600

Typical Range: $1,000 to $25,000
Disclosure Period: fiscal year ending February 28, 1992

RECENT GRANTS

42,600 Teen Challenge of Ozarks, Springfield, MO — capital improvements

26,176 Springfield Victory Mission, Springfield, MO — capital improvements

25,000 Colorado Masons Benevolent Fund, Denver, CO — scholarships

20,000 Skaggs Community Hospital, Branson, MO — building fund

20,000 Young Life, Branson, MO

15,000 Shriners Hospital for Crippled Children, Tampa, FL

14,900 Ozark Christian Counseling, Springfield, MO — start-up costs new counseling center

10,000 Diabetes Foundation, Springfield, MO

8,000 Full Gospel Business Men's Fellowship, International, Cosa Mesa, CA

5,000 Agape House of Springfield, Springfield, MO

Small Educational and Charitable Trust, Rita H.

CONTACT
Carl M. Franklin
Trustee
Rita H. Small Educational and Charitable Trust
5966 Abernathy Drive
Los Angeles, CA 90045-1622

FINANCIAL SUMMARY
Recent Giving: $0 (1990)
Assets: $2,886,847 (1990)
EIN: 95-4287547

GIVING OFFICERS
Carl M. Franklin: trust
Sterling Franklin: trust

GRANTS ANALYSIS
Total Grants: $0
Disclosure Period: 1990

Smart Family Foundation

CONTACT
Raymond Smart
President
Smart Family Foundation
15 Benders Dr.
Greenwich, CT 06831
(203) 531-1474

FINANCIAL SUMMARY
Recent Giving: $2,400,000 (1992 approx.); $2,400,000 (1991); $2,319,179 (1990)
Assets: $63,000,000 (1992 est.); $49,216,276 (1990); $52,244,756 (1989); $44,973,841 (1988)
EIN: 36-6008282

CONTRIBUTIONS SUMMARY
Donor(s): The Smart Family Foundation was established in 1951. Donors are members of the Smart family.
Typical Recipients: • *Arts & Humanities:* museums/galleries, public broadcasting, theater • *Education:* colleges & universities, elementary education
Grant Types: project and research
Geographic Distribution: broad geographic distribution

GIVING OFFICERS
Joan Feitler: mem
Robert Feitler: chmn *B* Chicago IL 1930 *ED* Univ PA BS 1951; Harvard Univ LLB 1954 *CURR EMPL* pres: Weyco Group *CORP AFFIL* chmn: Hynite Corp; dir: Assn Banc Corp, Assn Commerce Bank, Champion Parts, Kelley Co, TC Mfg Co; pres: Weyenberg Shoe Mfg Co *NONPR AFFIL* pres: Milwaukee Art Mus; trust: Newberry Library Univ Chicago
Ellen Oswald: mem
Edgar Richards: mem
Mary Smart: secy
Nancy Smart: mem
Raymond Smart: pres
Sue Smart Stone: mem

APPLICATION INFORMATION
Initial Approach: Informal letters of application should be addressed to the foundation's president.
Letters should outline the project and include the purpose for which aid is sought, resources needed, list of personnel involved, description of the methods to be used in completing the project, detailed proposed budget, and IRS determination letter of tax-exempt status. Proposals should arrive at least three months prior to board meetings held in March and September.

GRANTS ANALYSIS
Total Grants: $2,319,179
Number of Grants: 25
Highest Grant: $1,000,000
Typical Range: $5,000 to $25,000 and $50,000 to $100,000
Disclosure Period: 1990
Note: Average grant figure does not include foundation's highest grant of $1,000,000. Recent grants are derived from a 1990 Form 990.

RECENT GRANTS
1,000,000 Columbia University-Phase II, New York, NY
327,300 Princeton University-Nadelmann, Princeton, NJ
119,829 University of North Carolina, Chapel Hill, NC — Strands Project
109,750 David and Alfred Smart Museum of Art, Chicago, IL
103,600 Wells-Ogunguit School District
100,000 Hebrew Union College, Cincinnati, OH
78,528 University of Chicago-Graduate Business School, Chicago, IL
75,000 Hebrew Union College-Stirball Museum
73,000 Bayshore School District
67,922 Little Orchestra Society, New York, NY

Smeal Foundation, Mary Jean & Frank P.

CONTACT
Goldman, Sachs & Co.
85 Broad St.
New York, NY 10004-2454
(212) 902-6897

FINANCIAL SUMMARY
Recent Giving: $310,128 (fiscal 1992); $500,093 (fiscal 1991); $586,310 (fiscal 1990)
Assets: $1,789,323 (fiscal year ending February 28, 1992); $1,872,519 (fiscal 1991); $2,219,792 (fiscal 1990)
EIN: 13-3318167

CONTRIBUTIONS SUMMARY
Donor(s): Frank P. Smeal
Typical Recipients: • *Arts & Humanities:* history/historic preservation, libraries, museums/galleries, theater • *Civic & Public Affairs:* economics, philanthropic organizations • *Education:* colleges & universities • *Health:* health organizations, mental health, pediatric health • *Social Services:* aged, child welfare, disabled, drugs & alcohol, youth organizations
Grant Types: general support and scholarship
Geographic Distribution: focus on the Northeast

GIVING OFFICERS
Frank P. Smeal: trust *B* Sykesville PA 1918 *ED* PA St Univ 1942 *CURR EMPL* ltd ptnr: Goldman Sachs & Co *CORP AFFIL* ltd ptnr: Goldman Sachs & Co *NONPR AFFIL* dir: Citizens Budget Comm NY
Mary Jean Smeal: trust

APPLICATION INFORMATION
Initial Approach: Send brief letter of inquiry describing program or project. There are no deadlines.
Restrictions on Giving: Does not support individuals or provide loans.

GRANTS ANALYSIS
Number of Grants: 39
Highest Grant: $100,000
Typical Range: $100 to $5,000
Disclosure Period: fiscal year ending February 28, 1992

RECENT GRANTS
100,000 Daytop Village, New York, NY
40,000 Citizens Budget Commission, New York, NY
40,000 Citizens Budget Commission, New York, NY
25,000 American Foundation on Aging Research (AFAR), New York, NY
25,000 Business Executives for National Security, Washington, DC
10,060 Pennsylvania State University, University Park, PA
10,000 Boy Scouts of America, New York, NY
10,000 Brooklyn Museum, Brooklyn, NY
8,333 YMCA, Red Bank, NJ
5,000 National Center for Disability Services, Albertson, NY

Smith and W. Aubrey Smith Charitable Foundation, Clara Blackford

CONTACT
Jane Ayers
Trust Officer
Clara Blackford Smith and W. Aubrey Smith Charitable Fdn.
c/o NationsBank
300 West Main St.
Denison, TX 75020
(903) 465-2131

FINANCIAL SUMMARY
Recent Giving: $1,006,572 (fiscal 1992); $401,367 (fiscal 1991); $674,474 (fiscal 1990)
Assets: $13,929,717 (fiscal year ending June 30, 1992); $13,901,288 (fiscal 1991); $14,329,388 (fiscal 1990)
EIN: 75-6314114

CONTRIBUTIONS SUMMARY
Donor(s): The foundation was established in 1985 by the late Clara Blackford Smith.
Typical Recipients: • *Arts & Humanities:* history/historic preservation, libraries, museums/galleries • *Civic & Public Affairs:* municipalities • *Education:* colleges & universities, community & junior colleges, medical education, public education (precollege) • *Health:* health funds, hospitals, medical research, nursing services • *Religion:* churches • *Social Services:* child welfare, recreation & athletics, united funds, youth organizations
Grant Types: capital and general support
Geographic Distribution: focus on Denison, TX

GIVING OFFICERS
Jane Ayres: chmn, trust off
Wayne E. Delaney: dir
Donald Harper: dir
Jack Lilley: dir
Robby Roberts: secy
H. W. Totten, Jr.: dir

APPLICATION INFORMATION

Initial Approach:
The foundation requests applicants contact the foundation for a formal application form. The foundation has no deadline for submitting proposals.

GRANTS ANALYSIS

Total Grants: $1,006,572
Number of Grants: 28
Highest Grant: $400,000
Typical Range: $2,000 to $25,000
Disclosure Period: fiscal year ending June 30, 1992
Note: Average grant figure does not include the highest grant of $400,000. Recent grants are derived from a fiscal 1992 grants list.

RECENT GRANTS

400,000 Texoma Medical Center, Denison, TX — ICU
250,000 Texoma Medical Foundation, Denison, TX — fund drive
62,265 Grayson County College, Denison, TX — lab learning center
58,000 M.D. Anderson Cancer Center, Houston, TX
53,500 Grayson County Rehabilitation Center, Sherman, TX — computer network
50,000 Denison Community, Denison, TX — renovation
25,270 Grayson County College, Denison, TX — nursing program
25,000 Austin College, Sherman, TX
25,000 Grayson County Crisis Center, Sherman, TX — capital expenses
23,876 Teen Challenge of Grayson County, Sherman, TX — transportation

Smith Barney, Harris Upham & Co.

Revenue: $1.63 billion
Employees: 7,150
Parent Company: Smith Barney
Headquarters: New York, NY
SIC Major Group: Security & Commodity Brokers

CONTACT

Henry Harris, Jr.
Vice Chairman
Smith Barney, Harris Upham & Co.
1345 Avenue of the Americas, 21st Fl.
New York, NY 10105
(212) 698-6140

CONTRIBUTIONS SUMMARY

In 1990, the Smith Barney Foundation merged with the Primerica and Commercial Credit Companies Foundation. Company interests include united funds, higher education, business education, youth organizations, urban and community affairs, and the arts and humanities.

Typical Recipients: • *Arts & Humanities:* general • *Civic & Public Affairs:* urban & community affairs • *Education:* general • *Social Services:* youth organizations

Operating Locations: NY (New York)

CORP. OFFICERS

Lewis L. Glucksman: *CURR EMPL* vchmn, dir: Smith Barney Harris Upham & Co

Jeffrey B. Lane: *CURR EMPL* vchmn, dir: Smith Barney Harris Upham & Co

John J. McAtee, Jr.: *CURR EMPL* vchmn, dir: Smith Barney Harris Upham & Co

Michael B. Panitch: *CURR EMPL* vchmn, dir: Smith Barney Harris Upham & Co

Frank Gustave Zarb: *B* Brooklyn NY 1935 *ED* Hofstra Univ 1957; Hofstra Univ 1961 *CURR EMPL* chmn, pres, ceo, dir: Smith Barney Harris Upham & Co *CORP AFFIL* dir: Am Stock Exchange, BMD Holdings, Securities Investor Protection Corp; mem: NY Stock Exchange; vchmn, dir: Primerica Corp *NONPR AFFIL* mem: Am Soc Pub Admin, Counc Foreign Rels, Natl Counc US-China Trade, Securities Indus Assn; trust: Gerald R Ford Fdn, Hofstra Univ

APPLICATION INFORMATION

Initial Approach: Contributes to preselected organizations; applications not accepted.

Smith Benevolent Association, Buckingham

CONTACT

A.J. McGhin, Jr.
Secretary-Treasurer
Buckingham Smith Benevolent Association
100 Arricola Ave.
St. Augustine, FL 32084
(904) 824-2881

FINANCIAL SUMMARY

Recent Giving: $176,965 (1990); $132,736 (1989); $174,835 (1988)
Assets: $4,646,952 (1990); $4,524,515 (1989); $3,929,174 (1988)
EIN: 59-6137514

CONTRIBUTIONS SUMMARY

Typical Recipients: • *Health:* health funds, hospitals, nursing services • *Social Services:* food/clothing distribution
Grant Types: emergency
Geographic Distribution: limited to St. Augustine, FL

GIVING OFFICERS

Loren Brown: trust
K. C. Bullard: trust
Arthur E. Fisher: vp
A. J. McGhin, Jr.: secy, treas
Reuben J. Plant: pres
Darrel Poli: trust
C. E. Walker: trust

APPLICATION INFORMATION

Initial Approach: Contributes only to preselected organizations.

GRANTS ANALYSIS

Number of Grants: 2
Disclosure Period: 1990

RECENT GRANTS

104,096 Flagler Hospital, St. Augustine, FL — medical care of needy
72,869 St. Johns County Welfare Federation of St. Augustine, St. Augustine, FL — nursing care, medical care, emergency food and utilities for needy

Smith Charitable Foundation, Lou and Lutza

CONTACT

Deborah Cowan
Program Director
Lou and Lutza Smith Charitable Fdn.
c/o New Hampshire Charitable Fund
One South St.
Concord, NH 03301
(603) 225-6641

FINANCIAL SUMMARY

Recent Giving: $504,330 (1990); $737,700 (1989); $431,351 (1988)
Assets: $3,300,752 (1990); $3,836,121 (1989); $3,746,631 (1988)
EIN: 23-7162940

CONTRIBUTIONS SUMMARY

Donor(s): Lutza Smith, Louis Smith Marital Trust
Typical Recipients: • *Arts & Humanities:* arts centers, history/historic preservation • *Civic & Public Affairs:* environmental affairs • *Health:* hospitals, pediatric health • *Social Services:* child welfare, shelters/homelessness, united funds, youth organizations
Grant Types: capital and project
Geographic Distribution: focus on NH

GIVING OFFICERS

Charles A. DeGrandpre: trust
Kenneth F. Graf: trust
Louise K. Newman: trust

APPLICATION INFORMATION

Initial Approach: Send brief letter of inquiry describing program or project. Deadlines are February 1, May 1, August 1, and November 1.
Restrictions on Giving: Does not support individuals.

OTHER THINGS TO KNOW

Publications: Informational Brochure (including application guidelines)

GRANTS ANALYSIS

Number of Grants: 35
Highest Grant: $50,000
Typical Range: $1,500 to $10,000
Disclosure Period: 1990

RECENT GRANTS

50,000 New Hampshire Community Loan Fund, Concord, NH — permanent capital

50,000 Seacoast Science Center, Rye, NH — build new facility

50,000 United Way, Manchester, NH

35,000 Mayhew Program, Bristol, NH — equipment and reconstruct facility

33,333 WEVO, Concord, NH — capital campaign

25,000 Crotched Mountain Community Care, Greenfield, NH — Alzheimer project

23,500 Boys and Girls Club, Salem, NH

20,000 Easter Seal Society, Manchester, NH

15,000 Upper Valley Support Group, Hanover, NH — parent support network

13,000 Friends Program, Concord, NH

Smith Charitable Fund, Eleanor Armstrong

CONTACT
Eleanor A. Smith
Trustee
Eleanor Armstrong Smith Charitable Fund
1100 National City Bank Bldg.
Cleveland, OH 44114
(216) 566-5500

FINANCIAL SUMMARY
Recent Giving: $92,153 (1991); $361,250 (1990); $128,335 (1989)
Assets: $3,873,703 (1991); $3,489,313 (1990); $3,558,166 (1989)
EIN: 23-7374137

CONTRIBUTIONS SUMMARY
Donor(s): the late Kelvin Smith
Typical Recipients: • *Arts & Humanities:* libraries, museums/galleries, music, performing arts • *Civic & Public Affairs:* environmental affairs, urban & community affairs, zoos/botanical gardens • *Education:* colleges & universities, private education (precollege) • *Health:* health organizations, hospitals, medical research, nursing services, single-disease

health associations • *Social Services:* child welfare, community centers, disabled, family planning, united funds
Grant Types: general support
Geographic Distribution: focus on the Cleveland, OH, area

GIVING OFFICERS
Eleanor A. Smith: trust

APPLICATION INFORMATION
Initial Approach: Send brief letter of inquiry describing program or project. There are no deadlines.
Restrictions on Giving: Does not support individuals.

GRANTS ANALYSIS
Number of Grants: 20
Highest Grant: $40,000
Typical Range: $100 to $1,000*
Disclosure Period: 1991

RECENT GRANTS

40,000 Head and Neck Medicine and Surgery Foundation, Cleveland, OH

20,000 Johns Hopkins Hospital, Baltimore, MD

10,000 Musical Arts Association, Cleveland, OH

5,000 Smith College, Northampton, MA

5,000 United Way, Cleveland, OH

2,500 Cleveland Skilled Industries, Cleveland, OH

2,000 Phillips Brooks School, Menlo Park, CA

2,000 University Hospitals of Cleveland, Cleveland, OH

1,000 Holden Arboretum, Mentor, OH

1,000 University Circle, Cleveland, OH

Smith Charitable Trust

CONTACT
Smith Charitable Trust
628 N. First St.
Rockford, IL 61107
(815) 965-0772

FINANCIAL SUMMARY
Recent Giving: $166,000 (1989); $156,575 (1988)
Assets: $3,429,047 (1989); $3,034,709 (1988)

Gifts Received: $30,000 (1989); $32,000 (1988)
EIN: 36-6078557

CONTRIBUTIONS SUMMARY
Donor(s): Smith Oil Corp., the late Carl A. Smith, Byron C. Marlowe
Typical Recipients: • *Education:* colleges & universities, private education (precollege), religious education • *Health:* hospitals • *Social Services:* child welfare, disabled, recreation & athletics, united funds, youth organizations
Grant Types: capital and general support
Geographic Distribution: limited to IL

GIVING OFFICERS
Howard Bell: trust
David S. Paddock: trust
C. Gordon Smith: trust

APPLICATION INFORMATION
Initial Approach: Contributes only to preselected organizations.
Restrictions on Giving: Does not support individuals.

GRANTS ANALYSIS
Number of Grants: 86
Highest Grant: $25,750
Typical Range: $50 to $1,000
Disclosure Period: 1989

RECENT GRANTS

25,750 Arts and Science Park, Rockford, IL

20,000 Rockford College, Rockford, IL

14,800 United Way, Rockford, IL

14,600 Keith Country Day School, Rockford, IL

10,200 Girl Scouts of America, Rockford, IL

9,700 Rockford Area Convention and Visitors Bureau, Rockford, IL

5,600 Second Congregational Church, Rockford, IL

5,050 Rosecrane Memorial Home for Children, Rockford, IL

5,000 Rockford Memorial Hospital, Rockford, IL

4,500 YMCA, Rockford, IL

Smith Charitable Trust, W. W.

CONTACT
Bruce M. Brown
Administrator
W. W. Smith Charitable Trust
101 Bryn Mawr Avenue, Ste. 200
Bryn Mawr, PA 19010
(215) 525-9667

FINANCIAL SUMMARY
Recent Giving: $4,000,000 (fiscal 1993 est.); $6,556,398 (fiscal 1992); $5,321,534 (fiscal 1991)
Assets: $103,000,000 (fiscal year ending June 30, 1992); $98,959,466 (fiscal 1991); $94,000,000 (fiscal 1990)
EIN: 23-6648841

CONTRIBUTIONS SUMMARY
Donor(s): The trust was established in 1977 from funds bequeathed by the will of William Wikoff Smith (d. 1976). Mr. Smith, a successful businessman in the oil and chemical industries, was president and chief executive officer of Kewanee Industries, formerly Kewanee Oil Company. He participated in educational, health, and charitable organizations. He also had a great love of the sea and ships and building ship models.
Typical Recipients: • *Education:* colleges & universities, student aid • *Health:* geriatric health, health organizations, hospitals, medical research, nursing services • *Social Services:* aged, child welfare, community centers, community service organizations, disabled, emergency relief, food/clothing distribution, homes, shelters/homelessness, youth organizations
Grant Types: capital, challenge, emergency, fellowship, general support, multiyear/continuing support, operating expenses, project, research, scholarship, and seed money
Geographic Distribution: Delaware Valley area

GIVING OFFICERS
Bruce M. Brown: adm *CURR EMPL* vp (charitable trusts): CoreStates NA *NONPR AFFIL* co-pres, dir: Brooke Valley Conservancy Assn; dir: Bermuda Artworks Fdn; mem: DE Valley Grantmakers, Natl Trust

Historic Preservation, Union League Philadelphia

G. Morris Dorrance, Jr.: trust rep CoreStates NA *B* Philadelphia PA 1922 *ED* Univ PA AB 1949; Univ PA Wharton Sch MBA 1951 *CORP AFFIL* dir: RR Donnelley & Sons Co, Penn VA Corp, Provident Mutual Life Ins Co, Rohm & Haas Co *NONPR AFFIL* trust: Univ PA

Louise A. Havens: grant adm

Nancy L. Myers: programs coordinator

Mary L. Smith: trust *NONPR AFFIL* dir: Planned Parenthood Mid-Iowa, US Inst Peace; mem: Am Med Assn Womens Auxiliary, Kappa Alpha Theta, Natl Conf Christians & Jews, PEO, UN Assn; mem adv bd: Natl Womens Political Caucus; trust: Drake Univ

APPLICATION INFORMATION

Initial Approach:

Grant applications should be submitted in writing to the trust. Requests for medical research grants must be submitted on the trust's application form. Specific guidelines for all programs are available from the trust office.

Applications should include description and justification of the project; all published material concerning the proposed project; purpose and activities of the organization; project budget and timetable; list of other sources of funds; list of officers and board members; audited financial statement for most recent fiscal year; current operating budget; and evidence of tax-exempt and non-private foundation status.

Applications are accepted throughout the year. Requests from colleges and universities for scholarship funds must be received by May 1 for consideration at the June meeting. Requests for clothing and shelter for children and the aged are considered at the March and September meetings. Applications for hospital care for the needy are due by February 1 for the March meeting. Heart research proposals must be received by September 15 to be considered at the December meeting. Cancer and AIDS research applications are due on June 15 for decision in September.

Applications are reviewed throughout the year by the staff. If interested, the trust may request more detailed information or a meeting.

Restrictions on Giving:

Grants are not made to individuals or for deficit financing. The trust does not provide loans. No more than one request may be submitted or funded each year. Funding is limited to a three-year maximum period. Hospital and college grants are by invitation only. There is no retroactive funding for non-medical emergencies.

OTHER THINGS TO KNOW

CoreStates, N.A., is the corporate trustee and fiduciary agent for the trust. The trust reports that it is affiliated with the Mary L. Smith Charitable Lead Trust in Pennsylvania. Proposal writing assistance is offered by the trust. Delaware Valley Grantmakers (RAG) proposal format accepted. The trust requires pre-award site visits and post-grant financial and narrative reports.

Publications: biennial report

GRANTS ANALYSIS

Total Grants: $6,556,398

Number of Grants: 113*

Highest Grant: $300,000*

Typical Range: $10,000 to $100,000

Disclosure Period: fiscal year ending June 30, 1992

Note: Figures for number of grants, average grant, and highest grant are from fiscal 1991. Recent grants are derived from a partial fiscal 1992 grants list.

RECENT GRANTS

286,000 Wistar Institute, Philadelphia, PA

277,000 Graduate Hospital, Philadelphia, PA

245,000 University of Pennsylvania, Philadelphia, PA

242,000 Milton S. Hershey Medical Center, Philadelphia, PA

233,000 Temple University School of Medicine, Philadelphia, PA

213,000 Milton S. Hershey Medical Center

210,000 Temple University, Philadelphia, PA

192,000 Johns Hopkins University School of Medicine, Baltimore, MD

184,000 Wistar Institute, Philadelphia, PA

150,000 University of Pennsylvania, Philadelphia, PA

Smith Charities, John

CONTACT

Wilbur Bridges
President
John Smith Charities
c/o NCNB South Carolina, Trust Department
PO Box 608
Greenville, SC 29602
(803) 271-5847

FINANCIAL SUMMARY

Recent Giving: $942,992 (fiscal 1990); $905,047 (fiscal 1989)

Assets: $16,511,799 (fiscal year ending July 31, 1990); $15,443,674 (fiscal 1989)

Gifts Received: $415,869 (fiscal 1990); $1,058,159 (fiscal 1989)

Fiscal Note: In 1990, contributions were received from the estate of John I. Smith.

EIN: 57-0806327

CONTRIBUTIONS SUMMARY

Donor(s): The foundation was established in 1985 by the late John I. Smith.

Typical Recipients: • *Arts & Humanities:* music • *Civic & Public Affairs:* philanthropic organizations • *Education:* colleges & universities, private education (precollege), religious education • *Health:* hospitals, single-disease health associations • *Religion:* religious organizations • *Social Services:* counseling, food/clothing distribution, homes

Grant Types: capital, emergency, endowment, general support, and scholarship

Geographic Distribution: focus on Greenville, SC

GIVING OFFICERS

Wilbur Y. Bridges: pres, secy

Jefferson V. Smith III: dir

W. Thomas Smith: vp, treas

APPLICATION INFORMATION

Initial Approach:

Applicants are requested to write the foundation for formal guidelines on submitting proposals.

GRANTS ANALYSIS

Total Grants: $942,992

Number of Grants: 25

Highest Grant: $250,000

Typical Range: $10,000 to $30,000

Disclosure Period: fiscal year ending July 31, 1990

Note: Average grant figure does not include the highest grant of $250,000. Recent grants are derived from a fiscal 1990 grants list.

RECENT GRANTS

250,000 Davidson College, Davidson, NC

140,000 Columbia Theological Seminary, New York, NY

136,450 Presbyterian College, Clinton, SC

100,000 Community Foundation for Public Housing, Greenville, SC

50,000 Furman University, Greenville, SC

50,000 Meals on Wheels, Greenville, SC

50,000 St. Frances Hospital, Greenville, SC

25,000 Family Counseling Center, Greenville, SC

20,000 Foundation Center, New York, NY

20,000 Pendleton Place, Greenville, SC

Smith Corona Corp.

Sales: $383.4 million
Employees: 3,399
Parent Company: Hanson PLC
Headquarters: Cortland, NY
SIC Major Group: Industrial Machinery & Equipment

CONTACT

Joyce Warner
Director, Employee Relations
Smith Corona Corp.
PO Box 2020
Cortland, NY 13045
(607) 753-6011

CONTRIBUTIONS SUMMARY

Operating Locations: NY (Cortland)

CORP. OFFICERS

William D. Henderson: *CURR EMPL* pres, coo: Smith Corona Corp

G. Lee Thompson: *CURR EMPL* chmn, ceo: Smith Corona Corp

Smith Corp., A.O. / Smith Foundation, A.O.

Sales: $1.04 billion
Employees: 10,300
Headquarters: Milwaukee, WI
SIC Major Group: Fabricated Metal Products, Industrial Machinery & Equipment, Rubber & Miscellaneous Plastics Products, and Transportation Equipment

CONTACT
Edward J. O'Connor
Secretary
A.O. Smith Fdn.
PO Box 23975
Milwaukee, WI 53223
(414) 359-4100

FINANCIAL SUMMARY
Recent Giving: $630,822 (fiscal 1991); $598,655 (fiscal 1990); $536,126 (fiscal 1989)
Assets: $116,659 (fiscal year ending June 30, 1991); $788,300 (fiscal 1990); $14,766 (fiscal 1989)
Fiscal Note: Company gives primarily through the foundation.
EIN: 39-6076724

CONTRIBUTIONS SUMMARY
Typical Recipients: • *Arts & Humanities:* arts funds, dance, history/historic preservation, libraries, museums/galleries, music, performing arts • *Civic & Public Affairs:* business/free enterprise, civil rights, economic development, environmental affairs, nonprofit management, safety, urban & community affairs • *Education:* business education, colleges & universities, community & junior colleges, economic education, education funds, engineering education, literacy, medical education, minority education, student aid • *Health:* emergency/ambulance services, hospitals, medical rehabilitation, mental health, public health • *Social Services:* aged, child welfare, community centers, community service organizations, disabled, drugs & alcohol, family services, homes, recreation & athletics, shelters/homelessness, united funds, youth organizations
Grant Types: capital, employee matching gifts, general support, operating expenses, project, and scholarship

Nonmonetary Support Types: donated equipment, donated products, in-kind services, loaned employees, and loaned executives
Note: Estimated value of non-cash support is unavailable and is not included in figures above.
Geographic Distribution: primarily in communities where company has manufacturing facilities
Operating Locations: AR (Little Rock), CA (Irvine), IL (Chicago, DeKalb, Granite City), KY (Florence, Mount Sterling), MI (Farmington Hills), NC (Mebane), OH (Tipp City, Upper Sandusky), SC (McBee), TN (Milan), TX (El Paso, Irving), WA (Seattle), WI (Milwaukee)
Note: Also operates in Bermuda, Canada, Ireland, Mexico, and the Netherlands.

CORP. OFFICERS
Thomas Ironside Dolan: *B* Hastings MI 1927 *ED* Univ MI BSME 1949 *CURR EMPL* dir: Smith Corp (AO) *CORP AFFIL* trust: Northwestern Mutual Life Ins Co; dir: First WI Natl Bank *NONPR AFFIL* corporate mem: Milwaukee Sch Engg; mem: Bus Counc, Intl Exec Svc Corps, Milwaukee Assn Commerce; trust: Highway Users Fed; mem: Bus Roundtable, Greater Milwaukee Comm, Soc Automotive Engrs; mem exec comm: Machinery Allied Products Inst
Robert J. O'Toole: *B* Chicago IL 1941 *ED* Loyola Univ 1961 *CURR EMPL* pres, ceo, chmn: Smith Corp (AO) *CORP AFFIL* dir: Agristor Credit Corp, First WI Natl Bank, Metalsa SA, Smith Fiberglass Products, AO Smith Harvestore Products *NONPR AFFIL* dir: Metro Milwaukee Assn Commerce; mem: Bus Roundtable, Competitive WI, Greater Milwaukee Comm, Mfrs Alliance Productivity & Innovation; mem exec comm: WI Mgrs & Commerce Assn

GIVING OFFICERS
Thomas Ironside Dolan: vp, dir *CURR EMPL* dir: Smith Corp (AO) (see above)
Edward J. O'Connor: secy, dir *B* St Louis MO *ED* St Louis Univ 1962 *CURR EMPL* vp (human resources & pub affairs): Smith (AO) Corp
Robert J. O'Toole: vp *CURR EMPL* pres, ceo, chmn: Smith Corp (AO) (see above)

Thomas W. Ryan: treas *B* Detroit MI 1947 *ED* Wayne St Univ BSBA 1969 *CURR EMPL* vp, treas: Smith (AO) Corp *CORP AFFIL* treas, real estate mgr: Smith Fiberglass Products *NONPR AFFIL* bd dirs: Greater Milwaukee Healthcare Network; mem: Fin Execs Inst, Natl Assn Accts
Arthur O. Smith: vp, dir *CURR EMPL* chmn: Arthur Smith Indus *CORP AFFIL* chmn: Smith Investment Co; dir: Smith (AO) Corp
Lloyd Bruce Smith: pres, dir *B* Milwaukee WI 1920 *ED* Yale Univ 1942 *CORP AFFIL* dir: Deere & Co, First WI Corp, Goodyear Tire & Rubber Co; dir, mem bus counc: AO Smith Corp; vp, dir: Smith Investment Co *NONPR AFFIL* dir: Med Coll WI; mem: Bus Counc

APPLICATION INFORMATION
Initial Approach: *Initial Contact:* letter or proposal on organization's letterhead *Include Information On:* name, location, and description of the organization; proof of tax-exempt status; geographic area served; explanation of activity for which support is sought; amount requested; description of benefits to be achieved and who will receive them; budget; other sources of income; plans for reporting results *When to Submit:* by March 30 to be considered for following year's budget; requests reviewed in order received *Note:* Also forward any printed materials describing organization that may lend support to application.
Restrictions on Giving: Foundation does not make contributions to politically active organizations seeking to influence legislation.

OTHER THINGS TO KNOW
A.O. Smith employees are encouraged to take an active part in civic affairs.

GRANTS ANALYSIS
Total Grants: $630,822
Number of Grants: 107
Highest Grant: $210,000
Typical Range: $500 to $5,000
Disclosure Period: fiscal year ending June 30, 1991
Note: Recent grants are derived from a fiscal 1991 Form 990.

RECENT GRANTS
210,000 United Way of Greater Milwaukee, Milwaukee, WI
35,000 United Performing Arts Fund, Milwaukee, WI — to assist in meeting the operating expenses of the performing arts organizations
32,500 Zoological Society of Milwaukee County, Milwaukee, WI — to maintain membership with the Platypus Society
20,000 Children's Hospital of Wisconsin, Milwaukee, WI — to aid in the purchase of an Echocardiograph Machine
20,000 Medical College of Wisconsin, Milwaukee, WI — in support of medical education, teaching and research
16,000 Sinai Samaritan Medical Center, Milwaukee, WI — in support of the Commitment for Tomorrow program
15,000 Marquette University, Milwaukee, WI — in support of an engineering school renovation project
15,000 Milwaukee Institute of Art and Design, Milwaukee, WI — to aid in the purchase and renovation of the terminal building
10,000 Boys and Girls Club of Milwaukee, Milwaukee, WI — in support of the capitol campaign Mission Possible
10,000 Junior Achievement of Southeastern Wisconsin, Milwaukee, WI — in support of the pacesetter campaign

Smith Family Foundation, Charles E.

CONTACT
E. Matthew Hause
Trustee
Charles E. Smith Family Fdn.
2345 Crystal Dr.
Arlington, VA 22202
(703) 920-8500

FINANCIAL SUMMARY
Recent Giving: $2,923,833 (fiscal 1992); $4,120,534 (fiscal 1991); $619,800 (fiscal 1990)
Assets: $14,915 (fiscal year ending February 28, 1992); $80,862 (fiscal 1991); $136,601 (fiscal 1990)
Gifts Received: $2,855,483 (fiscal 1992); $4,051,999 (fiscal 1991); $752,500 (fiscal 1990)
Fiscal Note: In 1992, contributions were received from Robert P. Kogod ($705,538), Robert H. Smith ($705,538), and Charles E. Smith Trust ($1,444,408).
EIN: 52-0800784

CONTRIBUTIONS SUMMARY
Donor(s): Charles E. Smith, Robert H. Smith, Robert P. Kogod.
Typical Recipients: • *Arts & Humanities:* history/historic preservation, museums/galleries, public broadcasting • *Civic & Public Affairs:* ethnic/minority organizations • *Education:* colleges & universities, minority education, private education (precollege), religious education • *Religion:* religious organizations • *Social Services:* community centers, community service organizations, disabled, united funds
Grant Types: general support
Geographic Distribution: focus on MD and Washington, DC

GIVING OFFICERS
Arlene R. Kogod: dir
Robert P. Kogod: vp, dir
Charles E. Smith: pres, dir
Clarice R. Smith: dir
Robert Howard Smith: secy, treas *B* Glendale CA 1935 *ED* Univ Southern CA 1957; Van Norman Univ 1966 *CURR EMPL* pres, ceo, dir: Security Pacific Corp *CORP AFFIL*

chmn: Security Pacific Natl Bank

APPLICATION INFORMATION
Initial Approach: The foundation reports it only makes contributions to preselected charitable organizations.
Restrictions on Giving: Does not support individuals.

GRANTS ANALYSIS
Number of Grants: 50
Highest Grant: $500,000
Typical Range: $2,500 to $25,000
Disclosure Period: fiscal year ending February 28, 1992

RECENT GRANTS
500,000 United Jewish Appeal Federation of Jewish Philanthropies, Rockville, MD
500,000 United Jewish Appeal Federation of Jewish Philanthropies, Rockville, MD
350,000 United Jewish Appeal Federation of Jewish Philanthropies, Rockville, MD
350,000 United Jewish Appeal Federation of Jewish Philanthropies, Rockville, MD
333,333 American Friends of Hebrew University, New York, NY
200,000 C.E. Smith Jewish Day School, Rockville, MD
125,000 Greater Washington Jewish Community Foundation, Rockville, MD
80,500 WETA Television, Washington, DC
70,000 Hebrew Day Institute, Rockville, MD
35,000 Junior Chamber of Commerce, Rockville, MD

Smith Family Foundation, Theda Clark

CONTACT
Michael Mahlik
Theda Clark Smith Family Fdn.
c/o Associated First Neenah Bank
100 West Wisconsin Ave.
Neenah, WI 54956
(414) 722-3321

FINANCIAL SUMMARY
Recent Giving: $206,407 (1990); $79,100 (1989); $76,300 (1988)
Assets: $1,846,932 (1990); $1,986,569 (1989); $1,794,886 (1988)
EIN: 39-6125329

CONTRIBUTIONS SUMMARY
Typical Recipients: • *Arts & Humanities:* arts centers, history/historic preservation, museums/galleries • *Civic & Public Affairs:* philanthropic organizations • *Education:* colleges & universities, private education (precollege) • *Health:* health organizations, nursing services • *Social Services:* community service organizations, united funds, youth organizations
Grant Types: general support
Geographic Distribution: focus on WI

GIVING OFFICERS
Clark R. Smith: pres
Tablin C. Smith: vp

APPLICATION INFORMATION
Initial Approach: Send brief letter describing program. There are no deadlines.
Restrictions on Giving: Does not support individuals.

GRANTS ANALYSIS
Number of Grants: 22
Highest Grant: $30,000
Typical Range: $1,000 to $5,000
Disclosure Period: 1990

RECENT GRANTS
30,000 University of Wisconsin, Madison, WI
15,000 Madison Art Center, Madison, WI
15,000 Neenah Historical Society, Neenah, WI
15,000 University of Wisconsin Law

School, Madison, WI — Minority Scholarship Fund
11,757 Fountain Valley School, CO
10,000 Best Friends of Neenah-Menasha, Neenah, WI
10,000 Maritime Museum
10,000 Sarah Lawrence College, Bronxville, NY — endowment fund
10,000 Shore Country Day School — endowment fund
10,000 YMCA

Smith Food & Drug
Headquarters: Salt Lake City, UT

CONTACT
Shelley Thomas
Director, Public Affairs
Smith Management Corp.
1550 South Redwood Rd.
Salt Lake City, UT 84104
(801) 974-1400

CONTRIBUTIONS SUMMARY
Nonmonetary Support Types: cause-related marketing & promotion, donated equipment, donated products, in-kind services, loaned employees, loaned executives, and workplace solicitation
Operating Locations: UT (Salt Lake City)

Smith Foundation

CONTACT
Joseph H. Barber
Secretary-Treasurer
Smith Fdn.
210 Fairlamb Ave.
Havertown, PA 19083
(215) 446-4651

FINANCIAL SUMMARY
Recent Giving: $365,975 (1991); $393,743 (1990); $364,250 (1989)
Assets: $6,680,109 (1991); $6,256,790 (1990); $6,384,473 (1989)
EIN: 23-6238148

CONTRIBUTIONS SUMMARY
Donor(s): the late W. Hinckle Smith, the late H. Harrison Smith
Typical Recipients: • *Arts & Humanities:* arts centers, arts institutes, public broadcasting • *Education:* colleges & universities • *Health:* hospitals, medi-

cal research, pediatric health, single-disease health associations • *Social Services:* animal protection, child welfare, community service organizations, disabled, shelters/homelessness, youth organizations
Grant Types: capital, general support, operating expenses, and project
Geographic Distribution: limited to southeastern PA

GIVING OFFICERS
Joseph H. Barber: secy, treas, dir
Philip C. Burnham: dir
Howard Busch: dir
Martin Evoy: dir
William Buchanan Gold, Jr.: dir
Lewis R. Good: dir
Roger P. Hollingsworth: pres, dir
Julia F. Menard: off
Robert L. Strayer: vp, dir
Francis Veale: dir

APPLICATION INFORMATION
Initial Approach: Contributes only to preselected organizations.
Restrictions on Giving: Does not support individuals.

OTHER THINGS TO KNOW
Publications: Annual Report

GRANTS ANALYSIS
Number of Grants: 42
Highest Grant: $25,000
Typical Range: $2,000 to $7,500
Disclosure Period: 1991

RECENT GRANTS
25,000 Children's Hospital Medical Center, Philadelphia, PA
25,000 St. Christopher's Hospital for Children, Philadelphia, PA
15,000 Fox Chase Cancer Center, Philadelphia, PA
15,000 Pennsylvania Academy of Fine Arts, Philadelphia, PA
15,000 University of Pennsylvania, Philadelphia, PA
15,000 Wistar Institute, Philadelphia, PA — Rabies Vaccine for Wildlife and Herpes Zoster Research
12,500 Kearsley-Christ Church Hospital, Philadelphia, PA

10,000 Chestnut Hill Hospital, Philadelphia, PA
10,000 Holy Redeemer Hospital and Medical Center, Medowbrook, PA
10,000 Pennsylvania Hospital, Philadelphia, PA

Smith Foundation, Bob and Vivian

CONTACT
Suzanne R. Benson
Secretary
Bob and Vivian Smith Fdn.
1900 West Loop South, Ste. 1050
Houston, TX 77027
(713) 622-8611

FINANCIAL SUMMARY
Recent Giving: $390,000 (1991); $335,900 (1990); $350,000 (1989)
Assets: $7,746,110 (1991); $7,249,571 (1990); $7,057,276 (1989)
EIN: 23-7029052

CONTRIBUTIONS SUMMARY
Donor(s): R.E. Smith, Vivian L. Smith.
Typical Recipients: • *Arts & Humanities:* museums/galleries • *Civic & Public Affairs:* ethnic/minority organizations, philanthropic organizations • *Education:* colleges & universities, private education (precollege) • *Health:* health organizations, hospitals, medical research, mental health, nursing services, pediatric health • *Social Services:* youth organizations
Grant Types: general support
Geographic Distribution: focus on Houston, TX

GIVING OFFICERS
Suzanne R. Benson: secy
Bobby Smith Cohn: trust
Sandra Smith Dompier: trust
W. N. Finnegan III: trust
Vivian L. Smith: pres, trust

APPLICATION INFORMATION
Initial Approach: Send cover letter and full proposal. There are no deadlines.
Restrictions on Giving: Does not support individuals.

GRANTS ANALYSIS
Number of Grants: 21
Highest Grant: $60,000
Typical Range: $5,000 to $25,000

Disclosure Period: 1991

RECENT GRANTS
60,000 Texas Children's Hospital, Houston, TX
50,000 Museum of Fine Arts, Houston, TX
45,000 Kelsey Seybold Clinic, Houston, TX
25,000 Hundred Club of Houston, Houston, TX
25,000 Special Camps for Special Kids, Dallas, TX
25,000 St. Luke's Episcopal Hospital, Houston, TX
20,000 Texas A&M Development Fund, College Station, TX
20,000 United Jewish Appeal Federation of Jewish Philanthropies, Houston, TX
15,000 Good Samaritan Foundation, Houston, TX
15,000 Kelsey Seybold Clinic, Houston, TX

Smith Foundation, Gordon V. and Helen C.

CONTACT
Gordon V. Smith
Director
Gordon V. and Helen C. Smith Fdn.
8716 Crider Brook Way
Potomac, MD 20854
(301) 469-8597

FINANCIAL SUMMARY
Recent Giving: $446,949 (1991); $976,777 (1990); $510,473 (1989)
Assets: $5,064,001 (1991); $4,953,302 (1990); $7,085,951 (1989)
Gifts Received: $579,848 (1991); $10,280 (1990); $1,772,991 (1989)
EIN: 52-1440846

CONTRIBUTIONS SUMMARY
Donor(s): Gordon V. Smith, Helen C. Smith, Miller and Smith, Inc.
Typical Recipients: • *Education:* colleges & universities, religious education • *Health:* health organizations • *Religion:* churches, religious organizations • *Social Services:* youth organizations
Grant Types: general support

GIVING OFFICERS
Cynthia Skarbek: dir
Bruce G. Smith: dir
Douglas I. Smith: dir
Gordon V. Smith: dir
Helen C. Smith: dir

APPLICATION INFORMATION
Initial Approach: Send brief letter of inquiry describing program or project. There are no deadlines.

GRANTS ANALYSIS
Number of Grants: 40
Highest Grant: $400,000
Typical Range: $1,000 to $15,000
Disclosure Period: 1991

RECENT GRANTS
400,000 Ohio Wesleyan University, Delaware, OH
13,000 Wesley Theological Seminary, Washington, DC
12,328 Ohio Wesleyan University, Delaware, OH
5,600 Bethesda United Methodist Church, Bethesda, MD
3,708 Boys and Girls Club, Washington, DC
2,500 Boy Scouts of America, Washington, DC
2,000 Jamestown Foundation, Washington, DC
1,498 American Red Cross, Washington, DC
1,422 Trinity Episcopal Church, Wheaton, IL
1,150 Operation Smile, Norfolk, VA

Smith Foundation, Julia and Albert

CONTACT
Julia and Albert Smith Foundation
1360 Post Oak Boulevard, Suite 2450
Houston, TX 77042
(713) 871-8271

FINANCIAL SUMMARY
Recent Giving: $20,000 (fiscal 1990)
Assets: $1,957,067 (fiscal year ending November 30, 1990)
Gifts Received: $569,104 (fiscal 1990)
Fiscal Note: Fiscal 1990 contributions received from Albert

J., Jr. and Julia C. Smith, and Albert J. Smith III.
EIN: 76-0207247

CONTRIBUTIONS SUMMARY
Typical Recipients: • *Health:* medical research • *Social Services:* community service organizations
Grant Types: general support and research

GIVING OFFICERS
Albert J. Smith, Jr.: secy, treas
Albert J. III Smith, Jr.: dir
Julia C. Smith, Jr.: pres
Wm. C. Smith, Jr.: dir
Julia A. Stuckey, Jr.: dir

APPLICATION INFORMATION
Initial Approach: The foundation reports it only makes contributions to preselected organizations and does not accept unsolicited requests for funds.

GRANTS ANALYSIS
Total Grants: $20,000
Number of Grants: 2
Highest Grant: $10,000
Disclosure Period: fiscal year ending November 30, 1990

RECENT GRANTS
10,000 Casa De Esperanza, TX
10,000 Houston Ear Research Foundation, Houston, TX

Smith Foundation, Kelvin and Eleanor

CONTACT
Douglas W. Richardson
President
Kelvin and Eleanor Smith Foundation
29425 Chagrin Blvd., Ste. 303
Pepper Pike, OH 44122
(216) 591-1404

FINANCIAL SUMMARY
Recent Giving: $2,129,278 (fiscal 1991); $1,208,817 (fiscal 1990); $1,271,783 (fiscal 1989)
Assets: $57,458,687 (fiscal year ending October 31, 1991); $48,109,433 (fiscal 1990); $34,096,651 (fiscal 1989)
Gifts Received: $14,920,981 (fiscal 1990); $713,436 (fiscal 1989); $651,727 (fiscal 1988)
Fiscal Note: In fiscal year ending October 31, 1990, the foundation received $14,920,981 from the estate of Kelvin Smith.

EIN: 34-6555349

CONTRIBUTIONS SUMMARY
Donor(s): The foundation was established in 1955 by the late Kelvin Smith.
Typical Recipients: • *Arts & Humanities:* arts associations, dance, libraries, museums/galleries, opera, performing arts, public broadcasting • *Civic & Public Affairs:* environmental affairs, professional & trade associations, public policy • *Education:* arts education, business education, career/vocational education, colleges & universities, education funds, private education (precollege), special education, student aid • *Social Services:* child welfare, disabled, drugs & alcohol, food/clothing distribution, youth organizations
Grant Types: capital, general support, project, and scholarship
Geographic Distribution: focus on the greater Cleveland, OH, area

GIVING OFFICERS
John L. Dampeer: chmn, treas, trust *B* Cleveland OH 1916 *ED* Harvard Univ SB; Harvard Univ LLB *CORP AFFIL* dir: Monarch Machine Tool Co, Van Dorn Co *NONPR AFFIL* mem: Am Bar Assn, Greater Cleveland Bar Assn, OH Bar Assn, Phi Beta Kappa
Ellen Mavec: secy, trust
Lucia S. Nash: vp, trust
Douglas W. Richardson: pres, trust
Cara S. Stirn: vp, trust
Ralph S. Tyler, Jr.: trust

APPLICATION INFORMATION
Initial Approach:
An initial written application should be submitted to the foundation. Telephone inquiries are discouraged.
The application should identify the applicant and its tax status, the nature of the project, its budget requirements, and the amount and scope of the requested grant. If the project appears to be of interest, but additional information is required, the foundation will request such information before taking action on the application. Personal interviews may be scheduled by appointment in some instances. There are no deadlines for submitting proposals. The

board usually meets in May and October.
Final notification usually takes 2 to 3 months.
Restrictions on Giving: The foundation does not make grants to private foundations or to individuals for scholarships, fellowships, loans, prizes, or similar benefits.

OTHER THINGS TO KNOW
Publications: application guidelines

GRANTS ANALYSIS
Total Grants: $2,129,278
Number of Grants: 35
Highest Grant: $1,000,000
Typical Range: $1,000 to $5,000 and $25,000 to $50,000
Disclosure Period: fiscal year ending October 31, 1991
Note: The average grant figure excludes the largest grant of $1,000,000. Recent grants are derived from a fiscal 1991 grants list.

RECENT GRANTS
1,000,000 Case Western Reserve University, Cleveland, OH — Kelvin Smith Library
225,000 Cleveland Museum of Art, Cleveland, OH — art exhibit
150,000 Hathaway Brown School, Shaker Heights, OH — capital campaign
150,000 Musical Arts Association, Cleveland, OH — artistic initiative
133,333 Sea Research Foundation, Cleveland, OH
100,000 Musical Arts Association, Cleveland, OH
75,000 Cleveland Institute of Music, Cleveland, OH — violin scholarships
55,000 Great Lakes Theatre Festival, Cleveland, OH
50,445 Cleveland Society for the Blind, Cleveland, OH — computerization
30,000 Hale Farm and Village, Bath, OH — fireplace at gatehouse

Smith Foundation, Kenneth L. and Eva S.

CONTACT
Thomas K. Jones
Trustee
Kenneth L. and Eva S. Smith Fdn.
1000 King Highway, Ste. 200, Bldg. C
Overland Park, KS 66210

FINANCIAL SUMMARY
Recent Giving: $155,031 (1991); $155,025 (1990); $222,000 (1989)
Assets: $5,133,923 (1991); $4,446,675 (1990); $4,521,619 (1989)
EIN: 48-6142517

CONTRIBUTIONS SUMMARY
Donor(s): the late Kenneth L. Smith
Typical Recipients: • *Health:* hospitals, pediatric health • *Social Services:* homes
Grant Types: general support and multiyear/continuing support
Geographic Distribution: focus on the greater Kansas City, MO, area

GIVING OFFICERS
Thomas K. Jones: trust
Eva S. Smith: trust

APPLICATION INFORMATION
Initial Approach: Contributes only to preselected organizations.
Restrictions on Giving: Does not support individuals.

GRANTS ANALYSIS
Number of Grants: 4
Highest Grant: $50,000
Disclosure Period: 1991

RECENT GRANTS
50,000 Children's Mercy Hospital, Kansas City, MO
50,000 St. Luke's Hospital, Kansas City, MO
30,000 Lakemary Center, Paola, KS
25,000 Spofford Home, Kansas City, MO

Smith Foundation, Lon V.

CONTACT
Marguerite M. Murphy
Secretary-Treasurer
Lon V. Smith Fdn.
9440 Santa Monica Blvd., Ste. 300
Beverly Hills, CA 90210-4201

FINANCIAL SUMMARY
Recent Giving: $806,100 (1991); $818,942 (1990); $736,450 (1989)
Assets: $20,175,737 (1991); $18,827,945 (1990); $17,408,653 (1989)
EIN: 95-6045384

CONTRIBUTIONS SUMMARY
Donor(s): The foundation was established in 1952.
Typical Recipients: • *Arts & Humanities:* arts institutes, libraries, museums/galleries, music • *Civic & Public Affairs:* philanthropic organizations • *Health:* hospitals, medical research, pediatric health, single-disease health associations • *Religion:* religious organizations • *Social Services:* aged, child welfare, community service organizations, counseling, disabled, family services, food/clothing distribution, homes, united funds, youth organizations
Grant Types: general support
Geographic Distribution: focus on Los Angeles, CA

GIVING OFFICERS
Stefan A. Kantardjieff: pres
John L. Lahn: vp
Donald R. Mellert: vp
Marguerite M. Murphy: secy, treas
Alexander Rados: vp

APPLICATION INFORMATION
Initial Approach: Restrictions on Giving: The foundation supports preselected organizations and does not accept unsolicited requests for funds. The foundation does not make grants to individuals.

GRANTS ANALYSIS
Total Grants: $806,100
Number of Grants: 82
Highest Grant: $40,000
Typical Range: $1,000 to $20,000
Disclosure Period: 1991

Note: Recent grants are derived from a 1991 grants list.

RECENT GRANTS
40,000 Child S.H.A.R.E. Program, Los Angeles, CA
40,000 United Way of Greater Los Angeles, Los Angeles, CA
25,000 American Lung Association, Los Angeles, CA
25,000 American Medical Flight Team, Los Angeles, CA
25,000 Boy Scouts of America, Los Angeles, CA
25,000 Maple Center of Beverly Hills, Beverly Hills, CA
25,000 Santa Marta Hospital Foundation, Los Angeles, CA
25,000 St. Vincent Senior Citizens Nutrition Program, New York, NY
25,000 World Research, Los Angeles, CA
22,000 American Diabetes Foundation, Washington, DC

Smith Foundation, Richard and Susan

CONTACT
Susan F. Smith
Trustee
Richard and Susan Smith Fdn.
27 Boylston St.
Chestnut Hill, MA 02167
(617) 232-8200

FINANCIAL SUMMARY
Recent Giving: $959,024 (fiscal 1991); $777,762 (fiscal 1990); $735,531 (fiscal 1989)
Assets: $3,668,805 (fiscal year ending April 30, 1991); $3,532,303 (fiscal 1990); $3,349,690 (fiscal 1989)
Gifts Received: $820,000 (fiscal 1991); $1,550,231 (fiscal 1990); $1,808,521 (fiscal 1989)
Fiscal Note: In 1991, contributions were received from the Richard A. Smith 1976 Charitable Trust ($390,000), the Marian Smith 1976 Charitable Trust ($195,000), the Richard A. Smith 1986 Charitable Trust ($125,000), and Richard H. Smith ($110,000).
EIN: 23-7090011

CONTRIBUTIONS SUMMARY
Donor(s): the late Marian Smith, Richard A. Smith
Typical Recipients: • *Arts & Humanities:* history/historic preservation, museums/galleries • *Civic & Public Affairs:* philanthropic organizations • *Education:* colleges & universities, private education (precollege) • *Health:* health organizations, hospitals, medical research, pediatric health, single-disease health associations • *Religion:* churches, synagogues • *Social Services:* child welfare, food/clothing distribution
Grant Types: capital, fellowship, general support, and project
Geographic Distribution: focus on Boston, MA

GIVING OFFICERS
Amy S. Berylson: trust
Debra S. Knez: trust
Robert A. Smith: trust
Susan F. Smith: trust

APPLICATION INFORMATION
Initial Approach: Send brief letter of inquiry describing program or project. There are no deadlines. Board meets in fall and spring.
Restrictions on Giving: Does not support individuals or deficit financing.

OTHER THINGS TO KNOW
Publications: Application Guidelines

GRANTS ANALYSIS
Number of Grants: 54
Highest Grant: $320,000
Typical Range: $500 to $15,000
Disclosure Period: fiscal year ending April 30, 1991

RECENT GRANTS
320,000 Combined Jewish Philanthropies, Boston, MA
150,000 Project Bread Walk for Hunger, MA
101,500 Children's Hospital, MA
75,000 Falmouth Hospital Association, Falmouth, MA
37,500 Jackson Laboratory, Bar Harbor, ME
34,525 Park School, Brooklandville, MD
24,500 Facing History and Ourselves, Boston, MA
20,500 Dana Farber Cancer Institute, Boston, MA
16,668 Massachusetts General Hospital, Boston, MA
10,000 Concord Museum, Concord, MA

Smith Fund, George D.

CONTACT
Lawrence W. Milas
Vice President
George D. Smith Fund
805 Third Avenue, 20th Fl.
New York, NY 10022
(212) 702-5700

FINANCIAL SUMMARY
Recent Giving: $1,346,433 (1991); $1,355,900 (1990); $1,337,847 (1989)
Assets: $29,298,811 (1991); $27,845,181 (1990); $26,844,305 (1989)
EIN: 13-6138728

CONTRIBUTIONS SUMMARY
Donor(s): The foundation was incorporated in 1956 by the late George D. Smith, Sr.
Typical Recipients: • *Arts & Humanities:* public broadcasting • *Education:* colleges & universities, medical education, public education (precollege) • *Health:* health funds • *Social Services:* family planning
Grant Types: research
Geographic Distribution: focus on California, New York, and Utah

GIVING OFFICERS
Lawrence W. Milas: vp
Camilla M. Smith: asst secy, asst treas
George D. Smith, Jr.: pres, secy, treas, trust

APPLICATION INFORMATION
Initial Approach: Restrictions on Giving: The foundation supports preselected organizations and does not accept unsolicited requests for funds.

GRANTS ANALYSIS
Total Grants: $1,346,433
Number of Grants: 8
Highest Grant: $693,333
Typical Range: $25,000 to $100,000

Disclosure Period: 1991
Note: Average grant figure does not include the highest grant of $693,333. Recent grants are derived from a 1991 grants list.

RECENT GRANTS

693,333 Stanford University Medical Center, Stanford, CA

373,000 Foundation for Medicine, San Francisco, CA

80,000 University of Utah, Salt Lake City, UT

75,000 CODESH, New York, NY

75,000 Planned Parenthood Federation of America, New York, NY — national assistance family planning

25,000 East Harlem Block Schools, New York, NY

25,000 National Public Radio, New York, NY

Smith Fund, Horace

CONTACT

Philip T. Hart
Executive Secretary
Horace Smith Fund
Box 3034
Springfield, MA 01101
(413) 739-4222

FINANCIAL SUMMARY

Recent Giving: $570,506 (fiscal 1991); $513,475 (fiscal 1990); $401,673 (fiscal 1989)
Assets: $6,121,343 (fiscal year ending March 31, 1991); $5,887,341 (fiscal 1990); $5,514,016 (fiscal 1989)
EIN: 04-2235130

CONTRIBUTIONS SUMMARY

Donor(s): Horace Smith
Grant Types: fellowship, loan, and scholarship
Geographic Distribution: limited to Hampden County, MA, residents or high school seniors in specified towns

GIVING OFFICERS

Benjamin Bump: treas
Richard C. Garvey: trust
Philip T. Hart: exec secy
Richard S. Milstein: trust
Harry Nelson: trust

APPLICATION INFORMATION

Initial Approach: Application form required. Deadlines are

February 1 for fellowships; June 15 for loans for college students; July 1 for loans for high school seniors; December 31 for scholarships.

OTHER THINGS TO KNOW

Provides scholarships, educational loans, and fellowships to residents of Hampden County, MA.

Smith Golden Rule Trust Fund, Fred G.

CONTACT

Ruth Skonecki
Trust Officer
Fred G. Smith Golden Rule Trust Fund
c/o Union National Bank of Mount Carmel
Third and Oak Streets
Mount Carmel, PA 17851-0000
(717) 339-1040

FINANCIAL SUMMARY

Recent Giving: $207,531 (1991); $187,153 (1990)
Assets: $3,533,297 (1991); $3,487,083 (1990)
EIN: 23-2394466

CONTRIBUTIONS SUMMARY

Typical Recipients: • *Education:* colleges & universities • *Health:* single-disease health associations
Grant Types: general support

APPLICATION INFORMATION

Initial Approach: The foundation reports no specific application guidelines. Send a brief letter of inquiry, including statement of purpose, amount requested, and proof of tax-exempt status.

GRANTS ANALYSIS

Number of Grants: 4
Highest Grant: $197,021
Typical Range: $2,327 to $4,850
Disclosure Period: 1991

RECENT GRANTS

179,385 Bloomsburg University, PA

3,418 Pennsylvania College of Technology, PA

2,500 Central Pennsylvania Business School, PA

1,000 GKM Associate Trade School

850 Geisinger Medical School, Danville, PA

Smith Horticultural Trust, Stanley

CONTACT

James Cullen
Trustee
Stanley Smith Horticultural Trust
Cory Lodge, PO Box 365
Cambridge CB2 1H4, England

FINANCIAL SUMMARY

Recent Giving: $332,800 (1990); $311,150 (1989); $331,188 (1988)
Assets: $7,808,229 (1990); $8,063,439 (1989); $6,851,029 (1988)
EIN: 94-6209165

CONTRIBUTIONS SUMMARY

Donor(s): May Smith
Typical Recipients: • *Arts & Humanities:* museums/galleries • *Civic & Public Affairs:* women's affairs, zoos/botanical gardens • *Education:* colleges & universities
Grant Types: capital, operating expenses, project, and research

GIVING OFFICERS

John P. Collins, Sr.: trust
Barbara de Brye: trust
James R. Gibbs: trust
May Smith: trust
George Taylor: trust

APPLICATION INFORMATION

Initial Approach: Send cover letter and full proposal. There are no deadlines.
Restrictions on Giving: Does not support individuals.

GRANTS ANALYSIS

Number of Grants: 17
Highest Grant: $50,000
Typical Range: $5,000 to $25,000
Disclosure Period: 1990

RECENT GRANTS

50,000 University of California Berkeley, Berkeley, CA

31,000 Eastwood Hill Arboretum, Gisborne, New Zealand — construction of a building

30,000 Bellevue Botanical Garden Society, Bellevue, WA — building expansion

30,000 San Mateo Arboretum Society, San Mateo, CA — landscaping and planting

30,000 Worcester County Horticultural Society, Boylston, MA — development of visitor center and library

25,000 Bernice P. Bishop Museum, Honolulu, HI — publication of a book

23,000 J.R. O'Neal Arboretum Society, Tortola, VI — landscaping and planting

20,300 American Association of Botanic Gardens and Arboreta, Wayne, PA — payroll

19,000 Missouri Botanical Garden, St. Louis, MO

15,000 Israeli Society for Coastal and Sand Vegetation, Kiryat Chayia, Israel

Smith International

Employees: 2,500
Parent Company: Smith International Inc.
Revenue: $403.1 million
Headquarters: Houston, TX
SIC Major Group: Industrial Machinery & Equipment, Miscellaneous Repair Services, and Oil & Gas Extraction

CONTACT

Kathy Sanford
Director, Compensations and Benefits
Smith International
16740 Hardy St.
Houston, TX 77032
(713) 233-5920

CONTRIBUTIONS SUMMARY

Grant Types: matching
Operating Locations: OK (Ponca City), TX (Houston)

CORP. OFFICERS

Douglas L. Rock: *CURR EMPL* chmn, ceo: Smith Intl

APPLICATION INFORMATION

Initial Approach: Request application.

Smith, Jr. Charitable Trust, Jack J.

CONTACT
Nancy C. Gurney
Executive Assistant
Jack J. Smith, Jr. Charitable Trust
c/o The Central Trust Co., N.A.
PO Box 1198
Cincinnati, OH 45201
(513) 651-8377

FINANCIAL SUMMARY
Recent Giving: $294,293 (fiscal 1991); $82,170 (fiscal 1990); $187,064 (fiscal 1989)
Assets: $4,816,882 (fiscal year ending September 30, 1991); $4,251,887 (fiscal 1990); $4,190,290 (fiscal 1989)
Gifts Received: $41,081 (fiscal 1990)
EIN: 31-0912146

CONTRIBUTIONS SUMMARY
Donor(s): the late Jack J. Smith, Jr.
Typical Recipients: • *Education:* private education (precollege), public education (precollege) • *Health:* hospitals, pediatric health • *Social Services:* child welfare, community centers, community service organizations, disabled, homes, religious welfare, united funds, youth organizations
Grant Types: capital, project, and seed money
Geographic Distribution: limited to the greater Cincinnati, OH, area

GIVING OFFICERS
Central Trust Company, N.A.: trust

APPLICATION INFORMATION
Initial Approach: Send brief letter of inquiry describing program or project.
Restrictions on Giving: Does not support individuals or provide loans.

OTHER THINGS TO KNOW
Publications: Informational Brochure (including application guidelines)

GRANTS ANALYSIS
Number of Grants: 29
Highest Grant: $40,000
Typical Range: $5,000 to $10,000

Disclosure Period: fiscal year ending September 30, 1991

RECENT GRANTS
40,000 Jewish Hospital of Cincinnati, Cincinnati, OH
30,000 Jewish Hospital of Cincinnati, Cincinnati, OH
23,250 Children's Hospital Medical Center, Cincinnati, OH
15,000 YMCA, Cincinnati, OH
12,500 Museum Center Foundation, Cincinnati, OH
10,000 Boy Scouts of America, Cincinnati, OH
10,000 Cincinnati Association for the Blind, Cincinnati, OH
10,000 Greater Cincinnati for Matching Funds, Cincinnati, OH
10,000 St. Francis Seraph School, Cincinnati, OH
10,000 St. Joseph Home, Cincinnati, OH

Smith, Jr. Foundation, M. W.

CONTACT
Kenneth E. Niemeyer
M. W. Smith, Jr. Fdn.
c/o AmSouth Bank, N.A.
PO Drawer 1628
Mobile, AL 36629
(205) 438-8260

FINANCIAL SUMMARY
Recent Giving: $68,500 (fiscal 1992); $141,000 (fiscal 1990); $109,675 (fiscal 1989)
Assets: $1,918,570 (fiscal year ending June 30, 1992); $1,877,717 (fiscal 1990); $1,891,791 (fiscal 1989)
EIN: 63-6018078

CONTRIBUTIONS SUMMARY
Donor(s): the late M. W. Smith, Jr.
Typical Recipients: • *Arts & Humanities:* community arts, dance, history/historic preservation, libraries, museums/galleries • *Civic & Public Affairs:* zoos/botanical gardens • *Social Services:* child welfare, community service organizations, disabled, united funds, youth organizations
Grant Types: capital, emergency, endowment, general support, multiyear/continuing support, operating expenses, project, research, scholarship, and seed money
Geographic Distribution: focus on southwest AL

GIVING OFFICERS
Louis M. Finlay, Jr.: mem
John Martin: mem
Maida Pearson: chmn
Mary M. Riser: secy

APPLICATION INFORMATION
Initial Approach: Send brief letter describing program. There are no deadlines.
Restrictions on Giving: Does not support individuals.

GRANTS ANALYSIS
Number of Grants: 5
Highest Grant: $50,000
Typical Range: $3,000 to $10,000
Disclosure Period: fiscal year ending June 30, 1992

RECENT GRANTS
50,000 Mobile College, Mobile, AL — education
10,000 Mobile Association for Retarded Citizens, Mobile, AL — community welfare
3,500 Jackson Public Library, Jackson, MS — education
3,000 Mobile Area Boys Scouts, Mobile, AL — community welfare
2,000 Ballet and Theatre Arts, Mobile, AL — community welfare

Smith Memorial Fund, Ethel Sergeant Clark

CONTACT
Bruce M. Brown
Vice President
Corestates Bank, N A
PO Box 7618
Philadelphia, PA 19101
(215) 973-2792

FINANCIAL SUMMARY
Recent Giving: $232,200 (fiscal 1992); $421,400 (fiscal 1991); $649,225 (fiscal 1990)
Assets: $11,852,378 (fiscal year ending May 31, 1992); $11,284,806 (fiscal 1991); $10,882,862 (fiscal 1990)
EIN: 23-6648857

CONTRIBUTIONS SUMMARY
Donor(s): the late Ethel Sergeant Clark Smith
Typical Recipients: • *Arts & Humanities:* arts centers, community arts, history/historic preservation, libraries, music • *Civic & Public Affairs:* environmental affairs, housing • *Education:* colleges & universities • *Health:* health organizations • *Religion:* religious organizations • *Social Services:* child welfare, community centers, community service organizations, disabled, domestic violence, united funds, youth organizations
Grant Types: capital, emergency, general support, multi-year/continuing support, operating expenses, project, research, scholarship, and seed money
Geographic Distribution: limited to Delaware County, PA

APPLICATION INFORMATION
Initial Approach: Send cover letter and full proposal. Deadlines are March 1 and September 1 for completed proposals.
Restrictions on Giving: Does not support individuals or provide loans.

OTHER THINGS TO KNOW
Publications: Multi-year report (including Application Guidelines)

GRANTS ANALYSIS
Number of Grants: 16
Highest Grant: $30,000
Typical Range: $2,500 to $15,000
Disclosure Period: fiscal year ending May 31, 1992

RECENT GRANTS
30,000 Widener University, Chester, PA
25,000 Delco Blind/Sight Center, Chester, PA
25,000 Domestic Abuse Project of Delaware County, Media, PA
25,000 Media-Providence Friends School, Media, PA
25,000 Wayne Art Center, Wayne, PA
20,000 Better Housing for Chester, Chester, PA
20,000 Woodlynde School, Strafford, PA
10,000 Chester Education Foundation, Chester, PA

10,000 Colonial Pennsylvania Plantation, Media, PA

10,000 Marble Public Library, Broomall, PA

Smith Oil Corp.

Sales: $14.6 million
Employees: 50
Headquarters: Rockford, IL
SIC Major Group: Automotive Dealers & Service Stations, Food Stores, Miscellaneous Retail, and Wholesale Trade—Nondurable Goods

CONTACT

William Breeland
President
Smith Oil Corp.
2120 16th St.
PO Box 3275
Rockford, IL 61106
(815) 229-8100

CONTRIBUTIONS SUMMARY

Operating Locations: IL (Rockford)

CORP. OFFICERS

William Breeland: *CURR EMPL* pres: Smith Oil Corp
Kaylon Smith: *CURR EMPL* cfo: Smith Oil Co

GIVING OFFICERS

William Breeland: pres *CURR EMPL* pres: Smith Oil Corp (see above)

OTHER THINGS TO KNOW

Company is an original donor to the Smith Charitable Trust.

Smith 1980 Charitable Trust, Kelvin

CONTACT

John L. Dampeer
Trustee
Kelvin Smith 1980 Charitable Trust
1100 National City Bank Bldg.
Cleveland, OH 44114
(216) 566-5500

FINANCIAL SUMMARY

Recent Giving: $180,000 (fiscal 1992); $175,000 (fiscal 1990); $150,000 (fiscal 1989)
Assets: $3,094,499 (fiscal year ending May 31, 1992); $2,956,310 (fiscal 1990); $2,884,364 (fiscal 1989)
EIN: 34-6789395

CONTRIBUTIONS SUMMARY

Donor(s): the late Kelvin Smith
Typical Recipients: • *Civic & Public Affairs:* environmental affairs • *Science:* scientific organizations
Grant Types: operating expenses, project, and research
Geographic Distribution: focus on Cleveland, OH

GIVING OFFICERS

John L. Dampeer: trust *B* Cleveland OH 1916 *ED* Harvard Univ SB; Harvard Univ LLB *CORP AFFIL* dir: Monarch Machine Tool Co, Van Dorn Co *NONPR AFFIL* mem: Am Bar Assn, Greater Cleveland Bar Assn, OH Bar Assn, Phi Beta Kappa
Howard F. Stirn: trust

APPLICATION INFORMATION

Initial Approach: Send brief letter describing program. There are no deadlines.
Restrictions on Giving: Does not support individuals.

GRANTS ANALYSIS

Number of Grants: 1
Highest Grant: $180,000
Disclosure Period: fiscal year ending May 31, 1992

RECENT GRANTS

180,000 Sea Research Foundation, Cleveland, OH

Smith 1963 Charitable Trust, Don McQueen

CONTACT

Don McQueen Smith 1963 Charitable Trust
c/o First Alabama Bank of Montgomery
PO Box 511
Montgomery, AL 36134

FINANCIAL SUMMARY

Recent Giving: $89,220 (1989); $153,350 (1988)
Assets: $1,902,732 (1989); $1,869,993 (1988)
EIN: 63-6049793

CONTRIBUTIONS SUMMARY

Typical Recipients: • *Civic & Public Affairs:* environmental affairs • *Education:* colleges & universities, private education (precollege) • *Health:* hospitals, medical research, single-disease health associations • *Social Services:* united funds, youth organizations
Grant Types: general support
Geographic Distribution: focus on AL and FL

GIVING OFFICERS

Don McQueen Smith: trust

APPLICATION INFORMATION

Initial Approach: Contributes only to preselected organizations. Applications not accepted.
Restrictions on Giving: Does not support individuals.

GRANTS ANALYSIS

Number of Grants: 18
Highest Grant: $17,360
Typical Range: $500 to $10,000
Disclosure Period: 1989

RECENT GRANTS

17,360 Community School of Naples, Naples, FL

16,320 Montgomery YMCA, Montgomery, AL

12,000 Prattville YMCA, Prattville, AL

10,000 Marco Island YMCA, Marco Island, FL

10,000 United Way, Prattville, AL

5,000 Bascom Palmer Eye Institute, Miami, FL

5,000 Gator Boosters, Gainesville, FL

4,200 Providenciales Health Medical Clinic, Miami, FL

2,000 University of Florida Foundation, Gainesville, FL

1,600 Seacrest School, Naples, FL

Smith Trust, May and Stanley

CONTACT

John P. Collins, Sr.
Trustee
May and Stanley Smith Trust
49 Geary St., Ste. 244
San Francisco, CA 94108
(415) 391-0292

FINANCIAL SUMMARY

Recent Giving: $176,800 (1990); $1,329,000 (1989); $144,400 (1988)
Assets: $3,616,538 (1990); $145,613,504 (1989); $3,024,903 (1988)
Gifts Received: $134,616,738 (1989)
EIN: 94-6435244

CONTRIBUTIONS SUMMARY

Donor(s): May Smith

GIVING OFFICERS

John P. Collins, Jr.: trust
John P. Collins, Sr.: trust
J. Ronald Gibbs: trust

APPLICATION INFORMATION

Initial Approach: Send brief letter of inquiry describing program or project.

GRANTS ANALYSIS

Number of Grants: 38
Highest Grant: $5,000
Typical Range: $3,500 to $5,000
Disclosure Period: 1990

RECENT GRANTS

5,000 Ahead With Horses, Sun Valley, CA — general budget

5,000 Bishop's Ranch, Healdsburg, CA — expansion and refurbishment of retreat center

5,000 Caring for Children, San Francisco, CA — program for emotionally disturbed children

5,000 Center for Aged and Visually Handicapped, Richmond, VA — general budget

5,000 Disabled Children's Computer Group, Berkeley, CA — individual consultation program

5,000 Emergency Housing Consortium of Santa Clara County, San Jose, CA — general budget

5,000 Evangelical Lutheran Church in America, San Francisco, CA — senior outreach ministry program

5,000 In Spirit, Woodacre, CA — general budget

5,000 Lighthouse for the Blind and Visually Impaired, San Francisco, CA — to send children to Enchanted Hills Camp

5,000 Tri-Cities Children's Center, Fremont, CA — services for abused and neglected children

Smithers Foundation, Christopher D.

CONTACT
R. Brinkley Smithers
President
Christopher D. Smithers Fdn.
PO Box 67
Oyster Bay Rd.
Mill Neck, NY 11765
(516) 676-0067

FINANCIAL SUMMARY
Recent Giving: $624,198 (1991); $338,956 (1990); $1,186,081 (1989)
Assets: $6,735,620 (1991); $6,415,119 (1990); $6,576,010 (1989)
Gifts Received: $137,721 (1991); $129,108 (1990); $32,366 (1989)
Fiscal Note: In 1991, contributions were received from R. Brinkley Smithers ($100,000), Shirley B. Kluesener ($10,000), and miscellaneous ($27,741).
EIN: 13-1861928

CONTRIBUTIONS SUMMARY
Donor(s): the late Christopher D. Smithers, the late Mrs. Mabel B. Smithers, R. Brinkley Smithers
Typical Recipients: • *Education:* colleges & universities, education associations, medical education • *Health:* health organizations, medical research, nursing services, single-disease health associations • *Social Services:* child welfare, disabled, domestic violence, drugs & alcohol, family planning, shelters/homelessness, united funds, youth organizations
Grant Types: conference/seminar, operating expenses, project, and research

GIVING OFFICERS
M. Elizabeth Brothers: vp, dir
Shirley B. Klusener: dir
Adele C. Smithers: pres, dir
Charles F. Smithers, Jr.: treas, dir
Christopher B. Smithers: dir
R. Brinkley Smithers: chmn, dir
Henry Steinway Ziegler: secy, dir *B* Utica NY 1933 *ED* Harvard Univ AB 1955; Columbia

Univ LLB 1958 *CURR EMPL* ptnr: Shearman & Sterling *CORP AFFIL* dir: North Central Oil Corp, RI Corp; ptnr: Shearman & Sterling *NONPR AFFIL* dir: Lincoln Ctr Performing Arts; hon trust: St Lukes-Roosevelt Hosp Ctr; mem: NY Bar Assn, NY City Bar Assn; mem bd regents: Am Coll Trust Estate Counc; vchmn: Lincoln Ctr Chamber Music Soc

APPLICATION INFORMATION
Initial Approach: Send cover letter and full proposal. There are no deadlines.
Restrictions on Giving: Does not support individuals or provide loans.

OTHER THINGS TO KNOW
Publications: Annual Report

GRANTS ANALYSIS
Number of Grants: 43
Highest Grant: $250,000
Typical Range: $1000 to $15,000
Disclosure Period: 1991

RECENT GRANTS
250,000 National Council on Alcoholism, New York, NY
75,000 University of California Regents, Los Angeles, CA
40,919 Johns Hopkins University, Baltimore, MD
30,964 Foundation's Own Project
25,000 Caribbean Institute on Alcoholism, St. Thomas, Virgin Islands of the United States
15,000 Gratitude House, West Palm Beach, FL
14,850 New York Medical College, Valhalla, NY
11,300 Robert and William Smith College, Geneva, NY
10,000 Alcoholism Council/Fellowship Center, New York, NY
10,000 American Associates of Ben Gurion University, New York, NY

SmithKline Beecham / SmithKline Beecham Foundation
Sales: $3.73 billion
Employees: 54,800
Headquarters: London,
SIC Major Group: Chemicals & Allied Products, Engineering & Management Services, and Holding & Other Investment Offices

CONTACT
Elizabeth A. Tyson
Chairperson
Smithkline Beecham Foundation
One Franklin Plz.
PO Box 7929
Philadelphia, PA 19101
(215) 751-3574

FINANCIAL SUMMARY
Recent Giving: $4,300,000 (1993 est.); $4,572,941 (1992); $4,310,484 (1991)
Assets: $1,649,506 (1991); $4,400,000 (1990); $6,649,415 (1988)
Gifts Received: $4,399,795 (1991)
Fiscal Note: Company gives directly and through the foundation. Above giving figures are for foundation only.
EIN: 23-2120418

CONTRIBUTIONS SUMMARY
Typical Recipients: • *Arts & Humanities:* arts centers, dance, history/historic preservation, museums/galleries, music, performing arts • *Civic & Public Affairs:* economic development, law & justice, public policy, urban & community affairs • *Education:* colleges & universities, education associations, medical education • *Health:* health funds, health organizations, single-disease health associations • *International:* international organizations • *Social Services:* disabled, volunteer services, youth organizations
Grant Types: employee matching gifts and project
Geographic Distribution: where company has major facilities
Operating Locations: PA (Philadelphia, Pittsburgh)

CORP. OFFICERS
Robert Bauman: *CURR EMPL* ceo: Smithkline Beecham

Norman Harris Blanchard: *B* Pittsfield MA 1930 *CURR EMPL* pres (animal health div): Smithkline Beecham
Ralph Christoffersen: *B* Elgin IL 1937 *ED* Cornell Univ BS 1959; IN Univ PhD 1963 *CURR EMPL* vp (res): Smithkline Beecham *NONPR AFFIL* chmn: Alliance Aging Res; dir: Keystone Ctr, Univ CA Los Angeles Symposia; fellow: Am Inst Chemists; mem: Am Chem Soc, Am Physical Soc, Intl Soc Quantum Biology, Pharmaceutical Mfrs Assn, US Biotech Adv Bd; mem bd assessment: Natl Inst Science Tech
Thomas Milton Landin: *B* Bradford PA 1937 *CURR EMPL* vp (govt & pub aff): Smithkline Beecham *NONPR AFFIL* dir: Am Music Theatre Festival, Citizens Crime Commn, Mfrs Assn DE Valley, Pub Aff Counc, YMCA Greater Philadelphia; mem: Am Bar Assn, DC Bar Assn; trust: Caribbean/Latin Am Action
Jan Leschley: *CURR EMPL* coo: SmithKline Beechan
Richard Torrenzano: *B* New York NY 1950 *ED* NY Inst Tech BS 1972; Stanford Univ *CURR EMPL* sr vp (corp aff): Smithkline Beecham *NONPR AFFIL* mem: Intl Pub Rels Assn, Pub Rels Soc Am
Henry Wendt: *B* Neptune City NJ 1933 *ED* Princeton Univ AB 1955 *CURR EMPL* chmn: Smithkline Beecham *CORP AFFIL* chmn: SmithKline Beecham plc; dir: Allergan Inc, ARCO, Beckman Indus, Wiggins Teape & Appleton *NONPR AFFIL* chmn, mem: US-Japan Bus Counc; mem: Japan Soc; mem adv counc: Princeton Univ; trust: Philadelphia Mus Art

GIVING OFFICERS
John Dent: dir
J. P. Garnier: dir
Henry J. King: treas
V. Stoochton: dir
Richard Torrenzano: pres *CURR EMPL* sr vp (corp aff): Smithkline Beecham (see above)
Elizabeth A. Tyson: chmn
Albert J. White: secy *B* Boston MA 1933 *CURR EMPL* sr vp, secy, gen couns: SmithKline Beecham Corp
J. B. Ziegler: dir

APPLICATION INFORMATION

Initial Approach: *Initial Contact:* by letter to foundation chairman

Restrictions on Giving: Foundation does not support capital campaigns, chairs, endowments, general operating expenses, deficit financing, debt retirement, conferences, symposia, individuals, fundraising events, and associated advertising.

GRANTS ANALYSIS

Total Grants: $4,310,484*

Number of Grants: 155*

Highest Grant: $500,000*

Typical Range: $1,000 to $75,000

Disclosure Period: 1991

Note: Figures for total grants, number of grants, average grant, and highest grant do not include matching gifts. Recent grants are derived from a 1991 Form 990.

RECENT GRANTS

500,000 Associated United Ways of Pennsylvania and New Jersey, Philadelphia, PA

500,000 Temple University, Philadelphia, PA

350,000 American Association of Colleges of Pharmacy, Bethesda, MD

200,000 Philadelphia Orchestra Association, Philadelphia, PA

150,000 American Association of Colleges of Osteopathic Medicine, Rockville, MD

100,000 American Enterprise Institute for Public Policy Research, Washington, DC

100,000 Pharmaceutical Manufacturers Association Foundation, Washington, DC

80,000 Pennsylvania Academy of the Fine Arts, Philadelphia, PA

60,000 Urban Foundation (USA), New York, NY

50,000 Bristol Regional Rehabilitation Center, Bristol, TN

Smitty's Super Valu, Inc.

Sales: $619.79 million
Employees: 6,000
Headquarters: Phoenix, AZ
SIC Major Group: Food Stores, General Merchandise Stores, and Primary Metal Industries

CONTACT

Mary Anne Black
Executive Secretary
Smitty's Super Valu, Inc.
2626 South 7th St.
Phoenix, AZ 85034
(602) 262-1000

FINANCIAL SUMMARY

Fiscal Note: Annual Giving Range: $100,000 to $250,000

CONTRIBUTIONS SUMMARY

Majority goes to health and human services; limited support for community affairs organizations.

CORP. OFFICERS

Jean-Roch Vachon: *CURR EMPL* chmn, dir: Smittys Super Valu

GIVING OFFICERS

Mary Anne Black: *CURR EMPL* exec secy: Smittys Super Valu

Smock Foundation, Frank and Laura

CONTACT

Alice Kopfer
Vice President
Frank and Laura Smock Fdn.
c/o Lincoln National Bank and Trust Co.
116 East Berry St.
Ft. Wayne, IN 46802
(219) 461-6444

FINANCIAL SUMMARY

Recent Giving: $363,836 (1991); $289,277 (1990); $269,998 (1989)
Assets: $10,417,491 (1991); $8,621,496 (1990); $8,264,217 (1989)
EIN: 35-6011335

CONTRIBUTIONS SUMMARY

Donor(s): the late Mrs. Laura L. Smock
Typical Recipients: • *Education:* colleges & universities • *Health:* geriatric health, hospices • *Religion:* churches • *So-*

cial Services: aged, disabled, homes
Grant Types: general support
Geographic Distribution: limited to IN

GIVING OFFICERS

Richard Hutchison: mem adv comm
John Walley: mem adv comm

APPLICATION INFORMATION

Initial Approach: Contributes only to preselected organizations.

OTHER THINGS TO KNOW

Publications: Application Guidelines

GRANTS ANALYSIS

Number of Grants: 9
Highest Grant: $151,214
Typical Range: $1,000 to $10,000
Disclosure Period: 1991
Note: 1991 does not include grants to individuals.

RECENT GRANTS

151,214 Peabody Retirement Community, North Manchester, IN

22,000 Hanover College, Hanover, IN

15,500 First Presbyterian Church, Ft. Wayne, IN

10,000 Samaritan Pastoral Center, Ft. Wayne, IN

9,931 Bethany Presbyterian Church, Ft. Wayne, IN

9,865 Westminster Presbyterian Church, South Bend, IN

4,223 Charleston Presbyterian Church, Charleston, IN

2,200 Calvary Presbyterian Church, Ft. Wayne, IN

2,190 Baptist Homes of Indiana, Ft. Wayne, IN

Smoot Charitable Foundation

CONTACT

Thomas J. Kennedy
Secretary-Treasurer
Smoot Charitable Fdn.
710 United Bldg.
PO Box 2567
Salina, KS 67402
(913) 825-4674

FINANCIAL SUMMARY

Recent Giving: $347,044 (fiscal 1992); $348,191 (fiscal 1991); $315,681 (fiscal 1990)
Assets: $7,651,596 (fiscal year ending June 30, 1992); $7,218,145 (fiscal 1991); $7,138,199 (fiscal 1990)
EIN: 48-0851141

CONTRIBUTIONS SUMMARY

Typical Recipients: • *Arts & Humanities:* community arts, music • *Civic & Public Affairs:* municipalities • *Education:* colleges & universities • *Social Services:* emergency relief, employment/job training, recreation & athletics, united funds, youth organizations
Grant Types: general support
Geographic Distribution: limited to Saline County, KS

GIVING OFFICERS

Joe C. Cloud: pres
Thomas J. Kennedy: secy, treas
Dr. Robert W. Weber: vp

APPLICATION INFORMATION

Initial Approach: Send brief letter of inquiry describing program or project. There are no deadlines.
Restrictions on Giving: Does not support individuals.

GRANTS ANALYSIS

Number of Grants: 19
Highest Grant: $173,544
Typical Range: $1,000 to $4,000
Disclosure Period: fiscal year ending June 30, 1992

RECENT GRANTS

173,544 YMCA, Salina, KS

85,000 Kansas Wesleyan University, Salina, KS

30,000 United Way, Salina, KS

25,000 YWCA, Salina, KS

10,000 City of Salina Baseball Facility, Salina, KS

4,000 Occupational Center of Central Kansas, Salina, KS

3,000 Salina Celtics, Salina, KS

2,500 Counseling and Growth center, Salina, KS

2,500 Crisis Hot Line Dial-Help, Salina, KS

2,500 Emergency Aid, Salina, KS

Smucker Co., J.M.

Sales: $550.0 million
Employees: 2,000
Headquarters: Orrville, OH
SIC Major Group: Food & Kindred Products

CONTACT

Cathy Hogan
Manager, Employee Training and Development
J.M. Smucker Co.
PO Box 280
Orrville, OH 44667
(216) 682-0015

FINANCIAL SUMMARY

Recent Giving: $605,000 (1993 est.); $600,000 (1992 approx.); $500,000 (1991)
Fiscal Note: Figure for 1991 does not include an estimated $394,000 in nonmonetary support. Company gives directly.

CONTRIBUTIONS SUMMARY

Typical Recipients: • *Arts & Humanities:* performing arts, public broadcasting • *Civic & Public Affairs:* urban & community affairs • *Education:* colleges & universities, elementary education • *Health:* health organizations • *Social Services:* community service organizations
Grant Types: general support
Nonmonetary Support Types: cause-related marketing & promotion and donated products
Note: Nonmonetary support for 1991 included approximately $244,000 in products, and $150,000 in marketing and sales, which totaled $394,000. In 1992, nonmonetary support totaled $391,000 and is not included in the above giving figures.
Geographic Distribution: emphasis on five-county area surrounding headquarters and communities where plant facilities are located
Operating Locations: CA (Chico, Oxnard, Salinas, Wat-

sonville), OH (Orrville), OR (Woodburn), PA (New Bethlehem), TN (Memphis), WA (Grandview), WI (Ripon)

CORP. OFFICERS

Paul Highnam Smucker: *B* Orrville OH 1917 *ED* Miami Univ BS 1939 *CURR EMPL* chmn exec comm, ceo, dir: JM Smucker Co *CORP AFFIL* chmn: AF Murch Co; dir: Natl Bank Orrville; trust: WK Kellogg Fdn Trust *NONPR AFFIL* dir: Grocery Mfrs Am; mem: Am Academy Achievement, Am Mgmt Assn, Natl Preservers Assn, Phi Delta Theta
Richard Kim Smucker: *ED* Miami Univ BS 1970; Univ PA Wharton Sch Bus MBA 1972 *CURR EMPL* pres, dir: JM Smucker Co *CORP AFFIL* dir: Bill Knapps Michigan, Sherwin-Williams Co, William Wrigley Jr Co; vp: AF Murch Co *NONPR AFFIL* trust: Cleveland Orchestra, Miami Univ Fdn
Timothy Paul Smucker: *B* Wooster OH 1944 *ED* Coll Wooster BA 1967; Univ PA Wharton Sch Bus MBA 1969 *CURR EMPL* chmn, dir: JM Smucker Co *CORP AFFIL* dir: Huntington Bancshares, Kellogg Co; pres: AF Murch Co *NONPR AFFIL* dir: Second Harvest; life trust: Coll Wooster; mem: Comm Econ Devel, Govs OH Devel Adv Counc; mem natl adv panel: Natl Ctr Adult Literacy

APPLICATION INFORMATION

Initial Approach: *Initial Contact:* brief letter or proposal *Include Information On:* description of the organization, amount requested, purpose for which funds are sought, recently audited financial statement, proof of tax-exempt status *When to Submit:* any time

OTHER THINGS TO KNOW

Company's goal is to donate 2% of pretax profits to charitable activities.

GRANTS ANALYSIS

Total Grants: $600,000*
Typical Range: $500 to $2,000
Disclosure Period: 1992
Note: Total grants figure is approximate and does not include nonmonetary support.

Smucker Co., J.M. / Smucker Foundation, Willard E.

Sales: $455.0 million
Employees: 1,900
Headquarters: Orrville, OH
SIC Major Group: Food & Kindred Products

CONTACT

Paul Smucker
President
Willard E. Smucker Foundation
2026 Wayne St.
Orrville, OH 44667
(216) 682-3000

FINANCIAL SUMMARY

Recent Giving: $203,608 (1991); $143,283 (1989)
Assets: $7,626,020 (1991); $3,914,411 (1989)
Gifts Received: $126,000 (1991); $89,000 (1989)
Fiscal Note: In 1991, contributions were received from J. M. Smucker Company.
EIN: 34-6610889

CONTRIBUTIONS SUMMARY

Typical Recipients: • *Arts & Humanities:* community arts, music • *Education:* agricultural education, colleges & universities • *Health:* hospitals • *Religion:* churches • *Social Services:* aged, child welfare, community service organizations, food/clothing distribution, shelters/homelessness, united funds, youth organizations
Grant Types: general support
Geographic Distribution: focus on OH
Operating Locations: CA (Watsonville), OH (Orrville)

CORP. OFFICERS

Paul Highnam Smucker: *B* Orrville OH 1917 *ED* Miami Univ BS 1939 *CURR EMPL* chmn exec comm, ceo, dir: JM Smucker Co *CORP AFFIL* chmn: AF Murch Co; dir: Natl Bank Orrville; trust: WK Kellogg Fdn Trust *NONPR AFFIL* dir: Grocery Mfrs Am; mem: Am Academy Achievement, Am Mgmt Assn, Natl Preservers Assn, Phi Delta Theta

GIVING OFFICERS

H. Ray Clark: vp, trust
Marcella S. Clark: exec vp, trust

Steven J. Ellcessor: secy *CURR EMPL* secy, gen coun: Smucker (JM) Co *CORP AFFIL* secy, gen coun: Smucker (JM) Co
Lorraine E. Smucker: vp, trust
Paul Highnam Smucker: pres, treas *CURR EMPL* chmn exec comm, ceo, dir: JM Smucker Co (see above)
Richard Kim Smucker: trust *ED* Miami Univ BS 1970; Univ PA Wharton Sch Bus MBA 1972 *CURR EMPL* pres, dir: JM Smucker Co *CORP AFFIL* dir: Bill Knapps Michigan, Sherwin-Williams Co, William Wrigley Jr Co; vp: AF Murch Co *NONPR AFFIL* trust: Cleveland Orchestra, Miami Univ Fdn
Timothy Paul Smucker: trust *B* Wooster OH 1944 *ED* Coll Wooster BA 1967; Univ PA Wharton Sch Bus MBA 1969 *CURR EMPL* chmn, dir: JM Smucker Co *CORP AFFIL* dir: Huntington Bancshares, Kellogg Co; pres: AF Murch Co *NONPR AFFIL* dir: Second Harvest; life trust: Coll Wooster; mem: Comm Econ Devel, Govs OH Devel Adv Counc; mem natl adv panel: Natl Ctr Adult Literacy
Philip Yuschak: asst treas

APPLICATION INFORMATION

Initial Approach: The foundation reports that it only makes contributions to preselected charitable organizations and does not accept unsolicited applications for funds.
Initial Approach: Send brief letter describing program. There are no deadlines.

GRANTS ANALYSIS

Number of Grants: 32
Highest Grant: $33,334
Typical Range: $1,000 to $5,000
Disclosure Period: 1991

RECENT GRANTS

33,334 Dunlap Memorial Hospital, Orrville, OH

25,000 College of Wooster, Wooster, OH

25,000 Miami University, Oxford, OH

13,334 Wooster Community Hospital, Wooster, OH

10,000 Ohio State University, Columbus, OH — agriculture

8,334 Salvation Army, Orrville, OH
7,000 Salvation Army, Phoenix, AZ
6,000 St. Mary's Food Bank, Phoenix, AZ
5,500 Orrville Boys and Girls, Orrville, OH
5,000 First Church of Christ, Wooster, OH

Smysor Memorial Fund, Harry L. and John L.

CONTACT
Michael Hagen
Harry L. and John L. Smysor Memorial Fund
c/o First National Bank
1515 Charleston Ave.
Martoon, IL 61938-3932
(217) 234-7454

FINANCIAL SUMMARY
Recent Giving: $181,000 (fiscal 1992); $170,970 (fiscal 1991); $216,625 (fiscal 1990)
Assets: $3,220,484 (fiscal year ending May 31, 1992); $3,356,319 (fiscal 1991); $3,160,452 (fiscal 1990)
Gifts Received: $70,000 (fiscal 1992); $90,000 (fiscal 1991); $100,000 (fiscal 1990)
EIN: 37-1160678

CONTRIBUTIONS SUMMARY
Donor(s): the late John L. Smysor
Grant Types: scholarship
Geographic Distribution: focus on IL

GIVING OFFICERS
First National Bank of Chicago: trust
Clarence Doehring: trust

APPLICATION INFORMATION
Initial Approach: Application form available from Windsor, IL, high school or from trustee bank. Deadline is April 15.

OTHER THINGS TO KNOW
Provides scholarships to individuals for higher education.

GRANTS ANALYSIS
Disclosure Period: fiscal year ending May 31, 1992
Note: In fiscal 1992, all individual scholarships.

Smyth Trust, Marion C.

CONTACT
John H. Griffin, Jr.
Chairman
Marion C. Smyth Trust
875 Elm St.
Manchester, NH 03101
(603) 623-3420

FINANCIAL SUMMARY
Recent Giving: $289,458 (1991); $226,750 (1990); $180,928 (1989)
Assets: $4,497,853 (1991); $4,246,247 (1990); $4,333,830 (1989)
EIN: 02-6005793

CONTRIBUTIONS SUMMARY
Donor(s): the late Marion C. Smyth
Typical Recipients: • *Arts & Humanities:* community arts, music, public broadcasting • *Education:* arts education, colleges & universities
Grant Types: multiyear/continuing support and scholarship
Geographic Distribution: limited to NH, primarily Manchester

GIVING OFFICERS
Alan C. Akeson: trust
T. William Bigelow: trust
John H. Griffin, Jr.: chmn, trust

APPLICATION INFORMATION
Initial Approach: Application form required for student scholarships.

GRANTS ANALYSIS
Number of Grants: 60
Highest Grant: $30,000
Typical Range: $1,000 to $10,000
Disclosure Period: 1991

RECENT GRANTS
30,000 University of New Hampshire, Durham, NH — music department
28,000 University of New Hampshire, Durham, NH — scholarships
15,000 Plymouth State College, Plymouth, MA — music department
13,000 Derryfield School, NH — music department
11,100 Daniel Webster Council, Manches-

ter, NH — explorers music post 934
10,500 New Hampshire Music Festival, Manchester, NH
10,500 New Hampshire Public Television, Manchester, NH
10,000 New Hampshire Symphony Orchestra, Manchester, NH
10,000 St. Anselm's College, Manchester, NH — music department
6,000 Keene State College, Keene, NH — scholarships

Snap-on Tools Corp.
Revenue: $881.59 million
Employees: 6,045
Headquarters: Kenosha, WI
SIC Major Group: Fabricated Metal Products, Industrial Machinery & Equipment, Lumber & Wood Products, and Wholesale Trade—Durable Goods

CONTACT
Berge Widmore
Community Relations
Snap-on Tools Corp.
2801 80th St.
Kenosha, WI 53141
(414) 656-5165

FINANCIAL SUMMARY
Fiscal Note: Annual Giving Range: less than $250,000

CONTRIBUTIONS SUMMARY
Geographic Distribution: in headquarters and operating communities
Operating Locations: CA (Escondido, San Jose), WI (Kenosha)

CORP. OFFICERS
Robert A. Cornog: *B* Philadelphia PA 1940 *ED* IL Inst Tech 1961; Univ Chicago Grad Sch Bus Admin 1966 *CURR EMPL* chmn, ceo, pres: Snap-On Tools Corp

Snayberger Memorial Foundation, Harry E. and Florence W.

CONTACT
James J. Corrigan
Sr. Vice President and Trust Officer
Harry E. and Florence W. Snayberger Memorial Fdn.
c/o Pennsylvania National Bank and Trust Co.
One South Centre St.
Pottsville, PA 17901-3003
(717) 622-4200

FINANCIAL SUMMARY
Recent Giving: $229,000 (fiscal 1992); $268,684 (fiscal 1991); $263,391 (fiscal 1990)
Assets: $3,790,626 (fiscal year ending March 31, 1992); $3,787,936 (fiscal 1991); $3,591,930 (fiscal 1990)
EIN: 23-2056361

CONTRIBUTIONS SUMMARY
Donor(s): the late Harry E. Snayberger
Grant Types: scholarship
Geographic Distribution: limited to Schuylkill County, PA

APPLICATION INFORMATION
Initial Approach: Send letter requesting application form. Deadline is February 28.

OTHER THINGS TO KNOW
Provides scholarships to individuals for higher education.
Disclosure Period: fiscal year ending March 31, 1992

SNC Manufacturing Co. / SNC Foundation
Sales: $22.0 million
Employees: 580
Headquarters: Oshkosh, WI
SIC Major Group: Electronic & Other Electrical Equipment

CONTACT
John L. Vette, III
Manager
SNC Foundation
101 Waukau Ave.
Oshkosh, WI 54901
(414) 231-7370

FINANCIAL SUMMARY
Recent Giving: $75,000 (1993 est.); $58,770 (1991); $8,370 (1990)
Assets: $37,918 (1991); $55,365 (1990)
Gifts Received: $40,000 (1991); $60,000 (1990)
Fiscal Note: In 1991, contributions were received from SNC Manufacturing Co., Inc. ($15,000), and Mrs. Janet Vette ($25,000).
EIN: 39-1384595

CONTRIBUTIONS SUMMARY
Typical Recipients: • *Arts & Humanities:* general, opera • *Civic & Public Affairs:* general • *Education:* general • *Health:* general, health organizations, public health • *Social Services:* general
Grant Types: general support
Geographic Distribution: focus on WI
Operating Locations: WI (Oshkosh)

CORP. OFFICERS
John L. Vette III: *CURR EMPL* ceo: SNC Mfg Co

GIVING OFFICERS
Timothy M. Dempsey: dir
John L. Vette III: dir *CURR EMPL* ceo: SNC Mfg Co (see above)

APPLICATION INFORMATION
Initial Approach: Send brief letter describing program. There are no deadlines.

GRANTS ANALYSIS
Number of Grants: 36
Highest Grant: $16,667
Typical Range: $100 to $500
Disclosure Period: 1991

RECENT GRANTS
16,667 EAA Aviation Foundation, Oshkosh, WI
7,787 United Way, Oshkosh, WI
7,500 Mercy Medical Center Foundation, Oshkosh, WI
4,000 Boys and Girls Club, Oshkosh, WI
3,400 Regional Domestic Abuse, Neenah, WI
2,500 Wisconsin Foundation of Independent Colleges, Milwaukee, WI
2,000 Palo Alto Community Health Care Foundation, Emmetsburg, IA
1,750 Fox Valley Technical Institute Foundation, Appleton, WI
1,100 Grand Opera House Foundation, Oshkosh, WI
1,000 Winnebagoland Council of Campfire, Menasha, WI

Snee-Reinhardt Charitable Foundation

CONTACT
Snee-Reinhardt Charitable Fdn.
c/o Mellon Bank, N.A.
PO Box 185
Pittsburgh, PA 15230

FINANCIAL SUMMARY
Recent Giving: $231,425 (1991); $226,370 (1990); $126,954 (1989)
Assets: $5,404,891 (1991); $3,878,309 (1990); $3,099,004 (1989)
Gifts Received: $662,143 (1991); $20,265 (1990); $29,276 (1989)
Fiscal Note: In 1991, contributions were received from C. Volkenant-Crut ($290,343), and the Estate of Viola Tortorice ($371,798).
EIN: 25-6292908

CONTRIBUTIONS SUMMARY
Typical Recipients: • *Arts & Humanities:* community arts, libraries, theater • *Civic & Public Affairs:* environmental affairs, housing, zoos/botanical gardens • *Health:* geriatric health, health organizations, hospitals, medical research, pediatric health, single-disease health associations • *Science:* scientific institutes • *Social Services:* aged, community service organizations, united funds, youth organizations
Grant Types: general support
Geographic Distribution: Does not support individuals.

GIVING OFFICERS
Virginia Davis: trust
Karen I. Heasley: trust
Paul A. Heasley: dir, chmn
Timothy Heasley: trust
James Ummer: dir
Richard T. Vale: trust

APPLICATION INFORMATION
Initial Approach: Contributes only to preselected organizations. Applications not accepted.

GRANTS ANALYSIS
Number of Grants: 28
Highest Grant: $25,000
Typical Range: $2,000 to $15,000
Disclosure Period: 1991

RECENT GRANTS
25,000 Carnegie, Pittsburgh, PA
25,000 Ohio Valley General Hospital, McKees Rock, PA
20,000 Zoological Society, Pittsburgh, PA
15,000 Children's Hospital, Pittsburgh, PA
14,000 City Theatre Company, Pittsburgh, PA
11,500 Pittsburgh Opera, Pittsburgh, PA
10,000 California Center, California, PA
10,000 Citizen's Library, Washington, PA
10,000 Pennsylvania Humanities Council Film Project, Pittsburgh, PA
10,000 Sisters of Holy Spirit, Pittsburgh, PA — nursing home expansion

SNET
Sales: $1.61 billion
Employees: 12,647
Headquarters: New Haven, CT
SIC Major Group: Communications

CONTACT
Daisy Rodriguez
Manager, Contributions/Community Relations
SNET
227 Church St.
New Haven, CT 06506
(203) 771-2546

FINANCIAL SUMMARY
Recent Giving: $1,500,000 (1993 est.); $1,500,000 (1992 approx.); $1,500,000 (1991 approx.)
Fiscal Note: Company gives directly.

CONTRIBUTIONS SUMMARY
Typical Recipients: • *Arts & Humanities:* arts associations, arts centers, arts festivals, arts funds, community arts, dance, ethnic arts, history/historic preservation, libraries, museums/galleries, music, performing arts, public broadcasting, theater • *Civic & Public Affairs:* better government, business/free enterprise, civil rights, consumer affairs, economic development, environmental affairs, law & justice, professional & trade associations, public policy, safety, urban & community affairs, women's affairs, zoos/botanical gardens • *Education:* business education, colleges & universities, community & junior colleges, continuing education, education associations, elementary education, engineering education, literacy, minority education, private education (precollege), science/technology education • *Health:* health care cost containment, health organizations, hospitals, mental health, single-disease health associations • *Social Services:* aged, child welfare, community service organizations, delinquency & crime, disabled, drugs & alcohol, united funds, volunteer services, youth organizations
Grant Types: capital, challenge, employee matching gifts, general support, project, and seed money
Nonmonetary Support Types: donated equipment, in-kind services, and loaned executives
Note: In 1992, nonmonetary support was valued at $200,000 and is not included in the above figures.
Geographic Distribution: Connecticut
Operating Locations: CT (New Haven)

CORP. OFFICERS
Dan Miligin: *CURR EMPL* pres, ceo: SNET
Walter H. Monteith, Jr.: *B* Framingham MA 1930 *CURR EMPL* chmn: SNET *CORP AFFIL* dir: CT Natl Bank, Hartford Natl Corp, Kaman Corp *NONPR AFFIL* chmn: Yale-New Haven Hosp; dir: Citizens Crime Commn, CT Bus Indus Assn, CT Econ Devel Corp, CT World Trade Assn, Long Wharf Theater; vchmn: CT Pub Expenditures Counc

GIVING OFFICERS
Toni Bouleay: staff assoc (matching gifts)
Linda D. Hershman: *B* Pittsburgh PA 1947 *ED* Univ Pittsburgh 1967; Univ CT Sch Law 1970 *CURR EMPL* vp (corp rels): SNET *CORP AFFIL* mem bd dir: Colony Savings Bank *NONPR AFFIL* mem: Am Bar Assn, Cheshire Democratic Town Comm, CT Bar Assn, Greater Hartford Chamber Commerce, Hartford Womens Network, Natl Policies Panel, St Govt Rels Comm, St Legislation Comm, Temple Beth David, USTA; mem bd dir: Hartford Advocates for Arts; mem bd trust: Univ CT Law Sch Fdn
Daisy Rodriguez: mgr (corporate contributions)

APPLICATION INFORMATION
Initial Approach: *Initial Contact:* letter or proposal *Include Information On:* description of the organization, amount requested, purpose for which funds are sought, recently audited financial statement, proof of tax-exempt status, and other corporate funding sources *When to Submit:* any time
Restrictions on Giving: Company does not support endowments; fraternal, political, or religious organizations; member agencies of united funds; goodwill advertising; or individuals.

GRANTS ANALYSIS
Total Grants: $1,500,000
Typical Range: $500 to $1,000
Disclosure Period: 1992

Snider Foundation

CONTACT
Sanford Lipstein
Secretary-Treasurer
Snider Fdn.
1804 Rittenhouse Sq.
Philadelphia, PA 19103
(215) 875-5204

FINANCIAL SUMMARY
Recent Giving: $764,265 (fiscal 1992); $594,719 (fiscal 1991); $839,455 (fiscal 1990)
Assets: $636,331 (fiscal year ending April 30, 1992); $548,629 (fiscal 1991); $1,180,050 (fiscal 1990)
Gifts Received: $803,939 (fiscal 1992); $434,063 (fiscal 1990); $305,280 (fiscal 1989)

EIN: 23-2047668

CONTRIBUTIONS SUMMARY
Donor(s): Edward M. Snider
Typical Recipients: • *Arts & Humanities:* arts centers, arts institutes, history/historic preservation, museums/galleries, music, theater • *Civic & Public Affairs:* business/free enterprise, environmental affairs, ethnic/minority organizations • *Education:* colleges & universities • *Health:* geriatric health, hospices, pediatric health • *Religion:* religious organizations • *Science:* scientific institutes • *Social Services:* aged, animal protection, child welfare, community service organizations, recreation & athletics
Grant Types: general support
Geographic Distribution: focus on Philadelphia, PA

GIVING OFFICERS
Sanford Lipstein: secy, treas
Fred A. Shabel: trust
Edward Malcolm Snider: pres *B* Washington DC 1933 *ED* Univ MD BS *CURR EMPL* fdr: Spectacor *CORP AFFIL* Chmn: Philadelphia Flyers Hockey Club *NONPR AFFIL* cofdr: Ayn Rand Inst; dir: Hahnemann Cancer Inst, JYC W branch, Philadelphia Assn Retarded Children, Police Athletic League

APPLICATION INFORMATION
Initial Approach: Contributes only to preselected organizations.
Restrictions on Giving: Does not support individuals.

GRANTS ANALYSIS
Number of Grants: 91
Highest Grant: $300,000
Typical Range: $60 to $5,000
Disclosure Period: fiscal year ending April 30, 1992

RECENT GRANTS
300,000 Simon Wiesenthal Center, Los Angeles, CA
160,000 Federation of Allied Jewish Appeal, Philadelphia, PA
100,000 Sol C. Snider Entrepreneurial Center, Philadelphia, PA
50,000 University of Pennsylvania, Philadelphia, PA
30,000 Hahnemann University, Philadelphia, PA

12,500 Foreign Policy Research Institute, Philadelphia, PA
11,500 National Museum of American Jewish History, Philadelphia, PA
10,100 Police Athletic League, Philadelphia, PA
10,000 Philadelphia Geriatric Center, Philadelphia, PA
10,000 Philadelphia Museum of Art, Philadelphia, PA

Snite Foundation, Fred B.

CONTACT
Terrance J. Dillon
President
Fred B. Snite Fdn.
550 Frontage Rd.
North Field, IL 60093
(708) 446-7705

FINANCIAL SUMMARY
Recent Giving: $475,500 (fiscal 1991); $311,000 (fiscal 1990); $316,500 (fiscal 1989)
Assets: $9,688,058 (fiscal year ending June 30, 1991); $9,502,874 (fiscal 1990); $8,905,141 (fiscal 1989)
EIN: 36-6084839

CONTRIBUTIONS SUMMARY
Donor(s): the late Fred B. Snite, Local Loan Co.
Typical Recipients: • *Arts & Humanities:* opera • *Education:* colleges & universities, private education (precollege), religious education • *Health:* hospitals, single-disease health associations • *Religion:* churches, missionary activities, religious organizations • *Social Services:* disabled, religious welfare, united funds, youth organizations
Grant Types: general support

GIVING OFFICERS
Teresa Bratton: vp, dir
Mary L. Dillon: vp, dir
Terrance J. Dillon: pres, dir
Allen E. Eliot: treas
Harry B. Holmes, Jr.: secy
Nicholas Rassas: dir
Margaret Sackley: vp, dir
Katherine B. Williams: vp, dir

APPLICATION INFORMATION
Initial Approach: Send cover letter and proposal. There are no deadlines.

GRANTS ANALYSIS
Number of Grants: 70
Highest Grant: $50,000
Typical Range: $1,000 to $25,000
Disclosure Period: fiscal year ending June 30, 1991

RECENT GRANTS
50,000 Catholic Relief Services, Los Angeles, CA
30,000 Rosary College, Chicago, IL
25,000 Big Shoulders Fund, Chicago, IL
25,000 Loyola University, Chicago, IL
25,000 Ravinia Festival Association, Highland Park, IL
25,000 Sisters of Mercy of New Jersey, Watchung, NJ
25,000 St. Ignatius College Preparatory, Chicago, IL
15,000 Santa Barbara Christian School, Santa Barbara, CA
10,000 ABC Club, Chicago, IL
10,000 De La Salle School, Chicago, IL

Snow Foundation, John Ben

CONTACT
Vernon F. Snow
President
John Ben Snow Fdn.
PO Box 376
Pulaski, NY 13142
(315) 298-6401

FINANCIAL SUMMARY
Recent Giving: $180,065 (fiscal 1992); $957,300 (fiscal 1991); $192,350 (fiscal 1990)
Assets: $4,891,492 (fiscal year ending March 31, 1992); $18,563,279 (fiscal 1991); $4,510,364 (fiscal 1990)
EIN: 13-6112704

CONTRIBUTIONS SUMMARY
Donor(s): the late John Ben Snow
Typical Recipients: • *Arts & Humanities:* history/historic preservation, libraries, museums/galleries • *Civic & Public Affairs:* environmental affairs • *Education:* colleges & universities, elementary education, legal education, private education (precollege), public education (precollege) • *Health:* hospitals, public health • *Religion:*

churches, religious organizations • *Social Services:* child welfare, community service organizations, disabled, youth organizations

Grant Types: capital, fellowship, project, and scholarship

Geographic Distribution: limited to central NY, with focus on Oswego County

GIVING OFFICERS
Allen R. Malcolm: exec vp, secy, dir
Bruce Malcolm: dir
Rollan Melton: dir
Royle Melton: dir
Joseph C. Mitchell: dir
David H. Snow: dir
Vernon F. Snow: pres, dir

APPLICATION INFORMATION
Initial Approach: Send brief letter requesting application form.
Restrictions on Giving: Does not support individuals.

OTHER THINGS TO KNOW
Publications: Annual Report (including application guidelines)

GRANTS ANALYSIS
Number of Grants: 18
Highest Grant: $35,000
Typical Range: $6,000 to $15,000
Disclosure Period: fiscal year ending March 31, 1992

RECENT GRANTS
35,000 Central School District 1, Pulaski, NY — Recycling Program
20,000 Northfield Mount Hermon School, East Northfield, MA
15,000 Clarkson University, Potsdam, NY
15,000 Keuka College, Keuka, NY
15,000 Salmon River Fine Arts Center, Pulaski, NY
15,000 St. Lawrence University, Canton, NY
15,000 Syracuse University, Syracuse, NY
15,000 Syracuse University, Syracuse, NY
15,000 Syracuse University, Syracuse, NY
8,000 Northern Oswego County Health Services, Pulaski, NY

Snow Memorial Trust, John Ben

CONTACT
Vernon F. Snow
Trustee
John Ben Snow Memorial Trust
PO Box 378
Pulaski, NY 13142
(315) 298-6401

FINANCIAL SUMMARY
Recent Giving: $917,100 (1991); $1,050,554 (1989); $836,840 (1988)
Assets: $19,854,043 (1991); $18,964,617 (1989); $16,940,550 (1988)
EIN: 13-6633814

CONTRIBUTIONS SUMMARY
Donor(s): The foundation was incorporated in 1948 by the late John Ben Snow.
Typical Recipients: • *Arts & Humanities:* arts centers, history/historic preservation, libraries, museums/galleries, theater • *Civic & Public Affairs:* environmental affairs, municipalities, philanthropic organizations, professional & trade associations, women's affairs • *Education:* business education, colleges & universities, journalism education, legal education • *Health:* health funds • *Social Services:* day care, delinquency & crime, youth organizations
Grant Types: fellowship, matching, project, research, scholarship, and seed money
Geographic Distribution: focus on eastern United States

GIVING OFFICERS
Allen R. Malcolm: trust
Rollan D. Melton: trust
Vernon F. Snow: trust

APPLICATION INFORMATION
Initial Approach:
The foundation requests applications be made in writing. The deadline for submitting proposals is April 15.
Restrictions on Giving: The foundation does not make grants to individuals or to support operating budgets, endowment funds, or contingency financing.

OTHER THINGS TO KNOW
Publications: annual report including application guidelines

GRANTS ANALYSIS
Total Grants: $917,100
Number of Grants: 39
Highest Grant: $57,500
Typical Range: $8,000 to $25,000
Disclosure Period: 1991
Note: Recent grants are derived from a 1991 grants list.

RECENT GRANTS
57,500 New York Law School, New York, NY
50,000 Central New York Community Foundation Greater Pulaski Fund, Syracuse, NY
50,000 New York University School of Law, New York, NY
50,000 New York University Stern School of Business and Public Administration, New York, NY
50,000 Northern Nevada Community College, Elko, NV
45,000 Lincoln Center Institute, New York, NY
35,000 American Museum of Natural History, New York, NY
35,000 Cornell University, Ithaca, NY
35,000 Frost Valley YMCA, Claryville, NY
35,000 Pulaski Baptist Church, Pulaski, NY

Snyder Charitable Fund, W. P.

CONTACT
John K. Foster
Trustee
W. P. Snyder Charitable Fund
3720 One Oliver Plaza
Pittsburgh, PA 15222
(412) 471-1331

FINANCIAL SUMMARY
Recent Giving: $452,204 (1989); $452,700 (1986)
Assets: $9,605,231 (1989); $8,845,363 (1986)
EIN: 25-6034967

CONTRIBUTIONS SUMMARY
Donor(s): the late W. P. Snyder, Jr., W. P. Snyder III, The Shenango Furnace Co.
Typical Recipients: • *Arts & Humanities:* arts centers, arts festivals, community arts, history/historic preservation, libraries • *Civic & Public Affairs:* municipalities, urban & community affairs • *Education:* colleges & universities, minority education • *Health:* hospitals • *Social Services:* community service organizations, family services, united funds, youth organizations
Grant Types: general support
Geographic Distribution: focus on PA

GIVING OFFICERS
John K. Foster: trust
G. Whitney Snyder: trust
CURR EMPL pres: Shenango Furnace Co
William Penn Snyder III: trust *B* Pittsburgh PA 1918 *ED* Univ Pittsburgh *CURR EMPL* Wilpen Group *CORP AFFIL* dir: HJ Heinz Co, Natl Forge Co, Whitney Holding Corp, Whitney Natl Bank New Orleans *NONPR AFFIL* chmn: Allegheny Health, Ed, Res Fdn; dir: PA Economy League; trust: Carnegie Hero Fund Comm, Carnegie Inst, Carnegie Mellon Univ, Western Res Hist Soc; vp, mgr: Allegheny Cemetery

APPLICATION INFORMATION
Initial Approach: Send brief letter of inquiry describing program or project. There are no deadlines.

GRANTS ANALYSIS
Number of Grants: 39
Highest Grant: $50,000
Typical Range: $1,000 to $15,000
Disclosure Period: 1989

RECENT GRANTS
50,000 Lehigh University, Bethlehem, PA
50,000 The Carnegie, Pittsburgh, PA
35,000 Goodwill Industries, Pittsburgh, PA
25,000 Valley Care Association, Sewickley, PA
25,000 Western Reserve Historical Society, Cleveland, OH
24,500 Carnegie-Mellon University, Pittsburgh, PA
15,000 Allegheny Health Services, Pittsburgh, PA
15,000 Mary and Alexander Laughlin Children's Center, Pittsburgh, PA
15,000 Sewickley Academy, Sewickley, PA

12,500 Canterbury Place, Pittsburgh, PA

Snyder Foundation, Frost and Margaret

CONTACT
John A. Cunningham
Trust Officer
Frost and Margaret Snyder Fdn.
c/o Puget Sound National Bank,
Trust Dept.
PO Box 11500
Tacoma, WA 98411-5052
(206) 593-3832

FINANCIAL SUMMARY
Recent Giving: $379,137 (1990); $418,362 (1989); $281,897 (1988)
Assets: $7,362,868 (1990); $7,508,465 (1989); $6,557,492 (1988)
EIN: 91-6030549

CONTRIBUTIONS SUMMARY
Donor(s): the late Frost Snyder and the late Margaret Snyder
Typical Recipients: • *Education:* colleges & universities, medical education, private education (precollege), public education (precollege), religious education • *Health:* medical research • *Religion:* churches, religious organizations • *Social Services:* community service organizations
Grant Types: general support
Geographic Distribution: focus on WA

GIVING OFFICERS
Catherine S. Brockert: trust
Margaret S. Cunningham: trust
August Von Boecklin: trust

APPLICATION INFORMATION
Initial Approach: Send brief letter of inquiry describing program or project. Deadline is September 1.
Restrictions on Giving: Does not support individuals.

GRANTS ANALYSIS
Number of Grants: 17
Highest Grant: $50,000
Typical Range: $5,000 to $30,000
Disclosure Period: 1990

RECENT GRANTS
50,000 Archdiocese of Seattle, Seattle, WA
48,462 Seattle University, Seattle, WA

32,000 Bellarmine Preparatory School, Tocoma, WA
30,000 Blessed Sacrament Church, Warren, OH
30,000 Central Catholic High School
25,000 John F. Kennedy High School
25,000 St. Martins College
20,000 Franciscan Foundation
20,000 O'Dea High School
17,250 Pastoral Life Services

Snyder Foundation, Harold B. and Dorothy A.

CONTACT
Audrey Snyder
Executive Director
Harold B. and Dorothy A. Snyder Fdn.
PO Box 671
Moorestown, NJ 08057
(609) 273-9745

FINANCIAL SUMMARY
Recent Giving: $275,000 (fiscal 1991); $210,237 (fiscal 1990); $179,926 (fiscal 1989)
Assets: $7,582,013 (fiscal year ending September 30, 1991); $6,779,258 (fiscal 1990); $5,520,840 (fiscal 1989)
Gifts Received: $160,229 (fiscal 1991); $6,805 (fiscal 1990); $322,948 (fiscal 1989)
Fiscal Note: In 1991, contributions were received from Audrey Snyder ($1,625), Arline Critese ($595), Ethlyn Allison ($600), Holly Roeck ($200), Bernard Professional Center ($6,765), and the Estate of Harold B. Snyder.
EIN: 22-2316043

CONTRIBUTIONS SUMMARY
Donor(s): the late Harold B. Snyder, Sr.
Typical Recipients: • *Civic & Public Affairs:* urban & community affairs • *Education:* religious education, science/technology education • *Health:* health organizations, hospitals, single-disease health associations • *Religion:* churches, religious organizations • *Social Services:* community service organizations, disabled, homes, religious welfare, shelters/homelessness
Grant Types: general support, loan, multiyear/continuing support, operating expenses, project, and seed money
Geographic Distribution: focus on the Union County, NJ, area

GIVING OFFICERS
Ethelyn Allison: trust
Arline Snyder Cortese: trust
Robert G. Longaker: trust
Lillian Palumbo: trust
Audrey Snyder: trust
Phyllis Johnson Snyder: trust

APPLICATION INFORMATION
Initial Approach: Scholarships paid through institutions only. Application form not required. There are no deadlines.
Restrictions on Giving: Does not support individuals.

GRANTS ANALYSIS
Number of Grants: 30
Highest Grant: $37,743
Typical Range: $500 to $15,000
Disclosure Period: fiscal year ending September 30, 1991
Note: 1991 figures do not include $39,356 in scholarships to individuals.

RECENT GRANTS
37,743 Deborah Hospital Foundation, Browns Mills, NJ
26,995 ARC Union County, Plainfield, NJ
25,000 Union Hospital Foundation, Union, NJ
20,504 Muhlenberg Foundation, Plainfield, NJ
20,000 Habitat for Humanity, Plainfield, NJ
15,250 Stevens Institute of Technology, Hoboken, NJ
15,000 Elizabethport Presbyterian Center, Elizabeth, NJ
11,675 Stevens Institute of Technology, Hoboken, NJ
11,417 Princeton Theological Seminary, Princeton, NJ
8,000 Cerebral Palsy Association, Edison, NJ

Snyder Fund, Valentine Perry

CONTACT
Hildy Simmons
Senior Vice President
Valentine Perry Snyder Fund
c/o Morgan Guaranty Trust Co. of New York
60 Wall St.
New York, NY 10260-0060
(212) 648-9664

FINANCIAL SUMMARY
Recent Giving: $217,500 (1991); $221,000 (1990); $224,150 (1989)
Assets: $6,785,599 (1991); $5,605,241 (1990); $5,933,476 (1989)
Gifts Received: $62,008 (1991)
EIN: 13-6036765

CONTRIBUTIONS SUMMARY
Donor(s): the late Mrs. Sheda T. Snyder
Typical Recipients: • *Arts & Humanities:* arts centers • *Civic & Public Affairs:* civil rights, environmental affairs, ethnic/minority organizations, zoos/botanical gardens • *Education:* literacy • *Religion:* churches • *Social Services:* aged, community centers, community service organizations, disabled, recreation & athletics, shelters/homelessness, youth organizations
Grant Types: capital, emergency, endowment, general support, multiyear/continuing support, operating expenses, project, and seed money
Geographic Distribution: focus on the New York, NY, metropolitan area

GIVING OFFICERS
Morgan Guaranty Trust Company of New York: trust

APPLICATION INFORMATION
Initial Approach: Send brief letter of inquiry describing program or project. There are no deadlines.
Restrictions on Giving: Does not support individuals or provide scholarships or loans.

GRANTS ANALYSIS
Number of Grants: 16
Highest Grant: $20,000
Typical Range: $10,000 to $20,000
Disclosure Period: 1991

RECENT GRANTS

20,000 Brooklyn in Touch Information Center, Brooklyn, NY

20,000 Hope Program, New York, NY

20,000 Union Settlement Association, New York, NY

15,000 Friends and Relatives of Institutionalized Aged, New York, NY

15,000 Mind Builders Creative Arts Center, New York, NY

15,000 New York Interface Development Project for Professional Development Laboratory School Project, New York, NY

15,000 Playing to Win, New York, NY

15,000 Sunnyside Community Services, New York, NY

15,000 United Neighborhood Houses of New York, New York, NY

12,500 Women in Need, New York, NY

Snyder General Corp.

Sales: $800.0 million
Employees: 7,000
Headquarters: Dallas, TX
SIC Major Group: Industrial Machinery & Equipment

CONTACT

Bart Bailey
Vice President, Administration
Snyder General Corp.
3219 McKinney Ave.
Dallas, TX 75204
(214) 754-0500

CONTRIBUTIONS SUMMARY

Operating Locations: TX (Dallas)

CORP. OFFICERS

B.W. Bonnivier: *CURR EMPL* pres, coo: Snyder Gen Corp
Richard Wesley Snyder: *B* Kansa City MO 1938 *ED* IN Univ BS 1960; Univ Detroit MBA 1964 *CURR EMPL* fdr, pres, ceo: SnyderGen

Society Corp.

Assets: $24.97 billion
Employees: 12,451
Headquarters: Cleveland, OH
SIC Major Group: Business Services, Depository

Institutions, and Holding & Other Investment Offices

CONTACT

Bruce H. Akers
Vice President, Public Affairs
Society Corp.
800 Superior Ave.
Cleveland, OH 44114
(216) 689-3000

FINANCIAL SUMMARY

Fiscal Note: Company gives directly. It does not release giving figures.

CONTRIBUTIONS SUMMARY

Typical Recipients: • *Arts & Humanities:* performing arts • *Civic & Public Affairs:* business/free enterprise, economic development, general, urban & community affairs • *Education:* business education, colleges & universities • *Health:* hospitals • *Social Services:* community centers, united funds

Grant Types: capital, employee matching gifts, general support, and operating expenses

Nonmonetary Support Types: in-kind services

Geographic Distribution: primarily headquarters area

Operating Locations: DE (Wilmington), FL (Tampa), IL (Chicago), IN (Elkhart, Franklin, Howe, Ligonier, Martinsville, Noblesville, Shelbyville, Syracuse), MI (Sturgis), NY (New York), OH (Cincinnati, Cleveland, Columbus, Dayton), TX (Dallas)

CORP. OFFICERS

Robert W. Gillespie: *B* Cleveland OH 1944 *ED* Wesleyan Univ 1966; Case Western Reserve Univ Sch Bus Admin 1968 *CURR EMPL* chmn, ceo, dir: Soc Natl Bank *CORP AFFIL* chmn, pres, ceo: Soc Corp
James W. Wert: *B* Chicago IL 1946 *ED* MI St Univ 1971; Northwestern Univ Sch Bus Admin *CURR EMPL* pres, coo: Soc Natl Bank *CORP AFFIL* vchmn, cfo: Soc Corp

APPLICATION INFORMATION

Initial Approach: *Initial Contact:* brief letter of inquiry *Include Information On:* description of the organization, amount requested, purpose for which funds are sought, budget information, and proof of tax-

exempt status *When to Submit:* any time

Restrictions on Giving: Does not fund individuals, religious organizations for sectarian purposes, or political groups.

OTHER THINGS TO KNOW

In 1992, Ameritrust merged with Society Corp.

Society for Savings

Assets: $2.48 billion
Employees: 525
Parent Company: Society for Savings Bancorp Inc.
Headquarters: Hartford, CT
SIC Major Group: Depository Institutions and Holding & Other Investment Offices

CONTACT

Robert W. Beggs
Senior Vice President, Corporate Communications
Society for Savings
31 Pratt St.
Hartford, CT 06103
(203) 727-5486

FINANCIAL SUMMARY

Fiscal Note: Company gives directly. Annual Giving Range: $250,000 to $500,000

CONTRIBUTIONS SUMMARY

Typical Recipients: • *Arts & Humanities:* general • *Civic & Public Affairs:* environmental affairs, ethnic/minority organizations, general, housing • *Education:* general • *Health:* general, health organizations • *Social Services:* aged, disabled, general, united funds

Grant Types: general support

Geographic Distribution: in headquarters and operating communities

Operating Locations: CT (Hartford)

CORP. OFFICERS

Lawrence Connell: *CURR EMPL* pres, ceo: Soc Savings

GIVING OFFICERS

Robert W. Beggs: *CURR EMPL* sr vp corp commun: Soc Savings

APPLICATION INFORMATION

Initial Approach: *Initial Contact:* concise proposal in the form of a cover letter with the necessary supportive documents *Include Information On:* a description of organization,

amount requested, purpose of funds sought, current list of board of directors, budget, other funding applied for or received, contingency plans in the event that requested funding is unavailable, and proof of tax-exempt status *When to Submit:* requests should be received before early Fall for consideration in the following year's budget

Restrictions on Giving: Does not support partisan political organizations; United Way or other federated drives outside of service communities; capital fund drives outside of service communities; individuals; organizations not designated tax-exempt; religious organizations for purely sectarian purposes; or scholarships for individuals.

OTHER THINGS TO KNOW

Publications: corporate contributions and public involvement policy statement

GRANTS ANALYSIS

Typical Range: $1,000 to $2,500

Society for the Increase of the Ministry

CONTACT

J. S. Zimmerman
Executive Director
Society for the Increase of the Ministry
120 Sigourney St.
Hartford, CT 06105
(203) 677-2543

FINANCIAL SUMMARY

Recent Giving: $150,000 (fiscal 1991); $146,000 (fiscal 1990); $114,815 (fiscal 1989)

Assets: $2,558,109 (fiscal year ending August 31, 1991); $2,304,737 (fiscal 1990); $2,371,885 (fiscal 1989)

Gifts Received: $36,544 (fiscal 1991); $40,582 (fiscal 1990); $30,790 (fiscal 1989)

Fiscal Note: In fiscal 1991, contributions were received from membership contributions ($23,309), S. N. Pardee Trust Fund ($12,235), and the Van Winkle Fund ($1,000).

EIN: 06-6053077

CONTRIBUTIONS SUMMARY

Donor(s): Sarah Norton Pardee Trust

Typical Recipients: • *Education:* colleges & universities, religious education • *Religion:* religious organizations • *Social Services:* homes

Grant Types: scholarship

Geographic Distribution: limited to the United States

GIVING OFFICERS

Rev. John Bishop: secy

Howard W. Bornholm: treas

Rev. Stephen H. Gushee: vp

Rev. Bordern W. Painter: pres

Rev. William N. Penfield: exec dir

APPLICATION INFORMATION

Initial Approach: Contact financial aid officer of each accredited theological seminary of the Episcopal Church. The deadline is March 1.

OTHER THINGS TO KNOW

Publications: Application Guidelines, Informational Brochure

GRANTS ANALYSIS

Number of Grants: 11

Highest Grant: $34,000

Typical Range: $2,600 to $20,000

Disclosure Period: fiscal year ending August 31, 1991

RECENT GRANTS

34,000 Theological Seminary, Alexandria, VA

20,410 Theological Seminary, Alexandria, VA

16,833 Church Divinity School of Pacific, Berkeley, CA

15,808 Seabury-Western, Evanston, IL

13,972 Church Divinity School of Pacific, Berkeley, CA

12,470 SEWANEE

11,207 Nashotah House

10,157 Episcopal Theological Seminary, Austin, TX

6,819 Trinity Episcopal School

5,628 Bexley Hall, Rochester, NY

Sofia American Schools

CONTACT

Sofia American Schools
850 Third Ave.
New York, NY 10022
(212) 319-2453

FINANCIAL SUMMARY

Recent Giving: $116,552 (fiscal 1991); $105,882 (fiscal 1990); $125,389 (fiscal 1989)

Assets: $2,870,044 (fiscal year ending June 30, 1991); $2,815,507 (fiscal 1990); $2,715,924 (fiscal 1989)

EIN: 13-6400773

CONTRIBUTIONS SUMMARY

Typical Recipients: • *Education:* agricultural education, colleges & universities, international exchange, medical education, private education (precollege) • *International:* foreign educational institutions, international health care

Grant Types: general support and scholarship

Geographic Distribution: focus on Greece and Turkey

GIVING OFFICERS

Corrine M. Black: trust

John H. Clymer: clerk

Carl S. Dorn: trust

Stephen Grant: off

Alfred H. Howell: trust

Robert C. Hubbard: vp

William B. Jones: trust

Edward M. Marwell: trust

Elizabeth Michaels: trust

Donald B. Murphy: treas

Sol Polansky: trust

Walter Prosser: secy

John Rigas: asst treas

Richard C. Robarts: trust

Peter W. Rupprecht: asst treas

Irwin T. Sanders: pres

Joel Studebaker: trust

Richard Van Bolt: secy

Roger Whitaker: trust

William J. Williams, Jr.: trust

APPLICATION INFORMATION

Initial Approach: Send brief letter of inquiry describing program. Deadline is February 1.

GRANTS ANALYSIS

Number of Grants: 9

Highest Grant: $25,000

Typical Range: $3,000 to $6,500

Disclosure Period: fiscal year ending June 30, 1991

RECENT GRANTS

25,000 Anatolia College, Thessaloniki, Greece

19,000 Robert College of Istanbul, Istanbul, Turkey

15,000 American Hospital of Istanbul, Istanbul, Turkey

9,000 Anatolia College, Thessaloniki, Greece

6,500 American Farm School, Thessaloniki, Greece

5,300 American Farm School, Thessaloniki, Greece

5,000 American Hospital of Istanbul School of Nursing, Istanbul, Turkey

3,050 Robert College of Istanbul, Istanbul, Turkey

2,652 Bulgarian Studies Project

Soft Sheen Products Co.

Sales: $92.1 million

Employees: 535

Headquarters: Chicago, IL

SIC Major Group: Chemicals & Allied Products

CONTACT

Edward Gardner
Chairman
Soft Sheen Products Co.
1000 East 87th St.
Chicago, IL 60619
(312) 978-0700
Note: Bettianne Gardner, co-chairperson, is another contact person at the same address.

CONTRIBUTIONS SUMMARY

Operating Locations: IL (Chicago)

CORP. OFFICERS

Betty A. Gardner: *CURR EMPL* co-chmn, secy: Soft Sheen Products Co

Edward G. Gardner: *CURR EMPL* chmn, ceo: Soft Sheen Products Co

Gary E. Gardner: *CURR EMPL* pres, coo: Soft Sheen Products Co

Software Toolworks

Sales: $66.0 million

Employees: 240

Headquarters: Novato, CA

SIC Major Group: Business Services

CONTACT

Tracy Eagan
Public Relations
Software Toolworks
60 Lervoni Ct.
Novato, CA 94947
(415) 883-3000

CORP. OFFICERS

Les Crane: *CURR EMPL* pres, chmn: Software Toolworks

Margo Hober: *CURR EMPL* cfo: Software Toolworks

Sogem Holding Ltd.

Sales: $500.0 million

Employees: 55

Headquarters: New York, NY

SIC Major Group: Holding & Other Investment Offices, Wholesale Trade—Durable Goods, and Wholesale Trade—Nondurable Goods

CONTACT

Maria Macchiarolo
Office Manager
Sogem Holding Ltd.
1212 Avenue of the Americas
New York, NY 10036
(212) 764-0880

CONTRIBUTIONS SUMMARY

Operating Locations: NY (New York)

CORP. OFFICERS

Steve Springer: *CURR EMPL* cfo: Sogem Holding Ltd

Robert Todewils: *CURR EMPL* ceo, pres: Sogem Holding Ltd

Solheim Foundation

CONTACT

Louise C. Solheim
Trustee
Solheim Fdn.
501 West Wakonda Lane
Phoenix, AZ 85023
(602) 863-3333

FINANCIAL SUMMARY

Recent Giving: $2,442,000 (fiscal 1992); $2,686,000 (fiscal 1991); $3,060,000 (fiscal 1990)

Assets: $926,741 (fiscal year ending June 30, 1992);

$1,308,163 (fiscal 1991); $507,289 (fiscal 1990)
Gifts Received: $2,000,000 (fiscal 1992); $3,315,000 (fiscal 1991)
Fiscal Note: In 1992, contributions were received from Karsten Manufacturing Corporation.
EIN: 74-2378207

CONTRIBUTIONS SUMMARY
Donor(s): Karsten Solheim and Louise C. Solheim
Typical Recipients: • *Arts & Humanities:* community arts, music • *Education:* colleges & universities, religious education • *Religion:* churches, missionary activities, religious organizations • *Social Services:* community service organizations, united funds, youth organizations
Grant Types: general support

GIVING OFFICERS
Allan O. Solheim: trust
John A. Solheim: trust
K. Louis Solheim: trust
Karsten Solheim: trust *B* Berger Norway 1911 *ED* Univ WA *CURR EMPL* fdr, chmn, pres, treas: Karsten Mfg Corp
Louise C. Solheim: trust

APPLICATION INFORMATION
Initial Approach: The foundation reports it only makes contributions to preselected charitable organizations.
Restrictions on Giving: Does not support individuals.

GRANTS ANALYSIS
Number of Grants: 12
Highest Grant: $1,000,000
Typical Range: $10,000 to $100,000
Disclosure Period: fiscal year ending June 30, 1992

RECENT GRANTS
1,000,000 Dallas Theological Seminary, Dallas, TX
500,000 Grand Canyon University, Phoenix, AZ
500,000 Moody Bible Institute, Chicago, IL
300,000 Arizona College of the Bible, Phoenix, AZ
100,000 Phoenix Gospel Mission, Phoenix, AZ
75,000 International Foundation, Washington, DC
60,000 Shepherd Ministries, Irving, TX
50,000 Neues Leben International, Phoenix, AZ
46,000 Navigators, Colorado Springs, CO
25,000 Inter-Varsity Christian Fellowship, Madison, WI

Soling Family Foundation

CONTACT
Soling Family Fdn.
c/o Solico
142 East 39th St., Rm. 300
New York, NY 10016

FINANCIAL SUMMARY
Recent Giving: $33,658 (fiscal 1991); $57,050 (fiscal 1990); $157,412 (fiscal 1989)
Assets: $2,333,053 (fiscal year ending May 31, 1991); $2,597,910 (fiscal 1990); $2,216,593 (fiscal 1989)
EIN: 13-3288798

CONTRIBUTIONS SUMMARY
Donor(s): Chester Song
Typical Recipients: • *Arts & Humanities:* arts festivals, community arts, museums/galleries, performing arts, theater • *Civic & Public Affairs:* municipalities • *Education:* colleges & universities • *Health:* health organizations • *Social Services:* counseling, day care
Grant Types: general support and multiyear/continuing support
Geographic Distribution: focus on MA and NY

GIVING OFFICERS
Caytha Jentis: trust
Carole Song: secy
Chester Song: pres

APPLICATION INFORMATION
Initial Approach: Contributes only to preselected organizations.
Restrictions on Giving: Does not support individuals.

GRANTS ANALYSIS
Number of Grants: 17
Highest Grant: $19,400
Typical Range: $55 to $2,500
Disclosure Period: fiscal year ending May 31, 1991

RECENT GRANTS
19,400 Main Street Child Care, New York, NY
5,900 Mount Holyoke College, South Hadley, MA
4,133 Savannah on Stage, Savannah, GA
1,250 Lucas Theatre, Savannah, GA
1,070 Williamstown Theatre Festival, Williamstown, NY
500 Red Cross
395 Syracuse University, Syracuse, NY
300 Metropolitan Museum of Art, New York, NY
200 Williamstown Community, Williamstown, NY
135 Williamstown Advocate, Williamstown, NY

Solo Cup Co. / Solo Cup Foundation
Sales: $450.0 million
Employees: 3,000
Parent Company: SCC Holding Co.
Headquarters: Highland Park, IL
SIC Major Group: Paper & Allied Products and Rubber & Miscellaneous Plastics Products

CONTACT
Ronald L. Whaley
Treasurer & Foundation Administrator
Solo Cup Fdn.
1700 Old Deerfield Rd.
Highland Park, IL 60035
(708) 831-4800

FINANCIAL SUMMARY
Recent Giving: $1,149,400 (fiscal 1991); $587,800 (fiscal 1990); $80,500 (fiscal 1989)
Assets: $7,057,519 (fiscal year ending March 31, 1991); $7,541,724 (fiscal 1990); $7,771,305 (fiscal 1989)
Gifts Received: $7,732,473 (fiscal 1989)
Fiscal Note: In 1989, contributions were from SCC Holding Stock; substantial contributor is estate of Dorothy (Hall) Hulseman.
EIN: 36-6062327

CONTRIBUTIONS SUMMARY
Typical Recipients: • *Civic & Public Affairs:* philanthropic organizations • *Education:* private education (precollege), religious education • *Health:* hospitals, single-disease health associations • *Religion:* churches, missionary activities • *Social Services:* aged, community centers, disabled, drugs & alcohol, religious welfare, youth organizations
Grant Types: capital, general support, operating expenses, project, research, and scholarship
Geographic Distribution: primarily Illinois
Operating Locations: IL (Highland Park)

CORP. OFFICERS
Robert L. Hulseman: *B* 1932 *CURR EMPL* pres, dir, ceo: Solo Cup Co *CORP AFFIL* pres: Premore; pres, ceo: SCC Holding Co

GIVING OFFICERS
E.L. Carter: secy *CURR EMPL* vp, real estate off: Solo Cup Co
J. F. Hulseman: vp *CURR EMPL* vp, secy, dir: Solo Cup Co *CORP AFFIL* vp, secy, dir: Solo Cup Co
Robert L. Hulseman: pres *CURR EMPL* pres, dir, ceo: Solo Cup Co (see above)
Ronald L. Whaley: treas *CURR EMPL* vp, treas, dir: Solo Cup Co *CORP AFFIL* vp: Bus Leases, Quality Inks, SCC Holding Co; vp, treas, dir: Solo Cup Co

APPLICATION INFORMATION
Initial Approach: *Initial Contact:* full proposal *Include Information On:* description of the organization, amount requested, purpose of funds sought, audited financial statement, and proof of tax-exempt status *When to Submit:* any time
Restrictions on Giving: Does not support individuals or political or lobbying groups.

GRANTS ANALYSIS
Total Grants: $1,149,400
Number of Grants: 36
Highest Grant: $200,000
Typical Range: $5,000 to $35,000
Disclosure Period: fiscal year ending March 31, 1991
Note: Recent grants are derived from a fiscal 1991 Form 990.

RECENT GRANTS
200,000 St. Scholastica High School, Chicago, IL — general support

160,000 Benedictine School Foundation, Ridgely, MD — capital improvement

150,000 Salvation Army, Baltimore, MD — food for the needy

77,000 Faith, Hope and Charity Church, Winnetka, IL — general support

50,000 Casa Experanza, Albuquerque, NM — general support

50,000 Hazelden, Center City, MN — general support

50,000 Little Sisters of the Poor, Newark, DE — general support

50,000 Maria Joseph Manor, Danville, PA — general support

50,000 Misericordia Heart of Mercy, Chicago, IL — general support

50,000 Old St. Patrick's Renaissance Campaign, Chicago, IL — general support

Solomon Foundation, Sarah M.

CONTACT
Jane C. Williams
Sarah M. Solomon Fdn.
c/o First National Bank of Chicago
One First National Plaza
Ste. 0111
Chicago, IL 60670-0111
(312) 732-5586

FINANCIAL SUMMARY
Recent Giving: $180,000 (1991); $170,400 (1989); $168,700 (1988)
Assets: $3,857,475 (1991); $3,378,595 (1989); $2,658,395 (1988)
EIN: 36-6613406

CONTRIBUTIONS SUMMARY
Typical Recipients: • *Arts & Humanities:* arts institutes • *Education:* colleges & universities, medical education
Grant Types: general support
Geographic Distribution: focus on Chicago, IL

GIVING OFFICERS
L. Roy Papp: trust

APPLICATION INFORMATION
Initial Approach: Contributes only to preselected organizations. Applications not accepted.
Restrictions on Giving: Does not support individuals.

GRANTS ANALYSIS
Number of Grants: 3
Highest Grant: $85,000
Disclosure Period: 1991

RECENT GRANTS
85,000 University of Chicago, Chicago, IL
67,000 Brandeis University, Waltham, MA
28,000 Roosevelt University, Chicago, IL

Solow Foundation

CONTACT
Sheldon H. Solow
President
Solow Fdn.
9 West 57th St.
New York, NY 10019-2601
(212) 935-7529

FINANCIAL SUMMARY
Recent Giving: $274,001 (fiscal 1990); $554,416 (fiscal 1989); $2,104,750 (fiscal 1988)
Assets: $7,576,339 (fiscal year ending October 31, 1990); $7,254,232 (fiscal 1989); $7,201,167 (fiscal 1988)
EIN: 13-2950685

CONTRIBUTIONS SUMMARY
Donor(s): Sheldon H. Solow
Typical Recipients: • *Arts & Humanities:* arts centers, community arts, ethnic arts, libraries, museums/galleries, performing arts • *Education:* colleges & universities, education associations, religious education • *Social Services:* community service organizations, united funds, youth organizations
Grant Types: general support

GIVING OFFICERS
Steven Cherniak: treas
Leonard Lazarus: secy
Sheldon Henry Solow: don, pres *B* 1928
Rosalie S. Wolff: vp

APPLICATION INFORMATION
Initial Approach: Send brief letter of inquiry describing program or project. There are no deadlines.

GRANTS ANALYSIS
Number of Grants: 39
Highest Grant: $40,000
Typical Range: $1,000 to $5,000
Disclosure Period: fiscal year ending October 31, 1990

RECENT GRANTS
40,000 Center for African Art, New York, NY
28,200 Educational Alliance, New York, NY
25,000 American Friends of Israel Philharmonic Orchestra, Chicago, IL
25,000 Columbia Grammar and Preparatory School, New York, NY
25,000 New York Public Library, New York, NY
16,666 Children's Museum of Manhattan, New York, NY
10,000 National Multiple Sclerosis Society
10,000 New School for Social Research, New York, NY
10,000 New York Bar Foundation, New York, NY
10,000 Whitehouse Endowment Fund

Solow Foundation, Sheldon H.

CONTACT
Sheldon H. Solow
President
Sheldon H. Solow Fdn.
9 West 57th St.
New York, NY 10019-2601
(212) 751-1100

FINANCIAL SUMMARY
Recent Giving: $135,000 (fiscal 1991); $550,000 (fiscal 1990); $328,000 (fiscal 1989)
Assets: $6,878,979 (fiscal year ending November 30, 1991); $6,445,847 (fiscal 1990); $6,917,866 (fiscal 1989)
EIN: 13-3386646

CONTRIBUTIONS SUMMARY
Donor(s): Sheldon H. Solow
Typical Recipients: • *Arts & Humanities:* arts centers, arts funds, public broadcasting • *Education:* colleges & universities, education associations • *Health:* medical research • *Social Services:* united funds, youth organizations
Grant Types: general support

GIVING OFFICERS
Steven M. Cherdiak: vp, treas
Margaret E. Hewitt: secy
Sheldon Henry Solow: pres, treas *B* 1928

APPLICATION INFORMATION
Initial Approach: Send brief letter of inquiry describing program or project. There are no deadlines.

GRANTS ANALYSIS
Number of Grants: 3
Highest Grant: $100,000
Disclosure Period: fiscal year ending November 30, 1991

RECENT GRANTS
100,000 Soumui Art and Architecture Foundation
25,000 WGBH Educational Foundation, Boston, MA
10,000 Educational Broadcasting, New York, NY

Somers Corp. (Mersman/ Waldron)

Sales: $.0 thousand
Employees: 5
Headquarters: Navesink, NJ
SIC Major Group: Business Services and Furniture & Fixtures

CONTACT
Willard C. Somers
President
Somers Corp. (Mersman/Waldron)
500 Hwy. 36
Navesink, NJ 07752
(908) 291-4000

CONTRIBUTIONS SUMMARY
Company sponsors employee matching gift program; also supports community organizations.
Typical Recipients: • *Arts & Humanities:* general • *Civic & Public Affairs:* general • *Education:* general • *Health:* general • *Social Services:* general
Grant Types: matching
Geographic Distribution: primarily headquarters area
Operating Locations: NJ (Navesink)

CORP. OFFICERS
W. Somers: *CURR EMPL* pres: Somers Corp

APPLICATION INFORMATION

Initial Approach: Send brief letter of inquiry. There are no deadlines.

Somers Foundation, Byron H.

CONTACT

Byron H. Somers Fdn.
5814 Reed Rd.
Ft. Wayne, IN 46835

FINANCIAL SUMMARY

Recent Giving: $241,200 (fiscal 1991); $41,812 (fiscal 1990); $196,172 (fiscal 1989)
Assets: $4,276,334 (fiscal 1990); $4,213,002 (fiscal 1989); $4,010,390 (fiscal 1988)
EIN: 35-1410969

CONTRIBUTIONS SUMMARY

Typical Recipients: • *Arts & Humanities:* arts associations, arts funds, community arts, history/historic preservation, museums/galleries, music • *Education:* private education (precollege) • *Health:* health organizations • *Religion:* religious organizations • *Social Services:* child welfare, community service organizations, united funds, youth organizations
Grant Types: capital and multi-year/continuing support
Geographic Distribution: focus on Fort Wayne, IN

GIVING OFFICERS

Druscilla S. Doehrman: trust
Robert W. Gibson: trust

APPLICATION INFORMATION

Initial Approach: Contributes only to preselected organizations.

GRANTS ANALYSIS

Number of Grants: 15
Highest Grant: $50,000
Typical Range: $2,000 to $10,000
Disclosure Period: fiscal year ending November 30, 1991

RECENT GRANTS

50,000 YMCA, Ft. Wayne, IN
50,000 YWCA, Ft. Wayne, IN
25,000 Fine Arts Foundation, Ft. Wayne, IN
25,000 Fort Wayne Philharmonic, Ft. Wayne, IN
25,000 Lindenwood Historical Foundation, Ft. Wayne, IN — historic preservation
17,000 Canterbury School, Ft. Wayne, IN — equipment
10,000 Crossroads, Ft. Wayne, IN — diagnostic/treatment center
10,000 Washington House Treatment Center, Ft. Wayne, IN
9,000 Very Special Arts Indiana, Indianapolis, IN
4,500 Allen County-Fort Wayne Historical Society, Ft. Wayne, IN

Sonat / Sonat Foundation

Sales: $1.42 billion
Employees: 5,700
Headquarters: Birmingham, AL
SIC Major Group: Electric, Gas & Sanitary Services, Holding & Other Investment Offices, and Oil & Gas Extraction

CONTACT

J. Lisa Burge
Secretary
Sonat Fdn.
PO Box 2563
Birmingham, AL 35202
(205) 325-7460

FINANCIAL SUMMARY

Recent Giving: $1,300,000 (1993 est.); $1,200,000 (1992 approx.); $1,300,000 (1991 approx.)
Assets: $5,042,487 (1991); $5,089,984 (1990); $6,200,000 (1988)
Gifts Received: $1,000,000 (1991)
Fiscal Note: Company gives through foundation only.
EIN: 63-0830299

CONTRIBUTIONS SUMMARY

Typical Recipients: • *Arts & Humanities:* arts associations, arts centers, arts festivals, history/historic preservation, libraries, museums/galleries, music, opera, performing arts, public broadcasting, theater • *Civic & Public Affairs:* business/free enterprise, economic development, economics, philanthropic organizations, professional & trade associations, urban & community affairs, zoos/botanical gardens • *Education:* business education, colleges & universities, continuing education, economic education, education associations, education funds, engineering education, legal education, liberal arts education, literacy, medical education, minority education, science/technology education • *Health:* health care cost containment, health funds, health organizations, hospitals, single-disease health associations • *Science:* scientific institutes • *Social Services:* aged, animal protection, child welfare, community centers, community service organizations, disabled, drugs & alcohol, employment/job training, food/clothing distribution, homes, recreation & athletics, shelters/homelessness, youth organizations
Grant Types: employee matching gifts, general support, project, and seed money
Nonmonetary Support Types: donated equipment, in-kind services, and loaned executives
Note: Nonmonetary support is provided by the foundation and the company. Estimated value of nonmonetary support for 1991 is not available. For more information, contact J. Lisa Burge.
Geographic Distribution: communities where company operates, with emphasis on Birmingham, AL
Operating Locations: AL (Birmingham), GA, LA, TX (Houston)

CORP. OFFICERS

John Robert Doody: *B* Joplin MO 1930 *ED* Univ MO 1957 *CURR EMPL* exec vp fin & admin: Sonat *CORP AFFIL* chmn: Sonat Exploration Co; dir: Sherman Intl Corp, Sonat Offshore Drilling, Southern Natural Gas Co, First AL Bank Birmingham, Maritrans Partners LP *NONPR AFFIL* mem: Am Inst CPAs, Fin Execs Inst
Ronald L. Kuehn, Jr.: *B* Brooklyn NY 1935 *ED* Fordham Univ BS 1957; Fordham Univ LLB 1964 *CURR EMPL* chmn, pres, ceo, dir: Sonat *CORP AFFIL* dir: Am South Bancorp, Protective Life Corp, Sonat Exploration Co, Sonat Offshore Drilling, Southern Natural Gas Co, Teleco Oilfield Svcs, Union Carbide Corp *NONPR AFFIL* dir: Gas Res Inst, Interstate Natural Gas Assn, Natl Petroleum Counc; mem: Am Bar Assn, Am Gas Assn, Assn Bar City NY, Bretton Woods Comm, Fed Energy Bar Assn, Newcomen Soc US, NY St Bar Assn; mem pres counc: Univ AL Birmingham; trust: Birmingham Southern Coll, Boys Clubs Am

GIVING OFFICERS

Ms J. Lisa Burge: secy
Edie James: treas
Leria L. Jordan: vp
Beverly Turner Krannich: pres *B* Mobile AL 1951 *ED* Rhodes Coll 1973; Samford Univ Law Sch 1976 *CURR EMPL* vp, secy: SONAT
L.David Mathews: VP
William A. Smith: vp

APPLICATION INFORMATION

Initial Approach: *Initial Contact:* brief letter or proposal *Include Information On:* description of the organization, amount requested, list of corporate and foundation support, purpose for which funds are sought, recently audited financial statement, proof of tax-exempt status *When to Submit:* submission deadline is February 1
Restrictions on Giving: Foundation does not make grants to individuals; organizations already receiving United Way support; or political, religious, fraternal, or veterans organizations.

OTHER THINGS TO KNOW

Scholarships are awarded only to children of active, retired, disabled or deceased employees of Sonat, Inc. and its subsidiaries and affiliates.

GRANTS ANALYSIS

Total Grants: $1,300,000
Number of Grants: 146*
Highest Grant: $202,500
Typical Range: $1000 to $10,000
Disclosure Period: 1991
Note: Number of grants and average grant figures include matching gifts. Recent grants are derived from a 1991 Form 990.

RECENT GRANTS

202,500 University of Alabama Medical and Education, Birmingham, AL — general support

153,026 Vanderbilt University, Nashville, TN — capital campaign

83,706 Metropolitan Arts Council, Birmingham, AL — general support

77,125 Birmingham Southern College, Birmingham, AL — general support

30,325 Samford University, Birmingham, AL — capital campaign; matching gift

25,125 Children's Hospital, Birmingham, AL — capital campaign

25,000 Metropolitan Development Board, Birmingham, AL — general support

25,000 Robert W. Woodruff Arts Center, Birmingham, AL — general support

25,000 University of Alabama School of Law, Tuscaloosa, AL — general support

22,500 Boys Clubs of America New York, New York, NY — general support

Sonat Exploration

Sales: $270.0 million
Employees: 830
Headquarters: Houston, TX
SIC Major Group: Oil & Gas Extraction

CONTACT
Charles Gauthiery
Human Resources
Sonat Exploration
4 Greenway Plz.
Houston, TX 77046
(713) 940-4000

CONTRIBUTIONS SUMMARY
Primarily support United Way and employee matching gifts.
Typical Recipients: • *Social Services:* united funds
Grant Types: matching
Geographic Distribution: headquarters area
Operating Locations: TX (Houston)

CORP. OFFICERS
Ron B. Pruet, Jr.: *CURR EMPL* cfo: Sonat Exploration
Don G. Russell: *CURR EMPL* chmn: Sonat Exploration

APPLICATION INFORMATION
Initial Approach: Applications not accepted.

Sonat Offshore Drilling

Sales: $200.0 million
Employees: 1,500
Parent Company: Sonat
Headquarters: Houston, TX
SIC Major Group: Oil & Gas Extraction

CONTACT
Dennis Heagney
Vice President, Controller & Treasurer
Sonat Offshore Drilling
PO Box 1513
Houston, TX 77251-1513
(713) 871-7500

CONTRIBUTIONS SUMMARY
Operating Locations: TX (Houston)

CORP. OFFICERS
W. Dennis Heagney: *CURR EMPL* pres: Sonat Offshore Drilling
William C. O'Malley: *CURR EMPL* chmn, ceo: Sonat Offshore Drilling

Sonesta International Hotels Corp. / Sonesta Charitable Foundation

Revenue: $49.9 million
Employees: 1,444
Headquarters: Boston, MA
SIC Major Group: Hotels & Other Lodging Places

CONTACT
Paul Sonnabend
President
Sonesta Charitable Foundation
200 Clarendon St.
Boston, MA 02116-5021
(617) 421-5450

FINANCIAL SUMMARY
Recent Giving: $0 (1991)
Assets: $100,000 (1991)
Gifts Received: $100,000 (1991)
Fiscal Note: In 1991, contributions were received from Sonesta International Hotels Corporation.
EIN: 04-6169167

CONTRIBUTIONS SUMMARY
Geographic Distribution: principally near operating locations and to national organizations
Operating Locations: FL (Key Biscayne, Orlando), LA (New Orleans), MA (Boston, Cambridge)

CORP. OFFICERS
Paul Sonnabend: *CURR EMPL* pres, dir: Sonesta Intl Hotels Corp
Roger P. Sonnabend: *CURR EMPL* chmn, ceo, dir: Sonesta Intl Hotels Corp

GIVING OFFICERS
Joseph L. Bower: dir
Brian T. Owen: vp, treas, dir
William J. Poorvu: dir
Paul Sonnabend: vp, dir *CURR EMPL* pres, dir: Sonesta Intl Hotels Corp (see above)
Peter J. Sonnabend: clerk, dir
Roger P. Sonnabend: pres, dir *CURR EMPL* chmn, ceo, dir: Sonesta Intl Hotels Corp (see above)

APPLICATION INFORMATION
Initial Approach: Send brief letter of inquiry.
Restrictions on Giving: Does not support individuals.

GRANTS ANALYSIS
Typical Range: $50 to $1,000

Sonoco Products Co. / Sonoco Products Foundation

Sales: $1.69 billion
Employees: 14,490
Headquarters: Hartsville, SC
SIC Major Group: Chemicals & Allied Products, Lumber & Wood Products, Paper & Allied Products, and Rubber & Miscellaneous Plastics Products

CONTACT
Jim Shelley
Chairman, Sonoco Foundation
Sonoco Products Co.
PO Box 160
Hartsville, SC 29550
(803) 383-7000

FINANCIAL SUMMARY
Recent Giving: $996,148 (1990); $569,465 (1989)
Assets: $952,994 (1990); $667,142 (1989)
Gifts Received: $1,050,000 (1990); $600,000 (1989)
Fiscal Note: 1990 contribution received from Sonoco Products Co.
EIN: 57-0752950

CONTRIBUTIONS SUMMARY
Typical Recipients: • *Arts & Humanities:* arts centers, arts institutes, community arts, dance, general, history/historic preservation, libraries, music, opera, performing arts, public broadcasting, theater • *Civic & Public Affairs:* better government, economic development, environmental affairs, ethnic/minority organizations, general, safety, urban & community affairs, women's affairs • *Education:* business education, colleges & universities, community & junior colleges, economic education, elementary education, engineering education, faculty development, health & physical education, minority education, science/technology education • *Health:* emergency/ambulance services, general, health organizations, hospitals, medical rehabilitation, medical research, mental health, single-disease health associations • *Science:* science exhibits & fairs • *Social Services:* community centers, domestic violence, drugs & alcohol, emergency relief, general, recreation & athletics, shelters/homelessness, volunteer services, youth organizations
Grant Types: emergency, employee matching gifts, endowment, general support, multiyear/continuing support, project, research, and scholarship
Nonmonetary Support Types: donated equipment and donated products
Geographic Distribution: focus on South Carolina, concentrating in counties in which employees reside
Operating Locations: GA (Marietta), NC (Statesville), SC (Hartsville)

CORP. OFFICERS
Charles W. Coker: *B* Florence SC 1933 *ED* Princeton Univ BA 1955; Harvard Univ MBA 1957 *CURR EMPL* chmn, pres, ceo, dir: Sonoco Products Co *CORP AFFIL* dir: Carolina Power Light Co, NCNB Corp, Sara Lee Corp, Springs Indus,

State Capital Corp *NONPR AFFIL* mem: Palmetto Bus Forum
Russell C. King, Jr.: *CURR EMPL* pres, coo, dir: Sonoco Products Co
Jim Shelley:

GIVING OFFICERS
Charles W. Coker: trust *CURR EMPL* chmn, pres, ceo, dir: Sonoco Products Co (see above)
T. C. Coxe III: trust *B* Darlington SC 1930 *CURR EMPL* exec vp, dir: Sonoco Products Co *CORP AFFIL* dir: SC Natl Corp *NONPR AFFIL* mem: Am Inst Banking
F. Trent Hill, Jr.: trust *B* Greensboro NC 1952 *CURR EMPL* vp (products div): Sonoco Products Co
Russell C. King, Jr.: trust *CURR EMPL* pres, coo: Sonoco Products Co
F. B. Williams: trust

APPLICATION INFORMATION
Initial Approach: *Initial Contact:* The foundation reports that it only makes contributions to pre-selected organizations.
Restrictions on Giving: The foundation reports that it only makes contributions to pre-selected organizations.

GRANTS ANALYSIS
Total Grants: $996,148
Number of Grants: 445
Highest Grant: $200,000
Typical Range: $500 to $2,500
Disclosure Period: 1990
Note: Figure for average grant excludes a single grant for $200,000. Recent grants are derived from a 1990 Form 990.

RECENT GRANTS
200,000 Sonovista School — Science and Math
100,000 Coker College, Hartsville, SC
100,000 South Carolina Independent College Fund, Taylors, SC
52,000 Hartsville United Way, Hartsville, SC
42,975 Darlington County School System, SC
37,846 Darlington County School Anti-Drug, SC
27,000 Darlington County School District, SC
20,000 Hartsville YMCA, Hartsville, SC

16,668 Hartsville Downtown Development, Hartsville, SC
15,000 Thomas Hart Academy

Sony Corp. of America / Sony USA Foundation
Former Foundation Name: Sony Corp. of America Foundation
Sales: $5.46 billion
Employees: 78,900
Parent Company: Sony Corp. Tokyo
Headquarters: Park Ridge, NJ
SIC Major Group: Electronic & Other Electrical Equipment, Industrial Machinery & Equipment, Instruments & Related Products, and Wholesale Trade—Durable Goods

CONTACT
c/o Corporate Communications
Sony Electronics, Inc.
1 Sony Dr., MD 3B8
Park Ridge, NJ 07656
(212) 418-9404
Note: The company does not list a specific contact person.

FINANCIAL SUMMARY
Recent Giving: $1,250,000 (1993 est.); $1,500,000 (1992); $1,200,000 (1991 approx.)
Assets: $1,102,690 (1991); $1,853,760 (1989)
Fiscal Note: Company gives primarily through the foundation. Also runs a limited and informal direct giving program. Above figures represent Sony U.S. electronics operations only. Company's subsidiaries operate own giving program. See "Other Things You Should Know" for more details.
EIN: 23-7181637

CONTRIBUTIONS SUMMARY
Typical Recipients: • *Arts & Humanities:* ethnic arts, public broadcasting • *Civic & Public Affairs:* ethnic/minority organizations, urban & community affairs • *Education:* arts education, career/vocational education, colleges & universities, minority education, private education (precollege), public education (precollege), religious education, science/technology education • *Health:* health organizations, hospitals • *Social Services:* community service organiza-

tions, disabled, united funds, youth organizations
Grant Types: employee matching gifts, general support, project, and scholarship
Nonmonetary Support Types: donated equipment
Note: Nonmonetary support is provided by the company and is estimated at $135,000 for 1992. This amount is included in the above total giving figures.
Geographic Distribution: nationally, with emphasis on communities where Sony has a presence
Operating Locations: AL (Dothan), CA (San Diego, San Jose), FL (Boca Raton), GA (Atlanta), HI (Honolulu), IL (Chicago), NJ (Paramus, Park Ridge, Teaneck), NY (New York), TX (San Antonio)
Note: Operates 122 sites in 25 states.

CORP. OFFICERS
Kuri Ando: *CURR EMPL* pres: Sony Engring Mfg Am
John Briesch: *CURR EMPL* deputy pres (sales & mktg): Sony Corp Am
Masaaki Morita: *CURR EMPL* chmn, ceo, dir: Sony Corp Am *CORP AFFIL* dep pres, rep dir, dir: Sony Corp (Japan)
Michael Peter Schulhof: *B* New York NY 1942 *ED* Grinnell Coll BA 1964; Cornell Univ MS 1967; Brandeis Univ PhD 1970; Grinnell Coll DSc 1990 *CURR EMPL* vchmn, ceo, pres: Sony Corp Am *CORP AFFIL* chmn: Digital Audio Disc Corp, Quadriga Art, Sony Video Software; chmn, ceo, dir: Sony Music Entertainment; chmn, mem exec comm, dir: CBS Records; dir: Columbia Pictures Entertainment, Materials Res Corp, Sony Corp Japan; pres, dir: Sony Software Corp; pres, mem exec comm, dir: Sony Corp NY City *NONPR AFFIL* corp mem: Counc Foreign Rels; dir: Computer Bus Equipment Mfrs Assn; fellow: Natl Science Fdn; mem: Aircraft Owners Pilots Assn, Am Physics Soc, Am Radio Relay League, Guggenheim Mus, Whitney Mus Am Art; trust: Brandeis Univ
Shinichi Takagi: *CURR EMPL* pres: Sony Recording Media AM

GIVING OFFICERS
H. Paul Burak: secy, dir

Masaaki Morita: chmn, dir *CURR EMPL* chmn, ceo, dir: Sony Corp Am (see above)
Kenneth L. Nees: pres, asst secy, dir
Michael Peter Schulhof: dir *CURR EMPL* vchmn, ceo, pres: Sony Corp Am (see above)

APPLICATION INFORMATION
Initial Approach: *Initial Contact:* brief letter *Include Information On:* description of the organization, amount requested, purpose for which funds are sought, recently audited financial statement, and proof of tax-exempt status *When to Submit:* any time
Restrictions on Giving: No grants are made to individuals.

OTHER THINGS TO KNOW
Foundation will not consider more than one proposal per organization per year.
Sony Pictures Entertainment administers an independent program, which is currently under review. Requests for information must be in writing and can be sent to Janice Pober, Vice President, Corporate Affairs, Sony Pictures Entertainment, 10202 W Washington Blvd., Culver City, CA, 90232-3195. Sony Music Entertainment also administers an independent program. Request for information must be in writing and can be sent to Public Relations, 500 Madison Ave., 20th Fl., New York, NY, 10022-3211.

GRANTS ANALYSIS
Total Grants: $1,500,000*
Number of Grants: 740
Highest Grant: $70,000
Typical Range: $100 to $3,000
Disclosure Period: 1992
Note: Total grants is approximate. Assets are from 1991. Recent grants are derived from a 1991 Form 990.

RECENT GRANTS
55,000 United Way-Gergen County, Oradell, NJ
50,000 Armed Forces Relief Trust
50,000 Armed Forces Relief Trust
50,000 National Action Council-Minorities in Engineering
50,000 New York City Opera, New York, NY

50,000 Satellite Educational Resources Consortium
50,000 United Way-Dothan
35,000 New York Community Trust, New York, NY
33,333 Lincoln Center Building Campaign, New York, NY
33,333 Lincoln Center for the Performing Arts, New York, NY

Sooner Pipe & Supply Corp. / Sooner Pipe & Supply Corp. Foundation

Sales: $226.0 million
Employees: 804
Headquarters: Tulsa, OK
SIC Major Group: Wholesale Trade—Durable Goods

CONTACT
J. W. Kirby
Secretary-Treasurer
Sooner Pipe & Supply Corp.
P.O. Box 1530
Tulsa, OK 74101
(918) 587-3391
Note: Company is located at 401 South Boston, Suite 1000, Tulsa, Oklahoma 74103.

FINANCIAL SUMMARY
Recent Giving: $561,350 (fiscal 1992); $760,200 (fiscal 1991)
Assets: $1,067,870 (fiscal year ending July 31, 1992); $899,316 (fiscal 1991)
Gifts Received: $655,998 (fiscal 1992); $500,000 (fiscal 1991)
Fiscal Note: Contributes through foundation only. In fiscal 1992, contributions were received from Sooner Pipe & Supply Corp.
EIN: 73-1332141

CONTRIBUTIONS SUMMARY
Typical Recipients: • *Arts & Humanities:* arts associations, museums/galleries, opera, performing arts • *Civic & Public Affairs:* better government, philanthropic organizations, professional & trade associations, urban & community affairs • *Education:* colleges & universities, education associations, private education (precollege), religious education • *Health:*

geriatric health, health funds, health organizations, hospices, hospitals, medical research, mental health, single-disease health associations • *Religion:* religious organizations • *Social Services:* aged, child welfare, community centers, community service organizations, community service organizations, drugs & alcohol, family services, food/clothing distribution, volunteer services, youth organizations
Grant Types: general support and operating expenses
Nonmonetary Support Types: in-kind services and loaned employees
Note: Company also provides office space.
Geographic Distribution: primarily in Tulsa, OK
Operating Locations: OK (Tulsa)

CORP. OFFICERS
Henry H. Zarrow: *CURR EMPL* pres: Sooner Pipe & Supply Corp

GIVING OFFICERS
J. W. Kerby: secy-treas
Henry H. Zarrow: pres *CURR EMPL* pres: Sooner Pipe & Supply Corp (see above)

APPLICATION INFORMATION
Initial Approach: *Initial Contact:* brief letter of inquiry *Include Information On:* a description of organization, amount requested, purpose of funds sought, recently audited financial statement, and proof of tax-exempt status *When to Submit:* any time
Restrictions on Giving: Does not make grants to individuals.

GRANTS ANALYSIS
Total Grants: $561,350
Number of Grants: 54
Highest Grant: $250,000
Typical Range: $500 to $10,000
Disclosure Period: fiscal year ending July 31, 1992
Note: Recent grants are derived from a fiscal 1992 grants list.

RECENT GRANTS
250,000 Congregational B'Nai Emman Endowment Fund, Tulsa, OK
51,000 Crohn's and Colitis Foundation of America, Tulsa, OK

27,000 Goodwill Industries of Tulsa, Tulsa, OK
25,000 Schumpert Medical Center, Shreveport, LA
20,000 Holland Hall School, Tulsa, OK
20,000 Menninger Foundation, Topeka, KS
18,600 University of Oklahoma Foundation, Norman, OK
11,500 Project Get Together, Tulsa, OK
10,000 American Diabetes Association, Tulsa, OK
10,000 Town and Country School, Tulsa, OK

Sordoni Enterprises

Revenue: $80.0 million
Employees: 200
Headquarters: Wilkes-Barre, PA
SIC Major Group: General Building Contractors, Holding & Other Investment Offices, Industrial Machinery & Equipment, and Wholesale Trade—Nondurable Goods

CONTACT
Angie Edgar
Administration Assistant, Construction
Sordoni Enterprises
45 Owen St.
Wilkes-Barre, PA 18704
(717) 287-3161

CONTRIBUTIONS SUMMARY
Operating Locations: PA (Forty Fort, Wilkes-Barre)

CORP. OFFICERS
Andrew J. Sordoni III: *B* Pratt KS 1943 *ED* Kings Coll BA 1967 *CURR EMPL* chmn, dir: C-TEC Corp *CORP AFFIL* chmn, dir: C-TEC Corp, Commonwealth Telephone Co; dir: Harsco Corp, Sordoni Enterprises *NONPR AFFIL* mem: PA Chamber Bus Indus, Pennsylvanians Effective Govt
William B. Sordoni: *CURR EMPL* ceo: Sordoni Enterprises

GIVING OFFICERS
William B. Sordoni: dir *CURR EMPL* ceo: Sordoni Enterprises (see above)

Sordoni Foundation

CONTACT
Benjamin Badman, Jr.
Exec. Vice President
Sordoni Fdn.
45 Owen St.
Forty Ft., PA 18704
(717) 283-1211

FINANCIAL SUMMARY
Recent Giving: $194,700 (fiscal 1992); $1,048,562 (fiscal 1991); $589,833 (fiscal 1990)
Assets: $6,553,518 (fiscal year ending July 31, 1992); $6,310,814 (fiscal 1991); $7,538,907 (fiscal 1990)
Gifts Received: $51,025 (fiscal 1992); $47,000 (fiscal 1991); $170,667 (fiscal 1990)
EIN: 24-6017505

CONTRIBUTIONS SUMMARY
Donor(s): the late Andrew J. Sordoni, Sr., the late Andrew J. Sordoni, Jr., Andrew J. Sordoni III, the late Mrs. Andrew J. Sordoni, Sr., the late Mrs. Andrew J. Sordoni, Jr., Mrs. Andrew J. Sordoni III
Typical Recipients: • *Arts & Humanities:* community arts, libraries, museums/galleries, music, public broadcasting, theater • *Civic & Public Affairs:* economic development, municipalities, public policy, urban & community affairs • *Education:* colleges & universities, education funds • *Health:* health organizations, medical research • *Religion:* religious organizations • *Social Services:* child welfare, youth organizations
Grant Types: capital, endowment, general support, multi-year/continuing support, project, and seed money
Geographic Distribution: focus on northeastern PA

GIVING OFFICERS
Richard Allen: dir
Jule Ayers: dir
Benjamin Badman, Jr.: exec vp, secy, treas, dir
Ruth Hitchner: asst secy
Roy Edward Morgan: dir *B* Nanticoke PA 1908 *ED* PA St Univ BA 1931; PA St Univ MA 1935 *CURR EMPL* pres: WY Valley Broadcasting Co *CORP AFFIL* pres: Wyoming Valley Broadcasting Co; treas: Ra-Tel Realty Co *NONPR AFFIL* chmn emeritus exec comm: ABC Radio Network Affiliates

Comm; dir: Econ Devel Counc Northeastern PA; mem pres counc: Kings Coll; trust: Hosp Assn PA

Patrick Solano: dir

Andrew J. Sordoni III: pres, dir *B* Pratt KS 1943 *ED* Kings Coll BA 1967 *CURR EMPL* chmn, dir: C-TEC Corp *CORP AFFIL* chmn, dir: C-TEC Corp, Commonwealth Telephone Co; dir: Harsco Corp, Sordoni Enterprises *NONPR AFFIL* mem: PA Chamber Bus Indus, Pennsylvanians Effective Govt

Stephen Sordoni: dir

Susan F. Sordoni: dir

William James Umphred: dir *B* Wilkes-Barre PA 1928 *ED* Wilkes Coll 1952 *CURR EMPL* sr vp: C-TEC Corp *CORP AFFIL* dir: Franklin Fed Savings & Loan Assn, PA Millers Mutual Ins co; sr vp: C-TEC Corp

APPLICATION INFORMATION

Initial Approach: Send brief letter of inquiry describing program or project. There are no deadlines.

Restrictions on Giving: Does not support individuals or provide scholarships.

GRANTS ANALYSIS

Number of Grants: 30
Highest Grant: $60,000
Typical Range: $100 to $5,000
Disclosure Period: fiscal year ending July 31, 1992

RECENT GRANTS

    60,000 Geisinger Foundation, Danville, PA
    55,000 Collegiate Museum of Art, Wilkes-Barre, PA
    35,000 University of Scranton, Scranton, PA
    10,000 WVIA Channel 44, Jenkins Township, PA
     5,000 College Misercordia, Dallas, PA
     5,000 Committee for Economic Growth, Wilkes-Barre, PA
     5,000 Marywood College, Scranton, PA
     5,000 Northeast Pennsylvania Philharmonic, Avoca, PA
     5,000 Osterhout Free Library, Wilkes-Barre, PA
     2,500 United Rehabilitation Services, Wilkes-Barre, PA

Soref Foundation, Samuel M. Soref and Helene K.

CONTACT

Belinda Pontow
Tax Officer
Samuel M. Soref and Helene K. Soref Fdn.
First Union National Bank
PO Box 44245 FL0720
Jacksonville, FL 32231-4245
(904) 361-1352

FINANCIAL SUMMARY

Recent Giving: $1,115,000 (1990); $246,500 (1989); $76,321 (1987)
Assets: $20,644,818 (1990); $7,844,945 (1989); $2,498,711 (1987)
Gifts Received: $10,476,056 (1990); $2,517,093 (1989); $489,172 (1987)
EIN: 59-2246963

CONTRIBUTIONS SUMMARY

Donor(s): The foundation was established in 1983.
Typical Recipients: • *Arts & Humanities:* public broadcasting • *Civic & Public Affairs:* philanthropic organizations • *Education:* colleges & universities, religious education • *Religion:* religious organizations, synagogues • *Social Services:* child welfare, community service organizations, homes, shelters/homelessness, united funds, youth organizations
Grant Types: capital, operating expenses, and research
Geographic Distribution: California, Florida, and Israel

GIVING OFFICERS

Benjamin F. Breslaver: trust
Helene M. Soref: trust

APPLICATION INFORMATION

Initial Approach: Restrictions on Giving: The foundation supports preselected organizations and does not accept unsolicited requests for funds. The foundation does not make grants to individuals.

GRANTS ANALYSIS

Total Grants: $1,115,000
Number of Grants: 4
Highest Grant: $500,000
Typical Range: $250,000 to $500,000
Disclosure Period: 1990
Note: Recent grants are derived from a 1990 grants list.

RECENT GRANTS

    500,000 Jewish National Fund, Los Angeles, CA
    360,000 Jewish Federation of Greater Fort Lauderdale, Fort Lauderdale, FL
    250,000 Boys Town, Jerusalem, Israel
      5,000 Cumberland College, Williamsburg, KY

Soros Foundation-Hungary

CONTACT

Elizabeth Agocs
Secretary-Treasurer
Soros Fdn-Hungary
888 Seventh Avenue, Ste. 3301
New York, NY 10106

FINANCIAL SUMMARY

Recent Giving: $5,390,557 (1990); $3,903,812 (1989); $3,624,967 (1988)
Assets: $3,345,080 (1990); $5,662,186 (1989); $3,548,599 (1988)
Gifts Received: $3,322,149 (1990); $5,474,964 (1989); $4,577,604 (1988)
EIN: 13-3210361

CONTRIBUTIONS SUMMARY

Donor(s): George Soros, George Soros Charitable Lead Trust, Tivadar Charitable Lead Trust
Typical Recipients: • *Civic & Public Affairs:* international affairs • *Education:* medical education • *Health:* hospitals, medical research • *International:* international organizations
Grant Types: research

GIVING OFFICERS

Elizabeth Agocs: secy, treas
Philip Mayer Kaiser: vp, dir *B* Brooklyn NY 1913 *ED* Univ WI AB 1935; Oxford Univ Balliol Coll MA 1939 *CURR EMPL* sr consultant: SRI Intl *CORP AFFIL* sr consultant: SRI Intl *NONPR AFFIL* mem: Counc Am Ambassadors, Counc Foreign Rels, Intl Inst Strategic Studies, Intl Res Exchanges Bd
George Soros: pres, dir *B* Budapest Hungary 1931 *ED* London Sch Econ *CURR EMPL* fdr, chmn: Quantum Fund *CORP AFFIL* dir: Crystal Oil Co; owner: Am Equine Pro-

ducts, Autofinance Group, Digicon Inc, ERC Indus, Gataas-Larsen Shipping Corp, Harkin Energy Corp, Mueller Indus, Pansophic Sys, Paradyne Corp, Receptech Corp, Spectrum Digital Corp, Triangle Indus, Triton Energy Corp
William David Zabel: vp, dir *B* Omaha NE 1936 *ED* Princeton Univ AB 1958; Harvard Univ LLB 1961 *CURR EMPL* ptnr: Schulte Roth & Zabel *CORP AFFIL* ptnr: Schulte Roth & Zabel *NONPR AFFIL* mem: Am Bar Assn, Am Coll Trust Estate Counc, Am Law Inst, FL Bar Assn, Lawyers Comm Human Rights, NY Bar Assn, NY City Bar Assn

APPLICATION INFORMATION

Initial Approach: Send brief letter of inquiry describing program or project. There are no deadlines.

GRANTS ANALYSIS

Number of Grants: 315
Highest Grant: $750,000
Typical Range: $200 to $10,000
Disclosure Period: 1990

RECENT GRANTS

    750,000 Consultrade, Budapest, Hungary
    554,022 HAS-Soros Foundation Secretariat, Wallingford, CT
    362,244 HAS-Soros Foundation Secretariat, Budapest, Hungary
    250,000 Kisvallaklozo's Orszagos Szovestsege, Budapest, Hungary
    232,604 University of Pennsylvania, Philadelphia, PA
    216,645 National Szechenyi Library, Budapest, Hungary
    146,341 Student Advising Center, Budapest, Hungary
    100,000 East-West Management Institute Foundation, Budapest, Hungary
    100,000 Free Trade Union Foundation, Budapest, Hungary
    100,000 University of Texas Summer Travel, Budapest, Hungary

Sosland Foundation

CONTACT
Morton Sosland
President
Sosland Foundation
4800 Main St., 100
Kansas City, MO 64112-2504
(816) 756-1000

FINANCIAL SUMMARY
Recent Giving: $1,250,000
(1993 est.); $1,397,725 (1992);
$1,250,000 (1991)
Assets: $23,183,940 (1992);
$21,646,805 (1991);
$20,234,296 (1989)
EIN: 44-6007129

CONTRIBUTIONS SUMMARY
Donor(s): The foundation was established in 1955 by members of the Sosland family.
Typical Recipients: • *Arts & Humanities:* arts associations, dance, museums/galleries, music, opera, public broadcasting, theater • *Civic & Public Affairs:* economic development, environmental affairs, international affairs, philanthropic organizations, urban & community affairs, zoos/botanical gardens • *Education:* arts education, colleges & universities, education funds, elementary education, medical education, minority education, preschool education, private education (precollege), special education • *Health:* hospitals, mental health • *Religion:* religious organizations • *Social Services:* aged, child welfare, community centers, community service organizations, emergency relief, employment/job training, family services, recreation & athletics, religious welfare, united funds, youth organizations
Grant Types: general support and project
Geographic Distribution: primarily the Metropolitan Kansas City, MO, area

GIVING OFFICERS
Morton I. Sosland: pres, dir *B* Kansas City MO 1925 *ED* Harvard Univ 1946 *CURR EMPL* pres, treas, dir: Sosland Cos *CORP AFFIL* dir: H&R Block, Brown Group, Commerce Bancshares, Hallmark Cards, Ingredient Tech Corp, Kansas City Southern Indus, TW Svcs
Neil Sosland: secy/treas, dir

Melanie Townsend: asst secy, asst treas

APPLICATION INFORMATION
Initial Approach:
The foundation does not have formal application forms. Applicants may submit a grant request in letter form.
There are no deadlines for requesting funds.

GRANTS ANALYSIS
Total Grants: $1,397,725
Number of Grants: 243
Highest Grant: $400,000
Typical Range: $100 to $5,000 and $10,000 to $50,000
Disclosure Period: 1992
Note: Recent grants are derived from a 1992 grants list.

RECENT GRANTS
368,069 Jewish Federation, Kansas City, MO
140,000 Children's Mercy Hospital, Kansas City, MO — capital campaign pledge
107,334 Jewish Federation, Kansas City, MO — Operation E
50,000 Greater Kansas City Community Foundation, Kansas City, MO — Take Part
50,000 Jewish Community Foundation, Kansas City, MO — fund for Jewish education
50,000 Jewish Theological Seminary, Rochester, NY
30,000 Salvation Army of Kansas City, Kansas City, MO — capital campaign
25,000 Nelson Gallery Foundation, Kansas City, MO
20,000 Greater Kansas City Community Foundation, Kansas City, MO — Kauffman Book Fund Pledge
16,000 Truman Medical Center Foundation, Kansas City, MO

Sotheby's
Sales: $300.0 million
Employees: 450
Headquarters: New York, NY
SIC Major Group: Business Services, Holding & Other Investment Offices, and Real Estate

CONTACT
Katherine Ross
Vice President, Museum Services
Sotheby's
1334 York Ave.
New York, NY 10021
(212) 606-7303

FINANCIAL SUMMARY
Fiscal Note: Company gives directly. Annual Giving Range: $250,000 to $500,000

CONTRIBUTIONS SUMMARY
Typical Recipients: • *Arts & Humanities:* arts associations • *Education:* arts education • *Social Services:* youth organizations
Grant Types: project and scholarship
Nonmonetary Support Types: cause-related marketing & promotion and in-kind services
Geographic Distribution: headquarters only
Operating Locations: MI (Bloomfield), NV (La Vegas, Reno), NY (New York)

CORP. OFFICERS
Diana D. Brooks: *CURR EMPL* pres, ceo: Sothebys
John L. Marion: *B* New York NY 1933 *ED* Fordham Univ BS 1956; Columbia Univ 1960-61 *CURR EMPL* chmn, dir: Sothebys *NONPR AFFIL* chmn fine arts comm: NY City Div Am Cancer Soc

GIVING OFFICERS
Katherine Ross: *CURR EMPL* vp museum svcs: Sothebys

APPLICATION INFORMATION
Initial Approach: *Initial Contact:* brief letter of inquiry *Include Information On:* description of the organization, amount requested, purpose of funds sought, audited financial statement, and proof of tax-exempt status *When to Submit:* any time
Restrictions on Giving: Does not support individuals, religious organizations for sectarian purposes, or political or lobbying groups.

GRANTS ANALYSIS
Typical Range: $2,500 to $10,000

Souers Charitable Trust, Sidney W. and Sylvia N.

CONTACT
Sidney W. and Sylvia N. Souers Charitable Trust
c/o Boatmen's Trust Co.
510 Locust St.
St. Louis, MO 63178
(314) 436-9263

FINANCIAL SUMMARY
Recent Giving: $547,000 (1988)
Assets: $10,659,865 (1988)
EIN: 43-6079817

CONTRIBUTIONS SUMMARY
Donor(s): Sylvia N. Souers
Typical Recipients: • *Civic & Public Affairs:* zoos/botanical gardens • *Education:* colleges & universities • *Health:* health organizations, hospitals, medical research, single-disease health associations • *Religion:* churches • *Social Services:* disabled, united funds, youth organizations
Grant Types: general support
Geographic Distribution: focus on MO and Washington, DC

GIVING OFFICERS
Sylvia N. Souers: grantor

APPLICATION INFORMATION
Initial Approach: Send brief letter of inquiry describing program or project. There are no deadlines.

GRANTS ANALYSIS
Number of Grants: 27
Highest Grant: $100,000
Typical Range: $1,000 to $10,000
Disclosure Period: 1988

RECENT GRANTS
100,000 George Washington University, Washington, DC
100,000 Washington University, St. Louis, MO
100,000 Washington University, St. Louis, MO
50,000 Miami University, Miami, FL
38,000 Barnes Hospital Fund, St. Louis, MO
20,000 St. Louis Childrens Hospital, St. Louis, MO
20,000 St. Lukes Hospital, St. Louis, MO

15,000 Missouri Botanical
Garden, St. Louis,
MO
10,000 Bethesda General
Hospital, Bethesda,
MD
10,000 Central Presbyte-
rian Church, St.
Louis, MO

Soundesign Corp.

Sales: $220.0 million
Employees: 1,200
Headquarters: Jersey City, NJ
SIC Major Group: Electronic &
Other Electrical Equipment
and Wholesale
Trade—Durable Goods

CONTACT
Leslie Switzer
Director of Administration
Soundesign Corp.
Harbor Financial Center, 400
Plz. II
Jersey City, NJ 07311
(201) 434-1050

CONTRIBUTIONS
SUMMARY
Operating Locations: NJ (Jer-
sey City)

CORP. OFFICERS
Ely E. Ashkenazi: *CURR
EMPL* chmn: Soundesign Corp
Morris Franco: *CURR EMPL*
pres: Soundesign Corp

South Bend Tribune / Schurz Communications Foundation, Inc.

Sales: $22.0 million
Employees: 450
Parent Company: Schurz
Communications
Headquarters: South Bend, IN
SIC Major Group: Printing &
Publishing

CONTACT
Schurz Communications Fdn.,
Inc.
225 West Colfax Ave.
South Bend, IN 46601
(219) 287-1001

FINANCIAL SUMMARY
Recent Giving: $136,883
(1991); $153,734 (1990);
$213,204 (1989)
Assets: $1,126,714 (1991);
$1,138,121 (1990); $1,156,560
(1989)
Gifts Received: $50,321
(1991); $50,282 (1990);
$52,630 (1989)

Fiscal Note: In 1991, contribu-
tions were received from South
Bend Tribune ($33,633), and
WSBT ($16,688).
EIN: 35-6024357

CONTRIBUTIONS
SUMMARY
Typical Recipients: • *Arts &
Humanities:* history/historic
preservation, libraries • *Education:* business education, colleges & universities, education
funds • *Health:* hospices • *Social Services:* united funds,
youth organizations
Grant Types: general support
Geographic Distribution: limited to South Bend, IN
Operating Locations: IN
(South Bend)

CORP. OFFICERS
John J. McGann: *CURR
EMPL* pres, publ, dir: South
Bend Tribune

GIVING OFFICERS
John J. McGann: vp *CURR
EMPL* pres, publ, dir: South
Bend Tribune (see above)
James Montgomery Schurz:
pres, dir *B* South Bend IN 1933
ED Stanford Univ 1956 *CURR
EMPL* vp, dir: Schurz Com-
muns
E. Berry Smith: secy, treas

APPLICATION
INFORMATION
Initial Approach: Send brief
letter of inquiry. There are no
deadlines.

GRANTS ANALYSIS
Number of Grants: 20
Highest Grant: $50,000
Typical Range: $500 to $1,000
Disclosure Period: 1991

RECENT GRANTS
50,000 Civic Foundation
(Purdue University
at IUSB), South
Bend, IN
33,633 United Way, South
Bend, IN
15,000 University of Notre
Dame, Notre
Dame, IN
11,000 United Way, South
Bend, IN
5,000 Northern Indiana
Historical Society,
South Bend, IN
5,000 Stanley Clark
School, IN
5,000 YMCA, South
Bend, IN
4,000 Junior Achieve-
ment, South Bend,
IN
1,000 United Way, IN

1,000 United Way, Niles,
IN

South Branch Foundation

CONTACT
Peter S. Johnson
South Branch Fdn.
c/o Gillen and Johnson
PO Box 477
Somerville, NJ 08876
(201) 722-6400

FINANCIAL SUMMARY
Recent Giving: $410,000
(1990); $480,000 (1989);
$440,500 (1988)
Assets: $9,326,940 (1990);
$9,853,370 (1989); $7,978,014
(1988)
EIN: 22-6029434

CONTRIBUTIONS
SUMMARY
Donor(s): J. Seward Johnson,
J. Seward Charitable Trust
Typical Recipients: • *Arts &
Humanities:* arts centers, community arts, dance, history/his-
toric preservation, libraries,
music, public broadcasting
• *Civic & Public Affairs:* civil
rights, environmental affairs,
zoos/botanical gardens • *Education:* arts education, colleges &
universities • *Social Services:*
animal protection, community
service organizations
Grant Types: fellowship, mul-
tiyear/continuing support, project, research, and scholarship
Geographic Distribution:
focus on NY, NJ, and MA

GIVING OFFICERS
Jennifer U. Johnson Duke: dir
Esther U. Johnson: trust
James L. Johnson: trust *B* Ver-
non TX 1927 *ED* TX Tech
Univ BBA 1949 *CURR EMPL*
chmn, ceo: GTE Corp *CORP
AFFIL* dir: Bloomington Unlim-
ited, British Columbia Telecom-
munications, First Fed Savings
& Loan Assn, Mutual Life Ins
Co NY *NONPR AFFIL* dir: IL
Telephone Assn, McLean
County Assn Commerce Indus;
mem: Fin Execs Inst, Natl Assn
Accts, Wesleyan Assocs,
Wesleyan Univ; mem adv
counc: IL St Univ Coll Bus;
trust, mem adv counc: Mennon-
ite Hosp
John Duncan Mack: trust *B*
New York NY 1924 *ED* St
Johns Annapolis Coll 1948;
Harvard Univ 1950 *CURR
EMPL* pres (Carter Products):

Carter-Wallace *CORP AFFIL*
dir: Cuisinart's

APPLICATION
INFORMATION
Initial Approach: Send cover
letter and full proposal. Deadline is December 31.
Restrictions on Giving: Does
not support individuals.

GRANTS ANALYSIS
Number of Grants: 32
Highest Grant: $150,000
Typical Range: $1,000 to
$10,000
Disclosure Period: 1990

RECENT GRANTS
150,000 Matheny School,
Peapack, NJ
125,000 Nature Conser-
vancy, Pottersville,
NJ
100,000 Massachusetts
Audubon Society,
Lincoln, MA
50,000 Julliard School,
New York, NY
20,000 New Jersey Historical Society, New-
ark, NJ
11,500 Hunterdon Art Cen-
ter, Clinton, NJ —
preservation and
promotion of art
10,000 Vermont Studio
School, Johnson,
VT
5,000 Bach Choir of
Bethlehem, Bethle-
hem, PA
3,000 Help for Un-
claimed Dogs, Far
Hills, NJ — animal
protection

South Carolina Electric & Gas Co. / Summer Foundation

Assets: $3.74 billion
Employees: 4,600
Parent Company: SCANA
Headquarters: Columbia, SC
SIC Major Group: Electric, Gas
& Sanitary Services

CONTACT
Cathy Novinger
Executive Director
Summer Foundation
1426 Main St.
Columbia, SC 29201
(803) 748-3030

FINANCIAL SUMMARY
Recent Giving: $71,000
(1991); $47,900 (1990);
$47,500 (1989)

Assets: $1,056,573 (1991); $1,054,903 (1990); $557,629 (1989)
Gifts Received: $500,300 (1990); $940 (1989); $105,681 (1988)
Fiscal Note: In 1990, contributions were received from the Scana Corp.
EIN: 57-0784136

CONTRIBUTIONS SUMMARY
Typical Recipients: • *Civic & Public Affairs:* environmental affairs, municipalities, urban & community affairs • *Education:* colleges & universities, science/technology education, student aid • *Health:* public health • *Religion:* religious organizations • *Social Services:* community service organizations, united funds, youth organizations
Grant Types: general support
Geographic Distribution: focus on SC
Operating Locations: SC (Columbia)

CORP. OFFICERS
Lawrence Gressette: *CURR EMPL* ceo, chmn: South Carolina Electric & Gas Co
Bruce D. Kenyon: *CURR EMPL* pres, coo: SC Electric & Gas Co

GIVING OFFICERS
Lawrence M. Gressette, Jr.: trust *B* St Matthews SC 1932 *ED* Clemson Univ 1954 *CURR EMPL* chmn, pres, ceo: SCANA Corp
R.D. Hazel: trust
Bruce D. Kenyon: vp *CURR EMPL* pres, coo: SC Electric & Gas Co (see above)
James H. Kirkland: secy, treas
Randolph R. Mahan: trust
Kevin B. Marsh: trust
Thomas C. Nicols, Jr.: vp
Cathy B. Novinger: exec dir
Cathy B. Novinger: exec dir
John A. Warren: pres

APPLICATION INFORMATION
Initial Approach: Send brief letter describing program. There are no deadlines.

GRANTS ANALYSIS
Number of Grants: 20
Highest Grant: $12,500
Typical Range: $1,000 to $5,000
Disclosure Period: 1991

RECENT GRANTS
12,500 Richland County Health Department, Columbia, SC — health facility equipment
5,000 Center Place, Columbia, SC — operating fund
5,000 City of Abbeville, Abbeville, SC — building fund
5,000 Claflin College, Orangeburg, SC — honors program scholarship endowment
5,000 Conway Hospital Foundation, Conway, SC — annual funding raising
5,000 Edgefield County Council, Edgefield, SC — rural fire departments improvements
5,000 Hitchcock Rehabilitation Center, Aiken, SC — building fund
5,000 Town of Edgefield, Edgefield, SC — downtown development
3,000 Florence-Darlington Technical College, Florence, SC
2,500 Palmetto Partnership, Columbia, SC — Teen Institute for Alcohol and Drug Abuse

South Coast Foundation

CONTACT
South Coast Foundation
1217 Bel Air Drive
Santa Barbara, CA 93105

FINANCIAL SUMMARY
Recent Giving: $160,146 (1990); $68,285 (1989)
Assets: $2,124,589 (1990); $2,131,955 (1989)
EIN: 77-0177830

GIVING OFFICERS
Franklin C. Cook: vp
Kathleen M. Cook: pres
Susan V. Cook: treas
William H. Cook: secy

APPLICATION INFORMATION
Initial Approach: The foundation reports it only makes contributions to preselected organizations and does not accept unsolicited requests for funds.

GRANTS ANALYSIS
Total Grants: $160,146
Number of Grants: 14
Highest Grant: $31,600
Disclosure Period: 1990

South Jersey Industries
Assets: $446.4 million
Employees: 1,040
Headquarters: Folsom, NJ
SIC Major Group: Electric, Gas & Sanitary Services, Holding & Other Investment Offices, Nonmetallic Minerals Except Fuels, and Oil & Gas Extraction

CONTACT
Joe McCullough
Senior Vice President
South Jersey Industries
One South Jersey Plaza, Rte. 54
Folsom, NJ 08037
(609) 561-9000

CONTRIBUTIONS SUMMARY
Operating Locations: NJ (Folsom)

CORP. OFFICERS
Gerald S. Levitt: *CURR EMPL* vp, cfo: South Jersey Indus
William F. Ryan: *CURR EMPL* pres, ceo, coo: South Jersey Indus

South Plains Foundation

CONTACT
Robert P. Anderson, Ph.D.
Executive Director, Secretary, and Treas
South Plains Foundation
3716 21st Street
Lubbock, TX 79410-1231
(806) 792-9915

FINANCIAL SUMMARY
Recent Giving: $131,149 (fiscal 1991); $124,557 (fiscal 1990)
Assets: $3,108,826 (fiscal year ending June 30, 1991); $3,020,286 (fiscal 1990)
Gifts Received: $4,441 (fiscal 1990)
Fiscal Note: In fiscal 1990, the foundation received contributions of $4,250 from the estate of Mildred Jones and $191 from miscellaneous donors.
EIN: 75-2294100

CONTRIBUTIONS SUMMARY
Typical Recipients: • *Education:* colleges & universities, medical education • *Health:* hospitals, medical research, mental health • *Social Services:* drugs & alcohol
Grant Types: fellowship, project, research, scholarship, and seed money
Geographic Distribution: Texas

GIVING OFFICERS
Robert P. Anderson, Ph.D.: exec dir, secy, treas
Max L. Ince: pres, dir
C. E. Merkt, Ph.D.: dir
Howard Moore: vp, dir
Jim S. Moore, Ph.D.: dir
Evelyn Wilson, Ph.D.: dir

APPLICATION INFORMATION
Initial Approach: The foundation reports that proposals in the research grant program must be concerned with basic research in an area of health care; clinical investigations related to the rehabilitation of persons with chronic illnesses; or applied research problems focused on the treatment of persons with behavioral, mental, or physical problems. Grants in this area are limited to $10,000.L The foundation has no standard application form for either the research grant program or the small grants program: however, proposals should be a maximum of five pages and include the title of the study or project; name of the sponsoring institution; principal investigator or coordinator, with curriculum vitae attached for research grants; and abstract of the proposed study or project, not to exceed 100 words.L Additionally, research grant proposals should include a statement of purpose, objectives, and goals of the study; review of relevant background research; procedures to be followed and populations being studied; procedures to be followed in analyzing results; expected outcomes; and an outline of the proposed budget.L Small grant program proposals should also include a statement of purpose, objectives, and goals; description of the project, how it is to be carried out, equipment and personnel needs, and target population; and outline of the proposed

budget, with a list of other funding sources.L There are no deadlines; however, applicants are encouraged to submit proposals at least five weeks prior to quarterly board meetings held in March, June, September, and December. Three copies of the application must be submitted. Research proposals should be mailed to the above address. Small grant proposals should be sent to the foundation at P.O. Box 93377, Lubbock, TX 79493-3377.

GRANTS ANALYSIS

Total Grants: $131,149
Number of Grants: 10
Highest Grant: $28,657
Typical Range: $4,000 to $25,000
Disclosure Period: fiscal year ending June 30, 1991
Note: Incomplete grants list provided for fiscal year 1991.

RECENT GRANTS

28,657 Crosbyton Clinic, Crosbyton, TX — for equipment
25,000 Lubbock General Hospital, Lubbock, TX — William Gordon lectures
25,000 Texas Tech University, Lubbock, TX — W. T. Campbell scholarship
11,650 Texas Tech University Health Science Center, Lubbock, TX — endogenous digitalis
10,300 Selco/Roosevelt ISD, Slaton, Slaton, TX — drug abuse prevention
9,550 Texas Tech University Health Science Center, Lubbock, TX
5,000 University of Texas Health Science Center, Houston, TX — vasoactive peptides in renal transplant
4,000 Texas Tech University, Lubbock, TX — fellowship in psychology
4,000 Texas Tech University, Department of Psychology, Lubbock, TX — risk taking adolescents/young adults
1,400 Texas Special Olympics, Lubbock, TX — Special Olympics aquatics

South Texas Charitable Foundation

CONTACT
Rayford L. Keller
Secretary-Treasurer
South Texas Charitable Fdn.
PO Box 2549
Victoria, TX 77902
(512) 573-4383

FINANCIAL SUMMARY
Recent Giving: $708,100 (fiscal 1991); $423,300 (fiscal 1990); $403,884 (fiscal 1989)
Assets: $13,616,898 (fiscal year ending November 30, 1991); $7,848,700 (fiscal 1990); $7,608,382 (fiscal 1989)
Gifts Received: $5,000,000 (fiscal 1991)
Fiscal Note: In 1991, contributions were received from Maude O'Connor Williams.
EIN: 74-2148107

CONTRIBUTIONS SUMMARY
Donor(s): The foundation was established in 1981 by Maude O'Connor Williams.
Typical Recipients: • *Civic & Public Affairs:* municipalities, safety • *Education:* colleges & universities • *Health:* hospitals, single-disease health associations • *Religion:* churches, religious organizations • *Social Services:* domestic violence, emergency relief, food/clothing distribution, shelters/homelessness, volunteer services
Grant Types: general support
Geographic Distribution: focus on Texas

GIVING OFFICERS
Rayford L. Keller: secy, treas
Maude O'Connor Williams: pres
Roger P. Williams: vp

APPLICATION INFORMATION
Initial Approach:
The foundation reports all distributions have been made to 501(c)(3) organizations. If the foundation adopts a grant, it will develop appropriate forms and procedures at that time.
Restrictions on Giving: The foundation does not make grants to individuals.

GRANTS ANALYSIS
Total Grants: $708,100
Number of Grants: 20
Highest Grant: $240,000

Typical Range: $5,000 to $40,000
Disclosure Period: fiscal year ending November 30, 1991
Note: Recent grants are derived from a fiscal 1991 grants list.

RECENT GRANTS
240,000 Our Lady of Victory Cathedral, Victoria, TX
125,000 Covenant House, Houston, TX
50,000 Spohn Hospital, Corpus Christi, TX
50,000 Victoria College, Victoria, TX
40,000 Our Lady of Victory Cathedral TV Fund, Victoria, TX
30,000 Affectionate Arms, Victoria, TX
30,000 Christ's Kitchen, Victoria, TX
30,000 Meals on Wheels, Victoria, TX
25,000 Our Lady of Victory Parish Education Endowment Fund, Victoria, TX
20,000 Victoria Preservation, Victoria, TX

South Waite Foundation

CONTACT
Thomas P. Demeter
South Waite Fdn.
Ameritrust Co., N.A.
900 Euclid Ave.
Cleveland, OH 44101
(216) 737-3159

FINANCIAL SUMMARY
Recent Giving: $139,000 (1991); $138,000 (1990); $137,332 (1989)
Assets: $2,203,958 (1991); $1,944,337 (1990); $2,238,351 (1989)
EIN: 34-6526411

CONTRIBUTIONS SUMMARY
Donor(s): the late Francis M. Sherwin, Margaret H. Sherwin
Typical Recipients: • *Arts & Humanities:* arts associations, history/historic preservation, museums/galleries • *Civic & Public Affairs:* environmental affairs • *Education:* health & physical education, private education (precollege) • *Health:* health organizations, hospitals, medical research • *Science:* scientific institutes • *Social Services:* community service organizations, drugs & alcohol,

united funds, youth organizations
Grant Types: capital, multi-year/continuing support, and operating expenses
Geographic Distribution: limited to the Cleveland, OH, area

GIVING OFFICERS
Sherman Dye: mem *B* Portland OR 1915 *ED* Oberlin Coll AB 1937; Case Western Reserve Univ LLB 1940 *CURR EMPL* ptnr: Baker & Hostetler *NONPR AFFIL* mem: Am Bar Assn, Cleveland Bar Assn, OH Bar Assn; trust: PACE Assn; trust, chmn: First Baptist Church Greater Cleveland; trust, treas: Am Cancer Soc Cleveland
Donald W. Gruetner: trust, secy, treas
Brian Sherwin: trust, pres
Dennis Sherwin: mem
Margaret H. Sherwin: trust, vp
Peter Sherwin: mem

APPLICATION INFORMATION
Initial Approach: Contributes only to preselected organizations.
Restrictions on Giving: Does not support individuals, or provide funds for scholarships.

GRANTS ANALYSIS
Number of Grants: 30
Highest Grant: $25,000
Typical Range: $2,000 to $5,000
Disclosure Period: 1991

RECENT GRANTS
25,000 Cleveland Health Education Museum, Cleveland, OH
12,000 United Way, Cleveland, OH
8,000 Alcoholism Services of Cleveland, Cleveland Heights, OH
8,000 Jackson Laboratory, Bar Harbor, ME
8,000 Willoughby Fine Arts Association, Willoughby, OH
7,000 Cleveland Clinic Foundation, Cleveland, OH
6,000 Jackson Laboratory, Bar Harbor, ME
5,000 Cleveland Health Education, Cleveland, OH
5,000 Nature Conservancy, Columbus, OH

5,000 Nature Conservancy, Columbus, OH

South-Western Publishing Co.

Sales: $110.0 million
Employees: 600
Parent Company: Thomson Corp.
Headquarters: Cincinnati, OH
SIC Major Group: Printing & Publishing

CONTACT
Diane M. Kleinfelter
Human Resource Specialist
South-Western Publishing Co.
5101 Madison Rd.
Cincinnati, OH 45227
(513) 527-6388

CONTRIBUTIONS SUMMARY
Company provides employee matching gifts only.
Grant Types: matching
Operating Locations: MA (Boston), OH (Cincinnati)

CORP. OFFICERS
Elmer Kaising: *CURR EMPL* cfo: South-Wester Publ Co
Chester C. Lucido, Jr.: *CURR EMPL* pres, ceo: South-Western Publ Co

Southdown, Inc.

Sales: $506.9 million
Employees: 3,200
Headquarters: Houston, TX
SIC Major Group: Electric, Gas & Sanitary Services, Holding & Other Investment Offices, and Stone, Clay & Glass Products

CONTACT
Joe Devine
Vice President, Human Resources
Southdown, Inc.
1200 Smith St., Ste. 2400
Houston, TX 77002
(713) 650-6200

CONTRIBUTIONS SUMMARY
Operating Locations: CA (Los Angeles), FL (Tampa), TX (Houston)

CORP. OFFICERS
Clarence C. Comer: *B* Charleston WV 1948 *ED* Lamar Univ 1971 *CURR EMPL* pres, ceo: Southdown *CORP AFFIL* chmn, ceo: Moore McCormack Resources

W. Joseph Conway: *CURR EMPL* vchmn, dir: Southdown
G. Walter Loewenbaum III: *CURR EMPL* chmn, dir: Southdown

Southern Bell

Sales: $7.3 billion
Employees: 46,000
Headquarters: Atlanta, GA
SIC Major Group: Communications

CONTACT
Pam Arledge
Manager
Southern Bell
675 West Peachtree St. NE, 35-C-52 Southern Bell Center
Atlanta, GA 30375
(404) 529-2435

CONTRIBUTIONS SUMMARY
Support provided in the following major categories: United Way and American Red Cross, Health and Welfare, Youth Organizations, Civic and Cultural, and Education. Preference is given capital campaigns of community hospitals, agencies which receive operating funds through United Ways, and colleges and universities with both capital and operating fund needs. Company also gives through the Bell-South Foundation. Southern Bell also has a Volunteer Service Grant program which provides for monetary contributions to a charitable organization after an employee has volunteered a specific number of hours.
Typical Recipients: • *Arts & Humanities:* arts festivals • *Civic & Public Affairs:* civil rights • *Education:* career/vocational education • *Health:* geriatric health • *Social Services:* aged
Grant Types: capital, general support, matching, multi-year/continuing support, and scholarship
Nonmonetary Support Types: in-kind services, loaned executives, and workplace solicitation
Geographic Distribution: communities within service region
Operating Locations: GA (Atlanta)

CORP. OFFICERS
R. Franklin Skinner: *CURR EMPL* pres, ceo: Southern Bell

APPLICATION INFORMATION
Initial Approach: Send brief letter of inquiry, including a description of the organization, amount requested, purpose of funds sought, audited financial statement, and proof of tax-exempt status. There are no deadlines.
Restrictions on Giving: Does not support individuals; organizations that are not tax-exempt; discriminatory organizations; political organizations or campaigns; churches; goodwill advertising; operating expenses of United Way organizations; fraternal, veteran, or labor organizations.

OTHER THINGS TO KNOW
Publications: Southern Bell's Contributions Policy

Southern California Edison Co.

Parent Company: SCECorp
Revenue: $8.04 billion
Parent Employees: 17,236
Headquarters: Rosemead, CA
SIC Major Group: Electric, Gas & Sanitary Services

CONTACT
Rebecca S. Jones
Director, Charitable Contributions
Southern California Edison Co.
2244 Walnut Grove Ave.
PO Box 800
Rosemead, CA 91770
(818) 302-3841

FINANCIAL SUMMARY
Recent Giving: $4,500,000 (1992 approx.); $4,000,000 (1991 approx.); $3,800,000 (1990 approx.)
Fiscal Note: Company gives directly.

CONTRIBUTIONS SUMMARY
Typical Recipients: • *Arts & Humanities:* arts associations, arts centers, arts institutes, community arts, dance, ethnic arts, history/historic preservation, libraries, museums/galleries, music, opera, performing arts, public broadcasting, theater • *Civic & Public Affairs:* better government, business/free enterprise, civil rights, consumer affairs, economic development, economics, environmental af-

fairs, housing, law & justice, professional & trade associations, public policy, safety, urban & community affairs, women's affairs, zoos/botanical gardens • *Education:* business education, career/vocational education, colleges & universities, economic education, engineering education, faculty development, literacy, minority education, private education (precollege), science/technology education, special education • *Health:* geriatric health, health organizations, hospices, hospitals, nursing services • *Science:* science exhibits & fairs, scientific institutes, scientific organizations • *Social Services:* aged, child welfare, community centers, community service organizations, counseling, disabled, drugs & alcohol, emergency relief, family services, recreation & athletics, united funds, volunteer services, youth organizations
Grant Types: capital, challenge, endowment, general support, project, and scholarship
Nonmonetary Support Types: donated equipment, in-kind services, and loaned executives
Note: Above figures include nonmonetary support, valued at $80,000 in 1989.
Geographic Distribution: primarily in southern California service area; limited giving elsewhere
Operating Locations: CA (Brea, Irvine, Rosemead, Seal Beach)
Note: Also, operates in 800 cities and communities in Southern California.

CORP. OFFICERS
John E. Bryson: *B* New York NY 1943 *ED* Stanford Univ BA 1965; Freie Univ Berlin 1965-66; Yale Univ JD 1969 *CURR EMPL* chmn, ceo: Southern CA Edison Co *CORP AFFIL* dir: Pacific Am Income Shares, Times Mirror Co *NONPR AFFIL* mem: CA Bar Assn, DC Bar Assn, Natl Assn Regulatory Utility Comrs, OR Bar Assn, Phi Beta Kappa, Stanford Univ Alumni Assn; mem bd editors, assoc editor: Yale Univ Law Journal; trust: CA Environmental Trust, Claremont Univ Ctr, Stanford Univ Grad Sch Alumni Assn, World Resources Inst

GIVING OFFICERS
Rebecca S. Jones: dir charitable contributions

APPLICATION INFORMATION
Initial Approach: *Initial Contact:* brief letter or proposal *Include Information On:* description of the organization, amount requested, purpose for which funds are sought, recently audited financial statement, proof of tax-exempt status *When to Submit:* any time **Restrictions on Giving:** Company does not support fraternal, political, veterans, religious organizations, or public agencies.

GRANTS ANALYSIS
Total Grants: $4,000,000*
Typical Range: $500 to $1,000
Disclosure Period: 1991
Note: Total grants figure is approximate. Recent grants are derived from a 1993 grants list.

RECENT GRANTS
3,500,000 Puzzle Factory — for production of a national public-education campaign for a new daily children's television series on PBS

Southern California Gas Co.
Sales: $2.92 billion
Employees: 9,562
Parent Company: Pacific Enterprises
Headquarters: Los Angeles, CA
SIC Major Group: Electric, Gas & Sanitary Services and Oil & Gas Extraction

CONTACT
Carolyn R. Williams
Community Outreach and Contributions Manager
Southern California Gas Co.
Terminal Annex ML 110H
PO Box 3249
Los Angeles, CA 90051
(213) 244-2555
Note: Contact above also handles noncash requests. See "Other Things You Should Know" for more details.

FINANCIAL SUMMARY
Recent Giving: $1,300,000 (1992 approx.); $1,400,000 (1991); $2,500,000 (1990)
Fiscal Note: Company gives directly.

CONTRIBUTIONS SUMMARY
Typical Recipients: • *Civic & Public Affairs:* environmental affairs, ethnic/minority organizations, urban & community affairs, women's affairs • *Education:* career/vocational education, engineering education, literacy, minority education, public education (precollege), science/technology education • *Health:* health funds • *Science:* science exhibits & fairs
Grant Types: general support and project
Geographic Distribution: awards grants only to organizations and activities located in company's service area in central and southern California
Operating Locations: CA (Fresno, Kern, Kings, Los Angeles, Orange, Riverside, San Luis Obispo, Santa Barbara, Ventura)

CORP. OFFICERS
Richard Donald Farman: *B* San Francisco CA 1935 *ED* Stanford Univ 1957; Stanford Univ 1963 *CURR EMPL* chmn, ceo, dir: Southern CA Gas Co *CORP AFFIL* dir: Assoc Electric & Gas Ins Svcs, Pacific Enterprises, Union Bank *NONPR AFFIL* dir: LA Sports Counc, Pub Svc Television Station KCET; exec comm: Central City Assn Los Angeles; mem: CA Bar Assn, Los Angeles Area Chamber Commerce, Pacific Coast Gas Assn, Town Hall CA, US Chamber Commerce; mem exec comm, dir: Am Gas Assn; mem: Am Bar Assn
Warren I. Mitchell: *B* Los Angeles CA 1937 *ED* Pepperdine Univ 1963; Pepperdine Univ 1965 *CURR EMPL* pres, dir: Southern CA Gas Co *NONPR AFFIL* dir: Gas Res Inst, Inst Gas Tech, Merchants & Mfrs Assn; mem: Am Gas Assn, Pacific Coast Gas Assn

GIVING OFFICERS
Carolyn R. Williams: contributions adm

APPLICATION INFORMATION
Initial Approach: *Initial Contact:* letter *Include Information On:* background of organization, including objectives, target groups, programs, and accomplishments to date; purpose for which funds are sought; recently audited financial statement and budget forecasts for current fiscal year; proof of tax-exempt status; provision of evaluative criteria; list of board members and affiliations, total budgets past and present, explanation of how previous donations made by Southern California Gas have helped fulfill organization's objectives, name and phone number of a contact in the organization *When to Submit:* any time
Restrictions on Giving: Does not fund endowments or contribute furniture, equipment, appliances, or salvaged material. Does not support individuals, commercial profit-making groups, fraternal groups, goodwill advertising, sectarian religious institutions, political organizations, or groups that already receive substantial support from the United Way. Arts support was discontinued in 1988.

OTHER THINGS TO KNOW
Company rarely makes multi-year grants; recreational programs rarely receive support. Southern California Gas Company stresses that the vast majority of grants are less than $1,000.
Contributions usually are unrestricted. Occasionally, company makes grants for capital improvements.
Southern California Gas had traditionally made grants on behalf of Pacific Enterprises. In 1988, Pacific Enterprises began administering an independent contributions program, totaling approximately $1.4 million annually. Its focuses are private education and arts in the Los Angeles area. For more information, contact Arnie Berghoff, Director, External Affairs, Pacific Enterprises, 633 West Fifth Street, Los Angeles, CA 90071-2006.
Southern California Gas Company has nine divisions which give locally. Larger grants are handled by Ms. Williams.

GRANTS ANALYSIS
Total Grants: $2,500,000
Number of Grants: 2,000*
Highest Grant: $35,000
Typical Range: $1,000 to $5,000
Disclosure Period: 1990
Note: Number of grants figure is approximate.

Southern Co. Services
Sales: $4.28 billion
Employees: 6,500
Parent Company: Southern Co.
Headquarters: Birmingham, AL
SIC Major Group: Electric, Gas & Sanitary Services and Engineering & Management Services

CONTACT
Dora Brandt
Community Affairs
Southern Co. Services, Inc.
PO Box 2625
Birmingham, AL 35202
(205) 870-6011

FINANCIAL SUMMARY
Fiscal Note: Company gives directly. Annual Giving Range: $1 million to $5 million

CONTRIBUTIONS SUMMARY
Typical Recipients: • *Civic & Public Affairs:* general • *Education:* general • *Health:* general • *Social Services:* general
Grant Types: employee matching gifts and general support
Nonmonetary Support Types: donated equipment, in-kind services, and loaned employees
Geographic Distribution: in headquarters and operating communities
Operating Locations: AL (Birmingham)

CORP. OFFICERS
Edward L. Addison: *B* Cottageville SC 1930 *ED* Univ SC BEE 1950 *CURR EMPL* chmn, dir: Southern Co Svcs *CORP AFFIL* dir: AL Power Co, CSX Corp, First Atlanta Corp, First Natl Bank Atlanta, GA Power Co, Gulf Power Co, MS Power Co, Phelps Dodge Corp, Protective Life Corp, Savannah Electric & Power Co, Southern Electric Generating Co, Southern Electric Intl, Southern Nuclear Operating Co, Wachovia Bank GA, Wachovia Corp; pres, ceo: Southern Co
H. Allen Franklin: *B* 1945 *ED* Univ AL BEE 1966 *CURR EMPL* pres, ceo, dir: Southern Co Svcs

GIVING OFFICERS
Dora Brandt: *CURR EMPL* commun aff: Southern Co Svcs

APPLICATION INFORMATION

Initial Approach: *Initial Contact:* one page letter *Include Information On:* contact name, address, and phone number; IRS classification; description of the organization and its objectives; amount sought; its intended purpose *When to Submit:* any time

Restrictions on Giving: Does not contribute to individuals; political organizations, candidates or activities; lobbying organizations; labor organizations; veteran, or fraternal, organizations; religious organizations, unless project benefits the entire community; and organizations without 501 (c)(3) status.

Also does not make grants in the form of advertising, deficit reduction, or to colleges and universities other than matching gifts.

OTHER THINGS TO KNOW

Each of the five electric utilities—Alabama Power Co., Georgia Power Co., Gulf Power Co., Mississippi Power Co., and Savannah Electric and Power—has its own chariable contributions program, which are carried on independently with their own applications and guidelines.

Publications: charitable contributions policy statement and application guidelines

Southern Connecticut Gas Co.

Sales: $179.0 million
Employees: 618
Parent Company: Connecticut Energy Corp.
Headquarters: Bridgeport, CT
SIC Major Group: Electric, Gas & Sanitary Services

CONTACT

Romilda R. Anderson
Director, Public Affairs
Southern Connecticut Gas Co.
885 Main St.
Bridgeport, CT 06601
(203) 382-8111

CONTRIBUTIONS SUMMARY

Operating Locations: CT
(Bridgeport)

CORP. OFFICERS

J. R. Crespo: *CURR EMPL* chmn, pres, ceo, dir: Southern CT Gas Co

Southern Furniture Co. / Bolick Foundation

Sales: $60.0 million
Employees: 900
Headquarters: Conover, NC
SIC Major Group: Furniture & Fixtures

CONTACT

Jerome W. Bolick
Trustee
Bolick Foundation
PO Box 307
Conover, NC 28613

FINANCIAL SUMMARY

Recent Giving: $121,400 (1990); $113,500 (1989)
Assets: $2,957,939 (1990); $2,682,534 (1989)
Gifts Received: $100,000 (1990); $50,000 (1989)
Fiscal Note: In 1990, contributions were received from Southern Furniture Co. of Conover.
EIN: 56-6086348

CONTRIBUTIONS SUMMARY

Typical Recipients: • *Civic & Public Affairs:* public policy • *Health:* hospices • *Religion:* churches, religious organizations • *Social Services:* community service organizations, recreation & athletics, united funds, youth organizations
Grant Types: general support
Operating Locations: NC (Conover)

CORP. OFFICERS

Jerome W. Bolick: *CURR EMPL* pres: Southern Furniture Co

GIVING OFFICERS

Jerome W. Bolick: trust *CURR EMPL* pres: Southern Furniture Co (see above)
O. W. Bolick: trust

APPLICATION INFORMATION

Initial Approach: Contributes only to preselected organizations.

GRANTS ANALYSIS

Number of Grants: 50
Highest Grant: $33,500
Typical Range: $500 to $2,500
Disclosure Period: 1990

RECENT GRANTS

33,500	Christian Education Funds, St. Louis, MO
19,000	Concordia Lutheran Church, Austin, TX
10,000	Concordia Seminary, St. Louis, MO
10,000	Hospice, St. Louis, MO
6,000	YMCA
5,000	Kairos Community Service, St. Louis, MO
3,000	Jesse Helms Center Foundation
2,500	K.C.M.S. Together We Can, St. Louis, MO
2,000	Camp Linn Haven, St. Louis, MO
2,000	Grace Lutheran Church, Ft. Lauderdale, FL

Southern Indiana Gas & Electric Co.

Sales: $747.4 million
Employees: 975
Headquarters: Evansville, IN
SIC Major Group: Electric, Gas & Sanitary Services

CONTACT

Greg McManus
Vice President and Dir. of Govt. Rel.
Southern Indiana Gas & Electric Co.
20 Northwest 4th St.
Evansville, IN 47741
(812) 424-6411

FINANCIAL SUMMARY

Fiscal Note: Annual Giving Range: $100,000 to $250,000

CONTRIBUTIONS SUMMARY

Company reports 30% of contributions support the arts; 30% to education; 20% to health and welfare; 10% to civic and public affairs; and 10% to other organizations.
Typical Recipients: • *Arts & Humanities:* general • *Civic & Public Affairs:* general • *Education:* general • *Social Services:* general
Grant Types: general support
Nonmonetary Support Types: cause-related marketing & promotion and loaned executives
Operating Locations: IN (Evansville)

CORP. OFFICERS

Ronald G. Reherman: *B* Evansville IN 1935 *ED* Univ Evansville 1958; IA St Univ Sch Bus Admin 1971 *CURR EMPL* pres, ceo, dir: Southern IN Gas & Electric Co *CORP AFFIL* dir: Natl City Bancshares *NONPR AFFIL* dir: IN Gas Assn

Norman P. Wagner: *B* Newark NJ 1924 *ED* Clemson Univ 1949 *CURR EMPL* chmn, dir: Southern IN Gas & Electric Co *CORP AFFIL* dir: Community Natural Gas, Evansville Brewing Co, IN KY Electric Corp, OH Valley Electric Co; mem, dir: CNB Bancshares; mem exec comm, dir: Intl Steel Co *NONPR AFFIL* dir: IN Electric Assn

APPLICATION INFORMATION

Initial Approach: Send brief letter of inquiry. There are no deadlines.

Southern Pacific Transportation Co.

Revenue: $2.5 billion
Employees: 22,000
Parent Company: Rio Grande Industries Inc.
Headquarters: San Francisco, CA
SIC Major Group: Railroad Transportation and Trucking & Warehousing

CONTACT

Nancy Russell
Manager, Administration
Southern Pacific Transportation Co.
One Market Plz.
San Francisco, CA 94105
(415) 541-2101

CONTRIBUTIONS SUMMARY

Operating Locations: CA (San Francisco)

CORP. OFFICERS

D. M. Mohan: *CURR EMPL* pres: Southern Pacific Transportation Co

Southland Corp.

Sales: $8.1 billion
Employees: 45,665
Headquarters: Dallas, TX
SIC Major Group: Food & Kindred Products, Food Stores, Holding & Other Investment Offices, and Wholesale Trade—Nondurable Goods

CONTACT
John Rodgers
Sr. Vice President, Chief
  Administrative Officer
The Southland Corporation
2711 North Haskell Ave.
Dallas, TX 75204
(214) 828-7255

FINANCIAL SUMMARY
Recent Giving: $1,000,000
(1992 approx.); $554,000
(1991); $800,000 (1990)
Fiscal Note: Company gives directly.

CONTRIBUTIONS SUMMARY
Typical Recipients: • *Arts & Humanities:* general • *Civic & Public Affairs:* general • *Education:* general, literacy • *Health:* general • *Social Services:* general

Grant Types: award, conference/seminar, emergency, general support, multiyear/continuing support, research, and scholarship

Nonmonetary Support Types: cause-related marketing & promotion, donated equipment, donated products, in-kind services, and workplace solicitation

Geographic Distribution: Dallas, TX and operating locations

Operating Locations: CA (Brea, La Mesa, Pleasanton), CO (Englewood), FL (Orlando), MI (Novi), NV (Los Vegas), NY (Smithtown), OR (Portland), PA (Willow Grove), TX (Dallas), VA (Alexandria, Virginia Beach)

CORP. OFFICERS
S. R. Dole: *CURR EMPL* exec vp, coo: Southland Corp *CORP AFFIL* coo: 7-Eleven Stores
Frank J. Gangi: *B* Passaic NJ 1941 *CURR EMPL* sr vp, cfo: Southland Corp *CORP AFFIL* div mgr: Singer Co; sr acct: Intl Bus Machines Corp
Masatoshi Ito: *B* 1924 *CURR EMPL* chmn: Southland Corp *CORP AFFIL* chmn: Dennys Japan Co Ltd, Famil Co, Marudai Co, Maryann Co, Seven Eleven Japan Co Ltd, Stepe Co, Umeya Co, York Keibi Co, York Mart Co; chmn, dir: IYG Holding Corp, Southland Corp; dir: Seven Eleven Hawaii, Shop Am Ltd; pres: Oshmans Japan Co, Robinsons Japan Co, York Matausakaya Co
Stephen B. Krumholz: *B* Peoria IL 1949 *CURR EMPL* sr vp

7-Eleven Stores: Southland Corp
Clark J. Matthews II: *B* Arkansas City KS 1936 *CURR EMPL* ceo, pres, dir: Southland Corp *NONPR AFFIL* mem: Alpha Tau Omega, Am Bar Assn, Am Judicature Soc, Dallas Bar Assn, Pi Alpha Delta, TX Bar Assn

GIVING OFFICERS
John Hunter Rodgers: sr vp, chief admin off, gen couns, secy *B* Lubbock TX 1944 *ED* TX A&M Univ BA 1966; Univ TX JD 1969 *CURR EMPL* sr vp, chief admin off, gen couns, secy: Southland Corp *NONPR AFFIL* dir: Jr Achievement Dallas; mem: Am Bar Assn, Dallas Bar Assn, Dallas Citizens Counc, Southwestern Legal Fdn, TX A&M Univ Visual Arts Comm, TX Bar Assn; trust: Boys & Girls Clubs Am

APPLICATION INFORMATION
Initial Approach: *Initial Contact:* brief letter of inquiry *Include Information On:* description of the organization, amount requested, purpose for which funds are sought, recently audited financial statement, and proof of tax-exempt status *When to Submit:* any time
Restrictions on Giving: Does not make political contributions.

GRANTS ANALYSIS
Total Grants: $554,000
Typical Range: $1,000 to $2,500
Disclosure Period: 1991
Note: Recent grants are derived from a 1991 grants list.

RECENT GRANTS
100 Boys and Girls Club, Dallas, TX
100 Dallas County Adult Literacy Council, Dallas, TX
100 Dallas County Community College District, Dallas, TX
100 Dallas Museum of Art, Dallas, TX
100 Junior Achievement, Dallas, TX
100 National Commission Against Drunk Driving, Washington, DC
100 National Crime Prevention Council, Washington, DC

100 Richardson Medical Center, Richardson, TX
100 Texas Foundation for Visually Impaired Children, Dallas, TX

Southmark Corp. / Southmark Foundation on Gerontology
Sales: $62.3 million
Employees: 147
Headquarters: Dallas, TX
SIC Major Group: Holding & Other Investment Offices and Real Estate

CONTACT
Richard P. Conard
Vice President
Southmark Fdn. on Gerontology
2711 LBJ Fwy., Ste. 900
Dallas, TX 75234
(813) 792-7572

CONTRIBUTIONS SUMMARY
Operating Locations: FL (Bradenton), TX (Dallas)

CORP. OFFICERS
Glen Adams: *CURR EMPL* ceo, pres: Southmark Corp
Donald W. Hair: *CURR EMPL* vp, cfo: Southmark Corp

Southtrust Corp.
Assets: $10.15 billion
Employees: 6,000
Headquarters: Birmingham, AL
SIC Major Group: Depository Institutions and Holding & Other Investment Offices

CONTACT
Lisa Moorer
Personnel
Southtrust Corp.
PO Box 2554
Birmingham, AL 35290
(205) 254-5509

FINANCIAL SUMMARY
Fiscal Note: Annual Giving Range: $100,000 to $250,000

CONTRIBUTIONS SUMMARY
Company reports 75% of contributions support health and welfare; and 25% to the arts.
Typical Recipients: • *Arts & Humanities:* general • *Social Services:* general
Grant Types: general support

Nonmonetary Support Types: cause-related marketing & promotion, loaned employees, loaned executives, and workplace solicitation
Operating Locations: AL (Alexander City, Anniston, Auburn, Bay Minette, Birmingham, Boaz, Cullman, Dothan, Elba, Florence, Gadsden, Hartselle, Heflin, Huntsville, Jasper, Lineville, Mobile, Montgomery, Northport, Ozark, Phenix City, Roanoke, Selma, Sulacauga), FL (Jacksonville, Marianna, Ocala, Sarasota, South Daytona, St. Petersburg, Tampa), SC (Charleston), TN (Nashville)
Note: Operating names have the city or county attached to the bank, such as SouthTrust Bank of Mobile.

CORP. OFFICERS
Roy W. Gilbert, Jr.: *CURR EMPL* pres, dir: Southtrust Corp
Wallace D. Malone, Jr.: *B* Dothan AL 1936 *ED* Univ AL 1957; Univ PA 1960 *CURR EMPL* chmn, ceo, dir: Southtrust Corp

APPLICATION INFORMATION
Initial Approach: Send brief letter of inquiry. There are no deadlines.

Southways Foundation

CONTACT
Don Morrison
Vice President and Treasurer
Southways Fdn.
c/o Sargent Management Co.
1300 TCF Tower
Minneapolis, MN 55402
(612) 338-3871

FINANCIAL SUMMARY
Recent Giving: $441,726
(1990); $721,198 (1989)
Assets: $5,548,023 (1990); $6,043,540 (1989)
Gifts Received: $1,417 (1990)
EIN: 41-6018502

CONTRIBUTIONS SUMMARY
Donor(s): the late John S. Pillsbury and family
Typical Recipients: • *Arts & Humanities:* arts centers, arts institutes, community arts, music, theater • *Civic & Public Affairs:* urban & community affairs • *Education:* colleges &

universities, legal education, private education (precollege) • *Health:* single-disease health associations • *Social Services:* animal protection, child welfare, youth organizations
Grant Types: capital, endowment, and general support
Geographic Distribution: focus on MN

GIVING OFFICERS
Ella P. Crosby: trust
Lucy C. Mitchell: trust
Donald K. Morrison: vp, treas
George Sturgis Pillsbury: secy, trust *B* Crystal Bay MN 1921 *ED* Yale Univ AB 1943 *CURR EMPL* chmn: Sargent Mgmt Co *CORP AFFIL* chmn: Sargent Mgmt Co
Mrs. John S. Pillsbury: trust
John S. Pillsbury III: vp, trust
John S. Pillsbury, Jr.: pres, trust
Jane P. Resor: trust

APPLICATION INFORMATION
Initial Approach: Send cover letter and full proposal. There are no deadlines.

GRANTS ANALYSIS
Number of Grants: 100
Highest Grant: $50,000
Typical Range: $500 to $10,000
Disclosure Period: 1990

RECENT GRANTS
50,000　Minneapolis Institute of Arts, Minneapolis, MN
32,000　United Way, Minneapolis, MN
20,500　Blake School, Hopkins, MN
20,000　St. Paul's School, Concord, NH
16,150　Walker Art Center, Minneapolis, MN
15,000　Guthrie Theater, Minneapolis, MN
11,000　Smith College, Northampton, MA
10,000　Guthrie Theater, Minneapolis, MN
10,000　Walker Art Center, Minneapolis, MN
7,500　Albany Symphony Orchestra, New York, NY

Southwest Airlines Co.
Revenue: $1.31 billion
Employees: 9,778
Headquarters: Dallas, TX
SIC Major Group:
　Transportation by Air

CONTACT
Colleen C. Barrett
Vice President, Administration
Southwest Airlines Co.
PO Box 36611,
Dallas, TX 75235-1611
(214) 904-5559

CONTRIBUTIONS SUMMARY
Operating Locations: TX (Dallas)

CORP. OFFICERS
Gary A. Barron: *CURR EMPL* exec vp, coo: Southwest Airlines Co
Herbert D. Kelleher: *CURR EMPL* chmn, pres, ceo: Southwest Airlines Co

Southwest Gas Corp. / Southwest Gas Corp. Foundation
Assets: $794.79 million
Employees: 2,243
Headquarters: Las Vegas, NV
SIC Major Group: Depository Institutions, Electric, Gas & Sanitary Services, and Real Estate

CONTACT
Delores Nielsen
Assistant to the Chairman
Southwest Gas Corp.
PO Box 98510
Las Vegas, NV 89193-8510
(702) 876-7299

FINANCIAL SUMMARY
Recent Giving: $350,002 (1991); $145,894 (1989)
Assets: $502,325 (1991); $784,480 (1989)
Gifts Received: $382,000 (1991); $497,808 (1989)
Fiscal Note: Contributes through foundation only. In 1991, contributions were received from the Southwest Gas Corporation.
EIN: 94-2988564

CONTRIBUTIONS SUMMARY
Typical Recipients: • *Arts & Humanities:* community arts, museums/galleries, performing

arts, theater • *Education:* colleges & universities, legal education • *Social Services:* community service organizations, united funds, youth organizations
Grant Types: general support
Geographic Distribution: in headquarters and operating communities
Operating Locations: NV (Boulder City, Carson City, Gardnerville, Las Vegas, Reno, Sparks)

CORP. OFFICERS
Kenny C. Guinn: *B* 1936 *ED* Fresno Univ MA; UT St Univ PhD *CURR EMPL* chmn, ceo: PriMerit Bank *CORP AFFIL* chmn, ceo: Southwest Gas Corp; chmn, ceo, dir: Southwest Gas Corp
Michael Otis Maffie: *B* Los Angeles CA 1948 *ED* Univ Southern CA BS 1969; Univ Southern CA MBA 1971 *CURR EMPL* pres, coo, dir: Southwest Gas Corp *CORP AFFIL* pres, coo, dir: Southwest Gas Corp

GIVING OFFICERS
Fred W. Cover: trust *B* San Diego CA 1942 *ED* Univ San Diego 1964; Univ Dallas *CURR EMPL* sr vp: Southwest Gas Corp *CORP AFFIL* sr vp: Southwest Gas Corp *NONPR AFFIL* mem: Am Gas Assn, Am Mgmt Assn
Kenny C. Guinn: trust *CURR EMPL* chmn, ceo: PriMerit Bank (see above)
Michael Otis Maffie: trust *CURR EMPL* pres, coo, dir: Southwest Gas Corp (see above)

APPLICATION INFORMATION
Initial Approach: *Initial Contact:* brief letter of inquiry *Include Information On:* description of the organization, amount requested, recently audited financial statement, and proof of tax-exempt status *When to Submit:* any time

GRANTS ANALYSIS
Total Grants: $350,002
Number of Grants: 220
Highest Grant: $60,408
Typical Range: $250 to $2,500
Disclosure Period: 1991
Note: Recent grants are derived from a 1991 grants list.

RECENT GRANTS
60,408　United Way, Las Vegas, NV

29,225　University of Nevada Las Vegas Foundation, Las Vegas, NV
25,000　Arizona State University, Tempe, AZ
20,000　University of Arizona, Tucson, AZ
6,500　Las Vegas Symphony Orchestra, Las Vegas, NV
6,350　Salvation Army, Las Vegas, NV
6,000　Community Food Bank, Las Vegas, NV
6,000　Phoenix Symphony, Phoenix, AZ
5,000　Adopt-A-Family, Las Vegas, NV
5,000　Brewery Arts Center, Carson City, NV

Southwestern Bell Corp. / Southwestern Bell Foundation
Revenue: $10.01 billion
Employees: 59,500
Headquarters: St. Louis, MO
SIC Major Group:
　Communications

CONTACT
Charles DeRiemer
Executive Director
Southwestern Bell Fdn.
175 E Houston, Ste. 200
San Antonio, TX 78205
(210) 351-2208

FINANCIAL SUMMARY
Recent Giving: $14,000,000 (1992 approx.); $14,896,466 (1991); $15,716,000 (1990)
Assets: $34,300,000 (1991); $40,735,576 (1989); $33,903,516 (1988)
Fiscal Note: Some company departments make contributions directly from corporate funds. This amount is not included in the figures above.
EIN: 43-1353948

CONTRIBUTIONS SUMMARY
Typical Recipients: • *Arts & Humanities:* arts appreciation, arts associations, arts centers, arts festivals, arts funds, arts institutes, cinema, community arts, dance, ethnic arts, history/historic preservation, libraries, museums/galleries, music, opera, performing arts, public broadcasting, theater • *Civic & Public Affairs:* economic development, public

policy, urban & community affairs, zoos/botanical gardens • *Education:* arts education, business education, career/vocational education, colleges & universities, education funds, engineering education, faculty development, literacy, minority education, public education (precollege), science/technology education, special education • *Social Services:* aged, child welfare, community service organizations, disabled, drugs & alcohol, family services, recreation & athletics, shelters/homelessness, united funds, volunteer services, youth organizations

Grant Types: employee matching gifts and project

Geographic Distribution: nationally, with emphasis on corporate operating locations

Operating Locations: AR, KS, MO, NJ, OK, TX

CORP. OFFICERS

James R. Adams: *B* Jefferson TX 1939 *ED* TX A&M Univ BA; Univ TX MBA *CURR EMPL* pres, ceo: Southwestern Bell Telephone

Gerald D. Blatherwick: *B* Kansas City MO 1936 *ED* Univ KS BS 1958 *CURR EMPL* vchmn, dir: Southwestern Bell Corp *CORP AFFIL* chmn: Asset Mgmt Inc; dir: Centerre Trust Co, Metromedia Paging Svcs, Southwestern Bell Mobile Sys Inc, Southwestern Bell Telephone *NONPR AFFIL* chmn: Am Counc Arts; chmn emeritus: Dance St Louis; dir: Arthur W Page Soc, Mary Inst St Louis, Natl Action Counc Minorities Engg, Natl Assn Mfrs, St Louis Symphony Orchestra, St Louis Variety Club, US Telephone Assn

Robert G. Pope: *B* Greenville TX 1935 *ED* Southern Methodist Univ BSME 1958 *CURR EMPL* vchmn, cfo, dir: Southwestern Bell Corp *CORP AFFIL* dir: Boatmens Bancshares *NONPR AFFIL* mem: MO Soc Professional Engrs, NSPE; mem adv bd: Battery Ventures; mem gov bd: Lutheran Med Ctr; trust: Maryville Coll

Edward E. Whitacre, Jr.: *B* Ennis TX 1941 *ED* TX Tech Univ BS 1964 *CURR EMPL* chmn, ceo, dir: Southwestern Bell Corp *CORP AFFIL* dir: Anheuser-Busch Cos, May Dept Stores Co, Mercantile Bancorp *NONPR AFFIL* dir:

Boy Scouts Am, St Louis Art Mus

GIVING OFFICERS

James R. Adams: dir *CURR EMPL* pres, ceo: Southwestern Bell Telephone (see above)

Larry J. Alexander: pres

Gerald D. Blatherwick: pres, dir *CURR EMPL* vchmn, dir: Southwestern Bell Corp (see above)

Royce S. Caldwell: dir

Charles O. DeRiemer: vp, exec dir

James D. Ellis: dir *B* 1943 *CURR EMPL* sr exec vp, gen coun: Southwestern Bell Corp

Charles E. Foster: dir

Robert G. Pope: dir *CURR EMPL* vchmn, cfo, dir: Southwestern Bell Corp (see above)

Harold E. Rainbolt: vp, secy *B* Norman OK 1929 *ED* Univ OK 1951 *CURR EMPL* chmn: BancFirst Corp *CORP AFFIL* dir: First Natl Bank, Trend Venture Corp; owner: Trencor

Roger W. Wohlert: vp, treas

APPLICATION INFORMATION

Initial Approach: *Initial Contact:* grant requests of a local or statewide nature should be sent to local subsidiary or division; requests of a regional or national nature should be addressed directly to the Foundation's executive director *Include Information On:* proof of tax-exempt status; brief statement of history and accomplishments; statement of current objectives, including problem being addressed, program budget and amount sought; linkage of project's goals to the Foundation's priorities; timetable for implementation and description of expected results; details of fund-raising plans, including sources, amounts, and commitments; plans for sustaining activities after conclusion of foundation support; annual report or budget for organization, showing all income sources and expenditures; list of board members; list of accrediting agencies *When to Submit:* any time; however, organizations are asked not to submit a proposal more than once in a 12-month period

Restrictions on Giving: Foundation does not support private foundations or organizations without tax-exempt status; organizations that practice discrimination by race, color,

creed, sex, age, or national origin; hospital operating funds or capital funds; organizations supported by United Way; individuals; political activities or organizations; religious organizations; fraternal, veterans, or labor groups when serving only their membership; or special occasion goodwill advertising and ticket or dinner purchases.

OTHER THINGS TO KNOW

Foundation states a preference for organizations that operate in corporate operating locations and in communities where a significant number of employees live; project-oriented proposals rather than requests for grants to underwrite operating or capital budgets; projects that promote citizen participation and voluntarism; projects that generate public awareness and offer opportunities to leverage contributions; projects that address human needs and whose services are provided directly rather than through intermediary organizations; and projects that develop leadership skills.

Publications: contributions guidelines

GRANTS ANALYSIS

Total Grants: $14,896,466

Number of Grants: 1,933

Highest Grant: $817,000

Typical Range: $1,000 to $10,000

Disclosure Period: 1991

Note: Recent grants are derived from a 1990 Form 990.

RECENT GRANTS

700,000 Grand Center, St. Louis, MO

300,000 Education Commission of the States, Denver, CO

300,000 St. Louis Science Center, St. Louis, MO

300,000 St. Louis Zoological Society, St. Louis, MO

250,000 National Gallery of Art, Washington, DC — Paul Strand Exhibition

205,000 Kansas University Endowment Association, Lawrence, KS

200,000 Missouri Botanical Garden, St. Louis, MO

200,000 University of Missouri, Columbia, MO — Columbia

200,000 Washington University, St. Louis, MO

179,500 Texas Independent College Fund, Ft. Worth, TX

Southwestern Electric Power Co.

Assets: $1.85 billion

Employees: 1,959

Parent Company: Central & South West Corp.

Headquarters: Shreveport, LA

SIC Major Group: Electric, Gas & Sanitary Services

CONTACT

Michael Heard

Vice President, Operations

Southwestern Electric Power Co.

PO Box 21106

Shreveport, LA 71156

(318) 222-2141

CONTRIBUTIONS SUMMARY

Operating Locations: LA (Shreveport)

CORP. OFFICERS

Richard H. Bremer: *CURR EMPL* ceo, pres: Southwestern Electric Power Co

Southwestern Life Insurance Co.

Premiums: $124.4 million

Employees: 558

Parent Company: I.C.H. Corp.

Headquarters: Dallas, TX

SIC Major Group: Insurance Carriers and Security & Commodity Brokers

CONTACT

Mary Lindle

Corporate Tax Department

Southwestern Life Insurance Co.

PO Box 2699, Rm. 1219

Dallas, TX 75221

(214) 954-7111

CONTRIBUTIONS SUMMARY

Operating Locations: TX (Dallas)

CORP. OFFICERS

Thomas Brophy: *CURR EMPL* pres, dir: Southwestern Life Ins Co

Southwestern Public Service Co.

Assets: $1.67 billion
Employees: 2,026
Headquarters: Amarillo, TX
SIC Major Group: Electric, Gas & Sanitary Services

CONTACT
Lewis Thomas
District Manager
Southwestern Public Service Co.
PO Box 1261
Amarillo, TX 79170
(806) 378-2121

FINANCIAL SUMMARY
Fiscal Note: Annual Giving Range: $100,000 to $250,000

CONTRIBUTIONS SUMMARY
Company reports 71% of contributions support civic and public affairs; 18% to education; 9% to health and welfare; and 1% to the arts.
Typical Recipients: • *Arts & Humanities:* general • *Civic & Public Affairs:* general • *Education:* general • *Social Services:* general
Grant Types: general support
Nonmonetary Support Types: donated equipment and loaned executives
Operating Locations: TX (Amarillo)

CORP. OFFICERS
Bill D. Helton: *B* Wheeler TX 1938 *ED* TX Tech Univ 1964 *CURR EMPL* pres, coo, dir: Southwestern Pub Svc Co

APPLICATION INFORMATION
Initial Approach: Send brief letter of inquiry. There are no deadlines.

Southwire Co.

Sales: $1.33 billion
Employees: 5,000
Headquarters: Carrolton, GA
SIC Major Group: Primary Metal Industries

CONTACT
Cheryl Stephenson
Asst. V.P., Corporate Communications
Southwire Co.
PO Box 1000
Carrolton, GA 30119
(404) 832-4242
Note: Cheryl Stephenson's extension is 4512.

FINANCIAL SUMMARY
Fiscal Note: Annual Giving Range: less than $100,000

CONTRIBUTIONS SUMMARY
Small program focusing on community needs.
Nonmonetary Support Types: donated equipment and donated products
Operating Locations: GA (Carrollton)

CORP. OFFICERS
Roy Richards, Jr.: *CURR EMPL* ceo, pres: Southwire Co

Spahn & Rose Lumber Co. / Spahn & Rose Lumber Co. Charitable Foundation

Employees: 195
Headquarters: Dubuque, IA

CONTACT
C. D. Spahn
President
Spahn & Rose Lumber Co.
c/o First National Bank of Dubuque
Seventh at Town Clock Plaza
Dubuque, IA 52001
(319) 582-3606

FINANCIAL SUMMARY
Recent Giving: $45,540 (fiscal 1992); $53,275 (fiscal 1990)
Assets: $693,324 (fiscal year ending January 31, 1992); $566,653 (fiscal 1990)
Gifts Received: $75,000 (fiscal 1992); $55,000 (fiscal 1990)
Fiscal Note: In fiscal 1992, contributions were received from Spahn and Rose Lumber Company.
EIN: 42-6234027

CONTRIBUTIONS SUMMARY
Typical Recipients: • *Civic & Public Affairs:* rural affairs • *Education:* colleges & universities, public education (precollege) • *Health:* hospitals • *Social Services:* united funds, youth organizations
Grant Types: general support
Geographic Distribution: giving primarily in Dubuque, IA
Operating Locations: IA (Dubuque)

CORP. OFFICERS
F.C. Altman: *CURR EMPL* chmn, ceo: Spahn & Rose Lumber Co
C.D. Spahn: *CURR EMPL* pres: Spahn & Rose Lumber Co

GIVING OFFICERS
R.K. Gutherie: dir
C.D. Spahn: dir *CURR EMPL* pres: Spahn & Rose Lumber Co (see above)

APPLICATION INFORMATION
Initial Approach: Applications not accepted. The foundation reports it supports preselected organizations.

GRANTS ANALYSIS
Number of Grants: 41
Highest Grant: $6,300
Typical Range: $500 to $2,000
Disclosure Period: fiscal year ending January 31, 1992

RECENT GRANTS
6,300 United Way, Dubuque, IA
5,000 Loras College, Dubuque, IA
5,000 University of Dubuque, Dubuque, IA
4,000 Clarke College, Dubuque, IA
2,500 Finley Hospital, Dubuque, IA
2,000 Boys Club of America, Dubuque, IA
2,000 Iowa College Foundation, Des Moines, IA
1,750 Wahlert High School, Dubuque, IA
1,500 Albrecht Acre, Sherrill, IA
1,500 Mercy Medical Center, Cedar Rapids, IA

Spalding Health Care Trust

CONTACT
Spalding Health Care Trust
c/o First Union National Bank, Trust Tax Department
Charlotte, NC 28288-0000

FINANCIAL SUMMARY
Recent Giving: $757,133 (1990)
Assets: $8,081,213 (1990)
Gifts Received: $688,626 (1990)
EIN: 58-1657005

CONTRIBUTIONS SUMMARY
Typical Recipients: • *Health:* hospitals
Grant Types: general support

APPLICATION INFORMATION
Initial Approach: The foundation reports it only makes contributions to preselected organizations and does not accept unsolicited requests for funds.

GRANTS ANALYSIS
Total Grants: $757,133
Number of Grants: 1
Highest Grant: $757,133
Disclosure Period: 1990

RECENT GRANTS
757,133 AMI Hospital, GA

Spang & Co. / Spang & Co. Charitable Trust

Sales: $87.0 million
Employees: 1,200
Headquarters: Butler, PA
SIC Major Group: Electronic & Other Electrical Equipment and Stone, Clay & Glass Products

CONTACT
C.R. Dorsch
Vice President, Finance
Spang & Co. Charitable Trust
c/o Union National Bank of Pittsburgh, PO Box 751
Butler, PA 16003-0751
(412) 287-8781

FINANCIAL SUMMARY
Recent Giving: $73,611 (1991); $71,986 (1990); $76,003 (1989)
Assets: $976,877 (1991); $905,973 (1990); $882,426 (1989)

Gifts Received: $15,365 (1991); $14,710 (1990); $15,800 (1989)
Fiscal Note: In 1991, contributions were received from employees of Spang & Co.
EIN: 25-6020192

CONTRIBUTIONS SUMMARY
Typical Recipients: • *Civic & Public Affairs:* economics • *Education:* colleges & universities, medical education, special education • *Health:* hospitals, medical research, pediatric health, single-disease health associations • *Social Services:* child welfare, community service organizations, disabled, united funds, youth organizations
Grant Types: general support
Geographic Distribution: focus on PA
Operating Locations: PA (Butler)

CORP. OFFICERS
Frank E. Rath: *CURR EMPL* chmn, dir: Spang & Co
Frank E. Rath, Jr.: *CURR EMPL* pres, dir: Spang & Co
Robert A. Rath: *CURR EMPL* vchmn: Spang & Co

GIVING OFFICERS
Frank E. Rath, Jr.: trust *CURR EMPL* pres, dir: Spang & Co (see above)

APPLICATION INFORMATION
Initial Approach: Send brief letter describing program. There are no deadlines.

GRANTS ANALYSIS
Number of Grants: 61
Highest Grant: $20,000
Typical Range: $100 to $1,000
Disclosure Period: 1991

RECENT GRANTS
20,000 United Way, Butler, PA
10,000 Johns Hopkins University Hospital, Baltimore, MD
5,000 Easter Seal Society, Butler, PA
5,000 Girl Scouts of America, Butler, PA
5,000 Presbyterian University Hospital, Pittsburgh, PA
5,000 West Penn Hospital, Pittsburgh, PA
1,500 Pittsburgh Public Theatre, Pittsburgh, PA
1,342 Children's Hospital, Pittsburgh, PA
1,000 School for Blind Children, Pittsburgh, PA
700 Pennsylvania Economic League, Butler, PA

Sparton Corp.
Sales: $214.4 million
Employees: 2,500
Headquarters: Jackson, MI
SIC Major Group: Electronic & Other Electrical Equipment, Fabricated Metal Products, Instruments & Related Products, and Oil & Gas Extraction

CONTACT
John J. Smith
Chairman
Sparton Corp.
2400 East Ganson St.
Jackson, MI 49202
(517) 787-8600

CONTRIBUTIONS SUMMARY
Operating Locations: MI (Jackson)

CORP. OFFICERS
David W. Hockenbrocht: *CURR EMPL* pres, coo: Sparton Corp
John J. Smith: *CURR EMPL* chmn, ceo: Sparton Corp

Spartus Corp.
Sales: $68.0 million
Employees: 700
Parent Company: Hanson Industries
Headquarters: Arlington Heights, IL
SIC Major Group: Electronic & Other Electrical Equipment and Instruments & Related Products

CONTACT
Kevin Crosthwaite
Chief Executive Officer
Spartus Corp.
3250 North Arlington Heights Rd.
Arlington Heights, IL 60004
(708) 870-7777

CONTRIBUTIONS SUMMARY
Operating Locations: IL (Arlington Heights)

CORP. OFFICERS
Kevin C. Crosthwaite: *CURR EMPL* pres: Spartus Corp
Wilfred E. Gustafson: *CURR EMPL* chmn, ceo: Spartus Corp

OTHER THINGS TO KNOW
Company is an original donor to the Galter Foundation.

Speas Foundation, Victor E.

CONTACT
David P. Ross
Senior Vice President
Victor E. Speas Foundation
c/o Boatmen's First National Bank of Kansas City
14 West Tenth St.
Kansas City, MO 64183
(816) 221-2800

FINANCIAL SUMMARY
Recent Giving: $1,277,125 (1990); $1,262,212 (1989); $1,057,376 (1988)
Assets: $21,097,613 (1990); $18,296,135 (1989); $18,955,082 (1988)
Gifts Received: $6,165 (1989); $17,769 (1987)
EIN: 44-6008346

CONTRIBUTIONS SUMMARY
Donor(s): Victor E. Speas, the late chairman of Speas Company, established the foundation bearing his name as a trust in 1947. Both Mr. Speas and the Speas Company, a vinegar and apple products manufacturing firm, contributed to the foundation.
Typical Recipients: • *Education:* colleges & universities, health & physical education, medical education, science/technology education • *Health:* emergency/ambulance services, geriatric health, health funds, health organizations, hospitals, medical rehabilitation, mental health, nursing services, nutrition & health maintenance, outpatient health care delivery, pediatric health, public health, single-disease health associations • *Social Services:* aged, child welfare, community centers, disabled, drugs & alcohol, family services, homes, shelters/homelessness, volunteer services
Grant Types: capital, challenge, general support, project, and seed money
Geographic Distribution: metropolitan Kansas City, MO

GIVING OFFICERS
David P. Ross: bank rep, contact person *CURR EMPL* sr vp:

Boatmens First Natl Bank Kansas City

APPLICATION INFORMATION
Initial Approach:
An initial phone call is suggested. There are no formal application forms.
Initial applications should be no more than three pages and should include the appropriate attachments. Eligible grantees will be asked to submit one copy of a full proposal. Interviews may be requested if the foundation is interested in a submitted proposal.
There are no application deadlines; the board meets on a bimonthly basis.
Notification, if funding will be provided, normally takes about two months.
Restrictions on Giving: Funding is restricted to improving the quality of health care in the Kansas City area. Grants are not made for endowment campaigns.

OTHER THINGS TO KNOW
Boatmen's First National Bank of Kansas City serves as a corporate trustee for the foundation. The Victor E. Speas Foundation and the John W. and Effie E. Speas Memorial Trust are affiliated.

GRANTS ANALYSIS
Total Grants: $1,277,125
Number of Grants: 73
Highest Grant: $100,000
Typical Range: $10,000 to $50,000
Disclosure Period: 1990
Note: The average grant figure excludes grants of $100,000; $75,000; and $71,000. Recent grants are derived from a 1990 Form 990.

RECENT GRANTS
100,000 Avila College, Kansas City, MO — support of strategic response to nursing in 90's
75,000 Greater Kansas City Community Foundation, Kansas City, MO — assist funding a comprehensive health clinic
71,000 Ozanam Home for Boys, Kansas City, MO — support joint special consultation team program unit

50,000 Kansas City Association for the Blind, Kansas City, MO — for purchase of plastic blow molding equipment

50,000 Rockhurst College, Kansas City, MO — support of revolving loan fund for accelerated nursing degree options

50,000 William Jewell College, Liberty, MO — scientific teaching equipment

42,000 Truman Medical Center, Kansas City, MO — support of nursing services Manpower Development Program

39,250 Sharenet Association, Independence, MO — support of Phase II of telecommunications system

33,000 Community Blood Center of Greater Kansas City, Kansas City, MO — clinical research

30,000 Adolescent Resources, Kansas City, MO — support health track coalition

Speas Memorial Trust, John W. and Effie E.

CONTACT
David P. Ross
Senior Vice President
John W. and Effie E. Speas Memorial Trust
c/o Boatmen's First National Bank of Kansas City
PO Box 419038
Kansas City, MO 64183
(816) 221-2800

FINANCIAL SUMMARY
Recent Giving: $1,254,160 (1990); $1,189,129 (1989); $1,159,862 (1988)
Assets: $21,107,140 (1990); $21,725,953 (1989); $18,721,268 (1988)
EIN: 44-6008249

CONTRIBUTIONS SUMMARY
Donor(s): The John W. and Effie E. Speas Memorial Trust was established in 1947. Both this foundation and the Victor E. Speas Foundation, also established in 1947, reflect the philanthropic concerns of members of the Speas family.
Typical Recipients: • *Education:* community & junior colleges, medical education • *Health:* health organizations, hospitals, medical research, medical training, mental health, nursing services • *Social Services:* child welfare, community centers, shelters/homelessness
Grant Types: capital, challenge, general support, project, research, and seed money
Geographic Distribution: Jackson, Clay, Platte, and Cass counties, MO; and Wyandotte and Johnson counties, KS

GIVING OFFICERS
David P. Ross: bank rep, contact person *CURR EMPL* sr vp: Boatmens First Natl Bank Kansas City

APPLICATION INFORMATION
Initial Approach:
A preliminary phone call is requested. If interested, the trust will request a complete project proposal.
The board meets twice a month; applications should be in the form of a three page letter with the appropriate attachments and may be submitted any time.
Notification follows about two months after receipt of proposal.
Restrictions on Giving: The trust does not fund individuals or endowments.

OTHER THINGS TO KNOW
Boatmen's First National Bank of Kansas City serves as the corporate trustee. The John W. and Effie E. Speas Memorial Trust and the Victor E. Speas Foundaton are affiliated.

GRANTS ANALYSIS
Total Grants: $1,254,160
Number of Grants: 26
Highest Grant: $250,000
Typical Range: $12,000 to $75,000
Disclosure Period: 1990
Note: Recent grants are derived from a 1990 grants list..

RECENT GRANTS
250,000 Children's Mercy Hospital, Kansas City, MO — support of capital campaign

109,144 Adolescent Resources Corporation, Kansas City, MO — support of health track

100,000 St. Luke's Hospital Foundation, Kansas City, MO — to establish a geriatric assessment program

92,000 Research Foundation, Kansas City, MO — in support of research project involving implantable insulin pumps

80,000 Samuel U. Rodgers Community Health Center, Kansas City, MO — in support of development of comprehensive eye center

80,000 University of Kansas Endowment Fund, Kansas City, KS — in support of strengthen nutrition education programs

79,000 Menorah Medical Center, Kansas City, MO — to renovate and furnish their new mother/baby unit

75,000 St. Joseph Health Center Foundation, Kansas City, MO — for construction of new community center for health education

60,000 Spelman Memorial Hospital, Smithville, MO — to establish older adult memory assessment program

50,000 Excelsior Springs Medical Center, Excelsior Springs, MO — for expansion of out-patient addition

Special People In Need

CONTACT
Gary H. Kline
Secretary
Special People In Need
500 West Madison St., Ste. 3700
Chicago, IL 60661
(312) 715-5000

FINANCIAL SUMMARY
Recent Giving: $83,605 (1990); $98,100 (1989)
Assets: $2,549,564 (1990); $2,586,641 (1989)
Gifts Received: $200 (1990); $5,902 (1989)
EIN: 58-1483651

CONTRIBUTIONS SUMMARY
Donor(s): Josephine M. Thompson, Katherine Morningstar Irrevocable Trust
Typical Recipients: • *Arts & Humanities:* arts funds, performing arts, theater • *Civic & Public Affairs:* environmental affairs • *Education:* education funds, private education (precollege), religious education • *Health:* hospices • *Religion:* churches • *Social Services:* aged, child welfare, community service organizations, homes, youth organizations
Grant Types: general support, project, and scholarship

GIVING OFFICERS
Kenneth A. Algozin: asst treas, secy, dir
Kent Chandler, Jr.: trust *B* Chicago IL 1920 *ED* Yale Univ BA 1942; Univ MI JD 1949 *CURR EMPL* ptnr: Wilson & McIlvaine *NONPR AFFIL* mem: Am Bar Assn, Chicago Bar Assn, IL Bar Assn, Lake County Bar Assn, Lake County Bar Assn, Legal Club Chicago
Larry D. Gerbaz: dir, vp
Molly M. Gerbaz: dir, chmn
Gary H. Kline: dir, secy
John M. Morningstar: dir, vchmn
Leslie H. Morningstar: dir, vp
Thomas A. Polachek: dir, treas
Josephine H. Thompson: dir, pres

APPLICATION INFORMATION
Initial Approach: Send brief letter of inquiry describing program. There are no deadlines.

GRANTS ANALYSIS
Number of Grants: 19
Highest Grant: $12,000
Typical Range: $1,000 to $7,500
Disclosure Period: 1990

RECENT GRANTS
12,000 Eagles Mount, Chicago, IL

7,500 National Center for Effective Schools, Chicago, IL

7,500 Prince of Peace United Methodist Church, Chicago, IL

6,500 Courage Center, Golden Valley, MN

6,000 Cornerstone Christian School, Chicago, IL
6,000 Greater Yellowstone Coalition, Bozeman, MT
6,000 Sound of Sight
5,000 Ellington Fund
5,000 Francis W. Parker Schools
5,000 Hospices of North Shore, Wilmette, IL

Specialty Restaurants Corp.
Sales: $141.0 million
Employees: 4,000
Headquarters: Anaheim, CA
SIC Major Group: Eating & Drinking Places

CONTACT
David Tallichet
President
Specialty Restaurants Corp.
4155 East LaPalma Avenue, Ste. 250
Anaheim, CA 92807
(714) 579-3900

CONTRIBUTIONS SUMMARY
Operating Locations: CA (Anaheim)

CORP. OFFICERS
David Tallichet: *CURR EMPL* chmn, ceo, pres: Specialty Restaurants Corp

Spectra-Physics Analytical
Sales: $300.0 million
Employees: 250
Parent Company: Spectra-Physics Inc.
Headquarters: San Jose, CA
SIC Major Group: Electronic & Other Electrical Equipment and Instruments & Related Products

CONTACT
Stan Dunlap
Vice President, Human Resources
Spectra-Physics Analytical
45757 North Port Loop West
Fremont, CA 94537
(510) 657-1100

FINANCIAL SUMMARY
Recent Giving: $80,000 (1990); $90,000 (1989); $75,000 (1988)

CONTRIBUTIONS SUMMARY
The company's priorities are arts and humanities, education, health, and social services, with an emphasis on programs for women and minorities. The majority of arts funding goes to performing arts and community arts organizations. Education grants primarily support colleges and universities. Single disease health associations, the United Way, and youth organizations also are supported.

Typical Recipients: • *Arts & Humanities:* community arts, performing arts • *Civic & Public Affairs:* civil rights, professional & trade associations, women's affairs • *Education:* colleges & universities • *Health:* single-disease health associations • *Social Services:* united funds, youth organizations

Grant Types: emergency, general support, matching, and multiyear/continuing support

Nonmonetary Support Types: loaned employees and loaned executives

Geographic Distribution: near headquarters and operating locations

Operating Locations: CA (Fremont, San Jose), CO, GA, MI, NJ, OH, OR, WA

CORP. OFFICERS
Mark Harrington: *CURR EMPL* sr vp, cfo: Spectra-Physics Analytical
William Offenberg: *CURR EMPL* pres, gen mgr: Spectra-Physics Analytical

GIVING OFFICERS
Stan Dunlap: *CURR EMPL* vp (human resources): Spectra-Physics Analytical

APPLICATION INFORMATION
Initial Approach: Applicants should apply in writing by early fall for funding the following year. Initial letter should include a description of the organization, amount requested, purpose for which funds are sought, a recently audited financial statement, and proof of tax-exempt status.

Restrictions on Giving: Does not support fraternal organizations or religious organizations for sectarian purposes.

GRANTS ANALYSIS
Typical Range: $1,000 to $2,500

Speer Foundation, Roy M.

CONTACT
Roy M. Speer Foundation
1803 U.S. Highway 19
Holiday, FL 34691-5536
(813) 938-8521

FINANCIAL SUMMARY
Recent Giving: $40,000 (fiscal 1991); $35,000 (fiscal 1990)
Assets: $2,006,083 (fiscal year ending June 30, 1991); $1,988,671 (fiscal 1990)
EIN: 59-2785945

CONTRIBUTIONS SUMMARY
Typical Recipients: • *Arts & Humanities:* libraries • *Education:* colleges & universities, religious education • *Health:* hospitals, pediatric health, single-disease health associations • *Religion:* churches, religious organizations • *Social Services:* religious welfare
Grant Types: endowment, general support, and research

GIVING OFFICERS
Richard W. Baker: trust

APPLICATION INFORMATION
Initial Approach: The foundation reports no specific application guidelines. Send a brief letter of inquiry, including statement of purpose, amount requested, and proof of tax-exempt status.

GRANTS ANALYSIS
Total Grants: $40,000
Highest Grant: $25,000
Disclosure Period: fiscal year ending June 30, 1991

Spencer Foundation

CONTACT
John H. Barcroft
Vice President
Spencer Foundation
900 North Michigan Avenue, Ste. 2800
Chicago, IL 60611
(312) 337-7000

FINANCIAL SUMMARY
Recent Giving: $7,100,000 (fiscal 1993 est.); $9,293,501 (fiscal 1992); $8,580,767 (fiscal 1991)
Assets: $225,000,000 (fiscal 1993 est.); $224,776,532 (fiscal year ending March 31, 1992); $212,746,234 (fiscal 1991 est.); $210,439,249 (fiscal 1990)
EIN: 36-6078558

CONTRIBUTIONS SUMMARY
Donor(s): The Spencer Foundation was established in 1962 with funds donated by the late Lyle M. Spencer. Mr. Spencer was the founder of Science Research Associates (SRA), a leading publisher of educational tests, guidance programs, and curriculum materials. Mr. Spencer bequeathed the majority of his estate to the foundation.

Mr. Spencer was especially interested in the educational process. On several occasions he described himself as "a businessman looking in over the rim of education." During his life, his major philanthropic gifts were made in the field of education, and in notes found after his death he expressed the feeling that, since the Spencer family fortune had been earned in educational publishing, "...much of this money should be returned eventually to investigating ways in which education, broadly conceived, can be improved around the world."

Typical Recipients: • *Education:* colleges & universities • *International:* foreign educational institutions
Grant Types: research
Geographic Distribution: national and international

GIVING OFFICERS
John H. Barcroft: vp
Frank L. Bixby: dir *B* New Richmond WI 1928 *ED* Harvard Univ AB 1950; Univ WI LLB 1953 *CURR EMPL* ptnr: Sidley & Austin *NONPR AFFIL* dir: Voices for Ill Children; mem: Am Bar Assn, Chicago Bar Assn, Chicago Counc Foreign Rels, Chicago Counc Lawyers, FL Bar Assn, IL Bar Assn, WI Bar Assn; vp, dir: Chicago Urban League
Linda Darling-Hammond: dir
Marion M. Faldet: vp, secy
Patricia Albjerg Graham, PhD: pres, dir *B* Lafayette IN 1935 *ED* Purdue Univ BS 1955; Purdue Univ MS 1957; Columbia Univ PhD 1964

CORP AFFIL trust: Northwestern Mutual Life Ins Co *NONPR AFFIL* dir: Carnegie Fdn Advancement Teaching, Natl Inst Ed; mem: Am Historical Assn, Natl Academy Ed, Phi Beta Kappa, Science Res Assocs; Warren prof: Harvard Univ Grad Sch Ed *PHIL AFFIL* dir: Carnegie Foundation Advancement Teaching, Johnson Foundation

Robert A. LeVine: dir
Coralie A. Novotny: asst secy
George A. Ranney, Jr.: dir
John Shepard Reed: dir *B* Chicago IL 1939 *ED* Washington & Jefferson Coll BA 1959; MA Inst Tech BS 1961; MA Inst Tech MS 1965 *CURR EMPL* chmn, ceo: Citicorp & Citibank NA *CORP AFFIL* dir: Monsanto Co, Philip Morris Co, Un Techs Corp; mem bd: Rand Corp *NONPR AFFIL* chmn: Coalition Svc Indus, NY Blood Ctr, Svcs Policy Adv Comm US Trade Rep; mem bd: Ctr Advanced Study Behavioral Sciences, MA Inst Tech, Meml Sloan-Kettering Cancer Ctr, Woodrow Wilson Intl Ctr Scholars; mem policy comm: Bus Roundtable; vchmn: Bus Counc
Linda M. Schumacher: treas
Donna Edna Shalala: dir *B* Cleveland OH 1941 *ED* Western Coll AB 1962; Syracuse Univ MS 1968; Syracuse Univ PhD 1970 *CORP AFFIL* dir: M & I Madison *NONPR AFFIL* dir: Am Ditchley Fdn, Childrens Defense Fund, Inst Intl Econs; mem: Am Political Science Assn, Am Soc Pub Admin, Counc Foreign Rels, Knight Comm Intercollegiate Sports, Natl Academy Ed, Natl Academy Pub Admin, Trilateral Comm; prof political science, chancellor: Univ WI Madison; trust: Brookings Inst, Comm Econ Devel, Teachers Ins Annuity Assn
Lee S. Shulman: dir
David S. Tatel: dir *CURR EMPL* ptnr: Hogan & Hartson
William Julius Wilson: dir *B* Derry Township PA 1935 *ED* Wilberforce Univ BA 1958; Bowling Green St Univ MA 1961; WA St Univ PhD 1966 *NONPR AFFIL* chmn dept sociology, prof: Univ Chicago; dir: Ctr Advanced Study Behavioral Sciences, Ctr Natl Policy; dir, mem: Chicago Urban League; fellow: Am Academy Arts & Sciences, Am Assn Advancement Science; mem: Am

Philosophical Soc, Am Sociological Assn, Intl Sociological Assn, Lucy Flower Univ, Soc Study Social Problems, Sociological Res Assn; mem adv bd: Environmental Devel Pub Policy, Social Science Book Club; mem natl bd dirs: Inst Res Poverty, Randolph Inst (A Philip); trust: Spelman Coll

APPLICATION INFORMATION

Initial Approach:
Applicants should send a letter or preliminary proposal. Inquiries concerning the Small Grants Program and procedures for submitting proposals under the program should be addressed to Coralie Novotny, assistant secretary, and administrator of the Small Grants Program.

The preliminary proposal should include the curriculum vitae of the principal investigator, estimated budget, time schedule, description of project, and important telephone numbers. If the project falls within foundation guidelines, five detailed proposals will be requested. These should include a detailed description of the project, budget, time schedule, information on investigations, methods, relevant literature, expected new knowledge, and how it will benefit education. Applicants also must submit a short summary proposal of 300 to 500 words.

Final proposal deadlines are March 1, June 1, September 1, or December 1. Grant decisions are made at board meetings in July, October, January, and April.

The internal staff reviews the project to check the competency of the investigators, validity of new knowledge, cost of the project, and the budget. External consultant opinions will be sought on the research value of a project. A proposal then can be recommended for consideration by the board of trustees. When the board makes its decision, notification is immediate.

Restrictions on Giving: The foundation does not give grants for capital purposes, operating support, or ongoing program expenses; neither does it support service, training, or curriculum development; or travel funds, fellowships, or sabbatical supplements. No grants are made to individuals.

OTHER THINGS TO KNOW
Publications: annual report, general brochure, small grants brochure, newsletter

GRANTS ANALYSIS
Total Grants: $9,293,501
Number of Grants: 85
Highest Grant: $345,100
Typical Range: $1,000 to $7,500 and $25,000 to $200,000
Disclosure Period: fiscal year ending March 31, 1992
Note: Recent grants are derived from a fiscal 1992 annual report.

RECENT GRANTS
350,000 New York University, New York, NY — Inquiries in Cultural Psychology
345,100 University of California at Berkeley, Berkeley, CA — Psychological Theory and Educational Reform: From the Committee of Ten to the Bush Initiatives
345,000 Michigan State University, Ann Arbor, MI — practices of teaching and learning authentic mathematics for understanding in school
343,150 University of California at Berkeley, Berkeley, CA — the dynamics of local change in intuitive conceptions in physics
333,000 University of Georgia, Athens, GA — Child Competence, Parenting, and Family Transactions in Rural Black Families
300,000 Harvard University, Cambridge, MA — Writing Development and Instruction in the English-writing World
300,000 University of Chicago, Chicago, IL — consortium on Chicago School Research
299,100 Ontario Institute for Studies in Education — learning through talk
297,400 University of Pennsylvania, University Park, IL — lan-

guage diversity and cognitive development
279,900 Harvard University — ethnic differences in American educational attainments, 1880-1990

Sperry Fund
Former Foundation Name: S & H Foundation

CONTACT
Frederick W. Beinecke
Sperry Fund
420 Lexington Avenue, Ste. 3020
New York, NY 10170
(212) 370-1144

FINANCIAL SUMMARY
Recent Giving: $660,000 (fiscal 1992); $299,500 (fiscal 1991); $265,500 (fiscal 1990)
Assets: $10,094,194 (fiscal year ending June 30, 1992); $9,693,576 (fiscal 1991); $9,321,704 (fiscal 1990)
EIN: 13-6114308

CONTRIBUTIONS SUMMARY
Typical Recipients: • *Education:* colleges & universities • *Social Services:* recreation & athletics, youth organizations
Grant Types: project and scholarship

GIVING OFFICERS
Frederick W. Beinecke: pres, dir *B* Stamford CT 1943 *ED* Yale Univ BA 1966; Univ VA JD 1972 *CURR EMPL* pres, dir: Antaeus Enterprises *CORP AFFIL* dir: Catalina Mktg Corp, Long Lake Energy Corp, Nature Food Ctrs, Rehab Clinics *NONPR AFFIL* mem: Assn Bar City New York; trust: NY Zoological Soc, Phillips Academy, Trudeau Inst; dir: Outward Bound; vp, dir: NY City Ballet
William S. Beinecke: vp, dir *B* New York NY 1914 *ED* Yale Univ BA 1936; Columbia Univ LLB 1940 *CURR EMPL* co-fdr: Casey Beinecke & Chase *CORP AFFIL* dir: Antaeus Enterprises *NONPR AFFIL* chmn: Hudson River Fdn Scientific Environmental Res; mem: Counc Foreign Rels; mem bd mgrs: NY Botanical Garden
Thane Benefit III: secy, dir
R. Scott Greathead: dir
Melvyn L. Shaffir: dir
Michael A. Yesko: treas

APPLICATION INFORMATION

Initial Approach: College or university must be invited to nominate juniors for scholarship program. Application form required.

OTHER THINGS TO KNOW

Provides scholarships to college juniors for support during two years of graduate education.

Publications: Informational Brochure (including application guidelines)

GRANTS ANALYSIS

Highest Grant: $30,000

Disclosure Period: fiscal year ending June 30, 1992

RECENT GRANTS

30,000	Beloit College, Beloit, WI
30,000	Brown University, Providence, RI
30,000	Bryn Mawr College, Bryn Mawr, PA
30,000	Georgetown University, Washington, DC
30,000	Harvard University, Cambridge, MA
30,000	Harvard University, Cambridge, MA
30,000	Occidental College/Oxford University, Los Angeles, CA
30,000	Stanford University, Stanford, CA
30,000	University of North Carolina, Chapel Hill, NC
30,000	Wellesley College, Wellesley, MA

Speyer Foundation, Alexander C. and Tillie S.

CONTACT

A. C. Speyer, Jr.
Manager
Alexander C. and Tillie S. Speyer Fdn.
1202 Benedum Trees Bldg.
Pittsburgh, PA 15222
(412) 281-7225

FINANCIAL SUMMARY

Recent Giving: $152,135 (1991); $167,639 (1990); $163,327 (1989)

Assets: $3,710,891 (1991); $3,424,008 (1990); $3,797,828 (1989)

EIN: 25-6051650

CONTRIBUTIONS SUMMARY

Donor(s): members of the Speyer family

Typical Recipients: • *Arts & Humanities:* arts associations, arts institutes, community arts, libraries, museums/galleries • *Civic & Public Affairs:* environmental affairs, ethnic/minority organizations • *Education:* arts education, colleges & universities, education funds • *Religion:* religious organizations, synagogues • *Social Services:* united funds

Grant Types: general support

GIVING OFFICERS

A.C. Speyer, Jr.: trust

Darthea Speyer: trust

APPLICATION INFORMATION

Initial Approach: Send brief letter describing program. There are no deadlines.

GRANTS ANALYSIS

Number of Grants: 63

Highest Grant: $13,100

Typical Range: $100 to $8,000

Disclosure Period: 1991

RECENT GRANTS

13,100	United Jewish Appeal Federation of Jewish Philanthropies, Pittsburgh, PA
11,850	Carnegie Museum of Art, Pittsburgh, PA
11,000	Carnegie-Mellon University, Pittsburgh, PA
10,000	Rodef Shalom, Pittsburgh, PA
8,000	Art Institute of Chicago, Chicago, IL
8,000	United Way, Pittsburgh, PA
7,000	New York School of Drawing, New York, NY
7,000	Provincetown Art Association, Provincetown, MA
7,000	Textile Museum, Washington, DC
6,000	Fine Arts Work Center, Provincetown, MA

Spiegel

Sales: $1.98 billion
Employees: 5,500
Headquarters: Downers Grove, IL
SIC Major Group: Apparel & Accessory Stores, Furniture & Homefurnishings Stores, and Miscellaneous Retail

CONTACT

Lynn White
Contributions Manager
Spiegel, Inc.
3500 Lacey Rd.
Downers Grove, IL 60515
(708) 769-2251

FINANCIAL SUMMARY

Fiscal Note: Company gives directly. Annual Giving Range: $250,000 to $500,000

CONTRIBUTIONS SUMMARY

Typical Recipients: • *Civic & Public Affairs:* business/free enterprise, civil rights, urban & community affairs, women's affairs • *Education:* career/vocational education • *Religion:* religious organizations • *Social Services:* aged, child welfare, community centers, community service organizations, disabled, domestic violence, drugs & alcohol, employment/job training, family services, religious welfare, united funds, youth organizations

Grant Types: general support

Nonmonetary Support Types: donated products, loaned employees, loaned executives, and workplace solicitation

Geographic Distribution: no geographic restrictions

Operating Locations: DE (Wilmington), GA, IL (Downers Grove, Oakbrook Terrace), NV, PA, WA (Redmond)

CORP. OFFICERS

Henry A. Johnson: *B* Chicago IL 1919 *ED* Univ Chicago MBA 1964 *CURR EMPL* vchmn, dir: Spiegel *NONPR AFFIL* mem: Direct Mail Mktg Assn, Natl Retail Merchants Assn; mem natl exec bd: Boy Scouts Am

John J. Shea: *B* Newark NJ 1938 *ED* LaSalle Coll BS; Univ Pittsburgh MBA *CURR EMPL* pres, ceo, dir: Spiegel

GIVING OFFICERS

Lynn White: *CURR EMPL* contributions mgr: Spiegel

APPLICATION INFORMATION

Initial Approach: *Initial Contact:* send a brief letter and full proposal *Include Information On:* description of the organization, amount requested, purpose for which funds are sought, and proof of tax-exempt status *When to Submit:* requests may be submitted year-round; however, the best time to apply is the beginning of the year

OTHER THINGS TO KNOW

Spiegel provides nonmonetary support primarily in the form of donated clothing. The value of this support is not available.

Spiegel Family Foundation, Jerry and Emily

Former Foundation Name: Jerry Spiegel Foundation

CONTACT

Jerry and Emily Spiegel Family Fdn.
2 East 88th St.
New York, NY 10128

FINANCIAL SUMMARY

Recent Giving: $175,946 (fiscal 1992); $280,359 (fiscal 1991); $334,821 (fiscal 1990)

Assets: $5,715,801 (fiscal year ending March 31, 1992); $5,151,322 (fiscal 1991); $2,383,572 (fiscal 1990)

Gifts Received: $500,000 (fiscal 1992); $1,035,000 (fiscal 1991); $58,000 (fiscal 1990)

Fiscal Note: Company gives directly. In fiscal 1992, contributions were received from Jerry and Emily Spiegel.

EIN: 11-6006020

CONTRIBUTIONS SUMMARY

Donor(s): Jerry Spiegel

Typical Recipients: • *Arts & Humanities:* dance, museums/galleries, music, opera • *Civic & Public Affairs:* ethnic/minority organizations • *Education:* colleges & universities, legal education • *Health:* health organizations, hospitals, medical research, single-disease health associations • *Religion:* religious organizations, synagogues • *Social Services:* community service organizations

Grant Types: general support

Geographic Distribution: focus on NY

GIVING OFFICERS
Arthur D. Sanders: treas
Emily Spiegel: vp
Jerry Spiegel: pres
Lise Spiegel: secy, treas

APPLICATION INFORMATION
Initial Approach: Contributes only to preselected organizations.
Restrictions on Giving: Does not support individuals.

GRANTS ANALYSIS
Number of Grants: 77
Highest Grant: $20,000
Typical Range: $500 to $5,000
Disclosure Period: fiscal year ending March 31, 1992

RECENT GRANTS

20,000	Temple Beth-El, Great Neck, NY
17,185	Metropolitan Opera Guild, New York, NY
15,250	Hofstra University School of Law, Hempstead, NY
15,050	United Jewish Appeal Federation of Jewish Philanthropies, New York, NY
10,500	Museum of Modern Art, New York, NY
10,000	Road Runners Club of America, New York, NY
6,200	United Jewish Y's of Long Island, New York, NY
5,000	Greenwich Hospital Association, Greenwich, NY
5,000	J. Gurwin Foundation, New York, NY
4,256	Temple Sholom, New York, NY

Spingold Foundation, Nate B. and Frances

CONTACT
Daniel L. Kurtz
President
Nate B. and Frances Spingold Fdn.
c/o Lankenau & Bickford
1740 Broadway
New York, NY 10019
(212) 489-8230

FINANCIAL SUMMARY
Recent Giving: $186,400 (fiscal 1991); $233,067 (fiscal 1990); $222,400 (fiscal 1989)

Assets: $7,665,360 (fiscal year ending November 30, 1991); $6,468,970 (fiscal 1990); $9,762,999 (fiscal 1989)
Gifts Received: $20,000 (fiscal 1991); $10,000 (fiscal 1989)
EIN: 13-6107659

CONTRIBUTIONS SUMMARY
Donor(s): the late Frances Spingold, the late Nathan Breither Spingold
Typical Recipients: • *Arts & Humanities:* arts centers, museums/galleries, opera • *Civic & Public Affairs:* ethnic/minority organizations • *Education:* colleges & universities • *Health:* hospitals, medical research • *International:* international development/relief • *Religion:* religious organizations, synagogues • *Social Services:* aged, community service organizations, disabled, youth organizations
Grant Types: conference/seminar, fellowship, professorship, project, research, and scholarship
Geographic Distribution: focus on the New York, NY, metropolitan area and in Israel

GIVING OFFICERS
James R. Halperin: off
Sherry Klein Heitler: vp, secy
Lorance Hockert: vp, treas
Daniel L. Kurtz: pres, ceo
Melvyn C. Levitan: off

APPLICATION INFORMATION
Initial Approach: Send cover letter and full proposal. There are no deadlines.
Restrictions on Giving: Does not support individuals or provide loans.

OTHER THINGS TO KNOW
Publications: Annual Report (including application guidelines)

GRANTS ANALYSIS
Number of Grants: 19
Highest Grant: $75,000
Typical Range: $1,000 to $10,000
Disclosure Period: fiscal year ending November 30, 1991

RECENT GRANTS

75,000	Long Island Jewish Medical Center, New Hyde Park, NY
25,000	Jerusalem Foundation, New York, NY
25,000	North Shore Synagogue, New York, NY
12,400	American Friends of Haifa University, New York, NY
10,000	American Associates of Ben Gurion University, New York, NY
10,000	Sid Jacobson North Shore YWCA, New York, NY
6,000	Samuel Field YM/YWHA, New York, NY
3,500	Fordham Law School, New York, NY
2,500	Jewish Home and Hospital for the Aged, New York, NY
2,250	Open Housing Center, New York, NY

Spiritus Gladius Foundation

Former Foundation Name: D.C. Foundation

CONTACT
Nadenia H. Hartley
President
Spiritus Gladius Fdn.
c/o Meyer Handelman Co.
PO Box 817
Purchase, NY 10577-0817

FINANCIAL SUMMARY
Recent Giving: $174,750 (fiscal 1991); $178,650 (fiscal 1990); $136,650 (fiscal 1989)
Assets: $2,637,527 (fiscal year ending August 31, 1991); $2,468,795 (fiscal 1990); $2,574,668 (fiscal 1989)
EIN: 13-6113272

CONTRIBUTIONS SUMMARY
Donor(s): Nedenia H. Hartley
Typical Recipients: • *Arts & Humanities:* arts centers, museums/galleries, performing arts, theater • *Education:* colleges & universities • *Health:* hospitals, medical research, single-disease health associations • *Social Services:* child welfare, community service organizations, youth organizations
Grant Types: general support
Geographic Distribution: focus on NY, CT, and MA

GIVING OFFICERS
Nedenia R. Craig: trust
Donald E. Handelman: vp, secy, treas
Joseph W. Handelman: trust

William Handelman: asst secy, treas
Nedinia H. Hartley: pres
Heather M. Robertson: trust
Stanley H. Rumbough: trust

APPLICATION INFORMATION
Initial Approach: Contributes only to preselected organizations.
Restrictions on Giving: Does not support individuals.

GRANTS ANALYSIS
Number of Grants: 21
Highest Grant: $35,000
Typical Range: $1,000 to $10,000
Disclosure Period: fiscal year ending August 31, 1991

RECENT GRANTS

35,000	Eugene O'Neill Theater Center, Waterford, CT
16,000	Museum of Broadcasting, New York, NY
10,000	Sundance Institute for Film and Television, Salt Lake City, UT
5,000	Circle in the Square, New York, NY
5,000	John F. Kennedy Center for the Performing Arts, Washington, DC
2,500	National Theater Network, New York, NY
1,500	WNET Thirteen, New York, NY
1,000	Guild Hall, East Hampton, NY
1,000	Musical Theater Works, New York, NY
200	South Bronx 2000 Local Development, New York, NY

Spiro Foundation, Donald W.

CONTACT
Donald W. Spiro Foundation
7 World Trade Center
New York, NY 10048-1100

FINANCIAL SUMMARY
Recent Giving: $43,156 (fiscal 1991)
Assets: $2,088,588 (fiscal year ending August 30, 1991)
Gifts Received: $970,000 (fiscal 1991)

Fiscal Note: Fiscal 1991 contribution received from Donald Spiro.
EIN: 22-2770724

CONTRIBUTIONS SUMMARY

Typical Recipients: • *Health:* hospices, hospitals, single-disease health associations • *International:* international development/relief • *Religion:* churches • *Social Services:* aged, child welfare
Grant Types: general support

GIVING OFFICERS

Donald W. Spiro: trust

APPLICATION INFORMATION

Initial Approach: The foundation reports it only makes contributions to preselected organizations and does not accept unsolicited requests for funds.

GRANTS ANALYSIS

Total Grants: $43,156
Number of Grants: 16
Highest Grant: $29,000
Typical Range: $500 to $5,625
Disclosure Period: fiscal year ending August 30, 1991

RECENT GRANTS

29,000 Salvation Army, NY
5,625 Gates County Flag GIA- Wagner College, NY
2,500 St. Patrick's Home for the Aged, NY
1,176 Save the Children, NY
1,000 Chilton Hospital Foundation, NJ
1,000 Hospice of Morris County, NJ
755 Community Church of Smoke Rise, NJ
500 International Rescue Committee, NY
250 National Kidney Foundation, NY

Sprague Educational and Charitable Foundation, Seth

CONTACT

Maureen Augusciak
Senior Vice President
Seth Sprague Educational and Charitable Foundation
U.S. Trust Company of New York
114 West 47th St.
New York, NY 10036
(212) 852-3683
Note: Anne L. Smith-Ganey, assistant vice president, may also be contacted for information. The foundation lists an additional number: 212-852-3686.

FINANCIAL SUMMARY

Recent Giving: $1,600,000 (1992 approx.); $1,819,500 (1991); $1,556,500 (1990)
Assets: $40,558,000 (1992 est.); $41,082,406 (1991); $36,831,033 (1990); $41,124,151 (1989)
EIN: 13-6071886

CONTRIBUTIONS SUMMARY

Donor(s): Established in 1939 by Seth Sprague, the Sprague Educational and Charitable Foundation is administered by three trustees and the United States Trust Company of New York. All of the trustees were either associates of Mr. Sprague or familiar with his philanthropic pursuits.
Seth Sprague was a graduate of Norwich Academy and a lifetime employee of F. H. Foster and Company, a Boston cotton processing corporation of which he eventually became president. Mr. Sprague died in 1941.
Typical Recipients: • *Arts & Humanities:* arts funds, arts institutes, cinema, dance, ethnic arts, history/historic preservation, libraries, literary arts, museums/galleries, music, opera, performing arts, public broadcasting, theater • *Civic & Public Affairs:* business/free enterprise, economic development, environmental affairs, law & justice, professional & trade associations, public policy, urban & community affairs, women's affairs, zoos/botanical gardens • *Education:* arts education, colleges & universities, education

associations, education funds, journalism education, legal education, medical education, minority education, private education (precollege), public education (precollege), religious education, special education, student aid • *Health:* emergency/ambulance services, geriatric health, health funds, health organizations, hospices, hospitals, medical rehabilitation, medical training, mental health, nursing services, pediatric health, single-disease health associations • *Religion:* churches • *Science:* scientific institutes • *Social Services:* aged, animal protection, child welfare, community centers, community service organizations, counseling, delinquency & crime, disabled, domestic violence, drugs & alcohol, employment/job training, family planning, recreation & athletics, religious welfare, shelters/homelessness, volunteer services, youth organizations
Grant Types: challenge, general support, operating expenses, project, and seed money
Geographic Distribution: primarily New York and Massachusetts

GIVING OFFICERS

Maureen O. Augusciak: contact person *CURR EMPL* sr vp: US Trust Co NY
Walter G. Dunnington, Jr.: trust *B* New York NY 1927 *ED* Univ VA BA 1948; Univ VA LLB 1950 *CORP AFFIL* dir: Brittainia Indus (India) *NONPR AFFIL* bd govs: NY Hosp; mem: Am Bar Assn, Assn Bar City NY, NY St Bar Assn; trust: Algernon Sydney Sullivan Fdn, Boys Club NY, Woodberry Forest Sch
Arline Ripley Greenleaf: trust
Jacqueline DeNeuflize Simpkins: trust
Anne L. Smith-Ganey: contact person *CURR EMPL* asst vp: US Trust Co NY

APPLICATION INFORMATION

Initial Approach:
Initial contact should be a written request.
Applications should include a summary (two pages), budget, audited financial statement, and an IRS determination letter. The board of directors meets in March, June, September, and November. Deadlines for applications are April 15 and Octo-

ber 1. Grants are made in June and December.
Restrictions on Giving: The foundation does not give grants for research or capital expenditures. In addition, the foundation does not make grants to individuals or for organizations located outside the United States.

OTHER THINGS TO KNOW

Most grants benefit organizations within the New York and Massachusetts areas. There are exceptions, and support is usually unrestricted.

GRANTS ANALYSIS

Total Grants: $1,819,500
Number of Grants: 417
Highest Grant: $45,000
Typical Range: $1,000 to $5,000
Disclosure Period: 1991
Note: Recent grants are derived from a 1991 Form 990.

RECENT GRANTS

45,000 Woodberry Forest School, Woodberry Forest, VA
30,000 Rockport Apprenticeshop, Rockport, ME
30,000 Rockport Apprenticeshop, Rockport, ME
28,000 Birth Right Forces, Bath, ME
25,000 Birth Right Forces, Bath, ME
25,000 Riley School, Glen Cove, ME
25,000 Riley School, Glen Cove, ME
25,000 Society of the New York Hospital, New York, NY
20,000 Atlantic Challenge Foundation
20,000 Society of the New York Hospital, New York, NY

Sprague, Jr. Foundation, Caryll M. and Norman F.

CONTACT
Norman F. Sprague, Jr., M.D.
Trustee
Caryll M. and Norman F.
Sprague, Jr. Fdn.
2049 Century Park East, No. 2760
Los Angeles, CA 90067-3202
(213) 387-7311

FINANCIAL SUMMARY
Recent Giving: $193,810 (1990); $156,780 (1989); $174,350 (1988)
Assets: $3,815,086 (1990); $3,806,603 (1989); $3,458,261 (1988)
EIN: 95-6021187

CONTRIBUTIONS SUMMARY
Donor(s): Caryll M. Sprague, Norman F. Sprague, Jr., M.D.
Typical Recipients: • *Arts & Humanities:* arts centers, museums/galleries • *Civic & Public Affairs:* environmental affairs • *Education:* colleges & universities, medical education, private education (precollege) • *Health:* hospitals, medical research, pediatric health • *Religion:* churches
Grant Types: general support
Geographic Distribution: focus on CA

GIVING OFFICERS
Cynthia S. Connolly: trust
Caryll S. Mingst: trust
Charles Thomas Munger: trust *B* Omaha NE 1924 *CURR EMPL* pres: Wesco Fin Corp *CORP AFFIL* chmn, pres: Wesco Fin Corp; vchmn: Berkshire Hathaway
Norman F. Sprague III: trust
Norman Frederick Sprague, Jr., M: trust *B* Los Angeles CA 1914 *ED* Univ CA AB 1933; Harvard Univ MD 1937 *NONPR AFFIL* asst clinical prof: Univ CA Los Angeles; mem: Am Cattlemans Assn, Am Med Assn, CA Med Assn; mem bd visitors: Univ CA Los Angeles Med Sch

APPLICATION INFORMATION
Initial Approach: Contributes only to preselected organizations.
Restrictions on Giving: Does not support individuals.

GRANTS ANALYSIS
Number of Grants: 37
Highest Grant: $29,050
Typical Range: $1,000 to $10,000
Disclosure Period: 1990

RECENT GRANTS
29,050   Southwest Museum, Los Angeles, CA
26,350   Music Center Unified Fund, Los Angeles, CA
12,550   Harvey Mudd College, Claremont, CA
10,000   Regents of the University of California, Berkeley, CA
7,500   University of Southern California School of Medicine/C.J. Berne Professorship, Los Angeles, CA
6,500   Children's Institute International, Los Angeles, CA
5,000   Cate School, Carpinteria, CA
5,000   Harvard School, Cambridge, MA
5,000   Los Angeles County Museum of Art, Los Angeles, CA
5,000   Nature Conservancy, San Francisco, CA

Sprague Memorial Institute, Otho S. A.

CONTACT
Thomas E. Macior
Manager
Otho S. A. Sprague Memorial Institute
c/o Harris Trust and Savings Bank
190 South LaSalle St., Fourth Fl.
PO Box 755
Chicago, IL 60690
(312) 461-7054

FINANCIAL SUMMARY
Recent Giving: $1,000,000 (1992 approx.); $695,000 (1990); $625,000 (1989)
Assets: $14,952,513 (1990); $15,631,920 (1989); $13,028,669 (1988)
Gifts Received: $173,758 (1989); $150,000 (1988)
EIN: 36-6068723

CONTRIBUTIONS SUMMARY
Donor(s): The foundation was incorporated in 1910 by members of the Sprague family.
Typical Recipients: • *Civic & Public Affairs:* economic development, professional & trade associations, urban & community affairs • *Education:* medical education • *Health:* hospitals • *Social Services:* emergency relief
Grant Types: project and research
Geographic Distribution: limited to Chicago, IL

GIVING OFFICERS
Whitney Wood Addington: trust
Vernon Armour: pres, trust
Harry N. Beaty, MD: trust *B* Brookfield MO 1932 *ED* Univ WA MD 1950-1954 *NONPR AFFIL* fellow: Am Coll Physicians; mem: Am Soc Clinical Investigation, Assn Am Med Colls, Assn Profs Medicine, Infectious Diseases Soc Am
Charles F. Clarke, Jr.: treas, trust
Steward Strawn Dixon: secy, trust *B* Chicago IL 1930 *ED* Yale Univ BA 1952; Univ MI JD 1955 *CURR EMPL* ptnr: Wildman Harold Allen & Dixon *CORP AFFIL* dir: Lord Abbett & Co Managed Mutual Funds; ptnr: Wildman Harold Allen & Dixon *NONPR AFFIL* dir: Otho Sprague Inst; mem: Am Bar Assn, Am Law Inst, Chicago Bar Assn, IL Bar Assn; trust: Chicago Historical Soc
Charles C. Haffner III: vp, trust *B* Chicago IL 1928 *CURR EMPL* ret vchmn: RR Donnelley & Sons Co *CORP AFFIL* dir: DuKane Corp, Protection Mutual Ins Co; dir, chmn: Lakeside Bank *NONPR AFFIL* chmn: Morton Arboretum, Newberry Library; trust: Art Inst Chicago, Brooks Sch, Chicago City Day Sch, IL Cancer Counc, Lincoln Park Zoological Soc, Sprague Fdn
Leo M. Henikoff, Jr.: trust *B* Chicago IL 1939 *ED* Univ IL MD 1963 *CURR EMPL* prof pediatrics, prof medicine: Rush Med Coll Chicago *CORP AFFIL* chmn: Mid-America Health Programs; dir: Harris Bankcorp, Harris Trust & Savings Bank, Rush/Copley Health Care Sys, Rush North Shore Health Svcs, Savings & Profit Sharing Fund Sears Employees *NONPR AFFIL* chmn-elect: Philadelphia County Med Soc; diplomat: Am Bd Pediatrics; dir: Assn Academy Health Ctrs, JR Bowman Health Ctr; fellow: Am Academy Pediatrics, Am Coll Physician Execs, Coll Physicians Philadelphia, Inst Medicine Chicago; mem: Am Med Assn, Assn Am Med Colls, Counc Teaching Hosps, PA Med Sch Deans Comm, PA Med Soc; mem adv bd: Univ Village Assn; pres: Rush Univ; pres, trust, ceo: Rush-Presbyterian-St Lukes Med Ctr; sr attending: Presbyterian-St Lukes Hosp
E. Wayne Robinson: trust

APPLICATION INFORMATION
Initial Approach:
The foundation requests applications be made in writing.
Written applications should state the purpose of the organization and its activities.
The foundation reports the deadline for submitting proposals is the end of the calendar year.
The board meets in May and December.
Restrictions on Giving: The foundation makes grants to private institutions involved in investigating and preventing disease and human suffering. No grants are made to individuals, or for building or endowment funds, general purposes, scholarships, fellowships, matching funds, or loans.

OTHER THINGS TO KNOW
Publications: annual report

GRANTS ANALYSIS
Total Grants: $695,000
Number of Grants: 9
Highest Grant: $175,000
Typical Range: $20,000 to $175,000
Disclosure Period: 1990
Note: Recent grants are derived from a 1990 grants list.

RECENT GRANTS
175,000   Northwestern University Medical School, Evanston, IL
175,000   Rush Presbyterian, Chicago, IL — St. Lukes Medical Center
175,000   University of Chicago Medical School, Chicago, IL
50,000   Lawndale Christian Health Center, Chicago, IL
30,000   Metropolitan Planning Council, Chicago, IL

30,000 Travelers and Immigrants Aid, Chicago, IL

25,000 Visiting Nurse Association, Chicago, IL

20,000 American Red Cross, Chicago, IL

15,000 Chicago Institute of Urban Poverty, Chicago, IL

Spring Arbor Distributors

Sales: $120.0 million
Employees: 620
Headquarters: Belleville, MI
SIC Major Group: Wholesale Trade—Durable Goods and Wholesale Trade—Nondurable Goods

CONTACT
Iris Young
Assistant Controller
Spring Arbor Distributors
10885 Textile Rd.
Belleville, MI 48111
(313) 481-0900

FINANCIAL SUMMARY
Fiscal Note: Annual Giving Range: less than $100,000.

CONTRIBUTIONS SUMMARY
Company reports 99% of contributions support Christian educational organizations and nondenominational Christian ministries.
Typical Recipients: • *Religion:* missionary activities, religious organizations
Grant Types: matching
Operating Locations: MI (Belleville)

CORP. OFFICERS
James E. Carlson: *CURR EMPL* vchmn, dir: Spring Arbor Distributors
Thomas B. Murphy: *B* Brockton MA 1927 *ED* Boston Coll 1950; Univ MI 1953 *CURR EMPL* chmn, dir: Spring Arbor Distributors *CORP AFFIL* dir: Flex Ban *NONPR AFFIL* mem: Soc Actuaries
Richard Pigott: *CURR EMPL* pres: Spring Arbor Distributors

APPLICATION INFORMATION
Initial Approach: Send a full proposal including a description of the organization, amount requested, purpose of funds sought, and proof of tax exempt status.

Restrictions on Giving: Does not support individuals, or political or lobbying groups.

GRANTS ANALYSIS
Typical Range: $10 to $1,000

Springs Foundation

CONTACT
Charles A. Bundy
President
Springs Foundation
PO Drawer 460
Lancaster, SC 29721
(803) 286-2196
Note: The foundation is located at 104 East Springs Street, Lancaster, SC.

FINANCIAL SUMMARY
Recent Giving: $1,625,699 (1991); $938,528 (1990); $1,401,548 (1989)
Assets: $20,326,869 (1992 est.); $20,141,262 (1991); $20,141,262 (1990); $20,737,827 (1989)
EIN: 57-0426344

CONTRIBUTIONS SUMMARY
Donor(s): Colonel Elliott White Springs (1896-1959) was the founder of Springs Industries, one of the largest textile manufacturers in the United States. He established the foundation, formerly called the Elliott White Springs Foundation, in 1942. His wife, Frances Ley Springs, continued her husband's philanthropic interests through her work at the foundation. "Her estate provided the means for expanded philanthropic work over a wider geographic area. Those funds began what is now called the Close Foundation."
Typical Recipients: • *Arts & Humanities:* arts associations, community arts, libraries • *Civic & Public Affairs:* economic development, environmental affairs, law & justice, municipalities • *Education:* colleges & universities, public education (precollege), student aid • *Health:* health organizations, hospitals, mental health • *Religion:* churches • *Social Services:* community service organizations, drugs & alcohol, recreation & athletics, united funds, youth organizations
Grant Types: capital, challenge, endowment, project, scholarship, and seed money

Geographic Distribution: Lancaster County, Chester Township of Chester County, and Fort Mill Township of York County, SC

GIVING OFFICERS
Lillian Crandall Close Bowles: vp, treas, dir *B* 1948 *CURR EMPL* pres: Springs Co *CORP AFFIL* dir: Duke Power Co, Richmond Fed Reserve Bank, Springs Indus; dir SC bd: SC Natl Bank
James Bradley: dir
Charles Alan Bundy: pres, dir *B* Cheraw SC 1930 *ED* Wofford Coll BA 1951 *NONPR AFFIL* dir: Elliott White Spring Meml Hosp; mem: Counc Fdns, Lancaster County Chamber Commerce; chmn: SC Dept Parks Recreation Tourism Comm; mem: SC Coordinating Counc Econ Devel; trust: SC Fdn Independent Colls
Anne Springs Close: don, chmn, dir
Derick Springsteen Close: dir
Elliot Springs Close: dir
Hugh William Close, Jr.: dir
Katherine Anne Close: dir
Leroy Springs Close: dir
Pat Close: dir *PHIL AFFIL* dir: Close Foundation
Frances Close Hart: dir
James H. Hodges: secy

APPLICATION INFORMATION
Initial Approach:
Initial contact should take the form of a brief letter. Letters should provide a brief statement of need. The president researches the proposal for merit, eligibility, and priority status. Recommendations are then presented to the board for approval.

OTHER THINGS TO KNOW
Publications: annual report

GRANTS ANALYSIS
Total Grants: $1,625,699
Number of Grants: 51
Highest Grant: $775,000
Typical Range: $1,000 to $50,000
Disclosure Period: 1991
Note: Recent grants are derived from a 1991 annual report.

RECENT GRANTS
775,000 Leroy Springs and Company, Lancaster, SC — operation/maintenance

355,050 Leroy Springs and Company, Lan-

caster, SC — Springmaid Beach $4 Million Project

150,000 Elliott White Springs Memorial Hospital, Lancaster, SC — radiology equipment

50,000 Lancaster County Healthy Mothers/Healthy Babies Coalition, Lancaster, SC

29,745 School Assistance Programs, Lancaster, SC — Lancaster County School District

25,000 South Carolina Foundation of Independent Colleges, Taylors, SC

25,000 Town of Kershaw, Kershaw, SC — fire truck

20,277 School Assistance Programs, Chester, SC — Chester County Department of Education

20,000 Lancaster County Recreation Commission, Lancaster, SC

20,000 United Way of Lancaster County, Lancaster, SC

Springs Industries

Sales: $1.96 billion
Employees: 20,000
Headquarters: Fort Mill, SC
SIC Major Group: Apparel & Other Textile Products and Textile Mill Products

CONTACT
Robert L. Thompson
Vice President, Public Affairs
Springs Industries
PO Box 70
Ft. Mill, SC 29716
(803) 547-3736

FINANCIAL SUMMARY
Recent Giving: $850,000 (1993 est.); $1,070,000 (1992); $945,000 (1991)
Fiscal Note: All contributions are made directly by the company. Figure for 1992 includes nonmonetary support.

CONTRIBUTIONS SUMMARY
Typical Recipients: • *Arts & Humanities:* arts associations, arts festivals, community arts, history/historic preservation, museums/galleries, visual arts • *Civic & Public Affairs:* business/free enterprise, economic development, environmental af-

fairs, professional & trade associations, public policy • *Education:* arts education, business education, career/vocational education, colleges & universities, community & junior colleges, continuing education, economic education, education associations, elementary education, faculty development, liberal arts education, literacy, minority education, preschool education, public education (precollege) • *Health:* health care cost containment, hospices, hospitals, single-disease health associations • *Science:* science exhibits & fairs • *Social Services:* aged, child welfare, community centers, drugs & alcohol, emergency relief, employment/job training, family services, united funds, volunteer services, youth organizations

Grant Types: employee matching gifts and multiyear/continuing support

Nonmonetary Support Types: donated products

Note: Estimated value of nonmonetary support is unavailable but is included in figures above.

Geographic Distribution: near operating locations, national organizations

Operating Locations: AL (Piedmont), CA (Fullerton), GA (Calhoun, Cleveland, Dalton, Washington), IL (Naperville), NC (Aberdeen, Biscoe, Laurel Hill, Statesville), NV (Sparks), NY (New York, White Plains), PA (Montgomery), SC (Anderson, Chester, Columbia, Fort Mill, Gaffney, Honea Path, Lancaster, Lyman, Union), TN (Nashville), WI (Middleton)

CORP. OFFICERS

Walter Y. Elisha: *B* 1932 *ED* Wabash Coll; Harvard Univ Sch Bus Admin *CURR EMPL* chmn, ceo, dir: Springs Indus

GIVING OFFICERS

Crandall C. Bowles: vp *CURR EMPL* vp (textile mfg): Springs Indus

C. Powers Dorsett: *CURR EMPL* vp (gen coun): Springs Indus

William K. Easley: mem (pub affairs comm) *CURR EMPL* pres: Grey Mfg

Richard D. Foster: *CURR EMPL* vp (human resources): Springs Indus

Stephen Paul Kelbley: *B* Tiffin OH 1942 *CURR EMPL* exec vp, cfo: Springs Indus *NONPR AFFIL* mem: Fin Execs Inst

Robert W. Moser: mem (pub affairs comm) *B* Rock Hill SC 1938 *CURR EMPL* exec vp: Springs Indus *NONPR AFFIL* mem: SC Textile Mfrs Assn

Robert L. Thompson: *B* Adel GA 1937 *CURR EMPL* vp (pub aff): Springs Indus

J. Spratt White: mem (pub affairs comm) *B* Rock Hill SC 1941 *ED* Wofford Coll 1963; Univ SC JD 1968 *CURR EMPL* sr vp, pres: Diversified Products Group

APPLICATION INFORMATION

Initial Approach: *Initial Contact:* brief letter *Include Information On:* description of the organization, amount requested, purpose for which funds are sought, recently audited financial statement, proof of tax-exempt status, relationship to company interests *When to Submit:* any time

Restrictions on Giving: Does not give to dinners or special events, fraternal organizations, goodwill advertising, individuals, member agencies of united funds, political or lobbying groups, or religious organizations.

GRANTS ANALYSIS

Total Grants: $1,070,133
Number of Grants: 697
Typical Range: $500 to $1,000
Disclosure Period: 1992

Sprint / Sprint Foundation

Former Foundation Name: United Telecommunications Fdn
Sales: $9.2 billion
Employees: 43,000
Headquarters: Westwood, KS
SIC Major Group: Business Services, Communications, Holding & Other Investment Offices, and Industrial Machinery & Equipment

CONTACT

Don Forsythe
Vice President
Sprint
2330 Shawnee Mission Pkwy.
Westwood, KS 66205
(913) 624-3343

FINANCIAL SUMMARY

Recent Giving: $2,687,000 (1993 est.); $2,215,919 (1992); $1,917,926 (1991)
Assets: $11,364,022 (1992); $9,604,379 (1990); $12,566,000 (1989)
Fiscal Note: The Sprint Foundation began operating in 1989. Figures above represent combined contributions by company and foundation. The foundation currently handles approximately 80% of total contributions.
EIN: 48-1062018

CONTRIBUTIONS SUMMARY

Typical Recipients: • *Arts & Humanities:* performing arts, public broadcasting • *Civic & Public Affairs:* business/free enterprise, economic development • *Education:* business education, colleges & universities, community & junior colleges, economic education, education associations, engineering education, literacy, minority education, private education (precollege), public education (precollege), science/technology education • *Social Services:* community service organizations, drugs & alcohol, united funds, youth organizations

Grant Types: capital, employee matching gifts, general support, operating expenses, and project

Nonmonetary Support Types: cause-related marketing & promotion, donated equipment, in-kind services, and loaned executives

Note: Estimated value of nonmonetary support was $268,000 in 1991 and $23,000 in 1990 and is not included in giving totals above.

Geographic Distribution: areas where the corporation and its subsidiaries have major concentrations of employees

Operating Locations: CA (Burlingame, Sacramento), DC, FL (Altamonte Springs, Ft. Myers, Ocala), GA (Atlanta), IN (Warsaw), KS (Industrial Airport, Junction City, Kansas City, Lenexa, Overland Park, Westwood), MN (Chaska), MO (Jefferson City, Kansas City), NC (Tarboro), NE (Scottsbluff), NJ (Clinton), NY (New York), OH (Mansfield), OR (Hood River), PA (Carlisle), SC, TN (Bristol), TX (Athens, Dallas), VA (Reston), WA, WY

CORP. OFFICERS

William Todd Esrey: *B* Philadelphia PA 1940 *ED* Denison Univ BA 1961; Harvard Univ MBA 1964 *CURR EMPL* chmn, ceo: Sprint *CORP AFFIL* chmn, ceo: Un Telecom Commun; dir: Equitable Life Assurance Soc US, Gen Mills; pres, ceo: Un Telecommunications; pres, dir: Panhandle Eastern Corp; trust: Midwest Res Comm Econ Devel; pres, dir: Un MO Bank *NONPR AFFIL* mem: Phi Beta Kappa

GIVING OFFICERS

James Richard Devlin: dir *B* Camden NJ 1950 *CURR EMPL* exec vp external affs, gen couns: Sprint Corp *NONPR AFFIL* mem: Am Bar Assn, Fed Comun Bar Assn

Donald G. Forsythe: *B* Emmetsburg IA 1938 *ED* Univ IA 1960; Rockhurst Coll 1978 *CURR EMPL* vp: Sprint

Richard C. Smith: dir *CURR EMPL* Un Telecommunications

M. Jeannie Strandjord: dir *B* Kansas City MO 1945 *ED* Kansas City Univ 1968 *CURR EMPL* vp, copmtr: Un Telecommunications Inc *NONPR AFFIL* mem: Am Inst CPAs, Fin Execs Inst; mem exec comm, acct adv counc: KS Univ Lawrence; treas: St Health Ctr Fdn

APPLICATION INFORMATION

Initial Approach: *Initial Contact:* brief letter or proposal *Include Information On:* description of the organization, description of project which the funding will support, current financial reports, proof of tax-exempt status *When to Submit:* any time

Restrictions on Giving: Company does not support fraternal organizations, individuals, political or lobbying groups, or religious organizations for sectarian purposes.

OTHER THINGS TO KNOW

Subsidiaries and regional offices administer their own charitable giving programs. Contact the public relations department of the nearest office for more information.

GRANTS ANALYSIS

Total Grants: $2,215,919
Number of Grants: 599
Highest Grant: $305,000
Typical Range: $500 to $10,000
Disclosure Period: 1992
Note: Recent grants are derived from a 1992 grants list.

RECENT GRANTS

305,000 Learning Exchange, Kansas City, MO
180,000 Heart of America United Way, Kansas City, MO
100,000 Kansas City Museum, Kansas City, MO
75,000 Kansas City Symphony, Kansas City, MO
59,000 Lyric Opera of Kansas City, Kansas City, MO
50,000 University of Kansas Endowment Association, Lawrence, KS
40,000 American Royal Association, Kansas City, MO
35,000 Kansas City Public Television, Kansas City, MO
30,213 Full Employment Council, Kansas City, MO
30,000 Sister Cities Association of Greater Kansas City, Kansas City, MO

Sprint United Telephone

Employees: 710
Parent Company: Sprint Corp.
Parent Sales: $9.23 billion
Headquarters: Mansfield, OH
SIC Major Group: Communications

CONTACT

John Eitelgeorge
Manager, Public Relations for Corporate Contributions
Sprint United Telephone
PO Box 3555
Mansfield, OH 44907
(419) 755-8370

FINANCIAL SUMMARY

Recent Giving: $330,000 (1993)

Fiscal Note: Company gives directly.

CONTRIBUTIONS SUMMARY

Typical Recipients: • *Arts & Humanities:* general • *Civic & Public Affairs:* general • *Education:* general • *Health:* general • *Social Services:* general

Grant Types: employee matching gifts and general support

Geographic Distribution: no geographic restrictions.

Operating Locations: IN (Warsaw), OH (Mansfield)

CORP. OFFICERS

Darrell Kelley: *CURR EMPL* pres: Sprint Un Telephone

GIVING OFFICERS

John Eitelgeorge: *CURR EMPL* mgr publ rels corp contributions: Sprint Un Telephone

APPLICATION INFORMATION

Initial Approach: *Initial Contact:* brief letter of inquiry *Include Information On:* description of the organization, amount requested, purpose of funds sought, recently audited financial statements, and proof of tax-exempt status *When to Submit:* any time

Restrictions on Giving: Does not support individuals or religious organizations for sectarian purposes.

OTHER THINGS TO KNOW

Sprint United Telephone's giving program is separate from the Sprint Foundation in Westwood, KS.

GRANTS ANALYSIS

Typical Range: $1,000 to $2,500

SPS Technologies / SPS Foundation

Sales: $374.5 million
Employees: 4,709
Headquarters: New Town, PA
SIC Major Group: Fabricated Metal Products, Industrial Machinery & Equipment, and Primary Metal Industries

CONTACT

John McGrath
Vice President, Industrial Relations
SPS Fdn.
PO Box 1000
New Town, PA 18940

FINANCIAL SUMMARY

Recent Giving: $175,184 (1991); $243,016 (1990); $239,281 (1989)
Assets: $513,085 (1991); $564,492 (1990); $749,896 (1989)
Gifts Received: $260,060 (1989)
EIN: 23-6294553

CONTRIBUTIONS SUMMARY

Typical Recipients: • *Arts & Humanities:* arts centers, arts institutes, music • *Civic & Public Affairs:* environmental affairs, law & justice, safety • *Education:* colleges & universities, private education (precollege) • *Health:* health organizations, hospitals, medical research, pediatric health, single-disease health associations • *International:* international development/relief • *Social Services:* community service organizations, delinquency & crime, united funds, youth organizations

Grant Types: general support

Geographic Distribution: focus on PA

Operating Locations: PA (New Town)

CORP. OFFICERS

John R. Selby: *B* Des Moines IA 1929 *ED* IA St Univ 1956 *CURR EMPL* chmn, ceo: SPS Techs

Harry J. Wilkinson: *B* Philadelphia PA 1937 *ED* Temple Univ 1965 *CURR EMPL* pres, coo: SPS Techs

GIVING OFFICERS

John D. McGrath: trust
John R. Selby: trust *CURR EMPL* chmn, ceo: SPS Techs (see above)

APPLICATION INFORMATION

Initial Approach: Send brief letter describing program. There are no deadlines.

GRANTS ANALYSIS

Number of Grants: 145
Highest Grant: $63,000
Typical Range: $25 to $1,500
Disclosure Period: 1991

RECENT GRANTS

63,000 United Way, Philadelphia, PA
5,000 Franklin Institute, Philadelphia, PA
5,000 Holy Redeemer Hospital, Meadowbrook, PA
5,000 Philadelphia Orchestra, Philadelphia, PA
4,140 St. Joseph's Preparatory School, Philadelphia, PA
3,000 Citizens Crime Commission of Delaware Valley, Philadelphia, PA
2,500 Doylestown Hospital, Doylestown, PA
1,025 Beaver College, Glenside, PA
1,000 Abington Memorial Hospital, Abington, PA
1,000 American Red Cross, Langhorne, PA

Spunk Fund

CONTACT

Anna Matheny-Cartier
Executive-Director
Spunk Fund
675 Third Avenue, Ste. 1510
New York, NY 10017
(212) 972-8330

FINANCIAL SUMMARY

Recent Giving: $1,415,940 (fiscal 1991); $443,081 (fiscal 1990); $725,086 (fiscal 1989)
Assets: $10,381,086 (fiscal year ending June 30, 1991); $11,421,905 (fiscal 1990); $10,731,123 (fiscal 1989)
Gifts Received: $520,000 (fiscal 1991); $600,000 (fiscal 1990); $600,000 (fiscal 1989)
Fiscal Note: In 1991, contributions were received from Marianne Gerschel.
EIN: 13-3116094

CONTRIBUTIONS SUMMARY

Donor(s): Marianne Gerschel
Typical Recipients: • *Arts & Humanities:* dance, literary

arts, museums/galleries, public broadcasting • *Education:* colleges & universities • *Health:* health organizations, medical research, mental health • *Social Services:* child welfare, community service organizations, disabled, drugs & alcohol, family services, youth organizations
Grant Types: general support and research
Geographic Distribution: focus on NY

GIVING OFFICERS
Joseph Erdman: secy
Marianne Gerschell: pres, treas
Anna Metheny-Cartier: exec dir

APPLICATION INFORMATION
Initial Approach: Only contributes to preselected organizations.

OTHER THINGS TO KNOW
Publications: Informational Brochure (including application guidelines)

GRANTS ANALYSIS
Number of Grants: 69
Highest Grant: $85,645
Typical Range: $10,000 to $44,500
Disclosure Period: fiscal year ending June 30, 1991

RECENT GRANTS
85,645 Columbia University, New York, NY
64,800 Handicap International, New York, NY — physical therapist/nurse in Thailand
50,000 Harvard University School of Public Health, Boston, MA — international health training program
48,000 Handicap International, New York, NY — physical therapist/nurse in Thailand
44,892 International Rescue Committee, New York, NY — women's training and housing
44,000 Yale University School of Medicine, New Haven, CT — medical research
41,631 International Rescue Committee, New York, NY —

women's agricultural project
40,756 National Arts Education Research Center/New York University - - education, New York, NY
40,000 Stanford University Medical Center, Stanford, CA — postdoctoral research
40,000 Yale University School of Medicine, New Haven, CT — abuse/neglect prevention

SPX Corp. / SPX Foundation
Former Foundation Name: Sealed Power Foundation
Sales: $673.5 million
Employees: 5,100
Headquarters: Muskegon, MI
SIC Major Group: Fabricated Metal Products, Industrial Machinery & Equipment, Primary Metal Industries, and Transportation Equipment

CONTACT
James M. Sheridan
President
SPX Fdn.
700 Ter. Point Dr.
Muskegon, MI 49443
(616) 724-5826

FINANCIAL SUMMARY
Recent Giving: $235,058 (1991); $310,118 (1990); $416,873 (1989)
Assets: $657 (1991); $24,748 (1990); $132,600 (1989)
Gifts Received: $205,948 (1991); $196,269 (1990); $134,102 (1989)
Fiscal Note: In 1991, contributions were received from SPX Corporation.
EIN: 38-6058308

CONTRIBUTIONS SUMMARY
Typical Recipients: • *Arts & Humanities:* music, performing arts, public broadcasting, theater • *Civic & Public Affairs:* economic development, municipalities • *Education:* business education, colleges & universities, minority education, public education (precollege), science/technology education • *Health:* hospitals, pediatric health • *Religion:* religious organizations • *Social Services:* community service organizations, family services,

united funds, youth organizations
Grant Types: general support and matching
Geographic Distribution: primarily in plant communities
Operating Locations: IL (Des Plaines), IN (Auburn, La Grange, Rochester), KY (Franklin), MI (Alma, Dowagiac, Jackson, Kalamazoo, Muskeogon, Ravenna, Saint Johns, Warren, Whitehall, Zeeland), MN (Owatonna, St. Paul), MS (Olive Branch), OH (Montpelier), WI (New Berlin)

CORP. OFFICERS
Curtis T. Atkisson, Jr.: *CURR EMPL* pres, coo: SPX Corp
Dale A. Johnson: *CURR EMPL* chmn, ceo, dir: SPX Corp

GIVING OFFICERS
D.A. Johnson: trust
D.H. Johnson: treas, trust
S.A. Lison: vp, trust
J.M. Sheridan: pres, trust
R.D. Tuttle: trust
J.D. Tyson: secy, trust
R.B. Werner: trust

APPLICATION INFORMATION
Initial Approach: Send brief letter of inquiry. There are no deadlines.

GRANTS ANALYSIS
Number of Grants: 37
Highest Grant: $37,000
Typical Range: $100 to $5,000
Disclosure Period: 1991
Note: 1991 figures do not include $42,198 in matching gift donations.

RECENT GRANTS
37,000 United Way, Detroit, MI
34,748 United Way, Detroit, MI
20,000 Y Family Christian Association, MI
15,000 West Shore Symphony, Scottville, MI
12,000 Owatonna Foundation, MI
10,000 Southeastern Minnesota Initiative, MI
8,333 Muskegon County Catholic, MI
7,700 Blue Lake Public Radio, MI
6,064 United Way, Detroit, MI
5,000 Junior Achievement, MI

Square D Co. / Square D Foundation
Sales: $1.65 billion
Employees: 11,571
Parent Company: Schneider S.A.
Headquarters: Palatine, IL
SIC Major Group: Electronic & Other Electrical Equipment, Fabricated Metal Products, and Instruments & Related Products

CONTACT
Charlie Hutchinson
Secretary
Square D Fdn.
1415 S Roselle
Palatine, IL 60067
(708) 397-2600

FINANCIAL SUMMARY
Recent Giving: $2,101,490 (1993 est.); $1,294,947 (1992); $1,909,057 (1991)
Assets: $2,084,433 (1992); $1,502,806 (1990); $1,456,322 (1989)
Fiscal Note: Total giving figures above are for foundation only. Contributions primarily made through the foundation; company occasionally makes direct contributions.
EIN: 36-6054195

CONTRIBUTIONS SUMMARY
Typical Recipients: • *Arts & Humanities:* arts associations, arts centers, arts festivals, arts funds, arts institutes, dance, libraries, museums/galleries, music, opera, public broadcasting, theater • *Civic & Public Affairs:* business/free enterprise, environmental affairs, professional & trade associations, rural affairs, safety • *Education:* arts education, business education, colleges & universities, community & junior colleges, economic education, education funds, engineering education, minority education, student aid • *Health:* emergency/ambulance services, health funds, hospitals, medical research, mental health, single-disease health associations • *Social Services:* aged, child welfare, community centers, community service organizations, disabled, emergency relief, food/clothing distribution, homes, united funds, youth organizations
Grant Types: capital, conference/seminar, department, employee matching gifts, fellow-

ship, general support, research, and scholarship

Nonmonetary Support Types: donated equipment

Note: The foundation does not specify the value of nonmonetary support. Individual plants and plant managers should be contacted for nonmonetary support.

Geographic Distribution: areas where Square D Co. maintains manufacturing facilities

Operating Locations: AL (Clanton, Leeds), CA (Costa Mesa), CO, FL (Clearwater, Pinellas Park), IA (Cedar Rapids), IL (Niles, Palatine, Schiller Park), IN (Huntington, Peru), KY (Florence, Lexington), MO (Columbia), NC (Asheville, Knightdale, Monroe, Raleigh), NE (Lincoln), OH (Dublin, Middletown, Oxford), SC (Columbia, Seneca), TN (Elkton, Memphis, Nashville, Smyrna), TX (Dallas, Ft. Worth, Mesquite), WI (Milwaukee, Oshkosh)

CORP. OFFICERS

Charley W. Denny: *CURR EMPL* coo: Square D Co *CORP AFFIL* coo: Schneider NA

GIVING OFFICERS

W. P. Brink: treas, dir
R. P. Fiorani: vp, dir
Philip H. Francis: vp, dir *B* San Diego CA 1938 *CURR EMPL* vp (tech), chief tech off: Square D Co
Charles Hutchinson: secy
W. W. Kurczewski: pres, dir *CURR EMPL* vp, secy, gen coun: Square D Co

APPLICATION INFORMATION

Initial Approach: *Initial Contact:* brief letter or proposal *Include Information On:* description of the organization, amount requested, evaluative plans, purpose for which funds are sought, recently audited financial statement, proof of tax-exempt status, operating budget for the current year showing breakdown of expenses and sources of income, members of the agency's governing board, and corporate and foundation contributors and amount each has contributed in the last calendar year *When to Submit:* to local Square D facilities/plants between June and August for funding the next calendar year

Restrictions on Giving: Does not make contributions to religious organizations (except where support used for nondenominational social service); political groups and organizations; labor unions and organizations; organizations making requests by telephone; organizations listed by the U.S. Attorney General as subversive or front organizations; or individuals.

Since foundation supports United Way in corporate communities, donations normally are not made to organizations receiving support through United Way.

OTHER THINGS TO KNOW

Square D was purchased by Group Schneider in mid-1991. Information on how giving program will be affected is not available.

GRANTS ANALYSIS

Total Grants: $1,294,947
Number of Grants: 321
Highest Grant: $50,000
Typical Range: $1,000 to $5,000
Disclosure Period: 1992
Note: Recent grants are derived from a fiscal 1991 Form 990.

RECENT GRANTS

150,000 Community Youth Creative Learning Experience, Palatine, IL
125,000 North Carolina A&T State University, Greensboro, NC
100,000 American-Ireland Fund
100,000 University of Iowa Foundation, Iowa City, IA
75,000 Northern Illinois University, DeKalb, IL
75,000 Twin Brook YMCA
50,000 Glenwood School for Boys, Glenwood, IL
50,000 International Circus Hall of Fame
50,000 Mount Mercy College, Cedar Rapids, IA
33,000 EAA Aviation Foundation

Stabler Cos., Inc.

Sales: $100.0 million
Employees: 1,500
Headquarters: Harrisburg, PA
SIC Major Group: Electronic & Other Electrical Equipment, Heavy Construction Except Building Construction, Nonmetallic Minerals Except Fuels, and Stone, Clay & Glass Products

CONTACT

Cyril Dunmire
Senior Vice President and Secretary
Stabler Cos., Inc.
635 Lucknow Rd.
Harrisburg, PA 17110
(717) 234-3106

CONTRIBUTIONS SUMMARY

Operating Locations: PA (Harrisburg)

CORP. OFFICERS

Donald B. Stabler: *CURR EMPL* chmn, ceo, pres: Stabler Cos

OTHER THINGS TO KNOW

Company is an original donor to the Doanls B. & Dorothy L. Stabler Foundation.

Stabler Foundation, Donald B. and Dorothy L.

CONTACT

William King
Chairman, Board of Trustees
Donald B. and Dorothy L. Stabler Fdn.
c/o Dauphin Deposit Bank and Trust Co.
213 Market St.
Harrisburg, PA 17105
(717) 255-2121

FINANCIAL SUMMARY

Recent Giving: $532,525 (1991); $471,980 (1990); $373,800 (1989)
Assets: $6,795,507 (1991); $6,429,083 (1990); $6,047,881 (1989)
Gifts Received: $138,500 (1991); $422,800 (1990); $1,198,850 (1989)
Fiscal Note: In 1991, contributions were received from Cyril Dunmire ($300), R. E. Jordan ($200), and Donald B. and Dorothy L. Stabler ($138,000).
EIN: 23-6422944

CONTRIBUTIONS SUMMARY

Donor(s): Stabler Companies
Typical Recipients: • *Arts & Humanities:* libraries, music, public broadcasting • *Education:* colleges & universities, community & junior colleges, education funds, private education (precollege), student aid • *Health:* hospices, hospitals • *Religion:* churches, religious organizations • *Social Services:* child welfare, community service organizations, united funds, youth organizations
Grant Types: capital, endowment, general support, multiyear/continuing support, operating expenses, professorship, and scholarship
Geographic Distribution: focus on PA

GIVING OFFICERS

Richard E. Jordan: trust
William Joseph King: chmn, trust *B* Philadelphia PA 1929 *ED* Univ PA 1954; La Salle Univ MBA 1980 *CURR EMPL* chmn, ceo: Dauphin Deposit Corp *CORP AFFIL* chmn, ceo: Dauphin Deposit Bank & Trust Co; dir: Bank PA, Hempt Bros, Millers Mutual Ins Co
David Schaper: trust
Frank A. Sinon: secy, trust
Richard Zimmerman: trust

APPLICATION INFORMATION

Initial Approach: Send brief letter of inquiry describing program or project. There are no deadlines.
Restrictions on Giving: Does not support individuals or provide loans.

GRANTS ANALYSIS

Number of Grants: 71
Highest Grant: $100,000
Typical Range: $500 to $10,000
Disclosure Period: 1991

RECENT GRANTS

100,000 Woods School, Langhorne, PA
50,000 Harrisburg Area Community College, Harrisburg, PA
50,000 Lehigh University Scholarship Fund, Bethlehem, PA
50,000 Messiah College Scholarship Fund, Harrisburg, PA
45,000 Catholic Diocese of Allentown Scholarship Fund, Allentown, PA

45,000 Catholic Diocese
of Harrisburg
Scholarship Fund,
Harrisburg, PA

40,000 Elizabethtown College Library Fund,
Elizabethtown, PA

20,000 Susquehanna University, Selinsgrove, PA —
Fisher Science Hall

10,000 United Way, Harrisburg, PA

10,000 Wilson College,
Chambersburg, PA

Stackner Family Foundation

CONTACT
Patrick W. Cotter
Executive Director
Stackner Family Fdn.
411 East Wisconsin Avenue,
2500
Milwaukee, WI 53202
(414) 277-5000

FINANCIAL SUMMARY
Recent Giving: $906,000 (fiscal 1991); $1,200,445 (fiscal 1990); $1,212,158 (fiscal 1989)
Assets: $10,999,236 (fiscal year ending August 31, 1991); $10,382,943 (fiscal 1990); $11,941,568 (fiscal 1989)
EIN: 39-6097597

CONTRIBUTIONS SUMMARY
Donor(s): the late John S. Stackner, the late Irene M. Stackner
Typical Recipients: • *Arts & Humanities:* arts institutes, community arts, museums/galleries, theater • *Civic & Public Affairs:* zoos/botanical gardens • *Education:* colleges & universities, elementary education, public education (precollege) • *Health:* health organizations, medical research, single-disease health associations • *Religion:* churches • *Social Services:* child welfare, community service organizations, youth organizations
Grant Types: capital, conference/seminar, general support, multiyear/continuing support, operating expenses, project, research, scholarship, and seed money
Geographic Distribution: limited to the greater Milwaukee, WI, area

GIVING OFFICERS
Patrick William Cotter: secy, exec dir

David Lee MacGregor: treas, dir *B* Cedar Rapids IA 1932 *ED* Univ WI BBA 1954; Univ WI LLB 1956 *CURR EMPL* ptnr: Quarles & Brady *CORP AFFIL* ptnr: Quarles & Brady *NONPR AFFIL* fellow: Am Coll Probate Couns; mem: Am Bar Assn, Milwaukee Bar Assn, Natl Assn Estate Planning Councs, WI Bar Assn
John A. Treiber: vp, dir
Patricia S. Treiber: pres, dir
Phillip A. Treiber: vp, dir

APPLICATION INFORMATION
Initial Approach: Send cover letter and full proposal. Deadlines are March 31 and August 31. Board meets in April and September. Decisions are made three weeks after board meetings.
Restrictions on Giving: Does not support individuals or provide scholarships or loans.

GRANTS ANALYSIS
Number of Grants: 141
Highest Grant: $150,000
Typical Range: $1,000 to $5,000
Disclosure Period: fiscal year ending August 31, 1991

RECENT GRANTS
150,000 Milwaukee Repertory Theater, Milwaukee, WI

60,000 Carroll College, Waukesha, WI

60,000 University Lake School, Hartland, WI

60,000 University Lake School, Hartland, WI

60,000 Zoological Society, Milwaukee, WI

40,000 Friends of Museum, Milwaukee, WI

26,000 Methodist Manor Health Center, Milwaukee, WI

20,000 Lake Geneva Charitable Sailing Trust, Lake Geneva, WI — Olympic Entry

17,000 Milwaukee Art Museum, Milwaukee, WI

17,000 Montessori School of Waukesha, Waukesha, WI

Stackpole-Hall Foundation

CONTACT
William C. Conrad
Executive Secretary
Stackpole-Hall Foundation
44 South St. Marys St.
St. Marys, PA 15857
(814) 834-1845

FINANCIAL SUMMARY
Recent Giving: $841,843 (1991); $606,357 (1990); $659,768 (1989)
Assets: $14,867,242 (1991); $17,852,116 (1990); $17,738,312 (1989)
EIN: 25-6006650

CONTRIBUTIONS SUMMARY
Donor(s): The Stackpole-Hall Foundation was established as a trust in Pennsylvania in 1951, with funds donated by the late L. G. Hall, J. H. Stackpole, Mrs. Adelaide Stackpole, and by Harrison C. Stackpole. James Hall Stackpole (1902-1964), son of Harrison C. Stackpole and the former Sallie Hall, was chairman of Stackpole Carbon Company. A portion of the foundation's funds is restricted by the donors through specific bequests to designated religious organizations.
Typical Recipients: • *Arts & Humanities:* arts associations, history/historic preservation, libraries • *Civic & Public Affairs:* economic development, environmental affairs, municipalities, nonprofit management, urban & community affairs • *Education:* colleges & universities, education associations, private education (precollege) • *Health:* emergency/ambulance services, hospitals, mental health, nursing services • *Religion:* churches, religious organizations • *Social Services:* community centers, drugs & alcohol, employment/job training, recreation & athletics, united funds, youth organizations
Grant Types: capital, general support, project, and seed money
Geographic Distribution: focus on Elk County, PA, area

GIVING OFFICERS
William C. Conrad: exec secy

Douglas R. Dobson: trust *CURR EMPL* vchmn, dir: Stackpole Corp
Helen Hall Drew: trust
Lyle G. Hall: trust *B* 1929 *ED* Yale Univ 1948-1951; Harvard Univ 1969; Boston Univ BS 1975; Episcopal Divinity Sch M 1978 *CURR EMPL* chmn, dir: Stackpole Corp *NONPR AFFIL* mem diocesan counc: Episcopal Church Diocese Erie; rector: St Dunstans Episcopal Church; trust: Church Home Soc, Dana Hall Sch, Episcopal Divinity Sch
J. M. Hamlin Johnson: trust *B* Ridgeway PA 1925 *ED* Grove City Coll BS 1949; PA St Univ 1969 *CORP AFFIL* asst treas: Pure Indus; dir: Hamlin Bank & Trust Co; ptnr, treas: J & B Co; vp, dir: Stackpole Corp; asst treas: Stackpole Ltd; treas, asst secy: Stackpole Components Co *NONPR AFFIL* dir: Un Fund St Mary; mem: Natl Assn Accts; trust: A Kaul Meml Hosp; dir, treas: ELCAM Vocational Rehab Ctr
Alexander Sheble-Hall: trust
Harrison Clinton Stackpole: chmn, trust *B* Ridgeway PA 1914 *ED* Yale Univ *CORP AFFIL* dir: Stackpole Corp
R. Dauer Stackpole: trust *CORP AFFIL* dir: Stackpole Corp

APPLICATION INFORMATION
Initial Approach:
The foundation accepts brief letters of inquiry. If the board is interested in a project, it will request a more complete proposal.
Applicants should include a history of the organization, description of the proposed project, proposed budget, most recent financial statement, evidence of need for the project, and organizational staff list.
The board meets in February, May, August, and December. Proposals should be received by January, April, July, or November.
Restrictions on Giving: No grants are made to individuals.

GRANTS ANALYSIS
Total Grants: $841,843
Number of Grants: 68
Highest Grant: $150,000
Typical Range: $1,000 to $8,000 and $30,000 to $50,000
Disclosure Period: 1991
Note: Figure for average grant excludes two grants totaling

$238,663. Recent grants are derived from a 1991 Form 990.

RECENT GRANTS

150,000 Elk County Development Foundation Loan Fund, St. Marys, PA — community economic development

88,663 Grace Episcopal Church, Ridgway, PA — unrestricted

68,202 Episcopal Diocese of Northwest Pennsylvania, Erie, PA — unrestricted

50,000 Episcopal Divinity School, Cambridge, MA — program development

29,251 Ridgway Area School District, Ridgway, PA — Votech educaton feasibility study

27,280 Andrew Kaul Memorial Hospital, St. Marys, PA — unrestricted

27,280 Boy Scouts of America-Bucktail Council, DuBois, PA — unrestricted

27,280 Hotchkiss School, Lakeville, CT — unrestricted

27,280 St. Agnes Episcopal Church, St. Marys, PA — unrestricted

27,280 Yale University, New Haven, CT — unrestricted

Stacy Foundation, Festus

CONTACT
Festus Stacy
Trustee
Festus Stacy Fdn.
c/o McMillan, Unruh and Davis
1941 West Oakland Park Blvd.
Ft. Lauderdale, FL 33311-1572
(305) 739-5633

FINANCIAL SUMMARY
Recent Giving: $460,055 (fiscal 1991); $371,428 (fiscal 1990); $127,000 (fiscal 1988)
Assets: $10,543,674 (fiscal year ending October 31, 1991); $8,194,417 (fiscal 1990); $3,927,378 (fiscal 1988)
Gifts Received: $352,750 (fiscal 1990); $1,094,350 (fiscal 1988)
EIN: 59-6698852

CONTRIBUTIONS SUMMARY
Donor(s): Festus Stacy

Typical Recipients: • *Arts & Humanities:* public broadcasting • *Health:* health organizations, mental health, single-disease health associations • *Religion:* churches, missionary activities, religious organizations • *Social Services:* community service organizations, community service organizations
Grant Types: general support

GIVING OFFICERS
Festus Stacy: trust
Helen Stacy: trust
Virlee Stacy Stepelton: trust

APPLICATION INFORMATION
Initial Approach: Contributes only to preselected organizations.
Restrictions on Giving: Does not support individuals.

GRANTS ANALYSIS
Number of Grants: 31
Highest Grant: $307,555
Typical Range: $2,000 to $20,000
Disclosure Period: fiscal year ending October 31, 1991

RECENT GRANTS

307,555 First Presbyterian Church, Ft. Lauderdale, FL

20,000 Irene Stacy Community Mental Health, Butler, PA

15,000 Salvation Army, Ft. Lauderdale, FL

12,000 Trinity Broadcasting Network, Santa Ana, CA

8,000 Coral Ridge Ministries, Coral Ridge Presbyterian Church, Ft. Lauderdale, FL

7,500 First Christian Church, Princeton, NJ

7,500 Mount Zion Baptist Church, Los Angeles, CA

6,000 American Cancer Society, Ft. Lauderdale, FL

6,000 American Heart Association, Ft. Lauderdale, FL

Staley Foundation, Thomas F.

CONTACT
Thomas F. Staley
President
Thomas F. Staley Fdn.
Four Chatsworth Avenue, No. 3
Larchmont, NY 10538-2932
(914) 834-2669

FINANCIAL SUMMARY
Recent Giving: $201,112 (1991); $198,531 (1990); $205,433 (1989)
Assets: $5,804,296 (1991); $4,903,073 (1990); $5,226,976 (1989)
Gifts Received: $100 (1991)
EIN: 13-6071888

CONTRIBUTIONS SUMMARY
Donor(s): the late Thomas F. Staley, Shirley H. Hunter
Typical Recipients: • *Education:* colleges & universities, religious education

GIVING OFFICERS
Rev. Joseph P. Bishop: trust
Robert G. Howard: treas
Shirley H. Hunter: trust
Rev. Peter C. Moore: trust
Thomas F. Staley: pres
Alfred Sunderwirth: trust

APPLICATION INFORMATION
Initial Approach: Contributes only to preselected organizations.

OTHER THINGS TO KNOW
Provides grants for Christian scholar lectureship programs on college campuses.
Publications: Informational Brochure (including application guidelines)

GRANTS ANALYSIS
Number of Grants: 139
Highest Grant: $3,200
Typical Range: $1,000 to $1,600
Disclosure Period: 1991

RECENT GRANTS

3,200 Virginia Intermont College, Richmond, VA

3,188 Covenant College, Lookout Mountain, TN

3,105 Concordia College, Moorehead, MN

3,063 Pepperdine University, Malibu, CA

2,900 Averett College, Danville, VA

2,834 Dallas Baptist University, Dallas, TX

2,807 Southern Nazarene University, Bethany, OK

2,387 Dordt College, Sioux City, IA

2,375 National Student Prayer Breakfast

1,900 Bethel College, North Newton, KS

Staley, Jr. Foundation, A. E.

CONTACT
J. W. Penn
Manager
A. E. Staley, Jr. Fdn.
c/o First of America Trust Company
Decatur, IL 62525
(217) 424-2010

FINANCIAL SUMMARY
Recent Giving: $309,435 (1990); $223,230 (1989); $147,026 (1988)
Assets: $4,076,682 (1990); $4,502,321 (1989); $4,113,219 (1988)
EIN: 37-6023961

CONTRIBUTIONS SUMMARY
Donor(s): Augustus Eugene Staley, Jr.
Typical Recipients: • *Arts & Humanities:* museums/galleries • *Civic & Public Affairs:* environmental affairs, zoos/botanical gardens • *Education:* colleges & universities, community & junior colleges, education funds • *Health:* health organizations, hospitals, medical research, single-disease health associations • *Social Services:* child welfare, community service organizations, united funds, youth organizations
Grant Types: general support
Geographic Distribution: focus on IL

GIVING OFFICERS
First of America Bank: trust

APPLICATION INFORMATION
Initial Approach: Contributes only to preselected organizations.

GRANTS ANALYSIS
Number of Grants: 45
Highest Grant: $80,750
Typical Range: $400 to $8,700

Disclosure Period: 1990

RECENT GRANTS

80,750 Millikin University, Decatur, IL

74,250 Decatur Memorial Hospital, Decatur, IL

62,500 United Way, Decatur, IL

15,000 American Cancer Society, Decatur, IL

10,000 Richland Community College, Richland, IL

10,000 St. Theresa Educational Foundation, IL

8,750 Macon County Heart Association, Decatur, IL

7,500 St. Theresa Educational Foundation, IL

5,000 Decatur Area Children's Museum, Decatur, IL

5,000 University of Pennsylvania, Philadelphia, PA

Staley Manufacturing Co., A.E. / Staley Company Foundation

Sales: $1.1 billion
Employees: 2,815
Headquarters: Decatur, IL
SIC Major Group: Food & Kindred Products

CONTACT

J. Patrick Mohan
Executive Vice President, Administration
A.E. Staley Manufacturing Co.
2200 East Eldorado St.
Decatur, IL 62525
(217) 423-4411

FINANCIAL SUMMARY

Recent Giving: $265,000 (fiscal 1991)
Assets: $217,929 (fiscal year ending August 31, 1991); $455,351 (fiscal 1990)
EIN: 37-1106376

CONTRIBUTIONS SUMMARY

Typical Recipients: • *Arts & Humanities:* arts associations, museums/galleries • *Civic & Public Affairs:* economics • *Education:* colleges & universities, community & junior colleges • *Health:* general • *Social Services:* community service organizations, youth organizations

Grant Types: general support and project

Geographic Distribution: headquarters and operating locations

Operating Locations: IL (Decatur)

CORP. OFFICERS

Douglas Lapins: *CURR EMPL* pres, ceo, dir: AE Staley Mfg Co

GIVING OFFICERS

J. Patrick Mohan: *CURR EMPL* exec vp (admin): A.E. Staley Mfg Co

APPLICATION INFORMATION

Initial Approach: Send letter of inquiry. There are no deadlines.

GRANTS ANALYSIS

Number of Grants: 14
Highest Grant: $75,000
Typical Range: $1,000 to $10,000
Disclosure Period: fiscal year ending August 31, 1991

RECENT GRANTS

75,000 Purdue Foundation, West Lafayette, IN — Whistler Center for Carbohydrate Research

40,000 Richland Community College, Decatur, IL — Staley Scholarships

40,000 University of Tennessee, Knoxville, TN — engineering department

25,000 Associated Colleges of Illinois, Chicago, IL — Millikin University

20,000 St. Teresa Education Foundation, Decatur, IL

18,000 American Association of Cereal Chemists Scholarship Endowment Fund, St. Paul, MN

12,500 Decatur Memorial Foundation, Decatur, IL

10,000 Decatur Swim Club, Decatur, IL

10,000 Friends of St. Mary's Hospital Foundation, Decatur, IL — obstetrics department

5,000 Decatur Area Arts Council, Decatur, IL

Stamps Foundation, James L.

CONTACT

Delores J. Boutault
Manager
James L. Stamps Fdn.
PO Box 250
Downey, CA 90241
(310) 861-3112

FINANCIAL SUMMARY

Recent Giving: $790,286 (1991); $807,639 (1990); $548,548 (1989)
Assets: $21,298,374 (1991); $18,755,181 (1990); $18,528,015 (1989)
Gifts Received: $499,376 (1991)
Fiscal Note: In 1991, contributions were received from the trust for the estate of James L. Stamps.
EIN: 95-6086125

CONTRIBUTIONS SUMMARY

Donor(s): The foundation was incorporated in 1963 by the late James L. Stamps.
Typical Recipients: • *Civic & Public Affairs:* municipalities, public policy • *Education:* colleges & universities, religious education • *Health:* public health • *Religion:* churches, missionary activities, religious organizations • *Social Services:* food/clothing distribution, youth organizations
Grant Types: capital, emergency, matching, operating expenses, and project
Geographic Distribution: limited to Southern California

GIVING OFFICERS

Delores J. Boutalt: mgr
E. C. Boutalt: pres, trust
Kenneth E. Gail: secy, treas, trust
I. W. Johnson: trust
Willis R. Leach: trust
Thomas P. Lynch: vp, trust

APPLICATION INFORMATION

Initial Approach:
The foundation requests applications be made in writing.
The foundation requests a brief inquiry describing the organization and the project for which funds are sought. Further information will be requested by the foundation.
The foundation has no deadline for submitting proposals.

Restrictions on Giving: The foundation supports Christian-based organizations. Some support is given for hospital equipment, medical research, and local public service organizations. No grants are made to individuals, or for conferences, endowment funds, deficit financing, fellowships, publications, or scholarships.

OTHER THINGS TO KNOW

Publications: application guidelines

GRANTS ANALYSIS

Total Grants: $790,286
Number of Grants: 67
Highest Grant: $65,000
Typical Range: $5,000 to $15,000
Disclosure Period: 1991
Note: Recent grants are derived from a 1991 grants list.

RECENT GRANTS

65,000 City of Downey, Downey, CA — purchase of organ

50,000 Forest Home Christian Conference Center, Forest Falls, CA

38,000 First Baptist Church, Downey, CA — choir tour

30,000 Kare Youth League, Arcadia, CA — building of cabins at Wrightwood Camp

25,225 Valley Baptist Fellowship, Yucalpa, CA

25,000 First Baptist Church, Downey, CA — intern program

25,000 Mission Aviation Fellowship, Redlands, CA — purchase of radios for safety training pilots

25,000 Youth for Christ/San Gabriel and Inland Valleys, San Dimas, CA

24,000 Azusa Pacific University, Azusa, CA — scholarships

24,000 Biola University, La Mirada, CA — scholarships

Standard Brands Paint Co.

Sales: $253.0 million
Employees: 2,014
Headquarters: Torrance, CA
SIC Major Group: Building
    Materials & Garden Supplies,
    Chemicals & Allied Products,
    Furniture & Homefurnishings
    Stores, and Wholesale
    Trade—Nondurable Goods

CONTACT
Susan Guillaume
Secretary to V.P. of Finance
Standard Brands Paint Co.
4300 West 190th St.
Torrance, CA 90509
(310) 214-2411

FINANCIAL SUMMARY
Fiscal Note: Annual Giving
Range: $100,000 to $250,000

CONTRIBUTIONS SUMMARY
Company reports 60% of contributions support health and welfare; 20% to the arts; 10% to civic and public affairs; and 10% to education.
Typical Recipients: • *Arts & Humanities:* general • *Civic & Public Affairs:* general • *Education:* general • *Social Services:* general
Grant Types: general support
Nonmonetary Support Types: donated products, in-kind services, and loaned executives
Operating Locations: CA (Carson, Torrance)

CORP. OFFICERS
Stuart Buchalter: *B* Los Angeles CA 1937 *ED* Univ CA Berkeley 1959; Harvard Univ Law Sch 1962 *CURR EMPL* chmn, dir: Standard Brands Paint Co
Richard Loeffler: *CURR EMPL* pres, coo, dir: Standard Brands Paint Co

APPLICATION INFORMATION
Initial Approach: Send brief letter of inquiry. There are no deadlines.

Standard Chartered Bank New York

Headquarters: New York, NY
SIC Major Group: Depository
    Institutions

CONTACT
Tina Xydiaris
Officer, Accounts Payable
Standard Chartered Bank New
    York
160 Water St.
New York, NY 10038
(212) 269-3100

FINANCIAL SUMMARY
Fiscal Note: Annual Giving
Range: $50,000 annually

CONTRIBUTIONS SUMMARY
General manager makes funding decisions. In the past, has supported all the major categories of giving: arts and humanities, civic and public affairs, education, health, and social services.
Typical Recipients: • *Arts & Humanities:* museums/galleries, music • *Civic & Public Affairs:* professional & trade associations • *Health:* hospitals • *Social Services:* community service organizations
Grant Types: general support
Nonmonetary Support Types: donated equipment
Geographic Distribution: in the New York area and to local chapters of national organizations
Operating Locations: FL, GA, IL, NY (New York), WA

CORP. OFFICERS
Peter Dobson: *CURR EMPL* pres, gen mgr North Am: Standard Chartered Bank NY

GIVING OFFICERS
Tina Xydiaris: *CURR EMPL* off (accounts payable): Standard Chartered Bank NY

APPLICATION INFORMATION
Initial Approach: Send letter any time.

GRANTS ANALYSIS
Typical Range: $200 to $300

Standard Federal Bank

Assets: $9.51 billion
Employees: 2,400
Headquarters: Troy, MI
SIC Major Group: Depository
    Institutions

CONTACT
William Yaw, Jr.
Senior Vice President, Marketing
Standard Federal Bank
2600 West Big Beaver Rd.
Troy, MI 48084
(313) 643-9600

CONTRIBUTIONS SUMMARY
Operating Locations: MI
(Troy)

CORP. OFFICERS
Joseph Krul: *CURR EMPL* sr vp, cfo: Standard Fed Bank
Thomas R. Ricketts: *CURR EMPL* chmn, pres: Standard Fed Bank

Standard Motor Products, Inc.

Sales: $534.8 million
Employees: 3,400
Headquarters: Long Island City, NY
SIC Major Group: Electronic & Other Electrical Equipment, Industrial Machinery & Equipment, and Transportation Equipment

CONTACT
Sandford Kay
Vice President, Human Relations
Standard Motor Products, Inc.
37-18 Northern Blvd.
Long Island City, NY 11101
(718) 392-0200

CONTRIBUTIONS SUMMARY
Operating Locations: NY
(Long Island City)

CORP. OFFICERS
Bernard Fife: *CURR EMPL* co-chmn, co-ceo, dir: Standard Motor Products
Lawrence I. Sills: *CURR EMPL* pres, coo, dir: Standard Motor Products
Nathaniel L. Sills: *CURR EMPL* co-chmn, co-ceo, dir: Standard Motor Products

Standard Pacific Corp.

Revenue: $299.1 million
Employees: 553
Headquarters: Costa Mesa, CA
SIC Major Group: Depository
    Institutions, Furniture & Fixtures, General Building Contractors, and Stone, Clay & Glass Products

CONTACT
Victor Loeza
Corporate Tax
Standard Pacific Corp.
1565 West MacArthur Blvd.
Costa Mesa, CA 92626
(714) 546-1161

CONTRIBUTIONS SUMMARY
Operating Locations: CA
(Costa Mesa)

CORP. OFFICERS
Ronald R. Foell: *CURR EMPL* pres: Standard Pacific Corp
Arthur Svendsen: *CURR EMPL* chmn, ceo: Standard Pacific Corp

Standard Products Co. / Standard Products Co. Foundation

Sales: $592.0 million
Employees: 7,543
Headquarters: Cleveland, OH
SIC Major Group: Rubber & Miscellaneous Plastics Products and Transportation Equipment

CONTACT
Thomas A. Harker
Vice President, Finance & Trustee
Standard Products
2130 West 110th St.
Cleveland, OH 44102
(216) 281-8300

FINANCIAL SUMMARY
Recent Giving: $77,000 (1990); $51,750 (1989)
Assets: $1,364,423 (1990); $1,056,954 (1989)
Gifts Received: $291,248 (1990)
Fiscal Note: In 1990, contributions were received from Standard Products Co.
EIN: 34-1440117

CONTRIBUTIONS SUMMARY
Typical Recipients: • *Civic & Public Affairs:* environmental affairs, municipalities • *Education:* colleges & universities, education funds • *Health:* health organizations, hospitals, medical research, single-disease health associations • *Social Services:* community service organizations, food/clothing distribution, united funds, youth organizations
Grant Types: general support

Geographic Distribution:
focus on OH
Operating Locations: CA
(Oakland), KY (Lexington), MI
(Dearborn, Gaylord), NC
(Goldsboro, Rocky Mount),
NY (Schenectady), OH (Cleveland, Port Clinton), SC (Winnsboro)
Note: List includes division
and plant locations.

CORP. OFFICERS
James Sims Reid, Jr.: *B* Cleveland OH 1926 *ED* Harvard
Univ AB 1948; Harvard Univ
JD 1951 *CURR EMPL* chmn,
ceo, dir: Standard Products Co
CORP AFFIL dir: Soc Corp,
Soc Natl Bank Cleveland
NONPR AFFIL mem: MI Bar
Assn, OH Bar Assn; trust: John
Carroll Univ, Musical Arts
Assn Cleveland

GIVING OFFICERS
Edward B. Brandon: trust *B*
Davenport IA 1931 *ED* Northwestern Univ BS 1953; Univ
PA Wharton Sch MBA 1956
CURR EMPL chmn, ceo, dir:
Natl City Corp *CORP AFFIL*
chmn, dir: Natl City Bank
Cleveland; dir: First KY Natl
Corp; mem audit comm: Premier Indus Corp; mem (audit &
compensation comm): Standard
Products Co; mem compensation comm: RPM Inc *NONPR
AFFIL* bd advs, mem exec
comm: Notre Dame Coll OH;
mem: Am Bankers Assn, Assn
Reserve City Bankers, OH
Bankers Assn; trust: John
Carroll Univ, Greater Cleveland Roundtable, Natl Conf
Christians Jews, St Vincent
Charity Hosp, Un Way Svcs;
trust, mem exec comm: Greater
Cleveland Growth Assn;
vchmn, mem exec comm:
YMCA Greater Cleveland
James Edward Chapman:
secy, trust *B* Wadsworth OH
1927 *ED* OH St Univ BBA
1953; OH St Univ JD 1954
CURR EMPL secy: Preformed
Line Products Co *CORP
AFFIL* dir: Euclid Indus,
McGean-Rohco Inc; ptnr:
Baker & Hostetler; secy: Preformed Line Products Co
NONPR AFFIL mem: Am Bar
Assn, Cleveland Bar Assn,
Great Lakes Historical Soc,
Natl Assn Mental Health, Natl
Maritime Historical Soc, OH
Bar Assn, Shaker Symphony
Orchestra, Suburban Symphony Orchestra, US Naval
Inst; trust: Mystic Seaport Mus

Robert C. Jacob: vp, trust
CORP AFFIL vp, secy: Standard Products Co
James Sims Reid, Jr.: pres,
trust *CURR EMPL* chmn, ceo,
dir: Standard Products Co (see
above)
Joseph A. Robinson: treas,
trust *B* Kenton OH 1938 *ED*
Univ Cincinnati 1961 *CURR
EMPL* vp: Standard Products
Co *CORP AFFIL* vp: Standard
Products Co *NONPR AFFIL*
mem: Am Inst CPAs, Fin Execs
Inst

APPLICATION INFORMATION
Initial Approach: Contributes
only to preselected organizations.

GRANTS ANALYSIS
Number of Grants: 143
Highest Grant: $35,000
Typical Range: $250 to $2,000
Disclosure Period: 1990

RECENT GRANTS
35,000 Cleveland Initiative for Education, Cleveland, OH
35,000 Musical Arts Association, Cleveland, OH
17,025 John Carroll University, University Heights, OH
14,050 United Way, Cleveland, OH
10,000 Case Associates Program, Cleveland, OH
8,000 University Hospitals of Cleveland, Cleveland, OH
7,020 Baldwin-Wallace College, Berea, OH
5,000 American Red Cross, Cleveland, OH
5,000 Boys Club of Rocky Mount, Rocky Mount, NC
2,500 South Carolina Council on Economic Education, Columbia, SC

Standard Register Co. / Sherman-Standard Register Foundation
Sales: $693.7 million
Employees: 5,852
Headquarters: Dayton, OH
SIC Major Group: Industrial
Machinery & Equipment,

Paper & Allied Products, and
Printing & Publishing

CONTACT
Bill Sherman
President
Sherman Fdn.
PO Box 1167
Dayton, OH 45401-1167
(513) 443-1000

FINANCIAL SUMMARY
Recent Giving: $194,858
(1990)
Assets: $759,251 (1990)
Gifts Received: $203,600
(1990); $203,600 (1989)
Fiscal Note: In 1990, contributions were received from Standard Register Co.
EIN: 31-6026027

CONTRIBUTIONS SUMMARY
Typical Recipients: • *Arts &
Humanities:* arts funds, community arts • *Civic & Public Affairs:* women's affairs
• *Health:* hospitals • *Social
Services:* community service organizations, united funds,
youth organizations
Grant Types: general support
Geographic Distribution:
focus on NY and OH
Operating Locations: IN
(Shelby), OH (Cincinnati, Dayton, Newark), PA (Bedford,
York), TN (Murfreesboro), TX
(Houston), VT (Middlebury)
Note: List includes plant locations

CORP. OFFICERS
John K. Darragh: *CURR
EMPL* pres, ceo: Standard Register Co

GIVING OFFICERS
Craig J. Brown: treas
J. L. Sherman: vp
William P. Sherman: pres
Otto F. Stock: secy

APPLICATION INFORMATION
Initial Approach: Send brief
letter describing program.
There are no deadlines.

GRANTS ANALYSIS
Number of Grants: 44
Highest Grant: $8,500
Typical Range: $500 to $1,000
Disclosure Period: 1990

RECENT GRANTS
8,500 United Way
5,000 United Fund, Fayetteville, AR
4,725 United Way

4,000 Arts Dayton, Dayton, OH
2,700 United Way, Rochester, NY
2,700 United Way
2,670 United Way
2,500 Hanford Community Hospital Fund, Hanford, CA
2,000 United Way
2,000 Womanline, Dayton, OH

Standard Steel Speciality Co. / Standard Steel Speciality Co. Foundation
Sales: $40.0 million
Employees: 300
Headquarters: Beaver Falls, PA
SIC Major Group: Fabricated
Metal Products, Industrial
Machinery & Equipment, and
Primary Metal Industries

CONTACT
R.E. Conley
Secretary & Teasurer
Standard Steel Speciality Co.
Foundation
PO Box 20
Beaver Falls, PA 15010
(412) 846-7600
Note: Foundation is located at
c/o Equibank, Financial
Management Department, Two
Oliver Plaza, Pittsburgh, PA,
15222-2711.

FINANCIAL SUMMARY
Recent Giving: $7,300 (1991)
Assets: $70,334 (1991)
EIN: 25-6038268

CONTRIBUTIONS SUMMARY
Typical Recipients: • *Education:* general • *Social Services:*
community service organizations, united funds, youth organizations
Grant Types: general support
Geographic Distribution:
headquarters area
Operating Locations: PA
(Beaver Falls)

CORP. OFFICERS
T. G. Armstrong: *CURR
EMPL* pres, ceo: Standard
Steel Speciality Co
R.E. Conley: *CURR EMPL*
cfo: Standard Steel Speciality
Co

GIVING OFFICERS
Integra Bank/North: trust

APPLICATION INFORMATION

Initial Approach: Foundation supports preselected organizations.

GRANTS ANALYSIS

Disclosure Period: 1991
Note: 1991 grants list not provided.

Standard Textile Co., Inc.

Sales: $140.0 million
Employees: 1,000
Headquarters: Cincinnati, OH
SIC Major Group: Apparel & Other Textile Products, Textile Mill Products, and Wholesale Trade—Nondurable Goods

CONTACT

Ernest Frankel
Controller & Secretary
Standard Textile Co., Inc.
One Knollcrest Dr.
Cincinnati, OH 45222
(513) 761-9255

CONTRIBUTIONS SUMMARY

Operating Locations: OH (Cincinnati)

CORP. OFFICERS

Gary Heiman: *CURR EMPL* pres: Standard Textile Co
Paul Heiman: *CURR EMPL* chmn, ceo: Standard Textile Co

Standex International Corp. / Standex International Foundation

Sales: $481.7 million
Employees: 5,000
Headquarters: Salem, NH
SIC Major Group: Fabricated Metal Products, Industrial Machinery & Equipment, Miscellaneous Manufacturing Industries, and Printing & Publishing

CONTACT

Thomas King
President
Standex International Fdn.
6 Manor Pkwy.
Salem, NH 03079
(603) 893-9701

FINANCIAL SUMMARY

Recent Giving: $103,098 (1988)
Assets: $53,492 (1988)

EIN: 04-6173127

CONTRIBUTIONS SUMMARY

Typical Recipients: • *Civic & Public Affairs:* urban & community affairs • *Education:* general • *Health:* hospitals
Grant Types: matching
Geographic Distribution: primarily Salem, NH
Operating Locations: NH (Salem)

CORP. OFFICERS

T.L. King: *CURR EMPL* pres, ceo: Standex Intl Corp

APPLICATION INFORMATION

Initial Approach: Application form is required for all submissions. There are no deadlines.

GRANTS ANALYSIS

Highest Grant: $10,500
Typical Range: $1,000 to $2,500
Disclosure Period: 1988

Stanford Theater Foundation

CONTACT

Stanford Theater Foundation
P.O. Box 1330
Los Altos, CA 94023-1330

FINANCIAL SUMMARY

Recent Giving: $0 (1990)
Assets: $8,976,257 (1990)
Gifts Received: $305,100 (1990)
EIN: 77-0197543

GRANTS ANALYSIS

Total Grants: $0
Disclosure Period: 1990

Stanhome Inc.

Sales: $710.0 million
Employees: 4,700
Headquarters: Westfield, MA
SIC Major Group: Chemicals & Allied Products, Miscellaneous Manufacturing Industries, Miscellaneous Retail, and Wholesale Trade—Durable Goods

CONTACT

Ronald Jalbert
Vice President, Human Resources
Stanhome Inc.
333 Western Ave.
Westfield, MA 01085
(413) 562-3631

CONTRIBUTIONS SUMMARY

Grant Types: matching
Operating Locations: MA (Westfield)

CORP. OFFICERS

H.L. Tower: *CURR EMPL* chmn, dir: Stanhome
Alejandro Diaz Vargas: *CURR EMPL* pres, ceo, coo, dir: Stanhome

Stanley Charitable Foundation, A. W.

CONTACT

James Lemeris
A. W. Stanley Charitable Fdn.
1 Exchange Pl.
Waterbury, CT 06721
(203) 548-3125

FINANCIAL SUMMARY

Recent Giving: $446,250 (1991); $443,950 (1990); $458,092 (1989)
Assets: $12,663,001 (1991); $10,235,055 (1990); $10,620,756 (1989)
EIN: 06-0724195

CONTRIBUTIONS SUMMARY

Donor(s): the late Alix W. Stanley
Typical Recipients: • *Arts & Humanities:* community arts, museums/galleries, music, performing arts, public broadcasting • *Civic & Public Affairs:* housing • *Education:* colleges & universities • *Health:* hospitals • *Social Services:* child welfare, community service organizations, family planning, family services, religious welfare, united funds, youth organizations
Grant Types: capital, emergency, and multiyear/continuing support
Geographic Distribution: focus on New Britain, CT, and surrounding areas

GIVING OFFICERS

William E. Attwood: pres
Donald Walter Davis: trust *B* Springfield MA 1921 *ED* PA St Univ AB; Harvard Univ MBA

CORP AFFIL chmn exec comm, dir: Stanley Works; dir: Allied-Signal, Northeast Utilities, Pitney Bowes *NONPR AFFIL* dir: CT Pub TV, Natl Captioning Inst, Natl Inst Dispute Resolution, New Britain Gen Hosp; mem: Natl Assn Mfrs; vchmn bd regents: Univ Hartford
Timothy Grace: off
Marie S. Gustin: trust
James R. Lemeris: secy, treas
Susan Rathgeber: trust
Catherine Rogers: trust
John W. Shumaker: trust
Rev. James A. Simpson: trust
Talcott Stanley: trust

APPLICATION INFORMATION

Initial Approach: Send brief letter describing program. There are no deadlines.
Restrictions on Giving: Does not support individuals.

GRANTS ANALYSIS

Number of Grants: 15
Highest Grant: $125,000
Typical Range: $3,000 to $30,000
Disclosure Period: 1991

RECENT GRANTS

125,000 United Way, New Britain, CT
69,500 New Britain Museum of American Art, New Britain, CT
55,000 Friendship Center, New Britain, CT
50,000 YWCA, New Britain, CT
30,000 Catholic Family Services, New Britain, CT
30,000 Constructive Workshop, New Britain, CT
30,000 Family Services, New Britain, CT
15,000 New Britain Symphony, New Britain, CT
12,500 Connecticut Public Broadcasting, New Britain, CT
10,750 Prudence Crandall Center, New Britain, CT

Stanley Consultants / Stanley Consultants Charitable Foundation

Revenue: $24.0 million
Employees: 460
Parent Company: SC Companies
Headquarters: Muscatine, IA
SIC Major Group: Engineering & Management Services

CONTACT

Kathleen K. Johnson
Secretary
Stanley Consultants Charitable Foundation
225 Iowa Ave.
Muscatine, IA 52761-3764
(319) 264-6600

FINANCIAL SUMMARY

Recent Giving: $7,450 (fiscal 1991)
Assets: $614 (fiscal year ending March 30, 1991)
Gifts Received: $6,200 (fiscal 1991)
Fiscal Note: In 1991, contributions were received from Stanley Consultants.
EIN: 42-1186325

CONTRIBUTIONS SUMMARY

Typical Recipients: • *Education:* colleges & universities • *Social Services:* united funds
Operating Locations: IA (Muscatine)

CORP. OFFICERS

Richard H. Stanley: *B* Muscatine IA 1932 *ED* IA St Univ BS; Univ IA MS *CURR EMPL* vchmn, dir: HON Indus *CORP AFFIL* chmn, dir: Stanley Consulting *NONPR AFFIL* bd govs: IA St Univ Achievement Fdn; dir: Northeast-Midwest Inst, Univ Dubuque; mem: Am Soc Engring Ed, Am Soc Mechanical Engrs, Chamber Commerce, Consulting Engrs Counc IA, IA Engring Soc, Inst Electrical Electronics Engrs, Muscatine Chamber Commerce, Natl Soc Professional Engrs; mem industrial adv counc: IA St Univ Coll Engring; mem pres counc: IA St Univ; pres, dir: Muscatine Health Support Fdn, Stanley Fdn
Gregs G. Thomopulos: *CURR EMPL* pres: Stanley Consultants

GIVING OFFICERS

Ronald E. Barrett: vp, dir
Kathleen K. Johnson: secy, dir
Richard C. Smith: treas, dir
Richard H. Stanley: pres, dir *CURR EMPL* vchmn, dir: HON Indus (see above)

OTHER THINGS TO KNOW

In fiscal 1991 Stanley Consultants Charitable Foundation had $7,450 in qualifying distributions.
Disclosure Period: fiscal year ending March 30, 1991

Stanley Works / Stanley Works Foundation

Sales: $2.21 billion
Employees: 18,464
Headquarters: New Britain, CT
SIC Major Group: Fabricated Metal Products, Industrial Machinery & Equipment, Primary Metal Industries, and Wholesale Trade—Durable Goods

CONTACT

Ronald F. Gilrain
Vice President, Public Affairs
Stanley Works
1000 Stanley Dr.
New Britain, CT 06053
(203) 225-5111

FINANCIAL SUMMARY

Recent Giving: $1,680,000 (1993 est.); $1,600,000 (1992 approx.); $1,560,826 (1991)
Assets: $1,468,588 (1991); $1,691,390 (1990); $1,955,283 (1989)
Fiscal Note: Above figures include direct giving, which totals about $255,000 annually.
EIN: 06-6088099

CONTRIBUTIONS SUMMARY

Typical Recipients: • *Arts & Humanities:* community arts, dance, libraries, museums/galleries, music, opera, performing arts, public broadcasting, theater • *Civic & Public Affairs:* business/free enterprise, economics, environmental affairs, housing, urban & community affairs • *Education:* business education, colleges & universities, economic education, elementary education, literacy, minority education, public education (precollege), science/technology education • *Health:* hospitals • *Science:*

science exhibits & fairs • *Social Services:* community service organizations, disabled, family services, homes, shelters/homelessness, united funds, youth organizations
Grant Types: capital, challenge, employee matching gifts, general support, and seed money
Nonmonetary Support Types: donated equipment and in-kind services
Note: Nonmonetary support is valued at $150,000 annually. This support is included in above figures.
Geographic Distribution: primarily in communities in which company has operating locations
Operating Locations: CA (Monrovia, Rancho Cucamonga, San Dimas, Visalia), CT (Farmington, New Britain), GA (Covington), KS (Lenexa), MI (Novi, Troy), MO (St. Louis), NC (Charlotte), OH (Cleveland, Covington, Georgetown, Sabina, Washington Court House), OR (Milwaukie), PA (Allentown, York), RI (East Greenwich), TN (Shelbyville), TX (Dallas, Wichita Falls), VA (Richmond), VT (Shaftsbury)

CORP. OFFICERS

Richard H. Ayers: *B* Newton MA 1942 *ED* MA Inst Tech BS 1965; MA Inst Tech MS 1965 *CURR EMPL* pres, ceo, dir: Stanley Works *CORP AFFIL* assoc: Perkin Elmer Corp; dir: CT Mutual Investment Accounts, Southern New England Telecommunications Corp *NONPR AFFIL* dir: New Britain Gen Hosp; mem: Econ Club NY, Hand Tools Inst, Hartford Bus Econ Advs, Natl Assn Mfrs; trust: Hartford Grad Ctr

GIVING OFFICERS

Ronald F. Gilrain: vp (pub affairs) *B* Elizabeth NJ 1927 *ED* Seton Hall Univ BS 1949; Rutgers Univ MBA 1953 *CURR EMPL* vp (pub aff): Stanley Works *NONPR AFFIL* mem: Machinery Allied Products Inst
Edward J. Leary: dir

APPLICATION INFORMATION

Initial Approach: *Initial Contact:* brief letter or proposal *Include Information On:* description of the organization and how it will affect Stanley em-

ployees, amount requested, purpose for which funds are sought, recently audited financial statement, proof of 501(c)(3) tax-exempt status, identification of company employees involved with organization *When to Submit:* any time
Restrictions on Giving: Foundation does not fund endowments. Generally does not support United Way-supported organizations, individuals, political organizations, dinners, special events, fraternal organizations, goodwill advertising, athletic events, or religious organizations for sectarian purposes.

OTHER THINGS TO KNOW

Foundation particularly supports capital projects and funding for building, equipment, or seed money projects in Stanley communities.

GRANTS ANALYSIS

Total Grants: $1,306,826*
Number of Grants: 1,100
Highest Grant: $75,000
Typical Range: $2,000 to $5,000
Disclosure Period: 1991

Note: Fiscal information for foundation only. Figures include matching gifts and scholarships. Recent grants are derived from a 1991 Form 990.

RECENT GRANTS

75,000	Boys Club of New Britain, New Britain, CT
50,000	Constructive Workshops
50,000	Friendship Service Center
32,000	United Way/CHA
32,000	United Way/CHA
25,000	New Britain Museum of American Art, New Britain, CT
23,063	United Way of Southeastern New England
20,000	Greater Hartford Arts Council, Hartford, CT
10,000	AIDS Project Greater New Britain, New Britain, CT
10,000	Central Connecticut State University Foundation

Stans Foundation

CONTACT

Maurice H. Stans
Chairman
Stans Fdn.
350 West Colorado Blvd.
Pasadena, CA 91105
(818) 795-5947

FINANCIAL SUMMARY

Recent Giving: $175,640 (1990); $179,437 (1989); $220,000 (1988)
Assets: $4,694,494 (1990); $4,470,232 (1989); $4,300,000 (1988)
EIN: 36-6008663

CONTRIBUTIONS SUMMARY

Donor(s): Maurice H. Stans, the late Kathleen C. Stans
Typical Recipients: • *Arts & Humanities:* history/historic preservation, museums/galleries • *Education:* colleges & universities • *Health:* hospices, hospitals, medical research, single-disease health associations • *Religion:* religious organizations • *Social Services:* united funds
Grant Types: capital, conference/seminar, general support, multiyear/continuing support, and research
Geographic Distribution: focus on CA

GIVING OFFICERS

Mary C. Elia: secy
Maureen Stans Helmick: vp, dir
Walter Helmick: dir
Terrell Stans Manley: dir
William Manley: vp, dir
Diane Stans: dir
Maurice Hubert Stans: chmn, treas, dir *B* Shakopee MN 1908 *ED* Northwestern Univ 1925-28; Columbia Univ 1929-30; IL Wesleyan Univ LLD 1954; Northwestern Univ 1960; DePaul Univ 1960; Parsons Coll 1960; Grove City Coll LLD 1969; St Anselms Coll 1969; Univ San Diego 1970; Gustavus Adolphus Coll 1970; Pomona Coll 1971; Maryville Coll 1971; Rio Grande Coll 1972; Natl Univ 1979; Pepperdine Univ 1984 *CORP AFFIL* chmn, dir: Weatherby Inc; dir: Uniglobe Travel Intl *NONPR AFFIL* dir: Chinese Am Med Assistance Fdn, Eisenhower World Affs Inst, Huntington Meml Library, Huntington Meml Res Inst; fin chmn,

dir: Nixon Presidential Library; founding dir: African Wildlife Fdn; hon mem: DC Soc CPAs, HI Soc CPAs, Iron Molders & Foundry Workers Union, Natl Assn Postmasters; mem: Am Accounting Assn, Am Inst CPAs, Fed Govt Accts Assn, IL Soc CPAs, Natl Assn Mfrs
Steven H. Stans: pres, dir
Susan Stans: dir
Theodore M. Stans: vp, dir

APPLICATION INFORMATION

Initial Approach: Funds fully committed for next 4 to 6 years.
Restrictions on Giving: Does not support individuals or provide loans.

GRANTS ANALYSIS

Number of Grants: 135
Highest Grant: $36,826
Typical Range: $500 to $5,000
Disclosure Period: 1990

RECENT GRANTS

36,826	Museum of York County, Rock Hill, SC
25,000	Murphys Landing
6,500	Nixon Library and Birthplace, Washington, DC
3,500	Huntington Memorial Hospital, Huntington, CA
2,500	Miller Center
2,500	Purdue University Foundation, West Lafayette, IN
2,100	Natural History Museum of Los Angeles County, Los Angeles, CA
2,100	Shikar Safari Foundation
2,000	Shakopee Schools
2,000	Sisters of Notre Dame

Stanton Fund, Ruth and Frank

CONTACT

Ruth and Frank Stanton Fund
Reminick Aarons & Co.
685 Third Ave.
New York, NY 10017
(212) 697-6900

FINANCIAL SUMMARY

Recent Giving: $100,000 (1992)
Assets: $2,011,201 (1992); $1,887,122 (1991)
EIN: 13-3598005

GIVING OFFICERS

Frank Stanton: trust
Andrew H. Weiss: trust

GRANTS ANALYSIS

Number of Grants: 1
Highest Grant: $100,000
Disclosure Period: 1992

Star Bank, N.A. / Star Bank, N.A., Cincinnati Foundation

Assets: $7.71 billion
Parent Company: Star Banc Corp.
Parent Employees: 3,696
Headquarters: Cincinnati, OH
SIC Major Group: Depository Institutions

CONTACT

Peggy Woods
Director, Public Affairs
Star Bank, N.A.
PO Box 1038
Mail Location 5165
Cincinnati, OH 45201
(513) 632-4610

FINANCIAL SUMMARY

Recent Giving: $792,866 (1991); $580,673 (1990); $615,519 (1989)
Assets: $1,666,981 (1991); $1,538,835 (1990); $1,117,944 (1989)
Fiscal Note: The bank also maintains a direct giving program of about $80,000 annually. This support is not included in above figures. See "Other Things You Should Know" for more information.
EIN: 31-6079013

CONTRIBUTIONS SUMMARY

Typical Recipients: • *Arts & Humanities:* arts festivals, arts funds, history/historic preservation, museums/galleries, music, public broadcasting, theater • *Civic & Public Affairs:* better government, business/free enterprise, ethnic/minority organizations, housing, municipalities, philanthropic organizations, professional & trade associations, zoos/botanical gardens • *Education:* arts education, business education, career/vocational education, colleges & universities, economic education, education associations, education funds, medical education, private education (precollege), public education (precollege), special education • *Health:* health organizations, hospitals, single-disease health associations • *Social Services:* aged, child wel-

fare, community centers, disabled, food/clothing distribution, recreation & athletics, religious welfare, united funds, youth organizations
Grant Types: capital, endowment, general support, operating expenses, professorship, project, and scholarship
Nonmonetary Support Types: cause-related marketing & promotion, donated equipment, in-kind services, loaned employees, and loaned executives
Note: Value of nonmonetary support is unavailable and is not included in above figures.
Geographic Distribution: emphasis on greater Cincinnati area and the state of Ohio
Operating Locations: IN (Lawrenceburg, Richmond), KY (Newport), OH (Cincinnati, Easton, Elmwood Place, Gallipolis, Hamilton, Hillsborough, Ironton, Lockland, Miamitown, Norwood, Portsmouth, Troy, Worthington, Yellow Springs)

CORP. OFFICERS

Samuel M. Cassidy: *B* Lexington KY 1932 *ED* Duke Univ 1958; Univ Cincinnati 1962 *CURR EMPL* pres, ceo, dir: Star Bank NA *CORP AFFIL* dir: Leyman Corp; exec vp: Star Banc Corp *NONPR AFFIL* dir: Cincinnati Chamber Commerce; trust: Cincinnati Better Bus Bur; vchmn: Un Appeal Cincinnati
Charles S. Mechem, Jr.: *B* Nelsonville OH 1930 *ED* Miami Univ AB 1952; Yale Univ LLB 1955 *CURR EMPL* dir: Star Bank Cincinnati *CORP AFFIL* dir: Eagle Picher Indus, First Natl Bank Cincinnati, Great Am Communs Co, Mead Corp, Myers Y Cooper Co, OH Natl Life Ins Co, Philips Indus, Smucker Co (JM), Star Bank Cincinnati, US Shoe Corp *NONPR AFFIL* dir: Childrens Home Cincinnati, Cincinnati Bus Comm, Family Svc; mem: Cincinnati Chamber Commerce
Oliver Wendell Waddell: *B* Covington KY 1930 *ED* Duke Univ 1954; Rutgers Univ 1969 *CURR EMPL* chmn, dir: Star Bank *CORP AFFIL* chmn, pres, ceo: Star Banc Corp; dir: Cincinnati Gas Electric Co, Myers Y Cooper Co, OH Natl Ins Co *NONPR AFFIL* dir: INROADS, OH Bankers Assn; mem: Am Inst Banking, Cincinnati Bus

Comm, Greater Cincinnati Chamber Commerce

GIVING OFFICERS

Raymond Beck: trust

James R. Bridgeland, Jr.: trust *CORP AFFIL* dir: First Natl Bank Cincinnati, First Natl Cincinnati Corp

Samuel M. Cassidy: pres, trust *CURR EMPL* pres, ceo, dir: Star Bank NA (see above)

Joseph Page Hayden, Jr.: trust *B* Cincinnati OH 1929 *ED* Miami Univ BSBA 1951; Univ Cincinnati 1952 *CURR EMPL* chmn, ceo, dir: Midland Co *CORP AFFIL* dir: Fed Natl Mortgage Assn, Star Banc Corp, Star Banc NA *NONPR AFFIL* mem: Bankers Club, Bankers Club; mem bd trust: Miami Univ Fdn; mem bus adv comm: Miami Univ; mem pres counc: Xavier Univ

Thomas J. Klinedinst: trust

William Newton Liggett: trust

Charles S. Mechem, Jr.: trust *CURR EMPL* dir: Star Bank Cincinnati (see above)

Thomas E. Petry: trust *B* Cincinnati OH 1939 *ED* Univ Cincinnati; Harvard Univ MBA *CURR EMPL* chmn, pres, ceo, dir: Eagle-Picher Indus *CORP AFFIL* dir: Cincinnati Gas & Electric Co, Star Bancorp, Star Bank NA, Union Central Life Ins Co, William Powell Co

William Portman: trust

Oliver Wendell Waddell: vp, trust *CURR EMPL* chmn, dir: Star Bank (see above)

William Walton Wommack: trust *B* Winston-Salem NC 1922 *ED* NC St Univ BChE 1943; Harvard Univ MBA 1948 *CORP AFFIL* dir: Chem Lawn Corp, Clark Equipment Corp, Mead Corp, Rand McNally Co, Robbins & Myers Inc, Star Bancorp, Star Bank

APPLICATION INFORMATION

Initial Approach: *Initial Contact:* brief letter or proposal *Include Information On:* description of the organization, amount requested, description of project/activity for which funds are sought, recently audited financial statement, proof of tax-exempt status, size of project budget, other funding sources (including contributions of other companies), whether request is for one-time contribution or ongoing support *When to Submit:* any time

Restrictions on Giving: Contributions will not be made to partisan political organizations, religious organizations for services limited to their membership, controversial social causes, agencies that are beneficiaries of united appeal and fine arts funds (with the exeception of capital grants), individuals, or institutions supported principally by taxes (except specific programs at publicly funded educational institutions), or organizations which discriminate on the basis of race, creed, color, sex, age, or national origin.

Grants will generally not be made to organizations outside the greater Cincinnati, Cleveland and Hamilton areas.

OTHER THINGS TO KNOW

Company declined to furnish updated contributions data.

GRANTS ANALYSIS

Total Grants: $792,866

Number of Grants: 62

Highest Grant: $225,000

Typical Range: $1,000 to $10,000

Disclosure Period: 1991

Note: Average grant excludes two grants totaling $325,000. Recent grants are derived from a 1991 Form 990.

RECENT GRANTS

225,000	United Way, Cincinnati, OH
100,000	Ohio Center for the Arts, Cincinnati, OH
78,370	Miami University, Oxford, OH
37,500	Boy Scouts of America, Cincinnati, OH
35,000	Fine Arts Fund, Cincinnati, OH
30,000	Greater Cincinnati Chamber of Commerce, Cincinnati, OH — Blue Chip campaign
20,000	Franciscan Sisters of the Poor Foundation, Brooklyn Heights, NY
20,000	Museum Center at Cincinnati Union Terminal, Cincinnati, OH
16,000	Cincinnati Youth Collaborative, Cincinnati, OH
15,000	Hebrew Union College, Cincinnati, OH

Star Enterprise

Sales: $8.05 billion

Employees: 5,000

Headquarters: Houston, TX

SIC Major Group: Automotive Dealers & Service Stations, Petroleum & Coal Products, and Wholesale Trade—Nondurable Goods

CONTACT

Marlene Bradley
Human Resources Assistant
Star Enterprise
12700 Northborough
Houston, TX 77067
(713) 874-7983

CONTRIBUTIONS SUMMARY

Company provides employee matching gifts only.

Grant Types: matching

Operating Locations: TX (Houston)

CORP. OFFICERS

D.H. Schmude: *CURR EMPL* pres, ceo: Star Enterprise

Lester Wilkes: *CURR EMPL* coo: Star Enterprise

Star Markets Co.

Employees: 6,000

Parent Company: American Superstores Inc.

Headquarters: Cambridge, MA

SIC Major Group: Food Stores

CONTACT

Lisa Corbett
Public Relations
Star Markets Co.
PO Box 9122
Cambridge, MA 02238-9122
(617) 661-2200

CONTRIBUTIONS SUMMARY

Operating Locations: MA (Cambridge)

CORP. OFFICERS

James C. Horn: *CURR EMPL* pres: Star Markets Co

Stare Fund

CONTACT

Harry Mansfield
Trustee
Stare Fund
c/o Ropes and Gray
One International Pl.
Boston, MA 02110
(617) 951-7704

FINANCIAL SUMMARY

Recent Giving: $75,001 (fiscal 1991); $85,131 (fiscal 1990); $74,953 (fiscal 1989)

Assets: $2,196,626 (fiscal year ending November 30, 1991); $1,880,679 (fiscal 1990); $1,907,761 (fiscal 1989)

Gifts Received: $1,000 (fiscal 1991); $34,250 (fiscal 1990); $1,000,000 (fiscal 1989)

Fiscal Note: In 1991, contributions were received from Mary S. Wilkinson.

EIN: 04-6026648

CONTRIBUTIONS SUMMARY

Donor(s): Frederick J. Stare

Typical Recipients: • *Arts & Humanities:* community arts, libraries, music, public broadcasting • *Education:* colleges & universities, health & physical education • *Health:* health organizations, medical research, nutrition & health maintenance • *Science:* scientific organizations

Grant Types: general support

GIVING OFFICERS

Harry K. Mansfield: trust

David S. Stare: trust

Fredrick John Stare: trust *B* Columbus WI 1910 *ED* Univ WI BS 1931; Univ WI MS 1932; Univ WI PhD 1934; Univ Chicago MD 1941; Suffolk Univ DSc 1963 *CORP AFFIL* dir: Continental Group *NONPR AFFIL* co-fdr, dir: Am Counc Sci Health; fellow: Am Pub Health Assn, Royal Irish Coll Physicians; mem: Am Academy Arts Sciences, Am Chemical Soc, Am Dietetic Assn, Am Inst Nutrition, Am Med Assn, Am Soc Arteriosclerosis, Am Soc Biological Chemists, Am Soc Clinical Investigation, Biochemical Soc Am, Soc Nutrition Ed; prof nutrition emeritus: Harvard Univ Sch Pub Health; trust: New England Conservatory Music

Irene M. Stare: trust

Mary S. Wilkinson: trust

APPLICATION INFORMATION

Initial Approach: Send brief letter describing program. There are no deadlines.

GRANTS ANALYSIS

Number of Grants: 41
Highest Grant: $20,000
Typical Range: $500 to $2,000
Disclosure Period: fiscal year ending November 30, 1991

RECENT GRANTS

20,000 Harvard College Department of Human Nutrition, Cambridge, MA

15,000 New England Conservatory of Music, Boston, MA

5,000 Harvard College of Public Health, Cambridge, MA

5,000 New England Conservatory of Music, Boston, MA

2,500 Boston Symphony Orchestra, Boston, MA

2,000 American Council in Science and Health, Boston, MA

2,000 American Council on Science and Health, Boston, MA

2,000 Harvard College Countway Library, Cambridge, MA

2,000 Pathfinder Fund, Boston, MA

1,250 New England Conservatory of Music, Boston, MA

Stark Foundation, Nelda C. and H. J. Lutcher

CONTACT

Clyde V. McKee, Jr.
Secretary-Treasurer
Nelda C. and H. J. Lutcher Stark Foundation
PO Box 909
Orange, TX 77631-0909
(409) 883-3513

FINANCIAL SUMMARY

Recent Giving: $354,100 (fiscal 1992); $168,730 (fiscal 1991); $128,210 (fiscal 1990)
Assets: $98,497,838 (fiscal year ending February 28, 1992); $90,088,307 (fiscal 1991); $82,483,621 (fiscal 1990)
Gifts Received: $1,500,011 (fiscal 1992); $2,000,000 (fiscal 1990); $1,636,470 (fiscal 1989)

Fiscal Note: The foundation receives gifts from Nelda C. Stark, chairman, donor, and trustee of the foundation.
EIN: 74-6047440

CONTRIBUTIONS SUMMARY

Donor(s): The Nelda C. and H. J. Lutcher Stark Foundation was established in 1961 with funds donated by H. J. Lutcher Stark and his wife, Nelda Childers Stark. Mr. Stark's business included the Lutcher & Moore Lumber Company, the First National Bank of Orange, and Vinton Petroleum. After Mr. Stark's death in 1965, the foundation received the Starks' sizeable art collection, including American Western art of the nineteenth and twentieth centuries, Native American artifacts, and a selection of decorative arts including a collection of Steuben glass. The entire collection is now housed in the Stark Museum of Art, owned and operated by the foundation. The art museum is part of a civic and cultural center in downtown Orange, TX, that also includes the W. H. Stark House, the Frances Ann Lutcher Theater for the Performing Arts, a church, and a park. The W. H. Stark House, a restored Victorian mansion built in 1894, is open to the public for tours. The foundation built the Frances Ann Lutcher Theater for the Performing Arts for the City of Orange, TX, as the major forum for the performing arts in Orange County. In 1986, the foundation assumed responsibility for the facility's operating expenses.
Typical Recipients: • *Arts & Humanities:* arts associations, history/historic preservation, museums/galleries • *Education:* student aid • *Health:* single-disease health associations
Grant Types: general support, project, and scholarship
Geographic Distribution: emphasis on Texas

GIVING OFFICERS

Eunice R. Benckenstein: vchmn, trust
William J. Butler: trust *B* Brighton MA 1924 *NONPR AFFIL* chmn adv comm: Univ Cincinnati Sch Law Inst Human Rights; dir emeritus: Intl League Human Rights, NY Civil Liberties Union; intl legal observer: Intl Human Rights Org; mem: Am Bar Assn, Am Soc Intl Law, Assn Bar City New York, Counc Foreign Rels, Inter-Am Assn Democracy Freedom, Intl Commn Jurists, Intl Law Assn; mem exec comm: League Abolish Capital Punishment; mem standing comm human rights: World Peace Through Law Ctr
Clyde V. McKee, Jr.: secy-treas, trust
Sidney H. Phillips: trust
Walter G. Riedel III: trust
John C. Sargent: trust
Nelda Childers Stark: chmn *B* Orange TX 1909 *ED* Denton Coll

APPLICATION INFORMATION

Initial Approach:
The foundation does not have an application form. Initial contact should be by letter. Include a brief description of the purpose and objectives of the requested grant, operational procedures, personnel and financial resources available, amount of financial assistance needed, and proof of tax-exempt status under IRS Section 501(c)(3).
Applications may be submitted any time. The foundation board usually meets monthly.
Restrictions on Giving: No grants are made to individuals or for endowment or operating budgets. The trustees prefer not to make grants for capital costs.

GRANTS ANALYSIS

Total Grants: $354,100
Number of Grants: 14
Highest Grant: $143,600
Typical Range: $15,000 to $25,000
Disclosure Period: fiscal year ending February 28, 1992
Note: Average grant figure excludes $143,600 in scholarships. Recent grants are derived from a fiscal 1992 grants list.

RECENT GRANTS

143,600 Texas Interscholastic League Foundation, Austin, TX — scholarship program

50,000 St. James Historical Society, Grammercy, LA — permanent scholarship endowment

25,000 Houston Grand Opera, Houston, TX — underwrite production of Annie Get Your Gun

25,000 Houston Grand Opera, Houston, TX — underwrite production of My Fair Lady

25,000 Mid America Arts Alliance, Kansas City, MO — general support grant

10,000 Texans, Austin, TX — Environmental Defense Fund; establish a Texas Office of the Environmental Defense Fund

10,000 Texas Energy Museum Foundation, Beaumont, TX — renovation expense

5,000 Retina Research Foundation, Houston, TX — retina research

2,500 Southeast Texas Hospice, Orange, TX — hospice care for 45 days

Starling Foundation, Dorothy Richard

CONTACT

Allen Weatherby
Manager
Dorothy Richard Starling Fdn.
PO Box 66527
Houston, TX 77266
(713) 651-9102

FINANCIAL SUMMARY

Recent Giving: $508,500 (1991); $570,000 (1990); $528,000 (1989)
Assets: $16,319,577 (1991); $14,373,583 (1990); $14,672,847 (1989)
EIN: 74-6121656

CONTRIBUTIONS SUMMARY

Donor(s): The foundation was established in 1969 by the late Frank M. Starling.
Typical Recipients: • *Arts & Humanities:* arts festivals, arts institutes, music • *Education:* arts education, colleges & universities, private education (precollege)
Grant Types: endowment, general support, and scholarship
Geographic Distribution: nationally

GIVING OFFICERS

Robert K. Jewett: trust
A. C. Speyer, Jr.: trust

Jack M. Watson: consultant
H. Allen Weatherby: trust

APPLICATION INFORMATION

Initial Approach:
The foundation requests applications be made in writing. Proposals should be in essay form and include the name and address of the organization, proof of 501(c)(3) organization and that it is not operating as a private foundation, the purpose of the grant, and the percentage of the total funding sought by the foundation.
The foundation has no deadline for submitting proposals.
Restrictions on Giving: The foundation only makes grants for purposes of instruction and study of classical violin.

GRANTS ANALYSIS

Total Grants: $508,500
Number of Grants: 7
Highest Grant: $336,000
Typical Range: $1,500 to $30,000
Disclosure Period: 1991
Note: Average grant figure does not include the highest grant of $336,000. Recent grants are derived from a 1991 grants list.

RECENT GRANTS

336,000 Julliard School, New York, NY — funding for the Dorothy Richard Starling Chair for violin studies

91,000 University of Cincinnati, College of Conservation of Music, Cincinnati, OH — funding for the Dorothy Richard Starling Chair for Violin Studies

30,000 Aspen Music Festival, Aspen, CO — for general funding, advancement of listening pleasure of violin

25,000 Rice University, Houston, TX

15,000 Music Festival at Roundtop, Roundtop, TX — for general funding, advancement of listening pleasure of violin

10,000 University of Houston, Houston, TX — funding for scholarships for violin students

1,500 Carnegie Museum, Pittsburgh, PA

Starr Foundation

CONTACT

Ta Chun Hsu
President
Starr Foundation
70 Pine St.
New York, NY 10270
(212) 770-6880

FINANCIAL SUMMARY

Recent Giving: $33,034,519 (1991); $30,804,045 (1990); $19,764,187 (1989)
Assets: $780,052,477 (1991); $616,002,007 (1990); $687,307,919 (1989)
Gifts Received: $2,000,023 (1991); $4,001,500 (1990); $16,120 (1988)
Fiscal Note: In 1988, the foundation received gifts of $13,620 from Mansfield Freeman and $2,500 from John S. Galinato. In 1990, the foundation received $4,000,000 from the estate of Howard L. Kleinoeder and $1,500 from John S. Galinato. In 1991, the foundation received $2,000,000 from the estate of Howard L. Kleinoeder.
EIN: 13-6151545

CONTRIBUTIONS SUMMARY

Donor(s): Cornelius Vander Starr (1892-1968) established the foundation in New York in 1955. Mr. Starr attended the University of California, and passed the California Bar exam at age 21. After serving in World War I, he resided in China, and established the Asia Life and American Asiatic Life Insurance Companies. By the 1930s, his insurance activities and investments in real estate and automobiles extended throughout the Far East. After World War II, he renamed the companies the American Life Insurance Company. At the time of his death, his operations expanded to a group of 100 insurance companies in about 130 countries. Since the 1970s, the foundation has received considerable donations of stock from the corporate directors of American International Group.
Typical Recipients: • *Arts & Humanities:* arts associations, arts centers, arts festivals, arts funds, arts institutes, dance, ethnic arts, history/historic preservation, libraries, museums/galleries, music, opera,

public broadcasting, theater
• *Civic & Public Affairs:* civil rights, economics, environmental affairs, international affairs, law & justice, nonprofit management, philanthropic organizations, public policy, rural affairs, women's affairs, zoos/botanical gardens • *Education:* arts education, business education, colleges & universities, economic education, education associations, health & physical education, international exchange, journalism education, legal education, medical education, minority education, private education (precollege), religious education, science/technology education, special education, student aid • *Health:* hospices, hospitals, medical research, medical training, nursing services, outpatient health care delivery, pediatric health, single-disease health associations • *International:* foreign educational institutions, international health care, international organizations • *Religion:* churches • *Social Services:* aged, child welfare, community centers, community service organizations, counseling, disabled, drugs & alcohol, emergency relief, employment/job training, family planning, family services, food/clothing distribution, recreation & athletics, refugee assistance, religious welfare, shelters/homelessness, youth organizations
Grant Types: capital, emergency, endowment, general support, multiyear/continuing support, professorship, project, and scholarship
Geographic Distribution: national and international, with emphasis on metropolitan New York City

GIVING OFFICERS

Marion I. Breen: vp, dir
Houghton Freeman: dir *B* People's Republic of China 1921 *ED* Wesleyan Univ 1943 *CURR EMPL* vchmn, dir: Am Intl Group *CORP AFFIL* dir: Bank Tokyo Trust Co; sr vp, dir: Am Intl Group
Ida E. Galler: secy
Maurice Raymond Greenberg: chmn bd, dir *B* New York NY 1925 *ED* Univ Miami BA 1948; NY Univ Law Sch JD 1950 *CURR EMPL* chmn: Am Intl Group *CORP AFFIL* chmn bd govs: NY Hosp; dir, dep chmn: Fed Reserve Bank

NY *NONPR AFFIL* mem: ASEAN-US Bus Adv Counc, Coalition Svc Indus, Counc Foreign Rels, Foreign Policy Assn, Hoover Inst, NY Bar Assn, NY City Partnership, Police Athletic League, Sigma Alpha Mu, US-USSR Trade Econ Counc; pres adv comm: Ctr Strategic Intl Studies *PHIL AFFIL* chmn, dir: Maurice R & Corinne Greenberg Foundation
Ta Chun Hsu: pres, dir
Edwin Alfred Grenville Manton: dir *B* Essex England 1909 *ED* London Univ 1925-1927 *CURR EMPL* sr adv, dir: Am Intl Group *CORP AFFIL* chmn: Am Intl MAR Agency NY; dir: AIV Ins Co, Am Home Assurance, Birmingham Fire & Ins Co PA; hon dir: CV Starr & Co; vchmn, dir: Starr Tech Risks Agency; dir: AIG Oil Rig, Am Intl Aviation Agency, Starr Intl Co *NONPR AFFIL* trust: St Lukes-Roosevelt Hosp; vp: St Georges Soc
John Joseph Roberts: dir *B* Montreal Canada 1922 *ED* Princeton Univ BA 1947 *CURR EMPL* chmn, ceo, dir: Am Intl Underwriters *CORP AFFIL* dir: Adams Express Co, AIG Mktg, AIG Risk Mgmt, Am Intl Marine Agency, Am Intl Reinsurance Co, CV Starr & Co, Petroleum & Resources Corp, Starr Intl Co, Starr Tech Risks Agency; vice chmn, dir: Am Intl Group *NONPR AFFIL* chmn: Bus Counc Intl Understanding, US Secy Hungarian US Bus Counc; chmn intl corp counc: Columbia Univ Sch Intl & Pub Affs; mem: Counc Foreign Rels; trust: Counc Ams, Juilliard Sch Music, Mason Early Ed Fdn
Ernest Edward Stempel: dir *B* New York NY 1916 *ED* Manhattan Coll AB 1938; Fordham Univ LLB 1946; NY Univ LLM 1949; NY Univ DJS 1951 *CURR EMPL* vchmn, dir: Am Intl Group *CORP AFFIL* chmn, dir: Am Intl Assurance Co, Am Intl Co, Am Intl Reinsurance Co, Australian Am Assurance Co, Phillipine Am Life Ins Co; dir: AIG Life Ins Co, Am Intl Life Assurance Co, Am Intl Reinsurance Co, Am Intl Underwriters, Am Life Ins Co, DE Am Life Ins Co, La Interamericana, Mt Mansfield Co, Pacific Union Assurance Co, Seguros Interamericana SA, Seguros Venezuela, CV Starr & Co, Underwriters Adjustment Co; pres, dir: Starr Intl Co *NONPR*

AFFIL mem: Am Bar Assn, NY Bar Assn
Frank R. Tengi: treas
Gladys R. Thomas: vp

APPLICATION INFORMATION

Initial Approach:
Applications should be submitted in writing. There are no formal application forms.
The foundation requests only basic information on letters of application.
There are no deadlines for submitting proposals.

OTHER THINGS TO KNOW

Grants to individuals are limited to four scholarship programs. Those programs are the Starr Foundation Scholarship Program for "American International" Children (U.S.), the Starr Foundation Scholarship Program for "American International" Children (overseas), the Brewster Starr Scholarship Program, and the Lower Manhattan Starr Scholarship Program.
Publications: annual report

GRANTS ANALYSIS

Total Grants: $31,534,482*
Number of Grants: 387
Highest Grant: $6,250,000
Typical Range: $10,000 to $50,000 and $100,000 to $250,000
Disclosure Period: 1991
Note: Total grant figure excludes $1,500,037 in scholarships. Average grant figure excludes four grants that total $9,250,000. Recent grants are derived from a 1991 Form 990.

RECENT GRANTS

6,250,000 New York Hospital, New York, NY — in support of its Major Modernization Campaign
1,000,000 Brown University, Providence, RI — to augment the C. V. Starr National Service Fellowship at Brown
1,000,000 St. Luke's/Roosevelt Center, New York, NY — in support of C. V. Starr Hand Surgery Center
1,000,000 Yale University, New Haven, CT — in support of renovation and redesign of the Sterling Library Reference Center

875,000 Metropolitan Museum of Art, New York, NY — in support of C. V. Starr Conservatorship in Asian Art at The Met
500,000 Center for Strategic and International Studies, Washington, DC — renewed support
500,000 Dartmouth-Hitchcock Medical Center, Hanover, NH — to establish the C. V. Starr Center for Magnetic Resonance Imaging
500,000 Hebrew Home for the Aged at Riverdale, Riverdale, NY — in support of renovation and expansion project
500,000 New York Downtown Hospital, New York, NY — in support of Chinese patients
500,000 New York Historical Society, New York, NY — in support of New Study/Storage Center for the Permanent Collections

Starrett Co., L.S. / Starrett Co. Charitable Foundation, L.S.

Sales: $188.4 million
Employees: 2,653
Headquarters: Athol, MA
SIC Major Group: Chemicals & Allied Products, Fabricated Metal Products, and Industrial Machinery & Equipment

CONTACT

R.C. Wellington, Jr.
Director
L.S. Starrett Co. Charitable Foundation
121 Crescent St.
Athol, MA 01331-1915
(508) 249-3551

FINANCIAL SUMMARY

Recent Giving: $103,988 (1990); $121,920 (1989)
Assets: $265,577 (1990); $347,594 (1989)
Gifts Received: $50,000 (1990)
Fiscal Note: In 1990, contributions were received from the Starrett Co.
EIN: 04-6054780

CONTRIBUTIONS SUMMARY

Typical Recipients: • *Civic & Public Affairs:* municipalities • *Education:* colleges & universities, education funds, public education (precollege), science/technology education • *Health:* hospitals, medical research, single-disease health associations • *Social Services:* community centers, community service organizations, disabled, united funds, youth organizations
Grant Types: general support and scholarship
Geographic Distribution: focus on MA
Operating Locations: MA (Athol)

CORP. OFFICERS

Douglas R. Starrett: *CURR EMPL* pres: LS Starrett Co
Roger U. Wellington, Jr.: *CURR EMPL* cfo, treas: LS StarrettCo

GIVING OFFICERS

D. A. Starrett: dir
Douglas R. Starrett: dir *CURR EMPL* pres: LS Starrett Co (see above)
Roger U. Wellington, Jr.: dir *CURR EMPL* cfo, treas: LS StarrettCo (see above)

APPLICATION INFORMATION

Initial Approach: Send brief letter describing program. There are no deadlines.

GRANTS ANALYSIS

Number of Grants: 20
Highest Grant: $30,000
Typical Range: $100 to $3,000
Disclosure Period: 1990

RECENT GRANTS

25,000 Phillipston Youth Center, Baldwinville, MA
22,010 United Way, Athol, MA
20,000 Athol Memorial Hospital, Athol, MA
15,000 Worcester Polytechnic Institute, Worcester, MA
10,000 Franklin Medical Center, Greenfield, MA
8,000 Athol High School Scholarship Association, Athol, MA
5,000 Reeves Community Center, Mount Airy, NC

3,000 Orange Scholarship Association, Orange, MA
2,000 Boy Scouts of America, Mount Airy, NC
2,000 Rockford College, Rockford, IL

Starrett Housing Corp.

Sales: $102.8 million
Employees: 1,500
Headquarters: New York, NY
SIC Major Group: General Building Contractors, Heavy Construction Except Building Construction, and Real Estate

CONTACT

Louis Weinfeld
Chief Financial Officer
Starrett Housing Corp.
909 Third Avenue, 16th Fl.
New York, NY 10022
(212) 751-3100

CONTRIBUTIONS SUMMARY

Operating Locations: NY (New York)

CORP. OFFICERS

Richard Bassuk: *CURR EMPL* pres, coo: Starrett Housing Corp
Henry Benach: *CURR EMPL* chmn, ceo: Starrett Housing Corp

State Farm Mutual Automobile Insurance Co. / State Farm Cos. Foundation

Parent Company: State Farm Mutual Automobile Insurance Co.
Parent Sales: $21.5 billion
Parent Employees: 60,786
Headquarters: Bloomington, IL
SIC Major Group: Insurance Carriers

CONTACT

Dave Polzin
Assistant Vice President
State Farm Cos. Fdn.
One State Farm Plz.
Bloomington, IL 61710
(309) 766-2161

FINANCIAL SUMMARY

Recent Giving: $6,300,000 (1993 est.); $2,889,000 (1992 approx.); $3,243,000 (1991)

Assets: $4,400,000 (1992); $13,651,700 (1991); $6,800,000 (1990)

Fiscal Note: Other company departments make contributions from corporate funds, however the above figures only reflect foundation giving. There is no determined budget for company contributions. Contact for this support is Bruce Callis, Vice President. **EIN:** 36-6110423

CONTRIBUTIONS SUMMARY

Typical Recipients: • *Civic & Public Affairs:* economics, ethnic/minority organizations, law & justice, professional & trade associations, safety • *Education:* business education, colleges & universities, economic education, education associations, minority education, student aid • *Health:* hospitals • *Social Services:* community service organizations, united funds

Grant Types: capital, employee matching gifts, and scholarship

Nonmonetary Support Types: donated equipment, in-kind services, and loaned executives

Note: Estimated value of nonmonetary support is unavailable and is not included in figures above. Support is provided by the company. For information contact Steve Stockton, Vice President, Administrations Services Department.

Geographic Distribution: near major offices

Operating Locations: AL, AZ, CA, CO, FL, GA, IL (Bloomington), IN, LA, MD, MI, MN, MO, NE, NJ, NY, OH, OK, OR, PA, TN, TX, VA

CORP. OFFICERS

Edward B. Rust, Jr.: *B* Chicago IL 1950 *ED* IL Wesleyan Univ BS; IL Wesleyan Univ 1972; Southern Methodist Univ MBA; Southern Methodist Univ JD 1975 *CURR EMPL* chmn, pres, ceo: St Farm Ins Co *CORP AFFIL* dir, mem exec comm, mem invest comm: St Farm Fire & Casualty, St Farm Gen, St Farm Life Ins Co, St Farm Mutual Auto Ins Co; dir, mem exec comm, mem investment comm: St Farm Annuity & Life Ins Co, St Farm Mutual Auto Ins Co; pres, dir: St Farm Intl Svcs Inc, St Farm Investment Mgmt Corp

NONPR AFFIL mem: Am Bar Assn, Am Inst Property Liability Underwriters, IL Bar Assn, Ins Inst Am, Inst Civil Justice, TX St Bar Assn; mem adv counc: Stanford Univ Grad Sch Bus; mem bus adv counc: Univ IL Coll Commerce & Bus Admin; trust: Wesleyan Univ

GIVING OFFICERS

Bruce Callis: dir *B* Sedalia MO 1939 *ED* Univ MO BS 1961 *CURR EMPL* vp, dir: St Farm Mutual Automobile Ins Co *CORP AFFIL* dir: St Farm Annuity Co, St Farm Gen Ins Co, St Farm Intl Svcs, St Farm Life & Accident Ins *NONPR AFFIL* mem: Am Soc Pers Admin, IL Wesleyan Univ Assocs, Ins Inst Highway Safety, McLean County Assn, Westminster Coll Alumni Assocs

John Coffey: vp

Robert Spence Eckley: dir *B* Kankakee IL 1921 *ED* Bradley Univ BS 1942; Univ MN MBA 1943; Harvard Univ MA 1948; Harvard Univ PhD 1949 *CORP AFFIL* dir: St Farm Mutual Automobile Ins Co, Central IL Pub Svc Co *NONPR AFFIL* mem: Am Econ Assn, Am Statistical Assn, Natl Assn Bus Economists

Charles O. Galvin: dir *CORP AFFIL* dir: St Farm Mutual Automobile Ins Co

Roger Joslin: asst treas *B* Bloomington IL 1936 *ED* Miami Univ BS 1958; Univ IL JD 1961 *CURR EMPL* sr vp, treas: St Farm Mutual Automobile Ins Co *CORP AFFIL* chmn: St Farm Fire & Casualty Co; dir: Annuity & Life Ins Co, Life & Accident Assurance Co, St Farm Life Ins Co; treas: St Farm County Mutual Ins Co TX; vp, dir: St Farm Gen Ins Co; vp, treas, dir: St Farm Balanced Fund, St Farm Growth Fund, St Farm Interim Fund, St Farm Intl Svcs, St Farm Investment Mgmt Corp, St Farm Lloyds, St Farm Municipal Bond Fund *NONPR AFFIL* mem: Am Bar Assn, IL Bar Assn, IL Soc CPAs, McLean County Bar Assn, Miami Univ Alumni Assn

Dave Polzin: asst vp (programs)

Edward B. Rust, Jr.: pres, treas *CURR EMPL* chmn, pres, ceo: St Farm Ins Co (see above)

Laura Sullivan: vp, secy, dir *B* Des Moines IA 1947 *ED* Cornell Univ BA 1971; Drake Univ JD 1972 *CURR EMPL*

secy, coun, vp: St Farm Mutual Automobile Ins Co *CORP AFFIL* asst secy: St Farm Indemnity Co; secy: St Farm Annuity & Life Ins Co, St Farm Life Ins Co, St Farm Lloyds; secy, dir: St Farm Life & Accident Assurance Co; secy, vp, couns: St Farm & Casualty Co; secy, vp, couns, dir: St Farm Gen Ins Co *NONPR AFFIL* dir: Scott Ctr; mem: Am Bar Assn, Am Corp Counc Assn, IA Bar Assn, Natl Assn Women Lawyers; trust: John M Scott Indus Sch Trust

Vincent Trosino: asst secy *B* Upland PA 1940 *ED* Villanova Univ 1962; IL St Univ 1973 *CURR EMPL* exec vp, chief admin off, dir: St Farm Mutual Automobile Ins Co *CORP AFFIL* dir: St Farm Fire Casualty Co, St Farm Gen Ins Co, St Farm Intl Svcs, St Farm Investment Mgmt Corp, St Farm Life Accident Assurance Co, St Farm Life Ins Co *NONPR AFFIL* mem: NJ Ins News Svc, NJ Joint Underwriting Assn

Donna Vincent: asst secy

APPLICATION INFORMATION

Initial Approach: *Initial Contact:* brief letter or proposal *Include Information On:* description of the organization, amount requested, purpose for which funds are sought, recently audited financial statement, proof of tax-exempt status, fund-raising plan *When to Submit:* any time

Restrictions on Giving: Does not support dinners or special events, fraternal organizations, goodwill advertising, operating budgets, individuals, political or lobbying groups, or religious organizations for sectarian purposes.

OTHER THINGS TO KNOW

Scholarship, fellowship, and doctoral program grants have specific deadlines for submission. These dates can be obtained from the foundation.

GRANTS ANALYSIS

Total Grants: $2,889,000*

Number of Grants: 75

Highest Grant: $1,000,000

Typical Range: $2,000 to $50,000

Disclosure Period: 1992

Note: Company reports median grant at $10,000. Total grant figure excludes direct giving.

Recent grants are derived from a 1990 grants list.

RECENT GRANTS

449,811 National Merit Scholarship Corporation, Evanston, IL

300,000 McLean County Illinois Historical Society, IL

150,000 Illinois State University, Normal, IL — presidential scholarship program

100,000 BroMenn Foundation, Bloomington, IL

87,096 Illinois State University, Normal, IL

86,500 McLean County United Way, IL

83,333 YWCA of McLean County, Bloomington, IL — Expansion '89

50,395 Illinois Wesleyan University, Bloomington, IL — minority opportunity program

50,000 Drake University Insurance Center, Des Moines, IA — Kenneth W. Smith Memorial Fund

50,000 Illinois Wesleyan University, Bloomington, IL — Interactive Learning Center

---

State Mutual Life Assurance Co. / State Mutual Life Charitable Trust

Premiums: $1.96 billion
Employees: 3,429
Headquarters: Worcester, MA
SIC Major Group: Insurance Carriers

CONTACT

David Portney
Second Vice President, Public Relations
State Mutual Life Assurance Co. of America
440 Lincoln St., MS A9
Worcester, MA 01605
(508) 855-1000

FINANCIAL SUMMARY

Recent Giving: $500 (1991)
Assets: $248,470 (1991)
Gifts Received: $249,044 (1991)

Fiscal Note: Annual Giving Range: $250,000 to $500,000 In 1991, contributions were received from the State Mutual Life Assurance Co.

EIN: 04-3105650

CONTRIBUTIONS SUMMARY

Typical Recipients: • *Arts & Humanities:* general • *Civic & Public Affairs:* general • *Education:* general • *Health:* general • *Social Services:* general

Grant Types: general support

Nonmonetary Support Types: donated equipment, in-kind services, loaned executives, and workplace solicitation

Geographic Distribution: headquarters and operating locations

Operating Locations: MA (Worcester)

CORP. OFFICERS

John O'Brien: *CURR EMPL* pres, ceo: State Mutual Cos Am

GIVING OFFICERS

David Portney: *CURR EMPL* second vp pub rels: State Mutual Life Assurance Co

APPLICATION INFORMATION

Initial Approach: *Initial Contact:* brief letter of inquiry *Include Information On:* description of the organization, amount requested, purpose of funds sought, audited financial statement, and proof of tax-exempt status *When to Submit:* any time

OTHER THINGS TO KNOW

At time of publication, David Portney reported that State Mutual Life Assurance Co. was in the process of establishing a new foundation, but he declined to provide any further information on it.

State Street Bank & Trust Co. / State Street Foundation

Assets: $16.48 billion
Parent Company: State Street Boston Corp.
Parent Employees: 9,338
Headquarters: Boston, MA
SIC Major Group: Depository Institutions and Holding & Other Investment Offices

CONTACT

George A. Bowman, Jr.
Vice President
State Street Bank & Trust Co.
225 Franklin St.
12th Fl.
Boston, MA 02101
(617) 654-3381

FINANCIAL SUMMARY

Recent Giving: $2,800,000 (1992 approx.); $1,981,385 (1991); $1,872,187 (1990)
Assets: $5,645,225 (1991); $4,588,854 (1990); $2,987,615 (1989)
Fiscal Note: Company gives through foundation only. The 1991 giving figure includes the matching gift program.
EIN: 04-6401847

CONTRIBUTIONS SUMMARY

Typical Recipients: • *Arts & Humanities:* arts associations, arts centers, arts institutes, community arts, dance, ethnic arts, history/historic preservation, museums/galleries, music, opera, performing arts, theater • *Civic & Public Affairs:* civil rights, economic development, economics, housing, law & justice, nonprofit management, safety, urban & community affairs, women's affairs, zoos/botanical gardens • *Education:* arts education, colleges & universities, continuing education, education funds, elementary education, literacy, minority education, public education (precollege), science/technology education, student aid • *Health:* health care cost containment, health organizations, hospitals, mental health, outpatient health care delivery • *Social Services:* child welfare, community centers, community service organizations, counseling, delinquency & crime, employment/job training, family services, homes, recreation & athletics, refugee assistance, religious welfare, shelters/homelessness, united funds, youth organizations

Grant Types: capital, challenge, employee matching gifts, general support, operating expenses, and project

Nonmonetary Support Types: cause-related marketing & promotion, donated equipment, in-kind services, loaned employees, and loaned executives

Note: Estimated value of nonmonetary support is unavail-

able and is not included in figures above.

Geographic Distribution: priority to greater Boston area, emphasis on Suffolk County

Operating Locations: MA (Boston, Quincy), NY (New York)

CORP. OFFICERS

William Skelton Edgerly: *B* Lewiston ME 1927 *ED* MA Inst Tech 1949; Harvard Univ MBA 1955 *CURR EMPL* chmn: St Street Boston Corp *CORP AFFIL* chmn: St Street Bank & Trust Co; dir: Arkwright-Boston Ins Co, Depository Trust Co, Fed Reserve Bank Boston *NONPR AFFIL* dir: Boston Housing Partnership Inc, Boston Pvt Indus Counc, Inst Foreign Policy Analysis, Jobs MA, MA Bus Roundtable; mem: Harvard Bus Sch Assn, MA Inst Tech Alumni Assn; mem bd dirs: Assn Reserve City Bankers; mem (corp): Northeastern Univ; trust, vchmn: Comm Econ Devel; mem: MA Inst Tech Corp Devel Comm; mem (corp): Mus Science & Indus; mem fed adv counc: Fed Reserve Bd; trust, overseer: Childrens Hosp Med Ctr

Peter E. Madden: *B* Wellesley MA 1942 *ED* Babson Coll BS 1964; Harvard Univ 1977 *CURR EMPL* pres, dir: St Street Boston Corp *CORP AFFIL* dir: Boston Fin Data Svcs, Depository Trust Co, VISA USA *NONPR AFFIL* dir: Family Counseling Guidance Ctrs, Greater Boston Chamber Commerce; mem: Assn Reserve City Bankers, Corp Northeastern Univ; trust: Babson Coll, Clinic Fdn, Lahey Clinic Fdn

GIVING OFFICERS

George A. Bowman, Jr.: vp
George A. Russell, Jr.: chmn, dir

APPLICATION INFORMATION

Initial Approach: *Initial Contact:* proposal on organization's letterhead, not to exceed 8 pages *Include Information On:* proof of tax-exempt status, audited financial statement for at least two years, detailed budget for proposed project, budget projections for two years; explanation regarding specific request for support;

list of board of directors *When to Submit:* any time

Restrictions on Giving: Foundation does not support dinners, special events, fraternal organizations, goodwill advertising, individuals including scholarships, member agencies of united funds, political or lobbying groups, religious organizations for sectarian purposes, research, or groups outside New England.

Foundation is reluctant to make grants to solve emergency cash flow situations.

Foundation seldom makes multi-year grants. Organizations should re-apply annually.

OTHER THINGS TO KNOW

Foundation seeks to respond to range of issues and needs, particularly those aiding the poor in inner-city neighborhoods. Particular interest in neighborhood revitalization through low-income housing intiatives. Another strong interest of the foundation is organizations that deal with violence and crime reduction.

GRANTS ANALYSIS

Total Grants: $1,981,385
Number of Grants: 115
Highest Grant: $530,000
Typical Range: $3,000 to $20,000
Disclosure Period: 1991
Note: Average grant figure excludes a $530,000 grant. Recent grants are derived from a 1991 Form 990.

RECENT GRANTS

530,000 United Way of Massachusetts Bay, Boston, MA — annual corporate gift for 1991

70,000 Metropolitan Boston Housing Partnership, Boston, MA — expansion of tenant involvement initiative of the Partnership

50,000 Massachusetts Institute of Technology, Cambridge, MA — scientific research

50,000 Sail Boston 1992, Boston, MA — co-sponsorship of the tall ships in bicentennial celebration

40,000 Northeastern University, Boston, MA — participation in the Century Fund campaign

30,000 Boys and Girls
Clubs of Boston,
Boston, MA — con-
struction of a new
facility in Dorches-
ter

30,000 Massachusetts Gen-
eral Hospital, Bos-
ton, MA — support
emergency room fa-
cilities

30,000 Youth Build Bos-
ton, Boston, MA —
takes inner-city
youth and teaches
them trade skills
through the reha-
bilitation of afford-
able housing units
in their neighbor-
hoods

25,000 Dimock Commu-
nity Health Center,
Roxbury, MA — of-
fering comprehen-
sive health, mental
health services, vo-
cational training fa-
cility for maternal
health care for cor-
rectional facility in-
mates

25,000 Lena Park Commu-
nity Development
Corporation, Dor-
chester, MA — de-
veloping an ex-
panded
library/reading pro-
gram also Family
Impact Project
which brings social
services to the resi-
dents of affordable
housing units they
manage

Statesman Group, Inc.

Assets: $2.95 billion
Employees: 285
Headquarters: Des Moines, IA
SIC Major Group: Depository
Institutions, Holding & Other
Investment Offices, Insurance
Carriers, and Nondepository
Institutions

CONTACT
John Matovina
Treasurer
Statesman Group, Inc.
PO Box 394
Des Moines, IA 50302
(515) 284-7500

CONTRIBUTIONS SUMMARY
Operating Locations: IA (Des Moines)

CORP. OFFICERS
D. J. Noble: *CURR EMPL*
chmn, pres, ceo: Statesman
Group

Statler Foundation

CONTACT
William J. Cunningham Jr.
Chairman
Statler Foundation
Statler Towers, Ste. 508
Buffalo, NY 14202
(716) 852-1104

FINANCIAL SUMMARY
Recent Giving: $949,215
(1991); $964,745 (1990);
$1,151,229 (1989)
Assets: $28,906,710 (1991);
$25,872,158 (1990);
$25,659,414 (1989)
EIN: 13-1889077

CONTRIBUTIONS SUMMARY
Donor(s): Ellsworth Milton
Statler, founder of the Statler
hotel chain, contributed 10,000
shares of common stock from
the Statler Hotels Company to
form the Statler Foundation in
1934. The foundation designated the Statler Hotel Management School of Cornell University as its principal beneficiary.
Typical Recipients: • *Civic &
Public Affairs:* professional &
trade associations • *Education:*
career/vocational education,
colleges & universities,
science/technology education,
student aid • *Health:* hospitals
• *Social Services:* community
service organizations,
food/clothing distribution
Grant Types: capital, professorship, and scholarship
Geographic Distribution:
principally New York state

GIVING OFFICERS
William J. Cunningham, Jr.:
chmn
M. Robert Koren: trust
Arthur F. Musarra: trust

APPLICATION INFORMATION
Initial Approach:
Applications may be requested
from the foundation by means
of a letter of inquiry.
Organizations should submit
applications by April 1.
The foundation reviews and
processes all requests for support as quickly as possible.
Restrictions on Giving: The
foundation makes grants in the

hospitality field (hotels, mo-
tels, and food service) only.

GRANTS ANALYSIS
Total Grants: $949,215
Number of Grants: 19
Highest Grant: $360,000
Typical Range: $10,000 to
$50,000
Disclosure Period: 1991
Note: The average grant figure
excludes the highest grant total-
ing $360,000. Recent grants
are derived from a 1991 Form
990.

RECENT GRANTS
360,000 Cornell University,
Ithaca, NY

194,195 Hotel/Motel Asso-
ciation, New York,
NY

83,750 Western New York
Scholarship
Awards Commit-
tee, Buffalo, NY

62,150 Lynn University

50,000 Florida Interna-
tional University,
Miami, FL

40,425 International Food
Service Executive
Association, Chi-
cago, IL

25,600 New York State Ag-
ricultural Child
Care Program, NY

25,000 University of Buf-
falo, Buffalo, NY

20,000 Jewish Family
Service, Buffalo,
NY

20,000 Maplebrook
School, Anemia,
NY

Statter Foundation, Amy Plant

CONTACT
John H. Reilly, Jr.
Trustee
Amy Plant Statter Fdn.
598 Madison Avenue, 9th Fl.
New York, NY 10022
(212) 943-7000

FINANCIAL SUMMARY
Recent Giving: $228,500
(1991); $168,200 (1990);
$152,000 (1989)
Assets: $2,918,648 (1991);
$2,711,404 (1990); $2,785,404
(1989)
EIN: 13-6152801

CONTRIBUTIONS SUMMARY
Donor(s): Amy Plant Statter
Clark
Typical Recipients: • *Arts &
Humanities:* community arts,

museums/galleries • *Education:* colleges & universities
• *Health:* hospitals, medical research, single-disease health associations • *Social Services:*
child welfare, community service organizations, counseling,
disabled, food/clothing distribution, shelters/homelessness,
united funds, youth organizations
Grant Types: general support

GIVING OFFICERS
Amy Plant Statter Clark: trust
John H. Reilly, Jr.: trust

APPLICATION INFORMATION
Initial Approach: Contributes
only to preselected organizations.

GRANTS ANALYSIS
Number of Grants: 49
Highest Grant: $10,000
Typical Range: $1,000 to
$6,000
Disclosure Period: 1991

RECENT GRANTS
10,000 Chatham Hall,
Chatham, VA

10,000 Ethel Walker
School, Simsbury,
CT

10,000 Pomfret School,
Pomfret, CT

10,000 Wheaton College,
Wheaton, IL

8,000 United Hospital of
Portchester, Port-
chester, NY

7,000 Salvation Army,
New York, NY

6,000 Rippowam Cisqua
School

5,000 Professional Chil-
dren's School, New
York, NY

5,000 Recording for the
Blind, New York,
NY

5,000 University Hospi-
tal, Seattle, WA

Stauffer Charitable Trust, John

CONTACT
H. Jess Senecal
Trustee
John Stauffer Charitable Trust
301 North Lake Avenue, 10th Fl.
Pasadena, CA 91101
(818) 793-9400

FINANCIAL SUMMARY
Recent Giving: $1,000,000
(fiscal 1993 est.); $1,381,500
(fiscal 1992); $1,272,800 (fis-
cal 1991)

Assets: $37,304,448 (fiscal year ending May 31, 1992); $34,437,412 (fiscal 1991); $31,852,038 (fiscal 1990)
EIN: 23-7434707

CONTRIBUTIONS SUMMARY
Donor(s): The terms of the late John Stauffer's will established the John Stauffer Charitable Trust in 1974. John Stauffer was an officer and director of the Stauffer Chemical Company. He was particularly interested in educational concerns and hospitals.
Typical Recipients: • *Education:* colleges & universities, science/technology education • *Health:* hospitals, pediatric health
Grant Types: endowment, fellowship, and general support
Geographic Distribution: primarily California

GIVING OFFICERS
Carl M. Franklin: co-trust
H. Jess Senecal: co-trust
Michael S. Whalen: co-trust

APPLICATION INFORMATION
Initial Approach:
All proposals must be submitted to the trust in writing. Personal interviews are discouraged. Guidelines are available upon request.
Proposals should include the amount requested; an explanation of the need for the subject of the grant; the goals; the manner in which John Stauffer's name will be memorialized; full financial information, including a detailed budget for the project to be assisted by the grant; and a statement of whether other sources of funding are being sought, and if so, which other sources are providing funding.
All applications must be executed by an officer of the grantee institution. Applications signed by a division or department head must be approved and countersigned by the head of the organization or institution, or by an officer thereof.
Applicants should submit the latest IRS tax-exempt determination letter, stating that the grantee is not a private foundation, as well as the latest audited balance sheet and statement of income and expenditures. In addition, the trust would like to see a tax-exempt

letter from the State of California. Letters of support from authorities and/or organizations in the applicant's field are encouraged.
All proposals and letters should be submitted in three copies, one for each of the trustees. An applicant desiring the material to be returned in the event of a rejection should state so.
The board meets bimonthly, and accepts applications any time.
If the proposal needs amplification or clarification, the trust will request the needed information in writing. Applicants are notified in writing whether or not the grant is being given. Decisions are made within six to nine months.
Restrictions on Giving:
Grants are not made to organizations which, in turn, distribute them to others at their own discretion. Recipients may be required to provide matching funds. Also, large grants may be distributed over a period of two or more years.
Those receiving grants are required to send a report on the use of the funds to the trust, including a certification that the funds have been used for the purpose for which the grant was made. The trust reserves the right to call for a reasonable audit of the use of grant funds conducted by its representatives at its own expense.
If grants were used for purposes other than that for which the grant was made, the total amount of the grant must be returned.
Grants are usually for one calendar year; however, there may be exceptions in unusual situations.

OTHER THINGS TO KNOW
Those denied a grant may submit a new application in the future, but should not request reinstatement of a prior request which has been denied. The trust prefers to participate with other donors when making grants.
Publications: policy guidelines

GRANTS ANALYSIS
Total Grants: $1,381,500
Number of Grants: 16
Highest Grant: $200,000
Typical Range: $50,000 to $200,000

Disclosure Period: fiscal year ending May 31, 1992
Note: Recent grants are derived from a fiscal 1992 Form 990.

RECENT GRANTS
200,000 University of California at Los Angeles Law School, Los Angeles, CA — for expansion of law library
150,000 Stanford University, Stanford, CA — for renovation of Stauffer Laboratories
150,000 University of California at Berkeley, Berkeley, CA — expansion of Law School and renovation of seminar room
125,000 University of Redlands, Redlands, CA — equipment fund for Chemistry Department
100,000 University of Southern California, Los Angeles, CA — Loker Hydrocarbon Institute; for transformer and spectrometer
83,000 Queen of Angels, Los Angeles, CA — Hollywood Presbyterian Foundation; Emergency Center capital fund
75,000 Pepperdine University, Malibu, CA — for expansion of Odell McConnell Law Center
75,000 University of California at Irvine, Irvine, CA — to establish John Stauffer Radiopharmaceutical Laboratory
75,000 University of California at Irvine, Irvine, CA — to establish John Stauffer Radiopharmaceutical Laboratory
72,500 Queen of Angels, Los Angeles, CA — Hollywood Presbyterian Foundation; pneumatic tube system

Stauffer Communications / Stauffer Communications Foundation
Sales: $134.0 million
Employees: 2,300
Headquarters: Topeka, KS
SIC Major Group:
Communications and Printing & Publishing

CONTACT
Stanley H. Stauffer
Foundation Chairman
Stauffer Communications Foundation
616 Jefferson
Topeka, KS 66607
(913) 295-1111

FINANCIAL SUMMARY
Recent Giving: $89,490 (1991); $120,612 (1990); $146,907 (1989)
Assets: $1,081,236 (1991); $960,686 (1990); $853,526 (1989)
Gifts Received: $50,000 (1991); $50,000 (1990); $125,000 (1989)
Fiscal Note: In 1991, contributions were received from Stauffer Communications.
EIN: 48-6212412

CONTRIBUTIONS SUMMARY
Typical Recipients: • *Arts & Humanities:* community arts, public broadcasting • *Civic & Public Affairs:* law & justice, municipalities, urban & community affairs • *Education:* colleges & universities, religious education • *Health:* health organizations • *Religion:* religious organizations • *Social Services:* community service organizations, religious welfare, united funds, youth organizations
Grant Types: general support
Geographic Distribution: focus on OK and KS
Operating Locations: FL (Winter Haven), KS (Topeka), MN (Brainerd), MO (Independence), OK (Shawnee), SD (Brookings)

CORP. OFFICERS
John H. Stauffer: *CURR EMPL* chmn, pres, ceo, dir: Stauffer Communs

GIVING OFFICERS
William Duckworth: secy
John H. Stauffer: mem

Stanley H. Stauffer: chmn

APPLICATION INFORMATION

Initial Approach: Send brief letter describing program. There are no deadlines.

GRANTS ANALYSIS

Number of Grants: 37
Highest Grant: $15,000
Typical Range: $500 to $5,000
Disclosure Period: 1991

RECENT GRANTS

15,000 Menninger Foundation, Topeka, KS
10,000 Kansas University, Lawrence, KS — Campaign Kansas
5,000 Capper Foundation Residence Hall, Topeka, KS
5,000 Kansas Bar Association, KS — Bill of Rights
5,000 Topeka Community Foundation, Topeka, KS
4,000 Rescue Mission, KS
3,000 Salvation Army, KS
2,850 Baker University FM Station, Baldwin City, KS
2,500 Aboretum in City Park, Topeka, KS
2,500 Washburn Law Library, Topeka, KS

Stauffer Foundation, John and Beverly

CONTACT

Laurence Gold
John and Beverly Stauffer Fdn.
333 S. Hope St. 48th floor
Los Angeles, CA 90071
(213) 381-3933

FINANCIAL SUMMARY

Recent Giving: $169,130 (1991); $191,620 (1990); $171,615 (1989)
Assets: $3,596,838 (1991); $3,513,642 (1990); $3,444,847 (1989)
EIN: 95-2241406

CONTRIBUTIONS SUMMARY

Donor(s): the late John Stauffer and Beverly Stauffer
Typical Recipients: • *Arts & Humanities:* museums/galleries, music • *Civic & Public Affairs:* philanthropic organizations, zoos/botanical gardens • *Education:* colleges & universities, private education (prec-ollege) • *Health:* health organi-

zations, hospitals, medical research, single-disease health associations • *Religion:* churches, religious organizations • *Social Services:* child welfare, community service organizations, drugs & alcohol, food/clothing distribution, shelters/homelessness, youth organizations
Grant Types: capital, general support, multiyear/continuing support, and scholarship
Geographic Distribution: focus on the southern CA, area

GIVING OFFICERS

Leslie Sheridan Bartleson: dir
Harriette Hughes: dir
Katherine Stauffer Sheridan: dir
Thomas C. Towse: treas, dir

APPLICATION INFORMATION

Initial Approach: Send brief letter of inquiry describing program or project. There are no deadlines.
Restrictions on Giving: Does not support individuals or fund endowments or operating budgets.

GRANTS ANALYSIS

Number of Grants: 37
Highest Grant: $20,000
Typical Range: $100 to $7,500
Disclosure Period: 1991

RECENT GRANTS

20,000 Wellness Community, Pasadena, CA
15,350 Hospitaller Foundation of California, Los Angeles, CA
11,500 Childhelp USA, Pasadena, CA
10,000 Foundation Endowment, Pasadena, CA
9,500 Our Lady of Guadalupe, Pasadena, CA
8,500 La Jolla Youth, La Jolla, CA
8,000 Boys and Girls Club, Hollywood, CA
7,000 Kelter Center, Pasadena, CA
6,500 Youth Development, Pasadena, CA
6,000 Palm Springs Museum, Palm Springs, CA

Staunton Farm Foundation

CONTACT

Marilyn Ingalls
Grants Administrator
Staunton Farm Foundation
Center City Tower, Ste. 240
650 Smithfield St.
Pittsburgh, PA 15222
(412) 281-8020

FINANCIAL SUMMARY

Recent Giving: $750,000 (1992 approx.); $793,025 (1991); $761,500 (1990)
Assets: $21,500,000 (1992 est.); $27,603,590 (1991); $22,497,072 (1990); $22,246,877 (1989)
Gifts Received: $5,428 (1987)
EIN: 25-0965573

CONTRIBUTIONS SUMMARY

Donor(s): The Staunton Farm Foundation was established in Pennsylvania in 1937, with funds donated by Mrs. Matilda S. McCready (born Matilda Staunton Craig). Mrs. McCready original wish was that funds from the foundation would be used to erect a home for the mentally ill. However, her estate lacked the necessary funds for such an undertaking. Mrs. McCready realized her original intentions may not always be practical and stated, "In the event that advances in medical sciences or in social conditions render carrying on of the home...impractical, the directors of Staunton Farm may, with the consent of Orphan's Court of Allegheny County, PA, change its character so as to suit the needs of the times, keeping always in view the effort to alleviate the conditions of the sick and unfortunate."
Typical Recipients: • *Education:* colleges & universities • *Health:* hospitals • *Religion:* churches • *Social Services:* aged, child welfare, counseling, delinquency & crime, family services, recreation & athletics, shelters/homelessness
Grant Types: general support, professorship, and project
Geographic Distribution: Southwestern Pennsylvania

GIVING OFFICERS

Albert H. Burchfield III: pres, dir
Albert B. Craig III: dir

Joseph D. Dury, Jr.: dir
Rev. David C. Frederick: dir
Andrea Q. Griffiths: vp, dir
Nancy E. Gruner: dir
Carolyn S. Hammer: dir
Alexander A. Henkels, Jr.: dir
Marilyn Ingalls: grants admin
Kathleen C. Knight: dir
Hope S. Linge: dir
Lee C. Lundback: dir
Barbara Robinson: secy/treas
Thomas L. Wentling, Jr.: dir

APPLICATION INFORMATION

Initial Approach:
A letter of inquiry should be sent describing the organization and proposed project. After initial review, prospective grantees may be asked to make a formal application for consideration by the Foundation's Project Committee. Formal applications are due in the middle of January, April, July and October. Prospective grantees should plan accordingly.

GRANTS ANALYSIS

Total Grants: $793,025
Number of Grants: 28
Highest Grant: $250,000
Typical Range: $5,000 to $50,000
Disclosure Period: 1991
Note: Recent grants are derived from a 1991 grants list.

RECENT GRANTS

250,000 University of Pittsburgh, Pittsburgh, PA — for the endowment of a chair of professor of pediatrics and psychiatry
250,000 University of Pittsburgh, Pittsburgh, PA — payment to endow the chair of the professor of pediatrics and psychiatry
80,000 Mon Yough Human Services, McKeesport, PA — for the program for Angora Gardens
75,000 Three Rivers Youth, Pittsburgh, PA — for the program for renovating and upgrading the intensive treatment unit
40,000 Mental Health Association in Westmoreland County, Greensburg, PA — for external advocacy services

35,000 Children's Hospital of Pittsburgh, Pittsburgh, PA — for the Family Advocate program

33,000 Arsenal Family and Children's Center, Pittsburgh, PA — for therapy for emotionally deprived children

33,000 South Hills Interfaith Ministries, Bethel Park, PA — for a one year extension of the Morgan Project program

26,000 Alpha House, Pittsburgh, PA — for the re-entry program

25,000 Saltworks, Pittsburgh, PA — for the prevention/intervention program on sexual abuse

Steadley Memorial Trust, Kent D. and Mary L.

CONTACT
Linda M. Hedge
Kent D. and Mary L. Steadley Memorial Trust
c/o Boatmen's Bank of Carthage
231 South Main
Carthage, MO 64836
(417) 358-9011

FINANCIAL SUMMARY
Recent Giving: $373,271 (1990); $389,758 (1989); $254,800 (1987)
Assets: $7,161,181 (1990); $7,394,203 (1989); $5,062,376 (1987)
EIN: 43-6120866

CONTRIBUTIONS SUMMARY
Typical Recipients: • *Arts & Humanities:* arts centers, libraries • *Civic & Public Affairs:* municipalities, urban & community affairs • *Social Services:* recreation & athletics
Grant Types: capital and general support
Geographic Distribution: limited to Carthage, MO

APPLICATION INFORMATION
Initial Approach: Contributes only to preselected organizations.

GRANTS ANALYSIS
Number of Grants: 6
Highest Grant: $272,008

Typical Range: $20,000 to $50,000
Disclosure Period: 1990

RECENT GRANTS
272,008 City of Carthage, Carthage, MO
50,000 Victorian Carthage, Carthage, MO
20,500 Carthage R-9 School District, Carthage, MO
20,000 Art Central, Carthage, MO
4,000 City of Carthage, Carthage, MO
676 Joplin Family Y, Joplin, MO

Stearns Charitable Foundation, Anna B.

CONTACT
Katherine Babson
Anna B. Stearns Charitable Fdn.
Hutchins and Wheeler
101 Federal St.
Boston, MA 02110

FINANCIAL SUMMARY
Recent Giving: $644,100 (1991); $462,541 (1990); $118,800 (1989)
Assets: $8,578,950 (1991); $7,045,544 (1990); $2,440,300 (1989)
Gifts Received: $1,036,795 (1991); $4,869,374 (1990)
Fiscal Note: In 1991, contributions were received from the estate of Anna B. Stearns.
EIN: 04-6144732

CONTRIBUTIONS SUMMARY
Typical Recipients: • *Civic & Public Affairs:* environmental affairs, municipalities, philanthropic organizations • *Health:* single-disease health associations • *Social Services:* child welfare, community service organizations, counseling, employment/job training, family planning, family services, recreation & athletics, united funds, youth organizations
Grant Types: general support

GIVING OFFICERS
Katherine Babson: clerk
Gwen Harper: trust
Ralph B. Hersey, Jr.: pres
Leonard Johnson: treas
Joseph R. Watkins: trust

APPLICATION INFORMATION
Initial Approach: Send brief letter describing program. There are no deadlines.

GRANTS ANALYSIS
Number of Grants: 32
Highest Grant: $295,000
Typical Range: $5,000 to $10,000
Disclosure Period: 1991

RECENT GRANTS
295,000 Northern New Hampshire Foundation, NH
66,441 Nature Conservancy, Boston, MA
12,000 Planned Parenthood Federation of America, Cambridge, MA
10,000 COPE, Boston, MA
10,000 Massachusetts Committee For Children and Youth, Boston, MA
7,500 Bridge Over Troubled Waters, Boston, MA
7,500 Judge Baker Children's Center, Boston, MA
7,500 Samaritans, Boston, MA
6,000 Careers For Later Years, Boston, MA
5,000 East End House, Boston, MA

Stearns Trust, Artemas W.

CONTACT
Clifford E. Elias, Esq.
Trustee
Artemas W. Stearns Trust
70 East St.
Methuen, MA 01844
(508) 687-0151

FINANCIAL SUMMARY
Recent Giving: $185,500 (1991); $173,888 (1989); $161,125 (1988)
Assets: $3,420,256 (1991); $3,138,619 (1989); $2,884,969 (1988)
EIN: 04-2137061

CONTRIBUTIONS SUMMARY
Donor(s): the late Artemas W. Stearns
Typical Recipients: • *Civic & Public Affairs:* municipalities • *Education:* private education (precollege), religious education • *Health:* hospitals • *Social Services:* child welfare, community service organizations,

counseling, disabled, food/clothing distribution, recreation & athletics, shelters/homelessness, united funds, youth organizations
Grant Types: capital, emergency, general support, project, and scholarship
Geographic Distribution: limited to the greater Lawrence, MA, area

GIVING OFFICERS
Clifford E. Elias: trust
Marsha K. Elias: off
Vincent P. Morton, Jr.: trust
Marsha E. Rich: trust

APPLICATION INFORMATION
Initial Approach: Contributes only to preselected organizations.
Restrictions on Giving: Does not support individuals.

OTHER THINGS TO KNOW
Publications: Application Guidelines

GRANTS ANALYSIS
Number of Grants: 28
Highest Grant: $30,000
Typical Range: $2,000 to $5,000
Disclosure Period: 1991

RECENT GRANTS
30,000 Holy Family Hospital, Lawrence, MA
30,000 Lawrence General Hospital, Lawrence, MA
20,000 Merrimack Valley United Fund, Lawrence, MA
12,000 Big Brothers and Big Sisters, Lawrence, MA
10,000 Brooks School, Lawrence, MA
10,000 Central Catholic High School, Lawrence, MA
10,000 YMCA, Lawrence, MA
5,500 Bread and Roses, Lawrence, MA
5,000 Boys Club of America, Lawrence, MA
5,000 CLASS, Lawrence, MA

Steel Heddle Manufacturing Co.

Sales: $70.0 million
Employees: 850
Headquarters: Greenville, SC
SIC Major Group: Industrial Machinery & Equipment and Primary Metal Industries

CONTACT

W. R. Rogers
Manager, Human Resources
Steel Heddle Manufacturing Co.
PO Box 1867
Greenville, SC 29602
(803) 244-4110

CONTRIBUTIONS SUMMARY

Company sponsors employee matching gift program; also supports community organizations.
Typical Recipients: • *Arts & Humanities:* general • *Civic & Public Affairs:* general • *Education:* general • *Health:* general • *Social Services:* general
Grant Types: matching
Geographic Distribution: primarily headquarters area
Operating Locations: SC (Greenville)

CORP. OFFICERS

James B. Bowen: *CURR EMPL* chmn, dir: Steel Heddle Mfg Co
Hugh I. Cash: *CURR EMPL* pres: Steel Heddle Manufacturing Co

APPLICATION INFORMATION

Initial Approach: Send brief letter of inquiry. There are no deadlines.

Steel, Sr. Foundation, Marshall

CONTACT

Marshall Steel, Jr.
Trustee
Marshall Steel, Sr. Fdn.
685 Market St., Ste. 910
San Francisco, CA 94105

FINANCIAL SUMMARY

Recent Giving: $1,826,787 (1991); $282,440 (1990); $421,750 (1989)
Assets: $4,108,568 (1990); $3,975,506 (1989)
EIN: 94-6080053

CONTRIBUTIONS SUMMARY

Donor(s): members of the Steel family and family-related businesses
Typical Recipients: • *Arts & Humanities:* museums/galleries, music, opera, public broadcasting • *Civic & Public Affairs:* environmental affairs, municipalities, zoos/botanical gardens • *Education:* colleges & universities • *Health:* hospitals • *Social Services:* animal protection, child welfare, family planning, youth organizations
Grant Types: emergency and general support
Geographic Distribution: focus on CA

GIVING OFFICERS

Eric Steel: trust
Gordon Steel: trust
Jane Steel: trust
Lauri Steel: trust
Marshall Steel, Jr.: trust

APPLICATION INFORMATION

Initial Approach: Send brief letter of inquiry describing program or project. There are no deadlines.
Restrictions on Giving: Does not support individuals.

OTHER THINGS TO KNOW

All assets of the Marshall Steel, Sr. Foundation have been transferred to the San Francisco Foundation.

GRANTS ANALYSIS

Number of Grants: 2
Highest Grant: $1,826,587
Disclosure Period: 1991

RECENT GRANTS

1,826,587 San Francisco Foundation, San Francisco, CA
200 SPCA, San Francisco, CA

Steelcase / Steelcase Foundation

Sales: $1.88 billion
Employees: 20,700
Headquarters: Grand Rapids, MI
SIC Major Group: Business Services, Furniture & Fixtures, and Industrial Machinery & Equipment

CONTACT

Kate Pew Wolters
Executive Director
Steelcase Fdn.
PO Box 1967
Grand Rapids, MI 49501
(616) 246-4695

FINANCIAL SUMMARY

Recent Giving: $3,380,000 (fiscal 1992); $3,900,000 (fiscal 1991); $4,600,000 (fiscal 1990)
Assets: $60,552,600 (fiscal year ending November 30, 1992); $52,848,728 (fiscal 1991); $41,411,600 (fiscal 1989)
Fiscal Note: Company gives primarily through the foundation.
EIN: 38-6050470

CONTRIBUTIONS SUMMARY

Typical Recipients: • *Arts & Humanities:* arts centers, arts institutes, dance, ethnic arts, history/historic preservation, literary arts, museums/galleries, music, opera, performing arts, public broadcasting, theater • *Civic & Public Affairs:* economic development, housing, women's affairs, zoos/botanical gardens • *Education:* arts education, colleges & universities, community & junior colleges, education funds, private education (precollege) • *Health:* health care cost containment, health organizations, hospices, medical rehabilitation, mental health, nutrition & health maintenance, single-disease health associations • *Social Services:* aged, child welfare, community centers, community service organizations, counseling, delinquency & crime, disabled, domestic violence, drugs & alcohol, family planning, family services, food/clothing distribution, homes, shelters/homelessness, united funds, youth organizations
Grant Types: capital, challenge, general support, project, and seed money
Nonmonetary Support Types: donated products and in-kind services
Note: Nonmonetary support in fiscal 1990 was valved at approximately $700,000.
Geographic Distribution: exclusively in communities in which company has manufacturing operations

Operating Locations: AL (Athens), CA (Orange County, Tustin), MI (Grand Rapids, Kent County, Kentwood, Lowell, Ottawa County), NC (Fletcher, Highpoint)

CORP. OFFICERS

Frank Henry Merlotti: *B* Herrin IL 1926 *CURR EMPL* dir, chmn exec comm: Steelcase *CORP AFFIL* dir: CMS Energy Corp
Jerry K. Myers: *CURR EMPL* ceo: Steelcase
Robert Cunningham Pew II: *B* Syracuse NY 1923 *CURR EMPL* chmn, ceo, dir: Steelcase *CORP AFFIL* dir: Old Kent Fin Corp *NONPR AFFIL* bd control: Grand Valley St Coll; dir: Econ Devel Corp Grand Rapids
Peter M. Wege: *B* Grand Rapids MI 1920 *ED* Univ MI *CURR EMPL* vchmn, dir: Steelcase

GIVING OFFICERS

David Dyer Hunting, Jr.: trust *B* Grand Rapids MI 1926 *ED* Univ MI 1948 *CURR EMPL* vchmn, dir: Steelcase
Roger L. Martin: trust *CURR EMPL* vp (community rels): Steelcase Inc
Frank Henry Merlotti: trust *CURR EMPL* dir, chmn exec comm: Steelcase (see above)
Jerry K. Myers: trust *CURR EMPL* ceo: Steelcase (see above)
Robert Cunningham Pew II: trust *CURR EMPL* chmn, ceo, dir: Steelcase (see above)
Peter M. Wege: trust *CURR EMPL* vchmn, dir: Steelcase (see above)
Kate Pew Wolters: exec dir

APPLICATION INFORMATION

Initial Approach: *Initial Contact:* letter and request for application *Include Information On:* project description, statement of objectives and duration, budget covering income and expenses, proof of tax-exemption, list of board members and business affiliations *When to Submit:* any time; allow at least 90 days for grant decision
Restrictions on Giving: The foundation does not make grants to individuals, fraternal organizations, political or lobbying groups, or to dinners or special events.
Donations to religiously affiliated programs are made only

when the objectives benefit the entire community. Programs with substantial religious overtones of a sectarian nature are not considered.

OTHER THINGS TO KNOW

The foundation and company endeavor to support organizations in which company employees are board members, volunteers, or clients, or where employees are part of the benefiting community.

The foundation prefers to participate with others in providing financial support for a project and occasionally will structure its grants to encourage broad support by others. Old Kent Bank and Trust Company serves as a corporate trustee for the foundation. Foundation requires reports from recipients detailing financial accounting of grant expenditures and accomplishments.

Publications: annual report

GRANTS ANALYSIS

Total Grants: $3,380,000
Number of Grants: 115
Highest Grant: $500,000
Typical Range: $10,000 to $30,000

Disclosure Period: fiscal year ending November 30, 1992

Note: Average grant figure excludes a $500,000 grant. Recent grants are derived from a fiscal 1992 annual report.

RECENT GRANTS

500,000 John Ball Zoo Society — funding for Phase II and III Zoo construction and renovation

375,000 United Way of Kent County, Grand Rapids, MI — 1992 Campaign

200,000 YWCA, Grand Rapids, Grand Rapids, MI — funding for building renovation and creation of Grand Rapids Center for Women

125,000 Kent Intermediate School District, Grand Rapids, MI — start up funding for Instructional Delivery System

106,000 Inner City Christian Federation — seed money for Capital Revolving Loan Fund for housing lease for purchase program for people who are economically disadvantaged

100,000 Dwelling place of Grand Rapids, Grand Rapids, MI — support for the renovation and rehabilitation of Goodrich Apartments for people of low income

100,000 Grand Rapids Christian School Association, Grand Rapids, MI — expansion and renovation of classroom facilities

100,000 Mary Free Bed Hospital and Rehabilitation Center, Grand Rapids, MI — funding to create Biomotion Analysis Laboratory to aid persons with impaired mobility

100,000 St. Andrew's School, Laurinburg, NC — support to enhance the school's math and science program

100,000 West Michigan Public Broadcasting, Grand Rapids, MI — support for capital campaign to expand and improve public radio and television stations

---

Steele Foundation

CONTACT

Daniel F. Cracchiolo
President
Steele Fdn.
702 East Osborn Rd.
Phoenix, AZ 85014-5215
(602) 230-2038

FINANCIAL SUMMARY

Recent Giving: $739,427 (1990); $998,925 (1989); $838,700 (1988)
Assets: $18,451,880 (1990); $20,263,650 (1989); $17,540,104 (1988)
Gifts Received: $302,050 (1990); $361,091 (1989); $475,130 (1988)
Fiscal Note: In 1990, contributions were received from Ethel Steele.
EIN: 95-3466880

CONTRIBUTIONS SUMMARY

Donor(s): The foundation was established in 1980 by Ethel Steele and the late Horace Steele.

Typical Recipients: • *Arts & Humanities:* music, performing arts, theater • *Civic & Public Affairs:* philanthropic organizations • *Education:* colleges & universities • *Health:* health organizations, single-disease health associations • *Social Services:* community service organizations, disabled, youth organizations

Grant Types: capital and general support

Geographic Distribution: focus on Phoenix, AZ, and California

GIVING OFFICERS

Joseph F. Anselmo: secy
Burt Caldwell: treas
Dr. Andrea Cracchiolo III: dir
Daniel Cracchiolo: pres

APPLICATION INFORMATION

Initial Approach: Restrictions on Giving: The foundation supports preselected organizations and does not accept unsolicited requests for funds.

GRANTS ANALYSIS

Total Grants: $739,427
Number of Grants: 20
Highest Grant: $201,200
Typical Range: $5,000 to $50,000
Disclosure Period: 1990
Note: Recent grants are derived from a 1990 grants list.

RECENT GRANTS

201,200 Phoenix Symphony, Phoenix, AZ
200,000 Foundation for the Performing Arts, San Louis Obispo, CA
60,000 Arizona Community Foundation, Children's Action Alliance, Phoenix, AZ
50,000 Arizona Theatre Company, Tucson, AZ
50,000 Sun Angel Foundation, Phoenix, AZ
34,222 Compas, St. Paul, MN
25,000 Rancho YMCA
20,000 John Wayne Cancer Clinic, Los Angeles, CA
10,000 American Heart Association, Washington, DC
10,000 Southwest Leadership Foundation

Steele Foundation, Harry and Grace

CONTACT

Marie F. Kowert
Assistant Secretary
Harry and Grace Steele Foundation
441 Old Newport Blvd., Ste. 301
Newport Beach, CA 92663
(714) 631-9158

FINANCIAL SUMMARY

Recent Giving: $5,925,555 (fiscal 1991); $5,065,383 (fiscal 1990); $8,317,646 (fiscal 1989)
Assets: $50,100,764 (fiscal year ending October 31, 1991); $41,327,823 (fiscal 1990); $45,701,382 (fiscal 1989)
EIN: 95-6035879

CONTRIBUTIONS SUMMARY

Donor(s): The Harry and Grace Steele Foundation, formerly the Harry G. Steele Foundation, was established in California in 1953 by the late Grace C. Steele in memory of her husband, Harry G. Steele. The trustees of the foundation seek to perpetuate Mr. Steele's legacy of social consciousness and philanthropy. The trustees elected to change the name of the foundation to the Harry and Grace Steele Foundation. Mrs. Steele bequeathed the major portion of her estate to the foundation upon her death in 1974.

Typical Recipients: • *Arts & Humanities:* arts institutes, museums/galleries, music, opera, performing arts, public broadcasting • *Civic & Public Affairs:* environmental affairs, nonprofit management, public policy, zoos/botanical gardens • *Education:* private education (precollege), special education, student aid • *Health:* hospitals, pediatric health • *International:* international organizations • *Social Services:* aged, disabled, family planning, food/clothing distribution, recreation & athletics, youth organizations

Grant Types: capital, challenge, endowment, general support, multiyear/continuing support, professorship, project, and scholarship

Geographic Distribution: primarily Orange County, CA

GIVING OFFICERS

Alphonse A. Burnand III: secy *PHIL AFFIL* pres: Burnand (Alphonse A) Med and Ed Foundation

Audrey Steele Burnand: pres

Marie F. Kowert: asst secy

Richard Steele: treas

Barbara Steele Williams: asst secy

APPLICATION INFORMATION

Initial Approach:

The foundation has no formal application forms; send a single copy of a concise letter with supporting documentation and signed by an officer of the organization.

Letters of application should be signed by an officer of the organization and include a copy of IRS letter showing section 501(c)(3) status and classification of the organization as "not a private foundation"; current list of officers, directors, or trustees; evidence of need for services or facilities to be funded; list of other outstanding potential sources of support; time schedule for reporting the manner of expenditure and results obtained from foundation funding; analysis of expenditures disbursed for fund raising and administrative costs against amount expended for the purposes intended; and the amount requested from the foundation.

There are no specific deadlines for receipt of proposals. The trustees meet several times a year to consider grant requests. Grantees will not be considered for grants more often than once every three or four years. Proposals are initially reviewed by staff to see if they conform to legal requirements and foundation guidelines, and contain all essential information. Based on the information in the application, the trustees may request a visit with the applicant and will on occasion request a personal interview. Applicants should allow approximately six months for decisions on proposals.

Restrictions on Giving: The foundation does not make donations to tax-supported organizations or private foundations. No grants are given to individuals or for loans. The foundation requires progress and financial reports from recipients.

OTHER THINGS TO KNOW

Publications: annual report, program policy statement

GRANTS ANALYSIS

Total Grants: $5,925,555

Number of Grants: 48

Highest Grant: $750,000

Typical Range: $5,000 to $25,000 and $200,000 to $500,000

Disclosure Period: fiscal year ending October 31, 1991

Note: Recent grants are derived from a fiscal 1991 annual report.

RECENT GRANTS

750,000 International Projects Assistance Services, Chapel Hill, NC — continued support

649,688 Pomona College, Claremont, CA — faculty leave program

516,875 Orange County Performing Arts Center, Costa Mesa, CA — funding to underwrite Opera

500,000 Mills College, Oakland, CA — scholarship fund

500,000 Planned Parenthood Federation of America, New York, NY — general support

500,000 Scripps College, Claremont, CA — capital improvements

500,000 Zoological Society of San Diego, San Diego, CA — Heart of the Zoo project

268,669 Newport Harbor Art Museum, Newport Beach, CA — capital improvement

250,000 Planned Parenthood/Orange and San Bernardino Counties, Santa Ana, CA — general support

242,985 Newport Beach Public Library Foundation, Newport Beach, CA — capital improvement

Steele-Reese Foundation

CONTACT

William T. Buice III
Trustee
Steele-Reese Foundation
c/o Davidson, Dawson and Clark
330 Madison Avenue, 35th Fl.
New York, NY 10017
(212) 557-7700

Note: Southern Appalachia applicants should address inquiries to Dr. John R. Bryden, 760 Malabu Drive, Lexington, KY 40502. Northwest applicants should address inquiries to: Mrs. Christine N. Brady, P.O. Box 7263, Boise, ID 83707. High school seniors in Lemhi and Custer Counties, ID, are invited to apply for foundation undergraduate scholarships through their schools.

FINANCIAL SUMMARY

Recent Giving: $1,104,821 (fiscal 1991); $1,186,839 (fiscal 1990); $1,020,750 (fiscal 1988)

Assets: $29,965,358 (fiscal year ending August 31, 1991); $26,855,942 (fiscal 1990); $23,179,853 (fiscal 1988)

EIN: 13-6034763

CONTRIBUTIONS SUMMARY

Donor(s): The foundation was established in 1955 by Eleanor Steele Reese, whose father Charles Steele was a partner of J.P. Morgan. Eleanor Steele was born in New York City in 1893. After pursuing a career as an opera singer and recitalist in Europe and the United States for two decades, she moved to the western United States. She met and married Emmet P. Reese in 1941. At the time of their marriage, he and Eleanor bought and operated a small working ranch near Shoup, ID. In the mid-1950s, they moved to a large ranch in Salmon, ID, which they operated until a few years before her death in 1977. Emmet P. Reese died in 1982. The original trustees of the foundation were Sidney W. Davidson and J.P. Morgan & Co., Inc.

Typical Recipients: • *Arts & Humanities:* history/historic preservation, libraries • *Civic & Public Affairs:* philanthropic organizations, urban & community affairs • *Education:* colleges & universities, education associations, private education (precollege), student aid • *Health:* hospices, hospitals, single-disease health associations, single-disease health associations • *Social Services:* family planning, food/clothing distribution, homes, shelters/homelessness, youth organizations

Grant Types: general support and scholarship

Geographic Distribution: primarily Southern Appalachia, particularly Kentucky; and the Northwest, particularly Idaho

GIVING OFFICERS

William T. Buice III: co-trust

Robert T. H. Davidson: co-trust

APPLICATION INFORMATION

Initial Approach:

Applicants should review the foundation's policy and criteria, available upon request, in detail. If a proposal seems warranted, applicants should write a succinct factual letter of no more than several pages. Any brief printed material that is pertinent to an application should also be included.

There are no application deadlines.

The officers meet as necessary to review proposals. Grant installments are generally paid in February and August of each year.

Restrictions on Giving: No grants are made to individuals, virtually none for research or planning, and few for construction. The foundation seeks grantees which have "special experience in their fields, unusually talented staff, an imaginative and courageous approach toward pursuing their goals, or some other essential quality." The foundation generally does not fund projects where its funds would be the major contribution or where evidence of strong community support is lacking. Other preferred qualities include teamwork and financial responsibility. In addition, the foundation "avoids organizations which seem to pivot on a single manager who could not be replaced with smooth continuity."

OTHER THINGS TO KNOW

Morgan Guaranty Trust Company of New York serves as the corporate trustee for the foundation.

The individual trustees share the responsibility for grant determination. To reduce overhead costs, the foundation does not maintain an office or a full-time staff. Trustees are assisted with grant decisions in Southern Appalachia by Dr. John R. Bryden of Lexington, KY; in the Northwest by Mrs. Christine N. Brady of Carmen, ID; and in the scholarship program in Idaho by Mrs. Lydia Schofield of Salmon, ID.

Publications: annual report includes detailed grant application information

GRANTS ANALYSIS

Total Grants: $1,104,821
Number of Grants: 43
Highest Grant: $81,250
Typical Range: $10,000 to $50,000
Disclosure Period: fiscal year ending August 31, 1991
Note: Recent grants are derived from a fiscal 1991 grants list.

RECENT GRANTS

81,250 Whitman College, Walla Walla, WA
80,000 Steele Memorial Benefit Association, Salmon, ID
75,000 Teachers and Writers Collaborative, New York, NY
50,000 Davidson College, Davidson, NC
50,000 Hospice of Big Sandy, Paintsville, KY
50,000 Idaho Foodbank Warehouse, Boise, ID
50,000 Kentucky Valley Educational Cooperative, Hazard, KY
50,000 Lexington Bluegrass Chapter of the Alzheimers Disease and Related Disorders Association, Lexington, KY
50,000 Midway College, Midway, KY
50,000 Natural Resources Defense Council, New York, NY

Steiger Memorial Fund, Albert

CONTACT

Albert Steiger Memorial Fund
1477 Main St.
Springfield, MA 01101
(413) 781-4211

FINANCIAL SUMMARY

Recent Giving: $96,000 (1991); $109,350 (1990); $112,850 (1989)

Assets: $2,355,779 (1991); $1,999,730 (1990); $2,033,611 (1989)

EIN: 04-6051750

CONTRIBUTIONS SUMMARY

Donor(s): Ralph A. Steiger, Chauncey A. Steiger, Albert Steiger, Inc.

Typical Recipients: • *Arts & Humanities:* arts associations, arts funds, public broadcasting, theater • *Education:* colleges & universities, education funds • *Health:* health organizations, hospitals • *Social Services:* community centers, community service organizations, homes, united funds, youth organizations

Grant Types: capital and project

Geographic Distribution: focus on Hampden County, MA

GIVING OFFICERS

Richard Sherman Milstein: clerk *B* Westfield MA 1926 *ED* Harvard Univ BA 1948; Boston Univ JD 1952 *CURR EMPL* ptnr: Ely & King *CORP AFFIL* consulting dir: MA Continuing Legal Ed; ptnr: Chaplin & Milstein *NONPR AFFIL* chmn adv comm: Springfield Fine Arts Mus; fellow: Am Coll Probate Couns, MA Bar Fdn; life mem, trust: WGBY Pub TV Springfield; mem: Am Bar Fdn, Am Law Inst, Springfield Library Mus Assn; trust, gen coun: Springfield Symphony Orchestra

Albert E. Steiger, Jr.: pres, dir

Albert E. Steiger III: dir

Albert E. Steiger, Jr.: pres, dir (see above)

Allen Steiger: treas

Phillip C. Steiger, Jr.: trust

Ralph A. Steiger, Jr.: vp

Robert K. Steiger: trust

APPLICATION INFORMATION

Initial Approach: Send brief letter describing program. There are no deadlines.
Restrictions on Giving: Does not support individuals.

GRANTS ANALYSIS

Number of Grants: 14
Highest Grant: $42,000
Typical Range: $1,000 to $11,500
Disclosure Period: 1991

RECENT GRANTS

42,000 United Way, Springfield, MA
15,000 Business Friends for the Arts, Springfield, MA
5,000 Community Foundation of Western Massachusetts, Springfield, MA
3,500 Ronald McDonald House, Springfield, MA
3,500 WGBY-TV Channel 57, Springfield, MA
3,000 Baystate Health Systems, Springfield, MA — Women and Infants Unit
3,000 Grandmother's Garden Trust Fund, Springfield, MA
2,500 Stagewest, Springfield, MA
2,000 Valley Land Fund, Springfield, MA

Steiger Tractor

Sales: $80.0 million
Employees: 319
Parent Company: Case IH
Headquarters: Fargo, ND
SIC Major Group: Industrial Machinery & Equipment, Nondepository Institutions, and Wholesale Trade—Durable Goods

CONTACT

Ann Eveslage
Benefits & Compensation Administrator
Steiger Tractor
3401 1st Ave. North
PO Box 6006
Fargo, ND 58108
(701) 293-4425

CONTRIBUTIONS SUMMARY

Company provides employee matching gifts only.
Grant Types: matching
Operating Locations: ND (Fargo)

CORP. OFFICERS

James K. Ashford: *B* Starkville MS 1937 *ED* MS St Univ 1958 *CURR EMPL* ceo, pres: Tenneco Automotive *CORP AFFIL* exec vp, dir: Tenneco; pres: JI Case Co, Steiger Tractor *NONPR AFFIL* mem: Automotive Information Counc

OTHER THINGS TO KNOW

Compnay acquired by J.J. Case of Tenneco

Steigerwaldt Foundation, Donna Wolf

CONTACT

Donna Wolf Steigerwaldt Fdn.
200 North LaSalle St., Ste. 2100
Chicago, IL 60601-1095

FINANCIAL SUMMARY

Recent Giving: $146,674 (fiscal 1990); $122,121 (fiscal 1989)

Assets: $2,178,796 (fiscal year ending October 31, 1990); $1,872,154 (fiscal 1989)

Gifts Received: $300,000 (fiscal 1990); $10,000 (fiscal 1989)

EIN: 36-3104409

CONTRIBUTIONS SUMMARY

Donor(s): Donna Wolf Steigerwaldt, Jockey International, Inc.

Typical Recipients: • *Arts & Humanities:* community arts, museums/galleries, music, opera, theater • *Education:* colleges & universities, education associations • *Health:* hospitals

Grant Types: capital, multi-year/continuing support, and scholarship

Geographic Distribution: focus on WI, FL, and IL

GIVING OFFICERS

Linda Steigerwaldt Davis: trust

Michael R. Shelist: trust

Donna Wolf Steigerwaldt: pres, treas, dir *B* Chicago IL 1929 *ED* CO Coll BA 1950 *CURR EMPL* chmn, ceo, dir: Jockey Intl *NONPR AFFIL* dir: Asolo Performing Arts Ctr, Century Club Sarasota Meml Hosp, FL W Coast Symphony, New Coll Fdn, Sarasota Meml Hosp Assn, Sarasota Opera Assn; governing mem: Art Inst Chicago; mem: Am Apparel Mfrs Assn, Concerned Citizens Drug & Alcohol Coalition,

Evanston Hosp-Glenbrook
Hosp Corp, Glenview Histori-
cal Soc, Infant Welfare Soc,
NW Commun Hosp Auxiliary;
mem adv bd: Boy Scouts Am
SE WI Counc; vchmn:
Carthage Coll; mem: Aid Ani-
mals Northern IL, Exec
Women Rotary Intl, Navy
League US
Donna Wolf Steigerwaldt:
pres, treas, dir *CURR EMPL*
chmn, ceo, dir: Jockey Intl (see
above)
William Steigerwaldt: dir, vp
Debra Steigerwaldt Waller:
dir, vp
Noreen A. Wilkinson: dir, secy

APPLICATION INFORMATION

Initial Approach: Contributes
only to preselected organizations.

GRANTS ANALYSIS

Number of Grants: 60
Highest Grant: $15,000
Typical Range: $500 to $5,000
Disclosure Period: fiscal year
ending October 31, 1990

RECENT GRANTS

15,000 St. Francis Hospi-
tal, Evanston, IL
14,000 Sarasota Opera As-
sociation, Sarasota,
FL
12,500 New College Foun-
dation, Sarasota, FL
12,500 New College Foun-
dation, Sarasota, FL
10,000 Kemper Center,
Kenosha, WI
10,000 Lakeside Players,
Kenosha, WI
10,000 Sarasota Memorial
Hospital Founda-
tion, Sarasota, FL
6,200 New College Foun-
dation, Sarasota, FL
5,000 Carthage College,
Kenosha, WI
5,000 Carthage College,
Kenosha, WI

Stein Foundation, Joseph F.

CONTACT

Melvin M. Stein
President
Joseph F. Stein Fdn.
28 Aspen Rd.
Scarsdale, NY 10583
(914) 725-1770

FINANCIAL SUMMARY

Recent Giving: $624,019
(1991); $935,129 (1990);
$870,593 (1989)

Assets: $9,959,828 (1991);
$8,380,834 (1990); $9,860,856
(1989)
Gifts Received: $399,997
(1991); $623,781 (1990);
$491,681 (1989)
EIN: 13-6097095

CONTRIBUTIONS SUMMARY

Donor(s): the late Joseph F.
Stein, the late Allen A. Stein,
Esq.
Typical Recipients: • *Arts &
Humanities:* history/historic
preservation, museums/galler-
ies • *Civic & Public Affairs:*
ethnic/minority organizations
• *Education:* colleges & universities, legal education • *Health:*
health organizations, medical
research, single-disease health
associations • *Religion:* religious organizations, synagogues
• *Social Services:* community
centers, community service organizations, united funds,
youth organizations
Grant Types: general support,
research, and scholarship
Geographic Distribution:
focus on NY and FL.

GIVING OFFICERS

Melvin M. Stein: pres, dir
Stuart M. Stein: secy, dir

APPLICATION INFORMATION

Initial Approach: The foundation reports it only makes contributions to preselected charitable organizations.
Restrictions on Giving: Does
not support individuals.

GRANTS ANALYSIS

Number of Grants: 140
Highest Grant: $268,160
Typical Range: $100 to $1,000
Disclosure Period: 1991

RECENT GRANTS

268,160 United Jewish Ap-
peal Federation of
Jewish Philanthro-
pies, New York, NY
80,000 Hillcrest Jewish
Center, Flushing,
NY
17,100 Westchester Jewish
Center, Westches-
ter, NY
13,350 American Jewish
Congress, New
York, NY
11,750 Jewish Theological
Seminary, New
York, NY
11,100 United Home for
Aged Hebrews
10,368 Temple Israel Cen-
ter, New York, NY

10,000 Duke University
School of Law,
Durham, NC
10,000 Ohr Someyach,
New York, NY
10,000 Syracuse Cancer
Research Institute,
Syracuse, NY

Stein Foundation, Jules and Doris

CONTACT

Linda L. Valliant
Secretary
Jules and Doris Stein Foundation
PO Box 30
Beverly Hills, CA 90213
(310) 276-2101

FINANCIAL SUMMARY

Recent Giving: $714,600
(1992); $3,154,500 (1991);
$4,132,617 (1990)
Assets: $56,000,000 (1993
est.); $46,617,284 (1991);
$41,723,746 (1990);
$38,756,749 (1989)
Gifts Received: $4,409,266
(1990); $3,453,217 (1989);
$3,930,828 (1988)
Fiscal Note: The foundation re-
ceives contributions from the
Doris Jones Stein Charitable
Lead Trusts (1-4).
EIN: 95-3708961

CONTRIBUTIONS SUMMARY

Donor(s): The foundation was
established in 1981 in California, and was formerly named
the Doris Jones Stein Foundation.
Typical Recipients: • *Arts &
Humanities:* arts institutes,
dance, libraries, literary arts,
museums/galleries, music,
opera, performing arts, theater
• *Civic & Public Affairs:* civil
rights, environmental affairs,
urban & community affairs,
zoos/botanical gardens • *Education:* colleges & universities,
education funds • *Health:* medical rehabilitation, medical research • *Social Services:* child
welfare, delinquency & crime,
employment/job training, family planning, family services,
legal aid, religious welfare,
shelters/homelessness, youth
organizations
Grant Types: capital, endowment, general support, project,
and research
Geographic Distribution: primarily in Los Angeles, CA;
Kansas City, MO; and New
York, NY

GIVING OFFICERS

Gerald H. Oppenheimer:
pres, dir
Hamilton G. Oppenheimer:
dir
Andrew Shiva: vp, dir
Jean Stein: vp, dir
Mrs. Linda Valliant: secy
Lew Robert Wasserman:
chmn *B* Cleveland OH 1913
CURR EMPL chmn, ceo, dir,
mem exec comm: MCA *CORP
AFFIL* dir: Am Airlines
NONPR AFFIL bd govs:
Ronald Reagan Presidential
Fdn; chmn: Res Prevent Blind-
ness Fdn; chmn emeritus: Assn
Motion Picture Television Pro-
ducers; dir: Amateur Athletic
Fdn Los Angeles, Los Angeles
Ctr Fdn; hon chmn: Ctr Theatre
Group Los Angeles Music Ctr;
trust: CA Inst Tech, Carter
Presidential Ctr, John F
Kennedy Ctr Performing Arts,
John F Kennedy Library, LBJ
Fdn, Jules Stein Eye Inst

APPLICATION INFORMATION

**Initial Approach: Restric-
tions on Giving:** The foundation is fulfilling a pledge to
build the Doris Stein Eye Research Center and is not solicit-
ing any new grant applications
through the 1994 calendar year.
Prospective applicants must
complete the foundation's
Grant Application Summary
form and submit it with a copy
of the IRS determination letter
verifying tax-exempt status.
Applicants should provide a description of the purpose for
which funds are sought. Funding requests for a special program or project receive more
consideration than proposals
for the general operating
budget. Supporting information
may be provided at the applicant's discretion. Also enclose
pertinent financial data, including a statement of current assets and liabilities, as well as
the source and application of
funds. Applicants also should
provide information on qualifications of the professional and
volunteer staff, organizational
history, performance record,
and future goals.
Applications may be sent any
time.
The grant review committee
meets periodically to review
new grant applications and
make recommendations to the
board of directors. Applicants

are notified of funding decisions as soon as possible. Grant applications are not held over for consideration at a subsequent time; however, applicants may re-apply and receive consideration. The foundation does not provide grants for individuals or political campaigns.

OTHER THINGS TO KNOW

Grant recipients are responsible for reporting on the progress of their programs and verifying the use of grant funds. Reports are due at six-month intervals during grant fund utilization, and a final report of fund application must be submitted.
Publications: guidelines

GRANTS ANALYSIS

Total Grants: $3,154,500
Number of Grants: 263
Highest Grant: $743,110
Typical Range: $1,000 to $20,000
Disclosure Period: 1991
Note: Recent grants are derived from a 1991 Form 990.

RECENT GRANTS

743,110 Jules Stein Eye Institute, Los Angeles, CA — Susan Stein Shiva Memorial Fund

144,950 New York Foundation for the Arts, New York, NY — general operating fund

125,000 Lyric Opera of Kansas City, Kansas City, MO — general support for program; performance subsidy

125,000 Research to Prevent Blindness, New York, NY — general support for program

75,000 New York Shakespeare Festival, New York, NY

62,000 Nature Conservancy, St. Louis, MO — general support for program; preserving threatened species and ecosystems; land conservation in Missouri

61,500 Riverhills Christian School, Tampa, FL — building of a library

57,550 Costume Council of LACMA, Los Angeles, CA — Doris Stein Re-

search and Design Center for Costumes and Textiles

55,500 Harvard Law School, Cambridge, MA — Harvard Law School Fund

54,000 Trees for Life, Wichita, KS — provides funding, management and expertise worldwide planting food bearing trees

---

Stein Foundation, Louis

CONTACT
Louis Stein
Trustee
Louis Stein Fdn.
1700 Walnut St., Ste. 925
Philadelphia, PA 19103
(215) 546-8100

FINANCIAL SUMMARY
Recent Giving: $293,098 (1991); $277,222 (1990); $269,055 (1989)
Assets: $2,979,581 (1991); $2,831,184 (1990); $2,298,543 (1989)
Gifts Received: $443,596 (1991); $123,834 (1990); $333,973 (1989)
EIN: 23-6395253

CONTRIBUTIONS SUMMARY
Donor(s): Louis Stein, Walter Liventhal, Stanley Merves, Stein, Stein and Engel
Typical Recipients: • *Civic & Public Affairs:* municipalities • *Education:* colleges & universities • *Health:* health organizations, hospitals, medical research, pediatric health, single-disease health associations • *International:* foreign educational institutions • *Religion:* religious organizations, synagogues • *Social Services:* aged, community service organizations
Grant Types: general support

GIVING OFFICERS
Marilyn Bellet: trust
Louis Stein: trust

APPLICATION INFORMATION
Initial Approach: Send brief letter of inquiry describing program or project. There are no deadlines.

GRANTS ANALYSIS
Number of Grants: 67
Highest Grant: $5,000
Typical Range: $50 to $5,000
Disclosure Period: 1991
Note: 1991 grants list was incomplete.

RECENT GRANTS
5,000 Elmira College, Elmira, NY

5,000 Jewish Theological Seminary, New York, NY

5,000 Miami Jewish Federation, Miami, FL

5,000 Tel Aviv University, Tel Aviv, Israel

2,500 Fordham University, New York, NY

Stein Roe & Farnham Investment Council / Stein Roe & Farnham Foundation

Headquarters: Chicago, IL

CONTACT
James W. Atkinson
Vice President
Stein Roe & Farnham Foundation
One South Wacker Drive
Room 3300
Chicago, IL 60606-4103
(312) 368-7890

FINANCIAL SUMMARY
Recent Giving: $38,500 (1991); $40,500 (1989)
Assets: $44,474 (1991); $28,209 (1989)
Gifts Received: $50,000 (1991); $41,000 (1989)
Fiscal Note: In 1991, contributions were received from Stein Roe & Farnham, Inc.
EIN: 36-6117895

CONTRIBUTIONS SUMMARY
Typical Recipients: • *Education:* general • *Social Services:* general
Grant Types: general support, matching, and research
Geographic Distribution: giving primarily in IL
Operating Locations: IL (Chicago)

CORP. OFFICERS
Timothy A. Schlindwein: *CURR EMPL* pres: Stein Roe & Farnham Investment Council

GIVING OFFICERS
James W. Atkinson: vp, treas

H. Kent Mergler: pres
Keith J. Rudolf: secy

APPLICATION INFORMATION
Initial Approach: The foundation supports preselected organizations and does not accept unsolicited requests for funds.

GRANTS ANALYSIS
Disclosure Period: 1991
Note: Grant list for 1991 not included.

Steinbach Fund, Ruth and Milton

CONTACT
John Klingenstein
Vice President
Ruth and Milton Steinbach Fund
c/o Klingstein, Fields & Co., L.P.
787 Seventh Ave.
New York, NY 10019-6016
(212) 492-6190

FINANCIAL SUMMARY
Recent Giving: $200,000 (fiscal 1991); $501,000 (fiscal 1990); $364,000 (fiscal 1989)
Assets: $15,815,614 (fiscal year ending October 31, 1991); $13,025,991 (fiscal 1990); $7,627,000 (fiscal 1989)
Gifts Received: $7,000,000 (fiscal 1990)
Fiscal Note: In 1990, contributions were received from Ruth A. Steinbach.
EIN: 13-6028785

CONTRIBUTIONS SUMMARY
Donor(s): the late Milton Steinbach
Typical Recipients: • *Arts & Humanities:* libraries • *Civic & Public Affairs:* ethnic/minority organizations • *Education:* business education, colleges & universities, special education • *Health:* hospitals, medical research, single-disease health associations • *Religion:* religious organizations • *Social Services:* disabled, united funds
Grant Types: general support and research
Geographic Distribution: focus on NY

GIVING OFFICERS
Kenneth H. Fields: asst treas
Frederick A. Klingenstein: vp, secy, dir *B* New York NY 1931 *ED* Yale Univ BA 1953; Harvard Univ *CURR EMPL* chmn: Klingenstein Fields & W LP *NONPR AFFIL* chmn: Mt

Sinai Med Ctr; trust: Am Mus Natural History

John Klingenstein: pres, treas, dir *CURR EMPL* mng dir: Wertheim-Schroder & Co

Patricia D. Klingenstein: dir

Sharon L. Klingenstein: dir

APPLICATION INFORMATION

Initial Approach: Send brief letter of inquiry describing program or project. There are no deadlines.

GRANTS ANALYSIS

Number of Grants: 9
Highest Grant: $100,000
Typical Range: $5,000 to $15,000
Disclosure Period: fiscal year ending October 31, 1991

RECENT GRANTS

100,000   Lighthouse, New York, NY

35,000   Rensselaerville Institute, Rensselaerville, NY

15,000   New York Public Library, New York, NY

10,000   Eye Bank for Sight Restoration, New York, NY

10,000   Guiding Eyes for the Blind, New York, NY

10,000   National Society to Prevent Blindness, New York, NY

10,000   Seeing Eye, New York, NY

5,000   Fidelco Guide Dog Foundation, New York, NY

5,000   New York Institute for Special Education, New York, NY

Steinberg Family Foundation, Meyer and Jean

Former Foundation Name: Meyer Steinberg Foundation

CONTACT

Meyer Steinberg
President
Meyer and Jean Steinberg Family Fdn.
11 East 44th St.
New York, NY 10017
(212) 867-6899

FINANCIAL SUMMARY

Recent Giving: $651,044 (1991); $145,050 (1990); $491,470 (1989)

Assets: $4,287,379 (1991); $4,257,410 (1990); $4,160,772 (1989)

Gifts Received: $336,650 (1991); $100,000 (1990); $500,000 (1989)

Fiscal Note: In 1991, contributions were received from Meyer Steinberg.

EIN: 13-6199973

CONTRIBUTIONS SUMMARY

Donor(s): Meyer Steinberg

Typical Recipients: • *Arts & Humanities:* history/historic preservation, museums/galleries, music • *Civic & Public Affairs:* ethnic/minority organizations • *Education:* colleges & universities, education associations, private education (precollege) • *Health:* hospitals, medical research, pediatric health, single-disease health associations • *Religion:* religious organizations, synagogues • *Social Services:* aged, community service organizations, disabled, family planning, united funds, youth organizations

Grant Types: general support

GIVING OFFICERS

Jean Steinberg: vp, secy
Meyer Steinberg: pres, treas

APPLICATION INFORMATION

Initial Approach: Send brief letter of inquiry describing program or project. There are no deadlines.

GRANTS ANALYSIS

Number of Grants: 116
Highest Grant: $531,362
Typical Range: $100 to $1,000
Disclosure Period: 1991

RECENT GRANTS

531,362   United Jewish Appeal Federation of Jewish Philanthropies, New York, NY

12,030   Anti-Defamation League, New York, NY

7,000   American Friends of Israel Philharmonic Orchestra, New York, NY

6,005   Park Avenue Synagogue, New York, NY

6,000   Boys and Girls Club, New York, NY

5,500   Jewish Theological Seminary, New York, NY

5,025   Brandeis University, Waltham, MA

5,000   American Associates of Ben Gurion University, New York, NY

5,000   Metropolitan Museum of Art, New York, NY

4,000   CLAL, New York, NY

Steiner Charitable Fund, Albert

CONTACT

L. G. Sherman, Jr.
Trustee
Albert Steiner Charitable Fund
3451 Paces Ferry Rd., N.W.
Atlanta, GA 30327
(404) 237-8736

FINANCIAL SUMMARY

Recent Giving: $136,500 (1991); $154,000 (1990); $150,000 (1989)

Assets: $1,754,517 (1991); $1,718,538 (1990); $1,673,893 (1989)

EIN: 58-6030063

CONTRIBUTIONS SUMMARY

Donor(s): the late Albert Steiner

Typical Recipients: • *Education:* colleges & universities, medical education • *Health:* health organizations, hospitals, medical rehabilitation, medical research, public health, single-disease health associations • *Religion:* religious organizations • *Social Services:* aged, homes

Grant Types: general support, multiyear/continuing support, and research

Geographic Distribution: focus on Atlanta, GA

GIVING OFFICERS

Joyce O. Happ: trust

Bernard L. Lipman, M.D.: trust *B* St Joseph MO 1920 *ED* Washington Univ AB 1941; Washington Univ MD 1944 *NONPR AFFIL* clinical prof emeritus: Emory Univ Sch Med; fellow: Am Coll Cardiology, Am Coll Physicians; mem: Am Federation Clinical Res, Am Heart Assn, Am Soc Internal Medicine; mem staff: Emory Univ Hosp, Grady Hosp, Piedmont Hosp, St Joseph Hosp, West Paces Ferry Hosp

L.G. Sherman, Jr.: trust

APPLICATION INFORMATION

Initial Approach: Send brief letter describing program. There are no deadlines.

Restrictions on Giving: Does not support individuals.

GRANTS ANALYSIS

Number of Grants: 17
Highest Grant: $20,000
Typical Range: $500 to $5,000
Disclosure Period: 1991

RECENT GRANTS

20,000   Central Health Center, Atlanta, GA

17,000   Our Lady of Perpetual Hope Home, Atlanta, GA

16,000   Sheperd Spinal Center, Atlanta, GA

15,000   Emory University School of Medicine, Atlanta, GA

15,000   Grady Memorial Hospital, Atlanta, GA

15,000   St. Joseph's Hospital Foundation, Atlanta, GA

7,500   Ben Massell Dental Clinic, Atlanta, GA

5,000   Alzheimer's Disease and Related Disorders Association, Atlanta, GA

5,000   Grant Park Family Health Center, Atlanta, GA

5,000   Jewish Home for the Aged, Atlanta, GA

Steiner Corp. / Steiner Foundation

Revenue: $350.0 million
Employees: 6,900
Headquarters: Salt Lake City, UT
SIC Major Group: Business Services, Fabricated Metal Products, Food & Kindred Products, and Personal Services

CONTACT

Tim Weiler
Treasurer
Steiner Fdn.
PO Box 2317
Salt Lake City, UT 84110
(801) 328-8831

FINANCIAL SUMMARY

Recent Giving: $209,112 (1991); $112,357 (1989)

Assets: $2,212,993 (1991); $2,274,900 (1989)

EIN: 87-6119190

CONTRIBUTIONS SUMMARY

Typical Recipients: • *Arts & Humanities:* community arts, dance, history/historic preservation, museums/galleries, music • *Civic & Public Affairs:* zoos/botanical gardens • *Social Services:* community service organizations, recreation & athletics, united funds, youth organizations

Grant Types: general support

Geographic Distribution: focus on UT

Operating Locations: CA (San Francisco), ID (Payette), IL (Aurora, Chicago), OR (Nyssa), TN (Cleveland), UT (Salt Lake City)
Note: List includes division locations.

CORP. OFFICERS

Richard R. Steiner: *B* Chicago IL 1923 *ED* Dartmouth Coll 1948 *CURR EMPL* pres, ceo: Steiner Corp

GIVING OFFICERS

Kevin K. Steiner: pres, dir
Timothy L. Weiler: secy, dir

APPLICATION INFORMATION

Initial Approach: Send brief letter describing program. There are no deadlines.

Steinhagen Benevolent Trust, B. A. and Elinor

CONTACT

Pam Parish
Trust Officer
B. A. and Elinor Steinhagen Benevolent Trust
c/o First City, Texas-Beaumont, N.A.
PO Box 3391
Beaumont, TX 77701

FINANCIAL SUMMARY

Recent Giving: $151,000 (fiscal 1991); $114,500 (fiscal 1990); $228,870 (fiscal 1989)
Assets: $3,954,505 (fiscal year ending August 31, 1991); $3,453,538 (fiscal 1990); $3,393,149 (fiscal 1989)
EIN: 74-6039544

CONTRIBUTIONS SUMMARY

Donor(s): the late B.A. Steinhagen, the late Elinor Steinhagen

Typical Recipients: • *Arts & Humanities:* arts associations, community arts, history/historic preservation, libraries, museums/galleries • *Health:* geriatric health, medical research, mental health, single-disease health associations • *Social Services:* aged, child welfare, community service organizations, religious welfare, shelters/homelessness, youth organizations

Grant Types: capital, endowment, research, and seed money

Geographic Distribution: limited to Jefferson County, TX

GIVING OFFICERS

First City, Texas Beaumont, N.A.: trust

APPLICATION INFORMATION

Initial Approach: Application form required. Deadline is May 31. Decisions are made by the end of August.

Restrictions on Giving: Does not support individuals or provide scholarships or loans.

OTHER THINGS TO KNOW

Publications: Application Guidelines

GRANTS ANALYSIS

Number of Grants: 10
Highest Grant: $50,000
Typical Range: $2,500 to $20,000
Disclosure Period: fiscal year ending August 31, 1991

RECENT GRANTS

50,000 Texas Energy Museum, Beaumont, TX
35,000 Boys Haven of America, Beaumont, TX
20,000 Catholic Charities, TX
15,000 St. Elizabeth Hospital, TX
10,000 Some Other Place, TX
8,000 South Texas Art Council, TX
8,000 South Texas Art Council, TX
5,000 Foundation for Interfaith, TX
3,000 YMCA, Beaumont, TX
2,500 Young Life, TX

Steinhardt Foundation, Judy and Michael

CONTACT

Michael Steinhardt
Trustee
Judy and Michael Steinhardt Fdn.
c/o Goldstein Golub Kessler & Company, P.C.
1185 Avenue of the Americas
New York, NY 10036
(212) 523-1200

FINANCIAL SUMMARY

Recent Giving: $1,381,570 (fiscal 1991); $1,480,395 (fiscal 1990); $1,339,705 (fiscal 1989)
Assets: $1,734,335 (fiscal year ending September 30, 1991); $3,102,930 (fiscal 1990); $3,425,571 (fiscal 1989)
Gifts Received: $84,875 (fiscal 1991); $1,084,875 (fiscal 1990); $36,870 (fiscal 1989)
Fiscal Note: 1991 contribution received from The Sol Steinhardt Charitable Trust.
EIN: 13-3357500

CONTRIBUTIONS SUMMARY

Typical Recipients: • *Arts & Humanities:* arts centers, museums/galleries • *Civic & Public Affairs:* ethnic/minority organizations, international affairs, public policy, zoos/botanical gardens • *Education:* colleges & universities, religious education • *International:* international health care, international organizations • *Religion:* religious organizations, synagogues • *Social Services:* community service organizations, disabled, youth organizations

Grant Types: general support

GIVING OFFICERS

Judith Steinhardt: trust
Michael Steinhardt: trust

APPLICATION INFORMATION

Initial Approach: The foundation reports it only makes contributions to preselected charitable organizations.

GRANTS ANALYSIS

Number of Grants: 62
Highest Grant: $354,025
Typical Range: $1,000 to $10,000
Disclosure Period: fiscal year ending September 30, 1991

RECENT GRANTS

354,025 United Jewish Appeal Federation of Jewish Philanthropies, New York, NY
300,000 Brooklyn Botanic Garden, Brooklyn, NY
239,550 American Friends of Israel Museum, New York, NY
100,000 Anti-Defamation League, New York, NY
62,000 Dalton School, New York, NY
52,500 PEF Israel Endowment Fund, New York, NY
37,150 Hebrew Union College, Cincinnati, OH
25,000 Sanz Medical Center
20,000 American Committee for the Tel Aviv Foundation, New York, NY
19,350 YMCA, New York, NY

Steinhauer Charitable Foundation

CONTACT

Steinhauer Charitable Foundation
P.O. Box 389
Madison, WI 53701-0389
(608) 256-5561

FINANCIAL SUMMARY

Recent Giving: $21,660 (1990); $17,280 (1989)
Assets: $3,586,886 (1990); $344,544 (1989)
Gifts Received: $58,562 (1990)
EIN: 39-1600091

CONTRIBUTIONS SUMMARY

Typical Recipients: • *Arts & Humanities:* arts centers, arts festivals, performing arts, theater • *Civic & Public Affairs:* urban & community affairs, zoos/botanical gardens • *Education:* colleges & universities, minority education • *Social Services:* family services

Grant Types: general support

APPLICATION INFORMATION

Initial Approach: The foundation reports it only makes contributions to preselected organizations and does not accept unsolicited requests for funds.

GRANTS ANALYSIS

Total Grants: $21,660

Number of Grants: 23
Highest Grant: $5,000
Typical Range: $1,000 to
$5,000
Disclosure Period: 1990

RECENT GRANTS

5,000 Madison Civic Center, Madison, WI
2,000 Family Services
1,500 Madison Festival of the Lakes, Madison, WI
1,200 United Negro College Fund
1,000 Children's Theater of Madison, Madison, WI
1,000 Edgewood College, WI
1,000 Madison Art Center, Madison, WI
1,000 Madison Boys Choir, Madison, WI
1,000 Madison Civic Center, Madison, WI
1,000 Olbrich Botanical Garden

Steiniger Charitable Foundation, Edward & Joan

CONTACT
Hollister Reid
Edward and Joan Steiniger
  Charitable Foundation
153 East 53rd Street, 5th Floor
New York, NY 10003

FINANCIAL SUMMARY
Recent Giving: $0 (1990)
Assets: $9,146,771 (1990)
Gifts Received: $9,246,652 (1990)
EIN: 13-3585674

CONTRIBUTIONS SUMMARY
Typical Recipients: • *Religion:* religious organizations
• *Social Services:* religious welfare

GRANTS ANALYSIS
Total Grants: $0
Disclosure Period: 1990

Steinman Foundation, James Hale
Headquarters: Lancaster, PA

CONTACT
M. Steven Weaver
Secretary
James Hale Steinman Fdn.
8 West King St.
Lancaster, PA 17603
(717) 291-8607

FINANCIAL SUMMARY
Recent Giving: $439,649 (1991); $449,275 (1990); $429,562 (1989)
Assets: $8,886,638 (1991); $7,589,485 (1990); $7,668,821 (1989)
Gifts Received: $440,000 (1991); $740,000 (1990); $300,000 (1989)
Fiscal Note: In 1991, contributions were received from Lancaster Newspapers ($160,000), Intelligencer Printing Company ($160,000), and Delmarva Broadcasting Company ($120,000).
EIN: 23-6266377

CONTRIBUTIONS SUMMARY
Donor(s): the late James Hale Steinman, the late Louise Steinman von Hess, Lancaster Newspapers, Inc.
Typical Recipients: • *Arts & Humanities:* community arts, history/historic preservation, music, opera • *Civic & Public Affairs:* municipalities, philanthropic organizations • *Education:* colleges & universities, education associations, private education (precollege) • *Health:* hospitals, medical research, single-disease health associations • *Religion:* churches, religious organizations • *Social Services:* community service organizations, disabled, family planning, united funds, youth organizations
Grant Types: capital, general support, and scholarship
Geographic Distribution: focus on Lancaster, PA

GIVING OFFICERS
John M. Buckwalter: trust *B* Lancaster PA 1931 *ED* Franklin & Marshall Coll 1952; Harvard Univ Sch Bus Admin 1954 *CURR EMPL* pres, ceo: Lancaster Newspapers *CORP AFFIL* dir: Hamil-

ton Bank, Intelligencer Printing Co
Jack S. Gerhart: trust
Dennis A. Getz, Jr.: secy, trust *CURR EMPL* vp, contr: Lancaster Newspapers *CORP AFFIL* vp, contr: Lancaster Newspapers Inc
Caroline N. Hill: trust *CORP AFFIL* dir: Intelligencer Printing Co, Lancaster Newspapers Inc
Hale S. Krasne: trust *CORP AFFIL* dir: Intelligencer Printing Co, Lancaster Newspapers Inc
Caroline S. Nunan: chmn, trust *CORP AFFIL* dir: Intelligencer Printing Co, Lancaster Newspapers Inc
Willis Weidman Shenk: treas, trust *B* Manheim PA 1915 *CURR EMPL* chmn, dir: Lancaster Newspapers *CORP AFFIL* chmn: Delmarva Broadcasting Co, Steinman Mgmt Corp; chmn, dir: Intelligencer Printing Co, Lancaster Newspapers Inc
Beverly R. Steinman: vchmn, trust *CORP AFFIL* dir: Intelligencer Printing Co, Lancaster Newspapers Inc

APPLICATION INFORMATION
Initial Approach: Application form available for employee-related scholarships. Deadline for scholarships is February 28 of senior year of high school.

GRANTS ANALYSIS
Number of Grants: 39
Highest Grant: $293,374
Typical Range: $250 to $6,000
Disclosure Period: 1991
Note: 1991 figures do not include $37,000 in scholarships to individuals.

RECENT GRANTS
293,374 Conestoga House Foundation, Lancaster, PA
40,000 United Fund, Lancaster, PA
16,125 Heritage Center of Lancaster, Lancaster, PA
10,000 Episcopal Diocese of Pennsylvania, Lancaster, PA
5,000 Boys Club of America, Lancaster, PA
3,500 James Buchanan Foundation, Lancaster, PA
2,500 Lancaster Foundation for Education and Enrichment, Lancaster, PA

2,500 Planned Parenthood Federation of America, Lancaster, PA
2,500 St. James Church, Lancaster, PA
2,000 Lancaster Summer Arts, Lancaster, PA

Steinman Foundation, John Frederick

CONTACT
Jay H. Wenrich
Secretary
John Frederick Steinman Fdn.
8 West King St.
Lancaster, PA 17603
(717) 291-8607

FINANCIAL SUMMARY
Recent Giving: $505,750 (1991); $477,533 (1990); $950,964 (1989)
Assets: $12,516,565 (1991); $10,850,484 (1990); $11,373,565 (1989)
Gifts Received: $160,000 (1991); $160,000 (1990); $300,000 (1989)
Fiscal Note: In 1991, contributions were received from Intelligencer Printing Company.
EIN: 23-6266378

CONTRIBUTIONS SUMMARY
Donor(s): the late John Frederick Steinman, the late Shirley W. Steinman, Lancaster Newspapers, Inc.
Typical Recipients: • *Arts & Humanities:* arts appreciation, community arts, opera • *Education:* arts education, colleges & universities, religious education • *Health:* hospices, hospitals, medical research, mental health, single-disease health associations • *Religion:* churches, religious organizations • *Social Services:* family planning, shelters/homelessness, united funds, youth organizations
Grant Types: capital, fellowship, and general support
Geographic Distribution: focus on PA, with emphasis on the Lancaster area

GIVING OFFICERS
John M. Buckwalter: trust *B* Lancaster PA 1931 *ED* Franklin & Marshall Coll 1952; Harvard Univ Sch Bus Admin 1954 *CURR EMPL* pres, ceo: Lancaster Newspapers *CORP AFFIL* dir: Hamil-

ton Bank, Intelligencer Printing Co

Jack S. Gerhart: trust

Dennis A. Getz, Jr.: secy, trust *CURR EMPL* vp, contr: Lancaster Newspapers *CORP AFFIL* vp, contr: Lancaster Newspapers Inc

Henry Pildner, Jr.: trust *CORP AFFIL* dir: Intelligencer Printing Co

Willis Weidman Shenk: treas *B* Manheim PA 1915 *CURR EMPL* chmn, dir: Lancaster Newspapers *CORP AFFIL* chmn: Delmarva Broadcasting Co, Steinman Mgmt Corp; chmn, dir: Intelligencer Printing Co, Lancaster Newspapers Inc

Pamela M. Thye: chmn, trust *CORP AFFIL* dir: Intelligencer Printing Co

APPLICATION INFORMATION

Initial Approach: Application for fellowship program available upon request. The deadline is February 1.

GRANTS ANALYSIS

Number of Grants: 95

Highest Grant: $60,000

Typical Range: $500 to $15,000

Disclosure Period: 1991

Note: 1991 figures do not include $30,000 in fellowship grants to individuals.

RECENT GRANTS

60,000 Moravian Manor, Lancaster, PA

40,000 Girls Club of Lancaster, Lancaster, PA

38,500 United Fund, Lancaster, PA

25,000 Lancaster Bible College, Lancaster, PA

25,000 Lancaster Theological Seminary, Lancaster, PA

25,000 Pennsylvania School of Arts, Lancaster, PA

15,000 HARB, Lancaster, PA — Adult

15,000 Parish Resource Center, Lancaster, PA

12,500 Habitat for Humanity, Lancaster, PA

12,500 Lancaster Mennonite High School, Lancaster, PA

Steinsapir Family Foundation, Julius L. and Libhie B.

CONTACT

Samuel Horovitz
Trustee
Julius L. and Libhie B.
 Steinsapir Family Fdn.
900 Lawyers Bldg.
Pittsburgh, PA 15219
(412) 391-2920

FINANCIAL SUMMARY

Recent Giving: $92,855 (fiscal 1991); $87,245 (fiscal 1990); $97,975 (fiscal 1988)

Assets: $1,922,471 (fiscal year ending January 31, 1991); $1,884,718 (fiscal 1990); $1,759,780 (fiscal 1988)

EIN: 25-6104248

CONTRIBUTIONS SUMMARY

Donor(s): I. H. Steinsapir the late Standard Emblem Jewelers

Typical Recipients: • *Civic & Public Affairs:* ethnic/minority organizations • *Education:* colleges & universities, religious education • *Religion:* religious organizations, synagogues • *Social Services:* aged, community centers, community service organizations, homes, united funds, youth organizations

Grant Types: general support

Geographic Distribution: focus on PA

GIVING OFFICERS

Samuel Horovitz: trust
Albert C. Shapira: trust
Lewis Silverboard: trust

APPLICATION INFORMATION

Initial Approach: Send brief letter describing program. There are no deadlines.

Restrictions on Giving: Does not support individuals.

GRANTS ANALYSIS

Number of Grants: 51

Highest Grant: $15,000

Typical Range: $200 to $1,000

Disclosure Period: fiscal year ending January 31, 1991

RECENT GRANTS

15,000 Yeshiva Achei Tmimim School, Pittsburgh, PA

10,515 R.C. Franciscan Fathers, Pittsburgh, PA

10,000 Sheareth Israel Synagogue, Atlanta, GA

5,000 Ahavath Achim Congregation, Atlanta, GA

5,000 B'nai Israel Congregation, Pittsburgh, PA

5,000 Duquesne University, Pittsburgh, PA

5,000 Epstein Solomon Schechter School, Atlanta, GA

5,000 Riverside Center for Jewish Seniors, Pittsburgh, PA

4,000 United Jewish Appeal Federation of Jewish Philanthropies, Pittsburgh, PA

3,200 United Jewish Appeal Federation of Jewish Philanthropies, Pittsburgh, PA

Stella D'Oro Biscuit Co. / Kresevich Foundation

Sales: $53.0 million
Employees: 600
Headquarters: Bronx, NY
SIC Major Group: Food & Kindred Products and Wholesale Trade—Nondurable Goods

CONTACT

Charles J. Ferrara
Vice President, Administration
Kresevich Foundation
184 West 237th St.
Bronx, NY 10463
(212) 549-3700

FINANCIAL SUMMARY

Recent Giving: $24,600 (fiscal 1991); $23,061 (fiscal 1990); $104,971 (fiscal 1989)

Assets: $443,390 (fiscal year ending November 30, 1991); $443,428 (fiscal 1990); $437,057 (fiscal 1989)

EIN: 13-6082003

CONTRIBUTIONS SUMMARY

Typical Recipients: • *Education:* private education (precollege) • *Health:* hospitals • *Religion:* churches, religious organizations • *Social Services:* community service organizations, homes, recreation & athletics, united funds, youth organizations

Grant Types: general support

Geographic Distribution: focus on NY

Operating Locations: CA (San Leandro), IL (St. Elmo), NY (Bronx)

CORP. OFFICERS

E. Val Cerrutti: *CURR EMPL* pres: Stella DOro Biscuit Co
Angela Kresevich: *CURR EMPL* chmn: Stella DOro Biscuit Co
Felice M. Zambetti: *CURR EMPL* ceo: Stella DOro Biscuit Co

GIVING OFFICERS

Charles J. Ferrara: dir(admin)
Felice M. Zambetti: pres, dir *CURR EMPL* ceo: Stella DOro Biscuit Co (see above)

APPLICATION INFORMATION

Initial Approach: Send brief letter including a description of the organization, amount requested, purpose of funds sought, audited financial statement, and proof of tax-exempt status. There are no deadlines.

Restrictions on Giving: Does not support individuals or political or lobbying groups.

GRANTS ANALYSIS

Disclosure Period: fiscal year ending November 30, 1991

Note: 1991 grants list not provided.

RECENT GRANTS

30,000 Verona Fathers, Verona, Italy — Sons of the Sacred Heart

30,000 Verona Fathers, Verona, Italy — Sons of the Sacred Heart

16,000 Downstate Research Foundation

15,000 Presbyterian Hospital Foundation, New York, NY

3,100 Verona Fathers, Verona, Italy — Sons of the Sacred Heart

1,400 A.I.F.C.R.

1,000 Father Oliver Brancreci

1,000 St. Gabriels Church

1,000 St. Margarets Church, Rumford, RI

1,000 Third Order of St. Francis

Stemmons Foundation

CONTACT
Ann M. Roberts
Secretary-Treasurer
Stemmons Fdn.
2700 Stemmons Fwy.
1200 Tower East
Dallas, TX 75207
(214) 631-7910

FINANCIAL SUMMARY
Recent Giving: $206,961
(1991); $328,099 (1990);
$208,100 (1989)
Assets: $3,602,258 (1991);
$3,544,601 (1990); $3,569,810
(1989)
EIN: 75-6039966

CONTRIBUTIONS SUMMARY
Typical Recipients: • *Arts &
Humanities:* community arts,
dance, history/historic preservation, music, opera, public
broadcasting • *Education:* colleges & universities, education
funds, public education (precollege) • *Health:* hospitals, medical research, pediatric health,
single-disease health associations • *Religion:* churches • *Social Services:* animal protection, community service
organizations, disabled, family
services, youth organizations
Grant Types: general support
and scholarship
Geographic Distribution:
focus on Dallas, TX

GIVING OFFICERS
Ann M. Roberts: secy, treas
Allison S. Simon: vp
Heinz K. Simon: vp
John M. Stemmons, Jr.: secy,
treas
John M. Stemmons, Sr.: pres
Ruth T. Stemmons: vp

APPLICATION INFORMATION
Initial Approach: Send cover
letter and full proposal. There
are no deadlines.

GRANTS ANALYSIS
Number of Grants: 60
Highest Grant: $25,000
Typical Range: $1,000 to
$5,000
Disclosure Period: 1991

RECENT GRANTS
25,000 United Way, Dal-
las, TX
12,500 Shelter Ministries,
Dallas, TX
10,500 YMCA, Dallas, TX

10,000 Children's Medical
Center, Dallas, TX
10,000 Dallas Opera, Dal-
las, TX
10,000 Dallas Symphony
Association, Dal-
las, TX
10,000 Parkland Founda-
tion, Dallas, TX
10,000 SPCA of Texas, Ft.
Worth, TX
10,000 Young Audiences,
Dallas, TX
8,000 Texas Interscholas-
tic League Fund,
Austin, TX

Stepan Co.
Sales: $414.1 million
Employees: 1,317
Headquarters: Northfield, IL
SIC Major Group: Chemicals &
Allied Products

CONTACT
Joan Kusher
Contributions Coordinator
Stepan Co.
22 West Frontage Rd.
Northfield, IL 60093
(708) 446-7500

FINANCIAL SUMMARY
Fiscal Note: Company does
not disclose contributions figures

CONTRIBUTIONS SUMMARY
Company does not release in-
formation regarding corporate
contributions.
Operating Locations: IL
(Northfield)

CORP. OFFICERS
F. Quinn Stepan: *CURR
EMPL* chmn, pres, coo, ceo,
dir: Stepan Co

Stephens Foundation Trust

CONTACT
Stephens Fdn Trust
Rte. 5, Pasquo Rd.
Nashville, TN 37221

FINANCIAL SUMMARY
Recent Giving: $131,200 (fis-
cal 1990); $115,900 (fiscal
1989)
Assets: $3,703,512 (fiscal year
ending July 31, 1990);
$2,737,301 (fiscal 1989)
Gifts Received: $10,000 (fis-
cal 1990); $145,495 (fiscal
1989)
EIN: 62-6201842

CONTRIBUTIONS SUMMARY
Donor(s): W.E. Stephens, Jr.,
Juanita Stephens, Stephens
Foundation
Typical Recipients: • *Educa-
tion:* colleges & universities,
religious education • *Religion:*
churches, missionary activities,
religious organizations • *Social
Services:* community service or-
ganizations
Grant Types: general support
Geographic Distribution:
focus on TN

GIVING OFFICERS
Greg Hardeman: trust
Walter C. Leaver III: trust
Juanita Stephens: trust
W.E. Stephens, Jr.: trust, chmn
James Vandiver: trust

APPLICATION INFORMATION
Initial Approach: Contributes
only to preselected organizations.

GRANTS ANALYSIS
Number of Grants: 42
Highest Grant: $50,000
Typical Range: $150 to $2,500
Disclosure Period: fiscal year
ending July 31, 1990

RECENT GRANTS
50,000 Pepperdine Univer-
sity, Malibu, CA
12,200 Eastern European
Missions, Houston,
TX
10,500 David Lipscomb
University, Nash-
ville, TN
9,150 Agape, Nashville,
TN
7,900 World Christian
Broadcasting,
Abilene, TX
7,500 Lakeshore Home,
Nashville, TN
7,500 World Bible
School, Austin, TX
7,250 Hillsboro Church
of Christ, Nash-
ville, TN
2,500 Columbia Chris-
tian College, Port-
land, OR
2,500 Ohio Valley Chris-
tian College, Park-
ersburg, WV

Sterkel Trust, Justine

CONTACT
Justine Sterkel Trust
c/o Bank One, Mansfield
28 Park Ave.
West Mansfield, OH 44901
(419) 525-5532

FINANCIAL SUMMARY
Recent Giving: $136,760
(1991); $134,200 (1990);
$133,000 (1989)
Assets: $3,490,624 (1991);
$3,470,483 (1990); $2,961,338
(1989)
EIN: 34-6576810

CONTRIBUTIONS SUMMARY
Donor(s): Justine Sterkel
Typical Recipients: • *Arts &
Humanities:* community arts,
music • *Education:* religious
education • *Health:* geriatric
health, health organizations,
medical research, pediatric
health • *Religion:* churches
• *Social Services:* child welfare, family planning, family
services, united funds, youth organizations
Grant Types: general support
Geographic Distribution:
focus on OH

GIVING OFFICERS
Bank One Mansfield: trust

APPLICATION INFORMATION
Initial Approach: Send brief
letter describing program.
There are no deadlines.

GRANTS ANALYSIS
Number of Grants: 7
Highest Grant: $59,380
Typical Range: $2,000 to
$10,000
Disclosure Period: 1991

RECENT GRANTS
59,380 Rehabilitation Services of North Cen-
tral Ohio, Mans-
field, OH
42,000 Center for Individual and Family
Services, Mans-
field, OH
22,380 Raintree Pediatric
Development Cen-
ter, Mansfield, OH
7,500 YWCA, Mansfield,
OH
2,500 Richland Preg-
nancy Services,
Mansfield, OH

2,000 Richland Country
Children Services,
Mansfield, OH
1,000 Mansfield Symphony Society,
Mansfield, OH

Sterling Inc.

Sales: $398.89 million
Employees: 10,000
Headquarters: Akron, OH
SIC Major Group: Fabricated
Metal Products, Industrial
Machinery & Equipment,
Miscellaneous Retail, and
Transportation Equipment

CONTACT
George Frankovich
In-House Attorney
Sterling Inc.
375 Ghent Rd.
Akron, OH 44333
(216) 668-5000

CONTRIBUTIONS SUMMARY
Sterling Inc. supports charitable organizations in the communities in which its stores are located. Areas of interest include the arts and humanities, civic and public affairs, and health and social service organizations. Funding priorities include civic groups concentrating on law, justice, or national security; hospitals; and health organizations.
Typical Recipients: • *Arts & Humanities:* arts associations, arts centers, arts funds, history/historic preservation, music, performing arts, theater • *Civic & Public Affairs:* economic development, law & justice, safety • *Health:* health funds, health organizations, hospitals, medical research • *Social Services:* aged, child welfare, community service organizations, domestic violence, drugs & alcohol, family services, united funds, youth organizations
Grant Types: capital, general support, and seed money
Nonmonetary Support Types: donated equipment and donated products
Geographic Distribution: principally near operating locations and to national organizations
Operating Locations: OH

CORP. OFFICERS
Nathan Light: *CURR EMPL* chmn, pres, ceo: Sterling
Richard Miller: *CURR EMPL* sr vp, cfo: Sterling

GIVING OFFICERS
George Frankovich: *CURR EMPL* in-house atty: Sterling

APPLICATION INFORMATION
Initial Approach: Initial letter may be submitted at any time and should include a description of the organization and purpose for which funds are sought.
Restrictions on Giving: Sterling does not make contributions to individuals, political or lobbying groups, or religious organizations for sectarian purposes.

Sterling Chemicals Inc.

Sales: $543.0 million
Employees: 950
Headquarters: Texas City, TX
SIC Major Group: Chemicals & Allied Products

CONTACT
David Heaney
Vice President, Finance
Sterling Chemicals Inc.
P. O. Box 1311
Texas City, TX 77592
(713) 650-3700

CONTRIBUTIONS SUMMARY
Operating Locations: TX (Houston, Texas City)

CORP. OFFICERS
Douglas W. Metten: *CURR EMPL* vp, cfo: Sterling Chemicals
J. Virgil Waggoner: *CURR EMPL* ceo, pres: Sterling Chemicals

Sterling Software Inc.

Sales: $224.4 million
Employees: 1,800
Headquarters: Dallas, TX
SIC Major Group: Business Services

CONTACT
Sam Wyly
Chairman
Sterling Software Inc.
8080 North Central Expressway, Ste. 1100
Dallas, TX 75206
(214) 891-8600

CONTRIBUTIONS SUMMARY
Operating Locations: TX (Dallas)

CORP. OFFICERS
Sterling L. Williams: *CURR EMPL* pres, ceo, dir: Sterling Software
Charles Joseph Wyly, Jr.: *B* Lake providence LA 1933 *ED* LA Polytechnic Inst BS 1956 *CURR EMPL* co-fdr, vchmn, dir: Sterling Software *CORP AFFIL* bd mem: TX High-Speed Rail Authority; chmn: USA Cafes; co-fdr: Photomatrix; co-fdr, vchmn, dir: Michaels Stores; fdr: Earth Resources Co *NONPR AFFIL* dir: Dallas County Un Way Fund; mem: Am Mgmt Assn, Beta Gamma Sigma, Delta Sigma Pi, Omicron Delta Kappa, Phi Kappa Alpha
Sam Wyly: *CURR EMPL* chmn, dir: Sterling Software

Sterling Winthrop

Sales: $2.3 billion
Employees: 12,000
Parent Company: Eastman Kodak Co.
Headquarters: New York, NY
SIC Major Group: Chemicals & Allied Products

CONTACT
Heather Hollowell
Director, Community Relations
Sterling Winthrop
90 Park Ave.
New York, NY 10016
(212) 907-3087

FINANCIAL SUMMARY
Recent Giving: $1,500,000 (1993 est.); $1,300,000 (1992); $1,400,000 (1991)
Fiscal Note: Company gives directly. Figures above do not include an estimated $1,000,000 worth of nonmonetary support.

CONTRIBUTIONS SUMMARY
Typical Recipients: • *Arts & Humanities:* arts centers, community arts, dance, libraries, museums/galleries, music, performing arts, theater • *Civic & Public Affairs:* better government, business/free enterprise, civil rights, consumer affairs, ethnic/minority organizations, municipalities, nonprofit management, professional & trade associations, public policy, urban & community affairs, zoos/botanical gardens • *Education:* career/vocational education, colleges & universities, continuing education, education associations, education funds, elementary education, faculty development, health & physical education, liberal arts education, medical education, minority education, science/technology education • *Health:* health care cost containment, health funds, health organizations, hospices, hospitals, medical research, medical training, nursing services, nutrition & health maintenance, outpatient health care delivery, pediatric health, public health • *Science:* scientific organizations • *Social Services:* aged, child welfare, community centers, community service organizations, disabled, drugs & alcohol, emergency relief, employment/job training, family services, food/clothing distribution, homes, shelters/homelessness, united funds, volunteer services, youth organizations
Grant Types: employee matching gifts, general support, and project
Nonmonetary Support Types: donated products
Note: Contact person for noncash support is Heather Holowell. Estimated value of noncash support in 1991 was $1.0 million, which is not included in the total giving figure above. See "Other Things You Should Know" for more information.
Geographic Distribution: principally to organizations in the New York City metropolitan area
Operating Locations: IL (Des Plaines), KS (McPherson), NY (New York, Rensselaer), PA (Great Valley, Myerstown)

CORP. OFFICERS
Louis Price Mattis: *CURR EMPL* chmn, pres, ceo: Sterling Winthrop

GIVING OFFICERS
Heather Hollowell: *CURR EMPL* dir (community rels): Sterling Winthrop

APPLICATION INFORMATION

Initial Approach: *Initial Contact:* brief letter or proposal *Include Information On:* description of the organization, amount requested, purpose for which funds are sought, recently audited financial statement or annual report, disclosure of how funds used, proof of tax-exempt status, list of board of directors, and list of other corporate donors *When to Submit:* any time; requests reviewed quarterly
Restrictions on Giving: Generally, no commitment will be made for more than one year. Company does not support fraternal organizations, labor organizations, or religious denominations whose primary purpose is the propagation of a particular religious faith or creed. Company rarely supports testimonial dinners. No goodwill advertising; no grants to individuals.

OTHER THINGS TO KNOW

Sterling donates reasonable quantities of salable nonprescription and certain prescription products to a select group of recognized, U.S.-based international and domestic health and relief agencies. It is not anticipated that the list of approved organizations will expand in the near future, so unsolicited requests for grants are discouraged.

GRANTS ANALYSIS

Total Grants: $1,400,000
Number of Grants: 185*
Highest Grant: $50,000
Typical Range: $1,500 to $10,000
Disclosure Period: 1991
Note: Figure for number of grants does not include matching gifts.

Stern Family Foundation, Alex

CONTACT

W. R. Amundson
Trustee
Alex Stern Family Fdn.
Bill Stern Bldg., Ste. 202
609 1/2 First Avenue, North
Fargo, ND 58102
(701) 237-0170

FINANCIAL SUMMARY

Recent Giving: $349,120 (1990); $343,323 (1989)
Assets: $7,472,724 (1990); $7,257,823 (1989)
EIN: 45-6013981

CONTRIBUTIONS SUMMARY

Donor(s): the late William Stern, the late Sam Stern, the late Edward A. Stern
Typical Recipients: • *Arts & Humanities:* history/historic preservation, opera, public broadcasting • *Education:* colleges & universities, education funds, public education (precollege) • *Health:* single-disease health associations • *Religion:* churches, religious organizations • *Social Services:* community service organizations, disabled, family planning, family services, recreation & athletics, united funds, youth organizations
Grant Types: general support, operating expenses, and project
Geographic Distribution: focus on Fargo, ND

GIVING OFFICERS

W. R. Amundson: trust
A. M. Eriksmoen: exec dir, trust
J. L. McCormick: trust
Ed Preston: trust

APPLICATION INFORMATION

Initial Approach: Telephone to request application guidelines. Application is a full proposal (three copies required). Submit application preferably between April and December; no set deadline.

OTHER THINGS TO KNOW

Publications: Application Guidelines

GRANTS ANALYSIS

Number of Grants: 52
Highest Grant: $50,000

Typical Range: $1,000 to $10,000
Disclosure Period: 1990

RECENT GRANTS

50,000 St. Lukes Foundation, Fargo, ND — first installment on a five-year grant of $250,000 designated for the Roger Maris Cancer Center
30,000 North Dakota State University Foundation, Fargo, ND — fourth installment on five-year grant of $150,000, equipment for Biotechnical Center
10,000 Eventide Foundation, Moorehead, ND — assistance with construction and related expenses for Alzheimer Unit at Eventide Nursing Home
10,000 Grace Lutheran School, Fargo, ND — matching grant to assist in purchase of a new school bus
10,000 Hospice, Fargo, ND
10,000 Moorehead State University Foundation, Fargo, ND — honors apprenticeship program
10,000 Prairie Public Television, Fargo, ND — program support/local programming
10,000 Shanley High School, Fargo, ND — purchase of computer related equipment
10,000 Share House of Fargo and Moorehead, Fargo, ND — assistance with salary costs of an addiction counselor for Share House
10,000 YMCA, Fargo, ND

Stern Family Foundation, Harry

CONTACT

Jerome Stern
Secretary
Harry Stern Family Fdn.
PO Box 23034
Philadelphia, PA 19124
(215) 744-0100

FINANCIAL SUMMARY

Recent Giving: $234,504 (1991); $248,131 (1989); $754,342 (1987)
Assets: $6,071,053 (1991); $5,946,789 (1989); $5,692,128 (1987)
EIN: 23-6806751

CONTRIBUTIONS SUMMARY

Donor(s): members of the Stern family
Typical Recipients: • *Civic & Public Affairs:* ethnic/minority organizations • *Education:* colleges & universities, private education (precollege), religious education • *Health:* health organizations, hospitals, medical research • *International:* international organizations • *Religion:* religious organizations, synagogues • *Social Services:* community service organizations, youth organizations
Grant Types: general support
Geographic Distribution: focus on the greater Philadelphia, PA, area

GIVING OFFICERS

Rebecca Stern Herschkopf: dir
Sheva Stern Mann: dir
Sareva Stern Naor: dir
Amram Stern: dir
Harry Stern: pres
I. Jerome Stern: secy, dir
Zelda Stern: dir

APPLICATION INFORMATION

Initial Approach: Send brief letter of inquiry describing program or project. There are no deadlines.

GRANTS ANALYSIS

Number of Grants: 277
Highest Grant: $25,218
Typical Range: $25 to $1,500
Disclosure Period: 1991

RECENT GRANTS

25,218 Camp Ramah in the Poconos, PA
21,900 Jewish Theological Seminary, New York, NY

19,250 P.E.F. Israel Endowment Funds, New York, NY
11,500 American Jewish Committee, New York, NY
10,500 Yeshiva Darchel Torah, New York, NY
7,850 American Foundation for Boys Town of Jerusalem, New York, NY
7,410 Torah Academy of Greater Philadelphia, Philadelphia, PA
5,972 Union of Orthodox Jewish Congregations of America/Orthodox Congregation, New York, NY
5,475 Congregation Adath Jeshurun, Elkins Park, PA
5,100 Ramaz School, New York, NY

Stern Family Fund

Former Foundation Name: Philip M. Stern Family Fund

CONTACT
Betsy Taylor
Stern Family Fund
6930 Carroll Avenue, Ste. 500
Takoma Park, MD 20912

FINANCIAL SUMMARY
Recent Giving: $498,977 (fiscal 1992); $561,365 (fiscal 1991); $706,265 (fiscal 1990)
Assets: $560,806 (fiscal year ending June 30, 1991); $673,756 (fiscal 1990); $681,945 (fiscal 1989)
Gifts Received: $525,000 (fiscal 1991); $691,303 (fiscal 1990); $597,350 (fiscal 1989)
Fiscal Note: In 1992, contributions were received from Philip M. Stern ($550,000), Michael P. S. Stern ($45,000), and David M. Stern ($70,000).
EIN: 52-6037658

CONTRIBUTIONS SUMMARY
Donor(s): Philip M. Stern and other members of the Stern family
Typical Recipients: • *Arts & Humanities:* performing arts, public broadcasting • *Civic & Public Affairs:* better government, civil rights, economics, environmental affairs, ethnic/minority organizations, international affairs, law & justice, public policy, women's affairs • *Health:* health organi-

zations • *Social Services:* youth organizations
Grant Types: general support and project

GIVING OFFICERS
Anne A. Plaster: secy, dir
Walter Slocombe: vp, dir
Philip M. Stern: pres, treas, dir

APPLICATION INFORMATION
Initial Approach: Send cover letter and full proposal. There are no deadlines. Board meets quarterly.

OTHER THINGS TO KNOW
Publications: Application Guidelines

GRANTS ANALYSIS
Number of Grants: 100
Highest Grant: $25,000
Typical Range: $1,000 to $10,000
Disclosure Period: fiscal year ending June 30, 1991

RECENT GRANTS
25,000 Center for Economic Conversion
25,000 Center for Public Integrity, Washington, DC
25,000 Environmental Support Center
20,000 National Insurance Consumer Organization
15,000 20/20 Vision Education Fund
10,000 Environmental Action Foundation
10,000 Jewish Fund for Justice
10,000 Partnership for Democracy
10,000 Women's Legal Defense Fund, Washington, DC

Stern Foundation, Bernice and Milton

CONTACT
Bernice Stern
President
Bernice and Milton Stern Fdn.
437 Madison Ave.
New York, NY 10022
(212) 503-1701

FINANCIAL SUMMARY
Recent Giving: $696,515 (fiscal 1992); $611,250 (fiscal 1991); $374,500 (fiscal 1990)
Assets: $14,199,741 (fiscal year ending April 30, 1992);

$13,301,592 (fiscal 1991); $11,955,596 (fiscal 1990)
Gifts Received: $5,381,068 (fiscal 1990); $5,000,000 (fiscal 1987)
EIN: 51-0264122

CONTRIBUTIONS SUMMARY
Typical Recipients: • *Arts & Humanities:* museums/galleries • *Civic & Public Affairs:* ethnic/minority organizations, philanthropic organizations • *Education:* literacy • *Health:* health organizations, hospitals, medical research, single-disease health associations • *Religion:* religious organizations • *Social Services:* child welfare, community centers, community service organizations
Grant Types: general support

GIVING OFFICERS
Wendy S. Pesky: vp
Bernice Stern: pres

APPLICATION INFORMATION
Initial Approach: Send brief letter describing program. There are no deadlines.

GRANTS ANALYSIS
Number of Grants: 8
Highest Grant: $275,000
Disclosure Period: fiscal year ending April 30, 1992

RECENT GRANTS
275,000 Memorial Sloan-Kettering Cancer Center, New York, NY
100,560 Children's Aid Society, New York, NY
100,500 Stern Center for Language and Learning, Winooski, VT
100,000 US Holocaust Memorial Museum, Washington, DC
75,000 Knightsbridge Heights Community Center, Bronx, NY
20,000 M and M Stern Foundation, New York, NY
15,100 Helping Hands, Boston, MA
10,000 Ezra Lemarpeh Association, Brooklyn, NY

Stern Foundation for the Arts, Richard J.

CONTACT
Christopher Blair
Richard J. Stern Fdn for the Arts
Commerce Bank of Kansas City, N.A.
Kansas City, MO 64141
(816) 234-2000

FINANCIAL SUMMARY
Recent Giving: $401,200 (fiscal 1991); $245,000 (fiscal 1990); $300,150 (fiscal 1989)
Assets: $3,854,851 (fiscal year ending June 30, 1991); $3,933,683 (fiscal 1990); $3,901,239 (fiscal 1989)
EIN: 43-6313811

CONTRIBUTIONS SUMMARY
Typical Recipients: • *Arts & Humanities:* arts institutes, community arts, museums/galleries, music, opera, performing arts
Grant Types: general support
Geographic Distribution: limited to the greater Kansas City, MO, area

GIVING OFFICERS
Commerce Bank of Kansas City, N.A.: trust

APPLICATION INFORMATION
Initial Approach: Send brief letter of inquiry describing program or project. There are no deadlines.
Restrictions on Giving: Does not support private foundations or individuals.

GRANTS ANALYSIS
Number of Grants: 3
Highest Grant: $301,200
Typical Range: $50,000 to $301,200
Disclosure Period: fiscal year ending June 30, 1991

RECENT GRANTS
301,200 Lyric Opera of Chicago, Chicago, IL
50,000 Kansas City Art Institute, Kansas City, MO
50,000 Kansas Symphony, Kansas City, MO

Stern Foundation, Gustav and Irene

Former Foundation Name:
Gustav Stern Foundation

CONTACT
Irene Stern
Principal Manager
Gustav and Irene Stern Fdn.
c/o Braver Stern Securities
641 Lexington Avenue, 24th Fl.
New York, NY 10022
(212) 319-9110

FINANCIAL SUMMARY
Recent Giving: $440,858 (fiscal 1991); $117,390 (fiscal 1990); $35,106 (fiscal 1989)
Assets: $9,218,382 (fiscal year ending March 31, 1991); $8,929,179 (fiscal 1990); $458,511 (fiscal 1989)
EIN: 13-6121155

CONTRIBUTIONS SUMMARY
Donor(s): James O. Herland, Ray Stern
Typical Recipients: • *Arts & Humanities:* dance • *Civic & Public Affairs:* ethnic/minority organizations • *Education:* elementary education, private education (precollege) • *Health:* single-disease health associations • *Religion:* religious organizations, synagogues • *Social Services:* community service organizations
Grant Types: general support and scholarship

GIVING OFFICERS
Joyce Herland: secy, treas
Irene Stern: pres
Roy Stern: treas
Steven Stern: vp
Ralph Suskind: dir

APPLICATION INFORMATION
Initial Approach: Send brief letter of inquiry describing program or project. There are no deadlines.

GRANTS ANALYSIS
Number of Grants: 142
Highest Grant: $75,000
Typical Range: $500 to $10,000
Disclosure Period: fiscal year ending March 31, 1991

RECENT GRANTS
75,000　Memorial Sloan-Kettering Cancer Center, New York, NY
50,000　United Jewish Appeal Federation of Jewish Philanthropies, New York, NY
25,000　Memorial Sloan-Kettering Cancer Center, New York, NY
25,000　Ohr Torah, New York, NY
18,000　Memorial Sloan-Kettering Cancer Center, New York, NY
18,000　United Jewish Appeal Federation of Jewish Philanthropies, New York, NY
15,000　Ballet Theater Foundation, New York, NY
15,000　Lincoln Square Synagogue, New York, NY
5,000　Ohr Torah, New York, NY

Stern Foundation, Irvin

CONTACT
Rae W. Epstein
Secretary
Irvin Stern Fdn.
2710 W. Peterson
Chicago, IL 60659
(312) 786-9355

FINANCIAL SUMMARY
Recent Giving: $454,682 (fiscal 1990); $506,500 (fiscal 1989); $491,500 (fiscal 1988)
Assets: $7,718,686 (fiscal year ending September 30, 1990); $8,432,666 (fiscal 1989); $7,327,820 (fiscal 1988)
EIN: 36-6047947

CONTRIBUTIONS SUMMARY
Donor(s): the late Irvin Stern
Typical Recipients: • *Civic & Public Affairs:* ethnic/minority organizations, municipalities • *Education:* colleges & universities, private education (precollege) • *Religion:* religious organizations, synagogues • *Social Services:* aged, child welfare, community centers, community service organizations, food/clothing distribution, youth organizations
Grant Types: conference/seminar, emergency, multiyear/continuing support, operating expenses, and scholarship
Geographic Distribution: focus on Chicago, IL; New York, NY; and San Diego, CA

GIVING OFFICERS
E. Allan Epstein: trust
Jeffrey Epstein: trust
Rae W. Epstein: secy
Stuart Epstein: trust
Arthur Winter: trust
Dorothy G. Winter: trust
Stanley Winter: trust

APPLICATION INFORMATION
Initial Approach: Application form required. Deadlines are April 1 and September 1.

OTHER THINGS TO KNOW
Publications: Application Guidelines

GRANTS ANALYSIS
Number of Grants: 42
Highest Grant: $110,000
Typical Range: $1,000 to $5,000
Disclosure Period: fiscal year ending September 30, 1990

RECENT GRANTS
110,000　Jewish United Fund, Chicago, IL
109,000　Jewish Federation, San Diego, CA
50,000　United Jewish Appeal Federation of Jewish Philanthropies, New York, NY
25,000　Thresholds, New York, NY
20,000　University of Michigan, Ann Arbor, MI
17,000　Jewish Federation, San Diego, CA
17,000　United Jewish Appeal Federation of Jewish Philanthropies, New York, NY
15,000　Citizens Committee for New York City, New York, NY
12,500　Peoples Reinvestment and Development Effort-PRIDE, New York, NY
12,000　Providence-St. Mel School, New York, NY

Stern Foundation, Leonard N.

CONTACT
Leonard N. Stern
Principal Manager
Leonard N. Stern Fdn.
400 Plaza Drive
Secaucus, NJ 07096-1411
(201) 348-1200

FINANCIAL SUMMARY
Recent Giving: $626,983 (1991); $1,209,011 (1990); $1,806,430 (1989)
Assets: $2,343 (1991); $5,639 (1990); $230,908 (1989)
Gifts Received: $625,000 (1991); $987,000 (1990); $1,957,500 (1989)
Fiscal Note: In 1991, contributions were received from Leonard N. Stern.
EIN: 13-6149990

CONTRIBUTIONS SUMMARY
Donor(s): Leonard N. Stern
Typical Recipients: • *Arts & Humanities:* community arts, libraries, museums/galleries • *Civic & Public Affairs:* women's affairs, zoos/botanical gardens • *Education:* colleges & universities, education funds, public education (precollege) • *Health:* health organizations, hospitals, medical research, pediatric health, single-disease health associations • *Religion:* churches, religious organizations, synagogues • *Social Services:* child welfare, community centers, community service organizations, shelters/homelessness, united funds, youth organizations
Grant Types: general support, multiyear/continuing support, operating expenses, project, and seed money
Geographic Distribution: focus on the New York, NY, metropolitan area

GIVING OFFICERS
Ronald Catalina: asst treas
Carol Kellermann: off
Armand Lindenbaum: vp
Frank Roscitt: asst secy
Curtis Schwartz: secy, treas *CURR EMPL* vp, dir: Hartz Mountain Corp *CORP AFFIL* vp, dir: Hartz Mountain Corp
Leonard Norman Stern: pres, dir *B* New York NY 1938 *ED* NY Univ BS 1956; NY Univ MBA 1957 *CURR EMPL* owner, chmn, ceo: Hartz Group *CORP AFFIL* chmn, ceo: Hartz Mountain Indus; dir: Rite Aid Corp; mem adv bd: Chemical Bank; publ: Village Voice *NONPR AFFIL* dir: Jewish Ctr, Manhattan Day Sch; fdr: Albert Einstein Coll Medicine; mem: Natl Assn Pet Indus, NY Holocaust Meml Comm

APPLICATION INFORMATION
Initial Approach: Contributes only to preselected organizations.

GRANTS ANALYSIS

Number of Grants: 44
Highest Grant: $166,666
Typical Range: $750 to $12,000
Disclosure Period: 1991

RECENT GRANTS

166,666 New York Public Library, New York, NY

150,000 United Jewish Appeal Federation of Jewish Philanthropies, New York, NY

100,000 Homes for the Homeless Summer Camp, New York, NY

32,000 Homes for the Homeless, New York, NY

25,000 Fund for New York City Public Education, New York, NY

16,668 Children's Museum of Manhattan, New York, NY

15,000 Fund for Aging Services, New York, NY

12,500 City Parks Foundation, New York, NY

12,500 New York City Partnership Foundation, New York, NY

10,000 National Jewish Center for Immunology and Respiratory Medicine, Denver, CO

Stern Foundation, Marjorie and Michael

CONTACT

Marjorie and Michael Stern Foundation
c/o Yohalem, Gillman & Company
477 Madison Avenue
New York, NY 10022-5802

FINANCIAL SUMMARY

Recent Giving: $124,026 (1990)
Assets: $3,895,367 (1990)
EIN: 13-3440362

GIVING OFFICERS

Erica Stern: dir
Marjorie Stern: secy
Mark Stern: dir
Michael Stern: pres, treas

APPLICATION INFORMATION

Initial Approach: The foundation reports it only makes contributions to preselected organizations and does not accept unsolicited requests for funds.

GRANTS ANALYSIS

Total Grants: $124,026
Highest Grant: $60,000
Disclosure Period: 1990

Stern Foundation, Max

CONTACT

Leonard N. Stern
President
Max Stern Fdn.
400 Plaza Drive
PO Box 1411
Secaucus, NJ 07096
(201) 617-5007

FINANCIAL SUMMARY

Recent Giving: $656,018 (fiscal 1991); $532,969 (fiscal 1990); $497,905 (fiscal 1989)
Assets: $2,606,372 (fiscal year ending September 30, 1990); $2,976,376 (fiscal 1989)
EIN: 13-6161280

CONTRIBUTIONS SUMMARY

Donor(s): the late Max Stern, Stanley Stern
Typical Recipients: • *Education:* colleges & universities, religious education • *Religion:* religious organizations, synagogues • *Social Services:* community centers, community service organizations
Grant Types: multiyear/continuing support

GIVING OFFICERS

Ronald Catalina: asst treas
Armand Lindenbaum: secy, dir
Curtis B. Schwartz: treas
Ghity Stern: dir
Leonard Norman Stern: pres, dir *B* New York NY 1938 *ED* NY Univ BS 1956; NY Univ MBA 1957 *CURR EMPL* owner, chmn, ceo: Hartz Group *CORP AFFIL* chmn, ceo: Hartz Mountain Indus; dir: Rite Aid Corp; mem adv bd: Chemical Bank; publ: Village Voice *NONPR AFFIL* dir: Jewish Ctr, Manhattan Day Sch; fdr: Albert Einstein Coll Medicine; mem: Natl Assn Pet Indus, NY Holocaust Meml Comm

APPLICATION INFORMATION

Initial Approach: The foundation reports it only makes contributions to preselected charitable organizations.

GRANTS ANALYSIS

Number of Grants: 94
Highest Grant: $125,000
Typical Range: $100 to $1,000
Disclosure Period: fiscal year ending September 30, 1990

RECENT GRANTS

125,000 Yeshiva University Scholars Program, New York, NY

125,000 Yeshiva University Scholars Program, New York, NY

100,000 New York Holocaust Memorial Commission, New York, NY

30,000 Jewish Center, New York, NY

20,000 92nd Street YM and YWHA, New York, NY

20,000 Jewish Center, New York, NY

15,000 Friends of Yeshiva Harav Amiel, New York, NY

10,000 American Friends Rab Kol Torah, New York, NY

10,000 Yeshiva University, New York, NY — Stern College

5,000 Greater New York Council on Religion, New York, NY

Stern Foundation, Percival

CONTACT

Walter L. Brown
President
Percival Stern Fdn.
3901 Tulane Avenue, Ste. 103
New Orleans, LA 70119
(504) 482-9622

FINANCIAL SUMMARY

Recent Giving: $1,325 (1991); $80,306 (1986)
Assets: $3,041,180 (1991); $3,246,848 (1990); $3,448,225 (1989)
EIN: 72-0545551

CONTRIBUTIONS SUMMARY

Donor(s): the late Percival Stern, Elsie Kahn Stern

GIVING OFFICERS

Perry S. Brown: vp, trust
Mrs. Walter L. Brown: trust
Walter L. Brown, Jr.: pres, trust
Louis G. Lemk: secy, treas, trust
Dr. Clarence Shep: trust *B* Houston TX 1915 *ED* Rice Inst BA 1935; Columbia Univ MS
1936; LA St Univ PhD 1943 *NONPR AFFIL* mem: Natl Assn Coll Univ Bus Offs, Southern Assn Coll Univ Bus Offs; secy: Tulane Univ
Mark S. Stein: trust

APPLICATION INFORMATION

Initial Approach: Send brief letter of inquiry. There are no deadlines.

GRANTS ANALYSIS

Disclosure Period: 1991
Note: No grants were provided in 1991.

Stern Memorial Trust, Sidney

CONTACT

Sue Boling
Vice President
Sidney Stern Memorial Trust
Board of Advisory, PO Box 893
Pacific Palisades, CA 90272
(213) 253-3154

FINANCIAL SUMMARY

Recent Giving: $1,272,187 (fiscal 1991); $1,108,971 (fiscal 1990); $964,750 (fiscal 1989)
Assets: $20,418,989 (fiscal year ending August 31, 1991); $18,560,149 (fiscal 1990); $19,361,279 (fiscal 1989)
EIN: 95-6495222

CONTRIBUTIONS SUMMARY

Donor(s): The foundation was established in 1974 by the late S. Sidney Stern.
Typical Recipients: • *Arts & Humanities:* museums/galleries, public broadcasting • *Civic & Public Affairs:* better government, civil rights, environmental affairs, ethnic/minority organizations, first amendment issues, international affairs, law & justice, public policy • *Education:* colleges & universities, literacy, medical education, private education (precollege), religious education, science/technology education • *Health:* hospitals, medical research, public health, single-disease health associations • *Religion:* religious organizations, synagogues • *Social Services:* aged, child welfare, community centers, counseling, day care, drugs & alcohol, employment/job training, family planning, family services, homes,

legal aid, shelters/homelessness, youth organizations
Grant Types: capital, emergency, endowment, matching, operating expenses, project, research, scholarship, and seed money
Geographic Distribution: focus on California

GIVING OFFICERS

Ira E. Bilson: secy, mem bd advs
Betty Hoffenberg: mem bd advs
Marvin Hoffenberg: chmn bd advs *B* Buffalo NY 1914 *ED* OH St Univ BSc 1939; OH St Univ MA 1940 *NONPR AFFIL* comr: Los Angeles County Economy & Efficiency Commn; dir: Reiss-Davis Child Study Ctr, Vista Del Mar Child Ctr; dir Los Angeles chapter: Am Jewish Comm; fellow: Am Academy Advancement Science; mem: Am Econ Assn; prof emeritus: Univ CA Los Angeles
Peter H. Hoffenberg: mem bd advs
Edith Lessler: mem bd advs
Howard O. Wilson: mem bd advs

APPLICATION INFORMATION

Initial Approach:
The foundation has no formal grant application procedure or application form.
Written applications for grants must contain the following information: a brief background description of the organization, its purposes, and the target population; a description of its governing board and professional staff; the organization's most recent audited financial statement and its current total operating budget, including the percent of operating costs expended on fundraising, the budget for the proposed activity, and other sources of support; evidence of federal and (where applicable) California tax-exempt status; and the means for continuing the support of specific programs or activities after the expiration of the requested grant.
The foundation's board accepts, reviews, and votes on applications for grants throughout the year.
Normally, requests for grants are considered at each regularly scheduled meeting. Most of the first scheduled meeting

of the year is reserved for planning, operational review, and deciding on the substantive areas for major allocations during the upcoming year. Since the processing of a proposal by the board entails considerable study, and because a large number of proposals await review during the year, an applicant should allow a considerable period of time for a decision. Presentations by applicants at the monthly board meetings are not invited.
Restrictions on Giving: All funds must be used within the United States, and grants are not made to individuals. Grants also are not made to political candidates or campaigns, lobbying projects, programs to directly influence legislation, continuing support, publications, conferences, or for loans.

OTHER THINGS TO KNOW
Publications: informational brochure and application guidelines

GRANTS ANALYSIS
Total Grants: $1,272,187
Number of Grants: 202
Highest Grant: $33,000
Typical Range: $1,000 to $21,000
Disclosure Period: fiscal year ending August 31, 1991
Note: Recent grants are derived from a fiscal 1991 grants list.

RECENT GRANTS
33,000 Simon Wiesenthal Center of Holocaust, Los Angeles, CA
31,330 University of California Los Angeles, Los Angeles, CA
30,000 Planned Parenthood Federation of America, Los Angeles, CA
27,500 American Jewish College, New York, NY
25,000 San Francisco Senators, San Francisco, CA
21,500 California State University, CA
20,000 Exceptional Children's Foundation, Los Angeles, CA
20,000 Home-Safe Child Care Center, Los Angeles, CA
20,000 KCET Community Television, Los Angeles, CA

20,000 Swarthmore College/Foundation, Swarthmore, PA

Stern Private Charitable Foundation Trust, Charles H. and Anna S.

CONTACT
Melitta L. Fleck
Charles H. and Anna S. Stern Private Charitable Foundation Trust
1200 Prospect Street, Suite 575
La Jolla, CA 92037-3608
(619) 456-3088

FINANCIAL SUMMARY
Recent Giving: $193,260 (1991); $139,732 (1990)
Assets: $3,740,174 (1991); $3,166,293 (1990)
EIN: 95-6878433

CONTRIBUTIONS SUMMARY
Typical Recipients: • *Education:* colleges & universities, medical education
Grant Types: general support

GIVING OFFICERS
Christopher C. Calkins: trust
Frederick De La Vega: trust
Barbara Durban: trust
William W. Gordon: pres
Frank Nielsen: treas

GRANTS ANALYSIS
Number of Grants: 4
Highest Grant: $50,000
Typical Range: $44,280 to $50,000
Disclosure Period: 1991

RECENT GRANTS
50,000 Whittier Institute, La Jolla, CA
49,932 Creighton University School of Medicine, CA
39,800 University of California San Diego, La Jolla, CA — School of Medicine

Sternberger Foundation, Sigmund

CONTACT
Robert O. Klepfer, Jr.
Executive Director
Sigmund Sternberger Fdn.
PO Box 3111
Greensboro, NC 27402
(919) 373-1500

FINANCIAL SUMMARY
Recent Giving: $636,664 (fiscal 1991); $428,815 (fiscal 1990); $433,128 (fiscal 1989)
Assets: $9,930,738 (fiscal year ending March 31, 1991); $9,536,523 (fiscal 1990); $8,810,326 (fiscal 1989)
EIN: 56-6045483

CONTRIBUTIONS SUMMARY
Donor(s): the late Sigmund and Rosa Sternberger Williams
Typical Recipients: • *Arts & Humanities:* arts festivals, community arts, history/historic preservation, libraries • *Education:* colleges & universities, education funds, student aid • *Social Services:* child welfare, community service organizations, united funds, youth organizations
Grant Types: capital, general support, and scholarship
Geographic Distribution: focus on Guilford County, NC

GIVING OFFICERS
Howard E. Carr: dir
Robert O. Klepfer, Jr.: exec dir
Charles M. Reid: dir
Sidney J. Stern, Jr.: secy, dir
Mrs. A. J. Tannenbaum: pres, dir
Jeanne Tannenbaum: dir
Sigmund I. Tannenbaum, MD: dir
Rabbi Arnold S. Task: dir

APPLICATION INFORMATION
Initial Approach: Send letter requesting application form. There are no deadlines.

OTHER THINGS TO KNOW
Publications: Application Guidelines

GRANTS ANALYSIS
Number of Grants: 62
Highest Grant: $100,000
Typical Range: $1,000 to $10,000

Disclosure Period: fiscal year ending March 31, 1991

RECENT GRANTS

100,000 Guildord Battle-ground, NC

55,000 Duke University, Durham, NC — scholarships

50,000 Natural Science Center, NC — drug and nutrition exhibits

25,000 Eastern Music Festival, Greensboro, NC

25,000 Links Adolescent Services Foundation, Greensboro, NC

25,000 University of North Carolina School of Social Works, Chapel Hill, NC

25,000 YMCA, Greensboro, NC

20,000 United Arts Council, Greensboro, NC

16,666 Greensboro College, Greensboro, NC — library renovation

15,000 Greensboro Urban Ministry, Greensboro, NC

Sterne-Elder Memorial Trust

CONTACT

Sterne-Elder Memorial Trust
c/o United Bank of Denver, NA
1700 Broadway
Denver, CO 80274-0081

FINANCIAL SUMMARY

Recent Giving: $282,500 (fiscal 1992); $255,000 (fiscal 1991); $173,700 (fiscal 1990)
Assets: $4,281,794 (fiscal year ending March 31, 1992); $4,258,589 (fiscal 1991); $4,334,272 (fiscal 1990)
EIN: 84-6143172

CONTRIBUTIONS SUMMARY

Donor(s): Charles S. Sterne
Typical Recipients: • *Arts & Humanities:* museums/galleries, music, opera, public broadcasting • *Civic & Public Affairs:* zoos/botanical gardens • *Health:* health organizations, hospices, hospitals, pediatric health, single-disease health associations • *Religion:* churches • *Social Services:* child welfare, family planning, united funds, youth organizations
Grant Types: general support

Geographic Distribution: focus on CO

GIVING OFFICERS

Dorothy Elder Sterne: dir

APPLICATION INFORMATION

Initial Approach: Contributes only to preselected organizations.

GRANTS ANALYSIS

Number of Grants: 46
Highest Grant: $100,000
Typical Range: $1,000 to $5,000
Disclosure Period: fiscal year ending March 31, 1992

RECENT GRANTS

100,000 Colorado Symphony Association, Denver, CO

50,000 St. Joseph Hospital Foundation, Denver, CO

30,000 Central City Opera Association, Denver, CO

25,000 United Way, Denver, CO

10,000 St. John Cathedral of Denver, Denver, CO

5,000 Bridge Trust, Denver, CO

5,000 Callae McIntosh Duke Memorial Scholarship Fund, Englewood, CO

5,000 Children's Hospital Foundation, Denver, CO

2,500 South Suburban Park, Littleton, CO

2,000 Girl Scouts of America, Denver, CO

Steuart Petroleum Co.

Sales: $910.0 million
Employees: 1,400
Headquarters: Washington, DC
SIC Major Group: Automotive Dealers & Service Stations, Miscellaneous Retail, Stone, Clay & Glass Products, and Wholesale Trade—Nondurable Goods

CONTACT

Steuart Petroleum Co.
4646 40th St., NW
Washington, DC 20016
(202) 537-8900

FINANCIAL SUMMARY

Fiscal Note: Annual Giving Range: less than $100,000

CONTRIBUTIONS SUMMARY

Company reports 30% of contributions support the arts; 30% to health and welfare; 20% to education; 10% to civic and public affairs; and 10% to other organizations.
Typical Recipients: • *Arts & Humanities:* general • *Civic & Public Affairs:* general • *Education:* general • *Social Services:* general
Grant Types: general support
Nonmonetary Support Types: donated products
Operating Locations: DC (Washington)

CORP. OFFICERS

John C. Johnson: *CURR EMPL* pres, ceo, dir: Steuart Petroleum Co

APPLICATION INFORMATION

Initial Approach: Send brief letter of inquiry. There are no deadlines.

Stevens Foundation, Abbot and Dorothy H.

CONTACT

Elizabeth A. Beland
Administrator
Abbot and Dorothy H. Stevens Fdn.
PO Box 111
North Andover, MA 01845
(508) 688-7211

FINANCIAL SUMMARY

Recent Giving: $614,806 (1991); $474,280 (1990); $624,848 (1989)
Assets: $14,086,783 (1991); $12,374,528 (1990); $12,484,272 (1989)
EIN: 04-6107991

CONTRIBUTIONS SUMMARY

Donor(s): The foundation was established in 1953 by the late Abbot Stevens.
Typical Recipients: • *Arts & Humanities:* dance, history/historic preservation, libraries, museums/galleries, music, opera • *Civic & Public Affairs:* business/free enterprise, environmental affairs, municipalities, philanthropic organizations, safety, zoos/botanical gardens • *Education:* colleges & universities, community & junior colleges, education associations, education funds, private education (precollege) • *Health:* hospitals, medical research • *International:* foreign educational institutions • *Religion:* churches • *Social Services:* aged, community service organizations, delinquency & crime, disabled, homes, united funds, youth organizations
Grant Types: capital, endowment, matching, multiyear/continuing support, operating expenses, project, and seed money
Geographic Distribution: limited to Massachusetts, with an emphasis on Greater Lawrence area

GIVING OFFICERS

Phebe S. Miner: trust
Christopher W. Rogers: trust
Samuel S. Rogers: trust

APPLICATION INFORMATION

Initial Approach:
The foundation requests applications be made in writing and do not exceed 10 pages. Appendices may be attached.
formal applications should include a copy of an IRS determination letter, proof of incorporation in Massachusetts, the names of the organization's officers and directors, the most recent annual financial statement, institutional income and an expense budget for the current fiscal year, a detailed program budget for which support is requested, the starting and completion dates of the project and the proposed cash flow, and the current status of fundraising program and anticipated sources.
Proposals may be submitted throughout the year.
Restrictions on Giving: No grants will be made to individuals, state or federal agencies, annual campaigns, deficit financing, exchange programs, internships, fellowships, professorships, scholarships, loans, or to organizations for the use of another agency that has not been determined tax-exempt. The trustees will not normally consider more than one application from an agency in the same calendar year.

OTHER THINGS TO KNOW

Publications: program policy statement and application guidelines

GRANTS ANALYSIS
Total Grants: $614,806
Number of Grants: 92
Highest Grant: $50,000
Typical Range: $1,000 to $8,000
Disclosure Period: 1991
Note: Recent grants are derived from a 1991 grants list.

RECENT GRANTS
50,000 Merrimack College, North Andover, MA
35,500 Greater Law Community Foundation, Boston, MA
35,000 First Calvary Baptist Church, Boston, MA
25,000 Holy Family Hospital, Boston, MA
25,000 MGH Institution/Health Professions, Boston, MA
25,000 Northeast Document Conservation Center, Boston, MA
25,000 Pine Manor College, Boston, MA
20,000 Law Boys Club, Boston, MA
18,000 Children's Museum, Boston, MA
18,000 South Church, Boston, MA — Andover

Stevens Foundation, John T.

CONTACT
John T. Stevens Fdn.
PO Box 158
Kershaw, SC 29067

FINANCIAL SUMMARY
Recent Giving: $199,938 (fiscal 1991); $150,470 (fiscal 1990); $163,279 (fiscal 1989)
Assets: $3,803,300 (fiscal year ending May 31, 1990); $3,699,360 (fiscal 1989)
EIN: 57-6005554

CONTRIBUTIONS SUMMARY
Donor(s): John T. Stevens
Typical Recipients: • *Arts & Humanities:* arts associations, arts centers, libraries • *Civic & Public Affairs:* municipalities • *Education:* public education (precollege) • *Religion:* churches • *Social Services:* united funds, youth organizations
Grant Types: general support
Geographic Distribution: focus on SC

GIVING OFFICERS
John S. Davison: pres, secy, treas
Douglas Williams: treas
Steve L. Williams: vp

APPLICATION INFORMATION
Initial Approach: Send brief letter of inquiry describing program or project.

GRANTS ANALYSIS
Number of Grants: 26
Highest Grant: $29,600
Typical Range: $1,000 to $6,000
Disclosure Period: fiscal year ending May 31, 1990

RECENT GRANTS
29,600 Town of Kershaw, Kershaw, SC
20,000 Health Science Foundation, Charleston, SC
18,000 Unity Baptist Church, Kershaw, SC
13,937 Lancaster County Library, Kershaw, SC
8,000 Kershaw Methodist Church, Kershaw, SC
6,700 Clinton Chapel African Methodist Episcopal Church, Clinton, SC
5,800 Kershaw Second Baptist Church, Kershaw, SC
5,000 Buffalo Baptist Church, Buffalo, SC
5,000 Crossroads Baptist Church, Kershaw, SC
5,000 North Carolina Performing Arts Center, Charlotte, NC

Stevens Foundation, Nathaniel and Elizabeth P.

CONTACT
Elizabeth A. Beland
Administrator
Nathaniel and Elizabeth P. Stevens Fdn.
PO Box 111
North Andover, MA 01845
(508) 688-7211

FINANCIAL SUMMARY
Recent Giving: $349,528 (1991); $537,925 (1990); $506,066 (1989)
Assets: $9,616,626 (1990); $9,737,306 (1989)
EIN: 04-2236996

CONTRIBUTIONS SUMMARY
Donor(s): the late Nathaniel Stevens
Typical Recipients: • *Arts & Humanities:* history/historic preservation, libraries, museums/galleries, music • *Education:* private education (precollege), public education (precollege) • *Health:* hospitals • *Religion:* churches • *Social Services:* youth organizations
Grant Types: capital, conference/seminar, emergency, endowment, general support, multiyear/continuing support, operating expenses, and project
Geographic Distribution: limited to MA, with emphasis on the greater Lawrence area

GIVING OFFICERS
Joshua L. Miner IV: trust
Phebe S. Miner: trust
Samuel S. Rogers: trust

APPLICATION INFORMATION
Initial Approach: Contributes only to preselected organizations.
Restrictions on Giving: Does not support individuals.

OTHER THINGS TO KNOW
Publications: Application Guidelines

GRANTS ANALYSIS
Number of Grants: 89
Highest Grant: $100,000
Typical Range: $1,000 to $5,000
Disclosure Period: 1991

RECENT GRANTS
100,000 Museum of American Textile History, Lawrence, MA
32,000 Holy Family Hospital and Medical Center, Lawrence, MA
25,000 Lawrence Boys Club, Lawrence, MA
20,000 Centro Panamericano-Ecuatorio, Lawrence, MA
16,910 Bread and Roses Heritage Committee, Lawrence, MA
15,000 Northfield Mount Hermon, Northfield, MA
15,000 YWCA, Lawrence, MA
10,000 Academy of Notre Dame, Lawrence, MA
10,000 House of Hope, Lawrence, MA
10,000 Lowell General Hospital, Lowell, MA

Stewards Fund

CONTACT
Nancy B. Faircloth
President
Stewards Fund
PO Box 17845
Raleigh, NC 27619
(919) 782-8410

FINANCIAL SUMMARY
Recent Giving: $111,000 (1990); $86,500 (1989)
Assets: $2,697,018 (1990); $2,908,392 (1989)
Gifts Received: $59,675 (1990); $194,350 (1989)
Fiscal Note: In 1990, contributions were received from Nancy B. Faircloth.
EIN: 56-1482138

CONTRIBUTIONS SUMMARY
Donor(s): Nancy B. Faircloth, Anne B. Faircloth
Typical Recipients: • *Education:* private education (precollege) • *Health:* hospices • *Religion:* churches, missionary activities, religious organizations • *Social Services:* community service organizations, food/clothing distribution, shelters/homelessness, united funds, youth organizations
Grant Types: general support, multiyear/continuing support, operating expenses, and project
Geographic Distribution: focus on Raleigh, NC

GIVING OFFICERS
Albert G. Edwards: vp
Anne B. Faircloth: vp
Nancy B. Faircloth: pres
Alton E. Howard: secy, treas

APPLICATION INFORMATION
Initial Approach: Send brief letter of inquiry describing program. There are no deadlines.
Restrictions on Giving: Does not support individuals.

GRANTS ANALYSIS
Number of Grants: 13
Highest Grant: $45,000
Typical Range: $2,500 to $10,000
Disclosure Period: 1990

RECENT GRANTS

45,000 Habitat for Humanity, Raleigh, NC
15,000 Tammy Lynn Center, Raleigh, NC
10,000 Habitat for Humanity, Raleigh, NC
10,000 Salvation Army, Raleigh, NC
5,000 Frankie Lemmon School, Raleigh, NC
5,000 Halifax Court Day Care, Raleigh, NC
5,000 Raleigh Rescue Mission, Raleigh, NC
3,500 Goodwill Industries, Raleigh, NC
3,000 Urban Ministries, Raleigh, NC
2,500 Hospice, Raleigh, NC

Stewardship Foundation

CONTACT
George S. Kovats
Executive Director
Stewardship Foundation
PO Box 1278
Tacoma, WA 98401
(206) 272-8336

FINANCIAL SUMMARY
Recent Giving: $4,000,000 (1991 est.); $4,186,842 (1990); $3,991,409 (1989)
Assets: $70,000,000 (1991 est.); $73,725,192 (1989)
Gifts Received: $300,000 (1991 est.); $300,017 (1989)
EIN: 91-1405117

CONTRIBUTIONS SUMMARY
Donor(s): The foundation was established in 1962 by Charles Davis Weyerhaeuser, a son of the late Frederick Edward Weyerhaeuser, former president of Weyerhaeuser Timber Company.
Typical Recipients: • *Civic & Public Affairs:* civil rights, environmental affairs, law & justice, urban & community affairs • *Education:* colleges & universities, international exchange, private education (precollege), religious education • *Religion:* churches, missionary activities, religious organizations • *Social Services:* child welfare, community centers, delinquency & crime, disabled, domestic violence, drugs & alcohol, employment/job training, family planning, religious welfare, youth organizations
Grant Types: capital, challenge, fellowship, general support, operating expenses, and project
Geographic Distribution: no geographical restrictions

GIVING OFFICERS
Louis A. Flora: dir
Carl T. Fynbone: dir
James R. Hanson: secy, dir
George S. Kovats: exec dir
Annette Thayer Black Weyerhaeuser: vp, treas, dir
Charles Davis Weyerhaeuser: don, pres, treas, dir *B* St Paul MN *ED* Yale Univ BA 1933 *CORP AFFIL* dir: Weyerhaeuser Timber Co *NONPR AFFIL* chmn: YMCA Campaign; trust: Fuller Theological Seminary, Inter-Varsity Christian Fellowship, Moody Bible Inst, Whitworth Coll, Young Life; vchmn: Natl Alliance Businessmen
William Toycen Weyerhaeuser: dir *B* Tacoma WA 1943 *ED* Stanford Univ 1966; Fuller Grad Sch Psychology PhD 1975 *CURR EMPL* owner, chmn: Yelm Telephone Co *CORP AFFIL* dir: Potlatch Corp *NONPR AFFIL* mem: Am Psychological Assn; vchmn: Univ Puget Sound

APPLICATION INFORMATION
Initial Approach:
Potential applicants should send a brief letter to the foundation.
Letters should include a description of the proposed project along with the organization's budget and sources of revenue. If a program falls within foundation interests, an application form will be sent. Trustees meet quarterly and an organization making a request will usually receive a response from the foundation within three months from the time of the request.
Restrictions on Giving:
Grants generally are not made for the following purposes: seed funding for start-up organizations; scholarships or fellowships to individuals; endowments; debt retirement; media time and program production; or for propagandizing or influencing elections or legislation. Grants are not made to churches, but only to parachurch organizations, as well as to a few local, secular, community-based organizations.

Grants are primarily made in support of operating expenses rather than for capital projects.

GRANTS ANALYSIS
Total Grants: $3,991,409
Number of Grants: 349
Highest Grant: $187,500
Typical Range: $1,000 to $25,000
Disclosure Period: 1989
Note: Recent grants are derived from a 1989 grants list.

RECENT GRANTS

187,500 Fuller Theological Seminary, Pasadena, CA — scholarship endowment
156,250 Focus on the Family, Pomona, CA — DeMoss music project
125,000 ISSACHAR, Seattle, WA
100,000 African Enterprise, Pasadena, CA
90,000 Young Life Campaign, Colorado Springs, CO — mission advance fund
87,500 Fuller Theological Seminary, Pasadena, CA — scholarship endowment and unrestricted funds
85,000 Fuller Theological Seminary, Pasadena, CA
75,000 Crista Ministries, Seattle, WA — world concern
75,000 Slavic Gospel Association, Wheaton, IL
75,000 Whitworth College, Spokane, WA

Stewart Alexander Foundation

CONTACT
Stewart Alexander Fdn.
c/o Mellon Bank (East), N.A.
PO Box 7236
Philadelphia, PA 19101
(215) 585-3690

FINANCIAL SUMMARY
Recent Giving: $192,952 (fiscal 1991); $188,909 (fiscal 1990); $214,136 (fiscal 1989)
Assets: $3,973,250 (fiscal year ending June 30, 1991); $3,755,652 (fiscal 1990); $3,451,095 (fiscal 1989)
EIN: 23-6732616

CONTRIBUTIONS SUMMARY
Grant Types: scholarship
Geographic Distribution: focus on Shippensburg, PA

APPLICATION INFORMATION
Initial Approach: Send brief letter requesting application. Deadline is April 1.

GRANTS ANALYSIS
Number of Grants: 22
Highest Grant: $31,272
Typical Range: $1,000 to $10,000
Disclosure Period: fiscal year ending June 30, 1991
Note: Grants list for fiscal year 1991 was incomplete.

Stewart Educational Foundation, Donnell B. and Elizabeth Dee Shaw

CONTACT
J.D. Lampros
Trust Officer
Donnell B. and Elizabeth Dee Shaw Stewart Educational Fdn.
c/o First Security Bank of Utah, N.A.
PO Box 9936
Ogden, UT 84409
(801) 626-9533

FINANCIAL SUMMARY
Recent Giving: $169,475 (1991); $127,400 (1990); $2,093 (1989)
Assets: $3,778,056 (1991); $3,022,540 (1990); $1,224,983 (1989)
Gifts Received: $3,976 (1991)
EIN: 87-6179880

CONTRIBUTIONS SUMMARY
Donor(s): Elizabeth D. S. Stewart
Typical Recipients: • *Arts & Humanities:* dance, music • *Civic & Public Affairs:* environmental affairs, municipalities • *Education:* colleges & universities • *Health:* health organizations, single-disease health associations • *Religion:* churches • *Social Services:* disabled, youth organizations
Grant Types: capital and scholarship
Geographic Distribution: focus on Ogden, UT

GIVING OFFICERS
Dean W. Hurst: mem

Donnell B. Stewart: vchmn
Elizabeth D.S. Stewart: chmn

APPLICATION INFORMATION
Initial Approach: Send brief letter describing program. There are no deadlines.

GRANTS ANALYSIS
Number of Grants: 20
Highest Grant: $55,000
Typical Range: $500 to $1,000
Disclosure Period: 1991

RECENT GRANTS
55,000 McKay-Dee Hospital Foundation, Ogden, UT
53,000 Weber State University, Ogden, UT
20,000 Utah Girl Scout Council, Ogden, UT
10,000 Ogden Discovery Center, Ogden, UT
10,000 Ogden Symphony Ballet Foundation, Ogden, UT
5,000 Utah Downs Syndrome Foundation, Ogden, UT
5,000 Utah North Mission 2000, Ogden, UT
2,000 Ogden Nature Center, Ogden, UT
1,000 Ogden Weber AVC Foundation, Ogden, UT
1,000 Union Station Foundation, Ogden, UT

Stewart Memorial Trust, J. C.

CONTACT
Robert S. Hoyert
Trustee
J. C. Stewart Memorial Trust
7718 Finns Lane
Lanham, MD 20706
(301) 459-4200

FINANCIAL SUMMARY
Recent Giving: $16,500 (fiscal 1991); $36,476 (fiscal 1990); $10,500 (fiscal 1989)
Assets: $5,796,411 (fiscal year ending November 30, 1991); $5,143,740 (fiscal 1990); $6,204,030 (fiscal 1989)
EIN: 23-7357104

CONTRIBUTIONS SUMMARY
Donor(s): the late Anna L. Stewart
Grant Types: loan and scholarship

Geographic Distribution: focus on MD

GIVING OFFICERS
Robert S. Hoyert: trust
Bill I. Yoho: trust

APPLICATION INFORMATION
Initial Approach: Contact foundation for application form. There are no deadlines.

OTHER THINGS TO KNOW
Provides student loans and scholarships to MD residents.
Disclosure Period: fiscal year ending November 30, 1991

Stewart & Stevenson Services

Sales: $686.3 million
Employees: 2,612
Headquarters: Houston, TX
SIC Major Group: Electronic & Other Electrical Equipment, Industrial Machinery & Equipment, Transportation Equipment, and Wholesale Trade—Durable Goods

CONTACT
C. Jim Stewart, Jr.
Chairman
Stewart & Stevenson Services
PO Box 1637
Houston, TX 77251-1637
(713) 868-7700

FINANCIAL SUMMARY
Fiscal Note: Annual Giving Range: less than $100,000

CONTRIBUTIONS SUMMARY
Typical Recipients: • *Arts & Humanities:* general • *Civic & Public Affairs:* general • *Education:* general • *Health:* general • *Social Services:* general
Grant Types: general support
Geographic Distribution: primarily headquarters area
Operating Locations: TX (Houston)

CORP. OFFICERS
Bob H. O'Neal: *CURR EMPL* pres, dir: Stewart & Stevenson Svcs
C. Jim Stewart II: *CURR EMPL* chmn, dir: Stewart & Stevenson Svcs

APPLICATION INFORMATION
Initial Approach: Send brief letter of inquiry. There are no deadlines.

Stewart Trust under the will of Helen S. Devore, Alexander and Margaret

CONTACT
Ruth C. Shaw
Secretary
Alexander and Margaret Stewart Trust (under the will of Helen S. Devore)
c/o First American Bank, N.A., Trust Department
740 15th St., NW
Washington, DC 20005
(202) 637-7887

FINANCIAL SUMMARY
Recent Giving: $1,212,100 (1991); $1,346,375 (1990); $1,552,243 (1989)
Assets: $32,537,971 (1991); $27,281,588 (1990); $26,678,426 (1989)
EIN: 52-6020271

CONTRIBUTIONS SUMMARY
Donor(s): The Alexander and Margaret Stewart Trust was established in the District of Columbia in 1947 under the terms of the will of the late Helen S. Devore.
Typical Recipients: • *Education:* colleges & universities, medical education, special education • *Health:* hospitals, medical rehabilitation, mental health, outpatient health care delivery, pediatric health • *Social Services:* child welfare, disabled, drugs & alcohol, family services, youth organizations
Grant Types: general support, multiyear/continuing support, operating expenses, project, and seed money
Geographic Distribution: primarily the Washington, DC, area

GIVING OFFICERS
Francis G. Addison III: trust
George E. Hamilton III: trust
Ruth C. Shaw: secy *PHIL AFFIL* secy: Stewart (Alexander and Margaret) Trust (under the will of Mary E Stewart)

APPLICATION INFORMATION
Initial Approach:
There are no set guidelines for application. A letter of inquiry outlining the project is the preferred method of initial contact.

The letter should include the qualifications of the staff, budget, list of other funding sources, board participation in fund-raising efforts, proof of tax-exempt status, and a copy of the most recent audit report. There are no application deadlines.
The board meets in March, June, September, November, and December.
Restrictions on Giving: The trust does not support individuals or endowment funds, annual campaigns, capital campaigns, or building funds. Funding is not provided for conferences, scholarships, or fellowships.

OTHER THINGS TO KNOW
First American Bank serves as a corporate trustee for the trust. The Alexander and Margaret Stewart Trust (created under the will of the late Helen S. Devore) is jointly administered with the Alexander and Margaret Stewart Trust (created under the will of the late Mary E. Stewart).

GRANTS ANALYSIS
Total Grants: $1,212,100
Number of Grants: 23
Highest Grant: $292,000
Typical Range: $15,000 to $60,000
Disclosure Period: 1991
Note: Average grant figure does not include two grants totaling $492,000. Recent grants are derived from a 1991 Form 990.

RECENT GRANTS
292,000 Children's Hospital National Medical Center, Washington, DC — cancer care program
200,000 Children's Hospital National medical Center, Washington, DC — AIDS diagnostic and care center
100,000 District of Columbia Institute for Mental Health, Washington, DC — care/treatment of sick or handicapped children
65,000 Community of Hope, Washington, DC — care/treatment of sick or handicapped children
60,000 Child Development Center of Northern

Virginia, Falls Church, VA — care/treatment of sick or handicapped children

58,300 St. Ann's Infant and Maternity Home, Hyattsville, MD — respite care program

44,800 Reginald S. Lourie Center for Infants and Young Children, Rockville, MD — diagnostic nursery project

42,000 St. John's Child Development Center, Washington, DC — summer autistic program

40,000 Easter Seal Society of DC, Washington, DC — care/treatment of sick or handicapped children

40,000 Providence Hospital, Washington, DC — neonatal services

Stewart Trust under the will of Mary E. Stewart, Alexander and Margaret

CONTACT
Doris Lustine
Executive Secretary
Alexander and Margaret Stewart Trust (u/w/o Mary E. Stewart)
20 Chevy Chase Circle, NW, Ste. 200
Washington, DC 20015
(202) 686-1552

FINANCIAL SUMMARY
Recent Giving: $1,385,450 (1992); $1,518,639 (1991); $1,058,893 (1990)
Assets: $29,162,002 (1991); $24,827,401 (1990); $25,099,510 (1989)
EIN: 52-6020260

CONTRIBUTIONS SUMMARY
Donor(s): The Alexander and Margaret Stewart Trust was established in the District of Columbia under the terms of the will of the late Mary E. Stewart.
Typical Recipients: • *Health:* hospices, hospitals, nursing services, outpatient health care delivery, single-disease health associations
Grant Types: general support, operating expenses, and seed money

Geographic Distribution: primarily metropolitan Washington, DC, area

GIVING OFFICERS
Francis G. Addison III: trust
George E. Hamilton III: trust
Doris Lustine: exec secy

APPLICATION INFORMATION
Initial Approach:
The applicant should contact the foundation for guidelines and an application form. Grants extend for one-year at a time and may be renewed upon reapplication. A site visit and interview may be required as part of the application process. Applications may be submitted at any time during the year. Those received by the close of business on September 15th are generally assured of decision before the end of the year.
Restrictions on Giving: The trust makes grants only to organizations that are able to produce evidence of tax exemption under the Internal Revenue Service Code Section 501(c)(3) and public charity status under the Section 509. The trust also does not fund endowments, building programs or capital campaigns. It does not award scholarships to individuals or to institutions on behalf of individuals. The trust rarely funds cancer research, or the education of students or doctors engaged in cancer research.

OTHER THINGS TO KNOW
The trust also lists First American Bank in Washington, DC, as a trustee. The bank is represented by Ruth C. Shaw, group vice president, personal trust. The trust is affiliated with the Alexander and Margaret Stewart Trust under the will of the Helen S. Devore in Washington, DC.
Publications: application forms and guidelines

GRANTS ANALYSIS
Total Grants: $1,385,450
Number of Grants: 17
Highest Grant: $220,000
Typical Range: $40,000 to $95,000
Disclosure Period: 1992
Note: Recent grants are derived from a 1991 Form 990.

RECENT GRANTS
316,906 Georgetown University, Washing-

ton, DC — cancer home care program

220,000 Washington Hospital Center, Washington, DC — care of cancer patients needy sick fund

170,000 George Washington University, Washington, DC — cancer home care program

110,000 American Cancer Society, Washington, DC — cancer aid plan

90,000 Providence Hospital, Washington, DC — cancer clinic

80,000 Visiting Nurse Association of Northern Virginia, Arlington, VA — care of cancer patients

80,000 Visiting Nurse Association of the District of Columbia, Washington, DC — care of cancer patients

79,400 Hospice Council of Metropolitan Washington, Washington, DC — hospital liaison program

55,000 Hospice of Northern Virginia, Arlington, VA — care of cancer patients

55,000 Washington Home Hospice, Washington, DC — hospice unit-care of cancer patients and national conference

Stieren Foundation, Arthur T. and Jane J.

CONTACT
Arthur T. and Jane J. Stieren Fdn.
D-101 Petroleum Center
San Antonio, TX 78209
(512) 828-0740

FINANCIAL SUMMARY
Recent Giving: $100,000 (1991); $100,000 (1990); $100,000 (1989)

Assets: $2,729,658 (1991); $2,466,068 (1990); $2,418,957 (1989)

Gifts Received: $75,000 (1989); $300,000 (1988)

Fiscal Note: 1989 contribution from Arthur T. and Jane J. Stieren.

EIN: 74-2346000

CONTRIBUTIONS SUMMARY
Donor(s): Arthur T. Stieren, Jane J. Stieren
Typical Recipients: • *Arts & Humanities:* opera
Grant Types: general support
Geographic Distribution: focus on TX and NM

GIVING OFFICERS
Arthur T. Stieren: trust
Jane J. Stieren: trust

APPLICATION INFORMATION
Initial Approach: Contributes only to preselected organizations.
Restrictions on Giving: Does not support individuals.

GRANTS ANALYSIS
Number of Grants: 2
Highest Grant: $50,000
Disclosure Period: 1991

RECENT GRANTS
50,000 Santa Fe Opera, Santa Fe, NM
50,000 Santa Fe Opera Foundation, Santa Fe, NM

Stillwell Charitable Trust, Glen and Dorothy

CONTACT
Glen and Dorothy Stillwell Charitable Trust
301 N. Lake Avenue, 10th floor
Pasadena, CA 91101

FINANCIAL SUMMARY
Recent Giving: $105,525 (fiscal 1991); $88,650 (fiscal 1990); $93,141 (fiscal 1989)
Assets: $1,897,754 (fiscal year ending November 30, 1991); $1,725,300 (fiscal 1990); $1,771,021 (fiscal 1989)
EIN: 95-6751888

CONTRIBUTIONS SUMMARY
Donor(s): Glen Stillwell, Dorothy Stillwell
Typical Recipients: • *Civic & Public Affairs:* law & justice • *Health:* health organizations, medical research, pediatric health, single-disease health associations • *Social Services:* child welfare, disabled, family services, youth organizations
Grant Types: general support
Geographic Distribution: limited to Orange County, CA

GIVING OFFICERS
John F. Bradley: trust
Stanley C. Lagerlof: trust,
chmn *B* Minneapolis MN 1915
ED Univ MN AB 1936; Univ
Southern CA JD 1939 *CURR
EMPL* atty: Lagerlof Senecal
Drescher & Swift
H. Jess Senecal: trust

APPLICATION INFORMATION
Initial Approach: Send brief
letter describing program.
There are no deadlines.

GRANTS ANALYSIS
Number of Grants: 10
Highest Grant: $12,500
Typical Range: $10,000 to
$12,000
Disclosure Period: fiscal year
ending November 30, 1991

RECENT GRANTS
12,500 Orange County Bar
Association,
Irvine, CA
12,075 Dale McIntosh Center for the Disabled, Anaheim,
CA
12,000 Children's Bureau
of Los Angeles,
Los Angeles, CA
12,000 High Hopes Head
Injury Program,
Costa Mesa, CA
12,000 Pilgrimage County
Center, Santa Ana,
CA
10,000 Alzheimer's Disease and Related
Disorders Association, Costa Mesa,
CA
10,000 Florence Crittenton
Services, Fullerton, CA
10,000 St. Joseph Hospital
Foundation, Orange, CA
9,850 Stop-Gap, Santa
Ana, CA
5,100 Boys Republic,
Chino, CA

Stirtz, Bernards & Co.
Headquarters: Edina, MN

CONTACT
Kurt Williams
Comptroller
Stirtz, Bernards & Co.
Financial Plaza, 7200 Metro
Blvd.
Edina, MN 55439
(612) 831-6499

FINANCIAL SUMMARY
Fiscal Note: Annual Giving
Range: less than $100,000

CONTRIBUTIONS SUMMARY
Company reports 40% of contributions support health and
welfare; 30% to the arts; 20%
to civic and public affairs; and
10% to education.
Typical Recipients: • *Arts &
Humanities:* general • *Civic &
Public Affairs:* general • *Education:* general • *Social Services:*
general
Grant Types: general support
Nonmonetary Support Types:
cause-related marketing & promotion
Operating Locations: MN
(Edina)

APPLICATION INFORMATION
Initial Approach: Send brief
letter of inquiry. There are no
deadlines.

Stock Foundation, Paul

CONTACT
Charles G. Kepler
President
Paul Stock Fdn.
1135 Fourteenth St.
Cody, WY 82414
(307) 587-5275

FINANCIAL SUMMARY
Recent Giving: $677,414
(1991); $372,857 (1989)
Assets: $11,388,650 (1991);
$9,692,274 (1989)
EIN: 83-0185157

CONTRIBUTIONS SUMMARY
Donor(s): the late Paul Stock,
Eloise J. Stock
Typical Recipients: • *Arts &
Humanities:* history/historic
preservation, museums/galleries • *Education:* colleges & universities, public education
(precollege) • *Social Services:*
child welfare, recreation & athletics, recreation & athletics,
youth organizations
Grant Types: general support
and operating expenses
Geographic Distribution:
focus on WY; student aid limited to those who have resided
in WY for one year or more

GIVING OFFICERS
Esther C. Brumage: vp
Charles G. Kepler: pres
Donald M. Robirds: secy, treas

APPLICATION INFORMATION
Initial Approach: Application
form and instructions for educational grants only. Send brief
letter of inquiry describing program or project. Deadline is
June 30 and November 30 for
educational grants. Board
meets in July and December.

OTHER THINGS TO KNOW
Awards scholarships and educational grants to individuals.

GRANTS ANALYSIS
Number of Grants: 21
Highest Grant: $60,000
Typical Range: $500 to
$10,000
Disclosure Period: 1991

RECENT GRANTS
60,000 Salk Institute for
Biological Studies,
San Diego, CA
56,000 University of Wyoming, Laramie, WY
30,000 Buffalo Bill Memorial Association,
Cody, WY — stock
residence upkeep
30,000 Northwest College,
Powell, WY —
scholarships
25,000 Buffalo Bill Memorial Association,
Cody, WY — Cody
Firearms museum
10,000 Cathedral Home
for Children,
Laramie, WY
6,259 Buffalo Bill Memorial Association,
Cody, WY — Jack
Richards Photo
Collection
5,000 Gottsche Foundation, Thermopolis,
WY
5,000 Park County
Search and Rescue,
Cody, WY
1,000 Crook County
School District No.
1, Laramie, WY

Stocker Foundation

CONTACT
Sara Jane Norton
Secretary-Treasurer
Stocker Fdn.
209 6th St., Ste. 25
Lorain, OH 44052
(216) 246-5719

FINANCIAL SUMMARY
Recent Giving: $501,095 (fiscal 1991); $546,571 (fiscal
1990); $602,625 (fiscal 1989)
Assets: $9,901,660 (fiscal year
ending September 30, 1991);
$8,334,216 (fiscal 1990);
$8,542,375 (fiscal 1989)
Gifts Received: $225,000 (fiscal 1991); $200,000 (fiscal
1990); $125,000 (fiscal 1989)
Fiscal Note: In 1991, contributions were received from Beth
K. Stocker.
EIN: 34-1293603

CONTRIBUTIONS SUMMARY
Donor(s): Beth K. Stocker
Typical Recipients: • *Arts &
Humanities:* dance, museums/galleries, music • *Civic &
Public Affairs:* environmental
affairs, urban & community affairs, zoos/botanical gardens
• *Education:* community & junior colleges, private education
(precollege), public education
(precollege) • *Health:* health organizations, hospices, medical
research, mental health, pediatric health, single-disease
health associations • *Social
Services:* aged, child welfare,
community service organizations, disabled, drugs & alcohol, family planning, family
services, legal aid, united
funds, youth organizations
Grant Types: capital, emergency, endowment, multiyear/continuing support, operating expenses, project, research,
scholarship, and seed money
Geographic Distribution:
focus on Lorain County, OH,
and Tucson, AZ

GIVING OFFICERS
Mary Ann Dobras: trust
Sara Jane Norton: secy, treas,
dir, trust
Mrs. Beth K. Stocker: pres,
trust
Anne Woodling: trust
Nancy Elizabeth Woodling:
trust

APPLICATION INFORMATION

Initial Approach: Send brief letter describing program. Deadlines are February 1, May 15, and October 1.

Restrictions on Giving: Does not support individuals or provide loans.

OTHER THINGS TO KNOW

Publications: Application Guidelines, Informational Brochure (including application guidelines)

GRANTS ANALYSIS

Number of Grants: 94

Highest Grant: $20,000

Typical Range: $1,000 to $10,000

Disclosure Period: fiscal year ending September 30, 1991

RECENT GRANTS

20,000 Lorain County Community College, Lorain, OH

15,000 Heart of Texas Hospice, Belton, TX

12,500 Tucson Shalom House, Tucson, AZ

10,026 Vocational Guidance Services, Cleveland, OH

10,000 Alliance for the Mentally Ill, Tucson, AZ

10,000 Legal Aid Society, Elyria, OH

6,500 Community Foundation of Greater Lorain County, Lorain, OH

5,525 Cleveland Ballet, Cleveland, OH

5,510 Family Services Association of Lorain, Lorain, OH

5,500 Community Foundation of Greater Lorain County, Lorain, OH

Stockham Valves & Fittings / Stockham Foundation, William H. & Kate F.

Sales: $120.0 million
Employees: 1,350
Headquarters: Birmingham, AL
SIC Major Group: Fabricated Metal Products and Primary Metal Industries

---

CONTACT

Herbert Stockham
Secretary
Stockham Valves & Fittings
PO Box 10326
Birmingham, AL 35202
(205) 592-6361

FINANCIAL SUMMARY

Recent Giving: $311,128 (1991); $364,081 (1990); $331,456 (1989)

Assets: $3,498,025 (1991); $3,466,793 (1990); $3,856,540 (1989)

Gifts Received: $112,396 (1989)

Fiscal Note: Contributes through foundation only.

EIN: 63-6049787

CONTRIBUTIONS SUMMARY

Typical Recipients: • *Arts & Humanities:* museums/galleries • *Civic & Public Affairs:* better government, business/free enterprise, law & justice, philanthropic organizations, professional & trade associations • *Education:* career/vocational education, colleges & universities, community & junior colleges, student aid • *Social Services:* united funds

Grant Types: award, capital, challenge, emergency, multiyear/continuing support, and scholarship

Geographic Distribution: giving primarily in Alabama

Operating Locations: AL (Birmingham)

CORP. OFFICERS

Larry Kinderman: *CURR EMPL* exec vp, coo: Stockham Valves & Fittings

Herbert C. Stockham: *B* 1928 *ED* Lehigh Univ BS 1949 *CURR EMPL* chmn: Stockham Valves & Fittings *CORP AFFIL* dir: Southtrust Bank, Southtrust Corp

GIVING OFFICERS

Larry Kinderman: trust *CURR EMPL* exec vp, coo: Stockham Valves & Fittings (see above)

Virginia S. Ladd: trust

Charles E. Stockham: trust

Herbert C. Stockham: chmn, trust *CURR EMPL* chmn: Stockham Valves & Fittings (see above)

Kate Stockham: trust

Richard J. Stockham, Jr.: trust *CURR EMPL* dir: Stockham Valves & Fittings *CORP*

AFFIL dir: Stockham Valves & Fittings Inc

APPLICATION INFORMATION

Initial Approach: *Initial Contact:* a brief letter of inquiry *Include Information On:* a description of organization, amount requested, purpose of funds sought, and proof of tax-exempt status *When to Submit:* any time

Restrictions on Giving: Awards are expressly limited to religious, charitable, scientific, literary, or educational purposes primarily for the benefit of needy persons; and religious, educational, scientific, and charitable institutions, within the United States and primarily to the Southeastern section. Scholarships and fellowships are limited to employees past, present and future, and their dependents.

GRANTS ANALYSIS

Total Grants: $311,128

Number of Grants: 47*

Highest Grant: $65,000

Typical Range: $500 to $10,000

Disclosure Period: 1991

Note: Number of grants and average grant figures do not include scholarships and fellowships to individuals totaling $38,093. Recent grants are derived from a 1991 grants list.

RECENT GRANTS

65,000 United Way, Birmingham, AL

50,000 Birmingham Southern College, Birmingham, AL

25,000 Children's Hospital of Alabama, Birmingham, AL

15,000 Birmingham Museum of Art, Birmingham, AL

12,875 Stockham Literacy Program, Stockham, AL

10,000 Junior Achievement, Birmingham, AL

10,000 National Right to Work Legal Defense Foundation, Springfield, VA

10,000 Samford University, Tuscaloosa, AL

10,000 YMCA, Birmingham, AL

5,000 American Security Council Education Foundation, Boston, MA

Stoddard Charitable Trust

CONTACT

Warren S. Fletcher
Secretary and Treasurer
Stoddard Charitable Trust
370 Main St., 12th Fl.
Worcester, MA 01608
(508) 798-8621

FINANCIAL SUMMARY

Recent Giving: $2,470,000 (1991); $3,205,500 (1990); $3,109,000 (1989)

Assets: $37,379,556 (1991); $39,164,894 (1990); $51,689,534 (1989)

Gifts Received: $170,586 (1991); $2,037,201 (1990); $7,500 (1989)

Fiscal Note: In 1990 and 1991, the foundation received gifts from the estate of Paris Fletcher.

EIN: 04-6023791

CONTRIBUTIONS SUMMARY

Donor(s): Harry G. Stoddard established the Stoddard Charitable Trust in 1939 and was its principal donor. Mr. Stoddard (d. 1969) was chairman of Wyman Gordon Company and of the *Worcester Telegram and Gazette.* He was president of the Worcester Community Chest and a director of the Worcester YMCA and the Worcester Boys Club.

Typical Recipients: • *Arts & Humanities:* arts centers, history/historic preservation, museums/galleries, music, performing arts, public broadcasting, theater • *Civic & Public Affairs:* business/free enterprise, environmental affairs, housing, professional & trade associations • *Education:* arts education, colleges & universities, private education (precollege), science/technology education • *Social Services:* animal protection, child welfare, community service organizations, homes, shelters/homelessness, united funds, youth organizations

Grant Types: general support

Geographic Distribution: Worcester, MA, area

GIVING OFFICERS

Allen W. Fletcher: trust

Marion S. Fletcher: trust, asst treas, don daughter

Warner S. Fletcher: chmn, trust *B* Worcester MA 1945 *ED*

Williams Coll BA 1967; Boston Univ JD 1973 *CURR EMPL* atty: Fletcher Tilton Whipple *NONPR AFFIL* mem: Am Bar Assn, MA Bar Assn, Worcester County Bar Assn
Judith S. King: trust, treas
Valerie S. Loring: trust, secy
Helen E. Stoddard: vchmn, trust

APPLICATION INFORMATION
Initial Approach:
The trust does not provide application forms or publish application guidelines. Initial contact should be by letter.
Four copies of a proposal must be submitted. They should include a description of the requesting organization and its total budget, amount needed, and a projected budget. Proof of tax exemption also should be included.
Applications may be submitted any time. There are no deadlines for requests.
The trust acknowledges receipt of an application. An interview may be required. The decision-making process takes about three months.
Restrictions on Giving: The trust makes no grants to individuals. It rarely makes grants to organizations outside the Worcester, MA, area.

GRANTS ANALYSIS
Total Grants: $2,470,000
Number of Grants: 70
Highest Grant: $325,000
Typical Range: $1,000 to $50,000 and $100,000 to $250,000
Disclosure Period: 1991
Note: Recent grants are derived from a fiscal 1991 Form 990.

RECENT GRANTS
325,000 Worcester Polytechnic Institute, Worcester, MA
300,000 Worcester Art Museum, Worcester, MA
150,000 New England Science Center, Worcester, MA
150,000 Salem Community Corporation, Worcester, MA
100,000 Clark University, Worcester, MA
100,000 Worcester County Horticultural Society, Boylston, MA
100,000 YWCA of Central Massachusetts, Worcester, MA

75,000 Nichols College, Dudley, MA
75,000 Trustees of Reservations, Beverly, MA
75,000 Worcester Girls Club, Worcester, MA

Stokely, Jr. Foundation, William B.

CONTACT
William B. Stokely, III
President
William B. Stokely, Jr. Fdn.
620 Campbell Sta. Rd., Ste. 27
Knoxville, TN 37922
(615) 966-4878

FINANCIAL SUMMARY
Recent Giving: $466,943 (1991); $410,504 (1990); $406,855 (1989)
Assets: $9,120,682 (1991); $7,873,714 (1990); $8,230,909 (1989)
EIN: 35-6016402

CONTRIBUTIONS SUMMARY
Donor(s): the late William B. Stokely, Jr
Typical Recipients: • *Arts & Humanities:* arts festivals, community arts, libraries, museums/galleries, music • *Civic & Public Affairs:* environmental affairs • *Education:* colleges & universities • *Health:* hospitals, medical research, pediatric health, single-disease health associations • *Religion:* churches • *Social Services:* child welfare, recreation & athletics, shelters/homelessness, youth organizations
Grant Types: general support
Geographic Distribution: focus on eastern TN

GIVING OFFICERS
Horace Burnett: off
Stacy S. Byerly: dir
Kay H. Stokely: exec vp, dir
William B. Stokely III: pres, dir
William B. Stokely IV: dir
Cathlin E. Sullivan: asst treas, asst secy
Andrea A. White-Randall: vp, secy, treas

APPLICATION INFORMATION
Initial Approach: Send letter of inquiry or full proposal. Submit proposal preferably in the

fall. Board meets in February, May, August, and November.
Restrictions on Giving: Does not support individuals.

GRANTS ANALYSIS
Number of Grants: 92
Highest Grant: $75,000
Typical Range: $500 to $5,000
Disclosure Period: 1991

RECENT GRANTS
75,000 University of Tennessee, Knoxville, TN
50,000 Little League Baseball, Williamsport, TN
40,000 Knoxville Museum of Art, Knoxville, TN
25,000 East Tennessee Foundation, Knoxville, TN
15,000 University of Tennessee, Knoxville, TN
15,000 University of Tennessee, Knoxville, TN
12,500 Indianapolis Museum of Art, Indianapolis, IN
10,000 Knoxville Symphony Orchestra, Knoxville, TN
10,000 United Way, Knoxville, TN
5,000 Carter Center, Atlanta, GA

Stokes Foundation, Lydia B.

CONTACT
Joyce N. Portnoy
Lydia B. Stokes Fdn.
3400 Centre Sq. West
Philadelphia, PA 19102
(215) 981-2383

FINANCIAL SUMMARY
Recent Giving: $142,000 (1990)
Assets: $3,106,546 (1990)
EIN: 21-6016107

CONTRIBUTIONS SUMMARY
Geographic Distribution: focus on the NJ and Philadelphia, PA area

APPLICATION INFORMATION
Initial Approach: Send brief letter requesting application. There are no deadlines.

GRANTS ANALYSIS
Disclosure Period: 1990

Note: No grants list was provided for 1990.

Stone Charitable Foundation

CONTACT
Stephen A. Stone
President
Stone Charitable Fdn.
PO Box 728
Wareham, MA 02571
(508) 759-3503

FINANCIAL SUMMARY
Recent Giving: $352,650 (fiscal 1991); $368,950 (fiscal 1989); $351,486 (fiscal 1988)
Assets: $6,408,031 (fiscal year ending November 30, 1991); $5,912,485 (fiscal 1989); $5,236,726 (fiscal 1988)
Gifts Received: $450,000 (fiscal 1991)
Fiscal Note: In 1991, contributions were received from Stephen A. Stone ($25,000), Thelma Finn ($35,000), and the Estate of Anne Stone ($400,000).
EIN: 04-6114683

CONTRIBUTIONS SUMMARY
Donor(s): the late Dewey D. Stone, Stephen A. Stone, Anne A. Stone, Thelma Finn, Jack Finn, the late Harry K. Stone
Typical Recipients: • *Arts & Humanities:* history/historic preservation, libraries, museums/galleries, music • *Civic & Public Affairs:* ethnic/minority organizations, philanthropic organizations • *Education:* colleges & universities, education associations • *Health:* health organizations, hospitals • *Religion:* religious organizations • *Social Services:* child welfare, family planning, family services, youth organizations
Grant Types: capital, endowment, and general support
Geographic Distribution: focus on MA

GIVING OFFICERS
Alford P. Rudnick: treas, trust
Stephen A. Stone: pres, trust *ED* Univ MI 1938; Harvard Univ 1939 *CURR EMPL* pres: Agawam Farms *CORP AFFIL* dir: Malden Trust Co; pres: Agawam Farms Inc
Theodore Herzl Teplow: secy, trust *ED* US Merchant Marine Academy BS 1950; Harvard Univ MBA 1953 *CORP AFFIL* consultant: Crosby Valve &

Gage Co *NONPR AFFIL* trust: Am Merchant Marine Mus Fdn; vchmn, trust: Hebrew Coll MA

APPLICATION INFORMATION

Initial Approach: Send brief letter of inquiry describing program or project. There are no deadlines.
Restrictions on Giving: Does not support individuals.

GRANTS ANALYSIS

Number of Grants: 48
Highest Grant: $65,000
Typical Range: $250 to $5,000
Disclosure Period: fiscal year ending November 30, 1991

RECENT GRANTS

65,000 American Committee for the Weizmann Institute, New York, NY
60,000 New Israel Fund, Boston, MA
42,000 Jewish Family and Children's Services, Boston, MA
40,000 Hebrew College, Boston, MA
15,000 Americans for Peace Now, New York, NY
15,000 Project Nishma, Boston, MA
11,000 Tobey Health Systems, Boston, MA
10,000 American Friends of Hebrew University, New York, NY
10,000 Brandeis University, Waltham, MA
10,000 Fuller Museum of Art, Boston, MA

Stone Container Corp. / Stone Foundation

Sales: $5.55 billion
Employees: 31,000
Headquarters: Chicago, IL
SIC Major Group: Industrial Machinery & Equipment, Oil & Gas Extraction, Paper & Allied Products, and Rubber & Miscellaneous Plastics Products

CONTACT

Jerome N. Stone
Vice President, Secretary, Treasurer
Stone Fdn.
150 N Michigan Ave.
Chicago, IL 60601
(312) 346-6600

FINANCIAL SUMMARY

Recent Giving: $943,537 (1990); $723,643 (1989); $732,825 (1988)
Assets: $3,375,991 (1990); $1,382,766 (1989)
Fiscal Note: Company gives through foundation only.
EIN: 36-6063761

CONTRIBUTIONS SUMMARY

Typical Recipients: • *Arts & Humanities:* arts centers, arts institutes, history/historic preservation, museums/galleries, music, opera, public broadcasting, theater • *Civic & Public Affairs:* business/free enterprise, economic development, environmental affairs, ethnic/minority organizations, international affairs, philanthropic organizations, urban & community affairs, women's affairs, zoos/botanical gardens • *Education:* arts education, business education, career/vocational education, colleges & universities, economic education, education associations, education funds, legal education, minority education, private education (precollege), science/technology education, student aid • *Health:* hospitals, medical rehabilitation, medical research, mental health, pediatric health, single-disease health associations • *Social Services:* child welfare, community centers, disabled, family planning, food/clothing distribution, legal aid, religious welfare, shelters/homelessness, united funds, volunteer services, youth organizations
Grant Types: capital, general support, and project
Geographic Distribution: emphasis on Chicago, IL, area; also to national organizations
Operating Locations: AL (Birmingham), AR (Jacksonville, Little Rock, Rogers), AZ (Phoenix, Snowflake, Tempe), CA (City of Industry, Santa Fe Springs), CO (Denver), CT (Torrington, Uncasville), FL (Cantonment, Orlando, Panama City, Yulee), GA (Atlanta, Lithonia, Port Wentworth, Sa-

vannah), IA (Des Moines, Keokuk, Sioux City), IL (Bedford Park, Chicago, Herrin, Joliet, North Chicago, Oak Brook, Zion), IN (Columbus, Indianapolis, Mishawaka), KY (Louisville), LA (Arcadia, Hodge, Martinsville, New Orleans), MA (Westfield), MD (Savage), MI (Detroit, Melvindale, Ontonagon), MN (Minneapolis, Rochester, St. Cloud, St. Paul), MO (Blue Springs, Kansas City, Liberty, St. Joseph, St. Louis), MS (Jackson, Tupelo), NC (Charlotte, Lexington), NJ (Teterboro), NM (Albuquerque), OH (Cleveland, Coshocton, Mansfield, New Philadelphia, Worthington), OK (Sand Springs), OR (Jefferson, Medford), PA (Philadelphia, Williamsport, York), SC (Columbia, Florence, Orangeburg), TN (Chattanooga, Clarksville), TX (Dallas, El Paso, Grand Prairie, Tyler), UT (Salt Lake City), VA (Hopewell, Martinsville, Richmond, Sandston)

CORP. OFFICERS

Roger Warren Stone: *B* Chicago IL 1935 *ED* Univ PA BS 1957 *CURR EMPL* chmn, ceo, dir: Stone Container Corp *CORP AFFIL* chmn: Stone-Consolidated; dir: Am Appraisal Assocs, First Chicago Corp, First Natl Bank Chicago, Gen Tel & Electric Corp, GTE Corp, McDonalds Corp, Morton Intl, Thiokol Corp; vp: Intl Design Corp *NONPR AFFIL* bd overseers: Univ PA Wharton Sch Bus; fellow: Lake Forest Academy; mem: Chicago Comm, Chicago Counc Foreign Rels, Mid-Am Comm; trust: Chicago Symphony Orchestra Assn, Inst Paper Science Tech

GIVING OFFICERS

Jerome N. Stone: vp, secy, treas *B* Chicago IL 1913 *ED* Northwestern Univ 1934; DePaul Univ *CORP AFFIL* dir: GRI Corp, Lypho-Med, Solar Press
Marvin N. Stone: dir *B* Chicago IL 1909 *ED* Northwestern Univ
Roger Warren Stone: pres *CURR EMPL* chmn, ceo, dir: Stone Container Corp (see above)

APPLICATION INFORMATION

Initial Approach: *Initial Contact:* brief letter or proposal *In-*

clude Information On: description of the organization, amount requested, purpose for which funds are sought, recently audited financial statement, proof of tax-exempt status *When to Submit:* any time *Note:* Deadline for scholarship applications is April 1.
Restrictions on Giving: Scholarships are available only to children of active, full-time employees with more than two years service to the company.

GRANTS ANALYSIS

Total Grants: $943,537
Number of Grants: 84*
Highest Grant: $254,150
Typical Range: $1,000 to $5,000
Disclosure Period: 1990
Note: Number of grants and average grant figures do not reflect 36 scholarships to employee children totaling $55,000. Recent grants are derived from a 1990 Form 990.

RECENT GRANTS

369,333 Jewish United Fund of Metropolitan Chicago, Chicago, IL
141,800 Jewish Community Centers
73,087 United Way
40,000 Orchestral Association
16,667 Leadership for Quality Education, Chicago, IL
10,500 Boys Clubs of America
10,000 Alzheimers Disease Association
10,000 Chicago Library Foundation, Chicago, IL
10,000 Governor's School of Science and Mathematics
10,000 St. Joseph's Hospital

Stone Family Foundation, Jerome H.

CONTACT

Jerome H. Stone Family Fdn.
150 North Michigan Ave.
Chicago, IL 60601

FINANCIAL SUMMARY

Recent Giving: $84,914 (1990); $171,349 (1989); $128,297 (1988)
Assets: $2,010,779 (1990); $3,056,850 (1989); $3,202,546 (1988)

EIN: 36-6061300

CONTRIBUTIONS SUMMARY
Donor(s): Jerome H. Stone, Cynthia Raskin
Typical Recipients: • *Arts & Humanities:* arts festivals, museums/galleries, opera, theater • *Education:* business education, colleges & universities • *Health:* medical research, mental health, single-disease health associations • *Religion:* religious organizations • *Social Services:* community service organizations, united funds
Grant Types: general support

GIVING OFFICERS
Ellen Stone Belic: dir
Cynthia Stone Raskin: secy
James Howard Stone: vp *B* Chicago IL 1939 *ED* Harvard Univ AB 1060; Harvard Univ MBA 1962 *CURR EMPL* fdr, pres, ceo: Stone Mgmt Corp *CORP AFFIL* chmn: Stone Petroleum Corp; dir: Hibernia Corp, Sheridan Beverage Co, Stone Container Corp *NONPR AFFIL* co-chmn: Natl Conf Christians Jews; co-chmn, planning comm: Hadley Sch Blind; mem: Chicago Comm, Harvard Univ Bus Sch Alumni Assn, Mid-Am Comm; mem visitor comm library: Univ Chicago; trust exec comm: Roosevelt Univ
Jerome H. Stone: pres *B* Chicago IL 1913 *ED* Northwestern Univ 1934; DePaul Univ *CORP AFFIL* chmn emeritus: Stone Container Corp; dir: GRI Corp, Lypho-Med, Solar Press *NONPR AFFIL* pres: Alzheimers Disease Related Disorders Assn

APPLICATION INFORMATION
Initial Approach: Contributes only to preselected organizations.

GRANTS ANALYSIS
Number of Grants: 78
Highest Grant: $16,667
Typical Range: $100 to $5,000
Disclosure Period: 1990

RECENT GRANTS
16,667 Stone Foundation
10,000 Alzheimer's Disease and Related Disorders Association, Chicago, IL — general purpose
7,000 Jewish United Fund, Chicago, IL
5,000 June Institute
5,000 Winnetka Public School Nursery, Winnetka, IL
4,660 Museum of Contemporary Art, Chicago, IL
3,160 Palm Springs Desert Museum, Palm Springs, CA
2,500 Lyric Opera of Chicago, Chicago, IL
2,400 Ravinia Festival Association, Highland Park, IL
2,000 Institute for Psychoanalysis, Chicago, IL

Stone Family Foundation, Norman H.

CONTACT
Marvin N. Stone
Norman H. Stone Family Fdn.
c/o Stone Container Corp.
150 North Michigan Ave.
Chicago, IL 60601
(312) 580-4632

FINANCIAL SUMMARY
Recent Giving: $111,352 (1990); $113,558 (1989); $88,938 (1988)
Assets: $1,786,671 (1990); $2,095,343 (1989); $1,905,643 (1988)
EIN: 36-6061301

CONTRIBUTIONS SUMMARY
Donor(s): the late Norman H. Stone, Ira Stone, Alan Stone
Typical Recipients: • *Civic & Public Affairs:* ethnic/minority organizations • *Health:* mental health • *Religion:* religious organizations, synagogues • *Social Services:* child welfare, community service organizations, food/clothing distribution, recreation & athletics, shelters/homelessness, united funds, youth organizations
Grant Types: general support
Geographic Distribution: focus on IL

GIVING OFFICERS
Judi H. Stern: vp
Alan Stone: pres, don *B* Chicago IL 1928 *ED* Univ PA BSE 1951 *CURR EMPL* sen vp, gen mgr, dir: Stone Container Corp *CORP AFFIL* pres: Abbyville & Grimes RR, Apache RR, Atlanta & St Andrews RR *NONPR AFFIL* trust: Brewster Academy
Ida F. Stone: dir, vp

Ira N. Stone: vp, secy *B* 1932 *ED* Univ PA BSE 1954 *CURR EMPL* svp, dir: Stone Container Corp *CORP AFFIL* pres: Stone Container Intl

APPLICATION INFORMATION
Initial Approach: Contributes only to preselected organizations. Applications not accepted.

GRANTS ANALYSIS
Number of Grants: 90
Highest Grant: $40,460
Typical Range: $50 to $1,000
Disclosure Period: 1990

RECENT GRANTS
40,460 Emergency Fund for Needy People, Chicago, IL
15,000 US Emergency Appeal Stone Foundation, Chicago, IL
10,500 GIRF, Chicago, IL
6,865 Jewish United Fund, Chicago, IL
6,350 Congregational Kol Ami, Chicago, IL
6,087 United Way, Chicago, IL
5,000 U of C for Emotional Disturbed Children, Chicago, IL
3,250 Alzheimer's and Related Disorders Association, Chicago, IL
2,500 Brewster Academy, Chicago, IL
2,000 Ravinia Festival Association, Highland Park, IL

Stone Forest Industries
Sales: $210.0 million
Employees: 1,450
Parent Company: Stone Container Corp.
Headquarters: Chicago, IL
SIC Major Group: Lumber & Wood Products

CONTACT
Gerald M. Freeman
President
Stone Forest Industries
150 North Michigan Ave.
Chicago, IL 60601
(312) 346-6600

CONTRIBUTIONS SUMMARY
Operating Locations: IL (Chicago)

CORP. OFFICERS
Gerald M. Freeman: *CURR EMPL* pres: Stone Forest Indus
Roger Warren Stone: *B* Chicago IL 1935 *ED* Univ PA BS 1957 *CURR EMPL* chmn, ceo, dir: Stone Container Corp *CORP AFFIL* chmn: Stone-Consolidated; dir: Am Appraisal Assocs, First Chicago Corp, First Natl Bank Chicago, Gen Tel & Electric Corp, GTE Corp, McDonalds Corp, Morton Intl, Thiokol Corp; vp: Intl Design Corp *NONPR AFFIL* bd overseers: Univ PA Wharton Sch Bus; fellow: Lake Forest Academy; mem: Chicago Comm, Chicago Counc Foreign Rels, Mid-Am Comm; trust: Chicago Symphony Orchestra Assn, Inst Paper Science Tech

OTHER THINGS TO KNOW
Publications: Policy on Contributions

Stone Foundation

CONTACT
Robert B. Milligan, Jr.
Secretary-Treasurer
Stone Fdn.
25 Ford Rd., Ste. 200
Westport, CT 06880
(203) 227-2000

FINANCIAL SUMMARY
Recent Giving: $188,818 (1991); $254,415 (1990); $231,242 (1989)
Assets: $10,220,079 (1991); $8,180,354 (1990); $8,540,984 (1989)
EIN: 23-7148468

CONTRIBUTIONS SUMMARY
Donor(s): the late Marion H. Stone, the late Charles Lynn Stone
Typical Recipients: • *Civic & Public Affairs:* philanthropic organizations, zoos/botanical gardens • *Education:* colleges & universities, medical education, private education (precollege) • *Health:* nursing services • *Social Services:* drugs & alcohol
Grant Types: capital, endowment, and general support
Geographic Distribution: focus on CT and NY

GIVING OFFICERS
Paul W. Adams: trust
Robert B. Milligan, Jr.: trust, secy, treas

Mary Stone Payson: trust
Charles Lynn Stone, Jr.: trust, pres
Edward Eldredge Stone: trust, vp
Sara S. Stone: trust

APPLICATION INFORMATION

Initial Approach: Funds presently committed; grant requests only from qualified medical schools, colleges, and universities.
Restrictions on Giving: Does not support individuals.

OTHER THINGS TO KNOW

Publications: Application Guidelines

GRANTS ANALYSIS

Number of Grants: 7
Highest Grant: $50,000
Typical Range: $7,500 to $25,000
Disclosure Period: 1991

RECENT GRANTS

50,000 Bok Tower Gardens
50,000 Columbia School of Nursing
37,500 East Woods School
26,761 Alcoholism and Drug Dependency
16,357 Norwalk Maritime Center, Norwalk, CT
7,500 Hastings College, Omaha, NE
700 Foundation Center

Stone Foundation, David S.

CONTACT

Shelton Binstock
President
David S. Stone Fdn.
1140 Connecticut Avenue, N.W. Ste. 703
Washington, DC 20036
(202) 785-1111

FINANCIAL SUMMARY

Recent Giving: $116,400 (1991); $112,000 (1990); $145,000 (1989)
Assets: $2,463,142 (1991); $2,272,488 (1990); $2,351,944 (1989)
EIN: 52-1120708

CONTRIBUTIONS SUMMARY

Typical Recipients: • *Arts & Humanities:* history/historic preservation, museums/galleries • *Civic & Public Affairs:* ethnic/minority organizations

• *Education:* private education (precollege) • *Health:* pediatric health • *International:* international organizations • *Religion:* religious organizations • *Social Services:* aged, child welfare, community centers, homes, youth organizations
Grant Types: general support
Geographic Distribution: focus on Washington, DC; Toledo, OH; and Boca Raton, FL

GIVING OFFICERS

Irving Adler: dir, vp
Shelton M. Binstock: dir, pres
Ralph Cohen: dir, secy, treas *B* Bridgeport CT 1919 *CURR EMPL* co-chmn intl bd: Ampal Am Israil Corp *CORP AFFIL* dir: Israel Ampal Indus Devel Bank Ltd, Moriah Hotels Ltd *NONPR AFFIL* bd govs: Weizmann Inst; dir: New Outlook; trust: Israel Ctr Peace Middle East
David A. Katz: dir, vp

APPLICATION INFORMATION

Initial Approach: Send letter requesting application form. There are no deadlines.

GRANTS ANALYSIS

Number of Grants: 8
Highest Grant: $50,000
Typical Range: $5,000 to $10,000
Disclosure Period: 1991

RECENT GRANTS

50,000 Florence Fuller Child Development Center, Boca Raton, FL
25,000 Chelsea School, Chelsea, MA
10,000 National Holocaust Museum, Washington, DC
10,000 Toledo Community Jewish Fund, Toledo, OH
6,000 Bethesda Academy of Performing Arts, Bethesda, MD
5,400 Israel Tennis Centers Association, New York, NY
5,000 Make-A-Wish Foundation
5,000 Metro Police Boys and Girls Club

Stone Foundation, France

CONTACT

Joseph S. Heyman
President
France Stone Fdn.
1000 National Bank Bldg.
Toledo, OH 43604
(419) 241-2201

FINANCIAL SUMMARY

Recent Giving: $234,500 (1991); $412,950 (1989); $313,200 (1988)
Assets: $8,996,217 (1990); $7,766,446 (1989); $7,324,876 (1988)
EIN: 34-6523033

CONTRIBUTIONS SUMMARY

Donor(s): the late George A. France, The France Stone Co., and subsidiaries
Typical Recipients: • *Arts & Humanities:* community arts, museums/galleries, music, opera • *Education:* colleges & universities, medical education, private education (precollege) • *Health:* health organizations • *Religion:* churches • *Social Services:* child welfare, homes, united funds, youth organizations
Grant Types: capital, general support, multiyear/continuing support, research, and scholarship
Geographic Distribution: focus on OH, MI, and IN

GIVING OFFICERS

Andrew E. Anderson: secy, treas, trust
Joseph S. Heyman: pres, trust
Ollie J. Risner: vp, trust

APPLICATION INFORMATION

Initial Approach: Send cover letter and full proposal. There are no deadlines.
Restrictions on Giving: Does not support individuals.

GRANTS ANALYSIS

Number of Grants: 21
Highest Grant: $121,000
Typical Range: $1,000 to $5,000
Disclosure Period: 1991

RECENT GRANTS

121,000 Medical College of Ohio Foundation, Toledo, OH
22,500 Colorado State University, Ft. Collins, CO

22,000 Toledo Museum of Art, Toledo, OH
10,000 St. Patricks Historic Church, Toledo, OH
5,000 America College of Dentists Foundation, Bethesda, MD
5,000 Boys and Girls Club, Toledo, OH
5,000 Cummings Zucker Center, Toledo, OH
5,000 Friendly Center, Toledo, OH
5,000 Grady Home, Toledo, OH
5,000 St. Luke's Hospital Foundation, Toledo, OH

Stone Foundation, W. Clement and Jessie V.

CONTACT

Maree G. Bullock
Executive Director
W. Clement and Jessie V. Stone Fdn.
PO Box 649
Lake Forest, IL 60045
(708) 615-0228

FINANCIAL SUMMARY

Recent Giving: $140,000 (1990); $124,200 (1989)
Assets: $2,972,576 (1990); $2,359,082 (1989)
Gifts Received: $767,896 (1990); $800,445 (1989)
Fiscal Note: In 1989, contributions were received from W. Clement and Jessie V. Stone.
EIN: 36-2498125

CONTRIBUTIONS SUMMARY

Donor(s): W. Clement Stone, Jessie V. Stone
Typical Recipients: • *Social Services:* community service organizations, food/clothing distribution, shelters/homelessness
Grant Types: general support
Geographic Distribution: limited to Chicago, IL

GIVING OFFICERS

Maree G. Bullock: dir, exec dir
Sandra Stone Knecht: trust
James Thomas Rhind: trust *B* Chicago IL 1922 *ED* OH St Univ AB 1944; Harvard Univ LLB 1950 *CURR EMPL* ptnr: Bell Boyd & Lloyd *CORP AFFIL* dir: Griffith Labs, Kewaunee Scientific Corp, Lindberg Corp, Microseal Corp *NONPR AFFIL* comr: Un Presbyterian Church Gen Assem-

bly; life trust: Childrens Home
Aid Soc; mem: Am Bar Assn,
Chicago Bar Assn, Chicago
Counc Foreign Rels, Fed Bar
Assn, IL Bar Assn, Japan Am
Soc, Law Club Chicago, Legal
Club Chicago; trust: Presbyte-
rian Home, Univ Chicago
Hosps; vchmn, trust: Hamilton
Coll, Northwestern Univ As-
socs, Univ Chicago
Linda E. Rupp: trust
Barbara Stone: dir, vp
Barbara West Stone: trust
Jessie V. Stone: dir, vp
Michael Stone: trust
Norah Sharp Stone: trust
Steven Stone: dir, vp, secy,
treas
William Clement Stone: dir,
chmn *B* Chicago IL 1902 *ED*
Monmouth Coll JD 1963; Inter-
lochen Arts Academy HHD
1964; DePaul Univ LHD 1970;
Whittier Coll LLD 1973; De-
troit Coll Law LLD 1983
CURR EMPL chmn emeritus,
dir: Aon Corp *CORP AFFIL*
chmn: Walter V Clark & Assocs, Combined Life Ins Co
Am, Combined Life Ins Co Ireland, Combined Life Ins Co
NY, Health Res Corp, W Clement Stone PMA Commun; dir:
Alberto-Culver Co *NONPR
AFFIL* chmn bd trusts: Interlochen Arts Academy, Religious Heritage Am; hon chmn
bd: Chicago Boys Girls Club;
life dir: Insts Religion Health;
life mem bd mgrs: Robert R
McCormick Chicago Boys
Club; mem: Intl Assn Health
Underwriters; mem exec
comm: Intl Federation Keystone Youth Org; natl exec
comm: Religious Heritage Am

**APPLICATION
INFORMATION**
Initial Approach: Contributes
only to preselected organizations.
Restrictions on Giving: Does
not support individuals.

**OTHER THINGS TO
KNOW**
Publications: Annual Report,
Informational Brochure

GRANTS ANALYSIS
Number of Grants: 6
Highest Grant: $42,000
Typical Range: $5,000 to
$35,000
Disclosure Period: 1990

RECENT GRANTS
42,000 St. Martin de Por-
res House of Hope,

Chicago, IL — gen-
eral support
40,000 Community Sup-
portive Living Sys-
tems, Chicago, IL
— general support
35,000 Chicago Coalition
for the Homeless,
Chicago, IL — gen-
eral support
10,000 Housing Opportuni-
ties for Women,
Chicago, IL — gen-
eral support
8,000 New Moms, Chi-
cago, IL — general
support
5,000 Lakefront Single
Room Occupancy
Corporation, Chi-
cago, IL — general
support

Stone Fund, Albert
H. and Reuben S.

CONTACT
Carlton E. Nichols
Trustee
Albert H. and Reuben S. Stone
Fund
c/o Mechanics Bank
PO Box 15073
Worcester, MA 01615-0073
(617) 632-2770

FINANCIAL SUMMARY
Recent Giving: $168,350
(1991); $209,375 (1990);
$138,900 (1989)
Assets: $3,051,518 (1991);
$2,886,033 (1990); $3,126,744
(1989)
EIN: 04-6050419

**CONTRIBUTIONS
SUMMARY**
Grant Types: scholarship
Geographic Distribution: lim-
ited to residents of Gardner,
MA

GIVING OFFICERS
James Kenary: trust
Carlton E. Nichols, Jr.: trust
Carlton E. Nichols, Sr.: trust

**APPLICATION
INFORMATION**
Initial Approach: Send letter
requesting application form.
Deadline is early in the second
semester.

**OTHER THINGS TO
KNOW**
Provides higher education
scholarships for local residents.

GRANTS ANALYSIS
Disclosure Period: 1991

Note: 1991 grants list not
provided.

Stone Trust, H.
Chase

CONTACT
H. Chase Stone Trust
c/o Affiliated National Bank
PO Box 1699
Colorado Springs, CO 80942
(719) 471-5000

FINANCIAL SUMMARY
Recent Giving: $99,608
(1991); $102,400 (1990);
$90,512 (1989)
Assets: $2,558,360 (1991);
$2,226,155 (1990); $2,226,548
(1989)
EIN: 84-6066113

**CONTRIBUTIONS
SUMMARY**
Typical Recipients: • *Arts &
Humanities:* arts centers, muse-
ums/galleries, music, opera
• *Civic & Public Affairs:* municipalities • *Education:* colleges & universities, private
education (precollege)
• *Health:* health organizations,
medical research, single-disease health associations • *Social Services:* community service organizations, united funds,
youth organizations
Grant Types: general support
Geographic Distribution: limited to El Paso County, CO.

GIVING OFFICERS
**Affiliated National Bank
Trust Department:** trust

**APPLICATION
INFORMATION**
Initial Approach: Send brief
letter describing program.
Deadlines are April 30 and Oc-
tober 31.
Restrictions on Giving: Does
not support individuals.

GRANTS ANALYSIS
Number of Grants: 21
Highest Grant: $15,000
Typical Range: $1,000 to
$10,000
Disclosure Period: 1991

RECENT GRANTS
15,000 Colorado College,
Colorado Springs,
CO
10,000 Penrose-St. Francis
Healthcare Founda-
tion, Colorado
Springs, CO — for
Penrose Cancer
Center

10,000 Pikes Peak Chapter
American Red
Cross, Colorado
Springs, CO — for
operating expenses
10,000 Webb-Waring Lung
Institute, Denver,
CO
6,523 University of Colo-
rado, Boulder, CO
5,000 Assistance League
of Colorado
Springs, Colorado
Springs, CO — to
provide clothing
for needy school
children
5,000 Colorado Opera
Festival, Colorado
Springs, CO — for
the 1991 summer
production ex-
penses
5,000 Pikes Peak Y/USO,
Colorado Springs,
CO — for the city-
wide Gulf War Pro-
gram
5,000 Pikes Peak Y/USO,
Colorado Springs,
CO — for the
Youth Leadership
Institute
5,000 United Sates Space
Foundation, Colo-
rado Springs, CO
— for teacher edu-
cation program

Stone & Webster,
Inc.

Revenue: $273.24 million
Employees: 8,000
Headquarters: New York, NY
SIC Major Group: Engineering
& Management Services,
General Building Contractors,
Heavy Construction Except
Building Construction, and
Trucking & Warehousing

CONTACT
Laura Campbell
Secretary, Contributions
Committee
Stone & Webster, Inc.
PO Box 1244
New York, NY 10116
(212) 290-7462

FINANCIAL SUMMARY
Recent Giving: $500,000
(1991); $600,000 (1990)
Fiscal Note: Company gives directly.

**CONTRIBUTIONS
SUMMARY**
Typical Recipients: • *Arts &
Humanities:* arts centers
• *Civic & Public Affairs:* busi-
ness/free enterprise • *Educa-
tion:* business education

• *Health:* health organizations
• *Social Services:* community centers
Grant Types: department, matching, multiyear/continuing support, professorship, and scholarship
Nonmonetary Support Types: loaned executives
Geographic Distribution: primarily New York, NY
Operating Locations: NY (New York)

CORP. OFFICERS
William Frederick Allen, Jr.: *B* North Kingstown RI 1919 *CURR EMPL* chmn, ceo, dir, pres: Stone & Webster *NONPR AFFIL* fellow: Am Soc Mechanical Engrs; mem: Engg Soc New England, Natl Academy Engg, Sigma Xi, Tau Beta Pi; natl bd mem: Jr Achievement; trust: Northeastern Univ
Walter F. Sullivan: *CURR EMPL* pres, dir: Stone & Webster

APPLICATION INFORMATION
Initial Approach: *Initial Approach:* Send brief letter of inquiry *Include Information On:* description of the organization, amount requested, purpose of funds sought, audited financial statement, and proof of tax-exempt status. *When to Submit:* Any time
Restrictions on Giving: Does not support political or lobbying groups.

GRANTS ANALYSIS
Total Grants: $500,000
Typical Range: $1,000 to $2,500
Disclosure Period: 1991

Stonecutter Mills Corp. / Stonecutter Foundation
Sales: $78.0 million
Employees: 1,200
Headquarters: Spindale, NC
SIC Major Group: Textile Mill Products and Wholesale Trade—Nondurable Goods

CONTACT
V. H. Lonan
Treasurer
Stonecutter Foundation
300 Dallas St.
Spindale, NC 28160
(704) 286-2341

FINANCIAL SUMMARY
Recent Giving: $230,000 (fiscal 1992); $162,855 (fiscal 1991); $249,162 (fiscal 1990)
Assets: $6,297,447 (fiscal year ending March 31, 1992); $6,080,752 (fiscal 1991); $5,493,547 (fiscal 1990)
Gifts Received: $39,700 (fiscal 1992); $26,155 (fiscal 1991); $27,574 (fiscal 1990)
Fiscal Note: In 1991, contributions were received from Stonecutter Mills Corporation.
EIN: 56-6044820

CONTRIBUTIONS SUMMARY
Typical Recipients: • *Civic & Public Affairs:* civil rights • *Education:* colleges & universities, community & junior colleges, education associations, education funds, elementary education, private education (precollege), religious education • *Religion:* churches, religious organizations • *Social Services:* child welfare, community service organizations, homes, united funds, youth organizations
Grant Types: general support
Operating Locations: NC (Spindale)

CORP. OFFICERS
Ivy Cowan, Sr.: *CURR EMPL* sr chmn: Stonecutter Mills Corp
James R. Cowan: *CURR EMPL* chmn, ceo: Stonecutter Mills Corp
James M. Perry: *CURR EMPL* pres: Stonecutter Mills Corp

GIVING OFFICERS
James R. Cowan: vp, dir *CURR EMPL* chmn, ceo: Stonecutter Mills Corp (see above)
H. W. Crenshaw: dir
Z. E. Dobbins: pres, dir
V. H. Lonan: treas
Adin Henry Rucker, Jr.: vp, dir *B* Rutherfordton NC 1937 *ED* Univ NC 1959-1960 *CURR EMPL* sr vp, treas, cfo: Stonecutter Mills Corp *CORP AFFIL* sr vp, treas, cfo: Stonecutter Mills Corp
Mark L. Summey: dir
K. S. Tanner, Jr.: dir *CORP AFFIL* dir: Stonecutter Mills Corp

T. P. Walker: secy *CURR EMPL* sr vp, secy, dir: Stonecutter Mills Corp *CORP AFFIL* sr vp, secy, dir: Stonecutter Mills Corp

APPLICATION INFORMATION
Initial Approach: Send brief letter describing program. There are no deadlines.

GRANTS ANALYSIS
Number of Grants: 53
Highest Grant: $100,000
Typical Range: $1,000 to $5,000
Disclosure Period: fiscal year ending March 31, 1992
Note: Above does not include scholarships to individuals.

RECENT GRANTS
100,000	Isothermal Community College Foundation, Spindale, NC
12,500	Gardner-Webb College, Boiling Springs, NC
10,000	National Right to Work Legal Defense Fund, Springfield, VA
10,000	Spindale First United Methodist Church, Spindale, NC
7,000	Spindale Elementary School, Spindale, NC
5,000	Main Street Baptist Church, NC
5,000	Southmountain Children's Home, NC
5,000	Spencer Baptist Church, NC
5,000	Students for America
5,000	Warren Wilson College, Swannanoa, NC

Stoneman Charitable Foundation, Anne and David

CONTACT
Ala H. Reid
Treasurer
Anne and David Stoneman Charitable Fdn.
c/o Grants Mgmt. Associates
230 Congress St.
Boston, MA 02110
(617) 426-7172

FINANCIAL SUMMARY
Recent Giving: $244,550 (fiscal 1991); $157,618 (fiscal 1990); $357,877 (fiscal 1989)
Assets: $1,952,781 (fiscal year ending July 31, 1991); $1,946,145 (fiscal 1990); $1,844,806 (fiscal 1989)
Gifts Received: $166,218 (fiscal 1991); $159,465 (fiscal 1990); $135,923 (fiscal 1989)
Fiscal Note: In 1991, contributions were received from the Stoneman Charitable Lead Trust.
EIN: 04-6047379

CONTRIBUTIONS SUMMARY
Donor(s): Anne Stoneman
Typical Recipients: • *Arts & Humanities:* community arts, music • *Civic & Public Affairs:* civil rights, ethnic/minority organizations, municipalities, philanthropic organizations • *Education:* colleges & universities • *Health:* hospitals • *Religion:* churches, religious organizations • *Social Services:* community service organizations, youth organizations
Grant Types: general support

GIVING OFFICERS
Elizabeth DeKnatel: trust
Jean R. Fitzpatrick: trust
William G. Michael: clerk
Ala H. Reid: treas
Alan Rottenberg: trust
Robert Smith: trust
Eric Stein: trust
Jane Stein: trust
Miriam H. Stoneman: pres

APPLICATION INFORMATION
Initial Approach: Send brief letter describing program. There are no deadlines.
Restrictions on Giving: Does not support individuals.

GRANTS ANALYSIS
Number of Grants: 61
Highest Grant: $17,000
Typical Range: $250 to $10,000
Disclosure Period: fiscal year ending July 31, 1991

RECENT GRANTS

- 17,000 Jewish Federation, Boston, MA
- 16,500 Combined Jewish Philanthropies, Boston, MA
- 15,000 Dimock Community Hospital, Dimock, MA
- 15,000 Dudley Street Neighborhood, Boston, MA
- 15,000 Wilson Community, Boston, MA
- 12,500 Boston Community, Boston, MA
- 12,000 Presbyterian Church, Boston, MA
- 10,000 Steppingstone Foundation, Boston, MA
- 10,000 Teens As Community, Boston, MA
- 10,000 Youthbuild Boston, Boston, MA

Stonestreet Trust, Eusebia S.

CONTACT
Eusebia S. Stonestreet Trust
c/o NationsBank of Texas
PO Box 1317
Ft. Worth, TX 76101
(817) 390-6954

FINANCIAL SUMMARY
Recent Giving: $381,331 (fiscal 1991); $325,757 (fiscal 1990); $319,325 (fiscal 1989)
Assets: $5,423,566 (fiscal year ending October 31, 1991); $4,712,094 (fiscal 1990); $4,337,743 (fiscal 1988)
EIN: 75-6009142

CONTRIBUTIONS SUMMARY
Typical Recipients: • *Religion:* religious organizations • *Social Services:* child welfare, community service organizations, homes, youth organizations
Grant Types: general support
Geographic Distribution: focus on Fort Worth, TX

GIVING OFFICERS
NationsBank of Texas, N.A.: trust

APPLICATION INFORMATION
Initial Approach: Contributes only to preselected organizations.

GRANTS ANALYSIS
Number of Grants: 2
Highest Grant: $190,666
Disclosure Period: fiscal year ending October 31, 1991

RECENT GRANTS

- 190,666 All Church Home for Children, Ft. Worth, TX
- 190,665 Trinity Terrance, Ft. Worth, TX

Stony Wold Herbert Fund

CONTACT
Cheryl S. Friedman
Executive Director
Stony Wold Herbert Fund
136 East 57th St., Rm. 1705
New York, NY 10022
(212) 753-6565

FINANCIAL SUMMARY
Recent Giving: $209,111 (1991); $208,010 (1990); $180,070 (1989)
Assets: $5,128,763 (1991); $4,344,865 (1990); $4,540,139 (1989)
Gifts Received: $2,550 (1990); $16,575 (1989); $3,582 (1987)
EIN: 13-2784124

CONTRIBUTIONS SUMMARY
Typical Recipients: • *Education:* colleges & universities • *Health:* health organizations, hospitals, medical research
Grant Types: conference/seminar, fellowship, multiyear/continuing support, project, and research
Geographic Distribution: focus on NY

GIVING OFFICERS
Mrs. Phillip Davidson: pres
Ashton Harvy: treas
Mrs. George Moore: secy
Mrs. Charles Whitman, Jr.: vp

APPLICATION INFORMATION
Initial Approach: Send letter requesting application form or telephone. Deadline is October 15 for fellowship grants; March 1 for community service proposals.

Restrictions on Giving: No matching gifts or loans.

OTHER THINGS TO KNOW
Provides research grants to doctors studying respiratory diseases.
Publications: Application Guidelines

GRANTS ANALYSIS
Number of Grants: 15
Highest Grant: $25,000
Disclosure Period: 1991

RECENT GRANTS

- 25,000 New York Hospital Cornell Medical Center, New York, NY
- 21,000 St. Luke's-Roosevelt Hospital Center, New York, NY
- 10,440 St. Luke's-Roosevelt Hospital Center, New York, NY
- 10,000 Columbia University, New York, NY
- 10,000 St. Clare's Hospital and Health Center, New York, NY
- 8,000 Spence-Chapin Services to Family and Children, New York, NY
- 6,300 Mt. Sinai Medical Center, New York, NY
- 5,000 Beth Israel Medical Center, New York, NY
- 5,000 Lenox Hill Hospital, New York, NY
- 3,000 New York Lung Association, New York, NY

Storage Technology Corp. / StorageTek Foundation

Sales: $1.52 billion
Employees: 9,300
Headquarters: Louisville, CO
SIC Major Group: Industrial Machinery & Equipment

CONTACT
Arlyce K. Lewis
Manager, Corporate Communications
Storage Technology Corp.
2270 South 88th St., MS-4310
Louisville, CO 80028-4310
(303) 673-6833

FINANCIAL SUMMARY
Recent Giving: $785,000 (1992)

Fiscal Note: Contributes through foundation only.

CONTRIBUTIONS SUMMARY
Typical Recipients: • *Arts & Humanities:* arts appreciation, general, performing arts, public broadcasting • *Civic & Public Affairs:* general • *Education:* business education, colleges & universities, continuing education, elementary education, engineering education, general, literacy, minority education, science/technology education • *Health:* general, hospices, nutrition & health maintenance • *Social Services:* community service organizations, drugs & alcohol, food/clothing distribution, general, shelters/homelessness, youth organizations
Grant Types: award and general support
Nonmonetary Support Types: donated equipment and in-kind services
Geographic Distribution: only in headquarters area
Operating Locations: CO (Longmont, Louisville), FL (Palm Bay), IL (Crestwood, Hinsdale), PR (Mayaguez, Ponce), TX (El Paso)

CORP. OFFICERS
R. R. Poppa: *B* Wahpeton ND 1933 *ED* Claremont Mens Coll BBA 1957 *CURR EMPL* chmn, pres, ceo: Storage Technology Corp *NONPR AFFIL* fdr: Charles Babbage Inst; mem: Am Electronics Assn, Chief Execs Org, Chmns Circle CO Reps, Computer & Commun Indus Assn, Electronic Mfrs Club, World Bus Counc; trust: Claremont Mens Coll

GIVING OFFICERS
Arlyce K. Lewis: *CURR EMPL* mgr corp commun: Storage Tech Corp

APPLICATION INFORMATION
Initial Approach: *Initial Contact:* brief letter of inquiry and a full proposal *Include Information On:* a description of organization, amount requested, purpose of funds sought, recently audited financial statement, and proof of tax-exempt status *When to Submit:* any time
Restrictions on Giving: Does not support individuals, religious organizations for sectarian

purposes, or political or lobbying groups.

GRANTS ANALYSIS
Typical Range: $1,000 to $2,500

Note: No grants list provided for 1992.

Storer Communications Inc.

Sales: $600.0 million
Employees: 2,875
Parent Company: SCI Holdings, Inc.
Headquarters: Miami, FL
SIC Major Group: Communications

CONTACT
William Whelan
President
Storer Communications
12000 Biscayne Blvd.
Miami, FL 33181
(305) 899-1000

FINANCIAL SUMMARY
Fiscal Note: Annual Giving Range: $100,000 to $250,000

CONTRIBUTIONS SUMMARY
Support goes to local education, health and human service, arts, and civic organizations.

Typical Recipients: • *Arts & Humanities:* general • *Civic & Public Affairs:* general • *Education:* general • *Health:* general • *Social Services:* general

Grant Types: general support

Nonmonetary Support Types: cause-related marketing & promotion, donated products, in-kind services, and workplace solicitation

Geographic Distribution: primarily headquarters area

Operating Locations: FL (Miami)

CORP. OFFICERS
William Whelan: *CURR EMPL* pres: Storer Communs

APPLICATION INFORMATION
Initial Approach: Send brief letter of inquiry. There are no deadlines.

Storer Foundation, George B.

CONTACT
Peter Storer
President
George B. Storer Foundation
PO Box 1270
Saratoga, WY 82331
(307) 326-8308

FINANCIAL SUMMARY
Recent Giving: $2,401,750 (1991); $2,400,000 (1990); $2,132,000 (1989)
Assets: $58,466,423 (1991); $51,161,141 (1990); $51,113,243 (1989)
Gifts Received: $20,865 (1986)
EIN: 59-6136392

CONTRIBUTIONS SUMMARY
Donor(s): The foundation was established in 1955.
Typical Recipients: • *Arts & Humanities:* arts associations • *Civic & Public Affairs:* environmental affairs • *Education:* colleges & universities, private education (precollege), student aid • *Health:* hospitals, single-disease health associations • *Social Services:* disabled, homes, recreation & athletics, religious welfare, united funds, youth organizations
Grant Types: capital, department, general support, project, and scholarship
Geographic Distribution: emphasis on the Miami, FL, area

GIVING OFFICERS
Bill Michaels: vp, dir
James Storer: secy, dir
Peter Storer: pres, treas, dir

APPLICATION INFORMATION
Initial Approach: Proposals should be addressed to the president of the foundation.
Proposals should include descriptive literature, purpose for which funds are requested, and a copy of the IRS determination letter of tax-exempt status. Proposals should be sent to the foundation by November 15; grants are made annually in December. The foundation reports that the best time to submit proposals is from October 15 to November 15.

GRANTS ANALYSIS
Total Grants: $2,401,750
Number of Grants: 88

Highest Grant: $150,000
Typical Range: $1,000 to $5,000 and $10,000 to $50,000
Disclosure Period: 1991
Note: Recent grants are derived from a 1991 Form 990.

RECENT GRANTS
150,000 Kenyon College, Ganbier, OH — Asia study
150,000 Musical Arts Association
150,000 TNC Florida Chapter, Miami, FL
100,000 Miami Heart Institute, Miami, FL
100,000 University of Miami, Miami, FL
100,000 University of Miami, Miami, FL
100,000 University of Miami, Miami, FL
90,000 TNC Idaho Chapter, Boise, ID
80,000 TNC-Wyoming Chapter, Sweetwater, WY
75,000 Cleveland Sight Center, Cleveland, OH

Storer Scholarship Foundation, Oliver W.

CONTACT
Charles G. Retherford
Partner
Oliver W. Storer Scholarship Fdn.
c/o Beasly, Gilkinson, Retherford and Buckles
110 East Charles St.
Muncie, IN 47305
(317) 289-0661

FINANCIAL SUMMARY
Recent Giving: $148,808 (fiscal 1991); $192,775 (fiscal 1990); $224,456 (fiscal 1989)
Assets: $4,018,893 (fiscal year ending February 28, 1991); $3,705,716 (fiscal 1990); $3,464,903 (fiscal 1989)
EIN: 35-6012044

CONTRIBUTIONS SUMMARY
Grant Types: scholarship
Geographic Distribution: limited to Delaware County, IN

APPLICATION INFORMATION
Initial Approach: Send brief letter of inquiry describing program or project. Deadline is 60 days prior to beginning of school year.

OTHER THINGS TO KNOW
Provides scholarship grants for higher education to high school graduates of Delaware County, IN.

Storz Foundation, Robert Herman

CONTACT
Robert Herman Storz Fdn.
Kiewit Plaza, 8th Fl.
Omaha, NE 68131

FINANCIAL SUMMARY
Recent Giving: $305,510 (1990); $244,067 (1989); $34,355 (1987)
Assets: $6,653,618 (1990); $6,447,818 (1989); $5,645,509 (1987)
Gifts Received: $500,000 (1989); $250,000 (1987)
EIN: 47-6025980

CONTRIBUTIONS SUMMARY
Donor(s): Robert Herman Storz
Typical Recipients: • *Arts & Humanities:* community arts, dance, museums/galleries, opera, theater • *Education:* colleges & universities • *Health:* hospitals • *Social Services:* community service organizations, united funds
Grant Types: general support
Geographic Distribution: focus on NE

GIVING OFFICERS
Susan Storz Butler: trust
Robert Herman Storz: trust

APPLICATION INFORMATION
Initial Approach: Contributes only to preselected organizations.

GRANTS ANALYSIS
Number of Grants: 42
Highest Grant: $160,736
Typical Range: $1,000 to $10,531
Disclosure Period: 1990

RECENT GRANTS
160,736 Omaha Community Playhouse, Omaha, NE
25,000 Boy Scouts of America, Omaha, NE
22,000 United Way, Omaha, NE
10,531 Trinity Cathedral, Omaha, NE
3,000 Progress, Omaha, NE

2,700 Clarkson Hospital Fashion Production, Omaha, NE

2,500 Fontenelle Forest, Bellevue, NE

1,000 National Conference of Christians and Jews, New York, NY

1,000 Palm Springs Friends of the Los Angeles Philharmonics, Los Angeles, CA

1,000 University of Nebraska, Omaha, NE

Storz Instrument Co.

Sales: $83.0 million
Employees: 937
Parent Company: American Cyanamid Co.
Headquarters: St. Louis, MO
SIC Major Group: Instruments & Related Products

CONTACT

Carla Young
Executive Assistant to the V.P.
Storz Instrument Co.
3365 Tree Court Industrial Blvd.
St. Louis, MO 63122
(314) 225-5051

CONTRIBUTIONS SUMMARY

Operating Locations: MO (St. Louis)

CORP. OFFICERS

Robert H. Blankemeyer: *CURR EMPL* coo, dir: Storz trument Co
J. Donald Gaines: *CURR EMPL* pres, dir: Storz trument Co

RECENT GRANTS

57,900 Ohio State University, Columbus, OH — donated equipment for the Department of Opthamology

Stott Foundation, Louis L.

CONTACT

William P. Wood
Trustee
Louis L. Stott Fdn.
2000 One Logan Sq.
Philadelphia, PA 19103

FINANCIAL SUMMARY

Recent Giving: $128,500 (fiscal 1991); $113,500 (fiscal 1990)

Assets: $2,411,531 (fiscal year ending September 30, 1991); $2,238,898 (fiscal 1990)
EIN: 23-7009027

CONTRIBUTIONS SUMMARY

Donor(s): Martha Stott Diener
Typical Recipients: • *Education:* colleges & universities, private education (precollege) • *Health:* hospitals • *Social Services:* community service organizations, drugs & alcohol, family planning, youth organizations
Grant Types: general support

GIVING OFFICERS

Brady Oliver Bryson: trust *B* Overton NV 1915 *ED* Western MD Coll AB 1935; Western MD Coll LLD 1973; Columbia Univ LLD 1938 *CORP AFFIL* chmn: Locust Wines Ltd; dir: IN Publs *NONPR AFFIL* mem: Am Bar Assn, DC Bar Assn, NY Bar Assn, PA Bar Assn, Philadelphia Bar Assn
Martha Stott Diener: trust, chmn
Benjamin W. Stott: trust
Edward Barrington Stott: trust
Jonathan D. Stott: trust
William Philler Wood: trust, secy *B* Bryn Mawr PA 1927 *ED* Harvard Univ AB 1949; Harvard Univ JD 1955 *CURR EMPL* counselor: Morgan Lewis Bockius *CORP AFFIL* dir: Church & Dwight Co, McArdle Desco Corp *NONPR AFFIL* chmn: LaNapoule Art Fdn Henry Clews Meml; chmn exec comm: Philadelphia Mus Art; mem: Am Bar Assn, PA Bar Assn, Philadelphia Bar Assn; pres, trust: Genesee Valley Conservancy; trust, vp: Fairmount Park Art Assn

APPLICATION INFORMATION

Initial Approach: Send brief letter requesting application. There are no deadlines.

GRANTS ANALYSIS

Number of Grants: 39
Highest Grant: $20,000
Typical Range: $1,000 to $5,000
Disclosure Period: fiscal year ending September 30, 1991

RECENT GRANTS

20,000 Planned Parenthood, New York, NY

20,000 Sheriff's Meadow Foundation, Vineyard Haven, MA

10,000 Woods Schools, Langhorne, PA — general fund

8,000 Planned Parenthood, Harrisburg, PA

5,000 Bryn Mawr College, Bryn Mawr, PA — for research

5,000 Calvary Fund, Bronx, NY — for scholarship fund

5,000 Freedom from Chemical Dependency Foundation, Needham, MA — general fund

5,000 Planned Parenthood, Reading, PA

5,000 Wilkes University, Wilkes-Barre, PA — Donald Carpenter Memorial Fund

4,000 Oregon Acupuncture Association, Hood River, OR — general fund

Stott Foundation, Robert L.

CONTACT

Robert L. Stott
President
Robert L. Stott Fdn.
c/o Wagner, Stott and Co.
20 Broad St.
New York, NY 10005

FINANCIAL SUMMARY

Recent Giving: $132,500 (1991); $157,000 (1990); $149,900 (1989)
Assets: $2,784,435 (1991); $2,769,984 (1990); $2,747,097 (1989)
EIN: 13-6061943

CONTRIBUTIONS SUMMARY

Donor(s): the late Robert L. Stott

Typical Recipients: • *Arts & Humanities:* history/historic preservation, libraries • *Civic & Public Affairs:* environmental affairs, zoos/botanical gardens • *Education:* business education, colleges & universities, education funds • *Health:* hospitals, medical research, single-disease health associations • *Religion:* churches • *Social Services:* recreation & athletics
Grant Types: general support
Geographic Distribution: focus on NY and in Palm Beach, FL

GIVING OFFICERS

Donald B. Stott: dir, secy, treas
Robert L. Stott, Jr.: dir, pres

APPLICATION INFORMATION

Initial Approach: Contributes only to preselected organizations.
Restrictions on Giving: Does not support individuals.

GRANTS ANALYSIS

Number of Grants: 33
Highest Grant: $25,000
Typical Range: $1,000 to $10,000
Disclosure Period: 1991

RECENT GRANTS

25,000 St. Bartholomew's Church, New York, NY

10,000 Billfish Foundation, Riviera Beach, FL

10,000 New York Hospital, New York, NY

10,000 Parkinson Support Group Fund, Memphis, TN

10,000 St. Bartholomew's Church, New York, NY

10,000 Wharton School of University of Pennsylvania, Philadelphia, PA

5,000 Church of Holy Trinity, Greenport, NY

5,000 Foundation for the Care and Cure of Huntington's Disease, Islamorada, FL

5,000 International Game Fish Association, Ft. Lauderdale, FL

5,000 World Rehabilitation Fund, New York, NY

Stowe, Jr. Foundation, Robert Lee

CONTACT

Daniel Harding Stowe
President
Robert Lee Stowe, Jr. Fdn.
100 North Main St.
PO Box 351
Belmont, NC 28012
(704) 825-5314

FINANCIAL SUMMARY

Recent Giving: $172,433 (1991); $164,974 (1990); $251,697 (1989)

Assets: $3,125,706 (1991); $2,668,050 (1990); $2,725,042 (1989)

Gifts Received: $100,000 (1987)

EIN: 56-6034773

CONTRIBUTIONS SUMMARY

Donor(s): Robert Lee Stowe, Jr., Robert Lee Stowe III, R. L. Stowe Mills

Typical Recipients: • *Arts & Humanities:* community arts, dance, opera • *Education:* colleges & universities, religious education • *Health:* single-disease health associations • *Religion:* churches • *Social Services:* community service organizations, family planning, united funds, youth organizations

Grant Types: general support

Geographic Distribution: focus on NC

GIVING OFFICERS

Jean H. Gibson: secy, treas
David M. McConnell: vp
Daniel Harding Stowe: pres
Richmond H. Stowe: vp
Robert Lee Stowe III: vp

APPLICATION INFORMATION

Initial Approach: Send brief letter of inquiry describing program. There are no deadlines.

GRANTS ANALYSIS

Number of Grants: 50
Highest Grant: $41,500
Typical Range: $1,000 to $5,000
Disclosure Period: 1991

RECENT GRANTS

41,500 Belmont Abbey College, Belmont, NC

21,666 First Presbyterian Church, Belmont, NC

20,000 Davidson College, Davidson, NC

10,000 University of North Carolina at Charlotte Foundation, Charlotte, NC

7,613 Crafted With Pride In USA Council, Washington, DC

6,660 Belmont Community Organization, Belmont, NC

6,000 North Carolina Dance Theatre, Winston-Salem, NC

5,835 Science Museums of Charlotte, Charlotte, NC

5,200 Clemson IPTAY Club, Clemson, SC

5,000 Lineberger Comprehensive Cancer Center, Chapel Hill, NC

Stowers Foundation

CONTACT

Stowers Foundation
P.O. Box 419385
Kansas City, MO 64141-6385
(816) 531-5575

FINANCIAL SUMMARY

Recent Giving: $55,000 (1990); $44,400 (1989)

Assets: $1,805,743 (1990); $1,461,272 (1989)

Gifts Received: $500,000 (1990)

Fiscal Note: 1990 contribution received from James E. Stowers, Jr.

EIN: 43-1465279

CONTRIBUTIONS SUMMARY

Typical Recipients: • *Health:* medical research

Grant Types: general support and research

GIVING OFFICERS

Linda T. Killion, Jr.: dir
James E. Stowers, Jr.: dir, pres
James E. III Stowers, Jr.: dir, secy
Virginia G. Stowers, Jr.: dir, treas

APPLICATION INFORMATION

Initial Approach: The foundation reports no specific application guidelines. Send a brief letter of inquiry, including statement of purpose, amount requested, and proof of tax-exempt status.

GRANTS ANALYSIS

Total Grants: $55,000
Number of Grants: 1
Highest Grant: $55,000
Disclosure Period: 1990

RECENT GRANTS

55,000 St. Luke's Hospital Foundation, Kansas City, MO — urologic oncology fellowship program

Strake Foundation

CONTACT

George W. Strake, Jr.
President
Strake Foundation
712 Main St., Ste. 3300
Houston, TX 77002-3291
(713) 546-2400

FINANCIAL SUMMARY

Recent Giving: $1,250,000 (1993 est.); $1,420,300 (1992); $1,399,300 (1991)

Assets: $25,000,000 (1993 est.); $26,542,676 (1991); $22,733,775 (1990); $23,230,117 (1989)

Gifts Received: $21,608 (1985)

EIN: 76-0041524

CONTRIBUTIONS SUMMARY

Donor(s): George W. Strake, an independent oil operator, and his wife, Susan K. Strake, founded Strake Charities Foundation in 1952. It was renamed the Strake Foundation in 1957, and chartered as a Texas non-profit corporation in 1982. The Strakes and their children are the principal donors.

Typical Recipients: • *Arts & Humanities:* arts associations, dance, history/historic preservation, museums/galleries, music, theater • *Civic & Public Affairs:* better government, business/free enterprise, civil rights, economic development, environmental affairs, ethnic/minority organizations, first amendment issues, national security, philanthropic organizations, public policy, urban & community affairs, zoos/botanical gardens • *Education:* business education, colleges & universities, education associations, education funds, medical education, minority education, private education (precollege), religious education, special education • *Health:* health organizations, hospices, hospitals, medical rehabilitation, mental health, single-disease health associations • *Religion:* churches, religious organizations • *Science:* scientific organizations • *Social Services:* child welfare, community centers, community service organizations, disabled, drugs & alcohol, family services, homes, recreation & athletics, religious welfare, shelters/homelessness, united

funds, volunteer services, youth organizations

Grant Types: capital, general support, and project

Geographic Distribution: primarily Texas

GIVING OFFICERS

Willie S. Alexander: trust
Kathleen D. Covey: trust
Sandra P. Moffet: trust
Joseph F. Niehaus: trust
Georganna S. Parsley: vp, secy
Michele S. Sommerfield: trust
George W. Strake, Jr.: pres, treas *B* Houston TX 1935 *ED* Univ Notre Dame AB; Harvard Univ MBA *CURR EMPL* pres: Strake Trading Co
Linda D. Walsh: trust

APPLICATION INFORMATION

Initial Approach:
The foundation has no formal application form; one copy of a brief request letter together with supporting data is sufficient.

Requests should include a brief description of the need or problem; simple statement of what is to be accomplished; project budget; amount raised to date, sources of support, amount raised locally, and plans to raise balance; current status of project and how long it will take to complete; specific sum requested from foundation, specific purpose for which it is needed, and miminum amount that would be of practical assistance; plans for placing continuing projects on a self-sustaining basis and when that will be accomplished; and a copy of the organization's IRS determination letter of tax-exempt status and latest audited financial statements.

The board of trustees meets twice a year, usually about May/June and November/December. Applications may be submitted any time, but should be received one month prior to board meetings.

Restrictions on Giving: The foundation does not make grants to individuals, elementary schools, or international projects.

GRANTS ANALYSIS

Total Grants: $1,399,300
Number of Grants: 220
Highest Grant: $115,000
Typical Range: $1,000 to $10,000

Disclosure Period: 1991
Note: Average grant excludes a
$115,000 grant. Recent grants
are derived from a 1991 Form
990.

RECENT GRANTS

115,000	St. Joseph Hospital Foundation, Houston, TX
60,000	San Jacinto Museum of History Association, LaPorte, TX
36,000	Boy Scouts of America, Houston, TX — Sam Houston Area Council
30,000	University of St. Thomas, Houston, TX
28,500	Diocese of Galveston-Houston, Houston, TX
25,000	Concerned Women for America, Washington, DC
25,000	Hospice at the Texas Medical Center, Houston, TX
25,000	St. Vincent de Paul Church, Houston, TX
22,000	Institute for Rehabilitation and Research Foundation, Houston, TX
20,000	Archdiocese for the Military Services, USA, Silver Spring, MD

Stranahan Foundation

CONTACT
Charles G. Yeager
Director and Trustee
Stranahan Foundation
4149 Holland-Sylvania Rd.
Toledo, OH 43623
(419) 882-6575

FINANCIAL SUMMARY
Recent Giving: $3,700,000
(1993 est.); $3,300,000 (1992
approx.); $4,145,297 (1991)
Assets: $53,947,070 (1991);
$47,152,215 (1990);
$50,570,622 (1989)
EIN: 34-6514375

CONTRIBUTIONS SUMMARY
Donor(s): The Stranahan Foundation was established as a family trust in Ohio in 1944.
Robert A. Stranahan, former president and chairman of the Champion Spark Plug Company, and his brother, Frank, were two of the foundation's

original benefactors. Robert A. Stranahan, Jr., and Duane Stranahan have since contributed substantially to the foundation. Members of the Stranahan family still serve on the board of trustees.

Typical Recipients: • *Arts & Humanities:* dance, museums/galleries, music, opera, performing arts, public broadcasting • *Civic & Public Affairs:* economics, environmental affairs, law & justice, philanthropic organizations, public policy, urban & community affairs • *Education:* business education, colleges & universities, economic education, education associations, education funds, medical education, religious education • *Health:* geriatric health, hospitals, pediatric health • *Religion:* religious organizations • *Social Services:* aged, animal protection, child welfare, community service organizations, disabled, homes, united funds, youth organizations

Grant Types: capital and general support

Geographic Distribution: Toledo, OH, area; some national giving

GIVING OFFICERS
Diana Foster: trust
Gerald Miller: trust *B* Columbus OH 1941 *CURR EMPL* pres: Typographic Printing Co
Frances Parry: trust
Dinny Stranahan: trust
Duane Stranahan: trust *B* Toledo OH *ED* Harvard Univ BA 1926; Brookline Univ MA *CORP AFFIL* dir: Champion Spark Plug Co *NONPR AFFIL* mem: Aircraft Owners Pilots Assn
Duane Stranahan, Jr.: trust *CURR EMPL* dir: Champion Spark Plug Co
Mark Stranahan: trust
Mescal Stranahan: trust
Robert A. Stranahan, Jr.: trust *B* Toledo OH 1915 *CURR EMPL* chmn, pres, dir: Champion Spark Plug Co *CORP AFFIL* chmn: Anderson Co, Baron Drawn Steel Corp, Bougie Champion SA Paris, Champion Spark Plug Europe SA; dir: Champion Spark Plug Co (South Africa); pres: Champion Fuel Sys; pres, dir: IA Indus
Charles G. Yeager: dir, trust

APPLICATION INFORMATION
Initial Approach:
The foundation requests an initial letter of inquiry. If interested, it will require a single copy of the project proposal. The proposal deadline is October 1.
Decisions on proposals take approximately four months.

GRANTS ANALYSIS
Total Grants: $4,145,297
Number of Grants: 48
Highest Grant: $500,000
Typical Range: $5,000 to $75,000
Disclosure Period: 1991
Note: The average grant figure excludes the foundation's three highest grants totaling $1,300,000. Recent grants are derived from a 1991 Form 990.

RECENT GRANTS

500,000	United Way of Greater Toledo, Toledo, OH
400,000	Medical College of Ohio Foundation, Toledo, OH
400,000	Youth for Christ/USA, OH
250,000	Living Bibles International, Naperville, IL
250,000	Toledo Hospital, Toledo, OH
225,000	Hillsdale College, Hillsdale, MI
200,000	Bowling Green State University, Bowling Green, OH — Social Philosophy and Policy Center
200,000	Campus Crusade for Christ, San Bernadino, CA
200,000	Lutheran Orphans' and Old Folks' Home Society
165,000	Public Broadcasting Foundation of Northwest Ohio, Toledo, OH

Stratford Foundation

CONTACT
Peter A. Wilson
Executive Director
Stratford Foundation
53 State St., 17th Fl.
Boston, MA 02109-2809
(617) 248-7426

FINANCIAL SUMMARY
Recent Giving: $5,660,985
(1992); $6,040,708 (1991);
$9,002,127 (1990)
Assets: $90,957,967 (1991);
$95,486,067 (1990);
$152,542,550 (1989)
Gifts Received: $124,200
(1991); $57,875 (1990);
$47,800 (1989)
Fiscal Note: In 1991, the foundation received $124,200 from Kenneth H. Olsen, its donor.
EIN: 22-2524023

CONTRIBUTIONS SUMMARY
Donor(s): Kenneth H. Olsen, founder and former president of Digital Equipment Corporation, donated $80 million in Digital stock to establish the Stratford Foundation in 1983. Digital, the second largest computer company in the United States, produces digital computers, circuit modules, and memory electronic systems and components.

Typical Recipients: • *Arts & Humanities:* arts associations, history/historic preservation, museums/galleries, public broadcasting • *Education:* colleges & universities, engineering education, private education (precollege), religious education, science/technology education • *Health:* health funds, hospitals, medical research, pediatric health, single-disease health associations • *International:* international development/relief • *Religion:* churches, religious organizations • *Social Services:* community service organizations, drugs & alcohol, homes, recreation & athletics, religious welfare, shelters/homelessness

Grant Types: general support
Geographic Distribution: national, with emphasis on the Boston metropolitan area

GIVING OFFICERS
Ava-Lisa Memmen: trust
Eeva-Liisa Aulikki Olsen: trust

Kenneth H. Olsen: don, trust *B* Bridgeport CT 1926 *ED* MA Inst Tech BSEE 1950; MA Inst Tech MS 1952 *CURR EMPL* co-fdr, pres, ceo: Digital Equipment Corp *CORP AFFIL* dir: Ford Motor Co, Polaroid Corp *NONPR AFFIL* adv vp, mem: Joslin Diabetes Fdn; fellow: Inst Electrical Electronics Engrs; mem: Computer Science Engring Bd, Natl Academy Engring, Natl Academy Sciences; mem corp: MA Inst Tech, Wentworth Inst Boston; trust: Gordon Coll

Richard J. Testa: trust *B* Marlboro MA 1939 *ED* Assumption Coll 1959; Harvard Univ 1962 *CURR EMPL* ptnr: Testa Hurwitz & Thibeault *CORP AFFIL* dir: Boston Five Cents Savings Bank, Teradyne

Peter A. Wilson: exec dir *CURR EMPL* sr vp: Shawmut Bank Boston

APPLICATION INFORMATION

Initial Approach:
Applicants should send a letter to the foundation.
Grant applications should include an explanation of the proposed project and goals for use of the requested funds, limited to two pages.
There are no deadlines.
The foundation's trustees meet periodically.
Restrictions on Giving: No grants are made to individuals.

GRANTS ANALYSIS
Total Grants: $6,040,708
Number of Grants: 68
Highest Grant: $895,125
Typical Range: $10,000 to $50,000 and $100,000 to $500,000
Disclosure Period: 1991
Note: Recent grants are derived from a 1991 grants list.

RECENT GRANTS
895,125 Project Reach
504,562 Museum of Science
429,625 Gordon College, Wenham, MA
419,893 Good News Publishers
327,318 Living Bibles International
276,850 Project Reach
267,250 Arizona-Sonora Desert Museum, Tucson, AZ
240,075 Chicago Educational Television Association
184,331 Gordon-Conwell Theological Semi-

nary, South Hamilton, MA
156,000 Project Reach

Straub Estate, Gertrude S.

CONTACT
Caroline Sharman
Admin.
Gertrude S. Straub Estate
c/o Hawaii Community Foundation
212 Merchant St., Ste. 330
Honolulu, HI 96813
(808) 537-6333

FINANCIAL SUMMARY
Recent Giving: $216,150 (fiscal 1990); $176,235 (fiscal 1989)
Assets: $3,954,800 (fiscal year ending March 31, 1990); $3,588,711 (fiscal 1989)
EIN: 99-6003243

CONTRIBUTIONS SUMMARY
Donor(s): the late Gertrude S. Straub
Grant Types: scholarship
Geographic Distribution: focus on HI

APPLICATION INFORMATION
Initial Approach: Application form required. Deadline is March. Board meets in April.

OTHER THINGS TO KNOW
Publications: Application Guidelines

Straus Foundation, Aaron and Lillie

CONTACT
Jan Rivitz
Executive Director
Aaron and Lillie Straus Foundation
101 West Mount Royal Ave.
Baltimore, MD 21201
(301) 539-8308

FINANCIAL SUMMARY
Recent Giving: $3,115,300 (1991); $3,093,883 (1990); $2,302,829 (1989)
Assets: $51,219,676 (1991); $45,587,552 (1990); $48,350,954 (1989)
EIN: 52-0563083

CONTRIBUTIONS SUMMARY
Donor(s): Aaron and Lillie Straus, owners of Reliable Stores (a chain of retail furniture and jewelry stores) and establishers of two Baltimore area camps for children, established the Straus Foundation in 1926.
Typical Recipients: • *Arts & Humanities:* museums/galleries, music, opera, performing arts • *Civic & Public Affairs:* housing, nonprofit management, philanthropic organizations, public policy, urban & community affairs • *Education:* literacy, preschool education, public education (precollege) • *Health:* hospitals, pediatric health, public health • *Social Services:* child welfare, community service organizations, disabled, employment/job training, family planning, family services, homes, religious welfare, united funds, youth organizations
Grant Types: capital, general support, loan, multiyear/continuing support, project, and seed money
Geographic Distribution: primarily Baltimore, MD, and Washington, DC, area

GIVING OFFICERS
Richard M. Barnett: chmn, pres
Alfred I. Coplan: secy, treas, trust *B* Baltimore MD 1925 *ED* Univ VA BA 1944 *CURR EMPL* chmn, ceo: Reliable Stores Corp *CORP AFFIL* dir: Webster Clothes *NONPR AFFIL* dir: Assoc Jewish Charities Welfare Fund, Baltimore Chamber Orchestra, Baltimore Hebrew Congregation, Baltimore Symphony Orchestra, Levindale Geriatric Home Hosp; vp: Baltimore Goodwill Indus
Darrell Friedman: trust
Jan Rivitz: exec dir, trust

APPLICATION INFORMATION
Initial Approach:
Interested parties may send one copy of a detailed proposal to the foundation.
The foundation does not use standard application forms, nor do they define official guidelines for this procedure. Therefore, information pertinent to the applicant organization's structure and project should be included, at the applicant's dis-

cretion. A letter of intent is required as to the use of the funds requested.
Applications may be submitted any time; however, recommended dates for proposal submissions are the first of February, May, August, and November. Early submittal of requests is advisable to permit ample review time.
The board meets in March, June, September, and December.
Restrictions on Giving: The foundation does not contribute to endowments or to national organizations.

GRANTS ANALYSIS
Total Grants: $3,115,300
Number of Grants: 48
Highest Grant: $1,121,500
Typical Range: $1,000 to $50,000
Disclosure Period: 1991
Note: The average grant figure excludes two grants totaling $2,121,500. Recent grants are derived from a 1991 grants list.

RECENT GRANTS
1,121,500 Associated Jewish Charities and Welfare Fund, Baltimore, MD
1,000,000 Operation Exodus, Baltimore, MD
153,429 Camp Airy, Baltimore, MD — Camp Louise Vacation Fund
120,000 Advocates for Children and Youth, Baltimore, MD
105,000 Maryland Association of Non-Profit Organizations, Baltimore, MD
100,000 Baltimore Reads, Baltimore, MD
100,000 Maryland Committee for Children, Baltimore, MD
100,000 Volunteers for Medical Engineering, Baltimore, MD
50,000 Partners for Giving, Baltimore, MD
50,000 United Way of Central Maryland, Baltimore, MD

Straus Foundation, Martha Washington Straus and Harry H.

CONTACT
Roger J. King
Secretary
Martha Washington Straus and
 Harry H. Straus Fdn.
52 Gramercy Park, Ste. 1705
New York, NY 10010
(212) 533-6246

FINANCIAL SUMMARY
Recent Giving: $226,000
(1991); $219,100 (1990);
$206,800 (1989)
Assets: $4,512,873 (1991);
$3,990,461 (1990); $3,919,756
(1989)
Gifts Received: $27,938
(1991); $28,950 (1989);
$27,263 (1988)
Fiscal Note: In 1991, contributions were received from Louise S. King.
EIN: 56-0645526

CONTRIBUTIONS SUMMARY
Donor(s): the late Harry H.
Strains, Sr.
Typical Recipients: • *Civic &
Public Affairs:* ethnic/minority
organizations • *Education:* colleges & universities, medical
education • *Health:* hospitals,
medical research, pediatric
health, single-disease health associations • *Religion:* churches
• *Social Services:* child welfare, community service organizations, disabled, religious welfare, united funds, youth
organizations
Grant Types: emergency, general support, and research
Geographic Distribution:
focus on NY

GIVING OFFICERS
Louise Straus King: pres, trust
Roger J. King: secy, treas,
trust
Betty B. Straus: vp, trust
Harry H. Straus III: trust

APPLICATION INFORMATION
Initial Approach: Contributes
only to preselected organizations.
Restrictions on Giving: Does
not support individuals.

GRANTS ANALYSIS
Number of Grants: 117
Highest Grant: $25,000

Typical Range: $500 to $3,000
Disclosure Period: 1991

RECENT GRANTS
25,000 White Plains Hospital Medical Center,
White Plains, NY
20,000 Columbia University College of
Physicians and Surgeons, New York,
NY
15,000 Jewish Guild for
the Blind, New
York, NY
10,000 Columbia Presbyterian Medical Center, Clinical Oncology Fund, New
York, NY
10,000 United Jewish Appeal Federation of
Jewish Philanthropies, New York, NY
7,000 Georgetown University Hospital,
Washington, DC
5,000 Lynchburg College, Lynchburg,
VA
5,000 State University of
New York School
of Management,
Binghamton, NY
5,000 Vanderbilt University, Nashville, TN
4,000 Cardinal's Appeal
for Charity, Washington, DC

Straus Foundation, Philip A. and Lynn

CONTACT
Philip A. Straus
President
Philip A. and Lynn Straus Fdn.
1037 Constable Dr. South
Mamaroneck, NY 10543

FINANCIAL SUMMARY
Recent Giving: $1,045,920
(fiscal 1991); $920,305 (fiscal
1990); $670,900 (fiscal 1989)
Assets: $11,584,117 (fiscal
year ending March 31, 1991);
$12,614,611 (fiscal 1990);
$12,518,481 (fiscal 1989)
EIN: 13-6161223

CONTRIBUTIONS SUMMARY
Donor(s): Philip A. Strains
Typical Recipients: • *Arts &
Humanities:* museums/galleries, public broadcasting • *Civic
& Public Affairs:* civil rights
• *Education:* colleges & universities • *Social Services:* child
welfare, community service organizations, disabled, family
planning, united funds, youth
organizations

Grant Types: general support
Geographic Distribution:
focus on NY

GIVING OFFICERS
John W. Hertz: secy, trust
Lynn G. Straus: vp, treas, trust
Philip A. Straus: pres, trust

APPLICATION INFORMATION
Initial Approach: Contributes
only to preselected organizations.
Restrictions on Giving: Does
not support individuals.

GRANTS ANALYSIS
Number of Grants: 84
Highest Grant: $55,000
Typical Range: $3,000 to
$20,000
Disclosure Period: fiscal year
ending March 31, 1991

RECENT GRANTS
55,000 National Center for
Clinical Infant Programs, New York,
NY
50,000 Renaissance Project, New York, NY
28,500 Museum of Modern Art, New York,
NY
25,000 New York State
Council of
Churches, New
York, NY
25,000 Vassar College,
Poughkeepsie, NY
10,000 Very Special Arts
Massachusetts,
Boston, MA
6,000 Hudson Guild,
Hudson, NY
6,000 People for the
American Way,
Washington, DC
5,000 Parents Place, New
York, NY
5,000 Planned Parenthood, New York,
NY

Strauss Foundation

CONTACT
Judy Prendergast
Administrator
Strauss Fdn.
c/o Fidelity Bank, N.A.
Broad and Walnut St.s
Philadelphia, PA 19109
(215) 985-8031

FINANCIAL SUMMARY
Recent Giving: $1,438,371
(1991); $1,190,380 (1989);
$1,681,344 (1988)
Assets: $40,389,983 (1991);
$29,812,506 (1989);
$30,922,264 (1988)

Gifts Received: $66,431 (1991)
EIN: 23-6219939

CONTRIBUTIONS SUMMARY
Donor(s): The foundation was
established in 1951 by Maurice
L. Strauss.
Typical Recipients: • *Arts &
Humanities:* arts institutes, cinema, community arts, museums/galleries, music, opera,
performing arts, public broadcasting • *Civic & Public Affairs:* philanthropic organizations, zoos/botanical gardens
• *Education:* colleges & universities, legal education, private
education (precollege)
• *Health:* geriatric health, hospices, hospitals, medical research, pediatric health, singledisease health associations
• *Religion:* religious organizations, synagogues • *Social Services:* child welfare, community
centers, community service organizations, recreation & athletics, shelters/homelessness,
united funds, youth organizations
Grant Types: general support
and research
Geographic Distribution:
focus on Pennsylvania and California

GIVING OFFICERS
Henry A. Gladstone: trust
Scott R. Isdaner: trust
Sandra S. Krause: trust
Benjamin Strauss: trust
Robert Perry Strauss: trust

APPLICATION INFORMATION
Initial Approach:
The foundation requests applications be made in writing.
The foundation has no deadline
for submitting proposals.
Restrictions on Giving: The
foundation reports grants are
made only to public charities
and unsolicited requests are
generally not encouraged. The
foundation does not make
grants to individuals.

GRANTS ANALYSIS
Total Grants: $1,438,371
Number of Grants: 406
Highest Grant: $200,000
Typical Range: $1,000 to
$10,000
Disclosure Period: 1991
Note: Recent grants are derived from a 1991 grants list.

RECENT GRANTS
200,000 RCNO
100,000 Camp Max Strauss

50,000 Harrison Youth Boosters
25,000 Cedars-Sinai Medical Center, Los Angeles, CA
25,000 Cedars-Sinai Medical Center, Los Angeles, CA
25,000 Cedars-Sinai Medical Center, Los Angeles, CA
25,000 Harrison Youth Boosters
25,000 Harrison Youth Boosters
25,000 Harrison Youth Boosters
25,000 Jewish Federation of Palm Beach, Palm Beach, FL

Strauss Foundation, Judy and Howard E.

CONTACT
Howard E. Strauss
President
Judy and Howard E. Strauss Fdn.
Nine Broadmoor Dr.
Rumson, NJ 07760

FINANCIAL SUMMARY
Recent Giving: $818,682 (fiscal 1990); $25,391 (fiscal 1989)
Assets: $818,652 (fiscal year ending June 30, 1990); $1,098,895 (fiscal 1989)
EIN: 13-6161012

CONTRIBUTIONS SUMMARY
Typical Recipients: • *Religion:* religious organizations • *Social Services:* animal protection
Grant Types: general support

APPLICATION INFORMATION
Initial Approach: Send brief letter of inquiry describing program or project. Deadline is September 1.

OTHER THINGS TO KNOW
In previous years, supported Jewish welfare funds and animal welfare. No grants list was provided for 1990.

Strauss Foundation, Leon

CONTACT
Robert P. Vossler
Trustee
Leon Strauss Fdn.
5332 Harbor Street
Commerce, CA 90040
(213) 728-5440

FINANCIAL SUMMARY
Recent Giving: $400,000 (1990)
Assets: $6,546,156 (1989)
Gifts Received: $6,476,359 (1990)
Fiscal Note: In fiscal 1990, contributions were received from the late Leon Strauss.
EIN: 51-0205308

CONTRIBUTIONS SUMMARY
Donor(s): the late Leon Strauss
Typical Recipients: • *Health:* health organizations, medical research, single-disease health associations • *Religion:* churches • *Social Services:* youth organizations
Grant Types: endowment and general support

GIVING OFFICERS
Tom Breeze: trust
Charles Curley: trust
Paul Simon: trust
Robert P. Vossler: trust

APPLICATION INFORMATION
Initial Approach: Send brief letter of inquiry including purpose and I.R.S. identification number. There are no deadlines.
Restrictions on Giving: Does not provide grants to individuals.

GRANTS ANALYSIS
Number of Grants: 35
Highest Grant: $100,000
Typical Range: $1,000 to $30,000
Disclosure Period: 1990

RECENT GRANTS
100,000 Boys and Girls Club
30,000 City of Hope, Los Angeles, CA
30,000 City of Hope, Los Angeles, CA
26,000 California Parkinson's Foundation, Los Angeles, CA
26,000 California Parkinson's Foundation, Los Angeles, CA

20,000 Boys Club of America
18,000 Redwood Presbyterian Church
10,000 Guardsman — endowment fund
10,000 National Jewish Center for Immunology and Respiratory Medicine, Denver, CO
10,000 St. Francis Foundation

Strawbridge & Clothier
Sales: $967.79 million
Employees: 7,749
Headquarters: Philadelphia, PA
SIC Major Group: General Merchandise Stores

CONTACT
Steven L. Strawbridge
Vice President, Treasurer & Secretary
Strawbridge & Clothier
801 Market St., 10th Fl.
Philadelphia, PA 19107-3199
(215) 629-6000

FINANCIAL SUMMARY
Fiscal Note: Company gives directly. Annual Giving Range: $500,000 to $1 million

CONTRIBUTIONS SUMMARY
Typical Recipients: • *Arts & Humanities:* general • *Civic & Public Affairs:* urban & community affairs • *Education:* general • *Health:* general • *Social Services:* general
Grant Types: general support
Geographic Distribution: specifically in Philadelphia, but covers the entire Delaware Valley
Operating Locations: PA (Philadelphia)

CORP. OFFICERS
Francis R. Strawbridge III: *B* Bryn Mawr PA 1937 *ED* Princeton Univ AB *CURR EMPL* chmn: Strawbridge & Clothier *CORP AFFIL* dir: Mellon Bank *NONPR AFFIL* chmn bd trusts: Princeton Univ Store; mem: Am Retail Fed, Assoc Merchandising Corp, Greater Philadelphia Chamber Commerce, Natl Retail Merchants Assn; vchmn, bd mgrs: Germantown Hosp
Peter S. Strawbridge: *B* Philadelphia PA 1938 *ED* Hamilton Coll BA *CURR EMPL* pres: Strawbridge & Clothier *CORP AFFIL* dir: Assoc Merchandis-

ing Corp, CoreStates Fin Corp; mem bd mgrs: PA Hosp

GIVING OFFICERS
Steven L. Strawbridge: *CURR EMPL* vp, treas, secy: Strawbridge & Clothier

APPLICATION INFORMATION
Initial Approach: *Initial Contact:* brief letter of inquiry *Include Information On:* description of the organization, amount requested, purpose of funds sought, audited financial statement, and proof of tax-exempt status *When to Submit:* any time
Restrictions on Giving: Does not support individuals, or give funding for nominal gifts such as door prizes and gift certificates.

GRANTS ANALYSIS
Typical Range: $1,000 to $2,500

Strawbridge Foundation of Pennsylvania I, Margaret Dorrance

CONTACT
Diana S. Norris
Margaret Dorrance Strawbridge Fdn of Pennsylvania I
Bldg. 3, Ste. 108
125 Strafford Ave.
Wayne, PA 19067

FINANCIAL SUMMARY
Recent Giving: $200,500 (1990); $122,000 (1989); $208,000 (1988)
Assets: $4,600,729 (1990); $4,316,181 (1989); $3,812,987 (1988)
Gifts Received: $113,460 (1990); $139,334 (1989); $160,917 (1988)
EIN: 23-2373081

CONTRIBUTIONS SUMMARY
Donor(s): Margaret Dorrance Strawbridge Foundation
Typical Recipients: • *Arts & Humanities:* arts centers, museums/galleries • *Civic & Public Affairs:* environmental affairs • *Education:* colleges & universities, religious education • *Health:* hospitals, medical research
Grant Types: general support

GIVING OFFICERS

George Strawbridge, Jr.: pres, sec *B* 1937 *ED* Trinity Coll BA 1960; Univ PA PhD 1979 *CORP AFFIL* dir: Buffalo Sabres, Campbell Soup Co, DE Trust Co, Fairhill Training Ctr, Highland Med Ctr, Meridian Bancorp; pres: Augustin Co, Augustin Stables, GAR Inc *NONPR AFFIL* pres: Natl Steeplechase & Hunt Assn
Nina S. Strawbridge: vp, secy

APPLICATION INFORMATION

Initial Approach: Contributes only to preselected organizations.
Restrictions on Giving: Does not support individuals.

GRANTS ANALYSIS

Highest Grant: $100,000
Typical Range: $2,000 to $10,000
Disclosure Period: 1990

RECENT GRANTS

100,000 Trinity College, Hartford, CT
20,000 International Steeplechase Group, Brentwood, TN
17,000 Memorial Sloan-Kettering Cancer Center, New York, NY
11,000 Aspen Foundation, Aspen, CO
10,000 Brandywine Conservancy Brandywine River Museum, Chadds Ford, PA
5,000 Backstretch Employee Assistance Team, Jamaica, NY
5,000 St. Davids Episcopal Church, Radnor, PA
5,000 Trustees of the University of Pennsylvania, Kennett Square, PA — Bolton Center
5,000 Upland Country Day School, Kennett Square, PA
5,000 Widener University, Chester, PA

Strawbridge Foundation of Pennsylvania II, Margaret Dorrance

CONTACT

Diana Strawbridge Norris
President
Margaret Dorrance Strawbridge Fdn of Pennsylvania II
125 Strafford Ave.
Bldg. 3, Ste. 108
Wayne, PA 19087-3367
(215) 688-0743

FINANCIAL SUMMARY

Recent Giving: $266,380 (1991); $180,165 (1990); $314,715 (1989)
Assets: $3,376,865 (1991); $3,221,846 (1990); $3,161,685 (1989)
Gifts Received: $108,954 (1991); $109,887 (1990); $106,124 (1989)
Fiscal Note: In 1991, contributions were received from the trusts of Diana S. Norris.
EIN: 23-2371943

CONTRIBUTIONS SUMMARY

Donor(s): Margaret Dorrance Strawbridge Foundation
Typical Recipients: • *Arts & Humanities:* arts associations, community arts, history/historic preservation, music • *Civic & Public Affairs:* environmental affairs, zoos/botanical gardens • *Education:* agricultural education, colleges & universities, private education (precollege) • *Health:* hospices, hospitals, medical research, pediatric health, single-disease health associations • *Social Services:* animal protection, child welfare, family planning
Grant Types: general support, multiyear/continuing support, operating expenses, and research
Geographic Distribution: focus on the eastern U.S., especially PA and FL

GIVING OFFICERS

Charles S. Norris, Jr.: off
Diana Strawbridge Norris: pres *B* 1939

APPLICATION INFORMATION

Initial Approach: Send brief letter of inquiry describing program or project. There are no deadlines.

Restrictions on Giving: Does not support individuals or provide loans.

GRANTS ANALYSIS

Number of Grants: 76
Highest Grant: $13,000
Typical Range: $500 to $10,000
Disclosure Period: 1991

RECENT GRANTS

13,000 Pennsylvania Horticultural Society, Philadelphia, PA
11,000 Planned Parenthood Federation of America, West Palm Beach, FL
10,000 Church Farm School, Paoli, PA
10,000 Garden Club of America, New York, NY
10,000 Good Samaritan Hospital, West Palm Beach, FL
10,000 Memorial Sloan-Kettering Cancer Center, New York, NY
10,000 Palm Beach Day School, Palm Beach, FL
10,000 Society of Four Arts, Palm Beach, FL
7,000 Hospice Guild of Palm Beach, Palm Beach, FL
6,000 Children's Hospital Foundation, Philadelphia, PA

Stride Rite Corp. / Stride Rite Charitable Foundation

Sales: $585.92 million
Employees: 3,000
Headquarters: Cambridge, MA
SIC Major Group: Apparel & Accessory Stores and Leather & Leather Products

CONTACT

Ellen Sahl
Assistant to the Chairman
Stride Rite Charitable Fdn.
400 Atlantic Ave.
Boston, MA 02110
(617) 574-4169

FINANCIAL SUMMARY

Recent Giving: $2,747,000 (fiscal 1993 est.); $1,911,854 (fiscal 1992); $1,797,711 (fiscal 1991)
Assets: $9,252,673 (fiscal 1991); $5,666,177 (fiscal 1990); $4,402,083 (fiscal 1989)

Fiscal Note: Figures are for foundation giving. No monetary support is given directly from company. 1993 figure includes foundation giving and nonmonetary support.
EIN: 04-6059887

CONTRIBUTIONS SUMMARY

Typical Recipients: • *Arts & Humanities:* arts associations, arts centers, community arts, dance, museums/galleries, music, opera, performing arts, theater • *Civic & Public Affairs:* economic development, law & justice, urban & community affairs, women's affairs, zoos/botanical gardens • *Education:* arts education, colleges & universities, public education (precollege) • *Health:* hospitals, nursing services • *Social Services:* child welfare, community centers, community service organizations, counseling, disabled, drugs & alcohol, family services, homes, shelters/homelessness, united funds, volunteer services
Grant Types: capital, employee matching gifts, multi-year/continuing support, operating expenses, and scholarship
Nonmonetary Support Types: donated equipment
Note: In 1992, the company reported nonmonetary support totaling $930,740.
Geographic Distribution: to organizations in Massachusetts, with emphasis on the greater Boston area
Operating Locations: MA (Boston, Cambridge, New Bedford), MO (Fulton, Hamilton, Tipton)

CORP. OFFICERS

John J. Phelan: *CURR EMPL* vchmn, treas, cfo, dir: Stride Rite Corp *CORP AFFIL* chmn, ceo: NY Stock Exchange; dir: Eastman Kodak Co, JWP Inc, Merrill Lynch & Co, Metro Life Ins Co, Sonat
Ervin Shames: *B* Des Moines IA 1940 *CURR EMPL* pres, ceo, chmn: Stride Rite Corp *CORP AFFIL* dir: First Brands Corp; pres: Kendall Co *NONPR AFFIL* bd visitors: Duke Univ Fuqua Sch Bus, Univ Northeastern Coll Bus Admins; mem: Harvard Bus Sch Alumni Assn

GIVING OFFICERS

Arnold S. Hiatt: chmn, dir *B* Worcester MA 1927 *ED* Harvard Univ BA 1948 *CORP AFFIL* dir: Dreyfus Fund, New Republic Magazine; chmn: Stride Rite Corp *NONPR AFFIL* bd dirs: Bus Social Responsibility; bd overseers: Boston Symphony Orchestra; bd regents higher ed: Commonwealth MA; dir: MA Advocacy Ctr; mem: Am Footwear Indus Assn, Young Pres Org; mem visiting comm: Boston Univ Med Sch; trust: Boston Plan Excellence Pub Schs, Isabella Stewart Gardner Mus, Northeastern Univ; bd overseers: Harvard Univ

Marcia C. Morris: clerk, dir *CURR EMPL* sr vp, secy, gen coun, clerk: Stride Rite Corp

APPLICATION INFORMATION

Initial Approach: *Initial Contact: letter Include Information On:* funding proposal, detailed description of services provided, plans for the allocated funds from Stride Rite, descriptions of goals to date, list of volunteers and their salaries, list of sources of income, copy of the IRS letter that approves your nonprofit status, detailed budget and most recent audited financial statement *When to Submit:* any time

Restrictions on Giving: Organizations must be tax-exempt under IRS standards. Does not fund advertising, building projects, special events, fundraisers, or funds for single-disease health organizations.

GRANTS ANALYSIS

Total Grants: $1,911,854*
Number of Grants: 85
Highest Grant: $1,355,000
Typical Range: $500 to $3,000
Disclosure Period: fiscal year ending September 30, 1992
Note: Total grant figure is from 1992. All other figures are from 1990. Recent grants are derived from a 1990 grants list. Assets are from 1991.

RECENT GRANTS

67,550 Harvard University Scholarship Program, Cambridge, MA

5,000 Big Brother Association of Boston, Boston, MA

5,000 Cambridge Fund for Housing the Homeless, Cambridge, MA

3,000 Children's Hospital League, Boston, MA

2,500 Boston Museum of Science, Boston, MA

2,500 Boys and Girls Clubs of Boston, Boston, MA

2,500 Cambridge Partnership for Public Education, Cambridge, MA

2,500 New England Aquarium, Boston, MA

2,500 Northeastern University, Boston, MA

2,000 New Bedford Women's Center, New Bedford, MA

Stroehmann Bakeries

Sales: $275.0 million
Employees: 3,900
Headquarters: Horsham, PA
SIC Major Group: Food & Kindred Products

CONTACT

Robert Gansel
Vice President, Finances
Stroehmann Bakeries
255 Business Center Dr., Ste. 200
Horsham, PA 19044
(215) 672-8010
Note: Art Smith, Controller, may also be used as a contact name.

CONTRIBUTIONS SUMMARY

Operating Locations: NJ, PA (Horsham), VA

CORP. OFFICERS

David Collins: *CURR EMPL* pres: Stroehmann Bakeries
Robert Gansel: *CURR EMPL* vp (fin & admin): Stroehmann Bakeries
D.T. Robinson: *CURR EMPL* vp (mktg): Stroehmann Bakeries

GIVING OFFICERS

Robert Gansel: *CURR EMPL* vp (fin & admin): Stroehmann Bakeries (see above)

Stroh Brewery Co.

Sales: $1.4 billion
Employees: 3,500
Headquarters: Detroit, MI
SIC Major Group: Food & Kindred Products

CONTACT

R. Sue Smith
Manager, Alcohol Education
Stroh Brewery Co.
100 River Pl.
Detroit, MI 48207
(313) 446-2194

CONTRIBUTIONS SUMMARY

The Stroh Brewery Foundation was disbanded in September 1989. Company continues a direct giving program targeting local organizations.
Typical Recipients: • *Arts & Humanities:* general • *Civic & Public Affairs:* general • *Education:* general • *Health:* general • *Social Services:* general
Grant Types: general support
Geographic Distribution: headquarters and operating locations
Operating Locations: MI (Detroit)

CORP. OFFICERS

R. Friedholm: *CURR EMPL* pres: Stroh Brewery Co
Christopher Sortwell: *CURR EMPL* cfo: Stroh Brewery Co
Peter Wetherill Stroh: *B* Detroit MI 1927 *ED* Princeton Univ BA 1951; US Brewers Academy *CURR EMPL* chmn, ceo: Stroh Cos *CORP AFFIL* chmn, ceo: Stroh Brewery Co; dir: NBD Bancorp *NONPR AFFIL* chmn: Detroit Renaissance; dir: Atlantic Salmon Fed, Beer Inst, Conservation Intl, Econ Alliance MI, Natl Audubon Soc; trust: Inst Resource Mgmt, New Detroit; vchmn: Detroit Econ Growth Corp, Detroit Med Ctr

APPLICATION INFORMATION

Initial Approach: Send letter of inquiry. There are no deadlines.

Strong Foundation, Hattie M.

CONTACT

Barbara B. Cantrell
Director of Loans
Hattie M. Strong Fdn.
1735 Eye St., NW, Ste. 705
Washington, DC 20006
(202) 331-1619

FINANCIAL SUMMARY

Recent Giving: $761,645 (fiscal 1991); $772,125 (fiscal 1990); $776,550 (fiscal 1989)

Assets: $17,855,823 (fiscal year ending August 31, 1991); $16,086,535 (fiscal 1990); $16,166,117 (fiscal 1989)
Gifts Received: $1,820 (fiscal 1990); $1,560 (fiscal 1989)
EIN: 53-0237223

CONTRIBUTIONS SUMMARY

Donor(s): The foundation was incorporated in 1928 by the late Hattie M. Strong.
Typical Recipients: • *Arts & Humanities:* performing arts, public broadcasting • *Civic & Public Affairs:* philanthropic organizations, women's affairs • *Education:* education funds, health & physical education, minority education, public education (precollege) • *Religion:* churches, religious organizations • *Social Services:* aged, child welfare, community service organizations, disabled, employment/job training, family services, shelters/homelessness, united funds, volunteer services, youth organizations
Grant Types: loan and project
Geographic Distribution: focus on the Washington, DC, metropolitan area

GIVING OFFICERS

Barbara B. Cantrell: secy, treas, dir
Olive W. Covington: dir
Judith Cyphers: asst secy, dir
Thelma L. Eichman: dir
Charles H. Fleischer: dir
Richard S. T. Marsh: treas, dir
Patricia Mascari: dir
John A. Nevius: dir
Vincent Emory Reed: dir *B* St Louis MO 1928 *ED* WV St Coll BS 1952; Howard Univ MA 1965 *CORP AFFIL* dir: Home Fed Savings & Loan Assn *NONPR AFFIL* asst sec ed: US Dept Ed; dir: DC Goodwill Indus, Twelve Neediest Kids, YMCA; mem: Am Assn Sch Pers Adms, Am Soc Bus Officials, DC PTA, Kappa Alpha Psi, NAACP, Natl Assn Sch Security Offs, Natl Assn Secondary Sch Prins, Natl Ed Assn, Phi Delta Kappa, Washington Sch; mem staff: DC Pub Schs; volunteer: SE Boys Club, SE Youth Football Assn; volunteer worker: SE Boys Club, SE Youth Football Assn
C. Peter Strong: dir
Henry Strong: chmn, pres, dir *B* Rochester NY 1923 *ED* Williams Coll AB 1949 *NONPR AFFIL* dir: Mt Vernon Coll, Natl Symphony Orchestra

Assn; vchmn bd trusts, hon trust: John F Kennedy Ctr Performing Arts
Henry L. Strong: vp, dir
Robin C. Tannet: asst secy, asst treas

APPLICATION INFORMATION
Initial Approach:
For the loan program, students should sent an initial letter to the foundation. For the grant program, organizations interested in submitting a proposal should first contact the foundation and request written materials explaining proposal procedures and requirements.

For the loan program, students should send an initial letter providing a brief personal history and identification of the educational institution attended, the subjects studied, the date studies are expected to be completed, and the amount of funds needed. If the student qualifies for consideration, application forms are then sent out to be completed and returned to the foundation. For the grant program, organizations should follow the foundation's proposal procedures and requirements as directed.

Students should apply between January 1 and March 31 for loans covering the academic year beginning the following September. Deadlines for grant proposals are January 15, April 15, July 15, and October 15 to be considered in March, June, September, and December, respectively.

Loan applicants are normally notified of the foundation's decision in late June or early July. After a full review of grant proposals by foundation staff, including personal interviews if necessary, proposals are presented to the board for action. Applicants are notified in writing of the board's decision.

Restrictions on Giving: For the loan program, foreign students temporarily in the United States do not qualify. For the grant program, the foundation generally does not support building or endowment funds, requests for equipment, research, conferences, projects designed to educate the general public, or programs of national or international scope. The foundation does not make

grants to individuals or provide scholarships.

OTHER THINGS TO KNOW
Publications: annual report and informational brochure including application guidelines

GRANTS ANALYSIS
Total Grants: $761,645
Number of Grants: 46
Highest Grant: $12,500
Typical Range: $3,000 to $10,000
Disclosure Period: fiscal year ending August 31, 1991
Note: Recent grants are derived from a fiscal 1991 grants list.

RECENT GRANTS
12,500 Bell Multicultural High School (ADVANCE), Washington, DC — evening prevention dropout program

10,000 Federal City Council, Washington, DC — DC Committee on Public Education's implementation of recommendations made by the Committee to improve the local public schools

10,000 For Love of Children (FLOC), Washington, DC — education advocacy component for at-risk, school-age children living in Hope and A Home Housing units

10,000 Network of Educators on Central America, Washington, DC — books project

8,500 Boys and Girls Club, Washington, DC

7,500 Columbia Hospital for Women (Teen Health Center), Washington, DC — health education outreach program providing classes and workshops to DC schools and the community, targeting young women ages 13-19

7,500 Good Shepherd Ministries, Washington, DC — educational, mentoring, and vocational programs provided to at-risk, low-income youth ages

13 through 18 at Teen Center

7,500 Higher Achievement Program (HAP), Washington, DC — HAP's six week academic summer enrichment program for highly motivated and talented low-income students in grades 5-8

7,500 Martha's Table, Washington, DC — educational after school program for homeless children

6,000 Anacostia Coordinating Council, Washington, DC — neighborhood planning enrichment course for 8th and 9th graders at Kramer Junior High School

---

Strosacker Foundation, Charles J.

CONTACT
Patricia E. McKelvey
Secretary
Charles J. Strosacker Foundation
PO Box 471
Midland, MI 48640-0471
(517) 832-0066

FINANCIAL SUMMARY
Recent Giving: $1,300,000 (1992 approx.); $1,303,140 (1991); $1,299,120 (1990)
Assets: $29,500,000 (1992 est.); $29,560,650 (1991); $26,066,852 (1990); $34,664,521 (1989)
EIN: 38-6062787

CONTRIBUTIONS SUMMARY
Donor(s): The foundation was established in 1957 by the late Charles J. Strosacker (1882-1963), one of the pioneers of the Dow Chemical Company.
Typical Recipients: • *Arts & Humanities:* arts centers • *Civic & Public Affairs:* housing • *Education:* colleges & universities • *Social Services:* community centers, community service organizations, united funds
Grant Types: general support
Geographic Distribution: focus on Michigan, with emphasis on the city of Midland

GIVING OFFICERS
David J. Arnold: trust

Martha G. Arnold: pres, trust
Lawrence E. Burks: treas, trust
Ralph A. Cole: vp, trust
John Samuel Ludington: asst treas, trust *B* Detroit MI 1928 *ED* Albion Coll BS 1951; Saginaw Valley St Coll JD 1977 *CURR EMPL* chmn, dir: Dow Corning Corp *CORP AFFIL* dir: Bank-Midland Comerica *NONPR AFFIL* chmn bd trusts: Albion Coll; dir: Am Industrial Health Counc; mem fin comm: Chemical Mfrs Assn; trust: Midland Commun Ctr
Patricia E. McKelvey: secy
Hon Donna T. Morris: asst secy, trust
Charles J. Thrune: asst vp, trust
Eugene C. Yehle: chmn, trust

APPLICATION INFORMATION
Initial Approach:
Send full proposal. All correspondence must be in writing, unless the foundation initiates a personal interview.

The proposal should describe the purpose of the project, amount required, timetable for funding and completion of the project, a list of other income sources, and a list of major expenditures. The proposal should also include copies of the IRS letter granting tax-exempt status to the applicant and the organization's latest financial statements.

Requests should be received by October of the year preceding the time payment is desired.
Restrictions on Giving: The foundation does not make grants to individuals.

OTHER THINGS TO KNOW
Publications: annual report (including application guidelines)

GRANTS ANALYSIS
Total Grants: $1,303,140
Number of Grants: 59
Highest Grant: $277,500
Typical Range: $1,000 to $15,000
Disclosure Period: 1991
Note: Average grant figure excludes the foundation's two highest grants of $277,500 and $200,300. Recent grants are derived from a 1991 grants list.

RECENT GRANTS
277,500 United Way of Midland County, Midland, MI

200,300 City of Midland-Riverside Place, Midland, MI
100,500 Cooley Law School
100,000 Midland Community Center, Midland, MI
75,000 Saginaw Valley State University, University Center, MI
60,500 Kalamazoo College, Kalamazoo, MI
41,000 Baldwin-Wallace College, Berea, OH
40,000 Central Michigan University, Mount Pleasant, MI
40,000 David Reece Fund, MI
31,200 Midland Foundation, Midland, MI

Stroud Foundation

CONTACT
W. B. Dixon Stroud
Manager
Stroud Fdn.
c/o Mellon Bank (East), N.A.
PO Box 7236
Philadelphia, PA 19101
(215) 553-2557

FINANCIAL SUMMARY
Recent Giving: $241,050 (1991); $244,900 (1990); $333,500 (1988)
Assets: $3,325,617 (1991); $2,856,624 (1990); $2,662,414 (1988)
Gifts Received: $84,621 (1991); $62,431 (1990); $352,927 (1988)
Fiscal Note: In 1991, contributions were received from Wilmington Trust.
EIN: 23-6255701

CONTRIBUTIONS SUMMARY
Donor(s): Joan M. Stroud.
Typical Recipients: • *Arts & Humanities:* libraries, music, theater • *Civic & Public Affairs:* environmental affairs • *Education:* colleges & universities, private education (precollege) • *Health:* pediatric health • *Religion:* churches • *Science:* scientific institutes, scientific organizations
Grant Types: capital, emergency, endowment, general support, multiyear/continuing support, research, scholarship, and seed money

GIVING OFFICERS
Joan S. Blaine: mgr
T. Sam Means: mgr

Joan M. Stroud: mgr
Morris W. Stroud: mgr
W. B. Dixon Stroud: mgr
Truman Welling: mgr

APPLICATION INFORMATION
Initial Approach: Send brief letter of inquiry describing program or project. There are no deadlines.
Restrictions on Giving: Does not support individuals.

GRANTS ANALYSIS
Number of Grants: 16
Highest Grant: $120,000
Typical Range: $500 to $13,000
Disclosure Period: 1991

RECENT GRANTS
120,000 Academy of Natural Sciences, Philadelphia, PA
65,000 Marine Environmental Research, New York, NY
24,000 Upland Day School, Kennett Square, PA
13,000 Harpischord Music Society, Whitestone, NY
5,000 Harvard University, Cambridge, MA
4,000 Smithsonian Institution, Washington, DC
3,500 Northeast Harbor Library, Northeast Harbor, ME
2,000 Sarah Lawrence College, Bronxville, NY
1,000 Delaware Theater Company, Wilmington, DE
1,000 Groton School, Groton, MA

Strouse, Greenberg & Co. / Strouse, Greenberg & Co. Charitable Fund
Headquarters: Philadelphia, PA
SIC Major Group: Real Estate

CONTACT
Howard Abrams
Director
Strouse, Greenberg & Co. Charitable Fund
1626 Locust St.
Philadelphia, PA 19103
(215) 985-1100

FINANCIAL SUMMARY
Recent Giving: $16,500 (1989)

Assets: $4,891 (1990); $4,648 (1989)
Gifts Received: $14,500 (1989)
Fiscal Note: In 1989, contributions were received from Strouse, Greenberg & Co.
EIN: 23-6298227

CONTRIBUTIONS SUMMARY
Typical Recipients: • *Education:* colleges & universities • *Health:* mental health • *Religion:* religious organizations
Grant Types: general support
Geographic Distribution: focus on PA
Operating Locations: PA (Philadelphia)

CORP. OFFICERS
Joseph Strauss, Jr.: *CURR EMPL* chmn: Strouse Greenberg & Co
Samuel Switzenbaum: *CURR EMPL* pres: Strouse Greenberg & Co

GIVING OFFICERS
Howard Abrams: dir
Archie Hampton: dir
Joseph Strauss, Jr.: dir *CURR EMPL* chmn: Strouse Greenberg & Co (see above)

APPLICATION INFORMATION
Initial Approach: Send brief letter describing program. There are no deadlines.

GRANTS ANALYSIS
Disclosure Period: 1990
Note: No grants were provided in 1990.

RECENT GRANTS
14,500 Allied Jewish Appeal, Philadelphia, PA
1,000 Philadelphia Psychiatric Center, Philadelphia, PA
1,000 University of Pennsylvania, Philadelphia, PA

Stry Foundation, Paul E.

CONTACT
Paul E. Stry Foundation
311 Main Street
La Crosse, WI 54601-3251
(608) 782-1148

FINANCIAL SUMMARY
Recent Giving: $177,191 (1990); $159,322 (1989)
Assets: $3,556,788 (1990); $3,746,608 (1989)

EIN: 39-1598681

CONTRIBUTIONS SUMMARY
Typical Recipients: • *Civic & Public Affairs:* environmental affairs • *Education:* colleges & universities • *Religion:* churches • *Social Services:* family services, homes, recreation & athletics
Grant Types: general support

GIVING OFFICERS
Robert Sramo: vp
Robert Swartz: pres

APPLICATION INFORMATION
Initial Approach: The foundation reports it only makes contributions to preselected organizations and does not accept unsolicited requests for funds.

GRANTS ANALYSIS
Total Grants: $177,191
Highest Grant: $97,670
Typical Range: $660 to $14,307
Disclosure Period: 1990

RECENT GRANTS
97,670 University of Wisconsin, WI — La Crosse Foundation
50,000 Hixon Forest Nature Center
14,307 City of La Crosse, La Crosse, WI
5,382 Bethesda Lutheran Home
4,650 La Crosse Park and Recreation
2,641 Nature Conservancy
1,321 First Evangelical Lutheran Church
660 Coulee Region Sierra Club
660 Family and Children's Center

Stuart Center Charitable Trust, Hugh

CONTACT
Hugh Stuart Center Charitable Trust
152 North Third St., Ste. 400
San Jose, CA 95115-0024
(408) 293-0463

FINANCIAL SUMMARY
Recent Giving: $442,235 (1989); $382,680 (1988)
Assets: $8,193,816 (1989); $7,822,482 (1988)
EIN: 94-2455308

CONTRIBUTIONS SUMMARY

Donor(s): the late Hugh Stuart Center

Typical Recipients: • *Arts & Humanities:* community arts, museums/galleries, music, performing arts, theater • *Education:* colleges & universities • *Health:* hospitals • *Religion:* churches, religious organizations • *Social Services:* child welfare, community centers, community service organizations, disabled, food/clothing distribution, shelters/homelessness, united funds, youth organizations

Grant Types: general support

Geographic Distribution: focus on San Jose, CA

GIVING OFFICERS

Arthur K. Lund: trust
Louis O'Neal: trust

APPLICATION INFORMATION

Initial Approach: Contributes only to preselected organizations.

GRANTS ANALYSIS

Number of Grants: 178
Highest Grant: $50,000
Typical Range: $500 to $3,000
Disclosure Period: 1989

RECENT GRANTS

50,000 O'Connor Hospital Foundation Society, San Jose, CA — general fund

26,000 Crippled Children's Society, Santa Clara, CA — general fund

25,000 Peninsula Center for the Blind, Palo Alto, CA

25,000 Technology Center, San Jose, CA — general fund

20,000 American Inns of Court Foundation, Washington, DC — general fund

15,000 Peninsula Center for the Blind, Palo Alto, CA

15,000 University of California Santa Cruz Foundation, Santa Cruz, CA — general fund

11,500 O'Connor Hospital Foundation Society, San Jose, CA — general fund

10,000 Santa Clara University, Santa Clara, CA — general fund

10,000 University of California Berkeley

Foundation, Class of 1950, Berkeley, CA — general fund

Stuart Foundation

CONTACT

James M. Stuart
Treasurer
Stuart Fdn.
126 East 56th St.
New York, NY 10022
(212) 753-0800

FINANCIAL SUMMARY

Recent Giving: $125,443 (1991); $112,820 (1990); $101,543 (1989)
Assets: $2,953,539 (1991); $2,444,458 (1990); $2,613,357 (1989)
EIN: 13-6066191

CONTRIBUTIONS SUMMARY

Donor(s): members of the Stuart family

Typical Recipients: • *Arts & Humanities:* libraries, opera, public broadcasting • *Civic & Public Affairs:* municipalities • *Education:* colleges & universities, private education (precollege) • *Health:* hospitals, medical research • *Religion:* religious organizations, synagogues • *Social Services:* community service organizations, recreation & athletics, united funds, youth organizations

Grant Types: general support

Geographic Distribution: focus on NY and New England.

GIVING OFFICERS

Ronda H. Lubin: secy
Edward Polito: asst secy
Alan L. Stuart: dir, vp, secy
Carolyn A. Stuart: dir
James M. Stuart, Sr.: pres, dir
James M. Stuart, Jr.: dir
James M. Stuart, Sr.: pres, dir (see above)

APPLICATION INFORMATION

Initial Approach: Contributes only to preselected organizations.

GRANTS ANALYSIS

Number of Grants: 43
Highest Grant: $84,448
Typical Range: $100 to $1,500
Disclosure Period: 1991

RECENT GRANTS

84,448 Brown University, Providence, RI

6,550 Congregation Emanuel Westches-

ter, Westchester, NY

5,000 Metropolitan Opera Association, New York, NY

5,000 United Jewish Appeal Federation of Jewish Philanthropies, New York, NY

4,000 Rye Country Day School, Rye, NY

1,638 United Way, New York, NY

1,620 Congregation Emanuel, New York, NY

1,100 Hudson Guild, New York, NY

1,000 Brown Sports Foundation, New York, NY

1,000 White Plains Hospital Medical Center, White Plains, NY

Stuart Foundation, Edward C.

CONTACT

Margrette M. Stuart
President
Edward C. Stuart Fdn.
PO Box 250
Bartow, FL 33830

FINANCIAL SUMMARY

Recent Giving: $337,606 (fiscal 1991); $331,197 (fiscal 1990); $453,732 (fiscal 1989)
Assets: $2,667,078 (fiscal year ending May 31, 1991); $2,764,685 (fiscal 1990); $2,936,803 (fiscal 1989)
EIN: 59-6142151

CONTRIBUTIONS SUMMARY

Donor(s): William H. Stuart, and family

Typical Recipients: • *Education:* colleges & universities, science/technology education

Grant Types: general support, multiyear/continuing support, scholarship, and seed money

GIVING OFFICERS

C.A. Boswell: secy, treas
Stuart Lane: trust
Margrette M Stuart: pres
Nancy S. Stuart: trust
William H. Stuart: trust
William H. Stuart, Jr.: vp

APPLICATION INFORMATION

Initial Approach: Send brief letter describing program. There are no deadlines.

Restrictions on Giving: Does not support individuals.

OTHER THINGS TO KNOW

Publications: Annual Report, Application Guidelines

GRANTS ANALYSIS

Number of Grants: 13
Highest Grant: $240,455
Typical Range: $500 to $4,000
Disclosure Period: fiscal year ending May 31, 1991

RECENT GRANTS

240,455 Erskine College, Due West, SC — scholarship program

68,651 Davidson College, Davidson, NC

12,500 Nancy Fulwood Hospital, Greenville, SC — Pakistan orthopaedic project

4,000 Harvard University, Cambridge, MA — academic tournament

3,500 Massachusetts Institute of Technology, Cambridge, MA — academic tournament

2,000 Florida FFA Foundation, Tallahassee, FL — leadership program

2,000 Rose-Hulman Institute of Technology, Terre Haute, IN

1,000 Auburn University, Auburn, AL — academic tournament

1,000 Princeton University, Princeton, NJ — academic tournament

1,000 Turnaround, Winter Haven, FL — adolescent drug rehabilitation program

Stuart Foundation, Elbridge and Evelyn

CONTACT

Bill August
Vice President
Bank of America
333 S. Hope St.
Los Angeles, CA 90071
(213) 613-4877

FINANCIAL SUMMARY

Recent Giving: $530,000 (1991); $470,000 (1990); $440,000 (1989)
Assets: $8,755,058 (1991); $8,073,654 (1990); $8,011,476 (1989)
EIN: 95-6014019

CONTRIBUTIONS SUMMARY

Typical Recipients: • *Education:* agricultural education, business education, colleges & universities, religious education • *Health:* hospitals, pediatric health • *Religion:* churches, religious organizations
Geographic Distribution: focus on CA

GIVING OFFICERS
Bank of America: trust

APPLICATION INFORMATION
Initial Approach: Send brief letter of inquiry describing program or project. There are no deadlines.

GRANTS ANALYSIS
Number of Grants: 39
Highest Grant: $140,000
Typical Range: $1,000 to $10,000
Disclosure Period: 1991

RECENT GRANTS
140,000 Stanford University, Stanford, CA
50,000 American Graduate School of International Management, Los Angeles, CA
50,000 J. Paul Getty Trust, Los Angeles, CA
40,000 Stanford University, Stanford, CA
26,000 Episcopal Diocese of Los Angeles, Los Angeles, CA
25,000 St. Matthew's Church, Los Angeles, CA
20,000 Children's Hospital Medical Center, Los Angeles, CA
18,500 University of Redlands, Redlands, CA
10,000 St. John's Hospital, Los Angeles, CA
10,000 Winrock International, Los Angeles, CA

Stuart Foundations

CONTACT
Theodore E. Lobman
President
Stuart Foundations
188 The Embarcadero, Ste. 420
San Francisco, CA 94105
(415) 495-1144

FINANCIAL SUMMARY
Recent Giving: $7,300,000 (1993 est.); $7,300,000 (1992 approx.); $7,600,000 (1991)
Assets: $202,600,000 (1992); $197,000,000 (1991); $167,000,000 (1990)
Fiscal Note: The above asset and giving figures represent the combined figures for the three Stuart foundations.

CONTRIBUTIONS SUMMARY
Donor(s): The Stuart Foundations combine three family trusts: the Elbridge Stuart Foundation, the Elbridge and Mary Stuart Foundation, and the Mary Horner Stuart Foundation. The foundations were created by the late Elbridge A. Stuart, who in 1899 founded the Pacific Coast Condensed Milk Company, which later became the Carnation Company, headquartered in Los Angeles. Previously administered by the company, in 1985 the three Stuart Trusts were transferred to San Francisco to be administered together, on an independent basis, as the Stuart Foundations.
Typical Recipients: • *Civic & Public Affairs:* public policy • *Education:* education associations, elementary education, preschool education, public education (precollege) • *Social Services:* child welfare, family services
Grant Types: general support and project
Geographic Distribution: primarily California and Washington

GIVING OFFICERS
Ellen Hershey: program off
Theodore E. Lobman: pres
Amelia B. Loomis: program off
Pat Reynolds: program off

APPLICATION INFORMATION
Initial Approach:
Applicants should obtain a copy of the detailed grantmaking guidelines before applying, which can be requested by phone.
Letters of request should include a description of the organization, problem to be solved, expected outcome, activities to be supported, and the amount requested. In addition, include a current financial statement and operating budget with an expense and income budget for the program to be funded; a list of the board of directors, showing compensation received and their principal outside affiliations; a description of the criteria by which the program fund can be evaluated; and a copy of the IRS letter indicating tax-exempt status. Proposals should arrive at least three months prior to the board meetings. The board usually meets in March, June, September, and December.
All applications received will be acknowledged, and applicants will be advised if further information or a visit is necessary. Applicants may inquire by telephone on the assessment of a proposal's chances of approval. After initiation of the grant, the organization must provide narrative and financial reports of how the funds were spent.
Restrictions on Giving: Grant requests for political or lobbying activities, general support of endowment, building or annual giving campaigns, support of individuals, or audio/visual programs are discouraged.

OTHER THINGS TO KNOW
Publications: Grantmaking Guidelines Brochure

GRANTS ANALYSIS
Total Grants: $7,300,000
Number of Grants: 134
Highest Grant: $500,000
Typical Range: $25,000 to $200,000
Disclosure Period: 1992
Note: Recent grants are derived from a 1991 grants list.

RECENT GRANTS
250,000 California Foundation for the Improvement of Employer-Employee Relations, Sacramento, CA — to provide training, networking, and research services
245,000 Kaiser Family Foundation, Health Promotion Program, Menlo Park, CA — to continue community-wide pregnancy and substance abuse prevention programs
240,636 Children's Hospital and Health Center, San Diego, CA — to create in interagency collaborative system
220,000 Developmental Studies Center, San Ramon, CA — to extend the Child Development Project
218,363 University of Southern California, School of Social Work, Los Angeles, CA — for an evaluation of in-home family support programs
201,745 Santa Monica Hospital Medical Center, Rape Treatment Center, Santa Monica, CA — for start-up and operating expenses
157,370 ETR Associates, Santa Cruz, CA — to establish and manage a training system
150,000 Children's Bureau of Los Angeles, Los Angeles, CA — for continued support of the Family Connection Program
150,000 Hathaway Children's Services, Sylmar, CA — for continued support of the In-Home Services Project
150,000 Los Angeles Educational Partnership, Los Angeles, CA — for Humanitas program

Stubblefield, Estate of Joseph L.

CONTACT
H. H. Hayner
Trustee
Estate of Joseph L. Stubblefield
249 West Alder St.
PO Box 1757
Walla Walla, WA 99362
(509) 527-3500

FINANCIAL SUMMARY
Recent Giving: $137,353 (1991); $126,868 (1990); $119,965 (1989)

Assets: $3,208,909 (1991);
$2,926,963 (1990); $2,858,330
(1989)

EIN: 91-6031350

CONTRIBUTIONS SUMMARY

Donor(s): the late Joseph L.
Stubblefield

Typical Recipients: • *Arts &
Humanities:* music • *Education:* colleges & universities
• *Health:* hospices • *Religion:*
churches • *Social Services:*
community service organizations, counseling, homes,
united funds, youth organizations

Grant Types: scholarship

Geographic Distribution: limited to WA and OR

GIVING OFFICERS

H. H. Hayner: trust

James K. Hayner: trust

Robert O. Kenyon: trust

APPLICATION INFORMATION

Initial Approach: Send brief
letter describing program.
There are no deadlines.

GRANTS ANALYSIS

Number of Grants: 24

Highest Grant: $15,000

Typical Range: $500 to $5,000

Disclosure Period: 1991

RECENT GRANTS

15,000 Whitman College,
Walla Walla, WA
11,000 Walla Walla Community Hospice,
Walla Walla, WA
10,000 Walla Walla College, Walla Walla,
WA
10,000 YMCA, Walla
Walla, WA
10,000 YWCA, Walla
Walla, WA
7,500 United Way, Walla
Walla, WA
5,200 Children's Home
Society, Walla
Walla, WA
5,000 Pacific Lutheran
University, Tacoma, WA
5,000 Seattle Pacific University, Seattle, WA
5,000 Walla Walla Symphony Guild, Walla
Walla, WA

Student Loan Marketing Association

Assets: $45.32 billion
Employees: 865
Headquarters: Washington, DC
SIC Major Group:
 Nondepository Institutions

CONTACT

Robin Kennedy
Compensations
Student Loan Marketing
 Association
1050 Thomas Jefferson St. N.W.
Washington, DC 20007
(202) 298-2541

CONTRIBUTIONS SUMMARY

Support goes to local education, human service, arts, and
civic organizations. Company
promotes voluntarism through
employee matching contribution program, employee publications that contain volunteer
information, and a recognition
program for employees who
volunteer.

Typical Recipients: • *Arts &
Humanities:* general • *Civic &
Public Affairs:* general • *Education:* general • *Social Services:*
general

Grant Types: matching

Geographic Distribution: primarily at headquarters and operating locations

Operating Locations: DC
(Washington)

CORP. OFFICERS

Lawrence Alan Hough: *B* Janesville WI 1944 *ED* Stanford
Univ 1966; MA Inst Tech 1973
CURR EMPL pres, ceo: Student Loan Mktg Assn *CORP
AFFIL* chmn: Shakespeare Theatre Co

Harry R. King: *CURR EMPL*
chmn, dir: Student Loan Mktg
Assn

Albert L. Lord: *CURR EMPL*
exec vp, coo: Student Loan
Mktg Assn

APPLICATION INFORMATION

Initial Approach: Send brief
letter of inquiry, including a description of the organization,
amount requested, purpose of
funds sought, recently audited
financial statements, and proof
of tax-exempt status. There are
no deadlines.

Restrictions on Giving: Does
not support religious organiza-

tions for sectarian purposes, or
political or lobbying groups.

GRANTS ANALYSIS

Typical Range: $1,000 to
$2,500

Stulsaft Foundation, Morris

CONTACT

Joan Nelson Dills
Administrator
Morris Stulsaft Foundation
100 Bush St., Ste. 825
San Francisco, CA 94104
(415) 986-7117

FINANCIAL SUMMARY

Recent Giving: $1,070,420
(1991); $1,075,253 (1990);
$1,170,777 (1989)
Assets: $22,066,766 (1991);
$19,520,853 (1990);
$19,201,846 (1989)
Gifts Received: $1,162,463
(1991); $1,300,056 (1990);
$1,298,656 (1989)
Fiscal Note: The foundation receives contributions from the
Morris Stulsaft Testamentary
Trust.
EIN: 94-6064379

CONTRIBUTIONS SUMMARY

Donor(s): The Morris Stulsaft
Foundation was established in
California in 1953 by the Morris Stulsaft Testamentary Trust.
Its primary aim is to aid San
Francisco organizations for
needy and deserving children,
without regard to race, creed,
or age.

Typical Recipients: • *Arts &
Humanities:* arts appreciation,
dance, museums/galleries,
music, opera, performing arts,
public broadcasting • *Civic &
Public Affairs:* zoos/botanical
gardens • *Education:* arts education, career/vocational education, education associations,
elementary education, faculty
development, literacy, minority
education, special education,
student aid • *Health:* hospitals,
medical research, mental
health, nursing services, pediatric health, single-disease
health associations • *Science:*
scientific institutes • *Social
Services:* child welfare, community centers, community
service organizations, counseling, day care, delinquency &
crime, disabled, domestic violence, drugs & alcohol, employment/job training, family plan-

ning, family services, homes,
recreation & athletics, refugee
assistance, shelters/homelessness, volunteer services, youth
organizations

Grant Types: capital, general
support, operating expenses,
and project

Geographic Distribution: six
counties of the San Francisco
Bay Area (Alameda, Conta
Costa, Marin, San Francisco,
San Mateo, and Santa Clara)

GIVING OFFICERS

Roy L. Bouque: dir

J. Boatner Chamberlain:
pres, dir

Mrs. Robert Corvin: dir

William Corvin: vp, dir

Joan Nelson Dills: adm

Andrew C. Gaither: dir

Raymond Marks: secy, treas,
dir *B* 1922

Edward A. Miller: dir

Isadore Pivnick: dir

Yori Wada: dir

APPLICATION INFORMATION

Initial Approach:
The foundation provides an application form. The foundation
application form must be used.
The grant application should include project title; date submitted; legal name of organization, address, city, zip code,
and telephone number; funds
requested; project budget; total
agency budget; signature of
authorized organization representative; project summary (including purposes, objectives
and methodology, number of
people served, and how funds
would be used if granted);
brief description of the organization; list of other funding
sources contacted and funds
committed or pending; and a
listing of previous application(s) to the foundation. With
the completed application
form, include the proof of tax
exemption from the IRS and
the Franchise Tax Board; IRS
letter classifying the organization as not a private foundation; most recent Form 990, including all attached schedules;
organization's articles of incorporation, bylaws, and all
amendments; latest financial
statement, audited if possible;
organization budget, including
income and expenses; current
list of officers, including occupations and affiliations; and an
organizational brochure.

Applications are accepted any time. The board meets in January, March, May, July, September, and November.

If interested, the board of directors may require a representative from the applying organization to provide a presentation (of not more than half an hour) to a committee of the board. All applications are acknowledged. Notice of approval or rejection, or requests for more information are usually made in about eight months.

Restrictions on Giving: No grants are made to individuals or for emergency funds, endowments, or sectarian purposes. The foundation does not provide ongoing support.

OTHER THINGS TO KNOW

Publications: biennial report and application guidelines

GRANTS ANALYSIS

Total Grants: $1,070,420
Number of Grants: 144
Highest Grant: $55,000
Typical Range: $2,500 to $10,000
Disclosure Period: 1991
Note: Recent grants are derived from a 1990-1991 biennial report.

RECENT GRANTS

55,000 United Jewish Community Centers, San Francisco, CA — to provide daycare/day camp at thirteen sites in Marin, San Mateo and San Francisco counties

25,000 Dominican College of San Rafael, San Rafael, CA — for multicultural focus for student-teaching candidates

25,000 Jewish Family and Children Services, San Francisco, CA — for partnership to improve learning for troubled youth

25,000 Mount St. Joseph's/St. Elizabeth's, San Francisco, CA — to expand the shelter for crack babies and teen mothers

25,000 New Children's Shelter Fund, San Jose, CA — toward construction of a residential cottage for abused and neglected children

25,000 University of California, San Francisco, San Francisco, CA — for the Clearinghouse for Drug Exposed Infants and Children

20,000 Bill Wilson Counseling Center, Santa Clara, CA — for purchase and construction of a twelve-bed youth shelter

15,000 Center to Prevent Handgun Violence, San Mateo, CA — to help Oakland students to prevent firearm violence

15,000 Children's Council of San Francisco, San Francisco, CA — for coordinator for Bayview/Hunters Point children's programs

15,000 Santa Clara County Office of Education, San Jose, CA — for Regional Office of Child Care to increase quality of care

---

Stupp Brothers Bridge & Iron Co. / Stupp Brothers Bridge & Iron Co. Foundation

Sales: $50.0 million
Employees: 350
Headquarters: St. Louis, MO
SIC Major Group: Fabricated Metal Products and Primary Metal Industries

CONTACT

Erwin P. Stupp, Jr.
Trustee
Stupp Brothers Bridge & Iron Co. Foundation
PO Box 6600
St. Louis, MO 63125
(314) 638-5000

FINANCIAL SUMMARY

Recent Giving: $325,980 (fiscal 1991); $323,120 (fiscal 1990); $351,505 (fiscal 1989)

Assets: $7,183,450 (fiscal year ending October 31, 1991); $6,319,439 (fiscal 1990); $6,420,314 (fiscal 1989)

Fiscal Note: Contributes through foundation only.

EIN: 23-7412437

CONTRIBUTIONS SUMMARY

Typical Recipients: • *Civic & Public Affairs:* economic development, municipalities, zoos/botanical gardens • *Education:* colleges & universities, private education (precollege) • *Health:* health organizations, hospitals, medical research, single-disease health associations • *Religion:* churches, religious organizations • *Social Services:* child welfare, community service organizations, homes, recreation & athletics, united funds

Grant Types: general support

Geographic Distribution: focus on Missouri

Operating Locations: MO (St. Louis)

CORP. OFFICERS

Robert P. Stupp: *B* St. Louis MO 1930 *ED* Washington Univ 1952 *CURR EMPL* pres, ceo, dir: Stupp Brothers Bridge & Iron Co *CORP AFFIL* dir: Laclede Gas Co; pres: Builders Engr Co; pres, dir: Stupp Brothers; sr vp: Stupp Corp *NONPR AFFIL* fellow: Am Soc Civil Engrs; mem: Am Inst Steel Construction, Am Soc Testing & Materials

GIVING OFFICERS

Erwin P. Stupp, Jr.: trust *CURR EMPL* chmn, dir: Stupp Brothers Bridge & Iron Co *CORP AFFIL* chmn, dir: Stupp Brothers Bridge & Iron Co

John P. Stupp, Jr.: trust *CURR EMPL* exec vp, secy, dir: Stupp Brothers Bridge & Iron Co *CORP AFFIL* exec vp, secy, dir: Stupp Brothers Bridge & Iron Co

Robert P. Stupp: trust *CURR EMPL* pres, ceo, dir: Stupp Brothers Bridge & Iron Co (see above)

APPLICATION INFORMATION

Initial Approach: *Note:* The foundation supports preselected organizations and does not accept unsolicited requests for funds.

GRANTS ANALYSIS

Total Grants: $325,980
Number of Grants: 163
Highest Grant: $47,000
Typical Range: $200 to $1,500
Disclosure Period: fiscal year ending October 31, 1991
Note: Recent grants are derived from a fiscal 1991 grants list.

RECENT GRANTS

47,000 United Way, St. Louis, MO

41,500 Washington University, St. Louis, MO

17,500 Capital Area United Givers Campaign, St. Louis, MO

15,900 Tower Grove Park, St. Louis, MO

14,000 Church of St. Michael and St. George, St. Louis, MO

11,500 St. Louis Country Day School, St. Louis, MO

11,250 Mary Institute, St. Louis, MO

8,200 St. Louis Mercantile Library Association, St. Louis, MO

7,700 St. Louis Zoo Association, St. Louis, MO

7,500 State of St. Louis Foundation, St. Louis, MO

Stupp Foundation, Norman J.

CONTACT

John W. North
Vice President
Norman J. Stupp Fdn.
Commerce Bank
8000 Forsyth Blvd.
Clayton, MO 63105
(314) 746-7220

FINANCIAL SUMMARY

Recent Giving: $531,249 (fiscal 1991); $509,708 (fiscal 1990); $457,333 (fiscal 1989)

Assets: $11,967,051 (fiscal year ending June 30, 1991); $11,776,001 (fiscal 1990); $10,746,817 (fiscal 1989)

EIN: 43-6027433

CONTRIBUTIONS SUMMARY

Donor(s): the late Norman J. Stupp

Typical Recipients: • *Arts & Humanities:* history/historic preservation, museums/galleries, public broadcasting • *Civic & Public Affairs:* municipalities, zoos/botanical gardens • *Education:* colleges & universities, community & junior colleges, medical education • *Health:* hospitals, medical research • *Science:* scientific institutes • *Social Services:* child welfare, community service organizations, united funds, youth organizations

Grant Types: capital, endowment, operating expenses, project, research, and scholarship
Geographic Distribution: focus on St. Louis, MO

GIVING OFFICERS
Commerce Bank of St. Louis: trust

APPLICATION INFORMATION
Initial Approach: Send brief letter describing program. There are no deadlines.

GRANTS ANALYSIS
Number of Grants: 44
Highest Grant: $93,333
Typical Range: $1,500 to $7,500
Disclosure Period: fiscal year ending June 30, 1991

RECENT GRANTS
    93,333 Washington University, St. Louis, MO
    55,000 Missouri Botanical Garden, St. Louis, MO
    50,000 Bethesda Building Fund, St. Louis, MO
    50,000 Bethesda General Hospital and Homes, St. Louis, MO
    30,000 St. Louis Science Center, St. Louis, MO
    28,000 YMCA, St. Louis, MO
    25,000 St. Louis Children's Hospital, St. Louis, MO
    20,000 Epworth Children's Home, St. Louis, MO
    20,000 St. Louis Art Museum, St. Louis, MO
    15,000 KETC Channel 9, St. Louis, MO

Sturgis Charitable and Educational Trust, Roy and Christine

CONTACT
Katie Speer
Roy and Christine Sturgis Charitable and Educational Trust
P. O. Box 92
Melvern, AR 72104
(501) 332-3899

FINANCIAL SUMMARY
Recent Giving: $530,624 (fiscal 1991); $1,536,159 (fiscal 1990); $2,010,892 (fiscal 1989)

Assets: $38,000,000 (fiscal 1993 est.); $38,000,000 (fiscal 1992 approx.); $37,315,690 (fiscal year ending September 30, 1991); $34,616,372 (fiscal 1990); $32,134,850 (fiscal 1989)

Gifts Received: $317,755 (fiscal 1988); $3,888,507 (fiscal 1986)

Fiscal Note: The foundation has received contributions from the estate of Christine Sturgis which is now closed.
EIN: 75-6331832

CONTRIBUTIONS SUMMARY
Donor(s): The trust was established in 1981 from the estate of Christine Sturgis. There is a Roy and Christine Sturgis Charitable and Educational Trust in Arkansas, as well as a Roy and Christine Sturgis Foundation, also in Arkansas.

Typical Recipients: • *Arts & Humanities:* music, performing arts • *Civic & Public Affairs:* nonprofit management • *Education:* colleges & universities, elementary education • *Health:* health organizations, pediatric health • *Social Services:* child welfare, domestic violence, family services, religious welfare, youth organizations

Grant Types: capital, endowment, general support, project, and research

Geographic Distribution: primarily Arkansas and Texas with some giving nationally

GIVING OFFICERS
Harry C. Mayer: trust off *CURR EMPL* sr vp (trusts): NCNB TX Natl Bank

APPLICATION INFORMATION
Initial Approach:
Potential applicants must request application form by mail. Application form should be filled out completely. Information that should be included with application is copy of IRS 501(c)(3) IRS letter; brief history of organization, its purpose and the people it serves; an one page budget outline; list of board members; and previous audited financial statement.
Proposals must be postmarked by February 1.
Grant decision meetings are held in late April. Receipients must wait one year after final payment to reapply.
Restrictions on Giving: The trust does not fund individuals, scholarship for individuals, seminars, loans, or political organizations.

OTHER THINGS TO KNOW
NationsBank of Texas serves as corporate trustee for the trust. Trustees consider grant requests which do not exceed $200,000. Funding for amounts above $200,000 will be considered on very limited basis. Charitable organizations which received a one payment grant must skip a year before applying for a new grant. Organizations which receive multiyear support cannot apply again while receiving payments and must skip a year from the date last payment is received.
The foundation designates 65% of funds for the state of Arkansas and 35% for the state of Texas and other areas.

GRANTS ANALYSIS
Total Grants: $2,177,200
Number of Grants: 34
Highest Grant: $700,000
Typical Range: $5,000 to $75,000
Disclosure Period: fiscal year ending September 30, 1991
Note: Average grant excludes two grants totaling $900,000. Recent grants are derived from a fiscal 1991 grants list.

RECENT GRANTS
    700,000 University of Arkansas at Fayetteville, Fayetteville, AR
    200,000 Easter Seal Society of Dallas, Dallas, TX
    200,000 YMCA of Metropolitan Dallas, Dallas, TX
    150,000 Arkansas Repertory Theatre Company, Little Rock, AR
    100,000 Centers for Youth and Families, Little Rock, AR
    100,000 Hendrix College, Conway, AR
    100,000 University of Arkansas-Monticello, Monticello, AR — Department of Forest Resources
     65,000 Kingsland Public Schools, Kingsland, AR
     60,000 Arkansas Advocates for Children and Families, Little Rock, AR
     60,000 Arkansas Rice Depot, Little Rock, AR

Subaru-Isuzu Automotive Inc.
Sales: $250.0 million
Employees: 1,908
Headquarters: Lafayette, IN
SIC Major Group:
   Transportation Equipment

CONTACT
Ann McConnell
Community Relations Manager
Subaru-Isuzu Automotive Inc.
5500 State Rd. 38 East
Post Office Box 5689
Lafayette, IN 47905
(317) 449-1111

FINANCIAL SUMMARY
Fiscal Note: Giving Range: approximately $100,000 annually

CONTRIBUTIONS SUMMARY
Company is actively involved in community organizations. Focus is on education, children, and arts and culture. Also supports the homeless, minorities, and the less fortunate.
Typical Recipients: • *Arts & Humanities:* community arts, music, public broadcasting • *Education:* colleges & universities • *Social Services:* child welfare, community service organizations, shelters/homelessness
Grant Types: capital, general support, and project
Nonmonetary Support Types: loaned employees
Geographic Distribution: primarily in headquarters community

Operating Locations: IN (Lafayette)

CORP. OFFICERS
Katsuya Utada: *CURR EMPL* exec vp, cfo: Subaru-Isuzu Automotive
Tamon Yamamoto: *CURR EMPL* pres: Subaru-Isuzu Automotive

APPLICATION INFORMATION
Initial Approach: Send letter of inquiry, including a description of the organization, amount requested, purpose of funds sought, and proof of tax-exempt status. A six-person contributions committee meets quarterly to review requests.

GRANTS ANALYSIS
Typical Range: $100 to $1,000

Subaru of America Inc. / Subaru of America Foundation

Revenue: $1.72 billion
Employees: 1,000
Headquarters: Cherry Hill, NJ
SIC Major Group: Wholesale Trade—Durable Goods

CONTACT
Denise L. Schwartz
Foundation Manager
Subaru of America Fdn.
Subaru Plz.
PO Box 6000
Cherry Hill, NJ 08034
(609) 488-5099

FINANCIAL SUMMARY
Recent Giving: $244,923 (1991); $400,000 (1990); $416,838 (1989)
Assets: $853,805 (1991); $1,246,778 (1989)
Fiscal Note: Figures for foundation only and do not include company direct giving.
EIN: 22-2531774

CONTRIBUTIONS SUMMARY
Typical Recipients: • *Arts & Humanities:* arts centers, community arts, dance, museums/galleries, music, performing arts, theater • *Civic & Public Affairs:* environmental affairs, safety, urban & community affairs, women's affairs, zoos/botanical gardens • *Education:* business education, colleges & universities, education associations, international ex-

change, literacy • *Health:* health organizations, hospitals, pediatric health, single-disease health associations • *Social Services:* child welfare, community service organizations, domestic violence, family services, united funds, youth organizations
Grant Types: employee matching gifts, general support, operating expenses, project, and seed money
Nonmonetary Support Types: donated products and loaned executives
Geographic Distribution: primarily supports organizations in and around company's Cherry Hill, NJ, headquarters; to a lesser degree, foundation supports organizations in regional office locations: Aurora, CO; Addison, IL; Moorestown, NJ; Austell, GA; and Portland, OR

CORP. OFFICERS
Takeshi Higurashi: *CURR EMPL* chmn, pres, ceo, dir: Subaru of Am
George T. Muller: *CURR EMPL* exec vp, dir: Subaru of Am
Charles T. Worrell: *CURR EMPL* exec vp, dir: Subaru of Am

GIVING OFFICERS
Denise L. Schwartz: fdn mgr

APPLICATION INFORMATION
Initial Approach: The foundation requires no special application forms. Grant requests are accepted year-round with application deadline dates on the first working day of March, July, and October. The foundation's contributions committee, trustees, and staff meet in April, August, and November. Acknowledgment letters for qualified proposals are sent out within four weeks of receipt of request. Eligible applicants should allow five months for the entire review process. Final decisions are communicated in writing within three weeks of each trimester meeting. Proposals that are accepted for review are assigned to the appropriate member of the employee contribution committee, who will often contact the applicant directly. Committee members are assigned specific categories and are responsible for evaluating proposals and making fund-

ing recommendations to the foundation trustees. In order that a proposal be considered, it must contain the following information upon submission: brief description of the organization including objectives, activities, and specified area of service; summary of the proposed project, how the project will improve the situation, and expected outcomes of the proposed project; indication of the level of support requested and other project supporters, if appropriate; most recent audited financial statements, including sources and amounts of financial support; detailed organizational budget for the current operating year; budget of the proposed project for which funding is requested; list of governing board, including their primary affiliations; and proof of 501(c)(3) status. Organizations are asked not to submit a proposal more than once in any 12-month period. Repeat requests will not be considered in the same year. A grant does not necessarily indicate that continued support will be awarded. Unless specified as a multiyear commitment, funding requests must be submitted annually.
Restrictions on Giving: Grants are limited to organizations that are tax-exempt under IRC section 501(c)(3). Does not support individuals; veteran, fraternal and/or labor organizations; direct support of churches, religious groups, or sectarian groups; social, membership, or other groups that serve the special interests of their constituency; advertising in charitable publications; fund raising campaigns or athletic events; political organizations/campaigns or candidates; or organizations that benefit individuals or groups outside the United States. The foundation makes no vehicle donations (Occasionally, howvever, Subaru of America may choose to participate in the support of an organization through these means).

OTHER THINGS TO KNOW
The foundation makes a limited number of grants to national organizations that have a direct impact on the foundation's goals. Determination of eligibility for national organizations is

at the discretion of the foundation staff, contributions committee, and trustees.
Publications: Policies and Guidelines

GRANTS ANALYSIS
Number of Grants: 95
Highest Grant: $10,400
Typical Range: $1,000 to $5,000
Disclosure Period: 1991

RECENT GRANTS
104,047 United Way, Camden, NJ
15,000 Rutgers University Foundation, Camden, NJ
8,333 Academy of Natural Sciences, Philadelphia, PA — capital campaign
8,333 Franklin Institute, Philadelphia, PA — three year grant toward Futures Center capital campaign
8,000 Philadelphia Orchestra Association, Philadelphia, PA
6,000 Academy of Natural Sciences, Philadelphia, PA
5,000 Camden County Council of Girl Scouts, Cherry Hill, NJ — capital campaign for "Subaru" trail
5,000 Glassboro State College Development Fund, Glassboro, NJ — towards college's Provost Lecture Series 1992
5,000 Kennedy Health Care Foundation, Sewell, NJ — toward expansion and upgrading of the Cherry Hill Division's Emergency Room
5,000 Mothers Against Drunk Driving, Dallas, TX — for MADD Student Library

Suburban Propane
Sales: $571.6 million
Employees: 3,000
Parent Company: Quantum Chemical Corp.
Headquarters: New York, NY

CONTACT
Arden Melick
Director, Corporate
Communications
Quantum Chemical
99 Park Ave.
New York, NY 10016
(212) 949-5000
Note: Suburban Propane Gas is
located at P.O. Box 206,
Whippany, NY 07981.

FINANCIAL SUMMARY
Fiscal Note: Annual Giving
Range: less than $100,000

CONTRIBUTIONS SUMMARY
Contributions are made
through parent company.
Geographic Distribution:
grants are awarded in headquarters and operating communities
Operating Locations: NY
(New York, Whippany)

CORP. OFFICERS
Dennis J. Spina: *CURR EMPL*
pres: Suburban Propane Gas
Corp
Dennis J. Spina: *CURR EMPL*
pres: Suburban Propane Gas
Corp

APPLICATION INFORMATION
Initial Approach: Company
does not accept proposals at
this time.

GRANTS ANALYSIS
Typical Range: $10 to $1,000

RECENT GRANTS
EMS Squad, Cedar Knolls, NJ
EMS Squad, Lony Valley, NJ

Sudbury Inc.
Sales: $376.2 million
Employees: 3,957
Headquarters: Cleveland, OH
SIC Major Group: Chemicals &
Allied Products, Fabricated
Metal Products, Primary Metal
Industries, and Rubber &
Miscellaneous Plastics Products

CONTACT
Carol Egan
Executive Secretary
Sudbury Inc.
25800 Science Park Dr.
Cleveland, OH 44122
(216) 464-7026

CONTRIBUTIONS SUMMARY
Operating Locations: OH
(Cleveland)

CORP. OFFICERS
Russell B. Every: *CURR
EMPL* pres: Sudbury
Thomas M. Lynch: *CURR
EMPL* exec vp, cfo: Sudbury
Tinkham Veale II: *CURR
EMPL* chmn: Sudbury

Sudix Foundation

CONTACT
Wesley Moon Dixon, Jr.
President
Sudix Fdn.
400 Skokie Boulevard, Ste. 675
Northbrook, IL 60062
(708) 291-9790

FINANCIAL SUMMARY
Recent Giving: $160,000
(1990); $163,000 (1989);
$150,000 (1987)
Assets: $3,453,458 (1990);
$3,349,949 (1989); $3,168,567
(1987)
EIN: 36-3377946

CONTRIBUTIONS SUMMARY
Donor(s): Wesley M. Dixon, Jr.
Typical Recipients: • *Arts &
Humanities:* museums/galleries
• *Civic & Public Affairs:* environmental affairs • *Education:*
education associations, private
education (precollege),
science/technology education
• *Health:* hospitals, medical research • *Religion:* churches
• *Social Services:* animal protection
Grant Types: general support
Geographic Distribution:
focus on IL

GIVING OFFICERS
Suzanne Searle Dixon: vp,
secy, treas *B* 1931 *NONPR
AFFIL* trust: Northwestern
Meml Hosp
Wesley Moon Dixon, Jr.: pres
B Evanston IL 1927 *ED* Yale
Univ BA 1950 *CURR EMPL*
vp: Earl-Kinship Capital Corp
CORP AFFIL dir: Northern
Trust Co, Searle (GD) & Co;
vp: Earl-Kinship Capital Corp
NONPR AFFIL dir: Lake Forest Hosp, Rehab Inst Chicago,
Up With People; mem: Chicago Counc Foreign Rels;
trust: Art Inst Chicago, Lake
Forest Coll
Susan R. Piggott: dir

APPLICATION INFORMATION
Initial Approach: Contributes
only to preselected organizations.

GRANTS ANALYSIS
Number of Grants: 7
Highest Grant: $60,000
Typical Range: $5,000 to
$25,000
Disclosure Period: 1990

RECENT GRANTS
60,000 Brain Research
Foundation, Chicago, IL
30,000 First Presbyterian
Church, Lake Forest, IL
25,000 Woodside School,
Woodside, CA
20,000 Lake Forest Hospital, Lake Forest, IL
15,000 Lambs, Chicago, IL
5,000 American Friends
of Game Conservation, Chicago, IL
5,000 Chicago Foundation for Education,
Chicago, IL

Sullivan Foundation, Algernon Sydney

CONTACT
William E. Bardusch, Jr.
President
Algernon Sydney Sullivan Fdn.
53 Maple Ave.
Morristown, NJ 07960
(201) 267-8856

FINANCIAL SUMMARY
Recent Giving: $549,350
(1991); $544,350 (1990);
$429,350 (1989)
Assets: $11,075,443 (1991);
$9,610,507 (1990); $9,375,028
(1989)
Gifts Received: $15,000
(1991); $10,000 (1990)
Fiscal Note: In 1991, contributions were received from Vera
H. Armstrong.
EIN: 13-6084596

CONTRIBUTIONS SUMMARY
Donor(s): the late Mrs. Algernon Sydney Sullivan, the late
George Hammond Sullivan, the
late Zilph P. Devereaux
Typical Recipients: • *Education:* colleges & universities
Grant Types: scholarship
Geographic Distribution:
focus on the Southeast

GIVING OFFICERS
William E. Bardusch, Jr.:
pres, trust
John S. Chapman, Jr.: off
Charles W. Cook: secy, trust
Nancy Cortner: trust

Walter G. Dunnington, Jr.:
trust *B* New York NY 1927 *ED*
Univ VA BA 1948; Univ VA
LLB 1950 *CORP AFFIL* dir:
Brittainia Indus (India)
NONPR AFFIL bd govs: NY
Hosp; mem: Am Bar Assn,
Assn Bar City NY, NY St Bar
Assn; trust: Algernon Sydney
Sullivan Fdn, Boys Club NY,
Woodberry Forest Sch
Hiram B. Ely, Jr.: trust
R. Bruce McBratney: trust
Myles C. Morrison IV: trust
Frederick L. Redpath: treas,
trust
Gray Williams, Jr.: trust
Emmett Wright, Jr.: trust

APPLICATION INFORMATION
Initial Approach: Send brief
letter of inquiry describing program or project. There are no
deadlines.
Restrictions on Giving: Does
not support individuals.

GRANTS ANALYSIS
Number of Grants: 29
Highest Grant: $22,500
Typical Range: $4,500 to
$13,000
Disclosure Period: 1991

RECENT GRANTS
22,500 Berea College,
Berea, KY
16,000 Lincoln Memorial
University, Harrogate, TN
16,000 Mary Baldwin College, Staunton, VA
14,750 Randolph-Macon
College, Ashland,
VA
13,500 Warren Wilson College, Swannanoa,
NC
13,250 Hampden-Sydney
College, Hampden-Sydney, VA
13,250 University of
South, Sewanee,
TN
12,250 Cumberland College, Williamsburg, KY
12,250 Erskine College,
Due West, SC
12,250 Furman University,
Greenville, SC

Sullivan Foundation, Ray H. and Pauline

CONTACT
John J. Curtin
Ray H. and Pauline Sullivan Fdn.
c/o Connecticut National Bank
250 Captain's Walk
New London, CT 06320
(203) 447-6132

FINANCIAL SUMMARY
Recent Giving: $496,800 (fiscal 1991); $436,425 (fiscal 1990); $336,935 (fiscal 1989)
Assets: $8,849,111 (fiscal year ending July 31, 1991); $8,419,338 (fiscal 1990); $8,541,566 (fiscal 1989)
EIN: 06-6141242

CONTRIBUTIONS SUMMARY
Donor(s): the late Ray H. Sullivan
Typical Recipients: • *Education:* private education (precollege), religious education • *Health:* hospitals • *Religion:* churches, missionary activities, religious organizations • *Social Services:* community service organizations, counseling, food/clothing distribution
Grant Types: general support and scholarship
Geographic Distribution: focus on the diocese of Norwich, CT

GIVING OFFICERS
Virginia M. Calanquin: trust
David C. Kavicke: trust
James McGuire: trust
Msgr. Paul J. St. Onge: trust

APPLICATION INFORMATION
Initial Approach: Application form required. Deadline is May 1.

OTHER THINGS TO KNOW
Primarily provides scholarships to individuals for higher education.

GRANTS ANALYSIS
Number of Grants: 46
Highest Grant: $22,000
Typical Range: $2,000 to $10,000
Disclosure Period: fiscal year ending July 31, 1991

RECENT GRANTS
22,000 St. Bernard High School
22,000 St. Bernard High School
22,000 St. Bernard High School
22,000 St. Bernard High School
22,000 St. Bernard High School
20,000 Lawrence and Memorial Hospital
20,000 Mt. St. John School for Boys
20,000 St. Joseph School
20,000 St. Joseph School
20,000 St. Joseph School

Sullivan Musical Foundation, William Matheus

CONTACT
David Lloyd
Executive Director
William Matheus Sullivan Musical Fdn.
251 West 89th St
New York, NY 10024
(201) 238-3489

FINANCIAL SUMMARY
Recent Giving: $111,749 (1991); $184,186 (1990); $64,350 (1989)
Assets: $3,635,569 (1991); $3,218,182 (1990); $3,372,092 (1989)
Gifts Received: $1,250 (1991)
EIN: 13-6069096

CONTRIBUTIONS SUMMARY
Donor(s): the late William Matheus Sullivan, the late Arcie Lubetkin
Typical Recipients: • *Arts & Humanities:* opera
Grant Types: project

GIVING OFFICERS
Rose Bampton: trust
Spencer Byard: trust
Bruce Donnell: trust
Edward O. Downes: trust
Barbara B. Last: trust, pres
David Lloyd: trust, exec dir
Peter J. Merrill: trust, treas
Jose T. Moscoso: trust, secy
Stanley Reese: trust
Lee Schaenen: trust

APPLICATION INFORMATION
Initial Approach: Requests for New York auditions should be accompanied by resume and copy of contract for at least one engagement with full orchestra after November; San Francisco and Chicago auditions in early November, New York auditions in mid-November.

OTHER THINGS TO KNOW
Provides grants to advance the careers of gifted young singers who have completed their formal music training.
Publications: Application Guidelines

GRANTS ANALYSIS
Number of Grants: 23
Highest Grant: $17,083
Typical Range: $250 to $750
Disclosure Period: 1991
Note: Incomplete grants list provided in 1991.

RECENT GRANTS
17,083 Opera America, New York, NY

Sulzberger Foundation

CONTACT
Marian S. Heiskell
President
Sulzberger Fdn.
229 West 43rd St.
New York, NY 10036
(212) 556-1750

FINANCIAL SUMMARY
Recent Giving: $1,001,147 (1991); $1,018,865 (1990); $839,819 (1989)
Assets: $21,955,901 (1991); $18,531,197 (1990); $18,628,326 (1989)
Gifts Received: $28,953 (1990); $1,500,000 (1989); $1,547,490 (1988)
Fiscal Note: In 1990, contributions were received from the Sarah Christy Trust.
EIN: 13-6083166

CONTRIBUTIONS SUMMARY
Donor(s): The foundation was incorporated in 1956 by the late Arthur Hays Sulzberger and the late Iphigene Ochs Sulzberger.
Typical Recipients: • *Arts & Humanities:* arts associations, arts funds, history/historic preservation, libraries, museums/galleries, music, opera, public broadcasting • *Civic & Public Affairs:* economic development, environmental affairs, municipalities, philanthropic organizations, professional & trade associations, zoos/botanical gardens • *Education:* colleges & universities, education funds, international studies, medical education, private education (precollege) • *Health:* hospitals, medical research • *Religion:* religious organizations, synagogues • *Social Services:* recreation & athletics, shelters/homelessness, united funds

Grant Types: capital, conference/seminar, emergency, endowment, fellowship, general support, operating expenses, professorship, project, scholarship, and seed money

Geographic Distribution: national

GIVING OFFICERS
Marian Sulzberger Heiskell: pres, dir *B* New York NY 1918 *ED* Frobeleague Kindergarten Teaching Sch 1941 *CORP AFFIL* dir: Consolidated Edison Co NY, Ford Motor Co, Merck & Co, NY Times Co *NONPR AFFIL* chmn: Citizens Westway Park Adv Comm, Counc Environment NY City, Gateway Natl Recreation Area Adv Comm; co-chmn: We Care About NY; dir: Natl Audubon Soc, NY Citizens Balanced Transportation, NYC Partnership, Regional Plan Assn; exec comm: NY Botanical Gardens; mem: Natl Parks System Adv Bd, St Park Recreation Comm City NY; mem, dir: Inter Am Press Assn; trust: Parks Counc

Ruth Sulzberger Holmberg: vp, dir *B* New York NY 1921 *ED* Smith Coll AB 1943 *CURR EMPL* publ, dir: Chattanooga Times *CORP AFFIL* dir: NY Times Co *NONPR AFFIL* dir: Hunter Mus Art, Reading Is Fundamental, Southern Ctr Intl Studies; sustaining mem: Jr League; trust: Univ Chattanooga Fdn

Frederick T. Mason: asst secy, asst treas

Arthur Ochs Sulzberger, Sr.: vp, secy, treas, dir *B* New York NY 1926 *ED* Columbia Univ BA 1951 *CURR EMPL* chmn, ceo: NY Times Co *CORP AFFIL* dir: Times Printing Co *NONPR AFFIL* chmn, trust: Metro Mus Art; mem: Newspaper Publs Assn, Sons Am Revolution; mem, dir: Bur Newspaper Advertising; trust: Columbia Univ

Judith P. Sulzberger: vp, dir *NONPR AFFIL* attending physician: St Luke's-Roosevelt Hosp Ctr

APPLICATION INFORMATION

Initial Approach:
The foundation has no formal grant application procedure or application form.

The foundation has no deadline for submitting proposals.

Restrictions on Giving: The foundation makes grants only to public charities described in IRS section 501(c)(3). No grants are made to individuals, or for matching gifts or loans.

GRANTS ANALYSIS

Total Grants: $1,001,147
Number of Grants: 192
Highest Grant: $77,150
Typical Range: $500 to $10,000
Disclosure Period: 1991
Note: Recent grants are derived from a 1991 grants list.

RECENT GRANTS

77,150 Metropolitan Museum of Art, New York, NY
64,500 Council on the Environment of New York City, New York, NY
40,000 Tennessee Aquarium, Chattanooga, TN
30,000 American Foundation for AIDS Research, New York, NY
30,000 Columbia College of Physicians and Surgeons, New York, NY
25,000 Allied Arts Fund of Greater Chattanooga, Chattanooga, TN
25,000 Chattanooga Symphony and Opera Association, Chattanooga, TN
25,000 Mount Sinai Medical Center, New York, NY
25,000 New York Public Library, New York, NY
21,500 New York Botanical Garden, Bronx, NY

Sulzer Brothers Inc.

Sales: $460.0 million
Employees: 4,000
Headquarters: New York, NY
SIC Major Group: Chemicals & Allied Products, Engineering & Management Services, Industrial Machinery &

Equipment, and Primary Metal Industries

CONTACT
Susan Leech
Controller
Sulzer Brothers Inc.
200 Park Ave.
New York, NY 10166
(212) 949-0999

CONTRIBUTIONS SUMMARY
Operating Locations: NY (New York)

CORP. OFFICERS
Fritz Fahrni: *CURR EMPL* pres, ceo, dir: Sulzer Brothers

Sulzer Family Foundation

CONTACT
Sulzer Family Fdn.
1940 West Irving Park Rd.
Chicago, IL 60613

FINANCIAL SUMMARY
Recent Giving: $213,600 (1989); $200,100 (1988)
Assets: $3,270,088 (1989); $3,634,546 (1988)
EIN: 36-2466016

CONTRIBUTIONS SUMMARY
Donor(s): Grace E. Sulzer
Typical Recipients: • *Arts & Humanities:* history/historic preservation, libraries • *Education:* colleges & universities • *Health:* hospices • *Religion:* churches • *Social Services:* recreation & athletics, shelters/homelessness, united funds, youth organizations
Grant Types: multiyear/continuing support, operating expenses, and scholarship
Geographic Distribution: focus on IL; emphasis on the Ravenswood and Lakeview areas of Chicago

GIVING OFFICERS
Richard Bjorklund: dir
John J. Hoellen: pres
Robert B. Hoellen: dir
Rev. George Rice: secy
Arthur Teleser: treas
Sherwin Willens: dir

APPLICATION INFORMATION
Initial Approach: Only contributes to preselected organizations.

GRANTS ANALYSIS
Number of Grants: 85
Highest Grant: $15,000
Typical Range: $1,000 to $5,000
Disclosure Period: 1989

RECENT GRANTS
15,000 Neighborhood Boys Club, Chicago, IL
15,000 Sulzer Regional Library, Chicago, IL
10,000 North Park College, Chicago, IL
3,500 St. Benedict High School, Chicago, IL
3,500 WTTW, Chicago, IL
2,500 Our Lady of Lourdes Grade School, Chicago, IL
2,500 Queen of Angels Grade School, Chicago, IL
2,500 Salvation Army, Chicago, IL
1,000 Swedish American Museum, Chicago, IL
1,000 Uptown Fellowship, Chicago, IL

Sumitomo Bank of California

Assets: $5.41 billion
Employees: 1,589
Headquarters: San Francisco, CA
SIC Major Group: Depository Institutions

CONTACT
Mike Crawford
Administration
Sumitomo Bank of California
320 California St.
8th Fl.
San Francisco, CA 94104
(415) 445-8000

FINANCIAL SUMMARY
Recent Giving: $335,000 (1993)
Fiscal Note: Company gives directly.

CONTRIBUTIONS SUMMARY
Typical Recipients: • *Arts & Humanities:* community arts, libraries, museums/galleries, music, public broadcasting • *Civic & Public Affairs:* economic development, housing, municipalities, urban & community affairs • *Education:* business education, colleges & universities, community & junior colleges, public education (precollege) • *Health:* health organizations • *Social Services:*

community service organizations, disabled, employment/job training, family services, united funds, youth organizations
Grant Types: department, employee matching gifts, general support, and project
Geographic Distribution: contributions restricted to headquarters area

GIVING OFFICERS
Mike Crawford: *CURR EMPL* admin: Sumitomo Bank CA
Michele Dixon: *CURR EMPL* pub aff rep: Sumitomo Bank CA

APPLICATION INFORMATION
Initial Approach: *Initial Contact:* brief letter of inquiry *Include Information On:* description of the organization and name of contact person, a statement of purpose, a request for a specific amount of funding, an explanation of why it is needed and how it will be used, a list of contributors, and a recently audited financial statement* *When to Submit:* any time *Note:* Individual branches administer small budgets; large grants are referred to headquarters.
Restrictions on Giving: Does not support individuals, religious organizations for sectarian purposes, political or lobbying groups, or organizations outside operating areas.

GRANTS ANALYSIS
Total Grants: $335,000
Typical Range: $1,000 to $2,500
Disclosure Period: 1993
Note: Grants listed below were provided by the company in 1993.

RECENT GRANTS
Big Brothers/Big Sisters of East Bay, CA
La Familia Counseling Center, Sacramento, CA
Low-Income Housing Fund, San Francisco, CA
Neighborhood Housing Service, CA
Nonprofit Housing Assistance, San Francisco, CA
Ronald McDonald House, San Francisco, CA
San Francisco Symphony Orchestra, San Francisco, CA
United Way, CA

Sumitomo Corp. of America

Sales: $10.0 billion
Employees: 1,400
Headquarters: New York, NY
SIC Major Group: Holding &
Other Investment Offices, Real
Estate, Wholesale
Trade—Durable Goods, and
Wholesale Trade—Nondurable
Goods

CONTACT

K. Okamoto
General Manager, General
Affairs
Sumitomo Corp. of America
345 Park Ave.
New York, NY 10154
(212) 207-0700

FINANCIAL SUMMARY

Fiscal Note: Giving Range:
$300,000 annually

CONTRIBUTIONS SUMMARY

Contributions are handled on a
case-by-case basis. Highest priority is education. Other recipients have included arts centers,
music, colleges and universities, and single-disease health
associations. Also has funded
little league baseball games between Japanese and American
teams.

Typical Recipients: • *Arts &
Humanities:* arts centers, music
• *Education:* colleges & universities, international exchange,
international studies • *Health:*
single-disease health associations • *Social Services:* youth
organizations

Grant Types: general support
Geographic Distribution: primarily metropolitan New York
City
Operating Locations: NY
(New York)

CORP. OFFICERS

Masahiro Ishikawa: *CURR
EMPL* vp, gen mgr, treas,
acctg: Sumitomo Corp of Am
Kenji Sadao Miyahara:
CURR EMPL pres, ceo: Sumitomo Corp of Am
Tadasu Takagi: *CURR EMPL*
exec vp: Sumitomo Corp of Am

GIVING OFFICERS

Y. Yamane: *CURR EMPL* gen
mgr, gen aff: Sumitomo Corp
of Am

APPLICATION INFORMATION

Initial Approach: Send a proposal at any time, including a
description of the organization
and the amount requested.

GRANTS ANALYSIS

Typical Range: $1,000 to
$5,000

Sumitomo Trust & Banking Co., Ltd.

Employees: 308
Headquarters: New York, NY
SIC Major Group: Depository
Institutions

CONTACT

David Warren
Vice President and Manager,
Community Affairs
Sumitomo Trust & Banking Co.,
Ltd.
527 Madison Ave.
8th Fl.
New York, NY 10022
(212) 418-4813

FINANCIAL SUMMARY

Fiscal Note: Giving Range:
$100,000 to $150,000

CONTRIBUTIONS SUMMARY

Sumitomo targets middle
school reform within the immediate communities which it
serves, with an emphasis on
mathematics, science, and english. Company is currently involved in education reform projects with the Fund for New
York City Public Education,
Bank Street College, and Castle Hill Middle School in the
Bronx. Sumitomo Trust also is
active in adopting classes from
local community schools.

Typical Recipients: • *Arts &
Humanities:* general • *Civic &
Public Affairs:* international affairs
Grant Types: project
Nonmonetary Support Types:
loaned executives
Geographic Distribution:
near operating locations only
Operating Locations: NY
(New York)

CORP. OFFICERS

Hiromasa Yakushiji: *CURR
EMPL* dir, gen mgr: Sumitomo
Trust & Banking Co Ltd

GIVING OFFICERS

Ray Kuchler: *CURR EMPL*
asst vp (commun): Sumitomo
Trust & Banking Co Ltd

David Warren: *CURR EMPL*
vp, mgr commun affs: Sumitomo Trust & Banking Co Ltd

APPLICATION INFORMATION

Initial Approach: Initial letter
may be submitted at any time
and should include a description and brief history of the organization, the amount requested, the purpose for which
funds are sought, and any timing constraints.

Summa Development Corp.

Revenue: $28.0 million
Employees: 135
Headquarters: Las Vegas, NV
SIC Major Group: Real Estate

CONTACT

Gary Ray
Chairman, Public Affairs
Committee
Summa Development Corp.
PO Box 14000
Las Vegas, NV 89114
(702) 791-4000

CONTRIBUTIONS SUMMARY

Operating Locations: NV
(Las Vegas)

CORP. OFFICERS

John L. Goolsby: *CURR
EMPL* ceo, pres: Summa Devel
Corp

Summerfield Foundation, Solon E.

CONTACT

Joseph A. Tiano
Secretary
Solon E. Summerfield
Foundation
270 Madison Avenue, Rm. 1201
New York, NY 10016
(212) 685-5529

FINANCIAL SUMMARY

Recent Giving: $1,498,171
(1991); $1,415,483 (1990);
$1,435,729 (1989)
Assets: $34,933,160 (1991);
$34,364,057 (1990);
$34,346,768 (1989)
EIN: 13-1797260

CONTRIBUTIONS SUMMARY

Donor(s): The foundation was
established in 1939 by the late

Solon E. Summerfield (1877-
1947).

Typical Recipients: • *Arts &
Humanities:* arts associations,
arts festivals, libraries, museums/galleries, music, performing arts, public broadcasting,
theater • *Civic & Public Affairs:* environmental affairs,
ethnic/minority organizations,
law & justice, philanthropic organizations, professional &
trade associations, public policy • *Education:* arts education,
business education, colleges &
universities, community & junior colleges, education associations, education funds, legal
education, medical education,
minority education, private education (precollege), student aid
• *Health:* geriatric health,
health funds, hospitals, medical
research, nursing services, outpatient health care delivery, single-disease health associations
• *Religion:* churches, religious
organizations • *Social Services:*
aged, child welfare, community
centers, community service organizations, counseling, disabled, family services,
food/clothing distribution, recreation & athletics, religious
welfare, shelters/homelessness,
youth organizations
Grant Types: endowment, general support, and scholarship
Geographic Distribution: emphasis on the Northeast especially New York, NY

GIVING OFFICERS

William W. Prager: pres, trust
Joseph A. Tiano: secy, treas,
trust
Clarence R. Treeger: vp, trust

APPLICATION INFORMATION

Initial Approach:
Send initial letter of inquiry.
Grant proposals require general
information about the proposed
project and the applicant.
There are no deadlines for submitting proposals.
Restrictions on Giving: Almost 80% of the foundation's
funds are set aside for preselected organizations

GRANTS ANALYSIS

Total Grants: $1,498,171*
Number of Grants: 115*
Highest Grant: $20,000
Typical Range: $10,000 to
$20,000
Disclosure Period: 1991
Note: Figure for total grants includes $1,071,171 in undis-

closed grants. Number of grants figure is partial. Figure for average grants is based on 115 grants given. An undisclosed number of grants were made in addition to the ones disclosed. All of above figures are based on grants given between January 27, 1991 and January 26, 1992. Recent grants are derived from a 1991 Form 990.

RECENT GRANTS

- 20,000 Kansas University Endowment Association, Lawrence, KS
- 12,500 Levine School of Music, Washington, DC
- 12,000 Visions, Washington, DC
- 10,000 American University, Washington, DC
- 10,000 Barnard College, New York, NY
- 10,000 Bennington College, Bennington, VT
- 10,000 Brandeis University, Waltham, MA
- 10,000 Brown University, Providence, RI
- 10,000 Bryn Mawr College, Bryn Mawr, PA
- 10,000 Columbia College, New York, NY

Summerlee Foundation

CONTACT
David D. Jackson
Vice President
Summerlee Fdn.
8222 Douglas Avenue, Ste. 580
Dallas, TX 75225

FINANCIAL SUMMARY
Recent Giving: $598,727 (fiscal 1990); $13,500 (fiscal 1989)
Assets: $7,984,267 (fiscal year ending June 30, 1990); $4,121,070 (fiscal 1989)
Gifts Received: $4,011,212 (fiscal 1990); $4,014,356 (fiscal 1989)
EIN: 75-8314010

CONTRIBUTIONS SUMMARY
Donor(s): Annie Lee Roberts
Typical Recipients: • *Arts & Humanities:* history/historic preservation, museums/galleries • *Civic & Public Affairs:* environmental affairs • *Education:* private education (precollege) • *Religion:* relig-

ious organizations • *Social Services:* animal protection
Grant Types: general support
Geographic Distribution: focus on TX and SD

GIVING OFFICERS
Mary Lavinia Griffith: vp
David D. Jackson: vp, secy, treas, mgr
Anne Lee Roberts: pres

APPLICATION INFORMATION
Initial Approach: Send brief letter of inquiry describing program or project. Deadlines are December 15, March 15, June 15, and September 15. Board meets in January, April, July, and October.
Restrictions on Giving: Does not support individuals or provide loans.

GRANTS ANALYSIS
Number of Grants: 29
Highest Grant: $250,000
Typical Range: $2,500 to $20,000
Disclosure Period: fiscal year ending June 30, 1990

RECENT GRANTS

- 250,000 St. Josephs Indian School, Chamberlain, SD
- 90,000 San Jacinto Museum of History, La Porte, TX
- 41,000 San Jacinto Museum of History, La Porte, TX
- 40,000 Society for the Prevention of Cruelty to Animals, Dallas, TX
- 21,000 Daughters of the Republic of Texas Library, San Antonio, TX
- 19,844 Emergency Animal Relief Fund, Dallas, TX
- 18,500 Animal Connection of Texas, Dallas, TX
- 18,000 Animal Protection Institute, Sacramento, CA
- 15,575 Physicians Committee for Responsible Medicine, Washington, DC
- 13,000 South Texas Primate Observation, Dilley, TX

Summit Bancorporation
Assets: $3.76 billion
Employees: 1,760
Headquarters: Chatham, NJ
SIC Major Group: Depository Institutions and Holding & Other Investment Offices

CONTACT
Laurie Friedman
Public Relations Director
Summit Bancorporation
One Maine St.
Chatham, NJ 07928
(201) 701-2638

CONTRIBUTIONS SUMMARY
Operating Locations: NJ (Chatham, Flemington, Maplewood, Point Pleasant Beach, Princeton, Ship Bottom, Short Hills, Somerville, Summit)

CORP. OFFICERS
Robert G. Cox: *B* Watertown NY 1941 *ED* Mohawk Valley Community Coll 1960 *CURR EMPL* pres, dir: Summit Bancorp *CORP AFFIL* ceo, dir, pres: Summit Trust Co *NONPR AFFIL* mem: Am Inst Real Estate Appraisers
John R. Feeney: *CURR EMPL* exec vp, cfo: Summit Bancorp
Thomas D. Sayles, Jr.: *B* Newton Center MA 1932 *ED* Dartmouth Coll 1954; NY Univ Sch Bus Admin 1961 *CURR EMPL* chmn, ceo, dir: Summit Bancorp *CORP AFFIL* dir: Selective Ins Group; mem: Robert Morris Assocs

Sumners Foundation, Hatton W.

CONTACT
Gordon R. Carpenter
Executive Director
Hatton W. Sumners Fdn.
3333 NCNB Center Tower II
Dallas, TX 75201
(214) 220-2128

FINANCIAL SUMMARY
Recent Giving: $1,483,042 (1991); $1,370,300 (1989); $1,306,500 (1988)
Assets: $36,397,720 (1991); $31,559,876 (1989); $29,634,279 (1988)
Gifts Received: $5,150 (1991); $12,000 (1989); $6,000 (1988)
EIN: 75-6003490

CONTRIBUTIONS SUMMARY
Donor(s): The foundation was established in 1949 by the late Hatton W. Sumners for the teaching and science of self-government. Hatton Sumners served as a U.S. Senator from Texas for 34 years before his voluntary retirement in 1947.
Typical Recipients: • *Arts & Humanities:* museums/galleries, public broadcasting • *Civic & Public Affairs:* law & justice, municipalities • *Education:* colleges & universities, economic education, legal education, religious education, social sciences education • *Health:* medical research • *Social Services:* child welfare, community service organizations, youth organizations
Grant Types: endowment and general support
Geographic Distribution: focus on Texas and Oklahoma

GIVING OFFICERS
Gordon R. Carpenter: exec dir, trust
David Bourne Long: trust
Alfred P. Murrah, Jr.: trust
William C. Pannell: trust
J. Cleo Thompson, Jr.: trust
Thomas S. Walker: trust

APPLICATION INFORMATION
Initial Approach:
Grant applications must be in writing but need not be formal. Letters of application should include the full name of the organization and the date when it was founded; a brief narrative of the primary purpose and work of the organization; a list of trustees or directors and the principal administrative officer; evidence of the organization's tax-exempt status; a brief description of the specific program for which funds are requested, together with an expression of how this conforms to the foundation's purpose; a budget, or proposed budget, for the project or program; the grant amount requested; and date the funds are needed. Brief and concise applications are preferred. If any of the requested information is contained within an annual report or another document, simply refer to the document and enclose a copy.
Proposals must be received by August 15 to be considered by the trustees in October.

Applicants will be acknowledged as promptly as possible once the funding decisions are made.

Restrictions on Giving: The foundation does not make loans, grants-in-aid, scholarships, or fellowships directly to individuals. Grants for such purposes are made to selected schools, colleges, and universities, and each school administers the grant funds. The foundation is non-political and non-partisan; none of its funds are to be used for political or propagandistic purposes.

GRANTS ANALYSIS

Total Grants: $1,483,042
Number of Grants: 40
Highest Grant: $407,679
Typical Range: $5,000 to $50,000
Disclosure Period: 1991
Note: Recent grants are derived from a 1991 grants list.

RECENT GRANTS

407,679 Oklahoma City University School of Law, Oklahoma City, OK — Sumners scholarship endowment

201,554 Schreiner College, Kerrville, TX — Sumners scholarship endowment

100,809 Southern Methodist University School of Law, Dallas, TX — Sumners scholarship endowment

100,000 Howard Payne University, Brownwood, TX — student center building

75,000 Law Focused Education, Austin, TX — teachers training seminars

55,000 Texas Wesleyan University, Fort Worth, TX — Sumners scholars program

50,000 Austin College, Sherman, TX — Sumners scholars endowment

50,000 Because We Care, Fort Worth, TX — counseling program in schools

50,000 Thrive Program, Oklahoma City, OK

36,000 Southern Methodist University, Dallas, TX — undergraduate scholarships

Sun Banks Inc. / Sun Bank Foundation

Assets: $17.76 billion
Employees: 8,018
Parent Company: Suntrust Banks Inc.
Headquarters: Orlando, FL
SIC Major Group: Depository Institutions, Insurance Agents, Brokers & Service, and Nondepository Institutions

CONTACT

Frank Nelson
Trustee
Sun Banks of Florida
PO Box 3838
Orlando, FL 32802
(407) 237-5063

FINANCIAL SUMMARY

Recent Giving: $300,000 (fiscal 1993 est.); $109,850 (fiscal 1991); $391,250 (fiscal 1990)
Assets: $4,425,457 (fiscal year ending June 30, 1991); $4,349,821 (fiscal 1990)
Fiscal Note: Contributes through foundation only.
EIN: 59-6877429

CONTRIBUTIONS SUMMARY

Typical Recipients: • *Arts & Humanities:* community arts • *Civic & Public Affairs:* economics • *Education:* colleges & universities
Grant Types: general support
Geographic Distribution: primarily Florida
Operating Locations: FL (Brooksville, Cape Coral, Daytona Beach, Ft. Lauderdale, Gainesville, Jacksonville, Miami, Naples, Ocala, Orlando, Panama City, Pensacola, Plant City, Port Charlotte, Sarasota, Sebring, Tallahassee, Tampa, Vero Beach, Winter Haven, Zephyrhills)
Note: Sun Bank has 17 branches in locations with geographic predicates, such as Sun Bank of Gainesville.

CORP. OFFICERS

Wendell H. Colson: *CURR EMPL* pres: Sun Banks
Buell G. Duncan, Jr.: *B* Orlando FL 1928 *ED* Emory Univ 1950 *CURR EMPL* chmn: Sun Banks *CORP AFFIL* dir: Columbian Mutual Life Ins Co

GIVING OFFICERS

Sunbank, N.A.: trust

APPLICATION INFORMATION

Initial Approach: *Initial Contact:* brief letter *Include Information On:* tax-exempt status of organization *When to Submit:* any time
Restrictions on Giving: Foundation gives specifically to scientific, literary, and educational institutions.

GRANTS ANALYSIS

Total Grants: $109,850
Number of Grants: 4
Highest Grant: $100,000
Typical Range: $1,250 to $6,700
Disclosure Period: fiscal year ending June 30, 1991
Note: Average grant figure does not include the highest grant of $100,000. Recent grants are derived from a fiscal 1991 grants list.

RECENT GRANTS

100,000 University of Central Florida, Orlando, FL — scholar chair in banking

6,700 TMH Foundation, Tallahassee, FL — diabetes center

1,900 Senior Society Planning Council, Tallahassee, FL

1,250 Tallahassee YMCA, Tallahassee, FL

Sun Chemical Corp.

Sales: $890.0 million
Employees: 5,600
Parent Company: Dainippon Ink & Chemicals Inc.
Headquarters: Fort Lee, NJ
SIC Major Group: Chemicals & Allied Products

CONTACT

Salvatore Cacace
Vice President, Finance
Sun Chemical
222 Bridge Plaza, South
Ft. Lee, NJ 07024
(201) 224-4600

FINANCIAL SUMMARY

Fiscal Note: Annual Giving Range: $100,000 to $250,000

CONTRIBUTIONS SUMMARY

Operating Locations: IL (Northlake), NJ (Fort Lee), OH (Cincinnati)

CORP. OFFICERS

E. E. Barr: *B* Reading PA 1937 *ED* NY Univ 1957; Univ MI 1959 *CURR EMPL* ceo, pres: Sun Chem
Biag Vignolo, Jr.: *CURR EMPL* cfo: Sun Chem

Sun Co.

Sales: $10.44 billion
Employees: 14,219
Headquarters: Philadelphia, PA
SIC Major Group: Coal Mining, Oil & Gas Extraction, Pipelines Except Natural Gas, and Wholesale Trade—Nondurable Goods

CONTACT

Richard Jackman
Vice President, Communications
Sun Co.
1801 Market St.
Philadelphia, PA 19103
(215) 977-6524
Note: Eileen Impriano, Director of Contributions, is also a contact person.

FINANCIAL SUMMARY

Recent Giving: $3,200,000 (1993 est.); $4,000,000 (1992 approx.); $4,900,000 (1991 approx.)
Fiscal Note: Company gives directly.

CONTRIBUTIONS SUMMARY

Typical Recipients: • *Arts & Humanities:* arts associations, arts centers, dance, museums/galleries, music, performing arts • *Civic & Public Affairs:* business/free enterprise, economic development, public policy, urban & community affairs • *Education:* business education, colleges & universities, education associations, engineering education, literacy, minority education, public education (precollege), science/technology education, student aid • *Health:* hospitals, outpatient health care delivery, public health • *Social Services:* aged, community service organizations, disabled, drugs & alcohol, emergency relief, employment/job training, united funds, youth organizations
Grant Types: employee matching gifts, general support, project, and scholarship
Note: Company reports that employee matching gifts are suspended for 1993.
Nonmonetary Support Types: in-kind services

Note: Company reports that it offers in-house printing and use of conference facilities to nonprofits. Estimated value of support for 1991 was $100,000 and is not included in above giving totals.
Geographic Distribution: gives local in scope, primarily in Philadelphia and operating locations, gives very few nationally
Operating Locations: OH (Toledo), OK (Tulsa), PA (Marcus Hook, Philadelphia)
Note: Also operates in Puerto Rico.

CORP. OFFICERS
Robert Henderson Campbell: *B* Pittsburgh PA 1937 *ED* Princeton Univ BS 1959; Carnegie-Mellon Univ MS 1961; MA Inst Tech MA 1978 *CURR EMPL* chmn, ceo, pres: Sun Co *CORP AFFIL* bd dirs: Philadelphia Natl Bank; pres: Sun Refining & Mktg Co *NONPR AFFIL* mem: Am Petroleum Inst

GIVING OFFICERS
Eileen A. Impriano: mem *CURR EMPL* dir (contributions): Sun Co
Richard Jackman: mem *CURR EMPL* vp (commun): Sun Co

APPLICATION INFORMATION
Initial Approach: *Initial Contact:* letter to Richard Jackman or to local Sun facility *Include Information On:* brief history of organization, list of key management and board, number of paid employees and volunteers, annual report or update of activities, latest audited financial report, current operating budget and sources of income, and copy of current tax-exempt status; requests for program support also should include purpose and objective, need addressed, population served, plan of action and time frame, qualifications of administrators, total funding required and projected sources, evaluative criteria, and utilization of results *When to Submit:* any time *Note:* See "Other Things You Should Know" for more details.
Restrictions on Giving: Company does not support political parties or candidates, individuals, or organizations that are not tax-exempt; generally does not support veterans, labor, re-

ligious, fraternal, or athletic groups; goodwill advertising or benefit fund raisers; or funding to cover continuing operating deficits.

OTHER THINGS TO KNOW
Contributions program focuses on needs of company's operating locations, primarily in the Philadelphia area. In view of the company's restructuring and budget reductions, new grant applications were not encouraged at time of publication.

GRANTS ANALYSIS
Total Grants: $4,000,000
Disclosure Period: 1992
Note: Recent grants are derived from a 1992 grants list.

RECENT GRANTS
40,000 American Red Cross Disaster Relief Campaign

Sun-Diamond Growers of California
Sales: $602.9 million
Employees: 2,500
Headquarters: Pleasanton, CA
SIC Major Group: Agricultural Services, Food & Kindred Products, and Wholesale Trade—Nondurable Goods

CONTACT
Richard Douglas
Senior Vice President, Corporate Affairs
Sun-Diamond Growers of California
PO Box 9024
Pleasanton, CA 94566
(510) 463-8200

CONTRIBUTIONS SUMMARY
Operating Locations: CA (Pleasanton, Stockton)

CORP. OFFICERS
Larry Busboom: *CURR EMPL* pres: Sun-Diamond Growers of CA

Sun Electric Corp.
Sales: $220.4 million
Employees: 2,205
Headquarters: Crystal Lake, IL
SIC Major Group: Automotive Dealers & Service Stations, Industrial Machinery & Equipment, Instruments &

Related Products, and Miscellaneous Repair Services

CONTACT
H. A. Stark
Senior Vice President, Human Resources
Sun Electric Corp.
One Sun Pkwy.
Crystal Lake, IL 60014
(815) 459-7700

CONTRIBUTIONS SUMMARY
Operating Locations: IL (Crystal Lake)

CORP. OFFICERS
Martin M. Ellen: *CURR EMPL* exec vp, cfo: Sun Electric Corp
Gerald A. Kien: *CURR EMPL* chmn, pres, ceo: Sun Electric Corp

Sun Life Assurance Co. of Canada (U.S.)
Assets: $5.11 billion
Parent Employees: 1,500
Headquarters: Wellesley Hills, MA
SIC Major Group: Insurance Carriers

CONTACT
Paul Vaskas
Public Relations Officer
Sun Financial Group
One Sun Life Executive Park, SC 1385
Wellesley Hills, MA 02181
(617) 237-6030

FINANCIAL SUMMARY
Fiscal Note: Annual Giving Range: $100,000 to $250,000

CONTRIBUTIONS SUMMARY
Supports health and human services, medical research, and education; arts and cultural organizations receive limited support. Contributions range is for U.S. operations only.
Operating Locations: MA (Wellesley Hills)

CORP. OFFICERS
Thomas Bell: *CURR EMPL* asst vp (group insurance): Sun Fin Group
John R. Gardner: *CURR EMPL* pres: Sun Life Assurance Co Canada (US)
David Horn: *CURR EMPL* gen mgr: Sun Life Assurance Co Canada

John D. McNeil: *CURR EMPL* chmn: Sun Life Assurance Co Canada (US)

GIVING OFFICERS
Paul Vaskas: *CURR EMPL* pub rels mgr: Sun Fin Group

Sun Microsystems / Sun Microsystems Foundation
Sales: $3.62 billion
Employees: 12,500
Headquarters: Mountain View, CA
SIC Major Group: Business Services and Industrial Machinery & Equipment

CONTACT
Sun Microsystems Fdn.
2550 Garcia Ave.
Mailstop PAL1-516
Mountain View, CA 94043
(415) 336-5337
Note: Company does not list a contact person.

FINANCIAL SUMMARY
Recent Giving: $1,400,000 (1993 est.); $1,489,739 (1992 approx.); $1,208,480 (1991)
Assets: $3,000,000 (1993 approx.); $1,854,445 (1991)
Gifts Received: $3,011,000 (1991)
Fiscal Note: Above figures are for the foundation only and do not include nonmonetary support. Contact for such support is Connie Brobeck, Manager, Academic Equipment Grants.
EIN: 77-0244198

CONTRIBUTIONS SUMMARY
Typical Recipients: • *Civic & Public Affairs:* business/free enterprise, economic development, urban & community affairs • *Education:* business education, career/vocational education, minority education, public education (precollege) • *Social Services:* employment/job training
Grant Types: employee matching gifts and project
Nonmonetary Support Types: donated products and in-kind services
Note: Estimate for nonmonetary support is not available. Contact for product donation for research is Emil Sarpa. Contact for education product donations is Connie Brobeck. Company also offers workplace solicitation for several feder-

ated campaigns. See "Other Things You Should Know" for more details.

Geographic Distribution: the south San Francisco Bay, CA, area and the Merrimack Valley, MA

Operating Locations: CA (Milpitas, Mountain View), MA (Chelmsford)

Note: Company also has sales, services, and other support in 83 locations throughout the U.S. and sales, services, and distributors in 63 foreign countries, including Brazil, China, Japan, Norway, Peru, Singapore, and the United Kingdom.

CORP. OFFICERS

Scott G. McNealy: *B* Columbus IN 1954 *ED* Harvard Univ BA 1976; Stanford Univ Grad Sch Bus MBA 1980 *CURR EMPL* co-fdr, chmn, pres, ceo, dir: Sun Microsystems *CORP AFFIL* chmn: Sun Microsystems Fed; pres: Sun Microsystems Computer Corp

GIVING OFFICERS

Ken Alveres: pres
Richard Barker: cfo
Michael H. Morris: secy, dir *CURR EMPL* vp, gen coun, secy: Sun Microsystems
Mark Vermillion: exec dir

APPLICATION INFORMATION

Initial Approach: *Initial Contact:* one- to two-page concept letter *Include Information On:* description of the organization, its goals, and project; project duration; budget; qualifications of staff; and proof of tax-exempt status *When to Submit:* deadline for concept letters are February 15, May 15, August 15, and November 15

Restrictions on Giving: Gives only to organizations in south San Francisco Bay area, CA, and the Merrimack Valley, MA. Does not support individuals, religious or political organizations, or fund-raising events. Also does not make grants for corporate sponsorship.

OTHER THINGS TO KNOW

Company also offers matching gifts and payroll deductions for any U.S. nonprofit or federated campaign. Company matches employees' donations up to $1,000 per year per employee. Company offers workplace solicitation to United Way chap-

ters, Progressive Way, Earth Share/Environmental Federation, International Services Agencies, Combined Health Appeal, and Community Works.

Publications: *Sun Corporate Affairs Community Involvement Programs*

GRANTS ANALYSIS

Total Grants: $1,489,739*
Highest Grant: $50,000
Typical Range: $10,000 to $20,000
Disclosure Period: 1992

Note: Total grants figure is an approximate and does not include matching gifts. Assets are as of January 1993. Recent grants are derived from a 1991 annual report.

RECENT GRANTS

50,000 Brandeis University's Heller School, Waltham, MA — Career Beginnings

50,000 East Palo Alto Youth Development Center, East Palo Alto, CA — Hispanic Mentor Advocates

49,973 Opportunities Industrialization Center West, Menlo Park, CA — The Industry Specific Training Program

44,000 Coalition for a Better Acre, Lowell, MA — Hispanic Empowerment and Leadership Program

36,000 Mid-Peninsula YWCA, Palo Alto, CA — Women Entrepreneurs Program

35,000 YWCA of Greater Lawrence, Lawrence, MA — YWCA Study Center

34,320 Boys and Girls Club, Menlo Park, CA — The Key Council

32,562 Catholic Charities, Santa Clara, CA — job placement for the mentally ill

31,471 Lawrence Youth Commission, Lawrence, MA — adult leadership development program

30,300 Massachusetts Advanced Studies Program of Milton Academy, Milton, MA — Merrimack Valley Initiative

Sunbeam-Oster

Parent Company: Allegheny International Inc.
Headquarters: Providence, RI
SIC Major Group: Electronic & Other Electrical Equipment

CONTACT

Sunbeam-Oster
One Citizens Plaza, Sixth floor
Providence, RI 02903
(401) 831-0050

CONTRIBUTIONS SUMMARY

At time of publication, the contributions program had been temporarily suspended.
Operating Locations: PA (Pittsburgh)

CORP. OFFICERS

Paul B. Kazarian: *CURR EMPL* chmn, pres, ceo: Sunbeam-Oster

APPLICATION INFORMATION

Initial Approach: Does not accept applications.

Sunburst Foundation

CONTACT

James M. Hankins
President
Sunburst Fdn.
855 South Federal Highway, Ste. 212
Boca Raton, FL 33432
(407) 368-0376

FINANCIAL SUMMARY

Recent Giving: $115,700 (fiscal 1991); $93,320 (fiscal 1990); $93,320 (fiscal 1989)
Assets: $2,157,288 (fiscal year ending June 30, 1991); $2,123,069 (fiscal 1990); $2,123,069 (fiscal 1989)
Gifts Received: $20,000 (fiscal 1990)
EIN: 59-2637289

CONTRIBUTIONS SUMMARY

Donor(s): Fred Lieberman
Grant Types: scholarship
Geographic Distribution: focus on FL

GIVING OFFICERS

Donald E. Baker: treas, trust
James M. Hankins: trust, pres
Paul R. Rugo: trust, secy *B* Boston MA 1933 *ED* Harvard Univ AB 1955; Harvard Univ JD 1958 *CURR EMPL* ptnr:

Goodwin Procter & Hoar *CORP AFFIL* dir: First Mutual Boston, FW Dixon Co, Instron Corp, Mutual Adv Corp, Vicor Corp; trust: Batterymarch Fin Mgmt *NONPR AFFIL* mem: Am Bar Assn, Boston Bar Assn, MA Bar Assn, Marshall St Historical Soc; trust: Harid Conservatory

APPLICATION INFORMATION

Initial Approach: Application form required.

Sunderland Foundation, Lester T.

CONTACT

James P. Sunderland
Vice President
Lester T. Sunderland Fdn.
8080 Ward Pkwy., Ste. 155
Kansas City, MO 64114
(913) 451-8900

FINANCIAL SUMMARY

Recent Giving: $693,924 (1990); $613,637 (1989)
Assets: $13,874,306 (1990); $14,491,360 (1989)
EIN: 44-6011082

CONTRIBUTIONS SUMMARY

Donor(s): The foundation was incorporated in 1945 by the late Lester T. Sunderland.
Typical Recipients: • *Arts & Humanities:* arts centers, community arts, opera, performing arts • *Civic & Public Affairs:* zoos/botanical gardens • *Education:* colleges & universities, private education (precollege) • *Health:* hospitals • *Religion:* churches • *Social Services:* child welfare, community service organizations, homes, united funds, youth organizations
Grant Types: capital, emergency, endowment, operating expenses, and seed money
Geographic Distribution: focus on MO

GIVING OFFICERS

James P. Sunderland: vp, secy, dir *B* Springfield MO 1928 *ED* Washington & Lee Univ BS 1950; Washington Univ LLB 1952 *CURR EMPL* chmn: Ash Grove Cement Co *CORP AFFIL* dir: Boatmens First Natl Bank Kansas City, TK Communs, Ash Grove Materials Corp; pres: Century Concrete, Vinton Corp *NONPR AFFIL* mem: MO Bar Assn

Paul Sunderland: pres, trust *B* Omaha NE 1896 *ED* Univ WI 1916-1917; Univ WI 1919-1920; Drury Coll LLD (hon)

Robert Sunderland: vp, treas, dir *B* Omaha NE 1921 *ED* Washington Univ BS 1947 *CURR EMPL* hon chmn: Ash Grove Cement Co *CORP AFFIL* dir: Boatmens Bancshares, TK Communs; vp, treas: Vinton Corp *NONPR AFFIL* mem: Greater KS Chamber Commerce, Sigma Chi

APPLICATION INFORMATION

Initial Approach:

The foundation requests applications be made in writing.

The foundation has no deadline for submitting proposals.

Restrictions on Giving: The foundation does not support individuals or provide loans.

GRANTS ANALYSIS

Total Grants: $693,924

Number of Grants: 100

Highest Grant: $50,000

Typical Range: $100 to $10,000

Disclosure Period: 1990

Note: Recent grants are derived from a 1990 grants list.

RECENT GRANTS

50,000 University of Kansas, Lawrence, KS

50,000 University of Missouri at Kansas City, Kansas City, MO

40,000 American Royal Association, Kansas City, MO

35,000 Baker University, Baldwin, KS

30,000 Greater Kansas Community Foundation, Kansas City, MO

30,000 Kansas City Rescue Mission, Kansas City, MO

30,000 National Right to Work Legal Defense Foundation, Springfield, VA

25,000 Bellevue College, Belevue, NE

25,000 Depot Restoration Project, Chanute, KS

25,000 Drury College, Springfield, MO

Sundet Foundation

CONTACT
Steve Erbstoesser
Sundet Fdn.
9231 Penn Ave. South
Minneapolis, MN 55431

FINANCIAL SUMMARY
Recent Giving: $186,591 (1990); $139,865 (1988)

Assets: $3,360,155 (1990); $2,504,588 (1988)

Gifts Received: $489,377 (1990); $673,241 (1988)

Fiscal Note: In 1990, contributions were received from Century Manufacturing ($300,000), Fountain Industries ($103,589), Goodall Manufacturing ($15,788), and Leland and Louise Sundet ($70,000).

EIN: 41-1378654

CONTRIBUTIONS SUMMARY
Donor(s): Century Manufacturing Co., Fountain Industries Co., Goudall Manufacturing Co.

Grant Types: scholarship

Geographic Distribution: focus on MN

GIVING OFFICERS
Leland N. Sundet: pres
Louise C. Sundet: vp
Scott A. Sundet: secy, treas

APPLICATION INFORMATION
Initial Approach: Application form required for scholarships. Deadline is February 28.

GRANTS ANALYSIS
Number of Grants: 86
Highest Grant: $31,000
Typical Range: $300 to $5,000
Disclosure Period: 1990
Note: Complete 1990 grants list not provided.

Sundstrand Corp. / Sundstrand Corp. Foundation

Sales: $1.69 billion
Employees: 12,800
Headquarters: Rockford, IL
SIC Major Group: Fabricated Metal Products, Industrial Machinery & Equipment, Instruments & Related Products, and Transportation Equipment

CONTACT
Carolyn Thomas
Secretary
Sundstrand Corp. Fdn.
4949 Harrison Ave.
PO Box 7003
Rockford, IL 61125
(815) 226-6310

FINANCIAL SUMMARY
Recent Giving: $1,300,000 (fiscal 1993 est.); $1,200,000 (fiscal 1992 approx.); $1,491,479 (fiscal 1991)

Assets: $3,239,141 (fiscal 1991); $2,409,834 (fiscal 1990); $1,787,458 (fiscal 1989)

Fiscal Note: Company gives through foundation only.

EIN: 36-6072477

CONTRIBUTIONS SUMMARY
Typical Recipients: • *Arts & Humanities:* museums/galleries, performing arts • *Education:* colleges & universities, community & junior colleges, economic education, engineering education, literacy, minority education • *Health:* hospitals • *Social Services:* community centers, food/clothing distribution, homes, united funds, youth organizations

Grant Types: capital, employee matching gifts, and general support

Geographic Distribution: primarily Illinois, with emphasis on the Rockford area; areas where Sundstrand has a significant presence

Operating Locations: AZ (Phoenix), CA (Brea, San Diego), CO (Arvada, Denver, Grand Junction), IL (Rockford), IN (Michigan City), NV (York), OH (Lima), WA (Redmond), WI (Milwaukee)

CORP. OFFICERS
Harry C. Stone-Cipher: *CURR EMPL* chmn, pres, ceo, dir: Sundstrand Corp *CORP AFFIL* chmn, pres, ceo: Pre-Paid Legal Svcs Inc *NONPR AFFIL* chmn: Pre-Paid Legal Agency

GIVING OFFICERS
Gary Hedges: vp
Don R. O'Hare: pres, dir *B* Joliet IL 1922 *ED* Univ MN BS 1943 *CORP AFFIL* dir: M&I Corp, Modine Mfg Co, Sauer Inc, Sunstrand Corp
Richard M. Schilling: dir *B* Green Bay WI 1937 *CURR EMPL* vp, secy, gen coun: Sun-

strand Corp *NONPR AFFIL* mem: Am Bar Assn
Carolyn Thomas: secy
Claude Vernam: dir *CURR EMPL* dir communications & pub rels: Sunstrand Corp
Jim White: treas

APPLICATION INFORMATION
Initial Approach: *Initial Contact:* brief letter; if interested, a full proposal is requested *Include Information On:* description of the organization, amount requested, purpose for which funds are sought, budget and recently audited financial statement, proof of tax-exempt status, and list of board of directors *When to Submit:* any time; board meets in March, June, September, and December

Restrictions on Giving: Foundation generally will not support individuals, operating funds, projects of a religious or political nature, or organizations that receive funding from the United Way.

GRANTS ANALYSIS
Total Grants: $1,200,000
Number of Grants: 100*
Highest Grant: $200,000
Typical Range: $5,000 to $10,000
Disclosure Period: fiscal year ending October 31, 1992
Note: Number of grants and average grant figures are approximate and exclude about $120,000 in matching gifts. Assets are from fiscal 1991. Recent grants are derived from a fiscal 1991 Form 990.

RECENT GRANTS
500,000 River Front Museum Park, Rockford, IL — capital

167,500 United Way-Rockford, Rockford, IL — operating

33,000 United Way-Milwaukee, Milwaukee, WI — operating

28,000 United Way-Mile High, Denver, CO — operating

26,700 The Mill, Rockford, IL — capital

25,000 Girl Scouts-Rock River Valley Council, Rockford, IL — capital

25,000 Institute for Illinois, Washington, DC — operating

25,000 Rockford College, Rockford, IL — capital

25,000 YMCA Camp Winnebago, Rockford, IL

22,000 United Way of King County, Seattle, WA — operating

Sunkist Growers / Bodine-Sunkist Memorial Scholarship, A.W.

Sales: $956.0 million
Employees: 800
Headquarters: Van Nuys, CA
SIC Major Group: Food & Kindred Products and Wholesale Trade—Nondurable Goods

CONTACT

A. W. Bodine
Administrator
Sunkist Growers
PO Box 7888
Van Nuys, CA 91409
(818) 986-4800

FINANCIAL SUMMARY

Recent Giving: $63,000 (1991)
Assets: $393,389 (1991)
Gifts Received: $46,000 (1991)
EIN: 95-3958439

CONTRIBUTIONS SUMMARY

Typical Recipients: • *Education:* agricultural education
Grant Types: scholarship
Operating Locations: CA (Van Nuys)

CORP. OFFICERS

Thomas N. Dungan: *CURR EMPL* chmn: Sunkist Growers

Russell L. Hanlin: *CURR EMPL* pres, ceo, coo: Sunkist Growers

Disclosure Period: 1991

Sunmark Capital Corp. / Sunmark Foundation

Parent Sales: $150.0 million
Parent Employees: 900
Headquarters: St. Louis, MO
SIC Major Group: Food & Kindred Products

CONTACT

Menlo F. Smith
Trustee
Sunmark Fdn.
1600 South Brentwood Blvd., Ste. 770
St. Louis, MO 63144
(314) 961-3001

FINANCIAL SUMMARY

Recent Giving: $310,500 (fiscal 1991); $291,231 (fiscal 1990); $239,000 (fiscal 1989)
Assets: $1,255,263 (fiscal year ending January 31, 1991); $1,169,630 (fiscal 1990); $1,081,616 (fiscal 1989)
Gifts Received: $304,706 (fiscal 1991); $300,000 (fiscal 1990); $717,407 (fiscal 1989)
Fiscal Note: Contributes through foundation only. In fiscal 1991, contributions were received from Menlo F. Smith (1,134 shares of British Petroleum ADR and 4,834 shares of Abbott Laboratories).
EIN: 43-6061564

CONTRIBUTIONS SUMMARY

Typical Recipients: • *Arts & Humanities:* public broadcasting • *Civic & Public Affairs:* better government, business/free enterprise, civil rights, economics, international affairs, law & justice, national security, public policy, public policy, rural affairs • *Education:* business education, colleges & universities, economic education, education funds, journalism education, social sciences education • *Religion:* religious organizations • *Social Services:* community service organizations, legal aid
Grant Types: general support
Geographic Distribution: nationally
Operating Locations: MO (St. Louis)

CORP. OFFICERS

James P. Gaglairducci: *CURR EMPL* pres, ceo: Sunmark Inc

GIVING OFFICERS

John Prentiss: trust
John Reed: trust
Menlo F. Smith: trust

APPLICATION INFORMATION

Initial Approach: *Initial Contact:* full proposal *Include Information On:* clearly defined need for funds in education or research, most recent annual report and budget, names of officers and directors and their major affiliations, verification of tax-exempt status, copy of most recent newsletter, recently audited financial statement, one-page listing of the four or five most significant accomplishments within the past year, and a condensed summary of news articles or media attention generated by the organization regarding issues of concern *When to Submit:* any time
Restrictions on Giving: The foundation supports tax-exempt organizations for research purposes only. The foundation does not make grants to individuals.

OTHER THINGS TO KNOW

The foundation supports organizations that work to preserve and develop the free enterprise system and its basic underlying principles of individual freedom and responsibility, private property, and limited constitutional government. It does not support activities outside this field of interest and does not support general charity appeals.

GRANTS ANALYSIS

Total Grants: $310,500
Number of Grants: 44
Highest Grant: $50,000
Typical Range: $1,000 to $8,000
Disclosure Period: fiscal year ending January 31, 1991
Note: Recent grants are derived from a fiscal 1991 grants list.

RECENT GRANTS

50,000 National Right to Work Legal Defense Foundation, Springfield, VA

30,000 Heritage Foundation, Washington, DC

25,000 Brigham Young University, Provo, UT

25,000 Center of National Labor Policy, Washington, DC

25,000 National Institute for Labor Relations

15,000 Landmark Legal Foundation

10,000 Atlas Economic Research Foundation, Fairfax, VA

10,000 Christian Anti-Communism Crusade, Washington, DC

8,000 Capital Research Center, Washington, DC

6,000 Heartland Institute, Chicago, IL

Sunnen Foundation

CONTACT

Sunnen Foundation
7910 Manchester Ave.
St. Louis, MO 63143
(314) 781-2100
Note: The foundation does not list a specific contact person.

FINANCIAL SUMMARY

Recent Giving: $725,000 (1992 approx.); $689,632 (1991); $920,324 (1990)
Assets: $15,000,000 (1992 est.); $15,129,159 (1991); $12,255,563 (1990); $13,465,328 (1989)
Gifts Received: $1,053 (1989)
Fiscal Note: In 1989, a gift was received from the Sunnen Foundation Trust.
EIN: 43-6029156

CONTRIBUTIONS SUMMARY

Donor(s): The Sunnen Foundation was established in Missouri in 1953 by Joseph Sunnen, founder of Sunnen Products Company, a manufacturer of high precision tools and gauges.
Typical Recipients: • *Civic & Public Affairs:* economics, first amendment issues, public policy, urban & community affairs, women's affairs • *Education:* colleges & universities, special education • *Social Services:* domestic violence, family planning, family services, food/clothing distribution, youth organizations
Grant Types: project
Geographic Distribution: principally to national organizations

GIVING OFFICERS

James K. Berthold: vp, dir, asst treas *CURR EMPL* pres, dir: Sunnen Products Co
C. Diane Boulware: secy, dir *CURR EMPL* secy,treas: Sunnen Products Co
Esther S. Kreider: dir, fdr daughter
Paul E. Slaten: tresa, dir
Helen S. Sly: pres, dir, fdr daughter
Ms. Wanda Taylor: adm asst

APPLICATION INFORMATION

Initial Approach:
Initial contact should be in the form of a brief letter.

Applicants should include purpose for which grant is desired, rationale behind proposed project, outline of the solution and method of evaluation, evidence of applicant's ability to carry out the project, and total budget.

The annual deadline for applications is August 1. The board meets in October to consider proposals.

Restrictions on Giving: With the exception of specific projects related to its areas of main concern, grants are not made to general fund-raising drives, religious bodies, educational institutions, environmental organizations, hospitals or medical charities, charities with broad based appeal, or to the arts. No scholarship, research, or travel grants are made to or for specific individuals.

GRANTS ANALYSIS

Total Grants: $689,632
Number of Grants: 31
Highest Grant: $125,000
Typical Range: $2,000 to $50,000
Disclosure Period: 1991
Note: Recent grants are derived from a 1990 grants list.

RECENT GRANTS

165,000 People for the American Way, Washington, DC

110,000 National Abortion Rights Action League Foundation, Washington, DC

100,000 Catholics for a Free Choice, Washington, DC

75,000 Planned Parenthood - St. Louis, St. Louis, MO

75,000 Religious Coalition for Abortion Rights, Washington, DC

50,000 Communications Consortium, Washington, DC

50,000 YMCA of the Ozarks, MO

45,000 Missouri Religious Coalition for Abortion Rights, St. Louis, MO

33,000 Planned Parenthood of Alabama, Birmingham, AL

30,000 National Family Planning and Reproductive Health Association, Washington, DC

Sunshine Biscuits / Sunshine Biscuits Foundation Trust

Sales: $350.0 million
Employees: 4,000
Parent Company: GF Industries, Inc.
Headquarters: Woodbridge, NJ
SIC Major Group: Food & Kindred Products

CONTACT

Sunshine Biscuits Foundation Trust
Wells Fargo Bank, Trust Tax Dept.
PO Box 63954
San Francisco, CA 94163
(310) 491-8118

FINANCIAL SUMMARY

Recent Giving: $7,500 (1991); $76,460 (1990)

Assets: $148,212 (1991); $60,000 (1990); $80,766 (1989)

Gifts Received: $60,000 (1991); $60,000 (1990)

Fiscal Note: In 1991, contributions were received from Sunshine Biscuits.

EIN: 41-6019763

CONTRIBUTIONS SUMMARY

Typical Recipients: • *Health:* hospitals, pediatric health • *International:* international development/relief • *Social Services:* united funds

Operating Locations: NJ (Woodbridge), OR (Portland)

CORP. OFFICERS

Arthur G. Murray: *CURR EMPL* pres, coo: Sunshine Biscuits

Wilfred Uytengsu: *CURR EMPL* chmn, ceo: Sunshine Biscuits

GIVING OFFICERS

Wells Fargo Bank, N.A.: trust

GRANTS ANALYSIS

Number of Grants: 1

Highest Grant: $7,500

Disclosure Period: 1991

RECENT GRANTS

7,500 Children's Hospital, Stanford, CA

Sunwest Bank of Albuquerque, N.A.

Assets: $1.93 billion
Employees: 1,500
Parent Company: Sunwest Financial Services
Headquarters: Albuquerque, NM
SIC Major Group: Depository Institutions

CONTACT

Ike Kalangis
President & Ceo
Sunwest Bank of Albuquerque, N.A.
PO Box 25500
Albuquerque, NM 87125-0500
(505) 765-2403

CONTRIBUTIONS SUMMARY

Operating Locations: NM (Albuquerque)

CORP. OFFICERS

Ike Kalangis: *CURR EMPL* ceo: Sunwest Bank Albuquerque NA

Tim Marquardt: *CURR EMPL* cfo: Sunwest Bank Albuquerque NA

RECENT GRANTS

250,000 University of New Mexico, Albuquerque, NM

Super Food Services

Revenue: $1.82 billion
Employees: 2,480
Headquarters: Dayton, OH
SIC Major Group: Wholesale Trade—Nondurable Goods

CONTACT

Robert Koogler
Treasurer
Super Food Services
PO Box 2323
Dayton, OH 45429
(513) 439-7500

CONTRIBUTIONS SUMMARY

Operating Locations: OH (Dayton)

CORP. OFFICERS

John Demos: *CURR EMPL* vchmn: Super Food Svcs

Sam Robinson: *CURR EMPL* pres, coo: Super Food Svcs

Jack Twyman: *CURR EMPL* chmn, ceo: Super Food Svcs

Super Valu Stores

Sales: $10.63 billion
Employees: 24,400
Headquarters: Eden Prairie, MN
SIC Major Group: Food & Kindred Products, Food Stores, and Wholesale Trade—Nondurable Goods

CONTACT

John Seltzer
Corporate Planning Manager
Super Valu Stores
PO Box 990
Eden Prairie, MN 55440
(612) 828-4000

FINANCIAL SUMMARY

Fiscal Note: Company gives directly. Annual Giving Range: $500,000 to $1 million

CONTRIBUTIONS SUMMARY

Typical Recipients: • *Arts & Humanities:* community arts • *Civic & Public Affairs:* environmental affairs, law & justice • *Education:* colleges & universities • *Social Services:* disabled, drugs & alcohol, employment/job training, youth organizations

Grant Types: general support and matching

Nonmonetary Support Types: in-kind services

Geographic Distribution: geographic areas will have priority in the order listed: Twin Cities area, state of Minnesota, basic service area, national

Operating Locations: AL (Anniston), CO (Aurora), GA (Atlanta), IA (Des Moines), IL (Urbana), IN (Fort Wayne), MN (Chaska, Eden Prairie, Hopkins, Minneapolis, Stillwater), MS (Indianola), MT (Billings), ND (Bismarck, Fargo), OH (Xenia), OR (Salem), PA (New Station), WA (Spokane, Tacoma), WI (Green Bay, Pleasant Prairie)

CORP. OFFICERS

Michael W. Wright: *CURR EMPL* chmn, pres, ceo, dir: Super Valu Stores

GIVING OFFICERS

John Seltzer: *CURR EMPL* mgr corp planning: Super Valu Stores

APPLICATION INFORMATION

Initial Approach: *Initial Contact:* brief letter of inquiry *Include Information On:* brief history, objectives, and current activities of the organization; description of the program or activity for which funds are being requested, and verification of its need; proposed method of evaluating the program or activity; amount of request, including other funding sources and funds received; copy of the organization's most recent financial report, audited if possible; current operating budget and a proposed budget if the project will occur during the following fiscal year; list of the organization's board of directors and their affiliations; brief resume of the individual who serves as administrator for the program; and proof of tax-exempt status *When to Submit:* requests for support should be made during August and September for disbursement in the following year

Restrictions on Giving: Does not support political or lobbying groups; religious organizations for sectarian purposes; veteran, fraternal, and labor organizations; advertising; individuals; and capital funds for education.

OTHER THINGS TO KNOW

Publications: program guidelines

Superior Tube Co. / Superior-Pacific Fund

Sales: $40.0 million
Employees: 800
Headquarters: Wynnewood, PA
SIC Major Group: Primary Metal Industries

CONTACT

Paul E. Kelly
President
Superior-Pacific Fund
Seven Wynnewood Rd.
Wynnewood, PA 19096
(215) 647-2701

FINANCIAL SUMMARY

Recent Giving: $527,524 (1991); $675,594 (1990); $631,637 (1989)

Assets: $12,402,442 (1991); $10,592,160 (1990); $10,965,005 (1989)

Fiscal Note: Contributes through foundation only.
EIN: 23-6298237

CONTRIBUTIONS SUMMARY

Typical Recipients: • *Arts & Humanities:* community arts, music • *Education:* colleges & universities, private education (precollege) • *Health:* hospitals • *Religion:* churches, religious organizations • *Social Services:* community service organizations, united funds, youth organizations

Grant Types: general support
Geographic Distribution: focus on Pennsylvania
Operating Locations: PA (Wynnewood)

CORP. OFFICERS

Donald C. Reilly: *CURR EMPL* pres, ceo: Superior Tube Co

GIVING OFFICERS

Paul E. Kelly, Jr.: dir *CURR EMPL* pres: Cawsl Corp
Paul Edward Kelly: pres, dir *B* Philadelphia PA 1912 *ED* St Josephs Coll BS 1934 *CURR EMPL* chmn, ceo: Superior Tube Co *CORP AFFIL* asst treas, dir: Johnson & Hoffman Mfg Corp, Pacific Tube Co; chmn, ceo: Cawsl Corp, Superior Tube Co; dir: Drever Co, Lease Financing Corp, Oxford First Corp, Swepco Tube Corp, Tubesales, Western Pneumatic Tube Co, Williams & Co; pres, dir: Improvement Leasing Co; secy, dir: Molecu-Wire Corp; treas, dir: Gen Bindery Co; vp, dir: Anchor/Darling Indus, Sharp Corp *NONPR AFFIL* dir: Merry Catholic Med Ctr; mem: Welded Steel Tube Inst
William G. Warden III: dir *CURR EMPL* vp, dir: Superior Tube Co *CORP AFFIL* vp, dir: Superior Tube Co

APPLICATION INFORMATION

Initial Approach: *Initial Contact:* for grants, submit brief letter; for scholarships, written request for application guidelines *Include Information On:* brief description of program *When to Submit:* for grants, any time; for scholarships, completed application must be submitted by January fourth
Restrictions on Giving: Foundation makes scholarship awards to children of employees of Superior Tube Company only.

GRANTS ANALYSIS

Total Grants: $527,524

Number of Grants: 87*
Highest Grant: $125,000
Typical Range: $100 to $2,500
Disclosure Period: 1991
Note: Number of grants and average grant figures do not include scholarships to individuals totaling $13,000. Recent grants are derived from a 1991 grants list.

RECENT GRANTS

125,000 St. Joseph's Preparatory School, Philadelphia, PA
90,000 Bryn Mawr Hospital, Bryn Mawr, PA
75,000 St. Joseph's University, Philadelphia, PA
45,000 Academy of Vocal Arts, Philadelphia, PA
25,000 Mercy Catholic Medical Center, Darby, PA
20,000 Historical Society of Trappe, Trappe, PA
18,491 United Fund, Philadelphia, PA
15,000 Paoli Memorial Hospital, Paoli, PA
12,000 Johns Hopkins University, Baltimore, MD
5,500 World Affairs Council of Philadelphia, Philadelphia, PA

Superior's Brand Meats

Headquarters: Massillon, OH

CONTACT

Bill Baxter
Director, Sales & Marketing
Superior's Brand Meats
1600 Harmont NE
Canton, OH 44711-8440
(216) 832-7491

CONTRIBUTIONS SUMMARY

Operating Locations: OH (Canton, Massillon)

Support Systems International

Sales: $2.0 million
Employees: 25
Headquarters: Charleston Heights, SC
SIC Major Group: Industrial Machinery & Equipment and Primary Metal Industries

CONTACT

Ann Garves
Personnel
Support Systems International
4349 Corporate Rd.
Charleston Heights, SC 29405
(803) 740-8002

CONTRIBUTIONS SUMMARY

Operating Locations: SC (Charleston Heights)

CORP. OFFICERS

B. Parsons: *CURR EMPL* pres: Support Sys Intl Corp

RECENT GRANTS

25,000 Nell Hodgson Woodruff School of Nursing at Emory University, Atlanta, GA

Surdna Foundation

CONTACT

Edward Skloot
Executive Director
Surdna Foundation
1155 Avenue of the Americas, 16th Fl.
New York, NY 10036-2711
(212) 730-0030

FINANCIAL SUMMARY

Recent Giving: $11,373,942 (fiscal 1991); $16,844,753 (fiscal 1990); $18,205,839 (fiscal 1989)
Assets: $319,795,450 (fiscal year ending June 30, 1991); $318,279,856 (fiscal 1990); $277,858,760 (fiscal 1989)
Gifts Received: $1,571,993 (fiscal 1991); $1,560,590 (fiscal 1990); $1,524,072 (fiscal 1989)
Fiscal Note: The foundation receives gifts from the John E. Andrus Residuary and the Andrus Liquidating Trust.
EIN: 13-6108163

CONTRIBUTIONS SUMMARY

Donor(s): The foundation was established in 1917 by John E. Andrus. "Born in 1841, Mr. Andrus was a graduate of Wesleyan University. His successful ventures which amassed his fortune included pharmaceuticals, real estate, timber, and gold mining. A long-term resident of Yonkers, NY, he served that city as mayor and was a four-term representative of his district in the U.S. Congress." He was also a major stockholder in Standard

Oil. Upon his death in 1934, he left a considerable fortune to the Surdna Foundation. His daughter, Helen Andrus Benedict (1888-1969), served as the foundation's president from the time of her father's death in 1934 until 1968.

Typical Recipients: • *Arts & Humanities:* music, public broadcasting • *Civic & Public Affairs:* environmental affairs, nonprofit management • *Education:* colleges & universities, student aid • *Health:* public health • *Social Services:* aged, child welfare, youth organizations

Grant Types: general support and project

Geographic Distribution: emphasis on New York and the northeastern United States; some funding nationwide

GIVING OFFICERS

John E. Andrus III: chmn emeritus, dir B Fergus Falls MN 1909 *ED* Wesleyan Univ BA 1933 *NONPR AFFIL* dir: John E Andrus Meml, Julia Dyckman Andrus Meml
Julia A. Moon Aubry: dir
Peter B. Benedict: chmn, dir
Christopher F. Davenport: dir
Lawrence S. C. Griffith: vp, dir B Washington DC 1937 *CURR EMPL* prof medicine: Johns Hopkins Univ *NONPR AFFIL* consult: Program Surgery Control Hyperlipidemias Univ MN, VA Cooperative Study Surgery Coronary Artery Disease; dir: Julia Dyckman Andrus Meml Home Aged; fellow: Am Coll Cardiology, Am Coll Physicians, Counc Clinical Cardiology Am Heart Assn; mem: Alpha Omega Alpha
Sandra T. Kaupe: dir
Elizabeth A. Kelly: dir
John J. Lynagh: secy, dir B Brooklyn NY 1942 *ED* Fordham Univ BA 1963; Harvard Univ JD 1971 *CURR EMPL* ptnr: Kelley Drye Warren *NONPR AFFIL* mem: FL St Bar, NY St Bar
Frederick F. Moon III: treas, dir
Edward Skloot: exec dir
Edith D. Thorpe: dir
Samuel S. Thorpe III: pres, dir *PHIL AFFIL* treas, dir: Thorpe (James R) Foundation

APPLICATION INFORMATION

Initial Approach: Applicants should submit a two- or three-page preliminary letter outlining a grant proposal. This letter must precede requests for appointments. The preliminary letter should include a concise description of the project; purpose and objectives; cost estimate; and plans for funding the entire project, showing commitments to date. If the proposal appears suitable for the foundation, additional information will be requested.

There are no deadlines for submitting requests.

The board meets quarterly.

Restrictions on Giving: The foundation generally does not fund individuals, capital campaigns, or building funds.

OTHER THINGS TO KNOW

Publications: annual report, grant guidelines and application procedures

GRANTS ANALYSIS

Total Grants: $11,373,942
Number of Grants: 67
Highest Grant: $5,411,973
Typical Range: $25,000 to $200,000
Disclosure Period: fiscal year ending June 30, 1991
Note: The average grant figure excludes a $5,411,973 grant to the John E. Andrus Memorial and the Julia Dyckman Andrus Memorial. Recent grants are derived from a fiscal 1991 annual report.

RECENT GRANTS

500,000 Local Initiatives Support Corporation and Child Care, New York, NY — for technical assistance to 12-15 community development organizations
300,000 Environmental Defense Fund, New York, NY
225,000 South Bronx 2000, Bronx, NY — to fund the stabilization and expansion of environmental and housing enterprises
200,000 Conservation Law Foundation of New England, Boston, MA — to expand transportation planning, advocacy and litigation activities
175,000 Cooper Union for the Advancement of Science and Art, New York, NY —

to create an Infrastructure Institute to advocate, design and teach solutions to New York City's transportation program
163,000 Center for Community Change/National CRA Coalition, Washington, DC — establishment of a national coalition
160,000 1000 Friends of Oregon, Portland, OR — to partially fund a land use/transportation project that would find alternatives to the Western Bypass Freeway plan for Portland and apply the lessons nationally
160,000 Blackside/Civil Rights Project, Boston, MA — toward production of a six part series "The War on Poverty"
125,000 Center for Community Change, Washington, DC — general support for this national technical assistance/policy/advocacy organization
125,000 Center for Marine Conservation, Washington, DC — to conserve marine biological diversity and improve fisheries conservation and management

Surgical Science Foundation for Research and Development

CONTACT

Surgical Science Fdn for Research and Development
c/o First Wisconsin National Bank
One South Pickney St.
Madison, WI 53703

FINANCIAL SUMMARY

Recent Giving: $750,000 (1990); $251,542 (1989); $35,143 (1987)
Assets: $7,247,009 (1989); $4,648,393 (1987)
Gifts Received: $438,242 (1989); $840,000 (1987)
EIN: 93-0846339

CONTRIBUTIONS SUMMARY

Typical Recipients: • *Education:* medical education
Grant Types: general support
Geographic Distribution: focus on WI

GIVING OFFICERS

Folkert Belzer, M.D.: trust
Herbert Berkoff, M.D.: trust
David Dibbell, M.D.: trust
Manucher J. Javid, M.D.: trust
Andrew A. McBeath, M.D.: trust
James R. Starling, M.D.: trust
David Vehling, M.D.: trust
Charles E. Yale, M.D.: trust

APPLICATION INFORMATION

Initial Approach: Contributes only to preselected organizations.

GRANTS ANALYSIS

Number of Grants: 2
Highest Grant: $131,542
Typical Range: $120,000 to $131,542
Disclosure Period: 1989

RECENT GRANTS

131,542 University of Wisconsin Foundation, Madison, WI
120,000 University of Wisconsin Foundation, Madison, WI

Surrena Memorial Fund, Harry and Thelma

CONTACT

Henry A. Burgess
Trustee
Harry and Thelma Surrena Memorial Fund
PO 888
Sheridan, WY 82801
(307) 672-0300

FINANCIAL SUMMARY

Recent Giving: $201,176 (fiscal 1991); $203,548 (fiscal 1990); $203,820 (fiscal 1989)
Assets: $3,510,836 (fiscal year ending October 31, 1991); $3,240,535 (fiscal 1990); $3,348,439 (fiscal 1989)
EIN: 23-7435554

CONTRIBUTIONS SUMMARY

Typical Recipients: • *Religion:* churches • *Social Services:* child welfare, community service organizations, disabled,

united funds, youth organizations
Grant Types: general support
Geographic Distribution: focus on WY

GIVING OFFICERS
Henry A. Burgess: trust
Ralph C. Robinson: trust

APPLICATION INFORMATION
Initial Approach: Send written application form. There are no deadlines.

GRANTS ANALYSIS
Disclosure Period: fiscal year ending October 31, 1991
Note: 1991 grants list not provided.

RECENT GRANTS
    31,999 Children's Center,
           Sheridan, WY
    27,200 Children's Center,
           Sheridan, WY
    25,000 Children's Center,
           Sheridan, WY
     6,684 Methodist Church,
           Buffalo, NY

Susquehanna Corp.
Sales: $100.0 million
Employees: 725
Headquarters: Charlotte, NC
SIC Major Group: Rubber & Miscellaneous Plastics Products

CONTACT
Eugene Thordahl
Business Consultant
Susquehanna Corp.
1727-8A Sardis Rd. North, Ste. 168
Charlotte, NC 28270
(704) 366-8895

CONTRIBUTIONS SUMMARY
Operating Locations: NC (Charlotte)

CORP. OFFICERS
Fred L. Pundsack: *CURR EMPL* chmn, pres, ceo, dir: Susquehanna Corp

Susquehanna Investment Group
Employees: 95
Headquarters: Philadelphia, PA
SIC Major Group: Security & Commodity Brokers

CONTACT
Brian Sullivan
Program Administrator
Susquehanna Investment Group
1900 Market St., Ste. 600
Philadelphia, PA 19103
(215) 963-7400

CONTRIBUTIONS SUMMARY
Company provides employee matching gifts only.
Typical Recipients: • *Arts & Humanities:* history/historic preservation, performing arts • *Civic & Public Affairs:* rural affairs • *Education:* private education (precollege) • *Health:* hospitals • *Social Services:* united funds, youth organizations
Grant Types: matching
Operating Locations: PA (Philadelphia)

RECENT GRANTS
    44,000 United Way, York,
           PA
    35,000 Strand-Capitol Per-
           forming Arts Cen-
           ter, Harrisburg, PA
    25,000 United Way,
           Syracuse, NY
    20,000 York Hospital,
           York, PA
    12,000 Historic York,
           York, PA
    10,000 York City 250th
           Anniversary Cele-
           bration, York, PA
     8,000 Pennsylvania State
           York Campaign,
           York, PA
     5,000 York Catholic High
           School, York, PA
     5,000 York County Farm-
           land Trust, York,
           PA
     5,000 YWCA, York, PA

Susquehanna-Pfaltzgraff Co. / Susquehanna-Pfaltzgraff Foundation
Employees: 5,000
Headquarters: York, PA

CONTACT
John L. Finlayson
Susquehanna-Pfaltzgraff Foundation
140 East Market Street
York, PA 17401
(717) 852-2303

FINANCIAL SUMMARY
Recent Giving: $227,475 (1991); $148,258 (1989)

Assets: $386,065 (1991); $457,468 (1989)
Gifts Received: $100,000 (1991); $198,500 (1989)
Fiscal Note: In 1991, contributions were received from the Pfaltzgraff Co. ($70,000) and the Susquehanna Cable Co. ($30,000).
EIN: 23-6420008

CONTRIBUTIONS SUMMARY
Typical Recipients: • *Arts & Humanities:* general • *Social Services:* general, youth organizations
Grant Types: general support
Operating Locations: PA (York)

CORP. OFFICERS
Louis J. Appell: *CURR EMPL* pres: Susquehanna-Pfaltzgraff Co

GIVING OFFICERS
George N. Appell: vp
Louis J. Appell, Jr.: pres, treas
Helen A. Norton: vp
William H. Simpson: secy

APPLICATION INFORMATION
Initial Approach: Submit a brief letter of inquiry. There are no deadlines.

GRANTS ANALYSIS
Number of Grants: 47
Highest Grant: $44,000
Typical Range: $500 to $2,500
Disclosure Period: 1991

RECENT GRANTS
    44,000 United Way of
           York County, York,
           PA
    35,000 United Way of
           Adams County,
           York, PA
    25,000 United Way of
           Syracuse,
           Syracuse, NY
    20,000 York Hospital,
           York, PA — Cen-
           tury Project
    12,000 Historic York,
           York, PA
    10,000 York City 250th
           Anniversary Cele-
           bration, York, PA
     8,000 Penn State York
           Campaign, York,
           PA
     5,000 Lutheran Social
           Services, York, PA
     5,000 York County Farm-
           land Trust, York,
           PA
     5,000 YWCA, York, PA
           — Child Care Cen-
           ter

Sussman Fund, Edna Bailey

CONTACT
Dorothy Bertine
Administrator
Edna Bailey Sussman Fund
75 Cos Cob Ave. 10
Cos Cob, CT 06807

FINANCIAL SUMMARY
Recent Giving: $192,788 (fiscal 1992); $173,824 (fiscal 1990); $161,962 (fiscal 1989)
Assets: $3,934,559 (fiscal year ending April 30, 1992); $3,586,146 (fiscal 1990); $3,472,335 (fiscal 1989)
EIN: 13-3187064

CONTRIBUTIONS SUMMARY
Donor(s): the late Arthur H. Dean, Edward S. Miller
Typical Recipients: • *Civic & Public Affairs:* environmental affairs • *Education:* colleges & universities, education associations, science/technology education
Grant Types: general support

GIVING OFFICERS
Robert H. Frey: trust
Edward S. Miller: trust

APPLICATION INFORMATION
Initial Approach: Stipends disbursed to institution on behalf of intern selected by fund trustees. Application form required. There are no deadlines.

GRANTS ANALYSIS
Number of Grants: 9
Highest Grant: $40,037
Typical Range: $15,000 to $20,000
Disclosure Period: fiscal year ending April 30, 1992

RECENT GRANTS
    40,037 Duke University
           School of Forestry
           and Environmental
           Studies, Durham,
           NC
    36,500 Virginia Polytech-
           nic Institute and
           State University,
           Blacksburg, VA
    32,553 State University of
           New York College
           of Environmental
           Science and For-
           estry, Syracuse, NY
    22,473 Graduate School
           Cornell University,
           Ithaca, NY

21,300 Colorado School of Mines Foundation, Golden, CO

20,170 University of Michigan School of Natural Resources, Ann Arbor, MI

16,225 University of Colorado Foundation, Boulder, CO

8,000 Yale University, New Haven, CT

570 Pennsylvania State University School of Forest Resources, University Park, PA

Sussman Trust, Otto

CONTACT
Edward S. Miller
Trustee
Otto Sussman Trust
PO Box 1374
Trainsmeadow Sta.
Flushing, NY 11370-9998

FINANCIAL SUMMARY
Recent Giving: $184,691 (1991); $182,397 (1990); $65,606 (1989)

Assets: $3,631,905 (1991); $3,193,877 (1990); $3,392,039 (1989)

EIN: 13-6075849

CONTRIBUTIONS SUMMARY
Donor(s): the late Otto Sussman

Geographic Distribution: limited to residents of NY, NJ, OK, and PA

GIVING OFFICERS
Edward S. Miller: trust
Alice M. Ullmann: trust
Erwin A. Weil: trust

APPLICATION INFORMATION
Initial Approach: Applicants must be recommended by agencies known to the trustees.

Sutcliffe Foundation, Walter and Louise

CONTACT
Walter and Louise Sutcliffe Foundation
c/o First Fidelity Bank, N.A., N.J.
765 Broad Street
Newark, NJ 07102

FINANCIAL SUMMARY
Recent Giving: $200,000 (1990); $0 (1989)

Assets: $2,599,716 (1990); $2,025,401 (1989)

Gifts Received: $820,900 (1990)

EIN: 65-0078683

CONTRIBUTIONS SUMMARY
Typical Recipients: • *Education:* colleges & universities
Grant Types: general support

APPLICATION INFORMATION
Initial Approach: The foundation reports no specific application guidelines. Send a brief letter of inquiry, including statement of purpose, amount requested, and proof of tax-exempt status.

GRANTS ANALYSIS
Total Grants: $200,000
Number of Grants: 1
Highest Grant: $200,000
Disclosure Period: 1990

RECENT GRANTS
200,000 University of Florida, FL — nursing

Sutherland Foundation

CONTACT
Sutherland Foundation
7001 U.S. 42
Lyndon, KY 40222-0000

FINANCIAL SUMMARY
Recent Giving: $132,115 (fiscal 1991)

Assets: $1,818,387 (fiscal year ending March 31, 1991)

Gifts Received: $799,984 (fiscal 1991)

Fiscal Note: Fiscal 1991 contribution received from Laura Lee Brown Deters.

EIN: 61-6175862

GIVING OFFICERS
Laura Lee Brown Deters: pres

Laura Lee Lyons Deters: secy
David W. Henderman: treas

APPLICATION INFORMATION
Initial Approach: The foundation reports it only makes contributions to preselected organizations and does not accept unsolicited requests for funds.

GRANTS ANALYSIS
Total Grants: $132,115
Number of Grants: 35
Highest Grant: $41,000
Disclosure Period: fiscal year ending March 31, 1991

Sutton Foundation

CONTACT
Elis S. Sutton
President
Sutton Fdn.
115 Kennedy Dr.
Sayreville, NJ 08872
(201) 721-0022

FINANCIAL SUMMARY
Recent Giving: $323,488 (fiscal 1991); $250,473 (fiscal 1990); $323,300 (fiscal 1989)

Assets: $3,802,781 (fiscal year ending July 31, 1991); $3,135,422 (fiscal 1990); $1,897,357 (fiscal 1989)

Gifts Received: $682,614 (fiscal 1991); $1,306,658 (fiscal 1990); $979,220 (fiscal 1989)

EIN: 23-7387217

CONTRIBUTIONS SUMMARY
Donor(s): Elie S. Sutton, Ralph S. Sutton, Joseph S. Sutton

Typical Recipients: • *Civic & Public Affairs:* ethnic/minority organizations • *Education:* colleges & universities, private education (precollege), religious education • *Religion:* religious organizations, synagogues • *Social Services:* community service organizations

Grant Types: general support

GIVING OFFICERS
Altoon Sutton: treas
Elie S. Sutton: pres
Joseph S. Sutton: vp
Ralph S. Sutton: secy

APPLICATION INFORMATION
Initial Approach: Send brief letter of inquiry describing program or project. There are no deadlines.

GRANTS ANALYSIS
Number of Grants: 298
Highest Grant: $15,000
Typical Range: $500 to $3,000
Disclosure Period: fiscal year ending July 31, 1991

RECENT GRANTS
15,000 Yeshiva Kehilath, New York, NY

10,000 Kollel Bnei Yeshivot, New York, NY

10,000 Sherrae Torah High School, New York, NY

8,000 Magen David Yeshiva, New York, NY

7,500 United Jewish Appeal Federation of Jewish Philanthropies, New York, NY

5,435 Congregation Beth Torah, New York, NY

5,200 Shephardic Community, New York, NY

5,200 Shetilei Zetim, New York, NY

5,200 Yakirei Yerushalaim, New York, NY

5,000 Beth Torah Congregation, New York, NY

Swalm Foundation

CONTACT
Jo Beth Camp Swalm
President
Swalm Fdn.
8707 Katy Fwy., Ste. 300
Houston, TX 77024
(713) 464-1321

FINANCIAL SUMMARY
Recent Giving: $187,400 (fiscal 1991); $1,125,466 (fiscal 1990); $291,625 (fiscal 1989)

Assets: $30,023,624 (fiscal year ending November 30, 1991); $19,604,112 (fiscal 1990); $12,813,020 (fiscal 1989)

Gifts Received: $7,650,000 (fiscal 1991); $7,578,032 (fiscal 1990); $4,452,018 (fiscal 1989)

Fiscal Note: In 1991, contributions were received from Dave Swalm ($2,500,000), Texas Olefins Company ($2,000,000), Texas Petrochemicals Corporation ($2,500,000), and Clark Swalm ($650,000).

EIN: 74-2073420

CONTRIBUTIONS SUMMARY

Donor(s): The foundation was established in 1980 by Dave C. Swalm, Ron Woliver, and Texas Olefins Co.

Typical Recipients: • *Arts & Humanities:* libraries, museums/galleries • *Civic & Public Affairs:* urban & community affairs • *Education:* colleges & universities, elementary education, private education (precollege), special education, student aid • *Health:* hospices, hospitals, mental health • *Religion:* religious organizations • *Social Services:* child welfare, community service organizations, disabled, drugs & alcohol, family services, food/clothing distribution, shelters/homelessness, united funds, youth organizations

Grant Types: capital, emergency, endowment, general support, matching, operating expenses, and scholarship

Geographic Distribution: focus on Texas

GIVING OFFICERS

Mark C. Mendelovitz: secy, trust
Dave C. Swalm: vp, trust
Jo Beth Camp Swalm: pres, trust

APPLICATION INFORMATION

Initial Approach: The foundation requests applications be made in writing. The foundation has no deadline for submitting proposals.

Restrictions on Giving: The foundation makes grants only to charitable organizations.

OTHER THINGS TO KNOW

Publications: informational brochure including application guidelines

GRANTS ANALYSIS

Total Grants: $187,400
Number of Grants: 10
Highest Grant: $60,000
Typical Range: $5,000 to $20,000
Disclosure Period: fiscal year ending November 30, 1991
Note: Recent grants are derived from a fiscal 1991 grants list.

RECENT GRANTS

60,000 Young People in Action Ministry, Jackson, MS — operating expenses

40,000 Bay Area Rehabilitation Center, Baytown, TX — capital campaign

20,000 Center Incorporated, Houston, TX — mortgage retirement and co-compliance renovation of properties used for housing and rehabilitation of low-income and indigent substance abusers, building purchase

16,500 Mental Health Association of Houston and Harris County, Houston, TX — for publishing a manual to assist the clergy in understanding mental health issues and community resources

15,000 Boy Scouts of America, Houston, TX

10,000 Family Service Center, Baytown, TX — scholarship for art therapy program for abused children

10,000 Kent School, Baytown, TX — scholarships for needy dyslexic students

6,000 Houston Hospice, Houston, TX — general operating

5,000 National Vitiligo Foundation, Tyler, TX — operating expenses

4,900 Palmer Drug Abuse Program, Pasadena, TX — providing rehabilitation programs to substance abusers

---

Swank, Inc.

Revenue: $128.06 million
Employees: 2,300
Headquarters: Attleboro, MA
SIC Major Group: Apparel & Other Textile Products, Leather & Leather Products, and Miscellaneous Manufacturing Industries

CONTACT

Andrew Corsini
Senior Vice President & Treasurer, CFO
Swank, Inc.
6 Hazel St.
Attleboro, MA 02703-2962
(508) 222-3400

CONTRIBUTIONS SUMMARY

Primarily provides matching gifts and donated products (building supplies) valued at approximately $500,000 in 1989.

Grant Types: matching
Nonmonetary Support Types: donated products
Operating Locations: MA (Attleboro)

CORP. OFFICERS

Andrew C. Corsini: *CURR EMPL* sr vp, cfo: Swank
Marshall Tulin: *CURR EMPL* pres, coo, ceo, dir: Swank

APPLICATION INFORMATION

Initial Approach: Applications not accepted.

Swanson Family Foundation, Dr. W.C.

CONTACT

Lew Costley
Trustee
Dr. W.C. Swanson Family Fdn.
257 37th Street
Ogden, UT 84405
(801) 399-5837

FINANCIAL SUMMARY

Recent Giving: $942,835 (1991)
Assets: $24,689,851 (1991)
EIN: 94-2478549

CONTRIBUTIONS SUMMARY

Donor(s): the late W.C. Swanson E.W. "Al" Thrasher

Typical Recipients: • *Arts & Humanities:* history/historic preservation • *Civic & Public Affairs:* municipalities, philanthropic organizations • *Education:* private education (precollege), public education (precollege) • *Religion:* religious organizations • *Social Services:* youth organizations

Grant Types: general support
Geographic Distribution: giving primarily in Utah, with emphasis on Ogden giving on a domestic and international basis

GIVING OFFICERS

Victor L. Brown: exec comm
Aileen H. Clyde: exec comm
Lew Costley: trust
Isaac C. Ferguson: exec comm
Addie Fuhriman: exec comm
Harry L. Gibbons: exec comm
Glenn L. Pace: chmn, exec comm
W. Charles Swanson: mgr
E.W. Al Thrasher: vchmn, exec comm

APPLICATION INFORMATION

Initial Approach: Send brief letter of inquiry. There are no deadlines.

Initial Approach: Contact by telephone or send brief letter of inquiry, followed by a four-page prospectus. After initial prospectus review, applicant is notified whether a full proposal is requested. If so, an application kit is provided. Submit eight copies of proposal. There are no deadlines.board meetings are held in May and November. Final notification is given in six to nine months.

Restrictions on Giving: Does not provide grants to individuals. no support given for studies in the areas of abortion, reproductive physiology, contraceptive technology, or sexually transmitted diseases

OTHER THINGS TO KNOW

Publications: multi-year report (including application guidelines), informational brochure

GRANTS ANALYSIS

Number of Grants: 55
Highest Grant: $300,000
Typical Range: $1,000 to $25,000
Disclosure Period: 1991

RECENT GRANTS

300,000 Weber School Foundation, Ogden, UT

100,000 Roy Historical Foundation, Roy, UT

90,000 St. Annes Center, Ogden, UT

46,000 Ogden School Foundation, Ogden, UT

40,000 Primary Children's Hospital, Salt Lake City, UT

26,000 Enable, Ogden, UT

26,000 Your Community Foundation, Ogden, UT

25,000 St. Peters School, Clearfield, UT

25,000 Utah Girl Scout Council, Ogden, UT

Swanson Foundation

CONTACT
Arthur Rosenthal
Trust
Swanson Fdn.
122 East 42nd St.
New York, NY 10168
(212) 687-8360

FINANCIAL SUMMARY
Recent Giving: $130,008 (1991); $27,850 (1990); $197,800 (1989)
Assets: $4,184,869 (1991); $3,829,231 (1990); $3,930,257 (1989)
EIN: 13-6108509

CONTRIBUTIONS SUMMARY
Donor(s): Glen E. Swanson
Typical Recipients: • *Health:* health organizations, hospitals, medical research, pediatric health, single-disease health associations • *Social Services:* community service organizations, disabled, united funds, youth organizations
Grant Types: general support and research
Geographic Distribution: focus on southern CA

GIVING OFFICERS
Arthur Rosenthal: trust
Glen E. Swanson: don

APPLICATION INFORMATION
Initial Approach: Send brief letter describing program. There are no deadlines.

GRANTS ANALYSIS
Number of Grants: 4
Highest Grant: $100,000
Typical Range: $5,000 to $25,000
Disclosure Period: 1991

RECENT GRANTS
100,000 Mt. Sinai Medical Center, New York, NY
25,000 Memorial Sloan-Kettering Cancer Center, New York, NY
20,000 Dr. School College, Chicago, IL
5,000 International Foundation of Dermatology

Swasey Fund for Relief of Public School Teachers of Newburyport

CONTACT
Jean MacDonald
Treasurer
Swasey Fund for Relief of Public School Teachers of Newburyport
23 Summitt Pl.
Newburyport, MA 01950
(508) 462-2784

FINANCIAL SUMMARY
Recent Giving: $124,670 (fiscal 1990); $7,008 (fiscal 1989)
Assets: $2,240,194 (fiscal year ending April 30, 1990); $2,208,475 (fiscal 1989)
EIN: 04-6044618

GIVING OFFICERS
Irene Grant: trust
Jean Kirkpatrick: pres
Jean Macisonald: treas
Carol Mullen: trust
John H. Pramberg, Jr.: trust
Margaret Taranda: secy

APPLICATION INFORMATION
Initial Approach: Assistance limited to individuals who have taught in Newburyport, MA

Sweatt Foundation, Harold W.

CONTACT
Karen McGlynn
Harold W. Sweatt Fdn.
1500 Bracketts Point Rd.
Wayzata, MN 55391
(612) 473-9200

FINANCIAL SUMMARY
Recent Giving: $110,250 (fiscal 1991); $114,162 (fiscal 1990); $105,263 (fiscal 1989)
Assets: $2,615,501 (fiscal year ending February 28, 1991); $2,205,570 (fiscal 1990); $1,973,251 (fiscal 1989)
EIN: 41-6075860

CONTRIBUTIONS SUMMARY
Typical Recipients: • *Arts & Humanities:* history/historic preservation • *Civic & Public Affairs:* environmental affairs, zoos/botanical gardens • *Education:* colleges & universities, private education (precollege) • *Health:* health organizations,

hospitals • *International:* international organizations • *Religion:* churches, religious organizations • *Social Services:* community service organizations, united funds, youth organizations
Grant Types: general support

GIVING OFFICERS
A. Lachlan Reed: trust
Harold S. Reed: trust
Martha S. Reed: trust
William S. Reed: trust

APPLICATION INFORMATION
Initial Approach: Send brief letter describing program. There are no deadlines.

GRANTS ANALYSIS
Number of Grants: 118
Highest Grant: $20,000
Typical Range: $100 to $2,500
Disclosure Period: fiscal year ending February 28, 1991

RECENT GRANTS
20,000 Physicians for Peace, Norfolk, VA
10,000 International College, New York, NY
10,000 University of Connecticut, Storrs, CT
5,000 Abbott Northwestern, Minneapolis, MN
5,000 Andover, Andover, MA
3,000 United Way, Minneapolis, MN
2,500 Maderia, McLean, VA
2,000 Benjamin School, North Palm Beach, FL
2,000 Middle East Institute, Washington, DC
2,000 St. David School, Minneapolis, MN

Sweet Life Foods / Sweet Life Foundation

Sales: $1.0 billion
Employees: 2,800
Headquarters: Windsor Locks, CT
SIC Major Group: Holding & Other Investment Offices and Wholesale Trade—Nondurable Goods

CONTACT
Julian Leavitt
Manager
Sweet Life Foundation
PO Box 385
Windsor Locks, CT 06096
(203) 623-1681

FINANCIAL SUMMARY
Recent Giving: $550 (fiscal 1992); $200 (fiscal 1991); $300 (fiscal 1990)
Assets: $990 (fiscal year ending June 30, 1992); $952 (fiscal 1991); $552 (fiscal 1990)
Gifts Received: $1,000 (fiscal 1992); $1,000 (fiscal 1991); $11,000 (fiscal 1990)
Fiscal Note: In fiscal 1992, contributions were received from Springfield Sugar and Products Company.
EIN: 06-6067918

CONTRIBUTIONS SUMMARY
Typical Recipients: • *Education:* private education (precollege) • *Health:* health organizations, medical research • *Religion:* religious organizations • *Social Services:* community service organizations, food/clothing distribution, youth organizations
Grant Types: general support
Geographic Distribution: focus on CT
Operating Locations: CT (Suffield, Windsor Locks)

CORP. OFFICERS
Julian J. Leavitt: *CURR EMPL* pres: Sweet Life Foods

GIVING OFFICERS
Julian Leavitt: mgr, trust

APPLICATION INFORMATION
Initial Approach: Send brief letter describing program. There are no deadlines.

GRANTS ANALYSIS
Number of Grants: 4
Highest Grant: $250
Typical Range: $100 to $250
Disclosure Period: fiscal year ending June 30, 1992

RECENT GRANTS
250 St. Clement's Parish Development Fund, Suffield, CT
100 Alzheimer's Disease and Related Disorders Association, Suffield, CT
100 American Heart Association, Suffield, CT

100 Suffield High School Safe Parties, Suffield, CT

Swensrud Charitable Trust, Sidney A.

CONTACT
Nancy S. Anthony
Trustee
Sidney A. Swensrud Charitable Trust
24 Federal St., Ste. 400
Boston, MA 02110

FINANCIAL SUMMARY
Recent Giving: $309,570 (1990); $317,950 (1989); $296,300 (1988)
Assets: $6,803,731 (1990); $6,893,177 (1989); $5,377,027 (1988)
Gifts Received: $39,895 (1990); $459,895 (1989); $336,674 (1988)
EIN: 25-6050238

CONTRIBUTIONS SUMMARY
Typical Recipients: • *Civic & Public Affairs:* environmental affairs, ethnic/minority organizations, public policy, zoos/botanical gardens • *Health:* hospitals • *Social Services:* family planning
Grant Types: general support and project
Geographic Distribution: focus on FL and Washington, DC

GIVING OFFICERS
Nancy S. Anthony: trust
Steven B. Swensrud: trust

APPLICATION INFORMATION
Initial Approach: Contributes only to preselected organizations.
Restrictions on Giving: Does not support individuals.

GRANTS ANALYSIS
Number of Grants: 46
Highest Grant: $75,000
Typical Range: $500 to $1,500
Disclosure Period: 1990

RECENT GRANTS
75,000 Conservancy, Naples, FL
5,000 Children's Hospital Medical Center, Boston, MA
3,000 Association for Voluntary Surgical Contraception, New York, NY
3,000 Population Communications International, New York, NY
2,500 Foundation for Endowment, Alexandria, VA
2,000 Population Environment Balance, Washington, DC
1,800 Planned Parenthood, Naples, FL
1,500 Foundation for Mental Health, Naples, FL
1,500 U.S. English, Washington, DC
1,000 Naples Community Hospital, Naples, FL

Swift Co. Inc., John S. / Swift Co. Inc. Charitable Trust, John S.

Sales: $15.0 million
Employees: 300
Parent Company: J.S.S. Co. Inc.
Headquarters: Chicago, IL
SIC Major Group: Printing & Publishing

CONTACT
Bryan Swift
Trustee
John S. Swift Co. Inc.
17 North Loomis St.
Chicago, IL 60607
(312) 666-7020

FINANCIAL SUMMARY
Recent Giving: $143,380 (1990); $42,130 (1989); $84,405 (1988)
Assets: $1,923,096 (1990); $1,430,492 (1989); $1,351,042 (1988)
Gifts Received: $500,000 (1990)
Fiscal Note: In 1990, contributions were received from John S. Swift Co.
EIN: 43-6020812

CONTRIBUTIONS SUMMARY
Typical Recipients: • *Arts & Humanities:* libraries, museums/galleries, public broadcasting • *Education:* colleges & universities, medical education • *Health:* hospitals, medical research • *Social Services:* drugs & alcohol, united funds, youth organizations
Grant Types: challenge and general support
Geographic Distribution: primarily in MO and IL.

Operating Locations: IL (Chicago), MO (St. Louis)

CORP. OFFICERS
Hampden M. Swift: *CURR EMPL* pres, treas, dir: John S Swift Co

GIVING OFFICERS
Ben Heckel: trust
Hampden M. Swift: trust *CURR EMPL* pres, treas, dir: John S Swift Co (see above)

APPLICATION INFORMATION
Initial Approach: Send brief letter of inquiry. There are no deadlines.

GRANTS ANALYSIS
Number of Grants: 44
Highest Grant: $8,500
Typical Range: $100 to $1,000
Disclosure Period: 1990

RECENT GRANTS
8,500 St. Lawrence University, St. Lawrence, NY — annual fund and Hewlett Challenge
5,000 St. Louis Art Museum, St. Louis, MO
3,000 United Way, St. Louis, MO
2,000 School of the Ozarks, Point Lookout, MO
2,000 United Way, Chicago, IL
1,250 Museum of Contemporary Art, Chicago, IL
1,000 Anti-Drug Abuse Education Fund, Chicago, IL
1,000 Arts and Education Council of St. Louis, St. Louis, MO
1,000 Lake Forest College, Lake Forest, IL
1,000 Washington University Department of Dermatology,, St. Louis, MO

Swift-Eckrich Inc.

Sales: $2.0 billion
Employees: 6,500
Headquarters: Downers Groves, IL
SIC Major Group: Food & Kindred Products and Wholesale Trade—Nondurable Goods

CONTACT
Swift-Eckrich Inc.
2001 Butterfield Rd.
Downers Groves, IL 60515
(708) 512-1000

CONTRIBUTIONS SUMMARY
Operating Locations: IL (Downers Groves)

CORP. OFFICERS
Lee Lochmann: *CURR EMPL* pres: Swift-Eckrich

Swift Memorial Health Care Foundation

CONTACT
Emma M. Orr
Chairman of Awards Committee
Swift Memorial Health Care Fdn.
PO Box 7048
Oxnard, CA 93031
(805) 385-3650

FINANCIAL SUMMARY
Recent Giving: $133,315 (fiscal 1992); $207,260 (fiscal 1991); $161,644 (fiscal 1990)
Assets: $2,548,096 (fiscal year ending June 30, 1992); $2,513,096 (fiscal 1991); $2,403,705 (fiscal 1990)
Gifts Received: $100 (fiscal 1992)
EIN: 77-0132512

CONTRIBUTIONS SUMMARY
Typical Recipients: • *Health:* health organizations, hospitals, medical research, single-disease health associations • *Religion:* religious organizations • *Social Services:* child welfare, community service organizations, domestic violence, drugs & alcohol, homes, religious welfare
Grant Types: general support and loan
Geographic Distribution: focus on Ventura County, CA

GIVING OFFICERS
Allen Camp: trust
Jack Erbeck: trust
Lester E. Jacobson: trust
Robert E. Jordan, M.D.: trust
Robert Juarez: trust
Frank Leiblein: trust
R. Blinn Maxwell: trust
Ray Swift: trust
Jessica White: trust

APPLICATION INFORMATION
Initial Approach: Application form required. There are no deadlines.

OTHER THINGS TO KNOW
Publications: Occasional report

GRANTS ANALYSIS
Number of Grants: 31
Highest Grant: $18,990
Typical Range: $1,000 to $5,000
Disclosure Period: fiscal year ending June 30, 1992

RECENT GRANTS
18,990 City of Oxnard
5,500 Primary Purpose
5,000 AHA
5,000 Catholic Charities
5,000 Long Term Care Ombudsman
5,000 Salvation Army
4,000 Caregivers, Manchester, NH
4,000 Khepera House
4,000 Pediatric Diagnostic Center
3,500 Casa Pacifica

Swig Charity Foundation, Mae and Benjamin

CONTACT
Melvin M. Swig
Trustee
Mae and Benjamin Swig Charity Fdn.
220 Montgomery Sreet
San Francisco, CA 94104
(415) 291-1100

FINANCIAL SUMMARY
Recent Giving: $672,868 (1991); $892,200 (1990); $1,769,604 (1989)
Assets: $9,176,671 (1991); $8,975,625 (1990); $8,892,136 (1989)
Gifts Received: $20,000 (1990)
Fiscal Note: In 1990, contributions were received from Melvin M. Swig.
EIN: 23-7416746

CONTRIBUTIONS SUMMARY
Typical Recipients: • *Arts & Humanities:* arts associations, community arts, dance, libraries, museums/galleries, opera, public broadcasting • *Civic & Public Affairs:* ethnic/minority organizations, municipalities • *Education:* colleges & univer-

sities, religious education • *Health:* hospitals • *Religion:* religious organizations, synagogues • *Social Services:* child welfare, community centers, community service organizations, domestic violence, family services, recreation & athletics, united funds, youth organizations
Grant Types: emergency and general support
Geographic Distribution: focus on the San Francisco Bay Area, CA

GIVING OFFICERS
Richard S. Dinner: trust *B* 1921
Melvin M. Swig: trust *B* 1917 *CURR EMPL* vchmn, dir: Fairmont Hotel Mgmt Co *CORP AFFIL* chmn: Swig Weiler & Dinner Devel Co; dir: Atalanta Sosnoff Capital Corp
Richard L. Swig: trust *B* Boston MA 1925 *ED* Univ San Francisco *CURR EMPL* pres, mng dir: Fairmont Hotel Mgmt Co

APPLICATION INFORMATION
Initial Approach: Send brief letter of inquiry describing program or project. There are no deadlines.

GRANTS ANALYSIS
Number of Grants: 57
Highest Grant: $100,000
Typical Range: $750 to $50,000
Disclosure Period: 1991
Note: $100,000

RECENT GRANTS
100,000 Congregation Emanuel, San Francisco, CA
50,000 San Francisco Symphony, San Francisco, CA
50,000 US Holocaust Memorial Museum, Washington, DC
50,000 Vail Valley Foundation
45,000 American Society for Technion, New York, NY
40,000 San Jose Museum of Art, San Jose, CA
40,000 Technology Center of Silicon Valley, Los Angeles, CA
35,000 University of San Francisco, San Francisco, CA
30,000 Hebrew Union College, Cincinnati, OH

25,000 Fort Mason

Swig Foundation

CONTACT
Nat Starr
Executive Director
Swig Fdn.
220 Montgomery St.
San Francisco, CA 94104
(415) 291-1100

FINANCIAL SUMMARY
Recent Giving: $870,837 (1991); $1,054,620 (1990); $1,906,495 (1989)
Assets: $16,620,591 (1991); $15,729,353 (1990); $15,296,191 (1989)
EIN: 94-6065205

CONTRIBUTIONS SUMMARY
Donor(s): The foundation was established in 1957 by the late Benjamin H. Swig and members of the Swig family.
Typical Recipients: • *Arts & Humanities:* arts associations, arts centers, community arts, dance, museums/galleries, music, opera, public broadcasting • *Civic & Public Affairs:* municipalities, philanthropic organizations, public policy, zoos/botanical gardens • *Education:* colleges & universities • *Health:* health funds, medical research • *Religion:* churches, religious organizations, synagogues • *Social Services:* community service organizations, family services, homes, recreation & athletics, united funds, youth organizations
Grant Types: general support
Geographic Distribution: focus on the San Francisco Bay area, CA

GIVING OFFICERS
Richard S. Dinner: trust *B* 1921
Nat Starr: exec dir
Richard L. Swig: trust *B* Boston MA 1925 *ED* Univ San Francisco *CURR EMPL* pres, mng dir: Fairmont Hotel Mgmt Co

APPLICATION INFORMATION
Initial Approach:
The foundation requests applications be made in writing. The foundation has no deadline for submitting proposals.
Restrictions on Giving: The foundation makes grants only to organizations exempt under

section 501(c)(3). The foundation does not make grants to individuals. The foundation does not support conferences, seminars, or workshops.

GRANTS ANALYSIS
Total Grants: $870,837
Number of Grants: 81
Highest Grant: $20,000
Typical Range: $500 to $30,000
Disclosure Period: 1991
Note: Recent grants are derived from a 1991 grants list.

RECENT GRANTS
20,000 San Francisco Conservatory of Music, San Francisco, CA
20,000 San Francisco Zoological Society, San Francisco, CA
12,500 US Department of State, Washington, DC
10,000 Palace of Fine Arts, San Francisco, CA
10,000 San Francisco Conservatory of Music, San Francisco, CA
10,000 San Francisco Conservatory of Music, San Francisco, CA
5,000 San Francisco Museum of Modern Art, San Francisco, CA
5,000 United Service Organization, Washington, DC
4,000 San Francisco Chamber of Commerce, San Francisco, CA
3,000 San Francisco Ballet, San Francisco, CA

Swim Foundation, Arthur L.

CONTACT
Arthur L. Swim Fdn.
1095 South 800 East, Ste. 4
Orem, UT 84058

FINANCIAL SUMMARY
Recent Giving: $677,000 (1991); $251,000 (1989); $65,000 (1988)
Assets: $11,728,517 (1991); $10,084,000 (1989); $8,457,025 (1988)
EIN: 82-6007432

CONTRIBUTIONS SUMMARY
Typical Recipients: • *Civic & Public Affairs:* civil rights, rural affairs • *Education:* busi-

ness education, colleges & universities, medical education • *Health:* hospitals, medical research, public health • *Religion:* religious organizations
Grant Types: general support, operating expenses, research, and scholarship

GIVING OFFICERS
Marilyn S. Lenahan: trust
Gaylord K. Swim: trust
Katherine M. Swim: trust
Roger C. Swim: trust

APPLICATION INFORMATION
Initial Approach: Contributes only to preselected organizations.
Restrictions on Giving: Does not support individuals.

GRANTS ANALYSIS
Number of Grants: 17
Highest Grant: $155,000
Typical Range: $5,000 to $30,000
Disclosure Period: 1991

RECENT GRANTS
155,000 Corporation of Presiding Bishop, Salt Lake City, UT
135,000 Benson Institute, Provo, UT — farmer assistance
100,000 National Right to Work Legal Defense Fund, Springfield, VA
100,000 Rural Health Care Foundation, Nephi, UT — rural health care
70,000 Rockford Institute, Rockford, IL — educational
30,000 LDS Business College, Salt Lake City, UT — capital improvements
20,000 Hillsdale College, Hillsdale, MI
6,000 Heritage Society, Provo, UT — genealogical research
5,000 Deseret International, Salt Lake City, UT — medical care
5,000 Washington Legal Foundation, Washington, DC

Swinerton & Walberg Co.
Revenue: $380.0 million
Employees: 780
Headquarters: San Francisco, CA
SIC Major Group: General Building Contractors and Special Trade Contractors

CONTACT
James B. Swinerton
Manager, Strategic Planning
Swinerton & Walberg Co.
580 California St., Ste. 1200
San Francisco, CA 94104
(415) 421-2980

FINANCIAL SUMMARY
Fiscal Note: Annual Giving Range: less than $100,000

CONTRIBUTIONS SUMMARY
Nonmonetary Support Types: donated equipment, loaned employees, loaned executives, and workplace solicitation
Geographic Distribution: only in headquarters area
Operating Locations: CA (San Francisco)

CORP. OFFICERS
James R. Gillette: *CURR EMPL* cfo: Swinerton & Walberg Co
David H. Grubb: *B* Wheeling WV 1936 *ED* Princeton Univ 1958; Stanford Univ 1962 *CURR EMPL* pres: Swinerton & Walberg Co

Swisher Foundation, Carl S.

CONTACT
E. A. Middlebrooks, Jr.
Secretary-Treasurer
Carl S. Swisher Fdn.
PO Box 14790
Jacksonville, FL 32238-1790
(904) 389-8320

FINANCIAL SUMMARY
Recent Giving: $484,500 (1991); $465,000 (1990); $499,000 (1989)
Assets: $6,785,523 (1990); $6,804,540 (1989); $6,612,123 (1988)
EIN: 59-0998262

CONTRIBUTIONS SUMMARY
Donor(s): the late Carl S. Swisher
Typical Recipients: • *Education:* colleges & universities, medical education • *Health:*

hospitals, medical research
• *Social Services:* aged, child welfare, community service organizations, food/clothing distribution, united funds, youth organizations
Grant Types: capital, general support, project, and scholarship
Geographic Distribution: focus on the Jacksonville, FL, area

GIVING OFFICERS
Kenneth G. Anderson: trust
George S. Coulter: pres, trust
E. A. Middlebrooks, Jr.: secy, treas, trust
Harold W. Smith: vp, trust

APPLICATION INFORMATION
Initial Approach: Send brief letter of inquiry or full proposal. There are no deadlines. Board meets quarterly.
Restrictions on Giving: Does not support individuals.

GRANTS ANALYSIS
Number of Grants: 92
Highest Grant: $100,000
Typical Range: $1,000 to $2,500
Disclosure Period: 1990

RECENT GRANTS
100,000 University of Florida Foundation, Gainesville, FL — neurosurgery pediatrics
50,000 St. Lukes Hospital Foundation, Jacksonville, FL — therapy equipment
12,000 St. Marks Epis Day School, Jacksonville, FL — general support
10,000 University of North Florida Foundation, Jacksonville, FL — scholarship fund American music
8,000 Wesleyan College, Macon, GA — scholarship fund
6,000 University of Alabama at Birmingham, Birmingham, AL
5,000 Salvation Army, Jacksonville, FL — hungry fund
5,000 SOU Scholarship Foundation, Tallahassee, FL — scholarship fund
5,000 St. Johns River City Band, Jacksonville, FL — general support

3,000 Young Life, Jacksonville, FL — general support

Swiss American Securities, Inc.
Employees: 140
Headquarters: New York, NY
SIC Major Group: Security & Commodity Brokers

CONTACT
John Pulaski
Vice President, Chief Executive Officer
Swiss American Securities, Inc.
100 Wall St., Fifth Fl.
New York, NY 10005
(212) 612-8700

CONTRIBUTIONS SUMMARY
The program is unstructured, flexible, and responsive to the needs of the community.
Typical Recipients: • *Arts & Humanities:* museums/galleries • *Health:* hospitals, single-disease health associations • *Social Services:* youth organizations
Grant Types: general support and matching
Geographic Distribution: primarily in the New York area
Operating Locations: CA, FL, GA, IL, NY (New York), TX

CORP. OFFICERS
George J. Helwig: *CURR EMPL* pres, ceo: Swiss Am Securities
Hans Peter Sorg: *CURR EMPL* chmn: Swiss Am Securities

GIVING OFFICERS
John Pulaski: *CURR EMPL* vp: Swiss Am Securities

APPLICATION INFORMATION
Initial Approach: Decisions are made quarterly, but applications may be submitted at any time. Send a letter, including a description of the organization, amount and purpose of funds sought, a recently audited financial statement, and proof of tax-exempt status.
Restrictions on Giving: Program does not support individuals, fraternal or religious organizations, or political or lobbying groups.

Swiss Bank Corp.

Employees: 1,500
Headquarters: New York, NY
SIC Major Group: Depository
Institutions

CONTACT
Joan Moschello
Vice President
Swiss Bank Corp.
PO Box 395, Church St. Sta.
New York, NY 10008
(212) 574-3000

CONTRIBUTIONS SUMMARY
Program supports all traditional categories of giving: arts and humanities, civic and public affairs, education, health, and social services.
Typical Recipients: • *Arts & Humanities:* arts centers, arts funds, dance, ethnic arts, history/historic preservation, libraries, museums/galleries, music, performing arts, theater • *Civic & Public Affairs:* zoos/botanical gardens • *Education:* colleges & universities, private education (precollege) • *Health:* hospitals, single-disease health associations • *Social Services:* united funds, youth organizations
Grant Types: general support
Geographic Distribution: in the eight cities with operating branches: New York, Miami, Atlanta, Chicago, Houston, Dallas, San Francisco, and Los Angeles
Operating Locations: CA, FL, GA, IL, NY (New York), TX

CORP. OFFICERS
Walter G. Frehner: *CURR EMPL* pres, gen mgr: Swiss Bank Corp
Franz Galliker: *CURR EMPL* chmn: Swiss Bank Corp

GIVING OFFICERS
Joan Moschello: *CURR EMPL* vp: Swiss Bank Corp
Bonnie Sweeney: *CURR EMPL* asst treas: Swiss Bank Corp

APPLICATION INFORMATION
Initial Approach: Send a letter any time including a description of the organization, amount and purpose of funds sought, recently audited financial statement, and proof of tax-exempt status.
Restrictions on Giving: Does not support individuals, member agencies of united funds, political or lobbying groups, or religious organizations for sectarian purposes.

GRANTS ANALYSIS
Typical Range: $1,000 to $5,000

Switzer Foundation

CONTACT
Ann Swander
Trustee
Switzer Fdn.
2000 Huntington Bldg.
Cleveland, OH 44115
(216) 696-4700

FINANCIAL SUMMARY
Recent Giving: $396,843 (fiscal 1991); $445,414 (fiscal 1990); $278,471 (fiscal 1988)
Assets: $8,226,469 (fiscal year ending June 30, 1991); $8,001,396 (fiscal 1990); $6,974,835 (fiscal 1988)
EIN: 34-1504501

CONTRIBUTIONS SUMMARY
Donor(s): members of the Switzer family
Typical Recipients: • *Civic & Public Affairs:* environmental affairs, municipalities • *Education:* colleges & universities
Grant Types: endowment, research, and scholarship
Geographic Distribution: focus on CA and northern New England

GIVING OFFICERS
Lincoln Reavis: trust
Ann P. Swander: trust
Fred E. Switzer: trust
Marge Switzer: trust
Patricia D. Switzer: trust
Paul E. Switzer: trust
Robert Switzer: trust

APPLICATION INFORMATION
Initial Approach: Contributes only to preselected organizations.
Restrictions on Giving: Does not support individuals.

OTHER THINGS TO KNOW
Publications: Application Guidelines

GRANTS ANALYSIS
Number of Grants: 2
Highest Grant: $226,843
Typical Range: $170,000 to $226,843
Disclosure Period: fiscal year ending June 30, 1991

RECENT GRANTS
226,843 New Hampshire Charitable Fund, Concord, NH
170,000 San Francisco Foundation, San Francisco, CA

Switzer Foundation

CONTACT
Mary D. Butler
Secretary-Treasurer
Switzer Fdn.
350 Hudson St.
New York, NY 10014
(212) 989-9393

FINANCIAL SUMMARY
Recent Giving: $190,000 (1991); $189,000 (1990); $179,600 (1989)
Assets: $4,804,832 (1991); $4,220,929 (1990); $4,292,451 (1989)
EIN: 13-5596831

CONTRIBUTIONS SUMMARY
Donor(s): the late Margaret Switzer, the late Sarah Switzer
Typical Recipients: • *Education:* colleges & universities, medical education • *Health:* hospitals, nursing services
Grant Types: scholarship
Geographic Distribution: focus on the New York, NY, metropolitan area

GIVING OFFICERS
John D. Bamonte: vp
Mary D. Butler: secy, treas
John A. Pileski: pres

APPLICATION INFORMATION
Initial Approach: Send brief letter of inquiry describing program or project. There are no deadlines.
Restrictions on Giving: Does not support individuals.

OTHER THINGS TO KNOW
Publications: Informational Brochure

GRANTS ANALYSIS
Number of Grants: 36
Highest Grant: $10,000
Typical Range: $2,500 to $8,000
Disclosure Period: 1991

RECENT GRANTS
10,000 Manhattan College, Riverdale, NY
10,000 St. Vincent's School of Nursing, New York, NY
9,500 Mountainside Hospital, New York, NY
9,000 Pratt Institute, New York, NY
8,500 Felician College, New York, NY
8,000 Pace University, New York, NY
7,000 Rider College, New York, NY
7,000 Wagner College, New York, NY
6,000 Bridgeport Hospital, Bridgeport, CT
6,000 Christ Hospital, New York, NY

Sylvester Foundation, Harcourt M. and Virginia W.

CONTACT
Nevin B. Gilpatrick
Trust Officer
Harcourt M. and Virginia W. Sylvester Fdn.
c/o Nations Bank, Trust Department
PO Box 407090 FL59010203
Ft. Lauderdale, FL 33340-7090
(407) 393-5194

FINANCIAL SUMMARY
Recent Giving: $5,500,000 (fiscal 1990); $5,513,000 (fiscal 1989)
Assets: $27,911,664 (fiscal year ending July 31, 1990); $31,184,726 (fiscal 1989)
EIN: 59-2018824

CONTRIBUTIONS SUMMARY
Donor(s): The foundation was established in 1980 by the late Harcourt M. Sylvester and the late Virginia W. Sylvester.
Typical Recipients: • *Education:* continuing education, education funds, medical education, science/technology education
Grant Types: endowment
Geographic Distribution: Miami, FL

GIVING OFFICERS
Gary King: dir
James J. Linus: dir
Harcourt M. Sylvester II: pres, dir

APPLICATION INFORMATION
Initial Approach:

The foundation requests applications be made in writing. Applications should include the names of the organization's directors and the purpose of the grant.

The foundation has no deadline for submitting proposals.

Restrictions on Giving: The foundation makes grants only to organizations exempt under section 501(c)(3). The foundation does not make grants to individuals.

GRANTS ANALYSIS

Total Grants: $5,500,000
Number of Grants: 1
Highest Grant: 5,500,000
Disclosure Period: fiscal year ending July 31, 1990
Note: Recent grants are derived from a fiscal 1990 grants list.

RECENT GRANTS

5,500,000 University of Miami Medical School, Miami, FL — endowment

Symmes Foundation, F. W.

CONTACT

Thomas Decrardsvich
F. W. Symmes Fdn.
c/o South Carolina National Bank Trust
Ste. 501
1401 Main St.
Columbia, SC 29226-9365
(803) 239-6842

FINANCIAL SUMMARY

Recent Giving: $633,500 (fiscal 1992); $468,800 (fiscal 1990); $446,000 (fiscal 1989)
Assets: $9,488,315 (fiscal year ending March 31, 1992); $8,385,832 (fiscal 1990); $8,154,423 (fiscal 1989)
EIN: 57-6017472

CONTRIBUTIONS SUMMARY

Donor(s): the late F.W. Symmes
Typical Recipients: • *Arts & Humanities:* arts centers, history/historic preservation, libraries, performing arts • *Civic & Public Affairs:* environmental affairs, municipalities • *Education:* colleges & universities, literacy • *Health:* hospitals • *Social Services:* food/clothing distribution, homes
Grant Types: capital and project

Geographic Distribution: focus on Greenville, SC

GIVING OFFICERS

William H. Orders: trust

Wilson C. Wearn: trust *ED* Clemson Univ BEE 1941 *CORP AFFIL* chmn emeritus: Multimedia Inc; dir: NCNB Corp *NONPR AFFIL* mem: Natl Assn Broadcasters, Natl Assn Securities Dealers; trust: Presbyterian Coll

F. McKinnon Wilkinson: trust

APPLICATION INFORMATION

Initial Approach: Send brief letter of inquiry describing program or project. There are no deadlines.

Restrictions on Giving: Does not support individuals.

OTHER THINGS TO KNOW

Publications: Application Guidelines, Informational Brochure

GRANTS ANALYSIS

Number of Grants: 14
Highest Grant: $250,000
Typical Range: $5,000 to $25,000
Disclosure Period: fiscal year ending March 31, 1992

RECENT GRANTS

250,000 Peace Center, Greenville, SC
100,000 Furman University, Greenville, SC
88,000 Rosewood House of Recovery, Greenville, SC
50,000 Greenville County Library, Greenville, SC
50,000 Miracle Hill Ministries, Greenville, SC
25,000 Community Foundation of Greater Greenville, Greenville, SC
22,000 Phyllis Wheatley Association, Greenville, SC
12,500 South Carolina Governor's School For the Arts, Columbia, SC
10,000 Greenville Literacy Association, Greenville, SC
10,000 United Way, Greenville, SC

Synovus Financial Corp. / Synovus Charitable Trust

Former Foundation Name: CB & T Charitable Trust
Assets: $5.18 billion
Employees: 4,000
Headquarters: Columbus, GA
SIC Major Group: Business Services, Depository Institutions, Holding & Other Investment Offices, and Security & Commodity Brokers

CONTACT

William L. Slaughter, Jr.
Trust Officer
Synovus Charitable Trust
PO Box 120
Columbus, GA 31902
(404) 649-2679

FINANCIAL SUMMARY

Recent Giving: $480,000 (1992 approx.); $480,000 (1991); $480,000 (1990)
Assets: $40,314 (1989)
Gifts Received: $415,000 (1989)
Fiscal Note: Contributes through foundation only.
EIN: 23-7024198

CONTRIBUTIONS SUMMARY

Typical Recipients: • *Arts & Humanities:* arts centers, museums/galleries • *Civic & Public Affairs:* better government, economic development, philanthropic organizations, urban & community affairs, zoos/botanical gardens • *Education:* colleges & universities, economic education, education associations, education funds, private education (precollege), student aid • *Health:* geriatric health, health organizations, hospices, hospitals, mental health, pediatric health, single-disease health associations • *Religion:* churches, religious organizations • *Social Services:* aged, community centers, community service organizations, counseling, family services, homes, recreation & athletics, shelters/homelessness, united funds, youth organizations
Grant Types: general support
Geographic Distribution: limited to Columbus, GA
Operating Locations: AL (Fort Rucker, Phenix City), FL (Fernandina Beach, Pensacola, Quincy, Tallahassee, Valparaiso), GA (Albany, Americus, Brunswick, Carrollton,

Chatsworth, Columbus, Hazleburst, LaGrange, Monroe, Newman, Statesboro, Thomasville, Tifton, Valdosta, Warner Robins)

CORP. OFFICERS

Joe E. Beverly: *CURR EMPL* vchmn, dir: Synovus Fin Corp
James H. Blanchard: *B* Augusta GA 1941 *ED* Univ GA 1963-1965 *CURR EMPL* chmn, dir: Synovus Fin Corp
Stephen L. Burts, Jr.: *CURR EMPL* pres, treas, cfo: Synovus Fin Corp
James D. Yancey: *CURR EMPL* vchmn, dir: Synovus Fin Corp

GIVING OFFICERS

William Slaughter: trust off

APPLICATION INFORMATION

Initial Approach: *Initial Contact:* brief letter of inquiry *Include Information On:* description of the organization, amount requested, purpose of funds sought, audited financial statement, and proof of tax-exempt status *When to Submit:* any time
Restrictions on Giving: Does not support non-tax-exempt organizations or groups not directly benefiting the Columbus, GA, area.

GRANTS ANALYSIS

Total Grants: $482,212
Number of Grants: 61
Highest Grant: $96,000
Typical Range: $500 to $5,000
Disclosure Period: 1990
Note: Recent grants are derived from a 1990 grants list.

RECENT GRANTS

96,000 United Way, Columbus, GA
58,850 St. Luke Child Development Center, Columbus, GA
50,000 Bradley Center, Columbus, GA
50,000 Columbus Medical Center, Columbus, GA
25,000 Springer Society, Columbus, GA
21,250 YMCA, Columbus, GA
20,000 Callaway Gardens, Columbus, GA
16,667 Family Counseling Center, Columbus, GA
16,000 Columbus Museum, Columbus, GA

12,500 Columbus Community Center, Columbus, GA

Syntex Corp.
Sales: $2.08 billion
Employees: 9,500
Headquarters: Palo Alto, CA
SIC Major Group: Agricultural Production— Crops and Chemicals & Allied Products

CONTACT
Suzanne Ward
Director, Community Affairs
Syntex Corp.
3401 Hillview Ave.
Palo Alto, CA 94304
(415) 855-6111

FINANCIAL SUMMARY
Recent Giving: $6,000,000 (fiscal 1993 est.); $6,000,000 (fiscal 1992 approx.); $3,327,576 (fiscal 1991 approx.)
Fiscal Note: Company gives directly.

CONTRIBUTIONS SUMMARY
Typical Recipients: • *Arts & Humanities:* arts centers, opera, performing arts, visual arts • *Civic & Public Affairs:* public policy • *Education:* colleges & universities, elementary education, science/technology education • *Science:* science exhibits & fairs
Grant Types: award, employee matching gifts, fellowship, and general support
Nonmonetary Support Types: donated products and in-kind services
Note: Value of company nonmonetary support was $4,000,000 in 1992 and is included in the figures above. In addition to donating products and in-kind services, Syntex also makes conference facilities available for limited use by nonprofits during evenings and weekends.
Geographic Distribution: near operating locations, nationally and internationally
Operating Locations: CA (Cupertino, Mountain View, Palo Alto, San Jose), CO (Boulder), DC, IA (Des Moines), MO (Springfield, Verona)
Note: Syntex and its subsidiaries also have facilities in the Bahamas, Bermuda, Brazil, Canada, England, Ireland, Mexico, Panama, Puerto Rico, and Scotland.

CORP. OFFICERS
Paul E. Freiman: *B* New York NY 1934 *CURR EMPL* chmn, ceo: Syntex Corp
James N. Wilson: *CURR EMPL* chmn, coo: Syntex Corp

GIVING OFFICERS
Gwynn Akin: mem contributions comm
Paul E. Freiman: *CURR EMPL* chmn, ceo: Syntex Corp (see above)
Darlene Friedman: mem contributions comm
Kathleen N. Gary: mem contributions comm *B* Long Beach CA 1945 *ED* Univ WA 1967 *CURR EMPL* vp (pub affairs & communications): Syntex Corp *NONPR AFFIL* mem: Natl Investor Rels Inst, Pharmaceutical Mfrs Assn, Publ Rels Soc Am
Thomas L. Gutshall: mem contributions comm *B* Huntingdon PA 1938 *ED* Univ DE BS 1960 *CURR EMPL* exec vp, pres (diagnostics div): Syntex Corp *NONPR AFFIL* chmn: City Team Ministries; mem: Am Inst Chem Engrs, Am Social Health Assn, Tau Beta Pi
Cindy Mansfield: admin asst *CURR EMPL* admin asst: Syntex Corp
Richard P. Powers: mem contributions comm *CURR EMPL* sr vp, cfo: Syntex Corp
Robert Roe: mem contributions comm
Virgil Thompson: mem contributions comm *CURR EMPL* exec vp: Syntex Laboratories
Virginia Turner: contributions coordinator *CURR EMPL* volunteer coordinator: Syntex Corp
Suzanne Ward: *CURR EMPL* dir pub aff: Syntex Corp

APPLICATION INFORMATION
Initial Approach: *Initial Contact:* letter or proposal *Include Information On:* organization, including list of staff and board members, annual budget, and audit, if available; program or project for which funds are sought, including detailed expense breakdown; list of other funding commitments; copy of IRS determination of tax-exempt status; list of Syntex employees or family members involved with organization *When to Submit:* any time
Restrictions on Giving: Syntex does not contribute to for-profit organizations; program advertisements; telephone solicitations; testimonials; athletic fund raisers; emergency funds; benefit events, unless Syntex is directly involved with the sponsoring organization; community organizations outside company communities; united fund agencies, other than for special projects not eligible for united funds; individuals; goodwill advertising; fraternal organizations; religious organizations for sectarian purposes; or organizations that discriminate on the basis of age, disability, race, religion, ethnic origin, gender, or sex preference.

OTHER THINGS TO KNOW
Geographically, 80% of contributions are disbursed in United States and Puerto Rico; 20% to other countries.
Publications: guidelines

GRANTS ANALYSIS
Total Grants: $6,000,000
Number of Grants: 400*
Highest Grant: $180,000*
Typical Range: $1,000 to $10,000
Disclosure Period: fiscal year ending July 31, 1992
Note: Figure for number of grants is approximate. Highest grant was to the Pediatric AIDS Foundation in Los Angeles, CA. Recent grants are derived from a fiscal 1991 grants list.

RECENT GRANTS
290,000 University of California San Francisco, San Francisco, CA
165,000 Stanford University, Stanford, CA
67,500 PMA Foundation Pharmacology Fellowships, Philadelphia, PA
52,508 CSFA Syntex Employee Children's Scholarships
37,500 American Medical Association Education and Research Foundation, Chicago, IL
35,000 San Jose Museum of Art, San Jose, CA
30,000 Valley Medical Center Foundation, Fresno, CA
25,000 Clean Sites, Alexandria, VA
25,000 El Camino Hospital Foundation, Mountain View, CA
25,000 Science Screen Reports

Sysco Corp.
Sales: $8.14 billion
Employees: 21,000
Headquarters: Houston, TX
SIC Major Group: Wholesale Trade—Nondurable Goods

CONTACT
Bill Delaney
Treasurer
Sysco Corp.
1390 Enclave Pkwy.
Houston, TX 77077-2027
(713) 584-1390

CONTRIBUTIONS SUMMARY
Operating Locations: TX (Houston)

CORP. OFFICERS
John F. Baugh: *CURR EMPL* sr chmn: Sysco Corp
Herbert Irving: *B* 1917 *ED* Univ PA BA 1938; Univ PA MBA 1940 *CURR EMPL* vchmn, chmn fin comm, dir: Sysco Corp
Bill M. Lindig: *CURR EMPL* pres, coo: Sysco Corp
John F. Woodhouse: *CURR EMPL* chmn, ceo: Sysco Corp

T & T United Truck Lines
Employees: 200
Headquarters: Spokane, WA
SIC Major Group: Trucking & Warehousing

CONTACT
Nicky Doyle
Vice President, Administration
T & T United Truck Lines
PO Box 3845
Spokane, WA 99220
(509) 535-2980

CONTRIBUTIONS SUMMARY
Washington State University Foundation
Operating Locations: WA (Spokane)

T.T.X. Co.
Sales: $621.5 million
Employees: 1,400
Parent Company: Conrail
Headquarters: Chicago, IL
SIC Major Group: Real Estate and Transportation Services

CONTACT

John Colson
Director, Personnel for
  Corporate Comm.
T.T.X. Co.
101 North Wacker Dr.
Chicago, IL 60606
(312) 984-3701

CONTRIBUTIONS SUMMARY

Company sponsors employee matching gift program; also supports community organizations.
Typical Recipients: • *Arts & Humanities:* general • *Civic & Public Affairs:* general • *Education:* general • *Health:* general • *Social Services:* general
Grant Types: matching
Geographic Distribution: primarily headquarters area
Operating Locations: IL (Chicago)

CORP. OFFICERS

R.C. Burton, Jr.: *CURR EMPL* ceo, pres: Trailer Train Co

APPLICATION INFORMATION

Initial Approach: Send brief letter of inquiry. There are no deadlines.

Taconic Foundation

CONTACT

Jane Lee Eddy
Executive Director and Secretary
Taconic Foundation
745 Fifth Avenue, Ste. 1608
New York, NY 10151
(212) 758-8673

FINANCIAL SUMMARY

Recent Giving: $762,500 (1991); $822,183 (1990); $758,000 (1989)
Assets: $21,263,256 (1991); $17,507,638 (1990); $19,363,192 (1989)
Gifts Received: $112,699 (1988); $278,791 (1985)
Fiscal Note: The 1988 gift of $112,699 was the remainder of the interest matured under the will of Stephen Currier.
EIN: 13-1873668

CONTRIBUTIONS SUMMARY

Donor(s): The Taconic Foundation was established in 1958 by the late Mr. and Mrs. Stephen R. Currier. Mrs. Currier, the former Audrey Mellon Bruce, was the daughter of Ailsa Mellon, who was the sister of Paul Mellon and the daughter of Andrew Mellon. Mr. and Mrs. Currier, who were lost in the Caribbean on an airplane flight in 1967, left a fund having a current market value of approximately $15 million to carry on their charitable activities.
Typical Recipients: • *Civic & Public Affairs:* better government, civil rights, economic development, housing, law & justice, philanthropic organizations • *Education:* colleges & universities, education associations, literacy • *Social Services:* child welfare, counseling, employment/job training, family planning
Grant Types: general support and project
Geographic Distribution: national, with emphasis on New York City

GIVING OFFICERS

Sheila M. Bautz: asst treas
Mrs. Jane Lee Eddy: secy, exec dir, trust *NONPR AFFIL* chmn, trust: Corp for Youth Energy Corps; pres, trust: Smokey House Project
John Gerald Simon: pres, treas, trust *B* New York NY 1928 *ED* Harvard Univ AB 1950; Yale Univ LLB 1953 *NONPR AFFIL* mem: Phi Beta Kappa; mem grad bd: Harvard Crimson; prof: Yale Univ Law Sch; trust: Fdn Ctr; trust, secy: Potomac Inst; vchmn: Coop Assistance Fund; vp, trust: Smokey House Project; chmn program nonprofit orgs: Yale Univ

APPLICATION INFORMATION

Initial Approach:
Prospective applicants should send a letter to the foundation. The letter should briefly describe the intended project. If the foundation is interested, one copy of a proposal will be requested.
The board meets four to six times a year, and there are no deadlines for submitting requests.
Final notification comes within two to three months.
Restrictions on Giving: No grants are given for higher education, art and cultural programs, mass media, crime and justice, health, medicine, mental health, ecology and the environment, individual economic development projects, or local community programs outside New York City. The foundation also makes no grants to individuals or to building or endowment funds. It rarely makes grants for research or loans.

OTHER THINGS TO KNOW

Publications: biennial report

GRANTS ANALYSIS

Total Grants: $762,500
Number of Grants: 35
Highest Grant: $265,000
Typical Range: $5,000 to $20,000
Disclosure Period: 1991
Note: Average grant figure excludes the largest grant of $265,000. Recent grants are derived from a 1991 Form 990.

RECENT GRANTS

265,000 Smokey House Project, Danby, VT — general support
28,000 Potomac Institute, Washington, DC — general support
25,000 Corporation for Youth Energy Corps, Bronx, NY — loan converted to grant
25,000 Public Education Association, New York, NY — general support
20,000 Business and Professional People for the Public Interest, Chicago, IL — to develop new ways to implement outcomes in the Gautreaux litigation
20,000 Center for Community Change, Washington, DC — in support of the Housing Trust Fund
20,000 Council of New York Law Associates (now Lawyers' Alliance), New York, NY — in support of the Community Development Legal Assistance Center program
20,000 Enterprise Foundation, Columbia, MD — general support
20,000 Lower East Side Mutual Housing Association, New York, NY — in general support
20,000 South Bronx 2000 Local Development Corporation, Bronx, NY — general support

Tai and Co., J. T. / Tai and Co. Foundation, J. T.

Headquarters: New York, NY

CONTACT

Ping Y. Tai
Officer
J.T. Tai & Company Foundation
  Inc.
18 East 67th St.
New York, NY 10021
(212) 288-5242

FINANCIAL SUMMARY

Recent Giving: $429,986 (1991); $541,748 (1990); $507,487 (1989)
Assets: $13,810,007 (1991); $11,964,070 (1990); $12,391,432 (1989)
Gifts Received: $788 (1991); $4,286 (1990); $3,200 (1989)
Fiscal Note: Contributes through foundation only.
EIN: 13-3157279

CONTRIBUTIONS SUMMARY

Typical Recipients: • *Education:* colleges & universities, medical education • *Health:* health organizations, hospitals, medical research • *Religion:* churches, religious organizations
Grant Types: general support
Geographic Distribution: northeastern United States, focus on New York
Operating Locations: NY (New York)

GIVING OFFICERS

F. Richard Hsu: secy
Jun Tset Tai: pres, mang dir
Ping Y. Tai: off

APPLICATION INFORMATION

Initial Approach: *Initial Contact:* detailed letter *Include Information On:* description of program and proposed utilization of funds *When to Submit:* any time

GRANTS ANALYSIS

Total Grants: $429,986
Number of Grants: 43
Highest Grant: $108,150
Typical Range: $1,000 to $10,000
Disclosure Period: 1991
Note: Recent grants are derived from a 1991 grants list.

RECENT GRANTS

108,150 New York University, New York, NY

72,065 Columbia University, New York, NY
40,000 Chemotherapy Foundation, New York, NY
20,000 Chinese Institute in America, New York, NY
16,000 Harvard Medical School, Cambridge, MA
15,000 Chinese Bible Church, New York, NY
12,000 Cornell University Medical College, Ithaca, NY
10,000 Church in New York, New York, NY
10,000 Department of Urology, New York, NY — Cancer Research
10,000 Madison Avenue Presbyterian Church, Madison, WI

Tait Foundation, Frank M.

CONTACT
Frank M. Tait Fdn.
Courthouse Plaza, S.W., 9th fl.
Dayton, OH 45402
(513) 222-2401

FINANCIAL SUMMARY
Recent Giving: $259,625 (1991); $267,925 (1990); $231,114 (1989)
Assets: $5,897,962 (1991); $4,827,019 (1990); $5,019,768 (1989)
EIN: 31-6037499

CONTRIBUTIONS SUMMARY
Donor(s): the late Frank M. Tait, the late Mrs. Frank M. Tait
Typical Recipients: • *Arts & Humanities:* arts institutes, community arts, history/historic preservation, museums/galleries, music, opera, performing arts, public broadcasting, theater • *Civic & Public Affairs:* municipalities • *Education:* colleges & universities • *Social Services:* community service organizations, youth organizations
Grant Types: general support
Geographic Distribution: focus on Montgomery County, OH

GIVING OFFICERS
Richard F. Beach: pres, trust *CURR EMPL* dir commun rels: NCR Corp

Peter Hans Forster: dir *B* Berlin Germany 1942 *ED* Univ WI BS 1964; Columbia Univ JD 1972 *CURR EMPL* chmn: Dayton Power & Light Co *CORP AFFIL* chmn, ceo, pres: DPL; dir: Amcast Indus Corp, Bank One Dayton, CH Gosiger Machinery Co, Comair Inc *NONPR AFFIL* dir: Miami Valley Hosp, Pub Ed Fund Gov Bd, Un Negro Coll Fund; mem: Am Bar Assn, Dayton Area Chamber Commerce, Dayton Bar Assn, Edison Electric Inst, OH Bar Assn; trust: Comm Econ Devel, Med Am Health Sys
Robert J. Kegerreis: trust
Susan T. Rankin: secy, treas, exec dir
Frederick W. Schantz: vp
Alexander J. Williams: trust

APPLICATION INFORMATION
Initial Approach: Send brief letter of inquiry describing program. Deadline is October 1.
Restrictions on Giving: Does not support individuals.

GRANTS ANALYSIS
Number of Grants: 42
Highest Grant: $25,000
Typical Range: $1,000 to $5,000
Disclosure Period: 1991

RECENT GRANTS
25,000 Boys and Girls Club, Dayton, OH
20,000 Arts Center Foundation, Dayton, OH
20,000 Dayton Museum of Natural History, Dayton, OH
20,000 Dayton Museum of Natural History, Dayton, OH
19,000 Arts Center Foundation, Dayton, OH
19,000 United Way, Dayton, OH
10,000 Dayton Art Institute, Dayton, OH
10,000 Dayton Foundation, Dayton, OH
10,000 Dayton Opera, Dayton, OH
10,000 Victoria Theatre Association, Dayton, OH

Talley Industries, Inc. / Talley Foundation

Sales: $332.6 million
Employees: 3,114
Headquarters: Phoenix, AZ
SIC Major Group: Instruments & Related Products, Miscellaneous Manufacturing Industries, Rubber & Miscellaneous Plastics Products, and Transportation Equipment

CONTACT
William Bonnell
Director, Human Resources
Talley Industries, Inc.
2800 North 44th St., Ste. 900
Phoenix, AZ 85008
(602) 957-7711

FINANCIAL SUMMARY
Recent Giving: $89,880 (1991); $90,580 (1990); $63,217 (1989)
Assets: $468,903 (1991); $449,634 (1990); $513,347 (1989)
EIN: 06-6090371

CONTRIBUTIONS SUMMARY
Typical Recipients: • *Arts & Humanities:* community arts, dance, museums/galleries, music • *Civic & Public Affairs:* zoos/botanical gardens • *Education:* community & junior colleges, education funds • *Health:* health organizations, medical research, single-disease health associations • *Social Services:* youth organizations
Grant Types: general support and scholarship
Nonmonetary Support Types: donated products
Geographic Distribution: focus on AZ
Operating Locations: AZ (Phoenix), CT (Waterbury), IL (Rolling Meadows), NC (Davidson), NY (New York), OH (Toledo), SC (Hartsville)

CORP. OFFICERS
Jack C. Crim: *B* Cleveland OH 1930 *ED* Purdue Univ 1954 *CURR EMPL* pres, coo: Talley Indus
William H. Mallender: *B* Birmingham MI 1935 *ED* Yale Univ 1957; Univ MI 1960 *CURR EMPL* chmn, ceo: Talley Indus

GIVING OFFICERS
Mark S. Dickerson: secy, dir

William H. Mallender: pres, dir *CURR EMPL* chmn, ceo: Talley Indus (see above)
Daniel P. Mullen: vp, treas, dir

APPLICATION INFORMATION
Initial Approach: Send a brief letter of inquiry and a full proposal. Include a description of organization, amount requested, purpose of funds sought, recently audited financial statement, and proof of tax-exempt status. There are no deadlines.

GRANTS ANALYSIS
Number of Grants: 23
Highest Grant: $11,200
Typical Range: $2,000 to $10,000
Disclosure Period: 1991

RECENT GRANTS
11,200 Phoenix Zoo, Phoenix, AZ
10,000 Ballet Arizona, Phoenix, AZ
7,700 Thunderbirds, Phoenix, AZ
7,000 American Heart Association, Phoenix, AZ
6,000 Maricopa Colleges Foundation, Phoenix, AZ
5,000 Local Initiatives Support Corporation, Phoenix, AZ
5,000 Phoenix Symphony, Phoenix, AZ
4,000 Phoenix Art Museum, Phoenix, AZ
3,500 Rising STAR, Scottsdale, AZ
2,500 Congressional Charity Golf Tournament, Washington, DC

Tamaki Foundation

CONTACT
Tamaki Foundation
4739 University Way, NE, Suite 1638
Seattle, WA 98105-4412

FINANCIAL SUMMARY
Recent Giving: $241,924 (1990)
Assets: $4,313,190 (1990)
EIN: 94-3099647

GRANTS ANALYSIS
Total Grants: $241,924
Disclosure Period: 1990

Tamarkin Co. / Tamarkin Foundation

Sales: $50.0 million
Employees: 727
Headquarters: Youngstown, OH
SIC Major Group: Food Stores and Wholesale Trade—Nondurable Goods

CONTACT

Bertram Tamarkin
President
Tamarkin Foundation
20 Federal Plz.
Youngstown, OH 44503
(216) 743-1786
Note: Nathan H. Monus, secretary, is another contact.

FINANCIAL SUMMARY

Recent Giving: $265,430 (1990); $205,260 (1989)
Assets: $379,814 (1990); $423,856 (1989)
Gifts Received: $200,000 (1990); $200,000 (1989)
Fiscal Note: In 1990, contributions were received from Giant Eagle Markets, Inc.
EIN: 34-1023645

CONTRIBUTIONS SUMMARY

Typical Recipients: • *Arts & Humanities:* arts centers, arts institutes, community arts, music • *Civic & Public Affairs:* ethnic/minority organizations • *Education:* colleges & universities • *Health:* geriatric health, hospitals, medical research, single-disease health associations • *Religion:* religious organizations, synagogues • *Social Services:* aged, community service organizations, religious welfare
Grant Types: general support
Operating Locations: OH (Youngstown), PA (Pittsburgh)

CORP. OFFICERS

David Shapira: *CURR EMPL* pres, ceo: Tamarkin Co

GIVING OFFICERS

Arthur N. K. Friedman: trust
Michael I. Monus: dir
Nathan H. Monus: secy, trust
Bertram Tamarkin: pres, trust
Jack B. Tamarkin: treas, trust
Jerry P. Tamarkin: vp, trust

APPLICATION INFORMATION

Initial Approach: Send brief letter describing program. There are no deadlines.

GRANTS ANALYSIS

Number of Grants: 30
Highest Grant: $90,000
Typical Range: $300 to $1,000
Disclosure Period: 1990

RECENT GRANTS

90,000 Jewish Federation, Palm Beach, FL
70,000 Youngstown Area Jewish Federation, Youngstown, OH
3,000 Joseph L. Morse Geriatrics Center, West Palm Beach, FL
2,000 Oblate Sisters SHJ, Youngstown, OH
2,000 Palm Beach Community Foundation, Palm Beach, FL
1,500 Temple Israel, Youngstown, OH
1,500 Temple Israel, Youngstown, OH
1,250 Jewish National Fund, Pittsburgh, PA
1,000 Good Samaritan Hospital, Palm Beach, FL
1,000 St. Mary's Hospital, Palm Beach, FL

Tambrands Inc.

Sales: $660.7 million
Employees: 3,800
Headquarters: White Plains, NY
SIC Major Group: Paper & Allied Products

CONTACT

Marian Gryzlo
Corporate Contributions, Human Resources
Tambrands Inc.
777 Westchester Ave.
White Plains, NY 10604
(914) 696-6060

CONTRIBUTIONS SUMMARY

Grant Types: matching
Operating Locations: NY (Lake Success, White Plains)

CORP. OFFICERS

Martin F.C. Emmett: *CURR EMPL* chmn, ceo, dir: Tambrands

Tamko Asphalt Products / Craig Foundation, E. L.

Sales: $200.0 million
Employees: 1,340
Headquarters: Joplin, MO
SIC Major Group: Petroleum & Coal Products

CONTACT

J. P. Humphreys
President
Tamko Asphalt Products
PO Box 1404
Joplin, MO 64802
(417) 624-6644

FINANCIAL SUMMARY

Recent Giving: $297,114 (fiscal 1991); $306,300 (fiscal 1990); $85,549 (fiscal 1989)
Assets: $4,945,980 (fiscal year ending July 31, 1991); $4,689,747 (fiscal 1990); $4,550,465 (fiscal 1989)
Gifts Received: $200,000 (fiscal 1991); $100,000 (fiscal 1990); $100,000 (fiscal 1989)
Fiscal Note: Contributes through foundation only. In fiscal 1991, contributions were received from Tamko Asphalt Products, Inc.
EIN: 44-6015127

CONTRIBUTIONS SUMMARY

Typical Recipients: • *Arts & Humanities:* music • *Civic & Public Affairs:* better government, civil rights, economics, housing, international affairs, law & justice, public policy, rural affairs, urban & community affairs • *Education:* colleges & universities, economic education, private education (precollege), private education (precollege), public education (precollege), social sciences education • *Health:* hospitals, medical research, single-disease health associations • *Religion:* churches • *Social Services:* community service organizations, food/clothing distribution, legal aid, youth organizations
Grant Types: research
Geographic Distribution: nationally, with a focus on Joplin, MO
Operating Locations: MO (Joplin)

CORP. OFFICERS

Jay P. Humphreys: *CURR EMPL* pres: Tamko Asphalt Products

John Patrick Humphreys: *CURR EMPL* pres: Tamko Asphalt Products

GIVING OFFICERS

Ethel Mae Craig Humphreys: trust
John Patrick Humphreys: pres, dir *CURR EMPL* pres: Tamko Asphalt Products (see above)

APPLICATION INFORMATION

Initial Approach: *Note:* The foundation supports preselected organizations and does not accept unsolicited requests for funds.
Restrictions on Giving: Company does not support individuals.

GRANTS ANALYSIS

Total Grants: $297,114
Number of Grants: 32
Highest Grant: $101,000
Typical Range: $100 to $1,000
Disclosure Period: fiscal year ending July 31, 1991
Note: Recent grants are derived from a fiscal 1991 grants list.

RECENT GRANTS

101,000 First Community Church, Joplin, MO
50,000 CATO Institute, Washington, DC
50,000 Council for a Sound Economy Foundation, Washington, DC
20,000 Advocates for Self-Government, Fresno, CA
10,000 Heartland Institute of Missouri, St. Louis, MO
10,000 Institute for Humane Studies, Fairfax, VA
10,000 National Right to Work Legal Defense Foundation, Springfield, VA
7,800 Pathfinder School
6,250 Boy Scouts of America, Tuscaloosa, AL
5,000 Boy Scouts of America, Joplin, MO

Tampa Electric

Revenue: $988.0 million
Employees: 3,228
Parent Company: Teco Energy
Inc.
Headquarters: Tampa, FL
SIC Major Group: Electric, Gas
& Sanitary Services

CONTACT

Julius Hobbes
Director, Community Relations
Tampa Electric
PO Box 111
Tampa, FL 33601
(813) 228-4273

FINANCIAL SUMMARY

Recent Giving: $1,000,000
(1993 est.); $1,000,000 (1992
approx.); $1,000,000 (1991)
Fiscal Note: Company gives directly.

CONTRIBUTIONS SUMMARY

Typical Recipients: • *Civic &
Public Affairs:* general • *Education:* general • *Health:* general
• *Social Services:* general
Grant Types: general support
Geographic Distribution: in
headquarters and operating
communities
Operating Locations: FL
(Tampa)

CORP. OFFICERS

G.F. Anderson: *CURR EMPL*
pres, coo: Tampa Electric
CORP AFFIL dir: Sun Bank
Tampa Bay, TECO Energy

GIVING OFFICERS

Julius Hobbes: *CURR EMPL*
dir commun rels: Tampa Electric

APPLICATION INFORMATION

Initial Approach: *Initial Contact:* brief letter of inquiry *Include Information On:* a description of organization,
amount requested, purpose of
funds sought, recently audited
financial statement, and proof
of tax-exempt status *When to
Submit:* any time
Restrictions on Giving: Does
not support individuals, religious organizations for sectarian
purposes, political or lobbying
groups, or organizations outside operating areas.

OTHER THINGS TO KNOW

Publications: contributions
guidelines, community improvement partnership brochure, and fact sheet

GRANTS ANALYSIS

Typical Range: $50 to $1,000

Tandem Computers

Sales: $2.03 billion
Employees: 11,167
Headquarters: Cupertino, CA
SIC Major Group: Business
Services, Industrial Machinery
& Equipment, and Wholesale
Trade—Durable Goods

CONTACT

Mary Kelly
Community Affairs/Corporate
Grants
Tandem Computers Incorporated
10435 N Tantau Ave., Loc.
200-47
Cupertino, CA 95014-0709
(408) 285-2703

FINANCIAL SUMMARY

Recent Giving: $400,000
(1993 est.); $400,000 (1992 approx.); $545,000 (1991 approx.)
Fiscal Note: All contributions
are made directly by the company. Figures above are approximate. Value of nonmonetary support is included in
figures above.

CONTRIBUTIONS SUMMARY

Typical Recipients: • *Civic &
Public Affairs:* environmental
affairs, urban & community affairs, women's affairs • *Education:* business education, colleges & universities,
community & junior colleges,
elementary education, engineering education, literacy, minority education, science/technology education • *Health:*
hospices • *Social Services:*
aged, child welfare, community service organizations, disabled, drugs & alcohol, family
services, food/clothing distribution, volunteer services, youth
organizations
Grant Types: general support
and research
Nonmonetary Support Types:
donated equipment, in-kind
services, and loaned employees
Note: Nonmonetray amount for
1992 is unavailable. The contact for used donated equipment is Wanda Cavanaugh.
Geographic Distribution:
near headquarters in San Francisco and Santa Clara valley;
giving is limited in areas where
Tandem has a local presence

Operating Locations: AR (Little Rock), AZ (Phoenix, Tucson), CA (Culver City, Los Angeles, Oakland, Sacramento,
San Diego, San Francisco, San
Jose, Santa Ana, Santa Clara),
CO (Englewood), CT (Hartford, Norwalk), FL (Jacksonville, Miami, Orlando, Tampa),
GA (Atlanta), HI (Honolulu),
IA (Bettendorf, Cedar Rapids,
Des Moines), IL (Chicago,
Itasca, Palatine), IN (Ft.
Wayne, Indianapolis), KY (Louisville), LA (Metairie), MA
(Newton), MD (Linthicum), MI
(Detroit, Flint, Lansing), MN
(Minneapolis), MO (Creve
Coeur), NC (Charlotte), NE
(Omaha), NJ (Cherry Hill, Hasbrouck Heights), NM (Albuquerque), NV (Las Vegas), NY
(Amherst, Jericho, New York
City), OH (Cincinnati, Cleveland, Columbus, Dayton), OK
(Oklahoma City, Tulsa), PA
(Allentown, Horsham, Philadelphia, Pittsburgh), TN (Memphis), TX (Austin, Dallas, Ft.
Worth, Houston, Plano), UT
(Salt Lake City), VA (Reston,
Richmond), WA (Olympia,
Salem, Seattle), WI (Milwaukee)
Note: Also operates in Australia, Austria, Belgium, Canada,
Denmark, France, Hong Kong,
Italy, Japan, the Netherlands,
New Zealand, Norway, Singapore, Spain, Sweden, Switzerland, the United Kingdom, and
West Germany.

CORP. OFFICERS

Robert C. Marshall: *B* Berwyn IL 1931 *ED* Heald Engr
Coll 1956; Pepperdine Univ
1976 *CURR EMPL* sr vp, coo,
dir: Tandem Computers
David J. Rynne: *B* Buffalo NY
1940 *ED* State Univ NY 1963
CURR EMPL sr vp, cfo: Tandem Computers

GIVING OFFICERS

Mary Kelly: *CURR EMPL* mgr
corp grants & community affairs: Tandem Computers

APPLICATION INFORMATION

Initial Approach: *Initial Contact:* one-page letter of intent
Include Information On: description of the organization,
amount requested, purpose for
which funds are sought, statement of need for proposed project, sources and status of other
funding, key personnel and
qualifications of staff, detailed
budget showing how cash grant
will be spent, current financial
statement, proof of tax-exempt
status
Restrictions on Giving: Company does not support political
activities, national programs;
religious and fraternal organizations; arts organizations; memberships; clubs or sponsorships; breakfasts, luncheons,
dinners, dances, advertisements, or tickets; or individuals.

GRANTS ANALYSIS

Total Grants: $400,000*
Typical Range: $1,000 to
$5,000
Disclosure Period: 1992
Note: Total grants figure is approximate and reflects cash
contributions only. Recent
grants are derived from a 1989
Corporate Contributions Report.

RECENT GRANTS

California Polytechnic State
University, San Luis Obispo,
CA
Emergency Housing
Consortium, San Jose, CA —
to shelter and assist the
homeless
Exploratorium, San Francisco,
CA — for activities at science
museum
Hospice of the Valley, San Jose,
CA
Opportunities Industrialization
Center West, Menlo Park, CA
— for employment training
work with minorities
Project Hired, Sunnyvale, CA —
for work with the disabled
San Jose Youth at Risk, San
Jose, CA
San Jose YWCA Villa Nueva
Project, San Jose, CA
Valley Medical Center
Foundation, Santa Clara
Valley, Santa Clara, CA

Tandon Corp.

Sales: $461.3 million
Employees: 1,656
Headquarters: Moorpark, CA
SIC Major Group: Industrial
Machinery & Equipment and
Wholesale Trade—Durable
Goods

CONTACT

Brenda Turner
Human Resources
Tandon Corp.
609 Science Dr.
Moorpark, CA 93021
(805) 523-0340
Note: Contributions suspended
through at least 1994.

CONTRIBUTIONS
SUMMARY

Operating Locations: CA
(Moorpark, San Jose, Santa
Clara, Simi Valley)

CORP. OFFICERS

Sirjang Lal Tandon: *CURR
EMPL* chmn, pres, ceo: Tandon
Corp
Denis J. Trafecanty: *CURR
EMPL* vp, cfo: Tandon Corp

Tandy Corp.

Sales: $4.68 billion
Employees: 41,000
Headquarters: Ft. Worth, TX
SIC Major Group: Furniture &
Homefurnishings Stores and
Wholesale Trade—Durable
Goods

CONTACT

John Burnam
Vice President
Tandy Corp.
1800 One Tandy Ctr.
Ft. Worth, TX 76102
(817) 390-3270

FINANCIAL SUMMARY

Fiscal Note: Company does
not disclose financial information.

CONTRIBUTIONS
SUMMARY

Typical Recipients: • *Arts &
Humanities:* performing arts
• *Education:* general, private
education (precollege), public
education (precollege) • *Social
Services:* child welfare
Grant Types: employee match-
ing gifts and general support
Note: Company does not offer
multiyear/continuing support.
Operating Locations: CA
(Santa Clara, Stockton), IA

(Burlington), MO (Lamar), TX
(Azle, Ft. Worth)

CORP. OFFICERS

Thomas J. Perkins: *B* Oak
Park IL 1932 *ED* MA Inst Tech
BS 1953; Harvard Univ MBA
1957 *CURR EMPL* chmn:
Tandy Corp *CORP AFFIL* dir:
Collagen Corp, Corning Glass
Works, Econics Corp, Hy-
britech, LSI Logic Corp, Spec-
tra Physics, Vitatink Comm
Corp *NONPR AFFIL* trust: San
Francisco Ballet
James G. Treybig: *B* Claren-
don TX 1940 *ED* Rice Univ
1964; Stanford Univ 1968
CURR EMPL pres, ceo, dir:
Tandy Corp

GIVING OFFICERS

John Burnam: *CURR EMPL*
vp: Tandy Corp

APPLICATION
INFORMATION

Initial Approach: *Initial Contact:* brief letter *When to Submit:* before October 31
Restrictions on Giving: Company funds only 501(c)(3) organizations.

OTHER THINGS TO
KNOW

Company is not accepting any
new grant applications for
1993 and is currently funding
prior committments. Tandy
also is not initiating new program areas. The company reports that grant applications for
1994 should be received by October 31, 1993.
Tandy Direct Marketing, a division of Tandy Corp., sponsors
the Tandy Multimedia Users
Group (TMMUG). TMMUG, a
group of 10 public high schools
and two universities nationwide, goal is to show the practi-
cality of multimedia in education.

RECENT GRANTS

300,000 Cougar Valley, TX

Tandy Foundation, Anne Burnett and Charles

CONTACT

Thomas F. Beech
Executive Vice President
Anne Burnett and Charles Tandy
Foundation
801 Cherry St., Ste. 1400
Ft. Worth, TX 76102
(817) 877-3344

FINANCIAL SUMMARY

Recent Giving: $10,400,000
(1992 approx.); $7,871,511
(1991); $6,472,108 (1990)
Assets: $220,000,000 (1993
est.); $209,000,000 (1992 est.);
$209,288,944 (1991);
$171,733,884 (1990);
$186,007,603 (1989)
EIN: 75-1638517

CONTRIBUTIONS
SUMMARY

Donor(s): The foundation was
established in 1978 by Anne
Burnett Tandy in memory of
her husband, Charles D. Tandy
(d. 1978). Mr. Tandy bought
Radio Shack in 1963 and built
it from a debt-ridden chain of
nine electronics stores to a national chain with over 7,000
outlets.
Typical Recipients: • *Arts &
Humanities:* arts associations,
dance, history/historic preservation, museums/galleries, music,
visual arts • *Civic & Public Affairs:* housing, zoos/botanical
gardens • *Education:* colleges
& universities, education associations, private education
(precollege), public education
(precollege) • *Health:* hospitals, mental health, pediatric
health, single-disease health associations • *Social Services:*
child welfare, disabled, drugs
& alcohol, emergency relief,
employment/job training, family planning, food/clothing distribution, legal aid, religious
welfare, shelters/homelessness,
united funds, youth organizations
Grant Types: capital, challenge, endowment, general support, project, and seed money
Geographic Distribution: primarily Texas, with emphasis on
the Ft. Worth metropolitan area

GIVING OFFICERS

Perry R. Bass: vp, trust *B*
Wichita Falls TX 1914 *ED* Yale
Univ BS 1937 *CURR EMPL*

pres, dir: Perry R Bass Inc
CORP AFFIL chmn: Sid Rich-
ardson Carbon & Gas Co; dir:
Bass Brothers Enterprises
NONPR AFFIL chmn: TX
Parks Wildlife Comm; mem:
All Am Wildcatters, Am Assn
Petroleum Geologists, Inde-
pendent Petroleum Assn Am,
Longhorn Counc Boy Scouts
Am; mem ad hoc comm: TX
Energy Natural Resources Adv
Comm; mem adv comm bd visi-
tors: Univ Cancer Fdn MD An-
derson Hosp Tumor Inst; mem
bd govs: Ochsner Med Fdn;
mem exec comm: Am
Petroleum Inst, Natl Oil Policy
Comm Future Petroleum Prob-
lems, Natl Petroleum Counc,
TX Mid-Continent Oil & Gas
Assn
Thomas F. Beech: exec vp
Benjamin J. Fortson: vp,
trust, treas
Edward R. Hudson, Jr.: vp,
trust, secy
Anne W. Marion: pres, trust
John L. Marion: trust *B* New
York NY 1933 *ED* Fordham
Univ BS 1956; Columbia Univ
1960-61 *CURR EMPL* chmn,
dir: Sothebys *NONPR AFFIL*
chmn fine arts comm: NY City
Div Am Cancer Soc
Anne W. Phillips: adv trust

APPLICATION
INFORMATION

Initial Approach:
Applicants should write a succinct letter of inquiry describing the organization, the specific program to be considered,
the amount requested, and a
budget summary.
A detailed application form
will be sent if the program fits
within the foundation's guidelines and priorities.
There are no application deadlines.
Grant review meetings normally are held in February,
June, and November.
Restrictions on Giving: Funding is limited to organizations
with 501(c)(3) status. Individual scholarships are not given.
The foundation will not fund religious organizations for sectarian purposes.

OTHER THINGS TO
KNOW

Publications: annual report

GRANTS ANALYSIS

Total Grants: $7,871,511
Number of Grants: 67
Highest Grant: $1,250,000

Typical Range: $20,000 to $50,000 and $100,000 to $300,000
Disclosure Period: 1991
Note: Recent grants are derived from a 1991 annual report.

RECENT GRANTS

1,250,000 Amon Carter Museum of Western Art, Ft. Worth, TX — purchase of the Thomas Eakins painting

1,200,000 Memorial Sloan-Kettering Cancer Center, New York, NY — capital campaign

1,000,000 Ft. Worth Zoological Association, Ft. Worth, TX — capital campaign

650,000 Texas Christian University, Ft. Worth, TX — Burnett Ranches Endowed Professorship

500,000 Miss Porter's School, Farmington, CT — capital and endowment campaign

456,617 City of Ft. Worth/Burnett Park, Ft. Worth, TX — support of maintenance and landscaping of Burnett Park

285,000 Ft. Worth Modern Art Museum Association, Ft. Worth, TX — general operating expenses

250,000 United Way of Metropolitan Tarrant County/Tarrant County Housing Partnership, Ft. Worth, TX

250,000 White House Endowment Fund, Washington, DC — permanent endowment for historical preservation of the public rooms

150,000 Child Study Center, Ft. Worth, TX — operating expenses; capital campaign

Tandy Foundation, David L.

CONTACT
David L. Tandy Fdn.
PO Box 101477
Ft. Worth, TX 76185
(817) 877-0665

FINANCIAL SUMMARY
Recent Giving: $129,500 (fiscal 1992); $152,500 (fiscal 1990); $143,000 (fiscal 1989)
Assets: $3,229,017 (fiscal year ending May 31, 1992); $2,683,184 (fiscal 1990); $3,060,992 (fiscal 1989)
EIN: 75-6083140

CONTRIBUTIONS SUMMARY
Typical Recipients: • *Arts & Humanities:* community arts, history/historic preservation, museums/galleries, music, public broadcasting • *Civic & Public Affairs:* ethnic/minority organizations, women's affairs, women's affairs • *Education:* colleges & universities, private education (precollege), religious education • *Social Services:* aged, child welfare, community service organizations, food/clothing distribution, shelters/homelessness, youth organizations
Grant Types: general support
Geographic Distribution: focus on TX

GIVING OFFICERS
Emmett Duemke: dir, pres
William H. Michero: dir, vp, secy
B.R. Roland: dir, vp, treas
A.R. Tandy, Jr.: vp
Mrs. E.C. Whitney: vp

APPLICATION INFORMATION
Initial Approach: Send brief letter describing program. There are no deadlines.

GRANTS ANALYSIS
Number of Grants: 39
Highest Grant: $7,000
Typical Range: $1,000 to $5,000
Disclosure Period: fiscal year ending May 31, 1992

RECENT GRANTS

7,000 Texas Christian University, Ft. Worth, TX

5,000 Casa Manana, Ft. Worth, TX

5,000 Happy Hill Farm, Granbury, TX

5,000 Meals on Wheels, Ft. Worth, TX

5,000 North Texas Public Broadcasting, Dallas, TX

5,000 Presbyterian Night Shelter, Ft. Worth, TX

5,000 Women's Haven of Tarrant County, Ft. Worth, TX

4,000 Fort Worth Museum of Science and History, Ft. Worth, TX

4,000 Fort Worth Symphony Orchestra Association, Ft. Worth, TX

4,000 Junior Achievement, Ft. Worth, TX

Tang Foundation

CONTACT
Leslie Schilling
Chief Financial Officer-Secretary
Tang Fdn.
944 Market St., Ste. 610
San Francisco, CA 94102-4010

FINANCIAL SUMMARY
Recent Giving: $368,667 (fiscal 1991); $610,015 (fiscal 1990); $411,000 (fiscal 1989)
Assets: $3,752,676 (fiscal year ending October 31, 1991); $3,808,848 (fiscal 1990); $4,246,050 (fiscal 1989)
EIN: 94-2963249

CONTRIBUTIONS SUMMARY
Donor(s): members of the Tang family
Typical Recipients: • *Civic & Public Affairs:* civil rights, ethnic/minority organizations • *Education:* colleges & universities, public education (precollege), science/technology education • *Social Services:* community service organizations, family services, youth organizations
Grant Types: general support and project
Geographic Distribution: focus on the San Francisco Bay Area, CA

GIVING OFFICERS
Leslie W. Schilling: cfo, secy
Jack C. C. Tang: pres, dir
Madeleine H. Tang: vp
Martin Y. Tang: vp

APPLICATION INFORMATION
Initial Approach: Send brief letter of inquiry describing program or project. There are no deadlines.

GRANTS ANALYSIS
Number of Grants: 5
Highest Grant: $300,000
Typical Range: $5,000 to $10,000
Disclosure Period: fiscal year ending October 31, 1991

RECENT GRANTS

300,000 Massachusetts Institute of Technology, Cambridge, MA

10,000 Chinese for Affirmative Action, San Francisco, CA

10,000 University of California, Berkeley, CA

5,205 Japanese Community Youth Council, San Francisco, CA

5,000 Community Educational Services, San Francisco, CA

Tanner Cos. / Tanner Foundation
Headquarters: Rutherfordton, NC

CONTACT
Lloyd Wood
Treasurer
Tanner Foundation
Oak Springs Road
Rutherfordton, NC 28139-2115
(704) 287-4205

FINANCIAL SUMMARY
Recent Giving: $32,710 (fiscal 1992); $36,774 (fiscal 1990)
Assets: $232,933 (fiscal year ending May 31, 1992); $265,454 (fiscal 1990)
Gifts Received: $100,000 (fiscal 1990)
EIN: 51-0151695

CONTRIBUTIONS SUMMARY
Typical Recipients: • *Arts & Humanities:* arts associations • *Civic & Public Affairs:* professional & trade associations • *Education:* education funds, elementary education • *Religion:* religious organizations • *Social Services:* united funds, youth organizations
Grant Types: capital, general support, and research
Geographic Distribution: giving primarily in NC
Operating Locations: NC (Rutherfordton)

CORP. OFFICERS
James T. Tanner: *CURR EMPL* pres, ceo: Tanner Companies

GIVING OFFICERS
Tom Downs: dir
James T. Tanner: pres *CURR EMPL* pres, ceo: Tanner Companies (see above)
Michael S. Tanner: secy
Simpson B. Tanner III: vp
Lloyd Wood: treas

APPLICATION INFORMATION
Initial Approach: Send a full proposal. Deadline is May 31.

GRANTS ANALYSIS
Number of Grants: 27
Highest Grant: $8,500
Typical Range: $500 to $1,000
Disclosure Period: fiscal year ending May 31, 1992

RECENT GRANTS
8,500 United Way
3,000 Chancellor's Club
2,500 Asheville School — capital fund
2,000 W N C W
1,500 096 Chaplaincy
1,500 Rutherford County Arts Council
1,250 Independent College Fund
1,000 Noah's House/Path
1,000 Rutherfordton Elementary School
1,000 South Mountain Boy's Home

Taper Foundation, Mark

CONTACT
Raymond F. Reisler
Executive Director
Mark Taper Fdn.
12011 San Vicente Blvd., Ste. 401
Los Angeles, CA 90049
(310) 476-5413

FINANCIAL SUMMARY
Recent Giving: $1,856,500 (fiscal 1992); $1,689,827 (fiscal 1991); $461,350 (fiscal 1990)
Assets: $8,259,157 (fiscal year ending June 30, 1992); $9,801,894 (fiscal 1991); $10,103,917 (fiscal 1990)
EIN: 95-6027846

CONTRIBUTIONS SUMMARY
Donor(s): S. Mark Taper
Typical Recipients: • *Civic & Public Affairs:* ethnic/minority organizations, philanthropic organizations • *Education:* colleges & universities, legal education • *Health:* geriatric health, health organizations, medical research, single-disease health associations • *Social Services:* aged, child welfare, community service organizations, counseling, homes
Grant Types: capital, general support, and project
Geographic Distribution: focus on CA

GIVING OFFICERS
Janice Taper Lazarof: vp, treas, dir
Ruth Stegall: asst secy
Barry H. Taper: vp, secy, dir
Sydney Mark Taper: pres, dir *B* Warsaw Poland 1901

APPLICATION INFORMATION
Initial Approach: Contributes only to preselected organizations.
Restrictions on Giving: Does not support individuals.

OTHER THINGS TO KNOW
Publications: Application Guidelines

GRANTS ANALYSIS
Highest Grant: $500,000
Typical Range: $5,000 to $20,000
Disclosure Period: fiscal year ending June 30, 1992

RECENT GRANTS
500,000 Los Angeles Free Clinic, Los Angeles, CA
400,000 Child Victims in Court Foundation, Los Angeles, CA
250,000 Organization for the Needs of Elderly, Van Nuys, CA
250,000 Santa Monica Senior Health and Peer Counseling Center, Santa Monica, CA
200,000 Children's Hospital, Los Angeles, CA
150,000 Hadassah, New York, NY
100,000 American Red Cross, Los Angeles, CA
5,000 Los Angeles County Museum of Art, Los Angeles, CA
1,000 Alzheimer's Disease and Related Disorders Association, Los Angeles, CA
500 Council on Foundations, Washington, DC

Taper Foundation, S. Mark

CONTACT
S. Mark Taper Foundation
12011 San Vicente Boulevard, Suite 400
Los Angeles, CA 90049-4986
(213) 476-5413

FINANCIAL SUMMARY
Recent Giving: $1,689,827 (fiscal 1991)
Assets: $9,801,894 (fiscal year ending June 30, 1991)
EIN: 95-4245076

CONTRIBUTIONS SUMMARY
Typical Recipients: • *Arts & Humanities:* museums/galleries • *Education:* colleges & universities, legal education • *Religion:* religious organizations • *Social Services:* aged, community service organizations
Grant Types: general support

GIVING OFFICERS
Janice A. Lazarof: vp, treas, dir
Ruth Stegall: asst secy
Barry H. Taper: vp, secy, dir
S. Mark Taper: pres, dir

APPLICATION INFORMATION
Initial Approach: The foundation reports no specific application guidelines. Send a brief letter of inquiry, including statement of purpose, amount requested, and proof of tax-exempt status.

GRANTS ANALYSIS
Total Grants: $1,689,827
Highest Grant: $1,299,727
Typical Range: $5,000 to $250,000
Disclosure Period: fiscal year ending June 30, 1991

RECENT GRANTS
1,299,727 Hadassah, The Women's Zionist Organization of America, NY
250,000 Santa Monica Senior Health and Peer Counseling Center, Santa Monica, CA
100,000 American Red Cross, CA
35,000 Stanford University Law School, Stanford, CA
5,000 Los Angeles County Museum, Los Angeles, CA
100 Hebrew Union College, CA

Target Stores
Sales: $6.0 billion
Employees: 80,000
Parent Company: Dayton-Hudson Corp.
Headquarters: Minneapolis, MN
SIC Major Group: General Merchandise Stores

CONTACT
Sherry Smith
Manager, Community Relations
Target Stores
PO Box 1392
Minneapolis, MN 55440
(612) 370-6098
Note: Gail Dorn, Director, Communications and Community Relations also is a contact.

FINANCIAL SUMMARY
Recent Giving: $8,000,000 (1993 est.); $7,500,000 (1992); $7,000,000 (1991)
Fiscal Note: Company gives directly.

CONTRIBUTIONS SUMMARY
Typical Recipients: • *Arts & Humanities:* arts festivals, community arts, dance, ethnic arts, museums/galleries, music, opera, performing arts, public broadcasting, theater, visual arts • *Social Services:* child welfare, domestic violence, domestic violence, family services
Grant Types: multiyear/continuing support and project
Geographic Distribution: headquarters and operating locations
Operating Locations: AR, AZ, CA, CO, FL, GA, IA, ID, IL, IN, KS, KY, LA, MI, MN (Minneapolis), MO, MT, NC, ND, NE, NM, NV, OH, OK, OR, SC, SD, TN, TX, WA, WI, WY

CORP. OFFICERS
Robert J. Ulrich: *CURR EMPL* chmn, ceo: Target Stores

GIVING OFFICERS
Sherry Smith: *CURR EMPL* mgr commun rels: Target Stores

APPLICATION INFORMATION

Initial Approach: *Initial Contact:* letter or phone call requesting application guidelines; if your organization and project meet criteria, submit a grant proposal to the local Target store manager *Include Information On:* two- to three-page project description, including a description of the activity, event, or project; the need for the program; how the program will enrich and strengthen families in Target communities; a description of the organization's main audience; an explanation of the expected outcome or result of the program; program impact; how results will be measured and evaluated; the proposed time frame; project budget information that details the various expenses and anticipated income sources; and plans if Target is unable to fund the full amount requested* *When to Submit:* while grants are made throughout the year, applicants are encouraged to submit proposals between March 1 and November 1 *Note:* Attach the following supporting documents: a current, annual operating budget for the organization that lists income and expenses; a list of major business donors that includes their contributions level; a list of the organization's board of directors; the most recent audited financial statement for the organization; and a copy of the IRS ruling on the organization's nonprofit status.

Restrictions on Giving: Does not make grants to programs outside Target communities; community foundations; endowment funds or capital fund drives; religious organizations; healthcare rehabilitation organizations; housing programs; treatment programs, i.e., medical, substance abuse, or alcohol abuse; individuals; athletic teams or events; fundraisers or tickets for benefit dinners; or advertising purposes.

Social service agencies with religious affiliations are eligible for grants if the proposed project does not advocate religious beliefs or practices, or restrict participation on the basis of religion.

Merchandise contributions, discounts, or gift certificates are not provided in lieu of grants.

OTHER THINGS TO KNOW

Company donates 5% of federally taxable income to programs that meet social and cultural needs. Target is the largest operating company of the Dayton Hudson Corp. (see separate entry).

Company also participates in a national program that donates usable damaged goods to local Goodwill Industries agencies, helping reduce potential waste and supporting Goodwill's job training program. Also hosts an annual holiday shpping event for senior citizens and disabled persons.

Most grants support specific programs, but general operating support will be considered when an organization's overall mission matches company's funding guidelines.

Will consider requests for multiyear support if the organization has a funding history with Target. Grants are renewable, based upon an evaluation of achieved results, continuing need, and available funds. Organizations that are funded by United Way are not excluded from applying for a grant.

Publications: contributions guidelines

GRANTS ANALYSIS

Typical Range: $2,000 to $10,000

Tarmac America Inc.

Sales: $600.0 million
Employees: 3,800
Parent Company: Tarmac PLC
Headquarters: Herndon, VA
SIC Major Group: Nonmetallic Minerals Except Fuels, Stone, Clay & Glass Products, and Wholesale Trade—Durable Goods

CONTACT

Stuart Fishkin
Treasurer
Tarmac America Inc.
13873 Park Center Rd.
Herndon, VA 22071
(703) 481-3104

FINANCIAL SUMMARY

Recent Giving: $10,000 (1993 est.)

CONTRIBUTIONS SUMMARY

Company reports 75% of contributions go to civic and public affairs and 25% go to health and human services.

Typical Recipients: • *Civic & Public Affairs:* law & justice • *Health:* health organizations, hospices, medical research, single-disease health associations • *Social Services:* community service organizations, disabled, domestic violence, drugs & alcohol

Grant Types: general support

Nonmonetary Support Types: donated equipment

Note: Also donates office equipment and bricks.

Geographic Distribution: principally near operating locations and to national organizations

Operating Locations: FL (Deerfield Beach), VA (Herndon, Norfolk)

CORP. OFFICERS

Ian McPherson: *CURR EMPL* pres: Tarmac Am

Laurence Prud'homme: *CURR EMPL* cfo: Tarmac Am

GIVING OFFICERS

Stuart Fishkin: *CURR EMPL* treas: Tarmac Am

APPLICATION INFORMATION

Initial Approach: Send a brief letter of inquiry. Include a description of the organization, amount requested, purpose of funds sought, and proof of tax-exempt status.

Restrictions on Giving: Does not support individuals, religious organizations for sectarian purposes, or political or lobbying groups.

GRANTS ANALYSIS

Typical Range: $50 to $1,000

RECENT GRANTS

American Cancer Society
Amvets
Angel Planes
Cal Pava National Brain Tumor Fund
Hospice of Northern Virginia
March of Dimes
Salvation Army
St. Jude's Hospital

Tartt Scholarship Fund, Hope Pierce

CONTACT

Pat Day
Vice-Chairman
Hope Pierce Tartt Scholarship Fund
PO Box 1964
Marshall, TX 75671
(214) 938-6622

FINANCIAL SUMMARY

Recent Giving: $455,000 (fiscal 1992); $503,000 (fiscal 1990); $491,000 (fiscal 1989)
Assets: $8,225,550 (fiscal year ending May 31, 1992); $7,692,163 (fiscal 1990); $7,454,743 (fiscal 1989)
EIN: 75-6263272

CONTRIBUTIONS SUMMARY

Donor(s): the late Hope Pierce Tartt
Grant Types: scholarship
Geographic Distribution: focus on Harrison, Gregg, Marion, Panola, and Upshur counties, TX

GIVING OFFICERS

Rev. R. Pat Day: vchmn
Robert L. Duvall: secy, treas
William L. Gaw: vchmn
James Heflin: vchmn
E. N. Smith, Jr.: chmn

APPLICATION INFORMATION

Initial Approach: Application form required. There are no deadlines. Board meets in February.

OTHER THINGS TO KNOW

Provides higher education scholarships for east Texas students at private institutions in TX and LA.
Publications: Application Guidelines
Disclosure Period: fiscal year ending May 31, 1992

Tasty Baking Co. / Tasty Baking Foundation

Sales: $287.9 million
Employees: 1,500
Headquarters: Philadelphia, PA
SIC Major Group: Food & Kindred Products, Instruments & Related Products, and Wholesale Trade—Nondurable Goods

CONTACT

Kathleen M. Grim
Advertising Manager
Tasty Baking Fdn.
2801 Hunting Park Ave.
Philadelphia, PA 19129
(215) 221-8500

FINANCIAL SUMMARY

Recent Giving: $152,080 (1991); $165,475 (1990)
Assets: $64,252 (1991); $63,128 (1990); $75,505 (1989)
Gifts Received: $150,000 (1991); $102,000 (1990)
Fiscal Note: In 1991, contributions were received from Tasty Baking Company.
EIN: 23-6271018

CONTRIBUTIONS SUMMARY

Typical Recipients: • *Arts & Humanities:* dance, general, museums/galleries, music • *Civic & Public Affairs:* zoos/botanical gardens • *Education:* colleges & universities • *Health:* health funds, pediatric health, single-disease health associations • *Social Services:* community service organizations, disabled, united funds
Grant Types: general support
Nonmonetary Support Types: donated products
Geographic Distribution: Philadelphia metropolitan area
Operating Locations: PA (Philadelphia)

CORP. OFFICERS

John M. Pettine: *CURR EMPL* vp, cfo: Tasty Baking Co
Carl S. Watts: *CURR EMPL* pres, ceo: Tasty Baking Co

GIVING OFFICERS

Philip J. Baur, Jr.: trust, chmn
Elizabeth H. Gemmill: trust *B* Philadelphia PA 1945 *ED* Bryn Mawr Coll 1967; Boston Univ 1970 *CURR EMPL* vp, secy: Tasty Baking Co *CORP AFFIL* dir: Am Water Works Co; vp, secy: Tasty Baking Co

John M. Pettine: trust, secy, treas *CURR EMPL* vp, cfo: Tasty Baking Co (see above)
Carl S. Watts: trust *CURR EMPL* pres, ceo: Tasty Baking Co (see above)

APPLICATION INFORMATION

Initial Approach: Send a full proposal. Include a description of organization, amount requested, purpose of funds sought, recently audited financial statement, and proof of tax-exempt status.
Restrictions on Giving: Does not support individuals, religious organizations for sectarian purposes, political or lobbying groups, or organizations outside operating areas.

GRANTS ANALYSIS

Number of Grants: 87
Highest Grant: $15,000
Typical Range: $250 to $5,000
Disclosure Period: 1991

RECENT GRANTS

15,000 Pioneers, Sterling, VA
10,000 Juvenile Diabetes Foundation, Philadelphia, PA
7,300 United Way, Philadelphia, PA
5,500 Academy of Natural Sciences, Philadelphia, PA
5,000 Academy of Music, Philadelphia, PA
5,000 Blind Relief Fund, Philadelphia, PA
5,000 Franklin Institute, Philadelphia, PA
5,000 Pennsylvania Ballet Association, Philadelphia, PA
5,000 Philadelphia Museum of Art, Philadelphia, PA
5,000 Philadelphia Zoological Society, Philadelphia, PA

Tate & Lyle Inc.

Sales: $454.2 million
Employees: 7,920
Headquarters: Wilmington, DE
SIC Major Group: Engineering & Management Services, Holding & Other Investment Offices, Wholesale Trade—Durable Goods, and Wholesale Trade—Nondurable Goods

CONTACT

Pat Scott
Assistant Treasurer
Tate & Lyle Inc.
1403 Foulk Rd., Ste. 102
Wilmington, DE 19803-2755
(302) 478-4773

CONTRIBUTIONS SUMMARY

Operating Locations: DE (Wilmington)

CORP. OFFICERS

Paul J. Mirsky: *CURR EMPL* pres: Tate & Lyle
Lynton R. Wilson: *CURR EMPL* chmn: Tate & Lyle

Taub Foundation

CONTACT

Henry J. N. Taub
Trustee
Taub Fdn.
Texan Bldg.
333 West Loop North, 4th Fl.
Houston, TX 77024
(713) 688-2426

FINANCIAL SUMMARY

Recent Giving: $172,201 (fiscal 1992); $279,370 (fiscal 1990); $25,407 (fiscal 1989)
Assets: $3,817,059 (fiscal year ending June 30, 1992); $3,621,679 (fiscal 1990); $3,365,126 (fiscal 1989)
Gifts Received: $10,000 (fiscal 1992)
Fiscal Note: In fiscal 1992, contributions were received from Stedman Adams.
EIN: 74-6060216

CONTRIBUTIONS SUMMARY

Donor(s): Henry J. N. Taub, Ben Taub
Typical Recipients: • *Arts & Humanities:* community arts, libraries, museums/galleries, music, performing arts • *Civic & Public Affairs:* civil rights, environmental affairs, ethnic/minority organizations • *Education:* colleges & universities, community & junior colleges, medical education • *Health:* health organizations, hospitals, medical research, pediatric health, single-disease health associations • *International:* foreign educational institutions • *Religion:* religious organizations • *Social Services:* animal protection, child welfare, community service organizations, drugs & alcohol, united funds, youth organizations
Grant Types: general support
Geographic Distribution: focus on TX

GIVING OFFICERS

Gail Hendryx: trust
H. Ben Taub: trust
Henry J. N. Taub: trust
Henry J. N. Taub II: trust
Marcy E. Taub: trust

APPLICATION INFORMATION

Initial Approach: Contributes only to preselected organizations.

GRANTS ANALYSIS

Number of Grants: 140
Highest Grant: $131,000
Typical Range: $100 to $250
Disclosure Period: fiscal year ending June 30, 1992

RECENT GRANTS

131,000 Baylor College of Medicine, Houston, TX
4,500 Society for the Performing Arts, Houston, TX
3,050 Institute of International Education, Houston, TX
2,300 Museum of Fine Arts, Houston, TX
2,000 Ben Taub General Hospital, Houston, TX
1,250 Park People, Houston, TX
1,225 Brookwood Community, Brookshire, TX
1,150 Baylor Medical Foundation, Houston, TX
1,050 Anderson, M.D. Cancer Center, Houston, TX
1,000 Challenger Center for Space Science Education, Houston, TX

Taub Foundation, Henry and Marilyn

CONTACT
Henry Taub
President
Henry and Marilyn Taub Fdn.
c/o Wiss and Co.
354 Eisenhower Pkwy.
Livingston, NJ 07039
(201) 994-9400

FINANCIAL SUMMARY
Recent Giving: $1,769,371 (1991); $1,992,430 (1990); $1,574,422 (1989)
Assets: $17,133,685 (1991); $14,888,070 (1990); $15,220,523 (1989)
Gifts Received: $387,784 (1991); $794,262 (1990); $816,494 (1989)
Fiscal Note: In 1991, contributions were received from the Henry Taub Charitable Trust No. 1 ($95,307), the Henry Taub Charitable Trust No. 2 ($148,102), and the Henry Taub Charitable Trust No. 3 ($144,375).
EIN: 22-6100525

CONTRIBUTIONS SUMMARY
Donor(s): The foundation was established in 1967 by Henry Taub.
Typical Recipients: • *Arts & Humanities:* arts centers, arts festivals, museums/galleries, opera • *Civic & Public Affairs:* ethnic/minority organizations, municipalities, philanthropic organizations, professional & trade associations • *Education:* colleges & universities, education funds, private education (precollege), religious education • *Health:* hospitals • *International:* international organizations • *Religion:* religious organizations, synagogues • *Social Services:* community centers, employment/job training, united funds, youth organizations
Grant Types: general support
Geographic Distribution: eastern United States; focus on New York and New Jersey

GIVING OFFICERS
Fred Seymour Lafer: secy *B* Passaic NJ 1929 *ED* NY Univ BIE 1950; NY Univ JD 1961 *CURR EMPL* sr vp, secy, gen couns: Automatic Data Processing *NONPR AFFIL* mem: Am Bar Assn, Assn Data Processing Svc Orgs, Computer Law

Assn; mem exec comm: Washington Inst Near East Policy; pres: Am Friends Hebrew Univ; trust: Patterson (William) Coll
Henry Taub: pres, dir *B* Paterson NJ 1927 *ED* NY Univ BS 1947 *CURR EMPL* fdr, hon chmn, chmn exec comm, dir: Automatic Data Processing *CORP AFFIL* dir: Bank Leumi Trust Co NY, Hasbro, Rite Aid Corp *NONPR AFFIL* assoc chmn: Am Technion Soc; dir: Am Friends Hebrew Univ, Interfaith Hunger Appeal, New York Shakespeare Festival, NY Shakespeare Festival, UN Jewish Appeal, UN Jewish Fund; mem: Paterson Alumni Assn; pres: Am Jewish Joint Distribution Comm, NY Chapter Hemophilia Fdn; trust: NY Univ; chmn: Bus Employment Fdn
Marilyn Taub: treas, dir

APPLICATION INFORMATION
Initial Approach: Restrictions on Giving: The foundation supports preselected organizations and does not accept unsolicited requests for funds.

GRANTS ANALYSIS
Total Grants: $1,769,371
Number of Grants: 99
Highest Grant: $989,366
Typical Range: $500 to $10,000
Disclosure Period: 1991
Note: Average grant figure does not include the highest grant of $989,366. Recent grants are derived from a 1991 grants list.

RECENT GRANTS
989,366 United Jewish Community of Bergen County, River Edge, NJ
75,000 American Society for Technion, New York, NY
32,485 Temple Sinai, Tenafly, NJ
30,500 Paterson Alumni Association, Paterson, NJ
30,000 American Friends of Hebrew University, New York, NY
25,000 Harvard University, Cambridge, MA
25,000 New York Shakespeare Festival, New York, NY
20,080 United Jewish Appeal Federation, New York, NY

20,000 Operation Independence, New York, NY
15,100 Jewish Community Center on the Palisades, Tenafly, NJ

Taub Foundation, Joseph and Arlene

CONTACT
Joseph and Arlene Taub Fdn.
c/o Wiss and Co.
354 Eisenhower Pkwy.
Livingston, NJ 07039

FINANCIAL SUMMARY
Recent Giving: $289,458 (1990); $492,132 (1989); $217,674 (1988)
Assets: $2,514,965 (1990); $3,066,598 (1989); $2,867,083 (1988)
EIN: 22-6104545

CONTRIBUTIONS SUMMARY
Donor(s): Joseph Taub
Typical Recipients: • *Arts & Humanities:* libraries, museums/galleries • *Civic & Public Affairs:* international affairs • *Education:* colleges & universities • *Health:* medical research, pediatric health, single-disease health associations • *Religion:* churches, religious organizations, synagogues • *Social Services:* community service organizations, united funds
Grant Types: general support

GIVING OFFICERS
Fred S. Lafer: dir, secy
Abraham H. Nechemie: trust
Arlene Taub: dir, treas
Joseph Taub: dir, pres

APPLICATION INFORMATION
Initial Approach: Contributes only to preselected organizations.

GRANTS ANALYSIS
Number of Grants: 42
Highest Grant: $158,115
Typical Range: $25 to $10,000
Disclosure Period: 1990

RECENT GRANTS
158,115 United Jewish Appeal Federation of Jewish Philanthropies, New York, NY
20,505 Paterson Alumni Association, Paterson, NJ
15,000 Easter Seal Society

13,000 Maurice Stokes Basketball Foundation
12,750 Solomon Schechter Day School
10,000 Montefiore Foundation, New York, NY
10,000 Washington Institute for Near East Policy, Washington, DC
7,100 Temple Emanu-el
5,500 Georgia Tech Catholic Center, Atlanta, GA
5,500 New York Basketball Hall of Fame, New York, NY

Taube Family Foundation

CONTACT
Thaddeus N. Taube
President
Taube Family Fdn.
1050 Ralston Ave.
Belmont, CA 94002
(415) 592-3960

FINANCIAL SUMMARY
Recent Giving: $421,245 (fiscal 1991); $178,615 (fiscal 1990); $299,359 (fiscal 1989)
Assets: $4,459,572 (fiscal year ending November 30, 1991); $3,738,306 (fiscal 1990); $3,060,467 (fiscal 1989)
Gifts Received: $188,240 (fiscal 1991); $668,532 (fiscal 1990); $112,383 (fiscal 1989)
Fiscal Note: In fiscal 1991, contributions were received from the Taube Family Trust.
EIN: 94-2702180

CONTRIBUTIONS SUMMARY
Donor(s): members of the Taube family
Typical Recipients: • *Arts & Humanities:* museums/galleries • *Civic & Public Affairs:* ethnic/minority organizations • *Education:* colleges & universities, education associations, religious education • *Religion:* religious organizations • *Social Services:* community service organizations, community service organizations, disabled, family services, united funds
Grant Types: general support

GIVING OFFICERS
Anita T. Hirsch: vp, dir
Robert Hirsch: dir
Kenneth A. Moline: secy, treas
Thaddeus N. Taube: pres, dir

APPLICATION INFORMATION

Initial Approach: The foundation reports it only makes contributions to preselected charitable organizations.

GRANTS ANALYSIS

Number of Grants: 79
Highest Grant: $250,000
Typical Range: $100 to $1,200
Disclosure Period: fiscal year ending November 30, 1991

RECENT GRANTS

250,000 United Way, San Francisco, CA
100,000 Jewish Community Federation, San Francisco, CA
10,000 US Holocaust Memorial Museum, Washington, DC
7,500 US Holocaust Memorial Museum, Washington, DC
5,300 College of Notre Dame, Belmont, CA
5,000 American Friends of Hebrew University, New York, NY
5,000 Jewish Community Endowment Fund, San Francisco, CA
3,000 Stanford University, Stanford, CA
1,500 Pacific Graduate School of Psychology, Los Angeles, CA
1,500 Peninsula Center for the Blind, Palo Alto, CA

Tauber Foundation

CONTACT
Laszlo N. Tauber, M.D.
Director
Tauber Fdn.
5110 Ridgefield Rd.
Bethesda, MD 20816-1424
(301) 657-2030

FINANCIAL SUMMARY
Recent Giving: $419,740 (1991); $410,187 (1990); $269,987 (1989)
Assets: $7,658,111 (1991); $9,176,037 (1990); $8,451,036 (1989)
EIN: 52-6054648

CONTRIBUTIONS SUMMARY
Typical Recipients: • *Arts & Humanities:* history/historic preservation, museums/galleries • *Civic & Public Affairs:* ethnic/minority organizations • *Education:* colleges & universities, medical education, private education (precollege) • *Health:* medical research • *Religion:* religious organizations, synagogues

Grant Types: capital and general support

GIVING OFFICERS
Laszlo Nandor Tauber: don, pres *B* Budapest Hungary 1915 *ED* Univ Budapest MD 1938 *CURR EMPL* dir dept surgery: Jefferson Meml Hosp *NONPR AFFIL* fellow: ACS Intl Coll Surgeons, Am Soc Abdominal Surgeons, Hungarian Bd Gen Surgery, Southeastern Surgical Congress; mem: NY Med Soc; trust: Am Univ DC

Temziye G. Turker: treas

Dr. Judah Weinberger: vp

APPLICATION INFORMATION
Initial Approach: Send brief letter of inquiry describing program or project. The deadline is December 10.

GRANTS ANALYSIS
Number of Grants: 20
Highest Grant: $191,300
Typical Range: $1,500 to $10,000
Disclosure Period: 1991

RECENT GRANTS
191,300 Neutrophic Research Fund, Brookline, MI
57,000 Georgetown University, Washington, DC
50,000 Museum of Jewish Heritage, New York, NY
11,000 American Academy of Achievement, Malibu, CA
10,000 American University, Washington, DC
10,000 Anti-Defamation League, New York, NY
10,000 Archdiocese of Washington, Washington, DC
10,000 Holton Arms School, Bethesda, MD
10,000 Kiryat Ungvar Synagogue, New York, NY
10,000 St. Bonaventure University, St. Bonaventure, NY

Tauber Oil Co.

Sales: $950.0 million
Employees: 57
Headquarters: Houston, TX
SIC Major Group: Electronic & Other Electrical Equipment and Wholesale Trade—Nondurable Goods

CONTACT
Virginia Wininger
Supervisor of Administration
Tauber Oil Co.
PO Box 4645
Houston, TX 77210
(713) 869-8700

CONTRIBUTIONS SUMMARY
Operating Locations: TX (Houston)

CORP. OFFICERS
O. J. Tauber, Jr.: *CURR EMPL* pres: Tauber Oil Co

Taubman Foundation, A. Alfred

CONTACT
John Sullivan
A. Alfred Taubman Fdn.
PO Box 200
200 East Long Lake Rd.
Bloomfield Hills, MI 48303-0200
(313) 258-6800

FINANCIAL SUMMARY
Recent Giving: $1,799,160 (fiscal 1990); $2,027,402 (fiscal 1989)
Assets: $3,931 (fiscal year ending July 31, 1990); $2,064 (fiscal 1989)
Gifts Received: $1,800,673 (fiscal 1990); $2,027,912 (fiscal 1989)
Fiscal Note: In 1990, contributions were received from A. Alfred Taubman.
EIN: 38-2219625

CONTRIBUTIONS SUMMARY
Donor(s): A. Alfred Taubman
Typical Recipients: • *Arts & Humanities:* history/historic preservation, libraries • *Civic & Public Affairs:* better government, environmental affairs, international affairs, public policy, women's affairs • *Health:* health organizations, hospitals, medical research, single-disease health associations • *Religion:* religious organizations • *Science:* science exhibits & fairs • *Social Services:* aged, community service organizations, disabled, drugs & alcohol, family planning, family services, united funds, youth organizations

Grant Types: operating expenses and research
Geographic Distribution: focus on MI, with emphasis on Detroit

GIVING OFFICERS
Max Martin Fisher: pres, trust *B* Pittsburgh PA 1908 *ED* OH St Univ BS 1930 *CORP AFFIL* chmn: Chiquita Brands Intl; dir: Mfrs Natl Corp, Taubman Co *NONPR AFFIL* chmn bd: Detroit Renaissance; dir: Sinai Hosp Detroit; hon chmn: Un Fdn Detroit; mem: Petroleum Inst

Gayle T. Kalisman: trust

Jeffrey H. Miro: secy, trust *CURR EMPL* secy: Sothebys Holdings *CORP AFFIL* dir: Taubman Co, Woodward & Lothrop Inc; secy: Sotheby's Holdings

Dean Eugene Richardson: trust *B* West Branch MI 1927 *CORP AFFIL* dir: Detroit Edison Co, Ford Holdings, Tecumseh Products Co *NONPR AFFIL* chmn: AAA MI; mem: Detroit Bar Assn, MI Bar Assn

A. Alfred Taubman: chmn, treas, trust *B* Pontiac MI 1925 *ED* Univ MI; Lawrence Inst Tech *CURR EMPL* chmn: Taubman Co *CORP AFFIL* chmn: A&W Restaurants Inc, Sothebys Holdings; dir: Chase Manhattan Corp, Detroit Renaissance, RH Macy & Co; owner: Woodward & Lothrop Co *NONPR AFFIL* chmn: Univ PA Wharton Real Estate Ctr; chmn emeritus: Smithsonian Inst Am Art; dir: Detroit Symphony Orchestra, Econ Club Detroit, Friends Art Preservation Embassies, Natl Realty Comm; mem: City Detroit Arts Comm; nat bd: Smithsonian Assocs; prin benefactor: A Alfred Taubman Health Care Ctr, A Alfred Taubman Med Library Univ MI; trust: Ctr Creative Studies, Detroit Inst Art, Harper-Grace Hosp, Urban Land Inst, Whitney Mus Am Art

Robert S. Taubman: trust *CURR EMPL* pres, ceo, dir: Taubman Co *CORP AFFIL* dir: A&W Restaurants Inc, Mfrs Natl Bank Detroit, Woodward & Lothrop Inc; pres, ceo, dir: Taubman Co *NONPR AFFIL* dir: Sinai Hosp; mem: Intl

Counc Shopping Ctrs; mem bd govs: Cranbrook Sch
William S. Taubman: trust
CORP AFFIL dir: A&W Restaurants Inc

APPLICATION INFORMATION
Initial Approach: Send brief letter of inquiry describing program or project. There are no deadlines.

GRANTS ANALYSIS
Number of Grants: 112
Highest Grant: $1,020,000
Typical Range: $100 to $5,000
Disclosure Period: fiscal year ending July 31, 1990

RECENT GRANTS
1,020,000 Jewish Welfare Organization of Detroit, Detroit, MI
  38,875 Royal National Institute for the Blind, London, England
  35,000 Memorial Sloan-Kettering Cancer Center, New York, NY
  20,000 American Jewish Committee, New York, NY
  20,000 Hanley Hazelden Foundation, West Palm Beach, FL
  10,000 Blenheim Foundation, New York, NY
  10,000 Catherine McAuley Health Center, Ann Arbor, MI
  10,000 Historic Charleston Foundation, Charleston, SC
  10,000 Hutzel Hospital/Kresge Eye Institute, Detroit, MI
  10,000 National Abortion Rights League Foundation, Washington, DC

Taubman Foundation, Herman P. and Sophia

CONTACT
Morris Taubman
Trustee
Bank of Oklahoma N. A. Agent
PO Box 2300
Tulsa, OK 74103
(918) 588-6318

FINANCIAL SUMMARY
Recent Giving: $278,626 (1991); $525,451 (1990); $209,135 (1989)
Assets: $4,857,425 (1991); $3,028,721 (1990); $4,132,958 (1989)
EIN: 73-6092820

CONTRIBUTIONS SUMMARY
Donor(s): the late Herman P. Taubman, the late Sophia Taubman
Typical Recipients: • *Civic & Public Affairs:* ethnic/minority organizations • *Education:* colleges & universities, religious education • *Health:* hospitals, medical research, single-disease health associations • *Religion:* religious organizations, synagogues • *Social Services:* aged, community service organizations, religious welfare, united funds, youth organizations
Grant Types: capital, general support, research, and scholarship
Geographic Distribution: focus on OK

GIVING OFFICERS
David Fist: trust
Lois Taubman: trust
Morris G. Taubman: trust

APPLICATION INFORMATION
Initial Approach: Send brief letter of inquiry describing program or project. There are no deadlines.
Restrictions on Giving: Does not support individuals.

GRANTS ANALYSIS
Number of Grants: 23
Highest Grant: $51,000
Typical Range: $1,000 to $10,000
Disclosure Period: 1991

RECENT GRANTS
  51,000 Operation Exodus, Studio City, CA
  50,000 Southern Methodist University, Dallas, TX
  40,000 Dallas Home for Jewish Aged, Dallas, TX
  25,000 American Society for Technion, New York, NY
  12,000 Jewish Federation, Tulsa, OK
  10,000 Hillel Hebrew Academy, Beverly Hills, CA
  10,000 Jewish Welfare Federation, San Francisco, CA
  10,000 United Jewish Welfare Fund, Los Angeles, CA
  10,000 United Jewish Welfare Fund, Palm Springs, CA
  10,000 United Jewish Welfare Fund, San Diego, CA

Taylor Charitable Trust, Jack DeLoss

CONTACT
Catherine Taylor, PhD.
Trustee
Jack DeLoss Taylor Charitable Trust
1414 Price Drive
Cape Girardeau, MO 63701
Note: The foundation's mailing address is P.O. Box 1378, Madison, WI 53701.

FINANCIAL SUMMARY
Recent Giving: $55,000 (fiscal 1991)
Assets: $3,214,215 (fiscal year ending June 30, 1991)
EIN: 39-6510710

CONTRIBUTIONS SUMMARY
Typical Recipients: • *International:* international development/relief, international health care • *Social Services:* child welfare
Grant Types: general support

GIVING OFFICERS
Christopher Bugg: trust
Lyle Larson: trust
Catherine Taylor: trust

GRANTS ANALYSIS
Total Grants: $55,000
Number of Grants: 18
Highest Grant: $4,500
Typical Range: $1,500 to $4,500
Disclosure Period: fiscal year ending June 30, 1991

RECENT GRANTS
  7,300 CARE
  4,500 United Way, Madison, WI
  4,000 3 Gaits
  3,200 Scheckinah Ministries
  3,000 Downtown Rotary, Madison, WI
  3,000 Salvation Army, Madison, WI
  2,000 Catholic Social Services, Madison, WI
  2,000 Children's Service Society of Wisconsin, WI
  1,500 Deerfield Food Pantry, Deerfield, WI
  1,500 McFarland Food Pantry, McFarland, WI

Taylor Corp.
Sales: $250.0 million
Employees: 5,000
Headquarters: North Mankato, MN
SIC Major Group: Holding & Other Investment Offices and Printing & Publishing

CONTACT
Al Fallenstein
Executive Vice President of Finance
Taylor Corp.
1725 Row Crest
North Mankato, MN 56003
(507) 625-2828

CONTRIBUTIONS SUMMARY
Operating Locations: MN (North Mankato)

CORP. OFFICERS
Al Fallenstein: *CURR EMPL*
cfo: Taylor Corp
Glenn Taylor: *CURR EMPL*
pres: Taylor Corp

Taylor Family Foundation, Jack

CONTACT
Jack Taylor Family Fdn.
1111 Kane Concourse, Ste. 619
Bay Harbor Islands, FL 33154

FINANCIAL SUMMARY
Recent Giving: $414,656 (1990); $474,116 (1989); $306,664 (1988)
Assets: $10,908,229 (1990); $10,339,699 (1989); $9,062,630 (1988)
Gifts Received: $325,957 (1990); $612,200 (1989); $102,200 (1988)
Fiscal Note: In 1990, contributions were received from Taylor and Sons and Jack Taylor.
EIN: 59-6205187

CONTRIBUTIONS SUMMARY
Donor(s): Taylor Development Corp., Jack Taylor, and other members of the Taylor family
Typical Recipients: • *Civic & Public Affairs:* housing • *Education:* colleges & universities, medical education • *Health:* hospitals, medical research, single-disease health associations • *Religion:* religious organiza-

tions, synagogues • *Social Services:* aged
Grant Types: general support, project, and scholarship

GIVING OFFICERS
Norman A. Arkin: dir
Victor Denbrow: dir
Ilene B. Eefting: treas
Saul S. Silverman: dir
Elly Taylor: vp, dir
Jack Taylor: pres, dir
Mitchell Taylor: secy, dir
Harold Zinn: dir

APPLICATION INFORMATION
Initial Approach: Contributes only to preselected organizations.

GRANTS ANALYSIS
Number of Grants: 28
Highest Grant: $100,000
Typical Range: $10,000 to $50,000
Disclosure Period: 1990

RECENT GRANTS
100,000 Mayo Foundation, Rochester, MN
81,200 Mount Sinai Medical Foundation, New York, NY
25,000 American Cancer Society
25,000 Newport Adolescents Programs
22,800 Miami BSOP, Miami, FL
15,000 Temple Emanu-el
12,500 Mayo Medical School, Rochester, MN
10,000 Miami Beach Housing Authority, Miami, FL
10,000 Womens Cancer League
8,356 University of Miami, Coral Gables, FL

Taylor Foundation

CONTACT
Robert T. Taylor
President
Taylor Fdn.
6969 Tidewater Dr.
Norfolk, VA 23509
(804) 853-4351

FINANCIAL SUMMARY
Recent Giving: $120,900 (1991); $205,400 (1990); $152,200 (1989)
Assets: $2,031,716 (1991); $1,760,526 (1990); $1,923,239 (1989)
EIN: 54-0555235

CONTRIBUTIONS SUMMARY
Donor(s): West India Fruit and Steamship Co., Inc., members of the Taylor family
Typical Recipients: • *Civic & Public Affairs:* safety • *Education:* colleges & universities, education funds, private education (precollege), religious education, student aid • *Health:* emergency/ambulance services, hospitals • *Religion:* churches, religious organizations • *Social Services:* community service organizations, homes, united funds, youth organizations
Grant Types: general support and project
Geographic Distribution: focus on NC, VA, and the Southeast

GIVING OFFICERS
T.A. Bennett: trust
Susan T. Kirkpatrick: trust
I. Lewis Rawls, Jr.: secy
Leslie M. Taylor: vp
Robert T. Taylor: pres

APPLICATION INFORMATION
Initial Approach: Send brief letter of inquiry describing program. Deadline is December 1.
Restrictions on Giving: Does not support individuals.

GRANTS ANALYSIS
Number of Grants: 43
Highest Grant: $10,000
Typical Range: $500 to $5,000
Disclosure Period: 1991

RECENT GRANTS
10,000 Cape Henry Collegiate School, Virginia Beach, VA
10,000 East Carolina Education Foundation, Greenville, NC
6,000 Norfolk Christian School, Norfolk, VA
6,000 Old Dominion University Intercollegiate, Norfolk, VA
6,000 United Way, Norfolk, VA
5,000 Campbell University, Buies Creek, NC
5,000 Hebron Colony and Grace Home, Boone, NC
5,000 North Carolina State University, Raleigh, NC
5,000 Sea Level Fire and Rescue Squad, Sea Level, NC
1,000 Student Aid Foundation of Virginia, University of Virginia, Charlottesville, VA

Taylor Foundation, Fred and Harriett

CONTACT
Fred and Harriett Taylor Fdn.
c/o Chase Lincoln First Bank, N.A.
PO Box 1412
Rochester, NY 14603

FINANCIAL SUMMARY
Recent Giving: $459,600 (1990); $422,750 (1989); $468,584 (1988)
Assets: $6,299,820 (1990); $6,531,572 (1989); $5,897,313 (1988)
EIN: 16-6205365

CONTRIBUTIONS SUMMARY
Donor(s): the late Fred C. Taylor
Typical Recipients: • *Education:* education funds • *Health:* health organizations, hospitals, medical research, single-disease health associations • *Religion:* churches • *Social Services:* child welfare, community service organizations, food/clothing distribution, youth organizations
Grant Types: general support and research
Geographic Distribution: limited to the Hammondsport, NY, area

APPLICATION INFORMATION
Initial Approach: Contributes only to preselected organizations.

GRANTS ANALYSIS
Number of Grants: 46
Highest Grant: $100,000
Typical Range: $1,000 to $10,000
Disclosure Period: 1990

RECENT GRANTS
100,000 Ira Davenport Memorial Hospital
80,000 Independent College Fund of New York, Binghamton, NY
40,000 Hammondsport Central School Board
32,000 Beautification Committee, New York, NY
28,000 Boy Scouts of America
20,000 Citizens Hose Company, New York, NY
20,000 Pleasant Valley Cemetery, Pleasant Valley, NY
17,000 Hamm Volunteer Ambulance
14,000 Reginald Wood Memorial
10,000 Chemung Valley Arts Council, Elmira, NY

Taylor Foundation, Ruth and Vernon

CONTACT
Friday A. Green
Trustee
Ruth and Vernon Taylor Foundation
1670 Denver Club Bldg.
Denver, CO 80202
(303) 893-5284

FINANCIAL SUMMARY
Recent Giving: $1,254,930 (fiscal 1992); $1,317,382 (fiscal 1991); $1,216,000 (fiscal 1990 est.)
Assets: $25,915,006 (fiscal year ending June 30, 1992); $26,252,629 (fiscal 1991); $21,150,000 (fiscal 1990 est.)
Gifts Received: $958,125 (fiscal 1985)
EIN: 84-6021788

CONTRIBUTIONS SUMMARY
Donor(s): The Colorado-based foundation was established in 1950 by Ruth and Vernon Taylor. Vernon F. Taylor (1888-1972) was president of Peerless Oil and Gas Company (San Antonio) and chairman of Wytana Cattle Company. He was a director of Trinity University and Tulane University. Three of the four members of the current board of trustees are members of the Taylor family, the children of the foundation's donors.
Typical Recipients: • *Arts & Humanities:* arts associations, arts institutes, cinema, dance, history/historic preservation, libraries, museums/galleries, opera, public broadcasting • *Civic & Public Affairs:* better government, environmental affairs, ethnic/minority organizations, international affairs, philanthropic organizations, public policy, zoos/botanical gardens • *Education:* arts education, colleges & universities, education administration, edu-

cation funds, international studies, preschool education, private education (precollege), religious education, science/technology education, student aid • *Health:* emergency/ambulance services, health funds, health organizations, hospitals, medical rehabilitation, medical research, pediatric health, single-disease health associations • *Social Services:* aged, disabled, drugs & alcohol, emergency relief, family planning, homes, recreation & athletics, religious welfare, youth organizations

Grant Types: general support
Geographic Distribution: national, with some preference for Texas, Colorado, Wyoming, Montana, Illinois, and the Mid-Atlantic states

GIVING OFFICERS
Ruth Taylor Campbell: trust, don daughter
Friday A. Green: trust
Sara Taylor Swift: trust, don daughter
Vernon F. Taylor, Jr.: trust, don son *B* 1916 *ED* Dartmouth Coll 1938 *CORP AFFIL* dir: CO Natl Bankshares, Peerless Co, Westhoma Oil Co *NONPR AFFIL* bd mgr: Denver Boys Club, Presbyterian Hosp

APPLICATION INFORMATION
Initial Approach:
The foundation suggests that initial contact be made in writing. There are no official application guidelines. Only one proposal copy should be sent. Proposal deadline is April 30. The board of directors meets in May and August. Final notification takes about 30 days.

GRANTS ANALYSIS
Total Grants: $1,254,930
Number of Grants: 151
Highest Grant: $135,000
Typical Range: $1,000 to $15,000
Disclosure Period: fiscal year ending June 30, 1992
Note: Recent grants are derived from a fiscal 1992 Form 990.

RECENT GRANTS
135,000 Madeira School, McLean, VA
85,000 St. Mary's Hall, San Antonio, TX
73,750 Sublette County Historical Society, Pinedale, WY

73,750 Sublette County Retirement Center, Pinedale, WY
66,100 Museum of the Rockies, Bozeman, MT
50,000 Montana 4-H Foundation, Bozeman, MT
45,000 Emerson Cultural Center, Bozeman, MT
30,000 Mountain States Legal Foundation, Denver, CO
25,000 Heritage Foundation, Washington, DC
25,000 World Wildlife Fund, Grenwich, CT

Taylor Trust, Lydia M.

CONTACT
Lydia M. Taylor Trust
c/o First National Bank
PO Box 2458
Zanesville, GA 43702

FINANCIAL SUMMARY
Recent Giving: $187,635 (1991); $198,523 (1990); $188,654 (1989)
Assets: $4,527,862 (1991); $3,840,514 (1990); $4,079,414 (1989)
EIN: 31-6307982

CONTRIBUTIONS SUMMARY
Typical Recipients: • *Arts & Humanities:* history/historic preservation • *Health:* hospitals
Grant Types: general support and research

GIVING OFFICERS
FirStar Bank Burlington, N.A.: trust

APPLICATION INFORMATION
Initial Approach: Contributes only to preselected organizations.

GRANTS ANALYSIS
Number of Grants: 2
Highest Grant: $184,635
Typical Range: $5,000 to $184,635
Disclosure Period: 1991

RECENT GRANTS
184,635 Bethesda Hospital, Zanesville, OH
5,000 Pioneer Historical Society, Zanesville, OH

TBG, Inc.
Sales: $900.0 million
Employees: 10,000
Headquarters: New York, NY
SIC Major Group: Electronic & Other Electrical Equipment, Industrial Machinery & Equipment, and Transportation Equipment

CONTACT
Eugene Gross
Vice President, Human Resources
TBG Inc.
1211 Avenue of the Americas
New York, NY 10036
(212) 556-8500

CONTRIBUTIONS SUMMARY
Company annually supports the United Way; limited support in other areas.
Typical Recipients: • *Social Services:* united funds
Operating Locations: NY (New York)

CORP. OFFICERS
Jack E. Haegele: *CURR EMPL* ceo: TBG

GIVING OFFICERS
Eugene Gross: *CURR EMPL* vp (human resources): TBG

APPLICATION INFORMATION
Initial Approach: Send letter of inquiry describing organization and need. There are no deadlines.

TCF Banking & Savings, FSB / TCF Foundation
Employees: 2,351
Parent Company: TCF Financial Corp.
Assets: $4.04 billion
Headquarters: St. Paul, MN
SIC Major Group: Depository Institutions

CONTACT
Neil I. Whitehouse
President
TCF Foundation
405 North Robert St., Ste. 200
St. Paul, MN 55101
(612) 298-4097

FINANCIAL SUMMARY
Recent Giving: $429,994 (1991); $293,594 (1990)
Assets: $21,682 (1990)
Gifts Received: $315,276 (1990)

Fiscal Note: Contributes through foundation only. In 1990, contributions were received from TCF Bank Savings FSB.
EIN: 41-1659826

CONTRIBUTIONS SUMMARY
Typical Recipients: • *Arts & Humanities:* arts associations, arts centers, arts institutes, general, libraries, museums/galleries, music, opera, performing arts, public broadcasting • *Civic & Public Affairs:* general, housing, philanthropic organizations, urban & community affairs, women's affairs • *Education:* business education, colleges & universities, community & junior colleges, education administration, education associations, faculty development, general, minority education, public education (precollege) • *Health:* general • *Science:* observatories & planetariums • *Social Services:* aged, child welfare, community centers, drugs & alcohol, food/clothing distribution, general, refugee assistance, shelters/homelessness, united funds, youth organizations
Grant Types: employee matching gifts, general support, and operating expenses
Geographic Distribution: in headquarters and operating communities
Operating Locations: IL, MN (St. Paul)

CORP. OFFICERS
Joseph P. Clifford: *B* 1943 *ED* Detroit Inst Tech DBA 1967; Detroit Coll Law JD 1972 *CURR EMPL* vchmn, dir: TCF Bank Savings FSB
William A. Cooper: *B* Detroit MI 1943 *ED* Wayne St Univ BS 1967 *CURR EMPL* chmn, ceo, dir: TCF Bank Savings FSB *CORP AFFIL* chmn, ceo: TCF Fin Corp *NONPR AFFIL* mem: Am Inst CPAs
Robert E. Evans: *CURR EMPL* pres, coo, dir: TCF Bank Savings FSB

GIVING OFFICERS
Henry F. Fischer: vp
Lynn A. Nagorske: treas
Gregory J. Pulles: secy
Neil Whitehouse: pres

APPLICATION INFORMATION
Initial Approach: *Initial Contact:* letter of inquiry *Include*

2631

Information On: brief description of the organization; list of board members; information about people who will manage the activities; audited financial statements, current budget, and next year's budget; mission statement and summary of long-range plans; purpose of contribution requested and relationship to plans; sources of income, current and planned; copy of IRS 501(c)(3) tax exemption determination letter*
When to Submit: any time
Note: Request a copy of the foundation's guidelines prior to submitting a full proposal.
Restrictions on Giving: The foundation does not make grants to individuals, political parties or candidates, individual churches or strictly sectarian organizations, or for social events of otherwise qualified organizations.
Support will be given only to organizations that are able to provide evidence of 501(C)(3) tax-exempt status. Exceptions may be made in the case of local organizations and projects that are clearly nonprofitable and charitable in nature.

GRANTS ANALYSIS
Total Grants: $293,594
Number of Grants: 185*
Highest Grant: $20,000
Typical Range: $250 to $3,500
Disclosure Period: 1990
Note: Number of grants and average grant figures do not include matching gifts totaling $11,910. Recent grants are derived from a 1990 grants list.

RECENT GRANTS
20,000 Twin Cities Neighborhood, St. Paul, MN
17,500 Minnesota Private Colleges, St. Paul, MN
11,800 Patrick Henry High School, St. Paul, MN
11,800 Patrick Henry High School, St. Paul, MN
11,000 Patrick Henry High School, St. Paul, MN
10,000 Downtown Council, St. Paul, MN
10,000 Illusion Theater, St. Paul, MN
10,000 Patrick Henry High School, St. Paul, MN
6,250 Institute of Social, St. Paul, MN

5,000 Minnesota Meeting, Minneapolis, MN

TDK Corp. of America
Headquarters: Skokie, IL
SIC Major Group: Electronic & Other Electrical Equipment

CONTACT
Lisa Messina
Assistant, Human Resources
TDK Corp. of America
1600 Feehanville Dr.
Mt. Prospect, IL 60056
(708) 803-6100

CONTRIBUTIONS SUMMARY
TDK has no formal giving program and no set budget for contributions. While the company has no established geographic restrictions on its giving, most donations go to local organizations to which TDK has contributed in the past.
Typical Recipients: • *Arts & Humanities:* community arts • *Civic & Public Affairs:* civil rights, international affairs • *Education:* international exchange • *Social Services:* employment/job training, united funds, youth organizations
Geographic Distribution: no geographic restrictions
Operating Locations: IL (Mt. Prospect, Skokie)

CORP. OFFICERS
Takeshi Owada: *CURR EMPL* pres: TDK Corp Am

GIVING OFFICERS
Lisa Messini: *CURR EMPL* asst human resources: TDK Corp Am
Deborah Togut: *CURR EMPL* supv (advertising): TDK Corp of Am

APPLICATION INFORMATION
Initial Approach: Initial contact should be by letter early in the year. Applications should include a description of the organization, amount requested, and purpose for which funds are sought.

GRANTS ANALYSIS
Typical Range: $10 to $500

Teac America, Inc.
Sales: $280.0 million
Employees: 190
Headquarters: Montebello, CA
SIC Major Group: Wholesale Trade—Durable Goods

CONTACT
Bill Mohrhoff
Marketing & Media Manager
Teac America, Inc.
7733 Telegraph Rd.
Montebello, CA 90640
(213) 726-0303

CONTRIBUTIONS SUMMARY
Operating Locations: CA (Montebello)

CORP. OFFICERS
Norio Tamura: *CURR EMPL* chmn, pres: TEAC Am

GIVING OFFICERS
Bill Stevens: *CURR EMPL* mgr, marketing & media: TEAC Am

Teagle Foundation

CONTACT
Richard W. Kimball
President
Teagle Foundation
30 Rockefeller Plaza, Rm. 2835
New York, NY 10112
(212) 247-1946

FINANCIAL SUMMARY
Recent Giving: $4,700,000 (fiscal 1993 est.); $4,761,694 (fiscal 1992); $3,981,073 (fiscal 1991)
Assets: $99,000,000 (fiscal 1993 est.); $96,810,728 (fiscal year ending May 31, 1992); $93,855,526 (fiscal 1991); $89,847,911 (fiscal 1990)
Gifts Received: $275 (fiscal 1991)
EIN: 13-1773645

CONTRIBUTIONS SUMMARY
Donor(s): The Teagle Foundation was established in 1944 by Walter C. Teagle, former president and chairman of the Standard Oil Company (New Jersey), now Exxon Corporation. The foundation's assets also come from bequests from Mr. Teagle's wife, Rowena Lee Teagle, and their son, Walter C. Teagle, Jr.
Typical Recipients: • *Education:* colleges & universities, engineering education, faculty

development, liberal arts education, religious education, science/technology education • *Social Services:* community service organizations, united funds, youth organizations
Grant Types: challenge, general support, multiyear/continuing support, project, and seed money
Geographic Distribution: national, with limited giving in Canada

GIVING OFFICERS
James C. Anderson: treas, contr
Donald M. Cox: chmn, dir
Richard W. Kimball: ceo, pres, dir
Margaret B. Sullivan: secy

APPLICATION INFORMATION
Initial Approach:
Applicants should submit a brief preliminary letter to the foundation. Applications for the Exxon scholarship program are available within Exxon; assistance to needy Exxon annuitants or their surviving spouses is initiated by Exxon management.
The letter should describe the grant seeker and outline the scope and purpose of the proposed grant.
Applications may be submitted any time.
If initial reaction is favorable, a more detailed proposal will be requested. The board meets in November, February, and May to review requests.
Restrictions on Giving: The foundation makes no grants to individuals unconnected with Exxon and no grants for scholarships except for its Exxon scholarship program. It does not make grants for building funds; seminars or lectureships; the arts; research; primary or secondary schools; or community service organizations outside New York City. It does not fund college-based programs for pre-college youth, including partnerships with public school systems. Activities of U.S.-based organizations which take place outside the U.S. are also not funded.

OTHER THINGS TO KNOW
Publications: annual report

GRANTS ANALYSIS
Total Grants: $4,671,694

Number of Grants: 290*

Highest Grant: $100,000

Typical Range: $20,000 to $65,000

Disclosure Period: fiscal year ending May 31, 1992

Note: This figure comprises payments to 214 colleges and universities for scholarships awarded under the Exxon scholarship program and 76 grants to institutions of higher education, community service organizations, and foundation-related organizations, representing in the aggregate, 99% of the foundation's grant expenditures. The average grant figure is not applicable. Recent grants are derived from a fiscal 1992 annual report.

RECENT GRANTS

1,471,500 Exxon Scholarship Program — to the children of employees of Exxon Corporation and its affiliates which can be applied to any accredited institution in the United States or Canada

100,000 Polytechnic University, Brooklyn, NY — for faculty renewal in materials science and engineering

100,000 Salvation Army of Greater New York, New York, NY — to establish the Mary R. Williams Memorial Endowment which will assist cadets from the New York Division with the cost of attending its officers' training school

91,000 North Carolina Agricultural and Technical State University, Greensboro, NC

90,000 Hampton University, Hampton, VA

90,000 Medical University of South Carolina, Charleston, SC

90,000 Otterbein College, Westerville, OH

90,000 Salem State College, Salem, MA

90,000 San Jose State University, San Jose, CA

90,000 University of Nebraska College of Nursing, Kearney, NE

Team Bancshares Inc.

Assets: $5.4 billion
Employees: 2,700
Parent Company: Team Bancshares
Headquarters: Dallas, TX
SIC Major Group: Depository Institutions and Holding & Other Investment Offices

CONTACT
Dave Perdue
Regional Chairman
Team Bancshares Inc.
3300 Oaklawn, PO Box 190667
Dallas, TX 75219
(214) 290-7840

CONTRIBUTIONS SUMMARY
Operating Locations: TX (Dallas)

CORP. OFFICERS
Gary W. Cage: *CURR EMPL* cfo: Team Bancshares
Terry Kelley: *CURR EMPL* coo: Team Bancshares
Ronald G. Steinhart: *CURR EMPL* chmn, ceo: Team Bancshares

Team Bank Houston

Employees: 2,310
Parent Company: Team Bancshares
Headquarters: Houston, TX
SIC Major Group: Depository Institutions

CONTACT
Mike Balasses
Regional Chairman
Team Bank Houston
2800 Post Oak Blvd.
Houston, TX 77056
(713) 626-3420

CONTRIBUTIONS SUMMARY
Operating Locations: TX (Houston)

CORP. OFFICERS
Mike Balasses: *CURR EMPL* regional chmn: Team Bank Houston

Technical Foundation of America

CONTACT
Gene Martin
Vice President
Technical Fdn of America
206 Oak Ridge
San Marcos, TX 78666

FINANCIAL SUMMARY
Recent Giving: $253,216 (fiscal 1991); $216,090 (fiscal 1990); $178,179 (fiscal 1989)
Assets: $4,530,054 (fiscal year ending June 30, 1991); $4,589,903 (fiscal 1990); $4,461,753 (fiscal 1989)
EIN: 36-0730670

CONTRIBUTIONS SUMMARY
Typical Recipients: • *Education:* career/vocational education, colleges & universities, science/technology education • *Social Services:* recreation & athletics
Grant Types: project, research, and seed money
Geographic Distribution: national

GIVING OFFICERS
John Eames: secy, treas, trust
David E. Hall: pres, trust *B* Big Rapids MI 1937 *ED* Wheaton Coll 1959; DePaul Univ 1971 *CURR EMPL* pres, dir: Scripture Press Publs *CORP AFFIL* pres, dir: Scripture Press Publs *NONPR AFFIL* dir: Christian Booksellers Assn, Evangelical Christian Publs Assn
G. Eugene Martin: vp, trust

APPLICATION INFORMATION
Initial Approach: Send cover letter and full proposal (two copies). There are no deadlines.

OTHER THINGS TO KNOW
Publications: Application Guidelines

GRANTS ANALYSIS
Number of Grants: 22
Highest Grant: $48,854
Typical Range: $1,400 to $10,000
Disclosure Period: fiscal year ending June 30, 1991

RECENT GRANTS
48,854 Texas A&M University, College Station, TX
45,000 National Vocational Industrial Clubs of America
43,600 National Vocational Industrial Clubs of America
24,048 Technology Student Association
19,353 James Madison University, Harrisonburg, VA
14,015 Texas A&M University, College Station, TX
10,966 TFA Program
10,402 TFA Program
8,123 Oklahoma State University, Stillwater, OK
8,000 California State University, Fresno, CA

Technical Training Foundation

CONTACT
Ibrahim Hefni
Trustee
Technical Training Fdn.
c/o Bay Bank Merrimac Valley
588 Essex St.
Lawrence, MA 01845
(508) 682-1900

FINANCIAL SUMMARY
Recent Giving: $118,200 (fiscal 1990); $58,627 (fiscal 1989)
Assets: $5,502,963 (fiscal year ending August 30, 1990); $7,151,855 (fiscal 1989)
EIN: 04-2864138

CONTRIBUTIONS SUMMARY
Typical Recipients: • *Education:* career/vocational education, colleges & universities, science/technology education
Grant Types: research and scholarship

GIVING OFFICERS
Denis Hamboyan: trust
Ibrahim Hefni: trust
Wensley Hefni: trust

APPLICATION INFORMATION
Initial Approach: Send brief letter of inquiry describing program or project. There are no deadlines.

GRANTS ANALYSIS
Number of Grants: 4
Highest Grant: $100,000
Typical Range: $625 to $5,825

Disclosure Period: fiscal year ending August 30, 1990

RECENT GRANTS

100,000 Howard University, Washington, DC
5,825 Merrimack College, North Andover, MA
625 Lowell University, Lowell, MA

Tecumseh Products Co. / Herrick Foundation

Sales: $1.19 billion
Employees: 12,483
Headquarters: Tecumseh, MI
SIC Major Group: Industrial Machinery & Equipment and Transportation Equipment

CONTACT

Kenneth Herrick
Chairman, Director
Tecumseh Products Co.
150 West Jefferson, Ste. 2500
Detroit, MI 48226
(313) 496-7656

FINANCIAL SUMMARY

EIN: 38-6041517

CONTRIBUTIONS SUMMARY

Operating Locations: MI (Detroit, Tecumseh)

CORP. OFFICERS

Kenneth G. Herrick: *B* Jackson MI 1921 *CURR EMPL* chmn, dir: Tecumseh Products Co *CORP AFFIL* dir: Mfrs Natl Bank Detroit *NONPR AFFIL* mem exec adv bd: St Jude Childrens Hosp

Todd Wesley Herrick: *B* Tecumseh MI 1942 *ED* Univ Notre Dame 1967 *CURR EMPL* pres, ceo: Tecumseh Products Co *CORP AFFIL* dir: OH Citizens Trust Co, Sharon Mfg Co, Tecnamotor, Un Savings Bank; pres: Tecumseh Products Intl *NONPR AFFIL* dir: Sociedad Intercontinental Compressores Hermitocos; mem: Am Soc Heating Refrigerating Air Conditioning Engrs, Am Soc Metals

OTHER THINGS TO KNOW

A majority of the Herrick Foundation's assets consist of shares of the Tecumseh Products Co.

Teichert / Teichert Foundation

Employees: 1,300
Headquarters: Sacramento, CA

CONTACT

Frederick Teichert
Executive Director
Teichert Foundation
3500 American River Drive
Sacramento, CA 95864
(916) 484-3344

FINANCIAL SUMMARY

Recent Giving: $139,994 (fiscal 1992); $0 (fiscal 1990)
Assets: $535,371 (fiscal year ending March 31, 1992); $500,000 (fiscal 1990)
Gifts Received: $100,000 (fiscal 1992); $500,000 (fiscal 1990)
Fiscal Note: In fiscal 1992, contributions were received from A. Teichert & Sons Inc.
EIN: 68-0212355

CONTRIBUTIONS SUMMARY

Typical Recipients: • *Arts & Humanities:* libraries, music • *Civic & Public Affairs:* environmental affairs, safety • *Education:* colleges & universities • *Social Services:* child welfare, youth organizations
Grant Types: general support
Operating Locations: CA (Sacramento)

CORP. OFFICERS

Louis V. Riggs: *CURR EMPL* pres, ceo: Teichert

GIVING OFFICERS

Thomas J. Hammer: dir
Anne S. Haslam: secy
Judson T. Riggs: dir
Bruce Stimson: cfo
Erma M. Teichert: dir
Frederick Teichert: exec dir
Frederick A. Teichert: exec dir,

APPLICATION INFORMATION

Initial Approach: Application form required. Applicants should submit a description of the organization; population served; plans for cooperation with other organizations, if any; principal source of support for project in the past; listing of board of directors, trustees, officers and other key people and their affiliations; copy of most recent annual reports; copy of current year's organizational budget and/or project budget; qualifications of key personnel; detailed description of project and amount of funding requested; statement of problem project will address; timetable for implementation and evaluation of project; how project will be sustained once foundation support is completed; how project's results will be evaluated or measured.
Restrictions on Giving: No support for religious, political or fraternal organizations, or for national fundraising campaigns. No grants to individuals, or for courtesy advertising, benefits, telephone solicitations.

GRANTS ANALYSIS

Number of Grants: 64
Highest Grant: $10,000
Typical Range: $500 to $5,000
Disclosure Period: fiscal year ending March 31, 1992

RECENT GRANTS

10,000 Sacramento Public Library, Sacramento, CA
10,000 Sacramento Symphony Association, Sacramento, CA
6,155 Stanford Home for Children, Sacramento, CA
5,000 Center for Natural Lands Management, Sacramento, CA
5,000 River Oak Center for Children, Sacramento, CA
5,000 Sacramento Citizens Crime Alert Reward Program, Sacramento, CA — "California Crackdown
5,000 Sacramento Police Athletic League, Sacramento, CA
5,000 University of California Davis Presents, Davis, CA
4,800 Neighborhood Study Centers, Sacramento, CA
4,000 El Dorado School, Stockton, CA

Teitel Charitable Trust, Ben N.

CONTACT

Gerald S. Cook
Ben N. Teitel Charitable Trust
2290 First National Building
Detroit, MI 48226-3583
(313) 256-7800

FINANCIAL SUMMARY

Recent Giving: $778,500 (fiscal 1990)
Assets: $8,820,331 (fiscal year ending September 30, 1990)
Gifts Received: $467 (fiscal 1990)
Fiscal Note: Fiscal 1990 contribution received from the Estate of Ben N. Teitel.
EIN: 38-6512136

GIVING OFFICERS

Gerald S. Cook: trust

APPLICATION INFORMATION

Initial Approach: The foundation reports it only makes contributions to preselected organizations and does not accept unsolicited requests for funds.

GRANTS ANALYSIS

Total Grants: $778,500
Highest Grant: $300,000
Disclosure Period: fiscal year ending September 30, 1990

Tektronix / Tektronix Foundation

Sales: $1.29 billion
Employees: 13,005
Headquarters: Beaverton, OR
SIC Major Group: Industrial Machinery & Equipment and Instruments & Related Products

CONTACT

Jill Powers Kirk
Executive Director
Tektronix Fdn.
PO Box 1000
Wilsonville, OR 97070-1000
(503) 685-4000

FINANCIAL SUMMARY

Recent Giving: $1,723,492 (1991); $2,000,000 (1990); $1,760,082 (1989)
Assets: $2,964,094 (1991); $1,840,121 (1990); $2,604,827 (1988)
Fiscal Note: Company gives directly and through the foundation. Figures for 1989 and 1990 reflect both direct and founda-

tion giving. The figure for 1991 is for the foundation only. EIN: 93-6021540

CONTRIBUTIONS SUMMARY

Typical Recipients: • *Arts & Humanities:* arts institutes, music, performing arts, public broadcasting • *Civic & Public Affairs:* economics • *Education:* arts education, colleges & universities, economic education, engineering education, minority education, private education (precollege), public education (precollege), science/technology education, student aid • *Social Services:* united funds

Grant Types: employee matching gifts, general support, project, research, and scholarship

Nonmonetary Support Types: donated equipment and donated products

Note: In 1990, estimated value of nonmonetary support was $4,000,000. This support is not included in above figures.

Geographic Distribution: primarily in northwestern Oregon

Operating Locations: CA (Grass Valley), OR (Forest Grove, Portland, Redmond, Wilsonville)

Note: Company also operates 35 sales and service offices in 23 states and the District of Columbia. Also operates internationally.

CORP. OFFICERS

Lawrence R. Kaplan: *B* Mount Vernon NY 1950 *ED* Univ WI 1973; Rutgers Univ 1978 *CURR EMPL* vp (tv sys group): Tektronix

Jerome J. Meyer: *B* Caledonia MN 1938 *CURR EMPL* chmn, pres, ceo: Tektronix *CORP AFFIL* dir: Honeywell Erickson Devel Co, Keycom Electronic Devel Co, Magnetic Data

GIVING OFFICERS

Paul E. Bragdon: trust *B* Portland ME 1927 *ED* Amherst Coll BA 1950 *NONPR AFFIL* chmn: OR Partnership Intl Ed; mem: Beta Theta Pi, Phi Beta Kappa; pres: Med Res Fdn OR; trust: OR Grad Ctr Science & Tech

Charles H. Frost: vchmn *B* 1936 *ED* Willamette Univ; Portland St Univ *CURR EMPL* vp (admin): Tektronix

Richard S. Hill: trust

Lawrence R. Kaplan: sec *CURR EMPL* vp (tv sys group): Tektronix (see above)
Jill Powers Kirk: trust
William Spivey: trust
Mrs. Jean E. Vollum: chmn, trust
William D. Walker: trust *B* Howell County MO 1930 *ED* MO Sch Mines & Metallurgy BSEE 1958 *CURR EMPL* exec vp: Tektronix *CORP AFFIL* chmn, ceo, dir: Electro Scientific Indus; dir: Sony/Tektronix Corp *NONPR AFFIL* mem: Am Electronics Assn, Intl Electrotechnical Comm; tech adv: Natl Science Fdn

APPLICATION INFORMATION

Initial Approach: *Initial Contact:* full proposal *Include Information On:* description of the organization, amount requested, purpose for which funds are sought, recently audited financial statement, and proof of tax-exempt status *When to Submit:* allow four months lead time since Foundation meets quarterly but not on a regular schedule

GRANTS ANALYSIS

Total Grants: $1,723,492*
Number of Grants: 42*
Highest Grant: $200,000*
Typical Range: $5,000 to $45,000
Disclosure Period: 1991
Note: Total grants is for the foundation only. Figures for number of grants and average grant exclude seven scholarships grants totaling $17,500. Recent grants are derived from a 1991 Form 990.

RECENT GRANTS

200,000	United Way
141,200	Portland State University, Portland, OR
100,000	Oregon State University, Portland, OR
96,182	Portland State University, Portland, OR
80,000	Oregon Independent College Foundation, Portland, OR
45,000	Oregon Museum of Science and Industry, Portland, OR
40,000	St. Vincent, Portland, OR
30,000	Portland State University Foundation, Portland, OR
28,803	Oregon State University, Portland, OR
25,000	Oregon Museum of Science and Industry, Portland, OR

Tele-Communications, Inc.

Sales: $3.82 billion
Employees: 33,000
Headquarters: Denver, CO
SIC Major Group: Communications and Motion Pictures

CONTACT

Gary Bracken
Senior Vice President and Controller
Tele-Communications, Inc.
PO Box 5630
Denver, CO 80217
(303) 721-5500

CONTRIBUTIONS SUMMARY

Operating Locations: CO (Denver), IA (Des Moines), IN (Warsaw), OH (Cincinnati), TX (Dallas)

CORP. OFFICERS

Brendan R. Clouston: *CURR EMPL* coo: Tele-Commun

Bob John Magness: *B* Clinton OK 1924 *ED* Southwestern St Coll 1949 *CURR EMPL* chmn, dir: Tele-Commun *CORP AFFIL* chmn: Community Tele-Commun; dir: Gen Commun, Liberty Media Corp, Republic Pictures Corp, Un Artists Commun, WestMarc Commun

John Charles Custer Malone: *B* Milford CT 1941 *ED* Yale Univ BS 1963; Johns Hopkins Univ MS 1964; Johns Hopkins Univ PhD 1969 *CURR EMPL* pres, ceo, dir: Tele-Communs *CORP AFFIL* chmn, dir: Liberty Media Corp, TCI East, Un Artists Entertainment; dir: Bank NY Co, BET Holdings, Black Entertainment Television, McCaw Cellular Communs, QVC Network, Turner Broadcasting Sys, Westmore Communs; pres, ceo, dir: Heritage Communs; pres, dir: Commun Reality, Heritage Cablevision CA, TCI Cablevision OH, TCI Cablevision UT, TCI Devel Corp, TCI Holdings, TCI Northeast, Televent Group

Telecom Corp.

Sales: $51.9 million
Employees: 557
Headquarters: Dallas, TX
SIC Major Group: Holding & Other Investment Offices, Industrial Machinery & Equipment, and Wholesale Trade—Durable Goods

CONTACT

Larry Merrick
Executive Vice President & CFO
Telecom Corp.
1545 West Mockingbird Ln., Ste. 7000
Dallas, TX 75235
(214) 638-0638

CONTRIBUTIONS SUMMARY

Operating Locations: TX (Dallas)

CORP. OFFICERS

Lawrence Schumann: *CURR EMPL* chmn, pres, coo, dir: Telecom Corp

Teledyne / Teledyne Charitable Trust Foundation

Parent Sales: $2.89 billion
Parent Employees: 33,200
Headquarters: Los Angeles, CA
SIC Major Group: Holding & Other Investment Offices, Insurance Carriers, Rubber & Miscellaneous Plastics Products, and Transportation Equipment

CONTACT

Gary A. Zitterbart
Treasurer
Teledyne Charitable Trust Fdn.
1901 Avenue of the Stars
Los Angeles, CA 90067
(310) 277-3311

FINANCIAL SUMMARY

Recent Giving: $1,387,548 (1991); $1,430,580 (1990); $1,944,957 (1989)
Assets: $1,200 (1991); $81,000 (1990); $185,997 (1989)
Gifts Received: $1,387,548 (1991)
Fiscal Note: Figures for foundation only. Operating companies also administer limited contributions programs.
EIN: 25-6074705

CONTRIBUTIONS SUMMARY

Typical Recipients: • *Arts & Humanities:* arts associations, arts centers, arts funds, community arts, history/historic preservation, libraries, museums/galleries, music, opera, performing arts, public broadcasting, theater, visual arts • *Civic & Public Affairs:* better government, business/free enterprise, consumer affairs, economic development, environmental affairs, ethnic/minority organizations, international affairs, law & justice, national security, professional & trade associations, public policy, safety, urban & community affairs, women's affairs • *Education:* business education, career/vocational education, colleges & universities, community & junior colleges, economic education, education associations, education funds, minority education, private education (precollege), public education (precollege), science/technology education, student aid • *Health:* health organizations, hospitals, medical research, pediatric health, single-disease health associations • *Social Services:* child welfare, community service organizations, drugs & alcohol, emergency relief, family services, food/clothing distribution, homes, recreation & athletics, refugee assistance, religious welfare, shelters/homelessness, united funds, youth organizations

Grant Types: capital, employee matching gifts, general support, project, research, and scholarship

Nonmonetary Support Types: donated equipment and in-kind services

Note: Value of nonmonetary support is not available and is not included in above figures. Operating companies provide such support on a case-by-case basis.

Geographic Distribution: primarily in areas of company operating facilities

Operating Locations: AL (Huntsville, Mobile), CA (Arcadia, Burbank, City of Industry, Fresno, Gardena, Hawthorne, Hollister, Los Angeles, Mountain View, Newbury Park, North Hollywood, Northridge, Palo Alto, Pomona, Redlands, Redwood City, San Diego, San Marcos, Santa Clara, Saratoga, Solana Beach, Torrance, Whittier), CO (Denver, Fort Collins), CT (Ansonia), IL (Aurora, Chicago, Crystal Lake, Des Plaines, Elk Grove Village, Peoria), IN (Elkhart, Indianapolis, La Porte, Portland), KS (Shawnee Mission), LA (Lafayette), MA (Cambridge, Canton, Dedham, New Bedford, Waltham, Woburn), MD (Timonium), MI (Benton Harbor, Howell, Muskegon), MN (Fairmont), MO (Neosho), MS (Gulfport), NC (Elm City, Monroe, Rocky Mount), NH (Hudson), NJ (Clifton, Palisades Park, Union, Warren, Westwood), NY (Buffalo, New Rochelle, North Tonawanda, Troy), OH (Brecksville, Canal Winchester, Cincinnati, Cleveland, Hartville, Lima, Toledo, Wickliffe), OR (Alany), PA (Carnegie, Chester, Edinboro, Latrobe, Mohnton, Monaca, Pittsburgh, Reading, Waynesboro, York), TN (Cookeville, Dyer, Garland, La Vergne, Lewisburg, Memphis), TX (Dallas, Galveston, Garland, Houston), VA (Charlottesville, Hampton), WI (Milwaukee, Owen, Waukesha)

CORP. OFFICERS

George Adam Roberts: *B* Uniontown PA 1919 *ED* US Naval Academy 1937; Carnegie Inst Tech BS 1939; Carnegie Inst Tech MS 1941; Carnegie Inst Tech 1942 *CURR EMPL* chmn, ceo, dir: Teledyne *NONPR AFFIL* fellow: Am Inst Mining Metallurgical Petroleum Engrs, Am Soc Metals; mem: Am Iron Steel Inst, Metal Powder Indus Fed, Natl Academy Engg, Soc Mfg Engrs; trust: Carnegie-Mellon Univ

William Rutledge: *B* 1942 *CURR EMPL* pres, ceo, dir: Teledyne

GIVING OFFICERS

Berkley J. Baker: trust

Jack H. Hamilton: trust *B* Lubbock TX 1941 *CURR EMPL* ceo: CGF Indus *CORP AFFIL* dir: Bank IV Topeka *NONPR AFFIL* dir: Automobile Assoc Am KS; mem: Topeka Chamber Commerce

George Adam Roberts: trust *CURR EMPL* chmn, ceo, dir: Teledyne (see above)

Gilbert A. Zitterbart: treas, trust

APPLICATION INFORMATION

Initial Approach: *Initial Contact:* letter *Include Information On:* description of the organization, amount requested, purpose for which funds are sought, recently audited financial statement, and proof of tax-exempt status *When to Submit:* any time

Restrictions on Giving: Foundation does not make grants to individuals; political or purely social organizations; or to religious organizations for sectarian purposes.

GRANTS ANALYSIS

Total Grants: $1,387,548

Number of Grants: 640

Highest Grant: $34,000

Typical Range: $500 to $5,000

Disclosure Period: 1992

Note: Recent grants are derived from a 1991 Form 990. Assets are for 1991.

RECENT GRANTS

34,000	United Way Campaign, Los Angeles, CA
34,000	United Way Campaign, Los Angeles, CA
34,000	United Way Campaign, Los Angeles, CA
34,000	United Way Campaign, Los Angeles, CA
33,400	Westminster Christian Academy, Huntsville, AL
28,991	Ft. Collins United Way, Ft. Collins, CO
25,000	Foundation for the Carolinas, Charlotte, NC
25,000	Foundation for the Carolinas, Charlotte, NC
24,906	Auburn University Foundation, Auburn, AL
23,000	Music Center Unified Fund, Los Angeles, CA

Teleflex Inc. / Teleflex Foundation

Sales: $479.5 million
Employees: 6,800
Headquarters: Plymouth Meeting, PA
SIC Major Group: Electronic & Other Electrical Equipment, Fabricated Metal Products, Industrial Machinery & Equipment, and Rubber & Miscellaneous Plastics Products

CONTACT
Bob Bertschy
Treasurer
Teleflex Foundation
155 South Limerick Rd.
Limerick, PA 19468
(215) 948-5100

FINANCIAL SUMMARY
Fiscal Note: Annual Giving Range: $100,000 to $250,000
EIN: 23-2104782

CONTRIBUTIONS SUMMARY
Typical Recipients: • *Arts & Humanities:* arts associations, arts centers, arts funds, arts institutes, community arts, dance, ethnic arts, history/historic preservation, libraries, literary arts, museums/galleries, music, opera, performing arts, theater • *Civic & Public Affairs:* urban & community affairs, women's affairs, zoos/botanical gardens • *Health:* hospices, hospitals • *Science:* observatories & planetariums • *Social Services:* community centers, drugs & alcohol, youth organizations

Grant Types: employee matching gifts

Geographic Distribution: in headquarters and operating communities

Operating Locations: CA (Compton, Oxnard), CT (Suffield, Windsor), FL (Boynton Beach, Sarasota), MI (Hillsdale), NH (Jaffrey), OH (Van Wert), PA (King of Prussia, Limerick, North Wales, Plymouth Meeting), TX (Sugar Land), UT (Spanish Fork)

Note: Sermatech International Inc. operates 4 plants in locations.

CORP. OFFICERS
Lennox K. Black: *B* Montreal Canada 1930 *ED* Royal Naval Coll 1949; McGill Univ BC 1952 *CURR EMPL* chmn, ceo: Teleflex *CORP AFFIL* chmn, ceo: Penn VA Corp; dir: Envirite Corp, Pep Boys, Quaker Chemical Corp, TFX Engg, Westmoreland Coal Co

David S. Boyer: *CURR EMPL* pres: Teleflex

Harold L. Zuber, Jr.: *CURR EMPL* vp, cfo: Teleflex

GIVING OFFICERS
Lennox K. Black: pres *CURR EMPL* chmn, ceo: Teleflex (see above)

APPLICATION INFORMATION

Initial Approach: Submit a full proposal that includes a a description of organization, amount requested, purpose of funds sought, recently audited financial statement, and proof of tax-exempt status.
Restrictions on Giving: Does not support individuals, religious organizations for sectarian purposes, political or lobbying groups, organizations outside operating areas, or advertisements.

GRANTS ANALYSIS

Typical Range: $1,000 to $2,500

Teleklew Productions / Welk Foundation, Lawrence

Headquarters: Santa Monica, CA

CONTACT

Shirley Fredricks
Executive Director
Lawrence Welk Foundation
1299 Ocean Avenue, Ste. 800
Santa Monica, CA 90401
(213) 451-5727

FINANCIAL SUMMARY

Recent Giving: $291,075 (1991)
Fiscal Note: In 1991, contributions were received from The Welk Group.
EIN: 95-6064646

CONTRIBUTIONS SUMMARY

Typical Recipients: • *Civic & Public Affairs:* economic development, housing, women's affairs • *Social Services:* aged, child welfare, community centers, community service organizations, counseling, day care, delinquency & crime, domestic violence, employment/job training, family planning, family services, shelters/homelessness, youth organizations
Grant Types: capital, challenge, general support, multiyear/continuing support, operating expenses, project, and seed money
Nonmonetary Support Types: donated equipment
Geographic Distribution: in headquarters and operating communities
Operating Locations: CA (Santa Monica)

GIVING OFFICERS

Shirley Fredrickson: exec dir
Donna Mack: dir
Lawrence L. Welk: dir

APPLICATION INFORMATION

Initial Approach: Send brief letter of inquiry by July 1 (completed applications are due September 1). Include a description of the organization, amount requested, purpose of funds sought, recently audited financial statement, and proof of tax-exempt status.
Restrictions on Giving: Does not support individuals, political or lobbying groups, or organizations outside operating areas.

OTHER THINGS TO KNOW

Publications: Application Guidelines

GRANTS ANALYSIS

Number of Grants: 76
Highest Grant: $30,000
Typical Range: $100 to $15,000
Disclosure Period: 1990
Note: No grants list provided for 1991.

RECENT GRANTS

30,000 Welk Heritage, Santa Monica, CA
15,000 Casa de Amparo, Santa Monica, CA
15,000 St. Johns Hospital, Santa Monica, CA
10,000 Proyecto Pastoral, Santa Monica, CA
10,000 Senior Health and Peer and Wise, Santa Monica, CA
10,000 St. Joseph Center, Santa Monica, CA
9,600 Boys Club, Santa Monica, CA
9,000 University of California Los Angeles, Santa Monica, CA
8,000 Catholic Health Association of the United States, Santa Monica, CA

Telinde Trust, Richard W.

CONTACT

Richard W. Telinde Trust
c/o First National Bank of Maryland, P.O. Box 1596
Baltimore, MD 21203
(410) 244-4600

FINANCIAL SUMMARY

Recent Giving: $334,384 (1991); $285,842 (1990)
Assets: $6,861,460 (1991); $5,859,988 (1990)
EIN: 52-6458357

CONTRIBUTIONS SUMMARY

Typical Recipients: • *Education:* medical education

GIVING OFFICERS

First National Bank of Maryland: trust

GRANTS ANALYSIS

Number of Grants: 1
Highest Grant: $334,384
Disclosure Period: 1991

RECENT GRANTS

285,842 Johns Hopkins University School of Medicine, Baltimore, MD — to endow a chair of gynecological pathology

Tell Foundation

CONTACT

Ron L. Lewis
Administrator
Tell Fdn.
4020 North 38th Ave.
Phoenix, AZ 85019

FINANCIAL SUMMARY

Recent Giving: $136,700 (fiscal 1992); $188,313 (fiscal 1990); $167,035 (fiscal 1989)
Assets: $2,737,380 (fiscal 1991); $2,498,688 (fiscal 1990); $2,371,977 (fiscal 1989)
Gifts Received: $112,200 (fiscal 1992); $51,300 (fiscal 1990); $27,000 (fiscal 1989)
Fiscal Note: In fiscal 1992, contributions were received from Mary Tell ($45,000), Tell Land Co. ($62,500), and Ranald and Lydia Lewis($4,700).
EIN: 86-6050214

CONTRIBUTIONS SUMMARY

Donor(s): the late Andrew P. Tell, Mary J. Tell
Typical Recipients: • *Education:* colleges & universities, private education (precollege), religious education • *Religion:* churches, missionary activities, religious organizations • *Social Services:* community service organizations, family services
Grant Types: general support
Geographic Distribution: focus on AZ

GIVING OFFICERS

Marilyn P. Hamman: vp, treas, dir
Elizabeth P. Hirshberg: secy, dir
Lydia Lewis: dir
Ronald L. Lewis: admin, dir
Benny Rhodes: dir
Esther Rhodes: dir
Mary J. Tell: pres, dir

APPLICATION INFORMATION

Initial Approach: Contributes only to preselected organizations.
Restrictions on Giving: Does not support individuals.

GRANTS ANALYSIS

Number of Grants: 47
Highest Grant: $41,000
Typical Range: $1,000 to $6,000
Disclosure Period: fiscal year ending June 30, 1992

RECENT GRANTS

41,000 Phoenix Christian High School, Phoenix, AZ
25,000 Southwestern College, Phoenix, AZ
19,100 Conservative Baptist Foreign Mission Society, Wheaton, IL
15,000 Living Bibles International, Naperville, IL
7,400 Christian Family Care Agency, Phoenix, AZ
6,638 Gideons International, Nashville, TN
6,000 Tonto Rim Baptist Camp, Valley Forge, PA
5,400 Grand Canyon University, Phoenix, AZ
5,150 Scotsdale Christian Academy, Phoenix, AZ
5,000 Youth With a Mission, Salem, OR

Temple Foundation, T. L. L.

CONTACT
Phillip M. Leach
Executive Director
T. L. L. Temple Foundation
109 Temple Blvd.
Lufkin, TX 75901
(409) 639-5197

FINANCIAL SUMMARY
Recent Giving: $11,000,000 (fiscal 1993 est.); $10,500,000 (fiscal 1992 approx.); $10,950,000 (fiscal 1991)
Assets: $275,000,000 (fiscal 1993 est.); $270,000,000 (fiscal year ending November 30, 1992 est.); $240,000,000 (fiscal 1991 approx.); $220,000,000 (fiscal 1990 approx.)
Gifts Received: $100,000 (fiscal 1991 est.); $100,000 (fiscal 1990); $100,000 (fiscal 1989)
Fiscal Note: In fiscal 1990, the foundation received a contribution of $100,000 from the estate of Katherine S. Temple.
EIN: 75-6037406

CONTRIBUTIONS SUMMARY
Donor(s): In 1894, Thomas Lewis Latane Temple started a sawmill and began acquiring timberland in east Texas. Arthur Temple, one of his sons, eventually served as president of Temple Industries. He was later succeeded by his son, Arthur Temple, Jr.
By 1973, the Temples owned 50% of Temple Industries stock. That same year, they merged their company into Time Inc., and in return, the Temple family received 15% of Time stock, worth over $60 million. In 1984, Time spun off Temple-Inland, a holding company of which Arthur Temple, Jr., is chairman.
The T. L. L. Temple Foundation was established in 1962, with donations from the late Georgia T. Munz and the late Katherine S. Temple.
Typical Recipients: • *Arts & Humanities:* libraries • *Civic & Public Affairs:* safety, urban & community affairs • *Education:* agricultural education, colleges & universities, elementary education, minority education, special education • *Health:* hospices, hospitals, medical rehabilitation, medical research, mental health • *Social*

Services: aged, community service organizations, day care, domestic violence, drugs & alcohol, employment/job training, shelters/homelessness, united funds, volunteer services, youth organizations
Grant Types: capital, general support, project, and scholarship
Geographic Distribution: primarily to the East Texas Pine Timber Belt area

GIVING OFFICERS
Ward R. Burke: trust
Phillip M. Leach: exec dir, gen couns, trust
Arthur Temple, Jr.: chmn, trust *B* Texarkana AR 1920 *ED* Univ TX 1937-1938; Williams Coll *CORP AFFIL* chmn: Exeter Investment Co, Lufkin Pineland St Bank; chmn bd: T&T Corp; dir: AMCA Intl Ltd, Austin Crest Hotel, Contractors Supplies, Great Am Restaurant Ins Co, Henley Mfg Corp, Lufkin, Lufkin Block, Lumbermans Investment Corp, Signal Cos, Sunbelt Ins Co, Temple-Eastex, Temple-Inland Properties; dir, chmn emeritus: Temple-Inland; exec vp, dir: Temple-White Co; mem exec comm, dir: Republic Bank Corp; pres bd regents, dir: TX Southeastern RR; pres, dir: John E Gray Inst; ptnr: Dallas Cowboys *NONPR AFFIL* dir: Lumberman Merchants Assn, Natl Forest Products Assn, Natl Park Fdn, Southern Forest Products Assn, St Michael Hosp Fdn; trust: Am Forest Products Assn *PHIL AFFIL* trust: Temple Foundation; trust comm: Temple Industries Pension Trust
Arthur (Buddy) Temple III: trust
W. Temple Webber: vchmn
M. F. Zeagler: asst exec dir, contr

APPLICATION INFORMATION
Initial Approach:
Prospective applicants should send a written request to the foundation.
Applicants should furnish the following information: name, address, phone number, charter, articles of incorporation, constitution and by-laws; copy of exemption letters; names and addresses of officers and directors; brief, factual resume of the operations of the appli-

cant; and an explanation of the request, with evidence of need. Applicants should detail the services to be rendered and explain the benefits to members of the public; and include copies of present and prior year budgets and financial statements reflecting sources and amounts of receipts and disbursements, and an audit for the prior year, if available.
There are no application deadlines. The foundation board meets as case load demands.
Restrictions on Giving: The foundation gives only to governmental units, exempt under the Internal Revenue Code, or to nonprofit, charitable organizations having exempt status under Section 501(c)(3) of the Internal Revenue Code evidencing that it is such an organization and is not classified as a "Private Foundation."
No grants are made to churches, religious organizations, or other entities for the propagation of religious faith and/or practices. Grants also are not made to individuals for scholarships, research, or other purposes.

GRANTS ANALYSIS
Total Grants: $10,500,000
Number of Grants: 140
Highest Grant: $4,970,000
Typical Range: $15,000 to $75,000
Disclosure Period: fiscal year ending November 30, 1992
Note: Average grant figure excludes a single grant for $4,970,000. Recent grants are derived from a fiscal 1991 grants list.

RECENT GRANTS
1,693,000 Methodist Retirement Services, The Woodlands, TX — construction of retirement facility
1,410,149 Memorial Medical Center of East Texas, Lufkin, TX — Magnetic Resonance Image facility
1,000,000 University of Texas System, Houston, TX — M. D. Anderson Cancer Center; Golden Jubilee campaign
521,260 University of Texas at Austin, Austin, TX — engineering education excellence

500,000 St. Stephen's Episcopal School, Austin, TX — construction and renovations
476,120 Memorial Medical Center of East Texas, Lufkin, TX — Stewart Blood Center; Lufkin Branch
323,000 Angelina County Exposition Center, Lufkin, TX — capital improvements
265,000 Foundation for the Retarded, Houston, TX — Willow River Farms project
255,500 City of Lufkin, Lufkin, TX — Jones Park improvements
252,425 City of Lufkin, Lufkin, TX — Phase I and Phase II/recycling program

Temple-Inland / Temple-Inland Foundation
Sales: $2.71 billion
Employees: 14,000
Headquarters: Diboll, TX
SIC Major Group: Building Materials & Garden Supplies, Holding & Other Investment Offices, Lumber & Wood Products, and Paper & Allied Products

CONTACT
James R. Wash
Secretary & Treasurer
Temple-Inland Fdn.
303 S Temple Dr.
PO Box N
Diboll, TX 75941
(409) 829-1314

FINANCIAL SUMMARY
Recent Giving: $2,519,404 (fiscal 1992); $1,930,757 (fiscal 1991); $1,453,156 (fiscal 1990)
Assets: $14,508,325 (fiscal year ending June 30, 1992); $10,283,014 (fiscal 1989)
Fiscal Note: Company gives through foundation only. A subsidiary, Inland Container Corp., sponsors its own independent foundation.
EIN: 75-1977109

CONTRIBUTIONS SUMMARY
Typical Recipients: • *Arts & Humanities:* libraries, museums/galleries • *Civic & Public*

Affairs: municipalities • *Education:* colleges & universities, elementary education, private education (precollege), public education (precollege) • *Social Services:* drugs & alcohol, united funds, youth organizations

Grant Types: employee matching gifts, general support, and scholarship

Geographic Distribution: primarily near company headquarters

Operating Locations: AL (Monroeville), AR (Ft. Smith), CA (Los Angeles, Newark, Ontario, Santa Fe Springs, Tracy), CO (Denver), FL (Orlando), GA (Macon, Rome, Thomson), IL (Chicago), TX (Austin, Dallas, Diboll, Evadale, Houston, Irving, Killeen, Temple)

CORP. OFFICERS

Clifford J. Grum: *B* Davenport IA 1934 *ED* Austin Coll BA 1956; Univ PA Wharton Sch MBA 1958 *CURR EMPL* chmn, ceo: Temple-Inland *CORP AFFIL* dir: Cooper Indus, Premark Intl *NONPR AFFIL* trust: Austin Coll

GIVING OFFICERS

Glenn Chancellor: dir *B* Nacogdoches TX 1937 *CURR EMPL* vp (forest group): Temple Inland Group *CORP AFFIL* chmn: Am Pulpwood Assn; dir: Sabine River & Northern Railroad

Roger Delwin Ericson: dir *B* Moline IL 1934 *CURR EMPL* vp, gen couns, sec: Temple-Inland Inc *CORP AFFIL* corp secy: El Moro Corrugated Box Co, Indisk Inc, Inland Intl Inc; corp secy, dir: Inland Container Corp, Inland-Orange Inc, Inland Real Estate Investments Inc, Temple-Inland Realty Inc; dir: Easter Paellaging Inc; vchmn, pres, dir: GK Investments Inc, Kraft Land Svcs; vp, dir: Guaranty Holdings Inc, Temple-Inland Fdn, Temple-Inland Forest Products; vp, secy, bd dirs: Inland-Rome Inc *NONPR AFFIL* dir: Stetson Univ; mem: Am Bar Assn, Am Paper Inst, Am Soc Corp Secys, Chicago Bar Assn, FL Bar Assn, IL Bar Assn, IN Bar Assn, Indianapolis Bar Assn, Indianapolis Chamber Commerce, Omicron Delta Kappa, Phi Delta Phi

Clifford J. Grum: dir *CURR EMPL* chmn, ceo: Temple-Inland (see above)

Kenneth M. Jastrow II: dir
Robert Grant Luttrell: pres, dir *B* Eagletown OK 1937 *ED* Univ TX 1960; Southern Methodist Univ 1981 *CURR EMPL* vp admin, treas: Temple-Inland Forest Products Corp
Harold Maxwell: dir
Evonne Nerren: vp
Arthur Temple, Jr.: dir *B* Texarkana AR 1920 *ED* Univ TX 1937-1938; Williams Coll *CORP AFFIL* chmn: Exeter Investment Co, Lufkin Pineland St Bank; chmn bd: T&T Corp; dir: AMCA Intl Ltd, Austin Crest Hotel, Contractors Supplies, Great Am Restaurant Ins Co, Henley Mfg Corp, Lufkin, Lufkin Block, Lumbermans Investment Corp, Signal Cos, Sunbelt Ins Co, Temple-Eastex, Temple-Inland Fin Svcs, Temple-Inland Properties; dir, chmn emeritus: Temple-Inland; exec vp, dir: Temple-White Co; mem exec comm, dir: Republic Bank Corp; pres bd regents, dir: TX Southeastern RR; pres, dir: John E Gray Inst; ptnr: Dallas Cowboys *NONPR AFFIL* dir: Lumberman Merchants Assn, Natl Forest Products Assn, Natl Park Fdn, Southern Forest Products Assn, St Michael Hosp Fdn; trust: Am Forest Products Assn
James R. Wash: secy, treas *B* 1930 *CURR EMPL* secy: Temple-Inland Forest Products Corp *CORP AFFIL* asst secy: Temple Inland

APPLICATION INFORMATION

Initial Approach: *Initial Contact:* brief letter *Include Information On:* description of the organization; amount requested; purpose for which funds are sought; recently audited financial statements; proof of tax-exempt status *When to Submit:* any time
Restrictions on Giving: Does not provide support to individuals; fraternal or veterans organizations; political or lobbying groups; or religious organizations.

GRANTS ANALYSIS

Total Grants: $2,519,404
Number of Grants: 1,327
Highest Grant: $249,868
Typical Range: $1,000 to $20,000
Disclosure Period: fiscal year ending June 30, 1992
Note: Recent grants are derived from a fiscal 1991 Form

990. The average grant excludes three grants totaling $469,187.

RECENT GRANTS

249,868 City of Diboll, Diboll, TX
119,116 Texas A&M University, College Station, TX
100,202 United Way, Dallas, TX
75,000 City of Jasper, Jasper, TX
45,000 Diboll Booster Club, Diboll, TX
43,466 University of Texas, Houston, TX
30,000 Alcohol and Drug Abuse Council, Lufkin, TX
29,000 Youth Young Adult Fellowship, Silsbee, TX
25,075 City of Pineland, Pineland, TX
25,000 Center for Housing Resources, Dallas, TX

Templeton Foundation, Herbert A.

CONTACT
Ruth B. Richmond
President
Herbert A. Templeton Fdn.
1717 S.W. Park Ave.
Portland, OR 97201
(503) 223-0036

FINANCIAL SUMMARY
Recent Giving: $285,400 (1991); $300,300 (1990); $298,350 (1989)
Assets: $5,804,144 (1991); $4,630,624 (1990); $4,712,644 (1989)
EIN: 93-0505586

CONTRIBUTIONS SUMMARY
Donor(s): the late Herbert A. Templeton, members of the Templeton family.
Typical Recipients: • *Arts & Humanities:* community arts, museums/galleries, music, opera, theater • *Civic & Public Affairs:* environmental affairs • *Education:* colleges & universities, public education (precollege) • *Religion:* churches, religious organizations • *Social Services:* child welfare, community service organizations, day care, drugs & alcohol, family services, united funds, youth organizations

Grant Types: emergency, general support, multiyear/continuing support, operating expenses, project, scholarship, and seed money
Geographic Distribution: limited to OR

GIVING OFFICERS
James E. Bryson: trust
Jane T. Bryson: vp, trust
John Bryson: mem
Bess Cristman: mem
John Robert Olsen: trust *B* Portland OR 1928 *ED* Univ OR 1950 *CURR EMPL* sr vp: Standard Co *CORP AFFIL* dir: Legacy Health Sys; sr vp: Standard Ins Co *NONPR AFFIL* chmn, mem exec comm: Holiday Park Med Ctr
Terrence Russell Pancoast: secy, treas *B* Everett WA 1942 *ED* Whitman Coll AB 1965; Harvard Univ LLB 1968 *CURR EMPL* ptnr: Stoel Rives Boley Fraser & Wyse *CORP AFFIL* ptnr: Stoel Rives Boley Fraser & Wyse *NONPR AFFIL* dir: OR Art Inst; dir (Portland OR): Planned Parenthood Assn; mem: Am Bar Assn, OR Bar Assn, World Affs Counc; mem bd overseers: Whitman Coll
Ruth B. Richmond: pres, trust
Hall Templeton: trust
Robert Templeton: mem
William B. Webber: trust

APPLICATION INFORMATION
Initial Approach: Send proposal describing program or project. Deadline is October 1.
Restrictions on Giving: Does not support individuals or provide loans.

OTHER THINGS TO KNOW
Publications: Program policy statement (including Application Guidelines)

GRANTS ANALYSIS
Number of Grants: 101
Highest Grant: $15,000
Typical Range: $1,000 to $3,000
Disclosure Period: 1991

RECENT GRANTS
15,000 United Way, Portland, OR
10,000 Albina Ministerial Alliance, Albina, OR — neighborhood connections
10,000 Augustana Lutheran Church, Portland, OR — peer support network

10,000 Beaverton School District 48, Beaverton, OR — home-school project

7,500 YWCA, Portland, OR

6,500 Oregon Museum of Science and Industry, Portland, OR

6,000 Salvation Army, Portland, OR

5,000 Boy Scouts of America, Columbia, OR

5,000 Ecumenical Ministries of Oregon, Portland, OR

5,000 Tri-County Youth Services Consortium, Portland, OR

Templeton Foundation, John

CONTACT
Ann Cameron
Treasurer
John Templeton Fdn.
900 Can-Tex Dr.
Sewanee, TN 37375-2835
(615) 598-0565

FINANCIAL SUMMARY
Recent Giving: $460,719 (fiscal 1992); $399,500 (fiscal 1991); $591,296 (fiscal 1990)
Assets: $4,931,414 (fiscal year ending March 31, 1992); $3,112,603 (fiscal 1991); $1,290,144 (fiscal 1990)
Gifts Received: $2,031,000 (fiscal 1992); $2,010,000 (fiscal 1991)
Fiscal Note: In fiscal 1992, contributions were received from John Templeton ($2,000,000)and Templeton Foundation, Inc. ($31,000).
EIN: 62-1322826

CONTRIBUTIONS SUMMARY
Donor(s): John Marks Templeton
Typical Recipients: • *Civic & Public Affairs:* public policy • *Education:* colleges & universities, religious education • *Health:* health organizations • *Religion:* churches, religious organizations • *Social Services:* family services
Grant Types: general support

GIVING OFFICERS
Ann Templeton Cameron: treas
Harvey Maxwell Templeton III: secy
John Marks Templeton, Jr.: pres

APPLICATION INFORMATION
Initial Approach: The foundation reports it only makes contributions to preselected charitable organizations.

GRANTS ANALYSIS
Number of Grants: 13
Highest Grant: $102,000
Typical Range: $13,000 to $25,000
Disclosure Period: fiscal year ending March 31, 1992

RECENT GRANTS
102,000 Association of Unity Churches, Lee's Summit, MO

96,000 Association of Unity Churches, Lee's Summit, MO

80,000 Association of Unity Churches, Lee's Summit, MO

44,745 Christian Medical and Dental Society, Richardson, TX — to support their training module

24,600 Eastern College, St. David's, PA — to complete a bibliography of research by scientists on spiritual subjects

23,360 Christian Medical and Dental Society, Richardson, TX — to support Phase I bibliography

20,000 American Family Association, Tupelo, MS — to support the Biblical ethic of decency in American Society with emphasis on TV and other media

20,000 Association of Unity Churches, Lee's Summit, MO — to support religion through radio media

17,500 Association of Unity Churches, Lee's Summit, MO — to promote Cadre of Patrons

13,412 Association of Unity Churches, Lee's Summit, MO — to promote Templeton institute

Tennant Co. / Tennant Co. Foundation

Sales: $198.6 million
Employees: 1,738
Headquarters: Minneapolis, MN
SIC Major Group: Chemicals & Allied Products and Industrial Machinery & Equipment

CONTACT
Paul Brunelle
President
Tennant Co. Fdn.
PO Box 1452
Minneapolis, MN 55440-1452
(617) 540-1207
Note: For scholarships, contact Tennant Scholarship Program, Citizens' Scholarship Foundation of America, Inc., P.O. Box 297, St. Peter, MN 56082.

FINANCIAL SUMMARY
Recent Giving: $292,954 (1990); $362,808 (1989)
Assets: $506,436 (1990); $85,638 (1989)
Gifts Received: $690,931 (1990); $424,787 (1989)
Fiscal Note: In 1990, contributions were received from Tennant Co.
EIN: 23-7297045

CONTRIBUTIONS SUMMARY
Typical Recipients: • *Arts & Humanities:* arts centers, museums/galleries, music, opera, public broadcasting, theater • *Civic & Public Affairs:* environmental affairs, women's affairs, zoos/botanical gardens • *Education:* colleges & universities, education funds, student aid • *Health:* health care cost containment, mental health, single-disease health associations • *Social Services:* child welfare, domestic violence, family planning, refugee assistance, united funds, youth organizations
Grant Types: capital, general support, matching, and scholarship
Geographic Distribution: primarily in areas where Tennant Co. employees live and work; support depends on the extent to which the applicant offers its services to Tennant Co. communities in Minneapolis and the Hennepin County, MN, area
Operating Locations: MN (Hennepin County, Minneapolis), NY (Niagara Falls)

CORP. OFFICERS
Roger L. Hale: *B* Plainfield NJ 1934 *ED* Brown Univ 1956; Harvard Univ Sch Bus Admin 1961 *CURR EMPL* pres, ceo, dir: Tennant Co *CORP AFFIL* dir: Dayton Hudson Corp, Donaldson Co, First Bank Sys, St Paul Cos Inc *NONPR AFFIL* dir: Bus Execs for Natl Security; mem: Machinery Allied Products Inst; vchmn: MN Bus Partnership
Richard A. Snyder: *CURR EMPL* vp, cfo, treas: Tennant Co

GIVING OFFICERS
Richard Adams: dir
Chandlee M. Barksdale: dir
Paul E. Brunelle: pres
Roger Loucks Hale: dir *B* Plainfield NJ 1934 *ED* Brown Univ BA 1956; Harvard Univ MBA 1961 *CURR EMPL* pres, ceo, dir: Tennant Co *CORP AFFIL* dir: Dayton Hudson Corp, Donaldson Co, First Bank Sys, MN Bus Partnership, St Paul Cos; pres, ceo, dir: Tennant Co *NONPR AFFIL* co-chmn: MN Quality Counc; dir: Bus Execs for Natl Security; mem: Machinery Allied Products Inst
George Tennant Pennock: dir *B* Minneapolis MN 1912 *ED* Univ MN BBA 1934 *CORP AFFIL* dir: Tennant Co *NONPR AFFIL* life dir: Minneapolis Orchestra Assn
Joseph A. Shaw: treas, dir

APPLICATION INFORMATION
Initial Approach: Send proposal or call requesting guidelines. Deadlines are four weeks prior to board meetings on February 16, May 4, September 10, and December 14. Scholarship deadline for children of employees is March 15-May 15.
Restrictions on Giving: Does not support agencies funded through umbrella organizations, religious organizations for religious purposes. No support for travel, benefit tickets, or courtesy advertising. Does not support political organizations or national organizations without active local chapters.

OTHER THINGS TO KNOW
Publications: Annual Report (including Application Guidelines)

GRANTS ANALYSIS
Number of Grants: 178
Highest Grant: $27,600
Typical Range: $1,000 to $3,000
Disclosure Period: 1990
Note: Number, size, and range of grants figures do not include matching gifts.

RECENT GRANTS
27,600 United Way, Minneapolis, MN
9,000 Minnesota Private College Fund, St. Paul, MN
8,500 Minnesota Opera, St. Paul, MN
8,350 College of St. Thomas, St. Paul, MN
6,000 Citizens Scholarship Foundation of America, St. Peter, MN
5,500 Minnesota Orchestral Association, Minneapolis, MN
5,100 Walker Art Center, Minneapolis, MN
5,000 Sharing and Caring Hands, St. Paul, MN
4,500 Guthrie Theater, Minneapolis, MN
4,200 Senior Resources, Minneapolis, MN

Tenneco
Sales: $13.6 billion
Parent Company: Tenneco, Inc.
Headquarters: Houston, TX
SIC Major Group: Chemicals & Allied Products, Holding & Other Investment Offices, Industrial Machinery & Equipment, and Pipelines Except Natural Gas

CONTACT
Jo Ann Swinney
Director, Community Affairs
Tenneco Inc.
PO Box 2511
Houston, TX 77252
(713) 757-3930
Note: Mrs. Swinney handles Houston area and national activities; all other requests handled by contributions coordinator at the divisional company operating most prominently in the geographic area.

FINANCIAL SUMMARY
Recent Giving: $4,801,050 (1993 est.); $5,042,067 (1992); $7,191,000 (1991)
Assets: $400,000 (1992); $400,000 (1991); $202,000 (1990)

Fiscal Note: Company gives directly. Figures include international contributions.

CONTRIBUTIONS SUMMARY
Typical Recipients: • *Arts & Humanities:* arts associations, arts centers, arts festivals, arts funds, community arts, dance, history/historic preservation, libraries, museums/galleries, music, opera, performing arts, public broadcasting, theater, visual arts • *Civic & Public Affairs:* business/free enterprise, environmental affairs, ethnic/minority organizations, housing, law & justice, professional & trade associations, public policy, safety, urban & community affairs, women's affairs, zoos/botanical gardens • *Education:* business education, career/vocational education, colleges & universities, community & junior colleges, economic education, education associations, education funds, engineering education, faculty development, literacy, minority education, public education (precollege), science/technology education, student aid • *Health:* emergency/ambulance services, health organizations, hospices, hospitals, medical research, mental health, nutrition & health maintenance, single-disease health associations • *Science:* science exhibits & fairs • *Social Services:* aged, animal protection, community centers, community service organizations, delinquency & crime, disabled, drugs & alcohol, emergency relief, employment/job training, food/clothing distribution, shelters/homelessness, united funds, volunteer services, youth organizations

Grant Types: capital, challenge, department, fellowship, professorship, project, research, and scholarship

Nonmonetary Support Types: cause-related marketing & promotion, donated equipment, donated products, in-kind services, loaned employees, and loaned executives

Note: In 1992, estimated value of nonmonetary support was $350,000. This amount is not included in the figure above. Nonmonetary support is suppliedby the company. Contact person for this support is Ms. Swinney.

Geographic Distribution: near operating locations; limited nationally

Operating Locations: CT (Hartford), IL (Chicago, Deerfield, Evanston, Lincolnshire, Wheeling), IN (Blufton), KS (Wichita), LA (Lafayette, Westwego), MI (Monroe), NC (Arden), ND (Fargo, Valley City), NJ (Norwood, Old Tappon, Orange), OH (Perry), OK (Pryor), PA (Pittsburgh, Springfield), TN (Counce, Greeneville, Knoxville, Nashville), TX (Houston), VA (Charlottesville, Newport News), WA (Brookfield), WI (Racine, Wausau)

CORP. OFFICERS
Dana George Mead: *B* Cresco IA 1936 *CURR EMPL* pres, coo, dir: Tenneco
Michael H. Walsh: *B* Binghamton NY 1942 *CURR EMPL* chmn, ceo: Tenneco *NONPR AFFIL* mem: San Diego Bar Assn, St Bar CA; trust: Stanford Univ

GIVING OFFICERS
Jo Ann Swinney: *CURR EMPL* dir (community affairs): Tenneco

APPLICATION INFORMATION
Initial Approach: *Initial Contact:* brief letter or proposal on organization's letterhead to contributions coordinator at divisional company operating most prominently in the geographic area; for Houston area and national activities, send brief letter or proposal to Jo Ann Swinney *Include Information On:* description of the organization, amount requested, purpose for which funds are sought, proof of tax-exempt status, financial report, board of directors, budget for project *When to Submit:* prior to August 15
Restrictions on Giving: Company does not give to political or lobbying groups; religious organizations; or individuals

OTHER THINGS TO KNOW
Each operating location administers its own contributions program. Together these local programs account for around 50% of overall Tenneco giving. Tenneco has considered reactivating the Tenneco Foundation

for educational/scholarship purposes.

GRANTS ANALYSIS
Total Grants: $5,042,067
Highest Grant: $475,000
Typical Range: $1,000 to $10,000
Disclosure Period: 1992
Note: Recent grants are derived from a 1992 grants list.

RECENT GRANTS
250,000 Houston Host Committee Fund, Houston, TX — for construction cost inside the Astrodome for GOP national convention
250,000 Houston Host Committee Fund, Houston, TX — for construction cost inside the Astrodome for GOP national convention

Tension Envelope Corp. / Tension Envelope Foundation
Sales: $155.0 million
Employees: 1,750
Headquarters: Kansas City, MO
SIC Major Group: Paper & Allied Products

CONTACT
Eliot S. Berkley
Secretary
Tension Envelope Foundation
819 East 19th St., 5th Fl.
Kansas City, MO 64108
(816) 471-3800

FINANCIAL SUMMARY
Recent Giving: $295,362 (1989)
Assets: $2,680,911 (1989)
EIN: 44-6012554

CONTRIBUTIONS SUMMARY
Typical Recipients: • *Arts & Humanities:* arts institutes, community arts • *Civic & Public Affairs:* better government, environmental affairs • *Education:* colleges & universities • *Religion:* religious organizations • *Social Services:* child welfare, community service organizations, disabled, united funds, youth organizations
Grant Types: general support
Geographic Distribution: focus on MO

Operating Locations: CA (Santa Fe Springs), IA (Des Moines), KS (Marysville), MN (Minneapolis), MO (Kansas City, St. Louis), NC (Winston-Salem), NJ (Hackensack), TN (Memphis), TX (Fort Worth)
Note: Listing includes plant locations.

CORP. OFFICERS
William S. Berkley: *CURR EMPL* pres, ceo, dir: Tension Envelope Corp

GIVING OFFICERS
E. Bertram Berkley: treas
Eliot S. Berkley: secy
Richard L. Berkley: pres
Walter L. Hiersteiner: vp
Abraham E. Margolin: dir

APPLICATION INFORMATION
Initial Approach: Send brief letter describing program. There are no deadlines.

GRANTS ANALYSIS
Number of Grants: 155
Highest Grant: $30,094
Typical Range: $250 to $1,000
Disclosure Period: 1989

RECENT GRANTS
30,094 Jewish Federation of Kansas City, Kansas City, MO
30,094 Jewish Federation of Kansas City, Kansas City, MO
20,000 United Way, Kansas City, MO
20,000 United Way, Kansas City, MO
8,000 UMKC New Horizons, Iowa City, IA
5,000 Smith College, Northhampton, MA
4,500 Jewish Federation of Des Moines, Des Moines, IA
3,000 Smith College, Northhampton, MA
2,875 United Way, Des Moines, IA
2,500 Nelson Gallery Foundation, Kansas City, MO

Teradyne, Inc.
Sales: $508.9 million
Employees: 4,300
Headquarters: Boston, MA
SIC Major Group: Electronic & Other Electrical Equipment and Instruments & Related Products

CONTACT
Frederick Van Veen
Vice President, Corporate Relations
Teradyne, Inc.
321 Harrison Ave.
Boston, MA 02118
(617) 482-2700

CONTRIBUTIONS SUMMARY
Operating Locations: CA (Agoura Hills, Walnut Creek), IL (Deerfield), MA (Boston), NH (Nashua)
Note: Seven divisions of Teradyne Inc. can be found in operating cities.

CORP. OFFICERS
Alexander V. d'Arbeloff: *B* New Rochelle NY 1928 *ED* MA Inst Tech BS *CURR EMPL* co-fdr, chmn, pres: Teradyne *CORP AFFIL* dir: BTU Intl, Stratus Computer *NONPR AFFIL* mem corp: MA Inst Tech; trust, mem corp: MA Gen Hosp

OTHER THINGS TO KNOW
Publications: Guidelines Sheet

Terner Foundation

CONTACT
Emmanuel M. Terner
Chairman
Terner Fdn.
PO Box 340
Oakhurst, NJ 07755

FINANCIAL SUMMARY
Recent Giving: $676,335 (fiscal 1991); $902,320 (fiscal 1990); $202,000 (fiscal 1988)
Assets: $4,841,047 (fiscal year ending July 31, 1991); $4,837,152 (fiscal 1990); $2,701,774 (fiscal 1988)
Gifts Received: $300,000 (fiscal 1991)
EIN: 22-1605265

CONTRIBUTIONS SUMMARY
Donor(s): Emmanuel M. Terner, Mathida Terner
Typical Recipients: • *Arts & Humanities:* cinema, museums/galleries • *Civic & Public Affairs:* municipalities • *Education:* religious education • *Health:* geriatric health, health organizations, hospitals, medical research, mental health, single-disease health associations • *Social Services:* child welfare, community serv-

ice organizations, disabled, united funds, youth organizations
Grant Types: general support

GIVING OFFICERS
Nancy Behrman: vp
Elaine Cooper: vp, secy
Carol Lederman: vp
Winifred A. Packard: vp
Emmanuel M Terner: chmn
Mathilda Terner: pres, treas

APPLICATION INFORMATION
Initial Approach: Send brief letter of inquiry describing program. There are no deadlines.

GRANTS ANALYSIS
Number of Grants: 95
Highest Grant: $300,000
Typical Range: $100 to $10,000
Disclosure Period: fiscal year ending July 31, 1991

RECENT GRANTS
300,000 St. Marys Hospital Foundation
25,000 Brown University, Providence, RI
25,000 Hospice, Palm Beach, FL
25,000 Solomon R. Guggenheim Museum, New York, NY
25,000 Tufts University School of Medicine, Medford, MA
22,000 Monmouth Health Care Foundation, Monmouth, NJ
12,100 United Jewish Appeal Federation of Jewish Philanthropies, New York, NY
12,000 American Jewish Committee
10,000 Joseph L. Morse Geriatric Center, West Palm Beach, FL
10,000 Rutgers Foundation, New Brunswick, NJ

Terra Industries
Sales: $1.06 billion
Employees: 6,204
Headquarters: Sioux City, IA
SIC Major Group: Chemicals & Allied Products, Coal Mining, Holding & Other Investment Offices, and Metal Mining

CONTACT
Jane Rice
Corporate Secretary
Terra Industries
600 Fourth St.
Sioux City, IA 51101
(712) 277-1340

CONTRIBUTIONS SUMMARY
Supports civic affairs, libraries, literacy, and voluntarism.
Typical Recipients: • *Civic & Public Affairs:* general • *Education:* literacy • *Social Services:* volunteer services
Operating Locations: IA (Sioux City)
Note: company operates over 300 retail centers in 30 states

CORP. OFFICERS
Burton M. Joyce: *CURR EMPL* pres, ceo, dir: piration Resources Corp
Reuben F. Richards: *B* New York NY 1929 *ED* Harvard Univ 1952 *CURR EMPL* chmn, dir: Engelhard Corp *CORP AFFIL* chmn: Inspiration Resources Corp, Minorco USA; chmn, pres, ceo, dir: Inspiration Resources Corp; dir: Adobe Resources Corp, Ecolab, Independence Mining Co, Potlatch Corp

APPLICATION INFORMATION
Initial Approach: Send brief letter of inquiry and descriptive information.

Terry Foundation

CONTACT
Howard L. Terry
Trustee
Terry Fdn.
600 Jefferson, Ste. 1600
Houston, TX 77002

FINANCIAL SUMMARY
Recent Giving: $439,836 (1991); $373,000 (1990); $356,250 (1989)
Assets: $9,065,538 (1991); $6,530,359 (1990); $4,877,401 (1989)
Gifts Received: $1,182,500 (1991); $1,771,455 (1990); $1,582,071 (1989)
Fiscal Note: In 1991, contributions were received from H. L. Terry.
EIN: 76-0224312

CONTRIBUTIONS SUMMARY
Donor(s): Howard L. Terry

Typical Recipients: • *Education:* agricultural education, colleges & universities
Grant Types: scholarship
Geographic Distribution: limited to TX

GIVING OFFICERS
Rhett Campbell: trust
Carter Overton: trust
Darrell K. Royal: trust *B* Hollis OK 1924 *ED* Univ OK BS 1950 *NONPR AFFIL* asst to pres: Univ TX
John W. Storms: trust
Howard L. Terry: trust *CORP AFFIL* dir: First Interstate Bank TX

APPLICATION INFORMATION
Initial Approach: Contact the University of Texas at Austin and Texas A&M University for deadlines. Application form required.

GRANTS ANALYSIS
Number of Grants: 2
Highest Grant: $279,086
Disclosure Period: 1991

RECENT GRANTS
279,086 University of Texas, Austin, TX — scholarships
160,750 Texas A&M University, College Station, TX

Terry Foundation, C. Herman

CONTACT
C. Herman Terry Fdn.
1301 Gulf Life Dr., Ste. 2216
Jacksonville, FL 32207

FINANCIAL SUMMARY
Assets: $2,089,924 (1989)
EIN: 59-2241642

CONTRIBUTIONS SUMMARY
Donor(s): C. Herman Terry
Typical Recipients: • *Religion:* churches, religious organizations • *Social Services:* community service organizations, youth organizations
Grant Types: general support

GIVING OFFICERS
Kenneth Alan Barnebey: trust *B* Fremont NE 1931 *ED* Univ MD 1950; Univ Tampa 1951; Univ WA BA 1953; Harvard Univ 1977 *CORP AFFIL* dir: Community Bank Holding Co, Dependable Ins Group Inc Am, Exmart *NONPR AFFIL* adv

counc: FL St Univ; dir: Am Academy Achievement, Asolo St Theatre, Manatee Jr Coll; mem: Am Mgmt Assn, FL Canners Assn, FL Counc 100, Manatee County Chamber Commerce, Natl Assn Mfrs
Hugh T. Nelson: trust
C. Herman Terry: trust
Mary Virginia Terry: trust
James H. Winston: trust

APPLICATION INFORMATION
Initial Approach: Send brief letter describing program. There are no deadlines.

Tesoro Petroleum Corp.
Revenue: $996.5 million
Employees: 1,669
Headquarters: San Antonio, TX
SIC Major Group: Oil & Gas Extraction, Petroleum & Coal Products, and Wholesale Trade—Nondurable Goods

CONTACT
James Duncan
Vice President of Corporate Development
Tesoro Petroleum Corp.
8700 Tesoro Dr.
San Antonio, TX 78217
(210) 828-8484

FINANCIAL SUMMARY
Fiscal Note: Annual Giving Range: $50,000 to $100,000

CONTRIBUTIONS SUMMARY
Priorities are health and human services, and education. Also support the arts, civic affairs, and science organizations.
Typical Recipients: • *Arts & Humanities:* arts associations • *Civic & Public Affairs:* economic development • *Education:* business education • *Health:* health organizations • *Social Services:* aged
Grant Types: general support, matching, and scholarship
Nonmonetary Support Types: donated equipment, in-kind services, loaned employees, and loaned executives
Geographic Distribution: communities where company employees live
Operating Locations: AK (Anchorage), LA (Harahan), TX (San Antonio)

CORP. OFFICERS
Michael Burke: *CURR EMPL* pres, ceo: Tesoro Petroleum Corp

APPLICATION INFORMATION
Initial Approach: brief letter of inquiry
Include Information On: description of the organization, amount requested, purpose of funds sought, audited financial statement, and proof of tax-exempt status
When to Submit: any time

GRANTS ANALYSIS
Typical Range: $500 to $2,000

Tetley, Inc.
Sales: $325.0 million
Employees: 1,325
Headquarters: Shelton, CT
SIC Major Group: Food & Kindred Products

CONTACT
Dorothy Young
Contributions Committee
Tetley, Inc.
100 Commerce Dr.
Shelton, CT 06484
(203) 929-9200

FINANCIAL SUMMARY
Recent Giving: $100,000 (1990); $60,000 (1989); $50,000 (1988)

CONTRIBUTIONS SUMMARY
Emphasis of support goes to health; also funds the arts, social services, and civic affairs. Colleges and universities are supported via an educational matching grant program. Limited support to local chapters of national organizations. Company's charitable contributions policy states, "It is the policy of the Company to participate in the betterment of the society in which the Company conducts its business affairs. The Company acknowledges its responsibiliy to assist in the preservation of values which form the basis of the free enterprise system. The Company also acknowledges its commitment to help the citizens of our society fulfill their human needs. A means by which the Company can fulfill its social responsibility and act upon its commitment is to make cash contributions to charitable, not-for-profit organizations

which engage in activities consistent with the Company's stated policy."
Typical Recipients: • *Arts & Humanities:* arts centers, community arts, dance, history/historic preservation, libraries, museums/galleries, music, performing arts, public broadcasting • *Civic & Public Affairs:* better government, economic development, safety • *Education:* colleges & universities • *Health:* hospitals, medical research, mental health, pediatric health, single-disease health associations • *Social Services:* aged, community centers, community service organizations, domestic violence, drugs & alcohol, united funds, youth organizations
Grant Types: general support, matching, and multiyear/continuing support
Nonmonetary Support Types: loaned employees
Geographic Distribution: primarily near headquarters and operating locations; limited support to national organizations
Operating Locations: CT (Shelton), FL, GA, MO, NJ, NY, PA

CORP. OFFICERS
Henry F. McInerney: *CURR EMPL* ceo, pres: Tetley

GIVING OFFICERS
Pat Leary: *CURR EMPL* contact: Tetley

APPLICATION INFORMATION
Initial Approach: Send letter in spring or fall including a description of the organization, amount and purpose of funds sought, and proof of tax-exempt status.

Restrictions on Giving: Program does not support political or religious groups; groups which receive contributions from United Way offices to which the company has made a contribution; or groups that do not qualify as exempt under section 501 (c)(3) of the Internal Revenue Code, unless there is an overriding community interest involved.

GRANTS ANALYSIS
Typical Range: $100 to $5,000

Teubert Charitable Trust, James H. and Alice

CONTACT
Jimelle Bowen
Executive Director
James H. and Alice Teubert
Charitable Trust
PO Box 2131
Huntington, WV 25701
(304) 525-6337

FINANCIAL SUMMARY
Recent Giving: $529,236 (fiscal 1992); $606,944 (fiscal 1990); $409,100 (fiscal 1989)
Assets: $14,323,946 (fiscal year ending September 30, 1992); $13,339,992 (fiscal 1990); $11,385,577 (fiscal 1989)
EIN: 55-6101813

CONTRIBUTIONS SUMMARY
Typical Recipients: • *Arts & Humanities:* libraries • *Education:* colleges & universities, public education (precollege), special education • *Health:* hospitals • *Social Services:* disabled, recreation & athletics, youth organizations
Grant Types: general support
Geographic Distribution: focus on Cabell and Wayne Counties, WV

GIVING OFFICERS
Jimelle Bowen: exec dir

APPLICATION INFORMATION
Initial Approach: Send letter requesting application form. Deadlines are October 1 and March 1. Board meets in April and November.

GRANTS ANALYSIS
Number of Grants: 12
Highest Grant: $338,819
Typical Range: $5,000 to $20,000
Disclosure Period: fiscal year ending September 30, 1992

RECENT GRANTS
338,819   Cabell Wayne Association of Blind, Huntington, WV
59,283   West Virginia Lions Sight Conservation Foundation, Huntington, WV
40,668   Marshall University Research, Huntington, WV
40,000   Blind Ambition, Huntington, WV
34,492   Cabell County Public Schools, Huntington, WV
11,045   YMCA, Huntington, WV
10,000   West Virginia School for the Deaf and Blind, Huntington, WV
6,603   Marshall University, Huntington, WV
5,000   Little League of Huntington, Huntington, WV
4,550   St. Mary's Hospital Link to Life, Huntington, WV

Texaco / Texaco Foundation

Sales: $37.13 billion
Employees: 54,481
Headquarters: Harrison, NY
SIC Major Group: Oil & Gas Extraction, Petroleum & Coal Products, Pipelines Except Natural Gas, and Wholesale Trade—Nondurable Goods

CONTACT
C. B. Davidson
President
Texaco Fdn.
2000 Westchester Ave.
White Plains, NY 10650
(914) 253-4150

FINANCIAL SUMMARY
Recent Giving: $11,600,000 (1992 approx.); $11,081,269 (1991); $9,421,189 (1990)
Assets: $36,314,975 (1991); $48,600,000 (1989)
Fiscal Note: Figures reflect foundation giving only. In 1991, company gave $13,380,918 in direct grants.
EIN: 13-3007516

CONTRIBUTIONS SUMMARY
Typical Recipients: • *Arts & Humanities:* arts centers, arts festivals, arts funds, community arts, dance, ethnic arts, history/historic preservation, libraries, museums/galleries, music, opera, performing arts, public broadcasting • *Civic & Public Affairs:* business/free enterprise, civil rights, economics, environmental affairs, international affairs, law & justice, public policy, safety, urban & community affairs, women's affairs • *Education:* business education, career/vocational education, colleges & universities, economic education, education associations, education funds, engineering education, health & physical education, international studies, journalism education, legal education, medical education, minority education, science/technology education, social sciences education, special education, student aid • *Health:* health organizations, hospices, hospitals, medical rehabilitation, medical research, medical training, public health • *International:* foreign educational institutions, international development/relief, international health care • *Science:* scientific organizations • *Social Services:* aged, child welfare, community centers, community service organizations, delinquency & crime, disabled, drugs & alcohol, employment/job training, legal aid, united funds, volunteer services, youth organizations
Grant Types: challenge, department, employee matching gifts, fellowship, general support, project, research, and scholarship
Geographic Distribution: national organizations and organizations near operating locations
Operating Locations: CA (Los Angeles, Universal City), CO (Denver), FL (Coral Gables), KS (North Wichita, Wichita), LA (New Orleans), NY (White Plains), OK (Tulsa), PR (San Juan), TX (Bellaire, Houston, Port Arthur)
Note: Also operates internationally.

CORP. OFFICERS
Alfred Charles DeCrane, Jr.: *B* Cleveland OH 1931 *ED* Univ Notre Dame BA 1953; Georgetown Univ JD 1959 *CURR EMPL* chmn: Texaco *CORP AFFIL* dir: CIGNA Corp *NONPR AFFIL* dir: Am Petroleum Inst; mem: Am Bar Assn; trust: Conf Bd, Counc Econ Devel, Univ Notre Dame
James Wesley Kinnear III: *B* Pittsburgh PA 1928 *ED* US Naval Academy BS 1950 *CURR EMPL* pres, ceo, dir: Texaco *CORP AFFIL* dir: ASARCO, Corning Inc; vchmn: Texaco USA *NONPR AFFIL* dir: Am Petroleum Inst, Bus Counc NY; mem: Bus Counc, Bus Roundtable, US Naval Inst; pres bd trusts: St Pauls Sch; trust: Natl Petroleum Counc

GIVING OFFICERS
C. A. Brooks: asst secy
D. C. Crikelair: treas
Carl Barry Davidson: pres, dir *B* Trenton NJ 1933 *ED* Rutgers Univ AB 1954; Rutgers Univ LLB 1957 *CURR EMPL* vp, corp secy: Texaco *NONPR AFFIL* mem: Am Soc Corp Secs Inc
Patrick J. Lynch: dir *B* Jersey City NJ 1937 *ED* Iona Coll BBA 1959 *CURR EMPL* comptr, vp: Texaco *NONPR AFFIL* mem: Fin Execs Inst
Maria Mike-Mayer: secy
George Parker, Jr.: dir *B* Tulsa OK 1920 *ED* Princeton Univ BA 1943; Univ Michigan LLB 1949 *CORP AFFIL* dir: Texaco *NONPR AFFIL* fellow: JP Morgan Library; mem: Chevalier Des Arts et des Lettres, Phi Delta Phi, Societe des Amis De Versailles; sustaining mem: Dallas Mus Fine Arts; vp: International Committee La Demure Historique
L. Stanton Williams: dir

APPLICATION INFORMATION
Initial Approach: *Initial Contact:* cover letter highlighting the following: description, timetable, and objectives of project; reason why Texaco is appropriate donor; amount requested; any prior history of Texaco funding; Texaco operations in vicinity; part played in applicant's organization by Texaco employee or director volunteers; description of how Texaco's support will be acknowledged *Note:* If of local or regional scope, apply directly to Community Relations Committee at local plant. *Include Information On:* background in the form of enclosures describing the following: budget for project or event with reasonable breakout of costs and sources already committed or expected; size and composition of the population to be served by the project; explanation of how efforts do not duplicate efforts of other agencies or institutions in the same or related fields; instrument and method of evaluating success; description of overall purpose and objectives of organization; list of names and primary professional affiliations of members of organization's board of trustees; copy of certification of IRS Code Section 501(c)(3) tax-exempt status; most recently audited financial statement; organization's gen-

eral funding sources by category and, if available, a list of contributors and the size of their contributions *When to Submit:* any time

Restrictions on Giving: The foundation generally does not provide funds for unrestricted operating support or capital campaigns. Giving is directed more toward specific activities, programs, and events.

The foundation normally does not support individuals; private foundations; non tax-exempt organizations; social functions, commemorative journals, or meetings; religious, fraternal, social, or veterans organizations; political or partisan organizations or candidates; endowments; organizations attempting to influence legislation or elections; or organizations established to influence the outcome of any specific election or to carry on any voter-registration drive.

GRANTS ANALYSIS

Total Grants: $11,081,269
Number of Grants: 478*
Highest Grant: $500,000*
Typical Range: $1,000 to $5,000 and $10,000 to $25,000
Disclosure Period: 1991
Note: Number of grants and highest grant do not include the following: $1,564,300 to united funds nationwide; multi-year grants to Metropolitan Opera (1991-93) for $1,500,000 and the United Negro College Fund (1991-94) for $1,000,000; $693,900 to Texaco Foundation Scholarship Program; or $288,019 to Texaco Star Academic Challenge and Championship Programs. Recent grants are derived from a 1991 Form 990.

RECENT GRANTS

1,564,300 United Funds
500,000 Metropolitan Opera Association, New York, NY
400,000 United Negro College Fund, New York, NY
200,000 Louisiana State University, Environmental Engineering, Baton Rouge, LA
150,000 Memorial Sloan-Kettering Cancer Society, New York, NY
106,400 Texas A&M University, Petroleum Engineering Department, College Station, TX
100,000 American Forestry Association, Washington, DC
100,000 California Institute of Technology, Pasadena, CA
100,000 Massachusetts Institute of Technology, Chemical Engineering Department, Cambridge, MA
100,000 Texas Children's Hospital, Houston, TX

Texas Commerce Bank Houston, N.A. / Texas Commerce Bank Houston Foundation

Employees: 4,000
Parent Company: Texas Commerce Bancshares
Headquarters: Houston, TX
SIC Major Group: Depository Institutions

CONTACT

Glenn Baird
Community Relations Director
Texas Commerce Bank-Houston, N.A.
PO Box 2558
Houston, TX 77252
(713) 216-4004

FINANCIAL SUMMARY

Recent Giving: $1,163,000 (1993 est.); $1,163,432 (1992); $1,000,566 (1991)
Assets: $539,071 (1991); $644,000 (1989)
Gifts Received: $1,023,781 (1991)
Fiscal Note: Total includes contributions by subsidiaries. Company gives primarily through the foundation, and reports that the budget for direct giving programs is $40,000.
EIN: 74-6036696

CONTRIBUTIONS SUMMARY

Typical Recipients: • *Arts & Humanities:* arts associations, arts centers, arts funds, community arts, history/historic preservation, libraries, museums/galleries, music, opera, performing arts, public broadcasting, theater • *Civic & Public Affairs:* economic development, economics, ethnic/minority organizations,
housing, nonprofit management, women's affairs, zoos/botanical gardens • *Education:* business education, colleges & universities, education funds, literacy, minority education • *Health:* health organizations, hospices, hospitals, medical research, medical training, mental health, pediatric health, single-disease health associations • *Science:* science exhibits & fairs • *Social Services:* aged, community service organizations, delinquency & crime, disabled, drugs & alcohol, employment/job training, food/clothing distribution, homes, recreation & athletics, shelters/homelessness, united funds, volunteer services, youth organizations

Grant Types: capital, employee matching gifts, general support, professorship, and project

Nonmonetary Support Types: in-kind services

Note: Value of noncash support is unavailable and is not included in figures above.

Geographic Distribution: limited to Houston, TX
Operating Locations: TX (Houston)

CORP. OFFICERS

Marc J. Shapiro: *B* Houston TX 1947 *ED* Harvard Univ 1969; Stanford Univ 1971 *CURR EMPL* chmn, pres, ceo: TX Commerce Bank Houston

GIVING OFFICERS

Glenn Baird: community relations dir *CURR EMPL* community rels coordinator: TX Commerce Bank Houston
Marilyn Chappelear: acct mgr
Beverly McCaskill: vp, treas
Shelby Rogers: secy *B* Jackson MS 1949 *CURR EMPL* sr vp, gen couns, dir regulatory affairs: TX Commerce Bankshares *NONPR AFFIL* mem: Am Bar Assn
Marc J. Shapiro: trust *CURR EMPL* chmn, pres, ceo: TX Commerce Bank Houston (see above)
Marshall Clay Tyndall: exec vp *B* Wilmington DE 1943 *CURR EMPL* exec vp: TX Commerce Bank *CORP AFFIL* vp mktg: TX Commerce Bancshares Inc *NONPR AFFIL* chmn: Greater Houston Convention & Visitors Bur; dir: Houston Grand Opera, Houston Symphony; mem: Bank Mktg
Assn, Houston Chamber Commerce, TX Bankers Assn

APPLICATION INFORMATION

Initial Approach: *Initial Contact:* proposal *Include Information On:* description of the organization, budget, amount requested, purpose for which funds are sought, recently audited financial statement, proof of tax-exempt status, list of board members, and recent contributions *When to Submit:* by the 15th of each month

Restrictions on Giving: Grants are not made to support political or lobbying groups, or individuals.

GRANTS ANALYSIS

Total Grants: $1,163,432
Number of Grants: 272
Highest Grant: $425,000*
Typical Range: $500 to $5,000
Disclosure Period: 1992
Note: The highest grant represents a United Way grant. The next highest grant was $20,000. Recent grants are derived from a 1991 Form 990. Assets are from 1991.

RECENT GRANTS

405,000 United Way of the Texas Gulf Coast, Houston, TX
72,000 New Foundation, Houston, TX
30,000 Houston Committee for Private Sector Initiatives, Houston, TX
15,000 Salvation Army - Houston Cammand, Houston, TX
14,535 Children's Museum of Houston, Houston, TX
11,863 Boy Scouts of America Sam Houston Area Council, Houston, TX
10,400 Houston Ballet Foundation, Houston, TX
10,250 Houston Citizens Chamber of Commerce, Houston, TX
10,000 Baylor College of Medicine, Houston, TX
10,000 Depelchin Children's Center Cullen Bayou Place, Houston, TX

Texas Energy Museum

CONTACT
Texas Energy Museum
801 Main Street
Beaumont, TX 77701-3548

FINANCIAL SUMMARY
Recent Giving: $0 (1990)
Assets: $2,915,703 (1990)
Gifts Received: $458,225 (1990)
Fiscal Note: 1990 contributions received from Chevron USA ($52,800), City of Beaumont ($154,800), Harles & Montgomery ($5,000), Rosine B. McFaddin ($10,000), Stark Foundation ($20,000), Texaco Philanthropic Foundation ($63,850), TEM Endowment income ($121,274), and Rosine M. Wilson ($11,602).
EIN: 76-0225927

GIVING OFFICERS
Melanie Dishman, Jr.: secy
Billy Franklin: pres
David Hitt, Jr.: treas
Ted E. Moor, Jr.: vp

GRANTS ANALYSIS
Total Grants: $0
Disclosure Period: 1990

Texas Gas Transmission Corp.
Sales: $464.0 million
Employees: 1,185
Parent Company: Transco Energy
Headquarters: Owensboro, KY
SIC Major Group: Electric, Gas & Sanitary Services

CONTACT
Thomas E. Lewis
Director, Company
  Communications
Texas Gas Transmission Corp.
3800 Frederica St.
Owensboro, KY 42301
(502) 926-8686

FINANCIAL SUMMARY
Recent Giving: $950,000 (1993 est.); $950,000 (1992); $1,050,000 (1991)

CONTRIBUTIONS SUMMARY
Typical Recipients: • *Arts & Humanities:* arts associations, arts centers, arts festivals, arts funds, community arts, dance, museums/galleries, music, theater • *Civic & Public Affairs:* better government, economic development,

economics, ethnic/minority organizations, housing, urban & community affairs • *Education:* business education, colleges & universities, community & junior colleges • *Health:* general • *Social Services:* aged, child welfare, community service organizations, counseling, day care, delinquency & crime, disabled, domestic violence, drugs & alcohol, food/clothing distribution, recreation & athletics, shelters/homelessness, united funds, volunteer services, youth organizations
Grant Types: general support, matching, multiyear/continuing support, and operating expenses
Nonmonetary Support Types: donated equipment, donated products, loaned employees, and workplace solicitation
Geographic Distribution: headquarters and operating locations
Operating Locations: KY (Owensboro)

CORP. OFFICERS
Robert W. Best: *B* Nappanee IN 1946 *ED* IN St Univ BS 1968; IN Univ JD 1974 *CURR EMPL* pres, ceo: Texas Gas Transmission Corp *CORP AFFIL* dir: Cardinal Fed Savings Bank *NONPR AFFIL* dir: Brescia Coll, KY-IN Coll Fund, Leadership Owensboro, Mercy Hosp, Un Way Owensboro—Daveiss County; mem: Am Bar Assn, Fed Energy Bar Assn, IN Bar Assn, KY Bar Assn, KY Econ Devel Corp; mem exec comm: Strategies Tomorrow

GIVING OFFICERS
Thomas E. Lewis: *CURR EMPL* dir co commun: TX Gas Transmission Corp

APPLICATION INFORMATION
Initial Approach: *Initial Contact:* brief letter of inquiry *Include Information On:* purpose of funds sought and proof of tax-exempt status *When to Submit:* any time
Restrictions on Giving: Company does not support religious organizations for sectarian purposes.

Texas Industries, Inc. / Texas Industries Foundation
Sales: $654.4 million
Employees: 2,800
Headquarters: Dallas, TX
SIC Major Group: Primary Metal Industries and Stone, Clay & Glass Products

CONTACT
Texas Industries, Inc.
7610 Stemmons Fwy., Ste. 200
Dallas, TX 75247
(214) 647-6700

FINANCIAL SUMMARY
Recent Giving: $20,077 (1991); $25,915 (1990); $136,315 (1989)
Assets: $1,989 (1991); $622 (1990)
Gifts Received: $21,454 (1991); $25,915 (1990)
Fiscal Note: In 1991, contributions were received from Texas Industries.
EIN: 75-6043179

CONTRIBUTIONS SUMMARY
Typical Recipients: • *Education:* student aid
Grant Types: general support and scholarship
Geographic Distribution: in headquarters and operating communities
Operating Locations: LA (Alexandria, Bossier City, Harahan, Monroe), TX (Austin, Dallas, Fort Worth, Houston)

CORP. OFFICERS
Robert D. Rogers: *B* Hartford CT 1936 *ED* Yale Univ 1958; Harvard Univ 1962 *CURR EMPL* ceo, pres: TX Indus

GIVING OFFICERS
R.M. Fowler: vp, treas
J.R. McCraw: contr
R.C. Moore: secy
R.B. Rogers: chmn

APPLICATION INFORMATION
Initial Approach: Send letter of inquiry.

OTHER THINGS TO KNOW
Provides scholarships to individuals for higher education.

GRANTS ANALYSIS
Highest Grant: $25,000
Typical Range: $5,000 to $25,000

Disclosure Period: 1991

RECENT GRANTS
25,000 Colby College, Waterville, ME
18,300 United Way, Dallas, TX
12,750 United Way, Ft. Worth, TX
8,400 United Way, Artesia, MI
7,600 United Way, Houston, TX
5,900 United Way, Alexandria, LA
5,875 United Way, Bridgeport, TX
5,000 Dallas Museum of Art, Dallas, TX
5,000 University of Dallas, Dallas, TX
4,669 Georgia Institute of Technology, Atlanta, GA

Texas Instruments / Texas Instruments Foundation
Sales: $7.47 billion
Employees: 62,939
Headquarters: Dallas, TX
SIC Major Group: Electronic & Other Electrical Equipment, Industrial Machinery & Equipment, and Instruments & Related Products

CONTACT
L. M. Rice, Jr.
President
Texas Instruments Fdn.
PO Box 650311, M/S 3906
Dallas, TX 75265
(214) 917-4505
Note: Inquiries about foundation giving also may be addressed to Ann Minnis, Grants Administrator, at the address below. Address inquiries concerning companies direct giving program to Ms. Karen Johnson, Manager, Corporate University Relations, PO Box 655474, M/S 8219 (214)-995-7268, or to Ms. Linda Coumelis, Manager, Corporate Community Relations, PO Box 655474, M/S 271.

FINANCIAL SUMMARY
Recent Giving: $10,501,126 (1992); $10,500,000 (1991); $10,500,000 (1990)
Assets: $12,780,721 (1992); $13,336,910 (1991); $10,800,000 (1990)
Fiscal Note: Total contributions include foundation giving ($1,501,126 in 1992)and direct

contributions (approximately $9.0 million (retail) in 1992).
EIN: 75-6038519

CONTRIBUTIONS SUMMARY

Typical Recipients: • *Arts & Humanities:* arts centers, arts funds, museums/galleries, music, public broadcasting • *Civic & Public Affairs:* business/free enterprise, civil rights, economics, international affairs, law & justice, municipalities, national security, urban & community affairs • *Education:* business education, colleges & universities, community & junior colleges, economic education, education associations, education funds, elementary education, engineering education, medical education, minority education, private education (precollege), science/technology education, student aid • *Health:* health funds, hospitals, medical research, pediatric health, single-disease health associations • *Science:* science exhibits & fairs, scientific institutes • *Social Services:* community centers, community service organizations, counseling, drugs & alcohol, emergency relief, food/clothing distribution, shelters/homelessness, united funds, youth organizations

Grant Types: capital, department, employee matching gifts, endowment, general support, project, research, and scholarship

Nonmonetary Support Types: donated equipment, donated products, loaned employees, and loaned executives
Note: Nonmonetary support is provided under company's direct giving program. Texas Instruments sponsors a $1.2 million cost-sharing program for equipment and products with Texas colleges and universities. Value of nonmonetary support included in above totals.

Geographic Distribution: nationally, with emphasis on Texas-based groups

Operating Locations: CO (Colorado Springs), KY (Versailles), MA (Attleboro), TN (Johnson City), TX (Abilene, Austin, Dallas, Houston, Lewisville, Lubbock, McKinney, Midland, Sherman, Temple)

CORP. OFFICERS

Jerry Ray Junkins: *B* Ft. Madison IA 1937 *ED* IA St

Univ 1958; Southern Methodist Univ MS 1968 *CURR EMPL* chmn, pres, ceo, dir: TX Instruments *CORP AFFIL* dir: Caterpillar Inc, Procter & Gamble Co *NONPR AFFIL* dir: Dallas Citizens Counc; mem: Natl Academy Engg

GIVING OFFICERS

Richard John Agnich: dir *B* Eveleth MN 1943 *ED* Stanford Univ AB Econ 1965; Univ TX JD 1969 *CURR EMPL* sr vp, secy, gen coun: TX Instruments *CORP AFFIL* bd visitors: Southern Methodist Univ Sch Law; mem: Assn Gen Couns *NONPR AFFIL* dir: Un Way; mem: Am Bar Assn, Am Soc Corp Secs, Dallas Bar Assn, Southwestern Legal Fdn, TX Bar Assn; mem adv counc sch social sciences: Univ TX Dallas; mem: Dallas Assembly, TX St Bar

William Andrew Aylesworth: treas *B* Gary IN 1942 *ED* Cornell Univ 1965; Carnegie-Mellon Univ 1967 *CURR EMPL* sr vp, treas, cfo: TX Instruments *CORP AFFIL* dir: Arkwright-Boston Ins Co, Corp Off Dirs Assurance Holding Ltd, Halliburton Geophysical Svcs Inc, KTI Semiconductor Ltd, TX Instruments-Acer Inc *NONPR AFFIL* dir: Children's Med Ctr Dallas, Corp Offs Dirs Assn, Natl Assn Corp Treas; mem: Fin Execs Inst, Tau Beta Pi

Linda Coumelis: *CURR EMPL* mgr corp community rels: TX Instruments

Jerry Fronterhouse: dir

Karen Johnson: *CURR EMPL* mgr corp univ rels: TX Instruments

Jerry Ray Junkins: dir *CURR EMPL* chmn, pres, ceo, dir: TX Instruments (see above)

Ann Minnis: grants admin

Bill Mitchell: dir

Liston Mike Rice, Jr.: pres, dir *B* Dallas TX 1927 *ED* Univ TX 1949 *CURR EMPL* vp (corp communications & mktg): TX Instruments

Joseph N. Richardson: secy

Mark Shepherd, Jr.: dir *B* Dallas TX 1923 *ED* Southern Methodist Univ BSEE 1942; Univ IL MS 1947 *CORP AFFIL* dir: RepublicBank Corp, TX Instruments, USX Corp; mem intl counc: Morgan Guaranty Trust Co *NONPR AFFIL* councillor: Conf Bd; fellow: Inst Electrical Electronics Engrs; mem: Bus Counc, Counc Foreign Rels, Dallas

Citizens Counc, Eta Kappa Nu, Natl Academy Engg, Newcomen Soc, Sigma Xi, Soc Exploration Geophysicists, TX Science Tech Counc, US-Japan Bus Counc, US-Korean Bus Counc; mem adv comm trade negotiations: Off US Trade Reps; mem adv counc: Am Ditchley Fdn; mem natl bd: Comm Present Danger; trust: Am Enterprise Inst, Comm Econ Devel, Southern Methodist Univ

William Weber: vp, dir *B* 1940 *ED* Lamar Univ BS 1962; Southern Methodist Univ MS 1966 *CURR EMPL* exec vp, dir: TX Instruments

APPLICATION INFORMATION

Initial Approach: *Initial Contact:* brief letter (no longer than two pages) *Include Information On:* description of the organization, amount requested, purpose for which funds are sought, recently audited financial statement, copy of tax-exempt status letter *When to Submit:* any time; board meets four times a year: March, June, September, December; applicants notified of grant decision within three weeks *Note:* Deadline for application for Founders Prize is December 31.

Restrictions on Giving: Foundation does not support individuals or make loans.

GRANTS ANALYSIS

Total Grants: $1,501,126*
Number of Grants: 45
Highest Grant: $450,000
Typical Range: $2,500 to $25,000
Disclosure Period: 1992

Note: Total grants for foundation only. The average grant figure excludes the two highest foundation grants totaling $666,600. Recent grants are for the foundation only. Recent grants are derived from a 1992 Form 990.

RECENT GRANTS

450,000	United Way of Metropolitan Dallas, Dallas, TX
216,600	Head Start of Greater Dallas, Dallas, TX
55,000	United Way of Eastern New England-Attleboro, Boston, MA

40,000	United Way of Grayson County, Sherman, TX
34,000	University of Texas at Arlington, Arlington, TX
30,000	Daytop Village Foundation, Dallas, TX
27,000	United Way of the Texas Gulf Coast, Houston, TX
25,000	Junior Achievement-Dallas, Dallas, TX
25,000	United Way of Austin-Capital, Austin, TX
25,000	University of Texas at Dallas, Dallas, TX

Texas-New Mexico Power Co.

Revenue: $441.34 million
Employees: 1,104
Parent Company: TNP Enterprises Inc.
Headquarters: Fort Worth, TX
SIC Major Group: Electric, Gas & Sanitary Services

CONTACT

Maxie Davie
Vice President
Texas-New Mexico Power Co.
4100 International Plz.
Ft. Worth, TX 76109
(817) 731-0099

FINANCIAL SUMMARY

Fiscal Note: Annual Giving Range: less than $100,000

CONTRIBUTIONS SUMMARY

Small program focusing on community needs.

Nonmonetary Support Types: cause-related marketing & promotion, in-kind services, and loaned executives

Geographic Distribution: company service area

Operating Locations: NM (Silver City), TX (Bremond, Clifton, Fort Worth, Lewisville, Pecos, Texas City)
Note: Company operates five divisions in operating locations.

CORP. OFFICERS

James M. Tarpley: *B* Leonard TX 1934 *ED* Southern Methodist Univ 1963 *CURR EMPL* pres, ceo: Texas-New Mexico Power Co *CORP AFFIL* dir: Bayport Cogeneration, TNP Operating Co, TX Generating Co; pres, ceo, dir: TNP Enterprises

R.D. Woofter: *B* Lewis County WV 1923 *ED* WV Univ 1950 *CURR EMPL* chmn: Texas-New Mexico Power Co

APPLICATION INFORMATION
Initial Approach: Send inquiry letter.

Texas Olefins Co. / Swalm Foundation
Sales: $68.7 million
Employees: 300
Headquarters: Houston, TX
SIC Major Group: Chemicals & Allied Products, Petroleum & Coal Products, and Wholesale Trade—Nondurable Goods

CONTACT
Mimi Minkoff
Contribution Coordinator
Texas Olefins Co.
8707 Katy Fwy., Ste. 300
Houston, TX 77024
(713) 464-1321

CONTRIBUTIONS SUMMARY
Operating Locations: TX (Houston)

CORP. OFFICERS
David C. Swalm: *CURR EMPL* chmn, pres, ceo: Texas Olefins Co

OTHER THINGS TO KNOW
Company is an original donor to the Swalm Foundation.

Textron / Textron Charitable Trust
Sales: $8.34 billion
Employees: 60,000
Headquarters: Providence, RI
SIC Major Group: Instruments & Related Products, Insurance Carriers, Printing & Publishing, and Stone, Clay & Glass Products

CONTACT
Elizabeth W. Monahan
Contributions Coordinator
Textron Charitable Trust
PO Box 878
Providence, RI 02901
(401) 457-2430

FINANCIAL SUMMARY
Recent Giving: $2,729,845 (1991); $3,000,000 (1989); $2,601,795 (1988)

Assets: $12,206,827 (1991); $12,715,514 (1990); $12,630,000 (1989)
Fiscal Note: Company gives through charitable trust only.
EIN: 25-6115832

CONTRIBUTIONS SUMMARY
Typical Recipients: • *Arts & Humanities:* arts appreciation, arts associations, arts centers, arts funds, arts institutes, community arts, dance, history/historic preservation, libraries, museums/galleries, music, opera, performing arts, public broadcasting, theater • *Civic & Public Affairs:* business/free enterprise, civil rights, economic development, economics, environmental affairs, international affairs, law & justice, municipalities, national security, professional & trade associations, public policy, safety, urban & community affairs, women's affairs, zoos/botanical gardens • *Education:* arts education, business education, career/vocational education, colleges & universities, community & junior colleges, economic education, education associations, education funds, engineering education, international studies, legal education, medical education, minority education, private education (precollege), public education (precollege), science/technology education, student aid • *Health:* health care cost containment, health organizations, hospices, hospitals, pediatric health, single-disease health associations • *International:* international development/relief • *Science:* science exhibits & fairs, scientific institutes • *Social Services:* aged, child welfare, community centers, community service organizations, counseling, disabled, drugs & alcohol, emergency relief, employment/job training, family planning, food/clothing distribution, legal aid, recreation & athletics, refugee assistance, religious welfare, shelters/homelessness, united funds, volunteer services, youth organizations
Grant Types: capital, employee matching gifts, general support, and scholarship
Geographic Distribution: primarily in areas where company operates
Operating Locations: AL (Huntsville), CA (Anaheim,

Irvine, Santa Ana, Santa Fe Springs, Valencia), CT (Newington, Stratford), FL (Cocoa, Orlando), GA (Americus, Augusta), IL (Harvard, Rockford), IN (Angola, Berne, Elwood, Pendleton, Vevay), LA (New Orleans), MA (Danvers, Lowell, Wilmington, Winchester, Worcester), MI (Ann Arbor, Detroit, Holland, Melvindale, Muskegon, Owosso, Traverse City, Walled Lake, Warren, Wyandotte, Zeeland), MN (St. Paul), NC (Charlotte, Hickory, Swannanoa), NH (Dover, Portsmouth), NY (Niagara Falls), OH (Blufton, Cincinnati, Cleveland, Fostoria, Greenville, Lima), PA (Williamsport), RI (Providence), SC (Greer), TN (Athens, Cookeville, Nashville), TX (Fort Worth, Houston), VT (Springfield), WI (Racine)

CORP. OFFICERS
James F. Hardymon: *B* Maysville KY 1934 *CURR EMPL* pres, ceo: Textron
Dennis Gage Little: *B* Cambridge MA 1935 *ED* Harvard Univ 1956; Harvard Univ 1961 *CURR EMPL* exec vp, cfo: Textron *CORP AFFIL* dir: BICC USA, Paul Revere Corp, Russell Reynold Assocs, Avco Fin Svcs *NONPR AFFIL* dir: Pine St Fund; mem: Fin Execs Inst; trust: Bryant Coll

GIVING OFFICERS
Raymond William Caine, Jr.: chmn (contributions comm) *B* Fall River MA 1932 *ED* Providence Coll BS 1956 *CURR EMPL* vp (corp communications): Textron *NONPR AFFIL* dir: Providence Fdn, RI Commodores, RI Pub Transit Authority; mem: Machinery Allied Products Inst, Pub Rels Soc Am; mem exec adv comm: Bryant Coll RI; mem exec com, trust: Salve Regina Coll
Elizabeth W. Monahan: contributions coordinator, secy (contributions comm)

APPLICATION INFORMATION
Initial Approach: *Initial Contact:* brief letter or proposal *Include Information On:* statement of purposes and objectives of the organization; history of the programs of the organization; list of the organization's officers, board of directors, and staff; annual operating budget for the organization

for the year in which the project will occur; audited financial statements for the most recently completed year; description of the program or project that is the subject of the proposal and how it relates to the needs of the community; budget for the program or project that is the subject of the proposal; dollar level of support requested; copy of tax-exempt determination letter from the Internal Revenue Service; list of other sources approached for financial assistance and amounts received *When to Submit:* any time
Restrictions on Giving: Does not support individuals, including political candidates; endowment funds; educational or hospital capital or operating expenses; requests intended to reduce operating deficits; fundraising appeals from churches, seminaries, or other directly related religious organizations; operating funds of United Way member agencies; or organizations that are not 501(c)(3) tax-exempt.

OTHER THINGS TO KNOW
Grant recipients are required to complete a post-grant application form and adhere to terms of the grant. A fiscal and program summary must be submitted upon completion of the project.
Officer titles are likely to change.
Rhode Island Hospital Trust National Bank serves as a corporate trustee of the trust.

GRANTS ANALYSIS
Total Grants: $2,729,845
Number of Grants: 1,720
Highest Grant: $89,000
Typical Range: $1,000 to $5,000
Disclosure Period: 1991
Note: Recent grants are derived from a 1991 Form 990.

RECENT GRANTS
89,000 United Way of Eastern Fairfield County, Bridgeport, CT
55,480 National Merit Scholarship Corporation
48,256 United Way of Southeastern New England, Providence, RI
40,000 Brown University, Providence, RI

33,500 Educational Testing Service, Princeton, NJ

31,250 Tarrant County United Way, Ft. Worth, TX

31,250 Tarrant County United Way, Ft. Worth, TX

31,250 Tarrant County United Way, Ft. Worth, TX

31,250 Tarrant County United Way, Ft. Worth, TX

26,250 United Way of Central Massachusetts, Worcester, MA

Thagard Foundation

CONTACT
Richard O' Connor
Secretary-Treasurer
Thagard Fdn.
PO Box 171
Fullerton, CA 92532
(714) 738-7349

FINANCIAL SUMMARY
Recent Giving: $196,000 (fiscal 1992); $217,000 (fiscal 1991); $171,200 (fiscal 1990)
Assets: $3,167,507 (fiscal year ending April 30, 1992); $3,132,736 (fiscal 1991); $3,005,189 (fiscal 1990)
EIN: 95-6225425

CONTRIBUTIONS SUMMARY
Typical Recipients: • *Education:* colleges & universities • *Health:* hospitals, medical research, pediatric health, single-disease health associations • *Social Services:* child welfare, community service organizations, disabled, united funds, youth organizations
Grant Types: general support and research
Geographic Distribution: focus on CA

GIVING OFFICERS
John C. Bagwell: trust
Belle I. Ellis: trust
William H. Godel: trust
Richard L. O'Connor: trust, secy, treas
William N. Ratkovic: trust
Roy Reynolds: trust, vp
George F. Thagard, Jr.: trust, pres
Raymond G. Thagard, Sr.: trust, vp

APPLICATION INFORMATION
Initial Approach: Send brief letter describing program. There are no deadlines.

GRANTS ANALYSIS
Number of Grants: 13
Highest Grant: $80,000
Typical Range: $1,000 to $5,000
Disclosure Period: fiscal year ending April 30, 1992

RECENT GRANTS
80,000 University of Southern California Scholarship Fund, Los Angeles, CA

65,000 Center for Neurological Study, Los Angeles, CA

10,000 Salvation Army, Los Angeles, CA

10,000 Scottish Rite Aphasia Fund

5,000 Boy Scouts of America, Los Angeles, CA

5,000 For Children Foundation of Oakridge

5,000 Shriners Hospital for Crippled Children

3,500 High Sky Girls Ranch, Midland, TX

3,500 West Texas Boys Ranch, TX

3,000 Memorial Trust Foundation of DCH

Thalheimer Foundation, Alvin and Fanny Blaustein

CONTACT
Louis B. Thalheimer
President
Alvin and Fanny Blaustein Thalheimer Fdn.
Blaustein Bldg.
PO Box 238
Baltimore, MD 21203
(410) 685-4230

FINANCIAL SUMMARY
Recent Giving: $701,066 (fiscal 1992); $819,316 (fiscal 1991); $327,715 (fiscal 1989)
Assets: $12,628,024 (fiscal year ending February 28, 1992); $11,109,810 (fiscal 1991); $9,564,003 (fiscal 1989)
Gifts Received: $333,500 (fiscal 1992); $333,500 (fiscal 1991); $240,000 (fiscal 1989)
Fiscal Note: In 1992, contributions were received from American Trading and Production Corporation.
EIN: 52-6038383

CONTRIBUTIONS SUMMARY
Donor(s): American Trading and Production Corp.
Typical Recipients: • *Arts & Humanities:* community arts, museums/galleries, music, performing arts • *Civic & Public Affairs:* ethnic/minority organizations, law & justice, municipalities • *Education:* colleges & universities, private education (precollege) • *Health:* hospitals • *Religion:* religious organizations, synagogues • *Social Services:* community service organizations, religious welfare, united funds, youth organizations
Grant Types: general support
Geographic Distribution: focus on Baltimore, MD

GIVING OFFICERS
Marjorie Thalheimer Coleman: trust
Dale E. Maxson: asst secy
Henry A. Rosenberg, Jr.: vp *B* Pittsburgh PA 1929 *ED* Hobart Coll BA 1952 *CURR EMPL* chmn, chmn exec comm, ceo, dir: Crown Central Petroleum Corp *CORP AFFIL* dir: Am Trading & Production Corp, Signet Banking Corp, US Fidelity & Guaranty Co; mem listed co adv comm: Am Stock Exchange *NONPR AFFIL* chmn, dir, mem exec comm: Natl Petroleum Refiners Assn; dir: Crohn's & Colitis Fdn, Goucher Coll, Johns Hopkins Hosp, McDonogh Sch, Natl Aquarium, Natl Aquarium Baltimore, Natl Flag Day Fdn, Un Way Central MD, YMCA Greater Baltimore; mem: Am Petroleum Inst, Natl Petroleum Counc, Twenty-Five Year Club Petroleum Indus; mem adv bd: William Donald Schaefer Ctr Pub Policy; mem natl exec bd: Boy Scouts Am
Ruth Blaustein Rosenberg: trust *CORP AFFIL* dir: Am Trading & Production Corp
Frank A. Strzelczyk: secy, treas
Louis B. Thalheimer: pres, trust
Elizabeth T. Wachs: trust

APPLICATION INFORMATION
Initial Approach: Send brief letter of inquiry describing program or project. There are no deadlines. Board meets six times a year.
Restrictions on Giving: Does not support individuals.

GRANTS ANALYSIS
Number of Grants: 11
Highest Grant: $347,566
Typical Range: $5,000 to $20,000
Disclosure Period: fiscal year ending February 28, 1992

RECENT GRANTS
347,566 Associated Jewish Charities and Welfare Fund, Baltimore, MD

110,000 Amherst College, Amherst, MA

100,000 Sarah Lawrence College, Bronxville, NY

62,500 Baltimore Museum of Art, Baltimore, MD

25,000 Maryland Institute, Baltimore, MD

20,000 Peabody Institute, Baltimore, MD

18,000 Baltimore Symphony Orchestra, Baltimore, MD

7,500 Johns Hopkins Hospital, Baltimore, MD

5,000 Jewish Fund for Justice, New York, NY

5,000 Mazon A Jewish Response to Hunger, Los Angeles, CA

Thalhimer and Family Foundation, Charles G.

CONTACT
Charles Thalhimer
President
Charles G. Thalhimer and Family Fdn.
PO Box 26788
Richmond, VA 23261
(804) 643-4211

FINANCIAL SUMMARY
Recent Giving: $176,875 (fiscal 1990); $121,285 (fiscal 1989); $128,223 (fiscal 1988)
Assets: $2,064,055 (fiscal year ending October 31, 1990); $2,156,687 (fiscal 1989); $2,065,551 (fiscal 1988)
EIN: 54-6047108

CONTRIBUTIONS SUMMARY

Donor(s): members of the Thalhimer family

Typical Recipients: • *Arts & Humanities:* arts institutes, community arts, music, theater • *Civic & Public Affairs:* municipalities • *Education:* colleges & universities • *Religion:* religious organizations • *Social Services:* child welfare, community service organizations, united funds, youth organizations

Grant Types: general support

Geographic Distribution: focus on VA

GIVING OFFICERS

Charles G. Thalhimer, Jr.: vp
Charles G. Thalhimer, Sr.: pres, dir
Harry R. Thalhimer: vp
Rhonda R. Thalhimer: secy, treas
William B. Thalhimer, Jr.: vp *B* Richmond VA 1914 *CORP AFFIL* dir: Fidelity Bankers Life Ins Co

APPLICATION INFORMATION

Initial Approach: Send brief letter describing program. There are no deadlines.
Restrictions on Giving: Does not support individuals.

GRANTS ANALYSIS

Number of Grants: 68
Highest Grant: $70,000
Typical Range: $100 to $6,000
Disclosure Period: fiscal year ending October 31, 1990

RECENT GRANTS

70,000 Jewish Community Federation, Richmond, VA
35,000 United Way, Richmond, VA
15,000 Richmond Symphony, Richmond, VA
6,000 Carpenter Center for the Performing Arts, Richmond, VA
6,000 Virginia Foundation for Independent Colleges, Richmond, VA
5,000 James Madison University, Harrisonburg, VA
5,000 Metropolitan Richmond Chamber of Commerce, Richmond, VA
5,000 Theatre IV, Richmond, VA

5,000 Virginia Commonwealth University, Richmond, VA
5,000 Virginia Commonwealth University, Richmond, VA

Thalhimer Brothers Inc. / Thalhimer Brothers Foundation

Sales: $156.0 million
Employees: 6,600
Parent Company: May Department Stores
Headquarters: Richmond, VA
SIC Major Group: General Merchandise Stores

CONTACT

James E. Branson
Secretary & Treasurer
Thalhimer Brothers Foundation
615 East Broad St.
Richmond, VA 23219
(804) 643-4211

FINANCIAL SUMMARY

Recent Giving: $244,350 (1990)
Assets: $429 (1990)
Gifts Received: $247,050 (1990)
Fiscal Note: In 1990, contributions were received from Thalhimer Brothers Inc.
EIN: 54-6047107

CONTRIBUTIONS SUMMARY

Typical Recipients: • *Arts & Humanities:* community arts, music • *Education:* colleges & universities, education funds • *Health:* single-disease health associations • *Religion:* religious organizations • *Social Services:* community service organizations, shelters/homelessness, united funds

Grant Types: general support

Geographic Distribution: focus on VA

Operating Locations: VA (Richmond)

CORP. OFFICERS

Howard Lahrer: *CURR EMPL* pres: Thalhimer Brothers
William B. Thalhimer, Jr.: *B* Richmond VA 1914 *CORP AFFIL* dir: Fidelity Bankers Life Ins Co

GIVING OFFICERS

James E. Branson: secy, treas, dir
William B. Thalhimer III: dir

William B. Thalhimer, Jr.: pres, dir, dn (see above)
Michael C. Weisberg: vp, dir

APPLICATION INFORMATION

Initial Approach: Send brief letter describing program. There are no deadlines.

GRANTS ANALYSIS

Number of Grants: 76
Highest Grant: $70,000
Typical Range: $100 to $5,000
Disclosure Period: 1990

RECENT GRANTS

70,000 Jewish Community Federation, Richmond, VA
35,000 United Way, Richmond, VA
15,000 Richmond Symphony, Richmond, VA
6,000 Virginia Foundation for Independent Colleges, Richmond, VA
5,000 James Madison University, Harrisonburg, VA
5,000 Richmond Metropolitan Chamber of Commerce, Richmond, VA
5,000 Virginia Commonwealth University, Richmond, VA — Thalhimer Family Fund
5,000 Virginia Commonwealth University Special Fund Raising Campaign, Richmond, VA
4,500 United Way, Memphis, TN
4,000 Emergency Shelter, Richmond, VA

Thalhimer, Jr. and Family Foundation, William B.

CONTACT

Robert L. Thalhimer
Vice President
William B. Thalhimer, Jr. and Family Fdn.
1513 Hearthglow Ln.
Richmond, VA 23233
(804) 780-2992

FINANCIAL SUMMARY

Recent Giving: $146,560 (fiscal 1991); $251,973 (fiscal 1990); $92,098 (fiscal 1989)
Assets: $2,067,421 (fiscal year ending October 31, 1991);

$1,822,110 (fiscal 1990); $1,923,101 (fiscal 1989)
Gifts Received: $50,000 (fiscal 1991); $160,953 (fiscal 1990); $5,284 (fiscal 1989)
EIN: 54-6047110

CONTRIBUTIONS SUMMARY

Donor(s): William B. Thalhimer, Jr., Barbara J. Thalhimer

Typical Recipients: • *Arts & Humanities:* community arts, history/historic preservation, music, performing arts, theater • *Education:* colleges & universities • *Religion:* religious organizations, synagogues • *Social Services:* community service organizations, youth organizations

Grant Types: general support

Geographic Distribution: focus on VA

GIVING OFFICERS

Barbara J. Thalhimer: dir, secy, treas
Robert L. Thalhimer: dir, vp
William B. Thalhimer III: vp
William B. Thalhimer, Jr.: vp, dir, don *B* Richmond VA 1914 *CORP AFFIL* dir: Fidelity Bankers Life Ins Co

APPLICATION INFORMATION

Initial Approach: Send brief letter describing program. There are no deadlines.
Restrictions on Giving: Does not support individuals.

GRANTS ANALYSIS

Number of Grants: 72
Highest Grant: $50,500
Typical Range: $100 to $1,000
Disclosure Period: fiscal year ending October 31, 1991

RECENT GRANTS

50,500 Collegiate Schools, Richmond, VA
50,000 St. Marys Hospital Foundation, Richmond, VA
10,000 Virginia Historical Society, Richmond, VA
5,000 Richmond Forum, Richmond, VA
3,450 Virginia Museum Foundation, Richmond, VA
2,400 Richmond Symphony, Richmond, VA
2,300 Arts Council of Richmond, Richmond, VA
1,710 Jewish Community Federation, Richmond, VA

1,295 Theatre Virginia, Richmond, VA

1,070 Congregation Beth Ahabah, Richmond, VA

Thanksgiving Foundation

CONTACT
Thanksgiving Fdn.
c/o Fiduciary Trust Co.
Two World Trade Center
New York, NY 10048

FINANCIAL SUMMARY
Recent Giving: $245,500 (fiscal 1991); $232,731 (fiscal 1990); $217,500 (fiscal 1989)
Assets: $5,854,454 (fiscal year ending July 31, 1991); $5,393,097 (fiscal 1990); $5,268,073 (fiscal 1989)
EIN: 13-6861874

CONTRIBUTIONS SUMMARY
Donor(s): Thomas M. Peters, Marion Post Peters
Typical Recipients: • *Arts & Humanities:* history/historic preservation, museums/galleries, music • *Civic & Public Affairs:* environmental affairs, zoos/botanical gardens • *Education:* colleges & universities, private education (precollege) • *Health:* nursing services • *Religion:* churches, religious organizations • *Social Services:* child welfare, community service organizations, disabled, family planning, family services, religious welfare, united funds, youth organizations
Grant Types: general support
Geographic Distribution: focus on NY and NJ

GIVING OFFICERS
Thomas Henry Stine: trust
Mark C. Winmill: trust

APPLICATION INFORMATION
Initial Approach: Contributes only to preselected organizations.
Restrictions on Giving: Does not support individuals.

GRANTS ANALYSIS
Number of Grants: 56
Highest Grant: $25,000
Typical Range: $2,000 to $10,000
Disclosure Period: fiscal year ending July 31, 1991

RECENT GRANTS
25,000 Sheltering Arms Children's Service, New York, NY

22,000 Delbarton School, Morristown, NJ

20,000 Broad Jump Prep for Prep, New York, NY

10,000 International Rescue Committee, New York, NY

10,000 St. Michael's Episcopal Church, New York, NY

7,500 American Frontier Culture Foundation, Staunton, VA

6,500 St. George's School, Newport, RI

5,500 Federation of Protestant Welfare Agencies, New York, NY

5,000 American Commission for Keep, Evanston, IL

5,000 Somerset Hills Community Chest, Basking Ridge, NJ

Thatcher Foundation

CONTACT
Bernadine Hardin
Thatcher Fdn.
c/o Minnequa Bank of Pueblo
Pueblo, CO 81004
(719) 545-2345

FINANCIAL SUMMARY
Recent Giving: $284,991 (1991); $265,364 (1990); $274,001 (1989)
Assets: $3,395,502 (1991); $3,098,467 (1990); $3,281,750 (1989)
EIN: 84-0581724

CONTRIBUTIONS SUMMARY
Typical Recipients: • *Arts & Humanities:* arts centers, museums/galleries, music • *Civic & Public Affairs:* municipalities, zoos/botanical gardens • *Education:* colleges & universities • *Social Services:* community service organizations, family services, united funds
Grant Types: general support and scholarship
Geographic Distribution: limited to Pueblo County, CO

GIVING OFFICERS
Adrian Comer: trust
Lester L. Ward, Jr.: secy, treas
Helen T. White: trust, vp
Mahlon T. White III: trust

APPLICATION INFORMATION
Initial Approach: Applications accepted only for scholarships; contributions to organizations are preselected.

GRANTS ANALYSIS
Number of Grants: 40
Highest Grant: $42,250
Typical Range: $1,000 to $10,000
Disclosure Period: 1991

RECENT GRANTS
42,250 Sangre de Christo Arts and Conference Center, Pueblo, CO

40,000 United Way, Pueblo, CO

30,100 Pueblo Zoological Society, Pueblo, CO

20,000 City of Pueblo, Pueblo, CO

20,000 University of Colorado, Boulder, CO

10,500 El Pueblo Museum, Pueblo, CO

10,000 Pueblo Symphony Association, Pueblo, CO

10,000 Thatcher Learning Center at Parkview, Pueblo, CO

8,000 Family Counseling Center, Pueblo, CO

7,500 KTSC Channel 8 Auction, Pueblo, CO

Thendara Foundation

CONTACT
Thendara Fdn.
1800 Star Bank Center
425 Walnut St.
Cincinnati, OH 45202-3957
(513) 381-2838

FINANCIAL SUMMARY
Recent Giving: $141,600 (1991); $76,467 (1990); $68,000 (1989)
Assets: $2,775,507 (1991); $2,361,989 (1990); $2,200,893 (1989)
Gifts Received: $40,000 (1991); $225,000 (1990); $731,731 (1989)
Fiscal Note: In 1991, contributions were received from C. Lawson Reed.
EIN: 31-1126072

CONTRIBUTIONS SUMMARY
Donor(s): C. Lawson Reed, Dorothy Reed

Typical Recipients: • *Arts & Humanities:* arts centers, arts funds, history/historic preservation, museums/galleries • *Civic & Public Affairs:* environmental affairs • *Education:* private education (precollege) • *Health:* single-disease health associations • *Social Services:* community service organizations, united funds
Grant Types: general support
Geographic Distribution: focus on Cincinnati, OH

GIVING OFFICERS
James M. Anderson: trust
Janet Reed Goss: trust
Dorothy Reed Hagist: trust
C. Lawson Reed: trust
C.L. Reed III: trust
Dorothy W. Reed: trust
Foster A. Reed: trust
Peter S. Reed: trust

APPLICATION INFORMATION
Initial Approach: Contributes only to preselected organizations.
Restrictions on Giving: Does not support individuals.

GRANTS ANALYSIS
Number of Grants: 19
Highest Grant: $40,000
Typical Range: $1,000 to $5,000
Disclosure Period: 1991

RECENT GRANTS
40,000 Concrete Foundation, New York, NY

25,000 Cincinnati Art Museum, Cincinnati, OH

15,000 Fine Arts Fund, Cincinnati, OH

10,600 Collage Children's Museum, Boulder, CO

10,000 AIDS Volunteers of Cincinnati, Cincinnati, OH

10,000 Whitney Museum of American Art, New York, NY

5,000 Aspen Country Day School, Aspen, CO

5,000 Contemporary Arts Center, Cincinnati, OH

5,000 Joy Outdoor Education Center, Clarksville, OH

5,000 San Francisco School, San Francisco, CA

Thermo Electron Corp. / Thermo Electron Foundation

Sales: $805.5 million
Employees: 5,954
Headquarters: Waltham, MA
SIC Major Group: Industrial Machinery & Equipment and Instruments & Related Products

CONTACT

Linda C. Nordberg
Manager, Corporate Contributions
Thermo Electron Fdn.
c/o Thermo Electron Corporation
81 Wyman St.
Waltham, MA 02254
(617) 622-1000

FINANCIAL SUMMARY

Recent Giving: $125,000 (1993 est.); $71,500 (1990)
Assets: $371,989 (1990)
Gifts Received: $125,000 (1990)
Fiscal Note: In 1990, contributions were received from Thermo Electron Corporation.
EIN: 22-2778152

CONTRIBUTIONS SUMMARY

Typical Recipients: • *Arts & Humanities:* arts centers, dance, museums/galleries, performing arts, public broadcasting • *Civic & Public Affairs:* better government, business/free enterprise, civil rights, economic development, economics, environmental affairs, professional & trade associations, public policy • *Education:* business education, career/vocational education, colleges & universities, community & junior colleges, economic education, literacy, science/technology education • *Health:* hospices, hospitals • *International:* international development/relief • *Science:* observatories & planetariums, science exhibits & fairs • *Social Services:* aged, child welfare, counseling, disabled, emergency relief, employment/job training, food/clothing distribution, shelters/homelessness, united funds
Grant Types: award, capital, challenge, general support, and scholarship
Geographic Distribution: focus on headquarters area
Operating Locations: MA (Waltham)

CORP. OFFICERS

G.N. Hatsopoulos: *CURR EMPL* chmn, pres: Thermo Electron Corp
John N. Hatsopoulos: *CURR EMPL* exec vp, cfo: Thermo Electron Corp

APPLICATION INFORMATION

Initial Approach: Send letter of inquiry. Include a description of organization, amount requested, purpose of funds sought, recently audited financial statement, and proof of tax-exempt status. There are no deadlines.
Restrictions on Giving: Does not support individuals or organizations outside operating areas.

GRANTS ANALYSIS

Number of Grants: 25
Highest Grant: $10,000
Typical Range: $1,000 to $5,000
Disclosure Period: 1990

RECENT GRANTS

10,000   Massachusetts General Hospital, Boston, MA
10,000   Museum of Science, Boston, MA
5,000   Boston Symphony Orchestra, Boston, MA
5,000   DeCordova Museum, Lincoln, MA
5,000   Institute for International Economics, Washington, DC
5,000   Massachusetts Institute of Technology, Cambridge, MA
4,000   United Way, Boston, MA
3,000   Museum of Fine Arts, Boston, MA
2,500   Alliance to Save Energy, Washington, DC
2,500   National Conference of Christians and Jews, New York, NY

Third National Corp.

Assets: $5.73 billion
Employees: 2,709
Parent Company: Suntrust Banks Inc.
Headquarters: Nashville, TN
SIC Major Group: Depository Institutions, Holding & Other Investment Offices, and Nondepository Institutions

CONTACT

Julie Clay
Director, Contributions & Donations
Third National Corp.
PO Box 30511
Nashville, TN 37230-5110
(615) 748-4821

CONTRIBUTIONS SUMMARY

Operating Locations: GA (Atlanta), TN (Chattanooga, Cleveland, Clinton, Johnson City, Knoxville, Lawrenceburg, Lebannon, Lenoir City, Morristown, Murfreesboro, Nashville, Pulaski, Savannah, Sevierville)
Note: Third National Bank operates 6 branches in locations.

CORP. OFFICERS

John W. Clay, Jr.: *B* Americus GA 1913 *ED* Vanderbilt Univ 1937 *CURR EMPL* chmn, pres, dir: Third Natl Corp
Scott L. Probasco, Jr.: *CURR EMPL* vchmn, dir: Third Natl Corp
John E. Southwood: *B* Evansville IN 1929 *ED* Vanderbilt Univ 1952 *CURR EMPL* vchmn, dir: Third Natl Corp

Thirty-Five Twenty, Inc.

Headquarters: Indianapolis, IN

CONTACT

Helen Garlotte
Thirty-Five Twenty, Inc.
7440 North Shadeland
Indianapolis, IN 46250
(317) 842-0880

FINANCIAL SUMMARY

Recent Giving: $75,000 (1992); $70,000 (1990); $60,000 (1989)
Assets: $2,180,880 (1992); $1,878,754 (1990); $1,811,482 (1989)
EIN: 35-6056960

CONTRIBUTIONS SUMMARY

Donor(s): Enid Goodrich
Typical Recipients: • *Arts & Humanities:* arts festivals, community arts, music • *Civic & Public Affairs:* economics, international affairs, municipalities, public policy • *Education:* education associations, education funds, student aid • *Social Services:* animal protection, community service organizations
Grant Types: general support

GIVING OFFICERS

Ruth E. Connolly: trust
Helen W. Garlotte: secy
Enid Goodrich: vchmn
W.W. Hill: pres, treas
Ralph W. Husted: trust
Chris I. Talley: trust

APPLICATION INFORMATION

Initial Approach: Send brief letter describing program. There are no deadlines.

GRANTS ANALYSIS

Number of Grants: 9
Highest Grant: $20,000
Typical Range: $2,500 to $7,500
Disclosure Period: 1992

RECENT GRANTS

20,000   Festival Music Society of Indiana, Indianapolis, IN
9,000   American Spectator Educational Foundation, Arlington, VA
8,000   Foundation for Research on Economics and the Environment, Bozeman, MT
7,500   Competitive Enterprise Institute, Washington, DC
7,500   Institute for Political Economy, Washington, DC
6,500   Centre for Research into Communist Economies
6,500   Philadelphia Society, North Adams, MI
5,000   Eisenhower Memorial Scholarship Foundation, Bloomington, IN
5,000   Pacific Research Institute for Public Policy, San Francisco, CA

Thoman Foundation, W. B. and Candace

CONTACT
Benjamin O. Schwendener, Jr.
President and Secretary
W. B. and Candace Thoman Fdn.
222 N. Washington Sq., Ste. 400
Lansing, MI 48933-1800
(517) 484-8282

FINANCIAL SUMMARY
Recent Giving: $127,500 (1991); $98,975 (1990); $216,450 (1989)
Assets: $2,378,237 (1991); $2,300,361 (1990); $2,305,640 (1989)
Gifts Received: $37,714 (1990); $37,715 (1989)
Fiscal Note: In 1990, contributions were received from the W.B. Thoman Trust.
EIN: 23-7029842

CONTRIBUTIONS SUMMARY
Donor(s): the late W. B. Thoman, the late Candace Thoman
Typical Recipients: • *Arts & Humanities:* community arts, dance, performing arts, theater • *Education:* colleges & universities, education funds, public education (precollege) • *Health:* single-disease health associations • *Social Services:* child welfare, community service organizations
Grant Types: project, scholarship, and seed money
Geographic Distribution: focus on Ingham, Eaton, and Clinton counties, MI. No support for political organizations, churches, or religious organizations or programs.

GIVING OFFICERS
John Hannah: trust, vp
Louis Legg, Jr.: trust
Benjamin O. Schwendener: trust, pres, secy
Lillian Smucker: trust
Ronald E. Weger: trust, treas

APPLICATION INFORMATION
Initial Approach: Send brief letter of inquiry describing program. There are no deadlines.

OTHER THINGS TO KNOW
Publications: Application Guidelines

GRANTS ANALYSIS
Number of Grants: 6

Highest Grant: $45,000
Typical Range: $2,500 to $25,000
Disclosure Period: 1991

RECENT GRANTS
45,000 Ingham Intermediate School District, Mason, MI
40,000 Michigan Dyslexia Institute, Lansing, MI
25,000 Capitol Region Community Foundation, Lansing, MI
10,000 Olivet College, Olivet, MI
5,000 Happendance, Lansing, MI
2,500 Opera Company of Mid-Michigan, Lansing, MI

Thomas & Betts Corp. / Thomas & Betts Charitable Trust

Sales: $1.05 billion
Employees: 7,600
Headquarters: Bridgewater, NJ
SIC Major Group: Electronic & Other Electrical Equipment

CONTACT
Janice H. Way
Trust Administrator
Thomas & Betts Charitable Trust
1001 Frontier Rd.
Bridgewater, NJ 08807
(908) 685-1600

FINANCIAL SUMMARY
Recent Giving: $185,000 (1993 est.); $310,262 (1992 approx.); $428,177 (1991)
Assets: $23,529 (1991); $196,061 (1990)
Gifts Received: $250,000 (1991); $500,000 (1990)
Fiscal Note: Figure for 1992 includes $60,000 contributed by Electrical Division, which makes direct contributions. The remainder is distributed through the foundation. In 1991, contributions were received from the Thomas & Betts Corporation.
EIN: 22-6032533

CONTRIBUTIONS SUMMARY
Typical Recipients: • *Arts & Humanities:* arts associations, arts centers, museums/galleries • *Civic & Public Affairs:* economic development, international affairs, professional & trade associations, safety • *Education:* colleges & universities, community & junior colleges, education associations, education funds, minority education, private education (precollege), science/technology education, student aid • *Health:* emergency/ambulance services, health funds, health organizations, hospices, hospitals, nursing services • *Science:* science exhibits & fairs, scientific institutes • *Social Services:* community centers, united funds, youth organizations
Grant Types: capital, employee matching gifts, and general support
Geographic Distribution: primarily headquarters and operating locations, some nationally
Operating Locations: CT (Monroe), NJ (Bridgewater), SC (Greenville), TN (Memphis)

CORP. OFFICERS
T. Kevin Dunnigan: *B* Montreal Canada 1928 *ED* Loyola Univ BA 1971 *CURR EMPL* chmn, pres, ceo: Thomas & Betts Corp *CORP AFFIL* dir: Natl Starch & Chem Corp *NONPR AFFIL* mem: Electronics Indus Assn

GIVING OFFICERS
Robert V. Berry: trust *B* Newark NJ 1933 *ED* Dartmouth Coll BA 1954 *CURR EMPL* sr vp: Thomas & Betts Corp *CORP AFFIL* dir: Ames Rubber Corp *NONPR AFFIL* Carrier Fdn Psychiatric Hosp
John F. Walsh: trust
Janice H. Way: trust *CURR EMPL* secy: Thomas & Betts Corp *CORP AFFIL* secy: Thomas & Betts Corp

APPLICATION INFORMATION
Initial Approach: *Initial Contact:* brief letter or phone call *Include Information On:* description of the organization, amount requested, purpose of funds sought, audited financial statement, proof of tax-exempt status *When to Submit:* before October 15 for consideration at the time the budget is prepared; applications for grants will be considered at other times during the year if there are unallocated funds available
Restrictions on Giving: Does not support individuals, religious organizations for sectarian purposes, or political or lobbying groups.

OTHER THINGS TO KNOW
Publications: annual report

GRANTS ANALYSIS
Total Grants: $310,262*
Number of Grants: 36*
Highest Grant: $20,000
Typical Range: $1,000 to $5,000
Disclosure Period: 1992
Note: Number of grants and average grant figures do not include matching gifts totaling $14,662. Total grants figure includes $60,000 distributed through a division as direct contributions. Recent grants are derived from a 1992 grants list.

RECENT GRANTS
20,000 Liberty Science Center, NJ
20,000 Matheny School, NJ
17,000 Somerset Valley YMCA, NJ
15,000 United Way - Eastern Fairfield County, CT
14,000 Rutgers University Foundation, New Brunswick, NJ
13,000 Rolling Hills Girl Scout Council, NJ
12,000 Somerset Medical Center, NJ
12,000 United Way - Union County, NJ
10,000 St. Elizabeth Hospital Foundation, NJ
10,000 United Way - North Penn, PA

Thomas Built Buses L.P. / Thomas Foundation

Sales: $200.0 million
Employees: 1,450
Headquarters: High Point, NC
SIC Major Group: Transportation Equipment

CONTACT
Doug Harrison
Secretary
Thomas Foundation
PO Box 2450
High Point, NC 27261
(919) 889-4871

FINANCIAL SUMMARY
Recent Giving: $30,000 (1991); $27,500 (1990); $30,000 (1989)
Assets: $357,607 (1991); $322,437 (1990); $342,982 (1989)
EIN: 51-0189803

CONTRIBUTIONS SUMMARY

Typical Recipients: • *Education:* colleges & universities • *Health:* hospices, mental health • *Social Services:* aged, drugs & alcohol, family services, food/clothing distribution, united funds, youth organizations

Grant Types: general support
Operating Locations: NC (High Point)

CORP. OFFICERS

W. P. Duncan, Jr.: *CURR EMPL* cfo, treas: Thomas Built Buses LP

John W. Thomas, Jr.: *B* High Point NC 1927 *ED* AL Polytech Inst 1949 *CURR EMPL* chmn, pres, ceo: Thomas Built Buses LP

GIVING OFFICERS

D.M. Harrison: secy
R. A. Price: trust
Albert L. Thomas: trust
B. L. Thomas: trust
James E. Thomas: secy, trust
John W. Thomas, Jr.: treas, trust *CURR EMPL* chmn, pres, ceo: Thomas Built Buses LP (see above)
P. A. Thomas: trust

APPLICATION INFORMATION

Initial Approach: Send brief letter describing program. There are no deadlines.

GRANTS ANALYSIS

Number of Grants: 13
Highest Grant: $6,000
Typical Range: $1,000 to $3,000
Disclosure Period: 1991

RECENT GRANTS

6,000 Independent College Fund of North Carolina, Winston-Salem, NC
3,500 Salvation Army, High Point, NC
3,000 High Point Arts Council, High Point, NC
3,000 Piedmont School, High Point, NC
2,500 Boys and Girls Club, High Point, NC
2,500 YMCA, Archdale, NC
2,000 Boy Scouts of America, High Point, NC
2,000 High Point College, High Point, NC

2,000 YMCA, High Point, NC
1,000 Alcoholics Home, Jamestown, NC

Thomas Foundation, Dorothy

CONTACT

Dorothy Thomas Fdn.
PO Box 3436
Tampa, FL 33601

FINANCIAL SUMMARY

Recent Giving: $186,800 (1991); $574,650 (1990); $212,300 (1989)
Assets: $2,447,204 (1991); $2,365,512 (1990); $2,862,050 (1989)
Gifts Received: $428,000 (1989); $17,286 (1988)
EIN: 59-6059765

CONTRIBUTIONS SUMMARY

Donor(s): the late Wayne Thomas, Robert Thomas, Port Sutton

Typical Recipients: • *Education:* colleges & universities, private education (precollege) • *Religion:* churches, religious organizations • *Social Services:* child welfare, community service organizations, disabled, food/clothing distribution, homes, united funds, youth organizations

Grant Types: general support and multiyear/continuing support

Geographic Distribution: focus on FL

GIVING OFFICERS

Michael Thomas: dir, chmn, treas
Robert Thomas: dir, vchmn
Henry Toland: secy

APPLICATION INFORMATION

Initial Approach: Contributes only to preselected organizations.

GRANTS ANALYSIS

Number of Grants: 14
Highest Grant: $60,000
Typical Range: $5,000 to $25,000
Disclosure Period: 1991

RECENT GRANTS

60,000 Children's Home Society of Florida, Tampa, FL

25,000 Metropolitan Ministries, Tampa, FL
25,000 Prison Crusade, Tampa, FL
15,000 Abilities of Florida, Clearwater, FL
15,000 Self Reliance, Tampa, FL — apartments for the disabled
10,000 Alpha, Tampa, FL
10,000 Tampa United Methodist Centers, Tampa, FL
5,000 Alpha, Tampa, FL
5,000 Children's Home, Tampa, FL
5,000 Divine Providence Food Bank, Tampa, FL

Thomas Foundation, Joan and Lee

CONTACT

Lee B. Thomas, Jr.
Director
Joan and Lee Thomas Foundation
601 West Market Street, Suite 402
Louisville, KY 40202-2745
(502) 584-6724

FINANCIAL SUMMARY

Recent Giving: $210,000 (fiscal 1991); $138,000 (fiscal 1990)
Assets: $10,793,746 (fiscal year ending June 30, 1991); $9,910,970 (fiscal 1990)
Gifts Received: $250,000 (fiscal 1991); $9,469,600 (fiscal 1990)
EIN: 61-1166955

CONTRIBUTIONS SUMMARY

Donor(s): the donor is Lee B. Thomas, Jr., a director of the foundation

Typical Recipients: • *Arts & Humanities:* arts centers • *Civic & Public Affairs:* first amendment issues, international affairs, law & justice, urban & community affairs • *Education:* colleges & universities, literacy • *Social Services:* family services, religious welfare, youth organizations

Grant Types: general support
Geographic Distribution: primarily Kentucky

GIVING OFFICERS

Glenn E. Thomas, Jr.: dir
Joan E. Thomas, Jr.: dir
Lee B. Thomas, Jr.: don, dir

GRANTS ANALYSIS

Total Grants: $210,000
Number of Grants: 5
Highest Grant: $80,000
Typical Range: $5,000 to $50,000
Disclosure Period: fiscal year ending June 30, 1991

RECENT GRANTS

80,000 Westtown School
50,000 Lincoln Foundation
50,000 National Center for Family Literacy
25,000 Family and Children's Agency
5,000 Louisville Urban League

Thomas Industries / Thomas Foundation

Sales: $347.58 million
Employees: 3,170
Headquarters: Louisville, KY

CONTACT

Phillip J. Stuecker
Secretary-Treasurer
Thomas Foundation
4360 Brownsboro Road
Suite 300
Louisville, KY 40207
(502) 893-4600

FINANCIAL SUMMARY

Recent Giving: $25,100 (1991); $47,965 (1989)
Assets: $8,765 (1991); $23,149 (1989)
Gifts Received: $29,500 (1991); $70,000 (1989)
Fiscal Note: In 1991, contributions were received from Thomas Industries, Inc.
EIN: 39-6075230

CONTRIBUTIONS SUMMARY

Typical Recipients: • *Civic & Public Affairs:* economic development • *Education:* community & junior colleges, economic education, education funds • *Health:* health funds • *Social Services:* united funds, youth organizations

Grant Types: capital and general support
Operating Locations: KY (Louisville)

CORP. OFFICERS

Walter S. Davis: *CURR EMPL* chmn: Thomas Indus
Thomas R. Fuller: *CURR EMPL* pres, ceo: Thomas Indus

GIVING OFFICERS

C. Barr Schuler: vp

Phillip J. Stuecker: secy-treas

APPLICATION INFORMATION
Initial Approach: Submit a brief letter of inquiry. There are no deadlines.

GRANTS ANALYSIS
Number of Grants: 12
Highest Grant: $5,000
Typical Range: $1,000 to $5,000
Disclosure Period: 1991

RECENT GRANTS
5,000 NAED Education Fund, Louisville, KY
5,000 University of Kentucky Community College, Lexington, KY
3,600 Jewish Hospital Foundation, Louisville, KY
3,500 Boy Scouts of America, Louisville, KY
3,000 Metro United Way, Louisville, KY
1,000 Kentucky Council on Economic Education, Louisville, KY
1,000 Kentucky Independent College Fund, Louisville, KY
1,000 Louisville Development Foundation, Louisville, KY
750 March of Dimes, Louisville, KY
500 Volunteers of America, Louisville, KY

Thomas Medical Foundation, Roy E.

CONTACT
Roy E. Thomas Medical Fdn.
c/o Security Pacific National Bank
PO Box 3189 Terminal Annex
Los Angeles, CA 90051
(213) 613-7141

FINANCIAL SUMMARY
Recent Giving: $100,000 (1991); $110,000 (1990); $100,000 (1989)
Assets: $2,219,741 (1991); $2,018,783 (1990); $2,208,967 (1989)
EIN: 95-3190677

CONTRIBUTIONS SUMMARY
Donor(s): the late Roy E. Thomas, the late Georgia Seaver Thomas

Typical Recipients: • *Health:* hospitals, single-disease health associations
Grant Types: general support
Geographic Distribution: focus on CA

GIVING OFFICERS
Bank of America: trust
Seaver T. Page: trust

APPLICATION INFORMATION
Initial Approach: Contributes only to preselected organizations. Applications not accepted.

GRANTS ANALYSIS
Number of Grants: 10
Highest Grant: $75,000
Disclosure Period: 1991

RECENT GRANTS
75,000 Hospital of Good Samaritan, Los Angeles, CA
25,000 Hospital of Good Samaritan, Los Angeles, CA

Thomas Memorial Foundation, Theresa A.

CONTACT
Charles L. Reed
President
Theresa A. Thomas Memorial Fdn.
PO Box 1122
Richmond, VA 23208
(804) 697-1200

FINANCIAL SUMMARY
Recent Giving: $823,968 (fiscal 1991); $369,628 (fiscal 1990); $1,415,641 (fiscal 1988)
Assets: $11,157,198 (fiscal year ending August 31, 1991); $10,012,688 (fiscal 1990); $8,938,355 (fiscal 1988)
Gifts Received: $127,111 (fiscal 1990); $34,611 (fiscal 1988)
EIN: 51-0146629

CONTRIBUTIONS SUMMARY
Typical Recipients: • *Education:* colleges & universities, medical education • *Health:* emergency/ambulance services • *Religion:* religious organizations • *Social Services:* child welfare, community service organizations, family planning, homes, united funds, youth organizations
Grant Types: operating expenses and scholarship

Geographic Distribution: focus on VA

GIVING OFFICERS
Thomas P. Carr: secy, dir
Charles L. Reed: pres, treas, dir
James C. Roberts: vp, dir

APPLICATION INFORMATION
Initial Approach: Send brief letter of inquiry describing program or project. There are no deadlines.

GRANTS ANALYSIS
Number of Grants: 18
Highest Grant: $250,000
Typical Range: $3,000 to $5,000
Disclosure Period: fiscal year ending August 31, 1991

RECENT GRANTS
250,000 Medical College of Virginia Foundation, Richmond, VA — Virginia Commonwealth University
250,000 University of Virginia Health Sciences Center, Charlottesville, VA — nursing fellowship
100,000 Westminster-Canterbury Foundation, Richmond, VA — fellowship endowment
76,000 Alderson-Broaddus College, Philippi, WV — student aid
25,000 American Cancer Society, Glen Allen, VA
25,000 Kilmarnock-Lancaster County Volunteer Rescue Squad, Kilmarnock, VA
25,000 National Foundation for Infectious Diseases, Bethesda, MD
20,000 Alderson-Broaddus College, Philippi, WV — student aid
16,666 Elk Hill Farm, Goochland, VA
8,303 St. Charles Health Council, St. Charles, VA — capital improvements

Thomaston Mills, Inc.

Sales: $201.5 million
Employees: 2,368
Headquarters: Thomaston, GA
SIC Major Group: Apparel & Other Textile Products and Textile Mill Products

CONTACT
Dan Tripp
Vice President, Human Resources
Thomaston Mills, Inc.
115 East Main St.
Thomaston, GA 30286-0311
(706) 647-7131

CONTRIBUTIONS SUMMARY
Operating Locations: GA (Thomaston)

CORP. OFFICERS
Neil H. Hightower: *B* Atlanta GA 1940 *ED* GA Inst Tech BS 1963; Harvard Univ 1974 *CURR EMPL* pres, ceo, dir: Thomaston Mills *NONPR AFFIL* dir: Am Textile Mfrs Inst, GA Textile Mfrs Assn; mem: Am Yarn Spinners Assn; mem natl adv bd: GA Inst Tech

OTHER THINGS TO KNOW
Company is an original donor to the Community Enterprises

Thomasville Furniture Industries / Thomasville Furniture Industries Foundation

Sales: $417.9 million
Employees: 8,000
Parent Company: Armstrong World Industries
Headquarters: Thomasville, NC
SIC Major Group: Furniture & Fixtures

CONTACT
Carlyle Nance, Jr.
Secretary
Thomasville Furniture Industries Fdn.
PO Box 339
Thomasville, NC 27361-0339
(919) 472-4000

FINANCIAL SUMMARY
Recent Giving: $250,000 (1993 est.); $250,000 (1991); $269,311 (1990)
Assets: $3,248,376 (1990); $3,381,806 (1989); $3,169,423 (1988)
EIN: 56-6047870

CONTRIBUTIONS SUMMARY
Typical Recipients: • *Arts & Humanities:* community arts, libraries, museums/galleries, performing arts, theater • *Education:* colleges & universities, public education (precollege) • *Social Services:* community service organizations, united funds, youth organizations
Grant Types: general support
Nonmonetary Support Types: donated products
Geographic Distribution: focus on NC
Operating Locations: MS (Fayette), NC (Statesville, Thomasville), TN (Johnson City)

CORP. OFFICERS
Frederick B. Starr: *CURR EMPL* pres, ceo: Thomasville Furniture Indus

GIVING OFFICERS
Carlyle A. Nance, Jr.: adm comm
Charles G. O'Brien: adm comm
Frederick B. Starr: chmn, mem adm comm *CURR EMPL* pres, ceo: Thomasville Furniture Indus (see above)

APPLICATION INFORMATION
Initial Approach: Send a brief letter of inquiry and a full proposal. There are no deadlines.
Restrictions on Giving: Does not support individuals, religious organizations for sectarian purposes, political or lobbying groups, or organizations outside operating areas.

GRANTS ANALYSIS
Number of Grants: 106
Highest Grant: $20,000
Typical Range: $100 to $5,000
Disclosure Period: 1990

RECENT GRANTS
25,000 Community General Hospital of Thomasville, Thomasville, NC
20,000 Davidson County Library Foundation, Lexington, NC
18,000 YMCA, Thomasville, NC
15,000 YMCA, Thomasville, NC
10,000 Arts Council for Davidson County, Lexington, NC
10,000 YMCA, Statesville, NC
8,000 Ashe County Performing Arts Building Committee, West Jefferson, NC
7,000 Reynolda House Museum of American Art, Winston-Salem, NC
5,779 YMCA, Statesville, NC
5,000 Habitat for Humanity of Thomasville, Thomasville, NC

Thompson Charitable Foundation

CONTACT
Thompson Charitable Foundation
P.O. Box 10516
Knoxville, TN 37939-0516
(615) 588-0491

FINANCIAL SUMMARY
Recent Giving: $4,230,000 (fiscal 1990)
Assets: $17,503,147 (fiscal year ending June 30, 1990)
Gifts Received: $4,350,000 (fiscal 1990)
Fiscal Note: Fiscal 1990 contribution received from the Estate of B. R. Thompson, Sr.

CONTRIBUTIONS SUMMARY
Typical Recipients: • *Arts & Humanities:* music • *Civic & Public Affairs:* housing • *Education:* colleges & universities • *Health:* hospitals
Grant Types: department and general support

GIVING OFFICERS
Carl Ensor: dir
B. Ray Thompson, Jr.: dir
Jesse J. Thompson: dir
Merle Wolfe: dir
Lindsay Young: dir

APPLICATION INFORMATION
Initial Approach: The foundation reports no specific application guidelines. Send a brief letter of inquiry, including statement of purpose, amount requested, and proof of tax-exempt status.

GRANTS ANALYSIS
Total Grants: $4,230,000
Number of Grants: 6
Highest Grant: $3,380,000
Typical Range: $20,000 to $150,000
Disclosure Period: fiscal year ending June 30, 1990

RECENT GRANTS
3,380,000 Thompson Cancer Survival Center, Knoxville, TN — purchase of MRI equipment
500,000 University of Tennessee Athletic Department, Knoxville, TN — football facility
150,000 Knoxville Symphony, TN
100,000 Helen Ross McNabb Foundation, Knoxville, TN — youth center
50,000 Maryville College, Maryville, TN
30,000 Kentucky Mountain Housing Development, KY
20,000 Memorial Hospital Foundation — expansion of emergency room facilities

Thompson Charitable Foundation, Marion G.

CONTACT
Lowell C. Bernard
Trustee
Marion G. Thompson Charitable Fdn.
6140 Plumas St.
Reno, NV 89505-6060

FINANCIAL SUMMARY
Recent Giving: $290,000 (fiscal 1992); $255,000 (fiscal 1991); $255,000 (fiscal 1990)
Assets: $2,723,048 (fiscal year ending March 31, 1992); $2,759,017 (fiscal 1991); $2,738,787 (fiscal 1990)
EIN: 88-6042564

CONTRIBUTIONS SUMMARY
Typical Recipients: • *Education:* colleges & universities, community & junior colleges, private education (precollege) • *Health:* pediatric health • *Religion:* religious organizations • *Social Services:* child welfare, disabled
Grant Types: general support
Geographic Distribution: focus on NV and CA

GIVING OFFICERS
Lowell C. Bernard: trust

APPLICATION INFORMATION
Initial Approach: Contributes only to preselected organizations.

GRANTS ANALYSIS
Number of Grants: 11
Highest Grant: $44,000
Typical Range: $10,000 to $30,000
Disclosure Period: fiscal year ending March 31, 1992

RECENT GRANTS
44,000 Our Lady of Snows School, Reno, NV — tuition assistance program
40,000 Sisters of St. Dominic, San Rafael, CA — intensive care nursery
30,000 Eagle Valley Children's Home, Reno, NV — respite care program
25,000 Eagle Valley Children's Home, Reno, NV — general
25,000 Shriner's Hospital for Crippled Children, San Francisco, CA — general
25,000 Truckee Meadows Community College, Reno, NV — technical building fund
25,000 University of Nevada Reno, Reno, NV — scholarship fund
23,000 Our Lady of Snows School, Reno, NV — heating and air conditioning system
20,000 Our Lady of Snows School, Reno, NV
18,000 Our Lady of Snows School, Reno, NV — general

Thompson Charitable Trust, Sylvia G.

CONTACT
Sylvia G. Thompson Charitable Trust
P.O. Box 1546
Sedalia, MO 65302

FINANCIAL SUMMARY
Recent Giving: $0 (1990)
Assets: $3,310,331 (1990)
Gifts Received: $3,203,469 (1990)
EIN: 43-6368333

CONTRIBUTIONS SUMMARY
Typical Recipients: • *Social Services:* aged
Grant Types: project

GIVING OFFICERS
Adam B. Fischer: trust
Henry Lamm: trust
Opal Rinebarger: trust
William Shumake: trust

GRANTS ANALYSIS
Total Grants: $0
Disclosure Period: 1990

Thompson Family Fund, Lucille S.

CONTACT
Lucille S. Thompson Family Fund
c/o Northern Trust Company
50 South La Salle Street
Chicago, IL 60675-0001
(312) 630-6000

FINANCIAL SUMMARY
Recent Giving: $355,103 (fiscal 1990)
Assets: $16,299,582 (fiscal year ending February 28, 1990); $16,299,582 (fiscal 1989)
EIN: 58-1788548

GIVING OFFICERS
Archer W. Bishop, Jr.: chmn
Archer W. III Bishop, Jr.: trust comm mem
Baker O'Neil Bishop, Jr.: trust comm mem
Kristen Kohlhase Bishop, Jr.: Trust comm mem
Sandra K. Bishop, Jr.: trust comm mem
Thompson Alexander Bishop, Jr.: trust comm mem
Lucille S. Thompson: emeritus chmn

APPLICATION INFORMATION
Initial Approach: The foundation reports no specific application guidelines. Send a brief letter of inquiry, including statement of purpose, amount requested, and proof of tax-exempt status.

GRANTS ANALYSIS
Total Grants: $355,103
Number of Grants: 23
Highest Grant: $100,000
Disclosure Period: fiscal year ending February 28, 1990

Thompson Trust, Thomas

CONTACT
Daniel W. Fawcett
Trustee
Thomas Thompson Trust
31 Milk St., Ste. 201
Boston, MA 02109
(617) 723-4535

FINANCIAL SUMMARY
Recent Giving: $345,340 (fiscal 1990); $395,938 (fiscal 1989)
Assets: $9,426,325 (fiscal year ending May 31, 1990); $8,036,339 (fiscal 1989)
EIN: 03-0179429

CONTRIBUTIONS SUMMARY
Donor(s): the late Thomas Thompson
Typical Recipients: • *Arts & Humanities:* community arts, history/historic preservation • *Health:* health funds, hospitals, mental health • *Social Services:* aged, homes, recreation & athletics
Grant Types: capital, emergency, general support, and project
Geographic Distribution: limited to Brattleboro, VT and Rhinebeck, NY, and surrounding areas

GIVING OFFICERS
Daniel W. Fawcett: trust
William B. Tyler: trust

APPLICATION INFORMATION
Initial Approach: Initial contact by telephone. Grants awarded only to organizations that have been in operation for three consecutive years. Application form required. Approach foundation by telephone. There are no deadlines. Board meets monthly except in August. Decisions are made within six weeks.

GRANTS ANALYSIS
Number of Grants: 17
Highest Grant: $100,000
Typical Range: $5,000 to $10,000
Disclosure Period: fiscal year ending May 31, 1990

RECENT GRANTS
100,000 Northern Dutchess Hospital, Rhinebeck, NY
50,000 Brattleboro Memorial Hospital, Brattleboro, VT
35,000 Brattleboro Mutual Aid Association, Brattleboro, VT
20,004 Rhinebeck Community Center, Brattleboro, VT
18,000 Winston L. Prouty Center, Brattleboro, VT
10,000 Greater Brattleboro Teen Community, Brattleboro, VT
10,000 Mental Health Services of S.E. Vermont, Brattleboro, VT
10,000 Putney Cares, Putney, VT
10,000 Rockingham Community Land Trust, Rockingham, NH
8,000 Preservation Trust of Vermont, Windsor, VT

Thomson Information Publishing Group

Sales: $87.0 million
Employees: 975
Parent Company: Thomson Holdings
Headquarters: New York, NY
SIC Major Group: Printing & Publishing and Security & Commodity Brokers

CONTACT
Gerald Tenser
Vice President
Thomson Information Publishing
One Sta. Pl.
Stamford, CT 06902
(203) 969-8700

FINANCIAL SUMMARY
Fiscal Note: Annual Giving Range: $50,000 to $100,000

CONTRIBUTIONS SUMMARY
Supports education, primarily colleges and universities and student aid. Also support the arts and social service organizations.

Typical Recipients: • *Arts & Humanities:* libraries • *Education:* colleges & universities • *Social Services:* general

Grant Types: general support and scholarship

Nonmonetary Support Types: donated products

Geographic Distribution: primarily in headquarters area

Operating Locations: CT (Stamford)

CORP. OFFICERS
George Landgrebe: *CURR EMPL* pres: Thomson Information Publ Group

APPLICATION INFORMATION
Initial Approach: Send brief letter or proposal, including information on the organization, the amount requested, purpose of the grant, and proof of tax-exempt status. Company accepts applications at any time, but the best time to apply is mid-year for funding the following year.

GRANTS ANALYSIS
Typical Range: $500 to $1,500

Thomson Newspapers Corp.

Sales: $750.0 million
Employees: 9,600
Headquarters: Des Plaines, IL
SIC Major Group: Printing & Publishing

CONTACT
Joseph Barletta
Senior Vice President and COO
Thomson Newspapers Corp.
3150 Des Plaines Ave.
Des Plaines, IL 60018
(708) 299-5544

CONTRIBUTIONS SUMMARY
Operating Locations: IL (Des Plaines)

CORP. OFFICERS
W. Johnston: *CURR EMPL* pres: Thomson Newspapers

Thor Industries, Inc.

Sales: $140.9 million
Employees: 1,199
Headquarters: Jackson Center, OH
SIC Major Group: Holding & Other Investment Offices and Transportation Equipment

CONTACT

Larry Huttle
President
Thor Industries, Inc.
419 West Pke. St.
Jackson Center, OH 45334
(513) 596-6849

CONTRIBUTIONS SUMMARY

Operating Locations: OH (Jackson Center)

CORP. OFFICERS

P.B. Orthwein: *CURR EMPL* vchmn, treas: Thor Indus
W. F. B. Thompson: *CURR EMPL* chmn, pres, ceo, dir: Thor Indus

RECENT GRANTS

Henry Ford Museum and Greenfield Village, Dearborn, MI

Thoresen Foundation

CONTACT

George V. Berger
Trustee
Thoresen Fdn.
2881 La Concha Dr.
Clearwater, FL 34622

FINANCIAL SUMMARY

Recent Giving: $2,070,000 (fiscal 1992); $2,083,375 (fiscal 1991); $342,971 (fiscal 1990)
Assets: $18,943,513 (fiscal year ending February 28, 1992); $4,253,753 (fiscal 1991); $6,151,820 (fiscal 1990)
Gifts Received: $13,479,464 (fiscal 1992); $420,330 (fiscal 1991); $686,044 (fiscal 1990)
Fiscal Note: In 1992, contributions were received from Ann Stillman Trust ($26,406) and the estate of Catherine Thoresen ($13,453,058).
EIN: 36-6102493

CONTRIBUTIONS SUMMARY

Donor(s): The foundation was established in 1952 by William E. Thoresen and Catherine E. Thoresen.

Typical Recipients: • *Arts & Humanities:* arts institutes, opera • *Education:* colleges & universities • *Health:* health organizations

Grant Types: general support

Geographic Distribution: focus on Florida, Illinois, and Virginia

GIVING OFFICERS

George V. Berger: trust
Catherine Culver: trust
Paul O' Connell: trust
Michael Thoresen: trust

APPLICATION INFORMATION

Initial Approach: Restrictions on Giving: The foundation supports preselected organizations and does not accept unsolicited requests for funds. The foundation does not make grants to individuals or for scholarships.

GRANTS ANALYSIS

Total Grants: $2,070,000
Number of Grants: 4
Highest Grant: $2,000,000
Typical Range: $5,000 to $50,000
Disclosure Period: fiscal year ending February 28, 1992
Note: Average grant figure does not include the highest grant of $2,000,000. Recent grants are derived from a fiscal 1992 grants list.

RECENT GRANTS

2,000,000 Randolph-Macon Woman's College, Ashland, VA
50,000 Lyric Opera Company, Chicago, IL
15,000 American Heart Association, St. Petersburg, FL
5,000 Art Institute of Chicago, Chicago, IL

Thorn Apple Valley, Inc.

Sales: $817.3 million
Employees: 3,060
Headquarters: Southfield, MI
SIC Major Group: Food & Kindred Products

CONTACT

Kim Aschione
Thorn Apple Valley, Inc.
18800 West Ten Mile Rd.
Southfield, MI 48075
(313) 552-0700

CONTRIBUTIONS SUMMARY

Operating Locations: MA (Chelsea), MI (Detroit, Grand Rapids, Southfield), NC (Holly Ridge), UT (Hyrum)

Note: Company opertes six divisions in locations.

CORP. OFFICERS

Henry S. Dorfman: *CURR EMPL* chmn, ceo, dir: Thorn Apple Valley
Joel Dorfman: *CURR EMPL* ceo, dir: Thorn Apple Valley

Thorn, Jr. Foundation, Columbus W.

CONTACT

Columbus W. Thorn, Jr. Fdn.
109 East Main St.
Elkton, MD 21921
(410) 398-0611

FINANCIAL SUMMARY

Recent Giving: $265,900 (1990); $244,159 (1989)
Assets: $5,576,622 (1990); $5,796,886 (1989)
Gifts Received: $134,435 (1990); $124,534 (1989)
EIN: 23-7153983

CONTRIBUTIONS SUMMARY

Donor(s): the late Columbus W. Thorn
Grant Types: loan
Geographic Distribution: limited to residents of Cecil County, MD

GIVING OFFICERS

Charles L. Scott: trust
Doris P. Scott: trust

APPLICATION INFORMATION

Initial Approach: Application form required. Deadline is August 15.

Thorne Foundation

CONTACT

Miriam A. Thorne
President
Thorne Fdn.
435 East 52nd St.
New York, NY 10022
(212) 758-2425

FINANCIAL SUMMARY

Recent Giving: $463,954 (1991); $386,213 (1990); $306,080 (1989)
Assets: $2,206,527 (1991); $2,350,640 (1990); $2,642,549 (1989)
EIN: 13-6109955

CONTRIBUTIONS SUMMARY

Donor(s): the late Landon K. Thorne, the late Julia L. Thorne
Typical Recipients: • *Arts & Humanities:* history/historic preservation, libraries, museums/galleries, public broadcasting • *Civic & Public Affairs:* zoos/botanical gardens • *Education:* colleges & universities • *Health:* medical research • *Social Services:* child welfare, community service organizations, family services, homes, united funds, youth organizations
Grant Types: general support
Geographic Distribution: focus on NY

GIVING OFFICERS

John B. Jessup: secy, treas
David H. Thorne: vp
Miriam A. Thorne: pres

APPLICATION INFORMATION

Initial Approach: Send brief letter of inquiry describing program. There are no deadlines.

GRANTS ANALYSIS

Number of Grants: 53
Highest Grant: $100,000
Typical Range: $300 to $10,000
Disclosure Period: 1991

RECENT GRANTS

100,000 Pierpont Morgan Library, New York, NY
52,500 Metropolitan Museum of Art, New York, NY
52,250 New York Zoological Society, New York, NY
40,000 Frick Collection, New York, NY
30,000 National Foundation for Facial Re-

construction, New York, NY
25,000 American Museum of Natural History, New York, NY
25,000 Thirteen, New York, NY
20,000 Manhattan Eye and Ear, New York, NY
10,650 Boys and Girls Club, New York, NY
10,000 Educational Fund, New York, NY

Thornton Foundation

CONTACT
Charles B. Thornton, Jr.
President
Thornton Fdn.
523 West Sixth St., Ste. 636
Los Angeles, CA 90016
(213) 629-3867

FINANCIAL SUMMARY
Recent Giving: $330,600 (1991); $347,500 (1990); $310,000 (1988)
Assets: $7,799,116 (1991); $6,304,248 (1990); $7,222,076 (1988)
EIN: 95-6037178

CONTRIBUTIONS SUMMARY
Donor(s): the late Charles B. Thornton, Flora I.Thornton
Typical Recipients: • *Arts & Humanities:* libraries, museums/galleries, public broadcasting • *Education:* colleges & universities, private education (precollege), science/technology education • *Health:* hospitals • *Religion:* churches • *Social Services:* day care, youth organizations
Grant Types: operating expenses
Geographic Distribution: focus on CA

GIVING OFFICERS
Robert E. Novell: secy
Charles B. Thornton, Jr.: pres, trust
William Laney Thornton: vp, trust

APPLICATION INFORMATION
Initial Approach: Send brief letter of inquiry describing program or project. There are no deadlines.
Restrictions on Giving: Does not support individuals.

GRANTS ANALYSIS
Number of Grants: 38
Highest Grant: $105,000
Typical Range: $1,000 to $5,000
Disclosure Period: 1991

RECENT GRANTS
105,000 Fine Arts Museum of San Francisco, San Francisco, CA
52,500 San Francisco University High School, San Francisco, CA
25,000 Harvard-Westlake School, Los Angeles, CA
25,000 San Francisco Opera, San Francisco, CA
20,000 Stanford University, Stanford, CA
15,000 Texas Tech University, Lubbock, TX
11,000 San Francisco Museum of Modern Art, San Francisco, CA
10,000 Education Foundation
10,000 Greenbelt Alliance
10,000 KCET, San Francisco, CA

Thornton Foundation, Flora L.

CONTACT
Flora L. Thornton
Trustee
Flora L. Thornton Fdn.
c/o Edward A. Landry
4444 Lakeside Dr., Ste. 300
Burbank, CA 91505
(213) 842-1645

FINANCIAL SUMMARY
Recent Giving: $805,500 (fiscal 1991); $1,580,550 (fiscal 1990); $502,450 (fiscal 1989)
Assets: $4,652,471 (fiscal year ending November 30, 1991); $3,823,625 (fiscal 1990); $4,579,357 (fiscal 1989)
Gifts Received: $874,428 (fiscal 1991); $1,014,000 (fiscal 1990)
EIN: 95-3855595

CONTRIBUTIONS SUMMARY
Donor(s): Flora L. Thornton
Typical Recipients: • *Arts & Humanities:* museums/galleries, opera, public broadcasting • *Education:* colleges & universities, private education (precollege), public education (precollege) • *Health:* hospitals,

medical research, pediatric health • *Religion:* churches • *Social Services:* shelters/homelessness, united funds
Grant Types: general support

GIVING OFFICERS
Edward A. Landry: trust *B* New Orleans LA 1939 *ED* LA St Univ BA 1961; Univ CA Los Angeles JD 1964 *CURR EMPL* atty: Musick Peeler & Garrett *NONPR AFFIL* mem: Am Bar Assn, Am Coll Probate Couns, CA Bar Assn, Los Angeles County Bar Assn
Glen P. McDaniel: trust
Flora L. Thornton: trust
William Laney Thornton: trust

APPLICATION INFORMATION
Initial Approach: Send brief letter of inquiry describing program or project. There are no deadlines.

GRANTS ANALYSIS
Number of Grants: 32
Highest Grant: $200,000
Typical Range: $1,000 to $10,000
Disclosure Period: fiscal year ending November 30, 1991

RECENT GRANTS
200,000 Los Angeles Music Center Opera Association, Los Angeles, CA
200,000 University of Southern California Comprehensive Cancer Center, Los Angeles, CA
107,500 San Francisco Day School, San Francisco, CA
100,000 St. Johns Hospital and Health Center Foundation
50,000 KCET, San Francisco, CA
30,000 St. John's Hospital
15,000 Santa Fe Opera, Sante Fe, NM
10,000 Library of Congress, James Madison National Council, Washington, DC
10,000 San Francisco Day School, San Francisco, CA
10,000 United Way, San Francisco, CA

Thornton Foundation, John M. and Sally B.

CONTACT
John M. and Sally B. Thornton Fdn.
2125 Evergreen St.
San Diego, CA 92106

FINANCIAL SUMMARY
Recent Giving: $703,232 (fiscal 1991); $1,244,165 (fiscal 1990); $293,149 (fiscal 1989)
Assets: $2,124,601 (fiscal year ending September 30, 1991); $1,180,842 (fiscal 1990); $2,295,706 (fiscal 1989)
Gifts Received: $5,000 (fiscal 1991)
EIN: 95-3800986

CONTRIBUTIONS SUMMARY
Typical Recipients: • *Arts & Humanities:* arts centers, arts funds, community arts, museums/galleries, opera, performing arts, public broadcasting • *Civic & Public Affairs:* zoos/botanical gardens • *Education:* colleges & universities • *Health:* hospices, hospitals, medical research, single-disease health associations • *Social Services:* united funds
Grant Types: operating expenses
Geographic Distribution: focus on San Diego, CA

GIVING OFFICERS
John McBride Thornton: secy, dir
Mark B. Thornton: dir
Sally B. Thornton: pres, dir
Steven B. Thornton: dir

APPLICATION INFORMATION
Initial Approach: Contributes only to preselected organizations.

GRANTS ANALYSIS
Number of Grants: 56
Highest Grant: $500,000
Typical Range: $1,000 to $7,000
Disclosure Period: fiscal year ending September 30, 1991

RECENT GRANTS
500,000 University of California San Diego, San Diego, CA
100,420 San Diego Museum of Art, San Diego, CA

15,000 San Diego Foundation for the Arts, San Diego, CA

11,966 San Diego Opera, San Diego, CA

6,350 Los Angeles Music Center Opera Association, Los Angeles, CA

6,100 Zoological Society, San Diego, CA

5,000 San Diego Natural History Museum, San Diego, CA

5,000 Whittier Institute, San Diego, CA

4,195 Old Globe Theatre, San Diego, CA

3,000 La Jolla Playhouse, La Jolla, CA

Thorpe Foundation, James R.

CONTACT
Edith D. Thorpe
President
James R. Thorpe Fdn.
8085 Wayzata Blvd.
Minneapolis, MN 55426-1499
(612) 545-1111

FINANCIAL SUMMARY
Recent Giving: $368,070 (fiscal 1991); $349,970 (fiscal 1990); $371,555 (fiscal 1989)
Assets: $7,552,800 (fiscal year ending November 30, 1991); $6,881,982 (fiscal 1990); $7,463,568 (fiscal 1989)
EIN: 41-6175293

CONTRIBUTIONS SUMMARY
Donor(s): the late James R. Thorpe
Typical Recipients: • *Arts & Humanities:* community arts, history/historic preservation, public broadcasting, theater • *Education:* colleges & universities, education funds, private education (precollege) • *Health:* medical research, pediatric health, single-disease health associations • *Social Services:* aged, child welfare, community centers, youth organizations
Grant Types: capital, general support, operating expenses, project, research, scholarship, and seed money
Geographic Distribution: focus on MN, especially Minneapolis and St. Paul

GIVING OFFICERS
Leonard M. Addington: vp, dir
Mary C. Boos: secy, dir

Samuel A. Cote: vp, dir
Elizabeth A. Kelly: vp, dir
Edith D. Thorpe: pres, dir
Samuel S. Thorpe III: treas, dir

APPLICATION INFORMATION
Initial Approach: Send brief letter of inquiry and outline of proposal. Deadines are March 1 and September 1. Board meets in May and November.
Restrictions on Giving: Does not support individuals, deficit financing land acquisition, matching gifts, or publications.

OTHER THINGS TO KNOW
Publications: Biennial Report

GRANTS ANALYSIS
Number of Grants: 52
Highest Grant: $20,000
Typical Range: $1,000 to $5,000
Disclosure Period: fiscal year ending November 30, 1991

RECENT GRANTS
20,000 Minnesota Private College Fund, St. Paul, MN

10,000 Children's Cancer Research Fund, Minneapolis, MN

7,500 Loft, Minneapolis, MN

7,500 Minnesota Public Radio, Minneapolis, MN

5,000 Biomedical Research Institute, Minneapolis, MN

5,000 Dunwoody Institute, Minneapolis, MN

5,000 Groves Learning Center, Minneapolis, MN

5,000 Minnesota Independent School Fund, Minneapolis, MN

5,000 Minnesota Vietnam Veterans Memorial, Minneapolis, MN

5,000 St. David's School for Child Development, Minneapolis, MN

Thorson Foundation

CONTACT
Thorson Fdn.
399 Fullerton Pkwy.
Chicago, IL 60614
(312) 327-2687

FINANCIAL SUMMARY
Recent Giving: $75,050 (1990); $70,875 (1989); $71,175 (1988)
Assets: $2,147,325 (1990); $2,152,070 (1989); $1,907,038 (1988)
EIN: 36-6051916

CONTRIBUTIONS SUMMARY
Donor(s): the late Robert D. Thorson, the late ReubenThorson, Dorothy W. Thorson
Typical Recipients: • *Arts & Humanities:* community arts, history/historic preservation, museums/galleries • *Civic & Public Affairs:* environmental affairs, zoos/botanical gardens • *Education:* colleges & universities, private education (precollege) • *Health:* hospitals • *Social Services:* community service organizations, drugs & alcohol, youth organizations
Grant Types: capital, fellowship, multiyear/continuing support, and scholarship
Geographic Distribution: focus on Chicago, IL

GIVING OFFICERS
John C. Goodall III: dir, secy
Virginia T. Goodall: dir, vp, treas
Dorothy W. Thorson: dir, pres

APPLICATION INFORMATION
Initial Approach: Contributes only to preselected organizations. Applications not accepted.
Restrictions on Giving: Does not support individuals.

GRANTS ANALYSIS
Number of Grants: 52
Highest Grant: $20,000
Typical Range: $100 to $2,500
Disclosure Period: 1990

RECENT GRANTS
20,000 Lincoln Park Zoological Society, Chicago, IL — Koala Program

7,100 Historic Sites Foundation, Baraboo, WI

4,500 Northwestern Memorial Foundation, Chicago, IL

3,500 Field Museum of Natural History, Chicago, IL

2,750 Chicago Historical Society, Chicago, IL

2,500 Rehabilitation Institute Foundation, Chicago, IL

1,000 Academy of the Sacred Heart, Chicago, IL

1,000 Chicago Maternity Center of Prentice Womens Hospital, Chicago, IL

1,000 Children's Memorial Foundation, Chicago, IL

1,000 Palm Beach Patrol Christmas Fund, Palm Beach, FL

Three Swallows Foundation

CONTACT
Ross Main
Manager
Three Swallows Fdn.
8313 Persimmon Tree Rd.
Bethesda, MD 20817-2647

FINANCIAL SUMMARY
Recent Giving: $496,641 (fiscal 1990); $360,225 (fiscal 1989)
Assets: $5,495,044 (fiscal year ending October 31, 1990); $5,511,741 (fiscal 1989)
EIN: 52-1234546

CONTRIBUTIONS SUMMARY
Typical Recipients: • *Civic & Public Affairs:* ethnic/minority organizations • *Education:* colleges & universities • *International:* international organizations • *Religion:* religious organizations • *Science:* scientific institutes • *Social Services:* family planning, shelters/homelessness, youth organizations
Grant Types: fellowship and general support
Geographic Distribution: focus on the Washington, DC, metropolitan area

GIVING OFFICERS
D. Barry Abell: treas, dir
Pamela T. Abell: dir
Steven Greenberg: dir
Logan Kline: dir
Robin T. Kline: dir
Ross Main: mgr
Diane E. Temple: secy, dir
Nancy L. Temple: dir

Paul N. Temple, Jr.: pres, dir *ED* Princeton Univ 1944; Harvard Univ 1948 *CURR EMPL* sole proprietor: Energy Capital Co *CORP AFFIL* sole proprietor: Energy Capital Co
Thomas D. Temple: dir
Lise Temple-Greenberg: dir

APPLICATION INFORMATION
Initial Approach: Contributes only to preselected organizations.
Restrictions on Giving: Does not support individuals.

GRANTS ANALYSIS
Number of Grants: 60
Highest Grant: $116,896
Typical Range: $250 to $5,000
Disclosure Period: fiscal year ending October 31, 1990

RECENT GRANTS
- 116,896 Institute of Noetic Sciences, Sausalito, CA
- 102,920 International Foundation, Arlington, VA
- 63,000 Endowment for the Neurosciences, North Pellmore, NY
- 44,000 New York Fellowship, New York, NY
- 37,500 Health Research, RPCI Division, Buffalo, NY
- 20,000 D.C. Treas/2nd Street Shelter Project, Washington, DC
- 17,000 Refugees International, Washington, DC
- 13,000 Metropolitan Area Youth for Christ, Wayne, NJ
- 10,000 Society of St. Andrew, Big Island, VA
- 7,500 Amistad Foundation, Birmingham, AL

3M Co. / 3M Foundation
Sales: $13.88 billion
Employees: 87,015
Headquarters: St. Paul, MN
SIC Major Group: Chemicals & Allied Products, Paper & Allied Products, Rubber & Miscellaneous Plastics Products, and Textile Mill Products

CONTACT
Cynthia F. Kleven
Assistant Secretary, 3M Foundation
Community Affairs
591-30-02 3M Ctr.
St. Paul, MN 55144-1000
(612) 733-1721
Note: Inquiries from the St. Paul, MN, area should be addressed to the designated staff person at the above address. See "Other Things You Should Know" for more details.

FINANCIAL SUMMARY
Recent Giving: $40,000,000 (1993 est.); $40,000,000 (1992 approx.); $31,392,102 (1991)
Assets: $12,951,001 (1992); $18,000,000 (1991); $36,489,547 (1989)
Fiscal Note: Above figures include both foundation giving and direct contributions by the company. Foundation giving totaled $10,768,742 in 1992, $10,647,376 in 1991, and $9,758,307 in 1989. Figures included international contributions.
EIN: 41-6038262

CONTRIBUTIONS SUMMARY
Typical Recipients: • *Arts & Humanities:* arts centers, arts institutes, community arts, dance, ethnic arts, history/historic preservation, libraries, museums/galleries, music, opera, performing arts, public broadcasting, theater • *Civic & Public Affairs:* economic development, environmental affairs, housing, law & justice, nonprofit management, safety, urban & community affairs, women's affairs, zoos/botanical gardens • *Education:* arts education, business education, career/vocational education, colleges & universities, community & junior colleges, continuing education, economic education, education associations, education funds, engineering education, journalism education, legal education, liberal arts education, literacy, medical education, minority education, science/technology education, special education, student aid • *Health:* geriatric health, health care cost containment, health organizations, hospitals, medical rehabilitation, mental health, single-disease health associations • *International:* international develop-ment/relief • *Science:* science exhibits & fairs, scientific institutes, scientific organizations • *Social Services:* aged, child welfare, community centers, community service organizations, counseling, day care, delinquency & crime, disabled, domestic violence, drugs & alcohol, emergency relief, employment/job training, family services, food/clothing distribution, homes, legal aid, recreation & athletics, shelters/homelessness, united funds, volunteer services, youth organizations
Grant Types: challenge, employee matching gifts, fellowship, general support, multi-year/continuing support, operating expenses, project, and scholarship
Nonmonetary Support Types: donated equipment, donated products, in-kind services, loaned employees, loaned executives, and workplace solicitation
Note: Nonmonetary support is budgeted at $18,000,000 in 1993 and valued at $24,000,000 in 1992 and $14,000,000 in 1991. David Ginkel, Manager Special Community Projects, is the contact person for nonmonetary support.
Geographic Distribution: near headquarters and operating locations only
Operating Locations: AK (Anchorage), AL (Decatur, Guin, Huntsville), AR (Little Rock), AZ (Phoenix, Tucson), CA (Camarillo, Chico, Corona, Costa Mesa, Fresno, Irvine, Irwindale, Los Angeles, Monrovia, Mountain View, Northridge, Petaluma, Sacramento, San Francisco, Santa Barbara, Santa Clara), CO (Denver), CT (Hartford, Norwalk, Stamford, West Haven), DC, FL (Miami), GA (Atlanta, Norcross), HI (Honolulu), IA (Ames, Forest City, Knoxville), IL (Bedford Park, Bloomington, Chicago, Cordova, Dekalb, Hinsdale), IN (Hartford City, Indianapolis), KY (Cynthiana), MA (Boston, Burlington, Cambridge, Chelmsford, Wilmington), MD (College Park, Westminster), MI (Ann Arbor, Detroit, Midland, Southfield), MN (Alexandria, Arden Hills, Cottage Grove, Eagan, Fairmont, Hutchinson, Maplewood, New Brighton, New Ulm, Park Rapids, Pine City, St. Paul, Staples, Stillwater), MO (Columbia, Nevada, Springfield, St. Louis), NC (Burlington, High Point), ND (Wahpeton), NE (Norfolk, Valley), NJ (Belle Mead, Eatontown, Freehold, West Caldwell, West Deptford), NY (Albany, Honeoye, Long Island, New York, Rochester), OH (Baltimore, Beaver Creek, Cincinnati, Cleveland, Columbus, Grove City, Mentor), OK (Weatherford), OR (White City), PA (Bristol, Philadelphia, Pittsburgh), SC (Greenville), SD (Aberdeen, Brookings), TN (Chattanooga, Memphis), TX (Austin, Brownwood, Dallas, El Paso, Houston, Stafford), UT (Salt Lake City), VA (McLean), WA (Seattle), WI (Cumberland, Menomonie, Nekoosa, Prairie du Chien, Wausau, Wisconsin Rapids), WV (Middleway)

CORP. OFFICERS
Livio Diego DeSimone: *B* Montreal Canada 1936 *ED* McGill Univ BSChE 1957 *CURR EMPL* chmn, ceo, dir: 3M Co *CORP AFFIL* dir: Cray Res, Dayton Hudson Corp, Gen Mills, Vulcan Materials Co *NONPR AFFIL* dir: Jr Achievement, MN Bus Partnership; mem: Bus Roundtable; trust: Univ MN Fdn

GIVING OFFICERS
J. Marc Adam: dir *B* Montreal Canada 1938 *ED* Univ Ottawa *CURR EMPL* group vp (consumer products): 3M Co *CORP AFFIL* dir: Bird Products Corp
M. George Allen: dir *CURR EMPL* sr vp (research & devel): 3M Co
Elva E. Christiansen: secy *CURR EMPL* mgr commun aff: 3M Co
D. D. Davis: dir *CURR EMPL* staff vp, corp marketing & pub aff: 3M Co *CORP AFFIL* mng dir: 3M Italia SpA
Livio Diego DeSimone: dir *CURR EMPL* chmn, ceo, dir: 3M Co (see above)
Larry E. Eaton: dir *CURR EMPL* exec vp (information imagin & electronic sector): 3M Co
M. Kay Grenz: dir *CURR EMPL* human resoues oper: 3M Co
Harry Allan Hammerly: dir *B* St Paul MN 1934 *ED* Univ MN 1955 *CURR EMPL* exec vp (industrial & electronic sector): 3M Co *NONPR AFFIL* mem:

Fin Execs Inst, MAPI, Natl
Assn Accts, Natl Assoc Mfrs;
trust: Univ St Thomas
Richard E. Hanson: vp, dir
CURR EMPL dir (community
affairs): 3M Co
Barbara W. Kaufmann: dir
CURR EMPL supvr corp con-
tributions art & ed: 3M Co
Arlo Dane Levi: pres *B*
Zeeland ND 1933 *ED* SD St
Univ BS 1963; Univ MI JD
1966 *CURR EMPL* vp, secy:
3M Co *NONPR AFFIL* dir:
Long Lake Conservation Fdn;
mem: Am Bar Assn, Am Soc
Corp Secys, Corp Counc MN,
MN Bar Assn
William J. McLellan: dir
Ronald Allen Mitsch: dir *B* St
Paul MN 1934 *ED* Hamline
Univ BS 1956; Univ NE MS
CURR EMPL sr vp (research &
dev): 3M Co *CORP AFFIL* dir:
Medimorphics Inc, Shigematsu
Works Co Ltd *NONPR AFFIL*
mem: Am Chem Soc; trust:
Childrens Hosp, Hamline Univ
Dwight A. Peterson: treas *B*
Minneapolis MN 1933 *ED* Law-
rence Univ 1955; Harvard Univ
Sch Bus Admin 1957 *CURR
EMPL* vp, treas: 3M Co
NONPR AFFIL dir: Eastern
Heights St Bank
L. J. Schoenwetter: dir *B* Mil-
waukee WI 1939 *CURR EMPL*
vp, contr: 3M Co *NONPR
AFFIL* mem: Fin Exec Inst,
Inst Mng Accts, MAPI Fin
Counc II
John J. Ursu: dir *CURR
EMPL* gen couns: 3M Co

APPLICATION INFORMATION

Initial Approach: *Initial Contact:* letter of inquiry; no phone
requests are accepted but company will provide direction *Include Information On:* proof of
tax-exempt status, brief history
of organization, project description (need, objective, target
group), and specific contribution request *When to Submit:*
anytime
Restrictions on Giving: The
company does not support individuals; religious endeavors;
propaganda or lobbying efforts;
fraternal, social, political, veterans, or military organizations; for-profit organizations;
travel; subsidization of books,
magazines, or articles in professional journals (except those relating to other 3M-supported
projects); commercial advertising; or purchase of equipment
not manufactured by 3M.

Generally does not consider organizations and causes that do
not impact 3M communities;
workshops, symposia, conferences, seminars, and publication of proceedings; fund-raising, testimonial, and athletic
events; endowments; or emergency operating support.
Multiple proposals from one organization per calendar year
are discouraged.
The company will not normally
fund a program or project beyond three years, or support
more than 10% of an organization's campaign goal or annual
budget.

OTHER THINGS TO KNOW

In countries where 3M has subsidiary operations, requests
should be directed to that location.
3M sponsors a volunteer program called Community Action
Retired Employees Services
(CARES) for all community
projects.
After the initial inquiry, if further consideration is to be
given to the funding request, a
grant application form will be
sent which should be com-
pleted and include the following aditional information: pro-
gram/project timetable;
evaluation; sources and
amounts of other support; annual report; and listing of directors and officers and their affiliations.
Inquiries from the St. Paul,
MN, area should be addressed
to the designated staff person
at the above address. The contact people include the following: Wendell J. Butler, health
& human services at 612-736-
3781; David E. Ginkel,
civic/community and contribution of product and property at
612-733-1420; and Barbara W.
Kaufmann, arts and education
at 612-733-1241.
Publications: giving guidelines

GRANTS ANALYSIS

Total Grants: $40,000,000
Number of Grants: 2,000*
Typical Range: $5,000 to
$20,000
Disclosure Period: 1992
Note: Number of grants figure
is approximate. Recent grants
are derived from a 1992 Form
990.

RECENT GRANTS

1,403,940   Twin Cities Public Television, St. Paul, MN
1,088,000   United Way of St. Paul Area, St. Paul, MN
355,000   Science Museum of Minnesota, St. Paul, MN
285,000   Ordway Music Theatre, St. Paul, MN
260,000   St. Paul Chamber Orchestra, St. Paul, MN
201,794   United Way of St. Paul, St. Paul, MN
200,000   Junior Achievement
200,000   Minnesota Historical Society, St. Paul, MN
148,418   American Red Cross, St. Paul, MN
137,000   Minneapolis Institute of Arts, Minneapolis, MN

Thrift Drug, Inc.
Sales: $652.0 million
Employees: 9,000
Parent Company: JC Penney Co.
Headquarters: Pittsburgh, PA
SIC Major Group: Miscellaneous Retail

CONTACT
Janice Meikle
VP, Professional and Public Affairs
Thrift Drug, Inc.
615 Alpha Dr.
Pittsburgh, PA 15238
(412) 963-6600

CONTRIBUTIONS SUMMARY
Operating Locations: PA (Pittsburgh)

CORP. OFFICERS
Robert W. Hannan: *CURR EMPL* pres: Thrift Drug

RECENT GRANTS
50,000   Philadelphia College of Pharmacy and Science, Philadelphia, PA — over five years

---

Thrifty Corp.
Sales: $3.25 billion
Employees: 30,400
Parent Company: Pacific Enterprises
Headquarters: Los Angeles, CA
SIC Major Group: Miscellaneous Retail

CONTACT
Iris Hackett
Vice President, Govt. & Comm. Relations
Thrifty Corp.
3424 Wilshire Blvd.
Los Angeles, CA 90010
(213) 251-6531

CONTRIBUTIONS SUMMARY
Operating Locations: CA (Los Angeles)

CORP. OFFICERS
Joseph H. Coulombe: *CURR EMPL* co-chmn, dir: Thrifty Corp
Daniel A. Seigel: *CURR EMPL* pres, dir: Thrifty Corp
William E. Yingling: *CURR EMPL* chmn, ceo, dir: Thrifty Corp

---

Thrifty Oil Co.
Sales: $750.0 million
Employees: 1,000
Headquarters: Downey, CA
SIC Major Group: Automotive Dealers & Service Stations and Petroleum & Coal Products

CONTACT
Jerry Haight
Vice President, Marketing
Thrifty Oil Co.
10000 Lakewood Blvd.
Downey, CA 90240
(310) 923-9876

CONTRIBUTIONS SUMMARY
Operating Locations: CA (Downey)

CORP. OFFICERS
Jack Elgin: *CURR EMPL* cfo: Thrifty Oil Co
Ted Orden: *CURR EMPL* pres: Thrifty Oil Co

Thrush-Thompson Foundation
Former Foundation Name: H. A. Thrush Foundation

CONTACT
Thrush-Thompson Fdn.
PO Box 185
Peru, IN 46970
(317) 743-6765

FINANCIAL SUMMARY
Recent Giving: $163,185 (fiscal 1992); $156,610 (fiscal 1991); $136,321 (fiscal 1989)
Assets: $3,941,669 (fiscal year ending July 31, 1992);

$3,602,777 (fiscal 1991);
$3,422,082 (fiscal 1989)
EIN: 35-6018476

CONTRIBUTIONS SUMMARY

Donor(s): the late Homer A. Thrush

Typical Recipients: • *Civic & Public Affairs:* municipalities • *Education:* colleges & universities, education associations • *Health:* medical research, single-disease health associations • *Religion:* churches • *Science:* scientific institutes • *Social Services:* recreation & athletics, united funds, youth organizations

Grant Types: general support

Geographic Distribution: focus on IN

GIVING OFFICERS

Dean A. Thompson: vp, dir

Jerry T. Thompson: vp, dir

Paul F. Thompson: pres, treas, dir

Robert L. Thompson: secy, dir *B* Adel GA 1937 *CURR EMPL* vp (pub aff): Springs Indus

GRANTS ANALYSIS

Number of Grants: 48

Highest Grant: $28,740

Typical Range: $100 to $10,000

Disclosure Period: fiscal year ending July 31, 1992

RECENT GRANTS

28,740 YMCA, IN
20,195 United Way, IN
17,110 Circus City Festival, IN
16,000 Indiana University Foundation, Bloomington, IN
11,100 Carmel Lutheran Church, Indianapolis, IN
10,000 Associated Colleges of Indiana, Indianapolis, IN
10,000 Main Street United Methodist Church, IN
8,472 American Red Cross, IN
4,000 Honeywell Foundation, IN
3,900 Linus Pauling Institute of Science and Medicine, Palo Alto, CA

Thums Long Beach Co.

Sales: $130.0 million
Employees: 315
Parent Company: Atlantic Richfield Co.
Headquarters: Long Beach, CA
SIC Major Group: Oil & Gas Extraction

CONTACT

Bill McFarland
Corporate Planning
Thums Long Beach Co.
PO Box 2900
Long Beach, CA 90801
(310) 436-9211

CONTRIBUTIONS SUMMARY

Operating Locations: CA (Long Beach)

CORP. OFFICERS

Frank Brown: *CURR EMPL* pres, gen mgr: Thums Long Beach Co
Raymond L. Stapp: *CURR EMPL* treas, contrl: Thums Long Beach Co

Thurman Charitable Foundation for Children, Edgar A.

CONTACT

Mike Johnson
c/o Crestar Bank, Trust Division
PO Box 13888
Roanoke, VA 24038

FINANCIAL SUMMARY

Recent Giving: $267,700 (fiscal 1992); $259,280 (fiscal 1991); $246,600 (fiscal 1990)
Assets: $5,784,547 (fiscal year ending June 30, 1992); $5,504,926 (fiscal 1991); $5,447,132 (fiscal 1990)
EIN: 54-6113281

CONTRIBUTIONS SUMMARY

Donor(s): the late Edgar A. Thurman
Typical Recipients: • *Health:* pediatric health • *Religion:* churches, religious organizations • *Social Services:* child welfare, community service organizations, day care, family planning, family services, food/clothing distribution, homes, shelters/homelessness, united funds, youth organizations

Grant Types: general support and operating expenses
Geographic Distribution: limited to VA, with preference given to the Roanoke area

GIVING OFFICERS

G. Chapman Duffy: comm
Kenneth L. Neathery, Jr.: comm
Charles W. Walker: comm

APPLICATION INFORMATION

Initial Approach: Application form required. Deadline is June 30.
Restrictions on Giving: Does not support individuals.

OTHER THINGS TO KNOW

Publications: Application Guidelines

GRANTS ANALYSIS

Number of Grants: 43
Highest Grant: $12,500
Typical Range: $2,000 to $10,000
Disclosure Period: fiscal year ending June 30, 1992

RECENT GRANTS

12,500 Virginia Baptist Children's Home, Richmond, VA
12,000 City Rescue Mission of Roanoke, Roanoke, VA
12,000 Greenvale Nursery School, Greenvale, VA
12,000 Northwest Child Development Center, Richmond, VA
12,000 St. John's Episcopal Church, Richmond, VA
11,000 Family Service of Roanoke Valley, Roanoke, VA
10,000 Boy Scouts of America, Richmond, VA
10,000 Planned Parenthood Federation of America, Richmond, VA
10,000 Salvation Army, Richmond, VA
9,000 Achievement Center, Richmond, VA

Thurston Charitable Foundation

CONTACT

Bradley Henke
Thurston Charitable Fdn.
900 4th Avenue, 38th Fl.
Seattle, WA 98164
(206) 623-1031

FINANCIAL SUMMARY

Recent Giving: $170,000 (fiscal 1992); $190,300 (fiscal 1991); $114,300 (fiscal 1990)
Assets: $2,081,890 (fiscal year ending June 30, 1992); $1,853,128 (fiscal 1991); $1,783,239 (fiscal 1990)
Gifts Received: $104,310 (fiscal 1992); $89,248 (fiscal 1991); $102,248 (fiscal 1990)
Fiscal Note: In fiscal 1992, contributions were received from Ellen E. Thurston Loving Trust I ($52,248) and Ellen E. Thurston Loving Trust II ($52,062).
EIN: 91-6055032

CONTRIBUTIONS SUMMARY

Donor(s): the late Ellen E. Thurston
Typical Recipients: • *Arts & Humanities:* dance, museums/galleries, public broadcasting • *Education:* colleges & universities, private education (precollege) • *Health:* health organizations, hospitals • *Religion:* churches, religious organizations • *Social Services:* child welfare, counseling, united funds, youth organizations
Grant Types: general support
Geographic Distribution: focus on WA

GIVING OFFICERS

Robert H. Thurston: vp
Severt W. Thurston, Jr.: pres
Susan E. Thurston: treas
Sherrie Tossell: secy

APPLICATION INFORMATION

Initial Approach: Send brief letter describing program. There are no deadlines.
Restrictions on Giving: Does not support individuals.

GRANTS ANALYSIS

Number of Grants: 64
Highest Grant: $15,000
Typical Range: $500 to $5,000
Disclosure Period: fiscal year ending June 30, 1992

RECENT GRANTS

15,000 Seattle Art Museum, Seattle, WA

10,100 Pacific Northwest Ballet, Seattle, WA

10,000 KCTS Channel 9, Seattle, WA

9,000 Ruth Dykeman Children's Foundation, Seattle, WA

8,000 Love, Seattle, WA

8,000 Poncho, Seattle, WA

6,000 Overlake Hospital Foundation, Seattle, WA

6,000 Oysterville Foundation, Seattle, WA

5,000 Cystic Fibrosis Foundation, Seattle, WA

5,000 US Ski Education Foundation, Seattle, WA

Thyssen Specialty Steels

Sales: $47.4 million
Employees: 130
Headquarters: New York, NY
SIC Major Group: Primary Metal Industries and Wholesale Trade—Durable Goods

CONTACT

Renate Knoefel
Personnel Manager
Thyssen Specialty Steels
1114 Avenue of the Americas, 31st Fl.
New York, NY 10036
(212) 512-9764

CONTRIBUTIONS SUMMARY

Thyssen has no set giving priorities, and maintains a very general contributions program. Past areas of interest have included arts and humanities, civic and public affairs, education, health (single-disease health associations), and social services (united funds, youth organizations).

Typical Recipients: • *Arts & Humanities:* arts associations • *Civic & Public Affairs:* urban & community affairs • *Education:* education associations • *Health:* single-disease health associations • *Social Services:* united funds, youth organizations

Grant Types: general support
Geographic Distribution: no geographic restrictions
Operating Locations: CT, IL, MI, MN, NY, PA

CORP. OFFICERS

Holger Flieth: *CURR EMPL* pres, coo: Thyssen Specialty Steels

GIVING OFFICERS

Renate Knoefel: *CURR EMPL* pers mgr: Thyssen Specialty Steels

APPLICATION INFORMATION

Initial Approach: Initial letter may be submitted at any time, but the beginning of the calendar year is the best time to apply. Applications should include a description of the organization, amount requested, and the purpose for which funds are sought.

Tibstra Charitable Foundation, Thomas and Gertrude

CONTACT

Thomas and Gertrude Tibstra Charitable Fdn.
119 South Old Creek Rd.
Palos Park, IL 60464

FINANCIAL SUMMARY

Recent Giving: $218,000 (1990); $131,000 (1989); $107,000 (1988)
Assets: $5,955,352 (1990); $6,119,310 (1989); $2,853,756 (1988)
Gifts Received: $649,375 (1989)
EIN: 36-3215222

CONTRIBUTIONS SUMMARY

Typical Recipients: • *Education:* religious education • *Health:* hospitals, medical research • *Religion:* churches, missionary activities, religious organizations
Grant Types: general support
Geographic Distribution: focus on MI and IL

GIVING OFFICERS

Gertrude Tibstra: secy
Larry Tibstra: trust
Thomas Tibstra: pres

APPLICATION INFORMATION

Initial Approach: Contributes only to preselected organizations.
Restrictions on Giving: Does not support individuals

GRANTS ANALYSIS

Number of Grants: 11
Highest Grant: $35,000
Typical Range: $5,000 to $25,000
Disclosure Period: 1990

RECENT GRANTS

35,000 Cedar Lake Conference Grounds Religious Work, Cedar Lake, IN

25,000 Back to God Hour Religious Work, Palos Heights, IL

25,000 Moody Bible Institute Religious Work, Chicago, IL

25,000 Southwest Chicago Christian School Association Religious Education, Chicago, IL

20,000 Christian Reformed Work Missions Religious Work, Grand Rapids, MI

20,000 Reformed Bible College Religious Education, Grand Rapids, MI

18,000 St. Jude Childrens Research Hospital, Memphis, TN

15,000 Calvin College and Seminary Religious Work, Grand Rapids, MI

15,000 Kedvale Avenue Christian Reform Christian Education Church Education Fund, Chicago, IL

15,000 World Home Bible League, South Holland, MI

Tidewater, Inc.

Sales: $546.5 million
Employees: 6,400
Headquarters: New Orleans, LA
SIC Major Group: Industrial Machinery & Equipment, Oil & Gas Extraction, and Water Transportation

CONTACT

John P. Laborde
President and CEO
Tidewater, Inc.
PO Box 61117
New Orleans, LA 70161
(504) 568-1010

CONTRIBUTIONS SUMMARY

Operating Locations: CA (Santa Barbara), CO (Grand Junction), LA (Morgan City, New Orleans), PA (Cuddy), TX (Houston)

CORP. OFFICERS

John P. Laborde: *B* Marksville LA 1923 *ED* LA St Univ 1947 *CURR EMPL* chmn, pres, ceo, dir: Tidewater *CORP AFFIL* dir: Am Bankers Ins Group, Bellsouth Corp, Hibernia Corp, Hibernia Natl Bank of New Orleans, LaSalle Energy Corp *NONPR AFFIL* mem: Am Bar Assn
Ken C. Tamblyn: *CURR EMPL* exec vp, cfo: Tidewater

Tiger Foundation

CONTACT

Julian H. Robertson, Jr.
Trustee
Tiger Foundation
101 Park Avenue, 47th Floor
New York, NY 10178-0002
(212) 867-4350

FINANCIAL SUMMARY

Recent Giving: $1,828,500 (fiscal 1991); $10,000 (fiscal 1990)
Assets: $3,586,907 (fiscal year ending June 30, 1991); $2,772,997 (fiscal 1990)
Gifts Received: $2,569,651 (fiscal 1991); $2,510,642 (fiscal 1990)
Fiscal Note: Fiscal 1991 contribution received from Julian H. Robertson, Jr.
EIN: 13-3555671

CONTRIBUTIONS SUMMARY

Donor(s): the donor is Julian H. Robertson, Jr., a trustee of the foundation
Typical Recipients: • *Civic & Public Affairs:* philanthropic organizations
Grant Types: general support

GIVING OFFICERS

Patrick D. Duff, Jr.: trust
John A. Griffin, Jr.: trust
D. Christine King, Jr.: trust
Steven C. Olson, Jr.: trust
Julian H. Robertson, Jr.: don, trust
Timothy R. Schlit, Jr.: trust
Arnold H. Snider, Jr.: trust

APPLICATION INFORMATION

Initial Approach: The foundation reports that unsolicited requests for funds are not accepted.

GRANTS ANALYSIS

Number of Grants: 14
Highest Grant: $400,000

Disclosure Period: fiscal year ending June 30, 1991
Note: Incomplete grants list provided in fiscal 1991.

RECENT GRANTS

10,000 Foundation for New Era Philanthropy

Tigon Corp.

Sales: $30.0 million
Employees: 250
Parent Company: Ameritech Corp.
Headquarters: Dallas, TX
SIC Major Group: Business Services

CONTACT

Jill Boeschenskein
Communications Manager
Tigon Corp.
17080 Dallas Pkwy.
Dallas, TX 75248
(214) 733-2700

CONTRIBUTIONS SUMMARY

Considers support for a limited number of organizations that complement their business interests.
Operating Locations: TX (Dallas)

CORP. OFFICERS

Bruce Simpson: *CURR EMPL* pres, ceo: Tigon Corp

APPLICATION INFORMATION

Initial Approach: Send letter of inquiry to Ameritech requesting foundation annual report, which includes application guidelines and brief priorities for the foundation, Ameritech's Bell companies, and other Ameritech companies. Preliminary inquiries by telephone or personal visits are discouraged. To request a contribution from Ameritech operating companies, a letter of inquiry is suggested before submitting a formal proposal. There are no deadlines.

OTHER THINGS TO KNOW

Before applying for a contribution, grant seekers should match their needs with the interests and priorities of the specific Ameritech company being approached; each Ameritech company has its own contributions program.

Tilghman, Sr., Charitable Trust, Bell and Horace

CONTACT

Rae H. Ely
Trustee
Bell and Horace Tilghman, Sr., Charitable Trust
PO Box 1550
Louisa, VA 23093

FINANCIAL SUMMARY

Assets: $9,333,333 (1988)
Gifts Received: $9,333,333 (1988)
EIN: 22-2918521

CONTRIBUTIONS SUMMARY

Donor(s): the late Anne Tilghman Boyce

GIVING OFFICERS

Olivia Boyce-Abel: trust
Rae H. Ely: trust
Tyson B. van Auken: trust

APPLICATION INFORMATION

Initial Approach: Contributes only to preselected organizations.
Restrictions on Giving: Does not support individuals.

Tilles Nonsectarian Charity Fund, Rosalie

CONTACT

Susan Shrago
Vice President
Rosalie Tilles Nonsectarian Charity Fund
7050 Olive St., Ste. 906
St. Louis, MO 63101
(314) 231-1721

FINANCIAL SUMMARY

Recent Giving: $56,163 (fiscal 1990); $63,386 (fiscal 1989)
Assets: $2,521,320 (fiscal year ending June 30, 1990); $2,263,192 (fiscal 1989)
EIN: 43-6020833

CONTRIBUTIONS SUMMARY

Donor(s): Cap Andrew Tilles
Grant Types: scholarship
Geographic Distribution: limited to St. Louis City and St. Louis County, MO

GIVING OFFICERS

Richard W. Braun: trust

Archbishop John L. May: trust
Mark L. Shook: trust
Paul P. Weil: trust

APPLICATION INFORMATION

Initial Approach: Application Guidelines issued for University Scholarship Program; applications for transportation aid accepted only through authorized social service case workers. Deadline is March 1.

OTHER THINGS TO KNOW

Publications: Application Guidelines

Time Insurance Co. / Time Insurance Foundation

Employees: 2,000
Parent Company: Fortis
Headquarters: Milwaukee, WI
SIC Major Group: Insurance Carriers

CONTACT

Catherine E. Feierstein
Vice President and Secretary
Time Insurance Fdn.
501 West Michigan
Milwaukee, WI 53201
(414) 271-3011

FINANCIAL SUMMARY

Recent Giving: $350,000 (1993 est.); $696,880 (1992); $298,507 (1991)
Assets: $1,267,184 (1990); $448,786 (1989)
Gifts Received: $1,085,000 (1990)
Fiscal Note: Contributes through foundation only. In 1990, contributions were received from Time Insurance Co.
EIN: 23-7346436

CONTRIBUTIONS SUMMARY

Typical Recipients: • *Arts & Humanities:* music, performing arts • *Civic & Public Affairs:* economic development, ethnic/minority organizations, housing, nonprofit management, philanthropic organizations, public policy, zoos/botanical gardens • *Education:* health & physical education, minority education • *Health:* geriatric health, health care cost containment, mental health, nutrition & health maintenance, pediatric health, public health, single-dis-

ease health associations • *Social Services:* child welfare, community service organizations, disabled, domestic violence, drugs & alcohol, employment/job training, family planning, food/clothing distribution, united funds, youth organizations
Grant Types: emergency, employee matching gifts, operating expenses, project, and seed money
Nonmonetary Support Types: donated equipment, in-kind services, loaned employees, and loaned executives
Note: Nonmonetary support, provided by the company, was valued at $25,000 in 1992. This amount is not included in the contributions figure above.
Geographic Distribution: focus on Milwaukee, WI
Operating Locations: WI (Milwaukee)

CORP. OFFICERS

Carl Schramm: *CURR EMPL* pres: Time Ins Co

GIVING OFFICERS

Cathy E. Feierstein: vp, secy, dir
Bonnie Gauger: trust
Jack Gochenaur: trust
Gwen A. Johnson: trust
Spencer N. Smith: pres, treas, dir
Madeleine Turner: trust

APPLICATION INFORMATION

Initial Approach: *Initial Contact:* letter requesting grant application form *Include Information On:* application form requests information on organization's background, its mission, size, and history; description of proposed program, its purpose and goals; description of beneficiaries, including the approximate number of people who will be helped; and information on personnel, including qualifications for those personnel who play a key role in carrying out the objectives of the organization; attachements requested include financial statements for the past fiscal year and a copy of the most recent IRS ruling under senction 501(c)(3)* *When to Submit:* any time *Note:* Applicants also should indicate if they receive United Way funding.
Restrictions on Giving: Grants are not generally made to organizations that are primar-

ily political, religious, labor-related, or to hospitals. Generally does not provide grants for fund-raising events or multiyear grants, nor does it provide endowment grants. Foundation will not individually support operational grant requests from organizations that receive a substantial amount of their funding from United Way or UPAF.

OTHER THINGS TO KNOW

Publications: application guidelines and application form

GRANTS ANALYSIS

Total Grants: $318,936
Number of Grants: 123*
Highest Grant: $121,451
Typical Range: $100 to $5,000
Disclosure Period: 1990
Note: Number of grants and average grant figures do not include matching gifts totaling $9,382. Recent grants are derived from a 1990 grants list.

RECENT GRANTS

121,451 United Way, Milwaukee, WI
16,590 Channel 10/36, Milwaukee, WI
16,397 United Way, Milwaukee, WI
15,000 United Performing Arts Fund, Milwaukee, WI
10,000 Channel 10/36, Milwaukee, WI
10,000 Milwaukee Art Museum, Milwaukee, WI
10,000 Milwaukee Redevelopment Corporation, Milwaukee, WI
6,000 Wisconsin Foundation of Independent Colleges, Milwaukee, WI
5,000 DePaul Foundation, Milwaukee, WI — Mission of Hope
5,000 Greater Milwaukee Education Trust, Milwaukee, WI

Time Warner / Time Warner Foundation

Former Foundation Name: Warner Communications Foundation
Sales: $13.07 billion
Employees: 41,700
Headquarters: New York, NY
SIC Major Group: Communications, Electronic & Other Electrical Equipment,

Motion Pictures, and Printing & Publishing

CONTACT

Mary McCarthy
Director, Corporate Contributions
Time Warner Inc.
75 Rockefeller Plz.
New York, NY 10019
(212) 484-8022
Note: Emelda M. Cathcart, Time & Life Bldg., 4173 Rockefeller Ctr., New York, NY 10020, (212) 522-1212, also is a contact.

FINANCIAL SUMMARY

Recent Giving: $15,000 (1991); $30,000 (1990); $135,000 (1989)
Fiscal Note: Figures are for foundation only, which is basically inactive. Company does not disclose the figure for direct contributions.
EIN: 13-3131902

CONTRIBUTIONS SUMMARY

Typical Recipients: • *Arts & Humanities:* general • *Civic & Public Affairs:* general • *Education:* general • *Health:* general • *Social Services:* general
Grant Types: capital and general support
Geographic Distribution: primarily the New York City area
Operating Locations: CA (Burbank, Los Angeles), CT (Stamford), NY (New York), VA (Alexandria)

CORP. OFFICERS

Gerald Manuel Levin: *B* Philadelphia PA 1939 *ED* Haverford Coll BA 1960; Univ PA LLB 1963 *CURR EMPL* chmn, pres, ceo, dir: Time-Warner *CORP AFFIL* dir: IBM Corp, Whittle Communs Partnership *NONPR AFFIL* mem: Intl Radio TV Soc, Natl Counc Families Television, Phi Beta Kappa; trust: Hampshire Coll; trust, chmn: Haverford Coll; dir: NY Philharmonic Symphony

GIVING OFFICERS

Emelda M. Cathcart: pres *CURR EMPL* coordinator contributions: Time Warner
Gerald Manuel Levin: dir *CURR EMPL* chmn, pres, ceo, dir: Time-Warner (see above)

APPLICATION INFORMATION

Initial Approach: *Note:* The foundation and the company support preselected organiza-

tions and generally do not accept applications for support.

OTHER THINGS TO KNOW

Time Warner was created by the merger of Time Inc. and Warner Communications in July 1989. The contributions program has been in flux since then and, as of July 1993, was still under review.

Time Warner Cable

Sales: $714.39 million
Employees: 6,000
Parent Company: Time-Warner, Inc.
Headquarters: Stamford, CT
SIC Major Group: Communications

CONTACT

Joseph J. Collins
Chairman and Chief Executive Officer
Time Warner Cable
300 First Stamford Pl.
Stamford, CT 06902-6732
(203) 328-0600
Note: Joan Sawyer, coordinator of public affairs, is another contact person at the same address.

CONTRIBUTIONS SUMMARY

Company provides grants from local divisions for education (45% of contributions), health and community programs (45%), and the arts (10%). Company also administers a volunteer funds that makes $500 to $1,000 grants to organizations for which employees volunteer their time.
Typical Recipients: • *Arts & Humanities:* arts appreciation • *Education:* agricultural education • *Health:* emergency/ambulance services • *Social Services:* aged
Grant Types: award and matching
Nonmonetary Support Types: donated equipment, in-kind services, and workplace solicitation
Geographic Distribution: headquarters and operating locations
Operating Locations: CT (Stamford)

CORP. OFFICERS

Joseph J. Collins: *B* Troy NY 1944 *ED* Harvard Univ MBA 1966 *CURR EMPL* chmn, ceo, dir: Am Television & Commun

Corp *CORP AFFIL* chmn: Time Warner Cable; dir: TBS, Tristar Pictures *NONPR AFFIL* mem: Natl Cable TV Assn
James Doolittle: *CURR EMPL* pres, dir: Am Television & Communs Corp
Timothy F. Evard: *CURR EMPL* vp (mktg): Am Television & Communs Corp

APPLICATION INFORMATION

Initial Approach: brief letter of inquiry
Include Information On: description of the organization, amount requested, purpose of funds sought, audited financial statement, and proof of tax-exempt status
When to Submit: any time
Restrictions on Giving: Does not support individuals, religious organizations for sectarian purposes, or political or lobbying groups.

Times Mirror Co. / Times Mirror Foundation

Sales: $3.7 billion
Employees: 30,000
Headquarters: Los Angeles, CA
SIC Major Group: Communications, Paper & Allied Products, and Printing & Publishing

CONTACT

Cassandra Malry
Treasurer
Times Mirror Fdn.
Times Mirror Sq.
Los Angeles, CA 90053
(213) 237-3936
Note: Ms. Malry is contact for general information and for organizations in Southern California. Organizations outside of Southern California should apply for support first to the Times Mirror operating unit in their area.

FINANCIAL SUMMARY

Recent Giving: $8,351,463 (1992); $8,050,691 (1991); $9,523,694 (1990)
Assets: $9,523,694 (1990); $18,183,490 (1989)
Fiscal Note: Giving figures include foundation giving and direct contributions by the corporation and its operating units. In 1992, the foundation gave $3,684,750 while the corporation and its subsidiaries gave $4,666,713.

EIN: 95-6079651

CONTRIBUTIONS SUMMARY

Typical Recipients: • *Arts & Humanities:* arts associations, arts centers, arts funds, arts institutes, dance, history/historic preservation, libraries, museums/galleries, music, opera, performing arts, public broadcasting, theater • *Civic & Public Affairs:* civil rights, economic development, environmental affairs, ethnic/minority organizations, first amendment issues, nonprofit management, professional & trade associations, public policy, urban & community affairs, women's affairs, zoos/botanical gardens • *Education:* arts education, business education, career/vocational education, colleges & universities, continuing education, economic education, education associations, education funds, international studies, international studies, journalism education, legal education, liberal arts education, literacy, medical education, minority education, private education (precollege), science/technology education, student aid • *Health:* health funds, health organizations, hospices, hospitals, medical research, mental health, single-disease health associations • *Social Services:* aged, child welfare, community centers, community service organizations, counseling, disabled, employment/job training, family planning, family services, food/clothing distribution, homes, recreation & athletics, refugee assistance, religious welfare, shelters/homelessness, united funds, volunteer services, youth organizations

Grant Types: capital, employee matching gifts, general support, multiyear/continuing support, project, and scholarship

Nonmonetary Support Types: in-kind services

Geographic Distribution: to national organizations, in southern California, and in communities served by subsidiaries

Operating Locations: AL (Birmingham), CA (Irvine, Laguna Niguel, Long Beach, Los Angeles, San Jose, Santa Ana), CO (Englewood), CT (Greenwich, Hartford, Stamford), DC, IL (Chicago, Homewood), MA (Cambridge), MD (Baltimore), MO (St. Louis), NY (Buffalo, Elmira, Melville, New York, Riverhead, Syracuse), OR (Lake Oswego, Milwaukie, Motalla, Oregon City, Philomath, Sweet Home, Tillamook, Toledo), PA (Allentown, Harrisburg), TX (Austin, Dallas)

CORP. OFFICERS

Robert F. Erburu: *B* Ventura CA 1930 *ED* Univ Southern CA BA 1952; Harvard Univ LLB 1955 *CURR EMPL* chmn, ceo, dir: Times Mirror Co *CORP AFFIL* dir: Tejon Ranch Co; dir, dep chmn: Fed Reserve Bank San Francisco *NONPR AFFIL* dir: Am Newspaper Publs Assn; mem: Bus Counc, Bus Roundtable; mem bd dirs: Counc Foreign Rels, Los Angeles Festival; mem trust counc: Natl Gallery Art; trust: Art Collections & Botanical Gardens, Brookings Inst, Huntington Art Gallery, Huntington Library, Tomas Rivera Ctr

David Abram Laventhol: *B* Philadelphia PA 1933 *ED* Yale Univ AB 1957; Univ MN MA 1960 *CURR EMPL* pres: Times Mirror Co *CORP AFFIL* chmn: Newsday; dir: Hartford Courant Co, Los Angeles Times Post News Svc, Newspaper Advertising Bur; pres, ceo, publ: Los Angeles Times *NONPR AFFIL* chmn: Pulitzer Prize Bd; dir: Baltimore Sun Co, NY City Partnership; mem: Am Soc Newspaper Editors, Am Soc Newspaper Editors, Counc Foreign Rels; mem, dir: Am Press Inst; mem, trust: CA Mus Fdn, Mus Contemporary Art; secy, treas: Am Comm Intl Press Inst; trust: Hartford-Courant Fdn; vchmn: Intl Press Inst

Phillip L. Williams: *B* St Louis MO 1922 *ED* Harvard Univ 1943; Harvard Univ MBA 1948 *CURR EMPL* vchmn, dir: Times Mirror Co

GIVING OFFICERS

Shelby Coffey III: dir *CURR EMPL* editor, exec vp: Los Angeles Times

Robert F. Erburu: chmn, dir *CURR EMPL* chmn, ceo, dir: Times Mirror Co (see above)

Curtis Alan Hessler: dir *B* Berwyn IL 1943 *CURR EMPL* sr exec vp: Times Mirror Co

David Abram Laventhol: dir *CURR EMPL* pres: Times Mirror Co (see above)

Cassandra Malry: treas *CURR EMPL* mgr (corp contributions): Times Mirror Co

Stephen Charles Meier: secy, dir *B* Los Angeles CA 1950 *ED* Occidental Coll 1972; Harvard Univ MA 1977 *CURR EMPL* vp (admin & community affairs): Times Mirror Co

Lisa Cleri Reale: asst secy

Charles Robert Redmond: pres, ceo, dir *B* New Brunswick NJ 1926 *ED* Rutgers Univ 1950; Univ Southern CA MBA 1960 *CURR EMPL* exec vp: Times Mirror Co

Richard T. Schlosberg III: dir *CURR EMPL* group vp newspaper: Times Mirror Co

Phillip L. Williams: dir *CURR EMPL* vchmn, dir: Times Mirror Co (see above)

Donald Franklin Wright: dir *B* St Paul MN 1934 *ED* Univ MN BME 1957; Univ MN MBA 1958 *CURR EMPL* sr vp: Times Mirror Co *NONPR AFFIL* dir: Assocs CA Inst Tech, CA Newspaper Publs Assn, Univ MN Fdn; dir, mem: Univ MN Alumni Club; mem exec comm: Claremont Grad Sch Univ Ctr; vchmn: Boy Scouts Am Los Angeles Area Counc

APPLICATION INFORMATION

Initial Approach: *Initial Contact:* two- to three-page letter to foundation *Include Information On:* description of the organization, its purpose, programs, and project to be considered; proof of tax-exempt status; list of current supporting organizations and amount of support; organizational budget for current and upcoming fiscal years *When to Submit:* by May 1 or October 1; board meets in June and November *Note:* Organizations in areas served by Times Mirror subsidiaries should submit requests to subsidiary directly.

Restrictions on Giving: Company and foundation do not provide grants for religious or fraternal purposes, publications, conferences, television programs, or films, or to individuals. Foundation does not support fund-raising events.

Repeat grant requests will not be considered within a one-year time period.

OTHER THINGS TO KNOW

Grants requests to the Times Mirror Co. are considered as received. Company's grants are generally smaller than the foundation and may include support for fund-raising events. Application criteria and eligibility are similar to those for the foundation. Contact Ms. Malry for further information.

Times Mirror also gives through 26 operating units, including $510,628 by the Los Angeles Times, CA; $544,150, Newsday, Long Island, NY; and $477,303, Baltimore Sun Newspaper, MD. These figures are for 1990 and are included in giving figures above.

Publications: Contributions Annual Report

GRANTS ANALYSIS

Total Grants: $8,351,463
Number of Grants: 462
Highest Grant: $600,000
Typical Range: $5,000 to $30,000
Disclosure Period: 1992
Note: Asset figure is from 1990. Recent grants are derived from a 1992 grants list.

RECENT GRANTS

600,000 United Way of Los Angeles, Los Angeles, CA — annual support

185,000 Independent Colleges of Southern California, Los Angeles, CA — annual support

150,000 California Institute of Technology, Pasadena, CA — to establish the Earthquake Media and Exhibit Center

100,000 Music Center Unified Fund — annual support

100,000 Natural History Museum Foundation, Los Angeles, CA — for the Times Mirror Hall of Native American Cultures

100,000 Puente Learning Center — capital campaign

100,000 United Negro College Fund, New York, NY — to establish Campaign 2000, a scholarship assistance program for students in Los Angeles County

90,000 Los Angeles County Museum of

Art, Los Angeles, CA — annual support

80,000 United Way of Orange County, Irvine, CA — annual support

75,000 California State University, Los Angeles, CA — capital grant

Timex Corp.

Sales: $640.0 million
Employees: 7,500
Headquarters: Middlebury, CT
SIC Major Group: Electronic & Other Electrical Equipment and Instruments & Related Products

CONTACT
Robert Ricci
Director, Human Resources
Timex Corp.
PO Box 310
Middlebury, CT 06762-0310
(203) 573-5000

CONTRIBUTIONS SUMMARY
Nonmonetary Support Types: donated products
Operating Locations: CT (Middlebury)

CORP. OFFICERS
James W. Binns: *CURR EMPL* pres: Timex Corp
T. F. Olsen: *CURR EMPL* chmn: Timex Corp

Timken Co. / Timken Co. Charitable Trust

Sales: $1.64 billion
Employees: 18,860
Parent Company: Timken Co.
Headquarters: Canton, OH
SIC Major Group: Industrial Machinery & Equipment and Primary Metal Industries

CONTACT
Ward J. Timken
Vice President Office
Timken Co. Charitable Trust
1835 Dueber Ave. SW
Canton, OH 44706
(216) 471-4062

FINANCIAL SUMMARY
Recent Giving: $572,430 (1991); $582,355 (1990); $536,980 (1989)
Assets: $1,978,792 (1991); $2,033,355 (1990); $719,906 (1989)

Fiscal Note: Figures represent giving by Timken Charitable Trust only. Timken Co. gives a very small amount directly, usually through plant managers. An educational fund gives scholarships only to children of employees.
EIN: 34-6534265

CONTRIBUTIONS SUMMARY
Typical Recipients: • *Arts & Humanities:* arts associations, arts funds, museums/galleries • *Civic & Public Affairs:* business/free enterprise, law & justice, philanthropic organizations, zoos/botanical gardens • *Education:* business education, colleges & universities, education associations • *Health:* health organizations • *Social Services:* community service organizations, food/clothing distribution, united funds
Grant Types: capital, emergency, general support, multiyear/continuing support, project, and research
Note: Maximum multiyear support: 5 years.
Geographic Distribution: mostly in areas where company plants operate, with an emphasis on Ohio
Operating Locations: CA (Los Angeles), CO (Denver), CT (Hartford), GA (Atlanta), IL (Chicago, Moline, Peoria), KS (Kansas City), MI (Detroit), MN (Minneapolis), NC (Charlotte, Lincolnton), NV (Sparks), OH (Ashland, Bucyrus, Canton, Cincinnati, Cleveland, Columbus, New Philadelphia, Obetz, Pittsburgh), SC (Gaffney), TN (Memphis), TX (Dallas, Houston), WA (Seattle), WI (Milwaukee)

CORP. OFFICERS
Peter Jack Ashton: *B* Wolverhampton England 1935 *ED* Wolverhampton Coll Tech England 1935; Univ Aston England 1958 *CURR EMPL* exec vp (bearings), dir: Timken Co *NONPR AFFIL* mem: Anti-friction Bearings Mfrs Assn, Inst Electrical Engrs, Mfrs Alliance Productivity & Innovation, Soc Automotive Engrs, Soc Mfg Engrs
William Robert Timken, Jr.: *B* Canton OH 1938 *ED* Stanford Univ BA 1960; Harvard Univ MBA 1962 *CURR EMPL* chmn, chmn exec comm, chmn

fin comm, dir: Timken Co *CORP AFFIL* beneficial owner: Concurrent Computer Corp; dir: Diebold, LA Land & Exploration Co, Trinova Corp
Joseph Frederick Toot, Jr.: *B* Canton OH 1935 *ED* Princeton Univ AB 1957; Harvard Univ MBA 1961 *CURR EMPL* pres, dir: Timken Co *CORP AFFIL* dir: Latrobe Steel Co, Rockwell Intl Corp *NONPR AFFIL* chmn: Am Iron Steel Inst
Charles H. West: *B* 1934 *ED* Tri-State Univ BSME; Harvard Univ *CURR EMPL* exec vp, dir: Timken Co

GIVING OFFICERS
J. Kevin Ramsey: adv *B* Youngstown OH 1932 *ED* Youngstown St Univ 1954; Univ Akron Law Sch 1963 *CURR EMPL* vp (finance): Timken Co
J.J. Schubach: adv *CURR EMPL* vp (strategic mgmt): Timken Co
Ward J. Timken: off *CURR EMPL* vp, off: Timken Co

APPLICATION INFORMATION
Initial Approach: *Initial Contact:* by letter, including proposal *Include Information On:* description of the organization; amount and purpose of request; proof of tax exemption *When to Submit:* any time
Restrictions on Giving: Timken Co. Trust generally does not fund religious organizations.

OTHER THINGS TO KNOW
Very small amount of contributions is given directly by Timken Co., usually through plant managers. The Timken Co. Educational Fund provides scholarships only for children of employees.

GRANTS ANALYSIS
Total Grants: $572,430*
Number of Grants: 59
Highest Grant: $230,000
Typical Range: $500 to $20,000
Disclosure Period: 1991
Note: Figures based on 1991 Charitable Trust giving only. Recent grants are derived from a 1991 Form 990.

RECENT GRANTS
230,000 United Way of Central Stark County, Canton, OH

40,000 Ohio Foundation Independent Colleges, Cleveland, OH

33,500 United Arts Fund, Canton, OH

26,000 Bucyrus Area United Way, Bucyrus, OH

25,000 Associate Harvard Business School, Cambridge, MA

22,000 United Way of Westmoreland County, Greensburg, PA

20,000 Education Enhancement Partnership

20,000 Junior Achievement Stark County, Canton, OH

18,500 United Way Cherokee County, Gaffney, SC

16,000 Malone College, Canton, OH

Timken Foundation of Canton

CONTACT
Don D. Dickes
Secretary-Treasurer
Timken Foundation of Canton
236 Third St., S.W.
Canton, OH 44702
(216) 455-5281

FINANCIAL SUMMARY
Recent Giving: $6,000,000 (fiscal 1993 est.); $5,775,000 (fiscal 1992 approx.); $5,430,321 (fiscal 1991)
Assets: $125,000,000 (fiscal 1993 est.); $123,800,000 (fiscal 1992 est.); $125,651,551 (fiscal year ending September 30, 1991); $119,905,688 (fiscal 1990); $139,372,000 (fiscal 1989)
Gifts Received: $2,967,000 (fiscal 1988)
EIN: 34-6520254

CONTRIBUTIONS SUMMARY
Donor(s): The foundation was established in 1934. Donors are members of the Timken family. The Timken family fortune stems from Timken Company, a manufacturer of roller bearings and alloy steel.
Typical Recipients: • *Arts & Humanities:* arts centers, history/historic preservation, libraries, museums/galleries, theater • *Civic & Public Affairs:* better government, business/free enterprise, municipalities, philanthropic

organizations • *Education:* community & junior colleges, education funds, public education (precollege), student aid • *Health:* hospitals • *International:* international organizations • *Religion:* religious organizations • *Social Services:* community service organizations, recreation & athletics, youth organizations

Grant Types: capital, challenge, general support, and project

Geographic Distribution: broad geographic distribution, with emphasis on Canton, OH; some international giving

GIVING OFFICERS

Don D. Dickes: secy, treas, trust

Ward J. Timken: pres, trust *CURR EMPL* vp, off: Timken Co *PHIL AFFIL* pres: Timken International Fund

William R. Timken: vp, trust

William Robert Timken, Jr.: vp, trust *B* Canton OH 1938 *ED* Stanford Univ BA 1960; Harvard Univ MBA 1962 *CURR EMPL* chmn, chmn exec comm, chmn fin comm, dir: Timken Co *CORP AFFIL* beneficial owner: Concurrent Computer Corp; dir: Diebold, LA Land & Exploration Co, Trinova Corp *PHIL AFFIL* don, pres, trust: WR Timken Jr Family Foundation; trust: Edith M Timken Family Foundation, Timken Family Charitable Trust

APPLICATION INFORMATION

Initial Approach: Grant requests should be in writing.

No specific form of application is required; however, the application must include proof of tax-exempt status under Internal Revenue Code 501(c)(3). There are no deadlines for application.

GRANTS ANALYSIS

Total Grants: $5,430,321
Number of Grants: 46
Highest Grant: $625,000
Typical Range: $25,000 to $125,000
Disclosure Period: fiscal year ending September 30, 1991
Note: The average grant figure excludes a single grant for $625,000. Recent grants are derived from a fiscal 1991 Form 990.

RECENT GRANTS

625,000 Canton Scholarship Foundation, Canton, OH — scholarship fund

580,000 Stark County Foundation, Canton, OH — education enhancement partnership

500,000 Ohio Foundation of Independent Colleges, Columbus, OH — challenge funds

500,000 Stark Development Board, Canton, OH — operating expenses

387,027 Cherokee County School District, Gaffney, SC — support four projects to enhance quality of education

300,000 Adelphoi, Inc., Latrobe, PA — Latrobe Community Children's Center

250,000 Cleveland Clinic Foundation, Cleveland, OH — capital campaign

250,000 Limestone College, Gaffney, SC — renovate Montgomery Classroom Building

250,000 North Canton Medical Center, North Canton, OH — new facility

225,000 South Street Seaport Museum, New York, NY — annual operations

Timme Revocable Trust, Abigail S.

CONTACT

Abigail S. Timme Revocable Trust
236 Catalina Dr.
San Luis Obispo, CA 93401

FINANCIAL SUMMARY

Recent Giving: $100,000 (fiscal 1991); $80,000 (fiscal 1990); $75,000 (fiscal 1989)
Assets: $2,802,496 (fiscal year ending September 30, 1991); $2,692,051 (fiscal 1990); $2,592,611 (fiscal 1989)
EIN: 77-0182900

CONTRIBUTIONS SUMMARY

Typical Recipients: • *Education:* colleges & universities
Grant Types: general support

GIVING OFFICERS

Robert Enigleben: trust
Clifford Larsen: trust

APPLICATION INFORMATION

Initial Approach: Contributes only to preselected organizations.

GRANTS ANALYSIS

Number of Grants: 1
Highest Grant: $100,000
Disclosure Period: fiscal year ending September 30, 1991

RECENT GRANTS

100,000 Ferris State University, Big Rapids, MI

Timmis Foundation, Michael & Nancy

CONTACT

Frank M. Jerneycic
Manager
Michael & Nancy Timmis Fdn.
200 Talon Centre
Detroit, MI 48204
(313) 396-4300

FINANCIAL SUMMARY

Recent Giving: $1,984,588 (1991); $1,874,723 (1990); $1,846,844 (1989)
Assets: $23,461 (1991); $10,681 (1990); $5,407 (1989)
Gifts Received: $1,997,000 (1991); $1,879,000 (1990); $1,785,900 (1989)
Fiscal Note: In 1991, contributions were received from Michael T. Timmis.
EIN: 38-2519177

CONTRIBUTIONS SUMMARY

Typical Recipients: • *Arts & Humanities:* public broadcasting • *Civic & Public Affairs:* international affairs • *International:* international development/relief, international organizations • *Religion:* churches, missionary activities, religious organizations • *Social Services:* food/clothing distribution, youth organizations
Grant Types: general support
Geographic Distribution: focus on MI

GIVING OFFICERS

Wayne C. Inman: secy
Michael T. Timmis: pres, treas
Nancy E. Timmis: vp

APPLICATION INFORMATION

Initial Approach: The foundation reports it only makes contributions to preselected charitable organizations.

GRANTS ANALYSIS

Number of Grants: 67
Highest Grant: $977,808
Typical Range: $1,000 to $10,000
Disclosure Period: 1991

RECENT GRANTS

977,808 International Foundation, Washington, DC

202,150 Servant Ministries, Ann Arbor, MI

168,255 International Fellowship, Arlington, VA

140,000 Youth With A Mission, Washington, DC

78,000 Fellowship Foundation, Washington, DC

74,500 Joy of Jesus, Detroit, MI

58,000 Bonn House

50,000 Prison Fellowship Ministries, Washington, DC

40,000 Catholic Church

25,000 Genesis Foundation, Detroit, MI

Tinker Foundation

CONTACT

Martha T. Muse
Chairman of the Board, President
Tinker Foundation
55 East 59th St.
New York, NY 10022
(212) 421-6858
Note: An alternative contact is Renate Rennie, executive director of the foundation.

FINANCIAL SUMMARY

Recent Giving: $2,039,100 (1991); $1,770,233 (1990); $2,290,547 (1989)
Assets: $52,925,088 (1991); $48,778,149 (1990); $53,037,776 (1989)
EIN: 51-0175449

CONTRIBUTIONS SUMMARY

Donor(s): The foundation was established in 1959 by Edward Larocque Tinker (1881-1968). Dr. Tinker invested in real estate in New York City. After his death in 1968, his estate was bequeathed to the foundation. He originally set up the foundation in memory of his wife, father, and grandfather. "His lifelong devotion to the Iberian tradition in the Old and New Worlds gave definition to the foundation's overall purpose."

Typical Recipients: • *Civic & Public Affairs:* economic development, environmental affairs, international affairs, public policy • *Education:* colleges & universities, education funds, international exchange, international studies, minority education • *International:* foreign educational institutions, international development/relief, international organizations • *Science:* scientific institutes

Grant Types: conference/seminar, project, and research

Geographic Distribution: national, some international

GIVING OFFICERS

Raymond Lee Brittenham: secy, dir, mem exec, audit & fin comms *B* Moscow Union of Soviet Socialist Republics 1916 *ED* Principia Coll AB 1936; Kaiser Wilhelm Univ 1937; Harvard Univ LLB 1940 *CORP AFFIL* consultant: Lazard Freres & Co *NONPR AFFIL* mem: Am Bar Assn, Counc Foreign Rels; vchmn: Spanish Inst

William R. Chaney: dir *CURR EMPL* chmn, ceo: Tiffany & Co

John Nichol Irwin II: dir *B* Keokuk IA 1913 *ED* Princeton Univ AB 1937; Oxford Univ MA 1944; Fordham Univ LLB 1941 *CURR EMPL* ptnr: Patterson Belknap & Webb *CORP AFFIL* mem adv bd: IBM Corp *NONPR AFFIL* mem: Am Bar Assn, Am Mus Natural History, Bar Assn City NY, Counc Foreign Rels, Fed Bar Assn, NY Bar Assn, Pilgrims US; trust: Metro Mus Art, NY Zoological Soc; trust emeritus: Lawrenceville Sch, Princeton Univ

Grayson Louis Kirk: vp, dir, chmn exec comm, mem audit comm *B* Jeffersonville OH 1903 *ED* Miami Univ BA 1924; Clark Univ MA 1925; Univ WI PhD 1930 *CORP AFFIL* dir: Bullock Aggressive Growth Shares, Bullock Balanced Shares, Bullock Dividend Shares, Bullock Growth Shares, Bullock High Income Shares, Bullock Monthly Income Shares, Bullock Tax-Free Shares, Bullock US Govt Income Shares; mem adv bd: IBM Corp *NONPR AFFIL* chmn: Am Soc French Legion

Honor; dir: Academy Political Sciences, Lycee Francaise; mem: Academy Arts Sciences, Am Philosophical Soc, Counc Foreign Rels; pres emritus, trust emeritus: Columbia Univ; trust: French Inst; trust emeritus: Asia Fdn, Inst Intl Ed

Charles McC. Mathias, Jr.: dir *B* Frederick MD 1922 *ED* Haverford Coll BA 1944; Yale Univ LLB; Univ MD 1949 *CURR EMPL* ptnr: Jones Day Reavis & Pogue *NONPR AFFIL* chmn: Am Counc Germany; mem bd: Counc Foreign Rels

Martha Twitchell Muse: chmn, pres, dir *B* Dallas TX 1926 *ED* Barnard Coll BA 1948; Columbia Univ MA 1955 *CORP AFFIL* dir: Bank NY Audit & Examining Ctr, Bank NY Co, Bank NY Comm Reinvestment Accounting Ctr, Bank NY Trust & Investment Ctr, NYSE; mem bd: Irving Bank Corp, Irving Trust Co, May Dept Stores Co *NONPR AFFIL* mem: Advertising Counc, Hugnenof Soc, Intl Exec Svc Corps, Natl Soc Coll Dames, NY City Counc Foreign Rels, Pvt Sector Arts Commn US Information Agency, Woodrow Wilson Intl Ctr Scholars; mem adv comm: Ctr Strategic Intl Studies; mem adv counc: Lusa-Am Devel Fdn; mem bd dirs: Am Counc Germany, Am Fdn, Am Portuguese Soc, Am Soc, Intl Univ Fdn; mem bd visitors: Georgetown Univ Sch Foreign Svc; trust emeritus: Columbia Univ; vice chmn bd dirs: Spanish Inst

Renate Rennie: exec dir

Beatrice C. Treat: asst treas

Gordon T. Wallis: treas, chmn fin comm, mem exec comm *B* Salt Lake City UT 1919 *ED* Columbia Univ 1940; NY Univ LLB 1948 *CURR EMPL* chmn exec comm, dir: Irving Trust Co *CORP AFFIL* chmn exec comm, dir: Irving Bank Corp; dir: Banca della Svizzera Italiana Switzerland, GTE Corp, JWT Group, Sterling Drug

William Clarke Wescoe, MD: dir *B* Allentown PA 1920 *ED* Cornell Univ MD 1944; Muhlenberg Coll BS 1941; Muhlenberg Coll ScD 1957 *CORP AFFIL* dir: NY Stock Exchange, Phillips Petroleum Co; mem adv bd: Irving Bank Corp, Irving Trust Co *NONPR AFFIL* fellow: Am Coll Physicians; mem: Alpha Omega Alpha, Alpha Tau Omega, Am Soc

Pharmacology & Experimental Therapeutics, Nu Sigma Nu, Phi Beta Kappa, Sigma Xi; trust: Samuel Kress Fdn

APPLICATION INFORMATION

Initial Approach:
Applicants interested in institutional grants should send a complete proposal to the president of the foundation. Applicants interested in Tinker Field Research grants should send a letter of request for complete application instructions and forms to the foundation.

The proposal should include a single page description of the project, objectives, timetable, anticipated results, qualifications of project director and personnel, budget, copy of IRS classification form, 990 form, latest financial statement, list of staff and directors, and historical overview of the applying institution.

Applications are considered biennially. Deadline are March 1 for the summer meeting and October 1 for the winter meeting. If the project falls within the scope of the foundation's interests and funds are available, the president will invite a formal application to the foundation.

The board meets in June and December to review grant proposals.

Restrictions on Giving: The foundation will not consider institutional grant requests for annual fund raising, capital grants, individual research, funding related to health or medical issues, production costs for film and television projects, or general purpose endowments.

OTHER THINGS TO KNOW

Applications must be submitted in English.

Publications: annual report, application guidelines

GRANTS ANALYSIS

Total Grants: $2,039,100
Number of Grants: 52
Highest Grant: $107,000
Typical Range: $15,000 to $50,000
Disclosure Period: 1991
Note: The average grant figure excludes 10 grants totaling $347,093. Recent grants are derived from a 1991 annual report.

RECENT GRANTS

107,000 Americas Society, New York, NY — support of a two-part public affairs program focused on transitions in Latin America

100,000 Council on Foreign Relations, New York, NY — to examine and define the developing post-Cold War agenda for relations between the United States and Latin America

75,000 International Union for Conservation of Nature and Natural Resources-U.S., Washington, DC — a comprehensive review of the history of human impact on Antartica

75,000 World Resources Institute, Washington, DC — a forum for cooperation and exchange of ideas among representatives from North and South America

70,000 University of Florida Foundation, Gainesville, FL — addressing policy-relevant topics of conservation and development in Argentina and Chile

60,000 Environmental Law Institute, Washington, DC — partial support of project to strengthen environmental protection institutions in Latin America and the Caribbean through education and training

50,000 Conservation International Foundation, Washington, DC — issues of environmental and natural resource degradation in Central America

50,000 Institute for International Economics, Washington, DC — to promote closer trade and economic relations among the United States and its neighbors in the Western Hemisphere

50,000 Trustees of Columbia University, New York, NY —

support activities designated to bring Portuguese and Brazilian issues to the attention of the public

50,000 University of Texas at El Paso, El Paso, TX — to support an investigation into the contamination of ground water from agricultural irrigation with sewage

Tippens Foundation

CONTACT
George W. Tippens
Trustee
Tippens Fdn.
435 Butler St.
Etna, PA 15223
(412) 781-7800

FINANCIAL SUMMARY
Recent Giving: $194,000 (1991)
Assets: $88,383 (1991)
Gifts Received: $200,000 (1991)
EIN: 25-6282382

CONTRIBUTIONS SUMMARY
Typical Recipients: • *Civic & Public Affairs:* municipalities • *Education:* colleges & universities, education funds • *Health:* health organizations, medical rehabilitation • *Social Services:* community service organizations, united funds
Grant Types: general support

APPLICATION INFORMATION
Initial Approach: Send brief letter of inquiry. There are no deadlines.

GRANTS ANALYSIS
Number of Grants: 28
Highest Grant: $25,000
Typical Range: $1,000 to $10,000
Disclosure Period: 1991

RECENT GRANTS
25,000 Allegheny Trails Council, Pittsburgh, PA
25,000 United Way, Pittsburgh, PA
21,000 Allegheny College, Meadville, PA
20,000 Extra Mile Education Foundation, Pittsburgh, PA
20,000 Salvation Army, Pittsburgh, PA

10,000 American Red Cross, Pittsburgh, PA
10,000 Carnegie, Pittsburgh, PA
10,000 Rehabilitation Institute, Pittsburgh, PA
10,000 St. Margaret Memorial Hospital Foundation, Pittsburgh, PA
5,000 Shadyside Academy, Fox Chapel, PA

Tippit Charitable Trust, C. Carlisle and Margaret M.

CONTACT
C. Carlisle and Margaret M. Tippit Charitable Trust
2000 Huntington Building
Cleveland, OH 44115-1407
(216) 696-4700
Note: The trust lists no specific contact person.

FINANCIAL SUMMARY
Recent Giving: $184,600 (fiscal 1991); $89,000 (fiscal 1990)
Assets: $2,605,201 (fiscal year ending August 21, 1991); $2,492,998 (fiscal 1990)
Gifts Received: $2,558,676 (fiscal 1990)
Fiscal Note: In fiscal 1990, C. C. Tippit contributed assets with a fair market value of $2,558,676.
EIN: 34-1627297

CONTRIBUTIONS SUMMARY
Donor(s): the donor is C. C. Tippit
Typical Recipients: • *Education:* career/vocational education, colleges & universities, private education (precollege), religious education • *Health:* hospitals, public health • *Religion:* churches • *Social Services:* disabled, family planning, united funds
Grant Types: general support
Geographic Distribution: primarily Ohio

GIVING OFFICERS
James R. Bright: trust
Carl J. Tippit: trust

GRANTS ANALYSIS
Number of Grants: 21
Highest Grant: $28,000
Typical Range: $5,000 to $28,000
Disclosure Period: fiscal year ending August 21, 1991

Note: Incomplete grants list provided in fiscal 1991.

RECENT GRANTS
28,000 Orlando Regional Medical Center Foundation, Orlando, FL
25,000 Cleveland Clinic Foundation, Cleveland, OH
15,000 United Way Services, Cleveland, OH
13,850 University School, Hunting Valley, OH
10,900 Laurel School, Shaker Heights, OH
10,000 Smith College, Northhampton, MA
8,251 Planned Parenthood of Cleveland, Cleveland, OH
7,248 Rainbow Kids Cards, Chagrin Falls, OH
6,000 Fairmount Presbyterian Church, Cleveland Heights, Cleveland, OH
5,000 Shaker Schools Foundation, Shaker Heights, OH

Tisch Foundation

CONTACT
E. Jack Beatus
Secretary and Treasurer
Tisch Foundation
667 Madison Ave.
New York, NY 10021
(212) 545-2930

FINANCIAL SUMMARY
Recent Giving: $7,530,199 (1991); $7,322,033 (1990); $3,114,758 (1989)
Assets: $90,694,955 (1991); $79,108,351 (1990); $92,595,184 (1989)
EIN: 59-1002844

CONTRIBUTIONS SUMMARY
Donor(s): Laurence Alan Tisch and Preston Robert Tisch began restoring and building hotels with their father in 1946. Ten years later, they had built a 12-hotel chain, and in the following year constructed a $17 million Florida hotel. In 1959, they gained control of Loews Theatres, Inc.
In 1986, Laurence took over as head of CBS, and Robert, former U.S. Postmaster General, joined the CBS board in 1988.
The foundation donors were Hotel Americana, Tisch Hotels, Tisch family members, and

closely held corporations. Early in 1989, the Tisch brothers gave $30 million to New York University and its medical center, subsequently renamed Tisch Hospital.
Typical Recipients: • *Arts & Humanities:* arts appreciation, arts centers, arts funds, community arts, dance, ethnic arts, history/historic preservation, libraries, museums/galleries, music, performing arts, public broadcasting • *Civic & Public Affairs:* civil rights, environmental affairs, international affairs, public policy • *Education:* business education, colleges & universities, education associations, literacy, private education (precollege), religious education • *Health:* emergency/ambulance services, health funds, hospitals, medical research, outpatient health care delivery, pediatric health, single-disease health associations • *International:* international organizations • *Religion:* religious organizations, synagogues • *Social Services:* aged, child welfare, community centers, community centers, disabled, family services, recreation & athletics, united funds, volunteer services, youth organizations
Grant Types: award, capital, department, general support, operating expenses, project, and research
Geographic Distribution: national, with emphasis on New York City

GIVING OFFICERS
E. Jack Beatus: secy, treas, dir
Joan M. Tisch: dir, don wife
Laurence Alan Tisch: sr vp, don B New York NY 1923 *ED* NY Univ BSc 1942; Univ PA MA 1943; Harvard Univ Law Sch *CURR EMPL* chmn, pres, ceo, dir: CBS *CORP AFFIL* chmn: CNA Fin Corp; chmn, co-ceo: Loews Corp; dir: Automatic Data Processing Corp, Bulova Corp, Getty Oil Co, RH Macy & Co, NY Stock Exchange, Petrie Stores Corp *NONPR AFFIL* chmn bd trustees: NY Univ; dir: Un Jewish Appeal Fed Jewish Philanthropies Greater NY City; mem: Counc Foreign Rels, Mayors Comm Pub-Pvt Partnerships; trust: Metro Mus Art, NY Pub Library
Preston Robert Tisch: pres, don B Brooklyn NY 1926 *ED* Bucknell Univ; Univ MI BA

1948 *CURR EMPL* pres, co-ceo: Loews Corp *CORP AFFIL* chmn: Loews Hotels; dir: Bulova Corp, CBS, CNA Fin Corp, Hasbro, Healthco Intl, Rite Aid Corp; owner: NY Giants *NONPR AFFIL* chmn emeritus: NY Convention & Visitors Bur; mem: Govs Bus Adv Counc NY, Quadrennial Comm Exec Legislative Judicial Salaries, Sigma Alpha Mu, Travel Indus Assn Am; mem travel tourism adv bd: Dept Commerce; trust: NY Univ, Sales Mktg Execs Greater NY **Wilma S. Tisch:** dir, don wife

APPLICATION INFORMATION

Initial Approach:
The foundation contributes to preselected charitable organizations, and does not accept unsolicited applications for funds. The board meets in March, June, September, December, and as required.
Restrictions on Giving: The foundation does not make loans or grants to individuals. Endowment funds, scholarships, fellowships, and matching funds also are not supported.

GRANTS ANALYSIS

Total Grants: $7,530,199
Number of Grants: 143
Highest Grant: $2,000,000
Typical Range: $500 to $2,500 and $5,000 to $50,000
Disclosure Period: 1991
Note: The average grant figure excludes three large grants totaling $4,000,000. Recent grants are derived from a 1991 Form 990.

RECENT GRANTS

2,000,000 Tisch Hospital, New York, NY
1,000,000 Metropolitan Museum of Art, New York, NY
1,000,000 United Jewish Appeal-Federation of Jewish Philanthropies of New York, New York, NY — Operation Exodus
775,000 New York University-Tisch School of the Arts, New York, NY
628,413 United Jewish Appeal Federation, New York, NY
523,100 Mount Sinai Hospital, New York, NY
510,228 YM and YWHA-92nd Street, New York, NY

151,000 Gay Men's Health Crisis, New York, NY
115,000 Jewish Museum, New York, NY
100,000 Fund for Jewish Education, New York, NY

Tiscornia Foundation

CONTACT
Laurianne T. Davis
Secretary
Tiscornia Fdn.
1010 Main St., Ste. A
St. Joseph, MI 49085
(616) 926-0812

FINANCIAL SUMMARY
Recent Giving: $154,630 (1991); $173,575 (1990); $143,495 (1989)
Assets: $4,424,735 (1991); $3,746,286 (1990); $3,755,376 (1989)
EIN: 38-1777343

CONTRIBUTIONS SUMMARY
Donor(s): late James W. Tiscornia, the late Waldo V. Tiscornia, Auto Specialties Manufacturing Co., Lambert Brake Corp.
Typical Recipients: • *Arts & Humanities:* libraries, music • *Education:* colleges & universities • *Health:* health funds, health organizations, hospices • *Social Services:* community service organizations, family planning, recreation & athletics, youth organizations
Grant Types: capital, emergency, general support, multi-year/continuing support, scholarship, and seed money
Geographic Distribution: focus on MI

GIVING OFFICERS
Laurianne T. Davis: secy, trust
Howard H. Paxson: vp, trust
Henry H. Tippett: treas, trust
Bernice Tiscornia: trust
Edward Tiscornia: trust
Lester Clinton Tiscornia: pres, trust *ED* Coll Pacific AB 1932; Andrews Univ LLD 1971 *CURR EMPL* chmn, dir: Auto Specialties Mfg Co *CORP AFFIL* chmn, dir: Auto Specialties Mfg Co; dir: Peoples St Bank *NONPR AFFIL* mem: Soc Automotive Engrs; mem adv bd Twin Cities chapter: Salvation Army; pres: St Joseph Commun Chest

APPLICATION INFORMATION
Initial Approach: Scholarships only for Northern Berrien County high school students and children of Auto Specialties Manufacturing Co. employees. Deadline is April 1 for scholarships; October 1 for general grants.
Restrictions on Giving: Does not support individuals (except for employee-related scholarships).

GRANTS ANALYSIS
Number of Grants: 22
Highest Grant: $25,000
Typical Range: $1,000 to $7,500
Disclosure Period: 1991

RECENT GRANTS
25,000 Mercy Memorial Health Foundation, Benton Harbor, MI
20,000 CEDC, Benton Harbor, MI
12,000 YWCA, St. Joseph, MI
10,000 Lake Michigan College, Mendel Center, Benton, MI
7,500 Planned Parenthood Federation of America, Benton Harbor, MI
7,000 Andrews University, Berrien Springs, MI
6,000 Michigan Colleges Foundation, Southfield, MI
5,000 Calaveras Library, San Andreas, CA
5,000 Sarett Nature Center, Benton Harbor, MI
3,500 SWMI Symphony Orchestra, St. Joseph, MI

Titan Industrial Co. / Titan Industrial Foundation
Sales: $500.0 million
Employees: 350
Headquarters: New York, NY
SIC Major Group: Wholesale Trade—Durable Goods

CONTACT
Titan Industrial Fdn.
555 Madison Ave.
New York, NY 10022

FINANCIAL SUMMARY
Recent Giving: $108,802 (fiscal 1990); $113,477 (fiscal 1989)

Assets: $936,767 (fiscal year ending November 30, 1990); $849,563 (fiscal 1989)
Gifts Received: $150,000 (fiscal 1990); $200,000 (fiscal 1989)
Fiscal Note: In 1990, contributions were received from Titan Industrial Corp.
EIN: 13-6066216

CONTRIBUTIONS SUMMARY
Typical Recipients: • *Arts & Humanities:* arts centers, cinema, museums/galleries, theater • *Education:* business education, colleges & universities • *Health:* hospitals • *International:* international organizations • *Religion:* religious organizations, synagogues • *Social Services:* religious welfare, united funds
Grant Types: endowment and general support
Geographic Distribution: primarily in NY
Operating Locations: NY (New York)

CORP. OFFICERS
Michael S. Levin: *CURR EMPL* pres: Titan Indus Co
Walter Schroeder: *CURR EMPL* cfo: Titan Indus Co

APPLICATION INFORMATION
Initial Approach: Contributes only to preselected organizations. Applications not accepted.
Restrictions on Giving: Does not support individuals.

GRANTS ANALYSIS
Number of Grants: 98
Highest Grant: $10,500
Typical Range: $100 to $1,000
Disclosure Period: fiscal year ending November 30, 1990

RECENT GRANTS
10,500 Harvard University Business School Fund, Cambridge, MA
10,000 Institute for Contemporary Art, Flushing, NY
10,000 Open Space Institute, New York, NY
10,000 United Jewish Appeal Federation of Jewish Philanthropies, New York, NY
7,500 Usdan Center for the Performing Arts, New York, NY
7,000 United Jewish Appeal Federation of

Jewish Philanthropies, New York, NY

5,000 Brick Hawkins Dance Foundation, New York, NY

5,000 Institute for Contemporary Art, Flushing, NY

5,000 St. Lawrence College, Bronxville, NY

3,000 Princess Grace Foundation, New York, NY

Titmus Foundation

CONTACT
Edward B. Titmus
President
Titmus Fdn.
PO Box 10
Sutherland, VA 23885-0010
(804) 265-5834

FINANCIAL SUMMARY
Recent Giving: $480,767 (fiscal 1992); $483,018 (fiscal 1991); $458,779 (fiscal 1990)
Assets: $12,606,197 (fiscal year ending January 31, 1992); $10,437,511 (fiscal 1991); $10,588,733 (fiscal 1990)
EIN: 54-6051332

CONTRIBUTIONS SUMMARY
Donor(s): the late Edward Hutson Titmus, Sr.
Typical Recipients: • Arts & Humanities: history/historic preservation • Education: colleges & universities • Health: medical research, pediatric health, single-disease health associations • Religion: churches, missionary activities, religious organizations • Social Services: child welfare, community service organizations, disabled, homes, recreation & athletics, youth organizations
Grant Types: general support
Geographic Distribution: focus on VA

GIVING OFFICERS
Margaret V. Beck: off
George M. Modlin: vp
John J. Muldowney: treas
Edward T. Titmus: pres
John J. Whitt, Jr.: vp

APPLICATION INFORMATION
Initial Approach: Send cover letter and full proposal. There are no deadlines.
Restrictions on Giving: Does not support individuals.

GRANTS ANALYSIS
Number of Grants: 158
Highest Grant: $28,825
Typical Range: $200 to $5,000
Disclosure Period: fiscal year ending January 31, 1992

RECENT GRANTS
28,825 Second Baptist Church, Petersburg, VA

25,000 Jackson-Feild Homes, Richmond, VA

25,000 Jackson-Feild Homes, Richmond, VA

15,000 Virginia Historical Society, Richmond, VA

15,000 Virginia Historical Society Fifth Century Fund, Richmond, VA

15,000 YMCA, Petersburg, VA

10,700 End Baptist Church, Petersburg, VA

10,000 College of William and Mary, Williamsburg, VA — Carol Veazey Titmus Endowment

10,000 Lineberger Comprehensive Cancer Center, Chapel Hill, NC

10,000 Lineberger Comprehensive Cancer Center, Chapel Hill, NC

Titus Foundation, C. W.

CONTACT
C. W. Titus Fdn.
1801 Philtower Bldg.
Tulsa, OK 74103
(918) 582-8095

FINANCIAL SUMMARY
Recent Giving: $419,305 (1991); $368,124 (1990); $421,624 (1989)
Assets: $10,553,480 (1991); $9,521,425 (1990); $8,398,581 (1989)
EIN: 23-7016981

CONTRIBUTIONS SUMMARY
Typical Recipients: • Arts & Humanities: dance, history/historic preservation, museums/galleries, music, performing arts, public broadcasting • Education: private education (precollege) • Health: hospitals, medical research, pediatric health, single-disease health associations • Social Services: aged, animal protection, community service organizations, disabled, family services, food/clothing distribution, united funds, youth organizations
Grant Types: general support
Geographic Distribution: focus on OK and MO

GIVING OFFICERS
Timothy T. Reynolds: trust

APPLICATION INFORMATION
Initial Approach: Send brief letter of inquiry describing program or project. There are no deadlines.

GRANTS ANALYSIS
Number of Grants: 68
Highest Grant: $80,000
Typical Range: $1,000 to $6,250
Disclosure Period: 1991

RECENT GRANTS
80,000 Freeman Hospital, Joplin, MO — building fund

25,000 Tulsa Speech and Hearing Association, Tulsa, OK — building fund

25,000 United Way, Tulsa, OK

25,000 United Way, Broken Bow, OK

25,000 YMCA, Tulsa, OK

15,000 Tulsa Boys Home, Tulsa, OK

15,000 Wright Christian Academy, Tulsa, OK

10,000 Children's Mercy Hospital, Kansas City, MO

10,000 Fair Acres Family Y, Carthage, MO

10,000 Tender Loving Care, Ronald McDonald House, Tulsa, OK — building program

TJX Cos. / TJX Foundation
Sales: $3.26 billion
Employees: 30,000
Headquarters: Framingham, MA

CONTACT
Carla Bertonazzi
Community Affairs Administrator
TJX Fdn
770 Cochituate Rd.
Framingham, MA 01701
(508) 390-3199

FINANCIAL SUMMARY
Recent Giving: $541,800 (fiscal 1992); $500,000 (fiscal 1991 approx.); $524,580 (fiscal 1990)
Assets: $217,641 (fiscal year ending January 31, 1992); $737,464 (fiscal 1990); $173,834 (fiscal 1989)
Fiscal Note: Company gives primarily through foundation. The differential in giving figures is due to the fact that TJX Foundation is no longer Zayre Foundation, and is much smaller.
EIN: 04-2399760

CONTRIBUTIONS SUMMARY
Typical Recipients: • Arts & Humanities: arts centers, arts funds, arts institutes, community arts, dance, history/historic preservation, museums/galleries, performing arts, theater • Civic & Public Affairs: business/free enterprise, civil rights, ethnic/minority organizations, law & justice, philanthropic organizations, women's affairs • Education: business education, career/vocational education, colleges & universities, education associations, education funds, elementary education, legal education, medical education, minority education, public education (precollege) • Health: health organizations, hospices, hospitals, medical rehabilitation, mental health, pediatric health, public health, single-disease health associations • Social Services: child welfare, community centers, community service organizations, counseling, disabled, domestic violence, employment/job training, family services, religious welfare, shelters/homelessness, united funds, volunteer services, youth organizations
Grant Types: capital, challenge, endowment, general support, project, and scholarship
Nonmonetary Support Types: cause-related marketing & promotion, donated equipment, donated products, and workplace solicitation

Geographic Distribution: limited to geographical area of TJX operations
Operating Locations: DC, FL (Miami, Tampa), GA (Forest Park), IL (Chicago), MA (Framingham, Mansfield, Natick, Stoughton), NJ (Secaucus), NY (New York)

CORP. OFFICERS
Bernard Cammarata: *CURR EMPL* pres, ceo, dir: JJX Cos
Donald Campbell: *CURR EMPL* cfo: TJX Cos
Sumner Lee Feldberg: *B* Boston MA 1924 *ED* Harvard Univ BA 1947; Harvard Univ MBA 1949 *CURR EMPL* chmn: TJX Cos *CORP AFFIL* chmn: Waban Corp; trust: Massmutual Corp Investors, Massmutual Participation Investors; chmn: TJX Operating Cos *NONPR AFFIL* trust: Beth Israel Hosp Boston, Combined Jewish Philanthropies Greater Boston
Richard Lesser: *CURR EMPL* sr vp: TJX Cos
Arthur F. Loewy: *B* New York NY 1929 *ED* Univ CA Los Angeles BS 1952 *CURR EMPL* chmn (fin comm): TJX Cos *NONPR AFFIL* mem: Fin Execs Inst

GIVING OFFICERS
Bernard Cammarata: pres, dir *CURR EMPL* pres, ceo, dir: JJX Cos (see above)
Donald Campbell: treas, dir *CURR EMPL* cfo: TJX Cos (see above)
Sumner Lee Feldberg: dir *CURR EMPL* chmn: TJX Cos (see above)
Richard Lesser: vp, dir *CURR EMPL* sr vp: TJX Cos (see above)
Arthur F. Loewy: dir *CURR EMPL* chmn (fin comm): TJX Cos (see above)

APPLICATION INFORMATION
Initial Approach: *Initial Contact:* brief letter *Include Information On:* description of the organization and its purpose, objective of grant and its target group, evidence of need for such program, organizational experience with similar problems, method of evaluation, program budget and amount sought, IRS tax-exempt statement, most recent audited financial statement, current operating budget, list of board of directors, a list of contributors and amounts received in last

fiscal year *When to Submit:* any time
Restrictions on Giving: TJX generally will not support individuals, political groups, religious organizations for sectarian purposes, research projects, conferences, publications, or films.

OTHER THINGS TO KNOW
TJX Foundation had been Zayre Foundation until fiscal year 1989.

GRANTS ANALYSIS
Total Grants: $541,800
Number of Grants: 162
Highest Grant: $49,536
Typical Range: $1,000 to $5,000
Disclosure Period: fiscal year ending January 31, 1992
Note: Recent grants are derived from a fiscal 1992 Form 990.

RECENT GRANTS
49,536 Save the Children, Westport, CT
43,968 Save the Children, New York, NY
39,552 Save the Children, New York, NY
27,500 Great Woods Institute, Wreton, MA
26,800 United Way of Eastern New England, Boston, MA
25,000 Beth Israel Hospital, Boston, MA
25,000 Combined Jewish Philanthropies, Boston, MA
20,000 Wang Center for Performing Arts, Boston, MA
15,000 Massachusetts Easter Seal Society, Boston, MA
10,000 Framingham Union Hospital, Framingham, MA

TMZ Corp.
Headquarters: Irvine, CA

CONTACT
Robert James
Chief Financial Officer
Life Support Products
PO Box 19569
Irvine, CA 92713
(714) 727-2000

CONTRIBUTIONS SUMMARY
Operating Locations: CA (Irvine)

Tobin Foundation

CONTACT
Arnold Swartz
Trustee
Tobin Fdn.
PO Box 2101
San Antonio, TX 78297
(512) 223-6203

FINANCIAL SUMMARY
Recent Giving: $387,415 (1991); $142,963 (1990); $95,470 (1989)
Assets: $2,986,710 (1991); $2,474,115 (1990); $2,505,504 (1989)
Gifts Received: $600,000 (1991)
EIN: 74-6035718

CONTRIBUTIONS SUMMARY
Donor(s): the late Edgar G. Tobin, Margaret Batts Tobin
Typical Recipients: • *Arts & Humanities:* arts centers, community arts, libraries, museums/galleries, music, opera, public broadcasting • *Health:* medical research, single-disease health associations • *Religion:* churches • *Social Services:* community centers, community service organizations, united funds, youth organizations
Grant Types: general support
Geographic Distribution: limited to TX

GIVING OFFICERS
James T. Gasnell: secy
James T. Hart: trust
Arnold Swartz: trust
R.L.B. Tobin: pres

APPLICATION INFORMATION
Initial Approach: Send brief letter of inquiry describing program. There are no deadlines.
Restrictions on Giving: Does not support individuals.

GRANTS ANALYSIS
Number of Grants: 16
Highest Grant: $196,200
Typical Range: $100 to $5,000
Disclosure Period: 1991

RECENT GRANTS
196,200 Metropolitan Opera, New York, NY
50,000 McNay Art Museum, San Antonio, TX
37,500 United Way, San Antonio, TX

31,000 Cathedral Church of St. John, San Antonio, TX
30,000 Museum of Modern Art, New York, NY
20,000 Houston Grand Opera Association, Houston, TX
6,000 San Antonio Symphony, San Antonio, TX
5,000 Public Radio, San Antonio, TX
2,750 Carver Community Center, Carver, TX
2,500 San Antonio Public Library Foundation, San Antonio, TX

Todd Co., A.M. / Todd Co. Foundation, A.M.
Sales: $160.0 million
Employees: 266
Headquarters: Kalamazoo, MI
SIC Major Group: Chemicals & Allied Products and Food & Kindred Products

CONTACT
Ian D. Blair
Trustee
A.M. Todd Co. Foundation
Cash Manager
Box 50711
Kalamazoo, MI 49005
(616) 337-6940

FINANCIAL SUMMARY
Recent Giving: $38,300 (1991); $43,800 (1990); $30,700 (1989)
Assets: $234,706 (1991); $201,176 (1990); $189,498 (1989)
Gifts Received: $50,000 (1991); $40,000 (1990); $70,000 (1989)
Fiscal Note: In 1991, contributions were received from A.M. Todd Co.
EIN: 38-6055829

CONTRIBUTIONS SUMMARY
Typical Recipients: • *Arts & Humanities:* community arts, libraries, music • *Civic & Public Affairs:* environmental affairs, housing, zoos/botanical gardens • *Education:* colleges & universities, special education • *Health:* health organizations • *Social Services:* community service organizations, united funds, youth organizations
Grant Types: general support
Geographic Distribution: focus on Kalamazoo County

Operating Locations: MI
(Kalamazoo)

CORP. OFFICERS
A. J. Todd III: *CURR EMPL*
pres: AM Todd Co

GIVING OFFICERS
Ian D. Blair: trust
A. J. Todd III: trust *CURR
EMPL* pres: AM Todd Co (see
above)

APPLICATION
INFORMATION
Initial Approach: Send brief
letter describing program.
There are no deadlines.
Restrictions on Giving: Does
not support individuals, religious organizations for sectarian
purposes, political or lobbying
groups, or organizations outside operating areas.

OTHER THINGS TO
KNOW
Education support is primarily
provided directly by A.M.
Todd Co., not the foundation.

GRANTS ANALYSIS
Number of Grants: 31
Highest Grant: $7,700
Typical Range: $200 to $3,000
Disclosure Period: 1991

RECENT GRANTS
　7,700　United Way, Kala-
　　　　mazoo, MI
　5,000　Kalamazoo Founda-
　　　　tion, Kalamazoo,
　　　　MI
　3,000　CEO Council, Kala-
　　　　mazoo, MI
　3,000　Gateway Villa
　　　　Capital, Kalama-
　　　　zoo, MI
　3,000　Salvation Army,
　　　　Kalamazoo, MI
　2,500　Pride Place, Kala-
　　　　mazoo, MI
　2,500　YWCA, Kalama-
　　　　zoo, MI
　2,000　Kalamazoo Con-
　　　　sultation Center,
　　　　Kalamazoo, MI
　1,000　Shangri-La Corpo-
　　　　ration, Salem, OR
　1,000　Specific Language
　　　　Disability Center,
　　　　Kalamazoo, MI

Tokai Bank, Ltd.
Headquarters: New York, NY
SIC Major Group: Depository
　Institutions

CONTACT
T. Hoshida
Assistant Manager, General
　Affairs
Tokai Bank, Ltd.
Park Ave. Plz.
55 East 52nd St.
11th Fl.
New York, NY 10055
(212) 339-1200

CONTRIBUTIONS
SUMMARY
In early 1990, Japan's Tokai
Bank Ltd. awarded a $1 mil-
lion endowment to Northwestern University's Kellogg Graduate School of Management for
a chair in international finance.
The endowment is the first gift
of that magnitude to the university from a foreign corporation.
Tokai officials said the gift reflected a growing desire by
Japanese firms to reciprocate
the assistance and support they
have received from the United
States. The bank picked Northwestern because of Kellogg's
stature in global finance and to
cement an existing relationship: several Kellogg graduates
have gone on to become Tokai
employees. The gift represented the bank's first univer-
sity-directed giving in the
United States. Officials at Tokai's New York branch, which
celebrated its 25th year in business in 1990, expect the bank
to make other grants to higher
education, as well as to the
arts, but stress that they do not
maintain a formal giving program.
Typical Recipients: • *Education:* colleges & universities

CORP. OFFICERS
H. Hayashi: *CURR EMPL* asst
mgr (gen aff): Tokai Bank NY
Kaneo Takeda: *CURR EMPL*
gen mgr: Tokai Bank NY

GIVING OFFICERS
H. Hayashi: *CURR EMPL* asst
mgr (gen aff): Tokai Bank NY
(see above)

Tokheim Corp. /
Tokheim
Foundation
Sales: $162.2 million
Employees: 1,600
Headquarters: Fort Wayne, IN
SIC Major Group: Electronic &
　Other Electrical Equipment,
　Industrial Machinery &
　Equipment, Instruments &

Related Products, and
　Transportation Equipment

CONTACT
Douglas K. Pinner
Trustee
Tokheim Fdn.
PO Box 360
Ft. Wayne, IN 46801
(219) 423-2552

FINANCIAL SUMMARY
Recent Giving: $172,036 (fis-
cal 1991); $149,000 (fiscal
1990); $149,645 (fiscal 1989)
Assets: $57,900 (fiscal year
ending November 30, 1991);
$222,472 (fiscal 1990);
$352,548 (fiscal 1989)
Gifts Received: $75,000 (fis-
cal 1988)
EIN: 35-6043647

CONTRIBUTIONS
SUMMARY
Typical Recipients: • *Arts &
Humanities:* arts associations,
arts funds, theater • *Civic &
Public Affairs:* business/free en-
terprise • *Education:* business
education, colleges & universi-
ties • *Health:* health organiza-
tions • *Social Services:* united
funds, youth organizations
Grant Types: capital, endow-
ment, and general support
Geographic Distribution: pri-
marily in IN
Operating Locations: IL
(West Chicago), IN (Fremont,
Ft. Wayne, Washington), PA
(Lansdale), TN (Jasper), TX
(Dallas, Houston)
Note: Operating names of three
plants are city names where lo-
cated: Fremont, Ft. Wayne, and
Washington.

CORP. OFFICERS
Gerald H. Frieling, Jr.:
CURR EMPL chmn: Tokheim
Corp
Douglas K. Pinner: *CURR
EMPL* pres, ceo: Tokheim Corp

GIVING OFFICERS
Timothy R. Eastom: trust
Jess B. Ford: trust *CURR
EMPL* vp, cfo: Tokheim Corp
Bob F. Jesse: trust
Myron L. Marsh: trust
Douglas K. Pinner: trust
CURR EMPL pres, ceo: Tok-
heim Corp (see above)

APPLICATION
INFORMATION
Initial Approach: Send brief
letter of inquiry and proposal.
There are no deadlines.
Restrictions on Giving: Does
not support individuals, relig-

ious organizations for sectarian
purposes, or political or lobbying groups,

GRANTS ANALYSIS
Number of Grants: 82
Highest Grant: $77,056
Typical Range: $500 to $3,000
Disclosure Period: fiscal year
ending November 30, 1991

RECENT GRANTS
　77,056　United Way, Ft.
　　　　Wayne, IN
　10,178　Fort Wayne Urban
　　　　Enterprise Associa-
　　　　tion, Ft. Wayne, IN
　7,000　Arts United, Ft.
　　　　Wayne, IN
　7,000　Fort Wayne Fine
　　　　Arts Foundation,
　　　　Ft. Wayne, IN
　6,500　Associated Col-
　　　　leges of Indiana, In-
　　　　dianapolis, IN
　6,000　YWCA, Ft. Wayne,
　　　　IN
　4,025　Ball State Univer-
　　　　sity, Muncie, IN
　3,425　Junior Achieve-
　　　　ment, Ft. Wayne,
　　　　IN
　3,000　St. Francis Col-
　　　　lege, Ft. Wayne, IN
　　　　— endowment con-
　　　　tinuation
　2,415　Purdue University,
　　　　West Lafayette, IN

Toledo Edison Co.
Assets: $4.01 billion
Employees: 2,562
Parent Company: Centerior
　Energy Corp.
Headquarters: Toledo, OH
SIC Major Group: Electric, Gas
　& Sanitary Services

CONTACT
Tess Demko
Community Relations
Toledo Edison Co.
300 Madison Ave.
Toledo, OH 43652
(419) 249-5000

CONTRIBUTIONS
SUMMARY
Operating Locations: OH
(Toledo)

CORP. OFFICERS
Murray R. Edelman: *CURR
EMPL* pres: Toledo Edison Co
Robert J. Farling: *B* Cleve-
land OH 1936 *ED* Case Inst
Tech 1958; Case Western Re-
serve Univ MBA 1965 *CURR
EMPL* chmn, ceo, dir, pres:
Centerior Energy Corp *CORP
AFFIL* dir: Natl City Bank
Cleveland; chmn, ceo: Toledo

Edison Co; exec vp, dir: CCO
Co; pres, dir: Cleveland Electric Illuminating Co

Paul M. Smart: *CURR EMPL*
vchmn: Toledo Edison Co

Tombstone Pizza
Corp. / Tombstone
Pizza Foundation

Sales: $209.0 million
Employees: 1,400
Parent Company: Kraft General
  Foods
Headquarters: Glenview, IL
SIC Major Group: Food &
  Kindred Products

CONTACT
Thomas A. Tranetzki
President
Tombstone Pizza Foundation
Kraft Ct.
Glenview, IL 60015

FINANCIAL SUMMARY
EIN: 39-1471833

CONTRIBUTIONS
SUMMARY
Operating Locations: IL
(Glenview)

CORP. OFFICERS
Harold Reinhart: *CURR
EMPL* pres: Tombstone Pizza

R. L. Simek: *CURR EMPL*
ceo: Tombstone Pizza

GIVING OFFICERS
Julaine F. Anderson: secy, dir

Richard D. Pddy: treas, dir

D. David Sebod: vp, dir

Thomas A. Tranetzki: pres, dir

OTHER THINGS TO
KNOW
No grants were provided in
1990.

Tomen America, Inc.

Sales: $2.0 billion
Employees: 500
Headquarters: New York, NY
SIC Major Group: Wholesale
  Trade—Durable Goods and
  Wholesale Trade—Nondurable
  Goods

CONTACT
Eichi Yamori
Manager, General Affairs
Toyomenka America
1285 Avenue of the Americas,
  36th Fl.
New York, NY 10019
(212) 397-5751

CONTRIBUTIONS
SUMMARY
Operating Locations: NY
(New York)

CORP. OFFICERS
K. Miyaoka: *CURR EMPL*
pres: Tomen Am

Tomkins Industries,
Inc. / Tomkins
Corporation
Foundation

Former Foundation Name:
  Philips Industries Foundation
Sales: $930.0 million
Employees: 10,348
Headquarters: Dayton, OH
SIC Major Group: Fabricated
  Metal Products, Industrial
  Machinery & Equipment,
  Rubber & Miscellaneous
  Plastics Products, and
  Transportation Equipment

CONTACT
David T. Jeanmougin
Vice President
Tomkins Industries Fdn.
4801 Springfield St., PO Box 943
Dayton, OH 45401
(513) 253-7171

FINANCIAL SUMMARY
Recent Giving: $416,032 (fis-
cal 1992); $93,595 (fiscal
1991); $90,856 (fiscal 1990)
Assets: $4,304,594 (fiscal year
ending April 30, 1992);
$4,162,138 (fiscal 1991);
$3,925,740 (fiscal 1990)
Fiscal Note: Company gives
through foundation only.
EIN: 31-1207183

CONTRIBUTIONS
SUMMARY
Typical Recipients: • *Arts &
Humanities:* arts associations,
dance, music, public broadcasting • *Civic & Public Affairs:*
philanthropic organizations,
safety • *Education:* business
education, colleges & universities, education associations,
education funds, public education (precollege) • *Health:*
health organizations, hospitals,
single-disease health associations • *Social Services:* child

welfare, united funds, youth or-
ganizations
Grant Types: general support
Geographic Distribution: pri-
marily in the Dayton, OH, area
Operating Locations: AZ
(Tucson), CA (Anaheim, Irwin-
dale), IN (Albion, Bristol, Elk-
hart, Indianapolis, Lebanon),
KS (Kansas City), MI (Detroit,
Three Rivers), OH (Amelia,
Cleveland, Dayton, Malta), PA
(Selinsgrove), TX (Clarksville,
El Paso)

CORP. OFFICERS
Dennis Mulhall: *CURR EMPL*
cfo: Tomkins Indus
Steve Schneider: *CURR
EMPL* pres: Tomkins Indus

GIVING OFFICERS
Richard G. Carr: pres, trust
Ian Duncan: trust
Gregory Hutchings: trust
David T. Jeanmougin: vp *B*
Cincinnati OH 1940 *ED* Xavier
Univ 1962
Dennis Mulhall: vp *CURR
EMPL* cfo: Tomkins Indus (see
above)
Edwin L. Ryan, Jr: secy *B*
Chicago IL 1932 *ED* Univ
Notre Dame 1952; DePaul
Univ 1957
William R. Winkler: treas,
trust

APPLICATION
INFORMATION
Initial Approach: *Initial Contact:* Foundation does not accept unsolicited requests for
funds.

GRANTS ANALYSIS
Total Grants: $416,032
Number of Grants: 50*
Highest Grant: $160,000
Typical Range: $1,000 to
$5,000
Disclosure Period: fiscal year
ending April 30, 1992
Note: Number of grants and av-
erage grant figures do not in-
clude matching gifts totaling
$41,560. Recent grants are de-
rived from a fiscal 1992 grants
list.

RECENT GRANTS
160,000 Dayton Montgom-
        ery County Scholar-
        ship Fund, Dayton,
        OH
 97,380 United Way, OH
 25,000 Lawrence County
        Education Founda-
        tion, OH
 16,040 National Merit
        Scholarship
 13,500 Interfaith Hospital-
        ity Network

  5,000 Western New Eng-
        land College
  4,000 Fellowship of
        Christian Athletes,
        OH
  4,000 Junior Achieve-
        ment of Dayton,
        Dayton, OH
  4,000 Junior Achieve-
        ment of SE Michi-
        gan, MI
  3,500 Tennessee Founda-
        tion of Independent
        Colleges, TN

Tomlinson Family
Foundation

CONTACT
Barbara D. Tomlinson
President
Tomlinson Family Foundation
P.O. Box 590
Morristown, NJ 07963-0590

FINANCIAL SUMMARY
Recent Giving: $141,840
(1990)
Assets: $5,316,595 (1990);
$5,000,000 (1989)
Gifts Received: $5,000,000
(1989)
Fiscal Note: 1990 contribution
received from the Morristown
Daily Record.
EIN: 22-3014796

CONTRIBUTIONS
SUMMARY
Donor(s): the donor is the Morristown Daily Record

GIVING OFFICERS
Barbara Tomlinson: pres
Kate Tomlinson: treas
Norman Tomlinson: secy

APPLICATION
INFORMATION
Initial Approach: The foundation reports that requests for
funds should be in the form of
a written proposal of less than
three pages in length. The proposal should include information on the activity to be
funded, list trustees and principal officers, describe applicant's organization, and include proof of tax-exempt
status.

GRANTS ANALYSIS
Total Grants: $141,840
Highest Grant: $100,000
Disclosure Period: 1990

Tomlinson Foundation, Kate and Elwyn

CONTACT
Kathryn Bridges
Chairman
Kate and Elwyn Tomlinson Fdn.
3000 Habersham Rd., N.W.
Atlanta, GA 30305-2844
(404) 952-2277

FINANCIAL SUMMARY
Recent Giving: $131,800 (1990); $133,800 (1989); $135,700 (1988)
Assets: $2,583,194 (1990); $2,754,143 (1989); $2,474,850 (1988)
EIN: 58-0634727

CONTRIBUTIONS SUMMARY
Typical Recipients: • *Arts & Humanities:* dance, history/historic preservation • *Civic & Public Affairs:* environmental affairs, zoos/botanical gardens • *Education:* colleges & universities, private education (precollege) • *Health:* hospitals, medical research, single-disease health associations • *Religion:* churches • *Science:* observatories & planetariums • *Social Services:* community service organizations, united funds, youth organizations
Grant Types: general support
Geographic Distribution: focus on GA

GIVING OFFICERS
Kathryn T. Bridges: chmn
Mark P. Tomlinson: vchmn

APPLICATION INFORMATION
Initial Approach: Send brief letter of inquiry describing program. There are no deadlines.
Restrictions on Giving: Does not support individuals.

GRANTS ANALYSIS
Number of Grants: 51
Highest Grant: $30,000
Typical Range: $300 to $5,000
Disclosure Period: 1990

RECENT GRANTS
30,000 Atlanta Botanical Gardens, Atlanta, GA
10,000 Atlanta Historical Society, Atlanta, GA
7,000 United Way, Atlanta, GA
7,000 Woodruff Arts Center, Atlanta, GA
6,000 Ducks Unlimited, Long Grove, IL
6,000 Northside United Methodist Church, Atlanta, GA
4,000 Elks Admore Children's Center, Atlanta, GA
2,500 Georgia Foundation of Independent Colleges, Atlanta, GA
1,500 Atlanta Ballet Company, Atlanta, GA
1,500 Boy Scouts of America, Atlanta, GA

Toms Foundation

CONTACT
William C. Wilson
President
Toms Fdn.
Valley Fidelity Bank Bldg., Ninth Fl.
PO Box 2466
Knoxville, TN 37901
(615) 544-3000

FINANCIAL SUMMARY
Recent Giving: $11,400 (1990); $94,969 (1989)
Assets: $3,250,368 (1990); $3,138,716 (1989)
EIN: 62-6037668

CONTRIBUTIONS SUMMARY
Donor(s): the late W. P. Toms
Typical Recipients: • *Arts & Humanities:* community arts, opera • *Education:* colleges & universities • *Health:* medical research, single-disease health associations • *Social Services:* community service organizations, united funds, youth organizations
Grant Types: capital, emergency, research, and seed money
Geographic Distribution: focus on eastern TN

GIVING OFFICERS
Ronald L. Grimm: secy, treas, trust
Eleanor C. Krug: vp, trust
Mary Mayne Perry: trust
Dorothy B. Wilson: trust
William C. Wilson: chmn, pres, trust

APPLICATION INFORMATION
Initial Approach: Send letter of inquiry followed by proposal. Submit proposal preferably in June. Deadline is June 30. Board meets in August. De-cisions are made one month after annual meeting.
Restrictions on Giving: Does not support individuals.

OTHER THINGS TO KNOW
Publications: Annual Report

GRANTS ANALYSIS
Number of Grants: 11
Highest Grant: $4,000
Typical Range: $200 to $4,000
Disclosure Period: 1990
Note: 06/30

RECENT GRANTS
4,000 University of Tennessee, Memphis, TN
2,500 Thompson Cancer Center, Knoxville, TN
1,500 Boy Scouts of America, Knoxville, TN
750 Knoxville Zoological Park, Knoxville, TN
500 Arts Council of Knoxville, Knoxville, TN
500 Children's Family House, Knoxville, TN
500 Girls Club of Knoxville, Knoxville, TN
500 Tanasi Girl Scout Council, Knoxville, TN
250 Knoxville Opera Company, Knoxville, TN
200 Empty Stocking Fund, Knoxville, TN

Tom's of Maine
Sales: $17.0 million
Employees: 52
Headquarters: Kennebunk, ME
SIC Major Group: Chemicals & Allied Products

CONTACT
Coleen Meyers
Vice President of Community Life
Tom's of Maine
Railroad Ave.
PO Box 710
Kennebunk, ME 04043
(207) 985-2944

CONTRIBUTIONS SUMMARY
Operating Locations: ME (Kennebunk)

CORP. OFFICERS
Thomas M. Chappell: *CURR EMPL* pres, ceo: Toms of Maine

Tonkin Foundation, Tom and Helen

CONTACT
Elona Anderson
Tom and Helen Tonkin Fdn.
c/o Northwest Bank Trust Dept.
PO Box 2799
Casper, WY 82602
(307) 266-1100

FINANCIAL SUMMARY
Recent Giving: $109,784 (fiscal 1992); $91,825 (fiscal 1991); $103,932 (fiscal 1990)
Assets: $2,370,475 (fiscal year ending July 31, 1992); $2,166,497 (fiscal 1991); $2,041,578 (fiscal 1990)
EIN: 83-6002200

CONTRIBUTIONS SUMMARY
Donor(s): the late Helen B. Tonkin, the late T. C. Tonkin
Typical Recipients: • *Arts & Humanities:* history/historic preservation • *Civic & Public Affairs:* economic development, municipalities, urban & community affairs • *Health:* nutrition & health maintenance • *Religion:* churches • *Social Services:* child welfare, disabled, homes, recreation & athletics, youth organizations
Grant Types: emergency, operating expenses, and scholarship
Geographic Distribution: limited to WY, with emphasis on the Casper area

GIVING OFFICERS
James A. Barlow, Jr.: mem
Sheri Caelisle: mem
A.F. Haskey: chmn, mem
Warren A. Morton: mem
R.M. Robertson: mem

APPLICATION INFORMATION
Initial Approach: Send brief letter describing program. There are no deadlines.
Restrictions on Giving: Does not support individuals.

OTHER THINGS TO KNOW
Publications: 990-PF, Application Guidelines

GRANTS ANALYSIS
Number of Grants: 27
Highest Grant: $14,615

Typical Range: $2,000 to $8,000
Disclosure Period: fiscal year ending July 31, 1992

RECENT GRANTS

14,615 Hearing Education and Rehabilitation Service, Casper, WY

11,228 Handicapped Education and Referral Systems, Casper, WY

8,564 Hearing Education and Referral Service, Casper, WY

5,000 Caring Program for Children, Casper, WY

5,000 Children's Dental Fund, Casper, WY

4,720 HIRES, Casper, WY

4,128 Rawlins Day Care Center, Rawlins, WY

4,000 Community Recreation Foundation, Casper, WY

4,000 Special Friends of Rawlins, Rawlins, WY

3,900 Nutrition and Child Development, Casper, WY

Tonya Memorial Foundation

CONTACT
Maurice H. Martin
President
Tonya Memorial Fdn.
c/o American National Bank and Trust Co., Trust Dept.
736 Market St.
Chattanooga, TN 37402

FINANCIAL SUMMARY
Recent Giving: $3,623,939 (1991); $2,942,591 (1990); $2,229,924 (1989)
Assets: $8,943,988 (1991); $11,190,972 (1990); $13,870,063 (1989)
EIN: 62-6042269

CONTRIBUTIONS SUMMARY
Donor(s): the late Burkett Miller
Typical Recipients: • *Arts & Humanities:* libraries, public broadcasting • *Civic & Public Affairs:* municipalities, urban & community affairs, zoos/botanical gardens • *Education:* colleges & universities, private education (precollege) • *Social Services:* community centers, community service or-

ganizations, homes, united funds, youth organizations
Grant Types: capital and multi-year/continuing support
Geographic Distribution: focus on Chattanooga, TN

GIVING OFFICERS
H. Whitney Durand: secy, trust
James R. Hedges III: vp, asst secy, trust
Harry James Hitching: chmn, trust *B* New York NY 1909 *ED* Columbia Univ AB 1929; Columbia Univ LLB 1931; Columbia Univ JD 1969 *CURR EMPL* ptnr: Miller & Martin *CORP AFFIL* dir: Krystal Co; div coun: Vulcan Materials Co; gen coun: Skyland Intl Corp; ptnr: Miller & Martin *NONPR AFFIL* chmn adv bd: Salvation Army Chattanooga; dir: Chattanooga Ophthalmological Fdn; mem: Am Bar Assn, Chattanooga Bar Assn, Chattanooga Chamber Commerce, GA Bar Assn, Newcomen Soc North Am, TN Bar Assn
Maurice H. Martin: pres, treas, trust

APPLICATION INFORMATION
Initial Approach: Send brief letter of inquiry describing program or project. There are no deadlines.
Restrictions on Giving: Does not support individuals or provide loans.

GRANTS ANALYSIS
Number of Grants: 22
Highest Grant: $507,625
Typical Range: $5,000 to $25,000
Disclosure Period: 1991

RECENT GRANTS

507,625 Tennessee Aquarium Fund, Chattanooga, TN — aquarium fund

416,000 Girls Preparatory School, Chattanooga, TN — endowment

329,668 Enterprise Fund of Greater Chattanooga, Chattanooga, TN

300,000 McCallie School, Chattanooga, TN

299,675 Baylor School, Chattanooga, TN — for Hedges Library

167,000 City of Chattanooga, Chattanooga, TN — renovation of Memorial Auditorium

100,000 River City Company, Chattanooga, TN

65,000 Martin Luther King Boulevard Community Development Corporation, Chattanooga, TN — to fund Bessie Smith Hall

35,950 River City Company, Chattanooga, TN — partial payment for planning work on Riverwalk

25,000 Junior Achievement, Chattanooga, TN

Tootsie Roll Industries, Inc.
Sales: $207.9 million
Employees: 2,400
Headquarters: Chicago, IL
SIC Major Group: Food & Kindred Products

CONTACT
Ellen Gordon
President
Tootsie Roll Industries, Inc.
7401 South Cicero Ave.
Chicago, IL 60629
(312) 838-3400

CONTRIBUTIONS SUMMARY
Operating Locations: IL (Chicago)

CORP. OFFICERS
Ellen R. Gordon: *B* New York NY 1931 *ED* Brandeis Univ BA 1965; Vassar Coll; Harvard Univ *CURR EMPL* pres, coo, dir: Tootsie Roll Indus *CORP AFFIL* dir: CPC Intl; vp, dir: HDI Investment Corp *NONPR AFFIL* chp, pres: Comm 200 Fdn; mem: Natl Confectioners Assn; mem adv counc: Stanford Univ Grad Sch Bus; mem bd fellows: Harvard Univ Sch Med
Melvin J. Gordon: *CURR EMPL* chmn, ceo: Tootsie Roll Indus

Topps Company
Sales: $303.1 million
Employees: 1,000
Headquarters: Brooklyn, NY
SIC Major Group: Food & Kindred Products and Printing & Publishing

CONTACT
William O'Connor
Director, Personnel
Topps Chewing Gum, Inc.
254 36th St.
Brooklyn, NY 11232
(718) 768-8900

CONTRIBUTIONS SUMMARY
Operating Locations: NY (Brooklyn)

CORP. OFFICERS
John J. Langdon: *CURR EMPL* pres, coo: Topps Chewing Gum
Arthur T. Shorin: *CURR EMPL* chmn, ceo: Topps Chewing Gum

Tops Markets, Inc.
Sales: $1.82 billion
Employees: 15,000
Parent Company: RFS Buffalo Holding Corp.
Headquarters: Buffalo, NY
SIC Major Group: Food Stores

CONTACT
Doug Hartmayer
Director, Community Relations
Tops Markets, Inc.
60 Dingens St.
Buffalo, NY 14240-1027
(716) 827-3264

CONTRIBUTIONS SUMMARY
Nonmonetary Support Types: donated products
Operating Locations: NY (Buffalo)

CORP. OFFICERS
Armand J. Castellani: *CURR EMPL* chmn emeritus: Tops Markets
Lawrence P. Castellani: *CURR EMPL* pres, coo: Tops Markets
Savino P. Nanula: *CURR EMPL* chmn, ceo: Tops Markets

Torchmark Corp.
Revenue: $1.93 billion
Employees: 5,968
Headquarters: Birmingham, AL
SIC Major Group: Engineering & Management Services, Insurance Carriers, and Security & Commodity Brokers

CONTACT
Sam Upchurch
Vice President & General
Counsel
Torchmark Corp.
2001 Third Ave. S
Birmingham, AL 35233
(205) 325-4256

FINANCIAL SUMMARY
Recent Giving: $700,000
(1989 approx.); $700,000
(1988 approx.)
Fiscal Note: Company gives directly.

CONTRIBUTIONS SUMMARY
Typical Recipients: • *Arts & Humanities:* arts funds, community arts, dance, history/historic preservation, museums/galleries, music, opera, performing arts • *Civic & Public Affairs:* business/free enterprise, civil rights, consumer affairs, safety • *Education:* career/vocational education, colleges & universities • *Health:* health organizations, hospitals, medical rehabilitation, single-disease health associations • *Science:* science exhibits & fairs • *Social Services:* community service organizations, disabled, emergency relief, united funds, youth organizations
Grant Types: capital, general support, professorship, and project
Nonmonetary Support Types: cause-related marketing & promotion, donated equipment, and in-kind services
Note: All nonmonetary support provided by individual branches. Estimated value is unavailable and is not included in figures above.
Geographic Distribution: in the Birmingham area; very few contributions are made outside the state of Alabama
Operating Locations: AL (Birmingham), AR (Little Rock), CA (San Mateo), GA (Atlanta), MI (Bloomfield Hills), MO (Kansas City), NY (Corum, Liverpool), OK (Oklahoma City), RI (Providence), TX (Dallas, Houston, Irving)

CORP. OFFICERS
Ronald Kay Richey: *B* Erie KS 1926 *ED* Washburn Univ BA 1949; Washburn Univ LLB 1951 *CURR EMPL* chmn, ceo, dir: Torchmark Corp *CORP AFFIL* chmn: Global Life & Accident Ins Co, Liberty Mgmt

Svcs, Liberty Mgmt Svcs, Liberty Natl Reinsurance, Liberty Natl Reinsurance Co Ltd, Sheffield Ins Corp, Torchmark Devel Corp, Torchmark Devel Corp, Un Investors Mgmt Co, Vesta Ins, Vesta Ins Corp, Waddell & Reed; chmn, ceo: Un Investors Life Ins Co; chmn, dir: Liberty Natl Fire Ins Co, Sheffield Ins Corp; dir: Am Life & Accident Ins Co, Family Svcs Life Ins, First Un Am Ins Co, Sentinel Am Life Ins Co, Sentinel Am Life Ins Co, Un Am Ins Corp *NONPR AFFIL* dir: OK City Chamber Commerce; mem: Am Bar Assn, Am Counc Life Ins, OK Bar Assn
Keith A. Tucker: *B* Chicago IL 1945 *ED* Univ TX BBA 1967; Univ TX JD 1970 *CURR EMPL* dir: Torchmark Corp *CORP AFFIL* dir: Atlantis Group, Great Am Reserve Ins Co, Natl Fidelity Ins Co; mem audit comm: AMBAC Indemnity Corp; vchmn: Un Investigators Mgmt Co *NONPR AFFIL* dir: Natl Library Medicine; mem: Am Inst CPAs, Assn Corp Growth, Campaign Am, Intl Ins Soc, Mus Modern Art, Natl Assoc Life Cos, TX Bar Assn, TX Inst CPAs, YMCA Dallas

GIVING OFFICERS
Samuel Upchurch: *B* Birmingham AL 1952 *ED* Davidson Coll 1974; Univ AL 1978 *CURR EMPL* vp, gen couns, secy, dir: Torchmark Corp *CORP AFFIL* dir: Un Investors Mgmt Co *NONPR AFFIL* mem: AL St Bar Assn, Am Bar Assn, Birmingham Bar Assn

APPLICATION INFORMATION
Initial Approach: *Initial Contact:* brief letter or proposal *Include Information On:* budget, area served by project or organization, amount requested, purpose of organization, list of officers and directors, copy of letter with 501(c)(3) number, last annual report and financial statement *When to Submit:* February through November

GRANTS ANALYSIS
Total Grants: $700,000
Typical Range: $100 to $2,000
Disclosure Period: 1989

Toro Co.
Sales: $711.6 million
Employees: 3,500
Headquarters: Bloomington, MN
SIC Major Group: Fabricated Metal Products, Industrial Machinery & Equipment, and Rubber & Miscellaneous Plastics Products

CONTACT
Mary Elliott
Director, Public Affairs
Toro Co.
8111 Lyndale Avenue, South
Bloomington, MN 55420
(612) 888-8801

FINANCIAL SUMMARY
Fiscal Note: Annual Giving Range: Less than $100,000

CONTRIBUTIONS SUMMARY
Nonmonetary Support Types: cause-related marketing & promotion, donated equipment, donated products, in-kind services, and loaned employees
Operating Locations: CA (Riverside, Riverside), KS (Industrial Airport), MN (Bloomington, Mound, Shakopee, Windom), MS (Oxford, Sardis), WI (Plymouth, Tomah)
Note: Company operates 2 divsions and 3 plants in locations. Lunalite Inc.

CORP. OFFICERS
Kendrick B. Melrose: *B* Orlando FL 1940 *ED* Princeton Univ 1962; Univ Chicago 1967 *CURR EMPL* chmn, dir: Toro Co *CORP AFFIL* dir: Bio-Metric Sys, Donaldson Co, Link-Osborn Co, Valspar Corp, Vic Mfg *NONPR AFFIL* mem: Outdoor Power Equipment Inst
David H. Morris: *B* Trail, British Columbia Canada 1941 *ED* Univ British Columbia 1965 *CURR EMPL* pres, ceo: Toro Co *NONPR AFFIL* mem: British Columbia Chartered Accts
Robert A. Peterson: *B* Sioux City IA 1925 *ED* Univ MN BS 1946; Univ MN BBA 1947 *CURR EMPL* vp, pres: Toro Credit Co *CORP AFFIL* dir: Hector Turf & Garden, Tesco, Wesco Turf Products *NONPR AFFIL* mem: Fin Execs Inst

Torrington Co.
Sales: $1.21 billion
Employees: 11,000
Parent Company: Ingersoll-Rand Co.
Headquarters: Torrington, CT
SIC Major Group: Industrial Machinery & Equipment and Transportation Equipment

CONTACT
Jim Lussier
Torrington Co.
59 Field St.
Torrington, CT 06790
(203) 482-9511

CONTRIBUTIONS SUMMARY
Company sponsors employee matching gift program; also supports community organizations.
Typical Recipients: • *Arts & Humanities:* general • *Civic & Public Affairs:* general • *Education:* general • *Health:* general • *Social Services:* general
Grant Types: matching
Geographic Distribution: primarily headquarters area
Operating Locations: CT (Torrington)

CORP. OFFICERS
James S. Perrella: *CURR EMPL* pres: Torrington Co

APPLICATION INFORMATION
Initial Approach: Send brief letter of inquiry. There are no deadlines.

Tortuga Foundation

CONTACT
Tortuga Fdn.
c/o Siegel, Sacks & Co.
630 Third Avenue, 22nd Fl.
New York, NY 10017

FINANCIAL SUMMARY
Recent Giving: $550,000 (fiscal 1991); $500,000 (fiscal 1990); $450,000 (fiscal 1989)
Assets: $5,425,475 (fiscal year ending September 30, 1991); $4,291,434 (fiscal 1990); $4,481,140 (fiscal 1989)
Gifts Received: $600,000 (fiscal 1991); $600,000 (fiscal 1990); $600,025 (fiscal 1989)
EIN: 51-0245279

CONTRIBUTIONS SUMMARY
Donor(s): William C. Breed III, J. L. Tweedy

Typical Recipients: • *Civic & Public Affairs:* civil rights, environmental affairs, public policy, zoos/botanical gardens • *Health:* medical research, single-disease health associations • *Social Services:* community service organizations, family planning
Grant Types: general support

GIVING OFFICERS
George H. P. Dwight: pres, trust
Hugh J. Freund: vp, secy, treas, trust *B* Brno Czech Republic 1937 *ED* NY Univ 1960 *CURR EMPL* exec vp: Sandata *CORP AFFIL* exec vp: Sandata Inc
Patricia P. Livingston: vp, trust
Robert C. Livingston: trust
Millie L. Siceloff: trust

APPLICATION INFORMATION
Initial Approach: Contributes only to preselected organizations.
Restrictions on Giving: Does not support individuals.

GRANTS ANALYSIS
Number of Grants: 23
Highest Grant: $50,000
Typical Range: $5,000 to $30,000
Disclosure Period: fiscal year ending September 30, 1991

RECENT GRANTS
50,000 Nature Conservancy
50,000 New York Zoological Society, New York, NY
35,000 Environmental Support Center, Washington, DC
30,000 American Civil Liberties Union Foundation, New York, NY
30,000 Association of Forest Service Employees for Environmental Ethics
30,000 Center for Population Options, Washington, DC
30,000 National Toxics Campaign Fund, Boston, MA
25,000 Western Ancient Forest Campaign
20,000 Environmental Grantmakers Association
20,000 Rails to Trails Conservancy, Washington, DC

Tosco Corp. Refining Division
Sales: $370.0 million
Employees: 870
Parent Company: Tosco Corp.
Headquarters: Concord, CA
SIC Major Group: Oil & Gas Extraction, Petroleum & Coal Products, and Water Transportation

CONTACT
James Simmons
Director, Public Affairs
Tosco Corp. Refining Division
2300 Clayton Rd., Ste. 1100
Concord, CA 94520-2466
(510) 602-4000

FINANCIAL SUMMARY
Recent Giving: $250,000 (1991); $250,000 (1990)

CONTRIBUTIONS SUMMARY
Company reports 29% of contributions go to civic and public affairs; 34% to health and human services; 23% to education; 13% to the arts; and 1% to the environment. Company promotes employee voluntarism by notifying employees what groups have requested help.
Typical Recipients: • *Arts & Humanities:* arts centers, community arts, museums/galleries, public broadcasting, theater • *Civic & Public Affairs:* economic development, environmental affairs, ethnic/minority organizations, professional & trade associations, urban & community affairs • *Education:* education funds, elementary education, engineering education, minority education • *Health:* emergency/ambulance services, hospitals • *Social Services:* child welfare, community centers, community service organizations, domestic violence, drugs & alcohol, emergency relief, family services, recreation & athletics, united funds, youth organizations
Grant Types: multiyear/continuing support, project, and scholarship
Nonmonetary Support Types: cause-related marketing & promotion, donated equipment, donated products, and in-kind services
Geographic Distribution: primarily CA

Operating Locations: CA (Concord, Martinez, Pittsburg, Sacramento), CT (Stamford)

CORP. OFFICERS
John J. Lee: *CURR EMPL* pres, coo, dir: Tosco Corp
Thomas D. O'Malley: *CURR EMPL* chmn, ceo, dir: Tosco Corp

APPLICATION INFORMATION
Initial Approach: Send a brief letter of inquiry including a description of organization, amount requested, and purpose of funds sought. Apply between January and June for the following year.
Restrictions on Giving: Does not support individuals, religious organizations for sectarian purposes or political or lobbying groups.

GRANTS ANALYSIS
Typical Range: $100 to $2,500

RECENT GRANTS
Aquatic Habitat Institute, Richmond, CA
Bay Area Crisis Nursery, Concord, CA
Contra Costa Child Care Council, Concord, CA
Contra Costa County School Volunteer Program, Pleasant Hill, CA
Contra Costa Food Bank, Concord, CA
Golden State Minority Foundation, San Fransisco, CA
Hispanic Chamber of Commerce Scholarship, Concord, CA
Lindsay Museum, Walnut Creek, CA
Mount Diablo Council Boy Scouts of America, Walnut Creek, CA
Pre-School Coordinating Council, Pittsburgh, CA

Toshiba America, Inc. / Toshiba America Foundation
Sales: $3.4 billion
Employees: 7,500
Headquarters: New York, NY
SIC Major Group: Holding & Other Investment Offices

CONTACT
John Sumansky
President
Toshiba America Foundation
375 Park Ave.
New York, NY 10152
(212) 596-0600

FINANCIAL SUMMARY
Recent Giving: $312,000 (fiscal 1993); $275,012 (fiscal 1992); $275,000 (fiscal 1991)
Assets: $7,516,912 (fiscal year ending March 31, 1992); $6,398,641 (fiscal 1991)
Gifts Received: $1,184,113 (fiscal 1992); $6,000,000 (fiscal 1991)
Fiscal Note: Other company departments make contributions directly from corporate funds. The budget for such support is not available, and it is not included in the figures above. For more information, write Kenjiro Ishihara, Vice President. In fiscal 1992, contributions were received from Toshiba America.
EIN: 13-3596612

CONTRIBUTIONS SUMMARY
Typical Recipients: • *Education:* engineering education, private education (precollege), public education (precollege), science/technology education
Grant Types: project and seed money
Nonmonetary Support Types: donated products
Note: Contact Kenjiro Ishihara, Vice President, for noncash support information. Estimated value of this support is unavailable.
Geographic Distribution: foundation primarily, but not exclusively, supports organizations in operating locations, including local affiliates of national educational organizations
Operating Locations: CA (Irvine, South San Francisco, Tustin), HI (Honolulu), IL, NJ (Wayne), NY (Horseheads, New York), SD (Mitchell), TN (Lebanon), TX (Houston)
Note: Above lists locations where company has major manufacturing facilities; Toshiba America, Inc., and its subsidiaries operate in 30 states nationwide. See "Other Things You Should Know" for more details.

CORP. OFFICERS
Tadao Taguchi: *B* Miyagi Japan 1929 *ED* Tohoku Univ

CURR EMPL chmn, ceo:
Toshiba Am *CORP AFFIL* dir:
Toshiba Corp

GIVING OFFICERS
John Anderson: secy
Robyn T. Calisti: program off
Hiromu Matsuda: dir
Tomoyuki Nakayama: treas
Atsutoshi Nishida: dir
Hitoshi Ohashi: dir
Masaya Okumura: dir
John Sumansky: pres
Kunio Sumikawa: dir
Tadao Taguchi: chmn *CURR EMPL* chmn, ceo: Toshiba Am (see above)

APPLICATION INFORMATION
Initial Approach: *Initial Contact:* send letter requesting application guidelines before preparing a proposal *Include Information On:* no application form required; form and format for proposals is left to the discretion of applicant; foundation guidelines require the following information (in as few pages as possible): names, addresses, and phone numbers of the organization and its project officer(s); executive summary of entire proposal; student-oriented objectives of the project and how they are to be measured; time period for reaching objectives; management plan showing how people, money, facilities, and time will be managed to reach objectives; line item budget reflective of management plan; proposed evaluation of the success of the project; narrative establishing the credibility of the organization including proof of not-for-profit status* *When to Submit:* throughout the year for proposals of $5,000 or less; prior to February 1 for March meeting and prior to August 1 for September for larger grants *Note:* While certain information described above is required for proposal review, applicants may include additional information if it is essential to making the case for support. Application guidelines contain a section, "Beyond the Guidelines," to assist in evaluating foundation's mission in relation to proposed program.
Restrictions on Giving: Does not support dinners or special events; fraternal organizations; goodwill advertising; individuals; member agencies of united funds; political or lobbying

groups; religious organizations for sectarian purposes; or organizations that discriminate against women, minorities, older Americans, or the handicapped.
The foundation has a greater interest in supporting time-limited projects/programs and, therefore, is not likely to contribute to capital projects, endowments, or general operations. Also not likely to be favorably reviewed are requests for contributions for conferences, independent study, fund-raising events, or similar activities.

OTHER THINGS TO KNOW
The Toshiba America Foundation was established in April 1990 marking the 25th anniversary of Toshiba America, Inc. The foundation's endowment will reach $10 million by 1995. Financial support for the foundation has been provided by each of the five independent companies listed above.
The Toshiba America Foundation board of trustees includes the chairman of Toshiba America, Inc., and the presidents of the five independent companies. In addition, the board will include representatives from outside the corporation from professional educational groups representing the middle and upper grades.
Company also specializes in x-ray and diagnostic equipment; semiconductors, super TV picture tubes, and discrete devices; TVs, telephones, satellite receivers, camcorders, and various home electronic equipment; power plants, steel mills, water treatment facilities, digital instrumentation and switch gears, and factory automation products.

GRANTS ANALYSIS
Total Grants: $275,012
Number of Grants: 33
Highest Grant: $25,940
Typical Range: $5,000 to $10,000
Disclosure Period: fiscal year ending March 31, 1992
Note: Recent grants are derived from a fiscal 1992 grants list.

RECENT GRANTS
25,940 Los Angeles Educational Partnership, Los Angeles, CA — Students Explore

Science with Technology
20,000 Cumberland Science Museum, Nashville, TN — Toshiba scholarship days
20,000 San Francisco Unified School District, San Francisco, CA — Algebra GATE
20,000 San Francisco Unified School District, San Francisco, CA — Biotechnology in the Classroom
18,128 Cypress-Fairbanks Independent School District, Houston, TX — Biotechnology
17,688 Girls Incorporated, New York, NY — Toshiba Traveling SMART program
15,000 Los Angeles Educational Partnership, Los Angeles, CA — Interactive Mathematics
10,918 New York Zoological Society, Bronx, NY — Super Science Day
10,000 Poolesville High School, Poolesville, MD — wetlands
9,969 Mitchell School District No. 17-2, Mitchell, SD — Science, Technology and Society Out-Reach Program

---

Totsy Manufacturing Co. / Totsy Foundation
Sales: $10.0 million
Employees: 100
Headquarters: Holyoke, MA

CONTACT
Totsy Manufacturing Co.
1505 Riverview Road
P.O. Box 279
St. Peter, MN 56082
(413) 536-0510

FINANCIAL SUMMARY
Recent Giving: $61,350 (fiscal 1992); $58,750 (fiscal 1990)
Assets: $925,907 (fiscal year ending March 31, 1992); $777,492 (fiscal 1990)
Gifts Received: $25,000 (fiscal 1992); $50,000 (fiscal 1990)
Fiscal Note: In fiscal 1992, contributions were received from the Totsy Manufacturing Co., Inc.

EIN: 04-2785460

CONTRIBUTIONS SUMMARY
Typical Recipients: • *Arts & Humanities:* museums/galleries • *Civic & Public Affairs:* philanthropic organizations • *Education:* private education (precollege), student aid • *Health:* hospitals, pediatric health • *Social Services:* community centers

Grant Types: capital, endowment, general support, and scholarship

Geographic Distribution: giving primarily in western MA

Operating Locations: MA (Holyoke)

CORP. OFFICERS
Steven M. Feldman: *CURR EMPL* pres: Totsy Manufacturing Co

Shefford S. Goldband: *CURR EMPL* chmn: Totsy Manufacturing Co

GIVING OFFICERS
Steven M. Feldman: trust *CURR EMPL* pres: Totsy Manufacturing Co (see above)

APPLICATION INFORMATION
Initial Approach: Application form required.

GRANTS ANALYSIS
Number of Grants: 36
Highest Grant: $15,000
Typical Range: $500 to $1,000
Disclosure Period: fiscal year ending March 31, 1992

RECENT GRANTS
15,000 21st Century Endowment Fund
10,000 Citizens Scholarship
8,000 Springfield Jewish Community Center
5,000 US Holocaust Memorial Museum, Washington, DC
4,000 Heritage Academy
1,500 Friends of Holyoke
1,500 Holyoke Hospital, Holyoke, MA — capital fund
1,350 Jimmy Fund
1,000 Children's Hospital of Boston, Boston, MA
1,000 Willie Ross School

Towers Perrin

Revenue: $680.0 million
Employees: 5,000
Headquarters: New York, NY
SIC Major Group: Engineering
& Management Services

CONTACT

Rollie Stichweh
Vice President
Towers Perrin
245 Park Ave.
New York, NY 10167-0128
(212) 309-3878

CONTRIBUTIONS
SUMMARY

Company provides employee
matching gifts only.
Grant Types: matching
Operating Locations: NY
(New York)

CORP. OFFICERS

John T. Lynch: *CURR EMPL*
chmn, pres, ceo: Towers Perrin
Forster & Crosby

Towle
Manufacturing Co.

Sales: $90.0 million
Employees: 630
Headquarters: East Boston, MA
SIC Major Group: Miscellaneous
Manufacturing Industries,
Rubber & Miscellaneous
Plastics Products, Stone, Clay
& Glass Products, and
Wholesale Trade—Durable
Goods

CONTACT

Patti Felt
Senior Administrator
Towle Manufacturing Co.
175 McClellan Hwy.
East Boston, MA 02128
(617) 568-1300

FINANCIAL SUMMARY

Fiscal Note: Annual Giving
Range: less than $100,000

CONTRIBUTIONS
SUMMARY

Typical Recipients: • *Arts &
Humanities:* general • *Civic &
Public Affairs:* general • *Educa-
tion:* general • *Health:* general
• *Social Services:* general
Grant Types: general support
Nonmonetary Support Types:
cause-related marketing & pro-
motion and donated products
Geographic Distribution: pri-
marily headquarters area
Operating Locations: MA
(East Boston)

CORP. OFFICERS

Christopher McGillivary:
CURR EMPL pres, ceo: Towle
Mfg Co

APPLICATION
INFORMATION

Initial Approach: Send brief
letter of inquiry. There are no
deadlines.

Town & Country
Corp.

Sales: $272.2 million
Employees: 2,600
Headquarters: Chelsea, MA
SIC Major Group: Furniture &
Homefurnishings Stores,
Miscellaneous Manufacturing
Industries, and Miscellaneous
Retail

CONTACT

Irene Shea
Manager, Corporate
Communications
Town & Country Corp.
25 Union St.
Chelsea, MA 02150
(617) 884-8500

CONTRIBUTIONS
SUMMARY

Support goes to local educa-
tion, human services, arts, and
civic organizations. Includes
matching gifts.
Typical Recipients: • *Arts &
Humanities:* general • *Civic &
Public Affairs:* general • *Educa-
tion:* general • *Health:* general
Grant Types: general support
Geographic Distribution:
headquarters and operating lo-
cations
Operating Locations: MA
(Chelsea)

CORP. OFFICERS

C. William Carey: *CURR
EMPL* chmn, ceo: Town &
Country Corp
Francis X. Correra: *CURR
EMPL* sr vp, cfo: Town &
Country Corp

APPLICATION
INFORMATION

Initial Approach: Send letter
of inquiry.

Town Creek
Foundation

CONTACT

Christine Shelton
Executive Director
Town Creek Fdn.
PO Box 159
Oxford, MD 21654
(410) 226-5315

FINANCIAL SUMMARY

Recent Giving: $1,180,000
(1990); $1,056,000 (1989)
Assets: $20,165,755 (1990);
$21,512,321 (1989)
EIN: 52-1227030

CONTRIBUTIONS
SUMMARY

Donor(s): The foundation was
established in 1981 by Edmund
A. Stanley, Jr.
Typical Recipients: • *Arts &
Humanities:* public broadcasting • *Civic & Public Affairs:*
better government, environmental affairs, public policy,
women's affairs • *Education:*
social sciences education • *Social Services:* employment/job
training, recreation & athletics
Grant Types: multiyear/con-
tinuing support, operating expenses, project, and seed money
Geographic Distribution:
some national, with a focus on
Maryland

GIVING OFFICERS

Philip E. L. Dietz, Jr.: secy,
treas, trust
Edmund Allport Stanley, Jr.:
pres, exec dir, trust *B* New
York NY 1924 *ED* Princeton
Univ AB 1949 *CORP AFFIL*
dir: Bowne & Co, Venture Ad-
visers Mutual Fund Group
NONPR AFFIL pres: Town
Creek Fdn; trust: Law-
renceville Sch, South St Sea-
port Mus; trust, mem: Wilder-
ness Soc
Jennifer Stanley: vp
Lisa A. Stanley: trust
Gerald L. Stokes: trust

APPLICATION
INFORMATION

Initial Approach:
The foundation requests applications be made in writing.
The application should contain
a statement of the program, the
amount requested, and a brief
description of the organization.
The foundation has no deadline
for submitting proposals.
Restrictions on Giving: The
foundation does not make

grants to individuals, private organizations, primary or secondary schools, hospitals, health
care institutions, religious organizations, building fund campaigns, endowments, capital
funds, land acquisition, research, scholarships, conferences, publications, or the visual or performing arts.

OTHER THINGS TO
KNOW

Publications: informational
brochure including application
guidelines

GRANTS ANALYSIS

Total Grants: $1,180,000
Number of Grants: 84
Highest Grant: $125,000
Typical Range: $5,000 to
$15,000
Disclosure Period: 1990
Note: Recent grants are derived
from a 1990 grants list.

RECENT GRANTS

125,000 National Public
Radio, Washington,
DC
100,000 Wilderness Soci-
ety, Washington,
DC
85,000 Chesapeake Bay
Foundation, Anna-
polis, MD
60,000 WETA Public Tele-
vision, Washing-
ton, DC
25,000 American Rivers,
Washington, DC
25,000 Center for Marine
Conservation,
Washington, DC
25,000 National Audubon
Society, New York,
NY
20,000 Sierra Club Legal
Defense Fund, San
Francisco, CA
15,000 Adirondack Coun-
cil, Elizabethtown,
NY
15,000 Alaska Public
Radio Network, An-
chorage, AK

Towsley Foundation, Harry A. and Margaret D.

CONTACT
Margaret Ann Riecker
President
Harry A. and Margaret D.
Towsley Foundation
220 East Huron St., Ste. 670
City Center Bldg.
Ann Arbor, MI 48104
(313) 662-6777

FINANCIAL SUMMARY
Recent Giving: $1,577,623
(1990); $1,310,649 (1989);
$1,257,963 (1988)
Assets: $32,527,082 (1990);
$47,363,157 (1989);
$38,771,730 (1988)
Gifts Received: $100,000
(1985)
EIN: 38-6091798

CONTRIBUTIONS SUMMARY
Donor(s): Margaret Dow
Towsley established the foundation in 1959 in Michigan with a gift of Dow Chemical Company common stock.
Typical Recipients: • *Arts & Humanities:* arts associations, arts funds, arts institutes, museums/galleries, music • *Civic & Public Affairs:* philanthropic organizations • *Education:* colleges & universities, community & junior colleges, faculty development, medical education, minority education, preschool education, science/technology education • *Health:* medical rehabilitation, medical research, public health, single-disease health associations • *Social Services:* community service organizations, drugs & alcohol, family services, religious welfare, volunteer services, youth organizations
Grant Types: emergency, general support, multiyear/continuing support, operating expenses, project, and research
Geographic Distribution: Michigan, especially Ann Arbor and Washtenaw County

GIVING OFFICERS
Judith Dow Alexander: vp, trust
Robert L. Bring: trust
C. Wendell Dunbar: treas, trust
Lynn T. Hamblin: trust
Janis T. Poteat: trust
John E. Riecker: secy

Margaret Ann Riecker: pres, trust
Harry A. Towsley, MD: chmn, trust
Margaret Dow Towsley: vp, trust
Susan T. Wyland: trust

APPLICATION INFORMATION
Initial Approach:
Prospective applicants should submit a letter and proposal to the foundation. The foundation does not provide application forms for requests. Elaborate presentations are discouraged. Applicants should submit a copy of the tax-exempt letter from the IRS; letter establishing that the applicant is not a private foundation; amount requested, need, and intended use; and organization's latest financial statements with an operating budget and other funding sources.
Applications should be submitted between January 1 and March 31 of each year. Send two copies of proposals.
Final notification to applicants usually is made within 60 to 90 days.
Restrictions on Giving: The trustees do not conduct personal interviews with applicants except upon the foundation's initiative. Additional information is frequently requested by the foundation after the application is received. The foundation does not make direct grants to individuals, provide loan funds, make grants to students for scholarships, or make grants for travel and conferences.

OTHER THINGS TO KNOW
Publications: annual report, application guidelines

GRANTS ANALYSIS
Total Grants: $1,577,623
Number of Grants: 40
Highest Grant: $250,000
Typical Range: $5,000 to $50,000
Disclosure Period: 1990
Note: Recent grants are derived from a 1991 grants list.

RECENT GRANTS
250,000 Catherine McAuley Health Center (Systems), Ann Arbor, MI — (outpatient Oncology Treatment Facility)

250,000 University of Michigan-Center for the Education of Women, Ann Arbor, MI — scholarship fund (endowment)
200,000 Case Western Reserve, Cleveland, OH — Herbert Henry Dow Distinguished Professorship
150,000 Children's Play School, Ann Arbor, MI — (Preschool Education)
141,375 Carleton College, Northfield, MN — (Chair in Biology)
125,000 Greenhills School, Ann Arbor, MI — (endowment campaign)
100,000 Glacier Hills Nursing Center, Ann Arbor, MI — (Geriatric Teaching/Nursing Home and Adult Respite Day Care)
100,000 Michigan State University, East Lansing, MI — (College of Natural Sciences-Center for Science and Mathematics Teachers)
100,000 Starr Commonwealth Schools, Albion Campus, Albion, MI — (health, physical education and recreation center)
100,000 University of Michigan-Athletic Department-Center of Champions, Ann Arbor, MI — (replacement sports facility)

Toyota Motor Sales, U.S.A. / Toyota U.S.A. Foundation
Sales: $17.0 billion
Employees: 60,000
Headquarters: Torrance, CA
SIC Major Group: Wholesale Trade—Durable Goods

CONTACT
Christie Abe
Community Relations Supervisor
Toyota Motor Sales, U.S.A.
19001 S Western Ave.
Torrance, CA 90509
(310) 618-4000
Note: Ms. Abe is the contact person for corporate contributions. Patricia Hull is the contact for foundation

contributions, at address above. See "Other Things You Should Know" for more details.

FINANCIAL SUMMARY
Recent Giving: $1,900,000 (fiscal 1992 approx.); $1,900,000 (fiscal 1991 approx.); $1,600,000 (fiscal 1990 approx.)
Assets: $17,225,566 (fiscal year ending June 30, 1992); $17,000,000 (fiscal 1991); $15,033,674 (fiscal 1990)
Fiscal Note: Figures for 1990 and 1991 include corporate and foundation contributions from the California office. See Other Things You Should Know. Foundation contributions in 1991 were $754,808 and $684,305 in 1992.
EIN: 95-3255038

CONTRIBUTIONS SUMMARY
Typical Recipients: • *Arts & Humanities:* arts appreciation, arts associations, arts centers, arts institutes, museums/galleries, opera, performing arts, public broadcasting, theater • *Education:* colleges & universities, community & junior colleges, education funds, elementary education, engineering education, minority education, science/technology education • *Health:* nutrition & health maintenance • *Social Services:* child welfare, disabled, drugs & alcohol
Grant Types: employee matching gifts, general support, project, and scholarship
Note: Foundation primarily supports special projects. Other types of grants are disbursed through the corporate direct giving program.
Nonmonetary Support Types: donated products
Note: Value of nonmonetary support is $50,000 annually. This amount is not included in the total giving figures above.
Geographic Distribution: corporate contributions disbursed in headquarters and operating areas only; foundation contributions are national in scope; support is not available outside the U.S.
Operating Locations: CA (Torrance)

CORP. OFFICERS
Yukiyasu Togo: *B* Yokohama Japan 1924 *CURR EMPL* pres, ceo: Toyota Motor Sales USA *CORP AFFIL* pres: Canada

Auto Parts Toyota Inc, Toyota Aviation USA Inc, Toyota Motor Credit Corp, Toyota Motor Ins Svcs

GIVING OFFICERS
R. Best: group vp, secy, dir
M. Imai: vp, dir
S. Sakai: pres, dir
K. Usuda: vp, dir

APPLICATION INFORMATION
Initial Approach: *Initial Contact:* one-page summary for foundation; for corporate contributions, a one- to two-page summary *Include Information On:* for foundation, describe the project and the amount requested. This is a preliminary step to submitting a full proposal. For corporate contributions, describe the project, dollar amount requested, project budget, budget for current year, list of board of directors, copy of the IRS tax exemption letter, and the most recent IRS Form 990. *When to Submit:* any time
Restrictions on Giving: Toyota U.S.A. does not contribute to individuals, political campaigns or organizations, military groups, religious organizations or their affiliates, or unions.

Toyota U.S.A. Foundation does not fund routine institutional expenses, endowment campaigns, deficit reduction, fundraising dinners, advertising, seed money, challenge grants, or annual fund drives. Also excluded are trips, tours, and seminars; publication subsidies; grants to individuals; lobbying organizations; conduit charities; or fraternal, veterans, or labor groups.

OTHER THINGS TO KNOW
Requests for corporate contributions of up to $5,000 should be sent to Toyota's Corporate Employee Contribution Committee, Toyota Motor Sales, U.S.A., Inc., at the above address. All other requests should be submitted to the community relations department.
Toyota will consider only one request per year from an organization.
Elaborate and lengthy requests are not encouraged. Telephone inquires are accepted only to clarify Toyota contributions guidelines and verify mailing address information. Evalu-

ations of proposals are not made over the phone.
Meetings with organizations requesting contributions are not encouraged.
Toyota formalized a corporate giving and community relations program in 1973, contributing to various U.S. organizations and activities in support of the goals of the company and its employees. Total contributions in the United States in 1990 were $10.1 million. The three main centers for contributions are Toyota Motor Sales U.S.A., Torrance, CA; Toyota Corporate Services of North America, New York, NY; and Toyota Manufacturing U.S.A., Inc., Georgetown, KY. Toyota Motor Sales handles contributions from 13 regional offices and administers the foundation. Toyota Motor Corporate Services adminsters grants on behalf of its parent. Toyota Manufacuturing handles requests from the Georgetown area, site of Toyota's largest U.S. manufacturing facility.
Publications: separate application forms and guidelines for both foundation and corporate contributions

GRANTS ANALYSIS
Total Grants: $684,305*
Number of Grants: 24*
Highest Grant: $200,000*
Typical Range: $500 to $50,000*
Disclosure Period: fiscal year ending June 30, 1992
Note: Figures represent foundation giving only. Recent grants are derived from a fiscal 1992 Form 990.

RECENT GRANTS
200,000 Teach for America, New York, NY — to fund national teacher recruitment, training and placement program
168,300 Los Angeles Educational Partnership, Los Angeles, CA — to fund the 1992 Toyota Math and Science Grants for Teachers in the LAUSD
160,000 ASPIRA Association, Washington, DC — internships for Public Policy Leadership Program
100,000 Teach for America, New York, NY — to fund national teacher recruit-

ment, training and placement program
78,800 Los Angeles Educational Partnership, Los Angeles, CA — to fund the 1992 Toyota Math and Science Grants for Teachers in the LAUSD
66,700 Michigan State University, East Lansing, MI — to fund science courses/workshops for elementary teachers in Michigan
60,000 Ball State University, IN — to support the Center for Integrating Technology in Teaching Science in the Indiana Academy
50,000 California Academy of Mathematics and Science, Carson, CA — to support a four-year high school program dedicated to educating women and under-represented minorities in mathematics and science
50,000 Illinois Mathematics and Science Academy, Aurora, IL — to equip academy's video production lab
50,000 Illinois Mathematics and Science Academy, Aurora, IL — to equip academy's video production

Toys "R" Us, Inc.
Sales: $6.12 billion
Employees: 47,000
Headquarters: Paramus, NJ
SIC Major Group: Apparel & Accessory Stores and Miscellaneous Retail

CONTACT
Angela Baurdan
Public Relations Department
Toys "R" Us, Inc.
461 From Rd.
Paramus, NJ 07652
(201) 599-7897

CONTRIBUTIONS SUMMARY
Operating Locations: NJ (Paramus)

CORP. OFFICERS
Michael Goldstein: *CURR EMPL* vchmn, cfo: Toys R Us

Charles Lazarus: *B* Washington DC 1923 *CURR EMPL* fdr, chmn, ceo: Toys R Us *CORP AFFIL* dir: Automatic Data Processing, Wal Mart Stores

Tozer Foundation

CONTACT
Grant T. Waldref
President
Tozer Fdn.
c/o First Trust, N.A.
P. O. 64704
St. Paul, MN 55164-0704
(612) 291-5134

FINANCIAL SUMMARY
Recent Giving: $746,220 (fiscal 1990); $751,361 (fiscal 1989)
Assets: $15,767,854 (fiscal year ending October 31, 1990); $16,614,506 (fiscal 1989)
EIN: 41-6011518

CONTRIBUTIONS SUMMARY
Donor(s): The foundation was incorporated in 1946 by the late David Tozer.
Typical Recipients: • *Arts & Humanities:* arts associations, community arts, history/historic preservation, museums/galleries, music, opera, performing arts, public broadcasting, theater • *Civic & Public Affairs:* business/free enterprise, philanthropic organizations • *Education:* colleges & universities, economic education, education funds, elementary education, minority education, public education (precollege), religious education, student aid • *Health:* health organizations, hospitals • *Religion:* religious organizations • *Social Services:* community centers, counseling, family services, food/clothing distribution, homes, shelters/homelessness, united funds, volunteer services, youth organizations
Grant Types: general support and scholarship
Geographic Distribution: focus on Minnesota

GIVING OFFICERS
Robert S. Davis: vp, dir *B* Stillwater MN 1914 *ED* Univ MN 1934 *CURR EMPL* dir: HM Smyth Co *CORP AFFIL* dir: Chicago Milwaukee Corp, SPH Hotel Corp
James R. Oppenheimer: dir *B* St Paul MN 1921 *ED* Dartmouth Coll BA 1943; Yale

Univ JD 1948 *CURR EMPL* off couns: Oppenheimer Wolff & Donnelly *CORP AFFIL* dir: Blandin Paper Co *NONPR AFFIL* mem: Am Bar Assn, MN Bar Assn, Ramsey County Bar Assn, St Paul Chamber Commerce

J. Thomas Simonet: dir *B* Stillwater MN 1926 *CORP AFFIL* dir: Carondelet Life Care Corp, Donovan Cos, First Trust, Mairs & Power Funds *NONPR AFFIL* trust: St Paul Seminary

Earl C. Swanson: trust *CURR EMPL* dir: Andersen Corp *PHIL AFFIL* dir: Katzenberger Foundation

John F. Thoreen: dir

Grant T. Waldref: pres, dir

APPLICATION INFORMATION

Initial Approach:
The foundation requests applications be made in writing. Applications for scholarships may be received through high school guidance counselors. Grant applications must outline the nature of the request.
The foundation has no deadline for submitting proposals.
The board meets six to seven times per year to consider grant requests. Decisions are made immediately after the meeting.

GRANTS ANALYSIS

Total Grants: $746,220
Number of Grants: 39*
Highest Grant: $57,420
Typical Range: $1,000 to $10,000
Disclosure Period: fiscal year ending October 31, 1990
Note: Average grant and number of grants figures do not include scholarships to individuals totaling $491,400. Recent grants are derived from a fiscal 1990 grants list.

RECENT GRANTS

51,420 United Way, St. Paul, MN
20,000 Minnesota Orchestral Association, Minneapolis, MN
20,000 Ordway Music Theatre, St. Paul, MN
15,000 Courage Center, Golden Valley, MN
15,000 St. Paul Chamber Orchestra, St. Paul, MN
13,000 Boy Scouts of America, St. Paul, MN

10,000 Lakeview Memorial Hospital, Stillwater, MN
10,000 Stillwater School District, Stillwater, MN
8,500 United Negro College Fund, Minneapolis, MN
6,350 Family Service of St. Croix Area, Stillwater, MN

Tracor, Inc.

Sales: $261.8 million
Employees: 3,400
Headquarters: Austin, TX
SIC Major Group: Chemicals & Allied Products, Engineering & Management Services, Fabricated Metal Products, and Stone, Clay & Glass Products

CONTACT

Marian Kelley
Director, Public Relations
Tracor, Inc.
6500 Tracor Ln.
Austin, TX 78725-2006
(512) 926-2800

FINANCIAL SUMMARY

Fiscal Note: Annual Giving Range: Company does not disclose contributions figures, but generally total less than $100,000.

CONTRIBUTIONS SUMMARY

Support goes to local education, human services, arts, and civic organizations. Company also is involved with adopt-a-school and promotes employee voluntarism through an employee newsletter and bulletin boards.

Typical Recipients: • *Arts & Humanities:* museums/galleries, opera, performing arts, theater, visual arts • *Civic & Public Affairs:* business/free enterprise, consumer affairs, environmental affairs, ethnic/minority organizations, professional & trade associations, women's affairs • *Education:* colleges & universities, community & junior colleges, elementary education, engineering education, legal education, literacy, public education (precollege), science/technology education • *Health:* health organizations, hospices, hospitals, mental health, single-disease health associations • *Science:* science exhibits & fairs, scientific organizations • *Social Services:* child welfare, day care, dis-

abled, domestic violence, drugs & alcohol, emergency relief, employment/job training, family planning, family services, food/clothing distribution, homes, legal aid, shelters/homelessness, united funds, volunteer services, youth organizations

Grant Types: employee matching gifts and general support

Nonmonetary Support Types: donated equipment, in-kind services, loaned employees, and loaned executives
Note: Also provides printing services.

Geographic Distribution: in headquarters and operating communities

Operating Locations: AR (East Camden), CA (Mojave, Sunnyvale), MD (Rockville, St. Mary's County), NC (Lillington), NM (Holloman AFB), TX (Austin)

CORP. OFFICERS

Robert K. Floyd: *CURR EMPL* vp, cfo: Tracor
James B. Skaggs: *CURR EMPL* pres: Tracor

APPLICATION INFORMATION

Initial Approach: Send brief letter of inquiry, including a description of the organization, amount requested, purpose of funds sought, audited financial statement, and proof of tax-exempt status. There are no deadlines.

Restrictions on Giving: Does not support individuals, religious organizations for sectarian purposes, sports/athletic organizations/programs, or political or lobbying groups.

OTHER THINGS TO KNOW

Company also provides non-cash support through printing services.

Tractor & Equipment Co. / Tractor & Equipment Company Foundation

Sales: $48.0 million
Employees: 190
Headquarters: Birmingham, AL
SIC Major Group: Wholesale Trade—Durable Goods

CONTACT

Benny Winford
Secretary-Treasurer
Tractor & Equipment Co. Fdn.
5336 Airport Hwy
Birmingham, AL 35212
(205) 591-2131
Note: Address scholarship applications to: James W. Waitzman, Sr., President, Tractor & Equipment Co., P.O. Box 2326, Birmingham, AL 35201

FINANCIAL SUMMARY

Recent Giving: $130,901 (1992); $110,654 (1990); $120,528 (1989)
Assets: $229,957 (1990); $231,944 (1989); $187,639 (1987)
Gifts Received: $150,000 (1989)
Fiscal Note: In 1992, contributions were received from Tractor & Equipment Co., Inc.
EIN: 63-0718825

CONTRIBUTIONS SUMMARY

Typical Recipients: • *Education:* colleges & universities, student aid • *Health:* hospitals, mental health, single-disease health associations • *Religion:* churches, religious organizations • *Social Services:* united funds, youth organizations

Grant Types: general support and scholarship

Geographic Distribution: Gives primarily AL

Operating Locations: AL (Birmingham)

CORP. OFFICERS

John J. Harnish: *CURR EMPL* ceo: Tractor & Equipment Co
David L. Wendte: *CURR EMPL* cfo: Tractor & Equipment Co

GIVING OFFICERS

J. C. Durden: vp, dir
B. J. Roberts: vp, dir
James W. Waitzman, Jr.: pres, dir
B.F. Winford: dir
Benny F. Winford: secy-treas

APPLICATION INFORMATION

Initial Approach: Application form required for scholarship. Deadlines are March 1; May 20 for scholarships.

Restrictions on Giving: Does not support individuals (except for employee-related scholarships).

GRANTS ANALYSIS

Number of Grants: 67
Highest Grant: $10,000
Typical Range: $500 to $5,000
Disclosure Period: 1991
Note: Number, high, low, and range figures do not include scholarships to employees' children.

RECENT GRANTS

10,000 Episcopal Foundation of Jefferson County, Birmingham, AL
10,000 First Baptist Church of Center Point, Birmingham, AL
7,840 United Way, Birmingham, AL
7,500 Big Oak Ranch, Gadsden, AL
5,225 Birmingham Southern College, Birmingham, AL
5,000 St. Francis Xavier Church, Birmingham, AL
4,000 Boys and Girls Club, Birmingham, AL
4,000 Glenwood Mental Health Service, Birmingham, AL
4,000 YMCA, Birmingham, AL
1,000 Birmingham State University, Birmingham, AL

Trans-Apex

Sales: $235.1 million
Employees: 2,818
Headquarters: Tulsa, OK
SIC Major Group:
  Transportation Equipment

CONTACT

Russell D. McBroom
President
Trans-Apex
7136 South Yale, Ste. 300
Tulsa, OK 74136
(918) 492-1800

CONTRIBUTIONS SUMMARY

Company sponsors employee matching gift program; also supports community organizations.
Typical Recipients: • *Arts & Humanities:* general • *Civic & Public Affairs:* general • *Education:* general • *Health:* general • *Social Services:* general
Grant Types: matching
Geographic Distribution: primarily headquarters area
Operating Locations: OK (Tulsa)

CORP. OFFICERS

Russell D. McBroom: *CURR EMPL* pres: Facet Enterprises

APPLICATION INFORMATION

Initial Approach: Send brief letter of inquiry. There are no deadlines.

Trans World Airlines

Sales: $3.6 billion
Employees: 29,463
Parent Company: Icahn & Co. Inc.
Headquarters: Kansas City, MO
SIC Major Group:
  Transportation by Air

CONTACT

Chuck Thibaudeau
Senior Vice President, Employee Relation
Trans World Airlines
11500 Ambassador Dr., PO Box 20007
Kansas City, MO 64195
(816) 464-6601

CONTRIBUTIONS SUMMARY

Operating Locations: MO (Kansas City)

CORP. OFFICERS

Carl Celian Icahn: *B* Queens NY 1936 *ED* Princeton Univ BA 1957; NY Univ Sch Medicine *CURR EMPL* chmn, pres, ceo: Icahn & Co *CORP AFFIL* chmn, ceo: ACF Indus Inc; chmn, pres: Icahn Holding Corp; chmn, pres, ceo: Trans World Airlines; dir: Fairchild Corp

Glenn R. Zander: *CURR EMPL* sr vp, cfo: Trans World Airlines

---

Transamerica Corp. / Transamerica Fdn.

Revenue: $4.98 billion
Employees: 10,700
Headquarters: San Francisco, CA
SIC Major Group: Holding & Other Investment Offices

CONTACT

Mary Sawai
Assistant Secretary
Transamerica Fdn.
600 Montgomery St.
San Francisco, CA 94111
(415) 983-4333

FINANCIAL SUMMARY

Recent Giving: $3,013,000 (1991 approx.); $2,827,000 (1990); $2,935,990 (1989)
Assets: $28,774,177 (1991); $17,100,000 (1989)
Fiscal Note: Figures for 1990 and 1991 represent giving for foundation, corporation, and affiliates.
EIN: 94-3034825

CONTRIBUTIONS SUMMARY

Typical Recipients: • *Arts & Humanities:* libraries, museums/galleries, music, opera, performing arts, public broadcasting • *Civic & Public Affairs:* nonprofit management, urban & community affairs, zoos/botanical gardens • *Education:* economic education, education associations, education funds • *Health:* health funds, hospices, hospitals, mental health, single-disease health associations • *Social Services:* child welfare, community centers, community service organizations, family services, food/clothing distribution, legal aid, religious welfare, shelters/homelessness
Grant Types: employee matching gifts, general support, professorship, project, research, scholarship, and seed money
Nonmonetary Support Types: in-kind services
Note: Value of nonmonetary support estimated at $154,000 for 1989. This amount is included in contribution figure above.
Geographic Distribution: primarily in operating areas
Operating Locations: CA (Burbank, Irvine, Los Angeles, San Francisco), IL (Chicago), MI (Battle Creek), NY (White Plains)

CORP. OFFICERS

Burton Edward Broome: *B* New York NY 1935 *ED* Fordham Univ 1963; Univ CA 1964 *CURR EMPL* vp, contr: TransAmerica Corp *NONPR AFFIL* chmn adv counc: Univ Southern CA Securities Exchange Comm & Fin Reporting Inst; mem: Am Inst CPAs, CA Soc CPAs, Fin Execs Inst; mem professional account ing program: Univ CA Berkeley

Richard H. Finn: *B* Luanshya Zambia 1934 *ED* Oxford Univ 1956 *CURR EMPL* pres, ceo, dir: TransAmerica Fin Corp *CORP AFFIL* dir: TransAmerica Commercial Fin Corp, TransAmerica Leasing Inc, TransAmerica Life Cos

Edger H. Grubb: *B* Harrisburg PA 1939 *ED* PA St Univ BA 1961; CA St Univ Fullerton MBA 1967 *CURR EMPL* sr vp: TransAmerica Corp *NONPR AFFIL* bd dirs: Goodwill Indus; mem: Am Inst CPAs, CA Soc CPAs, Fin Execs Inst; trust: Mills Coll

James Ross Harvey: *B* Los Angeles CA 1934 *ED* Princeton Univ BS 1956; Univ CA Berkeley Sch Bus Admin MBA 1963 *CURR EMPL* chmn, dir: TransAmerica Corp *CORP AFFIL* dir: McKesson Corp, Pacific Telesis Group, Charles Schwab Corp, Sedgwick Group, SRI Intl, TransAmerica Fin Corp, TransAmerica Ins Co, TransAmerica Interway, TransAmerica Leasing, TransAmerica Occidental Life Ins, TransAmerica Title Ins *NONPR AFFIL* dir: Bay Area Counc, CA St Parks Fdn; mem: Presidio Counc; pres, dir: San Francisco Chamber Commerce; trust: Mt Land Reliance, Natl Park Fdn, Nature Conservancy, St Marys Coll, Univ CA Bus Sch

Frank Casper Herringer: *B* New York NY 1942 *ED* Dartmouth Coll AB 1964; Dartmouth Coll MBA 1965 *CURR EMPL* pres, ceo, dir: TransAmerica Corp *CORP AFFIL* dir: Fred S James Corp, Sedgwick Group, TransAmerica Equipment Leasing Co, TransAmerica Fin Corp, TransAmerica Ins Co, TransAmerica Interway, TransAmerica Occidental Life Ins, Unocal Corp, Unocal Exploration Corp *NONPR AFFIL* mem: Phi Beta Kappa; trust: CA Pacific Med Ctr, Dartmouth Coll (Amos Tuck Sch Bus Admin), Mills Coll, Pacific Presbyterian Med Ctr

James Blakeley Lockhart: *B* New York NY 1936 *ED* Boston Univ BS 1957; Boston Univ JD 1959 *CURR EMPL* vp (pub affairs): TransAmerica Corp *CORP AFFIL* dir: Budget Rent-a-Car Intl *NONPR AFFIL* chmn: Bay Area Urban League, KQED-FM, KQED-TV, St

Marys Coll Exec Symposium; chmn bus counc: Fine Arts Mus San Francisco; chmn pub affairs comm: San Francisco Chamber Commerce; dep: CA Bus Roundtable; dir: Downtown Assn San Francisco, Pub Aff Counc, Pub Broadcasting Svc Enterprises, Pvt Indus Counc San Francisco; mem: Am Bar Assn, Bay Area Counc, Car Truck Rental Leasing Assn Am, IL Bar Assn, Intl Franchise Assn, SC Bar Assn, World Aff Counc; vp, dir: Lawrence Hall Sch Boys; vp, dir, mem exec comm: Bd Episcopal Charities

GIVING OFFICERS
David R. Carpenter: exec vp, dir *B* Fort Wayne IN 1939 *ED* Univ MI BBA 1961; Univ MI MS 1962 *CURR EMPL* chmn, pres, ceo: TransAm Occidental Life Ins Co *NONPR AFFIL* bd dirs: Am Womens Econ Devel Corp, Century City Assn, Independent Colls Southern CA; chmn bd dirs: Ca Med Ctr Fdn; fellow: Soc Actuaries; gov bd: Fords Theatre; mem: Am Academy Actuaries, Assoc CA Life Ins Cos, Intl Ins Soc, Los Angeles Chamber Commerce; trust, founding mem: Alliance Aging Res
Richard H. Finn: dir *CURR EMPL* pres, ceo, dir: TransAmerica Fin Corp (see above)
Edger H. Grubb: dir *CURR EMPL* sr vp: TransAmerica Corp (see above)
James Ross Harvey: chmn, dir *CURR EMPL* chmn, dir: TransAmerica Corp (see above)
Frank Casper Herringer: dir *CURR EMPL* pres, ceo, dir: TransAmerica Corp (see above)
James Blakeley Lockhart: pres, dir *CURR EMPL* vp (pub affairs): TransAmerica Corp (see above)
Christopher M. McLain: vp, secy, dir
Richard Tatzer: vp, dir, chief investment off

APPLICATION INFORMATION
Initial Approach: *Initial Contact:* brief letter or proposal *Include Information On:* description of the organization, amount requested, purpose for which funds are sought, recently audited financial statement, proof of tax-exempt status, and a list of board of directors *When to Submit:* any time

Restrictions on Giving: Does not support individuals; political, religious, fraternal, or veterans organizations; advertisements in charitable publications; or loans.

OTHER THINGS TO KNOW
Company reports that certain aspects of the giving program are undergoing changes, and that giving may be somewhat curtailed in the future.

GRANTS ANALYSIS
Total Grants: $1,812,433*
Number of Grants: 2,571*
Highest Grant: $250,000*
Typical Range: $100 to $5,000
Disclosure Period: 1991
Note: Numbers above reflect foundation contributions only and include matching gifts. Recent grants are derived from a 1991 Form 990.

RECENT GRANTS
250,000 United Way of the Bay Area, San Francisco, CA
125,000 San Francisco Museum of Modern Art, San Francisco, CA
80,000 That Man May See, San Francisco, CA
65,070 National Merit Scholarship Corporation, Chicago, IL
55,000 United Way of the Bay Area, San Francisco, CA
50,000 St. Mary's College of California, Moraga, CA
30,000 Fine Arts Museum of San Francisco, San Francisco, CA
28,000 San Francisco Suicide Prevention, San Francisco, CA
25,000 Bridge Housing Corporation, San Francisco, CA
25,000 National Park Foundation, Washington, DC

Transamerica Occidental Life Insurance Co.
Assets: $48.62 billion
Employees: 3,300
Parent Company: Transamerica Insurance Corp. of California
Headquarters: Los Angeles, CA
SIC Major Group: Holding & Other Investment Offices and Insurance Carriers

CONTACT
Donald Shellgren
Senior Vice President
Transamerica Occidental Life Insurance Co.
1150 South Olive St.
Los Angeles, CA 90015
(213) 742-2742

CONTRIBUTIONS SUMMARY
Support goes to Los Angeles area health and wellness, elderly, education, youth, minority, homeless, arts, and civic organizations.

Geographic Distribution: only in headquarters area
Operating Locations: CA (Los Angeles)

CORP. OFFICERS
David R. Carpenter: *B* Fort Wayne IN 1939 *ED* Univ MI BBA 1961; Univ MI MS 1962 *CURR EMPL* chmn, pres, ceo: TransAm Occidental Life Ins Co *NONPR AFFIL* bd dirs: Am Womens Econ Devel Corp, Century City Assn, Independent Colls Southern CA; chmn bd dirs: Ca Med Ctr Fdn; fellow: Soc Actuaries; gov bd: Fords Theatre; mem: Am Academy Actuaries, Assoc CA Life Ins Cos, Intl Ins Soc, Los Angeles Chamber Commerce; trust, founding mem: Alliance Aging Res
John A. Fibiger: *CURR EMPL* exec vp, cfo: TransAm Occidental Life Ins Co

OTHER THINGS TO KNOW
Publications: Contributions Policy & Guidelines

Transco Energy Company
Sales: $2.74 billion
Employees: 4,345
Headquarters: Houston, TX
SIC Major Group: Coal Mining, Electric, Gas & Sanitary Services, Holding & Other Investment Offices, and Oil & Gas Extraction

CONTACT
Beth Anne Clay
Manager, Corporate Contributions
Transco Energy Company
PO Box 1396
Houston, TX 77251
(713) 439-2010

FINANCIAL SUMMARY
Recent Giving: $900,000 (1992 approx.); $914,000 (1991 approx.); $1,558,000 (1990)
Fiscal Note: Company gives directly. Figures above do not include a small amount of contributions given by the public relations department.

CONTRIBUTIONS SUMMARY
Typical Recipients: • *Arts & Humanities:* arts centers, community arts, dance, ethnic arts, libraries, museums/galleries, music, opera, performing arts, public broadcasting, theater, visual arts • *Civic & Public Affairs:* better government, business/free enterprise, economic development, economics, environmental affairs, ethnic/minority organizations, housing, law & justice, public policy, urban & community affairs, women's affairs, zoos/botanical gardens • *Education:* arts education, business education, colleges & universities, community & junior colleges, economic education, elementary education, engineering education, literacy, minority education, preschool education, public education (precollege), science/technology education • *Health:* hospices, hospitals, medical research, mental health, pediatric health • *Science:* science exhibits & fairs • *Social Services:* child welfare, community service organizations, delinquency & crime, disabled, domestic violence, drugs & alcohol, employment/job training, food/clothing distribution, recreation & athletics, shelters/homelessness, united funds, youth organizations
Grant Types: capital, employee matching gifts, endowment, general support, project, and scholarship
Nonmonetary Support Types: loaned employees and workplace solicitation
Note: Estimated value of nonmonetary support is not available and is not included in figures above.

Geographic Distribution:
near headquarters and operating locations only, 95% in Houston
Operating Locations: AL, GA, LA, MD, MS, NC, NJ, NY (New York), PA, SC, TX (Houston), VA
Note: Above represents major operating locations; company operates in the Gulf Coast and Atlantic Seaboard areas of the United States.

CORP. OFFICERS
J.P. DesBarres: *CURR EMPL* chmn, ceo, dir: Transco Energy Co

GIVING OFFICERS
Beth Anne Clay: mgr (corp contributions)
T. W. Spencer: chmn (contributions comm) *B* Tornado WV 1929 *CURR EMPL* sr vp, chief admin off: Transco Energy Co *CORP AFFIL* sr vp, chief admin off: Transco Exploration Co, Transco Exploration & Production Co, Transcontinetal Pipe Line Corp

APPLICATION INFORMATION
Initial Approach: *Initial Contact:* telephone call, brief letter, or proposal *Include Information On:* name of organization, address, and telephone number; contact person and title; name of executive director; names and affiliations of directors and trustees; general purpose of organization and people it serves; notation if organization is a United Way agency; type of organization (local, national, or local affiliate of national organization); most recent financial statement to include current and projected budget, preferably audited; sources and amount of organization's funding, both public and private; purpose for which organization is seeking contribution; amount requested; description of the organization's service to or use by company employees; 501(c)(3) exemption letter from IRS *When to Submit:* July through November
Restrictions on Giving: Company does not purchase benefit tickets; contribute to advertising space in souvenir books, programs, or benefit performances; offer loans or financial aid to individuals; or make grants to fraternal, political,

veterans, or religious organizations; or to member agencies of united funds.

OTHER THINGS TO KNOW
Company reports that grant-making will be suspended until 1993. The giving program is undergoing a massive reorganization, and certain priorities and guidelines can be expected to change.

No contribution is automatically renewable; company tries to rotate support in many categories among as many recipients as possible. Company suggests brief progress reports outlining use of contributions at 6-month intervals.

GRANTS ANALYSIS
Total Grants: $914,000*
Number of Grants: 201
Highest Grant: $285,438*
Typical Range: $1,000 to $5,000
Disclosure Period: 1991
Note: Figure for total grants is approximate. Figures for average grant and highest grant are from 1990.

TransOhio Savings Bank

Assets: $3.99 billion
Employees: 1,198
Parent Company: Transcapital Financial Corp.
Headquarters: Cleveland, OH
SIC Major Group: Depository Institutions

CONTACT
Jill Vavro
Branch Manager
TransOhio Savings Bank
PO Box 93449
2000 East 9th St.
Cleveland, OH 44115
(216) 579-7700

CONTRIBUTIONS SUMMARY
Operating Locations: OH (Cleveland)

CORP. OFFICERS
Judith Adam: *CURR EMPL* cfo: TransOhio Savings Bank
William Wooldredge: *CURR EMPL* pres, ceo: TransOhio Savings Bank

Transtar Inc.

Headquarters: Monroeville, PA
SIC Major Group: Holding & Other Investment Offices

CONTACT
Alice C. Saylor
Director, Public Affairs
Transtar Inc.
135 Jamison Ln., PO Box 68
Monroeville, PA 15146
(412) 829-3463

FINANCIAL SUMMARY
Fiscal Note: Annual Giving Range: $100,000 to $250,000

CONTRIBUTIONS SUMMARY
Support goes to local education, human service, arts, and civic organizations.
Typical Recipients: • *Arts & Humanities:* general • *Civic & Public Affairs:* general • *Education:* general • *Social Services:* general
Grant Types: matching
Geographic Distribution: primarily in PA
Operating Locations: PA (Monroeville)

APPLICATION INFORMATION
Initial Approach: Send brief letter of inquiry, including a description of the organization, amount requested, purpose of funds sought, recently audited financial statements, and proof of tax-exempt status. There are no deadlines.

GRANTS ANALYSIS
Typical Range: $1,000 to $2,500

Tranzonic Cos. / Tranzonic Foundation

Sales: $110.72 million
Employees: 924
Headquarters: Pepper Pike, OH
SIC Major Group: Furniture & Fixtures, Paper & Allied Products, and Textile Mill Products

CONTACT
Robert S. Reitman
Vice President
Tranzonic Foundation
30195 Chagrin Blvd., Ste. 224E
Pepper Pike, OH 44124
(216) 831-5757

FINANCIAL SUMMARY
Recent Giving: $369,500 (fiscal 1991); $252,550 (fiscal 1990); $230,000 (fiscal 1989)
Assets: $7,164 (fiscal year ending June 30, 1991); $1,164 (fiscal 1990); $1,164 (fiscal 1989)
Gifts Received: $369,500 (fiscal 1991); $258,550 (fiscal 1990); $230,575 (fiscal 1989)
Fiscal Note: Contributes through foundation only. In 1991, contributions were received from Tranzonic Companies.
EIN: 34-1193613

CONTRIBUTIONS SUMMARY
Typical Recipients: • *Arts & Humanities:* community arts, history/historic preservation, opera, performing arts, public broadcasting, theater • *Civic & Public Affairs:* ethnic/minority organizations, urban & community affairs • *Education:* colleges & universities, private education (precollege) • *Health:* hospitals • *Religion:* religious organizations • *Social Services:* community service organizations, disabled, homes, united funds
Grant Types: general support
Geographic Distribution: focus on Ohio
Operating Locations: OH (Highland Heights, Pepper Pike), TX (Dallas)
Note: Listing includes division locations

CORP. OFFICERS
Robert S. Reitman: *B* Fairmont WV 1933 *ED* WV Univ BS 1955; Case Western Reserve Univ JD 1958 *CURR EMPL* chmn, pres, ceo: Tranzonic Cos *NONPR AFFIL* del: Counc Jewish Feds; mem: Am Bar Assn, Case Western Univ Sch Law Soc, Cleveland Growth Assn; mem adv counc: Cleveland Opera; natl chmn: Un Jewish Appeal; secy, div chmn: Un Way Svcs; trust: Am Jewish Joint Distr Comm, Cleveland St Univ, Cleveland Zoological Soc, Greater Cleveland Roundtable, Jewish Comm Fed, Mt Sinai Med Ctr, Sta WVIZ, Un Israel Appeal

GIVING OFFICERS

James H. Berick: pres *B* Cleveland OH 1933 *ED* Columbia Univ AB 1955; Case Western Univ JD 1958 *CURR EMPL* chmn: Berick Pearlman & Mills Co *CORP AFFIL* dir: A Schulman Inc, Cleveland Browns, MBNA Am Bank, MBNA Corp, SA Horvitz Testamentary Trust, Sandusco, Transonic Cos; pres, ceo, coo, treas: Realty ReFund Trust *NONPR AFFIL* bd visitors: Columbia Coll; mem: Am Bar Assn, Columbia Coll Alumni Assn; trust emeritus: Mt Sinai Med Ctr

Samuel Pearlman: secy, treas
Robert S. Reitman: vp *CURR EMPL* chmn, pres, ceo: Tranzonic Cos (see above)

APPLICATION INFORMATION

Initial Approach: *Initial Contact:* brief letter *Include Information On:* description of program and intended use of funds *When to Submit:* any time
Restrictions on Giving: The foundation does not support individuals, political or lobbying groups, or organizations outside operating areas.

GRANTS ANALYSIS

Total Grants: $369,500
Number of Grants: 30
Highest Grant: $50,000
Typical Range: $500 to $20,000
Disclosure Period: fiscal year ending June 30, 1991
Note: Recent grants are derived from a fiscal 1991 grants list.

RECENT GRANTS

50,000 Jewish Community Federation of Cleveland, Cleveland, OH
25,000 Jewish Community Federation of Cleveland, Cleveland, OH
25,000 Jewish Community Federation of Cleveland, Cleveland, OH
25,000 Jewish Community Federation of Cleveland, Cleveland, OH
25,000 Jewish Community Federation of Cleveland, Cleveland, OH
25,000 Jewish Community Federation of Cleveland, Cleveland, OH
23,750 United Way, Cleveland, OH
20,000 Jewish Community Federation of Cleveland, Cleveland, OH
20,000 Jewish Community Federation of Cleveland, Cleveland, OH
20,000 Jewish Community Federation of Cleveland, Cleveland, OH
20,000 Jewish Community Federation of Cleveland, Cleveland, OH

Travelers Cos. / Travelers Cos. Foundation

Parent Company: Travelers Corp.
Revenue: $9.67 billion
Parent Employees: 30,000
Headquarters: Hartford, CT
SIC Major Group: Insurance Carriers

CONTACT

Debbie McCants
Foundation Assistant
Travelers Cos. Fdn.
One Tower Sq.—6SHS
Hartford, CT 06183
(203) 277-4070

FINANCIAL SUMMARY

Recent Giving: $3,660,000 (1992 approx.); $3,592,431 (1991); $4,412,686 (1990)
Assets: $5,385,501 (1991); $4,511,881 (1989)
Fiscal Note: Company gives through foundation only.
EIN: 22-2535386

CONTRIBUTIONS SUMMARY

Typical Recipients: • *Arts & Humanities:* arts funds, dance, libraries, museums/galleries, music, performing arts, public broadcasting, theater • *Education:* colleges & universities, elementary education, public education (precollege)
• *Health:* geriatric health, medical research, pediatric health
• *Social Services:* aged, community service organizations, united funds, youth organizations
Grant Types: capital, employee matching gifts, general support, multiyear/continuing support, project, and research
Nonmonetary Support Types: in-kind services
Note: Estimated value of nonmonetary support for 1991 is $346,930 and is not included in total contributions figure above. Contact Penny Brice,

Coordinator, Community Services, for nonmonetary suport.
Geographic Distribution: youth education and children's health grants are limited to Hartford, CT
Operating Locations: AL (Birmingham), AR (Little Rock), AZ (Phoenix), CA (Fresno, Los Angeles, Orange County, Sacramento, San Diego, San Jose, Walnut Creek), CO (Denver), CT (Hamden, Hartford), DC, FL (Ft. Lauderdale, Jacksonville, Orlando, Tampa), GA (Atlanta), HI (Honolulu), IA (Des Moines), IL (Chicago, Peoria), IN (Indianapolis), KS (Wichita), KY (Louisville), LA (New Orleans), MA (Boston, Springfield, Worcester), MD (Baltimore), MI (Grand Rapids, Southfield), MN (Minneapolis), MO (Kansas City, St. Louis), MS (Jackson), NC (Charlotte), NE (Omaha), NH (Manchester), NJ (Cherry Hill, Echelon, Morris Plains), NM (Albuquerque), NY (Albany, Buffalo, Garden City, New York, Rochester, Syracuse), OH (Cincinnati, Cleveland, Columbus, Dayton), OK (Oklahoma City), OR (Portland), PA (Erie, Philadelphia, Pittsburgh, Reading), RI (Providence), SC (Columbia), TN (Memphis, Nashville), TX (Dallas, Houston, Lubbock, San Antonio), UT (Salt Lake City), VA (Norfolk, Richmond), WA (Seattle), WI (Milwaukee), WV (Charleston)

CORP. OFFICERS

Edward Hey Budd: *B* Zanesville OH 1933 *ED* Tufts Univ BS 1955 *CURR EMPL* chmn, ceo: Travelers Corp *CORP AFFIL* dir: Charter Oak Fire Ins Co, Delta Air Lines, GTE Corp, Phoenix Ins Co, Travelers Indemnity Co, Travelers Indemnity Co Am, Travelers Indemnity Co RI, Travelers Ins Co *NONPR AFFIL* chmn bus comm: Natl Ctr St Courts; chmn pub awareness comm: CT Bus Ed Coalition; dir: Am Counc Life Ins, Health Ins Assn Am, Inst Living; fellow: Casualty Actuarial Soc; mem: Am Academy Actuaries, Am Ins Assn, Bus Counc, Bus Roundtable

GIVING OFFICERS

Stephen Barton: asst treas *CURR EMPL* vp (corp commun): North Am Reinsurance Corp

Michele Courton Brown: exec dir

Elliot Francis Gerson: dir *B* New Haven CT 1952 *CURR EMPL* sr vp: Travelers Corp *NONPR AFFIL* elector: Wadsworth Atheneum; mem: CT Bar Assn, Phi Beta Kappa; pres, dir: Hartford Stage Co; pres, trust: Hartford Courant Fed; secy: CT Rhodes Scholar Selection Comm; treas: Am S African Scholarship Assn
Thomas Helfrich: dir
Frank Peter Libassi: chmn *B* Brooklyn NY 1930 *ED* Colgate Univ BA 1951; Yale Univ LLB 1954 *CURR EMPL* sr vp (corp communications): Travelers Corp *NONPR AFFIL* bd advs: Natl Academy Aging; dir: Alliance Aging Res, Capitol Partnerships, Greater Hartford Chamber Commerce, Highway Loss Data Inst, Ins Inst Highway Safety, Mt Sinai Hosp; incorporator: Hartford Hosp, Inst Living; mem: Am Assn Retired Persons, Am Bar Assn, CT Bar Assn, Fed Bar Assn, Inst Med, NY Bar Assn, Pew Commn Future Health Professionals; mem comm elderly people living alone: Commonwealth Fund; mem health adv counc: Johns Hopkins Univ; mem pub rels policy comm: Health Ins Assn Am; trust: CT Pub Expenditure Counc
Debbie McCants: fdn asst
John Motley: dir
Michael Smiley: secy
Nancy Van Doren: pres
William White: treas, dir

APPLICATION INFORMATION

Initial Approach: *Initial Contact:* national and Hartford organizations should submit written request to the foundation *Include Information On:* description of the organization; brief statement of history, objectives, and accomplishments; purpose of grant; list of board members and affiliations; proof of tax-exempt status; copy of most recently audited financial statement; for project grants also include: statement of need, program objectives, expected benefits, constituency served, evaluative criteria, budget (including other sources of committed and pending financial support) *When to Submit:* any time
Restrictions on Giving: Grants will not be considered for individuals; mass mail ap-

peals; political organizations; testimonial dinners or memberships in business, professional and trade associations; religious sectarian activities; or fraternal, athletic, social, or veterans organizations. The Foundation also does not grant conferences, films, videos, advertising, or publication of books and magazines.
Multiple year commitments are made but must be evaluated annually.
Capital grants limited to greater Hartford area.

OTHER THINGS TO KNOW

Grants are usually awarded for one year only. Multiple year commitments are considered, but must be evaluated annually.

GRANTS ANALYSIS

Total Grants: $3,592,431
Number of Grants: 105*
Highest Grant: $925,000
Typical Range: $2,000 to $50,000
Disclosure Period: 1991
Note: Number of grants and average grant figures exclude matching gifts to the arts and higher education and contributions given by field offices. Recent grants are derived from a 1991 Form 990.

RECENT GRANTS

925,000 United Way of the Capital Area and Combined Health Appeal, Hartford, CT
250,000 University of Connecticut Foundation/Travelers Center on Aging, Storrs, CT
100,000 Greater Hartford Arts Council (GHAC), Hartford, CT
81,742 Hartford Public Schools, Hartford, CT — School Development Program (Comer Model)
80,000 Riverfront Recapture (RRI), Hartford, CT
75,000 American College, Bryn Mawr, PA
60,000 Hartford Public Schools, Hartford, CT — computer literacy
30,000 Connecticut Small Business Development Center, Storrs, CT
28,000 Junior Achievement of North Cen-

tral Connecticut (J.A.), Windsor Locks, CT
25,000 Community Renewal Team, Hartford, CT

Travelers Express Co.

Assets: $50.0 million
Employees: 1,000
Parent Company: Dial Corp.
Headquarters: Minneapolis, MN
SIC Major Group: Depository Institutions

CONTACT

Carol A. Poulson
Director, Public Relations
Travelers Express Co.
1550 Utica Ave. South
Minneapolis, MN 55416
(612) 591-3000
Note: Telephone extension is ext. 3337.

FINANCIAL SUMMARY

Fiscal Note: Annual Giving Range: less than $100,000

CONTRIBUTIONS SUMMARY

Company sponsors employee matching gift program; also supports community organizations.

Typical Recipients: • *Arts & Humanities:* general • *Civic & Public Affairs:* general • *Education:* general • *Health:* general • *Social Services:* general

Grant Types: employee matching gifts, general support, and matching

Geographic Distribution: primarily headquarters area

Operating Locations: MN (Minneapolis)

CORP. OFFICERS

James K. Bill: *CURR EMPL* pres, coo: Travelers Express Co

APPLICATION INFORMATION

Initial Approach: Send a brief letter of inquiry. Include a description of organization, purpose of funds sought, recently audited financial statement, and proof of tax-exempt status. There are no deadlines.
Restrictions on Giving: Does not support individuals, religious organizations for sectarian purposes, or political or lobbying groups.

Travelli Fund, Charles Irwin

CONTACT

Charles Irwin Travelli Fund
c/o Tyler and Reynolds
One Boston Pl.
Boston, MA 02108

FINANCIAL SUMMARY

Recent Giving: $546,275 (fiscal 1990); $629,650 (fiscal 1989)
Assets: $923,647 (fiscal year ending November 30, 1990); $845,876 (fiscal 1989)
Gifts Received: $702,210 (fiscal 1990); $598,791 (fiscal 1989)
Fiscal Note: In 1990, contributions were received from a trust created under the will of Emma R. Travelli.
EIN: 04-2260155

CONTRIBUTIONS SUMMARY

Donor(s): the late Charles I. Travelli, the late Emma R. Travelli
Typical Recipients: • *Arts & Humanities:* music • *Education:* colleges & universities, private education (precollege) • *Health:* hospitals • *Social Services:* united funds
Grant Types: scholarship
Geographic Distribution: focus on the New England area, emphasis on Boston

GIVING OFFICERS

Oliver R. Andrews, Jr.: exec dir *B* Montclair NJ 1917 *ED* Harvard Univ BS 1939; Middlebury Coll MA 1947; McGill Univ PhD 1956 *NONPR AFFIL* prof emeritus: Univ CT
Sumner R. Andrews: pres

APPLICATION INFORMATION

Initial Approach: Scholarship application forms available at participating educational institutions. For grants, send brief letter of inquiry describing program or project. There are no deadlines.

GRANTS ANALYSIS

Number of Grants: 27
Highest Grant: $80,000
Typical Range: $1,000 to $15,000
Disclosure Period: fiscal year ending November 30, 1990

RECENT GRANTS

80,000 Northeastern University, Boston, MA

56,000 Tufts University, Medford, MA
52,875 University of Vermont, Burlington, VT
52,000 Bowdoin College, Brunswick, ME
52,000 Colby College, Waterville, ME
51,000 Middlebury College, Middlebury, VT
47,000 Keene State College, Keene, NH
28,000 Bates College, Lewiston, ME
28,000 Clark University, Worcester, MA
27,000 University of Maine, Orono, ME

Treadwell Foundation, Nora Eccles

CONTACT

Patricia Canepa
President and Director
Nora Eccles Treadwell Foundation
239 Joaquin Ave.
San Leandro, CA 94577
(415) 775-2879

FINANCIAL SUMMARY

Recent Giving: $2,492,000 (1991); $2,610,606 (1990); $2,819,874 (1989)
Assets: $2,142,596 (1991); $1,934,232 (1990); $1,710,852 (1989)
Gifts Received: $2,659,432 (1991); $2,863,334 (1990); $2,924,803 (1989)
Fiscal Note: The foundation receives yearly gifts from the Nora Eccles Treadwell Charitable Trust, which had assets of $40,270,918 in 1990.
EIN: 23-7425351

CONTRIBUTIONS SUMMARY

Donor(s): The Nora Eccles Treadwell Foundation was established in 1962, with funds donated by the late Nora Eccles Treadwell Harrison.
Typical Recipients: • *Arts & Humanities:* arts centers • *Education:* colleges & universities, medical education • *Health:* health funds, health organizations, hospitals, medical research, mental health, single-disease health associations • *Social Services:* family planning

Grant Types: capital, general support, professorship, and research

Geographic Distribution: Utah and California

GIVING OFFICERS

Patricia Canepa: pres, dir

Spencer Fox Eccles: dir *B* Ogden UT 1934 *ED* Univ UT BS 1956; Columbia Univ MA 1959 *CURR EMPL* chmn, ceo, dir: First Security Corp *CORP AFFIL* chmn exec comm, dir: First Security Bank ID; dir: Anderson Lumber Co, First Security Ins, First Security Investment Mgmt Co, Union Pacific Corp, Zions Coop Mercantile Inst; pres, dir: First Security Cheque Corp, First Security Life Ins Co TX; vp, dir: First Security Computer Ctr *NONPR AFFIL* mem: Am Bankers Assn, Assn Bank Holding Cos, Assn Reserve City Bankers, Young Pres Org; mem adv counc: Univ UT Bus Coll

Lawrence Harrison: dir

Richard A. Harrison: vp, dir

W. D. Hilger, MD: secy, dir

Nicholas T. Prepouses: treas, dir

Alonzo Wallace Watson, Jr.: secy, dir *B* Salt Lake City UT 1922 *ED* Univ UT AB 1943; Univ UT JD 1950; Georgetown Univ BSFS 1947 *CURR EMPL* atty, pres: Ray Quinney & Nebeker (Salt Lake City) *CORP AFFIL* corp counsel, secy: First Security Corp *NONPR AFFIL* dir, exec comm: UT Symphony; mem: Am Bar Assn, CA Bar Assn, UT St Bar Assn; mem natl adv bd: Univ UT; trust: Westminster Coll

APPLICATION INFORMATION

Initial Approach: Applicants should send a letter of inquiry to the foundation. The foundation has no formal application requirements or procedures. Letters of inquiry should describe the organization and project for which funds are sought, provide a biography of the researcher, describe the type of research, and state the amount requested. There are no deadlines. Proposals are reviewed by the president, who then brings them to the board for final review.

Restrictions on Giving: The foundation reports that it is currently not accepting unsolicited

proposals. No grants are given to individuals.

GRANTS ANALYSIS

Total Grants: $2,492,000

Number of Grants: 35

Highest Grant: $800,000

Typical Range: $20,000 to $120,000

Disclosure Period: 1991

Note: The average grant figure excludes the largest grant of $800,000. Recent grants are derived from a 1991 Form 990.

RECENT GRANTS

800,000　University of Utah N.E. Harrison Cardiovascular Research and Training Institute, Salt Lake City, UT — cardiovascular electrophy

200,000　University of Utah N.E. Harrison Cardiovascular Research and Training Institute, Salt Lake City, UT — biochemistry

200,000　University of Utah N.E. Harrison Cardiovascular Research and Training Institute, Salt Lake City, UT — cardiovascular flow

200,000　University of Utah N.E. Harrison Cardiovascular Research and Training Institute, Salt Lake City, UT — cardiovascular pharm

125,000　University of California Los Angeles Medical Center, Los Angeles, CA — arthritis research

125,000　University of California Los Angeles Medical Center, Los Angeles, CA — diabetes research

125,000　University of California School of Medicine, San Francisco, CA — arthritis research

125,000　University of Utah Medical Center Development Fund, Salt Lake City, UT — diabetes research

125,000　University of Utah N.E. Harrison Cardiovascular Research and Training Institute, Salt Lake City, UT — cardio-electric mapping

125,000　University of Utal Medical Center,

Salt Lake City, UT — arthritis research

Treakle Foundation, J. Edwin

CONTACT

John Warren Cooke
President, Treasurer
J. Edwin Treakle Fdn.
PO Box 1157
Gloucester, VA 23061
(804) 693-0881

FINANCIAL SUMMARY

Recent Giving: $172,400 (fiscal 1992); $166,000 (fiscal 1991); $150,000 (fiscal 1990)

Assets: $4,852,529 (fiscal year ending April 30, 1992); $4,369,639 (fiscal 1991); $3,937,576 (fiscal 1990)

Gifts Received: $100,000 (fiscal 1992)

Fiscal Note: In 1992, contributions were received from the Estate of James B. Martin.

EIN: 54-6051620

CONTRIBUTIONS SUMMARY

Donor(s): the late J. Edwin Treakle

Typical Recipients: • *Arts & Humanities:* history/historic preservation, libraries, music • *Civic & Public Affairs:* environmental affairs, safety • *Education:* colleges & universities, private education (precollege) • *Health:* emergency/ambulance services, medical research, nursing services, single-disease health associations • *Religion:* churches • *Social Services:* community service organizations, youth organizations

Grant Types: capital, general support, multiyear/continuing support, research, and scholarship

Geographic Distribution: focus on VA

GIVING OFFICERS

John Warren Cooke: pres, treas

Harry E. Dunn: vp, dir

J. Kirkland Jarvis: secy, dir

APPLICATION INFORMATION

Initial Approach: Application form required. Deadlines are between January 1 and April 30.

Restrictions on Giving: Does not support individuals.

GRANTS ANALYSIS

Number of Grants: 46

Highest Grant: $22,200

Typical Range: $300 to $5,000

Disclosure Period: fiscal year ending April 30, 1992

RECENT GRANTS

22,200　Gloucester Volunteer Fire and Rescue Squad, Gloucester, VA

11,100　Abingdon Volunteer Fire Company, Bena, VA — equipment

11,100　Mathews Volunteer Fire Department, Mathews, VA

11,100　Mathews Volunteer Rescue Squad, Mathews, VA

11,100　Mathews Volunteer Rescue Squad, Mathews, VA — toward replacement of chassis for ambulance

10,650　Friends of Mathews Memorial Library, Mathews, VA — painting, blinds, equipment

10,650　Gloucester Library Endowment Foundation, Gloucester, VA

10,650　Mathews Memorial Library, Friends of, Mathews, VA

7,500　University of Richmond, Richmond, VA — building fund

7,500　Washington and Lee University, Lexington, VA — addition for law school

---

Treasure Chest Advertising Co.

Sales: $550.0 million

Employees: 2,700

Headquarters: Glendora, CA

SIC Major Group: Printing & Publishing

CONTACT

Robert J. Turner
Vice President, Human Resources
Treasure Chest Advertising Co.
511 West Citrus Edge
Glendora, CA 91740
(818) 914-3981

CONTRIBUTIONS SUMMARY

Operating Locations: CA (Glendora)

CORP. OFFICERS
Kenneth B. Erickson: *CURR EMPL* cfo: Treasure Chest Advertising Co
Sanford G. Scheller: *CURR EMPL* pres, ceo: Treasure Chest Advertising Co

Tredegar Industries
Sales: $473.9 million
Employees: 3,500
Headquarters: Richmond, VA
SIC Major Group: Fabricated Metal Products, Primary Metal Industries, Real Estate, and Rubber & Miscellaneous Plastics Products

CONTACT
Ed Cunningham
Manager, Corporate Communications
Tredegar Industries
1100 Boulders Pkwy.
Richmond, VA 23225
(804) 330-1000

CONTRIBUTIONS SUMMARY
Operating Locations: VA (Richmond)

CORP. OFFICERS
John D. Gottwald: *CURR EMPL* chmn, pres, ceo: Tredegar Indus
Norman A. Scher: *CURR EMPL* exec vp, cfo: Tredegar Indus

Trees Charitable Trust, Edith L.

CONTACT
James M. Ferguson III
Edith L. Trees Charitable Trust
c/o Pittsburgh National Bank
One Oliver Plaza, 29th Floor
Pittsburgh, PA 15265-0970
(412) 762-3808

FINANCIAL SUMMARY
Recent Giving: $1,159,721 (1991)
Assets: $32,310,916 (1991)
Gifts Received: $2,159,451 (1991)
Fiscal Note: In fiscal 1991, contributions were received from the Edith L. Trees Trust.
EIN: 25-6026443

CONTRIBUTIONS SUMMARY
Donor(s): the Edith L. Trees Trust
Typical Recipients: • *Civic & Public Affairs:* philanthropic or-

ganizations • *Education:* private education (precollege), religious education • *Social Services:* child welfare, community service organizations, employment/job training
Grant Types: endowment and general support
Geographic Distribution: giving primarily in Pennsylvania

GIVING OFFICERS
Henry A. Bergstrom: trust

APPLICATION INFORMATION
Initial Approach: Submit a written application that details services provided by the Agency, financial information for the previous three years, and a copy of IRS exemption letter. Deadline is November 30.
Restrictions on Giving: Does not provide grants to individuals.

GRANTS ANALYSIS
Number of Grants: 20
Highest Grant: $209,000
Typical Range: $15,000 to $150,000
Disclosure Period: 1991

RECENT GRANTS
209,000 ARC Allegheny County, Pittsburgh, PA
150,000 St. Peters Child Development, Pittsburgh, PA
150,000 Verland Foundation, Pittsburgh, PA — debt retirement
100,000 Celian Heights School, Greensburg, PA
100,000 Verland Foundation, Pittsburgh, PA — endowment
64,443 ARC Westmoreland Chapter, Greensburg, PA
58,000 Martha Lloyd Community Services, Troy, PA — sprinkler and air conditioning systems/motor vehicle
56,937 Goodwill Industries, Pittsburgh, PA
42,612 St. Anthony's School, Oakmont, PA — expressive therapies
34,390 Vocational Rehabilitation Center, Pittsburgh, PA — work activities programs

Tremco Inc. / Tremco Foundation
Sales: $332.0 million
Employees: 2,200
Headquarters: Beachwood, OH
SIC Major Group: Chemicals & Allied Products, Petroleum & Coal Products, and Special Trade Contractors

CONTACT
Mark A. Steinbock
Chief Financial Officer
Tremco Foundation
3735 Green Rd.
Beachwood, OH 44122
(216) 292-5000

FINANCIAL SUMMARY
Recent Giving: $155,472 (1992); $234,632 (1991); $185,299 (1990)
Assets: $2,448,822 (1991); $1,968,101 (1990); $1,936,482 (1989)
Gifts Received: $152,000 (1991); $173,000 (1990); $175,455 (1989)
Fiscal Note: In 1991, contributions were received from Tremco Inc.
EIN: 34-6527566

CONTRIBUTIONS SUMMARY
Typical Recipients: • *Arts & Humanities:* general • *Civic & Public Affairs:* general • *Education:* education associations, general • *Health:* general • *Religion:* religious organizations • *Social Services:* general
Grant Types: general support and matching
Geographic Distribution: focus on OH
Operating Locations: OH (Beachwood)

CORP. OFFICERS
Mark A. Steinbock: *CURR EMPL* vp, cfo: Tremco
H. David Warren: *CURR EMPL* pres, ceo: Tremco

GIVING OFFICERS
Mark A. Steinbock: trust *CURR EMPL* vp, cfo: Tremco (see above)

APPLICATION INFORMATION
Initial Approach: Contributes only to preselected organizations.

GRANTS ANALYSIS
Number of Grants: 15
Highest Grant: $73,000
Typical Range: $500 to $1,500

Disclosure Period: 1991

RECENT GRANTS
73,000 United Way, Ashland, OH
18,423 United Way, Cleveland, OH
15,000 WECO, Cleveland, OH
8,000 Ohio Foundation of Independent Colleges, Columbus, OH
7,528 United Way, Cleveland, OH
7,000 Educational Television, Cleveland, OH
7,000 Friends of Shakers, Cleveland, OH
6,250 Case Alumni Association, Cleveland, OH
6,000 Ashland University, Ashland, OH
6,000 Ashland University, Ashland, OH

Treuhaft Foundation

CONTACT
William C. Treuhaft
Chairman
Treuhaft Fdn.
1400 Hanna Bldg.
1422 Euclid Ave.
Cleveland, OH 44115
(216) 861-3810

FINANCIAL SUMMARY
Recent Giving: $4,250,000 (1991); $645,566 (1990); $787,760 (1989)
Assets: $18,018,141 (1991); $22,199,829 (1990); $21,842,950 (1989)
EIN: 34-1206010

CONTRIBUTIONS SUMMARY
Donor(s): Mrs. William C. Treuhaft, William C. Treuhaft
Typical Recipients: • *Arts & Humanities:* history/historic preservation, opera • *Civic & Public Affairs:* philanthropic organizations • *Education:* colleges & universities, legal education, private education (precollege) • *Health:* health funds, hospitals, medical research, mental health, single-disease health associations • *Religion:* religious organizations • *Social Services:* child welfare, day care, disabled, drugs & alcohol, homes, recreation & athletics, united funds, youth organizations
Grant Types: capital, conference/seminar, emergency, endowment, general support, op-

erating expenses, professorship, project, research, and seed money

Geographic Distribution: focus on the Cleveland, OH, area

GIVING OFFICERS

Irwin Miles Feldman: trust *B* Milwaukee WI 1939 *ED* Univ WI BBA 1961; Univ WI JD 1964 *CURR EMPL* ptnr: Squire Sanders & Dempsey *CORP AFFIL* ptnr: Squire Sanders & Dempsey *NONPR AFFIL* mem: Am Soc Hosp Attys, Cleveland Bar Assn, Natl Health Care Lawyers Assn, OH Bar Assn, WI Bar Assn

Isabel Marting: trust

Arthur W. Treuhaft: trust

Elizabeth M. Treuhaft: mgr, trust

Mrs. William C. Treuhaft: off

APPLICATION INFORMATION

Initial Approach: The foundation is not open to application.

Restrictions on Giving: Does not support individuals or provide funds for capital grants, deficit financing, or hardware or software equipment.

GRANTS ANALYSIS

Number of Grants: 1

Highest Grant: $4,250,000

Disclosure Period: 1991

Note: Total foundation contributions in 1991 went to the Treu-Mart Fund, a supporting organization of the Cleveland Foundation and the Jewish Community Federation of Cleveland.

RECENT GRANTS

260,000 Jewish Community Federation, Cleveland, OH

50,000 Cleveland Play House, Cleveland, OH

50,000 Girl Scouts of America, Cleveland, OH

40,000 Bellefaire Jewish Children's Bureau, Shaker Heights, OH

40,000 Case Western Reserve University, Cleveland, OH

35,000 United Way, Cleveland, OH

33,333 Montefiore Home, Cleveland, OH

24,000 Planned Parenthood, Cleveland, OH

20,000 Cleveland Music School Settlement, Cleveland, OH

15,000 Judson Retirement Community, Cleveland, OH

Trexler Foundation

CONTACT

Trexler Foundation
P.O. Box 32486
Charlotte, NC 28232-6083

FINANCIAL SUMMARY

Recent Giving: $53,999 (1990)

Assets: $1,986,626 (1990)

EIN: 56-1546464

GIVING OFFICERS

Alice E. Trexler: trust

C. Brent Trexler, Jr.: trust

Charles B. Trexler: trust

James Henry Trexler, Jr.: trust

John F. Trexler, Jr.: trust

Mary Margaret Trexler: trust

APPLICATION INFORMATION

Initial Approach: The foundation reports no specific application guidelines. Send a brief letter of inquiry, including statement of purpose, amount requested, and proof of tax-exempt status.

GRANTS ANALYSIS

Total Grants: $53,000

Number of Grants: 12

Highest Grant: $35,000

Disclosure Period: 1990

Trexler Trust, Harry C.

CONTACT

Thomas H. Christman
Secretary to the Trustees
Harry C. Trexler Trust
33 South Seventh St., Ste. 205
Allentown, PA 18101
(215) 434-9645

FINANCIAL SUMMARY

Recent Giving: $1,926,387 (fiscal 1992); $1,755,347 (fiscal 1991); $1,453,417 (fiscal 1990)

Assets: $69,825,825 (fiscal year ending March 31, 1992); $64,319,581 (fiscal 1991); $59,374,996 (fiscal 1990)

Gifts Received: $5,881 (fiscal 1992); $6,822 (fiscal 1990); $4,903 (fiscal 1989)

Fiscal Note: The trust received a contribution in fiscal 1990 from the Harry C. Trexler Fund.

EIN: 23-1162215

CONTRIBUTIONS SUMMARY

Donor(s): The trust was established in 1934, with Harry C. Trexler and Mary M. Trexler as donors. Mr. Trexler was president of Trexler Lumber Company (Allentown, PA) and chairman of Lehigh Portland Cement Company and Bell Telephone Company of Pennsylvania. He was a trustee of Allentown State Hospital, Sacred Heart Hospital (Allentown), St. Luke's Hospital, Lehigh University, Franklin and Marshall College, and Muhlenberg College.

The Trexler will stipulated that one-half of the trust's income be distributed to charitable organizations which serve the benefit of mankind in Lehigh County, one-fourth be paid to the City of Allentown for parks, and one-fourth be added to the foundation's investment assets.

Typical Recipients: • *Arts & Humanities:* arts associations, arts festivals, dance, history/historic preservation, libraries, museums/galleries, music, opera, theater • *Civic & Public Affairs:* environmental affairs, ethnic/minority organizations, municipalities • *Education:* arts education, colleges & universities, community & junior colleges, literacy, special education • *Health:* nursing services • *Social Services:* aged, child welfare, community centers, community service organizations, disabled, recreation & athletics, shelters/homelessness, youth organizations

Grant Types: capital, challenge, and general support

Geographic Distribution: Allentown and Lehigh County, PA, only

GIVING OFFICERS

Dexter F. Baker: trust *B* Worcester MA 1927 *ED* Lehigh Univ BS 1950; Lehigh Univ MBA 1957 *CURR EMPL* chmn, ceo, dir: Air Products & Chemicals *CORP AFFIL* dir: Air Products SA Ltd, Stearns Catalytic, World Corp *NONPR AFFIL* adv comm: Minsi Trails Boy Scouts Am; assoc: Muhlenberg Coll; dir: Pennsylvanians Effective Govt; dir, mem exec comm: Natl Assn Mfrs; head off: Chemical Indus Trade Advisor; mem: Am Inst Chemical Engrs, Am Mgmt Assn, Asa

Packer Soc Lehigh Univ, Bus Roundtable, Soc Chemical Indus, Theta Chi; trust: Harry C. Trexler Fdn, Lehigh Univ

Philip I. Berman: trust *B* Pennsburg PA 1915 *CURR EMPL* pres: Philip I Berman/DBA Fleetways *CORP AFFIL* underwriting mem: Lloyd's London *NONPR AFFIL* adv bd mgrs, mem compensaation comm: Morris Arboretum; chmn: PA St Pub TV Network Comm; dir: Am Friends Hebrew Univ, Lehigh Valley Ed TV-Channel 39, Pennsylvanians Effective Govt; fellow: Culinary Inst Am, Metro Mus Art, PA Academy Fine Arts; mem: Am Assn Music, Am Fed Arts, Am Retail Fed, Beta Gamma Sigma, Counc Consumer Information, Explorers Club NY, Metro Opera Guild, Polar Soc, Soc Automobile Engrs; mem bd govs: Shenkar Coll Fashion Textiles; mem exec bd: Lehigh County Counc Boy Scouts Am; mem exec comm: Philadelphia Mus Art; mem intl bd: Hebrew Univ; mem natl bd: Am Jewish Comm, Israel Bonds; pres, dir: Allentown Symphony Assn, PA Industrial Devel Corp, World Jewish Congress; trust: Keneseth Israel Congregation *PHIL AFFIL* pres: Berman (Philip and Muriel) Foundation

Thomas H. Christman: secy to trust

Carl J. W. Hessinger: trust *B* 1915 *ED* Muhlenberg Coll; Univ PA LLB *NONPR AFFIL* mem: Am Bar Assn

Katherine Stephanoff: trust *NONPR AFFIL* dir: Allentown Pub Library

Richard K. White: chmn

APPLICATION INFORMATION

Initial Approach:

Grant requests should be in letter form.

Letters should state the purpose for which funds are sought, the amount requested, and the anticipated public benefit. Proposals should also include a copy of the organization's articles of incorporation and by-laws, proof of IRS nonprofit status, most recent financial statements, an operating budget, a list of other sources of project support, and detailed program descriptions with current client statistics.

Applications must be received prior to January 31 for funding consideration.

Trustees meet on the third Tuesday of every month to discuss applications. In these meetings the trustees familiarize themselves with an organization's stated purposes and structure. They also subjectively compare organizations seeking funds, preferring to fund the organization demonstrating a more compelling benefit to the local community.

OTHER THINGS TO KNOW

The foundation reports that it also offers proposal writing assistance.
Publications: annual report

GRANTS ANALYSIS
Total Grants: $1,926,387
Number of Grants: 76
Highest Grant: $637,943
Typical Range: $5,000 to $50,000
Disclosure Period: fiscal year ending March 31, 1992
Note: The average grant figure excludes the largest grant of $637,943. Recent grants are derived from a fiscal 1992 Form 990.

RECENT GRANTS
625,811 City of Allentown, Allentown, PA — improve/extend/maintain parks
100,000 Lehigh County Conference of Churches, Lehigh, PA — Alliance Hall project
100,000 Muhlenberg College, Allentown, PA — debt reduction
75,000 Cedar Crest College, Allentown, PA — scholarships
70,000 Allentown Public Library, Allentown, PA — debt reduction
70,000 Boy Scouts of America — Minsi Trails Council; camp improvements
70,000 Holy Family Manor — building addition
50,000 Allentown College, Allentown, PA — scholarship aid
50,000 Phoebe Home, Allentown, PA — indigent care
49,727 Girls Club of Allentown, Allentown,

PA — debt reduction

Triangle Industries / Triangle Foundation
Sales: $2.67 billion
Employees: 2,100
Headquarters: New York, NY

CONTACT
Nelson Peltz
Director
Triangle Foundation
900 Third Avenue
31st Floor
New York, NY 10022
(212) 230-3000

FINANCIAL SUMMARY
Recent Giving: $120,183 (1990); $42,440 (1989)
Assets: $0 (1990); $101,227 (1989)
Gifts Received: $13,210 (1990)
EIN: 22-6064018

CONTRIBUTIONS SUMMARY
Typical Recipients: • *Civic & Public Affairs:* municipalities • *Social Services:* shelters/homelessness
Grant Types: general support
Operating Locations: NY (New York)

CORP. OFFICERS
Peter W. May: *CURR EMPL* pres, coo: Triangle Indus
Nelson Peltz: *CURR EMPL* chmn, ceo: Triangle Indus
William N. Sick: *CURR EMPL* vice-chmn: Triangle Indus

GIVING OFFICERS
Peter W. May: trust *CURR EMPL* pres, coo: Triangle Indus (see above)
Nelson Peltz: trust *CURR EMPL* chmn, ceo: Triangle Indus (see above)

APPLICATION INFORMATION
Initial Approach: Submit a brief letter of inquiry. There are no deadlines.
Restrictions on Giving: The foundation does not make grants to individuals.

GRANTS ANALYSIS
Number of Grants: 3
Highest Grant: $117,683
Typical Range: $500 to $2,000
Disclosure Period: 1990

RECENT GRANTS
117,683 Homeless in America Foundation
2,000 12 Hours for Tyson
500 Core

Trico Foundation

CONTACT
Trico Foundation
P.O. Box 2001
Bloomfield Hills, MI 48303-2001

FINANCIAL SUMMARY
Recent Giving: $52,944 (fiscal 1991)
Assets: $2,158,536 (fiscal year ending June 30, 1991)
EIN: 38-2702725

GRANTS ANALYSIS
Total Grants: $52,944
Disclosure Period: fiscal year ending June 30, 1991

Triford Foundation

CONTACT
Triford Fdn.
20446 Harper Ave.
Harper Woods, MI 48225
(313) 885-0812

FINANCIAL SUMMARY
Recent Giving: $126,000 (1991); $150,000 (1989); $126,000 (1988)
Assets: $2,745,815 (1991); $2,753,411 (1989); $2,389,525 (1988)
EIN: 23-7003478

CONTRIBUTIONS SUMMARY
Typical Recipients: • *Arts & Humanities:* history/historic preservation • *Civic & Public Affairs:* environmental affairs, public policy, urban & community affairs • *Education:* colleges & universities • *Health:* hospitals • *Religion:* churches • *Social Services:* animal protection, community service organizations, united funds
Grant Types: general support and multiyear/continuing support

GIVING OFFICERS
Frederick B. Ford: trust, vp, mgr
Frederick S. Ford: trust, pres, secy
Horace C. Ford: trust, vp, treas
James W. Ford: trust

APPLICATION INFORMATION
Initial Approach: Contributes only to preselected organizations.
Restrictions on Giving: Does not support individuals.

GRANTS ANALYSIS
Number of Grants: 68
Highest Grant: $6,000
Typical Range: $100 to $6,000
Disclosure Period: 1991

RECENT GRANTS
6,000 Hillsdale College, Hillsdale, MI
6,000 Northern Michigan Hospital Foundation, Petoskey, MI
5,600 Hillsdale College, Hillsdale, MI
5,500 Humane Society of Vero Beach, Vero Beach, FL
5,000 Taft School, Watertown, CT
5,000 Tip of the Mitt Watershed Council, Watertown, CT
5,000 Trinity Pulpit Trust, Wayland, MA
4,000 First United Presbyterian Church, Harbor Springs, MI
4,000 Pewabic Society, Detroit, MI
4,000 Red Cross Capital Campaign, Petoskey, MI

Trimble Family Foundation, Robert Mize and Isa White

CONTACT
Gerard Finneran
Trustee
Robert Mize and Isa White Trimble Family Fdn.
50 East 77th St.
Apt 12D
New York, NY 10021

FINANCIAL SUMMARY
Recent Giving: $96,000 (fiscal 1991); $110,000 (fiscal 1990); $103,000 (fiscal 1989)
Assets: $2,473,591 (fiscal year ending June 30, 1991); $2,421,212 (fiscal 1990); $2,333,386 (fiscal 1989)
EIN: 13-2972532

CONTRIBUTIONS SUMMARY
Donor(s): the late Mary Ray Finneran

Typical Recipients: • *Health:* hospitals, medical research, single-disease health associations • *Social Services:* aged, child welfare, community service organizations, disabled, homes, youth organizations

Grant Types: general support and research

Geographic Distribution: focus on NY

GIVING OFFICERS

Daniel J. Ashley: dir, vp

Gerard B. Finneran: trust

Gerard I. Finneran: dir, pres

Rita H. Rowan: dir, secy

APPLICATION INFORMATION

Initial Approach: Contributes only to preselected organizations.

Restrictions on Giving: Does not support individuals or provide funds for scholarships or fellowships.

GRANTS ANALYSIS

Number of Grants: 15

Highest Grant: $15,000

Typical Range: $1,000 to $5,000

Disclosure Period: fiscal year ending June 30, 1991

RECENT GRANTS

15,000 Hope Hill Children's Home, Hope, KY

15,000 St. Patricks Home for the Aged and Infirm, Bronx, NY

10,000 Covenant House, New York, NY

10,000 Missionary Sisters of Charity, New York, NY

10,000 Shriners Hospital for Crippled Children, Tampa, FL

6,000 Atonement Friars, Garrison, NY

5,000 Memorial Sloan-Kettering Cancer Center, New York, NY

5,000 National Jewish Center for Immunology and Respiratory Medicine, Denver, CO

5,000 St. Jude Childrens Research Hospital, Memphis, TN

5,000 St. Roses Home, New York, NY

Trinity Foundation

CONTACT
W. K. Atkinson
Secretary
Trinity Fdn.
PO Box 7008
Pine Bluff, AR 71611
(501) 534-7120

FINANCIAL SUMMARY
Recent Giving: $484,325 (fiscal 1991); $404,303 (fiscal 1990); $270,501 (fiscal 1989)
Assets: $12,519,784 (fiscal year ending September 30, 1991); $10,323,264 (fiscal 1990); $10,485,901 (fiscal 1989)
EIN: 71-6050288

CONTRIBUTIONS SUMMARY
Donor(s): Pine Bluff Sand and Gravel Co., McGeorge Contracting Co., Cornerstone Farm and Gin Co., Standard Investment Co., and the late Harvey W. McGeorge
Typical Recipients: • *Arts & Humanities:* arts centers • *Education:* colleges & universities, education associations, public education (precollege), science/technology education • *Health:* pediatric health • *Social Services:* disabled, recreation & athletics
Grant Types: scholarship
Geographic Distribution: focus on AR

GIVING OFFICERS
W. K. Atkinson: secy, treas
H. Tyndall Dickinson: pres
Haskell L. Dickinson: vp
W. Scott McGeorge: vp
Wallace P. McGeorge, Jr.: vp

APPLICATION INFORMATION
Initial Approach: Scholarship application information available at guidance offices of public high schools in Pine Bluff Little Rock, Benton, and Bauxite, AR. Make inquiry before April 10 of senior year in high school.

OTHER THINGS TO KNOW
Provides scholarships to individuals for higher education.

GRANTS ANALYSIS
Number of Grants: 34
Highest Grant: $170,000
Typical Range: $1,000 to $22,000

Disclosure Period: fiscal year ending September 30, 1991

RECENT GRANTS
170,000 Independent College Fund, Little Rock, AR

30,000 University of Arkansas Little Rock, Little Rock, AR

25,000 Aerospace Education Center, Little Rock, AR

22,000 Arkansas Arts Center, Little Rock, AR

16,716 Little Rock School District, Little Rock, AR

13,758 Pine Bluff Public Schools, Pine Bluff, AR

12,000 Pine Bluff Parks and Recreation, Pine Bluff, AR

10,000 Arkansas Association of Hearing Impaired Children, Little Rock, AR

10,000 Arkansas River Education Service, Little Rock, AR

Trinity Industries, Inc.

Sales: $1.19 billion
Employees: 10,500
Headquarters: Dallas, TX
SIC Major Group: Fabricated Metal Products and Transportation Equipment

CONTACT
Jack S. Cunningham
Vice President
Trinity Industries, Inc.
2525 Stemmons Fwy., Box 568887
Dallas, TX 75356-8887
(214) 631-4420

CONTRIBUTIONS SUMMARY
Operating Locations: TX (Dallas)

CORP. OFFICERS
W. Ray Wallace: *CURR EMPL* pres, ceo: Trinity Indus

TRINOVA Corp. / TRINOVA Foundation

Sales: $1.69 billion
Employees: 15,900
Headquarters: Maumee, OH
SIC Major Group: Fabricated Metal Products, Industrial Machinery & Equipment, Instruments & Related

Products, and Rubber & Miscellaneous Plastics Products

CONTACT
TRINOVA Corp.
3000 Strayer
PO Box 50
Maumee, OH 43537-0050
(419) 867-2294
Note: Contact will change every three months, on a rotating basis. Send all inquiries for northwest Ohio to Contributions Administrator at the above address. Outside northwest Ohio, requests need to be addressed to the closest Aeroquip or Vickers facility.

FINANCIAL SUMMARY
Recent Giving: $525,000 (1993 est.); $516,000 (1992); $460,000 (1991 approx.)
Assets: $2,942,616 (1992); $3,373,311 (1991); $3,122,600 (1990)
Fiscal Note: The Aeroquip Foundation merged with the TRINOVA Foundation in 1989. The company also makes limited gifts, approximately $100,000 annually, directly from corporate and operating company funds and only for organizations in proximity to operating locations. Decisions made locally.
EIN: 31-1276884

CONTRIBUTIONS SUMMARY
Typical Recipients: • *Arts & Humanities:* arts associations, arts funds, dance, libraries, museums/galleries, music, performing arts, public broadcasting, theater • *Civic & Public Affairs:* environmental affairs, law & justice, urban & community affairs • *Education:* business education, colleges & universities, community & junior colleges, economic education, education associations, engineering education • *Health:* health organizations, hospitals • *Social Services:* aged, community service organizations, disabled, drugs & alcohol, family services, united funds, youth organizations
Grant Types: capital, employee matching gifts, general support, and operating expenses
Nonmonetary Support Types: donated equipment and donated products
Note: No estimate is available for value of nonmonetary support, and it is not included above. There is no formal appli-

cation process; requests for this support are handled individually by local facilities. Support is provided by the company. **Geographic Distribution:** near headquarters and operating locations only **Operating Locations:** AL, AR, CA, GA, IL, IN, KY, MD, MI (Jackson, Mount Clemens, Troy), MS (Jackson), NC, NE, NJ, OH (Cincinnati, Maumee, Van Wert), OR, PA (Glenolden), TN, TX, VA, WI

CORP. OFFICERS

Darryl F. Allen: *B* Detroit MI 1943 *CURR EMPL* chmn, pres, ceo: TRINOVA Corp *CORP AFFIL* dir: First OH Bancshares *NONPR AFFIL* mem: Am Inst CPAs, MI Assn CPAs, Fin Execs Inst

GIVING OFFICERS

Darryl F. Allen: trust *CURR EMPL* chmn, pres, ceo: TRINOVA Corp (see above)
William Ammann: trust *B* Toledo OH 1941 *CURR EMPL* vp (admin): Trinova Corp
James Edward Kline: trust *B* Fremont OH 1941 *CURR EMPL* vp, gen couns: Trinova Corp *CORP AFFIL* dir: Essex Devel Group *NONPR AFFIL* adjunct prof: Univ Toledo Coll Law; fellow: OH Bar Fdn; mem: Am Bar Assn, Natl Assn Corp Dirs, OH Bar Assn, Toledo Area Chamber Commerce, Toledo Bar Assn; pres, dir: Toledo Zoological Soc; trust: Lourdes Coll, OH Fdn Independent Colls, Toledo Symphony Orchestra

APPLICATION INFORMATION

Initial Approach: *Initial Contact:* brief letter *Include Information On:* description of the organization, amount requested, purpose for which funds are sought, recently audited financial statement, proof of tax-exempt status *When to Submit:* any time **Restrictions on Giving:** Does not support dinners or special events, fraternal organizations, individuals, member agencies of united funds, political or lobbying groups, or religious organizations for sectarian purposes.

OTHER THINGS TO KNOW

Only requests for Northwest Ohio are directly accepted and

reviewed by the company or its foundation in Maumee. Organizations outside Northwest Ohio must begin their application process with the TRINOVA operating location closest to them.

GRANTS ANALYSIS

Total Grants: $516,000
Typical Range: $100 to $1,000
Disclosure Period: 1992
Note: Recent grants are derived from a 1991 Form 990.

RECENT GRANTS

29,950	United Way of Jackson County, Jackson, MI
19,435	United Way of the Midlands, Omaha, NE
16,460	United Way of the Capital Area, Jackson, MS
15,040	United Way of Van Wert County, Van Wert, OH
15,000	Ohio Foundation of Independent Colleges, Columbus, OH
14,000	Junior Achievement of Northwestern Ohio, Toledo, OH
10,000	Toledo Museum of Art, Toledo, OH
10,000	Toledo Museum of Art, Toledo, OH
10,000	Van Wert County YMCA, Van Wert, OH
9,935	United Way of White County, Searcy, AR

Trion / Trion Charitable Foundation

Sales: $51.98 million
Employees: 350
Headquarters: Sanford, NC

CONTACT

W. P. Glaser
Senior Vice President
Trion
P.O. Box 760
Sanford, NC 27331
(919) 775-2201

FINANCIAL SUMMARY

Recent Giving: $22,960 (1990); $27,312 (1989)
Assets: $181,229 (1990); $201,887 (1989)
Gifts Received: $25,000 (1989)
EIN: 25-6036489

CONTRIBUTIONS SUMMARY

Typical Recipients: • *Civic & Public Affairs:* housing, zoos/botanical gardens • *Education:* community & junior colleges, education funds • *Health:* health organizations • *Social Services:* animal protection, united funds
Grant Types: general support
Geographic Distribution: giving primarily in Lee County, NC
Operating Locations: NC (Sanford)

CORP. OFFICERS

Hugh E. Carr: *CURR EMPL* pres, ceo: Trion

GIVING OFFICERS

Hugh E. Carr: trust *CURR EMPL* pres, ceo: Trion (see above)
William P. Glaser: trust
J. Gary Waters: trust

APPLICATION INFORMATION

Initial Approach: The foundation supports preselected organizations and does not accept unsolicited requests for funds.

GRANTS ANALYSIS

Number of Grants: 72
Highest Grant: $2,500
Typical Range: $100 to $500
Disclosure Period: 1990

RECENT GRANTS

2,500	Independent College Fund of North Carolina, NC
2,000	Sandhills Community College, NC
1,015	United Fund, NC
1,000	CP and L for Project Share, NC
1,000	Lee County Emergency Food Pantry, NC
1,000	Medical Foundation of East Carolina University, NC
1,000	North Carolina Zoological Society, NC
1,000	San-Lee Humane, NC
500	Center for Independent Living, NC
500	Lee County Alzheimer's Disease Support Group, NC

Tripifoods / Tripifoods Foundation

Headquarters: Buffalo, NY

CONTACT

Natalie Gerling
Secretary
Tripifoods
c/o Hodgson, Russ et al.
1800 One M & T Plaza
Buffalo, NY 14203
(716) 853-7400

FINANCIAL SUMMARY

Recent Giving: $40,700 (fiscal 1992); $22,250 (fiscal 1990)
Assets: $101,208 (fiscal year ending June 30, 1992); $108,887 (fiscal 1990)
Gifts Received: $20,000 (fiscal 1992); $20,000 (fiscal 1990)
Fiscal Note: In fiscal 1992, contributions were received from Tripifoods, Inc.
EIN: 13-3399842

CONTRIBUTIONS SUMMARY

Typical Recipients: • *Education:* general • *Social Services:* general
Grant Types: general support
Geographic Distribution: giving primarily in NY
Operating Locations: NY (Buffalo)

CORP. OFFICERS

Robert E. Hillburger: *CURR EMPL* pres: Tripifoods
Carl J. Tripi: *CURR EMPL* ceo: Tripifoods

GIVING OFFICERS

Anthony Dutton: secy
Carl J. Tripi: dir *CURR EMPL* ceo: Tripifoods (see above)

APPLICATION INFORMATION

Initial Approach: The foundation supports preselected organizations and does not accept unsolicited requests for funds.

GRANTS ANALYSIS

Number of Grants: 9
Highest Grant: $25,000
Typical Range: $500 to $1,500
Disclosure Period: fiscal year ending June 30, 1992

RECENT GRANTS

25,000	Tom Haggai and Association Foundation, High Point, NC
7,000	Food Industry Crusade Against Hun-

ger, Washington,
DC
2,500 Canisius High
School, Buffalo,
NY
2,000 Franciscan Sisters
1,500 Sisters of St. Francis, Columbus, OH
1,500 St. Joseph Collegiate Institute, Buffalo, NY
500 Georgetown Annual Fund, Washington, DC
500 Holy Cross Foreign Missions, Notre Dame, IN
200 Ladies Auxiliary, Niagara Falls Memorial Medical Center, Lewiston, NY

Triskelion Ltd.
Headquarters: Albuquerque, NM

CONTACT
Douglas B. Quine
President
Triskelion Ltd.
PO Box 7822
Albuquerque, NM 87194-7822

FINANCIAL SUMMARY
Fiscal Note: Company does not disclose contributoions figures.

CONTRIBUTIONS SUMMARY
Company provides a 9:1 employee gift matching program.
Typical Recipients: • *Arts & Humanities:* dance, general, history/historic preservation, libraries, public broadcasting, theater • *Civic & Public Affairs:* first amendment issues, general, zoos/botanical gardens • *Education:* general • *Health:* general • *Science:* general • *Social Services:* general
Grant Types: employee matching gifts
Nonmonetary Support Types: donated equipment, loaned employees, and loaned executives
Geographic Distribution: nationally

CORP. OFFICERS
Douglas B. Quine: *CURR EMPL* pres: Triskelion Ltd

APPLICATION INFORMATION
Initial Approach: Company provides matching gifts of employees only.
Restrictions on Giving: Does not support individuals, religious organizations for sectarian

purposes, or political or lobbying groups.

Tropicana Products, Inc.
Sales: $540.0 million
Employees: 3,000
Headquarters: Bradenton, FL
SIC Major Group: Chemicals & Allied Products, Food & Kindred Products, Paper & Allied Products, and Stone, Clay & Glass Products

CONTACT
Terri L. McNorton
Director, Public Relations and Communications
Tropicana Products, Inc.
PO Box 338
Bradenton, FL 34206
(813) 747-4461

FINANCIAL SUMMARY
Fiscal Note: Annual Giving Range: Company does not disclose contributions figures.

CONTRIBUTIONS SUMMARY
Priorities include education and social services. Education funding is distributed over elementary, secondary, and vocational education areas, also interested in minority education. Also supports economic, business, and technical education. Contributions in the social services focus on United Way, children and families, and the elderly and disabled. Also supports programs concerned with delinquency and crime, domestic violence, and drug and alcohol rehabilitation. Also provides support to arts, civic, and health organizations.
Typical Recipients: • *Arts & Humanities:* community arts, museums/galleries, performing arts, theater • *Civic & Public Affairs:* civil rights, economic development, law & justice, professional & trade associations, public policy, safety, urban & community affairs • *Education:* business education, career/vocational education, colleges & universities, economic education, education associations, elementary education, engineering education, literacy, minority education, public education (precollege), science/technology education, student aid • *Health:* health care cost containment, health organizations, single-disease

health associations • *Science:* scientific organizations • *Social Services:* aged, child welfare, community centers, community service organizations, disabled, domestic violence, drugs & alcohol, employment/job training, family services, food/clothing distribution, united funds, youth organizations
Grant Types: capital, general support, project, and scholarship
Nonmonetary Support Types: donated equipment, donated products, in-kind services, loaned employees, and loaned executives, and workplace solicitation
Geographic Distribution: principally near headquarters and operating locations and to national organizations
Operating Locations: CA, FL, NJ, NY

CORP. OFFICERS
William G. Pietersen: *CURR EMPL* pres, dir: Tropicana Products

GIVING OFFICERS
Terri L. McNorton: *CURR EMPL* dir pub rels & commun: Tropicana Products

APPLICATION INFORMATION
Initial Approach: Send a letter and proposal at least one month before grant is needed. Include a description of the organization, purpose of funds, amount requested, and proof of tax-exempt status.

True North Foundation

CONTACT
Kerry K. Hoffman
True North Fdn.
2190 West Drake, No. 361
Ft. Collins, CO 80526
(503) 293-3348

FINANCIAL SUMMARY
Recent Giving: $642,588 (1991); $389,000 (1990); $328,005 (1989)
Assets: $6,898,494 (1991); $6,885,110 (1990); $6,676,598 (1989)
EIN: 74-2421528

CONTRIBUTIONS SUMMARY
Typical Recipients: • *Arts & Humanities:* opera, theater

• *Civic & Public Affairs:* environmental affairs • *Social Services:* community centers, community service organizations, family planning, family services, united funds
Grant Types: capital, emergency, general support, operating expenses, and project
Geographic Distribution: focus on CA and national environmental programs

GIVING OFFICERS
L. Jane Gallup: dir
Kerry K. Hoffman: pres, dir
Kathryn Fong Stephens: dir

APPLICATION INFORMATION
Initial Approach: Contributes only to preselected organizations.
Restrictions on Giving: Does not support individuals.

OTHER THINGS TO KNOW
Publications: Informational Brochure (including application guidelines)

GRANTS ANALYSIS
Number of Grants: 44
Highest Grant: $75,000
Typical Range: $2,500 to $25,000
Disclosure Period: 1991

RECENT GRANTS
75,000 Season of Sharing, San Francisco, CA — general fund
50,000 Planned Parenthood Federation of America, New York, NY
35,000 Environmental Defense Fund, New York, NY — waste reduction
25,000 Berkeley Repertory Theatre, Berkeley, CA — bridge to the future campaign
25,000 Center for Marine Conservation, Washington, DC — California marine debris action plan
25,000 Family School, San Francisco, CA — general fund
25,000 San Francisco Opera, San Francisco, CA — Western opera theatre
20,000 Natural Resources Defense Council, New York, NY
20,000 NRDC, San Francisco, CA — energy efficiency work

20,000 Oregon Environ-
mental Council,
Portland, OR —
clean air project

True Oil Co. / True Foundation

Headquarters: Casper, WY

CONTACT
H.A. True, Jr.
Trustee
True Foundation
PO Drawer 2360
Casper, WY 82602
(307) 237-9301

FINANCIAL SUMMARY
Recent Giving: $63,086
(1991); $148,800 (1990);
$153,025 (1989)
Assets: $3,114,147 (1991);
$507,828 (1990); $615,879
(1989)
Gifts Received: $2,512,000
(1991); $9,600 (1990); $9,600
(1989)
Fiscal Note: In 1991, contribu-
tions were received from True
Oil Company ($12,000) and
H.A. True, Jr. ($2,500,000).
EIN: 83-6004596

CONTRIBUTIONS SUMMARY
Typical Recipients: • *Arts & Humanities:* history/historic
preservation, museums/galler-
ies, music • *Civic & Public Affairs:* environmental affairs,
housing, law & justice • *Education:* colleges & universities,
community & junior colleges
• *Health:* hospitals • *Social Services:* community service organizations, united funds,
youth organizations
Grant Types: general support
Geographic Distribution:
focus on WY
Operating Locations: WY
(Casper)

CORP. OFFICERS
H. A. True, Jr.: *CURR EMPL*
chmn, pres: True Oil Co

GIVING OFFICERS
H. A. True, Jr.: trust *CURR
EMPL* chmn, pres: True Oil Co
(see above)

APPLICATION INFORMATION
Initial Approach: Send brief
letter describing program.
There are no deadlines.

GRANTS ANALYSIS
Number of Grants: 30
Highest Grant: $25,000

Typical Range: $100 to $1,000
Disclosure Period: 1991

RECENT GRANTS
25,000 Mountain States
Legal Foundation,
Denver, CO
18,386 United Way, Cas-
per, WY
4,500 University of Wyo-
ming, Laramie, WY
1,500 Dickinson State
College, Dickin-
son, ND
1,250 Wyoming State 4-
H Foundation,
Laramie, WY
1,100 Center for Science
Technology and
Political Thought,
Boulder, CO
1,000 Heritage Founda-
tion, Washington,
DC
1,000 Mother Seton Hous-
ing, Casper, WY
1,000 Weston County Me-
morial Hospital
Foundation, New-
castle, WY
750 Black Hills State
College, Spearfish,
SD

True Trust, Henry A.

CONTACT
John Kline Bartram
Trustee
Henry A. True Trust
146 East Center St.
Marion, OH 43302
(614) 387-6000

FINANCIAL SUMMARY
Recent Giving: $105,500
(1991); $110,000 (1990);
$95,500 (1989)
Assets: $3,555,163 (1991);
$3,431,780 (1990); $3,329,379
(1989)
EIN: 31-0679235

CONTRIBUTIONS SUMMARY
Typical Recipients: • *Arts & Humanities:* arts associations,
ethnic arts, history/historic pre-
servation, museums/galleries
• *Civic & Public Affairs:* urban
& community affairs • *Religion:* churches • *Social Services:* child welfare, community
service organizations,
food/clothing distribution,
united funds, youth organizations
Grant Types: general support
Geographic Distribution: limited to the Marion County, OH,
area

GIVING OFFICERS
John C. Bartram: trust
John Kline Bartram: trust
Joe D. Donithen: trust

APPLICATION INFORMATION
Initial Approach: Send brief
letter of inquiry describing program or project. There are no
deadlines.

GRANTS ANALYSIS
Number of Grants: 30
Highest Grant: $15,000
Typical Range: $1,000 to
$2,500
Disclosure Period: 1991

RECENT GRANTS
15,000 Stengel-True Mu-
seum, Marion, OH
10,000 First Presbyterian
Church, Marion,
OH
10,000 Palace Cultural
Arts Association,
Marion, OH
10,000 St. Paul's Episco-
pal Church,
Marion, OH
7,500 United Way,
Marion, OH
6,000 Lee Street Presbyterian Church,
Marion, OH
5,000 Marion Junior Serv-
ice Guild, Marion,
OH
5,000 Mobile Meals on
Marion County,
Marion, OH
5,000 YMCA, Marion,
OH
3,000 Noren Circle Trin-
ity Baptist Church,
Marion, OH

Truland Foundation

CONTACT
Robert W. Truland
Trustee
Truland Fdn.
3330 Washington Blvd.
Arlington, VA 22201
(703) 516-2600

FINANCIAL SUMMARY
Recent Giving: $112,347 (fis-
cal 1992); $109,381 (fiscal
1991); $101,581 (fiscal 1990)
Assets: $2,526,830 (fiscal year
ending March 31, 1992);
$2,479,530 (fiscal 1991);
$2,281,744 (fiscal 1990)
EIN: 54-6037172

CONTRIBUTIONS SUMMARY
Donor(s): Truland of Florida,
Inc., and members of the Truland family
Typical Recipients: • *Arts & Humanities:* arts centers, community arts, dance, literary
arts, museums/galleries, performing arts • *Civic & Public
Affairs:* environmental affairs,
housing, zoos/botanical gardens • *Education:* colleges &
universities, private education
(precollege) • *Health:* medical
research, pediatric health, single-disease health associations
• *Religion:* churches, religious
organizations • *Social Services:*
community service organizations, disabled
Grant Types: general support
Geographic Distribution:
focus on VA

GIVING OFFICERS
Alice O. Truland: trust
Robert W. Truland: trust
Walter R. Truland: trust
CURR EMPL pres, dir: Truland
Corp

APPLICATION INFORMATION
Initial Approach: Applications not accepted.

GRANTS ANALYSIS
Number of Grants: 78
Highest Grant: $25,000
Typical Range: $250 to $2,000
Disclosure Period: fiscal year
ending March 31, 1992

RECENT GRANTS
25,000 Chelonia Institute,
Arlington, VA
11,500 Smithsonian Institution, Washington,
DC
10,000 Barnesville School,
Barnesville, MD
5,110 St. Anslem's
Abbey School,
Washington, DC
5,000 D.C. Housing Eq-
uity Foundation,
Washington, DC
4,000 Solaris Dance Thea-
tre, New York, NY
2,500 American Cancer
Society, Vienna, VA
2,500 Caribbean Conser-
vation Fund,
Gainesville, FL
2,220 John F. Kennedy
Center for the Per-
forming Arts, Wash-
ington, DC
2,000 National Gallery of
Art, Washington,
DC

Truland Systems Corp.

Sales: $50.0 million
Employees: 300
Headquarters: Arlington, VA
SIC Major Group: Special Trade Contractors

CONTACT
Patti Ferrante
Secretary to the President
Truland Systems Corp.
3330 Washington Blvd.
Arlington, VA 22201
(703) 524-4900

CONTRIBUTIONS SUMMARY
Operating Locations: VA (Arlington)

CORP. OFFICERS
Walter R. Truland: *CURR EMPL* pres, dir: Truland Corp

OTHER THINGS TO KNOW
Company is an original donor to the Truland Foundation.

Trull Foundation

CONTACT
Colleen Claybourn
Executive Director
Trull Foundation
404 Fourth St.
Palacios, TX 77465
(512) 972-5241

FINANCIAL SUMMARY
Recent Giving: $696,475 (1992); $718,000 (1991); $690,560 (1990)
Assets: $18,500,000 (1993 est.); $18,000,000 (1992 est.); $17,612,905 (1991); $14,976,665 (1990)
Gifts Received: $9,126 (1987)
Fiscal Note: In 1987, the foundation received a gift of stock in Aberdeen 68.7 Ltd. from Rick Reese.
EIN: 23-7423943

CONTRIBUTIONS SUMMARY
Donor(s): The B. W. Trull Foundation was established in 1948 by B. W. and Florence M. Trull for religious, charitable, and educational purposes. Trustees were Robert B. Trull, Harry H. Sisson, and Ralph P. Newsom. By the terms of its indenture, the original foundation expired in 1973. In 1967, Florence M. Trull and her four children established a new foundation to receive the assets of the old foundation and to run until its assets were expended. The Trull family's fortune stems from farming, land management, and investments.
Typical Recipients: • *Arts & Humanities:* ethnic arts, history/historic preservation, libraries, museums/galleries, music, opera, performing arts, public broadcasting, theater, visual arts • *Civic & Public Affairs:* environmental affairs, housing, law & justice, nonprofit management • *Education:* colleges & universities, community & junior colleges, medical education, minority education, private education (precollege), public education (precollege), religious education, student aid • *Health:* mental health, pediatric health • *International:* international development/relief, international health care, international organizations • *Religion:* churches, missionary activities, religious organizations • *Science:* observatories & planetariums • *Social Services:* aged, child welfare, community centers, community service organizations, counseling, day care, delinquency & crime, domestic violence, drugs & alcohol, emergency relief, employment/job training, family planning, family services, homes, legal aid, refugee assistance, religious welfare, shelters/homelessness, united funds, youth organizations
Grant Types: conference/seminar, general support, multi-year/continuing support, operating expenses, project, scholarship, and seed money
Geographic Distribution: primarily Texas area, but no geographic restrictions; principally to national organizations

GIVING OFFICERS
Garland M. Brooking: fdr
Gladys Trull Brooking: fdr
Colleen Claybourn: secy, treas, trust, mem contributions comm, exec dir
Jean Trull Herlin: fdr, mem contributions comm, trust
Robert G. Herlin: fdr
J. Fred Huitt: vchmn bd trusts, mem investment comm
Rose C. Lancaster: trust, mem contributions comm
B. B. Shiflett: fdr
Laura Trull Shiflett: fdr
Robert B. Trull: fdr, chmn bd trusts, mem investment comm

APPLICATION INFORMATION
Initial Approach:
Send a brief proposal to the foundation. If additional information is needed for complete analysis, it will be requested. Information that may be requested includes background information, amount requested, other sources of support, and future plans; qualifications of personnel; budget from past year and for the proposed funding year; current audited financial statement; proof of IRS tax exemption; and newsclips detailing the project or the organization funded.
Applications may be submitted any time.
The grants committee meets monthly. Letters of approval or non-approval are sent four-to-six weeks after meetings.
Restrictions on Giving: Usually, funding is not provided for long-term commitments, capital expenses, endowments, grants longer than three years, or operating expenses (except for new organizations). There is no funding for individuals. There are no loans.

OTHER THINGS TO KNOW
The foundation supports established organizations to develop new programs, assists in proposal writing to work in coordination with other foundations, and conducts seminars/workshops.
The foundation expects periodic progress reports during the funding period.
Publications: biennial report

GRANTS ANALYSIS
Total Grants: $696,475
Number of Grants: 224
Highest Grant: $15,000
Typical Range: $1,500 to $5,000
Disclosure Period: 1992
Note: Recent grants are derived from a 1992 grants list for the month of December.

RECENT GRANTS
10,000 TAMU Development Foundation, College Station, TX — Rice Research Program
5,500 Hilliard High Alumni Association — purchase of display cases and laminator
5,000 Blessing Historical Foundation — rewiring the hotel building
5,000 Mujeres Project — HIV/AIDS and birth control education programs
5,000 Presbyterian Church (U.S.A.), Louisville, KY — Somalia relief efforts
5,000 Presbyterian Pan American School, Kingsville, TX — support of programs
5,000 Stillman College, Tuscaloosa, AL — support of programs
5,000 Stillman College, Tuscaloosa, AL — support of programs
5,000 Video Action Fund — production of documentaries
3,500 Zachary Scott Theatre Center, Austin, TX — two performances of "A Christmas Carol"

Truman Foundation, Mildred Faulkner

CONTACT
Irene C. Graven
Executive Director
Mildred Faulkner Truman Fdn.
212 Front St.
PO Box 236
Owego, NY 13827
(607) 687-1350

FINANCIAL SUMMARY
Recent Giving: $300,941 (fiscal 1989); $161,402 (fiscal 1988)
Assets: $5,258,806 (fiscal year ending August 31, 1989); $4,564,405 (fiscal 1988)
Gifts Received: $1,291 (fiscal 1989); $1,159,812 (fiscal 1988)
EIN: 16-6293320

CONTRIBUTIONS SUMMARY
Donor(s): Mildred Faulkner Truman
Typical Recipients: • *Arts & Humanities:* arts associations, community arts, history/historic preservation, music • *Civic & Public Affairs:* environmental affairs, municipalities, zoos/botanical gardens • *Education:* community & junior colleges • *Religion:* churches • *Social Services:* aged, child welfare, community service organizations, shel-

ters/homelessness, united funds, youth organizations
Grant Types: emergency, general support, and project
Geographic Distribution: focus on Tioga County, NY, with emphasis on the Owego, NY, area

GIVING OFFICERS
Edwin B. Bartow: vchmn
John J. Donnelly: dir
Dorothy Goodrich: treas
Irene C. Graver: exec dir
James V. Guido: dir
Fred R. McFadden: dir
John Reginald Murphy: dir *B* Gainesville GA 1934 *ED* Mercer Univ; Harvard Univ *NONPR AFFIL* chmn: Univ MD Friends Library Gallery; dir: Baltimore Urban League Exec Bd, Baltimore Washington Intl Airport Devel Counc, Econ Devel Counc, Johns Hopkins Univ Sch Medicine, Un Way Central MD, Washington Baltimore Regional Assn; mem: Johns Hopkins Ctr Metro Planning Res; trust: Johns Hopkins Hosp, Loyola Coll Baltimore
Carl Saddlemire: chmn
Robert Williams: secy

APPLICATION INFORMATION
Initial Approach: Contributes only to preselected organizations.

OTHER THINGS TO KNOW
Publications: Application Guidelines, Informational Brochure

GRANTS ANALYSIS
Number of Grants: 49
Highest Grant: $35,000
Typical Range: $500 to $12,500
Disclosure Period: fiscal year ending August 31, 1989

RECENT GRANTS
35,000 Village of Owego, Owego, NY
20,000 United Health Services, New York, NY
18,500 Family and Children's Services, New York, NY
15,346 Tioga Opportunities Program, Owego, NY
15,000 Day Care Center of Oswego, Oswego, NY
12,500 WSKG, New York, NY
10,513 Tioga County Squad Captains As-

sociation, Owego, NY
10,303 Tioga County Squad Captains Association, Owego, NY
10,000 SOS Shelter, New York, NY
10,000 Tompkins Wetland Community, New York, NY

Trump Group
Employees: 10,000
Headquarters: New York, NY
SIC Major Group: Holding & Other Investment Offices and Real Estate

CONTACT
James Lieb
Trump Group
4 Stagecoach Run
E. Brunswick, NJ 08816
(212) 838-1000

CONTRIBUTIONS SUMMARY
Operating Locations: NY (New York)

CORP. OFFICERS
Eddie Trump: *CURR EMPL* pres: Trump Group
Julius Trump: *CURR EMPL* chmn, treas: Trump Group

Trusler Foundation
CONTACT
Trusler Fdn.
PO Box 704
Emporia, KS 66801

FINANCIAL SUMMARY
Recent Giving: $297,666 (1991); $127,300 (1990); $143,000 (1989)
Assets: $2,439,861 (1991); $2,482,205 (1990); $2,559,259 (1989)
EIN: 48-6117374

CONTRIBUTIONS SUMMARY
Typical Recipients: • *Arts & Humanities:* arts associations, community arts • *Civic & Public Affairs:* zoos/botanical gardens • *Education:* colleges & universities • *Social Services:* shelters/homelessness, youth organizations
Grant Types: general support
Geographic Distribution: focus on Emporia, KS

GIVING OFFICERS
S. Richard Mellinger: secy
Tom Thomas: treas

Michael Turnball: pres

APPLICATION INFORMATION
Initial Approach: Contributes only to preselected organizations.

GRANTS ANALYSIS
Number of Grants: 4
Highest Grant: $160,166
Typical Range: $5,000 to $130,000
Disclosure Period: 1991

RECENT GRANTS
160,166 USD 253, Emporia, KS — land donated for use in the construction of a new junior high school
130,000 Emporia State University Endowment, Emporia, KS — build a sports complex for use by university students and the community
5,000 Girl Scouts of America, Emporia, KS
2,500 Emporia Arts Council, Emporia, KS — feasibility study for the development of a community cultural center

Trust Co. Bank / Trust Co. of Georgia Foundation
Employees: 5,000
Parent Company: Sun Trust Banks, Inc.
Headquarters: Atlanta, GA
SIC Major Group: Depository Institutions

CONTACT
Victor A. Gregory
Secretary
Trust Co. of Georgia Fdn.
Mail Code 041 PO Box 4418
Atlanta, GA 30302
(404) 588-8246

FINANCIAL SUMMARY
Recent Giving: $1,364,331 (1991 est.); $1,366,111 (1990); $1,274,119 (1989)
Assets: $10,936,385 (1990); $10,700,000 (1989)
Fiscal Note: Company gives primarily through the foundation.
EIN: 58-6026063

CONTRIBUTIONS SUMMARY
Typical Recipients: • *Arts & Humanities:* arts appreciation, arts associations, arts centers, arts festivals, arts funds, community arts, dance, ethnic arts, history/historic preservation, libraries, museums/galleries, music, opera, performing arts, public broadcasting, theater • *Civic & Public Affairs:* business/free enterprise, civil rights, consumer affairs, economic development, economics, environmental affairs, ethnic/minority organizations, housing, law & justice, municipalities, nonprofit management, public policy, safety, urban & community affairs, women's affairs, zoos/botanical gardens • *Education:* arts education, business education, colleges & universities, economic education, education funds, international exchange, international studies, legal education, medical education, minority education, private education (precollege), public education (precollege), religious education, science/technology education, special education • *Health:* geriatric health, health organizations, hospitals, medical rehabilitation, medical training, mental health, nursing services, pediatric health, single-disease health associations • *Science:* scientific institutes • *Social Services:* aged, child welfare, community centers, community service organizations, counseling, delinquency & crime, disabled, domestic violence, drugs & alcohol, emergency relief, employment/job training, family services, food/clothing distribution, homes, legal aid, recreation & athletics, shelters/homelessness, united funds, youth organizations
Grant Types: capital, employee matching gifts, project, and seed money
Geographic Distribution: metropolitan Atlanta area
Operating Locations: GA (Atlanta)
Note: Operates numerous branches in Fulton and Dekalb counties.

CORP. OFFICERS
Edward P. Gould: *B* Chattanooga TN 1931 *ED* Emory Univ 1953 *CURR EMPL* chmn: Trust Co Bank Atlanta *CORP AFFIL* chmn: Trust Co GA;

chmn, mem exec comm: Munich Am Reassurance Co *NONPR AFFIL* mem: Assn Reserve City Bankers

GIVING OFFICERS
Edward P. Gould: chmn *CURR EMPL* chmn: Trust Co Bank Atlanta (see above)
Victor A. Gregory: secy
Jesse Seaborn Hall: mem *B* Atlanta GA 1929 *ED* Emory Univ AB 1950; Emory Univ LLB 1955 *CURR EMPL* exec vp: SunTrust Banks *CORP AFFIL* dir: Crawford & Co; exec vp: SunTrust Banks, Trust Co Bank *NONPR AFFIL* mem: Am Bankers Assn, Trust Mgmt Assn; trust: Egleston (Henrietta) Hosp Children, Oglethorpe Univ
L. Phillip Humann: mem *CURR EMPL* chmn, dir: Trust Co Bank
Wade T. Mitchell: mem *B* Atlanta GA 1935 *ED* GA Inst Tech BS 1957; Harvard Univ MBA 1961 *CURR EMPL* exec vp: Trust Co Bank *CORP AFFIL* dir: Ivan Allen Co; mem adv comm: Pan Am Investment Co *NONPR AFFIL* dir: Metro Atlanta Am Red Cross, Pvt Indus Counc Atlanta, Un Way Metro Atlanta
John W. Spiegel: mem *B* Indianapolis IN 1941 *ED* Wabash Coll 1963; Emory Univ 1965 *CURR EMPL* exec vp, cfo: Sun Trust Banks *CORP AFFIL* dir: Rock Tenn Co; exec vp: Trust Co GA *NONPR AFFIL* dir: Atlanta Opera, High Mus Art Atlanta; dir, mem exec comm: Morehouse Sch Medicine; mem: Atlanta Chamber Commerce, Bank Admin Inst, Emory Univ Bus Sch Alumni Assn, Fin Exec Inst; mem adv bd: Young Audiences Atlanta; mem exec comm: Robert Woodruff Arts Ctr; mem exec comm, dir: Alliance Theatre Atlanta; trust: Leadership Atlanta; vp exec bd: Atlanta Area Counc Boy Scouts Am
James Bryan Williams: mem *B* Sewanee TN 1933 *ED* Emory Univ 1955 *CURR EMPL* chmn, ceo: SunTrust Banks *CORP AFFIL* dir: Boral Indus, Coca-Cola Co, GA Intl Life Ins Co, GA Pacific Corp, Genuine Parts Co, Rollins Inc, RPC Energy Svcs, Sonat; pres, dir: Trust Co Bank *NONPR AFFIL* chmn, trust: Henrietta Egleston Hosp Children; mem: Am Bankers Assn; mem bd visitors: Berry Coll; mem, dir: Reserve

City Bankers Assn; trust: Emory Univ, Robert W Woodruff Health Sciences Ctr, Westminster Schs, Woodruff Med Ctr

APPLICATION INFORMATION
Initial Approach: *Initial Contact:* call or write *Include Information On:* organization, objectives, amount requested, total amount needed, purpose for grant, proposed objective and community benefit, other contributors, financial data, annual report, list of board of directors and their affiliations, proof of tax-exempt status *When to Submit:* December 1, March 1, June 1, or September 1; board meets in January, April, July, and October
Restrictions on Giving: Foundation does not make loans or grants for maintenance or debt service. Does not support political organizations, churches, individuals, dinners or special events, or conferences.

OTHER THINGS TO KNOW
Nonmatching grants may be made to national organizations but must benefit the metropolitan Atlanta area.
The committee expects periodic program reports from recipients.
Publications: application guidelines

GRANTS ANALYSIS
Total Grants: $1,366,111*
Number of Grants: 150*
Highest Grant: $100,000
Typical Range: $3,000 to $5,000
Disclosure Period: 1990
Note: Total grants figure includes matching gifts. Number of grants figure excludes matching gifts. Recent grants are derived from a 1990 Form 990.

RECENT GRANTS
123,491   United Way of Metro Atlanta, Atlanta, GA
123,491   United Way of Metro Atlanta, Atlanta, GA — operating grant
123,491   United Way of Metro Atlanta, Atlanta, GA — operating grant
123,490   United Way of Metro Atlanta, Atlanta, GA — operating grant

115,250   United Way of Metro Atlanta, Atlanta, GA — operating
100,000   Woodruff Arts Center, Atlanta, GA
18,000   United Negro College Fund, New York, NY — operating grant
16,666   Atlanta Heritage Row, Atlanta, GA — operating grant
15,000   Oglethorpe University, Atlanta, GA — operating grant
15,000   Shepherd Spinal Clinic, Atlanta, GA — operating grant

---

Trust for Mutual Understanding

CONTACT
Richard S. Lanier
Director
Trust for Mutual Understanding
280 Madison Ave.
New York, NY 10016
(212) 632-3405

FINANCIAL SUMMARY
Recent Giving: $1,681,051 (fiscal 1992); $1,085,799 (fiscal 1991); $674,077 (fiscal 1990)
Assets: $43,559,975 (fiscal year ending April 30, 1992); $18,221,956 (fiscal 1991); $18,429,088 (fiscal 1990)
Gifts Received: $25,000,000 (fiscal 1992)
Fiscal Note: In 1992, contributions were received from an anonymous contributor c/o Elizabeth J. McCormack, Rockefeller Financial Services, 30 Rockefeller Plaza, New York, NY 10112.
EIN: 13-3212724

CONTRIBUTIONS SUMMARY
Donor(s): The foundation was established in 1984.
Typical Recipients: • *Arts & Humanities:* arts associations, arts festivals, dance, music, opera, performing arts, theater • *Civic & Public Affairs:* business/free enterprise, consumer affairs, environmental affairs, international affairs, law & justice, zoos/botanical gardens • *Education:* colleges & universities, international exchange • *Social Services:* community service organizations, food/clothing distribution, religious welfare
Grant Types: project

Geographic Distribution: national

GIVING OFFICERS
Richard Lanier: trust
Elizabeth J. McCormack: trust *CURR EMPL* assoc: Rockefeller Family & Assocs
Donal C. O'Brien, Jr.: trust

APPLICATION INFORMATION
Initial Approach:
Applicants are requested to submit an initial letter of inquiry. The deadline for submitting proposals is six months prior to the date of implementation of the activity for which the grant is requested.
Restrictions on Giving: The foundation supports exchanges between the United States, the former Soviet Union, and Eastern and Central Europe in the arts and environmental conservation. The foundation does not give grants to individuals, or for capital campaigns, general programs, operating costs, scholarships, or equipment purchases.

OTHER THINGS TO KNOW
Publications: application guidelines

GRANTS ANALYSIS
Total Grants: $1,681,051
Number of Grants: 59
Highest Grant: $150,000
Typical Range: $10,000 to $45,000
Disclosure Period: fiscal year ending April 30, 1992
Note: Recent grants are derived from a fiscal 1992 grants list.

RECENT GRANTS
150,000   National Audubon Society, New York, NY
100,000   Jacobs Pillow Dance Festival, Lee, MA
95,500   American Dance Festival, Durham, NC
88,800   Institute for International Education
75,000   Center for US/USSR Initiatives, San Francisco, CA
65,000   Natural Resources Defense Council, New York, NY
52,500   National Fish and Wildlife Foundation, Washington, DC

45,000 Middlebury College, Middlebury, CT

40,000 Paul Taylor Dance Company

36,000 Charter Seventy Seven, New York, NY

Trust Funds

CONTACT
Albert J. Steiss
President
Trust Funds
100 Broadway, 3rd Fl.
San Francisco, CA 94111
(415) 434-3323

FINANCIAL SUMMARY
Recent Giving: $290,225 (1991); $246,033 (1990); $210,942 (1989)
Assets: $4,048,050 (1991); $3,909,205 (1990); $3,956,252 (1989)
EIN: 94-6062952

CONTRIBUTIONS SUMMARY
Donor(s): Bartley P. Oliver
Typical Recipients: • *Civic & Public Affairs:* rural affairs • *Education:* private education (precollege), religious education • *Health:* pediatric health • *International:* international organizations • *Religion:* churches, religious organizations • *Social Services:* aged, community service organizations, family planning, family services, youth organizations
Grant Types: conference/seminar, emergency, general support, research, scholarship, and seed money
Geographic Distribution: focus on the San Francisco Bay area, CA

GIVING OFFICERS
James T. Healy: cfo, vp, dir
Albert J. Steiss: pres, dir
Rev. James J. Ward: vp, secy, dir

APPLICATION INFORMATION
Initial Approach: The foundation reports that a letter of application is acceptable. Information should include a description of the organization, purpose for which funds are sought, amount requested, recently audited financial statement, and proof of tax-exempt status. Grants are not awarded for buildings, endowments, annual funds, or to organizations

that draw substantial public support. A program policy statement can be obtained by writing Albert J. Steiss.
Restrictions on Giving: Does not support individuals.

OTHER THINGS TO KNOW
Publications: Application Guidelines

GRANTS ANALYSIS
Number of Grants: 61
Highest Grant: $18,000
Typical Range: $3,000 to $10,000
Disclosure Period: 1991

RECENT GRANTS
18,000 Sacramento Life Center, Sacramento, CA

15,000 Americans United for Life, Chicago, IL

15,000 Human Life Center, Steubenville, OH

12,000 Farm Subsidy, Wallace, SD

10,093 College of Notre Dame, Belmont, CA

10,000 Assumption Catholic Church, Northwest Territories, Canada

10,000 Berkeley Crisis Pregnancy Center, Berkeley, CA

10,000 St. Patrick's Seminary, Menlo Park, CA

10,000 St. Peter's School, San Francisco, CA

10,000 Their Turn SUCCEED, Sacramento, CA

Trustcorp, Inc. / Trustcorp Foundation
Assets: $557.0 million
Employees: 6,000
Headquarters: Toledo, OH
SIC Major Group: Transportation Equipment

CONTACT
James E. Lupe
Vice President, Foundations & Endowments
Trustcorp, Inc.
Three Sea Gate
Toledo, OH 43603
(419) 259-8217

FINANCIAL SUMMARY
EIN: 34-6504808

CONTRIBUTIONS SUMMARY
Operating Locations: OH (Toledo)

CORP. OFFICERS
Harry Lebensfeld: *CURR EMPL* ceo: Trustcorp

APPLICATION INFORMATION
Initial Approach: Applications not accepted.

Trustmark National Bank
Gross Operating Earnings: $240.04 million
Employees: 2,000
Parent Company: Trustmark Corp.
Headquarters: Jackson, MS
SIC Major Group: Depository Institutions

CONTACT
Charles Bailey
Executive Vice President
Trustmark National Bank
PO Box 291
Jackson, MS 39205
(601) 354-5863

FINANCIAL SUMMARY
Fiscal Note: Company gives directly. Annual Giving Range: $500,000 to $1 million

CONTRIBUTIONS SUMMARY
Typical Recipients: • *Arts & Humanities:* general • *Civic & Public Affairs:* general • *Education:* general • *Health:* general • *Social Services:* general
Grant Types: general support
Nonmonetary Support Types: cause-related marketing & promotion, donated equipment, in-kind services, loaned employees, and loaned executives
Geographic Distribution: in headquarters and operating communities
Operating Locations: MS (Jackson)

CORP. OFFICERS
David R. Carter: *B* Ashland KY 1951 *ED* Millsaps Coll BA 1972 *CURR EMPL* exec vp, cfo: Trustmark Natl Bank *CORP AFFIL* dir: Furst *NONPR AFFIL* dir: Millsaps Coll; mem: Am Inst CPAs, City Madison Chamber Commerce, Madison Ridgeland Academy Sch Bd, MS Soc CPAs

Frank Day: *CURR EMPL* chmn, ceo: Trustmark Natl Bank

GIVING OFFICERS
Charles Bailey: *CURR EMPL* exec vp: Trustmark Natl Bank

APPLICATION INFORMATION
Initial Approach: *Initial Contact:* brief letter of inquiry *Include Information On:* a description of organization, amount requested, purpose of funds sought, recently audited financial statement, and proof of tax-exempt status *When to Submit:* any time

TRW Corp. / TRW Foundation
Sales: $8.31 billion
Employees: 65,000
Headquarters: Cleveland, OH
SIC Major Group: Electronic & Other Electrical Equipment, Industrial Machinery & Equipment, and Transportation Equipment

CONTACT
Alan F. Senger
Vice President
TRW Fdn.
1900 Richmond Rd.
Cleveland, OH 44124
(216) 291-7160
Note: Laura L. Johnson, Manager, TRW Foundation, also is a contact person.

FINANCIAL SUMMARY
Recent Giving: $7,100,000 (1993 est.); $7,100,000 (1992 approx.); $8,118,005 (1991)
Assets: $19,333,044 (1990); $21,840,572 (1989); $20,976,217 (1988)
Fiscal Note: Figure for 1990 includes $7,952,000 from the foundation.
EIN: 34-6556217

CONTRIBUTIONS SUMMARY
Typical Recipients: • *Arts & Humanities:* community arts, museums/galleries, music, opera, performing arts, theater • *Civic & Public Affairs:* better government, business/free enterprise, consumer affairs, public policy • *Education:* colleges & universities, preschool education, public education (precollege), science/technology education • *Health:* health care cost containment, hospitals • *Science:* scientific organiza-

tions • *Social Services:* child welfare, food/clothing distribution, shelters/homelessness, united funds, youth organizations

Grant Types: capital, department, employee matching gifts, fellowship, general support, operating expenses, professorship, project, research, and scholarship

Geographic Distribution: in plant communities; to a select number of educational institutions with engineering, science, or business administration programs; and to selected national and international organizations

Operating Locations: AL (Huntsville), AZ (Mesa), CA (Berkeley, Los Angeles, Orange, San Bernadino, San Diego, Sunnyvale), CO (Colorado Springs, Denver), DC (Washington), IN (Lafayette), KY (Maysville), MA (Boston), MI (Detroit), MS (Louisville), NY (Union Springs), OH (Cleveland), TN, TX (Houston), UT (Ogden), VA (Fairfax) Note: TRW maintains facilities in nearly 100 U.S. communities.

CORP. OFFICERS

Edsel D. Dunford: *CURR EMPL* pres, coo, dir: TRW Corp

Joseph Tolle Gorman: *B* Rising Sun IN 1937 *ED* Kent St Univ 1959; Yale Univ JD 1962 *CURR EMPL* chmn, ceo: TRW Corp *CORP AFFIL* dir: Aluminum Co Am, Centran Corp, Soc Corp, Soc Natl Bank; mem (adv bd): BP Am *NONPR AFFIL* chmn adv comm: US-Japan Bus Counc; dir: Cleveland Counc World Aff, Cleveland Inst Arts, Cleveland Play House, Cleveland Tomorrow, Mus Arts Assn, Town Hall Cleveland, Univ Circle; mem: Bus Counc, Bus Roundtable, Conf Bd, Japan Import Bd, US Auto Elect Panel, US Chamber Commerce; mem exec comm: Yale Law Sch Assn; trust: Bus Higher Ed Forum, Cleveland Clinic Fdn, Comm Econ Devel, Greater Cleveland Roundtable, Un Way Svcs; trust, mem exec comm: Greater Cleveland Growth Assn; vchmn: US-Canada Automotive Select Panel

GIVING OFFICERS

Laura L. Johnson: mgr

Howard V. Knicely: pres *B* Parkersburg WV 1936 *CURR EMPL* exec vp human rels: TRW Inc *CORP AFFIL* dir:

Morrison Products *NONPR AFFIL* dir: Natl Fdn Study Equal Empl Policy; dir, trust: GMI Engg & Mgmt Inst, IN-ROADS; mem: Am Mgmt Assn, Am Soc Pers Admin, BRT Employee Rels Comm, Bus Roundtable, Conf Bd, Greater Cleveland Roundtable, Human Resources Assn Chicago, Labor Policy Assn, Soc Human Resource Mgmt; trust: Cleveland Ballet

Alan F. Senger: vp

APPLICATION INFORMATION

Initial Approach: *Initial Contact:* one- or two-page letter *Include Information On:* description of the organization (legal name, history, activities, governing board); purpose, amount of request, and listing of sources of financial support; audited financial statement; proof of tax-exempt status; statement of need; budget; benefits to community; additional staffing requirements; and evaluative criteria *When to Submit:* any time *Note:* Organizations currently receiving support should request renewal no later than September 1.

Restrictions on Giving: Grants are not made to groups with unusually high fund-raising expenses; fraternal, political, or labor organizations; religious organizations for sectarian purposes; individuals; or endowments (generally).

OTHER THINGS TO KNOW

Publications: annual report

GRANTS ANALYSIS

Total Grants: $8,118,005
Number of Grants: 272*
Highest Grant: $358,210
Typical Range: $10,000 to $50,000
Disclosure Period: 1991
Note: Number of grants and average grant figures exclude grants under $5,000 which were not itemized on the grants list. Recent grants are derived from a 1991 annual report. Assets are from 1990.

RECENT GRANTS

358,210 United Way, Cleveland, OH

350,000 United Way, Los Angeles, CA

240,000 Cleveland Initiative for Education, Cleveland, OH — payment on a $1.2

million pledge to support innovative educational programs in the Cleveland public schools

150,000 CalTech, Pasadena, CA — payment on $750,000 pledge to support the R. F. Mettler Chair of Engineering and Applied Science

145,000 University of California at Los Angeles, Los Angeles, CA — final payment on $400,000 pledge to support chair in electrical engineering, and graduate minority engineering program

125,000 Western Reserve Historical Society, Cleveland, OH — payment on $475,000 grant to help expand the Crawford Auto Museum

117,500 Musical Arts Association, Cleveland, OH — to provide general support for the Cleveland Orchestra and payment on $400,000 deficit reduction pledge

100,000 California State University, Dominguez Hills, CA — payment on $1 million pledge to support the establishment and continuing operation of the California Academy of Math and Science

100,000 University of Southern California, Pasadena, CA — payment on $1 million pledge to support construction of new Electrical Engineering center

75,000 Stanford University, Stanford, CA — payment on $300,000 pledge to support data communications system

Tsai Foundation, Gerald

CONTACT

Gerald Tsai Foundation
200 Park Avenue, Suite 3100
New York, NY 10166-0105

FINANCIAL SUMMARY

Recent Giving: $738,087 (1990)

Assets: $2,825,205 (1990)

Gifts Received: $490,066 (1990)

Fiscal Note: 1990 contribution received from Gerald Tsai, Jr.

EIN: 13-3513057

GIVING OFFICERS

Susan Kish, Jr.: secy

Cynthia Tsai, Jr.: trust

Gerald Tsai, Jr.: pres *B* Shangai People's Republic of China 1929 *ED* Boston Univ BA 1949; Boston Univ MA *CURR EMPL* dir: Delta Life *CORP AFFIL* dir: First Gibraltar Bank, Rite Aid Corp, Sequa Corp, Universal Matchbox Group Ltd, Zenith Natl Ins Corp *NONPR AFFIL* trust: Boston Univ, NY Univ Med Ctr

Maryalice Wolfe, Jr.: vp

APPLICATION INFORMATION

Initial Approach: The foundation reports no specific application guidelines. Send a brief letter of inquiry, including statement of purpose, amount requested, and proof of tax-exempt status.

GRANTS ANALYSIS

Total Grants: $738,087

Number of Grants: 13

Highest Grant: $550,000

Disclosure Period: 1990

TSC Stores, Inc.

Sales: $216.0 million
Employees: 1,300
Headquarters: Nashville, TN
SIC Major Group: Automotive Dealers & Service Stations and Building Materials & Garden Supplies

CONTACT
Tom Flood
Vice President, Administration
TSC Industries, Inc.
320 Plus Park Blvd.
Nashville, TN 37217
(615) 366-4600

CONTRIBUTIONS SUMMARY
Operating Locations: TN (Nashville)

CORP. OFFICERS
Thomas Hennesy: *CURR EMPL* chmn, ceo: TSC Indus
Joseph Scarlett: *CURR EMPL* pres, coo: TSC Indus

TU Electric Co.

Parent Company: Texas Utilities Co.
Revenue: $4.9 billion
Parent Employees: 10,687
Headquarters: Dallas, TX
SIC Major Group: Electric, Gas & Sanitary Services

CONTACT
Mike McKinney
Manager, Dallas Region Customer Service/Customer Operation
TU Electric Co.
1506 Commerce, Ste. 17 W
Dallas, TX 75201
(214) 812-4600
Note: TU Services, a company division, administers the contribution program.

FINANCIAL SUMMARY
Recent Giving: $750,000 (1991 est.); $1,000,000 (1990 approx.); $1,000,000 (1989 approx.)
Fiscal Note: All contributions are made directly by the company.

CONTRIBUTIONS SUMMARY
Typical Recipients: • *Arts & Humanities:* community arts, museums/galleries, performing arts, public broadcasting, theater • *Civic & Public Affairs:* business/free enterprise, economic development, environmental affairs, professional & trade associations, safety, urban & community affairs, zoos/botanical gardens • *Education:* colleges & universities, community & junior colleges • *Health:* hospitals • *Science:* scientific organizations • *Social Services:* united funds
Grant Types: general support

Geographic Distribution: near headquarters and operating locations
Operating Locations: TX (Dallas, Ft. Worth)

CORP. OFFICERS
Erle Nye: *B* Ft Worth TX 1937 *CURR EMPL* chmn, ceo, dir: TU Electric Co *CORP AFFIL* pres: TU Svcs; pres, dir: TX Utilities Co

GIVING OFFICERS
Terry Griffin: *CURR EMPL* sr vp: TU Svcs
Mike McKinney: *CURR EMPL* mgr: TU Svcs

APPLICATION INFORMATION
Initial Approach: *Initial Contact:* letter *Include Information On:* description of the organization, amount requested, purpose for which funds are sought, recently audited financial statement, proof of tax-exempt status *When to Submit:* any time

GRANTS ANALYSIS
Total Grants: $1,000,000
Disclosure Period: 1990

Tuch Foundation, Michael

CONTACT
Eugene Tuck
President
Michael Tuch Fdn.
122 East 42nd St., No. 2905
New York, NY 10168
(212) 986-9082

FINANCIAL SUMMARY
Recent Giving: $292,932 (1990); $278,816 (1989); $263,082 (1988)
Assets: $5,494,950 (1990); $5,679,651 (1989); $4,893,969 (1988)
Gifts Received: $27,078 (1990); $84,797 (1989); $62,677 (1988)
EIN: 13-6002848

CONTRIBUTIONS SUMMARY
Donor(s): the late Michael Tuch
Typical Recipients: • *Arts & Humanities:* community arts, music, opera, theater • *Civic & Public Affairs:* environmental affairs, zoos/botanical gardens • *Education:* colleges & universities • *Religion:* religious organizations • *Social Services:*

child welfare, community service organizations, disabled, united funds, youth organizations
Grant Types: fellowship, project, and scholarship
Geographic Distribution: focus on New York, NY

GIVING OFFICERS
Martha Rozell: 2nd vp
Jacques J. Stone: secy, treas
Elizabeth Tuck: 1st vp
Eugene Tuck: pres, exec dir

APPLICATION INFORMATION
Initial Approach: Send cover letter and full proposal. There are no deadlines.
Restrictions on Giving: Does not support individuals.

GRANTS ANALYSIS
Number of Grants: 115
Highest Grant: $10,000
Typical Range: $500 to $5,000
Disclosure Period: 1990

RECENT GRANTS
10,000 United Jewish Appeal Federation of Jewish Philanthropies, New York, NY
5,938 Brooklyn Public Library, Brooklyn, NY
5,000 Educational Alliance, New York, NY
5,000 Food for Survival, New York, NY
5,000 International Center for Intergrative Studies, New York, NY
5,000 New York City Food for Survival, New York, NY
5,000 New York City Opera, New York, NY
5,000 St. Matthews and St. Timothys Neighborhood Center, New York, NY
5,000 The Door, New York, NY
5,000 United Jewish Appeal Federation of Jewish Philanthropies, New York, NY

Tucker Anthony, Inc.

Sales: $120.0 million
Employees: 500
Parent Company: John Hancock Mutual Life Insurance Co.
Headquarters: New York, NY
SIC Major Group: Nondepository Institutions and Security & Commodity Brokers

CONTACT
Marge Fetowitz
Director of Personnel
Tucker, Anthony & R.L. Day, Inc.
1 World Finacial Center, 200 Liberty St.
New York, NY 10281
(212) 225-8000

CONTRIBUTIONS SUMMARY
Operating Locations: NY (New York)

CORP. OFFICERS
John H. Goldsmith: *CURR EMPL* pres, ceo: Tucker Anthony

Tucker Charitable Trust, Rose E.

CONTACT
Thomas B. Stoel
Trustee
Rose E. Tucker Charitable Trust
900 Southwest Fifth Avenue, 24th Fl.
Portland, OR 97204
(503) 224-3380

FINANCIAL SUMMARY
Recent Giving: $764,577 (fiscal 1991); $592,060 (fiscal 1990); $587,605 (fiscal 1988)
Assets: $14,777,238 (fiscal year ending June 30, 1991); $14,472,562 (fiscal 1990); $13,350,953 (fiscal 1988)
EIN: 93-6119091

CONTRIBUTIONS SUMMARY
Donor(s): The foundation was established in 1976 by the late Rose E. Tucker and the Max and Rose Tucker Foundation.
Typical Recipients: • *Arts & Humanities:* arts festivals, arts institutes, dance, museums/galleries, music, opera, public broadcasting • *Civic & Public Affairs:* economic development, environmental affairs, ethnic/minority organizations, municipalities, zoos/botanical

gardens • *Education:* colleges & universities, private education (precollege) • *Health:* health funds, hospitals, public health, single-disease health associations • *Religion:* religious organizations • *Social Services:* family planning, food/clothing distribution, legal aid, united funds, youth organizations
Grant Types: capital, general support, operating expenses, project, and scholarship
Geographic Distribution: focus on Oregon, with emphasis on Portland metropolitan area

GIVING OFFICERS

Milo Ormseth: trust *B* Wolf Point MT 1932 *ED* St Olaf Coll BA 1954; Harvard Univ LLB 1959 *CURR EMPL* ptnr: Stoel Rives Boley Fraser & Wyse *NONPR AFFIL* mem: OR Bar Assn
Thomas B. Stoel: trust *CORP AFFIL* secy, dir: Collins Pine Co *PHIL AFFIL* trust: Tucker (Rose E) Charitable Trust

APPLICATION INFORMATION

Initial Approach: The foundation has no formal grant application procedure or application form.
Restrictions on Giving: The foundation does not make grants to individuals, program-related loans or investments, organizations which unfairly descriminate, or efforts to carry on propaganda or to influence legislation. No grants are made for fellowships, operating budgets, or debt reduction.

OTHER THINGS TO KNOW

Publications: application guidelines and annual report

GRANTS ANALYSIS

Total Grants: $764,577
Number of Grants: 164
Highest Grant: $30,000
Typical Range: $500 to $10,000
Disclosure Period: fiscal year ending June 30, 1991
Note: Recent grants are derived from a fiscal 1991 grants list.

RECENT GRANTS

30,000 Lewis and Clark College, Portland, OR — scholarships
29,000 Portland State University, Portland,

OR — honors program and faculty development
25,000 Lewis and Clark College, Portland, OR — student scholarships
25,000 One Thousand Friends of Oregon, Portland, OR — computer system
25,000 Willamette University, Salem, OR
20,000 United Way of Columbia/Willamette, Columbia, OR — 1990 campaign
18,000 Tucker-Maxon Oral School, Portland, OR — current program
15,000 Linfield College, McMinnville, OR — renovation of Riley Hall
15,000 Natural Resources Defense Council, New York, NY — NW energy project
15,000 Oregon Museum of Science and Industry, Portland, OR — capital campaign

Tucker Foundation, Marcia Brady

CONTACT

Luther Tucker, Jr.
President
Marcia Brady Tucker Fdn.
11 South Washington St.
Easton, MD 21601
(410) 822-3155

FINANCIAL SUMMARY

Recent Giving: $440,920 (1990); $455,271 (1989)
Assets: $8,286,295 (1990); $8,354,869 (1989)
Gifts Received: $59,518 (1990); $81,000 (1989)
EIN: 13-6161561

CONTRIBUTIONS SUMMARY

Donor(s): the late Marcia Brady Tucker
Typical Recipients: • *Arts & Humanities:* community arts, dance, history/historic preservation, museums/galleries • *Civic & Public Affairs:* ethnic/minority organizations, zoos/botanical gardens • *Education:* private education (precollege), religious education • *Religion:* churches, missionary activities, religious organizations • *Social Services:* community service organizations, family planning,

united funds, youth organizations
Grant Types: capital, emergency, scholarship, and seed money

GIVING OFFICERS

Marcia T. Boogaard: dir
Anne Draper: dir
Carll Tucker III: treas, dir *ED* Yale Univ 1973 *CURR EMPL* publ, editor: Patent Trader Newspaper *CORP AFFIL* publ, editor: Patent Trader Newspaper
Gay Tucker: dir
Rev. Luther Tucker: dir
Luther Tucker, Jr.: pres, dir
Nicholas Tucker: dir
Stephanie Tucker: dir
Toinette Tucker: chmn, dir

APPLICATION INFORMATION

Initial Approach: Send brief letter of inquiry describing program. There are no deadlines.
Restrictions on Giving: Does not support individuals.

GRANTS ANALYSIS

Number of Grants: 36
Highest Grant: $30,000
Typical Range: $150 to $5,000
Disclosure Period: 1990

RECENT GRANTS

30,000 Phoenix House
25,000 Episcopal Divinity School
25,000 Planned Parenthood
25,000 St. Pauls School
20,000 Seven Hills Schools, Cincinnati, OH
20,000 St. Bartholomews Church, New York, NY
16,700 Children's Hospital Medical Center, Boston, MA
15,000 Central Park Conservancy, New York, NY
15,000 Katonah Art Gallery, Katonah, NY
10,000 Covenant House

Tucson Electric Power Co.

Sales: $589.29 million
Employees: 1,056
Headquarters: Tucson, AZ
SIC Major Group: Electric, Gas & Sanitary Services

CONTACT

Betsy Bolding
Director, Consumer and Community Affairs
Tucson Electric Power Co.
PO Box 711
Tucson, AZ 85702
(602) 571-4000

FINANCIAL SUMMARY

Recent Giving: $290,000 (1993); $368,000 (1991)
Fiscal Note: Company gives directly.

CONTRIBUTIONS SUMMARY

Typical Recipients: • *Arts & Humanities:* general • *Civic & Public Affairs:* general • *Education:* general • *Health:* general • *Social Services:* general, youth organizations
Grant Types: capital and general support
Nonmonetary Support Types: donated equipment
Note: Donated equipment is in the form of used power poles and used office equipment.
Geographic Distribution: company service area
Operating Locations: AZ (Tucson)

CORP. OFFICERS

Ira R. Adler: *CURR EMPL* sr vp, cfo: Tucson Electric Power Co
Charles E. Bayless: *B* Dunbar WV 1942 *ED* WV Inst Tech BSEE 1968; WV Univ MSEE 1972; WV Univ JD 1972; Univ MI MBA 1977 *CURR EMPL* chmn, pres, ceo, dir: Tucson Electric Power Co *CORP AFFIL* fin vp: Pub Svc NH *NONPR AFFIL* dir: Un Way Greater Manchester; exec bd: Boy Scouts Am Daniel Webster Council; mem: Am Bar Assn, Boy Scouts Am Philmont Ranch Comm Natl Counc, MI Bar Assn, WV Bar Assn; mem fin comm: Edison Electric Inst

GIVING OFFICERS

Betsy Bolding: *CURR EMPL* dir commun and consumer aff: Tucson Electric Power Co

APPLICATION INFORMATION

Initial Approach: *Initial Contact:* brief letter of inquiry *Include Information On:* description of the organization, amount requested, purpose of funds sought, recently audited financial statements, and proof of tax-exempt status *When to Submit:* by July 1 of year prior

       Directory of Corporate and Foundation Givers, 1994

to the year for which funds are being requested

Restrictions on Giving: Does not support individuals, religious organizations for sectarian purposes, political or lobbying groups, or unions.

Tucson Osteopathic Medical Foundation

CONTACT
Tucson Osteopathic Medical Foundation
4280 North Campbell Avenue, Suite 200
Tucson, AZ 85718
(602) 299-4545

FINANCIAL SUMMARY
Recent Giving: $290,561 (fiscal 1991); $43,863 (fiscal 1990)
Assets: $9,354,261 (fiscal year ending June 30, 1991); $8,336,757 (fiscal 1990)
Gifts Received: $1,234,819 (fiscal 1991)
Fiscal Note: Fiscal 1991 contribution received from Tucson Hospital Liquidating Corporation. Fiscal 1991 high grant and number of grants figures do not include grants to individuals.
EIN: 74-2449503

GRANTS ANALYSIS
Total Grants: $290,561
Highest Grant: $198,211
Disclosure Period: fiscal year ending June 30, 1991

Tull Charitable Foundation

CONTACT
Barbara Cleveland
Executive Director
Tull Charitable Foundation
230 Peachtree St., Ste. 1502
Atlanta, GA 30303
(404) 659-7079

FINANCIAL SUMMARY
Recent Giving: $2,085,000 (1992 approx.); $2,101,500 (1991); $2,002,900 (1990)
Assets: $43,800,000 (1992 est.); $35,000,000 (1991 approx.); $34,002,796 (1990); $31,776,617 (1989)
Gifts Received: $2,196,748 (1990); $22,111,070 (1987)
Fiscal Note: In 1990, the foundation received $2,196,748 from the Estate of John H. Tull.

EIN: 58-1687028

CONTRIBUTIONS SUMMARY
Donor(s): In 1953, Joseph McKeon Tull and the J. M. Tull Metal Company established the J. M. Tull Foundation to enable Mr. Tull and the company to respond to charitable and community needs. The Tull Charitable Foundation was established in 1984 to broaden the operating authority of the original foundation. It was at this time that the company was sold and the relationship between the company and the foundation was ended.

Joseph McKeon Tull was a successful businessman, civic leader, and a strong supporter of Christian education. A native of North Carolina, he moved to Atlanta early in his business career and established an industrial supply and metal distribution organization in 1914. The company operated with its facilities in Atlanta from its beginnings, but through the years expanded into the industrial centers of the Southeast. Mr. Tull held the firm belief that each citizen should feel a duty to financially support, to the appropriate extent, charitable and civic endeavors.

Both the Tull Charitable Foundation and the J. M. Tull Foundation continue to carry on the commitment to community service begun by Mr. Tull. They are governed by the same board of trustees that makes all decisions regarding grant requests.

Typical Recipients: • *Arts & Humanities:* arts centers, libraries, museums/galleries, theater, visual arts • *Civic & Public Affairs:* philanthropic organizations, zoos/botanical gardens • *Education:* colleges & universities, education associations, private education (precollege), public education (precollege) • *Health:* geriatric health, health organizations, medical research, pediatric health, single-disease health associations • *Social Services:* aged, community service organizations, disabled, family services, food/clothing distribution, shelters/homelessness, youth organizations

Grant Types: capital, endowment, scholarship, and seed money

Geographic Distribution: restricted to Georgia

GIVING OFFICERS
Barbara Cleveland: exec dir
John McIntyre: trust *B* Lowndes GA 1930 *ED* Emory Univ BBA 1951; Stanford Univ mgmt program 1966 *CORP AFFIL* dir: MasterCard Intl *NONPR AFFIL* dir: Atlanta Exec Svcs Corps, Bus Counc GA, City Atlanta, Fulton County Recreation Authority, GA Chamber Commerce, Kaiser Fdn Health Plan GA; mem: Assn Reserve City Bankers; mem bd sponsors: Atlanta Symphony Orchestra; trust: Emory Univ, Lovett Sch
Larry I. Prince: trust *CURR EMPL* chmn, ceo: Genuine Parts Co
Frank Skinner: trust
George E. Smith: chmn, trust *B* Athens GA 1916 *ED* GA St Univ 1939 *CORP AFFIL* dir: Am Heritage Life Ins Co, Haverty Furniture Cos, Laclede Steel Co, Trust Co GA
Walter J. Thomas: treas/secy, trust
John B. Zellars: trust *B* Hartwell GA 1924 *ED* Emory Univ 1950 *CURR EMPL* chmn: GA Fed Bank *CORP AFFIL* vchmn: Fed Home Loan Bank Atlanta

APPLICATION INFORMATION
Initial Approach:
Prior to submitting a full proposal, applicants should contact the foundation via a concise letter-of-intent or a brief visit to the office.
Initial letters should include a brief description of the applicant organization and project for which funding is being sought, total cost of the project and amount being requested, and a copy of the organization's 501(c)(3) certification. If the foundation determines that further consideration is to be given to the proposed project, additional information will be requested from the applicant, as needed.
A full proposal will generally include the name and address of the organization; brief history and statement of purpose; overview of programs, services, and people served; description of facilities and staff; list of directors; current operating budget; and a recent financial audit. Information on the

proposed project should include a statement on why the project is needed and who will benefit; brief overview of the project with objectives, plans, staffing, and timetable; budget; amount of support requested; list of other potential sources of support, both current and future; and, as appropriate, demonstration of community support.
Proposals must be received by the first day of the month in which quarterly meetings occur: January 1, April 1, July 1, or October 1.
The board of trustees meets quarterly to consider grant proposals. Each applicant will be notified in writing shortly after a decision on its proposal has been made. Grant recipients will be requested to submit a brief written report periodically and at the completion of the project describing what has been accomplished with funds granted.
Restrictions on Giving: The foundation does not make grants to individuals; projects of religious organizations that primarily benefit their own members or adherents; or retire accumulated debt; or for tickets to charitable events or dinners; scientific research; conferences and seminars; legislative lobbying or other political purposes; or to sponsor specific events or productions. The foundation does not make loans.

OTHER THINGS TO KNOW
Publications: application policies and guidelines

GRANTS ANALYSIS
Total Grants: $2,101,500
Number of Grants: 48
Highest Grant: $150,000
Typical Range: $25,000 to $50,000
Disclosure Period: 1991
Note: Recent grants are derived from a 1990 grants list.

RECENT GRANTS
150,000 Georgia State University, Atlanta, GA — capital grant
100,000 Atlanta Urban League, Atlanta, GA — capital grant
100,000 Morris Brown College, Atlanta, GA — capital grant
75,000 Scottish Rite Children's Medical Center Foundation, At-

lanta, GA — capital grant

62,500 University of Georgia, Athens, GA — capital campaign

60,000 Hillside, Atlanta, GA — capital grant

50,000 Alliance Theater Company, Atlanta, GA — capital grant

50,000 American Red Cross Metro Atlanta Chapter, Atlanta, GA — capital grant

50,000 Atlanta Historical Society, Atlanta, GA — capital grant

50,000 Atlanta International School, Atlanta, GA — capital grant

Tultex Corp.

Sales: $315.2 million
Employees: 6,405
Headquarters: Martinsville, VA
SIC Major Group: Apparel & Accessory Stores, Nondepository Institutions, and Textile Mill Products

CONTACT

Ron Cox
Personnel Director
Tultex Corp.
PO Box 5191
Martinsville, VA 24115
(703) 632-2961

CONTRIBUTIONS SUMMARY

Nonmonetary Support Types: donated products

Operating Locations: VA (Martinsville)

CORP. OFFICERS

Charles W. Davies: *CURR EMPL* pres, coo: Tultex Corp

John M. Franck: *CURR EMPL* chmn, ceo: Tultex Corp

William F. Franck: *CURR EMPL* chmn emeritus: Tultex Corp

Tuohy Foundation, Alice Tweed

CONTACT

Harris W. Seed
President
Alice Tweed Tuohy Fdn.
PO Box 2578
Santa Barbara, CA 93101
(805) 963-0675

FINANCIAL SUMMARY

Recent Giving: $483,372 (fiscal 1992); $516,152 (fiscal 1991); $391,165 (fiscal 1989)

Assets: $11,600,231 (fiscal year ending June 30, 1992); $11,298,526 (fiscal 1991); $11,688,202 (fiscal 1989)

EIN: 95-6036471

CONTRIBUTIONS SUMMARY

Donor(s): the late Alice Tweed Tuohy

Typical Recipients: • *Arts & Humanities:* history/historic preservation, museums/galleries, public broadcasting, theater • *Education:* colleges & universities, education funds, private education (precollege), public education (precollege), student aid • *Health:* medical research, single-disease health associations • *Social Services:* child welfare, family planning, family services, united funds, youth organizations

Grant Types: capital, scholarship, and seed money

Geographic Distribution: limited to the Santa Barbara, CA, area

GIVING OFFICERS

Lorenzo Dall'Armi, Jr.: dir
Paul W. Hartloff, Jr.: dir
John R. Mackall: dir
Harris Waller Seed: pres, dir *B* La Ceiba Honduras 1927 *ED* Univ CA 1949; Univ CA 1952 *CURR EMPL* ptnr: Seed Mackall Nida & Cole *CORP AFFIL* chmn: La Cumbre Savings Bank; dir: GRC Intl; ptnr: Seed Mackall Nida & Cole
Eleanor Van Cott: exec vp, secy, treas

APPLICATION INFORMATION

Initial Approach: Send brief letter of inquiry describing program or project.
Restrictions on Giving: Does not support individuals or provide loans.

OTHER THINGS TO KNOW

Publications: Annual Report (including application guidelines)

GRANTS ANALYSIS

Number of Grants: 35
Highest Grant: $50,000
Typical Range: $500 to $30,000
Disclosure Period: fiscal year ending June 30, 1992

RECENT GRANTS

50,000 Claremont McKenna College, Claremont, CA

49,827 University of Minnesota, Minneapolis, MN

40,000 Junior Statesman Foundation, Santa Barbara, CA

38,000 Westmont College, Santa Barbara, CA

30,000 Lobero Theater Foundation, Santa Barbara, CA

25,000 Las Positas Park Foundation, Santa Barbara, CA

25,000 Santa Barbara New House, Santa Barbara, CA

22,894 Santa Barbara Scholarship Foundation, Santa Barbara, CA

20,000 Trust for Historic Preservation, Santa Barbara, CA

Tupancy-Harris Foundation of 1986

CONTACT

Robert N. Karelitz
Vice President, Fiduciary Trust Co.
Tupancy-Harris Fdn of 1986
175 Federal St.
Boston, MA 02110
(617) 482-5270

FINANCIAL SUMMARY

Recent Giving: $439,995 (1991); $435,344 (1990); $669,632 (1989)

Assets: $11,771,416 (1991); $9,333,883 (1990); $193,661 (1989)

Gifts Received: $910,740 (1991); $8,215,374 (1990); $670,300 (1989)

Fiscal Note: In 1991, contributions were received from the estate of Oswald A. Tupancy.

EIN: 04-6547989

CONTRIBUTIONS SUMMARY

Donor(s): the late Oswald A. Tupancy

Typical Recipients: • *Arts & Humanities:* history/historic preservation, music, theater • *Civic & Public Affairs:* environmental affairs • *Education:* colleges & universities, community & junior colleges • *Health:* hospices, hospitals, single-disease health associations • *Social Services:* child welfare, youth organizations

Grant Types: general support

Geographic Distribution: focus on Nantucket, MA

GIVING OFFICERS

Fiduciary Trust Company: trust

APPLICATION INFORMATION

Initial Approach: Send brief letter of inquiry describing program or project. There are no deadlines.

GRANTS ANALYSIS

Number of Grants: 22
Highest Grant: $193,087
Typical Range: $1,000 to $3,000
Disclosure Period: 1991

RECENT GRANTS

193,087 Nantucket Conservation Foundation, Nantucket, MA

100,909 Nantucket Historical Association, Nantucket, MA

38,000 Nantucket College Hospital, Nantucket, MA

22,000 Boys and Girls Club, Nantucket, MA

18,000 A Safe Place, Nantucket, MA

18,000 Small Friends, Nantucket, MA

12,000 Nantucket AIDS Network, Nantucket, MA

10,000 Cape Cod Community College, Nantucket, MA

10,000 Nantucket Marra Mitchell Association, Nantucket, MA

6,000 Hospice Care of Nantucket, Nantucket, MA

Turner Broadcasting System

Sales: $1.48 billion
Employees: 4,370
Headquarters: Atlanta, GA
SIC Major Group: Amusement
& Recreation Services,
Communications, Motion
Pictures, and Real Estate

CONTACT
William Shaw
Vice President, Personnel
Turner Broadcasting System
One CNN Center, Ste. 1412
North Tower, PO Box 105366
Atlanta, GA 30348-5366
(404) 827-1700

CONTRIBUTIONS SUMMARY
Operating Locations: GA (Atlanta)

CORP. OFFICERS
William C. Bartholomay:
CURR EMPL vchmn: Turner
Broadcasting Sys
Ted Turner: *B* Cincinnati OH
1938 *ED* Brown Univ *CURR
EMPL* chmn, pres: Turner
Broadcasting Sys *CORP AFFIL*
ltd ptnr: Atlanta Hawks; owner:
Atlanta Braves; vp: Pantasote
NONPR AFFIL dir: Greater Yellowstone Coalition, Martin Luther King Ctr, Natl Cable TV
Assn; mem: Cousteau Soc,
NAACP Atlanta, Natl Audubon
Soc

Turner Charitable Foundation

CONTACT
Eyvonne Moser
Assistant Secretary
Turner Charitable Fdn.
811 Rusk, Ste. 205
Houston, TX 77002
(713) 237-1117

FINANCIAL SUMMARY
Recent Giving: $503,540 (fiscal 1991); $497,700 (fiscal 1990); $426,100 (fiscal 1989)
Assets: $18,709,720 (fiscal year ending February 28, 1991); $15,410,682 (fiscal 1990); $14,008,092 (fiscal 1989)
EIN: 74-1460482

CONTRIBUTIONS SUMMARY
Donor(s): The foundation was incorporated in 1956 by the late Isla Carroll Turner and the late P. E. Turner.
Typical Recipients: • *Arts & Humanities:* dance, history/historic preservation, museums/galleries, opera, public broadcasting, theater • *Civic & Public Affairs:* philanthropic organizations, zoos/botanical gardens • *Education:* colleges & universities, private education (precollege) • *Health:* hospices, hospitals, medical research, mental health, single-disease health associations • *Religion:* churches, religious organizations • *Social Services:* disabled, food/clothing distribution, homes, recreation & athletics
Grant Types: capital, conference/seminar, emergency, endowment, fellowship, general support, matching, multi-year/continuing support, operating expenses, professorship, project, research, scholarship, and seed money
Geographic Distribution: focus on Texas

GIVING OFFICERS
Thomas E. Berry: asst secy
Chaille W. Hawkins: trust
Christiana R. McConn: trust
Eyvonne Moser: asst secy, asst treas
Isla C. Reckling: asst secy
James S. Reckling: trust
T. R. Reckling III: pres, trust
Thomas R. Reckling IV: trust
Clyde J. Verheyden: secy, trust
Bert F. Winston, Jr.: vp, trust

APPLICATION INFORMATION
Initial Approach:
The foundation requests applications be made in writing. The application must include a copy of IRS code section 501(c)(3) exemption letter. The deadline for submitting applications is March 1. The board meets in April.
Restrictions on Giving: The foundation makes grants only to public charities. The foundation does not make grants to individuals.

GRANTS ANALYSIS
Total Grants: $503,540
Number of Grants: 58
Highest Grant: $75,000
Typical Range: $1,000 to $10,000
Disclosure Period: fiscal year ending February 28, 1991
Note: Recent grants are derived from a fiscal 1991 grants list.

RECENT GRANTS
75,000 Tennis A.C.E., Ingram, Ingram, TX
50,000 Holly Hall Building Fund, Houston, TX
50,000 Houston Grand Opera, Houston, TX
40,000 Hill Country Youth Ranch, Ingram, TX — campground headquarters
34,000 Center for the Retarded, Houston, TX
23,000 Good Samaritan Foundation, Houston, TX — nursing scholarships
15,000 St. Joseph Foundation, Houston, TX
10,000 DePelchin Children's Center, Houston, TX
10,000 Houston Ballet Foundation, Houston, TX
10,000 Institute of Religion, Houston, TX

Turner Charitable Foundation, Harry and Violet

CONTACT
Bernice Jones
Harry and Violet Turner Charitable Foundation
2130 Oak Knoll
Springfield, OH 45504-1035

FINANCIAL SUMMARY
Recent Giving: $56,966 (1991); $30,000 (1990)
Assets: $389,659 (1991); $291,751 (1990)
Gifts Received: $50,000 (1991)
Fiscal Note: 1991 contribution received from Harry Turner.
EIN: 31-1224184

GIVING OFFICERS
Sara Jane Turner Landers: trust
Judith Ann Turner Lorman: trust
Harry M. Turner: trust

APPLICATION INFORMATION
Initial Approach: The foundation reports it only makes contributions to preselected organizations and does not accept unsolicited requests for funds.

GRANTS ANALYSIS
Total Grants: $56,966
Highest Grant: $43,966
Disclosure Period: 1991

Turner Charitable Trust, Courtney S.

CONTACT
David P. Ross, Sr.
Vice President
Courtney S. Turner Charitable Trust
c/o Boatmen's First National Bank Trust Div.
14 West Tenth St.
Kansas City, MO 64105
(816) 691-7481

FINANCIAL SUMMARY
Recent Giving: $896,500 (1990); $1,079,776 (1989)
Assets: $15,782,009 (1990); $15,869,065 (1989)
EIN: 43-6316904

CONTRIBUTIONS SUMMARY
Donor(s): The foundation was established in 1986 by Courtney S. Turner.
Typical Recipients: • *Arts & Humanities:* museums/galleries, music, public broadcasting, theater • *Education:* colleges & universities • *Health:* public health • *Social Services:* drugs & alcohol, legal aid, youth organizations
Grant Types: capital, matching, project, and seed money
Geographic Distribution: focus on Kansas and Missouri

GIVING OFFICERS
Daniel C. Weary: trust

APPLICATION INFORMATION
Initial Approach:
Potential applicants should contact David Ross directly by phone before submitting applications.
The foundation requests applicants submit a letter no longer than three pages with the appropriate attachments.
The foundation has no deadline for submitting proposals.

GRANTS ANALYSIS
Total Grants: $896,500
Number of Grants: 24
Highest Grant: $174,840
Typical Range: $5,000 to $35,000
Disclosure Period: 1990
Note: Average grant figure does not include the highest grant of $174,840. Recent grants are derived from a 1990 grants list.

RECENT GRANTS

174,840 Benedictine College, Atchison, KS — final payment to rebuild their traditional student base

135,500 Nelson Atkins Museum of Art, Kansas City, MO — to underwrite 1990 Spring Impressionism Exhibit

100,000 University of Missouri at Kansas City, Kansas City, MO — to acquire computers and support equipment at Block Business School

50,000 Kansas University Endowment Association, Lawrence, KS — support Campaign Kansas Medical Center Program

50,000 KCPT Channel 19, Kansas City, MO — capital campaign

42,160 Benedictine College, Atchison, KS — partial payment to rebuild their traditional student base

35,000 Friends of Chamber Music, Kansas City, MO — underwrite their 1991 piano recital series

35,000 Mid Continent Council of Girl Scouts, Kansas City, MO — capital campaign

30,000 Crittenton Center, Kansas City, MO

30,000 Missouri Repertory Theatre, Kansas City, MO

Turner Construction Co. / Turner Construction Co. Foundation

Sales: $668.0 million
Employees: 3,000
Parent Company: Turner Corp.
Headquarters: New York, NY
SIC Major Group: Engineering & Management Services, General Building Contractors, and Heavy Construction Except Building Construction

CONTACT
Allen H. Wahlberg
President & Treasurer
Turner Construction Co. Fdn
375 Hudson St.
New York, NY 10014
(212) 229-6000

FINANCIAL SUMMARY
Assets: $895 (1991); $1,024 (1990)
EIN: 13-3072570

CONTRIBUTIONS SUMMARY
Operating Locations: CA (Los Angeles), CO (Denver), IL (Chicago), MA (Boston), MI (Detroit), NY (New York), VA (Arlington)
Note: List includes plant locations.

CORP. OFFICERS
Harold J. Parmelee: *CURR EMPL* pres, ceo: Turner Construction Co

GIVING OFFICERS
R Berk: vp, dir
J. V. VumbacCo.: secy, dir
Allen H. Wahlberg: pres, treas, dir *CURR EMPL* sr vp, cfo: Turner Corp

OTHER THINGS TO KNOW
No grants were provided in 1990.

Turner Corp.
Revenue: $2.67 billion
Employees: 2,806
Headquarters: New York, NY
SIC Major Group: Engineering & Management Services, General Building Contractors, Holding & Other Investment Offices, and Real Estate

CONTACT
Barbara McAllister
Marketing Manager
Turner Corp.
375 Hudson St.
New York, NY 10014
(212) 229-6000

CONTRIBUTIONS SUMMARY
Company sponsors employee matching gift program; also supports community organizations.
Typical Recipients: • *Arts & Humanities:* general • *Civic & Public Affairs:* general • *Educa-tion:* general • *Health:* general • *Social Services:* general
Grant Types: matching
Geographic Distribution: primarily headquarters area
Operating Locations: AL (Decatur), CA (Los Angeles, San Francisco), CO (Denver), FL (Miami, Tampa, Winter Park), GA (Atlanta), IL (Chicago), MA (Boston), MI (Detroit), NC (Charlotte), NY (New York), OH (Cincinnati, Cleveland, Columbus), PA (Philadelphia, Pittsburgh), TX (Houston, Temple), VA (Arlington), WA (Seattle)

CORP. OFFICERS
A.T. McNeil: *CURR EMPL* chmn, pres, ceo, dir: Turner Corp
Allen H. Wahlberg: *CURR EMPL* sr vp, cfo: Turner Corp

APPLICATION INFORMATION
Initial Approach: Send brief letter of inquiry. There are no deadlines.

Turner Foundation

CONTACT
Edward Harris
Treasurer
Turner Foundation
100 International Boulevard, Suite 300
Atlanta, GA 30303

FINANCIAL SUMMARY
Recent Giving: $0 (1990)
Assets: $11,250,000 (1990)
Gifts Received: $12,125,000 (1990)
Fiscal Note: 1990 contribution received from R.E. Turner III.
EIN: 58-1924590

GIVING OFFICERS
Tench C. Coxe: secy
Jane Fonda: dir
Ed Harris: treas
Laura Lee Turner: dir
R.E. III Turner: pres
Reed Beauregard Turner: dir
Rhett Lee Turner: dir
Sarah Jean Turner: dir

GRANTS ANALYSIS
Total Grants: $0
Disclosure Period: 1990

Turner Fund, Ruth

CONTACT
Gloria S. Neuwirth
Secretary
Ruth Turner Fund
360 Lexington Ave.
New York, NY 10017-6502

FINANCIAL SUMMARY
Recent Giving: $172,000 (1991); $172,000 (1990); $72,500 (1989)
Assets: $4,172,099 (1990); $4,200,504 (1989)
Gifts Received: $26,120 (1989)
EIN: 23-7240889

CONTRIBUTIONS SUMMARY
Donor(s): the late RuthTurner
Typical Recipients: • *Health:* health organizations, hospitals, medical research, nursing services, pediatric health • *Religion:* religious organizations • *Social Services:* animal protection, child welfare, community service organizations, disabled, united funds, youth organizations
Grant Types: research and scholarship
Geographic Distribution: focus on New York, NY

GIVING OFFICERS
Daniel L. Hartman: vp
William J. Kridel: pres
Gloria S. Neuwirth: secy

APPLICATION INFORMATION
Initial Approach: Send brief letter of inquiry describing program. There are no deadlines.
Restrictions on Giving: Does not support individuals.

GRANTS ANALYSIS
Number of Grants: 13
Highest Grant: $25,000
Typical Range: $2,700 to $6,600
Disclosure Period: 1990

RECENT GRANTS
25,000 American Foundation for AIDS Research, New York, NY
20,000 New York Association for the Blind, New York, NY
20,000 Recording for the Blind, New York, NY
17,000 Community Service Society, New York, NY
15,000 Catholic Charities, New York, NY

15,000 Federation of Jewish Philanthropies of New York, New York, NY

15,000 Mount Sinai Medical Center, New York, NY

10,000 Children's Immunology Research Fund, New York, NY

10,000 Mount Sinai Medical Center, New York, NY

8,000 Society for the Prevention of Cruelty to Animals, New York, NY

Turrell Fund

CONTACT
E. Belvin Williams
Executive Director
Turrell Fund
111 Northfield Ave.
West Orange, NJ 07052
(201) 325-5108

FINANCIAL SUMMARY
Recent Giving: $4,385,953 (1990); $4,030,654 (1989); $3,925,854 (1988)
Assets: $82,751,580 (1990); $87,033,575 (1989); $73,668,719 (1988)
Gifts Received: $4,575 (1989)
EIN: 22-1551936

CONTRIBUTIONS SUMMARY
Donor(s): The Turrell Fund was established in 1935 by Herbert and Margaret Turrell. Mr. Turrell was associated with Parke, Davis and Co. and American Home Products. The foundation has some of its assets in the latter company. Since its inception, the Turrell Fund has aided children and youth, a major interest of the Turrells during their lifetimes. Although the foundation originally was empowered to make grants to organizations in New York, New Jersey, and Vermont, the trustees have phased out giving in New York.
Typical Recipients: • *Arts & Humanities:* music • *Education:* career/vocational education, colleges & universities, education associations, education funds, elementary education, literacy, minority education, preschool education, private education (precollege), special education, student aid • *Social Services:* child welfare, community centers, com-

munity service organizations, counseling, day care, family services, food/clothing distribution, recreation & athletics, volunteer services, youth organizations
Grant Types: capital, challenge, general support, project, scholarship, and seed money
Geographic Distribution: New Jersey and Vermont

GIVING OFFICERS
Paul J. Christiansen: trust *B* Orange NJ 1906 *ED* Rutgers Univ LLB 1927 *CURR EMPL* ptnr: Christiansen Jube & Keegan
Ann G. Dinse: trust
Carl Gustaf Fjellman: trust *B* Cedar Rapids IA 1919 *ED* Augustana Coll BA 1941; Augustana Theological Seminary BD 1945; Drew Univ PhD 1955 *NONPR AFFIL* mem faculty: Upsala Coll
Robert H. Grasmere: pres, trust *CURR EMPL* mayor: Maplewood NJ
Frank Joseph Hoenemeyer: chmn, trust
Richard Ralston Hough: trust *B* Trenton NJ 1917 *ED* Princeton Univ BSE 1939; Princeton Univ BSEE 1940 *CORP AFFIL* dir: Alleghany Corp, Cyclops Indus, Dravo Corp, Midlantic Banks, Midlantic Natl Bank, Primerica Corp *NONPR AFFIL* fellow: IEEE; mem: Natl Academy Engring, Phi Beta Kappa, Princeton Engring Assn, Sigma Xi, Tau Beta Pi, Telephone Pioneers Am; trust: Morris Jr Mus, Morristown Meml Hosp, Morristown Presbyterian Church, Wilson Coll; charter trust: Princeton Univ; dir: Un Way Tri-State
Frank A. Hutson, Jr.: trust
S. Whitney Landon: trust *B* Burlington VT 1896 *ED* Princeton Univ BS 1917; Rutgers Univ LLB 1925; Rutgers Univ LLM 1926
Anne Marie Mills: treas
Larry Prendergast: trust
Vivian B. Shapiro: trust
E. Belvin Williams: exec dir, secy, trust *ED* Denver Univ; Columbia Univ MA; Columbia Univ MS; Columbia Univ PhD

APPLICATION INFORMATION
Initial Approach: Organizations that meet the foundation's geographic requirements and provide direct services for children and youth should submit a brief letter on

offical letterhead to the executive director.

The letter should describe the project, include a project budget, and be sent on the organization's letterhead, signed by an official on behalf of the governing board. If the request meets eligibility requirements, a more complete proposal will be requested. Information should include background on the organization, identification of board members, and staff qualifications; financial report, current budget, and project costs; copy of IRS letter granting tax exemption; and a description of project, its purpose, and its relation to other activities of the organization.

The fall deadline is September 1, and the spring deadline is February 1. For organizations that have previously received grants from the Turrell Fund, the deadlines are October 1 and March 1.

Proposals are screened by the grant committee, which then recommends selected proposals to the board of trustees for consideration and action. Evaluative criteria include evidence of need, organizational resources to meet the need, evidence of local support, prospects for future support, and plans for evaluation of the project. A visit by a fund representative may precede the final decision. Notice of the board's decision is sent out in late December and in late May. Progress reports and a final accounting of the use of funds is required of all grant recipients.
Restrictions on Giving: The fund does not encourage requests for support of cultural activities; and will not fund advocacy, research, endowment funds, grants to individuals, and most hospital and health care services.

OTHER THINGS TO KNOW
Publications: annual report

GRANTS ANALYSIS
Total Grants: $4,385,953
Number of Grants: 258
Highest Grant: $337,139
Typical Range: $10,000 to $25,000
Disclosure Period: 1990
Note: Recent grants are derived from a 1990 grants list.

RECENT GRANTS
337,139 Turrell Fund Scholarship Program — scholarships

75,000 Salvation Army, Newark, NJ — children's and youth services

75,000 YMCA-Oranges, Maplewood, West Essex and Sussex county, New Jersey, South Orange, NJ

65,000 Boys and Girls Clubs of Newark, Newark, NJ — general program

65,000 Newark Renaissance House, Newark, NJ — residential youth program

62,500 University of Medicine and Dentistry of New Jersey, Newark, NJ — special projects

58,500 Educational Information and Resource Center, Sewell, NJ — training program

50,000 Blair Academy, Blairstown, NJ — special

50,000 St. Johnsbury Academy, St. Johnsbury, VT — special

48,000 Princeton Center for Leadership Training, Princeton, NJ — Jersey City peer leadership project

Twentieth Century Insurance Co.
Revenue: $740.25 million
Employees: 1,800
Headquarters: Woodland Hills, CA
SIC Major Group: Holding & Other Investment Offices and Insurance Carriers

CONTACT
Shelly Boyd
Employee Relations Specialist
Twentieth Century Insurance Co.
6301 Owensmouth Ave.
Woodland Hills, CA 91367
(818) 704-3756

CONTRIBUTIONS SUMMARY
Company sponsors employee matching gift program; also supports community organizations.
Typical Recipients: • *Arts & Humanities:* general • *Civic & Public Affairs:* general • *Educa-*

tion: general • *Health:* general • *Social Services:* general
Grant Types: matching
Geographic Distribution: primarily headquarters area
Operating Locations: CA (Woodland Hills)

APPLICATION INFORMATION

Initial Approach: Send brief letter of inquiry. There are no deadlines.

21st Century Foods

Headquarters: Jamaica Plain, MA
SIC Major Group: Food & Kindred Products

CONTACT

Rudy Canale
Owner
21st Century Foods
30 A Germania St.
Jamaica Plain, MA 02130
(617) 522-7595

CONTRIBUTIONS SUMMARY

Company provides limited support to nonprofit organizations.
Operating Locations: MA (Jamaica Plain)

CORP. OFFICERS

Rudy Canale: *CURR EMPL* owner: 21st Century Foods

---

21 International Holdings / KIHI/21 International Holding Foundation

Sales: $1.93 billion
Employees: 19,600
Headquarters: New York, NY

CONTACT

Judith G. Hershon
KIHI/21 International Holding Fdn.
153 E 53rd St., Ste. 5900
New York, NY 10022
(212) 230-0400
Note: Foundation does not accept unsolicited requests for funds.

FINANCIAL SUMMARY

Recent Giving: $500,000 (1992 approx.); $646,017 (1991); $1,087,150 (1990)
Assets: $31,806 (1991); $116,160 (1988)
Fiscal Note: Company gives through foundation only.
EIN: 22-2518739

CONTRIBUTIONS SUMMARY

Typical Recipients: • *Arts & Humanities:* arts institutes, dance, ethnic arts, history/historic preservation, museums/galleries • *Civic & Public Affairs:* civil rights, ethnic/minority organizations, international affairs • *Education:* colleges & universities, private education (precollege), religious education • *Health:* hospitals, medical research, single-disease health associations • *Social Services:* animal protection, disabled, emergency relief, food/clothing distribution, refugee assistance, united funds, youth organizations
Grant Types: general support
Geographic Distribution: primarily in New York City area
Operating Locations: NY (New York)

CORP. OFFICERS

Marshall S. Cogan: *B* Boston MA 1937 *ED* Harvard Univ 1959; Harvard Univ MBA 1962 *CURR EMPL* chmn, ceo, dir: 21 Intl Holdings *CORP AFFIL* vchmn, chmn exec comm: Color Tile Inc
Saul Sherman: *CURR EMPL* vchmn, dir: 21 Intl Holdings

GIVING OFFICERS

Donald E. Betson: asst treas
Marshall S. Cogan: pres, dir *CURR EMPL* chmn, ceo, dir: 21 Intl Holdings (see above)
Joan M. Flood: asst treas
Judith G. Hershon: vp
Frank Murtagh: asst treas
Robert N. Nelson: treas
Philip N. Smith, Jr.: secy *CURR EMPL* vp, corp couns: 21 Intl Holdings

APPLICATION INFORMATION

Initial Approach: *Initial Contact:* Foundation does not accept unsolicited requests for funds.
Restrictions on Giving: Foundation does not accept unsolicited requests for funds.

OTHER THINGS TO KNOW

In addition to receiving contributions from 21 International Holdings, KIHI Foundation is funded from the profits of subsidiaries, such as Foamex Products Corp. and The "21st" Club Restaurant.

GRANTS ANALYSIS

Total Grants: $646,017
Number of Grants: 71
Highest Grant: $100,000
Typical Range: $1,000 to $10,000
Disclosure Period: 1991
Note: Recent grants are derived from a 1991 Form 990.

RECENT GRANTS

100,000 Rockefeller University, New York, NY
75,000 American Friends of Israel Museum, New York, NY
50,000 Goddard Riverside Children, New York, NY
50,000 Spastic Children's Endowment Foundation, Van Nuys, CA
50,000 United Cerebral Palsy/Spastic Children's Foundation of Los Angeles County, Van Nuys, CA
25,000 Carter Presidential Center, Atlanta, GA
25,000 Coro Foundation, New York, NY
25,000 Foundation for French Museums, New York, NY
25,000 Museum of Television and Radio, New York, NY
20,000 Lawyers Committee for Human Rights, New York, NY

28:19

CONTACT

28:19
7300 North Comanche
Oklahoma City, OK 73132
(405) 721-2797

FINANCIAL SUMMARY

Recent Giving: $412,511 (fiscal 1991); $509,235 (fiscal 1990); $199,899 (fiscal 1989)
Assets: $4,640,413 (fiscal year ending November 30, 1991); $4,921,854 (fiscal 1990); $5,105,751 (fiscal 1989)
Gifts Received: $44,819 (fiscal 1991); $228,831 (fiscal 1990)
EIN: 73-6091732

CONTRIBUTIONS SUMMARY

Typical Recipients: • *Civic & Public Affairs:* municipalities • *Education:* education associations • *Health:* nursing services • *Religion:* churches, mission-

ary activities, religious organizations
Grant Types: general support

GIVING OFFICERS

Don T. Glenn: secy, treas
John R. Repass: vp
Gene Warr: pres

APPLICATION INFORMATION

Initial Approach: Send letter describing program. There are no deadlines.

GRANTS ANALYSIS

Number of Grants: 338
Highest Grant: $75,000
Typical Range: $100 to $1,000
Disclosure Period: fiscal year ending November 30, 1991

RECENT GRANTS

75,000 Student Work Development Foundation
30,000 Campus Crusade for Christ, San Bernardino, CA
20,000 Samaritan's Purse
14,000 City of Warr Acres — Traffic Control
11,500 Covenant Community Church
10,000 Chapel on the Campus
10,000 Christian and Missionary Alliance
10,000 Eastern European Seminary
10,000 Luis Palau Evangeline Association
10,000 Samaritan's Purse

Tyco Laboratories, Inc.

Sales: $3.1 billion
Employees: 27,000
Headquarters: Exeter, NH
SIC Major Group: Fabricated Metal Products, Industrial Machinery & Equipment, Primary Metal Industries, and Special Trade Contractors

---

CONTACT

Irving Gutin
Senior Vice President
Tyco Laboratories, Inc.
1 Tyco Park
Exeter, NH 03833
(603) 778-9700

CONTRIBUTIONS SUMMARY

Operating Locations: NH (Exeter)

CORP. OFFICERS
John F. Fort: *CURR EMPL* chmn, pres, ceo: Tyco Laboratories
L. Dennis Kozlowski: *CURR EMPL* pres: Mueller Co *CORP AFFIL* pres: Grinnell Corp; pres, coo: Tyco Laboratories
Richard D. Power: *CURR EMPL* cfo: Tyco Laboratories

Tyler Corp. / Tyler Foundation
Sales: $266.4 million
Employees: 3,445
Headquarters: Dallas, TX
SIC Major Group: Automotive Dealers & Service Stations, Holding & Other Investment Offices, and Primary Metal Industries

CONTACT
R. W. Margerison
Tyler Corp.
2121 San Jacinto St., Ste. 3200
Dallas, TX 75201
(214) 754-7800

FINANCIAL SUMMARY
Recent Giving: $70,380 (1991); $101,900 (1990); $177,120 (1989)
Assets: $2,037,317 (1991); $1,892,282 (1989)
EIN: 23-7140526

CONTRIBUTIONS SUMMARY
Typical Recipients: • *Arts & Humanities:* arts appreciation, museums/galleries • *Education:* business education, colleges & universities, general • *Health:* general, health organizations • *Social Services:* general, recreation & athletics, united funds
Geographic Distribution: focus on TX
Operating Locations: TX (Dallas, Tyler)

CORP. OFFICERS
Joseph F. McKinney: *B* Philadelphia PA 1931 *ED* St Josephs Coll 1952; Harvard Univ Sch Bus Admin 1957 *CURR EMPL* chmn, ceo, pres, dir: Tyler Corp *CORP AFFIL* dir: Corstar Intl Inc, Cronus Indus Inc, InterFirst Bank Dallas NA, Kidde Inc

GIVING OFFICERS
Linda K. Hill: pres, dir
Rick W. Margerison: vp, dir
Joseph F. McKinney: chmn *CURR EMPL* chmn, ceo, pres, dir: Tyler Corp (see above)

Sandie D. Shepherd: secy

APPLICATION INFORMATION
Initial Approach: Send brief letter including a description of the organization, amount requested, purpose of funds sought, and proof of tax-exempt status. There are no deadlines.
Restrictions on Giving: Does not support individuals, or political or lobbying groups.

GRANTS ANALYSIS
Number of Grants: 31
Highest Grant: $20,000
Typical Range: $500 to $1,000
Disclosure Period: 1991

RECENT GRANTS
20,000 University of Texas at Dallas, Dallas, TX
10,000 Cooper Institute for Aerobics Research, Dallas, TX
5,000 Dallas Museum of Art, Dallas, TX
5,000 Notre Dame of Dallas Schools, Irving, TX
3,000 Ursuline Academy of Dallas, Dallas, TX
2,300 Dallas Museum of Art, Dallas, TX
2,000 Consortium for Graduate Study in Management, St. Louis, MO
2,000 Crystal Charity Ball, Dallas, TX
2,000 Restart Corporation, Dallas, TX
2,000 United Way, Dallas, TX

Tyndale House Foundation

CONTACT
Mary Kleine Yehling
Executive Director
Tyndale House Fdn.
351 Executive Dr.
Wheaton, IL 60188
(708) 668-8300

FINANCIAL SUMMARY
Recent Giving: $582,000 (1991); $566,900 (1990); $346,777 (1989)
Assets: $136,694 (1991); $135,051 (1990); $402,903 (1989)
Gifts Received: $474,583 (1991); $389,823 (1990); $589,646 (1989)
Fiscal Note: In 1991, contributions were received from the

Kenneth N. Taylor Charitable Trust ($333,987), and Howard Eklind ($140,000).
EIN: 36-2555516

CONTRIBUTIONS SUMMARY
Donor(s): Kenneth N. Taylor, Howard A. Elkind, ENB Charitable Trust.
Typical Recipients: • *International:* international organizations • *Religion:* churches, missionary activities, religious organizations • *Social Services:* youth organizations
Grant Types: general support

GIVING OFFICERS
Edwin L. Frizen, Jr.: pres, mgr
Mary Gieser: mgr
Peter Gunther: mgr
Wendell Charles Hawley: mgr *B* Priest River ID 1930 *ED* Univ OR 1954-1959 *CURR EMPL* sr vp: Tyndale House Publs *CORP AFFIL* sr vp: Tyndale House Publs
Elizabeth Knighton: mgr
Paul Mathews: mgr *CURR EMPL* vp, asst secy, dir: Tyndale House Publs *CORP AFFIL* vp, asst secy, dir: Tyndale House Publs
Kenneth Nathaniel Taylor: mgr *ED* Wheaton Coll BA 1938; Dallas Theological Seminary 1943; Northern Baptist Theological Seminary ThM 1944 *CURR EMPL* chmn, dir: Tyndale House Publs *CORP AFFIL* chmn, dir: Tyndale House Publs
Margaret W. Taylor: secy, treas, mgr *CORP AFFIL* dir: Tyndale House Publs
Mark D. Taylor: mgr *CURR EMPL* pres, ceo, dir: Tyndale House Publs *CORP AFFIL* pres, ceo, dir: Tyndale House Publs

APPLICATION INFORMATION
Initial Approach: Prospective grantee should write or call the foundation to request a copy of its application guidelines and program policy statement. The foundation usually does not fund building projects, libraries, scholarships, or personal support. The foundation may provide applicants with names of other foundations that are apt to be interested in projects which do not fit Tyndale's interests.
Restrictions on Giving: No support for libraries. No grants to individuals, building or en-

dowment funds, scholarships, fellowships, or personnel support.

GRANTS ANALYSIS
Number of Grants: 53
Highest Grant: $175,000
Typical Range: $2,000 to $10,000
Disclosure Period: 1991

RECENT GRANTS
175,000 Living Bibles International, Naperville, IL
150,000 South Park Church, Park Ridge, IL
100,000 South Park Church, Park Ridge, IL
75,000 Living Bibles International, Naperville, IL
15,000 Middle East Media, Lynnwood, WA
10,000 Christian World Publishers, Pleasant Hill, CA
10,000 Romanian Missionary Society, Wheaton, IL
10,000 Wheaton Youth Outreach Community Center, Wheaton, IL
10,000 World Relief, Wheaton, IL
9,000 Bible League, South Holland, IL

Tyson Foods, Inc. / Tyson Foundation
Sales: $3.92 billion
Employees: 44,000
Headquarters: Springdale, AR
SIC Major Group: Agricultural Production— Livestock, Food & Kindred Products, and Wholesale Trade—Nondurable Goods

CONTACT
Cheryl Tyson
Trustee
Tyson Fdn.
2210 West Oaklawn Dr.
PO Box 2020
Springdale, AR 72765-2020
(501) 756-4000

FINANCIAL SUMMARY
Recent Giving: $555,663 (1990); $307,140 (1989)
Assets: $10,925,408 (1990); $9,323,713 (1989)
Gifts Received: $250,000 (1990); $275,000 (1989)
Fiscal Note: Contributes through foundation only. In 1990, contributions were received from Tyson Foods, Inc.
EIN: 23-7087948

CONTRIBUTIONS SUMMARY

Typical Recipients: • *Arts & Humanities:* arts centers, community arts, museums/galleries • *Civic & Public Affairs:* business/free enterprise, economic development, economics, environmental affairs, municipalities, professional & trade associations, safety, urban & community affairs • *Education:* agricultural education, business education, colleges & universities, economic education, education funds, literacy, medical education, private education (precollege), science/technology education, student aid • *Health:* emergency/ambulance services, health organizations, pediatric health, single-disease health associations • *Social Services:* community centers, community service organizations, homes, recreation & athletics, united funds, youth organizations

Grant Types: general support

Geographic Distribution: focus on Arkansas

Operating Locations: AR (Springdale), CA (Santa Clara), IA (Des Moines, LeMars), MI (Holland), MN (Duluth), NC (Wilkesboro), NJ (Clifton), TN (Memphis), TX (Center, Garland), WA (Seattle)

CORP. OFFICERS

Leland E. Tollett: *B* Nashville AR 1937 *ED* Univ AR BSA 1958; Univ AR MSA 1959 *CURR EMPL* pres, ceo: Tyson Foods *CORP AFFIL* dir: Worthern Banking Corp; pres: Henry House Sales; pres, ceo: Holly Farms Food Svc; pres, coo: Tyson Farms TX; sr vp: Arctic Alaska Fisheries Corp; pres, coo: Eagle Distributing, Lane Farms, Lane Processing, Poultry Growers, Spring Valley Farms *NONPR AFFIL* mem, dir: Natl Broiler Counc

Donald John Tyson: *B* Olathe KS 1930 *ED* Univ AR *CURR EMPL* chmn, ceo, dir: Tyson Foods

GIVING OFFICERS

James B. Blair: trust

Harry C. Erwin: trust

Joe F. Starr: trust *CURR EMPL* vchmn, dir: Tyson Foods *CORP AFFIL* vchmn, dir: Tyson Foods Inc

Cheryl L. Tyson: trust

APPLICATION INFORMATION

Initial Approach: *Initial Contact:* written request for pre-printed application form and instructions *When to Submit:* any time

GRANTS ANALYSIS

Total Grants: $555,663
Number of Grants: 46
Highest Grant: $100,000
Typical Range: $100 to $5,000
Disclosure Period: 1990
Note: Recent grants are derived from a 1990 grants list.

RECENT GRANTS

100,000 Agriculture Development, AR
50,000 McCurtan County Sports Center, AR
50,000 Shiloh Museum, AR
40,000 International Billfish Foundation, Miami, FL
25,000 Arkansas Adult Literacy Foundation, Little Rock, AR
25,000 Southern Arkansas University, El Dorado, AR
20,000 Leukemia Society of America
20,000 University of Arkansas, Little Rock, AR
5,000 Institute for Advanced Studies
5,000 Ronald McDonald House

Tyson Fund

CONTACT

Tyson Fund
One Indiana Sq. No. 733
Indianapolis, IN 46266
(317) 266-6109

FINANCIAL SUMMARY

Recent Giving: $302,546 (1991); $277,172 (1990); $279,862 (1989)
Assets: $8,188,711 (1991); $6,970,757 (1990); $6,786,696 (1989)
EIN: 35-6009973

CONTRIBUTIONS SUMMARY

Donor(s): James H. Tyson
Typical Recipients: • *Arts & Humanities:* history/historic preservation, libraries • *Civic & Public Affairs:* municipalities, safety, urban & community affairs • *Health:* emergency/ambulance services, health organizations • *Religion:* churches • *Social Services:* aged

Grant Types: general support and project

Geographic Distribution: limited to Versailles, IN

APPLICATION INFORMATION

Initial Approach: Contributes only to preselected organizations.

GRANTS ANALYSIS

Number of Grants: 15
Highest Grant: $136,690
Typical Range: $3,000 to $15,000
Disclosure Period: 1991

RECENT GRANTS

136,690 Town of Versailles, Versailles, IN — sewer, water and equipment
55,000 Tyson Library, Versailles, IN
31,751 Southern Ripley Life Squad, Versailles, IN — equipment
25,000 Southern Ripley Life Squad, Versailles, IN — building
15,000 Versailles Fire Department, Versailles, IN — equipment
12,472 Tyson United Methodist Church, Versailles, IN — repairs
10,000 Ripley County Health Coalition, Versailles, IN — materials, services
5,000 Tyson United Methodist Church, Versailles, IN
3,000 Ripley County Historical Society, Versailles, IN — equipment
3,000 Versailles Senior Citizens, Versailles, IN — utilities, maintenance

Uarco Inc.

Sales: $692.0 million
Employees: 5,500
Headquarters: Barrington, IL
SIC Major Group: Printing & Publishing

CONTACT

J.K. Marshall
Senior Vice President & Treasurer
Uarco Inc.
700 West Main St.
Barrington, IL 60010
(708) 381-7000

CONTRIBUTIONS SUMMARY

Operating Locations: IL (Barrington)

CORP. OFFICERS

Herbert L. Koelling: *CURR EMPL* ceo: Uarco
Bruce H. Moses: *CURR EMPL* pres, coo: Uarco

Ucross Foundation

CONTACT

Ucross Foundation
c/o Apache Corporation
Route Ucross, Box 19
Ucross, WY 82835-0000

FINANCIAL SUMMARY

Recent Giving: $6,424,703 (1990)
Assets: $3,986,966 (1990)
Gifts Received: $1,506,451 (1990)
EIN: 74-2188539

GIVING OFFICERS

James Bauman: vp, treas
John Harris: vp, secy
Raymond Plank: bd chmn

GRANTS ANALYSIS

Total Grants: $642,470
Number of Grants: 1
Highest Grant: $642,470
Disclosure Period: 1990

UDC-Universal Development LP

Sales: $365.4 million
Employees: 500
Headquarters: Tempe, AZ
SIC Major Group: General Building Contractors, Nondepository Institutions, and Real Estate

CONTACT

Richard Kraemer
President
UDC-Universal Development LP
4812 South Mill Ave.
Tempe, AZ 85282
(602) 820-4488

CONTRIBUTIONS SUMMARY

Operating Locations: AZ (Tempe)

CORP. OFFICERS

Richard C. Kraemer: *CURR EMPL* pres, treas, coo: UDC-Universal Develo[D LP

Gary Aron Rosenberg: *B* Green Bay WI 1940 *ED* Northwestern Univ BS 1962; Northwestern Univ MBA 1963; Univ WI JD 1966 *CURR EMPL* chmn: UDC Homes *CORP AFFIL* chmn, ceo: UDC - Universal Devel LP *NONPR AFFIL* adv bd, adjunct prof: Northwestern Univ Kellogg Sch; fdr, chmn: Real Estate Res Ctr; mem: Natl Assn Home Builders

UGI Corp.

Assets: $1.0 billion
Employees: 3,812
Headquarters: Valley Forge, PA
SIC Major Group: Electric, Gas & Sanitary Services, Miscellaneous Retail, Oil & Gas Extraction, and Wholesale Trade—Nondurable Goods

CONTACT

Lynn J. McCwon
Manager, Employee Benefits
UGI Corp.
PO Box 858
Valley Forge, PA 19482
(215) 337-1000

CONTRIBUTIONS SUMMARY

Company provides employee matching gifts only.

Grant Types: matching

Operating Locations: CA (Sacramento), PA (King of Prussia, Valley Forge)

CORP. OFFICERS

James A. Sutton: *B* Gary IN 1934 *ED* Purdue Univ 1957 *CURR EMPL* chmn, pres, ceo, coo, dir: UGI Corp *CORP AFFIL* chmn: AmeriGas Inc; dir: Gilbert Associates Inc, Mellon Bank (East)

UIS, Inc.

Sales: $530.0 million
Employees: 5,900
Headquarters: New York, NY
SIC Major Group:
  Transportation Equipment

CONTACT

Joseph Arrigo
Vice President and Treasurer
Lebensfeld Fdn.
600 Fifth Ave.
New York, NY 10020
(212) 581-7660

CONTRIBUTIONS SUMMARY

Operating Locations: NY (New York)

CORP. OFFICERS

Harry Lebensfeld: *B* New York NY 1904 *CURR EMPL* pres, ceo: UIS *CORP AFFIL* chrmn: Automotive Accessory, Champion Laboratories, Flexible Lamps, Harlyn Indus, HKM CA Corp, Luber-Finer, Luber-Finer Europe, Mid South Mfg, Neapco, New England Confectionery Co, Sacks Electrical Supply, Three States Supply Co, US Export Corp, Wells Mfg Canada, Wells Mfg Corp

OTHER THINGS TO KNOW

Company is an original donor to the Lebensfeld Foundation.

UJB Financial Corp.

Sales: $311.57 million
Employees: 6,380
Headquarters: Princeton, NJ
SIC Major Group: Depository Institutions, Holding & Other Investment Offices, Nondepository Institutions, and Security & Commodity Brokers

CONTACT

Virginia Ibarra
Manager, Educational Matching Gifts
UJB Financial Corp.
PO Box 2066, 301 Carnegie Center
Princeton, NJ 08543
(609) 987-3413

CONTRIBUTIONS SUMMARY

Company sponsors employee matching gift program; also supports community organizations.

Typical Recipients: • *Arts & Humanities:* general • *Civic & Public Affairs:* general • *Education:* general • *Health:* general • *Social Services:* general

Grant Types: matching

Geographic Distribution: primarily headquarters area

Operating Locations: DE (Wilmington), NJ (Cherry Hill, Colonia, Dover, Hackensack,

Hazlet, Laurence Harbor, Paramus, Princeton, Randolph, Red Bank), NY (New York), PA (Allentown, Bethlehem, Hazleton, Whitehall, Wilkes-Barre)

CORP. OFFICERS

John G. Collins: *B* Jersey City NJ 1936 *ED* St Peters Coll 1958; Rutgers Univ 1965 *CURR EMPL* vchmn, dir: UJB Fin Corp

John R. Howell: *CURR EMPL* vchmn, dir: UJB Fin Corp

T. Joseph Semrod: *CURR EMPL* chmn, pres, ceo, dir: UJB Fin Corp

APPLICATION INFORMATION

Initial Approach: Send brief letter of inquiry. There are no deadlines.

Ukrop's Super Markets, Inc. / Ukrop Foundation

Sales: $350.0 million
Employees: 4,000
Headquarters: Richmond, VA
SIC Major Group: Food Stores

CONTACT

Gail Long
Assistant to the President
Ukrop's Super Markets, Inc.
600 Southlake Blvd.
Richmond, VA 23236
(804) 794-1321

FINANCIAL SUMMARY

Recent Giving: $208,033 (fiscal 1990); $188,290 (fiscal 1989)

Assets: $228,009 (fiscal 1990); $132,392 (fiscal 1989)

Gifts Received: $47,260 (fiscal 1989)

Fiscal Note: In 1989, contributions were received from Ukrop's Super Markets, Inc.

EIN: 54-1206389

CONTRIBUTIONS SUMMARY

Typical Recipients: • *Arts & Humanities:* arts funds, community arts, opera • *Civic & Public Affairs:* environmental affairs, municipalities, urban & community affairs, zoos/botanical gardens • *Education:* colleges & universities, education funds • *Health:* medical research, single-disease health associations • *Religion:* churches, religious organizations • *Social Services:* recreation & athlet-

ics, united funds, youth organizations

Grant Types: general support and scholarship

Geographic Distribution: focus on Richmond, VA

Operating Locations: VA (Richmond)

CORP. OFFICERS

James E. Ukrop: *CURR EMPL* pres, ceo: Ukrops Super Markets

Joseph Ukrop: *CURR EMPL* chmn: Ukrops Super Markets

Robert Ulkrop: *CURR EMPL* coo: Ukrops Super Markets

GIVING OFFICERS

J. Nelson Melton: treas, dir

Jacqueline L. Ukrop: secy, dir

James E. Ukrop: pres, dir *CURR EMPL* pres, ceo: Ukrops Super Markets (see above)

Joseph Ukrop: dir *CURR EMPL* chmn: Ukrops Super Markets (see above)

Robert S. Ukrop: vp, dir

APPLICATION INFORMATION

Initial Approach: Send brief letter describing program. There are no deadlines.

GRANTS ANALYSIS

Number of Grants: 124
Highest Grant: $30,033
Typical Range: $1,000 to $3,000
Disclosure Period: fiscal year ending June 30, 1991

RECENT GRANTS

30,033 United Way, Richmond, VA
26,635 William and Mary Athletic Education Foundation, Williamsburg, VA
14,560 University of Richmond, Richmond, VA — soccer scholarship fund
12,500 University of Virginia, Charlottesville, VA
10,000 Central American Mission International, Dallas, TX
10,000 Davidson College, Davidson, NC
10,000 Poplar Springs Baptist Church, Richmond, VA
6,000 Valentine Museum, Richmond, VA — capital improvements
6,000 Virginia Commonwealth University, Richmond, VA
5,000 Virginia Foundation for Inde-

pendent Colleges,
Richmond, VA

Ulrich Chemical, Inc.

Sales: $52.0 million
Employees: 110
Headquarters: Indianapolis, IN
SIC Major Group: Chemicals &
Allied Products and Wholesale
Trade—Nondurable Goods

CONTACT
Steve Hiatt
Vice President
Ulrich Chemical, Inc.
3111 North Post Rd.
Indianapolis, IN 46226
(317) 898-8632

CONTRIBUTIONS SUMMARY
Operating Locations: IN (Indianapolis)

CORP. OFFICERS
Edward M. Pitkin: *CURR EMPL* pres: Ulrich Chem
Joan C. Pitkin: *CURR EMPL* chmn: Ulrich Chem

RECENT GRANTS
Wabash College, Crawfordsville, IN

UNC, Inc.

Sales: $360.6 million
Employees: 3,852
Headquarters: Annapolis, MD
SIC Major Group: Fabricated
Metal Products, Miscellaneous
Repair Services,
Transportation by Air, and
Transportation Equipment

CONTACT
Mark Jartman
Vice President, Government
Affairs
UNC, Inc.
175 Admiral Cochrane Dr.
Annapolis, MD 21401
(410) 266-9101

CONTRIBUTIONS SUMMARY
Operating Locations: CA
(Burbank, Los Angeles), CO
(Grand Junction), CT (Norwich, Uncasville), FL (Mulberry), IN (Terre Haute), MD
(Annapolis), NJ (Millville),
NM (Albuquerque), NY (Bay
Shore, Ronkonkoma)

CORP. OFFICERS
Dan A. Colussy: *B* Pittsburgh
PA 1931 *ED* US Coast Guard
Academy 1953; Harvard Univ

Sch Bus Admin 1965 *CURR
EMPL* chmn, pres, ceo, dir:
UNC *CORP AFFIL* dir: Blue
Cross & Shield MD *NONPR
AFFIL* dir: Historic Annapolis
Robert L. Pevenstein: *CURR
EMPL* sr vp, cfo: UNC

Unger Foundation, Aber D.

CONTACT
Eugene M. Feinblatt
President
Aber D. Unger Fdn.
c/o Gordon, et al.
223 East Redwood St.
Baltimore, MD 21202
(410) 576-4211

FINANCIAL SUMMARY
Recent Giving: $120,010 (fiscal 1992); $95,250 (fiscal
1990); $79,850 (fiscal 1989)
Assets: $2,043,340 (fiscal year
ending February 28, 1992);
$1,849,972 (fiscal 1990);
$1,872,039 (fiscal 1989)
EIN: 52-6034758

CONTRIBUTIONS SUMMARY
Typical Recipients: • *Arts &
Humanities:* community arts,
music, theater • *Civic & Public
Affairs:* housing • *Education:*
colleges & universities
• *Health:* health organizations,
pediatric health • *Social Services:* community service organizations, disabled, food/clothing
distribution, shelters/homelessness
Grant Types: general support

GIVING OFFICERS
Eugene M. Feinblatt: pres,
treas
John Feinblatt: trust
Marjorie W. Feinblatt: trust
Paul C. Woman III: trust

APPLICATION INFORMATION
Initial Approach: Send brief
letter describing program.
There are no deadlines.

GRANTS ANALYSIS
Disclosure Period: fiscal year
ending February 28, 1992
Note: 1992 grants list not
provided.

RECENT GRANTS
25,000 Associated Jewish
Community Federation of Baltimore,
Baltimore, MD
19,000 Peabody Institute,
Baltimore, MD

16,000 Center Stage, Baltimore, MD
10,000 Theatre Project,
Baltimore, MD
5,000 Johns Hopkins University, Baltimore,
MD
5,000 Johns Hopkins University School of
Hygiene, Baltimore, MD
5,000 Mount Washington
Pediatric Hospital,
Baltimore, MD
2,500 Governor's Commission Healthcare
Policy, Baltimore,
MD
2,000 Learning Independence, Baltimore, MD
1,500 Association of Baltimore Area Grantmakers, Baltimore,
MD

Unifi, Inc.

Sales: $441.8 million
Employees: 5,271
Headquarters: Greensboro, NC
SIC Major Group: Textile Mill
Products

CONTACT
Robert Ward
Executive Vice President,
Finance
Unifi, Inc.
PO Box 19109
Greensboro, NC 27419
(919) 294-4410

CONTRIBUTIONS SUMMARY
Operating Locations: NC
(Greensboro)

CORP. OFFICERS
William T. Kretzer: *CURR
EMPL* pres, ceo: Unifi
G. Allen Mebane: *CURR
EMPL* chmn: Unifi

Uniform Tubes, Inc.

Sales: $30.0 million
Employees: 360
Parent Company: UTI Corp.
Headquarters: Collegeville, PA
SIC Major Group: Fabricated
Metal Products and Stone,
Clay & Glass Products

CONTACT
William Buck
Personnel Manager
Uniform Tubes, Inc.
PO Box 992
Collegeville, PA 19426
(215) 539-0700

CONTRIBUTIONS SUMMARY
Operating Locations: PA (Collegeville)

CORP. OFFICERS
Gordon B. Hattersley: *CURR
EMPL* pres, secy: Uniform
Tubes
A. Bruce Mainwaring: *CURR
EMPL* chmn, treas: Uniform
Tubes

Unigard Security Insurance Co.

Sales: $570.0 million
Employees: 575
Parent Company: John Hancock
Mutual Life Insurance Co.
Headquarters: Bellevue, WA
SIC Major Group: Insurance
Carriers

CONTACT
Catherine Kietzman
Assistant Secretary
Unigard Security Insurance Co.
PO Box 90701
Bellevue, WA 98009-0701
(206) 641-4321
Note: Ms. Barone's Extention is
5310.

FINANCIAL SUMMARY
Fiscal Note: Annual Giving
Range: $100,000 to $250,000

CONTRIBUTIONS SUMMARY
Support goes to local education, health and human service,
arts, and civic organizations.
Typical Recipients: • *Arts &
Humanities:* general • *Civic &
Public Affairs:* general • *Education:* general • *Health:* general
• *Social Services:* general
Grant Types: general support
Nonmonetary Support Types:
in-kind services
Geographic Distribution: primarily headquarters area
Operating Locations: WA
(Bellevue)

CORP. OFFICERS
Dale Abbrederis: *CURR
EMPL* cfo: Unigard Security
Ins Co
Laurence O'Connor: *CURR
EMPL* chmn, ceo: Unigard Security Ins Co

Donald K. Shanks: *CURR EMPL* pres: Unigard Security Ins Co

APPLICATION INFORMATION

Initial Approach: Send brief letter of inquiry. There are no deadlines.

UniGroup Inc.

Sales: $789.0 million
Employees: 950
Headquarters: Fenton, MO
SIC Major Group: Holding & Other Investment Offices, Transportation Services, and Trucking & Warehousing

CONTACT
David C. Erich
Director, Advertising & Promotions
UniGroup Inc.
One United Dr.
Fenton, MO 63026
(314) 326-3100

CONTRIBUTIONS SUMMARY
Operating Locations: MO (Fenton)

CORP. OFFICERS
Robert Baer: *CURR EMPL* ceo, pres: UniGroup *CORP AFFIL* cfo: Advance Carter Co
Doug Wilton: *CURR EMPL* cfo: UniGroup

Unilever United States / Unilever United States Foundation

Sales: $8.85 billion
Employees: 30,000
Parent Company: Unilever N.V. and Unilever P.L.C
Headquarters: New York, NY
SIC Major Group: Business Services

CONTACT
Ed Cheney
Manager, Corporate Affairs
Unilever United States Inc.
Lever House, 390 Park Ave.
New York, NY 10022
(212) 906-4685

FINANCIAL SUMMARY
Recent Giving: $899,252 (1991); $958,240 (1990); $688,872 (1989)
Assets: $287,797 (1991); $623,068 (1990); $578,181 (1989)

Gifts Received: $547,182 (1991); $915,629 (1990)
Fiscal Note: Figures include foundation contributions only. The Unilever United States Foundation gives on behalf of Unilever United States, Unilever Research U.S., and Vanden Bergh Foods Co.
EIN: 13-6122117

CONTRIBUTIONS SUMMARY
Typical Recipients: • *Arts & Humanities:* arts centers, libraries, museums/galleries, music, performing arts, public broadcasting, theater • *Civic & Public Affairs:* better government, business/free enterprise, civil rights, economic development, ethnic/minority organizations, municipalities, nonprofit management, professional & trade associations, public policy, safety, urban & community affairs, zoos/botanical gardens • *Education:* agricultural education, business education, career/vocational education, colleges & universities, economic education, education associations, elementary education, literacy, minority education, private education (precollege), science/technology education • *Health:* health organizations, hospitals, outpatient health care delivery, pediatric health, single-disease health associations • *Science:* scientific organizations • *Social Services:* community centers, community service organizations, day care, disabled, drugs & alcohol, employment/job training, food/clothing distribution, shelters/homelessness, united funds, youth organizations
Grant Types: emergency, general support, and matching
Nonmonetary Support Types: cause-related marketing & promotion, donated equipment, and donated products
Note: Value of nonmonetary support is unavailable and is not included in the figures above.
Geographic Distribution: primarily in communities where company has major facilities
Operating Locations: CA, CT (Greenwich), FL (Jacksonville), GA, IN, MD, MO, NJ (Englewood Cliffs), NY (New York), PR

CORP. OFFICERS
Richard A. Goldstein: *B* Boston MA 1942 *CURR EMPL* chmn, ceo: Unilever Canada

GIVING OFFICERS
Ed Cheney: mgr *CURR EMPL* mgr corp aff: Unilever United States
Rachel Greenstein: community affairs mgr *CURR EMPL* Unilever US

APPLICATION INFORMATION
Initial Approach: *Initial Contact:* letter or proposal *Include Information On:* proposal on organization's letterhead and signed by its chief executive officer, the grant's purpose, background information on the organization, the most recent annual report, a copy of the current operating budget, proof of tax-exempt status *When to Submit:* any time; budget is determined annually in February
Restrictions on Giving: The foundation does not support research activities; organizations or programs of international scope; project underwriting; purchase of advertising in benefit publications or for support of benefit events; political activities; capital campaigns (other than hospitals in communities where company employees are concentrated); organizations which espouse religious philosophies; operating funds of member agencies of United Way; individuals; or scholarships, except through the National Merit Scholarship Program.

GRANTS ANALYSIS
Total Grants: $899,252
Number of Grants: 221
Highest Grant: $66,530
Typical Range: $1,000 to $5,000
Disclosure Period: 1991
Note: Recent grants are derived from a 1991 Form 990.

RECENT GRANTS
66,530 National Merit Scholarship Corporation
35,000 United Way of Tri-State, New York, NY
30,000 Stevens Institute of Technology, Hoboken, NJ
20,500 Lake Area United Way, Griffith, IN
15,000 State Legislative Leaders Founda-

tion, Centerville, MA
14,000 National Urban League, New York, NY
14,000 United Way Central Maryland, Baltimore, MD
12,000 National Governors' Association Foundation, Washington, DC
12,000 New Jersey Business/Industry/Science/Education Consortium, Hoboken, NJ
10,000 Columbia Business School's Affiliated Business Fellowship Program

Union Bank / Union Bank Foundation

Assets: $16.84 billion
Employees: 7,303
Parent Company: Bank of Tokyo, Ltd., Tokyo, Japan
Headquarters: San Francisco, CA
SIC Major Group: Depository Institutions

CONTACT
Christopher I. M. Houser
President
Union Bank Fdn.
Terminal Annex
PO Box 3100
Los Angeles, CA 90051
(213) 236-5823

FINANCIAL SUMMARY
Recent Giving: $2,340,000 (1991 est.); $2,200,000 (1990); $1,263,615 (1989)
Assets: $862,144 (1991); $18,659 (1988)
Fiscal Note: Above figures include both foundation contributions and direct giving by the bank. Foundation giving in 1991 amounted to $1,269,843.
EIN: 95-6023551

CONTRIBUTIONS SUMMARY
Typical Recipients: • *Arts & Humanities:* arts centers, arts funds, dance, history/historic preservation, libraries, museums/galleries, music, opera, performing arts, theater • *Civic & Public Affairs:* economic development, environmental affairs, ethnic/minority organizations, housing, nonprofit management, urban & community affairs • *Education:* arts education, business education, colleges & universities, economic education, education

funds • *Health:* hospitals, medical rehabilitation, medical research, single-disease health associations • *Social Services:* community service organizations, disabled, domestic violence, family services, united funds, youth organizations
Grant Types: capital, general support, and project
Nonmonetary Support Types: donated equipment
Note: No estimate is available for value of nonmonetary support, and it is not included above.
Geographic Distribution: primarily in California
Operating Locations: CA (Los Angeles)

CORP. OFFICERS
Jiro Ishizaka: *B* Shanghai People's Republic of China 1927 *CURR EMPL* chmn, dir: Union Bank, Los Angeles *NONPR AFFIL* bd dirs: Intl Sta -KCET; bd govs: Music Ctr Los Angeles; bd overseers: Huntington Library & Botanical Gardens; dir: Japan-Am Cultural & Comm Ctr, Japan-Am Soc Los Angeles, Los Angeles Chamber Orchestra, World Aff Counc; mem: Los Angeles Chamber Commerce (bd dirs); trust: CA Inst Arts, Japanese-Am Nat Mus, Jr Achievement Los Angeles
Taisuke Shimizu: *B* Osaka Japan 1936 *CURR EMPL* pres, ceo: Union Bank

GIVING OFFICERS
Christopher I. M. Houser: pres *B* Los Angeles CA 1936

APPLICATION INFORMATION
Initial Approach: *Initial Contact:* brief letter or proposal *Include Information On:* description of the organization, amount requested, purpose for which funds are sought, recently audited financial statement, proof of tax-exempt status *When to Submit:* any time; board meets quarterly
Restrictions on Giving: Foundation does not support individuals, primary or secondary education, or religious or political organizations.

OTHER THINGS TO KNOW
The foundation lists Union Bank as a corporate trustee.

GRANTS ANALYSIS
Total Grants: $1,269,843*

Number of Grants: 254*
Highest Grant: $280,000*
Typical Range: $500* to $5,000
Disclosure Period: 1991
Note: Financial information is for the foundation only. The figure for average grant excludes three grants totaling $494,500. Recent grants are derived from a 1991 Form 990.

RECENT GRANTS
280,000 United Way, Los Angeles County, Los Angeles, CA
112,000 United Way, San Diego, San Diego, CA
102,500 Logan Heights Family Health Center, San Diego, CA
45,000 United Way, Bay Area, San Francisco, CA
25,000 California Educational Initiatives Fund, San Francisco, CA
25,000 Los Angeles Music Center Unified Fund, Los Angeles, CA
20,000 California Neighborhood Housing Services Foundation, San Francisco, CA
20,000 California Working Group
15,000 American Red Cross — East Bay Fire Fund
15,000 Independent Colleges of Southern California, Los Angeles, CA

Union Bank of Switzerland Los Angeles Branch
Headquarters: Los Angeles, CA

CONTACT
Viktor Uehlinger
Logistics Manager
Union Bank of Switzerland Los Angeles Branch
444 South Flower St., 45th Fl.
Los Angeles, CA 90071
(213) 489-0600

FINANCIAL SUMMARY
Recent Giving: $16,500 (1993 est.)

CONTRIBUTIONS SUMMARY
Contributions fall into three broad categories: community organizations, education, and social services. Community organizations are those with a concern for culture as well as civic affairs. Interest in education is confined solely to schooling in science and techology. Other donations support the social services.
Typical Recipients: • *Arts & Humanities:* arts appreciation, arts associations, arts centers, museums/galleries • *Civic & Public Affairs:* international affairs, nonprofit management, urban & community affairs, women's affairs, zoos/botanical gardens • *Education:* arts education, education funds, special education • *Health:* single-disease health associations • *International:* international organizations • *Science:* scientific organizations • *Social Services:* child welfare, community centers, community service organizations, counseling, delinquency & crime, disabled, domestic violence, emergency relief, food/clothing distribution, recreation & athletics, shelters/homelessness, united funds, volunteer services, youth organizations
Grant Types: emergency, endowment, and general support
Nonmonetary Support Types: donated products
Geographic Distribution: only in Southern California
Operating Locations: CA, IL, NY

CORP. OFFICERS
Roger Wacker: *CURR EMPL* sr vp: Union Bank of Switzerland Los Angeles

GIVING OFFICERS
Viktor Uehlinger: *CURR EMPL* vp: Union Bank Switzerland Los Angeles

APPLICATION INFORMATION
Initial Approach: Send a letter including a description of the organization, amount and purpose of funds sought, proof of tax-exempt status, and, for larger requests, a recently audited financial statement. Of importance to the program is that an organization be in real need, that it serve the local community, and that it somehow further a direct or indirect business interest. Letters sent earlier in the calendar year have a better chance of success.
Restrictions on Giving: Program does not support individuals, goodwill advertising, dinners or special events, or fraternal, political, or religious organizations.

GRANTS ANALYSIS
Typical Range: $100 to $1,000

RECENT GRANTS
Boy Scouts
Junior Achievement of Southern California
Music Center Unified Fund
National Neuro Fibromatosis
ROC/ROP Action Task Force
Save the Books
Union Bank/Heart of the City 3K Run
United Way
YMCA
Yosemite Fund

Union Bank of Switzerland New York Branch
Headquarters: New York, NY
SIC Major Group: Depository Institutions

CONTACT
Mike Snow
Senior Vice President
Union Bank of Switzerland New York Branch
299 Park Avenue, 4th Fl.
New York, NY 10171
(212) 715-3000

FINANCIAL SUMMARY
Fiscal Note: Annual Giving Range: $60,000 to $70,000

CONTRIBUTIONS SUMMARY
Supports corporate memberships; education, science, and culture; and community organizations. Small grants are decided on a case-by-case basis by the branch manager, while larger gifts must be approved by the home office in Switzerland. Some contributions are linked to improving Swiss-American relations, but most have no such criteria.
Typical Recipients: • *Arts & Humanities:* museums/galleries, music, performing arts, theater • *Civic & Public Affairs:* business/free enterprise • *Education:* international exchange • *Science:* scientific organizations
Grant Types: general support
Geographic Distribution: almost exclusively in the New York City area
Operating Locations: CA, IL, NY

CORP. OFFICERS

Markus Rohrbasser: *CURR EMPL* ceo: Un Bank Switzerland NY Branch

GIVING OFFICERS

Mike Snow: *CURR EMPL* sr vp: Union Bank Switzerland NY

APPLICATION INFORMATION

Initial Approach: Send a letter any time, including information on the purpose of funds sought, a list of other support, an explanation why Union Bank of Switzerland in particular is being solicited, and proof of tax-exempt status. Early in the calendar year is the best time to apply.
Restrictions on Giving: Union Bank of Switzerland does not support political or lobbying groups.

GRANTS ANALYSIS

Typical Range: $500 to $1,000

Union Camp Corp. / Union Camp Charitable Trust

Sales: $3.06 billion
Employees: 18,646
Headquarters: Wayne, NJ
SIC Major Group: Chemicals & Allied Products, Lumber & Wood Products, Paper & Allied Products, and Wholesale Trade—Durable Goods

CONTACT

Sydney N. Phin
Director, Human Resources
Union Camp Corp.
1600 Valley Rd.
Wayne, NJ 07470
(201) 628-2248

FINANCIAL SUMMARY

Recent Giving: $2,505,000 (1993 est.); $2,537,118 (1992); $2,410,000 (1991)
Assets: $1,641,007 (1991); $4,399,600 (1990); $2,251,486 (1988)
Fiscal Note: Figures represent foundation contributions only. Company also sponsors limited direct giving program.
EIN: 13-6034666

CONTRIBUTIONS SUMMARY

Typical Recipients: • *Arts & Humanities:* arts associations, arts festivals, arts funds, community arts, ethnic arts, his-tory/historic preservation, libraries, literary arts, museums/galleries, music, public broadcasting, visual arts
• *Civic & Public Affairs:* better government, business/free enterprise, consumer affairs, economic development, economics, environmental affairs, ethnic/minority organizations, law & justice, municipalities, professional & trade associations, public policy, safety, urban & community affairs, women's affairs, zoos/botanical gardens • *Education:* agricultural education, business education, career/vocational education, colleges & universities, community & junior colleges, continuing education, economic education, education administration, education associations, education funds, elementary education, engineering education, faculty development, legal education, liberal arts education, literacy, medical education, minority education, preschool education, private education (precollege), public education (precollege), religious education, science/technology education, social sciences education, special education, student aid
• *Health:* emergency/ambulance services, geriatric health, health funds, health organizations, hospices, hospitals, medical rehabilitation, medical research, medical training, mental health, nursing services, outpatient health care delivery, single-disease health associations • *Religion:* churches, religious organizations, synagogues • *Science:* science exhibits & fairs, scientific organizations • *Social Services:* aged, child welfare, community centers, community service organizations, counseling, day care, delinquency & crime, disabled, domestic violence, drugs & alcohol, emergency relief, employment/job training, family planning, family services, homes, legal aid, recreation & athletics, religious welfare, shelters/homelessness, united funds, volunteer services, youth organizations
Grant Types: capital, employee matching gifts, endowment, fellowship, general support, multiyear/continuing support, research, and scholarship

Nonmonetary Support Types: donated products and loaned employees
Note: In 1990, 1989, and 1988, estimated value of nonmonetary support was $20,000. This support is not included in total giving figures above. Nonmonetary support in the form of donated land also is given, but no estimate is available. A. Withington is the contact for nonmonetary support.
Geographic Distribution: principally near operating locations and to national organizations
Operating Locations: AL (Birmingham, Chapman, Cullman, Decatur, Montgomery, Opelika, Thorsby), AR (Conway, Monticello), CA (Hanford, Stockton), CO (Denver), CT (Newtown), FL (Jacksonville, Lakeland), GA (Atlanta, Folkston, Forest Park, Griffin, Meridian, Savannah, Statesboro, Tifton, Tucker, Valdosta, Waycross), IA (Sibley), IL (Cicago, Normal), IN (Seymour), KY (Shelbyville), LA (Lafayette), MA (Auburn), MI (Kalamazoo), MO (Kansas City, St. Louis), MS (Houston), NC (Asheville, Greensboro, Raleigh, Reidsville), NJ (Clifton, Englewood, Montvale, Moonachie, Morristown, Norwood, Princeton, Trenton, Wayne), OH (Centerville, Cleveland, Dover, Franklin), PA (Hazelton, Lancaster, Washington), SC (Eastover, Spartanburg), TN (Morristown), TX (Carrollton, Denton, Houston, Orange, San Antonio), VA (Franklin, Richmond), WI (Tomah)

CORP. OFFICERS

Raymond Eugene Cartledge: *B* Pensacola FL 1929 *ED* Univ AL BS 1952 *CURR EMPL* chmn, ceo, dir: Union Camp Corp *CORP AFFIL* dir: Delta Air Lines, Mutual Benefit Life Ins Co, NationsBank Corp, Sun Co; pres, ceo: Clevepak Corp
W. Craig McClelland: *B* Orange NJ 1934 *CURR EMPL* pres, coo, dir: Union Camp Corp *CORP AFFIL* dir: Allegheny Ludlum Corp, PNC Fin Corp, Quaker St Oil Refining Corp

GIVING OFFICERS

Russell W. Boekenheide: trust *B* St Louis MO 1930 *ED* Blackburn Coll 1952 *CURR EMPL* sr vp: Union Camp Corp *NONPR AFFIL* adv bd: Riegel & Emory Human Resources Res Ctr; mem: Am Paper Inst; mem empl & labor rels comm: Am Paper Inst; trust: Blackburn Coll, NJ Ind Coll Fund
Raymond Eugene Cartledge: trust *CURR EMPL* chmn, ceo, dir: Union Camp Corp (see above)
Sydney N. Phin: trust *CURR EMPL* dir (human resources): Union Camp Corp
James M. Reed: trust *B* New Sharon IA 1933 *ED* Simpson Coll 1954 *CURR EMPL* exec vp: Union Camp Corp *CORP AFFIL* dir: Allied Container Corp, AM Intl, Mark Controls Corp

APPLICATION INFORMATION

Initial Approach: *Initial Contact:* brief letter or proposal *Include Information On:* description of the organization, amount requested, purpose for which funds are sought, recently audited financial statement, proof of tax-exempt status *When to Submit:* any time
Restrictions on Giving: As of 1988, the trust no longer funds the arts.

GRANTS ANALYSIS

Total Grants: $2,537,118
Number of Grants: 1,700*
Typical Range: $500 to $10,000
Disclosure Period: 1992
Note: Number of grants is an approximate figure. Asset figure is from 1991. Recent grants are derived from a 1991 Form 990.

RECENT GRANTS

223,096 United Way of the Coastal Empire, Savannah, GA
50,000 Georgia Public Telecommunications Commission, Atlanta, GA
40,000 America's Clean Water Foundation, Washington, DC
40,000 United Way-Autauga County, Prattville, AL
32,000 United Way of the Midlands, Columbia, SC
31,822 Franklin Area United Way, Franklin, VA
25,000 Alabama Shakespeare Festival, Montgomery, AL
25,000 Earth Conservation Corps, Washington, DC

25,000 North Carolina
State University,
Raleigh, NC —
Pulp and Paper
Foundation
25,000 South Carolina
State Museum, Co-
lumbia, SC

Union Carbide Corp. / Union Carbide Foundation

Sales: $6.16 billion
Employees: 43,119
Headquarters: Danbury, CT
SIC Major Group: Chemicals &
Allied Products, Metal Mining,
and Rubber & Miscellaneous
Plastics Products

CONTACT
Judy H. Lavenka
Manager, Corporate
Contributions
Union Carbide Corp.
39 Old Ridgebury Rd.
C-2
Danbury, CT 06817
(203) 794-6484

FINANCIAL SUMMARY
Recent Giving: $2,500,000
(1992 approx.); $3,560,287
(1991); $4,116,563 (1990)
Assets: $50,000 (1991)
Fiscal Note: Company gives directly and through the foundation. Figure for 1991 does not
include $50,000 in foundation
giving.
EIN: 22-3064103

CONTRIBUTIONS SUMMARY
Typical Recipients: • *Civic &
Public Affairs:* business/free enterprise, environmental affairs,
law & justice, nonprofit management, safety • *Education:*
colleges & universities,
economic education, engineering education, public education
(precollege), science/technol-
ogy education • *Health:* hospices • *Social Services:* disabled, emergency relief, united
funds, volunteer services,
youth organizations
Grant Types: department, general support, multiyear/continu-
ing support, and project
Nonmonetary Support Types:
donated equipment, in-kind
services, and workplace solicitation
Note: In 1991, nonmonetary
support was valued at $50,000;
in 1989, $53,000. This support

is not included in above figures. Headquarters contact for
nonmonetary support is J.A.
Hlavenka, Manager Commu-
nity Affairs. For more information on nonmonetary support,
see "Other Things You Should
Know."
Geographic Distribution:
principally near operating locations and to national organizations; approximately 30% of
domestic giving is made
through location managers
Operating Locations: CA (Astoria, Hayward, Irvine, Long
Beach, Sunnyvale, Torrence),
CT (Danbury, North Haven),
DC (Washington), GA (At-
lanta), IL (Bensenville, Chicago, Robinson), KS (Ulysses),
KY (Henderson), LA (Greens-
burg, Taft), MA (Acushnet,
Boston, Norwood), MI (De-
troit, Ecorse), MN (Roseville),
MO (Kansas City), NH (Am-
herst), NJ (Bound Brook, Edi-
son, Hackensack, Roseland,
Somerset), NY (Tarrytown),
OH (Cincinnati), PA (New Cas-
tle), TN (Lawrenceburg), TX
(Carolltown, Dallas, Houston,
Seadrift, Texas City), WA
(Moses Lake, Washougal), WI
(Clear Lake), WV (Institute,
Sistersville, South Charleston)
Note: Also operates in 43 coun-
tries internationally, including
Canada, Europe, the Far East,
Latin America, Africa, and Aus-
tralia.

CORP. OFFICERS
Robert D. Kennedy: *B* Pittsburgh PA 1925 *ED* Cornell
Univ BS 1955 *CURR EMPL*
chmn, pres, ceo, dir: Union Carbide Corp *NONPR AFFIL*
chmn bd trusts: New Hampton
Sch; hon mem: Am Inst Chemists; mem: Chem Mfrs Assn;
vchmn, trust: INROADS

GIVING OFFICERS
P. T. Barker: *CURR EMPL*
mgr corporate contributions:
Union Carbide Corp
J. A. Hlavenka: *CURR EMPL*
mgr community affairs: Union
Carbide Corp
T.J. Neelen: mgr univ rels

APPLICATION INFORMATION
Initial Approach: *Initial Contact:* letter or proposal *Include
Information On:* goals of organization, project, and
budget; explanation of why project is important to Union Carbide *When to Submit:* any time

Restrictions on Giving: Company does not support fraternal
organizations; goodwill advertising; individuals; lobbying,
advertising, or capital campaigns; public-supported health
organizations; or religious organizations for sectarian purposes.

OTHER THINGS TO KNOW
Nonmonetary support is decentralized at various locations,
handled by plant managers, employee relations administrators,
and community affairs representatives.
Company prefers to initiate
contact with organizations
working in areas of interest,
rather than being contacted by
organizations.
The majority of international
giving went to the Foundation
for Social Justice in South Africa, and is not a normal part of
the giving program. There are
no plans to make additional
contributions to this entity.

GRANTS ANALYSIS
Total Grants: $3,560,287
Number of Grants: 1,300
Highest Grant: $135,000
Typical Range: $1,000 to
$10,000
Disclosure Period: 1991
Note: Recent grants are de-
rived from a 1991 Form 990.

RECENT GRANTS
50,000 Teach for America,
New York, NY

Union Central Life Insurance Co. / Union Central Charitable Contribution Trust

Assets: $3.09 billion
Employees: 800
Headquarters: Cincinnati, OH
SIC Major Group: Insurance
Carriers

CONTACT
David F. Westerbeck
Vice President & Secretary
Union Central Life Insurance Co.
PO Box 179
Cincinnati, OH 45201
(513) 595-2200

FINANCIAL SUMMARY
Recent Giving: $170,000
(1991); $260,000 (1990)

CONTRIBUTIONS SUMMARY
Typical Recipients: • *Arts &
Humanities:* community arts
• *Civic & Public Affairs:*
economic development • *Educa-
tion:* colleges & universities
• *Health:* hospitals • *Social
Services:* community service or-
ganizations
Grant Types: capital, general
support, and matching
Nonmonetary Support Types:
donated equipment and in-kind
services
Operating Locations: OH
(Cincinnati)

CORP. OFFICERS
Larry R. Pike: *CURR EMPL*
chmn, ceo, pres: Union Central
Life Ins Co

APPLICATION INFORMATION
Initial Approach: Send brief
letter of inquiry, including a description of the organization,
amount requested, purpose of
funds sought, audited financial
statement, and proof of tax-exempt status. There are no deadlines.
Restrictions on Giving: Does
not support individuals, religious organizations for sectarian
purposes, or political or lobbying groups.

Union City Body Co. / Union City Body Co. Foundation

Sales: $99.5 million
Employees: 600
Headquarters: Union City, IN
SIC Major Group:
Transportation Equipment

CONTACT
William L. Adlesperger
Chairman
Union City Body Co. Foundation
350 West Deerfield Rd., PO Box
190
Union City, IN 47390-1250
(317) 964-3121

FINANCIAL SUMMARY
Recent Giving: $16,110
(1991); $14,387 (1990);
$13,554 (1989)
Assets: $161,780 (1991);
$165,424 (1990); $166,096
(1989)
EIN: 23-7426420

CONTRIBUTIONS SUMMARY

Grant Types: scholarship
Geographic Distribution: focus on IN
Operating Locations: IN (Union City)

CORP. OFFICERS

Steven L. Adelsperger: *CURR EMPL* pres: Union City Body Co

GIVING OFFICERS

J. W. Adelsperger: dir
Steven L. Adelsperger: pres, dir *CURR EMPL* pres: Union City Body Co (see above)
D. Munger: dir
D. K. Shomber: dir
M. Vaupel: secy, dir
W. Westfall: dir
S.L. Woodward: dir

APPLICATION INFORMATION

Initial Approach: Request application form. Deadline is May 1.

OTHER THINGS TO KNOW

Provides scholarships for higher education to graduates of Union City, OH, high schools.

GRANTS ANALYSIS

Disclosure Period: 1991
Note: In 1991, all grants were individual scholarships.

Union Electric Co. / Union Electric Co. Charitable Trust

Revenue: $2.01 billion
Employees: 6,594
Headquarters: St. Louis, MO
SIC Major Group: Electric, Gas & Sanitary Services

CONTACT

Carlin Scanlan
Manager, Corporate Communications
Union Electric Co. Charitable Trust
PO Box 149
St. Louis, MO 63166
(314) 621-3222

FINANCIAL SUMMARY

Recent Giving: $3,000,000 (1993 est.); $3,300,000 (1992); $2,200,000 (1991 approx.)
Assets: $905,000 (1992); $3,000,000 (1991); $3,623,001 (1990)
Fiscal Note: Above figures include trust contributions and

noncash support provided by the company.
EIN: 43-6022693

CONTRIBUTIONS SUMMARY

Typical Recipients: • *Arts & Humanities:* arts associations, arts centers, arts festivals, arts funds, arts institutes, dance, history/historic preservation, libraries, museums/galleries, music, performing arts, theater, visual arts • *Civic & Public Affairs:* economic development, environmental affairs, ethnic/minority organizations, housing • *Education:* colleges & universities, community & junior colleges, economic education, education funds, elementary education, engineering education, private education (precollege), science/technology education • *Health:* health organizations • *Social Services:* aged, child welfare, community centers, community service organizations, delinquency & crime, disabled, emergency relief, food/clothing distribution, homes, shelters/homelessness, united funds, volunteer services, youth organizations
Grant Types: capital, employee matching gifts, general support, project, and scholarship
Nonmonetary Support Types: donated equipment and loaned executives
Note: Above figures include nonmonetary support, valued at $180,000 in 1992. See "Other Things You Should Know" for further information. Requests for nonmonetary support are handled by Susan B. Martel, supervisor of corporate commuications.
Geographic Distribution: near headquarters and operating locations
Operating Locations: IL, MO (Cape Girardeau, Jefferson City, Kirksville, St. Louis)

CORP. OFFICERS

William E. Cornelius: *B* Salt Lake City UT 1931 *ED* Univ MO BS 1953; Washington Univ MA *CURR EMPL* chmn, ceo, dir: Union Electric Co *CORP AFFIL* dir: Boatmens Bancshares, Centerre Bancorp, Centerre Bank Electric Energy, Gen Am Life Ins Co, INTERCO Inc, McDonnell Douglas Corp *NONPR AFFIL* dir: Mercantile Library, St Louis Childrens Hosp, WA

Univ, William Woods Coll; mem: Beta Theta Pi; mem, dir: Municipal Theatre Assn

GIVING OFFICERS

William E. Cornelius: trust *CURR EMPL* chmn, ceo, dir: Union Electric Co (see above)
Carlin Scanlan: mgr corp communications

APPLICATION INFORMATION

Initial Approach: *Initial Contact:* brief letter or full proposal and one copy on organization letterhead *Include Information On:* explanation of project for which funds are requested, statement of organization's purpose and services, fund-raising goal, amount sought, current status of fund raising for project, organization's current board-approved operating budget, audited financial statement for previous year, proof of tax-exempt status, roster of organization's governing board *When to Submit:* any time
Restrictions on Giving: Does not support individuals, political organizations, or religious organizations for sectarian purposes.
Company's electric service is not contributed.

OTHER THINGS TO KNOW

Items of salvage from company stock sometimes are donated to nonprofit organizations, including utility poles, office furnishings, and other surplus items. Organizations receiving such material must arrange pickup. Same general policies and procedures prevail as with monetary contributions.

GRANTS ANALYSIS

Total Grants: $3,300,000
Number of Grants: 1,130
Highest Grant: $520,000
Typical Range: $500 to $1,000
Disclosure Period: 1992
Note: Recent grants are derived from a 1992 annual report. Average grant figure provided by the company.

RECENT GRANTS

770,000 United Way-St. Louis, St. Louis, MO
250,000 Salvation Army-St. Louis, St. Louis, MO

250,000 St. Louis Science Center, St. Louis, MO
200,000 St. Louis Children's Hospital, St. Louis, MO
150,000 University of Missouri-Columbia Minority Engineering Program, Columbia, MO
110,000 Washington University, St. Louis, MO
80,000 St. Louis Archdiocese School System, St. Louis, MO
75,000 Provident Counseling
75,000 YMCA of the Ozarks, MO
60,000 Lincoln University

Union Equity Division of Farmland Industries

Sales: $1.24 billion
Employees: 485
Headquarters: Enid, OK
SIC Major Group: Food & Kindred Products and Wholesale Trade—Nondurable Goods

CONTACT

Ron Thompson
Administrator, Community Relations
Farmland Industries
PO Box 7305
Kansas City, MO 64116
(816) 459-3800

FINANCIAL SUMMARY

Fiscal Note: Annual Giving Range: $100,000 to $250,000

CONTRIBUTIONS SUMMARY

Company reports 70% of contributions support education; 10% to the arts; 10% to civic and public affairs; and 10% to health and welfare.
Typical Recipients: • *Arts & Humanities:* general • *Civic & Public Affairs:* general • *Education:* general • *Social Services:* general
Grant Types: general support
Nonmonetary Support Types: cause-related marketing & promotion, donated equipment, and in-kind services
Operating Locations: OK (Enid)

CORP. OFFICERS

William R. Allen, Jr.: *B* Fort Worth TX 1940 *ED* Phillips

Univ 1976 *CURR EMPL* pres, ceo: Union Equity Co-op Exchange *NONPR AFFIL* dir: Natl Counc Farmer Coops, Natl Grain Feed Assn, Natl Grain Trade Counc, North Am Export Grain Assn, U.S. Feeds Grains Counc; mem: Natl Freight Assn, Terminal Elevator Grain Merchants Assn
Erwin Duerksin: *CURR EMPL* chmn, dir: Union Equity Co-op Exchange
Darwin Francis: *CURR EMPL* vchmn, dir: Union Equity Co-op Exchange

APPLICATION INFORMATION
Initial Approach: Send brief letter of inquiry. There are no deadlines.

Union Foundation

CONTACT
William V. Engel
Secretary-Trustee
Union Fdn.
PO Box 4470
Warren, NJ 07060
(908) 753-2440

FINANCIAL SUMMARY
Recent Giving: $694,760 (fiscal 1991); $674,650 (fiscal 1990); $656,500 (fiscal 1989)
Assets: $10,222,317 (fiscal year ending November 30, 1991); $9,490,230 (fiscal 1990); $9,451,993 (fiscal 1989)
EIN: 22-6046454

CONTRIBUTIONS SUMMARY
Donor(s): the late Edward J. Grassmann and others
Typical Recipients: • *Arts & Humanities:* history/historic preservation • *Civic & Public Affairs:* environmental affairs, zoos/botanical gardens • *Education:* colleges & universities, education funds, medical education, private education (precollege) • *Health:* health funds, hospitals, medical research, mental health, nursing services • *Religion:* churches, religious organizations • *Social Services:* community service organizations, disabled, youth organizations
Grant Types: capital and endowment
Geographic Distribution: focus on Union County, NJ

GIVING OFFICERS
Suzanne B. Engel: secy

William V. Engel: secy, trust
Cynthia Fuller: trust
Haydn Herbert Murray: trust *B* Kewanee IL 1924 *ED* Univ IL BS 1948; Univ IL MS 1951; Univ IL PhD *NONPR AFFIL* fellow: Am Ceramic Soc, Geological Soc Am, Mineralogical Soc Am; mem: Am Assn Petroleum Geologists, Clay Minerals Soc; prof, chmn dept geology: Univ IN
William O. Wuester, MD: trust

APPLICATION INFORMATION
Initial Approach: Send cover letter and full proposal. Deadline is October 15.
Restrictions on Giving: Does not support individuals.

OTHER THINGS TO KNOW
Publications: Application Guidelines

GRANTS ANALYSIS
Number of Grants: 101
Highest Grant: $42,000
Typical Range: $4,000 to $10,000
Disclosure Period: fiscal year ending November 30, 1991

RECENT GRANTS
42,000 Elizabeth General Medical Center Foundation, Elizabeth, NJ
28,000 St. Elizabeth Hospital, Elizabeth, NJ
17,500 Indiana University Foundation, Bloomington, IN
17,000 Nature Conservancy, Pottersville, NJ
17,000 Overlook Hospital Foundation, Summit, NJ
15,000 Kent Place School, Summit, NJ
14,000 Covenant House, Newark, NJ
14,000 Mount St. Mary Academy, Plainfield, NJ
14,000 Renesselaerville Institute, Renesselaerville, NY
13,000 Muhlenberg Regional Medical Center, Plainfield, NJ

Union Manufacturing Co. / Chipman-Union Foundation
Headquarters: Union Point, GA

CONTACT
Chipman-Union Fdn.
500 Sibley Ave.
Union Point, GA 30669
(404) 486-2112

FINANCIAL SUMMARY
Recent Giving: $38,635 (1990); $80,519 (1989); $109,321 (1988)
Assets: $660,240 (1990); $598,306 (1989); $629,868 (1988)
Gifts Received: $35,300 (1990); $550 (1989); $110,000 (1988)
Fiscal Note: In 1990, contributions were received from Union Manufacturing Co.
EIN: 58-6034848

CONTRIBUTIONS SUMMARY
Typical Recipients: • *Education:* colleges & universities, education funds, student aid • *Health:* single-disease health associations • *Religion:* churches • *Social Services:* community service organizations, homes, youth organizations
Grant Types: general support and scholarship
Operating Locations: GA (Union Point)

CORP. OFFICERS
Albert P. Harris: *CURR EMPL* pres, treas: Union Mfg Co

GIVING OFFICERS
F. Sibley Bryan, Jr.: trust
Carl E. Hagen: trust
John M. Osborne: trust

APPLICATION INFORMATION
Initial Approach: Applications not accepted.
Restrictions on Giving: Foundation reports that it only makes contributions to preselected charitable organizations.

GRANTS ANALYSIS
Number of Grants: 56
Highest Grant: $12,000
Typical Range: $100 to $1,000
Disclosure Period: 1990
Note: Number, size, and range of grants figures do not include scholarships to individuals.

RECENT GRANTS
12,000 Georgia District Wesleyan Methodist Church, Atlanta, GA
2,500 Alexander Tharpe Fund, Atlanta, GA
2,000 Georgia Tech Foundation, Atlanta, GA
2,000 Now Generation Ministries
1,500 Fairfield University, Fairfield, CT
1,500 YMCA
1,250 First Baptist Church of Union Point
1,200 Bethel Baptist Church, Bradenton, FL
1,175 Greene Taliaferro Comprehensive High School
1,000 Joint Tech-Georgia Development Fund, Atlanta, GA

Union Mutual Fire Insurance Co.
Employees: 84
Headquarters: Montpelier, VT
SIC Major Group: Insurance Carriers

CONTACT
Jack McLaughlin
President
Union Mutual Fire Insurance Co.
139 State St.
Montpelier, VT 05602-0158
(802) 223-5261

CONTRIBUTIONS SUMMARY
Company provides employee matching gifts only.
Grant Types: matching
Operating Locations: VT (Montpelier)

CORP. OFFICERS
Lawrence H. Reilly: *B* Alburg VT 1928 *ED* Univ VT 1952 *CURR EMPL* pres, dir: Union Mutual Fire Ins Co *CORP AFFIL* dir: Banknorth Group, Central VT Railway, Champlain Casualty, First VT Bank & Trust Co; pres, dir: New England Guaranty Ins Co

Union Pacific Corp. / Union Pacific Foundation

Revenue: $7.29 billion
Employees: 46,039
Headquarters: Bethlehem, PA
SIC Major Group: Holding & Other Investment Offices, Metal Mining, Oil & Gas Extraction, and Petroleum & Coal Products

CONTACT
Judy L. Swantak
President
Union Pacific Fdn.
Martin Tower
8th & Eaton Ave.
Bethlehem, PA 18018
(215) 861-3225

FINANCIAL SUMMARY
Recent Giving: $7,200,000 (1993 est.); $7,162,000 (1992 approx.); $6,250,000 (1991 approx.)
Assets: $1,835,000 (1992); $1,031,353 (1990); $852,694 (1989)
Fiscal Note: Company gives only through the foundation. Contributions are expected to remain at the current level indefinitely.
EIN: 13-6406825

CONTRIBUTIONS SUMMARY
Typical Recipients: • *Arts & Humanities:* dance, history/historic preservation, museums/galleries, music, opera, performing arts, public broadcasting, theater • *Education:* colleges & universities, economic education, education funds, faculty development, literacy, minority education • *Health:* hospices, hospitals, medical rehabilitation, outpatient health care delivery, pediatric health • *Social Services:* aged, child welfare, community centers, community service organizations, disabled, domestic violence, drugs & alcohol, family services, food/clothing distribution, homes, shelters/homelessness, united funds, youth organizations
Grant Types: capital, challenge, employee matching gifts, general support, and project
Geographic Distribution: in communities served by Union Pacific's operating companies, principally in the western United States

Operating Locations: AR, CA, CO, ID, IL, KS, LA, MO, NE (Omaha), NV, OK, OR, PA (Bethlehem), TX (Ft. Worth), UT, WA

CORP. OFFICERS
Andrew Lindsay Lewis, Jr.: *B* Philadelphia PA 1931 *ED* Haverford Coll BS 1953; Harvard Univ MBA 1955 *CURR EMPL* chmn, pres, ceo, dir: Union Pacific Corp *CORP AFFIL* chmn exec comm, dir: Union Pacific Realty Co, Union Pacific Resources Co, Union Pacific RR; dir: Am Express Co, AT&T, Ford Motor Co, FPL Group, Gulfstream Aerospace Corp, Rockefeller Group, Smithkline Beechman, Westmark Sys *NONPR AFFIL* chmn: Bus Roundtable, Citizens Democracy Corps; mem: Union League Philadelphia; mem exec bd (Valley Forge Counc): Boy Scouts Am; trust: Comm Econ Devel

GIVING OFFICERS
Andrew Lindsay Lewis, Jr.: chmn, trust *CURR EMPL* chmn, pres, ceo, dir: Union Pacific Corp (see above)
Barbara C. Myers: mgr
Judy L. Swantak: pres, trust, secy *B* Bryn Mawr PA 1955 *CURR EMPL* secy: Union Pacific Corp *CORP AFFIL* secy: Union Pacific Railroad Co, Union Pacific Realty Co, Union Pacific Resources *NONPR AFFIL* mem: Am Soc Corp Secys

APPLICATION INFORMATION
Initial Approach: *Initial Contact:* letter *Include Information On:* description of the organization, purpose for which funds are sought *When to Submit:* formal application form, supplied by the foundation after receipt of initial inquiry, must be submitted by August 15 for consideration for the following year's budget (board meets annually in January)
Restrictions on Giving: Does not support organizations not eligible for tax-exempt status under Section 501(c)(3) of the Internal Revenue Code; specialized national health or welfare organizations other than through United Way; political organizations; organizations engaged in influencing legislation; religious organizations that are sectarian or denomina-

tional in purpose; veterans organizations, labor groups, social clubs, or fraternal organizations; individuals; dinners or special events; goodwill advertising; or grant-making organizations, except allied arts funds and independent college associations. Only reviews requests for support of capital projects from organizations funded by United Way.

GRANTS ANALYSIS
Total Grants: $7,162,000
Number of Grants: 800
Highest Grant: $230,000*
Typical Range: $1,000 to $5,000
Disclosure Period: 1992
Note: Highest grant was to United Way of Midlands (Omaha). Recent grants are derived from a 1991 grants list.

RECENT GRANTS
225,000 United Way of the Midlands, Omaha, NE
130,000 United Way of Greater St. Louis, St. Louis, MO
115,000 United Arts Omaha, Omaha, NE — final installment of a grant of $345,000, payable in three installments in 1989-91, inclusive, to provide continued support to this organization and the 30+ Omaha area arts group it supports
100,000 United Way of Metropolitan Tarrant County, Ft. Worth, TX
100,000 University of Minnesota, Minneapolis, MN — final installment of a grant of $500,000, payable in five equal installments in 1987-91, inclusive, to assist in the creation of a Center for Interdisciplinary Studies in Distribution/Logistics in the Carlson School of Management
85,000 Arts Council of Ft. Worth and Tarrant County, Ft. Worth, TX
65,000 United Way of Pulaski County, Little Rock, AR
60,000 Cottonwood Alta View Health Care Foundation, Murray, UT — third installment of a grant

of $300,000, payable in five equal installments in 1989-93, inclusive, to construct a building and therapy pool for the Back Institute/Work Hardening Program at Cottonwood Hospital
60,000 Heart of America United Way, Kansas City, MO
60,000 Texas Christian University, Ft. Worth, TX — final installment of a grant of $240,000, payable in four equal installments in 1988-91, inclusive, to help establish an Academic Services Center that will offer writing enhancement programs and academic advising to students

Union Planters Corp.

Assets: $3.78 billion
Employees: 2,327
Headquarters: Memphis, TN
SIC Major Group: Business Services, Depository Institutions, Holding & Other Investment Offices, and Insurance Agents, Brokers & Service

CONTACT
Ben Price
Marketing Director
Union Planters Corp.
7130 Goddelett Farms Pkwy.
Codorva, TN 38018
(901) 383-6000

CONTRIBUTIONS SUMMARY
Nonmonetary Support Types: in-kind services and workplace solicitation
Operating Locations: MS (Clarksdale), TN (Brydstown, Cookeville, Crossville, Cumberland City, Harriman, Hohenwald, Humboldt, Memphis, Trenton)

CORP. OFFICERS
Jackson W. Moore: *CURR EMPL* pres, dir: Union Planters Corp
Jack W. Parker: *CURR EMPL* exec vp, cfo: Union Planters Corp
Benjamin W. Rawlins, Jr.: *CURR EMPL* chmn, ceo, dir: Union Planters Corp

J. Armistead Smith: *CURR EMPL* vchmn, dir: Union Planters Corp

OTHER THINGS TO KNOW
Value of nonmonetary support is approximately $200,000.

Union Texas Petroleum
Sales: $125.1 million
Employees: 500
Parent Company: Union Texas Petroleum Holdings
Headquarters: Houston, TX
SIC Major Group: Electric, Gas & Sanitary Services and Oil & Gas Extraction

CONTACT
William L. Brabham
Vice President, Corporate Communications
Union Texas Petroleum
1330 Post Oak Blvd.
Houston, TX 77056
(713) 623-6544

CONTRIBUTIONS SUMMARY
Operating Locations: TX (Houston)

CORP. OFFICERS
A.C. Johnson: *CURR EMPL* chmn, ceo, dir: Union TX Petroleum

Union Trust
Assets: $3.47 billion
Employees: 1,710
Parent Company: Northeast Bancorp, Inc.
Headquarters: Stamford, CT
SIC Major Group: Depository Institutions

CONTACT
Steward Steiger
Executive Vice President, Human Resourc.
Union Trust
300 Main St.
PO Box 700
Stamford, CT 06904
(203) 348-6211

CONTRIBUTIONS SUMMARY
Operating Locations: CT (Stamford)

CORP. OFFICERS
George R. Kabureck: *CURR EMPL* pres, cfo: Union Trust
Frank J. Kugler, Jr.: *CURR EMPL* chmn, ceo: Union Trust

Peter V. Young: *CURR EMPL* vchmn: Union Trust

Uniroyal Chemical Co. Inc.
Sales: $980.0 million
Employees: 2,800
Headquarters: Middlebury, CT
SIC Major Group: Chemicals & Allied Products and Petroleum & Coal Products

CONTACT
Robert Petrausch
Director, Communications
Uniroyal Chemical Co. Inc.
World Headquarters
Middlebury, CT 06749
(203) 573-2000

CONTRIBUTIONS SUMMARY
Operating Locations: CT (Middlebury)

CORP. OFFICERS
Robert J. Mazaika: *CURR EMPL* pres, ceo: Uniroyal Chem Co

Unisys Corp.
Sales: $8.42 billion
Employees: 60,000
Headquarters: Blue Bell, PA
SIC Major Group: Business Services, Electronic & Other Electrical Equipment, and Industrial Machinery & Equipment

CONTACT
Lorraine Obrzut
Manager, Corporate Public Affairs
Unisys Corp.
One Unisys Pl., Rm. 4A01
Detroit, MI 48202
(313) 972-0124

FINANCIAL SUMMARY
Recent Giving: $2,500,000 (1993 est.); $1,700,000 (1992 approx.); $2,000,000 (1991 approx.)
Fiscal Note: Company gives directly.

CONTRIBUTIONS SUMMARY
Typical Recipients: • *Arts & Humanities:* museums/galleries, music • *Civic & Public Affairs:* business/free enterprise, economic development, public policy • *Education:* minority education, science/technology education • *Health:* health organizations • *Science:* science

exhibits & fairs • *Social Services:* united funds
Grant Types: general support
Nonmonetary Support Types: donated equipment and in-kind services
Note: Estimated value of nonmonetary support for 1993 was $500,000 and is included in the above giving figure.
Geographic Distribution: near headquarters and operating locations
Operating Locations: CA (Camarillo, Rancho Bernardo, San Diego, Santa Clara, Santa Monica, Woodland Hills), CO (Boulder), DC, GA (Atlanta), IL (Chicago), MI (Detroit), MN (Minnetonka, St. Paul), NY (Great Neck, Rochester), PA (Blue Bell, Paoli), TX (Houston), UT (Salt Lake City), VA (McLean)
Note: Also operates internationally.

CORP. OFFICERS
Reto Braun: *CURR EMPL* pres, coo, dir: Unisys Corp
James Arlen Unruh: *B* Goodrich ND 1941 *ED* Jamestown Coll BS 1963; Univ Denver MBA 1964 *CURR EMPL* chmn, ceo, dir: Unisys Corp *CORP AFFIL* dir: Convergent *NONPR AFFIL* bd overseers: Univ PA Wharton Sch Bus; dir: Detroit Renaissance Ctr, Greater Philadelphia First Corp; mem: Fin Execs Inst, Greater Philadelphia Chamber Commerce; mem exec comm: PA Bus Roundtable; mem visiting comm: Univ MI; trust: Franklin Inst, Jamestown Coll

GIVING OFFICERS
David R. Curry: staff vp (pub affairs)
Lorraine Oberzut: mgr (corporate pub affairs)

APPLICATION INFORMATION
Initial Approach: *Initial Contact:* brief letter to corporate headquarters *Include Information On:* background of organization (history, record of accomplishments, evidence of fulfilling definite existing need); structure and board of control of organization; campaign goal, other corporate support, timetable, method of solicitation, fund-raising costs as percentage of total budget; total annual budget; annual report, preferably independently audited, including sources and

use of funds (new organizations should provide certified public accountant's statement attesting to installation of proper financial system); and proof of tax-exempt status
When to Submit: before June 30
Restrictions on Giving: Company does not support individuals, dinners or special events, member agencies of united funds, political or lobbying groups, fraternal groups, or religious organizations for sectarian purposes.

OTHER THINGS TO KNOW
The company reports that it will not be accepting unsolicited requests for grants in 1993. The corporation will support the following types of grants: operating (undesignated funds given in general support); program (funds designated for implementation of a specific program); and major nonrecurring requests that will have significant impact on the community.

GRANTS ANALYSIS
Total Grants: $1,700,000
Number of Grants: 20
Highest Grant: $200,000
Typical Range: $10,000 to $200,000
Disclosure Period: 1992

United Airlines / United Airlines Foundation
Parent Company: UAL Inc.
Revenue: $12.88 billion
Parent Employees: 86,100
Headquarters: Elk Grove, IL
SIC Major Group: Transportation by Air

CONTACT
Eileen Younglove
Secretary & Contributions Manager
United Airlines Fdn
PO Box 66100
Chicago, IL 60666
(708) 952-5714

FINANCIAL SUMMARY
Recent Giving: $2,800,000 (1992 approx.); $2,830,135 (1991); $2,891,342 (1990)
Assets: $2,856,000 (1990); $7,950,887 (1989)
Fiscal Note: Figures are for foundation only. Company also maintains an annual direct giving program of about $500,000, and in-kind transpor-

tation donations of about $2 million.
EIN: 36-6109873

CONTRIBUTIONS SUMMARY

Typical Recipients: • *Arts & Humanities:* arts associations, dance, museums/galleries, music, opera • *Civic & Public Affairs:* business/free enterprise, civil rights, economic development, ethnic/minority organizations, safety, urban & community affairs, women's affairs • *Education:* arts education, business education, career/vocational education, literacy, minority education, public education (precollege), science/technology education • *Health:* hospitals, single-disease health associations • *Science:* observatories & planetariums • *Social Services:* community centers, employment/job training, united funds, youth organizations
Grant Types: general support and project
Nonmonetary Support Types: in-kind services
Note: Company contributes about $2 million in transportation costs annually. This figure is not included in the above total. In 1991, transportation costs was estimated at $2,000,000.
Geographic Distribution: primarily in Washington, DC; Los Angeles and San Francisco, CA; Denver, CO; Honolulu, HI; Chicago, IL; and Seattle, WA
Operating Locations: CA (Los Angeles, San Francisco), DC, HI (Honolulu), IL (Chicago), WA (Seattle)
Note: Also operates in London, England and Tokyo, Japan.

CORP. OFFICERS

John C. Pope: *B* Newark NJ 1949 *ED* Yale Univ BA 1971; Harvard Univ MBA 1973 *CURR EMPL* pres, dir, coo: Un Airlines *CORP AFFIL* dir: Federal-Mogul Corp; pres, coo, dir: UAL Corp; trust: WTTW *NONPR AFFIL* mem: Air Transport Assn
Stephen M. Wolf: *B* Oakland CA 1941 *ED* San Francisco St Univ BA 1965 *CURR EMPL* chmn, ceo, pres: UAL Corp *CORP AFFIL* chmn, ceo, pres: Un Airlines; dir: ConAgra; pres: Un Airlines Credit Corp *NONPR AFFIL* dir: Alzheimer's Disease & Related

Disorders Assn, Chicago Symphony Orchestra, ConAgra, Conf Bd NY, Mus Flight, Northwestern Univ Kellogg Sch Bus, Rush Presbyterian-St Lukes Med Ctr

GIVING OFFICERS

Paul George: vp, dir *CURR EMPL* sr vp (human resources): Un Airlines
James M. Guyette: dir *B* Fresno CA 1945 *CURR EMPL* exec vp (opers): Un Airlines *CORP AFFIL* chmn: Un Airlines Employees Credit Union; dir: Private Bancorp
Terry L. Hall: treas
Lawrence M. Nagin: dir *B* San Francisco CA 1941 *CURR EMPL* sr vp (corp & external affairs): Un Airlines *CORP AFFIL* sr vp, gen couns: Flying Tiger Line *NONPR AFFIL* mem: Am Bar Assn
Joseph R. O'Gorman: dir
John C. Pope: dir *CURR EMPL* pres, dir, coo: Un Airlines (see above)
Stephen M. Wolf: dir *CURR EMPL* chmn, ceo, pres: UAL Corp (see above)
Eileen M. Younglove: secy *CURR EMPL* contributions mgr: Un Airlines

APPLICATION INFORMATION

Initial Approach: *Initial Contact:* brief letter or proposal *Include Information On:* annual report; description of the organization; amount requested; current and proposed budget; purpose for which funds are sought; recently audited financial statement; proof of tax-exempt status; list of board of directors; past and present contributions; name, address, and telephone number of program's contact person *When to Submit:* 60 days prior to quarterly meetings in March, June, September, and December *Note:* Supporting documentation can not be returned.
Restrictions on Giving: The United Airlines Foundation does not provide in-kind gifts or funding in the following areas: capital or building grants, development campaigns, endowments, individuals, political organizations, United Way-funded agencies, individual public or private schools, churches, the purchase of tickets to dinners or other fund-raising events, or goodwill advertising.

GRANTS ANALYSIS

Total Grants: $2,891,342
Number of Grants: 245
Highest Grant: $300,000*
Typical Range: $1,000 to $10,000
Disclosure Period: 1991
Note: Highest grant went to a United Way chapter. Company reports that it donates to United Way chapters in 124 U.S. cities served by United Airlines. Assets are from 1990. Recent grants are derived from a 1990 grants list.

RECENT GRANTS

Adler Planetarium, Chicago, IL
Alexian Brothers Medical Center, Elk Grove Village, IL
American Enterprise Institute for Public Policy Research, Washington, DC
Archdiocese Education Foundation, Los Angeles, CA — Grant a Dream program
Ballet Chicago, Chicago, IL
Blue Ridge Hospice, Winchester, VA
Boy Scouts of America, Denver, CO
Boys and Girls Clubs of Chicago, Chicago, IL
Cardinal's Big Shoulder's Fund, Chicago, IL — inner-city school program
Catalyst, New York, NY

United Artists Theatre Circuits

Revenue: $697.0 million
Employees: 12,000
Headquarters: Woodland Hills, CA
SIC Major Group: Motion Pictures

CONTACT

Robert Vallone
Senior Vice President
United Artists Theatre Circuits
21700 Oxnord St., Ste. 1000
Woodland Hills, CA 91367
(818) 593-4000

CONTRIBUTIONS SUMMARY

Operating Locations: CA (Woodland Hills)

CORP. OFFICERS

Allen Pinsker: *CURR EMPL* pres: Un Artists Theatre Circuits

United Asset Management Corp.

Revenue: $226.6 million
Employees: 588
Headquarters: Boston, MA
SIC Major Group: Holding & Other Investment Offices and Security & Commodity Brokers

CONTACT

Richard Robie
Vice President
United Asset Management Corp.
One International Pl.
Boston, MA 02110
(617) 330-8900

CONTRIBUTIONS SUMMARY

Operating Locations: MA (Boston)

CORP. OFFICERS

Norton H. Reamer: *CURR EMPL* pres: Un Asset Mgmt Svcs

United Co. / United Coal Co. Charitable Foundation

Sales: $210.0 million
Employees: 1,100
Headquarters: Bristol, VA
SIC Major Group: Coal Mining and Wholesale Trade—Durable Goods

CONTACT

James W. McGlothlin
President
United Coal Co. Charitable Foundation
PO Box 1280
Bristol, VA 24203
(703) 466-3322

FINANCIAL SUMMARY

Recent Giving: $112,109 (1991); $128,086 (1990); $131,770 (1989)
Assets: $1,596,341 (1991); $1,431,754 (1990); $1,460,154 (1989)
EIN: 54-1390453

CONTRIBUTIONS SUMMARY

Typical Recipients: • *Social Services:* community service organizations, youth organizations
Grant Types: general support
Geographic Distribution: focus on VA
Operating Locations: VA (Bristol)

CORP. OFFICERS
James W. McGlothlin: *B* 1940
ED Coll William & Mary JD
CURR EMPL chmn, ceo, pres:
Un Co *CORP AFFIL* dir: Birmingham Steel Corp, CSX
Corp, Dominion Bankshares

GIVING OFFICERS
Wayne L. Bell: secy, dir
Lois A. Clarke: treas, dir
Boyd Fowler: vchmn, dir
James W. McGlothlin: pres, dir *CURR EMPL* chmn, ceo, pres: Un Co (see above)

APPLICATION INFORMATION
Initial Approach: Send brief letter describing program. There are no deadlines.

GRANTS ANALYSIS
Number of Grants: 1
Highest Grant: $112,109
Disclosure Period: 1991

RECENT GRANTS
112,109 YMCA, Grundy, VA

United Conveyor Corp. / United Conveyor Foundation
Sales: $50.0 million
Employees: 330
Headquarters: Waukegan, IL
SIC Major Group: Engineering & Management Services, Fabricated Metal Products, Industrial Machinery & Equipment, and Primary Metal Industries

CONTACT
Margret Dargatz
United Conveyor Fdn.
2100 Norman Dr. West
Waukegan, IL 60085
(708) 473-5900

FINANCIAL SUMMARY
Recent Giving: $100,000 (1993 est.); $86,700 (1992 approx.); $122,350 (1991)
Assets: $1,847,770 (1990); $2,008,423 (1989); $1,825,656 (1988)
Gifts Received: $40,000 (1989); $60,000 (1988)
EIN: 36-6033638

CONTRIBUTIONS SUMMARY
Typical Recipients: • *Arts & Humanities:* music, public broadcasting • *Education:* colleges & universities, engineering education, student aid
• *Health:* hospitals, mental health • *Social Services:* child welfare, community service organizations, family services, united funds, youth organizations
Grant Types: general support and scholarship
Geographic Distribution: emphasis on the Chicago, IL, area
Operating Locations: IL (Waukegan)

CORP. OFFICERS
Donald N. Basler: *CURR EMPL* pres, dir: Un Conveyor Corp

GIVING OFFICERS
Donald N. Basler: trust *CURR EMPL* pres, dir: Un Conveyor Corp (see above)
David S. Hoyem: trust

APPLICATION INFORMATION
Initial Approach: Application form required for scholarships (Deadline is July 1; recipients notified Aug.).

GRANTS ANALYSIS
Number of Grants: 48
Highest Grant: $35,000
Typical Range: $1,000 to $2,500
Disclosure Period: 1990
Note: Number, size, and range of grant figures do not include scholarships.

RECENT GRANTS
35,000 Grinnell College, Grinnell, IA
12,000 Chicago Child Care Society, Chicago, IL
6,000 Chicago Symphony Orchestra, Chicago, IL
3,500 Chicago Public Television WTTW, Chicago, IL
3,000 Illinois Institute of Technology, Chicago, IL
3,000 Milwaukee School of Engineering, Milwaukee, WI
3,000 Ravinia Festival Association, Highland Park, IL
3,000 United Way, Libertyville, IL
3,000 United Way, Chicago, IL
2,500 Glenwood School for Boys, Glenwood, IL

United Dominion Industries / AMCA Foundation
Headquarters: Charlotte, NC
SIC Major Group: Fabricated Metal Products, Heavy Construction Except Building Construction, Transportation Equipment, and Wholesale Trade—Durable Goods

CONTACT
Robert Shaffer
Vice President, Communications
United Dominion Industries
2300 One First Union Center
Charlotte, NC 28202-6039

FINANCIAL SUMMARY
Recent Giving: $80,000 (1990); $80,000 (1989); $80,000 (1988)
EIN: 39-6044275

CONTRIBUTIONS SUMMARY
Typical Recipients: • *Arts & Humanities:* arts centers, libraries, museums/galleries, public broadcasting • *Education:* colleges & universities, private education (precollege), public education (precollege)
• *Health:* hospitals, medical research, single-disease health associations • *Social Services:* aged, community service organizations, disabled, domestic violence, drugs & alcohol, united funds, youth organizations
Grant Types: capital, emergency, general support, project, and research
Geographic Distribution: near headquarters office only
Operating Locations: CA, CT, GA, IA, KY, MO, MS, NC, NY, OH, TX, WI

CORP. OFFICERS
John A. Davis: *CURR EMPL* sr vp, gen coun, secy: Un Dominion Indus
William R. Holland: *CURR EMPL* chmn, ceo: Un Dominion Indus
Robert C. Kelley: *CURR EMPL* pres, coo: Un Dominion Indus

GIVING OFFICERS
B. B. Burns: vp, dir
William Dries: vp, dir
Robert E. Drury: vp, dir
C. B. Mercer: secy, dir
Robert Shaffer: vp commun
Joseph F. Sherer: pres, dir

APPLICATION INFORMATION
Initial Approach: Initial letter may be submitted at any time and should include a description of the organization, a specific dollar request, the purpose for which funds are sought, and scope of the project. While applications are accepted throughout the year, the second half of the calendar year generally is the best time to apply.

GRANTS ANALYSIS
Typical Range: $500 to $2,000

RECENT GRANTS
20,000 United Way, Charlotte, NC
10,000 Arts and Science Council, Charlotte, NC

United Fire & Casualty Co.
Assets: $510.6 million
Employees: 594
Headquarters: Cedar Rapids, IA
SIC Major Group: Insurance Carriers and Nondepository Institutions

CONTACT
Marianna Hall
Director of Human Resources
United Fire & Casualty Co.
PO Box 73909
Cedar Rapids, IA 52407
(319) 399-5796

CONTRIBUTIONS SUMMARY
Company provides employee matching gifts only.
Grant Types: matching
Operating Locations: IA (Cedar Rapids)

CORP. OFFICERS
Kent G. Baker: *CURR EMPL* vp, cfo: Un Fire & Casualty Co
Gary L. Huber: *CURR EMPL* pres, coo: Un Fire & Casualty Co
Scott McIntyre, Jr.: *CURR EMPL* chmn, dir: Un Fire & Casualty Co

United Gas Pipe Line Co.

Revenue: $2.32 billion
Employees: 1,540
Parent Company: United Gas Holding Corp
Headquarters: Houston, TX
SIC Major Group: Electric, Gas & Sanitary Services and Petroleum & Coal Products

CONTACT

Rachel Lichenstein
United Gas Pipe Line Co.
PO Box 1478
Houston, TX 77251-1478
(713) 229-4082

FINANCIAL SUMMARY

Fiscal Note: Annual Giving Range: $250,000 to $500,000

CONTRIBUTIONS SUMMARY

Company reports 47% of contributions support health and welfare; 31% to education; 17% to the arts; and 5% to civic and public affairs.

Typical Recipients: • *Arts & Humanities:* general • *Civic & Public Affairs:* general • *Education:* general • *Social Services:* general

Grant Types: general support
Operating Locations: TX (Houston)

CORP. OFFICERS

John S. Davis: *B* Joneboro LA 1942 *ED* LA Tech Univ BS 1964; LA Tech Univ MBA 1965 *CURR EMPL* pres, coo: Un Gas Pipe Line Co *NONPR AFFIL* mem: Am Gas Assn, Am Inst CPAs, Am Mgmt Assn, LA Soc CPAs, TX Soc CPAs, World Energy Conf

C. William Pollock: *CURR EMPL* chmn, ceo, dir: Un Gas Pipe Line Co

APPLICATION INFORMATION

Send brief letter of inquiry
When to Submit: any time

OTHER THINGS TO KNOW

United Gas Pipe Line Co. has been acquired by Koch Industries Inc. of Witchita, KS. Contact the human resources department at PO Box 2256, Wichita, KS, 67201. The phone number is (316)832-5500.

United Grocers, Inc.

Sales: $882.0 million
Employees: 1,250
Headquarters: Portland, OR
SIC Major Group: Wholesale Trade—Nondurable Goods

CONTACT

Bev McPherson
Administrative Secretary
United Grocers, Inc.
6433 S.E. Lake Rd.
PO Box 2690187
Portland, OR 97222
(503) 653-6330

CONTRIBUTIONS SUMMARY

Operating Locations: OR (Portland)

CORP. OFFICERS

Craig Danielson: *CURR EMPL* chmn: Un Grocers

Alan C. Jones: *CURR EMPL* pres, ceo, secy, gen mgr: Un Grocers

Ray Nidiffer: *CURR EMPL* vchmn: Un Grocers

John White: *CURR EMPL* cfo: Un Grocers

RECENT GRANTS

Oregon Museum of Science and Industry, Portland, OR

United Industrial Corp.

Sales: $258.0 million
Employees: 2,700
Headquarters: New York, NY
SIC Major Group: Electronic & Other Electrical Equipment, Fabricated Metal Products, Holding & Other Investment Offices, and Rubber & Miscellaneous Plastics Products

CONTACT

Howard Bloch
Treasurer
United Industrial Corp.
18 East 48th St.
New York, NY 10017
(212) 752-8787

CONTRIBUTIONS SUMMARY

Operating Locations: NY (New York)

CORP. OFFICERS

Bernard Fein: *CURR EMPL* chmn, pres: Un Indus Corp

United Inns, Inc.

Revenue: $105.0 million
Employees: 2,601
Headquarters: Memphis, TN
SIC Major Group: Hotels & Other Lodging Places

CONTACT

Don Cockroft
President
United Inns, Inc.
5100 Poplar Ave.
Memphis, TN 38137
(901) 767-2880

CONTRIBUTIONS SUMMARY

Operating Locations: TN (Memphis)

CORP. OFFICERS

Don Cockroft: *CURR EMPL* pres: Un Inns

United Iron & Metal Co.

Sales: $24.0 million
Employees: 110
Headquarters: Baltimore, MD
SIC Major Group: Primary Metal Industries, Real Estate, and Wholesale Trade—Durable Goods

CONTACT

David Workum
General Manager
United Iron & Metal Co.
2545 Wilkens Ave.
Baltimore, MD 21223
(410) 947-8000

CONTRIBUTIONS SUMMARY

Operating Locations: MD (Baltimore)

CORP. OFFICERS

David Workum: *CURR EMPL* pres: Un Iron & Metal Co

OTHER THINGS TO KNOW

Company is an original donor to the Jocob S. Shapiro Foundation.

United Merchants & Manufacturers / United Merchants Foundation

Sales: $216.0 million
Employees: 3,400
Headquarters: Teaneck, NJ
SIC Major Group: Apparel & Other Textile Products, Miscellaneous Manufacturing Industries, Rubber & Miscellaneous Plastics Products, and Textile Mill Products

CONTACT

Uzi Ruskin
President
United Merchants Fdn.
1650 Palisade Ave.
Teaneck, NJ 07666
(201) 837-1700

FINANCIAL SUMMARY

Recent Giving: $33,482 (fiscal 1991); $42,090 (fiscal 1989); $116,533 (fiscal 1988)
Assets: $1,043,539 (fiscal year ending June 30, 1991); $1,019,609 (fiscal 1989); $1,152,850 (fiscal 1988)
EIN: 13-6077135

CONTRIBUTIONS SUMMARY

Typical Recipients: • *Civic & Public Affairs:* business/free enterprise, international affairs • *Education:* business education, colleges & universities, education associations, education funds • *Health:* hospitals • *Religion:* religious organizations • *Social Services:* religious welfare, united funds, youth organizations

Grant Types: general support
Geographic Distribution: primarily in NY
Operating Locations: GA (Clarkesville), MA (Fall River), MD (Baltimore), NJ (North Bergen, Teaneck), NY (Ft. Edward, New York), PA (Philadelphia), RI (Warwick), SC (Buffalo, Conway, Union)
Note: Company operates 11 plants in locations.

CORP. OFFICERS

Judith A. Nadzick: *CURR EMPL* exec vp, cfo: Un Merchants & Mfrs

Uzi Ruskin: *CURR EMPL* pres, ceo, coo, dir: Un Merchants & Mfrs

Martin J. Schwab: *CURR EMPL* chmn, dir: Un Merchants & Mfrs

GIVING OFFICERS

Uzi Ruskin: vp *CURR EMPL* pres, ceo, coo, dir: Un Merchants & Mfrs (see above)

Martin J. Schwab: vp *CURR EMPL* chmn, dir: Un Merchants & Mfrs (see above)

Edward Taffet: secy, treas

APPLICATION INFORMATION

Initial Approach: Foundation reports that it only makes contributions to preselected organizations and does not accept unsolicited requests for funds.
Restrictions on Giving: Does not support individuals.

GRANTS ANALYSIS

Number of Grants: 18
Highest Grant: $6,500
Typical Range: $500 to $3,200
Disclosure Period: fiscal year ending June 30, 1991

RECENT GRANTS

6,500 United Way, Fall River, MA
5,000 United Jewish Appeal Federation of Jewish Philanthropies, New York, NY
3,932 United Merchants and Manufacturers Employee Foundation
3,200 Southeastern Massachusetts University, MA
3,000 Business Council for the United Nations, New York, NY
2,000 Boy Scouts of America, New York, NY
2,000 United Hospital of Portchester, Portchester, NY
1,600 United Way, Elizabeth, NJ
1,500 N.A.D.A.P.
1,000 United Way

United Missouri Bancshares, Inc.

Assets: $4.69 billion
Employees: 3,200
Headquarters: Kansas City, MO
SIC Major Group: Depository Institutions and Holding & Other Investment Offices

CONTACT

Melinda Moss
Vice President & Director, Corp. Commun.
United Missouri Bancshares, Inc.
PO Box 419226
Kansas City, MO 64141
(816) 860-7000

CONTRIBUTIONS SUMMARY

Operating Locations: IL (Collinsville, Morrisonville), MO (Boonville, Brookfield, Carthage, Jefferson City, Joplin, Kansas City, Monett, Mon-

roe City, Paris, Peculiar, Springfield, St. Joseph, Warrensburg, Warsaw), NY (New York)
Note: Company operates 18 United Missouri Banks in operating locations.

CORP. OFFICERS

Malcolm M. Aslin: *B* Bloomfield MO 1947 *ED* Univ MO 1969; Univ MO 1972 *CURR EMPL* pres, coo, dir: Un MO Bancshares *CORP AFFIL* chmn: Un MO Bank South; dir: FCB Corp, Pioneer Svc Corp, Un MO Bank Hickman Mills, Un MO Bank USA; pres, dir: UMB Properties, Un MO Bank Kansas City NA, Un MO Ins Co
Peter J. Genovese: *CURR EMPL* vchmn, dir: Un MO Bancshares
Rufus Crosby Kemper, Jr.: *B* Kansas City MO 1927 *ED* Univ MO 1946-1950; Westminster Coll 1983 *CURR EMPL* chmn, ceo: Un MO Bancshares *CORP AFFIL* adv dir: Overland Park Bancshares, Overland Park Bank & Trust Co, Un MO Bank Boonville; chmn, dir: City Bankshares; dir: Chicago Title Ins Co, Kansas City Southern Indus, Un MO Bank St Joseph, Un MO City Bank, Un MO Mortgage Co; pres, dir: Kemper Realty Co, Pioneer Svc Corp *NONPR AFFIL* dir: Boy Scouts Am, Kansas City Indus Fdn, Mid-Am Arts Alliance, Un Way; faculty mem: Baker Univ; hon dir: Albrecht Art Mus; hon trust: YWCA; mem: Beta Theta Pi; mem commun adv counc: Childrens Mercy Hosp; mem dirs counc: Lyric Opera; mem natl comm: Whitney Mus Am Art; treas, dir: Metro Performing Arts Fund; trust: Freedom Fdn, Frury Coll, Kansas City Art Inst, Kemper Military Sch & Coll, Univ Kansas City, Univ MO Kansas City Conservatory; vp, dir: Am Royal Assn
William M Teiwes: *CURR EMPL* exec vp, cfo: Un MO Bancshares

United Parcel Service of America / UPS Foundation

Revenue: $16.54 billion
Employees: 267,000
Headquarters: Atlanta, GA
SIC Major Group: Holding & Other Investment Offices and Trucking & Warehousing

CONTACT

Clement E. Hanrahan
Executive Director
The UPS Fdn.
400 Perimeter Ctr.
Terraces North
Atlanta, GA 30346
(404) 913-6374

FINANCIAL SUMMARY

Recent Giving: $20,100,000 (1993 est.); $18,900,000 (1992 approx.); $15,900,000 (1991)
Assets: $45,000,000 (1992 est.); $41,764,741 (1990); $50,578,278 (1989)
Fiscal Note: About 33% of contributions is direct giving to United Way organizations. In 1992, $11.8 million was given through the foundation; $6.0 million was given through the company to United Ways; and $1.1 million was given in direct gifts from other company departments.
EIN: 13-6099176

CONTRIBUTIONS SUMMARY

Typical Recipients: • *Civic & Public Affairs:* business/free enterprise, ethnic/minority organizations, nonprofit management, public policy, urban & community affairs, women's affairs, zoos/botanical gardens • *Education:* business education, career/vocational education, colleges & universities, community & junior colleges, continuing education, economic education, education associations, education funds, engineering education, literacy, minority education, student aid • *Health:* health organizations • *Social Services:* aged, child welfare, community service organizations, family services, food/clothing distribution, shelters/homelessness
Grant Types: employee matching gifts, project, research, and scholarship
Nonmonetary Support Types: loaned executives and workplace solicitation

Note: Figures for nonmonetary support are not available and are not included in the above figures. Workplace solicitation is for United Ways only.
Geographic Distribution: nationally
Operating Locations: GA (Atlanta)
Note: Headquarters is in Atlanta, Georgia. Company operates both nationally and internationally.

CORP. OFFICERS

Kent Charles Nelson: *B* Kokomo IN 1937 *ED* Ball St Univ 1959 *CURR EMPL* chmn, ceo, dir: Un Parcel Svc Am

GIVING OFFICERS

Don R. Fischer: trust
Clement E. Hanrahan: exec dir *CURR EMPL* sr vp (pub rels): Un Parcel Svc Am
Edwin Jacoby: treas
John Kelley: vchmn
Donald W. Layden: trust
Kent Charles Nelson: chmn *CURR EMPL* chmn, ceo, dir: Un Parcel Svc Am (see above)
Richard B. Oehme: trust
Calvin E. Tyler: secy

APPLICATION INFORMATION

Initial Approach: *Initial Contact:* brief letter and proposal *Include Information On:* needs addressed by program, goals and objectives, how objectives will be achieved, standards by which to judge success or failure of project, total cost, amount requested, sources of future support, current budget, audited financial statement, annual report, and proof of tax-exempt status *When to Submit:* any time
Restrictions on Giving: Does not support individuals; fraternal organizations; political organizations; religious organizations, sectarian purposes, goodwill advertising; dinners or special events; member agencies of united funds; organizations located outside the United States and Canada; or organizations not certified as 501(c)(3).

GRANTS ANALYSIS

Total Grants: $11,800,000*
Number of Grants: 302
Highest Grant: $1,400,000*
Typical Range: $20,000 to $50,000
Disclosure Period: 1992

Note: Total grants does not include $6.0 million in United-Way corporate contributions and $1.1 million in direct corporate gifts. Highest grant was to National Merit Scholarship Corp. for the James E. Casey Scholarship Program. Recent grants are derived from a 1991 grants list.

RECENT GRANTS

Association for Community Based Education, Washington, DC — to support comprehensive literacy instructor training programs for community based organizations in eight communities

Literacy Action, Atlanta, GA — to support the establishment of family literacy programs at eight Head Start sites in Atlanta, Georgia

Literacy South, Norfolk, VA — to support "learner centered literacy" instructor training and model site development in three Southeastern states

Literacy Volunteers of America, Stamford, CT — to support the implementation of a strategic plan to improve the quality of literacy instruction while increasing the number of learners served

Metro United Way, Louisville, KY — to support the expanded implementation of its model workplace literacy curriculum and to provide training

United Way of America, Alexandria, VA — to support a second round of local United Way challenge grants to build the capacity of literacy efforts in up to 13 communities

United Way of Central Maryland, Baltimore, MD — to support the expanded implementation of its model computer-assisted instruction curriculum

United Way of Elkhart County, Elkhart, IN — to support the expanded implementation of its model critical thinking skills curriculum and new adult learner recruitment efforts

United Way of St. Paul Area, St. Paul, MN — to support the continuation of work with community based agencies on the use of technology and the development of multi-cultural family literacy programs

United Refining Co

Sales: $1.09 billion
Employees: 2,800
Headquarters: Warren, PA
SIC Major Group: Automotive Dealers & Service Stations, Food Stores, and Petroleum & Coal Products

CONTACT

Larry Loughlin
Vice President, Human Resouces
United Refining Co
PO Box 780
Warren, PA 16365
(814) 723-1500

CONTRIBUTIONS SUMMARY

Operating Locations: PA (Warren)

CORP. OFFICERS

John Andreas Catsimatidis: *B* Nissiros Greece 1948 *CURR EMPL* chmn, ceo: Red Apple Cos *CORP AFFIL* chmn: Florida Supermarket, Un Acquisition Corp; chmn, ceo: Un Refining Co; chmn, ceo, pres: Continental Bank Corp; chmn, ceo, pres, dir: Un Refining Co PA; chmn, ceo, treas: Designcraft Indus; chmn, pres: Kiantone Pipeline Corp; dir: First NY Bank Bus *NONPR AFFIL* mem: Westside Chamber Commerce

United Savings Association of Texas

Assets: $6.8 billion
Employees: 2,200
Headquarters: Houston, TX
SIC Major Group: Depository Institutions

CONTACT

Ruth Lack
Director of Public Relations
United Savings Association of Texas
3200 Southwest Fwy.,13th Fl.
Houston, TX 77027
(713) 963-6500

FINANCIAL SUMMARY

Fiscal Note: Annual Giving Range: $100,000 to $250,000

CONTRIBUTIONS SUMMARY

Operating Locations: TX (Houston)

CORP. OFFICERS

Barry Burkholder: *CURR EMPL* pres: Un Savings Assn TX

Anthony J. Nocella: *CURR EMPL* cfo: Meritor Fin Group *CORP AFFIL* cfo: Un Savings Assn TX

United Service Foundation

CONTACT

United Service Fdn.
P.O. Box 36
New Holland, PA 17577

FINANCIAL SUMMARY

Recent Giving: $218,317 (1991); $479,922 (1990)
Assets: $7,569,273 (1991); $6,634,799 (1990)
Gifts Received: $100,000 (1991)
Fiscal Note: In fiscal 1991, contributions were received from Edith M. Weaver.
EIN: 23-7038781

CONTRIBUTIONS SUMMARY

Donor(s): the late Victor F. Weaver, Edith M. Weaver, Dale M. Weaver, Irene M. Weaver and Larry Newswanger
Typical Recipients: • *Education:* religious education • *Religion:* churches, religious organizations • *Social Services:* homes, recreation & athletics, shelters/homelessness
Grant Types: general support and operating expenses

GIVING OFFICERS

Dale M. Weaver: mgr

APPLICATION INFORMATION

Initial Approach: Contributes only to preselected organizations. Applications not accepted.
Restrictions on Giving: Does not provide grants to individuals.

GRANTS ANALYSIS

Number of Grants: 15
Highest Grant: $100,000
Typical Range: $1,000 to $10,000
Disclosure Period: 1991

RECENT GRANTS

100,000 Eastern Mennonite Seminary — program support
30,000 Habitat for Humanity, Lancaster, PA

24,974 Camp Hebron, Halifax, PA — equipment fund
18,843 Camp Hebron, Halifax, PA — equipment fund
10,000 Mennonite Board of Education, Elkhart, IN — program support
10,000 Naaman Center, Elizabethtown, PA — program support
5,000 MEDA, Lancaster, PA
4,000 Beth Shalom, Lancaster, PA — program support
3,000 Spanish Mennonite Church, New Holland, PA — program support
2,000 Water Street Rescue, Lancaster, PA — operations fund

United Services Automobile Association / USAA Trust

Headquarters: San Antonio, TX
SIC Major Group: Insurance Carriers

CONTACT

William L. Patton
Executive Director
USAA Trust
USAA Bldg., B-01-W
San Antonio, TX 78288
(512) 498-0752

FINANCIAL SUMMARY

Recent Giving: $1,014,935 (fiscal 1990)
Assets: $3,295,375 (fiscal year ending June 30, 1990)
EIN: 74-636461

CONTRIBUTIONS SUMMARY

Grant Types: general support and matching
Operating Locations: TX (San Antonio)

APPLICATION INFORMATION

Initial Approach: Company supports preselected organizations and does not accept applications.
Disclosure Period: fiscal year ending June 30, 1990

U.S. Bank of Washington

Assets: $5.33 billion
Employees: 2,837
Parent Company: U.S. Bancorp
Headquarters: Seattle, WA
SIC Major Group: Depository
Institutions

CONTACT

Molly W. Reed
Vice President & Manager,
Communications
U.S. Bank of Washington
PO Box 720, WWH658
Seattle, WA 98111-0720
(206) 344-2360

CONTRIBUTIONS SUMMARY

Primarily supports social service and arts organizations in operating communities.

Typical Recipients: • *Arts & Humanities:* general • *Health:* general • *Social Services:* child welfare

Grant Types: capital, general support, and matching

Nonmonetary Support Types: in-kind services

Geographic Distribution: headquarters and operating locations

Operating Locations: WA (Seattle)

CORP. OFFICERS

Joshua Green III: *B* Seattle WA 1936 *ED* Harvard Univ 1958 *CURR EMPL* vchmn, ceo: US Bancorp *CORP AFFIL* chmn: Green (Joshua) Corp; chmn, ceo: US Bank WA; dir: SAFECO Corp; vchmn: US Bancorp *NONPR AFFIL* mem: Assn Reserve City Bankers

APPLICATION INFORMATION

Initial Approach: Send brief letter of inquiry, including a description of the organization, amount requested, purpose of funds sought, audited financial statement, and proof of tax-exempt status. There are no deadlines.

United States Borax & Chemical Corp.

Sales: $3.5 billion
Employees: 1,500
Headquarters: Los Angeles, CA
SIC Major Group: Chemicals & Allied Products, Nonmetallic Minerals Except Fuels, and Oil & Gas Extraction

CONTACT

Clay Lorah
Vice President
United States Borax & Chemical Corp.
PO Box 75128 Sanford Sta.
Los Angeles, CA 90075-0128
(213) 251-5400

CONTRIBUTIONS SUMMARY

The program supports the traditional categories of arts, civic, education, health, and social services.

Typical Recipients: • *Arts & Humanities:* community arts • *Civic & Public Affairs:* urban & community affairs • *Health:* health organizations • *Social Services:* united funds

Grant Types: capital and general support

Nonmonetary Support Types: donated products

Geographic Distribution: principally near operating locations and to some national organizations via local chapters

Operating Locations: CA, WV

CORP. OFFICERS

F. A. S. Lesser: *CURR EMPL* chmn: US Borax & Chem Corp

Glenn Swartz: *CURR EMPL* treas: US Borax & Chem Corp

I. L. White-Thomson: *CURR EMPL* pres: US Borax & Chem Corp

GIVING OFFICERS

Clay Lorah: *CURR EMPL* vp: US Borax & Chem Corp

APPLICATION INFORMATION

Initial Approach: Send a letter between June and December of the year prior to when support is needed. Include a description of the organization, amount and purpose of funds sought, a recently audited financial statement, and proof of tax-exempt status.

Restrictions on Giving: Program does not support individuals, political groups, or religious organizations. It rarely makes grants to agencies already receiving support from united funds.

U.S. Healthcare, Inc.

Assets: $758.2 million
Employees: 2,538
Headquarters: Blue Bell, PA
SIC Major Group: Health Services and Insurance Carriers

CONTACT

Lori Bookbinder
U.S. Healthcare, Inc.
1425 Union Meeting Rd.
Blue Bell, PA 19422
(215) 628-4800

CONTRIBUTIONS SUMMARY

Operating Locations: PA (Blue Bell)

CORP. OFFICERS

Leonard Abramson: *B* Philadelphia PA 1932 *ED* PA St Univ BA 1954; Philadelphia Coll Pharmacy & Science BsPh 1960; Nova Univ MPA 1978 *CURR EMPL* pres, dir: US HealthCare *NONPR AFFIL* mem: Big Brothers/Big Sisters Am, Philadelphia Orchestra Assn, Police Athletic League

Costas C. Nicolaides: *CURR EMPL* exec vp, cfo: US Healthcare

RECENT GRANTS

75,000 Philadelphia College of Pharmacy and Science, Philadelphia, PA — over five years

---

United States-Japan Foundation

CONTACT

Ronald Aqua
Vice President
United States-Japan Foundation
145 East 32nd St.
New York, NY 10016
(212) 481-8753
Note: FAX: (212) 481-8762

FINANCIAL SUMMARY

Recent Giving: $4,500,000 (1993 est.); $4,495,000 (1992 approx.); $5,267,989 (1991)
Assets: $83,000,000 (1993 est.); $82,877,008 (1992); $87,449,567 (1991); $81,830,619 (1990)
EIN: 13-3054425

CONTRIBUTIONS SUMMARY

Donor(s): The United States-Japan Foundation was incorporated in 1980 under the laws of New York as a private American philanthropic organization dedicated to the promotion of greater mutual knowledge between the people of Japan and the United States. It was founded by Ryoichi Sasakawa, chairman of the Japan Shipbuilding Industry Foundation, as a response to the increasingly competitive nature of bilateral relations between the United States and Japan. He expressed the hope that, through the foundation, "the mutual interests of the two societies would be more clearly recognized and better appreciated."

Typical Recipients: • *Civic & Public Affairs:* international affairs, public policy • *Education:* public education (precollege)

Grant Types: challenge and project

Geographic Distribution: United States and Japan

GIVING OFFICERS

Yoko Amari: adm asst Tokyo off

Ronald Aqua: vp

Thomas A. Bartlett: trust *B* Salem OR 1930 *ED* Stanford Univ AB 1951; Stanford Univ PhD 1959; Oxford Univ MA 1953 *CORP AFFIL* dir: Am Cast Iron Pipe Co, Security Mutual Life Ins Co *NONPR AFFIL* mem: Counc Foreign Rels, US-Egyptian Comm Cultural Exchanges, West AL Chamber Commerce; pres: OR St Sys Higher Ed Off; trust: Am Univ Cairo, US-Japan Fdn; chancellor: Univ AL system; mem natl bd examining Chaplains: Episcopal Church

Hiroko Bloch: exec secy, grant adm

Stephen W. Bosworth: pres, trust *B* Grand Rapids MI 1939 *ED* Dartmouth Coll AB 1961

Robin Chandler Duke: trust

William Denman Eberle: chmn bd trusts *B* Boise ID 1923 *ED* Stanford Univ BA 1945; Harvard Univ MBA 1947; Harvard Univ LLB 1949 *CORP AFFIL* chmn: EBCO, Holders Capital Corp; dir: Alexander Proudfoot Cos, Ampco-Pittsburgh Corp, Mitchell Energy & Devel Corp, Oak Indus; pres: Manchester Assocs *NONPR AFFIL* mem: Am Bar Assn, Aspen Inst Production US World Economy, Chief Execs Org, Counc Foreign Rels, ID Bar Assn, Intl Chamber Commerce, Intl Res Policy Comm, US Canada Comm, US

Counc Intl Bus, US Japan Fdn; trust: Atlantic Counc US, Comm Econ Devel, Un Nations Assn

Thomas J. Foran: sr program off

Shinji Fukukawa: trust

Jennifer Fulton: program off

Takeaki Hori: vp, dir

Tokeaki Hori: dir

Tadao Ishikawa: trust

Maximilian Walter Kempner: secy *B* Berlin Germany 1929 *ED* Harvard Univ BA 1951; Harvard Univ LLB 1954; Columbia Univ LLM 1957 *CURR EMPL* couns: McDermott Will & Emery *NONPR AFFIL* chmn: Counc Library Resources; dean: VT Law Sch South Royalton; fellow: Am Bar Fdn; mem: Am Bar Assn, Am Law Inst, Counc Foreign Rels, New York City Bar Assn, NY Bar Assn; mem adv comm: Yale Program Nonprofit Orgs; mem visitors comm: Columbia Univ; pres: Harvard Law Sch Assn NY City

Sander Lehrer: secy

Winston Lord: trust *NONPR AFFIL* adv: Fletcher Sch Law & Diplomacy; dir: Carnegie Endowment Natl Comm Am & New World, Natl Endowment Democracy, US Comm US-China Rels; distinguished fellow: Aspen Inst; mem: Asia Soc, Trilateral Commn

Christine Mayo: adm off

Robert Strange McNamara: trust *B* San Francisco CA 1916 *ED* Univ CA AB 1937; Harvard Univ MBA 1939 *CORP AFFIL* dir: BankAmerica Corp, Corning Glass Works, Intl Fin Corp, Transworld Corp, Washington Post Co; pres: Intl Devel Assn *NONPR AFFIL* dir: Brookings Inst, CA Inst Tech, Natl Comm Pub Svc, Overseas Devel Counc, Strategic Planning Assocs, Urban Inst; mem: Phi Beta Kappa; mem, trust: Enterprise Fdn

Moriyuki Motono: trust

Isao Nakauchi: trust

Robert W. Sarnoff: trust *CORP AFFIL* dir: Am Home Products Corp

Yohei Sasakawa: trust

Ryuzo Sejima: trust

Ayako Sono: trust

Phillips Talbot: trust *B* Pittsburgh PA 1915 *ED* Univ IL BA; Univ IL BS 1936; London Sch Oriental Studies 1938; Aligarh Muslim Univ 1939; Univ Chicago PhD 1954 *NONPR AFFIL* mem: Am Academy Diplomacy, Assn Asian Stud-ies, Counc Foreign Rels, Pilgrims US, Royal Soc Asian Affs; pres emeritus: Asia Soc; trust: China Inst Am, East Asian History Science, Inst Current World Affs, South-North News Svc, Un Bd Christian Higher Ed Asia, Univ Field Staff Intl

Yoshio Terasawa: trust

Joseph Davies Tydings: trust *B* Asheville NC 1928 *ED* Univ MD BA 1951; Univ MD LLB 1953 *CURR EMPL* ptnr: Anderson, Kill, Olick & Oshinsky *CORP AFFIL* dir: GAF Corp *NONPR AFFIL* co-chmn: Univ MD Population Crisis Comm; mem: Am Bar Assn, Baltimore Bar Assn, Baltimore Jr Bar Assn, DC Bar Assn, Fed Bar Assn, Hartford County Bar Assn, MD Bar Assn; special sr couns: Un Nations Fund Population Activities; vchmn bd regents: Univ MD

Jiro Ushio: vchmn bd trusts

John S. Wadsworth, Jr.: trust *B* Ft Thomas KY 1939 *ED* Williams Coll BA 1961; Univ Chicago MBA 1963 *CURR EMPL* pres: Morgan Stanley Japan Ltd Tokyo *CORP AFFIL* chmn: Littleford Brothers; mng dir: Morgan Stanley & Co *NONPR AFFIL* mem: Am Chamber Commerce Japan; mem Japan program adv counc: Asia Fdn; trust: Parker Collegiate Inst, US - Japan Fdn

Henry G. Walter, Jr.: trust *B* New York NY 1910 *ED* Columbia Univ BA 1931; Columbia Univ LLB 1934 *NONPR AFFIL* dir: Intl Atlantic Salmon Fdn; trust: Am Mus Natural History, Monell Chemical Senses Ctr, Neuroscience Res Fdn, Pierpont Morgan Library

APPLICATION INFORMATION

Initial Approach:

The foundation does not provide application forms. Requests for grants should be submitted by letter.

The initial letter should be no longer than three pages and should provide the following information: summary of the proposed project; description of the applicant organization, including tax-exempt status, if applicable; present sources of funds; and the amount of the requested grant. The foundation will notify the grantseeker if the proposed project is not of interest. If the foundation is in-terested, it will request a detailed prospectus of the project. Requests for grants may be inititated at any time. The grant review process takes from six to twelve months.

Restrictions on Giving: The foundation does not fund undergraduate education, student exchanges, sports exchanges, publication subventions, cultural performances, exhibitions, scientific research, or research conferences. It does not support capital campaigns, endowment funds, or deficit operations; nor does it make grants for the purchase of equipment. As a rule, it does not extend grants to individuals applying on their own behalf for independent study, research, travel, or participation in meetings.

OTHER THINGS TO KNOW

The foundation is governed by a board of trustees made up of representatives from the United States and Japan. The foundation's headquarters is in New York City, with a liaison office in Tokyo.

Publications: annual report and quarterly newsletter

GRANTS ANALYSIS

Total Grants: $4,495,000*

Number of Grants: 40

Highest Grant: $300,000

Typical Range: $50,000 to $200,000

Disclosure Period: 1992

Note: Recent grants are derived from a 1991 annual report. The total grants and average grant figures are approximate.

RECENT GRANTS

242,002 Fund for the City of New York, New York, NY — for exchange between officals and urban experts from three large metropolitan areas in the U.S. and their counterparts in Japan

218,536 University of Maryland Foundation, Adelphi, MD — for the Mid-Atlantic Region Japan-in-the-Schools Program for precollege educators in the District of Columbia, Maryland, Virginia, and West Virginia

200,000 Japan Society, New York, NY — to support the Commis-sion on U.S.-Japan Relations for the 21st Century

185,636 Carnegie Council on Ethics and International Affairs, New York, NY — to support the third year of the consultative group on U.S.-Japan economic cooperation in the Philippines

162,461 Institute of Public Administration, New York, NY — to support exchange between American and Japanese public works professionals

150,000 World Resources Institute, Washington, DC — for U.S.-Japan research on the transfer of environmental protection technology between developed and Third World countries

146,391 American Public Radio, Minneapolis, MN — to support coverage of business and economic news and issues from Japan through American Public Radio's weeknightly series, Marketplace

145,541 Five Colleges, Amherst, MA — to support the New England Program for Teaching About Japan for precollege educators in Connecticut, Maine, Massachusetts, New Hampshire, Rhode Island, and Vermont

141,050 Columbia Univesity, New York, NY — to support the second year of the U.S.-Japan consultative group on Indochina

140,000 United Nations Association of the USA, New York, NY — for US-Japan dialogue on regional crisis management and the United Nations

U.S. Leasing International

Sales: $547.5 million
Employees: 850
Parent Company: Ford Financial Services Group, which is a subsidiary of Ford Motor Co.
Headquarters: San Francisco, CA
SIC Major Group: Automobile Repair, Services & Parking and Business Services

CONTACT

Tom Donohue
Manager, Community Affairs
U.S. Leasing
733 Front St.
San Francisco, CA 94111
(415) 627-9000

FINANCIAL SUMMARY

Recent Giving: $500,000 (1993 est.); $484,830 (1992); $485,000 (1991 approx.)
Fiscal Note: Figures above for foundation only. Company also gives an unspecified amount of nonmonetary support.

CONTRIBUTIONS SUMMARY

Typical Recipients: • *Arts & Humanities:* ethnic arts, libraries, museums/galleries, music, opera, performing arts, public broadcasting, theater • *Civic & Public Affairs:* business/free enterprise, housing, public policy, women's affairs • *Education:* arts education, colleges & universities, education funds, elementary education, minority education • *Health:* hospices, single-disease health associations • *Social Services:* community centers, disabled, domestic violence, employment/job training, legal aid, shelters/homelessness, united funds, youth organizations
Grant Types: employee matching gifts and general support
Nonmonetary Support Types: donated equipment
Note: Contact for nonmonetary support is Ed Mazyck, Manager, Corporate administration at (415) 627-9000.
Geographic Distribution: near headquarters and operating locations
Operating Locations: CA (San Francisco, San Mateo)

CORP. OFFICERS

James George Duff: *B* Pittsburgh KS 1938 *CURR EMPL* chmn, ceo, dir: US Leasing Intl *CORP AFFIL* dir: Airlease Mgmt Svcs, US Fleet Leasing Inc, US Rail Svcs, USL Securities Corp *NONPR AFFIL* mem: Conf Bd, San Francisco Chamber Commerce; mem adv bd: Univ KS Sch Bus

GIVING OFFICERS

Tom Donohue: *CURR EMPL* mgr (commun aff): US Leasing Intl

APPLICATION INFORMATION

Initial Approach: *Initial Contact:* brief letter *Include Information On:* description of the organization and clients served, amount requested, purpose for which funds are sought, recently audited financial statement (including statement of income and expenses), list of board members, proof of tax-exempt status *When to Submit:* any time
Restrictions on Giving: Does not make contributions for political, religious, or sectarian activities.

OTHER THINGS TO KNOW

Gives priority to organizations in which company's employees are active in a regular volunteer capacity.
Publications: guidelines

GRANTS ANALYSIS

Total Grants: $484,830
Number of Grants: 88
Highest Grant: $60,000
Typical Range: $1,000 to $10,000
Disclosure Period: 1992
Note: Recent grants are derived from a 1992 contributions report.

RECENT GRANTS

60,000	Library Foundation of San Francisco, San Francisco, CA — capital campaign
18,250	San Francisco Museum of Modern Art, San Francisco, CA
15,500	San Francisco Symphony, San Francisco, CA
15,000	San Francisco Museum of Modern Art, San Francisco, CA — capital campaign
13,000	Fine Arts Museums of San Francisco, San Francisco, CA
11,500	San Francisco Opera, San Francisco, CA
8,750	Boy Scouts of the Bay Area, San Francisco, CA
8,000	San Francisco Ballet, San Francisco, CA
7,500	San Francisco AIDS Foundation
7,500	San Francisco Education Fund, San Francisco, CA

U.S. News & World Report

Sales: $140.0 million
Employees: 500
Headquarters: New York, NY
SIC Major Group: Printing & Publishing

CONTACT

Sandy Moore
Publicity Coordinator
U.S. News & World Report
599 Lexington Avenue, 12th Fl.
New York, NY 10022
(212) 326-5300

CONTRIBUTIONS SUMMARY

Operating Locations: NY (New York)

CORP. OFFICERS

Fred Drasner: *CURR EMPL* ceo: US News & World Report
Alice Rogoff: *CURR EMPL* cfo: US News & World Report

U.S. Oil/Schmidt Family Foundation, Inc.

CONTACT

U.S. Oil/Schmidt Family Fdn, Inc.
425 Washington St.
PO Box 25
Combined Locks, WI 54113-1049

FINANCIAL SUMMARY

Recent Giving: $328,111 (fiscal 1990); $196,810 (fiscal 1989)
Assets: $1,800,118 (fiscal year ending July 31, 1990); $1,633,956 (fiscal 1989)
Gifts Received: $7,187 (fiscal 1990); $36,165 (fiscal 1989)
EIN: 39-1540933

CONTRIBUTIONS SUMMARY

Donor(s): Raymond Schmidt, Arthur J. Schmidt, William Schmidt

Typical Recipients: • *Civic & Public Affairs:* municipalities • *Education:* private education (precollege), religious education • *Health:* health funds, health organizations, hospitals, pediatric health • *Religion:* churches, missionary activities, religious organizations • *Social Services:* community service organizations, community service organizations, food/clothing distribution, youth organizations
Grant Types: general support
Geographic Distribution: focus on WI

GIVING OFFICERS

Paul Bachman: trust
Arthur J. Schmidt: dir, pres
Raymond Schmidt: dir, secy
Thomas Schmidt: trust
William Schmidt: dir, vp

APPLICATION INFORMATION

Initial Approach: Contributes only to preselected organizations. Applications not accepted.
Restrictions on Giving: Does not support individuals.

GRANTS ANALYSIS

Number of Grants: 74
Highest Grant: $25,000
Typical Range: $1,000 to $10,000
Disclosure Period: fiscal year ending July 31, 1990

RECENT GRANTS

25,000	Salvatorian Mission Warehouse, New Holstein, WI
25,000	St. Paul Home, Kaukauna, WI
19,470	Community Foundation for the Region, Appleton, WI
5,620	Children's Hospital, Milwaukee, WI
5,000	Diocesan Mission, Kaukauna, WI — Dominican Republic, St. Al's Parish
5,000	Sisters of St. Francis of Holy Cross, Combined Locks, WI
5,000	Xavier High School, Appleton, WI
3,000	St. Elizabeth Hospital Foundation, Appleton, WI
3,000	St. Elizabeth Hospital Foundation, Appleton, WI
3,000	YMCA, Appleton, WI

U.S. Silica Co.

Sales: $85.0 million
Employees: 1,055
Parent Company: United States Borax and Chemical Corp.
Headquarters: Berkeley Springs, WV
SIC Major Group: Nonmetallic Minerals Except Fuels

CONTACT

Walter Pellish
Vice President, Administration
U.S. Silica Co.
PO Box 187
Berkeley Springs, WV 25411
(304) 258-2500

CONTRIBUTIONS SUMMARY

Support is given in the traditional contributions categories of the arts, education, health, civic and public affairs, and social services.
Typical Recipients: • *Arts & Humanities:* museums/galleries • *Civic & Public Affairs:* safety • *Education:* public education (precollege) • *Health:* hospitals • *Social Services:* youth organizations
Grant Types: general support
Geographic Distribution: near headquarters and operating locations only
Operating Locations: WV

CORP. OFFICERS

Richard Goodell: *CURR EMPL* pres: US Silica Co

GIVING OFFICERS

Walter Pellish: *CURR EMPL* vp (admin): US Silica Co

APPLICATION INFORMATION

Initial Approach: Send letter any time including a description of the organization and the amount and purpose of funds sought.

United States Sugar Corp. / United States Sugar Corporate Charitable Trust

Sales: $320.0 million
Employees: 2,550
Headquarters: Clewiston, FL
SIC Major Group: Agricultural Production— Crops and Food & Kindred Products

CONTACT

Atwood Dunwoody
Trustee
United States Sugar Corp. Charitable Trust
PO Box 1207
Clewiston, FL 33440
(813) 983-8121

FINANCIAL SUMMARY

Recent Giving: $377,671 (fiscal 1991); $488,615 (fiscal 1990); $362,808 (fiscal 1989)
Assets: $1,976,535 (fiscal year ending October 31, 1991); $1,922,168 (fiscal 1990); $2,385,862 (fiscal 1987)
Fiscal Note: Figures for fiscal year 1990 do not include direct giving by corporation. Company gives directly and through the foundation, but reports that direct giving is available only to organizations located near headquarters and is limited.
EIN: 59-6142825

CONTRIBUTIONS SUMMARY

Typical Recipients: • *Arts & Humanities:* arts associations • *Civic & Public Affairs:* better government, business/free enterprise, environmental affairs, municipalities, philanthropic organizations, professional & trade associations, public policy • *Education:* agricultural education, colleges & universities, economic education, education administration, education associations, education funds, elementary education, preschool education, public education (precollege), science/technology education • *Health:* emergency/ambulance services, health organizations, hospices, hospitals, single-disease health associations • *Social Services:* child welfare, community centers, community service organizations, disabled, family services, legal aid, recreation & athletics, shelters/homelessness, united funds, youth organizations
Grant Types: capital, emergency, fellowship, general support, professorship, and project
Geographic Distribution: in geographic areas near operating locations
Operating Locations: FL (Clewiston, South Bay)

CORP. OFFICERS

John Buckner Boy: *B* Johnson City TN 1917 *ED* GA Inst Tech 1938 *CURR EMPL* vchmn: US Sugar Corp *CORP AFFIL* dir:

FL Sugarcane League *NONPR AFFIL* dir: Am Soc Sugar Cane Technologists
Atwood Dunwody: *CURR EMPL* gen coun, dir: US Sugar Corp
J. Nelson Fairbanks: *CURR EMPL* pres, dir: US Sugar Corp
William Samuel White: *B* Cincinnati OH 1937 *ED* Dartmouth Coll BA 1959; Dartmouth Coll MBA 1960 *CURR EMPL* chmn, dir: US Sugar Corp *CORP AFFIL* dir: Continental Water Corp *NONPR AFFIL* chmn: Flint Area Focus Counc; dir: Counc on Fdns; mem exec comm: Daycroft Sch

GIVING OFFICERS

Fleming A. Barbour: trust *CORP AFFIL* dir: US Sugar Corp
John Buckner Boy: trust *CURR EMPL* vchmn: US Sugar Corp (see above)
Atwood Dunwody: trust *CURR EMPL* gen coun, dir: US Sugar Corp (see above)

APPLICATION INFORMATION

Initial Approach: *Initial Contact:* full proposal *Include Information On:* description of the organization, amount requested, purpose for which funds are sought, recently audited financial statement, proof of tax-exempt status *When to Submit:* any time; trustees meet four times a year

OTHER THINGS TO KNOW

United States Sugar Corp. reports that it gives directly only to organizations located near company's headquarters.

GRANTS ANALYSIS

Total Grants: $377,671
Number of Grants: 77
Highest Grant: $41,437
Typical Range: $1,000 to $5,000
Disclosure Period: fiscal year ending October 31, 1991
Note: Recent grants are derived from a fiscal 1991 Form 990.

RECENT GRANTS

41,436 Child Care of Southwest Florida, Ft. Myers, FL
31,934 Child Care of Southwest Florida, Ft. Myers, FL
25,000 Carroll County Tornado Disaster Relief Fund, Vaiden, MS

25,000 Hendry County District School Board, LaBelle, FL
13,200 YMCA of the Palm Beaches, West Palm Beach, FL
10,000 Friends of the Children's Inn at National Institute of Health, Washington, DC
10,000 Palm Beach Atlantic University, Palm Beach, FL
10,000 Planned Parenthood of the Palm Beach Area, Belle Glade, FL
7,500 Florida Future Farmers of America Foundation, Winter Haven, FL
7,500 Florida Taxwatch, Tallahassee, FL

United States Surgical Corp.

Sales: $843.55 million
Employees: 7,300
Headquarters: Norwalk, CT
SIC Major Group: Instruments & Related Products

CONTACT

Karen Violette
Manager, Community Relations
United States Surgical Corp.
150 Glover Ave.
Norwalk, CT 06856
(203) 845-1000

CONTRIBUTIONS SUMMARY

Operating Locations: CT (Norwalk)

CORP. OFFICERS

Leon Charles Hirsch: *B* Bronx NY 1927 *CURR EMPL* chmn, pres, ceo: US Surgical Corp *NONPR AFFIL* chmn adv bd, mem: Am Soc Colon Rectal Surgeons Res Fdn; mem: Am Bus Conf
Bruce S. Lustman: *CURR EMPL* exec vp (fin), coo: Un States Surgical Corp

RECENT GRANTS

5,000 St. Francis School, New Haven, CT

United States Trust Co. of New York / United States Trust Co. of New York Foundation

Revenue: $405.03 million
Employees: 2,200
Parent Company: U.S. Trust Corp.
Headquarters: New York, NY
SIC Major Group: Depository Institutions, Holding & Other Investment Offices, and Security & Commodity Brokers

CONTACT

Carol Strickland
Vice President & Secretary
United States Trust Co. of New York Fdn.
114 W 47th St.
New York, NY 10036
(212) 852-1330

FINANCIAL SUMMARY

Recent Giving: $551,981 (1991); $479,526 (1990); $471,171 (1989)

Assets: $164,303 (1991); $324,600 (1990); $32,715 (1988)

EIN: 13-6072081

CONTRIBUTIONS SUMMARY

Typical Recipients: • *Arts & Humanities:* arts centers, community arts, dance, museums/galleries, music, opera, performing arts, public broadcasting, theater, visual arts • *Civic & Public Affairs:* business/free enterprise, economic development, environmental affairs, housing, public policy, urban & community affairs, zoos/botanical gardens • *Education:* colleges & universities, literacy • *Health:* geriatric health, health care cost containment, health funds, health organizations, hospitals, medical rehabilitation, nursing services, nutrition & health maintenance, pediatric health • *Social Services:* aged, child welfare, community centers, community service organizations, delinquency & crime, disabled, drugs & alcohol, food/clothing distribution, homes, legal aid, shelters/homelessness, volunteer services, youth organizations

Grant Types: capital, employee matching gifts, and general support

Nonmonetary Support Types: donated equipment and in-kind services

Note: Value of nonmonetary support is not available and is not included in the giving figures above. For information on nonmonetary giving, contact Maureen Nuget, Vice President.

Geographic Distribution: primarily in the metropolitan New York area

Operating Locations: CA (Los Angeles), FL (West Palm Beach), MA (Boston), NY (New York), TX (Dallas)

CORP. OFFICERS

Jeffrey Stuart Maurer: *B* New York NY 1947 *ED* St Johns Univ *CURR EMPL* pres, dir: US Trust Co NY *NONPR AFFIL* mem: Am Bankers Assn, Am Bar Assn, Nassau County Bar Assn, NY Bar Assn, NY St Bankers Assn
Donald M. Roberts: *B* Paterson NJ 1935 *CURR EMPL* vchmn, treas, dir: US Trust Co NY *CORP AFFIL* dir: York Intl Corp *NONPR AFFIL* trust: Brick Presbyterian Church, St Bernards Sch
H. Marshall Schwarz: *B* New York NY *ED* Harvard Univ AB 1958; Harvard Univ MBA 1961 *CURR EMPL* chmn, ceo, dir: US Trust Co NY

GIVING OFFICERS

Carol A. Strickland: adm *B* Cold Spring NY 1949 *ED* Skidmore Coll 1972; NY Univ 1978 *CURR EMPL* sr vp, secy, dir (investor rels): US Trust Corp NY *NONPR AFFIL* mem: Am Soc Corp Secys

APPLICATION INFORMATION

Initial Approach: *Initial Contact:* proposal *Include Information On:* concise statement regarding project, agency, or program, including need or problem addressed; service area and beneficiaries; procedures and evaluative criteria of the project; detailed budget, including program costs and funds required for administrative and overhead expenses and two-year budget projections; past two-years' audited financial statements; proof of tax-exempt status; immediate and long-range goals; current and prospective sources of support, including foundations, corporations, and government grants; list of board members and officers *When to Submit:* all grants proposals for the Cultural & the Arts and Education must be received by April 1; for Health & Human Services and Civic & Community proposals must be received by July 1 *Note:* If additional information is necessary or meeting is desired, the organization will be contacted.

Restrictions on Giving: Foundation does not make contributions to individuals; veterans, fraternal, or labor organizations unless such organizations are nondiscriminatory and are engaged in significant work for the entire community; religious institutions, unless affiliated with educational or housing-related institutions; organizations, projects, or programs outside the United States; political organizations or activities; emergency cash flow situations; requests for goodwill advertising, fund-raising dinners, sponsorship in publications, or athletic teams; national associations; or member agencies of the United Way or other agencies supported by umbrella organizations.

GRANTS ANALYSIS

Total Grants: $551,981
Number of Grants: 85
Highest Grant: $50,000
Typical Range: $2,500 to $10,000
Disclosure Period: 1991
Note: Recent grants are derived from a 1991 Form 990.

RECENT GRANTS

50,000 United Way of New York City, New York, NY
20,000 Habitat for Humanity, New York, NY
16,000 Consumer-Farmer Foundation, New York, NY
15,000 Central Park Conservancy, New York, NY
15,000 Lincoln Center for the Performing Arts, New York, NY
15,000 New York University, New York, NY
15,000 Playing to Win, New York, NY
12,500 Cooper Union for the Advancement of Science and Art, New York, NY
10,000 Children's Health Fund, New York, NY
10,000 Children's Museum of Manhattan, New York, NY

United Stationers Inc. / United Stationers Foundation

Sales: $951.1 million
Employees: 2,800
Headquarters: Des Plaines, IL
SIC Major Group: Wholesale Trade—Durable Goods and Wholesale Trade—Nondurable Goods

CONTACT

Allen Kravis
Senior Vice President & CFO
United Stationers Inc.
2200 East Golf Rd.
Des Plaines, IL 60016
(708) 699-5000

FINANCIAL SUMMARY

Fiscal Note: Company does not disclose contributions figures.

CONTRIBUTIONS SUMMARY

Typical Recipients: • *Arts & Humanities:* general • *Civic & Public Affairs:* general • *Education:* general • *Health:* general • *Social Services:* general
Grant Types: general support
Operating Locations: IL (Des Plaines)

CORP. OFFICERS

Melvin L. Hecktman: *CURR EMPL* vchmn, dir: Un Stationers
Jeffrey K. Hewson: *CURR EMPL* pres, coo, dir: Un Stationers
Allen B. Kravis: *CURR EMPL* sr vp, cfo: Un Stationers
Joel D. Spungin: *CURR EMPL* chmn, ceo, dir: Un Stationers

APPLICATION INFORMATION

Initial Approach: Send brief letter of inquiry, including a description of the organization, amount requested, purpose of funds sought, and proof of tax-exempt status.

United Technologies, Automotive / United Technologies, Automotive

Former Foundation Name: Sheller-Globe Foundation
Sales: $2.1 billion
Employees: 32,000
Parent Company: United Technologies Corp.
Headquarters: Dearborn, MI
SIC Major Group: Electronic & Other Electrical Equipment, Industrial Machinery & Equipment, and Transportation Equipment

CONTACT
William H. Patterson
United Technologies, Automotive
c/o Sheller-Globe Corporation
1505 Jefferson Ave.
Toledo, OH 43603
(419) 255-8840

FINANCIAL SUMMARY
Recent Giving: $155,000 (1990); $21,625 (1989)
Assets: $172,812 (1989)
EIN: 34-6518486

CONTRIBUTIONS SUMMARY
Typical Recipients: • *Education:* colleges & universities • *Social Services:* community service organizations, united funds
Grant Types: general support
Geographic Distribution: focus on OH and IN
Operating Locations: MI (Dearborn)

CORP. OFFICERS
Norman R. Bodine: *CURR EMPL* pres: Un Techs Automotive

GIVING OFFICERS
Ohio Citizen's Bank: trust

APPLICATION INFORMATION
Initial Approach: Send brief letter including a description of the organization, amount requested, purpose of funds sought, audited financial statement, and proof of tax-exempt status. Deadline is August.
Restrictions on Giving: Does not support individuals or religious organizations for sectarian purposes.

GRANTS ANALYSIS
Number of Grants: 4
Highest Grant: $10,000
Typical Range: $375 to $10,000
Disclosure Period: 1989

RECENT GRANTS
10,000 Indiana University at Kokomo, Kokomo, IN
10,000 Toledo Red Cross, Toledo, OH
1,250 United Foundation Torch Drive
375 United Foundation Urban Progress Fund, Detroit, MI

United Technologies Corp.

Sales: $22.03 billion
Employees: 176,000
Headquarters: Hartford, CT
SIC Major Group: Business Services, Industrial Machinery & Equipment, Instruments & Related Products, and Transportation Equipment

CONTACT
Kenneth R. Green
Director, Contributions
United Technologies Corp.
One Financial Plz.
Hartford, CT 06101
(203) 728-7943
Note: Leah Bailey, Contributions and Matching Gifts Administrator, can be reached at address above.

FINANCIAL SUMMARY
Recent Giving: $11,480,000 (1993 est.); $10,898,894 (1992); $12,117,787 (1991)
Fiscal Note: Company gives directly.

CONTRIBUTIONS SUMMARY
Typical Recipients: • *Arts & Humanities:* arts appreciation, arts centers, community arts, history/historic preservation, museums/galleries, music, opera, performing arts • *Civic & Public Affairs:* better government, business/free enterprise, environmental affairs, ethnic/minority organizations, law & justice, public policy, urban & community affairs, women's affairs • *Education:* business education, career/vocational education, colleges & universities, community & junior colleges, engineering education, literacy, minority education, public education (precollege), science/technology education • *Health:* health care cost containment, health organizations, hospitals • *Science:* science exhibits & fairs • *Social Services:* aged, child welfare, community service organizations, disabled, drugs & alcohol, family services, food/clothing distribution, volunteer services, youth organizations
Grant Types: capital and employee matching gifts
Nonmonetary Support Types: in-kind services
Note: In 1990, estimated value of nonmonetary support was $5,800. This amount is not included in totals above.
Geographic Distribution: emphasis on communities where company operates (about one third of budget distributed in headquarters state); also international contributions in countries in which company has operations
Operating Locations: AL (Huntsville), CA (San Jose), CO (Colorado Springs), CT (East Hartford, Farmington, Hartford, Middletown, North Haven, Norwalk, Stonington, Stratford, Windsor, Windsor Locks), DC, FL (West Palm Beach), GA (Columbus), IN (Bloomington, Fort Wayne), MA, MI (Alma, Dearborn), MS, NY (Syracuse), TN, VA (Arlington)
Note: Also operates internationally.

CORP. OFFICERS
Robert Fisher Daniell: *B* Milton MA 1933 *ED* Boston Univ 1954 *CURR EMPL* chmn, ceo: Un Techs Corp *CORP AFFIL* dir: Shell Oil Co, The Travelers Corp *NONPR AFFIL* corporator: Inst Living Svcs Corp; fellow: Univ Bridgeport; mem: Bus Counc, Bus Roundtable, Conf Bd, CT Bus Ed Coalition; trust: Falcon Fdn, Boston Univ, Natl Aviation Mus Fdn

George L. David: *B* Bryn Mawr PA 1942 *ED* Harvard Univ BA 1965; Univ VA MBA 1967 *CURR EMPL* exec vp, pres (commercial & indus): Un Techs Corp *NONPR AFFIL* trust: Wadsworth Atheneum

GIVING OFFICERS
Kenneth R. Green: *CURR EMPL* dir (contributions): Un Techs Corp

APPLICATION INFORMATION
Initial Approach: *Initial Contact:* brief letter *Include Information On:* description of the organization; amount and purpose of grant requested; most recent financial statement; list of directors; how program objectives will be achieved, including evidence of need for project; proof that organization can achieve project's purpose; project budget; current major donor listing with dollar amounts and anticipated funding sources for future project support; proof of tax-exempt status *When to Submit:* by August 1, for consideration for following year *Note:* All funding applications must be made by mail.
Restrictions on Giving: Does not support partisan political organizations; individuals; religious organizations for sectarian purposes; controversial social causes on which there are strong differences of opinion; organizations which are the recipients of federated drives to which company already contributes; or endowment campaigns.

OTHER THINGS TO KNOW
Corporation also contributes to charitable organizations in many of the 62 countries outside the United States where it has operations.

GRANTS ANALYSIS
Total Grants: $10,898,894
Number of Grants: 2,500
Highest Grant: $3,500,000
Typical Range: $2,000 to $30,000
Disclosure Period: 1992
Note: Recent grants are derived from a 1989 grants list.

United Telephone Co. of Florida
Sales: $735.8 million
Employees: 4,700
Parent Company: Sprint Corp.
Headquarters: Altamonte Springs, FL
SIC Major Group: Communications and Engineering & Management Services

CONTACT

J. A. Schnell
Staff Manager, Public Relations
United Telephone Co. of Florida
PO Box 5000
Altamonte Springs, FL
32716-5000
(407) 889-6118

FINANCIAL SUMMARY

Fiscal Note: Annual Giving
Range: $250,000 to $500,000

CONTRIBUTIONS SUMMARY

Company reports 50% of contributions support health and welfare; 25% to the arts; 20% to civic and public affairs; and 5% to education.
Typical Recipients: • *Arts & Humanities:* general • *Civic & Public Affairs:* general • *Education:* general • *Social Services:* general
Grant Types: general support
Operating Locations: FL (Altamonte Springs)

CORP. OFFICERS

T. W. Todd: *B* Windsor NC 1928 *ED* VA Polytech Inst 1955 *CURR EMPL* chmn, ceo, dir: Un Telephone Co FL *CORP AFFIL* dir: Barnett Bank Central FL

APPLICATION INFORMATION

Initial Approach: Send brief letter of inquiry. There are no deadlines.

United Telephone System (Eastern Group)

Sales: $179.2 million
Employees: 1,600
Parent Company: United Telecommunications Inc.
Headquarters: Carlisle, PA
SIC Major Group: Communications

CONTACT

Sandra J. Castillo Jackson
Director, Public Relations
United Telephone System (Eastern Group)
PO Box 1201
Carlisle, PA 17013-0905
(717) 245-6312

FINANCIAL SUMMARY

Fiscal Note: Annual Giving
Range: $100,000 to $250,000

CONTRIBUTIONS SUMMARY

Company reports 38% of contributions support health and welfare; 20% to education; 22% to civic and public affairs; 6% to the arts; and 14% to other organizations.
Typical Recipients: • *Arts & Humanities:* general • *Civic & Public Affairs:* general • *Education:* general • *Health:* general • *Social Services:* general
Grant Types: capital, employee matching gifts, and general support
Nonmonetary Support Types: donated equipment
Geographic Distribution: in headquarters and operating communities
Operating Locations: PA (Carlisle)

CORP. OFFICERS

William K. Smith: *CURR EMPL* pres: Un Telephone Sys Eastern Group

APPLICATION INFORMATION

Initial Approach: Send a brief letter of inquiry and a full proposal. Include a description of organization, amount requested, purpose of funds sought, recently audited financial statement, and proof of tax-exempt status. There are no deadlines.

GRANTS ANALYSIS

Note: Company reports that grant size varies.

United Togs Inc. / United Togs Foundation

Sales: $10.0 million
Employees: 100
Headquarters: Long Island City, NY
SIC Major Group: Apparel & Other Textile Products

CONTACT

Sam Saporta
President
United Togs Foundation
27-01 Bridge Plz. North
Long Island City, NY 11101
(718) 937-6610

FINANCIAL SUMMARY

Recent Giving: $45,228 (1990); $34,213 (1989)
Assets: $1,433 (1990); $2,022 (1989)
Gifts Received: $44,700 (1990); $32,500 (1989)
Fiscal Note: In 1990, contributions were received from United Togs, Inc.
EIN: 13-6108520

CONTRIBUTIONS SUMMARY

Typical Recipients: • *Education:* colleges & universities, religious education, science/technology education • *Health:* hospitals • *Religion:* religious organizations, synagogues • *Social Services:* aged, community service organizations, homes, united funds, youth organizations
Grant Types: general support
Geographic Distribution: focus on NY
Operating Locations: NY (Long Island City)

CORP. OFFICERS

Sam Saporta: *CURR EMPL* pres: Un Togs

GIVING OFFICERS

Sam Saporta: pres, dir *CURR EMPL* pres: Un Togs (see above)
Barry Shecter: vp, dir
Myron Sprei: secy, dir

APPLICATION INFORMATION

Initial Approach: Send brief letter describing program. There are no deadlines.

GRANTS ANALYSIS

Number of Grants: 17
Highest Grant: $13,333
Typical Range: $100 to $3,000
Disclosure Period: 1990

RECENT GRANTS

13,333 Jerusalem College of Technology, New York, NY
7,600 Sid Jacobson North Shore YMHA and YWHA, East Hills, NY
5,000 Ben Gurion University, New York, NY
3,075 Sephardic Temple, Cedarhurst, NY
1,100 Lasha and The Sephardic Home
1,000 Mount Sinai Medical Center, New York, NY
700 Garment Industry Day Care Center of China, New York, NY
600 Thirteen, New York, NY
600 United Jewish Appeal Federation of Jewish Philanthropies, New York, NY
500 Yeshivoth Har Etzion, Cedarhurst, NY

United Van Lines, Inc.

Revenue: $681.0 million
Employees: 540
Parent Company: UniGroup, Inc.
Headquarters: Fenton, MO
SIC Major Group: Trucking & Warehousing

CONTACT

Dave Erich
Director, Advertising
United Van Lines, Inc.
One United Dr.
Fenton, MO 63026
(314) 326-3100

CONTRIBUTIONS SUMMARY

Operating Locations: MO (Fenton)

CORP. OFFICERS

Robert J. Baer: *CURR EMPL* pres, coo: Un Van Lines
Maurice Greenblatt: *CURR EMPL* chmn, ceo: Un Van Lines
Gerald P. Stadler: *CURR EMPL* vchmn: Un Van Lines
Douglas H. Wilton: *CURR EMPL* cfo: Un Van Lines

Unitrode Corp.

Revenue: $87.3 million
Employees: 760
Headquarters: Billerica, MA
SIC Major Group: Electronic & Other Electrical Equipment and Industrial Machinery & Equipment

CONTACT

S. Kelley MacDonald
V.P., Corp. Communication
Unitrode Corp.
8 Suburban Park Dr.
Billerica, MA 01821
(508) 670-9706

FINANCIAL SUMMARY

Recent Giving: $25,000 (1993 est.)

CONTRIBUTIONS SUMMARY

Company reports 35% of contributions support civic and public affairs; 30% to education; 25% to the arts; and 20% to health and welfare. Interests include the arts, united funds, support for local school systems, food pantries, and youth sport leagues.

Typical Recipients: • *Arts & Humanities:* community arts, libraries, museums/galleries, performing arts, theater • *Civic & Public Affairs:* economic development • *Education:* arts education, business education, career/vocational education, elementary education, literacy • *Social Services:* aged, community service organizations, delinquency & crime, drugs & alcohol, employment/job training, recreation & athletics, youth organizations

Grant Types: general support, operating expenses, and scholarship

Nonmonetary Support Types: donated equipment and workplace solicitation

Geographic Distribution: in headquarters and operating communities

Operating Locations: MA (Billerica, Worcester), NH (Merrimack), NY (Ronkonkoma)

CORP. OFFICERS

Robert L. Gable: *B* Baltimore MD 1930 *ED* Univ MD 1952; Univ MD Sch Bus Admin 1953 *CURR EMPL* chmn, pres, ceo, dir: Unitrode Corp *CORP AFFIL* chmn: NH Savings Bank Corp, Rockingham County Trust Co; dir: Apollo Computer, Fin Concepts, H K Webster Co, Symbolics Inc *NONPR AFFIL* vchmn: Outward Bound

Cosmo S. Trapani: *CURR EMPL* vp, cfo, treas: Unitrode Corp

APPLICATION INFORMATION

Initial Approach: Send brief letter of inquiry. There are no deadlines.

GRANTS ANALYSIS

Typical Range: $50 to $1,000

RECENT GRANTS

Boston Symphony Orchestra
Museum of Fine Arts
United Way

Univar Corp. / Univar Foundation

Sales: $1.55 billion
Employees: 3,268
Headquarters: Seattle, WA
SIC Major Group: Engineering & Management Services and Wholesale Trade—Nondurable Goods

CONTACT

Karen Cadle
Secretary
Univar Foundation
PO Box 34325
Seattle, WA 98124-1325
(206) 889-3419

FINANCIAL SUMMARY

Recent Giving: $169,490 (fiscal 1992); $168,000 (fiscal 1991); $199,450 (fiscal 1990)

Assets: $147,133 (fiscal year ending February 28, 1992); $166,605 (fiscal 1990)

Gifts Received: $180,000 (fiscal 1992); $151,500 (fiscal 1990)

Fiscal Note: In fiscal 1992, contributions were received from Univar Corporation.

EIN: 91-0826180

CONTRIBUTIONS SUMMARY

Typical Recipients: • *Arts & Humanities:* community arts, museums/galleries • *Education:* business education, colleges & universities, economic education • *Health:* health funds • *Social Services:* community service organizations, united funds

Grant Types: capital

Geographic Distribution: focus on Seattle, WA

Operating Locations: WA (Seattle)

CORP. OFFICERS

James W. Bernard: *B* Brainerd MN 1937 *ED* Univ OR 1960 *CURR EMPL* pres, ceo: Univar Corp

GIVING OFFICERS

James W. Bernard: pres, trust *CURR EMPL* pres, ceo: Univar Corp (see above)

Robert D. O'Brien: pres, dir

N. Stewart Rogers: treas, dir

APPLICATION INFORMATION

Initial Approach: Send brief letter of inquiry. Include a a description of organization, amount requested, purpose of funds sought, recently audited financial statement, and proof of tax-exempt status. There are no deadlines.

Restrictions on Giving: Does not support individuals, religious organizations for sectarian purposes, political or lobbying groups, or organizations outside operating areas. Also does not make grants for endowments.

GRANTS ANALYSIS

Number of Grants: 45

Highest Grant: $20,000

Typical Range: $1,000 to $10,000

Disclosure Period: fiscal year ending February 28, 1992

RECENT GRANTS

20,000 Seattle University, Seattle, WA
20,000 United Way, Seattle, WA
10,000 Catholic Community Center, Seattle, WA
10,000 Corporate Council of Arts, Seattle, WA
10,000 Seattle Art Museum, Seattle, WA
10,000 Tacoma Art Museum, Tacoma, WA
8,334 YMCA, Seattle, WA
5,000 Nature Conservancy, Seattle, WA
5,000 Tacoma Zoological Society, Tacoma, WA
5,000 United Way, Seattle, WA

Universal Foods Corp. / Universal Foods Foundation

Sales: $883.4 million
Employees: 5,400
Headquarters: Milwaukee, WI
SIC Major Group: Chemicals & Allied Products, Food & Kindred Products, and Wholesale Trade—Nondurable Goods

CONTACT

John Heinrich
Vice President
Universal Foods Fdn.
433 E Michigan St.
Milwaukee, WI 53202
(414) 271-6755

FINANCIAL SUMMARY

Recent Giving: $1,122,500 (fiscal 1993 est.); $1,573,322 (fiscal 1992); $1,395,692 (fiscal 1991)

Assets: $7,163,309 (fiscal year ending September 30, 1992); $7,725,969 (fiscal 1990); $6,076,205 (fiscal 1989)

Gifts Received: $350,000 (fiscal 1990); $730,000 (fiscal 1989)

Fiscal Note: Figures for fiscal 1991, fiscal 1992, and fiscal 1993 include foundation and direct corporate gifts and nonmonetary support. Foundation giving for fiscal 1991 was $476,660, and for fiscal 1992, $588,316. Foundation giving for fiscal 1993 was budgeted at $590,000. 1990 contribution received from Universal Foods Corp.

EIN: 39-6044488

CONTRIBUTIONS SUMMARY

Typical Recipients: • *Arts & Humanities:* arts institutes, community arts, history/historic preservation, museums/galleries, music, opera, performing arts, public broadcasting, theater • *Civic & Public Affairs:* business/free enterprise, economic development, ethnic/minority organizations, urban & community affairs, zoos/botanical gardens • *Education:* business education, career/vocational education, colleges & universities, continuing education, engineering education, literacy, medical education, science/technology education • *Health:* hospitals, medical research, mental health, single-disease health associations • *Science:* scientific organizations • *Social Services:* aged, child welfare, community service organizations, day care, delinquency & crime, disabled, drugs & alcohol, emergency relief, family planning, family services, food/clothing distribution, general, shelters/homelessness, united funds, volunteer services, youth organizations

Grant Types: capital, challenge, employee matching gifts, general support, multi-year/continuing support, operating expenses, project, research, and scholarship

Nonmonetary Support Types: donated products, loaned executives, and workplace solicitation

Note: Nonmonetary support was valued at $779,362 for fiscal 1992 and $852,131 for fiscal 1991. Nonmonetary support is included in total giving figures above.

Geographic Distribution: in headquarters and operating communities

Operating Locations: CA (Greenfield, Oakland, Turlock), ID (Boise, Twin Falls), IN (Indianapolis), MO (St. Louis), NJ (South Plainfield), WI (Milwaukee)

Note: List includes division location.

CORP. OFFICERS

Kenneth Paul Manning: *B* New York NY 1942 *ED* Rensselaer Polytech Inst BSME 1963; Am Univ MBA 1968 *CURR EMPL* chmn, coo, dir: Universal Foods Corp *NONPR AFFIL* dir: 1st WI Trust Co; mem: Greater Milwaukee Comm, Naval Reserve Assn, Navy League, US Naval Inst; mem adv counc: Marquette Univ; trust: Stritch Coll

Guy A. Osborn: *B* Evanston IL 1936 *ED* Northwestern Coll 1958 *CURR EMPL* pres, coo: Universal Foods Corp *CORP AFFIL* dir: First Star, First WI Natl Bank, Fleming Cos, WICOR

GIVING OFFICERS

John E. Heinrich: vp *B* Washington DC 1944 *ED* Univ WI 1969 *CURR EMPL* vp: Universal Foods Corp *NONPR AFFIL* dir: Channel 10/36 Friends

Kenneth Paul Manning: vp, dir *CURR EMPL* chmn, coo, dir: Universal Foods Corp (see above)

Guy A. Osborn: pres, dir *CURR EMPL* pres, coo: Universal Foods Corp (see above)

Carl L. Zaar: secy, treas, dir *CURR EMPL* dir internal audit: Universal Foods Corp

APPLICATION INFORMATION

Initial Approach: *Initial Contact:* brief letter *Include Information On:* description of program, amount requested, purpose for which funds are sought, and any other supporting documentation *When to Submit:* any time; board meets in January and June

OTHER THINGS TO KNOW

Company matches gifts made by its employees and board of directors.

GRANTS ANALYSIS

Total Grants: $588,316*
Number of Grants: 272
Highest Grant: $100,000
Typical Range: $25 to $1,000 and $5,000 to $20,000
Disclosure Period: fiscal year ending September 30, 1992
Note: Recent grants are derived from a fiscal 1991 Form 990.

RECENT GRANTS

68,850 United Way of Greater Milwaukee, Milwaukee, WI

25,000 Children's Hospital of Wisconsin, Milwaukee, WI

21,000 United Way of Magic Valley

20,000 Columbia Hospital, Milwaukee, WI

20,000 Milwaukee Foundation, Milwaukee, WI

20,000 Rx for Reading in Wisconsin, WI

16,600 United Way of Central Indiana, Indianapolis, IN

16,050 United Way of Greater St. Louis, St. Louis, MO

16,000 United Performing Arts Fund, Milwaukee, WI

15,000 Tything Place

Universal Health Services, Inc.

Sales: $690.9 million
Employees: 9,950
Headquarters: King of Prussia, PA
SIC Major Group: Health Services

CONTACT

Eileen Bove
Director, Human Resources
Universal Health Services, Inc.
367 South Gulph Rd.
King of Prussia, PA 19406
(215) 768-3300

FINANCIAL SUMMARY

Fiscal Note: Annual Giving Range: less than $100,000

CONTRIBUTIONS SUMMARY

Operating Locations: PA (King of Prussia)

CORP. OFFICERS

Alan B. Miller: *CURR EMPL* chmn, pres, ceo: Universal Health Svcs

Universal Leaf Tobacco Co. / Universal Leaf Foundation

Sales: $12.0 million
Employees: 14,100
Parent Company: Universal Corp.
Headquarters: Richmond, VA
SIC Major Group: Wholesale Trade—Nondurable Goods

CONTACT

Nancy Powell
Manager, Corporate Relations
Universal Leaf Fdn.
PO Box 25099
Richmond, VA 23260
(804) 359-9311
Note: Company is located at 1501 N. Hamilton St., Richmond, VA 23230.

FINANCIAL SUMMARY

Recent Giving: $393,447 (fiscal 1992); $379,555 (fiscal 1991); $443,504 (fiscal 1990)

Assets: $8,757,310 (fiscal year ending June 30, 1992); $6,450,135 (fiscal 1991); $309,984 (fiscal 1990)

Gifts Received: $1,500,000 (fiscal 1992); $4,949,278 (fiscal 1991); $372,500 (fiscal 1990)

Fiscal Note: Contributes through foundation only. In 1992, contributions were received from Universal Leaf Tobacco Co.
EIN: 51-0162337

CONTRIBUTIONS SUMMARY

Typical Recipients: • *Arts & Humanities:* arts associations, arts centers, arts festivals, community arts, dance, history/historic preservation, museums/galleries, music, performing arts, public broadcasting, theater • *Civic & Public Affairs:* environmental affairs, ethnic/minority organizations, housing, municipalities, philanthropic organizations, professional & trade associations, urban & community affairs, zoos/botanical gardens • *Education:* colleges & universities, colleges & universities, community & junior colleges, economic education, education funds, elementary education, minority education, private education (precollege), public education (precollege), religious education • *Health:* health funds, health organizations, pediatric health, single-disease health associations • *Religion:* religious organizations • *Social Services:* animal protection, child welfare, child welfare, community centers, community service organizations, disabled, employment/job training, family services, food/clothing distribution, homes, recreation & athletics, united funds, youth organizations

Grant Types: general support

Geographic Distribution: focus on VA and NC

Operating Locations: NC (Henderson, Smithfield, Wilson, Winston-Salem), PA (Lancaster), VA (Danville, Farmville, Petersburg, Richmond)

CORP. OFFICERS

Gordon L. Crenshaw: *B* Richmond VA 1922 *ED* Univ VA BA 1943 *CURR EMPL* chmn: Universal Leaf Tobacco Co *CORP AFFIL* chmn: Universal Corp; dir: Crestar Fin Corp, Lawyers Title Ins Co *NONPR AFFIL* bd govs: VA Home Boys; dir: Inter-Govt Inst, VA Fdn Independent Coll, VA Port Authority; mem: Tobacco Assn US; trust: Richmond Meml Hosp

Henry H. Harrell: *B* Richmond VA 1939 *CURR EMPL* pres: Universal Leaf Tobacco Co *CORP AFFIL* chmn, ceo: Universal Corp; dir: Jefferson Bankshares, Lawyers Title Ins Co

GIVING OFFICERS

Wallace Lee Chandler: vp, dir *B* Mecklenburg County VA 1926 *ED* Elon Coll AB 1949; Smithdeal Coll Law LLB 1953 *CURR EMPL* vchmn, dir: Universal Leaf Tobacco Co *CORP AFFIL* dir: Life VA Series Funds, Regency Bank, Taylor (JP) Co; mem exec comm, dir: Lawyers Title Ins Co; sr vp: KR Edwards Leaf Tobacco Co; sr vp, dir: Lancaster Leaf Tobacco Co, Southwestern Tobacco Co; vchmn, dir: Universal Corp, Universal Leaf Tobacco Co *NONPR AFFIL* mem: Am Bar Assn; mem bd govs: Tobacco Assn US; mem bd visitors: James Madison Univ; vchmn, trust: Elon Coll

Gordon L. Crenshaw: mem *CURR EMPL* chmn: Universal Leaf Tobacco Co (see above)

Ollin Kemp Dozier: treas *B* Rocky Mount NC 1929 *ED* US Military Academy 1953; Harvard Univ 1958 *CURR EMPL* vp, treas: Universal Corp *CORP AFFIL* dir: Deli-Universal; treas: Southern Processors, Southwestern Tobacco Co, Taylor (JP) Co, Tobacco Processors; vp, treas, dir: Universal Leaf Tobacco Co; vp, treas: Universal Corp *NONPR AFFIL* mem: Fin Execs Inst

Henry H. Harrell: dir *CURR EMPL* pres: Universal Leaf Tobacco Co (see above)

F. V. Lowden III: secy
Nancy G. Powell: vp, dir
T. R. Towers: pres, dir
J. M. White: gen couns

APPLICATION INFORMATION
Initial Approach: *Initial Contact:* written proposal *Include Information On:* amount, purpose, copy of tax exemption letter, description of the organization detailing its history and charitable purposes, and most recent audited financial statements *When to Submit:* any time
Restrictions on Giving: Foundation does not support individuals, political or lobbying efforts, or make loans.

GRANTS ANALYSIS
Total Grants: $393,447
Number of Grants: 509
Highest Grant: $43,500
Typical Range: $100 to $1,000
Disclosure Period: fiscal year ending June 30, 1992
Note: Recent grants are derived from a fiscal 1992 grants list.

RECENT GRANTS
43,500 AMF/Signet Open of Virginia, Richmond, VA
35,000 United Way of Greater Richmond, Richmond, VA
13,000 North Carolina Tobacco Foundation, NC
12,500 Independent College Fund of North Carolina, NC
11,000 Richmond Renaissance, Richmond, VA
10,000 James Madison University, Harrisonburg, VA
10,000 University of Richmond, Richmond, VA
10,000 Virginia Foundation of Independent Colleges, Richmond, VA
8,000 SPCA, Richmond, VA
7,500 SRC Housing Richmond, Richmond, VA

UNO-VEN Co.
Sales: $550.0 million
Employees: 1,100
Headquarters: Arlington Heights, IL
SIC Major Group: Automotive Dealers & Service Stations and Petroleum & Coal Products

CONTACT
Dave Henderson
Director, Public Relations
UNO-VEN Co.
3850 North Wilke Rd.
Arlington Heights, IL 60004
(708) 818-1800

CONTRIBUTIONS SUMMARY
Operating Locations: IL (Arlington Heights)

CORP. OFFICERS
Edward T. DiCorcia: *CURR EMPL* chmn, ceo: UNO-VEN Co

Unocal Corp. / Unocal Foundation
Sales: $10.1 billion
Employees: 14,687
Headquarters: Los Angeles, CA
SIC Major Group: Chemicals & Allied Products, Oil & Gas Extraction, Petroleum & Coal Products, and Wholesale Trade—Nondurable Goods

CONTACT
Judith Barker
President
Unocal Fdn.
1201 W 5th St.
Los Angeles, CA 90017
(213) 977-6171

FINANCIAL SUMMARY
Recent Giving: $3,093,000 (fiscal 1992 approx.); $4,012,550 (fiscal 1991); $3,804,802 (fiscal 1990)
Assets: $4,646,623 (fiscal 1991); $3,900,000 (fiscal 1990); $3,715,577 (fiscal 1989)
Fiscal Note: Figures are for the foundation only and do not include corporate contributions.
EIN: 95-6071812

CONTRIBUTIONS SUMMARY
Typical Recipients: • *Arts & Humanities:* arts centers, arts institutes, community arts, dance, history/historic preservation, libraries, museums/galleries, music, opera, performing arts, theater • *Civic & Public Affairs:* business/free enterprise, civil rights, economic development, economics, environmental affairs, international affairs, law & justice, nonprofit management, professional & trade associations, public policy, urban & community affairs, women's affairs • *Education:* agricultural education, arts education, business education, career/vocational education, colleges & universities, continuing education, economic education, education associations, education funds, faculty development, international exchange, international studies, legal education, medical education, minority education, public education (precollege), science/technology education, social sciences education, student aid • *Health:* health organizations, hospitals, medical rehabilitation, medical research, medical training, mental health, pediatric health, single-disease health associations • *Science:* science exhibits & fairs, scientific institutes • *Social Services:* community service organizations, drugs & alcohol, homes, legal aid, recreation & athletics, religious welfare, united funds, youth organizations
Grant Types: challenge, department, employee matching gifts, fellowship, general support, professorship, project, research, and scholarship
Geographic Distribution: nationally, with preference given to areas where Unocal maintains corporate facilities
Operating Locations: AK, CA, LA, TX

CORP. OFFICERS
Claude Stout Brinegar: *ED* Stanford Univ BA 1950; Stanford Univ MS 1951; Stanford Univ PhD 1954 *CURR EMPL* vchmn, exec vp, dir: Unocal Corp *CORP AFFIL* bd dirs: Maxicare Health Plans Inc; founding dir: Consolidated Rail Corp *NONPR AFFIL* chmn: CA Citizens Compensation Commn; mem: Am Petroleum Inst, Phi Beta Kappa
Richard Joseph Stegemeier: *B* Alton IL 1928 *ED* Univ MO BS 1950; TX A&M Univ MS 1951 *CURR EMPL* chmn, ceo, dir: Unocal Corp *CORP AFFIL* dir: First Interstate Bancorp, Northrop Corp, Outboard Marine Corp *NONPR AFFIL* bd govs: Music Ctr Los Angeles, Town Hall of CA; bd overseers: Exec Counc on Foreign Diplomats, Huntington Library; bd visitors: Univ CA Los Angeles Anderson Grad Sch, Univ MO; chmn: Boy Scouts Am Los Angeles Counc, Los Angeles World Aff Counc; dir: French Fdn Alzheimer Res, Los Angeles Philharmonic, Martin Luther Hosp Med Ctr, Natl Counc Bus Advs, Orange County Performing Arts Ctr, John Tracy Clinic, YMCA Los Angeles; mem: Am Inst Chem Engrs, Am Petroleum Inst, CA Bus Roundtable, CA Counc Science & Tech, Conf Bd, Counc Foreign Rels, Natl Academy Engg, Natl Assn Mfrs, Natl Petroleum Counc, Soc Petroleum Engrs, World Petroleum Congress; mem adv bd: Northwestern Univ Kellogg Sch Bus; mem chemistry adv counc: CA St Univ (Long Beach); trust: Comm for Econ Devel, Los Angeles Archdiocese Fdn, Loyola Marymount Univ, Harvey Mudd Coll, Hugh O'Brian Youth Fdn, Univ Southern CA

GIVING OFFICERS
Judith Barker: pres
MacDonald Becket: trust
Claude Stout Brinegar: trust *CURR EMPL* vchmn, exec vp, dir: Unocal Corp (see above)
Karen Ann Sikkema: trust *ED* Kalamazoo Coll 1968; Univ MI 1970 *CURR EMPL* vp (corp commun): Unocal Corp *NONPR AFFIL* dir: Alliance Bus Childcare Devel
Richard Joseph Stegemeier: trust *CURR EMPL* chmn, ceo, dir: Unocal Corp (see above)

APPLICATION INFORMATION
Initial Approach: *Initial Contact:* brief letter *Include Information On:* background of organization, goals and objectives; necessity/purpose of grant; amount budgeted for project; most recent audited financial statement and annual report; current year's budget; evaluative criteria; other organizations solicited and amounts received, pledged, or anticipated; copy of IRS determination letter; copy of most recent IRS Form 990 *When to Submit:* no deadlines
Restrictions on Giving: Foundation does not support grants to individuals; elementary or secondary education; political or lobbying groups; veterans,

fraternal, sectarian, social, religious, athletic, choral, band, or similar groups; courtesy advertising; conferences, films, or contests; supplemental operating support for organizations eligible for united funds; governmental agencies or departments; or trade, business, or professional associations; most capital campaigns or endowments.

Grants are not renewed automatically; a request for support must be submitted each year.

GRANTS ANALYSIS
Total Grants: $3,093,000*
Number of Grants: 200
Highest Grant: $100,000
Typical Range: $500 to $5,000
Disclosure Period: fiscal year ending January 31, 1993
Note: Fiscal information for foundation only. Foundation did not supply an average grant figure. Recent grants are derived from a 1991 Form 990. Asset figure is from 1991.

RECENT GRANTS
1,757,922 United Way Campaign
100,000 California Institute of Technology, Pasadena, CA
100,000 Stanford University, Stanford, CA
92,100 Citizens' Scholarship Foundation of America, St. Peter, MN
60,000 University of Oklahoma, Norman, OK — Petroleum and Geological Engineering
55,000 Southern California Building Funds, Los Angeles, CA
51,000 National Four-H Council, Chevy Chase, MD
50,000 Archdiocese of Los Angeles Education Foundation, Los Angeles, CA
50,000 Carter Center
50,000 Ford's Theater Society, Washington, DC

Unocal-Union Oil of California
Sales: $753.0 million
Employees: 1,310
Headquarters: Houston, TX
SIC Major Group: Oil & Gas Extraction

CONTACT
Carl Hebert
President
Unocal-Union Oil of California
PO Box 4551
Houston, TX 77210-4551
(713) 491-7600

CONTRIBUTIONS SUMMARY
Operating Locations: TX (Houston)

UNUM Corp. / UNUM Charitable Foundation
Revenue: $2.6 billion
Employees: 7,000
Headquarters: Portland, ME
SIC Major Group: Holding & Other Investment Offices and Insurance Carriers

CONTACT
Janine M. Manning
Manager
UNUM Charitable Fdn.
2211 Congress St.
Portland, ME 04122
(207) 770-4347

FINANCIAL SUMMARY
Recent Giving: $2,000,000 (1993 est.); $1,436,700 (1992); $1,562,015 (1991)
Assets: $3,656,864 (1992); $3,596,783 (1990); $3,255,747 (1989)
Fiscal Note: Company gives primarily through the foundation. Totals include giving by subsidiaries.
EIN: 23-7026979

CONTRIBUTIONS SUMMARY
Typical Recipients: • *Arts & Humanities:* dance, museums/galleries, music, performing arts • *Civic & Public Affairs:* economic development • *Education:* public education (precollege) • *Social Services:* aged, united funds
Grant Types: challenge, employee matching gifts, multiyear/continuing support, project, and seed money
Nonmonetary Support Types: donated equipment, in-kind services, and loaned employees
Note: Estimate for nonmonetary support is not available for 1991 and is not included in the above figures. Support is provided by the company. For information, contact Laurie Taylor, Grants Administrator.

Geographic Distribution: in order of priority: greater Portland, southern Maine, Maine, other communities where UNUM has a significant corporate presence; limited national and international funding for target grants
Operating Locations: ME (Portland)

CORP. OFFICERS
James F. Orr III: *B* Minneapolis MN 1943 *ED* Villanova Univ 1962; Boston Univ 1969 *CURR EMPL* pres: UNUM Life Ins Co *CORP AFFIL* ceo: Colonial Life & Accident Ins Co

GIVING OFFICERS
Ann Beadle: trust *CURR EMPL* vp oper long term care: UNUM Life Ins Co
Terry Cohen: trust *CURR EMPL* sr vp human resources: UNUM Life Ins Co
Karen Gervasoni: trust
Matthew Gilligan: trust
Kevin Healey: ed mgr
Janice Hird: dir corp pub involvement
Deborah Histen: adm asst
Rosemary Lavoie: trust *CURR EMPL* mgr field incentive compensation: UNUM Life Ins Co
Melinda Loring: trust *CURR EMPL* vp corp fin: UNUM Life Ins Co
Janine Manning: mgr
Richard McMurry: trust *CURR EMPL* vp corp strategic planning & devel: UNUM Life Ins Co
Donna Mundy: vp, trust *CURR EMPL* vp external aff: UNUM Life Ins Co
James F. Orr III: pres, trust *CURR EMPL* pres: UNUM Life Ins Co (see above)
James S. Orser: trust *CURR EMPL* vp life & health customer service: UNUM Life Ins Co
Cheryl Stewart: trust *CURR EMPL* vp private label markets: UNUM Life Ins Co
Laurie Taylor: grant adm
Janet Whitehouse: trust *CURR EMPL* vp corp devel: UNUM Life Ins Co
Deborah Winters: adm asst
Kathryn A. Yates: vp, trust *CURR EMPL* vp communications: UNUM Life Ins Co

APPLICATION INFORMATION
Initial Approach: *Initial Contact:* letter *Include Information On:* description of project and

sponsoring organization; statement of project's importance and relevance to foundation priorities; total project cost, sources of funding, and amount requested; list of organization's officers and board of directors; proof of IRS tax-exempt status *When to Submit:* any time *Note:* After initial evaluation of proposal, foundation may request additional information.
Restrictions on Giving: The foundation does not support individuals, political organizations or candidates, religious organizations or activities, athletics, events such as walk-athons, goodwill advertising, or United Way member agencies except in emergency circumstances.
The foundation supports capital campaigns only in the greater Portland, ME, area.

OTHER THINGS TO KNOW
Requests for noncash contributions program are reviewed by the foundation and the internal contributor whose services or skills are being requested.
The foundation sponsors a matching gifts program that awards grants of $50 to $500 to community organizations at which company employees volunteer, also matches gifts of $25 to $1,000 to higher education institutions and public broadcasting organizations.

GRANTS ANALYSIS
Total Grants: $1,436,700
Number of Grants: 105*
Highest Grant: $327,000
Typical Range: $5,000 to $20,000
Disclosure Period: 1992
Note: Number of grants includes 50 United Way organizations. Recent grants are derived from a 1991 annual report.

RECENT GRANTS
260,000 United Way of Greater Portland, Portland, ME
233,418 University of Southern Maine, Portland, ME — Southern Maine Partnership
137,350 Maine Aspirations Foundation, Augusta, ME — Community Compacts

90,000 YMCA of Portland, Portland, ME — capital campaign

75,564 United Way — Field Office Communities

65,000 Portland Museum of Art, Portland, ME

60,000 Family Planning Association, Augusta, ME — AIDS Education Program

50,000 Cumberland County Affordable Housing Venture, Portland, ME

46,134 Portland Public Schools, Portland, ME — Portland Partnership Program

44,000 UNUM Employee Scholarship Program, St. Peter, MN — Citizens' Scholarship Foundation of America

Upjohn California Fund

CONTACT
Eugene C. Wheary
President
Upjohn California Fund
8545 Carmel Valley Rd.
Carmel Valley, CA 93924
(408) 626-4828

FINANCIAL SUMMARY
Recent Giving: $50,250 (fiscal 1991); $36,700 (fiscal 1990); $84,750 (fiscal 1989)
Assets: $1,297,344 (fiscal year ending October 31, 1991); $2,332,479 (fiscal 1990); $2,400,444 (fiscal 1989)
EIN: 94-6065219

CONTRIBUTIONS SUMMARY
Typical Recipients: • *Arts & Humanities:* community arts, dance, museums/galleries, music, public broadcasting • *Education:* colleges & universities, private education (precollege) • *Health:* health organizations, hospices, hospitals, medical research, nursing services, single-disease health associations • *Social Services:* community service organizations, family services, united funds, youth organizations
Grant Types: general support
Geographic Distribution: focus on northern CA

GIVING OFFICERS
Barbara Gauntlet: dir
Cynthia W. Hertlein: dir, cfo, secy
Edwin W. Macrae: vp
G. Frederick Roll: dir
Eugene C. Wheary: dir, pres

APPLICATION INFORMATION
Initial Approach: Send brief letter describing program. There are no deadlines.
Restrictions on Giving: Does not support individuals.

GRANTS ANALYSIS
Number of Grants: 37
Highest Grant: $5,000
Typical Range: $500 to $1,000
Disclosure Period: fiscal year ending October 31, 1991

RECENT GRANTS
5,000 Community Hospital Foundation, Monterey, CA

5,000 Hospice of Monterey Peninsula, Monterey, CA

2,500 Goodwill Industries, Monterey, CA

2,500 Monterey Sports Center, Monterey, CA

2,500 Salvation Army, Monterey, CA

2,000 American Red Cross, Monterey, CA

2,000 Natividad Medical Foundation, Monterey, CA

1,500 American Red Cross, Monterey, CA

1,500 Boys and Girls Club, Monterey, CA

1,500 Central Coast Visiting Nurses Association, Monterey, CA

Upjohn Co. / Upjohn Co. Foundation
Sales: $3.66 billion
Employees: 19,100
Headquarters: Kalamazoo, MI
SIC Major Group: Agricultural Production— Crops and Chemicals & Allied Products

CONTACT
Vickie G. Heerlyn
Manager, Corporate Support Program
Upjohn Co.
7000 Portage Rd.
Kalamazoo, MI 49001
(616) 323-7017

FINANCIAL SUMMARY
Recent Giving: $7,622,500 (1991 approx.); $7,300,000 (1990 approx.); $5,700,000 (1989)
Assets: $23,316,516 (1991); $4,572,330 (1989); $411,600 (1988)
Fiscal Note: Above totals include both direct and foundation contributions. Although the Upjohn Co. Foundation was established in 1987; direct giving by the company remains the primary focus of Upjohn's contributions program. See "Other Things You Should Know" for more details.
EIN: 38-2784862

CONTRIBUTIONS SUMMARY
Typical Recipients: • *Arts & Humanities:* community arts, museums/galleries, music, performing arts, theater, visual arts • *Civic & Public Affairs:* business/free enterprise, ethnic/minority organizations, housing, urban & community affairs • *Education:* colleges & universities, education funds, health & physical education, medical education, minority education, science/technology education • *Health:* health organizations, hospitals, medical research • *Social Services:* united funds
Grant Types: capital, employee matching gifts, general support, project, and scholarship
Note: General support given in local communities only. Matching gifts made to educational institutions only.
Nonmonetary Support Types: donated equipment and donated products
Note: Nonmonetary support was valued at $9.9 million in 1991 and is not included in above figures. Support goes to a few selected international organizations that provide emergency relief. About $9.8 million was in product donation, and less than $100,000 in surplus office equipment to local organizations.

Geographic Distribution: almost entirely in major operating locations; about 55% of cash grants go to organizations in Kalamazoo, MI; product donations go only to Third World countries
Operating Locations: CT (North Haven), MI (Kalamazoo)
Note: Also operates in Puerto Rico.

CORP. OFFICERS
Theodore Cooper, MD: *B* Trenton NJ 1928 *ED* Georgetown Univ BS 1949; St Louis Univ MD 1954; St Louis Univ PhD 1956 *CURR EMPL* chmn, ceo, dir: Upjohn Co *CORP AFFIL* dir: Am Natl Holding Co, Borden, Bronson HealthCare Group, Harris Bank, Kellogg Co, Metro Life Ins Co *NONPR AFFIL* mem: Am Assoc Advancement Science, Am Assoc Univ Profs, Am Coll Cardiology, Am Coll Chest Physicians, Am Fed Clinical Res, Am Physiological Soc, Am Soc Artificial Internal Organs, Am Soc Clinical Investigation, Am Soc Pharmacology Experimental Therapeutics, Intl Cardiovascular Soc, Sigma Xi, Soc Experimental Biology Medicine; mem bd overseers: Meml Sloan-Kettering Cancer Ctr
Mark Novitch: *B* New London CT 1932 *ED* Yale Univ AB 1954; NY Med Coll MD 1958 *CURR EMPL* vchmn, dir: Upjohn Co *NONPR AFFIL* dir: Am Fdn Pharmaceutical Ed, Natl Fund Med Ed; mem: Am Med Assn, Am Pub Health Assn, Am Soc Clinical Pharmacology Therapeutics, Counc Excellence Govt, MA Med Soc, Overseas Devel Counc; pres: US Pharmacopeial Convention; trust: Kalamazoo Coll
William Upjohn Parfet: *B* Ann Arbor MI 1946 *ED* Lake Forest Coll BA 1972; Univ MI MBA 1975 *CURR EMPL* pres, dir: Upjohn Co *CORP AFFIL* dir: Old Kent Fin Corp *NONPR AFFIL* chmn: Kalamazoo CEO Counc, Western MI Univ Fdn; mem: Kalamazoo Inst Arts Fin Comm; trust: Lake Forest Coll
Ley S. Smith: *B* St. Thomas Canada 1934 *ED* Univ Western Ontario BA 1958 *CURR EMPL* vchmn, dir: Upjohn Co

GIVING OFFICERS

Vickie G. Heerlyn: exec dir, secy *CURR EMPL* mgr (corp support program): Upjohn Co
Mark Novitch: dir *CURR EMPL* vchmn, dir: Upjohn Co (see above)
Donald R. Parfet: pres *CURR EMPL* exec vp admin: Upjohn Co
William Upjohn Parfet: vp, treas *CURR EMPL* pres, dir: Upjohn Co (see above)
Ley S. Smith: dir *CURR EMPL* vchmn, dir: Upjohn Co (see above)

APPLICATION INFORMATION

Initial Approach: *Initial Contact:* letter *Include Information On:* programs in detail, budget records, goals and objectives, organization's efficiency, proof of tax-exempt status *When to Submit:* by August for contribution in following year
Restrictions on Giving: Does not give grants to individuals; social organizations; political action committees or candidates; sectarian religious institutions, churches, or veterans organizations; travel funds for tours, expeditions, or trips; tickets, tables, or any social events; or school-related sports or band events and activities. Grants are made for one year only, except in the case of capital grants.

OTHER THINGS TO KNOW

Upjohn considers applications from a medicinal/scientific/research perspective; generally does not support projects outside these areas.
Company's charitable giving focuses on local communities, where contributions can make a significant impact.
In 1991, company made approximately $6.5 million in cash gifts, and the Upjohn Foundation, a separate charitable entity, gave $1,122,500 in contributions. Company also donated almost $9.9 million in products and merchandise.

GRANTS ANALYSIS

Total Grants: $7,622,500*
Number of Grants: 21*
Highest Grant: $422,500*
Typical Range: $15,000 to $20,000
Disclosure Period: 1991
Note: Total grants figure is approximate. Number of grants,

average grant, and highest grant figures reflect 1991 foundation giving. For information on foundation giving, see "Other Things You Should Know." Assets reflect foundation only. Recent grants are derived from a 1991 Form 990.

RECENT GRANTS

　422,500 KVCC Foundation, Kalamazoo, MI
　200,000 University of Oklahoma, Oklahoma City, OK
　100,000 LISC-Kalamazoo, Kalamazoo, MI
　100,000 YWCA, Kalamazoo, MI
　50,000 Michigan Colleges Foundation, Detroit, MI
　35,000 Boys and Girls Club of Kalamazoo, Kalamazoo, MI
　30,000 Kalamazoo Institute of Arts, Kalamazoo, MI
　27,500 Kalamazoo Consultation Center, Kalamazoo, MI
　25,000 George Washington University Hospital, Washington, DC
　25,000 Kalamazoo Symphony, Kalamazoo, MI

Upjohn Foundation, Harold and Grace

CONTACT

Floyd L. Parks
Secretary-Treasurer
Harold and Grace Upjohn Fdn.
Mall Plaza, Ste. 90
157 South Kalamazoo Mall
Kalamazoo, MI 49007
(616) 344-2818

FINANCIAL SUMMARY

Recent Giving: $604,355 (fiscal 1991); $390,827 (fiscal 1990); $244,684 (fiscal 1989)
Assets: $7,672,786 (fiscal year ending October 31, 1991); $6,624,363 (fiscal 1990); $6,933,227 (fiscal 1989)
Gifts Received: $237,875 (fiscal 1991)
Fiscal Note: In 1991, contributions were received from Mary U. Meader.
EIN: 38-6052963

CONTRIBUTIONS SUMMARY

Donor(s): the late Grace G. Upjohn

Typical Recipients: • *Arts & Humanities:* libraries, music • *Civic & Public Affairs:* environmental affairs, housing, municipalities, philanthropic organizations, urban & community affairs • *Education:* colleges & universities, education associations, public education (precollege) • *Religion:* religious organizations • *Social Services:* child welfare, community service organizations, disabled, drugs & alcohol, recreation & athletics, united funds, youth organizations
Grant Types: capital, project, and seed money
Geographic Distribution: focus on MI

GIVING OFFICERS

Gene R. Conrad: off
Joseph J. Dunnigan: trust
William A. Kirkpatrick: off
Edwin E. Meader: trust
Mary U. Meader: trust
C. H. Mullin: trust
Floyd L. Parks: secy, treas

APPLICATION INFORMATION

Initial Approach: Application form available upon request.
Restrictions on Giving: Does not support individuals.

OTHER THINGS TO KNOW

Publications: Annual Report, Application Guidelines

GRANTS ANALYSIS

Number of Grants: 46
Highest Grant: $50,000
Typical Range: $3,000 to $10,000
Disclosure Period: fiscal year ending October 31, 1991

RECENT GRANTS

　50,000 Downtown Tomorrow, Kalamazoo, MI
　50,000 Kalamazoo Foundation-Arcadia Creek Project, Kalamazoo, MI
　50,000 Kalamazoo Valley Community College, Kalamazoo, MI
　40,000 University of Michigan, Ann Arbor, MI
　30,000 Kalamazoo Alcohol and Drug Abuse, Kalamazoo, MI
　30,000 Kalamazoo Public Schools, Kalamazoo, MI

　30,000 Kalamazoo Public Schools, Kalamazoo, MI
　25,000 Kalamazoo Foundation, Kalamazoo, MI
　25,000 Western Michigan University Foundation, Kalamazoo, MI
　25,000 YWCA, Kalamazoo, MI

Upton Charitable Foundation, Lucy and Eleanor S.

CONTACT

Thomas L. Morrissey
Trustee
Lucy and Eleanor S. Upton Charitable Fdn.
100 Mulberry St.
Newark, NJ 07102

FINANCIAL SUMMARY

Recent Giving: $228,000 (1990); $222,000 (1988)
Assets: $4,793,095 (1990); $4,353,153 (1988)
EIN: 22-6074947

CONTRIBUTIONS SUMMARY

Donor(s): the late Eleanor S. Upton
Typical Recipients: • *Arts & Humanities:* community arts, music • *Education:* colleges & universities • *Health:* hospitals, medical research • *Religion:* religious organizations • *Social Services:* child welfare, shelters/homelessness, youth organizations
Grant Types: fellowship, general support, and research
Geographic Distribution: focus on NJ

GIVING OFFICERS

William B. Cater: trust
Thomas L. Morrissey: trust
Samuel C. Williams, Jr.: trust
Samuel C. Williams, Jr.: trust

APPLICATION INFORMATION

Initial Approach: Contributes only to preselected organizations.

GRANTS ANALYSIS

Number of Grants: 11
Highest Grant: $96,560
Typical Range: $3,000 to $15,000
Disclosure Period: 1990

RECENT GRANTS

96,560 Princeton University, Princeton, NJ — Upton Fellowship Program

50,000 New Jersey Symphony Orchestra, Newark, NJ — general

25,000 Memorial Sloan-Kettering Cancer Center, New York, NY

15,000 Rutgers University Foundation, New Brunswick, NJ — Thomas Edison Papers

7,500 Green Hill Memorial Center, West Orange, NJ — general

7,500 House of the Good Shepherd, Hackettstown, NJ — general

7,500 House of the Holy Comforter, West Orange, NJ — general

5,000 Greater Newark Christmas Fund, 1990, Newark, NJ — general

5,000 Isaiah House, East Orange, NJ — general

5,000 Washington College, Chestertown, MD — general

Upton Foundation, Frederick S.

CONTACT
Stephen E. Upton
Chairman of the Board of Trustees
Frederick S. Upton Foundation
100 Ridgeway
St. Joseph, MI 49085
(616) 982-0272

FINANCIAL SUMMARY
Recent Giving: $733,439 (1990); $611,885 (1989); $518,440 (1988)
Assets: $18,132,915 (1990); $20,405,748 (1989); $14,196,411 (1988)
Gifts Received: $3,153,634 (1989); $5,000,000 (1988)
EIN: 36-6013317

CONTRIBUTIONS SUMMARY
Donor(s): The foundation was established in 1954, with Frederick S. Upton as donor. In 1911, Mr. Upton was a cofounder of the Upton Machine Company, the predecessor of the Whirlpool appliance company.

Typical Recipients: • *Arts & Humanities:* arts centers, arts funds, arts institutes, dance, history/historic preservation, libraries, music, visual arts • *Civic & Public Affairs:* environmental affairs, philanthropic organizations, urban & community affairs • *Education:* arts education, colleges & universities, education funds, minority education, religious education • *Religion:* religious organizations • *Social Services:* animal protection, child welfare, community centers, community service organizations, counseling, disabled, family services, religious welfare, united funds, youth organizations

Grant Types: general support, project, and scholarship

Geographic Distribution: primarily Michigan

GIVING OFFICERS
Priscilla U. Byrns: trust
David F. Upton: trust
Stephen E. Upton: chmn bd trusts *B* Benton Harbor MI 1924 *ED* Univ MI 1949 *CURR EMPL* sr vp: Whirlpool Corp
Sylvia Upton Wood: secy, trust

APPLICATION INFORMATION
Initial Approach:
Applicants should submit a letter of inquiry to the foundation. There are no formal application procedures or guidelines. Applications may be submitted any time. The board of trustees usually meets four to five times annually.

GRANTS ANALYSIS
Total Grants: $733,439
Number of Grants: 100
Highest Grant: $60,000
Typical Range: $1,000 to $10,000
Disclosure Period: 1990
Note: Recent grants are derived from a 1990 grants list.

RECENT GRANTS

60,000 Interlochen Center for the Arts, Interlochen, MI

51,000 Olivet College/Library Fund, Olivet, MI

50,200 YMCA, MI

50,000 Community Economic Development Corp, Benton Harbor, MI

50,000 Lake Michigan College Educational Foundation, Detroit, MI

50,000 Olivet College/Conservatory of Music, Olivet, MI

39,000 Kershaw City Fine Arts Center, Kershaw, MI

35,900 Southwest Michigan Symphony Orchestra, St. Joseph, MI

25,000 Kershaw County Humane Society, Kershaw, SC

22,500 University of Michigan Center of Champions Facility, Ann Arbor, MI

Urann Foundation

CONTACT
Howard Whelan
Administrator
Urann Fdn.
PO Box 1788
Brockton, MA 02403
(508) 588-7744

FINANCIAL SUMMARY
Recent Giving: $100,131 (1990); $90,780 (1989); $47,000 (1988)
Assets: $2,098,253 (1990); $2,140,134 (1989); $2,139,951 (1988)
EIN: 04-6115599

CONTRIBUTIONS SUMMARY
Grant Types: scholarship
Geographic Distribution: limited to MA and ME

GIVING OFFICERS
Balfour Bassett: trust
Reginald T. Cole: trust
Ellen Stillman: trust

APPLICATION INFORMATION
Initial Approach: Telephone during weekday mornings; scholarship applications also available at guidance offices of high schools.

Uris Brothers Foundation

CONTACT
Alice Paul
Executive Director and Secretary
Uris Brothers Foundation
300 Park Ave.
New York, NY 10022
(212) 355-7080

FINANCIAL SUMMARY
Recent Giving: $1,500,000 (fiscal 1993 est.); $1,450,874 (fiscal 1992); $1,492,228 (fiscal 1991)
Assets: $25,930,385 (fiscal year ending October 31, 1992); $25,234,507 (fiscal 1991); $22,004,587 (fiscal 1990)
EIN: 13-6115748

CONTRIBUTIONS SUMMARY
Donor(s): The foundation was established in 1956 in New York by Percy and Harold Uris, then co-owners of Uris Brothers Building Corporation of New York. During the building boom of the 1920s, the brothers ranked among the country's foremost builders of hotels and large apartment and office buildings. Their investment building firm remained successful until the Depression. By the 1970s, however, Uris Building's assets rose to $350 million.
Percy Uris, the elder brother and a trustee of Columbia University, died in 1971. Harold Uris died in 1982.

Typical Recipients: • *Arts & Humanities:* arts centers, libraries, museums/galleries, music, opera, performing arts, public broadcasting • *Civic & Public Affairs:* housing, professional & trade associations, urban & community affairs, zoos/botanical gardens • *Education:* arts education, faculty development, literacy, preschool education, special education • *Social Services:* child welfare, community service organizations, counseling, day care, domestic violence, employment/job training, family planning, food/clothing distribution, shelters/homelessness, youth organizations

Grant Types: capital, general support, loan, multiyear/continuing support, and project

Geographic Distribution: primarily New York City; limited support elsewhere

GIVING OFFICERS

Robert H. Abrams: dir
Robert L. Bachner: asst secy, dir *PHIL AFFIL* dir: Witco Foundation
Jane Bayard: vp, dir
Bernard Fisher: dir
Benjamin Gessula: treas
Susan Halpern: pres, dir
Alice Paul: exec dir, secy
Linda Sanger: vp, dir
Ruth Uris: chmn, dir

APPLICATION INFORMATION

Initial Approach:
A letter and a brief proposal is the recommended form of initial contact.
Letter of inquiry should include a description of the applicant organization, specific project, and budget.
There are no application deadlines. The board of directors meets quarterly.
Restrictions on Giving: The foundation is primarily interested in organizations within New York City. Grants are not made to individuals, for endowment funds, films, or studies. The foundation does not make loans to individuals.

OTHER THINGS TO KNOW

Besides making grants, the foundation provides technical assistance to grantees on fund raising and program development.

GRANTS ANALYSIS

Total Grants: $1,450,874
Number of Grants: 73
Highest Grant: $127,000
Typical Range: $5,000 to $50,000
Disclosure Period: fiscal year ending October 31, 1992
Note: Recent grants are derived from a fiscal 1992 Form 990.

RECENT GRANTS

127,000 New York Public Library, New York, NY
100,000 Local Initiatives Support Corporation, New York, NY
75,000 Surdna Foundation/CCRP-Multi Funders Account, New York, NY
50,000 Center for Collaborative Education, New York, NY
50,000 Federation of Jewish Philanthropies, New York, NY —

United Jewish Appeal
50,000 New York Community Trust/Community Funds, New York, NY
45,000 Brooklyn Botanic Garden Corporation, New York, NY
28,800 Goddard Riverside Community Center, New York, NY
27,174 SCAN New York Volunteer Parent Aides Association, New York, NY
27,000 Ramapo Anchorage Camp, Westchester, NY

US Bancorp

Assets: $20.74 billion
Employees: 9,872
Headquarters: Portland, OR
SIC Major Group: Depository Institutions and Holding & Other Investment Offices

CONTACT

Linda Wright
Secretary, Contributions Committee
US Bancorp
PO Box 8837
Portland, OR 97208
(503) 275-5776

FINANCIAL SUMMARY

Recent Giving: $5,200,000 (1993); $3,700,000 (1992 approx.); $2,800,000 (1991)
Fiscal Note: Company gives directly.

CONTRIBUTIONS SUMMARY

Typical Recipients: • *Arts & Humanities:* arts associations, arts institutes, general, museums/galleries, music, opera, performing arts, public broadcasting, theater, visual arts
• *Civic & Public Affairs:* economic development, environmental affairs, ethnic/minority organizations, general, housing, nonprofit management, philanthropic organizations, rural affairs, women's affairs
• *Education:* business education, colleges & universities, faculty development, general
• *Health:* general, hospices
• *Social Services:* aged, community centers, counseling, delinquency & crime, disabled, domestic violence, drugs & alcohol, employment/job training, general, united funds, youth organizations

Grant Types: capital, challenge, employee matching gifts, general support, and operating expenses
Nonmonetary Support Types: cause-related marketing & promotion, donated equipment, in-kind services, loaned employees, and loaned executives
Geographic Distribution: primarily at headquarters and operating locations
Operating Locations: CA, OR (Portland), WA

CORP. OFFICERS

Roger L. Breezley: *B* Williston ND 1938 *ED* Univ ND 1960 *CURR EMPL* chmn, ceo, dir: US Bancorp
Edmund P. Jensen: *B* Oakland CA 1937 *ED* Univ WA BA 1959; Univ Santa Clara *CURR EMPL* pres, coo: US Bancorp *CORP AFFIL* dir: US Bancorp, US Bank WA, US Natl Bank OR, VISA USA *NONPR AFFIL* bd dirs: Portland Art Mus; dir: Marylhurst Coll, OR Bus Counc, OR Downtown Devel Assn, OR Independent Coll Fdn, Saturday Academy; mem: Assn Portland Progress, Assn Reserve City Bankers, Portland Chamber Commerce

GIVING OFFICERS

Linda Wright: *CURR EMPL* secy contributions comm: US Bancorp

APPLICATION INFORMATION

Initial Approach: *Initial Contact:* letter requesting copy of guidelines* *When to Submit:* before February 28 for health and welfare; before May 31 for civic and public affairs; before August 31 for education *Note:* Proposals will not be reviewed if a copy of the guidelines has not been previously obtained.
Restrictions on Giving: Does not support individuals, religious organizations for sectarian purposes, or political or lobbying groups.

OTHER THINGS TO KNOW

Publications: contributions guidelines

GRANTS ANALYSIS

Typical Range: $1,000 to $5,000

RECENT GRANTS

Children's Hospital and Medical Center, Seattle, WA
Goodwill Industries, Portland, OR
Hutchinson Cancer Center, Seattle, WA
Independent Colleges Foundation — for funding in Oregon, Washington, and California
Oregon Shakespearean Association, Ashland, OR

US Shoe Corp.

Revenue: $2.72 billion
Employees: 49,500
Headquarters: Cincinnati, OH
SIC Major Group: Apparel & Accessory Stores, Holding & Other Investment Offices, Leather & Leather Products, and Wholesale Trade—Nondurable Goods

CONTACT

Robert Petrik
Vice President & Treasurer
US Shoe Corp.
One Eastwood Dr.
Cincinnati, OH 45227
(513) 527-7000

CONTRIBUTIONS SUMMARY

Nonmonetary Support Types: donated products
Operating Locations: OH (Cincinnati)

CORP. OFFICERS

Philip G. Barach: *CURR EMPL* chmn, dir: US Shoe Corp
Bannus B. Hudson: *CURR EMPL* pres, ceo, dir: US Shoe Corp

US WEST / US WEST Foundation

Revenue: $10.28 billion
Employees: 63,707
Headquarters: Englewood, CO
SIC Major Group: Communications and Holding & Other Investment Offices

CONTACT

Jane Prancan
Executive Director
U S WEST Fdn.
7800 E Orchard Rd., Ste. 300
Englewood, CO 80111
(303) 793-6245
Note: Proposals should be sent to the nearest of 14 foundation offices throughout the western United States; a list can be

obtained by contacting Ms. Prancan at the above address.

FINANCIAL SUMMARY

Recent Giving: $22,000,000 (1993 est.); $21,519,411 (1992); $24,379,813 (1991)
Fiscal Note: All contributions are made through the foundation.
EIN: 84-0978668

CONTRIBUTIONS SUMMARY

Typical Recipients: • *Arts & Humanities:* arts associations, history/historic preservation, museums/galleries, music, opera, public broadcasting, theater • *Civic & Public Affairs:* business/free enterprise, civil rights, economic development, environmental affairs, law & justice, nonprofit management, professional & trade associations, public policy, urban & community affairs, women's affairs • *Education:* business education, colleges & universities, economic education, education funds, engineering education, legal education, minority education, science/technology education, student aid • *Social Services:* child welfare, employment/job training, family services, united funds, youth organizations
Grant Types: employee matching gifts and general support
Nonmonetary Support Types: donated equipment, loaned employees, and loaned executives
Note: Value of nonmonetary support was estimated at $4.0 million in 1987, the last year for which this information was calculated. This support is not included in above figures.
Geographic Distribution: primarily in the West
Operating Locations: AZ, CO, IA, ID, MN, MT, ND, NE, NM, OR, SD, UT, WA, WY

CORP. OFFICERS

Richard David McCormick: *B* Ft Dodge IA 1940 *ED* IA St Univ BS 1961 *CURR EMPL* chmn, pres, ceo, dir: US WEST *CORP AFFIL* dir: Majers Corp, Norwest Bank MN, Norwest Corp, Prin Fin Group, Supervalu Stores *NONPR AFFIL* dir: Regis Coll; fdr: Osaga Initiatives; mem: Phi Gamma Delta

GIVING OFFICERS

Leon Marks: secy

Richard David McCormick: pres *CURR EMPL* chmn, pres, ceo, dir: US WEST (see above)
James Marvin Osterhoff: treas *B* Lafayette IN 1936 *CURR EMPL* exec vp, cfo: US West *CORP AFFIL* dir: GenCorp *NONPR AFFIL* dir, cfo: Pvt Sector Counc; mem: Conf Bd Fin Counc, Fin Execs Inst
Jane Prancan: exec dir *CURR EMPL* dir (corp community affairs): US West

APPLICATION INFORMATION

Initial Approach: *Initial Contact:* proposal not to exceed 12 pages *Include Information On:* name of organization, mailing address, telephone number, contact person, list of organization's board of directors, copy of IRS form 501(c)(3) *Note:* Foundation only accepts proposals for the general grants category of giving; unsolicited proposals submitted for other initiative areas are not considered. However, the foundation will accept concept papers of up to three pages concerning these giving areas.
Restrictions on Giving: Foundation does not fund political campaigns; individuals; fraternal organizations, clubs, school organizations, and school athletic funds; general operating budgets of organizations that receive more than 40% of their budget from the United Way; religious organizations for sectarian purposes; international organizations; national health agencies or their local affiliates; general operating budgets of tax-supported educational institutions; debt retirement or operational deficits; foudations that are themselves grantmaking bodies; or trips and tours. (Exceptions may be made.)

OTHER THINGS TO KNOW

In October 1987, the company announced a new educational support program that will contribute $20,000,000 over the next five years to support educational efforts in its 14-state service area. The U S WEST Educational Initiative began in 1988 with $2,000,000 in funding. Through the initiative, the company will support a number of programs to help ensure educational excellence at primary, secondary, and postsecondary levels. The company also has

announced the formation of the U S WEST Fellowship Program, which will recognize and stimulate excellence and innovation in teaching. Beginning in 1989, these programs are funded through the foundation. The U S WEST Foundation was formed in July 1988 and began making grants in 1989. The foundation serves to combine U S WEST's giving program with those of its subsidiaries, Mountain Bell, Pacific Northwest Bell, and Northwestern Bell, which have now been combined into one company, U S WEST Communications. The foundation also gives on behalf of the holding company's other subsidiaries, which include companies involved in cellular communications, advanced technologies, financial services, and real estate.
Publications: *U S West Foundation Review, U S West Community Involvement Program, Revive: Rural Economic Vitality Initiative*

GRANTS ANALYSIS

Total Grants: $21,519,411
Number of Grants: 2,138
Highest Grant: $210,000
Typical Range: $1,000 to $25,000
Disclosure Period: 1992
Note: Recent grants are derived from a 1991 annual report.

RECENT GRANTS

594,500 United Way of King County, Seattle, WA — for annual support and KidsPlace
530,616 United Way-Mile High, Denver, CO — for annual support
490,000 Osage Initiatives, Denver, CO — for program development
339,599 American Indian College Fund, New York, NY — operating support and advertising campaign
323,242 United Way Columbia-Willamette, Portland, OR — for annual support
282,700 United Way of Minneapolis Area, Minneapolis, MN — for annual support
282,178 U S WEST Outstanding Teacher Program — for the "Reaching Beyond Classroom Walls"

teacher recognition program
280,390 United Way of the Midlands, Omaha, NE — for annual support
250,000 University of Washington, Seattle, WA — first of a two-year $500,000 grant to develop educational uses for virtual reality technology
210,100 Arizona Hispanic Chamber of Commerce, Phoenix, AZ — first of a three-year $634,004 grant for REVIVE! Arizona, a rural development partnership

USF&G Co. / USF&G Foundation

Revenue: $3.66 billion
Employees: 7,400
Parent Company: USF&G Corp.
Headquarters: Baltimore, MD
SIC Major Group: Holding & Other Investment Offices and Insurance Carriers

CONTACT

Sue Lovell
Corporate Foundation Administrator
USF&G Fdn.
100 Light St.
Baltimore, MD 21202
(412) 547-3752

FINANCIAL SUMMARY

Recent Giving: $1,900,000 (1993 est.); $2,622,682 (1992); $2,150,000 (1991)
Assets: $13,212,490 (1992); $13,790,000 (1991); $14,620,000 (1989)
Fiscal Note: The 1992 figure includes matching gifts and branch office donations. Without these donations, total for 1992 was $1,657,000. Estimate for 1993 does not include matching gifts and branch office donations.
EIN: 52-1197155

CONTRIBUTIONS SUMMARY

Typical Recipients: • *Education:* arts education, business education, colleges & universities, education funds, private education (precollege)
• *Health:* hospitals, pediatric health, single-disease health associations • *Social Services:*

child welfare, delinquency & crime, disabled, drugs & alcohol, family planning, homes, united funds, youth organizations
Grant Types: capital, employee matching gifts, endowment, general support, operating expenses, and scholarship
Note: Scholarships apply to USFG employee children only.
Geographic Distribution: primarily in operating locations and to national organizations; also through their 34 branch offices throughout the United States
Operating Locations: MD (Baltimore)
Note: Maintains branches throughout the United States.

CORP. OFFICERS
Norman P. Blake, Jr.: *B* New York NY 1941 *CURR EMPL* chmn, pres, ceo: USF&G Corp *CORP AFFIL* chmn: Fidelity & Guaranty Life Ins; chmn, ceo: Heller Fin, Heller Overseas Corp; chmn, pres: Fidelity & Guaranty Ins Underwriters

GIVING OFFICERS
Norman P. Blake, Jr.: pres *CURR EMPL* chmn, pres, ceo: USF&G Corp (see above)
Joan Dillard: treas *B* Baltimore MD 1951 *CURR EMPL* vp, treas: USF & G Corp *NONPR AFFIL* mem: Am Fin Svcs Assn, Houston Cash Mgmt Assn, Natl Assn Corp Treas, Treas Mgmt Assn
John Hoffen: secy
Ms. Sue Lovell: corp fdn adm

APPLICATION INFORMATION
Initial Approach: *Initial Contact:* letter or proposal *Include Information On:* description of the organization, amount requested, purpose for which funds are sought, recently audited financial statement, proof of tax-exempt status
When to Submit: any time
Restrictions on Giving: Contributions are not made to political organizations or candidates for political office, religious organizations or activities for the propagation of a particular faith or creed, veterans organizations, tax-supported institutions, propaganda institutions, trade and industry associations, dinners or special events, goodwill advertising, or individuals. Contributions also are not made for the pur-

chase of advertising space, tickets, or similar purposes.

OTHER THINGS TO KNOW
Priority is given to special programs or projects rather than to providing support for ongoing activities.
Support for national organizations is limited to 25% of the annual contributions budget.
For the next two years of giving the Foundation will concentrate most of its efforts on education and human and community services.

GRANTS ANALYSIS
Total Grants: $1,657,000
Number of Grants: 92
Highest Grant: $28,000
Typical Range: $5,000 to $25,000
Disclosure Period: 1992
Note: Recent grants are derived from a 1992 grants list.

RECENT GRANTS
330,403 United Way of Central Maryland, Baltimore, MD
125,000 Loyola College, Baltimore, MD
58,955 Citizens' Scholarship Foundation of America, Fall River, MA
56,115 Citizen's Scholarship Foundation of America, Fall River, MA
50,000 Baltimore Museum of Art, Baltimore, MD
50,000 College Bound Foundation, Baltimore, MD
50,000 Peabody Institute, Baltimore, MD
37,500 Campaign for Our Children, Baltimore, MD
37,500 Villa Julie College, Stevenson, MD
35,000 Center Stage, Baltimore, MD

USG Corp. / USG Foundation
Sales: $1.77 billion
Employees: 11,800
Headquarters: Chicago, IL
SIC Major Group: Holding & Other Investment Offices, Paper & Allied Products, Rubber & Miscellaneous Plastics Products, and Stone, Clay & Glass Products

CONTACT
Harold Pendexter, Jr.
President
USG Fdn.
125 S Franklin
Chicago, IL 60606
(312) 606-4594

FINANCIAL SUMMARY
Recent Giving: $290,959 (1991); $500,000 (1990); $716,446 (1989)
Assets: $477,156 (1991); $1,011,359 (1989)
Fiscal Note: Since 1989 all contributions have, and will, come through the foundation only. Prior figures represent both foundation giving, which amounted to $740,620 in 1988, and contributions by the corporation and its plants, which totaled $311,485 in 1988.
EIN: 36-2984045

CONTRIBUTIONS SUMMARY
Typical Recipients: • *Arts & Humanities:* arts institutes, history/historic preservation, libraries, museums/galleries, opera, public broadcasting, theater • *Civic & Public Affairs:* economic development, law & justice, public policy, urban & community affairs, zoos/botanical gardens • *Education:* colleges & universities • *Health:* health organizations, hospices, hospitals, medical research, mental health • *Social Services:* community service organizations, disabled, emergency relief, food/clothing distribution, united funds, youth organizations
Grant Types: capital, employee matching gifts, general support, and scholarship
Geographic Distribution: nationally, with emphasis on Illinois and corporate operating locations
Operating Locations: CA (Plaster City), FL (Jacksonville), GA (Atlanta), IA (Fort Dodge), IL (Chicago), IN (Shoals), MN (Cloquet), NY (Stony Point), OH (Gypsum, Tipp City, Westlake), OK (Southard), TX (Dallas), WI (Walworth)
Note: Above is only a partial list of major plant and subsidiary locations.

CORP. OFFICERS
Eugene B. Connolly, Jr.: *B* New York NY 1932 *ED* Hofstra Univ BS 1954 *CURR EMPL* chmn, ceo: USG Corp

CORP AFFIL dir: BPB Indus, CGC Inc *NONPR AFFIL* dir: Natl Assn Mfrs, Un Way Chicago; mem: Mid-Am Comm
Richard Harrison Fleming: *B* Milwaukee WI 1947 *ED* Univ Pacific 1969; Dartmouth Coll 1971 *CURR EMPL* vp, treas: USG Corp
Harold E. Pendexter, Jr.: *CURR EMPL* sr vp (admin), chief admin off: USG Corp

GIVING OFFICERS
Paul D. Backer: trust
Richard Harrison Fleming: treas, trust *CURR EMPL* vp, treas: USG Corp (see above)
Mathew P. Gonring: trust
Harold E. Pendexter, Jr.: pres, dir *CURR EMPL* sr vp (admin), chief admin off: USG Corp (see above)
Donald E. Roller: vp
Deloris E. Stacy: trust
S. K. Torrey: secy

APPLICATION INFORMATION
Initial Approach: *Initial Contact:* full proposal *Include Information On:* statement of need or problem and summary of background; amount requested and how it will be used; copy of IRS determination letter and most recent financial statements; list of board members; detailed description of proposed project, its purpose, and qualifications of organization to obtain objectives; goals and plan to achieve goals; supporting literature
When to Submit: any time (board meets quarterly); foundation attempts to respond to all proposals within 2 months
Restrictions on Giving: The foundation does not contribute to sectarian organizations having an exclusively religious nature; individuals; political parties, offices, or candidates; fraternal or veterans organizations; primary or secondary schools; organizations that cannot provide adequate accounting records or procedures; or courtesy advertising. In general, organizations already receiving funds through united campaigns will not be considered for additional support.

OTHER THINGS TO KNOW
Company took on a substantial debt in 1988 while successfully resisting a hostile takeover attempt. As a result, contribu-

tions level decreased temporarily. Currently negotiating a new debt restructuring. Foundation activity is still down.

GRANTS ANALYSIS
Total Grants: $290,959
Number of Grants: 80
Highest Grant: $41,135
Typical Range: $500 to $5,000
Disclosure Period: 1991
Note: The average grant figure excludes a single grant totaling $41,135. Recent grants are derived from a 1991 Form 990.

RECENT GRANTS
41,135 National Merit Scholarship, Evanston, IL
25,282 United Way/Crusade of Mercy, Chicago, IL
5,000 University of Missouri-Rolla, Rolla, MO
4,800 Robert Morris College, Chicago, IL
3,000 Chicago Crime Commission, Chicago, IL
3,000 Chicago United, Chicago, IL
3,000 Chicago Urban League, Chicago, IL
3,000 City of Hope
2,500 Friends of Handicapped Riders, Chicago, IL
2,000 Chicago Council on Foreign Relations, Chicago, IL

Ushkow Foundation

CONTACT
Maurice A. Deane
Secretary
Ushkow Fdn.
c/o Sedco Industries
98 Cutter Mill Rd., Ste. 475
Great Neck, NY 11021

FINANCIAL SUMMARY
Recent Giving: $31,680 (fiscal 1991); $7,985 (fiscal 1990); $384,185 (fiscal 1989)
Assets: $3,008,867 (fiscal year ending October 31, 1991); $2,784,497 (fiscal 1990); $2,591,643 (fiscal 1989)
EIN: 11-6006274

CONTRIBUTIONS SUMMARY
Donor(s): Joseph Ushkow
Typical Recipients: • *Arts & Humanities:* museums/galleries • *Civic & Public Affairs:* international affairs • *Education:* colleges & universities

• *Health:* health organizations, hospitals, medical research, single-disease health associations • *Religion:* religious organizations • *Social Services:* child welfare, community service organizations, disabled
Grant Types: general support
Geographic Distribution: focus on NY

GIVING OFFICERS
Barbara Deane: vp
Maurice A. Deane: secy, treas
Jerome Serchuck: vp
Joan Serchuck: pres

APPLICATION INFORMATION
Initial Approach: Contributes only to preselected organizations.
Restrictions on Giving: Does not support individuals.

GRANTS ANALYSIS
Number of Grants: 38
Highest Grant: $2,500
Typical Range: $50 to $500
Disclosure Period: fiscal year ending October 31, 1991

RECENT GRANTS
2,500 Plastic Reconstructive Surgical Research
2,000 Hofstra University, Hempstead, NY
1,400 Temple Beth El
450 North Shore University Hospital, Manhasset, NY
380 Anti-Defamation League, New York, NY
250 Planned Parenthood
250 Washington Institute for Near East Policy, Washington, DC
200 CCAR Endowment Fund
100 Nassau County Museum of Art
100 North Shore Child and Family Guidance, New York, NY

Uslico Corp. / Uslico Foundation
Revenue: $393.31 million
Employees: 1,200
Headquarters: Arlington, VA
SIC Major Group: Holding & Other Investment Offices, Insurance Carriers, and Security & Commodity Brokers

CONTACT
Jeffrey N. Mason
Secretary
Uslico Corp.
PO Box 3700
Arlington, VA 22203
(703) 875-3600

FINANCIAL SUMMARY
Recent Giving: $60,000 (1993 est.); $160,000 (1992); $145,000 (1991)
Assets: $297,364 (1991); $745,244 (1990); $299,464 (1989)
Gifts Received: $120,000 (1991); $145,000 (1989)
Fiscal Note: Contributes through foundation only. In 1991, contributions were received from Bankers Security Life Insurance Society ($50,000), Provident Life Insurance Company ($10,000), United Olympic Insurance Company ($10,000), and United Services Life Insurance Company ($50,000).
EIN: 52-1276950

CONTRIBUTIONS SUMMARY
Typical Recipients: • *Civic & Public Affairs:* housing, international affairs • *Education:* colleges & universities • *Health:* hospitals • *Social Services:* community service organizations, drugs & alcohol, united funds, youth organizations
Grant Types: general support
Geographic Distribution: focus on Virginia
Operating Locations: DC (Washington), VA (Arlington), WA (Bellevue)

CORP. OFFICERS
Daniel J. Callahan III: *CURR EMPL* chmn, ceo, dir: Uslico Corp

GIVING OFFICERS
W. Alan Aument: pres, treas, dir
David W. Karsten: vp, contr, dir *B* Chicago IL 1947 *ED* Northwestern Univ 1968; Northwestern Univ 1974 *CURR EMPL* sr vp, contr: USLICO Corp *CORP AFFIL* sr vp: Un Svcs Life Ins Co *NONPR AFFIL* mem: Am Inst CPAs
Jeffrey N. Mason: secy, dir
Thomas Y. Moon: dir
J. Rodman Myers: dir
Peter M. Regan: dir
David H. Roe: chmn, dir

APPLICATION INFORMATION
Initial Contact: brief letter

Include Information On: description of the organization, amount requested, purpose of funds sought, and proof of tax-exempt status*
When to Submit: any time
Note: Requests for support are evaluated along the following guidelines: the contribution will benefit a nonprofit organization in the geographic area served by the company; the need is identified with the interests of the insurance industry in providing for and promoting the health and well-being of individuals; the contribution will support insurance-related activities in the areas of research, statistical or educational programs, or building funds; the recipient agency is an ongoing one that has demonstrated financial capability for handling and administering the funds in a responsible manner; support of the organization has been identified by a board member or an officer of one of the companies as within the interest of the public affairs of the corporation; and the contribution falls within the guidelines of Section 501(c)(3) and the IRS has ruled that the organization is an eligible charity for tax purposes.

OTHER THINGS TO KNOW
Publications: foundation guidelines

GRANTS ANALYSIS
Total Grants: $160,500
Number of Grants: 13
Highest Grant: 100,000
Typical Range: $1,000 to $2,500
Disclosure Period: 1992
Note: Recent grants are derived from a 1992 grants list.

RECENT GRANTS
100,000 University of Wisconsin, Madison, WI—LPS Endowment
40,000 United Way of the National Capital Area, Arlington, VA—paid in four installments in 1993
5,000 Washington Performing Arts Society, Washington, DC
3,500 American Red Cross, Arlington, VA—Arlington Chapter

2,500 Arlington Housing Corporation, Arlington, VA
2,000 Arlington Hospital Foundation, Arlington, VA
2,000 Cystic Fibrosis Foundation, Bethesda, MD
2,000 Life Underwriting Training Council Building Fund
1,000 Arlington Symphony, Arlington, VA—Ballston Pops '92
1,000 INSURE, Washington, DC—ACLI AIDS Initiative

USLIFE Corp.

Assets: $5.32 billion
Employees: 2,024
Headquarters: New York, NY
SIC Major Group: Holding & Other Investment Offices, Insurance Carriers, Real Estate, and Security & Commodity Brokers

CONTACT

John Kelly
Senior Vice President, Corporate Affairs
USLIFE Corp.
3600 Rte. 66
Neptune, NJ 07754
(212) 709-6301

CONTRIBUTIONS SUMMARY

Company provides employee matching gifts only.
Grant Types: matching
Operating Locations: CA (Pasadena), IL (Chicago, Schaumburg), NY (New York), PA (Reading), TX (Dallas), WI (Milwaukee)

CORP. OFFICERS

Gordon E. Crosby, Jr.: *B* Remsen IA 1920 *ED* Univ MO *CURR EMPL* chmn, ceo, dir: USLIFE Corp *CORP AFFIL* chmn: All Am Life Ins Co, Old Line Life Ins Co Am, Security of Am Life Ins Co, US Life Ins Co, USLIFE Advisers Inc, US-Life Agency Svcs Inc, USLIFE Credit Life Ins Co, USLIFE Equity Sales Corp, USLIFE Income Fund Inc, USLife Ins Svcs Corp, USLIFE Life Ins Co, USLIFE Real Estate Svcs Corp, USLIFE Real Estate Svcs Corp, USLIFE Realty Corp, USLIFE Sys Corp *NONPR AFFIL* dir: Am Counc Life Ins, Health Ins Assn Am; trust: Pace Univ

Greer F. Henderson: *B* Jersey City NJ 1932 *ED* St Peters Coll 1954; Rutgers Univ *CURR EMPL* vchmn, cfo, dir: USLIFE Corp
William A. Simpson: *CURR EMPL* pres, dir: USLIFE Corp

UST

Sales: $1.01 million
Employees: 3,337
Headquarters: Greenwich, CT
SIC Major Group: Food & Kindred Products, Holding & Other Investment Offices, and Wholesale Trade—Nondurable Goods

CONTACT

Geraldine K. Morgan
Manager, Corporate Contributions
UST, Inc.
100 W Putnam Ave.
Greenwich, CT 06830
(203) 622-3696

FINANCIAL SUMMARY

Recent Giving: $6,000,000 (1993 est.); $6,000,000 (1992 approx.); $5,000,000 (1991 approx.)
Fiscal Note: All contributions are made directly by the company.

CONTRIBUTIONS SUMMARY

Typical Recipients: • *Arts & Humanities:* public broadcasting, theater • *Civic & Public Affairs:* civil rights, law & justice, urban & community affairs • *Education:* colleges & universities, minority education • *Health:* health care cost containment, health organizations, medical research • *Science:* scientific organizations • *Social Services:* aged, child welfare, community centers, community service organizations, domestic violence, drugs & alcohol, family services
Grant Types: capital, challenge, employee matching gifts, general support, project, scholarship, and seed money
Geographic Distribution: near headquarters and operating locations only; on rare occasions will consider awards to national organizations
Operating Locations: CT (Greenwich), IL (Franklin Park), TN (Hopkinsville, Nashville), WA (Woodenville)

CORP. OFFICERS

Jack Africk: *B* NY 1928 *CURR EMPL* exec vp, dir: UST *CORP AFFIL* vchmn: UST

Louis Francis Bantle: *B* Bridgeport CT 1928 *ED* Syracuse Univ BS 1951 *CURR EMPL* chmn, ceo, pres, dir: UST *CORP AFFIL* dir: St Natl Bank CT, US Tobacco Co *NONPR AFFIL* chmn: Alcohol & Drug Abuse Counc; dir: Americares Fdn; mem: Statue Liberty-Ellis Island Comm; trust: Fairfield Univ, Syracuse Univ; dir: Boy Scouts Am Greenwich; mem: CT Alcohol & Drug Abuse Comm, Natl Assn Tobacco Distributors; mem, dir: Tobacco Inst

Vincent Andrew Gierer, Jr.: *B* Bronx NY 1947 *CURR EMPL* pres, coo, dir: US Tobacco *CORP AFFIL* coo, pres, dir: US Tobacco *NONPR AFFIL* mem: Am Inst CPAs, Am Mgmt Assn, Fin Execs Inst

Ralph L. Rossi: *B* Scranton PA 1928 *ED* Pace Coll *CURR EMPL* vchmn, dir: UST

GIVING OFFICERS

Edward D. Kratovil: mem (corp contributions comm) *B* New Bedford MA 1944 *CURR EMPL* sr vp: UST

Geraldine K. Morgan: *CURR EMPL* mgr (corp contributions): UST

Harry W. Peter III: mem (corp contributions comm) *CURR EMPL* vp: UST

Ralph L. Rossi: chmn (corp contributions comm) *CURR EMPL* vchmn, dir: UST (see above)

Joan Schreiner: dir (taxes)

APPLICATION INFORMATION

Initial Approach: *Initial Contact:* letter and proposal *Include Information On:* description of the organization, amount requested, purpose for which funds are sought, recently audited financial statement, proof of tax-exempt status *When to Submit:* any time
Restrictions on Giving: Company does not fund dinners or special events, fraternal organizations, goodwill advertising, individuals, political or lobbying groups, or religious organizations for sectarian purposes.

OTHER THINGS TO KNOW

Company changed its name from U.S. Tobacco Co. in January 1988.
Company does not provide nonmonetary support.

GRANTS ANALYSIS

Total Grants: $6,000,000
Typical Range: $1,000 to $2,500
Disclosure Period: 1992
Note: Recent grants are derived from a 1993 grants list.

RECENT GRANTS

500,000 Le Moyne College, Syracuse, NY — to endow student-aid funds for over a five year period

USX Corp. / USX Foundation

Sales: $17.84 billion
Employees: 45,582
Headquarters: Pittsburgh, PA
SIC Major Group: Coal Mining, Metal Mining, Oil & Gas Extraction, and Primary Metal Industries

CONTACT

James L. Hamilton III
General Manager
USX Foundation
USX Tower
600 Grant St., Rm. 2640
Pittsburgh, PA 15219-4776
(412) 433-5237

FINANCIAL SUMMARY

Recent Giving: $6,000,000 (fiscal 1993 est.); $6,178,778 (fiscal 1992); $6,441,971 (fiscal 1991)
Assets: $6,999,299 (fiscal year ending November 30, 1992); $12,292,814 (fiscal 1991); $8,612,307 (fiscal 1990)
Fiscal Note: USX gives only through its foundation.
EIN: 13-6093185

CONTRIBUTIONS SUMMARY

Typical Recipients: • *Arts & Humanities:* arts associations, arts centers, arts festivals, dance, history/historic preservation, museums/galleries, music, opera, performing arts, theater • *Civic & Public Affairs:* business/free enterprise, environmental affairs, public policy, urban & community affairs • *Education:* arts education, business education, career/vocational education, colleges &

universities, economic education, education associations, engineering education, minority education, science/technology education • *Health:* health organizations, medical rehabilitation, mental health, single-disease health associations • *Science:* scientific organizations • *Social Services:* aged, community centers, disabled, drugs & alcohol, employment/job training, united funds, youth organizations

Grant Types: capital, employee matching gifts, general support, project, and scholarship

Note: Matching grants are made for education only.

Geographic Distribution: U.S., with emphasis on communities where USX Corp. and its subsidiaries operate

Operating Locations: AL (Chickasaw, Fairfield), GA (Atlanta), IL (Joliet), IN (Gary), MN (Duluth), OH (Conneaut, Findlay), PA (Dravosburg, Monroeville, Pittsburgh), TX (Dallas, Garland, Houston, Wichita Falls), WV

CORP. OFFICERS

Charles A. Corry: *B* Wyoming OH 1932 *ED* Univ Cincinnati BA 1955; Univ Cincinnati JD 1959 *CURR EMPL* chmn, ceo, dir: USX Corp *CORP AFFIL* dir: Marathon Oil Co, Mellon Bank Corp, Transtar Inc, TX Oil & Gas Corp *NONPR AFFIL* mem: Am Bar Assn, Am Iron Steel Inst, Fin Execs Inst, Machinery Allied Products Inst, North Am Soc Corp Planning, OH Bar Assn, PA Chamber Commerce; trust: Presbyterian Univ Hosp, Univ Pittsburgh; vchmn, dir: PA Chamber Bus Indus; dir: Jr Achievement Southwestern PA

GIVING OFFICERS

Victor Gene Beghini: trust *B* Greensboro PA 1934 *ED* PA St Univ BS 1956; Harvard Univ 1974 *CURR EMPL* pres, dir: Marathon Oil *CORP AFFIL* dir: Texas Oil & Gas Corp; mem corp policy comm: USX Corp *NONPR AFFIL* chmn: Natural Gas Supply Assn; dir: Am Petroleum Inst; mem: Mid-Continent Oil Gas Assn, Soc Petroleum Engrs; mem bus adv comm: Northwestern Univ Transportation Ctr; trust: OH Northern Univ

M. Sharon Cassidy: asst secy

Charles A. Corry: chmn, trust *CURR EMPL* chmn, ceo, dir: USX Corp (see above)

Gary Allen Glynn: vp (investments) *B* Springfield VT 1946 *CURR EMPL* pres: US Steel *NONPR AFFIL* mem: Assn Investment Mgmt & Res, Fin Exec Inst, Soc Security Analysts

Gretchen R. Haggerty: vp, treas

James L. Hamilton III: gen mgr

Robert M. Hernandez: cfo *B* Pittsburgh PA 1944 *ED* Univ Pittsburgh 1966; Univ PA Wharton Sch 1968 *CURR EMPL* exec vp (fin), cfo, dir: USX Corp *CORP AFFIL* chmn: RMI Titanium Co; dir: Am Casualty Excess Ltd, Corp Offs & Dirs Assurance Ltd

Frank H. Jones: asst secy

David A. Lynch: asst secy

John T. Mills: tax coun

Peter Black Mulloney: pres, trust *B* Boston MA 1932 *ED* Yale Univ 1954 *CURR EMPL* vp, asst chmn: USX Corp *NONPR AFFIL* mem: Am Iron Steel Inst, Intl Iron & Steel Inst; mem adv bd, secy: Salvation Army Pittsburgh; vchmn: World Aff Counc Pittsburgh

John L. Richmond: asst treas

Dan D. Sandman: gen couns, secy

Thomas J. Usher: trust

Louis A. Valli: trust *B* Nemacolin PA 1932 *CURR EMPL* sr vp (employee rels): USX Corp

APPLICATION INFORMATION

Initial Approach: *Initial Contact:* one- or two-page letter *Include Information On:* description of project and its goals; amount requested and estimated cost of project, with full explanation of necessity of funds sought in relation to total requirements and resources; statement and amounts of other sources of aid, in-hand and anticipated; name of executive in charge of activities and names of members of board of directors or trustees; signature of authorized executive of organization; statement of approval signed by individual in charge of parent organization if application originates in subdivision; copy of current budget; copy of most recently audited financial report; proof of tax-exempt status under Section 501(c)(3) of the Internal Revenue Code *When to Submit:* by

January 15 for public, cultural, and scientific requests; by April 15 for aid to education; by July 15 for social services and medical/health requests *Note:* Personal interviews and on-site visits may be scheduled as staff scedules permit. It is not necessary or desirable that requests be expensively prepared.

Restrictions on Giving: The foundation does not support individuals, religious organizations for religious purposes; conferences, seminars, symposia, or travel; publishing of books, magazines, films, or television productions; dissemination of propaganda; or attempts to influence legislation.

OTHER THINGS TO KNOW

Company also includes leasing and financial services; mining; mineral resources management.

GRANTS ANALYSIS

Total Grants: $6,178,778
Number of Grants: 1,129
Highest Grant: $700,000
Typical Range: $1,000 to $25,000
Disclosure Period: fiscal year ending November 30, 1992
Note: Recent grants are derived from a 1992 annual report.

RECENT GRANTS

60,000 National Association of College and University Business Officers (NACUBO) — recognize proven cost reduction programs developed by colleges and universities

25,000 Pittsburgh Symphony, Pittsburgh, PA — capital for deficit reduction

25,000 Pittsburgh Symphony, Pittsburgh, PA — capital for deficit reduction

Accessible Space, St. Paul, MN — for equipment and a transportation van to assist physically disabled adults

Allegheny County Bar Foundation, Pittsburgh, PA — for computer hardware/software for its pro bono legal services program

Ashland University, Ashland, OH — for computer hardware and support of the Business and Student Dialogue Program

Birmingham Area Council, Boy Scouts of America — for

construction of a Council Service Center

Carnegie Library of Homestead, Homestead, PA — for renovations

Children's Museum of Houston, Houston, TX — for construction of a new building

Clairton High School, Clairton, PA — scholarships

Utah Power & Light Co.

Headquarters: Salt Lake City, UT

CONTACT

Kay Jordan
Public Relations Department
Utah Power & Light Co.
1407 West North Temple St.
Salt Lake City, UT 84140
(801) 220-2000

CONTRIBUTIONS SUMMARY

Operating Locations: UT (Salt Lake City)

Utica National Insurance Group / Utica National Group Foundation

Premiums: $489.0 million
Employees: 1,450
Parent Company: Utica Mutual Insurance Co.
Headquarters: Utica, NY
SIC Major Group: Insurance Agents, Brokers & Service and Insurance Carriers

CONTACT

John R. Zapisek
Treasurer
Utica National Group Foundation
PO Box 530
Utica, NY 13503
(315) 734-2521
Note: Carolyn L. Dalton, vice president of human resources, is another contact at Utica National Insurance Group at the same address.

FINANCIAL SUMMARY

Recent Giving: $78,154 (1991); $73,958 (1990); $47,681 (1989)

Assets: $1,930,108 (1991); $871,992 (1990); $856,254 (1989)

Gifts Received: $1,000,000 (1991); $25,000 (1990); $25,000 (1989)

Fiscal Note: In 1991, contributions were received from Utica Mutual Insurance Company.

EIN: 16-1313450

CONTRIBUTIONS SUMMARY
Typical Recipients: • *Arts & Humanities:* history/historic preservation, public broadcasting • *Civic & Public Affairs:* economic development, municipalities, urban & community affairs • *Health:* mental health • *Social Services:* community service organizations, disabled, family services, food/clothing distribution, shelters/homelessness, united funds
Grant Types: general support and matching
Geographic Distribution: focus on NY
Operating Locations: NY (Utica)

CORP. OFFICERS
W. Craig Heston: *B* Philadelphia PA 1935 *CURR EMPL* chmn, ceo: Utica Natl Corp Group
John R. Lanz: *CURR EMPL* sr vp, cfo: Utica Natl Ins Group
Wallace W. Watkins: *B* Utica NY 1936 *ED* Yale Univ 1956 *CURR EMPL* pres: Utica Natl Corp Group

GIVING OFFICERS
Robert M. Best: dir
Alfred E. Calligaris: dir
Edward W. Duffy: dir
John G. Haehl: dir
W. Craig Heston: pres, dir *CURR EMPL* chmn, ceo: Utica Natl Corp Group (see above)
Herbert P. Ladds, Jr.: dir
David R. Newcomb: dir
Randall H. Pakula: dir
Robert L. Tarnow: dir *B* Rochester NY 1924 *ED* Oberlin Coll 1949 *CURR EMPL* chmn: Goulds Pumps *CORP AFFIL* dir: Bausch & Lomb, Norstar Bancorp, Raymond Corp, Utica Mutual Ins
George P. Wardley III: secy
Wallace H. Watkins: vp, dir
John R. Zapisek: treas, dir

APPLICATION INFORMATION
Initial Approach: Send brief letter including a description of the organization, amount requested, purpose of funds sought, audited financial statement, and proof of tax-exempt status. Deadlines are quarterly.

GRANTS ANALYSIS
Number of Grants: 6
Highest Grant: $55,000
Typical Range: $3,500 to $5,000

Disclosure Period: 1991

RECENT GRANTS
55,000 United Way, Utica, NY
5,000 Association for Retarded Citizens, Utica, NY
5,000 Family Service of Greater Utica, Utica, NY
5,000 Oneida County Historical Society, Utica, NY
4,654 Neighborhood Center of Utica, Utica, NY
3,500 United Arts Fund of Mohawk Valley, Utica, NY

Utilicorp United / Utilicorp United Charitable Foundation

Sales: $732.0 million
Employees: 3,022
Headquarters: Kansas City, MO

CONTACT
Nancy Schulte
Secretary-Treasurer
Utilicorp United Charitable
 Foundation
911 Main Street
Kansas City, MO 64105
(816) 421-6600

FINANCIAL SUMMARY
Recent Giving: $142,617 (1991)
Assets: $2,378,279 (1991); $1,300,000 (1990)
Gifts Received: $883,680 (1991); $470,000 (1990)
EIN: 43-1481996

CONTRIBUTIONS SUMMARY
Typical Recipients: • *Arts & Humanities:* public broadcasting, theater • *Education:* colleges & universities, education funds • *Social Services:* child welfare, youth organizations
Grant Types: employee matching gifts and general support
Geographic Distribution: giving primarily in Kansas City, MO, Omaha, NE, and other areas of company operations
Operating Locations: MO (Kansas City)

CORP. OFFICERS
Avis Green Tucker: *CURR EMPL* chmn: Utilicorp United

GIVING OFFICERS
Richard C. Green, Jr.: vp
William I Owen: dir

Roger K. Sallee: secy-treas
Avis Green Tucker: pres *CURR EMPL* chmn: Utilicorp United (see above)

APPLICATION INFORMATION
Initial Approach: Submit a brief letter of inquiry. There are no deadlines.
Restrictions on Giving: The foundation does not make grants to individuals.

GRANTS ANALYSIS
Number of Grants: 50
Highest Grant: $25,000
Typical Range: $1,000 to $5,000
Disclosure Period: 1991

RECENT GRANTS
25,000 Dana College
10,000 Boy Scouts of America
10,000 Marillac Center for Children
8,000 Kansas City Public Television, Kansas City, KS
7,282 Girl Scouts of America
6,000 Missouri Colleges Fund, MO
5,000 Crittenton
5,000 De La Salle
5,000 Folley Theatre
5,000 Nelson Gallery Foundation, Kansas City, MO

Uvas Foundation

CONTACT
Uvas Fdn.
50 Fremont St., Ste. 3520
San Francisco, CA 94105-2230
(415) 768-6024

FINANCIAL SUMMARY
Recent Giving: $88,250 (fiscal 1992); $88,000 (fiscal 1991); $80,000 (fiscal 1990)
Assets: $2,005,009 (fiscal year ending June 30, 1992); $1,837,689 (fiscal 1991); $1,804,930 (fiscal 1990)
EIN: 94-2678808

CONTRIBUTIONS SUMMARY
Donor(s): Barbara B. Davies, I.D. Mateo, Paul Lewis Davies III, Paul I. Davies, Jr.
Typical Recipients: • *Arts & Humanities:* history/historic preservation • *Civic & Public Affairs:* environmental affairs, philanthropic organizations, zoos/botanical gardens • *Education:* colleges & universities,

education associations, medical education, private education (precollege) • *Health:* nursing services • *Religion:* churches • *Science:* scientific institutes
Grant Types: endowment and general support
Geographic Distribution: focus on CA

GIVING OFFICERS
Barbara B. Davies: dir, vp
P.H. Davies: dir, vp
Paul Lewis Davies III: dir, vp
Paul Lewis Davies, Jr.: dir, pres *B* San Jose CA 1930 *ED* Stanford Univ AB 1952; Harvard Univ JD 1957 *CURR EMPL* pres: Lakeside Corp *CORP AFFIL* dir: FMC Corp, FMC Gold Co, Indus Indemnity Co, Sumitomo Bank CA *NONPR AFFIL* bd regents: Univ Pacific; hon trust: CA Academy Sciences; mem: Am Bar Assn, CA Bar Assn
Laura Davies Mateo: dir, vp
Segundo Mateo: dir, vp
A. McDonald: secy

APPLICATION INFORMATION
Initial Approach: Contributes only to preselected organizations. Applications not accepted.
Restrictions on Giving: Does not support individuals.

GRANTS ANALYSIS
Number of Grants: 36
Highest Grant: $20,000
Typical Range: $1,000 to $5,000
Disclosure Period: fiscal year ending June 30, 1992

RECENT GRANTS
20,000 Piedmont Community Church, Piedmont, CA
12,500 California Academy of Sciences, San Francisco, CA
10,000 University of Virginia Alumni Association, Charlottesville, VA
5,000 University of California Chancellor's Circle, Berkeley, CA
2,500 Colonial Williamsburg Foundation, Williamsburg, VA
2,500 Head-Royce School, Oakland, CA
2,500 Samuel Merritt College of Nursing, Oakland, CA
2,000 Alta Bates Herrick Foundation, Berkeley, CA

2,000 Aurora School,
Oakland, CA
2,000 Aurora School,
Oakland, CA

V and V Foundation

CONTACT
Tinkham Veale II
Trustee
V and V Fdn.
Epping Rd.
Gates Mills, OH 44040

FINANCIAL SUMMARY
Recent Giving: $107,800
(1990); $348,650 (1989);
$79,975 (1988)
Assets: $3,507,784 (1990);
$3,406,621 (1989); $2,415,305
(1988)
Gifts Received: $100,000
(1990); $900,000 (1989);
$152,000 (1988)
Fiscal Note: In 1990, contributions were received from Tinkham Veale II and G.W. Veale.
EIN: 34-6565830

CONTRIBUTIONS SUMMARY
Donor(s): Tinkham Veale II
Typical Recipients: • *Arts & Humanities:* community arts, history/historic preservation, performing arts, theater • *Civic & Public Affairs:* zoos/botanical gardens • *Education:* colleges & universities, private education (precollege) • *Health:* hospitals
Grant Types: general support and research

GIVING OFFICERS
Helen V. Gelbach: trust
Harriet V. Leedy: trust
Harriet E. Veale: trust
Tinkham Veale III: trust
Tinkham Veale II: trust *CURR EMPL* chmn: Sudbury

APPLICATION INFORMATION
Initial Approach: Send brief letter describing program. There are no deadlines.

GRANTS ANALYSIS
Number of Grants: 33
Highest Grant: $25,000
Typical Range: $1,000 to $5,000
Disclosure Period: 1990

RECENT GRANTS
25,000 Hathaway Brown
School, Shaker
Heights, OH
25,000 Shipley School

6,500 Kenyon College,
Gambier, OH
5,000 Case Western Reserve University,
Cleveland, OH
5,000 Connecticut College, New London,
CT
5,000 Hillsdale College,
Hillsdale, MI
5,000 Lynchburg College, Lynchburg,
VA
5,000 University School,
Shaker Heights, OH
3,000 Fairmont Presbyterian Church
3,000 Garden Center of
Greater Cleveland,
Cleveland, OH

Valdese Manufacturing Co., Inc. / Valdese Manufacturing Co. Foundation

Sales: $30.0 million
Employees: 400
Headquarters: Valdese, NC
SIC Major Group: Textile Mill Products

CONTACT
William Galloway
President & Treasurer
Valdese Manufacturing Co.
Foundation
PO Drawer 10
Valdese, NC 28690-0010
(704) 874-2151

FINANCIAL SUMMARY
Recent Giving: $7,600 (1990);
$8,600 (1989)
Assets: $4,138 (1990); $8,297
(1989)
Gifts Received: $3,000 (1990);
$10,000 (1989)
Fiscal Note: In 1990, contributions were received from
Valdese Manufacturing Co.
EIN: 56-6061867

CONTRIBUTIONS SUMMARY
Typical Recipients: • *Arts & Humanities:* community arts, performing arts, theater • *Civic & Public Affairs:* municipalities, urban & community affairs • *Social Services:* united funds, youth organizations
Grant Types: general support
Geographic Distribution: focus on NC
Operating Locations: NC
(Valdese)

CORP. OFFICERS
Jack D. Grooms: *CURR EMPL* pres, treas: Valdese Mfg Co

GIVING OFFICERS
Jack D. Grooms: pres, treas, dir
Edward Pascal: vp, secy, dir

APPLICATION INFORMATION
Initial Approach: Send brief letter describing program. There are no deadlines.

GRANTS ANALYSIS
Number of Grants: 3
Highest Grant: $5,000
Typical Range: $500 to $5,000
Disclosure Period: 1990

RECENT GRANTS
5,000 Western Piedmont
Blueprint for Progress
2,100 Burke County
United Fund
500 Old Colony Players, Manteo, NC

Vale-Asche Foundation

CONTACT
Vale Asche Ackerman
President
Vale-Asche Fdn.
2001 Kirby Dr., Ste. 910
Houston, TX 77019
(713) 520-7334

FINANCIAL SUMMARY
Recent Giving: $202,196 (fiscal 1990); $177,735 (fiscal 1989); $207,006 (fiscal 1988)
Assets: $5,308,479 (fiscal year ending November 30, 1990);
$4,936,208 (fiscal 1989);
$4,467,063 (fiscal 1988)
EIN: 51-6015320

CONTRIBUTIONS SUMMARY
Donor(s): the late Ruby Vale, the late Fred B. Asche
Typical Recipients: • *Arts & Humanities:* museums/galleries • *Civic & Public Affairs:* environmental affairs, zoos/botanical gardens • *Health:* health organizations, medical research • *Religion:* churches, religious organizations • *Social Services:* aged, child welfare, community service organizations, food/clothing distribution, shelters/homelessness
Grant Types: operating expenses, project, and research

Geographic Distribution: focus on Houston, TX

GIVING OFFICERS
Asche Ackerman: trust
Mrs. Vale Asche Ackerman: pres, trust
Harry H. Hudson: secy, treas, trust
Bettyann Asche Murray: vp, trust

APPLICATION INFORMATION
Initial Approach: Contributes only to preselected organizations.
Restrictions on Giving: Does not support individuals.

GRANTS ANALYSIS
Number of Grants: 19
Highest Grant: $38,000
Typical Range: $1,000 to $10,000
Disclosure Period: fiscal year ending November 30, 1990

RECENT GRANTS
38,000 Palmer Memorial
Episcopal Church
35,000 Bayou Bend Collection, Houston, TX
35,000 Stahlin Foundation
19,000 Harris County
Emergency Corps,
Houston, TX
15,000 Wilhelm School
11,000 Adult Institute for
Independent Living
Skills
10,000 Houston School for
Deaf Children,
Houston, TX
5,000 Contemporary Arts
Museum, Houston,
TX
5,000 Cotulla Independent School District
5,000 Harris County Psychiatric Center,
Houston, TX

Vale Foundation, Ruby R.

CONTACT
Richard E. Menkiewicz
Sr. Trust Administrator
Ruby R. Vale Fdn.
c/o Bank of Delaware
300 Delaware Ave.
Wilmington, DE 19801

FINANCIAL SUMMARY
Recent Giving: $179,000
(1990); $218,000 (1989);
$180,000 (1987)
Assets: $2,772,385 (1990);
$2,818,331 (1989); $2,484,074
(1987)

EIN: 51-6018883

CONTRIBUTIONS SUMMARY
Donor(s): the late Ruby R. Vale
Typical Recipients: • *Education:* colleges & universities, legal education, private education (precollege) • *Social Services:* child welfare
Grant Types: general support

APPLICATION INFORMATION
Initial Approach: Send brief letter describing program. Deadline is September 1.

GRANTS ANALYSIS
Number of Grants: 15
Highest Grant: $40,000
Typical Range: $10,000 to $20,000
Disclosure Period: 1990

RECENT GRANTS
40,000 Dickinson School of Law, Carlisle, PA
25,000 Children's Bureau of Delaware, Wilmington, DE
25,000 Dartmouth College, Hanover, NH
25,000 Smith College, Northampton, MA
10,000 Delaware Nature Education, Hockessin, DE
10,000 Kiwanis Club of Melford
10,000 South Kent School, South Kent, CT
5,000 Berry College, Mount Berry, GA
5,000 Cumberland College, Williamsburg, KY
5,000 Easter Seal Society, Wilmington, DE

Valencia Charitable Trust

CONTACT
Valencia Charitable Trust
c/o Fleet Trust Company
159 East Main Street
Rochester, NY 14638
(716) 726-8053

FINANCIAL SUMMARY
Recent Giving: $219,244 (fiscal 1992); $210,000 (fiscal 1991); $210,000 (fiscal 1990)
Assets: $2,973,929 (fiscal year ending September 30, 1992); $1,843,414 (fiscal 1991); $2,700,067 (fiscal 1990)
Gifts Received: $10,000 (fiscal 1992)

EIN: 22-2908724

CONTRIBUTIONS SUMMARY
Typical Recipients: • *Religion:* religious organizations
Grant Types: general support

GIVING OFFICERS
Katherine M. Baker: trust
Carol Cifatte: trust
Margaret Rosita Kenny: trust
Daniel Marie McCabe: trust
Jean Sauntry: trust

GRANTS ANALYSIS
Number of Grants: 1
Highest Grant: $219,244
Disclosure Period: fiscal year ending September 30, 1992

RECENT GRANTS
210,000 Connecticut Province of the Sisters of St. Joseph of Chambery, CT

Valentine Foundation, Lawson

CONTACT
Alice P. Doyle
Trustee
Lawson Valentine Fdn.
998 Farmington Avenue, Suite 123
West Hartford, CT 06107
(203) 521-3108

FINANCIAL SUMMARY
Recent Giving: $266,278 (fiscal 1992); $369,225 (fiscal 1991)
Assets: $8,656,884 (fiscal year ending February 28, 1992); $7,802,298 (fiscal 1991)
EIN: 13-6920044

CONTRIBUTIONS SUMMARY
Donor(s): Alice P. Doyle
Typical Recipients: • *Arts & Humanities:* opera, theater • *Civic & Public Affairs:* municipalities • *Education:* colleges & universities, private education (precollege) • *Religion:* churches
Grant Types: general support

GIVING OFFICERS
Alice P. Doyle: trust
Allen Doyle: trust
Valentine Doyle: trust
Lucy Miller: trust
Paul E. Vawter: trust
William D. Zabel: trust

APPLICATION INFORMATION
Initial Approach: Send brief letter of inquiry. There are no deadlines.

GRANTS ANALYSIS
Number of Grants: 104
Highest Grant: $60,000
Typical Range: $50 to $5,000
Disclosure Period: fiscal year ending February 28, 1992

RECENT GRANTS
60,000 Bennington College Corporation, Bennington, WA
25,000 Non-Traditional Casting Project
25,000 University of Pennsylvania, Philadelphia, PA
20,000 Westminster Choir College, Princeton, NJ
16,000 St. Anne's School, Brooklyn, NY
11,200 Faith Seventh Day Adventist Church, Hartford, CT
10,000 In Fact, Boston, MA
5,000 Batoto Yetu
5,000 June Opera Festival of New Jersey, Princeton, NJ
4,000 Hartford Monthly Meeting of Friends, West Hartford, CT

Valero Energy Corp.
Sales: $1.23 billion
Employees: 1,831
Headquarters: San Antonio, TX
SIC Major Group: Electric, Gas & Sanitary Services, Oil & Gas Extraction, and Wholesale Trade—Durable Goods

CONTACT
Luis A. De La Garza
Vice President, Corporate Relations
Valero Energy Corp.
PO Box 500
San Antonio, TX 78292
(512) 246-2496

FINANCIAL SUMMARY
Recent Giving: $988,000 (fiscal 1991); $830,665 (fiscal 1990)

CONTRIBUTIONS SUMMARY
Typical Recipients: • *Arts & Humanities:* arts appreciation, general • *Civic & Public Affairs:* better government, environmental affairs • *Education:* agricultural education

• *Health:* emergency/ambulance services • *Social Services:* aged, food/clothing distribution
Grant Types: capital, challenge, emergency, endowment, fellowship, general support, multiyear/continuing support, project, research, and seed money
Nonmonetary Support Types: donated equipment, in-kind services, and loaned executives
Note: In-kind services consist of printing services for a number of nonprofit organizations in San Antonio.
Geographic Distribution: headquarters and operating locations
Operating Locations: TX (Brownsville, Corpus Christi, Houston, San Antonio)

CORP. OFFICERS
Edward C. Benninger: *B* 1942 *ED* TX Tech Univ BBA 1965 *CURR EMPL* exec vp, cfo: Valero Energy Corp *CORP AFFIL* exec vp, cfo: Valero Energy Corp Subs
William E. Greehey: *B* Ft Dodge IA 1936 *ED* St Marys Univ 1960 *CURR EMPL* chmn, ceo, dir: Valero Energy Corp
Palmer L. Moe: *CURR EMPL* pres, coo, dir: Valero Energy Corp

GIVING OFFICERS
Luis A. De La Garza: *CURR EMPL* vp corp rels: Valero Energy Corp

APPLICATION INFORMATION
Initial Approach: *Initial Contact:* brief letter of inquiry *Include Information On:* description of the organization, amount requested, purpose of funds sought, audited financial statement, and proof of tax-exempt status *When to Submit:* any time

Valley Bancorp / Valley Bank Charitable Contributions Distributions Trust
Assets: $318.7 million
Employees: 206
Headquarters: Chambersburg, PA
SIC Major Group: Depository Institutions and Holding & Other Investment Offices

CONTACT

Holly Kann
Marketing Manager
Valley Bancorp
PO Box 459
Chambersburg, PA 17201
(717) 263-2265

CONTRIBUTIONS SUMMARY

Operating Locations: PA
(Chambersburg)

CORP. OFFICERS

John C. Brugler: *CURR
EMPL* pres: Valley Bancorp
John C. McNew: *CURR EMPL*
exec vp, cfo: Valley Bancorp

Valley Foundation

CONTACT

Ervie L. Smith
Executive Director
Valley Foundation
PO Box 5129
San Jose, CA 95150
(408) 292-1124
Note: The foundation is located
at 333 West Santa Clara Street,
Suite 500, San Jose, CA, 95113.

FINANCIAL SUMMARY

Recent Giving: $2,000,000
(fiscal 1993 est.); $1,924,409
(fiscal 1992); $2,128,383 (fis-
cal 1991)
Assets: $44,616,716 (fiscal
1991)
EIN: 94-1584547

CONTRIBUTIONS SUMMARY

Donor(s): The Valley Foundation was formed in 1984 from
the proceeds of sale of the
Community Hospital of Los
Gatos and Saratoga, Inc. The
foundation seeks to provide
funding for nonprofit organizations in Santa Clara County,
CA, with an emphasis in the
medical field.
Typical Recipients: • *Arts &
Humanities:* museums/galler-
ies, opera, theater • *Civic &
Public Affairs:* philanthropic organizations • *Education:* business education, colleges & universities, medical education
• *Health:* health funds, hospices, hospitals, mental health,
pediatric health, public health,
single-disease health associations • *Science:* scientific organizations • *Social Services:*
aged, child welfare, community
centers, disabled, food/clothing
distribution, homes, shel-

ters/homelessness, volunteer
services, youth organizations
Grant Types: capital, matching, operating expenses, and
project
Geographic Distribution: restricted to Santa Clara County,
CA

GIVING OFFICERS

Warren Belanger, MD: trust
Phillip R. Boyce: chmn
Herbert Kain, MD: trust
Edgar G. LaVeque, MD: trust
Sydney Resnick: treas
Ralph Ross: vchmn
Richard Sieve, MD: secy
Walter Silberman, MD: trust

APPLICATION INFORMATION

Initial Approach:
Applicants should send a preliminary letter of one or two
pages in length.
The letter should describe the
general background and purpose of the sponsoring organization; individuals to be in-
vovled in the project; need to
be addressed; goals and anticipated results of the project; and
the total project budget including other sources of funding
and the amount requested from
the foundation. Applicants
should send the preliminary letter one month prior to submitting a full proposal. If the foundation determines that the
proposal falls within its current
areas of interest, submission of
a full proposal will be invited.
Deadlines for full proposals are
December 1, March 1, July 1,
and September 1.
Staff review of the proposal
will often include a site visit.
The board considers full proposals at its quarterly meetings
in February, May, September,
and December.
Restrictions on Giving: Applications for grants are accepted
only from qualified tax-exempt
charitable organizations. Applications will not be accepted for
the benefit of individuals or religious purposes.

OTHER THINGS TO KNOW

Publications: guidelines for
grant applications, annual report

GRANTS ANALYSIS

Total Grants: $1,924,409
Number of Grants: 48
Highest Grant: $100,000

Typical Range: $25,000 to
$75,000
Disclosure Period: fiscal year
ending September 30, 1992
Note: Recent grants are derived
from a fiscal 1992 annual report.

RECENT GRANTS

100,000 American Red
Cross, Santa Clara,
CA — funding to-
ward expansion of
the new facility
100,000 Art Fund Cam-
paign/Community
Foundation, Santa
Clara, CA — funds
to go toward the de-
velopment of a per-
manent endowment
for stability of the
arts in Santa Clara
County
100,000 California Parkinson's Foundation —
support to build a
neural tissue trans-
plantation program
100,000 City Team Minis-
tries, Los Angeles,
CA — funds to-
ward relocation
and program expan-
sion
100,000 Emergency Hous-
ing Consortium of
Santa Clara
County, Santa
Clara, CA — sup-
port toward the
Family Case Man-
agement Program
100,000 New Children's
Shelter Fund, Los
Angeles, CA — to
complete the con-
struction and equip-
ping of the new
shelter
100,000 Stanford Univer-
sity Medical Cen-
ter, Stanford, CA —
Department of
Gynecology/Obstet-
rics; funding for
the capital costs
segment of a Peri-
natal Community
Outreach Program
100,000 Valley Medical
Center Foundation,
Santa Clara, CA —
funding to provide
expanded and reno-
vated space for the
main pharmacy
52,489 Santa Clara University, Santa Clara,
CA — to provide
full-tuition scholar-
ships for four pre-
medical students
50,000 Bay and Valley
Habitat for Human-
ity — a matching
grant for securing
donations

Valley Foundation, Wayne and Gladys

CONTACT

Paul D. O'Connor
President and Executive Director
Wayne and Gladys Valley Fdn.
4000 Executive Pkwy., Ste. 535
San Ramon, CA 94583
(510) 275-9330

FINANCIAL SUMMARY

Recent Giving: $5,143,050
(fiscal 1991); $5,147,750 (fis-
cal 1990); $1,722,176 (fiscal
1989)
Assets: $146,403,671 (fiscal
year ending September 30,
1991); $118,022,608 (fiscal
1990); $70,159,697 (fiscal
1989)
Gifts Received: $13,972,000
(fiscal 1991); $52,460,000 (fis-
cal 1990); $31,295,000 (fiscal
1989)
Fiscal Note: In fiscal 1991, the
foundation received
$13,972,000 from the estate of
F. Wayne Valley, one of the
original donors.
EIN: 95-3203014

CONTRIBUTIONS SUMMARY

Donor(s): The foundation was
established by Mr. F. Wayne
Valley and Mrs. Gladys Valley
in 1977. After Mr. Valley's
death in 1986, the foundation
received substantial funds from
his estate and will continue to
receive funds over a period of
years.
Mr. Valley was the founder and
major owner of Citation Builders, headquartered in San Leandro, CA, which became one of
the largest single-family homebuilders in California. Besides
Citation, Mr. Valley's other
business activities included
part-ownership of the former
Oakland Raiders of the National Football League. Mrs.
Valley continues to serve as the
chairwoman of the foundation.
Typical Recipients: • *Civic &
Public Affairs:* philanthropic organizations, professional &
trade associations • *Education:*
colleges & universities, education associations, private education (precollege), religious education • *Health:* hospitals,
medical research • *Social Services:* religious welfare, youth
organizations
Grant Types: capital, general
support, matching, and research

Geographic Distribution:
focus on East Bay, CA, which
includes Alameda, Contra
Costa, and Santa Clara counties

GIVING OFFICERS
Robert C. Brown: dir
Stephen M. Chandler: dir
Edwin Austin Heafey, Jr.: dir
B Oakland CA 1930 *ED* Univ
Santa Clara AB 1952; Stanford
Univ LLB 1955 *CURR EMPL*
sr ptnr: Crosby Heafey Roach
& May *NONPR AFFIL* mem:
Alameda County Bar Assn, Am
Bar Fdn, Am Bd Trial Advo-
cates, Am Coll Trial Lawyers,
Assn Deaf Couns Northern CA,
Assn Trial Lawyers Am, CA
Bar Assn, CA Trial Lawyers
Assn, Intl Soc Barristers, San
Francisco Bar Assn; trust: Univ
Santa Clara
Richard M. Kingsland: vp
Paul Daniel O'Connor: pres *B*
Paterson NJ 1936 *ED* US Naval
Academy BS 1959; Univ VA
LLB 1965 *CURR EMPL* ceo:
Citation Builders *NONPR
AFFIL* mem: Am Horse Shows
Assn, NY City Bar Assn
John Stock: dir
Gladys Valley: chmn
Sonya Valley: dir
Tamara Valley: dir

APPLICATION INFORMATION
Initial Approach:
Applicants should submit a
two- to three-page summary letter.
The letter should include the
following: goal and purpose of
the project; description and
brief history of the sponsoring
organization; research references, if any, that shows the
need of the project or the effi-
cacy of the subject method; project time frame; amount requested from the foundation,
total project cost, and other
funding sources; brief biographies of project administrators;
and milestones by which progress or success will be measured. Other materials should be
attached to the summary letter
including income and expense
budget for the project and the
latest annual financial statement of the sponsoring organization; list of the board of directors of the sponsoring
organization; a copy of the IRS
tax-exempt determination letter; and a letter from the chief
officer of the sponsoring organization stating that tax-ex-

empt status has not been re-
voked or modified.
There are no deadlines for submitting proposals.
The board of directors meets
quarterly, and the foundation
promises a quick preliminary
response.
Restrictions on Giving: In
general, the foundation will not
provide funding to any of the
following: individuals; organizations for profit or profit-making enterprises of nonprofit
groups; veterans, fraternal,
labor, service club, military, or
similar organizations whose
principal activity is for the
benefit of members; lobbying,
propaganda, or other attempts
to influence legislation or other
partisan political activities;
fund-raising events, dinners, or
similar affairs, or for advertising; and private operating foundations.

OTHER THINGS TO KNOW
Publications: informational
brochure, application guidelines

GRANTS ANALYSIS
Total Grants: $5,143,050
Number of Grants: 27
Highest Grant: $2,000,000
Typical Range: $25,000 to
$400,000
Disclosure Period: fiscal year
ending September 30, 1991
Note: Average grant figure ex-
cludes a grant of $2,000,000.
Recent grants are derived from
a 1991 grants list.

RECENT GRANTS
2,000,000 University of Cali-
            fornia, Berkeley,
            Berkeley, CA
  400,000 Bellarmine College
            Prepratory School,
            Santa Clara, CA
  400,000 Mills College,
            Piedmont, CA
  390,000 Holy Names Col-
            lege, Oakland, CA
  325,000 Bishop O'Dowd
            High School, San
            Leandro, CA
  250,000 Oregon State Uni-
            versity, Corvallis,
            OR
  250,000 St. Mary's College,
            Moraga, CA
  250,000 University of Cali-
            fornia, San Fran-
            cisco, San Fran-
            cisco, CA
  200,000 Providence Hospi-
            tal, Oakland, CA
  100,000 East Bay Commu-
            nity Foundation,
            Oakland, CA

Valley Line Co. / Valley Line Co. Charitable Trust
Sales: $75.0 million
Employees: 420
Parent Company: Sequa Corp.
Headquarters: St. Louis, MO
SIC Major Group: Electric, Gas
  & Sanitary Services and Water
  Transportation

CONTACT
Valley Line Co. Charitable Trust
510 Locust St., PO Box 14737
St. Louis, MO 63178-4737
(314) 889-0100

FINANCIAL SUMMARY
Recent Giving: $265,527
(1990)
Assets: $2,561 (1990);
$273,894 (1989)
EIN: 43-6023507

CONTRIBUTIONS SUMMARY
Operating Locations: MO (St.
Louis)

CORP. OFFICERS
D. J. Marquitz: *CURR EMPL*
pres: Valley Line Co

GIVING OFFICERS
Boatmen's Trust Company:
trust

GRANTS ANALYSIS
Disclosure Period: 1990
Note: No grants list was
provided for 1990.

Valley National Bancorp
Assets: $2.4 billion
Employees: 700
Headquarters: Passaic, NJ
SIC Major Group: Depository
  Institutions and Holding &
  Other Investment Offices

CONTACT
Gerald Lipkin
Chairman
Valley National Bancorp
615 Main Ave.
Passaic, NJ 07055
(201) 777-1800

FINANCIAL SUMMARY
Recent Giving: $60,000 (1992)

CONTRIBUTIONS SUMMARY
Company reports 75% of contributions support health and
welfare; 15% to education; 5%
to the arts; and 5% to civic and
public affairs.

Typical Recipients: • *Arts &
Humanities:* general • *Civic &
Public Affairs:* general, housing • *Education:* elementary
education, student aid
• *Health:* hospitals, medical research • *Religion:* religious organizations, synagogues • *Social Services:* united funds,
youth organizations
Grant Types: general support
and research
Nonmonetary Support Types:
donated products, loaned employees, and workplace solicitation
Geographic Distribution: in
headquarters and operating
communities
Operating Locations: NJ
(Clifton)

CORP. OFFICERS
Gerald H. Lipkin: *B* Passaic
NJ 1941 *ED* Rutgers Univ
1963; NY Univ Sch Bus Admin
1966 *CURR EMPL* chmn, ceo,
dir: Valley Natl Bancorp *CORP
AFFIL* chmn, ceo, dir: Valley
Natl Bank
Peter Southway: *CURR EMPL*
pres: Valley Natl Bancorp

APPLICATION INFORMATION
Initial Approach: Send brief
letter of inquiry. There are no
deadlines.
Restrictions on Giving: Does
not support individuals, political or lobbying groups, or organizations outside operating
areas.

OTHER THINGS TO KNOW
Company and its employees
also are actively involved in
community volunteer activities, including sponsorship of
"Tomorrow's Children's Fund."

GRANTS ANALYSIS
Typical Range: $50 to $1,000
Note: Recent grants are derived from a 1992 list provided
by the company.

RECENT GRANTS
Beth Israel Hospital, Passaic,
NJ
Boys & Girls Club, Passaic, NJ
Eastern Christian Children's
Retreat, Wyckoff, NJ
Hispanic/American Chamber
of Commerce, Passaic, NJ
Passport Award for Staying in
School (PASS), Passaic, NJ
Respiratory Health Associa-
tion, Wyckoff, NJ
Tomorrow's Children Fund,
Hackensack, NJ

West Hudson Hospital, Kearny, NJ

YM-YMaa of North Jersey, Paterson, NJ

Valley National Bank of Arizona / Valley Bank Charitable Foundation

Parent Company: Valley National Corp.
Parent Employees: 7,913
Headquarters: Phoenix, AZ
SIC Major Group: Depository Institutions and Holding & Other Investment Offices

CONTACT
Lydia Lee
Chairperson, Contributions Committee
Valley Bank Charitable Fdn.
PO Box 71
Phoenix, AZ 85001
(602) 221-2230

FINANCIAL SUMMARY
Recent Giving: $2,200,000 (1993 est.); $2,252,000 (1992); $1,600,000 (1991 approx.)
Assets: $493,301 (1992); $1,256,039 (1989)
Fiscal Note: 1992 figure represents combined corporate and foundation giving. Value of direct giving is not available. Contact for such support is Brian Cooper.
EIN: 95-3330232

CONTRIBUTIONS SUMMARY
Typical Recipients: • *Arts & Humanities:* arts associations, arts centers, museums/galleries, performing arts, theater • *Civic & Public Affairs:* consumer affairs, urban & community affairs, women's affairs, zoos/botanical gardens • *Education:* business education, colleges & universities, continuing education, economic education • *Health:* health funds, hospitals, single-disease health associations • *Social Services:* child welfare, community centers, community service organizations, drugs & alcohol, employment/job training, food/clothing distribution, united funds, youth organizations
Grant Types: capital, employee matching gifts, general support, and project

Nonmonetary Support Types: donated equipment, in-kind services, loaned employees, and loaned executives
Note: Estimated value of non-cash support is unavailable and is not included in above figures.
Geographic Distribution: Arizona
Operating Locations: AZ (Phoenix)
Note: Operates approximately 260 branches statewide.

CORP. OFFICERS
Richard J. Lehmann: *B* Portland OR 1944 *ED* Univ WA BA 1967; Univ WA MBA 1969 *CURR EMPL* chmn, ceo, dir: Valley Natl Bank AZ *CORP AFFIL* chmn, ceo: Valley Natl Corp; mem banking comm, dir: Phoenix Econ Growth Corp; mem nominating comm, dir: MasterCard Intl *NONPR AFFIL* mem: Assn Reserve City Bankers; trust: Am Grad Sch Intl Mgmt-Thunderbird
Robert F. B. Logan: *B* 1932 *CURR EMPL* pres, coo: Valley Natl Bank *CORP AFFIL* pres, coo: Valley Natl Corp

GIVING OFFICERS
Neil H. Christensen: secy-treas
Michael Hard: bd mem
Lydia Lee: chairperson contributions comm
Robert Lloyd Matthews: bd mem *B* Omaha NE 1937 *ED* Univ NE BA 1959; Am Inst Banking 1968; Pacific Coast Banking Sch 1970 *CURR EMPL* pres, coo, dir: AZ Bank *CORP AFFIL* chmn, ceo, dir: Security Pacific Bank AZ; pres, coo, dir: AZ Bancwest Corp *NONPR AFFIL* adv dir: Valley Big Brothers; dir: AZ Cultural Devel, Pacific Coast Banking Sch, Sun Angel Fdn; mem: Am Bankers Assn, AZ Bankers Assn, Fiesta Bowl Adv Bd, Phoenix Metro Chamber Commerce, Phoenix Thunderbirds, Robert Morris Assn
Steve Roman: bd mem
Robert Wahlstrom: pres
John Westman: pres

APPLICATION INFORMATION
Initial Approach: *Initial Contact:* brief letter requesting application *Include Information On:* application requests description of the organization, amount requested, purpose for which funds are sought, recently audited financial state-

ment, proof of tax-exempt status *When to Submit:* any time
Restrictions on Giving: Foundation does not support individuals, religious organizations, political organizations, national health organizations, or private foundations. Also does not fund service club activities, scholarships, trips and tours, or research projects.

GRANTS ANALYSIS
Total Grants: $2,252,000*
Number of Grants: 270*
Highest Grant: $400,000
Typical Range: $1,000 to $20,000
Disclosure Period: 1992
Note: Figures are approximate and are supplied by foundation. Recent grants are derived from a partial 1992 grants list.

RECENT GRANTS
American Cancer Society
American Heart Association
Angel Charity for Children, Tucson, AZ
Area Agency on Aging
Arizona Clean and Beautiful, AZ
Arizona Educational Foundation, Phoenix, AZ
Arizona Hispanic Chamber of Commerce, Phoenix, AZ
Arizona Opera, Tucson, AZ
Arizona Preservation Foundation, AZ
Arizona Sonora Desert Museum, Tucson, AZ

Valmont Industries / Valmont Foundation

Revenue: $429.72 million
Employees: 4,320
Headquarters: Valley, NE
SIC Major Group: Fabricated Metal Products, Furniture & Homefurnishings Stores, Industrial Machinery & Equipment, and Primary Metal Industries

CONTACT
Robert B. Daugherty
Chairman
Valmont Industries, Inc.
PO Box 358
Valley, NE 68064
(402) 359-2201
Note: Garly L. Crouch is another contact name.

FINANCIAL SUMMARY
Recent Giving: $300,000 (fiscal 1993 est.); $263,750 (fiscal 1992); $335,591 (fiscal 1991)

Assets: $4,324 (fiscal year ending February 28, 1991); $13,178 (fiscal 1990); $9,073 (fiscal 1989)
Gifts Received: $325,041 (fiscal 1991); $270,000 (fiscal 1990); $260,000 (fiscal 1989)
Fiscal Note: Contributes through foundation only. In fiscal 1992, contributions were received from Valmont Industries.
EIN: 36-2895245

CONTRIBUTIONS SUMMARY
Typical Recipients: • *Arts & Humanities:* arts associations, libraries, museums/galleries, music, public broadcasting • *Civic & Public Affairs:* business/free enterprise, ethnic/minority organizations, professional & trade associations, women's affairs • *Education:* business education, colleges & universities, economic education, student aid • *Health:* single-disease health associations • *Religion:* religious organizations • *Social Services:* child welfare, recreation & athletics, united funds, youth organizations
Grant Types: general support
Geographic Distribution: primarily in Nebraska, limited nationally
Operating Locations: CO (Ft. Collins), IL (Danville), NE (Omaha, Valley)

CORP. OFFICERS
Robert B. Daugherty: *B* 1922 *CURR EMPL* chmn, dir: Valmont Indus *CORP AFFIL* dir: Conagra, FirsTier Financial, Peter Kiewit Sons, KN Energy *NONPR AFFIL* trust: Hastings Coll
William F. Welsh II: *B* Muskogee OK 1941 *ED* Univ Tulsa; Clemson Univ *CURR EMPL* pres, ceo, dir: Valmont Indus *CORP AFFIL* dir: Firstier Bank Omaha, Inacom Corp

GIVING OFFICERS
Melvin A. Bannister: dir
Gary L. Crouch: off, dir *B* Omaha NE 1941 *ED* Univ NE 1964 *CURR EMPL* vp (fin & accounting): Valmont Indus *NONPR AFFIL* mem: Am Inst CPAs, Fin Execs Inst
Robert B. Daugherty: pres *CURR EMPL* chmn, dir: Valmont Indus (see above)
Thomas P. Egan, Jr.: off
Brian C. Stanley: off *CORP AFFIL* vp, treas: Valmont Indus

William F. Welsh II: dir
CURR EMPL pres, ceo, dir:
Valmont Indus (see above)

APPLICATION INFORMATION
Initial Approach: *Initial Contact:* letter of solicitation *When to Submit:* any time

GRANTS ANALYSIS
Total Grants: $263,750
Number of Grants: 76
Highest Grant: $55,000
Typical Range: $250 to $5,500
Disclosure Period: fiscal year ending February 28, 1991
Note: Recent grants are derived from a fiscal 1991 grants list.

RECENT GRANTS
55,000 United Way, Omaha, NE
25,000 Creighton University, Omaha, NE
24,000 United Arts of Omaha, Omaha, NE
16,167 College of St. Mary, Omaha, NE
11,666 Midland Lutheran College, Fremont, NE
10,500 Zoofair VIII, Omaha, NE
10,000 Boy Scouts of America, Omaha, NE
10,000 Dana College Add Campaign, Blair, NE
10,000 Eugene T. Mahoney State Park, Omaha, NE
10,000 University of Nebraska Lincoln Foothold Facilities Fund, Lincoln, NE

Valspar Corp. / Valspar Foundation
Sales: $632.56 million
Employees: 2,500
Headquarters: Minneapolis, MN
SIC Major Group: Chemicals & Allied Products

CONTACT
Sam Guerrera
Chairperson, Charitable Contributions
Valspar Fdn.
1101 South Third St.
Minneapolis, MN 55415
(612) 375-7847

FINANCIAL SUMMARY
Recent Giving: $383,767 (fiscal 1991); $324,082 (fiscal 1990); $321,360 (fiscal 1989)
Assets: $430,226 (fiscal year ending September 30, 1991);
$363,343 (fiscal 1990); $47,955 (fiscal 1989)
Gifts Received: $430,000 (fiscal 1991); $625,000 (fiscal 1990); $340,000 (fiscal 1989)
Fiscal Note: Contributes through foundation only. In fiscal 1991, contributions were received from Valspar Corporation.
EIN: 41-1363847

CONTRIBUTIONS SUMMARY
Typical Recipients: • *Arts & Humanities:* arts funds, community arts, music, opera, performing arts, theater • *Education:* business education, colleges & universities • *Health:* hospitals, medical research, single-disease health associations • *Social Services:* community service organizations, disabled, united funds, youth organizations
Grant Types: general support
Geographic Distribution: provides grants throughout the United States
Operating Locations: FL (Tampa), IL (Carpentersville, Chicago, Rockford), MD (Baltimore), MN (Minneapolis), PA (Philadelphia), WI (Milwaukee)
Note: List includes plant and division locations.

CORP. OFFICERS
Robert E. Pajor: *B* 1937 *ED* Roosevelt Univ BS 1958; Univ CA Berkeley MBA 1964 *CURR EMPL* pres, coo, dir: Valspar Corp
C. A. Wurtele: *B* Minneapolis MN 1934 *ED* Yale Univ BA; Stanford Univ MBA *CURR EMPL* chmn, ceo: Valspar Corp *CORP AFFIL* dir: Donaldson Co, Gen Mills, Northwestern Natl Life Ins Co *NONPR AFFIL* dir: Walker Art Ctr; mem: Am Bus Conf, Natl Paint & Coatings Assn; mem adv counc: Stanford Univ Grad Sch Bus

GIVING OFFICERS
B. Eppel: asst treas
S. Guerrera: vp, treas, dir
D. C. Olfe: vp, secy, dir
C. A. Wurtele: pres, dir *CURR EMPL* chmn, ceo: Valspar Corp (see above)

APPLICATION INFORMATION
Initial Approach: *Initial Contact:* written request for application form *When to Submit:* by June 1 of each year

Restrictions on Giving: Scholarships are limited to children of employees of Valspar Corporation.

GRANTS ANALYSIS
Total Grants: $383,767
Number of Grants: 130*
Highest Grant: $17,000
Typical Range: $100 to $4,000
Disclosure Period: fiscal year ending September 30, 1991
Note: Number of grants and average grant figures do not include scholarships to individuals totaling $30,000. Recent grants are derived from a fiscal 1991 grants list.

RECENT GRANTS
17,000 City of Hope, Los Angeles, CA
13,250 United Way, Minneapolis, MN
13,250 United Way, Minneapolis, MN
13,250 United Way, Minneapolis, MN
13,250 United Way, Minneapolis, MN
11,496 United Way, Pittsburgh, PA
11,019 United Way, Baltimore, MD
10,000 College of St. Thomas, St. Paul, MN
10,000 Minneapolis Institute of Arts, Minneapolis, MN
10,000 Minnesota Opera, St. Paul, MN

Value City Furniture
Sales: $200.0 million
Employees: 825
Parent Company: Schottenstein Stores Co.
Headquarters: Columbus, OH
SIC Major Group: Furniture & Homefurnishings Stores and Wholesale Trade—Durable Goods

CONTACT
Elan Foundation
1800 Moler Rd.
Columbus, OH 43207
(614) 221-9200

CONTRIBUTIONS SUMMARY
Operating Locations: OH (Columbus)

CORP. OFFICERS
Jay L. Schottenstein: *CURR EMPL* vchmn, exec vp, dir: Schottenstein Stores Corp *CORP AFFIL* dir: Valley Fair Corp; exec vp, dir: Schottenstein Stores Corp; vchmn, exec vp: Value City Furniture

Jerome Schottenstein: *CURR EMPL* chmn, dir: Schottenstein Stores Corp

OTHER THINGS TO KNOW
Orginal donors include W.M. Whitney & Co. and Elyria City, Inc.

Valvoline Inc.
Sales: $700.0 million
Employees: 3,000
Parent Company: Ashland Oil Inc.
Headquarters: Lexington, KY
SIC Major Group: Automotive Dealers & Service Stations, Chemicals & Allied Products, Industrial Machinery & Equipment, and Petroleum & Coal Products

CONTACT
Martin A. Kish
Vice President, Public Affairs
Valvoline Inc.
PO Box 14000
Lexington, KY 40512
(606) 264-7777

CONTRIBUTIONS SUMMARY
Operating Locations: KY (Lexington)

CORP. OFFICERS
J. D. Barr: *CURR EMPL* pres, coo: Valvoline

van Ameringen Foundation

CONTACT
Henry van Ameringen
President and Chief Executive Officer
van Ameringen Foundation
509 Madison Ave.
New York, NY 10022
(212) 758-6221

FINANCIAL SUMMARY
Recent Giving: $1,682,487 (1991); $1,711,499 (1990); $1,960,934 (1989)
Assets: $42,100,266 (1991); $33,564,486 (1990); $32,909,798 (1989)
EIN: 13-6125699

CONTRIBUTIONS SUMMARY
Donor(s): The van Ameringen Foundation was established in 1950 by Arnold Louis van Ameringen, chairman of International Flavors and Fragrances. Mr. van Ameringen

died in 1966, leaving his family to continue his lifetime work in the field of mental health.

Typical Recipients: • *Education:* colleges & universities, medical education, special education • *Health:* geriatric health, health organizations, hospitals, medical research, medical training, mental health, single-disease health associations • *Social Services:* counseling, disabled, domestic violence, family services, legal aid, shelters/homelessness, youth organizations

Grant Types: general support, multiyear/continuing support, project, research, and seed money

Geographic Distribution: Northeastern United States

GIVING OFFICERS

Lily van Ameringen Auchincloss: vp

Harmon Duncombe: secy *B* Bogota NJ 1909 *ED* Harvard Univ BS 1931; Harvard Univ LLB 1935 *CURR EMPL* mem: Fulton Duncombe & Rowe *CORP AFFIL* dir: Intl Flavors & Fragrances

Patricia Kind: dir

Henry P. van Ameringen: pres *B* 1931 *CORP AFFIL* dir: Intl Flavors & Fragrances

Mrs. A. L. van Ameringen: hon chmn

Henry G. Walter, Jr.: dir *B* New York NY 1910 *ED* Columbia Univ BA 1931; Columbia Univ LLB 1934 *NONPR AFFIL* dir: Intl Atlantic Salmon Fdn; trust: Am Mus Natural History, Monell Chemical Senses Ctr, Neuroscience Res Fdn, Pierpont Morgan Library

APPLICATION INFORMATION

Initial Approach:

Applications may be sent to the foundation and addressed to the president. Although a concise statement of the aims and significance of a proposed project is sufficient, the foundation prefers to receive a full proposal.

Proposals must include a concise cover letter containing a description of the nature and purpose of the proposed project, major activities planned, amount requested, and a description of the organization itself. The proposal, not exceeding five pages, should include an outline of program design

and anticipated accomplishments during the proposed grant period; statement indicating the qualifications of the organization to complete the proposed project; statement of how the program will be evaluated; and a budget marking all anticipated expenditures, income, and sources of income. Each application must additionally contain a copy of the IRS letter indicating tax-exempt status; recent financial statement (preferably audited); current operating budget; list of the directors and officers; and the most recent annual report. Relevant documents, publications, or articles may be included.

The board meets in March, June, and November. Applications should be submitted two months in advance of the scheduled meeting at which funding decisions are made.

Grant recipients are notified in writing shortly after the board decision. Grant recipients are expected to submit periodic progress reports and a final report indicating financial activity and evaluated results.

Restrictions on Giving: The foundation does not fund any programs for mental retardation, physical disabilities, or drug and alcohol problems. No grants are given to individuals, for capital or endowment funds, to areas outside the mental health field, for annual fundraising drives, or in support of international organizations or activities. Grants are made only to charitable organizations that are tax-exempt under section 501(c)(3) of the IRS code.

OTHER THINGS TO KNOW

Short-term funding is favored over long-range commitments, although occasional multi-year grants are approved. Interviews may be arranged only after a proposal has been submitted.

Publications: annual report and program and application guidelines

GRANTS ANALYSIS

Total Grants: $1,682,487
Number of Grants: 48
Highest Grant: $80,000
Typical Range: $10,000 to $50,000
Disclosure Period: 1991
Note: Recent grants are derived from a 1991 annual report.

RECENT GRANTS

80,000 Fountain House, New York, NY — continued support for the research, training, and rehabilitation programs

73,195 Wediko Children's Services, Boston, MA — short-term residential diagnostic/treatment program for seriously disturbed children

60,000 Lower East Side Community School, New York, NY — social worker for the Parent-Pupil School-Based Support Team

53,689 Trustees of Columbia University in the City of New York Columbia University Community Services-The Rio, New York, NY — for social and mental-health services to formerly homeless families in residence at The Rio in Washington Heights

50,707 Institute for Experimental Psychiatry Research Foundation, Merion Station, PA — a clinical study of the effects of hypnosis on children in pain with sickle-cell disease

50,000 Contributors to the Pennsylvania Hospital Mill Creek School/The Institute of Pennsylvania Hospital, Philadelphia, PA — school for emotionally-disturbed adolescents

50,000 Federation of Parents and Friends of Lesbians and Gays, Washington, DC — The Family AIDS Support Program serves those with HIV/AIDS through a national network of volunteer organizers and educators

50,000 Green Door, Washington, DC — kitchen renovation and vocational equipment for the cafe in the clubhouse program for the recovering mentally ill

50,000 International Center for Integrative

Studies, (The Door), New York, NY — support of The Door's Counseling Center, which offers free services to at-risk adolescents from off the streets

50,000 Medical College of Pennsylvania, Philadelphia, PA — to start the Schizophrenic Diagnostic and Referral Center

Van Andel Foundation, Jay and Betty

CONTACT

Jay Van Andel
President
Jay and Betty Van Andel Fdn.
7575 E. Fulton Rd.
Ada, MI 49355
(616) 676-6224

FINANCIAL SUMMARY

Recent Giving: $4,792,800 (1991); $569,900 (1989); $610,410 (1987)
Assets: $11,778,326 (1989); $8,540,753 (1987)
Fiscal Note: In 1991, contributions wee received from the Amway Corporation.
EIN: 23-7066716

CONTRIBUTIONS SUMMARY

Donor(s): Jay Van Andel, Betty Van Andel
Typical Recipients: • *Arts & Humanities:* arts funds, community arts, museums/galleries, opera • *Civic & Public Affairs:* philanthropic organizations, public policy • *Education:* colleges & universities, religious education • *Health:* hospitals • *Religion:* missionary activities, religious organizations • *Social Services:* community service organizations, united funds, youth organizations
Grant Types: general support
Geographic Distribution: focus on MI

GIVING OFFICERS

James Roslonic: treas, trust
Otto Stolz: secy, trust *CURR EMPL* exec vp, secy, gen coun: Amway Corp
Betty Van Andel: vp, trust
Jay Van Andel: pres, trust *B* Grand Rapids MI 1924 *ED* Calvin Coll 1942-1946; Yale Univ 1944 *CURR EMPL* chmn, dir: Amway Intl *CORP AFFIL*

chmn: Amway Canada, Amway Hotel Corp, Amway Intl, Amway Properties Corp, Nutrilite Products; dir: MI Natl Corp, Van Andel & Flikkema Motor Sales *NONPR AFFIL* Omicron Delta Kappa; chmn: Jamestown Fdn; dir: Ctr Intl Private Enterprise, Gerald R. Ford Fdn, Grand Rapids Regional Bd, Heritage Fdn, Natl Endowment Democracy; mem: Direct Selling Assn; mem adv bd: Natl 4-H Fdn; mem exec comm: US Chamber Commerce; trust: Citizens Res Counc MI, Ferguson Hosp, Hillsdale Coll, Hudson Inst

APPLICATION INFORMATION

Initial Approach: Applicants should submit a letter of request to the foundation office. There are no deadlines.

GRANTS ANALYSIS

Number of Grants: 83
Highest Grant: $500,000
Typical Range: $1,000 to $10,000
Disclosure Period: 1989

RECENT GRANTS

500,000 Public Museum Foundation, Grand Rapids, MI
50,000 Heritage Foundation, Washington, DC
50,000 Jamestown Foundation, Washington, DC
40,000 Opera Grand Rapids, Grand Rapids, MI
35,000 Coral Ridge Ministries, Ft. Lauderdale, FL
30,000 Hour of Power
30,000 Pine Rest Christian Hospital Association, Chicago, IL
25,000 Jamestown Foundation, Washington, DC
25,000 Reformed Bible College, Grand Rapids, MI
20,000 Opera Grand Rapids, Grand Rapids, MI

Van Beuren Charitable Foundation

CONTACT

Van Beuren Charitable Foundation
P.O. Box 4098
Middletown, RI 02840-0010
(617) 232-1942

FINANCIAL SUMMARY

Recent Giving: $583,550 (1989)
Assets: $4,595,249 (1989)
EIN: 22-2773769

GRANTS ANALYSIS

Total Grants: $583,550
Disclosure Period: 1989

Van Buren Foundation

CONTACT

John A. Manning
Chairman
Van Buren Fdn.
c/o Farmers State Bank
Keosauqua, IA 52565
(319) 293-3794

FINANCIAL SUMMARY

Recent Giving: $181,411 (1990); $177,622 (1989); $146,191 (1988)
Assets: $2,435,085 (1990); $2,665,172 (1989); $2,393,384 (1988)
Gifts Received: $1,283 (1989); $1,206 (1988)
EIN: 42-6062589

CONTRIBUTIONS SUMMARY

Donor(s): the late Ralph S. Roberts
Typical Recipients: • *Civic & Public Affairs:* economic development, municipalities, urban & community affairs • *Education:* public education (precollege) • *Health:* health organizations, hospitals • *Social Services:* aged, recreation & athletics
Grant Types: capital, general support, project, and scholarship
Geographic Distribution: limited to Van Buren County, IA

GIVING OFFICERS

Richard H. Lytle: secy
John A. Manning: chmn
John R. Nickelson: vp
Arthur P. Ovrom: treas
Davis E. Pollock: pres

Rex Strait: vp
Norwood Teal: vchmn

APPLICATION INFORMATION

Initial Approach: Application forms for scholarships available from foundation or high school counselors in Van Buren County.

OTHER THINGS TO KNOW

Provides scholarships to individuals for higher education.

GRANTS ANALYSIS

Highest Grant: $92,081
Typical Range: $1,000 to $7,500
Disclosure Period: 1990
Note: Incomplete grants list provided for 1990.

RECENT GRANTS

92,081 Van Buren County Courthouse, Keosauqua, IA
17,700 City of Keosauqua, Keosauqua, IA
15,000 Van Buren County Memorial, Keosauqua, IA
5,000 Harmony Athletic Boosters, Bonaparte, IA
5,000 Van Buren County Agency on Aging, Keosauqua, IA
3,250 Bonaparte First Response, Bonaparte, IA
2,772 Van Buren High School, Keosauqua, IA
2,500 Riverview Club, Keosauqua, IA
2,000 Van Buren County Agency on Aging, Keosauqua, IA
2,000 Van Buren County Memorial Hospital, Keosauqua, IA

Van Camp Foundation

CONTACT

Fred Fox, Jr.
President
Van Camp Fdn.
6615 East Pacific Coast Highway, 115
Long Beach, CA 90803
(310) 430-5760

FINANCIAL SUMMARY

Recent Giving: $340,000 (1991); $310,640 (1990); $330,000 (1989)

Assets: $8,086,177 (1991); $7,334,667 (1990); $7,219,260 (1989)
EIN: 95-6039680

CONTRIBUTIONS SUMMARY

Donor(s): Gilbert C. Van Camp, Sr., Family Trust
Typical Recipients: • *Arts & Humanities:* arts institutes • *Education:* education funds • *International:* international organizations • *Social Services:* child welfare, domestic violence, family services, united funds, youth organizations
Grant Types: general support
Geographic Distribution: focus on CA

GIVING OFFICERS

Catherine Fairbank: dir
Fred Fox, Jr.: pres, treas, dir
Linda Van Camp: dir
Patricia Van Camp: dir
Christine Van Camp Zecca: vp, secy, dir

APPLICATION INFORMATION

Initial Approach: Contributes only to preselected organizations.

GRANTS ANALYSIS

Highest Grant: $150,000
Typical Range: $20,000 to $30,000
Disclosure Period: 1991
Note: Incomplete grants list provided in 1991.

RECENT GRANTS

150,000 Art Institute of Southern California, San Diego, CA
80,000 YMCA, San Diego, CA
70,000 Amity International Education Foundation, San Diego, CA
65,640 Amity International Foundation, San Diego, CA
35,000 Olympia Institute, San Diego, CA
30,000 Marin Abused Women Services, San Diego, CA
20,000 Children's Self-Help Center, San Diego, CA
20,000 Marin Therapy and Training Institute, San Diego, CA
15,000 Family Services, San Diego, CA
10,000 Children's Self Help, San Diego, CA

Van Evera Foundation, Dewitt Caroline

Former Foundation Name:
Dewitt Van Evera Foundation

CONTACT
Laura la Fond
Advisor
Dewitt Caroline Van Evera Fdn.
29710 Kipper Rd.
St. Joseph, MN 56374
(612) 363-8388

FINANCIAL SUMMARY
Recent Giving: $120,000
(1991); $116,000 (1990);
$107,000 (1989)
Assets: $2,697,092 (1991);
$2,384,469 (1990); $2,429,595
(1989)
EIN: 87-6117907

CONTRIBUTIONS SUMMARY
Donor(s): the late Dewitt Van
Evera, the late Caroline Irene
Van Evera
Typical Recipients: • *Arts &
Humanities:* libraries, public
broadcasting • *Education:* colleges & universities, private
education (precollege),
science/technology education
Grant Types: capital, endowment, general support, operating expenses, and scholarship
Geographic Distribution:
focus on MN, WI, and UT.

GIVING OFFICERS
First Interstate Bank, UT:
trust
**Laura Jane Van Evera la
Fond:** adv
Robert W. Van Evera: adv

APPLICATION INFORMATION
Initial Approach: Send brief
letter of inquiry describing program. There are no deadlines.
Restrictions on Giving: Does
not support individuals.

GRANTS ANALYSIS
Number of Grants: 9
Highest Grant: $40,000
Typical Range: $4,000 to
$25,000
Disclosure Period: 1991

RECENT GRANTS
40,000 Northland College,
Ashland, WI
25,000 Jessie F. Hallett
Memorial Library,
Crosby, MN
25,000 St. John's Preparatory School, Col-
legeville, MN
13,500 College of St.
Benedict, St.
Joseph, MO
4,000 College of St. Scholastica, Duluth, MN
4,000 Michigan Tech-
nological Univer-
sity, Houghton, MI
4,000 Westminster Col-
lege, Salt Lake
City, UT
3,000 St. Mark's School,
Salt Lake City, UT
1,500 KBPR/FM, Col-
legeville, MN

Van Every Foundation, Philip L.

CONTACT
Zean Jamison, Jr.
Director
Philip L. Van Every Foundation
c/o Lance, Inc.
PO Box 32368
Charlotte, NC 28232
(704) 554-1421

FINANCIAL SUMMARY
Recent Giving: $1,452,625
(1991); $1,445,150 (1990);
$1,541,683 (1989)
Assets: $22,766,958 (1991);
$22,022,740 (1990);
$10,612,688 (1989)
Gifts Received: $13,413
(1988); $14,530 (1987)
Fiscal Note: In 1988, the foun-
dation received a $13,413 con-
tribution from Lance, Inc. of
Charlotte, NC.
EIN: 56-6039337

CONTRIBUTIONS SUMMARY
Donor(s): The foundation was
established in 1961 by Philip
Van Every.
Typical Recipients: • *Arts &
Humanities:* arts associations,
history/historic preservation, libraries, museums/galleries
• *Civic & Public Affairs:* busi-
ness/free enterprise, environmental affairs, housing, municipalities, philanthropic
organizations, safety,
zoos/botanical gardens • *Education:* colleges & universities,
education associations, education funds, public education
(precollege) • *Health:* hospices, hospitals, medical research, single-disease health associations • *Religion:* churches,
religious organizations • *Social
Services:* child welfare, community service organizations,
homes, recreation & athletics,
religious welfare, shel-
ters/homelessness, united
funds, youth organizations
Grant Types: general support,
research, and scholarship
Geographic Distribution: primarily North Carolina

GIVING OFFICERS
J. W. Disher: mem bd adms
Thomas Borland Hurack:
mem bd adms *B* Durham NC
1946 *CURR EMPL* vp, secy,
treas, mem bd dirs: Lance Inc
Zean Jamison, Jr.: dir *B* Gas-
tonia NC 1932 *ED* Belmont
Abbey Coll 1959 *CURR EMPL*
dir human resources: Lance
J. S. Moore: mem bd adms
Albert Frazier Sloan: mem bd
adms *B* Charlotte NC 1929 *ED*
Presbyterian Coll 1955; Univ
NC 1969 *CURR EMPL* chmn,
dir: Lance *CORP AFFIL* dir:
Bassett Furniture Indus, Dr Pep-
per Co, PCA Intl
Paul Stroup: mem bd adms

APPLICATION INFORMATION
Initial Approach:
The foundation lists no specific
application procedures.
There are no application deadlines.
Restrictions on Giving: The
foundation reports no restrictions or limitations on giving.

OTHER THINGS TO KNOW
Nations Bank of North Carolina serves as corporate trustee
for the foundation.

GRANTS ANALYSIS
Total Grants: $1,452,652
Number of Grants: 123
Highest Grant: $150,000
Typical Range: $5,000 to
$50,000
Disclosure Period: 1991
Note: The average figure ex-
cludes two grants totaling
$250,000. Recent grants are de-
rived from a 1991 Form 990.

RECENT GRANTS
125,000 Charlotte-Mecklenburg Hospital,
Charlotte, NC
125,000 Charlotte-Mecklenburg Hospital,
Charlotte, NC
100,000 Hope Haven
75,000 Willingway Foun-
dation
50,000 Florence Crittenton
Services, Char-
lotte, NC
50,000 Mecklenburg
County Health De-
partment, NC
50,000 National Head In-
jury Foundation
50,000 Presbyterian Hospital, Charlotte, NC
35,000 Lineberger Cancer
Research
30,000 Nancy Henning
Lance Scholarship

Van Houten Charitable Trust

CONTACT
James S. Hohn
Vice President
Van Houten Charitable Trust
c/o First Fidelity Bank, N.A.,
New Jersey
765 Broad St.
Newark, NJ 07101
(201) 430-4500

FINANCIAL SUMMARY
Recent Giving: $836,018 (fis-
cal 1990)
Assets: $13,869,241 (fiscal
year ending November 30,
1990); $12,112,921 (fiscal
1989)
EIN: 22-6311438

CONTRIBUTIONS SUMMARY
Donor(s): The foundation was
established in 1979 by the late
Stella C. Van Houten.
Typical Recipients: • *Civic &
Public Affairs:* philanthropic organizations • *Education:* colleges & universities, education
funds, medical education, student aid • *Health:* health funds,
hospitals, pediatric health, single-disease health associations
• *Social Services:* child welfare, homes, youth organizations
Grant Types: capital, general
support, project, and seed
money
Geographic Distribution:
focus on Bergen and Passaic
counties, NJ

GIVING OFFICERS
First Fidelity, N.A.
corp trust

APPLICATION INFORMATION
Initial Approach:
The foundation requests applications be made in writing.
Proposals are accepted throughout the year, but no later than
April 31 for review in May.
Restrictions on Giving: The
foundation does not make
grants to individuals, churches,
or political organizations, or

for general operating needs or endowments. The foundation does not make loans.

OTHER THINGS TO KNOW
Publications: application guidelines.

GRANTS ANALYSIS
Total Grants: $836,018
Number of Grants: 30
Highest Grant: $100,000
Typical Range: $10,000 to $36,000
Disclosure Period: fiscal year ending November 30, 1990
Note: Average grant figure does not include the highest grant of $100,000. Recent grants are derived from a fiscal 1990 grants list.

RECENT GRANTS
```
100,000 St. Mary's Hospital
 65,000 Barnert Hospital
        Foundation, Pater-
        son, NJ
 60,000 St. Joseph Hospital
        and Medical Center
 50,514 Foundation of Uni-
        versity of Medi-
        cine and Dentistry,
        Newark, NJ
 50,000 Wayne General
        Hospital
 36,000 Aspire
 35,000 New Jersey HLA
        Registry, Newark,
        NJ
 30,000 Pellins College
 30,000 St. Peter's College,
        Jersey City, NJ
 25,000 Felician College
```

Van Huffel Foundation, I. J.

CONTACT
Crystal Hudspeth
I. J. Van Huffel Fdn.
PO Box 231
Warren, OH 44482
(216) 841-7820

FINANCIAL SUMMARY
Recent Giving: $112,500 (1991); $115,500 (1990); $107,900 (1989)
Assets: $1,964,898 (1991); $1,799,481 (1990); $1,839,089 (1989)
EIN: 34-6516726

CONTRIBUTIONS SUMMARY
Donor(s): Van Huffel Tube Corp.
Typical Recipients: • *Education:* colleges & universities, private education (precollege),

public education (precollege), religious education • *Health:* hospitals • *Religion:* churches, religious organizations • *Social Services:* community service organizations, food/clothing distribution, shelters/homelessness
Grant Types: general support
Geographic Distribution: focus on OH

GIVING OFFICERS
Joseph F. Dray: dir
Dianne Knappenberger: dir
Evelyn M. Reese: dir
Edgar A. Van Huffel: dir
Harold E. Van Huffel, Sr.: dir

APPLICATION INFORMATION
Initial Approach: Send brief proposal. There are no deadlines.

GRANTS ANALYSIS
Number of Grants: 43
Highest Grant: $20,100
Typical Range: $1,000 to $5,000
Disclosure Period: 1991

RECENT GRANTS
```
20,100 St. Joseph River-
       side Hospital, War-
       ren, OH
10,000 Trumbull County
       Catholic School,
       Warren, OH
 7,000 John F. Kennedy
       High School, War-
       ren, OH
 7,000 University of
       Notre Dame, Notre
       Dame, IN
 5,000 Blessed Sacrament
       Church, Warren,
       OH
 5,000 First Presbyterian
       Church, Niles, OH
 5,000 St. Mary Middle
       School, Warren, OH
 5,000 Trumbull Memo-
       rial Hospital, War-
       ren, OH
 4,000 Catholic Diocese
       of Youngstown,
       Youngstown, OH
 4,000 St. Mary's College,
       Madeleva Society,
       Notre Dame, IN
```

van Loben Sels - Eleanor Slate van Lobel Sels Charitable Foundation, Ernst D.

CONTACT
Claude H. Hogan
President
Ernst D. van Loben Sels -
Eleanor Slate van Lobel Sels
Charitable Fdn.
235 Montgomery St., No. 1635
San Francisco, CA 94104
(415) 983-1093

FINANCIAL SUMMARY
Recent Giving: $551,395 (1991); $438,900 (1990); $519,676 (1989)
Assets: $12,476,795 (1991); $9,031,686 (1990); $10,251,370 (1989)
EIN: 94-6109309

CONTRIBUTIONS SUMMARY
Donor(s): the late Ernst D. van Loben Sels
Typical Recipients: • *Civic & Public Affairs:* civil rights, ethnic/minority organizations, law & justice • *Education:* legal education • *Health:* medical research, mental health, public health, single-disease health associations • *Religion:* religious organizations • *Social Services:* community service organizations, counseling, disabled, family planning, family services, youth organizations
Grant Types: conference/seminar, emergency, project, research, and seed money
Geographic Distribution: limited to northern CA

GIVING OFFICERS
Claude Hollis Hogan: pres, dir *B* Bishop CA 1920 *ED* Coll Pacific AB 1942; Yale Univ LLB 1948 *CURR EMPL* ptnr: Pillsbury Madison & Sutro *CORP AFFIL* ptnr: Pillsbury Madison & Sutro *NONPR AFFIL* mem: Am Bar Assn, Am Judicature Soc, CA Chamber Commerce, Intl Fiscal Assn, San Francisco Bar Assn, San Francisco Lawyers Comm Urban Affs; trust: Lawyers Comm Civil Rights Under Law
Edward A. Nathan: vp, dir
Toni Rembe: secy, treas, dir *ED* Univ WA LLB 1960; NY Univ LLM 1961 *CURR EMPL*

ptnr: Pillsbury Madison & Sutro *CORP AFFIL* dir: Potlatch Corp, SAFECO Corp; ptnr: Pillsbury Madison & Sutro *NONPR AFFIL* mem: Am Bar Assn, Am Judicature Soc, San Francisco Bar Assn; trust: Mills Coll

APPLICATION INFORMATION
Initial Approach: Send cover letter and full proposal. There are no deadlines.
Restrictions on Giving: Does not support individuals or provide scholarships or fellowships.

OTHER THINGS TO KNOW
Publications: Annual Report, Program Policy Statement, Application Guidelines

GRANTS ANALYSIS
Number of Grants: 69
Highest Grant: $20,000
Typical Range: $2,000 to $10,000
Disclosure Period: 1991

RECENT GRANTS
```
20,000 Bay Area Institute,
       San Francisco, CA
       — Pacific News
       Service
20,000 Legal Aid Society,
       San Francisco, CA
20,000 University of Cali-
       fornia, Berkeley,
       CA
15,770 University of Cali-
       fornia, Berkeley,
       CA
15,700 Family Enrichment
       Network, San Fran-
       cisco, CA
15,000 Asian Law Caucus,
       San Francisco, CA
15,000 Center for Family
       in Transition, San
       Francisco, CA
10,000 Agricultural Work-
       ers Health Center,
       San Francisco, CA
10,000 American Civil
       Liberties Union
       Foundation, San
       Francisco, CA
10,000 Catholic Charities,
       San Francisco, CA
```

Van Nuys Charities, J. B. and Emily

CONTACT
Wilbur Warren
J. B. and Emily Van Nuys
  Charities
852 Via Somonte
Palos Verdes Estates, CA 90274
(310) 373-8521

FINANCIAL SUMMARY
Recent Giving: $632,296
(1991); $607,503 (1989);
$557,355 (1988)

Assets: $534,729 (1991);
$511,667 (1989); $438,806
(1988)

Gifts Received: $692,724
(1991); $733,102 (1989);
$681,001 (1988)

Fiscal Note: In 1991, contributions were received from J.
Benton Van Nuys Trust
($109,372)and Emily Van Nuys
Charitable Remainder Trust
($583,351).

EIN: 95-6096134

CONTRIBUTIONS SUMMARY
Donor(s): Emily Van Nuys, J.
Benton Van Nuys

Typical Recipients: • *Arts &
Humanities:* museums/galleries, music, public broadcasting,
theater • *Health:* health organizations, hospitals, medical research, pediatric health, single-disease health associations
• *Social Services:* aged, child
welfare, community service organizations, disabled, family
services, shelters/homelessness, united funds, youth organizations

Grant Types: general support

Geographic Distribution:
focus on southern CA

GIVING OFFICERS
Lawrence Chaffin: vp, trust

John M. Heidt: trust *B* Oceanside NY 1931 *ED* Stanford
Univ 1954; Univ Southern CA
Sch Bus Admin 1969 *CURR
EMPL* chmn, ceo: Multibank
Fin Svcs Group *CORP AFFIL*
chmn, ceo: Multibank Fin Svcs
Group; dir: Union Venture

Robert Gibson Johnson: pres,
trust

Franklin F. Moulton: secy,
treas, trust

Robert S. Warner: trust

APPLICATION INFORMATION
Initial Approach: Send cover
letter and full proposal. There
are no deadlines.

GRANTS ANALYSIS
Number of Grants: 133
Highest Grant: $25,000
Typical Range: $2,500 to
$12,000
Disclosure Period: 1991

RECENT GRANTS
25,000 Children's Hospital
  Medical Center,
  Los Angeles, CA
7,500 Foothill Family
  Service, Pasadena,
  CA
7,500 Marlborough
  School, Los Angeles, CA
7,000 Hathaway Children's Services,
  Sylmar, CA
5,000 American Center
  for Music Theater,
  Pasadena, CA
5,000 American Heart Association, Los Angeles, CA
5,000 American Red
  Cross, Los Angeles, CA
5,000 American Red
  Cross, Los Angeles, CA
5,000 American Red
  Cross, Washington,
  DC
5,000 Angeles Girl Scout
  Council, Los Angeles, CA

Van Nuys Foundation, I. N. and Susanna H.

CONTACT
I. N. and Susanna H. Van Nuys
Fdn.
444 South Flower St., Ste. 2340
Los Angeles, CA 90071

FINANCIAL SUMMARY
Recent Giving: $679,435 (fiscal 1992); $772,406 (fiscal
1991); $704,245 (fiscal 1990)
Assets: $11,716,305 (fiscal
year ending May 31, 1992);
$11,493,987 (fiscal 1991);
$10,401,549 (fiscal 1990)
EIN: 95-6006019

CONTRIBUTIONS SUMMARY
Typical Recipients: • *Arts &
Humanities:* history/historic
preservation, libraries, museums/galleries • *Education:* colleges & universities, private

education (precollege), public
education (precollege), student
aid • *Health:* hospitals • *Religion:* churches • *Social Services:* child welfare, disabled,
homes, youth organizations
Grant Types: general support
Geographic Distribution:
focus on CA

GIVING OFFICERS
George A. Bender: trust
Freeman Gates: trust
George H. Whitney: trust

APPLICATION INFORMATION
Initial Approach: Send brief
letter of inquiry describing program or project. There are no
deadlines.

GRANTS ANALYSIS
Number of Grants: 16
Highest Grant: $344,280
Typical Range: $5,000 to
$50,000
Disclosure Period: fiscal year
ending May 31, 1992

RECENT GRANTS
344,280 Hospital of Good
  Samaritan, Los Angeles, CA
72,857 Wellesley College,
  Wellesley, MA
43,724 Children's Hospital
  Medical Center,
  Los Angeles, CA
40,000 Braille Institute of
  America, Los Angeles, CA
36,429 California Institute
  of Technology,
  Pasadena, CA
25,000 Thacher School,
  Ojai, CA
25,000 Welb School of
  California, Los Angeles, CA
20,000 Hathaway Children's Service, Los
  Angeles, CA
14,571 Henry E. Huntington Library and Art
  Gallery, Los Angeles, CA
7,287 Los Angeles
  County Museum of
  Natural History
  Foundation, Los
  Angeles, CA

Van Schaick Scholarship Fund, Nellie

CONTACT
Mason Borgman
Nellie Van Schaick Scholarship
  Fund
c/o Valley National Bank of
  Arizona, Trust Dept.
5210 E. Williams Circle
Tucson, AZ 85732
(602) 792-7130

FINANCIAL SUMMARY
Recent Giving: $223,807 (fiscal 1992); $219,523 (fiscal
1991); $215,246 (fiscal 1990)
Assets: $4,140,082 (fiscal year
ending May 31, 1992);
$3,966,342 (fiscal 1991);
$3,770,115 (fiscal 1990)
EIN: 86-6090500

CONTRIBUTIONS SUMMARY
Typical Recipients: • *Civic &
Public Affairs:* rural affairs
• *Education:* colleges & universities, international studies • *International:* foreign educational institutions, international
organizations
Grant Types: scholarship
Geographic Distribution:
focus on the Philippines and
other developing East Asian
and Western Pacific countries

GIVING OFFICERS
Louis W. Barassi: trust

APPLICATION INFORMATION
Initial Approach: Send proposal. Deadline is May 1.

GRANTS ANALYSIS
Number of Grants: 8
Highest Grant: $84,328
Typical Range: $2,500 to
$9,000
Disclosure Period: fiscal year
ending May 31, 1992

RECENT GRANTS
84,328 Davao Medical
  School Foundation
  — pre-medical and
  medical students
  and community
  medicine scholarships
65,400 Xavier University,
  Cincinnati, OH —
  scholarships for
  pre-medical and
  medical students
27,560 St. Louis University, St. Louis, MO
  — scholarship for
  medical students

25,000 International Institute of Rural Reconstruction — scholarships for community medicine

9,000 Ateneo de Davao University — scholarships for pre-medical and medical students

7,800 University of Hong Kong, Hong Kong — scholarships for scholarship funding

2,436 Davad Medical School Foundation — scholarships for faculty development/training sessions

2,283 Davad Medical School Foundation — scholarships for fifth Asian course

Van Vleet Foundation

CONTACT
Fletcher Haaga
1st V.P. and Trust Officer
Van Vleet Fdn.
c/o National Bank of Commerce
One Commerce Sq.
Memphis, TN 38150

FINANCIAL SUMMARY
Recent Giving: $260,100 (1991); $255,163 (1990); $203,470 (1988)
Assets: $7,411,064 (1991); $6,470,644 (1990); $6,299,462 (1988)
EIN: 62-6034067

CONTRIBUTIONS SUMMARY
Donor(s): the late Harriet Smith Van Vleet
Typical Recipients: • *Arts & Humanities:* museums/galleries • *Education:* colleges & universities
Grant Types: scholarship
Geographic Distribution: limited to Memphis, TN

GIVING OFFICERS
National Bank of Commerce, Trust Division: trust
B. Snowden Boyle, Jr.: adv
Thomas C. Farnsworth: adv

APPLICATION INFORMATION
Initial Approach: Contributes only to preselected organizations.

GRANTS ANALYSIS
Number of Grants: 3

Highest Grant: $100,000
Typical Range: $60,000 to $100,000
Disclosure Period: 1991

RECENT GRANTS
100,000 Children's Museum of Memphis, Memphis, TN — exhibits endowment
100,000 University of Tennessee, Memphis, TN — computer equipment
60,100 Memphis State University, Memphis, TN — scholarships

Van Wert County Foundation

CONTACT
Robert W. Games
Executive Secretary
Van Wert County Fdn.
101 1/2 East Main St.
Van Wert, OH 45891
(419) 238-1743

FINANCIAL SUMMARY
Recent Giving: $545,943 (1991); $276,238 (1990); $297,291 (1989)
Assets: $10,152,048 (1991); $6,792,272 (1990); $6,827,919 (1989)
Gifts Received: $57,947 (1991); $19,905 (1990); $35,488 (1989)
Fiscal Note: In 1991, contributions were received from the Kerns and Margaret Wright Trust Fund ($5,122), the Van Wert Kiwanis Club Scholarship Fund ($2,000), the Alice H. Games Memorial Fund ($3,000), Mary Jane Culler Scholarship Trust Fund ($100), The Graduates of Van Wert County Hospital School of Nursing Memorial Fund ($20,000), the Benjamin H. and Lura Waitman Scholarship Fund ($25,000), the John F. Markley Trust ($450), and the Walter A. and Bruce C. Kennedy Trust ($2,0
EIN: 34-0907558

CONTRIBUTIONS SUMMARY
Donor(s): the late Charles F. Wassenberg, Gaylord Saltzgaber, the late John D. Ault, Kernan Wright, the late Richard L. Klein, the late Hazel Gleason, the late Constance Eirich
Typical Recipients: • *Arts & Humanities:* arts centers, arts institutes, history/historic preservation, museums/galleries,

music, performing arts, theater • *Civic & Public Affairs:* municipalities • *Education:* public education (precollege) • *Social Services:* child welfare, community service organizations, day care, disabled, recreation & athletics, united funds, youth organizations
Grant Types: general support
Geographic Distribution: limited to Van Wert County, OH

GIVING OFFICERS
D. L. Brumback, Jr.: secy
William S. Derry: trust
A. C. Diller: off
Robert W. Games: exec secy
Kenneth Koch: trust *ED* Univ PA 1976; OH St Univ 1979
Gaylord E. Leslie: trust
Watson Ley: trust
Paul W. Purmort, Jr.: trust
Charles F. Ross: trust
C. Allan Runser: trust
Donald C. Sutton: trust
Roger Kennedy Thompson: trust *ED* Rensselaer Polytech Inst 1951 *CURR EMPL* pres: Kennedy Mfg Co *CORP AFFIL* pres: Kennedy Mfg Co
Sumner J. Walters: trust
Larry L. Wendel: vp
G. Dale Wilson: trust
Michael R. Zedaker: trust

APPLICATION INFORMATION
Initial Approach: Application forms and guidelines issued for scholarship program.
Restrictions on Giving: Does not provide loans.

OTHER THINGS TO KNOW
Publications: Application Guidelines

GRANTS ANALYSIS
Number of Grants: 65
Highest Grant: $54,100
Typical Range: $1,000 to $10,000
Disclosure Period: 1991
Note: 1991 figures do not include grants given for individual scholarships.

RECENT GRANTS
54,100 Wassenburg Art Center, Van Wert, OH
54,100 YMCA, Van Wert, OH
53,131 Wassenburg Art Center, Van Wert, OH
16,914 Van Wert City Schools, Van Wert, OH

10,000 Crisis Care House of Transportation, Van Wert, OH
10,000 Van Wert Civic Theater, Van Wert, OH
10,000 Van Wert Historical Society, Van Wert, OH
9,500 Van Wert Extension Service, Van Wert, OH
7,000 Van Wert Community Concerts, Van Wert, OH
6,600 Van Wert City Schools, Van Wert, OH

Vance Charitable Foundation, Robert C.

CONTACT
Herbert E. Carlson, Jr.
President
Robert C. Vance Charitable Fdn.
21 Winesap Rd.
Kensington, CT 06037
(203) 828-6037

FINANCIAL SUMMARY
Recent Giving: $246,694 (fiscal 1992); $280,418 (fiscal 1990); $332,750 (fiscal 1988)
Assets: $5,910,051 (fiscal year ending November 30, 1990); $5,485,102 (fiscal 1988)
EIN: 06-6050188

CONTRIBUTIONS SUMMARY
Donor(s): the late Robert C. Vance
Typical Recipients: • *Arts & Humanities:* community arts, museums/galleries, music • *Education:* literacy, private education (precollege) • *Health:* hospitals, medical research • *Religion:* religious organizations • *Social Services:* child welfare, community centers, community service organizations, disabled, family planning, religious welfare, youth organizations
Grant Types: general support
Geographic Distribution: limited to the Berlin, CT, area

GIVING OFFICERS
Herbert E. Carlson, Jr.: pres

APPLICATION INFORMATION
Initial Approach: Send brief letter describing program. There are no deadlines.
Restrictions on Giving: Does not support individuals.

OTHER THINGS TO KNOW

Publications: Application Guidelines

GRANTS ANALYSIS

Number of Grants: 20
Highest Grant: $60,000
Typical Range: $500 to $10,000
Disclosure Period: fiscal year ending November 30, 1990
Note: No grants listed for fiscal 1992

RECENT GRANTS

60,000 United Community Services, New Britain, CT

30,000 Mooreland Hill School, New Britain, CT

28,000 Friendship Center, New Britain, CT

25,000 Boys and Girls Club, New Britain, CT

25,000 YMCA, New Britain, CT

18,694 CCSU Foundation, New Britain, CT

17,500 Catholic Family Services, New Britain, CT

15,000 Constructive Workshop, New Britain, CT

11,000 New Britain Institute, New Britain, CT

7,500 Family Services, New Britain, CT

Vanderbilt Trust, R. T.

CONTACT

Hugh B. Vanderbilt
Chairman
R. T. Vanderbilt Trust
30 Winfield St.
Norwalk, CT 06855
(203) 853-1400

FINANCIAL SUMMARY

Recent Giving: $310,065 (1991); $302,060 (1990); $288,085 (1989)
Assets: $7,849,861 (1991); $6,893,059 (1990); $6,846,917 (1989)
EIN: 06-6040981

CONTRIBUTIONS SUMMARY

Typical Recipients: • *Arts & Humanities:* history/historic preservation, libraries • *Civic & Public Affairs:* environmental affairs, zoos/botanical gardens • *Education:* colleges & universities • *Health:* hospitals, medical research, pediatric health, single-disease health associations • *Religion:* churches • *Social Services:* community service organizations, family planning, united funds, youth organizations
Grant Types: capital, endowment, and operating expenses
Geographic Distribution: focus on CT and NY

GIVING OFFICERS

Hugh Bedford Vanderbilt, Sr.: chmn, trust *B* New York NY 1921 *ED* Trinity Coll 1942 *CURR EMPL* chmn, ceo: Vanderbilt (RT) Co *CORP AFFIL* chmn, ceo: Vanderbilt (RT) Co *NONPR AFFIL* hon trust: Greenwich Historical Soc; mem: Chemical Mfrs Assn

Robert T. Vanderbilt, Jr.: trust

APPLICATION INFORMATION

Initial Approach: Send brief letter describing program. There are no deadlines.
Restrictions on Giving: Does not support individuals.

GRANTS ANALYSIS

Number of Grants: 104
Highest Grant: $86,000
Typical Range: $100 to $2,000
Disclosure Period: 1991

RECENT GRANTS

86,000 Historical Society of Town of Greenwich, Cos Cob, CT

70,000 Planned Parenthood Federation of America, New York, NY

11,500 Planned Parenthood Federation of America, New York, NY

10,000 Historic Deerfield, Deerfield, MA

10,000 Historical Society of Town of Greenwich, Cos Cob, CT

10,000 New York Zoological Society, New York, NY

5,000 National Audubon Society, New York, NY

5,000 Planned Parenthood Federation of America, New York, NY

4,000 Incarnation Parish, New York, NY

4,000 Our Lady of Sorrows Church, Essex, CT

Vanguard Group of Investment Cos.

Sales: $400.0 million
Employees: 2,300
Headquarters: Wayne, PA
SIC Major Group: Holding & Other Investment Offices and Security & Commodity Brokers

CONTACT

Brian Mattes
Vice President
Vanguard Group of Investment Cos.
1300 Morris Dr.
Wayne, PA 19087
(215) 648-6000

CONTRIBUTIONS SUMMARY

Operating Locations: PA (Wayne)

CORP. OFFICERS

John J. Brennan: *CURR EMPL* pres: Vanguard Group

RECENT GRANTS

George Washington University, Washington, DC

Vanneck-Bailey Foundation

CONTACT

John B. Vanneck
Vice President
Vanneck-Bailey Fdn.
100 Park Ave.
New York, NY 10017
(212) 725-2850

FINANCIAL SUMMARY

Recent Giving: $269,860 (1991); $247,600 (1990); $235,400 (1989)
Assets: $5,989,724 (1991); $5,606,335 (1990); $5,396,446 (1989)
EIN: 23-7165285

CONTRIBUTIONS SUMMARY

Donor(s): the late John Vanneck, Barbara Bailey Vanneck
Typical Recipients: • *Arts & Humanities:* libraries, museums/galleries • *Civic & Public Affairs:* environmental affairs, philanthropic organizations, urban & community affairs, zoos/botanical gardens • *Education:* colleges & universities, health & physical education • *Health:* hospitals, medical research • *Religion:* churches • *Social Services:* child welfare, community service organizations, recreation & athletics, united funds, youth organizations
Grant Types: multiyear/continuing support and research
Geographic Distribution: focus on NY

GIVING OFFICERS

Barbara Bailey Vanneck: pres
John B. Vanneck: vp
William P. Vanneck: treas
Jeanne M. Wiedenman: secy

APPLICATION INFORMATION

Initial Approach: Contributes only to preselected organizations.
Restrictions on Giving: Does not support individuals.

GRANTS ANALYSIS

Number of Grants: 101
Highest Grant: $42,000
Typical Range: $100 to $1,000
Disclosure Period: 1991

RECENT GRANTS

42,000 University of Vermont, Burlington, VT

25,000 Columbia University College of Physicians and Surgeons, New York, NY

20,000 Presbyterian Hospital, New York, NY

15,000 Bailey Arboretum, Friends of Nassau County, Locust Valley, NY

15,000 University of Texas, Houston, TX

10,800 Southern Charitable Foundation, Columbus, GA

10,500 Union College, Schenectady, NY

10,000 Brooklyn Botanic Garden, Brooklyn, NY

6,200 Freedom Institute, New York, NY

6,000 Hanley Hazelden Foundation, West Palm Beach, FL

Varian Associates

Sales: $1.38 billion
Employees: 9,300
Headquarters: Palo Alto, CA
SIC Major Group: Electronic & Other Electrical Equipment and Instruments & Related Products

CONTACT
Gary Simpson
Vice President, Marketing
Varian Associates
3050 Hansen Way
Palo Alto, CA 94304-1000
(415) 424-5782

FINANCIAL SUMMARY
Recent Giving: $375,000 (fiscal 1992); $450,000 (fiscal 1991 approx.); $500,000 (fiscal 1990 approx.)
Fiscal Note: Company gives directly. Figures include contributions by subsidiaries and exclude value of equipment donations.

CONTRIBUTIONS SUMMARY
Typical Recipients: • *Arts & Humanities:* arts appreciation, arts festivals, history/historic preservation, museums/galleries • *Civic & Public Affairs:* environmental affairs, ethnic/minority organizations, nonprofit management, public policy, women's affairs • *Education:* business education, colleges & universities, elementary education, engineering education, faculty development, minority education, public education (precollege), science/technology education, student aid • *Health:* health organizations, mental health, public health • *Science:* science exhibits & fairs, scientific organizations • *Social Services:* aged, child welfare, community service organizations, counseling, delinquency & crime, disabled, family services, recreation & athletics, shelters/homelessness, united funds, youth organizations
Grant Types: challenge, employee matching gifts, endowment, fellowship, general support, multiyear/continuing support, professorship, research, scholarship, and seed money
Nonmonetary Support Types: donated equipment, in-kind services, loaned employees, and loaned executives
Note: Estimated value of nonmonetary support is $350,000 to $1.0 million annually. Equipment donations are handled directly by divisions and subsidiaries. This support is not included in above figures.
Geographic Distribution: near headquarters and operating locations only

Operating Locations: AZ (Tempe), CA (Milpitas, Palo Alto, San Carlos, Santa Clara, Walnut Creek), MA (Beverly, Gloucester, Lexington), UT (Salt Lake City)

CORP. OFFICERS
J. Tracy O'Rourke: *B* Columbia SC 1935 *CURR EMPL* chmn, ceo, dir: Varian Assocs

GIVING OFFICERS
Gary Simpson: chmn contributions comm *B* Fresno CA 1937 *ED* CA St Univ Fresno 1959 *CURR EMPL* vp (corp communications): Varian Assocs

APPLICATION INFORMATION
Initial Approach: *Initial Contact:* proposal *Include Information On:* description of the organization, including history and overall purpose; need and amount requested, current financial statements and detailed budget showing how grant will be spent; other sources of funding and their current status; list of key personnel and staff qualifications; list of board of directors; evidence of tax-exempt status; relevance to evaluative criteria *When to Submit:* any time *Note:* Only written requests are considered; applicants are contacted if further information is needed.
Restrictions on Giving: Company does not support for-profit organizations; fraternal or religious groups; political organizations or candidates; individuals or their research projects; university-related affiliate programs; advertising campaigns under any circumstance; conferences, seminars, or meetings; disease-related organizations; or film or creative productions unless of direct benefit to the company. Grants made almost entirely according to links with the company, its employees, or its activities.

OTHER THINGS TO KNOW
Most grant awards are predetermined; yearly, less than $60,000 is available for new recipients.

GRANTS ANALYSIS
Total Grants: $375,000
Number of Grants: 75
Highest Grant: $20,000
Typical Range: $250 to $1,000

Disclosure Period: fiscal year ending September 30, 1992

Varlen Corp.
Sales: $230.5 million
Employees: 1,880
Headquarters: Naperville, IL
SIC Major Group: Fabricated Metal Products, Primary Metal Industries, Rubber & Miscellaneous Plastics Products, and Transportation Equipment

CONTACT
Loretta Ascher
Varlen Corp.
PO Box 3089
Naperville, IL 60566
(708) 420-0400
Note: An alternative address is P.O. Box 3089.

CONTRIBUTIONS SUMMARY
Operating Locations: IL (Naperville)

CORP. OFFICERS
Ernest H. Lorch: *CURR EMPL* chmn: Varlen Corp
Richard A. Nunemaker: *CURR EMPL* vp, cfo: Varlen Corp
Richard L. Wellek: *CURR EMPL* pres, ceo: Varlen Corp

Vaughan Foundation, Rachael and Ben

CONTACT
Ben F. Vaughan III
President
Rachael and Ben Vaughan Fdn.
PO Box 1579
Corpus Christi, TX 78403
(512) 241-2890

FINANCIAL SUMMARY
Recent Giving: $126,270 (fiscal 1991); $157,000 (fiscal 1990); $108,500 (fiscal 1989)
Assets: $2,539,380 (fiscal year ending November 30, 1991); $2,397,197 (fiscal 1990); $2,333,631 (fiscal 1989)
Gifts Received: $39,500 (fiscal 1991)
EIN: 74-6040479

CONTRIBUTIONS SUMMARY
Donor(s): the late Ben F. Vaughan, Jr., the late Rachael Vaughan
Typical Recipients: • *Arts & Humanities:* performing arts,

public broadcasting • *Civic & Public Affairs:* environmental affairs, public policy, women's affairs, zoos/botanical gardens • *Education:* literacy • *Religion:* religious organizations • *Social Services:* community service organizations, family planning, refugee assistance, united funds, youth organizations
Grant Types: capital, emergency, endowment, general support, multiyear/continuing support, operating expenses, professorship, project, and research
Geographic Distribution: limited to south and central TX

GIVING OFFICERS
Kleberg Eckhardt: vp, trust
Ben F. Vaughan III: pres, trust
Ben F. Vaughan IV: treas, vp
Daphne duPont Vaughan: trust, secy, treas
Genevieve Vaughan: vp, trust
William R. Ward, Jr.: asst secy, asst treas

APPLICATION INFORMATION
Initial Approach: Send cover letter and full proposal. Deadline is September 1.
Restrictions on Giving: Does not support individuals

OTHER THINGS TO KNOW
Publications: Application Guidelines

GRANTS ANALYSIS
Number of Grants: 42
Highest Grant: $4,000
Typical Range: $1,000 to $5,000
Disclosure Period: fiscal year ending November 30, 1991

RECENT GRANTS
4,000 Institute for Women's Policy Research, Washington, DC
3,400 Refugio Del Rio Grande, Harlingen, TX
2,000 La Mujer Obrera Program, El Paso, TX
2,000 New Radio and Performing Arts

Vaughn Foundation

CONTACT
James M. Vaughan
Director
Vaughn Fdn.
830 S. Beckham
Tyler, TX 75701

FINANCIAL SUMMARY
Recent Giving: $259,405
(1991); $257,222 (1990);
$51,100 (1989)
Assets: $6,453,950 (1991);
$5,763,110 (1990); $399,653
(1989)
EIN: 75-6008953

CONTRIBUTIONS SUMMARY
Donor(s): the late Edgar H.
Vaughn, Lillie Mae Vaughn
Typical Recipients: • *Arts &
Humanities:* music, public
broadcasting • *Education:* colleges & universities, legal education, public education (precollege) • *Health:* hospitals,
medical research • *Religion:*
churches • *Social Services:*
child welfare, community service organizations, family planning, food/clothing distribution, recreation & athletics,
united funds, youth organizations
Grant Types: general support
and research
Geographic Distribution:
focus on Tyler, TX

GIVING OFFICERS
Ameritrust Texas, N.A.: trust
James M. Vaughn: dir

APPLICATION INFORMATION
Initial Approach: Send brief
letter of inquiry describing program or project. Deadline is
March 1.
Restrictions on Giving: Does
not support individuals.

GRANTS ANALYSIS
Number of Grants: 105
Highest Grant: $18,000
Typical Range: $500 to $5,000
Disclosure Period: 1991

RECENT GRANTS
18,000 University of
Texas Medical
Branch at
Galveston,
Galveston, TX
16,300 Tyler Junior Col-
lege, Tyler, TX
15,000 Tyler Independent
School District,
Tyler, TX
13,000 First Presbyterian
Church, Tyler, TX
10,500 University of
Texas Health Cen-
ter, Tyler, TX
10,000 Path, Tyler, TX
10,000 Regional East
Texas Food Bank,
Tyler, TX
10,000 Tyler Baseball,
Tyler, TX

Vaughn, Jr. Foundation Fund, James M.

CONTACT
James M. Vaughn, Jr.
President
James M. Vaughn, Jr. Fdn Fund
2235 Brentwood
Houston, TX 77019

FINANCIAL SUMMARY
Recent Giving: $58,500
(1990); $122,535 (1988);
$298,777 (1986)
Assets: $2,564,725 (1990);
$2,812,325 (1988); $3,074,912
(1986)
EIN: 23-7166546

CONTRIBUTIONS SUMMARY
Typical Recipients: • *Arts &
Humanities:* arts centers, librar-
ies, museums/galleries • *Educa-
tion:* colleges & universities
• *Religion:* churches
Grant Types: fellowship and
research

GIVING OFFICERS
James M. Vaughn, Jr.: pres
Sally Vaughn: vp
Jan Werner: secy, treas

APPLICATION INFORMATION
Initial Approach: Send resume and cover letter. There
are no deadlines.

GRANTS ANALYSIS
Number of Grants: 14
Highest Grant: $10,000
Typical Range: $1,000 to $5,000
Disclosure Period: 1990

RECENT GRANTS
10,000 Museum of Fine
Arts, Houston, TX
10,000 National Gallery of
Art, Washington,
DC
10,000 Pierpont Morgan
Library, New York,
NY
6,500 Museum of Fine
Arts, Houston, TX
5,000 Contemporary Art
Museum of Hous-
ton, Houston, TX
5,000 D.A. Camera,
Houston, TX
5,000 Menlo College,
Houston, TX
1,500 Palmer Memorial
Church, Houston,
TX
1,000 Rice University,
Houston, TX
1,000 Stages Production
Company, Kirk-
wood, MO

Veritas Foundation

CONTACT
Diana Crow Leach
President
Veritas Fdn.
602 West 13th St.
Austin, TX 78701
(512) 472-1877

FINANCIAL SUMMARY
Recent Giving: $108,700
(1991); $257,448 (1990);
$102,796 (1989)
Assets: $2,198,872 (1991);
$1,867,749 (1990); $1,892,982
(1989)
EIN: 74-2254024

CONTRIBUTIONS SUMMARY
Donor(s): the late Joe Crow
Typical Recipients: • *Arts &
Humanities:* performing arts,
theater • *Civic & Public Affairs:* environmental affairs
• *Education:* colleges & universities, medical education, private education (precollege)
• *Health:* health organizations,
medical rehabilitation, mental
health, nursing services • *Religion:* churches • *Social Services:* aged, community service
organizations, domestic violence, united funds, youth organizations
Grant Types: general support
Geographic Distribution:
Provides grants in Austin, TX

GIVING OFFICERS
Chris Crow: treas
I.A. Crow: vp
Deborah A. Grote: secy
Diana Crow Leach: pres, exec
dir

APPLICATION INFORMATION
Initial Approach: Send brief
letter describing program.
There are no deadlines.
Restrictions on Giving: Does
not support individuals.

GRANTS ANALYSIS
Number of Grants: 29
Highest Grant: $15,000
Typical Range: $1,000 to
$5,000
Disclosure Period: 1991

RECENT GRANTS
15,000 University of
Texas School of
Nursing, San Anto-
nio, TX
7,500 Hyde Park Baptist
Church, Austin, TX
7,500 Salvation Army,
Austin, TX
6,000 Austin Center for
Battered Women,
Austin, TX
6,000 National Wild-
flower Research
Center, Austin, TX
5,500 Austin Center for
Attitudinal Heal-
ing, Austin, TX
5,000 Austin Groups for
the Elderly, Austin,
TX
5,000 Caritas of Austin,
Austin, TX
5,000 Southwest Neu-
ropsychiatric Insti-
tute, San Antonio,
TX
3,500 Vaughn House,
Austin, TX

Vermeer Charitable Foundation

Sales: $160.0 million
Employees: 1,200
Headquarters: Pella, IA
SIC Major Group: Industrial
Machinery & Equipment

CONTACT
Lois Vermeer
Director & Secretary
Vermeer Charitable Foundation
PO Box 200
Pella, IA 50219
(515) 628-3141

FINANCIAL SUMMARY
Recent Giving: $575,000
(1991); $558,000 (1990);
$300,495 (1989)
Assets: $3,686,248 (1989)
EIN: 42-1087640

CONTRIBUTIONS SUMMARY
Typical Recipients: • *Educa-
tion:* general • *Religion:* relig-
ious organizations • *Social
Services:* animal protection
Grant Types: general support
and seed money
Geographic Distribution: lim-
ited to IA
Operating Locations: IA
(Pella)

GIVING OFFICERS
Dale Andringa: dir
Mary Andringa: dir
Gary J. Vermeer: dir *CURR EMPL* pres: Vermeer Mfg Co *CORP AFFIL* pres: Vermeer Mfg Co
Lois J. Vermeer: dir
Matilda Vermeer: dir
Robert L. Vermeer: dir *CURR EMPL* ceo: Vermeer Mfg Co

APPLICATION INFORMATION
Initial Approach: Send letter requesting application form.
Restrictions on Giving: Does not support individuals, endowment funds, scholarships, or fellowships.

GRANTS ANALYSIS
Typical Range: $1,000 to $2,500

Vermeer Investment Company Foundation
Sales: $158.0 million
Employees: 1,200
Headquarters: Pella, IA
SIC Major Group: Industrial Machinery & Equipment

CONTACT
Vermeer Investment Company Fdn.
412 Franklin St.
Pella, IA 50219

FINANCIAL SUMMARY
Recent Giving: $155,500 (1990); $150,275 (1989); $275,092 (1988)
Assets: $2,130,194 (1990); $1,994,728 (1989); $2,948,112 (1988)
Gifts Received: $143,925 (1989); $465,794 (1988); $98,337 (1987)
Fiscal Note: In 1989, contributions were received from Harry G. Vermeer ($100,000), Michael Vermeer ($5,000), and Marion County State Bank ($38,925).
EIN: 51-0182729

CONTRIBUTIONS SUMMARY
Donor(s): Harry G. Vermeer, Michael Vermeer, Marion County State Bank
Typical Recipients: • *Education:* colleges & universities, private education (precollege), religious education • *Health:* hospitals • *Religion:* churches, missionary activities, religious organizations • *Social Services:* community service organizations, youth organizations
Grant Types: general support

GIVING OFFICERS
Bernice Vermeer: secy
Harry J. Vermeer: chmn, treas
Michael Vermeer: vchmn

GRANTS ANALYSIS
Number of Grants: 10
Highest Grant: $50,000
Typical Range: $1,000 to $10,000
Disclosure Period: 1990

RECENT GRANTS
50,000 Luke Society, Pella, IA
50,000 Pella Community Hospital, Pella, IA
25,000 Pella Historical Society, Pella, IA
10,000 Trinity College, IA
5,000 Bethel Mission, Des Moines, IA
5,000 Christian Schools International, Grand Rapids, MI
5,000 Pella Christian High School, Pella, IA
5,000 Reformed Bible College, Grand Rapids, MI
500 Iowa Fellowship of Christian Athletes, IA

Vermeer Manufacturing Co. / Vermeer Foundation Co.
Sales: $158.0 million
Employees: 1,200
Headquarters: Pella, IA
SIC Major Group: Industrial Machinery & Equipment

CONTACT
Lois Vermeer
Secretary
c/o Vermeer Manufacturing Company
PO Box 200
Pella, IA 50219
(515) 628-3141

FINANCIAL SUMMARY
Recent Giving: $219,051 (1989); $334,422 (1988); $1,101,638 (1987)
Assets: $362,551 (1989); $547,204 (1988); $831,569 (1987)
EIN: 42-6059566

CONTRIBUTIONS SUMMARY
Typical Recipients: • *Arts & Humanities:* opera • *Civic & Public Affairs:* safety • *Education:* colleges & universities, public education (precollege), religious education, student aid • *Health:* hospices • *Religion:* churches, religious organizations • *Social Services:* community centers, community service organizations
Grant Types: capital, general support, scholarship, and seed money
Geographic Distribution: primarily in Pella, IA
Operating Locations: IA (Pella)

CORP. OFFICERS
Gary Vermeer: *CURR EMPL* pres: Vermeer Mfg Co
Robert L. Vermeer: *CURR EMPL* ceo: Vermeer Mfg Co

GIVING OFFICERS
Lois J. Vermeer: secy, dir
Robert L. Vermeer: pres, dir *CURR EMPL* ceo: Vermeer Mfg Co (see above)

APPLICATION INFORMATION
Initial Approach: Send letter including background, tax-exempt status, purpose of request, financial statement of organization. Organization applying for substantial grant should plan to make a presentation to directors. Organizations must contact foundation to obtain standard application form. Formal application procedure may be waived in the case of applications for small (less than $2,500) grants. There are no deadlines. Applicants are promptly notified that their applications have been approved or rejected, or that additional information is needed.
Restrictions on Giving: Foundation does not accept applications from individuals.

GRANTS ANALYSIS
Number of Grants: 20
Highest Grant: $50,000
Typical Range: $100 to $1,000
Disclosure Period: 1989

RECENT GRANTS
50,000 Central College, Pella, IA
35,200 Pella Christian Grade School, Pella, IA
25,000 Dordt College, Sioux City, IA
25,000 Opera House, Pella, IA
19,576 Pella Christian High School, Pella, IA
15,000 Navigators, Pella, IA
11,000 Community Church of Los Angeles, Los Angeles, CA
6,350 Immanuel C.R.C, Pella, IA
5,000 Pella Pine Rest, Pella, IA
2,500 Crossroads of Pella, Pella, IA

Vernitron Corp. / Vernitron Foundation
Sales: $84.0 million
Employees: 974
Headquarters: New York, NY
SIC Major Group: Electronic & Other Electrical Equipment and Instruments & Related Products

CONTACT
Stephen Bershad
Chairman
Vernitron Corp.
645 Madison Ave.
New York, NY 10022
(212) 593-7900

FINANCIAL SUMMARY
EIN: 23-7038835

CONTRIBUTIONS SUMMARY
Operating Locations: NY (New York)

CORP. OFFICERS
Stephen Bershad: *CURR EMPL* chmn, ceo, dir: Vernitron Corp
Edward Murchie: *CURR EMPL* pres, coo, dir: Vernitron Corp

Vernon Fund, Miles Hodsdon

CONTACT
Robert C. Thomson, Jr.
President
Miles Hodsdon Vernon Fund
49 Beekman Ave.
North Tarrytown, NY 10591
(914) 631-4226

FINANCIAL SUMMARY
Recent Giving: $208,060 (1991); $221,450 (1990); $186,500 (1989)

Assets: $5,636,639 (1991); $4,809,305 (1990); $5,055,868 (1989)
EIN: 13-6076836

CONTRIBUTIONS SUMMARY
Donor(s): Miles Hodsdon Vernon, Martha Hodsdon Kinney, Louise Hodsdon
Typical Recipients: • *Arts & Humanities:* music, public broadcasting • *Education:* colleges & universities • *Health:* hospitals, medical research, single-disease health associations • *Social Services:* aged, child welfare, community service organizations, united funds, youth organizations
Grant Types: research and scholarship

GIVING OFFICERS
Dennis M. Fitzgerald: vp, secy, dir
Eleanor C. Thomson: dir
Robert C. Thomson, Jr.: pres, treas, dir
Gertrude Whalen: dir

APPLICATION INFORMATION
Initial Approach: Send cover letter and full proposal. There are no deadlines.

GRANTS ANALYSIS
Number of Grants: 52
Highest Grant: $30,000
Typical Range: $250 to $5,000
Disclosure Period: 1991

RECENT GRANTS
30,000 Columbia University College of Physicians and Surgeons, New York, NY — encephalitis research aid
15,000 Suburban Community Music Center — aid for educational programs
15,000 YMCA
10,000 Columbia-Presbyterian Medical Center, New York, NY — aid for research in oral diseases and viral infections of the mouth
10,000 Pingry School, Martinsville, NJ — scholarships
10,000 Wolfeboro Area Children's Center, Wolfeboro, NH — aid for maintenance of services of social worker
10,000 YMCA
6,000 YMCA

5,000 Old Dutch Church of Sleepy Hollow — aid for the preservation of an historical structure
5,000 Wolfeboro Area Children's Center, Wolfeboro, NH — aid for operating expenses

---

Vesper Corp. / Vesper Foundation
Sales: $135.0 million
Employees: 1,407
Headquarters: Bala-Cynwyd, PA

CONTACT
James Benenson, Jr.
Trustee
Vesper Corp.
Two Brecksville Commons
8221 Brecksville Road
Brecksville, OH 44141
(216) 838-4700

FINANCIAL SUMMARY
Recent Giving: $89,950 (1991); $34,700 (1989)
Assets: $1,250,797 (1991); $184,061 (1989)
Gifts Received: $1,200,000 (1991)
EIN: 23-6251198

CONTRIBUTIONS SUMMARY
Typical Recipients: • *Arts & Humanities:* libraries, museums/galleries • *Civic & Public Affairs:* municipalities, philanthropic organizations • *Education:* career/vocational education • *Social Services:* united funds, youth organizations
Grant Types: general support
Geographic Distribution: giving primarily in New York, NY
Operating Locations: PA (Bala-Cynwyd)

CORP. OFFICERS
James Benenson: *CURR EMPL* chmn, pres: Vesper Corp

GIVING OFFICERS
James Benenson, Jr.: trust
Sharen Benenson: trust
John V. Curci: trust

APPLICATION INFORMATION
Initial Approach: The foundation supports preselected organizations and does not accept unsolicited requests for funds.

GRANTS ANALYSIS
Number of Grants: 16
Highest Grant: $25,000

Typical Range: $1,000 to $5,000
Disclosure Period: 1991

RECENT GRANTS
25,000 Smith Cove Preservation Trust, Ellsworth, ME
15,000 Brooksville Free Public Library, Brooksville, ME
12,500 Society of the Cincinnati of New Hampshire, Cohasset, MA
5,000 American Independence Museum, Boston, MA
5,000 Casa Youth Shelter, Los Alamitos, CA
5,000 Horticultural Society of New York, New York, NY
5,000 Maine Maritime Academy, Castine, ME
4,500 United Way, Orange, CA
4,500 Wilson Museum, Castine, ME
3,000 Orange County Council, Costa Mesa, CA

Vesuvius Charitable Foundation
Sales: $130.0 million
Employees: 1,100
Headquarters: Pittsburgh, PA
SIC Major Group: Stone, Clay & Glass Products and Wholesale Trade—Durable Goods

CONTACT
John Culbertson
Vice President
Vesuvius Charitable Foundation
c/o Pittsburgh National Bank, Trust Div.
One Oliver Plaza, 27th Fl.
Pittsburgh, PA 15265
(412) 762-3390
Note: Corporation is located at: 305 E. Sherman Blvd., Naperville, IL 60540; Tel: (708) 717-0099.

FINANCIAL SUMMARY
Recent Giving: $100,000 (1991); $100,000 (1990); $105,425 (1989)
Assets: $2,120,177 (1990); $2,119,434 (1989)
EIN: 25-6076182

CONTRIBUTIONS SUMMARY
Typical Recipients: • *Arts & Humanities:* community arts, music • *Civic & Public Affairs:* environmental affairs • *Education:* colleges & universities • *Health:* hospices, hospitals, medical research, pediatric health • *Social Services:* family services, homes, united funds
Grant Types: general support
Geographic Distribution: focus on PA
Operating Locations: PA (Pittsburgh)

GIVING OFFICERS
Pittsburgh National Bank: trust

APPLICATION INFORMATION
Initial Approach: Send brief letter including a description of the organization, amount requested, purpose of funds sought, audited financial statement, and proof of tax-exempt status. There are no deadlines.
Restrictions on Giving: Does not support individuals or political or lobbying groups.

GRANTS ANALYSIS
Number of Grants: 24
Highest Grant: $25,000
Typical Range: $100 to $6,000
Disclosure Period: 1990

RECENT GRANTS
25,000 Rehabilitation Institute of Pittsburgh, Pittsburgh, PA
25,000 The Carnegie, Pittsburgh, PA
8,600 Greater Pittsburgh Guild for the Blind, Bridgeville, PA
8,000 Pittsburgh Youth Symphony Orchestra Association, Pittsburgh, PA
6,000 Carnegie-Mellon University, Pittsburgh, PA
6,000 Earthwatch, Pacific Palisades, CA
6,000 Foundation of Independent Colleges, Mechanicsburg, PA
5,000 Greater Pittsburgh Literacy Council, Pittsburgh, PA
5,000 United Way, Pittsburgh, PA
3,000 Southwest Services, Pittsburgh, PA

Vetlesen Foundation, G. Unger

CONTACT
George Rowe, Jr.
President
G. Unger Vetlesen Foundation
30 Rockefeller Plaza, Ste. 3217
New York, NY 10112
(212) 586-0700

FINANCIAL SUMMARY
Recent Giving: $2,155,349 (1991); $1,999,750 (1990); $1,700,827 (1989)
Assets: $53,175,742 (1991); $42,971,709 (1990); $42,781,914 (1989)
EIN: 13-1982695

CONTRIBUTIONS SUMMARY
Donor(s): The foundation was established in 1955 by the late George Unger Vetlesen.
Typical Recipients: • *Arts & Humanities:* libraries • *Civic & Public Affairs:* environmental affairs, ethnic/minority organizations, international affairs, zoos/botanical gardens • *Education:* colleges & universities, education funds, science/technology education • *International:* international organizations • *Religion:* churches • *Science:* scientific institutes
Grant Types: general support
Geographic Distribution: no geographic restrictions, with emphasis on New York and Massachusetts

GIVING OFFICERS
Harmon Duncombe: vp, treas *B* Bogota NJ 1909 *ED* Harvard Univ BS 1931; Harvard Univ LLB 1935 *CURR EMPL* mem: Fulton Duncombe & Rowe *CORP AFFIL* dir: Intl Flavors & Fragrances
Eugene Philip Grisanti: dir *B* Buffalo NY 1929 *ED* Holy Cross Coll AB 1951; Boston Univ LLB 1953; Harvard Univ LLM 1954 *CURR EMPL* chmn, pres, ceo, dir: Intl Flavors & Fragrances *NONPR AFFIL* dir: Cosmetic Toiletry Fragrance Assn, Fragrance Fdn
Joseph C. Hart: sec
George Rowe, Jr.: pres *B* Ossining NY 1922 *ED* Yale Univ AB 1943; Columbia Univ LLB 1948 *CURR EMPL* mem: Fulton Duncombe & Rowe
Henry G. Walter, Jr.: trust *B* New York NY 1910 *ED* Columbia Univ BA 1931; Columbia Univ LLB 1934 *NONPR AFFIL* dir: Intl Atlantic Salmon Fdn; trust: Am Mus Natural History, Monell Chemical Senses Ctr, Neuroscience Res Fdn, Pierpont Morgan Library

APPLICATION INFORMATION
Initial Approach:
Applicants should submit a simple letter outlining program or project to be funded, and amount of funding requested. Applications will be accepted at any time.

GRANTS ANALYSIS
Total Grants: $2,155,349
Number of Grants: 39
Highest Grant: $250,000
Typical Range: $5,000 to $50,000 and $100,000 to $500,000
Disclosure Period: 1991
Note: Average grant figure does not include two grants totaling $500,000. Recent grants are derived from a 1991 Form 990.

RECENT GRANTS
500,000 Columbia University, New York, NY
500,000 Scripps Oceanographic Institute, La Jolla, CA
400,000 Woods Hole Oceanographic Institute, Woods Hole, MA
250,000 Woods Hole Marine Biology Laboratory, Woods Hole, MA
163,500 University of Washington
100,000 Pierpont Morgan Library, New York, NY
75,000 Institute for Geophysics, Austin, TX
50,000 Norwegian Seaman's Church, New York, NY
50,000 Resources for the Future, Washington, DC
25,000 Columbia University, New York, NY

Vevay-Switzerland County Foundation

CONTACT
Ralph Tilley
President
Vevay-Switzerland County Fdn.
102 West Main St.
Vevay, IN 47043
(812) 427-2323

FINANCIAL SUMMARY
Recent Giving: $928,471 (1991); $254,844 (1990); $168,315 (1989)
Assets: $5,398,056 (1991); $5,723,040 (1990); $4,866,948 (1989)
Gifts Received: $1,000,000 (1991)
EIN: 35-1472069

CONTRIBUTIONS SUMMARY
Donor(s): Paul W. Ogle
Typical Recipients: • *Arts & Humanities:* arts appreciation, libraries, music • *Civic & Public Affairs:* municipalities, safety, urban & community affairs • *Health:* emergency/ambulance services • *Social Services:* aged
Grant Types: multiyear/continuing support and project
Geographic Distribution: limited to the town of Vevay and Switzerland County, IN

GIVING OFFICERS
Evelina Brown: treas
Martha Cole: secy
Jack Kitka: off
Woodie Reeves: vp
Ralph W. Tilley: pres

APPLICATION INFORMATION
Initial Approach: Application form required. There are no deadlines.

GRANTS ANALYSIS
Number of Grants: 29
Highest Grant: $319,500
Typical Range: $3,000 to $33,000
Disclosure Period: 1991

RECENT GRANTS
319,500 Town of Vevay Library, Vevay, IN
175,000 Town of Vevay, Vevay, IN
77,000 Town of Vevay, Vevay, IN
64,165 Town of Patriot, Patriot, IN
40,000 Town of Vevay, Vevay, IN
33,777 University of California Conservancy of Music, Berkeley, CA
25,000 Switzerland County Emergency Services
20,000 Town of Vevay, Vevay, IN
19,500 Town of Vevay, Vevay, IN
15,000 East Enterprise Fire Department, Enterprise, IN

VF Corp.
Sales: $2.95 billion
Employees: 49,000
Headquarters: Reading, PA
SIC Major Group: Apparel & Other Textile Products and Textile Mill Products

CONTACT
Laurie Tarnoski
Vice President & Corporate Secretary
VF Corp.
PO Box 1022
Reading, PA 19603
(215) 378-1151

CONTRIBUTIONS SUMMARY
Nonmonetary Support Types: donated products
Operating Locations: PA (Reading)

CORP. OFFICERS
Lawrence R. Pugh: *CURR EMPL* chmn, pres, ceo, dir: VF Corp

Viacom International Inc.
Revenue: $1.71 billion
Employees: 4,900
Parent Company: Viacom, Inc.
Headquarters: New York, NY
SIC Major Group: Communications, Holding & Other Investment Offices, and Motion Pictures

CONTACT
Raymond Boyce
Senior Vice President, Corporate Rels.
Viacom International Inc.
1515 Broadway
New York, NY 10036
(212) 258-6000

CONTRIBUTIONS SUMMARY
Operating Locations: NY (New York)

CORP. OFFICERS
Frank J. Biondi, Jr.: *CURR EMPL* pres, ceo, dir: Viacom Intl

Sumner Murray Redstone: *B* Boston MA 1923 *ED* Harvard Univ BA 1944; Harvard Univ LLB 1947 *CURR EMPL* chmn, dir: Viacom *CORP AFFIL* chmn, dir: Viacom Intl; chmn, pres, ceo, dir: Natl Amusements *NONPR AFFIL* chmn: Art Lending Library; dir: Boston Arts Festival, John F Kennedy Library Fdn; mem: Am Bar Assn, Am Congress Exhibitors, Am Judicature Soc, Boston Bar Assn, Harvard Univ Law Sch Assn, MA Bar Assn, Motion Picture Pioneers, Natl Assn Theatre Owners, Theatre Owners Am; mem adv comm: John F Kennedy Ctr Performing Arts; mem corp: New England Med Ctr; overseer: Boston Mus Fine Arts, Dana Farber Cancer Ctr; sponsor: Boston Mus Science; trust: Childrens Cancer Res Fdn; vp, mem exec comm: Will Rogers Meml Fund

Vicksburg Foundation

CONTACT
Nancy L. Grabiak
Secretary
Vicksburg Fdn.
c/o First of America
  Bank-Michigan N.A.
108 East Michigan Ave.
Kalamazoo, MI 49007
(616) 376-8016

FINANCIAL SUMMARY
Recent Giving: $193,113 (1991); $164,270 (1990); $92,020 (1989)
Assets: $4,220,616 (1991); $3,550,164 (1990); $3,453,746 (1989)
Gifts Received: $51,992 (1991)
Fiscal Note: In 1991, contributions were received from the Stanley J. Herman Charitable Unitrust.
EIN: 38-6065237

CONTRIBUTIONS SUMMARY
Typical Recipients: • *Arts & Humanities:* libraries • *Civic & Public Affairs:* municipalities, urban & community affairs • *Education:* colleges & universities, education funds, public education (precollege) • *Religion:* religious organizations • *Social Services:* community

centers, community service organizations, youth organizations
Grant Types: operating expenses and project
Geographic Distribution: focus on MI

GIVING OFFICERS
Maxwell D. Bardeen: off
Dennis Boyle: trust
Meredith Clarke: trust
Gordon Daniels: trust
Nancy L. Grabiak: secy, treas
Warren Lawrence: trust
William Oswalt: trust

APPLICATION INFORMATION
Initial Approach: Send brief letter of inquiry describing program. There are no deadlines.

GRANTS ANALYSIS
Number of Grants: 15
Highest Grant: $93,890
Typical Range: $2,000 to $8,000
Disclosure Period: 1991

RECENT GRANTS
93,890 Village of Vicksburg, Vicksburg, MI
25,000 Vicksburg Community Schools, Vicksburg, MI
10,000 Catholic Family Services, Vicksburg, MI
10,000 Schoolcraft Community Library, Vicksburg, MI
8,929 Vicksburg Community Library, Vicksburg, MI
8,000 United Way, Kalamazoo, MI
7,500 Vicksburg School Foundation, Vicksburg, MI
5,000 Kalamazoo Foundation, Kalamazoo, MI
5,000 Vicksburg Community Library, Vicksburg, MI
4,000 Kalamazoo College, Kalamazoo, MI

Vicksburg Hospital Medical Foundation

CONTACT
W. K. Purks
President
Vicksburg Hospital Medical Fdn.
PO Box 1578
Vicksburg, MS 39181
(601) 636-5514

FINANCIAL SUMMARY
Recent Giving: $373,000 (1991); $415,000 (1990); $365,000 (1989)
Assets: $7,094,376 (1991); $7,947,181 (1990); $8,212,110 (1989)
EIN: 64-6025312

CONTRIBUTIONS SUMMARY
Typical Recipients: • *Education:* colleges & universities, community & junior colleges, medical education • *Health:* health organizations, medical research, nursing services
Grant Types: endowment, research, and scholarship
Geographic Distribution: focus on MS and GA

GIVING OFFICERS
H. D. Andrews: trust
H. N. Gage, Jr.: trust
I. C. Knox, Jr.: vp
W. K. Purks, MD: pres
P. K. Watson: trust
Philip Watson, Jr.: secy, treas

APPLICATION INFORMATION
Initial Approach: Contributes only to preselected organizations.
Restrictions on Giving: Does not support individuals.

GRANTS ANALYSIS
Number of Grants: 6
Highest Grant: $143,000
Typical Range: $25,000 to $100,000
Disclosure Period: 1991

RECENT GRANTS
143,000 University of Mississippi, Jackson, MS
100,000 Millsaps College, Jackson, MS
50,000 Mississippi College, Clinton, MS
30,000 Vicksburg Patient Education, Vicksburg, MS
25,000 Hinds Community College, Raymond, MS

25,000 State Institute of Higher Learning, Jackson, MS

Victaulic Co. of America
Sales: $110.0 million
Employees: 1,200
Headquarters: Easton, PA
SIC Major Group: Business Services, Electronic & Other Electrical Equipment, Fabricated Metal Products, and Primary Metal Industries

CONTACT
George Naumann
Chairman
Victaulic Company of America
PO Box 31
Easton, PA 18044-0031
(215) 559-3300

CONTRIBUTIONS SUMMARY
Operating Locations: MA (Sutton), NJ (Stewartsville), PA (Easton)

CORP. OFFICERS
Joseph Trachtenberg: *CURR EMPL* pres: Victaulic Co Am

Victoria Foundation

CONTACT
Catherine M. McFarland
Secretary and Executive Officer
Victoria Foundation
40 South Fullerton Ave.
Montclair, NJ 07042
(201) 783-4450

FINANCIAL SUMMARY
Recent Giving: $7,080,000 (1993 est.); $6,942,800 (1992); $6,436,555 (1991)
Assets: $155,000,000 (1993 est.); $138,000,000 (1992 approx.); $149,000,000 (1991); $115,000,000 (1990)
EIN: 22-1554541

CONTRIBUTIONS SUMMARY
Donor(s): The Victoria Foundation was established in 1924 by Hendon Chubb.
Typical Recipients: • *Civic & Public Affairs:* economic development, environmental affairs, housing, nonprofit management • *Education:* minority education, private education (precollege), special education • *Social Services:* community service organizations, day care, drugs & alcohol, employment/job training, family plan-

ning, family services, youth organizations

Grant Types: capital, general support, matching, operating expenses, project, and research

Geographic Distribution: primarily Newark, NJ; with support for statewide environmental programs

GIVING OFFICERS

Charles Chapin III: trust

Corinne A. Chubb: trust

Percy Chubb III: pres of bd, trust *B* New York NY 1934 *ED* Yale Univ BA 1956 *CURR EMPL* vchmn: Chubb Corp *CORP AFFIL* dir: Am Fed Ins Co, Chubb Life Am, Colonial Life Ins Co Am; vchmn: Chubb & Son *NONPR AFFIL* mem: Downtown Assn

Sally Chubb: trust

Mary Coggeshall: trust

Robert Curvin, Ph.D.: trust

Haliburton Fales II: trust *B* New York NY 1919 *ED* Harvard Univ 1941; Columbia Univ LLB 1947 *CURR EMPL* White & Case *NONPR AFFIL* chmn dept discipline: NY St Supreme Ct; dir: Union Theological Seminary, Volunteers Legal Svc; fellow: Am Bar Fdn, Am Coll Trial Lawyers, Inst Judicial Admin, NY Bar Fdn; mem: Am Bar Assn, Am Judicature Soc, Am Law Inst, Am Soc Intl Law, Columbia Law Sch Assn, Gallatin (Albert) Assn, Intl Bar Assn, Intl Law Assn, Intl Legal Aid Defender Assn, NY Bar Assn, NY City Bar Assn, NY County Lawyers Assn, St Paul's Sch Alumni Assn; special master: Ny St Supreme Ct; trust: Pierpont Morgan Library, St Barnabas Hosp

Patricia Jenny: program off

Elliot D. Lee: program off

Catherine M. McFarland: exec off, secy

Gordon A. Millspaugh, Jr.: asst treas, trust

Margaret H. Parker: vp of bd, trust

Kevin Shanley: treas, trust *B* New York NY 1942 *ED* Univ PA 1964 *CORP AFFIL* dir: Bettlemead Devel Corp, Colonial Life Ins; pres, cfo, dir: Duro-Test Corp; vchmn, dir: Fidelity Union Bancorp *NONPR AFFIL* vp, trust: Newark Mus Assn

William Turnbull: trust

APPLICATION INFORMATION

Initial Approach:

Applicants should either phone or submit a 2-page letter outlining the project.

Application guidelines are available.

Proposals, except for elementary and secondary school proposals, must be received before February 1 for spring consideration or before September 1 for fall review. Elementary and secondary school proposals are due by March 1 for spring consideration. Any proposal received after the deadline will not be considered. Proposals will not be received by FAX. Each proposal is evaluated for its fit within the foundation interests. After initial screening, proposals are reviewed by trustee committees that make recommendations to the full board for decision. If a proposal falls within foundation guidelines and foundation priorities permit consideration of the grant request, additional information about the organization or project may be requested. As part of the evaluation process, staff members may make site visits to speak directly with project staff and/or board members to see the organization's work first-hand.

Restrictions on Giving: No grants are made to individuals, or for programs dealing with specific diseases, afflictions, geriatric needs, day care, or for multi-year funding.

OTHER THINGS TO KNOW

Projects are funded one year at a time. Occasionally, the foundation, by its own initiative, will fund an out-of-state agency. Elementary and secondary schools are asked to submit proposals during the spring cycle for the next school year. Grantees should demonstrate financial potential to sustain the project on a continuing basis after foundation funding is ended.

Publications: annual report, grant guidelines

GRANTS ANALYSIS

Total Grants: $6,942,800

Number of Grants: 174

Highest Grant: $500,000

Typical Range: $25,000 to $90,000

Disclosure Period: 1992

Note: Recent grants are derived from a 1992 grants list.

RECENT GRANTS

500,000 New Jersey Performing Arts Center, NJ — payable over five years. $1 million be used for leveraging; as a challenge grant to the newly created statewide Attorney's Campaign

400,000 New Community Corporation, Newark, NJ — to purchase and renovate the 201 Bergen Street facility

380,000 New Community Corporation, Newark, NJ — operating and expansion funds for the Employment Center

200,000 La Casa De Don Pedro, Newark, NJ — general operating support

139,000 Newark Public Library, Newark, NJ — to renovate the North End branch library and toward the position of coordinator

101,000 Protestant Community Center, Newark, NJ — general support; to fund a full time Education Coordinator

100,000 Boys and Girls Clubs of Newark, Newark, NJ — general operating support

100,000 Essex County College (For: Training), Newark, NJ — toward Training, operating costs

100,000 Liberty Science Center and Hall of Technology, Jersey City, NJ — toward the Victoria Environmental Education Center

100,000 Newark Museum, Newark, NJ — an emergency grant to help meet current budget deficit

---

Victory Markets, Inc.

Sales: $550.0 million

Employees: 3,500

Headquarters: Utica, NY

SIC Major Group: Automotive Dealers & Service Stations, Food & Kindred Products, Food Stores, and General Merchandise Stores

CONTACT

Pat Putnam

Consumer Advisor

Victory Markets, Inc.

PO Box 4200

Utica, NY 13504-4200

(315) 734-4200

CONTRIBUTIONS SUMMARY

Operating Locations: NY (Utica)

CORP. OFFICERS

Darryl R. Gregson: *CURR EMPL* pres, ceo, dir: Victory Markets

Jack Liberman: *CURR EMPL* chmn, dir: Victory Markets

Vidda Foundation

CONTACT

Gerald E. Rupp

Manager

Vidda Fdn.

10 East 40th St.

New York, NY 10016

(212) 696-4052

FINANCIAL SUMMARY

Recent Giving: $1,097,001 (fiscal 1992); $368,085 (fiscal 1991); $603,295 (fiscal 1990)

Assets: $1,700,351 (fiscal year ending May 31, 1992); $1,773,536 (fiscal 1991); $1,040,595 (fiscal 1990)

Gifts Received: $1,000,000 (fiscal 1992); $1,089,662 (fiscal 1991); $755,115 (fiscal 1990)

EIN: 13-2981105

CONTRIBUTIONS SUMMARY

Donor(s): Ursula Corning

Typical Recipients: • *Arts & Humanities:* arts centers, history/historic preservation, museums/galleries, music, opera, performing arts, theater • *Civic & Public Affairs:* environmental affairs, zoos/botanical gardens • *Education:* colleges & universities • *Health:* health organizations, hospitals, pediatric health • *Religion:* churches • *Social Services:* community service organizations, disabled, youth organizations

Grant Types: capital, endowment, general support, operating expenses, project, and research

Geographic Distribution: focus on NY

GIVING OFFICERS
Ann Fraser Brewer: trust
Ursula Corning: trust
Thomas T. Fraser: trust
Gerald E. Rupp: mgr, trust
Christophe Velay: trust

APPLICATION INFORMATION
Initial Approach: Send brief letter of inquiry describing program or project. There are no deadlines.
Restrictions on Giving: Does not support individuals.

GRANTS ANALYSIS
Number of Grants: 47
Highest Grant: $500,000
Typical Range: $5,000 to $25,000
Disclosure Period: fiscal year ending May 31, 1992

RECENT GRANTS
500,000 Columbia University, New York, NY
100,000 University Children's Medical Group, Los Angeles, CA — fellowship in pediatric plastic surgery
50,000 Laban Bartenieff Institute for Movement Studies, New York, NY
50,000 Theater for the New City Foundation, New York, NY
35,000 Metropolitan Museum of Art, New York, NY — department of paintings conservation
25,000 Church of Heavenly Rest, New York, NY
25,000 Fairleigh Dickinson University, Teaneck, NJ — research on Blackspot Disease of roses
25,000 Interschool Orchestras of New York, New York, NY
25,000 New York League for the Hard of Hearing, New York, NY
25,000 Student Conservation Association, Charleston, NH — publication of earth work

Video Software Dealers Association
Headquarters: Morestown, NJ

CONTACT
Victor Girardi
Controller
Video Software Dealers Association
303 Harper Dr.
Moorestown, NJ 08057-3229
(609) 231-7800

CONTRIBUTIONS SUMMARY
Operating Locations: NJ (Moorestown)

Vidinha Charitable Trust, A. and E.

CONTACT
Lois C. Loomis
Vice President
A. and E. Vidinha Charitable Trust
c/o Bishop Trust Co.
Box 2390
Honolulu, HI 96804-2390
(808) 523-2233

FINANCIAL SUMMARY
Recent Giving: $365,975 (fiscal 1992); $428,500 (fiscal 1991); $36,097 (fiscal 1990)
Assets: $4,608,670 (fiscal year ending June 30, 1992); $4,540,437 (fiscal 1991); $4,479,483 (fiscal 1990)
EIN: 99-0273993

CONTRIBUTIONS SUMMARY
Donor(s): the late Antone Vidinha and Edene Vidinha
Typical Recipients: • *Education:* colleges & universities • *Health:* hospitals, medical research, public health, single-disease health associations • *Religion:* churches • *Social Services:* community service organizations, counseling, disabled
Grant Types: general support, operating expenses, and scholarship
Geographic Distribution: focus on HI

APPLICATION INFORMATION
Initial Approach: Contributes only to preselected organizations.
Restrictions on Giving: Does not support individuals.

GRANTS ANALYSIS
Number of Grants: 23
Highest Grant: $67,550
Typical Range: $1,000 to $10,000
Disclosure Period: fiscal year ending June 30, 1992

RECENT GRANTS
67,550 University of Hawaii, Honolulu, HI
25,000 Chaminade University, Honolulu, HI
25,000 State of Hawaii Department of Health, Honolulu, HI
25,000 Wilcox Hospital Foundation, Lihue, HI
21,500 Koloa Missionary Church, HI
20,000 Hawaii Loa College, Kaneohe, HI
20,000 United Church of Christ, Honolulu, HI
19,300 Easter Seal Society, Honolulu, HI
16,500 State of Hawaii Department of Health, Honolulu, HI
15,000 Office of United Self Help, Honolulu, HI

Viele Scholarship Trust, Frances S.

CONTACT
Stevens Weller, Jr.
Manager
Frances S. Viele Scholarship Trust
502 Toro Canyon Rd.
Santa Barbara, CA 93108
(805) 565-1393

FINANCIAL SUMMARY
Recent Giving: $104,500 (fiscal 1992); $102,500 (fiscal 1991); $86,250 (fiscal 1990)
Assets: $2,029,512 (fiscal year ending May 31, 1992); $1,971,372 (fiscal 1991); $1,962,315 (fiscal 1990)
EIN: 95-3285561

CONTRIBUTIONS SUMMARY
Grant Types: scholarship

GIVING OFFICERS
Stevens Weller, Jr.: mgr

APPLICATION INFORMATION
Initial Approach: Request application form.

OTHER THINGS TO KNOW
Provides scholarships to members of Sigma Phi Society.
Disclosure Period: fiscal year ending May 31, 1992

Vilter Manufacturing Corp. / Vilter Foundation
Sales: $40.0 million
Employees: 345
Headquarters: Milwaukee, WI
SIC Major Group: Industrial Machinery & Equipment

CONTACT
A.A. Silverman
President
Vilter Foundation
2217 South First St.
Milwaukee, WI 53207

FINANCIAL SUMMARY
Recent Giving: $142,280 (1991); $172,096 (1990); $147,709 (1989)
Assets: $3,856,004 (1991); $3,693,727 (1990); $3,626,394 (1989)
EIN: 39-0678640

CONTRIBUTIONS SUMMARY
Typical Recipients: • *Arts & Humanities:* community arts, history/historic preservation, libraries, museums/galleries • *Health:* hospitals • *Religion:* religious organizations • *Social Services:* community service organizations, united funds, youth organizations
Grant Types: emergency and general support
Geographic Distribution: focus on WI
Operating Locations: FL (Altamonte Spring, Miami), WI (Milwaukee)

CORP. OFFICERS
A. A. Silverman: *CURR EMPL* chmn, pres: Vilter Mfg Corp
K. Wegner: *CURR EMPL* cfo: Vilter Mfg Corp

GIVING OFFICERS
R. A. Hall: dir
E. J. Kocher: vp, dir *CURR EMPL* sr vp, dir: Vilter Mfg Corp *CORP AFFIL* sr vp, dir: Vilter Mfg Corp
Albert A. Silverman: pres, dir *B* Copenhagen Denmark 1908 *ED* Northwestern Univ 1934; Central YMCA Coll AA 1936; Loyola Univ JD 1940 *CURR*

EMPL chmn, pres, dir: Vilter
Mfg Corp *CORP AFFIL* chmn,
pres, dir: Vilter Mfg Corp
NONPR AFFIL counc: Med
Coll WI; mem: Am Bar Assn,
Am Soc Heating Refrigerating
Air Conditioning Engrs, Chi-
cago Bar Assn, Loyola Univ
Alumni Assn, Master Brewers
Assn, Milwaukee Bar Assn, WI
Bar Assn; mem counc engring
sch: Marquette Univ

C. D. Wegener: secy, dir
CURR EMPL exec vp, cfo,
secy, dir: Vilter Mfg Corp
CORP AFFIL exec vp, cfo,
secy, dir: Vilter Mfg Corp

APPLICATION INFORMATION

Initial Approach: Send brief
letter describing program.
There are no deadlines.

GRANTS ANALYSIS

Number of Grants: 111
Highest Grant: $20,000
Typical Range: $250 to $1,000
Disclosure Period: 1991

RECENT GRANTS

20,000 United Way, Mil-
waukee, WI
10,000 St. Josephs Hospi-
tal, Milwaukee, WI
— for medical care
and treatment
7,500 DePaul University
College of Com-
merce, Chicago, IL
5,000 UW-O Foundation,
Oshkosh, WI —
for education and
research programs
in business
4,600 American Cancer
Society, Milwau-
kee, WI
4,000 American Cancer
Society, Milwau-
kee, WI
2,000 Historic Sites Foundation, Milwaukee,
WI — support of
1990 circus parade,
civic event
2,000 MPC Endowment,
Ltd, Milwaukee,
WI
2,000 Our House in Mil-
waukee, Wauwa-
tosa, WI — sup-
port for Ronald
McDonald House,
for families of hos-
pitalized children
2,000 Stanford Univer-
sity Hospital,
Friends of Radiol-
ogy, Stanford, CA
— for medial re-
search and care

Vincent Trust, Anna M.

CONTACT
Patricia M. Kling
Trust Officer
Anna M. Vincent Trust
c/o Mellon Bank (East), N.A.
PO Box 7899
Philadelphia, PA 19101-7899
(215) 553-3208

FINANCIAL SUMMARY
Recent Giving: $207,354 (fis-
cal 1990); $101,400 (fiscal
1987)
Assets: $3,994,508 (fiscal year
ending June 30, 1990);
$3,738,177 (fiscal 1987)
EIN: 23-6422666

CONTRIBUTIONS SUMMARY
Donor(s): the late Anna M.
Vincent
Grant Types: scholarship
Geographic Distribution: lim-
ited to the Delaware Valley,
PA, area

GIVING OFFICERS
Robert I. Whitelaw: trust

APPLICATION INFORMATION
Initial Approach: Application
forms available at high
schools. Send letter requesting
application form.

OTHER THINGS TO KNOW
Provides scholarships for
graduate or undergraduate
study at any recognized college, university, or other institution of higher learning.
Publications: Application
Guidelines

Vingo Trust II

CONTACT
Mary Sargent
Secretary
Vingo Trust II
c/o Ropes and Gray
One International Pl.
Boston, MA 02110-2624
(617) 951-7000

FINANCIAL SUMMARY
Recent Giving: $2,741,577
(1991); $517,224 (1990);
$484,579 (1989)
Assets: $4,673,321 (1991);
$11,459,902 (1990);
$11,362,311 (1989)
EIN: 04-6027982

CONTRIBUTIONS SUMMARY
Donor(s): the late Amory
Coolidge, WIlliam A. Coolidge
Typical Recipients: • *Arts &
Humanities:* history/historic
preservation, museums/galler-
ies, music • *Civic & Public Affairs:* environmental affairs,
ethnic/minority organizations,
zoos/botanical gardens • *Education:* colleges & universities,
medical education, private education (precollege), religious
education • *Religion:* churches,
religious organizations • *Social
Services:* counseling
Grant Types: capital, operating expenses, and project
Geographic Distribution: limited to Boston, Cambridge,
Somerville, and Chelsea, MA

GIVING OFFICERS
Francis Hardon Burr: trust *B*
Nahant MA 1914 *ED* Harvard
Univ AB 1935; Harvard Univ
LLB 1938; Harvard Univ LLD
1982 *CURR EMPL* coun:
Ropes & Gray *CORP AFFIL*
dir: Harvard Mgmt Co, Ray-
theon Co, State St Growth
Fund Inc, State St Investment
Corp; of coun: Ropes & Gray
NONPR AFFIL fellow: Har-
vard Coll; mem: Am Assn Ad-
vancement Science, Am Bar
Assn, Am Bar Fdn, Am Law
Inst, Boston Bar Assn; pres:
MA Gen Hosp
William A. Coolidge: trust
John Lastavica: trust

APPLICATION INFORMATION
Initial Approach: Contributes
only to preselected organizations.
Restrictions on Giving: Does
not support individuals or provide loans, scholarships, or fellowships.

OTHER THINGS TO KNOW
Publications: Informational
Brochure, Application Guide-
lines

GRANTS ANALYSIS
Number of Grants: 24
Highest Grant: $2,626,380
Typical Range: $1,000 to
$10,000
Disclosure Period: 1991

RECENT GRANTS
2,626,380 Trustees of Reservations, Beverly,
MA
60,000 Lamb of God

50,197 Associates for Re-
ligion and Intellec-
tual Life, Boston,
MA
5,000 Trinity Episcopal
Church of
Topsfield,
Topsfield, MA
5,000 Trinity Episcopal
Church of
Topsfield,
Topsfield, MA

Virginia Power Co.
Parent Company: Dominion
Resources
Revenue: $3.81 billion
Parent Employees: 12,220
Headquarters: Richmond, VA
SIC Major Group: Electric, Gas
& Sanitary Services

CONTACT
Kathryn M. Fessler
Contributions Administrator
Virginia Power Co.
PO Box 26666
Richmond, VA 23261
(804) 771-4417

FINANCIAL SUMMARY
Recent Giving: $1,496,000
(1993 est.); $1,615,000 (1992
approx.); $1,581,000 (1991 ap-
prox.)
Fiscal Note: All contributions
are made directly by the company. Figures for 1991 and
1992 include matching gifts.
Figure for 1991 does not include an estimated $325,000 in
nonmonetary support.

CONTRIBUTIONS SUMMARY
Typical Recipients: • *Arts &
Humanities:* arts associations,
arts centers, arts festivals, community arts, dance, libraries, literary arts, museums/galleries,
music, opera, performing arts,
public broadcasting, theater,
visual arts • *Civic & Public Affairs:* environmental affairs,
ethnic/minority organizations,
housing, safety, urban & community affairs, women's affairs
• *Education:* colleges & universities, economic education, education associations, education
funds, engineering education
• *Health:* emergency/ambu-
lance services, health organizations, hospices, hospitals, medical rehabilitation, mental
health, public health • *Social
Services:* aged, child welfare,
community centers, community
service organizations, counseling, delinquency & crime, disabled, drugs & alcohol, employ-

ment/job training, food/clothing distribution, homes, shelters/homelessness, volunteer services, youth organizations
Grant Types: capital, employee matching gifts, general support, project, and seed money
Nonmonetary Support Types: donated equipment, donated products, in-kind services, and loaned employees
Note: In 1991, estimated value of nonmonetary support was $325,500. This support is not included in above total. Contact person listed above handles requests for such support.
Geographic Distribution: organizations serving areas where company does business
Operating Locations: NC (Roanoke Rapids), VA (Alexandria, Charlottesville, Fairfax, Norfolk, Richmond), WV (Mount Storm)

CORP. OFFICERS
James Thomas Rhodes: *B* Lincolnton NC 1941 *ED* NC St Univ 1963; Purdue Univ 1972 *CURR EMPL* pres, ceo, dir: VA Power Co *CORP AFFIL* dir: Dominion Resources, NationsBank VA

GIVING OFFICERS
Thomas Edward Cupps: *B* Wilmington NC 1935 *CURR EMPL* vchmn, dir: Virginia Power Co *CORP AFFIL* dir: Bassett Furniture Indus Inc; pres, ceo, dir: Dominion Resources *NONPR AFFIL* mem: Am Bar Assn, Bd Bar Overseers, FL Bar Assn, MA Bar Assn, NC Bar Assn; trust: Univ NC Chapel Hill
Kathryn M. Fessler: *CURR EMPL* contributions adm: Virginia Power Co
R.H. Hill: mem (contributions comm)
James Thomas Rhodes: mem (contributions comm) *CURR EMPL* pres, ceo, dir: VA Power Co (see above)
Eva S. Teig: mem (contributions comm)

APPLICATION INFORMATION
Initial Approach: *Initial Contact:* letter or proposal to Kathryn Fessler, contributions administrator, for organizations serving broad areas where company does business; community organizations should apply to nearest division office of Virginia Power Co. or North Caro-

lina Power Co. *Include Information On:* organization's purpose and goals, most recent financial statement, proof of tax-exempt status, amount of grant requested and overall goal for contributions, purpose of grant *When to Submit:* any time
Restrictions on Giving: The company does not contribute to individuals, churches or religious organizations, national health and welfare agencies, political campaigns, landmark restoration, primary or secondary schools, individual Boy or Girl Scout troops unless not United Way supported, fraternal organizations, veterans' groups, groups which are United Way supported unless for capital contributions, goodwill advertising, or organizations to which the company has awarded capital funding until two years have elapsed since final payment.

OTHER THINGS TO KNOW
Local community organizations should apply to nearest company offices. Their addresses and phone numbers are listed in Virginia Power Company's Corporate Giving Program brochure, available upon request from contributions administrator.

GRANTS ANALYSIS
Total Grants: $1,581,000*
Number of Grants: 791
Highest Grant: $110,000
Typical Range: $1,000 to $5,000
Disclosure Period: 1991
Note: Figure for total grants includes matching gifts.

Visciglia Foundation, Frank

CONTACT
Frank Visciglia Fdn.
300 Raritan Center Pkwy.
Edison, NJ 08871

FINANCIAL SUMMARY
Recent Giving: $229,181 (1991); $181,462 (1990); $148,190 (1989)
Assets: $2,429,489 (1991); $2,126,232 (1990); $2,187,912 (1989)
Gifts Received: $155,000 (1991); $150,000 (1990); $236,670 (1989)
EIN: 51-0174975

CONTRIBUTIONS SUMMARY
Typical Recipients: • *Education:* colleges & universities, community & junior colleges, education funds, private education (precollege), religious education • *Health:* hospitals • *Religion:* churches, missionary activities, religious organizations • *Social Services:* community service organizations, food/clothing distribution
Grant Types: general support

GIVING OFFICERS
Frank D. Visceglia: mgr

APPLICATION INFORMATION
Initial Approach: Contributes only to preselected organizations. Applications not accepted.

GRANTS ANALYSIS
Number of Grants: 232
Highest Grant: $124,051
Typical Range: $250 to $1,000
Disclosure Period: 1991

RECENT GRANTS
124,051 National Conference of Christians and Jews
10,000 Immaculate College
10,000 Immaculate College
10,000 University of Notre Dame, Notre Dame, IN
9,000 Continue the Mission Campaign
6,000 Middleburg City College Foundation, Middleburg, VA
6,000 MJ Pride
5,000 Funds for Educational Advancement
5,000 Oak Crest School
5,000 St. Peters Medical Center

Vista Chemical Company
Sales: $705.3 million
Employees: 1,750
Headquarters: Houston, TX
SIC Major Group: Chemicals & Allied Products and Oil & Gas Extraction

CONTACT
Margarette Golatta
Vista Chemical Company
900 Threadneedle
Houston, TX 77079
(713) 588-3000

CONTRIBUTIONS SUMMARY
Operating Locations: TX (Houston)

CORP. OFFICERS
John D. Burns: *CURR EMPL* chmn, pres, ceo: Vista Chem Co

Vlasic Foundation

CONTACT
Robert Joseph Vlasic
President
Vlasic Fdn.
710 N. Woodward
Bloomfield Hills, MI 48304

FINANCIAL SUMMARY
Recent Giving: $133,175 (fiscal 1992); $346,604 (fiscal 1991); $37,475 (fiscal 1990)
Assets: $3,240,710 (fiscal year ending May 31, 1992); $3,697,568 (fiscal 1991); $2,799,299 (fiscal 1990)
EIN: 38-6077329

CONTRIBUTIONS SUMMARY
Donor(s): Robert J. Vlasic, Joseph Vlasic
Typical Recipients: • *Arts & Humanities:* arts institutes, community arts, music, performing arts • *Education:* private education (precollege), public education (precollege) • *Health:* health funds • *Religion:* religious organizations • *Social Services:* community service organizations, disabled, homes, recreation & athletics, religious welfare, united funds, youth organizations
Grant Types: general support

GIVING OFFICERS
James Vlasic: trust, secy, treas
Michael A. Vlasic: trust
Richard R. Vlasic: trust, vp
Robert Joseph Vlasic: pres, trust, don *B* Detroit MI 1926 *ED* Univ MI BS 1949 *CURR EMPL* chmn, chmn exec comm, dir: Campbell Soup Co *CORP AFFIL* dir: MI Natl Corp, Reynolds Metals Co *NONPR AFFIL* chmn bd trust: Henry Ford Hosp; mem: Cranbrook Ed Commun Bd
William Vlasic: trust, vp

APPLICATION INFORMATION

Initial Approach: Contributes only to preselected organizations.

GRANTS ANALYSIS

Number of Grants: 37
Highest Grant: $70,000
Typical Range: $100 to $5,000
Disclosure Period: fiscal year ending May 31, 1992

RECENT GRANTS

70,000 St. Hugo Completion Fund, MI
10,000 Catholic Services Appeal, MI
10,000 Henry Ford Health System, Detroit, MI
5,000 Rollins Fund, MI
5,000 Rose Hill Center, Bloomfield Hills, MI
5,000 United Way, Detroit, MI
2,850 Founders Society Detroit Institute of Arts, Detroit, MI
2,475 Northern High School, MI
2,000 Detroit Symphony Orchestra, Detroit, MI
2,000 Oakland County Special Olympics, MI

Voelkerding Charitable Trust, Walter and Jean

CONTACT

William J. Zollmann III
Trustee
Walter and Jean Voelkerding Charitable Trust
PO Box 81
Dutzow, MO 63342
(314) 433-5520

FINANCIAL SUMMARY

Recent Giving: $158,200 (fiscal 1992); $157,000 (fiscal 1991); $154,500 (fiscal 1990)
Assets: $3,422,571 (fiscal year ending February 28, 1991); $3,422,259 (fiscal 1990); $3,456,896 (fiscal 1987)
EIN: 23-7015780

CONTRIBUTIONS SUMMARY

Donor(s): the late Walter J. Voelkerding
Typical Recipients: • *Education:* private education (precollege) • *Religion:* churches, religious organizations • *Social Services:* youth organizations
Grant Types: general support

Geographic Distribution: limited to Warren County, MO

GIVING OFFICERS

William Marquart: trust
Steven J. Maune: trust
David J. Voelkerding: trust
William J. Zollman III: trust

APPLICATION INFORMATION

Initial Approach: The foundation reports it only makes contributions to preselected charitable organizations.

GRANTS ANALYSIS

Number of Grants: 4
Highest Grant: $115,000
Typical Range: $10,000 to $12,000
Disclosure Period: fiscal year ending February 28, 1991

RECENT GRANTS

115,000 North Dakota Boys Ranch, ND
20,000 Knights of Columbus, Dutzow, MO
12,000 St. Vincent de Paul Church, Dutzow, MO
10,000 St. Francis Borgia Regional High School, Washington, MO

Vogt Machine Co., Henry / Vogt Foundation, Henry

Sales: $110.0 million
Employees: 1,250
Headquarters: Louisville, KY
SIC Major Group: Fabricated Metal Products and Industrial Machinery & Equipment

CONTACT

Kent Oyler
Manager
Henry Vogt Fdn.
PO Box 1918
Louisville, KY 40201-1918
(502) 634-1511

FINANCIAL SUMMARY

Recent Giving: $200,000 (fiscal 1993 est.); $200,000 (fiscal 1991); $181,800 (fiscal 1990)
Assets: $1,800,429 (fiscal year ending June 30, 1990); $1,845,136 (fiscal 1989)
Gifts Received: $75,000 (fiscal 1990); $400,000 (fiscal 1989)
Fiscal Note: In 1989, contributions were received from Henry Vogt Machine Co.
EIN: 23-7416717

CONTRIBUTIONS SUMMARY

Typical Recipients: • *Arts & Humanities:* arts funds • *Education:* business education, career/vocational education, colleges & universities, economic education, education funds • *Health:* hospices • *Social Services:* community service organizations, drugs & alcohol, emergency relief, employment/job training, homes, shelters/homelessness, united funds, youth organizations
Grant Types: capital and multiyear/continuing support
Nonmonetary Support Types: donated equipment
Geographic Distribution: emphasis on the Louisville, KY, area
Operating Locations: KY (Louisville)

CORP. OFFICERS

Henry V. Heuser: *B* Louisville KY 1914 *ED* Purdue Univ 1936 *CURR EMPL* chmn, dir: Henry Vogt Machine Co *CORP AFFIL* dir: Enterprises Inc
Henry V. Heuser, Jr.: *CURR EMPL* pres, dir: Henry Vogt Machine Co

GIVING OFFICERS

Margaret S. Culver: secy
Henry V. Heuser: dir *CURR EMPL* chmn, dir: Henry Vogt Machine Co (see above)
Henry V. Heuser, Jr.: pres, dir *CURR EMPL* pres, dir: Henry Vogt Machine Co (see above)
Leland D. Schlegel, Jr.: vp, dir
David G. White: dir

APPLICATION INFORMATION

Initial Approach: Send brief letter of inquiry and concise proposal. Include amount requested and purpose of funds sought. There are no deadlines. Board meets in June.
Restrictions on Giving: No support for endowments, fellowships, matching gifts, scholarships, or loans. Generally, the foundation awards capital funds for projects that enhance computer or technical literacy in Jefferson County, KY.

GRANTS ANALYSIS

Number of Grants: 18
Highest Grant: $98,000
Typical Range: $500 to $50,000
Disclosure Period: fiscal year ending June 30, 1990

RECENT GRANTS

98,000 Jefferson County Public Education Foundation, Louisville, KY
29,000 United Way
10,000 Boy Scouts of America
10,000 DePaul School, Pepper Pike, OH
9,500 Kentucky Independent College Fund, Henderson, KY
5,000 Dare to Care, Louisville, KY
5,000 Home of the Innocents, Louisville, KY
5,000 Junior Achievement, Louisville, KY
2,500 Funds for the Arts
2,500 Operation Brightside, St. Louis, MO

Volen Charitable Trust, Benjamin

CONTACT

Benjamin Volen Charitable Trust
c/o Northern Trust Bank of Florida
700 Brickell Avenue
Miami, FL 33131-2804

FINANCIAL SUMMARY

Recent Giving: $1,282,896 (1990)
Assets: $9,085,390 (1990)
Gifts Received: $1,144,666 (1990)
EIN: 65-6018806

CONTRIBUTIONS SUMMARY

Donor(s): Benjamin Volen
Typical Recipients: • *Education:* colleges & universities • *Health:* hospitals • *Religion:* synagogues • *Social Services:* aged
Grant Types: general support
Geographic Distribution: giving primarily in Boca Raton, FL

GIVING OFFICERS

Northern Trust Bank of Florida: trust

APPLICATION INFORMATION

Initial Approach: Contributes only to preselected organizations. Applications not accepted.
Restrictions on Giving: Does not provide grants to individuals.

GRANTS ANALYSIS

Number of Grants: 4

Highest Grant: $574,950
Typical Range: $57,565 to $66,190
Disclosure Period: 1990

RECENT GRANTS
574,950 Mae Volen Senior Center, Boca Raton, FL
66,190 Boca Raton Community Hospital, Boca Raton, FL
66,190 Temple Beth-El, Boca Raton, FL
57,565 Brandeis University, Waltham, MA

Volkswagen of America, Inc.

Sales: $2.92 billion
Employees: 1,800
Headquarters: Auburn Hills, MI
SIC Major Group: Wholesale Trade—Durable Goods

CONTACT
Maria Leonhauser
Public Relations Manager
Volkswagen of America, Inc.
3800 Hamlin Rd.
Auburn Hills, MI 48326
(313) 340-5534

FINANCIAL SUMMARY
Recent Giving: $175,000 (1993 est.); $184,000 (1992 approx.); $175,000 (1991)

CONTRIBUTIONS SUMMARY
Support goes to local education, human services, arts, and civic organizations.
Typical Recipients: • *Arts & Humanities:* arts appreciation, arts associations, history/historic preservation, museums/galleries, public broadcasting, theater • *Civic & Public Affairs:* consumer affairs, ethnic/minority organizations, urban & community affairs • *Education:* business education, career/vocational education, colleges & universities, community & junior colleges, continuing education, economic education, engineering education, international exchange, international studies • *Health:* hospitals, medical research • *International:* foreign educational institutions, international organizations • *Social Services:* united funds
Grant Types: general support
Geographic Distribution: in headquarters and operating communities; some contributions to national organizations

Operating Locations: AZ, CA, CO, DC, DE, FL, GA, IL, MA, MD, MI, NJ, NY, OH, OR, RI, TX, WA

CORP. OFFICERS
John Kerr: *CURR EMPL* pres, ceo: Volkswagen AG
Ferdinand Piech: *CURR EMPL* chmn: Volkswagen AG

GIVING OFFICERS
Maria E. Leonhauser: *CURR EMPL* mgr pubic rels: Volkswagen Am

APPLICATION INFORMATION
Initial Approach: Send a full proposal. Include a description of the organization, amount requested, purpose of funds sought, recently audited financial statement, and proof of tax-exempt status.
Restrictions on Giving: Does not support individuals, religious organizations for sectarian purposes, or political or lobbying groups. Generally does not support organizations outside operating areas.

GRANTS ANALYSIS
Typical Range: $1,000 to $2,500

RECENT GRANTS
100 American Council on Germany, Washington, DC
100 American Institute for Contemporary German Studies, Washington, DC
100 Boys and Girls Club, MI
100 Detroit Symphony Orchestra, Detroit, MI
100 Salk Institute for Biological Studies, San Diego, CA
100 United Way

Vollbrecht Foundation, Frederick A.

CONTACT
Kenneth J. Klebba
President
Frederick A. Vollbrecht Fdn.
31700 Telegraph Rd., Ste. 220
Birmingham, MI 48025
(313) 646-7440

FINANCIAL SUMMARY
Recent Giving: $141,500 (1991); $114,500 (1989); $91,100 (1988)

Assets: $2,518,440 (1991); $2,342,004 (1989); $2,096,803 (1988)
EIN: 38-6056173

CONTRIBUTIONS SUMMARY
Donor(s): the late Frederick A. Vollbrecht
Typical Recipients: • *Education:* business education, career/vocational education, colleges & universities, community & junior colleges, literacy • *Health:* health organizations, hospitals, medical research, pediatric health • *Social Services:* child welfare, community service organizations, family services, food/clothing distribution, united funds, youth organizations
Grant Types: general support and research
Geographic Distribution: focus on MI

GIVING OFFICERS
Kenneth J. Klebba: trust, pres, treas
Richard E. Mida: trust, vp, secy

APPLICATION INFORMATION
Initial Approach: Send brief letter of inquiry describing program. There are no deadlines.
Restrictions on Giving: Does not support individuals.

OTHER THINGS TO KNOW
Publications: Annual Report

GRANTS ANALYSIS
Number of Grants: 37
Highest Grant: $30,000
Typical Range: $1,000 to $5,000
Disclosure Period: 1991

RECENT GRANTS
30,000 Walsh College of Accountancy and Business Administration, Troy, MI — capital campaign
15,000 Oakland Family Services, Pontiac, MI — preventive services program
10,000 Community House Association, Birmingham, MI
10,000 Walsh College of Accountancy and Business Administration, Troy, MI
5,000 Boysville of Michigan, Clinton, MI — St. Joseph Hall Fund

5,000 Children's Hospital Medical Center, Detroit, MI
5,000 Gleaners Community Food Bank, Detroit, MI
3,000 North Oakland SCAMP Funding Corporation, Clarkston, MI
3,000 Oakland Community College Foundation, Pontiac, MI
3,000 Oakland Literacy Council, Pontiac, MI

Vollmer Foundation

CONTACT
Albert L. Ennist
Assistant Secretary
Vollmer Fdn.
PO Box 704
Butler, NJ 07405
(201) 492-2309

FINANCIAL SUMMARY
Recent Giving: $8,295,283 (1991); $145,347 (1990); $184,240 (1989)
Assets: $17,801,411 (1991); $32,913,661 (1990); $8,152,030 (1989)
Gifts Received: $724,138 (1989)
EIN: 13-2620718

CONTRIBUTIONS SUMMARY
Donor(s): The foundation was incorporated in 1965 in New York. It was endowed by the late Alberto F. Vollmer of Caracas, Venezuela. The income of the foundation is derived from investments in the securities of Venezuelan corporations.
Typical Recipients: • *International:* foreign educational institutions, international organizations • *Religion:* churches
Grant Types: general support and multiyear/continuing support
Geographic Distribution: limited to Venezuela

GIVING OFFICERS
Carolina V. de Eseverri: secy
Ana Mercedes de Estrada: dir
Albert L. Ennist: asst secy
Ana Luisa Estrada: asst treas
Gustavo A. Vollmer: dir
Gustavo J. Vollmer: pres, dir

APPLICATION INFORMATION
Initial Approach: The foundation does not provide application forms and

there is no required procedure for applying for grants. Applications should include sufficient information to justify support of the proposal and to establish the eligibility of the applying organization. A copy of the organization's IRS determination letter should accompany the application. Grant requests should be sent in duplicate form.

The foundation accepts grant requests at any time.

Restrictions on Giving: In general, the foundation does not make grants to other private foundations. No grants are made to individuals, or for building funds, matching gifts, or loans.

OTHER THINGS TO KNOW

Publications: application guidelines

GRANTS ANALYSIS

Total Grants: $8,295,283
Number of Grants: 10
Highest Grant: $7,458,867
Typical Range: $8,000 to $124,000
Disclosure Period: 1991
Note: Average grant figure does not include the highest grant of $7,458,867. Recent grants are derived from a 1991 grants list.

RECENT GRANTS

7,458,867 Fundacion Palmar Banco del Orinoco, Caracas, Venezuela — capital grant

230,757 Dividendo Voluntario para la Comunidad, Caracas, Venezuela — construction and support rural schools

169,646 Asociacion Venezolana de Conciertos, Caracas, Venezuela — general purposes

145,908 Universidad Catolica Andres Bello, Caracas, Venezuela — general purposes

124,389 Academia Nacional de Medicina, Caracas, Venezuela — support for Venezuelan Medical programs

49,342 Universidad Catolica del Tachira, Estado Tachira, Venezuela — general purposes

46,711 Sociedad de Proteccion Benefica y So-

cial, Sol. Santa Maria Micaela, Calle F. Urb. Vista Alegre, Caracas, Venezuela — general purposes

44,992 A.C. Centro Medico Docente La Trinidad, Caracas, Venezuela — general purposes

16,447 Instituto de Estudios Superiores de Administracion, Caracas, Venezuela — general purposes of graduate school of Business Administration

8,224 Archdiocese of Caracas, Caracas, Venezuela — general purposes

Vollrath Co. / Windway Foundation, Inc.

Former Foundation Name: Vollrath Co. Foundation
Sales: $140.0 million
Employees: 2000
Parent Company: Windway Capital Corp.
Headquarters: Sheboygen, WI
SIC Major Group: Fabricated Metal Products, Miscellaneous Manufacturing Industries, Primary Metal Industries, and Rubber & Miscellaneous Plastics Products

CONTACT

Mary Kohler
Vice President
Windway Foundation, Inc.
PO Box 897
Sheboygen, WI 53082-0897
(414) 457-8600

FINANCIAL SUMMARY

Recent Giving: $240,000 (1992 approx.); $287,688 (1991); $208,506 (1989)
Assets: $46,224 (1991); $67,555 (1989)
Gifts Received: $240,000 (1991); $145,000 (1989)
Fiscal Note: 1981 contribution received from Windway Capital
EIN: 39-6046987

CONTRIBUTIONS SUMMARY

Typical Recipients: • *Civic & Public Affairs:* business/free enterprise, environmental affairs, public policy • *Education:* economic education • *Health:* health care cost containment
Grant Types: capital, challenge, conference/seminar,

matching, multiyear/continuing support, project, research, scholarship, and seed money
Nonmonetary Support Types: donated equipment
Geographic Distribution: focus on WI
Operating Locations: WI (Sheboygen)

GIVING OFFICERS

Charlotte M. Kohler: vp, dir
Mary S. Kohler: vp, dir
Terry J. Kohler: pres, dir
Roland M. Neumann, Jr.: treas, dir
Mary L. Ten Haken: secy, dir

APPLICATION INFORMATION

Initial Approach: Send a brief letter of inquiry, including a description of the organization, amount requested, purpose of funds sought, list of board of trustees, and proof of tax-exempt status.
Restrictions on Giving: The foundation prefers to give to public policy research; private education above the secondary level; and conservation, from the free market perspective. In general, preference is given to direct service projects and programs, as opposed to intermediary funding agencies. The foundation does not make grants to individuals; organizations that do not have tax-exempt status under section 501(c)(3) of the Internal Revenue Code; political or fraternal organizations; charitable dinners or fund raising events and related advertising; tax-supported organizations, public schools, and events or organizations connected with public schools; veterans organizations; or tickets. Projects generally outside foundation guidelines are travel costs for groups or individuals, secondary education, or religious organizations and/or endeavors.

OTHER THINGS TO KNOW

The foundation seeks to support organizations that demonstrate responsible management, provide timely reports to the directors of the foundation, and who acknowledge the foundation and thank it for its support.
Publications: Guidelines

GRANTS ANALYSIS

Number of Grants: 59
Highest Grant: $35,000

Typical Range: $200 to $5,000
Disclosure Period: 1991

RECENT GRANTS

35,000 Rockford Institute, Rockford, IL

25,000 Eric Voeglin Institute, Baton Rouge, LA

25,000 P.A.C.T., Spokane, WA

20,000 National Review Institute, New York, NY

20,000 Rockford Institute, Rockford, IL

15,000 C-Media, New York, NY

15,000 Rockford Institute, Rockford, IL

10,000 American Legislative Exchange Council, Washington, DC

10,000 American Legislative Exchange Council, Washington, DC

10,000 Ice Age Park and Trail, Madison, WI

Volvo North America Corp.

Sales: $11.0 million
Employees: 4,500
Headquarters: New York, NY
SIC Major Group: Nondepository Institutions, Transportation Equipment, and Wholesale Trade—Durable Goods

CONTACT

Nancy Fiesler
Communications Specialist
Volvo North America Corp.
535 Madison Avenue, 25th Fl.
New York, NY 10022
(212) 754-3300

CONTRIBUTIONS SUMMARY

Operating Locations: NY

CORP. OFFICERS

Albert R. Dowden: *CURR EMPL* pres, ceo: Volvo North Am Corp
David Korpics: *CURR EMPL* sr vp, cfo: Volvo North Am Corp

GIVING OFFICERS

Nancy Fiesler: *CURR EMPL* commun specialist: Volvo North Am Corp

APPLICATION INFORMATION

Restrictions on Giving: Company reports available funds for the next several years have been allocated. Discretionary budget is small and generally allocated to preselected organizations.

OTHER THINGS TO KNOW

Volvo GM Heavy Truck, P.O. Box 26115, Greensboro, NC 27402, (919) 279-2000, sponsors a limited direct giving program focusing on community development, education, health, and arts and culture. Contact the public relations department for more information.

Von der Ahe Foundation

CONTACT

Frederick T. Von der Ahe
Board Member
Von der Ahe Fdn.
4605 Lankershim Blvd., Ste. 707
North Hollywood, CA 91602

FINANCIAL SUMMARY

Recent Giving: $330,100 (1991); $315,000 (1990); $343,850 (1989)
Assets: $4,926,318 (1991); $4,060,894 (1990); $4,730,202 (1989)
EIN: 95-6051857

CONTRIBUTIONS SUMMARY

Donor(s): members of the Von der Ahe family, Von's Grocery Co.
Typical Recipients: • *Arts & Humanities:* arts centers, museums/galleries • *Civic & Public Affairs:* civil rights, international affairs • *Education:* colleges & universities, private education (precollege), religious education • *Health:* hospitals • *Religion:* churches, religious organizations • *Social Services:* child welfare, community service organizations, drugs & alcohol, religious welfare, shelters/homelessness, united funds, youth organizations
Grant Types: general support
Geographic Distribution: focus on CA

GIVING OFFICERS

Charles K. Von der Ahe: bd mem
Clyde W. Von der Ahe, MD: vp, dir
Frederick T. Von der Ahe: bd mem
Thomas R. Von der Ahe: bd mem

Vincent M. Von der Ahe: secy, treas, dir
Wilfred L. Von der Ahe: pres, dir

APPLICATION INFORMATION

Initial Approach: Contributes only to preselected organizations.
Restrictions on Giving: Does not support individuals.

GRANTS ANALYSIS

Number of Grants: 49
Highest Grant: $12,000
Typical Range: $1,000 to $10,000
Disclosure Period: 1991

RECENT GRANTS

12,000 Maryknoll Sisters of St. Dominic, Maryknoll, NY
10,000 Amnesty International, New York, NY
10,000 Campbell Hall School, North Hollywood, CA
10,000 Catholic Relief Services, Los Angeles, CA
10,000 Catholic Social Services, Los Angeles, CA
10,000 Christian Appalachian Project, Lancaster, KY
10,000 Community for Creative Non-Violence, Washington, DC
10,000 El Rescate, Los Angeles, CA
10,000 Friend of Our Little Brother, Tempe, AZ
10,000 Mount St. Marys College, Los Angeles, CA

Von der Ahe, Jr. Trust, Theodore Albert

CONTACT

Frederick T. Von der Ahe
Trustee
Theodore Albert Von der Ahe, Jr. Trust
3151 Airway Avenue, Ste. L-1
Costa Mesa, CA 92626
(714) 850-0376

FINANCIAL SUMMARY

Recent Giving: $144,000 (fiscal 1992); $140,000 (fiscal 1991); $112,000 (fiscal 1990)
Assets: $7,156,170 (fiscal year ending January 31, 1992);

$7,395,306 (fiscal 1991); $7,306,687 (fiscal 1990)
EIN: 95-3371127

CONTRIBUTIONS SUMMARY

Typical Recipients: • *Civic & Public Affairs:* civil rights, international affairs, law & justice, public policy, urban & community affairs • *International:* international development/relief, international organizations • *Religion:* churches, religious organizations • *Social Services:* community centers, community service organizations, religious welfare
Grant Types: general support

GIVING OFFICERS

Frederick T. Von der Ahe: trust

APPLICATION INFORMATION

Initial Approach: Contributes only to preselected organizations.

GRANTS ANALYSIS

Number of Grants: 21
Highest Grant: $10,000
Typical Range: $6,000 to $10,000
Disclosure Period: fiscal year ending January 31, 1992

RECENT GRANTS

10,000 Amnesty International, Washington, DC
10,000 Catholic Relief Services, Los Angeles, CA
10,000 Catholic Social Services, Los Angeles, CA
10,000 Christian Appalachian Project, Lancaster, KY
10,000 Community for Creative Non-Violence, Washington, DC
10,000 El Rescate, Los Angeles, CA
10,000 Oxfam-America, Boston, MA
8,000 Maryknoll Sisters of St. Dominic, Maryknoll, NY
6,000 Pacifica Foundation, Los Angeles, CA
6,000 Peace and Justice Center of Southern California, Los Angeles, CA

Von Rebay Foundation, Hilla

CONTACT

Francis P. Schiaroli
Hilla Von Rebay Fdn.
PO Box 120
Stamford, CT 06904

FINANCIAL SUMMARY

Recent Giving: $28,642 (1991); $40,128 (1990); $31,000 (1989)
Assets: $3,069,490 (1991); $2,928,592 (1990); $3,014,630 (1989)
EIN: 23-7112973

CONTRIBUTIONS SUMMARY

Typical Recipients: • *Arts & Humanities:* museums/galleries • *Civic & Public Affairs:* philanthropic organizations
Grant Types: general support

GIVING OFFICERS

Fleet Bank, N.A.: trust

APPLICATION INFORMATION

Initial Approach: Send brief letter of inquiry describing program or project. There are no deadlines.

GRANTS ANALYSIS

Number of Grants: 1
Highest Grant: $28,642
Disclosure Period: 1991

RECENT GRANTS

28,642 Hilla Rebay Foundation

Vons Cos., Inc.

Sales: $5.33 billion
Employees: 35,000
Headquarters: Arcadia, CA
SIC Major Group: Food & Kindred Products, Food Stores, and Wholesale Trade—Nondurable Goods

CONTACT

Gloria Winder
Consumer Affairs Representative
Vons Cos., Inc.
PO Box 3338
Los Angeles, CA 90051
(818) 821-7000

FINANCIAL SUMMARY

Fiscal Note: Annual Giving Range: Company does not disclose contribution figures.

CONTRIBUTIONS SUMMARY

Company supports local education, human service, arts, and civic organizations. A major corporate contribution is also given to the United Way.

Typical Recipients: • *Arts & Humanities:* general • *Civic & Public Affairs:* general • *Education:* general • *Social Services:* general

Geographic Distribution: headquarters only

Operating Locations: CA (Arcadia)

CORP. OFFICERS

Dennis K. Eck: *CURR EMPL* vchmn, coo, dir: Vons Cos

Roger E. Stangeland: *CURR EMPL* chmn, ceo, dir: Vons Cos

APPLICATION INFORMATION

Initial Approach: Send brief letter of inquiry, including a description of the organization, amount requested, purpose of funds sought, recently audited financial statements, and proof of tax-exempt status. Company requests that applicants allow 8 weeks for a decision.

GRANTS ANALYSIS

Note: Company reports that grant size varies.

Voplex Corp.

Sales: $56.55 million
Employees: 750
Headquarters: Troy, MI
SIC Major Group: Chemicals & Allied Products, Rubber & Miscellaneous Plastics Products, Textile Mill Products, and Transportation Equipment

CONTACT

Marie Jakubiak
Voplex Corp.
1455 Imlay City Rd.
Lapeer, MI 48446
(313) 584-2850

CONTRIBUTIONS SUMMARY

Operating Locations: MI (Troy)

CORP. OFFICERS

Richard Crawford: *CURR EMPL* pres, ceo: Voplex Corp

Raymond A. Lander, Jr.: *CURR EMPL* chmn: Voplex Corp

Vulcan Materials Co. / Vulcan Materials Co. Foundation

Sales: $1.07 billion
Employees: 6,300
Headquarters: Birmingham, AL
SIC Major Group: Chemicals & Allied Products, Nonmetallic Minerals Except Fuels, Petroleum & Coal Products, and Stone, Clay & Glass Products

CONTACT

Mary S. Russom
Community Affairs Representative
Vulcan Materials Co.
PO Box 530187
Birmingham, AL 35253-0187
(205) 877-3229

FINANCIAL SUMMARY

Recent Giving: $2,752,000 (1993 est.); $2,822,610 (1992); $2,319,191 (1991)
Assets: $1,529,158 (1992); $2,665,690 (1989)
Fiscal Note: Figures include foundation and direct contributions. Total for 1990 includes approximately $1,791,000 in foundation donations. Total for 1991 includes $460,000 in matching gifts.
EIN: 63-0971859

CONTRIBUTIONS SUMMARY

Typical Recipients: • *Arts & Humanities:* arts associations, arts centers, arts festivals, arts funds, arts institutes, community arts, dance, ethnic arts, history/historic preservation, libraries, literary arts, museums/galleries, music, opera, performing arts, public broadcasting, theater, visual arts • *Civic & Public Affairs:* business/free enterprise, economic development, economics, environmental affairs, municipalities, zoos/botanical gardens • *Education:* colleges & universities, economic education, education funds, elementary education, engineering education, literacy, minority education, public education (precollege), science/technology education, special education • *Health:* health organizations, mental health • *Science:* science exhibits & fairs • *Social Services:* aged, animal protection, child welfare, community centers, community service organizations, counseling, delinquency & crime, disabled, drugs & alcohol, emergency relief, food/clothing distribution, recreation & athletics, shelters/homelessness, united funds, youth organizations

Grant Types: capital, department, emergency, employee matching gifts, endowment, fellowship, general support, multiyear/continuing support, project, scholarship, and seed money

Nonmonetary Support Types: donated equipment, donated products, in-kind services, loaned employees, loaned executives, and workplace solicitation

Note: Estimated value of nonmonetary support is unavailable and is not included in above figures.

Geographic Distribution: in states where company has operations

Operating Locations: AL (Birmingham, Calera, Childersburg, Gadsder, Glencoe, Helena, Huntsville, Lacon, Madison, Ohatchee, Russelville, Scottsboro, Trinity, Tuscumbia), GA (Adairsville, Columbus, Dalton, Fairmount, Grayson, Kennesaw, LaGrange, Lithia Springs, Lithonia, Newman, Norcross, Rabun, Red Oak, Stockbridge, Villa Rica), IA (Camanche, Cedar Rapids, Garrison, Mentour, Robbins), IL (Casey, Crystal Lake, Decatur, Fairbury, Joliet, Kankakee, Lemont, McCook-Hodgkins, Momence, Pontiac, Weston), IN (Francesville, Lafayette, Monon, South Bend), KS (Wichita), KY (Brandenburg, Elizabethtown, Fort Knox, Lexington, Stephensburg), LA (Geismar), MI (Iuka), NC (Boone, Charlotte, Concord, East Forsyth, Elkin, Enka, Gold Hill, Henderson, Hendersonville, Morgantown, North Wilkesboro, Rockingham, Smith Grove, Winston-Salem), SC (Blacksburg, Gray Court, Greeneville, Liberty, Lyman, Pacolet), TN (Athens, Bristol, Chattanooga, Clarksville, Cleveland, Dayton, Franklin, Greeneville, Holladay, Kingsport, Knox County, Knoxville, Lebanon, Maryville, Morristown, Nashville, Parsons, Rogersville, Savannah, Sevierville, South Pittsburg, Tazewell, Waverly), TX (Abilene, Boyd, Bridgeport, Brownwood, Denison, Knippa, San Antonio, Uvalde), VA (Danville, Edgerton, Manassas, Occoquan, Richmond, South Boston, Stafford, Warrenton), WI (Milwaukee, Oconomowoc, Oshkosh, Port Edwards, Racine, Sussex)

CORP. OFFICERS

Herbert A. Sklenar: *B* Omaha NE 1931 *ED* Univ NE 1952; Harvard Univ MBA 1954 *CURR EMPL* chmn, pres, ceo, dir: Vulcan Materials Co *CORP AFFIL* dir: Am South Bancorp *NONPR AFFIL* mem: Am Inst CPAs, Delta Sigma Pi, Omicron Delta Kappa, Phi Eta Sigma, Phi Kappa Phi, US Chamber Commerce; trust: AL Symphony Assn, Birmingham Southern Coll, Southern Res Inst; vp bd dirs: YMCA Birmingham

GIVING OFFICERS

Peter J. Clemens III: vp, trust *CURR EMPL* sr vp: Vulcan Materials Co

John A. Heilala: trust

Daniel J. Leemon: trust

Raymond Morrieson Lord: vp, trust *CURR EMPL* sr vp human resources: Vulcan Materials Co *NONPR AFFIL* mem: Am Psychological Assn

Guy K. Mitchell, Jr.: trust

Terry W. Reese: asst treas *B* Huntsville AL 1942 *ED* Univ TN 1970 *CURR EMPL* asst treas & dir taxes: Vulcan Materials Co *NONPR AFFIL* mem: Inst Mgmt Accts, Natl Assn Accts, Tax Executives Inst

Mary S. Russom: secy, treas *CURR EMPL* community affairs rep: Vulcan Materials Co

Herbert A. Sklenar: chmn, trust *CURR EMPL* chmn, pres, ceo, dir: Vulcan Materials Co (see above)

E. Starke Sydnor: pres, trust *CURR EMPL* asst gen counc, dir publ affairs: Vulcan Materials Co

APPLICATION INFORMATION

Initial Approach: *Initial Contact:* letter or proposal to Mary S. Russom *Include Information On:* description of the organization, amount requested, purpose for which funds are sought, recently audited financial statement, proof of tax-exempt status *When to Submit:* any time; applications acted upon throughout the year *Note:* Company does not respond to telephone solicitations.

Restrictions on Giving: Does not give grants to individuals, fraternal organizations, member agencies of united funds, political or lobbying groups, or religious organizations for sectarian purposes; does not support goodwill advertising or dinners or special events.

GRANTS ANALYSIS
Total Grants: $2,822,610
Highest Grant: $133,000
Typical Range: $1,000 to $10,000
Disclosure Period: 1992
Note: Financial information is for foundation only; includes approximately $568,000 in matching gifts. Recent grants are derived from a 1989 grants list.

RECENT GRANTS
85,000 Metropolitan Arts Council, Birmingham, AL
78,333 Birmingham Southern College, Birmingham, AL
75,000 Civic Club Foundation, Birmingham, AL
66,666 University of Alabama, Birmingham, AL
51,500 United Way of Birmingham, Birmingham, AL
30,000 NAPA Education Foundation, Riverdale, MD
30,000 Samford University, Birmingham, AL
30,000 Tuskegee University, Tuskegee, AL
28,000 City Haysville Pride Community, Haysville, KS
25,000 Auburn University, Auburn, AL

W. L. T.
Revenue: $120.0 million
Employees: 2,800
Headquarters: Cleveland, OH
SIC Major Group: Apparel & Other Textile Products, Instruments & Related Products, and Paper & Allied Products

CONTACT
W. L. T.
PO Box 19009
Greensboro, NC 27419
(919) 299-5050

CONTRIBUTIONS SUMMARY
Operating Locations: OH (Cleveland)

CORP. OFFICERS
David J. Gallitano: *CURR EMPL* chmn: Work Wear Corp

OTHER THINGS TO KNOW
Company is an original donor to the Samuel Rosenthal Foundation.

W. W. W. Foundation

CONTACT
Linda J. Blinkenberg
Secretary
W. W. W. Fdn.
1260 Huntington Dr., Ste. 204
South Pasadena, CA 91030
(213) 259-0484

FINANCIAL SUMMARY
Recent Giving: $1,881,130 (fiscal 1991); $1,848,800 (fiscal 1990); $2,610,060 (fiscal 1988)
Assets: $9,578,324 (fiscal year ending July 31, 1991); $8,124,389 (fiscal 1990); $6,017,600 (fiscal 1988)
Gifts Received: $2,532,653 (fiscal 1991); $3,437,273 (fiscal 1990); $2,124,731 (fiscal 1988)
Fiscal Note: In 1991, contributions were received from the Helen W. Woodward Charitable Lead Trust ($2,493,646) and Michael Tennenbaum ($39,005).
EIN: 95-3694741

CONTRIBUTIONS SUMMARY
Donor(s): the late Helen W. Woodward
Typical Recipients: • *Arts & Humanities:* museums/galleries, music • *Education:* education funds, public education (precollege) • *Health:* hospitals • *Social Services:* animal protection, child welfare, delinquency & crime, youth organizations
Grant Types: capital and operating expenses
Geographic Distribution: focus on CA

GIVING OFFICERS
Linda J. Blinkenberg: secy
Marcia W. Constance: vp
Winifred W. Rhodes Bea: pres
Arlo G. Sorensen: cfo

APPLICATION INFORMATION
Initial Approach: Contributes only to preselected organizations.

GRANTS ANALYSIS
Number of Grants: 18
Highest Grant: $1,450,000
Typical Range: $5,000 to $20,000
Disclosure Period: fiscal year ending July 31, 1991

RECENT GRANTS
1,450,000 Helen Woodward Animal Care Center, Rancho Santa Fe, CA
200,000 Scripps Memorial Hospital Foundation, La Jolla, CA
46,200 Boys and Girls Club, Los Angeles, CA
40,000 Children Now, Los Angeles, CA
20,000 National Gallery of Art, Washington, DC
20,000 National Gallery of Art, Washington, DC
20,000 Ronald McDonald House, San Francisco, CA
20,000 Ronald McDonald House, San Francisco, CA
10,600 Youth Enrichment Adventures, Georgetown, SC
10,000 Charleston Symphony Orchestra, Charleston, SC

Wachovia Bank of Georgia, N.A. / Wachovia Foundation of Geaorgia
Former Foundation Name: First Atlanta Foundation
Parent Company: Wachovia Corp.
Assets: $33.36 billion
Parent Employees: 16,164
Headquarters: Atlanta, GA
SIC Major Group: Depository Institutions, Holding & Other Investment Offices, Insurance Agents, Brokers & Service, and Nondepository Institutions

CONTACT
William K. Hohlstein
Wachovia Bank of Georgia, N.A.
PO Box 4148, MC: 415
Atlanta, GA 30302
(404) 332-6439

FINANCIAL SUMMARY
Recent Giving: $1,200,000 (1992 approx.); $850,000 (1991 approx.); $1,042,082 (1990)
Assets: $7,200,000 (1992); $6,795,694 (1990); $6,520,261 (1989)
Gifts Received: $965,000 (1990)
Fiscal Note: Company also has a direct giving program, but did not disclose amount given. The contact for direct gifts is Ann Morris, Manager Public Affairs, at the above address. See also Wachovia Bank and Trust Co., N.A.
EIN: 58-1274979

CONTRIBUTIONS SUMMARY
Typical Recipients: • *Arts & Humanities:* arts centers, public broadcasting • *Civic & Public Affairs:* economic development, housing • *Education:* colleges & universities, community & junior colleges, literacy • *Health:* hospitals • *Social Services:* community service organizations, shelters/homelessness, united funds, youth organizations
Grant Types: capital, employee matching gifts, and project
Nonmonetary Support Types: donated equipment
Note: Value of nonmonetary support is not available, but is included in figures above. Contact for nonmonetary support is Lydia Batchelor.
Geographic Distribution: near operating locations in Georgia only
Operating Locations: GA (Americus, Atlanta, Augusta, Cartersville, Dalton, Gainesville, Macon, Savannah)

CORP. OFFICERS
Thomas E. Boland: *B* Columbus GA 1934 *ED* GA St Univ 1957 *CURR EMPL* chmn, dir: Wachovia Bank GA *CORP AFFIL* chmn: First Natl Bank Atlanta; dir: Atlanta Exec Svcs Corp, First Atlanta Leasing, First Natl Bldg Corp, Minbanc Capital Corp, Visa USA, Wachovia Auto Leasing Co GA; exec vp: First Wachovia Corp;

vp: First Atlanta Intl Corp *NONPR AFFIL* mem: Am Bankers Assn, Christian Life Comm, GA St Univ Alumni Assn, GA St Univ Fdn; rep natl counc: Boy Scouts Am; treas: GA Baptist Fdn; trust: Scottish Rite Children's Med Ctr, Robert W Woodruff Arts Ctr; trustres counc: Mercer Univ; mem: Southern Baptist Convention
Joseph Prendergast: *CURR EMPL* pres, dir: Wachovia Bank GA

GIVING OFFICERS
George W. P. Atkins, Jr.: treas, dir *B* Birmingham AL 1938 *ED* Vanderbilt Univ 1960 *CURR EMPL* exec vp, trust: Wachovia Bank Georgia
Beverly Blake: secy
Thomas E. Boland: dir *CURR EMPL* chmn, dir: Wachovia Bank GA (see above)
Ann Morris: contact *CURR EMPL* mgr (publ affairs): Wachovia Bank GA

APPLICATION INFORMATION
Initial Approach: *Initial Contact:* brief letter or proposal not to exceed two pages *Include Information On:* grant amount requested, background on organization and its needs and resources, copy of IRS determination letter, financial information, list of board members, and any other important information *When to Submit:* should be received at least 30 days before board meeting
Restrictions on Giving: Does not contribute to dinners or special events, fraternal organizations, goodwill advertising, individuals, political or lobbying groups, or religious organizations for sectarian purposes.

OTHER THINGS TO KNOW
Sponsoring company name changed from First Atlanta Corp. in 1991; foundation name changed from First Atlanta Foundation.

GRANTS ANALYSIS
Total Grants: $1,200,000
Number of Grants: 20*
Highest Grant: $577,000
Typical Range: $1,000 to $10,000
Disclosure Period: 1992
Note: Total grants figure includes matching gifts to educational and cultural programs. Number of grants exclude

matching gifts. Average grant figure supplied by foundation. Recent grants are derived from a 1990 Form 990.

RECENT GRANTS
482,000 United Way, Atlanta, GA — 89/90 pledge
100,000 Robert W. Woodruff Arts Center, Atlanta, GA — general support
75,000 Georgia Amateur Athletics Foundation, Atlanta, GA — 1996 summer olympics
50,000 Atlanta Chamber of Commerce, Atlanta, GA — final payment on a $150,000 pledge for the forward Atlanta campaign that began in 1986
50,000 Georgia Amateur Athletics Foundation, Atlanta, GA — final payment on a $150,000 pledge for the 1996 olympics
18,000 United Way of Northwest Georgia, Atlanta, GA — 1990 pledge
10,000 Boy Scouts of America, Savannah, GA — 3rd installment on capital campaign pledge of $45,000
10,000 Camp Best Friends 1990, Atlanta, GA — supporting camp best friends
10,000 Georgia Baptist Medical Center, Atlanta, GA — charitable contribution
6,000 United Way of Hall County, Gainesville, GA — 1990 pledge

---

Wachovia Bank & Trust Co., N.A. / Wachovia Foundation
Parent Company: Wachovia Corp.
Assets: $33.36 billion
Parent Employees: 16,164
Headquarters: Winston-Salem, NC
SIC Major Group: Depository Institutions

CONTACT
L. M. Baker, Jr.
President & Chief Executive Officer
Wachovia Bank & Trust Co., N.A.
PO Box 3099
Winston-Salem, NC 27150
(919) 770-5976

FINANCIAL SUMMARY
Recent Giving: $1,799,506 (1991); $3,470,000 (1990); $4,300,000 (1989)
Assets: $8,937,180 (1991); $7,000,000 (1990); $5,710,021 (1989)
Fiscal Note: All contributions are made by the bank or its holding company, Wachovia Corporation, but they pass through the Wachovia Foundation. Company stresses that the bank and the company are the only decision-making bodies; foundation is merely the funding vehicle. See also Wachovia Bank of Georgia, N.A.
EIN: 58-1485946

CONTRIBUTIONS SUMMARY
Typical Recipients: • *Arts & Humanities:* arts associations, arts centers, arts festivals, arts funds, community arts, dance, history/historic preservation, libraries, museums/galleries, opera, performing arts, public broadcasting • *Civic & Public Affairs:* better government, business/free enterprise, civil rights, economic development, environmental affairs, professional & trade associations, urban & community affairs, women's affairs, zoos/botanical gardens • *Education:* agricultural education, business education, career/vocational education, colleges & universities, community & junior colleges, economic education, education funds, elementary education • *Health:* health funds, health organizations, hospices, hospitals • *International:* international organizations • *Social Services:* child welfare, community centers, community service organizations, day care, delinquency & crime, drugs & alcohol, family planning, food/clothing distribution, recreation & athletics, united funds, youth organizations
Grant Types: capital, challenge, employee matching gifts, endowment, and general support

Nonmonetary Support Types: loaned executives
Note: Estimated value of nonmonetary support is $100,000, which is not included in figures above. Contact local bank office for nonmonetary support.
Geographic Distribution: exclusively in the state of North Carolina
Operating Locations: NC (Ahoskie, Andrews, Asheboro, Asheville, Aurora, Bayboro, Belhaven, Belmont, Bethel, Burlington, Chapel Hill, Charlotte, Durham, Eden, Elizabeth City, Elizabethtown, Fayetteville, Gastonia, Goldsboro, Greensboro, Greenville, Hendersonville, Hickory, High Point, Jacksonville, Kernersville, Kinston, Laurinburg, Lumberton, Marshall, Morehead, Morgantown, Murphy, New Bern, Raleigh, Reidsville, Robersonville, Rocky Mount, Salisbury, Statesville, Thomasville, Vanceboro, Washington, Williamston, Wilmington, Winston-Salem)
Note: Company operates in 87 communities in North Carolina.

CORP. OFFICERS
Leslie Mayo Baker, Jr.: *B* Brunswick MD 1942 *ED* Univ Richmond BA 1964; Univ VA MBA 1969 *CURR EMPL* pres: Wachovia Bank & Trust Co *CORP AFFIL* exec vp: Wachovia Corp; sr assoc: Robert Morris Assocs; trust: Piedmont Craftsmen *NONPR AFFIL* mem: Salvation Army Boys Club Counc
Anthony Lloyd Furr: *B* Albemarle NC 1944 *ED* Univ NC 1968; Am Grad Sch Intl Mgmt 1969 *CURR EMPL* cfo, exec vp: Wachovia Corp *CORP AFFIL* dir: Wachovia Intl Banking Corp *NONPR AFFIL* pres, mem exec comm, dir: Bankers Assn Foreign Trade
John Grimes Medlin, Jr.: *B* Benson NC 1933 *ED* Univ NC BSBA 1956 *CURR EMPL* chmn, dir: Wachovia Bank & Trust Co *CORP AFFIL* chmn: First Atlanta Corp, First Natl Bank Atlanta, Wachovia Bank GA, Wachovia Bank NC, Wachovia Corp GA, Wachovia Corp NC; chmn, pres, ceo, dir: Wachovia Corp; dir: Bell South Corp, First Wachovia Corp, Natl Svc Indus, Piedmont Aviation, RJR Nabisco, SC Natl Corp, USAir Group *NONPR AFFIL* dir: Ed Fdn, Kenan Inst Pvt Enterprise, NC Bus Counc

Mgmt & Devel; mem: Am
Bankers Assn, Assn Reserve
City Bankers, Order Holy
Grail, Order Old Well, Phi
Delta Theta; trust: Conference
Bd, Natl Humanities Ctr, Res
Triangle Fdn, Salem Academy
Coll, Wake Forest Univ

GIVING OFFICERS

Leslie Mayo Baker, Jr.: *CURR EMPL* pres: Wachovia Bank & Trust Co (see above)
John Grimes Medlin, Jr.: *CURR EMPL* chmn, dir: Wachovia Bank & Trust Co (see above)

APPLICATION INFORMATION

Initial Approach: *Initial Contact:* requests should be sent to officer in charge of nearest branch bank *Include Information On:* description of the organization, amount requested, purpose for which funds are sought, recently audited financial statement, proof of tax-exempt status, list of contributors *When to Submit:* any time
Restrictions on Giving: Does not support individuals, political or lobbying groups, good will advertising, or religious organizations for sectarian purposes.

GRANTS ANALYSIS

Total Grants: $1,799,506
Number of Grants: 147
Highest Grant: $100,000
Typical Range: $1,000 to $20,000
Disclosure Period: 1991
Note: Recent grants are derived from a 1991 Form 990.

RECENT GRANTS

100,000 American Red Cross Gulf Crisis Fund
100,000 North Carolina State University, Raleigh, NC
75,000 St. Augustine's College, Raleigh, NC
65,000 Arts Council
56,200 Winston-Salem Business and Technology Center, Winston-Salem, NC
50,000 Crosby Fund-Winston-Salem Foundation, Winston-Salem, NC
45,000 Independent College Fund of North Carolina, Winston-Salem, NC
37,500 North Carolina Association of Community Develop-

ment Corporation, NC
30,000 Pack Place Education Arts and Science Center, Asheville, NC
30,000 Technical College of Alamance Foundation

Wachtell, Lipton, Rosen & Katz / Wachtell, Lipton, Rosen & Katz Foundation

Sales: $110.0 million
Employees: 145
Headquarters: New York, NY
SIC Major Group: Legal Services

CONTACT

Hilary Rappaport
Vice President, Secretary
Wachtell, Lipton, Rosen & Katz Fdn.
299 Park Ave.
New York, NY 10171
(212) 371-9200
Note: Foundation does not accept unsolicited requests for funds.

FINANCIAL SUMMARY

Recent Giving: $1,550,000 (fiscal 1991); $4,899,564 (fiscal 1989); $2,478,907 (fiscal 1988)
Assets: $6,329,503 (fiscal year ending September 30, 1991); $6,845,767 (fiscal 1989)
Fiscal Note: Company gives through foundation only.
EIN: 13-3099901

CONTRIBUTIONS SUMMARY

Typical Recipients: • *Civic & Public Affairs:* ethnic/minority organizations, philanthropic organizations • *Education:* business education, colleges & universities • *Social Services:* religious welfare, united funds
Grant Types: general support
Geographic Distribution: primarily in metropolitan New York City
Operating Locations: NY (New York)

CORP. OFFICERS

Martin Lipton: *B* NJ 1931 *ED* Univ PA BS 1952; NY Univ LLB 1955 *CURR EMPL* ptnr: Wachtell Lipton Rosen & Katz *NONPR AFFIL* mem counc: Am Law Inst; pres, bd trust: NY Univ Law Sch; pres bd trusts: Law Ctr Fdn; treas: Inst

Judicial Admin; trust: NY Univ, Univ PA
Leonard M. Rosen: *CURR EMPL* ptnr: Wachtell Lipton Rosen & Katz
Herbert M. Wachtell: *CURR EMPL* ptnr: Wachtell Lipton Rosen & Katz

GIVING OFFICERS

Peter C. Canellos: asst vp
David M. Einhorn: asst vp
Martin Lipton: pres *CURR EMPL* ptnr: Wachtell Lipton Rosen & Katz (see above)
Hilary Rappaport: vp, secy
Herbert M. Wachtell: vp, treas *CURR EMPL* ptnr: Wachtell Lipton Rosen & Katz (see above)

APPLICATION INFORMATION

Initial Approach: *Initial Contact:* foundation does not accept unsolicited requests for funds
Restrictions on Giving: Foundation does not accept unsolicited requests for funds.

GRANTS ANALYSIS

Total Grants: $1,550,000
Number of Grants: 2
Highest Grant: $1,500,000
Disclosure Period: fiscal year ending September 30, 1991
Note: Recent grants are derived from a fiscal 1991 Form 990.

RECENT GRANTS

1,500,000 United Jewish Appeal-Federation of Jewish Philanthropies of New York, New York, NY
50,000 Harvard University-Graduate School or Business Administration, Boston, MA

Wade Endowment Fund, Elizabeth Firth

CONTACT

Patricia M. Brouard
Secretary-Treasurer
Elizabeth Firth Wade Endowment Fund
114 East De la Guerra St., No. 7
Santa Barbara, CA 93101
(805) 963-8822

FINANCIAL SUMMARY

Recent Giving: $113,500 (fiscal 1992); $113,306 (fiscal 1991); $87,250 (fiscal 1990)
Assets: $2,836,267 (fiscal year ending January 31, 1992);

$2,703,498 (fiscal 1991); $2,769,070 (fiscal 1990)
EIN: 95-3610694

CONTRIBUTIONS SUMMARY

Donor(s): the late Elizabeth Firth Wade
Typical Recipients: • *Arts & Humanities:* dance, performing arts • *Civic & Public Affairs:* zoos/botanical gardens • *Education:* private education (precollege) • *Social Services:* child welfare, community centers, community service organizations, family services, youth organizations
Grant Types: general support

GIVING OFFICERS

Steven M. Anders: vp
Patricia M. Brouard: secy, treas
Arthur R. Gaudi: pres

APPLICATION INFORMATION

Initial Approach: Send brief letter of inquiry describing program. There are no deadlines.

GRANTS ANALYSIS

Number of Grants: 14
Highest Grant: $20,000
Typical Range: $1,000 to $11,250
Disclosure Period: fiscal year ending January 31, 1992

RECENT GRANTS

20,000 Santa Barbara Contemporary Arts, Santa Barbara, CA
15,000 Ballet Theatre Foundation, New York, NY
11,250 Joseph H. Firth Youth Center, Phillipsburg, NJ
11,250 Joseph H. Firth Youth Center, Phillipsburg, NJ
11,250 Joseph H. Firth Youth Center, Phillipsburg, NJ
11,250 Joseph H. Firth Youth Center, Phillipsburg, NJ
10,000 Bishop Garcia Diego High School, Santa Barbara, CA
10,000 Santa Barbara County Vietnam Veterans, Santa Barbara, CA
5,000 City of Santa Barbara Rose Garden, Santa Barbara, CA
5,000 Joffrey Ballet, New York, NY

Waffle House, Inc. / Waffle House Foundation

Sales: $220.0 million
Employees: 6,200
Headquarters: Norcross, GA
SIC Major Group: Eating & Drinking Places and Holding & Other Investment Offices

CONTACT

Alice Johnson
President
Waffle House Foundation
PO Box 6450
Norcross, GA 30091
(404) 729-5700

FINANCIAL SUMMARY

Recent Giving: $242,315 (1990)
Assets: $151,630 (1989)
Gifts Received: $250,000 (1989)
Fiscal Note: In 1989, contributions were received from Waffle House, Inc.
EIN: 58-1477023

CONTRIBUTIONS SUMMARY

Typical Recipients: • *Social Services:* community service organizations, domestic violence, food/clothing distribution, youth organizations
Grant Types: project and scholarship
Geographic Distribution: focus on GA
Operating Locations: GA (Norcross)

CORP. OFFICERS

Thomas F. Forkner: *CURR EMPL* vchmn: Waffle House
Joe W. Rogers, Jr.: *CURR EMPL* pres: Waffle House
Joe W. Rogers, Sr.: *CURR EMPL* chmn: Waffle House

GIVING OFFICERS

Alice Johnson: pres
Roy Nelson: secy

APPLICATION INFORMATION

Initial Approach: Send brief letter including a description of the organization, amount requested, purpose of funds sought, audited financial statement, and proof of tax-exempt status. The deadline for college scholarship application is April 1.
Restrictions on Giving: Does not support individuals, religious organizations for sectarian purposes, political or lobbying groups, or organizations outside of Georgia.

GRANTS ANALYSIS

Number of Grants: 70
Highest Grant: $25,000
Typical Range: $100 to $1,000
Disclosure Period: 1990

RECENT GRANTS

25,000 Georgia Tech, Atlanta, GA — Love Chair
25,000 Georgia Tech Foundation, Atlanta, GA
20,000 CURE, Atlanta, GA — Emory Leukemia Research
10,000 Exodus/Cities in Schools, Atlanta, GA
10,000 Georgia Baptist Hospital, Atlanta, GA
8,643 Georgia Council on Child Abuse, Atlanta, GA
7,500 Feed the Hungry, Atlanta, GA
5,000 Atlanta Hospital Hospitality House, Atlanta, GA
5,000 Woodruff Arts Center, Atlanta, GA
5,000 YMCA, Atlanta, GA

Waggoner Charitable Trust, Crystelle

CONTACT

Darlene Mann
Vice President
Crystelle Waggoner Charitable Trust
c/o NCNB Texas National Bank
PO Box 1317
Ft. Worth, TX 76101
(817) 390-6114

FINANCIAL SUMMARY

Recent Giving: $412,070 (fiscal 1991); $315,485 (fiscal 1990); $286,224 (fiscal 1989)
Assets: $4,948,723 (fiscal year ending June 30, 1991); $4,796,321 (fiscal 1990); $4,564,302 (fiscal 1989)
EIN: 75-1881219

CONTRIBUTIONS SUMMARY

Donor(s): the late Crystelle Waggoner
Typical Recipients: • *Arts & Humanities:* arts associations, music, opera • *Civic & Public Affairs:* urban & community affairs • *Education:* colleges & universities • *Health:* health organizations, hospitals, medical research, single-disease health associations • *Religion:* churches • *Social Services:* aged, child welfare, community service organizations, disabled, domestic violence, food/clothing distribution, shelters/homelessness, united funds, youth organizations
Grant Types: capital, emergency, endowment, general support, multiyear/continuing support, operating expenses, professorship, project, research, scholarship, and seed money
Geographic Distribution: limited to TX, especially Fort Worth and Decatur

APPLICATION INFORMATION

Initial Approach: Send brief letter of inquiry describing program or project. Deadlines are March 31, June 30, September 30, and December 31. Board meets in January, April, July, and October. Decisions are made within six months.
Restrictions on Giving: Does not support individuals, or provide funds for challenge grants, consulting services, deficit financing, loans or conferences.

OTHER THINGS TO KNOW

Publications: Annual Report (including Application Guidelines)

GRANTS ANALYSIS

Number of Grants: 41
Highest Grant: $20,000
Typical Range: $500 to $10,000
Disclosure Period: fiscal year ending June 30, 1991

RECENT GRANTS

20,000 YWCA, Ft. Worth, TX
15,000 Child Study Center, Ft. Worth, TX
13,000 Arts Council of Fort Worth and Tarrant County, Ft. Worth, TX
11,000 Forth Worth Opera, Ft. Worth, TX
11,000 Planned Parenthood Federation of America, Ft. Worth, TX
11,000 YMCA, Ft. Worth, TX
10,500 Texas Boys Choir, Ft. Worth, TX
10,000 Hill School of Fort Worth, Ft. Worth, TX
10,000 Jewel Charity Ball, Ft. Worth, TX
10,000 Meals on Wheels, Ft. Worth, TX

Waggoner Foundation, E. Paul and Helen Buck

CONTACT

Gene W. Willingham
Director
E. Paul and Helen Buck Waggoner Fdn.
PO Box 2130
Vernon, TX 76384
(817) 552-2521

FINANCIAL SUMMARY

Recent Giving: $294,582 (fiscal 1992); $250,779 (fiscal 1991); $294,256 (fiscal 1990)
Assets: $6,375,241 (fiscal year ending April 30, 1992); $6,215,230 (fiscal 1991); $5,868,189 (fiscal 1990)
EIN: 75-1243683

CONTRIBUTIONS SUMMARY

Donor(s): the late E. Paul Waggoner, the late Helen Buck Waggoner
Typical Recipients: • *Arts & Humanities:* history/historic preservation, museums/galleries • *Civic & Public Affairs:* environmental affairs, municipalities • *Education:* agricultural education, colleges & universities, private education (precollege), religious education • *Health:* medical research, pediatric health, single-disease health associations • *Social Services:* community service organizations, homes, united funds, youth organizations
Grant Types: capital, research, and scholarship
Geographic Distribution: focus on TX

GIVING OFFICERS

Electra Waggoner Biggs: pres *B* Ft Worth TX 1916 *ED* TX Womens Christian Univ; Columbia Univ
Gene W. Willingham: dir
Helen Biggs Willingham: secy, treas
Charles F. Winston: dir
Elecra Biggs Winston: 1st vp, dir

APPLICATION INFORMATION

Initial Approach: Send cover letter and full proposal. There are no deadlines.

GRANTS ANALYSIS

Number of Grants: 10
Highest Grant: $200,000
Typical Range: $1,000 to $15,000
Disclosure Period: fiscal year ending April 30, 1992

RECENT GRANTS

200,000 Texas Christian University, Ft. Worth, TX
50,000 Texas A&M University, Vernon, TX
15,000 Midwestern State University, Wichita Falls, TX
8,745 Red River Valley Museum, Vernon, TX
7,000 Boys and Girls Club, Vernon, TX
5,000 Vernon Regional Junior College, Vernon, TX
5,000 Wilbarger County Welfare, Vernon, TX
1,837 Boys Club of America, Vernon, TX
1,000 City of Vernon, Vernon, TX
1,000 Masonic Home and School, Ft. Worth, TX

Wagnalls Memorial

CONTACT
Jerry W. Neff
Director
Wagnalls Memorial
150 East Columbus St.
Lithopolis, OH 43136
(614) 837-4765

FINANCIAL SUMMARY
Recent Giving: $244,100 (fiscal 1991); $253,900 (fiscal 1990); $255,767 (fiscal 1989)
Assets: $17,282,226 (fiscal year ending August 31, 1991); $15,989,705 (fiscal 1990); $16,874,285 (fiscal 1989)
EIN: 31-4379589

CONTRIBUTIONS SUMMARY

Donor(s): The foundation was incorporated in 1924 by the late Mabel Wagnalls Jones.
Typical Recipients: *Civic & Public Affairs:* urban & community affairs • *Education:* student aid
Grant Types: fellowship, matching, and scholarship
Geographic Distribution: limited to the Bloom Township in Fairfield County, OH, area

GIVING OFFICERS
George W. Boving: vchmn
Bonnie S. Butterbaugh: exec secy
Benjamin C. Humphrey: trust
Jerry W. Neff: exec dir
Robert L. Rager: chmn
Jerry A. Solt: trust
Dwayne R. Spence: secy, treas
John Watkins: trust
Edwin Wisner: trust

APPLICATION INFORMATION
Initial Approach:
The foundation requests scholarship applicants contact the foundation and meet with the director to obtain a formal application.
Applications for scholarship benefits are accepted between March 1 and May 15.
Restrictions on Giving: Scholarships and grants are made to residents and organizations in Bloom Township, OH.

OTHER THINGS TO KNOW
Publications: annual report, newsletter, biennial report, application guidelines, and informational brochure

GRANTS ANALYSIS
Total Grants: $244,100
Number of Grants: 2*
Highest Grant: $12,956
Disclosure Period: fiscal year ending August 31, 1991
Note: In fiscal 1991, scholarships totaled $228,144. Number of grants figure represents non-scholarships grants.

RECENT GRANTS
12,956 Lithapolis Community Projects, Lithapolis, OH — general support
3,000 Lithapolis Cemetery, Lithapolis, OH — operating funds

Wagner and George Hosser Scholarship Fund Trust, Edward

CONTACT
Suzette Fontaine Collins
Trust Administrator
Edward Wagner and George Hosser Scholarship Fund Trust
c/o Amoskeag Bank
875 Elm St.
Manchester, NH 03105
(603) 647-3614

FINANCIAL SUMMARY
Recent Giving: $157,300 (1990); $142,466 (1989)
Assets: $4,386,279 (1990); $3,968,184 (1989)
EIN: 02-6005491

CONTRIBUTIONS SUMMARY
Donor(s): the late Ottilie Wagner Hosser
Grant Types: scholarship
Geographic Distribution: limited to residents of Manchester, NH

APPLICATION INFORMATION
Initial Approach: Contact foundation for application. Deadline is April 30.

OTHER THINGS TO KNOW
Provides scholarship grants for college or professional education to worthy young men.

Wagner Foundation, Ltd., R. H.

CONTACT
Paul B. Edwards
Trustee
R. H. Wagner Fdn., Ltd.
441 Milwaukee Ave.
Burlington, WI 53105
(414) 763-7616

FINANCIAL SUMMARY
Recent Giving: $198,512 (fiscal 1991); $72,779 (fiscal 1989)
Assets: $4,596,684 (fiscal year ending June 30, 1991); $4,090,314 (fiscal 1989)
Gifts Received: $74,528 (fiscal 1991)
Fiscal Note: $198,512
EIN: 39-1311452

CONTRIBUTIONS SUMMARY
Donor(s): Richard H. Wagner, Roberta Wagner
Typical Recipients: • *Arts & Humanities:* history/historic preservation, public broadcasting • *Civic & Public Affairs:* professional & trade associations • *Education:* science/technology education • *Health:* hospitals, pediatric health • *International:* international development/relief, international health care, international organizations • *Religion:* religious organizations • *Social Services:* child welfare, food/clothing distribution, shelters/homelessness
Grant Types: operating expenses and scholarship

GIVING OFFICERS
Paul B. Edwards: trust
Richard H. Wagner: trust
Roberta Wagner: secy, treas

APPLICATION INFORMATION
Initial Approach: Send brief letter of inquiry describing program or project. There are no deadlines.

GRANTS ANALYSIS
Number of Grants: 32
Highest Grant: $53,282
Typical Range: $1,000 to $2,500
Disclosure Period: fiscal year ending June 30, 1991

RECENT GRANTS
53,282 Belize
24,226 Hogar De Fatima Orphanage
24,000 Rotary International
20,000 Brother Norman Memorial Fund
16,657 Sim Air
14,818 Food for Africa
8,652 Father Gould Fund
6,500 Amanda the Panda, Milwaukee, WI
4,200 Bolivia Medical Clinic
2,500 Children's Hospital Medical Center, Milwaukee, WI

Wagner Manufacturing Co., E. R. / Wagner Manufacturing Co. Foundation, E. R.

Sales: $44.0 million
Employees: 375
Headquarters: Milwaukee, WI
SIC Major Group: Electronic &
Other Electrical Equipment,
Fabricated Metal Products, and
Primary Metal Industries

CONTACT

Robert S. Wagner
Chairman
E.R. Wagner Manufacturing Co.
  Foundation
4611 North 32nd St.
Milwaukee, WI 53209-6023
(414) 871-5080

FINANCIAL SUMMARY

Recent Giving: $45,000
(1992); $43,850 (1989)
Assets: $485,113 (1989)
EIN: 39-6037097

CONTRIBUTIONS SUMMARY

Typical Recipients: • *Arts & Humanities:* community arts • *Education:* colleges & universities • *Health:* hospitals, medical research, single-disease health associations • *Social Services:* community service organizations, homes, united funds, youth organizations
Grant Types: general support
Geographic Distribution: focus on Milwaukee, WI
Operating Locations: WI (Milwaukee)

CORP. OFFICERS

Frank M. Sterner: *B* Lafayette IN 1935 *ED* Purdue Univ 1958; Purdue Univ 1962 *CURR EMPL* vchmn, ceo: ER Wagner Mfg Co
Robert S. Wagner: *B* Milwaukee WI 1908 *ED* Dartmouth Coll 1931 *CURR EMPL* chmn: ER Wagner Mfg Co

GIVING OFFICERS

Marna W. Fullerton: dir
Cynthia W. Kahler: dir
Bernard S. Kubale: vp, secy, dir
Robert S. Wagner: pres, dir *CURR EMPL* chmn: ER Wagner Mfg Co (see above)

APPLICATION INFORMATION

Initial Approach: Send a brief letter of inquiry. Include a description of organization, amount requested, purpose of funds sought, recently audited financial statement, and proof of tax-exempt status. There are no deadlines.

GRANTS ANALYSIS

Number of Grants: 41
Highest Grant: $8,500
Typical Range: $1,000 to $5,000
Disclosure Period: 1992

RECENT GRANTS

8,500 United Way, Milwaukee, WI
8,000 Children's Hospital of Wisconsin, Milwaukee, WI
5,000 MSOE Milwaukee School of Engineering, Milwaukee, WI
4,000 Milwaukee Repertory Theater, Milwaukee, WI
4,000 Neighborhood House of Milwaukee, Milwaukee, WI
2,000 Nashotah House, Nashotah, WI
1,200 Milwaukee Art Museum, Milwaukee, WI
1,200 Whitefish Bay, Milwaukee, WI
1,000 Cardinal Stritch Jubilee, Milwaukee, WI
1,000 Neighborhood House of Milwaukee, Milwaukee, WI

Wahlert Foundation

CONTACT

Robert H. Wahlert
President and Treasurer
Wahlert Fdn.
701 East 16th St.
Dubuque, IA 52001
(319) 588-5400

FINANCIAL SUMMARY

Recent Giving: $314,500 (fiscal 1991); $308,250 (fiscal 1990); $304,916 (fiscal 1989)
Assets: $4,375,613 (fiscal year ending November 30, 1991); $3,776,121 (fiscal 1990); $4,052,257 (fiscal 1989)
Gifts Received: $3,015 (fiscal 1991); $2,985 (fiscal 1990); $2,965 (fiscal 1989)

Fiscal Note: In 1991, contributions were received from McGladrey and Pullen.
EIN: 42-6051124

CONTRIBUTIONS SUMMARY

Donor(s): Dubuque Packing Co., FDL Foods, Inc., the late H.W. Wahlert, and officers of the foundation
Typical Recipients: • *Arts & Humanities:* history/historic preservation • *Education:* colleges & universities, education funds, public education (precollege), religious education • *Health:* health funds • *Religion:* religious organizations • *Social Services:* aged, community service organizations, religious welfare, shelters/homelessness, united funds, youth organizations
Grant Types: general support and scholarship
Geographic Distribution: focus on Dubuque, IA

GIVING OFFICERS

Al E. Hughes: secy, trust
A. J. Kisting: trust
Donald Strausse: trust
David Wahlert: trust
Donna Wahlert: trust
Jim Wahlert: trust
R. C. Wahlert: trust
R. C. Wahlert III: trust
Robert H. Wahlert: pres, treas, trust *B* Dubuque IA 1939 *ED* Univ IA 1961 *CURR EMPL* ceo, pres: FDL Foods *CORP AFFIL* chmn, dir: FDL Foods; dir: Banks IA, Edelcar, Key City Bank & Trust Co, Rigid-Pak

APPLICATION INFORMATION

Initial Approach: Contributes only to preselected organizations; does not accept unsolicited applications for funds.

GRANTS ANALYSIS

Number of Grants: 22
Highest Grant: $240,500
Typical Range: $1,000 to $3,000
Disclosure Period: fiscal year ending November 30, 1991

RECENT GRANTS

240,500 Wahlert High School, Dubuque, IA
14,000 Dubuque County Historical Society, Dubuque, IA
12,000 Stonehill Care Center, Dubuque, IA
7,500 Catholic Charities, Dubuque, IA
7,500 Dubuque Rescue Mission, Dubuque, IA
5,000 Visiting Nurse Association, Dubuque, IA
5,000 Wartburg Seminary, Dubuque, IA
2,500 Finley Health Foundation, Dubuque, IA
2,500 Iowa Scholarship Fund, Dubuque, IA
2,500 Mercy Health Center, Dubuque, IA

Wahlstrom Foundation

CONTACT

Eleonora W. McCabe
President
Wahlstrom Fdn.
PO Box 3276
Vero Beach, FL 32963
(407) 231-0373

FINANCIAL SUMMARY

Recent Giving: $218,792 (1990); $232,500 (1989); $223,220 (1988)
Assets: $5,310,291 (1990); $5,382,381 (1989); $4,833,836 (1988)
EIN: 06-6053378

CONTRIBUTIONS SUMMARY

Donor(s): the late Magnus Wahlstrom
Typical Recipients: • *Arts & Humanities:* arts centers, community arts, museums/galleries, theater • *Civic & Public Affairs:* municipalities • *Education:* colleges & universities, literacy • *Health:* hospitals, nursing services • *Religion:* churches • *Social Services:* shelters/homelessness
Grant Types: capital, endowment, multiyear/continuing support, project, research, scholarship, and seed money
Geographic Distribution: focus on Indian River County, FL, and CT

GIVING OFFICERS

Lois J. Hughes: vp, secy, dir
Bruce R. Johnson: vp, dir
Eleanora W. McCabe: pres, treas, dir

APPLICATION INFORMATION

Initial Approach: Send letter requesting application form.

Deadlines are May 1 and October 1.

Restrictions on Giving: Does not support individuals or provide funds for fellowships or operating budgets.

OTHER THINGS TO KNOW

Publications: Application Guidelines

GRANTS ANALYSIS

Number of Grants: 21
Highest Grant: $75,000
Typical Range: $1,000 to $5,000
Disclosure Period: 1990

RECENT GRANTS

75,000 Riverside Youth Playhouse, Vero Beach, FL — to provide support in the establishment of a home for the Riverside Children's Theatre

64,100 Bridgeport Area Foundation, Bridgeport, CT — to establish the Magnus Wahlstrom Leadership award fund

30,592 Center for the Arts, Vero Beach, FL — to support development activities and to provide a video film to be used as a development tool

20,000 Environmental Learning Center, Vero Beach, FL — to provide support in the establishment of a learning facility designed to create an informed electorate regarding environmental issues

7,500 Indian River Memorial Hospital, Vero Beach, FL — to provide opportunities for continuing education to nurses

6,750 Saratoga Performing Arts Center, Saratoga, NY — to support endowment and operating funds

1,000 Bridgeport Hospital Foundation, Bridgeport, CT — operational support for pastoral care

1,000 Citizens Scholarship Fund, Vero Beach, FL — scholarship support

1,000 Corporation of Yaddo, Saratoga Springs, NY — operational support

1,000 Friends of Riverside Theatre, Vero Beach, FL — operational support

Wal-Mart Stores / Wal-Mart Foundation

Sales: $55.48 billion
Employees: 425,000
Headquarters: Bentonville, AR
SIC Major Group: General Merchandise Stores

CONTACT

Ginger Cowherd
Assistant Director
Wal-Mart Fdn.
702 SW Eighth St.
Bentonville, AR 72716-8071
(501) 273-4000
Note: Company does not accept requests for direct contributions.

FINANCIAL SUMMARY

Recent Giving: $10,312,301 (fiscal 1992); $10,000,000 (fiscal 1991 approx.); $11,266,033 (fiscal 1990)
Assets: $15,681,286 (fiscal 1991); $9,332,875 (fiscal 1990); $7,464,586 (fiscal 1989)
Fiscal Note: Company gives through foundation only.
EIN: 71-6107283

CONTRIBUTIONS SUMMARY

Typical Recipients: • *Arts & Humanities:* arts festivals, community arts, dance, history/historic preservation, libraries, museums/galleries, music, public broadcasting, theater • *Civic & Public Affairs:* business/free enterprise, economic development, economics, environmental affairs, law & justice, municipalities, professional & trade associations, public policy, safety, urban & community affairs, women's affairs, zoos/botanical gardens • *Education:* agricultural education, business education, career/vocational education, colleges & universities, continuing education, economic education, education administration, education associations, education funds, elementary education, literacy, medical education, minority education, preschool education, public education (precollege), religious education, science/technology education, special education, student aid • *Health:* emergency/ambu-

lance services, geriatric health, health funds, health organizations, hospices, hospitals, medical rehabilitation, medical research, mental health, nutrition & health maintenance, outpatient health care delivery, pediatric health, public health, single-disease health associations • *Social Services:* aged, animal protection, child welfare, community centers, community service organizations, counseling, disabled, domestic violence, drugs & alcohol, emergency relief, food/clothing distribution, homes, recreation & athletics, religious welfare, shelters/homelessness, united funds, volunteer services, youth organizations
Grant Types: capital, general support, research, and scholarship
Geographic Distribution: in communities where stores are located
Operating Locations: AL, AR (Bentonville, Fayetteville, Ft. Smith, Rogers), AZ, CA, CO, FL, GA, IA, IL, IN, KS, KY, LA, MI, MN, MO, MS, NC, ND, NE, NM, OH, OK, SC, SD, TN, TX, VA, WI, WV, WY
Note: Operates over 1,400 stores in 29 states.

CORP. OFFICERS

David D. Glass: *B* New Liberty MO 1935 *ED* Southwest MO St Univ 1959 *CURR EMPL* pres, ceo, dir: Wal-Mart Stores *CORP AFFIL* dir: Bank Bentonville, Phillips Food Ctrs
Donald G. Soderquist: *B* Chicago IL 1934 *ED* Wheaton Coll BA 1955 *CURR EMPL* vchmn, coo, dir: Wal-Mart Stores *CORP AFFIL* dir: First Natl Bank Rogers AR *NONPR AFFIL* dir: Intl Mass Retail Assn
S. Robson Walton: *B* 1945 *ED* Columbia Univ JD 1969 *CURR EMPL* chmn: Wal-Mart Stores *CORP AFFIL* dir: Acxiom Corp, Cooper Communities; vchmn: North AR Wholesale Co

GIVING OFFICERS

Paul R. Carter: mem *B* Monticello AR 1940 *ED* Univ AR BA 1964 *CURR EMPL* exec vp (fin), cfo: Wal-Mart Stores *NONPR AFFIL* mem: Am Inst CPAs
Thomas Martin Coughlin: mem *B* Cleveland OH 1949 *ED* CA St Univ BS 1972 *CURR EMPL* sr vp (opers): Sams Wholesale Div (Wal-Mart

Stores) *NONPR AFFIL* dir: Students Free Enterprise; mem: Natl Mass Retail Inst
Bill Fields: mem *B* 1949 *CURR EMPL* exec vp (merchandising & sales): Wal-Mart Stores Inc
David D. Glass: trust *CURR EMPL* pres, ceo, dir: Wal-Mart Stores (see above)
Carrie Grammer: asst dir
Joe Hardin: mem *B* Nashville TN 1945 *ED* US Military Academy 1967; North TX St Univ 1972 *CURR EMPL* sr vp (distribution & transportation): Wal-Mart Stores
Bobby Martin: mem *B* Giddeon MO 1948 *ED* TX St Univ 1969 *CURR EMPL* sr vp: Wal-Mart Stores *CORP AFFIL* mem exec bd: I/S Adv Group IBM *NONPR AFFIL* exec dir: Gen Merchandise Adv Counc
Dean Sanders: mem
Thomas P. Seay: mem *B* Little Rock AR 1941 *ED* Univ AR BS 1963; Univ AR MBA 1975 *CURR EMPL* sr vp (real estate & construction): Wal-Mart Stores *NONPR AFFIL* mem adv counc: Univ AR Mktg Dept; trust: Intl Counc Shopping Ctrs
Donald Shinkel: mem
Donald G. Soderquist: trust *CURR EMPL* vchmn, coo, dir: Wal-Mart Stores (see above)
S. Robson Walton: mem *CURR EMPL* chmn: Wal-Mart Stores (see above)
Wesley Wright: mem *CURR EMPL* sr vp (special divs): Wal-Mart Stores

APPLICATION INFORMATION

Initial Approach: *Initial Contact:* brief letter or proposal to foundation; or contact local store for application *Include Information On:* description of the organization, amount requested, purpose for which funds are sought, recently audited financial statement, and proof of tax-exempt status *When to Submit:* any time *Note:* Company does not accept requests for direct grants.

Restrictions on Giving: Wal-Mart Foundation only supports organizations that in some way benefit the communities in which their stores are located.

The foundation does not give grants to individuals except student scholarships.

OTHER THINGS TO KNOW

Wal-Mart Foundation awards one scholarship per year to a graduating high school senior in each of its store communities.

The Wal-Mart "Community Involvement Program" (CIP) allows each store to hold local fundraisers on store premises for qualifying charities and organizations. Qualifying projects are matched up to $2,000. In 1989, distributions through this program totaled over $10.0 million, including funds raised at store level through the help of individual communities.

GRANTS ANALYSIS

Total Grants: $10,312,301
Number of Grants: 1,304
Highest Grant: $1,470,433
Typical Range: $100 to $2,000 and $10,000 to $20,000
Disclosure Period: fiscal year ending January 31, 1992
Note: Recent grants are derived from a fiscal 1992 Form 990. Assets are from 1991.

RECENT GRANTS

1,470,433 Children's Miracle Network, St. Paul, MN

120,000 Students in Free Enterprise, Springfield, MO

106,354 Children's Miracle Network, St. Paul, MN

55,260 Children's Miracle Network, St. Paul, MN

54,000 Texas A&M University, College Station, TX

50,404 Bentonville United Way, Bentonville, AR

43,000 National Future Farmers of America Foundation, Madison, WI

35,000 American Red Cross

31,000 University of North Carolina, Chapel Hill, NC

31,000 University of Texas, Austin, TX

Wal-Mart Stores, Inc. / Walton Foundation

Sales: $43.88 billion
Employees: 371,000
Headquarters: Bentonville, AR
SIC Major Group: Food Stores and General Merchandise Stores

CONTACT

Jan Ney
Walton Fdn.
125 West Central 210
Bentonville, AR 72712
(501) 273-5743
Note: Address for scholarship program for employees' children: Walton Scholarship Program, c/o Wal-Mart Stores, Inc., 702 S.W. 8th Street, Bentonville, AR 72716; direct questions to Wal-Mart Foundation, ext. 6878.

FINANCIAL SUMMARY

Recent Giving: $217,500 (fiscal 1990)
Assets: $717,914 (fiscal year ending January 31, 1990)
Gifts Received: $1,002,279 (fiscal 1990)
Fiscal Note: In 1990, contributions were received from the Helen R. Walton 1987 Nonqualified Charitable Remainder Trust and from Walton Enterprises, Inc.
EIN: 71-6091647

CONTRIBUTIONS SUMMARY

Typical Recipients: • *Education:* student aid
Grant Types: scholarship
Operating Locations: AR (Bentonville), KS (Topeka), TX (Arlington, Garland)

CORP. OFFICERS

David D. Glass: *B* New Liberty MO 1935 *ED* Southwest MO St Univ 1959 *CURR EMPL* pres, ceo, dir: Wal-Mart Stores *CORP AFFIL* dir: Bank Bentonville, Phillips Food Ctrs
A. L. Johnson: *CURR EMPL* coo, vchmn, dir: Wal-Mart Stores
Donald G. Soderquist: *B* Chicago IL 1934 *ED* Wheaton Coll BA 1955 *CURR EMPL* vchmn, coo, dir: Wal-Mart Stores *CORP AFFIL* dir: First Natl Bank Rogers AR *NONPR AFFIL* dir: Intl Mass Retail Assn
S. Robson Walton: *B* 1945 *ED* Columbia Univ JD 1969 *CURR*

EMPL chmn: Wal-Mart Stores *CORP AFFIL* dir: Acxiom Corp, Cooper Communities; vchmn: North AR Wholesale Co
Samuel M. Walton: *B* Kingfisher OK 1920 *ED* Univ MO 1940 *CURR EMPL* chmn, dir: Wal-Mart Stores *CORP AFFIL* dir: Winn-Dixie Stores; mem: Walton Enterprises

GIVING OFFICERS

Alice L. Walton: trust *B* 1949 *CURR EMPL* fdr: Llama Co
Helen Robson Walton: trust *ED* Univ OK 1941
James C. Walton: trust *B* 1948 *CURR EMPL* pres: Walton Enterprises
John T. Walton: trust *B* 1945
S. Robson Walton: trust *CURR EMPL* chmn: Wal-Mart Stores (see above)

APPLICATION INFORMATION

Initial Approach: Application form required for scholarships. Send brief letter of inquiry.
Disclosure Period: fiscal year ending January 31, 1990

Walbridge Aldinger Co.

Sales: $520.0 million
Employees: 1,470
Headquarters: Detroit, MI
SIC Major Group: Engineering & Management Services and General Building Contractors

CONTACT

Terry Merritt
Public Relations
Walbridge Aldinger Co.
613 Evett St.
Detroit, MI 48226-2521
(313) 963-8000

CONTRIBUTIONS SUMMARY

Operating Locations: MI (Detroit)

CORP. OFFICERS

Richard Haller: *CURR EMPL* cfo: Walbridge Aldinger Co
John Rakolta, Jr.: *CURR EMPL* chmn, pres: Walbridge Aldinger Co

Waldbaum, Inc.

Sales: $1.76 billion
Parent Company: Great Atlantic & Pacific Tea Co.
Parent Employees: 6,500
Headquarters: Central Islip, NY
SIC Major Group: Food Stores

CONTACT

Dee Perfido
Executive Secretary to the President
Waldbaum, Inc.
One Hemlock St.
Central Islip, NY 11722
(516) 233-8425

FINANCIAL SUMMARY

Fiscal Note: Annual Giving Range: $250,000 to $500,000

CONTRIBUTIONS SUMMARY

Typical Recipients: • *Arts & Humanities:* arts associations, community arts, museums/galleries, music • *Education:* colleges & universities, private education (precollege), student aid • *Religion:* religious organizations • *Social Services:* aged, child welfare, community service organizations, disabled, domestic violence, family services, united funds, youth organizations
Grant Types: general support, matching, project, and scholarship
Nonmonetary Support Types: donated products
Geographic Distribution: principally near operating locations and to national organizations
Operating Locations: NY (Central Islip)

CORP. OFFICERS

Stanley Lang: *CURR EMPL* pres: Waldbaum
Ira Waldbaum: *CURR EMPL* chmn, pres, dir: Waldbaum

GIVING OFFICERS

Dee Perfido: *CURR EMPL* exec secy to the pres: Waldbaum
Norma Valle: *CURR EMPL* admin asst: Waldbaum

APPLICATION INFORMATION

Initial Approach: *Initial Contact:* brief letter of inquiry* *Include Information On:* description of the organization, amount requested, and purpose for which the funds are sought
When to Submit: any time
Note: Initial letter of inquiry

must be on organization's letterhead.

Restrictions on Giving: Political and lobbying groups are not considered for charitable contributions.

Waldbaum Family Foundation, I.

CONTACT
Lawrence J. Waldman
I. Waldbaum Family Fdn.
3 Bostwick Ln.
Old Westburt, NY 11568

FINANCIAL SUMMARY
Recent Giving: $434,296 (1991); $377,417 (1990); $405,478 (1989)
Assets: $9,859,989 (1991); $8,568,263 (1990); $8,247,547 (1989)
Gifts Received: $7,300 (1991)
EIN: 13-6145916

CONTRIBUTIONS SUMMARY
Donor(s): Bernice Waldbaum, Ira Waldbaum, Waldbaum, Inc.
Typical Recipients: • *Civic & Public Affairs:* civil rights • *Health:* health funds, hospitals • *Religion:* religious organizations, synagogues • *Social Services:* child welfare, community centers, united funds, youth organizations
Grant Types: general support
Geographic Distribution: focus on the New York, NY, metropolitan area

GIVING OFFICERS
Randie Malinsky: dir
Bernice Waldbaum: treas
Ira Waldbaum: pres *CURR EMPL* chmn, pres, dir: Waldbaum
Julia Waldbaum: dir

APPLICATION INFORMATION
Initial Approach: Send cover letter and full proposal.

GRANTS ANALYSIS
Number of Grants: 50
Highest Grant: $150,000
Typical Range: $100 to $1,000
Disclosure Period: 1991

RECENT GRANTS
150,000 PPB Jewish Federation
 60,000 United Jewish Appeal Federation of Jewish Philanthropies, New York, NY
 36,000 United Jewish Appeal Federation of Jewish Philanthropies, New York, NY
 25,000 Gurwin Jewish Geriatric Center, New York, NY
 15,000 United Jewish Appeal Federation of Jewish Philanthropies, New York, NY
 10,000 Anti-Defamation League, New York, NY
 10,000 PPBC Jewish Federation Lions
  6,000 United Jewish Appeal Federation of Jewish Philanthropies, New York, NY
  5,000 Bar-Ilan University, New York, NY
  5,000 Department of Dermatology

Waldinger Corp. / Waldinger Corp. Foundation

Sales: $25.0 million
Employees: 300
Headquarters: Des Moines, IA

CONTACT
Tom Koehn
President
Waldinger Corp.
2601 Bell Avenue
P.O. Box 1612
Des Moines, IA 50306
(515) 284-1911

FINANCIAL SUMMARY
Recent Giving: $40,000 (fiscal 1992); $12,100 (fiscal 1990)
Assets: $0 (fiscal year ending May 31, 1992); $65,625 (fiscal 1990)
EIN: 42-1299671

CONTRIBUTIONS SUMMARY
Typical Recipients: • *Civic & Public Affairs:* housing • *Education:* medical education • *Health:* health organizations
Grant Types: general support
Geographic Distribution: giving limited to Des Moines, IA
Operating Locations: IA (Des Moines)

CORP. OFFICERS
Stephen E. Moses: *CURR EMPL* pres, treas: Waldinger Corp

GIVING OFFICERS
Thomas Koehn: pres, treas
Greg Roth: vp, secy

APPLICATION INFORMATION
Initial Approach: The foundation supports preselected organizations and does not accept unsolicited requests for funds.

GRANTS ANALYSIS
Number of Grants: 3
Highest Grant: $20,000
Typical Range: $1,500 to $20,000
Disclosure Period: fiscal year ending May 31, 1992

RECENT GRANTS
20,000 Iowa Osteopathic Education Foundation, Des Moines, IA — health care
18,500 Iowa Osteopathic Education Foundation, Des Moines, IA — health care
 1,500 HOME, Des Moines, IA — housing for the needy

Waldorf Educational Foundation

CONTACT
Stephen R. Starr
Waldorf Educational Fdn.
c/o The Glenmede Trust Co.
229 South 18th St.
Philadelphia, PA 19103
(215) 875-3200

FINANCIAL SUMMARY
Recent Giving: $497,200 (1991); $412,865 (1990); $410,200 (1989)
Assets: $8,885,992 (1991); $7,962,497 (1990); $8,622,210 (1989)
EIN: 23-6254206

CONTRIBUTIONS SUMMARY
Typical Recipients: • *Education:* business education, colleges & universities, faculty development, private education (precollege)
Grant Types: general support

GIVING OFFICERS
Samuel W. Morris: trust
Karin Myrin: trust

APPLICATION INFORMATION
Initial Approach: Send brief letter of inquiry describing program. There are no deadlines.

GRANTS ANALYSIS
Number of Grants: 12

Highest Grant: $200,000
Typical Range: $4,000 to $33,000
Disclosure Period: 1991

RECENT GRANTS
200,000 Waldorf School of Garden City, Garden City, NY
 78,000 Rudolph Steiner College, Fair Oaks, CA
 60,000 Waldorf Institute of Spring Valley, Spring Valley, NY
 38,700 Association of Waldorf Schools of North America, Great Barrington, MA
 37,000 Rudolf Steiner Institute, Takoma, MD
 33,000 Antioch New England Graduate School, Keene, NH
 12,000 Kimberton Waldorf School, Kimberton, PA
 11,500 Rudolf Steiner Centre, Ann Arbor, MI
 11,500 Waldorf Institute of Southern California, Northridge, CA
  6,500 Green Meadow Waldorf School, Chestnut Ridge, NY

Walgreen Co. / Walgreen Benefit Fund

Sales: $7.47 billion
Employees: 53,500
Headquarters: Deerfield, IL
SIC Major Group: Miscellaneous Retail

CONTACT
Kimary Lee
Corporate Manager, Public Affairs
Walgreen Co.
200 Wilmot Rd.
Deerfield, IL 60015
(708) 940-3156
Note: The contact for the Walgreen Benefit Fund is Edward H. King at the above address.

FINANCIAL SUMMARY
Recent Giving: $3,500,000 (fiscal 1992); $3,500,000 (fiscal 1990); $3,500,000 (fiscal 1989)
Assets: $11,750,177 (fiscal 1991); $10,461,323 (fiscal 1989)
Fiscal Note: Above figures include both fund giving and direct contributions by the com-

pany. Fund contributions are about $500,000 annually.
EIN: 36-6051130

CONTRIBUTIONS SUMMARY

Typical Recipients: • *Arts & Humanities:* arts institutes, museums/galleries, opera • *Civic & Public Affairs:* business/free enterprise, ethnic/minority organizations, municipalities, public policy, urban & community affairs, women's affairs, zoos/botanical gardens • *Education:* colleges & universities, economic education • *Health:* hospitals, mental health, single-disease health associations • *Social Services:* child welfare, disabled, drugs & alcohol, united funds, youth organizations
Grant Types: general support
Geographic Distribution: primarily areas of company operations, with emphasis on the Chicago metropolitan area
Operating Locations: AZ (Flagstaff, Phoenix), CA (San Francisco), CO (Denver), FL (Merrit Island, Orlando, Tampa), IL (Bedford Park, Berkeley, Chicago, Danville, Deerfield, Elk Grove Village), MA (Boston), MI (Kalamazoo), MN (Minneapolis), MO (St. Louis), NJ, OH, TN (Memphis), TX (Houston), WI (Menominee Falls, Windsor)
Note: Company operates more than 1,700 stores in 29 states and Puerto Rico.

CORP. OFFICERS

L. Daniel Jorndt: *B* Chicago IL 1941 *ED* Drake Univ BS 1963; Univ NM MBA 1974 *CURR EMPL* pres, coo, dir: Walgreen Co *NONPR AFFIL* dir: Chicago Assn Commerce Indus, Chicago Better Bus Bur; mem: Fin Execs Inst, Natl Assn Corp Treas; natl chmn: Drake Univ Pharmacy Alumni Fund
Charles Rudolph Walgreen III: *B* Chicago IL 1935 *ED* Univ MI BS 1958 *CURR EMPL* chmn, ceo, dir: Walgreen Co *NONPR AFFIL* dir: Am Pharmaceutical Assn, Jr Achievement Chicago; mem: Delta Sigma Phi, IL Pharmaceutical Assn, IL Retail Merchants Assn, Natl Assn Chain Drug Stores; mem bus adv counc: Chicago Urban League

GIVING OFFICERS

Richard E. Engler: dir
N. J. Godfrey: secy, treas, dir

Charles David Hunter: vp, dir *B* Alameda CA 1929 *ED* Modesto Jr Coll AA 1949; Univ CA Berkeley BS 1951; Univ CA Berkeley BA 1951 *CURR EMPL* vchmn, cfo, dir: Walgreen Co *NONPR AFFIL* mem: Am Inst CPAs, Chicago Retail Fin Execs Assn, Fin Execs Inst, IL Soc CPAs
Edward H. King: pres, dir
Kimary Lee: mgr pub affairs
John A. Rubino: asst secy, asst treas, dir *CURR EMPL* vp: Walgreen Co
William G. Thien: vp, dir *CURR EMPL* vp: Walgreen Co
Charles Rudolph Walgreen III: dir *CURR EMPL* chmn, ceo, dir: Walgreen Co (see above)

APPLICATION INFORMATION

Initial Approach: *Initial Contact:* letter *Include Information On:* description of the organization, amount requested, purpose for which funds are sought, current budget and audited financial statement, proof of tax-exempt status, list of directors, most recent contributors and amounts, list of accrediting agencies as appropriate *When to Submit:* any time; requests should be sent at least six weeks before funds are needed
Restrictions on Giving: Company does not make grants to individuals, religious organizations for sectarian purposes, or for research.

OTHER THINGS TO KNOW

Company's goal is to donate at least 2% of after-tax profits to charitable organizations. Grant amount rarely exceeds $5,000. The Walgreen Benefit Fund, established in the 1930s by an endowment from the company's founder, is officially independent of Walgreen Co. but continues to serve company employees.

GRANTS ANALYSIS

Total Grants: $3,500,000
Typical Range: $200 to $5,000
Disclosure Period: fiscal year ending April 30, 1992
Note: Total grants figure is for both company and fund. Assets are from 1991. Recent grants are derived from a fiscal 1991 Form 990 for the fund.

RECENT GRANTS

22,144 United Way of the Texas Gulf Coast, Houston, TX — general purpose fund

17,716 United Way of Dane County, Madison, WI — general purpose fund

9,620 United Way Greater St. Louis, St. Louis, MO — general purpose fund

9,338 United Way of Greater Milwaukee, Milwaukee, WI — general purpose fund

9,049 United Way of Eastern New England, Boston, MA — general purpose fund

8,921 United Way of Dade County, Miami, FL — general purpose fund

7,972 United Way of Greater Memphis, Memphis, TN — general purpose fund

7,600 United Way of Sun Valley, Phoenix, AZ — general purpose fund

7,281 United Way of Mile High, Denver, CO — general purpose fund

7,158 United Way Metropolitan Louisville, Louisville, KY — general purpose fund

---

Walker Co., Shaw

Parent Company: Westinghouse Electric Corp.
Headquarters: Muskegon, MI

CONTACT

Rick Vales
Vice President, Operations
Shaw Walker Co.
PO Box 209
Muskegon, MI 49443-0209
(616) 755-2270

CONTRIBUTIONS SUMMARY

Operating Locations: MI (Muskegon)

OTHER THINGS TO KNOW

Company is an original donor to the L.C. & Margaret Walker Foundation.

Walker Educational and Charitable Foundation, Alex C.

CONTACT

Henry C. Flood, Jr.
Alex C. Walker Educational and Charitable Fdn.
c/o Pittsburgh National Bank, Trust Div.
One Oliver Plz. 28th Fl.
Pittsburgh, PA 15265
(412) 762-3866

FINANCIAL SUMMARY

Recent Giving: $231,000 (1991); $224,200 (1990); $150,500 (1989)
Assets: $5,150,716 (1991); $4,460,378 (1990); $4,430,884 (1989)
EIN: 25-6109746

CONTRIBUTIONS SUMMARY

Donor(s): the late Alex C. Walker
Typical Recipients: • *Civic & Public Affairs:* business/free enterprise, economics, environmental affairs, philanthropic organizations, public policy • *Education:* colleges & universities, international studies, legal education • *Religion:* religious organizations
Grant Types: general support and research

GIVING OFFICERS

Pittsburgh National Bank: trust
Barrett C. Walker: trust

APPLICATION INFORMATION

Initial Approach: Send cover letter and full proposal. There are no deadlines.
Restrictions on Giving: Does not support individuals.

OTHER THINGS TO KNOW

Publications: Program policy statement

GRANTS ANALYSIS

Number of Grants: 22
Highest Grant: $65,000
Typical Range: $1,000 to $25,000
Disclosure Period: 1991

RECENT GRANTS

65,000 Heritage Foundation, Washington, DC

15,000 American Society for Technion, New York, NY

15,000 Competitive Enterprise Institute, Washington, DC

15,000 International Center for Economic Growth, San Francisco, CA

12,000 Santa Fe Institute, Santa Fe, NM

10,000 Brookings Institute, Washington, DC

10,000 CATO Institute, Washington, DC

10,000 George Mason University Law and Economic Center, Arlington, VA

10,000 Leadership Institute, Springfield, VA

10,000 Wilderness Society, Washington, DC

Walker Foundation, Archie D. and Bertha H.

CONTACT
David H. Griffith
President
Archie D. and Bertha H. Walker Fdn.
1121 Hennepin Ave.
Minneapolis, MN 55403
(612) 332-3556

FINANCIAL SUMMARY
Recent Giving: $366,870 (1990); $263,275 (1989)
Assets: $4,785,324 (1990); $5,023,898 (1989)
EIN: 41-6022758

CONTRIBUTIONS SUMMARY
Donor(s): the late Archie D. Walker, the late Bertha H. Walker
Typical Recipients: • *Arts & Humanities:* community arts, museums/galleries • *Civic & Public Affairs:* environmental affairs • *Education:* colleges & universities • *Religion:* churches • *Social Services:* community service organizations, counseling, domestic violence, drugs & alcohol, employment/job training
Grant Types: capital, conference/seminar, general support, operating expenses, project, and research
Geographic Distribution: focus on the seven-county Min-

neapolis-St. Paul, MN, metropolitan area

GIVING OFFICERS
Louise W. Davy: trust
Harriet W. Fitts: treas, trust
David H. Griffith: pres, trust
Katherine W. Griffith: trust
Teri M. Lamb: secy, trust
Dana D. McCannell: trust
Laurie H. McCannell: trust
Louise Walker McCannell: vp, trust
Abigail M. Walker: trust
Amy C. Walker: trust
Archie D. Walker III: trust
Archie D. Walker, Jr.: trust
Berta Walker: vp, trust
Elaine B. Walker: trust
Patricia Walker: trust
Walter W. Walker: vp, trust
Lita W. West: trust

APPLICATION INFORMATION
Initial Approach: Application form required. Send cover letter and full proposal. Deadline is December 1. Board meets in March. Decisions are made in June.
Restrictions on Giving: Does not support individuals.

OTHER THINGS TO KNOW
Publications: Annual Report (including application guidelines)

GRANTS ANALYSIS
Number of Grants: 38
Highest Grant: $120,000
Typical Range: $1,000 to $10,000
Disclosure Period: 1990

RECENT GRANTS
120,000 University of Minnesota Art Museum, Minneapolis, MN

100,000 Walker Art Center, Minneapolis, MN

38,000 Mental Health Association of Middlesex

25,000 Fine Arts Work Center, Provincetown, MA

10,000 Lincoln Street

7,200 Sobriety High

6,000 Vinland National Center, Loretto, MN

5,000 New Beginnings Womens Support Network, Springfield, VT

5,000 New Connections Programs, St. Paul, MN

5,000 New Visions Treatment Center

Walker Foundation, L. C. and Margaret

CONTACT
Shaw Walker
President
L. C. and Margaret Walker Fdn.
PO Box 660
Muskegon, MI 49443-0660
(616) 744-5294

FINANCIAL SUMMARY
Recent Giving: $509,703 (1991); $564,800 (1990); $434,289 (1989)
Assets: $12,181,155 (1991); $10,215,239 (1990); $12,278,390 (1989)
EIN: 38-6060045

CONTRIBUTIONS SUMMARY
Donor(s): the late Louis Carlisle Walker, Shaw Walker Co.
Typical Recipients: • *Arts & Humanities:* arts centers, museums/galleries, public broadcasting • *Civic & Public Affairs:* environmental affairs • *Education:* colleges & universities, literacy, private education (precollege), science/technology education • *Health:* health organizations, single-disease health associations • *Religion:* churches • *Social Services:* child welfare, community service organizations, united funds, youth organizations
Grant Types: general support

GIVING OFFICERS
Monica Bauman: secy
Walker McKinney: treas, trust
CORP AFFIL dir: Shaw-Walker Co
Tom Munroe: trust
Margaret Walker Spofford: vp, trust
Shaw Walker: pres, trust

APPLICATION INFORMATION
Initial Approach: Contributes only to preselected organizations.
Restrictions on Giving: Does not support individuals.

GRANTS ANALYSIS
Number of Grants: 80
Highest Grant: $79,000
Typical Range: $500 to $5,000
Disclosure Period: 1991

RECENT GRANTS
79,000 Literacy Volunteers of America

40,000 AIDS Fund

25,401 Mayo Foundation, Rochester, MN

25,000 Katonah Gallery

25,000 Marymount Manhattan College

25,000 Michigan Technological University, Houghton, MI

25,000 Princeton University, Princeton, NJ

20,000 Hotchkiss School

20,000 Muskegon Museum of Art

15,000 Interlochen Center for the Arts

Walker Foundation, Smith

CONTACT
Smith Walker Foundation
1260 Coast Vill Circle
Santa Barbara, CA 93108-0000
(805) 969-4764

FINANCIAL SUMMARY
Recent Giving: $195,801 (fiscal 1991)
Assets: $3,412,247 (fiscal year ending September 30, 1991); $3,126,126 (fiscal 1989)
EIN: 33-0327308

CONTRIBUTIONS SUMMARY
Typical Recipients: • *Arts & Humanities:* history/historic preservation, museums/galleries • *Health:* single-disease health associations • *Religion:* churches • *Social Services:* family planning, youth organizations
Grant Types: general support

APPLICATION INFORMATION
Initial Approach: The foundation reports it only makes contributions to preselected organizations and does not accept unsolicited requests for funds.

GRANTS ANALYSIS
Total Grants: $195,801
Number of Grants: 43
Highest Grant: $33,266
Typical Range: $5,000 to $18,000
Disclosure Period: fiscal year ending September 30, 1991

RECENT GRANTS
33,226 Santa Barbara Historical Society, CA

18,000 Boys Club of Palm Springs, Palm Springs, CA

18,000 Boys Club of Palm Springs, Palm Springs, CA

13,000 United Methodist Church, CA

10,000 Girls Incorporated of Greater Santa Barbara, Santa Barbara, CA

10,000 Newport Harbor Nautical Museum, CA

10,000 Planned Parenthood of Santa Barbara, Santa Barbara, CA

10,000 United Methodist Church, CA

7,500 Newport Harbor Art Museum, CA

5,000 Hoag Memorial Hospital, CA

Walker Foundation, T. B.

CONTACT
T. B. Walker Fdn.
PO Box 330112
San Francisco, CA 94133

FINANCIAL SUMMARY
Recent Giving: $135,000 (fiscal 1991); $201,000 (fiscal 1990); $234,000 (fiscal 1989)
Assets: $4,682,980 (fiscal year ending September 30, 1991); $4,477,386 (fiscal 1990); $4,803,127 (fiscal 1989)
EIN: 52-1078287

CONTRIBUTIONS SUMMARY
Donor(s): the late T. B. Walker and Gilbert M. Walker
Typical Recipients: • *Arts & Humanities:* arts centers, arts institutes, museums/galleries, music, performing arts, public broadcasting, theater • *Civic & Public Affairs:* environmental affairs • *Education:* colleges & universities, private education (precollege) • *Health:* medical research • *Social Services:* child welfare, community service organizations, family planning, family services, united funds, volunteer services, youth organizations
Grant Types: multiyear/continuing support, project, and research
Geographic Distribution: focus on CA

GIVING OFFICERS
Ann M. Hatch: trust
Harriet W. Henderson: 2nd vp, trust
Wellington S. Henderson, Jr.: trust
Colleen Marsh: secy, trust
Brooks Walker, Jr.: treas, trust *ED* Univ CA Berkeley BA 1950; Harvard Univ MBA 1957

CORP AFFIL dir: Gap Stores
NONPR AFFIL chmn: San Francisco Mus Modern Art; dir: Pacific Legal Fdn, San Francisco Opera Assn, Smith Kettlewell Eye Res Fdn
John C. Walker: pres, trust
R. Lance Walker: trust
S. Adrian Walker: trust
Jean W. Yeates: trust
Jeffrey L. Yeates: trust

APPLICATION INFORMATION
Initial Approach: Contributes only to preselected organizations.
Restrictions on Giving: Does not support individuals.

GRANTS ANALYSIS
Number of Grants: 45
Highest Grant: $15,000
Typical Range: $1,000 to $5,500
Disclosure Period: fiscal year ending September 30, 1991

RECENT GRANTS
15,000 Children's Health Council Summer Symphony, Palo Alto, CA

10,500 San Francisco Museum of Modern Art, San Francisco, CA

10,000 Peninsula Volunteers, Menlo Park, CA

8,000 Hunters Point Boys Club, San Francisco, CA

5,500 Davis Joint Unified School District, Davis, CA

5,500 San Francisco Museum of Modern Art, San Francisco, CA

4,500 Life on the Water, People's Theatre Coalition, San Francisco, CA

4,500 University of California Regents University Art Museum, Berkeley, CA

4,000 Pacific Presbyterian Family Therapy Clinic, San Francisco, CA

4,000 San Francisco Art Institute, San Francisco, CA

Walker Foundation, W. E.

CONTACT
John S. Jenkins
Trustee
W. E. Walker Fdn.
1675 Lakeland Dr.
Riverhill Tower, Ste. 400
Jackson, MS 39216
(601) 362-9895

FINANCIAL SUMMARY
Recent Giving: $2,212,071 (1991); $1,005,170 (1990); $841,499 (1989)
Assets: $6,682,477 (1991); $7,733,305 (1990); $8,499,631 (1989)
Gifts Received: $531,024 (1991)
Fiscal Note: 1991 contributionsreceived from W.E. Walker($500,000)and William E. Walker, Jr. Revocable Trust ($31,024)
EIN: 23-7279902

CONTRIBUTIONS SUMMARY
Donor(s): W. E. Walker, Jr., W. E. Walker Stores
Typical Recipients: • *Arts & Humanities:* dance • *Education:* colleges & universities, private education (precollege), religious education • *Health:* health organizations, hospitals, medical research, pediatric health, single-disease health associations • *Religion:* churches, religious organizations • *Social Services:* united funds, youth organizations
Grant Types: general support and scholarship
Geographic Distribution: focus on MS

GIVING OFFICERS
Edmund L. Brunini: trust
Baker Duncan: trust
Justina W. McLean: trust
Gloria M. Walker: trust
W. E. Walker, Jr.: trust

APPLICATION INFORMATION
Initial Approach: Application form required for scholarships. There are no deadlines.

GRANTS ANALYSIS
Number of Grants: 57
Highest Grant: $1,105,043
Typical Range: $100 to $1,000
Disclosure Period: 1991

RECENT GRANTS
1,105,043 McLean Foundation, Columbia, MS

295,000 Walker Education Enrichment Foundation, Jackson, MS

100,000 Diocese of Mississippi, MS — Gray Center Chapel

100,000 St. Andrews School, MS — teacher's salaries

94,600 Scripps Clinic and Research Foundation, La Jolla, CA

63,132 Children's Hospital, MS — AIDS project

50,000 Diocese of Mississippi, MS — Gray Center Assembly Building

50,000 Ecumenical Health Care Organization, MS

50,000 Trinity Episcopal School for Ministry, MS

50,000 Vanderbilt University, Nashville, TN — Owen Graduate School

Walker Wildlife Conservation Foundation

CONTACT
W. E. Walker, Jr.
Trustee
Walker Wildlife Conservation Fdn.
1675 Lakeland Dr., Ste. 400
Jackson, MS 39216

FINANCIAL SUMMARY
Recent Giving: $16,990 (1990); $380,660 (1989); $12,671 (1988)
Assets: $2,410,241 (1990); $2,288,074 (1989); $2,101,650 (1988)
Gifts Received: $500,000 (1989); $2,000,000 (1988)
EIN: 64-0697006

CONTRIBUTIONS SUMMARY
Donor(s): W. E. Walker Foundation
Typical Recipients: • *Civic & Public Affairs:* environmental affairs, zoos/botanical gardens
Grant Types: general support

GIVING OFFICERS
Edmund L. Brunini: trust
Justina W. McLean: trust
Gloria M. Walker: trust
W.E. Walker, Jr.: trust

APPLICATION INFORMATION

Initial Approach: Contributes only to preselected organizations.

GRANTS ANALYSIS

Number of Grants: 4
Highest Grant: $10,000
Typical Range: $200 to $6,750
Disclosure Period: 1990

RECENT GRANTS

10,000 Nature Conservancy, Jackson, MS
6,750 Atlantic Salmon Foundation, New York, NY
200 Soil Conservancy Service, Oxford, MS
40 National Wildlife Foundation, Washington, DC

Wallace Computer Services / Wallace Computer Services Foundation

Sales: $511.6 million
Employees: 2,993
Headquarters: Hillside, IL
SIC Major Group: Business Services, Miscellaneous Manufacturing Industries, Printing & Publishing, and Wholesale Trade—Nondurable Goods

CONTACT

Matthew Wedding
Secretary and Treasurer
Wallace Computer Services Fdn.
4600 Roosevelt Rd.
Hillside, IL 60162
(708) 449-8600

FINANCIAL SUMMARY

Recent Giving: $30,000 (1993 est.); $30,000 (1991); $31,395 (1990)
Assets: $311,301 (1990)
Gifts Received: $100,000 (1990)
Fiscal Note: In 1990, contributions were received from Wallace Computer Services.
EIN: 23-7380556

CONTRIBUTIONS SUMMARY

Typical Recipients: • *Civic & Public Affairs:* municipalities, urban & community affairs • *Education:* colleges & universities • *Health:* health organizations, hospitals • *Social Services:* community service organizations, united funds, youth organizations

Grant Types: general support
Nonmonetary Support Types: donated equipment and donated products
Geographic Distribution: focus on Chicago, IL
Operating Locations: IL (Hillside, St. Charles)

CORP. OFFICERS

Robert Cronin: *CURR EMPL* pres, ceo: Wallace Computer Svcs
Theodore Dimitriou: *B* Dayton OH 1926 *ED* Northwestern Univ 1969; Miami Univ 1970 *CURR EMPL* chmn, dir: Wallace Computer Svcs

GIVING OFFICERS

Robert Cronin: pres, dir *CURR EMPL* pres, ceo: Wallace Computer Svcs (see above)
Michael Duffield: vp, dir
Michael J. Halloran: vp, dir
Matthew Wedding: secy, treas, dir

APPLICATION INFORMATION

Initial Approach: Send a full proposal. a description of organization, amount requested, purpose of funds sought, recently audited financial statement, and proof of tax-exempt status There are no deadlines.
Restrictions on Giving: Does not support individuals, religious organizations for sectarian purposes, political or lobbying groups, or organizations outside operating areas.

GRANTS ANALYSIS

Number of Grants: 41
Highest Grant: $8,000
Typical Range: $100 to $2,000
Disclosure Period: 1990

RECENT GRANTS

8,000 United Way, Chicago, IL
2,000 Osage Community Chest, Osage, IA
2,000 United Way, Gastonia, NC
2,000 United Way, Clinton, IA
1,500 United Way, Statesboro, GA
1,500 United Way, San Luis Obispo, CA
1,000 Boys Club of America, Bellwood, IL
1,000 Burr and Burton Annual Fund, Manchester, NH
1,000 United Way, Ravenna, OH
800 United Way, Stockton, CA

Wallace Foundation, George R.

CONTACT

George R. Wallace Fdn.
One Boston Pl.
Boston, MA 02108
(617) 722-6818

FINANCIAL SUMMARY

Recent Giving: $265,000 (1991); $297,250 (1990); $244,750 (1989)
Assets: $6,938,454 (1991); $5,802,829 (1990); $5,766,431 (1989)
Gifts Received: $7,803 (1990)
EIN: 04-6130518

CONTRIBUTIONS SUMMARY

Donor(s): the late George R. Wallace
Typical Recipients: • *Arts & Humanities:* dance, history/historic preservation, libraries, museums/galleries • *Education:* colleges & universities, private education (precollege) • *Health:* hospitals • *Religion:* religious organizations • *Social Services:* child welfare, youth organizations
Grant Types: capital and endowment
Geographic Distribution: focus on MA

GIVING OFFICERS

John Grado, Jr.: trust
Henry B. Shepard, Jr.: trust
George R. Wallace III: trust

APPLICATION INFORMATION

Initial Approach: Send brief letter of inquiry and proposal. There are no deadlines. Board meets semiannually. Decisions are made within six months.
Restrictions on Giving: Does not support individuals.

GRANTS ANALYSIS

Number of Grants: 34
Highest Grant: $55,000
Typical Range: $500 to $5,000
Disclosure Period: 1991

RECENT GRANTS

55,000 Walnut Hill School, Natick, MA
26,000 Fitchburg Art Museum, Fitchburg, MA
25,000 Cushing Academy, Ashburnham, MA
25,000 Mount Holyoke College, South Hadley, MA
20,750 Fitchburg Public Library, Fitchburg, MA
20,000 Stoneleigh Burnham School, Greenfield, MA
12,500 Fitchburg State College, Fitchburg, MA
10,500 Naples Community Hospital, Naples, FL
10,000 MSPCC-Cape Cod, Hyannis, MA
10,000 University Christian Movement, Cambridge, MA

Wallace Genetic Foundation

CONTACT

Polly Lawrence
Research Secretary
Wallace Genetic Foundation
4801 Massachusetts Avenue, NW, Ste. 400
Washington, DC 20016
(202) 966-2932

FINANCIAL SUMMARY

Recent Giving: $2,336,628 (1991); $2,360,794 (1990); $2,517,231 (1988)
Assets: $89,368,409 (1991); $50,884,858 (1990); $46,974,737 (1988)
Gifts Received: $310,000 (1991); $310,000 (1990); $190,000 (1988)
Fiscal Note: The foundation receives contributions from Robert B. Wallace.
EIN: 13-6162575

CONTRIBUTIONS SUMMARY

Donor(s): The foundation was incorporated in 1959 in New York by the late Henry A. Wallace.
Typical Recipients: • *Arts & Humanities:* cinema, museums/galleries • *Civic & Public Affairs:* consumer affairs, economic development, economics, environmental affairs, international affairs, national security, philanthropic organizations, public policy, rural affairs, safety • *Education:* agricultural education, career/vocational education, colleges & universities, education funds, international studies • *Health:* single-disease health associations • *International:* international organizations • *Science:* scientific organizations

Grant Types: general support, project, and research
Geographic Distribution: national, international; no geographic restrictions

GIVING OFFICERS

Jean W. Douglas: dir
Stanley Rosenberg: asst secy
Henry B. Wallace: dir
Robert B. Wallace: don, dir *ED* IA St Univ 1940

APPLICATION INFORMATION

Initial Approach:
Applicants should send a brief letter of proposal to the foundation.
The foundation will provide an application form.
There are no deadlines for submitting applications.

GRANTS ANALYSIS

Total Grants: $2,336,628
Number of Grants: 62
Highest Grant: $523,000
Typical Range: $5,000 to $75,000
Disclosure Period: 1991
Note: Average grant figure excludes high grants of $523,000 and $131,411. Recent grants are derived from a 1991 grants list.

RECENT GRANTS

523,000 Population Crisis Committee, Washington, DC
131,411 University of Arizona Health Sciences Center, Tucson, AZ
125,000 Dermatology Foundation of Miami, Miami, FL
100,000 University of Illinois Foundation, Urbana, IL
90,000 Harlen E. Moore Heart Research Foundation, Champaign, IL
90,000 Institute for Alternative Agriculture, Greenbelt, MD
75,000 Natural Resources Defense Council, New York, NY
50,000 American Farmland Trust, Washington, DC
50,000 Cancer Research Council, Bethesda, MD
50,000 International Cancer Alliance, Bethesda, MD

Wallace-Reader's Digest Fund, DeWitt

CONTACT
M. Christine DeVita
President
DeWitt Wallace-Reader's Digest Fund
261 Madison Avenue, 24th Fl.
New York, NY 10016
(212) 953-1201

FINANCIAL SUMMARY
Recent Giving: $52,000,000 (1993 est.); $73,102,761 (1992); $33,443,295 (1991)
Assets: $1,133,982,206 (1992); $1,088,044,858 (1991); $761,826,602 (1990)
Gifts Received: $7,158 (1992); $7,158 (1991); $131,939 (1990)
EIN: 13-6183757

CONTRIBUTIONS SUMMARY
Donor(s): The fund's donor, DeWitt Wallace (1889-1981) was born in St. Paul, MN. His father was president of Macalester College, where Mr. Wallace studied for two years before transfering to the University of California at Berkeley. In 1922, Mr. Wallace and his wife, Lila Acheson Wallace, founded Reader's Digest with $5,000 in borrowed money. Upon his retirement in 1972, Reader's Digest was the world's most widely read magazine. "He was particularly interested in young people and education, and that continues to be reflected in the Fund's current grant program."
Typical Recipients: • *Arts & Humanities:* libraries • *Education:* career/vocational education, education associations, faculty development, minority education, private education (precollege), public education (precollege) • *Social Services:* employment/job training, youth organizations
Grant Types: general support, multiyear/continuing support, project, scholarship, and seed money
Geographic Distribution: no geographic restrictions and principally to national organizations

GIVING OFFICERS
William G. Bowen, PhD: dir *B* Cincinnati OH 1933 *ED*

Denison Univ BA 1955; Princeton Univ PhD 1958 *CORP AFFIL* dir: Am Express Co, Merck & Co, NCR Corp, Readers Digest Assn, Rockefeller Group *NONPR AFFIL* mem: Am Econ Assn, Counc Foreign Rels, Indus Rels Res Assn, Phi Beta Kappa; mem bd regents: Smithsonian Inst; trust: Ctr Advanced Study Behavioral Sciences; prof econ: Princeton Univ
Theodore F. Brophy: dir *B* New York NY 1923 *ED* Yale Univ BA 1944; Harvard Univ LLB 1949 *CORP AFFIL* dir: Irving Bank Corp, Irving Trust Co, JWP Inc, Procter & Gamble Co, Reader's Digest Assn; mem adv comm: NY Stock Exchange *NONPR AFFIL* dir: Un Way Tri-State; mem: Am Bar Assn, Brookings Inst, Bus Roundtable, Conf Bd Bus Counc, Fed Communs Bar Assn, Greeenwich Hosp Assn, Smith Coll Pres Comm; mem adv counc: Natl Urban Coalition; trust: Am Indian Coll Funds
Jessica Chao: vp
M. Christine DeVita: pres, dir
George V. Grune: chmn, dir *B* White Plains NY 1929 *ED* Duke Univ BA 1952; Univ FL 1955-1956 *CURR EMPL* chmn, pres, ceo, coo: Readers Digest Assn *CORP AFFIL* dir: Assoc Dry Goods, Avon Products, Chem Bank, Chem NY Corp, CPC Intl, GTE Corp, Sterling Drug *NONPR AFFIL* dir: Boys Club Am; mem bd overseers, bd mgrs: Counc Conservators NY Pub Library, Counc Fin Aid Ed, Counc Foreign Rels, Inst France, Meml Sloan Kettering Cancer Ctr; mem conf bd, dir: Metro Opera Assn; mem policy comm: Bus Roundtable; trust: Duke Univ, Metro Mus Art, NY Zoological Soc, Rollins Coll Roy E Crummer Grad Sch Bus
J. Edward Hall: dir
Melvin R. Laird: dir *B* Omaha NE 1922 *ED* Carleton Coll BA 1942 *CURR EMPL* sr counsellor (natl & intl affairs): Readers Digest Assn *CORP AFFIL* bd dirs: Commercial Credit Co, Commun Satellite Corp, IDS Mutual Fund Group, Martin Marietta Corp, Metro Life Ins Co, Northwest Airlines, Phillips Petroleum Co, Scientific Applications Intl Inc *NONPR AFFIL* mem: Am Legion, Military Order Purple Heart, Veterans Foreign Wars; mem bd

dirs: Am Inst CPAs, Boys Clubs Am, George Washington Univ, Laird Youth Leadership Fdn, Securities Exchange Comm Practice Section, World Rehab Fund; trust: John F Kennedy Ctr Performing Arts *PHIL AFFIL* dir: Airlie Foundation
Robert D. Nagel: treas
Jane Quinn: program dir
Laurance Spelman Rockefeller: dir *B* New York NY 1910 *ED* Princeton Univ BA 1932 *CORP AFFIL* chmn: Woodstock Resort Corp; dir: Readers Digest Assn *NONPR AFFIL* comr emeritus: Palisades Interstate Park Comm; hon chmn: NY Zoological Soc; hon trust: Natl Geographic Soc; trust emeritus: Princeton Univ *PHIL AFFIL* trust: Greenacre Foundation
Walter Vincent Shipley: dir *B* Newark NJ 1935 *ED* NY Univ BS 1960 *CURR EMPL* pres, coo: Chem Bank *CORP AFFIL* chmn: Chem NY Corp; dir: Champion Intl Corp, NYNEX Corp, Readers Digest Assn *NONPR AFFIL* dir: Assn Reserve City Bankers, Goodwill Indus Greater NY, Lincoln Ctr Performing Arts, NY Chamber Commerce Indus, NY City Partnership, Un Way Tri-St; mem: Bus Counc, Bus Roundtable, Counc Foreign Rels, English Speaking Union, Japan Soc, Pilgrims US; trust: NY Univ

APPLICATION INFORMATION
Initial Approach:
Initial approach should be through a brief letter of inquiry of no more than two pages. The fund requests no videotapes. The initial letter should describe the organization, proposed project and its goal, and include an estimated budget of project, and the portion of the budget requiring funding. If the request falls within fund interests, a formal proposal with detailed information will be requested.
There are no proposal deadlines.
The board meets four times a year to consider proposals. Proposals will be reviewed for the potential contribution to the field, the organization's ability to produce and sustain the proposed projects, plans for documenting both process and results, and the financial stability of the organization.

Restrictions on Giving:
Areas currently outside giving guidelines include health and medical services or research; scholarly research; capital campaigns, including but not limited to, buildings and endowments; religious, fraternal, or veterans organizations; and private foundations or individuals.

OTHER THINGS TO KNOW
The fund is closely affiliated with the Lila Wallace Reader's Digest Fund.

The fund has become more national and less local in its grant making. Generally the fund does not make grants under $100,000, or grants for long-term annual support of an organization. Multiyear funding will be considered relative to specific needs and the potential of a particular project. The fund will increasingly be initiating projects internally.

Publications: annual report includes application guidelines

GRANTS ANALYSIS
Total Grants: $73,102,761
Number of Grants: 132
Highest Grant: $3,672,242
Typical Range: $100,000 to $600,000
Disclosure Period: 1992
Note: Recent grants are derived from a 1991 annual report.

RECENT GRANTS
4,236,000 College Board, New York, NY
2,815,000 Fund for the City of New York, New York, NY
1,662,000 Boy Scouts of America, Irving, TX
1,367,000 New York Public Library, New York, NY
1,315,000 National 4-H Council, Chevy Chase, MD
1,029,000 Institute for Literacy Studies, Bronx, NY
965,000 National Endowment for the Humanities, Washington, DC
927,620 Woodrow Wilson National Fellowship Foundation, Princeton, NJ
925,000 Fund for New York City Public Education, New York, NY
900,000 Nonprofit Facilities Fund, New York, NY

Wallace Reader's Digest Fund, Lila

CONTACT
M. Christine DeVita
President
Lila Wallace-Reader's Digest Fund
261 Madison Avenue, 24th Fl.
New York, NY 10016
(212) 953-1200

FINANCIAL SUMMARY
Recent Giving: $42,000,000 (1993 est.); $40,048,145 (1992); $32,675,042 (1991)
Assets: $855,569,785 (1992); $821,550,514 (1991); $577,279,420 (1990)
Gifts Received: $44,094 (1992); $55,658 (1991); $128,311 (1989)
EIN: 13-6086859

CONTRIBUTIONS SUMMARY
Donor(s): Lila Wallace and her husband, DeWitt Wallace, founded Reader's Digest magazine in 1922 in New York City. The company has grown to be a leading global publisher direct-mail marketer of magazines, books, music, and video products. Lila Wallace was a social worker who established innovative programs in conjunction with the YMCA and the U.S. Department of Labor. She also was interested in the arts and supported various museums, performing arts organizations, and programs to beautify the environment.

She and her husband established four charitable foundations to support their interests. In 1987, the DeWitt Wallace Fund, L.A.W. Fund, Lakeview Fund, and High Winds Fund were merged into two funds known as the DeWitt Wallace-Reader's Digest Fund and the Lila Wallace-Reader's Digest Fund.

Typical Recipients: • *Arts & Humanities:* arts appreciation, arts associations, arts centers, arts festivals, arts institutes, dance, ethnic arts, literary arts, museums/galleries, music, opera, performing arts, theater, visual arts • *Civic & Public Affairs:* zoos/botanical gardens • *Education:* arts education, literacy
Grant Types: general support and project
Geographic Distribution: no geographic restrictions and principally to national organizations

GIVING OFFICERS
William G. Bowen, PhD: dir *B* Cincinnati OH 1933 *ED* Denison Univ BA 1955; Princeton Univ PhD 1958 *CORP AFFIL* dir: Am Express Co, Merck & Co, NCR Corp, Readers Digest Assn, Rockefeller Group *NONPR AFFIL* mem: Am Econ Assn, Counc Foreign Rels, Indus Rels Res Assn, Phi Beta Kappa; mem bd regents: Smithsonian Inst; trust: Ctr Advanced Study Behavioral Sciences; prof econ: Princeton Univ
Theodore F. Brophy: dir *B* New York NY 1923 *ED* Yale Univ BA 1944; Harvard Univ LLB 1949 *CORP AFFIL* dir: Irving Bank Corp, Irving Trust Co, JWP Inc, Procter & Gamble Co, Reader's Digest Assn; mem adv comm: NY Stock Exchange *NONPR AFFIL* dir: Un Way Tri-State; mem: Am Bar Assn, Brookings Inst, Bus Roundtable, Conf Bd Bus Counc, Fed Communs Bar Assn, Greeenwich Hosp Assn, Smith Coll Pres Comm; mem adv counc: Natl Urban Coalition; trust: Am Indian Coll Funds
Jessica Chao: vp
M. Christine DeVita: pres, dir
George V. Grune: chmn, dir *B* White Plains NY 1929 *ED* Duke Univ BA 1952; Univ FL 1955-1956 *CURR EMPL* chmn, pres, ceo, coo: Readers Digest Assn *CORP AFFIL* dir: Assoc Dry Goods, Avon Products, Chem Bank, Chem NY Corp, CPC Intl, GTE Corp, Sterling Drug *NONPR AFFIL* dir: Boys Club Am; mem bd overseers, bd mgrs: Counc Conservators NY Pub Library, Counc Fin Aid Ed, Counc Foreign Rels, Inst France, Meml Sloan Kettering Cancer Ctr; mem conf bd, dir: Metro Opera Assn; mem policy comm: Bus Roundtable; trust: Duke Univ, Metro Mus Art, NY Zoological Soc, Rollins Coll Roy E Crummer Grad Sch Bus
J. Edward Hall: dir
Melvin R. Laird: dir *B* Omaha NE 1922 *ED* Carleton Coll BA 1942 *CURR EMPL* sr counsellor (natl & intl affairs): Readers Digest Assn *CORP AFFIL* bd dirs: Commercial Credit Co, Commun Satellite Corp, IDS Mutual Fund Group, Martin Marietta Corp, Metro Life Ins Co, Northwest Airlines, Phillips Petroleum Co, Scientific Applications Intl Inc *NONPR AFFIL* mem: Am Legion, Military Order Purple Heart, Veterans Foreign Wars; mem bd dirs: Am Inst CPAs, Boys Clubs Am, George Washington Univ, Laird Youth Leadership Fdn, Securities Exchange Comm Practice Section, World Rehab Fund; trust: John F Kennedy Ctr Performing Arts *PHIL AFFIL* dir: Airlie Foundation
Robert D. Nagel: treas
Laurance Spelman Rockefeller: dir *B* New York NY 1910 *ED* Princeton Univ BA 1932 *CORP AFFIL* chmn: Woodstock Resort Corp; dir: Readers Digest Assn *NONPR AFFIL* comr emeritus: Palisades Interstate Park Comm; hon chmn: NY Zoological Soc; hon trust: Natl Geographic Soc; trust emeritus: Princeton Univ *PHIL AFFIL* trust: Greenacre Foundation
Holly Sedford: program dir
Walter Vincent Shipley: dir *B* Newark NJ 1935 *ED* NY Univ BS 1960 *CURR EMPL* pres, coo: Chem Bank *CORP AFFIL* chmn: Chem NY Corp; dir: Champion Intl Corp, NYNEX Corp, Readers Digest Assn *NONPR AFFIL* dir: Assn Reserve City Bankers, Goodwill Indus Greater NY, Lincoln Ctr Performing Arts, NY Chamber Commerce Indus, NY City Partnership, Un Way Tri-St; mem: Bus Counc, Bus Roundtable, Counc Foreign Rels, English Speaking Union, Japan Soc, Pilgrims US; trust: NY Univ

APPLICATION INFORMATION
Initial Approach:
Initial approach should be a letter of no more than three pages. The letter should describe the organization, proposed project and its goal, and include an estimated total budget for the project, and the relationship between the goals of the project and the mission of the Lila Wallace-Reader's Digest Fund. If the request falls within fund interests, a formal proposal with detailed information will be requested.

There are no proposal deadlines.

The board meets three times a year to consider proposals. Proposals will be reviewed for their potential contribution to the field, the organization's ability to produce the proposed project, the financial stability of the organization, and the potential furthering of the fund's goals.

Restrictions on Giving: Grants generally are not given to individuals, religious organizations, fraternal or veterans' groups, or private foundations.

OTHER THINGS TO KNOW
The fund generally will not make grants under $50,000, or for long-term annual support of an organization. The fund is closely affiliated with the DeWitt Wallace-Reader's Digest Fund-New York.
Publications: annual report includes application guidelines

GRANTS ANALYSIS
Total Grants: $40,028,635
Number of Grants: 131
Highest Grant: $7,000,000
Typical Range: $100,000 to $500,000
Disclosure Period: 1992
Note: Recent grants are derived from a 1991 annual report.

RECENT GRANTS
5,000,000 Brooklyn Academy of Music, Brooklyn, NY
2,000,000 Philadelphia Museum of Art, Philadelphia, PA
1,267,830 City Parks Foundation, Bronx, NY
1,100,000 Joyce Theater, New York, NY
1,000,000 Association of Performing Arts Presenters, Washington, DC
1,000,000 Association of Performing Arts Presenters, Washington, DC
1,000,000 Opera America, Washington, DC
979,809 Council of Literary Magazines and Presses, New York, NY
903,506 Arts International, New York, NY
884,000 New England Foundation for the Arts, Cambridge, MA

Wallace & Wallace Ltd.
Headquarters: Hingham, MA

CONTACT
Tom Wallace
President
Wallace & Wallace Ltd.
PO Box 243
Hingham, MA 02043
(617) 749-7474

CONTRIBUTIONS SUMMARY
Company provides employee matching gifts only.
Grant Types: matching
Operating Locations: MA (Hingham)

Wallach Foundation, Miriam G. and Ira D.

CONTACT
Miriam G. and Ira D. Wallach Fdn.
100 Park Ave.
New York, NY 10017

FINANCIAL SUMMARY
Recent Giving: $1,343,247 (fiscal 1990); $1,283,105 (fiscal 1989); $1,278,939 (fiscal 1988)
Assets: $13,012,768 (fiscal year ending October 31, 1990); $14,500,338 (fiscal 1989); $13,244,061 (fiscal 1988)
Gifts Received: $200,200 (fiscal 1990)
EIN: 13-6101702

CONTRIBUTIONS SUMMARY
Typical Recipients: • *Arts & Humanities:* arts associations, dance, libraries, museums/galleries, opera, public broadcasting • *Civic & Public Affairs:* environmental affairs, international affairs, public policy, zoos/botanical gardens • *Education:* colleges & universities • *Health:* hospitals • *International:* international organizations • *Religion:* religious organizations • *Social Services:* child welfare, community centers, community service organizations, disabled, family planning, united funds, youth organizations
Grant Types: general support
Geographic Distribution: focus on NY

GIVING OFFICERS
Benjamin Glowatz: treas
Peter C. Siegfried: secy
Edgar Wachenheim III: vp, dir
Sue W. Wachenheim: dir
Ira D. Wallach: pres, dir *ED* Columbia Univ AB 1929; Columbia Univ JD 1931 *CURR EMPL* chmn, dir: Central Natl - Gottesman *CORP AFFIL* chmn, dir: Central Natl - Gottesman *NONPR AFFIL* dir: People Am Way; mem: Am Bar Assn, NY City Bar Assn
James G. Wallach: vp, dir *CURR EMPL* pres, ceo: Central Natl - Gottesman *CORP AFFIL* pres, ceo: Central Natl - Gottesman
Kate B. Wallach: dir
Kenneth L. Wallach: vp, dir
Mary K. Wallach: dir
Miriam G. Wallach: vp, dir
Susan S. Wallach: dir

APPLICATION INFORMATION
Initial Approach: Contributes only to preselected organizations.

GRANTS ANALYSIS
Number of Grants: 112
Highest Grant: $150,000
Typical Range: $50 to $5,000
Disclosure Period: fiscal year ending October 31, 1990

RECENT GRANTS
150,000 Williams College, Williamstown, MA
143,529 Israel Museum, Jerusalem, Israel
90,000 Earthview Foundation, New York, NY
75,000 Internews Network, Arcadia, CA
65,000 People for the American Way, Washington, DC
55,000 World Policy Institute, New York, NY
50,000 Bryant Park Restoration Corporation, New York, NY
50,000 Moreshet Israel, New York, NY
41,250 New York Hospital-Cornell Medical Center, New York, NY
40,000 International Peace Academy, New York, NY

Wallestad Foundation

CONTACT
Wallestad Foundation
7101 York Avenue South
Edina, MN 55435

FINANCIAL SUMMARY
Recent Giving: $284,513 (fiscal 1990)
Assets: $4,536,165 (fiscal year ending November 30, 1990)
Gifts Received: $36,915 (fiscal 1990)
Fiscal Note: Fiscal 1990 contributions received from Fluoroware ($215,000), Victor C. Wallestad ($100,000), Phadoris Wallestad Estate ($38,735), Wayne and Ann Zitzloff ($8,000), and Bunkley, Bennett and Christensen, P.A. ($5,000).
EIN: 36-3485265

GIVING OFFICERS
Jay Bennett: dir, pres, treas
Sally Bennett: dir, vp, secy
Stanley Geyer: dir
Brad McNaught: exec dir
Victor C. Wallestad: dir
Jan Wright: dir
Wayne Zitzloff: dir

GRANTS ANALYSIS
Total Grants: $284,513
Number of Grants: 55
Highest Grant: $27,000
Disclosure Period: fiscal year ending November 30, 1990

Wallin Foundation

CONTACT
Wallin Foundation
c/o Winston R. Wallin
7022 Tupa Circle
Edina, MN 55435

FINANCIAL SUMMARY
Recent Giving: $80,150 (1990); $62,005 (1989)
Assets: $2,244,902 (1990); $1,434,161 (1989)
Gifts Received: $838,742 (1990)
EIN: 41-6283068

CONTRIBUTIONS SUMMARY
Typical Recipients: • *Arts & Humanities:* arts institutes • *Education:* colleges & universities • *Social Services:* child welfare, family planning, homes, united funds
Grant Types: general support and project

GRANTS ANALYSIS

Total Grants: $80,150
Number of Grants: 21
Typical Range: $1,800 to
$10,000
Disclosure Period: 1990

RECENT GRANTS

13,500 United Way
10,000 Carleton College,
MN
10,000 Children's Home
Society
10,000 Planned Parenthood
5,000 N.E.H.G.S. Sesqui-
centennial Fund
4,000 Presbyterian
Homes of Minne-
sota, MN
3,500 Minneapolis Insti-
tute of the Arts,
Minneapolis, MN
2,000 Abbott N.W. Asso-
ciates
2,000 Hopkins Project
1,800 Planned Parent-
hood of Minnesota,
MN

Walsh Charity Trust, Blanche M.

CONTACT

Robert F. Mushy, Jr.
Trustee
Blanche M. Walsh Charity Trust
174 Central St., Ste. 329
Lowell, MA 01852
(508) 454-5654

FINANCIAL SUMMARY

Recent Giving: $204,650
(1990); $183,165 (1988)
Assets: $2,622,808 (1990);
$2,532,507 (1988)
EIN: 04-6311841

CONTRIBUTIONS SUMMARY

Typical Recipients: • *Education:* private education (precollege) • *Health:* hospitals • *Religion:* religious organizations
• *Social Services:* aged,
food/clothing distribution
Grant Types: capital, operating expenses, scholarship, and
seed money

GIVING OFFICERS

Ruth F. Cowdrey: trust
John E. Leggat: trust
Robert F. Murphy, Jr.: trust

APPLICATION INFORMATION

Initial Approach: Applicants
should contact the trust, in writing, to obtain grant application
forms. Completed applications
must be sumbitted December 1.
The foundation makes grants to
Roman Catholic Charities only.
Restrictions on Giving: Does
not support individuals or provide funds for endowments.

OTHER THINGS TO KNOW

Publications: Application
Guidelines

GRANTS ANALYSIS

Number of Grants: 103
Highest Grant: $6,000
Typical Range: $1,000 to
$6,000
Disclosure Period: 1990

RECENT GRANTS

6,000 St. Vincent de Paul
Society, Lowell,
MA — operating
4,000 Bethany House,
Olive Hill, KY —
emergency assis-
tance to rural poor
3,500 Managers of the
Roman Catholic Or-
phan's Asylums,
St. Louis, MI — op-
erating
3,500 Merrimack Valley
Catholic Charities,
Lowell, MA —
emergency food
program
3,000 Academy of Notre
Dame, Tyngsboro,
MA — science de-
partment
3,000 Catholic Charities,
Palm Beach Gar-
dens, FL
3,000 Madonna Manor,
Villa Hills, NY —
day room for al-
zheimer patients
3,000 Sisters of Charity
of Nazareth Provin-
cial House,
Quincy, MA — op-
erating/ESL
3,000 St. Patricks
School, Lowell,
MA — social stud-
ies materials
2,500 St. Joseph Hospi-
tal, North Provi-
dence, RI — high-
risk family program

Walsh Foundation

CONTACT

F. Howard Walsh, Sr.
President
Walsh Fdn.
500 West 7th St., Ste. 1007
Ft. Worth, TX 76102
(817) 335-3741

FINANCIAL SUMMARY

Recent Giving: $331,725
(1991); $509,485 (1990);
$132,550 (1989)
Assets: $1,819,508 (1991);
$1,724,506 (1990); $1,917,452
(1989)
Gifts Received: $217,164
(1991); $236,435 (1990);
$432,887 (1989)
EIN: 75-6021726

CONTRIBUTIONS SUMMARY

Donor(s): Mary D. Walsh, F.
Howard Walsh, Sr.
Typical Recipients: • *Arts &
Humanities:* arts institutes,
community arts, dance, music,
opera, performing arts, theater
• *Education:* colleges & universities, private education (precollege) • *Religion:* churches • *Social Services:* child welfare,
united funds, youth organizations
Grant Types: general support,
multiyear/continuing support,
operating expenses, and project
Geographic Distribution:
focus on Fort Worth, TX

GIVING OFFICERS

Gary F. Goble: dir
G. Malcolm Louden: secy, dir
ED TX Christian Univ BBA
1967 *CURR EMPL* gen mgr:
Walsh Family Co
F. Howard Walsh, Sr.: pres,
don *B* Waco TX 1913 *ED* TX
Christian Univ BBA 1933
CORP AFFIL pres: Walsh &
Watts *NONPR AFFIL* guaran-
tor: Ft Worth Arts Counc, Ft
Worth Ballet, Ft Worth Opera,
Ft Worth Theatre, Schola Can-
torum, TX Boys' Choir; mem:
Am-Intl Charolais Assn, Inde-
pendent Petroleum Assn Am,
North TX Oil Gas Assn, TX
Christian Univ Ex-Lettermen
Assn, TX Independent Produc-
ers Royalty Owners Assn, TX
Mid-Continent Oil Gas Assn,
West Central TX Oil Gas Assn;
trust: TX Christian Univ
F. Howard Walsh, Sr.: asst
secy, asst treas *B* Waco TX
1913 *ED* TX Christian Univ
BBA 1933 *CORP AFFIL* pres:

Walsh & Watts *NONPR AFFIL*
dir: Southwestern Exposition
Fat Stock Show; guarantor: Ft
Worth Arts Counc, Ft Worth
Ballet, Ft Worth Opera, Ft
Worth Theatre, Schola Can-
torum, TX Boys' Choir; hon
trust: TX Christian Univ; mem:
Am-Intl Charolais Assn, Bap-
tist Bd Sr Deacons, Inde-
pendent Petroleum Assn, North
TX Oil & Gas Assn, TX Chris-
tian Univ Ex-Lettermen Assn,
TX Independent Producers &
Royalty Owners Assn, TX Mid-
Continent Oil & Gas Assn,
West Central TX Oil & Gas
Assn
Mary D. Walsh: vp

APPLICATION INFORMATION

Initial Approach: Send brief
letter of inquiry describing program or project. There are no
deadlines.

GRANTS ANALYSIS

Number of Grants: 81
Highest Grant: $90,000
Typical Range: $100 to
$10,000
Disclosure Period: 1991

RECENT GRANTS

90,000 Arts Council
Greater Fort
Worth, Ft. Worth,
TX
70,000 Broadway Baptist
Church, Ft. Worth,
TX
25,000 Jewel Charity Ball,
Ft. Worth, TX
19,000 Fort Worth Sym-
phony Orchestra
Association, Ft.
Worth, TX
15,000 Texas Christian
University, Ft.
Worth, TX
10,000 Fort Worth Ballet
Association, Ft.
Worth, TX
10,000 Fort Worth Opera
Association, Ft.
Worth, TX
10,000 Fort Worth Thea-
tre, Ft. Worth, TX
10,000 Texas Boys Choir,
Ft. Worth, TX
6,500 Van Cliburn Piano
Competition, Ft.
Worth, TX

Disney Co., Walt / Disney Co. Foundation, Walt

Sales: $7.63 billion
Employees: 60,000
Headquarters: Burbank, CA
SIC Major Group: Amusement
& Recreation Services, Motion
Pictures, and Real Estate

CONTACT

Doris A. Smith
Administrator
Walt Disney Co. Fdn.
500 S. Buena Vista St.
Burbank, CA 91521-0968
(818) 560-5151

FINANCIAL SUMMARY

Recent Giving: $1,737,238
(fiscal 1991); $1,508,560 (fiscal 1989); $599,172 (fiscal 1987)
Assets: $302,994 (fiscal year ending September 30, 1991); $134,118 (fiscal 1989)
Fiscal Note: Above figures are for the foundation only.
EIN: 95-6037079

CONTRIBUTIONS SUMMARY

Typical Recipients: • *Arts & Humanities:* arts centers, arts institutes, cinema, museums/galleries, music, performing arts, public broadcasting • *Civic & Public Affairs:* better government, business/free enterprise, environmental affairs, ethnic/minority organizations, international affairs, law & justice, philanthropic organizations, public policy, urban & community affairs, zoos/botanical gardens • *Education:* arts education, business education, colleges & universities, education funds, health & physical education, legal education, science/technology education • *Health:* hospitals, medical rehabilitation, single-disease health associations • *Social Services:* animal protection, community centers, disabled, food/clothing distribution, recreation & athletics, united funds, volunteer services, youth organizations
Grant Types: capital, challenge, general support, operating expenses, project, research, and scholarship
Note: Because the foundation does not release current giving information, some grant types are based on previous years.

Geographic Distribution: nationally to company operating areas, with emphasis on California (Los Angeles and Orange counties) and Florida (Orange and Osceola counties)
Operating Locations: CA (Anaheim, Burbank, Glendale), FL (Boca Raton, Lake Buena Vista, Miami, Orlando), NJ (Edison), NY (New York City)

CORP. OFFICERS

Roy Edward Disney: *B* Los Angeles CA 1930 *ED* Pomona Coll BA 1951 *CURR EMPL* vchmn, dir: Walt Disney Co *CORP AFFIL* dir: Shamrock Broadcasting; vchmn, dir: Walt Disney Co *NONPR AFFIL* dir: Big Bros Greater Los Angeles; mem: Dirs Guild Am, US Naval Academy Sailing Squadron; mem adv bd: St Joseph Med Ctr; trust: CA Inst Arts
Michael Dammann Eisner: *B* Mt Kisco NY 1942 *ED* Denison Univ BA 1964 *CURR EMPL* chmn, ceo, dir: Walt Disney Co *NONPR AFFIL* dir: Am Film Inst, CA Inst Arts, Denison Univ, Georgetown Univ, Performing Arts Counc Los Angeles Music Ctr
Frank G. Wells: *B* 1932 *ED* Pomona Coll BA 1953; Oxford Univ MA 1955; Stanford Univ LLB 1959 *CURR EMPL* pres, coo, dir: Walt Disney Co *NONPR AFFIL* bd overseers: RAND/Univ CA Los Angeles Ctr Study Soviet Behavior; mem: Am Bar Assn, Los Angeles County Bar Assn, Phi Beta Kappa, St Bar CA; mem svcs policy adv comm: US Trade Regulation; trust: CA Inst Tech, Natl Hist Mus, Pomona Coll, Sundance Inst

GIVING OFFICERS

Roy Edward Disney: trust *CURR EMPL* vchmn, dir: Walt Disney Co (see above)
Michael Dammann Eisner: pres, trust *CURR EMPL* chmn, ceo, dir: Walt Disney Co (see above)
Jack B. Lindquist: vp, trust *B* Chicago IL 1927 *ED* Univ Southern CA 1950 *CURR EMPL* pres: Disneyland *CORP AFFIL* chmn: Walt Disney Travel Co
Doris Anita Smith: secy *B* Elizabeth NJ 1935 *ED* Douglass Coll 1956; Univ CA Los Angeles *CURR EMPL* vp, secy: Walt Disney Co *NONPR AFFIL* dir: Los Angeles Emer-

gency Loan Fund; vp: Am Soc Corp Secys
Frank G. Wells: treas *CURR EMPL* pres, coo, dir: Walt Disney Co (see above)

APPLICATION INFORMATION

Initial Approach: *Initial Contact:* brief letter or proposal *Include Information On:* financial statements, preferably audited; list of major contributors, sources of income, and board members, including their affiliations; history of the organization; and proof of tax exemption *When to Submit:* any time; proposals should be submitted by December 31 to be evaluated the following spring
Restrictions on Giving: Foundation does not support individuals, sectarian organizations, or agency building campaigns; does not provide seed money or funds for medical research. Generally, foundation does not support public agencies, educational institutions, or other organizations that receive mostly tax dollars; or organizations receiving funds from United Way or other groups which the foundation supports.

OTHER THINGS TO KNOW

In past years, most grants have gone to repeat recipients.

GRANTS ANALYSIS

Total Grants: $1,521,310*
Number of Grants: 81*
Highest Grant: $500,000*
Typical Range: $1,000 to $20,000*
Disclosure Period: fiscal year ending September 30, 1991
Note: Figures do not include contributions from the company scholarship program totaling $215,928. Recent grants are derived from a fiscal 1991 Form 990.

RECENT GRANTS

500,000　California Institute of the Arts, Valencia, CA — general operations
150,000　California Institute of the Arts, Valencia, CA — matched ticket sales benefit premier "Rescuers Down Under"
100,000　Central Florida Capital Funds, Orlando, FL

100,000　Motion Picture and Television Fund, Woodland Hills, CA
100,000　United Arts of Central Florida, Orlando, FL
75,000　Orlando Regional Medical Center, Orlando, FL
50,000　Academy Foundation, Beverly Hills, CA
50,000　California Institute of the Arts, Valencia, CA — character animation program
50,000　California Institute of the Arts, Valencia, CA — character animation program equipment
50,000　Permanent Charities Committee of the Entertainment Industries, Los Angeles, CA

Walter Family Trust, Byron L.

CONTACT

Richard J. Blahnik
Byron L. Walter Family Trust
c/o Bank One Wisconsin Trust Co., N.A.
PO Box 19029
Green Bay, WI 54307-9029
(414) 436-2610

FINANCIAL SUMMARY

Recent Giving: $321,675 (fiscal 1992); $359,579 (fiscal 1991); $409,094 (fiscal 1990)
Assets: $8,816,144 (fiscal year ending April 30, 1992); $8,152,041 (fiscal 1991); $7,323,389 (fiscal 1990)
EIN: 39-6346563

CONTRIBUTIONS SUMMARY

Donor(s): the late Arlene B. Walter

Typical Recipients: • *Arts & Humanities:* history/historic preservation, museums/galleries, opera, performing arts, public broadcasting, theater • *Civic & Public Affairs:* environmental affairs • *Education:* colleges & universities • *Health:* hospitals, medical research, single-disease health associations • *Social Services:* animal protection, community service organizations, family planning, family services, food/clothing distribution, united funds, youth organizations

Grant Types: capital and project
Geographic Distribution: limited to Brown County, WI

GIVING OFFICERS
Bank One Wisconsin Trust Company: trust

APPLICATION INFORMATION
Initial Approach: Contributes only to preselected organizations.
Restrictions on Giving: Does not support individuals or provide loans.

OTHER THINGS TO KNOW
Publications: Application Guidelines

GRANTS ANALYSIS
Number of Grants: 23
Highest Grant: $32,000
Typical Range: $10,000 to $20,000
Disclosure Period: fiscal year ending April 30, 1992

RECENT GRANTS
32,000 St. Norbert College, De Pere, WI
32,000 St. Norbert College, De Pere, WI
30,000 Centre for the Performing Arts Fund, Green Bay, WI
30,000 Heritage Hill Foundation, Green Bay, WI
30,000 NEWIST, Green Bay, WI — Babies with AIDS project
25,000 Boys and Girls Club, Green Bay, WI
25,000 Bridge of Green Bay, Green Bay, WI
25,000 Our Lady of Charity Family Program, Green Bay, WI
25,000 St. Mary's Hospital, Green Bay, WI
20,000 YWCA, Green Bay, WI

Walter Industries / Walter Foundation

Former Foundation Name: Jim Walter Corp. Foundation
Sales: $1.36 billion
Employees: 8,000
Headquarters: Tampa, FL
SIC Major Group: Coal Mining, General Building Contractors, Primary Metal Industries, and Real Estate

CONTACT
W. Kendall Baker
Trustee
Walter Fdn.
1500 N. Dale Mabry
PO Box 31601
Tampa, FL 33631-3601
(813) 871-4168

FINANCIAL SUMMARY
Recent Giving: $392,608 (fiscal 1992); $507,975 (fiscal 1991); $293,675 (fiscal 1990)
Assets: $8,965,606 (fiscal year ending August 31, 1992); $8,198,470 (fiscal 1991); $7,335,161 (fiscal 1990)
Gifts Received: $338,600 (fiscal 1992); $375,725 (fiscal 1991); $380,000 (fiscal 1990)
Fiscal Note: Contributes through foundation only. In fiscal 1992, contributions were received from Walter Industries.
EIN: 59-6205802

CONTRIBUTIONS SUMMARY
Typical Recipients: • *Arts & Humanities:* arts centers • *Civic & Public Affairs:* business/free enterprise, economic development, environmental affairs • *Education:* business education, colleges & universities • *Health:* health organizations, hospitals, hospitals, single-disease health associations • *Social Services:* community service organizations, united funds, youth organizations
Grant Types: general support
Geographic Distribution: primarily in Tampa, FL; also gives near operating locations
Operating Locations: AL (Birmingham, Brookwood, Graysville), FL (Tampa), TN (Sweetwater)
Note: List includes locations of operating companies.

CORP. OFFICERS
G. Robert Durham: *B* West Frankfort IL 1929 *ED* Purdue Univ 1951 *CURR EMPL* pres, ceo: Walter Indus *CORP AFFIL* dir: Homestake Mining Co; trust: Mutual Life Ins Co NY
James W. Walter: *B* Lewes DE 1922 *CURR EMPL* chmn: Jim Walter Corp *CORP AFFIL* chmn, dir: Walter Indus; dir: Anchor Glass Container Corp, Beijer Indus, Calmar, Crown Indus, GTE Corp, Keller Indus

GIVING OFFICERS
W. K. Baker: trust

James W. Walter: trust *CURR EMPL* chmn: Jim Walter Corp (see above)
Robert A. Walter: trust

APPLICATION INFORMATION
Initial Approach: *Initial Contact:* brief letter or proposal *Include Information On:* brief description of the organization, purpose for which funding is needed, and amount requested *When to Submit:* any time
Restrictions on Giving: Grant must be received as a qualified charitable gift.

OTHER THINGS TO KNOW
In fiscal 1991, about 85% of foundation giving was on behalf of Walter Industries, approximately 8% of giving was on behalf of U.S. Pipe and Foundry Co., and 5% of giving was on behalf of Jim Walter Resources, Inc. Jim Walter Resources, Inc. and U.S. Pipe and Foundry Co. are subsidiaries of Walter Industries.
At this time, the foundation is not accepting new applications for grants. The foundation has curtailed back giving to only local organizations. Its sponsoring company has filed bankruptcy and is no longer contributing to the foundation.

GRANTS ANALYSIS
Total Grants: $392,608
Number of Grants: 72
Highest Grant: $100,000
Typical Range: $500 to $4,000
Disclosure Period: fiscal year ending August 31, 1992
Note: Recent grants are derived from a fiscal 1992 grants list.

RECENT GRANTS
100,000 Tampa Bay Performing Arts Center, Tampa, FL
50,000 University of South Florida, Tampa, FL
25,000 Eckerd Family Youth Alternatives, Eckerd, FL
25,000 Foundation for Leadership Quality and Ethics Practice, Tampa, FL
20,000 Boys and Girls Club, Tampa, FL
20,000 St. Leo College, St. Leo, FL
20,000 YMCA, Tampa, FL
10,000 Pediatric Pulmonary Research and Education Fund, Tampa, FL

10,000 Salvation Army, Tampa, FL
10,000 Salvation Army, Tampa, FL

Walthall Perpetual Charitable Trust, Marjorie T.

CONTACT
Paul Walthall
Trustee
Marjorie T. Walthall Perpetual Charitable Trust
112 W. Ridgewood
San Antonio, TX 78212
(512) 822-5433

FINANCIAL SUMMARY
Recent Giving: $113,500 (1991); $128,750 (1990); $88,000 (1989)
Assets: $2,464,763 (1991); $2,142,706 (1990); $2,247,964 (1989)
EIN: 51-0170313

CONTRIBUTIONS SUMMARY
Donor(s): Marjorie T. Walthall
Typical Recipients: • *Arts & Humanities:* community arts, museums/galleries • *Civic & Public Affairs:* women's affairs, zoos/botanical gardens • *Education:* medical education • *Health:* hospices, hospitals, medical research • *Religion:* churches • *Social Services:* animal protection, child welfare, community service organizations, counseling, homes
Grant Types: general support
Geographic Distribution: focus on San Antonio, TX

GIVING OFFICERS
Marjorie Walthall Fry: trust
Paul T. Walthall: trust
Wilson J. Walthall III: trust

APPLICATION INFORMATION
Initial Approach: Send brief letter describing program. Deadline is October 1.
Restrictions on Giving: Does not support individuals.

GRANTS ANALYSIS
Number of Grants: 33
Highest Grant: $10,000
Typical Range: $1,000 to $5,000
Disclosure Period: 1991

RECENT GRANTS
10,000 Christ Episcopal Church, San Antonio, TX

10,000 San Antonio College Nursing School, San Antonio, TX

5,000 Baptist Hospital School of Nursing, San Antonio, TX

5,000 Bexar County Women's Center, San Antonio, TX

5,000 Community Guidance Center, San Antonio, TX

5,000 Humane Society of Bexar County, San Antonio, TX

5,000 Ramparts, San Antonio, TX

5,000 San Antonio Museum Association, San Antonio, TX

5,000 San Antonio Zoological Society, San Antonio, TX

5,000 St. Jude's Home, San Antonio, TX

Walton Family Foundation

CONTACT
Jan Ney
Coordinator
Walton Family Foundation
125 West Central, Ste. 218
Bentonville, AR 72712
(501) 273-5743

FINANCIAL SUMMARY
Recent Giving: $2,470,105 (1990); $1,411,650 (1989)
Assets: $19,389,106 (1990); $3,080,083 (1989)
Gifts Received: $18,550,000 (1990)
Fiscal Note: In 1990, the foundation received $18,350,000 from the Sam M. Walton1987 Nonqualified Charitable Remainder Trust and $200,000 from the Helen R. Walton 1987 Nonqualified Charitable Remainder Trust.
EIN: 13-3441466

CONTRIBUTIONS SUMMARY
Donor(s): The Walton Family Foundation was established in 1987 by Sam M. Walton, founder of Wal-Mart Stores, one of the largest retailers in the country. Walton became a management trainee at JC Penny in 1940, and by 1945 was running his own franchise Ben Franklin store in Newport, AR, eventually managing nine stores by 1959. In 1962, he opened his own discount store, Wal-Mart Discount City in

Rogers, AR. In 1992, there were over 1,650 Wal-Marts and 200 Sam's Wholesale Clubs nationwide. Sam Walton died in April 1992.
Helen Robson Walton, the late Sam Walton's wife, and her four children, S. Robson, James C., John T., and Alice L., all serve as directors of the Walton Family Foundation. Additionally, Helen R. Walton and the four Walton children serve as trustees of the Walton Foundation and the Sam M. and Helen R. Walton Foundation.
Typical Recipients: • *Arts & Humanities:* public broadcasting • *Civic & Public Affairs:* public policy • *Education:* colleges & universities
Grant Types: general support
Geographic Distribution: primarily Arkansas

GIVING OFFICERS
Alice L. Walton: dir *B* 1949 *CURR EMPL* fdr: Llama Co *PHIL AFFIL* trust: Walton Foundation, Sam M & Helen R Walton Foundation
Helen Robson Walton: don, dir *ED* Univ OK 1941 *PHIL AFFIL* trust: Walton Foundation, Sam M & Helen R Walton Foundation
James C. Walton: dir *B* 1948 *CURR EMPL* pres: Walton Enterprises *PHIL AFFIL* trust: Walton Foundation, Sam M & Helen R Walton Foundation
John T. Walton: dir *B* 1945 *PHIL AFFIL* trust: Walton Foundation, Sam M & Helen R Walton Foundation
S. Robson Walton: dir *B* 1945 *ED* Columbia Univ JD 1969 *CURR EMPL* chmn: Wal-Mart Stores *CORP AFFIL* dir: Acxiom Corp, Cooper Communities; vchmn: North AR Wholesale Co *PHIL AFFIL* trust: Walton Foundation, Sam M & Helen R Walton Foundation

APPLICATION INFORMATION
Initial Approach:
Applicants should send a brief letter proposal of one to three pages to the foundation. The proposal should contain the following: proof of IRS 501(c)(3) nonprofit status; a short history of the organization and its purpose; a description of the project goal and the qualifications of the staff involved; the amount of funding requested; and anticipated long- and short-term advantages of

the project affecting the foundation as well as all others who stand to benefit.
There are no deadlines for application.

GRANTS ANALYSIS
Total Grants: $2,470,105
Number of Grants: 13
Highest Grant: $850,000
Typical Range: $10,000 to $50,000
Disclosure Period: 1990
Note: Average grant figure excludes three highest grants: $850,000; $675,000; and $625,000. Recent grants are derived from a 1990 Form 990.

RECENT GRANTS
850,000 Harding University, Searcy, AR

675,000 John Brown University, Siloam Springs, AR

625,000 University of the Ozarks, Clarksville, AR

110,000 Arkansas Business Council Foundation, Bentonville, AR — earmarked for grant to Westark Community College

86,105 Arkansas Business Council Foundation, Bentonville, AR — earmarked for grant to Southern Arkansas University Tech

50,000 EOA of Washington County, AR

25,000 Cookson Hills Christian School, Kansas, OK

15,000 American Educational Television Network

12,000 Independent College Fund of Arkansas, Little Rock, AR

10,000 University of Arkansas, Fayetteville, AR — KUAF radio station

Walton Monroe Mills
Sales: $516.0 million
Employees: 4,200
Headquarters: Monroe, GA
SIC Major Group: Textile Mill Products

CONTACT
Eugene Ashe
Director, Industrial Relations
Walton Monroe Mills
PO Box 1046
Monroe, GA 30655
(404) 267-9411

CONTRIBUTIONS SUMMARY
Operating Locations: GA (Monroe)

CORP. OFFICERS
G. Stephen Felker: *CURR EMPL* pres, ceo, treas: Walton Monroe Mills

George W. Felker III: *CURR EMPL* chmn: Walton Monroe Mills

Wang Laboratories, Inc.
Sales: $2.09 billion
Employees: 20,184
Headquarters: Lowell, MA
SIC Major Group: Business Services, Electronic & Other Electrical Equipment, and Industrial Machinery & Equipment

CONTACT
Paul Guzzi
Senior Vice President, Communications
Wang Laboratories, Inc.
One Industrial Avenue, M/S 019-B4A
Lowell, MA 01851
(508) 967-2356
Note: Edmund Pignone, Director, Public Relations, also is a contact.

CONTRIBUTIONS SUMMARY
Supports education, health, and the arts.

Typical Recipients: • *Arts & Humanities:* general • *Education:* general • *Health:* general

Geographic Distribution: primarily MA

Operating Locations: MA (Lowell)

CORP. OFFICERS
Harry H.S. Chou: *CURR EMPL* vchmn, dir: Wang Laboratories

Richard W. Miller: *CURR EMPL* chmn, pres, ceo, dir: Wang Laboratories

Ward Co., Joe L. / Ward Co. Ltd. Charitable Trust, Joe L.

Headquarters: Waco, TX

CONTACT
Joe L. Ward, Jr.
Trustee
Joe L. Ward Co. Ltd. Charitable Trust
4808 Lake Shore Dr.
Waco, TX 76710
(817) 772-1423

FINANCIAL SUMMARY
Recent Giving: $1,335 (1991); $700 (1990); $2,800 (1989)
Assets: $21,002 (1991); $21,218 (1990); $20,559 (1989)
EIN: 74-6047138

CONTRIBUTIONS SUMMARY
Typical Recipients: • *Arts & Humanities:* arts centers, history/historic preservation • *Civic & Public Affairs:* municipalities • *Social Services:* community service organizations, united funds, youth organizations
Grant Types: general support
Geographic Distribution: focus on TX
Operating Locations: TX (Waco)

CORP. OFFICERS
Joe L. Ward: *CURR EMPL* chmn: Joe L Ward Co

GIVING OFFICERS
Joe L. Ward, Jr.: trust

APPLICATION INFORMATION
Initial Approach: Send brief letter describing program.

GRANTS ANALYSIS
Number of Grants: 8
Highest Grant: $500
Typical Range: $100 to $500
Disclosure Period: 1991

RECENT GRANTS
500 YMCA, Waco, TX
200 Junior League of Waco, Waco, TX
150 Art Center, Waco, TX
125 Fort Griffin Fandangle, Albany, TX
100 Caritas of Waco, Waco, TX
100 Historic Waco, Waco, TX
100 Salvation Army, Waco, TX
60 KERA, Dallas, TX

Ward Foundation, A. Montgomery

CONTACT
M. C. Ryan
A. Montgomery Ward Fdn.
c/o Continental Bank, N.A.
30 North LaSalle St.
Chicago, IL 60697
(312) 828-1785

FINANCIAL SUMMARY
Recent Giving: $532,600 (fiscal 1990); $520,000 (fiscal 1989)
Assets: $9,272,456 (fiscal year ending June 30, 1989)
EIN: 36-2417437

CONTRIBUTIONS SUMMARY
Donor(s): the late Marjorie Montgomery Ward Baker
Typical Recipients: • *Arts & Humanities:* music, performing arts, public broadcasting • *Education:* colleges & universities, private education (precollege) • *Health:* hospitals • *Social Services:* aged, child welfare, homes, youth organizations
Grant Types: capital, operating expenses, and scholarship
Geographic Distribution: focus on Chicago, IL, and surrounding metropolitan areas

GIVING OFFICERS
Richard A. Beck: trust
John A. Hutchings: trust

APPLICATION INFORMATION
Initial Approach: Send brief letter of inquiry or proposal (two copies). Board meets in May and November.
Restrictions on Giving: Does not support individuals.

OTHER THINGS TO KNOW
Publications: Application Guidelines

GRANTS ANALYSIS
Number of Grants: 19
Highest Grant: $100,000
Typical Range: $5,000 to $25,000
Disclosure Period: fiscal year ending June 30, 1989

RECENT GRANTS
100,000 Children's Home and Aid Society of Illinois, Chicago, IL
75,000 Illinois Institute of Technology, Chicago, IL
35,000 Associated Colleges of Illinois, Chicago, IL
25,000 Chicago Symphony Orchestra, Chicago, IL
25,000 Northwestern University, Evanston, IL
25,000 Northwestern University, Evanston, IL
25,000 St. Ignatius College Preparatory, Chicago, IL
25,000 University of Chicago, Chicago, IL
20,000 St. Coletta's of Illinois, Palos Park, IL
20,000 United Charities of Chicago, Chicago, IL

Ward Foundation, Louis L. and Adelaide C.

CONTACT
Louis L. Ward
President
Louis L. and Adelaide C. Ward Fdn.
1000 Walnut St.
Kansas City, MO 64106
(816) 842-9240

FINANCIAL SUMMARY
Recent Giving: $382,010 (1990); $142,825 (1989); $143,901 (1988)
Assets: $4,780,665 (1990); $4,673,174 (1989); $4,491,364 (1988)
EIN: 43-6064548

CONTRIBUTIONS SUMMARY
Donor(s): Louis L. Ward, Adelaide C. Ward
Typical Recipients: • *Arts & Humanities:* music • *Health:* hospitals, medical research, medical research, single-disease health associations • *Religion:* churches • *Social Services:* child welfare, community service organizations, disabled, youth organizations
Grant Types: capital, endowment, general support, and scholarship
Geographic Distribution: focus on KS, MO, MT, and OH

GIVING OFFICERS
Scott Howard: secy
Adelaide C. Ward: vp, treas
Louis Larrick Ward: pres *B* Kansas City MO 1920 *ED* Stanford Univ BS 1941 *CURR EMPL* chmn, pres: Russell Sto-
ver Candies *CORP AFFIL* dir: First Natl Bank, Ward Paper Box Co

APPLICATION INFORMATION
Initial Approach: Send brief letter of inquiry describing program or project. Deadline is December 31.

GRANTS ANALYSIS
Number of Grants: 32
Highest Grant: $250,000
Typical Range: $100 to $5,000
Disclosure Period: 1990

RECENT GRANTS
250,000 Kansas University Endowment Association, Lawrence, KS
100,000 Nelson Art Gallery, Kansas City, MO
10,000 Williams Educational Fund, Lawrence, KS
5,000 Crippled Children's Nursery, Kansas City, MO
5,000 Red Cross, Kansas City, MO
1,000 Crippled Children's Nursery, Kansas City, MO
1,000 Gillis Home, Kansas City, MO
1,000 Mountain View Hospital, Billings, MT
1,000 Royal Night of Fashion, Kansas City, MO
1,000 Stanford University, Stanford, CA

Ward Heritage Foundation, Mamie McFaddin

CONTACT
Pamela K. Parish
Mamie McFaddin Ward Heritage Fdn.
PO Box 3391
Beaumont, TX 77704
(409) 838-9281

FINANCIAL SUMMARY
Recent Giving: $797,612 (1991); $856,035 (1990); $962,859 (1988)
Assets: $20,706,565 (1991); $20,263,661 (1990); $19,783,513 (1988)
EIN: 74-6260525

CONTRIBUTIONS SUMMARY

Donor(s): The foundation was established in 1976 by the late Mamie McFaddin Ward.

Typical Recipients: • *Civic & Public Affairs:* philanthropic organizations • *Social Services:* homes

Grant Types: general support and seed money

Geographic Distribution: limited to Jefferson County, TX

GIVING OFFICERS

Eugene H. B. McFaddin: trust
James L. C. McFaddin, Jr.: trust
Ida M. Pyle: trust
Rosine M. Wilson: trust

APPLICATION INFORMATION

Initial Approach: Applicants should write the foundation for a formal application.

The deadline for submitting proposals is May 15.

Restrictions on Giving: The foundation does not make grants to individuals.

GRANTS ANALYSIS

Total Grants: $797,612
Number of Grants: 2
Highest Grant: $749,517
Disclosure Period: 1991

Note: Recent grants are derived from a 1991 grants list.

RECENT GRANTS

749,517 McFaddin Ward House, Beaumont, TX

10,000 Beaumont Community Foundation, Beaumont, TX

Ward Machinery Co.

Sales: $33.0 million
Employees: 350
Headquarters: Cockeysville, MD
SIC Major Group: Industrial Machinery & Equipment

CONTACT

David Annon
Vice President, Finance
Ward Machinery Co.
10615 Beaver Dam Rd.
Cockeysville, MD 21030
(301) 584-7700

CONTRIBUTIONS SUMMARY

Operating Locations: MD (Cockeysville)

CORP. OFFICERS

David M. Annon: *CURR EMPL* cfo: Ward Machinery Co
Thomas M. Scanlan, Jr.: *CURR EMPL* pres: Ward Machinery Co

Wardlaw Fund, Gertrude and William C.

CONTACT

Gertrude and William C. Wardlaw Fund
c/o Trust Co. Bank
PO Box 4655
Atlanta, GA 30302

FINANCIAL SUMMARY

Recent Giving: $252,500 (1990); $184,000 (1989); $132,000 (1988)
Assets: $7,284,434 (1990); $6,572,152 (1989); $4,356,251 (1988)
EIN: 58-6026065

CONTRIBUTIONS SUMMARY

Donor(s): Gertrude Wardlaw, the late William C. Wardlaw, Jr.

Typical Recipients: • *Arts & Humanities:* arts centers, community arts • *Civic & Public Affairs:* zoos/botanical gardens • *Education:* colleges & universities, literacy • *Health:* hospitals, single-disease health associations • *Religion:* churches • *Social Services:* family planning, united funds, youth organizations

Grant Types: operating expenses

Geographic Distribution: focus on Atlanta, GA

GIVING OFFICERS

Trust Company Bank trust
Victor A. Gregory: trust
A. Pickney Straughn: secy, trust
Ednabelle Raine Wardlaw: chmn, trust
William C. Wardlaw III: trust

APPLICATION INFORMATION

Initial Approach: Send brief letter of inquiry describing program or project. There are no deadlines.

Restrictions on Giving: Does not support individuals.

GRANTS ANALYSIS

Number of Grants: 37
Highest Grant: $30,000

Typical Range: $1,000 to $5,000
Disclosure Period: 1990

RECENT GRANTS

30,000 Atlanta Speech School, Atlanta, GA

25,000 Boy Scouts of America, Atlanta, GA

20,000 United Way, Atlanta, GA

15,000 Scottish Rite Children's Hospital, Atlanta, GA

10,000 Raoul Foundation American Lung Association, Atlanta, GA

7,500 Emory University Hospital, Atlanta, GA

7,500 Shepherd Spinal Center, Atlanta, GA

7,500 Washington Peace Center, Washington, DC

7,500 Woodruff Arts Center, Atlanta, GA

6,000 Rural Advancement Fund, Atlanta, GA

Wardle Family Foundation

CONTACT

Robert V. Wardle
Principal Manager
Wardle Family Fdn.
380 Claremont Dr.
Lower Burrell, PA 15068-0744
(412) 335-0863

FINANCIAL SUMMARY

Recent Giving: $233,192 (1991); $222,924 (1990); $102,104 (1989)
Assets: $5,802,088 (1991); $4,890,926 (1990); $5,344,783 (1989)
Gifts Received: $2,571,563 (1989); $1,666,000 (1988)
Fiscal Note: 1989 contribution of 65,000 shares of Allegheny Ludlum Corporation stock from Robert V. Wardle.
EIN: 25-6290322

CONTRIBUTIONS SUMMARY

Donor(s): Robert V. Wardle

Typical Recipients: • *Arts & Humanities:* libraries • *Education:* colleges & universities • *Religion:* religious organizations • *Social Services:* child welfare, community service organizations, family planning, family services, food/clothing distribution, homes, religious

welfare, shelters/homelessness, united funds, youth organizations

Grant Types: general support

Geographic Distribution: focus on Pittsburgh, PA

GIVING OFFICERS

Corinne G. Wardle: trust
Robert V. Wardle: trust

APPLICATION INFORMATION

Initial Approach: Contributes only to preselected organizations.

Restrictions on Giving: Does not support individuals.

GRANTS ANALYSIS

Number of Grants: 31
Highest Grant: $75,000
Typical Range: $500 to $10,000
Disclosure Period: 1991

RECENT GRANTS

75,000 United Presbyterian Home for Children, Mars, PA

50,000 Hole in the Wall Gang Fund, New Haven, CT

15,000 Family House, Pittsburgh, PA

15,000 St. Elizabeth Shelter, Santa Fe, NM

10,768 Teen Pregnancy Childcare Training Program, Greensburg, PA

10,000 Los Nino's International Adoption Center, Austin, TX

10,000 United Way, Pittsburgh, PA

10,000 University of Pittsburgh, Pittsburgh, PA

7,500 Water Lines, Santa Fe, NM

5,000 United Way, Greensburg, PA

Ware Foundation

CONTACT

Rhoda C. Ware
Chairman
Ware Foundation
147 Alhambra Circle, Ste. 215
Coral Gables, FL 33134
(305) 443-8728

FINANCIAL SUMMARY

Recent Giving: $424,100 (1991); $902,000 (1990); $759,000 (1989)
Assets: $25,442,173 (1991); $16,235,835 (1990); $18,364,773 (1989)
EIN: 23-7286585

CONTRIBUTIONS SUMMARY

Donor(s): The Ware Foundation was founded in Pennsylvania in 1950 by John H. Ware, Jr. In recent years, the foundation has conducted its business operations in the Miami area.
Typical Recipients: • *Arts & Humanities:* cinema, history/historic preservation, public broadcasting • *Civic & Public Affairs:* public policy • *Education:* colleges & universities, international exchange, international studies, medical education, public education (precollege), religious education • *Health:* hospices, hospitals, medical research, nursing services • *Religion:* churches, missionary activities, religious organizations • *Social Services:* aged, child welfare, day care, drugs & alcohol, emergency relief, religious welfare, youth organizations
Grant Types: general support and research
Geographic Distribution: national

GIVING OFFICERS

Rhoda W. Cobb: trust
Martha Odem: trust
Nancy W. Pascal: trust
Rhoda C. Ware: chmn, trust

APPLICATION INFORMATION

Initial Approach:
Send all relevant information in writing to the foundation. The foundation does not accept telephone inquiries. Grant application forms are provided. A response will be provided only if a proposal is accepted by the board of directors.

OTHER THINGS TO KNOW

Previously funded programs may reapply. Multiple-year funding is not available.

GRANTS ANALYSIS

Total Grants: $424,100
Number of Grants: 32
Highest Grant: $55,000
Typical Range: $5,000 to $15,000
Disclosure Period: 1991
Note: Recent grants are derived from a 1991 Form 990.

RECENT GRANTS

55,000 Mission Research Training Center
50,000 Wake Forest University, Winston-Salem, NC
30,000 Mars Hill Productions, Stafford, TX
25,000 Interfaith Care Givers, Morristown, NJ
15,000 Mount Vernon Christian Academy, Atlanta, GA
15,000 Recovery Partnership, Whittier, CA
15,000 Village Seven Presbyterian Church
12,000 Haggai Institute, Atlanta, GA
10,000 American Red Cross
10,000 Campus Crusade for Christ, San Bernardino, CA

Wareheim Foundation, E. C.

CONTACT

William L. Mathers
Director
E. C. Wareheim Fdn.
PO Box 3444
Virginia Beach, VA 23454
(804) 481-3166

FINANCIAL SUMMARY

Recent Giving: $415,661 (1991); $405,803 (1990); $294,597 (1989)
Assets: $7,710,994 (1991); $7,078,842 (1990); $7,285,913 (1989)
Gifts Received: $17,471 (1991)
Fiscal Note: In 1991, contributions were received from Wareheim Annuity Trust.
EIN: 52-6033212

CONTRIBUTIONS SUMMARY

Typical Recipients: • *Civic & Public Affairs:* law & justice • *Education:* community & junior colleges, literacy • *Health:* hospitals, medical research, pediatric health, single-disease health associations • *Social Services:* child welfare, community service organizations, counseling, delinquency & crime, disabled, domestic violence, family services, united funds, volunteer services, youth organizations
Grant Types: general support

GIVING OFFICERS

First National Bank of Maryland
trust
William L. Mathers: exec dir, mgr

APPLICATION INFORMATION

Initial Approach: Send brief letter of inquiry describing program or project. There are no deadlines.

GRANTS ANALYSIS

Number of Grants: 40
Highest Grant: $40,000
Typical Range: $1,000 to $10,000
Disclosure Period: 1991

RECENT GRANTS

40,000 Boys and Girls Club, Norfolk, VA
30,300 YMCA, Chesapeake, VA
27,100 Junior League of Norfolk and Virginia Beach, Norfolk, VA
25,000 Tidewater Community College, Portsmouth, VA
24,400 Lady Maryland Foundation, Baltimore, MD
24,000 Chesapeake Volunteers in Youth Services, Chesapeake, VA
17,481 Chapel Hill Training Outreach Program, Chapel Hill, NC
15,000 Rappahannock CASA Program, Fredericksburg, VA
12,000 Sexual Assault Recovery Center, Baltimore, MD
10,000 Children's Hospital Medical Center, Norfolk, VA

Warfield Memorial Fund, Anna Emory

CONTACT

Charles B. Reeves
President
Anna Emory Warfield Memorial Fund
804 Merc. Bldg.
2 Hopkins Plz.
Baltimore, MD 21201
(301) 547-0612

FINANCIAL SUMMARY

Recent Giving: $164,450 (1991); $158,625 (1990); $150,800 (1989)
Assets: $3,774,685 (1991); $2,461,290 (1990); $3,632,641 (1989)
Gifts Received: $22,130 (1989)
EIN: 52-0785672

CONTRIBUTIONS SUMMARY

Donor(s): the late S. Davies Warfield
Typical Recipients: • *Civic & Public Affairs:* philanthropic organizations • *Social Services:* child welfare, family services
Geographic Distribution: focus on the Baltimore, MD, metropolitan area

GIVING OFFICERS

Mrs. W. Page Dame, Jr.: trust
Edward K. Dunn, Jr.: treas, trust *B* Baltimore MD 1935 *ED* Princeton Univ AB 1958; Harvard Univ MBA 1960 *CURR EMPL* chmn exec comm, dir: Mercantile-Safe Deposit & Trust Co *CORP AFFIL* chmn exec comm, dir: Mercantile-Safe Deposit & Trust Co; dir: Mercantile Bankshares Corp *NONPR AFFIL* trust: Johns Hopkins Hosp, Wilson (Thomas) Sanitarium
Mrs. William E. Grose: trust
Louis W. Hargrave: trust
Mrs. Thomas H. Maddux: trust
Braxton D. Mitchell: vp, trust
Thelma K. O'Neal: secy
Charles B. Reeves, Jr.: pres, trust *B* Baltimore MD 1923 *ED* Princeton Univ BA 1947; Univ VA LLB 1951 *CURR EMPL* ptnr: Venable Baetjer & Howard *CORP AFFIL* ptnr: Venable Baetjer & Howard *NONPR AFFIL* mem: Am Bar Assn, Am Judicature Soc, MD Bar Assn; pres: Kernan (James Lawrence) Hosp
Mrs. William F. Schmick, Jr.: trust
Mrs. John R. Sherwood: trust
Mrs. Lewis C. Strudwick: trust

APPLICATION INFORMATION

Initial Approach: Application form required. Approach foundation by telephone. There are no deadlines.

OTHER THINGS TO KNOW

Provides grants to individuals to alleviate poverty and human distress.
Publications: Application Guidelines

GRANTS ANALYSIS

Number of Grants: 2
Highest Grant: $1,200
Typical Range: $750 to $1,250
Disclosure Period: 1991

Note: Figures for 1991 do not reflect contributions to individuals.

RECENT GRANTS

    1,200 Family Children's
          Services
     750 Foundation Center

Warhol Foundation for the Visual Arts, Andy

CONTACT
Emily Todd
Program Director
Andy Warhol Foundation for the
Visual Arts
22 East 33rd St.
New York, NY 10016
(212) 683-6456
Note: Inquiries about the works of art of Andy Warhol that are the property of the foundation or the estate of the artist should be directed by letter to Jane Rubin, Administrator of Collections, at the above address.

FINANCIAL SUMMARY
Recent Giving: $4,290,000 (fiscal 1993 est.); $4,203,966 (fiscal 1992); $3,716,067 (fiscal 1990)
Assets: $122,480,076 (fiscal 1993 est.); $103,283,410 (fiscal year ending April 30, 1992); $30,065,794 (fiscal 1990)
Gifts Received: $24,615,034 (fiscal 1992); $5,295,700 (fiscal 1990)
Fiscal Note: On April 30, 1990, $5 million of the foundation's assets were in works of art. The foundation recieves gifts from the estate of Andy Warhol.
EIN: 13-3410749

CONTRIBUTIONS SUMMARY
Donor(s): The foundation was established in 1987, shortly after the death of pop artist Andy Warhol. Warhol was the artist who immortalized Marilyn Monroe, Jackie Kennedy Onassis, Campbell's soup cans, and other pop icons with his unique style of drawing and print making. He is often credited with starting a unique genre of art, called pop art, in the 1960s. Warhol died on February 22, 1987 from complications of surgery. The foundation was endowed with

Warhol's investments, art works, and other personal belongings, such as furniture and jewelry. Much of Warhol's personal belongings were sold at auction to create a permanent endowment for the foundation.
Typical Recipients: • *Arts & Humanities:* arts associations, arts centers, arts institutes, ethnic arts, history/historic preservation, museums/galleries, visual arts • *Civic & Public Affairs:* urban & community affairs • *Education:* arts education
Grant Types: general support and project
Geographic Distribution: no geographic restrictions

GIVING OFFICERS
Kinshasha Holman Conwill: dir
Peter P. McN. Gates: secy
Brendan Gill: chmn, dir *B* Hartford CT 1914 *CURR EMPL* archt critic: New Yorker *NONPR AFFIL* chmn emeritus: Inst Art Urban Resources, Landmarks Conservancy NY; dir: Film Soc Lincoln Ctr, MacDowell Colony, Metropolitan Art Soc; mem: Irish Georgian Soc, Victorian Soc Am
Archibald L. Gillies: pres, dir
Agnes Gund: dir *B* Cleveland OH 1938 *ED* CT Coll; Harvard Univ AM 1980 *NONPR AFFIL* fdr: Studios Sch Assn *PHIL AFFIL* trust: Agnes Gund Foundation
Kathy Halbreich: dir *CORP AFFIL* consult: Beacon Co, Frito Lay, New England Gen Svcs Admins *NONPR AFFIL* consult: Artist's Space, Capp St Project, Louis Comfort Tiffany Fdn, Mus Modern Art, Seattle Arts Comm, Southeastern Ctr Contemp Art, St Louis Art Mus, VA Art Arch Program; mem: Assn Art Mus Dirs; trust: MA Counc Arts & Humanities
Frederick W. Hughes: chmn emeritus, dir
James McCauley: treas, comptr
Anthony Solomon: dir
John Warhola: vp, dir

APPLICATION INFORMATION
Initial Approach:
Proposals should be submitted in the form of a one- to two-page letter.
Letters should include a brief descriptions of the project, a proposed budget, and a copy of

the organization's 501(c)(3) ruling.
Proposals must be postmarked by March 15 and September 15.
Grant notifications are mailed on July 1 and January 1.
Restrictions on Giving: The foundation generally makes grants on a one-time basis. The foundation does not support individual artists or filmmakers.

OTHER THINGS TO KNOW
Publications: annual report

GRANTS ANALYSIS
Total Grants: $1,167,615*
Number of Grants: 55
Highest Grant: $50,000
Typical Range: $5,000 to $50,000
Disclosure Period: fiscal year ending April 30, 1992
Note: Grants analysis is derived from a fiscal 1992 partial grants list. Recent grants are derived from a fiscal 1992 partial grants list.

RECENT GRANTS

    50,000 Asia Society, New
           York, NY
    50,000 Historic Hudson
           Valley, Tarrytown,
           NY
    50,000 Studio in a School,
           New York, NY
    25,000 Alliance for the
           Arts, New York,
           NY
    25,000 Aperture Founda-
           tion, New York, NY
    25,000 Architectural
           League of New
           York, New York,
           NY
    25,000 Art Awareness,
           Lexington, NY
    25,000 California Museum
           of Photography,
           Riverside, CA
    25,000 Capp Street Pro-
           ject, San Fran-
           cisco, CA
    25,000 Corcoran Gallery
           of Art, Washing-
           ton, DC

Warner Electric Brake & Clutch Co. / Warner Electric Foundation
Parent Company: Dana Corp.
Headquarters: South Beloit, IL

CONTACT
Frank E. Bauchiero
Trustee
Warner Electric Foundation
449 Gardner St.
South Beloit, IL 61080
(815) 389-3771

FINANCIAL SUMMARY
Recent Giving: $53,475 (1990); $101,530 (1989)
Assets: $221,370 (1990); $259,418 (1989)
EIN: 36-6142884

CONTRIBUTIONS SUMMARY
Typical Recipients: • *Arts & Humanities:* museums/galleries, music • *Education:* colleges & universities, private education (precollege), science/technology education • *Health:* hospitals • *Social Services:* community service organizations, united funds, youth organizations
Grant Types: general support
Geographic Distribution: focus on IL
Operating Locations: IL (South Beloit)

CORP. OFFICERS
Mike Carrigan: *CURR EMPL* vp, gm: Warner Electric Brake & Clutch Co

GIVING OFFICERS
Frank E. Bauchiero: trust
Michael Leopold: trust
Ronald McGregor: trust

APPLICATION INFORMATION
Initial Approach: Send brief letter describing program. There are no deadlines.

GRANTS ANALYSIS
Number of Grants: 17
Highest Grant: $15,750
Typical Range: $150 to $2,000
Disclosure Period: 1990

RECENT GRANTS

    15,750 United Way, Be-
           loit, WI
    10,000 Beloit College, Be-
           loit, WI
     6,400 Junior Achieve-
           ment, Rockford, IL
     3,200 Beloit Catholic
           High School, Be-
           loit, WI
     3,000 Milwaukee School
           of Engineering,
           Milwaukee, WI
     3,000 Rock County, Be-
           loit, WI
     2,500 Rockford Sym-
           phony Orchestra,
           Rockford, IL

1,500 Arts and Science
Park, Rockford, IL
1,125 Beloit Jamesville
Symphony Orches-
tra, Beloit, WI
1,125 Knights of Colum-
bus, Rockford, IL

Warner Foundation, Lee and Rose

CONTACT
Malcolm W. McDonald
Lee and Rose Warner Fdn.
444 Pine St.
St. Paul, MN 55101
(612) 228-4444

FINANCIAL SUMMARY
Recent Giving: $281,845
(1990); $260,000 (1989);
$287,648 (1988)
Assets: $6,725,703 (1990);
$6,884,351 (1989); $5,535,035
(1988)
EIN: 41-6011523

CONTRIBUTIONS SUMMARY
Donor(s): the late Rose Warner
Typical Recipients: • *Arts &
Humanities:* arts institutes, mu-
seums/galleries, music • *Educa-
tion:* colleges & universities
• *Health:* hospices, nursing
services • *Religion:* churches
Grant Types: general support
Geographic Distribution:
focus on MN

GIVING OFFICERS
Donald Gregory McNeely:
trust *B* St Paul MN 1914 *ED*
Yale Univ 1937 *CURR EMPL*
chmn: Space Center *CORP
AFFIL* chmn: Minneapolis Ter-
minal Warehouse Co, NYTCO
Inc, Space Center Inc; dir: Con-
wed Corp, Northwest Airlines,
Northwest Bancorp; pres, dir:
Ecologics Inc, Enterprise Inc,
MWF Co
Kevin McNeely: trust
Kevin Richey: trust
S. W. Richey: trust

APPLICATION INFORMATION
Initial Approach: Send brief
letter of inquiry and full pro-
posal. There are no deadlines.
Board meets in September and
December.
Restrictions on Giving: Does
not support individuals.

GRANTS ANALYSIS
Disclosure Period: 1990
Note: No grants list was
provided for 1990.

RECENT GRANTS
200,000 Science Museum
of Minnesota, St.
Paul, MN
20,000 Hospice, Monterey,
CA
15,000 Community Foun-
dation of Monterey
Peninsula, Mon-
terey, CA
5,000 College of St.
Benedict, St.
Joseph, MN
5,000 College of St. Scholastica, Duluth, MN
2,000 Claremont
McKenna College,
Claremont, CA
1,000 Home of the Good
Shepherd, Mon-
terey, CA
1,000 Monterey Institute
of International
Studies, Monterey,
CA
1,000 St. Johns Univer-
sity, Collegeville,
MN
1,000 University of Cali-
fornia Riverside,
Riverside, CA

Warner Fund, Albert and Bessie

CONTACT
Albert and Bessie Warner
Foundation
c/o Funding Exchange
666 Broadway Ste. 300
New York, NY 10011

FINANCIAL SUMMARY
Recent Giving: $186,501
(1991); $178,701 (1990);
$147,876 (1989)
Assets: $4,554,890 (1991);
$4,349,222 (1990); $4,063,102
(1989)
EIN: 13-6095213

CONTRIBUTIONS SUMMARY
Typical Recipients: • *Arts &
Humanities:* dance, muse-
ums/galleries • *Civic & Public
Affairs:* better government,
civil rights, environmental affairs, public policy, urban &
community affairs • *Health:*
hospitals • *Religion:* religious
organizations • *Social Services:*
child welfare, community service organizations, youth organizations
Grant Types: general support
Geographic Distribution:
focus on New York, NY

GIVING OFFICERS
Arthur J. Steele: trust
Lewis M. Steele: trust

Ruth M. Steele: trust

APPLICATION INFORMATION
Initial Approach: Send brief
letter of inquiry describing program or project. There are no
deadlines.
Restrictions on Giving: Does
not support individuals.

GRANTS ANALYSIS
Number of Grants: 33
Highest Grant: $50,000
Typical Range: $1,000 to
$10,000
Disclosure Period: 1991

RECENT GRANTS
50,000 Funding Exchange,
New York, NY
30,000 Funding Exchange,
New York, NY
15,000 Institute for Policy
Studies, New York,
NY
10,000 Center for Constitu-
tional Rights, New
York, NY
10,000 Institute for Policy
Studies, New York,
NY
10,000 Institute for Public
Affairs, New York,
NY
10,000 Robert Steel Foun-
dation, New York,
NY
8,000 Southampton Hos-
pital, New York,
NY
5,000 Americans for
Peace Now, New
York, NY
5,000 National Lawyers
Guild, New York,
NY

Warner-Lambert Co. / Warner-Lambert Charitable Foundation
Sales: $5.59 billion
Employees: 33,000
Headquarters: Morris Plains, NJ
SIC Major Group: Chemicals &
Allied Products and Food &
Kindred Products

CONTACT
Leslie Hare
Program Co-ordinator
Warner-Lambert Charitable Fdn.
201 Tabor Rd.
Morris Plains, NJ 07950
(201) 540-2243

FINANCIAL SUMMARY
Recent Giving: $6,000,000
(1992 approx.); $6,000,000

(1991 approx.); $7,000,000
(1990 approx.)
Assets: $2,500,000 (1991);
$2,287,628 (1990); $1,529,613
(1989)
Fiscal Note: Figures represent
foundation and direct giving.
In 1991, foundation contributions were $5,487,453.
EIN: 23-7038078

CONTRIBUTIONS SUMMARY
Typical Recipients: • *Arts &
Humanities:* arts centers, performing arts • *Civic & Public
Affairs:* economics, ethnic/mi-
nority organizations, professional & trade associations,
urban & community affairs
• *Education:* colleges & universities, education associations,
education funds, science/tech-
nology education • *Health:*
health funds, health organizations, hospitals, medical rehabilitation • *Social Services:*
aged, child welfare, disabled
Grant Types: capital, em-
ployee matching gifts, general
support, and project
Nonmonetary Support Types:
donated products and workplace solicitation
Note: Workplace solicitation is
for United Way only. Estimated
value of nonmonetary support
is not available and is not included in above figures.
Geographic Distribution: primarily where company maintains corporate facilities, especially near headquarters in
Morris Plains, NJ
Operating Locations: CT (Milford), MI (Ann Arbor), NJ
(Morris Plains), PR (Vega
Baja), SC (Greenwood)

CORP. OFFICERS
David C. Alton: *B* Atlantic
City NJ 1930 *CURR EMPL* vp,
gen tax couns: Warner-Lambert
Co *NONPR AFFIL* chmn tax
comm: Pharmaceutical Mfrs
Assn; dir: Childrens Special-
ized Hosp Fdn, Natl Foreign
Trade Counc
Lodewijk de Vink: *CURR
EMPL* pres US oper: Warner-
Lambert Co
Raymond M. Fino: *B* Plain-
field NJ 1942 *CURR EMPL* vp
(human resources): Warner-
Lambert Co *CORP AFFIL* mgr:
Continental Can Co; regional
pers dir: Sealtest Foods
Melvin Russell Goodes: *B*
Hamilton Canada 1935 *ED*
Queens Coll 1957; Univ Chi-
cago MBA 1960 *CURR EMPL*

chmn, ceo, dir: Warner-Lambert Co *CORP AFFIL* dir: Chem Bank, Chem Banking Corp, Unisys Corp *NONPR AFFIL* dir: Natl Alliance Bus; mem: Natl Assn Retail Druggists, Natl Wholesale Druggists Assn, Pharmaceutical Mfrs Assn, Proprietary Assn; mem exec adv counc: Natl Ctr Independent Retail Pharmacy; mem fin comm: Joint Counc Econ Ed; trust: Intl Exec Svc Corps, Queens Univ; dir: Counc Family Health

Ronald Edward Zier: *B* West New York NJ 1931 *ED* Univ Notre Dame AB 1952 *CURR EMPL* vp (pub affairs): Warner-Lambert Co

GIVING OFFICERS
David C. Alton: first vp *CURR EMPL* vp, gen tax couns: Warner-Lambert Co (see above)

Robert J. Dircks: pres *B* New York NY 1927 *ED* Fordham Univ BS 1951; City Univ NY MBA 1959 *CURR EMPL* exec vp, cfo: Warner-Lambert Co *CORP AFFIL* trust: SSM Healthcare Corp *NONPR AFFIL* mem: Am Accounting Assn, Natl Assn Accts

Raymond M. Fino: second vp *CURR EMPL* vp (human resources): Warner-Lambert Co (see above)

Stanley D. Grubman: secy

Richard W. Keelty: chmn

Evelyn Self: asst secy-treas *CURR EMPL* dir commun aff: Parke-Davis Group

Ronald Edward Zier: third vp *CURR EMPL* vp (pub affairs): Warner-Lambert Co (see above)

APPLICATION INFORMATION
Initial Approach: *Initial Contact:* brief letter or proposal *Include Information On:* description of the organization, amount requested, purpose for which funds are sought, recently audited financial statement, and proof of tax-exempt status *When to Submit:* any time

Restrictions on Giving: Must be exclusively for charitable, religious, scientific, literary, or educational purposes, either directly, or be contributions to organizations qualifying as exempt organizations.

GRANTS ANALYSIS
Total Grants: $5,487,453*
Number of Grants: 226*
Highest Grant: $300,000*

Typical Range: $2,000 to $20,000
Disclosure Period: 1991
Note: Financial information is for the foundation only. Recent grants are derived from a 1991 Form 990.

RECENT GRANTS
300,000 Liberty Science Center and Hall of Technology, Jersey City, NJ
300,000 United Way, Morris County, Morristown, NJ
270,000 American Heart Association
250,000 Columbia University, New York, NY
250,000 Harvard Medical School, Cambridge, MA
250,000 Rutgers University, New Brunswick, NJ
225,000 Morristown Memorial Hospital, Morristown, NJ
200,000 Seton Hall University-Peter Rodino Chair Law School, South Orange, NJ
200,000 United Negro College Fund, New York, NY
200,000 University of Medicine and Dentistry Foundation, Newark, NJ

Warren and Beatrice W. Blanding Foundation, Riley J. and Lillian N.

CONTACT
Henry L. Hulbert
Manager
Riley J. and Lillian N. Warren and Beatrice W. Blanding Fdn.
Six Ford Ave.
Oneonta, NY 13820
(607) 432-6720

FINANCIAL SUMMARY
Recent Giving: $189,000 (1991); $186,750 (1990); $184,500 (1989)
Assets: $5,612,847 (1991); $5,029,505 (1990); $5,079,738 (1989)
EIN: 23-7203341

CONTRIBUTIONS SUMMARY
Donor(s): Beatrice W. Blanding
Typical Recipients: • *Arts & Humanities:* libraries • *Education:* colleges & universities, private education (precollege), religious education • *Health:* hospitals • *Religion:* churches, religious organizations • *Social Services:* community service organizations, united funds
Grant Types: general support
Geographic Distribution: focus on NY

GIVING OFFICERS
Beatrice W. Blanding: trust
Robert A. Harlem: trust
Henry L. Hulbert: mgr, trust

APPLICATION INFORMATION
Initial Approach: Send brief letter of inquiry describing program or project. The deadline is November 1.

GRANTS ANALYSIS
Number of Grants: 24
Highest Grant: $75,000
Typical Range: $2,000 to $7,500
Disclosure Period: 1991

RECENT GRANTS
75,000 St. Mary's School
25,000 A.O. Fox Memorial Hospital, New York, NY
20,000 Hartwick College, Oneonta, NY
10,000 Siena College, Loudonville, NY
7,500 Huntington Memorial Library Foundation, San Marino, CA
7,500 Pathfinder Village
6,000 A.O. Fox Memorial Hospital Chaplaincy Program, New York, NY
6,000 United Way
5,000 Villanova University, Villanova, PA
3,000 St. Mary's Church

Warren Charite

CONTACT
W. R. Lissau
Warren Charite
PO Box 470372
Tulsa, OK 74147-0372
(918) 492-8100

FINANCIAL SUMMARY
Recent Giving: $348,125 (fiscal 1991); $366,050 (fiscal 1990); $371,283 (fiscal 1989)
Assets: $6,185,030 (fiscal year ending November 30, 1991); $6,312,639 (fiscal 1990); $5,790,353 (fiscal 1989)
Gifts Received: $200,000 (fiscal 1990)

Fiscal Note: In 1990, contributions were received from the William K. Warren Foundation.
EIN: 73-0776064

CONTRIBUTIONS SUMMARY
Donor(s): William K. Warren
Typical Recipients: • *Arts & Humanities:* community arts, history/historic preservation, museums/galleries, opera • *Civic & Public Affairs:* business/free enterprise • *Education:* colleges & universities, medical education, private education (precollege) • *Health:* hospitals, medical research • *Religion:* churches, religious organizations • *Social Services:* drugs & alcohol, united funds
Grant Types: general support
Geographic Distribution: focus on OK

GIVING OFFICERS
Patricia K. Griffith: secy
W. R. Lissau: dir, vp
William K. Warren: pres, dir
W. E. Weeks: treas, dir
D. B. Whitehill: asst secy

APPLICATION INFORMATION
Initial Approach: Send brief letter of inquiry describing program or project. There are no deadlines.

GRANTS ANALYSIS
Number of Grants: 48
Highest Grant: $85,000
Typical Range: $1,000 to $5,000
Disclosure Period: fiscal year ending November 30, 1991

RECENT GRANTS
85,000 Christ the King Church, Tulsa, OK
70,000 Augustinians, Olympia, IL
25,000 Oklahoma State Foundation, Stillwater, OK
20,000 Oklahoma Medical Research Foundation, Oklahoma City, OK
13,000 Cascia Hall, Tulsa, OK
10,000 All Saints Elementary School, Broken Arrow, OK
10,000 St. Mary's School, Tulsa, OK
10,000 Thomas Gilcrease Museum, Tulsa, OK
10,000 Tulsa Chamber of Commerce, Tulsa, OK

10,000 University of Notre Dame, Notre Dame, IN

Warren Co., S.D.

Sales: $1.48 billion
Employees: 4,000
Parent Company: Scott Paper Co,
Headquarters: Boston, MA
SIC Major Group: Paper &
  Allied Products

CONTACT
Christine Choate
Account Coordinator
S.D. Warren Co.
225 Franklin St.
Boston, MA 02110
(617) 423-7300

CONTRIBUTIONS SUMMARY
Operating Locations: MA
(Boston)

CORP. OFFICERS
Harry Johnson: *CURR EMPL*
cfo: SD WarrenCo
Richard Leaman: *CURR
EMPL* pres: SD WarrenCo

Warren Foundation, William K.

CONTACT
W. R. Lissau
President
William K. Warren Foundation
PO Box 470372
Tulsa, OK 74147-0372
(918) 492-8100

FINANCIAL SUMMARY
Recent Giving: $17,822,074
(1991); $18,359,249 (1990);
$15,372,500 (1989)
Assets: $297,295,926 (1990);
$299,890,994 (1989);
$269,743,325 (1988)
Gifts Received: $3,557,483
(1990); $3,713,335 (1989);
$605,537 (1988)
Fiscal Note: In 1990, major
contributions were received
from Natalie O. Warren, E. W.
Blankenship, Patricia W. Swin-
dle, Marilyn W. Vandever, Beth
Bryant Findell, Jean M. War-
ren, Dorothy W. King, Natalie
Bryant, and W. K. Warren, Jr.
EIN: 73-0609599

CONTRIBUTIONS SUMMARY
Donor(s): The foundation was
established in 1945. Donors to
the foundation are William K.
Warren, the Jean Warren Young
Trust A, Elizabeth Warren

Blankenship Trust A, Marilyn
Warren Vandever Trust A,
Dorothy Warren King Trust A,
W. K. Warren, Jr. Trust A, Na-
talie Warren Bryant Trust D-1,
Natalie Warren Bryant Trust D-
2, W. K. Warren, Jr., Natalie O.
Warren, Dorothy Warren King,
and Patricia Warren Swindle.
Typical Recipients: • *Arts &
Humanities:* arts associations
• *Civic & Public Affairs:* philanthropic organizations, professional & trade associations,
urban & community affairs
• *Education:* colleges & universities, education associations,
private education (precollege)
• *Health:* health organizations,
hospitals, medical research,
mental health, single-disease
health associations • *Religion:*
churches, religious organizations • *Social Services:* community service organizations,
drugs & alcohol, youth organizations
Grant Types: general support,
professorship, and project
Geographic Distribution: emphasis on Tulsa, OK

GIVING OFFICERS
John A. Gaberino, Jr.: dir
Patricia K. Griffith: asst secy
Dorothy Warren King: secy,
dir
John J. King, Jr.: dir
W. R. Lissau: pres, dir
John A. Naughton: vp, treas
Patricia Warren Swindle:
don, dir
Natalie O. Warren: don,
vchmn, dir
W. K. Warren, Jr.: vchmn, dir
W. E. Weeks: dir

APPLICATION INFORMATION
Initial Approach:
The foundation reports that applications should be in letter
form, and that they are accepted any time. The foundation notes that it gives "preference to local Catholic health
care facilities."

GRANTS ANALYSIS
Total Grants: $17,822,074
Number of Grants: 57
Highest Grant: $12,000,000
Typical Range: $1,000 to
$50,000
Disclosure Period: 1991
Note: Average grant size is cal-
culated without including two
large health grants totaling
$17,000,000. Recent grants are
derived from a 1991 grants list.

RECENT GRANTS
5,000,000 William K. Warren
  Medical Research
  Center, Tulsa, OK
144,000 Sister of the Incarnate Word, Hous-
  ton, TX
120,000 Bishop Kelley
  High School,
  Tulsa, OK
100,000 Boston Avenue
  Methodist Church,
  Tulsa, OK
100,000 Partnership of
  Quality Education,
  New York, NY
50,000 Citizen CPR-Criti-
  cal Link, Tulsa, OK
46,624 Diocese of Tulsa,
  Tulsa, OK
31,000 Tulsa Metropolitan
  Ministry, Tulsa, OK
20,000 Childrens Day
  Nursery, Tulsa, OK
20,000 Katrina Overall
  McDonald Memo-
  rial, Nashville, TN

Warsh-Mott Legacy

CONTACT
Maryanne T. Mott
President
Warsh-Mott Legacy
469 Bohemian Hwy.
Freestone, CA 95472-9579
(707) 874-2942

FINANCIAL SUMMARY
Recent Giving: $261,500 (fis-
cal 1990); $217,000 (fiscal
1989)
Assets: $4,616,998 (fiscal year
ending September 30, 1990);
$4,685,365 (fiscal 1989)
Gifts Received: $291,581 (fis-
cal 1990); $100,000 (fiscal
1989)
EIN: 68-0049658

CONTRIBUTIONS SUMMARY
Donor(s): Maryanne T. Mott
Typical Recipients: • *Civic &
Public Affairs:* civil rights, environmental affairs, international affairs, municipalities
• *Religion:* churches, religious
organizations • *Social Services:*
child welfare, youth organizations
Grant Types: general support,
multiyear/continuing support,
operating expenses, project,
and research

GIVING OFFICERS
Maryanne T. Mott: pres, don
Martin Tietel: vp, exec dir
Herman E. Warsh: secy, cfo

APPLICATION INFORMATION
Initial Approach: Send cover
letter and full proposal. Deadline is January 15, May 15, September 15, or following Monday if deadline falls on a
weekend.

Restrictions on Giving: Does
not support endowments, capital funds, or video or film production.

OTHER THINGS TO KNOW
Publications: Informational
Brochure (including applica-
tion guidelines)

GRANTS ANALYSIS
Number of Grants: 16
Highest Grant: $40,000
Typical Range: $5,000 to
$25,000
Disclosure Period: fiscal year
ending September 30, 1990

RECENT GRANTS
40,000 Children's Televi-
  sion and Research
  Education Center,
  San Francisco, CA
  — general support
20,000 Ecology Action,
  Willits, CA — gen-
  eral support
20,000 United Church of
  Christ, New York,
  NY — project sup-
  port
20,000 Washington Office
  on Latin America,
  Washington, DC —
  project support
15,000 Friends of the
  Earth International,
  Washington, DC —
  project support
15,000 Fund for Investigative Journalism,
  Washington, DC —
  project support
15,000 Institute for Energy
  and Environmental
  Research, Takoma
  Park, MD — pro-
  ject support
15,000 National Save the
  Family Farm Coali-
  tion, Washington,
  DC — project sup-
  port
10,000 Friends of the
  Earth, Washington,
  DC — project sup-
  port
10,000 George School,
  Newton, MA —
  general support

Warwick Foundation

CONTACT
Warwick Fdn.
108 West Court St.
Doylestown, PA 18901
(215) 348-3199

FINANCIAL SUMMARY
Recent Giving: $168,700 (1991); $114,700 (1990); $167,700 (1989)
Assets: $4,766,922 (1991); $3,515,428 (1990); $3,653,532 (1989)
EIN: 23-6230662

CONTRIBUTIONS SUMMARY
Donor(s): Helen H. Gemmill, Kenneth Gemmill
Typical Recipients: • *Arts & Humanities:* arts centers, history/historic preservation, music • *Civic & Public Affairs:* environmental affairs, zoos/botanical gardens • *Education:* colleges & universities, legal education, religious education • *Health:* hospitals • *Religion:* churches • *Social Services:* community service organizations, disabled, shelters/homelessness, united funds
Grant Types: operating expenses and scholarship
Geographic Distribution: focus on the Bucks County and Philadelphia, PA, areas

GIVING OFFICERS
Helen H. Gemmill: trust

APPLICATION INFORMATION
Initial Approach: Send brief letter of inquiry describing program or project. There are no deadlines.
Restrictions on Giving: Does not support individuals.

GRANTS ANALYSIS
Number of Grants: 43
Highest Grant: $30,000
Typical Range: $500 to $10,000
Disclosure Period: 1991

RECENT GRANTS
30,000 Pennsylvania Academy of Fine Arts, Philadelphia, PA
10,000 Bryn Mawr College, Bryn Mawr, PA
10,000 Bucks County Historical Society, Doylestown, PA
10,000 Princeton Theological Seminary, Princeton, NJ
10,000 Princeton University, Princeton, NJ
10,000 Princeton University, Princeton, NJ
10,000 University of Pennsylvania Law School, Philadelphia, PA
8,000 Neshaminy Warwick Presbyterian Church, Warminister, PA
6,000 United Way, Philadelphia, PA
5,000 Doylestown Hospital, Doylestown, PA

Washington Forrest Foundation

CONTACT
Lindsey D. Peete
Executive Director
Washington Forrest Fdn.
2300 South 9th St.
Arlington, VA 22204
(703) 920-3688

FINANCIAL SUMMARY
Recent Giving: $303,357 (fiscal 1992); $313,864 (fiscal 1991); $275,944 (fiscal 1990)
Assets: $7,930,148 (fiscal year ending June 30, 1992); $7,376,137 (fiscal 1991); $7,294,378 (fiscal 1990)
Gifts Received: $457,000 (fiscal 1992)
Fiscal Note: Major fiscal In 1992, contributions were received from The Virginia Smith Charitable Foundation.
EIN: 23-7002944

CONTRIBUTIONS SUMMARY
Donor(s): the late Benjamin M. Smith
Typical Recipients: • *Arts & Humanities:* community arts, dance • *Civic & Public Affairs:* philanthropic organizations, public policy, urban & community affairs • *Education:* colleges & universities, education funds, private education (precollege), religious education • *Health:* health organizations • *Religion:* churches, religious organizations • *Social Services:* child welfare, community service organizations, food/clothing distribution, recreation & athletics, united funds, youth organizations
Grant Types: capital, emergency, general support, multiyear/continuing support, operating expenses, scholarship, and seed money
Geographic Distribution: focus on northern VA

GIVING OFFICERS
Leslie Ariail: vp
Carolyn Dameron: secy
Deborah Lucckese: member
Lindsey Peete: exec dir
Margaret S. Peete: pres
Benjamin M. Smith, Jr.: secy, treas

APPLICATION INFORMATION
Initial Approach: Applicants must complete the foundation's application forms, which are available from the executive director. Applications are considered by the foundation board three times annually. Deadlines vary from year to year.
Restrictions on Giving: Does not support individuals.

OTHER THINGS TO KNOW
Publications: Program policy statement

GRANTS ANALYSIS
Number of Grants: 85
Highest Grant: $20,000
Typical Range: $1,000 to $10,000
Disclosure Period: fiscal year ending June 30, 1992

RECENT GRANTS
20,000 Linton Hall School, Bristow, VA
18,500 Arlington United Methodist Church, Arlington, VA
16,794 Arlington Food Assistance Center, Arlington, VA
15,000 Goodwin House, Alexandria, VA
13,863 Arlington County Department of Human Services, Arlington, VA
10,000 Christchurch School, Christchurch, VA — scholarships
10,000 Flint Hill School, Oakton, VA
7,500 Arlington Hospital Foundation, Arlington, VA — Cardiac Catherization Lab
7,500 Carpenter Shelter, Alexandria, VA
7,500 Virginia College Fund, Richmond, VA

Washington Foundation

Former Foundation Name: Church of Christ Foundation

CONTACT
Paul A. Hargis
President
Washington Fdn.
PO Box 159057
Nashville, TN 37215
(615) 244-0600

FINANCIAL SUMMARY
Recent Giving: $653,400 (1989); $682,450 (1988)
Assets: $12,929,536 (1989); $11,892,278 (1988)
EIN: 62-0649477

CONTRIBUTIONS SUMMARY
Donor(s): G.L. Comer
Typical Recipients: • *Education:* religious education • *Religion:* churches, missionary activities, religious organizations • *Social Services:* child welfare, community service organizations, counseling, shelters/homelessness, youth organizations
Grant Types: operating expenses
Geographic Distribution: focus on Nashville, TN

GIVING OFFICERS
Howard R. Amacher: trust
Andrew Bell Benedict, Jr.: trust *B* Nashville TN 1914 *ED* Vanderbilt Univ 1935; Rutgers Univ 1944 *CURR EMPL* sr chmn: First Am Natl Bank Nashville *CORP AFFIL* sr chmn: First Am Natl Bank Nashville
William Wells Berry: trust *B* Nashville TN 1917 *ED* Vanderbilt Univ BA 1938; Vanderbilt Univ LLB 1940 *CURR EMPL* ptnr: Bass Berry & Sims *CORP AFFIL* ptnr: Bass Berry & Sims *NONPR AFFIL* fellow: Am Bar Fdn, Am Coll Probate Couns, Intl Academy Trial Lawyers; mem: Am Bar Assn, Am Judicature Soc, Nashville Bar Assn, Nashville Chamber Commerce, Nashville Srs Golf Assn, TN Bar Assn, TN Bar Fdn
R. Hix Clark: secy, trust
James M. Denton III: trust
Paul A. Hargis: pres, trust
Neal L. Jennings: trust
E. M. Shepherd: vp, trust
Robert C. Taylor: trust
Paschall H. Young: treas, trust

APPLICATION INFORMATION

Initial Approach: Send brief letter of inquiry describing program. Deadline is December 1. Board meets quarterly.
Restrictions on Giving: Does not support individuals.

GRANTS ANALYSIS

Number of Grants: 160
Highest Grant: $60,000
Typical Range: $200 to $10,000
Disclosure Period: 1989

RECENT GRANTS

60,000 David Lipscomb University, Nashville, TN
50,000 United Way, Nashville, TN
30,000 Belmont College, Nashville, TN
20,000 Alive Hospice, Nashville, TN
20,000 Christ United Methodist Church, Franklin, TN
15,000 Watkins Institute, Nashville, TN
12,500 Lake Shore Home for Aged, Nashville, TN
10,000 Junior Achievement, Nashville, TN
10,000 Murci Home for Retarded, Nashville, TN
10,000 Youth Hobby Shop, Nashville, TN

Washington Mutual Savings Bank / Washington Mutual Savings Bank Foundation

Assets: $8.98 billion
Employees: 2,828
Headquarters: Seattle, WA
SIC Major Group: Depository Institutions

CONTACT

Tim Otani
Program Administration
Washington Mutual Savings Bank Fdn.
1201 Third Ave.
Seattle, WA 98101
(206) 461-4663

FINANCIAL SUMMARY

Recent Giving: $1,000,000 (1993 est.); $750,000 (1992 approx.); $655,876 (1991)
Assets: $1,349,640 (1991); $1,137,340 (1990); $924,842 (1989)

Fiscal Note: Giving figures reflect foundation contributions only and do not include non-monetary gifts (see below). All major contributions are made through the foundation. Contact person for company contributions is Margie Abolofla, vice president & manager, civic & investor relations.
EIN: 91-1070920

CONTRIBUTIONS SUMMARY

Typical Recipients: • *Arts & Humanities:* arts associations, arts centers, community arts, performing arts, theater • *Civic & Public Affairs:* housing • *Education:* colleges & universities, community & junior colleges, elementary education, literacy, public education (precollege) • *Social Services:* child welfare, community centers, united funds, volunteer services, youth organizations
Grant Types: award, capital, challenge, employee matching gifts, general support, loan, multiyear/continuing support, operating expenses, project, and seed money
Nonmonetary Support Types: donated equipment, donated products, in-kind services, loaned employees, loaned executives, and workplace solicitation
Note: Nonmonetary support was estimated at $52,000 in 1990, and is not included in above figure. Contact is Judy Whitehead, Coordinator, Civic Relations.
Geographic Distribution: primarily Washington state and other company operating areas
Operating Locations: ID, OR, WA

CORP. OFFICERS

Kerry K. Killinger: *CURR EMPL* pres, chmn, ceo: WA Mutual Savings Bank
William Arthur Longbrake: *B* Hershey PA 1943 *ED* Coll Wooster BA 1965; Univ WI MA 1968; Univ WI MBA 1969; Univ MD MBA 1976 *CURR EMPL* sr exec vp, cfo: WA Mutual Savings Bank *NONPR AFFIL* dir: Puget Sound Couns Fin Insts; mem: Am Econ Assn, Am Fin Assn, Coll Wooster Alumni Assn, Columbia Tower Club, Fin Mgmt Assn, Seattle Municipal League; mem adv comm: Univ WA Ctr Study Banking & Fin Markets; mem, chmn outreach & techassis-

tance comm: King County Housing Partnership; mem, dir, treas: Fin Execs Inst; mem exec comm, chmn fin &pers comm: Capitol Hill Housing Improvement Program Seattle; trust: Kenney Presbyterian Home, WA Savings League; trust, pres: Coll Wooster Alumni Assn Seattle Chapter; trust, treas: Intiman Theatre Co

GIVING OFFICERS

Sally S. Behnke: mem *CURR EMPL* dir: WA Mutual Savings Bank
Kerry Kent Killinger: mem *B* Des Moines IA 1949 *CURR EMPL* pres, ceo: WA Mutual Savings Bank *NONPR AFFIL* mem: Life Mgmt Inst, Seattle Chamber Commerce, Soc Fin Analysts
William Arthur Longbrake: mem *CURR EMPL* sr exec vp, cfo: WA Mutual Savings Bank (see above)
Deanna Oppenheimer: mem
Tim Otani: program adm

APPLICATION INFORMATION

Initial Approach: *Initial Contact:* by letter or phone to request application form *Include Information On:* completed grant application form along with any other fundraising efforts, most recent financial statement, a copy of IRS letter of nonprofit status, a copy of audited financial statements *When to Submit:* by January 1, to be notified by March 15, April 1, to be notified by June 15, July 1, to be notified by September 15, or October 1, to be notified by December 15 applications are reviewed at quarterly meetings
Restrictions on Giving: Does not support individuals; organizations without tax-exempt status; organizations which discriminate based on race, color, religion, creed, age, sex, national origin, or any reason; political organizations or groups that influence legislation; veterans organizations; labor organizations; or religious-oriented projects.
Does not provide funds, other than for capital campaigns, to organizations that already receive support from the United Way.
Accepts one application per organization per calendar year. Generally does not fund an or-

ganization for more than three successive years.
Foundation does not accept requests that are not made on application form.

OTHER THINGS TO KNOW

The foundation receives its funds from the financial services companies of the Washington Mutual Financial Group (WMFG), including: Washington Mutual Savings Bank; Benefit Service Corp.; Composite Research & Management Co.; Murphey Favre, Inc.; Mutual Travel, Inc.; Washington Mutual, a Federal Savings Bank; Washington Mutual Insurance Services; and WM Life Insurance Co.

GRANTS ANALYSIS

Total Grants: $655,876
Number of Grants: 278
Highest Grant: $107,775
Typical Range: $1,000 to $10,000
Disclosure Period: 1991
Note: Fiscal information reflects foundation giving only. Recent grants are derived from a 1991 Form 990.

RECENT GRANTS

107,775 United Way-King County, Seattle, WA
40,540 Seattle Art Museum, Seattle, WA
20,600 University of Puget Sound, WA
20,100 Visiting Nurse Services
20,000 Corporate Council for the Arts, Seattle, WA
20,000 Independent Colleges of Washington, Seattle, WA
17,000 United Way-Spokane, Spokane, WA
13,000 Heritage College, Toppenish, WA
10,225 Salvation Army-King County
10,150 YMCA-Greater Seattle, Seattle, WA

Washington National Insurance Co. / Washington National Foundation

Assets: $1.55 billion
Employees: 910
Parent Company: Washington National Corp.
Headquarters: Evanston, IL
SIC Major Group: Insurance Carriers

CONTACT

Terry Jenkins
Director
Washington National Foundation 20-NBD
1630 Chicago Ave.
Evanston, IL 60201
(708) 570-3622

FINANCIAL SUMMARY

Recent Giving: $200,000 (1992 approx.); $190,000 (1991)

CONTRIBUTIONS SUMMARY

Typical Recipients: • *Arts & Humanities:* general • *Civic & Public Affairs:* general • *Education:* general • *Social Services:* general

Geographic Distribution: headquarters and operating communities

Operating Locations: IL (Evanston)

CORP. OFFICERS

Robert Patin: *CURR EMPL* ceo: Washington Natl Ins Co

APPLICATION INFORMATION

Initial Approach: Send brief letter of inquiry, including a description of the organization, amount requested, purpose of funds sought, audited financial statement, and proof of tax-exempt status. There are no deadlines. Include a description of organization, amount requested, purpose of funds sought, recently audited financial statement, and proof of tax-exempt status.

Restrictions on Giving: Does not support individuals, religious organizations for sectarian purposes, or political or lobbying groups.

OTHER THINGS TO KNOW

Publications: Washington National Insurance Company Contributions Policy & Guidelines

GRANTS ANALYSIS

Typical Range: $1,000 to $2,500

Washington Natural Gas Co.

Revenue: $376.34 million
Employees: 1,550
Parent Company: Washington Energy Co.
Headquarters: Seattle, WA
SIC Major Group: Building Materials & Garden Supplies, Electric, Gas & Sanitary Services, Furniture & Homefurnishings Stores, and Special Trade Contractors

CONTACT

Jane Kilborn
Assistant Vice President of Public Affairs
Washington Natural Gas Co.
PO Box 1869
Seattle, WA 98111
(206) 622-6767
Note: Ms. Kilborn's extension is 2230.

FINANCIAL SUMMARY

Fiscal Note: Company gives directly. Annual Giving Range: $250,000 to $500,000

CONTRIBUTIONS SUMMARY

Typical Recipients: • *Arts & Humanities:* general • *Civic & Public Affairs:* general • *Education:* general • *Health:* general • *Social Services:* general

Grant Types: general support

Nonmonetary Support Types: cause-related marketing & promotion, donated equipment, donated products, in-kind services, loaned employees, and loaned executives

Geographic Distribution: gives only in five-county area around Seattle, WA

Operating Locations: WA (Seattle)

CORP. OFFICERS

Robert R. Golliver: *B* Silver Lake IN 1935 *ED* Purdue Univ 1957; IN Univ 1960 *CURR EMPL* pres, coo: WA Natural Gas Co *CORP AFFIL* pres: Thermal Energy; pres, ceo: Washington Energy Co; vchmn, ceo: Thermal Explora-

tion *NONPR AFFIL* trust: Assn Northwest Gas Utilities

James A. Thorpe: *B* Fall River MA 1929 *ED* Northeastern Univ BS *CURR EMPL* chmn, ceo: WA Natural Gas Co *CORP AFFIL* chmn, ceo: Thermal Efficiency, Thermal Energy, Washington Energy Resources; dir: Seafirst Corp, Unigard Ins Corp *NONPR AFFIL* dir: Salvation Army; mem: Am Gas Assn, Pacific Coast Gas Assn; trust: Univ Puget Sound

GIVING OFFICERS

Jane Kilborn: *CURR EMPL* asst vp publ aff: WA Natural Gas Co

APPLICATION INFORMATION

Initial Approach: *Initial Contact:* brief letter of inquiry *Include Information On:* a description of organization, amount requested, and purpose of funds sought *When to Submit:* any time

Restrictions on Giving: Does not support individuals, religious organizations for sectarian purposes, political or lobbying groups, or organizations outside operating areas.

Washington Post Co.

Sales: $1.46 billion
Employees: 6,100
Headquarters: Washington, DC
SIC Major Group: Communications and Printing & Publishing

CONTACT

Rima Calderon
Corporate Affairs Director
Washington Post Co.
1150 15th St., NW
Washington, DC 20071
(202) 334-6617

FINANCIAL SUMMARY

Recent Giving: $3,000,000 (1993 est.); $3,000,000 (1992 approx.); $3,000,000 (1991)
Assets: -$12,139 (1991); $1,496,500 (1990)
Gifts Received: $252,500 (1991)
Fiscal Note: Company gives majority of funding directly. Some contributions are also made through the Washington Post Company Educational Foundation. See "Other Things You Should Know" for more details.
EIN: 52-1545926

CONTRIBUTIONS SUMMARY

Typical Recipients: • *Arts & Humanities:* museums/galleries, music, opera, performing arts, public broadcasting • *Civic & Public Affairs:* public policy • *Education:* elementary education, faculty development, literacy, public education (precollege) • *Social Services:* child welfare, community service organizations, united funds, youth organizations

Grant Types: employee matching gifts, general support, multiyear/continuing support, operating expenses, project, and scholarship

Nonmonetary Support Types: cause-related marketing & promotion, donated equipment, donated products, in-kind services, and loaned executives
Note: Estimated value of nonmonetary support is unavailable.

Geographic Distribution: near headquarters and operating locations

Operating Locations: AZ (Phoenix), CA (Los Angeles), CT (Hartford), DC, FL (Jacksonville, Miami), MI (Detroit), MN (Minneapolis), NY (New York), PA (Philadelphia), VA (Alexandria, Ashland), WA (Everett)

CORP. OFFICERS

Donald E. Graham: *CURR EMPL* pres, ceo, dir: Washington Post Co

Katharine Meyer Graham: *B* New York NY 1917 *ED* Univ Chicago AB 1938 *CURR EMPL* chmn, dir: Washington Post Co *CORP AFFIL* co-chmn: Intl Herald Tribune; dir: Bowater Mersey Paper Co Ltd, Reuters Founders Share Co Ltd *NONPR AFFIL* dir: Counc Aid Ed, Fed City Counc, Urban Inst; fellow: Am Academy Arts & Sciences; hon trust: George Washington Univ; life trust: Univ Chicago; mem: Am Soc Newspaper Editors, Counc Foreign Rels, Natl Press Club, Overseas Devel Counc; mem sr adv bd: Joan Shorenstein Barone Ctr Press Politics Pub Policy, Harvard Univ

Alan Spoon: *B* Detroit MI 1951 *CURR EMPL* coo, exec vp, dir: Washington Post Co *CORP AFFIL* dir: Riggs Natl Bank WA; mem: Fin Execs Inst, Intl Newspapers Fin Execs *NONPR AFFIL* trust: WETA Pub Broadcasting

GIVING OFFICERS
Rima Calderon: corp affairs dir

APPLICATION INFORMATION
Initial Approach: *Initial Contact:* brief letter or proposal *Include Information On:* description of the organization, amount requested, purpose for which funds are sought, recently audited financial statement, proof of tax-exempt status *When to Submit:* any time *Note:* Each major business of the company administers its share of the total budget within policy guidelines. Company prefers to initiate action in areas of interest rather than respond to requests.
Restrictions on Giving: Generally, support is not awarded to individuals, for political or religious purposes, travel, or meeting or conference expenses.
Does not respond to form letters or mass-mailing appeals.

OTHER THINGS TO KNOW
Company donates approximately 2% of pretax earnings to charitable activities.
The company also makes contributions through the Washington Post Company Educational Foundation. In 1991, the foundation gave $138,630 for scholarships.

GRANTS ANALYSIS
Total Grants: $3,000,000*
Disclosure Period: 1991
Note: Company does not disclose precise contributions figures. Recent grants listed are for the Washington Post Company Foundation. Recent grants are derived from a 1991 Form 990.

RECENT GRANTS
3,600 District of Columbia Public Schools, Washington, DC — education award
3,600 Fairfax County Public Schools, Fairfax, VA
3,000 Anne Arundel County Public Schools, Annapolis, MD — education award
2,500 Morgan State University, Baltimore, MD — scholarship award
2,100 Arlington Public Schools, Arlington, VA — education award
2,100 Prince William County Public Schools, Manassas, VA — education award
2,000 Frederick County Public Schools, Frederick, MD — education award
2,000 Howard University, Washington, DC — scholarship award
2,000 Howard University, Washington, DC — scholarship award
2,000 University of the District of Columbia, Washington, DC — scholarship award

Washington Square Fund

CONTACT
Maurice F. Goodbody, Jr.
Washington Square Fund
PO Box 7938, F.D.R. Sta.
New York, NY 10150

FINANCIAL SUMMARY
Recent Giving: $106,540 (fiscal 1991); $119,500 (fiscal 1990); $105,200 (fiscal 1989)
Assets: $1,676,318 (fiscal year ending September 30, 1991); $2,364,072 (fiscal 1990); $2,559,891 (fiscal 1989)
EIN: 13-1624213

CONTRIBUTIONS SUMMARY
Typical Recipients: • *Education:* student aid • *Health:* health organizations, hospices, medical research, medical training, pediatric health, public health • *Social Services:* child welfare, community service organizations, family planning, family services, homes, youth organizations
Grant Types: general support, project, research, and scholarship
Geographic Distribution: limited to New York, NY

GIVING OFFICERS
Susan J. Baisley: treas
Louis Chinn: secy
James D. Johnson: trust
Mrs. James D. Johnson: trust
Margo Lynden: trust
L. Kirk Payne: pres
Theresa R. Schaff: vp
William Taggart: trust
Theresa Thompson: trust
Jeff Wallis: trust

APPLICATION INFORMATION
Initial Approach: Send brief letter describing program. There are no deadlines.
Restrictions on Giving: Does not support individuals or provide funds for operating funds.

GRANTS ANALYSIS
Number of Grants: 8
Highest Grant: $34,700
Typical Range: $7,500 to $15,000
Disclosure Period: fiscal year ending September 30, 1991

RECENT GRANTS
34,700 The Door, New York, NY — to provide health, vocational, recreational, and educational aid to children and young adults
21,000 Women In Need, New York, NY — to support a family therapist program
15,000 Family Dynamics, New York, NY — to support services to New York children in danger of abuse or neglect
15,000 Northside Center for Child Development, New York, NY — to support an educational and emotional support program for children aged 2-7
11,000 Enter, New York, NY — to provide monies for the direct expenses of operating a shelter
10,000 Youth Counseling League, New York, NY
7,500 Inwood House, New York, NY — to support an outreach service to counsel and guide teenagers in local high schools before problems develop
5,000 Seventh Avenue Windsor Place Community Association, New York, NY — to support the operations of a community hotline

Washington Square Health Foundation

CONTACT
Howard Nochumson
Executive Director
Washington Square Health Fdn.
875 North Michigan Avenue, Ste. 3516
Chicago, IL 60611
(312) 664-6488

FINANCIAL SUMMARY
Recent Giving: $855,860 (fiscal 1991); $856,800 (fiscal 1990); $812,993 (fiscal 1989)
Assets: $21,553,735 (fiscal year ending September 30, 1991); $14,007,810 (fiscal 1990); $20,235,567 (fiscal 1989)
Gifts Received: $18,014 (fiscal 1991)
EIN: 36-1210140

CONTRIBUTIONS SUMMARY
Donor(s): The foundation was established in in 1985 by Henrotin Hospital.
Typical Recipients: • *Education:* medical education • *Health:* health organizations, hospitals, medical research
Grant Types: project, research, and scholarship
Geographic Distribution: focus on the Chicago, IL, area

GIVING OFFICERS
Robert S. Bleier, MD: dir
Angelo P. Creticos, MD: vchmn, dir
L. B. Dillehay: pres, dir
William B. Friedman: dir
Robert Stephen Kirby: dir *B* Rochester IL 1925 *ED* Univ IL 1948-1950 *CURR EMPL* exec vp, secy: Whitman Corp *CORP AFFIL* vp, secy: IC Products Co *NONPR AFFIL* mem: Am Soc Corp Secys
James Lutz: chmn, dir
Arthur I. Margolis: secy, dir
Howard McDowell McCue III: dir *B* Sumter SC 1946 *ED* Princeton Univ AB 1968; Harvard Univ JD 1971 *CURR EMPL* ptnr: Mayer Brown & Platt *NONPR AFFIL* adj prof: Chicago Kent Coll Law; dir: Hall (Lawrence) Sch Boys, Northwestern Univ Library Counc, Ravinia Festival Assn; mem: Am Bar Assn, Am Coll Tax Couns, Am Coll Trust & Estate Couns, Chicago Bar Assn, Chicago Bar Fdn, Harvard Law Soc, IL Bar Assn,

Intl Academy Estate & Trust Law
Howard Nochumson: exec dir, dir
Bill G. Wiley III: dir
Mrs. Arthur M. Wirtz: vp, dir
John C. York: treas, dir

APPLICATION INFORMATION
Initial Approach:
The foundation requests applicants contact the foundation for a formal application form. The deadlines for submitting applications are June 1 and December 1.
Restrictions on Giving: The foundation does not support individuals, land acquisition projects, or general operating or adminstrative expenses.

OTHER THINGS TO KNOW
Publications: annual report and application guidelines

GRANTS ANALYSIS
Total Grants: $855,860*
Disclosure Period: fiscal year ending September 30, 1991
Note: Grant list not provided for 1991.

Washington Trust Bank / Washington Trust Bank Foundation
Assets: $409.0 million
Employees: 260
Parent Company: W.T.B. Financial Corp.
Headquarters: Spokane, WA
SIC Major Group: Depository Institutions

CONTACT
F. W. Scammell
Administrator and Trustee
Washington Trust Fdn.
c/o Washington Trust Bank, PO Box 2127
Spokane, WA 99210
(509) 353-3820

FINANCIAL SUMMARY
Recent Giving: $368,841 (1991); $405,631 (1990); $395,955 (1989)
Assets: $5,120 (1991); $9,327 (1990); $49,372 (1989)
Gifts Received: $364,634 (1991); $365,086 (1990); $445,792 (1989)
Fiscal Note: Contributes through foundation only. In 1991, contributions were received from Washington Trust Bank.
EIN: 91-1145506

CONTRIBUTIONS SUMMARY
Typical Recipients: • *Arts & Humanities:* community arts, music, performing arts • *Education:* colleges & universities, community & junior colleges, private education (precollege) • *Health:* hospitals • *Social Services:* community service organizations, food/clothing distribution, recreation & athletics, shelters/homelessness, united funds, youth organizations
Grant Types: general support
Geographic Distribution: emphasis on the greater Spokane, WA, area
Operating Locations: WA (Spokane)

CORP. OFFICERS
Peter F. Stanton: *CURR EMPL* pres, ceo: WA Trust Bank

GIVING OFFICERS
F. W. Scammell: trust, adm
Peter F. Stanton: trust *CURR EMPL* pres, ceo: WA Trust Bank (see above)
Philip H. Stanton: trust

APPLICATION INFORMATION
Initial Approach: *Initial Contact:* brief letter *Include Information On:* name and general purpose of the organization; proof of tax exemption; amount and purpose of funds requested; copy of current budget and the most recent finanical statements showing sources of grants, contributions and earned income, if any; and a list of officers and members of any advisory council or board *When to Submit:* any time
Restrictions on Giving: Does not support individuals, religious organizations for sectarian purposes, or political or lobbying groups.

GRANTS ANALYSIS
Total Grants: $368,841
Number of Grants: 55
Highest Grant: $69,250
Typical Range: $1,000 to $10,000
Disclosure Period: 1991
Note: Recent grants are derived from a 1991 grants list.

RECENT GRANTS
69,250 United Way, Spokane, WA
69,167 St. George's School, Spokane, WA
20,076 Spokane Symphony, Spokane, WA
20,000 Spokane Symphony, Spokane, WA — endowment fund
16,000 Community Colleges of Spokane, Spokane, WA
12,750 Inland Northwest Community Foundation, Spokane, WA
12,500 Gonzaga University, Spokane, WA — engineering building fund
10,000 Spokesman-Review, Spokane, WA — Christmas Fund
10,000 Washington State University, Pullman, WA
6,750 Allegro, Spokane, WA

Washington Water Power Co.
Revenue: $566.81 million
Employees: 1,401
Headquarters: Spokane, WA
SIC Major Group: Coal Mining, Electric, Gas & Sanitary Services, Nondepository Institutions, and Real Estate

CONTACT
Debbie Simock
Community Relations Coordinator
Washington Water Power Co.
PO Box 3727
Spokane, WA 99220
(509) 482-8031

FINANCIAL SUMMARY
Recent Giving: $500,000 (1993 approx.); $500,000 (1992 approx.); $500,000 (1991)
Fiscal Note: Company gives directly.

CONTRIBUTIONS SUMMARY
Typical Recipients: • *Arts & Humanities:* community arts, general, libraries, museums/galleries, music, performing arts, public broadcasting, theater, visual arts • *Civic & Public Affairs:* economic development, environmental affairs, ethnic/minority organizations, general, housing, philanthropic organizations, safety, urban & community affairs, women's affairs, zoos/botanical gardens • *Education:* business education, colleges & universities, community & junior colleges, economic education, elementary education, engineering education, faculty development, minority education, public education (precollege) • *Health:* general • *Science:* science exhibits & fairs, science exhibits & fairs • *Social Services:* aged, child welfare, community service organizations, delinquency & crime, drugs & alcohol, emergency relief, united funds, youth organizations
Grant Types: general support and project
Nonmonetary Support Types: donated equipment, in-kind services, and loaned executives
Geographic Distribution: eastern Washington and northern Idaho service area only
Operating Locations: WA (Spokane)

CORP. OFFICERS
James R. Harvey: *CURR EMPL* pres, coo, dir: Washington Water Power Co
Paul A. Redmond: *B* Lakeview OR 1937 *CURR EMPL* chmn, ceo, dir: Washington Water Power Co *CORP AFFIL* chmn: Devel Assocs, Devel Assocs, Northwest Telecom, Pentzer Corp, Pentzer Devel Corp, Pentzer Energy Post Street Corp, Pentzer Energy Scvs, Solganic Svc Corp, Widco Waste Svcs, WP Energy Co; chmn, ceo: WP Fin Co; chmn, ceo, pres: WA Irrigation & Devel; dir: Devel Assocs, Hecla Mining Co, Itron, Limestone Co, Security Pacific Bank WA, Spokane Indus Park, Water Power Impovement Co

GIVING OFFICERS
Debbie Simock: *CURR EMPL* commun rels coordinator: WA Water Power Co

APPLICATION INFORMATION
Initial Approach: *Initial Contact:* requests must be submitted in writing* *Include Information On:* a brief summary of the organization including date of establishment, history, mission statement, and objectives; copy of IRS letter designating the organization's 501(c)(3) status; current financial state-

ment; list of board of directors and key staff; a brief overview of the program/project for which funding is requested including purpose, targeted population, evaluation strategies, anticipated results, budget, other organizations providing support, and timeline; and current or past WWP involvement, if any, in the organization or program, including employee volunteers, board members, etc. *When to Submit:* any time *Note:* Applicants outside Spokane are encouraged to submit requests to regional offices. Contact headquarters for further information.

Restrictions on Giving: Generally does not contribute to individuals, team or extra-curricular school events, tournament fund raisers, trips or tours, churches or other religious organizations, organizations that discriminate for any reason, endowments or foundations, or hospital or patient care institution operating funds.

OTHER THINGS TO KNOW

Priority is given to requests that demonstrate partnerships and cooperative efforts between organizations and agencies and which directly benefit people within areas where company conducts business.
Publications: contributions guidelines

GRANTS ANALYSIS
Typical Range: $500 to $1,000

Wasie Foundation

CONTACT
Gregg D. Sjoquist
Executive Director
Wasie Foundation
909 Foshay Tower
Minneapolis, MN 55402
(612) 332-3883

FINANCIAL SUMMARY
Recent Giving: $650,000 (1993 est.); $450,000 (1992); $139,520 (1990)
Assets: $14,500,000 (1993 est.); $13,109,632 (1990); $12,281,549 (1989); $11,522,320 (1988)
Gifts Received: $60 (1989); $250 (1987); $8,000 (1985)
EIN: 41-0911636

CONTRIBUTIONS SUMMARY
Donor(s): Donald A. Wasie, Stanley L. Wasie, and Marie F. Wasie donated funds toward establishing the Wasie Foundation in 1966.
Typical Recipients: • *Education:* colleges & universities • *Health:* mental health
Grant Types: endowment, general support, operating expenses, project, research, and scholarship
Geographic Distribution: no geographic restrictions

GIVING OFFICERS
Jerome J. Choromanski: vp, treas, dir
Patrick F. Flaherty: dir
Andrew J. Leemhuis, MD: med dir, dir
David A. Odahowski: dir
Ina N. Reed: dir
Gregg D. Sjoquist: exec dir, secy, dir
Roy K. Sorensen: dir

APPLICATION INFORMATION
Initial Approach:
Initial contact should be a telephone inquiry. The foundation has eliminated its grant application guidelines and does not accept written applications. The foundation will discuss the proposed project over the telephone providing it falls within the foundation's scope of interest.

GRANTS ANALYSIS
Total Grants: $945
Number of Grants: 2
Highest Grant: $920
Disclosure Period: 1991
Note: Recent grants are derived from a 1990 grants list.

RECENT GRANTS
37,000 United Cerebral Palsy Broward County, Ft. Lauderdale, FL
26,000 Twin Cities Public Television/KTCA, St. Paul, MN
14,295 Church of St. Nicholas, New Market, MN
10,000 International Special Olympic Games, Minneapolis, MN
9,500 De La Salle High School, Minneapolis, MN — skills lab program
5,000 Listening House of St. Paul, St. Paul, MN

5,000 Little Brothers Friends of the Elderly, Minneapolis, MN
5,000 Minneapolis Crisis Nursery, Minneapolis, MN
5,000 Minnesota Orchestral Association, Minneapolis, MN
5,000 Rise, Spring Lake Park, MN

Wasily Family Foundation

CONTACT
Patrick N. Moloney
Wasily Family Foundation
230 Park Avenue, Suite 825
New York, NY 10169
(212) 490-2220

FINANCIAL SUMMARY
Recent Giving: $90,000 (fiscal 1991)
Assets: $3,093,432 (fiscal year ending June 30, 1991)
Gifts Received: $940,000 (fiscal 1991)
EIN: 13-3503227

CONTRIBUTIONS SUMMARY
Typical Recipients: • *Health:* health organizations • *Religion:* churches • *Social Services:* disabled, religious welfare, youth organizations
Grant Types: general support

APPLICATION INFORMATION
Initial Approach: The foundation reports no specific application guidelines. Send a brief letter of inquiry, including statement of purpose, amount requested, and proof of tax-exempt status.

GRANTS ANALYSIS
Total Grants: $90,000
Number of Grants: 6
Highest Grant: $15,000
Disclosure Period: fiscal year ending June 30, 1991

RECENT GRANTS
15,000 Alfred E. Smith Memorial Foundation, NY
15,000 Lighthouse, NY
15,000 Salvation Army, NY
15,000 Servants for Relief for Incurable Cancer, NY
15,000 St. Paul's Church, NY

15,000 Young Women's Christian Association, NY

Wasmer Foundation

CONTACT
Allan H. Toole
Trustee
Wasmer Fdn.
1100 U.S. Bank Bldg.
Spokane, WA 99201-0390
(509) 624-5265

FINANCIAL SUMMARY
Recent Giving: $99,700 (1991); $88,272 (1990); $91,725 (1989)
Assets: $2,864,519 (1991); $2,606,808 (1990); $2,598,454 (1989)
EIN: 91-1205115

CONTRIBUTIONS SUMMARY
Donor(s): the late Florence Wasmer
Typical Recipients: • *Arts & Humanities:* arts centers, community arts, dance, history/historic preservation, music, performing arts, theater • *Education:* arts education, community & junior colleges • *Religion:* churches, religious organizations • *Social Services:* community service organizations, food/clothing distribution, shelters/homelessness, youth organizations
Grant Types: endowment
Geographic Distribution: focus on Spokane, WA

GIVING OFFICERS
E.L. Rehn: trust
T.H. Richardson: trust
Allan H. Toole: trust *ED* Gonzaga Univ LLB 1948 *CURR EMPL* coun: Witherspoon Kelly Davenport & Tool *CORP AFFIL* coun: Witherspoon Kelly Davenport & Tool *NONPR AFFIL* fellow: Am Coll Trust Estate Counc; mem: Am Bar Assn, WA Bar Assn

APPLICATION INFORMATION
Initial Approach: Application form required. Deadlines are April 30 and October 31.
Restrictions on Giving: Does not support individuals.

OTHER THINGS TO KNOW
Publications: Application Guidelines

GRANTS ANALYSIS
Number of Grants: 17
Highest Grant: $35,000
Typical Range: $1,000 to
$6,000
Disclosure Period: 1991

RECENT GRANTS
35,000 Spokane Inland
Northwest Commu-
nity Foundation,
Spokane, WA —
music fund
17,500 Spokane Food
Bank, Spokane,
WA — food dis-
tribution
10,000 Spokane Art
School, Spokane,
WA — tuition assis-
tance
6,200 District 17 Commu-
nity College Foun-
dation, Spokane,
WA
5,000 Spokane Sym-
phony Society,
Spokane, WA
4,000 Eastern Washing-
ton Historical Soci-
ety, Spokane, WA
4,000 Full Gospel Mis-
sion, Spokane, WA
— youth summer
camp
3,500 Holy Names Music
Center, Spokane,
WA
2,500 Allegro-Baroque
and Beyond,
Spokane, WA
2,500 Spokane Chamber
Music Association,
Spokane, WA —
guest artist program

Wasserman Foundation

CONTACT
William J. Bird
Vice President
Wasserman Foundation
c/o Musick, Peeler & Garrett
One Wilshire Blvd. 2000
Los Angeles, CA 90017
(213) 629-7635

FINANCIAL SUMMARY
Recent Giving: $3,238,687
(1991); $1,280,381 (1990);
$2,475,958 (1989)
Assets: $38,294,393 (1990);
$31,168,300 (1989)
Gifts Received: $4,683,020
(1990); $1,126,125 (1989)
Fiscal Note: 1991 contribution
received from Lew R. Wasser-
man.
EIN: 95-6038762

CONTRIBUTIONS SUMMARY
Donor(s): The foundation was
established in 1956 by Lew A.
Wasserman, the current president. Mr. Wasserman is the
chairman and chief executive
officer of MCA, Inc., the
movie and entertainment company.
Typical Recipients: • *Arts &
Humanities:* arts centers, arts
funds, arts institutes, muse-
ums/galleries, public broadcasting, theater • *Civic & Public Affairs:* housing, international
affairs, philanthropic organizations, zoos/botanical gardens
• *Education:* arts education,
colleges & universities
• *Health:* hospitals, medical research, single-disease health associations • *International:* foreign educational institutions
• *Religion:* religious organizations, synagogues • *Social Services:* child welfare, religious
welfare
Grant Types: general support
Geographic Distribution: primarily Los Angeles, CA, and
New York, NY, areas

GIVING OFFICERS
William J. Bird: vp, asst secy
Edith Wasserman: vp, cfo,
secy
Lew Robert Wasserman: pres
B Cleveland OH 1913 *CURR
EMPL* chmn, ceo, dir, mem
exec comm: MCA *CORP
AFFIL* dir: Am Airlines
NONPR AFFIL bd govs:
Ronald Reagan Presidential
Fdn; chmn: Res Prevent Blind-
ness Fdn; chmn emeritus: Assn
Motion Picture Television Pro-
ducers; dir: Amateur Athletic
Fdn Los Angeles, Los Angeles
Ctr Fdn; hon chmn: Ctr Theatre
Group Los Angeles Music Ctr;
trust: CA Inst Tech, Carter
Presidential Ctr, John F
Kennedy Ctr Performing Arts,
John F Kennedy Library, LBJ
Fdn, Jules Stein Eye Inst

APPLICATION INFORMATION
**Initial Approach: Restric-
tions on Giving:** The foundation reports that it does not accept unsolicited proposals for
funds.

GRANTS ANALYSIS
Total Grants: $1,280,381
Number of Grants: 66
Highest Grant: $254,431
Typical Range: $1,000 to
$20,000

Disclosure Period: 1990
Note: Recent grants are derived from a 1990 grants list.
The average grant figure excludes the largest grant of
$254,431.

RECENT GRANTS
254,531 United Jewish
Fund, Los Angeles,
CA
204,000 Jerusalem Founda-
tion, New York, NY
113,125 Jules and Doris
Stein University of
California Los An-
geles Support
Group, Beverly
Hills, CA
113,125 Research to Pre-
vent Blindness,
New York, NY
100,000 Israel Heritage/Mo-
reshet Israel, New
York, NY
50,000 Academy Founda-
tion, Beverly Hills,
CA
50,000 United States Holocaust Memorial
Museum, Washing-
ton, DC
48,500 Motion Picture and
Television Fund,
Woodland Hills,
CA
29,200 John F. Kennedy
Center for the Per-
forming Arts,
Washington, DC
25,000 Cystic Fibrosis
Foundation, Los
Angeles, CA

Wasserman Foundation, George

CONTACT
Janice W. Goldsten
President
George Wasserman Fdn.
3134 Ellicott St., N.W.
Washington, DC 20005
(202) 966-3355

FINANCIAL SUMMARY
Recent Giving: $165,000
(1991); $56,100 (1990);
$245,150 (1989)
Assets: $2,913,873 (1991);
$2,821,931 (1990); $2,661,085
(1989)
EIN: 52-6035888

CONTRIBUTIONS SUMMARY
Donor(s): the late George Wasserman
Typical Recipients: • *Arts &
Humanities:* history/historic
preservation, museums/galler-
ies, public broadcasting • *Education:* colleges & universities,

public education (precollege),
religious education • *Religion:*
religious organizations, synagogues • *Social Services:* aged,
youth organizations
Grant Types: general support
Geographic Distribution:
focus on the Washington, DC
area

GIVING OFFICERS
Lisa Gill: vp, dir
Janice W. Goldsten: pres,
treas, dir
Carolyn Stopak: vp, secy, dir

APPLICATION INFORMATION
Initial Approach: Send brief
letter of inquiry describing program or project. There are no
deadlines.
Restrictions on Giving: Does
not support individuals.

GRANTS ANALYSIS
Disclosure Period: 1991
Note: 1991 grants list not
provided.

RECENT GRANTS
30,000 Washington He-
brew Synagogue,
Washington, DC
12,000 United States Holocaust Memorial
Museum, Washing-
ton, DC
10,000 Yeshiva High
School of Greater
Washington, Silver
Spring, MD
5,000 Zionist Organiza-
tion of America,
New York, NY
1,500 Raphael House,
Portland, OR
1,000 Adas Israel Mens
Club, Washington,
DC
1,000 B'nai B'rith, Wash-
ington, DC
500 Knesset Yenudo
Building Fund,
New York, NY
100 United States Com-
mittee, Philadel-
phia, PA — Sports
for Israel

Waste Management

Sales: $8.66 billion
Employees: 67,275
Headquarters: Oak Brook, IL
SIC Major Group: Electric, Gas
& Sanitary Services

CONTACT

Paul Pyrcik
Director of Community
  Investment
Waste Management, Inc.
3003 Butterfield Rd.
Oak Brook, IL 60521
(708) 572-3107
Note: Mr. Pyrcik is contact for
programs that are national in
scope or for the company's
headquarters area. Proposals
that are regional or state-wide
in impact should contact
regional offices. Local
organizations should contact
local operating divisions.

FINANCIAL SUMMARY

Recent Giving: $9,600,000
(1992); $7,900,000 (1991);
$7,500,000 (1990)
Fiscal Note: Total contributions figures for years prior to
1989 were not available. Company gives directly. In 1992,
corporate gi ving program accounted for 51% of contributions; local operating company
giving programs, 33%; and
matching gifts, 16%.

CONTRIBUTIONS
SUMMARY

Typical Recipients: • *Arts &
Humanities:* arts associations,
arts festivals, arts funds, arts institutes, history/historic preservation, museums/galleries,
music, opera, performing arts,
public broadcasting, theater
• *Civic & Public Affairs:* environmental affairs, ethnic/minor-
ity organizations, municipalities, professional & trade
associations, safety, urban &
community affairs, zoos/botani-
cal gardens • *Education:* colleges & universities, education
funds, elementary education,
engineering education, minority education, public education
(precollege), science/technol-
ogy education • *Health:* health
funds, hospitals, medical research, mental health, single-
disease health associations
Grant Types: employee matching gifts, general support, and
scholarship
Note: Company matches em-
ployee gifts to general charities, education, environmental

organizations, and for volunteer service. Company sponsors
two scholarship programs: a
general program and a minority
program, both for children of
employees.
Nonmonetary Support Types:
in-kind services
Note: Above figure includes
services donated by the company and its subsidiaries with
an estimated value of $765,000
in 1991 and $768,000 in 1992.
This amount is included in
above total giving figures.
Geographic Distribution:
near headquarters and operating locations and to some national organizations
Operating Locations: IL (Oak
Brook)
Note: Company operates in 48
states and in more than 20
countries overseas.

CORP. OFFICERS

Dean L. Buntrock: *B* Colum-
bia SD 1931 *ED* St Olaf Coll
1955 *CURR EMPL* chmn, ceo,
dir: Waste Mgmt *CORP AFFIL*
dir: Brand Cos, Chem Waste
Mgmt, Wheelabrator Techs
NONPR AFFIL dir: Natl Solid
Wastes Mgmt Assn; mem: Am
Pub Works Assn; mem bd trust:
Chicago Symphony Orchestra
Assn
Phillip B. Rooney: *B* Chicago
IL 1944 *ED* St Bernard Coll
1966 *CURR EMPL* pres, coo,
dir, mem exec comm: Waste
Mgmt *CORP AFFIL* chmn,
ceo: Wheelabrator Techs; dir:
Brand Cos, Chem Waste Mgmt,
First Natl Bank La Grange IL,
IL Tool Works, Servicemaster
Consumer Svcs *NONPR AFFIL*
active: Robert Crown Ctr; adv
bd: Hinsdale Commun House;
dir: Keep Am Beautiful, Lyric
Opera Chicago, Nazareth Acad-
emy; mem: Am Pub Works
Assn, Natl Solid Wastes Mgmt
Assn; trust: Denison Univ

GIVING OFFICERS

Paul Pyrcik: dir *CURR EMPL*
dir (commun investment):
Waste Mgmt

APPLICATION
INFORMATION

Initial Approach: *Initial Contact:* brief letter or proposal;
no telephone solicitations *Include Information On:* description of the organization, including history, mission statement,
purpose, and goals; amount requested; purpose for which
funds are sought, including

need and explanation of how it
fits within company's giving
guidelines; recently audited financial statements or annual report; approved operating
budget; project plan; method of
evaluation; list of current trustees and board members and
their affiliations; proof of tax-
exempt status *When to Submit:*
any time
Restrictions on Giving: Does
not support individuals; sectarian organizations; veterans'
and labor organizations; or organizations that discriminate
on the basis of race, sex, or religion.

OTHER THINGS TO
KNOW

Publications: charitable annual report

GRANTS ANALYSIS

Total Grants: $9,600,000
Disclosure Period: 1992
Note: Recent grants are derived
from a 1992 annual report.

RECENT GRANTS

Abraham Lincoln Centre,
  Chicago, IL
American Public Works
  Association, Chicago, IL
Art Institute of Chicago,
  Chicago, IL
Big Shoulders Fund, Chicago, IL
Boy Scouts of America-Hoover
  Outdoor Education Center,
  Chicago, IL
Broward Performing Arts
  Center, Ft. Lauderdale, FL
Calumet Area Family Fund,
  Chicago, IL
Center for Marine Conservation,
  Washington, DC
Chicago Educational Television
  Association/WTTW Channel
  11, Chicago, IL
Chicago Symphony Orchestra,
  Chicago, IL

Waterfowl Research
Foundation

CONTACT

Alexander Laughlin
Treasurer
Waterfowl Research Fdn.
140 Broadway
New York, NY 10005
(212) 504-4019

FINANCIAL SUMMARY

Recent Giving: $457,000
(1991); $977,508 (1990);
$310,000 (1989)

Assets: $8,761,157 (1991);
$5,432,901 (1990); $7,250,013
(1989)

Gifts Received: $12,500
(1989); $5,000 (1987)

EIN: 13-6122167

CONTRIBUTIONS
SUMMARY

Donor(s): the late M. E. Davis

Typical Recipients: • *Civic &
Public Affairs:* environmental
affairs • *Social Services:* animal protection

Grant Types: general support

GIVING OFFICERS

Henry E. Coe III: chmn, dir

Edward P. Donelan: asst treas

Edson I. Gaylord: pres, dir

Alexander M. Laughlin: treas

**Carroll Livingston Wain-
wright, Jr.:** vp, secy, dir *B*
New York NY 1925 *ED* Yale
Univ BA 1949; Harvard Univ
LLB 1952 *CURR EMPL* ptnr:
Milbank Tweed Hadley &
McCloy *CORP AFFIL* trust:
US Trust Corp *NONPR AFFIL*
mem: Am Bar Assn, Am Coll
Trust & Estate Couns, NY Bar
Assn, NY City Bar Assn; mem
gov bd: NY Commun Trust,
NY Commun Trust; mem univ
counc: Yale Univ; trust: Am
Mus Natural History; trust,
pres: Boys Club NY; trust,
vchmn: Cooper Union Advance-
ment Science Art

Robert Winthrop: off

APPLICATION
INFORMATION

Initial Approach: Contributes
only to preselected organizations.

GRANTS ANALYSIS

Number of Grants: 2

Highest Grant: $282,000

Typical Range: $175,000 to
$282,000

Disclosure Period: 1991

RECENT GRANTS

282,000 National Fish and
         Wildlife Founda-
         tion, Palatine, IL —
         prairie farming pro-
         gram
175,000 North American
         Wildlife Founda-
         tion, Palatine, IL —
         wild mallard pro-
         gram

Waters Charitable Trust, Robert S.

CONTACT
Barbara K. Robinson
Vice President
Robert S. Waters Charitable
  Trust
Three Mellon Bank Center
Pittsburgh, PA 15230
(412) 234-5784

FINANCIAL SUMMARY
Recent Giving: $267,250
(1991); $266,750 (1990);
$265,500 (1989)
Assets: $4,573,390 (1991);
$3,812,897 (1990); $4,076,648
(1989)
EIN: 25-6018986

**CONTRIBUTIONS
SUMMARY**
Donor(s): the late Robert S.
Waters
Typical Recipients: • *Arts &
Humanities:* arts centers, community arts, history/historic
preservation, music • *Civic &
Public Affairs:* environmental
affairs • *Education:* colleges &
universities • *Health:* hospitals
• *Social Services:* family services, homes
Grant Types: general support
Geographic Distribution:
focus on PA

GIVING OFFICERS
Mellon Bank, N.A.: trust

**APPLICATION
INFORMATION**
Initial Approach: Send letter
requesting application form.
There are no deadlines.
Restrictions on Giving: Does
not support individuals or provide loans.

GRANTS ANALYSIS
Number of Grants: 25
Highest Grant: $200,000
Typical Range: $500 to $5,000
Disclosure Period: 1991

RECENT GRANTS
  200,000 Carnegie, Pittsburgh, PA
    5,000 Family Social Services, Johnstown, PA
    5,000 Western Pennsylvania Historical Society, Pittsburgh, PA
    4,000 Cambria Free Library, Johnstown, PA
    4,000 Christian Home, Johnstown, PA
    4,000 Conamough Valley Hospital, Johnstown, PA
    4,000 Mercy Hospital, Johnstown, PA
    4,000 Southern Alleghenies Museum of Art, Loretto, PA
    3,500 Ellis School, Pittsburgh, PA
    3,500 Shady Side Academy, Pittsburgh, PA

Waters Foundation

CONTACT
James L. Waters
Trustee
Waters Fdn.
1153 Grove St.
Framingham, MA 01701
(508) 877-3791

FINANCIAL SUMMARY
Recent Giving: $527,600
(1991); $40,000 (1990); $1,000
(1988)
Assets: $4,860,680 (1991);
$4,520,259 (1990); $3,992,503
(1989)
Gifts Received: $600,000
(1990); $1,303,628 (1989);
$1,225,000 (1988)
Fiscal Note: In 1990, contributions were received from James
L. Waters.
EIN: 04-6115211

**CONTRIBUTIONS
SUMMARY**
Donor(s): James L. Waters
Typical Recipients: • *Civic &
Public Affairs:* environmental
affairs • *Education:* colleges &
universities • *Health:* public
health • *Religion:* churches
• *Science:* scientific institutes
• *Social Services:* community
service organizations, family
planning
Grant Types: general support

GIVING OFFICERS
Faith P. Waters: trust
James L. Waters: trust
Richard C. Waters: trust

**APPLICATION
INFORMATION**
Initial Approach: Send brief
letter describing program.
There are no deadlines.

**OTHER THINGS TO
KNOW**
No grants list was provided for
1990.

GRANTS ANALYSIS
Number of Grants: 27
Highest Grant: $157,500
Typical Range: $100 to $5,000
Disclosure Period: 1991

RECENT GRANTS
  157,500 Ideals Associated, MA
  150,000 Trinity College, MA
   41,600 Institute for Biospheric Research, MA
   40,000 Massachusetts Institute of Technology, Cambridge, MA
   35,000 CATO Institute, Washington, DC
   25,000 Northeastern University, Boston, MA
   15,000 Society of Analytical Chemists, MA
   10,000 First Parish Church of Framingham, MA
   10,000 Planned Parenthood Federation of America, Cambridge, MA
    7,000 Wellness Community Organization of Boston, Boston, MA

Watkins Associated Industries

Sales: $270.0 million
Employees: 3,500
Headquarters: Atlanta, GA
SIC Major Group: Agricultural
Production— Crops, Real
Estate, Trucking &
Warehousing, and Wholesale
Trade—Nondurable Goods

CONTACT
Ruth Anne Smith
Secretary to the Chairman
Watkins Associated Industries
1958 Monroe Dr., NE
Atlanta, GA 30324
(404) 872-3841

**CONTRIBUTIONS
SUMMARY**
Operating Locations: GA (Atlanta)

CORP. OFFICERS
Bill Watkins: *CURR EMPL*
chmn: Watkins Associated
Indus
George Watkins: *CURR
EMPL* pres: Watkins Associated Indus

**OTHER THINGS TO
KNOW**
Company is an original donor
to the Watkins Christian Foundation.

Watkins Christian Foundation

CONTACT
Bill Watkins
President
Watkins Christian Fdn.
1946 Monroe Dr., N.E.
Atlanta, GA 30324
(404) 872-3841

FINANCIAL SUMMARY
Recent Giving: $1,854,006
(1989); $938,327 (1988)
Assets: $3,070,398 (1989);
$3,915,545 (1988)
Gifts Received: $725,058
(1988)
EIN: 58-1494832

**CONTRIBUTIONS
SUMMARY**
Donor(s): Bill Watkins, Watkins Associated Industries
Typical Recipients: • *Health:*
hospitals • *Religion:* churches,
missionary activities, religious
organizations • *Social Services:* food/clothing distribution, united funds, youth organizations
Grant Types: general support
and multiyear/continuing support

GIVING OFFICERS
William A. Freeman: dir
CURR EMPL pres, dir: Zurn
Indus
George W. Ready, Jr.: secy,
treas, dir
Bill Watkins: pres, dir *CURR
EMPL* chmn: Watkins Associated Indus
George Watkins: vp, dir
CURR EMPL pres: Watkins Associated Indus

**APPLICATION
INFORMATION**
Initial Approach: The foundation reports it only makes contributions to preselected charitable organizations.

GRANTS ANALYSIS
Number of Grants: 50
Highest Grant: $1,165,000
Typical Range: $500 to $5,000
Disclosure Period: 1989

RECENT GRANTS
  1,165,000 Radio Training Network (Purchase Stations), Atlanta, GA
   120,000 Mount Paran Church, Atlanta, GA
    99,999 Real Life Ministries, Atlanta, GA

75,139 Real Life Ministry (Air Time), Atlanta, GA

57,600 Gospel Rescue Mission, Atlanta, GA

50,000 Smokerise Baptist Church, Smokerise, GA

43,500 Maranatha Church of God, Atlanta, GA

33,343 First Methodist Church Building Fund, Atlanta, GA

27,500 Boy Scouts of America, Atlanta, GA

23,568 Pure Praise Ministries, Atlanta, GA

Watkins-Johnson Co.

Sales: $277.5 million
Employees: 2,620
Headquarters: Palo Alto, CA
SIC Major Group: Electronic & Other Electrical Equipment, Industrial Machinery & Equipment, and Instruments & Related Products

CONTACT
Scott Buchanan
Treasurer
Watkins-Johnson Co.
3333 Hillview Ave.
Palo Alto, CA 94304
(415) 493-4141

CONTRIBUTIONS SUMMARY
Grant Types: matching
Operating Locations: CA (Palo Alto)

CORP. OFFICERS
H. Richard Johnson: *CURR EMPL* vchmn: Watkins-Johnson Co

W. Keith Kennedy, Jr.: *CURR EMPL* pres, ceo: Watkins-Johnson Co

Dean A. Watkins: *CURR EMPL* chmn: Watkins-Johnson Co

Watson Foundation, Thomas J.

CONTACT
Mary E. Brooner
Executive Director
Thomas J. Watson Foundation
217 Angell St.
Providence, RI 02906
(401) 274-1952

FINANCIAL SUMMARY
Recent Giving: $1,864,082 (fiscal 1992); $11,925,568 (fiscal 1991); $3,844,000 (fiscal 1990 approx.)
Assets: $43,331,287 (fiscal year ending May 31, 1992); $41,735,708 (fiscal 1991); $50,423,466 (fiscal 1990)
Gifts Received: $40,813 (fiscal 1991); $220,071 (fiscal 1988); $334,400 (fiscal 1987)
Fiscal Note: The foundation receives contributions from the Arthur K. Watson Trust in New York City.
EIN: 13-6038151

CONTRIBUTIONS SUMMARY
Donor(s): The Thomas J. Watson Foundation was founded in 1961 by Mrs. Watson, in honor of her husband who died in 1956. In 1914, Mr. Watson became president of a company that manufactured office machines. Ten years later, the company was renamed International Business Machines Corporation (IBM). Thomas Watson served as the company's president for almost forty years and was succeeded by his son, Thomas J. Watson, Jr. No family members are currently associated with IBM. Both Thomas Watson, Jr. and his brother, Arthur K. Watson, have donated additional funds to the foundation.
Typical Recipients: • *Education:* colleges & universities
Grant Types: fellowship
Geographic Distribution: national

GIVING OFFICERS
Mary E. Brooner: exec dir
Frances S. Cox: asst dir
Steven V. Licata: exec dir
David E. McKinney: exec secy, mem adv bd *B* Harriman TN 1934 *ED* Vanderbilt Univ 1952-53; Univ TN BS 1956 *CURR EMPL* pres: IBM World Trade Am/Far East Corp *CORP AFFIL* asst group exec: IBM Gen Bus Group; sr vp: IBM

Corp; vp, asst group exec: IBM Info Sys Group *NONPR AFFIL* dir: Gen Re Corp; mem: Intl Exec Svc Corps; trust: Am Univ Paris
Daniel L. Mosley: mem adv bd
Thomas J. Watson III: mem adv bd *B* New York NY 1933 *ED* St Bonaventure Univ 1956 *CURR EMPL* exec vp (mktg), dir: US Life Title Ins Co

APPLICATION INFORMATION
Initial Approach:
Gift-giving by the foundation is self-initiated, and not open to solicitation or application. Nominations for the Thomas J. Watson Fellowship may be made only by the participating colleges.
The foundation is concerned with qualities such as integrity, capacity for leadership, potential for creative achievement, and excellence within a chosen field. The board gives more weight to a candidate's record in his or her chosen field of special interest and proposed project. The project should reflect a demonstrated commitment on the part of the applicant. Completed applications must be accompanied by a statement of the proposed plan of study, a personal statement, two letters of recommendation, a recent photograph, and a college transcript.
Prospective Watson Fellows are nominated by their home college or university. Each participating institution may submit four (two for smaller colleges) fellowship nominations before the November 1 deadline. Completed applications and all other information should arrive by November 4. On-campus interviews of nominees by a representative of the foundation take place in the late fall and winter months. Sixty-five Watson Fellows generally are chosen each year. Grant recipients are announced by mid-March of the year following application.
All Watson Fellows are required to submit progress reports during their year abroad. They must also submit a final evaluation and an accounting of the fellowship funds at the end of the fellowship year.

OTHER THINGS TO KNOW
Morgan Guaranty Trust Company is listed as corporate trustee of the foundation.
Publications: fellowship program brochure

GRANTS ANALYSIS
Total Grants: $1,864,082
Number of Grants: 58
Highest Grant: $250,000
Typical Range: $10,000 to $100,000
Disclosure Period: fiscal year ending May 31, 1992
Note: Recent grants are derived from a fiscal 1992 grants list.

RECENT GRANTS
250,000 California Institute of Technology, Pasadena, CA
250,000 Camphill Soltane Grant, Glenmore, PA
100,000 Buckingham Browne and Nichols School, Cambridge, MA
100,000 Sea Education Association, Wood Hole, MA
60,000 American Philosophical Society, Philadelphia, PA
60,000 Ben Franklin Hall-American Phil Society Grant
39,000 Grinnell College, Grinnell, IA
39,000 Haverford College, Haverford, PA
37,626 University North Colorado Foundation Grant, Greenley, CO
31,000 Harvey Mudd College, Claremont, CA

Watson Foundation, Walter E. and Caroline H.

CONTACT
Herbert H. Pridham
Walter E. and Caroline H. Watson Fdn.
PO Box 450
Youngstown, OH 44501
(216) 744-9000

FINANCIAL SUMMARY
Recent Giving: $251,816 (1990); $239,319 (1989)
Assets: $4,580,271 (1990); $4,683,426 (1989)
EIN: 34-6547726

CONTRIBUTIONS SUMMARY

Donor(s): Walter E. Watson

Typical Recipients: • *Arts & Humanities:* community arts, music, theater • *Education:* colleges & universities • *Health:* health organizations, hospitals, medical research, pediatric health • *Social Services:* child welfare, community service organizations, family services, united funds, youth organizations

Grant Types: general support and project

Geographic Distribution: focus on OH

APPLICATION INFORMATION

Initial Approach: Send full proposal (three copies).

Restrictions on Giving: Does not support individuals.

GRANTS ANALYSIS

Number of Grants: 40

Highest Grant: $50,316

Typical Range: $1,000 to $5,000

Disclosure Period: 1990

RECENT GRANTS

50,316 Western Reserve Care System, Columbus, OH — general purposes

40,000 Henry H. Stombough Auditorium Association, Youngstown, OH — capital fund

40,000 Youngstown Symphony Society, Youngstown, OH — endowment campaign

30,000 United Way, Youngstown, OH

25,000 Rescue Missions, Youngstown, OH — capital campaign

5,000 Monday Musical Club, Youngstown, OH — 1990 programs

5,000 Youngstown Health Foundation, Canfield, OH — for children's hospital 1990 telethon

5,000 Youngstown Hearing and Speech Center, Youngstown, OH

5,000 Youngstown State University, Youngstown, OH

3,500 Park Vista Foundation, Youngstown, OH — annual life care fund

Watt Industry

Sales: $350.0 million
Employees: 400
Headquarters: Santa Monica, CA
SIC Major Group: Real Estate

CONTACT

Paula Tanoski
Vice President, Human Resources
Watt Industry
PO Box 2114
Santa Monica, CA 90406
(310) 450-0779

CONTRIBUTIONS SUMMARY

Operating Locations: CA (Santa Monica)

CORP. OFFICERS

James Maginn: *CURR EMPL* cfo: Watt Indus

J. Scott Watt: *CURR EMPL* ceo, vchmn: Watt Industry

Raymond A. Watt: *CURR EMPL* ceo: Watt Industry

Watumull Fund, J.

CONTACT

Gulab Watumull
President
J. Watumull Fund
1341 Kapiolani Blvd.
PO Box 3200
Honolulu, HI 96814
(808) 955-1144

FINANCIAL SUMMARY

Recent Giving: $314,366 (1990); $318,100 (1989); $220,000 (1988)

Assets: $6,507,864 (1990); $6,661,879 (1989); $5,785,813 (1988)

EIN: 51-0205431

CONTRIBUTIONS SUMMARY

Donor(s): Gulab Watumull, Watumull Brothers, Ltd.

Typical Recipients: • *Arts & Humanities:* arts centers, museums/galleries, theater • *Education:* colleges & universities • *Religion:* churches, religious organizations • *Social Services:* family planning, family services

Grant Types: capital, general support, multiyear/continuing support, and scholarship

Geographic Distribution: focus on HI

GIVING OFFICERS

Clinton Rutledge Ashford: secy, dir *B* Honolulu HI 1925

ED Univ CA Berkeley BA 1945; Univ MI JD 1950 *CURR EMPL* of coun: Ashford & Wriston *CORP AFFIL* of coun: Ashford & Wriston *NONPR AFFIL* fellow: Am Bar Fdn, Am Coll Probate Couns, Am Coll Real Estate Lawyers; mem: Am Bar Assn, Am Judicature Soc, Am Law Inst, HI Bar Assn

Gulab Watumull: pres, dir *CURR EMPL* pres, sec, treas: Watumull Brothers Ltd

Khubchand Watumull: vp, dir

Sundri R. Watumull: treas

APPLICATION INFORMATION

Initial Approach: Application form required. There are no deadlines. Decisions are made within two weeks.

GRANTS ANALYSIS

Number of Grants: 63

Highest Grant: $50,000

Typical Range: $1,000 to $6,000

Disclosure Period: 1990

RECENT GRANTS

50,000 Satya Narayah Mandir, New York, NY

50,000 Seva, Los Altos, CA — J. Watumull Memorial Scholarship

50,000 Vishwa Hindu Parishad of America, Staten Island, NY

12,356 Ghandi Memorial International Foundation, Walnut Creek, CA — Ghandi statue for Honolulu

10,000 Bishop Museum, Honolulu, HI — capital improvement program

10,000 Contemporary Museum, Honolulu, HI

6,000 Louisiana State University, Baton Rouge, LA — scholarships for foreign students of East Indian ancestry

6,000 Princeton University, Princeton, NJ — scholarships for foreign students of East Indian ancestry

5,000 Hanahauoli School, Honolulu, HI — scholarship fund

5,000 Honolulu Academy of Arts, Honolulu, HI — restoration of the academy of

art center at Linekona

Wausau Insurance Cos.

Sales: $1.5 billion
Employees: 5,592
Parent Company: Employers Insurance of Wausau Mutual Co.
Headquarters: Wausau, WI
SIC Major Group: Insurance Carriers

CONTACT

Lynn Korduf
Manager, Public Relations
Wausau Insurance Cos.
2000 Westwood Dr.
Wausau, WI 54401
800-826-9781

FINANCIAL SUMMARY

Recent Giving: $917,240 (1993)

Fiscal Note: Company gives directly only.

CONTRIBUTIONS SUMMARY

Typical Recipients: • *Arts & Humanities:* general • *Civic & Public Affairs:* general • *Education:* general • *Health:* general • *Social Services:* general

Grant Types: general support and matching

Nonmonetary Support Types: in-kind services

Geographic Distribution: primarily Wausau and Marathon Counties in Wisconsin, secondary to Wisconsin in general, some nationally

Operating Locations: WI (Wausau)

CORP. OFFICERS

John E. Fisher: *CURR EMPL* gen chmn, dir: Wausau Ins Cos

David O. Miller: *CURR EMPL* chmn, dir: Wausau Ins Cos *CORP AFFIL* dir: Nationwide Ins Cos

GIVING OFFICERS

Lynn Korduf: *CURR EMPL* mgr pub rels: Wausau Ins Co

APPLICATION INFORMATION

Initial Approach: *Initial Contact:* brief letter of inquiry *Include Information On:* description of the organization, amount requested, purpose of funds sought, audited financial statement, and proof of tax-exempt status *When to Submit:* any time

Restrictions on Giving: Does not support individuals, religious organizations for purely sectarian purposes, political or lobbying groups, agencies which receive funding from the United Way, labor groups, or "token requests."

Wausau Paper Mills Co. / Wausau Paper Mills Foundation

Sales: $350.4 million
Employees: 1,291
Headquarters: Wausau, WI
SIC Major Group: Paper & Allied Products

CONTACT
Larry Baker
Vice President, Administration
Wausau Paper Mills Co.
PO Box 1408
Wausau, WI 54402-1408
(715) 845-5266

FINANCIAL SUMMARY
Recent Giving: $175,418 (1991); $230,752 (1990)
Assets: $54,593 (1991); $131,397 (1990)
Gifts Received: $90,000 (1991)
Fiscal Note: In fiscal 1991, contributions were received from Wausau Paper Mills Company and Rhinelander Paper Company.
EIN: 39-6080502

CONTRIBUTIONS SUMMARY
Typical Recipients: • *Arts & Humanities:* community arts, performing arts, theater • *Civic & Public Affairs:* environmental affairs • *Education:* colleges & universities, public education (precollege) • *Health:* health organizations, hospitals, public health • *Religion:* religious organizations • *Social Services:* community service organizations, recreation & athletics, religious welfare, united funds, youth organizations
Grant Types: general support
Geographic Distribution: focus on WI
Operating Locations: WI (Rhinelander, Wausau)

CORP. OFFICERS
Arnold M. Nemirow: *CURR EMPL* pres, ceo: Wausau Paper Mills Co
Sam W. Orr, Jr.: *B* Madison WI 1941 *ED* Univ WI 1963;

Univ WI Law 1966 *CURR EMPL* chmn, dir: Wausau Paper Mills Co
Thomas B. Pitcher: *CURR EMPL* sr vp, sec, treas, cfo: Wausau Paper Mills Co

GIVING OFFICERS
Larry A. Baker: vp, adm, dir
John E. Forester: dir *B* Wauwatosa WI 1913 *ED* Univ WI 1934-1936 *CURR EMPL* pres, dir: Yawkey Lumber Co *CORP AFFIL* dir: Marathon Electric Mfg Corp, Wausau Paper Mills Co; pres, dir: Yawkey Lumber Co; vp, treas, dir: Woodson Fiduciary Corp *NONPR AFFIL* dir: Woodson (Leigh Yawkey) Art Mus
William L. Goggins: pres, ceo, dir
Daniel R. Olvey: vp, secy, treas, dir
Sam W. Orr, Jr.: dir *CURR EMPL* chmn, dir: Wausau Paper Mills Co (see above)
David Byron Smith: dir *B* Chicago IL 1936 *ED* Princeton Univ BSE 1958 *CURR EMPL* vp, treas: IL Tool Works
Stanley F. Staples, Jr.: dir

APPLICATION INFORMATION
Initial Approach: Send brief letter describing program. There are no deadlines.

GRANTS ANALYSIS
Number of Grants: 62
Highest Grant: $35,655
Typical Range: $25 to $2,000
Disclosure Period: 1991

RECENT GRANTS
35,655 United Way, Wausau, WI
24,200 YMCA, Wausau, WI
20,000 United Way, Rhinelander, WI
19,500 Wausau Area Community Foundation, Wausau, WI
12,500 St. Mary's Hospital Foundation, Rhinelander, WI
10,000 University of Wisconsin, Madison, WI
6,660 Trees for Tomorrow, Eagle River, WI
5,600 Good Samaritan Health Care Center Foundation, Merrill, WI
5,263 McDevco, Wausau, WI
5,000 Wausau Canoe and Kayak Corporation, Wausau, WI

Wauwatosa Savings & Loan Association / Wauwatosa Savings & Loan Foundation

Assets: $395.3 million
Employees: 70
Headquarters: Wauwatosa, WI
SIC Major Group: Depository Institutions

CONTACT
Raymond J. Perry
Trustee
Wauwatosa Savings & Loan Foundation
7500 West State St.
Wauwatosa, WI 53213
(414) 258-5880

FINANCIAL SUMMARY
Recent Giving: $100,703 (1991); $96,782 (1990); $97,958 (1989)
Assets: $1,978,586 (1991); $1,933,820 (1990); $1,882,007 (1989)
EIN: 39-1548588

CONTRIBUTIONS SUMMARY
Typical Recipients: • *Arts & Humanities:* public broadcasting • *Civic & Public Affairs:* economic development, housing • *Education:* colleges & universities, education funds • *Health:* hospitals, medical research, single-disease health associations • *Religion:* religious organizations • *Social Services:* community centers, community service organizations, disabled, drugs & alcohol, food/clothing distribution, homes, shelters/homelessness, youth organizations
Grant Types: general support
Geographic Distribution: focus on Milwaukee, WI
Operating Locations: WI (Wauwatosa)

CORP. OFFICERS
Charles A. Perry: *CURR EMPL* ceo: Wauwatosa Savings & Loan Assn
Raymond J. Perry, Jr.: *CURR EMPL* pres: Wauwatosa Savings & Loan Assn

GIVING OFFICERS
Charles A. Perry: trust *CURR EMPL* ceo: Wauwatosa Savings & Loan Assn (see above)
Raymond J. Perry: trust

APPLICATION INFORMATION
Initial Approach: Send brief letter describing program. There are no deadlines.

GRANTS ANALYSIS
Number of Grants: 150
Highest Grant: $5,000
Typical Range: $100 to $5,000
Disclosure Period: 1991

RECENT GRANTS
5,000 Boy Scouts of America, Waukesha, WI
5,000 Boy Scouts of America, Waukesha, WI
5,000 Channels 10/36, Milwaukee, WI
5,000 Oak Creek Community Center, Oak Creek, WI
4,000 Wauwatosa Economic Development Corporation, Wauwatosa, WI
2,750 Neighborhood Housing Services, Milwaukee, WI
2,500 Neighborhood Housing Services, Milwaukee, WI
2,100 Greater Milwaukee Open, Milwaukee, WI
2,000 Next Door Foundation, Milwaukee, WI
2,000 Oak Creek/Franklin Scholarship Fund, Oak Creek, WI

Wayne Steel Inc.

Sales: $49.9 million
Employees: 135
Headquarters: Wooster, OH
SIC Major Group: Primary Metal Industries and Wholesale Trade—Durable Goods

CONTACT
Tom Shapiro
President
Wayne Steel Inc.
1070 W. Liberty St. Extension
Wooster, OH 44691
(216) 264-8416

CONTRIBUTIONS SUMMARY
In 1991, provided equipment and materials for a Polish construction school.
Operating Locations: OH (Wooster)

CORP. OFFICERS
Robert W. Hagelin: *CURR EMPL* pres: Wayne Steel Co

WCVB-TV

Parent Company: Hearst Corp.
Headquarters: Boston, MA
SIC Major Group:
Communications

CONTACT
Donna Latson-Gittens
Vice President, Community
Programming
WCVB-TV
5 TV Pl., Needham
Needham, MA 02194
(617) 449-0400

CONTRIBUTIONS SUMMARY
In 1990, joined with Heinz
USA to produce television pro-
grams on family issues.

Operating Locations: MA
(Boston)

CORP. OFFICERS
S. James Coppersmith: *CURR
EMPL* vp, gen mgr: WCVB-TV

WEA Enterprises Co.

Sales: $2.4 million
Employees: 60
Headquarters: Brooklyn, NY
SIC Major Group: Holding &
Other Investment Offices and
Industrial Machinery &
Equipment

CONTACT
Eric M. Wunsch
Vice President
WEA Enterprises Co.
841 63rd St.
Brooklyn, NY 11220
(718) 238-2525

CONTRIBUTIONS SUMMARY
Operating Locations: NY
(Brooklyn)

CORP. OFFICERS
Eric M. Wunsch: *CURR
EMPL* vp: WEA Enterprises Co

Peter Wunsch: *CURR EMPL*
secy, treas: WEA Enterprises
Co

OTHER THINGS TO KNOW
Company is an original donor
to the Wunsch Foundation.

Wean Foundation, Raymond John

CONTACT
Raymond J. Wean, Jr.
Chairman
Raymond John Wean Foundation
PO Box 760
Warren, OH 44482
(216) 394-5600

FINANCIAL SUMMARY
Recent Giving: $2,472,531
(1991); $2,363,731 (1990);
$2,203,630 (1989)
Assets: $47,088,534 (1991);
$42,048,416 (1990);
$46,350,015 (1989)
Gifts Received: $1,325
(1989); $4,784,564 (1988)
Fiscal Note: In 1988, the foundation received a gift from the
estate of Sara R. Wean of Warren, Ohio.
EIN: 34-6505038

CONTRIBUTIONS SUMMARY
Donor(s): Raymond J. Wean
(1895-1980) established the
foundation in 1949. Mr. Wean
was chairman of Wean United
and the Second National Bank
of Warren, OH. He was also a
trustee of the Community
Chest of Palm Beach, American Institute of Economics,
Trinity College, and Carnegie-
Mellon University.
Typical Recipients: • *Arts &
Humanities:* arts associations,
arts centers, arts festivals, arts
funds, arts institutes, dance,
history/historic preservation, libraries, museums/galleries,
music, opera, public broadcasting, theater • *Civic & Public Affairs:* economic development,
environmental affairs, international affairs, municipalities,
professional & trade associations, public policy, safety,
urban & community affairs,
women's affairs, zoos/botani-
cal gardens • *Education:* arts
education, colleges & universities, education associations,
legal education, medical education, minority education, private education (precollege),
public education (precollege),
religious education,
science/technology education,
student aid • *Health:* health organizations, hospices, hospitals, medical rehabilitation,
mental health, nursing services, single-disease health associations • *Religion:* churches,
religious organizations • *Social*

Services: aged, animal protection, child welfare, disabled,
drugs & alcohol, employ-
ment/job training, family planning, food/clothing distribution, homes, recreation &
athletics, religious welfare,
united funds, youth organizations
Grant Types: capital, department, endowment, general support, project, research, and
scholarship
Geographic Distribution: national, emphasis on Ohio and
the eastern states

GIVING OFFICERS
Clara G. Petrosky: admin
Gordon B. Wean: mem bd
adms
Raymond J. Wean, Jr.: don,
chmn bd adms *B* Warren OH
1921 *ED* Yale Univ BA 1943
CURR EMPL chmn, ceo: Wean
Inc *CORP AFFIL* dir: Pitts-
burgh Natl Bank, Second Natl
Bank Warren OH, Wean Un
Canada Ltd *NONPR AFFIL*
trust: Blair Academy, Palm
Beach Day Sch
Raymond J. Wean III: vchmn
bd adms *CURR EMPL* pres,
coo: Wean Inc

APPLICATION INFORMATION
Initial Approach:
Applicants should send a letter
of inquiry. There are no formal
guidelines or application forms.
In the initial letter, applicants
should include an outline of
the proposed project and proof
of tax exemption.
A four-member board of administrators makes all decisions regarding applications.

GRANTS ANALYSIS
Total Grants: $2,472,531
Number of Grants: 674
Highest Grant: $250,000
Typical Range: $100 to
$10,000
Disclosure Period: 1991
Note: Recent grants are de-
rived from a 1991 Form 990.

RECENT GRANTS
250,000 Miss Porter's
School, Farming-
ton, CT — student
center
150,000 Carnegie-Mellon
University, Pitts-
burgh, PA — Uni-
versity Center
150,000 Pine Manor Col-
lege, Chestnut
Hill, MA — En-
dowment Senior

Faculty Professor-
ship
150,000 University School,
Chagria Falls, OH
— Wean Faculty
Development Fund
150,000 Yale University,
New Haven, CT —
Branford College
Entryway
125,000 Palm Beach Day
School, Palm
Beach, FL — capi-
tal campaign
125,000 Palm Beach Day
School, Palm
Beach, FL — en-
dowment fund
75,000 Palm Beach Day
School, Palm
Beach, FL — gen-
eral fund
75,000 Wooster School,
Wooster, CT —
transition to Full K-
2 Program
50,000 Babson College,
Babson Park, MA
— endowment fund

Weatherford International, Inc.

Revenue: $205.8 million
Employees: 2,063
Headquarters: Houston, TX
SIC Major Group: Building
Materials & Garden Supplies,
Industrial Machinery &
Equipment, Oil & Gas
Extraction, and Special Trade
Contractors

CONTACT
Monica Lora
Assistant to the President
Weatherford International, Inc.
PO Box 27608
Houston, TX 77227
(713) 439-9400

CONTRIBUTIONS SUMMARY
Operating Locations: TX
(Houston)

CORP. OFFICERS
Philip Burguieres: *CURR
EMPL* chmn, pres, ceo:
Weatherford Intl

Weatherhead Foundation

CONTACT
Thomas F. Allen
Treasurer
Weatherhead Fdn.
730 Ohio Savings Plaza
Cleveland, OH 44114
(216) 771-4000

FINANCIAL SUMMARY
Recent Giving: $2,020,000 (1991); $1,210,000 (1989); $1,255,000 (1988)
Assets: $5,078,828 (1990); $3,824,168 (1989); $2,850,314 (1988)
Gifts Received: $1,809,108 (1991); $1,293,453 (1989); $1,083,238 (1988)
Fiscal Note: In 1991, contributions were received from Albert J. Weatherhead, Jr. Trust.
EIN: 13-2711998

CONTRIBUTIONS SUMMARY
Donor(s): the late Albert I. Weatherhead, Jr.
Typical Recipients: • *Arts & Humanities:* museums/galleries • *Education:* colleges & universities, private education (precollege)
Grant Types: endowment, operating expenses, project, and research

GIVING OFFICERS
Thomas F. Allen: treas
Don K. Price: vp, trust *B* Middlesboro KY 1910 *ED* Vanderbilt Univ AB 1931; Oxford Univ BA 1934; Centre Coll LLD 1961 *NONPR AFFIL* fellow: Am Academy Arts Sciences; mem: Am Assn Advancement Science, Am Philosophical Soc; prof emeritus: Harvard Univ John F Kennedy Sch Govt; sr mem: Inst Medicine Natl Academy Sciences; trust: Vanderbilt Univ
Henry Rosovsky: vp, trust *B* Danzig Poland 1927 *ED* Coll William & Mary AB 1949; Coll William & Mary LLD 1976; Harvard Univ AM 1953; Harvard Univ PhD 1959 *CORP AFFIL* dir: Corning, PaineWebber Group *NONPR AFFIL* dir: Harvard Univ Corp; mem: Am Academy Arts Sciences, Am Econ Assn, Am Philosophical Soc, Assn Asian Studies; prof econ: Harvard Univ
Stanley Salmen: off *B* Olean NY 1914 *ED* Harvard Univ

1936 *CORP AFFIL* pres: Interbook Inc
Albert J. Weatherhead III: pres, trust *ED* Harvard Univ 1950-1952 *CURR EMPL* pres, dir: Weatherhead Indus *CORP AFFIL* pres, dir: Weatherhead Indus
Celia Weatherhead: vp, trust
Dwight S. Weatherhead: vp, secy, trust
John P. Weatherhead: vp, trust
Michael H. Weatherhead: vp, trust

APPLICATION INFORMATION
Initial Approach: Contributes only to preselected organizations.
Restrictions on Giving: Does not support individuals.

OTHER THINGS TO KNOW
Publications: Annual Report, Application Guidelines, Informational Brochure

GRANTS ANALYSIS
Number of Grants: 13
Highest Grant: $910,000
Typical Range: $5,000 to $10,000
Disclosure Period: 1991

RECENT GRANTS
910,000 Case Western Reserve University, Cleveland, OH
400,000 Case Western Reserve University, Cleveland, OH
350,000 Columbia University, New York, NY
260,000 School of American Research, Sante Fe, NM
35,000 University of California, Sausalito, CA
20,000 Mcalester College, St. Paul, MN
10,000 J.B. Speed Art, Louisville, KY
10,000 St. Francis College, Ft. Wayne, IN
7,500 Alternative Museum, New York, NY
5,000 St. Francis College, Ft. Wayne, IN

Weatherwax Foundation

CONTACT
Peter A. Weatherwax
Trustee
Weatherwax Fdn.
618 North Mechanic Street
P.O. Box 1111
Jackson, FL 49204
(517) 787-2117

FINANCIAL SUMMARY
Recent Giving: $82,880 (fiscal 1991)
Assets: $11,949,545 (fiscal year ending September 30, 1991)
Gifts Received: $9,983,940 (fiscal 1991)
Fiscal Note: In fiscal 1991, contributions were received from the K. A. Weatherwax Trust I.
EIN: 38-6439807

CONTRIBUTIONS SUMMARY
Donor(s): the K.A. Weatherwax Trust I
Typical Recipients: • *Arts & Humanities:* museums/galleries • *Civic & Public Affairs:* zoos/botanical gardens • *Education:* education associations, private education (precollege) • *Social Services:* animal protection, youth organizations
Grant Types: general support
Geographic Distribution: giving primarily in Jackson, MI

GIVING OFFICERS
Peter A. Weatherwax: trust

APPLICATION INFORMATION
Initial Approach: Send brief letter of inquiry including proof that the organization qualifies under Section 501 (C) (3) of the Internal Revenue Code. There are no deadlines.
Restrictions on Giving: Does not provide grants to individuals.

GRANTS ANALYSIS
Number of Grants: 10
Highest Grant: $65,000
Typical Range: $1,000 to $2,500
Disclosure Period: fiscal year ending September 30, 1991

RECENT GRANTS
65,000 Ella Sharp Museum Association, Jackson, MI

2,880 South Central Education Association, Jackson, MI
2,500 Cascades Humane Society, Jackson, MI
2,500 Culver Educational Foundation, Culver, IN
2,000 John George Home, Jackson, MI
2,000 Lumen Christi High School, Jackson, MI
2,000 Whistlestop Park Association, Grass Lake, MI
1,500 Boy Scouts of America, Jackson, MI
1,500 Leelanau Center for Education, Glenn Arbor, MI
1,000 Y Center, Jackson, MI

Weaver Foundation

CONTACT
Robert G. Kelley
Vice President
Weaver Fdn.
324 West Wendover Ave.
Greensboro, NC 27408
(919) 275-9600

FINANCIAL SUMMARY
Recent Giving: $525,100 (1991); $446,968 (1990); $170,382 (1989)
Assets: $13,126,422 (1991); $11,653,860 (1990); $11,293,808 (1989)
Gifts Received: $368,724 (1990); $198,339 (1989)
Fiscal Note: 1990 contribution recieved from R. H. Weaver Revocable Trust.
EIN: 56-6093527

CONTRIBUTIONS SUMMARY
Donor(s): the late W. H. Weaver, E. H. Weaver
Typical Recipients: • *Arts & Humanities:* arts associations, community arts, history/historic preservation, museums/galleries, opera • *Education:* colleges & universities, science/technology education • *Health:* hospices, hospitals, single-disease health associations • *Religion:* churches • *Social Services:* aged, child welfare, community service organizations, homes, united funds, youth organizations
Grant Types: general support
Geographic Distribution: focus on NC

GIVING OFFICERS
Robert G. Kelley: vp, secy, treas
Ashley E. Weaver: trust
Edith H. Weaver: trust
H. M. Weaver: pres, chmn, trust
Michele D. Weaver: trust

APPLICATION INFORMATION
Initial Approach: Send cover letter and full proposal. There are no deadlines.
Restrictions on Giving: Does not support individuals.

GRANTS ANALYSIS
Number of Grants: 44
Highest Grant: $148,000
Typical Range: $500 to $5,000
Disclosure Period: 1991

RECENT GRANTS
148,000 Well-Spring Retirement Community, NC
120,000 Project Uplift, NC
100,000 Greensboro Urban Ministry, Greensboro, NC
65,500 University of North Carolina at Greensboro, Greensboro, NC
13,000 Hospice at Greensboro, Greensboro, NC
10,000 First Presbyterian Church, Greensboro, NC
10,000 Links Adolescent Services, NC
10,000 North Carolina A&T University Foundation, NC
10,000 United Way, Greensboro, NC
5,250 Greensboro Historical Museum, Greensboro, NC

Weaver Foundation, Gil and Dody

CONTACT
Debbie Cain
Manager
Gil and Dody Weaver Fdn.
500 West Seventh St., Ste. 1714
Ft. Worth, TX 76102
(817) 877-1712

FINANCIAL SUMMARY
Recent Giving: $230,000 (fiscal 1991); $230,006 (fiscal 1990); $202,506 (fiscal 1989)
Assets: $3,936,872 (fiscal year ending September 30, 1991); $3,877,235 (fiscal 1990); $3,810,331 (fiscal 1989)
EIN: 75-1729449

CONTRIBUTIONS SUMMARY
Donor(s): Galbraith Weaver
Typical Recipients: • *Education:* colleges & universities, private education (precollege) • *Health:* health organizations, hospitals, mental health, pediatric health • *Religion:* churches, religious organizations • *Social Services:* aged, child welfare, community centers, community service organizations, disabled, food/clothing distribution, shelters/homelessness, united funds, youth organizations
Grant Types: multiyear/continuing support, operating expenses, project, and research
Geographic Distribution: focus on TX

GIVING OFFICERS
Galbraith Mc F. Weaver: trust
Eudora J. Weaver, trust: off
William R. Weaver, M.D.: trust

APPLICATION INFORMATION
Initial Approach: Send brief letter describing program. Deadline is July 31.
Restrictions on Giving: Does not support individuals.

GRANTS ANALYSIS
Number of Grants: 55
Highest Grant: $15,000
Typical Range: $800 to $10,000
Disclosure Period: fiscal year ending September 30, 1991

RECENT GRANTS
15,000 Harris Methodist Health System, Ft. Worth, TX
15,000 Meals on Wheels, Ft. Worth, TX
11,000 Lena Pope Home, Ft. Worth, TX
11,000 YWCA, Ft. Worth, TX
10,000 Food Bank of Greater Tarrant County, Ft. Worth, TX
10,000 St. John's Episcopal Church, Ft. Worth, TX
10,000 Tarrant County Hospital District, Ft. Worth, TX
9,000 Child Study Center, Ft. Worth, TX
9,000 Cook Fort Worth Children's Medical Center, Ft. Worth, TX
8,000 Presbyterian Night Shelter, Ft. Worth, TX

Webb Charitable Trust, Susan Mott

CONTACT
Kathryn W. Miree
Vice President and Trust
Susan Mott Webb Charitable Trust
c/o AmSouth Bank, N.A.
PO Box 11426
Birmingham, AL 35202
(205) 326-5396

FINANCIAL SUMMARY
Recent Giving: $378,666 (1991); $983,917 (1990); $459,333 (1989)
Assets: $9,224,303 (1991); $8,034,603 (1990); $8,675,261 (1989)
EIN: 63-6112593

CONTRIBUTIONS SUMMARY
Donor(s): the late Susan Mott Webb
Typical Recipients: • *Arts & Humanities:* arts institutes, history/historic preservation, museums/galleries, music • *Civic & Public Affairs:* urban & community affairs • *Education:* colleges & universities, religious education, special education • *Health:* mental health, pediatric health • *Religion:* churches • *Science:* scientific institutes • *Social Services:* child welfare, community service organizations, drugs & alcohol, family services, food/clothing distribution, shelters/homelessness, united funds, youth organizations
Grant Types: capital, general support, multiyear/continuing support, and project
Geographic Distribution: limited to the greater Birmingham, AL, area

GIVING OFFICERS
AmSouth Bank, N.A.: trust
Stewart Dansby: trust
Suzanne Dansby: trust
Charles B. Webb, Jr.: trust

APPLICATION INFORMATION
Initial Approach: Send brief letter of inquiry with copy of IRS determination letter. Deadline is May 15.
Restrictions on Giving: Does not support individuals.

GRANTS ANALYSIS
Number of Grants: 32
Highest Grant: $50,000
Typical Range: $2,500 to $25,000
Disclosure Period: 1991

RECENT GRANTS
50,000 Family and Child Services, Birmingham, AL
50,000 University of Alabama at Birmingham, Birmingham, AL
25,000 Boys and Girls Club, Birmingham, AL
25,000 Glenwood Mental Health, Birmingham, AL
25,000 Oncology Services of Alabama, Birmingham, AL
25,000 Southern Research Institute, Birmingham, AL
25,000 United Way, Birmingham, AL
25,000 YMCA, Birmingham, AL
16,666 Cathedral Church of Advent, Birmingham, AL
15,000 Resource Advisory, Birmingham, AL

Webb Educational and Charitable Trust, Torrey H. and Dorothy K.

CONTACT
Carl M. Franklin
Trustee
Torrey H. and Dorothy K. Webb Educational and Charitable Trust
5966 Abernathy Dr.
Los Angeles, CA 90045
(213) 740-7311

FINANCIAL SUMMARY
Recent Giving: $263,444 (1991); $558,300 (1989); $415,000 (1988)
Assets: $1,748,542 (1991); $2,282,766 (1989); $2,540,519 (1988)
EIN: 51-0188579

CONTRIBUTIONS SUMMARY
Donor(s): the late Torrey H. Webb
Typical Recipients: • *Education:* colleges & universities, education associations, science/technology education • *Health:* hospitals • *Religion:* religious organizations • *Social*

Services: child welfare, counseling, youth organizations
Grant Types: endowment
Geographic Distribution: focus on CA

GIVING OFFICERS
Carl M. Franklin: trust

APPLICATION INFORMATION
Initial Approach: Send brief letter of inquiry describing program or project. There are no deadlines.

GRANTS ANALYSIS
Number of Grants: 28
Highest Grant: $20,000
Typical Range: $1,000 to $14,000
Disclosure Period: 1991

RECENT GRANTS
20,000 Big Brothers and Big Sisters, Newport Beach, CA
10,000 Friends of Villa Aurora, Pacific Palisades, CA
10,000 Pathfinders of Palm Springs, Rancho Mirage, CA
10,000 Stanford University, Stanford, CA
10,000 Town and Gown of University of Southern California, Los Angeles, CA
10,000 Trojan League of Orange County, Corona del Mar, CA
10,000 University of Oklahoma Foundation, Norman, OK
10,000 Yale University, New Haven, CT
3,500 B'nai B'rith, Los Angeles, CA
2,000 Eisenhower Medical Center, Rancho Mirage, CA

Webb Foundation

CONTACT
Richard E. Fister
Secretary
Webb Fdn.
232 Kingshighway, Ste. 205
St. Louis, MO 63108
(314) 367-0232

FINANCIAL SUMMARY
Recent Giving: $420,500 (1990); $407,000 (1989)
Assets: $5,965,004 (1990); $6,285,302 (1989)
EIN: 23-7028768

CONTRIBUTIONS SUMMARY
Donor(s): the late Francis M. Webb, the late Pearl M. Webb
Typical Recipients: • *Education:* business education, colleges & universities, community & junior colleges
• *Health:* hospitals, medical research, single-disease health associations • *Religion:* religious organizations • *Social Services:* child welfare, community service organizations, disabled, family planning, family services, homes, united funds, youth organizations
Grant Types: capital, fellowship, general support, multi-year/continuing support, operating expenses, research, and seed money
Geographic Distribution: limited to the Midwest

GIVING OFFICERS
Richard E. Fister: secy, trust
Virginia M. Fister: mem adv comm, trust
Bernice Hock: mem adv comm, trust
Donald D. McDonald: mem adv comm, trust
Evelyn M. McDonald: mem adv comm, trust

APPLICATION INFORMATION
Initial Approach: Contributes only to preselected organizations.
Restrictions on Giving: Does not support individuals, deficit financing, land acquisition, matching gifts, special projects, or publications.

OTHER THINGS TO KNOW
Publications: Informational Brochure (including application guidelines)

GRANTS ANALYSIS
Number of Grants: 71
Highest Grant: $20,000
Typical Range: $1,000 to $5,000
Disclosure Period: 1990

RECENT GRANTS
20,000 Salvation Army, St. Louis, MO
20,000 Washington University School of Business, St. Louis, MO
15,000 Cardinal Glennon Children's Hospital, St. Louis, MO
15,000 Lutheran Child and Family Services, River Forest, IL
15,000 St. Louis University (Arts and Science), St. Louis, MO
12,000 Birthright Counseling, St. Louis, St. Louis, MO
10,000 Boys Club of St. Louis, St. Louis, MO
10,000 Girls Club of St. Louis, St. Louis, MO
10,000 Lewis and Clark Community College, Godfrey, IL
10,000 Oakland City College, Oakland, MO

Webb Foundation, Del E.

CONTACT
Robert H. Johnson
President and Director
Del E. Webb Foundation
2023 West Wickenburg Way
PO Box 20519
Wickenburg, AZ 85358
(602) 684-7223

FINANCIAL SUMMARY
Recent Giving: $2,152,000 (1991); $1,840,000 (1990); $1,608,300 (1989)
Assets: $50,187,601 (1991); $42,766,770 (1990); $43,515,363 (1989)
EIN: 86-6052737

CONTRIBUTIONS SUMMARY
Donor(s): Del E. Webb was best known for owning the New York Yankees as well as a network of Sunbelt hotels, office buildings, shopping malls, and subdivisions. A former semiprofessional baseball player, Del Webb moved his off-season carpentry business to Phoenix in 1928 after his hopes for a major-league career ended. There he established a building contracting venture that, by the end of World War II, had grown to a multi-million dollar national business, known as The Del Webb Corporation. Among Mr. Webb's best-known developments is Sun City, the retirement community outside Phoenix, Arizona. The corporation also owns and operates various commercial and leisure properties, including the Sahara Hotel and Casino in Las Vegas, NV, and developments and retirement communities concentrated in Arizona, California, Florida, Hawaii, and Nevada.
Mr. Webb purchased the New York Yankees in 1945 with Daniel Topping and Colonel Larry S. MacPhail. During the 20 years of Topping-Webb management, the team won 15 American League pennants and 10 World Series.
The Del E. Webb Foundation was incorporated in 1960 by Mr. Webb, his wife, Hazel L. Webb, and A. K. Steward. Its assets increased in 1977 upon receiving a gift of over $36 million from Mr. Webb's estate. One of its earliest large grants was a $3.8 million pledge to Loma Linda University for construction of the Del E. Webb Memorial Library.
Typical Recipients: • *Arts & Humanities:* history/historic preservation • *Education:* colleges & universities, medical education, science/technology education • *Health:* hospitals, medical research, single-disease health associations • *Social Services:* disabled
Grant Types: capital, general support, project, and research
Geographic Distribution: Arizona, Nevada, and California

GIVING OFFICERS
Owen F. Childress: vp
Robert H. Johnson: pres, dir *B* Phoenix AZ 1924 *CURR EMPL* chmn, pres, ceo: Del E Webb Corp *CORP AFFIL* dir: Webb Resources Inc *NONPR AFFIL* mem: Assn Gen Contractors Am
Marjorie Klinfelter: secy
W. D. Milliken: dir
Del V. Werderman: treas

APPLICATION INFORMATION
Initial Approach:
Applicants should contact the foundation with an initial letter of not more than two pages. In the preliminary letter, list the aims and specific needs of the proposed project. Formal applications must be submitted in quadruplicate and should include proof of IRS tax-exempt status; proof of valid state tax exemption in the state in which the applicant is organized; current, complete audited financial statement with original binding intact; current list of officers, directors, and trustees; detailed statement of the request with a complete budget, projected time schedule, and

other applicable details; statement of how the project would generally be of benefit; detailed statement defining the need for the services or facilities that would be provided by the requested funds; statement describing the manner and approximate schedule for reporting disbursement of monies and results obtained with requested funds; and a statement from the governing body of the organization authorizing the presentation of the application as a prime need within the scope and limitations of the foundation's policies.

The board of directors meets twice a year in May and December. Application deadlines are March 31 and October 31 for consideration at the following board meeting.

The foundation's board analyzes each application and evaluates it according to the following criteria: the serious current need for the facilities, research, or services proposed by the applicant's project and the extent to which the project would duplicate existing facilities, research, or services in the geographically affected area; the reasonableness of the budget for the project; the degree that the project will have efficient and economical management by persons who are experienced and competent; and the assurance that the results obtained by the project will be effectively communicated to and practically utilized by the persons whose needs are to be served.

Communications with individual board members of the Webb Foundation are not recommended, and can in no way benefit applicants.

Restrictions on Giving: No grants are made for programs operated by organizations other than the applicant. Grants are very seldom made to liquidate or reduce previously incurred obligations or operating deficits. The foundation does not support individuals, governmental agencies or subdivisions, or sectarian or religious organizations when their principal activity is for the benefit of their own members. Grants are made for nonpartisan, tax-exempt groups working in the public interest. Although the foundation may support scholarships, student aid, and medi-

cal assistance programs, it will not participate in their administration.

OTHER THINGS TO KNOW
Publications: application form and guidelines

GRANTS ANALYSIS
Total Grants: $2,152,000
Number of Grants: 30
Highest Grant: $500,000
Typical Range: $25,000 to $100,000
Disclosure Period: 1991
Note: The average grant figure excludes the largest grant of $500,000. Recent grants are derived from a 1991 grants list.

RECENT GRANTS
500,000　Del E. Webb Memorial Hospital, Sun City West, AZ — building fund campaign

250,000　House Ear Institute, Los Angeles, CA — building fund for Otologic Research Wing

200,000　Salk Institute, San Diego, CA — building fund to expand laboratory space

200,000　University of Southern California School of Medicine, Los Angeles, CA — for construction of a major laboratory suite in the new University of Southern California Center for Molecular Medicine

100,000　Children's Inn of Greater Las Vegas (Ronald McDonald House), Las Vegas, NV — funds for capital building program

100,000　Kingman Regional Medical Center Foundation, Kingman, AZ — partial funding to furnish additional operating room

100,000　Loma Linda University Medical Center, Loma Linda, CA — purchase of equipment for cancer treatment

90,000　Navajo Nation Health Foundation, Ganado, AZ — purchase trauma X-ray system for the Emergency Medical Service

75,000　California Institute of Technology,

Pasadena, CA — postdoctoral fellows support in neurology

69,000　St. Luke's Foundation, Phoenix, AZ — purchase of bone densitometry equipment

---

Webber Oil Co. / Webber Oil Foundation
Sales: $320.0 million
Employees: 500
Headquarters: Bangor, ME
SIC Major Group: Miscellaneous Retail and Wholesale Trade—Nondurable Goods

CONTACT
Linda F. Harnum
Trustee
Webber Oil Foundation
700 Main St.
Bangor, ME 04401-6810

FINANCIAL SUMMARY
Recent Giving: $61,250 (fiscal 1990)
Assets: $239,730 (fiscal year ending August 31, 1990)
Fiscal Note: Annual Giving Range: $50,000 to $100,000
EIN: 23-7046575

CONTRIBUTIONS SUMMARY
Typical Recipients: • *Arts & Humanities:* libraries, museums/galleries • *Civic & Public Affairs:* general, municipalities • *Education:* private education (precollege) • *Social Services:* general, youth organizations
Geographic Distribution: focus on Bangor, ME
Operating Locations: ME (Bangor)

CORP. OFFICERS
L. Mahaney: *CURR EMPL*
pres: Webber Oil Co

APPLICATION INFORMATION
Initial Approach: Send brief letter of inquiry.

GRANTS ANALYSIS
Number of Grants: 18
Highest Grant: $9,500
Typical Range: $1,000 to $6,000
Disclosure Period: fiscal year ending August 31, 1990

RECENT GRANTS
9,500　Holderness School, Plymouth, NH

7,000　YMCA, Bangor, ME

6,000　YMCA, Ellsworth, ME

5,000　John Baptist School, Bangor, ME

4,000　Maine Central Institute, Pittsfield, ME

2,500　Greater Bangor Chamber of Commerce, Bangor, ME

2,000　Bangor Outdoor Ice, Bangor, ME

2,000　Edythe Dyer Community Library, Hampden, ME

2,000　Maine Maritime Museum, Bath, ME

1,000　YMCA, Dover-Foxcroft, ME

Webcraft Technologies
Sales: $228.0 million
Employees: 1,700
Headquarters: North Brunswick, NJ
SIC Major Group: Printing & Publishing

CONTACT
Thomas Gardner
Controller
Webcraft Technologies
Rte. 1 & Adam Sta.
North Brunswick, NJ 08902
(908) 297-5100

CONTRIBUTIONS SUMMARY
Operating Locations: NJ (North Brunswick)

CORP. OFFICERS
Gilbert Osnos: *CURR EMPL*
pres: Webcraft Techs

Weber Charities Corp., Frederick E.

CONTACT
Mary Ann Dailey
President
Frederick E. Weber Charities Corp.
34 1/2 Beacon St.
Boston, MA 02108
(617) 523-1455

FINANCIAL SUMMARY
Recent Giving: $220,988 (fiscal 1992); $206,988 (fiscal 1991); $225,963 (fiscal 1990)
Assets: $4,364,982 (fiscal year ending March 31, 1992); $4,703,223 (fiscal 1991); $4,622,202 (fiscal 1990)

EIN: 04-2133244

CONTRIBUTIONS SUMMARY

Donor(s): the late Frederick E. Weber

Typical Recipients: • *Civic & Public Affairs:* philanthropic organizations, women's affairs • *Health:* hospitals, medical research, pediatric health • *Social Services:* child welfare, community service organizations, family planning, family services, recreation & athletics, united funds, youth organizations **Grant Types:** emergency, endowment, and scholarship **Geographic Distribution:** focus on the greater Boston, MA, area

GIVING OFFICERS

Robert H. Baldwin: dir
Lawrence Coolidge: dir *B* Boston MA 1936 *ED* Harvard Univ Sch Bus Admin 1962 *CURR EMPL* chmn: Seven Islands Land Co *CORP AFFIL* chmn: Seven Islands Land Co; dir: Big Sandy Co, Hollingsworth & Vose Co; trust: Loring Wolcott & Coolidge Off
Mary Ann Daily: pres, dir
Janet W. Eustis: clerk, dir
Franklin T. Hammond, Jr.: dir
William Francis Kehoe: dir *B* Stoneham MA 1933 *ED* Dartmouth Coll AB 1955; Yale Univ MA 1956; Harvard Univ LLB 1963 *CURR EMPL* ptnr: Gaston & Snow *CORP AFFIL* ptnr: Gaston & Snow *NONPR AFFIL* mem: Am Coll Trust Estate Counc, Boston Bar Assn
Daniel Anthony Phillips: vp, treas, dir *B* Boston MA 1938 *ED* Harvard Univ 1960-1963 *CURR EMPL* vp, mem exec comm, dir: Fiduciary Trust Co *CORP AFFIL* vp, mem exec comm, dir: Fiduciary Trust Co
Peter E. Reinhold: dir
Patrick V. Riley: dir
William C. Swan: dir
Daniel P. Wise: dir

APPLICATION INFORMATION

Initial Approach: Send brief letter of inquiry describing program or project. There are no deadlines.
Restrictions on Giving: No grants for research, capital projects, or equipment.

OTHER THINGS TO KNOW

Publications: Annual Report

GRANTS ANALYSIS

Number of Grants: 97
Highest Grant: $40,000
Typical Range: $500 to $5,000
Disclosure Period: fiscal year ending March 31, 1992

RECENT GRANTS

40,000	Associated Grantmakers of Massachusetts, Boston, MA
15,000	United Way, Boston, MA
10,000	Family Service of Greater Boston, Boston, MA
8,000	Children's Friend and Family Service Society, Salem, MA
5,410	Commonwealth of Massachusetts Department of Social Services, Boston, MA
5,000	Brigham and Women's Hospital, Boston, MA
5,000	Cambridge Camping Association, Cambridge, MA
5,000	Children's Hospital Medical Center, Boston, MA
5,000	New England Deaconess Hospital, Boston, MA
5,000	St. Elizabeth's Hospital Social Services Department, Brighton, MA

Webster Charitable Foundation

CONTACT

Eliza K. Webster
Webster Charitable Fdn.
13 Sunset Rock Rd.
Andover, MA 01810
(508) 686-4131

FINANCIAL SUMMARY

Recent Giving: $223,151 (1991); $95,500 (1990); $101,000 (1989)
Assets: $2,075,800 (1991); $1,820,303 (1990); $1,909,307 (1989)
Gifts Received: $131,801 (1991); $11,150 (1990); $70,779 (1989)
Fiscal Note: In 1991, contributions were received from R. Kingman Webster.
EIN: 04-6112387

CONTRIBUTIONS SUMMARY

Donor(s): H. K. Webster Co., members of the Webster Family

Typical Recipients: • *Arts & Humanities:* community arts, music, public broadcasting • *Civic & Public Affairs:* housing • *Education:* education funds • *Health:* health funds, hospitals • *Religion:* churches, religious organizations • *Social Services:* child welfare, community service organizations, food/clothing distribution, shelters/homelessness, united funds, youth organizations **Grant Types:** general support **Geographic Distribution:** focus on the greater Lawrence, MA, area

GIVING OFFICERS

Ralph W. Gilman: dir, treas
Dean K. Webster: off *CURR EMPL* pres: H K Webster Co
Eliza Webster: secy, dir
R. Kingman Webster: trust
Walter N. Webster: off *CURR EMPL* chmn: H K Webster Co

APPLICATION INFORMATION

Initial Approach: Send brief letter describing program. Deadlines are March 1 and October 1.

GRANTS ANALYSIS

Number of Grants: 50
Highest Grant: $55,301
Typical Range: $1,000 to $5,000
Disclosure Period: 1991

RECENT GRANTS

55,301	Greater Lawrence Community Foundation, Lawrence, MA — I Have A Dream
47,000	YMCA, Lawrence, MA
22,000	South Congregational Church, Lawrence, MA
20,000	Merrimack Valley United Fund, Lawrence, MA
5,000	Boys Club of America, Lawrence, MA
5,000	First Calvary Baptist Church, Lawrence, MA
5,000	Lawrence General Hospital Capital Campaign, Lawrence, MA
5,000	MECC Child Care Program, Lawrence, MA
5,000	YMCA, Lawrence, MA
4,000	Lawrence Neighborhood Housing Services, Lawrence, MA

Webster Co., H. K.

Sales: $120.0 million
Employees: 520
Headquarters: Lawrence, MA
SIC Major Group: Wholesale Trade—Nondurable Goods

CONTACT

Unis Veit
H. K. Webster Co.
32 West St.
Lawrence, MA 01842
(508) 686-4131

CONTRIBUTIONS SUMMARY

Operating Locations: MA (Lawrence)

CORP. OFFICERS

Dean K. Webster: *CURR EMPL* pres: H K Webster Co
Walter N. Webster: *CURR EMPL* chmn: H K Webster Co

OTHER THINGS TO KNOW

Company is an original donor to the Webster Charitable Foundation.

Webster Foundation, Edwin S.

CONTACT

Phil Hall
Administrator
Edwin S. Webster Fdn.
c/o Grants Management Associates
230 Congress St., 3rd Fl.
Boston, MA 02110
(617) 426-7172

FINANCIAL SUMMARY

Recent Giving: $800,000 (1990); $855,000 (1989); $701,000 (1988)
Assets: $19,599,070 (1990); $18,959,412 (1989); $15,470,970 (1988)
EIN: 04-6000647

CONTRIBUTIONS SUMMARY

Donor(s): The foundation was established in 1948 by the late Edwin S. Webster.

Typical Recipients: • *Arts & Humanities:* arts centers, arts institutes, museums/galleries, music, performing arts, theater • *Civic & Public Affairs:* environmental affairs, urban & community affairs, zoos/botanical gardens • *Education:* colleges & universities, minority education, private education (precollege), science/technology education, student aid • *Health:* health funds, hospitals, medical research, single-disease health associations • *Religion:* churches • *Science:* scientific institutes • *Social Services:* aged, child welfare, community centers, counseling, drugs & alcohol, employment/job training, family planning, family services, homes, shelters/homelessness, united funds, youth organizations

Grant Types: capital, endowment, operating expenses, project, and research

Geographic Distribution: focus on Massachusetts, New Hampshire, and New York

GIVING OFFICERS

Henry U. Harris III: trust
Henry Upham Harris, Jr.: trust *B* New York NY 1926 *ED* Stanford Univ 1951 *CURR EMPL* vchmn: Smith Barney Harris Upham & Co
Richard Harte, Jr.: trust
Edwin W. Hiam: trust

APPLICATION INFORMATION

Initial Approach: Applicants should contact foundation in writing.

Applicants must provide evidence of their tax-exempt status.

The foundation sets no deadline for the receipt of requests, but its preference months are March and September.

The trustees meet each year in early June and December to review requests and make distributions. Recipients are notified usually within 15 days of the meeting date.

Restrictions on Giving: Grants are not made outside the United States. The foundation does not make grants to individuals, or for loans, seed money, emergency funds, deficit financing, publications, or conferences.

OTHER THINGS TO KNOW

Publications: application guidelines

GRANTS ANALYSIS

Total Grants: $800,000
Number of Grants: 61
Highest Grant: $50,000
Typical Range: $5,000 to $15,000
Disclosure Period: 1990

Note: Recent grants are derived from a 1990 grants list.

RECENT GRANTS

```
50,000  Boys and Girls
        Club, Boston, MA
50,000  United Way, Bos-
        ton, MA
45,000  Museum of
        Science, Boston,
        MA
40,000  Massachusetts Gen-
        eral Hospital, Bos-
        ton, MA
28,000  Boston Symphony
        Orchestra, Boston,
        MA
25,000  Burke Rehabilita-
        tion Center, White
        Plains, NY
25,000  New England Con-
        servatory of Music,
        Boston, MA
25,000  United Negro Col-
        lege Fund, Boston,
        MA
20,000  Bostonian Society
        Corporation, Bos-
        ton, MA
20,000  Falmouth Hospital
        Foundation, Fal-
        mouth, MA
```

Weckbaugh Foundation, Eleanore Mullen

CONTACT

Edward J. Limes
President
Eleanore Mullen Weckbaugh Fdn.
PO Box 31678
Aurora, CO 80041
(303) 367-1545

FINANCIAL SUMMARY

Recent Giving: $418,280 (fiscal 1992); $416,980 (fiscal 1991); $425,080 (fiscal 1990)
Assets: $6,525,102 (fiscal year ending March 31, 1992); $6,426,823 (fiscal 1991); $6,343,088 (fiscal 1990)
EIN: 23-7437761

CONTRIBUTIONS SUMMARY

Donor(s): the late Eleanore Mullen Weckbaugh
Typical Recipients: • *Arts & Humanities:* libraries, public broadcasting • *Education:* colleges & universities, private education (precollege), public education (precollege) • *Health:* hospitals • *Religion:* churches, missionary activities, religious organizations • *Social Services:* child welfare, community centers, disabled,

food/clothing distribution, religious welfare, youth organizations

Grant Types: general support

Geographic Distribution: focus on CO

GIVING OFFICERS

Jean Guyton: secy
Samuel Percy Guyton: trust *B* Jackson MS 1937 *ED* MS St Univ BA 1959; Univ VA LLB 1965 *CURR EMPL* ptnr: Holland & Hart *CORP AFFIL* ptnr: Holland & Hart *NONPR AFFIL* dir: Genesis Jobs; fellow: Am Coll Tax Counc, Am Tax Policy Inst, CO Bar Fdn; mem: CO Bar Assn, Denver Bar Assn; trust: CO Historical Fdn
Edward J. Limes: pres, treas, trust
Michael Polakovic: trust
Teresa Polakovic: vp, trust

APPLICATION INFORMATION

Initial Approach: Send brief letter of inquiry describing program or project. There are no deadlines.

Restrictions on Giving: Does not support individuals.

GRANTS ANALYSIS

Number of Grants: 42
Highest Grant: $30,000
Typical Range: $1500 to $10,000
Disclosure Period: fiscal year ending March 31, 1992

RECENT GRANTS

```
30,000  Sacred Heart
        House, Denver, CO
23,980  Regis High School,
        Aurora, CO
22,700  St. Mary's Acad-
        emy, Englewood,
        CO
20,000  Regis College, Den-
        ver, CO
15,000  Genesis Jobs, Den-
        ver, CO
14,600  J.K. Mullen High
        School, Denver, CO
12,500  Jefferson County
        Adult ESL Pro-
        gram, Lakewood,
        CO
10,000  Church of Risen
        Christ, Denver, CO
10,000  Havern Center, Lit-
        tleton, CO
10,000  Migrant Workers
        Ministry, Denver,
        CO
```

Wedum Foundation

CONTACT

Mayo Johnson
President
Wedum Fdn.
PO Box 644
Alexandria, MN 56308
(612) 763-3407

FINANCIAL SUMMARY

Recent Giving: $391,745 (1990); $209,432 (1988)
Assets: $6,068,882 (1990); $6,288,012 (1988)
Gifts Received: $95,000 (1990)
EIN: 41-6025661

CONTRIBUTIONS SUMMARY

Donor(s): the late Maynard C. Wedum, the late John A. Wedum
Typical Recipients: • *Civic & Public Affairs:* environmental affairs • *Education:* business education, career/vocational education, education funds, private education (precollege), religious education, science/technology education • *Religion:* churches, religious organizations • *Social Services:* aged, child welfare, homes
Grant Types: conference/seminar and seed money
Geographic Distribution: focus on the Alexandria, MN, area

GIVING OFFICERS

Mayo Johnson: pres, treas
Gary Slette: vp
John A. Wedum: vp
Mary Beth Wedum: secy

APPLICATION INFORMATION

Initial Approach: Application form required; for education grant, include resume of academic qualifications. There are no deadlines.

GRANTS ANALYSIS

Number of Grants: 11
Highest Grant: $281,815
Typical Range: $2,000 to $12,000
Disclosure Period: 1990
Note: 1990 figures do not include scholarships to individuals.

RECENT GRANTS

```
281,815  Alexandria Techni-
         cal Foundation
 70,000  Lone Tree Bible
         Camp
 12,000  St. Anns School
  4,000  Pioneer Home
```

3,000 Williams Fund of Minn
2,000 Children's Chance
2,000 Ellsworth Dollars for Scholars
2,000 Hoffman Dollars for Scholars
2,000 Princeton Dollars for Scholars, Princeton, NJ
500 KTCA Public Radio

Weeden Foundation, Frank

CONTACT
Alan N. Weeden
President
Frank Weeden Fdn.
11 Broadway
New York, NY 10004
(212) 509-0579

FINANCIAL SUMMARY
Recent Giving: $1,028,380 (fiscal 1991); $1,861,875 (fiscal 1990); $810,000 (fiscal 1989)
Assets: $23,554,526 (fiscal year ending June 30, 1991); $23,568,558 (fiscal 1990); $21,633,085 (fiscal 1989)
EIN: 94-6109313

CONTRIBUTIONS SUMMARY
Donor(s): The foundation was established in 1963 by Alan N. Weeden, Donald E. Weeden, John D. Weeden, William F. Weeden, M.D., and the late Frank Weeden.
Typical Recipients: • *Arts & Humanities:* arts associations, museums/galleries, public broadcasting, theater • *Civic & Public Affairs:* environmental affairs, international affairs, professional & trade associations, public policy, women's affairs, zoos/botanical gardens • *Education:* colleges & universities, private education (precollege) • *Health:* health funds • *Social Services:* child welfare, family planning
Grant Types: general support and project
Geographic Distribution: national

GIVING OFFICERS
Alan Norman Weeden: pres, dir *B* Oakland CA 1924 *ED* Stanford Univ BA 1947
John D. Weeden: secy, treas, dir
William F. Weeden: vp, dir

APPLICATION INFORMATION
Initial Approach:
Grant requests should be in writing.
Requests should describe the purpose for which the grant is solicited in a clear and concise manner.
The board meets to consider grant requests four times per year, usually in early March, June, September, and December.
If the foundation is interested or needs more detailed information, it will contact the person or organization making the request. If the foundation is not interested, written notification to that effect will be given.
Restrictions on Giving: In general, the foundation will not make grants to individuals. The foundation also does not support buildings or publications of other organizations.

OTHER THINGS TO KNOW
Publications: annual report

GRANTS ANALYSIS
Total Grants: $1,028,380
Number of Grants: 93
Highest Grant: $100,000
Typical Range: $1,000 to $20,000
Disclosure Period: fiscal year ending June 30, 1991
Note: Recent grants are derived from a fiscal 1991 grants list.

RECENT GRANTS
100,000 Conservation Management Association
83,500 Stanford University, Stanford, CA
70,000 Charles Ives Center, Danbury, CT
52,700 Conservation International, Washington, DC
52,000 Nature Conservancy, Arlington, TX
51,000 Population Communications International, New York, NY
50,000 Natural Resources Defense Council, New York, NY
50,000 Nature Conservancy, Honolulu, HI
38,830 New York State Agricultural Experiment, Ithaca, NY
33,500 Nature Conservancy, San Francisco, CA

Weezie Foundation

CONTACT
Robert Schwecherl
Cotrustee, Advisory Committee
Weezie Fdn.
c/o Morgan Guaranty Trust Co. of New York
9 West 57th St.
New York, NY 10019
(212) 826-7607
Note: The alternate contact is Charles Davidson.

FINANCIAL SUMMARY
Recent Giving: $746,000 (1991); $711,500 (1990); $634,000 (1989)
Assets: $16,780,102 (1991); $14,644,034 (1990); $14,992,831 (1989)
EIN: 13-6090903

CONTRIBUTIONS SUMMARY
Donor(s): The foundation was established in 1961 by the late Adelaide T. Corbett.
Typical Recipients: • *Civic & Public Affairs:* environmental affairs • *Education:* arts education, colleges & universities, community & junior colleges, education associations, private education (precollege), religious education, student aid • *Health:* hospitals • *Religion:* churches, religious organizations • *Social Services:* community service organizations, counseling, homes, youth organizations
Grant Types: general support
Geographic Distribution: focus on northeastern United States

GIVING OFFICERS
Morgan Guaranty Trust Company of New York
trust
D. Nelson Adams: mem adv comm
Adelrick Benziger, Jr.: mem adv comm
Thomas W. Carroll: adv
James Francis Dolan: mem adv comm *B* Orange NJ 1930 *ED* Seton Hall Univ BS 1950; Columbia Univ LLB 1953 *CURR EMPL* ptnr: Davis Polk & Wardwell *NONPR AFFIL* mem: Am Bar Assn, NY Bar Assn, NY City Bar Assn
Mrs. William H. Hays III: mem adv comm
H. S. Graham McBride: adv
Robert Schwecherl: secy, treas, trust

Charles H. Theriot: mem adv comm

APPLICATION INFORMATION
Initial Approach:
The foundation requests applications be made in writing.

GRANTS ANALYSIS
Total Grants: $746,000
Number of Grants: 24
Highest Grant: $120,000
Typical Range: $10,000 to $50,000
Disclosure Period: 1991
Note: Recent grants are derived from a 1991 grants list.

RECENT GRANTS
120,000 Miss Porter's School, Farmington, CT
100,000 Human Resources Center, Albertson, NY
60,000 State Communities Aid Association, New York, NY
50,000 Cold Spring Harbor Laboratory, Cold Spring Harbor, NY
50,000 Leonard Morse Hospital, Natick, MA
50,000 Phoenix House Development Fund, New York, NY
50,000 St. Mark's School, Southborough, MA
45,000 Nantucket Boys and Girls Club, Nantucket, MA
35,000 Youth Counseling League, New York, NY
25,000 Cape Cod Community College Education Foundation, West Barnstable, MA

Wege Foundation

CONTACT
Peter M. Wege
President
Wege Fdn.
PO Box 6388
Grand Rapids, MI 49506
(616) 957-0480

FINANCIAL SUMMARY
Recent Giving: $350,549 (1991); $367,150 (1990); $386,850 (1989)
Assets: $6,703,784 (1991); $4,388,242 (1990); $5,155,824 (1989)
Gifts Received: $147,040 (1991); $50,000 (1990); $200,000 (1989)

Fiscal Note: In 1991, contributions were received from Peter M. Wege.
EIN: 38-6124363

CONTRIBUTIONS SUMMARY

Donor(s): Peter M. Wege
Typical Recipients: • *Arts & Humanities:* arts centers, community arts, museums/galleries, music • *Civic & Public Affairs:* environmental affairs • *Education:* colleges & universities, community & junior colleges, education funds, private education (precollege) • *Health:* health organizations, hospitals • *Social Services:* aged, child welfare, community service organizations, homes, youth organizations
Grant Types: general support
Geographic Distribution: focus on Greater Kent County, MI, with emphasis on the Grand Rapids area

GIVING OFFICERS

Charles Lundstrom: secy
Peter M. Wege II: vp
Peter M. Wege: pres *B* Grand Rapids MI 1920 *ED* Univ MI *CURR EMPL* vchmn, dir: Steelcase

APPLICATION INFORMATION

Initial Approach: Send cover letter and full proposal. There are no deadlines.

GRANTS ANALYSIS

Number of Grants: 30
Highest Grant: $200,000
Typical Range: $1,000 to $10,000
Disclosure Period: 1991

RECENT GRANTS

200,000 Blodgett/St. Mary's MRI, Grand Rapids, MI — MRI equipment
50,394 Center for Environmental Study, Grand Rapids, MI
15,000 Grand Rapids Public Educational Foundation, Grand Rapids, MI
10,000 Rivers Edge Environmental, Grand Rapids, MI
10,000 St. Cecilia Music Society, Grand Rapids, MI
7,500 American Red Cross, Grand Rapids, MI
7,500 Grand Rapids Art Museum, Grand Rapids, MI
5,000 Gerontology Network, Grand Rapids, MI
5,000 Grand Rapids Junior College Foundation, Grand Rapids, MI
5,000 National Bio Diversity Institute, Grand Rapids, MI

Wegener Foundation, Herman and Mary

CONTACT

Herman and Mary Wegener Fdn.
1711 First National Bldg.
Oklahoma City, OK 73102
(405) 235-7200

FINANCIAL SUMMARY

Recent Giving: $278,200 (1991); $278,200 (1990); $284,200 (1989)
Assets: $3,030,797 (1991); $2,879,770 (1990); $2,962,641 (1989)
Gifts Received: $25,475 (1990)
EIN: 73-6095407

CONTRIBUTIONS SUMMARY

Donor(s): the late Herman H. Wegener
Typical Recipients: • *Education:* colleges & universities, public education (precollege), religious education • *Health:* hospitals, medical research, pediatric health, single-disease health associations • *Religion:* religious organizations • *Social Services:* community service organizations, food/clothing distribution, united funds, youth organizations
Grant Types: capital, operating expenses, and project
Geographic Distribution: focus on Oklahoma City, OK

GIVING OFFICERS

Rosemary Fields: trust
Lee Holmes: trust, vp
Willis B. Sherin: trust, pres
Clenard Wegener: trust, treas
Kenneth Wegener: trust
Raymond Lee Wegener: trust
Willis B. Wegener: trust

APPLICATION INFORMATION

Initial Approach: Send brief letter of inquiry describing program. Deadline is November 1.
Restrictions on Giving: Does not support individuals.

GRANTS ANALYSIS

Number of Grants: 34
Highest Grant: $15,000
Typical Range: $5,000 to $10,000
Disclosure Period: 1991

RECENT GRANTS

15,000 Baptist Hospital, Oklahoma City, OK
15,000 Deaconess Hospital, Oklahoma City, OK
15,000 Mercy Hospital, Oklahoma City, OK
15,000 South Community Hospital, Oklahoma City, OK
15,000 St. Anthony Hospital, Oklahoma City, OK
10,000 Daily Living Center, Oklahoma City, OK
10,000 Midwest/Del City Schools, Del City, OK
10,000 Oklahoma Christian University, Oklahoma City, OK
10,000 Oklahoma City University, Oklahoma City, OK
10,000 Putnam City Schools, Oklahoma City, OK

Wehadkee Foundation

CONTACT

Bruce N. Lanier
Wehadkee Fdn.
PO Box 150
West Point, GA 31833
(404) 645-1331

FINANCIAL SUMMARY

Recent Giving: $78,900 (1991); $92,150 (1989); $110,950 (1988)
Assets: $1,969,897 (1991); $1,972,580 (1989); $1,628,860 (1988)
EIN: 63-6049784

CONTRIBUTIONS SUMMARY

Donor(s): D. A. Turner
Typical Recipients: • *Education:* colleges & universities, education associations, education funds, private education (precollege) • *Religion:* churches • *Social Services:* community service organizations, united funds, youth organizations
Grant Types: general support
Geographic Distribution: focus on GA

GIVING OFFICERS

G.P. Barnwell: trust
Ronnie Birchfield: secy, treas
Bruce N. Lanier, Jr.: vp
Bruce N. Lanier, Sr.: pres

APPLICATION INFORMATION

Initial Approach: Contributes only to preselected organizations.

GRANTS ANALYSIS

Number of Grants: 25
Highest Grant: $25,000
Typical Range: $500 to $4,000
Disclosure Period: 1991

RECENT GRANTS

25,000 Chattahoochee Valley Educational Society, Lannett, AL
7,000 Boy Scouts of America
5,000 Darlington School
5,000 Rock Mills Methodist Church
4,500 Alabama Independent Colleges, Birmingham, AL
4,000 Boy Scouts of America
4,000 Joint Tech-Georgia Development Fund, Atlanta, GA
4,000 United Fund
3,000 Georgia Foundation of Independent Colleges, Atlanta, GA
3,000 United Way

Wehr Foundation, Todd

CONTACT

Ralph G. Schulz
President
Todd Wehr Fdn.
111 East Wisconsin Avenue, Ste. 2100
Milwaukee, WI 53202
(414) 271-8210

FINANCIAL SUMMARY

Recent Giving: $488,500 (1990); $492,500 (1989); $522,000 (1988)
Assets: $9,931,609 (1990); $9,897,698 (1989); $9,023,495 (1988)
EIN: 39-6043962

CONTRIBUTIONS SUMMARY

Donor(s): the late C. Frederic Wehr
Typical Recipients: • *Civic & Public Affairs:* zoos/botanical gardens • *Education:* colleges & universities, science/technol-

ogy education • *Science:* scientific institutes
Grant Types: project
Geographic Distribution: limited to WI

GIVING OFFICERS
William J. Hardy: vp, treas, dir
Robert P. Harland: dir
Ralph G. Schulz: pres, dir
M. James Termondt: secy, dir
Winfred W. Wuesthoff: dir

APPLICATION INFORMATION
Initial Approach: Send brief letter of inquiry and full proposal. There are no deadlines.
Restrictions on Giving: Does not support individuals.

GRANTS ANALYSIS
Number of Grants: 10
Highest Grant: $156,000
Typical Range: $10,000 to $50,000
Disclosure Period: 1990

RECENT GRANTS
156,000 Museum of Science, Economics & Technology, Milwaukee, WI — general
100,000 Viterbo College, La Crosse, WI — general
80,000 Edgewood College, Madison, WI — general
50,000 Children's Hospital of Wisconsin, Milwaukee, WI — general
50,000 Zoological Society of Milwaukee County, Milwaukee, WI — general
15,000 Mayo Foundation, Rochester, MN — general
12,500 Marquette University, Milwaukee, WI
10,000 Cardinal Stritch College, Milwaukee, WI — general
10,000 Lawrence University, Appleton, WI
5,000 Boys and Girls Club, Milwaukee, WI

Weight Watchers International / Weight Watchers Foundation
Revenue: $1.6 billion
Employees: 7,500
Parent Company: H.J. Heinz Co.
Headquarters: Jericho, NY
SIC Major Group: Personal Services, Printing & Publishing, and Wholesale Trade—Nondurable Goods

CONTACT
Xavier P. Sunyer
Executive Director
Weight Watchers International
500 North Broadway
Jericho, NY 11753
(516) 939-0400

FINANCIAL SUMMARY
Recent Giving: $143,400 (1991); $122,163 (1989); $116,731 (1988)
Assets: $1,975 (1991); $3,577 (1989); $42,463 (1988)
Gifts Received: $141,610 (1991); $105,894 (1989); $137,259 (1988)
Fiscal Note: Major In 1991, contributions were received from Weight Watchers International.
EIN: 11-2165046

CONTRIBUTIONS SUMMARY
Typical Recipients: • *Education:* colleges & universities, medical education • *Health:* hospitals, medical research
Grant Types: conference/seminar and research
Geographic Distribution: no geographic restrictions
Operating Locations: NY (Jericho)

CORP. OFFICERS
Charles Berger: *CURR EMPL* chmn, dir: Weight Watchers Intl *CORP AFFIL* pres: WeightWatchers British Columbia Ltd
Lelio G. Parducci: *CURR EMPL* pres, ceo: Weight Watchers Intl

GIVING OFFICERS
Stephen Adams: dir
Charles Berger: chmn *CURR EMPL* chmn, dir: Weight Watchers Intl (see above)
George Christakis: dir
Joseph Folender: dir
Reve A. Frankle: dir
Stanley Lipman: dir
Florine Mark-Ross: dir
Barbara J. Moore: dir

Mildred Oppenheimer: dir
Lelio G. Parducci: dir *CURR EMPL* pres, ceo: Weight Watchers Intl (see above)
Brian Ruder: dir
David W. Sculley: dir
Henry Sebrell: exec dir emeritus
Xavier P. Sunyer: exec dir

APPLICATION INFORMATION
Initial Approach: Send a brief letter of inquiry and a full proposal. Include a description of organization, amount requested, purpose of funds sought, recently audited financial statement, and proof of tax-exempt status.
Restrictions on Giving: Does not support individuals, general support, building or endowment funds, scholarships, fellowships, matching gifts, overhead, or travel funds. Does not make loans.

GRANTS ANALYSIS
Number of Grants: 19
Highest Grant: $15,000
Typical Range: $7,500 to $15,000
Disclosure Period: 1991

RECENT GRANTS
15,000 Massachusetts General Hospital, Boston, MA
15,000 New York Hospital Cornell Medical Center, New York, NY
15,000 Stanford University, Stanford, CA
15,000 State University of New York at Stony Brook, Stony Brook, NY
15,000 University of Colorado Health Sciences Center, Boulder, CO
15,000 University of Washington, Seattle, WA
13,400 New England Medical Center Hospitals, Boston, MA
10,000 St. Luke's-Roosevelt Hospital Center, New York, NY
7,500 Rockefeller University, New York, NY
7,500 University of Vermont Metropolitan Health Medical Center, Burlington, VT

Weil, Gotshal & Manges Foundation

CONTACT
Jesse D. Wolff
Treasurer
Weil, Gotshal & Manges Fdn.
767 Fifth Ave.
New York, NY 10153
(212) 310-8000

FINANCIAL SUMMARY
Recent Giving: $920,750 (1990); $1,067,655 (1988)
Assets: $3,358,323 (1990); $2,824,950 (1989); $2,346,938 (1988)
Gifts Received: $1,300,000 (1990); $1,500,000 (1988)
Fiscal Note: In 1990, contributions were received from Weil, Gotshal & Manges.
EIN: 13-3158325

CONTRIBUTIONS SUMMARY
Donor(s): Robert Todd Lang, Ira M. Millstein, Harvey R. Miller
Typical Recipients: • *Arts & Humanities:* arts centers, dance, libraries, museums/galleries • *Civic & Public Affairs:* environmental affairs, law & justice, public policy • *Education:* colleges & universities, legal education • *Health:* medical research, single-disease health associations • *Religion:* religious organizations • *Social Services:* community service organizations, family planning, shelters/homelessness, united funds
Grant Types: general support
Geographic Distribution: focus on NY

GIVING OFFICERS
Robert Todd Lang: chmn, dir *B* New York NY 1924 *ED* Yale Univ 1945 *CURR EMPL* partner: Weil Gotschal & Manges *CORP AFFIL* partner: Weil Gotschal & Manges *NONPR AFFIL* mem: Am Bar Assn
Harvey R. Miller: secy, dir
Ira M. Millstein: pres, dir *B* New York NY 1926 *ED* Columbia Univ BS 1947; Columbia Univ LLB 1949 *CORP AFFIL* ptnr: Weil Gotschal & Manges *NONPR AFFIL* adjunct prof, dir: Columbia Univ Grad Sch Bus; chmn bd advs: Columbia Univ Ctr Law Econ Studies; mem: Am Bar Assn, NY Bar Assn; prof: Columbia Univ Ctr Law & Econ Studies; vchmn

bd overseers: Albert Einstein Coll Medicine
Jesse D. Wolff: treas, dir *ED* Dartmouth Coll BA 1935; Harvard Univ JD 1938 *CORP AFFIL* mem adv bd: Sotheby's Holdings *NONPR AFFIL* mem: Am Bar Assn; trust Greater NY chapter: Am Red Cross

APPLICATION INFORMATION

Initial Approach: Send brief letter of inquiry describing program or project. The deadline is November 1.

GRANTS ANALYSIS
Number of Grants: 51
Highest Grant: $500,000
Typical Range: $500 to $5,000
Disclosure Period: 1990

RECENT GRANTS
500,000 United Jewish Appeal Federation of Jewish Philanthropies, New York, NY
185,000 Legal Aid Society, New York, NY
25,000 United Jewish Campaign, Houston, TX
20,000 Planned Parenthood, New York, NY
17,500 Greater Miami Jewish Federation, Miami, FL
15,000 Lawyer's Committee for Civil Rights, Washington, DC
10,000 Columbia University, New York, NY
10,000 National Foundation for Ileitis and Colitis, New York, NY
10,000 Southern Methodist University, Dallas, TX
7,500 United Way, Miami, FL

Weiler Foundation

CONTACT
Bartlett Burnap
President
Weiler Fdn.
425 Alma St., Ste. 410
Palo Alto, CA 94301

FINANCIAL SUMMARY
Recent Giving: $118,250 (fiscal 1992); $227,650 (fiscal 1991); $699,002 (fiscal 1990)
Assets: $10,305,198 (fiscal year ending April 30, 1992); $9,838,395 (fiscal 1991); $7,202,733 (fiscal 1990)
EIN: 23-7418821

CONTRIBUTIONS SUMMARY
Donor(s): the late Ralph J. Weiler
Typical Recipients: • *Arts & Humanities:* arts centers, history/historic preservation, museums/galleries, public broadcasting • *Education:* colleges & universities, private education (precollege), religious education, science/technology education • *Health:* hospitals, medical research, pediatric health, public health, single-disease health associations • *Religion:* churches • *Social Services:* animal protection, disabled, family planning
Grant Types: general support
Geographic Distribution: focus on CA

GIVING OFFICERS
William Bullis: vp
Bartlett Burnap: pres
Elizabeth J. Kelly: secy, treas

APPLICATION INFORMATION
Initial Approach: Contributes only to preselected organizations.

OTHER THINGS TO KNOW
Publications: Application Guidelines.

GRANTS ANALYSIS
Number of Grants: 25
Highest Grant: $22,600
Typical Range: $2,000 to $5,000
Disclosure Period: fiscal year ending April 30, 1992

RECENT GRANTS
22,600 Natural History Museum, Los Angeles, CA
10,000 Los Angeles County Museum of Art, Los Angeles, CA
10,000 University of Southern California, Los Angeles, CA
8,000 KCSM TV, Los Angeles, CA
5,600 Diabetes Society, Los Angeles, CA
5,000 Americare, Los Angeles, CA
5,000 Immaculate Conception Academy, San Francisco, CA
5,000 K.A.R.A., Los Angeles, CA
5,000 Pacific Legal Foundation, Los Angeles, CA
5,000 San Francisco Art Museum, San Francisco, CA

Weiler Foundation, Theodore & Renee

CONTACT
Richard Kandel
Director, Secretary
Theodore & Renee Weiler Fdn.
24 Rock St.
Brooklyn, NY 11206
(718) 417-3600

FINANCIAL SUMMARY
Recent Giving: $648,825 (1991); $602,125 (1990); $395,700 (1989)
Assets: $12,972,087 (1991); $12,153,554 (1990); $11,225,799 (1989)
Gifts Received: $343,245 (1991); $594,593 (1990); $7,000,000 (1989)
Fiscal Note: In 1991, contributions were received from the Estate of Theodore R. Weiler.
EIN: 13-6181441

CONTRIBUTIONS SUMMARY
Donor(s): Theodore R. Weller
Typical Recipients: • *Arts & Humanities:* arts associations, arts centers, cinema, dance, libraries, museums/galleries, music, opera, performing arts • *Civic & Public Affairs:* environmental affairs, zoos/botanical gardens • *Education:* education funds, medical education • *Health:* hospitals, medical research, pediatric health, single-disease health associations • *Religion:* religious organizations • *Social Services:* aged, community centers, community service organizations, disabled
Grant Types: general support and scholarship
Geographic Distribution: focus on New York, NY, and Palm Beach, FL

GIVING OFFICERS
Richard Kandel: secy, treas
Alan Safir: pres
Rhoda Weiler: dir

APPLICATION INFORMATION
Initial Approach: Contributes only to preselected organizations.
Restrictions on Giving: Does not support individuals.

GRANTS ANALYSIS
Number of Grants: 171
Highest Grant: $91,500
Typical Range: $200 to $10,000
Disclosure Period: 1991

RECENT GRANTS
91,500 United Jewish Appeal Federation of Jewish Philanthropies, New York, NY
28,500 Blythedale Children's Hospital, Hawthorne, NY
26,500 Strand-Capitol Performing Arts Center, Harrisburg, PA
25,000 Carnegie Hall Society, New York, NY
25,000 Greenwich House, New York, NY
25,000 New York University Building Fund, New York, NY
20,000 Jewish Community Center, York, PA
17,000 American Film Institute, Los Angeles, CA
16,000 Samuel Waxman Cancer Research Foundation, New York, NY
11,500 New York City Ballet, New York, NY

Weinberg Foundation, Harry and Jeanette

CONTACT
Harry and Jeannette Weinberg Foundation
5518 Baltimore National Pke.
Baltimore, MD 21228
Note: The foundation does not list a specific contact person or a telephone number.

FINANCIAL SUMMARY

Recent Giving: $21,976,000 (fiscal 1992); $1,888,500 (fiscal 1991); $21,153,000 (fiscal 1990)

Assets: $762,808,000 (fiscal year ending February 29, 1992); $639,936,000 (fiscal 1991); $652,781,387 (fiscal 1990)

Gifts Received: $18,560,000 (fiscal 1992); $1,913,100 (fiscal 1991); $71,427,820 (fiscal 1990)

Fiscal Note: Gifts received were donated by the estate of Harry Weinberg and related companies.

EIN: 52-6037034

CONTRIBUTIONS SUMMARY

Donor(s): The foundation was established in 1959 by the late Harry and Jeanette Weinberg. Mr. Weinberg, who passed away in November 1990, was involved in real estate and investments throughout many areas of the United States, primarily in several of the Hawaiian Islands, Baltimore, MD, and Scranton, PA.

Typical Recipients: • *Social Services:* aged, food/clothing distribution

Grant Types: capital, endowment, and project

Geographic Distribution: no geographic restrictions

GIVING OFFICERS

Alvin Awaya: vp, asst secy, dir
Ted Gross: vp, asst secy
Robert Kelly: treas, dir
Gladys Lunasco: asst secy
Bernard Siegel: pres, dir
David Weinberg: asst treas *CURR EMPL* co-chmn: Fel-Pro
Nathan Weinberg: vp, secy, dir
William Weinberg: vp, dir
Joel Winegarden: vp, asst secy *B* New York NY 1938 *ED* NY Univ 1960 *CURR EMPL* vp, asst secy: Honolulu Ltd *CORP AFFIL* vp, asst secy: HRT Ltd; vp, asst secy, dir: Gutman Realty Corp, 3900 Corp

APPLICATION INFORMATION

Initial Approach: Restrictions on Giving: The foundation reports that it only makes contributions to preselected charitable organizations and does not accept unsolicited applications for funds.

GRANTS ANALYSIS

Total Grants: $21,976,000
Number of Grants: 106
Highest Grant: $2,000,000
Typical Range: $10,000 to $500,000
Disclosure Period: fiscal year ending February 29, 1992
Note: Recent grants are derived from a partial fiscal 1992 grants list.

RECENT GRANTS

1,524,000	Levindale Hebrew Geriatric Center
1,250,000	American Red Cross, Oahu, HI
1,025,000	Associated Catholic Charities, HI
525,000	Hospital For Sick Children, Washington, DC
500,000	Meals on Wheels
500,000	Sheppard and Enoch Pratt, Baltimore, MD
250,000	Associated Catholic Charities, Baltimore, MD
225,000	American Red Cross, Kauai, HI
200,000	Scranton Little Sisters of the Poor, Scranton, PA
150,000	Appalachia Service Project

Weinberg Foundation, John L.

CONTACT

Deborah Rogers
Secretary
John L. Weinberg Fdn.
c/o Goldman, Sachs & Co.
85 Broad St., 22nd Fl.
New York, NY 10004
(212) 902-8555

FINANCIAL SUMMARY

Recent Giving: $1,391,819 (fiscal 1992); $610,887 (fiscal 1991); $579,196 (fiscal 1990)
Assets: $20,763,612 (fiscal year ending April 30, 1992); $19,221,421 (fiscal 1991); $15,768,385 (fiscal 1990)
Gifts Received: $1,767,757 (fiscal 1992); $2,680,000 (fiscal 1991); $1,340,539 (fiscal 1990)
Fiscal Note: In 1992, contributions were received from John L. Weinberg.
EIN: 13-6028813

CONTRIBUTIONS SUMMARY

Donor(s): The foundation was established in 1959 by John L. Weinberg.

Typical Recipients: • *Arts & Humanities:* arts institutes, libraries, museums/galleries, public broadcasting • *Civic & Public Affairs:* environmental affairs, international affairs, philanthropic organizations, urban & community affairs • *Education:* business education, colleges & universities, community & junior colleges, education funds, private education (precollege) • *Health:* emergency/ambulance services, health funds, hospitals, medical research, single-disease health associations • *Religion:* churches, religious organizations • *Social Services:* aged, child welfare, community service organizations, counseling, employment/job training, recreation & athletics, united funds, youth organizations

Grant Types: general support

Geographic Distribution: focus on New York, NY, and Greenwich, CT

GIVING OFFICERS

Arthur Goodhart Altschul: trust *B* New York NY 1920 *ED* Yale Univ AB 1943 *CURR EMPL* ltd ptnr: Goldman Sachs Group *CORP AFFIL* chmn, dir: Gen Am Investors Co; dir: Assoc Dry Goods Corp, Boswell Energy Corp, Sunbelt Energy Corp, Wicat Sys *NONPR AFFIL* chmn: Intl Fdn Art Res; chmn bd trusts: Barnard Coll; fellow: Metro Mus Art; mem: Counc Foreign Rels; mem distribution comm: NY Commun Trust; mem gov bd: Yale Univ Art Gallery; mem natl bd: Smithsonian Assocs
Deborah Rogers: secy
Jean H. Weinberg: trust
John H. Weinberg: trust
John Livingston Weinberg: trust *B* New York NY 1925 *ED* Princeton Univ AB 1948; Harvard Univ MBA 1950 *CURR EMPL* sr chmn: Goldman Sachs & Co *CORP AFFIL* dir: BFGoodrich, Capital Holding Corp, Champion Intl Corp, EI du Pont de Nemours & Co, Knight-Ridder, Seagram Co Ltd *NONPR AFFIL* mem: Bus Counc, Chicago Bd Trade, Conf Bd, Counc Foreign Rels, Japan Soc, NY City Partnership; mem adv counc: Stanford Univ; mem bd govs, mem exec comm: NY Hosp-Cornell Med Ctr; trust: Princeton Univ
Sue Ann Weinberg: trust

APPLICATION INFORMATION

Initial Approach: Restrictions on Giving: The foundation supports preselected organizations and does not accept unsolicited requests for funds. The foundation does not make grants to individuals.

GRANTS ANALYSIS

Total Grants: $1,391,819
Number of Grants: 125
Highest Grant: $225,000
Typical Range: $100 to $15,000
Disclosure Period: fiscal year ending April 30, 1992
Note: Recent grants are derived from a fiscal 1992 grants list.

RECENT GRANTS

225,000	New York Hospital, New York, NY
225,000	Princeton University, Princeton, NJ
200,000	New York Hospital Major Modernization Campaign, New York, NY
160,000	Cystic Fibrosis Foundation, New York, NY
50,000	United Jewish Appeal, New York, NY
50,000	Vassar College, Ford Scholars Program, Poughkeepsie, NY
25,000	Hotchkiss School, Lakeville, CT
25,000	Inner-City Scholarship Fund, New York, NY
25,000	Scripps College, Claremont, CA
25,000	Teachers College, J.L. Weinberg Fellowship, New York, NY

Weinberg, Jr. Foundation, Sidney J.

CONTACT

Sydney J. Weinberg, Jr.
Trustee
Sidney J. Weinberg, Jr. Fdn.
c/o Goldman, Sachs & Co.
85 Broad St., Tax Department, 30th Fl.
New York, NY 11201
(212) 902-1000

FINANCIAL SUMMARY

Recent Giving: $981,890 (fiscal 1992); $1,118,400 (fiscal 1991); $1,166,850 (fiscal 1990)
Assets: $16,888,110 (fiscal year ending May 31, 1992); $14,732,497 (fiscal 1991); $12,134,936 (fiscal 1990)
Gifts Received: $1,945,923 (fiscal 1992); $2,000,082 (fiscal 1991); $2,015,175 (fiscal 1990)
Fiscal Note: In fiscal 1992, contributions were received from Sidney J. Weinberg.
EIN: 13-2998603

CONTRIBUTIONS SUMMARY

Donor(s): The foundation was established in 1979 by Sydney J. Weinberg, Jr.

Typical Recipients: • *Arts & Humanities:* dance, public broadcasting • *Civic & Public Affairs:* better government, economic development, economics, environmental affairs, municipalities, public policy • *Education:* arts education, business education, colleges & universities, international studies, private education (precollege), public education (precollege), religious education • *Health:* health funds, hospices, hospitals, medical research, mental health, pediatric health, single-disease health associations • *Religion:* churches, religious organizations • *Social Services:* aged, child welfare, disabled, recreation & athletics, united funds, youth organizations

Grant Types: general support

Geographic Distribution: nationally, with a focus on New York, NY

GIVING OFFICERS

Elizabeth W. Smith: trust

Peter A. Weinberg: trust

Sidney J. Weinberg, Jr.: trust *B* New York NY 1923 *ED* Princeton Univ 1945; Harvard Univ 1949 *CURR EMPL* ltd ptnr: Goldman Sachs Group LP *CORP AFFIL* dir: Eagle-Picher Indus, RH Macy & Co, Sigma_Aldrich Corp, Tejon Ranch Co

Sydney H. Weinberg: trust

APPLICATION INFORMATION

Initial Approach: Restrictions on Giving: The foundation supports preselected organizations and does not accept unsolicited requests for funds. The foundation does not make grants to individuals.

GRANTS ANALYSIS

Total Grants: $981,890

Number of Grants: 62

Highest Grant: $250,000

Typical Range: $500 to $10,000

Disclosure Period: fiscal year ending May 31, 1992

Note: Average grant figure does not include two grants of $250,000 each. Recent grants are derived from a fiscal 1992 grants list.

RECENT GRANTS

```
250,000  Carnegie Institute
         of Washington,
         Washington, DC
250,000  Presbyterian Hospi-
         tal, New York, NY
250,000  Scripps College,
         Claremont, CA
```

```
 25,000  Carnegie Institute
         of Washington,
         Washington, DC
 25,000  First Church of
         Round Hill, Green-
         wich, CT
 25,000  Presbyterian Hospi-
         tal, New York, NY
 15,000  New York City Bal-
         let, New York, NY
 15,000  Scripps College,
         Claremont, CA
 10,000  Committee for
         Economic Develop-
         ment, New York,
         NY
 10,000  Memorial Sloan-
         Kettering Cancer
         Center, New York,
         NY
```

Weiner Foundation

CONTACT

Leon Weiner
Secretary-Treasurer
Weiner Fdn.
PO Box 2612
Houston, TX 77252
(713) 688-1331

FINANCIAL SUMMARY

Recent Giving: $385,359 (1991); $384,086 (1990); $338,424 (1988)

Assets: $2,397,944 (1991); $2,439,547 (1990); $2,151,303 (1988)

Gifts Received: $291,224 (1991); $179,321 (1990); $206,830 (1988)

Fiscal Note: In 1991, contributions were received from Weiner's Stores, Inc..

EIN: 74-6060381

CONTRIBUTIONS SUMMARY

Donor(s): Weiner's Stores

Typical Recipients: • *Arts & Humanities:* community arts, opera • *Civic & Public Affairs:* civil rights, ethnic/minority organizations • *Religion:* religious organizations, synagogues • *Social Services:* community centers, community service organizations, united funds, youth organizations

Grant Types: general support

Geographic Distribution: focus on TX

GIVING OFFICERS

Leon Weiner: secy, treas, dir *CURR EMPL* chmn, ceo: Weiners Stores

Sol B. Weiner: vp, dir *CURR EMPL* pres: Weiners Stores

APPLICATION INFORMATION

Initial Approach: The foundation reports it only makes contributions to preselected charitable organizations.

GRANTS ANALYSIS

Number of Grants: 42

Highest Grant: $350,100

Typical Range: $100 to $1,000

Disclosure Period: 1991

RECENT GRANTS

```
350,100  Jewish Federation,
         Houston, TX
 15,000  American Jewish
         Committee, Hous-
         ton, TX
  7,750  Jewish Community
         Center, Houston,
         TX
  5,000  Greater Houston
         Partnership, Hous-
         ton, TX
  3,650  United Way, Hous-
         ton, TX
  2,500  National Confer-
         ence of Christians
         and Jews, Houston,
         TX
  1,554  Congregation Beth
         Yeshurun, Hous-
         ton, TX
  1,200  Anti-Defamation
         League, Houston,
         TX
  1,150  B'nai B'rith Foun-
         dation of US, Hous-
         ton, TX
  1,075  Seven Acres Geriat-
         ric Center, Hous-
         ton, TX
```

Weiner's Stores

Sales: $43.0 million
Employees: 500
Headquarters: Houston, TX
SIC Major Group: Apparel & Accessory Stores and General Merchandise Stores

CONTACT

Sol B. Weiner
President
Weiner's Stores
6005 Westview
Houston, TX 77055
(713) 688-1331

CONTRIBUTIONS SUMMARY

Operating Locations: TX (Houston)

CORP. OFFICERS

Leon Weiner: *CURR EMPL* chmn, ceo: Weiners Stores

Sol B. Weiner: *CURR EMPL* pres: Weiners Stores

OTHER THINGS TO KNOW

Company is an original donor to the Weiner Foundation.

Weingart Foundation

CONTACT

Charles W. Jacobson
President and Chief Administrative Officer
Weingart Foundation
PO Box 17982
Los Angeles, CA 90017-0982
(213) 688-7799

FINANCIAL SUMMARY

Recent Giving: $25,000,000 (fiscal 1993 est.); $24,381,251 (fiscal 1992); $22,893,357 (fiscal 1991)

Assets: $500,000,000 (fiscal 1993 est.); $478,969,848 (fiscal year ending June 30, 1992); $458,795,070 (fiscal 1991); $446,228,620 (fiscal 1990)

Gifts Received: $50,000 (fiscal 1992 est.); $12,142 (fiscal 1991); $12,906,340 (fiscal 1990)

Fiscal Note: The foundation received $10,428,992 from the distribution of the Ben Weingart Charitable Testamentary Trust and $1,876,981 from a revocable trust which terminated during the 1990 fiscal year.

EIN: 95-6054814

CONTRIBUTIONS SUMMARY

Donor(s): Ben Weingart (1888-1980) was a real estate developer in Southern California who help to create a new town, the City of Lakewood, during the 1950s. It was the first planned city in Southern California. Mr. Weingart was born in Atlanta, GA. He attended school through the eighth grade and arrived in Los Angeles when he was 18 years old. The Weingart Foundation was established in California in 1951 as the B. W. Foundation. The name of the foundation was changed in April 1978. Funds for the foundation's incorporation were donated by the late Ben and Stella Weingart, who bequeathed their estates to the foundation.

Typical Recipients: • *Arts & Humanities:* arts centers, libraries, museums/galleries, public broadcasting • *Civic & Public*

Affairs: better government, law & justice, public policy • *Education:* arts education, colleges & universities, elementary education, liberal arts education, literacy, minority education, preschool education, private education (precollege), special education, student aid • *Health:* hospices, hospitals, nursing services, outpatient health care delivery, pediatric health • *Social Services:* child welfare, community centers, community service organizations, counseling, delinquency & crime, disabled, drugs & alcohol, emergency relief, family services, food/clothing distribution, recreation & athletics, religious welfare, shelters/homelessness, volunteer services, youth organizations

Grant Types: capital, challenge, project, and seed money

Geographic Distribution: nine counties in Southern California

GIVING OFFICERS

Roy A. Anderson: dir *B* Ripon CA 1920 *ED* Stanford Univ AB 1947; Stanford Univ MBA 1949 *CURR EMPL* chmn emeritus: Lockheed Corp *CORP AFFIL* dir: ARCO, Avantek Inc, First Interstate Bancorp Los Angeles, First Interstate Bank CA, Southern CA Edison Co *NONPR AFFIL* dir: Los Angeles Music Ctr; trust: Stanford Univ

Steven D. Broidy: dir *CURR EMPL* ptnr: Loeb & Loeb

Lee A. DuBridge: adv to bd *B* Terre Haute IN 1901 *ED* Cornell Coll IA AB 1922; Univ WI AM 1924; Univ WI PhD 1926 *NONPR AFFIL* fellow: Am Physicians Soc; mem: Am Assn Advancement Science, Am Philosophical Soc, Eta Kappa Nu, Natl Academy Sciences, Phi Beta Kappa, Sigma Pi Sigma, Sigma Xi; pres emeritus: CA Inst Tech

Susan H. Grimes: corp secy, program off

John T. Gurash: dir, mem audit comm *B* Oakland CA 1910 *ED* Loyola Marymount Univ *CURR EMPL* chmn, dir: CertainTeed Corp *CORP AFFIL* chmn: Horace Mann Educators Corp; dir: Norton Co, Pic N Save Corp, Purex Indus *NONPR AFFIL* mem: Am Soc French Legion Honor, Knights Malta, Newcomen Soc North Am, PA Soc; trust: Ortho-

pedic Hosp; trust emeritus: Occidental Coll

Charles W. Jacobson: pres, chief adm off

Barbara Kese: program off

William J. McGill: dir *NONPR AFFIL* pres emeritus: Columbia Univ

Harvey L. Price: vp (grants)

Sol Price: dir *B* Chicago IL 1932 *ED* Northwestern Univ 1954 *CURR EMPL* chmn emeritus, dir: Price Co *PHIL AFFIL* pres, dir, don: Sol & Helen Price Foundation

Dennis Carothers Stanfill: dir *B* Centerville TN 1927 *ED* US Naval Academy BS 1949; Oxford Univ MA 1953 *CURR EMPL* co-chmn, ceo: MGM Pathe Commun *CORP AFFIL* dir: Carter Hawley Hale, Dial Corp *NONPR AFFIL* trust: CA Inst Tech, John F Kennedy Ctr Performing Arts

Ann L. Van Dormolen: vp, treas

Harry J. Volk: chmn, ceo, dir *B* Trenton NJ 1905 *ED* Rutgers Univ AB 1927; Rutgers Univ LLB 1930 *NONPR AFFIL* mem: CA Inst Tech, Los Angeles Chamber Commerce, Los Angeles County Mus Art Assocs, USC Assocs

Laurence A. Wolfe: vp (admin)

APPLICATION INFORMATION

Initial Approach:
Prospective applicants should send 15 copies of a test letter to the foundation.
The letter, not to exceed two pages, should contain a concise statement of the need for funds, amount sought, and enough factual information to enable the foundation to determine an initial response. Supporting data may be included. If the project meets the foundation's priorities, a formal application will be sent to the organization.
Applications are accepted throughout the year.
Final notification arrives three to four months after receiving the proposal.

Restrictions on Giving:
Grants are not made to carry out propaganda, to influence legislation or elections, to promote voter registration, or to support political candidates or political campaigns. The foundation does not make grants to federated appeals or to organizations that collect funds for redistribution to other nonprofit

groups. It does not make grants for support of national charities, for operating budgets of agencies served by the United Way or other federated sources (except for approved special projects), for operating expenses of performing arts organizations, or for the benefit of individuals or small groups. The foundation does not consider requests for support of projects that normally would be financed from government funds. It ordinarily does not make grants for operating expenses, endowment funds, contingencies, or deficits. As a general rule, it does not make grants for conferences, seminars, workshops, exhibits, travel, surveys, publishing activities, or films. Nor does the foundation encourage applications for funding the projects of environmental, consumer, refugee, and religious groups; international organizations; or governmental or quasi-governmental agencies. Applicant organizations must be tax-exempt under section 501(c)(3) of the IRS code.

OTHER THINGS TO KNOW
The foundation expects applicant organizations to show project support from internal sources as well as outside sources. Grants may cover a multiyear period in some cases, but the foundation generally does not make a grant to any organization on an annual basis.

Publications: annual report, guidelines, and application procedures

GRANTS ANALYSIS
Total Grants: $24,381,251
Number of Grants: 466
Highest Grant: $2,474,500
Typical Range: $25,000 to $100,000
Disclosure Period: fiscal year ending June 30, 1992
Note: Recent grants are derived from a fiscal 1992 Form 990.

RECENT GRANTS
2,474,500 YMCA-Metropolitan Los Angeles, Los Angeles, CA — expand early childhood programs
1,000,000 Children's Hospital of Los Angeles, Los Angeles, CA — toward construction costs of Imag-

ing and Diagnosis Center
600,000 City of Hope, Los Angeles, CA — support of medical services for children without insurance coverage
529,975 University of San Diego, San Diego, CA
500,000 KCET, Los Angeles, CA
500,000 UCSD, School of Medicine, La Jolla, CA — modernization/expansion of UCSD Medical Center-Hillcrest comp
500,000 USC-Library, Los Angeles, CA — toward library component of 21st Century Campaign
498,917 USD-Regulatory Commission, San Diego, CA — support of Children's Advocacy Institute
441,000 Loyola Marymount University, Los Angeles, CA
424,695 Pepperdine University, Malibu, CA

Weininger Foundation, Richard and Gertrude

CONTACT
Peter Simon
President
Richard and Gertrude Weininger Fdn.
c/o Stroock and Stroock and Lavan
7 Hanover Sq.
New York, NY 10004

FINANCIAL SUMMARY
Recent Giving: $115,000 (fiscal 1991); $113,000 (fiscal 1990); $107,000 (fiscal 1989)
Assets: $2,900,116 (fiscal year ending November 30, 1991); $2,687,694 (fiscal 1990); $2,749,016 (fiscal 1989)
EIN: 13-2362019

CONTRIBUTIONS SUMMARY
Donor(s): the late Gertrude Weininger
Typical Recipients: • *Arts & Humanities:* arts centers, museums/galleries, performing arts • *Education:* colleges & universities, religious education • *Health:* hospitals, medical research • *Religion:* churches, re-

ligious organizations • *Social Services:* community service organizations, youth organizations

Grant Types: general support

GIVING OFFICERS
William Alan Perlmuth: vp, secy *B* New York NY 1929 *ED* Wilkes Coll AB 1951; Columbia Univ LLB 1953 *CURR EMPL* ptnr: Stroock & Stroock & Lavan *CORP AFFIL* dir: Knogo Corp; ptnr: Stroock & Stroock & Lavan *NONPR AFFIL* mem: NY Bar Assn, NY City Bar Assn; trust: Hosp Joint Diseases Orthopedic Inst
Peter Simon: pres
T.J. Stevenson, Jr.: vp, treas

APPLICATION INFORMATION
Initial Approach: Contributes only to preselected organizations.

GRANTS ANALYSIS
Number of Grants: 14
Highest Grant: $18,000
Typical Range: $5,000 to $10,000
Disclosure Period: fiscal year ending November 30, 1991

RECENT GRANTS
18,000　92nd Street Y, New York, NY
15,000　City Parks Foundation, New York, NY
10,000　Hospital for Joint Diseases and Medical Center, New York, NY
10,000　International Sephardic Education Foundation, New York, NY
10,000　Lincoln Center for the Performing Arts, New York, NY
10,000　Museum of Modern Art, New York, NY
10,000　Wilkes College, Wilkes-Barre, PA
5,000　Blumenthal Jewish Home, Winston-Salem, NC
5,000　Georgetown University, Washington, DC
5,000　St. Ann Church, New York, NY

Weinstein Foundation, Alex J.

CONTACT
Alex J. Weinstein Fdn.
c/o Herbert Feinberg
60 Cutter Mill Rd., No. 504
Great Neck, NY 11021
(516) 466-6300

FINANCIAL SUMMARY
Recent Giving: $105,400 (fiscal 1991); $101,250 (fiscal 1990); $95,125 (fiscal 1989)
Assets: $2,526,613 (fiscal year ending November 30, 1991); $2,409,626 (fiscal 1990); $2,280,138 (fiscal 1989)
EIN: 13-6160964

CONTRIBUTIONS SUMMARY
Typical Recipients: • *Arts & Humanities:* performing arts • *Civic & Public Affairs:* women's affairs • *Education:* colleges & universities, legal education • *Health:* hospitals • *Religion:* religious organizations, synagogues
Grant Types: general support

GIVING OFFICERS
Herbert D. Feinberg: trust, dir
Barrie W. Selesko: trust, dir

APPLICATION INFORMATION
Initial Approach: Contributes only to preselected organizations.
Restrictions on Giving: Does not support individuals.

GRANTS ANALYSIS
Number of Grants: 25
Highest Grant: $35,000
Typical Range: $50 to $5,000
Disclosure Period: fiscal year ending November 30, 1991

RECENT GRANTS
35,000　Womens American ORT, New York, NY
10,000　Cornell Law School, Ithaca, NY
10,000　Lehigh University, Bethlehem, PA
10,000　Norwalk Hospital, Norwalk, CT
6,000　Long Island University, Brookville, NY
5,000　Bascom Palmer Eye Institute, Miami, FL
5,000　Community Hospital at Glen Cove, Glen Cove, NY

3,500　New York University Medical Center, New York, NY
2,700　Vitam Center, New York, NY
2,400　North Shore Synagogue, North Shore, NY

Weinstein Foundation, J.

CONTACT
J. Weinstein Fdn.
Rockridge Farm, Rte. 52
Carmel, NY 10512

FINANCIAL SUMMARY
Recent Giving: $147,908 (1991); $120,566 (1990); $259,166 (1989)
Assets: $4,274,720 (1991); $3,739,001 (1990); $3,853,781 (1989)
Gifts Received: $50,000 (1991); $30,000 (1990); $50,000 (1989)
EIN: 11-6003595

CONTRIBUTIONS SUMMARY
Donor(s): the late Joe Weinstein, J. W. Mays
Typical Recipients: • *Arts & Humanities:* museums/galleries • *Civic & Public Affairs:* urban & community affairs • *Education:* colleges & universities • *Health:* hospitals, single-disease health associations • *International:* international organizations • *Religion:* religious organizations, synagogues • *Science:* scientific institutes • *Social Services:* community service organizations, disabled
Grant Types: endowment, general support, and multiyear/continuing support
Geographic Distribution: focus on NY

GIVING OFFICERS
Melvin M. Kazdin: secy, dir
Lloyd J. Shulman: vp, dir *CURR EMPL* pres: JW Mays
Max L. Shulman: pres, dir *B* New York NY 1908 *ED* City Univ NY 1927; Natl Univ 1930 *CURR EMPL* chmn, ceo: JW Mays *CORP AFFIL* chmn, pres: Weinstein Enterprises; pres: Celwyn Co, Gailoyd Enterprises Corp
Sylvia W. Shulman: vp, dir

APPLICATION INFORMATION
Initial Approach: Contributes only to preselected organizations.

GRANTS ANALYSIS
Number of Grants: 38
Highest Grant: $61,551
Typical Range: $25 to $1,000
Disclosure Period: 1991

RECENT GRANTS
61,551　American Committee for the Weizmann Institute of Sciences, New York, NY
29,900　American Friends of the Israel Museum, New York, NY
5,000　Kent Schools Community Playground, Carmel, NY
4,760　Park Avenue Synagogue, New York, NY
2,100　Womens League for Israel, New York, NY
1,350　Putnam Association for Retarded Citizens, Carmel, NY
1,250　Putnam County Humane Society, Carmel, NY
1,000　Lake Carmel Fire Department, Carmel, NY
1,000　New York Branch Orton Dyslexia Society, New York, NY
1,000　Temple Beth Shalom, New York, NY

Weintraub Family Foundation, Joseph
Former Foundation Name: Weintraub-Landfield Charity Foundation

CONTACT
Joseph Weintraub
President
Joseph Weintraub Family Fdn.
200 S.E. 14th St., Ste. 901
Miami, FL 33131

FINANCIAL SUMMARY
Recent Giving: $225,150 (fiscal 1990); $263,211 (fiscal 1989)
Assets: $3,604,020 (fiscal year ending October 31, 1990); $4,992,023 (fiscal 1989)
EIN: 59-0975815

CONTRIBUTIONS SUMMARY

Donor(s): Joseph Weintraub

Typical Recipients: • *Education:* colleges & universities, legal education, medical education • *Health:* hospitals, single-disease health associations • *Religion:* religious organizations, synagogues • *Social Services:* aged, disabled, united funds

Grant Types: general support

GIVING OFFICERS

Hortense Weintraub: treas

Michael Weintraub: pres *B* Miami FL 1938 *ED* Univ VA BA; Univ VA JD *CORP AFFIL* chmn, pres: Gibson Security Corp; dir: Continental Corp, IVAX Corp, Nationsbank Corp *NONPR AFFIL* mem bus adv comm: Univ FL; mem: Am Bankers Assn, Am Bar Assn, Dade County Bar Assn, FL Bankers Assn, FL Bar Assn; mem adv bd: Variety Children's Hosp; trust: Miami Heart Inst, Univ Miami

APPLICATION INFORMATION

Initial Approach: Send brief letter of inquiry describing program or project. There are no deadlines.

GRANTS ANALYSIS

Number of Grants: 17

Highest Grant: $121,300

Typical Range: $100 to $10,000

Disclosure Period: fiscal year ending October 31, 1990

RECENT GRANTS

121,300 University of Miami, Coral Gables, FL

50,000 Mayo Clinic, Rochester, MN

15,000 JESCA

10,000 American Cancer Society

10,000 United Way

5,000 Miami Children's Hospital, Miami, FL

2,500 Boys Clubs of Miami, Miami, FL

2,500 Center for the Performing Arts

2,000 Cedars-Sinai Medical Center, Los Angeles, CA

1,200 Miami Lighthouse for the Blind, Miami, FL

Weir Foundation Trust

CONTACT

Charles D. Weir
Trustee
Weir Fdn Trust
1320 Fenwick Ln., Ste. 700
Silver Spring, MD 20910

FINANCIAL SUMMARY

Recent Giving: $128,190 (1991); $154,250 (1989); $106,850 (1988)

Assets: $2,106,248 (1991); $2,422,227 (1989); $2,177,943 (1988)

EIN: 52-6029328

CONTRIBUTIONS SUMMARY

Donor(s): the late Davis Weir

Typical Recipients: • *Arts & Humanities:* arts centers, community arts, history/historic preservation, museums/galleries • *Civic & Public Affairs:* philanthropic organizations • *Education:* colleges & universities • *Health:* mental health, pediatric health • *Religion:* churches • *Social Services:* community service organizations, community service organizations, food/clothing distribution, recreation & athletics, religious welfare, shelters/homelessness, united funds, youth organizations

Grant Types: capital, endowment, general support, multi-year/continuing support, operating expenses, and project

Geographic Distribution: focus on Washington, DC, MD, and VA

GIVING OFFICERS

Charles D. Weir: trust

APPLICATION INFORMATION

Initial Approach: Contributes only to preselected organizations.

Restrictions on Giving: Does not support individuals.

GRANTS ANALYSIS

Number of Grants: 56

Highest Grant: $23,020

Typical Range: $250 to $3,000

Disclosure Period: 1991

RECENT GRANTS

23,020 Boys and Girls Club, Silver Spring, MD

21,800 Bradley Hills Presbyterian Church, Bethesda, MD

9,500 Walters Art Gallery, Baltimore, MD

5,000 Service to Youth Awards, Silver Spring, MD

4,000 Baldwin Memorial United Methodist Church, Millersville, MD

3,550 Meals on Wheels, Baltimore, MD

3,500 Salvation Army, Austin, TX

3,000 Johns Hopkins Hospital Dementia Research, Baltimore, MD

3,000 Pyramid Atlantic, Riverdale, MD

2,500 Washington Charitable Fund, Silver Spring, MD

Weirton Steel Corp.

Sales: $1.03 billion

Employees: 6,979

Headquarters: Weirton, WV

SIC Major Group: Fabricated Metal Products and Primary Metal Industries

CONTACT

Charles Cronin
Director, Public Relations
Weirton Steel Corp.
400 Three Springs Dr.
Weirton, WV 26062
(304) 797-2000

CONTRIBUTIONS SUMMARY

Operating Locations: WV (Weirton)

CORP. OFFICERS

Herbert Elish: *CURR EMPL* chmn, pres, ceo: Weirton Steel Corp

Weisbrod Foundation Trust Dept., Robert and Mary

CONTACT

Robert and Mary Weisbrod Fdn Trust Dept.
c/o Integra Trust Company, N.A.
Pittsburgh, PA 15278

FINANCIAL SUMMARY

Recent Giving: $450,629 (1991); $454,715 (1990); $453,000 (1989)

Assets: $9,291,725 (1991); $8,200,824 (1990); $8,088,263 (1989)

Gifts Received: $146,569 (1991)

Fiscal Note: In 1991, contributions were received from Mary Weisbrod for Clayton and Dorothy Weisbrod.

EIN: 25-6105924

CONTRIBUTIONS SUMMARY

Donor(s): the late Mary E. Weisbrod

Typical Recipients: • *Arts & Humanities:* community arts, music, opera, theater • *Education:* special education • *Health:* hospitals, single-disease health associations • *Religion:* churches • *Social Services:* child welfare, community service organizations, disabled, shelters/homelessness, youth organizations

Grant Types: capital

Geographic Distribution: focus on the Pittsburgh, PA, area

GIVING OFFICERS

Integra Bank/Pittsburgh: trust

John R. Echement: off *B* Pittsburgh PA 1935 *CURR EMPL* exec vp, treas: Union Natl Corp *CORP AFFIL* exec vp: Integra Fin Corp; exec vp, treas: Union Natl Corp

Donald L. McCaskey: off

APPLICATION INFORMATION

Initial Approach: Send cover letter and full proposal. There are no deadlines.

GRANTS ANALYSIS

Number of Grants: 26

Highest Grant: $100,000

Typical Range: $1,000 to $25,000

Disclosure Period: 1991

RECENT GRANTS

100,000 Greater Pittsburgh Guild for the Blind, Bridgeville, PA

30,000 ARC Allegheny County, Pittsburgh, PA

25,000 City Theatre Company, Pittsburgh, PA

25,000 Manchester Youth Development Center, Pittsburgh, PA

25,000 Point Park College, Pittsburgh, PA

25,000 Smithfield United Church, Pittsburgh, PA

25,000 Try Again Homes, Washington, PA

25,000 West Pennsylvania School for the Deaf, Pittsburgh, PA

20,000 D.T. Watson Reha-
bilitation Services,
Sewickley, PA

20,000 Spina Bifida Asso-
ciation of West
Pennsylvania, Pitts-
burgh, PA

Weisman Art Foundation, Frederick R.

Former Foundation Name:
Frederick R. Weisman
Collection

CONTACT

Mitchell L. Reinschreiber
Executive Vice President and
CFO
Frederick R. Weisman Art Fdn.
10350 Santa Monica Blvd., Ste.
340
Los Angeles, CA 90025
(310) 553-8191

FINANCIAL SUMMARY

Recent Giving: $1,740,746
(fiscal 1991); $654,556 (fiscal
1990)
Assets: $22,895,790 (fiscal
year ending January 31, 1991);
$15,765,734 (fiscal 1990)
Gifts Received: $2,561,000
(fiscal 1991); $4,019,971 (fis-
cal 1990)
Fiscal Note: In 1991, contributions were received from the
Frederick Weisman Company
and the Frederick R. Weisman
Philanthropic Foundation.
EIN: 95-3767861

CONTRIBUTIONS SUMMARY

Donor(s): The foundation was
established in by Frederick R.
Weisman and Frederick Weisman Co.
Typical Recipients: • *Arts &
Humanities:* arts appreciation,
arts associations, arts centers,
arts institutes, museums/galler-
ies, visual arts • *Civic & Public
Affairs:* philanthropic organizations
Grant Types: general support
and research

GIVING OFFICERS

Henry Tyler Hopkins: exec
vp, trust *B* Idaho Falls ID 1928
ED Sch Art Inst BA 1952; Sch
Art Inst MA 1955 *NONPR
AFFIL* mem: Am Assn Muse-
ums, Assn Art Mus Dirs, Coll
Art Assn Am
Billie Milam: trust
Judith Pisar: trust
Mitchell L. Reinschreiber:
exec vp, cfo, trust

Lee Larssen Romaniello:
secy, trust
Edward Ruscha: trust *B*
Omaha NE 1937 *ED* Chouinard
Art Inst
Frederick R. Weisman: don *B*
1913 *CURR EMPL* pres, dir:
Frederick Weisman Co
Marcia S. Weisman: trust
Milton Wexler: trust

APPLICATION INFORMATION

Initial Approach: The foundation requests applications be
submitted in writing detailing
the purpose of the organization
seeking the grant.
Deadlines: The foundation has
no deadline for submitting proposals.
Note: The foundation makes
grants to improve the public's
understanding of modern art.

OTHER THINGS TO KNOW

Publications: occasional report

GRANTS ANALYSIS

Number of Grants: 27
Highest Grant: $816,791
Typical Range: $1,000 to
$1,800
Disclosure Period: fiscal year
ending January 31, 1991

RECENT GRANTS

816,791 San Diego Mu-
seum of Art, San
Diego, CA

600,000 University of Minnesota Foundation,
Minneapolis, MN

51,120 Birmingham Mu-
seum of Art, Bir-
mingham, AL

50,000 Contemporary Mu-
seum, Honolulu, HI

50,000 Menil Collection,
Houston, TX

50,000 Museum of Con-
temporary Art, Los
Angeles, CA

50,000 Whitney Museum
of American Art,
New York, NY

16,667 Israel Museum, Je-
rusalem, Israel

14,130 San Antonio Mu-
seum Association,
San Antonio, TX

12,273 Albuquerque Mu-
seum, Albuquer-
que, NM

Weiss Foundation, Stephen and Suzanne

CONTACT

Stephen Weiss
President
Stephen and Suzanne Weiss Fdn.
One New York Plz.
New York, NY 10004
(212) 908-9512

FINANCIAL SUMMARY

Recent Giving: $401,504
(1991); $39,010 (1990);
$134,121 (1989)
Assets: $3,200,175 (1991);
$2,797,236 (1990); $2,699,222
(1989)
Gifts Received: $1,450 (1991)
Fiscal Note: In 1991, contribu-
tions were received from
Stephen H. Weiss.
EIN: 13-3384021

CONTRIBUTIONS SUMMARY

Donor(s): Stephen Weiss
Typical Recipients: • *Arts &
Humanities:* arts centers,
dance, museums/galleries,
opera • *Civic & Public Affairs:*
philanthropic organizations
• *Education:* colleges & universities, private education (precollege) • *Health:* hospitals,
medical research, single-disease health associations • *Religion:* religious organizations
• *Social Services:* community
centers, community service organizations, recreation & athletics, youth organizations
Grant Types: general support
and research
Geographic Distribution:
focus on New York, NY

GIVING OFFICERS

Roger J. Weiss: secy, treas
Stephen Weiss: pres
Suzanne Weiss: vp

APPLICATION INFORMATION

Initial Approach: Contributes
only to preselected organizations.
Restrictions on Giving: Does
not support individuals.

GRANTS ANALYSIS

Number of Grants: 27
Highest Grant: $2,000
Typical Range: $25 to $1,000
Disclosure Period: 1991
Note: 1991 grants list was in-
complete.

RECENT GRANTS

2,000 Cambridge Col-
lege, Cambridge,
MA

2,000 Children's Mu-
seum of Manhat-
tan, New York, NY

1,500 Metropolitan
Opera, New York,
NY

1,000 Carson Newman
College, Jefferson
City, TN

1,000 Cystic Fibrosis
Foundation, New
York, NY

1,000 East Side Interna-
tional Community
Center, New York,
NY

1,000 National Associa-
tion for Southern
Poor

1,000 Nich and Marc
Buoniconti Fund,
Miami, FL

1,000 San Francisco Bal-
let, San Francisco,
CA

500 Jewish Guild for
the Blind, New
York, NY

Weiss Foundation, William E.

CONTACT

William E. Weiss Fdn.
3510 North Lake Creek Dr.
Jackson, WY 83001
(307) 733-1680

FINANCIAL SUMMARY

Recent Giving: $235,000 (fis-
cal 1992); $129,300 (fiscal
1991); $180,000 (fiscal 1990)
Assets: $5,508,758 (fiscal year
ending March 31, 1992);
$5,002,323 (fiscal 1991);
$4,396,813 (fiscal 1990)
EIN: 55-6016633

CONTRIBUTIONS SUMMARY

Donor(s): the late William E.
Weiss, Jr., the late Helene K
Brown
Typical Recipients: • *Arts &
Humanities:* history/historic
preservation, museums/galler-
ies, music • *Civic & Public Affairs:* environmental affairs
• *Education:* colleges & universities, private education (precollege), public education (precollege), science/technology
education • *Health:* mental
health • *Religion:* churches
• *Social Services:* food/cloth-
ing distribution, shelters/home-
lessness, united funds, youth organizations

Grant Types: capital, general support, multiyear/continuing support, project, and scholarship
Geographic Distribution: focus on NY, WV, and WY

GIVING OFFICERS
P. W. T. Brown: treas, dir
Lulu Hughes: secy, dir
Daryl Brown Uber: vp, dir
Mary K. Weiss: dir
William D. Weiss: pres, dir

APPLICATION INFORMATION
Initial Approach: Contributes only to preselected organizations.
Restrictions on Giving: Does not support individuals.

OTHER THINGS TO KNOW
Publications: Application Guidelines

GRANTS ANALYSIS
Number of Grants: 25
Highest Grant: $45,000
Typical Range: $2,000 to $10,000
Disclosure Period: fiscal year ending March 31, 1992

RECENT GRANTS
45,000 Buffalo Bill Memorial Association, Cody, WY
32,500 Buffalo Bill Historical Center, Cody, WY
30,000 Housatonic Mental Health Institute, Lakeville, CT
25,000 Teton Science School, Kelly, WY
23,000 Victorian Wheeling Foundation, Wheeling, WV
10,000 Center for Marine Conservation, Washington, DC
10,000 University of Wyoming, Laramie, WY
7,500 Partnership for the Homeless, New York, NY
5,000 Starlight Foundation, Boston, MA
5,000 Wildlife of American West Museum, Jackson, WY

Weiss Fund, Clara

CONTACT
David C. Weiss
Manager
Clara Weiss Fund
2225 Marks Rd.
Valley City, OH 44280
(216) 225-8514

FINANCIAL SUMMARY
Recent Giving: $90,700 (1991); $91,120 (1990); $90,820 (1989)
Assets: $2,190,735 (1991); $1,879,284 (1990); $2,011,413 (1989)
EIN: 34-6556158

CONTRIBUTIONS SUMMARY
Donor(s): L. C. Weiss, Mrs. L. C. Weiss
Typical Recipients: • *Education:* colleges & universities, private education (precollege) • *Health:* hospices, hospitals, medical research, single-disease health associations • *Social Services:* child welfare, community service organizations, disabled, family planning, homes, united funds, youth organizations
Grant Types: general support
Geographic Distribution: Provides grants in the Cleveland, OH, area

GIVING OFFICERS
Arthur D. Weiss: trust
David C. Weiss: trust, mgr
Robert L. Weiss: trust

APPLICATION INFORMATION
Initial Approach: Send brief letter describing program. There are no deadlines.
Restrictions on Giving: Does not support individuals.

GRANTS ANALYSIS
Number of Grants: 120
Highest Grant: $2,500
Typical Range: $100 to $1,000
Disclosure Period: 1991

RECENT GRANTS
2,500 Lake Ridge Academy, North Ridgeville, OH
2,500 Powhatan School, Boyce, VA
2,000 Holy Family Home
2,000 Hospice of Wayne County, Wooster, OH
1,500 Larlham Foundation, The Hattie
1,200 Project Hope, Boston, MA
1,000 Fairview General Hospital, Wooster, OH
1,000 Goodwill Industries
1,000 Goodwill Industries, Akron, OH
1,000 Planned Parenthood Federation of America

Weisz Foundation, David and Sylvia

CONTACT
Jay Grodin
Secretary
David and Sylvia Weisz Fdn.
1933 Broadway, Rm. 244
Los Angeles, CA 90007
(213) 749-7911

FINANCIAL SUMMARY
Recent Giving: $459,166 (fiscal 1992); $503,517 (fiscal 1991); $545,017 (fiscal 1990)
Assets: $5,578,441 (fiscal year ending October 31, 1991); $6,611,372 (fiscal 1990); $6,883,627 (fiscal 1989)
EIN: 95-3551424

CONTRIBUTIONS SUMMARY
Typical Recipients: • *Arts & Humanities:* museums/galleries, music, public broadcasting • *Education:* colleges & universities, religious education • *Health:* health organizations, hospitals, medical research, single-disease health associations • *Religion:* religious organizations, synagogues • *Social Services:* aged, religious welfare, united funds, youth organizations
Grant Types: general support

GIVING OFFICERS
Jay Grodin: secy, dir
Sylvia Weisz Hirschfield: pres, dir
Louis Leviton: treas, asst secy

APPLICATION INFORMATION
Initial Approach: The foundation reports it only makes contributions to preselected charitable organizations.

GRANTS ANALYSIS
Number of Grants: 48
Highest Grant: $202,650
Typical Range: $500 to $10,000
Disclosure Period: fiscal year ending October 31, 1991

RECENT GRANTS
202,650 Cedars-Sinai Medical Center, Los Angeles, CA
56,500 United Jewish Appeal Federation of Jewish Philanthropies, Los Angeles, CA
26,667 Operation Exodus, Los Angeles, CA
25,000 Music Center, Los Angeles, CA
20,200 Hebrew University, Los Angeles, CA
20,000 Los Angeles Free Clinic, Los Angeles, CA
11,000 Eye Research, Los Angeles, CA
10,000 City of Hope, Los Angeles, CA
10,000 Otis Parsons, Los Angeles, CA
10,000 Temple Israel, Los Angeles, CA

Weitz Corp.

Revenue: $470.0 million
Employees: 550
Headquarters: Des Moines, IA
SIC Major Group: General Building Contractors, Holding & Other Investment Offices, and Real Estate

CONTACT
Marilyn Wilson
Secretary to the CEO
Weitz Corp.
800 2nd Ave.
Des Moines, IA 50309
(515) 245-7600

CONTRIBUTIONS SUMMARY
Operating Locations: IA (Des Moines)

CORP. OFFICERS
Fred W. Weitz: *CURR EMPL* chmn, pres, ceo: Weitz Corp

RECENT GRANTS
George Washington University, Washington, DC

Welch Foods

Sales: $150.0 million
Employees: 1,200
Parent Company: National Grape Co-operative Association
Headquarters: Concord, MA
SIC Major Group: Food & Kindred Products

CONTACT
James Weidman III
Vice President, Corporate
  Communications
Welch Foods
100 Main St.
Concord, MA 01742
(508) 371-1000

CONTRIBUTIONS SUMMARY
Company sponsors employee
matching gift program; also
supports community organiza-
tions.
Typical Recipients: • *Arts &
Humanities:* general • *Civic &
Public Affairs:* general • *Educa-
tion:* general • *Health:* general
• *Social Services:* general
Grant Types: matching
Geographic Distribution: pri-
marily headquarters area

CORP. OFFICERS
Everett N. Baldwin: *CURR
EMPL* pres, ceo: Welch Foods

APPLICATION INFORMATION
Initial Approach: Send brief
letter of inquiry. There are no
deadlines.

Welch Foundation, Robert A.

CONTACT
Norbert Dittrich
Executive Manager
Robert A. Welch Foundation
4605 Post Oak Pl., Ste. 200
Houston, TX 77027
(713) 961-9884

FINANCIAL SUMMARY
Recent Giving: $13,897,895
(fiscal 1992); $12,753,527 (fis-
cal 1991); $12,617,545 (fiscal
1990)
Assets: $332,901,274 (fiscal
year ending August 31, 1992);
$302,765,612 (fiscal 1991);
$259,915,425 (fiscal 1990)
EIN: 74-1216248

CONTRIBUTIONS SUMMARY
Donor(s): Robert Alonzo
Welch, founder of the foundation, demonstrated a strong at-
tachment to the Texas community in which he made his
fortune. The Robert A. Welch
Foundation began operating in
1954 with funds from the will
of the founder.
Typical Recipients: • *Education:* science/technology education

Grant Types: award, confer-
ence/seminar, fellowship, and
research
Geographic Distribution: limited to Texas

GIVING OFFICERS
J. Evans Attwell: secy, dir
Norbert Dittrich: asst treas,
asst secy, exec mgr
Charles William Duncan, Jr.:
trust *B* Houston TX 1926 *ED*
Rice Univ BSCheE 1947; Univ
TX 1948-1949 *CORP AFFIL*
dir: Am Express Co, Chem
Banking Corp, Coca-Cola Co,
Panhandle Eastern Corp, TX
Commerce BancShares, Un
Tech Corp *NONPR AFFIL*
chmn bd trusts: Rice Univ;
mem: Counc Foreign Rels,
Sigma Alpha Epsilon, Sigma
Iota Epsilon; trust: Brookings
Inst
Dennis Ralph Hendrix: treas,
dir *B* Selmer TN 1940 *ED* Univ
TN BS 1962; GA St Univ MBA
1965 *CORP AFFIL* chmn, pres,
ceo: TX Eastern Corp; dir:
First City Bancorp TX; pres,
ceo, chmn, dir: Panhandle East-
ern Corp *NONPR AFFIL* dir:
Am Petroleum Inst, DePelchin
Childrens Ctr, Greater Houston
Partnership, Harris Co Chil-
drens Protective Svcs Fund,
Natl Jr Achievement, Natl
Ocean Indus Assn, TX Med
Ctr, TX South Coast Un Way,
Univ TN Devel Counc; mem:
Interstate Natural Gas Assn
Am, Natl Petroleum Counc,
TX Dept Corrections; mem adv
bd bus sch: GA St Univ; mem,
dir: Am Gas Assn, Counc
Higher Ed, Natl Assn Mfrs;
trust: Brescia Coll
Richard J. V. Johnson: pres,
dir *B* San Luis Potosi Mexico
1930 *ED* Univ TX BBA 1954
CURR EMPL pres, publ, dir:
Houston Chronicle Publ Co
CORP AFFIL dir: Am Gen
Corp, Mutual Ins Co Ltd,
Newspaper Advertising Bur,
TX Commerce Bank *NONPR
AFFIL* chmn bd visitors: Meth-
odist Hosp, Univ Cancer Fdn
MD Anderson Hosp Tumor
Inst; dir: Greater Houston Part-
nership, Soc Performing Arts,
TX Med Ctr; mem: Am News-
paper Publs Assn, Houston
Chamber Commerce, TX Daily
Newspaper Assn; trust: Un
Way TX Gulf Coast
Jack S. Josey: pres emeritus,
dir *B* Beaumont TX 1916 *ED*
Univ TX 1939 *CURR EMPL*
chmn, pres: Josey Oil Co
NONPR AFFIL dir: Univ TX

Fdn; lay dir: Physical Medicine
Rehab Ed Res Fdn; mem: Univ
TX Chancellors Counc, Univ
TX Ex-Students Assn, Univ TX
Excellence Comm; mem collec-
tor's comm: Natl Gallery Art;
mem dev bd: Univ TX Health
Ctr

APPLICATION INFORMATION
Initial Approach:
Application forms must be requested from the foundation.
Applications should include a
cover page with scientific summary, description of the project, biographical sketch of the
applicant, bibliography of the
applicant, and budget.
Applications for up to three
years of support may be submitted any time, but must be received by February 1 to be considered for the next grant year
(June 1-May 31).
The foundation will respond to
all grant applications. The foundation officers will transmit to
the scientific advisory board
all nominations received prior
to the deadline.
Restrictions on Giving: Applicants are restricted to universities, colleges, or other educational institutions within Texas.

OTHER THINGS TO KNOW
In addition to making grants,
foundation sponsors conferences and seminars/workshops.

GRANTS ANALYSIS
Total Grants: $13,897,895
Number of Grants: 335*
Highest Grant: $60,000*
Typical Range: $25,000 to
$60,000
Disclosure Period: fiscal year
ending August 31, 1992
Note: The figures for number
of grants, average grant, and
highest grant are from fiscal
1991. Recent grants are derived from a fiscal 1992 annual
report.

RECENT GRANTS
Baylor College of Medicine,
Houston, TX — Molecular
Immune Recognition of
Lysozyme
Baylor College of Medicine,
Houston, TX — Small Nuclear
Ribonucleoproteins
Baylor College of Medicine,
Houston, TX — The Role of
GTP Binding and Hydrolysis

Cycles in Regulating
Chromosome Structure
Southern Methodist University,
Dallas, TX — Synthesis of
Polycyclics by the Tandem
Addition-Rearrangement
Aryne Reaction
Texas A&M University, College
Station, TX — Chemisorption
and Growth on Semiconductor
Surfaces
Texas A&M University, College
Station, TX — Dating &
Chemical Characterization of
Rock Paintings
Texas A&M University, College
Station, TX — Interactions of
a Flavin Monooxygenase with
the Flavin Substrate
Texas A&M University, College
Station, TX — Ligand Control
of Reactivity in
Organometallic Chemistry
Texas A&M University, College
Station, TX — On the Kinetics
of Certain Electrode Reactions
Texas A&M University, College
Station, TX —
Photochemically Triggered
1,4-Diyl Formation: Design
and Applications

Welch Testamentary Trust, George T.

CONTACT
Bettie Loiacono
Assistant Vice President
George T. Welch Testamentary
  Trust
c/o Baker Boyer National Bank
PO Box 1796
Walla Walla, WA 99362
(509) 525-2000

FINANCIAL SUMMARY
Recent Giving: $184,983 (fis-
cal 1991); $155,859 (fiscal
1990); $149,234 (fiscal 1989)
Assets: $3,230,013 (fiscal year
ending September 30, 1991);
$2,866,194 (fiscal 1990);
$2,895,473 (fiscal 1989)
Gifts Received: $3,000 (fiscal
1991)
Fiscal Note: In 1991, contributions were received from Dennis L. King ($1,500), and the
Pelo Foundation ($1,500).
EIN: 91-6024318

CONTRIBUTIONS SUMMARY
Typical Recipients: • *Arts &
Humanities:* arts centers, com-
munity arts, dance, history/his-
toric preservation, libraries
• *Education:* colleges & univer-

sities, community & junior colleges, literacy • *Social Services:* child welfare, community service organizations, day care, family planning, food/clothing distribution, homes, recreation & athletics, shelters/homelessness

Grant Types: project and scholarship

Geographic Distribution: limited to Walla Walla County, WA

GIVING OFFICERS
Baker Boyer National Bank: trust

APPLICATION INFORMATION
Initial Approach: Send letter stating academic plans and financial resources. Deadline is May 1.

OTHER THINGS TO KNOW
Provides medical assistance and scholarships to individuals.
Publications: Application Guidelines

GRANTS ANALYSIS
Number of Grants: 12
Highest Grant: $20,000
Typical Range: $500 to $3,500
Disclosure Period: fiscal year ending September 30, 1991
Note: 1991 figures do not include $142,401 in grants to individuals.

RECENT GRANTS
20,000 Walla Walla Community College, Walla Walla, WA
4,000 Wildwood Park Project, Walla Walla, WA
3,750 Project Read of Walla Walla, Walla Walla, WA
3,650 Blue Mountain Area Foundation, Walla Walla, WA
2,315 Walla Walla Dance, Walla Walla, WA
2,200 Educare Center, Walla Walla, WA
1,780 Carnegie Art Center, Walla Walla, WA
1,575 Children's Home Society, Walla Walla, WA
1,500 Planned Parenthood Federation of America, Walla Walla, WA
1,050 Altrusa Club, Walla Walla, WA

Welfare Foundation

CONTACT
David Wakefield
Executive Secretary
Welfare Foundation
1004 Wilmington Trust Center
Wilmington, DE 19801
(302) 654-2477

FINANCIAL SUMMARY
Recent Giving: $2,000,000 (1993 est.); $2,000,000 (1992 approx.); $2,235,000 (1991)
Assets: $53,000,000 (1993 est.); $53,000,000 (1992 est.); $60,334,555 (1991); $37,489,892 (1990)
EIN: 51-6015916

CONTRIBUTIONS SUMMARY
Donor(s): The foundation was established in 1930 by the Pierre Samuel du Pont (d. 1954) to support initial plans for a public secondary school system. When that project was completed, the foundation turned its support to the community at large.
Du Pont family members are the descendants of Pierre Samuel du Pont de Nemours (1739-1817), a Frenchman who emigrated to America in 1800. His son, Eleuthere Irenee, founded a gunpowder factory in 1801 which was the precursor to E. I. du Pont de Nemours & Company, a manufacturer of chemicals, plastics, fibers, and specialty products. Edward B. du Pont, a treasurer of the foundation, is a director of the company.
Typical Recipients: • *Arts & Humanities:* libraries, museums/galleries • *Civic & Public Affairs:* environmental affairs • *Education:* colleges & universities, private education (precollege) • *Social Services:* aged, child welfare, community centers, counseling, day care, disabled, united funds, youth organizations
Grant Types: capital
Geographic Distribution: Delaware, with emphasis on the greater Wilmington area

GIVING OFFICERS
Robert C. Barlow: asst secy
Robert H. Bolling, Jr.: pres, trust *ED* Princeton Univ 1948 *CORP AFFIL* dir: Wilmington Trust Co
J. Simpson Dean, Jr.: vp, trust

Edward Bradford du Pont: treas, trust *B* Wilmington DE 1934 *ED* Yale Univ ED 1956; Harvard Univ MBA 1959 *CURR EMPL* chmn, dir: Atlantic Aviation Corp *CORP AFFIL* dir: EI du Pont de Nemours & Co; vp: Wilmington Trust Co *NONPR AFFIL* treas: Red Clay Reservation; trust: Easter Corp, Eleutherian Mills-Hagley Fdn, Hagley Mus & Library *PHIL AFFIL* treas, trust: Red Clay Reservation
Stephen A. Martinenza: asst treas
Mrs. W. Laird Stabler, Jr.: secy, trust
David Wakefield: exec secy

APPLICATION INFORMATION
Initial Approach:
Applicants should send a preliminary letter to the foundation.
Letters should state the reason for the grant request, and include pertinent financial statements and a copy of an IRS tax-exempt status letter.
The deadlines for submitting proposals are April 15 and November 1.

GRANTS ANALYSIS
Total Grants: $2,000,000*
Number of Grants: 45
Highest Grant: $100,000
Typical Range: $10,000 to $50,000
Disclosure Period: 1992
Note: Total grants figure is an estimate supplied by the foundation. Recent grants are derived from a 1991 grants list.

RECENT GRANTS
125,000 Boys Clubs of Delaware, Wilmington, DE — capital campaign
100,000 Brandywine Conservancy, Chadds Ford, PA — capital campaign
100,000 Community Legal Aid Society, Wilmington, DE — capital campaign
100,000 Delaware State College, Dover, DE — capital campaign
100,000 Middletown-Odessa-Townsend Senior Center, Middletown, DE — capital campaign
100,000 Opportunity Center, Wilmington, DE — capital campaign

75,000 Delaware Theatre Company, Wilmington, DE — endowment campaign
75,000 Hockessin Public Library, Hockessin, DE — capital campaign
75,000 Kent-Sussex Industries, Milford, DE — capital campaign
75,000 Wilmington Garden Center, Wilmington, DE — capital campaign

Weller Foundation

CONTACT
Weller Fdn.
East Hwy. 20
PO Box 636
Atkinson, NE 68713
(402) 925-2803

FINANCIAL SUMMARY
Recent Giving: $188,681 (fiscal 1991); $118,000 (fiscal 1990); $151,750 (fiscal 1989)
Assets: $3,781,949 (fiscal year ending October 31, 1991); $3,711,342 (fiscal 1990); $3,547,021 (fiscal 1989)
EIN: 47-0611350

CONTRIBUTIONS SUMMARY
Donor(s): E. C. Weller, Frances W. Weller
Typical Recipients: • *Education:* career/vocational education, medical education
Grant Types: scholarship
Geographic Distribution: focus on residents of Hot, Boyd, Brown, Rock, Keya Paha, and Garlield counties.

GIVING OFFICERS
Robert Clifford: vp
Dean Fleming: secy, treas
Clayton Goeke: dir
Ernest J. Gottschalk: pres
Paul Possnecker: dir
Robert Randall: dir
Frances W. Weller: dir

APPLICATION INFORMATION
Initial Approach: Application form required. Deadlines are June 1 for the Fall semester and November 1 for the Spring semester. Decisions are made within 30 days of the deadlines.
Restrictions on Giving: Does not provide grants for scholarships for education toward a Bachelor's degree.

OTHER THINGS TO KNOW

Provides scholarships for students attending technical community colleges in NE, particularly for nursing students.
Publications: Application Guidelines

Wellman Inc.

Sales: $805.7 million
Employees: 3,400
Headquarters: Shrewsbury, NJ
SIC Major Group: Chemicals & Allied Products, Textile Mill Products, and Wholesale Trade—Durable Goods

CONTACT

Frances Owens
Benefits Manager
Wellman Inc.
1040 Broad St.
Shrewsbury, NJ 07702
(908) 542-7300

CONTRIBUTIONS SUMMARY

Operating Locations: NJ (Shrewsbury)

CORP. OFFICERS

Thomas M. Duff: *CURR EMPL* pres, ceo: Wellman

Wellman Foundation, S. K.

CONTACT

R. Dugald Perrson
Executive Secretary
S. K. Wellman Fdn.
Leader Bldg., Rm. 548
Cleveland, OH 44114
(216) 696-4640

FINANCIAL SUMMARY

Recent Giving: $421,500 (1991); $356,000 (1989); $341,000 (1988)
Assets: $8,697,310 (1991); $7,743,755 (1989); $7,594,297 (1988)
EIN: 34-6520032

CONTRIBUTIONS SUMMARY

Donor(s): the late S. K. Wellman
Typical Recipients: • *Arts & Humanities:* arts institutes, community arts, history/historic preservation, museums/galleries • *Civic & Public Affairs:* environmental affairs, rural affairs • *Education:* colleges & universities, private education (precollege)

• *Health:* health organizations, medical research, pediatric health, single-disease health associations • *Social Services:* animal protection, child welfare, community service organizations
Grant Types: general support
Geographic Distribution: focus on OH

GIVING OFFICERS

Franklin B. Floyd: trust
Suzanne O'Gara: trust
R. Dugald Pearson: exec secy
John M. Wilson, Jr.: pres, trust
John M. Wilson, Jr.: pres, trust (see above)
Patricia W. Wilson: trust

APPLICATION INFORMATION

Initial Approach: Send brief letter of inquiry describing program or project. Deadline is December 31.
Restrictions on Giving: Does not support individuals.

OTHER THINGS TO KNOW

Publications: Application Guidelines

GRANTS ANALYSIS

Number of Grants: 79
Highest Grant: $24,000
Typical Range: $500 to $10,000
Disclosure Period: 1991

RECENT GRANTS

24,000 University School, Shaker Heights, OH
24,000 Wildlife Management Institute, Washington, DC
20,000 Home Health Care, Beachwood, OH
15,000 Bellefaire-Jewish Children's Bureau, Cleveland Heights, OH
15,000 Case Western Reserve University, Cleveland, OH
15,000 Cleveland Eye Bank, Cleveland, OH
15,000 Cleveland Institute of Art, Cleveland, OH
15,000 Cleveland Museum of Natural History, Cleveland, OH
15,000 Hale Farm and Village, Bath, OH
15,000 Nature Conservancy, Arlington, VA

Wellons Foundation

CONTACT

John H. Wellons, Sr.
President
Wellons Fdn.
PO Box 1254
Dunn, NC 28334
(919) 892-3123

FINANCIAL SUMMARY

Recent Giving: $21,703 (1991); $33,406 (1990); $25,195 (1989)
Assets: $2,232,006 (1991); $2,059,408 (1990); $2,020,997 (1989)
Gifts Received: $54,290 (1991); $35,388 (1990); $66,515 (1989)
EIN: 56-6061476

CONTRIBUTIONS SUMMARY

Typical Recipients: • *Civic & Public Affairs:* municipalities, public policy • *Education:* colleges & universities, religious education • *Religion:* religious organizations • *Social Services:* homes
Grant Types: loan

GIVING OFFICERS

Sylvia W. Craft: dir
Gene T. Jernigan: dir
Llewellyn Jernigan: dir
Donald Richard McCoy: dir, secy *B* Chicago IL 1928 *ED* Univ Denver BA 1949; Univ Chicago MA 1949; Am Univ PhD 1954 *NONPR AFFIL* fellow: Soc Am Archivists; mem: Am Historical Assn, KS Historical Soc, Org Am Historians; prof history: Univ KS
John H. Wellons, Jr.: dir, vp
John H. Wellons, Sr.: dir, pres

APPLICATION INFORMATION

Initial Approach: Application form required. There are no deadlines.

GRANTS ANALYSIS

Number of Grants: 19
Highest Grant: $11,275
Disclosure Period: 1991

RECENT GRANTS

11,275 Gospel Tabernacle, NC
5,000 Mount Olive College, Mount Olive, NC
2,500 Caramore Community, Caramore, NC
550 Christian Coalition, NC
300 Friends Home, NC

250 Emmanuel College, Mount Olive, NC
250 Oral Roberts University, Tulsa, OK
200 First Pentacostal Holiness, NC
200 Youth for Christ, NC
125 Gideons, NC

Wells Fargo & Co. / Wells Fargo Foundation

Assets: $52.53 billion
Employees: 21,300
Headquarters: San Francisco, CA
SIC Major Group: Depository Institutions and Holding & Other Investment Offices

CONTACT

Karen Wegmann
President
Wells Fargo Fdn.
420 Montgomery St.
San Francisco, CA 94163
(415) 396-3832
Note: Another contact address is Wells Fargo Community Development, Contributions Program, 394 Pacific Ave., 0107-033, San Francisco, CA 94163, (415) 396-3567 or (415) 396-5830.

FINANCIAL SUMMARY

Recent Giving: $4,200,000 (1993 est.); $6,685,000 (1992); $6,600,000 (1991)
Assets: $1,098,000 (1992); $2,600,000 (1991); $3,093,939 (1989)
Fiscal Note: Above figures include both foundation and direct giving. In 1992, the foundation gave $2,502,245. Other company departments also make contributions direclty form company funds. It is not included in above totals. There are various contact persons. Contact foundation for more information.
EIN: 94-2549743

CONTRIBUTIONS SUMMARY

Typical Recipients: • *Arts & Humanities:* performing arts • *Civic & Public Affairs:* economic development, housing, urban & community affairs • *Education:* business education, career/vocational education, economic education, education funds, elementary education, minority education, public education (precollege) • *Health:* single-disease health

associations • *Social Services:* aged, child welfare, community service organizations, disabled, employment/job training, family services, food/clothing distribution, united funds, volunteer services, youth organizations
Grant Types: challenge, employee matching gifts, general support, and project
Nonmonetary Support Types: cause-related marketing & promotion, donated equipment, donated products, and in-kind services
Note: Estimated value of nonmonetary support is unavailable and is not included in above figures.
Geographic Distribution: California communities where bank has offices
Operating Locations: CA, CO (Denver, Englewood), TX (Dallas, Houston, San Antonio)

CORP. OFFICERS
Michael Gillfillan: *CURR EMPL* vchmn: Wells Fargo & Co
Paul Mandeville Hazen: *B* Lansing MI 1941 *ED* Univ AZ BS 1963; Univ CA Berkeley MBA 1964 *CURR EMPL* pres, coo, dir: Wells Fargo & Co *CORP AFFIL* dir: Pacific Telesis Group, Phelps Dodge Corp, Safeway; pres, dir: Wells Fargo Bank; trust: Wells Fargo Mortgage & Equity Trust
Rodney Jacobs: *CURR EMPL* vchmn: Wells Fargo & Co
Charles M. Johnson: *B* 1941 *ED* OH St Univ BS 1963; Stanford Univ MA 1978 *CURR EMPL* vchmn: Wells Fargo & Co
Robert L. Joss: *CURR EMPL* vchmn: Wells Fargo & Co *CORP AFFIL* vchmn: Wells Fargo Bank
Clyde Ostler: *B* 1947 *CURR EMPL* vchmn: Wells Fargo & Co
Carl E. Reichardt: *B* Houston TX 1931 *ED* Univ Southern CA AB 1956; Stanford Univ 1965; Northwestern Univ 1965 *CURR EMPL* chmn, ceo, dir: Wells Fargo & Co *CORP AFFIL* chmn, ceo, dir: Wells Fargo Bank
William F. Zuendt: *B* 1946 *ED* Rensselaer Polytech Inst BA 1968; Stanford Univ MBA 1973 *CURR EMPL* vchmn, exec vp: Wells Fargo & Co *CORP AFFIL* vchmn: Wells Fargo Bank

GIVING OFFICERS
Elisa Arevalo Boone: vp
Michael Gillfillan: dir *CURR EMPL* vchmn: Wells Fargo & Co (see above)
Tim Hanlon: vp
Patricia Howze: dir
Rodney Jacobs: cfo *CURR EMPL* vchmn: Wells Fargo & Co (see above)
Mickey Jones: dir
Robert L. Joss: dir *CURR EMPL* vchmn: Wells Fargo & Co (see above)
Clyde Ostler: dir *CURR EMPL* vchmn: Wells Fargo & Co (see above)
Guy Rounsaville, Jr.: dir *CURR EMPL* exec vp, chief coun, secy: Wells Fargo & Co *CORP AFFIL* asst secy: Wells Fargo Investors Corp, Wells Fargo Lease Funding Corp, Wells Fargo Lease Holding Corp, Wells Fargo Lease Mgmt Corp, Wells Fargo Petrolease Inc; exec vp, chief coun, secy: Wells Fargo Bank; secy: Am Securities Co, ATC Realty Eight Inc, ATC Realty Eleven Inc, ATC Realty Fifteen Inc, ATC Realty Five Inc, ATC Realty Four Inc, ATC Realty Fourteen Inc, ATC Realty Nine Inc, ATC Realty One Inc, ATC Realty Seven Inc, ATC Realty Seventeen Inc, ATC Realty Six Inc, ATC Realty Sixteen Inc, ATC Realty Ten Inc, ATC Realty Thirteen Inc, ATC Realty Three Inc, ATC Realty Twelve Inc, ATC Realty Two Inc, Bishop Building Co Inc, Collin Equities Inc, Crocker Commercial Svcs Inc, Crocker Custody Corp, Crocker Equipment Leasing Inc, Crocker Holding Inc, Crocker Life Ins Co, Crocker Properties Inc, Crocker Securities Corp, Garces Water Co Inc, Royal Inns Am Reorganized Co Inc, Wells Fargo Ag Credit, Wells Fargo Agency Svcs Inc, Wells Fargo Capital Markets Inc, Wells Fargo Co, Wells Fargo Corp, Wells Fargo Corp Svcs Inc, Wells Fargo Credit Corp, Wells Fargo Fdn, Wells Fargo Fin Corp, Wells Fargo Foreign Lending Inc, Wells Fargo Ins Svcs, Wells Fargo Intl Affil Corp, Wells Fargo Leasing Corp, Wells Fargo Ltd, Wells Fargo Realty Advs, Wells Fargo Securities Clearance Corp, Wells Fargo Securities Inc, WF Ins Co Ltd, WF Investment Advisors; secy, dir: Wells Fargo Realty Fin Corp; vp, secy: ATC Building Co
Karen Wegmann: pres, dir

APPLICATION INFORMATION
Initial Approach: *Initial Contact:* brief letter *Include Information On:* description of the organization; name, address, and telephone number of contact person; short statement of purpose or objectives; request for a specific amount and how funds will be used; proof of tax-exempt status; list of board of directors and their affiliations; financial report showing overall budget, including past two years' income and expenses; assessment of need (if request is for specific program or project); scope of proposed project; geographical area and people served; evaluation plans and methods *When to Submit:* any time
Restrictions on Giving: Foundation does not provide repetitive annual grants or continuing support.

OTHER THINGS TO KNOW
Foundation may require recipient to provide year-end audited financial statements and periodic reports on the project.
Publications: contributions guidelines

GRANTS ANALYSIS
Total Grants: $6,685,000*
Number of Grants: 600*
Highest Grant: $1,800,000
Typical Range: $1,000 to $10,000
Disclosure Period: 1992
Note: Total grants figure includes foundation and direct giving. Number of grants, average grant, and total grants amounts are approximate and exclude matching gifts to education. Recent grants are derived from a 1991 Form 990 for the foundation.

RECENT GRANTS
1,400,000 United Way Bay Area, San Francisco, CA
125,000 Stanford Graduate School of Business, Stanford, CA
100,000 University of Southern California, Los Angeles, CA
94,930 United Way San Diego County, San Diego, CA
93,750 University of California Berkeley Graduate School of Business, Berkeley, CA
70,834 University of California at Los Angeles Graduate School of Business, Los Angeles, CA
65,175 United Way Orange County, Orange, CA
46,000 Los Angeles Music Center Foundation, Los Angeles, CA
40,480 United Way Sacramento Area, Sacramento, CA
40,000 California Society of Pioneers, San Francisco, CA

Wells Foundation, A. Z.

CONTACT
A. Z. Wells Fdn.
c/o Seattle-First National Bank
PO Box 3586
Seattle, WA 98124

FINANCIAL SUMMARY
Recent Giving: $489,585 (1991); $390,000 (1990); $525,000 (1989)
Assets: $11,305,314 (1991); $10,386,329 (1990); $10,374,806 (1989)
Gifts Received: $250,000 (1989)
EIN: 91-6026580

CONTRIBUTIONS SUMMARY
Donor(s): A.Z. Wells
Typical Recipients: • *Education:* community & junior colleges • *Health:* health organizations, hospitals • *Social Services:* child welfare, community service organizations, united funds, youth organizations
Grant Types: general support
Geographic Distribution: limited to north central WA

GIVING OFFICERS
Seattle First National Bank: trust

APPLICATION INFORMATION
Initial Approach: Contributes only to preselected organizations.

GRANTS ANALYSIS
Number of Grants: 9
Highest Grant: $71,060

Typical Range: $24,000 to $58,000
Disclosure Period: 1991

RECENT GRANTS

- 71,060 Hospital District Number Four of Okanogan County, WA
- 57,855 Chelan County Public Hospital, Okanogan, WA
- 57,855 Grant County Public Hospital District Number 1, WA
- 57,855 Grant County Public Hospital District Number 2, WA
- 57,855 Grant County Public Hospital District Number 3, WA
- 57,855 Okanogan County Public Hospital District Number 3, WA
- 57,855 Okanogan-Douglas County Hospital District Number 1, WA
- 47,440 Chelan County Public Hospital, Okanogan, WA
- 23,955 Community College District 15, WA

Wells Foundation, Franklin H. and Ruth L.

CONTACT
Miles J. Gibbons
Exec. Dir
Franklin H. and Ruth L. Wells Fdn.
4718 Old Gettysburg Rd., Ste. 405
Mechanicsburg, PA 17055-4325
(717) 763-1157

FINANCIAL SUMMARY
Recent Giving: $525,510 (fiscal 1992); $419,964 (fiscal 1991); $360,947 (fiscal 1990)
Assets: $5,341,769 (fiscal year ending May 31, 1992); $5,190,430 (fiscal 1991); $4,989,454 (fiscal 1990)
Gifts Received: $195,898 (fiscal 1992); $195,267 (fiscal 1991); $194,648 (fiscal 1990)
Fiscal Note: In 1992, contributions were received from the Ruth L. Wells Trust.
EIN: 22-2541749

CONTRIBUTIONS SUMMARY
Donor(s): Ruth L. Wells Annuity Trust, Frank Wells Marital Trust

Typical Recipients: • *Arts & Humanities:* arts associations, community arts, libraries, museums/galleries, music, theater • *Education:* colleges & universities, education funds, literacy, private education (precollege) • *Health:* health organizations, hospitals, medical research, mental health, pediatric health • *Religion:* religious organizations • *Social Services:* community service organizations, disabled, domestic violence, family planning, united funds, youth organizations
Grant Types: capital, emergency, project, and seed money
Geographic Distribution: focus on Dauphin, Cumberland, and Perry counties, PA

GIVING OFFICERS
Clifford S. Charles: comm mem
Gladys R. Charles: mem
Ellen R. Cramer: comm mem
Miles J. Gibbons, Jr.: exec dir

APPLICATION INFORMATION
Initial Approach: Send brief letter of inquiry describing program or project. There are no deadlines.
Restrictions on Giving: Does not provide support for religious activities, operating expenses, endowments, or debts.

GRANTS ANALYSIS
Number of Grants: 51
Highest Grant: $100,000
Typical Range: $1,000 to $25,000
Disclosure Period: fiscal year ending May 31, 1992

RECENT GRANTS
- 100,000 Monmouth College, Monmouth, IL
- 100,000 Tri-State University, Angola, IN
- 25,000 YWCA, Carlisle, PA
- 20,000 Harrisburg School District, Harrisburg, PA
- 18,313 Pennsylvania Higher Education Assistance Agency, Harrisburg, PA
- 17,500 Cumberland County Coalition for Shelter, Carlisle, PA — Safe Harbour
- 16,687 Council for Public Education, Harrisburg, PA
- 15,000 American Red Cross, Carlisle, PA

- 15,000 Edgewater Psychiatric Center, Harrisburg, PA
- 15,000 Greater Harrisburg Youth for Christ, Harrisburg, PA

Wells Foundation, Lillian S.

CONTACT
Barbara VanFleet
President
Lillian S. Wells Fdn.
PO Box 14338
Ft. Lauderdale, FL 33301
(305) 462-8639

FINANCIAL SUMMARY
Recent Giving: $228,000 (1990); $260,000 (1989); $226,000 (1988)
Assets: $5,845,615 (1990); $5,751,530 (1989); $5,058,475 (1988)
EIN: 23-7433827

CONTRIBUTIONS SUMMARY
Donor(s): Barbara W. Van Fleet; Preston A. Wells, Jr.
Typical Recipients: • *Education:* colleges & universities • *Health:* hospitals, medical research
Grant Types: endowment, general support, and research
Geographic Distribution: focus on FL

GIVING OFFICERS
Joseph E. Malecek: treas
Mary B. Moulding: secy
Barbara W. Van Fleet: pres
Preston A. Wells, Jr.: vp

APPLICATION INFORMATION
Initial Approach: Send brief letter of inquiry describing program or project. There are no deadlines.

GRANTS ANALYSIS
Number of Grants: 5
Highest Grant: $120,000
Typical Range: $10,000 to $60,000
Disclosure Period: 1990

RECENT GRANTS
- 120,000 University of Florida Foundation, Gainesville, FL
- 60,000 Children's Memorial Hospital, Chicago, IL
- 50,000 Memorial Sloan-Kettering Cancer Center, New York, NY

- 20,000 Broward Community College, Ft. Lauderdale, FL
- 10,000 Broward Center for Performing Arts, Ft. Lauderdale, FL

Wells Trust Fund, Fred W.

CONTACT
Fred W. Wells Trust Fund
Fleet Bank of Massachusetts
28 State St.
Boston, MA 02109

FINANCIAL SUMMARY
Recent Giving: $160,732 (fiscal 1992); $144,514 (fiscal 1991); $132,551 (fiscal 1990)
Assets: $3,158,327 (fiscal year ending June 30, 1992); $2,946,189 (fiscal 1991); $2,891,398 (fiscal 1990)
Gifts Received: $6,398 (fiscal 1992)
EIN: 04-6412350

CONTRIBUTIONS SUMMARY
Donor(s): the late Fred W. Wells
Typical Recipients: • *Education:* agricultural education • *Health:* health organizations, hospices, hospitals • *Social Services:* community service organizations
Grant Types: scholarship
Geographic Distribution: limited to Franklin County, MA; scholarships limited to residents of Greenfield, Deerfield, Shelburne, Ashfield, Montague, Buckland, Chariemont, Heath, Leyden, Gill, Northfield, Conway, Bernardston, Hawley, Rowe, and Monroe, MA

GIVING OFFICERS
Douglas A. Chandler: trust
Albert W. Charsky: trust
Jean B. Cummings: trust
Nancy Dole: trust
Laurel Ann Glocheski: trust
Ralph Haskins: trust
Thomas Heywood: trust
Jean Holdsworth: trust
Donald J. LaPierre: trust
Peter C. Mackin: trust
Theodore Penick: trust
Marsha Pratt: trust
Louis Scott: trust
Donald Smiaroski: trust

APPLICATION INFORMATION
Initial Approach: Application form required for education

grants. Deadline is May 1 for education grants.

OTHER THINGS TO KNOW

Provides scholarships to individuals for higher education.
Publications: Application Guidelines
Disclosure Period: fiscal year ending June 30, 1992

RECENT GRANTS

10,000 Hospice, Boston, MA
5,000 New England Learning Center for Women in Transition, Boston, MA
5,000 Visiting Nurses Association, Boston, MA
4,851 Franklin County Agricultural Society, Boston, MA
2,000 Mohawk Valley Medical Center, Boston, MA
1,500 Children with Attentional Deficit Disorders, Boston, MA
1,500 Western Massachusetts Food Bank, Boston, MA
800 Health Agricultural Society, Boston, MA

Wendt Foundation, Margaret L.

CONTACT

Robert J. Kresse
Secretary and Trustee
Margaret L. Wendt Foundation
40 Fountain Plaza, Ste. 277
Buffalo, NY 14202-2220
(716) 855-2146

FINANCIAL SUMMARY

Recent Giving: $1,616,294 (fiscal 1992); $2,555,379 (fiscal 1991); $1,891,521 (fiscal 1990)
Assets: $57,166,160 (fiscal year ending January 31, 1992); $47,737,307 (fiscal 1991); $46,698,856 (fiscal 1990)
EIN: 16-6030037

CONTRIBUTIONS SUMMARY

Donor(s): The Margaret L. Wendt Foundation was established in 1955, with funds donated by the late Margaret L. Wendt. The assets of the foundation more than doubled in the period between 1975 and 1980 because of the final dis-

tribution of Miss Wendt's bequest.
Typical Recipients: • *Arts & Humanities:* arts centers, dance, history/historic preservation, museums/galleries, opera, theater • *Civic & Public Affairs:* economic development, environmental affairs, ethnic/minority organizations • *Education:* arts education, colleges & universities, special education • *Health:* emergency/ambulance services, health funds, health organizations, hospitals, medical research, mental health, nursing services, single-disease health associations • *Religion:* churches, religious organizations • *Social Services:* animal protection, community service organizations, counseling, disabled, employment/job training, family services, homes, religious welfare, united funds, youth organizations
Grant Types: capital, challenge, general support, operating expenses, project, research, and seed money
Geographic Distribution: primarily Buffalo, and Western New York

GIVING OFFICERS

Robert J. Kresse: secy, trust
Ralph William Loew: trust *B* Columbus OH 1907 *ED* Capital Univ AB 1928; Hamma Divinity Sch M 1931; Wittenberg Univ DD 1947 *NONPR AFFIL* dir dept religion: Chautauqua Inst; trust: Chautauqua Inst
Thomas D. Lunt: trust

APPLICATION INFORMATION

Initial Approach:
Applicants should send four copies of a letter of request. Letters should include a description of the applicant organization, need or problem to be addressed, outline of the proposed project including total budget, specific amount requested, list of the board of directors, and the most recent copy of the organization's IRS determination letter of tax-exempt status.
Submit applications one month prior to the foundation's quarterly meetings.
Restrictions on Giving: The foundation does not make grants to individuals.

GRANTS ANALYSIS

Total Grants: $1,616,294

Number of Grants: 151
Highest Grant: $100,000
Typical Range: $4,000 to $50,000
Disclosure Period: fiscal year ending January 31, 1992
Note: Average grant figure does not include foundation's two highest grants totaling $172,000. Recent grants are derived from a fiscal 1992 Form 990.

RECENT GRANTS

100,000 Episcopal Church Home, Buffalo, NY — construction project
75,000 Alcoholism Services of Erie County, Buffalo, NY — construction of Adolescent Residential Treatment Facility
50,000 Greater Buffalo Athletic Corporation, Buffalo, NY — support of the World University Games Buffalo '93
50,000 Upstate New York Synod, ELCA, Syracuse, NY — conference center
47,300 Effective Parenting Information for Children, Buffalo, NY — program for targeted high-risk parents of infants and toddlers
46,000 United Way of Buffalo and Erie County, Buffalo, NY — annual grant
45,000 Erie County Sheriff's Department, Buffalo, NY — computer aided dispatch and emergency management system
35,000 Boys and Girls Clubs of Buffalo, Buffalo, NY — safety-related renovations to the five locations
30,160 Board of Education-City of Buffalo, Buffalo, NY — purchase of computers/software for high school
30,000 Western New York Heritage Institute, Buffalo, NY — funding for teacher's seminar, textbook project and summer cooperative program

Wendy's International, Inc.

Assets: $880.3 million
Employees: 39,000
Headquarters: Dublin, OH
SIC Major Group: Eating & Drinking Places and Holding & Other Investment Offices

CONTACT

Dennis Lynch
Vice President, Communications
Wendy's International, Inc.
4288 West Dublin-Granville Rd.
Dublin, OH 43017
(614) 764-3100

CONTRIBUTIONS SUMMARY

Nonmonetary Support Types: donated equipment and donated products
Operating Locations: CO (Denver), OH (Columbus, Dublin, Zanesville), TX (San Antonio)

CORP. OFFICERS

John K. Casey: *CURR EMPL* vchmn, cfo: Wendys Intl
James W. Near: *CURR EMPL* chmn, ceo, dir: Wendys Intl

Wenger Foundation, Henry L. and Consuelo S.

CONTACT

Shelly Raines
Principal Manager
Henry L. and Consuelo S. Wenger Fdn.
100 Renaissance Center
Detroit, MI 48226
(313) 567-1212

FINANCIAL SUMMARY

Recent Giving: $820,000 (1991); $600,800 (1990); $525,450 (1989)
Assets: $8,753,343 (1991); $7,508,823 (1990); $3,285,323 (1989)
EIN: 38-6077419

CONTRIBUTIONS SUMMARY

Donor(s): Consuelo S. Wenger
Typical Recipients: • *Arts & Humanities:* arts institutes, community arts, history/historic preservation, museums/galleries • *Civic & Public Affairs:* business/free enterprise, environmental affairs, women's affairs, zoos/botanical gardens • *Education:* colleges & universities, education

associations, private education (precollege) • *Health:* health organizations, hospitals • *Social Services:* child welfare, shelters/homelessness, youth organizations
Grant Types: general support

GIVING OFFICERS
Miles Jaffe: secy, dir
William E. Slaughter, Jr.: treas, dir *B* Chicago IL 1908 *ED* Northwestern Univ 1928; Detroit Inst Tech 1933 *NONPR AFFIL* mem: Am Petroleum Inst, MI Chamber Commerce, Natl Assn Mfrs; trust: Boys Girls Clubs Southeastern MI
Henry Penn Wenger: pres, dir
Diane Wenger Wilson: vp, dir

APPLICATION INFORMATION
Initial Approach: Contributes only to preselected organizations.
Restrictions on Giving: Does not support individuals.

GRANTS ANALYSIS
Number of Grants: 88
Highest Grant: $200,000
Typical Range: $1,000 to $5,000
Disclosure Period: 1991

RECENT GRANTS
200,000 Culver Educational Foundation, Culver, IN
100,000 Greenhills School, Ann Arbor, MI
75,000 DeTour School, DeTour, MI
50,000 Friends of Wilson Barn, Livonia, MI
50,000 Montana Land Reliance, Helena, MT
37,000 North Michigan Hospital Foundation, Petoskey, MI
25,000 Cranbrook Educational Community, Bloomfield Hills, MI
20,000 Nature Conservancy, Chicago, IL
15,000 DeTour Area Chamber of Commerce, DeTour, MI
10,000 Auxiliary Board Art Institute of Chicago, Chicago, IL

Wenner-Gren Foundation for Anthropological Research

CONTACT
Sydel Silverman
President
Wenner-Gren Foundation for Anthropological Research
220 Fifth Avenue, 16th Fl.
New York, NY 10001
(212) 683-5000

FINANCIAL SUMMARY
Recent Giving: $1,305,000 (1992 approx.); $1,418,002 (1991); $1,281,515 (1990)
Assets: $63,000,000 (1992 est.); $59,167,633 (1991); $54,236,833 (1990); $58,091,631 (1989)
EIN: 13-1813827

CONTRIBUTIONS SUMMARY
Donor(s): The Wenner-Gren Foundation for Anthropological Research, incorporated as the Viking Fund in 1941, assumed its present name in 1951. It is one of two foundations established by Axel L. Wenner-Gren (d. 1961), a Swedish philanthropist and founder of Electrolux, which manufactures vacuum cleaners and refrigerators.
Typical Recipients: • *Education:* colleges & universities • *Science:* scientific organizations
Grant Types: conference/seminar, fellowship, and research
Geographic Distribution: no geographic restrictions

GIVING OFFICERS
Nancy Y. Bekavac: trust
David Brigham: trust
George Brockway: trust *B* Portland ME 1915 *ED* Williams Coll BA 1936; Williams Coll LittD 1982; Yale Univ 1937 *CURR EMPL* columnist: New Leader *NONPR AFFIL* mem: Phi Beta Kappa, Soc Am Historians
Beverly Chase: trust
Marilyn Goldstein Fedak: trust, treas *B* New York NY 1947 *ED* Smith Coll BA 1968; Harvard Univ MBA 1972 *CURR EMPL* sr portfolio mgr: Stanford C Bernstein & Co
Robert Garrett: trust *B* Morristown NJ 1937 *ED* Princeton Univ AB 1959; Harvard Univ MBA 1965 *CURR EMPL* pres:

Robert Garrett & Sons *CORP AFFIL* dir: CA Home Brands Holdings, Continental Airlines Holdings, CR Gibson Co, Mickelberry Corp, Reich & Tang, TX Air Corp; pres: Admedia Corp Advisors *NONPR AFFIL* trust: Near East Fdn, NY Botanical Garden, Sch Am Res
Richard C. Hackney, Jr.: trust
Myra Jehlen: trust
Maugha Kenny: asst secy
George Dorland Langdon, Jr.: trust *B* Putnam CT 1933 *ED* Harvard Univ AB 1954; Amherst Coll MA 1957; Yale Univ PhD 1961 *NONPR AFFIL* dir: Quest Value Dual Purpose Fund; fellow: Pilgrim Soc; mem bd overseers: Harvard Coll; mem bus higher ed forum: Am Counc Ed; pres: Am Mus Natural History; pres emeritus: Colgate Univ; trust: Salisbury Sch, St Luke's/Roosevelt Hosp Ctr
Hiram Frederick Moody, Jr.: chmn, trust *B* Waterville ME 1935 *ED* Brown Univ AB 1957 *CURR EMPL* pres, ceo: Home Capital Svcs *CORP AFFIL* chmn, pres: Home Group Funds; dir: Chronogram Corp, Wardley Marine Intl Investment Mgmt; exec vp, chief investment off: Home Ins Co; pres: Marinvest *NONPR AFFIL* mem: Am Bankers Assn; pres: Wicopesset Mgmt Co
Dorothy K. Robinson: trust
Sydel Silverman: pres, secy, trust ex-officio
Frank W. Wadsworth: trust *B* New York NY 1919 *ED* Princeton Univ AB 1946; Princeton Univ PhD 1951 *NONPR AFFIL* mem: Am Soc Theatre Res, Malone Soc, Modern Language Assn, Phi Beta Kappa; prof literature emeritus: St Univ NY Purchase; trust: Rye County Day Sch, Woodrow Wilson Natl Fellowship Fdn
Curtis A. Williams: trust

APPLICATION INFORMATION
Initial Approach:
A program policy statement and grant application guidelines are available from the foundation. An application form will be supplied upon request for those wishing to apply for small grants. Conference grant inquiries should be initiated with a letter describing the conference, or by submission of a Conference Description Form (available from foundation).

All applications must include the name, address, affiliation, and title or degree status of the candidate.

The deadlines for small grants applications are May 1 and November 1. Conference grants applications must be submitted at least 6 months before the date of a decision is needed. The Developing Countries Training Fellowships deadline is no less than nine months prior to the starting date of training.
Restrictions on Giving: The foundation does not support large-scale projects, tuition, salary or fringe benefits, non-project personnel, travel to meetings, institutional overhead, or institutional support. Low priority is given to dissertation write-up or revision, publication, subvention, and filmmaking. Expenses incurred prior to the effective date of an award will not be considered.

OTHER THINGS TO KNOW
Publications: program information brochure

GRANTS ANALYSIS
Total Grants: $1,418,002
Number of Grants: 173
Highest Grant: $12,500
Typical Range: $1,000 to $10,000
Disclosure Period: 1991
Note: Recent grants are derived from a 1991 grants list.

RECENT GRANTS
12,000 Boston University, Boston, MA — aid research towards a machine-based Igbo Dictionary, Owere and Wari, Nigeria
12,000 University of Arizona, Tucson, AZ — aid Hopi Dictionary Project, Arizona
10,000 Arizona State University, Tempe, AZ — aid museum research on tooth morphology and prehistory of Australamelanesian populations, Australia
10,000 Case Western Reserve University, Cleveland, OH
10,000 Chicago Academy of Sciences, Chicago, IL — symposium was designed to review and integrate the rapidly

growing volume of research on the behavioral and ecological diversity of chimpanzees

10,000 City University of New York, New York, NY

10,000 City University of New York Graduate Center, New York, NY — aid field research on international uses of scientific models for the acquisition of immunodeficiency, Rio de Janeiro, Brazil

10,000 Princeton University, Princeton, NJ — conference focused on ritual, performing arts, plastic arts, and literary composition in Bali

10,000 University of Massachusetts, Amherst, MA — aid biocultural research on food storage options among the Hopi, Arizona

10,000 University of Pittsburgh, Pittsburgh, PA

Werblow Charitable Trust, Nina W.

CONTACT
Roger A. Goldman
Trustee
Nina W. Werblow Charitable Trust
c/o Hecht & Co. P.C.
1500 Broadway
New York, NY 10036
(212) 751-5959

FINANCIAL SUMMARY
Recent Giving: $215,000 (fiscal 1990); $215,000 (fiscal 1989)
Assets: $5,278,454 (fiscal year ending February 28, 1990); $4,758,674 (fiscal 1989)
EIN: 13-6742999

CONTRIBUTIONS SUMMARY
Donor(s): the late Nina W. Werblow
Typical Recipients: • *Arts & Humanities:* dance, history/historic preservation, muse-

ums/galleries, opera, public broadcasting • *Education:* colleges & universities, colleges & universities • *Health:* hospitals • *Religion:* religious organizations • *Social Services:* community service organizations, disabled
Grant Types: general support
Geographic Distribution: limited to New York, NY

GIVING OFFICERS
Lillian Ahrens Carver: trust
Joel S. Ehrenkranz: trust
Roger A. Goldman: trust

APPLICATION INFORMATION
Initial Approach: Send brief letter of inquiry describing program or project. Deadline is September 30

GRANTS ANALYSIS
Number of Grants: 50
Highest Grant: $25,000
Typical Range: $1,000 to $7,500
Disclosure Period: fiscal year ending February 28, 1990

RECENT GRANTS
25,000 United Jewish Appeal Federation of Jewish Philanthropies, New York, NY
15,000 New York University, New York, NY — fund to study Cognitive Decline of Elderly
11,000 Whitney Museum of American Art, New York, NY
9,000 Cornell University Medical Center, New York, NY
7,500 American Ballet Theatre, New York, NY
7,500 Beth Israel Medical Center, New York, NY
7,000 Metropolitan Museum of Art, New York, NY
7,000 Metropolitan Opera Association, New York, NY
7,000 New York Hospital-Cornell Medical Center, New York, NY

Werner Foundation, Clara and Spencer

CONTACT
W. Frank Wiggins
President
Clara and Spencer Werner Fdn.
711 South Main St.
PO Box 493
Paris, IL 61944
(217) 466-1215

FINANCIAL SUMMARY
Recent Giving: $95,000 (fiscal 1991); $157,000 (fiscal 1990); $2,327,360 (fiscal 1989)
Assets: $13,666,983 (fiscal year ending June 30, 1991); $12,389,699 (fiscal 1990); $11,077,807 (fiscal 1989)
EIN: 37-6046119

CONTRIBUTIONS SUMMARY
Donor(s): The foundation was incorporated in 1953 by the late Clara B. Werner, the late Spencer Werner, and Illinois Cereal Mills, Inc.
Typical Recipients: • *Education:* religious education • *Religion:* churches, religious organizations • *Social Services:* aged, community service organizations
Grant Types: capital, endowment, general support, matching, project, scholarship, and seed money
Geographic Distribution: focus on St. Louis, MO, and Chicago, IL

GIVING OFFICERS
J. D. Anderson: dir
Paul Coolley: dir
Robert L. Gibson: secy *CORP AFFIL* dir: IL Cereal Mills
Jerry L. Klug: treas
W. Frank Wiggins: pres, dir

APPLICATION INFORMATION
Initial Approach:
The foundation requests applications be made in writing. Applications should include a summary of why financial aid is requested, the amount needed, and personal contact information. The funding proposal should be short and include the following information about the organization: its purpose and history; objectives for the coming year and the activities necessary to carry them out; who will benefit from the project; a list of directors and their affiliations;

the projected income and expenses for the current fiscal year; an audited financial statement from the previous year; sources of income; proof of tax-exempt status; and a statement of the organization's qualifications for requesting funds for the specific project.
The foundation has no deadline for submitting proposals.
The board meets annually in October or November.
Restrictions on Giving: Grants are made solely to Lutheran charitable or religious organizations. No grants are made to individual churches, congregations, parochial schools, or individuals.

OTHER THINGS TO KNOW
Publications: application guidelines

GRANTS ANALYSIS
Total Grants: $95,000
Number of Grants: 4
Highest Grant: $50,000
Typical Range: $15,000 to $50,000
Disclosure Period: fiscal year ending June 30, 1991
Note: Recent grants are derived from a fiscal 1991 grants list.

RECENT GRANTS
50,000 Lutheran Church, IL — Central Illinois District
15,000 Concordia Theological Seminaries, St. Louis, MO
15,000 Concordia Theological Seminaries, St. Louis, MO
15,000 Lutheran School of Theology, Chicago, IL

Werthan Foundation

CONTACT
Herbert M. Shayne
Trustee
Werthan Fdn.
PO Box 1310
Nashville, TN 37202-1310
(615) 259-9331

FINANCIAL SUMMARY
Recent Giving: $519,600 (fiscal 1991); $568,520 (fiscal 1990); $571,290 (fiscal 1989)
Assets: $5,689,090 (fiscal year ending November 30, 1991); $5,244,676 (fiscal 1990); $6,760,451 (fiscal 1989)
Gifts Received: $329,439 (fiscal 1989)

Fiscal Note: In 1989, contributions were received from Werthan Packaging, Inc.
EIN: 62-6036283

CONTRIBUTIONS SUMMARY

Donor(s): Werthan Packaging, Inc., Bernard Werthan, Albert Werthan, Werthan Industries
Typical Recipients: • *Arts & Humanities:* community arts, music, performing arts • *Education:* colleges & universities • *International:* international organizations • *Religion:* religious organizations, synagogues • *Social Services:* community service organizations, family services, united funds, youth organizations
Grant Types: general support
Geographic Distribution: focus on TN

GIVING OFFICERS

Herbert M. Shayne: treas, asst secy *B* Montreal Quebec Canada 1926 *ED* McGill Univ 1947; Harvard Univ 1949 *CURR EMPL* chmn, ceo, dir: Werthan Indus *CORP AFFIL* chmn, ceo, dir: Werthan Indus; dir: Sovran Fin Corp
Albert Werthan: chmn
Bernard Werthan, Jr.: secy *ED* MA Inst Tech 1952 *CURR EMPL* chmn, pres, ceo, dir: Werthan Packaging Corp *CORP AFFIL* chmn, pres, ceo, dir: Werthan Packaging Corp
Morris Werthan II: asst secy

APPLICATION INFORMATION

Initial Approach: Send brief letter of inquiry describing program or project. There are no deadlines.
Restrictions on Giving: Does not support individuals.

GRANTS ANALYSIS

Number of Grants: 96
Highest Grant: $141,750
Typical Range: $100 to $5,000
Disclosure Period: fiscal year ending November 30, 1991

RECENT GRANTS

141,750	Jewish Federation, Nashville, TN
91,750	Jewish Federation, Nashville, TN
50,000	Jewish Federation, Nashville, TN
35,000	Vanderbilt University, Nashville, TN
10,000	Fisk University, Nashville, TN
10,000	United Way, Nashville, TN
8,500	Nashville Symphony Association, Nashville, TN
5,000	Girl Scouts of America, Nashville, TN
3,000	West End Synagogue, Nashville, TN
2,500	Project Pencil, Nashville, TN

Werthan Packaging, Inc.

Sales: $58.0 million
Employees: 450
Headquarters: Nashville, TN
SIC Major Group: Paper & Allied Products

CONTACT

Sue Daniels
Director of Personnel
Werthan Packaging, Inc.
PO Box 1310
Nashville, TN 37202-1310
(615) 259-9331

CONTRIBUTIONS SUMMARY

Operating Locations: TN (Nashville)

CORP. OFFICERS

Bernard Werthan, Jr.: *ED* MA Inst Tech 1952 *CURR EMPL* chmn, pres, ceo, dir: Werthan Packaging Corp *CORP AFFIL* chmn, pres, ceo, dir: Werthan Packaging Corp

OTHER THINGS TO KNOW

Company is an original donor to the Werthan Foundation.

Wertheim Foundation, Dr. Herbert A.

CONTACT

Herbert A. Wertheim
President
Dr. Herbert A. Wertheim Fdn.
4470 S.W. 74th Ave.
Miami, FL 33155
(305) 264-4465

FINANCIAL SUMMARY

Recent Giving: $204,793 (fiscal 1989); $114,574 (fiscal 1988)
Assets: $4,160,469 (fiscal year ending September 30, 1989); $3,351,330 (fiscal 1988)
EIN: 59-1778605

CONTRIBUTIONS SUMMARY

Donor(s): Herbert A. Wertheim
Typical Recipients: • *Arts & Humanities:* arts appreciation, community arts, dance • *Education:* medical education • *Health:* hospitals, medical research
Grant Types: research
Geographic Distribution: focus on FL and CO

GIVING OFFICERS

Herbert A. Wertheim: pres, dir
Nicole J. Wertheim: treas, dir

APPLICATION INFORMATION

Initial Approach: Contributes only to preselected organizations.

GRANTS ANALYSIS

Number of Grants: 27
Highest Grant: $24,340
Typical Range: $100 to $1,000
Disclosure Period: fiscal year ending September 30, 1989

RECENT GRANTS

24,340	Vail Valley Foundation, Vail, CO
24,340	Vail Valley Foundation, Vail, CO
2,700	University of Miami, Coral Gables, FL
2,700	University of Miami, Coral Gables, FL
1,270	Miami City Ballet, Miami, FL
1,270	Miami City Ballet, Miami, FL
500	Junior Achievement, Miami, FL
500	Junior Achievement, Miami, FL
450	Vail Valley Medical Center, Vail, CO
450	Vail Valley Medical Center, Vail, CO

Wertheimer Foundation

CONTACT

Wertheimer Foundation
100 Universal City Plaza Building
15th Floor
Universal City, CA 91608-1001
(818) 777-2956

FINANCIAL SUMMARY

Recent Giving: $76,405 (1991); $24,925 (1989)
Assets: $1,957,884 (1991); $329,355 (1989)
EIN: 95-4090231

GIVING OFFICERS

Douglas Wertheimer: cfo, dir
Elinor Wertheimer: secy, dir
Susan Wertheimer: secy, dir
Thomas Wertheimer: pres, dir

GRANTS ANALYSIS

Total Grants: $76,405
Number of Grants: 50
Highest Grant: $20,000
Disclosure Period: 1991

Wessinger Foundation

CONTACT

Wessinger Fdn.
121 SW Salmon Ste. 1100
Portland, OR 97204
(503) 274-4051

FINANCIAL SUMMARY

Recent Giving: $215,000 (fiscal 1991); $230,820 (fiscal 1989); $199,750 (fiscal 1988)
Assets: $4,790,752 (fiscal year ending September 30, 1991); $4,393,236 (fiscal 1989); $4,060,016 (fiscal 1988)
EIN: 93-0754224

CONTRIBUTIONS SUMMARY

Typical Recipients: • *Arts & Humanities:* arts institutes, history/historic preservation, opera, public broadcasting • *Civic & Public Affairs:* environmental affairs • *Education:* private education (precollege) • *Social Services:* family planning, youth organizations
Grant Types: general support
Geographic Distribution: limited to the Pacific Northwest, with emphasis on the Tri-County area

GIVING OFFICERS

Don Calvin Frisbee: dir *B* San Francisco CA 1923 *ED* Pomona Coll BA 1947; Harvard Univ MBA 1949 *CURR EMPL* chmn: PacifiCorp *CORP AFFIL* dir: First Interstate Bancorp, First Interstate Bank OR, Precision Castparts Corp, Standard Ins Co, Weyerhaeuser Co *NONPR AFFIL* cabinet mem: Boy Scouts Am; chmn bd trusts: Reed Coll; fdr: Am Leadership Forum OR Chap; mem: Intl Adv Comm, Japan-Western US Assn; mem exec comm: OR Partnership Intl Ed; trust: Greater Portland Trust Higher Ed, High Desert Mus, OR Indian Coll Fdn, Safari

Game Search Fdn; dir: OR Bus Counc; pres: OR Commun Fdn; trust: Comm Econ Devel, Whitman Coll

John C. Hampton: dir

Thomas B. Stoel: secy, dir *CORP AFFIL* secy, dir: Collins Pine Co

Fred G. Wessinger: vp, dir

W. W. Wessinger: pres, dir

APPLICATION INFORMATION

Initial Approach: Contributes only to preselected organizations.

GRANTS ANALYSIS

Number of Grants: 26

Highest Grant: $25,000

Typical Range: $1,000 to $10,000

Disclosure Period: fiscal year ending September 30, 1991

RECENT GRANTS

25,000 Catlin Gable School, Portland, OR

25,000 Oregon Shakespeare Festival, Ashland, OR

25,000 Pacific University, Forest Grove, OR

20,000 Boys and Girls Aid Society, Portland, OR

20,000 Salvation Army, Portland, OR

15,000 Oregon Museum of Science and Industry, Portland, OR

12,500 Boy Scouts of America, Portland, OR

12,500 Lewis and Clark College, Portland, OR

10,000 Nature Conservancy, Portland, OR

5,000 Columbia River Maritime Museum, Astoria, OR

West Co. / West Foundation, Herman O.

Sales: $338.2 million
Employees: 2,300
Headquarters: Phoenixville, PA
SIC Major Group: Fabricated Metal Products, Industrial Machinery & Equipment, Rubber & Miscellaneous Plastics Products, and Stone, Clay & Glass Products

CONTACT

George R. Bennyhoff
Senior Vice President, Trustee
Herman O. West Fdn.
1041 West Bridge St.
Phoenixville, PA 19460
(215) 935-4500
Note: Maureen Richards, Administrator, is another contact.

FINANCIAL SUMMARY

Recent Giving: $320,000 (1993 est.); $192,000 (1992 approx.); $230,864 (1991)

Assets: $216,556 (1991); $431,692 (1989)

Gifts Received: $44,334 (1991); $199,423 (1989)

Fiscal Note: Contributes through foundation only.

EIN: 23-7173901

CONTRIBUTIONS SUMMARY

Typical Recipients: • *Arts & Humanities:* arts appreciation, arts centers, arts funds, arts institutes, community arts, history/historic preservation, museums/galleries, performing arts, theater • *Civic & Public Affairs:* business/free enterprise, professional & trade associations, urban & community affairs, zoos/botanical gardens • *Education:* colleges & universities, community & junior colleges, education funds, medical education, minority education, student aid • *Health:* hospitals, medical research • *Religion:* religious organizations • *Science:* observatories & planetariums, science exhibits & fairs, scientific institutes • *Social Services:* aged, child welfare, community centers, community service organizations, counseling, drugs & alcohol, emergency relief, family services, shelters/homelessness, united funds, youth organizations

Grant Types: capital, emergency, employee matching gifts, general support, multiyear/continuing support, operating expenses, and scholarship

Geographic Distribution: in headquarters and operating communities

Operating Locations: FL (Clearwater, St. Petersburg), NC (Kinston), NE (Kearney), PA (Jersey Shore, Lititz, Montgomery, Phoenixville, Williamsport)

CORP. OFFICERS

William G. Little: *CURR EMPL* pres, ceo: West Co

William Stuart West: *B* Philadelphia PA 1927 *ED* Dartmouth Coll 1950 *CURR EMPL* chmn, dir: West Co *CORP AFFIL* dir: AMP Inc

GIVING OFFICERS

George R. Bennyhoff: trust

Maureen Richards: admin

Franklin West: trust

James A. West: trust *B* 1931 *CURR EMPL* pres: West Assocs *CORP AFFIL* dir: West Co

Victor E. Ziegler: trust

APPLICATION INFORMATION

Initial Approach: *Initial Contact:* submit a brief letter of intent and a full proposal *Include Information On:* a description of organization, amount requested, purpose of funds sought, recently audited financial statement, and proof of tax-exempt status *When to Submit:* any time

Restrictions on Giving: Foundation does not support individuals, political or lobbying groups, or organizations outside operating areas.

GRANTS ANALYSIS

Total Grants: $230,864

Number of Grants: 28*

Highest Grant: $37,500

Typical Range: $500 to $5,000

Disclosure Period: 1991

Note: Number of grants and average grant figures do not include $40,982 in scholarships or $10,630 in matching gifts. Recent grants are derived from a 1991 grants list.

RECENT GRANTS

37,500 Phoenxville YMCA, Phoenxville, PA

37,500 YMCA, Phoenixville, PA

26,000 United Way, Philadelphia, PA

20,000 Franklin Institute, Philadelphia, PA

20,000 Franklin Institute Futures Center, Philadelphia, PA

20,000 Philadelphia College Pharmacy, Philadelphia, PA

20,000 Philadelphia College Pharmacy, Philadelphia, PA

13,752 United Way, Philadelphia, PA

10,000 Phoenixville Hospital, Phoenixville, PA

10,000 Phoenixville Hospital, Phoenixville, PA

West Foundation

CONTACT

Stephen R. West
President
West Fdn.
4120 North Illinois St.
Indianapolis, IN 46208-4010
(317) 283-5525

FINANCIAL SUMMARY

Recent Giving: $121,228 (1990); $94,700 (1989); $102,075 (1988)

Assets: $1,957,640 (1990); $1,819,558 (1989); $1,700,359 (1988)

Gifts Received: $15,904 (1990)

EIN: 23-7416727

CONTRIBUTIONS SUMMARY

Donor(s): Stephen R. West

Typical Recipients: • *Civic & Public Affairs:* international affairs, urban & community affairs • *Health:* medical research, single-disease health associations • *International:* international development/relief • *Social Services:* community service organizations, drugs & alcohol, united funds, youth organizations

Grant Types: general support

GIVING OFFICERS

Phyllis West: vp, secy

Stephen R. West: pres, treas

APPLICATION INFORMATION

Initial Approach: Send brief letter describing program. There are no deadlines.

GRANTS ANALYSIS

Number of Grants: 34

Highest Grant: $25,000

Typical Range: $600 to $5,000

Disclosure Period: 1990

RECENT GRANTS

25,000 World Neighbors, Oklahoma City, OK

20,000 Media Indiana, IN

15,000 National Right to Work Legal Defense Foundation, Springfield, VA

10,000 Fairbanks Hospital, Indianapolis, IN

10,000 MAP International, Brunswick, GA

10,000 Meridian Kessler Development Corporation

5,000 Pleasant Run Children's Homes, Indianapolis, IN

5,000 Technoserve, Norwalk, CT

West Foundation

CONTACT
Charles B. West
President
West Fdn.
2865 Amwiler Rd.
Atlanta, GA 30360
(404) 447-0772

FINANCIAL SUMMARY
Recent Giving: $85,280
(1991); $46,724 (1989);
$102,895 (1988)
Assets: $4,569,612 (1991);
$4,712,911 (1989); $4,888,829
(1988)
EIN: 58-6073270

CONTRIBUTIONS SUMMARY
Typical Recipients: • *Arts & Humanities:* arts centers, history/historic preservation, museums/galleries • *Civic & Public Affairs:* zoos/botanical gardens • *Education:* arts education, colleges & universities, private education (precollege) • *Religion:* churches, missionary activities • *Social Services:* domestic violence
Grant Types: general support

GIVING OFFICERS
Charles B. West: chmn, pres, dir
Charles B. West, Jr.: vp, dir
Elizabeth D. West: vp, dir
G. Vincent West: vp, dir
Marian T. West: vp, dir
Marjorie E. West: vp, dir
Mark C. West: vp, dir
Marjorie West Wynne: secy, dir
Robert C. Wynne: vp, dir

APPLICATION INFORMATION
Initial Approach: Send brief letter of inquiry describing program or project. There are no deadlines.

GRANTS ANALYSIS
Number of Grants: 16
Highest Grant: $25,000
Typical Range: $500 to $5,000
Disclosure Period: 1991

RECENT GRANTS
25,000 Atlanta Historical Society, Atlanta, GA
25,000 Independent Schools, Atlanta, GA
7,500 Trinity Presbyterian Church, Atlanta, GA
5,000 George Walton Academy, Atlanta, GA
5,000 Pace Academy, Atlanta, GA
5,000 Woodruff Arts Center, Atlanta, GA
3,500 High Museum of Art, Atlanta, GA
3,000 Lovett School, Atlanta, GA
2,000 Schenck School, Atlanta, GA
1,000 Georgia Tech Foundation, Atlanta, GA

West Foundation

CONTACT
Reece A. West
President
West Fdn.
PO Box 1675
Wichita Falls, TX 76307

FINANCIAL SUMMARY
Recent Giving: $830,000 (fiscal 1992); $483,668 (fiscal 1991); $494,600 (fiscal 1990)
Assets: $18,475,421 (fiscal year ending September 30, 1992); $11,248,918 (fiscal 1991); $10,023,027 (fiscal 1990)
Gifts Received: $8,101,173 (fiscal 1992); $5,000 (fiscal 1989)
Fiscal Note: In 1992, contributions were received from Neva Watkins West.
EIN: 23-7332105

CONTRIBUTIONS SUMMARY
Donor(s): the late Gordon T. West, the late Ellen B. West, Gordon T. West, Jr.
Typical Recipients: • *Education:* colleges & universities, elementary education, public education (precollege)
Grant Types: award, research, and scholarship
Geographic Distribution: limited to the Wichita Falls, TX, area

GIVING OFFICERS
Joe Sherrill, Jr.: vp
Gordon T. West, Jr.: vp
Lane T. West: vp
Reece A. West: pres

APPLICATION INFORMATION
Initial Approach: Contributions only to preselected organizations.

OTHER THINGS TO KNOW
Provides awards to public school teachers and teaching institutes, and funds for faculty development and research.

GRANTS ANALYSIS
Number of Grants: 10
Highest Grant: $153,168
Disclosure Period: fiscal year ending September 30, 1992

RECENT GRANTS
153,168 Wichita Falls Independent School District, Wichita Falls, TX
50,000 Midwestern State University, Wichita Falls, TX
25,000 Wichita Falls Independent School District, Wichita Falls, TX
20,000 Midwestern State University, Wichita Falls, TX

West Foundation, Neva and Wesley

CONTACT
Marylene Weir
Neva and Wesley West Fdn.
PO Box 7
Houston, TX 77001
(713) 850-7911

FINANCIAL SUMMARY
Recent Giving: $780,000 (1990); $740,000 (1989); $625,000 (1988)
Assets: $8,282,003 (1990); $8,296,714 (1989); $7,593,286 (1988)
EIN: 74-6039393

CONTRIBUTIONS SUMMARY
Donor(s): the late Wesley West, Mrs. Wesley West
Typical Recipients: • *Education:* colleges & universities, literacy, medical education, private education (precollege), science/technology education • *Health:* emergency/ambulance services, hospitals, medical research, mental health, pediatric health • *Social Services:* child welfare
Grant Types: capital, general support, operating expenses, and research
Geographic Distribution: focus on TX

GIVING OFFICERS
W.H. Hodges: trust
Betty Ann West Stedman: trust
Stuart West Stedman: trust
Mrs. Wesley West: trust

APPLICATION INFORMATION
Initial Approach: Send brief letter describing program. There are no deadlines.
Restrictions on Giving: Does not support individuals.

OTHER THINGS TO KNOW
Publications: Annual Report

GRANTS ANALYSIS
Number of Grants: 16
Highest Grant: $250,000
Typical Range: $10,000 to $75,000
Disclosure Period: 1990

RECENT GRANTS
250,000 Baylor College of Medicine, Houston, TX
250,000 Texas Children's Hospital, Houston, TX — capital campaign
200,000 Texas A&M University, College Station, TX
75,000 Houston-Galveston Psychoanalytic Institute, Houston, TX
40,000 Texas A&I University, Kingsville, TX — research
5,000 Carrizo Springs Consolidated Independent School District, Carrizo Springs, TX
5,000 Service of Emergency, Kingsville, TX
5,000 Service of Emergency aid Resource Center for the Homeless, Houston, TX
2,500 Children's Fund, Houston, TX
250 Houston Read Commission, Houston, TX

West One Bancorp

Assets: $4.6 billion
Employees: 521
Headquarters: Boise, ID
SIC Major Group: Depository Institutions and Holding & Other Investment Offices

CONTACT

MelloDee Thornton
Manager, Community Affairs
West One Bancorp
PO Box 8247
Boise, ID 83702
(208) 383-7275
Note: An alternate address is 101
South Capital Boulevard,
Boise, ID 83733

FINANCIAL SUMMARY

Recent Giving: $850,000
(1993); $680,000 (1992 approx.); $670,000 (1991)
Fiscal Note: Company gives directly.

CONTRIBUTIONS SUMMARY

Typical Recipients: • *Arts & Humanities:* community arts, dance, general, libraries, museums/galleries, music, opera, performing arts, public broadcasting, theater, visual arts • *Civic & Public Affairs:* economics, general, housing, law & justice, women's affairs, zoos/botanical gardens • *Education:* agricultural education, arts education, business education, elementary education, general, literacy • *Health:* emergency/ambulance services, general, health care cost containment, hospitals • *Social Services:* community centers, community service organizations, disabled, domestic violence, general, homes, shelters/homelessness, united funds, youth organizations

Grant Types: capital, challenge, employee matching gifts, general support, multiyear/continuing support, and project

Nonmonetary Support Types: donated equipment, in-kind services, loaned employees, and loaned executives

Geographic Distribution: primarily at headquarters and operating locations

Operating Locations: ID (Boise), OR (Hillsboro, Portland), UT (Salt Lake City), WA (Bellevue)

CORP. OFFICERS

D. Michael Jones: *CURR EMPL* pres: West One Bancorp

Daniel R. Nelson: *B* Spokane WA 1937 *ED* WA St Univ 1962 *CURR EMPL* chmn, ceo, dir: West One Bancorp

GIVING OFFICERS

MelloDee Thornton: *CURR EMPL* mgr commun aff: West One Bancorp

APPLICATION INFORMATION

Initial Approach: *Initial Contact:* brief letter requesting copy of contributions request form* *Include Information On:* description of the organization; amount requested; purpose of funds sought; recently audited financial statements; list of board of directors; list of other corporate and major donors, including contribution amounts; and proof of tax-exempt status *When to Submit:* any time *Note:* Completed form is to be returned with other requested information.

Restrictions on Giving: Does not support individuals, private foundations, international and fraternal organizations, service or veteran's organizations, beauty or talent contests, general operating expenses of United Way organizations, athletic team events, direct support of religious groups, organizations outside of operating areas, or political or lobbying groups.

OTHER THINGS TO KNOW

Publications: contributions guidelines

GRANTS ANALYSIS

Typical Range: $1,000 to $2,500

West One Bank Idaho

Assets: $3.59 billion
Employees: 1,648
Parent Company: West One Bancorp
Headquarters: Boise, ID
SIC Major Group: Depository Institutions

CONTACT

Robert J. Lane
President & Chief Operating Officer
West One Bank Idaho
PO Box 8247
Boise, ID 83733
(208) 383-7000

CONTRIBUTIONS SUMMARY

Operating Locations: ID (Boise)

CORP. OFFICERS

Robert Lane: *CURR EMPL* ceo, pres: West One Bank ID

West Publishing Co.

Sales: $450.0 million
Employees: 4,000
Headquarters: St. Paul, MN
SIC Major Group: Printing & Publishing

CONTACT

J. M. Tostrud
Vice President & Asst. to the President
West Publishing Co.
610 Opperman Dr.
Eagan, MN 55123
(612) 687-7000

CONTRIBUTIONS SUMMARY

Operating Locations: MN (St. Paul)

CORP. OFFICERS

Grant Nelson: *CURR EMPL* cfo: West Publ Co

Dwight D. Opperman: *CURR EMPL* pres, ceo: West Publishing Co

RECENT GRANTS

American Bar Association Fund for Justice and Education, Chicago, IL

West Texas Corp., J. M.

CONTACT

J. M. West Texas Corp.
PO Box 491
Houston, TX 77001

FINANCIAL SUMMARY

Recent Giving: $264,000 (fiscal 1992); $252,500 (fiscal 1991); $247,500 (fiscal 1990)
Assets: $5,878,177 (fiscal year ending February 28, 1992); $5,737,312 (fiscal 1991); $5,414,681 (fiscal 1990)
EIN: 74-6040389

CONTRIBUTIONS SUMMARY

Typical Recipients: • *Arts & Humanities:* history/historic preservation, museums/galleries, music, opera • *Education:* colleges & universities, medical education, private education (precollege), science/technology education • *Health:* medical research, single-disease health associations • *Religion:* religious organizations

• *Science:* scientific institutes
• *Social Services:* recreation & athletics
Grant Types: general support
Geographic Distribution: focus on TX

GIVING OFFICERS

William B. Blakemore II: trust, pres

Margene West Lloyd: trust

William R. Lloyd, Jr.: trust, pres

Robert Horace Parsley: trust, secy, treas *B* Erwin TX 1923 *ED* Univ VA JDS *CURR EMPL* atty, ptnr: Butler & Binion *CORP AFFIL* dir: Stewart & Stevenson Svcs *NONPR AFFIL* dir: San Jose Clinic, Strake Jesuit Coll Prep, SW Law Enforcement Inst; fellow: TX Bar Fdn; mem: Am Bar Assn, Houston Bar Assn, TX Bar Assn

James A. Reichert: vp

Jack T. Trotter: vp, trust

APPLICATION INFORMATION

Initial Approach: Send brief letter of inquiry describing program. There are no deadlines.

GRANTS ANALYSIS

Number of Grants: 25
Highest Grant: $35,000
Typical Range: $5,000 to $15,000
Disclosure Period: fiscal year ending February 28, 1992

RECENT GRANTS

35,000 Briarwood-Brookwood, Brookshire, TX

20,000 John Cooper School, The Woodlands, TX

20,000 Museum of Southwest, Midland, TX

15,000 Houston Grand Opera Association, Houston, TX

15,000 University of Texas Health Science Center at San Antonio, San Antonio, TX

12,500 Kinkaid School, Houston, TX

10,000 Capital Area Radiation and Research Foundation, Austin, TX

10,000 City of Midland Swim Team, Midland, TX

10,000 Fay School, Houston, TX

10,000 Hermann Eye Fund, Houston, TX

West Texas Utilities Co.

Assets: $800.0 million
Employees: 1,294
Parent Company: Central &
   South West Corp.
Headquarters: Abilene, TX
SIC Major Group: Electric, Gas
   & Sanitary Services

CONTACT
Glen Files
President
West Texas Utilities Co.
PO Box 841
Abilene, TX 79604
(915) 674-7000

CONTRIBUTIONS SUMMARY
Operating Locations: TX
(Abilene)

CORP. OFFICERS
Glenn Files: *CURR EMPL*
pres, ceo: West TX Utilities Co

Westchester Health Fund

CONTACT
Ross M. Weale
Chairman
Westchester Health Fund
3010 Westchester Ave.
Purchase, NY 10577
(914) 694-2766

FINANCIAL SUMMARY
Recent Giving: $5,500 (1991);
$123,000 (1990); $73,941
(1989)
Assets: $2,178,241 (1991);
$1,994,126 (1990); $2,074,180
(1989)
EIN: 23-7071929

CONTRIBUTIONS SUMMARY
Typical Recipients: • *Education:* medical education
• *Health:* health funds, health
organizations, hospitals • *Social Services:* united funds
Grant Types: project
Geographic Distribution: limited to Westchester County, NY

GIVING OFFICERS
Sandra Brown: trust
**Richard Daniel Finucane,
MD:** dir, pres *B* Brooklyn NY
1926 *ED* Georgetown Univ
MD 1949 *CURR EMPL* dir
health services: Gen Foods
Corp *NONPR AFFIL* dir, pres:
Westchester Health Fund;
mem: Am Academy Occupa-

tional Medicine, Am Occupational Med Assn
Steven Galef: trust
Lisa M. Heskett: secy
S.J. Schulman: trust
Ivan G. Seidenberg: trust *B*
New York NY 1946 *ED* City
Univ NY BS 1972; Pace Univ
MBA 1980 *CURR EMPL*
vchmn: NYNEX Corp *NONPR
AFFIL* dir: US Telephone
Assn; mem: Rockland Bus
Counc
Harry L. Staley: secy, exec dir
Ross Weale: dir, chmn

APPLICATION INFORMATION
Initial Approach: Send brief
letter of inquiry describing program. There are no deadlines.

GRANTS ANALYSIS
Number of Grants: 1
Highest Grant: $5,500
Disclosure Period: 1991

RECENT GRANTS
   5,500 Hudson Valley
         Health Systems
         Agency, Tuxedo,
         NY

Westend Foundation

CONTACT
Raymond B. Witt, Jr.
Secretary-Treasurer
Westend Fdn.
1100 American National Bank
   Bldg.
Chattanooga, TN 37402
(615) 265-8881

FINANCIAL SUMMARY
Recent Giving: $208,250
(1990); $214,500 (1989);
$164,257 (1988)
Assets: $2,679,903 (1990);
$2,734,469 (1989); $2,479,370
(1988)
EIN: 62-6041060

CONTRIBUTIONS SUMMARY
Donor(s): the late George West
Typical Recipients: • *Arts &
Humanities:* arts funds • *Education:* colleges & universities,
education funds, private education (precollege) • *Health:*
medical research • *Religion:*
churches • *Social Services:*
community service organizations, food/clothing distribution, homes, shelters/homelessness, united funds, youth
organizations
Grant Types: general support
and scholarship

Geographic Distribution:
focus on the Chattanooga, TN,
area

GIVING OFFICERS
J. Burton Frierson, Jr.: vp,
trust
Daniel W. Oehmig: trust
L.W. Oehmig: pres, trust
Raymond B. Win, Jr.: trust,
secy, treas
Raymond B. Witt, Jr.: secy,
treas *ED* Univ Chattanooga AB
1937; Univ NC LLB 1939
CURR EMPL gen coun, dir:
Dixie Yarns *CORP AFFIL* gen
coun, dir: Dixie Yarns Inc;
ptnr: Witt Gaither Whitaker
NONPR AFFIL mem: Am Bar
Assn, TN Bar Assn, Univ Chattanooga Fdn

APPLICATION INFORMATION
Initial Approach: Application
form required. There are no
deadlines.

OTHER THINGS TO KNOW
Provides scholarships for
higher education.

GRANTS ANALYSIS
Highest Grant: $50,000
Disclosure Period: 1990

RECENT GRANTS
   50,000 RiverCity Company, Chattanooga,
          TN — third installment of $200,000
          pledge
   10,000 Chambliss Emergency Shelter,
          Chattanooga, TN —
          for general purposes
   10,000 Public Education
          Foundation, Chattanooga, TN — for
          general purposes
   10,000 University of Tennessee at Chattanooga, Chattanooga, TN — for
          the George R. West
          Chair of Excellence in Communications and Public
          Affairs
    8,000 United Way, Chattanooga, TN
    5,000 Chattanooga
          School for the Arts
          and Sciences, Chattanooga, TN — for
          school equipment
          fund
    5,000 Girls Preparatory
          School, Chattanooga, TN — for
          the sustaining fund
    5,000 McCallie School,
          Chattanooga, TN —

          for general purposes
    5,000 Northside Neighborhood House,
          Chattanooga, TN —
          for capital funds
          campaign
    5,000 St. Andrews - Sewanee, Sewanee,
          TN — final payment of three-year
          pledge

Westerman Foundation, Samuel L.

CONTACT
Martha Muir
Samuel L. Westerman Fdn.
14532 Indian Trails Dr.
Grand Haven, MI 49417
(313) 642-5770

FINANCIAL SUMMARY
Recent Giving: $354,550 (fiscal 1992); $303,350 (fiscal
1991); $301,725 (fiscal 1990)
Assets: $8,366,846 (fiscal year
ending January 31, 1992);
$7,503,520 (fiscal 1991);
$6,698,557 (fiscal 1990)
EIN: 23-7108795

CONTRIBUTIONS SUMMARY
Typical Recipients: • *Arts &
Humanities:* arts centers,
opera, theater • *Civic & Public
Affairs:* environmental affairs
• *Education:* colleges & universities, private education (precollege) • *Health:* hospitals,
medical research, pediatric
health, single-disease health associations • *Religion:* churches
• *Social Services:* animal protection, community centers,
community service organizations, disabled, united funds,
youth organizations
Grant Types: general support
and project

GIVING OFFICERS
Ruth H. Cooke: vp, secy
James H. LoPrete: pres
Keith H. Muir: treas

APPLICATION INFORMATION
Initial Approach: Send brief
letter of inquiry describing program or project. There are no
deadlines.
Restrictions on Giving: Does
not support individuals.

GRANTS ANALYSIS
Number of Grants: 94
Highest Grant: $20,000

Typical Range: $1,000 to $10,000
Disclosure Period: fiscal year ending January 31, 1992

RECENT GRANTS

20,000 Calvin College, Grand Rapids, MI
20,000 Leader Dogs for the Blind, Rochester, MI
14,100 Michigan Opera Theatre, Detroit, MI
11,000 First Baptist Church, Spring Lake, MI
10,500 Salvation Army, Detroit, MI
10,000 Arthritis Foundation, Southfield, MI
10,000 Capuchin Community Center, Detroit, MI
10,000 Children's Hospital Foundation, Columbus, OH
10,000 Michigan Eye Bank, Ann Arbor, MI
10,000 Optometric Institute and Clinic, Detroit, MI

Western Cardiac Foundation

CONTACT
Rexford Kennamer
President
Western Cardiac Fdn.
436 Roxbury Dr. 222
Beverly Hills, CA 90210
(310) 276-2379

FINANCIAL SUMMARY
Recent Giving: $131,000 (1991); $145,000 (1990); $187,500 (1988)
Assets: $4,594,984 (1991); $4,318,527 (1990); $2,870,335 (1988)
Gifts Received: $73,062 (1991); $62,324 (1990); $210,662 (1988)
EIN: 95-6116853

CONTRIBUTIONS SUMMARY
Donor(s): the late Katherine R. Vance
Typical Recipients: • *Education:* colleges & universities, medical education • *Health:* health organizations, hospitals, medical research, single-disease health associations
Grant Types: research

GIVING OFFICERS
Gladys Bishpo: secy

Rexford Kennamer, M.D.: pres
George Mercader: vp, fin off

APPLICATION INFORMATION
Initial Approach: Send brief letter describing program. There are no deadlines.
Restrictions on Giving: Does not support individuals.

GRANTS ANALYSIS
Number of Grants: 3
Highest Grant: $101,000
Disclosure Period: 1991

RECENT GRANTS

101,000 Cedars-Sinai Medical Center, Los Angeles, CA
75,000 University of California University of Medicine, Los Angeles, CA
5,000 Save-A-Heart Foundation, Los Angeles, CA

Western New York Foundation

CONTACT
Welles V. Moot, Jr.
President
Western New York Fdn.
1402 Main Seneca Bldg.
Buffalo, NY 14203
(716) 847-6440

FINANCIAL SUMMARY
Recent Giving: $212,000 (fiscal 1991); $212,504 (fiscal 1990); $195,731 (fiscal 1989)
Assets: $5,356,293 (fiscal year ending July 31, 1991); $5,158,319 (fiscal 1990); $4,696,329 (fiscal 1989)
EIN: 16-0845962

CONTRIBUTIONS SUMMARY
Donor(s): the late Welles V. Moot
Typical Recipients: • *Arts & Humanities:* arts associations, community arts, history/historic preservation, libraries • *Civic & Public Affairs:* zoos/botanical gardens • *Education:* elementary education, private education (precollege), public education (precollege) • *Social Services:* child welfare, community centers, community service organizations, disabled, drugs & alcohol, united funds, youth organizations
Grant Types: capital, conference/seminar, emergency, en-

dowment, loan, project, and seed money
Geographic Distribution: limited to the 8th Judicial District of NY (Erie, Niagara, Genesee, Wyoming, Allegany, Cattaraugus, and Chautauqua counties)

GIVING OFFICERS
Cecily M. Johnson: vp, trust
John R. Moot: secy, trust
Richard Moot: treas, trust
Welles V. Moot, Jr.: pres, trust
Karr Parker, Jr.: trust
Robert S. Scheu: vp, trust
John N. Walsh III: trust

APPLICATION INFORMATION
Initial Approach: Send brief letter of inquiry describing program or project. There are no deadlines.
Restrictions on Giving: Does not support individuals.

OTHER THINGS TO KNOW
Publications: Annual Report

GRANTS ANALYSIS
Number of Grants: 33
Highest Grant: $25,000
Typical Range: $1,000 to $10,000
Disclosure Period: fiscal year ending July 31, 1991

RECENT GRANTS

25,000 Kids Escaping Drugs, Buffalo, NY — construct facility
23,000 Wilson Free Library, Buffalo, NY — renovate library
20,000 Neighborhood Legal Services, Buffalo, NY — hotline for low income clients
15,000 Niagara Frontier Vocational Rehabilitation Center, Buffalo, NY — equipment
13,000 Shea's Buffalo Center for the Performing Arts, Buffalo, NY — market development
12,500 WNED-TV, Buffalo, NY
12,000 Bob Lanier Center for Education, Physical and Cultural Development, Buffalo, NY
10,000 Girl Scout Council, Buffalo, NY
10,000 Hospice, Buffalo, NY

9,500 Elmwood-Franklin School, Buffalo, NY

Western Publishing Co., Inc.

Sales: $480.0 million
Employees: 2,550
Parent Company: Western Publishing Group Inc.
Headquarters: Racine, WI
SIC Major Group: Miscellaneous Manufacturing Industries and Printing & Publishing

CONTACT
Bruce Bernberg
Senior Vice President, Finance & Admin.
Western Publishing Co., Inc.
1220 Mound Ave.
Racine, WI 53404
(414) 633-2431

CONTRIBUTIONS SUMMARY
Grant Types: matching
Operating Locations: WI (Racine)

CORP. OFFICERS
Bruce Bernberg: *CURR EMPL* cfo: Western Publ Co
Richard A. Bernstein: *CURR EMPL* chmn: Western Publishing Co
George Oess: *CURR EMPL* pres, ceo: Western Publ Co

Western Resources / Western Resources Foundation

Assets: $5.52 billion
Employees: 5,100
Headquarters: Topeka, KS
SIC Major Group: Electric, Gas & Sanitary Services

CONTACT
Thomas Sloan
Director, Corporate Communications
Western Resources, Inc.
PO Box 889
Topeka, KS 66601-0889
(913) 575-8350

FINANCIAL SUMMARY
Fiscal Note: Company gives directly. Annual Giving Range: $500,000 to $1,000,000

CONTRIBUTIONS SUMMARY
Typical Recipients: • *Civic & Public Affairs:* environmental affairs • *Health:* public health • *Social Services:* aged, commu-

nity service organizations, employment/job training, united funds, youth organizations
Geographic Distribution: in headquarters and operating communities
Operating Locations: KS, MO, OK
Note: western Missouri and northern Oklahoma

CORP. OFFICERS
John E. Hayes, Jr.: *CURR EMPL* chmn, pres, ceo, dir: KS Power & Light/KPL Gas Svc

GIVING OFFICERS
John E. Hayes, Jr.: chmn, pres, ceo *CURR EMPL* chmn, pres, ceo, dir: KS Power & Light/KPL Gas Svc (see above)

APPLICATION INFORMATION
Initial Approach: *Initial Contact:* brief letter of inquiry and full proposal *Include Information On:* a description of organization, amount requested, purpose of funds sought, recently audited financial statement, and proof of tax-exempt status *When to Submit:* any time
Restrictions on Giving: Does not support individuals, religious organizations for sectarian purposes, political or lobbying groups, or organizations outside operating areas.

OTHER THINGS TO KNOW
Foundation was established in 1991, grants information is not yet available.

Western Shade Cloth Charitable Foundation

CONTACT
William H. Regnery II
Trustee
Western Shade Cloth Charitable Foundation
5N251 White Thorn Road
P.O. Box 439
Wayne, IL 60184-0439
(708) 564-8880

FINANCIAL SUMMARY
Recent Giving: $102,600 (1989)
Assets: $2,862,382 (1989)
EIN: 36-3612613

CONTRIBUTIONS SUMMARY
Typical Recipients: • *Arts & Humanities:* public broadcast-

ing • *Civic & Public Affairs:* law & justice • *Education:* colleges & universities, public education (precollege) • *International:* international development/relief • *Religion:* churches, religious organizations • *Social Services:* animal protection, united funds, youth organizations
Grant Types: general support
Geographic Distribution: emphasis on Illinois

GIVING OFFICERS
Anne Regnery: trust
Patrick B. Regnery: trust
William H. II Regnery: trust

APPLICATION INFORMATION
Initial Approach: The foundation reports that unsolicited requests for grants will not be accepted.

GRANTS ANALYSIS
Total Grants: $102,600
Number of Grants: 21
Highest Grant: $25,300
Typical Range: $3,000 to $11,000
Disclosure Period: 1989

RECENT GRANTS
25,300 Amy E. Edgerton Foundation, IL
11,000 St. Augustine Center, IL
11,000 St. Augustine Center, IL
11,000 World Vision, Monrovia, CA
10,000 Happy Puppy, WI
8,000 Mercersburg Academy, Mercersburg, PA
5,500 Chicago Boys Club, Chicago, IL
5,500 House of the Good Shepard, IL
5,000 Intercollegiate Studies Institute, PA
3,000 Grace Church of Hinsdale, Hinsdale, IL

Western Southern Life Insurance Co. / Western-Southern Life Foundation
Employees: 5,590
Headquarters: Cincinnati, OH

CONTACT
J. Thomas Lancaster
Western-Southern Life Foundation
400 Broadway
Cincinnati, OH 45202-3341
(513) 629-1070

FINANCIAL SUMMARY
Recent Giving: $411,770 (fiscal 1990)
Assets: $2,760,806 (fiscal year ending March 31, 1990)
EIN: 31-1259670

CONTRIBUTIONS SUMMARY
Typical Recipients: • *Arts & Humanities:* museums/galleries • *Civic & Public Affairs:* business/free enterprise, civil rights, zoos/botanical gardens • *Education:* colleges & universities • *Health:* hospices, hospitals, mental health, single-disease health associations • *International:* international organizations • *Religion:* churches, religious organizations • *Social Services:* aged, child welfare, religious welfare, united funds
Grant Types: general support
Geographic Distribution: primarily Ohio
Operating Locations: OH (Cincinnati)

CORP. OFFICERS
William J. Williams: *CURR EMPL* chmn, ceo: Western-Southern Life Ins Co

GIVING OFFICERS
John F. Barrett: trust *CURR EMPL* pres, coo: Western-Southern Life Ins Co
Thomas L. Williams: trust

APPLICATION INFORMATION
Initial Approach: The foundation reports that there are no deadlines for grants, but that the requests must be written. The foundation also reports that there are no special restrictions on grants due to factors such as: the geographic location of grant seeker, charitable field, or kind of institution.

GRANTS ANALYSIS
Total Grants: $411,770
Number of Grants: 55
Highest Grant: $100,000
Typical Range: $10,000 to $100,000
Disclosure Period: fiscal year ending March 31, 1990

RECENT GRANTS
100,000 United Way
50,000 Xavier University, OH
35,150 Fine Arts Fund
35,000 Cincinnati Youth Collaborative, Cincinnati, OH
20,000 Bicentennial Commons Maintenance Trust
10,000 Cincinnati Zoo and Botany Garden, Cincinnati, OH
10,000 Dan Beard Council
10,000 Insure
10,000 St. Joseph Home
10,000 University of Notre Dame, Notre Dame, IN

Westinghouse Broadcasting Co.
Revenue: $850.0 million
Employees: 3,000
Parent Company: Westinghouse Electric Corp.
Headquarters: New York, NY
SIC Major Group: Communications

CONTACT
Paulette Carpenter
Director, Corporate Relations
Westinghouse Broadcasting Co.
888 Seventh Ave.
New York, NY 10106
(212) 307-3814

FINANCIAL SUMMARY
Fiscal Note: Annual Giving Range: $100,000 to $250,000

CONTRIBUTIONS SUMMARY
Supports education, journalism, civic affairs, and voluntarism, with emphasis on youth.
Typical Recipients: • *Civic & Public Affairs:* general • *Education:* journalism education • *Social Services:* volunteer services
Grant Types: general support and multiyear/continuing support
Geographic Distribution: operating communnities
Operating Locations: NY (New York)

CORP. OFFICERS
Burton B. Staniar: *CURR EMPL* ceo, chmn: Westinghouse Broadcasting Co

APPLICATION INFORMATION
Initial Approach: Send letter outlining program, amount requested, other sources of fund-

ing, and proof of tax-exempt status.

Westinghouse Electric Corp. / Westinghouse Foundation

Sales: $12.1 billion
Employees: 100,000
Headquarters: Pittsburgh, PA
SIC Major Group: Electronic & Other Electrical Equipment and Industrial Machinery & Equipment

CONTACT
Cheryl Kubelick
Manager, Contributions & Community Affairs
Westinghouse Fdn.
11 Stanwix St.
Pittsburgh, PA 15222-1384
(412) 642-6033

FINANCIAL SUMMARY
Recent Giving: $5,500,000 (1993 est.); $6,749,293 (1992); $8,205,242 (1991)
Assets: $3,703,725 (1992); $8,373,428 (1988)
Fiscal Note: Company cash contributions are made through the foundation only.
EIN: 25-1357168

CONTRIBUTIONS SUMMARY
Typical Recipients: • *Arts & Humanities:* arts centers, dance, music, opera, performing arts, public broadcasting, theater • *Civic & Public Affairs:* better government, civil rights, economic development, environmental affairs, housing, public policy, women's affairs • *Education:* colleges & universities, engineering education, faculty development, minority education, public education (precollege), science/technology education • *International:* foreign educational institutions • *Social Services:* child welfare, community service organizations, disabled, food/clothing distribution, recreation & athletics, united funds, youth organizations
Grant Types: capital, department, employee matching gifts, general support, project, and scholarship
Nonmonetary Support Types: donated equipment, in-kind services, loaned executives, and workplace solicitation
Note: Above figures do not include nonmonetary support, val-

ued at $7.0 million annually. Nonprofits can contact Ms. Cheryl Kubelick or individual plant managers for information.
Geographic Distribution: principally near operating locations and to national organizations
Operating Locations: AZ (Phoenix), CA (San Francisco, Sunnyvale), CT (Milford, Stamford), DC, FL (Naples, Orlando, Pensacola), MA (Boston), MD (Baltimore, Columbia, Hunt Valley), ME, MI (Grand Rapids), MN (Minneapolis), MO (St. Louis), NC (Asheville, Charlotte, Winston-Salem), NY (New Rochelle, New York, West Valley), OH (Cleveland, Lima), PA (Bridgeville, Monroeville, Pittsburgh, West Mifflin), SC (Aiken, Hampton), TX (College Station, Dallas, Round Rock), VA (Abingdon), WA (Richland)

CORP. OFFICERS
Gary M. Clark: *ED* GA Inst Tech BS 1957 *CURR EMPL* pres, ceo: Westinghouse Electric Corp
Thomas Patrick Costello: *ED* IL Inst Tech BSME 1956; Emory Univ 1971; Univ Coll Galway LLD 1989 *CURR EMPL* pres, dir: Thermo King Corp *CORP AFFIL* group pres: Westinghouse Electric Corp *NONPR AFFIL* chmn fund drive: Canisius Coll; chmn indus comm: Un Way Greater Buffalo; chmn pacesetter div: Un Way Minneapolis; mem: Serra Intl; mem bus adv comm: Northwestern Univ

GIVING OFFICERS
Louis J. Briskman: trust
G. Reynolds Clark: pres *CURR EMPL* dir (communication resources & community affairs): Westinghouse Electric Corp
Thomas Patrick Costello: trust *CURR EMPL* pres, dir: Thermo King Corp (see above)
Eric H. Dussling: treas
Frederick W. Hill: chmn, trust
Warren H. Hollinshead: trust
Cheryl L. Kubelick: secy *CURR EMPL* mgr (univ ed programs): Westinghouse Electric Corp
Richard A. Linder: trust *CURR EMPL* exec vp (electronic systems): Westinghouse Electric Corp
James S. Moore: trust
Maurice Charles Sardi: trust *B* Jamestown NY 1935 *CURR*

EMPL chmn, ceo: Knoll Group *NONPR AFFIL* dir: Allegheny County Commn Work-Force Excellence, Pittsburgh Ballet Theatre; mem: PA St Job Training Coordinating Counc
John B. Yasinsky: trust *B* Shenendoah PA 1939 *CURR EMPL* exec vp (intl): Westinghouse Electric Corp *NONPR AFFIL* mem: Am Nuclear Soc, Atomic Indus Forum, Natl Security Indus Assn, White House Fellows Assn

APPLICATION INFORMATION
Initial Approach: *Initial Contact:* letter and proposal *Include Information On:* purpose of organization, mission statement, program description, amount requested, purpose for which funds are sought, schedule of implementation, population served, name of person in charge with qualifications, recently audited financial statement, list of board members with their affiliations, proof of tax-exempt status *When to Submit:* any time
Restrictions on Giving: Westinghouse Foundation does not support the following groups or activities: organizations without nonprofit, tax-exempt status; individuals; political groups; specialized health, medical, or welfare programs that do not meet specific community needs; hospitals; religious groups; organizations which discriminate by race, color, creed, gender, or national origin; capital improvement or building projects at educational institutions; medical education programs; chairs or professorships; liberal arts, fine arts, or similar education programs; educational research programs; graduate education; or general endowment funds.

OTHER THINGS TO KNOW
Westinghouse Foundation is a consolidation of the Westinghouse Electric Fund, the Westinghouse Educational Foundation, and the Westinghouse International Education Foundation.

Average grants for education are approximately $30,000; average grants are about $15,000 for other areas.
Publications: Westinghouse Foundation Annual Report

GRANTS ANALYSIS
Total Grants: $6,749,293
Number of Grants: 195*
Highest Grant: $185,000
Typical Range: $1,000 to $50,000
Disclosure Period: 1992
Note: Number of grants and average grant figures exclude matching gifts and major united fund contribution. Recent grants are derived from a 1991 annual report.

RECENT GRANTS
1,000,000 United Way of Southwestern Pennsylvania, Pittsburgh, PA
525,000 Science Service (Westinghouse Science Talent Search), Washington, DC
375,000 United Way of Central Maryland and Columbia, Baltimore, MD
312,000 Westinghouse Family Scholarship, Pittsburgh, PA
290,000 University of Pittsburgh, Pittsburgh, PA
125,000 Westinghouse High School of Science and Mathematics, Pittsburgh, PA
117,000 United Way of Benton and Franklin Counties, Kennewick, WA
100,000 Extra Mile Education Foundation, Pittsburgh, PA
100,000 Pennsylvania State University, University Park, PA
100,000 Pittsburgh Ballet Theatre, Pittsburgh, PA

Westlake Scholarship Fund, James L. and Nellie M.

CONTACT
James L. and Nellie M. Westlake Scholarship Fund
111 South Bemiston Avenue, Ste. 412
Clayton, MO 63105-1954
(314) 725-6410
Note: The foundation does not report a specific contact person.

FINANCIAL SUMMARY
Recent Giving: $629,738 (fiscal 1990); $544,208 (fiscal 1989); $758,650 (fiscal 1988)

Assets: $14,100,665 (fiscal year ending June 30, 1990); $13,575,273 (fiscal 1989); $12,622,381 (fiscal 1988)
EIN: 43-6248269

CONTRIBUTIONS SUMMARY

Donor(s): The foundation was established in 1981 by the late James L. Westlake.

Typical Recipients: • *Education:* student aid

Grant Types: scholarship

Geographic Distribution: limited to high school graduates who are residents of MO

GIVING OFFICERS

Gary D. Clark: mem selection comm

Ronald L. Jackson: chmn selection comm

Newell S. Knight, Jr.: vchmn selection comm

Amy B. Murphy: mem selection comm

Lincoln Scott: mem selection comm

Emily F. Ullman: secy selection comm

APPLICATION INFORMATION

Initial Approach:
The foundation requests applicants write for a formal applications form.
The deadline is March 1.
Decisions are made in May.

Restrictions on Giving: The foundation does not make loans or support program-related investments.

OTHER THINGS TO KNOW

Publications: informational brochure including application guidelines

GRANTS ANALYSIS

Total Grants: $629,738*

Disclosure Period: fiscal year ending June 30, 1990

Note: The 1990 grants list consists of scholarship awards to individuals.

WestLB New York Branch

Headquarters: New York, NY
SIC Major Group: Depository Institutions

CONTACT
Gerard Barton
Vice President
WestLB New York Branch
1211 Avenue of the Americas
New York, NY 10036
(212) 852-6000

FINANCIAL SUMMARY
Fiscal Note: Annual Giving Range: $50,000 annually

CONTRIBUTIONS SUMMARY

Program is unstructured and fluid. All requests are forwarded to the headquarter office in Dusseldorf for approval.

Typical Recipients: • *Arts & Humanities:* libraries, museums/galleries, music • *Civic & Public Affairs:* professional & trade associations • *Education:* private education (precollege) • *Social Services:* united funds

Grant Types: general support

Geographic Distribution: only in the New York metropolitan area

Operating Locations: NY

CORP. OFFICERS

Horst T. Fuellkemper: *CURR EMPL* joint chmn N Am: WestLB NY Branch

John Paul Garber: *CURR EMPL* joint chmn N Am: WestLB NY Branch

H. Jurgen Schlichting: *CURR EMPL* joint chmn N Am: WestLB NY Branch

GIVING OFFICERS

Gerard Barton: *CURR EMPL* vp: WestLB NY Branch

APPLICATION INFORMATION

Initial Approach: Send letter, preferably in November, including a description of the organization, amount requested, and purpose of funds sought. All requests are forwarded to Dusseldorf for approval at the end of the year.

Westmoreland Coal Co.

Sales: $568.4 million
Employees: 1,226
Headquarters: Philadelphia, PA
SIC Major Group: Coal Mining

CONTACT
Steve Anderson
Director, Communications
Westmoreland Coal Co.
700 The Bellevue
200 South Broad St.
Philadelphia, PA 19102
(215) 545-2500

FINANCIAL SUMMARY
Fiscal Note: Annual Giving Range: less than $100,000

CONTRIBUTIONS SUMMARY

Operating Locations: KY (Banner), MT (Billings), PA (Philadelphia), VA (Big Stone Gap), WV (Clothier)
Note: Company has 2 operations in locations.

CORP. OFFICERS

Pemberton Hutchinson: *B* Charlotte NC 1931 *ED* Univ VA 1954; Univ VA 1963 *CURR EMPL* chmn, pres, ceo, dir: Westmoreland Coal Co

Larry Zalkin: *CURR EMPL* exec vp, cfo: Westmoreland Coal Co

Weston Associates/R.C.M. Corp. / Barrington Foundation

Headquarters: Great Barrington, MA

CONTACT
David H. Strassler
President
Barrington Foundation
PO Box 750
Great Barrington, MA 01230

FINANCIAL SUMMARY
Recent Giving: $503,400 (1991); $419,050 (1990); $425,200 (1989)
Assets: $2,614,985 (1991); $1,679,437 (1990); $1,958,285 (1989)
Gifts Received: $1,124,054 (1991); $48,130 (1990)
Fiscal Note: In 1991, contributions were received from Alan Strassler ($20,000), Karen Strassler ($20,000), Matthew Strassler ($20,000), David H. Strassler ($300,000), Robert B. Strassler ($500,000), and Weston Associates ($258,699).
EIN: 13-2930849

CONTRIBUTIONS SUMMARY

Typical Recipients: • *Arts & Humanities:* music • *Civic &*

Public Affairs: ethnic/minority organizations • *Social Services:* united funds
Grant Types: general support
Geographic Distribution: primarily MA
Operating Locations: MA (Great Barrington)

GIVING OFFICERS

David H. Strassler: pres
Robert B. Strassler: secy, treas

APPLICATION INFORMATION

Initial Approach: Send letter of inquiry. There are no deadlines.

GRANTS ANALYSIS

Number of Grants: 86
Highest Grant: $81,000
Typical Range: $500 to $6,000
Disclosure Period: 1991

RECENT GRANTS

81,000	Anti-Defamation League, New York, NY
80,000	Jewish Federation
60,000	Combined Jewish Philanthropies, Boston, MA
50,000	Simon's Rock
25,000	Simon's Rock
23,000	Aston-Magna/John HSU/Recording
18,000	Berkeley Friends of Baroque Music, Berkeley, CA
15,000	Harvard College Fund, Cambridge, MA
10,000	Ackerman Institute, New York, NY
10,000	Princeton Graduate Fellowship, Princeton, NJ

Westport Fund

CONTACT
Westport Fund
1815 Randolph St., N.W.
Washington, DC 20011

FINANCIAL SUMMARY
Recent Giving: $141,051 (1991); $157,207 (1990); $130,875 (1989)
Assets: $3,804,859 (1991); $3,063,560 (1990); $3,339,775 (1989)
Gifts Received: $20,292 (1991); $5,848 (1990)
Fiscal Note: In 1991, contributions were received from Jean McGreevy Green ($8,331) and Gail McGreevy Harmon ($11,961).
EIN: 44-6007971

CONTRIBUTIONS SUMMARY
Donor(s): the late Milton McGreevy
Typical Recipients: • *Arts & Humanities:* museums/galleries • *Civic & Public Affairs:* public policy, women's affairs • *Education:* colleges & universities, education funds, private education (precollege) • *International:* international organizations • *Religion:* churches • *Social Services:* community service organizations, family planning, united funds, youth organizations
Grant Types: capital, endowment, general support, multiyear/continuing support, operating expenses, research, and scholarship

GIVING OFFICERS
Jean McGreevy Green: vp, secy
Gail McGreevy Harmon: pres
Ann McGreevy Heller: treas
Barbara James McGreevy: trust
Thomas J. McGreevy: vp

APPLICATION INFORMATION
Initial Approach: Contributes only to preselected organizations.
Restrictions on Giving: Does not support individuals or provide funds for consulting services, deficit financing, exchange programs, or internships.

GRANTS ANALYSIS
Number of Grants: 66
Highest Grant: $16,000
Typical Range: $1,000 to $5,000
Disclosure Period: 1991

RECENT GRANTS
16,000 Population Services International, Washington, DC
14,000 Americans for Peace Now, New York, NY
13,500 Women's Legal Defense Fund, Washington, DC
12,500 Harvard College Fund, Cambridge, MA
11,000 Nelson Gallery Foundation, Kansas City, MO
8,000 Planned Parenthood Federation of America, Kansas City, MO
7,000 Salvation Army, Kansas City, MO
6,000 Vassar College, Poughkeepsie, NY
5,000 Pembroke School, Kansas City, MO
5,000 Santa Fe Mountain Center, Santa Fe, NM

WestStar Bank N.A.
Assets: $463.0 million
Employees: 240
Parent Company: First Bancshares Inc.
Headquarters: Bartlesville, OK
SIC Major Group: Depository Institutions

CONTACT
LeRoy Shepherd
Business Development Officer
WestStar Bank N.A.
PO Box 999
Bartlesville, OK 74005
(918) 337-3327

FINANCIAL SUMMARY
Fiscal Note: Annual Giving Range: less than $100,000

CONTRIBUTIONS SUMMARY
Company provides employee matching gifts only to schools of higher education.
Typical Recipients: • *Education:* colleges & universities
Grant Types: matching
Geographic Distribution: primarily in OK
Operating Locations: OK (Bartlesville)

CORP. OFFICERS
Walter V. Allison: *CURR EMPL* ceo, chmn: WestStar Bank NA

APPLICATION INFORMATION
Initial Approach: Send brief letter of inquiry, including a description of the organization, amount requested, purpose of funds sought, recently audited financial statements, and proof of tax-exempt status. Company requests applicants give it 2 to 3 weeks to make a decision.
Restrictions on Giving: Does not support individuals, religious organizations for sectarian purposes or political or lobbying groups.

Westvaco Corp. / Westvaco Foundation Trust
Sales: $2.34 billion
Employees: 14,440
Headquarters: New York, NY
SIC Major Group: Chemicals & Allied Products, Paper & Allied Products, and Real Estate

CONTACT
Roger Holmes
Secretary, Contributions Committee
Westvaco Corp.
299 Park Ave.
New York, NY 10171
(212) 688-5000

FINANCIAL SUMMARY
Recent Giving: $1,300,000 (fiscal 1993 est.); $1,300,000 (fiscal 1992 approx.); $1,210,119 (fiscal 1991)
Assets: $6,782,762 (fiscal year ending September 30, 1991); $3,486,861 (fiscal 1990); $4,615,655 (fiscal 1988)
Fiscal Note: Company gives primarily through the foundation. Local managers administer small discretionary budgets, cumulatively disbursing about $350,000 annually. This support is not included in above figures.
EIN: 13-6021319

CONTRIBUTIONS SUMMARY
Typical Recipients: • *Arts & Humanities:* arts centers, history/historic preservation, libraries, museums/galleries, performing arts, theater • *Civic & Public Affairs:* better government, business/free enterprise, civil rights, consumer affairs, economic development, economics, environmental affairs, international affairs, nonprofit management, professional & trade associations, public policy, safety, urban & community affairs, women's affairs, zoos/botanical gardens • *Education:* business education, colleges & universities, community & junior colleges, continuing education, education associations, education funds, elementary education, international studies, literacy, medical education, minority education, religious education, science/technology education • *Health:* health funds, health organizations, hospitals, medi-cal rehabilitation, medical research, single-disease health associations • *Social Services:* animal protection, community service organizations, counseling, disabled, drugs & alcohol, employment/job training, recreation & athletics, united funds, youth organizations
Grant Types: capital, challenge, employee matching gifts, endowment, general support, and multiyear/continuing support
Geographic Distribution: near headquarters and operating locations only
Operating Locations: DE (Newark), FL (Mulberry), LA (New Orleans), MA (Springfield), MD (Luke), NY (New York), PA (Tyrone), SC (Charleston, Summerville), VA (Covington, Richmond)

CORP. OFFICERS
David Lincoln Luke III: *B* Tyrone PA 1923 *ED* Yale Univ AB 1945 *CURR EMPL* chmn, pres, ceo: Westvaco Corp *CORP AFFIL* dir: BFGoodrich, Clupak, Grumman Corp, Irving Bank Corp, Irving Trust Co, McGraw-Hill *NONPR AFFIL* mem: Am Paper Inst, Inst Paper Chemistry; trust: Cold Springs Harbor Laboratory; trust emeritus: Hotchkiss Sch
John Anderson Luke: *B* Tyrone PA 1925 *ED* Yale Univ BA 1949 *CURR EMPL* pres, dir, ceo: Westvaco Corp *CORP AFFIL* dir: Arkwright Mutual Ins Co, Clupak, Discount Corp NY *NONPR AFFIL* dir: Am Arbitration Assn; mem: Am Paper Inst, Natl Assn Mfrs

GIVING OFFICERS
William S. Beaver: trust
George E. Cruser: trust *B* Princeton NJ 1930 *ED* Juniata Coll BA 1952; Univ PA Wharton Sch MBA 1954 *CURR EMPL* sr vp (fin), dir: Westvaco Corp
Roger Holmes: secy (contributions comm) *B* Princeton NJ 1930

APPLICATION INFORMATION
Initial Approach: *Initial Contact:* brief letter or proposal *Include Information On:* description of the organization, amount requested, purpose for which funds are sought, proof of tax-exempt status *When to Submit:* any time; best time of year is July *Note:* Program is

decentralized; recommended procedure is to apply through company operating units, rather than directly to the foundation.

GRANTS ANALYSIS

Total Grants: $1,210,119
Number of Grants: 173*
Highest Grant: $72,232*
Typical Range: $1,000 to $5,000
Disclosure Period: fiscal year ending September 30, 1991
Note: Number of grants, average grant, highest grant, and assets figures reflect 1990 giving. Recent grants are derived from a fiscal 1991 Form 990.

RECENT GRANTS

75,000 United Way
70,107 United Way of Tri-State, New York, NY
65,000 County United Way
50,000 National Geographic Education Foundation, Washington, DC
35,000 Cold Spring Harbor Laboratory, Cold Spring Harbor, NY
32,400 United Way of Greater Richmond, Richmond, VA
31,616 United Way of Pioneer Valley, Springfield, MA
30,000 Greater Alleghany United Fund
25,000 Medical University of South Carolina, Charleston, SC — capital campaign
24,750 United Way of Delaware, Wilmington, DE

Westwood Endowment

CONTACT

Richard A. West
President and Director
Westwood Endowment
3965 North Meridian Street
Indianapolis, IN 46208
(317) 925-9000

FINANCIAL SUMMARY

Recent Giving: $337,707 (fiscal 1991); $250,818 (fiscal 1990); $200,242 (fiscal 1989)
Assets: $3,511,307 (fiscal year ending November 30, 1991); $3,046,131 (fiscal 1990); $3,052,733 (fiscal 1989)
Gifts Received: $230,425 (fiscal 1991); $100,000 (fiscal 1990); $516,844 (fiscal 1989)

EIN: 31-1197125

CONTRIBUTIONS SUMMARY

Typical Recipients: • *Civic & Public Affairs:* environmental affairs, international affairs, public policy, rural affairs • *International:* international development/relief • *Religion:* churches, missionary activities, religious organizations • *Social Services:* religious welfare, youth organizations
Grant Types: general support
Geographic Distribution: national, with emphasis on California

GIVING OFFICERS

Alfred Burger: dir
Howard E. Luker: dir
Robin W. Wainwright: dir
Florence G. West: secy, dir
Richard A. West: pres, dir

GRANTS ANALYSIS

Total Grants: $337,707
Number of Grants: 13
Highest Grant: $149,207
Typical Range: $4,000 to $40,000
Disclosure Period: fiscal year ending November 30, 1991
Note: Grants list for 1991 was incomplete.

RECENT GRANTS

149,207 SIM, NC
40,000 World Vision, Monrovia, CA
30,000 International Rescue Committee, NY
30,000 Sentinal Group, WA
20,000 MAP International, GA
20,000 Prison Fellowship Ministries, Washington, DC
15,000 Mission Training and Resource Center, CA
10,000 Christian College Coalition, DC
10,000 World Concern, WA
4,000 American Leprosy Missions, SC

Wetterau

Sales: $5.77 billion
Employees: 16,100
Headquarters: Hazelwood, MO
SIC Major Group: Wholesale Trade—Nondurable Goods

CONTACT

Joyce Pinkowski
Contributions Coordinator
Wetterau Inc.
8920 Pershall Rd.
Hazelwood, MO 63042
(314) 524-5000

FINANCIAL SUMMARY

Recent Giving: $752,487 (fiscal 1990); $528,750 (fiscal 1989); $645,000 (fiscal 1988)
Fiscal Note: Company gives directly. Due to a recent takeover by Super Valu, figures for future giving are unavailable.

CONTRIBUTIONS SUMMARY

Typical Recipients: • *Arts & Humanities:* arts funds, museums/galleries, music, opera, performing arts • *Civic & Public Affairs:* economic development, housing, urban & community affairs, zoos/botanical gardens • *Education:* colleges & universities, education funds, elementary education, private education (precollege), public education (precollege) • *Health:* hospices, hospitals, medical research, single-disease health associations • *Science:* science exhibits & fairs • *Social Services:* emergency relief, recreation & athletics, shelters/homelessness, united funds, youth organizations
Grant Types: capital and general support
Nonmonetary Support Types: cause-related marketing & promotion, in-kind services, loaned employees, and loaned executives
Note: Estmated value of nonmonetary support is unavailable and is not included in above figures.
Geographic Distribution: national, with a focus on St. Louis, Missouri, and operating locations
Operating Locations: CA (Vernon), FL (Quincy), GA (Atlanta), IN (Bloomington), KY (Greenville, Lexington, Louisville), MA (Andover), MD (Hagerstown, Williamsport), ME (Portland, Presque Isle), MO (Desloge, Hazelwood, Kansas City, Mexico, Scott City, St. Louis), NH (Keene), OR (McKinnville), PA (Bell Vernon, Butler, Easton, Monroeville, Temple), RI (Providence), SC (Charleston), TN (Jackson), WV (Milton)

CORP. OFFICERS

Robert Keane Crutsinger: *B* St Louis MO 1930 *ED* Quincy Coll 1955 *CURR EMPL* chmn, chief exec off: Wetterau Properties *CORP AFFIL* ceo, chmn bd: Wetterau Properties; dir: Centerre Bank Florissant MO *NONPR AFFIL* mem: Am Mgmt Assn, Natl Am Wholesale Grocers Assn; trust: Quincy Coll
Robert E. Mohrmann: *CURR EMPL* vchmn, dir: Wetterau

GIVING OFFICERS

Joyce Pinkowski: *CURR EMPL* contributions coordinator: Wetterau

APPLICATION INFORMATION

Initial Approach: *Initial Contact:* brief letter requesting application form *Include Information On:* brief history, objectives, and current activities of the organization; description of the program or activity for which funds are requested, and verification of its need; proposed method of evaluating the program or activity; amount of request including where else funds are being sought and pledges to date *When to Submit:* any time, requests reviewed as received; requests in excess of $2,500 reviewed by board of directors at quarterly meetings (February, May, August, and November)
Restrictions on Giving: Company does not make contributions to individuals; political organizations or candidates; religious, fraternal, veterans, social, or similar groups; organizations deriving major support from government funding, or recipients of United Way, Arts & Education Council, or similar funding; organizations practicing discrimination on the basis of race, sex, or religion; or organizations outside the areas in which the company does business.

OTHER THINGS TO KNOW

Company has recently been bought out by Super Valu. As a result, priorities and guidelines may change in 1993.
Publications: application guidelines

GRANTS ANALYSIS

Total Grants: $752,487
Typical Range: $250 to $5,000

Disclosure Period: fiscal year ending March 31, 1990

Wexner Foundation

CONTACT
Maurice S. Corson
President
Wexner Fdn.
41 South High St., Ste. 3390
Columbus, OH 43215-6190
(614) 461-8112

FINANCIAL SUMMARY
Recent Giving: $4,820,553 (1991); $5,987,174 (1990); $3,567,949 (1989)
Assets: $122,340,758 (1991); $79,710,163 (1990); $83,377,690 (1989)
Gifts Received: $1,250,000 (1991); $600,000 (1990); $300,000 (1989)
EIN: 23-7320631

CONTRIBUTIONS SUMMARY
Donor(s): The foundation was established in 1973 by Leslie H. Wexner and Bella Wexner.
Typical Recipients: • *Education:* religious education • *Health:* hospitals, pediatric health • *Religion:* religious organizations, synagogues • *Social Services:* community service organizations
Grant Types: fellowship and project
Geographic Distribution: focus on OH

GIVING OFFICERS
Rabbi Maurice S. Corson: pres
Harold L. Levin: treas, trust
Stanley Schwartz, Jr.: secy
Bella Wexner: co-chmn, trust *CURR EMPL* dir, secy: The Ltd *PHIL AFFIL* pres, dir: Bella Wexner Charitable Foundation
Leslie Herbert Wexner: chmn, trust *B* Dayton OH 1937 *ED* OH St Univ BS 1959 *CURR EMPL* chmn, pres: The Ltd *CORP AFFIL* dir, mem exec comm: Banc One, Sothebys *NONPR AFFIL* co-chmn: Intl Un Jewish Appeal Comm; dir: Hebrew Immigrant Aid Soc; fdr: Columbus Fdn; founding mem: Columbus Capital Corp; mem adv counc, trust: OH St Univ; mem ex comm: Am Israel Pub Affs Comm, Am Jewish Joint Distribution Comm; natl vchmn: Un Jewish Appeal Federation; trust: Capitol South Commun Urban Devel Corp, Columbus Jewish Federation, Columbus Mus Art, Columbus Symphony Orchestra, Whitney Mus Am Art *PHIL AFFIL* chmn: Wexner Institutional Grants; chmn, trust: Wexner Heritage Foundation, Leslie H Wexner Charitable Fund; treas, dir: Bella Wexner Charitable Foundation

APPLICATION INFORMATION
Initial Approach:
For the Wexner Graduate Fellowship Program, call or write the foundation for an application. For the Institutional Grants for Graduate Professional Education Program and the Institutional Grants for Continuing Professional Education Program, send a letter of interest (two to three pages) to the director of the appropriate program. For the Wexner-Israel Fellowship Program, contact the program for an application form and further information. For the Wexner Graduate Fellowship Program, applicants should submit a completed application form, personal essays, transcripts of academic record, letters of recommendations and GRE General Test scores. Letters of interest for the Institutional Grants programs should answer the following questions: Upon what aspects of professional training will the project focus? On what basis was the need for this training determined to exist? How will the proposed project meet that need? What are the qualifications of your institution for carrying out the proposed project? What is the approximate amount of time and money required to carry out the proposed project? How will the effectiveness of the project be evaluated? If successful, how will the project be sustained once the grant has expired? Applicants should also list other sources of funding being sought and should briefly describe the relationship of the applying organization to the profession and professionals encompassed by the proposal. For the Wexner-Israel Fellowship Program, applicants should submit a completed application form, including personal essays (three copies), academic transcripts (one original and two copies), letters of recommendation, and scores from a standardized English proficiency test (check with fellowship office for details). It is strongly recommended but not required that results from a standardized test such as the GMAT or GRE also be submitted.

A full set of application materials for the Graduate Fellowship Program is due February 15 of each year. Letters of interest for the Institutional Grants programs are accepted throughout the year. If invited to do so, applicants should send formal project proposals by either November 1 or April 15. The last day to request materials for the Wexner-Israel Fellowship Program is November 25; completed applications and letters of recommendation are due by December 15.

For the Graduate Fellowship Program, fellows are selected by the Graduate Fellowship Committee, composed of leading academicians and professionals with expertise in the professional fields encompassed by the program. Awards are announced in early May for the ensuing academic year. For the Institutional Grants programs, the foundation determines the eligibility of the applicant and suitability of the contemplated project based on the letter of interest, then sends an invitation to submit a formal proposal, if appropriate. The Institutional Grants Committee evaluates the formal proposals and makes final funding decisions. Grants are announced by February 15 or August 15. All projects are expected to begin as soon as feasible, but no later than the start of the academic year following the foundation's approval. For the Wexner-Israel Fellowship Program, approximately 25 finalists are interviewed by the selection committee in February. The finalists are informed approximately two weeks before the interviews. A reception and orientation session are held for the new Wexner-Israel Fellows in April.

Restrictions on Giving: Under the Institutional Grants for Graduate Professional Education Program, the foundation does not contribute capital funds or support the purchase or maintenance of library, audio-visual, or computer equipment or supplies. Under the Institutional Grants Program for Continuing Profes-sional Education, the foundation does not contribute capital funds or operating funds for facilities.

OTHER THINGS TO KNOW
Publications: informational brochure and program policy statement

GRANTS ANALYSIS
Total Grants: $4,820,553
Number of Grants: 56
Highest Grant: $545,040
Typical Range: $2,000 to $80,000
Disclosure Period: 1991
Note: Average grant figure does not include the highest grant of $545,040. Recent grants are derived from a 1991 grants list.

RECENT GRANTS
545,040 Harvard University, Cambridge, MA
500,000 Wexner Heritage Foundation, Columbus, OH — educaitonal seminar
500,000 Wexner Heritage Foundation, Columbus, OH — educational seminar
500,000 Wexner Heritage Foundation, Columbus, OH — educational seminar
435,972 Hebrew Union College, Cincinnati, OH — fellowships
324,556 Jewish Theological Seminary, New York, NY
250,000 Wexner Heritage Foundation, Columbus, OH — educational seminar
206,776 Children's Hospital Foundation, Columbus, OH
156,500 Yeshiva University, New York, NY
100,000 Wexner Heritage Foundation, Columbus, OH — educational seminar

Weyerhaeuser Co. / Weyerhaeuser Co. Foundation
Sales: $9.25 billion
Employees: 39,022
Headquarters: Tacoma, WA
SIC Major Group: Chemicals & Allied Products, Lumber & Wood Products, Paper & Allied Products, and Real Estate

CONTACT
Elizabeth Crossman
Vice Presidnet
Weyerhaeuser Co. Fdn.
CH1F 31
Tacoma, WA 98477
(206) 924-3159

FINANCIAL SUMMARY
Recent Giving: $5,100,000 (1993 est.); $4,895,000 (1992); $4,600,000 (1991 approx.)
Assets: $9,207,547 (1992); $6,558,515 (1991); $1,688,726 (1989)
Fiscal Note: Above figures are for foundation contributions only. Local subsidiaries and operations also give directly. In 1992, this support was estimated at $1,000,000. Because these contribution programs are highly decentralized, detailed information is not available.
EIN: 91-6024225

CONTRIBUTIONS SUMMARY
Typical Recipients: • *Arts & Humanities:* arts associations, arts funds, arts institutes, community arts, dance, history/historic preservation, libraries, museums/galleries, music, opera, public broadcasting, theater • *Civic & Public Affairs:* business/free enterprise, economic development, economics, environmental affairs, housing, municipalities, nonprofit management, public policy, rural affairs, zoos/botanical gardens • *Education:* business education, colleges & universities, community & junior colleges, economic education, education associations, education funds, elementary education, engineering education, minority education, private education (precollege), public education (precollege), science/technology education • *Health:* emergency/ambulance services, health organizations, hospices, hospitals, medical rehabilitation, pediatric health, public health • *Social Services:* aged, child welfare, community centers, community service organizations, counseling, delinquency & crime, disabled, domestic violence, drugs & alcohol, employment/job training, family services, food/clothing distribution, recreation & athletics, shelters/homelessness, united funds, volunteer services, youth organizations

Grant Types: capital, employee matching gifts, general support, project, and research
Nonmonetary Support Types: in-kind services, loaned employees, and loaned executives
Note: Nonmonetary support is contributed directly through the company and no estimate of its value is available. Ms. Elizabeth Crossman, vice president, is the contact for nonmonetary support and may be reached at the above address.
Geographic Distribution: nationally and in Canada, with emphasis on communities, particularly remote communities, in which company has significant numbers of employees
Operating Locations: AL, AR (Hot Springs), CA (Alameda, Altadena, Anaheim, Belmont, City of Commerce, Colton, Emeryville, La Puente, Los Angeles, Modesto, Oceanside, Pleasanton, Rohnert Park, Salinas, San Francisco, San Jose, Santa Paula, West Sacramento), FL (Miami, Tampa), GA, HI (Honolulu), IA (Cedar Rapids, Waterloo), IL (Belleville, Elgin, Itasca, Rockford), KY (Franklin), MD (Dorsey, Millersville), ME (Westbrooke), MI (Warren), MN (Albert Lea, Austin, White Bear), MO (Clayton, St. Joseph, St. Louis), MS (Columbus, Jackson), NC (Charlotte, Durham, Greensboro, New Bern, Plymouth), NJ (Barrington, Closter, Marlton, Teaneck), OH (Columbus, Mount Vernon), OK (Oklahoma City, Valliant, Wright City), OR (Beaverton, Eugene, Klamath Falls, North Bend, Portland, Springfield), PA (Valley Forge), TX (Amarillo, Dallas, Grand Prairie, Houston, McAllen), VA (Lynchburg, Richmond), WA (Bellevue, Centralia, Chehalis, Cosmopolis, Everett, Federal Way, Kent, Longview, Olympia, Seattle, Tacoma, Union Gap, Vancouver), WI (Manitowoc, Rothschild)
Note: Also operates in Tokyo, Japan; and Beijing, China.

CORP. OFFICERS
John W. Creighton, Jr.: *B* Pittsburgh PA 1932 *ED* OH St Univ 1954; Univ Miami 1966 *CURR EMPL* pres, dir, ceo: Weyerhaeuser Co *CORP AFFIL* chmn bd dirs: Fed Home Loan Bank Seattle; dir: Am Paper Inst, MIP Properties, Mortgage Investments Plus

Inc, Portland Gen Corp, Puget Sound Bancorp, Quality Food Ctrs, WA Energy Co; pres: Weyerhaeuser Real Estate Co *NONPR AFFIL* dir: Natl Corp Housing Partnerships; dir, chief Seattle Coun: Boy Scouts Am, King County Un Way; trust: Univ Puget Sound
George Hunt Weyerhaeuser: *B* Seattle WA 1926 *ED* Yale Univ BS 1948 *CORP AFFIL* chmn: Weyerhaeuser Export; dir: Boeing Co, Chevron Corp, Fed Reserve Bank San Francisco, SAFECO Corp, Weyerhaeuser Real Estate Co; pres, dir: Weyerhaeuser Intl, Weyerhaeuser SA *NONPR AFFIL* mem: Bus Counc; mem adv bd: Bus Counc, Bus Roundtable, Univ WA Sch Bus Admin, WA St Bus Roundtable

GIVING OFFICERS
Charles W. Bingham: chmn, trust *B* Myrtle Point OR 1933 *ED* Harvard Univ BA 1955; Harvard Univ JD 1960 *CURR EMPL* exec vp: Weyerhaeuser Co *CORP AFFIL* dir: Puget Sound Power & Light Co *NONPR AFFIL* mem bd govs: Natl Forest Products Assn; mem: Soc Am Foresters
Mary L. Cabral: asst contr
John W. Creighton, Jr.: trust *CURR EMPL* pres, dir, ceo: Weyerhaeuser Co (see above)
Elizabeth Crossman: vp
Steven Richard Hill: trust *B* Oakland CA 1947 *CURR EMPL* sr vp human resources: Weyerhauser Co
N. E. Johnson: trust
C. Stephen Lewis: trust
Sandy D. McDade: asst secy (legal affairs)
William Howarth Meadowcroft: trust *ED* Univ Puget Sound; Harvard Univ MBA 1954 *CURR EMPL* asst to chmn: Weyerhaeuser Co *NONPR AFFIL* bd mem: Mus Flight; mem: Leukemia Soc Am, VA Mason Med Fdn, WA St Games Fdn; trust: Takoma Art Mus; trust, vchmn: Univ Puget Sound
Kenneth J. Stancato: contr *CURR EMPL* vp, contr: Weyerhaeuser Co
William Charles Stivers: treas, trust *B* Modesto CA 1938 *ED* Stanford Univ BA 1960; Univ Southern CA MBA 1963; Harvard Univ Sch Bus Admin 1977 *CURR EMPL* sr vp, cfo: Weyerhaeuser Co *CORP AFFIL* dir: First Interstate Bank WA, GNA Corp, Great

Northern Ins Annuity Co, Protection Mutual Ins Co, Republic Fed Savings & Loan; mem natl adv bd: Chem Banking Corp; pres, dir: S&S Land & Cattle Co *NONPR AFFIL* dir: Univ WA Ctr Study Banking Fin Markets; mem: Fin Execs Inst; mem fin comm: Am Paper Inst; trust, chmn: St Francis Hosp
Linda Terrien: asst treas
Karen L. Veitenhans: asst secy
J. H. Waechter: trust
George Hunt Weyerhaeuser: trust (see above)
Robert B. Wilson: trust

APPLICATION INFORMATION
Initial Approach: *Initial Contact:* brief letter or proposal *Include Information On:* description of project and sponsoring organization; statement of why project is consistent with foundation guidelines; project cost, sources of funding, and amount requested; evidence of tax-exempt status *When to Submit:* any time; requests received after September may not be considered until budgets are established for the following year *Note:* If further consideration is warranted, may ask for additional information or formal proposal; personal meetings or site visits are normally arranged only for projects that have passed initial letter of inquiry.
Restrictions on Giving: Does not support religious, sacramental, or theological functions; political campaigns; individuals; or direct grants to organizations already receiving foundation funds through an umbrella organization. Does not make grants for less than $1,000. Discourages applications seeking to cover operating deficits; for services that the public sector should reasonably be expected to provide; to purchase tables at fund-raising benefits; to establish endowments or to memorialize individuals; for research or conferences on topics outside the forest products industry; for hospital building of equipment campaigns that will result in significantly higher costs to health-care users; for services outside locales in which Weyerhaeuser has an operating facility or a significant number of employees; for general administrative expenses (with prior approval, direct

costs for reasonable levels of institutional support services may be included in the project's budget); or for amounts that are clearly unrealistic given the foundation's total annual budget (foundation follows accounting practices that require it to charge the full amount of a pledge against its current annual budget).

Grants will be made only to private, nonprofit, tax-exempt organizations with certified 501(c)(3) status, and to public entities qualifying under Section 170(c) of the Internal Revenue Code.

The foundation will not consider requests that do not meet its program and geographic criterion. If organizations are unsure about the presence of a Weyerhaeuser facility in their community, write or call the foundation for confirmation before submitting a grant request.

OTHER THINGS TO KNOW

Foundation makes cash grants only, with a $1,000 minimum. Normally, support is committed for one year at a time. Grants are given to eligible organizations primarily for special projects, with funding of general operations limited to a very small number of high-priority organizations.

Organizations receiving grants must practice equal opportunity.

Grants may be made to umbrella organizations or combined campaigns. Level of foundation support to such causes is influenced by the degree to which the organization rigorously reviews its annual priorities and allocations among member agencies; improves the efficiency of members' operations; provides leadership in responding to new needs; and evaluates the outcomes and impact of its members' activities.

Tends to make fewer but larger grants in order to concentrate sufficient resources to produce significant outcomes.

Foundation relies on advice of local review committees who represent company's regional operations. These volunteers establish local philanthropic priorities, review requests, recommend decisions, serve as grant monitors, and often assist with specific projects.

The Key University Program, initiated in 1987, is designed to concentrate resources at a few institutions that play major roles in education, research, or public service for the forest product industry.

Publications: biennial report and current guidelines, grant application, volunteer employee pamphlet

GRANTS ANALYSIS
Total Grants: $4,895,000
Number of Grants: 638
Highest Grant: $215,617
Typical Range: $1,000 to $10,000
Disclosure Period: 1992
Note: Average grant figure provided by the company. Recent grants are derived from a 1992 grants list.

RECENT GRANTS

295,000 Greater Tacoma Community Foundation, Tacoma, WA

215,617 National Merit Scholarship Corporation, Evanston, IL

134,032 United Way of Pierce County, Tacoma, WA

132,000 Saskatchewan Science Centre

125,000 Saskatchewan Science Centre

124,968 United Way of King County, Seattle, WA

112,030 Citizens Scholarship Foundation of America, St. Peter, MN

100,000 United Way of Pierce County, Tacoma, WA

95,000 Corporate Council for the Arts, Seattle, WA

77,674 Kamloops 1993 Canada Games Society

Weyerhaeuser Family Foundation
Former Foundation Name: Weyerhaeuser Foundation

CONTACT
Nancy N. Weyerhaeuser
President
Weyerhaeuser Family Fdn.
2100 First National Bank Bldg.
St. Paul, MN 55101
(612) 228-0935

FINANCIAL SUMMARY
Recent Giving: $377,625 (1990); $391,050 (1989); $371,438 (1988)
Assets: $8,162,148 (1990); $8,885,110 (1989); $8,146,710 (1988)
Gifts Received: $138,542 (1990); $135,452 (1989); $139,702 (1988)
EIN: 41-6012062

CONTRIBUTIONS SUMMARY
Donor(s): members of the Weyerhaeuser family
Typical Recipients: • *Arts & Humanities:* cinema, history/historic preservation • *Civic & Public Affairs:* environmental affairs, ethnic/minority organizations, international affairs, national security • *Education:* colleges & universities • *International:* international development/relief, international organizations • *Social Services:* animal protection, drugs & alcohol
Grant Types: emergency, project, and seed money

GIVING OFFICERS
Lynn Weyerhaeuser Day: trust, don
Elizabeth S. Driscoll: secy, trust
Rudolph W. Driscoll, Jr.: trust
Julia W. Heidman: trust
George Frederick Jewett, Jr.: don *B* Spokane WA 1927 *ED* Dartmouth Coll BA 1950; Harvard Univ MBA 1952 *CURR EMPL* vchmn, dir: Potlatch Corp *NONPR AFFIL* chmn: Pacific Presbyterian Med Fdn; dir: Carnegie Inst, San Francisco Ballet Assn; trust: Asia Fdn, Natl Gallery Art
Margaret King: trust
William Howarth Meadowcroft: trust *ED* Univ Puget Sound; Harvard Univ MBA 1954 *CURR EMPL* asst to chmn: Weyerhaeuser Co *NONPR AFFIL* bd mem: Mus Flight; mem: Leukemia Soc

Am, VA Mason Med Fdn, WA St Games Fdn; trust: Takoma Art Mus; trust, vchmn: Univ Puget Sound
J. S. Micallef: asst secy, asst treas
Elizabeth Davis Moorman: trust
Catherine W. Morley: trust
Robert J. Phares: trust
Lynn W. Piasecki: trust
Laura Rasmussen: trust
Walter Samuel Rosenberry III: treas, trust, don *ED* Harvard Univ AB 1953 *NONPR AFFIL* chmn: Denver Art Mus
Peter Titcomb: trust
Charles A. Weyerhaeuser: trust
Ginnie Weyerhaeuser: trust
Nancy Lane Neimeyer Weyerhaeuser: don, pres, trust
William Toycen Weyerhaeuser: trust *B* Tacoma WA 1943 *ED* Stanford Univ 1966; Fuller Grad Sch Psychology PhD 1975 *CURR EMPL* owner, chmn: Yelm Telephone Co *CORP AFFIL* dir: Potlatch Corp *NONPR AFFIL* mem: Am Psychological Assn; vchmn: Univ Puget Sound

APPLICATION INFORMATION
Initial Approach: Send letter requesting application form. Deadline is June 1.
Restrictions on Giving: Does not support individuals.

OTHER THINGS TO KNOW
Publications: Annual Report (including application guidelines)

GRANTS ANALYSIS
Number of Grants: 20
Highest Grant: $30,000
Typical Range: $10,000 to $25,000
Disclosure Period: 1990

RECENT GRANTS

30,000 Center for International Security and Strategic Studies, Mississippi State, MS

30,000 University of Minnesota Conflict and Change Center, Minneapolis, MN

25,000 Citizen Exchange Council, New York, NY

25,000 Conservation Fund, Arlington, VA

25,000 Coordination in Development, New York, NY

25,000 Institute for East/West Security Studies, New York, NY

25,000 National Fish and Wildlife Foundation, Washington, DC

25,000 Population Communications International, New York, NY

25,000 Southern African Freedom Through Education Foundation, Berkeley, CA

20,625 United Nations Association, New York, NY

Weyerhaeuser Foundation, Frederick and Margaret L.

CONTACT
Frederick T. Weyerhaeuser
President
Frederick and Margaret L. Weyerhaeuser Fdn.
2100 First National Bank Bldg.
St. Paul, MN 55101
(612) 228-0935

FINANCIAL SUMMARY
Recent Giving: $378,125 (fiscal 1991); $473,850 (fiscal 1990); $230,400 (fiscal 1989)
Assets: $2,028,806 (fiscal year ending June 30, 1991); $2,164,089 (fiscal 1990); $2,353,600 (fiscal 1989)
Gifts Received: $92,839 (fiscal 1991); $169,500 (fiscal 1990); $400,000 (fiscal 1989)
Fiscal Note: In 1991, contributions were received from Trust of C. L. Weyerhauser ($34,000), the Trust of Margaret W. Harmon ($18,500), and the Trust of Ginnie Weyerhauser ($40,338).
EIN: 41-6029036

CONTRIBUTIONS SUMMARY
Donor(s): Margaret Weyerhaeuser Harmon
Typical Recipients: • *Arts & Humanities:* arts institutes, libraries, music, theater • *Civic & Public Affairs:* environmental affairs, international affairs • *Education:* colleges & universities, religious education • *Health:* hospitals • *International:* foreign educational institutions • *Religion:* missionary activities, religious organizations • *Social Serv-*

ices: community centers, community service organizations, homes, united funds, youth organizations
Grant Types: capital, multiyear/continuing support, and project
Geographic Distribution: focus on MN

GIVING OFFICERS
Gordon E. Hed: dir, treas
Charles I. Weyerhaeuser: vp
Frederick Theodore Weyerhaeuser: pres, dir, don *B* Duluth MN 1931 *ED* Yale Univ BS 1953 *CURR EMPL* chmn, treas: Clearwater Mgmt Co *CORP AFFIL* chmn, treas: Clearwater Investment Trust; dir: Potlatch Corp; trust: MN Mutual Life Ins Co *NONPR AFFIL* chmn, trust: Macalester Coll; dir: Union Gospel Mission

APPLICATION INFORMATION
Initial Approach: Send brief letter describing program. There are no deadlines.

GRANTS ANALYSIS
Number of Grants: 35
Highest Grant: $50,000
Typical Range: $2,000 to $10,000
Disclosure Period: fiscal year ending June 30, 1991

RECENT GRANTS
50,000 Minneapolis Institute of Arts, Minneapolis, MN

50,000 Presbyterian Homes of Minnesota, St. Paul, MN

25,000 Macalester College, St. Paul, MN

25,000 Merriam Park Community Center, St. Paul, MN

25,000 Minnesota Landscape Arboretum Foundation, MN

20,000 American University in Cairo, New York, NY

20,000 Macalester College, St. Paul, MN

20,000 Minnesota Historical Society, St. Paul, MN

20,000 Ordway Music Theatre, St. Paul, MN

10,000 Center for Theological Inquiry, Princeton, NJ

Weyerhaeuser Memorial Foundation, Charles A.

CONTACT
Lucy R. McCarthy
President
Charles A. Weyerhaeuser Memorial Fdn.
2100 First National Bank Bldg.
St. Paul, MN 55101
(612) 228-0935

FINANCIAL SUMMARY
Recent Giving: $120,976 (fiscal 1991); $289,139 (fiscal 1990); $296,850 (fiscal 1989)
Assets: $3,704,020 (fiscal year ending February 28, 1991); $3,452,280 (fiscal 1990); $3,269,740 (fiscal 1989)
Gifts Received: $21,656 (fiscal 1991); $19,453 (fiscal 1990); $43,045 (fiscal 1989)
Fiscal Note: In 1991, contributions were received from Berkshire Hathaway ($1,236), Lucy R. McCarthy ($20,000), and the Carl A. Weyerhaeuser 1972 Trust ($420).
EIN: 41-6012063

CONTRIBUTIONS SUMMARY
Donor(s): Carl A. Weyerhaeuser Trusts
Typical Recipients: • *Arts & Humanities:* arts centers, community arts, libraries, music, performing arts, public broadcasting • *Civic & Public Affairs:* zoos/botanical gardens • *Education:* colleges & universities, elementary education • *Religion:* churches • *Social Services:* community service organizations, united funds
Grant Types: general support, multiyear/continuing support, and project
Geographic Distribution: focus on MN

GIVING OFFICERS
Elise R. Donohue: dir
Gordon E. Hed: dir
Lucy R. McCarthy: pres, dir
Joseph S. Micallef: secy, treas, dir
Charles W. Rosenberry II: dir
Walter Samuel Rosenberry III: off *ED* Harvard Univ AB 1953 *NONPR AFFIL* chmn: Denver Art Mus
Robert J. Sivertsen: vp, dir

APPLICATION INFORMATION
Initial Approach: Send cover letter and full proposal. There are no deadlines.
Restrictions on Giving: Does not support individuals.

GRANTS ANALYSIS
Number of Grants: 6
Highest Grant: $72,976
Typical Range: $1,000 to $25,000
Disclosure Period: fiscal year ending February 28, 1991

RECENT GRANTS
72,976 House of Hope Presbyterian Church, St. Paul, MN

25,000 Menninger Foundation, Topeka, KS

20,000 Minnesota Conservatory of Performing Arts, St. Paul, MN

1,000 Dr. Knight Science and Technology Magnet Elementary School, Randall, MN

1,000 Schubert Club, St. Paul, MN

1,000 United Way, St. Paul, MN

Whalley Charitable Trust

CONTACT
G. Lesko
Whalley Charitable Trust
1210 Graham Ave.
Windber, PA 15963
(814) 467-4000

FINANCIAL SUMMARY
Recent Giving: $156,090 (1991); $163,678 (1990); $175,846 (1989)
Assets: $3,683,628 (1991); $3,274,919 (1990); $3,546,827 (1989)
EIN: 23-7128436

CONTRIBUTIONS SUMMARY
Donor(s): John J. Whalley, John Whalley, Jr., Mary Whalley
Typical Recipients: • *Arts & Humanities:* history/historic preservation, museums/galleries • *Civic & Public Affairs:* municipalities • *Education:* colleges & universities • *Religion:* churches • *Social Services:* community service organizations, homes, united funds, youth organizations

Grant Types: general support
Geographic Distribution: focus on PA

GIVING OFFICERS
David Klementik: trust
Klementik G. Lesko: trust

APPLICATION INFORMATION
Initial Approach: Send brief letter describing program. There are no deadlines.

GRANTS ANALYSIS
Number of Grants: 52
Highest Grant: $22,639
Typical Range: $100 to $5,000
Disclosure Period: 1991

RECENT GRANTS
22,639 University of Pittsburgh, Johnstown, PA
22,639 University of Pittsburgh, Johnstown, PA
22,639 University of Pittsburgh, Johnstown, PA
10,000 Old Bedford Village, Bedford, PA
10,000 Windber Community Building, Windber, PA
8,325 University of Pittsburgh, Johnstown, PA
5,000 Automotive Hall of Fame, Midland, MI
5,000 Presbyterian Home of Redstone Presbyterian, Johnstown, PA
5,000 Windber Community Building, Windber, PA
5,000 Windber First Lutheran Church, Windber, PA

Wharton Foundation

CONTACT
J. B. Wharton
Manager
Wharton Fdn.
1400 112th Ave. S.E. 100
Bellevue, WA 98004
(206) 455-3257

FINANCIAL SUMMARY
Recent Giving: $187,457 (1991); $167,962 (1990); $193,093 (1989)
Assets: $3,748,747 (1991); $3,675,130 (1990); $3,684,946 (1989)
Gifts Received: $56,500 (1991); $184,500 (1990); $187,500 (1989)
Fiscal Note: In 1991, contributions were received from Sara

P. Wharton ($55,000), and The Wealden Company ($1,500).
EIN: 36-6130748

CONTRIBUTIONS SUMMARY
Typical Recipients: • *Arts & Humanities:* history/historic preservation, libraries, performing arts, public broadcasting • *Education:* colleges & universities, private education (precollege), religious education • *Religion:* churches, religious organizations • *Social Services:* animal protection, child welfare, community centers, community service organizations, domestic violence, family services, united funds, youth organizations
Grant Types: general support
Geographic Distribution: focus on AZ, IL, WA, CA, and FL.

GIVING OFFICERS
M. W. Minnich: vp, dir
J. W. Pettitt: vp, dir
Joseph B. Wharton III: secy, treas
M. W. Wharton: vp, dir
W. R. Wharton: pres, dir

APPLICATION INFORMATION
Initial Approach: Contributes only to preselected organizations.
Restrictions on Giving: Does not support individuals.

OTHER THINGS TO KNOW
Publications: Application Guidelines

GRANTS ANALYSIS
Number of Grants: 70
Highest Grant: $35,500
Typical Range: $300 to $5,000
Disclosure Period: 1991

RECENT GRANTS
35,500 Phoenix Country Day School, Seattle, WA
20,000 Medina Children's Service, Seattle, WA
20,000 University Presbyterian Church, Seattle, WA
12,400 Providence Foundation of Seattle, Seattle, WA
10,500 New Horizons Ministries, Seattle, WA
10,000 Future Leaders of America, Seattle, WA

10,000 Northwest Mediation Service, Seattle, WA
10,000 YMCA, Seattle, WA
5,000 Eastside Domestic Violence, Seattle, WA
5,000 Seattle University, Seattle, WA

Wharton Trust, William P.

CONTACT
Rhodes G. Lockwood
Trustee
William P. Wharton Trust
c/o Choate, Hall and Stewart
Exchange Pl., 34th Fl.
Boston, MA 02109-2808
(617) 227-5020

FINANCIAL SUMMARY
Recent Giving: $70,451 (fiscal 1992); $55,318 (fiscal 1991); $75,937 (fiscal 1990)
Assets: $1,922,750 (fiscal year ending September 30, 1992); $1,837,133 (fiscal 1991); $1,681,455 (fiscal 1990)
EIN: 04-6407797

CONTRIBUTIONS SUMMARY
Typical Recipients: • *Civic & Public Affairs:* environmental affairs, zoos/botanical gardens • *Science:* scientific institutes • *Social Services:* animal protection
Grant Types: project and research
Geographic Distribution: focus on MA and New England

GIVING OFFICERS
John M. Cornish: trust
Peter A. Fine: trust
Rhodes Greene Lockwood: trust *B* Buchanan VA 1919 *ED* Williams Coll BA 1941; Univ VA postgrad 1941-1942; Harvard Univ LLB 1949 *CURR EMPL* ptnr: Choate Hall & Stewart *NONPR AFFIL* mem: Am Law Inst, Am Soc Hosp Attys, Boston Bar Assn, Harvard Univ Law Sch Alumni Assn, MA Hosp Assn; secy, trust: Univ Hosps; trust: Brigham Womens Hosp

APPLICATION INFORMATION
Initial Approach: Funds limited to no more than $5,000 per application. Send brief letter describing program. Deadlines are April 15 and October 15.

OTHER THINGS TO KNOW
Publications: Informational Brochure (including application guidelines)

GRANTS ANALYSIS
Number of Grants: 17
Highest Grant: $5,000
Typical Range: $2,500 to $5,000
Disclosure Period: fiscal year ending September 30, 1992

RECENT GRANTS
5,000 Adirondack Conservation Council, Elizabethtown, NY
5,000 Appalachian Mountain Club, Boston, MA
5,000 Everglades Nature Center at Flamingo Gardens, Ft. Lauderdale, FL
5,000 Friends of Mount Auburn, Cambridge, MA
5,000 Maine Audubon Society, Portland, ME
4,000 Massachusetts Land League, Belchertown, MA
4,000 Merrimack River Watershed Council, West Newbury, MA
3,500 Massachusetts Forestry Association, Princeton, NJ
3,000 Audubon Society of New Hampshire, Concord, NH
3,000 Massachusetts Audubon Society, Lincoln, MA

Wheat First Securites / Wheat Foundation

Sales: $204.0 million
Employees: 1,100
Parent Company: WFS Financial Corp.
Headquarters: Richmond, VA
SIC Major Group: Security & Commodity Brokers

CONTACT
William V. Daniel
Director and Treasurer
Wheat Foundation
P. O. Box 1357
Richmond, VA 23211
(804) 649-2311

FINANCIAL SUMMARY
Recent Giving: $626,008 (fiscal 1992); $390,176 (fiscal 1991)

Assets: $1,227,870 (fiscal year ending March 31, 1992); $971,152 (fiscal 1990)
Gifts Received: $700,000 (fiscal 1992); $354,563 (fiscal 1990)
Fiscal Note: Contributes through foundation only. In 1992, contributions were received from Wheat, First Securities.
EIN: 54-6047119

CONTRIBUTIONS SUMMARY

Typical Recipients: • *Arts & Humanities:* arts funds, history/historic preservation, libraries, museums/galleries • *Civic & Public Affairs:* economic development, municipalities • *Education:* colleges & universities, community & junior colleges, education associations • *Health:* medical research, single-disease health associations • *Social Services:* community centers, community service organizations, disabled, united funds, youth organizations
Grant Types: capital and general support
Geographic Distribution: in headquarters and operating communities
Operating Locations: VA (Richmond)

CORP. OFFICERS

John Lee McElroy, Jr.: *B* Richmond VA 1931 *ED* Univ VA B 1953 *CURR EMPL* chmn, ceo, dir: Wheat First Securities *CORP AFFIL* dir: Piper Jaffray & Hopwood; vchmn, ceo, dir: WFS Fin Corp *NONPR AFFIL* dir: Central Richmond Assn, Childrens Home Soc; pres: VA Historical Soc; trust: St Pauls Episcopal Church Home
Marshall B. Wishnack: *CURR EMPL* pres, dir: Wheat First Securities *CORP AFFIL* pres, ceo, dir: WFS Fin Corp

GIVING OFFICERS

William V. Daniel: treas, dir *B* Philadelphia PA 1928 *ED* Univ VA 1950 *CURR EMPL* mng dir: Wheat First Securities *CORP AFFIL* dir: Fidelity Bankers Life Ins Co, James River Corp VA, WFS Fin Corp
Sharon L. Hobart: asst secy
Howard T. Macrae, Jr.: secy
John Lee McElroy, Jr.: pres, dir *CURR EMPL* chmn, ceo, dir: Wheat First Securities (see above)

James C. Wheat, Jr.: dir
Marshall B. Wishnack: dir *CURR EMPL* pres, dir: Wheat First Securities (see above)

APPLICATION INFORMATION

Initial Approach: *Initial Contact:* letter of inquiry *Include Information On:* Include a description of organization, amount requested, purpose of funds sought, recently audited financial statement, and proof of tax-exempt status. *When to Submit:* any time
Restrictions on Giving: Does not support individuals, religious organizations for sectarian purposes, political or lobbying groups, or organizations outside operating areas.

GRANTS ANALYSIS

Total Grants: $626,008
Number of Grants: 526
Highest Grant: $20,000
Typical Range: $50 to $1,000
Disclosure Period: fiscal year ending March 31, 1992
Note: Recent grants are derived from a fiscal 1992 grants list.

RECENT GRANTS

20,000 College of William and Mary, Williamsburg, VA — development fund
20,000 James Madison University, Harrisonburg, VA
20,000 University of Pennsylvania, Philadelphia, PA
20,000 University of Virginia, Charlottesville, VA — building program
20,000 Valentine Museum, Richmond, VA
20,000 Virginia Military Institute, Lexington, VA — endowment
15,000 University of Richmond, Richmond, VA
10,000 Capital Area Assembly, Richmond, VA
10,000 River Foundation, Roanoke, VA
10,000 Shenandoah University, Winchester, VA

Wheaton Industries

Sales: $480.0 million
Employees: 5,500
Parent Company: Wheaton, Inc.
Headquarters: Millville, NJ
SIC Major Group: Rubber & Miscellaneous Plastics Products and Stone, Clay & Glass Products

CONTACT

Earleen Charlesworth
Director, Public Relations
Wheaton Industries
1101 Wheaton Ave.
Millville, NJ 08332
(609) 825-1400

CONTRIBUTIONS SUMMARY

Operating Locations: NJ (Millville)

CORP. OFFICERS

Robert Veghte: *CURR EMPL* pres: Wheaton Indus

Wheeler Foundation

CONTACT

Samuel C. Wheeler
President
Wheeler Fdn.
1211 S.W. Fifth Avenue, Ste. 2906
Portland, OR 97204-1911
(503) 228-0261

FINANCIAL SUMMARY

Recent Giving: $252,600 (1991); $231,900 (1990); $225,700 (1989)
Assets: $5,415,668 (1991); $4,050,792 (1990); $5,291,225 (1989)
Gifts Received: $20,000 (1991); $20,000 (1990)
Fiscal Note: In 1991, contributions were received from the Coleman H. Wheeler Trust.
EIN: 93-0553801

CONTRIBUTIONS SUMMARY

Donor(s): the late Coleman H. Wheeler, Cornelia T. Wheeler
Typical Recipients: • *Arts & Humanities:* history/historic preservation, museums/galleries, music, theater • *Civic & Public Affairs:* environmental affairs • *Education:* colleges & universities, private education

(precollege), science/technology education • *Health:* hospitals • *Religion:* religious organizations • *Social Services:* food/clothing distribution, united funds, youth organizations
Grant Types: general support
Geographic Distribution: focus on OR

GIVING OFFICERS

Lil M. Hendrickson: asst secy
David A. Kekel: off
Charles B. Wheeler: vp, dir
Edward T. Wheeler: secy, dir
John C. Wheeler: vp, dir
Samuel C. Wheeler: pres, dir
Thomas K. Wheeler: treas, dir

APPLICATION INFORMATION

Initial Approach: Send brief letter of inquiry describing program or project. There are no deadlines.

GRANTS ANALYSIS

Number of Grants: 72
Highest Grant: $17,500
Typical Range: $1,000 to $5,000
Disclosure Period: 1991

RECENT GRANTS

17,500 Oregon Historical Society, Portland, OR
15,000 Marylhurst College, Marylhurst, OR
14,000 George Fox College, Newberg, OR
12,000 Sisters of Holy Names of Jesus and Mary, Marylhurst, OR
9,000 Lewis and Clark College, Portland, OR
8,000 DePaul Center, Portland, OR
8,000 Jesuit High School, Portland, OR
8,000 World Forestry Center, Portland, OR
5,500 Young Concert Artists, New York, NY
5,000 Jackson Laboratory, Bar Harbor, ME

Wheeler Foundation, Wilmot

CONTACT
Wilmot F. Wheeler, Jr.
President
Wilmot Wheeler Fdn.
PO Box 429
Southport, CT 06490
(203) 259-1615

FINANCIAL SUMMARY
Recent Giving: $70,925 (fiscal 1991); $62,100 (fiscal 1990); $52,950 (fiscal 1989)
Assets: $2,013,327 (fiscal year ending June 30, 1991); $2,024,506 (fiscal 1990); $1,771,812 (fiscal 1989)
EIN: 06-6039119

CONTRIBUTIONS SUMMARY
Donor(s): the late Wilmot F. Wheeler, Hulda C. Wheeler
Typical Recipients: • *Arts & Humanities:* community arts, music, opera, public broadcasting • *Civic & Public Affairs:* municipalities • *Education:* colleges & universities, private education (precollege) • *Health:* emergency/ambulance services • *Religion:* churches, religious organizations • *Social Services:* community service organizations, united funds, youth organizations
Grant Types: general support
Geographic Distribution: focus on CT

GIVING OFFICERS
Halsted W. Wheeler: secy
Wilmont F. Wheeler III: vp, treas
Wilmont Fitch Wheeler, Jr.: pres *B* Southport CT 1923 *ED* Yale Univ BA 1945; NY Univ postgrad 1947-1948 *CURR EMPL* chmn, dir: Jelliff Corp *CORP AFFIL* trust: Am Farm Sch, Peoples Mutual Holdings; vchmn: Manhattan Natl Corp *NONPR AFFIL* trust: Bridgeport Hosp, Univ Bridgeport

APPLICATION INFORMATION
Initial Approach: Send brief letter describing program. There are no deadlines.

GRANTS ANALYSIS
Number of Grants: 51
Highest Grant: $17,500
Typical Range: $300 to $3,000

Disclosure Period: fiscal year ending June 30, 1991

RECENT GRANTS
17,500 St. Lukes Parish
5,000 Rector Academy
5,000 St. Pauls Church
5,000 YMCA
3,000 United Way
2,950 St. Pauls School
2,500 Joffrey Ballet, New York, NY
2,000 Connecticut Grand Opera, Stamford, CT
2,000 Living Church Foundation, Boston, MA
2,000 Proctor Academy, Andover, NH

Wheeler Trust, Clara

CONTACT
Meg Armstrong
Trust Administrator
Clara Wheeler Trust
PO Box 5168
Colorado National Bank
Denver, CO 80217
(303) 893-1862

FINANCIAL SUMMARY
Recent Giving: $154,117 (1991); $163,870 (1990); $161,966 (1989)
Assets: $1,666,627 (1991); $1,770,974 (1990); $1,861,195 (1989)
EIN: 84-6018431

CONTRIBUTIONS SUMMARY
Typical Recipients: • *Education:* colleges & universities • *Health:* hospitals, medical research
Grant Types: research

APPLICATION INFORMATION
Initial Approach: Request application form. Deadline is March 15.

OTHER THINGS TO KNOW
Provides grants to individuals for cancer research.
Disclosure Period: 1991

Wheeling-Pittsburgh Corp.

Sales: $929.8 million
Employees: 5,000
Headquarters: New York, NY
SIC Major Group: Holding & Other Investment Offices and Primary Metal Industries

CONTACT
Charlotte Palmer
Director, Corporate Communications
Wheeling-Pittsburgh Corp.
110 E. 59th St.
New York, NY 10022
(304) 234-2223

FINANCIAL SUMMARY
Fiscal Note: Annual Giving Range: less than $100,000

CONTRIBUTIONS SUMMARY
Foundation disbanded in May 1990, however direct contributions may continue. At time of publication, company was in the process of evaluating contributions activities.
Operating Locations: OH (Canfield, Mingo Junction), WV (Omar, Wheeling)

CORP. OFFICERS
Robin Chenery: *CURR EMPL* chmn, ceo, dir: Wheeling-Pittsburgh Steel Corp
James L. Wareham: *CURR EMPL* pres, coo, dir: Wheeling-Pittsburgh Steel Corp

Wheelwright Scientific School

CONTACT
Josiah H. Welch
Secretary
Wheelwright Scientific School
c/o Woodstock Service Corporation
18 Tremont St.
Boston, MA 02108
(617) 462-4434

FINANCIAL SUMMARY
Recent Giving: $87,750 (fiscal 1990); $82,070 (fiscal 1989)
Assets: $2,776,424 (fiscal year ending June 30, 1990); $2,567,305 (fiscal 1989)
EIN: 04-6004390

CONTRIBUTIONS SUMMARY
Typical Recipients: • *Education:* science/technology education
Grant Types: scholarship

Geographic Distribution: limited to Newburyport, MA, residents

GIVING OFFICERS
Edward G. Malin: trust
John H. Pramberg, Jr.: trust
John W. Pramberg: trust
Douglas Sloane IV: treas
Josiah H. Welch: secy
James A. Zafris, Jr.: trust

APPLICATION INFORMATION
Initial Approach: Application form required.
Disclosure Period: fiscal year ending June 30, 1990

Wheless Foundation

CONTACT
Brett Josey
Wheless Fdn.
c/o Commercial National Bank Trust Department
PO Box 21119
Shreveport, LA 71152
(318) 429-1724

FINANCIAL SUMMARY
Recent Giving: $122,850 (fiscal 1991); $150,561 (fiscal 1990); $116,475 (fiscal 1989)
Assets: $3,365,556 (fiscal year ending October 31, 1991); $2,889,229 (fiscal 1990); $2,898,836 (fiscal 1989)
EIN: 72-6017724

CONTRIBUTIONS SUMMARY
Donor(s): the late N. Hobson Wheless
Typical Recipients: • *Arts & Humanities:* community arts, music • *Education:* colleges & universities, science/technology education • *Health:* health organizations, medical research • *Religion:* churches • *Social Services:* aged, child welfare, community service organizations, drugs & alcohol, united funds, youth organizations
Grant Types: general support
Geographic Distribution: focus on LA

GIVING OFFICERS
Commerce National Bank: trust
Elise W. Hogan: trust

APPLICATION INFORMATION
Initial Approach: Send brief letter of inquiry describing program. There are no deadlines.

GRANTS ANALYSIS
Number of Grants: 58
Highest Grant: $35,650
Typical Range: $100 to $2,000
Disclosure Period: fiscal year ending October 31, 1991

RECENT GRANTS
35,650 Centenary College, Shreveport, LA
15,500 United Way, Shreveport, LA
13,300 St. Mark's Episcopal Church, Shreveport, LA
10,000 Biomedical Research Foundation, Shreveport, LA
5,100 Glen Retirement Village, Shreveport, LA
5,000 Mothers Against Drugs, Shreveport, LA
3,100 YMCA, Shreveport, LA
3,000 Massachusetts Institute of Technology, Cambridge, MA
2,750 Boy Scouts of America, Shreveport, LA
2,700 US Pony Clubs, West Chester, PA

Whirlpool Corp. / Whirlpool Foundation
Sales: $7.09 billion
Employees: 38,500
Headquarters: Benton Harbor, MI
SIC Major Group: Electronic & Other Electrical Equipment and Industrial Machinery & Equipment

CONTACT
Colleen D. Keast
Executive Director
Whirlpool Fdn.
400 Riverview Dr.
Ste. 410
Benton Harbor, MI 49022
(616) 923-5112
Note: An alternative contact is Ms. Sharron Krieger.

FINANCIAL SUMMARY
Recent Giving: $5,300,000 (1993 est.); $4,100,000 (1992 approx.); $3,734,578 (1991)
Assets: $14,852,269 (1991); $5,614,000 (1990); $13,854,245 (1989)
Fiscal Note: Company gives directly and through the foundation; figures above represent combined giving.
EIN: 38-6077342

CONTRIBUTIONS SUMMARY
Typical Recipients: • *Arts & Humanities:* arts associations, arts centers, arts funds, arts institutes, community arts, dance, ethnic arts, history/historic preservation, libraries, museums/galleries, music, opera, performing arts, public broadcasting, theater, visual arts • *Civic & Public Affairs:* business/free enterprise, civil rights, consumer affairs, economic development, economics, environmental affairs, first amendment issues, housing, law & justice, municipalities, nonprofit management, professional & trade associations, public policy, safety, urban & community affairs, women's affairs, zoos/botanical gardens • *Education:* arts education, business education, career/vocational education, colleges & universities, community & junior colleges, economic education, education associations, education funds, elementary education, engineering education, international studies, liberal arts education, literacy, medical education, minority education, private education (precollege), public education (precollege), science/technology education, social sciences education, student aid • *Health:* geriatric health, health care cost containment, health funds, health organizations, hospices, hospitals, medical rehabilitation, medical research, mental health, outpatient health care delivery, pediatric health, single-disease health associations • *Religion:* churches, religious organizations • *Science:* science exhibits & fairs, scientific institutes, scientific organizations • *Social Services:* aged, animal protection, child welfare, community centers, community service organizations, counseling, delinquency & crime, disabled, domestic violence, drugs & alcohol, employment/job training, family planning, family services, food/clothing distribution, homes, recreation & athletics, religious welfare, shelters/homelessness, united funds, volunteer services, youth organizations
Grant Types: capital, department, employee matching gifts, fellowship, professorship, project, and scholarship
Nonmonetary Support Types: donated equipment and donated products
Note: Value of nonmonetary support is not available and is not included in total figures above.
Geographic Distribution: only areas where Whirlpool maintains manufacturing facilities
Operating Locations: AR (Fort Smith), IN (Evansville, La Porte), MI (Benton Harbor), OH (Clyde, Findlay, Marion), TN (Lavergne)

CORP. OFFICERS
David Ray Whitwam: *B* Stanley WI 1942 *ED* Univ WI BS 1967 *CURR EMPL* chmn, pres, ceo, dir: Whirlpool Corp *CORP AFFIL* dir: Combustion Engg *NONPR AFFIL* dir: Soup Kitchen; fellow: Aspen Inst; mem: Natl Counc Housing Indus

GIVING OFFICERS
Bradley Bell: treas *B* Chicago IL 1952 *ED* Univ IL 1974; Harvard Univ MBA 1978 *CURR EMPL* vp, treas: Whirlpool Corp
Bruce Berger: trust
Colleen D. Keast: exec dir *ED* OH St Univ BA
Sharron Krieger: program adm
Stephen E. Upton: pres, trust *B* Benton Harbor MI 1924 *ED* Univ MI 1949 *CURR EMPL* sr vp: Whirlpool Corp
Jay Van Den Berg: trust
Gloria Zamora: trust

APPLICATION INFORMATION
Initial Approach: *Initial Contact:* brief letter or telephone call to get guidelines and application form *Include Information On:* description of the organization, amount requested, purpose for which funds are sought, recently audited financial statement, and proof of tax-exempt status *When to Submit:* by January 30, April 30, July 31 or October 31
Restrictions on Giving: Does not support dinners or special events, fraternal organizations, goodwill advertising, individuals, political or lobbying groups, or religious organizations for sectarian purposes.

GRANTS ANALYSIS
Total Grants: $4,100,000
Number of Grants: 400
Highest Grant: $980,000
Typical Range: $1,000 to $25,000
Disclosure Period: 1992
Note: Average grant is from 1990 and is for foundation only. Assets are for 1991. Recent grants are derived from a 1991 Form 990.

RECENT GRANTS
980,000 Community Economic Development Corporation, Benton Harbor, MI
200,000 Lake Michigan College Educational Fund
142,660 United Way-Blossomland
110,000 University of Michigan, Ann Arbor, MI
107,214 Community Economic Development Corporation, Benton Harbor, MI
98,912 American Home Economics Association, Alexandria, VA
80,000 United Way-Southwestern Indiana, IN
70,000 United Way-Marion County
50,000 Berrien County Intermediate School District, MI
50,000 Purdue University, Lafayette, IN

Whitaker Charitable Foundation, Lyndon C.

CONTACT
Urban C. Bergbauer, Jr.
Trustee
Lyndon C. Whitaker Charitable Fdn.
120 South Central St., Ste. 1122
Clayton, MO 63105
(314) 726-5734

FINANCIAL SUMMARY
Recent Giving: $907,800 (fiscal 1992); $840,242 (fiscal 1991); $878,354 (fiscal 1990)
Assets: $22,121,889 (fiscal year ending April 30, 1992); $21,047,306 (fiscal 1991); $19,329,616 (fiscal 1990)
EIN: 51-0173109

CONTRIBUTIONS SUMMARY

Donor(s): The foundation was established in 1975 by the late Mae M. Whitaker.

Typical Recipients: • *Arts & Humanities:* arts funds, community arts, music, opera, performing arts, theater • *Civic & Public Affairs:* environmental affairs, philanthropic organizations, professional & trade associations, zoos/botanical gardens • *Education:* colleges & universities, medical education, private education (precollege) • *Health:* hospices, hospitals, medical research, single-disease health associations • *Religion:* religious organizations • *Science:* scientific organizations • *Social Services:* child welfare, community centers, community service organizations, disabled, homes, united funds, youth organizations

Grant Types: endowment, general support, and research
Geographic Distribution: focus on St. Louis, MO

GIVING OFFICERS
Urban C. Bergbauer, Jr.: trust

APPLICATION INFORMATION

Initial Approach:
Applications should be submitted in writing and state the purpose of the organization and the benefits of the project. Financial data should also be attached.

The foundation has no deadline for submitting proposals.

Restrictions on Giving:
Grants are made to organizations qualified under section 501(c)(3) of the IRS code. The foundation does not make grants to individuals.

GRANTS ANALYSIS
Total Grants: $907,800
Number of Grants: 85
Highest Grant: $150,000
Typical Range: $500 to $12,000
Disclosure Period: fiscal year ending April 30, 1992
Note: Recent grants are derived from a fiscal 1992 grants list.

RECENT GRANTS
150,000 Washington University, St. Louis, MO
100,000 Grand Center, St. Louis, MO
75,000 Opera Theatre of St. Louis, St. Louis, MO
55,000 CASA, St. Louis, MO
50,000 Opera Theatre of St. Louis, St. Louis, MO
50,000 Salk Institute, San Diego, CA
50,000 St. Louis Symphony Orchestra, St. Louis, MO
50,000 Washington University, St. Louis, MO
40,000 St. Louis Symphony Orchestra, St. Louis, MO
35,000 Paraquad, St. Louis, MO

Whitaker Foundation

CONTACT
Miles J. Gibbons, Jr.
President
Whitaker Foundation
4718 Old Gettysburg Rd., Ste. 405
Mechanicsburg, PA 17055-4380
(717) 763-1391

FINANCIAL SUMMARY
Recent Giving: $17,410,000 (1992 approx.); $15,007,433 (1991); $14,838,577 (1990)
Assets: $375,000,000 (1992 est.); $365,152,660 (1991); $293,966,316 (1990); $299,292,461 (1989)
Gifts Received: $2,109,460 (1990); $166,732 (1989); $216,811 (1988)
Fiscal Note: The foundation receives contributions from a trust account of Helen Whitaker. The foundation changed its disclosure period in 1987 from a fiscal year format ending February 28 to a calendar year format.
EIN: 22-2096948

CONTRIBUTIONS SUMMARY

Donor(s): The foundation was established as a trust in New York in 1975 by Mr. U. A. Whitaker. Mr. Whitaker founded Aircraft-Marine Products, now known as AMP, Inc., and was the former chairman of both the company and its operating subsidiaries abroad.

Typical Recipients: • *Arts & Humanities:* arts associations, community arts, museums/galleries, music, theater • *Education:* colleges & universities, community & junior colleges, medical education, private education (precollege), science/technology education • *Health:* emergency/ambulance services, hospices, hospitals, medical research • *Social Services:* community service organizations, employment/job training, religious welfare, united funds, volunteer services, youth organizations

Grant Types: capital, project, research, and seed money
Geographic Distribution: United States and Canada for research program, and Harrisburg, PA, area for regional program

GIVING OFFICERS
Allen W. Cowley, MD: comm mem
Eckley Coxe IV: comm mem
Miles J. Gibbons, Jr.: pres
G. Burtt Holmes, OD: comm mem
Ruth W. Holmes, PhD: chmn
Richard J. Johns: comm mem *B* Pendleton OR 1925 *CURR EMPL* physician, prof medicine: Johns Hopkins Hosp *CORP AFFIL* mem sci adv comm: Gen Motors Corp *NONPR AFFIL* bd sch engg: Duke Univ; chmn adv comm division health sciences & tech: Harvard-MA Inst Tech; fellow: ACP, Am Assoc Advancement Science, Am Inst Biological & Med Engg; mem: Alpha Omega Alpha, Am Clinical & Climatological Assn, Am Soc Clinical Investigation, Assn Am Physicians, Biomedical Engg Soc, IEEE, Inst Medicine Natl Academy Sciences, Johns Hopkins Med Soc, Nu Sigma Nu, Phi Kappa Psi, Sigma Xi; sec, vchmn, chmn med bd: Myasthenia Gravis Fdn
Peter Katuna, PhD: vp biomed engring program, comm mem
Portia W. Shumaker: comm mem

APPLICATION INFORMATION

Initial Approach:
Application guidelines for both biomedical engineering research grants and regional grants may be obtained by telephone or letter.

To apply for a biomedical engineering research grant, an investigator should submit a preliminary proposal containing an abstract of the proposed research, not to exceed two pages, and the curricula vitae of the investigators. The abstract should contain a brief statement of the significance of the proposed research and a paragraph describing the engineering involved. The curricula vitae should list all past and current research grants received by the investigators. If the preliminary proposal indicates that the project meets the foundation's requirements, an invitation to submit a formal applicaton will be sent.

Grant applications under the regional program do not have to be in any particular form. The application should state the objective and significance of the project and qualifications of the requesting organization and individuals responsible for the project, and contain a budget and a short statement of how the results will be evaluated. A copy of the letter from the IRS showing that the organization is tax-exempt under Section 501(c)(3), and that the organization is not a private foundation within the meaning of Section 509(a), should also be included.

In order to receive biomedical research grants by April 1, August 1, or December 1, preliminary proposals must be submitted by September 1, January 2, or May 1, respectively, followed by formal applications six weeks later.

Applications under the regional program should be submitted before the end of December, April, or August, respectively, in order to be placed on the agenda for the February, June, or October meeting of the foundation committee.

In judging eligibility for research grants, the foundation looks for two factors: the project must significantly involve the use of innovative engineering techniques, and the investigators must be relative beginners in their research careers. Regional program proposals should establish a demonstrated need and prove that the applicant organization has the ability to operate, complete, or provide for future operating expenses of the project. In most cases, it is preferred that costs be shared with other donors.

Restrictions on Giving: To obtain a biomedical research grant, the principal investigator must be a member of the faculty or research staff of the applicant institution, and have received a doctorate less than eight years prior to submitting a preliminary proposal, or have completed all residencies less than seven years before. Regional grants are not made to individuals, for sectarian religious purposes, nor solely for endowments. Grants generally will not be made to support operating expenses of established programs, nor to finance deficits.

OTHER THINGS TO KNOW

Publications: guidelines for regional program grant applications, biomedical engineering research grants applications and graduate student fellowship program.

GRANTS ANALYSIS

Total Grants: $15,007,433
Number of Grants: 277
Highest Grant: $1,650,000
Typical Range: $1,000 to $75,000
Disclosure Period: 1991
Note: Recent grants are derived from a 1991 grants list.

RECENT GRANTS

1,650,000 Whitaker Health Sciences Fund, Cambridge, MA

550,800 Johns Hopkins University, Baltimore, MD

517,139 University of Washington, Seattle, WA

200,000 Boston University School of Medicine, Boston, MA

100,000 Harrisburg Area Community College, Harrisburg, PA

100,000 Lebanon Valley College, Annville, PA

100,000 Messiah College, Grantham, PA

100,000 Naples Community Hospital, Naples, FL

100,000 Pennsylvania State University, Hershey, PA

100,000 Pennsylvania State University at Harrisburg, Middletown, PA

Whitaker Fund, Helen F.

CONTACT

Miles J. Gibbons, Jr.
Helen F. Whitaker Fund
4718 Old Gettysburg Rd., Ste. 405
Mechanicsburg, PA 17055-4325
(717) 763-1600

FINANCIAL SUMMARY

Recent Giving: $699,000 (fiscal 1991); $707,000 (fiscal 1990); $844,472 (fiscal 1989)
Assets: $23,643,445 (fiscal year ending July 31, 1991); $21,382,406 (fiscal 1990); $20,617,410 (fiscal 1989)
Gifts Received: $47,406 (fiscal 1991); $410,767 (fiscal 1990); $6,006,194 (fiscal 1989)
Fiscal Note: In 1991, contributions were received from the Helen F. Whitaker Trust.
EIN: 22-2459399

CONTRIBUTIONS SUMMARY

Donor(s): The fund was established in 1983 by the late Helen F. Whitaker.
Typical Recipients: • *Arts & Humanities:* arts associations, arts funds, music, opera, performing arts, public broadcasting
Grant Types: fellowship, project, research, and seed money
Geographic Distribution: national

GIVING OFFICERS

Carmelita Biggie: comm mem
Miles J. Gibbons, Jr.: comm mem
Ruth W. Holmes, PhD: comm mem

APPLICATION INFORMATION

Initial Approach:
The foundation requests applications be made in writing.
Written proposals should include a description of the project, information about the requesting organization, and the amount requested.
The foundation has no deadline for submitting proposals.
Restrictions on Giving:
Grants are made only to support the development of the professional careers of young classical musicians or to train administrators for classical music organizations.

GRANTS ANALYSIS

Total Grants: $699,000
Number of Grants: 6
Highest Grant: $200,000
Typical Range: $60,000 to $135,000
Disclosure Period: fiscal year ending July 31, 1991
Note: Recent grants are derived from a fiscal 1991 grants list.

RECENT GRANTS

200,000 American Symphony Orchestra League, Washington, DC

135,000 Naples/Marco Philharmonic, Naples, FL

104,000 National Public Radio, Washington, DC

100,000 Bay Area Women's Philharmonic, San Francisco, CA

100,000 Young Concert Artists, New York, NY

60,000 New York Philharmonic, New York, NY

White Castle System

Sales: $300.0 million
Employees: 9,700
Headquarters: Columbus, OH
SIC Major Group: Eating & Drinking Places and Fabricated Metal Products

CONTACT

Alice Ingram
Contributions Coordinator
White Castle System
555 West Goodale
Columbus, OH 43215
(614) 228-5781

CONTRIBUTIONS SUMMARY

Operating Locations: OH (Columbus)

CORP. OFFICERS

E.W. Ingram III: *CURR EMPL* pres, ceo: White Castle Sys

E.W. Ingram, Jr.: *CURR EMPL* chmn: White Castle Sys

OTHER THINGS TO KNOW

Company is an original donor to the Ingram-White Castle Foundation.

White Coffee Pot Family Inns / White Coffee Pot Restaurants Foundation

Sales: $21.0 million
Employees: 550
Headquarters: Baltimore, MD
SIC Major Group: Eating & Drinking Places and Food & Kindred Products

CONTACT

Alan Katz
President
White Coffee Pot Restaurants Foundation
137 South Warwick Ave.
Baltimore, MD 21223-2191
(301) 539-5474

FINANCIAL SUMMARY

Recent Giving: $50,000 (1991); $54,600 (1990); $66,100 (1989)
Assets: $368,259 (1991); $397,416 (1990); $372,783 (1989)
EIN: 52-6034788

CONTRIBUTIONS SUMMARY

Typical Recipients: • *Religion:* religious organizations
• *Social Services:* community service organizations, religious welfare
Grant Types: general support
Geographic Distribution: focus on MD
Operating Locations: MD (Baltimore)

CORP. OFFICERS

Allan R. Katz: *CURR EMPL* chmn, pres: White Coffee Pot Restaurants

GIVING OFFICERS

Barbara E. Judd: treas
Robert J. Katz: secy

APPLICATION INFORMATION

Initial Approach: Send brief letter describing program. There are no deadlines.

GRANTS ANALYSIS

Number of Grants: 2
Highest Grant: $49,000
Typical Range: $1,000 to $49,000
Disclosure Period: 1991

RECENT GRANTS

49,000 Associated Jewish Charities and Welfare Fund, Baltimore, MD

1,000 Lifesongs 1991,
Towson, MD

White Consolidated Industries / White Consolidated Industries Foundation

Sales: $400.0 million
Employees: 30,000
Headquarters: Cleveland, OH
SIC Major Group: Electronic & Other Electrical Equipment

CONTACT
Daniel R. Elliott
Chairman
White Consolidated Industries Fdn.
11770 Berea Rd.
Cleveland, OH 44111
(216) 252-8385

FINANCIAL SUMMARY
Recent Giving: $300,000 (1993 est.); $277,741 (1991); $329,000 (1990)
Assets: $649,888 (1991); $817,360 (1990)
Gifts Received: $56,480 (1991); $109,931 (1990)
Fiscal Note: Contributes through foundation only. In 1991, contributions were received from White Consolidated Industries.
EIN: 04-6032840

CONTRIBUTIONS SUMMARY
Typical Recipients: • *Arts & Humanities:* arts institutes, dance, museums/galleries, music, opera, theater • *Civic & Public Affairs:* civil rights, housing, law & justice, urban & community affairs, zoos/botanical gardens • *Education:* colleges & universities, economic education, education associations, elementary education, minority education • *Health:* hospitals, nutrition & health maintenance, pediatric health • *Social Services:* child welfare, community centers, food/clothing distribution, shelters/homelessness, united funds
Grant Types: employee matching gifts and endowment
Nonmonetary Support Types: donated products
Note: In 1990, nonmonetary support was valued at $20,000, which is not included in figure above.
Geographic Distribution: primarily Cleveland and Colum-

bus, OH, areas; other operating locations receive local requests
Operating Locations: AL (Cullman, Montgomery), AR (Conway), CT (Bridgeport), GA (Augusta), IA (Webster City), IL (Aurora, Bloomington, Itasca, Mattoon), IN (Elkhart), MA (Burlington), MI (Greenville), MN (St. Cloud), NJ (Edison), OH (Cleveland, Columbus, Mansfield), PA (Lake City, Pittsburgh), SC (Orangeburg), TN (Athens, Springfield)

CORP. OFFICERS
Donald C. Blasius: *B* Oakpark IL 1929 *ED* Northwestern Univ BSBA 1951 *CURR EMPL* pres: White Consolidated Indus *CORP AFFIL* dir: Bank One Mansfield, Natl Un Electric Corp, OH Edison Corp, Team Textile Svc Corp Domestic Sales Co; pres, dir: Getinge Intl, Husqvarna Motorcycle Co San Diego; vp, dir: Domestic Inc Soc Bank *NONPR AFFIL* trust: North Central Tech Coll
Anders Scharp: *B* 1934 *CURR EMPL* chmn, dir: White Consolidated Indus

GIVING OFFICERS
Donald C. Blasius: vp *CURR EMPL* pres: White Consolidated Indus (see above)
W. Greg Bleakley: trust *CURR EMPL* sr vp (human resources): White Consolidated Indus
Daniel Robert Elliott, Jr.: chmn *B* Cleveland OH 1939 *ED* Wesleyan Univ 1961; MI Univ JD 1964 *CURR EMPL* sr vp, secy, gen couns: White Consolidated Indus *NONPR AFFIL* mem: Am Bar Assn, Assn Home Appliance Mfrs; trust: Cleveland Poverty Commn, Judson Retirement Commun, Neighborhood Ctrs Assn; trust, fdr: Cleveland Tenants Org; mem: Am Corp Counc Assn; trust: Ctr Human Rels, Inst Child Advocacy
Wayne D. Schierbaum: trust

APPLICATION INFORMATION
Initial Approach: *Initial Contact:* brief letter or proposal *Include Information On:* description of the organization, amount requested, purpose for which funds are sought, recently audited financial statement, proof of tax-exempt status *When to Submit:* any time; foundation committee meets monthly

Restrictions on Giving: Does not support dinners or special events, fraternal organizations, goodwill advertising, individuals, member agencies of united funds, political or lobbying groups, or religious organizations for sectarian purposes.

GRANTS ANALYSIS
Total Grants: $277,741
Number of Grants: 63
Highest Grant: $78,000
Typical Range: $500 to $5,000
Disclosure Period: 1991
Note: Recent grants are derived from a 1991 grants list.

RECENT GRANTS
78,000 United Way, Cleveland, OH
25,000 Cleveland Orchestra, Cleveland, OH
20,000 Cleveland Initiative for Education, Cleveland, OH
20,000 United Way, St. Cloud, MN
18,411 Corporate Matching Gift-White Consolidated Industries, Inc. Foundation, Cleveland, OH
15,000 Case Western Reserve University Health Careers Enhancement Program, Cleveland, OH
10,000 John Carroll University, University Heights, OH
10,000 Lakewood Hospital, Cleveland, OH
7,260 United Way, Erie, PA
5,000 Cleveland Music School Settlement, Cleveland, OH

White Construction Co. / White Companies Charitable Trust

Headquarters: Auburn, MA

CONTACT
Leonard H. White
President
White Construction Co.
41 Central Street
Auburn, MA 01501-2304
(508) 832-3295

FINANCIAL SUMMARY
Recent Giving: $57,425 (fiscal 1992); $32,350 (fiscal 1990)
Assets: $280,364 (fiscal year ending April 30, 1992); $250,136 (fiscal 1990)

Gifts Received: $28,750 (fiscal 1992); $161,267 (fiscal 1990)
Fiscal Note: In fiscal 1992, contributions were received from R. H. White Contracting ($20,000) and Laurel Hill Realty ($8,750).
EIN: 04-2731784

CONTRIBUTIONS SUMMARY
Typical Recipients: • *Civic & Public Affairs:* philanthropic organizations • *Education:* colleges & universities, science/technology education • *Religion:* churches • *Social Services:* child welfare, united funds, youth organizations
Grant Types: general support
Geographic Distribution: giving primarily in MA
Operating Locations: MA (Auburn)

CORP. OFFICERS
David H. White: *CURR EMPL* pres: White Construction Co
Leonard H. White: *CURR EMPL* chmn: White Construction Co

GIVING OFFICERS
Sumner B. Tilton: treas
David H. White: vp *CURR EMPL* pres: White Construction Co (see above)
Leonard H. White: pres *CURR EMPL* chmn: White Construction Co (see above)

APPLICATION INFORMATION
Initial Approach: The foundation supports preselected organizations and does not accept unsolicited requests for funds.

GRANTS ANALYSIS
Number of Grants: 19
Highest Grant: $26,125
Typical Range: $100 to $1,000
Disclosure Period: fiscal year ending April 30, 1992

RECENT GRANTS
26,125 All Saints Church
15,125 Worcester Children's Friend Society, Worcester, MA
7,500 Virginia Polytechnic Institute and State University, Blacksburg, VA
2,100 United Way, Worcester, MA
1,400 Alliance for Education, Worcester, MA
1,000 Clark University
1,000 Endicott College
1,000 Fund for the Future

500 Salvation Army
500 YMCA

White Foundation, Erle and Emma

CONTACT
Erle and Emma White Fdn.
PO Box 4669
Wichita Falls, TX 76308

FINANCIAL SUMMARY
Recent Giving: $271,300 (1991); $236,650 (1990); $303,571 (1989)
Assets: $4,071,471 (1991); $3,784,904 (1990); $3,716,075 (1989)
EIN: 75-1781596

CONTRIBUTIONS SUMMARY
Typical Recipients: • *Arts & Humanities:* theater • *Civic & Public Affairs:* women's affairs • *Education:* colleges & universities, community & junior colleges • *Health:* hospices, hospitals, pediatric health, single-disease health associations • *Religion:* churches, religious organizations • *Social Services:* aged, child welfare, community service organizations, disabled, united funds, youth organizations
Grant Types: general support
Geographic Distribution: focus on the Wichita Falls, TX, area

GIVING OFFICERS
Carolyn Brown: trust
Marilyn Onstott: secy, treas
Steve Onstott: dir
Emma White: chmn

APPLICATION INFORMATION
Initial Approach: Contributes only to preselected organizations.
Restrictions on Giving: Does not support individuals.

GRANTS ANALYSIS
Number of Grants: 42
Highest Grant: $40,000
Typical Range: $1,000 to $5,000
Disclosure Period: 1991

RECENT GRANTS
40,000 Wichita Falls Hospice, Wichita Falls, TX
25,000 Midwestern State University, Wichita Falls, TX
25,000 North Texas Rehabilitation Center, Dallas, TX
20,000 Floral Heights United Methodist Church, TX — food pantry
15,000 Vernon Regional Junior College, Vernon, TX
14,000 Interfaith Ministries, TX
10,000 Bethania Regional Health Center, Bethania, TX
10,000 Children's Cancer Fund, Dallas, TX
10,000 Woman's Forum Trust Fund, TX
6,000 Senior Citizens Center, TX

White Foundation, W. P. and H. B.

CONTACT
Margaret Blandford
Executive Director
W. P. and H. B. White Fdn.
540 Frontage Rd., Ste. 3240
North Field, IL 60093
(708) 446-1441

FINANCIAL SUMMARY
Recent Giving: $1,020,375 (1991); $1,001,975 (1989)
Assets: $21,664,197 (1991); $20,063,721 (1989)
EIN: 36-2601558

CONTRIBUTIONS SUMMARY
Donor(s): The foundation was incorporated in 1958 by the late William P. White and the late Hazel B. White.
Typical Recipients: • *Education:* colleges & universities • *Health:* hospitals • *Social Services:* community service organizations
Grant Types: capital, emergency, general support, multi-year/continuing support, operating expenses, professorship, project, research, and scholarship
Geographic Distribution: focus on metropolitan Chicago, IL

GIVING OFFICERS
John H. McCortney: vp, treas, dir
Paul E. Plunkett: dir *B* Boston MA 1935 *ED* Harvard Univ BA; Harvard Univ LLB *NONPR AFFIL* adjunct faculty: John Marshall Law Sch; mem: Fed Bar Assn
Paul M. Plunkett: gen coun, dir *B* Chicago IL 1908 *ED* Loyola Univ 1930-1933 *CORP AFFIL* gen coun, dir: White Properties
Robert P. White: dir
Roger B. White: pres, dir
Steven R. White: secy, dir
William P. White, Jr.: dir

APPLICATION INFORMATION
Initial Approach: Send brief letter of inquiry describing program or project. There are no deadlines. Board meets in March, June, September, and December.
Note: The foundation does not make grants to individuals, or for land acquisition, building funds, endowments, publications, conferences, deficit, spending, matching gifts, or loans.

OTHER THINGS TO KNOW
Publications: application guidelines

White Trust, G. R.

CONTACT
Joe T. Lenamon
G. R. White Trust
c/o TeamBank
PO Box 2050
Ft. Worth, TX 76113
(817) 884-4162

FINANCIAL SUMMARY
Recent Giving: $360,522 (fiscal 1991); $359,072 (fiscal 1990); $364,072 (fiscal 1989)
Assets: $6,391,308 (fiscal year ending September 30, 1991); $7,211,843 (fiscal 1990); $7,587,031 (fiscal 1989)
EIN: 75-6094930

CONTRIBUTIONS SUMMARY
Donor(s): G.R. White
Typical Recipients: • *Civic & Public Affairs:* municipalities, safety • *Education:* agricultural education, colleges & universities, legal education, religious education, student aid • *Health:* hospitals, pediatric health • *Religion:* churches, religious organizations • *Social Services:* child welfare, disabled, united funds, youth organizations
Grant Types: capital, general support, and scholarship
Geographic Distribution: limited to TX

APPLICATION INFORMATION
Initial Approach: Send brief letter of inquiry describing program or project. Deadline is September 1.
Restrictions on Giving: Does not support individuals.

GRANTS ANALYSIS
Number of Grants: 42
Highest Grant: $75,000
Typical Range: $1,000 to $5,000
Disclosure Period: fiscal year ending September 30, 1991

RECENT GRANTS
75,000 University of Texas Law School, Austin, TX
63,631 Texas A&M Student Loan Fund, College Station, TX
25,000 Texas and Southwestern Cattle Raisers Foundation, Ft. Worth, TX
20,000 Texas Christian University, Ft. Worth, TX — Ranch Management Program
19,600 Texas A&M University Department of Agriculture Economics, College Station, TX
17,281 Rochelle Volunteer Fire Department, Rochelle, TX — truck purchase
10,000 Brady Presbyterian Church, Brady, TX
10,000 Mount Calvary Luthern Church, Brady, TX — building fund
10,000 Rochelle Baptist Church, Rochelle, TX — building fund
10,000 Texas Baptist Men, Dallas, TX

Whitehall Foundation

CONTACT
Laurel Baker
Contact Person
Whitehall Foundation
251 Royal Palm Way, Ste. 211
Palm Beach, FL 33480
(407) 655-4474

FINANCIAL SUMMARY
Recent Giving: $2,198,915 (fiscal 1992); $2,009,119 (fiscal 1991); $1,919,721 (fiscal 1990)
Assets: $56,073,514 (fiscal year ending September 30,

1992); $53,566,033 (fiscal 1991); $43,228,477 (fiscal 1990)
EIN: 13-5637595

CONTRIBUTIONS SUMMARY

Donor(s): The foundation was established in 1937 by George Monroe Moffett. Mr. Moffett was chairman of Corn Products Refining Company (now CPC International). He was an active supporter of the biology department at Princeton University, his alma mater. He also sponsored what became the Moffett Professorship of Agriculture and Business at Harvard University. Mr. Moffett's grandson, George M. Moffett II is the current president and treasurer of the foundation.
Typical Recipients: • *Education:* colleges & universities • *Science:* scientific institutes
Grant Types: research
Geographic Distribution: no geographic restrictions; primarily in the United States

GIVING OFFICERS

Warren Sanford Adams II: trust, gen coun *B* Cleveland OH 1910 *ED* Princeton Univ BA 1930; Harvard Univ LLB 1934; NY Univ JSD 1941 *NONPR AFFIL* mem: Am Bar Assn, English Speaking Union, The Pilgrims *PHIL AFFIL* dir emeritus: Washington Square Fund
Laurel T. Baker: secy
Kenneth S. Beall, Jr.: trust
Helen M. Brooks: trust
Van Vechten Burger: trust emeritus *B* East Orange NJ 1905 *ED* Yale Univ 1926 *CORP AFFIL* vchmn emeritus (Pershing Div): Donaldson Lufkin & Jenrette Securities Corp
Michael V. Dawes: trust
Peter Gibbons-Neff: trust
George M. Moffett II: pres, treas
J. Wright Rumbough, Jr.: vp

APPLICATION INFORMATION

Initial Approach:
Applicants should initiate the proposal process by writing a one-page letter to the foundation; if the foundation is interested it will forward a grant application.
The one-page letter should identify the nature of the research proposal and indicate whether the request is for a re-

search grant or a one-year grant-in-aid. Grant applications are divided into the following sections: applicant information, project title and field, budget, current and pending support (including amount and duration), publications pertinent to the project, letters of recommendation, and thesis abstract (for new researchers).
Letters of intent are accepted throughout the year. Deadlines will be defined when the application is sent to the investigator.
Technical advisors to the foundation determine the appropriateness of the proposed research project in light of the foundation's funding interests. The foundation holds three grant review sessions per year.
Restrictions on Giving: Funds are restricted to the support of research in neurobiology, specifically invertebrate and vertebrate (excluding clinical): investigations of neural mechanisms involved in sensory, motor, and other complex functions of the whole organism as these relate to behavior. Foundation funds may not be used for the following purposes: salary of the principal investigator, "bricks and mortar" projects or laboratory renovations, secretarial or office expenses, travel to scientific meetings, or tuition.

OTHER THINGS TO KNOW

Publications: descriptive brochure, guidelines

GRANTS ANALYSIS

Total Grants: $2,198,915
Number of Grants: 66
Highest Grant: $58,146
Typical Range: $25,000 to $50,000
Disclosure Period: fiscal year ending September 30, 1992
Note: Recent grants are derived from a fiscal 1992 grants list.

RECENT GRANTS

58,146 Harvard University, Cambridge, MA — perception and control of acoustic images in echo-locating bats

53,176 Louisiana State University, Baton Rouge, LA — functional organization of olfactory bulb circuits

47,140 Mount Sinai School of Medicine, New York, NY — functional role of peptidergic feedback regulation of neurotransmitter release

46,003 State University of New York, Albany, NY — genetic analysis of developmental plasticity in insects

45,000 University of California, Los Angeles, CA — olfactory perception: empirical honeybee studies and neural network models

44,632 University of Rochester, Rochester, NY — posterior parahippocampal gyrus

44,000 Weizmann Institute of Science, Jerusalem, Israel — cellular and molecular correlates of a gustatory memory engram: acquired gustatory representations in the rat

43,340 Boston University, Boston, MA — brain-immune system interactions: mechanisms of immuno-suppression in stressed mice

42,924 University of Hawaii, HI — electrical, biosynthetic and secretory characteristics in relation to morphogenesis of crustacean peptidergic neurons in culture

42,902 State University of New York, Syracuse, NY — effect of glucose-related changes in hypothalamic GABAergic Activity on feeding behavior

Whitehead Charitable Foundation

CONTACT

William F. Campbell
Whitehead Charitable Fdn.
100 First Stamford Pl., 4th Fl.
Stamford, CT 06912-0033
(914) 946-8027

FINANCIAL SUMMARY

Recent Giving: $5,000 (fiscal 1991); $590,450 (fiscal 1989); $571,950 (fiscal 1988)
Assets: $8,970,235 (fiscal year ending November 30, 1991); $6,464,558 (fiscal 1989); $3,067,746 (fiscal 1988)
Gifts Received: $3,000,000 (fiscal 1989); $1,000,000 (fiscal 1988)
Fiscal Note: In 1989, contributions were received from Edwin C. Whitehead.
EIN: 06-0956618

CONTRIBUTIONS SUMMARY

Donor(s): Edwin C. Whitehead
Typical Recipients: • *Arts & Humanities:* museums/galleries • *Education:* colleges & universities, medical education • *Health:* health organizations, medical research, single-disease health associations
Grant Types: endowment and research

GIVING OFFICERS

Arthur W. Brill: treas, dir
John J. Whitehead: pres, dir
Peter J. Whitehead: vp, dir
Rosalind C. Whitehead: secy, dir
Susan Whitehead: dir

APPLICATION INFORMATION

Initial Approach: The foundation has no set form of application. Organizations should submit a letter of inquiry, accompanied by basic information supporting the request, including tax status, program description, budget, and sources of support. Applications must be received by the end of September for consideration in November.

GRANTS ANALYSIS

Number of Grants: 1
Highest Grant: $5,000
Disclosure Period: fiscal year ending November 30, 1991

RECENT GRANTS

5,000 New York University, New York, NY

Whitehead Foundation

CONTACT
Denise Emmett
Grants Administrator
Whitehead Fdn.
65 East 55th St.
New York, NY 10022
(212) 755-3131

FINANCIAL SUMMARY
Recent Giving: $2,446,072 (fiscal 1991); $1,997,109 (fiscal 1990); $1,707,810 (fiscal 1989)
Assets: $17,616,045 (fiscal year ending June 30, 1991); $19,163,376 (fiscal 1990); $17,320,926 (fiscal 1989)
Gifts Received: $1,000,000 (fiscal 1991); $1,000,000 (fiscal 1990)
Fiscal Note: In 1991, contributions were received from John C. Whitehead.
EIN: 13-3119344

CONTRIBUTIONS SUMMARY
Donor(s): The foundation was established in 1982 by the John C. Whitehead Foundation.
Typical Recipients: • *Arts & Humanities:* arts associations, arts centers, dance, history/historic preservation, museums/galleries, opera, performing arts, theater • *Civic & Public Affairs:* better government, business/free enterprise, economic development, environmental affairs, housing, international affairs, law & justice, national security, urban & community affairs, women's affairs • *Education:* business education, colleges & universities, economic education, education funds, international studies • *Health:* medical research, single-disease health associations • *International:* international development/relief, international health care • *Religion:* churches • *Social Services:* child welfare, community service organizations, disabled, employment/job training, homes, recreation & athletics, shelters/homelessness, united funds, youth organizations
Grant Types: capital and general support

Geographic Distribution: national, with a focus on New York, NY

GIVING OFFICERS
Arthur Goodhart Altschul: trust *B* New York NY 1920 *ED* Yale Univ AB 1943 *CURR EMPL* ltd ptnr: Goldman Sachs Group *CORP AFFIL* chmn, dir: Gen Am Investors Co; dir: Assoc Dry Goods Corp, Boswell Energy Corp, Sunbelt Energy Corp, Wicat Sys *NONPR AFFIL* chmn: Intl Fdn Art Res; chmn bd trusts: Barnard Coll; fellow: Metro Mus Art; mem: Counc Foreign Rels; mem distribution comm: NY Commun Trust; mem gov bd: Yale Univ Art Gallery; mem natl bd: Smithsonian Assocs
Anne W. Crawford: trust
John Livingston Weinberg: trust *B* New York NY 1925 *ED* Princeton Univ AB 1948; Harvard Univ MBA 1950 *CURR EMPL* sr chmn: Goldman Sachs & Co *CORP AFFIL* dir: BFGoodrich, Capital Holding Corp, Champion Intl Corp, EI du Pont de Nemours & Co, Knight-Ridder, Seagram Co Ltd *NONPR AFFIL* mem: Bus Counc, Chicago Bd Trade, Conf Bd, Counc Foreign Rels, Japan Soc, NY City Partnership; mem adv counc: Stanford Univ; mem bd govs, mem exec comm: NY Hosp-Cornell Med Ctr; trust: Princeton Univ
John Cunningham Whitehead: trust *B* Evanston IL 1922 *ED* Haverford Coll BA 1943; Harvard Univ MBA 1947 *CURR EMPL* chmn: AEA Investors *CORP AFFIL* trust: Carnegie Corp *NONPR AFFIL* chmn: Asia Soc, Brookins Inst, Intl House, Intl Rescue Comm, UN Assn USA, Youth Understanding; mem: Counc Foreign Rels; pres: Boy Scouts Am Greater NY Counc; trust: Haverford Coll, J Paul Getty Trust, Lincoln Ctr Theater, Outward Bound, Phillips Collection, Rockefeller Univ, Schumann Fdn; trustees counc: Natl Gallery Art
John Gregory Whitehead: trust
Nancy D. Whitehead: trust

APPLICATION INFORMATION
Initial Approach: Restrictions on Giving: The foundation supports preselected organizations and does not

accept unsolicited requests for funds.

GRANTS ANALYSIS
Total Grants: $2,446,072
Number of Grants: 183
Highest Grant: $375,000
Typical Range: $1,000 to $25,000
Disclosure Period: fiscal year ending June 30, 1991
Note: Recent grants are derived from a fiscal 1991 grants list.

RECENT GRANTS

375,000 Haverford College, Haverford, PA
200,000 Outward Bound, Greenwich, CT
100,000 Asia Society, New York, NY
100,000 Boy Scouts of America, New York, NY
100,000 International Rescue Committee, New York, NY
100,000 New Jersey Historical Society, Newark, NJ
75,000 Daytop Village, New York, NY
50,000 Alpha Center for Public/Private Initiatives, Minneapolis, MN
50,000 Alpha Center for Public/Private Initiatives, Minneapolis, MN
50,000 American Women's Economic Development Corporation, New York, NY

Whitehead Foundation, Joseph B.

CONTACT
Charles H. McTier
President
Joseph B. Whitehead Foundation
50 Hurt Plaza, Ste. 1200
Atlanta, GA 30303
(404) 522-6755

FINANCIAL SUMMARY
Recent Giving: $20,164,000 (1992); $15,574,900 (1991); $11,621,577 (1990)
Assets: $531,004,683 (1992); $520,538,063 (1991); $353,487,542 (1990)
EIN: 58-6001954

CONTRIBUTIONS SUMMARY
Donor(s): The foundation was established in 1937 by the late

Joseph B. Whitehead, son of Mrs. Lettie Pate Evans. The foundation shares an office and staff with two other related foundations, the Lettie Pate Evans Foundation and the Lettie Pate Whitehead Foundation, established by Mr. Whitehead's mother and brother respectively.

Typical Recipients: • *Arts & Humanities:* arts centers • *Civic & Public Affairs:* philanthropic organizations, urban & community affairs • *Education:* colleges & universities, elementary education, private education (precollege), public education (precollege), special education • *Health:* hospitals • *Social Services:* aged, child welfare, community centers, disabled, homes, shelters/homelessness, volunteer services, youth organizations
Grant Types: capital
Geographic Distribution: metropolitan Atlanta, GA

GIVING OFFICERS
Roberto Crispulo Goizueta: trust *B* Havana Cuba 1931 *ED* Yale Univ BS 1953; Yale Univ BSChE 1953 *CURR EMPL* chmn, ceo, chmn exec bd, dir: Coca-Cola Co *CORP AFFIL* dir: Eastman Kodak Co, Ford Motor Co, Sonat, Suntrust Banks, Trust Co GA *NONPR AFFIL* mem: Bus Counc, Roundtable Policy Comm; mem, founding dir: Points Light Fdn; trust: Am Assembly, Boys Club Am, Emory Univ, Robert W Woodruff Arts Ctr
P. Russell Hardin: secy, treas *B* Charlotte NC 1931 *ED* Duke Univ BA 1952; Duke Univ JD 1954 *CORP AFFIL* dir: Mutual Benefit Life Ins Co, Shearson Daily Dividend, Summit Bankcorp *NONPR AFFIL* dir: Italy Fund
Joseph W. Jones: chmn, trust *B* Wilmington DE 1936 *ED* Univ FL BS 1959 *CURR EMPL* chmn, pres: Moms Best Cookies *CORP AFFIL* consult: Capital Co, Golden Distributors; mem bd dirs: Bordo Citrus Products; trust: Winter Park Meml Hosp; vchmn: YMCA Winter Park *NONPR AFFIL* mem: Assn Natl Advertisers, Sigma Nu; mem nuisance abatement bd: City Winter Park *PHIL AFFIL* chmn: Woodruff (Robert W) Foundation; secy: Coca-Cola Foundation
Charles H. McTier: pres

James Malcolm Sibley: vchmn, trust *B* Atlanta GA 1919 *ED* Princeton Univ AB 1941 *CURR EMPL* ptnr: King & Spalding *CORP AFFIL* chmn exec comm, dir: Trust Co GA; dir: Coca-Cola Co, GA US Corp, John H Harland Co, Rock-Tenn Co, Summit Indus, SunTrust Banks, Trust Company Bank; dir emeritus: Life Ins Co GA; trust: A G Rhodes Home *NONPR AFFIL* mem: Am Bar Assn, Am Bar Fdn, Am Coll Probate Couns, Am Law Inst, Atlanta Bar Assn, GA Bar Assn; mem bd dirs: Callaway Gardens Fdn; trust: Emory Univ, A G Rhodes Home

APPLICATION INFORMATION

Initial Approach:
There is no standard application form. The foundation requests an initial letter of inquiry followed by a formal application letter.

The application letter should include basic information on the project, tax status of the organization, description of program activities, budget with sources of support identified, and a list of officers and governing board.

The board meets in April and November; proposals submitted by February 1 and September 1 will be considered at the following meeting.

Restrictions on Giving:
Grants are restricted to the metropolitan Atlanta area. No grants are made to individuals, and grants for regular operating expenses are avoided.

GRANTS ANALYSIS

Total Grants: $20,164,000
Number of Grants: 58
Highest Grant: $5,000,000
Typical Range: $50,000 to $300,000
Disclosure Period: 1992
Note: The average grant calculation excludes the largest grant of $5,000,000. Recent grants are derived from a 1991 Form 990.

RECENT GRANTS

2,500,000 Henrietta Egleston Hospital, Atlanta, GA — capital expansion program

2,000,000 Metropolitan Atlanta Community Foundation, Atlanta, GA — coordinate services to at-risk youth

1,500,000 YMCA of Metropolitan Atlanta, Atlanta, GA — capital improvements at the Southwest, South DeKalb and Southeast Atlanta Branches

1,250,000 Salvation Army, Atlanta, GA — capital campaign for School for Officers' Training

750,000 Georgia Cities in Schools, Atlanta, GA — statewide development of the Cities in Schools program

500,000 Bridge Family Center of Atlanta, Atlanta, GA — provide temporary shelter and therapy services to runaway and homeless youth

500,000 Metropolitan Atlanta Community Foundation, Atlanta, GA — assess Georgia's health care system and shape public consensus on what values should guide

500,000 Metropolitan Atlanta Community Foundation, Atlanta, GA — fund for neighborhood planning in areas affected by construction of Olympic Venues

400,000 Boys and Girls Clubs of Metro Atlanta, Atlanta, GA — program development

400,000 North Georgia Presbyterian Homes, Atlanta, GA — for expansion of Presbyterian Village in Austell

Whitehead Foundation, Lettie Pate

CONTACT
Charles H. McTier
President
Lettie Pate Whitehead Foundation
50 Hurt Plaza, Ste. 1200
Atlanta, GA 30303
(404) 522-6755

FINANCIAL SUMMARY

Recent Giving: $10,500,000 (1993 est.); $10,399,167 (1992); $9,767,000 (1991)

Assets: $384,653,386 (1992); $371,889,178 (1991); $250,359,516 (1990)

EIN: 58-6012629

CONTRIBUTIONS SUMMARY

Donor(s): The foundation is one of a group of foundations located in Atlanta, GA, that share a common administrative arrangement; the other foundations in the group are the Lettie Pate Evans Foundation, the Joseph B. Whitehead Foundation, and the Robert W. Woodruff Foundation. All share the same staff.

Lettie Pate (1872-1953) married Joseph B. Whitehead in 1894. They had two sons: Joseph B. Whitehead, Jr., (1894-1936) and Conkey Pate Whitehead (1898-1940). In 1913, seven years after her husband's death, she married Colonel Arthur Kelly Evans, a retired Canadian army officer.

Following the death of her first husband, Lettie Pate Whitehead undertook the management of the Atlanta Coca-Cola Bottling Company, the Whitehead Holding Company and Whitehead Realty Company. She also served as a director of the Coca-Cola Company. She was trustee of the American Hospital in Paris, Museum of Fine Arts in Richmond, Emory University, and Agnes Scott College in Atlanta.

In 1945, Mrs. Evans established the Lettie Pate Evans Foundation with assets of about $2 million. After her death, her estate added almost $8 million to the foundation. The Joseph B. Whitehead Foundation was established under the will of Joseph B. Whitehead, Jr., as a memorial to his father. In like manner, Conkey Pate Whitehead set up the Lettie Pate Whitehead Foundation in honor of his mother. It was chartered in 1946.

Typical Recipients: • *Education:* colleges & universities, medical education, student aid • *Social Services:* aged, homes

Grant Types: general support and scholarship

Geographic Distribution: Alabama, Florida, Georgia, Louisiana, Mississippi, North Carolina, South Carolina, Tennessee, and Virginia

GIVING OFFICERS

Dr. Herbert A. Claiborne, Jr.: vchmn

Herbert A. Claiborne III: alternate trust

Lyons Gray: trust

P. Russell Hardin: secy, treas *B* Charlotte NC 1931 *ED* Duke Univ BA 1952; Duke Univ JD 1954 *CORP AFFIL* dir: Mutual Benefit Life Ins Co, Shearson Daily Dividend, Summit Bankcorp *NONPR AFFIL* dir: Italy Fund

Charles H. McTier: pres

Bolling P. Spalding: alternate trust

Hughes Spalding, Jr.: chmn *B* Atlanta GA *ED* Georgetown Univ; Univ GA *CURR EMPL* atty: King & Spalding (Atlanta GA)

APPLICATION INFORMATION

Initial Approach:
A preliminary letter of inquiry should be sent to the president. Educational institutions must submit the following information: proof of nonprofit educational status and tax exemption. The board meets in November. The foundation recommends applying by August.

Restrictions on Giving: The foundation does not make grants to individuals.

GRANTS ANALYSIS

Total Grants: $10,399,167
Number of Grants: 196
Highest Grant: $550,000
Typical Range: $30,000 to $95,000
Disclosure Period: 1992
Note: Recent grants are derived from a 1990 grants list.

RECENT GRANTS

550,000 Wesley Homes, Atlanta, GA — care of aged women

245,000 Emory University, Atlanta, GA — scholarships

150,000 Our Lady of Perpetual Help Cancer Home, Atlanta, GA — care of aged women

150,000 Penick Memorial Home, Southern Pines, NC — care of aged women

145,000 Westminster-Canterbury Foundation, Richmond, VA — care of aged women

125,000 Triad United Methodist Home, Win-

ston-Salem, NC —
care of aged women
124,000 University of
North Carolina,
Chapel Hill, NC —
scholarships
105,000 Clark Atlanta University, Atlanta,
GA — scholarships
90,000 University of Vir-
ginia Fund, Char-
lottesville, VA —
general scholarship
85,000 Bowman Gray
School of Medi-
cine, Winston-
Salem, NC —
scholarships

Whiteley Foundation, John and Elizabeth

CONTACT
Joseph A. Caruso
John and Elizabeth Whiteley Fdn.
c/o First of America
Bank-Central
101 South Washington Sq.
Lansing, MI 48933
(517) 374-5436

FINANCIAL SUMMARY
Recent Giving: $72,453
(1991); $75,668 (1990);
$81,717 (1989)
Assets: $1,981,985 (1991);
$1,813,894 (1990); $1,794,889
(1989)
EIN: 38-1558108

CONTRIBUTIONS SUMMARY
Donor(s): the late Nellie M.
Zimmerman
Typical Recipients: • *Religion:* churches, religious organizations • *Social Services:* community service organizations,
homes, united funds, youth organizations
Grant Types: general support
and scholarship
Geographic Distribution: limited to Ingham County, MI

GIVING OFFICERS
Richard F. Burmeister: vp
Douglas E. Gilman: vp
Romayne E. Hicks: treas
Richard P. Lyman: pres
Jonathan R. White: secy

APPLICATION INFORMATION
Initial Approach: Send brief
letter desribing program. There
are no deadlines.

GRANTS ANALYSIS
Number of Grants: 6

Highest Grant: $19,830
Typical Range: $3,000 to
$10,000
Disclosure Period: 1991
Note: Figures for 1991 do not
include scholarships to indi-
viduals.

RECENT GRANTS
19,830 YWCA
10,000 St. David's Episcopal Church
10,000 Trinity Episcopal
Church
5,000 St. Paul's Episco-
pal Church
2,993 St. Augustine Epis-
copal Church
900 Ingham County
Home Association

Whiteman Foundation, Edna Rider

CONTACT
Jack W. Whiteman
President
Edna Rider Whiteman Fdn.
PO Box 2985
Phoenix, AZ 85062
(602) 898-4300

FINANCIAL SUMMARY
Recent Giving: $83,196 (fiscal
1992); $100,217 (fiscal 1991);
$120,584 (fiscal 1990)
Assets: $2,389,501 (fiscal year
ending July 31, 1992);
$2,094,656 (fiscal 1991);
$5,921 (fiscal 1990)
Gifts Received: $10,000 (fis-
cal 1992); $60,000 (fiscal 1991)
Fiscal Note: In 1992, contribu-
tions were received from Jack
W. Whiteman.
EIN: 86-6052816

CONTRIBUTIONS SUMMARY
Donor(s): the late C. O. Whiteman
Typical Recipients: • *Arts &
Humanities:* community arts,
museums/galleries, music
• *Civic & Public Affairs:* environmental affairs, housing • *Social Services:* community service organizations, united funds,
youth organizations, youth organizations
Grant Types: capital, emergency, endowment, general support, multiyear/continuing support, operating expenses,
project, research, and seed
money
Geographic Distribution:
focus on the Phoenix, AZ,
metropolitan area

GIVING OFFICERS
Lynne Denton: trust
Louise Kleinz: trust
E. R. Strahm: secy
Jack W. Whiteman: pres
Jeffrey Whiteman: trust

APPLICATION INFORMATION
Initial Approach: Send brief
letter describing program.
There are no deadlines.
Restrictions on Giving: Does
not support individuals.

OTHER THINGS TO KNOW
Publications: Informational
Brochure (including Applica-
tion Guidelines)

GRANTS ANALYSIS
Number of Grants: 70
Highest Grant: $10,000
Typical Range: $250 to $5,000
Disclosure Period: fiscal year
ending July 31, 1992

RECENT GRANTS
10,000 Phoenix Art Mu-
seum, Phoenix, AZ
6,000 Phoenix Sym-
phony, Phoenix, AZ
5,000 Arizona Historical
Society Centennial
Foundation, Phoe-
nix, AZ
5,000 Arizona Museum
for Youth, Phoenix,
AZ
5,000 Heard Museum,
Phoenix, AZ
5,000 Homeward Bound,
Phoenix, AZ
3,750 Boys and Girls
Club, Phoenix, AZ
3,000 Childsplay, Tempe,
AZ
2,500 Coconino Center
for the Arts, Flag-
staff, AZ
2,000 Herberger Theatre
Center, Phoenix,
AZ

Whitener Foundation

CONTACT
Whitener Fdn.
1941 English Rd., Box E
High Point, NC 27260

FINANCIAL SUMMARY
Recent Giving: $141,450
(1990); $136,200 (1989);
$134,920 (1988)
Assets: $3,041,062 (1990);
$3,008,443 (1989); $2,747,815
(1988)
EIN: 52-1467548

CONTRIBUTIONS SUMMARY
Typical Recipients: • *Arts &
Humanities:* theater • *Education:* colleges & universities
• *Health:* medical research, pediatric health, single-disease
health associations • *Religion:*
churches, missionary activities,
religious organizations • *Social
Services:* child welfare, homes,
youth organizations
Grant Types: general support
Geographic Distribution:
focus on NC

GIVING OFFICERS
Marshall Pittman: vp
Loraine Ward: secy, treas
Orin Whitener: pres

APPLICATION INFORMATION
Initial Approach: Send brief
letter of inquiry describing program. There are no deadlines.

GRANTS ANALYSIS
Number of Grants: 64
Highest Grant: $20,000
Typical Range: $500 to $5,000
Disclosure Period: 1990

RECENT GRANTS
20,000 Catawba College,
Salisbury, NC
15,000 Children's Home
Society of North
Carolina, Greens-
boro, NC
15,000 United Cerebral
Palsy Association,
Raleigh, NC
10,000 Boy Scouts of
America, Gastonia,
NC
10,000 University of
North Carolina
Educational Foun-
dation, Chapel
Hill, NC
6,000 Catawba College,
Salisbury, NC
6,000 University of
North Carolina
Educational Foun-
dation, Chapel
Hill, NC
5,000 American Chil-
dren's Home,
Raleigh, NC
5,000 Central Baptist As-
sociation, NC
4,000 North Carolina
Shakespeare Festi-
val, High Point, NC

Whiteside Scholarship Fund, Robert B. and Sophia

CONTACT
C. F. Baker
Robert B. and Sophia Whiteside
Scholarship Fund
c/o First Bank, N.A.
130 West Superior St.
Duluth, MN 55801
(218) 723-2888

FINANCIAL SUMMARY
Recent Giving: $291,200
(1990); $384,100 (1989);
$436,900 (1988)
Assets: $2,097,422 (1990);
$2,435,617 (1989); $2,105,603
(1988)
EIN: 41-1288761

CONTRIBUTIONS SUMMARY
Grant Types: scholarship
Geographic Distribution: limited to Duluth, MN

APPLICATION INFORMATION
Initial Approach: Application form required. Submit applications Fall of senior year directly to Duluth High School counselors.

OTHER THINGS TO KNOW
Provides scholarships to individuals graduating in the top 10 percent of their high school class (must be residents of Duluth, MN).
Disclosure Period: 1990

Whiting Foundation

CONTACT
Donald E. Johnson, Jr.
Secretary
Whiting Fdn.
901 Citizens Bank Bldg.
328 South Saginaw St.
Flint, MI 48502
(313) 767-3600

FINANCIAL SUMMARY
Recent Giving: $426,350 (fiscal 1992); $545,412 (fiscal 1991); $512,800 (fiscal 1990)
Assets: $14,593,768 (fiscal year ending June 30, 1992); $12,273,920 (fiscal 1991); $11,301,900 (fiscal 1990)
Gifts Received: $100,000 (fiscal 1990); $133,000 (fiscal 1988)

Fiscal Note: In 1990, contributions were received from the Estate of Donald E. Johnson.
EIN: 38-6056693

CONTRIBUTIONS SUMMARY
Donor(s): members of the Johnson family
Typical Recipients: • *Arts & Humanities:* arts institutes, music • *Civic & Public Affairs:* environmental affairs • *Education:* colleges & universities, education funds, public education (precollege) • *Health:* geriatric health, hospitals, medical research, single-disease health associations • *Religion:* churches • *Social Services:* aged, child welfare, community service organizations, disabled, family services, homes, united funds, youth organizations
Grant Types: general support, project, and research
Geographic Distribution: focus on MI

GIVING OFFICERS
Mary Alice J. Heaton: trust
Donald E. Johnson: secy, treas, trust
Donald E. Johnson, Jr.: pres, trust *CORP AFFIL* pres: Advertisers Press
John T. Lindholm: trust
Linda W. J. Utley: trust

APPLICATION INFORMATION
Initial Approach: Send full proposal. Deadline is April 30.

GRANTS ANALYSIS
Number of Grants: 57
Highest Grant: $78,000
Typical Range: $250 to $11,000
Disclosure Period: fiscal year ending June 30, 1992

RECENT GRANTS
78,000 University of Michigan, Flint, MI
35,000 New Paths, Fenton, MI
30,000 St. Paul's Episcopal Church, Flint, MI
29,500 Flint Board of Education, Flint, MI
26,000 Flint College and Cultural Development, Flint, MI
25,000 Flint Institute of Music, Flint, MI
22,800 Flint Institute of Arts, Flint, MI
20,000 Center for Gerontology, Flint, MI
15,000 Whaley Children's Center, Flint, MI

12,750 United Way, Flint, MI

Whiting Foundation, Macauley and Helen Dow

CONTACT
Macauley Whiting
President
Macauley and Helen Dow
Whiting Fdn.
PO Box 1980
Sun Valley, ID 83353

FINANCIAL SUMMARY
Recent Giving: $233,462
(1991); $162,193 (1990);
$276,951 (1989)
Assets: $4,122,871 (1991);
$3,846,646 (1990); $4,885,697
(1989)
EIN: 23-7418814

CONTRIBUTIONS SUMMARY
Typical Recipients: • *Arts & Humanities:* dance, libraries, music, public broadcasting • *Civic & Public Affairs:* environmental affairs, municipalities, zoos/botanical gardens • *Education:* colleges & universities, economic education, private education (precollege) • *Health:* hospitals
Grant Types: general support
Geographic Distribution: gives throughout the United States

GIVING OFFICERS
Helen Dow Whiting: treas, trust
Mary MacAuley Whiting: secy, trust
McCauley Whiting: pres, trust
Sara Whiting: trust

APPLICATION INFORMATION
Initial Approach: Send brief letter of inquiry describing program or project. There are no deadlines.
Restrictions on Giving: Does not support individuals.

GRANTS ANALYSIS
Number of Grants: 19
Highest Grant: $57,500
Typical Range: $2,000 to $15,000
Disclosure Period: 1991

RECENT GRANTS
57,500 Hotchkiss School, Lakeville, CT

25,000 College of Southern Idaho, Twin Falls, ID
25,000 Trinity Preparatory School
25,000 Winter Park Public Library
16,000 Morritz Community Hospital
15,000 Nature Conservancy, ME
15,000 Northwood Institute, Midland, MI
10,000 Ballet School
10,000 Methodist Hospital
6,000 Foundation for Teaching Economics

Whiting Foundation, Mrs. Giles

CONTACT
Robert H. M. Ferguson
Secretary
Mrs. Giles Whiting Fdn.
30 Rockefeller Plz.
New York, NY 10112
(212) 698-2500

FINANCIAL SUMMARY
Recent Giving: $1,301,300
(fiscal 1991); $1,213,500 (fiscal 1990); $1,069,600 (fiscal 1989)
Assets: $23,322,422 (fiscal year ending November 30, 1991); $20,943,797 (fiscal 1990); $22,209,026 (fiscal 1989)
EIN: 13-6154484

CONTRIBUTIONS SUMMARY
Donor(s): The foundation was incorporated in 1963 by the late Mrs. Giles Whiting.
Typical Recipients: • *Arts & Humanities:* literary arts • *Education:* colleges & universities, education funds
Grant Types: fellowship
Geographic Distribution: national

GIVING OFFICERS
Robert Lamont Belknap: trust *B* New York NY 1929 *ED* Princeton Univ AB 1951; Columbia Univ MA 1954; Russian Inst PhD 1960 *NONPR AFFIL* prof: Columbia Univ
Mary St. John Douglas: vp, trust
Robert Harry Munro Ferguson: secy, treas *B* New York NY 1937 *ED* Yale Univ BA 1959; Harvard Univ LLB 1964 *CURR EMPL* assoc: Patterson

Belknap Webb & Tyler *NONPR AFFIL* mem: Am Bar Assn, NY Bar Assn; trust: Pierce (John B) Laboratory

Harry W. Havemeyer: vp, trust

John N. Irwin III: trust

Robert M. Pennoyer: pres, trust *B* New York NY 1925 *ED* Harvard Univ BA 1946; Columbia Univ LLB 1950 *NONPR AFFIL* mem: Am Bar Assn, Counc Foreign Rels, New York City Bar Assn, NY Bar Assn; trust: Metro Mus Art, Pierpont Morgan Library, Carnegie Inst, Columbia Univ, St Gaudens Meml

APPLICATION INFORMATION

Initial Approach: Restrictions on Giving: The foundation supports preselected organizations and does not accept unsolicited requests for funds. The foundation does not make grants to individuals, or for general support, capital funds, matching gifts, research, special projects, publications, conferences, or loans.

OTHER THINGS TO KNOW

Publications: multiyear report

GRANTS ANALYSIS

Total Grants: $1,301,300
Number of Grants: 9*
Highest Grant: $340,000
Typical Range: $50,000 to $217,500

Disclosure Period: fiscal year ending November 30, 1991
Note: Average grant and number of grants figures do not include Whiting Writer's Awards to individuals totaling $300,000. Recent grants are derived from a fiscal 1991 grants list.

RECENT GRANTS

340,000 Columbia University, New York, NY
217,500 Princeton University, Princeton, NJ
175,000 Harvard University, Cambridge, MA
105,000 Stanford University, Stanford, CA
105,000 University of Chicago, Chicago, IL
50,000 Bryn Mawr College, Bryn Mawr, PA
5,000 Pierpont Morgan Library, New York, NY
2,000 Poets & Writers, New York, NY

1,800 Council on Foundations, Washington, DC

Whiting Memorial Foundation, Henry and Harriet

CONTACT
Franklin H. Moore, Jr.
Trustee
Henry and Harriet Whiting Memorial Fdn.
200 South Riverside
St. Clair, MI 48079
(313) 329-2244

FINANCIAL SUMMARY
Recent Giving: $92,283 (1991); $88,500 (1990); $78,000 (1989)
Assets: $2,043,706 (1991); $1,849,339 (1990); $1,951,998 (1989)
EIN: 38-6091633

CONTRIBUTIONS SUMMARY
Donor(s): the late Harriet Clark Whiting
Typical Recipients: • *Civic & Public Affairs:* municipalities • *Health:* health organizations, mental health • *Religion:* churches, religious organizations • *Social Services:* child welfare, community service organizations, united funds, youth organizations
Grant Types: general support and operating expenses
Geographic Distribution: focus on MI

GIVING OFFICERS
Charles F. Moore: trust
Franklin Hall Moore, Jr.: pres, treas *B* Camden NJ 1937 *CURR EMPL* ptnr: Shearman & Sterling *NONPR AFFIL* mem: NY Bar Assn, NY City Bar Assn
Frederick S. Moore: trust
Charles Staiger: secy

APPLICATION INFORMATION
Initial Approach: Contributes only to preselected organizations.
Restrictions on Giving: Does not support individuals.

GRANTS ANALYSIS
Number of Grants: 28
Highest Grant: $11,000
Typical Range: $1,000 to $5,000
Disclosure Period: 1991

RECENT GRANTS
11,000 St. Clair Community Foundation, Port Huron, MI
10,000 St. Vincent de Paul, Marysville, MI
7,000 Teen Ranch, Marlette, MI
5,000 American Red Cross, Port Huron, MI
5,000 Mental Health Association, Southfield, MI
5,000 Mental Health Association, Southfield, MI
5,000 YMCA, Port Huron, MI
4,000 United Way, Port Huron, MI
3,500 Boy Scouts of America, Port Huron, MI
3,000 Blue Water Child Guidance Clinic, Port Huron, MI

Whitman Corp. / Whitman Corp. Foundation

Sales: $2.39 billion
Employees: 14,703
Headquarters: Rolling Meadows, IL
SIC Major Group: Holding & Other Investment Offices

CONTACT
Charles H. Connolly
President
Whitman Corp. Fdn.
3501 Algonquin Rd.
Rolling Meadows, IL 60008
(312) 565-3000

FINANCIAL SUMMARY
Recent Giving: $650,000 (1992 approx.); $736,148 (1991); $700,000 (1990 approx.)
Assets: $2,980,683 (1991); $3,347,300 (1989)
Fiscal Note: Whitman Corp. gives entirely through the foundation, which was founded in mid-1988.
EIN: 36-3610784

CONTRIBUTIONS SUMMARY
Typical Recipients: • *Arts & Humanities:* music, opera • *Civic & Public Affairs:* ethnic/minority organizations, urban & community affairs • *Education:* colleges & universities, minority education

Grant Types: capital, general support, multiyear/continuing support, and project
Note: Challenge grants are admistered through the foundation's matching gifts program, for which only directors, directors emeriti, and employees of Whitman Corporation, excluding subsidiaries, are eligible.
Geographic Distribution: nationwide, with emphasis on midwestern states
Operating Locations: IL (Chicago)
Note: Whitman subsidiaries operate in various other locations.

CORP. OFFICERS
Bruce Stanley Chelberg: *B* Chicago IL 1934 *ED* Univ IL BS 1956; Univ IL LLB 1958 *CURR EMPL* chmn, ceo, dir: Whitman Corp *CORP AFFIL* dir: First Midwest Bank Corp, Hussmann Corp, Midas Intl Corp, Northfield Labs, Pepsi-Cola Gen Bottlers Inc; mem adv bd: Schwinn Bicycle Co *NONPR AFFIL* dir higher ed: St IL; mem: Am Bar Assn, IL Bar Assn, Intl Exec Svc Corps

GIVING OFFICERS
Charles H. Connolly: pres *B* New York NY 1934 *CURR EMPL* vp corp communications: Whitman Corp *NONPR AFFIL* dir: Chicago Un
William B. Moore: secy

APPLICATION INFORMATION
Initial Approach: *Initial Contact:* letter *Include Information On:* description of the organization, amount of funds requested, purpose for which funds are sought, and proof of 501(c)(3) status *When to Submit:* any time *Note:* Foundation mandates no specific procedure for applications, and offers no written guidelines.
Restrictions on Giving: Recipients must be nonprofit organizations under IRS standards.

GRANTS ANALYSIS
Total Grants: $736,148
Number of Grants: 146
Highest Grant: $100,000
Typical Range: $500 to $10,000
Disclosure Period: 1991
Note: Recent grants are derived from a 1991 From 990.

RECENT GRANTS

100,000 Commercial Club Foundation, Chicago, IL
69,000 United Way of Chicago, Chicago, IL
36,474 Lyric Opera of Chicago, Chicago, IL
30,000 Corporate/Community Schools of America, Chicago, IL
30,000 Greenville College, Greenville, IL
22,000 St. Joseph's College, Rensselaer, IN
20,050 Northwestern University, Evanston, IL
20,000 Executive Council on Foreign Diplomats, Armonk, NY
16,000 University of Michigan, Ann Arbor, MI
15,000 Luther College, Decorah, IA

Whitney Benefits

CONTACT
Jack R. Hufford
Secretary-Treasurer
Whitney Benefits
PO Box 691
Sheridan, WY 82801
(307) 674-7303

FINANCIAL SUMMARY
Recent Giving: $147,378 (1991); $221,914 (1990); $109,463 (1989)
Assets: $9,877,939 (1991); $9,062,639 (1990); $9,619,255 (1989)
EIN: 83-0168511

CONTRIBUTIONS SUMMARY
Donor(s): the late Edward A. Whitney
Typical Recipients: • *Social Services:* community service organizations, youth organizations
Grant Types: loan
Geographic Distribution: limited to Sheridan County, WY

GIVING OFFICERS
Henry A. Burgess: vp, trust
John P. Chase: trust
William E. Cook: pres, trust
George E. Ewan: trust
George Gligorea: trust
Jack R. Hufford: secy, treas, trust
Ray V. Johnston: trust
Dorothy King: trust
C. B. Metz: trust
Nels A. Nelson, Jr.: trust
R. David Parker: trust

Jane S. Schroeder: trust
Homer A. Scott, Sr.: trust
David Withrow: trust

APPLICATION INFORMATION
Initial Approach: Applications accepted for loan program only. Foundation does not fund grants. Application form required.

OTHER THINGS TO KNOW
Provides interest-free student loans to graduates of Sheridan County, WY, high schools (for baccalaureate degrees only).
Publications: Annual Report

GRANTS ANALYSIS
Number of Grants: 1
Highest Grant: $147,378
Disclosure Period: 1991

RECENT GRANTS
147,378 YMCA, Sheridan, WY

Whitney Foundation, Helen Hay

CONTACT
Barbara M. Hugonnet
Administrative Director
Helen Hay Whitney Foundation
450 East 63rd St.
New York, NY 10021-7999
(212) 751-8228

FINANCIAL SUMMARY
Recent Giving: $1,257,586 (fiscal 1991); $1,304,464 (fiscal 1990); $1,302,319 (fiscal 1989)
Assets: $28,832,360 (fiscal year ending June 30, 1991); $27,679,850 (fiscal 1990); $26,182,856 (fiscal 1989)
Gifts Received: $50,000 (fiscal 1991); $75,000 (fiscal 1990); $50,000 (fiscal 1989)
Fiscal Note: Contributions were given by Merck, Sharpe and Dohme Research Laboratory.
EIN: 13-1677403

CONTRIBUTIONS SUMMARY
Donor(s): The Helen Hay Whitney Foundation was established and endowed by Mrs. Charles S. Payson (the former Joan Whitney) in 1947, and named in honor of her mother, Helen Hay Whitney. The current Postdoctoral Research Fel-

lowship Program was begun in 1956.
Typical Recipients: • *Education:* colleges & universities, medical education • *Health:* medical research
Grant Types: fellowship and research
Geographic Distribution: North America

GIVING OFFICERS
Alexander G. Bearn, MD: trust, mem *B* Surrey England 1923 *ED* Univ London MB; Univ London BS 1946; Univ London MD 1951 *CORP AFFIL* former sr vp (med & scientific affairs): Merck Sharp Dohme Intl *NONPR AFFIL* adjunct prof, trust: Rockefeller Univ; dir: Royal Soc Medicine; fellow: Am Assn Advancement Science, Royal Coll Physicians; mem: Am Assn History Medicine, Am Philosophical Soc, Am Soc Biological Chemists, Am Soc Clinical Investigation, Am Soc Human Genetics, Assn Am Physicians, Assn Physicians Great Britain Ireland, Genetics Soc Am, Harvey Soc, Inst Medicine, Med Res Soc Great Britain, Med Soc London, Natl Academy Sciences, Soc Experimental Biology Medicine; mem bd science ocerseers: Jackson Lab; prof emeritus: Cornell Univ; trust: Howard Hughes Med Inst *PHIL AFFIL* dir: Jr Foundation
Charles Leigh Christian, MD: trust, mem *B* Wichita KS 1926 *ED* Wichita St Univ BS 1949; Case Western Reserve Univ MD 1953 *NONPR AFFIL* adjunct prof: Rockefeller Univ; chmn: Natl Arthritis Adv Bd; mem: Am Rheumatism Assn; prof: Cornell Univ Med Coll
Sandra de Roulet: trust, treas, mem
Frank James Dixon: mem scientific adv comm *B* St Paul MN 1920 *ED* Univ MN BS 1941; Univ MN MB 1943; Univ MN MD 1944 *CURR EMPL* dir emeritus: Scripps Clinic & Res Fdn *NONPR AFFIL* adjunct prof: Univ CA San Diego; fellow: Am Coll Allergists; mem: Alpha Omega Alpha, Am Academy Allergists, Am Academy Arts Sciences, Am Assn Advancement Science, Am Assn Cancer Res, Am Assn Immunologists, Am Bd Pathology, Am Heart Assn, Am Soc Clinical Investigation, Am Soc Experimental Pathology, Assn Am Physicians,

Counc Kidney Cardiovascular Disease, Fed Am Scientists, Harvey Soc, Inter Urban Pathology Soc, Intl Academy Pathology, Japanese Soc Nephrology, Natl Academy Sciences, Nu Sigma Nu, NY Academy Sciences W Assn Physicians, Scandinavian Soc Immunology, Sigma Xi, Soc Experimental Biology Medicine, Transplant Soc, US Academy Pathologists, Western Soc Clinical Res; mem adv comm: Irvington House Inst, Lupus Res Inst, MA Gen Hosp, Natl Multiple Sclerosis Soc, Harold C Simmons Arthritis Res Ctr; mem expert adv panel immunology: World Health Org; science adv: Christ Hosp Inst, Natl Inst Health, Natl Kidney Fdn, St Judes Med Ctr
Jerome Gross, MD: trust, mem, mem scientific adv comm *B* New York NY 1917 *ED* MA Inst Tech BS 1939; NY Univ MD 1943 *CURR EMPL* biologist: MA Gen Hosp *NONPR AFFIL* dir science affairs comm: W Alton Jones Science Ctr; mem: Am Academy Arts Sciences, Am Soc Biological Chemists, Am Soc Cell Biology, Histochemistry Soc, Inst Medicine, Natl Academy Sciences; prof medicine emeritus: Harvard Univ Med Sch; sr investigator: Cutaneous Res Ctr Dept Dermatology MA Gen Hosp
David S. Hogness: mem scientific adv comm
Barbara M. Hugonnet: adm dir
Maclyn McCarty, MD: vp, trust, mem, chmn scientific adv comm *B* South Bend IN 1911 *ED* Stanford Univ AB 1933; Johns Hopkins Univ MD 1937 *NONPR AFFIL* chmn, dir: Pub Health Res Inst NY; mem: Am Academy Arts Sciences, Am Assn Immunologists, Am Philosophical Soc, Am Soc Clinical Investigation, Assn Am Physicians, Harvey Soc, Natl Academy Sciences, NY Academy Medicine, NY Heart Assn, Soc Am Bacteriologists, Soc Experimental Biology Medicine; prof, mem: Rockefeller Univ
Thomas A. Melfe: secy, mem
Mrs. Henry B. Middleton: pres, trust, mem
Gerald Mayer Rubin: mem scientific adv comm *B* Boston MA 1950 *ED* MA Inst Tech BS 1971; Cambridge Univ PhD 1974 *NONPR AFFIL* investiga-

tor: Howard Hughes Med Inst; mem: Natl Academy Sciences; prof biochemistry: Univ CA Berkeley

Lucille Shapiro: mem scientific adv comm *B* New York NY 1940 *ED* Brooklyn Coll BA 1961; Albert Einstein Coll Medicine PhD 1966 *CURR EMPL* chmn dept devel biology sch medicine: Stanford Univ *NONPR AFFIL* ed: Trends in Genetics; fellow: Am Academy Arts & Sciences; mem: Am Heart Assn, Am Soc Biochemistry & Molecular Biology, Am Soc Biological Chemists, Am Soc Cell Biologists, Genetics Soc Am, Harvey Soc, Inst Medicine Natl Academy Sciences, NY Academy Sciences; mem science adv bd: MA Gen Hosp; mem science bd: Whitehead Inst MIT; prof: Columbia Univ Coll Physicians & Surgeons; trust: Scientists Inst Publ Info; mem visiting comm, bd overseers: Harvard Univ

Lisa Amelia Steiner, MD: trust, mem *B* Vienna Austria 1933 *ED* Swarthmore Coll BA 1954; Radcliffe Coll MA 1956; Yale Univ MD 1959 *NONPR AFFIL* chmn bd overseers: Brandeis Univ; mem: Am Assn Immunologists, Am Soc Biological Chemists; prof: MA Inst Tech

W. Perry Welch: trust, mem

APPLICATION INFORMATION

Initial Approach:
Application forms are available from the foundation, and may be requested by writing the foundation's administrative director.
Submitted applications must be postmarked by August 15; late applications will not be considered.
Applications are initially screened by the scientific advisory committee. Those selected will be contacted by an assigned member for an interview in October or early November. Those declined for an interview will be informed on or about October 1. In December, the scientific advisory committee makes its recommendations to the board. The board of trustees votes fellowship awards at its annual meeting in January. July 1 is the usual activation date of the fellowship.
Restrictions on Giving: Candidates must hold an M.D.,

Ph.D., or equivalent degree, and must be seeking to begin postdoctoral training in basic biomedical research. Established scientists and advanced fellows or applicants who plan tenure of the fellowship in the same laboratory in which they have already received extensive predoctoral or postdoctoral training will not be considered. Applicants who have already had one year's postdoctoral laboratory training at time of application are usually not considered. The foundation usually does not make more than one award in any one year for training with a given supervisor. Candidates are expected to be under 35 years of age. U.S. citizens may train abroad but non-citizens must train in the United States. The foundation provides funds for travel expenses; however, no payment is made for transportation of household goods.

OTHER THINGS TO KNOW

Publications: annual report, descriptive brochure

GRANTS ANALYSIS

Total Grants: $1,257,586
Number of Grants: 68
Highest Grant: $24,603
Typical Range: $11,000 to $23,500
Disclosure Period: fiscal year ending June 30, 1991
Note: Recent grants are derived from a fiscal 1992 grants list.

RECENT GRANTS

31,750 National Institutes of Health, Bethesda, MD
25,375 Harvard University, Boston, MA
25,262 University of California, San Francisco, San Francisco, CA
25,250 Roche Institute of Molecular Biology, Rochester, NY
25,000 Harvard Medical School, Boston, MA
25,000 Harvard Medical School, Boston, MA
25,000 Harvard University, Boston, MA
25,000 Massachusetts Institute of Technology, Cambridge, MA

25,000 National Institutes of Health, Bethesda, MD
25,000 Stamford University, Stamford, CT

Whitney Fund, David M.

CONTACT

Peter P. Thurber
President
David M. Whitney Fund
150 West Jefferson, Ste. 2500
Detroit, MI 48226
(313) 963-6420

FINANCIAL SUMMARY

Recent Giving: $299,200 (1991); $187,650 (1990); $85,000 (1989)
Assets: $22,887,915 (1991); $20,072,637 (1990); $9,271,564 (1989)
Gifts Received: $3,433,351 (1989); $80,532 (1988)
EIN: 38-6040080

CONTRIBUTIONS SUMMARY

Donor(s): The foundation was established in 1949.
Typical Recipients: • *Arts & Humanities:* arts centers, community arts, libraries, music, opera • *Civic & Public Affairs:* zoos/botanical gardens • *Education:* colleges & universities, minority education, private education (precollege) • *Health:* hospitals, single-disease health associations • *Religion:* religious organizations • *Science:* scientific organizations • *Social Services:* child welfare, community centers, community service organizations, food/clothing distribution, homes, recreation & athletics, shelters/homelessness, united funds, youth organizations
Grant Types: general support
Geographic Distribution: focus on Detroit, MI

GIVING OFFICERS

Richard B. Gushee: vp, treas *B* Detroit MI 1926 *ED* Williams Coll BA 1947; Univ MI JD 1950
George E. Parker III: vp, secy *B* Detroit MI 1934 *ED* Princeton Univ AB; Univ MI JD *NONPR AFFIL* trust: Hannan House
Peter P. Thurber: pres *B* Detroit MI 1928 *ED* Williams Coll BA; Harvard Univ JD *NONPR AFFIL* dir: Detroit Symphony Orchestra; mem:

Am Bar Assn, MI Bar Assn; trust: Counc MI Fdns

APPLICATION INFORMATION

Initial Approach:
The foundation requests applications be made in writing. Written proposals should briefly state the specific purpose of the request and a complete explanation of the necessity. A copy of the organization's tax exemption and foundation status letter from the IRS should also be included.
The foundation has no deadline for submitting proposals.
Restrictions on Giving: The foundation makes grants only to tax-exempt organizations. The foundation does not make grants to individuals.

GRANTS ANALYSIS

Total Grants: $299,200
Number of Grants: 39
Highest Grant: $66,000
Typical Range: $1,000 to $10,000
Disclosure Period: 1991
Note: Recent grants are derived from a 1991 grants list.

RECENT GRANTS

66,000 Detroit Symphony Orchestra, Detroit, MI
35,000 Crossroads, Detroit, MI
20,000 St. Peter's Home for Boys, Detroit, MI
20,000 University of Michigan, Ann Arbor, MI — gold course restoration fund
15,000 Boys and Girls Club, Detroit, MI
11,000 WTVS/Channel 56, Detroit Public Television, Detroit, MI
10,000 Boy Scouts of America, Detroit, MI
10,000 Capuchin Community Center, Detroit, MI
10,000 Michigan Opera Theatre, Detroit, MI
10,000 Salvation Army, Southfield, MO

Whitney National Bank

Sales: $2.85 billion
Employees: 1,513
Parent Company: Whitney Holding Corp.
Headquarters: New Orleans, LA
SIC Major Group: Depository Institutions

CONTACT
Bill Marks
Chief Executive Officer & Chairman
Whitney National Bank of New Orleans
PO Box 61260
New Orleans, LA 70161
(504) 586-7272

CONTRIBUTIONS SUMMARY
Operating Locations: LA (New Orleans)

CORP. OFFICERS
William L. Marks: *CURR EMPL* chmn, ceo: Whitney Natl Bank of New Orleans
R. King Milling: *CURR EMPL* pres: Whitney Natl Bank of New Orleans

Whittaker Corp.

Sales: $158.5 million
Employees: 1,000
Headquarters: Los Angeles, CA
SIC Major Group: Instruments & Related Products

CONTACT
Joe Alibrandi
Chairman & Chief Executive Officer
Whittaker Corp.
10880 Wilshire Blvd.
Los Angeles, CA 90024
(310) 475-9411

CONTRIBUTIONS SUMMARY
Priorities are health and community service organizations, education, and civic affairs.
Typical Recipients: • *Civic & Public Affairs:* general • *Education:* general • *Health:* general • *Social Services:* general
Grant Types: general support and matching
Geographic Distribution: operating communities
Operating Locations: CA (Los Angeles)

CORP. OFFICERS
Joseph Francis Alibrandi: *CURR EMPL* chmn, ceo, dir: Whittaker Corp

Daniel Hofman: *CURR EMPL* vp, cfo: Whittaker Corp
Gregory T. Parkos: *CURR EMPL* pres, coo, dir: Whittaker Corp

APPLICATION INFORMATION
Initial Approach: Send brief letter of inquiry, including a description of the organization, amount requested, purpose of funds sought, audited financial statement, and proof of tax-exempt status. There are no deadlines.

OTHER THINGS TO KNOW
Publications: Policy and Procedure Guide

Whittell Trust for Disabled Veterans of Foreign Wars, Elia

CONTACT
Kenneth J. Ashcraft
Trustee
Elia Whittell Trust for Disabled Veterans of Foreign Wars
180 Montgomery St., 1900
San Francisco, CA 94104
(415) 705-5615

FINANCIAL SUMMARY
Recent Giving: $175,000 (fiscal 1991); $175,000 (fiscal 1990); $135,000 (fiscal 1989)
Assets: $2,496,334 (fiscal year ending November 30, 1991); $2,363,336 (fiscal 1990); $2,492,600 (fiscal 1989)
EIN: 94-6449253

CONTRIBUTIONS SUMMARY
Donor(s): the late Elia Whittell
Typical Recipients: • *Health:* health organizations • *International:* international organizations
Grant Types: multiyear/continuing support and project
Geographic Distribution: limited to France

GIVING OFFICERS
Kenneth J. Ashcraft: trust
Edward Ridley Finch, Jr.: trust *B* Westhampton Beach NY 1919 *ED* Princeton Univ AB 1941; NY Univ JD 1947 *CURR EMPL* gen couns: Am Intl Petroleum Corp *NONPR AFFIL* fellow: Am Bar Fdn; mem: Am Arbitration Assn, Am Bar Assn, Am Inst Aeronautics Astronau-

tics, Am Judicature Soc, Am Law Inst, Fed Bar Assn, FL Bar Assn, Inter-Am Bar Assn, Intl Astronautical Academy, Intl Bar Assn, Judge Advocates Assn, NY Bar Assn, PA Bar Assn; mem faculty adv comm: Princeton Univ; pres: Crippled Childrens Friendly Aid Assn, Finch Trusts; pres, dir: NY Inst Special Ed, St Nicholas Soc NY; trust: Cathedral St John Divine, St Andrews Dune Church

APPLICATION INFORMATION
Initial Approach: Contributes only to preselected organizations.
Restrictions on Giving: Does not support individuals.

GRANTS ANALYSIS
Number of Grants: 6
Highest Grant: $40,000
Typical Range: $20,000 to $40,000
Disclosure Period: fiscal year ending November 30, 1991

RECENT GRANTS
40,000 ASUNOR, Paris, France
40,000 L'Office National des Anciens Cobbattan et Vitimes deGuerre, Paris, France
30,000 Union National Des Combattants, Paris, France
25,000 Association du Foeyer de l'Institution, Paris, France
20,000 Foundation De France, Paris, France — Legion d'Honneur
20,000 Union de Aveugles de Guerre, Paris, France

Whittenberger Foundation, Claude R. and Ethel B.

CONTACT
William J. Rankin
Chairman
Claude R. and Ethel B. Whittenberger Fdn.
PO Box 1073
Caldwell, ID 83606
(208) 459-0091

FINANCIAL SUMMARY
Recent Giving: $205,189 (1990); $183,147 (1989)
Assets: $2,884,376 (1990); $3,502,848 (1989)

EIN: 23-7092604

CONTRIBUTIONS SUMMARY
Donor(s): the late Ethel B. Whittenberger

Typical Recipients: • *Arts & Humanities:* community arts, dance, music • *Civic & Public Affairs:* municipalities • *Education:* colleges & universities, education funds, public education (precollege) • *Social Services:* child welfare, community service organizations, day care, family services, united funds, youth organizations
Grant Types: general support and scholarship
Geographic Distribution: limited to ID

GIVING OFFICERS
Margaret Gigray: vchmn
Robert A. Johnson: trust
D. Whitman Jones: trust
Joe Miller: secy
William J. Rankin: chmn

APPLICATION INFORMATION
Initial Approach: Send outline and budget of project. There are no deadlines.

OTHER THINGS TO KNOW
Publications: Application Guidelines, Informational Brochure

GRANTS ANALYSIS
Number of Grants: 35
Highest Grant: $41,000
Typical Range: $625 to $7,200
Disclosure Period: 1990

RECENT GRANTS
41,000 College of Idaho, Caldwell, ID
20,000 Idaho Community Foundation, Boise, ID
20,000 State Department of Education, Boise, ID
10,100 School District 132, ID
9,600 American Fest Ballet, Boise, ID
8,785 School District 135, ID
8,720 Hope House, ID
7,128 Children's Voices, Boise, ID
6,260 Mercy House, ID
5,500 Caldwell Fine Arts, Caldwell, ID

Whittier Foundation, L. K.

CONTACT
Linda J. Blinkenberg
Secretary
L. K. Whittier Foundation
1260 Huntington Dr., Ste. 204
South Pasadena, CA 91030
(213) 259-0484

FINANCIAL SUMMARY
Recent Giving: $2,907,334 (fiscal 1992); $3,035,754 (fiscal 1991); $3,287,387 (fiscal 1990)
Assets: $41,425,889 (fiscal year ending April 30, 1992); $38,148,998 (fiscal 1991); $33,143,094 (fiscal 1990)
Gifts Received: $2,553,228 (fiscal 1992); $2,553,228 (fiscal 1991); $2,553,228 (fiscal 1990)
Fiscal Note: The foundation receives gifts from the Leland K. Whittier Charitable Lead Trust.
EIN: 95-6027493

CONTRIBUTIONS SUMMARY
Donor(s): Leland Whittier and other members of the Whittier family established the foundation in 1955. The founders are descendants of Mericos H. Whittier, who began Belridge Oil in 1911. In 1979, Shell Oil purchased the company for $3.6 billion.
Typical Recipients: • *Arts & Humanities:* libraries, museums/galleries, public broadcasting • *Civic & Public Affairs:* zoos/botanical gardens • *Education:* colleges & universities, elementary education, science/technology education • *Health:* medical research • *Social Services:* youth organizations
Grant Types: endowment, project, and seed money
Geographic Distribution: primarily Southern California area

GIVING OFFICERS
Linda J. Blinkenberg: cfo, secy, contact person
Arlo G. Sorensen: vp
Laura-Lee Whittier Woods: pres

APPLICATION INFORMATION
Initial Approach:
Organizations seeking support from the foundation should submit a brief letter of inquiry.

In the preliminary letter, include an outline of the proposed project, amount requested, purpose for which grant is sought, and proof of tax-exempt status.
Requests are accepted any time.
Restrictions on Giving: Due to restrictions on funding, the foundation manager prefers to initiate grants made by the foundation.

GRANTS ANALYSIS
Total Grants: $2,907,334
Number of Grants: 49
Highest Grant: $500,000
Typical Range: $10,000 to $50,000
Disclosure Period: fiscal year ending April 30, 1992
Note: Recent grants are derived from a 1992 Form 990. Average grant figure excludes a $500,000 grant and $495,410 grant.

RECENT GRANTS
500,000　KCET Los Angeles, Los Angeles, CA — support "The Human Quest" program
495,410　California Institute of Technology, Pasadena, CA — support Whittier Advanced Geophysical Observatory
300,707　University of California at Los Angeles, Los Angeles, CA — support Human Values and Communications in Medicine program
250,000　University of Southern California, Los Angeles, CA — support Petroleum Engineering Fellowship program
200,000　California Institute of Technology, Pasadena, CA — support development of Gene Analyzer for DNA research
127,739　J. David Gladstone Foundation, Irvine, CA — support research in genetic mutation and blood cholesterol
125,000　Huntington Medical Research Institute, Pasadena, CA
83,333　Harvard Medical School, Boston, MA — support medical science graduate fellowships

77,295　Johns Hopkins University, Baltimore, MD — support educational science programs
75,000　Los Angeles Planned Parenthood, Los Angeles, CA — support medical equipment for South Bay clinic

Wickes Foundation, Harvey Randall

CONTACT
James V. Finkbeiner
President
Harvey Randall Wickes Foundation
4800 Fashion Sq. Blvd.
Plaza North, Rm. 472
Saginaw, MI 48604
(517) 799-1850

FINANCIAL SUMMARY
Recent Giving: $1,241,416 (1992); $1,100,855 (1991); $1,090,249 (1990)
Assets: $26,469,466 (1991); $24,355,937 (1990); $24,539,852 (1989)
EIN: 38-6061470

CONTRIBUTIONS SUMMARY
Donor(s): The foundation was established in 1945 in Michigan with donations primarily from Harvey Randall Wickes. Mr. Wickes was president and later chairman of Wickes Corporation, which has diversified interests including the merchandising of building supplies.
Typical Recipients: • *Arts & Humanities:* dance, libraries, museums/galleries, music • *Civic & Public Affairs:* urban & community affairs, zoos/botanical gardens • *Education:* colleges & universities, education funds, minority education, student aid • *Health:* health organizations, hospitals, medical rehabilitation • *Social Services:* child welfare, community service organizations, disabled, employment/job training, family services, food/clothing distribution, recreation & athletics, shelters/homelessness, united funds, youth organizations
Grant Types: capital, operating expenses, and scholarship
Geographic Distribution: Saginaw, MI

GIVING OFFICERS
Frank N. Andersen: trust
Robert G. App: trust
Hugo E. Braun, Jr.: vp, secy, trust *B* Saginaw MI 1932 *ED* Yale Univ BA 1954; Univ MI LLB 1957 *CURR EMPL* atty: Braun Kendrick Finkbeiner Schafer Murphy *NONPR AFFIL* mem: Am Academy Hosp Attys, Natl Health Lawyers Assn
James V. Finkbeiner: pres, trust *B* Green Bay WI 1914 *ED* Univ MI BA 1935; Univ MI JD 1937 *CURR EMPL* atty: Braun Kendrick Finkbeiner Schafer Murphy *NONPR AFFIL* fellow: Am Coll Probate Couns
Craig W. Horn: trust
Frank M. Johnson: trust
William W. Kessel: trust
William F. Nelson, Jr.: trust
David Wallace: trust
Jane Wierman: asst secy
Lloyd J. Yeo: treas, trust
Melvin J. Zahnow: chmn, trust

APPLICATION INFORMATION
Initial Approach:
Applications should be in letter form.
Letters should include specific details as to the proposed use of funds. The foundation will request additional information if necessary.
Information should be submitted three weeks prior to the first of January, April, June, and October.
The board of trustees meets in January, April, June, and October.
Restrictions on Giving: The foundation does not make grants to individuals or churches.

GRANTS ANALYSIS
Total Grants: $1,100,855
Number of Grants: 38
Highest Grant: $128,511
Typical Range: $20,000 to $100,000
Disclosure Period: 1991
Note: Recent grants are derived from a 1991 grants list.

RECENT GRANTS
128,511　Saginaw Valley State University Foundation, Saginaw, MI — expansion of Valley Library Consortium
100,000　Saginaw General Hospital Foundation, Saginaw, MI — endoscopy

equipment and refurbishing

100,000 Saginaw Township Soccer Association, Saginaw, MI — soccer fields

100,000 Saginaw Township-H. R. Wickes Recreation Complex, Saginaw, MI — land development

100,000 St. Luke's Hospital Foundation — toward the purchase of a CT scanner

88,400 Saginaw Valley Zoological Society, Saginaw, MI — new entrance to the Saginaw zoo

50,000 Saginaw Valley State University Foundation, Saginaw, MI — conference center

50,000 Salvation Army, Saginaw, MI — renovations

50,000 Visiting Nurse Association of Saginaw — renovations

35,500 United Way of Saginaw County, Saginaw, MI — operations

Wickson-Link Memorial Foundation

CONTACT
Lloyd J. Yeo
President
Wickson-Link Memorial Fdn.
PO Box 3275
3023 Davenport St.
Saginaw, MI 48605
(519) 793-9830

FINANCIAL SUMMARY
Recent Giving: $160,045 (1991); $161,170 (1990); $129,900 (1989)
Assets: $3,870,251 (1991); $3,403,555 (1990); $3,475,000 (1989)
EIN: 38-6083931

CONTRIBUTIONS SUMMARY
Donor(s): the late James Wickson, the late Meta Wickson
Typical Recipients: • *Arts & Humanities:* history/historic preservation, libraries, museums/galleries, music • *Civic & Public Affairs:* municipalities, zoos/botanical gardens • *Education:* colleges & universities • *Health:* hospitals, nursing services • *Religion:* churches • *Social Services:* child wel-

fare, community service organizations, recreation & athletics, shelters/homelessness, united funds, youth organizations
Grant Types: general support
Geographic Distribution: focus on Saginaw County, MI

GIVING OFFICERS
B. J. Humphreys: vp, secy
C. Ward Lauderbach: dir
Lloyd J. Yeo: pres, treas

APPLICATION INFORMATION
Initial Approach: Send cover letter and full proposal. There are no deadlines.

GRANTS ANALYSIS
Number of Grants: 36
Highest Grant: $18,500
Typical Range: $500 to $10,000
Disclosure Period: 1991

RECENT GRANTS
18,500 Saginaw County Youth Protection Council, Saginaw, MI

16,000 Opportunity Industrial Center, Saginaw, MI

10,000 Saginaw Community Foundation, Saginaw, MI

10,000 Saginaw Township Soccer Association, Saginaw, MI

10,000 Saginaw Zoological Society, Saginaw, MI

10,000 Visiting Nurses Association, Saginaw, MI

8,300 St. Lorenz Building Fund, Frankenmuth, MI

7,000 James E. Wickson Memorial Library, Frankenmuth, MI

6,500 City Rescue Mission, Saginaw, MI

6,050 United Way, Saginaw, MI

WICOR, Inc. / WICOR Foundation

Revenue: $681.71 million
Employees: 3,406
Headquarters: Milwaukee, WI
SIC Major Group: Electric, Gas & Sanitary Services, Holding & Other Investment Offices, Industrial Machinery & Equipment, and Oil & Gas Extraction

CONTACT
Carolyn Simpson
Foundation Coordinator
WICOR Foundation
626 East Wisconsin Ave.
Milwaukee, WI 53202
(414) 291-6565

FINANCIAL SUMMARY
Recent Giving: $600,000 (1993 est.); $600,000 (1992 approx.); $581,963 (1991)
Assets: $429,018 (1990); $354,078 (1989)
Gifts Received: $684,890 (1990); $687,194 (1989)
Fiscal Note: Contributes through foundation only. In 1990, contributions were received from the Wisconsin Gas Company ($600,000) and Sta-Rite Industries ($84,890).
EIN: 39-1522073

CONTRIBUTIONS SUMMARY
Typical Recipients: • *Arts & Humanities:* libraries, museums/galleries, music, opera, performing arts • *Civic & Public Affairs:* environmental affairs, ethnic/minority organizations, housing, nonprofit management, urban & community affairs, women's affairs, zoos/botanical gardens • *Education:* business education, colleges & universities, economic education, elementary education, engineering education, literacy, minority education, public education (precollege) • *Health:* emergency/ambulance services, general, health care cost containment • *Social Services:* community centers, domestic violence, drugs & alcohol, employment/job training, general, recreation & athletics, united funds, youth organizations
Grant Types: capital and general support
Nonmonetary Support Types: donated equipment
Geographic Distribution: giving largely limited to WICOR plant locations and service territory
Operating Locations: CA (Oxnard), WI (Delavan, Milwaukee, Racine)

CORP. OFFICERS
Stuart W. Tisdale: *B* Leominster MA 1928 *ED* Yale Univ BA *CURR EMPL* chmn, ceo: WICOR *CORP AFFIL* chmn: STARITE Indus; chmn, dir: WI Gas Co; dir: Marshall & Ilsley Bank, Marshall & Ilsley Corp,

Modine Mfg Co, Twin Disc *NONPR AFFIL* dir: Columbia Hosp; pres: Greater Milwaukee Comm
Joseph Wenzler: *B* Fond du Lac WI 1942 *ED* Marquette Univ BS 1964; Univ WI MBA 1983 *CURR EMPL* pres, coo, dir: WICOR *CORP AFFIL* dir: WI Gas Co; pres, coo, dir: Sta-Rite Indus Inc

GIVING OFFICERS
James C. Donnelly: vp, dir *B* Boston MA 1945 *ED* Northeastern Univ BS 1969; Suffolk Univ JD 1978 *CURR EMPL* vp, treas, cfo: WI Gas Co *CORP AFFIL* cfo, vp: WICOR Inc; vp, treas, cfo: WI Gas Co *NONPR AFFIL* mem: Am Gas Assn, Fin Exec Inst, New England Gas Assn, Treas Club Boston
Thomas F. Schrader: vp, dir *B* Indianapolis IN 1950 *ED* Princeton Univ BS 1972; Princeton Univ MS 1978 *CURR EMPL* pres, ceo, dir: WI Gas Co *CORP AFFIL* dir: First WI Trust Co, Milwaukee Mgmt Support Org, Portal Indus, Sta-Rite Indus, Wexco DE, WI Utilities Assn; vp, dir: WICOR *NONPR AFFIL* dir: Goodwill Indus; head: New Hope Project
Carolyn Simpson: coordinator
Stuart W. Tisdale: pres, dir *CURR EMPL* chmn, ceo: WICOR (see above)
George E. Wardeberg: dir
Joseph Wenzler: secy, treas *CURR EMPL* pres, coo, dir: WICOR (see above)

APPLICATION INFORMATION
Initial Approach: *Initial Contact:* written proposal *Include Information On:* legal name, address, and telephone number of organization; name of representative who can be contacted by telephone; statement of purpose and a brief history of organization, including past projects; description of overall program, including any collaboration with other nonprofit organizations; an explanation regarding specific request for support; most recent audited financial statement; itemized annual and project budget with projected revenues and expenses; list of funding sources contacted and funds received; copy of tax-exempt letter; list of current board of directors; description of unique facets of request and what differentiates

it from other projects of the same nature; and a description of how results will be measured *When to Submit:* there are four deadlines a year: January 31, April 30, July 31, and October 31
Restrictions on Giving: Does not support individuals, religious organizations for sectarian purposes, political or lobbying groups, or organizations outside operating areas.

OTHER THINGS TO KNOW
Publications: fact sheet

GRANTS ANALYSIS
Total Grants: $646,920
Number of Grants: 159
Highest Grant: $50,000
Typical Range: $500 to $5,000
Disclosure Period: 1990
Note: Recent grants are derived from a 1990 grants list.

RECENT GRANTS
50,000 Marquette University, Milwaukee, WI
40,000 United Performing Arts Fund, Milwaukee, WI
35,000 United Performing Arts Fund, Milwaukee, WI
32,875 United Way, Milwaukee, WI
32,875 United Way, Milwaukee, WI
31,878 United Way, Milwaukee, WI
24,710 United Way, Milwaukee, WI
20,000 Children's Hospital of Wisconsin, Milwaukee, WI
20,000 Medical College of Wisconsin, Milwaukee, WI
15,412 Delavan Darien UWAY, Milwaukee, WI

Widgeon Foundation

CONTACT
George V. Strong, Jr.
Director
Widgeon Fdn.
PO Box 1084
Easton, MD 21601
(410) 822-7707

FINANCIAL SUMMARY
Recent Giving: $91,465 (1990); $98,200 (1989); $94,261 (1988)
Assets: $2,008,790 (1990); $2,053,139 (1989); $1,767,839 (1988)

EIN: 13-6113927

CONTRIBUTIONS SUMMARY
Donor(s): Elizabeth H. Robinson

Typical Recipients: • *Arts & Humanities:* arts centers • *Civic & Public Affairs:* urban & community affairs, zoos/botanical gardens • *Education:* colleges & universities • *Religion:* churches, religious organizations • *Social Services:* community service organizations, united funds, youth organizations
Grant Types: general support
Geographic Distribution: focus on MD

GIVING OFFICERS
Elizabeth H. Robinson: dir, pres, treas
Richard Robinson: dir, vp
George V. Strong, Jr.: dir, secy

APPLICATION INFORMATION
Initial Approach: Send brief proposal. There are no deadlines.
Restrictions on Giving: Does not support individuals.

GRANTS ANALYSIS
Number of Grants: 36
Highest Grant: $15,000
Typical Range: $750 to $5,000
Disclosure Period: 1990

RECENT GRANTS
15,000 University of Maryland Foundation, College Park, MD
13,250 Elwyn Institute, Elwyn, PA
10,000 Jamestown 4-H Center, Jamestown, VA
10,000 University of Richmond, Richmond, VA
5,000 Pennsylvania Horticultural Society, Philadelphia, PA
5,000 Salisbury State University, Salisbury, MD
5,000 Virginia Commonwealth University, Richmond, VA
5,000 Washington College, Chestertown, MD
4,500 YMCA, Cambridge, MD
2,200 Salvation Army

Widow's Society

CONTACT
Dorothy Johnson
Widow's Society
20 Bayberry Lane
Avon, CT 06001
(203) 678-9660

FINANCIAL SUMMARY
Recent Giving: $135,390 (fiscal 1991); $134,385 (fiscal 1990); $122,824 (fiscal 1989)
Assets: $2,488,171 (fiscal year ending August 31, 1991); $2,176,240 (fiscal 1990); $2,294,756 (fiscal 1989)
Gifts Received: $32,053 (fiscal 1991); $33,024 (fiscal 1990); $25,766 (fiscal 1989)
Fiscal Note: In 1991, contributions were received from the Sarah N. Pardee Trust ($9,177), Eleanor Parkman Estate ($9,276), and the City of Hartford ($13,589).
EIN: 06-6026060

CONTRIBUTIONS SUMMARY
Donor(s): City of Hartford, Sarah W. Pardee Fund
Geographic Distribution: focus on Hartford, CT

GIVING OFFICERS
Barbara Ashton: secy
Mary Hoffer: vp
Dorothy Johnson: pres

APPLICATION INFORMATION
Initial Approach: Applications generally referred through public or private social service agency.

OTHER THINGS TO KNOW
Provides aid to needy women and children.
Disclosure Period: fiscal year ending August 31, 1991

Wieboldt Foundation

CONTACT
Anne C. Hallett
Executive Director
Wieboldt Foundation
53 West Jackson Blvd., Ste. 838
Chicago, IL 60604
(312) 786-9377

FINANCIAL SUMMARY
Recent Giving: $600,000 (1992 approx.); $590,100 (1991); $639,900 (1990 approx.)
Assets: $18,000,000 (1992 est.); $14,878,024 (1991); $13,593,244 (1990 approx.); $15,401,448 (1989)
EIN: 36-2167955

CONTRIBUTIONS SUMMARY
Donor(s): The Wieboldt Foundation was founded in 1921 by William A. and Anna K. Wieboldt. Mr. Wieboldt (1857-1954) was chairman of Wieboldt Stores. The foundation was established with the hope of supporting "charities designed to put an end to the need for charity." The present directors of the foundation remain committed to preserving the founders' ideals, now translated into a concentration on community organizations.
Typical Recipients: • *Civic & Public Affairs:* economic development, environmental affairs, housing, law & justice, public policy, urban & community affairs, women's affairs • *Education:* education administration, education associations • *Social Services:* community service organizations
Grant Types: general support
Geographic Distribution: metropolitan Chicago

GIVING OFFICERS
Anita Straub Darrow: pres, dir
John Straub Darrow: vp, dir *CURR EMPL* vp: Northern Trust Co *NONPR AFFIL* trust: North Shore Country Day Sch
T. Lawrence Doyle: treas, dir *CURR EMPL* vp (mktg & sales Personal Trust): Am Natl Bank & Trust Co Chicago
Diane Glenn: dir
Anne C. Hallett: exec dir, secy
Ms. Nydia Hohf: dir
Benjamin Kendrick: dir
John Kretzmann: dir
Carol Larson: dir
Henry Mendoza: dir
Mary W. Sample: dir
Dolores J. Smith: asst secy, dir *CURR EMPL* pres: DJ Smith Enterprises *NONPR AFFIL* chmn: Midwest Womens Ctr
Ms. Jennifer Straub: dir
Anne L. Wieboldt: dir
Ms. Nancy Wieboldt: dir

APPLICATION INFORMATION
Initial Approach:

The foundation does not provide application forms for grants. Organizations should submit a detailed application of not more than ten pages. For a program related investment, organizations must submit a pre-application form, which is available from the foundation. If interested, the foundation will request a full application. Applications for grants should include a summary page briefly describing the organization, request, budget, and amount of request. Also required is a more detailed description of the organization, which must include its history, membership, structure, staff, and programs. Applications must list officers and directors with their work and community affiliations; indicate how the organization chooses issues, makes decisions, benefits the community, and provides skills to leaders and staff members; and provide current and anticipated budgets of income and expenses, a financial report showing actual income and expenses for the most recently completed budget year, a copy of the most recent audit, and information proving tax-exempt status. Final applications for a program related investment should include a description of the project, including analysis of need, goals, objectives, affected population, expected outcomes, and amount and terms requested; business plan, if appropriate; brief description of the applicant's organization; list of board members; full financial information; tax-exempt status information; repayment plan; and a description of collateral, if appropriate.

The application deadline for grants is the last working day of the month. Applications will be considered two months later. The deadline for submitting pre-applications for program related investments is the 15th of any month, except July and November. For final full applications, the deadline is the end of any month, except July and November.

Board members typically meet monthly except in August, and December. Characteristics of organizations that the foundation considers important are the ability to organize communities and develop leadership, the demonstrated competence of staff and leadership, the effectiveness in dealing with issues identified in conjunction with community residents, and evidence of local fund-raising efforts. Organizing efforts in the poorest urban neighborhoods will receive special consideration.

Program related investment pre-applications will receive a response by the end of the following month with a request for a full application or a denial of the request for assistance.

Restrictions on Giving: The foundation generally does not fund individuals, studies and research, conferences, capital development, or direct service programs.

OTHER THINGS TO KNOW

The board of directors believes that it is important to know personally the groups they fund. Most directors make site visits and attempt to meet the heads of the groups supported by the foundation. In 1987, the board scheduled four meetings in neighborhood locations where leaders of local organizations were invited to make presentations about their work.

The board also takes time once a year, in addition to grant-making meetings, to discuss policies, practices, and new initiatives. In January 1987, the board held its retreat to review grants, both for the past year and for the preceding ten-year period, and to reflect on the grant-making program. The board also initiated a new policy of program related investments to help the foundation increase the variety of support offered and leverage grant dollars. This program, begun in 1988, will use funds from the foundation portfolio and from the grant-making budget.

Publications: annual report

GRANTS ANALYSIS

Total Grants: $590,100
Number of Grants: 76
Highest Grant: $25,000
Typical Range: $5,000 to $15,000
Disclosure Period: 1991
Note: Recent grants are derived from a 1991 annual report.

RECENT GRANTS

25,000 Special Fund for 1991 LSC Elections, Chicago, IL — grants to community organizations

15,000 Catholic Community of Pilsen, Chicago, IL — general operating support

15,000 Center for Neighborhood Technology, Chicago, IL — general operating support

15,000 Interfaith Citizens Organization, Hammond, IN — general operating support

15,000 Interfaith Organizing Project of Greater Chicago, Chicago, IL — general operating support

15,000 Logan Square Neighborhood Association, Chicago, IL — general operating support

15,000 Organization of the Northeast, Chicago, IL — general operating support

12,500 Cicero, Berwyn, Stickney Interfaith Leadership Project, Cicero, IL — general operating support

10,000 Center for Community and Leadership Development, Chicago, IL — community organizing project

10,000 Chicago Acorn, Chicago, IL — general operating support

Wiegand Foundation, E. L.

CONTACT
Joanne C. Hildahl
Vice President, Grants Program
E. L. Wiegand Foundation
Wiegand Center
165 West Liberty St.
Reno, NV 89501
(702) 333-0310

FINANCIAL SUMMARY
Recent Giving: $3,600,000 (fiscal 1993); $3,819,785 (fiscal 1992); $3,962,086 (fiscal 1991)
Assets: $80,000,000 (fiscal 1993 est.); $78,000,000 (fiscal year ending October 31, 1991); $76,152,114 (fiscal 1990); $79,466,446 (fiscal 1989)
Gifts Received: $43,454 (fiscal 1991); $22,142 (fiscal 1990); $31,235 (fiscal 1989)
EIN: 94-2839372

CONTRIBUTIONS SUMMARY

Donor(s): Edwin L. Wiegand was born in Dover, OH, in 1891. He experimented with electricity as a boy and concluded that the use of electricity for heating afforded the most important growth potential for the future. In 1915, he obtained his first patent on a metal sheathed refractory insulated electric heating element, and two years later founded the Edwin L. Wiegand Company in Pittsburgh. In a small room with one employee, he manufactured the first successful resistance heating units. Under the trade name "Chromalox", Mr. Wiegand developed and manufactured heating elements for home appliances and industrial uses that are still the heart of many electric appliances today. In 1968, he merged his company with Emerson Electric Company of St. Louis, MO. He moved to Reno, NV, in 1971 and became an active participant in Miami Oil Producers, especially in their development of oil and gas properties. He served on the Miami board until his death at the age of 88.

The foundation was initiated in 1982 by the late Ann K. Wiegand and Edwin L. Wiegand, Jr. To foster the religious beliefs of E.L. Wiegand, a part of the annual grants are made to Roman Catholic charitable institutions.

Typical Recipients: • *Arts & Humanities:* arts centers, arts institutes, dance, museums/galleries, music, performing arts, theater • *Civic & Public Affairs:* public policy • *Education:* arts education, business education, colleges & universities, elementary education, legal education, medical education, private education (precollege), religious education • *Health:* hospitals, medical research • *Social Services:* community service organizations, youth organizations

Grant Types: capital and project

Geographic Distribution: for education: Nevada, California, Oregon, Idaho, Utah, and Arizona; for health and medical research: Nevada, California, Oregon, Idaho, Utah, and Arizona; for public affairs: Nevada, California, District of Columbia, and New York City; for civic and community affairs: Nevada and California; and for arts and cultural affairs: Nevada and California

GIVING OFFICERS
Kristen A. Avansino: pres
Raymond C. Avansino, Jr.: trust
James T. Carrico: treas
Frank J. Fahrenkopf, Jr.: trust
Harvey C. Fruehauf, Jr.: trust *B* Grosse Pointe Park MI 1929 *ED* Univ MI 1952 *CURR EMPL* pres, dir: HCF Enterprises *CORP AFFIL* chmn: Miami Oil Producers; dir: GA Pacific Corp; pres, treas, dir: HCF Realty
Mario J. Gabelli: trust
Joanne C. Hildahl: vp (grants program)

APPLICATION INFORMATION
Initial Approach:
Upon request, the foundation provides an informational booklet. Applicants initially must submit a brief letter of inquiry describing the organization and the proposed request.
Proposals must be submitted with an original Application for Grant form, a description of the project, an itemized budget for the project, project starting date and schedule, qualifications of key personnel, a brief history of the institution, a list of officers and their affiliations, the name of any employee or officer of the foundation who is associated with the applicant, a copy of the IRS tax-exempt determination letter, a copy of current documentary evidence from the organization's state classifying the applicant as tax-exempt, a copy of the most recent 990, current audited financial statements, current interim financial statements, a financial budget for the current year, a statement of the applicant's major sources of support for the last five years, and an indication of how the program will be evaluated upon its completion.
Applications are accepted throughout the year. Upon receiving the Application for Grant Form, applicants are notified of deadlines.
The board usually meets three times a year, generally in February, June and October.
Restrictions on Giving:
Grants will not be given for the following purposes: endow-

ments; debt retirement or operating deficits; general, ordinary, and normal operations or their extension, including the repair and maintenance of facilities; emergency funding; general fundraising events, appeals, campaigns, dinners, or mass mailings; loans; distribution of funds to beneficiaries; the influence of legislation or elections; multi-year grants, production of documentaries, publications, films, or media presentations; religious institutions for the construction or restoration of buildings; or to institutions that have been in existence for less than five years; federal, state, or local government agencies or institutions; institutions supported by public tax funds; institutions served by the United Way; or individuals.

OTHER THINGS TO KNOW
A portion of the foundation's fund balance is held as a special fund for the benefit of Roman Catholic charitable organizations.
Publications: informational booklet

GRANTS ANALYSIS
Total Grants: $3,819,785
Number of Grants: 97
Highest Grant: $360,000
Typical Range: $5,000 to $75,000
Disclosure Period: fiscal year ending October 31, 1991
Note: Average grant figure was supplied by the foundation. Recent grants are derived from a fiscal 1991 Form 990.

RECENT GRANTS
350,000 UNR Foundation-College of Agriculture, Reno, NV — experimental sheep project equipment
110,000 Monastery of St. Gertrude, Cottonwood, ID — fire alarm system
102,000 Roman Catholic Diocese of Reno-Las Vegas, Las Vegas, NV — chapel furnishings
100,000 National Judicial College, Reno, NV — library equipment
100,000 St. Rose Dominican Hospital, Henderson, NV — operating room equipment

85,000 Providence Milwaukee Hospital, Milwaukee, OR — angiodynograph system
75,000 Nevada Museum of Art, Reno, NV — general support
74,000 O'Conner Hospital, San Jose, CA — cardiac equipment
73,500 Seton Medical Center, San Francisco, CA — cardiac imaging system
73,000 Marylhurst College, Marylhurst, OR — science equipment

Wien Foundation, Lawrence A.

CONTACT
Lawrence A. Wien
President
Lawrence A. Wien Fdn.
60 East 42nd St.
New York, NY 10165
(212) 687-8700

FINANCIAL SUMMARY
Recent Giving: $640,591 (fiscal 1991); $794,504 (fiscal 1990); $630,687 (fiscal 1989)
Assets: $5,091,582 (fiscal year ending June 30, 1992); $5,530,237 (fiscal 1990); $4,568,451 (fiscal 1989)
EIN: 13-6095927

CONTRIBUTIONS SUMMARY
Donor(s): Lawrence A. Wien, Mae L. Wien
Typical Recipients: • *Arts & Humanities:* arts centers, history/historic preservation, music, performing arts • *Civic & Public Affairs:* zoos/botanical gardens • *Education:* colleges & universities, minority education • *Health:* hospitals, medical research • *Religion:* religious organizations, synagogues • *Social Services:* community service organizations, disabled, family planning
Grant Types: general support
Geographic Distribution: focus on New York, NY

GIVING OFFICERS
Isabel W. Malkin: dir
Peter Laurence Malkin: secy, dir *B* New York NY 1934 *ED* Harvard Univ AB 1955; Harvard Univ LLB 1958 *CURR EMPL* ptnr: Wien Malkin & Bettex *CORP AFFIL* mem: Empire St Bldg Assocs; mem natl

adv bd: Chemical Bank; ptnr: Wien Malkin & Bettex *NONPR AFFIL* del: Un Jewish Appeal Federation Jewish Philanthropies Greater NY; dir, mem exec comm: Lincoln Ctr Performing Arts; mem: Am Arbitration Assn, Am Bar Assn, CT Bar Assn, NY Bar Assn, NY City Bar Assn; mem devel comm: NY Pub Library; mem exec comm: Assn Better NY, Harvard Univ; overseer Wien intl scholarship program: Brandeis Univ; trust: Citizens Budget Comm NY, Natl Trust Historic Preservation
Enid W. Morse: dir
Lester S. Morse, Jr.: dir

APPLICATION INFORMATION
Initial Approach: Send brief letter describing program. There are no deadlines.

GRANTS ANALYSIS
Number of Grants: 162
Highest Grant: $110,000
Typical Range: $1,000 to $5,000
Disclosure Period: fiscal year ending June 30, 1992

RECENT GRANTS
110,000 New York Historical Society, New York, NY
66,000 Lincoln Center for the Performing Arts, New York, NY
59,200 New York City Opera, New York, NY
40,000 Yale University, New Haven, CT
25,000 International Festival of the Arts, New York, NY
25,000 National Trust for Historic Preservation, Washington, DC
25,000 New York Public Library, New York, NY
21,980 Parks Council, New York, NY
20,000 United Jewish Appeal Federation of Jewish Philanthropies, New York, NY
15,125 Brandeis University, Waltham, MA

Wiener Foundation, Malcolm Hewitt

CONTACT

Adelaide Lewis
c/o The Millburn Corporation
1270 Avenue of the Americas,
  11th Fl.
New York, NY 10020
(212) 397-8817

FINANCIAL SUMMARY

Recent Giving: $1,023,000
(1991); $730,975 (1990);
$1,298,243 (1989)
Assets: $28,536,574 (1991);
$22,067,043 (1990);
$23,339,337 (1989)
EIN: 13-3250321

CONTRIBUTIONS SUMMARY

Donor(s): The foundation was
incorporated in 1984 by Malcolm H. Wiener.
Typical Recipients: • *Arts &
Humanities:* arts funds, his-
tory/historic preservation, libraries, literary arts, muse-
ums/galleries • *Civic & Public
Affairs:* economics, environmental affairs, ethnic/minority
organizations, first amendment
issues, international affairs,
public policy, zoos/botanical
gardens • *Education:* colleges
& universities, education
funds, social sciences education • *Health:* hospitals, single-
disease health associations • *International:* international
organizations • *Social Services:*
child welfare, family planning,
family services, food/clothing
distribution, united funds
Grant Types: general support
and project
Geographic Distribution:
some national; focus on New
York, NY

GIVING OFFICERS

Harvey Beker: vp, dir
George Crapple: vp, dir
Thomas R. Moore: secy, dir
Martin J. Whitman: dir *ED*
Syracuse Univ 1949; New Sch
Social Research 1956 *CURR
EMPL* dir: Natl Am Co *CORP
AFFIL* dir: KCP Holding Co,
Natl Am Ins Co; managing
ptnr: Whitman Hefferman
Rhein & Co
Carolyn S. Wiener: dir
Malcolm Hewitt Wiener: don,
pres, treas *B* Tsingtao People's
Republic of China 1935 *ED*
Harvard Univ BA 1957; Har-
vard Univ JD 1963 *CURR
EMPL* chmn: Millburn Corp

CORP AFFIL chmn: Millburn
Ridge Field Corp, Share InVest
NONPR AFFIL dir: Intl Fdn
Art Res, NY Landmarks Preser-
vation Fdn; mem visitation
comm: Harvard Univ John F
Kennedy Sch Govt; trust: Am
Sch Classical Studies Athens;
vchmn: Metro Mus Art

APPLICATION INFORMATION

**Initial Approach: Restric-
tions on Giving:** The foundation supports preselected organizations and does not accept
unsolicited requests for funds.
The foundation does not make
grants to individuals.

GRANTS ANALYSIS

Total Grants: $1,023,000
Number of Grants: 41
Highest Grant: $186,000
Typical Range: $1,000 to
$25,000
Disclosure Period: 1991
Note: Average grant figure
does not include the highest
grant of $186,000. Recent
grants are derived from a 1991
grants list.

RECENT GRANTS

186,000 Winston Founda-
  tion for World
  Peace, New York,
  NY
110,000 Institute of Fine
  Arts, New York,
  NY
100,000 Family in Trust Appeal, Northampton,
  England
94,500 Metropolitan Mu-
  seum of Art, New
  York, NY
92,000 Harvard Univer-
  sity, Cambridge,
  MA
75,000 Gay Men's Health
  Crisis, New York,
  NY
62,000 Council on Foreign
  Relations, New
  York, NY
60,000 New York Hospital
  Cornell Medical
  Center, New York,
  NY
26,000 Columbia Univer-
  sity, New York, NY
25,000 Amnesty Interna-
  tional, New York,
  NY

Wiggins Memorial Trust, J. J.

CONTACT

J. J. Wiggins Memorial Trust
PO Drawer 1111
Moore Haven, FL 33471
(813) 946-0881

FINANCIAL SUMMARY

Recent Giving: $105,863 (fis-
cal 1992); $170,048 (fiscal
1991); $149,150 (fiscal 1990)
Assets: $5,715,337 (fiscal year
ending April 30, 1992);
$5,407,647 (fiscal 1991);
$5,440,619 (fiscal 1990)
Gifts Received: $1,482,367
(fiscal 1990); $2,060,993 (fis-
cal 1989)
EIN: 59-2675273

CONTRIBUTIONS SUMMARY

Donor(s): the late J. J. Wiggins
Typical Recipients: • *Civic &
Public Affairs:* law & justice,
municipalities, safety • *Education:* colleges & universities,
community & junior colleges,
elementary education, public
education (precollege) • *Social
Services:* youth organizations
Grant Types: capital, operating expenses, and scholarship
Geographic Distribution:
focus on Glades County, FL

GIVING OFFICERS

John M. Hathaway: trust
John Holbrook: trust
J. C. Sealey: trust
A. E. Wells: trust

APPLICATION INFORMATION

Initial Approach: Scholarship
applicants must be nominated
by high school or college level
educators. Application form required. Deadline is May 1.

GRANTS ANALYSIS

Number of Grants: 40
Highest Grant: $12,000
Typical Range: $1,200 to
$2,400
Disclosure Period: fiscal year
ending April 30, 1992

RECENT GRANTS

12,000 Edison Community
  College, Edison, NJ
7,950 University of Cen-
  tral Florida, Or-
  lando, FL
6,350 Glades County
  Youth Livestock,
  FL
6,000 South Florida Com-
  munity College, FL

6,000 Troy State Univer-
  sity, Troy, GA
4,400 College of Palm
  Beaches, Palm
  Beach, FL
4,043 Glades County
  Sheriff Depart-
  ment, FL
3,600 Florida A&M Uni-
  versity, FL
3,600 Nova University,
  Ft. Lauderdale, FL
3,600 Palm Beaches Com-
  munity College,
  Palm Beach, FL

Wigwam Mills / Wigwam Mills Fund

Sales: $10.0 million
Employees: 400
Headquarters: Sheboygan, WI

CONTACT

R. E. Chesebro, Jr.
President
Wigwam Mills
P.O. Box 818
Sheboygan, WI 53082-0818
(414) 457-5551

FINANCIAL SUMMARY

Recent Giving: $23,600 (fiscal
1991); $25,930 (fiscal 1989)
Assets: $28,178 (fiscal year
ending November 30, 1991);
$14,300 (fiscal 1989)
Gifts Received: $33,333 (fis-
cal 1991); $30,000 (fiscal 1989)
Fiscal Note: In fiscal 1991,
contributions were received
from Wigwam Mills, Inc.
EIN: 39-6053425

CONTRIBUTIONS SUMMARY

Typical Recipients: • *Arts &
Humanities:* arts centers
• *Civic & Public Affairs:* urban
& community affairs • *Educa-
tion:* colleges & universities
• *Health:* health organizations
• *Social Services:* united funds,
youth organizations
Grant Types: capital and gen-
eral support
Geographic Distribution: giv-
ing primarily in Sheboygan, WI
Operating Locations: WI (She-
boygan)

CORP. OFFICERS

R.E. Chesebro: *CURR EMPL*
chmn: Wigwam Mills

GIVING OFFICERS

R.E. Chesebro, Jr.: pres
E.H. Oeschger: vp
J.F. Wilke: secy-treas

APPLICATION INFORMATION
Initial Approach: The foundation supports preselected organizations and does not accept unsolicited requests for funds.

GRANTS ANALYSIS
Number of Grants: 14
Highest Grant: $6,000
Typical Range: $100 to $3,500
Disclosure Period: fiscal year ending November 30, 1991

RECENT GRANTS
6,000 Sheboygan Area United Way, Sheboygan, WI
5,600 Kiddies Camp Corporation, Sheboygan, WI
3,500 John Michael Kohler Arts Center, Sheboygan, WI
2,800 Lakeland College, Sheboygan, WI
2,600 YMCA, Sheboygan, WI
1,000 Community Core Group, Sheboygan, WI
600 American Cancer Society, Sheboygan, WI
500 American Heart Association, Sheboygan, WI
300 Boy Scouts of America, Menasha, WI
300 Sheboygan Symphony Orchestra, Sheboygan, WI

Wilber National Bank
Employees: 172
Headquarters: Oneonta, NY
SIC Major Group: Depository Institutions

CONTACT
Nancy Miller
Marketing Department
Wilber National Bank
PO Box 430
Oneonta, NY 13820
(607) 432-1700

CONTRIBUTIONS SUMMARY
Typical Recipients: • *Education:* colleges & universities
Grant Types: general support
Operating Locations: NY (Oneonta)

CORP. OFFICERS
R. W. Moyer: *CURR EMPL* pres, ceo: Wilber Corp

RECENT GRANTS
100,000 Hartwick College, Oneonta, NY

Wilbur-Ellis Co. / Wilbur Foundation, Brayton
Sales: $750.0 million
Employees: 1,400
Headquarters: San Francisco, CA
SIC Major Group: Wholesale Trade—Nondurable Goods

CONTACT
Brayton Wilbur, Jr.
President
Wilbur-Ellis
320 California St., 2nd Fl.
San Francisco, CA 94104
(415) 772-4006

FINANCIAL SUMMARY
Recent Giving: $225,877 (1991)
Assets: $4,792,083 (1991)
Gifts Received: $75,000 (1991)
Fiscal Note: In 1991, contributions were received from the Wilbur-Ellis Company.
EIN: 94-6088667

CONTRIBUTIONS SUMMARY
Typical Recipients: • *Arts & Humanities:* arts associations, general, museums/galleries • *Civic & Public Affairs:* environmental affairs, general • *Education:* colleges & universities, public education (precollege) • *Health:* health organizations • *International:* international organizations • *Social Services:* general, united funds
Grant Types: general support
Operating Locations: CA (San Francisco), IA (West Burlington), TX (Edinburg)

CORP. OFFICERS
Brayton Wilbur, Jr.: *CURR EMPL* pres: Wilbur-Ellis Co

GIVING OFFICERS
Carter P. Thacher: vp, dir
Herbert B. Tully: secy, treas, dir
Brayton Wilbur, Jr.: pres, dir *CURR EMPL* pres: Wilbur-Ellis Co (see above)

APPLICATION INFORMATION
Initial Approach: Send brief letter of inquiry; there are no deadlines.

GRANTS ANALYSIS
Number of Grants: 49
Highest Grant: $52,500
Typical Range: $500 to $7,500
Disclosure Period: 1991

RECENT GRANTS
52,500 San Francisco Museum of Modern Art, San Francisco, CA
15,000 California Pacific Medical Center Foundation, San Francisco, CA
15,000 University of California, San Francisco, CA
12,500 Claremont University Center, Claremont, CA
12,000 Cate School, Carpenteria, CA
10,000 Asia Foundation, San Francisco, CA
10,000 Center for Asian-Pacific Affairs, San Francisco, CA
10,000 United Way, San Francisco, CA
7,566 Asian Art Museum Foundation, San Francisco, CA
7,000 USSALEP, Washington, DC

Wilbur Foundation, Marguerite Eyer

CONTACT
Gary R. Ricks
Chief Executive Officer
Marguerite Eyer Wilbur Fdn.
PO Box 3370
Santa Barbara, CA 93130-3370

FINANCIAL SUMMARY
Recent Giving: $130,800 (fiscal 1992); $146,300 (fiscal 1991); $136,484 (fiscal 1990)
Assets: $2,845,116 (fiscal year ending June 30, 1992); $2,791,203 (fiscal 1991); $2,872,198 (fiscal 1990)
EIN: 51-0168214

CONTRIBUTIONS SUMMARY
Donor(s): the late Marguerite Eyer Wilbur
Typical Recipients: • *Arts & Humanities:* music • *Civic & Public Affairs:* law & justice, municipalities, rural affairs • *Education:* colleges & universities, education associations • *Social Services:* community service organizations, youth organizations
Grant Types: endowment, operating expenses, project, research, and seed money

GIVING OFFICERS
Regis C. Ginn: secy, dir
Russell Kirk: trust, pres
William Longstreth: trust, vp
Gary R. Ricks: trust, ceo
William Rusher: treas, dir

APPLICATION INFORMATION
Initial Approach: Send brief letter describing program. There are no deadlines.
Restrictions on Giving: Does not provide funds for deficit financing or land acquisition.

OTHER THINGS TO KNOW
Publications: Application Guidelines

GRANTS ANALYSIS
Number of Grants: 18
Highest Grant: $20,000
Typical Range: $1,000 to $5,000
Disclosure Period: fiscal year ending June 30, 1992
Note: The above does not include individual scholarships for fiscal 1992.

RECENT GRANTS
20,000 Intercollegiate Studies Institute, Bryn Mawr, PA
5,000 Music Academy of West, Santa Barbara, CA
5,000 Young America's Foundation, Herndon, VA
4,500 Center for Judicial Studies, Richmond, VA
4,000 Rockford Institute, Rockford, IL
2,500 Salisbury Review, London, England
2,000 Hillsdale Review, Front Royal, VA
1,000 FARMS, Provo, UT
1,000 Touchstone, Chicago, IL
1,000 University Professors for Academic Order, Wichita, KS

Wilcox General Trust, George N.

CONTACT
Lois C. Looms
V.P. and Corp. Secretary
George N. Wilcox General Trust
c/o Bishop Trust Co., Ltd.
PO Box 2390
Honolulu, HI 96804-2390
(808) 523-2233

FINANCIAL SUMMARY
Recent Giving: $706,393
(1990); $804,377 (1989)
Assets: $12,654,752 (1990);
$13,646,780 (1989)
EIN: 99-6002445

CONTRIBUTIONS SUMMARY
Donor(s): the late George N. Wilcox
Typical Recipients: • *Arts & Humanities:* arts institutes, public broadcasting, theater • *Civic & Public Affairs:* urban & community affairs • *Education:* private education (precollege), science/technology education • *Health:* hospices, hospitals, single-disease health associations • *Religion:* churches • *Social Services:* child welfare, community service organizations, disabled, united funds, youth organizations
Grant Types: capital, general support, multiyear/continuing support, operating expenses, and project
Geographic Distribution: limited to HI

GIVING OFFICERS
Gale Fisher Carswell: mem comm beneficiaries
Edwin L. Carter: chmn comm beneficiaries *CORP AFFIL* dir: HEI
Aletha Kaohi: mem comm beneficiaries

APPLICATION INFORMATION
Initial Approach: Make initial inquiry by telephone. Followed by full proposal, if requested.

OTHER THINGS TO KNOW
Publications: Annual Report (including application guidelines)

GRANTS ANALYSIS
Number of Grants: 74
Highest Grant: $50,000
Typical Range: $1,000 to $10,000

Disclosure Period: 1990

RECENT GRANTS
- 50,000 Wilcox Hospital, Kauai, HI
- 39,500 Salvation Army, Honolulu, HI
- 25,000 Chaminade University, Honolulu, HI
- 15,000 Hawaii Theatre, Honolulu, HI
- 15,000 St. Francis Medical Center
- 12,000 United Church Board
- 10,000 Boys and Girls Club
- 10,000 Hina Mauka, Waipahu, HI
- 10,000 St. Louis Education
- 10,000 YMCA

Wilcox Trust, S. W.

CONTACT
David W. Pratt
Trustee
S. W. Wilcox Trust
PO Box 2096
Puhi-Rural Sta.
Lihue, HI 96766
(808) 245-2822

FINANCIAL SUMMARY
Recent Giving: $233,500
(1991); $225,000 (1990);
$253,000 (1989)
Assets: $4,442,345 (1991);
$3,938,000 (1990); $4,478,701
(1989)
EIN: 99-6002547

CONTRIBUTIONS SUMMARY
Donor(s): the late Samuel Whitney Wilcox
Typical Recipients: • *Arts & Humanities:* history/historic preservation, museums/galleries, theater • *Civic & Public Affairs:* environmental affairs • *Education:* colleges & universities, private education (precollege) • *Health:* hospitals • *Religion:* churches • *Social Services:* animal protection, community service organizations, united funds, youth organizations
Grant Types: capital, general support, multiyear/continuing support, and operating expenses
Geographic Distribution: limited to HI

GIVING OFFICERS
Bishop Trust Company, Ltd.: agent
Gale Fisher Carswell: trust
Pam Dohrman: trust

APPLICATION INFORMATION
Initial Approach: Send brief letter of inquiry describing program or project. There are no deadlines.

GRANTS ANALYSIS
Number of Grants: 13
Highest Grant: $112,000
Typical Range: $5,000 to $25,000
Disclosure Period: 1991

RECENT GRANTS
- 112,000 Island School, HI
- 25,000 Salvation Army, HI
- 25,000 Wilcox Hospital Foundation, Lihue, HI
- 12,000 YMCA, Kauai, HI
- 10,000 Kauai Museum, Kauai, HI
- 10,000 Lyman House Memorial Museum, HI
- 9,500 Winners Camp, HI — scholarships
- 5,000 Hawaii Pacific University, HI
- 5,000 Kauai Community Players Children's Theater, Kauai, HI
- 5,000 Salvation Army, HI

Wilder Foundation

CONTACT
Rita Wilder
President
Wilder Fdn.
PO Box 99
Key Biscayne, FL 33149

FINANCIAL SUMMARY
Recent Giving: $106,206
(1991); $97,681 (1990);
$99,811 (1989)
Assets: $2,652,191 (1991);
$2,655,909 (1990); $2,598,382
(1989)
EIN: 74-6049547

CONTRIBUTIONS SUMMARY
Donor(s): the late Candace Mossler, Jacques Mossler
Typical Recipients: • *Arts & Humanities:* community arts, history/historic preservation, museums/galleries • *Civic & Public Affairs:* environmental affairs • *Education:* colleges & universities, religious education • *Health:* health organizations, hospitals • *Social Services:* community service organizations
Grant Types: capital, endowment, general support, research, and scholarship

Geographic Distribution: focus on FL

GIVING OFFICERS
Gary Wilder: vp
Rita Wilder: pres

APPLICATION INFORMATION
Initial Approach: Send brief letter describing program. There are no deadlines.
Restrictions on Giving: Does not support individuals.

GRANTS ANALYSIS
Number of Grants: 24
Highest Grant: $80,000
Typical Range: $500 to $1,000
Disclosure Period: 1991

RECENT GRANTS
- 80,000 Southern Methodist University, Dallas, TX
- 6,500 Houston Museum, Houston, TX
- 2,126 Beach Preservation Committee
- 2,000 Kinkaid School, Houston, TX
- 2,000 Miami Heart Institute, Miami, FL
- 1,100 WPBT 2, Miami, FL
- 1,000 Goodwill Industries
- 1,000 Methodist Hospital Foundation
- 1,000 Parish School
- 1,000 Save Venice

Wildermuth Foundation, E. F.

CONTACT
Homer W. Lee
Treasurer
E. F. Wildermuth Fdn.
4770 Indianola Avenue, Ste. 240
Columbus, OH 43214
(614) 846-5838

FINANCIAL SUMMARY
Recent Giving: $180,039
(1991); $175,048 (1990);
$178,775 (1989)
Assets: $3,271,310 (1991);
$3,001,871 (1990); $3,173,226
(1989)
Gifts Received: $35,000
(1989); $50,000 (1988)
EIN: 31-6050202

CONTRIBUTIONS SUMMARY
Typical Recipients: • *Arts & Humanities:* dance • *Education:* colleges & universities, medical education • *Health:* health organizations, hospitals, pediatric health • *Religion:*

churches, religious organizations • *Social Services:* child welfare, community service organizations, united funds, youth organizations
Grant Types: general support
Geographic Distribution: focus on OH

GIVING OFFICERS
Faurest Borton: vp
Karl Borton: trust
J. Patrick Campbell: trust
Genevieve Connable: trust
W. Daniel Driscoll: off
H. Ward Ewalt: pres
Bettie A. Kalb: secy
Homer W. Lee: treas
Robert W. Lee: trust
David R. Patterson: asst to pres, trust
David T. Patterson: trust
Phillip N. Phillipson: trust

APPLICATION INFORMATION
Initial Approach: Send brief letter describing program. Deadline is August 1.

GRANTS ANALYSIS
Number of Grants: 23
Highest Grant: $50,000
Typical Range: $1,000 to $5,000
Disclosure Period: 1991

RECENT GRANTS
50,000 Ohio State University, Columbus, OH
35,000 Pennsylvania College of Optometry, Philadelphia, PA
25,539 Wildermuth Memorial Church
10,000 Ballet Met, Columbus, OH
8,000 Illinois College of Optometry, Chicago, IL
7,500 Buckeye Boys Ranch, Grove City, OH
7,000 Big Brothers and Big Sisters
7,000 Pilot Dogs
5,000 American Heart Association, Philadelphia, PA
3,400 Childhood League

Wiley & Sons, Inc., John
Sales: $248.2 million
Employees: 1,700
Headquarters: New York, NY
SIC Major Group: Printing & Publishing

CONTACT
Deborah Wiley
Vice Chairman
John Wiley & Sons, Inc.
605 Third Ave.
New York, NY 10158
(212) 850-6000

FINANCIAL SUMMARY
Recent Giving: $100,000 (1992 approx.); $115,000 (1991)

CONTRIBUTIONS SUMMARY
Support goes to arts (40%), education (20%), health and human services (20%), and civic (20%) organizations.
Typical Recipients: • *Arts & Humanities:* arts institutes, dance, libraries, museums/galleries, opera, performing arts, public broadcasting • *Civic & Public Affairs:* civil rights, first amendment issues, zoos/botanical gardens • *Education:* colleges & universities, literacy • *Health:* single-disease health associations • *Social Services:* community service organizations, shelters/homelessness
Grant Types: conference/seminar, employee matching gifts, general support, and matching
Nonmonetary Support Types: donated products and workplace solicitation
Geographic Distribution: headquarters area
Operating Locations: NY (New York)

CORP. OFFICERS
Charles R. Ellis: *CURR EMPL* pres, ceo: John Wiley & Sons
W. Bradford Wiley: *CURR EMPL* chmn: John Wiley & Sons

APPLICATION INFORMATION
Initial Approach: Send brief letter of inquiry, including a description of the organization, amount requested, purpose of funds sought, audited financial statement, and proof of tax-exempt status. There are no deadlines.
Restrictions on Giving: Does not support individuals, film projects, religious organizations for sectarian purposes, or political or lobbying groups.

GRANTS ANALYSIS
Typical Range: $1,000 to $2,500

Wilf Family Foundation

CONTACT
Joseph Wilf
Trustee
Wilf Family Fdn.
820 Morris Tpke.
Short Hills, NJ 07078
(201) 467-0300

FINANCIAL SUMMARY
Recent Giving: $1,397,023 (fiscal 1991); $1,188,600 (fiscal 1990); $788,352 (fiscal 1989)
Assets: $28,618,853 (fiscal year ending October 31, 1991); $21,839,210 (fiscal 1990); $18,534,540 (fiscal 1989)
Gifts Received: $5,197,412 (fiscal 1991); $3,287,011 (fiscal 1990); $4,205,905 (fiscal 1989)
Fiscal Note: In 1991, contributions were received from Harry Wilf ($2,178,581), Joseph Wilf ($2,178,581), Leonard Wilf ($400,000), Zygmond Wilf ($250,000), Mark Wilf ($150,000), the Leonard Wilf Charitable Trust ($23,125), and the Zygmond Wilf Charitable Trust ($17,125).
EIN: 22-6075840

CONTRIBUTIONS SUMMARY
Donor(s): The foundation was established in 1964 by Harry Wilf and Joseph Wilf.
Typical Recipients: • *Arts & Humanities:* history/historic preservation, museums/galleries • *Civic & Public Affairs:* ethnic/minority organizations, philanthropic organizations • *Education:* colleges & universities, medical education, private education (precollege), religious education • *International:* foreign educational institutions, international development/relief • *Religion:* religious organizations • *Social Services:* aged, community centers, family services, youth organizations
Grant Types: general support
Geographic Distribution: national, with focus on the eastern United States

GIVING OFFICERS
Elizabeth Wilf: trust
Harry Wilf: pres
Joseph Wilf: secy
Judith Wilf: trust

APPLICATION INFORMATION
Initial Approach: Restrictions on Giving: The foundation supports preselected organizations and does not accept unsolicited requests for funds. The foundation does not make grants to individuals.

GRANTS ANALYSIS
Total Grants: $1,397,023
Number of Grants: 75
Highest Grant: $424,350
Typical Range: $250 to $15,000
Disclosure Period: fiscal year ending October 31, 1991
Note: Average grant figure does not include the highest grant of $424,350. Recent grants are derived from a fiscal 1991 grants list.

RECENT GRANTS
424,350 United Jewish Appeal Federation of New York, New York, NY
260,120 Jewish Educational Center, Elizabeth, NJ
250,000 Yeshiva University, New York, NY
200,000 US Holocaust Memorial Museum, Washington, DC
50,000 Harvard Medical School, Cambridge, MA
50,000 Rabbinical College of America, Morris Township, NJ
15,000 American Jewish Friends of Ungvar, Brooklyn, NY
12,500 Elie Wiesel Humanitarian Foundation, New York, NY
10,000 Park East Day School, New York, NY
10,000 Yeshiva Beth Shearim, Brooklyn, NY

Wilkof Foundation, Edward and Ruth

CONTACT
Harry Mestel
President
Edward and Ruth Wilkof Foundation
c/o Harry Mestel and Company
220 East Tuscarawas Street
Canton, OH 44702
(216) 452-9788

FINANCIAL SUMMARY
Recent Giving: $203,869 (fiscal 1991); $83,553 (fiscal 1990)

Assets: $2,296,141 (fiscal year ending June 30, 1991); $1,352,724 (fiscal 1990)
Gifts Received: $1,000,000 (fiscal 1991); $320,853 (fiscal 1990)
Fiscal Note: In fiscal 1990, the foundation received $320,853 from Edward and Ruth Wilkof.
EIN: 34-1536119

CONTRIBUTIONS SUMMARY

Donor(s): the donors are Edward and Ruth Wilkof
Typical Recipients: • *Arts & Humanities:* arts centers, music • *Civic & Public Affairs:* economic development, ethnic/minority organizations, philanthropic organizations, urban & community affairs • *Education:* colleges & universities, education associations, religious education • *International:* international organizations • *Religion:* religious organizations, synagogues • *Social Services:* child welfare, community service organizations, family services, food/clothing distribution, united funds, volunteer services, youth organizations
Grant Types: general support
Geographic Distribution: Sarasota, FL, and Ohio

GIVING OFFICERS

Frank H. Harvey, Jr.: secy, treas
Harry Mestel: pres
Richard Wilkof, Jr.: trust

APPLICATION INFORMATION

Initial Approach: The foundation reports that it only considers written proposals from 501(c)(3) organizations and does not support individuals. There are no specific application guidelines.

GRANTS ANALYSIS

Total Grants: $203,869
Number of Grants: 23
Highest Grant: $72,000
Typical Range: $3,500 to $27,500
Disclosure Period: fiscal year ending June 30, 1991
Note: Incomplete grants list provided for fiscal year 1991.

RECENT GRANTS

27,500 Sarasota Jewish Federation, Sarasota, FL
6,350 Cultural Center for the Arts, Canton, OH
5,950 Cleveland Orchestra, Cleveland, OH
5,000 Child Development Center, Sarasota, FL
5,000 Florida West Coast Music, Sarasota, FL
5,000 Van Wezel Foundation, Sarasota, FL
4,313 Canton Symphony, Canton, OH
3,750 Shaaray Torah
3,640 Temple Israel
3,500 United Way

Willamette Industries, Inc.

Sales: $2.0 billion
Employees: 11,350
Headquarters: Portland, OR
SIC Major Group: Lumber & Wood Products and Paper & Allied Products

CONTACT

Susanne C. Davis
Manager, Employee Benefits
Willamette Industries, Inc.
3800 First Interstate Tower
1300 S.W. Fifth Ave.
Portland, OR 97201
(503) 227-5581

CONTRIBUTIONS SUMMARY

Operating Locations: IN (Indianapolis), OR (Albany, Lebanon, Portland, Tualatin, Woodburn)

Note: Willamette Industries Building Materials Group operates 4 divisions in operating locations.

CORP. OFFICERS

J. A. Parsons: *CURR EMPL* exec vp, cfo: Willamette Indus

William Swindells, Jr.: *B* Oakland CA 1930 *ED* Stanford Univ BS 1953 *CURR EMPL* chmn, ceo, dir: Willamette Indus *CORP AFFIL* chmn, dir: Bohemia Inc; dir: OR Bank, Standard Ins Co

Willard Foundation, Helen Parker

CONTACT

Helen Parker Willard Fdn.
c/o Crestar Bank N.A.
15th St. and New York Avenue, N.W.
Washington, DC 20005
(202) 879-6337

FINANCIAL SUMMARY

Recent Giving: $154,500 (1991); $91,000 (1990); $145,500 (1989)
Assets: $2,496,188 (1991); $2,250,671 (1990); $2,181,451 (1989)
EIN: 52-6036750

CONTRIBUTIONS SUMMARY

Typical Recipients: • *Education:* colleges & universities • *Health:* hospitals, medical research, single-disease health associations • *Religion:* churches, missionary activities • *Social Services:* community service organizations, disabled, family planning, food/clothing distribution, united funds, youth organizations
Grant Types: capital, endowment, research, and scholarship
Geographic Distribution: focus on Washington, DC

GIVING OFFICERS

Sarah Willard Taylor: dir, vp
Henry A. Willard II: dir, secy, treas
William B. Willard: dir, pres

APPLICATION INFORMATION

Initial Approach: Send brief letter describing program. There are no deadlines.

GRANTS ANALYSIS

Number of Grants: 29
Highest Grant: $10,000
Typical Range: $2,000 to $7,000
Disclosure Period: 1991

RECENT GRANTS

10,000 Central Union Mission, Washington, DC
10,000 Martha's Table, Washington, DC
10,000 Salvation Army, Washington, DC
5,000 Boys and Girls Club, Washington, DC
5,000 Nantucket Cottage Hospital, Nantucket, MA
5,000 Planned Parenthood Federation of America, Washington, DC
5,000 Washington Cathedral, Washington, DC
5,000 Washington Ear, Washington, DC
5,000 YMCA, Washington, DC
5,000 YWCA, Washington, DC

Willard Helping Fund, Cecilia Young

CONTACT

Cecilia Young Willard Helping Fund
c/o Broadway National Bank, Trust Div.
1177 N.E. Loop 410
San Antonio, TX 78209
(512) 283-6700

FINANCIAL SUMMARY

Recent Giving: $203,900 (fiscal 1991); $225,791 (fiscal 1989); $31,593 (fiscal 1988)
Assets: $4,203,727 (fiscal year ending May 31, 1991); $3,789,903 (fiscal 1989); $2,002,566 (fiscal 1988)
Gifts Received: $24,021 (fiscal 1991); $150,000 (fiscal 1989); $2,004,571 (fiscal 1988)
EIN: 74-6350893

CONTRIBUTIONS SUMMARY

Donor(s): Celia Young Willard Trust
Typical Recipients: • *Arts & Humanities:* arts institutes, community arts, libraries, music • *Civic & Public Affairs:* municipalities • *Education:* colleges & universities • *Religion:* churches, religious organizations • *Social Services:* child welfare, community service organizations, homes, youth organizations
Grant Types: operating expenses
Geographic Distribution: focus on NC

APPLICATION INFORMATION

Initial Approach: Funding limited to only those organizations that Dr. Willard contributed to during her lifetime. Does not solicit grant requests.

GRANTS ANALYSIS

Number of Grants: 42

Highest Grant: $42,642
Typical Range: $500 to $5,500
Disclosure Period: fiscal year ending May 31, 1991

RECENT GRANTS
42,642 First Presbyterian Church, Hickory, NC
25,586 Crossnore School, Crossnore, NC
25,586 Grandfather Home for Children, Banner Elk, NC
25,586 Lees-McRae College, Banner Elk, NC
9,375 Lenoir Rhyne College, Hickory, NC
5,000 New Brounfels Art League
5,000 San Antonio Museum Association, San Antonio, TX
5,000 Symphony Society of San Antonio, San Antonio, TX
4,000 Friends of the Bourne Public Library, Bourne, TX
3,750 Mountain Retreat Association

Williams Charitable Trust, John C.

CONTACT
Bruce Bickel
John C. Williams Charitable Trust
c/o Pittsburgh National Bank, Trust Div.
One Oliver Plaza, 27th Fl.
Pittsburgh, PA 15265
(412) 762-3502

FINANCIAL SUMMARY
Recent Giving: $150,000 (1991); $359,580 (1990); $175,909 (1989)
Assets: $4,804,924 (1991); $4,059,844 (1990); $4,226,394 (1989)
Gifts Received: $5,142 (1991)
EIN: 25-6024153

CONTRIBUTIONS SUMMARY
Donor(s): the late John C. Williams
Typical Recipients: • *Arts & Humanities:* libraries • *Civic & Public Affairs:* municipalities • *Education:* colleges & universities • *Health:* emergency/ambulance services, hospitals • *Religion:* religious organizations • *Social Services:* community service organizations, youth organizations
Grant Types: capital and general support

Geographic Distribution: limited to Steubenville, OH, and Weirton, WV

GIVING OFFICERS
Pittsburgh National Bank: trust

APPLICATION INFORMATION
Initial Approach: Send brief letter of inquiry describing program. There are no deadlines.
Restrictions on Giving: Does not support individuals.

OTHER THINGS TO KNOW
Publications: Application Guidelines

GRANTS ANALYSIS
Number of Grants: 1
Highest Grant: $150,000
Disclosure Period: 1991

RECENT GRANTS
150,000 Franciscan University of Steubenville, Steubenville, OH

Williams Charitable Trust, Mary Jo

CONTACT
Michael E. Collins
Trustee
Mary Jo Williams Charitable Trust
P.O. Box 439
Garden City, KS 67846-0439
(316) 276-3203

FINANCIAL SUMMARY
Recent Giving: $116,150 (1990); $112,000 (1989)
Assets: $2,223,721 (1990); $2,187,098 (1989)
EIN: 48-6276428

CONTRIBUTIONS SUMMARY
Typical Recipients: • *Civic & Public Affairs:* housing, professional & trade associations • *Education:* arts education, community & junior colleges, education funds • *Social Services:* aged, community service organizations, united funds
Grant Types: emergency, endowment, general support, and scholarship
Geographic Distribution: Garden City, KS

GIVING OFFICERS
Michael E. Collins: trust
Leonard Rich: trust
Jack Williamson: trust

APPLICATION INFORMATION
Initial Approach: The foundation reports that only written proposals are considered for religious, charitable, scientific, literary, or educational purposes or for the prevention of cruelty to children or animals. The foundation does not support athletics or athletic competitions.

GRANTS ANALYSIS
Total Grants: $116,150
Number of Grants: 8
Highest Grant: $65,650
Disclosure Period: 1990
Note: Information for 1990 was incomplete.

RECENT GRANTS
80,000 Garden City Community College Endowment Association, Garden City, KS — establishment of a learning center and an endowed scholarship
10,000 Finney County United Way, Garden City, KS
5,000 American Red Cross, Garden City, KS — disaster relief
5,000 Emmaus House, Garden City, KS — aid to needy
5,000 Salvation Army, Garden City, KS — aid to needy
5,000 Salvation Army, Garden City, KS — disaster relief
1,000 Garden City Piano Teachers League, Garden City, KS
1,000 Senior Citizens Christmas Telethon, Dodge City, KS — aid to elderly

Williams Cos. / Williams Cos. Foundation

Sales: $1.82 billion
Employees: 3,800
Headquarters: Tulsa, OK
SIC Major Group: Electric, Gas & Sanitary Services, Nondepository Institutions, and Pipelines Except Natural Gas

CONTACT
Hannah Davis Robson
Managing Director
Williams Cos. Fdn.
PO Box 2400
Tulsa, OK 74102
(918) 588-2106

FINANCIAL SUMMARY
Recent Giving: $3,041,143 (1991); $2,048,945 (1989); $1,762,913 (1988)
Assets: $8,276,553 (1991); $7,497,508 (1990); $8,085,000 (1989)
Fiscal Note: Figures include direct and foundation contributions. 1991 Figure also includes nonmonetary support.
EIN: 23-7413843

CONTRIBUTIONS SUMMARY
Typical Recipients: • *Arts & Humanities:* arts associations, arts centers, arts institutes, dance, history/historic preservation, libraries, museums/galleries, music, opera, performing arts, theater • *Civic & Public Affairs:* business/free enterprise, economic development, environmental affairs, ethnic/minority organizations, housing, international affairs, law & justice, philanthropic organizations, professional & trade associations, public policy, rural affairs, safety, urban & community affairs, women's affairs, zoos/botanical gardens • *Education:* business education, career/vocational education, colleges & universities, community & junior colleges, economic education, education associations, education funds, elementary education, private education (precollege), public education (precollege), science/technology education • *Health:* health funds, health organizations, hospitals, single-disease health associations • *Science:* science exhibits & fairs, scientific organizations • *Social Services:* child welfare, community service organizations, disabled, domestic violence, drugs & alcohol, emergency relief, family planning, family services, homes, recreation & athletics, shelters/homelessness, united funds, youth organizations
Grant Types: capital, employee matching gifts, endowment, and general support
Nonmonetary Support Types: in-kind services, loaned execu-

tives, and workplace solicitation

Note: Above figures include nonmonetary support valued at $61,081 in 1989 and $75,890 in 1988.

Geographic Distribution: exclusively in areas near company headquarters and operating locations

Operating Locations: KS, LA, MO (St. Louis), OK (Tulsa), UT (Salt Lake City), WY

CORP. OFFICERS

Joseph Hill Williams: *B* Tulsa OK 1933 *ED* Yale Univ BA 1956 *CURR EMPL* chmn, ceo, dir: Williams Cos *CORP AFFIL* dir: Am Express Co, BancOklahoma Corp, Northwest Pipeline Corp, Parker Drilling Co, Peabody Holding Co, TX Gulf, Williams Natural Gas Co *NONPR AFFIL* bd govs: Nature Conservancy; dir: Am Petroleum Inst, Indus Tulsa, OK Chamber Commerce, Un Way Tulsa Area; mem: Bus Counc, Bus Roundtable, Conf Bd, Counc Foreign Rels, Natl Petroleum Counc, Young Pres Org; mem, dir: Tulsa Chamber Commerce; trust: Yale Corp

GIVING OFFICERS

Keith E. Bailey: pres, dir *B* Kansas City MO 1942 *ED* MO Sch Mines & Metallurgy BS 1964; Univ MO 1981 *CURR EMPL* pres: Williams Cos *CORP AFFIL* chmn, dir: Williams Pipe Line Co; pres, coo, dir: Williams Natural Gas Co *NONPR AFFIL* mem: Interstate Natural Gas Assn, Am Petroleum Inst, Assn Oil Pipe Lines, Natl Assn Corrosion Engrs, Natl Soc Professional Engrs, Southern Gas Assn

John C. Baumgarner, Jr.: dir *CURR EMPL* sr vp: Williams Cos

David M. Higbee: secy, treas *B* Cedar City UT 1944 *ED* Brigham Young Univ 1968; Univ Chicago 1971 *CURR EMPL* secy: Williams Cos

John Furman Lewis: dir *B* Ft Worth TX 1934 *ED* Rice Univ BA 1956; Univ TX 1962 *CURR EMPL* sr vp, gen coun: Williams Cos *NONPR AFFIL* mem: Am Bar Assn, Arts & Humanities Counc Tulsa, Intl Oil & Gas Ed Ctr Southwestern Legal Fdn, OH Bar Assn, OK Bar Assn, Tulsa County Bar Assn, TX Bar Assn; mem adv bd: Intl Comparative Law Ctr

Southwestern Legal Fdn; mem, gen law comm: Am Petroleum Inst

Hannah Davis Robson: mng dir

Joseph Hill Williams: chmn, dir *CURR EMPL* chmn, ceo, dir: Williams Cos (see above)

APPLICATION INFORMATION

Initial Approach: *Initial Contact:* brief letter and proposal (one copy) *Include Information On:* description of the organization, amount requested, purpose for which funds are sought, recently audited financial statement, and proof of tax-exempt status *When to Submit:* any time (board meets semiannually in June and December)

Restrictions on Giving: Does not support fraternal organizations, goodwill advertising, individuals, political or lobbying groups, or religious organizations for sectarian purposes.

GRANTS ANALYSIS

Total Grants: $1,506,781*
Number of Grants: 281*
Highest Grant: $510,463*
Typical Range: $1,000 to $10,000
Disclosure Period: 1991
Note: Financial information is for the foundation only and does not include direct gifts. The average grant figure excludes a single grant totaling $510,463. Recent grants are derived from a 1991 Form 990.

RECENT GRANTS

510,463	Tulsa Area United Way, Tulsa, OK
70,000	Tulsa Ballet Theatre, Tulsa, OK
51,000	Thomas Gilcrease Museum Association, Tulsa, OK
41,666	Tulsa Zoo Development, Tulsa, OK
33,334	Oklahoma State University Foundation, Stillwater, OK
33,334	University of Oklahoma Foundation, Norman, OK
33,333	Kansas University Endowment Association
30,000	St. John Medical Center Foundation, Tulsa, OK
30,000	Tulsa Performing Arts Center Trust, Tulsa, OK
27,500	YMCA, Tulsa, OK

Williams Family Foundation

CONTACT
Edward L. Zorn
Trustee
Williams Family Fdn.
317 Ensign St.
Ft. Morgan, CO 80701
(303) 867-5621

FINANCIAL SUMMARY
Recent Giving: $266,288 (1991); $207,150 (1990); $237,755 (1989)
Assets: $6,636,191 (1991); $5,826,695 (1990); $5,900,936 (1989)
EIN: 84-6023379

CONTRIBUTIONS SUMMARY
Donor(s): the late A. F. Williams and Mrs. A. F. Williams
Typical Recipients: • *Arts & Humanities:* history/historic preservation, public broadcasting • *Education:* colleges & universities, public education (precollege), student aid • *Health:* hospitals, pediatric health, single-disease health associations • *Social Services:* aged, disabled, united funds
Grant Types: general support, research, and scholarship
Geographic Distribution: focus on CO

GIVING OFFICERS
Catherine M. Woodward: trust
Paul E. Woodward: trust
Edward L. Zorn: trust

APPLICATION INFORMATION
Initial Approach: Send brief letter of inquiry describing program or project. There are no deadlines. Scholarship recipients are nominated by school district.

GRANTS ANALYSIS
Number of Grants: 23
Highest Grant: $88,750
Typical Range: $1,000 to $10,000
Disclosure Period: 1991

RECENT GRANTS

88,750	School District 3, Ft. Morgan, CO — scholarship
64,500	School District 2, Brush, CO — scholarship
22,613	Fort Morgan Hospital, Ft. Morgan, CO
16,500	School District 50, Wiggins, CO — scholarship
5,000	Heritage Foundation, Washington, DC
5,000	National Jewish Center for Immunology and Respiratory Medicine, Denver, CO
5,000	Salk Institute for Biological Studies, San Diego, CA
3,000	School District 20, Weldona, CO — scholarship
2,250	Children's Hospital, Denver, CO
2,000	Webb-Waring Lung Institute, Denver, CO

Williams Family Foundation of Georgia

Former Foundation Name: Marguerite N. and Thomas L. Williams, Jr., Foundation

CONTACT
Williams Family Fdn of Georgia
Old Monticello Rd.
PO Box 378
Thomasville, GA 31799

FINANCIAL SUMMARY
Recent Giving: $406,429 (fiscal 1990); $321,575 (fiscal 1989)
Assets: $5,332,140 (fiscal year ending November 30, 1990); $5,429,511 (fiscal 1989)
Gifts Received: $45,087 (fiscal 1990)
EIN: 58-1414850

CONTRIBUTIONS SUMMARY
Donor(s): Diane W. Parker, Marguerite N. Williams, Thomas L. Williams III, the late Bennie G. Williams

Typical Recipients: • *Arts & Humanities:* community arts, history/historic preservation, public broadcasting • *Civic & Public Affairs:* environmental affairs • *Education:* colleges & universities, private education (precollege), public education (precollege) • *Religion:* churches • *Social Services:* community service organizations, disabled, united funds, youth organizations
Grant Types: general support
Geographic Distribution: focus on GA

GIVING OFFICERS
Joseph E. Beverly: dir
Frederick Eansor Cooper: dir
B Thomasville GA 1942 *ED*
Washington & Lee Univ BA
1964; Univ GA JD 1967 *CURR
EMPL* of coun: Jones Day
Reavis & Pogue *CORP AFFIL*
dir: Flowers Indus; of coun:
Jones Day Reavis & Pogue
Bernard Lanigan, Jr.: treas,
dir
Diane W. Parker: secy, dir
Thomas H. Vann, Jr.: dir
Marguerite N. Williams: pres,
dir
Thomas L. Williams III: dir

GRANTS ANALYSIS
Number of Grants: 30
Highest Grant: $100,000
Typical Range: $500 to $2,500
Disclosure Period: fiscal year
ending November 30, 1990

RECENT GRANTS
100,000 Brookwood
   School, Thomas-
   ville, GA
 60,000 Florida State University Foundation,
   Tallahassee, FL
 50,000 Washington and
   Lee University,
   Lexington, VA
 27,000 Thomasville Cul-
   tural Center, Tho-
   masville, GA
 25,000 Georgia Trust for
   Historic Preserva-
   tion, Atlanta, GA
 25,000 Georgia Trust for
   Historic Preserva-
   tion, Atlanta, GA
 15,000 Thomasville Cul-
   tural Center, Tho-
   masville, GA
 12,512 YMCA, Thomas-
   ville, GA
 12,500 Archbold Founda-
   tion, Thomasville,
   GA
 10,000 Florida State University Foundation,
   Tallahassee, FL

Williams Foundation, Arthur Ashley

CONTACT
Frederick Cole
Chairman
Arthur Ashley Williams Fdn.
PO Box 665
Framingham, MA 01701
(508) 429-1149

FINANCIAL SUMMARY
Recent Giving: $70,170
(1991); $108,313 (1990);
$144,223 (1989)
Assets: $3,166,992 (1991);
$2,930,357 (1990); $3,008,764
(1989)
EIN: 04-6044714

CONTRIBUTIONS SUMMARY
Donor(s): the late Arthur A.
Williams
Typical Recipients: • *Arts &
Humanities:* arts festivals, community arts, history/historic
preservation, literary arts,
music, theater • *Education:* agricultural education, education
funds • *Health:* hospitals, medical research, single-disease
health associations • *Social
Services:* community service organizations, youth organizations
Grant Types: general support
and scholarship

GIVING OFFICERS
Frederick Cole: trust, chmn
Clement T. Lambert: trust,
treas
Elbert G. Tuttle: trust, secy
David S. Williams: trust
Hayden R. Wood: trust

APPLICATION INFORMATION
Initial Approach: Send letter
requesting application form.

OTHER THINGS TO KNOW
Publications: Application
Guidelines

GRANTS ANALYSIS
Number of Grants: 15
Highest Grant: $7,000
Typical Range: $500 to $5,000
Disclosure Period: 1991

RECENT GRANTS
 7,000 Mount Kearsarge
   Indian Museum
 5,000 Colby College, Wa-
   terville, ME

 5,000 David S. Williams
   Quarter Century
   Club
 5,000 Framingham Court
   Mediation, Fram-
   ingham, MA
 5,000 Pair Foods, MA
 3,000 Community Luther
   Church of Enfield,
   MA
 3,000 East Andover Vil-
   lage Preschool and
   Kindergarten, An-
   dover, MA
 3,000 Framingham Court
   Mediation, Fram-
   ingham, MA
 3,000 Southeastern Con-
   necticut AIDS Pro-
   ject, New Haven,
   CT
 3,000 St. James Parish

Williams Foundation, C. K.

CONTACT
Joan R. Rhame
President
C. K. Williams Fdn.
c/o Mellon Bank (East), N.A.
PO Box 7236
Philadelphia, PA 19101-7236
(215) 553-2557

FINANCIAL SUMMARY
Recent Giving: $185,918
(1991); $185,512 (1990);
$200,100 (1989)
Assets: $7,523,221 (1991);
$4,594,379 (1990); $4,185,205
(1989)
EIN: 23-6292772

CONTRIBUTIONS SUMMARY
Typical Recipients: • *Arts &
Humanities:* arts centers, public broadcasting • *Civic & Public Affairs:* housing • *Education:* colleges & universities
• *Health:* hospitals • *Religion:*
churches • *Social Services:*
youth organizations
Grant Types: general support
Geographic Distribution:
focus on PA

GIVING OFFICERS
Joan W. Rhame: pres, secy, dir
Charles K. Williams: dir
Josephine C. Williams: dir

APPLICATION INFORMATION
Initial Approach: Contributes
only to preselected organizations.

GRANTS ANALYSIS
Number of Grants: 13
Highest Grant: $70,000

Typical Range: $1,000 to
$5,000
Disclosure Period: 1991

RECENT GRANTS
 70,000 American School
   of Classical Stud-
   ies, New York, NY
 50,000 WNET Thirteen,
   New York, NY
 25,000 Easton Pennsylva-
   nia Hospital, Eas-
   ton, PA
 10,000 Marquis Society,
   Easton, PA
 10,000 Smith College,
   Northampton, MA
  5,000 Boys and Girls
   Club, Easton, PA
  5,000 Caramoor Arts Center, Katonah, NY
  5,000 Wilmington Gar-
   den Center, Wil-
   mington, DE
  2,000 Meadow Lakes
   Christmas Fund,
   Hightstown, NJ
  1,100 Fargo Methodist
   Church, Fargo, GA

Williams Foundation, Edna Sproull

CONTACT
James Burke
Trustee
Edna Sproull Williams Fdn.
2046 Eventide Rd.
Switzerland, FL 32043
(904) 287-0101

FINANCIAL SUMMARY
Recent Giving: $606,039
(1991); $859,643 (1990);
$687,761 (1989)
Assets: $15,206,535 (1991);
$14,080,282 (1990);
$16,330,131 (1989)
Gifts Received: $100,000
(1990); $700,000 (1989)
Fiscal Note: In 1990, contribu-
tions were received from estate
of Edna Sproull Williams.
EIN: 51-0198606

CONTRIBUTIONS SUMMARY
Donor(s): The foundation was
established by the late Edna
Sproull Williams.
Typical Recipients: • *Education:* colleges & universities,
education funds, private education (precollege) • *Health:*
health funds, single-disease
health associations • *Religion:*
churches, religious organizations • *Social Services:* family
services, united funds, youth organizations

Grant Types: general support
Geographic Distribution: focus on Florida

GIVING OFFICERS
J. W. Burke: trust
William J. Hamrick: trust
Edward McCarthy, Jr.: trust
Charles J. Williams III: trust
Patrick M. Williams: trust *B*
Bonne Terre MO 1939 *ED*
Duke Univ BA; Univ CO PhD
(hon) *NONPR AFFIL* mem:
Academy Motion Picture Arts
& Sciences, Academy Record-
ing Arts & Sciences, Academy
TV Arts & Sciences, Broadcast
Music

APPLICATION INFORMATION
**Initial Approach: Restric-
tions on Giving:** The foundation supports preselected organizations and does not accept
unsolicited requests for funds.
The foundation does not make
grants to individuals.

GRANTS ANALYSIS
Total Grants: $606,039
Number of Grants: 28
Highest Grant: $54,000
Typical Range: $5,000 to
$25,000
Disclosure Period: 1991
Note: Recent grants are derived
from a 1991 grants list.

RECENT GRANTS
54,000 Edward Waters Col-
lege President's
Fund, Jacksonville,
FL
50,000 Alzheimer's Care
and Research Cen-
ter
50,000 Cummer Museum
Foundation, Jack-
sonville, FL
50,000 PACE
50,000 Presbytery of St.
Augustine, St.
Augustine, FL
50,000 YMCA, FL
50,000 Young Life, Jack-
sonville, FL
32,000 Jacksonville Uni-
versity, Jackson-
ville, FL
25,000 Family Health
Services
25,000 United Way

Williams Foundation, Kemper and Leila

CONTACT
Fred M. Smith
Secretary-Treasurer
Kemper and Leila Williams Fdn.
c/o First National Bank of
Commerce
533 Royal St.
New Orleans, LA 70130
(504) 523-4162

FINANCIAL SUMMARY
Recent Giving: $78,604 (fiscal
1991); $75,359 (fiscal 1990)
Assets: $70,560,751 (fiscal
year ending March 31, 1991);
$67,042,259 (fiscal 1990)
Gifts Received: $133,372 (fis-
cal 1991)
Fiscal Note: In 1991, contributions were received from the
Horace W. Goldsmith Foundation ($25,000), Jane Sargent
($5,200), School of Design
($5,100), Edmund E. Richard-
son ($38,577), Jeff Feibleman
($5,000), and John B. Sewell
and Granville H. Sewell
($7,650).
EIN: 23-7336090

CONTRIBUTIONS SUMMARY
Donor(s): the late L. Kemper
Williams, the late Leila M. Wi-
liiams
Typical Recipients: • *Civic &
Public Affairs:* law & justice,
municipalities
Grant Types: project and
scholarship
Geographic Distribution:
focus on New Orleans, LA

GIVING OFFICERS
Mary Lou M. Christovich:
vp, dir
Francis C. Doyle: off
G. Henry Pierson, Jr.: dir
Joanne P. Platou: museum dir
Fred M. Smith: secy, treas, dir
John E. Walker: dir
Benjamin W. Yancey: pres, dir

APPLICATION INFORMATION
Initial Approach: Contributes
only to preselected organizations.

GRANTS ANALYSIS
Number of Grants: 7
Highest Grant: $76,921
Typical Range: $5,000 to
$10,000
Disclosure Period: fiscal year
ending March 31, 1991

Note: Information for fiscal
1991 was incomplete.

RECENT GRANTS
76,921 St. Mary Parish Police Jury, Franklin,
LA

Williams, Jr. Family Foundation, A. L.

CONTACT
D. Jack Sawyer, Jr.
Secretary and Treasurer
A. L. Williams, Jr. Family
Foundation
c/o Arden Group
11 Piedmont Center, Suite 405L
3495 Piedmont Road, NE
Atlanta, GA 30305
(404) 231-2340

FINANCIAL SUMMARY
Recent Giving: $124,000 (fis-
cal 1991); $60,798 (fiscal 1990)
Assets: $2,663,576 (fiscal year
ending June 30, 1990)
Gifts Received: $2,629,642
(fiscal 1990)
Fiscal Note: In fiscal 1990, the
foundation received $2,629,642
in stocks from Dorothy B.
Bancker.
EIN: 58-1868577

CONTRIBUTIONS SUMMARY
Donor(s): the donor is Dorothy
B. Bancker, a trustee for the
foundation
Typical Recipients: • *Educa-
tion:* colleges & universities
• *Health:* nursing services • *In-
ternational:* international
health care
Grant Types: project
Geographic Distribution:
Washington, DC

GIVING OFFICERS
Walter Akerman, Jr.: chmn,
trust
Dorothy B. Bancker: trust, don
D. Jack Sawyer, Jr.: secy,
treas, trust

GRANTS ANALYSIS
Total Grants: $60,798
Number of Grants: 1
Highest Grant: $60,798
Disclosure Period: fiscal year
ending June 30, 1990

RECENT GRANTS
60,798 American College
of Nurse-Mid-
wives, Washington,
DC — to assist
midwives in train-
ing for medical as-
sistance in Ghana

Williamson Co. / Williamson Co. Foundation
Sales: $50.0 million
Employees: 575
Headquarters: Cincinnati, OH
SIC Major Group: Fabricated
Metal Products, Industrial
Machinery & Equipment, and
Transportation Equipment

CONTACT
W.D. Wilder
Trustee
Williamson Co. Foundation
3500 Madison Rd.
Cincinnati, OH 45209-1185

FINANCIAL SUMMARY
Fiscal Note: Annual Giving
Range: $50,000 to $75,000
EIN: 31-6031985

CONTRIBUTIONS SUMMARY
Typical Recipients: • *Arts &
Humanities:* theater • *Educa-
tion:* colleges & universities
• *Social Services:* united funds
Geographic Distribution:
focus on Cincinnati, OH
Operating Locations: OH
(Cincinnati)

CORP. OFFICERS
John D. Carroll: *CURR EMPL*
pres, ceo: Williamson Co

APPLICATION INFORMATION
Initial Approach: Contributes
to preselected organizations;
applications not accepted.

GRANTS ANALYSIS
Typical Range: $100 to $1,000

Willits Foundation

CONTACT
Emily O. Lawrence
Secretary-Treasurer
Willits Fdn.
730 Central Ave.
Murray Hill, NJ 07974
(201) 277-8259

FINANCIAL SUMMARY
Recent Giving: $278,207
(1991); $322,590 (1989);
$278,665 (1987)
Assets: $7,616,169 (1991);
$6,135,462 (1989); $4,179,851
(1987)
Gifts Received: $147,534
(1991)
EIN: 22-6063106

CONTRIBUTIONS SUMMARY

Donor(s): members of the Willits family

Typical Recipients: • *Education:* colleges & universities, medical education, religious education • *Health:* health organizations, hospitals • *Religion:* churches • *Social Services:* child welfare, community service organizations, united funds, youth organizations

Grant Types: general support and scholarship

Geographic Distribution: focus on NJ

GIVING OFFICERS

Barbara W. Evans: vp
John H. Evans: trust
Rev. William H. Felmeth: trust
Emily D. Lawrence: secy, treas
Harris L. Willits: pres
Itto A. Willits: trust
John F. Willits: trust

APPLICATION INFORMATION

Initial Approach: Send cover letter and full proposal.
Restrictions on Giving: Does not support individuals.

GRANTS ANALYSIS

Number of Grants: 116
Highest Grant: $15,000
Typical Range: $1,000 to $5,000
Disclosure Period: 1991
Note: 11/30

RECENT GRANTS

15,000 Cape Cod Hospital, Hyannis, MA
15,000 Morristown Memorial Hospital, Morristown, NJ
15,000 Overlook Hospital, Summit, NJ
15,000 Wayside House, Delray Beach, FL
12,000 Presbyterian Church, Basking Ridge, NJ
10,000 Matheny School and Hospital, Peapack, NJ
10,000 Mrs. Wilson's, Morristown, NJ
6,000 Presbyterian Church, Basking Ridge, NJ
5,000 St. Bernards School, Bernardsville, NJ
5,000 University of Medicine and Dentistry of New Jersey, Newark, NJ

Willmott Foundation, Fred & Floy

CONTACT

Fred & Floy Willmott Fdn.
c/o Marine Midland Bank
PO Box 4203
Buffalo, NY 14240
(212) 841-5472

FINANCIAL SUMMARY

Recent Giving: $337,864 (1991); $264,390 (1990); $272,550 (1989)
Assets: $5,187,060 (1991); $4,598,254 (1990); $4,837,285 (1989)
EIN: 22-2587484

CONTRIBUTIONS SUMMARY

Typical Recipients: • *Education:* colleges & universities, public education (precollege) • *Religion:* churches • *Social Services:* aged, disabled, shelters/homelessness, youth organizations
Geographic Distribution: focus on NY

GIVING OFFICERS

Marine Midland Bank, N.A.: trust

APPLICATION INFORMATION

Initial Approach: Contributes only to preselected organizations.
Restrictions on Giving: Does not support individuals.

GRANTS ANALYSIS

Number of Grants: 48
Highest Grant: $16,025
Typical Range: $2,000 to $5,000
Disclosure Period: 1991

RECENT GRANTS

16,025 Grace United Methodist Church, Greenport, NY
10,000 Monroe County Council on Aging
10,000 Roberts Wesleyan College, Rochester, NY
10,000 University of Rochester, Rochester, NY
9,700 Habitat for Humanity
7,000 Rochester City School District, Rochester, NY
5,000 Independent Living for Seniors

5,000 Junior Achievement, Rochester, NY
5,000 National Braille Association
5,000 Statewide Youth Advocacy

Willmott Foundation, Peter S.

CONTACT

J. Noble
Secretary
Peter S. Willmott Foundation
919 North Michigan, Ste. 1220
Chicago, IL 60611
(312) 337-5591

FINANCIAL SUMMARY

Recent Giving: $498,000 (fiscal 1991); $256,750 (fiscal 1990); $0 (fiscal 1989)
Assets: $1,552,082 (fiscal year ending May 31, 1991); $1,922,401 (fiscal 1990); $2,057,813 (fiscal 1989)
Gifts Received: $7,850 (fiscal 1990); $2,057,813 (fiscal 1989)
Fiscal Note: Fiscal 1990 contribution received from Peter S. Willmott.
EIN: 36-3651342

CONTRIBUTIONS SUMMARY

Donor(s): the donor is Peter S. Willmott, the foundation's president and treasurer
Typical Recipients: • *Arts & Humanities:* music • *Civic & Public Affairs:* economic development • *Education:* colleges & universities, education associations, private education (precollege) • *Social Services:* youth organizations
Grant Types: general support

GIVING OFFICERS

Glen E. Hess: vp
Joan L. Noble: secy
Peter S. Willmott: pres, treas, don

GRANTS ANALYSIS

Number of Grants: 3
Highest Grant: $53,000
Typical Range: $20,000 to $53,000
Disclosure Period: fiscal year ending May 31, 1991

RECENT GRANTS

130,000 Williams College, Williamstown, MA
50,000 St. Mary's Episcopal School, Memphis, TN

30,000 Associated Colleges of Illinois, Chicago, IL
25,000 Memphis University School, Memphis, TN
10,000 Knox College, Galesburg, IL
5,000 North Adams Community Development Corp., North Adams, MA
2,750 Chicago Symphony Orchestra Society, Chicago, IL
1,000 Boys Club of Memphis, Memphis, TN
1,000 Henry Meers Fund for Television Excellence, Chicago, IL
1,000 University of Mississippi, University, MS

Wills Foundation

CONTACT

Alice Evans Pratt
President
Wills Fdn.
3436 Overbrook
Houston, TX 77027
(713) 965-9043

FINANCIAL SUMMARY

Recent Giving: $227,794 (fiscal 1991); $212,804 (fiscal 1990); $115,000 (fiscal 1989)
Assets: $5,160,735 (fiscal year ending July 31, 1991); $4,816,225 (fiscal 1990); $4,538,094 (fiscal 1989)
Gifts Received: $232,859 (fiscal 1991); $80,521 (fiscal 1990); $443,662 (fiscal 1989)
EIN: 74-6078200

CONTRIBUTIONS SUMMARY

Donor(s): Fletcher S. Pratt, Mrs. Fletcher S. Pratt, and others
Typical Recipients: • *Health:* medical research, single-disease health associations
Grant Types: endowment and research

GIVING OFFICERS

Charles Dillingham: chmn
Charlotte B. Ferguson: trust
Michael J. Murray, M.D.: trust
Alice Evans Pratt: pres, treas
Peter E. Pratt: vp, secy
St. Clare Pratt Seifert: trust

APPLICATION INFORMATION

Initial Approach: Send cover letter and proposal. There are no deadlines.

OTHER THINGS TO KNOW

Provides grants to individuals for research on hereditary diseases, particularly Huntington's Chorea.

GRANTS ANALYSIS

Highest Grant: $47,000
Disclosure Period: fiscal year ending July 31, 1991

RECENT GRANTS

47,000 University of California Regents, San Francisco, CA
30,804 University of California Regents, San Francisco, CA
30,000 University of California Regents, San Francisco, CA
30,000 University of California Regents, San Francisco, CA
25,000 Albert Einstein College of Medicine, New York, NY
25,000 University of California Regents, San Francisco, CA
25,000 University of California Regents, San Francisco, CA

Wilmington Trust Co. / Wilmington Trust Co. Foundation

Assets: $4.06 billion
Employees: 1,984
Headquarters: Wilmington, DE
SIC Major Group: Depository Institutions

CONTACT

Beryl A. Barmore
Trustee
Wilmington Trust Co.
Wilmington Trust Center,
 Rodney Sq. North
Wilmington, DE 19890
(302) 651-1462

FINANCIAL SUMMARY

Recent Giving: $213,780 (1991); $327,500 (1990); $481,987 (1989)
Assets: $635 (1991); $2,496 (1990); $20,601 (1989)
Gifts Received: $211,739 (1991); $308,287 (1990); $469,937 (1989)

Fiscal Note: In 1991, contributions were received from Wilmington Trust Co.
EIN: 51-6021540

CONTRIBUTIONS SUMMARY

Typical Recipients: • *Arts & Humanities:* community arts, libraries, museums/galleries, music, opera, performing arts, public broadcasting, theater • *Civic & Public Affairs:* environmental affairs, ethnic/minority organizations, zoos/botanical gardens • *Education:* colleges & universities • *Social Services:* community centers, community service organizations, united funds, youth organizations
Grant Types: general support
Geographic Distribution: focus on DE
Operating Locations: DE (Wilmington)

CORP. OFFICERS

Ted T. Cecala, Jr.: *CURR EMPL* cfo: Wilmington Trust Co
Bernard J. Taylor II: *ED* Univ PA 1949 *CURR EMPL* chmn, ceo, dir: Wilmington Trust Co *CORP AFFIL* chmn, ceo, dir: Wilmington Trust Co

GIVING OFFICERS

Beryl Barmore: trust
Bernard J. Taylor II: trust *CURR EMPL* chmn, ceo, dir: Wilmington Trust Co (see above)

APPLICATION INFORMATION

Initial Approach: Send brief letter describing program. There are no deadlines.

GRANTS ANALYSIS

Number of Grants: 60
Highest Grant: $17,000
Typical Range: $1,000 to $8,000
Disclosure Period: 1991

RECENT GRANTS

17,000 Winterthur Museum and Gardens, Winterthur, DE
13,500 Delaware Symphony Association, Wilmington, DE
10,500 University of Delaware, Newark, DE
10,000 Delaware State College, Dover, DE
9,000 Goldey-Beacon College, Wilmington, DE

8,500 Delaware Theatre Company, Wilmington, DE
8,500 Milford Public Library Building Fund, Milford, DE
8,500 Museum Trustee Association 1991 Fall Conference, DE
8,500 Newark Day Nursery, Newark, DE
8,000 Wesley College, Wilmington, DE

Wilsey Bennet Co. / Wilsey Foundation

Revenue: $26.0 million
Employees: 600
Headquarters: San Francisco, CA
SIC Major Group: Business Services

CONTACT

Wilsey Foundation
PO Box 3532
San Francisco, CA 94119
(415) 391-4150

FINANCIAL SUMMARY

Recent Giving: $117,200 (fiscal 1992); $104,800 (fiscal 1990); $77,700 (fiscal 1989)
Assets: $1,509,492 (fiscal year ending March 31, 1992); $1,224,349 (fiscal 1990); $966,788 (fiscal 1989)
Gifts Received: $45,000 (fiscal 1992); $145,000 (fiscal 1990); $200,000 (fiscal 1989)
Fiscal Note: In fiscal 1992, contributions were received from H & W Foods ($40,000) and Alfred Wilsey, Sr. ($5,000).
EIN: 94-6098720

CONTRIBUTIONS SUMMARY

Typical Recipients: • *Civic & Public Affairs:* municipalities, philanthropic organizations • *Education:* colleges & universities, private education (precollege), religious education • *Religion:* churches, religious organizations • *Social Services:* community service organizations, food/clothing distribution, religious welfare
Grant Types: general support
Geographic Distribution: focus on CA
Operating Locations: CA (San Francisco)

CORP. OFFICERS

Michael W. Wilsey: *CURR EMPL* chmn, pres, dir: Wilsey Bennet Co

GIVING OFFICERS

Jerome P. Solari: treas
A.S. Wilsey: pres
Alfred S. Wilsey, Jr.: secy
Diane B. Wilsey: vp
Michael W. Wilsey: vp *CURR EMPL* chmn, pres, dir: Wilsey Bennet Co (see above)

APPLICATION INFORMATION

Initial Approach: Send brief letter describing program. There are no deadlines.

GRANTS ANALYSIS

Number of Grants: 79
Highest Grant: $7,500
Typical Range: $1,000 to $5,000
Disclosure Period: fiscal year ending March 31, 1992

RECENT GRANTS

7,500 Immaculate Conception Academy, San Francisco, CA
6,000 University of Notre Dame, Notre Dame, IN
5,000 Central City Hospitality House, San Francisco, CA
5,000 Delancey Street Foundation, San Francisco, CA
5,000 Justin-Siena High School, Napa, CA
5,000 Pacific Vision Foundation, San Francisco, CA
5,000 St. John's Educational Threshhold's Center, San Francisco, CA
5,000 University California San Francisco Foundation, San Francisco, CA
3,000 Episcopal Community Services of San Francisco, San Francisco, CA
3,000 Our Lady of Mercy Church, Daly City, CA

Wilson Foundation, Elaine P. and Richard U.

CONTACT
Elaine P. and Richard U. Wilson Fdn.
c/o Chase Lincoln First Bank, N.A.
PO Box 1412
Rochester, NY 14603

FINANCIAL SUMMARY
Recent Giving: $404,000 (1990); $189,400 (1989); $375,941 (1988)
Assets: $5,445,005 (1990); $5,874,458 (1989); $5,305,459 (1988)
EIN: 16-6042023

CONTRIBUTIONS SUMMARY
Donor(s): the late Katherine M. Wilson
Typical Recipients: • *Arts & Humanities:* museums/galleries, music, visual arts • *Civic & Public Affairs:* zoos/botanical gardens • *Education:* colleges & universities • *Religion:* churches • *Social Services:* child welfare, united funds, youth organizations
Grant Types: general support
Geographic Distribution: focus on NY

APPLICATION INFORMATION
Initial Approach: Contributes only to preselected organizations.

GRANTS ANALYSIS
Number of Grants: 21
Highest Grant: $80,000
Typical Range: $2,500 to $9,500
Disclosure Period: 1990

RECENT GRANTS
```
80,000  Rochester Philhar-
        monic Orchestra,
        Rochester, NY —
        music festival
78,554  University of Roch-
        ester, Rochester,
        NY
40,000  Al Sigl Center for
        Rehabilitation
        Agencies, Roches-
        ter, NY
40,000  St. John Fisher Col-
        lege, NY — build-
        ing fund
30,000  Seneca Zoological
        Society, Seneca,
        NY — staff posi-
        tion
25,000  Memorial Art Gal-
        lery, New York, NY
21,446  University of Roch-
        ester, Rochester,
        NY
15,000  Harley School, NY
13,000  United Way, Roch-
        ester, NY
10,000  Rochester Museum
        and Science Cen-
        ter, Rochester, NY
```

Wilson Foundation, Frances Wood

CONTACT
W. T. Wingfield
President
Frances Wood Wilson Foundation
PO Box 33188
Decatur, GA 30033
(404) 634-3363
Note: The foundation can be contacted directly at 1501 Clairmont Road, Suite 222, Decatur, GA, 30033.

FINANCIAL SUMMARY
Recent Giving: $1,614,089 (fiscal 1993 est.); $1,604,410 (fiscal 1992); $1,630,104 (fiscal 1991)
Assets: $34,000,000 (fiscal 1993 est.); $33,857,278 (fiscal year ending May 31, 1992); $32,515,549 (fiscal 1991); $31,144,152 (fiscal 1990)
EIN: 58-6035441

CONTRIBUTIONS SUMMARY
Donor(s): The foundation was established in 1954 by the late Fred B. Wilson and Mrs. Frances W. Wilson.
Typical Recipients: • *Arts & Humanities:* museums/galleries • *Civic & Public Affairs:* housing, zoos/botanical gardens • *Education:* colleges & universities • *Health:* hospitals, single-disease health associations • *Religion:* churches • *Social Services:* child welfare, food/clothing distribution, shelters/homelessness
Grant Types: general support and scholarship
Geographic Distribution: Georgia

GIVING OFFICERS
T. Cecil Myers: vp, trust
J. M. Pate: vp, trust
W. T. Wingfield: pres, trust

APPLICATION INFORMATION
Initial Approach: Applicants should submit a written proposal to the foundation.
Proposals should include the following: a brief history of the organization; relevant experience of the applicant's administrators; the purpose and amount of the grant; current financial statements; and a copy of the applicant's IRS tax-exempt determination letter. There are no deadlines for submitting grant applications.

OTHER THINGS TO KNOW
Publications: application guidelines

GRANTS ANALYSIS
Total Grants: $1,604,410
Number of Grants: 53
Highest Grant: $650,000
Typical Range: $1,000 to $20,000
Disclosure Period: fiscal year ending May 31, 1992
Note: Average grant figure excludes two grants totaling $850,000. Recent grants are derived from a fiscal 1992 grants list.

RECENT GRANTS
```
650,000  Young Harris Col-
         lege, Young Harris,
         GA
200,000  Wesley Homes, At-
         lanta, GA
180,000  Henrietta Egleston
         Hospital, Atlanta,
         GA
 75,000  Roosevelt Warm
         Springs, Warm
         Springs, GA
 32,500  Scottish Rite Medi-
         cal Center, Atlanta,
         GA
 25,345  Shepherd Spinal
         Center, Atlanta, GA
 25,000  Chestnut Hill Be-
         nevolent Associa-
         tion, Boston, MA
 23,180  American Cancer
         Society, Atlanta,
         GA
 22,510  Elks-Ardmore Chil-
         drens Home, Cony-
         ers, GA
 20,000  Georgia North Civi-
         tan Foundation, At-
         lanta, GA
```

Wilson Foundation, H. W.

CONTACT
Leo M. Weins
President
H. W. Wilson Fdn.
950 University Ave.
Bronx, NY 10452
(212) 588-8400

FINANCIAL SUMMARY
Recent Giving: $487,091 (fiscal 1991); $421,000 (fiscal 1990); $369,750 (fiscal 1989)
Assets: $8,512,273 (fiscal year ending November 30, 1991); $6,454,534 (fiscal 1990); $6,339,240 (fiscal 1989)
EIN: 23-7418062

CONTRIBUTIONS SUMMARY
Donor(s): the late H. W. Wilson, the late Mrs. H. W. Wilson, the H. W. Wilson Co.
Typical Recipients: • *Arts & Humanities:* history/historic preservation, libraries, museums/galleries • *Civic & Public Affairs:* environmental affairs, public policy, zoos/botanical gardens • *Education:* colleges & universities, literacy • *Health:* hospitals • *Social Services:* disabled
Grant Types: research and scholarship

GIVING OFFICERS
Florence A. Arnold: dir
Howard Haycraft: chmn, dir
James Humphrey III: vp, dir *CORP AFFIL* dir: Wilson (HW) Co
Rutherford David Rogers: dir *B* Jesup IA 1915 *ED* Univ Northern IA BA 1936; Univ Northern IA LittD 1977; Columbia Univ MA 1937; Columbia Univ BS 1938 *CORP AFFIL* dir: Wilson (HW) Co *NONPR AFFIL* fdr, chmn: Res Libraries Group; fellow: Am Academy Arts Sciences; mem: Am Assn Univ Profs, Am Librarians Assn, Assn Res Libraries, Bibliographical Soc Am; univ librarian emeritus: Stanford Univ
Leo M. Weins: pres, treas, dir *ED* Loyola Univ 1936; Northwestern Univ 1947; Univ Chicago 1938 *CURR EMPL* pres, treas, dir: Wilson (HW) Co *CORP AFFIL* pres, treas, dir: Wilson (HW) Co *NONPR AFFIL* mem: Am Antiquarian Soc, Am Librarians Assn, Foreign Policy Assn

William Alexander Ziegler:
secy, dir *B* New York NY 1924
ED Harvard Univ AB 1944;
Harvard Univ JD 1949 *CORP
AFFIL* dir: Wilson (HW) Co
NONPR AFFIL mem: Am Bar
Assn, NY Bar Assn, NY City
Bar Assn; secy, dir: Foreign
Policy Assn

APPLICATION INFORMATION

Initial Approach: Send brief
letter of inquiry describing program or project. There are no
deadlines. Foundation primarily supports libraries and a
scholarship program.

GRANTS ANALYSIS

Number of Grants: 44
Highest Grant: $35,000
Typical Range: $1,000 to
$10,000
Disclosure Period: fiscal year
ending November 30, 1991

RECENT GRANTS

35,000 Columbia Univer-
sity, New York, NY
30,000 Association of Re-
search Libraries
22,000 American Antiquar-
ian Society,
Worcester, MA
20,000 Clarion University
of Pennsylvania,
Clarion, PA
16,666 University of California, Berkeley,
CA
15,000 Northeast Docu-
ment Conservation
Center
12,500 Wave Hill
10,000 Atlanta University,
Atlanta, GA
10,000 Brigham Young
University, Provo,
UT
10,000 University of Maryland, College Park,
MD

Wilson Foundation, Hugh and Mary

CONTACT
John R. Wood
President
Hugh and Mary Wilson Fdn.
c/o Wood and Seitl
240 North Washington Blvd.,
Ste. 460
Sarasota, FL 34236-5929
(813) 954-2155

FINANCIAL SUMMARY
Recent Giving: $231,918
(1990); $238,291 (1989)
Assets: $4,869,308 (1990);
$4,955,997 (1989)
EIN: 59-2243926

CONTRIBUTIONS SUMMARY
Donor(s): the late Hugh H. Wilson and Mary P. Wilson
Typical Recipients: • *Arts &
Humanities:* community arts
• *Civic & Public Affairs:* environmental affairs • *Education:*
colleges & universities
• *Health:* single-disease health
associations • *Religion:*
churches, religious organizations • *Social Services:* aged,
child welfare, united funds,
youth organizations
Grant Types: capital, confer-
ence/seminar, general support,
and scholarship
Geographic Distribution:
focus on the Sarasota, FL, area
and the Lewisburg-Danville,
PA, area

GIVING OFFICERS
George Fraley: treas, dir
Harry Klinger: vp, dir
John R. Wood: pres, dir
Sadie L. Wood: secy, dir
Susan Wood: dir

APPLICATION INFORMATION
Initial Approach: Send brief
letter of inquiry or full proposal (two copies). There are
no deadlines. Board meets in
March, June, and September.
Decisions are made in October.

OTHER THINGS TO KNOW
Publications: Informational
Brochure (including applica-
tion guidelines)

GRANTS ANALYSIS
Number of Grants: 18
Highest Grant: $50,000
Typical Range: $1,000 to
$5,000

Disclosure Period: 1990

RECENT GRANTS

50,000 Payne Chapel, Sarasota, FL — provide
and expand serv-
ices in Newtown
and liquidate mort-
gage at Barnett
Bank
45,000 Diocese of Venice
in Florida, Venice,
FL — assist in of-
fice expenses and
program develop-
ment
21,300 John and Mable
Ringling Museum
of Art foundation,
Sarasota, FL — art
program for senior
citizens
20,000 Manatee River
Youth Ranch,
Bradenton, FL —
construction of resi-
dent facility
20,000 Pines of Sarasota,
Sarasota, FL — as-
sist in remodeling
service center
18,000 Sarasota AIDS Sup-
port, Sarasota, FL
— assist in resi-
dent facility ex-
penses
11,245 Sarasota County
Twelfth Judicial
Circuit, Sarasota,
FL
10,000 Life Is For Every-
one, Osprey, FL —
scholarship assis-
tance for drug pro-
gram
10,000 Southeastern Guide
Dogs, Palmetto, FL
— help construct
80 dog kennel
5,000 Southern Scholar-
ship Foundation,
Tallahassee, FL —
assist in scholar-
ship house expenses

Wilson Foundation, John and Nevils

CONTACT
Joseph N. Sherrill, Jr.
Vice President
John and Nevils Wilson Fdn.
1100 Hamilton Bldg
Wichita Falls, TX 76301
(817) 322-3145

FINANCIAL SUMMARY
Recent Giving: $135,050 (fis-
cal 1991); $123,250 (fiscal
1990); $40,000 (fiscal 1989)
Assets: $2,961,724 (fiscal year
ending November 30, 1991);
$2,856,760 (fiscal 1990);
$2,747,125 (fiscal 1989)
Gifts Received: $50 (fiscal
1991)
EIN: 75-6080151

CONTRIBUTIONS SUMMARY
Donor(s): the late J. H. Wilson
Typical Recipients: • *Educa-
tion:* colleges & universities
• *Health:* health funds • *Relig-
ion:* churches
Grant Types: capital and gen-
eral support
Geographic Distribution:
focus on Wichita County, TX

GIVING OFFICERS
Earle W. Crawford: trust
Evelyn Wilson Egan: trust,
pres
Virginia Wilson Ewing: vp,
trust
David A. Kimbell: trust
Joseph N. Sherrill, Jr.: trust,
vp

APPLICATION INFORMATION
Initial Approach: Send brief
letter describing program.
Deadline is November 30.
Restrictions on Giving: Does
not support individuals.

GRANTS ANALYSIS
Number of Grants: 13
Highest Grant: $70,000
Typical Range: $1,000 to
$5,000
Disclosure Period: fiscal year
ending November 30, 1991

RECENT GRANTS
70,000 First Presbyterian
Church, Wichita
Falls, TX
11,800 Presbyterian
Manor, Wichita
Falls, TX
10,000 Episcopal Church
of the Holy Trinity,
Midland, TX

6,800 Interfaith Ministries, Wichita Falls, TX
6,800 North Central Texas Medical Foundation, Wichita Falls, TX
6,800 Pastoral Counseling Center, Wichita Falls, TX
-5,000 Maryville College, Maryville, TN
4,000 Wellesley College, Wellesley, MA
1,000 Trinity University, San Antonio, TX
750 Ingram Fire Department, Ingram, TX

Wilson Foundation, Marie C. and Joseph C.

CONTACT
Ruth H. Fleischmann
Executive Director
Marie C. and Joseph C. Wilson Fdn.
160 Allens Creek Rd.
Rochester, NY 14618
(716) 461-4699

FINANCIAL SUMMARY
Recent Giving: $1,240,959 (1991); $515,609 (1990); $565,793 (1989)
Assets: $11,097,986 (1991); $10,113,851 (1990); $11,160,077 (1989)
EIN: 16-6042022

CONTRIBUTIONS SUMMARY
Donor(s): the late Katherine M. Wilson, the late Joseph C. Wilson
Typical Recipients: • *Arts & Humanities:* museums/galleries, performing arts • *Civic & Public Affairs:* urban & community affairs • *Education:* colleges & universities, literacy, private education (precollege), science/technology education • *Health:* health organizations, hospitals, medical research, single-disease health associations • *Social Services:* aged, child welfare, disabled, domestic violence, food/clothing distribution, united funds, youth organizations
Grant Types: capital, conference/seminar, emergency, endowment, fellowship, general support, multiyear/continuing support, operating expenses, project, research, scholarship, and seed money

Geographic Distribution: focus on Rochester, NY

GIVING OFFICERS
Joan W. Dalbey: mem bd mgrs
R. Thomas Dalbey, Jr.: mem bd mgrs
Katherine Dalbey Ensign: off
Ruth H. Fleischmann: exec dir
Deirdre Wilson Garton: mem bd mgrs
Breckenridge Kling: mem bd mgrs
Judith W. Martin: mem bd mgrs
Katherine W. Roby: chmn bd mgrs
Katherine W. Roby: chmn
Janet C. Wilson: pres bd mgrs
Joseph R. Wilson: mem bd mgrs

APPLICATION INFORMATION
Initial Approach: Send brief letter of inquiry describing program.
Restrictions on Giving: Does not support individuals.

OTHER THINGS TO KNOW
Publications: Annual Report (includes application guidelines)

GRANTS ANALYSIS
Number of Grants: 47
Highest Grant: $896,707
Typical Range: $500 to $10,000
Disclosure Period: 1991

RECENT GRANTS
896,707 Wilson Commencement Park, Rochester, NY
82,500 Wilson Commencement Park, Rochester, NY
25,000 Anthony L. Jordan Health Center, Rochester, NY
20,000 International Museum of Photography, Rochester, NY
15,000 Notre Dame High School, Elmira, NY
14,450 Neighborhood HOPE, Rochester, NY
12,000 Rochester Institute of Technology, Rochester, NY
10,000 Action for a Better Community, Rochester, NY
10,000 Council on Economic Priorities, New York, NY
10,000 Rochester Association of Performing Arts, Rochester, NY

Wilson Fund, Matilda R.

CONTACT
Frederick C. Nash
President
Matilda R. Wilson Foundation
100 Renaissance Center Ste. 3377
Detroit, MI 48243
(313) 259-7777

FINANCIAL SUMMARY
Recent Giving: $1,345,622 (1990); $1,393,841 (1989); $1,241,557 (1988)
Assets: $32,598,493 (1990); $33,001,707 (1989); $28,372,728 (1988)
Gifts Received: $204,127 (1985)
EIN: 38-6087665

CONTRIBUTIONS SUMMARY
Donor(s): The foundation was incorporated in 1944 in Michigan. The donors were the late Matilda R. Wilson and Alfred G. Wilson.
Typical Recipients: • *Arts & Humanities:* arts centers, history/historic preservation, museums/galleries, public broadcasting, theater • *Civic & Public Affairs:* business/free enterprise, economic development, philanthropic organizations • *Education:* arts education, career/vocational education, colleges & universities, engineering education, science/technology education, special education • *Social Services:* community service organizations, homes, youth organizations
Grant Types: capital and operating expenses
Geographic Distribution: national, with emphasis on Michigan

GIVING OFFICERS
Pierre V. Heftler: vp, trust *B* Paris France 1910 *ED* Dartmouth Coll AB 1930; Univ MI BS Engring 1931; Univ MI JD 1934 *CURR EMPL* atty, mem: Bodman & Longley *NONPR AFFIL* mem: Am Bar Assn, Detroit Bar Assn, MI Bar Assn
Frederick C. Nash: pres, trust
Robert M. Surdam: treas, trust *B* Albany NY 1917 *ED* Williams Coll BA 1939 *CORP AFFIL* dir: NBD Bancorp

APPLICATION INFORMATION
Initial Approach: Prospective applicants should submit a letter explaining the need and use of requested funds.
The foundation reports no application deadlines.
The board meets quarterly to consider proposals, usually in January, April, July, and October.
Restrictions on Giving: The foundation does not make loans or grants to individuals.

GRANTS ANALYSIS
Total Grants: $1,345,662
Number of Grants: 32
Highest Grant: $415,291
Typical Range: $4,000 to $50,000
Disclosure Period: 1990
Note: Average grant figure excludes the high grant of $415,291. Recent grants are derived from a 1990 grants list.

RECENT GRANTS
415,291 Oakland University, Rochester, MI — capital
250,000 Beloit College, Beloit, WI — capital
100,000 Salvation Army, Southfield, MI — capital
62,500 Interlochen Center for the Arts, Interlochen, MI — capital
60,000 Hillsdale College, Hillsdale, MI — operating expenses
56,371 Detroit Public Library, Detroit, MI — capital
40,000 Boys and Girls Club of Southeastern Michigan, Detroit, MI — capital
40,000 High Scope Educational Research Foundation, Ypsilanti, MI — operating expenses
31,000 Center for Creative Studies, Detroit, MI — operating expenses
25,500 Detroit Association of Phi Beta Kappa, Detroit, MI — operating expenses

Wilson Public Trust, Ralph

CONTACT
Ralph Wilson Public Trust
5006 Sunflower Ln.
Temple, TX 76502

FINANCIAL SUMMARY
Recent Giving: $217,000 (1991); $212,500 (1990); $202,500 (1989)
Assets: $2,867,130 (1991); $2,594,326 (1990); $2,579,978 (1989)
EIN: 23-7351606

CONTRIBUTIONS SUMMARY
Donor(s): the late Ralph Wilson
Typical Recipients: • *Arts & Humanities:* arts institutes, community arts, theater • *Civic & Public Affairs:* public policy • *Religion:* religious organizations • *Social Services:* child welfare, community service organizations, counseling, homes, religious welfare, youth organizations
Grant Types: general support
Geographic Distribution: focus on TX

GIVING OFFICERS
Jamie Clements: trust
Ross Fairweather: trust
George Hester: trust
Bonnie McIninch: trust
Kaye Miron: trust
Johnny Payne: trust
Betty Prescott: trust, secy
William Reeder: trust
Phillip Snyder: vp
James Wilson: trust
Jim Wilson: pres
Sunny Wilson: hon chmn

APPLICATION INFORMATION
Initial Approach: Send brief letter describing program. There are no deadlines.

GRANTS ANALYSIS
Number of Grants: 7
Highest Grant: $150,000
Typical Range: $8,000 to $15,000
Disclosure Period: 1991

RECENT GRANTS
150,000 Ralph Wilson Youth Club, Dallas, TX
15,000 Bell Company Society Fund for Crippled Children, Dallas, TX
15,000 Christian Farms, Dallas, TX
15,000 Cultural Activities Center, Dallas, TX
10,000 Temple Civic Theatre, Temple, TX
8,000 Teens Off the Street, Dallas, TX
4,000 Alternatives to Abortion, Dallas, TX

Wilson Sanitarium for Children of Baltimore City, Thomas

CONTACT
Charles I. Stout
President
Thomas Wilson Sanitarium for Children of Baltimore City
Alex Brown and Sons
135 East Baltimore St.
Baltimore, MD 21202
(301) 727-1700

FINANCIAL SUMMARY
Recent Giving: $148,100 (fiscal 1990); $130,000 (fiscal 1989)
Assets: $3,484,592 (fiscal year ending January 31, 1990); $3,293,856 (fiscal 1989)
EIN: 52-6044885

CONTRIBUTIONS SUMMARY
Donor(s): the late Thomas Wilson
Typical Recipients: • *Education:* colleges & universities • *Health:* hospitals, medical research, single-disease health associations • *Social Services:* disabled
Grant Types: general support and research
Geographic Distribution: limited to Baltimore, MD

GIVING OFFICERS
Perry J. Bolton: trust
Edward K. Dunn, Jr.: trust *B* Baltimore MD 1935 *ED* Princeton Univ AB 1958; Harvard Univ MBA 1960 *CURR EMPL* chmn exec comm, dir: Mercantile-Safe Deposit & Trust Co *CORP AFFIL* chmn exec comm, dir: Mercantile-Safe Deposit & Trust Co; dir: Mercantile Bankshares Corp *NONPR AFFIL* trust: Johns Hopkins Hosp, Wilson (Thomas) Sanitarium
Nina Gardner: trust
Kenneth Schuberth: trust
Melchijah Spragins: trust
Charles I. Stout: dir, pres

Francis Trimble: trust
William C. Trimble, Jr.: dir, secy, treas
Frederick Whitridge: trust
Ralph N. Willis: trust
Kinloch N. Yellott III: dir, vp

APPLICATION INFORMATION
Initial Approach: Send brief letter describing program. There are no deadlines.

GRANTS ANALYSIS
Number of Grants: 12
Highest Grant: $17,600
Typical Range: $5,000 to $10,000
Disclosure Period: fiscal year ending January 31, 1990

RECENT GRANTS
17,600 University of Maryland, Baltimore, MD
16,000 John F. Kennedy Institute, Baltimore, MD
15,000 Johns Hopkins Hospital, Baltimore, MD
15,000 Johns Hopkins Hospital, Baltimore, MD
15,000 Johns Hopkins Hospital, Baltimore, MD
12,500 University of Maryland, Baltimore, MD
12,000 Maryland School for the Blind, Baltimore, MD
10,000 Ed Block Courage Awards Foundation, Baltimore, MD
10,000 George Williams Browne Molecular Genetic Facility, Baltimore, MD
10,000 University of Maryland, Baltimore, MD

Wilson Trust, Lula C.

CONTACT
Frederick H. Gravelle
Vice President
Lula C. Wilson Trust
c/o National Bank of Detroit
611 Woodward
Detroit, MI 48226
(313) 645-6600

FINANCIAL SUMMARY
Recent Giving: $97,650 (1991); $131,000 (1990); $93,550 (1989)

Assets: $2,015,613 (1991); $1,807,048 (1990); $1,840,224 (1989)
EIN: 38-6058895

CONTRIBUTIONS SUMMARY
Donor(s): Lula C. Wilson
Typical Recipients: • *Arts & Humanities:* community arts • *Civic & Public Affairs:* philanthropic organizations • *Education:* colleges & universities, private education (precollege) • *Health:* hospitals • *Social Services:* community service organizations, disabled, domestic violence, homes, recreation & athletics, united funds, youth organizations
Grant Types: capital, emergency, multiyear/continuing support, operating expenses, and seed money
Geographic Distribution: limited to Pontiac and Oakland County, MI

GIVING OFFICERS
NBD Bank, N.A.: trust

APPLICATION INFORMATION
Initial Approach: Send brief letter describing program. There are no deadlines.
Restrictions on Giving: Does not support individuals.

GRANTS ANALYSIS
Number of Grants: 20
Highest Grant: $10,000
Typical Range: $1,000 to $7,500
Disclosure Period: 1991

RECENT GRANTS
10,000 Beaumont Foundation, Royal Oak, MI
10,000 New Horizons of Oakland County, Birmingham, MI
9,800 Insight Recovery Center, Birmingham, MI
7,500 Oakland Family Services, Pontiac, MI
7,500 Oakland University Meadow Brook, Rochester, MI
5,000 Boys and Girls Club, Royal Oak, MI
5,000 Child Abuse and Neglect Council County of Oakland, Pontiac, MI
5,000 Community Services of Oakland, Pontiac, MI
5,000 Eton Academy, Bloomfield Hills, MI

5,000 OIC of Oakland County, Pontiac, MI

Wimpey Inc., George / Wimpey Charitable Trust, George

Parent Company: George Wimpey PLC
Headquarters: Escondido, CA
SIC Major Group: General Building Contractors and Real Estate

CONTACT
Penny Halpin
Assistant to the President
George Wimpey Inc.
508 West Mission Ave.
Excondido, CA 92025
(619) 741-1903

FINANCIAL SUMMARY
Recent Giving: $34,000 (1992 approx.)

CONTRIBUTIONS SUMMARY
Typical Recipients: • *Arts & Humanities:* general, history/historic preservation • *Civic & Public Affairs:* general • *Education:* general • *Health:* general, health care cost containment, hospices, medical rehabilitation • *Social Services:* child welfare, community centers, community service organizations, drugs & alcohol, family planning, general, recreation & athletics, shelters/homelessness, youth organizations
Grant Types: general support
Geographic Distribution: emphasis on San Diego, CA, area
Operating Locations: CA (San Diego)

CORP. OFFICERS
Russell Hayes: *CURR EMPL* pres: George Wimpey
Richard Papworth: *CURR EMPL* cfo: George Wimpey

APPLICATION INFORMATION
Initial Approach: Submit a brief letter of inquiry that includes a description of organization and amount requested.
Restrictions on Giving: Does not support religious organizations for sectarian purposes, political or lobbying groups, or organizations outside operating areas.

GRANTS ANALYSIS
Typical Range: $1,000 to $5,000

Winchell's Donut Houses Operating Company

Sales: $124.0 million
Employees: 4,200
Headquarters: La Mirada, CA
SIC Major Group: Food Stores

CONTACT
Avril Wood
Director of Marketing
Winchell's Donut Houses Operating Company
16424 Valley View Ave.
La Mirada, CA 90638
(714) 670-5300

CONTRIBUTIONS SUMMARY
Operating Locations: CA (La Mirada)

CORP. OFFICERS
Brad Bond: *CURR EMPL* chmn: Winchell Donut Houses
Robert Galastro: *CURR EMPL* pres, ceo: Winchell Donut Houses

Winchester Foundation

CONTACT
Don E. Welch
Chairman
Winchester Fdn.
100 South Meridian St.
Winchester, IN 47394
(317) 584-3501

FINANCIAL SUMMARY
Recent Giving: $103,447 (1991); $113,283 (1990); $86,933 (1989)
Assets: $2,813,946 (1991); $2,529,322 (1990); $2,636,239 (1989)
Gifts Received: $51,210 (1991)
Fiscal Note: In 1991, contributions were received from Virginia Davis Craw Weber ($50,000), Winchester Athena Club ($610), and Winchester Rotary Club ($500).
EIN: 23-7422941

CONTRIBUTIONS SUMMARY
Typical Recipients: • *Arts & Humanities:* arts associations, community arts, libraries, music • *Education:* colleges & universities, education funds

• *Social Services:* community service organizations
Grant Types: general support and scholarship
Geographic Distribution: focus on IN

GIVING OFFICERS
Ruth Connally: trust
Helen Garlotte: trust
Enid Goodrich: vchmn
Robert G. Jones: off
Terri E. Matchett: trust
Linda Pugh: asst secy
Chris L. Talley: secy
Don E. Welch: chmn

APPLICATION INFORMATION
Initial Approach: Send brief letter describing program. There are no deadlines.

GRANTS ANALYSIS
Number of Grants: 12
Highest Grant: $20,000
Typical Range: $1,000 to $3,000
Disclosure Period: 1991
Note: 1991 figures do not include scholarships to individuals.

RECENT GRANTS
20,000 Institute for Humane Studies, Fairfax, VA
15,000 Winchester Community Library, Winchester, IN
10,000 Hillsdale College, Hillsdale, MI
8,000 Ensemble Music Society of Indianapolis, Indianapolis, IN
7,500 Foundation for Economic Education, Irvington-on-Hudson, NY
7,000 Festival Music Society of Indianapolis, Indianapolis, IN
5,000 Intercollegiate Studies Institute, Bryn Mawr, PA
5,000 Randolph County Art Association
2,000 Harding University, Searcy, AR
1,500 Winchester Community High School, Winchester, IN

Winkler Foundation, Mark and Catherine

CONTACT
Lynne S. Bromley
Mark and Catherine Winkler Fdn.
4900 Seminary Rd., No. 900
Alexandria, VA 22311
(703) 998-0400

FINANCIAL SUMMARY
Recent Giving: $808,950 (fiscal 1991); $591,982 (fiscal 1990); $521,689 (fiscal 1988)
Assets: $2,264,073 (fiscal year ending January 31, 1991); $1,959,060 (fiscal 1990); $1,716,076 (fiscal 1988)
Gifts Received: $607,000 (fiscal 1990)
Fiscal Note: In fiscal 1990, contributions were received from Hamlet North Trust ($300,000), Southern Towers Hamlet North Trust ($300,000), and Catherine W. Herman ($7,000).
EIN: 54-6054383

CONTRIBUTIONS SUMMARY
Donor(s): the late Catherine and Mark Winkler
Typical Recipients: • *Civic & Public Affairs:* environmental affairs, municipalities, zoos/botanical gardens • *Education:* colleges & universities • *Health:* nursing services • *Religion:* churches • *Social Services:* community service organizations
Grant Types: general support
Geographic Distribution: focus on VA

GIVING OFFICERS
Margaret W. Hecht: vp, dir
Catherine W. Herman: chmn, dir
Kathleen W. Wennesland: pres, dir
Carolyn Winkler: secy, dir

APPLICATION INFORMATION
Initial Approach: Application form provided for scholarship applicants. Send brief letter of inquiry requesting application. There are no deadlines.

GRANTS ANALYSIS
Number of Grants: 41
Highest Grant: $130,000
Typical Range: $1,000 to $5,000
Disclosure Period: fiscal year ending January 31, 1991

RECENT GRANTS

130,000 Winkler Botanical Preserve, Alexandria, VA — general funding

100,000 George Mason University, Fairfax, VA — single parent scholarship fund

100,000 Harvard University, Cambridge, MA — single parent scholarship fund

100,000 University of Washington, Seattle, WA — single parent scholarship fund

75,000 Georgetown University, Washington, DC — refugee medicine program

50,000 Fairfax Bar Association, Fairfax, VA — legal aid fund

30,000 Shining Mountain School, Richmond, VA — scholarship fund

25,000 Colorado College, Colorado Springs, CO — presidential fund

25,000 Natural Resources Defense Council, New York, NY — ozone protection plan

25,000 Washington Hospital Center, Washington, DC — building fund

Winn-Dixie Stores / Winn-Dixie Stores Foundation

Sales: $10.33 billion
Employees: 102,000
Headquarters: Jacksonville, FL
SIC Major Group: Food Stores

CONTACT

L. H. May
President
Winn-Dixie Stores Fdn.
Box B
Jacksonville, FL 32203
(904) 783-5000

FINANCIAL SUMMARY

Recent Giving: $2,000,000 (1993 est.); $1,982,113 (1991); $1,800,000 (1990 approx.)

Assets: $1,963,486 (1991); $2,648,599 (1989)

Fiscal Note: All contributions are made through the foundation.

EIN: 59-0995428

CONTRIBUTIONS SUMMARY

Typical Recipients: • *Arts & Humanities:* public broadcasting • *Civic & Public Affairs:* ethnic/minority organizations, women's affairs • *Education:* colleges & universities, medical education, minority education, student aid • *Health:* hospices, hospitals, single-disease health associations • *Social Services:* child welfare, disabled, food/clothing distribution, united funds, youth organizations

Grant Types: employee matching gifts, general support, and scholarship

Geographic Distribution: primarily in the company's 13-state trade area; generally within the southeastern United States

Operating Locations: AL (Montgomery), FL (Jacksonville, Miami, Orlando, Pompano Beach, Tampa), GA (Atlanta), IN, KY (Louisville), LA (Harahan, Jefferson Parish, New Orleans), MS, NC (Charlotte, Raleigh), OK, SC (Greenville, Taylors), TN, TX (Fort Worth), VA

CORP. OFFICERS

Andrew Dano Davis: *B* Henderson AR 1945 *ED* Stetson Univ *CURR EMPL* chmn, ceo, dir: Winn-Dixie Stores *CORP AFFIL* dir: First Union Natl Bank FL; ptnr: Dixie Darling Bakers, Winn-Dixie Charlotte
James Kufeldt: *CURR EMPL* pres, dir: Winn-Dixie Stores

GIVING OFFICERS

D. H. Bragin: treas, asst secy, dir *CURR EMPL* treas: Winn-Dixie Stores *NONPR AFFIL* dir: Jr Achievement Jacksonville; fundraiser: Un Way Jacksonville; mem: Am Inst CPAs, N FL Cash Mgmt Assn, Natl Assn Accts, Natl Corp Cash Mgmt Assn
Andrew Dano Davis: vp, dir *CURR EMPL* chmn, ceo, dir: Winn-Dixie Stores (see above)
James Kufeldt: vp, dir *CURR EMPL* pres, dir: Winn-Dixie Stores (see above)
Larry H. May: pres, dir *CURR EMPL* vp, dir assoc rels & human resources: Winn-Dixie Stores
C. H. McKellar: vp, dir
T. L. Qualls: asst secy
W. E. Ripley, Jr.: secy

APPLICATION INFORMATION

Initial Approach: *Initial Contact:* letter *Include Information On:* description of the organization, amount requested, purpose for which funds are sought, recently audited financial statement, and proof of tax-exempt status *When to Submit:* any time, board meets quarterly
Restrictions on Giving: Funds only 501(c)(3) organizations near Winn-Dixie operating locations.

OTHER THINGS TO KNOW

In 1992, company pledged $1.25 million to the Red Cross to support relief efforts following Hurricane Andrew.

GRANTS ANALYSIS

Total Grants: $1,982,113
Number of Grants: 446*
Highest Grant: $60,043
Typical Range: $100 to $5,000
Disclosure Period: 1991
Note: Number of grants and average grant figures exclude matching gifts totaling $1,294,266. Recent grants are derived from a 1991 Form 990.

RECENT GRANTS

60,043 American Cancer Society-Duval County, Jacksonville, FL

44,071 American Cancer Celeb. Bagging, Orlando, FL

30,000 NAACP Special Contribution Fund, Jacksonville, FL

21,100 American Cancer Society, Jacksonville, FL

20,000 Museum Science and History, Jacksonville, FL

14,349 American Cancer Society, Jacksonville, FL

11,667 Central Florida Capital Funds, Orlando, FL

10,000 Amateur Athletes Society, Montgomery, AL

10,000 Florida History Associates, FL

10,000 Florida Tax Watch, Jacksonville, FL

Winn Educational Trust, Fanny Edith

CONTACT

Fanny Edith Winn Educational Trust
P.O. Drawer 307
Crowley, LA 70527-0307

FINANCIAL SUMMARY

Recent Giving: $140,950 (1991)
Assets: $2,072,610 (1991)
EIN: 72-6130364

GIVING OFFICERS

Sidney L. Broussard: trust
Stephen A. Stefanski: trust

GRANTS ANALYSIS

Total Grants: $140,950
Number of Grants: 17
Highest Grant: $44,250
Disclosure Period: 1991
Note: Information for 1991 was incomplete.

Winnebago Industries, Inc. / Winnebago Industries Foundation

Sales: $222.6 million
Employees: 2,279
Headquarters: Forest City, IA
SIC Major Group: Transportation Equipment

CONTACT

Elsie Felland
Secretary
Winnebago Industries Fdn.
PO Box 152
Forest City, IA 50436
(515) 582-3535

FINANCIAL SUMMARY

Recent Giving: $54,100 (1992 approx.); $46,544 (1991); $44,390 (1990)
Assets: $1,040,610 (1991); $985,013 (1990)
EIN: 23-7174206

CONTRIBUTIONS SUMMARY

Typical Recipients: • *Arts & Humanities:* arts centers, arts festivals, community arts • *Civic & Public Affairs:* municipalities, urban & community affairs • *Health:* emergency/ambulance services • *Social Services:* community centers, community service organizations, drugs & alcohol,

united funds, youth organizations
Grant Types: general support
Geographic Distribution: focus on IA
Operating Locations: IA (Forest City)

CORP. OFFICERS
Fred G. Dohrmann: *CURR EMPL* pres, coo, dir: Winnebago Indus
John K. Hanson: *B* Thor IA 1913 *ED* Waldorf Coll AA 1932; Univ MN BS 1934 *CURR EMPL* chmn, ceo, dir: Winnebago Indus

GIVING OFFICERS
Gerald E. Boman: trust
Keith Elwick: trust
Luise V. Hanson: trust
Paul D. Hanson: trust

APPLICATION INFORMATION
Initial Approach: Send a full proposal Include a description of organization, amount requested, purpose of funds sought, recently audited financial statement, and proof of tax-exempt status. There are no deadlines.
Restrictions on Giving: Does not support individuals, religious organizations for sectarian purposes, political or lobbying groups, or organizations outside operating areas.

GRANTS ANALYSIS
Number of Grants: 81
Highest Grant: $2,000
Typical Range: $200 to $2,000
Disclosure Period: 1991
Note: Specific grants list for 1991 not provided.

RECENT GRANTS
2,000 Waldorf College, Forest City, IA
2,000 West Hancock Ambulance Service, Britt, IA
2,000 YMCA, Forest City, IA
1,500 Forest City United Fund, Forest City, IA
1,000 Chemical Dependency Services of North Iowa, Mason City, IA
1,000 City of Forest City, Forest City, IA
1,000 City of Lorimor, Lorimor, IA
1,000 Forest City Fire Department, Forest City, IA
1,000 Puckerbrush Days, Forest City, IA
1,000 Robertelle Center, Forest City, IA

Winona Corporation

CONTACT
Patricia K. Healy
Principal Manager
Winona Corporation
200 South Michigan Avenue, Ste. 1100
Chicago, IL 60604
(312) 372-4000

FINANCIAL SUMMARY
Recent Giving: $360,000 (1990); $348,000 (1989); $340,100 (1988)
Assets: $5,183,208 (1990); $4,793,226 (1989); $4,687,294 (1988)
EIN: 36-6132949

CONTRIBUTIONS SUMMARY
Donor(s): the late Marjorie M. Kelly
Typical Recipients: • *Arts & Humanities:* arts institutes, history/historic preservation, museums/galleries • *Civic & Public Affairs:* environmental affairs • *Education:* agricultural education, colleges & universities, private education (precollege) • *Health:* hospitals, medical research • *Science:* observatories & planetariums, scientific institutes • *Social Services:* child welfare, community service organizations, family planning, united funds, youth organizations
Grant Types: general support
Geographic Distribution: focus on IL and MA

GIVING OFFICERS
Patricia K. Healy: pres, dir
Thomas A. Kelly: secy, dir
Marjorie K. Webster: vp, treas, dir

APPLICATION INFORMATION
Initial Approach: Contributes only to preselected organizations.

GRANTS ANALYSIS
Number of Grants: 35
Highest Grant: $125,000
Typical Range: $2,000 to $15,000
Disclosure Period: 1990

RECENT GRANTS
125,000 Penobscot Marine Museum, Searsport, ME
30,000 Smith College Alumni Fund, Northampton, MA
20,000 Chicago Horticulture Society, Glencoe, IL
20,000 Phillips Academy, Andover, MA
15,000 Westover School, Middlebury, CT
10,000 Evanston Hospital, Evanston, IL
10,000 Field Museum of Natural History, Chicago, IL
10,000 Nature Conservancy, Arlington, VA
10,000 World Wildlife Fund, Washington, DC
8,000 Rush Presbyterian St. Luke's Memorial Hospital, Chicago, IL

Winship Memorial Scholarship Foundation

CONTACT
Frances A. Hanson Moore
Executive Director
Winship Memorial Scholarship Fdn.
c/o Comerica Bank-Battle Creek, Trust Div.
25 West Michigan Mall
Battle Creek, MI 49016
(616) 966-6340

FINANCIAL SUMMARY
Recent Giving: $103,356 (1991); $93,515 (1990); $89,543 (1989)
Assets: $3,013,074 (1991); $2,514,898 (1990); $2,571,341 (1989)
EIN: 38-6092543

CONTRIBUTIONS SUMMARY
Grant Types: scholarship
Geographic Distribution: limited to Battle Creek, MI

GIVING OFFICERS
Paul Bauman: trust
Richard I. Brown: dir, pres
Richard L. Brown: trust
Margo S. Brush: secy
Joseph A. Davio: trust
Charles W. Elliott: trust
Arlon Elser: trust
Frances A. Hanson: exec dir
George Lindenberg: trust
Robert D. McFee: vp, trust
Al Murray: trust
Thomas A. Oatsman: dir, treas
Bruce Sellers: trust
Bruce Shurtz: trust
William S. Ticknor: trust
John Wagner: trust

APPLICATION INFORMATION
Initial Approach: Application form required. Applications processed through local high schools. Deadline is November 15.

OTHER THINGS TO KNOW
Provides scholarships for graduates of Battle Creek, MI, area high schools.
Publications: Annual Report, Informational Brochure, Application Guidelines

GRANTS ANALYSIS
Disclosure Period: 1991
Note: In 1991, all grants were for individual scholarships.

Winslow Foundation

CONTACT
Samuel W. Lambert III
Trustee
Winslow Foundation
P.O. Box 627
Princeton, NJ 08542-3712
(609) 921-6336

FINANCIAL SUMMARY
Recent Giving: $105,000 (1990); $65,000 (1989)
Assets: $1,670,608 (1989)
EIN: 22-2778703

CONTRIBUTIONS SUMMARY
Donor(s): the donor is the estate of Julia D. Winslow
Typical Recipients: • *Social Services:* drugs & alcohol
Grant Types: general support
Geographic Distribution: Skillman, NJ

GIVING OFFICERS
Theresa Heinz: trust
Samuel W. III Lambert: trust
Betty A. Ottinber: dir
Wren W. Wirth: trust

GRANTS ANALYSIS
Total Grants: $65,000
Number of Grants: 1
Highest Grant: $65,000
Disclosure Period: 1989

RECENT GRANTS
65,000 Crawford House, Skillman, NJ

Winston Foundation, Norman and Rosita

CONTACT
Julian S. Perlman
Director
Norman and Rosita Winston
Foundation
1740 Broadway
New York, NY 10019
(212) 757-0707

FINANCIAL SUMMARY
Recent Giving: $2,800,000
(1993 est.); $2,803,000 (1992);
$2,712,000 (1991)
Assets: $54,500,000 (1991
est.); $48,111,020 (1990);
$49,319,830 (1989)
Gifts Received: $500,268
(1987)
Fiscal Note: In 1987, the foun-
dation received a contribution
of $500,268 from the estate of
N. K. Winston.
EIN: 13-6161672

CONTRIBUTIONS SUMMARY
Donor(s): The foundation was
established in 1954. Its donor
was the late Norman K. Winston.
Typical Recipients: • *Arts &
Humanities:* arts centers, arts
festivals, dance, history/his-
toric preservation, libraries,
museums/galleries, music,
opera, theater, visual arts
• *Civic & Public Affairs:* civil
rights, ethnic/minority organizations, urban & community affairs • *Education:* colleges &
universities, legal education,
medical education, social
sciences education • *Health:*
hospitals, medical research
• *Religion:* synagogues • *Social
Services:* aged, employ-
ment/job training, recreation &
athletics, youth organizations
Grant Types: fellowship, general support, professorship, project, research, and scholarship
Geographic Distribution: principally New York

GIVING OFFICERS
Arthur Levitt, Jr.: dir *B*
Brooklyn NY 1931 *ED* Wil-
liams Coll BA 1952 *CURR
EMPL* chmn: Levitt Media Co
CORP AFFIL chmn: Levitt
Media Co, NY City Econ
Devel Corp; dir: Baker & Tay-
loy Distr, FDM Holdings, First
Empire St Corp, NY Daily
News, Shared Med Sys Corp;

trust: East NY Savings Bank
NONPR AFFIL chmn: Am Bus
Counc, Task Force Future
Devel W Side Manhattan;
mem: Am Bus Conf, Equitable
Life Assurance Soc US, NY St
Counc Arts; trust: Williams
Coll *PHIL AFFIL* dir: Dole
Foundation
Julian S. Perlman: dir
Richard Rifkind: dir
Simon H. Rifkind: chmn
emeritus, dir *B* Meretz Union
of Soviet Socialist Republics
1901 *ED* City Coll NY BS
1922; Columbia Univ LLB
1925; Jewish Theological Semi-
nary Am 1950; Brandeis Univ
1977; City Coll NY 1978; He-
brew Univ Jerusalem JD 1980
CURR EMPL ptnr: Paul Weiss
Rifkind Wharton & Garrison
CORP AFFIL dir: Sterling Ban-
corp, Sterling Natl Bank
NONPR AFFIL dir, emeritus:
Beth Israel Med Ctr; hon chmn
exec comm: Jewish Theological Seminary; mem: Am Bar
Assn City NY, Am Coll Trial
Lawyers, Phi Beta Kappa *PHIL
AFFIL* pres, dir: Tudor Foundation

APPLICATION INFORMATION
Initial Approach:
Currently, proposals should be
directed to Julian S. Perlman.
There is no prescribed form for
applications.
There is no deadline for submit-
ting proposals.

GRANTS ANALYSIS
Total Grants: $2,803,000
Number of Grants: 135
Highest Grant: $140,000
Typical Range: $1,000 to
$50,000
Disclosure Period: 1992
Note: Recent grants are derived
from a 1992 grants list.

RECENT GRANTS
140,000 Jewish Theological
Seminary of Amer-
ica, New York, NY
100,000 American Friends
of Hebrew Univer-
sity, New York, NY
100,000 City College
Simon H. Rifkind
Center, New York,
NY
100,000 Cornell University
Medical College
Biomedical Re-
search, New York,
NY
100,000 Fordham Univer-
sity Law School,
New York, NY —

Sidney C. Norris
Chair of Law
100,000 Memorial Sloan-
Kettering Cancer
Center, New York,
NY — biomedical
research
100,000 Mitchell Ginsberg
Chair
100,000 Rockefeller University, New York, NY
99,000 Williams College
— Van Alan Clark
Professorship
65,000 Harvard Univer-
sity, Cambridge,
MA — Law School

Winston Research Foundation, Harry

CONTACT
Ronald Winston
President
Harry Winston Research Fdn.
718 Fifth Ave.
New York, NY 10019
(212) 245-2000

FINANCIAL SUMMARY
Recent Giving: $761,550
(1991); $872,815 (1990);
$432,070 (1989)
Assets: $9,941,633 (1991);
$9,512,089 (1990);
$11,384,952 (1989)
EIN: 13-6168266

CONTRIBUTIONS SUMMARY
Donor(s): the late Harry Winston, Ronald Winston
Typical Recipients: • *Arts &
Humanities:* dance, muse-
ums/galleries, opera • *Education:* colleges & universities,
private education (precollege)
• *Health:* hospitals, medical research, single-disease health associations • *Religion:* religious
organizations, synagogues • *Social Services:* disabled, homes,
united funds, youth organizations
Grant Types: research
Geographic Distribution:
focus on NY

GIVING OFFICERS
Richard Copaken: secy
Robert Holtzman: vp
Ronald Winston: pres

APPLICATION INFORMATION
Initial Approach: Contributes
only to preselected organizations.

GRANTS ANALYSIS
Number of Grants: 21

Highest Grant: $325,200
Typical Range: $1,000 to
$10,000*
Disclosure Period: 1991

RECENT GRANTS
325,200 Genetic Research
Trust, Hamilton,
Bermuda
319,200 Rockefeller University, New York, NY
47,805 Stonwin Medical
Conference, Scars-
dale, NY
12,000 American Founda-
tion for AIDS Re-
search, New York,
NY
10,000 Anti-Defamation
League, New York,
NY
10,000 Houston Grand
Opera, Houston, TX
10,000 Zale Lipsny University Hospital, Dal-
las, TX
5,000 Boy Scouts of
America, New
York, NY
5,000 Handicapped Scout-
ing, New York, NY
5,000 Riverdale School,
Bronx, NY

Winter Construction Co.
Revenue: $40.0 million
Employees: 110
Headquarters: Atlanta, GA
SIC Major Group: General
Building Contractors

CONTACT
Patty Nally
Marketing Director
Winter Construction Co.
530 Means St. NW, Ste. 200
Atlanta, GA 30318-5730
(404) 588-3300

FINANCIAL SUMMARY
Recent Giving: $30,000 (1992
approx.); $30,000 (1991)

CONTRIBUTIONS SUMMARY
Company reports 75% of contributions support the arts; and
25% to civic and public affairs.
Typical Recipients: • *Arts &
Humanities:* arts appreciation,
arts associations, arts centers,
arts festivals, arts funds, community arts, dance, ethnic arts,
history/historic preservation, libraries, literary arts, muse-
ums/galleries, music, opera,
performing arts, theater, visual
arts • *Civic & Public Affairs:*
environmental affairs, eth-
nic/minority organizations, philanthropic organizations,

safety, urban & community affairs, zoos/botanical gardens • *Education:* arts education, business education, career/vocational education, continuing education • *Social Services:* community centers, volunteer services

Grant Types: award and general support

Nonmonetary Support Types: donated equipment, in-kind services, loaned employees, and loaned executives

Geographic Distribution: in headquarters and operating communities

Operating Locations: GA (Atlanta)

CORP. OFFICERS

Mike Lanier: *CURR EMPL* vp preconstruction svcs: Winter Construction Co

Martin Sickles: *CURR EMPL* cfo: Winter Construction Co

Arnold P. Silverman: *CURR EMPL* pres, coo: Winter Construction Co

Robert L. Silverman: *CURR EMPL* chmn, ceo: Winter Construction Co

APPLICATION INFORMATION

Initial Approach: Send brief letter of inquiry. There are no deadlines. Include a description of organization, amount requested, and purpose of funds sought.

Restrictions on Giving: Does not support individuals.

GRANTS ANALYSIS

Typical Range: $1,000 to $2,500

Winthrop Trust, Clara B.

CONTACT

Richard Olney III
Clara B. Winthrop Trust
c/o Welch and Forbes
45 School St.
Boston, MA 02108
(617) 523-1635

FINANCIAL SUMMARY

Recent Giving: $86,700 (1991); $85,100 (1990); $87,328 (1989)

Assets: $2,394,745 (1991); $2,011,961 (1990); $1,949,346 (1989)

EIN: 04-6039972

CONTRIBUTIONS SUMMARY

Typical Recipients: • *Arts & Humanities:* community arts, history/historic preservation, museums/galleries, music, public broadcasting • *Civic & Public Affairs:* municipalities, urban & community affairs • *Education:* colleges & universities, education associations • *Health:* hospitals

Grant Types: general support

Geographic Distribution: focus on MA

GIVING OFFICERS

F. Murray Forbes, Jr.: trust

APPLICATION INFORMATION

Initial Approach: Send brief letter describing program. There are no deadlines.

Restrictions on Giving: Does not support individuals.

GRANTS ANALYSIS

Number of Grants: 24
Highest Grant: $7,000
Typical Range: $1,300 to $5,229
Disclosure Period: 1991

RECENT GRANTS

7,000 WGBH Educational Foundation, Boston, MA
7,000 Winsor School, MA
6,800 Beverly Hospital, Beverly, MA
6,000 Peabody Museum of Salem, Salem, MA
5,000 Town of Manchester-by-the-Sea, Manchester, MA
4,500 Trustees of Reservations, Beverly, MA
4,200 Friends of Manchester Trees, Manchester, NH
4,200 Massachusetts Historical Society, Boston, MA
4,200 New England Conservatory of Music, Boston, MA
4,000 English Speaking Union, MA

Wiremold Co. / Wiremold Foundation

Sales: $100.0 million
Employees: 530
Headquarters: West Hartford, CT
SIC Major Group: Electronic & Other Electrical Equipment

CONTACT

Joan Johnson
Secretary
Wiremold Foundation.
60 Woodlawn St.
West Hartford, CT 06110
(203) 523-3620
Note: John Davis Murphy, chairman, is also listed as a contact at the same address but at telephone number 203-233-6251.

FINANCIAL SUMMARY

Recent Giving: $190,660 (1989)
Assets: $640,620 (1989)
EIN: 06-6089445

CONTRIBUTIONS SUMMARY

Typical Recipients: • *Arts & Humanities:* general • *Civic & Public Affairs:* general • *Education:* general • *Health:* general • *Social Services:* general

Grant Types: general support and matching

Geographic Distribution: primarily headquarters area

Operating Locations: CT (West Hartford)

CORP. OFFICERS

John Davis Murphy: *CURR EMPL* chmn, dir: Wiremold Co

Robert H. Murphy: *CURR EMPL* vchmn, dir: Wiremold Co

Watten C. Packard: *CURR EMPL* pres, dir: Wiremold Co

GIVING OFFICERS

Joan L. Johnson: secy

APPLICATION INFORMATION

Initial Approach: Send brief letter of inquiry. There are no deadlines.

GRANTS ANALYSIS

Number of Grants: 97
Highest Grant: $58,300
Typical Range: $250 to $7,000
Disclosure Period: 1989

RECENT GRANTS

58,300 United Way, Hartford, CT
17,000 Greater Hartford Arts Council, Hartford, CT
10,000 University of Hartford, West Hartford, CT
7,000 YMCA, Hartford, CT
5,000 National Association of Electrical Distributors Educational Foundation, Hartford, CT
4,800 Junior Achievement, Windsor Locks, CT
4,500 Hartford Area Training Center, Hartford, CT
4,000 New England Colleges Fund, Boston, MA
3,500 WHC-TV W. Hartford Community TV 26 Access, Hartford, CT
3,000 Walks Foundation, Hartford, CT

Wisconsin Bell, Inc.

Revenue: $1.06 billion
Employees: 5,500
Parent Company: Ameritech Corp.
Headquarters: Milwaukee, WI
SIC Major Group: Communications

CONTACT

Peggy Larson
Director, Corporate Contributions
Wisconsin Bell, Inc.
722 North Broadway, 13th Fl.
Milwaukee, WI 53202
(414) 678-2945

FINANCIAL SUMMARY

Recent Giving: $2,200,000 (1992); $2,300,000 (1991); $1,800,000 (1990)

Fiscal Note: Company gives directly.

CONTRIBUTIONS SUMMARY

Typical Recipients: • *Arts & Humanities:* arts centers, general, history/historic preservation, public broadcasting • *Civic & Public Affairs:* ethnic/minority organizations, general, zoos/botanical gardens • *Education:* colleges & universities, general • *Health:* general • *Social Services:* drugs & alcohol, employment/job training, general, united funds

Grant Types: capital, general support, matching, and project

Nonmonetary Support Types: donated equipment, loaned employees, and loaned executives

Geographic Distribution: headquarters and operating locations

Operating Locations: WI (Milwaukee)

CORP. OFFICERS

Barry K. Allen: *CURR EMPL* pres, ceo: WI Bell

GIVING OFFICERS

Peggy Larson: *CURR EMPL*
dir corp contributions: WI Bell

APPLICATION INFORMATION

Initial Approach: *Initial Contact:* call or write for the Wisconsin Bell Contribution Request Form *Include Information On:* description of the organization, audited financial statement, list of the board of directors, approximate number of face-to-face board meetings held each year, and proof of tax-exempt status *When to Submit:* any time

Restrictions on Giving: Does not support individuals; individual scholarships; organizations benefiting only a few persons; organizaitons that are not tax-exempt; organizations that receive more than 50% of their funding from government sources; organizations that discriminate by race, color, creed, or national origin; United Way agencies that receive more than 25% of funding from the United Way; affiliates of labor organizations; religious organizations for sectarian purposes; nursing or retirement homes; national health organizations; veteran or military organizations; athletic or sports programs; national and international organizations; service clubs raising money for community purposes, and all other second-party giving; foundations that are themselves grantmaking bodies; or advertising programs such as ads in yearbooks and program brochures. Wisconsin Bell, by law, is unable to donate its telecommunications products or services.

OTHER THINGS TO KNOW

Publications: Trend (newspaper)

Wisconsin Centrifugal / Wisconsin Centrifugal Charitable Foundation

Employees: 450
Headquarters: Waukesha, WI

CONTACT

Robert J. Smickley
President
Wisconsin Centrifugal
 Charitable Foundation
905 East St. Paul Avenue
Waukesha, WI 53188-3898
(414) 544-7777

FINANCIAL SUMMARY

Recent Giving: $34,184 (fiscal 1992); $46,608 (fiscal 1990)
Assets: $235,132 (fiscal year ending June 30, 1992); $261,671 (fiscal 1990)
EIN: 39-1591534

CONTRIBUTIONS SUMMARY

Typical Recipients: • *Civic & Public Affairs:* professional & trade associations, safety • *Education:* education funds • *Health:* health organizations, hospitals • *Social Services:* united funds, youth organizations
Grant Types: general support
Geographic Distribution: giving primarily in WI
Operating Locations: WI (Waukesha)

CORP. OFFICERS

Robert J. Smickley: *CURR EMPL* pres: Wisconsin Centrifugal

GIVING OFFICERS

Wayne R. Buske: secy-treas
Carter Paden, Jr.: chmn
Robert J. Smickley: pres *CURR EMPL* pres: Wisconsin Centrifugal (see above)

APPLICATION INFORMATION

Initial Approach: The foundation supports preselected organizations and does not accept unsolicited requests for funds.
Restrictions on Giving: The foundation does not make grants to individuals.

GRANTS ANALYSIS

Total Grants: $34,184
Number of Grants: 17
Highest Grant: $22,500
Typical Range: $100 to $2,000
Disclosure Period: fiscal year ending June 30, 1992

RECENT GRANTS

22,500	United Way
3,000	Foundry Educational Foundation, Des Plaines, IL
2,000	Partners of Education
2,000	St. Joseph's Medical/Dental Clinic
2,000	Waukesha Memorial Hospital, Waukesha, WI
500	Girl Scouts of America
500	Potawatomi Council 651
300	YMCA
300	YMCA
265	National Fire Safety Council

Wisconsin Energy Corp. / Wisconsin Energy Corp. Foundation

Sales: $1.54 billion
Employees: 5,678
Headquarters: Milwaukee, WI
SIC Major Group: Electric, Gas & Sanitary Services and Holding & Other Investment Offices

CONTACT

Jerry G. Remmel
Treasurer
Wisconsin Energy Corp. Fdn., Inc.
231 W Michigan St.
PO Box 2046
Milwaukee, WI 53201
(414) 221-2105

FINANCIAL SUMMARY

Recent Giving: $3,700,000 (1993 est.); $3,500,000 (1992 approx.); $2,916,848 (1991)
Assets: $27,000,000 (1992 approx.); $31,299,035 (1991); $30,717,619 (1990)
Fiscal Note: All contributions are made through the foundation.
EIN: 39-1433726

CONTRIBUTIONS SUMMARY

Typical Recipients: • *Arts & Humanities:* arts associations, arts funds, community arts, history/historic preservation, museums/galleries, music, performing arts, public broadcasting, theater • *Civic & Public Affairs:* business/free enterprise, civil rights, economic development, environmental affairs, urban & community affairs, zoos/botanical gardens • *Education:* arts education, business education, colleges & universities, economic education, education associations, education funds, engineering education, liberal arts education, minority education, private education (precollege), public education (precollege),

science/technology education, social sciences education • *Health:* health organizations, hospitals, medical rehabilitation, medical research, mental health, single-disease health associations • *Science:* scientific organizations • *Social Services:* aged, child welfare, community centers, community service organizations, disabled, family services, homes, shelters/homelessness, united funds, youth organizations
Grant Types: capital, employee matching gifts, general support, and research
Nonmonetary Support Types: donated equipment, loaned employees, and workplace solicitation
Note: Value of nonmonetary support is not known and is not included in above totals. Nonmonetary support is provided through the company.
Geographic Distribution: almost exclusively in company's service area, but grants may be made in other states
Operating Locations: WI (Fox Valley)
Note: Company also has operating locations throughout southeastern Wisconsin.

CORP. OFFICERS

Richard A. Abdoo: *B* Port Huron MI 1944 *ED* Univ Dayton 1965; Univ Detroit 1969 *CURR EMPL* chmn, ceo, pres: WI Energy Co *CORP AFFIL* chmn, ceo: WI Natural Gas Co, Wisconsin Electric Power Co; dir: Agridata Resources, M & I Marshall & Ilsley Bank, Syndesis Devel Corp
John William Boston: *B* Boise ID 1933 *ED* OR St Univ 1958 *CURR EMPL* pres, coo, dir: WI Energy Co *CORP AFFIL* vp, dir: WI Energy Corp

GIVING OFFICERS

Richard A. Abdoo: pres, dir *CURR EMPL* chmn, ceo, pres: WI Energy Co (see above)
John William Boston: dir *CURR EMPL* pres, coo, dir: WI Energy Co (see above)
John Hubert Goetsch: secy *B* Merrill WI 1933 *ED* Univ Notre Dame 1955; IN Univ 1956 *CURR EMPL* vp, secy: WI Electric Power CO *CORP AFFIL* secy: Badger Svc Co, Syndesis Corp, WI Energy Corp, WI MI Investment Corp, WI Natural Gas Co, Wispark Corp, Wisvest Corp, Witech

Corp *NONPR AFFIL* mem: Am
Soc Corp Secys
Sally A. Newton: asst treas,
asst secy
Jerry G. Remmel: treas, dir
CURR EMPL vp, treas: WI
Electric Power Co *CORP
AFFIL* treas: WI Energy Corp;
treas, dir: WI Natural Gas Co
Gordon A. Willis: asst treas,
asst secy *B* Milwaukee WI
1938 *CURR EMPL* treas: WI
Electronic Power Co *CORP
AFFIL* asst treas: WI Energy
Corp, WI Tech, WISPARK,
WISVEST; treas: WI Natural
Gas Co

APPLICATION INFORMATION
Initial Approach: *Initial Contact:* brief letter or proposal *Include Information On:* description of the organization, amount requested, purpose for which funds are sought, recently audited financial statement, proof of tax-exempt status *When to Submit:* any time

OTHER THINGS TO KNOW
Company's subsidiaries, Wisconsin Natural Gas Co. and Wisconsin Electric Power Co., also contribute to the foundation.

GRANTS ANALYSIS
Total Grants: $3,500,000
Number of Grants: 500
Highest Grant: $650,000
Typical Range: $100 to $7,500
Disclosure Period: 1992
Note: Recent grants are derived from a 1991 Form 990.

RECENT GRANTS
600,000 United Way of Greater Milwaukee, Milwaukee, WI
245,000 United Performing Arts Fund, Milwaukee, WI
100,000 Marquette University, Milwaukee, WI
80,000 University of Wisconsin-Madison, Madison, WI
70,000 Children's Hospital of Wisconsin, Milwaukee, WI
60,000 Milwaukee Foundation, Milwaukee, WI
50,000 Medical College of Wisconsin, Milwaukee, WI
50,000 Riveredge Nature Center, Newburg, WI

40,000 University of Wisconsin-Milwaukee, Milwaukee, WI
36,500 Racine Area United Way, Racine, WI

Wisconsin Power & Light Co. / Wisconsin Power & Light Foundation
Sales: $651.7 million
Employees: 3,000
Parent Company: WPL Holdings, Inc.
Headquarters: Madison, WI
SIC Major Group: Electric, Gas & Sanitary Services

CONTACT
Donald R. Piepenburg
Vice President
Wisconsin Power & Light Fdn.
PO Box 192
Madison, WI 53701
(608) 252-3181

FINANCIAL SUMMARY
Recent Giving: $1,068,500 (1993 est.); $991,600 (1992 approx.); $943,404 (1991)
Assets: $6,596,900 (1992); $6,887,141 (1991); $5,194,139 (1990)
Fiscal Note: Above figures do not include company direct giving of approximately $250,000 annually to local social services agencies for a community fuel fund. Company gives primarily through the foundation.
EIN: 39-1444065

CONTRIBUTIONS SUMMARY
Typical Recipients: • *Arts & Humanities:* arts festivals, community arts, history/historic preservation, libraries, museums/galleries, music, performing arts, theater • *Civic & Public Affairs:* business/free enterprise, economic development, environmental affairs, ethnic/minority organizations, safety, urban & community affairs • *Education:* colleges & universities • *Health:* health organizations, hospitals, nursing services, single-disease health associations • *Social Services:* child welfare, community service organizations, disabled, family services, food/clothing distribution, shelters/homelessness, united funds, youth organizations

Grant Types: capital, employee matching gifts, general support, operating expenses, scholarship, and seed money
Nonmonetary Support Types: donated equipment, loaned employees, and loaned executives Note: In 1992, estimated value of the company's nonmonetary support was $23,200. This support is not included in the figures above.
Geographic Distribution: principally near headquarters and service areas (Central and South-Central WI)
Operating Locations: WI (Madison, South & Central regions)

CORP. OFFICERS
Errol Brown Davis, Jr.: *B* Pittsburgh PA 1944 *ED* Carnegie-Mellon Univ 1965; Univ Chicago MBA 1967 *CURR EMPL* pres, ceo: WI Power & Light Co *CORP AFFIL* dir: WPL Sentry Ins; pres, dir: WPL Holdings *NONPR AFFIL* bd regents: Univ WI; commnr: Madison Police & Fire Commn; dir: Am Gas Assn, Amoco Corp, Competitive WI, Higher Ed AIDS Bd, Un Way Dane County, Un Way Dane County, WI Assn Mfrs & Commerce, WI Utilities Assn; mem: Am Assn Blacks in Energy, Selective Svc Bd

GIVING OFFICERS
A. J. Amato: pres, dir *B* Madison WI 1951 *CURR EMPL* vp (mktg, commun & environmental affs): Wisconsin Power & Light Co
Donald R. Piepenburg: vp *B* Oshkosh WI 1933 *ED* Univ WI 1955 *CURR EMPL* vp, exec dir: WI Power & Light Co

APPLICATION INFORMATION
Initial Approach: *Initial Contact:* brief letter or proposal *Include Information On:* name and history of organization, overview of proposed project, purpose for which funds are sought, proof of tax-exempt status, audited financial statement *When to Submit:* by September 1 for funding the next year

GRANTS ANALYSIS
Total Grants: $991,600
Number of Grants: 1,200
Highest Grant: $61,900
Typical Range: $250 to $1,000

Disclosure Period: 1992
Note: Recent grants are derived from a 1991 Form 990.

RECENT GRANTS
61,900 United Way of Dane County, Madison, WI
30,970 Citizens Scholarship Foundation of America, St. Peter, MN
26,000 WFIC
25,000 Menominee Indian Trust
20,000 WFIC
16,500 Board of Regents
15,000 American Players Theater, Spring Green, WI
15,000 Madison Urban League, Madison, WI — YES scholarship
12,500 March of Dimes
12,000 Madison Urban League, Madison, WI — YES scholarship

Wisconsin Public Service Corp. / Wisconsin Public Service Foundation
Revenue: $634.8 million
Employees: 2,631
Headquarters: Green Bay, WI
SIC Major Group: Electric, Gas & Sanitary Services

CONTACT
D. A. Bollom
President & CEO
Wisconsin Public Service Fdn.
700 North Adams St.
PO Box 19001
Green Bay, WI 54307-9001
(414) 433-1464

FINANCIAL SUMMARY
Recent Giving: $484,650 (1993 est.); $481,506 (1992); $627,000 (1991)
Assets: $10,227,000 (1992); $7,471,717 (1990); $7,452,153 (1989)
Gifts Received: $200,000 (1990)
EIN: 39-6075016

CONTRIBUTIONS SUMMARY
Typical Recipients: • *Arts & Humanities:* arts festivals, general, libraries, museums/galleries, performing arts • *Civic & Public Affairs:* general, zoos/botanical gardens • *Education:* agricultural education, business education, career/vocational education, colleges &

universities, engineering education • *Health:* hospitals, single-disease health associations • *Social Services:* aged, community centers, drugs & alcohol, food/clothing distribution, united funds, youth organizations

Grant Types: capital, emergency, fellowship, general support, and scholarship

Nonmonetary Support Types: donated equipment and loaned employees

Note: Estimated value of nonmonetary support is not available and is not included in figures above.

Geographic Distribution: northeast Wisconsin and parts of upper Michigan

Operating Locations: WI (Green Bay)

CORP. OFFICERS
Daniel Arthur Bollom: *B* Oshkosh WI 1936 *CURR EMPL* pres, ceo, dir: WI Pub Svc Corp *CORP AFFIL* dir: Prime Fed Bank *NONPR AFFIL* mem: WI Bd Certified Pub Accts

GIVING OFFICERS
D. P. Bittner: treas *CURR EMPL* vp, treas: WI Pub Svc Corp
Daniel Arthur Bollom: pres *CURR EMPL* pres, ceo, dir: WI Pub Svc Corp (see above)
Robert H. Knuth: secy *B* Manitowoc WI 1933 *ED* Univ WI 1960 *CURR EMPL* asst vp, secy: WI Pub Svc Corp *NONPR AFFIL* mem: Am Soc Corp Secys
Patrick D. Schrickel: mem bd *CURR EMPL* sr vp (opers): WI Pub Svc Corp

APPLICATION INFORMATION
Initial Approach: *Initial Contact:* brief letter *Include Information On:* organization name, explanation of organization, funds desired, and reason for request *When to Submit:* any time **Restrictions on Giving:** Only supports 501(c)3 organizations.

OTHER THINGS TO KNOW
Company reports that its funding through 1995 is committed.

GRANTS ANALYSIS
Total Grants: $481,506
Number of Grants: 105
Highest Grant: $70,500
Typical Range: $500 to $1,500
Disclosure Period: 1992

Note: Recent grants are derived from a 1991-1992 grants list.

RECENT GRANTS
70,500   United Way of Brown County, Green Bay, WI
66,500   United Way of Brown County, Green Bay, WI
25,000   St. Norbert College, Green Bay, WI
23,350   University of Wisconsin, Madison, WI
22,000   Marquette University, Milwaukee, WI
20,000   Heritage Hill State Park Foundation, Green Bay, WI
20,000   Heritage Hill State Park Foundation, Green Bay, WI
20,000   St. Vincent Hospital, Green Bay, WI
20,000   St. Vincent Hospital, Green Bay, WI
20,000   Trees for Tomorrow, Eagle River, WI

Wisdom Foundation, Mary F.

CONTACT
Steven W. Usdin
Trustee
Mary F. Wisdom Fdn.
c/o Stone, Pigman, Walther, Wirtman and Hutchinson
546 Carondelet St.
New Orleans, LA 70130

FINANCIAL SUMMARY
Recent Giving: $151,300 (fiscal 1992); $126,200 (fiscal 1991); $46,000 (fiscal 1990)
Assets: $3,201,905 (fiscal year ending April 30, 1992); $2,921,099 (fiscal 1991); $2,557,243 (fiscal 1990)
EIN: 72-6123208

CONTRIBUTIONS SUMMARY
Typical Recipients: • *Arts & Humanities:* community arts, dance, museums/galleries, music, performing arts • *Civic & Public Affairs:* environmental affairs, zoos/botanical gardens • *Education:* colleges & universities • *Religion:* religious organizations • *Social Services:* animal protection, religious welfare
Grant Types: general support

Geographic Distribution: focus on New Orleans, LA

GIVING OFFICERS
Adelaide W. Benjamin: secy
Helen Wisdom Collins: treas
Steven W. Usdin: trust
Mary E. Wisdom: pres

APPLICATION INFORMATION
Initial Approach: Send brief letter of inquiry describing program. There are no deadlines.

GRANTS ANALYSIS
Number of Grants: 23
Highest Grant: $20,000
Typical Range: $5,000 to $10,000
Disclosure Period: fiscal year ending April 30, 1992

RECENT GRANTS
20,000   Louisiana Philharmonic Society, New Orleans, LA
10,000   Boys Hope, New Orleans, LA
10,000   Louisa McGehee School, New Orleans, LA
10,000   Louisiana Museum Foundation, New Orleans, LA
10,000   Lusher School, New Orleans, LA
10,000   Nature Conservancy, Baton Rouge, LA
10,000   Project Lazarus, New Orleans, LA
7,500   Audubon Institute, New Orleans, LA
6,500   Metairie Park Country Day School, Metairie, LA
6,000   Little Sisters of Poor, New Orleans, LA

Wise Foundation and Charitable Trust, Watson W.

CONTACT
George T. Griffin
General Manager
Watson W. Wise Foundation and Charitable Trust
372 Fair Foundation Building
Tyler, TX 75702
(903) 597-5945

FINANCIAL SUMMARY
Recent Giving: $0 (1991); $2,500 (1990)
Assets: $985,183 (1990)
EIN: 75-6064539

CONTRIBUTIONS SUMMARY
Donor(s): the donor is the estate of Watson W. Wise
Typical Recipients: • *Social Services:* youth organizations
Grant Types: general support
Geographic Distribution: Tyler, TX

GIVING OFFICERS
Calvin Clyde: trust
Herman A. Engel: trust
Will Knight: trust
Emma F. Wise: trust

APPLICATION INFORMATION
Initial Approach: The foundation reports that there is no specific application form. The foundation is temporarily inactive until further notice.

GRANTS ANALYSIS
Number of Grants: 1
Highest Grant: $2,500
Disclosure Period: 1990

RECENT GRANTS
2,500   Boy Scouts of America

Wiseheart Foundation

CONTACT
Malcolm B. Wiseheart, Jr.
President
Wiseheart Fdn.
2840 S.W. Third Ave.
Miami, FL 33129
(305) 285-1222

FINANCIAL SUMMARY
Recent Giving: $37,655 (1991); $48,134 (1990); $50,317 (1989)
Assets: $2,364,925 (1991); $2,373,488 (1990); $2,469,789 (1989)
EIN: 59-0992871

CONTRIBUTIONS SUMMARY
Donor(s): the late Malcolm B. Wiseheart, the late Dorothy A. Wiseheart
Typical Recipients: • *Arts & Humanities:* community arts, dance, history/historic preservation, museums/galleries, opera, public broadcasting • *Civic & Public Affairs:* environmental affairs • *Education:* colleges & universities, private education (precollege) • *Religion:* churches, religious organizations
Grant Types: general support

Geographic Distribution: focus on FL, with a strong preference for the Dade County metropolitan area

GIVING OFFICERS
Elizabeth W. Joyce: vp
Carolyn W. Milne: trust
Malcolm B. Wiseheart, Jr.: pres

APPLICATION INFORMATION
Initial Approach: Send brief letter describing program. There are no deadlines.
Restrictions on Giving: Does not support individuals.

GRANTS ANALYSIS
Number of Grants: 42
Highest Grant: $7,000
Typical Range: $500 to $1,000
Disclosure Period: 1991

RECENT GRANTS
7,000 St. Thomas Episcopal Parish School
3,020 Greater Miami Opera Association, Miami, FL
2,500 Dance Alive
1,500 Elisabeth Morrow School
1,500 First Presbyterian Church
1,000 Cowboy Artists of America Museum, Kerrville, TX
1,000 Deering Estate Foundation
1,000 Flat Rock Brook Nature Center
1,000 Miami Choral Society, Miami, FL
1,000 Middlesex School

Witco Corp. / Wishnick Foundation, Robert I.
Former Foundation Name: Witco Foundation
Sales: $1.73 billion
Employees: 7,267
Headquarters: New York, NY
SIC Major Group: Chemicals & Allied Products, Petroleum & Coal Products, and Wholesale Trade—Nondurable Goods

CONTACT
William Wishnick
President, Director
Robert I. Wishnick Fdn.
375 Park Ave.
New York, NY 10152
(212) 371-1844

FINANCIAL SUMMARY
Recent Giving: $621,750 (1991); $564,065 (1990); $516,880 (1989)
Assets: $9,174,665 (1991); $8,919,752 (1990); $8,353,492 (1989)
Gifts Received: $500,000 (1989); $18,106 (1988)
Fiscal Note: Contributes through foundation only. In 1989, contributions were received from Witco Corporation.
EIN: 13-6068668

CONTRIBUTIONS SUMMARY
Typical Recipients: • *Arts & Humanities:* arts centers, libraries, museums/galleries, music, performing arts • *Civic & Public Affairs:* civil rights, ethnic/minority organizations, law & justice, national security • *Education:* business education, colleges & universities, engineering education, medical education, private education (precollege), student aid • *Health:* hospitals, single-disease health associations • *Religion:* religious organizations • *Science:* scientific organizations • *Social Services:* community service organizations, religious welfare, united funds, youth organizations
Grant Types: conference/seminar, endowment, fellowship, general support, research, and scholarship
Geographic Distribution: operating communities
Operating Locations: AL (Phenix City), CA (City of Industry, Commerce, Los Angeles, Oildale, Rancho Dominguez, Richmond, Santa Fe Springs), FL (Jacksonville), IA (Spencer), IL (Blue Island, Chicago, Melrose Park), IN (Indianapolis), KS (Olathe), LA (Gretna, Harahan, Taft), MI (Highland Park), MS (Philadelphia), NE (Omaha), NJ (Newark, Perth Amboy), NV (Las Vegas), NY (Beacon, Brooklyn, New York), OK (Ponca City), OR (Klamath Falls), PA (Bakerstown, Bradford, Petrolia, Trainer), TN (Memphis), TX (Fort Worth, Houston, Marshall), WA (Quincy)

CORP. OFFICERS
Denis Andreuzzi: *B* New York NY 1931 *ED* Columbia Univ BA 1953; NY Univ MBA 1958 *CURR EMPL* chmn exec comm, vchmn, pres, coo, dir: Witco Corp *CORP AFFIL* dir: Witco BV (Holland) *NONPR AFFIL* mem: Chem Mfrs Assn, IN Lubricant Mfrs Assn, Natl Petroleum Refiners Assn
William R. Toller: *B* Fort Smith AR 1930 *ED* Univ AR 1956; Stanford Univ 1971 *CURR EMPL* chmn, ceo, dir: Witco Corp *NONPR AFFIL* mem: Am Chem Soc, Am Petroleum Inst, Chem Mfrs Assn, Fin Execs Inst

GIVING OFFICERS
Robert L. Bachner: dir
Simeon Brinberg: dir
Lisa Wishnick: dir
William Wishnick: pres, dir *B* Brooklyn NY 1924 *ED* Univ TX BBA 1949; Carnegie Inst Tech *CURR EMPL* mem exec comm, dir: Witco Corp *CORP AFFIL* chmn: Aero Oil Co; chmn, dir: Continental Carbon Co *NONPR AFFIL* fellow: Polytech Inst NY; mem: Am Chem Assn, Am Chem Soc, Am Petroleum Inst, NY Paint Varnish & Lacquer Assn, Salesmans Assn, Tau Delta Phi; trust: Carnegie Mellon Univ, Mt Sinai Hosp; fellow: Polytechnic Univ; mem: NY Rubber Group, Young Pres Org

APPLICATION INFORMATION
Initial Approach: *Initial Contact:* brief letter* *Include Information On:* description of program, amount of funds requested *When to Submit:* any time *Note:* Requests from outside New York City must be forwarded through local offices of the corporation.
Restrictions on Giving: Foundation does not support individuals (except for employee-related scholarships) or matching gifts. Loans are not made.

GRANTS ANALYSIS
Total Grants: $621,750
Number of Grants: 41
Highest Grant: $110,000
Typical Range: $1,000 to $10,000
Disclosure Period: 1991
Note: Recent grants are derived from a 1991 grants list.

RECENT GRANTS
110,000 United Jewish Appeal Federation, New York, NY
100,000 Hospital for Joint Diseases and Medical Center, New York, NY
100,000 Jerusalem Foundation, New York, NY
75,000 Garlits Museum of Drag Racing
30,000 Mt. Sinai School of Medicine, New York, NY
25,000 National Foundation for the History of Chemistry, New York, NY
17,000 EAA Aviation Foundation, Oshkosh, WI
15,000 Los Angeles Philharmonic Association, Los Angeles, CA
12,500 Circle Repertory Company, New York, NY
10,000 Bradford Library Building Fund, Bradford, MA

Witte, Jr. Foundation, John H.

CONTACT
Robert C. Matsch
Sr. Vice President
John H. Witte, Jr. Fdn.
c/o First National Bank
201 Jefferson St.
Burlington, IA 52601
(319) 752-2761

FINANCIAL SUMMARY
Recent Giving: $256,560 (fiscal 1991); $245,261 (fiscal 1990); $214,114 (fiscal 1989 est.)
Assets: $5,922,645 (fiscal year ending August 31, 1991); $5,396,478 (fiscal 1990); $5,810,447 (fiscal 1989)
EIN: 42-6297940

CONTRIBUTIONS SUMMARY
Donor(s): the late John H. Witte, Jr.
Typical Recipients: • *Arts & Humanities:* arts associations, community arts, history/historic preservation • *Civic & Public Affairs:* economic development, environmental affairs • *Education:* colleges & universities, community & junior colleges, private education (precollege) • *Health:* hospitals

• *Social Services:* aged, family planning, family services, united funds, youth organizations

Grant Types: capital, endowment, general support, and scholarship

Geographic Distribution: focus on the Burlington, IA, area

GIVING OFFICERS

FirStar Bank Burlington, N.A.: trust

APPLICATION INFORMATION

Initial Approach: Send brief letter of inquiry describing program or project. There are no deadlines.

GRANTS ANALYSIS

Number of Grants: 20
Highest Grant: $75,000
Typical Range: $1,000 to $10,000
Disclosure Period: fiscal year ending August 31, 1991

RECENT GRANTS

75,000 Burlington High School, Burlington, IA
50,000 Girl Scouts of America, Burlington, IA
33,000 United Way, Burlington, IA
21,500 Burlington Medical Center, Burlington, IA
16,000 Hope Haven Area Development Center, Burlington, IA
10,000 Burlington Area Catholic Schools, Burlington, IA
10,000 Southeastern Community College, West Burlington, IA
5,000 Burlington Area Arts Council, Burlington, IA
5,000 Burlington Medical Center, Burlington, IA
5,000 Des Moines County Historical Society, Burlington, IA

Witter Foundation, Dean

CONTACT

Lawrence I. Kramer, Jr.
Administrative Director
Dean Witter Fdn.
601 Montgomery St., Ste. 900
San Francisco, CA 94111
(415) 788-8855

FINANCIAL SUMMARY

Recent Giving: $328,300 (fiscal 1991); $424,600 (fiscal 1990); $285,586 (fiscal 1989)

Assets: $9,938,935 (fiscal year ending November 30, 1991); $6,813,026 (fiscal 1990); $7,545,715 (fiscal 1989)

Gifts Received: $36,925 (fiscal 1989); $9,500 (fiscal 1988)

EIN: 94-6065150

CONTRIBUTIONS SUMMARY

Donor(s): the late Dean Witter, Mrs. Dean Witter, Dean Witter and Co.

Typical Recipients: • *Arts & Humanities:* history/historic preservation, museums/galleries • *Civic & Public Affairs:* environmental affairs, public policy, zoos/botanical gardens • *Education:* business education, colleges & universities • *Social Services:* animal protection, community service organizations

Grant Types: capital and project

Geographic Distribution: limited to northern CA

GIVING OFFICERS

James Ramsey Bancroft: vp *B* Ponca City OK *ED* Univ CA Berkeley AB 1940; Univ CA Berkeley MBA 1941; Hastings Coll JD 1949 *CURR EMPL* chmn: Adams Capital Mgmt Co *CORP AFFIL* chmn: Adams Capital Mgmt Co; mem: CA Consumers Inc, Canadian Ins Co CA; of coun: Bancroft Avery & McAlister; owner, mgr: Bancroft Vineyard; pres: Madison Properties Inc *NONPR AFFIL* dir: CA Urology Fdn, Fdn Res Ed Orthopedic Surgery, Pacific Vascular Res Fdn; mem: Am Bar Assn

Edmond S. Gillette, Jr.: trust

Stephen Nessier: trust

Frank Roberts: trust

Dean Witter III: pres, dir

William D. Witter: secy, treas

APPLICATION INFORMATION

Initial Approach: Send brief letter of inquiry describing program or project.

Restrictions on Giving: Does not support individuals or provide endowment funds.

OTHER THINGS TO KNOW

Publications: Annual Report (including application guidelines)

GRANTS ANALYSIS

Number of Grants: 20
Highest Grant: $60,000
Typical Range: $2,500 to $10,000
Disclosure Period: fiscal year ending November 30, 1991

RECENT GRANTS

60,000 Walter Haas School of Business, Berkeley, CA
50,000 Center for Economic Policy Research, Stanford, CA
25,000 Long Marine Laboratory Visitors Center, Santa Cruz, CA
20,000 California Waterfowl Association, San Francisco, CA
15,000 Pacific Research Institute for Public Policy, San Francisco, CA
13,000 Suisun Conservation Fund, San Francisco, CA
12,500 Golden Gate National Park Association, San Francisco, CA
11,800 Sempervirens Fund, San Francisco, CA
9,700 Environment Action Committee of West Marin, San Francisco, CA
7,500 Trust for Public Land, San Francisco, CA

WJLA Inc.

Revenue: $11.0 million
Employees: 180
Parent Company: Albritton Communications Company
Headquarters: Washington, DC
SIC Major Group: Communications

CONTACT

Beverly Hassell
Director, Community Relations
WJLA-TV
3007 Tilden, NW
Washington, DC 20008
(202) 364-7881

CONTRIBUTIONS SUMMARY

Operating Locations: DC (Washington)

CORP. OFFICERS

John D. Sawhill: *CURR EMPL* pres, ceo: WJLA

Wodecroft Foundation

CONTACT

H. Truxtun Emerson, Jr.
Secretary
Wodecroft Fdn.
1900 Chemed Center
Cincinnati, OH 45202
(513) 977-8250

FINANCIAL SUMMARY

Recent Giving: $356,100 (1991); $300,000 (1990); $300,000 (1989)

Assets: $11,193,351 (1991); $8,489,866 (1990); $7,163,650 (1989)

EIN: 31-6047601

CONTRIBUTIONS SUMMARY

Donor(s): Roger Drackett

Typical Recipients: • *Arts & Humanities:* museums/galleries, music • *Civic & Public Affairs:* environmental affairs • *Education:* colleges & universities, literacy, minority education, private education (precollege) • *Health:* health organizations, hospices, hospitals, medical research, single-disease health associations • *Social Services:* united funds, youth organizations

Grant Types: general support
Geographic Distribution: focus on OH

GIVING OFFICERS

Richard W. Barrett: chmn, trust

Jeanne H. Drackett: secy, trust

H. Truxton Emerson, Jr.: secy, trust

APPLICATION INFORMATION

Initial Approach: Send brief letter of inquiry describing program or project. There are no deadlines.

Restrictions on Giving: Does not support individuals.

GRANTS ANALYSIS
Number of Grants: 49
Highest Grant: $50,000
Typical Range: $1,000 to $10,000
Disclosure Period: 1991

RECENT GRANTS
50,000 Naples/Marco Philharmonic, Naples, FL
35,000 Conservancy
15,000 Children's Hospital Medical Center, Boston, MA
15,000 Fairfield Country Day School, Fairfield, CT
15,000 Seven Hills School, Lynchburg, VA
10,000 Carpenter-Briggs Radiation Therapy Center, Cincinnati, OH
10,000 Christ Hospital
10,000 Collier County Conservancy, Cincinnati, OH
10,000 Foundation for Mental Health, Naples, FL
10,000 United Way

Woldenberg Foundation

CONTACT
Dorothy Woldenberg
President
Woldenberg Fdn.
301 Magazine St., 2nd Fl.
New Orleans, LA 70130

FINANCIAL SUMMARY
Recent Giving: $1,190,950 (1991); $309,550 (1990); $232,850 (1989)
Assets: $2,009,786 (1991); $2,750,176 (1990); $3,006,481 (1989)
Gifts Received: $1,000,500 (1989); $803,000 (1988)
EIN: 72-6022665

CONTRIBUTIONS SUMMARY
Donor(s): Malcolm Woldenberg, Magnolia Liquor Co., Sazerac Co., Great Southern Liquor Co., Duval Spirits
Typical Recipients: • *Arts & Humanities:* arts funds, opera • *Education:* colleges & universities • *Health:* hospitals • *Religion:* religious organizations, synagogues • *Social Services:* united funds
Grant Types: general support

Geographic Distribution: focus on LA and FL

GIVING OFFICERS
Stephen Goldring: vp *B* 1908 *CURR EMPL* chmn, dir: N Goldring Corp
C. Halpern: secy, treas
Dorothy Woldenberg: pres

APPLICATION INFORMATION
Initial Approach: Send brief letter of inquiry describing program. There are no deadlines.
Restrictions on Giving: Does not support individuals.

GRANTS ANALYSIS
Number of Grants: 43
Highest Grant: $1,042,500
Typical Range: $1,000 to $5,000
Disclosure Period: 1991

RECENT GRANTS
1,042,500 Jewish Federation, New Orleans, LA
25,000 Tulane University, New Orleans, LA
15,000 United Way, New Orleans, LA
12,500 World Jewish Congress, New York, NY
10,000 Metropolitan Arts Foundation, New Orleans, LA
7,000 Anti-Defamation League, New Orleans, LA
5,000 B'nai B'rith Florida State Chapter, Miami, FL
5,000 Covenant House, New Orleans, LA
5,000 Foundation for Conservative Judaism in Israel, New York, NY
5,000 Greater Miami Opera Association, Miami, FL

Wolens Foundation, Kalman and Ida

CONTACT
Dean Milkes
President
Kalman and Ida Wolens Fdn.
513 East Seventh Ave.
PO Box 2235
Corsicana, TX 75151-2235
(214) 874-2961

FINANCIAL SUMMARY
Recent Giving: $240,031 (fiscal 1992); $155,666 (fiscal 1991); $134,207 (fiscal 1990)
Assets: $4,387,628 (fiscal year ending July 31, 1992);

$4,460,935 (fiscal 1991); $4,300,459 (fiscal 1990)
EIN: 23-7222516

CONTRIBUTIONS SUMMARY
Donor(s): the late Louis Wolens
Typical Recipients: • *Arts & Humanities:* arts associations • *Education:* colleges & universities, public education (precollege), religious education • *International:* international organizations • *Religion:* religious organizations, synagogues • *Social Services:* community service organizations
Grant Types: endowment, project, research, and scholarship
Geographic Distribution: focus on TX and Israel

GIVING OFFICERS
Cheryl Jerome: dir
Dean Milkes: pres, dir
Marjorie Milkes: secy, treas, dir
Bette Miller: vp, dir

APPLICATION INFORMATION
Initial Approach: Send brief letter of inquiry and full proposal. There are no deadlines.
Restrictions on Giving: Does not support individuals.

GRANTS ANALYSIS
Number of Grants: 27
Highest Grant: $35,500
Typical Range: $1,000 to $10,000
Disclosure Period: fiscal year ending July 31, 1992

RECENT GRANTS
35,500 Congregation Agudas Achim, Corsicana, TX
25,000 American Friends of Hebrew University, New York, NY
25,000 American Society for Technion, New York, NY
25,000 Corsicana Independent School District, Corsicana, TX
25,000 Dallas Home for Jewish Aged, Dallas, TX
21,500 Zionist Organization of America, New York, NY
16,666 Jewish Federation, Dallas, TX
10,000 National Council of Jewish Women, New York, NY
5,000 Community Services, Corsicana, TX

5,000 Retina Foundation of SW, Dallas, TX

Wolf Foundation, Benjamin and Fredora K.

CONTACT
David A. Horowitz
Administrator
Benjamin and Fredora K. Wolf Fdn.
Park Towne Pl. - North Bldg. 1205
Pkwy. at 22nd St.
Philadelphia, PA 19130
(215) 787-6079

FINANCIAL SUMMARY
Recent Giving: $122,750 (fiscal 1992); $116,139 (fiscal 1991); $95,855 (fiscal 1990)
Assets: $2,140,614 (fiscal year ending May 31, 1992); $2,137,419 (fiscal 1991); $2,008,014 (fiscal 1990)
EIN: 23-6207344

CONTRIBUTIONS SUMMARY
Donor(s): the late Fredora K. Wolf
Typical Recipients: • *Education:* student aid
Grant Types: scholarship
Geographic Distribution: limited to Philadelphia, PA, area residents

GIVING OFFICERS
Richard I. Abrahams: treas
Virginia Wolf Briscoe: trust
Alexandra Wolf Fogel: secy
Mrs. J. Ronald Gray: trust
Mary Wolf Hurtig: secy
Mary Wolf Hurtig: secy (see above)
Max Kohn: pres
John Tuton: trust
Flora Barth Wolf: trust

APPLICATION INFORMATION
Initial Approach: Application form required. There are no deadlines.

OTHER THINGS TO KNOW
Provides scholarships to individuals for higher education.

GRANTS ANALYSIS
Highest Grant: $9,250
Disclosure Period: fiscal year ending May 31, 1992

RECENT GRANTS

9,250 National Merit Scholarship, Evanston, IL

Wolf Foundation, Melvin and Elaine

CONTACT

Melvin Wolf
President
Melvin and Elaine Wolf Fdn.
1560 Broadway, Ste. 1000
Denver, CO 80202
(303) 830-8880

FINANCIAL SUMMARY

Recent Giving: $298,257 (fiscal 1992); $280,125 (fiscal 1991); $272,564 (fiscal 1990)
Assets: $6,762,804 (fiscal year ending June 30, 1992); $6,300,983 (fiscal 1991); $6,052,055 (fiscal 1990)
EIN: 84-0797937

CONTRIBUTIONS SUMMARY

Donor(s): Melvin Wolf, Elaine Wolf
Typical Recipients: • *Arts & Humanities:* museums/galleries • *Civic & Public Affairs:* ethnic/minority organizations, international affairs, women's affairs, zoos/botanical gardens • *Education:* colleges & universities • *Health:* hospices, hospitals, pediatric health, single-disease health associations • *Religion:* religious organizations • *Social Services:* child welfare, domestic violence, united funds, youth organizations
Grant Types: general support and operating expenses
Geographic Distribution: focus on CO

GIVING OFFICERS

Henry Reckler: secy, treas, dir
Elaine Wolf: vp, dir
Melvin Wolf: pres, dir

APPLICATION INFORMATION

Initial Approach: Contributes only to preselected organizations.
Restrictions on Giving: Does not support individuals.

GRANTS ANALYSIS

Number of Grants: 51
Highest Grant: $75,000
Typical Range: $1,000 to $10,000
Disclosure Period: fiscal year ending June 30, 1992

RECENT GRANTS

75,000 Rose Medical Center, Denver, CO
56,537 University of Colorado, Boulder, CO
10,000 Anti-Defamation League, Denver, CO
10,000 Children's Hospital, Denver, CO
10,000 Easter Seal Society, Littleton, CO
10,000 National Jewish Center for Immunology and Respiratory Medicine, Denver, CO
10,000 University of Wyoming, Laramie, WY
5,063 Alzheimer's Disease and Related Disorders Association, Denver, CO
5,000 Allied Housing, Denver, CO
5,000 Gateway Battered Women's Center, Aurora, CO

Wolff Foundation, John M.

CONTACT

John W. North
Vice President and Trust
John M. Wolff Fdn.
c/o Commerce Bank of St. Louis, N.A.
8000 Forsyth
Clayton, MO 63105
(314) 726-3600

FINANCIAL SUMMARY

Recent Giving: $268,000 (1989); $108,500 (1988)
Assets: $2,351,263 (1989); $2,136,610 (1988)
EIN: 43-6026247

CONTRIBUTIONS SUMMARY

Donor(s): the late John M. Wolff
Typical Recipients: • *Arts & Humanities:* community arts, performing arts • *Education:* colleges & universities • *Health:* hospitals, hospitals • *Science:* observatories & planetariums • *Social Services:* community service organizations, counseling, food/clothing distribution, homes, united funds, youth organizations
Grant Types: operating expenses and research
Geographic Distribution: focus on St. Louis, MO

GIVING OFFICERS

John M. Wolff III: trust

APPLICATION INFORMATION

Initial Approach: Send brief letter describing program. Deadline is October 1.

GRANTS ANALYSIS

Number of Grants: 23
Highest Grant: $143,500
Typical Range: $1,000 to $10,000
Disclosure Period: 1989

RECENT GRANTS

143,500 Lowell Observatory, Flagstaff, AZ
25,000 Salvation Army, St. Louis, MO
20,000 Bethesda General Hospital and Homes, St. Louis, MO
10,000 Care and Counseling, St. Louis, MO
10,000 St. Louis University, St. Louis, MO
7,000 Cardinal Glennon Memorial Hospital, St. Louis, MO
7,000 Shriners Hospital for Crippled Children, Tampa, FL
5,000 Phoenix Special Programs, Phoenix, AZ
5,000 Principia, St. Louis, MO
5,000 St. Louis Area Food Bank, St. Louis, MO

Wolff Memorial Foundation, Pauline Sterne

CONTACT

Robert H. Richardson, Jr.
Custodian
Pauline Sterne Wolff Memorial Fdn.
Texas Commerce Bank
PO Box 2558
Houston, TX 77252
(713) 236-4407

FINANCIAL SUMMARY

Recent Giving: $626,836 (1991); $602,433 (1990); $508,723 (1989)
Assets: $15,910,737 (1991); $12,792,893 (1990); $13,698,686 (1989)
Gifts Received: $597,074 (1991)
Fiscal Note: In 1991, contributions were received from the Estate of Blanche McMullen Green.
EIN: 74-1110698

CONTRIBUTIONS SUMMARY

Typical Recipients: • *Education:* medical education, private education (precollege) • *Health:* geriatric health, hospitals, pediatric health • *Religion:* religious organizations • *Social Services:* aged, child welfare, community centers, community service organizations, family planning, family services, homes
Grant Types: general support
Geographic Distribution: focus on Harris County, TX

GIVING OFFICERS

Jenard M. Gross: trust
Marc J. Shapiro: trust *B* Houston TX 1947 *ED* Harvard Univ 1969; Stanford Univ 1971 *CURR EMPL* chmn, pres, ceo: TX Commerce Bank Houston
Henry J. N. Taub: trust
Henry J. N. Taub II: trust

APPLICATION INFORMATION

Initial Approach: The foundation reports it only makes contributions to preselected charitable organizations.

GRANTS ANALYSIS

Number of Grants: 6
Highest Grant: $350,000
Typical Range: $5,000 to $20,000
Disclosure Period: 1991

RECENT GRANTS

350,000 Jewish Geriatric Center, Houston, TX
161,836 Jewish Community Center, Houston, TX
70,000 Jewish Family Services, Houston, TX
25,000 DePelchin Children's Center, Houston, TX
10,000 Baylor College of Medicine, Houston, TX
10,000 Texas Children's Hospital, Houston, TX

Wolff Shoe Co. / Wolff Shoe Foundation

Sales: $34.0 million
Employees: 50
Headquarters: Fenton, MO
SIC Major Group: Leather & Leather Products and

Wholesale Trade—Nondurable
Goods

CONTACT
William Wolff
Manager
Wolff Shoe Foundation
1705 Larkin Wiliams Rd.
Fenton, MO 63026-2024
(314) 343-7770

FINANCIAL SUMMARY
Recent Giving: $61,790 (1989)
Assets: $704,872 (1989)
Gifts Received: $100,000 (1989)
Fiscal Note: In 1989, contributions were received from William and Elaine Wolff.
EIN: 43-1345719

CONTRIBUTIONS SUMMARY
Typical Recipients: • *Arts & Humanities:* community arts, music • *Education:* private education (precollege), religious education • *Health:* medical research, single-disease health associations • *Religion:* religious organizations, synagogues • *Social Services:* community service organizations
Grant Types: general support
Geographic Distribution: focus on MO and NY
Operating Locations: MO (Fenton)

CORP. OFFICERS
William Wolff: *CURR EMPL* pres: Wolff Shoe Co

GIVING OFFICERS
Elaine Wolff: dir
William Wolff: mgr, dir *CURR EMPL* pres: Wolff Shoe Co (see above)

APPLICATION INFORMATION
Initial Approach: Contributes only to preselected organizations.

GRANTS ANALYSIS
Number of Grants: 12
Highest Grant: $50,000
Typical Range: $50 to $650
Disclosure Period: 1989

RECENT GRANTS
50,000 Jewish Federation of St. Louis, St. Louis, MO
5,000 J.C.C.A., St. Louis, MO
2,500 Diabetes Foundation, St. Louis, MO
2,500 National Kidney Foundation, St. Louis, MO
650 St. Louis Country Day School, St. Louis, MO
280 Memorial Sloan-Kettering Cancer Center, New York, NY
260 B'nai Amoona Congregation, St. Louis, MO
200 St. Louis Symphony Orchestra, St. Louis, MO
100 American Society for Technion, New York, NY
100 Moolah Temple Shrine Circus, St. Louis, MO

Wolfson Family Foundation

CONTACT
Cecil Wolfson
Principal Manager
Wolfson Family Fdn.
3733 University Blvd. West, Ste. 110
Jacksonville, FL 32217
(904) 731-7942

FINANCIAL SUMMARY
Recent Giving: $119,850 (fiscal 1991); $1,137,250 (fiscal 1990); $132,450 (fiscal 1989)
Assets: $4,380,440 (fiscal year ending September 30, 1991); $4,320,999 (fiscal 1990); $4,573,581 (fiscal 1989)
Gifts Received: $200 (fiscal 1991)
EIN: 59-0995431

CONTRIBUTIONS SUMMARY
Donor(s): Louis E. Wolfson, the late Sam W. Wolfson, Saul Wolfson, the late Florence M. Wolfson, Cecil Wolfson
Typical Recipients: • *Civic & Public Affairs:* civil rights, ethnic/minority organizations • *Education:* colleges & universities • *Health:* health organizations, medical research, single-disease health associations • *Religion:* religious organizations • *Social Services:* aged, community service organizations, homes, united funds
Grant Types: capital and operating expenses
Geographic Distribution: focus on FL

GIVING OFFICERS
Joe I. Degen: trust
Sylvia W. Degen: trust
Edith W. Edwards: trust
Morris D. Edwards: trust
Robert O. Johnson: treas
Rabbi Sidney M. Lefkowitz: trust
M. C. Tomberlin: secy, dir
Cecil Wolfson: chmn, dir
Gary L. Wolfson: trust
Nathan Wolfson: trust
Stephen P. Wolfson: trust

APPLICATION INFORMATION
Initial Approach: Contributes only to preselected organizations.

GRANTS ANALYSIS
Number of Grants: 33
Highest Grant: $75,000
Typical Range: $100 to $2,500
Disclosure Period: fiscal year ending September 30, 1991

RECENT GRANTS
75,000 Jacksonville Jewish Federation, Jacksonville, FL
12,000 Anti-Defamation League, Jacksonville, FL
8,180 Memorial Sloan-Kettering Cancer Center, New York, NY
5,500 United Way, Jacksonville, FL
5,000 Children's Support Group
2,500 Jewish Community Alliance, Jacksonville, FL
2,500 Mosaic, Maitland, FL
1,500 National Conference of Christians and Jews
1,000 American Red Cross, New York, NY
1,000 Joslin Diabetes Center, Boston, MA

Wolfson Foundation, Louis E.

CONTACT
Paul Bishop
Manager
c/o Mintz, Levin, Cohn, Ferris, Glovsky, Popeo
One Financial Center
Boston, MA 02111
(617) 542-6000

FINANCIAL SUMMARY
Recent Giving: $900,000 (fiscal 1991); $900,000 (fiscal 1990); $900,000 (fiscal 1989)
Assets: $17,562,777 (fiscal year ending June 30, 1991); $17,919,720 (fiscal 1990); $17,645,758 (fiscal 1989)
EIN: 04-6053295

CONTRIBUTIONS SUMMARY
Donor(s): The foundation was established in 1951 by the late Louis E. Wolfson, M.D.
Typical Recipients: • *Education:* medical education, student aid
Grant Types: endowment and scholarship
Geographic Distribution: Cambridge, Medford, and Boston, MA

GIVING OFFICERS
Henry H. Banks: trust *B* Boston MA 1921 *ED* Harvard Univ AB 1942; Tufts Univ MD 1945 *NONPR AFFIL* mem: Am Academy Cerebral Palsy, Am Academy Orthopedic Surgeons, Am Med Assn, Intl Soc Orthopedic Surgery Traumatology, MA Med Soc, New England Surgical Soc; prof: Tufts Univ Sch Medicine; trust: Kennedy Meml Hosp
Allie Cohen: trust
James Cohen: trust
Albert F. Cullen, Jr.: trust
Daniel D. Federman: trust *B* New York NY 1928
John Penn: trust
John I. Sandson: trust *B* Jeanette PA 1927 *ED* Washington Univ MD 1953 *NONPR AFFIL* dean emeritus, prof: Boston Univ Med Sch; fellow: Am Rheumatism Assn; mem: Alzheimers Disease Related Disorders Assn, Am Assn Advancement Science, Am Med Assn, Am Soc Clinical Investigation, Assn Am Physicians, MA Med Soc, MA Soc Med Res; pres MA chapter: Arthritis Fdn; trust: Whitaker Health Sciences Fund

APPLICATION INFORMATION
Initial Approach:
Applications should be made in writing and include a detailed explaination of the proposal and any supporting materials necessary.
The foundation has no deadline for submitting proposals.
Applications are acknowledged within one month after the board receives them, and a decision is made within three months. Grants are generally paid in late summer and in Decemeber or January.
Restrictions on Giving: Grants are made only to tax-ex-

empt organizations and are not made to individuals.

OTHER THINGS TO KNOW
Publications: application guidelines

GRANTS ANALYSIS
Total Grants: $900,000
Number of Grants: 3
Highest Grant: $300,000
Disclosure Period: fiscal year ending June 30, 1991
Note: Recent grants are derived from a fiscal 1991 grants list.

RECENT GRANTS
300,000 Boston University School of Medicine, Boston, MA
300,000 Harvard Medical School, Cambridge, MA
300,000 Tufts University School of Medicine, Medford, MA

Wollenberg Foundation

CONTACT
Marc H. Monheimer
Trustee
Wollenberg Fdn.
235 Montgomery St., Ste. 2700
San Francisco, CA 94104
(415) 981-1300

FINANCIAL SUMMARY
Recent Giving: $1,356,000 (1991); $1,194,000 (1990); $992,000 (1989)
Assets: $31,442,579 (1991); $23,805,727 (1990); $29,932,484 (1989)
EIN: 94-6072264

CONTRIBUTIONS SUMMARY
Donor(s): The foundation was established in 1952 by the late H. L. Wollenberg.
Typical Recipients: • *Arts & Humanities:* museums/galleries, music • *Civic & Public Affairs:* civil rights, law & justice, professional & trade associations, public policy • *Education:* business education, colleges & universities, education funds, legal education, literacy, medical education, minority education, public education (precollege) • *Health:* hospices, single-disease health associations • *Religion:* religious organizations • *Science:* observatories & planetariums • *Social Services:* child welfare, community serv-

ice organizations, disabled, family planning, food/clothing distribution, recreation & athletics, united funds, youth organizations
Grant Types: endowment, general support, operating expenses, and project
Geographic Distribution: national

GIVING OFFICERS
Marc H. Monheimer: trust
J. Roger Wollenberg: trust *B* New York NY 1919 *ED* Univ CA Berkeley BA; Univ CA Berkeley LLB *NONPR AFFIL* mem: Am Bar Assn, Fed Communs Commn Bar Assn
Richard Peter Wollenberg: trust *B* Juneau AK 1915 *ED* Univ CA Berkeley BSME 1936; Harvard Univ MBA 1938 *CURR EMPL* chmn, pres, ceo: Longview Fibre Co *CORP AFFIL* dir: Crabbe-Huson, Pacific NW Capital Group; trust: Inst Paper & Science Tech *NONPR AFFIL* mem: WA St Roundtable; pres: Pacific Coast Assn Pulp & Paper Mfrs; trust: Reed Coll

APPLICATION INFORMATION
Initial Approach: The foundation does not publish an annual report or any giving guidelines.
Restrictions on Giving: The foundation supports preselected organizations and does not accept unsolicited requests for funds. It does not support sectarian organizations, religiously affiliated institutions, or individuals. The foundation does not make loans.

GRANTS ANALYSIS
Total Grants: $1,356,000
Number of Grants: 40
Highest Grant: $650,000
Typical Range: $6,000 to $55,000
Disclosure Period: 1991
Note: Recent grants are derived from a 1991 grants list.

RECENT GRANTS
650,000 Reed College, Portland, OR — new science building, Hewlitt Foundation Challenge, endowment, and annual fund
85,000 Harvard Business School Fund, Boston, MA
85,000 United Negro College Fund, Oakland, CA

75,000 Meharry Medical College, Nashville, TN
55,000 Independent Colleges of Washington, Seattle, WA
35,000 National Fund for Medical Education, Boston, MA
30,000 Longview Public Schools, Longview, WA — head start program at St. Helens Elementary School
30,000 Lower Columbia Head Start, Longview, MA — playground surfacing and storage
30,000 Oregon Museum of Science and Industry, Portland, OR
30,000 Washington Pulp and Paper Foundation, Seattle, WA

Woltman Foundation, B. M.

CONTACT
Robert H. McCanne
Acting President
B. M. Woltman Fdn.
2200 West Loop South, Ste. 810
Houston, TX 77027
(713) 623-6448

FINANCIAL SUMMARY
Recent Giving: $248,900 (1991); $233,100 (1990); $237,100 (1989)
Assets: $5,090,196 (1990); $5,092,320 (1989); $4,749,980 (1986)
Gifts Received: $1,252 (1990)
Fiscal Note: In 1990, contributions were received from Franks, Branum & Co., P.C.
EIN: 74-1402184

CONTRIBUTIONS SUMMARY
Donor(s): the late B. M. Woltman, Woltman Furniture Co.
Typical Recipients: • *Education:* religious education • *Religion:* churches, missionary activities, religious organizations • *Social Services:* community service organizations
Grant Types: scholarship
Geographic Distribution: limited to TX

GIVING OFFICERS
Rev. Donald G. Black: trust
Richard D. Chandler, Jr.: trust
Rev. Gerald B. Kieschnick: trust
Robert H. McCanne: mgr

William Carloss Morris, Jr.: secy, treas, trust *B* Galveston TX 1915 *ED* Rice Univ BA 1938; Univ TX LLB 1939 *CURR EMPL* atty: Morris Tinsley & Snowden *NONPR AFFIL* fellow: Am Bar Fdn, TX Bar Fdn; mem: Am Bar Assn, TX Bar Assn; pres: Star Hope Mission; trust: Baylor Coll Medicine
Rev. Louis Pabor: trust
Michael Richter: trust
W. J. Woltman: pres, trust

APPLICATION INFORMATION
Initial Approach: Application forms provided for scholarships. The deadline is before school term begins for scholarships.

GRANTS ANALYSIS
Number of Grants: 33
Highest Grant: $121,000
Typical Range: $1,000 to $4,500
Disclosure Period: 1990
Note: 1991 grants list not provided.

RECENT GRANTS
121,000 Lutheran High School Association, Houston, TX
32,700 Concordia Lutheran College, Austin, TX
5,400 Lutheran Outdoor Ministry, Austin, TX
4,000 Concordia Theological Seminary, Ft. Wayne, IN
3,000 Christ the King Lutheran Church, New Braunfels, TX
3,000 Concordia Theological Seminary, Ft. Wayne, IN
3,000 Concordia Theological Seminary, Ft. Wayne, IN
3,000 Emmanuel Lutheran Church, Odessa, TX
3,000 New Black Ministry Lutheran Church, Houston, TX
2,500 Concordia Lutheran College, Austin, TX

Wolverine World Wide, Inc. / Wolverine World Wide Foundation

Sales: $313.8 million
Employees: 4,747
Headquarters: Rockford, MI
SIC Major Group: Leather &
Leather Products

CONTACT

Robert Sedrowski
Director, Human Resources
Wolverine World Wide, Inc.
c/o NBD Bank N.A.
200 Ottawa NW
Grand Rapids, MI 49503
(616) 771-7340

FINANCIAL SUMMARY

Recent Giving: $73,435
(1991); $91,820 (1990);
$70,059 (1989)
Assets: $180,161 (1991);
$179,312 (1990); $190,041
(1989)
Gifts Received: $54,061
(1991); $60,000 (1990);
$50,100 (1989)
Fiscal Note: In 1991, contributions were received from Wolverine World Wide.
EIN: 38-6056939

CONTRIBUTIONS SUMMARY

Typical Recipients: • *Arts &
Humanities:* community arts, libraries, museums/galleries,
music, performing arts, theater
• *Education:* colleges & universities, private education (precollege), science/technology
education • *Health:* emergency/ambulance services, hospitals • *Religion:* religious organizations • *Social Services:*
community service organizations, disabled, recreation &
athletics, united funds, youth
organizations
Grant Types: general support
Geographic Distribution:
focus on MI
Operating Locations: AR
(Jonesboro), MI (Rockford),
NY (Malone, St. Johnsville),
PA (Hanover), PR (Aguadilla)
Note: List includes division locations.

CORP. OFFICERS

Geoffrey B. Bloom: *CURR
EMPL* pres, coo: Wolverine
World Wide
Thomas D. Gleason: *B* St.
Louis MO 1936 *ED* Holy Cross
Coll 1957; Harvard Univ Bus A

1959 *CURR EMPL* chmn, ceo:
Wolverine World Wide

GIVING OFFICERS

NBD Bank, N.A.: trust

APPLICATION INFORMATION

Initial Approach: Send a brief
letter of inquiry and a full proposal. Include a description of
organization, amount requested, purpose of funds
sought, and proof of tax-exempt status. There are no deadlines.
Restrictions on Giving: Does
not support individuals, religious organizations for sectarian
purposes, political or lobbying
groups, or organizations outside operating areas.

GRANTS ANALYSIS

Number of Grants: 98
Highest Grant: $7,500
Typical Range: $50 to $5,500
Disclosure Period: 1991

RECENT GRANTS

7,500	Grand Rapids Symphony, Grand Rapids, MI
5,000	North Kent Service Center
5,000	Public Museum Building Fund, Grand Rapids, MI
5,000	United Way
5,000	United Way
5,000	United Way
2,500	Kent County Emergency Medical Services
2,000	United Way, Columbus, OH
1,500	Rockford High School, Rockford, MI
1,000	United Way

Woman's Seamen's Friend Society of Connecticut

CONTACT

Henry Burdick, III
Executive Director
Woman's Seamen's Friend
Society of Connecticut
74 Forbes Ave.
New Haven, CT 06502
(203) 467-3887

FINANCIAL SUMMARY

Recent Giving: $207,049
(1991); $56,573 (1988); $9,400
(1987)
Assets: $3,214,113 (1991);
$2,879,391 (1988); $2,148,181
(1987)

EIN: 06-0655133

CONTRIBUTIONS SUMMARY

Donor(s): the late Betsy
Forbes Bradley
Typical Recipients: • *Arts &
Humanities:* history/historic
preservation • *Health:* health
organizations • *Religion:* religious organizations
Grant Types: project, research, and scholarship
Geographic Distribution: limited to CT

GIVING OFFICERS

Kitty Barclay: trust, vp
Jane Hooker: trust, secy
Nancy Johnstone: trust
Nancy Pugsley: trust, vp
Floyd Shumway: trust, treas
Carol Stancliff: trust
Dorothy Venter: trust, pres

APPLICATION INFORMATION

Initial Approach: Send letter
requesting application form.

OTHER THINGS TO KNOW

Provides scholarship to aid to
students majoring in marine
science.

GRANTS ANALYSIS

Number of Grants: 33
Highest Grant: $53,000
Typical Range: $1,250 to
$12,000
Disclosure Period: 1991

RECENT GRANTS

53,000	Schooner, New Haven, CT
21,800	Fort Nathan Hale Restoration Project, New Haven, CT
20,000	North American Maritime Ministry Association, New Haven, CT
18,500	Massachusetts Maritime, Boston, MA
13,910	Sound School, New Haven, CT
12,200	New Haven Colony Historical Society, New Haven, CT
10,153	Project Oceanology, New Haven, CT
10,000	American Red Cross, New York, NY
6,000	Seaman's Church Institute, New Haven, CT
3,800	Long Island Sound Keeper Fund, NY

Women's Project Foundation

CONTACT

Joyce K. Alexander
Women's Project Fdn.
c/o Ameritrust Co., N.A.
PO Box 5937
Cleveland, OH 44101
(216) 737-3165

FINANCIAL SUMMARY

Recent Giving: $336,000 (fiscal 1991); $316,000 (fiscal
1989)
Assets: $7,504,021 (fiscal year
ending November 30, 1991);
$7,061,842 (fiscal 1989)
EIN: 13-3417304

CONTRIBUTIONS SUMMARY

Typical Recipients: • *Arts &
Humanities:* arts institutes
• *Civic & Public Affairs:* philanthropic organizations, urban
& community affairs, women's
affairs • *Social Services:* family planning
Grant Types: general support

GIVING OFFICERS

Louise L. Gund: trust
Maximillian Walter Kempner:
trust *B* Berlin Germany 1929
ED Harvard Univ BA 1951;
Harvard Univ LLB 1954; Columbia Univ LLM 1957 *CURR
EMPL* couns: McDermott Will
& Emery *NONPR AFFIL*
chmn: Counc Library Resources; dean: VT Law Sch
South Royalton; fellow: Am
Bar Fdn; mem: Am Bar Assn,
Am Law Inst, Counc Foreign
Rels, New York City Bar Assn,
NY Bar Assn; mem adv comm:
Yale Program Nonprofit Orgs;
mem visitors comm: Columbia
Univ; pres: Harvard Law Sch
Assn NY City

APPLICATION INFORMATION

Initial Approach: Send brief
letter of inquiry describing program or project. There are no
deadlines.

GRANTS ANALYSIS

Number of Grants: 4
Highest Grant: $160,000
Typical Range: $60,000 to
$100,000
Disclosure Period: fiscal year
ending November 30, 1991

RECENT GRANTS

160,000	Ms. Foundation for Women, New York, NY — for incest re-

lated projects and violence in families
105,000 Funding Exchange, New York, NY — for funding documentaries
60,000 Women's Foundation, San Francisco, CA
11,000 Women's Community Fund, Cleveland, OH — for Renewal Program

Wood Charitable Trust, W. P.

CONTACT
Steve Garner
Manager
W. P. Wood Charitable Trust
PO Box 127
Shawnee, OK 74802
(405) 273-2880

FINANCIAL SUMMARY
Recent Giving: $323,100 (1991); $263,225 (1990); $229,500 (1989)
Assets: $2,117,166 (1991); $2,292,979 (1990); $2,202,631 (1989)
EIN: 73-6152038

CONTRIBUTIONS SUMMARY
Typical Recipients: • *Arts & Humanities:* community arts, history/historic preservation • *Civic & Public Affairs:* municipalities • *Education:* colleges & universities, religious education • *Religion:* churches, religious organizations • *Social Services:* child welfare, community service organizations, drugs & alcohol, family planning, family services, united funds, youth organizations
Grant Types: capital, operating expenses, research, and scholarship
Geographic Distribution: focus on OK

GIVING OFFICERS
Steve Garner: mgr, trust
Gerald D. McGehee: trust
Lindsay Peters: trust

APPLICATION INFORMATION
Initial Approach: Send cover letter and full proposal. There are no deadlines.
Restrictions on Giving: Does not support individuals.

GRANTS ANALYSIS
Number of Grants: 16
Highest Grant: $72,000
Typical Range: $3,000 to $25,000
Disclosure Period: 1991

RECENT GRANTS
72,000 St. Gregory's Abbey, Shawnee, OK
50,000 YMCA, Shawnee, OK
50,000 Youth and Family Center, Shawnee, OK
25,000 South Central Sheltered Workshop, Shawnee, OK
25,000 United Way, Broken Bow, OK
23,400 Gateway to Drug Prevention, Shawnee, OK
17,200 Oklahoma Baptist University, Shawnee, OK
17,200 Pott County Telecom Corporation, Shawnee, OK
10,000 Central Oklahoma Economic Development District, Shawnee, OK
6,500 Pott County Historical Society, Shawnee, OK

Wood-Claeyssens Foundation

CONTACT
James Hurley, Jr.
Secretary
Wood-Claeyssens Fdn.
PO Box 99
Santa Barbara, CA 93102-0099
(805) 682-4775

FINANCIAL SUMMARY
Recent Giving: $564,000 (fiscal 1992); $572,700 (fiscal 1991); $465,500 (fiscal 1990)
Assets: $8,566,487 (fiscal year ending March 31, 1992); $8,220,431 (fiscal 1991); $7,715,245 (fiscal 1990)
Gifts Received: $5,000 (fiscal 1992)
EIN: 95-3514017

CONTRIBUTIONS SUMMARY
Donor(s): Ailene B. Claeyssens, Pierre P. Claeyssens
Typical Recipients: • *Arts & Humanities:* community arts, music, public broadcasting • *Health:* health organizations, hospitals, medical research, single-disease health associations • *Social Services:* community service organizations, family planning, family services, shelters/homelessness, united funds, youth organizations
Grant Types: general support
Geographic Distribution: focus on CA

GIVING OFFICERS
Ailene B. Claeyssens: pres, dir
Pierre P. Claeyssens: 1st vp, dir
Charles C. Gray: treas
James H. Hurley, Jr.: secy
Cynthia S. Wood: 2nd vp, dir

APPLICATION INFORMATION
Initial Approach: Send brief letter of inquiry describing program or project. Deadline is August 31.
Restrictions on Giving: Does not support individuals.

GRANTS ANALYSIS
Number of Grants: 70
Highest Grant: $30,000
Typical Range: $1,000 to $20,000
Disclosure Period: fiscal year ending March 31, 1992

RECENT GRANTS
30,000 Rehabilitation Institute, Santa Barbara, CA
20,000 Alzheimer's Disease and Related Disorders Association, Santa Barbara, CA
20,000 American Heart Association, Philadelphia, PA
20,000 Cancer Foundation of Santa Barbara, Santa Barbara, CA
10,000 CALM
10,000 Casa Serena
10,000 Community Arts Music Association, Santa Barbara, CA
10,000 Direct Relief International
10,000 Family Service Agency, Santa Barbara, CA
10,000 Goleta Valley Community Hospital

Wood Foundation, Lester G.

CONTACT
Patricia W. Baer
Secretary-Treasurer
Lester G. Wood Fdn.
3290 Vista Rd.
Green Bay, WI 54301-2632
(414) 336-1222

FINANCIAL SUMMARY
Recent Giving: $230,675 (1990); $112,650 (1989); $154,965 (1988)
Assets: $3,896,049 (1989); $3,698,917 (1988)
EIN: 39-6055567

CONTRIBUTIONS SUMMARY
Donor(s): members of the Baer and Lea families
Typical Recipients: • *Arts & Humanities:* arts festivals, arts institutes, community arts, music • *Education:* colleges & universities, education funds, medical education • *Social Services:* community service organizations, united funds, youth organizations
Grant Types: general support
Geographic Distribution: focus on IL and WI

GIVING OFFICERS
F.E. Baer: vp, dir
Patricia W. Baer: secy, treas, dir
L. Bates Lea: pres, dir
Marcia W. Lea: trust

APPLICATION INFORMATION
Initial Approach: Send brief letter describing program. There are no deadlines.
Restrictions on Giving: Does not support individuals.

GRANTS ANALYSIS
Number of Grants: 35
Highest Grant: $50,000
Typical Range: $300 to $5,000
Disclosure Period: 1989

RECENT GRANTS
50,000 University of Wisconsin at Green Bay Performing Arts Center, Green Bay, WI
5,000 Art Institute of Chicago, Chicago, IL
5,000 Chicago Symphony Orchestra, Chicago, IL
5,000 Salvation Army, Green Bay, WI

5,000 United Charities of Chicago, Chicago, IL

3,000 Bellin College of Nursing, Green Bay, WI

3,000 Heritage Hill Foundation, Green Bay, WI

3,000 N. W. T. C. Scholarship Fund, Green Bay, WI

3,000 Ravinia Festival Association, Highland Park, IL

3,000 YWCA, Green Bay, WI

Wood Foundation of Chambersburg, PA

CONTACT
C.O. Woods III
Trustee
Wood Fdn of Chambersburg, PA
273 Lincoln Way East
Chambersburg, PA 17201
(717) 267-3174

FINANCIAL SUMMARY
Recent Giving: $271,742 (fiscal 1991)
Assets: $6,773,734 (fiscal year ending May 31, 1991)
EIN: 25-1607838

CONTRIBUTIONS SUMMARY
Donor(s): Max Zimmer
Typical Recipients: • *Arts & Humanities:* museums/galleries • *Civic & Public Affairs:* environmental affairs, municipalities • *Education:* colleges & universities, private education (precollege) • *Health:* hospitals • *Social Services:* community service organizations
Grant Types: general support
Geographic Distribution: giving primarily in Chambersburg and Franklin counties, Pennsylvania

GIVING OFFICERS
Nathan Krems: secy
Emilie W. Myers: trust
C.O. Wood III: trust
Davis S. Wood: trust
Miriam M. Wood: trust
Max Zimmer: pres

APPLICATION INFORMATION
Initial Approach: Submit proposal. There are no deadlines.
Initial Approach: Contributes only to preselected organizations. Applications not accepted.

Restrictions on Giving: Does not provide grants to individuals.

GRANTS ANALYSIS
Number of Grants: 61
Highest Grant: $50,000
Typical Range: $1,000 to $25,000
Disclosure Period: fiscal year ending May 31, 1991

RECENT GRANTS
50,000 Henry Francis du Pont Winterthur Museum, Wilmington, DE

25,000 Chambersburg Hospital Health Services, Chambersburg, PA

25,000 Shippensburg University Foundation, Shippensburg, PA

20,000 Salvation Army, Chambersburg, PA

10,000 C.R.O.S.S., Shippensburg, VA — special campaign

10,000 Menno Haven, Chambersburg, PA

10,000 Mercersburg Academy, Mercersburg, PA

7,500 Wellesley College Office of Resources, Wellesley, MA

7,500 Wellesley College Office of Resources, Wellesley, MA

5,881 Falling Spring Greenway, Chambersburg, PA — preservation of Falling Spring Creek

Woodard Family Foundation

CONTACT
Woodard Family Fdn.
1580 Valley River Dr., Ste. 110
Eugenee Grove, OR 97440
(503) 343-9402

FINANCIAL SUMMARY
Recent Giving: $96,236 (fiscal 1991); $199,580 (fiscal 1990); $89,892 (fiscal 1989)
Assets: $2,738,223 (fiscal year ending June 30, 1990); $2,391,985 (fiscal 1989)
EIN: 93-6026550

CONTRIBUTIONS SUMMARY
Typical Recipients: • *Arts & Humanities:* museums/galleries • *Civic & Public Affairs:* municipalities • *Education:* colleges & universities, private education (precollege), private education (precollege) • *Religion:* churches • *Social Services:* community service organizations, united funds, youth organizations
Grant Types: general support
Geographic Distribution: focus on OR

GIVING OFFICERS
Carlton Woodard: pres
Dutee Woodard: vp
Kim Woodard: secy, treas

APPLICATION INFORMATION
Initial Approach: Send brief letter describing program. There are no deadlines.

GRANTS ANALYSIS
Number of Grants: 37
Highest Grant: $100,000
Typical Range: $100 to $2,500
Disclosure Period: fiscal year ending June 30, 1990

RECENT GRANTS
100,000 Oregon Community Foundation, Portland, OR

30,000 National Environmental Education Development, Portland, OR

20,000 Lewis and Clark College, Portland, OR

7,600 Portland Children's Museum, Portland, OR

5,474 Boy Scouts of America, Eugene, OR

4,000 Oregon Independent Colleges Foundation, Portland, OR

2,750 United Way, Eugene, OR

2,000 Oregon Aviation Museum, Cottage Grove, OR

1,025 First Presbyterian Church, Cottage Grove, OR

1,000 Menlo School, Atherton, CA

Woodland Foundation

CONTACT
Winthrop Rutherfurd, Jr.
Secretary
Woodland Fdn.
1155 Avenue of the Americas
New York, NY 10036
(212) 819-8200

FINANCIAL SUMMARY
Recent Giving: $170,000 (1991); $148,500 (1990); $185,500 (1989)
Assets: $4,333,176 (1991); $3,821,977 (1990); $3,826,521 (1989)
EIN: 13-6018244

CONTRIBUTIONS SUMMARY
Donor(s): William Durant Campbell
Typical Recipients: • *Civic & Public Affairs:* zoos/botanical gardens • *Education:* colleges & universities, minority education, private education (precollege) • *Health:* hospitals • *Religion:* churches • *Social Services:* child welfare, community service organizations, disabled, family planning, food/clothing distribution, united funds, youth organizations
Grant Types: capital, endowment, and general support

GIVING OFFICERS
Jeremiah M. Bogert: vp, trust
Margot C. Bogert: pres, trust
Milicient D. Bogert: trust
Harvey G. Burney: treas, trust
William Durant Campbell: trust
George W. Knight: trust
Frank J. Nulty: trust
Winthrop Rutherfurd, Jr.: trust

APPLICATION INFORMATION
Initial Approach: Contributes only to preselected organizations.
Restrictions on Giving: Does not support individuals.

GRANTS ANALYSIS
Number of Grants: 39
Highest Grant: $25,000
Typical Range: $1,000 to $10,000
Disclosure Period: 1991

RECENT GRANTS
25,000 Sarah Lawrence College, Bronxville, NY

15,000 Whiby School
10,000 Planned Parenthood Federation of America
10,000 Salvation Army
10,000 US Foundation for International Scouting
6,000 Sarah Lawrence College, Bronxville, NY
5,000 International Center for the Disabled, New York, NY
5,000 Project Open Hand, San Francisco, CA
5,000 Skin Disease Society
5,000 Wilton Meals on Wheels

Woodner Family Collection, Ian

CONTACT
Jennifer Jones
Curator
Ian Woodner Family Collection
745 Fifth Ave.
New York, NY 10151
(212) 644-0630

FINANCIAL SUMMARY
Recent Giving: $243,688 (fiscal 1991); $203,912 (fiscal 1990); $262,339 (fiscal 1989)
Assets: $43,891,216 (fiscal year ending June 30, 1991); $43,138,410 (fiscal 1990); $37,494,674 (fiscal 1989)
Gifts Received: $8,102,113 (fiscal 1990); $7,717,000 (fiscal 1989)
EIN: 13-3317928

CONTRIBUTIONS SUMMARY
Donor(s): The foundation was incorporated in 1986 by the late Ian Woodner and the Shipley Corp.
Typical Recipients: • *Education:* arts education, colleges & universities • *International:* foreign educational institutions
Grant Types: research
Geographic Distribution: focus on Washington, DC, and New York, NY

GIVING OFFICERS
Barry H. Dimson: ceo
Andrea Woodner: pres, secy, treas
Dian Woodner: pres, secy, treas

APPLICATION INFORMATION
Initial Approach:
The foundation requests applications be made in writing.
The foundation has no deadline for submitting proposals.
Restrictions on Giving: The foundation does not make grants to individuals.

GRANTS ANALYSIS
Total Grants: $243,688
Number of Grants: 16
Highest Grant: $72,440
Typical Range: $1,000 to $25,000
Disclosure Period: fiscal year ending June 30, 1991
Note: Recent grants are derived from a fiscal 1991 grants list.

RECENT GRANTS
72,440 Howard University, Washington, DC
46,750 Howard University, Washington, DC
40,000 Phillips Collection, Washington, DC
25,491 Royal Academy
17,187 Renata Surbone
12,600 Birke Artist Patron
6,900 British Museum
5,500 Museum of Modern Art, New York, NY
5,000 Holocaust Museum, Washington, DC
5,000 Triange Art School

Woodruff Foundation, Robert W.

CONTACT
Charles H. McTier
President
Robert W. Woodruff Foundation
50 Hurt Plaza, Ste. 1200
Atlanta, GA 30303
(404) 522-6755

FINANCIAL SUMMARY
Recent Giving: $53,355,206 (1992); $33,372,418 (1991); $26,448,375 (1990)
Assets: $1,529,005,324 (1992); $1,495,163,067 (1991); $995,893,546 (1990)
Gifts Received: $47,736,224 (1990); $192,765,504 (1989); $111,540,312 (1988)
Fiscal Note: In 1990, the foundation received $47,736,224 from the Estate of Robert W. Woodruff.
EIN: 58-1695425

CONTRIBUTIONS SUMMARY
Donor(s): The foundation was established in 1937 by the late Robert W. Woodruff. Mr. Woodruff became president of the Coca-Cola Company in the 1920s and was instrumental in building the soft drink company into an international business. Mr. Woodruff was generally recognized as one of America's leading philanthropists. He was a major benefactor of Emory University in Atlanta. Mr. Woodruff had no children. When he died in 1985, he left almost his entire estate to the foundation.
Typical Recipients: • *Arts & Humanities:* arts centers, community arts, history/historic preservation, museums/galleries, public broadcasting • *Civic & Public Affairs:* environmental affairs, nonprofit management • *Education:* colleges & universities, medical education • *Health:* outpatient health care delivery • *Social Services:* youth organizations
Grant Types: capital and project
Geographic Distribution: emphasis on Georgia, specifically the metropolitan Atlanta area

GIVING OFFICERS
Ivan Allen, Jr.: trust *B* Atlanta GA 1911 *ED* GA Inst Tech 1933 *CURR EMPL* chmn: Ivan Allen Co *CORP AFFIL* dir: Equitable Life Assurance Soc *NONPR AFFIL* area pres, mem natl exec bd: Boy Scouts Am; mem: Atlanta Chamber Commerce, Natl Stationery Off Equipment Assn; trust: GA Tech Fdn
P. Russell Hardin: secy, treas *B* Charlotte NC 1931 *ED* Duke Univ BA 1952; Duke Univ JD 1954 *CORP AFFIL* dir: Mutual Benefit Life Ins Co, Shearson Daily Dividend, Summit Bankcorp *NONPR AFFIL* dir: Italy Fund
Joseph West Jones: chmn, trust *B* Georgetown DE 1912 *ED* Beacom Coll BA 1932 *CURR EMPL* sr vp, asst treas, dir: Coca-Cola Co *CORP AFFIL* dir: Great Southern Enterprises *NONPR AFFIL* gov: Woodward Academy
Wilton Looney: trust
Charles H. McTier: pres
James Malcolm Sibley: vchmn, trust *B* Atlanta GA 1919 *ED* Princeton Univ AB 1941 *CURR EMPL* ptnr: King & Spalding *CORP AFFIL* chmn exec comm, dir: Trust Co GA; dir: Coca-Cola Co, GA US Corp, John H Harland Co, Rock-Tenn Co, Summit Indus, SunTrust Banks, Trust Company Bank; dir emeritus: Life Ins Co GA; trust: A G Rhodes Home *NONPR AFFIL* mem: Am Bar Assn, Am Bar Fdn, Am Coll Probate Couns, Am Law Inst, Atlanta Bar Assn, GA Bar Assn; mem bd dirs: Callaway Gardens Fdn; trust: Emory Univ, A G Rhodes Home
James Bryan Williams: trust *B* Sewanee TN 1933 *ED* Emory Univ 1955 *CURR EMPL* chmn, ceo: SunTrust Banks *CORP AFFIL* dir: Boral Indus, Coca-Cola Co, GA Intl Life Ins Co, GA Pacific Corp, Genuine Parts Co, Rollins Inc, RPC Energy Svcs, Sonat; pres, dir: Trust Co Bank *NONPR AFFIL* chmn, trust: Henrietta Egleston Hosp Children; mem: Am Bankers Assn; mem bd visitors: Berry Coll; mem, dir: Reserve City Bankers Assn; trust: Emory Univ, Robert W Woodruff Health Sciences Ctr, Westminster Schs, Woodruff Med Ctr

APPLICATION INFORMATION
Initial Approach:
Organizations seeking support should submit a letter to the foundation. No specific application form is required.
The letter should include a descriptive statement about the program, proof of the organization's tax-exempt status, basic information supporting the request, budget with sources of support, and a list of officers and governing board.
Applications may be submitted any time; however, the deadlines for consideration at board meetings held in April and November, are February 1 and September 1, respectively.
If the foundation is interested in the program, the applicant will be contacted and asked to submit a full proposal.
Restrictions on Giving: The foundation does not make grants for general operating expenses or to individuals.

OTHER THINGS TO KNOW
The foundation shares a common administrative arrangement with the Lettie Pate Evans Foundation, the Lettie

Pate Whitehead Foundation, and the Joseph B. Whitehead Foundation.

GRANTS ANALYSIS
Total Grants: $53,355,206
Number of Grants: 42
Highest Grant: $5,000,000
Typical Range: $25,000 to $2,000,000
Disclosure Period: 1992
Note: Recent grants are derived from a 1990 grants list.

RECENT GRANTS
7,023,500 Fernbank, Atlanta, GA — toward $30 million campaign to build the Fernbank Museum of Natural History

5,000,000 Atlanta Historical Society, Atlanta, GA — $15 million capital campaign for the Museum of Atlanta History

5,000,000 Emory University, Atlanta, GA — for $00 million capital campaign

3,000,000 Oglethorpe University, Atlanta, GA — renovation and expansion of main library to be named for the late Dr. Philip C. Weltner, former president of the University

1,650,000 Georgia Tech Foundation, Atlanta, GA — $3.3 million cost of property at 575 14th Street to house the Institute of Paper Science and Technology

1,000,000 Buffalo Bill Historical Center, Cody, WY — to complete funding of the Museum's $6.4 million capital campaign

1,000,000 Ichauway, Inc., Newton, GA — for establishment of Joseph W. Jones Ecological Research Center and general operating expenses

500,000 Bradley Center, Columbus, GA — $4.9 million capital campaign to build an adolescent residential treatment center and a multi-purpose activity center

500,000 Emory University, Atlanta, GA —$3 million capital campaign for The Aquinas Center

500,000 Georgia Research Alliance, Atlanta, GA — initial operating support for a new organization designed to leverage the combined research activity of Georgia's universities into broad-based economic development

---

Woods Charitable Fund

CONTACT
Jean Rudd
Executive Director
Woods Charitable Fund
3 First National Plz.
Ste. 2010
Chicago, IL 60602
(312) 782-2698
Note: Illinois applicants may also contact Ken Rolling at the address above. Nebraska applicants should direct inquiries to Pam Baker, P.O. Box 81309, Lincoln, NE 68501 ph. (402) 474-0707.

FINANCIAL SUMMARY
Recent Giving: $2,600,000 (1993 est.); $2,600,000 (1992 approx.); $2,506,644 (1991)
Assets: $52,000,000 (1992 est.); $33,500,000 (1991 est.); $32,373,521 (1990); $31,543,537 (1989)
EIN: 47-6032847

CONTRIBUTIONS SUMMARY
Donor(s): Frank H. Woods, his wife, Nelle Cochrane Woods, and their three sons founded the Woods Charitable Fund in Nebraska in 1941. The fund received substantial support in 1952 from Frank H. Woods before his death later that year. In 1955, the fund received one-third of the net residuary estate of Nelle C. Woods. Over the years, the family-owned Sahara Coal Company has contributed to the fund's assets. Although the five founders are now deceased, other family members continue to serve as officers and trustees of the fund.
Typical Recipients: • *Arts & Humanities:* arts associations, arts centers, community arts, dance, history/historic preservation, museums/galleries, music, opera, performing arts, theater • *Civic & Public Affairs:* better government, civil rights, economic development, ethnic/minority organizations, housing, law & justice, municipalities, nonprofit management, public policy, rural affairs, urban & community affairs, women's affairs • *Education:* arts education, colleges & universities, education administration, education associations, preschool education, public education (precollege) • *Social Services:* aged, child welfare, community centers, community service organizations, counseling, delinquency & crime, disabled, domestic violence, drugs & alcohol, family planning, family services, united funds, youth organizations
Grant Types: general support, multiyear/continuing support, operating expenses, project, and seed money
Geographic Distribution: focus on metropolitan Lincoln, NE, and Chicago, IL

GIVING OFFICERS
Pam Baker: dir (Lincoln Off)
Sydney Beane: trust
Mary Decker: trust
Marie Fischer: trust
George Kelm: vp, trust *B* Chicago IL 1928 *ED* Northwestern Univ BS 1951; Northwestern Univ JD 1954 *CURR EMPL* pres, dir: Sahara Coal Co *CORP AFFIL* dir: AM Intl, Lincoln Telecommunications Corp, Lincoln Telephone & Telegraph Co, Rolf Jensen & Assocs
Lucia Woods Lindley: pres, trust
Ken Rolling: assoc dir
Jean Rudd: exec dir
Charles N. Wheatley: treas, trust
Thomas C. Woods III: vp, trust *CURR EMPL* chmn: Lincoln Telecommunications Co *CORP AFFIL* dir: Lincoln Tel & Tel Co, Sahara Coal Co

APPLICATION INFORMATION
Initial Approach:
There is no standard application form. Applicants should contact the fund for a copy of guidelines, procedures, and timetables. Applicants should then send a two-page summary request and budget, or contact the fund by telephone to determine whether the project falls within funding guidelines.
If the fund requests a full proposal, an organization must provide a cover letter containing the request for funding, a one- to two-page summary of the purpose for the request, and a complete proposal of not more than ten pages.
The proposal may be in any format, but must specify the project's purpose, strategies, timeframes, and needs to be addressed. It may include workplans, and it must include a brief description of the organization's history, a summary of current activities, and a listing of staff members. The fund also requires a copy of an IRS determination letter of tax-exempt status; listing of board members, with addresses and phone numbers; audited financial statement for the last fiscal year; income and expense budgets for the current fiscal year and for the year for which support is sought; organization and project budgets, listing of actual commitments toward projected budget; itemization of other sources of support; and an IRS Form 990 if annual budget exceeds $500,000.
Organizations must submit applications between March 1 and April 15 for the June meeting, between June 1 and July 15 for the September meeting, and between September 1 and October 15 for the December board meeting.
Chicago arts organizations should apply between March 1 and April 15.
Proposals arriving well before a given deadline are given more careful review. An application not clearly within the fund's priorities, but not clearly ineligible, will be reviewed by local board members.
Restrictions on Giving: The fund occasionally reviews proposals from outside of Lincoln and Chicago if the proposed activities have statewide impact or are designed for wide application.
Both the Lincoln and Chicago programs do not make grants for individual needs, endowments, scholarships, fellowships, medical or scientific research, fund-raising benefits, program advertising, or religious programs. They also do not fund national health, welfare, educational, or cultural organizations or their state or local affiliates.
Additionally, the Lincoln grant program does not fund capital

projects in health care institutions, or college or university proposals that do not directly involve faculty or students in applied projects that benefit the region.

The Chicago grant program does not fund clinics, residential care, counseling programs, or recreational programs. It also does not support social services except for special projects having a clear public policy strategy or for projects expressly planned for wide duplication. The fund does not support capital projects or campaigns or housing or economic development initiatives, with the exception of policy initiatives.

Buildings and equipment acquisition, expansion, and renovation projects are low priorities for the fund. They are only considered at the final board meeting each year. Applicants must have a written ruling from the IRS that they are classified as 509(a)(1), (2), or (3). The fund occasionally considers proposals from private 501(c)(3) operating foundations; in unusual cases, it may consider fiscal agent and expenditure responsibility grants.

OTHER THINGS TO KNOW

Organizations receiving grants must present written reports informing the board of the use of funds in relation to the original proposal objectives, and the results. Some grantees are asked to participate in a post-grant evaluation to compare program accomplishments with proposed objectives. The foundation offers proposal writing assistance.
Publications: annual report and fund guidelines

GRANTS ANALYSIS
Total Grants: $2,506,644
Number of Grants: 174
Highest Grant: $100,000
Typical Range: $5,000 to $25,000
Disclosure Period: 1991
Note: Average grant figure excludes the two highest grants totaling $200,000. Recent grants are derived from a 1991 annual report.

RECENT GRANTS
100,000 Community Renewal Society — fiscal agent for Parental Involvement

Demonstration Project; public/private funding to improve welfare-to-work policy for fathers on General Assistance
100,000 University of Nebraska Foundation, Lincoln, NE — sixth payment of ten-year $1,000,000 grant for land acquisition, building construction costs and landscaping costs for Lied Performing Arts Center
50,000 Centers for New Horizons — first payment of three-year $130,000 grant for management restructuring
50,000 Designs for Change, Chicago, IL — second payment of $150,000 renewal grant for SCHOOLWATCH, a program of parent organizing, advocacy and technical assistance to local school counils, community groups and parents c
50,000 Legal Assistance Foundation of Chicago, Chicago, IL — first payment of two-year $100,000 renewal grant restricted to costs of staff attorney to specialize in welfare-to-work policy issues in Illinois
50,000 Voices for Illinois Children, IL — grant matching new and increased donors to agency engaged in policy, research and advocacy work on issues affecting the welfare of Illinois' children
45,000 Chicago Area Project, Chicago, IL — Women for Economic Security, a welfare recipient-based initiative to train welfare-to-work reform advocates and spearhead a campaign to improve welfare and employment in Illinois
40,000 Chicago Panel on Public School Policy and Finance, Chicago, IL — second payment of

three-year $120,000 support for Monitoring School Reform in Chicago project
39,000 Day Care Action Council of Illinois, Chicago, IL — first payment to improve day care policies and child care provisions in Illinois Department of Public Aid system
35,000 Chicago Commons Association — renewal support

Woods Foundation, James H.

CONTACT
James H. Woods, Jr.
Trustee
James H. Woods Fdn.
1228 South Mason Rd.
St. Louis, MO 63131
(314) 436-9048

FINANCIAL SUMMARY
Recent Giving: $439,093 (fiscal 1990); $380,798 (fiscal 1989); $389,500 (fiscal 1988)
Assets: $8,989,328 (fiscal year ending November 30, 1990); $8,699,180 (fiscal 1989); $8,050,140 (fiscal 1988)
EIN: 43-6024866

CONTRIBUTIONS SUMMARY
Donor(s): the late James H. Woods
Typical Recipients: • *Arts & Humanities:* history/historic preservation • *Civic & Public Affairs:* environmental affairs, national security • *Education:* colleges & universities, private education (precollege). • *Religion:* churches, religious organizations • *Social Services:* child welfare, community service organizations, recreation & athletics, united funds, youth organizations
Grant Types: capital, endowment, general support, operating expenses, scholarship, and seed money
Geographic Distribution: focus on the Midwestern states

GIVING OFFICERS
Boatmen's Trust Company: trust

APPLICATION INFORMATION
Initial Approach: Send brief letter of inquiry describing pro-

gram or project. There are no deadlines.

GRANTS ANALYSIS
Number of Grants: 35
Highest Grant: $60,000
Typical Range: $1,000 to $10,000
Disclosure Period: fiscal year ending November 30, 1990

RECENT GRANTS
60,000 Camping and Education Foundation, Cincinnati, OH
25,000 Church of Jesus Christ Latter Day Saints, Salt Lake City, UT
25,000 Winchester Club of America
18,470 Buffalo Bill Memorial Association, Cody, WY
15,000 St. Barnabas on the Desert, Scottsdale, AZ
10,000 American Defense Institute, Washington, DC
10,000 American Youth Foundation, St. Louis, MO
10,000 Central Christian Counseling
10,000 Rocky Mountain Elk Foundation
10,000 St. Barnabas on the Desert, Scottsdale, AZ

Woods-Greer Foundation

CONTACT
Peter T. Cooper
Secretary-Treasurer
Woods-Greer Fdn.
c/o American National Bank and Trust Co., Trust Dept.
736 Market St.
Chattanooga, TN 37401
(615) 757-3203

FINANCIAL SUMMARY
Recent Giving: $96,500 (fiscal 1991); $63,000 (fiscal 1990); $81,000 (fiscal 1989)
Assets: $2,043,013 (fiscal year ending May 31, 1991); $1,954,555 (fiscal 1990); $1,822,609 (fiscal 1989)
EIN: 62-6126272

CONTRIBUTIONS SUMMARY
Donor(s): the late C. Cecil Woods
Typical Recipients: • *Arts & Humanities:* community arts, music • *Education:* colleges & universities, private education

(precollege), religious education • *Religion:* churches, religious organizations • *Social Services:* community service organizations
Grant Types: capital, multiyear/continuing support, operating expenses, and scholarship
Geographic Distribution: focus on the southeastern U.S.

GIVING OFFICERS
William Gardner Brown: trust *B* Chicago IL 1942 *ED* Princeton Univ BA 1964; Harvard Univ LLB 1967 *CURR EMPL* ptnr: Bell Boyd & Lloyd *CORP AFFIL* dir: Knowsledge Data Sys, LaSalle Lake View Bank, Medicus Sys Corp, LE Myers Co Group *NONPR AFFIL* dir: Brain Res Fdn; mem: Am Bar Assn, Union Internationale des Avocates; trust: Better Govt Assn, Chicago Orchestral Assn, Ravinia Festival Assn
Peter T. Cooper: secy, treas
Margaret C. Woods Denkler: trust
Ellen Woods Polansky: trust
Kathleen Woods Van Devender: trust
Carolyn Taylor Woods: trust
Marie Cartinhour Woods: vchmn
Very Rev C. Cecil Woods, Jr.: chmn

APPLICATION INFORMATION
Initial Approach: Send brief letter describing program. There are no deadlines.
Restrictions on Giving: Does not support individuals.

GRANTS ANALYSIS
Number of Grants: 18
Highest Grant: $30,000
Typical Range: $1,000 to $10,000
Disclosure Period: fiscal year ending May 31, 1991

RECENT GRANTS
30,000 Prairie Creek Community School, Northfield, MN
10,000 University of the South, Sewanee, TN — science building
7,000 Allied Arts Fund of Greater Chattanooga, Chattanooga, TN
5,000 Association for Religion and Intelligent Life, New Rochelle, NY
5,000 Churches Center for Theology and Public Policy, Washington, DC
5,000 Presiding Bishop's Fund for World Relief
5,000 Siskin Memorial Foundation, Chattanooga, TN
5,000 St. Agnes School, Alexandria, VA
5,000 St. Andrews, Sewanee, TN
5,000 Virginia Theological Seminary, Alexandria, VA

Woodson Foundation, Aytchmonde

CONTACT
San W. Orr, Jr.
Treasurer
Aytchmonde Woodson Fdn.
PO Box 65
Wausau, WI 54402-0065
(714) 845-9201

FINANCIAL SUMMARY
Recent Giving: $233,919 (fiscal 1990); $243,526 (fiscal 1989)
Assets: $8,835,152 (fiscal year ending June 30, 1990); $8,654,381 (fiscal 1989)
EIN: 39-1017853

CONTRIBUTIONS SUMMARY
Donor(s): members of the Woodson family
Typical Recipients: • *Arts & Humanities:* museums/galleries
Grant Types: general support and operating expenses
Geographic Distribution: focus on Wausau, WI

GIVING OFFICERS
John M. Coates: dir
Frederick W. Fisher: dir
Alice Woodson Forester: vp, dir
John E. Forester: secy, dir *B* Wauwatosa WI 1913 *ED* Univ WI 1934-1936 *CURR EMPL* pres, dir: Yawkey Lumber Co *CORP AFFIL* dir: Marathon Electric Mfg Corp, Wausau Paper Mills Co; pres, dir: Yawkey Lumber Co; vp, treas, dir: Woodson Fiduciary Corp *NONPR AFFIL* dir: Woodson (Leigh Yawkey) Art Mus
San Watterson Orr, Jr.: treas, dir *B* Madison WI 1941 *ED* Univ WI BBA 1963; Univ WI JD 1966 *CURR EMPL* secy, treas, dir: Yawkey Lumber Co *CORP AFFIL* chmn: Mosinee Paper Corp, Wausau Paper Mills Co; chmn, secy: Marathon Electric Mfg Corp; dir: M&I First Am Natl Bank, M&I Marshall & Illsey Bank, Wausau Health Sys, Wausau Ins Cos; pres, dir: ARY Inc, Forewood Inc, Woodson Fiduciary Corp; secy, treas, dir: Yawkey Lumber Co; vp, secy, treas, dir: Marathon Improvement Co *NONPR AFFIL* dir: Competitive WI, Woodson (Leigh Yawkey) Art Mus, YMCA Wausau Fdn; mem: Am Bar Assn, Am Law Inst, Univ WI Alumni Assn, WI Bar Assn; mem bd visitors: Univ WI Sch Bus Admin
Lyman J. Spire: dir
Nancy Woodson Spire: pres, dir

APPLICATION INFORMATION
Initial Approach: Send brief letter of inquiry and full proposal. Board meets in September.
Restrictions on Giving: Does not support individuals.

GRANTS ANALYSIS
Number of Grants: 9
Highest Grant: $100,000
Typical Range: $1,000 to $8,000
Disclosure Period: fiscal year ending June 30, 1990

RECENT GRANTS
100,000 Leigh Yawkey Woodson Art Museum, Wausau, WI — general operations
75,000 Leigh Yawkey Woodson Art Museum, Wausau, WI — general operations
21,000 Leigh Yawkey Woodson Art Museum, Wausau, WI — collections acquisitions
19,600 Leigh Yawkey Woodson Art Museum, Wausau, WI — collections acquisitions
7,085 Leigh Yawkey Woodson Art Museum, Wausau, WI — office equipment
5,117 Leigh Yawkey Woodson Art Museum, Wausau, WI — communications services office
1,697 Leigh Yawkey Woodson Art Museum, Wausau, WI — office equipment, software
1,503 Leigh Yawkey Woodson Art Museum, Wausau, WI — collections acquisitions
417 Leigh Yawkey Woodson Art Museum, Wausau, WI — hygrothermograph

Woodward Fund

CONTACT
Samuel A. Curtis, Jr.
Woodward Fund
c/o Norstar Trust Co.
One East Ave.
Rochester, NY 14638
(716) 546-9093

FINANCIAL SUMMARY
Recent Giving: $125,750 (fiscal 1991); $110,000 (fiscal 1990); $140,000 (fiscal 1989)
Assets: $2,297,275 (fiscal year ending November 30, 1991); $2,124,335 (fiscal 1990); $2,171,283 (fiscal 1989)
Fiscal Note: $2,297,275
EIN: 16-6064221

CONTRIBUTIONS SUMMARY
Donor(s): Florence S. Woodward
Typical Recipients: • *Arts & Humanities:* arts funds, museums/galleries • *Civic & Public Affairs:* women's affairs, zoos/botanical gardens • *Education:* colleges & universities, private education (precollege) • *Health:* hospices, hospitals, medical research, single-disease health associations • *Social Services:* child welfare, community service organizations, youth organizations
Grant Types: general support and research
Geographic Distribution: focus on AZ and ME

GIVING OFFICERS
Barbara W. Piel: mgr
Reid T. Woodward: off
Stephen S. Woodward: mgr
William S. Woodward: mgr
William S. Woodward: trust

APPLICATION INFORMATION
Initial Approach: Contributes only to preselected organizations.
Restrictions on Giving: Does not support individuals.

GRANTS ANALYSIS
Number of Grants: 41
Highest Grant: $10,000
Typical Range: $1,000 to $5,000
Disclosure Period: fiscal year ending November 30, 1991

RECENT GRANTS
10,000 Heifer Project International, Little Rock, AR
7,000 Carmel High School Padre Parents
7,000 Piscataquis Regional WMCA
6,000 American Arts Heritage Fund for the University Museum
5,000 Arizona Boys Ranch, Boys Ranch, AZ
5,000 Gompers Rehabilitation Center
5,000 Maine Audubon Society, Portland, ME
5,000 Unity College, New York, NY
5,000 Women Care of Aegis Association
5,000 Women's Board, Barrow Neurological Foundation

Woodward Fund-Atlanta, David, Helen, Marian

CONTACT
Beverly Blake
Principal Manager
David, Helen, Marian Woodward Fund-Atlanta
c/o Wachovia Bank of Georgia
PO Box 4148
MC 705
Atlanta, GA 30302
(404) 332-6677
Note: Also known as the Marian Ottley Foundation-Atlanta

FINANCIAL SUMMARY
Recent Giving: $1,023,001 (fiscal 1991)
Assets: $30,567,176 (fiscal year ending May 31, 1991)
EIN: 58-6222004

CONTRIBUTIONS SUMMARY
Donor(s): The foundation was established in 1975 by the late Marian W. Ottley.
Typical Recipients: • *Arts & Humanities:* arts centers, history/historic preservation, opera, performing arts, public broadcasting, theater • *Civic &*

Public Affairs: environmental affairs, housing, professional & trade associations • *Education:* colleges & universities, education associations, international studies, literacy, private education (precollege), public education (precollege), religious education • *Health:* health organizations, hospitals, pediatric health, public health, single-disease health associations • *Religion:* churches, religious organizations • *Social Services:* child welfare, community service organizations, disabled, drugs & alcohol, employment/job training, food/clothing distribution, homes, recreation & athletics, religious welfare, united funds
Grant Types: capital and general support
Geographic Distribution: Georgia and neighboring states with an emphasis on Atlanta, GA

GIVING OFFICERS
William D. Ellis, Jr.: comm mem *CURR EMPL* pres, ceo, dir: Southern Mills
Robert L. Foreman, Jr.: comm mem
Joseph Hilsman: comm mem
Horace Holden Sibley: comm mem *B* Philadelphia PA 1939 *ED* Vanderbilt Univ BA 1961; Univ GA LLD 1964; GA St Univ MBA 1971 *CURR EMPL* ptnr: King & Spalding *NONPR AFFIL* mem: Am Bar Assn, Atlanta Bar Assn, GA Bar Assn, Japan-Am Soc; trust, mem exec comm: Egleston (Henrietta) Hosp Children
Edward D. Smith: chmn *B* Birmingham AL 1912 *ED* Emory Univ AB 1932; Harvard Univ JD 1935 *CURR EMPL* atty: Hansell & Post *NONPR AFFIL* mem: Am Bar Assn, Atlanta Bar Assn, Lawyers Club Atlanta

APPLICATION INFORMATION
Initial Approach:
Applicants should send a written grant request.
The proposal should include a cover letter of not more than two pages which gives basic information about the organization, a copy of the IRS letter showing tax status, financial information, a list showing names of board members, and any other information the applicant considers important.
Written grant requests should be received by the trustee at

least 30 days prior to the semi-annual board meetings in June and December.
Restrictions on Giving: Applications restricted to charitable organizations located and operating within Georgia and neighboring states.

OTHER THINGS TO KNOW
Wachovia Bank of Georgia serves as the corporate trustee of the foundation.

GRANTS ANALYSIS
Total Grants: $1,023,001
Number of Grants: 45
Highest Grant: $150,000
Typical Range: $10,000 to $20,000
Disclosure Period: fiscal year ending May 31, 1991
Note: Average grant figure excludes the foundation's two largest grants of $150,000 and $100,000. Recent grants are derived from a 1991 grants list.

RECENT GRANTS
150,000 Henrietta Egleston Hospital for Children, Atlanta, GA
100,000 Scottish Rite Hospital for Crippled Children, Atlanta, GA
75,000 Fernbank, Atlanta, GA
50,000 American Red Cross Blood Services
35,000 Robert W. Woodruff Arts Center, Atlanta, GA
35,000 Tommy Nobis Center, Marietta, GA
35,000 United Way of Metropolitan Atlanta, Atlanta, GA
30,000 Atlanta AIDS Fund, Metropolitan Atlanta Community Foundation, Atlanta, GA
25,000 Alliance Theatre
25,000 Atlanta Executive Services Corps, Atlanta, GA

Woodward Fund-Watertown, David, Helen, and Marian

Former Foundation Name:
Marian W. Ottley
Trust-Watertown

CONTACT
E. Edward Thompson
Member, Selection Committee
David, Helen, and Marian Woodward Fund-Watertown
Box 817
Watertown, CT 06795

FINANCIAL SUMMARY
Recent Giving: $377,900 (fiscal 1990); $370,919 (fiscal 1989)
Assets: $8,842,907 (fiscal year ending May 31, 1990); $8,145,021 (fiscal 1989)
EIN: 58-6222005

CONTRIBUTIONS SUMMARY
Donor(s): the late Marian W. Ottley
Typical Recipients: • *Education:* colleges & universities, private education (precollege) • *Health:* health organizations, hospitals, pediatric health, single-disease health associations • *Social Services:* child welfare, community service organizations, united funds, youth organizations
Grant Types: capital, endowment, and scholarship
Geographic Distribution: focus on New England

GIVING OFFICERS
M. Heminway Merriman II: mem selection comm
Edith Pelletier: mem selection comm
E. Edward Thompson: mem selection comm

APPLICATION INFORMATION
Initial Approach: Send brief letter of inquiry and full proposal (three copies). Deadline is 30 days prior to board meetings. Board meets in June and December.
Restrictions on Giving: Does not support individuals.

GRANTS ANALYSIS
Number of Grants: 42
Highest Grant: $250,000
Typical Range: $25 to $10,000
Disclosure Period: fiscal year ending May 31, 1990

RECENT GRANTS
250,000 Atlanta Historical Society, Atlanta, GA
100,000 Taft School, Watertown, CT
60,000 St. Margarets-McTernan School, New Haven, CT

50,000 American Red Cross, New Haven, CT
50,000 Southern Center for International Studies, Atlanta, GA
50,000 Trident Community Foundation, Charleston, SC
45,000 Easter Seal Rehabilitation Center of Greater Waterbury, Waterbury, CT
37,500 Vassar College, Poughkeepsie, NY
30,000 United Way, Atlanta, GA
25,000 YWCA, Waterbury, CT

Woodward Governor Co. / Woodward Governor Co. Charitable Trust

Sales: $361.92 million
Employees: 3,953
Headquarters: Rockford, IL
SIC Major Group: Electronic & Other Electrical Equipment, Industrial Machinery & Equipment, and Transportation Equipment

CONTACT
Harry Tallacksen
Contribution Committee Chairman
Woodward Governor Company
5001 N Second St.
Rockford, IL 61125
(815) 877-7441

FINANCIAL SUMMARY
Recent Giving: $467,265 (1991); $688,678 (1989); $450,566 (1988)
Assets: $7,922,499 (1991); $9,132,463 (1989)
Fiscal Note: All information reflects foundation contributions only.
EIN: 84-6025403

CONTRIBUTIONS SUMMARY
Typical Recipients: • *Arts & Humanities:* history/historic preservation, museums/galleries, performing arts, public broadcasting • *Civic & Public Affairs:* environmental affairs, ethnic/minority organizations, housing, law & justice, philanthropic organizations, safety, urban & community affairs • *Education:* colleges & universities, literacy, private education (precollege) • *Health:*

emergency/ambulance services, geriatric health, hospices, hospitals, medical rehabilitation, medical research, mental health, single-disease health associations • *Social Services:* aged, child welfare, community centers, counseling, disabled, emergency relief, family services, food/clothing distribution, legal aid, recreation & athletics, shelters/homelessness, united funds, volunteer services, youth organizations
Grant Types: capital, emergency, multiyear/continuing support, operating expenses, and seed money
Geographic Distribution: primarily in areas where company operates
Operating Locations: CO (Ft. Collins), IL (Rockford)

CORP. OFFICERS
Vern H. Cassens: *CURR EMPL* sr vp, treas: Woodward Governor Co
Calvin C. Covert: *B* Rockford IL 1924 *CURR EMPL* chmn, ceo, pres: Woodward Governor Co
Mark E. Leum: *CURR EMPL* pres, coo: Woodward Governor Co

GIVING OFFICERS
Edward Abegg: trust
Duane Miller: trust
Maurice Nelson: trust
Leo Powelson: trust
Robert Reuterfors: trust
Dick Robbins: trust
Harry Tallacksen: chmn contrib comm

APPLICATION INFORMATION
Initial Approach: *Initial Contact:* letter *Include Information On:* description of the organization and how it meets community needs and copy of unexpired IRS letter proving that contributions to organization are tax deductible *When to Submit:* any time
Restrictions on Giving: The foundation does not give to individuals, endowment funds, research, scholarships, fellowships, special projects, publications, or conferences. The foundation does not give matching gifts or loans.
Almost all grants go to organizations in company operating areas.

GRANTS ANALYSIS
Total Grants: $467,265

Number of Grants: 70
Highest Grant: $87,000
Typical Range: $1,000 to $20,000
Disclosure Period: 1991
Note: The average grant figure excludes two grants totaling $157,000. Recent grants are derived from a 1991 Form 990.

RECENT GRANTS
87,000 United Way-Rockford, Rockford, IL
70,000 United Way-Ft. Collins Area, Ft. Collins, CO
27,000 United Way-Portage County, Stevens Point, WI
25,000 P. A. Peterson Home, Rockford, IL
25,000 Profit Sharing Research Foundation, Chicago, IL
24,688 Crusader Clinic, Rockford, IL
20,000 The Mill, Rockford, IL
18,000 Wisconsin Eye Bank, Madison, WI
14,000 Eye Bank Association of America, Madison, WI
12,600 Hunger Connection, Rockford, IL

Woolf Foundation, William C.

CONTACT
Nicholas H. Wheiess, Jr.
Chairman
William C. Woolf Fdn.
PO Box 21119
Shreveport, LA 71152

FINANCIAL SUMMARY
Recent Giving: $105,875 (fiscal 1992); $163,162 (fiscal 1991); $142,960 (fiscal 1990)
Assets: $4,663,438 (fiscal year ending February 28, 1992); $3,889,638 (fiscal 1991); $3,412,644 (fiscal 1990)
EIN: 72-6020630

CONTRIBUTIONS SUMMARY
Donor(s): the late William C. and Geraldine H. Woolf
Typical Recipients: • *Arts & Humanities:* music • *Education:* colleges & universities, private education (precollege) • *Religion:* churches, religious organizations • *Social Services:* aged, drugs & alcohol, religious welfare, united funds, youth organizations
Grant Types: general support

Geographic Distribution: focus on Shreveport, LA

GIVING OFFICERS
Bobby L. Miller: secy
Claude G. Rives III: trust
C. Lane Sartor: trust
Nicholas Hobson Wheless, Jr.: chmn, trust *ED MA Inst Tech SB 1938 CURR EMPL* chmn, dir: Commercial Natl Bank Shreveport *CORP AFFIL* chmn, dir: Commercial Natl Bank Shreveport, Wheless Indus *NONPR AFFIL* dir: LA St Fair Assn, Mid-Continent Oil Gas Assn; trust: Centenary Coll

APPLICATION INFORMATION
Initial Approach: Contributes only to preselected organizations.

GRANTS ANALYSIS
Number of Grants: 38
Highest Grant: $15,125
Typical Range: $500 to $5,000
Disclosure Period: fiscal year ending February 28, 1992

RECENT GRANTS
15,125 United Way, Shreveport, LA
10,000 Loyola College Preparatory School, Shreveport, LA
7,500 Boy Scouts of America, Shreveport, LA
5,000 First Presbyterian Church, Shreveport, LA
5,000 Glen Retirement System, Shreveport, LA
5,000 Mothers Against Drugs, Shreveport, LA
5,000 Noel Memorial Methodist Church, Shreveport, LA
5,000 Southfield School, Shreveport, LA
5,000 St. Mark's Foundation, Shreveport, LA
5,000 YMCA, Shreveport, LA

Woolley Foundation, Vasser

CONTACT
Benjamin T. White
Vasser Woolley Fdn.
c/o Alston and Bird, One
 Atlantic Center
1201 West Peachtree St.
Atlanta, GA 30309-3424
(404) 881-7000

FINANCIAL SUMMARY
Recent Giving: $236,000
(1990); $169,167 (1989);
$196,667 (1988)
Assets: $5,648,883 (1990);
$5,913,173 (1989); $5,049,486
(1988)
EIN: 58-6034197

CONTRIBUTIONS SUMMARY
Donor(s): the late Vasser Woolley
Typical Recipients: • *Arts & Humanities:* community arts, history/historic preservation, museums/galleries, music, theater • *Civic & Public Affairs:* law & justice • *Education:* colleges & universities, legal education, private education (precollege) • *Health:* hospitals • *Social Services:* child welfare, united funds, youth organizations
Grant Types: department, general support, and multiyear/continuing support
Geographic Distribution: focus on the Atlanta, GA, area

GIVING OFFICERS
R. Neal Batson: trust *B* Nashville TN 1941 *ED* Vanderbilt Univ BA 1963; Vanderbilt Univ JD 1966 *CURR EMPL* ptnr: Alston & Bird *CORP AFFIL* ptnr: Alston & Bird *NONPR AFFIL* fellow: Am Coll Bankruptcy, Am Coll Trial Lawyers; mem: Am Law Inst, Atlanta Bar Assn, Southeastern Bankruptcy Law Inst; mem, dir: Am Bankruptcy Inst
Alexander Pendleton Gaines: trust *B* Atlanta GA 1910 *ED* Univ GA AB 1932; Emory Univ LLB 1935 *CURR EMPL* mem: Alston & Bird *CORP AFFIL* mem: Alston & Bird *NONPR AFFIL* fellow: Am Coll Probate Couns; mem: Am Bar Assn, Atlanta Bar Assn, DC Bar Assn, GA Bar Assn; trust: Piedmont Hosp Fdn; trust emeritus: Agnes Scott Coll, Berry Schs, Univ GA Fdn

George Conley Ingram: trust *ED* Emory Univ AB 1949; Emory Univ LLB 1951 *CURR EMPL* ptnr: Alston & Bird *CORP AFFIL* ptnr: Alston & Bird *NONPR AFFIL* mem: Am Bar Assn, Am Bar Fdn, Am Coll Trial Lawyers, Am Law Inst, Assn Trial Lawyers Am, GA Bar Assn, GA Bar Fdn; trust: Emory Univ
John R. Seydel: trust
Paul V. Seydel: trust
Benjamin T. White: secy, treas, trust
L. Neil Williams, Jr.: chmn, trust *ED* Duke Univ AB 1958; Duke Univ JD 1961 *CURR EMPL* mng ptnr: Alston & Bird *CORP AFFIL* dir: Natl Data Corp; managing ptnr: Alston & Bird *NONPR AFFIL* dir: Atlanta Symphony Orchestra; mem: Am Bar Assn, Am Law Inst; mem bd couns: Central Atlanta Progress Assn; pres: Woodruff Arts Ctr; trust: Duke Univ

APPLICATION INFORMATION
Initial Approach: Send brief letter of inquiry describing program or project. There are no deadlines.
Restrictions on Giving: Does not support individuals.

OTHER THINGS TO KNOW
Publications: Informational Brochure, Application Guidelines

GRANTS ANALYSIS
Number of Grants: 15
Highest Grant: $50,000
Typical Range: $2,500 to $10,000
Disclosure Period: 1990

RECENT GRANTS
50,000 University of Georgia School of Law, Athens, GA
30,000 Atlanta Symphony Orchestra, Atlanta, GA
30,000 Georgia Tech Foundation, Atlanta, GA — Vasser Woolley Chair in Chemistry
25,000 Alliance Theatre Company, Atlanta, GA
25,000 Science and Technology Museum of Atlanta, Atlanta, GA
20,000 Atlanta International School, Atlanta, GA

20,000 PCS Urban Ministries
15,000 Boy Scouts of America, Atlanta, GA
10,000 Robert W. Woodruff Arts Center, Atlanta, GA
10,000 Scottish Rite Children's Hospital, Atlanta, GA

Woolworth Co., F.W.
Sales: $2.08 billion
Employees: 32,000
Parent Company: Woolworth Corporation
Headquarters: New York, NY
SIC Major Group: General Merchandise Stores

CONTACT
Frances E. Trachter
Vice President, Public Affairs
F.W. Woolworth Co.
Woolworth Bldg., 233 Broadway
New York, NY 10279
(212) 553-2392

CONTRIBUTIONS SUMMARY
Operating Locations: NY (New York)

CORP. OFFICERS
William K. Lavin: *CURR EMPL* exec vp, cfo: Woolworth Co
Harold E. Sells: *CURR EMPL* chmn, ceo: FW Woolworth Co

Word Investments

CONTACT
Clare De Graaf
President
Word Investments
3366 Burton St. Southeast
Grand Rapids, MI 49546
(616) 942-0041

FINANCIAL SUMMARY
Recent Giving: $384,893
(1991); $463,842 (1990);
$425,848 (1989)
Assets: $5,218,286 (1991);
$5,265,070 (1990); $5,821,974 (1989)
Gifts Received: $440,905
(1991); $85,855 (1990);
$147,850 (1989)
Fiscal Note: In 1991, contributions were received from Joint Heirs Foundation ($1,300), Norm De Nooyer ($300), Gary Jaarda ($2,305), Ted Etheridge ($373,000), David Byker

($5,000), and Clare De Graaf ($59,000).
EIN: 38-2470907

CONTRIBUTIONS SUMMARY
Typical Recipients: • *Religion:* churches, missionary activities, religious organizations • *Social Services:* community service organizations, youth organizations
Grant Types: general support
Geographic Distribution: focus on MI

GIVING OFFICERS
Clare De Graaf: pres, treas
Susan De Graaf: secy

APPLICATION INFORMATION
Initial Approach: Send brief letter of inquiry describing program or project. There are no deadlines.
Restrictions on Giving: Does not support individuals.

GRANTS ANALYSIS
Number of Grants: 15
Highest Grant: $104,295
Typical Range: $800 to $20,000
Disclosure Period: 1991

RECENT GRANTS
104,295 Bethany Christian Services, Grand Rapids, MI
27,244 Good Shepherd Orphanage
25,000 Mission India
20,050 Campus Crusade for Christ, San Bernardino, CA
18,865 Christian Home Missions
12,250 Christian Learning Center
10,000 Calvary Church
9,000 Christian Business Men's Committee
7,000 Young Life
6,000 Bible League, South Holland, IL

World Book Inc.
Sales: $311.5 million
Employees: 8,000
Parent Company: Scott Fetzer Co.
Headquarters: Elk Grove Village, IL
SIC Major Group: Miscellaneous Retail and Printing & Publishing

CONTACT

Steven Fuller
Chairman & Chief Executive
  Officer
World Book Inc.
101 Northwest Point Blvd.
Elk Grove Village, IL 60007
(708) 290-5300

CONTRIBUTIONS
SUMMARY

Operating Locations: IL (Elk
Grove)

CORP. OFFICERS

Steven Fuller: *CURR EMPL*
chmn: World Book

World Carpets /
World Carpets
Foundation

Sales: $380.0 million
Employees: 3,000
Headquarters: Dalton, GA
SIC Major Group: Textile Mill
  Products

CONTACT

Ken Beandoin
Personnel
World Carpets
PO Box 1448
Dalton, GA 30722
(706) 278-8000

FINANCIAL SUMMARY

Fiscal Note: Annual Giving
Range: less than $100,000
EIN: 23-7248425

CONTRIBUTIONS
SUMMARY

Operating Locations: GA
(Cartersville, Columbus, Dalton, Rome)

CORP. OFFICERS

David Polley: *CURR EMPL*
pres: World Carpets

APPLICATION
INFORMATION

Restrictions on Giving: Company only supports employee's
dependents.

GRANTS ANALYSIS

Typical Range: $1,000 to
$2,500

World Savings &
Loan Association

Assets: $23.98 billion
Employees: 4,416
Parent Company: Golden West
  Financial Corp.
Headquarters: Oakland, CA
SIC Major Group: Depository
  Institutions

CONTACT

Hazel Quisumbing
Employee Relations
World Savings & Loan
  Association
1901 Harrison St.
Oakland, CA 94612
(510) 446-3055

CONTRIBUTIONS
SUMMARY

Company contributes to United
Way only.

Nonmonetary Support Types:
donated products

Operating Locations: CA
(Oakland)

CORP. OFFICERS

J. L. Helvey: *CURR EMPL* sr
vp, cfo: World Savings & Loan
Assn

Herbert M. Sandler: *B* New
York NY 1931 *ED* City Univ
NY 1951; Columbia Univ 1954
CURR EMPL chmn, ceo: World
Savings & Loan Assn *CORP
AFFIL* chmn, ceo: World Savings & Loan Assn; chmn, ceo,
dir: Golden West Fin Corp; dir:
Fed Home Loan Bank San Francisco

Wornall Charitable
Trust and
Foundation,
Kearney

CONTACT

Kearney Wornall Charitable
  Trust and Fdn.
PO Box 419226
Kansas City, MO 64141

FINANCIAL SUMMARY

Recent Giving: $237,850 (fiscal 1991); $94,800 (fiscal
1990); $85,350 (fiscal 1989)
Assets: $4,272,278 (fiscal year
ending September 30, 1991);
$3,906,721 (fiscal 1989)
Gifts Received: $3,692,505
(fiscal 1990); $2,752,653 (fiscal 1989)
EIN: 44-6013874

CONTRIBUTIONS
SUMMARY

Donor(s): the late Kearney
Wornall

Typical Recipients: • *Arts &
Humanities:* community arts,
history/historic preservation,
museums/galleries, theater
• *Education:* colleges & universities, education funds, private
education (precollege)
• *Health:* hospitals, pediatric
health • *Religion:* churches, religious organizations • *Social
Services:* child welfare, community service organizations,
counseling, disabled, united
funds, youth organizations
Grant Types: general support
and scholarship
Geographic Distribution:
focus on the Kansas City, MO,
area

APPLICATION
INFORMATION

Initial Approach: Contributes
only to preselected organizations.
Restrictions on Giving: Does
not support individuals.

GRANTS ANALYSIS

Number of Grants: 35
Highest Grant: $86,000
Typical Range: $500 to $5,000
Disclosure Period: fiscal year
ending September 30, 1991

RECENT GRANTS

```
86,000  American Royal
        Association, Kan-
        sas City, MO
30,000  United Way, Kan-
        sas City, MO
25,000  Society for the Pre-
        servation of John
        Wornall House Mu-
        seum, Kansas City,
        MO
12,500  Missouri Repertory
        Theatre, Kansas
        City, MO
10,000  Cradles and Cray-
        ons, Kansas City,
        MO
 7,500  Midwest Christian
        Counseling, Kan-
        sas City, MO
 6,000  Children's Mercy
        Hospital, Kansas
        City, MO
 5,000  Boys and Girls
        Club, Kansas City,
        MO
 5,000  St. Luke's Hospi-
        tal, Kansas City,
        MO
 5,000  St. Thomas Aqui-
        nas High School,
        Overland Park, KS
```

Wortham
Foundation

CONTACT

Barbara J. Snyder
Grants Administrator
Wortham Foundation
2727 Allen Pkwy., Ste. 2000
Wortham Tower
Houston, TX 77019
(713) 526-8849

FINANCIAL SUMMARY

Recent Giving: $7,736,784
(fiscal 1993 est.); $7,681,540
(fiscal 1992); $8,251,168 (fiscal 1991)
Assets: $154,632,553 (fiscal
1991); $134,251,953 (fiscal
1990); $139,209,452 (fiscal
1989)
EIN: 74-1334356

CONTRIBUTIONS
SUMMARY

Donor(s): The Wortham Foundation was established in 1958
by Mr. and Mrs. Gus S.
Wortham, both deceased. Mr.
Wortham was a partner of John
L. Wortham & Son, which organized the American General
Insurance Company (now
American General Corporation). Mr. Wortham was active
in civic, educational, and cultural affairs. He was on the
board of governors of Rice University and active in fund-raising activities for Rice Stadium,
the Houston Symphony Society, Houston Grand Opera, and
the Society for the Performing
Arts. His wife, Lyndall Finley
Wortham, was a member of the
board of regents of the University of Houston, and a board
member of the Houston Grand
Opera Association.
Typical Recipients: • *Arts &
Humanities:* arts associations,
music, opera, performing arts,
theater • *Civic & Public Affairs:* zoos/botanical gardens
• *Social Services:* youth organizations
Grant Types: capital and general support
Geographic Distribution:
Houston, TX

GIVING OFFICERS

H. Charles Boswell: vp, treas
Fred C. Burns: vp, asst treas
Allen H. Carruth: chmn, pres
Brady F. Carruth: vp, asst
treas
William V. H. Clarke: exec
secy

Barbara J. Snyder: grants adm, secy

E. A. Stumpf III: vp, asst treas

R. W. Wortham III: vp, asst treas

APPLICATION INFORMATION

Initial Approach:

Send a brief letter to the foundation requesting its Application for Grant Form.

The application form requests such information as the name and address of the organization; administrator of the proposed project; evidence of tax-exempt status; budget; copy of the organization's Form 990 or financial statement; description of activities; list of governing board and principal staff; amount requested; date needed; how the funds will be used; and the beneficiaries of the grant.

Applications should be received no later than the first week in January, April, July, or October.

Proposals are considered at the foundation's board meetings held in mid-February, May, August, and November. The staff will review and respond to requests within four weeks.

OTHER THINGS TO KNOW

Publications: annual report, grant application form

GRANTS ANALYSIS

Total Grants: $7,681,540

Number of Grants: 48

Highest Grant: $1,600,000

Typical Range: $5,000 to $25,000 and $50,000 to $250,000

Disclosure Period: fiscal year ending September 30, 1992

Note: Average grant figure excludes the foundation's highest grant of $1,600,000. Recent grants are derived from a fiscal 1991 grants list.

RECENT GRANTS

2,288,006 Texas Medical Center, Houston, TX

750,000 Houston Symphony Society, Houston, TX

750,000 Space Center Houston, Houston, TX

500,000 Galveston Historical Society, Galveston, TX

500,000 Houston Ballet, Houston, TX

500,000 Houston Museum of Natural Science, Houston, TX

300,000 Hospice, Houston, TX

263,000 Harris County Heritage Society, Houston, TX

240,000 Houston Grand Opera, Houston, TX

200,000 Houston Grand Opera, Houston, TX

Worthing Scholarship Fund

CONTACT

Carl W. Schumacher, Jr.

Sr. Vice President and Trust Officer

Worthing Scholarship Fund

c/o NCNB Texas National Bank

PO Box 2518

Houston, TX 77252-2518

(713) 652-6230

FINANCIAL SUMMARY

Recent Giving: $206,250 (fiscal 1991); $181,000 (fiscal 1990); $172,250 (fiscal 1989)

Assets: $3,824,844 (fiscal year ending September 30, 1991); $3,429,130 (fiscal 1990); $3,756,247 (fiscal 1989)

EIN: 74-1160916

CONTRIBUTIONS SUMMARY

Grant Types: scholarship

Geographic Distribution: limited to Houston, TX

GIVING OFFICERS

NCNB Texax National Bank: trust

APPLICATION INFORMATION

Initial Approach: Application form required. Deadline is May 1.

OTHER THINGS TO KNOW

Provides scholarships to high school graduates of the Houston Independent School District who plan to attend college in TX.

Disclosure Period: fiscal year ending September 30, 1991

Worthington Industries, Inc.

Sales: $974.2 million

Employees: 6,000

Headquarters: Columbus, OH

SIC Major Group: Primary Metal Industries and Rubber & Miscellaneous Plastics Products

CONTACT

Linda Derringer

Contributions Coordinator

Worthington Industries, Inc.

1205 Dearborn Dr.

Columbus, OH 43085

(614) 438-3210

Note: Joseph Stegmayer, vice president and chief financial officer, also is a contact.

CONTRIBUTIONS SUMMARY

Operating Locations: OH (Columbus, London), PA (Paoli)

CORP. OFFICERS

Donald H. Malenick: *CURR EMPL* pres, coo, dir: Worthington Indus

John Henderson McConnell: *B* New Manchester WV 1923 *ED* MI St Univ BA 1949 *CURR EMPL* fdr, chmn, ceo, dir: Worthington Indus *CORP AFFIL* chmn, ceo: Worthington Custom Plastics; dir: Alltel Corp, Anchor Hocking, Natl City Corp *NONPR AFFIL* dir: Childrens Hospital Columbus OH; mem: Columbus Area Chamber Commerce; trust: Ashland Coll

John P. McConnell: *CURR EMPL* vchmn: Worthington Indus

Wouk Foundation, Abe

CONTACT

Herman Wouk

President

Abe Wouk Fdn.

3255 N St., N.W

Washington, DC 20007

FINANCIAL SUMMARY

Recent Giving: $245,860 (1990); $173,860 (1988)

Assets: $1,930,816 (1990); $1,844,786 (1988)

Gifts Received: $3,295 (1990); $782,600 (1988)

EIN: 13-6155699

CONTRIBUTIONS SUMMARY

Donor(s): Betty Sarah Wouk, Herman Wouk

Typical Recipients: • *Civic & Public Affairs:* zoos/botanical gardens • *Education:* religious education • *Religion:* missionary activities, religious organizations, synagogues • *Social Services:* animal protection, community service organizations, united funds

Grant Types: general support

Geographic Distribution: focus on CA, NY, and Washington, DC

GIVING OFFICERS

Charles Rembar: trust *B* Oceanport NJ 1915 *ED* Harvard Univ AB 1935; Columbia Univ LLB 1938 *NONPR AFFIL* mem: NY City Bar Assn

Suzanne Stein: secy

Betty Saraha Wouk: treas

Herman Wouk: pres, trust *ED* Columbia Univ AB 1934 *NONPR AFFIL* mem: Poets Playrights Editors Essayists Novelists

Joseph Wouk: vp, trust

Nathaniel Wouk: vp

APPLICATION INFORMATION

Initial Approach: Send brief letter describing program. There are no deadlines.

GRANTS ANALYSIS

Number of Grants: 56

Highest Grant: $50,000

Typical Range: $100 to $5,000

Disclosure Period: 1990

RECENT GRANTS

50,000 Jewish Federation of Palm Springs, Palm Springs, CA

15,000 Animal Welfare Institute, Washington, DC

15,000 Jewish Federation of Palm Springs, Palm Springs, CA

12,000 Town Club Foundation, New York, NY

11,000 Library of Congress, Washington, DC

10,000 Bar-Ilan University, New York, NY

10,000 California Wildlife Protection, Sacramento, CA

10,000 U.S. Holocaust Memorial Museum Campaign, Washington, DC

5,000 Yeshiva Torah Vodnath and Mesivta, New York, NY

4,000 Torah Education in Israel, New York, NY

Wrap-On Co.

Sales: $8.0 million
Employees: 100
Parent Company: McArdle Ltd.
Headquarters: Chicago, IL
SIC Major Group: Electronic & Other Electrical Equipment

CONTACT

Al Dudycha
Comptroller
Wrap-On Co.
5550 West 70th Pl.
Chicago, IL 60638
(708) 496-2150

CONTRIBUTIONS SUMMARY

Operating Locations: IL (Chicago)

CORP. OFFICERS

James Binder: *CURR EMPL*
pres, ceo: Wrap-On Co

OTHER THINGS TO KNOW

Wrap-On Co., Inc., and Huron & Orleans Building Corp. are original donors to the Tom Russell Charitable Foundation.

Wrape Family Charitable Trust

CONTACT

W. R. Wrape
Manager
Wrape Family Charitable Trust
PO Box 193455
Little Rock, AR 72219-3455
(501) 565-9301

FINANCIAL SUMMARY

Recent Giving: $1,871,959 (1991); $283,550 (1989); $268,535 (1988)
Assets: $3,615,154 (1991); $4,189,699 (1989); $4,150,423 (1988)
Gifts Received: $1,215,773 (1991)
Fiscal Note: In 1991, contributions were received from the estate of Marie Wrape.
EIN: 71-6050323

CONTRIBUTIONS SUMMARY

Donor(s): the late Regina Sellmeyer, the late A. M. Wrape, and members of the Wrape family
Typical Recipients: • *Education:* colleges & universities, private education (precollege), religious education • *Religion:* religious organizations

Geographic Distribution: focus on AR

GIVING OFFICERS

A. J. Wrape, Jr.: mgr, trust
A. J. Wrape III: trust
Tom Wrape: trust
W. R. Wrape II: trust

APPLICATION INFORMATION

Initial Approach: The foundation reports that grant requests should state the purpose for which the grant is requested, including information on the specific project of program. Evidence of tax-exempt status and public charity status and a copy of Schedule A of Form 990 from the preceding year should also be included.

GRANTS ANALYSIS

Number of Grants: 35
Highest Grant: $836,217
Typical Range: $500 to $3,000
Disclosure Period: 1991

RECENT GRANTS

836,217 Carmelite Fathers, Little Rock, AR
305,000 Carmelite Fathers, Little Rock, AR
264,351 Notre Dame University, Notre Dame, IN
135,691 Carmelite Sisters, Little Rock, AR
118,500 Diocese of Little Rock, Little Rock, AR
105,743 St. Louis University, St. Louis, MO
43,127 Carmelite Sisters, Little Rock, AR
10,580 Marquette University, Milwaukee, WI
5,000 Catholic High School
5,000 Mount St. Mary's

Wright Foundation, Lola

CONTACT

Patrick H. O'Donnell
President
Lola Wright Fdn.
PO Box 550
Austin, TX 78789

FINANCIAL SUMMARY

Recent Giving: $876,585 (1991); $935,643 (1990); $424,508 (1989)
Assets: $11,671,486 (1991); $8,812,301 (1990); $8,470,238 (1989)
EIN: 74-6054717

CONTRIBUTIONS SUMMARY

Donor(s): the late Miss Johnie E. Wright
Typical Recipients: • *Arts & Humanities:* community arts, libraries, museums/galleries, music, performing arts • *Civic & Public Affairs:* women's affairs • *Education:* colleges & universities, literacy • *Health:* hospitals • *Religion:* churches • *Social Services:* aged, child welfare, community centers, community service organizations, disabled, domestic violence, family planning, food/clothing distribution, homes, shelters/homelessness, youth organizations
Grant Types: capital, endowment, multiyear/continuing support, project, and research
Geographic Distribution: limited to TX

GIVING OFFICERS

Texas Commerce Bank Trust: agent
Financial Consultants, Inc. agent
Wilford Flowers: dir
Linda H. Guerrero: dir
William Hilgers: vp, dir
James Meyers: dir
Patrick H. O'Donnell: pres, dir
Carole Rylander: dir

APPLICATION INFORMATION

Initial Approach: Send brief letter of inquiry describing program or project. Deadlines are April 1 and October 1.
Restrictions on Giving: Does not support individuals.

OTHER THINGS TO KNOW

Publications: Application Guidelines, Annual Report

GRANTS ANALYSIS

Number of Grants: 68
Highest Grant: $51,850
Typical Range: $5,000 to $25,000
Disclosure Period: 1991

RECENT GRANTS

51,850 Ebenezer Child Development Center, Austin, TX — purchase of vans
50,000 Austin Police Activities, Austin, TX — purchase of vans
50,000 Salvation Army, Austin, TX
35,000 James Dick Foundation for the Performing Arts, Austin, TX
30,000 United Fund, Austin, TX
26,000 Paramount Theatre, Austin, TX — restoration
25,000 Austin Habitat for Humanity, Austin, TX — build house for needy family
25,000 Karl Folkers Foundation for Biomedical and Clinical Research, Austin, TX — research
25,000 Southwestern University, Georgetown, TX — partial funding of Tower library
25,000 St. Edward's University, Austin, TX — library automation project

Wrigley Co., Wm. Jr. / Wrigley Co. Foundation, Wm. Jr.

Sales: $1.3 billion
Employees: 5,850
Headquarters: Chicago, IL
SIC Major Group: Food & Kindred Products

CONTACT

William M. Piet
President
Wm. Wrigley Jr. Co. Fdn.
410 N Michigan Ave.
Chicago, IL 60611
(312) 645-3950

FINANCIAL SUMMARY

Recent Giving: $1,081,500 (1991 est.); $1,038,500 (1990); $956,000 (1989)
Assets: $13,000,000 (1990); $10,000,000 (1989)
Fiscal Note: All contributions are made through the foundation.
EIN: 36-3486958

CONTRIBUTIONS SUMMARY

Typical Recipients: • *Civic & Public Affairs:* civil rights, environmental affairs, nonprofit management • *Education:* community & junior colleges, education funds, minority education • *Health:* health funds, health organizations, nursing services, single-disease health associations • *Social Services:* aged, child welfare, community service organizations, delinquency & crime, disabled, domestic violence, drugs & alcohol, employment/job training, food/clothing distribution, united funds, youth organizations

Grant Types: general support

Geographic Distribution: nationally, with an emphasis on the Chicago area

Operating Locations: CA (Santa Cruz), GA (Gainesville), IL (Chicago)

CORP. OFFICERS

William Wrigley: *B* Chicago IL 1933 *ED* Yale Univ BA 1954 *CURR EMPL* pres, ceo, dir: Wm Wrigley Jr Co *CORP AFFIL* chmn, ceo, dir, mem exec comm: Santa Catalina Island Co; dir: Am Home Products Corp, Wrigley Co Ltd HK, Wrigley Co Ltd Japan, Wrigley Co Ltd Kenya, Wrigley Co Ltd NZ, Wrigley Co Ltd UK, Wrigley Co Propriety Ltd, Wrigley Co Propriety Ltd Australia, Wrigley Co Propriety Ltd New Guinea, Wrigley Phillipines, Zeno Air; dir, mem comm non mgmt dirs, mem nominating comm: Texaco; dir, mem compensation comm: Natl Blvd Bank Chicago *NONPR AFFIL* dir: Cowboy Artists Am Mus, Wrigley Meml Garden Fdn; dir, mem exec comm: Geneva Lake Water Safety Comm; dir, mem personnel comm: Northwestern Meml Hosp Benefactor; mem: Catalina Island Mus Soc, Chicago Historical Soc, Delta Epsilon Sigma, Field Mus, Navy League, Santa Catalina Island Conservancy, Univ Southern CA Oceanographic Assns, Wolfs Head Soc; mem adv bd: Ctr Sports Medicine, Northwestern Univ Med Sch; mem audit comm: Grocery Mfrs Am; trust: Chicago Latin Sch Fdn, Univ Southern CA

GIVING OFFICERS

Mark Monroe: secy

Hollis Weaver Moyse: treas *B* New Brunswick NJ 1930 *ED* Univ CA Los Angeles 1955 *CURR EMPL* treas: Wrigley (Wm Jr) Co *NONPR AFFIL* mem: Natl Assn Corp Treas

William M. Piet: pres, dir *CURR EMPL* vp (corp affairs) & secy: Wrigley (Wm Jr) Co *CORP AFFIL* dir: IL World Trade Ctr, L A Dreyfus Co, Santa Catalina Island Co

William Wrigley, Jr.: vp, dir *CURR EMPL* asst to pres, dir: Wrigley (Wm Jr) Co

APPLICATION INFORMATION

Initial Approach: *Initial Contact:* brief letter and proposal *Include Information On:* summary of program, audited financial statement, annual report, list of current contributors, IRS letter of tax-exempt certification *When to Submit:* October 1 for consideration for the following year; considers emergency requests throughout the year

Restrictions on Giving: Does not support individuals, fraternal organizations, political or lobbying groups, religious organizations for sectarian purposes, member agencies of united funds, or goodwill advertising.

OTHER THINGS TO KNOW

Organizations must be certified by the state in which they operate and must qualify under IRS 501(c)(3) tax-exempt status.

GRANTS ANALYSIS

Total Grants: $1,038,500

Number of Grants: 63

Highest Grant: $60,000

Typical Range: $3,000 to $15,000

Disclosure Period: 1990

Note: Recent grants are derived from a 1990 grants list.

RECENT GRANTS

81,900 United Way Crusade of Mercy, Chicago, IL

81,900 United Way Crusade of Mercy, Chicago, IL

60,000 American Fund for Dental Health

56,600 United Way of Hall County, Gainesville, GA

50,000 Juvenile Diabetes Foundation International, New York, NY

37,500 WGBH Educational Foundation, Boston, MA

35,000 Northwestern Memorial Foundation, Chicago, IL

32,800 United Way of Santa Cruz County, Capitola, CA

27,500 United Negro College Fund, New York, NY

25,000 Gainesville College, Gainesville, GA

WSP&R Charitable Trust Fund

CONTACT

Michael V. Sterlacci
Trustee
WSP&R Charitable Trust Fund
1 Battery Park Plz.
New York, NY 10004
(212) 858-1000

FINANCIAL SUMMARY

Recent Giving: $92,500 (1991)

Assets: $892,559 (1991)

Gifts Received: $87,000 (1991)

EIN: 51-0243782

CONTRIBUTIONS SUMMARY

Typical Recipients: • *Civic & Public Affairs:* law & justice

Grant Types: general support

GIVING OFFICERS

Michael V. Sterlacci: trust

APPLICATION INFORMATION

Initial Approach: Send brief letter of inquiry. There are no deadlines.

GRANTS ANALYSIS

Number of Grants: 1

Highest Grant: $92,500

Disclosure Period: 1991

RECENT GRANTS

92,500 Legal Aid Society, New York, NY

Wunsch Foundation

CONTACT

Eric M. Wunsch
President
Wunsch Fdn.
841 63rd St.
Brooklyn, NY 11220
(718) 238-2525

FINANCIAL SUMMARY

Recent Giving: $236,631 (1991); $209,000 (1990); $196,701 (1989)

Assets: $5,471,946 (1991); $5,022,710 (1990); $4,863,201 (1989)

Gifts Received: $500 (1991); $340,300 (1989); $40,000 (1988)

EIN: 11-6006013

CONTRIBUTIONS SUMMARY

Donor(s): Joseph W. Wunsch, Eric M. Wunsch, Samuel Wunsch, WEA Enterprises Co.

Typical Recipients: • *Arts & Humanities:* arts appreciation, arts institutes, history/historic preservation, museums/galleries • *Education:* colleges & universities, education funds • *Health:* hospitals, pediatric health • *International:* international development/relief, international organizations • *Religion:* churches, religious organizations

Grant Types: emergency and general support

GIVING OFFICERS

Eric M. Wunsch: pres *CURR EMPL* vp: WEA Enterprises Co

Ethel Wunsch: secy

APPLICATION INFORMATION

Initial Approach: Contributes only to preselected organizations.

Restrictions on Giving: Does not support individuals.

GRANTS ANALYSIS

Number of Grants: 24

Highest Grant: $60,000

Typical Range: $500 to $7,000

Disclosure Period: 1991

RECENT GRANTS

60,000 Polytechnic University, Brooklyn, NY

43,333 Rhode Island School of Design, Providence, RI

30,000 Israel Emergency Fund

18,300 New York State Museum, New York, NY

13,250 Brooklyn Museum, Brooklyn, NY

13,250 Centre College Annual Fund, Danville, KY

12,500 University of Texas, Austin, TX

10,750 Baltimore Museum of Art, Baltimore, MD

7,500 American Society for Technion, New York, NY

7,348 New York University Medical center, New York, NY

Wurlitzer Foundation, Farny R.

CONTACT
William A. Rolting
President
Farny R. Wurlitzer Fdn.
PO Box 387
Sycamore, IL 60178
(815) 895-2923

FINANCIAL SUMMARY
Recent Giving: $146,400 (1990); $130,900 (1989)
Assets: $3,179,539 (1990); $3,130,410 (1989)
EIN: 16-6023172

CONTRIBUTIONS SUMMARY
Donor(s): the late Farny R. Wurlitzer, the late Grace K. Wurlitzer
Typical Recipients: • *Arts & Humanities:* arts centers, arts institutes, community arts, music, opera, public broadcasting • *Education:* colleges & universities, minority education
Grant Types: capital, emergency, endowment, general support, multiyear/continuing support, operating expenses, and research
Geographic Distribution: focus on IL and the Midwest

GIVING OFFICERS
H. L. Evans: trust
H.L. Hollingsworth: trust
J.D. Ovitz: dir, secy
William A. Rolting: dir, pres
W.S. Turner: dir, vp, treas

APPLICATION INFORMATION
Initial Approach: Send brief letter of inquiry describing program. There are no deadlines.
Restrictions on Giving: Does not support individuals.

GRANTS ANALYSIS
Number of Grants: 37
Highest Grant: $16,000
Typical Range: $2,000 to $5,000
Disclosure Period: 1990

RECENT GRANTS
16,000 Music Teachers National Association, Chicago, IL
8,500 Indiana Wesleyan University, Marion, IN
8,000 North Park College, Chicago, IL
7,500 WTTW, Chicago, IL

6,000 Merit Music Program, Chicago, IL
5,000 Concordia University, Mequon, WI
5,000 Hillsdale College, Hillsdale, MI
5,000 Interlochen Arts Academy, Interlochen, MI
5,000 Lyric Opera of Chicago, Chicago, IL
5,000 United Negro College Fund, Chicago, IL

Wurts Memorial, Henrietta Tower

CONTACT
Cecilia Lumsden
Henrietta Tower Wurts Memorial
c/o Fidelity Bank, N.A.
Broad and Walnut Sts.
Philadelphia, PA 19109
(215) 985-8712

FINANCIAL SUMMARY
Recent Giving: $135,794 (1991); $137,200 (1990); $144,702 (1989)
Assets: $3,413,397 (1991); $2,841,814 (1990); $2,800,727 (1989)
EIN: 23-6297977

CONTRIBUTIONS SUMMARY
Donor(s): the late Henrietta Tower Wurts
Typical Recipients: • *Civic & Public Affairs:* municipalities, women's affairs • *Health:* health organizations, pediatric health • *Religion:* religious organizations • *Social Services:* child welfare, community service organizations, domestic violence, family planning, family services, religious welfare, united funds, youth organizations
Grant Types: capital, emergency, general support, multiyear/continuing support, and operating expenses
Geographic Distribution: limited to Philadelphia, PA

GIVING OFFICERS
Fidelity Bank, N.A.: trust
Mrs. H. Carton Dittmann, Jr.: off
Howard Kellogg: off
Pamela G. Model: off
Mrs. Henry T. Reath: off
Sidney N. Repplier: off
S. Stoney Simmons: off

APPLICATION INFORMATION
Initial Approach: Application form required. Deadlines are January 1, May 1, and September 1.
Restrictions on Giving: Does not support individuals.

OTHER THINGS TO KNOW
Publications: Application Guidelines

GRANTS ANALYSIS
Number of Grants: 61
Highest Grant: $5,000
Typical Range: $1,000 to $5,000
Disclosure Period: 1991

RECENT GRANTS
5,000 Education for Parenting, Philadelphia, PA
5,000 Episcopal Community Services, Philadelphia, PA
5,000 Metropolitan Career Center, Philadelphia, PA
5,000 Planned Parenthood Federation of America, Philadelphia, PA
5,000 St. Gabriel's System, Philadelphia, PA
5,000 Women Organized Against Rape, Philadelphia, PA
4,000 Center for Early Childhood Services, Philadelphia, PA
4,000 Philadelphia Refugee Service Center, Philadelphia, PA
4,000 Southwest Community Enrichment Program Project, Philadelphia, PA
3,500 Big Sisters of Philadelphia, Philadelphia, PA

Wurzburg, Inc. / Wurzburg Foundation, Reginald

Former Foundation Name: Reginald Brothers Wurzburg Foundation
Sales: $82.7 million
Employees: 340
Headquarters: Memphis, TN
SIC Major Group: Paper & Allied Products, Printing & Publishing, Wholesale Trade—Durable Goods, and Wholesale Trade—Nondurable Goods

CONTACT
National Bank of Commerce Trustee
Reginald Wurzburg Foundation
One Commerce Sq.
Memphis, TN 38150
(901) 523-3680

FINANCIAL SUMMARY
Recent Giving: $77,720 (1991); $74,750 (1990); $57,250 (1989)
Assets: $806,066 (1991); $708,112 (1990); $699,496 (1989)
Gifts Received: $50,000 (1991); $50,000 (1990); $50,000 (1989)
Fiscal Note: In 1991, contributions were received from Wurzburg Brothers, Inc.
EIN: 62-6048546

CONTRIBUTIONS SUMMARY
Typical Recipients: • *Arts & Humanities:* community arts, music • *Civic & Public Affairs:* business/free enterprise, zoos/botanical gardens • *Education:* colleges & universities, religious education • *Health:* hospitals • *Religion:* religious organizations, synagogues • *Social Services:* aged, community service organizations, food/clothing distribution, youth organizations
Grant Types: general support
Geographic Distribution: focus on TN
Operating Locations: TN (Memphis)

CORP. OFFICERS
Reginald Wurzburg: *B* Memphis TN 1901 *CURR EMPL* ceo, vp: Wurzburg Brothers

GIVING OFFICERS
National Bank of Commerce, Trust Division: trust

APPLICATION INFORMATION
Initial Approach: Company reported in May 1993 that foundation grantmaking is suspended.

GRANTS ANALYSIS
Number of Grants: 55
Highest Grant: $28,500
Typical Range: $250 to $2,000
Disclosure Period: 1991

RECENT GRANTS

28,500 Memphis Jewish Federation, Memphis, TN
7,000 Memphis Rotary Foundation, Memphis, TN
5,000 B'nai B'rith Home and Hospital Building Fund, Memphis, TN
5,000 Memphis Zoo, Memphis, TN
2,400 Christian Brothers College, Memphis, TN
2,000 Memphis Food Bank, Memphis, TN
2,000 Temple Israel, Memphis, TN
1,000 American Society for Technion, Memphis, TN
1,000 Conference for Christians and Jews, Memphis, TN
1,000 St. Jude Children's Research Hospital, Memphis, TN

WWF Paper Corp.

Sales: $750.0 million
Employees: 550
Headquarters: Bala-Cynwyd, PA
SIC Major Group: Wholesale Trade—Nondurable Goods

CONTACT

Donald H. Palmer
Senior Vice President
WWF Paper Corp.
Two Bala Plaza, 2nd Fl.
Bala Cynwyd, PA 19004
(215) 667-9210

FINANCIAL SUMMARY

Fiscal Note: Annual Giving Range: less than $100,000

CONTRIBUTIONS SUMMARY

Support equally divided among local education, human service, arts, V.A. organizations, and civic organizations.
Typical Recipients: • *Arts & Humanities:* public broadcasting • *Civic & Public Affairs:* ethnic/minority organizations • *Education:* student aid • *Health:* emergency/ambulance services • *Social Services:* animal protection
Grant Types: general support
Nonmonetary Support Types: donated products and loaned employees
Geographic Distribution: headquarters community
Operating Locations: PA (Bala Cynwyd)

CORP. OFFICERS

Edward V. Furlong, Jr.: *CURR EMPL* pres: WWF Paper Corp

APPLICATION INFORMATION

Initial Approach: Send brief letter of inquiry, including a description of the organization, amount requested, purpose of funds sought, audited financial statement, and proof of tax-exempt status. There are no deadlines.

GRANTS ANALYSIS

Typical Range: $50 to $1,000

Wyatt Energy, Inc.

Employees: 100
Headquarters: Branford, CT
SIC Major Group: Wholesale Trade—Nondurable Goods

CONTACT

Kirk Blanchard
President & Treasurer
Wyatt Energy, Inc.
322 East Main St.
Branford, CT 06405-3105
(203) 483-4400

CONTRIBUTIONS SUMMARY

Operating Locations: CT (Branford)

CORP. OFFICERS

Dudley F. Blanchard: *CURR EMPL* chmn, dir: Wyatt Energy
George K. Blanchard: *CURR EMPL* hon chmn, dir: Wyatt Energy
Kirk F. Blanchard: *CURR EMPL* pres, treas: Wyatt Energy

Wyle Laboratories

Revenue: $453.4 million
Employees: 1,900
Headquarters: El Segundo, CA
SIC Major Group: Engineering & Management Services and Wholesale Trade—Durable Goods

CONTACT

James Bowers
Senior Vice President, Business Admin.
Wyle Laboratories
128 Maryland St.
El Segundo, CA 90245
(310) 322-1763

CONTRIBUTIONS SUMMARY

Operating Locations: CA (El Segundo)

CORP. OFFICERS

Charles M. Clough: *CURR EMPL* chmn, ceo, dir: Wyle Laboratories
Ralph L. Ozorkiewicz: *CURR EMPL* pres, coo: Wyle Laboratories
Stanley A. Wainer: *CURR EMPL* chmn exec comm: Wyle Laboratories

Wyman-Gordon Co. / Wyman-Gordon Foundation

Revenue: $355.39 million
Employees: 3,000
Headquarters: Worcester, MA
SIC Major Group: Fabricated Metal Products and Primary Metal Industries

CONTACT

Wallace F. Whitney, Jr.
Secretary-Treasurer
Wyman-Gordon Fdn.
244 Worcester St.
North Grafton, MA 01536-8001
(508) 756-5111

FINANCIAL SUMMARY

Recent Giving: $325,000 (1992 approx.); $349,646 (1991); $328,894 (1990)
Assets: $5,070,436 (1991); $4,771,215 (1990); $4,981,947 (1989)
Fiscal Note: Contributes through foundation only.
EIN: 04-6142600

CONTRIBUTIONS SUMMARY

Typical Recipients: • *Arts & Humanities:* general, history/historic preservation, museums/galleries • *Civic & Public Affairs:* general • *Education:* colleges & universities, community & junior colleges, continuing education, economic education, education associations, general • *Health:* general, health organizations, hospitals • *Science:* scientific organizations • *Social Services:* aged, community service organizations, general, united funds, youth organizations
Grant Types: capital, employee matching gifts, fellowship, general support, research, and scholarship
Nonmonetary Support Types: donated equipment, loaned employees, and loaned executives
Geographic Distribution: principally near operating locations and to national organizations

Operating Locations: CA (Mojave, San Leandro), CT (Groton), MA (North Grafton, Worcester), NH (Franklin, Tilton)

CORP. OFFICERS

John M. Nelson: *B* New York NY 1931 *ED* Wesleyan Univ 1953; Harvard Univ 1959 *CURR EMPL* chmn, ceo: Wyman-Gordon Co *CORP AFFIL* dir: Brown & Sharpe Mfg Co, Cambridge Biotech Corp, TSI Corp

GIVING OFFICERS

James E. Coyne: vp
Henry Dormitzer II: vp, dir *B* Medford MA 1935 *ED* Harvard Univ AB 1956 *CURR EMPL* exec vp, dir: Wyman-Gordon Co *CORP AFFIL* trust: Commonwealth Energy Sys; exec vp, dir: Wyman-Gordon Co *NONPR AFFIL* trust: Central MA Health Care; mem: Am Soc Metals, Fin Execs Inst, Worcester Area Chamber Commerce; trust: St Vincents Hosp
William S. Hurley: vp, dir
John M. Nelson: pres *CURR EMPL* chmn, ceo: Wyman-Gordon Co (see above)
Richard L. Stevens: secy, treas, dir
Wallace F. Whitney, Jr.: secy, treas

APPLICATION INFORMATION

Initial Approach: *Initial Contact:* formal proposal *Include Information On:* description of program, purpose of funds requested *When to Submit:* any time
Restrictions on Giving: Does not support individuals, religious organizations for sectarian purposes, or political or lobbying groups.

GRANTS ANALYSIS

Total Grants: $349,646
Number of Grants: 33
Highest Grant: $187,500
Typical Range: $1,000 to $10,000
Disclosure Period: 1991
Note: Recent grants are derived from a 1991 grants list.

RECENT GRANTS

187,500 United Way, Boston, MA
18,295 Worcester Polytechnic Institute, Worcester, MA
12,941 United Way, Danville, MA

10,553 United Way, Boston, MA
10,000 Clark University, Worcester, MA
10,000 Diabetes Foundation Fund, Boston, MA
10,000 Forging Industry Educational and Research Foundation, Boston, MA
10,000 Worcester Foundation for Experimental Biology, Worcester, MA
10,000 Worcester Historical Museum, Worcester, MA
10,000 Worcester Polytechnic Institute, Worcester, MA

Wyman Youth Trust

CONTACT
Wyman Youth Trust
304 Pioneer Bldg.
Seattle, WA 98104
(206) 682-2255

FINANCIAL SUMMARY
Recent Giving: $203,936 (1991); $187,511 (1990); $163,851 (1989)
Assets: $3,485,639 (1991); $3,070,653 (1990); $3,230,181 (1989)
EIN: 91-6031590

CONTRIBUTIONS SUMMARY
Donor(s): members of the Wyman family
Typical Recipients: • *Arts & Humanities:* arts centers, community arts, dance, history/historic preservation, libraries, museums/galleries, theater • *Education:* colleges & universities, private education (precollege) • *Health:* hospitals, pediatric health • *Social Services:* community service organizations, counseling, united funds, youth organizations
Grant Types: general support
Geographic Distribution: limited to King County, WA, and York County, NE.

GIVING OFFICERS
Ann McCall Wyman: off
David C. Wyman: trust
David E. Wyman: trust
Deehan M. Wyman: off
Hal Wyman: off

APPLICATION INFORMATION
Initial Approach: Send brief letter describing program. There are no deadlines.

Restrictions on Giving: Does not support individuals.

OTHER THINGS TO KNOW
Publications: Application Guidelines

GRANTS ANALYSIS
Number of Grants: 140
Highest Grant: $20,000
Typical Range: $40 to $5,000
Disclosure Period: 1991

RECENT GRANTS
20,000 Overlake Hospital Foundation, Seattle, WA
10,000 Bush School, Seattle, WA
7,000 Lakeside School Alumni Fund, WA
5,000 Lakeside School, WA
5,000 New Horizons for Learning, Seattle, WA
5,000 Pacific Arts Center, WA
5,000 Pacific Northwest Ballet, Seattle, WA
5,000 University of Washington, Seattle, WA
4,000 Children's Hospital Foundation, WA

Wyne Foundation

CONTACT
Thomas L. Rosenow
President
Wyne Fdn.
17490 Timber Rd.
Sterling, IL 61081
(312) 645-3950

FINANCIAL SUMMARY
Recent Giving: $70,000 (1990); $48,100 (1989); $28,690 (1988)
Assets: $1,984,673 (1990); $1,992,161 (1989); $1,730,640 (1988)
EIN: 36-6116114

CONTRIBUTIONS SUMMARY
Donor(s): Jeanerte C. Wyne Trust
Typical Recipients: • *Arts & Humanities:* arts institutes, community arts, music, theater • *Civic & Public Affairs:* environmental affairs, municipalities, zoos/botanical gardens • *Education:* colleges & universities • *Religion:* churches, religious organizations • *Social Services:* animal protection
Grant Types: general support
Geographic Distribution: focus on IL

GIVING OFFICERS
Laura R. Knie: trust
Mary V. Rosenow: dir, secy
Thomas L. Rosenow: dir, pres, treas

APPLICATION INFORMATION
Initial Approach: Contributes only to preselected organizations. Applications not accepted.
Restrictions on Giving: Does not support individuals.

GRANTS ANALYSIS
Number of Grants: 17
Highest Grant: $12,000
Typical Range: $100 to $2,500
Disclosure Period: 1990

RECENT GRANTS
12,000 Tisch School of the Arts of New York University, New York, NY
11,500 Opera Music Theatre International, Newark, NJ
7,500 United Way, Sterling, IL
5,000 First Congregational Church, Sterling, IL
5,000 Pittsburgh Opera Company, Pittsburgh, PA
5,000 Tri-County Humane Society, Dixon, IL
3,800 First Baptist Church, Sterling, IL
3,500 Romani Opera Foundation, Los Angeles, CA
3,000 Circle in the Square Theatre, New York, NY
3,000 Eastern Illinois University, Charleston, IL

Wynn's International, Inc.

Sales: $274.0 million
Employees: 1,924
Headquarters: Orange, CA
SIC Major Group: Industrial Machinery & Equipment, Petroleum & Coal Products, and Transportation Equipment

CONTACT
Dorothy Frey
Administrative Secretary
Wynn's International, Inc.
PO Box 14143
Orange, CA 92613-1543
(714) 938-3700

FINANCIAL SUMMARY
Fiscal Note: Annual Giving Range: less than $100,000

CONTRIBUTIONS SUMMARY
Limited support to local education, human service, arts, and civic organizations. Company does not have a formal policy for charitable contributions.
Typical Recipients: • *Arts & Humanities:* general • *Civic & Public Affairs:* general • *Education:* general • *Social Services:* general
Geographic Distribution: headquarters only
Operating Locations: AZ (Tempe), CA (Azusa, Compton, Fullerton, Orange), TN (Lebanon), TX (Ft. Worth), VA (Lynchburg)

CORP. OFFICERS
Wesley E. Bellwood: *CURR EMPL* chmn, dir: Wynns Intl
James Carroll: *CURR EMPL* pres, ceo, dir: Wynns Intl

APPLICATION INFORMATION
Initial Approach: Send brief letter of inquiry, including a description of the organization, amount requested, purpose of funds sought, audited financial statement, and proof of tax-exempt status. There are no deadlines.

Wyomissing Foundation

CONTACT
Alfred G. Hemmerich
Secretary
Wyomissing Fdn.
1015 Penn Ave.
Wyomissing, PA 19610
(215) 376-7494

FINANCIAL SUMMARY
Recent Giving: $554,525 (1991); $961,950 (1990); $437,250 (1989)
Assets: $17,153,565 (1991); $14,637,128 (1990); $14,352,905 (1989)
EIN: 23-1980570

CONTRIBUTIONS SUMMARY

Donor(s): The foundation was incorporated in 1929 by the late Ferdinand Thun and family.

Typical Recipients: • *Arts & Humanities:* arts associations, arts festivals, community arts, dance, history/historic preservation, libraries, museums/galleries, music, performing arts • *Civic & Public Affairs:* economic development, economics, environmental affairs, international affairs, municipalities, zoos/botanical gardens • *Education:* colleges & universities, literacy, science/technology education, special education • *Health:* health funds, health organizations, hospitals, medical rehabilitation • *Religion:* religious organizations • *Social Services:* community centers, community service organizations, family planning, family services, legal aid, united funds, youth organizations

Grant Types: capital, emergency, matching, multiyear/continuing support, operating expenses, and seed money

Geographic Distribution: focus on Berks County, PA, and contiguous counties

GIVING OFFICERS

Thomas A. Beaver: trust
Julia Buckman: trust
Victoria F. Guthrie: trust
Alfred Hemmerich: secy, trust
Sidney D. Kline, Jr.: trust
Marlin Miller, Jr.: pres, trust
Nicholas Muhlenberg: trust
Paul Robert Roedel: trust *B* Millville NJ 1927 *ED* Rider Coll BS 1949 *CURR EMPL* chmn, ceo, pres: Carpenter Technology Corp *CORP AFFIL* dir: Gen Pub Utilities Corp, Meridian Bancorp *NONPR AFFIL* dir: Childrens Home; dir Hawk Mountain counc: Boy Scouts Am; mem: Fin Execs Inst, Mfrs Assn Berks County, Reading-Berks Chamber Commerce, Stainless Steel Indus US; trust: Gettysburg Coll, PA Bus Roundtable
David L. Thun: trust
Ferdinand Thun: trust
Louis Thun: trust
Peter Thun: vp, dir

APPLICATION INFORMATION

Initial Approach:
The foundation requests applications be made in writing.

The foundation has no deadline for submitting proposals.

Restrictions on Giving: The foundation does not make grants to individuals, or for endowments, deficit financing, land acquisition, publications, conferences, scholarships, fellowships, or loans.

OTHER THINGS TO KNOW

Publications: application guidelines, annual report, program policy statement, and financial statement

GRANTS ANALYSIS

Total Grants: $554,525
Number of Grants: 50
Highest Grant: $74,500
Typical Range: $1,000 to $15,000
Disclosure Period: 1991
Note: Recent grants are derived from a 1991 grants list.

RECENT GRANTS

74,500 United Way, Reading, PA
50,000 Pennsylvania State University, Reading, PA
50,000 Williams College, Williamstown, PA
25,000 Albright College, Reading, PA
25,000 Foundation for the Reading Public Museum and Art Gallery, Reading, PA
25,000 Hawk Mountain Sanctuary Association, Kempton, PA
25,000 Lehigh University, Bethlehem, PA
25,000 Schuylkill River Greenway Association, Wyomissing, PA
25,000 St. Joseph's Hospital, Reading, PA
25,000 Wyomissing Public Library, Wyomissing, PA

Wyss Foundation

CONTACT
Wyss Foundation
111 Southwest Fifth Avenue
Portland, OR 97204-3604

FINANCIAL SUMMARY
Recent Giving: $103,250 (fiscal 1991)
Assets: $1,894,457 (fiscal year ending April 30, 1991)
EIN: 93-1010019

CONTRIBUTIONS SUMMARY

Typical Recipients: • *Arts & Humanities:* public broadcasting • *Education:* colleges & universities • *Religion:* churches, religious organizations • *Social Services:* child welfare, family planning

Grant Types: endowment and general support

GRANTS ANALYSIS
Total Grants: $103,250
Number of Grants: 40
Highest Grant: $35,000
Typical Range: $1,000 to $5,000
Disclosure Period: fiscal year ending April 30, 1991

RECENT GRANTS

35,000 Harvard College Fund, MA
35,000 Harvard College Fund, MA
5,000 St. Paul's Episcopal Church
2,000 Oregon Public Broadcasting, OR
2,000 PNCA Endowment
2,000 Westminster Presbyterian
1,500 Alumni Fund of Occidental
1,500 Greek Orthodox Common
1,000 Fosterling Fund
1,000 Planned Parenthood

Xerox Corp. / Xerox Foundation

Sales: $18.26 billion
Employees: 110,000
Headquarters: Stamford, CT
SIC Major Group: Business Services, Industrial Machinery & Equipment, and Wholesale Trade—Durable Goods

CONTACT
Robert H. Gudger
Vice President
Xerox Fdn.
PO Box 1600
Stamford, CT 06904
(203) 968-3306

FINANCIAL SUMMARY
Recent Giving: $15,000,000 (1992 approx.); $15,400,000 (1991); $13,693,506 (1990)
Assets: $245,867 (1991)
Fiscal Note: Above figures include direct giving. In 1991 foundation giving alone was $7,735,841.
EIN: 06-0996443

CONTRIBUTIONS SUMMARY

Typical Recipients: • *Arts & Humanities:* arts associations, arts centers, arts funds, arts institutes, dance, history/historic preservation, libraries, museums/galleries, music, opera • *Civic & Public Affairs:* better government, business/free enterprise, civil rights, economic development, economics, environmental affairs, housing, international affairs, law & justice, professional & trade associations, public policy, urban & community affairs, women's affairs • *Education:* arts education, business education, career/vocational education, colleges & universities, community & junior colleges, continuing education, economic education, education associations, education funds, elementary education, engineering education, faculty development, international exchange, international studies, liberal arts education, literacy, minority education, preschool education, private education (precollege), public education (precollege), science/technology education, special education • *Health:* health care cost containment, hospices, hospitals, medical research, public health • *International:* foreign educational institutions, international development/relief • *Science:* scientific organizations • *Social Services:* aged, child welfare, community service organizations, disabled, domestic violence, drugs & alcohol, employment/job training, recreation & athletics, shelters/homelessness, united funds, youth organizations

Grant Types: capital, department, employee matching gifts, fellowship, general support, project, and scholarship

Nonmonetary Support Types: in-kind services and loaned employees

Note: Estimated value of nonmonetary support for 1990 was $500,000. This support is included in above figure.

Geographic Distribution: nationally and internationally, with emphasis on operating locations

Operating Locations: CA (Anaheim, El Segundo, Hayward, Los Angeles, Palo Alto, Pasadena, Sacramento, San Francisco, Santa Clara, Sunnyvale), CO (Boulder), CT (Greenwich, Stamford), DC, GA (Atlanta), IL (Chicago, Lisle, Mundelein, Naperville), IN (Indianapolis), LA (Metarie), MA (Cambridge), MO (Kansas City), NJ (Basking Ridge, Morristown), NY (New York, Rochester, Webster), PA (Pittsburgh), TX (Dallas, Houston), VA (Arlington, Leesburg)

CORP. OFFICERS

Paul Arthur Allaire: *B* Worcester MA 1938 *ED* Worcester Polytech Inst BSEE 1960; Carnegie-Mellon Univ MSIA 1966 *CURR EMPL* chmn, dir, ceo: Xerox Corp *CORP AFFIL* dir: Crum & Forster, Fuji Xerox Co, Rank Xerox Ltd, Sara Lee Corp; mem investment policy advcomm: US Trade Rep; trust: Worchester Polytech Inst *NONPR AFFIL* mem: Eta Kappa Nu, Tau Beta Pi; trust: Natl Planning Assn

Melvin Howard: *B* Boston MA 1935 *ED* Univ MA BA 1957; Columbia Univ MBA 1959 *CURR EMPL* vchmn, dir: Xerox Corp *CORP AFFIL* chmn: Xerox Credit Corp; chmn, ceo, dir: Xerox Fin Svcs; chmn exec comm, dir: Crum & Forster; dir: Bond Investors Group, Goulds Pumps, LMH Fund, Furman Selz Holding Corp, Van Kampin Merritt, VMS Realty Partners; pres, ceo: Benson Eyecare Corp, Ehrlich Boben Fin Corp *NONPR AFFIL* dir: Am Ins Assn; mem: Am Mgmt Assn, Conf Bd, Counc Fin Execs, Fin Execs Inst, Planning Execs Inst; trust: Norwalk Hosp

David Todd Kearns: *B* Rochester NY 1930 *ED* Univ Rochester BS 1952 *CURR EMPL* chmn, chmn exec comm, ceo, dir: Xerox Corp *CORP AFFIL* dir: Chase Manhattan Bank, Chase Manhattan Corp, Crum & Forster, Dayton Hudson Corp, Fuji Xerox Co, Rank Xerox Ltd, Ryder Sys, Time-Warner, Westmark Sys *NONPR AFFIL* bd visitors: Duke Univ Fuqua Sch Bus; chmn: Natl Urban League, Pres Comm Exec Exchange; chmn natl bd dirs: Jr Achievement; dir: Univ Rochester; mem: Bus Roundtable, Counc Foreign Rels, Natl Action Counc Minorities Engg; trust: Inst Aerobics Res, Stamford Hosp

GIVING OFFICERS

Robert H. Gudger: vp *CURR EMPL* mgr (corp responsibility): Xerox Corp
David Todd Kearns: trust *CURR EMPL* chmn, chmn exec comm, ceo, dir: Xerox Corp (see above)
Allan Z. Senter: treas *B* Brooklyn NY 1941 *ED* Univ RI 1963; Univ Chicago MBA 1965 *CURR EMPL* vp (fin): Xerox Corp *CORP AFFIL* dir: Exel Ins, Xerox Realty Corp
Marty Wagner: secy

APPLICATION INFORMATION

Initial Approach: *Initial Contact:* two- to three-page letter *Include Information On:* legal name of organization, official contact person, proof of tax-exempt status, brief description of the organization's activities and programs, purpose for which funds are sought, benefits expected, plans for evaluation, projected budget, amount of funds needed and expected sources, copy of latest audited financial statement, any other pertinent information *When to Submit:* any time
Restrictions on Giving: Foundation does not support individuals; community colleges; organizations supported by the United Way unless permission has been granted by the United Way to conduct a capital fund drive or special benefit; political organizations or candidates; religious or sectarian groups; or municipal, county, state, federal, or quasi-government agencies.
Foundation does not provide capital grants (except in preselected locations with major company facilities), endowments, in-kind services, or Xerox equipment.
Foundation does not make grants for continuing support; grants may be approved for one to three years, but all requests from organizations that have previously received support will be evaluated as new proposals.

GRANTS ANALYSIS
Total Grants: $7,735,831*
Highest Grant: $1,000,000
Typical Range: $5,000 to $30,000
Disclosure Period: 1991
Note: Figures above are for foundation only. Figures for number of grants and average

grant are not available. Recent grants are derived from a 1991 Form 990.

RECENT GRANTS

1,000,000	University of Rochester, Rochester, NY
436,000	United Way of Tri-State, New York, NY
436,000	United Way of Tri-State, New York, NY
355,000	United Way, Los Angeles, CA
300,000	Rochester Institute of Technology, Rochester, NY
150,000	National Science Center Foundation, Augusta, GA
100,000	Smithsonian National Museum of American History, Washington, DC
93,000	United Way of Metropolitan Dallas, Dallas, TX
90,000	United Way of the National Capitol Area
82,000	United Way of the Bay Area, San Francisco, CA

XTEK Inc. / XTEK Foundation

Sales: $51.0 million
Employees: 404
Headquarters: Cincinnati, OH
SIC Major Group: Industrial Machinery & Equipment and Primary Metal Industries

---

CONTACT
James D. Kiggen
President
XTEK Foundation
11451 Reading Rd.
Cincinnati, OH 45241
(513) 733-7800

FINANCIAL SUMMARY
Recent Giving: $63,000 (1991); $75,175 (1990); $84,220 (1989)
Assets: $207,420 (1991); $245,358 (1990); $280,093 (1989)
Gifts Received: $10,806 (1991); $19,825 (1990); $18,725 (1989)
Fiscal Note: In 1991, contributions were received from James D. Kiggen.
EIN: 31-6029606

CONTRIBUTIONS SUMMARY
Typical Recipients: • *Arts & Humanities:* arts funds • *Educa-*

tion: arts education, colleges & universities, economic education, religious education • *Religion:* religious organizations • *Social Services:* community service organizations, united funds, youth organizations
Grant Types: general support
Geographic Distribution: focus on OH
Operating Locations: OH (Cincinnati)

CORP. OFFICERS
James D. Kiggen: *B* Cleveland OH 1932 *ED* Harvard Univ 1954; Harvard Univ Bus A 1956 *CURR EMPL* chmn, pres, ceo: XTEK

GIVING OFFICERS
James D. Kiggen: pres, dir *CURR EMPL* chmn, pres, ceo: XTEK (see above)
Robert C. Wood: secy, dir

APPLICATION INFORMATION
Initial Approach: Send brief letter describing program. There are no deadlines.

GRANTS ANALYSIS
Number of Grants: 23
Highest Grant: $30,000
Typical Range: $300 to $10,000
Disclosure Period: 1991

RECENT GRANTS

30,000	United Way, Cincinnati, OH
10,500	Fine Arts Fund, Cincinnati, OH
3,700	Xavier University, Cincinnati, OH
3,000	Blue Chips Campaign, Cincinnati, OH
500	College of Mt. St. Joseph, Cincinnati, OH
500	Greater Cincinnati Center for Economic Education, Cincinnati, OH
500	School for Creative and Performing Arts, Cincinnati, OH
500	Spire Foundation, Cincinnati, OH
300	Hebrew Union College, Cincinnati, OH
300	National Conference of Christians and Jews, Cincinnati, OH

Xtra Corp. / Xtra Corp. Charitable Foundation

Revenue: $208.9 million
Employees: 604
Headquarters: Boston, MA
SIC Major Group: Automobile Repair, Services & Parking

CONTACT
Mike Soja
Vice President, Finance
Xtra Corp. Charitable Fdn.
60 State St., 9th Fl.
Boston, MA 02109
(617) 367-5000

FINANCIAL SUMMARY
Recent Giving: $37,375 (fiscal 1990)
Assets: $573,470 (fiscal year ending September 30, 1990)
EIN: 04-2686410

CONTRIBUTIONS SUMMARY
Typical Recipients: • *Arts & Humanities:* community arts, museums/galleries, music, opera • *Education:* colleges & universities, legal education, private education (precollege) • *Health:* hospitals, medical research, pediatric health, single-disease health associations • *Religion:* religious organizations • *Social Services:* united funds
Grant Types: general support
Geographic Distribution: focus on MA
Operating Locations: DE (Wilmington), MA (Boston), ME (Portland), MI (Detroit), MO (St. Louis)

CORP. OFFICERS
Robert B. Georgen: *B* Buffalo NY 1938 *ED* Univ Rochester 1960; Univ PA Wharton Sch 1962 *CURR EMPL* chmn, dir: Xtra Corp
Robert Gintel: *CURR EMPL* vchmn, dir: Xtra Corp
John J. Lee: *CURR EMPL* chmn exec comm, dir: Xtra Corp
Lewis Rubin: *CURR EMPL* pres, ceo, dir: Xtra Corp

GIVING OFFICERS
Robert B. Kaye: trust
Selwyn A. Kudish: trust
Edward P. Roberts: trusts

APPLICATION INFORMATION
Initial Approach: Send brief letter describing program. There are no deadlines.

GRANTS ANALYSIS
Number of Grants: 36
Highest Grant: $12,500
Typical Range: $100 to $3,000
Disclosure Period: fiscal year ending September 30, 1990

RECENT GRANTS
12,500 Boston College Law School, Chestnut Hill, MA
3,000 Children's Mercy Hospital, Kansas City, MO — golf classic
3,000 Millbrook School, Millbrook, NY
2,000 Dedham Choral Society, Boston, MA
2,000 Shake-A-Leg, Newport, RI
1,250 Bentley College, Waltham, MA
1,000 Boston Museum of Science, Boston, MA
1,000 Cardinal Cushing School and Training, Boston, MA
1,000 Pope John XXIII, Boston, MA
1,000 United Way, Boston, MA

Y.K.K. (U.S.A.) Inc.

Sales: $100.0 million
Employees: 1,500
Headquarters: Macon, GA
SIC Major Group: Miscellaneous Manufacturing Industries and Textile Mill Products

CONTACT
Bill Wiley
Senior Vice President, Human Resources
Y.K.K. (U.S.A.) Inc.
3920 Arkwaigh Rd.
Ste. 350
Macon, GA 31210
(912) 744-6350

FINANCIAL SUMMARY
Fiscal Note: Annual Giving Range: $25,000 to $50,000

CONTRIBUTIONS SUMMARY
Approximately one-fifth of the contributions budget goes to United Way. The remaining funds support organizations on a case-by-case basis. Contributions have gone to all the traditional categories of philanthropy: arts and humanities, civic and public affairs, education, health, and social services.
Typical Recipients: • *Arts & Humanities:* arts centers, general • *Civic & Public Affairs:* general • *Education:* general • *Health:* general • *Social Services:* general
Grant Types: general support
Geographic Distribution: headquarters and operating locations

CORP. OFFICERS
Norio Tsubokawa: *CURR EMPL* pres: YKK (USA)

GIVING OFFICERS
Bill Wiley: *CURR EMPL* sr vp (industrial rels): YKK (USA) Inc

APPLICATION INFORMATION
Initial Approach: Applicants may send a brief letter of inquiry, however, unsolicited requests are not encouraged.
Restrictions on Giving: Y.K.K. (U.S.A.) Inc. gives to nonprofits by region. Contact nearest division for more information.

Yale Security Inc.

Sales: $200.0 million
Employees: 2,500
Parent Company: Williams Holdings, Inc.
Headquarters: Charlotte, NC
SIC Major Group: Electronic & Other Electrical Equipment and Fabricated Metal Products

CONTACT
Kathy Drye
Employee Relations Manager
Yale Security Inc.
PO Box 25288
Charlotte, NC 28229-8010
(704) 375-1734

CONTRIBUTIONS SUMMARY
Operating Locations: NC, OH

CORP. OFFICERS
Patrick J. McCord: *CURR EMPL* pres: Yale Security

GIVING OFFICERS
Kathy Drye: *CURR EMPL* employee rels mgr: Yale Security

Yamaichi International (America) Inc.

Revenue: $31.78 million
Employees: 280
Headquarters: New York, NY
SIC Major Group: Security & Commodity Brokers

CONTACT
John Schulten
Director Human Resources
Yamaichi International (America) Inc.
Two World Trade Center
Ste. 9650
New York, NY 10048
(212) 912-6400

CORP. OFFICERS
Scott E. Pardee: *CURR EMPL* chmn, dir: Yamaichi Intl Am
Genji Sugiyama: *CURR EMPL* pres, ceo, dir: Yamaichi Intl Am

GIVING OFFICERS
John Schulten: *CURR EMPL* dir human resources: Yamaichi Intl (Am)

Yassenoff Foundation, Leo

CONTACT
Cynthia A. Cecil-Lazarus
Executive Director
Leo Yassenoff Fdn.
37 North High St., Ste. 304
Columbus, OH 43215
(614) 221-4315

FINANCIAL SUMMARY
Recent Giving: $514,733 (1991); $666,368 (1990); $1,315,987 (1989)
Assets: $5,193,525 (1991); $5,770,026 (1990); $6,438,047 (1989)
EIN: 31-0829426

CONTRIBUTIONS SUMMARY
Donor(s): the late Leo Yassenoff
Typical Recipients: • *Arts & Humanities:* community arts • *Education:* arts education, colleges & universities • *Health:* hospitals, medical research, single-disease health associations • *Religion:* churches, missionary activities, religious organizations, synagogues • *Social Services:* aged, child welfare, community centers, community service organizations, disabled, homes, youth organizations
Grant Types: capital, emergency, project, and seed money
Geographic Distribution: limited to Franklin County, OH

GIVING OFFICERS
Frederick E. Dauterman, Jr.: vchmn, trust
Cynthia A. Cecil Lazarus: exec dir

Melvin L. Schottenstein:
chmn, trust

APPLICATION INFORMATION

Initial Approach: Request
foundation guidelines. Board
meets quarterly. Decisions are
made within three months.
Restrictions on Giving: Does
not support individuals or provide operating support, endowments, deficit financing, debt
reduction, or loans.

OTHER THINGS TO KNOW

Publications: Annual Report,
Application Guidelines

GRANTS ANALYSIS

Number of Grants: 101
Highest Grant: $140,000
Typical Range: $1,000 to
$6,000
Disclosure Period: 1991

RECENT GRANTS

140,000   Ohio State University Development
Fund, Columbus,
OH
50,000   Trilogy Fund, Columbus, OH
34,633   Heilel Foundation,
Columbus, OH
30,000   Ohio State University, Columbus,
OH — Leo Yassen-
off Chair
25,500   Gladden Commu-
nity Center, Colum-
bus, OH
20,000   Columbus Jewish
Foundation, Colum-
bus, OH
15,000   Faith Mission, Columbus, OH
10,500   Vascon Center of
Central Ohio, Co-
lumbus, OH
10,000   Buckeye Boys
Ranch, Grove City,
OH
10,000   Ohio State University College of
Arts, Columbus,
OH

Yawkey Foundation II

CONTACT

John L. Harrington
Executive Director
Yawkey Fdn II
990 Washington St.
Dedham, MA 02026-6716
(617) 329-7470

FINANCIAL SUMMARY

Recent Giving: $352,000 (fis-
cal 1991); $325,000 (fiscal
1990); $107,000 (fiscal 1987)
Assets: $9,224,703 (fiscal year
ending June 30, 1991);
$7,181,651 (fiscal 1990);
$2,137,610 (fiscal 1987)
Gifts Received: $1,839,665
(fiscal 1991); $1,532,400 (fis-
cal 1990); $1,257,643 (fiscal
1987)
Fiscal Note: 1991 contribution
from Jean R. Yawkey.
EIN: 04-2768239

CONTRIBUTIONS SUMMARY

Donor(s): Jean R. Yawkey
Typical Recipients: • *Arts &
Humanities:* community arts,
museums/galleries • *Education:* private education (precollege) • *Health:* hospitals • *Social Services:* child welfare,
community service organizations, disabled, recreation &
athletics, united funds, youth
organizations
Grant Types: general support
Geographic Distribution:
focus on MA, with emphasis
on the greater metropolitan
Boston area

GIVING OFFICERS

William P. Baldwin: trust
William O. Gutfarb: secy,
treas
John L. Harrington: exec dir
Edward F. Kenney: trust
Jean R. Yawkey: trust

APPLICATION INFORMATION

Initial Approach: Send brief
letter describing program.
There are no deadlines.

GRANTS ANALYSIS

Number of Grants: 14
Highest Grant: $150,000
Typical Range: $2,000 to
$30,000
Disclosure Period: fiscal year
ending June 30, 1991

RECENT GRANTS

150,000   National Baseball
Hall of Fame and

Museum, Cooper-
stown, NY
50,000   Massachusetts General Hospital, Bos-
ton, MA
40,000   Yale University,
New Haven, CT
25,000   Por Christo, Boston, MA
20,000   Boys and Girls
Club, Boston, MA
20,000   Tara Hall, Georgetown, SC — public
school operations
10,000   Boston Aid to the
Blind, Boston, MA
10,000   Friends of
C.A.S.A., Boston,
MA
10,000   Second Helping
Program, Boston,
MA
5,000   Boston Pops Or-
chestra, Boston,
MA

Yeager Charitable Trust, Lester E.

CONTACT

William Wilson
Trustee
Lester E. Yeager Charitable Trust
P.O. Box 964
Owensboro, KY 42302-0964
(502) 686-8254

FINANCIAL SUMMARY

Recent Giving: $222,527
(1990); $233,552 (1989)
Assets: $3,824,457 (1990);
$2,465,722 (1989)
Gifts Received: $148,947
(1990); $531,595 (1989)
Fiscal Note: 1990 contribution
received from the Estate of Lester E. Yeager.
EIN: 61-1159548

CONTRIBUTIONS SUMMARY

Donor(s): the donor is the estate of Lester E. Yeager
Typical Recipients: • *Arts &
Humanities:* museums/galler-
ies, music • *Civic & Public Affairs:* municipalities, urban &
community affairs, zoos/botani-
cal gardens • *Education:* ca-
reer/vocational education, colleges & universities, education
associations, education funds,
private education (precollege)
• *Health:* hospices, hospitals
• *Religion:* churches • *Social
Services:* child welfare, community centers, disabled,
homes, recreation & athletics,
shelters/homelessness, united
funds, youth organizations
Grant Types: general support

Geographic Distribution: primarily in Daviess County, KY

GIVING OFFICERS

Ruth F. Adkins: trust
Donald W. Haas: trust
William L. Wilson: trust

APPLICATION INFORMATION

Initial Approach: The trust reports that grants are limited to
501 (c)(3) organizations with
priority in Daviess County,
KY; second priority in Henderson County, KY; third priority
in the state of Kentucky; and
fourth priority in the Southern
Indiana area that borders Kentucky. Applications for grants
are available from the trust.
There are no deadlines.

GRANTS ANALYSIS

Total Grants: $222,527

Number of Grants: 31

Highest Grant: $20,000

Typical Range: $2,000 to
$20,000

Disclosure Period: 1990

RECENT GRANTS

20,000   College Founda-
tion, NY
14,950   Cliff Hagan Boys
Club
13,600   Girls
10,000   Brescia College,
KY
10,000   Green River Educational Foundation
10,000   Kentucky
Wesleyan College,
KY
10,000   Owensboro Area
Museum
10,000   Owensboro Mu-
seum of Fine Art
10,000   YMCA
2,000   Riverpark Center

Yellow Corp. / Yellow Corporate Foundation

Former Foundation Name:
Yellow Freight System
Revenue: $2.26 billion
Employees: 28,800
Headquarters: Overland Park, KS
SIC Major Group: Holding &
Other Investment Offices and
Trucking & Warehousing

CONTACT

Mike Kelley
Vice President
Yellow Corporate Fdn.
10777 Barkley
Overland Park, KS 66211
(913) 967-4351

Note: The Yellow Corporate Foundation was formerly the Yellow Freight System Foundation.

FINANCIAL SUMMARY

Recent Giving: $2,100,000 (1992 approx.); $2,100,000 (1991); $900,785 (1990)

Assets: $2,400,000 (1992); $3,728,966 (1990); $3,559,969 (1989)

Fiscal Note: Figures above include both direct and foundation giving.

EIN: 23-7004674

CONTRIBUTIONS SUMMARY

Typical Recipients: • *Arts & Humanities:* arts centers, arts institutes, community arts, dance, history/historic preservation, museums/galleries, music, opera, performing arts, public broadcasting, theater, visual arts • *Civic & Public Affairs:* economic development, urban & community affairs • *Education:* arts education, business education, colleges & universities, community & junior colleges, economic education • *Social Services:* united funds

Grant Types: capital, employee matching gifts, general support, multiyear/continuing support, operating expenses, and project

Nonmonetary Support Types: in-kind services and workplace solicitation

Note: Estimated value of nonmonetary support for 1993 is $40,000. This amount is included in the above figures. Workplace solicitations are offered only for the United Way.

Geographic Distribution: near headquarters and operating locations only; major emphasis on Kansas City, MO, area

Operating Locations: KS

CORP. OFFICERS

George Everett Powell III: *B* Kansas City MO 1948 *ED* IN Univ BSBA *CURR EMPL* pres, ceo, dir: Yellow Corp *NONPR AFFIL* bd govs: Regular Common Carrier Conf; chmn: Public Television 19, Inc; mem:

Young Pres Org; trust: Midwest Res Inst

George Everett Powell, Jr.: *B* Kansas City MO 1926 *ED* Northwestern Univ 1946 *CURR EMPL* chmn, dir: Yellow Corp *CORP AFFIL* dir: Butler Mfg Co, First Natl Charter Corp *NONPR AFFIL* assoc trust: Nelson Atkins Mus Art; bd govs: Kansas City Art Inst; dir: Kansas City Symphony; mem: Kansas City Chamber Commerce, Northwestern Univ Bus Adv Comm Trans Ctr; trust, mem exec comm: MidWest Res Inst

GIVING OFFICERS

Daniel L. Hornbeck: asst secy
Mike Kelley: mng dir
George Everett Powell, Jr.: trust *CURR EMPL* chmn, dir: Yellow Corp (see above)
George Everett Powell III: trust *CURR EMPL* pres, ceo, dir: Yellow Corp (see above)
Phillip A. Spangler: treas, secy *CURR EMPL* vp, treas: Yellow Freight Sys
Mark J. Spencer: trust

APPLICATION INFORMATION

Initial Approach: *Initial Contact:* letter *Include Information On:* description of the organization, amount requested, purpose for which funds are sought, recently audited financial statement, proof of tax-exempt status *When to Submit:* any time

Restrictions on Giving: Foundation does not support fraternal organizations, goodwill advertising, individuals, political or lobbying groups, or religious organizations for sectarian purposes.

Majority of support is given in the Kansas City area.

GRANTS ANALYSIS

Total Grants: $2,100,000
Number of Grants: 115
Highest Grant: $212,000
Typical Range: $1,000 to $2,500
Disclosure Period: 1992
Note: Recent grants are derived from a 1990 Form 990.

RECENT GRANTS

194,000 Kansas City Symphony, Kansas City, MO
193,825 Nelson Gallery Acquisition Funding, Kansas City, MO
100,000 Health and Social Services

100,000 Kansas City Public Television, Kansas City, MO — capital campaign over five years
37,500 Nelson Gallery of Art, Kansas City, MO — museum continuity
30,000 Lyric Opera, Kansas City, MO
25,000 State Ballet of Missouri, Kansas City, MO
22,000 Greater Kansas City Foundation Marketing Study, Kansas City, MO
15,000 Kansas City Public Television, Kansas City, MO — general operations
15,000 Missouri Repertory Theatre, Kansas City, MO

York Barbell Co. / Hoffman Foundation, Bob

Sales: $10.0 million
Employees: 100
Headquarters: York, PA
SIC Major Group: Miscellaneous Manufacturing Industries

CONTACT

John Terpak, Sr.
Trustee
Bob Hoffman Foundation
PO Box 1707
York, PA 17405
(717) 767-6481

FINANCIAL SUMMARY

Recent Giving: $77,126 (1992); $65,000 (1991); $45,083 (1990)
Assets: $1,575,705 (1992); $1,547,632 (1990)
EIN: 23-6298674

CONTRIBUTIONS SUMMARY

Typical Recipients: • *Civic & Public Affairs:* municipalities, urban & community affairs • *Education:* colleges & universities, private education (precollege) • *Social Services:* community service organizations, youth organizations
Grant Types: general support
Geographic Distribution: focus on PA
Operating Locations: PA (York)

CORP. OFFICERS

Victor J. Standish: *B* New York NY 1936 *ED* Franklin & Marshall Coll 1961 *CURR*

EMPL pres, treas: York Barbell Co

John B. Terpaik, Sr.: *CURR EMPL* chmn: York Barbell Co

GIVING OFFICERS

Alda Ketterman: trust

APPLICATION INFORMATION

Initial Approach: Send brief letter describing program. There are no deadlines.

Restrictions on Giving: Does not support individuals, religious organizations for sectarian purposes, political or lobbying groups, or organizations outside operating areas. Recipient organizations must be not-for-profit to qualify for support.

GRANTS ANALYSIS

Number of Grants: 21
Highest Grant: $10,500
Typical Range: $200 to $5,000
Disclosure Period: 1992

RECENT GRANTS

10,500 Crispus Attucks Community Cantor, York, PA
10,400 Mercersburg Academy, Mercersburg, PA — scholarship
8,140 Brookside Park, Dover, PA
5,741 YMCA, Dover, PA
5,000 Penn Laurel Girl Scout Council, York, PA
4,000 YMCA, York, PA
1,500 Pennsylvania Engineering Foundation, Philadelphia, PA
1,000 York College of Pennsylvania, York, PA
721 Springfield College, Springfield, MA
500 Community Progress Council, York, PA

York International Corp.

Sales: $1.65 billion
Employees: 11,500
Parent Company: York Holdings Corp.
Headquarters: York, PA
SIC Major Group: Industrial Machinery & Equipment

CONTACT
Robert Chattin
Vice President, Human
  Resources
York International Corp.
631 South Richland Ave.
York, PA 17403
(717) 771-7890

CONTRIBUTIONS SUMMARY
Operating Locations: CA
(Santa Fe Springs), PA (Waynesboro, York), TX (San Antonio), VA (Bristol)

CORP. OFFICERS
Dean T. DuCray: *CURR
EMPL* vp, cfo: York Intl Corp
Robert N. Pokelwaldt: *CURR
EMPL* pres, ceo: York Intl Corp

Yosemite Asset Management
Sales: $5,000.0 thousand
Employees: 2
Headquarters: Glendale, CA

CONTACT
Stephen K. Bache
Chief Financial Accountant
Yosemite Asset Management
411 N. Central, Ste. 270
Glendale, CA 91203
(818) 241-5066

FINANCIAL SUMMARY
Fiscal Note: Annual Giving
Range: less than $100,000

CONTRIBUTIONS SUMMARY
Company provides employee
matching gifts only with 100%
of contributions supporting education.
Typical Recipients: • *Education:* colleges & universities
Grant Types: matching
Geographic Distribution: primarily in CA
Operating Locations: CA
(Glendale)

CORP. OFFICERS
Stephen K. Bache: *CURR
EMPL* pres: Yosemite Asset
Mgmt

APPLICATION INFORMATION
Initial Approach: Send brief
letter of inquiry, including a description of the organization,
amount requested, purpose of
funds sought, recently audited
financial statements, and proof
of tax-exempt status.

Restrictions on Giving: Does
not support individuals or
political or lobbying groups.

Yost Trust, Elizabeth Burns

CONTACT
Lee Roy Lookabill
Administrator
Elizabeth Burns Yost Trust
c/o Southern National Bank of
  North Carolina
P.O. Box 111
Wadesboro, NC 28170
(704) 694-6521

FINANCIAL SUMMARY
Recent Giving: $199,391
(1990); $93,333 (1989)
Assets: $2,281,068 (1990);
$2,244,462 (1989)
Gifts Received: $101,415
(1990); $2,193,328 (1989)
Fiscal Note: 1990 contribution
received from the Estate of
Elizabeth B. Yost.
EIN: 56-6355993

CONTRIBUTIONS SUMMARY
Donor(s): the donor is the estate of Elizabeth B. Yost
Typical Recipients: • *Arts &
Humanities:* arts associations,
community arts • *Civic & Public Affairs:* safety • *Education:*
elementary education, public
education (precollege)
• *Health:* emergency/ambulance services, health organizations, hospitals, nutrition &
health maintenance, public
health • *Social Services:* child
welfare, community service organizations, recreation & athletics, united funds
Grant Types: capital, department, general support, and project
Geographic Distribution:
Anson County, NC

GRANTS ANALYSIS
Total Grants: $199,391
Number of Grants: 28
Highest Grant: $50,000
Typical Range: $6,500 to
$22,087
Disclosure Period: 1990

RECENT GRANTS
50,000 Anson County Hospital
22,087 Anson Senior High
  School — for business lab
19,267 Anson County
  School — for attendance counselor

11,500 Anson County
  Health Department
  — nutritionist, insulin program
10,000 J.R. Falson Center
  — "At Risk Children in Falson
  Community"
9,829 Anson County
  Schools — for attendance counselor
7,700 Anson County
  Schools — preservation of permanent school records
6,900 Anson County
  Schools — for
  "Anson County
  Schools Project
  Academics"
6,600 Anson County Arts
  Council
6,500 Anson County
  Health Department

Young Charity Trust Northern Trust Company

CONTACT
Young Charity Trust Northern
  Trust Company
50 South La Salle Street
Chicago, IL 60675-0001
(312) 630-6000

FINANCIAL SUMMARY
Recent Giving: $444,123 (fiscal 1991); $120,950 (fiscal
1990)
Assets: $16,255,695 (fiscal
year ending April 30, 1991);
$13,919,643 (fiscal 1990)
Gifts Received: $1,032,357
(fiscal 1991); $11,251,167 (fiscal 1990)
Fiscal Note: Fiscal 1991 contribution received from the
Trust of Oriet Margaret Young.
EIN: 36-6897850

CONTRIBUTIONS SUMMARY
Typical Recipients: • *Social
Services:* recreation & athletics
Grant Types: general support
Geographic Distribution:
Michigan

GIVING OFFICERS
Charles Hamacher, Jr.: trust
Ralph Schindler, Jr.: trust

APPLICATION INFORMATION
Initial Approach: The foundation reports no specific application guidelines. Send a brief letter of inquiry, including
statement of purpose, amount

requested, and proof of tax-exempt status.

GRANTS ANALYSIS
Total Grants: $444,123
Number of Grants: 1
Highest Grant: $444,123
Disclosure Period: fiscal year
ending April 30, 1991

RECENT GRANTS
444,123 George Young Recreational Complex,
  Iron River, MI

Young Foundation, H and B
Former Foundation Name:
  Morgan City Fund

CONTACT
H and B Young Fdn.
PO Box 889
Morgan City, LA 70380

FINANCIAL SUMMARY
Recent Giving: $224,050
(1990); $235,100 (1989);
$254,500 (1988)
Assets: $6,363,658 (1989);
$6,205,451 (1988)
EIN: 72-6029365

CONTRIBUTIONS SUMMARY
Donor(s): the late Byrnes M.
Young
Typical Recipients: • *Arts &
Humanities:* history/historic
preservation, libraries, music
• *Civic & Public Affairs:* municipalities, zoos/botanical gardens • *Education:* private education (precollege), public
education (precollege) • *Social
Services:* recreation & athletics
Grant Types: general support
and scholarship
Geographic Distribution: limited to Morgan City, LA

GIVING OFFICERS
C. R. Brownell, Jr.: pres, dir
Eugene B. Garber: vp, dir
Charles F. Sanber: treas, dir
Anna Pearl Squires: secy, dir

APPLICATION INFORMATION
Initial Approach: Contributes
only to preselected organizations.

GRANTS ANALYSIS
Number of Grants: 21
Highest Grant: $97,666
Typical Range: $1,000 to
$26,632
Disclosure Period: 1989
Note: No grants list was
provided in 1990.

RECENT GRANTS

97,666 Swamp Garden, Morgan City, LA

26,632 Turn of the Century House, Morgan City, LA

17,200 Archives Commission, Morgan City, LA

16,000 Lake End Park, Morgan City, LA

12,500 Lakewood Hospital, Lakewood, LA

12,302 Morgan City Auditorium, Morgan City, LA

10,000 Morgan City Garden Club, Morgan City, LA

10,000 Morgan City Public Library, Morgan City, LA

5,000 Morgan City High School, Morgan City, LA

Young Foundation, Hugo H. and Mabel B.

CONTACT
R. D. Mayer
Secretary-Treasurer
Hugo H. and Mabel B. Young Fdn.
416 North Wood St.
Loudonville, OH 44842
(419) 994-4501

FINANCIAL SUMMARY
Recent Giving: $241,495 (fiscal 1992); $253,952 (fiscal 1991); $231,126 (fiscal 1990)
Assets: $4,159,779 (fiscal year ending April 30, 1992); $4,055,165 (fiscal 1991); $3,808,815 (fiscal 1990)
EIN: 34-6560664

CONTRIBUTIONS SUMMARY
Typical Recipients: • *Arts & Humanities:* community arts, music • *Civic & Public Affairs:* rural affairs, safety • *Education:* public education (precollege), student aid • *Health:* health organizations, hospitals • *Social Services:* aged, community service organizations, disabled, youth organizations
Grant Types: capital and scholarship
Geographic Distribution: focus on Ashland County, OH

GIVING OFFICERS
Robert Dubler: trust
James Dudte: pres, trust
Avery Hand: vp, trust
John Kirkpatrick: trust

R. D. Mayer: secy, treas, trust
Phillip A. Ranney: chmn, trust

APPLICATION INFORMATION
Initial Approach: Contributes only to preselected organizations.
Restrictions on Giving: Does not support individuals or provide loans.

GRANTS ANALYSIS
Number of Grants: 11
Highest Grant: $82,812
Disclosure Period: fiscal year ending April 30, 1992

RECENT GRANTS

82,812 Kettering Mohican Area Medical Center, Londonville, OH

49,139 West Holmes School, Loudonville, OH

35,185 Loudonville-Perrysville School, Loudonville, OH

30,000 Michigan Area Growth Foundation, Loudonville, OH

22,157 Loudonville Fire Department, Loudonville, OH

4,500 Ashland Symphony Orchestra Association, Ashland, OH

4,000 Boy Scouts of America, Loudonville, OH

4,000 Loudonville-Perrysville Scholarship Fund, Loudonville, OH

3,702 Londonville Swim Team Boosters, Loudonville, OH

3,500 Londonville Agricultural Society, Londonville, OH

Young Foundation, Irvin L.

CONTACT
Fern D. Young
President-Treasurer
Irvin L. Young Fdn.
Snow Valley Ranch
Palmyra, WI 53156
(414) 495-2568

FINANCIAL SUMMARY
Recent Giving: $1,110,623 (1990); $501,188 (1989); $1,089,642 (1988)
Assets: $7,840,191 (1990); $8,586,001 (1989); $8,035,749 (1988)
EIN: 39-6077858

CONTRIBUTIONS SUMMARY
Donor(s): the late Irvin L. Young
Typical Recipients: • *Arts & Humanities:* libraries • *Civic & Public Affairs:* international affairs • *Education:* colleges & universities, religious education • *International:* international development/relief, international organizations • *Religion:* churches, missionary activities, religious organizations • *Social Services:* food/clothing distribution, shelters/homelessness, youth organizations
Grant Types: capital, general support, operating expenses, and scholarship

GIVING OFFICERS
L. Arden Almquist: dir
James H. Bird: dir
David S. Fisher: dir
Mary Longbrake: vp, dir
Robert W. Reninger: secy, dir
Fern D. Young: pres, treas, dir

APPLICATION INFORMATION
Initial Approach: Send brief letter of inquiry and full proposal. There are no deadlines.
Restrictions on Giving: Does not support individuals.

GRANTS ANALYSIS
Number of Grants: 41
Highest Grant: $500,000
Typical Range: $10,000 to $40,000
Disclosure Period: 1990

RECENT GRANTS

500,000 Whitewater Public Library Board — construct Young library

50,000 Mission Aviation Fellowship, Redlands, CA — used plane for Mexico

44,500 Foreign Missionary Society Grace Brethren Bangui Building Fund

35,400 Grace Ministries International — medical and motorcycle

31,500 Evangelical Covenant Church, Chicago, IL — guesthouse

30,000 Girl Scouts of America

27,800 Foreign Missionary Society Grace Brethren Bata Schools

26,500 Evangelical Covenant Church, Chicago, IL — hous-

ing, services, and AIDS protection

25,000 International Aid, Spring Lake, MI

25,000 Mission Aviation Fellowship, Redlands, CA — plane for New Guinea

Young Foundation, R. A.

CONTACT
Raymond A. Young
President
R. A. Young Fdn.
6401 North Pennsylvania Avenue, Ste. 209
Oklahoma City, OK 73116
(405) 840-4444

FINANCIAL SUMMARY
Recent Giving: $649,457 (fiscal 1991); $201,660 (fiscal 1990); $196,640 (fiscal 1989)
Assets: $3,164,212 (fiscal year ending November 30, 1991); $3,123,632 (fiscal 1990); $3,717,810 (fiscal 1989)
EIN: 73-6092654

CONTRIBUTIONS SUMMARY
Donor(s): Raymond A. Young, Verna N. Young
Typical Recipients: • *Arts & Humanities:* community arts, history/historic preservation, museums/galleries • *Education:* colleges & universities, education associations, science/technology education • *Health:* hospitals • *Religion:* churches, religious organizations • *Social Services:* community service organizations, united funds, youth organizations
Grant Types: general support
Geographic Distribution: focus on OK

GIVING OFFICERS
Carolyn Young Hodnett: vp, trust
Alsadean Jeffery: asst secy, treas
Raymond A. Young: pres, trust
Verna N. Young: secy, treas, trust

APPLICATION INFORMATION
Initial Approach: Send brief letter of inquiry describing program or project. There are no deadlines.
Restrictions on Giving: Does not support individuals.

GRANTS ANALYSIS
Number of Grants: 22
Highest Grant: $563,050
Typical Range: $200 to $2,500
Disclosure Period: fiscal year ending November 30, 1991

RECENT GRANTS
563,050 First Baptist Church, Oklahoma City, OK
25,453 YMCA, Oklahoma City, OK
25,000 Baptist Foundation of Oklahoma, Oklahoma City, OK
8,500 Oklahoma State University Foundation, Stillwater, OK
5,400 Oklahoma City Art Museum, Oklahoma City, OK
5,000 Salvation Army, Oklahoma City, OK
3,990 United Way, Oklahoma City, OK
3,990 Wentworth Institute of Technology, Oklahoma City, OK
2,614 Oklahoma University, Norman, OK
2,500 Baptist Student Union, Oklahoma City, OK

Young Foundation, Robert R.

CONTACT
David W. Wallace
President
Robert R. Young Foundation
P. O. Box 1423
Greenwich, CT 06830
Note: The foundation does not list a telephone number.

FINANCIAL SUMMARY
Recent Giving: $703,125 (1991); $745,900 (1990); $1,049,000 (1989)
Assets: $29,412,405 (1990); $30,152,779 (1989)
Gifts Received: $6,863,706 (1989)
Fiscal Note: The foundation received $6,863,706 from the Estate of Anita O'Keefe Young.
EIN: 13-6131394

CONTRIBUTIONS SUMMARY
Donor(s): The foundation was established by the late Anita O'Keefe Young.
Typical Recipients: • *Arts & Humanities:* libraries, music • *Civic & Public Affairs:* women's affairs • *Education:* colleges & universities, legal education, minority education

• *Health:* hospitals, medical research, mental health • *Religion:* churches • *Social Services:* drugs & alcohol, food/clothing distribution, united funds, youth organizations
Grant Types: general support and research
Geographic Distribution: New York and New England

GIVING OFFICERS
David William Wallace: pres, trust *B* New York NY 1924 *ED* Yale Univ BS 1948; Harvard Univ JD 1951 *CORP AFFIL* ceo, chmn, dir, mem exec comm: Lone Star Indus; chmn: Natl Securities and Res Corp, Piper Acceptance Corp, Piper Aircraft Corp; dir: Aitken Hume Intl, BV Capital Corp, Eastern Air Lines, Emigrant Savings Bank, Producers Cotton Oil Co, Putnam Trust Co, SCM Corp, UMC Electronics, Zurn Indus; mem: Lloyds of London *NONPR AFFIL* bd govs: NY Hosp; trust: Smith Coll *PHIL AFFIL* vp, trust: Robert R. Young Foundation
Jean W. Wallace: dir

APPLICATION INFORMATION
Initial Approach:
Applications should be in letter form.
Letters should include a description of the organization requesting funds, qualifications of individuals responsible for program or project, and an outline of proposed use of funds.
Applications are accepted any time.
Applicants may expect a reply, usually within three months.

GRANTS ANALYSIS
Total Grants: $745,900
Number of Grants: 35
Highest Grant: $505,000
Typical Range: $500 to $10,000
Disclosure Period: 1990
Note: Recent grants are derived from a 1990 grants list. The average grant figure excludes the largest grant of $505,000.

RECENT GRANTS
505,000 Smith College, Northampton, MA — education
45,000 Salve Regina College, Portsmouth, RI — education
30,000 Boys and Girls Club of Newport,

Newport, RI — public welfare
30,000 New York Hospital-Cornell Medical Center, New York, NY — medical research
25,000 Christ Church, Trumbull, CT — religious
15,000 United Way of Greenwich, Greenwich, CT — general charities
15,000 Yale University, New Haven, CT — education
10,000 Brick Presbyterian Church, New York, NY — public welfare
10,000 Clubhouse of Suffolk, Kings Park, NY — public welfare
5,000 Cathedral of St. John Divine, New York, NY — religious

Young Memorial Fund, John B. and Brownie

CONTACT
John B. and Brownie Young Memorial Fund
c/o Owensboro National Bank, Trust Dept.
230 Frederica St.
Owensboro, KY 42301
(502) 926-3232

FINANCIAL SUMMARY
Recent Giving: $219,600 (1991); $138,465 (1990); $201,850 (1989)
Assets: $4,375,936 (1991); $3,206,010 (1990); $3,115,924 (1989)
Gifts Received: $214,265 (1990); $176,420 (1989); $141,685 (1987)
EIN: 61-6025137

CONTRIBUTIONS SUMMARY
Grant Types: scholarship
Geographic Distribution: focus on Owensboro, Daviess, and McClean counties, KY

GIVING OFFICERS
Owensboro National Bank: trust

APPLICATION INFORMATION
Initial Approach: Application form required. There are no deadlines.

OTHER THINGS TO KNOW
Provides higher education scholarships for students from the school districts of Owensboro, Daviess, and McClean counties, KY.

GRANTS ANALYSIS
Number of Grants: 4
Highest Grant: $75,000
Typical Range: $69,000 to $75,000
Disclosure Period: 1991

Young & Rubicam / Young & Rubicam Foundation

Sales: $1.0 billion
Employees: 900
Headquarters: New York, NY
SIC Major Group: Business Services

CONTACT
R. John Cooper
President
Young & Rubicam Fdn.
285 Madison Ave.
Tax Department
New York, NY 10017
(212) 210-3000

FINANCIAL SUMMARY
Recent Giving: $541,650 (1991); $567,415 (1990); $490,156 (1989)
Assets: $59,576 (1991); $25,521 (1990); $76,874 (1989)
Gifts Received: $541,650 (1991); $513,979 (1990); $110,700 (1989)
Fiscal Note: Contributes through foundation only. In 1991, contributions were received from Young and Rubicam.
EIN: 13-6156199

CONTRIBUTIONS SUMMARY
Typical Recipients: • *Arts & Humanities:* arts centers, dance, museums/galleries, music, public broadcasting • *Civic & Public Affairs:* international affairs, professional & trade associations, urban & community affairs • *Education:* business education, colleges & universities, education funds, student aid • *Health:* single-disease health associations • *Religion:* religious organizations • *Social Services:* disabled, drugs & alcohol, employment/job training, recreation & athletics, united funds, youth organizations

Grant Types: general support and matching
Geographic Distribution: emphasis on New York
Operating Locations: CA (San Francisco), IL (Lombard), NY (New York)

CORP. OFFICERS

David E. Greene: *B* Bloomington IN 1949 *ED* IN Univ BS 1971; IN Univ ND 1973 *CURR EMPL* cfo, exec vp: Young & Rubicam *NONPR AFFIL* mem: Am Inst CPAs, Natl Assn Corp Treas, Tax Execs Inst
Alexander S. Kroll: *CURR EMPL* chmn, ceo: Young & Rubicam

GIVING OFFICERS

Deborah Carroll: secy
R. John Cooper III: pres, dir *B* East Orange NJ 1942 *ED* Amherst Coll AB 1964; Harvard Univ JD 1968 *CURR EMPL* gen coun, secy, dir: Young & Rubicam *CORP AFFIL* dir: Dentsu Young & Rubican Ptnrships, DWD, Y & R Sovero; gen coun, secy, dir: Young & Rubicam Inc; dir: HOM Inc *NONPR AFFIL* chmn: Millburn-Short Hills Cable Television Comm; mem: Am Assn Advertising Agencies, Am Bar Assn, NY City Bar Assn
David E. Greene: treas, dir *CURR EMPL* cfo, exec vp: Young & Rubicam (see above)
Joan L. Hafey: vp, dir
Mark Edwin Stroock II: vp, dir *B* New York NY 1922 *ED* Bard Coll BA 1947 *CURR EMPL* sr vp, dir (corp rels): Young & Rubicam *NONPR AFFIL* mem mktg & commun div exec comm: Anti-Defamation League Bnai Brith; mem: Pub Affs Counc; trust: Ailey (Alvin) Am Dance Theater, Covenant House NY City, Friends Theatre Mus NY City, NY Urban League

APPLICATION INFORMATION

Initial Approach: *Note:* The foundation supports preselected organizations and does not accept unsolicited requests for funds.
Restrictions on Giving: Does not support individuals, capital or endowment funds, scholarships, fellowships, operating budgets, continuing support, annual campaigns, seed money, emergency funds, deficit financing, special projects, re-search, publications, or conferences. Does not make loans.

GRANTS ANALYSIS

Total Grants: $541,650
Number of Grants: 110*
Highest Grant: $109,177
Typical Range: $500 to $5,000
Disclosure Period: 1991
Note: Number of grants and average grant figures do not include matching gifts totaling $126,805. Recent grants are derived from a 1991 grants list.

RECENT GRANTS

109,177 United Way, New York, NY
33,697 United Way, New York, NY
15,000 Advertising Council, New York, NY
10,000 Advertising Council, New York, NY
10,000 Bank Street College of Education, New York, NY
10,000 Hugh O'Brian Youth Foundation, St. Louis, MO
8,200 Jobs for Youth, New York, NY
7,500 Council on Foreign Relations, New York, NY
7,500 Lincoln Center for the Performing Arts, New York, NY
6,000 YWCA, New York, NY

Younkers, Inc. / Younkers Foundation

Revenue: $330.0 million
Employees: 4,300
Parent Company: Equitable of Iowa Cos.
Headquarters: Des Moines, IA
SIC Major Group: General Merchandise Stores

CONTACT

Jolene Radke
Younkers Inc.
Seventh and Walnut Sts.
Des Moines, IA 50309
(515) 247-7120

FINANCIAL SUMMARY

Recent Giving: $208,362 (1990); $231,573 (1989)
Assets: -$88,221 (1990); $1,348 (1989); $1,438 (1987)
Gifts Received: $230,200 (1989); $302,943 (1987)
EIN: 42-0937873

CONTRIBUTIONS SUMMARY

Typical Recipients: • *Arts & Humanities:* arts centers, music, public broadcasting, theater • *Civic & Public Affairs:* zoos/botanical gardens • *Education:* business education, colleges & universities • *Health:* single-disease health associations • *Science:* scientific organizations • *Social Services:* family services, united funds
Grant Types: general support
Geographic Distribution: emphasis on IA
Operating Locations: IA (Des Moines)

CORP. OFFICERS

W. Thomas Gould: *B* Greensboro FL 1946 *ED* FL St Univ 1968 *CURR EMPL* chmn, dir: Younkers *CORP AFFIL* prin: Frederick Atkins *NONPR AFFIL* dir: Am Retail Assn, Natl Retail Merchants Assn
Robert Mosco: *CURR EMPL* pres, dir: Younkers

GIVING OFFICERS

William Thomas Gould: pres *B* Greensboro FL 1946 *ED* FL St Univ 1968 *CURR EMPL* pres, ceo: Younkers *CORP AFFIL* pres, ceo: Younkers Inc; prin: Atkins (Frederick) Inc *NONPR AFFIL* dir: Am Retail Assn, Natl Retail Merchants Assn
Richard Luse: secy, treas *CURR EMPL* vp, cfo: Younkers
Jack Warren Prouty: vp *B* Chippewa Falls WI 1946 *ED* Univ CA Santa Barbara 1968; Univ CA Los Angeles 1971 *CURR EMPL* sr vp, secy, treas, cfo, dir: Younkers *CORP AFFIL* sr vp, secy, treas, cfo, dir: Younkers Inc
Gerald Bart Roth: vp *B* New York NY 1941 *CURR EMPL* exec vp: Younkers *CORP AFFIL* exec vp: Younkers Inc *NONPR AFFIL* vchmn: Downtown Des Moines
Donald Thomas: vp
Carl Ziltz: vp

APPLICATION INFORMATION

Initial Approach: Send letter of request which includes information as to need and use of funds.
Restrictions on Giving: Geographical area limited to the five-state region in which company operates retail stores. Does not support individuals.

GRANTS ANALYSIS

Number of Grants: 82
Highest Grant: $40,000
Typical Range: $200 to $2,000
Disclosure Period: 1990

RECENT GRANTS

40,000 United Way, Des Moines, IA
15,000 Omaha Community Playhouse, Omaha, NE
10,174 Arthritis Foundation
10,000 Homes of Oak-ridge, Des Moines, IA — building fund
10,000 Iowa Children's and Family Services, Des Moines, IA
10,000 Science Center of Iowa, Des Moines, IA
10,000 Smoother Sailing, Des Moines, IA
10,000 United Way, Omaha, NE
8,000 Arthritis Foundation
7,800 Quad City Arts, Davenport, IA

Youth Foundation

CONTACT

Edward F. L. Bruen
Vice President
Youth Fdn.
36 West 44th St.
New York, NY 10036

FINANCIAL SUMMARY

Recent Giving: $172,750 (1991); $147,000 (1990); $131,000 (1989)
Assets: $6,123,608 (1991); $5,108,597 (1990); $5,002,288 (1989)
Gifts Received: $11,785 (1991); $12,616 (1990); $4,365 (1989)
EIN: 13-6093036

CONTRIBUTIONS SUMMARY

Donor(s): the late Alexander M. Hadden, the late Mrs. Alexander M. Hadden
Typical Recipients: • *Civic & Public Affairs:* municipalities • *Education:* colleges & universities, religious education • *Religion:* religious organizations • *Social Services:* child welfare, shelters/homelessness, youth organizations
Grant Types: scholarship
Geographic Distribution: focus on NY

GIVING OFFICERS
Edward F. L. Bruen: vp, dir
Mrs. C. Kenneth Clinton: dir
John L. Fenton: dir
James W. Gerard: dir
Jean S. Gerard: dir
John Campbell Henry: dir
Mrs. Donald M. Liddell, Jr.: dir
Henry S. Middendorf, Jr.: secy, dir
Asa E. Phillips, Jr.: dir
Harry Roberts: dir
Mrs. Guy Norman Robinson: pres, dir
Horace B. B. Robinson: dir
Jack L. Rubin: treas, dir
Allan David Russell: dir *B* Cleveland OH 1924 *ED* Yale Univ BA 1945; Yale Univ LLB 1951 *NONPR AFFIL* dir, vp: Twain (Mark) Library; mem: Am Soc Corp Secys, CT Bar Assn, NY City Bar Assn, St Nicholas Soc NY, Yale Univ Alumni Assn

APPLICATION INFORMATION
Initial Approach: All entries must include self-addressed stamped envelope. Send letter requesting application form with recommendation. Deadline is April 15. Decisions are made in June.
Restrictions on Giving: Does not support post-graduate studies.

OTHER THINGS TO KNOW
Publications: Application Guidelines

GRANTS ANALYSIS
Number of Grants: 90
Highest Grant: $1,000
Typical Range: $500 to $1,000
Disclosure Period: 1991

RECENT GRANTS
1,000 ASTA
1,000 Billy Graham Evangelistic Association, Minneapolis, MN
1,000 Boys Brotherhood
1,000 Campus Crusade for Christ, San Bernardino, CA
1,000 Covenant House, New York, NY
1,000 Focus
1,000 Freedom Foundation at Valley Forge, Valley Forge, PA
1,000 Hillsdale College, Hillsdale, MI
1,000 Sheltering Arms
1,000 Teen Challenge

Yulman Trust, Morton and Helen

CONTACT
Morton and Helen Yulman Trust
c/o First Union Nfational Bank
PO Box 44245
Jacksonville, FL 30231-4245

FINANCIAL SUMMARY
Recent Giving: $175,482 (1991); $170,207 (1990); $223,700 (1989)
Assets: $2,601,320 (1991); $2,382,502 (1990); $2,387,343 (1989)
EIN: 14-6015572

CONTRIBUTIONS SUMMARY
Donor(s): Morton Yulman, Helen Yulman
Typical Recipients: • *Civic & Public Affairs:* ethnic/minority organizations • *Education:* colleges & universities, religious education • *Health:* hospitals • *Religion:* religious organizations, religious organizations • *Social Services:* community service organizations, youth organizations
Grant Types: general support
Geographic Distribution: focus on upstate NY and FL

GIVING OFFICERS
Helen Morton Yulman: investment mgr

APPLICATION INFORMATION
Initial Approach: Contributes only to preselected organizations.

GRANTS ANALYSIS
Number of Grants: 29
Highest Grant: $16,666
Typical Range: $250 to $5,000
Disclosure Period: 1991

RECENT GRANTS
16,666 Greater Miami Jewish Federation, Miami, FL
16,666 Jewish Federation, Palm Beach, FL
15,000 Greater Miami Jewish Federation, Miami, FL
15,000 Greater Miami Jewish Federation, Miami, FL
15,000 Jewish Federation, Palm Beach, FL
15,000 Jewish Federation, Palm Beach, FL
12,500 Anti-Defamation League, Miami, FL

12,500 University at Albany Fund, Albany, NY
12,500 University of Albany Fund, Albany, NY
10,000 Union College Annual Fund, Schenectady, NY

Zaban Foundation

CONTACT
Marshall Dinerman
Secretary
Zaban Fdn.
335 Green Glen Way
Atlanta, GA 30327
(404) 850-3838

FINANCIAL SUMMARY
Recent Giving: $263,250 (fiscal 1992); $320,275 (fiscal 1991); $210,828 (fiscal 1990)
Assets: $3,296,502 (fiscal year ending June 30, 1991); $3,697,306 (fiscal 1990); $3,320,955 (fiscal 1989)
Fiscal Note: In fiscal 1992, contributions received from Erwin Zaban.
EIN: 58-6034590

CONTRIBUTIONS SUMMARY
Donor(s): Erwin Zaban
Typical Recipients: • *Arts & Humanities:* history/historic preservation • *Civic & Public Affairs:* zoos/botanical gardens • *Education:* private education (precollege) • *Health:* medical research, single-disease health associations • *Religion:* religious organizations, synagogues • *Social Services:* community service organizations
Grant Types: general support
Geographic Distribution: focus on Atlanta, GA

GIVING OFFICERS
Marshall Dinerman: secy
Erwin Zaban: pres, treas *B* Atlanta GA 1921 *CURR EMPL* chmn, dir: Natl Svc Indus *CORP AFFIL* dir: Engraph Inc, First Wachovia Corp

APPLICATION INFORMATION
Initial Approach: Contributes only to preselected organizations.
Restrictions on Giving: Does not support individuals.

GRANTS ANALYSIS
Number of Grants: 17
Highest Grant: $105,500

Typical Range: $1,000 to $15,000
Disclosure Period: fiscal year ending June 30, 1991
Note: Grants list not provided for fiscal 1992.

RECENT GRANTS
105,500 Atlanta Jewish Federation, Atlanta, GA
58,025 Atlanta Jewish Federation, Atlanta, GA
54,750 Atlanta Jewish Federation, Atlanta, GA
25,000 Atlanta Jewish Federation, Atlanta, GA
25,000 Carter Presidential Library, Atlanta, GA
20,000 Atlanta Historical Society, Atlanta, GA
12,500 M.D. Anderson Cancer Center, San Antonio, TX
5,000 American Jewish Committee
5,000 Camp Twin Lakes
2,000 P.A.L. Program

Zacharia Foundation, Isaac Herman

CONTACT
Isaac Herman Zacharia
President
Isaac Herman Zacharia Fdn.
Rd 31 KM 24 HMG
Rico Blanco, PR

FINANCIAL SUMMARY
Recent Giving: $105,000 (1991); $67,486 (1990); $95,815 (1989)
Assets: $3,307,845 (1991); $3,157,671 (1990); $3,085,433 (1989)
EIN: 51-0108212

CONTRIBUTIONS SUMMARY
Donor(s): Isaac Herman Zacharia
Typical Recipients: • *Arts & Humanities:* history/historic preservation • *Education:* religious education • *Religion:* religious organizations, synagogues • *Social Services:* aged, community service organizations, disabled
Grant Types: general support
Geographic Distribution: focus on NY

GIVING OFFICERS
Issac Herman Zacharia: pres

APPLICATION INFORMATION
Initial Approach: Send brief letter of inquiry describing program. There are no deadlines.

GRANTS ANALYSIS
Number of Grants: 30
Highest Grant: $50,000
Typical Range: $200 to $1,000
Disclosure Period: 1991

RECENT GRANTS
50,000 Bobover Yeshivah B'nai Zion, New York, NY
25,000 Mosdos Bobov, New York, NY
5,500 Sephardic Temple, Cedarhurst, NY
5,000 Sephardic Home for the Aged, Brooklyn, NY
3,000 Jewish Guild for the Blind, New York, NY
1,050 Community Research Institute, New York, NY
1,000 Minds for History, New York, NY
800 Dorot, New York, NY
800 National Trust for Historic Preservation, Washington, DC
750 Shaarey Zedeck Synagogue, New York, NY

Zachry Co., H. B. / Zachry Foundation

CONTACT
Pat O'Connor
H. B. Zachry Co.
2500 Tower Life Bldg.
San Antonio, TX 78205
(512) 554-4666

FINANCIAL SUMMARY
Recent Giving: $402,995 (1991); $280,850 (1990); $541,500 (1989)
Assets: $7,118,852 (1991); $6,837,307 (1990); $6,516,316 (1989)
Gifts Received: $4,561,968 (1989); $1,090,000 (1988)
EIN: 74-1485544

CONTRIBUTIONS SUMMARY
Typical Recipients: • *Arts & Humanities:* arts associations, libraries, music, public broadcasting • *Civic & Public Affairs:* international affairs,

zoos/botanical gardens • *Education:* colleges & universities, religious education • *Social Services:* united funds
Grant Types: capital, endowment, general support, multi-year/continuing support, project, research, and scholarship
Geographic Distribution: limited to TX, with emphasis on San Antonio

CORP. OFFICERS
Emma Leigh Carter:
Charles E. Ebrom: *CURR EMPL* exec vp, dir: Zachry (HB) Co *CORP AFFIL* exec vp, dir: Zachry (HB) Co
Murray Lloyd Johnston, Jr.: *B* Lake Charles LA 1940 *ED* Austin Coll 1962; Univ TX 1965 *CURR EMPL* vp, secy, gen coun, dir: Zachry (HB) Co *CORP AFFIL* vp, secy, gen coun, dir: Zachry (HB) Co *NONPR AFFIL* mem: Am Bar Assn, Am Judicature Soc, Intl Assn Defense Counc
Dorothy G. Martin:
Henry Bartell Zachry, Jr.: *B* Laredo TX 1933 *ED* TX A&M Univ BS 1954; Harvard Bus Sch *CURR EMPL* chmn, dir: Zachry (HB) Co *CORP AFFIL* chmn, dir: Zachry (HB) Co; chmn, pres, dir: Capitol Aggregates; dir: Southwest Res Inst
Mollie S. Zachry:

APPLICATION INFORMATION
Initial Approach: Send cover letter and full proposal. Deadline is one month prior to quarterly board meetings.
Restrictions on Giving: Does not support individuals.

GRANTS ANALYSIS
Number of Grants: 43
Highest Grant: $64,000
Typical Range: $1,000 to $10,000
Disclosure Period: 1991

RECENT GRANTS
64,000 University of Texas at San Antonio, San Antonio, TX
36,500 St. Mary's University, San Antonio, TX
30,000 San Antonio Symphony, San Antonio, TX
25,000 Alamo Community College, San Antonio, TX
25,000 TSTO Development Foundation, Waco, TX

25,000 University of Texas, Austin, TX — J.J. Pickle Scholarship Program
25,000 University of Texas, Austin, TX — McDonald Observatory
20,000 Cancer Therapy and Research Foundation of South Texas, San Antonio, TX
16,000 World Affairs Council of San Antonio, San Antonio, TX
15,000 Grandparents Outreach, San Antonio, TX

Zachry Co., H.B.
Revenue: $700.0 million
Employees: 10,000
Headquarters: San Antonio, TX
SIC Major Group: Heavy Construction Except Building Construction

CONTACT
Cathy Obriotti Green
Vice President of Public Affairs
H.B. Zachry Co.
310 S. St. Mary, Ste. 2500
San Antonio, TX 78205
(512) 223-4061

FINANCIAL SUMMARY
Fiscal Note: Annual Giving Range: 100,000 to $250,000

CONTRIBUTIONS SUMMARY
Operating Locations: TX (San Antonio)

CORP. OFFICERS
Bruce B. Cloud: *CURR EMPL* pres: HB ZachryCo
Henry Bartell Zachry, Jr.: *B* Laredo TX 1933 *ED* TX A&M Univ BS 1954; Harvard Bus Sch *CURR EMPL* chmn, dir: Zachry (HB) Co *CORP AFFIL* chmn, dir: Zachry (HB) Co; chmn, pres, dir: Capitol Aggregates; dir: Southwest Res Inst

APPLICATION INFORMATION
Initial Approach: Send a letter of inquiry which includes a description of organization, amount requested, purpose of funds sought, proof of tax-exempt status, list of other contributors, and breakdown of administration/fundraising costs.
Restrictions on Giving: Does not support individuals, relig-

ious organizations for sectarian purposes, or organizations outside operating areas.

Zale Corp.
Sales: $1.34 billion
Employees: 10,000
Headquarters: Irving, TX
SIC Major Group: Miscellaneous Retail

CONTACT
Reg Garrett
Vice President, Human Resources
Zale Corp.
901 W. Walnut Hill Ln.
Irving, TX 75038
(214) 580-4000

CONTRIBUTIONS SUMMARY
Company reports contributions suspended until April 1992.
Operating Locations: TX (Irving)

CORP. OFFICERS
Dean Groussman: *CURR EMPL* chmn, pres, ceo: Zale Corp

GIVING OFFICERS
Reg Garrett: *CURR EMPL* vp (human resources): Zale Corp

Zale Foundation

CONTACT
Michael F. Romaine
President
Zale Foundation
3102 Maple Avenue, Ste. 160
Dallas, TX 75201
(214) 855-0627

FINANCIAL SUMMARY
Recent Giving: $929,300 (1992 approx.); $1,016,296 (1991); $860,492 (1990)
Assets: $19,774,000 (1992 approx.); $18,942,841 (1991); $16,438,499 (1990); $16,567,816 (1989)
Gifts Received: $346,300 (1991); $384,145 (1990); $31,625 (1989)
Fiscal Note: In 1990, the foundation received contributions from Abe Zale ($250,000), the Jewish Community Foundation ($58,250), Leo Fields ($21,845), Donald Zale ($13,125), Gloria Landsberg ($112,750), Temple Sholom ($5,250), Steven Landsberg ($5,000), and other miscellaneous contributors.
EIN: 75-6037429

CONTRIBUTIONS SUMMARY

Donor(s): The Zale Foundation was established in 1951 with gifts from the founding family of the Zale Corporation, a chain of jewelry and general merchandise stores.

Typical Recipients: • *Arts & Humanities:* museums/galleries, opera, public broadcasting • *Civic & Public Affairs:* civil rights, economic development, ethnic/minority organizations, philanthropic organizations • *Education:* colleges & universities, private education (precollege) • *Health:* hospitals, pediatric health • *International:* international health care • *Religion:* religious organizations, synagogues • *Social Services:* child welfare, community centers, community service organizations, day care, family services, food/clothing distribution, shelters/homelessness, youth organizations

Grant Types: challenge, project, and seed money

Geographic Distribution: no geographic restrictions

GIVING OFFICERS

Leo Fields: dir *B* Wichita Falls TX 1928 *ED* Univ TX *CURR EMPL* chmn: Leo Fields Interests *CORP AFFIL* pres, adv: Weisbart & Fields *NONPR AFFIL* pres: Dallas Home Jewish Aged Fdn; vchmn: Inst Soc & Econ Policy Middle East

Gloria Landsberg: dir

Bruce Lipshy: dir *B* 1941 *ED* Univ TX BBA 1963; Univ TX LLD 1965 *CORP AFFIL* dir: Interfirst Bank *NONPR AFFIL* dir: Goodwill Indus, Temple Shalom, Un Way Dallas; mem: Dallas Bar Assn, TX Bar Assn

Michael F. Romaine: pres, dir *B* Brooklyn NY 1939 *ED* Millersville St Coll 1966; PA St Univ 1970 *CURR EMPL* vp (community rels): Zale Corp *NONPR AFFIL* pres: Univ Med Ctr

George Tobolowsky: secy, treas

Abe Zale: dir

David Zale: dir

Donald Zale: chmn bd dirs *B* 1933 *ED* Southern Methodist Univ BBA 1954

APPLICATION INFORMATION

Initial Approach:
Applicants should send a brief proposal letter introducing their organization.

Proposals must include a concise description of the proposed project, its purpose, and significance; timetable; budget listing other sources of support; qualifications of key project personnel; plan for continuing project after foundation funding is completed; proof of tax-exempt status; listing of other philanthropic sources approached for funding; and background of applicant organization.

There are no deadlines for submitting requests.

The grant review committee meets one month prior to board meetings to discuss applications.

Restrictions on Giving: The foundation generally avoids endowments, building funds, operating budgets, and ongoing project support. Funding generally is limited to a period of not more than three to five years.

GRANTS ANALYSIS

Total Grants: $1,016,296
Number of Grants: 92
Highest Grant: $250,000
Typical Range: $2,000 to $15,000
Disclosure Period: 1991
Note: Recent grants are derived from a 1991 Form 990.

RECENT GRANTS

250,000 UT Southwestern Medical Center, Dallas, TX
200,000 Operation Exodus, Dallas, TX
84,700 Greenhill School, Dallas, TX
60,000 Temple Shalom, Dallas, TX
37,500 Harvard University, Cambridge, MA
31,000 University of Texas at Dallas, Richardson, TX
25,000 South Palm Beach Jewish Federation-Early Childhood Learing Center, Boca Raton, FL
25,000 Vogel Alcove, Dallas, TX
15,500 Lift, Dallas, TX
14,750 United Way of Metro Dallas, Dallas, TX

Zale Foundation, William and Sylvia

CONTACT
Joe Bock
Trustee
William and Sylvia Zale Fdn.
PO Box 223566
Dallas, TX 75222
(214) 821-2130

FINANCIAL SUMMARY
Recent Giving: $331,288 (fiscal 1991); $591,029 (fiscal 1990); $239,644 (fiscal 1989)
Assets: $3,699,737 (fiscal year ending August 31, 1991); $3,716,930 (fiscal 1990); $3,989,818 (fiscal 1989)
EIN: 75-6037591

CONTRIBUTIONS SUMMARY
Typical Recipients: • *Civic & Public Affairs:* urban & community affairs • *Education:* private education (precollege) • *Health:* hospitals, pediatric health • *Religion:* religious organizations, synagogues • *Social Services:* community centers, community service organizations
Grant Types: general support
Geographic Distribution: focus on Dallas, TX

GIVING OFFICERS
Eugene Zale: trust
Lew D. Zale: trust
Theodore Zale: trust

APPLICATION INFORMATION
Initial Approach: The foundation reports it only makes contributions to preselected charitable organizations.
Restrictions on Giving: Does not support individuals or provide scholarships or loans.

GRANTS ANALYSIS
Number of Grants: 46
Highest Grant: $50,000
Typical Range: $1,000 to $10,000
Disclosure Period: fiscal year ending August 31, 1991

RECENT GRANTS
50,000 Jewish Federation, Dallas, TX
50,000 Jewish Federation, Dallas, TX
34,000 Children's Medical Foundation of Texas, Dallas, TX
33,000 Jewish Federation, Dallas, TX

20,000 Congregation Sherith Israel, Dallas, TX
12,000 Jewish Community Center, Dallas, TX
10,000 Dallas Foundation Committee for Excellence in Education, Dallas, TX
10,000 Jewish Family Services, Dallas, TX
10,000 Parkland Foundation, Dallas, TX
10,000 United Way, Dallas, TX

Zamoiski Co. / Zamoiski Foundation

Sales: $75.0 million
Employees: 75
Headquarters: Baltimore, MD
SIC Major Group: Wholesale Trade—Durable Goods and Wholesale Trade—Nondurable Goods

CONTACT
Calman J. Zamoiski, Jr.
President
Zamoiski Foundation
3000 Waterview Ave.
Baltimore, MD 21230
(410) 539-3000

FINANCIAL SUMMARY
Recent Giving: $84,543 (1991); $132,764 (1990); $144,227 (1989)
Assets: $385,786 (1991); $399,456 (1990); $514,687 (1989)
EIN: 52-6043231

CONTRIBUTIONS SUMMARY
Typical Recipients: • *Arts & Humanities:* arts festivals, community arts, museums/galleries, music • *Civic & Public Affairs:* environmental affairs, urban & community affairs • *Education:* private education (precollege) • *Health:* health organizations, hospitals • *Religion:* religious organizations • *Social Services:* community service organizations
Grant Types: endowment and general support
Geographic Distribution: focus on Baltimore, MD
Operating Locations: MD (Baltimore)

CORP. OFFICERS
William Kitchell: *CURR EMPL* cfo: Zamoiski Co

Calman J. Zamoiski: *CURR EMPL* chmn, pres, ceo: Zamoiski Co

GIVING OFFICERS
Calman J. Zamoiski, Jr.: pres, dir

APPLICATION INFORMATION
Initial Approach: Send brief letter describing program. There are no deadlines.

GRANTS ANALYSIS
Number of Grants: 21
Highest Grant: $23,693
Typical Range: $250 to $2,500
Disclosure Period: 1991

RECENT GRANTS
23,693 Johns Hopkins University, Baltimore, MD
11,500 Baltimore Museum of Art, Baltimore, MD
10,000 Baltimore Symphony Orchestra, Baltimore, MD
10,000 United Way, Baltimore, MD
6,950 Johns Hopkins University, Baltimore, MD
3,500 Baltimore Festival of Arts, Baltimore, MD
3,500 Baltimore School for the Arts, Baltimore, MD
3,000 Har Sinai Congregation, Baltimore, MD
2,000 Catholic Charities, Baltimore, MD
2,000 Harbor Hospital, Baltimore, MD

Zapata Corp.
Sales: $93.4 million
Employees: 2,200
Headquarters: Houston, TX
SIC Major Group: Oil & Gas Extraction and Water Transportation

CONTACT
Mary Cashiola
Manager, Corporate Services
Zapata Corp.
PO Box 4240
Houston, TX 77210-4240
(713) 940-6100

FINANCIAL SUMMARY
Fiscal Note: Annual Giving Range: less than $100,000

CONTRIBUTIONS SUMMARY
Company reports 28% of contributions support civic and

public affairs; 28% to education; 23% to the arts; and 21% to health and welfare.
Typical Recipients: • *Arts & Humanities:* general • *Civic & Public Affairs:* general • *Education:* general • *Social Services:* general
Grant Types: general support
Operating Locations: LA (Abbeville, Cameron, Hammond), MS (Moss Point), TX (Houston), VA (Reedville)

CORP. OFFICERS
Ronald C. Lassiter: *B* Houston TX 1932 *ED* Rice Univ 1955; Harvard Univ Sch Bus Admin 1964 *CURR EMPL* chmn, ceo, dir: Zapata Corp *CORP AFFIL* dir: Daniel Indus, Pesquera Zapata SA, Zapata Exploration Co, Zapata Gulf Marine Corp, Zapata Haynie Corp, Zapata Off-Shore Co

APPLICATION INFORMATION
Initial Approach: Send brief letter of inquiry. There are no deadlines.

Zarkin Memorial Foundation, Charles

CONTACT
Constance Monte
Secretary
Charles Zarkin Memorial Fdn.
c/o Wachtell, Lipton, Rosen & Katz
299 Park Ave.
New York, NY 10171
(212) 371-9200

FINANCIAL SUMMARY
Recent Giving: $240,250 (1991); $128,500 (1989); $143,000 (1987)
Assets: $3,877,256 (1991); $4,663,681 (1989); $3,778,819 (1987)
EIN: 23-7149277

CONTRIBUTIONS SUMMARY
Donor(s): the late Fay Zarkin
Typical Recipients: • *Civic & Public Affairs:* zoos/botanical gardens • *Health:* hospitals • *Religion:* religious organizations • *Social Services:* child welfare, community service organizations, youth organizations
Grant Types: general support

Geographic Distribution: focus on New York, NY

GIVING OFFICERS
Martin Lipton: pres, treas, trust *B* NJ 1931 *ED* Univ PA BS 1952; NY Univ LLB 1955 *CURR EMPL* ptnr: Wachtell Lipton Rosen & Katz *NONPR AFFIL* mem counc: Am Law Inst; pres, bd trust: NY Univ Law Sch; pres bd trusts: Law Ctr Fdn; treas: Inst Judicial Admin; trust: NY Univ, Univ PA
Susan Lipton: trust
Robert B. McKay: off *ED* Univ KS BS 1940; Yale Univ JD 1947 *NONPR AFFIL* dir: Am Arbitration Assn, Mexican Am Legal Defense Ed Fund, Vera Inst Justice; mem: Am Bar Assn, NY Bar Assn, NY City Bar Assn; prof law: NY Univ; sr fellow, dir (justice & soc seminars): Aspen Inst Humanistic Studies
Constance Monte: secy
Estelle Oleck: off
Lester Pollack: off *B* New York NY 1933 *ED* City Univ NY 1957; NY Univ 1965 *CURR EMPL* ptnr: Lazard Freres & Co *CORP AFFIL* chmn fin comm, mem exec comm, dir: CNA Fin Corp; dir: Kaufman & Broad Home Corp, Loews Corp, Paramount Commun, Polaroid Corp, Transco Energy Co; ptnr: Lazard Freres & Co
Leonard M. Rosen: vp, trust *CURR EMPL* ptnr: Wachtell Lipton Rosen & Katz

APPLICATION INFORMATION
Initial Approach: Contributes only to preselected organizations.
Restrictions on Giving: Does not support individuals.

GRANTS ANALYSIS
Number of Grants: 9
Highest Grant: $50,000
Typical Range: $10,000 to $50,000
Disclosure Period: 1991

RECENT GRANTS
50,000 Mount Sinai Medical Center, New York, NY
50,000 New York Zoological Society, New York, NY
50,000 Temple Emanu-El, New York, NY
25,000 Brearley School, New York, NY

25,000 Prep for Prep, New York, NY
25,000 United Jewish Appeal Federation of Jewish Philanthropies, New York, NY
10,000 Early Steps, New York, NY
5,000 University of Miami School of Law, Miami, FL
250 British American Education Foundation, Worcester, MA

Zarrow Foundation, Anne and Henry

CONTACT
Judith Z. Kishner
Director
Anne and Henry Zarrow Fdn.
PO Box 1530
Tulsa, OK 74101
(918) 587-3391

FINANCIAL SUMMARY
Recent Giving: $309,100 (1991); $359,000 (1990); $288,700 (1989)
Assets: $4,103,348 (1991); $4,073,179 (1990); $4,110,287 (1989)
EIN: 73-1286874

CONTRIBUTIONS SUMMARY
Donor(s): Henry Zarrow
Typical Recipients: • *Arts & Humanities:* community arts • *Civic & Public Affairs:* law & justice, municipalities • *Education:* minority education • *Health:* mental health, pediatric health • *Social Services:* aged, community service organizations, day care, family planning, family services, food/clothing distribution, united funds, youth organizations
Grant Types: emergency and general support
Geographic Distribution: focus on Tulsa, OK, area

GIVING OFFICERS
Robert H. Elliot: secy, dir
Judith Z. Kishner: dir
Robert A. Mulholland: treas, dir
Anne Zarrow: vp, dir
Henry Zarrow: pres, dir
Stuart A. Zarrow: dir

APPLICATION INFORMATION
Initial Approach: Send brief letter of inquiry describing pro-

gram or project. There are no deadlines.

GRANTS ANALYSIS
Number of Grants: 24
Highest Grant: $60,000
Typical Range: $1,000 to $10,000
Disclosure Period: 1991

RECENT GRANTS
60,000 Oklahoma Arts Institute, Oklahoma City, OK
45,000 Tulsa Center for Physically Limited, Tulsa, OK
23,000 Tulsa Meals on Wheels, Tulsa, OK
20,000 Mayo Foundation for Medical Research, Rochester, MN
12,500 Catholic Charities, Tulsa, OK
10,000 Little Light House, Tulsa, OK
10,000 Salvation Army, Tulsa, OK
10,000 Town and Country School, Tulsa, OK
6,000 John 3:16 Mission, Tulsa, OK
5,000 Oklahoma Medical Research Foundation, Oklahoma City, OK

Zebco/Motorguide Corp.

Sales: $32.0 million
Employees: 550
Parent Company: Brunswick Corp.
Headquarters: Tulsa, OK
SIC Major Group: Electronic & Other Electrical Equipment, Industrial Machinery & Equipment, and Miscellaneous Manufacturing Industries

CONTACT
Wayne Paulison
Director of Human Resources
Zebco/Motorguide Corp.
PO Box 270
Tulsa, OK 74101
(918) 836-5581

CONTRIBUTIONS SUMMARY
Operating Locations: OK (Tulsa)

CORP. OFFICERS
J.W. Dawson: *CURR EMPL* pres: Zebco/Motorguide Corp

OTHER THINGS TO KNOW
Company is a major donor to the FishAmerica Foundation.

Zellerbach Family Fund

CONTACT
Edward A. Nathan
Executive Director
Zellerbach Family Fund
120 Montgomery St., Ste. 2125
San Francisco, CA 94104
(415) 421-2629

FINANCIAL SUMMARY
Recent Giving: $2,078,343 (1993 est.); $1,939,360 (1992); $1,765,413 (1991)
Assets: $47,300,000 (1993 est.); $47,141,337 (1991 approx.); $40,067,331 (1990); $41,414,451 (1989)
Gifts Received: $65,000 (1993 est.); $110,000 (1991); $215,000 (1990); $203,261 (1989)
Fiscal Note: In 1988, the fund received a $302,126 contribution from the Marin Community Foundation.
EIN: 94-6069482

CONTRIBUTIONS SUMMARY
Donor(s): The fund was established in 1956, with the late Jennie B. Zellerbach as donor. The Zellerbach family started a paper business in the latter part of the nineteenth century, which became the Crown Zellerbach Corporation through mergers and acquisitions.
Typical Recipients: • *Arts & Humanities:* arts associations, arts centers, cinema, community arts, dance, ethnic arts, music, opera, performing arts, theater • *Civic & Public Affairs:* ethnic/minority organizations, nonprofit management, public policy • *Education:* literacy, social sciences education • *Health:* mental health • *Social Services:* child welfare, family services, youth organizations
Grant Types: general support and project
Geographic Distribution: San Francisco Bay Area

GIVING OFFICERS
Stewart E. Adams: dir
Jeanette M. Dunckel: dir
Philip S. Ehrlich, Jr.: secy, dir
Sharon Fujii: dir
Linda Howe: arts adm, gen adm *CURR EMPL* mgr (commun rels): Alexander & Baldwin

George B. James II: dir *B* Haverhill MA 1937 *ED* Harvard Univ AB 1959; Stanford Univ MBA 1962 *CURR EMPL* sr vp, cfo: Levi Strauss & Co *CORP AFFIL* dir: Basic Vegetable Products, Pacific States Indus, Sequoia Pacific Sys, Supertex; mem adv bd: Canned Foods, Protection Mutual Ins Co *NONPR AFFIL* chmn: Towle Trust Fund; chmn bd trusts: San Francisco Ballet Assn; dir: Stanford Univ Hosp; mem: Andover Town Comm, Fin Execs Inst, Newcomen Soc North Am, San Francisco Comm Foreign Rels, San Francisco Film Commun, Select Congressional Comm World Hunger; mem adv counc: CA St Employees Pension Fund; trust: Cate Sch, Mid-Peninsula High Sch, Natl Corp Fund Dance, Stein Grove Festival Assn *PHIL AFFIL* chmn bd dirs: Towle Trust Fund; trust: Levi Strauss Foundation
Edward A. Nathan: exec dir
Louis Saroni II: vp, treas, dir
Robert E. Sinton: vp, dir
Anne Spence: dir
Verneice D. Thompson: dir
Ellen Walker: program exec
John W. Zellerbach: vp, dir
Thomas H. Zellerbach: dir
William Joseph Zellerbach: pres; *B* San Francisco CA 1920 *ED* Univ PA Wharton Sch BS 1942; Harvard Univ 1958 *CORP AFFIL* dir: Lloyds Bank CA *NONPR AFFIL* mem: Natl Paper Trade Assn
Nancy Zellerbach-Boschwitz: dir

APPLICATION INFORMATION
Initial Approach:
Initial approach for a grant application may be made by phone or written proposal. The proposal for an arts project should include a brief summary of the purpose of the program, its goals, number of persons participating, the audience or persons to whom the efforts are directed, and information about the organization's leadership. Press clippings and a few statements from community groups or experts in the field who appreciate the program should also be sent. In addition, requests should include the most recent financial statement, detailed project budget, listing of contributions and grants as well as a list of other groups that have received or will re-

ceive a request, and proof of tax-exempt status.
Those seeking art-related grants should call the office to inquire about up-coming deadlines.
Board meetings are held quarterly. Final notification of action taken on a grant proposal is made within one week for non-arts applications, and two weeks after the board meeting for arts applications.
Restrictions on Giving: The fund discourages mail solicitation (except in the area of San Francisco community arts projects), and initiates most of its own projects.

OTHER THINGS TO KNOW
The fund is interested in new ideas even though very few new projects can be supported. The fund discourages mail solicitation (except in the area of San Francisco community arts projects), and initiates most of its contributions.
Publications: annual report

GRANTS ANALYSIS
Total Grants: $1,765,413
Number of Grants: 251
Highest Grant: $98,398
Typical Range: $1,000 to $10,000
Disclosure Period: 1991
Note: Recent grants are derived from a 1991 annual report.

RECENT GRANTS
98,398 Community Task Force on Homes for Children, San Francisco, CA — a Bay Area regional project to recruit and improve services for foster and adoptive parents
85,000 San Francisco Study Center — to strengthen dissemination, graphics and expansion capacity of community projects
82,294 Parent Services Project, Fairfax, CA — PSP brings mutual support, leadership development and other activities to low-income parents with children in child care centers in Alameda, Marin and San Francisco counties

72,357 Mental Health Client Self-Help Projects — a cooperative effort to enable client mental health groups in four Bay Area counties to operate programs in the interest of their members

69,273 New Faces of Liberty and Voices of Liberty — to develop curriculum materials that enhance refugee and immigrant students' self-esteem and increase all students' understanding of newcomers' culture

66,502 Parent Empowerment Project, San Francisco, CA — (Mission Reading Clinic); to fund a program of support groups, educational activities and leadership training for parents of elementary and middle school children

65,200 Neighborhood Family Service Organization — to provide guidance to the California Legislature in developing pilot projects that establish Center for Integrated Services for Families and Neighborhoods

51,100 Family Outreach Project, San Mateo County, San Mateo, CA — to support public health-mental health-social services collaborative approach to providing outreach and in-home services to at-risk families

41,625 New Ways to Work, San Francisco, CA — to develop a monograph on "Work and the Family," practical suggestions on how to deal with work-related issues that increase family stress

41,500 Solid Foundation, Mandela House, Oakland, CA — to support family maintenance and reunification, healthy child development and community outreach programs for drug-addicted mothers and their infants

Zemurray Foundation

CONTACT
Walter J. Belsom, Jr.
Treasurer
Zemurray Fdn.
1436 Whitney Bldg.
New Orleans, LA 70130
(504) 525-0091

FINANCIAL SUMMARY
Recent Giving: $2,241,610 (1991); $1,714,370 (1989); $1,730,420 (1988)
Assets: $49,118,090 (1991); $48,673,314 (1989); $38,162,515 (1988)
EIN: 72-0539603

CONTRIBUTIONS SUMMARY
Donor(s): The foundation was incorporated in 1951 by Sarah W. Zemurray.
Typical Recipients: • *Arts & Humanities:* arts associations, arts centers, community arts, dance, history/historic preservation, museums/galleries, opera, performing arts • *Civic & Public Affairs:* environmental affairs, municipalities, zoos/botanical gardens • *Education:* agricultural education, colleges & universities, education funds, private education (precollege) • *Health:* hospitals, medical research • *International:* international organizations • *Religion:* churches • *Science:* scientific institutes • *Social Services:* aged, animal protection, family planning, homes
Grant Types: general support
Geographic Distribution: focus on New Orleans, LA

GIVING OFFICERS
Walter J. Belsom, Jr.: treas, dir
Thomas Berthelot Lemann: secy, dir *B* New Orleans LA 1926 *ED* Harvard Univ AB 1949; Harvard Univ LLB 1952; Tulane Univ MCL 1953 *CURR EMPL* ptnr: Monroe & Lemann *CORP AFFIL* dir: B Lemann & Bros, Mermenteau Mineral & Land Co, Riviana Foods *NONPR AFFIL* mem: Am Bar Assn, Am Law Inst, LA Bar Assn, New Orleans Bar Assn, NY City Bar Assn, Phi Beta Kappa, Soc Bartolus; mem counc: LA St Law Inst
Doris Zemurray Stone: pres *B* New Orleans LA 1909 *ED* Radcliffe Coll AB 1930 *NONPR AFFIL* bd mgrs: Sch Am Res; bd visitors: Tulane Univ; fellow: Am Anthropological Assn, Am Ethnological Soc, Soc Am Archaeology; hon life trust: New Orleans Mus Art; mem: Am Ethnographical Soc, Am Geographical Soc, Royal Anthropology Inst, Soc Women Geographers; mem bd: Natl Mus Costa Rica; mem natl counc: Mus Am Indian; pres: Thirty-Third Intl Congress Americanists; trust: Radcliffe Coll
Samuel Z. Stone: vp, dir

APPLICATION INFORMATION
Initial Approach: Restrictions on Giving: The foundation supports preselected organizations and does not accept unsolicited requests for funds. The foundation does not make grants to individuals.

GRANTS ANALYSIS
Total Grants: $2,241,610
Number of Grants: 46
Highest Grant: $550,000
Typical Range: $1,000 to $30,000
Disclosure Period: 1991
Note: Average grant figure does not include a grant for $550,000 and a grant for $415,000. Recent grants are derived from a 1991 grants list.

RECENT GRANTS
550,000 Greater New Orleans Foundation, New Orleans, LA
415,000 Tulane University, New Orleans, LA
352,500 New Orleans Museum of Art, New Orleans, LA
221,000 Ciapa (Centra de Investicacion y Adiestramiento Politico Administrativo), New Orleans, LA
206,000 Union College, Barbourville, KY
102,500 Audubon Institute, New Orleans, LA
56,000 Louisiana Nature and Science Center, New Orleans, LA
50,000 School of American Research, New Orleans, LA
45,000 Arts Council of New Orleans, New Orleans, LA
40,000 Christ Church Retirement Home, New Orleans, LA

Zenkel Foundation

CONTACT
Lois Zenkel
President
Zenkel Fdn.
15 West 53rd St.
New York, NY 10019-5410
(212) 333-5730

FINANCIAL SUMMARY
Recent Giving: $245,096 (1991); $202,353 (1990); $205,135 (1989)
Assets: $4,883,919 (1991); $3,820,567 (1990); $3,872,358 (1989)
EIN: 13-3380631

CONTRIBUTIONS SUMMARY
Typical Recipients: • *Arts & Humanities:* dance, libraries, museums/galleries, public broadcasting, theater, visual arts • *Civic & Public Affairs:* environmental affairs • *Education:* colleges & universities, medical education • *Health:* medical research, single-disease health associations • *Religion:* religious organizations • *Social Services:* community service organizations, food/clothing distribution
Grant Types: capital, general support, and scholarship
Geographic Distribution: focus on NY

GIVING OFFICERS
Bruce L. Zenkel: treas, dir
Daniel R. Zenkel: secy, dir
Gary B. Zenkel: dir
Lisa R. Zenkel: dir
Lois S. Zenkel: pres, dir

APPLICATION INFORMATION
Initial Approach: Contributes only to preselected organizations.
Restrictions on Giving: Does not support individuals.

GRANTS ANALYSIS
Number of Grants: 113
Highest Grant: $100,000
Typical Range: $250 to $1,000
Disclosure Period: 1991

RECENT GRANTS
100,000 Greenwich Hospital, Greenwich, CT

50,000 United Jewish Appeal Federation of Jewish Philanthropies, New York, NY

35,000 University of Michigan, Ann Arbor, MI

25,000 International Center of Photography, New York, NY

10,000 Metropolitan Museum of Art, New York, NY

10,000 National Urban League, New York, NY

5,000 American Jewish Congress, New York, NY

5,000 Connecticut College, New London, CT

5,000 Dartmouth College, Hanover, NH

5,000 Doral-Ryder Open Foundation, Miami, FL — American Cancer Society

Ziegler Foundation

CONTACT
Bernard C. Ziegler
President
Ziegler Fdn.
215 North Main St.
West Bend, WI 334-5521

FINANCIAL SUMMARY
Recent Giving: $321,814 (1989); $275,000 (1988)
Assets: $5,497,562 (1989); $4,800,000 (1988)
EIN: 39-6044762

CONTRIBUTIONS SUMMARY
Donor(s): members of the Ziegler family
Typical Recipients: • *Arts & Humanities:* arts funds • *Civic & Public Affairs:* environmental affairs • *Education:* colleges & universities • *Health:* hospitals, medical research • *Religion:* churches • *Social Services:* child welfare, community service organizations, disabled, united funds, youth organizations
Grant Types: general support and scholarship
Geographic Distribution: focus on the West Bend, WI, area

GIVING OFFICERS
Harrold J. McComas: vp, dir
Bernard C. Ziegler: pres, dir *CORP AFFIL* dir: Ziegler Co
R. Douglas Ziegler: vp, secy, treas, dir *B* Milwaukee WI 1927 *ED* Northwestern Univ 1949 *CURR EMPL* chmn: Ziegler Co *CORP AFFIL* chmn: BC Ziegler & Co, Ziegler Asset Mgmt Co; dir: Applied Power, Johnson Controls, Maxicare Health Plans, Prin Preservation Portfolios, Ziegler Fin Corp, Ziegler Leasing Corp, Ziegler Securities, Ziegler Thrift Trading

APPLICATION INFORMATION
Initial Approach: Send brief letter of inquiry describing program or project. There are no deadlines. Board meets in May and November.
Restrictions on Giving: Does not support individuals.

GRANTS ANALYSIS
Number of Grants: 22
Highest Grant: $50,000
Disclosure Period: 1990

RECENT GRANTS

50,000 Blood Center of Southeastern Wisconsin, Milwaukee, WI

40,000 Riveredge Nature Center, Newburg, WI

37,500 St. Joseph's Community Hospital, West Bend, WI

35,000 Kettle Moraine YMCA, West Bend, WI

15,000 West Bend Gallery of Fine Arts, West Bend, WI

15,000 West Bend Gallery of the Arts, West Bend, WI

3,000 United Performing Arts Fund, Milwaukee, WI

2,500 Milwaukee Zoological Society, Milwaukee, WI

2,200 Citizen Advocacy, West Bend, WI

2,000 Kettle Moraine YMCA, West Bend, WI

Ziegler Foundation for the Blind, E. Matilda

CONTACT
William Ziegler III
President
E. Matilda Ziegler Fdn for the Blind
250 Harbor Dr.
PO Box 10128
Stamford, CT 06904
(203) 356-9000

FINANCIAL SUMMARY
Recent Giving: $540,750 (1990); $450,500 (1989); $497,475 (1988)
Assets: $10,573,780 (1990); $11,743,016 (1989); $10,126,356 (1988)
EIN: 13-6086195

CONTRIBUTIONS SUMMARY
Donor(s): the late Mrs. William Ziegler
Typical Recipients: • *Arts & Humanities:* museums/galleries • *Education:* colleges & universities • *Religion:* religious organizations • *Social Services:* disabled
Grant Types: general support and multiyear/continuing support

GIVING OFFICERS
Lawrence G. Bodkin, Jr.: dir
Cynthia Zeigler Brighton: dir
Charles Beckwith Cook, Jr.: dir *B* Buffalo NY 1929 *ED* Yale Univ BA 1952 *CURR EMPL* vchmn: Janney Montgomery Scott *CORP AFFIL* dir: Am Fructose Co, Am Maize Products Co, Westbury Fed Savings & Loan; vchmn: Janney Montgomery Scott
James J. Marett: dir
Beatrice H. Page: treas
Frank K. Sanders, Jr.: dir
Eric M. Steinkraus: dir
Helen Z. Steinkraus: secy, dir
William Ziegler III: pres, dir *B* New York NY 1928 *ED* Harvard Univ BA 1950; Columbia Univ MBA 1962 *CURR EMPL* chmn, ceo, dir: Am Maize Products Co *CORP AFFIL* chmn, ceo: Helme Tobacco Co, Lloyd Lumber Div Am Maise Products; chmn, ceo, chmn exec comm: Am Fructose Co; chmn, ceo, pres, chmn exec comm, dir: Park Avenue Operating Co; chmn, chmn exec comm: Jon H Swisher & Son; dir: Foresight Inc; pres, dir: GIH Corp; secy, dir: Matilda Ziegler Publ Co Blind *NONPR AFFIL* dir: Maritime Ctr Norwalk, Project ORBIS, Southwestern Area Commerce Indus Assn; mem natl adv counc: Hampshire Coll; trust: Lavelle Sch Blind; trust, dir: YMCA Darien Commun

APPLICATION INFORMATION
Initial Approach: Send cover letter and full proposal. There are no deadlines.
Restrictions on Giving: Does not support individuals or provide loans.

GRANTS ANALYSIS
Number of Grants: 19
Highest Grant: $230,000
Typical Range: $1,000 to $8,000
Disclosure Period: 1990

RECENT GRANTS

230,000 Matilda Ziegler Publishing Company for the Blind, Stamford, CT

65,000 Yale University, New Haven, CT

35,000 Foresight, New Haven, CT

25,000 Explorer Post 53-Emergency Medical Service, Darien, CT

25,000 Maritime Center at Norwalk, South Norwalk, CT

10,000 Lighthouse, New York, NY

8,000 State of Connecticut Department of Human Resources, Wetherfield, CT

5,000 Harvard University, Cambridge, MA

5,000 Music Foundation for the Handicapped of Connecticut, Bridgeport, CT

5,000 Recording for the Blind, Princeton, NJ

Ziegler Foundation, Ruth/Allen

CONTACT
David Rose
Ruth/Allen Ziegler Foundation
c/o Gumbiner, Savett, Friedman
& Rose
1723 Cloverfield Boulevard
Santa Monica, CA 90404
(213) 828-9798

FINANCIAL SUMMARY
Recent Giving: $1,056,977
(fiscal 1991); $707,411 (fiscal
1990)
Assets: $6,028,450 (fiscal year
ending November 30, 1991);
$636,001 (fiscal 1990)
Gifts Received: $6,988,500
(fiscal 1991); $1,084,744 (fis-
cal 1990)
Fiscal Note: In 1990, Ruth and
Allen Ziegler donated
$1,084,744 in cash and stock to
the foundation.
EIN: 95-4113690

CONTRIBUTIONS SUMMARY
Donor(s): the donors are Ruth
B. and Allen S. Ziegler, the
foundation's secretary and the
foundation's president
Typical Recipients: • *Arts &
Humanities:* history/historic
preservation, music, public
broadcasting • *Civic & Public
Affairs:* municipalities • *Education:* colleges & universities,
religious education • *Health:*
outpatient health care delivery
• *International:* foreign educational institutions, international
health care, international organizations • *Religion:* religious organizations, synagogues
• *Social Services:* community
service organizations, disabled,
religious welfare, united funds
Grant Types: general support
Geographic Distribution: emphasis on California

GIVING OFFICERS
Allen S. Ziegler: don, pres
Ruth B. Ziegler: don, secy

APPLICATION INFORMATION
Initial Approach: The foundation reports that it donates only
to preselected charitable organizations. Unsolicited requests
for funds are not accepted.

GRANTS ANALYSIS
Total Grants: $1,056,977
Number of Grants: 18
Highest Grant: $295,313

Typical Range: $26,883 to
$99,241
Disclosure Period: fiscal year
ending November 30, 1991

RECENT GRANTS
295,313	University of Juda-ism, CA
193,898	University of Juda-ism, CA
99,241	University of Juda-ism, CA
98,435	University of Juda-ism, CA
59,398	City of Hope, Du-arte, CA
49,042	Jewish Federation Council, CA
28,123	American Youth Symphony, CA
27,948	Jewish Federation Council, CA
26,883	United Way, CA
26,883	Venice Family Clinic, Venice, CA

Ziemann Foundation

CONTACT
Lila Pierce
Secretary-Director
Ziemann Fdn.
PO Box 1408
Waukesha, WI 53187-1408
(414) 542-4996

FINANCIAL SUMMARY
Recent Giving: $81,000
(1990); $60,750 (1989)
Assets: $1,752,432 (1990);
$1,818,497 (1989)
EIN: 39-6069677

CONTRIBUTIONS SUMMARY
Donor(s): the late Lillian Ziemann, the late N.J. Ziemann,
the late Mrs. N. J. Ziemann
Typical Recipients: • *Civic &
Public Affairs:* housing • *Education:* colleges & universities,
private education (precollege)
• *Social Services:* community
service organizations, disabled
Grant Types: capital, multi-
year/continuing support, operating expenses, and scholarship
Geographic Distribution:
focus on WI

GIVING OFFICERS
Cynthia Linnan: dir, vp, treas
Lila Pierce: dir, secy
Pam Praulins: trust
Robert Veenendall: trust
Carolyn Wright: dir, pres

APPLICATION INFORMATION
Initial Approach: Send brief
letter describing program.
Deadline is September 30.

Restrictions on Giving: Does
not support individuals.

OTHER THINGS TO KNOW
Publications: Application
Guidelines

GRANTS ANALYSIS
Number of Grants: 13
Highest Grant: $30,000
Typical Range: $500 to $7,500
Disclosure Period: 1990

RECENT GRANTS
30,000	St. Colettas School, Jefferson, WI
25,000	A.R.C. Campaign Housing Start, Mil-waukee, WI
7,500	Medical College of Wisconsin, Milwau-kee, WI
4,000	Channel 10/36 Friends, Milwau-kee, WI
2,500	Center for Deaf-Blind Persons, Mil-waukee, WI
2,500	Children's Outing Association, Mil-waukee, WI
2,500	Literacy Service, Milwaukee, WI
2,500	Penfield Children's Center, Milwaukee, WI
1,000	Marilyn O'Brien Fund, Milwaukee, WI
1,000	St. Norbert Col-lege, West Du Prai-rie, WI

Ziff Communications Co.

Sales: $430.0 million
Employees: 2,573
Headquarters: New York, NY
SIC Major Group: Printing &
Publishing

CONTACT
Scott Greggs
President
Ziff Communications Co.
One Park Ave.
New York, NY 10016
(212) 503-3500

CONTRIBUTIONS SUMMARY
Operating Locations: NY
(New York)

CORP. OFFICERS
William Bernard Ziff, Jr.: *B*
1930 *CURR EMPL* chmn: Ziff
Communs Co *CORP AFFIL*
pres, chmn: Ziff-Davis Publ Co

Zigler Foundation, Fred B. and Ruth B.

CONTACT
Paul E. Brummett
President
Fred B. and Ruth B. Zigler Fdn.
PO Box 986
Jennings, LA 70546
(318) 824-2413

FINANCIAL SUMMARY
Recent Giving: $279,807
(1991); $251,896 (1989);
$136,518 (1988)
Assets: $6,096,761 (1991);
$6,005,536 (1989); $5,849,926
(1988)
EIN: 72-6019403

CONTRIBUTIONS SUMMARY
Donor(s): the late Fred B. and
Ruth B. Zigler
Typical Recipients: • *Arts &
Humanities:* museums/galleries
• *Education:* colleges & universities, private education (precollege) • *Social Services:* drugs
& alcohol, youth organizations
Grant Types: capital, endowment, general support, operating expenses, project, and
scholarship
Geographic Distribution:
focus on Jefferson Davis Parish, LA; scholarships restricted
to graduating seniors of Jefferson Davis Parish High Schools

GIVING OFFICERS
Paul E. Brummett: pres, trust
Margaret Cormier: secy,
treas, trust
Dave Elmore: trust
John Michael Elmore: trust
Mark Fehl: trust
A. J. M. Oustalet: trust
John Pipkin: trust

APPLICATION INFORMATION
Initial Approach: Scholarship
application forms available
through Parish High Schools.
Deadline is three weeks prior
to board meetings; scholarship
deadline March 10. Board
meets bimonthly.
Restrictions on Giving: Does
not support individuals (except
individual scholarships).

OTHER THINGS TO KNOW
Publications: Annual Report

GRANTS ANALYSIS
Number of Grants: 37

Highest Grant: $62,203
Typical Range: $1,000 to $6,000
Disclosure Period: 1991

RECENT GRANTS

62,203 McNeese State University, Lake Charles, LA

30,000 Louisiana State University, Baton Rouge, LA

25,000 Zigler Museum Foundation, Jennings, LA

22,500 University of Southwestern Louisiana, Lafayette, LA

10,220 Zigler Museum Foundation, Jennings, LA

10,000 City of Jennings, Jennings, LA

10,000 Louisiana State University, Baton Rouge, LA

9,000 Jennings High School, Jennings, LA

6,000 Boy Scouts of America, Lake Charles, LA

6,000 Louisiana Boys and Girls Village, Lake Charles, LA

Zilkha & Sons / Zilkha Foundation

Headquarters: New York, NY

CONTACT

Ezra K. Zilkha
President
Zilkha Fdn.
30 Rockefeller Plz.
New York, NY 10112-0153
(212) 632-8440

FINANCIAL SUMMARY

Recent Giving: $601,863 (fiscal 1992); $421,447 (fiscal 1991); $317,578 (fiscal 1989)
Assets: $2,797,961 (fiscal year ending August 31, 1992); $3,029,854 (fiscal 1991); $170,190 (fiscal 1989)
Gifts Received: $3,090,375 (fiscal 1991); $320,000 (fiscal 1989)
Fiscal Note: Contributes through foundation only. In fiscal year 1991, contributions were received from Ezra K. Zilkha.
EIN: 13-6090739

CONTRIBUTIONS SUMMARY

Typical Recipients: • *Arts & Humanities:* dance, history/historic preservation, muse-
ums/galleries, opera, public broadcasting • *Civic & Public Affairs:* international affairs, public policy • *Education:* arts education, colleges & universities • *Health:* hospitals • *Religion:* religious organizations • *Social Services:* child welfare, disabled, religious welfare, united funds
Grant Types: general support
Geographic Distribution: emphasis on New York, NY
Operating Locations: NY (New York)

CORP. OFFICERS

Ezra Khedouri Zilkha: *B* Baghdad Iraq 1925 *ED* Wesleyan Univ AB 1947 *CURR EMPL* pres: Zilkha & Sons *CORP AFFIL* chmn: Union Holdings; dir: Cambridge Assocs, Chicago Milwaukee Corp, CIGNA Corp, Fortune Fin Group, Merchants Grain & Transportation, Newhall Land & Farming Co *NONPR AFFIL* trust: Brookings Inst, Intl Ctr Disabled, Lycee Francais; trust emeritus: Wesleyan Univ

GIVING OFFICERS

Kathleen Quinlan: asst secy
Cecile E. Zilkha: vp, secy
Ezra Khedouri Zilkha: pres, treas *CURR EMPL* pres: Zilkha & Sons (see above)

APPLICATION INFORMATION

Initial Approach: *Note:* The foundation supports preselected organizations and does not accept unsolicited requests for funds.
Restrictions on Giving: Foundation does not support individuals.

GRANTS ANALYSIS

Total Grants: $601,863
Number of Grants: 49
Highest Grant: $200,000
Typical Range: $500 to $5,000
Disclosure Period: fiscal year ending August 31, 1992
Note: Recent grants are derived from a fiscal 1992 grants list.

RECENT GRANTS

200,000 Waterford Institute, New York, NY

125,000 Brookings Institute, New York, NY

58,333 CD, New York, NY

52,683 Metropolitan Opera, New York, NY

43,333 Hospital for Special Surgery, New York, NY

32,185 Congregation Shearith Israel, New York, NY

20,000 Ronald Reagan Library Foundation, Washington, DC

10,000 Federation of Jewish Philanthropies, New York, NY

10,000 Wesleyan University, Middleton, CT

5,000 Memorial Sloan Kettering Cancer Center, New York, NY

Zimmer Inc.

Sales: $990.0 million
Employees: 5,700
Parent Company: Bristol-Myers Squibb Company
Headquarters: Warsaw, IN
SIC Major Group: Instruments & Related Products

CONTACT

Deb Newman
Secretary of Public Relations
Zimmer Inc.
PO Box 708
Warsaw, IN 46580
(219) 267-6131

CONTRIBUTIONS SUMMARY

Operating Locations: IN (Warsaw)

CORP. OFFICERS

R. L. Davis: *CURR EMPL* pres: Zimmer

Zimmerman Family Foundation, Raymond

CONTACT

Jack Byrd
Raymond Zimmerman Family Fdn.
3818 Cleghorn Avenue, Ste. 200
Nashville, TN 37215

FINANCIAL SUMMARY

Recent Giving: $252,091 (fiscal 1992); $178,984 (fiscal 1989); $15,000 (fiscal 1987)
Assets: $8,486,106 (fiscal year ending May 31, 1992); $5,317,439 (fiscal 1989); $2,550,171 (fiscal 1987)
EIN: 62-6166380

CONTRIBUTIONS SUMMARY

Donor(s): Raymond Zimmerman

Typical Recipients: • *Arts & Humanities:* community arts, music, performing arts, theater • *Education:* colleges & universities • *Religion:* religious organizations, synagogues • *Social Services:* community service organizations, united funds
Grant Types: general support

GIVING OFFICERS

Arlene G. Zimmerman: trust
Fred E. Zimmerman: trust
Raymond Zimmerman: trust *B* Memphis TN 1933 *ED* Univ Miami; Memphis St Univ *CURR EMPL* pres, chmn, ceo, dir: Svc Merchandise Co *CORP AFFIL* dir: The Limited, Third Natl Bank *NONPR AFFIL* dir: TN Performing Arts Fdn; mem: Nashville Chamber Commerce, Natl Assn Catalog Showroom Merchandisers; trust: Ensworth Sch, Leo N Levi Natl Arthritis Hosp
Robyn Zimmerman: trust

APPLICATION INFORMATION

Initial Approach: Contributes only to preselected organizations.

GRANTS ANALYSIS

Number of Grants: 60
Highest Grant: $100,000
Typical Range: $100 to $7,500 and $10,000 to $15,000
Disclosure Period: fiscal year ending May 31, 1992

RECENT GRANTS

100,000 Vanderbilt Divinity School, Nashville, TN

30,000 Facing History and Ourselves, Boston, MA

24,299 Temple, Nashville, TN

16,000 Nashville Symphony, Nashville, TN

12,100 United Way, Nashville, TN

10,000 Cheekwood, Nashville, TN

10,000 Hebrew Union College, Cincinnati, OH

10,000 National Jewish Center for Learning and Leadership, Nashville, TN

6,000 American Israel Public Affairs Com-

mission, Nashville, TN
5,015 Tennessee Performing Arts Center, Nashville, TN

Zimmerman Foundation, Hans and Clara Davis

CONTACT
Caroline Sharman
Hans and Clara Davis Zimmerman Fdn.
c/o Hawaiian Trust Co., Ltd.
PO Box 3170
Honolulu, HI 96802
(808) 537-6333

FINANCIAL SUMMARY
Recent Giving: $363,300 (1989); $336,975 (1988)
Assets: $6,976,980 (1989); $6,205,880 (1988)
EIN: 99-6006669

CONTRIBUTIONS SUMMARY
Donor(s): the late Hans and Clara Zimmerman
Grant Types: scholarship
Geographic Distribution: focus on HI

GIVING OFFICERS
Mary V. Coyne: mem scholarship comm
Leon Julian: mem scholarship comm
Harold Nicolaus: mem scholarship comm
Jetta M. Zimmerman: chmn scholarship comm

APPLICATION INFORMATION
Initial Approach: Request application forms by February 1. Send cover letter. Deadline is March 1. Board meets in May.

OTHER THINGS TO KNOW
Provides scholarships to individuals for higher education.
Publications: Application Guidelines
Disclosure Period: 1991

Zimmerman Foundation, Mary and George Herbert

CONTACT
Elaine Z. Peck
President
Mary and George Herbert Zimmerman Fdn.
220 Bagley Avenue, Ste. 408
Detroit, MI 48226
(313) 963-9604

FINANCIAL SUMMARY
Recent Giving: $68,100 (1991); $84,425 (1990); $3,600 (1989)
Assets: $2,482,569 (1991); $2,126,454 (1990); $2,173,117 (1989)
EIN: 38-1685880

CONTRIBUTIONS SUMMARY
Donor(s): members of the Zimmerman family
Typical Recipients: • *Education:* colleges & universities, religious education • *Religion:* churches
Grant Types: general support

GIVING OFFICERS
Andrew G. Bato: dir, vp
Doris S. Bato: dir, secy
Elaine Z. Peck: dir, exec vp
Sheila Pette: dir, sr. vp
G.H. Zimmerman: treas
Louis G. Zimmerman: dir, pres

APPLICATION INFORMATION
Initial Approach: Contributes only to preselected organizations.
Restrictions on Giving: Does not support individuals.

GRANTS ANALYSIS
Number of Grants: 28
Highest Grant: $12,500
Typical Range: $500 to $7,500
Disclosure Period: 1991

RECENT GRANTS
12,500 Bon Secours Hospital, Detroit, MI
11,200 St. Paul's Church, Detroit, MI
7,000 Capuchin Community Center, Detroit, MI
5,000 Grosse Pointe Academy, Grosse Pointe, MI
3,000 Children's Hospital Medical Center, Detroit, MI
3,000 Guest House, Detroit, MI
2,650 St. Vincent de Paul Society, Detroit, MI
2,250 Little Sisters of Poor, Detroit, MI
1,500 Oxford University
1,500 United Foundation, Detroit, MI

Zimmermann Fund, Marie and John

CONTACT
Anne L. Smith-Ganey
Assistant Vice President
Marie and John Zimmermann Fund
c/o U.S. Trust Co. of New York
114 West 47th St.
New York, NY 10036-1532
(212) 852-1000

FINANCIAL SUMMARY
Recent Giving: $190,000 (1989)
Assets: $5,321,367 (1989)
EIN: 13-6158767

CONTRIBUTIONS SUMMARY
Donor(s): Marie Zimmermann, Frank A. Zunio, Jr.
Typical Recipients: • *Education:* colleges & universities, medical education
Grant Types: general support

GIVING OFFICERS
John Robert Buchanan, MD: dir *B* Newark NJ 1928 *ED* Amherst Coll AB 1950; Cornell Univ MD 1954 *NONPR AFFIL* dir: Charles River Breeding Labs; fellow: Am Coll Physicians, Am Pub Health Assn; mem: Am Pub Health Assn, Assn Am Med Colls, Assn Am Med Colls, Assn Med Schs NY & NJ, Harvey Soc, IL Hosp Assn, Inst Medicine Natl Academy Sciences, MA Hosp Assn, Natl Academy Sciences, NJ St Med Soc, NY Academy Medicine, NY Academy Science, NY Academy Sciences, NY County Med Soc, Private Indus Counc, Voluntary Hosps Am; mem coordinating comm: Boston Bus Roundtable; prof: Harvard Univ Sch Medicine; trust: Ed Commn Foreign Medicine Grads; trust, vchmn: China Med Bd NY
Henry W. Grady, Jr.: dir
Anne C. Heller: dir
A. Parks McCombs: dir
Thomas Harry Meikle, Jr.,MD: dir *B* Troy NY *ED* Cornell Univ AB 1951; Cornell Univ MD 1954 *NONPR AFFIL* mem: Am Physiological Soc, Soc Neuroscience
Robert Perret, Jr.: dir
Anne L. Smith-Ganey: treas, dir *CURR EMPL* asst vp: US Trust Co NY
John C. Zimmermann III: pres, dir

APPLICATION INFORMATION
Initial Approach: Contributes only to preselected organizations.
Restrictions on Giving: Does not support individuals.

GRANTS ANALYSIS
Number of Grants: 3
Highest Grant: $110,700
Typical Range: $31,300 to $48,000
Disclosure Period: 1989

RECENT GRANTS
110,700 Cornell University Medical Center, New York, NY
48,000 Wellesley College, Wellesley, MA
31,300 Dartmouth Medical School, Hanover, NH

Zink Foundation, John Steele

CONTACT
Jacqueline A. Zink
Trustee
John Steele Zink Fdn.
1259 East 26th Street
Tulsa, OK 74114
(918) 742-8249

FINANCIAL SUMMARY
Recent Giving: $1,780,809 (fiscal 1991)
Assets: $37,804,820 (fiscal year ending October 31, 1991)
EIN: 23-7246964

CONTRIBUTIONS SUMMARY
Donor(s): the late John Steele Zink and Jacqueline A. Zink
Typical Recipients: • *Arts & Humanities:* dance, museums/galleries • *Civic & Public Affairs:* philanthropic organizations, zoos/botanical gardens • *Education:* colleges & universities • *Religion:* churches • *Social Services:* united funds, youth organizations
Grant Types: general support
Geographic Distribution: giving primarily in Tulsa, Oklahoma

GIVING OFFICERS
Horace Ballaine: trust
Swannie Zink Tarbel: trust
Jacqueline A. Zink: trust
John Smith Zink: trust

APPLICATION INFORMATION
Initial Approach: Send brief letter of inquiry or contact by telephone. There are no deadlines.

GRANTS ANALYSIS
Number of Grants: 81
Highest Grant: $620,000
Typical Range: $1,000 to $60,000
Disclosure Period: fiscal year ending October 31, 1991

RECENT GRANTS
620,000 John Zink Foundation, Tulsa, OK
176,667 Tulsa Ballet Theatre, Tulsa, OK
173,867 Philbrook Museum of Art, Tulsa, OK
110,000 Park Friends, Tulsa, OK
60,500 Resonance, Tulsa, OK
50,000 Ronald McDonald House, Tulsa, OK
46,500 Tulsa University, Tulsa, OK
40,000 United Way, Tulsa, OK
35,000 St. Simeon's, Tulsa, OK
30,000 Boy Scouts of America, Tulsa, OK

Zions Bancorp.
Assets: $3.35 billion
Employees: 2,405
Headquarters: Salt Lake City, UT
SIC Major Group: Depository Institutions and Holding & Other Investment Offices

CONTACT
Harris Simmons
President and CEO
Zions Bancorp.
1 Main St.
Salt Lake City, UT 84130
(801) 524-4787
Note: An alternative address is P.O. Box 30709.

CONTRIBUTIONS SUMMARY
Operating Locations: UT (Salt Lake City)

CORP. OFFICERS
Harris H. Simmons: *CURR EMPL* pres, ceo, dir: Zions Bancorp

Roy W. Simmons: *CURR EMPL* chmn, dir: Zions Bancorp

Zippo Manufacturing Co.
Sales: $60.0 million
Employees: 800
Headquarters: Bradford, PA
SIC Major Group: Miscellaneous Manufacturing Industries

CONTACT
Rob Jackson
Controller
Zippo Manufacturing Co.
33 Barbour
Bradford, PA 16701
(814) 362-4541

CONTRIBUTIONS SUMMARY
Operating Locations: PA (Bradford)

CORP. OFFICERS
Michael Schuler: *CURR EMPL* chmn, pres, dir: Zippo Mfg Co

OTHER THINGS TO KNOW
Company is an original donor to the Philo & Sarah Blaisdell Foundation.

Zlinkoff Fund for Medical Research and Education, Sergei S.

CONTACT
Jerome J. Cohen
Director
Sergei S. Zlinkoff Fund for Medical Research and Education
c/o Carter, Ledyard & Milburn
2 Wall St.
New York, NY 10005

FINANCIAL SUMMARY
Recent Giving: $235,000 (fiscal 1991); $278,500 (fiscal 1990); $210,000 (fiscal 1989)
Assets: $2,510,845 (fiscal year ending October 31, 1991); $2,099,581 (fiscal 1990); $2,644,842 (fiscal 1989)
EIN: 13-6094651

CONTRIBUTIONS SUMMARY
Donor(s): Sergei S. Zlinkoff
Typical Recipients: • *Arts & Humanities:* libraries • *Educa-*

tion: colleges & universities, medical education • *Health:* hospitals • *Social Services:* disabled, family planning
Grant Types: general support
Geographic Distribution: focus on NY

GIVING OFFICERS
Iris B. Alster: secy
Jerome J. Cohen: secy
Robert Goldstein, MD: dir
Milton Hamolsky, MD: pres
Sandra Hamolsky: dir
Ralph Emil Hansmann: vp, treas *B* Utica NY 1918 *ED* Hamilton Coll AB 1940; Harvard Univ MBA 1942 *CURR EMPL* investment assoc: Harold F Linder, William T Golden NYC *CORP AFFIL* dir: First Eagle Fund Am, Schroder Capital Funds, Verde Exploration Ltd *NONPR AFFIL* life trust: Hamilton Coll; mem visitors comm: New Sch Grad Faculty; trust, treas: Inst Advanced Study, NY Pub Library
John O. Lipkin: vp
Mack Lipkin, Jr.: vp *B* New York NY 1943 *ED* Harvard Univ AB 1965; Harvard Univ MD 1970 *CORP AFFIL* editor: Frontiers Primary Medicine *NONPR AFFIL* assoc prof medicine: NY Univ Sch Medicine; fellow: NY Academy Medicine; mem: Am Assn Advancement Science, Am Psychosomatic Soc, Intl Epidemiology Assn, North Am Primary Care Res Group, Phi Beta Kappa, Primary Care Internal Medicine, Soc Gen Internal Medicine, Task Force Doctor & Patient

APPLICATION INFORMATION
Initial Approach: Contributes only to preselected organizations.
Restrictions on Giving: Does not support individuals.

GRANTS ANALYSIS
Number of Grants: 10
Highest Grant: $40,000
Typical Range: $10,000 to $25,000
Disclosure Period: fiscal year ending October 31, 1991

RECENT GRANTS
40,000 Ashoka, Washington, DC
35,000 Columbia University School of Nursing, New York, NY
35,000 Planned Parenthood Federation of

America, New York, NY
25,000 Good Samaritan Hospital, Portland, OR
25,000 Marion A. Buckley School of Nursing, Garden City, NY
25,000 New York Graduate School of Public Service, New York, NY
20,000 Center for Research on Population Control, Chapel Hill, NC
15,000 New York Public Library, New York, NY
10,000 Brown University, Providence, RI — program in medicine
5,000 Hamilton College, Clinton, NY

Zock Endowment Trust

CONTACT
Sara M. Zock
Trust
Zock Endowment Trust
506 Crescent Pkwy.
Sea Girt, NJ 08750
(201) 449-3618

FINANCIAL SUMMARY
Recent Giving: $172,941 (fiscal 1989); $122,000 (fiscal 1988)
Assets: $4,111,307 (fiscal year ending September 30, 1989); $3,910,415 (fiscal 1988)
EIN: 22-6093288

CONTRIBUTIONS SUMMARY
Typical Recipients: • *Arts & Humanities:* libraries • *Health:* health organizations, medical research, single-disease health associations • *Religion:* churches • *Social Services:* community service organizations
Grant Types: general support
Geographic Distribution: focus on NJ, MD, and PA.

GIVING OFFICERS
Robert A. Zock: trust
Sara M. Zock: trust

APPLICATION INFORMATION
Initial Approach: Send brief letter of inquiry describing program or project. There are no deadlines.
Restrictions on Giving: Does not support individuals.

GRANTS ANALYSIS
Number of Grants: 28
Highest Grant: $150,000
Typical Range: $50 to $1,000
Disclosure Period: fiscal year ending September 30, 1989

RECENT GRANTS
150,000 Sea Girt Library, Sea Girt, NJ
10,000 Salem Lutheran Church, Bethel, PA
2,000 Asian Relief, Riverdale, MD
2,000 Salvation Army, Hazlet, NJ
1,000 Church Farm School, Paoli, PA
1,000 Jersey Shore Medical Center, Neptune, NJ
1,000 Manasquan First Aid, Manasquan, NJ
1,000 Monmouth County Heart Association, Freehold, NJ
1,000 Salem Lutheran Church, Bethel, PA
500 American Cancer Society, Wall, NJ

Zollner Foundation

CONTACT
Alice Kopfer
Zollner Fdn.
PO Box 960
Ft. Wayne, IN 46801
(219) 461-6000

FINANCIAL SUMMARY
Recent Giving: $230,415 (1990); $234,428 (1989); $220,370 (1988)
Assets: $6,711,394 (1990); $7,415,787 (1989); $4,619,105 (1988)
EIN: 35-6381471

CONTRIBUTIONS SUMMARY
Typical Recipients: • *Arts & Humanities:* libraries, public broadcasting • *Education:* career/vocational education, colleges & universities • *Social Services:* united funds, youth organizations
Grant Types: general support
Geographic Distribution: focus on IN

APPLICATION INFORMATION
Initial Approach: Send brief letter of inquiry describing program or project. There are no deadlines.

GRANTS ANALYSIS
Number of Grants: 19

Highest Grant: $50,000
Typical Range: $5,000 to $10,000
Disclosure Period: 1990

RECENT GRANTS
50,000 United Way, IN
30,500 Tri-State University, Angola, IN
25,000 Naismith Basketball Hall of Fame, Springfield, MA
11,000 Indiana University, Bloomington, IN — Purdue University at Ft. Wayne
10,000 Allen County Public Library Foundation, Ft. Wayne, IN
10,000 Indiana Institute of Technology, Ft. Wayne, IN
10,000 Indiana Vocational Technical College, Kokomo, IN
8,400 Junior Achievement, IN
8,015 Ft. Wayne Public Television, Ft. Wayne, IN
7,500 Boy Scouts of America, IN

Zonas Trust, Steven K.

CONTACT
Steven K. Zonas Trust
c/o Central Trust Company, N.A.
P.O. Box 1198
Cincinnati, OH 45201-1198
(513) 651-8310
Note: The trust does not list a contact person.

FINANCIAL SUMMARY
Recent Giving: $0 (1990); $50,060 (1989)
Assets: $1,952,703 (1989)
Gifts Received: $1,766,263 (1989)
Fiscal Note: In 1989, the estate of Steven Zonas donated $1,766,263 in cash and securities.
EIN: 31-6363744

CONTRIBUTIONS SUMMARY
Donor(s): the donor is the estate of Steven K. Zonas
Typical Recipients: • *International:* international organizations • *Social Services:* child welfare
Grant Types: general support
Geographic Distribution: Meyiates, Greece

APPLICATION INFORMATION
Initial Approach: The trust reports that it donates only to a preselected charitable organization. Unsolicited requests for funds are not accepted. The trust lists Central Trust Co., N.A., as a trustee.

GRANTS ANALYSIS
Total Grants: $0
Number of Grants: 1
Highest Grant: $50,060
Disclosure Period: 1989

RECENT GRANTS
50,060 Village of Meyiates, Greece — for child care services

Zuckerberg Foundation, Roy J.

CONTACT
Roy J. Zuckerberg
Trustee
Roy J. Zuckerberg Fdn.
c/o Goldman, Sachs & Co.
85 Broad St., Tax Department, 30th Fl.
New York, NY 10004-2408
(212) 902-6897

FINANCIAL SUMMARY
Recent Giving: $684,845 (fiscal 1991); $288,560 (fiscal 1990); $376,580 (fiscal 1989)
Assets: $1,973,727 (fiscal year ending September 30, 1991); $1,791,423 (fiscal 1990); $1,413,000 (fiscal 1989)
Gifts Received: $600,000 (fiscal 1991); $598,539 (fiscal 1990); $456,281 (fiscal 1989)
Fiscal Note: In 1991, contributions were received from Roy J. Zuckerberg.
EIN: 13-3052489

CONTRIBUTIONS SUMMARY
Donor(s): Roy J. Zuckerberg
Typical Recipients: • *Arts & Humanities:* history/historic preservation, museums/galleries • *Education:* colleges & universities • *Health:* hospitals, mental health, single-disease health associations • *Religion:* churches, religious organizations, synagogues • *Social Services:* child welfare, disabled, united funds, youth organizations
Grant Types: general support
Geographic Distribution: focus on NY

GIVING OFFICERS
James C. Kautz: trust
Barbara Zuckerberg: trust
Dina R. Zuckerberg: trust
Lloyd P. Zuckerberg: trust
Roy J. Zuckerberg: trust *B* New York NY 1936 *ED* Lowell Technological Inst BS 1958 *CURR EMPL* head div: Goldman Sachs & Co *NONPR AFFIL* mem bd overseers: Albert Einstein Coll Medicine; trust: Brooklyn Mus, Long Island Hearing Speech Soc, Long Island Jewish Med Ctr

APPLICATION INFORMATION
Initial Approach: Contributes to preselected organizations.
Restrictions on Giving: Does not support individuals.

GRANTS ANALYSIS
Number of Grants: 136
Highest Grant: $100,000
Typical Range: $500 to $7,500
Disclosure Period: fiscal year ending September 30, 1991

RECENT GRANTS
100,000 Long Island Jewish Medical Center, New Hyde Park, NY
70,000 Jewish Museum, New York, NY
30,000 United Jewish Appeal Federation of Jewish Philanthropies, New York, NY
25,000 Brooklyn Museum, Brooklyn, NY
25,000 Long Island Jewish Medical Center, New Hyde Park, NY

Zurn Industries

Revenue: $596.5 million
Employees: 3,600
Headquarters: Erie, PA
SIC Major Group: Engineering & Management Services, Fabricated Metal Products, Heavy Construction Except Building Construction, and Stone, Clay & Glass Products

CONTACT
James A. Zurn
Senior Vice President
Zurn Industries
PO Box 2000
Erie, PA 16514
(814) 452-2111

FINANCIAL SUMMARY
Recent Giving: $450,000 (1993 est.)

Fiscal Note: Company gives directly.

CONTRIBUTIONS SUMMARY

Typical Recipients: • *Arts & Humanities:* general • *Civic & Public Affairs:* general • *Education:* general • *Health:* general • *Social Services:* general
Grant Types: capital, challenge, emergency, endowment, general support, matching, and seed money

Geographic Distribution: primarily in Pennsylvania
Operating Locations: AL (Birmingham), CA (City of Industry, Gardena, Paso Robles, Upland), FL (Tampa), GA (Augusta), IL (La Grange), ME (South Portland), NJ (Woodbridge), PA (Erie), WA (Redmond)

CORP. OFFICERS

William A. Freeman: *CURR EMPL* pres, dir: Zurn Indus

Charles L. Hedrick: *CURR EMPL* vchmn, dir: Zurn Indus
George H. Schofield: *CURR EMPL* chmn, ceo, dir: Zurn Indus

GIVING OFFICERS

James A. Zurn: *CURR EMPL* sr vp: Zurn Indus

APPLICATION INFORMATION

Initial Approach: *Initial Contact:* brief letter of inquiry *Include Information On:* description of the organization, amount requested, purpose of funds sought, and recently audited financial statements *When to Submit:* any time
Restrictions on Giving: Does not support individuals, religious organizations for sectarian purposes, or political or lobbying groups.

GRANTS ANALYSIS

Typical Range: $1,000 to $2,500

Glossary

501(C)3
Section of the Internal Revenue Code which defines nonprofit, charitable, tax-exempt organizations. Organizations qualifying under this section of the Code include religious, education, charitable, amateur athletic, scientific or literary groups, and private foundations.

990-PF
See Form 990-PF.

ACTION GRANT
A grant made to examine an operating program or project, as opposed to a research grant.

ANNUAL REPORT
Voluntary yearly report of financial and structural conditions prepared by the management of an organization. Although the term is sometimes used to refer to a report on the contributions activities of a foundation or corporation, "annual report" is more frequently applied to a corporation's annual report to shareholders.

ASSETS
The overall property or resources of the funding organization, including cash, real property, stocks, bonds, etc.

AWARD GRANT
A specific type of grant bestowed as an award for meeting a goal or other special accomplishment.

BENEFACTOR
Donor, usually at the highest level.

BENEFICIARY
Person or organization named by an insured to receive benefits upon death of insured--either primary or secondary.

BEQUEST
Cash, securities, or other personal property, transferred by will. A bequest may consist of a set amount, a percentage, or a residual amount of tangible property.

BRICKS AND MORTAR
Describes construction materials, equipment, and/or funds used to provide the basic "building blocks" for a building or construction project. See also *capital grant*.

CAPITAL GRANT
Grant provided to fund a *capital expenditure*, usually, for physical plant construction or equipment. See also *bricks and mortar*.

CAPITAL EXPENDITURE
An expenditure to acquire an asset with an expected useful life of more than one year.

CAUSE-RELATED MARKETING AND PROMOTION
Support provided by a for-profit corporation in which the company's donations are directly linked to marketing efforts to benefit the company. One examples would be a case in which an airline contributed $5 to a city's symphony orchestra for every passenger who booked a flight on the airline from that city; another example would be a company-sponsored foot race in which part of the fee for entering the race helps support a local charity.

CHALLENGE GRANT
A grant that is paid on the condition that the recipient organization is able to raise additional funds from other donors.

CHARITABLE REMAINDER ANNUITY TRUST
Provides a fixed amount of income to donor for life or for a term of years; upon death, the remainder reverts to the named charity.

CHARITY
Non-profit organization, institution or agency created to carry out programs or projects or to operate activities for the public good. Under section 501(c)3 of the Internal Revenue Code, organizations applying for tax-exempt

status are required to meet certain criteria which distinguish them as a "public charity" rather than a private foundation.

COMBINED GIVING PROGRAM
A corporate contributions program which consists of both a *direct giving program* and a *corporate foundation*. Because the direct giving program and the corporate foundation may each have distinct fields of interest, it is important to target proposals to the individual program or foundation based on its explicit funding priorities.

COMMUNITY FUND
An organization or program which conducts annual campaigns to support local health and social service agencies. See also *united fund*.

COMMUNITY FOUNDATION
An organization established to provide grants in a specific community or geographic area; typically, funds are pooled from multiple donors and donor organizations and independently administered.

COMPANY-SPONSORED FOUNDATION
See *corporate foundation*.

CONFERENCE/SEMINAR GRANT
A grant awarded to fund a conference or seminar.

CONTRIBUTION
Gift or donation in various forms to a non-profit organization for which no tangible value is received.

CONTRIBUTIONS COMMITTEE
The board responsible for making the grant decisions in a company or foundation.

CORPORATE DIRECT GIVING PROGRAM
A program established within the body of a for-profit corporation to coordinate the charitable interests of the corporation. Unlike a *corporate foundation*, a corporate direct giving program typically does not exist as a 501(c)(3) organization and is not subject to the same laws/regulations as a corporate or independent foundation.

CORPORATE FOUNDATION
Philanthropic organization established to coordinate the charitable interests of a sponsoring corporation. Most corporate foundations are themselves 501(c)(3) organizations and, as such, are legally required to file a 990-PF each year.

CORPORATE GIVING PROGRAM
A *direct giving program*, *foundation*, or *combined giving program* sponsored by a for-profit company. The giving program may be sponsored by a private or publicly owned corporation.

DEFERRED GIVING
Contributions to an organization other than through current gifts; fund reverts to organization at a later date.

DEPARTMENT GRANT
A grant awarded on the basis that it be used to support a specific academic department, usually in a college or university.

DIRECT GRANT
A monetary award made directly to the recipient organization, as contrasted with noncash support, in-kind contributions, or other nonmonetary grants.

DISCLOSURE PERIOD
Period of time to which the source information in a profile applies; may be based on fiscal or calendar year. Data provided in a Form 990-PF whose disclosure period is January 1 through December 31 of a given year refer to the financial and organizational condition of the foundation during that particular calendar year.

DISTRIBUTION COMMITTEE
See *contributions committee*.

DONATED EQUIPMENT
Equipment donated by a company to a nonprofit organization in lieu of cash support.

DONATED PRODUCTS
Products donated by a company to a nonprofit organization in lieu of cash support.

DONEE
The grant recipient.

DONOR
Person who contributes to a non-profit organization; synonymous with contributor or giver.

EMERGENCY GRANT
Funds provided for emergency purposes, such as disaster aid.

EMPLOYEE MATCHING GIFT
A contribution made by a company employee and matched by a like gift from the employer.

EMPLOYER IDENTIFICATION NUMBER (EIN)
A nine-digit code used to identify a foundation on its annual 990-PF filing.

ENDOWMENT
The process whereby a donor provides funds to an organization or institution to run a program or facility; typically, the program or facility is named after the donor.

ENDOWMENT CAMPAIGN
A campaign to solicit funds to establish or supplement an organization's endowment fund.

ESTATE
Degree, quality, nature and extent of one's interest in, or ownership of land, property, real estate, securities, royalties, insurance, cash, treasures, etc.

FAMILY FOUNDATION
A foundation which receives its funds solely from members of a single family. Generally, family members serve as officers or board members and influence grantmaking decisions.

FEDERATED CAMPAIGN
Fund raising campaign conducted by one agency or group for many paticipating or member organizations. See also *united fund*.

FEDERATED GIVING PROGRAM
See *united fund*.

FELLOWSHIP
An endowment, or money paid from such an endowment, for the support of a graduate student in a university or college.

FORM 990-PF
Financial report filed annually by a private or corporate foundation in accordance with federal and state tax laws. Items listed in the 990-PF include foundation assets, receipts, expenditures, compensation of officers, and grants.

FUNDING ORGANIZATION
Any type of donor organization -- corporate foundation or direct giving program; community, independent, family, private, or operating foundation; charitable trust, etc.

GENERAL PURPOSE FOUNDATION
An independent private foundation that awards grants in many different fields of interest.

GENERAL SUPPORT
A grant made to support the general work of an organization, rather than a specific project or goal. (Opposite of a *restricted grant*).

GRANT
Allocation of money by foundation, corporation, government, or organization to a person, agency, or institution for a general or specific purpose.

IN-KIND CONTRIBUTION
A contribution of equipment, supplies, or other property in lieu of cash. See also *nonmonetary support*.

IN-KIND SERVICES
Contribution of services, such as printing, data processing, or technical assistance, in lieu of money.

INDEPENDENT FOUNDATION
Any grantmaking, non-operating foundation.

LOAN
Funds awarded with the understanding that the amount of the loan be repaid over a period of time.

LOANED EMPLOYEES
Company employees whose time is donated in lieu of a monetary grant.

LOANED EXECUTIVES
Company employees whose time is donated in lieu of a monetary grant.

MEMORIAL
A gift intended to preserve the memory of a person or event. Memorial gifts are made to nonprofit organizations to memorialize deceased individuals; memorial trusts are established as an interest-bearing investment to memorialize the deceased.

MISSION STATEMENT
Concise description of the purpose of an organization.

MULTIYEAR/CONINUING SUPPORT
Grants awarded in several installments over a period of two or more years.

NONMONETARY SUPPORT
Contributions in lieu of cash grants, such as equipment, supplies, and services.

OPERATING FOUNDATION
A foundation established for the purpose of conducting scientific research or other highly focused programs, usually within the aegis of its own organizational structure. Funds are generally restricted to the foundation's own projects and not provided as grants to other organizations.

OPERATING EXPENSE GRANT
A grant to support the day-to-day administrative, staffing, and other operational costs of a program or organization.

PLEDGE
Promise made by a potential donor to pay a specific sum over a set period; property or fund paid at a later date.

PRIVATE FOUNDATION
An independent grantmaking organization operated by a private group, such as a family or private board. The Taft Group defines private foundations as family and general purpose foundations, rather than corporate, community, or operating foundations.

PROFESSORSHIP GRANT
Funds which help establish or support an ongoing professorship position within a college or university.

PROFILE
A description of pertinent details about a prospective donor gathered through prospect research.

PROGRAM-RELATED INVESTMENT
A loan or other investment made for a project related to the donor's specific interests, usually with the agreement that the recipient repay the funds over a period of time.

PROJECT GRANT
Funding for a stated project.

PROPOSAL
A written request or application for a gift or grant that includes why the project or progam is needed, who will carry it out, and how much it will cost.

PUBLIC CHARITY
A nonprofit organization that solicits funds from the general public and uses the funds to sponsor or aid social, educational, or religious activities, or engage in activities that provide relief for distressed or underprivileged individuals. Public charities are defined in Section 509(a)(1-4) of the Internal Revenue Code. Some public charities use the term "foundation" in their names but are not classified by the Internal Revenue Service as a foundation.

QUERY LETTER
Brief, preliminary letter describing an organization and proposed grant request, usually sent prior to initiating a full proposal.

RECENT GRANT
In Taft publications, a listing of recent grants may include grants awarded and paid during the *disclosure period* and/or one year immediately preceding the disclosure period.

RESEARCH GRANT
Funds awarded for specific research projects, usually at a college or university.

RESTRICTED GRANT
A contribution which specifies the purposes of the gift or how it must be used.

RFP
Request for Proposal. A solicitation of grant proposals. RFPs are used mainly by government agencies and are not often issued by corporate or private foundations.

SCHOLARSHIP GRANT
Funds provided to support a scholarship or scholarship program at a college or university.

SEED MONEY
Funds given for the support of a new program or organization.

SINGLE-DISEASE HEALTH ASSOCIATION
A nonprofit organization devoted to addressing a specific health care issue, such as heart disease, leukemia, etc.

SPECIAL PURPOSE FOUNDATION
A private foundation established to support specific areas of interest.

TECHNICAL ASSISTANCE
Support in the form of expert aid or advice, sometimes donated to a nonprofit organization in lieu of a cash grant.

TESTAMENTARY TRUST
A trust established by a last will and testament.

TRUST FUND
Everything (real or personal property, money or any assets) held by one entity for management by another.

TRUSTEE
Member of a board appointed to manage the affairs of a foundation, corporation, trust, or nonprofit.

UNITED FUND
A fundraising program administered by one agency or group for many participating or member organizations.

WORKPLACE SOLICITATION
An organized program which makes appeals to the employees of a corporation or other organization in the workplace.

Indexes

How to Use the Indexes

The *Directory of Corporate and Foundation Givers (CFG)* has nine indexes to assist in targeting your research. These indexes can be used to locate grant makers by geographic region, areas of interest, types of support, industry affiliation, officers and directors, and more than 45,000 organizations that have already received support.

The following example illustrates how to use the indexes. A prospect researcher needs a contribution to support a research project at a college in California. The researcher can use the **Index to Corporations and Foundations by Headquarters State** and the **Index to Grant Recipients by State** to locate donors that fund projects in California. The researcher then cross-checks the California corporations and foundations with the **Index to Corporations and Foundations by Grant Type** to find which ones contribute to research. The new list is then cross-referenced with the **Index to Corporations and Foundations by Recipient Type** to compile a list of donors with a history of giving to colleges and universities. If the research has application to a particular type of company, the **Index to Corporations by Major Products/Industry** should also be checked to see if a match can be made with a donor along business interests.

In the sample indexes provided below, one prospective funding possibility is the Chevron Corp. located in San Francisco. The researcher can now go back to *CFG's* profile section and find out about Chevron and its contributions program. If the company looks like it might be interested in your research project, call the company to request its guidelines and begin the application process. When broadening your search or strengthening your match, use the **Index to Corporations and Foundations by Operating Location** and the **Index to Officers and Directors** to identify additional links between your organization and the donor community.

The nine indexes in *CFG* are:

Corporations and Foundations by Headquarters State: Arranges companies and foundations by the state in which their main office is located.

Corporations and Foundations by Operating Location: Lists companies and foundations alphabetically within state of their headquarters and major operating locations.

Corporations and Foundations by Grant Type: Lists corporations by the types of funding they generally prefer or are required by their charters to endorse.

Corporations by Nonmonetary Support Type: Lists corporations that provide up to seven alternative sources of support other than cash.

Corporations and Foundations by Recipient Type: Arranges companies and foundations by the types of nonprofit programs and organizations they currently support or have a history of funding.

Corporations by Major Products/Industry: Lists companies by major field of business based on their two-digit SIC codes.

Officers and Directors: Arranges officers, trustees, directors, managers, and contact people in alphabetical order with the name of the company or foundation for which the serve

Grant Recipient by State: Lists all grant recipients located in the profile section by state, including the grant amount and the donor foundation or corporation.

Master Index to Corporations and Foundations: Alphabetically arranges all corporations and foundations profiled in the directory with page numbers.

Illustration of How to Cross-Reference Indexes

Index to Corporations and Foundations by Headquarters State
    California
    Chartwell Foundation
⇒   Chevron Corp.
    Chiron Corp.
    Christie Electric Corp.

Index to Grant Recipients by State
    California
    Stanford University ($100,000) *see* Cantor
      Foundation, Iris and B. Gerald
⇒   Stanford University ($73,650) *see* Chevron Corp.
    Stanford University — scholarship funds ($5,834)
      see Educational Communications

Index to Corporations and Foundations by Grant Type
    Research
    Charles River Laboratories
    Chernow Trust for the Benefit of Charity, Michael

Research (cont.)
⇒   Chevron Corp.
    Childs Memorial Fund for Medical Research
    Chiles Foundation

Index to Corporations and Foundations by Recipient Type
    Education — *Colleges and Universities*
    Cherokee Foundation
    Chesebrough-Pond's
⇒   Chevron Corp.
    Chicago Title and Trust Co.
    Childress Foundation, Francis and Miranda

Index to Corporations by Major Products/Industry
    Petroleum & Coal Products
    CertainTeed Corp.
⇒   Chevron Corp.
    Clark Oil & Refining

Index to Corporations and Foundations by Headquarters State

California (cont.)

Columbia Savings Charitable Foundation
Columbia Savings & Loan Association
Community Psychiatric Centers
Comprecare Foundation
Compton Foundation
Computer Sciences Corp.
Confidence Foundation
Connell Foundation, Michael J.
Conner Peripherals
Consolidated Electrical Distributors
Consolidated Freightways
Cook Brothers Educational Fund
Cook Family Trust
Copley Press
Cornnuts, Inc.
Cow Hollow Foundation
Cowell Foundation, S. H.
Crail-Johnson Foundation
Cramer Foundation
Crean Foundation
Crocker Trust, Mary A.
Crummer Foundation, Roy E.
Cubic Corp.
Curtin-Palohermo Charitable Remainder Trust
Dai-Ichi Kangyo Bank of California
Daily News
Daly Charitable Foundation Trust, Robert and Nancy
Darling Foundation, Hugh and Hazel
Dataproducts Corp.
Davies Charitable Trust
Day Foundation, Willametta K.
de Dampierre Memorial Foundation, Marie C.
Del Monte Foods
Deutsch Co.
DFS Group Limited
DHL Airways Inc.
Diamond Walnut Growers
Diasonics, Inc.
Diener Foundation, Frank C.
Digital Sciences Corp.
DiRosa Foundation, Rene and Veronica
Disney Family Foundation, Roy
Doelger Charitable Trust, Thelma
Doheny Foundation, Carrie Estelle
Dole Food Company, Inc.
Dole Fresh Vegetables
Domino of California
Douglas Charitable Foundation
Downey Savings & Loan Association
Downing Foundation, J. C.
Dreyer's & Edy's Grand Ice Cream
Drown Foundation, Joseph
Drum Foundation
Ducommun Inc.
Dunning Foundation
Durfee Foundation
Early Medical Research Trust, Margaret E.
Easton Aluminum
Eaton Foundation, Edwin M. and Gertrude S.
Ebell of Los Angeles Rest Cottage Association
Ebell of Los Angeles Scholarship Endowment Fund
Eisenberg Foundation, Ben B. and Joyce E.
Elixir Industries
Emery Worldwide
EMI Records Group
Environment Now
Ernest & Julio Gallo Winery
Erteszek Foundation
Essick Foundation

Everest & Jennings International
Exchange Bank
Factor Family Foundation, Max
Fairfield Foundation, Freeman E.
Falk Foundation, Elizabeth M.
Famous Amos Chocolate Chip Cookie Co.
Fantastic Foods
Far West Financial Corp.
Farallon Foundation
Farmers Group, Inc.
Fedco, Inc.
Feintech Foundation
Fellner Memorial Foundation, Leopold and Clara M.
Femino Foundation
Fidelity Federal Savings & Loan
Financial Corp. of Santa Barbara
Fireman's Fund Insurance Co.
First American Financial Corp.
First Fruit
First Interstate Bank of California
Fleetwood Enterprises, Inc.
Fleishhacker Foundation
Flintridge Foundation
Floyd Family Foundation
Fluor Corp.
Foothills Foundation
Forest Lawn Foundation
Foster Farms
Fox Inc.
Fox Foundation, John H.
Freedom Newspapers Inc.
Friedman Bag Co.
Friedman Family Foundation
Fritz Cos.
Frozfruit Corp.
Fujitsu America, Inc.
Fujitsu Systems of America, Inc.
Furth Foundation
Fusenot Charity Foundation, Georges and Germaine
G.A.G. Charitable Corporation
G.P.G. Foundation
Gallo Foundation, Ernest
Gallo Foundation, Julio R.
Gap, The
Garland Foundation, John Jewett and H. Chandler
Geffen Foundation, David
Gellert Foundation, Carl
Gellert Foundation, Celia Berta
Gellert Foundation, Fred
Genentech
Gensler Jr. & Associates, M. Arthur
Gerbode Foundation, Wallace Alexander
Getty Foundation, Ann and Gordon
Getty Trust, J. Paul
Ghidotti Foundation, William and Marian
Gildred Foundation
Gilmore Foundation, Earl B.
Gilmore Foundation, William G.
Girard Foundation
Gleason Foundation, James
Gleason Foundation, Katherine
Glendale Federal Bank
Global Van Lines
Gluck Foundation, Maxwell H.
Goel Foundation
Golden Grain Macaroni Co.
Golden State Foods Corp.
Golden West Financial Corp.
Golden West Foundation
Goldman Fund, Richard and Rhoda
Goldrich Family Foundation
Goldsmith Family Foundation
Goldwyn Foundation, Samuel
Goodman Foundation, Edward and Marion
Grand Auto, Inc.
Great American First Savings Bank, FSB

Great Western Financial Corp.
Green Foundation, Burton E.
Greenville Foundation
Greiner Trust, Virginia
Gross Charitable Trust, Stella B.
Grousbeck Family Foundation
Gumbiner Foundation, Josephine
Haas Fund, Miriam and Peter
Haas Fund, Walter and Elise
Haas, Jr. Fund, Evelyn and Walter
Hafif Family Foundation
Haigh-Scatena Foundation
Hale Foundation, Crescent Porter
Halsell Foundation, O. L.
Hammer United World College Trust, Armand
Hancock Foundation, Luke B.
Hannon Foundation, William H.
Harden Foundation
Harman Foundation, Reed L. and Nan H.
Harper Group
Hayden Foundation, William R. and Virginia
Haynes Foundation, John Randolph and Dora
Hedco Foundation
Helms Foundation
Hench Foundation, John C.
Herbst Foundation
Hertz Foundation, Fannie and John
Hewlett Foundation, William and Flora
Hewlett-Packard Co.
Hexcel Corp.
Hills Fund, Edward E.
Hilton Hotels Corp.
Hoag Family Foundation, George
Hoffman Foundation, H. Leslie Hoffman and Elaine S.
Hofmann Co.
Hogan Foundation, Royal Barney
Holmes & Narver Services Inc.
Holt Foundation, William Knox
Home Savings of America, FA
Homeland Foundation
Homestake Mining Co.
Homestead Financial Corp.
Hoover, Jr. Foundation, Margaret W. and Herbert
Howe and Mitchell B. Howe Foundation, Lucile Horton
Huck International Inc.
Hughes Aircraft Co.
Hume Foundation, Jaquelin
Hyundai Motor America
I Have A Dream Foundation - Los Angeles
Imagine Foods
Imperial Bancorp
Imperial Corp. of America
In His Name
Institute for Research on Learning
Intel Corp.
Intermark, Inc.
International Aluminum Corp.
International Rectifier Corp.
Ira-Hiti Foundation for Deep Ecology
Irmas Charitable Foundation, Audrey and Sydney
Irvine Foundation, James
Irvine Health Foundation
Irvine Medical Center
Irwin Charity Foundation, William G.
Ishiyama Foundation
Jackson Family Foundation, Ann
Jacobs Engineering Group
Jacoby Foundation, Lela Beren and Norman
Jafra Cosmetics, Inc. (U.S.)
Jameson Foundation, J. W. and Ida M.

Janeway Foundation, Elizabeth Bixby
Jefferson Endowment Fund, John Percival and Mary C.
Jeffries & Co.
Jerome Foundation
Jewett Foundation, George Frederick
Johnson Foundation, Walter S.
Jones Foundation, Fletcher
Jorgensen Co., Earle M.
Joslyn Foundation, Marcellus I.
Kaiser Aluminum & Chemical Corp.
Kaiser Cement Corp.
Kaiser Family Foundation, Henry J.
Kaiser Steel Resources
Kaisertech Ltd.
Kal Kan Foods, Inc.
Kasler Corp.
Kaufman & Broad Home Corp.
Kawasaki Motors Corp., U.S.A.
Keck Foundation, W. M.
Keck, Jr. Foundation, William M.
Kenwood U.S.A. Corp.
Kerr Foundation, A. H.
Kerr Glass Manufacturing Corp.
Kest Family Foundation, Sol and Clara
Kikkoman International, Inc.
Kingsley Foundation, Lewis A.
Kirchgessner Foundation, Karl
Kirkhill Rubber Co.
Knudsen Foundation, Tom and Valley
Kohl Charitable Foundation, Allen D.
Komes Foundation
Koret Foundation
Korn/Ferry International
Koulaieff Educational Fund, Trustees of Ivan Y.
Kraft Foodservice
Kyocera International Inc.
L. L. W. W. Foundation
L.A. Gear
Lakeside Foundation
Landmark Land Co., Inc.
Langendorf Foundation, Stanley S.
Lannan Foundation
Layne Foundation
Leavey Foundation, Thomas and Dorothy
Lebus Trust, Bertha
Ledler Corp.
LEF Foundation
Leonardt Foundation
Levi Strauss & Co.
Levine Family Foundation, Hyman
Levinson Foundation, Max and Anna
Levy Foundation, Hyman Jebb
Levy-Markus Foundation
Lewis Homes of California
Lincy Foundation
Liquid Air Corp.
Littlefield Foundation, Edmund Wattis
Litton Industries
Livingston Memorial Foundation
Llagas Foundation
Lockheed Corp.
Long Foundation, J.M.
Longs Drug Stores
LSI Logic Corp.
Lucas Cancer Foundation, Richard M.
Lucky Stores
Lund Foundation
Lurie Foundation, Louis R.
Luster Family Foundation
Lux Foundation, Miranda
Lyon Co., William
Lytel Foundation, Bertha Russ
M. E. G. Foundation

MacKenzie Foundation
Magnatek
Magowan Family Foundation
Maguire Thomas Partners
Makita U.S.A., Inc.
Management Compensation Group/Dulworth Inc.
Mann Foundation, Ted
Margoes Foundation
Mariani Nut Co.
Marshburn Foundation
Martin Foundation, Della
Masserini Charitable Trust, Maurice J.
Matson Navigation Co.
Mattel
Max Charitable Foundation
Maxfield Foundation
Maxicare Health Plans
Maxtor Corp.
May Foundation, Wilbur
Mayacamas Corp.
Mazda Motors of America (Central), Inc.
Mazda North America
MCA
McAlister Charitable Foundation, Harold
McBean Charitable Trust, Alletta Morris
McBean Family Foundation
McConnell Foundation
McDonnell Douglas Corp.-West
McKenzie Family Foundation, Richard
McKesson Corp.
Mead Foundation, Giles W. and Elise G.
Measurex Corp.
Meland Outreach
Mericos Foundation
Mervyn's
Metropolitan Theatres Corp.
Meyer Fund, Milton and Sophie
Microdot, Inc.
MicroSim Corp.
Milken Family Medical Foundation
Milken Foundation, L. and S.
Milken Institute for Job and Capital Formation
Miller Brewing Company/California
Miller Foundation, Earl B. and Loraine H.
Mitchell Family Foundation, Edward D. and Anna
Mitsubishi Electric America
Mitsubishi Motor Sales of America, Inc.
Modglin Family Foundation
Monterey Bay Aquarium Foundation
Montgomery Street Foundation
Moore Family Foundation
Mosher Foundation, Samuel B.
Moskowitz Foundation, Irving I.
Moss Foundation
Muller Foundation
Munger Foundation, Alfred C.
Murdock Development Co.
Murdy Foundation
Murphey Foundation, Lluella Morey
Murphy Foundation, Dan
Muth Foundation, Peter and Mary
Nakamichi Foundation, E.
National Dollar Stores, Ltd.
National Medical Enterprises
National Metal & Steel
National Pro-Am Youth Fund
National Semiconductor Corp.
Natural Heritage Foundation
NEC Electronics, Inc.
Nelson Foundation, Florence
Nestle U.S.A. Inc.
Neutrogena Corp.

Connecticut (cont.)

Advo System Inc.
Aetna Life & Casualty Co.
Air Express International Corp.
Alpert & Co., Inc., Herman
American Brands
American Maize Products
American National Bank
American Tobacco Co.
Ames Department Stores
Amstar Corp.
Anchor Fasteners
Arbor Acres Farm, Inc.
Asea Brown Boveri
Auerbach Foundation, Beatrice Fox
Baker Foundation, Elinor Patterson
Bank of Boston Connecticut
Barden Corp.
Barnes Foundation
Barnes Group
Bennett Foundation, Carl and Dorothy
Berbecker Scholarship Fund, Walter J. and Lille
Bingham Trust, The
Bissell Foundation, J. Walton
Bodine Corp.
Bowater Inc.
Brakeley, John Price Jones Inc.
Bristol Savings Bank
Burndy Corp.
Cadbury Beverages Inc.
Carey Industries
Carstensen Memorial Foundation, Fred R. and Hazel W.
Carter Co., William
Casey Foundation, Annie E.
Chadwick Fund, Dorothy Jordan
Champion International Corp.
Chapin Foundation, Frances
Chapman Foundation, William H.
Chase Packaging Corp.
Chesebrough-Pond's
Childs Memorial Fund for Medical Research, Jane Coffin
Citizens Utilities Co.
Clabir Corp.
CM Alliance Cos.
Community Cooperative Development Foundation
Connecticut General Corp.
Connecticut Natural Gas Corp.
Connecticut Savings Bank
Crompton & Knowles Corp.
Crystal Brands
Culpeper Foundation, Charles E.
Culpeper Memorial Foundation, Daphne Seybolt
Day Foundation, Nancy Sayles
Dell Foundation, Hazel
Deloitte & Touche
Dennett Foundation, Marie G.
Devon Group
Dexter Corp.
Dibner Fund
Dreyfus Corp., Louis
Duracell International
Duty Free International
Echlin Inc.
Eder Foundation, Sidney and Arthur
Educational Foundation of America
EIS Foundation
Ellis Fund
Engelberg Foundation
Ensign-Bickford Industries
Ensworth Charitable Foundation
EnviroSource
Fairchild Foundation, Sherman
FIP Corp.
First Brands Corp.
Fisher Foundation

FKI Holdings Inc.
Fleet Bank
Fleet Bank N.A.
Folsom Foundation, Maud Glover
Foster-Davis Foundation
Fox Foundation Trust, Jacob L. and Lewis
Fox Steel Co.
Franks Nursery and Crafts
Freas Foundation
General Electric Co.
General Reinsurance Corp.
General Signal Corp.
Grolier, Inc.
GTE Corp.
Harcourt Foundation, Ellen Knowles
Hartford Courant Foundation
Hartford Steam Boiler Inspection & Insurance Co.
Heritage Foundation
Herzog Foundation, Carl J.
Heublein
Hoffman Foundation, Maximillian E. and Marion O.
Howmet Corp.
Howmet Corp., Winstead Machining
Hubbell Inc.
Huisking Foundation
Hydraulic Co.
Industrial Risk Insurers
ITT Hartford Insurance Group
ITT Rayonier
IU International
Jones and Bessie D. Phelps Foundation, Cyrus W. and Amy F.
Jones Fund, Paul L.
Jost Foundation, Charles and Mabel P.
Kaman Corp.
Kohn-Joseloff Fund
Koopman Fund
Kreitler Foundation
Krieble Foundation, Vernon K.
Landis & Gyr, Inc.
Larrabee Fund Association
Lender Family Foundation
Lender's Bagel Bakery
Leonhardt Foundation, Frederick H.
Library Association of Warehouse Point
Loctite Corp.
Long Foundation, George A. and Grace
LPL Technologies Inc.
Lydall, Inc.
MacCurdy Salisbury Educational Foundation
Mazer Foundation, Jacob and Ruth
Meek Foundation
Meserve Memorial Fund, Albert and Helen
Middlesex Mutual Assurance Co.
Miles Inc., Pharmaceutical Division
Moore Charitable Foundation, Marjorie
Moore Foundation, Edward S.
Moore McCormack Resources
Moore Medical Corp.
Mosbacher, Jr. Foundation, Emil
Napier Co.
New England Aircraft Products Co.
Newman's Own
Newmil Bancorp
Nirenberg Family Charitable Foundation
Northeast Savings, FA
Northeast Utilities
Oaklawn Foundation
Obernauer Foundation
Olin Corp.
Otis Elevator Co.

Palmer-Fry Memorial Trust, Lily
Palmer Fund, Frank Loomis
Patterson and Clara Guthrie Patterson Trust, Robert Leet
Pechiney Corp.
People's Bank
Pepperidge Farm, Inc.
Perkin-Elmer Corp.
Pfriem Foundation, Norma F.
Phibro Energy
Phoenix Home Life Mutual Insurance Co.
Pirelli Armstrong Tire Corp.
Pitney Bowes
Pittston Co.
Preston Trust, Evelyn W.
Price Foundation, Lucien B. and Katherine E.
Psychists
Publicker Industries, Inc.
Rich Co., F.D.
Risdon Corp.
Robinson Fund, Charles Nelson
Rockfall Foundation
Rogers Corp.
Rogow Birken Foundation
Rosenthal Foundation, Richard and Hinda
S.T.J. Group, Inc.
Saunders Charitable Foundation, Helen M.
Savin Corp.
Schiro Fund
Senior Services of Stamford
Simkins Industries, Inc.
Smart Family Foundation
SNET
Society for Savings
Society for the Increase of the Ministry
Southern Connecticut Gas Co.
Stanley Charitable Foundation, A. W.
Stanley Works
Stone Foundation
Sullivan Foundation, Ray H. and Pauline
Sussman Fund, Edna Bailey
Sweet Life Foods
Tetley, Inc.
Time Warner Cable
Timex Corp.
Torrington Co.
Travelers Cos.
Union Carbide Corp.
Union Trust
Uniroyal Chemical Co. Inc.
United Illuminating Co.
United States Surgical Corp.
United Technologies Corp.
UST
Valencia Charitable Trust
Valentine Foundation, Lawson
Vance Charitable Foundation, Robert C.
Vanderbilt Trust, R. T.
Von Rebay Foundation, Hilla
Wheeler Foundation, Wilmot
Whitehead Charitable Foundation
Widow's Society
Wiremold Co.
Woman's Seamen's Friend Society of Connecticut
Woodward Fund-Watertown, David, Helen, and Marian
Wyatt Energy, Inc.
Xerox Corp.
Young Foundation, Robert R.
Ziegler Foundation for the Blind, E. Matilda

Delaware

AGFA Division of Miles Inc.
Amsterdam Foundation, Jack and Mimi Leviton
Beneficial Corp.

Birch Foundation, Stephen and Mary
Bishop Trust for the SPCA of Manatee County, Florida, Lillian H.
Borkee Hagley Foundation
Carpenter Foundation
Common Wealth Trust
Crestlea Foundation
Crystal Trust
Curran Foundation
Delmarva Power & Light Co.
Devonwood Foundation
Downs Perpetual Charitable Trust, Ellason
du Pont de Nemours & Co., E. I.
duPont Foundation, Chichester
Fair Play Foundation
Falcon Foundation
Gerard Foundation, Sumner
Glencoe Foundation
Good Samaritan
Gordy Family Educational Trust Fund, George E.
Hamel Family Charitable Trust, D. A.
Harrington Charitable Trust, Charles J.
Hercules Inc.
Himont Inc.
ICI Americas
Julia Foundation, Laura
Kao Corp. of America (DE)
Kent Foundation, Ada Howe
Kent-Lucas Foundation
Kingsley Foundation
Kutz Foundation, Milton and Hattie
Laffey-McHugh Foundation
Lalor Foundation
Longwood Foundation
Lovett Foundation
Lynch Scholarship Foundation, John B.
Marmot Foundation
Mercantile Stores Co.
Milliken Foundation, Agnes G.
Norton Simon Inc.
Raskob Foundation, Bill
Raskob Foundation for Catholic Activities
RLC Corp.
Rollins Environmental Services, Inc.
Romill Foundation
Schwartz Foundation, Bernard Lee
Tate & Lyle Inc.
Vale Foundation, Ruby R.
Welfare Foundation
Wilmington Trust Co.

District of Columbia

Acacia Mutual Life Insurance Co.
American Telephone & Telegraph Co./Washington, DC, Region
Appleby Foundation
Appleby Trust, Scott B. and Annie P.
Arca Foundation
Arcana Foundation
Beldon Fund
Bender Foundation
Benton Foundation
Bernstein Foundation, Diane and Norman
Bloedorn Foundation, Walter A.
Brownley Trust, Walter
Cafritz Foundation, Morris and Gwendolyn
Carr Real Estate Services
Chesapeake & Potomac Telephone Co.
Cohen Foundation, Manny and Ruthy
Colonial Parking

Communications Satellite Corp. (COMSAT)
Covington and Burling
Danaher Corp.
DelMar Foundation, Charles
Dimick Foundation
Dweck Foundation, Samuel R.
Federal National Mortgage Assn., Fannie Mae
Felburn Foundation
Folger Fund
Foundation for Middle East Peace
Fowler Memorial Foundation, John Edward
Freed Foundation
GEICO Corp.
Gelman Foundation, Melvin and Estelle
German Marshall Fund of the United States
Glen Eagles Foundation
Goldman Foundation, Aaron and Cecile
Gottesman Fund
Graham Fund, Philip L.
Gudelsky Family Foundation, Isadore and Bertha
Gumenick Foundation, Nathan and Sophie
Healy Family Foundation, M. A.
Higginson Trust, Corina
Hill-Snowdon Foundation
Himmelfarb Foundation, Paul and Annetta
Hitachi
Japanese American Agon Friendship League
Jerusalem Fund for Education and Community Development
Johnston Trust for Charitable and Educational Purposes, James M.
Kapiloff Foundation, Leonard
Kaplan Foundation, Charles I. and Mary
Kennedy, Jr. Foundation, Joseph P.
Kiplinger Foundation
Kiplinger Washington Editors
Koch Charitable Foundation, Charles G.
Lambe Charitable Foundation, Claude R.
Lea Foundation, Helen Sperry
Lehrman Foundation, Jacob and Charlotte
Loughran Foundation, Mary and Daniel
Loyola Foundation
Marpat Foundation
Marriott Foundation, J. Willard
MCI Communications Corp.
Meyer Foundation, Eugene and Agnes E.
Nationale-Nederlanden North America Corp.
Post Foundation of D.C., Marjorie Merriweather
Potomac Electric Power Co.
Public Welfare Foundation
Reasoner, Davis & Fox
Replogle Foundation, Luther I.
Riggs National Bank
Ross Foundation, Walter G.
Sea-Land Service
Steuart Petroleum Co.
Stewart Trust under the will of Helen S. Devore, Alexander and Margaret
Stewart Trust under the will of Mary E. Stewart, Alexander and Margaret
Stone Foundation, David S.
Strong Foundation, Hattie M.
Student Loan Marketing Association
Wallace Genetic Foundation
Washington Post Co.

Wasserman Foundation, George
Westport Fund
Willard Foundation, Helen Parker
WJLA Inc.
Wouk Foundation, Abe

Florida

Abraham Foundation, Anthony R.
Action Products International
Adams Foundation, Arthur F. and
Alice E.
Aldeen Charity Trust, G. W.
Amaturo Foundation
American Bankers Insurance
Group
American Capital Corp.
American Savings & Loan
Association of Florida
Anchor Glass Container Corp.
APL Corp.
Applebaum Foundation
Appleman Foundation
Archbold Expeditions
Aurora Foundation
Bacardi Imports
Bairnco Corp.
Baker Foundation, George T.
Barnett Banks
Bastien Memorial Foundation,
John E. and Nellie J.
Batchelor Foundation
Bay Branch Foundation
BCR Foundation
Beattie Foundation Trust,
Cordelia Lee
Beveridge Foundation, Frank
Stanley
Bible Alliance
Bickerton Charitable Trust,
Lydia H.
Blair Foundation, John
Blank Family Foundation
Bradish Trust, Norman C.
Brennan Foundation Trust
Breyer Foundation
Briggs Family Foundation
Broad Foundation, Shepard
Brown Charitable Trust, Peter D.
and Dorothy S.
Burdines
Burger King Corp.
Bush Charitable Foundation,
Edyth
Butler Foundation, Alice
Carnival Cruise Lines
Catlin Charitable Trust, Kathleen
K.
Celotex Corp.
Chastain Charitable Foundation,
Robert Lee and Thomas M.
Chatlos Foundation
Childress Foundation, Francis
and Miranda
Citizens & Southern National
Bank of Florida
Cobb Family Foundation
Cohen Foundation, George M.
Community Health Association
Conn Memorial Foundation
Cottrell Foundation
Coulter Corp.
Crane Foundation, Raymond E.
and Ellen F.
Davis Family - W.D. Charities,
James E.
Davis Family - W.D. Charities,
Tine W.
Davis Foundations, Arthur Vining
Day Charitable Foundation,
Harry M.
Delacorte Fund, George
Deltona Corp.
Dettman Foundation, Leroy E.
Dodge Foundation, P. L.
Dubow Family Foundation
Dunspaugh-Dalton Foundation
duPont Foundation, Alfred I.

duPont Fund, Jessie Ball
DWG Corp.
Eagles Memorial Foundation
Eastern Air Lines
Ebert Charitable Foundation,
Horatio B.
Echlin Foundation
Eckerd Corp., Jack
Einstein Fund, Albert E. and
Birdie W.
Ellis Foundation
Falk Foundation, David
Fireman Charitable Foundation,
Paul and Phyllis
First Union National Bank of
Florida
Fish Foundation, Bert
Florida East Coast Industries
Florida Power Corp.
Florida Power & Light Co.
Florida Rock Industries
Florida Steel Corp.
Ford III Memorial Foundation,
Jefferson Lee
Fort Pierce Memorial Hospital
Scholarship Foundation
Fortin Foundation of Florida
Fortune Bank
Foulds Trust, Claiborne F
Friends' Foundation Trust, A.
Frueauff Foundation, Charles A.
Gann Charitable Foundation,
Joseph and Rae
Garner Charitable Trust, James
G.
General Development Corp.
Genius Foundation, Elizabeth
Morse
Gerson Trust, B. Milfred
Gillett Foundation, Elesabeth
Ingalls
Goldstein Foundation, Alfred
and Ann
Gooding Charitable Foundation,
Luca
Goodwin Foundation, Leo
Gore Family Memorial
Foundation
Grace & Co., W.R.
Grader Foundation, K. W.
Greater Construction Corp.
Charitable Foundation, Inc.
Griffin, Sr., Foundation, C. V.
Grobstein Charitable Trust No.
2, Ethel
Gronewaldt Foundation, Alice
Busch
Gulf Power Co.
Gulfstream Housing Corp.
Halmos Foundation
Hanley Family Foundation
Harcourt Brace Jovanovich
Harris Corp.
Harris Foundation, John H. and
Lucille
Haven Charitable Foundation,
Nina
Hayward Foundation Charitable
Trust, John T. and Winifred
Holmes Foundation
Houck Foundation, May K.
Hovnanian Foundation, Hirair
and Anna
Howell Foundation, Eric and
Jessie
Hughes Supply, Inc.
Huizenga Family Foundation
Isaly Klondike Co.
Jaharis Family Foundation
Jenkins Foundation, George W.
Jennings Foundation, Alma
Jones Intercable, Inc.
Keating Family Foundation
Kelly Tractor Co.
Kennedy Family Foundation,
Ethel and W. George
Kirbo Charitable Trust, Thomas
M. and Irene B.

Kloster Cruise Ltd.
Knight Foundation, John S. and
James L.
Knight-Ridder, Inc.
Koch Foundation
Koger Properties
Kohl Foundation, Sidney
Kugelman Foundation
Landegger Charitable Foundation
Larsh Foundation Charitable
Trust
Lattner Foundation, Forrest C.
Lauffer Trust, Charles A.
Law Foundation, Robert O.
Lennar Corp.
Leu Foundation, Harry P.
Lewis Foundation, Frank J.
Link Foundation
Lipton Foundation
Loren Industries Inc.
Lost Tree Charitable Foundation
Lowe Foundation, Joe and Emily
Luria's
Lynn Foundation, E. M.
MacLeod Stewardship
Foundation
Magruder Foundation, Chesley
G.
Mann Foundation, John Jay
Markey Charitable Trust, Lucille
P.
May Mitchell Royal Foundation
McIntosh Foundation
Messing Foundation, Morris M.
and Helen F.
Meyer Foundation, Baron de
Hirsch
Meyer Foundation, Bert and
Mary
Mida Foundation
Mills Charitable Foundation,
Henry L. and Kathryn
Mineral Trust
Moore Foundation, Martha G.
Morgan Foundation, Louie R.
and Gertrude
NVF Co.
Overstreet Foundation
Overstreet Investment Co.
Parsons - W.D. Charities, Vera
Davis
Paulucci Family Foundation
Pearce Foundation, Dr. M. Lee
Phillips Foundation, A. P.
Phillips Foundation, Dr. P.
Picower Foundation, Jeffrey M.
and Barbara
Pope Foundation, Lois B.
Posnack Family Foundation of
Hollywood
Poynter Fund
Publix Supermarkets
Pyramid Foundation
Racal-Milgo
Rales and Ruth Rales
Foundation, Norman R.
Reinhold Foundation, Paul E.
and Ida Klare
Rice Family Foundation, Jacob
and Sophie
Rinker Materials Corp.
Rinker, Sr. Foundation, M. E.
River Branch Foundation
Rosenberg Family Foundation,
William
Rosenberg Foundation, William
J. and Tina
Royal Crown Cos., Inc.
Rumbaugh Foundation, J. H. and
F. H.
Russell Memorial Foundation,
Robert
Ryder System
St. Joe Paper Co.
Saunders Foundation
Schecter Private Foundation,
Aaron and Martha
Schering Laboratories

Schultz Foundation
Scotty's, Inc.
Selby and Marie Selby
Foundation, William G.
Sentinel Communications Co.
Servico, Inc.
Shapiro Foundation, Carl and
Ruth
Simon Foundation, Sidney,
Milton and Leoma
Smith Benevolent Association,
Buckingham
Soref Foundation, Samuel M.
Soref and Helene K.
Speer Foundation, Roy M.
Stacy Foundation, Festus
Storer Communications Inc.
Stuart Foundation, Edward C.
Sun Banks Inc.
Sunburst Foundation
Swisher Foundation, Carl S.
Sylvester Foundation, Harcourt
M. and Virginia W.
Tampa Electric
Taylor Family Foundation, Jack
Terry Foundation, C. Herman
Thomas Foundation, Dorothy
Thoresen Foundation
Tropicana Products, Inc.
United States Sugar Corp.
United Telephone Co. of Florida
Volen Charitable Trust, Benjamin
Wahlstrom Foundation
Walter Industries
Ware Foundation
Weatherwax Foundation
Weintraub Family Foundation,
Joseph
Wells Foundation, Lillian S.
Wertheim Foundation, Dr.
Herbert A.
Whitehall Foundation
Wiggins Memorial Trust, J. J.
Wilder Foundation
Williams Foundation, Edna
Sproull
Wilson Foundation, Hugh and
Mary
Winn-Dixie Stores
Wiseheart Foundation
Wolfson Family Foundation
Yulman Trust, Morton and Helen

Georgia

Abreu Charitable Trust u/w/o
May P. Abreu, Francis I.
AEC Trust
AFLAC
Alumax
American Business Products, Inc.
American Security Bank
American Telephone &
Telegraph Co./Atlanta Region
Anderson Foundation, Peyton
APAC Inc.
Arnold Fund
Atlanta Foundation
Atlanta Gas Light Co.
Atlanta Journal & Constitution
Atlantic Realty Co.
Baker Foundation, Clark and
Ruby
Bank South Corp.
Beck Foundation, Lewis H.
BellSouth Corp.
Bellsouth Telecommunications,
Inc.
Beloco Foundation
Bibb Co.
Blue Circle Inc.
Bradley-Turner Foundation
Burke Foundation, Thomas C.
Callaway Foundation
Callaway Foundation, Fuller E.
Camp Younts Foundation
Campbell Foundation, J. Bulow
Challenge Foundation

Charter Medical Corp.
Chatham Valley Foundation
Cherokee Foundation
Chick-Fil-A, Inc.
Churches Homes Foundation
Cobb Educational Fund, Ty
Coca-Cola Co.
Colonial Oil Industries, Inc.
Community Enterprises
Cook Batson Foundation
Courts Foundation
Cox Enterprises
Cox, Jr. Foundation, James M.
Crawford & Co.
Creel Foundation
Day Foundation, Cecil B.
Delta Air Lines
Digital Communications
Associates, Inc.
Dodson Foundation, James
Glenwell and Clara May
Dorminy Foundation, John Henry
Elkin Memorial Foundation, Neil
Warren and William Simpson
English Memorial Fund,
Florence C. and H. L.
Equifax
Evans Foundation, Lettie Pate
Exposition Foundation
First National Bank of Atlanta
Flagler Co.
Flowers Industries, Inc.
Foundation for Advancement of
Chiropractic Education
Franklin Foundation, John and
Mary
Fuqua Foundation, J. B.
Fuqua Industries, Inc.
Gage Foundation, Philip and
Irene Toll
Garden Foundation, Allan C. and
Lelia J.
Genuine Parts Co.
Georgia Gulf Corp.
Georgia Health Foundation
Georgia-Pacific Corp.
Georgia Pork Producers
Association
Georgia Power Co.
Georgia Scientific and Technical
Research Foundation
Gholston Trust, J. K.
Gilbert, Jr. Charitable Trust, Price
Glancy Foundation, Lenora and
Alfred
Glenn Memorial Foundation,
Wilbur Fisk
Gold Kist, Inc.
Graves Foundation
Gulfstream Aerospace Corp.
Haley Foundation, W. B.
Harland Charitable Foundation,
John and Wilhelmina D.
Harland Co., John H.
Haverty Furniture Cos., Inc.
Health 1st Foundation
Herndon Foundation, Alonzo F.
Herndon and Norris B.
Hill and Family Foundation,
Walter Clay
Hodge Foundation
Hollis Foundation
Home Depot
Howell Fund
Illges Foundation, John P. and
Dorothy S.
Illges Memorial Foundation, A.
and M. L.
Imlay Foundation
Interface Inc.
Jinks Foundation, Ruth T.
Johnson, Lane, Space, Smith &
Co., Inc.
Kuse Foundation, James R.
Lane Memorial Foundation,
Mills Bee
Langdale Co.
Lanier Brothers Foundation

Georgia (cont.)

Lanier Business Products, Inc.
Law Companies Group
Lee Foundation, Ray M. and Mary Elizabeth
Life Insurance Co. of Georgia
Livingston Foundation
Loridans Foundation, Charles
Love Foundation, Gay and Erskine
Marion Fabrics
Marshall Foundation, Mattie H.
Marshall Trust in Memory of Sanders McDaniel, Harriet McDaniel
McCamish Foundation
McCarthy Foundation, John and Margaret
Miller Brewing Company/Georgia
Mizuno Corporation of America
Moore Foundation, Roy C.
Moore Memorial Foundation, James Starr
Murata Erie North America
Murphy Foundation, Katherine and John
National Data Corp.
National Distributing Co., Inc.
National Service Industries
Oxford Foundation
Oxford Industries, Inc.
Parker, Jr. Foundation, William A.
Patterson-Barclay Memorial Foundation
Pickett and Hatcher Educational Fund
Piggly Wiggly Southern
Pitts Foundation, William H. and Lula E.
Pittulloch Foundation
Porter Testamentary Trust, James Hyde
Primerica Financial Services
Printpack, Inc.
Racetrac Petroleum
Ragan Charitable Foundation, Carolyn King
Raleigh Linen Service/National Distributing Co.
Rich Foundation
Robinson Foundation, J. Mack
Roddenbery Co., Inc., W.B.
Rollins Inc.
RTM
Saab Cars USA, Inc.
Savannah Electric & Power Co.
Schwob Foundation, Simon
Scientific-Atlanta
Senior Citizens Foundation
Sewell Foundation, Warren P. and Ava F.
Shaw Industries
Southern Bell
Southwire Co.
Steiner Charitable Fund, Albert
Synovus Financial Corp.
Taylor Trust, Lydia M.
Thomaston Mills, Inc.
Tomlinson Foundation, Kate and Elwyn
Trust Co. Bank
Tull Charitable Foundation
Turner Broadcasting System
Turner Foundation
Union Manufacturing Co.
United Parcel Service of America
Waffle House, Inc.
Walton Monroe Mills
Wardlaw Fund, Gertrude and William C.
Watkins Associated Industries
Watkins Christian Foundation
Wehadkee Foundation
West Foundation

Whitehead Foundation, Joseph B.
Whitehead Foundation, Lettie Pate
Williams Family Foundation of Georgia
Williams, Jr. Family Foundation, A. L.
Wilson Foundation, Frances Wood
Winter Construction Co.
Woodruff Foundation, Robert W.
Woodward Fund-Atlanta, David, Helen, Marian
Woolley Foundation, Vasser
World Carpets
Y.K.K. (U.S.A.) Inc.
Zaban Foundation

Hawaii

Alexander & Baldwin, Inc.
Amfac/JMB Hawaii
Atherton Family Foundation
Baldwin Memorial Foundation, Fred
Bancorp Hawaii
BHP Pacific Resources
Brewer and Co., Ltd., C.
Castle & Cooke
Castle Foundation, Harold K. L.
Castle Foundation, Samuel N. and Mary
Castle Trust, George P. and Ida Tenney
Cooke Foundation
First Hawaiian
Frear Eleemosynary Trust, Mary D. and Walter F.
Hawaii National Bank
Hawaiian Telephone Co.
HEI Inc.
Hobart Memorial Fund, Marion W.
Holy Land Charitable Trust
Hopper Foundation, May Templeton
McInerny Foundation
Moore Foundation, O. L.
Oceanic Cablevision Foundation
Persis Corp.
Servco Pacific
Straub Estate, Gertrude S.
Vidinha Charitable Trust, A. and E.
Watumull Fund, J.
Wilcox General Trust, George N.
Wilcox Trust, S. W.
Zimmerman Foundation, Hans and Clara Davis

Idaho

Albertson's
American Microsystems, Inc.
Beckman Foundation, Leland D.
Boise Cascade Corp.
CHC Foundation
Cunningham Foundation, Laura Moore
Daugherty Foundation
First Security Bank of Idaho N.A.
Hecla Mining Co.
Intermountain Gas Industries
Kasiska Family Foundation
Morrison Foundation, Harry W.
Morrison-Knudsen Corp.
Ore-Ida Foods, Inc.
Simplot Co., J.R.
West One Bancorp
West One Bank Idaho
Whiting Foundation, Macauley and Helen Dow
Whittenberger Foundation, Claude R. and Ethel B.

Illinois

Abbott Laboratories
Ace Hardware Corp.

Acorn Corrugated Box Co.
Aigner
Akzo America
Akzo Chemicals Inc.
Alberto-Culver Co.
Allen-Heath Memorial Foundation
Allstate Insurance Co.
Allyn Foundation
Alsdorf Foundation
AMCORE Bank, N.A. Rockford
American Decal & Manufacturing Co.
American National Bank & Trust Co. of Chicago
American National Can Co.
American Telephone & Telegraph Co./Chicago Region
Ameritech Corp.
Ameritech Development
Ameritech Information Systems
Ameritech International
Ameritech Mobile Communications
Ameritech Services
Amoco Corp.
Amsted Industries
Andersen Foundation, Arthur
Anderson Industries
Andreas Foundation
Andrew Corp.
AON Corp.
APV Crepaco Inc.
Archer-Daniels-Midland Co.
Atwood Foundation
Atwood Industries
AXIA Incorporated
Azteca Foods, Inc.
Balcor Co.
Banc One Illinois Corp.
Bang & Olufsen of America, Inc.
Bankers Life & Casualty Co.
Barber-Colman Co.
Barber-Greene Co.
Bates Memorial Foundation, George A.
Bauer Foundation, M. R.
Baum Family Fund, Alvin H.
Baxter International
Beidler Charitable Trust, Francis
Bell Federal Savings & Loan Association
Beloit Foundation
Benefit Trust Life Insurance Co.
Bere Foundation
Berger Foundation, Albert E.
Bergstrom Manufacturing Co.
Bersted Foundation
Best Foundation, Walter J. and Edith E.
Beverly Bank
Binks Manufacturing Co.
Bitco Corp.
Bjorkman Foundation
Blair and Co., William
Blowitz-Ridgeway Foundation
Blum Foundation, Harry and Maribel G.
Blum Foundation, Nathan and Emily S.
Blum-Kovler Foundation
Bock Charitable Trust, George W.
Boler Co.
Boothroyd Foundation, Charles H. and Bertha L.
Boots Pharmaceuticals, Inc.
Borg-Warner Corp.
Borwell Charitable Foundation
Bosch Corp., Robert
Boulevard Bank, N.A.
Bound to Stay Bound Books Foundation
Bowyer Foundation, Ambrose and Gladys
Brach Foundation, Edwin I.
Brach Foundation, Helen
Brand Cos.

Brown & Associates, Clayton
Brunner Foundation, Fred J.
Brunswick Corp.
Buchanan Family Foundation
Buehler Foundation, A. C.
Butler Family Foundation, George W. and Gladys S.
Butz Foundation
Caestecker Foundation, Charles and Marie
Camp and Bennet Humiston Trust, Apollos
Carus Corp.
Carylon Foundation
Castle & Co., A.M.
Caterpillar
CBI Industries
Ceco Corp.
Centel Corp.
Central Illinois Public Service Co.
Centralia Foundation
Chamberlain Manufacturing Corp.
Chanin Family Foundation, Paul R.
Chapin-May Foundation of Illinois
Cheney Foundation, Elizabeth F.
Chicago Board of Trade
Chicago City Bank & Trust Co.
Chicago Milwaukee Corp.
Chicago Resource Center
Chicago Sun-Times, Inc.
Chicago Title and Trust Co.
Chicago Tribune Co.
Chicago White Metal Casting
CLARCOR
CNA Insurance Cos.
Cohn Family Foundation, Robert and Terri
Cole Taylor Financial Group
Coleman Foundation
Combs Foundation, Earle M. and Virginia M.
Comer Foundation
Commerce Clearing House
Commonwealth Edison Co.
Commonwealth Industries Corp.
Continental Bank N.A.
Cooper Charitable Trust, Richard H.
Corroon & Black of Illinois
Costain Holdings Inc.
Cotter & Co.
Country Cos.
Cox Charitable Trust, A. G.
CR Industries
Credit Agricole
CRI Charitable Trust
CRL Inc.
Crowell Trust, Henry P. and Susan C.
Crown Charitable Fund, Edward A.
Crown Memorial, Arie and Ida
Cuneo Foundation
Curtis Industries, Helene
Dalgety Inc.
Dartnell Corp.
Davee Foundation
Dean Foods Co.
Deere & Co.
DeKalb Genetics Corp.
Demos Foundation, N.
DeSoto
Dick Family Foundation
Dickey-John Corp.
Dillon Foundation
Donnelley Foundation, Elliott and Ann
Donnelley Foundation, Gaylord and Dorothy
Donnelley & Sons Co., R.R.
Dower Foundation, Thomas W.
Driehaus Foundation, Richard H.
Duchossois Industries

Duplex Products, Inc.
Eisenberg Foundation, George M.
Elco Charitable Foundation
Elgin Sweeper Co.
Encyclopaedia Britannica, Inc.
Epaphroditus Foundation
Erickson Charitable Fund, Eben W.
Eureka Co.
Fabyan Foundation
Fairview Foundation
Falk Medical Research Foundation, Dr. Ralph and Marian
Fanuc U.S.A. Corp.
Farley Industries
Farmers & Mechanics Bank
Fearn International, Inc.
Feinberg Foundation, Joseph and Bessie
Fel-Pro Incorporated
Field Foundation, Jamee and Marshall
Field Foundation of Illinois
First Chicago
First National Bank of Evergreen Park
First National Bank & Trust Co. of Rockford
Fleming Charitable Trust, Joseph F.
Florsheim Shoe Co.
FMC Corp.
Foote, Cone & Belding Communications
Forest Fund
Foster and Gallagher
Four Wheels, Inc.
Fraida Foundation
Frank Fund, Zollie and Elaine
Frankel Foundation
Franklin Life Insurance Co.
Fruit of the Loom, Inc.
Fry Foundation, Lloyd A.
Fullerton Metals Co.
Galter Foundation
Galvin Foundation, Robert W.
GATX Corp.
Gavin Foundation, James and Zita
Gaylord Container Corp.
Geifman Family Foundation
Geneseo Foundation
Getz Foundation, Emma and Oscar
Gillespie Memorial Fund, Boynton
Goldberg Family Foundation, Milton D. and Madeline L.
Goldenberg Foundation, Max
Goldman Foundation, Morris and Rose
Graham Foundation for Advanced Studies in the Fine Arts
Grainger Foundation
Grainger, W.W.
Grant Thornton
Grenzebach & Associates, John
Griffith Laboratories Foundation, Inc.
Griswold Trust, Jessie
Growmark, Inc.
H. B. B. Foundation
Haffner Foundation
Hales Charitable Fund
Hales Foundation, William M.
Hammer Foundation, Armand
Hanson Testamentary Charitable Trust, Anna Emery
Harper Foundation, Philip S.
Harris Family Foundation, Hunt and Diane
Harris Foundation, H. H.
Harris Foundation, J. Ira and Nicki
Harris Trust & Savings Bank
Harrison Foundation, Fred G.

Hartmarx Corp.
Hay Foundation, John I.
Heed Ophthalmic Foundation
Heller Financial
Heller Foundation, Walter E.
Henry Foundation
Herald News
Heritage Pullman Bank & Trust
Hermann Foundation, Grover
Hobbs Foundation
Hoffer Plastics Corp.
Hoover Foundation, H. Earl
Hopper Memorial Foundation, Bertrand
Household International
Huizenga Foundation, Jennie
I and G Charitable Foundation
Ideal Industries
IDEX Corp.
Illinois Bell
Illinois Central Railroad Co.
Illinois Cereal Mills
Illinois Consolidated Telephone Co.
Illinois Power Co.
Illinois Tool Works
IMCERA Group Inc.
Ingersoll Milling Machine Co.
Inland Steel Industries
Interstate National Corp.
James & Co., Fred S.
Jim Beam Brands Co.
Johnson Foundation, A. D.
Joslyn Corp.
Joyce Foundation
Jupiter Industries, Inc.
Kaplan Foundation, Mayer and Morris
Kapoor Charitable Foundation
Katten, Muchin, & Zavis
Katy Industries Inc.
Kearney Inc., A.T.
Keebler Co.
Keeney Trust, Hattie Hannah
Kelco Industries, Inc.
Kellstadt Foundation
Kelly Foundation, Donald P. and Byrd M.
Kelly Foundation, T. Lloyd
Kemper Educational and Charitable Fund
Kemper Investors Life Insurance Co.
Kemper National Insurance Cos.
Kendall Foundation, George R.
Kern Foundation Trust
Kirkland & Ellis
Klein Tools
Kline Trust IV, Harry L.
Knowles Foundation
Kraft General Foods
La-Co. Industries, Inc.
Lapham-Hickey Steel Corp.
LaSalle Bank Lake View
LaSalle National Bank
Lasalle National Corp.
Lawson Products, Inc.
Lederer Foundation, Francis L.
Lehmann Foundation, Otto W.
Leo Burnett Co.
Levinson's, Inc.
Levy Circulating Co., Charles
Levy Foundation, Charles and Ruth
Linde Foundation, Ronald and Maxine
Lizzadro Family Foundation, Joseph
Logan Foundation, E. J.
Lord Educational Fund
Louis Foundation, Michael W.
Lumpkin Foundation
Lurie Family Foundation
MacArthur Foundation, J. Roderick
MacArthur Foundation, John D. and Catherine T.

MacLean-Fogg Co.
Manilow Foundation, Nathan
Mansfield Foundation, Albert and Anne
Mark Controls Corp.
Marmon Group, Inc.
Marshall Field's
Martin-Brower Co., The
Martin Foundation, Bert William
Mason Charitable Foundation
Masonite Corp.
Material Service Corp.
Mayer Charitable Trust, Oscar G. & Elsa S.
Mazza Foundation
McCormick Foundation, Chauncey and Marion Deering
McCormick Tribune Foundation, Robert R.
McDonald's Corp.
McFarland Charitable Foundation
McGraw Foundation
McIntosh Foundation
Mellinger Educational Foundation, Edward Arthur
Mercer, William M.
Merrion Foundation
Metropolitan Bank & Trust Co.
Miami Corp.
Midas International Corp.
MidCon Corp.
Midway Airlines
Millard Charitable Trust, Adah K.
Miller & Co.
Milwaukee Golf Development Co.
Mitchell Family Foundation, Bernard and Marjorie
Molex, Inc.
Montgomery Elevator Co.
Montgomery Ward & Co.
Monticello College Foundation
Moore Business Forms, Inc.
Moorman Manufacturing Co.
Morton International
Morton Memorial Fund, Mark
Motorola
Mueller Co.
Nalco Chemical Co.
National Manufacturing Co.
Navistar International Corp.
Neese Family Foundation
Negaunee Foundation
New Prospect Foundation
Newell Co.
Nicor, Inc.
Nielsen Co., A.C.
Norris Foundation, Dellora A. and Lester J.
Northern Illinois Gas Co.
Northern Trust Co.
Northwestern Golf Co.
Northwestern Steel & Wire Co.
Norton Memorial Corporation, Geraldi
NutraSweet Co.
Nuveen & Co., Inc., John
Offield Family Foundation
Old Republic International Corp.
Oppenheimer Family Foundation
Outboard Marine Corp.
Packaging Corporation of America
Payne Foundation, Frank E. and Seba B.
Peoples Energy Corp.
Pepper Cos.
Perina Corp
Perkins Foundation, Edwin E.
Pesch Family Foundation
Petersen Foundation, Esper A.
Pick, Jr. Fund, Albert
Pittway Corp.
Playboy Enterprises, Inc.
Portec, Inc.
Premark International
Prentice Foundation, Abra

Prince Trust, Abbie Norman
Pritzker Foundation
Pullman Educational Foundation, George M.
Quaker Oats Co.
Quality Metal Finishing Foundation
Quincy Newspapers
R. F. Foundation
Ragen, Jr. Memorial Fund Trust No. 1, James M.
Rand McNally and Co.
Reade Industrial Fund
Reflector Hardware Corp.
Regenstein Foundation
Relations Foundation
Retirement Research Foundation
Rhoades Fund, Otto L. and Hazel E.
Rice Foundation
Ringier-America
Robin Family Foundation, Albert A.
Rockford Acromatics Products Co./Aircraft Gear Corp.
Rockford Products Corp.
Rosenbaum Foundation, Paul and Gabriella
Rosenthal Foundation, Benjamin J.
Rothschild Foundation, Hulda B. and Maurice L.
Royal Insurance Co. of America
Russell Charitable Foundation, Tom
Rust-Oleum Corp.
Ryan Foundation, Patrick G. and Shirley W.
Safety-Kleen Corp.
St. Paul Federal Bank for Savings
Salwil Foundation
Sang Foundation, Elsie O. and Philip D.
Santa Fe Pacific Corp.
Sara Lee Corp.
Schiff, Hardin & Waite
Schmidt Charitable Foundation, William E.
Schmitt Foundation, Arthur J.
Schneider Foundation, Robert E.
Scholl Foundation, Dr.
Scott, Foresman & Co.
Seabury Foundation
Searle & Co., G.D.
Sears, Roebuck and Co.
Seeley Foundation
Seid Foundation, Barre
ServiceMaster Co. L.P.
Shapiro Family Foundation, Soretta and Henry
Shapiro Foundation, Charles and M. R.
Shaw Foundation, Walden W. and Jean Young
Shirk Foundation, Russell and Betty
Silver Spring Foundation
Silvestri Corp.
Simpson Foundation, John M.
Siragusa Foundation
Sjostrom & Sons
Skidmore, Owings & Merrill
Smith Charitable Trust
Smith Oil Corp.
Smysor Memorial Fund, Harry L. and John L.
Snite Foundation, Fred B.
Soft Sheen Products Co.
Solo Cup Co
Solomon Foundation, Sarah M.
Spartus Corp.
Special People In Need
Spencer Foundation
Spiegel
Sprague Memorial Institute, Otho S. A.
Square D Co.
Staley, Jr. Foundation, A. E.

Staley Manufacturing Co., A.E.
State Farm Mutual Automobile Insurance Co.
Steigerwaldt Foundation, Donna Wolf
Stein Roe & Farnham Investment Council
Stepan Co.
Stern Foundation, Irvin
Stone Container Corp.
Stone Family Foundation, Jerome H.
Stone Family Foundation, Norman H.
Stone Forest Industries
Stone Foundation, W. Clement and Jessie V.
Sudix Foundation
Sulzer Family Foundation
Sun Electric Corp.
Sundstrand Corp.
Swift Co. Inc., John S.
Swift-Eckrich Inc.
T.T.X. Co.
TDK Corp. of America
Thompson Family Fund, Lucille S.
Thomson Newspapers Corp.
Thorson Foundation
Tibstra Charitable Foundation, Thomas and Gertrude
Tombstone Pizza Corp.
Tootsie Roll Industries, Inc.
Tyndale House Foundation
Uarco Inc.
United Airlines
United Conveyor Corp.
United Stationers Inc.
UNO-VEN Co.
USG Corp.
Varlen Corp.
Walgreen Co.
Wallace Computer Services
Ward Foundation, A. Montgomery
Warner Electric Brake & Clutch Co.
Washington National Insurance Co.
Washington Square Health Foundation
Waste Management
Werner Foundation, Clara and Spencer
Western Shade Cloth Charitable Foundation
White Foundation, W. P. and H. B.
Whitman Corp.
Wieboldt Foundation
Willmott Foundation, Peter S.
Winona Corporation
Woods Charitable Fund
Woodward Governor Co.
World Book Inc.
Wrap-On Co.
Wrigley Co., Wm. Jr.
Wurlitzer Foundation, Farny R.
Wyne Foundation
Young Charity Trust Northern Trust Company

Indiana

AMAX Coal Industries
Ameribank
American General Finance
American Red Ball World Wide Movers
American United Life Insurance Co.
Anacomp, Inc.
Anderson Foundation, John W.
Arvin Industries
Ayres Foundation, Inc.
Ball Brothers Foundation
Ball Corp.

Ball Foundation, George and Frances
Ball-InCon Glass Packaging Corp.
Basic American Medical, Inc.
Bierhaus Foundation
Bindley Western Industries
Biomet
Boehringer Mannheim Corp.
Bowsher-Booher Foundation
Brink Unitrust, Julia H.
Bronstein Foundation, Sol and Arlene
Central Newspapers, Inc.
Central Soya Co.
Citizens Gas & Coke Utility
Clark Equipment Co.
Clowes Fund
Coachmen Industries
Cole Foundation, Olive B.
Coleman Scholarship Trust, Lillian R.
Cosco, Inc.
Countrymark Cooperative
Crescent Plastics
Crown International, Inc.
CTS Corp.
Cummins Engine Co.
DCB Corp.
Decio Foundation, Arthur J.
Dekko Foundation
Delco Electronics Corp.
Delta Tau Delta Educational Fund
Dow Elanco Inc.
Duncan Trust, James R.
English-Bonter-Mitchell Foundation
Excel Industries (Elkhart, Indiana)
First Source Corp.
Foellinger Foundation
Ford Meter Box Co.
Forum Group, Inc.
Franklin Electric Company Inc. (Bluffton, Indiana)
Froderman Foundation
General Housewares Corp.
Glick Foundation, Eugene and Marilyn
Globe Valve Corp.
Goodman Jewelers, Inc.
Graphic Printing Co.
Great Lakes Chemical Corp.
Griffith Foundation, W. C.
Habig Foundation, Arnold F.
Hand Industries
Harris Stores, Paul
Hillenbrand Industries
Hook Drug
Huber, Hunt & Nichols
Hutzell Foundation
Indiana Bell Telephone Co.
Indiana Desk Co.
Indiana Gas and Chemical Corp.
Indiana Gas Co.
Indiana Insurance Cos.
Indianapolis Newspapers, Inc.
Indianapolis Water Co.
Inland Container Corp.
IPALCO Enterprises
Jasper Desk Co.
Jasper Seating Co.
Jasper Table Co.
Jasper Wood Products Co.
JOFCo., Inc.
Jordan Foundation, Arthur
Journal Gazette Co.
Keller-Crescent Co.
Kilbourne Residuary Charitable Trust, E. H.
Kimball International
Koch Sons, George
Kuehn Foundation
Kuhne Foundation Trust, Charles
La Porte Casting Division
Lassus Brothers Oil
Leighton-Oare Foundation

Indiana (cont.)

Liberty National Bank
Lilly & Co., Eli
Lilly Endowment
Lincoln National Corp.
Marathon Oil, Indiana Refining Division
Marsh Supermarkets, Inc.
Martin Foundation
Maxon Charitable Foundation
Mayflower Group
McGill Manufacturing Co.
McMillen Foundation
Meridian Insurance Group Inc.
Metropolitan Health Council of Indianapolis
MidAmerica Radio Co.
Minnetrista Cultural Foundation
Moore Foundation
Morrill Charitable Foundation
National City Bank
National City Bank of Evansville
National City Bank of Indiana
NBD Bank, N.A.
NIBCO Inc.
Noll Foundation
Northern Indiana Fuel & Light Co.
Northern Indiana Public Service Co.
Noyes, Jr. Memorial Foundation, Nicholas H.
Oakley Foundation, Hollie and Anna
O'Brien Foundation, Cornelius and Anna Cook
O'Connor Foundation, Magee
Ogle Foundation, Paul
Old National Bank in Evansville
Oliver Memorial Trust Foundation
Ontario Corp.
Patrick Industries Inc.
Plumsock Fund
Pott Foundation, Robert and Elaine
PSI Energy
Raker Foundation, M. E.
Ransburg Corp.
Raper Foundation, Tom
Reilly Industries
Rieke Corp.
Saemann Foundation, Franklin I.
Schust Foundation, Clarence L. and Edith B.
Sherman Educational Fund
Skyline Corp.
Smock Foundation, Frank and Laura
Somers Foundation, Byron H.
South Bend Tribune
Southern Indiana Gas & Electric Co.
Storer Scholarship Foundation, Oliver W.
Subaru-Isuzu Automotive Inc.
Thirty-Five Twenty, Inc.
Thrush-Thompson Foundation
Tokheim Corp.
Tyson Fund
Ulrich Chemical, Inc.
Union City Body Co.
Vevay-Switzerland County Foundation
West Foundation
Westwood Endowment
Winchester Foundation
Zimmer Inc.
Zollner Foundation

Iowa

Adler Foundation Trust, Philip D. and Henrietta B.
American Investment Co.
Arbie Mineral Feed Co.
Bandag, Inc.

Bechtel Charitable Remainder Uni-Trust, Harold R.
Bechtel Charitable Remainder Uni-Trust, Marie H.
Bechtel Testamentary Charitable Trust, H. R.
Blank Fund, Myron and Jacqueline
Bohen Foundation
Brenton Banks Inc.
Carver Charitable Trust, Roy J.
Central Life Assurance Co.
Century Companies of America
Citizens First National Bank
Cowles Foundation, Gardner and Florence Call
Demco Charitable Foundation
Dexter Co.
E and M Charities
Employers Mutual Casualty Co.
Fahrney Education Foundation
FDL Foods/Dubuque Packing Co.
Forster Charitable Trust, James W. and Ella B.
Gazette Co.
Glazer Foundation, Madelyn L.
Grinnell Mutual Reinsurance Co.
Guaranty Bank & Trust Co.
Hall Foundation
Hanson Foundation
Harper Brush Works
Hawkeye Bancorporation
Hawley Foundation
HON Industries
Hy-Vee Food Stores
IES Industries
IMT Insurance Co.
Inter-State Assurance Co.
Interstate Power Co.
Iowa-Illinois Gas & Electric Co.
Iowa Savings Bank
Iowa State Bank
Jensen Construction Co.
K-Products
Kinney-Lindstrom Foundation
Kuyper Foundation, Peter H. and E. Lucille Gaass
Lee Enterprises
Life Investors Insurance Company of America
Lindstrom Foundation, Kinney
Maytag Corp.
Maytag Family Foundation, Fred
McDonald Industries, Inc., A. Y.
McElroy Trust, R. J.
Meredith Corp.
Mid-Iowa Health Foundation
Midwest Gas Co.
Midwest Resources
National By-Products
National Travelers Life Co.
Owen Industries, Inc.
Pella Corp.
Pioneer Hi-Bred International
Preferred Risk Mutual Insurance Co.
Principal Financial Group
Quad City Osteopathic Foundation
Ruan Foundation Trust, John Sheaffer Inc.
Sherman Educational Fund, Mabel E.
Spahn & Rose Lumber Co.
Stanley Consultants
Statesman Group, Inc.
Terra Industries
United Fire & Casualty Co.
Van Buren Foundation
Vermeer Charitable Foundation
Vermeer Investment Company Foundation
Vermeer Manufacturing Co.
Wahlert Foundation
Waldinger Corp.
Weitz Corp.
Winnebago Industries, Inc.

Witte, Jr. Foundation, John H.
Younkers, Inc.

Kansas

Abell Education Trust, Jennie G. and Pearl
Baehr Foundation, Louis W. and Dolpha
Bank IV
Baughman Foundation
Beech Aircraft Corp.
Beren Foundation, Robert M.
Breidenthal Foundation, Willard J. and Mary G.
Cessna Aircraft Co.
Coleman Co.
Davis Foundation, James A. and Juliet L.
DeVore Foundation
Dillons Super Markets
Dreiling and Albina Dreiling Charitable Trust, Leo J.
Duckwall-Alco Stores
Excel Corp.
Fink Foundation
First National Bank in Wichita
Forster-Powers Charitable Trust
Fourth Financial Corp.
Garvey Fund, Jean and Willard
Garvey Kansas Foundation
Garvey Trust, Olive White
Gault-Hussey Charitable Trust
Graham Charitable Trust, William L.
Hansen Foundation, Dane G.
Hedrick Foundation, Frank E.
Hesston Corp.
Insurance Management Associates
Jellison Benevolent Society
Jones Foundation, Walter S. and Evan C.
Kansas City Power & Light Co.
Kansas Power & Light/Western Resources
Kauffman Foundation, Muriel McBrien
Kejr Foundation
Kice Industries, Inc.
Koch Charitable Trust, David H.
Koch Industries
Law Company, Inc.
Learjet Inc.
Lee Apparel Co.
Marley Co.
Mingenback Foundation, Julia J.
Misco Industries
O'Connor Co.
Pizza Hut
Powell Family Foundation
Rice Foundation, Ethel and Raymond F.
Ross Foundation
Salgo Charitable Trust, Nicholas M.
Schowalter Foundation
Scroggins Foundation, Arthur E. and Cornelia C.
Sealright Co., Inc.
Security Benefit Life Insurance Co.
Security State Bank
Smith Foundation, Kenneth L. and Eva S.
Smoot Charitable Foundation
Sprint
Stauffer Communications
Trusler Foundation
Western Resources
Williams Charitable Trust, Mary Jo
Yellow Corp.

Kentucky

Abel Construction Co.
Ashland Oil
Bank of Louisville

Blue Cross & Blue Shield of Kentucky Foundation
Brown-Forman Corp.
Brown Foundation, James Graham
Brown Foundation, W. L. Lyons
Brown & Williamson Tobacco Corp.
C. E. and S. Foundation
Capital Holding Corp.
Collins Co.
Commonwealth Life Insurance Co.
Cooke Foundation Corporation, V. V.
Courier-Journal & Louisville Times
Cralle Foundation
Dairymen, Inc.
Diederich Educational Trust Fund, John T. and Ada
Enterprise Coal Co.
Ferre Revocable Trust, Joseph C.
Gardner Charitable Foundation, Edith D.
Gheens Foundation
Glenmore Distilleries Co.
Greenebaum, Doll & McDonald
Haywood Foundation
Hope Memorial Fund, Blanche and Thomas
Houchens Foundation, Ervin G.
Humana
ICH Corp.
Kentucky Central Life Insurance
Kentucky Foundation for Women
Kentucky Fried Chicken Corp.
Kentucky Utilities Co.
Kuhlman Corp.
LaViers Foundation, Harry and Maxie
Levy's Lumber & Building Centers
Louisville Gas & Electric Co.
Michael-Walters Industries
Million Memorial Park Trust, E. C.
Mills Foundation, Ralph E.
Norton Foundation Inc.
Ogden College Fund
Pinkerton Tobacco Co.
Porter Paint Co.
Reed Foundation
Robinson Mountain Fund, E. O.
Rosenthal Foundation
Roth Foundation, Louis T.
Scheirich Co., H.J.
Schneider Foundation Corp., Al J.
Sutherland Foundation
Texas Gas Transmission Corp.
Thomas Foundation, Joan and Lee
Thomas Industries
Valvoline Inc.
Vogt Machine Co., Henry
Yeager Charitable Trust, Lester E.
Young Memorial Fund, John B. and Brownie

Louisiana

Arkla
Avondale Industries, Inc.
Azby Fund
Babcock & Wilcox Co.
Beaird Foundation, Charles T.
Boh Brothers Construction Co.
Booth-Bricker Fund
Brown Foundation, Joe W. and Dorothy Dorsett
Burton Foundation, William T. and Ethel Lewis
Cahn Family Foundation
Community Coffee Co.
Copolymer Rubber & Chemical Corp.

Coughlin-Saunders Foundation
Entergy Corp.
First Commerce Corp.
Frazier Foundation
Freeman Foundation, Ella West
Freeport-McMoRan
German Protestant Orphan Asylum Association
Glazer Foundation, Jerome S.
Goldring Family Foundation
Helis Foundation
Heymann Special Account, Mr. and Mrs. Jimmy
Heymann-Wolf Foundation
Hibernia Corp.
Hurley Foundation, Ed E. and Gladys
Jones Family Foundation, Eugenie and Joseph
Keller Family Foundation
Kraus Co., Ltd.
Lakeside National Bank
Lamar Corp.
Libby-Dufour Fund, Trustees of the
Louisiana Gas Services
Louisiana Land & Exploration Co.
Louisiana Power & Light Co./New Orleans Public Service
Lupin Foundation
Lykes Brothers Steamship Co.
McDermott
McIlhenny and Sons Corp
Middle South Utilities
Monroe Foundation (1976), J. Edgar
Offshore Logistics
Pan-American Life Insurance Co.
Pennington Foundation, Irene W. and C. B.
Poindexter Foundation
Powers Foundation
Premier Bank
Premier Bank Lafayette
Premier Bank of South Louisiana
Reily & Co., William B.
RosaMary Foundation
Schlieder Educational Foundation, Edward G.
Shreveport Publishing Corp.
Southwestern Electric Power Co.
Stern Foundation, Percival
Tidewater, Inc.
Wheless Foundation
Whitney National Bank
Williams Foundation, Kemper and Leila
Winn Educational Trust, Fanny Edith
Wisdom Foundation, Mary F.
Woldenberg Foundation
Woolf Foundation, William C.
Young Foundation, H and B
Zemurray Foundation
Zigler Foundation, Fred B. and Ruth B.

Maine

Bangor Savings Bank
Bean, L.L.
Casco Northern Bank
Central Maine Power Co.
Davenport Trust Fund
Dexter Shoe Co.
Eastern Fine Paper, Inc.
Fleet Bank of Maine
Fraser Paper Ltd.
Gannett Publishing Co., Guy
Gardiner Savings Institution FSB
Key Bank of Maine
Mearl Corp.
Moosehead Manufacturing Co.
Mulford Trust, Clarence E.
Peoples Heritage Savings Bank
Rivers and Trails North East

Sewall Foundation, Elmina
Tom's of Maine
UNUM Corp.
Webber Oil Co.

Maryland

Abell Foundation, Charles S.
Abell Foundation, The
Abramson Family Foundation
AEGON USA, Inc.
American Trading & Production Corp.
Arcata Graphics Co.
B & O Railroad Museum
Baker, Jr. Memorial Fund, William G.
Baker Trust, Clayton
Baker, Watts & Co.
Baldwin, Jr. Foundation, Summerfield
Baltimore Bancorp.
Baltimore Gas & Electric Co.
Baltimore Life Insurance Co.
Bank Foundation, Helen and Merrill
Banner Life Insurance Co.
Barlow Family Foundation, Milton A. and Gloria G.
Barton-Gillet Co.
Beitzell & Co.
Beretta U.S.A. Corp.
Black & Decker Corp.
Blaustein Foundation, Jacob and Hilda
Blaustein Foundation, Louis and Henrietta
Blaustein Foundation, Morton K. and Jane
Blum Foundation, Lois and Irving
Brown, Jr. Charitable Trust, Frank D.
Brown & Sons, Alex
Campbell Foundation
Casey Foundation, Eugene B.
Chevy Chase Savings Bank FSB
Clark Charitable Foundation
Clark-Winchcole Foundation
Cohen Foundation, Naomi and Nehemiah
Commercial Credit Co.
Crown Books Foundation, Inc.
Crown Central Petroleum Corp.
Dart Group Corp.
Discovery Channel/Cable Education Network
Eastern Stainless Corp.
Egenton Home
First Maryland Bancorp
Fisher Foundation, Gramma
Foundation for Iranian Studies
France Foundation, Jacob and Annita
Freeman Foundation, Carl M.
Giant Food
Goldseker Foundation of Maryland, Morris
Gordon Charitable Trust, Peggy and Yale
Grady Management
Gross Foundation, Louis H.
Gudelsky Family Foundation, Homer and Martha
Hechinger Co.
Hecht-Levi Foundation
Hirschhorn Foundation, David and Barbara B.
Hobbs Foundation, Emmert
Hoffberger Foundation
Hughes Medical Institute, Howard
Hyman Construction Co., George
Isaacs Foundation, Harry Z.
Kelly, Jr. Memorial Foundation, Ensign C. Markland
Kerr Fund, Grayce B.
Knapp Educational Fund

Knapp Foundation
Knott Foundation, Marion I. and Henry J.
Legg Mason Inc.
Leidy Foundation, John J.
Levitt Foundation, Richard S.
Life Sciences Research Foundation
Loats Foundation
M.E. Foundation
Macht Foundation, Morton and Sophia
Manger and Audrey Cordero Plitt Trust, Clarence
Manor Care
Marriott Corp.
Martin Marietta Corp.
Maryland Casualty Co.
McCormick & Co.
McGregor Foundation, Thomas and Frances
Mechanic Foundation, Morris A.
Mercantile Bankshares Corp.
Merrick Foundation, Robert G. and Anne M.
Merry-Go-Round Enterprises, Inc.
Meyerhoff Foundation, Lyn P.
Meyerhoff Fund, Joseph
Middendorf Foundation
MNC Financial
Moriah Fund
Mulford Foundation, Vincent
Mullan Foundation, Thomas F. and Clementine L.
Myers and Sons, D.
Nathan Foundation
Number Ten Foundation
OMNI Construction
O'Neil Foundation, W.
Oxford Development Group
Pearlstone Foundation, Peggy Meyerhoff
Perdue Farms
PHH Corp.
Polinger Foundation, Howard and Geraldine
Poole & Kent Co.
Potomac Edison Co.
Preston Trucking Co., Inc.
Price Associates, T. Rowe
Procter & Gamble Cosmetic & Fragrance Products
Quality Inn International
Rollins Luetkemeyer Charitable Foundation
Rosenberg Foundation, Henry and Ruth Blaustein
Rosenbloom Foundation, Ben and Esther
Rosenthal-Statter Foundation
Rouse Co.
Ryan Family Charitable Foundation
Ryland Group
Sachs Electric Corp.
SCM Chemicals Inc.
Shapiro, Inc.
Shapiro Fund, Albert
Sheridan Foundation, Thomas B. and Elizabeth M.
Signet Bank/Maryland
Smith Foundation, Gordon V. and Helen C.
Stern Family Fund
Stewart Memorial Trust, J. C.
Straus Foundation, Aaron and Lillie
Tauber Foundation
Telinde Trust, Richard W.
Thalheimer Foundation, Alvin and Fanny Blaustein
Thorn, Jr. Foundation, Columbus W.
Three Swallows Foundation
Town Creek Foundation
Tucker Foundation, Marcia Brady
UNC, Inc.

Unger Foundation, Aber D.
United Iron & Metal Co.
USF&G Co.
Ward Machinery Co.
Warfield Memorial Fund, Anna Emory
Weinberg Foundation, Harry and Jeanette
Weir Foundation Trust
White Coffee Pot Family Inns
Widgeon Foundation
Wilson Sanitarium for Children of Baltimore City, Thomas
Zamoiski Co.

Massachusetts

Acushnet Co.
Adams Trust, Charles E. and Caroline J.
Addison-Wesley Publishing Co.
Affiliated Publications, Inc.
Agape Foundation
Alden Trust, George I.
Alden Trust, John W.
Alden's Inc.
Algonquin Energy, Inc.
Alpha Industries
Amdur Braude Riley, Inc.
American Biltrite
American Mutual Insurance Cos.
American Optical Corp.
American Saw & Manufacturing Co.
Amoskeag Co.
Analog Devices
Analogic Corp.
Ansin Private Foundation, Ronald M.
Apollo Computer Inc.
Arakelian Foundation, Mary Alice
Arkwright-Boston Manufacturers Mutual
Astra Pharmaceutical Products, Inc.
Augat, Inc.
Ayling Scholarship Foundation, Alice S.
Azadoutioun Foundation
Babson Foundation, Paul and Edith
Babson-Webber-Mustard Fund
Bachrach, Inc.
Bacon Trust, Charles F.
Badger Co., Inc.
Bailey Wildlife Foundation
Balfour Foundation, L. G.
Bank of Boston Corp.
BayBanks
Beaucourt Foundation
Benfamil Charitable Trust
Berenson Charitable Foundation, Theodore W. and Evelyn
Bird Inc.
Birmingham Foundation
Blake Foundation, S. P.
Blanchard Foundation
Bolten Charitable Foundation, John
Boston Co., Inc.
Boston Edison Co.
Boston Fatherless and Widows Society
Boston Gas Co.
Boston Mutual Life Insurance Co.
Boynton Fund, John W.
Braitmayer Foundation
Bright Charitable Trust, Alexander H.
Bull HN Information Systems Inc.
Bushee Foundation, Florence Evans
Cabot Corp.
Cabot Family Charitable Trust

Cabot-Saltonstall Charitable Trust
Cabot Stains
Cambridge Mustard Seed Foundation
Campbell and Adah E. Hall Charity Fund, Bushrod H.
Carteh Foundation
Charles River Laboratories
Charlesbank Homes
Charlton, Jr. Charitable Trust, Earle P.
Chase Charity Foundation, Alfred E.
Chase Trust, Alice P.
Childs Charitable Foundation, Roberta M.
Chomerics, Inc.
Clark Charitable Trust
Clark Home for Aged People, Ella
Clipper Ship Foundation
Colgan Scholarship Fund, James W.
Commonwealth Energy System
Connell LP
Continental Wingate Co., Inc.
Country Curtains, Inc.
Courier Corp.
Cove Charitable Trust
Cowan Foundation Corporation, Lillian L. and Harry A.
Cox Charitable Trust, Jessie B.
Cox Foundation
Crane & Co.
Crapo Charitable Foundation, Henry H.
Cumberland Farms
Cummings Properties Management, Inc.
Damon Corp.
Daniels Foundation, Fred Harris
Demoulas Supermarkets
Dennison Manufacturing Co.
Devereaux Foundation
Devonshire Associates
Dewar, A.W.G.
Dewing Foundation, Frances R.
Dexter Charitable Fund, Eugene A.
Digital Equipment Corp.
Doyle Charitable Foundation
Dunkin' Donuts
Dunn Foundation, Elizabeth Ordway
Dynatech Corp.
Eastern Bank Foundation
Eastern Enterprises
Eastman Gelatine Corp.
Eaton Memorial Fund, Georgiana Goddard
Edgerton Foundation, Harold E.
Edwards Scholarship Fund
EG&G Inc.
Ellison Foundation
Ellsworth Foundation, Ruth H. and Warren A.
Erving Paper Mills
Factory Mutual Engineering Corp.
Farm Credit Banks of Springfield
Farnsworth Trust, Charles A.
Fay Charitable Fund, Aubert J.
Feldberg Family Foundation
Fiduciary Trust Co.
Filene Foundation, Lincoln and Therese
Filene's Sons Co., William
First Petroleum Corp.
Fisher Foundation
Flatley Foundation
Fletcher Foundation
FMR Corp.
Foley, Hoag & Eliot
Ford Foundation, Joseph F. and Clara
Foster Foundation, Joseph C. and Esther

Fraser Foundation, Richard M. and Helen T.
French Foundation
Friendly Ice Cream Corp.
Friendship Fund
Fuller Foundation, George F. and Sybil H.
Galileo Electro-Optics Corp.
GCA Corp.
Gear Motion
Genetics Institute
GenRad
Gerondelis Foundation
Gillette Co.
Globe Newspaper Co.
Goddard Homestead
Goldberg Family Foundation
Goldberg Family Foundation, Israel and Matilda
Gordon Foundation
Gorin Foundation, Nehemiah
Grass Foundation
Grass Instrument Co.
Gulf USA Corp.
Hagler Foundation, Jon L.
Hampden Papers
Hanover Insurance Co.
Harcourt General
Harrington Foundation, Francis A. and Jacquelyn H.
Harrington Trust, George
Harvard Apparatus Foundation
Harvard Musical Association
Hayden Recreation Center, Josiah Willard
Henderson Foundation
Henderson Foundation, George B.
Heritage Travel Inc./Thomas Cook Travel
Heydt Fund, Nan and Matilda
Higgins Foundation, Aldus C.
Hills Department Stores, Inc.
Hixon Fund for Religion and Education, Alexander & Adelaide
HMK Enterprises
Hoche-Scofield Foundation
Hoffman Foundation, John Ernest
Holyoke Mutual Insurance Co. in Salem
Home for Aged Men
Hood Foundation, Charles H.
Hood Inc., H.P.
Hopedale Foundation
Hornblower Fund, Henry
Horne Trust, Mabel
Houghton Mifflin Co.
Housatonic Curtain Co.
House Educational Trust, Susan Cook
Howard Benevolent Society
Humane Society of the Commonwealth of Massachusetts
Hyams Foundation
Hyde Manufacturing Co.
Iacocca Foundation
Index Technology Corp.
Instron Corp.
Insurance Systems, Inc.
International Data Group
Island Foundation
Jackson Charitable Trust, Marion Gardner
John Hancock Mutual Life Insurance Co.
Johnson Foundation, Howard
Johnson Fund, Edward C.
Kapor Family Foundation
Kayem Foods, Inc.
Kelley and Elza Kelley Foundation, Edward Bangs
Kendall Foundation, Henry P.
Kendall Health Care Products
Keyport Life Insurance Co.
Killam Trust, Constance
Kilmartin Industries

Massachusetts (cont.)

King Trust, Charles A.
Knowles Trust A, Leonora H.
Kraft Foundation
Ladd Charitable Corporation, Helen and George
Lechmere
Levy Foundation, June Rockwell
Liberty Mutual Insurance Group/Boston
Linnell Foundation
Lipsky Foundation, Fred and Sarah
Little, Arthur D.
Little Brown & Co., Inc.
Little Family Foundation
Litton/Itek Optical Systems
LoJack Corp.
Loomis House
Loomis-Sayles & Co.
Lotus Development Corp.
Lowell Institute, Trustees of the
Luce Charitable Foundation, Stephen C.
M/A-COM, Inc.
Macom-Venitz
Malden Mills Industries
Marshalls Inc.
Massachusetts Charitable Mechanics Association
Massachusetts Mutual Life Insurance Co.
McCarthy Memorial Trust Fund, Catherine
McEvoy Foundation, Mildred H.
Mechanics Bank
Memorial Foundation for the Blind
Merck Fund, John
Mifflin Memorial Fund, George H. and Jane A.
Millipore Corp.
Milton Bradley Co.
Mitre Corp.
Morgan Construction Co.
Morse Foundation, Richard P. and Claire W.
Morse Shoe, Inc.
Naurison Scholarship Fund, James Z.
NEC Technologies, Inc.
Nellie Mae
New Balance Athletic Shoe
New Cycle Foundation
New England Biolabs Foundation
New England Business Service
New England Electric System
New England Foundation
New England Grocer Supply
New England Mutual Life Insurance Co.
New England Telephone Co.
Noonan Memorial Fund under the will of Frank Noonan, Deborah Munroe
Norton Co.
NRC, Inc.
Oak Industries
O'Brien Foundation, James W.
Ocean Spray Cranberries
Orchard Foundation
Pappas Charitable Foundation, Bessie
Pappas Charitable Foundation, Thomas Anthony
Parexel International Corp.
Parker Brothers and Company Inc.
Parker Foundation, Theodore Edson
Peabody Charitable Fund, Amelia
Peabody Foundation
Peabody Foundation, Amelia
Pellegrino-Realmuto Charitable Foundation
Perini Corp.
Perini Foundation, Joseph

Perpetual Benevolent Fund
Perpetual Trust for Charitable Giving
Phillips Trust, Edwin
Pierce Charitable Trust, Harold Whitworth
Pilgrim Foundation
Pioneer Group
Polaroid Corp.
Poorvu Foundation, William and Lia
Prime Computer, Inc.
Property Capital Trust
Prouty Foundation, Olive Higgins
Putnam Prize Fund for the Promotion of Scholarship, William Lowell
Quabaug Corp.
Rabb Charitable Foundation, Sidney and Esther
Rabb Charitable Trust, Sidney R.
Ramlose Foundation, George A.
Rand-Whitney Packaging-Delmar Corp.
Ratshesky Foundation, A. C.
Raytheon Co.
Reebok International Ltd.
Reed Publishing USA
Reisman Charitable Trust, George C. and Evelyn R.
Rice Charitable Foundation, Albert W.
Riley Foundation, Mabel Louise
Riley Stoker Co.
River Road Charitable Corporation
Rodgers Trust, Elizabeth Killam
Rogers Family Foundation
Rowland Foundation
Rubenstein Charitable Foundation, Lawrence J. and Anne
Rubin Family Fund, Cele H. and William B.
Russell Trust, Josephine G.
Sacharuna Foundation
Sailors' Snug Harbor of Boston
Saint Johnsbury Trucking Co.
Salem News Publishing Co.
Saltonstall Charitable Foundation, Richard
Sanders Trust, Charles
Sawyer Charitable Foundation
Schrafft and Bertha E. Schrafft Charitable Trust, William E.
Seaboard Corp.
Seiler Corp.
Shapiro Charity Fund, Abraham
Shaw Foundation, Gardiner Howland
Shaw Fund for Mariner's Children
Shawmut Bank of Franklin County
Shawmut National Corp.
Shawmut Needham Bank, N.A.
Shawmut Worcester County Bank, N.A.
Shaw's Supermarkets
Sherman Family Charitable Trust, George and Beatrice
Simplex Time Recorder Co.
Smith Foundation, Richard and Susan
Smith Fund, Horace
Sonesta International Hotels Corp.
Stanhome Inc.
Star Markets Co.
Stare Fund
Starrett Co., L.S.
State Mutual Life Assurance Co.
State Street Bank & Trust Co.
Stearns Charitable Foundation, Anna B.
Stearns Trust, Artemas W.
Steiger Memorial Fund, Albert

Stevens Foundation, Abbot and Dorothy H.
Stevens Foundation, Nathaniel and Elizabeth P.
Stoddard Charitable Trust
Stone Charitable Foundation
Stone Fund, Albert H. and Reuben S.
Stoneman Charitable Foundation, Anne and David
Stratford Foundation
Stride Rite Corp.
Sun Life Assurance Co. of Canada (U.S.)
Swank, Inc.
Swasey Fund for Relief of Public School Teachers of Newburyport
Swensrud Charitable Trust, Sidney A.
Technical Training Foundation
Teradyne, Inc.
Thermo Electron Corp.
Thompson Trust, Thomas
TJX Cos.
Totsy Manufacturing Co.
Towle Manufacturing Co.
Town & Country Corp.
Travelli Fund, Charles Irwin
Tupancy-Harris Foundation of 1986
21st Century Foods
United Asset Management Corp.
Unitrode Corp.
Urann Foundation
Vingo Trust II
Wallace Foundation, George R.
Wallace & Wallace Ltd.
Walsh Charity Trust, Blanche M.
Wang Laboratories, Inc.
Warren Co., S.D.
Waters Foundation
WCVB-TV
Weber Charities Corp., Frederick E.
Webster Charitable Foundation
Webster Co., H. K.
Webster Foundation, Edwin S.
Welch Foods
Wells Trust Fund, Fred W.
Weston Associates/R.C.M. Corp.
Wharton Trust, William P.
Wheelwright Scientific School
White Construction Co.
Williams Foundation, Arthur Ashley
Winthrop Trust, Clara B.
Wolfson Foundation, Louis E.
Wyman-Gordon Co.
Xtra Corp.
Yawkey Foundation II

Michigan

Abitibi-Price
Abrams Foundation, Talbert and Leota
Acustar Inc.
Alma Piston Co.
Alro Steel Corp.
American Natural Resources Co.
Americana Foundation
Ameritech Publishing
Amway Corp.
Asgrow Seed Co.
Auto Specialties Manufacturing Co.
Awrey Bakeries
Baldwin Foundation
Bank of Alma
Bargman Foundation, Theodore and Mina
Barstow Foundation
Barton-Malow Co.
Batts Foundation
Bauervic Foundation, Charles M.
Bauervic-Paisley Foundation
Beldon II Fund

Bentley Foundation, Alvin M.
Besser Co.
Besser Foundation
Bierlein Family Foundation
Bishop Charitable Trust, A. G.
Blue Cross/Blue Shield of Michigan
Borman's
Boutell Memorial Fund, Arnold and Gertrude
Bray Charitable Trust, Viola E.
Budd Co.
Cablevision of Michigan
Cadillac Products
Chamberlin Foundation, Gerald W.
Chrysler Corp.
Citizens Commercial & Savings Bank
Cold Heading Co.
Comerica
Consumers Power Co.
Cook Charitable Foundation
Dalton Foundation, Dorothy U.
Dart Foundation
Davenport Foundation, M. E.
Delano Foundation, Mignon Sherwood
DeRoy Foundation, Helen L.
DeRoy Testamentary Foundation
Deseranno Educational Foundation
Detroit Edison Co.
DeVlieg Foundation, Charles
DeVos Foundation, Richard and Helen
Dexter Industries
Difco Laboratories
Domino's Pizza
Douglas & Lomason Company
Dow Chemical Co.
Dow Corning Corp.
Dow Foundation, Herbert H. and Barbara C.
Dow Foundation, Herbert H. and Grace A.
Dow Fund, Alden and Vada
Earhart Foundation
Earl-Beth Foundation
Eddy Family Memorial Fund, C. K.
Eden Foods
Erb Lumber Co.
Ewald Foundation, H. T.
Fabri-Kal Corp.
Farwell Foundation, Drusilla
Federal-Mogul Corp.
Federal Screw Works
Fibre Converters
First Federal of Michigan
First of America Bank Corp.
Fisher Foundation, Max M. and Marjorie S.
Ford Fund, Benson and Edith
Ford Fund, Eleanor and Edsel
Ford Fund, Walter and Josephine
Ford Fund, William and Martha
Ford II Fund, Henry
Ford Motor Co.
Franklin Bank
Fruehauf Foundation
Gast Manufacturing Corp.
General Motors Corp.
Gerber Products Co.
Gershenson Foundation, Charles H.
Gerstacker Foundation, Rollin M.
Gilmore Foundation, Irving S.
Grand Rapids Label Co.
Grand Trunk Corp.
Great Lakes Bancorp, FSB
Great Lakes Casting Corp.
Greater Lansing Foundation
Green Charitable Trust, Leslie H. and Edith C.
Guardian Industries Corp.
Hammond Machinery

Handleman Co.
Harding Foundation, Charles Stewart
Haworth, Inc.
Hayes Albion Industries
Herman Foundation, John and Rose
Herrick Foundation
Hess Charitable Trust, Myrtle E. and William C.
Hiram Walker & Sons Inc.
Holden Fund, James and Lynelle
Holley Foundation
Holman
Honigman Foundation
Hudson-Webber Foundation
Hudson's
Hunter Foundation, Edward and Irma
Hurst Foundation
Imerman Memorial Foundation, Stanley
India Foundation
Intelligent Controls
Isuzu Motors America Inc.
Jackson National Life Insurance Co.
Jacobson Stores, Inc.
Jeffers Memorial Fund, Michael
JSJ Corp.
Kantzler Foundation
Karmazin Products Corp.
Kasle Steel Corp.
Kaufman Endowment Fund, Louis G.
Kaufman Memorial Trust, Chaim, Fanny, Louis, Benjamin, and Anne Florence
Keeler Fund, Miner S. and Mary Ann
Kellogg Foundation, W. K.
Kellogg's
Kelly Services
KitchenAid Inc.
Kmart Corp.
Kolene Corp.
Kowalski Sausage Co.
Kresge Foundation
Kysor Industrial Corp.
La-Z-Boy Chair Co.
Levy Co., Edward C.
Levy Foundation, Edward C.
Lincoln Health Care Foundation
Loeb Charitable Trust, Stella and Frederick S.
Loutit Foundation
Maas Foundation, Benard L.
Manat Foundation
Manoogian Foundation, Alex and Marie
Manufacturers National Bank of Detroit
Mardigian Foundation
Masco Corp.
McGregor Fund
McIntyre Foundation, B. D. and Jane E.
McIntyre Foundation, C. S. and Marion F.
McLouth Steel-An Employee Owned Co.
Meijer Inc.
Mendel Foundation
Merillat Foundation, Orville D. and Ruth A.
Merkley Charitable Trust
Mette Foundation
Michigan Bell Telephone Co.
Michigan Consolidated Gas Co.
Michigan Gas Utilities
Michigan Mutual Insurance Corp.
Michigan National Corp.
Michigan Wheel Corp.
Miller Charitable Foundation, C. John and Reva
Miller Foundation
Miller Inc., Herman
Mills Fund, Frances Goll

Monroe Auto Equipment Co.
Monroe-Brown Foundation
Moore Foundation, C. F.
Morley Brothers Foundation
Mott Foundation, Charles Stewart
Mott Fund, Ruth
National Standard Co.
NBD Bank
NBD Genesee Bank
Old Kent Bank & Trust Co.
Oleson Foundation
Padnos Iron & Metal Co., Louis
Pardee Foundation, Elsa U.
Penske Corp.
Perry Drug Stores
Peterson & Co. Consulting
PHM Corp.
PK Lumber Co.
Plante & Moran, CPAs
Plym Foundation
Polk & Co., R.L.
Prentis Family Foundation,
    Meyer and Anna
Prince Corp.
Protherapy of America
R&B Tool Co.
Ransom Fidelity Company
Ratner Foundation, Milton M.
Robertson Brothers
Rohlik Foundation, Sigmund and
    Sophie
Rouge Steel Co.
Sage Foundation
Scherer Foundation, Karla
Scientific Brake & Equipment
    Co.
Sebastian Foundation
Sehn Foundation
Seidman Family Foundation
Seymour and Troester Foundation
Shapero Foundation, Nate S. and
    Ruth B.
Shelden Fund, Elizabeth, Allan
    and Warren
Shiffman Foundation
Silverman Fluxus Collection
    Foundation, Gilbert and Lila
Simone Foundation
Simpson Foundation
Simpson Industries
Skillman Foundation
Sparton Corp.
Spring Arbor Distributors
SPX Corp.
Standard Federal Bank
Steelcase
Stroh Brewery Co.
Strosacker Foundation, Charles J.
Taubman Foundation, A. Alfred
Tecumseh Products Co.
Teitel Charitable Trust, Ben N.
Thoman Foundation, W. B. and
    Candace
Thorn Apple Valley, Inc.
Timmis Foundation, Michael &
    Nancy
Tiscornia Foundation
Todd Co., A.M.
Towsley Foundation, Harry A.
    and Margaret D.
Trico Foundation
Triford Foundation
United Technologies, Automotive
Upjohn Co.
Upjohn Foundation, Harold and
    Grace
Upton Foundation, Frederick S.
Van Andel Foundation, Jay and
    Betty
Vicksburg Foundation
Vlasic Foundation
Volkswagen of America, Inc.
Vollbrecht Foundation, Frederick
    A.
Voplex Corp.
Walbridge Aldinger Co.
Walker Co., Shaw

Walker Foundation, L. C. and
    Margaret
Wege Foundation
Wenger Foundation, Henry L.
    and Consuelo S.
Westerman Foundation, Samuel
    L.
Whirlpool Corp.
Whiteley Foundation, John and
    Elizabeth
Whiting Foundation
Whiting Memorial Foundation,
    Henry and Harriet
Whitney Fund, David M.
Wickes Foundation, Harvey
    Randall
Wickson-Link Memorial
    Foundation
Wilson Fund, Matilda R.
Wilson Trust, Lula C.
Winship Memorial Scholarship
    Foundation
Wolverine World Wide, Inc.
Word Investments
Zimmerman Foundation, Mary
    and George Herbert

Minnesota

ADC Telecommunications
AHS Foundation
Alliant Techsystems
Alliss Educational Foundation,
    Charles and Ellora
Alworth Memorial Fund,
    Marshall H. and Nellie
American Amusement Arcades
American Linen Supply Co.
Andersen Corp.
Andersen Foundation
Andersen Foundation, Hugh J.
Apogee Enterprises Inc.
Athwin Foundation
Bauervic Foundation, Peggy
Beim Foundation
Bemis Company
Bigelow Foundation, F. R.
Bio-Medicus, Inc.
Blandin Foundation
Blue Cross and Blue Shield of
    Minnesota Foundation Inc.
BMC Industries
Boulevard Foundation
Bremer Foundation, Otto
Bush Foundation
Business Incentives
Butler Family Foundation,
    Patrick and Aimee
C.P. Rail Systems
Cargill
Caring and Sharing Foundation
Carlson Cos.
Carolyn Foundation
CENEX
Chadwick Foundation
Cherne Foundation, Albert W.
Cochrane Memorial Trust, 1988
    Irrevocable
Control Data Corp.
Cowles Media Co.
Cray Research
Dain Bosworth/Inter-Regional
    Financial Group
Davis Foundation, Edwin W. and
    Catherine M.
Dayton Hudson Corp.
Dayton's
Deluxe Corp.
Donaldson Co.
Douglas Corp.
Driscoll Foundation
Ecolab
Eddy Foundation
Edwards Memorial Trust
Ellerbe Becket
Faribault Foods
Farmstead Foods
Federated Life Insurance Co.

Fingerhut Corp.
Fingerhut Family Foundation
First Bank System
Fiterman Charitable Foundation,
    Miles and Shirley
Foldcraft Co.
Fortis Benefits Insurance
    Company/Fortis Financial
    Group
Fuller Co., H.B.
General Mills
Getsch Family Foundation Trust
GNB Inc.
Good Value Home, Inc.
Graco
Gray Charitable Trust, Mary S.
Griggs and Mary Griggs Burke
    Foundation, Mary Livingston
Grossman Foundation, N. Bud
Grotto Foundation
Groves & Sons Co., S.J.
Hallett Charitable Trust
Hallett Charitable Trust, Jessie F.
Hartz Foundation
Harvest States Cooperative
Heilicher Foundation, Menahem
Hersey Foundation
Hiawatha Education Foundation
Honeywell
Hormel & Co., George A.
Hotchkiss Foundation, W. R.
Hubbard Broadcasting
Hubbard Milling Co.
Hudson Jewellers, J.B.
Hulings Foundation, Mary
    Andersen
IDS Financial Services
Independent Financial Corp.
International Dairy Queen, Inc.
International Multifoods Corp.
Jerome Foundation
Johnson Co., E. F.
Jostens
Kasal Charitable Trust, Father
Krelitz Industries
Land O'Lakes
Liberty Diversified Industries
    Inc.
Lieberman Enterprises
Lilly Foundation, Richard Coyle
Lutheran Brotherhood
    Foundation
Mankato Citizens Telephone Co.
Marbrook Foundation
Mardag Foundation
McKnight Foundation
McKnight Foundation, Sumner T.
McNeely Foundation
McVay Foundation
Meadowood Foundation
Medtronic
MEI Diversified, Inc.
Merrill Corp.
Metroquip
Minnegasco
Minnesota Foundation
Minnesota Mutual Life
    Insurance Co.
Minnesota Power & Light Co.
Mitchell, Jr. Trust, Oscar
Moore, Costello & Hart
Mortenson Co., M.A.
MSI Insurance
MTS Systems Corp.
Munsingwear, Inc.
Mutual Service Life Insurance
    Cos.
Nash-Finch Co.
Nash Foundation
National Car Rental System, Inc.
National Computer Systems
Neilson Foundation, George W.
North American Life & Casualty
    Co.
North Star Research Foundation
North Star Steel Co.
North Star Universal Inc.

Northern Star Foundation
Northern States Power Co.
Northwest Airlines, Inc.
Northwest Area Foundation
Northwestern National Life
    Insurance Co.
Norwest Corp.
Oakleaf Foundation
O'Brien Foundation, Alice M.
Onan Corp.
Onan Family Foundation
O'Neil Foundation, Casey Albert
    T.
Ordean Foundation
O'Shaughnessy Foundation, I. A.
Pax Christi Foundation
Pearson Foundation, E. M.
Pentair
Phillips Family Foundation, Jay
    and Rose
Pillsbury Co.
Piper Jaffray Cos.
Polaris Industries, LP
Quebecor Printing (USA) Inc.
Quinlan Foundation, Elizabeth C.
Red Wing Shoe Co.
Reell Precision Manufacturing
Regis Corp.
Remmele Engineering, Inc.
Rodman Foundation
Rosemount, Inc.
Saint Croix Foundation
Saint Paul Cos.
Schering Trust for Arthritis
    Research, Margaret Harvey
Schott Foundation
Schwan's Sales Enterprises
Security Life Insurance Co. of
    America
Sexton Foundation
Sheily Co., J.L.
Sheldahl Inc.
SIT Investment Associates, Inc.
Southways Foundation
Stirtz, Bernards & Co.
Sundet Foundation
Super Valu Stores
Sweatt Foundation, Harold W.
Target Stores
Taylor Corp.
TCF Banking & Savings, FSB
Tennant Co.
Thorpe Foundation, James R.
3M Co.
Toro Co.
Tozer Foundation
Travelers Express Co.
Valspar Corp.
Van Evera Foundation, Dewitt
    Caroline
Walker Foundation, Archie D.
    and Bertha H.
Wallestad Foundation
Wallin Foundation
Warner Foundation, Lee and
    Rose
Wasie Foundation
Wedum Foundation
West Publishing Co.
Weyerhaeuser Family Foundation
Weyerhaeuser Foundation,
    Frederick and Margaret L.
Weyerhaeuser Memorial
    Foundation, Charles A.
Whiteside Scholarship Fund,
    Robert B. and Sophia

Mississippi

Armstrong Foundation
Baird Charitable Trust, William
    Robert
Bryan Foods
Community Foundation
Croft Metals
Deposit Guaranty National Bank
Eastover Bank for Savings
Eastover Corp.

Eka Nobel
Feild Co-Operative Association
First Mississippi Corp.
Hardin Foundation, Phil
Ingalls Shipbuilding
Irby Construction Co.
Johnson Day Trust, Carl and
    Virginia
Kyle Educational Trust, S. H.
    and D. W.
Luckyday Foundation
McRae Foundation
Mississippi Chemical Corp.
Mississippi Power Co.
Mississippi Power & Light Co.
Oster/Sunbeam Appliance Co.
Schillig Trust, Ottilie
Trustmark National Bank
Vicksburg Hospital Medical
    Foundation
Walker Foundation, W. E.
Walker Wildlife Conservation
    Foundation

Missouri

ACF Industries, Inc.
Angelica Corp.
Anheuser-Busch Cos.
Apex Oil Co.
Arch Mineral Corp.
Barrows Foundation, Geraldine
    and R. A.
Bartlett & Co.
Black & Veatch
Bloch Foundation, Henry W. and
    Marion H.
Block Family Charitable Trust,
    Ephraim
Block Family Foundation,
    Emphraim
Block, H&R
Boatmen's Bancshares
Bohan Foundation, Ruth H.
Brisley and Noma Brisley
    Phillips Scholarship Loan
    Fund, Ella Frances
Bromley Residuary Trust, Guy I.
Brown Foundation, George
    Warren
Brown Group
Brown Shoe Co.
Bush Family Foundation, Peter
    W.
Business Men's Assurance Co. of
    America
Butler Manufacturing Co.
Chemtech Industries
Clark Oil & Refining Corp.
Columbia Terminals Co.
Commerce Bancshares, Inc.
Comprehensive Care Corp.
Cowden Foundation, Louetta M.
CPI Corp.
Danforth Foundation
Deer Creek Foundation
Diversified Industries, Inc.
Edison Brothers Stores
Edison Foundation, Harry
Edison Foundation, Irving and
    Beatrice C.
Edwards & Sons, A.G.
Emerson Electric Co.
Empire District Electric Co.
Enright Foundation
Enterprise Rent-A-Car Co.
Fabick Tractor Co., John
Farm & Home Savings
    Association
Farmland Industries, Inc.
Ferrell Cos.
Flarsheim Charitable
    Foundation, Louis and
    Elizabeth
Food Barn Stores, Inc.
Francis Families Foundation
Fru-Con Construction Corp.

Missouri (cont.)

Fulbright and Monroe L. Swyers Foundation, James H.
Garvey Memorial Foundation, Edward Chase
Gateway Apparel
Gaylord Foundation, Clifford Willard
General American Life Insurance Co.
Grant Charitable Trust, Elberth R. and Gladys F.
Graybar Electric Co.
Green Foundation, Allen P. and Josephine B.
Green Industries, A. P.
Group Health Plan Inc.
Guth Lighting Co.
Hall Family Foundations
Hallmark Cards
Hamilton Foundation, Florence P.
Harvard Interiors Manufacturing Co.
Helzberg Foundation, Shirley and Barnett
Herschend Family Foundation
Ingram Trust, Joe
Interco
Interstate Brands Corp.
Jefferson Smurfit Corp.
Jordan and Ettie A. Jordan Charitable Foundation, Mary Ranken
Kahn Memorial Trust
Kansas City Southern Industries
Kellwood Co.
Kelty Pack, Inc.
Kemper Charitable Lead Trust, William T.
Kemper Charitable Trust, William T.
Kemper Foundation, Enid and Crosby
Kemper Foundation, William T.
Kemper Memorial Foundation, David Woods
Korte Construction Co.
Laclede Gas Co.
Laclede Steel Co.
Leader Foundation
Leggett & Platt, Inc.
Lichtenstein Foundation, David B.
Loose Trust, Carrie J.
Loose Trust, Harry Wilson
Lopata Foundation, Stanley and Lucy
Love Charitable Foundation, John Allan
Lowenstein Brothers Foundation
Mallinckrodt, Jr. Foundation, Edward
Mallinckrodt Specialty Chemicals Co.
Marion Merrell Dow
Maritz Inc.
May Department Stores Co.
McBride & Son Associates
McCourtney Trust, Flora S.
McCray Lumber Co.
McDonnell Douglas Corp.
McDonnell Foundation, James S.
McGee Foundation
Mercantile Bancorp
Messick Charitable Trust, Harry F.
Messing Family Charitable Foundation
Mid-America Dairymen
Miller-Mellor Association
Millstone Foundation
Missouri Farmers Association
Missouri Public Service
Monsanto Co.
Moog Automotive, Inc.
Morgan Charitable Residual Trust, W. and E.

Moss Charitable Trust, Finis M.
Nichols Co., J.C.
Old American Insurance Co.
Olin Charitable Trust, John M.
Olin Foundation, Spencer T. and Ann W.
Oppenstein Brothers Foundation
Orchard Corp. of America.
Orscheln Co.
Paxton Co., Frank
Payless Cashways Inc.
Peabody Holding Company Inc.
Pendergast-Weyer Foundation
Pet
Petrolite Corp.
Pettus, Jr. Foundation, James T.
Pillsbury Foundation
Pitzman Fund
Plaster Foundation, Robert W.
Pott Foundation, Herman T. and Phenie R.
Pulitzer Publishing Co.
Ralston Purina Co.
Reliable Life Insurance Co.
Reynolds Foundation, J. B.
Rhoden Charitable Foundation, Elmer C.
Roblee Foundation, Joseph H. and Florence A.
Sachs Fund
Schnuck Markets
Share Foundation
Shaw Foundation, Arch W.
Shelter Mutual Insurance Co.
Sherwood Medical Co.
Shoenberg Foundation
Shughart, Thomson & Kilroy, P.C.
Sigma-Aldrich Corp.
Slusher Charitable Foundation, Roy W.
Sosland Foundation
Souers Charitable Trust, Sidney W. and Sylvia N.
Southwestern Bell Corp.
Speas Foundation, Victor E.
Speas Memorial Trust, John W. and Effie E.
Steadley Memorial Trust, Kent D. and Mary L.
Stern Foundation for the Arts, Richard J.
Storz Instrument Co.
Stowers Foundation
Stupp Brothers Bridge & Iron Co.
Stupp Foundation, Norman J.
Sunderland Foundation, Lester T.
Sunmark Capital Corp.
Sunnen Foundation
Tamko Asphalt Products
Taylor Charitable Trust, Jack DeLoss
Tension Envelope Corp.
Thompson Charitable Trust, Sylvia G.
Tilles Nonsectarian Charity Fund, Rosalie
Trans World Airlines
Turner Charitable Trust, Courtney S.
UniGroup Inc.
Union Electric Co.
United Missouri Bancshares, Inc.
United Van Lines, Inc.
Utilicorp United
Valley Line Co.
Voelkerding Charitable Trust, Walter and Jean
Ward Foundation, Louis L. and Adelaide C.
Webb Foundation
Westlake Scholarship Fund, James L. and Nellie M.
Wetterau
Whitaker Charitable Foundation, Lyndon C.
Wolff Foundation, John M.
Wolff Shoe Co.

Woods Foundation, James H.
Wornall Charitable Trust and Foundation, Kearney

Montana

Bair Memorial Trust, Charles M.
First Interstate Bancsystem of Montana
Gallagher Family Foundation, Lewis P.
Haynes Foundation
Heisey Foundation
Knowles Charitable Memorial Trust, Gladys E.
Lee Endowment Foundation
Montana Power Co.

Nebraska

AG Processing Inc.
Ameritas Life Insurance Corp.
Armour Food Co.
Baer Foundation, Alan and Marcia
Beef America Inc.
Berkshire Hathaway
Buckley Trust, Thomas D.
Buffett Foundation
Commercial Federal Corp.
ConAgra
Cooper Foundation
Cox Foundation, James M.
Criss Memorial Foundation, Dr. C.C. and Mabel L.
Faith Charitable Trust
Farr Trust, Frank M. and Alice M.
FirsTier Bank N.A. Omaha
Giger Foundation, Paul and Oscar
Great West Casualty Co.
Hitchcock Foundation, Gilbert M. and Martha H.
IBP, Inc.
Keene Trust, Hazel R.
Kiewit Foundation, Peter
Kiewit Sons, Peter
Lane Foundation, Winthrop and Frances
Lincoln Family Foundation
Lincoln Telecommunications Co.
Livingston Foundation, Milton S. and Corinne N.
Metromail Corp.
Mutual of Omaha Insurance Co.
Norwest Bank Nebraska
Pamida, Inc.
Physicians Mutual Insurance
Quivey-Bay State Foundation
Reynolds Foundation, Edgar
Richardson County Bank and Trust Co.
Rogers Foundation
Scott, Jr. Charitable Foundation, Walter
Scoular Co.
Storz Foundation, Robert Herman
Valmont Industries
Weller Foundation

Nevada

Bally's - Las Vegas
Bing Fund
Buck Foundation, Carol Franc
Circus Circus Enterprises
Cord Foundation, E. L.
Gabelli Foundation
Harrah's Hotels & Casinos
Hawkins Foundation, Robert Z.
Hilton Foundation, Conrad N.
Lied Foundation Trust
Mirage Casino-Hotel
Nevada Power Co.
Porsche Cars North America, Inc.
PriMerit F.S.B.
Redfield Foundation, Nell J.
Rochlin Foundation, Abraham and Sonia

Sierra Pacific Resources
Southwest Gas Corp.
Summa Development Corp.
Thompson Charitable Foundation, Marion G.
Wiegand Foundation, E. L.

New Hampshire

Abex Inc.
Barker Foundation
Bean Foundation, Norwin S. and Elizabeth N.
Benz Trust, Doris L.
Chubb Life Insurance Co. of America
Cogswell Benevolent Trust
Dingman Foundation, Michael D.
Eastman Foundation, Alexander
First NH Banks, Inc.
Fitch Trust f/b/o Cheshire Health Foundation, Leon M. and Hazel E.
Fleet Bank of Keene
Foundation for Seacoast Health
Freygang Foundation, Walter Henry
Fuller Foundation
Greenspan Foundation
Grinnell Corp.
Hubbard Farms
Hunt Foundation, Samuel P.
Jameson Trust, Oleonda
Kingsbury Corp.
Kollsman Instrument Co.
Lincolnshire
Lindsay Trust, Agnes M.
Lockheed Sanders
Lord Scholarship Fund Trust, Henry C.
Markem Corp.
Mascoma Savings Bank
Monadnock Paper Mills
MPB Corp.
Nashua Trust Co.
New Hampshire Ball Bearings
Page Belting Co.
Peerless Insurance Co.
Phillips Foundation, Ellis L.
Putnam Foundation
Smith Charitable Foundation, Lou and Lutza
Smyth Trust, Marion C.
Standex International Corp.
Tyco Laboratories, Inc.
Wagner and George Hosser Scholarship Fund Trust, Edward

New Jersey

Abrams Foundation
Air & Water Technologies Corp.
Alfa-Laval, Inc.
Allied Educational Foundation Fund
AlliedSignal
American Cyanamid Co.
American Re-Insurance Co.
American Telephone & Telegraph Co./New Jersey Region
American Water Works Co., Inc.
Anderson Foundation
Armco Inc.
Athlone Industries, Inc.
Atlantic Foundation
Ausimont, U.S.A.
Automatic Data Processing, Inc.
Ballet Makers
Barbour Foundation, Bernice
Bard, C. R.
BASF Corp.
Beck Foundation, Elsie E. & Joseph W.
Becton Dickinson & Co.
Beekman Memorial Home
Bell Communications Research

Bell Laboratories
Bergen Foundation, Frank and Lydia
Bergen Record Corp.
Berlex Laboratories
Berrie Foundation, Russell
Block Drug Co.
BMW of North America, Inc.
BOC Group
Bonner Foundation, Corella and Bertram
Borden Memorial Foundation, Mary Owen
Brady Foundation
Brennan Foundation, Robert E.
Brody Foundation, Frances
Brother International Corp.
Brundage Charitable, Scientific, and Wildlife Conservation Foundation, Charles E. and Edna T.
Buehler Foundation, Emil
Bunbury Company
Campbell Soup Co.
Cape Branch Foundation
Capita Charitable Trust, Emil
Caspersen Foundation for Aid to Health and Education, O. W.
Chubb Corp.
Church & Dwight Co.
Ciba-Geigy Corp. (Pharmaceuticals Division)
Clarion Hotel
Colonial Stores
Colt Foundation, James J.
Concord Chemical Co.
Connell Rice & Sugar Co.
Continental Can Co.
CPC International
Crane Fund for Widows and Children
Crum and Forster
Curtiss-Wright Corp.
Darby Foundation
Diabetes Research and Education Foundation
Dodge Foundation, Geraldine R.
Drueding Foundation
Duke Foundation, Doris
Edison Fund, Charles
Egan Machinery Co.
Elastimold Corp.
Elizabethtown Gas Co.
Elizabethtown Water Co.
Emerson Radio Corp.
Engelhard Foundation, Charles
Fanwood Foundation
Fedders Corp.
Federal Paper Board Co.
First Fidelity Bancorporation
Foodarama Supermarkets, Inc.
Formosa Plastics Corp. U.S.A.
Foster Wheeler Corp.
Frelinghuysen Foundation
Friedland Family Foundation, Samuel
Friedman Brothers Foundation
Fund for New Jersey
GAF Corp.
General Color Co.
General Public Utilities Corp.
Gindi Associates Foundation
Goodall Rubber Co.
Goya Foods
GrandMet Consumer Products, Inc.
Grassmann Trust, E. J.
Great Atlantic & Pacific Tea Co. Inc.
Gucci America Inc.
Gulton Foundation
Gund Foundation
Hackett Foundation
Harris Brothers Foundation
Hartz Mountain Corp.
Harvard Industries
Havens Foundation, O. W.

Hite Foundation
Hoechst Celanese Corp.
Hoffmann-La Roche
Holzer Memorial Foundation, Richard H.
Homasote Co.
Hovnanian Enterprises Inc., K.
Howard Savings Bank
Howson-Algraphy, Inc.
Huber Corp., J.M.
Huber Foundation
Hunt Chemical Corp., Phillip A.
Hyde and Watson Foundation
IMO Industries Inc.
Ingersoll-Rand Co.
Innovating Worthy Projects Foundation
International Foundation
IPCO Corp.
Ise America
Jamesway Corp.
Jaqua Foundation
Jaydor Corp.
Jersey Central Power & Light Co.
Jockey Hollow Foundation
Johnson Foundation, Barbara P.
Johnson Foundation, Robert Wood
Johnson & Johnson
Jones Fund, Blanche and George
Kajima International, Inc.
Kaplen Foundation
Kellogg Foundation, Peter and Cynthia K.
Kennedy Foundation, John R.
Kennedy Foundation, Quentin J.
Kerney Foundation, James
Ketchum & Co.
Kirby Foundation, F. M.
Klipstein Foundation, Ernest Christian
Knistrom Foundation, Fanny and Svante
Koh-I-Noor Rapidograph Inc.
KSM Foundation
L & F Products
Large Foundation
Lasky Co.
Laura Ashley Inc.
Lautenberg Foundation
Lazarus Charitable Trust, Helen and Charles
Lehigh Press, Inc.
Levin Foundation, Philip and Janice
Lionel Corp.
Lummus Crest, Inc.
Maneely Fund
Martin Family Fund
Martini Foundation, Nicholas
Matchbox Toys (USA) Ltd.
Matsushita Electric Corp. of America
Mayfair Super Markets
McCutchen Foundation
McGraw Foundation, Curtis W.
McMurray-Bennett Foundation
Melitta North America Inc.
Mennen Co.
Mercedes-Benz of North America, Inc.
Merck & Co.
Metallurg, Inc.
Metromedia Co.
Mettler Instrument Corp.
Meyer Memorial Foundation, Aaron and Rachel
Midlantic Banks, Inc.
Minolta Corp.
Moore & Co., Benjamin
Nabisco Foods Group
National Starch & Chemical Corp.
National Westminster Bank New Jersey
New Jersey Bell Telephone Company

New Jersey Manufacturers Insurance Co.
New Jersey National Bank
New Jersey Resources Corp.
New Valley
Newcombe Foundation, Charlotte W.
Newhouse Publication Corp.
NUI Corp.
Oakite Products
Ohl, Jr. Trust, George A.
Oki America Inc.
Okonite Co.
Olivetti Office USA, Inc.
Openaka Corp.
Orange Orphan Society
Ortho Diagnostic Systems, Inc.
Ortho-McNeil Pharmaceutical
Paddington Corp.
Pantasote Polymers
Parke-Davis Group
Parthenon Sportswear
Peridot Chemicals (NJ)
Polychrome Corp.
Prince Manufacturing, Inc.
Prudential Insurance Co. of America
Public Service Electric & Gas Co.
Quaker Hill Foundation
Read Foundation, Charles L.
Reckitt & Colman
Red Devil
Research-Cottrell Inc.
Reviva Labs
Rhone-Poulenc Inc.
Ricoh Corp.
Rippel Foundation, Fannie E.
Rosenhaus Peace Foundation, Sarah and Matthew
Rukin Philanthropic Foundation, David and Eleanore
Rutgers Community Health Foundation
Sagamore Foundation
Samsung America Inc.
Sandy Hill Foundation
Sanyo Fisher U.S.A. Corp.
Schamach Foundation, Milton
Schenck Fund, L. P.
Schering-Plough Corp.
Schimmel Foundation
Schindler Elevator Corp.
Schultz Foundation
Schumann Foundation, Florence and John
Schumann Fund for New Jersey
Schwartz Foundation, Arnold A.
Sealed Air Corp.
Seton Co.
Sharp Electronics Corp.
Shepherd Foundation
Siemens Medical Systems Inc.
Simon Foundation, William E. and Carol G.
Singer Company
Snyder Foundation, Harold B. and Dorothy A.
Somers Corp. (Mersman/Waldron)
Sony Corp. of America
Soundesign Corp.
South Branch Foundation
South Jersey Industries
Stern Foundation, Leonard N.
Stern Foundation, Max
Strauss Foundation, Judy and Howard E.
Subaru of America Inc.
Sullivan Foundation, Algernon Sydney
Summit Bancorporation
Sun Chemical Corp.
Sunshine Biscuits
Sutcliffe Foundation, Walter and Louise
Sutton Foundation

Taub Foundation, Henry and Marilyn
Taub Foundation, Joseph and Arlene
Terner Foundation
Thomas & Betts Corp.
Tomlinson Family Foundation
Toys "R" Us, Inc.
Turrell Fund
UJB Financial Corp.
Union Camp Corp.
Union Foundation
United Merchants & Manufacturers
Upton Charitable Foundation, Lucy and Eleanor S.
Valley National Bancorp
Van Houten Charitable Trust
Victoria Foundation
Video Software Dealers Association
Visciglia Foundation, Frank
Vollmer Foundation
Warner-Lambert Co.
Webcraft Technologies
Wellman Inc.
Wheaton Industries
Wilf Family Foundation
Willits Foundation
Winslow Foundation
Zock Endowment Trust

New Mexico

Bellamah Foundation, Dale J.
Continental Divide Electric Co-op
Frost Foundation
Furr's Supermarkets
Lea County Electric Co-op
Maddox Foundation, J. F.
Navajo Refining Co.
Phillips Foundation, Waite and Genevieve
Public Service Co. of New Mexico
Sandia National Laboratories
Sunwest Bank of Albuquerque, N.A.
Triskelion Ltd.

New York

Aarque Cos.
Abelard Foundation
Abeles Foundation, Joseph and Sophia
Abraham Foundation
Abraham & Straus
Abrams Foundation, Benjamin and Elizabeth
Abrons Foundation, Louis and Anne
Achelis Foundation
Ada Foundation, Julius
Adams Memorial Fund, Emma J.
Adler Foundation
Advertising Checking Bureau
Aeroflex Foundation
Agway
Air France
AKC Fund
Ala Vi Foundation of New York
Albany International Corp.
Alexander & Alexander Services, Inc.
Alexander Foundation, Joseph
Allegheny Power System, Inc.
Allen Brothers Foundation
Allen & Co.
Allen Foundation, Frances
Allen Foundation, Rita
Alliance Capital Management Corp.
Allyn Foundation
Altman Foundation
Altschul Foundation
AMAX

Amerada Hess Corp.
American Express Co.
American Home Products Corp.
American International Group, Inc.
American Standard
American Stock Exchange
American Telephone & Telegraph Co.
American Telephone & Telegraph Co./New York City Region
American Telephone & Telegraph Co./New York Region
Ampacet Corp.
Andal Corp.
Anderson Foundation
Apple and Eve
Apple Bank for Savings
Archbold Charitable Trust, Adrian and Jessie
Arell Foundation
Arkell Hall Foundation
Aron Charitable Foundation, J.
Arrow Electronics, Inc.
Asahi Glass America, Inc.
ASARCO
Associated Food Stores
Associated Products
Astor Foundation, Vincent
Atalanta/Sosnoff Capital Corp.
Atlantic Foundation of New York
Atlantic Mutual Cos.
Atran Foundation
AVI CHAI - A Philanthropic Foundation
Avis Inc.
Avnet, Inc.
Avon Products
Axe-Houghton Foundation
Ayco Corp.
Ayer Inc., N.W.
Baccarat Inc.
Bachmann Foundation
Backer Spielvogel Bates U.S.
Badgeley Residuary Charitable Trust, Rose M.
Bag Bazaar, Ltd.
Baier Foundation, Marie
Baird Foundation
Baird Foundation, Cameron
Baker Trust, George F.
Baldwin Foundation, David M. and Barbara
Ball Chain Manufacturing Co.
Bally Inc.
Banbury Fund
Banca Commerciale Italiana, New York Branch
Banco Portugues do Atlantico, New York Branch
Banfi Vintners
Bank Hapoalim B.M.
Bank Leumi Trust Co. of New York
Bank of New York
Bank of Tokyo Trust Co.
Bankers Trust Co.
Banque Francaise du Commerce Exterieur
Bantam Doubleday Dell Publishing Group, Inc.
Barclays Bank of New York
Barker Foundation, J. M. R.
Barker Welfare Foundation
Barnett Charitable Foundation, Lawrence and Isabel
Barth Foundation, Theodore H.
Bartsch Memorial Trust, Ruth
Bass and Edythe and Sol G. Atlas Fund, Sandra Atlas
Bausch & Lomb
Bay Foundation
Bayne Fund, Howard
BBDO Worldwide
Beck Foundation
Bedford Fund

Bedminster Fund
Beinecke Foundation
Beir Foundation
Belding Heminway Co.
Belfer Foundation
Belmont Metals
Benenson Foundation, Frances and Benjamin
Benetton
Bennett Memorial Corporation, James Gordon
Bennett Scholarship Fund, Margaret A. and Lawrence J.
Berkowitz Family Foundation, Louis
Berlin Charitable Fund, Irving
Bernstein & Co., Sanford C.
Biddle Foundation, Margaret T.
Bidermann Industries
Big V Supermarkets
Bill Communications
Bingham Second Betterment Fund, William
Blackmer Foundation, Henry M.
Blackstone Group LP
Bleibtreu Foundation, Jacob
Blinken Foundation
Bloomingdale's
Bluhdorn Charitable Trust, Charles G. and Yvette
Blum Foundation, Edith C.
Blum Foundation, Edna F.
Bobst Foundation, Elmer and Mamdouha
Bodman Foundation
Boehm Foundation
Boisi Family Foundation
Booth Ferris Foundation
Borden
Bostwick Foundation, Albert C.
Botwinick-Wolfensohn Foundation
Bowne Foundation, Robert
Bozell, Inc.
Brace Foundation, Donald C.
Branta Foundation
Bravmann Foundation, Ludwig
Brencanda Foundation
Bristol-Myers Squibb Co.
British Airways
Brody Foundation, Carolyn and Kenneth D.
Brookdale Foundation
Brooklyn Benevolent Society
Brooklyn Union Gas Co.
Brooks Brothers
Brooks Fashion Stores Inc.
Brooks Foundation, Gladys
Brown Brothers Harriman & Co.
Bruner Foundation
Brunner Foundation, Robert
Buffalo Color Corp.
Buffalo Forge Co.
Bugher Foundation
Buhl Family Foundation
Bulova Fund
Burchfield Foundation, Charles E.
Burden Foundation, Florence V.
Burnham Donor Fund, Alfred G.
Burns Foundation, Jacob
Butler Foundation, J. Homer
Bydale Foundation
Cablevision Systems Corp.
Calder Foundation, Louis
Caldwell Manufacturing Co.
Callanan Industries
Canadian Imperial Bank of Commerce
Candlesticks Inc.
Canon U.S.A., Inc.
Cantor Foundation, Iris and B. Gerald
Capital Cities/ABC
Carlisle Cos.
Carnahan-Jackson Foundation

New York (cont.)

Carnegie Corporation of New York
Carrier Corp.
Carrols Corp.
Carter-Wallace
Cartier, Inc.
Carvel Foundation, Thomas and Agnes
Cary Charitable Trust, Mary Flagler
CBS Inc.
Center for Educational Programs
Central Hudson Gas & Electric Corp.
Central National-Gottesman
Central Trust Co.
Chait Memorial Foundation, Sara
Champion Products, Inc.
Chapman Charitable Corporation, Howard and Bess
Charina Foundation
Charitable Foundation of the Burns Family
Chase Lincoln First Bank, N.A.
Chase Manhattan Bank, N.A.
Chazen Foundation
Cheatham Foundation, Owen
Chemical Bank
Chernow Trust for the Benefit of Charity Dated 3/13/75, Michael
Chicago Pneumatic Tool Co.
Children's Foundation of Erie County
China Medical Board of New York
China Times Cultural Foundation
Chisholm Foundation
Choice Courier Systems Inc.
Christian Dior New York, Inc.
Christie, Manson & Woods International, Inc.
Christodora
CIBA-GEIGY Corp.
Cintas Foundation
CIT Group Holdings
Citicorp
Claiborne Art Ortenberg Foundation, Liz
Clark Charitable Trust, Frank E.
Clark Family Charitable Trust, Andrew L.
Clark Foundation
Clark Foundation, Edna McConnell
Clark Foundation, Robert Sterling
Clover Foundation
Cohen Family Foundation, Saul Z. and Amy Scheuer
Cohen Foundation, Wilfred P.
Cohn Foundation, Herman and Terese
Cohn Foundation, Peter A. and Elizabeth S.
Coleman Foundation
Coleman, Jr. Foundation, George E.
Coles Family Foundation
Colgate-Palmolive Co.
Collins Foundation, Joseph
Coltec Industries
Commerzbank AG, New York
Common Giving Fund
Commonwealth Fund
Community National Bank & Trust Co. of New York
Computer Associates International
Concord Fabrics, Inc.
Conde Nast Publications, Inc.
Consolidated Edison Co. of New York Inc.
Consumer Farmer Foundation
Contempo Communications
Continental Corp.
Continental Grain Co.

Cook & Co., Frederic W.
Cook Foundation
Coopers & Lybrand
CooperVision, Inc.
Coral Reef Foundation
Cornell Trust, Peter C.
Corning Incorporated
Corporate Printing Co.
Cosmair, Inc.
Cowles Charitable Trust
Craigmyle Foundation
Crane Co.
Cranshaw Corporation
Crary Foundation, Bruce L.
Credit Suisse
Creditanstalt-Bankverein, New York
Crossland Savings FSB
CT Corp. System
Culbro Corp.
Culver Foundation, Constans
Cummings Foundation, James H.
Cummings Foundation, Nathan
Cummings Memorial Fund Trust, Frances L. and Edwin L.
Curtice-Burns Foods
Dahesh Museum
Dairylea Cooperative Inc.
Daiwa Securities America Inc.
Dammann Fund
Dana Charitable Trust, Eleanor Naylor
Dana Foundation, Charles A.
Danforth Co., John W.
Daniel & Co., Gerard
Daniel Foundation, Gerard and Ruth
D'Arcy Masius Benton & Bowles Inc.
Darrah Charitable Trust, Jessie Smith
Davenport-Hatch Foundation
David-Weill Foundation, Michel
Davis Foundation, Shelby Cullom
Davis Foundation, Simon and Annie
Day Family Foundation
DCNY Corp.
DDB Needham Worldwide
de Hirsch Fund, Baron
de Kay Foundation
De Lima Co., Paul
de Rothschild Foundation, Edmond
Dean Witter Discover
DeCamp Foundation, Ira W.
Deer Valley Farm
Delany Charitable Trust, Beatrice P.
Delavan Foundation, Nelson B.
Delaware North Cos.
Dellwood Foods, Inc.
Dent Family Foundation, Harry
Dentsu, Inc., NY
Deutsche Bank AG
Dewar Foundation
Diamond Foundation, Aaron
Dickenson Foundation, Harriet Ford
Dime Savings Bank of New York
DNP (America), Inc.
Dobson Foundation
Dodge Foundation, Cleveland H.
Doherty Charitable Foundation, Henry L. and Grace
Dolan Family Foundation
Dollar Dry Dock Bank
Dollard Charitable Trust
Donaldson Charitable Trust, Oliver S. and Jennie R.
Donaldson, Lufkin & Jenrette
Donner Foundation, William H.
Donovan, Leisure, Newton & Irvine
Dorot Foundation
Dorr Foundation

Doty Family Foundation
Dover Corp.
Dow Jones & Co.
Doyle Dane Bernback Group
Dreitzer Foundation
Dreyfus Corp.
Dreyfus Foundation, Camille and Henry
Dreyfus Foundation, Jean and Louis
Dreyfus Foundation, Max and Victoria
Dula Educational and Charitable Foundation, Caleb C. and Julia W.
Dun & Bradstreet Corp.
Dunlop Tire Corp.
Durst Foundation
Dyson Foundation
Dyson-Kissner-Moran Corp.
Eastern Star Hall and Home Foundation
Eastman Kodak Co.
Eckman Charitable Foundation, Samuel and Rae
Edmonds Foundation, Dean S.
Edouard Foundation
Edwards Foundation, O. P. and W. E.
Ehrman Foundation, Fred and Susan
Elf Aquitaine, Inc.
Ellsworth Trust, W. H.
Emerson Foundation, Fred L.
Eni-Chem America, Inc.
Entenman's Inc.
Equitable Life Assurance Society of the U.S.
Equitable Variable Life Insurance Co.
Ernst & Young
Erpf Fund, Armand G.
Essel Foundation
Esselte Pendaflex Corp.
Ettinger Foundation
European American Bank
Evans Foundation, Edward P.
Evans Foundation, T. M.
Everett Charitable Trust
FAB Industries
Faith Home Foundation
Falk Foundation, Michael David
Faulkner Trust, Marianne Gaillard
Fay's Incorporated
Feil Foundation, Louis and Gertrude
Fein Foundation
Ferkauf Foundation, Eugene and Estelle
Ferriday Fund Charitable Trust
Fiat U.S.A., Inc.
Fife Foundation, Elias and Bertha
Fink Foundation
First Boston
First Empire State Corp.
Fischbach Foundation
Fischel Foundation, Harry and Jane
Fish Foundation, Vain and Harry
Fisher Brothers
Fisher-Price
Fishoff Family Foundation
Fisons Corp.
Fleet Bank of New York
Flemm Foundation, John J.
Fogel Foundation, Shalom and Rebecca
Food Emporium
Foote Mineral Co.
Forbes
Forbes Charitable Trust, Herman
Forchheimer Foundation
Ford Foundation
Fortis Inc.
Foundation for Child Development

Foundation for the Needs of Others
Frank Foundation, Ernest and Elfriede
Frankel Foundation, George and Elizabeth F.
Frasch Foundation for Chemical Research (under the will of Elizabeth B. Frasch), Herman
Freeman Charitable Trust, Samuel
Frese Foundation, Arnold D.
Frey Trust f/b/o YMCA, Harry D.
Fribourg Foundation
Friedman Foundation, Stephen and Barbara
Frohlich Charitable Trust, Ludwig W.
Fruchthandler Foundation, Alex and Ruth
Frumkes Foundation, Alana and Lewis
Fuchsberg Family Foundation
Fuchsberg Family Foundation, Abraham
Fuld Health Trust, Helene
Gaisman Foundation, Catherine and Henry J.
Garfinkle Family Foundation
Gebbie Foundation
Geist Foundation
Gelb Foundation, Lawrence M.
General Atlantic Partners L.P.
General Railway Signal Corp.
General Steel Fabricators
Gerschel Foundation, Patrick A.
Gifford Charitable Corporation, Rosamond
Gilder Foundation
Gilman Foundation, Howard
Gilman Investment Co.
Gilman Paper Co.
Ginsberg Family Foundation, Moses
Gitano Group
Givenchy, Inc.
Glanville Family Foundation
Gleason Memorial Fund
Gleason Works
Glenn Foundation for Medical Research, Paul F.
Glickenhaus & Co.
Gloeckner Foundation, Fred
Goldberger Foundation, Edward and Marjorie
Golden Family Foundation
Goldie-Anna Charitable Trust
Goldman & Brothers, Inc., William P.
Goldman Charitable Trust, Sol
Goldman Foundation, Herman
Goldman Sachs & Co.
Goldome F.S.B
Goldsmith Foundation, Horace W.
Goldsmith Foundation, Nathan and Louise
Goldstein Foundation, Leslie and Roslyn
Golub Corp.
Goode Trust, Mae Stone
Goodman Family Foundation
Goodman Memorial Foundation, Joseph C. and Clare F.
Goodstein Family Foundation, David
Goodyear Foundation, Josephine
Gordon/Rousmaniere/Roberts Fund
Gottlieb Foundation, Adolph and Esther
Gould Foundation, Florence J.
Gould Foundation for Children, Edwin
Goulds Pumps
Grant Foundation, Charles M. and Mary D.
Grant Foundation, William T.
Graphic Controls Corp.

Grateful Foundation
Great Lakes Carbon Corp.
Greater New York Savings Bank
Green Fund
Greenberg Foundation, Alan C.
Greene Foundation, David J.
Greene Foundation, Jerome L.
Greene Foundation, Robert Z.
Greentree Foundation
Greenwall Foundation
Grenfell Association of America
Greve Foundation, William and Mary
Griffis Foundation
Grigg-Lewis Trust
Grow Group
Gruber Research Foundation, Lila
Grumman Corp.
Gruss Charitable and Educational Foundation, Oscar and Regina
Gruss Charitable Foundation, Emanuel and Riane
Gruss Petroleum Corp.
Guardian Life Insurance Co. of America
Guggenheim Foundation, Daniel and Florence
Guggenheim Foundation, Harry Frank
Guggenheim Memorial Foundation, John Simon
Gund Foundation, Geoffrey
Gurwin Foundation, J.
Gutman Foundation, Edna and Monroe C.
Guttag Foundation, Irwin and Marjorie
Guttman Foundation, Stella and Charles
Hagedorn Fund
Hall & Co. Inc., Frank B.
Halloran Foundation, Mary P. Dolciani
Handy & Harman
Hang Seng Bank
Hansen Memorial Foundation, Irving
Hanson Office Products
Harding Educational and Charitable Foundation
Harkness Ballet Foundation
Harkness Foundation, William Hale
HarperCollins Publishers
Harriman Foundation, Gladys and Roland
Harriman Foundation, Mary W.
Harrison Foundation Trust, Francena T.
Hartford Foundation, John A.
Hartman Foundation, Jesse and Dorothy
Hatch Charitable Trust, Margaret Milliken
Hauser Foundation
Hayden Foundation, Charles
Hazeltine Corp.
Hazen Foundation, Edward W.
Hearst Corp.
Hearst Foundation
Hearst Foundation, William Randolph
Hebrew Technical Institute
Heckscher Foundation for Children
Heffernan & Co.
Heineman Foundation for Research, Educational, Charitable, and Scientific Purposes
Hendrickson Brothers
Hess Foundation
Hettinger Foundation
Heyward Memorial Fund, DuBose and Dorothy
Hidary Foundation, Jacob
Hilliard Corp.

Hillman Family Foundation, Alex
Hirschl Trust for Charitable
    Purposes, Irma T.
HKH Foundation
Hobbs Charitable Trust, John H.
Hoffman Foundation, Marion O.
    and Maximilian
Holtzmann Foundation, Jacob L.
    and Lillian
Home Box Office
Homeland Foundation
Hooper Handling
Hopkins Foundation, Josephine
    Lawrence
Horncrest Foundation
Horowitz Foundation, Gedale B.
    and Barbara S.
House of Gross
Howard and Bush Foundation
Hoyt Foundation, Stewart W. and
    Willma C.
Hudson Neckwear
Hughes Memorial Foundation,
    Charles Evans
Hugoton Foundation
Hultquist Foundation
Hunt Alternatives Fund, Helen
Hunt Trust for Episcopal
    Charitable Institutions, Virginia
Hurford Foundation
Hutchins Foundation, Mary J.
Hyde, Jr. Scholarship Fund, J.R.
I. and L. Association
IBM Corp.
IBM South Africa Projects Fund
Icahn Foundation, Carl C.
ICC Industries
Industrial Bank of Japan Trust
    Co.
Innisfree Foundation
Innovation Packaging
Instrument Systems Corp.
Integrated Resources
Intercontinental Hotels Corp.
International Flavors &
    Fragrances
International Fund for Health
    and Family Planning
International Paper Co.
International Standard Electric
    Corp.
Interpublic Group of Cos.
Iroquois Avenue Foundation
Israel Discount Bank of New
    York
Israel Foundation, A. Cremieux
ISS International Service System
Itoh (C.) International
    (America), Inc.
ITT Corp.
Ittleson Foundation
Ix & Sons, Frank
J C S Foundation
J.P. Morgan & Co.
Jackson Hole Preserve
Jacobson & Sons, Benjamin
Jephson Educational Trust No. 1
Jephson Educational Trust No. 2
Jesselson Foundation
Jewish Foundation for Education
    of Women
JJJ Foundation
JM Foundation
Jockey Club Foundation
Johnson Inc., Axel
Johnson Charitable Trust, Keith
    Wold
Johnson Endeavor Foundation,
    Christian A.
Johnson Foundation, Willard T.
    C.
Johnson & Higgins
Jones Foundation, Daisy Marquis
Joselow Foundation
Josephson International Inc.
Joukowsky Family Foundation
Joy Family Foundation

Joyce Foundation, John M. and
    Mary A.
JTB International, Inc.
Julia R. and Estelle L.
    Foundation
Jurodin Fund
Jurzykowski Foundation, Alfred
Kade Foundation, Max
Kane-Miller Corp.
Kane Paper Corp.
Kanematsu-Gosho U.S.A. Inc.
Kaplan Foundation, Rita J. and
    Stanley H.
Kaplan Fund, J. M.
Kaplun Foundation, Morris J.
    and Betty
Katzenberger Foundation
Kaufman Foundation, Henry &
    Elaine
Kaufmann Foundation, Henry
Kaufmann Foundation, Marion
    Esser
Kautz Family Foundation
Kawaler Foundation, Morris and
    Nellie L.
Kaye, Scholer, Fierman, Hays &
    Handler
Keefe, Bruyette & Woods
Kellogg Foundation, J. C.
Kennedy Foundation, Ethel
Kenworthy - Sarah H. Swift
    Foundation, Marion E.
Kepco, Inc.
Kern Foundation, Ilma
Kevorkian Fund, Hagop
Key Food Stores Cooperative Inc.
KH Foundation
Kidder, Peabody & Co.
Killough Trust, Walter H. D.
Kimmelman Foundation, Helen
    & Milton
King Kullen Grocery Co., Inc.
Kingspoint Industries
Kingston Foundation
Klau Foundation, David W. and
    Sadie
Klee Foundation, Conrad and
    Virginia
Klingenstein Fund, Esther A. and
    Joseph
Klosk Fund, Louis and Rose
Knox Family Foundation
Knox Foundation, Seymour H.
Kopf Foundation
Kopf Foundation, Elizabeth
    Christy
KPMG Peat Marwick
Kramer Foundation
Kramer Foundation, C. L. C.
Kravis Foundation, Henry R.
Kremer Foundation Trust, George
Kress Foundation, Samuel H.
Krimendahl II Foundation, H.
    Frederick
Kunstadter Family Foundation,
    Albert
L and L Foundation
Ladies' Home Journal Magazine
Laerdal Foundation, Asmund S.
Lambda Electronics Inc.
Lambert Memorial Foundation,
    Gerard B.
Lang Foundation, Eugene M.
Langeloth Foundation, Jacob and
    Valeria
Larsen Fund
Lasdon Foundation
Lastfogel Foundation, Abe and
    Frances
Lauder Foundation
Lavanburg-Corner House
Lawrence Foundation, Alice
Lawyers Co-operative
    Publishing Co.
Lazar Foundation
Lazard Freres & Co.
LeaRonal, Inc.
LeBrun Foundation

Ledwith Charitable Trust Bank,
    Mary B.
Lee Foundation, James T.
Lehman Foundation, Edith and
    Herbert
Lehman Foundation, Robert
Leibovitz Foundation, Morris P.
Lemberg Foundation
Leonhardt Foundation, Dorothea
    L.
Leslie Fay Cos., Inc.
Leucadia National Corp.
Levinson Foundation, Morris L.
Leviton Manufacturing Co.
Levy Foundation, Betty and
    Norman F.
Levy Foundation, Jerome
Liberman Foundation, Bertha &
    Isaac
Lincoln Fund
Lindner Foundation, Fay J.
Lingnan Foundation
Link, Jr. Foundation, George
Linus Foundation
Lipchitz Foundation, Jacques
    and Yulla
Lipton, Thomas J.
List Foundation, Albert A.
Littauer Foundation, Lucius N.
Litwin Foundation
Liz Claiborne
Loeb Foundation, Frances and
    John L.
Loeb Partners Corp.
Loewenberg Foundation
Loews Corp.
Loewy Family Foundation
Long Island Lighting Co.
Loral Corp.
Lord & Taylor
Lorillard Tobacco Inc.
Lounsbery Foundation, Richard
Lowenstein Foundation, Leon
Lubo Fund
Luce Charitable Trust, Theodore
Luce Foundation, Henry
Lurcy Charitable and
    Educational Trust, Georges
MacAndrews & Forbes Holdings
MacDonald Foundation, James A.
MacDonald Foundation, Marquis
    George
MacKall and Evanina Evans Bell
    MacKall Trust, Paul
Maclellan Foundation, Robert L.
    and Kathrina H.
Macmillan, Inc.
Macy & Co., R.H.
Macy, Jr. Foundation, Josiah
Madison Mutual Insurance Co.
Mailman Family Foundation, A.
    L.
Mailman Foundation
Mamiye Brothers
Mandeville Foundation
Manning and Emma Austin
    Manning Foundation, James
    Hilton
Mapplethorpe Foundation, Robert
Marcade Group, Inc.
Marcus Brothers Textiles Inc.
Marine Midland Banks
Mark IV Industries
Markle Foundation, John and
    Mary R.
Marks Family Foundation
Marsh & McLennan Cos.
Marubeni America Corp.
Marx Foundation, Virginia &
    Leonard
Mastronardi Charitable
    Foundation, Charles A.
Mather Fund, Richard
Mathers Charitable Foundation,
    G. Harold and Leila Y.
Mathis-Pfohl Foundation
Mattus Foundation, Reuben and
    Rose

Matz Foundation — Edelman
    Division
Mayer Foundation, Louis B.
Mays , Inc., J.W.
MBIA, Inc.
McCann Foundation
McCarthy Charities
McCarthy Foundation, Michael
    W.
McConnell Foundation, Neil A.
McCrory Corp.
McDonald Foundation, J. M.
McGonagle Foundation, Dextra
    Baldwin
McGraw Foundation, Donald C.
McGraw-Hill
MCJ Foundation
McKinsey & Co.
Meenan Oil Co., Inc.
Mellam Family Foundation
Mellon Foundation, Andrew W.
Melohn Foundation
Melville Corp.
Memton Fund
Menschel Foundation, Robert
    and Joyce
Mercury Aircraft
Mercy, Jr. Foundation, Sue and
    Eugene
Meridien Hotels
Merrill Lynch & Co.
Mertz Foundation, Martha
Mertz-Gilmore Foundation, Joyce
Metallgesellschaft Corp.
Metropolitan Life Insurance Co.
Mex-Am Cultural Foundation
Meyer Foundation
Midland Montagu
Milbank Foundation, Dunlevy
Miles Inc., Diagnostic Division
Millbrook Tribute Garden
Miller Brewing Company/New
    York
Miller Fund, Kathryn and Gilbert
Milliken & Co.
Milstein Family Foundation
Milton Gordon Foundation
Mitrani Family Foundation
Mitsubishi Heavy Industries
    America
Mitsubishi International Corp.
Mitsubishi Kasei America
Mitsui & Co. (U.S.A.)
Mnuchin Foundation
Model Foundation, Leo
Modern Maid Food Products, Inc.
Monell Foundation, Ambrose
Moog, Inc.
Morania Foundation
Morgan Stanley & Co.
Morgenstern Foundation, Morris
Morris Foundation, Norman M.
Morris Foundation, William T.
Morse-Diesel International
Morse, Jr. Foundation, Enid and
    Lester S.
Moses Fund, Henry and Lucy
Mostyn Foundation
Mott Charitable Trust/Spectemur
    Agendo, Stewart R.
Mulligan Charitable Trust, Mary
    S.
Murphy Charitable Fund, George
    E. and Annette Cross
Murray, Jr. Foundation, John P.
Mutual of America Life
Mutual of New York
Nathan Berkman & Co.
National Broadcasting Co., Inc.
National Center for Automated
    Information Retrieval
National Fuel Gas Co.
National Spinning Co.
NEC USA
Nelco Sewing Machine Sales
    Corp.
Nepera Inc.

Neu Foundation, Hugo and Doris
Neuberger Foundation, Roy R.
    and Marie S.
New-Land Foundation
New & Sons, Hugo
New Street Capital Corp.
New World Foundation
New York Foundation
New York Life Insurance Co.
New York Marine & General
    Insurance Co.
New York Mercantile Exchange
New York Post Corp.
New York Racing Association
New York State Electric & Gas
    Corp.
New York Stock Exchange
New York Telephone Co.
New York Times Co.
The New Yorker Magazine, Inc.
Newbrook Charitable Foundation
Newhouse Foundation, Samuel I.
Newman Assistance Fund,
    Jerome A. and Estelle R.
News America Publishing Inc.
Newsweek, Inc.
Niagara Mohawk Power Corp.
Nias Foundation, Henry
Nichimen America, Inc.
Nichols Farmhouse
Nichols Foundation
Nippon Life Insurance Co.
Noble Charitable Trust, John L.
    and Ethel G.
Noble Foundation, Edward Joh..
Nomura Securities International
Norcross Wildlife Foundation
Norman Foundation
Normandie Foundation
North American Philips Corp.
North American Reinsurance
    Corp.
Norton & Co., W.W.
Noyes Foundation, Jessie Smith
N've Shalom Foundation
NYNEX Corp.
O'Connor Foundation, A.
    Lindsay and Olive B.
Odyssey Partners
Oestreicher Foundation, Sylvan
    and Ann
Ogden Corp.
Ogden Foundation, Ralph E.
Ogilvy & Mather Worldwide
Olin Foundation, F. W.
Olin Foundation, John M.
Olive Bridge Fund
Olsten Corp.
Olympus Corp.
Oneida Ltd.
O'Neil Foundation, Cyril F. and
    Marie E.
Open Society Fund
Oppenheimer and Flora
    Oppenheimer Haas Trust, Leo
Oppenheimer & Co., Inc.
Oppenheimer Management Corp.
Orange & Rockland Utilities, Inc.
Orion Capital Corp.
Osborn Charitable Trust, Edward
    B.
Osceola Foundation
Osram Corp.
O'Sullivan Children Foundation
O'Toole Foundation, Theresa
    and Edward
Outokumpu-American Brass Co.
Overbrook Foundation
Overseas Shipholding Group
PaineWebber
Paley Foundation, William S.
Palisades Educational Foundation
Palisano Foundation, Vincent
    and Harriet
Pall Corp.
Palmer Fund, Francis Asbury
Paramount Communications Inc.

New York (cont.)

Park Communications Inc.
Parnes Foundation, E. H.
Parshelsky Foundation, Moses L.
Parsons and Whittemore Inc.
Patrina Foundation
Paul and C. Michael Paul
 Foundation, Josephine Bay
Penguin USA Inc.
Penney Foundation, James C.
Penzance Foundation
PepsiCo
Perkin Fund
Perkins Memorial Foundation,
 George W.
Perley Fund, Victor E.
Pettus Crowe Foundation
Pfizer
Pforzheimer Foundation, Carl
 and Lily
Philip Morris Cos.
Philippe Foundation
Phillips-Van Heusen Corp.
Phipps Foundation, Howard
Piankova Foundation, Tatiana
Pincus Family Fund
Pines Bridge Foundation
Pinewood Foundation
Pinkerton Foundation
Pioneer Fund
Plant Memorial Fund, Henry B.
Pluta Family Foundation
Ply-Gem Industries, Inc.
Pollock-Krasner Foundation
Pope Foundation
Porter Foundation, Mrs. Cheever
Potts Memorial Foundation
Pratt & Lambert, Inc.
Price Foundation, Louis and
 Harold
Price Waterhouse-U.S.
Primerica Corp.
Pritchard Charitable Trust,
 William E. and Maude S.
Propp Sons Fund, Morris and
 Anna
Prospect Hill Foundation
Prudential-Bache Securities
Quantum Chemical Corp.
Ramapo Trust
Randolph Foundation
Random House Inc.
Rankin and Elizabeth Forbes
 Rankin Trust, William
Raskin Foundation, Hirsch and
 Braine
Rauch Foundation
Raymond Corp.
Reader's Digest Association
Reed Foundation
Reed Foundation, Philip D.
Reich & Tang L.P.
Reicher Foundation, Anne &
 Harry J.
Reliance Group Holdings, Inc.
Republic New York Corp.
Research Institute of America
Resnick Foundation, Jack and
 Pearl
Restaurant Associates, Inc.
Revlon
Revson Foundation, Charles H.
Reynolds Foundation,
 Christopher
Rhodebeck Charitable Trust
Rich Products Corp.
Richardson Charitable Trust,
 Anne S.
Richardson Foundation, Frank E.
 and Nancy M.
Richardson Foundation, Smith
Richmond Foundation, Frederick
 W.
Ridgefield Foundation
Ritter Foundation

Ritter Foundation, May Ellen
 and Gerald
RJR Nabisco Inc.
Robinson Fund, Maurice R.
Robison Foundation, Ellis H. and
 Doris B.
Roche Relief Foundation,
 Edward and Ellen
Rochester Community Savings
 Bank
Rochester Gas & Electric Corp.
Rochester Midland Corp.
Rochester Telephone Corp.
Rockefeller Brothers Fund
Rockefeller Family & Associates
Rockefeller Family Fund
Rockefeller Foundation
Rockefeller Fund, David
Rodgers Foundation, Richard &
 Dorothy
Rohatyn Foundation, Felix and
 Elizabeth
Rose Foundation, Billy
Rosen Foundation, Joseph
Rosenberg Foundation, Sunny
 and Abe
Rosenkranz Foundation
Rosenstiel Foundation
Rosenthal Foundation, Ida and
 William
Rosenthal Foundation, Richard
 and Lois
Rosenwald Family Fund, William
Ross Foundation, Arthur
Ross Foundation, Lyn & George
 M.
Rubin Foundation, Rob E. &
 Judith O.
Rubin Foundation, Samuel
Rubinstein Foundation, Helena
Rudin Foundation
Rudin Foundation, Louis and
 Rachel
Rudin Foundation, Samuel and
 May
Ruffin Foundation, Peter B. &
 Adeline W.
Russ Togs
Ryan Foundation, Nina M.
Sage Foundation, Russell
St. Faith's House Foundation
St. Giles Foundation
Saks Fifth Ave.
Salomon
Salomon Foundation, Richard &
 Edna
Saltz Foundation, Gary
Samuels Foundation, Fan Fox
 and Leslie R.
Sandoz Corp.
Sanwa Bank Ltd. New York
Sasco Foundation
Saul Foundation, Joseph E. &
 Norma G.
Schaffer Foundation, H.
Schaffer Foundation, Michael &
 Helen
Schapiro Fund, M. A.
Schepp Foundation, Leopold
Scherman Foundation
Scheuer Family Foundation, S.
 H. and Helen R.
Schieffelin Residuary Trust,
 Sarah I.
Schieffelin & Somerset Co.
Schiff Foundation
Schiff Foundation, Dorothy
Schlegel Corp.
Schloss & Co., Marcus
Schlumberger Ltd.
Schneiderman Foundation,
 Roberta and Irwin
Scholastic Inc.
Schulman Management Corp.
Schwartz Foundation, David
Schwartz Fund for Education
 and Health Research, Arnold
 and Marie

Seagram & Sons, Joseph E.
Sedgwick James Inc.
Seevak Family Foundation
Seneca Foods Corp.
Sequa Corp.
Sharp Foundation
Sharp Foundation, Evelyn
Shatford Memorial Trust, J. D.
Sheafer Charitable Trust, Emma
 A.
Shearson, Lehman & Hutton
Sheinberg Foundation, Eric P.
Sheldon Foundation, Ralph L.
Shubert Foundation
Silverburgh Foundation, Grace,
 George & Judith
Silverman Foundation, Marty
 and Dorothy
Silverweed Foundation
Simon & Schuster Inc.
Sinsheimer Fund, Alexandrine
 and Alexander L.
Skadden, Arps, Slate, Meagher
 and Flom Fellowship
 Foundation
Skandia America Reinsurance
 Corp.
Skirball Foundation
Slant/Fin Corp.
Slaughter Foundation, Charles
Slifka Foundation, Alan B.
Slifka Foundation, Joseph and
 Sylvia
Sloan Foundation, Alfred P.
Smeal Foundation, Mary Jean &
 Frank P.
Smith Barney, Harris Upham &
 Co.
Smith Corona Corp.
Smith Fund, George D.
Smithers Foundation,
 Christopher D.
Snow Foundation, John Ben
Snow Memorial Trust, John Ben
Snyder Fund, Valentine Perry
Sofia American Schools
Sogem Holding Ltd.
Soling Family Foundation
Solow Foundation
Solow Foundation, Sheldon H.
Soros Foundation-Hungary
Sotheby's
Sperry Fund
Spiegel Family Foundation, Jerry
 and Emily
Spingold Foundation, Nate B.
 and Frances
Spiritus Gladius Foundation
Spiro Foundation, Donald W.
Sprague Educational and
 Charitable Foundation, Seth
Spunk Fund
Staley Foundation, Thomas F.
Standard Chartered Bank New
 York
Standard Motor Products, Inc.
Stanton Fund, Ruth and Frank
Starr Foundation
Starrett Housing Corp.
Statler Foundation
Statter Foundation, Amy Plant
Steele-Reese Foundation
Stein Foundation, Joseph F.
Steinbach Fund, Ruth and Milton
Steinberg Family Foundation,
 Meyer and Jean
Steinhardt Foundation, Judy and
 Michael
Steiniger Charitable Foundation,
 Edward & Joan
Stella D'Oro Biscuit Co.
Sterling Winthrop
Stern Foundation, Bernice and
 Milton
Stern Foundation, Gustav and
 Irene
Stern Foundation, Marjorie and
 Michael

Stone & Webster, Inc.
Stony Wold Herbert Fund
Stott Foundation, Robert L.
Straus Foundation, Martha
 Washington Straus and Harry
 H.
Straus Foundation, Philip A. and
 Lynn
Stuart Foundation
Suburban Propane
Sullivan Musical Foundation,
 William Matheus
Sulzberger Foundation
Sulzer Brothers Inc.
Sumitomo Corp. of America
Sumitomo Trust & Banking Co.,
 Ltd.
Summerfield Foundation, Solon
 E.
Surdna Foundation
Sussman Trust, Otto
Swanson Foundation
Swiss American Securities, Inc.
Swiss Bank Corp.
Switzer Foundation
Taconic Foundation
Tai and Co., J. T.
Tambrands Inc.
Taylor Foundation, Fred and
 Harriett
TBG, Inc.
Teagle Foundation
Texaco
Thanksgiving Foundation
Thomson Information Publishing
 Group
Thorne Foundation
Thyssen Specialty Steels
Tiger Foundation
Time Warner
Tinker Foundation
Tisch Foundation
Titan Industrial Co.
Tokai Bank, Ltd.
Tomen America, Inc.
Topps Company
Tops Markets, Inc.
Tortuga Foundation
Toshiba America, Inc.
Towers Perrin
Triangle Industries
Trimble Family Foundation,
 Robert Mize and Isa White
Tripifoods
Truman Foundation, Mildred
 Faulkner
Trump Group
Trust for Mutual Understanding
Tsai Foundation, Gerald
Tuch Foundation, Michael
Tucker Anthony, Inc.
Turner Construction Co.
Turner Corp.
Turner Fund, Ruth
21 International Holdings
UIS, Inc.
Unilever United States
Union Bank of Switzerland New
 York Branch
United Industrial Corp.
United States-Japan Foundation
U.S. News & World Report
United States Trust Co. of New
 York
United Togs Inc.
Uris Brothers Foundation
Ushkow Foundation
USLIFE Corp.
Utica National Insurance Group
van Ameringen Foundation
Vanneck-Bailey Foundation
Vernitron Corp.
Vernon Fund, Miles Hodsdon
Vetlesen Foundation, G. Unger
Viacom International Inc.
Victory Markets, Inc.
Vidda Foundation

Volvo North America Corp.
Wachtell, Lipton, Rosen & Katz
Waldbaum, Inc.
Waldbaum Family Foundation, I.
Wallace-Reader's Digest Fund,
 DeWitt
Wallace Reader's Digest Fund,
 Lila
Wallach Foundation, Miriam G.
 and Ira D.
Warhol Foundation for the Visual
 Arts, Andy
Warner Fund, Albert and Bessie
Warren and Beatrice W.
 Blanding Foundation, Riley J.
 and Lillian N.
Washington Square Fund
Wasily Family Foundation
Waterfowl Research Foundation
WEA Enterprises Co.
Weeden Foundation, Frank
Weezie Foundation
Weight Watchers International
Weil, Gotshal & Manges
 Foundation
Weiler Foundation, Theodore &
 Renee
Weinberg Foundation, John L.
Weinberg, Jr. Foundation, Sidney
 J.
Weininger Foundation, Richard
 and Gertrude
Weinstein Foundation, Alex J.
Weinstein Foundation, J.
Weiss Foundation, Stephen and
 Suzanne
Wendt Foundation, Margaret L.
Wenner-Gren Foundation for
 Anthropological Research
Werblow Charitable Trust, Nina
 W.
Westchester Health Fund
Western New York Foundation
Westinghouse Broadcasting Co.
WestLB New York Branch
Westvaco Corp.
Wheeling-Pittsburgh Corp.
Whitehead Foundation
Whiting Foundation, Mrs. Giles
Whitney Foundation, Helen Hay
Wien Foundation, Lawrence A.
Wiener Foundation, Malcolm
 Hewitt
Wilber National Bank
Wiley & Sons, Inc., John
Willmott Foundation, Fred &
 Floy
Wilson Foundation, Elaine P. and
 Richard U.
Wilson Foundation, H. W.
Wilson Foundation, Marie C.
 and Joseph C.
Winston Foundation, Norman
 and Rosita
Winston Research Foundation,
 Harry
Witco Corp.
Woodland Foundation
Woodner Family Collection, Ian
Woodward Fund
Woolworth Co., F.W.
WSP&R Charitable Trust Fund
Wunsch Foundation
Yamaichi International
 (America) Inc.
Young & Rubicam
Youth Foundation
Zarkin Memorial Foundation,
 Charles
Zenkel Foundation
Ziff Communications Co.
Zilkha & Sons
Zimmermann Fund, Marie and
 John
Zlinkoff Fund for Medical
 Research and Education,
 Sergei S.
Zuckerberg Foundation, Roy J.

North Carolina

Abernethy Testamentary Charitable Trust, Maye Morrison
Acme-McCrary Corp.
Aeroglide Corp.
Alcatel NA Cable Systems, Inc.
American Otological Society
American Schlafhorst Foundation, Inc.
Anderson Foundation, Robert C. and Sadie G.
Babcock Foundation, Mary Reynolds
BarclaysAmerican Corp.
BB&T Financial Corp.
Belk Stores
Biddle Foundation, Mary Duke
Blue Bell, Inc.
Bossong Hosiery Mills
Brad Ragan, Inc.
Branch Banking & Trust Co.
Brenner Foundation
Brooke Group Ltd.
Broyhill Family Foundation
Bryan Family Foundation, Kathleen Price and Joseph M.
Bryan Foundation, James E. and Mary Z.
Burlington Industries
Burress, J.W.
Burroughs Wellcome Co.
Cannon Foundation
Carlyle & Co. Jewelers
Carolina Power & Light Co.
Carolina Steel Corp.
Carolina Telephone & Telegraph Co.
Carter Charitable Trust, Wilbur Lee
CCB Financial Corp.
Christian Training Foundation
Classic Leather
Coffey Foundation
Cole Foundation
Collins & Aikman Corp.
Collins & Aikman Holdings Corp.
Cone Mills Corp.
Connemara Fund
Covington Foundation, Marion Stedman
Dalton Foundation, Harry L.
Davis Charitable Foundation, Champion McDowell
Davis Hospital Foundation
Dickson Foundation
Dillard Paper Co.
Dove-Knight & Associates, P.A., Architects
Dover Foundation
Duke Endowment
Duke Power Co.
Durham Corp.
Durham Merchants Association Charitable Foundation
Fast Food Merchandisers
Ferebee Endowment, Percy O.
Fieldcrest Cannon
Finch Foundation, Doak
Finch Foundation, Thomas Austin
Finley Foundation, A. E.
First Citizens Bank and Trust Co.
First Union Corp.
Fletcher Foundation, A. J.
Food Lion Inc.
Giles Foundation, Edward C.
Gilmer-Smith Foundation
Ginter Foundation, Karl and Anna
Glaxo
Glenn Foundation, Carrie C. & Lena V.
Goody's Manufacturing Corp.
Guilford Mills
Halstead Foundation

Hampton Industries
Hanes Foundation, John W. and Anna H.
Harris Foundation, James J. and Angelia M.
Harris-Teeter Super Markets
Harvey Foundation, Felix
Hemby Foundation, Alex
Henredon Furniture Industries
Hillsdale Fund
Holding Foundation, Robert P.
Holzman USA, Philipp
Hurley Foundation, J. F.
Janirve Foundation
Jefferson-Pilot
Jefferson-Pilot Communications
Jones Construction Co., J.A.
Kellenberger Historical Foundation, May Gordon Latham
Kenan Family Foundation
Kenan, Jr. Charitable Trust, William R.
Lamb Foundation, Kirkland S. and Rena B.
Lance, Inc.
Lane Charitable Trust, Melvin R.
Laporte Inc.
Liberty Hosiery Mills
Livingstone Charitable Foundation, Betty J. and J. Stanley
Love Foundation, Martha and Spencer
Lowe's Cos.
Magee Christian Education Foundation
Marsh Furniture Co.
Martin Marietta Aggregates
Mast Drug Co.
McClure Educational and Development Fund, James G. K.
McDevitt Street Bovis Inc.
Mebane Packaging Corp.
Miller Brewing Company/North Carolina
Millis Foundation, James H. and Jesse E.
Mitsubishi Semiconductor America, Inc. Funds
Moore & Sons, B.C.
Morehead Foundation, John Motley
Morgan Trust for Charity, Religion, and Education
Morris Charitable Foundation, E. A.
Nanney Foundation, Charles and Irene
National Gypsum Co.
NationsBank Corp.
News & Observer Publishing Co.
North Carolina Foam Foundation
Nucor Corp.
Palin Foundation
Pepsi-Cola Bottling Co. of Charlotte
Perkins Memorial Fund, James J. and Marie Richardson
Perry-Griffin Foundation
Piedmont Natural Gas Co., Inc.
Poole Equipment Co., Gregory
Preyer Fund, Mary Norris
Prickett Fund, Lynn R. and Karl E.
R. L. Stowe Mills Inc.
Radiator Specialty Co.
Randleigh Foundation Trust
Reichhold Chemicals, Inc.
Rexham Inc.
Reynolds Charitable Trust, Kate B.
Reynolds Foundation, Z. Smith
Richardson Fund, Grace
Richardson Fund, Mary Lynn
Rixson Foundation, Oscar C.
Rogers Charitable Trust, Florence

Rose's Stores, Inc.
Ross, Johnston & Kersting
Royal Group Inc.
Ruddick Corp.
Sara Lee Hosiery
Scrivner of North Carolina Inc.
Shelton Cos.
Southern Furniture Co.
Spalding Health Care Trust
Sternberger Foundation, Sigmund
Stewards Fund
Stonecutter Mills Corp.
Stowe, Jr. Foundation, Robert Lee
Susquehanna Corp.
Tanner Cos.
Thomas Built Buses L.P.
Thomasville Furniture Industries
Trexler Foundation
Trion
Unifi, Inc.
United Dominion Industries
Valdese Manufacturing Co., Inc.
Van Every Foundation, Philip L.
Wachovia Bank & Trust Co., N.A.
Weaver Foundation
Wellons Foundation
Whitener Foundation
Yale Security Inc.
Yost Trust, Elizabeth Burns

North Dakota

Leach Foundation, Tom & Frances
MDU Resources Group, Inc.
Myra Foundation
Steiger Tractor
Stern Family Foundation, Alex

Ohio

ABB Process Automation
Access Energy Corp.
Acme-Cleveland Corp.
AGA Gas, Inc.
Albrecht Grocery Co., Fred W.
Alcan Aluminum Corp.
Alms Trust, Eleanora
Amcast Industrial Corp.
American Aggregates Corp.
American Electric Power
American Financial Corp.
American Foundation Corporation
American Greetings Corp.
American Society of Ephesus
American Welding & Manufacturing Co.
Anderson Foundation, William P.
Andersons Management Corp.
Andrews Foundation
Armco Steel Co.
Armington Fund, Evenor
Austin Memorial Foundation
Baird Brothers Co.
Baker Charitable Foundation, Jessie Foos
Bank One, Cambridge, NA
Bank One, Cleveland, NA
Bank One, Columbus, NA
Bank One, Coshocton, NA
Bank One, Dayton, NA
Bank One, Dover, NA
Bank One, Portsmouth, NA
Bank One, Sidney, NA
Bank One, Youngstown, NA
Bardes Corp.
Barry Corp., R. G.
Battelle
Baumker Charitable Foundation, Elsie and Harry
Bearings, Inc.
Beecher Foundation, Florence Simon
Beeghly Fund, Leon A.
Beerman Foundation

Belden Brick Co., Inc.
Benua Foundation
Berkman Co., Louis
Berkman Foundation, Louis and Sandra
Berry & Co., L.M.
Berry Foundation, Loren M.
BFGoodrich
Bicknell Fund
Bingham Foundation, William
Blade Communications
Bob Evans Farms
BP America
BP Exploration
Britton Fund
Browning Masonic Memorial Fund, Otis Avery
Bruening Foundation, Eva L. and Joseph M.
Brush Foundation
Brush Wellman Inc.
Calhoun Charitable Trust, Kenneth
Cayuga Foundation
Centerior Energy Corp.
Champion Spark Plug Co.
Charities Foundation
Chemed Corp.
Chiquita Brands Co.
Cincinnati Bell
Cincinnati Enquirer
Cincinnati Financial Corp.
Cincinnati Foundation for the Aged
Cincinnati Gas & Electric Co.
Cincinnati Milacron
Cincom Systems, Inc.
Cleveland-Cliffs
Clopay Corp.
Codrington Charitable Foundation, George W.
Cole National Corp.
Columbia Gas Distribution Cos.
Columbus Dispatch Printing Co.
Columbus Life Insurance Co.
Columbus Southern Power Co.
Commercial Intertech Corp.
Community Mutual Insurance Co.
Cooper Tire & Rubber Co.
Copeland Corp.
Copperweld Steel Co.
Corbett Foundation
Corbin Foundation, Mary S. and David C.
Crandall Memorial Foundation, J. Ford
CSC Industries
Dana Corp.
Danis Industries
Dater Foundation, Charles H.
Dauch Foundation, William
Davey Tree Expert Co.
Dayton Foundation Depository
Dayton Power and Light Co.
Dayton-Walther Corp.
DeBartolo Corp., Edward J.
Debartolo Foundation, Marie P.
Deuble Foundation, George H.
Didier Taylor Refractories Corp.
Diebold, Inc.
Dively Foundation, George S.
Duriron Co., Inc.
Eagle-Picher Industries
Easco Corp.
East Ohio Gas Co.
Eaton Corp.
Eaton Foundation, Cyrus
Ebco Manufacturing Co.
Edwards Industries
El-An Foundation
Electric Power Equipment Co.
Emery Memorial, Thomas J.
English Foundation, Walter and Marian
Enterprises Inc.

Epp Fund B Charitable Trust, Otto C.
Ernsthausen Charitable Foundation, John F. and Doris E.
Evans Foundation, Thomas J.
Eyman Trust, Jesse
Federated Department Stores and Allied Stores Corp.
Ferro Corp.
Fifth Third Bancorp
Figgie International
Finnegan Foundation, John D.
Firan Foundation
Firestone, Jr. Foundation, Harvey
Flickinger Memorial Trust
Flowers Charitable Trust, Albert W. and Edith V.
Ford and Ada Ford Fund, S. N.
Forest City Enterprises
Foss Memorial Employees Trust, Donald J.
Fox Charitable Foundation, Harry K. & Emma R.
Frankino Charitable Foundation, Samuel J. and Connie
French Oil Mill Machinery Co.
Frisch's Restaurants Inc.
Frohman Foundation, Sidney
Frohring Foundation, Paul & Maxine
Frohring Foundation, William O. and Gertrude Lewis
GAR Foundation
Gardner Foundation
GenCorp
General Tire Inc.
Generation Trust
Gerlach Foundation
Gerson Family Foundation, Benjamin J.
Glidden Co.
Goerlich Family Foundation
Goodyear Tire & Rubber Co.
Gould Inc.
Gradison & Co.
Green Acres Foundation
Greif Brothers Corp.
Gries Charity Fund, Lucile and Robert H.
Gries Family Foundation
Grimes Foundation
Griswold Foundation, John C.
Gross Charitable Trust, Walter L. and Nell R.
Gund Foundation, George
H.C.S. Foundation
Hankins Foundation
Hanna Co., M.A.
Hartzell Industries, Inc.
Haskell Fund
Hauserman, Inc.
Hauss-Helms Foundation
Hayfields Foundation
Hershey Foundation
Hobart Corp.
Homewood Corp.
Honda of America Manufacturing, Inc.
Hoover Foundation
Hoover Fund-Trust, W. Henry
Hosler Memorial Educational Fund, Dr. R. S.
Huffy Corp.
Humphrey Fund, George M. and Pamela S.
Huntington Bancshares Inc.
Huntington Fund for Education, John
Iddings Benevolent Trust
Imperial Electric
Ingalls Foundation, Louise H. and David S.
Ireland Foundation
Irwin-Sweeney-Miller Foundation

Ohio (cont.)

Jarson-Stanley and Mickey Kaplan Foundation, Isaac & Esther
Jasam Foundation
Jennings Foundation, Martha Holden
Jergens Foundation, Andrew
Kangesser Foundation, Robert E., Harry A., and M. Sylvia
Kaplan Trucking Co.
KDI Corp.
Kenridge Fund
Kettering Family Foundation
Kettering Fund
Kibble Foundation
Kilcawley Fund, William H.
Kling Trust, Louise
Kobacker Co.
Kramer Foundation, Louise
Kuhns Investment Co.
Kulas Foundation
Lamson & Sessions Co.
Lancaster Colony
Laub Foundation
LDI Charitable Foundation
Leaseway Transportation Corp.
Lennon Foundation, Fred A.
Libbey-Owens Ford Co.
The Limited, Inc.
Lincoln Electric Co.
Lippitt Foundation, Katherine Kenyon
Lubrizol Corp.
Lyons Physician's Supply Co.
M.T.D. Products
MalCo Products Inc.
Mandel Foundation, Jack N. and Lilyan
Mandel Foundation, Joseph and Florence
Mandel Foundation, Morton and Barbara
Markey Charitable Fund, John C.
Massie Trust, David Meade
Mather and William Gwinn Mather Fund, Elizabeth Ring
Mather Charitable Trust, S. Livingston
Mauger Insurance Co.
Mayerson Foundation, Manuel D. and Rhoda
McAlonan Trust, John A.
McDonald & Co. Securities
McFawn Trust No. 2, Lois Sisler
McIntire Educational Fund, John
McMaster Foundation, Harold and Helen
Mead Corp.
Mead Fund, Nelson
Mellen Foundation
Messenger Publishing Co.
Midland Co.
Midland Mutual Life Insurance Co.
Midmark Corp.
Mill-Rose Co.
Miller Brewing Company/Ohio
Miller Charitable Trust, Lewis N.
Miller Memorial Trust, George Lee
Miniger Memorial Foundation, Clement O.
Minster Machine Co.
Mirapaul Foundation
Monarch Machine Tool Co.
Montgomery Foundation
Mooney Chemicals
Moores Foundation, Harry C.
Mor-Flo Industries, Inc.
Morgan Foundation, Burton D.
Motch Corp.
Murch Foundation
Murphy Foundation, John P.
Musson Charitable Foundation, R. C. and Katharine M.
NACCO Industries

Nason Foundation
National City Bank, Columbus
National City Corp.
National Machinery Co.
Nationwide Insurance Cos.
NCR Corp.
New Orphan Asylum Scholarship Foundation
Nord Family Foundation
Nordson Corp.
North American Coal Corp.
NuTone Inc.
O'Bleness Foundation, Charles G.
Oglebay Norton Co.
Ohio Bell Telephone Co.
Ohio Casualty Corp.
Ohio Citizens Bank
Ohio Edison Corp.
Ohio National Life Insurance Co.
Ohio Road Paving Co.
Ohio Savings Bank
Ohio Valley Foundation
1525 Foundation
O'Neil Foundation, M. G.
O'Neill Charitable Corporation, F. J.
O'Neill Foundation, William J. and Dorothy K.
Ormet Corp.
Osborn Manufacturing Co.
OsCo. Industries
Owens-Corning Fiberglas Corp.
Owens-Illinois
Palm Beach Co.
Park National Bank
Park-Ohio Industries Inc.
Parker-Hannifin Corp.
Paulstan
Penn Central Corp.
Perkins Charitable Foundation
Peterloon Foundation
Philips Foundation, Jesse
Picker International
PMI Food Equipment Group Inc.
Pollock Company Foundation, William B.
Ponderosa, Inc.
Powell Co., William
Powers Higher Educational Fund, Edward W. and Alice R.
Preformed Line Products Co.
Premier Industrial Corp.
Prentiss Foundation, Elisabeth Severance
Procter & Gamble Co.
Progressive Corp.
Ranco, Inc.
Ranney Foundation, P. K.
RB&W Corp.
Reeves Foundation
Reinberger Foundation
Reliance Electric Co.
Renner Foundation
Republic Engineered Steels
Reynolds & Reynolds Co.
Rice Foundation, Helen Steiner
Riser Foods
Ritchie Memorial Foundation, Charles E. and Mabel M.
Ritter Charitable Trust, George W. & Mary F.
Roadway Services, Inc.
Robbins & Myers, Inc.
Rosenthal Foundation, Samuel
Ross Corp.
Ross Laboratories
Rotterman Trust, Helen L. and Marie F.
RPM, Inc.
Rubbermaid
Rupp Foundation, Fran and Warren
Russell Charitable Trust, Josephine S.
Saint Gerard Foundation
Sandusky International Inc.

Sapirstein-Stone-Weiss Foundation
Schermer Charitable Trust, Frances
Schey Foundation
Schiff Foundation, John J. and Mary R.
Schlink Foundation, Albert G. and Olive H.
Schmidlapp Trust No. 1, Jacob G.
Schmidlapp Trust No. 2, Jacob G.
Schottenstein Foundation, Jerome & Saul
Schottenstein Stores Corp.
Schulman Inc., A.
Scott and Fetzer Co.
Scripps Co., E.W.
Sealy, Inc.
Sears Family Foundation
Seasongood Good Government Foundation, Murray and Agnes
Seaway Food Town
Second Foundation
Semple Foundation, Louise Taft
Shafer Foundation, Richard H. and Ann
Sheadle Trust, Jasper H.
Sherwin-Williams Co.
Shinnick Educational Fund, William M.
Sifco Industries Inc.
Slemp Foundation
Smith Charitable Fund, Eleanor Armstrong
Smith Foundation, Kelvin and Eleanor
Smith, Jr. Charitable Trust, Jack J.
Smith 1980 Charitable Trust, Kelvin
Smucker Co., J.M.
Smucker Co., J.M.
Society Corp.
South Waite Foundation
South-Western Publishing Co.
Sprint United Telephone
Standard Products Co.
Standard Register Co.
Standard Textile Co., Inc.
Star Bank, N.A.
Sterkel Trust, Justine
Sterling Inc.
Stocker Foundation
Stone Foundation, France
Stranahan Foundation
Sudbury Inc.
Super Food Services
Superior's Brand Meats
Switzer Foundation
Tait Foundation, Frank M.
Tamarkin Co.
Thendara Foundation
Thor Industries, Inc.
Timken Co.
Timken Foundation of Canton
Tippit Charitable Trust, C. Carlisle and Margaret M.
Toledo Edison Co.
Tomkins Industries, Inc.
TransOhio Savings Bank
Tranzonic Cos.
Tremco Inc.
Treuhaft Foundation
TRINOVA Corp.
True Trust, Henry A.
Trustcorp, Inc.
TRW Corp.
Turner Charitable Foundation, Harry and Violet
Union Central Life Insurance Co.
US Shoe Corp.
V and V Foundation
Value City Furniture
Van Huffel Foundation, I. J.
Van Wert County Foundation
W. L. T.
Wagnalls Memorial

Watson Foundation, Walter E. and Caroline H.
Wayne Steel Inc.
Wean Foundation, Raymond John
Weatherhead Foundation
Weiss Fund, Clara
Wellman Foundation, S. K.
Wendy's International, Inc.
Western Southern Life Insurance Co.
Wexner Foundation
White Castle System
White Consolidated Industries
Wildermuth Foundation, E. F.
Wilkof Foundation, Edward and Ruth
Williamson Co.
Wodecroft Foundation
Women's Project Foundation
Worthington Industries, Inc.
XTEK Inc.
Yassenoff Foundation, Leo
Young Foundation, Hugo H. and Mabel B.
Zonas Trust, Steven K.

Oklahoma

Altec Lansing Corp.
American Fidelity Corp.
Anthony Co., C.R.
Bank of Oklahoma, N.A.
Beatty Trust, Cordelia Lunceford
Bernsen Foundation, Grace and Franklin
Boatmen's First National Bank of Oklahoma
Bovaird Foundation, Mervin
Brand Foundation, C. Harold and Constance
Broadhurst Foundation
Campbell Foundation
Chapman Charitable Trust, H. A. and Mary K.
Collins Foundation, George and Jennie
Collins, Jr. Foundation, George Fulton
Cuesta Foundation
First Interstate Bank & Trust Co.
Fleming Companies, Inc.
Goddard Foundation, Charles B.
Grace Petroleum Corp.
Grimes Foundation, Otha H.
Gussman Foundation, Herbert and Roseline
Hadson Corp.
Harmon Foundation, Pearl M. and Julia J.
Harris Foundation
Helmerich Foundation
Helmerich & Payne Inc.
Johnson Educational and Benevolent Trust, Dexter G.
Jones Foundation, Montfort Jones and Allie Brown
Kaiser Foundation, Betty E. and George B.
Kerr Foundation
Kerr Foundation, Robert S. and Grayce B.
Kerr-McGee Corp.
Kirkpatrick Foundation
Kirkpatrick Oil Co.
Liberty Glass Co.
Lyon Foundation
Mabee Foundation, J. E. and L. E.
Mapco Inc.
McCasland Foundation
McGee Foundation
McMahon Foundation
Merrick Foundation
Noble Affiliates, Inc.
Noble Foundation, Samuel Roberts
Noble Foundation, Vivian Bilby
Occidental Oil & Gas Corp.

Oklahoma Gas & Electric Co.
Oklahoman Foundation
ONEOK Inc.
Parker Drilling Co.
Parman Foundation, Robert A.
Phillips Petroleum Co.
Phoenix Resource Cos.
Public Service Co. of Oklahoma
Puterbaugh Foundation
Rapp Foundation, Robert Glenn
Sarkeys Foundation
Scrivner, Inc.
Share Trust, Charles Morton
Sooner Pipe & Supply Corp.
Taubman Foundation, Herman P. and Sophia
Titus Foundation, C. W.
Trans-Apex
28:19
Union Equity Division of Farmland Industries
Warren Charite
Warren Foundation, William K.
Wegener Foundation, Herman and Mary
WestStar Bank N.A.
Williams Cos.
Wood Charitable Trust, W. P.
Young Foundation, R. A.
Zarrow Foundation, Anne and Henry
Zebco/Motorguide Corp.
Zink Foundation, John Steele

Oregon

Autzen Foundation
Bend Millwork Systems
Bohemia Inc.
Carpenter Foundation
Chiles Foundation
Clark Foundation
Clemens Foundation
Collins Foundation
Collins-McDonald Trust Fund
Collins Medical Trust
Commercial Bank
Corroon & Black of Oregon
Corvallis Clinic
Crestar Food Products, Inc.
Failing Fund, Henry
First Interstate Bank NW Region
First Interstate Bank of Oregon
Fohs Foundation
Ford Foundation, Kenneth W.
Frank Family Foundation, A. J.
Frank Lumber Co.
Freightliner Corp.
Friendly Rosenthal Foundation
Gunderson Trust, Helen Paulson
Higgins Charitable Trust, Lorene Sails
Hunt Charitable Trust, C. Giles
Hyster-Yale
Jackson Foundation
Jantzen, Inc.
JELD-WEN, Inc.
Kelley Family Foundation Trust, Lora L. and Martin N.
Key Bank of Oregon
Louisiana-Pacific Corp.
Medford Corp.
Mentor Graphics
Merlo Foundation, Harry A.
Meyer, Inc., Fred
Meyer Memorial Trust
Nerco, Inc.
Nike Inc.
Northwest Natural Gas Co.
Northwest Publishing Co. — Portland
OCRI Foundation
Oregon Cutting Systems
Oregon Mutual Insurance Co.
OSF International, Inc.
PacifiCorp
PayLess Drug Stores

Peterson Memorial Fund, Chris and Mary L.
Pioneer Trust Bank, NA
Pope & Talbot, Inc.
Portland Food Products Co.
Portland General Electric Co.
Precision Castparts Corp.
Roseburg Forest Products Co.
Tektronix
Templeton Foundation, Herbert A.
Tucker Charitable Trust, Rose E.
United Grocers, Inc.
US Bancorp
Wessinger Foundation
Wheeler Foundation
Willamette Industries, Inc.
Woodard Family Foundation

Pennsylvania

Acme Markets
Action Industries, Inc.
Air Products & Chemicals
Akzo Salt Co.
Alco Standard Corp.
Allegheny Foundation
Allegheny Ludlum Corp.
Aluminum Co. of America
Amerigas
Ames Charitable Trust, Harriett
AMETEK
AMP
Amsco International
Annenberg Foundation
ARA Services
Arcadia Foundation
ARCO Chemical
Aristech Chemical Corp.
Armstrong World Industries Inc.
Arronson Foundation
Asplundh Foundation
Aydin Corp.
Baker Foundation, Dexter F. and Dorothy H.
Barnes & Roche
Barra Foundation
Bartol Foundation, Stockton Rush
Bell Atlantic Corp.
Benedum Foundation, Claude Worthington
Beneficia Foundation
Berkman Charitable Trust, Allen H. and Selma W.
Berry Foundation, Archie W. and Grace
Berwind Corp.
Bethlehem Steel Corp.
Betts Industries
Betz Foundation Trust, Theodora B.
Betz Laboratories
Billy Penn Corp
Binney & Smith Inc.
Binswanger Co.
Bishop Foundation, Vernon and Doris
Blair Corp.
Bozzone Family Foundation
Brodart Co.
Bronstein Foundation, Soloman and Sylvia
Bryn Mawr Trust Co.
Buhl Foundation
Burron Medical
Calgon Corp.
Cameron Memorial Fund, Alpin J. and Alpin W.
Campbell Foundation, Charles Talbot
Caplan Charity Foundation, Julius H.
Cardinal Industries
Carpenter Foundation, E. Rhodes and Leona B.
Carpenter Technology Corp.
Carthage Foundation

Cassett Foundation, Louis N.
Cawsl Corp.
CertainTeed Corp.
Chambers Development Co.
Charitable Fund
CIGNA Corp.
Claneil Foundation
Clapp Charitable and Educational Trust, George H.
Coen Family Foundation, Charles S. and Mary
Colket Foundation, Ethel D.
Colonial Penn Group, Inc.
Comcast Corp.
Commodore International Ltd.
Conair, Inc.
Connelly Foundation
Consol Energy Inc.
Consolidated Natural Gas Co.
Consolidated Rail Corp. (Conrail)
Conston Corp.
Continental Bancorp, Inc.
Contraves USA
Copernicus Society of America
Copperweld Corp.
Corestates Bank
Crawford Estate, E. R.
Crels Foundation
Crown Cork & Seal Co., Inc.
Dalsimer Fund, Craig
Dauphin Deposit Corp.
Decision Data Computer Corp.
DeMoss Foundation, Arthur S.
Dentsply International, Inc.
Development Dimensions International
Diamond State Telephone Co.
Dick Corp.
Dietrich Foundation, William B.
Donnelly Foundation, Mary J.
Douty Foundation
Driscoll Co., L.F.
Duquesne Light Co.
Dynamet, Inc.
Eastern Foundry Co.
Eberly Foundation
Eccles Foundation, Ralph M. and Ella M.
Eden Hall Foundation
Edgewater Steel Corp.
Educators Mutual Life Insurance Co.
Elf Atochem North America
Ellis Grant and Scholarship Fund, Charles E.
Emergency Aid of Pennsylvania Foundation
Equimark Corp.
Equitable Resources
Fair Oaks Foundation, Inc.
Falk Medical Fund, Maurice
Federation Foundation of Greater Philadelphia
Feinstein Foundation, Myer and Rosaline
Fels Fund, Samuel S.
Female Association of Philadelphia
Ferranti Tech
Fidelity Bank
Fidelity Mutual Life Insurance Co.
Finley Charitable Trust, J. B.
Firestone Foundation, Roger S.
First Fidelity Bank
First Pennsylvania Bank NA
First Valley Bank
Fischer & Porter Co.
Foerderer Foundation, Percival E. and Ethel Brown
Foster Charitable Trust
Foster Co., L.B.
Fourjay Foundation
Fox Foundation, Richard J.
Franklin Mint Corp.
Freeport Brick Co.

Frick Educational Commission, Henry C.
Frick Foundation, Helen Clay
Gahagen Charitable Trust, Zella J.
Garrigues Trust, Edwin B.
General Accident Insurance Co. of America
General Machine Works
Gershman Foundation, Joel
Giant Eagle
Giant Food Stores
Gibson Foundation, Addison H.
Gilbert Associates, Inc.
Glatfelter Co., P.H.
Glencairn Foundation
Glenmede Trust Corp.
Glosser Foundation, David A.
Goldman Foundation, William
Grable Foundation
Grass Family Foundation
Greenfield Foundation, Albert M.
Groome Beatty Trust, Helen D.
Gruen Marketing
Grumbacher Foundation, M. S.
Grundy Foundation
Hall Charitable Trust, Evelyn A. J.
Hall Foundation
Hallowell Foundation
Hambay Foundation, James T.
Hamilton Bank
Harleysville Mutual Insurance Co.
Harsco Corp.
Hazen Charitable Trust, Lita Annenberg
Heinz Co., H.J.
Heinz Endowment, Howard
Heinz Endowment, Vira I.
Heinz Family Foundation
Heinz Foundation, Drue
Henkel Corp.
Herr Foods
Hershey Entertainment & Resort Co.
Hershey Foods Corp.
High Foundation
Hillman Co.
Hillman Foundation
Hillman Foundation, Henry L.
Holdeen Fund 55-10
Holdeen Fund 50-10
Holdeen Fund 45-10
Hooker Charitable Trust, Janet A.
Hooper Foundation, Elizabeth S.
Hopwood Charitable Trust, John M.
Houghton & Co., E.F.
Hoyt Foundation
Hulme Charitable Foundation, Milton G.
Hunt Foundation
Hunt Foundation, Roy A.
Hunt Manufacturing Co.
Huston Charitable Trust, Stewart
Huston Foundation
IMS America Ltd.
Independence Foundation
Institute for Bio-Information Research
Integra Bank
Integra Bank/South
J. D. B. Fund
J&L Specialty Products Corp.
Janssen Foundation, Henry
Jennings Foundation, Mary Hillman
Jessop Steel Co.
Jewish Healthcare Foundation of Pittsburgh
Johnson Matthey Investments
Justus Trust, Edith C.
Kavanagh Foundation, T. James
Kelley Foundation, Kate M.
Kellmer Co., Jack
Kennametal

Ketchum Communications
Keystone Weaving Mills
Klein Charitable Foundation, Raymond
Kline Foundation, Charles and Figa
Kline Foundation, Josiah W. and Bessie H.
Knudsen Charitable Foundation, Earl
Korman Family Foundation, Hyman
Kulicke & Soffa Industries
Kunkel Foundation, John Crain
Kynett Memorial Foundation, Edna G.
LamCo. Communications
Lancaster Newspapers
Laros Foundation, R. K.
Laurel Foundation
Lebanon Mutual Insurance Co.
Lebovitz Fund
Lehigh Portland Cement Co.
Lesher Foundation, Margaret and Irvin
Levee Charitable Trust, Polly Annenberg
Levitt Foundation
Lockhart Iron & Steel Co.
Lord Corp.
Love Foundation, George H. and Margaret McClintic
Ludwick Institute
Lukens
Mack Foundation, J. S.
Magee Carpet Co.
Mandell Foundation, Samuel P.
Masland & Sons, C.H.
Massey Charitable Trust
Matthews International Corp.
McCormick Trust, Anne
McCune Charitable Trust, John R.
McCune Foundation
McFeely-Rogers Foundation
McKaig Foundation, Lalitta Nash
McKee Poor Fund, Virginia A.
McKenna Foundation, Katherine Mabis
McKenna Foundation, Philip M.
McLean Contributionship
McMannis and A. Haskell McMannis Educational Fund, William J.
McNeil Consumer Products
McNeil, Jr. Charitable Trust, Robert L.
McShain Charities, John
Measey Foundation, Benjamin and Mary Siddons
Mellon Bank Corp.
Mellon Foundation, Richard King
Mellon PSFS
Mellon Stuart Construction Inc.
Mengle Foundation, Glenn and Ruth
Merck Human Health Division
Meridian Bancorp
Merit Oil Corp.
Meritor Financial Group
Metal Industries
Michaels Scholarship Fund, Frank J.
Miles Inc.
Miller Charitable Foundation, Howard E. and Nell E.
Millstein Charitable Foundation
Mine Safety Appliances Co.
Morris Charitable Trust, Charles M.
Motter Printing Press Co.
Muller Foundation, C. John and Josephine
Murphy Co., G.C.
National Forge Co.
National Steel
Neville Chemical Co.
New Penn Motor Express

Novotny Charitable Trust, Yetta Deitch
Nutri/System Inc.
Oberkotter Family Foundation
Oberlaender Foundation, Gustav
1957 Charity Trust
Oxford Foundation
Packer Foundation, Horace B.
Paley Foundation, Goldie
Patterson Charitable Fund, W. I.
Penn Foundation, William
Penn Industrial Chemical Corp.
Penn Mutual Life Insurance Co.
Penn Savings Bank, a division of Sovereign Bank Bank of Princeton, a division of Sovereign Bank
Penn Traffic Co.
Pennbank
Pennsylvania Dutch Co.
Pennsylvania General Insurance Co.
Pennsylvania Knitted Outerwear Manufacturing Association
Pennsylvania Power & Light
Pep Boys
Peters Foundation, Charles F.
Pew Charitable Trusts
Philadelphia Electric Co.
Philadelphia Industries
Phillips Charitable Trust, Dr. and Mrs. Arthur William
Piedmont Health Care Foundation
Pilgrim Industries
Pine Tree Foundation
Piper Foundation
Pitt-Des Moines Inc.
Pittsburgh Child Guidance Foundation
Pittsburgh National Bank
Plankenhorn Foundation, Harry
PMA Industries
PNC Bank
PNC Bank
Polk Foundation
Pottstown Mercury
PPG Industries
PQ Corp.
Premier Dental Products Co.
Presser Foundation
Provident Mutual Life Insurance Co. of Philadelphia
Quaker Chemical Corp.
Quaker State Corp.
Raymark Corp.
Raytheon Engineers & Constructors
Reedman Car-Truck World Center
Reidler Foundation
Reliance Insurance Cos.
Rhone-Poulenc Rorer
Rider-Pool Foundation
Rite Aid Corp.
Rittenhouse Foundation
Rochester & Pittsburgh Coal Co.
Rock Foundation, Milton and Shirley
Rockwell Foundation
Rodale Press
Rohm and Haas Company
Rosenberg Foundation, Alexis
Rosenbluth Travel Agency
Roth Foundation
Rudy, Jr. Trust, George B.
Safeguard Scientifics Foundation
St. Mary's Catholic Foundation
Sanyo Audio Manufacturing (U.S.A.) Corp.
Sargent Electric Co.
Scaife Family Foundation
Scaife Foundation, Sarah
Schautz Foundation, Walter L.
Schmidt & Sons, C.
Scholler Foundation
Schoonmaker J-Sewkly Valley Hospital Trust

Pennsylvania (cont.)

Schwartz and Robert Schwartz Foundation, Bernard
Scott Paper Co.
SECO
Servistar Corp.
Seybert Institution for Poor Boys and Girls, Adam and Maria Sarah
Shaffer Family Charitable Trust
Shared Medical Systems Corp.
Sharon Steel Corp.
Sheppard Foundation, Lawrence B.
Shoemaker Co., R.M.
Shoemaker Fund, Thomas H. and Mary Williams
Shoemaker Trust for Shoemaker Scholarship Fund, Ray S.
Shore Fund
Shuster Memorial Trust, Herman
SICO Foundation
Simmons Family Foundation, R. P.
Simon Charitable Trust, Esther
SKF USA, Inc.
Smith Charitable Trust, W. W.
Smith Foundation
Smith Golden Rule Trust Fund, Fred G.
Smith Memorial Fund, Ethel Sergeant Clark
Snayberger Memorial Foundation, Harry E. and Florence W.
Snee-Reinhardt Charitable Foundation
Snider Foundation
Snyder Charitable Fund, W. P.
Sordoni Enterprises
Sordoni Foundation
Spang & Co.
Speyer Foundation, Alexander C. and Tillie S.
SPS Technologies
Stabler Cos., Inc.
Stabler Foundation, Donald B. and Dorothy L.
Stackpole-Hall Foundation
Standard Steel Speciality Co.
Staunton Farm Foundation
Stein Foundation, Louis
Steinman Foundation, James Hale
Steinman Foundation, John Frederick
Steinsapir Family Foundation, Julius L. and Libhie B.
Stern Family Foundation, Harry
Stewart Alexander Foundation
Stokes Foundation, Lydia B.
Stott Foundation, Louis L.
Strauss Foundation
Strawbridge & Clothier
Strawbridge Foundation of Pennsylvania I, Margaret Dorrance
Strawbridge Foundation of Pennsylvania II, Margaret Dorrance
Stroehmann Bakeries
Stroud Foundation
Strouse, Greenberg & Co.
Sun Co.
Superior Tube Co.
Susquehanna Investment Group
Susquehanna-Pfaltzgraff Co.
Tasty Baking Co.
Teleflex Inc.
Thrift Drug, Inc.
Tippens Foundation
Transtar Inc.
Trees Charitable Trust, Edith L.
Trexler Trust, Harry C.
UGI Corp.
Uniform Tubes, Inc.
Union Pacific Corp.

Unisys Corp.
United Refining Co
United Service Foundation
U.S. Healthcare, Inc.
United Telephone System (Eastern Group)
Universal Health Services, Inc.
USX Corp.
Valley Bancorp
Vanguard Group of Investment Cos.
Vesper Corp.
Vesuvius Charitable Foundation
VF Corp.
Victaulic Co. of America
Vincent Trust, Anna M.
Waldorf Educational Foundation
Walker Educational and Charitable Foundation, Alex C.
Wardle Family Foundation
Warwick Foundation
Waters Charitable Trust, Robert S.
Weisbrod Foundation Trust Dept., Robert and Mary
Wells Foundation, Franklin H. and Ruth L.
West Co.
Westinghouse Electric Corp.
Westmoreland Coal Co.
Whalley Charitable Trust
Whitaker Foundation
Whitaker Fund, Helen F.
Williams Charitable Trust, John C.
Williams Foundation, C. K.
Wolf Foundation, Benjamin and Fredora K.
Wood Foundation of Chambersburg, PA
Wurts Memorial, Henrietta Tower
WWF Paper Corp.
Wyomissing Foundation
York Barbell Co.
York International Corp.
Zippo Manufacturing Co.
Zurn Industries

Puerto Rico

Zacharia Foundation, Isaac Herman

Rhode Island

Allendale Mutual Insurance Co.
Almac's, Inc.
Alperin/Hirsch Family Foundation
Ann & Hope
Armbrust Chain Co.
Attleboro Pawtucket Savings Bank
Bafflin Foundation
Ballou & Co., B.A.
Brown Inc., John
Brown & Sharpe Manufacturing Co.
Carol Cable Co.
Champlin Foundations
Citizens Bank
Clarke Trust, John
Cookson America
Cranston Print Works
Cross Co., A.T.
DeBlois Oil Co.
Dimeo Construction Co.
Eastland Bank
ETCO Inc.
Fleet Financial Group
Ford Foundation, Edward E.
Galkin Charitable Trust, Ira S. and Anna
Genesis Foundation
Gilbane Building Co.
Gilbane Foundation, Thomas and William
Haffenreffer Family Fund
Hasbro

Hassenfeld Foundation
Jaffe Foundation
Johnstone and H. Earle Kimball Foundation, Phyllis Kimball
Kenney Manufacturing Co.
Kimball Foundation, Horace A. Kimball and S. Ella
Koffler Family Foundation
Leesona Corp.
Littlefield Memorial Trust, Ida Ballou
Nortek, Inc.
Peoples Drug Stores Inc.
Providence Energy Corp.
Providence Journal Company
Rhode Island Hospital Trust National Bank
Sunbeam-Oster
Textron
Van Beuren Charitable Foundation
Watson Foundation, Thomas J.

South Carolina

Abney Foundation
Alice Manufacturing Co.
Arkwright Foundation
Bailey Foundation
Bailey & Son, Bankers, M.S.
Baker & Baker
Bannon Foundation
Belk Stores
Budweiser of Columbia
Builder Marts of America
Chapin Foundation of Myrtle Beach, South Carolina
Cline Co.
Close Foundation
Coats & Clark Inc.
Colonial Life & Accident Insurance Co.
County Bank
Delta Woodside Industries
Evening Post Publishing Co.
Fairey Educational Fund, Kittie M.
Fuller Foundation, C. G.
Fullerton Foundation
Greenwood Mills
Gregg-Graniteville Foundation
Hopewell Foundation
Horne Foundation, Dick
Inman Mills
Jackson Mills
Liberty Corp.
Love Foundation, Lucyle S.
Merck Family Fund
Michelin North America
Mount Vernon Mills
Multimedia, Inc.
Rock Hill Telephone Co.
Roe Foundation
SCANA Corp.
Scurry Foundation, D. L.
Self Foundation
Siebe North Inc.
Simpson Foundation
Smith Charities, John
Sonoco Products Co.
South Carolina Electric & Gas Co.
Springs Foundation
Springs Industries
Steel Heddle Manufacturing Co.
Stevens Foundation, John T.
Support Systems International
Symmes Foundation, F. W.

South Dakota

Hatterscheidt Foundation
Sioux Steel Co.

Tennessee

AFG Industries, Inc.
Aladdin Industries, Incorporated

American General Life & Accident Insurance Co.
Ansley Foundation, Dantzler Bond
Belz Foundation
Benwood Foundation
Bradford & Co., J.C.
Bridgestone/Firestone
Briggs Foundation, T. W.
Brinkley Foundation
Brown Charitable Trust, Dora Maclellan
Caldwell Foundation, Hardwick
Cartinhour Foundation
Chattem, Inc.
Christy-Houston Foundation
Citizens Union Bank
Cole Foundation, Robert H. and Monica H.
Constar International Inc.
Conwood Co. L.P.
Currey Foundation, Brownlee
Danner Foundation
Davis Foundation, Joe C.
Dean Foods, Jimmy
Dixie-Portland Flour Mills
Dixie Yarns, Inc.
Dollar General Corp.
Dover Elevator Systems Inc.
Eastman Chemical Co.
Federal Express Corp.
First American Corp. (Nashville, Tennessee)
First Tennessee Bank
Foster Charitable Foundation, M. Stratton
Genesco
Goldsmith Foundation
Gordon Family Foundation, Joel C. and Bernice W.
H. R. H. Family Foundation
Heil Co.
Helena Chemical Co.
Hospital Corp. of America
Hurlbut Memorial Fund, Orion L. and Emma S.
Hutcheson Foundation, Hazel Montague
Hyde Foundation, J. R.
Ingram Book Co.
Ingram Industries
Interstate Packaging Co.
Jewell Memorial Foundation, Daniel Ashley and Irene Houston
Leu Foundation
Lowenstein Foundation, William P. and Marie R.
Lyndhurst Foundation
Maclellan Charitable Trust, R. J.
Maclellan Foundation
Magic Chef
Massengill-DeFriece Foundation
Massey Foundation, Jack C.
Memphis Light Gas & Water Division
Morristown Casting Support Division
Murray Ohio Manufacturing Co.
North American Royalties
Northern Telecom Inc.
Oak Hall, Inc.
1939 Foundation
Plough Foundation
Potter Foundation, Justin and Valere
Precision Rubber Products
Promus Cos.
Provident Life & Accident Insurance Co.
Red Food Stores, Inc.
Reflection Riding
Republic Automotive Parts, Inc.
Reynolds Foundation, Eleanor T.
Schadt Foundation
Schilling Motors
SCT Yarns
Shoney's Inc.

Stephens Foundation Trust
Stokely, Jr. Foundation, William B.
Templeton Foundation, John
Third National Corp.
Thompson Charitable Foundation
Toms Foundation
Tonya Memorial Foundation
TSC STores, Inc.
Union Planters Corp.
United Inns, Inc.
Van Vleet Foundation
Washington Foundation
Werthan Foundation
Werthan Packaging, Inc.
Westend Foundation
Woods-Greer Foundation
Wurzburg, Inc.
Zimmerman Family Foundation, Raymond

Texas

Abell-Hanger Foundation
Abercrombie Foundation
Adams Resources & Energy, Inc.
Alcon Laboratories, Inc.
Alexander Foundation, Robert D. and Catherine R.
American General Corp.
American National Insurance
American Telephone & Telegraph Co./Dallas Region
AMR Corp.
Anadarko Petroleum Corp.
Anderson Charitable Trust, Josephine
Anderson Foundation, M. D.
Apache Corp.
Associated Milk Producers, Inc.
Austin Industries
Aviall, Inc.
Baker Hughes Inc.
Bank One, Texas-Houston Office
Bank One, Texas, NA
Barnes Scholarship Trust, Fay T.
Baroid Corp.
Bass Corporation, Perry and Nancy Lee
Bass Foundation
Bass Foundation, Harry
Baumberger Endowment
Beal Foundation
Beasley Foundation, Theodore and Beulah
Behmann Brothers Foundation
Bell Helicopter Textron
Bell Trust
Belo Corp., A.H.
Beren Trust D, Harry H.
Bertha Foundation
Big Three Industries
Biological Humanics Foundation
Bonner & Moore Associates
Bordeaux Foundation
Bosque Foundation
Bowers Foundation
Brackenridge Foundation, George W.
Braniff International Airlines
Bridwell Foundation, J. S.
Brinker Girls' Tennis Foundation, Maureen Connolly
Brochsteins Inc.
Brown and C. A. Lupton Foundation, T. J.
Brown Foundation
Brown Foundation, M. K.
Brown & Root, Inc.
Brown Inc., Tom
Browning-Ferris Industries
Bryce Memorial Fund, William and Catherine
Burkitt Foundation
Burlington Northern Inc.
Business Records Corp.
C.I.O.S.
Cactus Feeders Inc.

Cain Foundation, Effie and Wofford
Cain Foundation, Gordon and Mary
Caleb Brett U.S.A. Inc.
Caltex Petroleum Corp.
Cameron Foundation, Harry S. and Isabel C.
Campbell Taggart, Inc.
Carter Foundation, Amon G.
Caston Foundation, M. C. and Mattie
Cauthorn Charitable Trust, John and Mildred
Centex Corp.
Central Power & Light Co.
Central & South West Services
Chilton Foundation Trust
Church's Fried Chicken, Inc.
Cimarron Foundation
Clarity Holdings Corp.
Clayton Fund
Clements Foundation
Coastal Corp.
Cockrell Foundation
Collins Foundation, Carr P.
Collins Foundation, James M.
Commercial Metals Co.
Community Hospital Foundation
Compaq Computer Corp.
Conoco Inc.
Constantin Foundation
Continental Airlines
Contran Corp.
Cook Foundation, Loring
Cook, Sr. Charitable Foundation, Kelly Gene
Cooper Industries
Cooper Oil Tool
Corpus Christi Exploration Co.
Cox Charitable Trust, Opal G.
Craig Foundation, J. Paul
CRC Evans Pipeline International, Inc.
CRS Sirrine Engineers
Crump Fund, Joe and Jessie
Cullen Foundation
Cullen/Frost Bankers
Cullum Cos.
Davidson Family Charitable Foundation
Davis Foundation, Ken W.
Delhi Gas Pipeline Co.
Diamond Shamrock
Digicon
Dishman Charitable Foundation Trust, H. E. and Kate
Dodge Jones Foundation
Doss Foundation, M. S.
Dougherty, Jr. Foundation, James R.
Dresser Industries
DSC Communications Co.
Dues Charitable Foundation, Cesle C. and Mamie
Dunagan Foundation
Duncan Foundation, Lillian H. and C. W.
Dunn Research Foundation, John S.
E-Systems
Early Foundation
EDS Corp.
Edwards Foundation, Jes
Electronic Data Systems Corp.
Elkins Foundation, J. A. and Isabel M.
Elkins, Jr. Foundation, Margaret and James A.
Ellwood Foundation
Enron Corp.
Enserch Corp.
Enterra Corp.
Entex
Exxon Corp.
Fair Foundation, R. W.
Farish Fund, William Stamps
Fashion Bar

Fasken Foundation
Favrot Fund
Feldman Foundation
Ferguson Family Foundation, Kittie and Rugeley
Fifth Avenue Foundation
Fikes Foundation, Leland
FINA, Inc.
First Interstate Bank of Texas, N.A.
Fish Foundation, Ray C.
Fleming Foundation
Florence Foundation
Fondren Foundation
Fort Worth Star Telegram
Foxmeyer Corp.
Franklin Charitable Trust, Ershel
Frees Foundation
Friona Industries L.P.
Frito-Lay
Frost National Bank
Fuller Foundation
Garvey Texas Foundation
George Foundation
Gill Foundation, Pauline Allen
Gilman and Gonzalez-Falla Theatre Foundation
Gilman, Jr. Foundation, Sondra and Charles
Glaze Foundation, Robert and Ruth
Gordon Foundation, Meyer and Ida
Grant-Norpac, Inc.
Green Foundation
Griffin Foundation, Rosa May
Grocers Supply Co.
GSC Enterprises
Haas Foundation, Paul and Mary
Hachar Charitable Trust, D. D.
Haggar Apparel Corp.
Haggar Foundation
Haggerty Foundation
Haghenbeck Foundation, Antonio Y. De La Lama
Halff Foundation, G. A. C.
Hall Financial Group
Hallberg Foundation, E. L. and R. F.
Halliburton Co.
Halsell Foundation, Ewing
Hamman Foundation, George and Mary Josephine
Hammill Foundation, Donald D.
Hankamer Foundation, Curtis and Doris K.
Harrington Foundation, Don and Sybil
Harte-Hanks Communications, Inc.
Hawn Foundation
HCB Contractors
Heath Foundation, Ed and Mary
Henry Foundation, Patrick
Hervey Foundation
Herzstein Charitable Foundation, Albert and Ethel
Hightower Foundation, Walter
Hillcrest Foundation
Hobby Foundation
Hoblitzelle Foundation
Hofheinz Foundation, Irene Cafcalas
Hofheinz Fund
Hofstetter Trust, Bessie
Houston Endowment
Houston Industries
Houston Post Co.
Howell Corp.
Howmet Corp., Wichita Falls Casting Division
Howmet Corp., Wichita Falls Refurbishment Center
Hubbard Foundation, R. Dee and Joan Dale
Huffington Foundation
Hugg Trust, Leoia W. and Charles H.

Humphreys Foundation
Hunt Oil Co.
Huthsteiner Fine Arts Trust
Imperial Holly Corp.
Independent Bankshares
Intercraft Co., Inc.
Iroquois Brands, Ltd.
JCPenney Co.
JMK-A M Micallef Charitable Foundation
Johnson Foundation, Burdine
Johnson Foundation, M. G. and Lillie A.
Jones Foundation, Helen
Jonsson Foundation
Justin Industries, Inc.
Kahn Dallas Symphony Foundation, Louise W. and Edmund J.
Kaneb Services, Inc.
Kayser Foundation
Keith Co., Ben E.
Keith Foundation Trust, Ben E.
Kellogg Co., M.W.
Kempner Fund, Harris and Eliza
Kenedy Memorial Foundation, John G. and Marie Stella
Keystone International
Killson Educational Foundation, Winifred and B. A.
Kilroy Foundation, William S. and Lora Jean
Kimberly-Clark Corp.
King Foundation, Carl B. and Florence E.
King Ranch
Kleberg Foundation for Wildlife Conservation, Caesar
Kleberg, Jr. and Helen C. Kleberg Foundation, Robert J.
Klein Fund, Nathan J.
Knox, Sr., and Pearl Wallis Knox Charitable Foundation, Robert W.
Koehler Foundation, Marcia and Otto
La Quinta Motor Inns
Lard Trust, Mary Potishman
LBJ Family Foundation
LDB Corp.
Lennox International, Inc.
Levit Family Foundation, Joe
Lewis Foundation, Lillian Kaiser
Lightner Sams Foundation
Lincoln Property Co.
Lindsay Student Aid Fund, Franklin
Lomas Financial Corp.
Lone Star Gas Co.
Los Trigos Fund
Lowe Foundation
LTV Corp.
Luby's Cafeterias
Luchsinger Family Foundation
Luse Foundation, W. P. and Bulah
Luttrell Trust
Lux Trust, Dr. Konrad and Clara
Lyondell Petrochemical Co.
Lyons Foundation
M/A/R/C Inc.
Maddox Trust, Web
Maguire Oil Co.
Mary Kay Cosmetics
Mary Kay Foundation
Maxus Energy Corp.
Mayborn Foundation, Frank W.
Mayer Foundation, James and Eva
Mayor Foundation, Oliver Dewey
McAshan Foundation
McCullough Foundation, Ralph H. and Ruth J.
McDermott Foundation, Eugene
McDonald Foundation, Tillie and Tom
McGovern Foundation, John P.
McGovern Fund for the Behavioral Sciences

McKee Foundation, Robert E. and Evelyn
McMillan, Jr. Foundation, Bruce
McNutt Charitable Trust, Amy Shelton
Meadows Foundation
Memorex Telex Corp.
Menil Foundation
Meredith Foundation
Mesa Inc.
Meyer Family Foundation, Paul J.
Meyer Foundation, Alice Kleberg Reynolds
Mid-Continent Supply Co.
Miller Brewing Company/Texas
Millhollon Educational Trust Estate, Nettie
Mitchell Energy & Development Corp.
Mobility Foundation
Moncrief Foundation, William A. and Elizabeth B.
Moody Foundation
Moores Foundation
MorningStar Foods
Morris Foundation
Morrison Trust, Louise L.
Moss Foundation, Harry S.
Moss Heart Trust, Harry S.
Munson Foundation, W. B.
Murfee Endowment, Kathryn
National Convenience Stores, Inc.
NationsBank Texas
Navarro County Educational Foundation
NCH Corp.
Neiman Marcus
Norman Foundation, Summers A.
Northen, Mary Moody
NorthPark National Bank
O'Connor Foundation, Kathryn
O'Donnell Foundation
Oldham Little Church Foundation
O'Quinn Foundation, John M. and Nancy C.
Orleans Trust, Carrie S.
Oshman's Sporting Goods, Inc.
Overlake Foundation
Owen Trust, B. B.
Owsley Foundation, Alvin and Lucy
Oxy Petrochemicals Inc.
Pangburn Foundation
Panhandle Eastern Corp.
Pay 'N Save Inc.
Pearle Vision
Pennzoil Co.
Perkins Foundation, Joe and Lois
Perkins-Prothro Foundation
Permian Corp.
Perot Foundation
Pier 1 Imports, Inc.
Pilgrim's Pride Corp.
Pineywoods Foundation
Pioneer Concrete of America Inc.
Piper Foundation, Minnie Stevens
Placid Oil Co.
Pogo Producing Co.
Pool Energy Services Co.
Potts and Sibley Foundation
Priddy Foundation
Pro-line Corp.
Puett Foundation, Nelson
Quanex Corp.
Rachal Foundation, Ed
Rainwater Charitable Foundation
Reading & Bates Corp.
Recognition Equipment
Redman Foundation
Redman Industries
Republic Financial Services, Inc.
Rexene Products Co.
RGK Foundation
Richardson Foundation, Sid W.

Rienzi Foundation
River Blindness Foundation
Riviana Foods
Roberts Foundation, Dora
Roberts Foundation, Summerfield G.
Robinson Foundation
Rockwell Fund
Rogers Foundation
Rowan Cos., Inc.
RSR Corp.
Sammons Enterprises
Sams Foundation, Earl C.
Sarofim Foundation
Scaler Foundation
Scott Foundation, William E.
Scurlock Foundation
Seay Charitable Trust, Sarah M. and Charles E.
Security Capital Corp.
Sedco Inc.
Seibel Foundation, Abe and Annie
Semmes Foundation
Service Corp. International
Seymour Foundation, W. L. and Louise E.
SGS-Thomson Microelectronics Inc.
Sharp Foundation, Charles S. and Ruth C.
Shell Oil Co.
Six Flags Theme Parks Inc.
Skaggs Alpha Beta Co.
Sky Chefs, Inc.
Smith and W. Aubrey Smith Charitable Foundation, Clara Blackford
Smith Foundation, Bob and Vivian
Smith Foundation, Julia and Albert
Smith International
Snyder General Corp.
Sonat Exploration
Sonat Offshore Drilling
South Plains Foundation
South Texas Charitable Foundation
Southdown, Inc.
Southland Corp.
Southmark Corp.
Southwest Airlines Co.
Southwestern Life Insurance Co.
Southwestern Public Service Co.
Star Enterprise
Stark Foundation, Nelda C. and H. J. Lutcher
Starling Foundation, Dorothy Richard
Steinhagen Benevolent Trust, B. A. and Elinor
Stemmons Foundation
Sterling Chemicals Inc.
Sterling Software Inc.
Stewart & Stevenson Services
Stieren Foundation, Arthur T. and Jane J.
Stonestreet Trust, Eusebia S.
Strake Foundation
Summerlee Foundation
Sumners Foundation, Hatton W.
Swalm Foundation
Sysco Corp.
Tandy Corp.
Tandy Foundation, Anne Burnett and Charles
Tandy Foundation, David L.
Tartt Scholarship Fund, Hope Pierce
Taub Foundation
Tauber Oil Co.
Team Banchares Inc.
Team Bank Houston
Technical Foundation of America
Telecom Corp.
Temple Foundation, T. L. L.
Temple-Inland

Texas (cont.)

Tenneco
Terry Foundation
Tesoro Petroleum Corp.
Texas Commerce Bank Houston, N.A.
Texas Energy Museum
Texas Industries, Inc.
Texas Instruments
Texas-New Mexico Power Co.
Texas Olefins Co.
Tigon Corp.
Tobin Foundation
Tracor, Inc.
Transco Energy Company
Trinity Industries, Inc.
Trull Foundation
TU Electric Co.
Turner Charitable Foundation
Tyler Corp.
Union Texas Petroleum
United Gas Pipe Line Co.
United Savings Association of Texas
United Services Automobile Association
Unocal-Union Oil of California
Vale-Asche Foundation
Valero Energy Corp.
Vaughan Foundation, Rachael and Ben
Vaughn Foundation
Vaughn, Jr. Foundation Fund, James M.
Veritas Foundation
Vista Chemical Company
Waggoner Charitable Trust, Crystelle
Waggoner Foundation, E. Paul and Helen Buck
Walsh Foundation
Walthall Perpetual Charitable Trust, Marjorie T.
Ward Co., Joe L.
Ward Heritage Foundation, Mamie McFaddin
Weatherford International, Inc.
Weaver Foundation, Gil and Dody
Weiner Foundation
Weiner's Stores
Welch Foundation, Robert A.
West Foundation
West Foundation, Neva and Wesley
West Texas Corp., J. M.
West Texas Utilities Co.
White Foundation, Erle and Emma
White Trust, G. R.
Willard Helping Fund, Cecilia Young
Wills Foundation
Wilson Foundation, John and Nevils
Wilson Public Trust, Ralph
Wise Foundation and Charitable Trust, Watson W.
Wolens Foundation, Kalman and Ida
Wolff Memorial Foundation, Pauline Sterne
Woltman Foundation, B. M.
Wortham Foundation
Worthing Scholarship Fund
Wright Foundation, Lola
Zachry Co., H. B.
Zachry Co., H.B.
Zale Corp.
Zale Foundation
Zale Foundation, William and Sylvia
Zapata Corp.

Utah

Amalgamated Sugar Co.
American Stores Co.
Bamberger and John Ernest Bamberger Memorial Foundation, Ruth Eleanor
Browning
Browning Charitable Foundation, Val A.
Caine Charitable Foundation, Marie Eccles
Callister Foundation, Paul Q.
Dee Foundation, Annie Taylor
Dee Foundation, Lawrence T. and Janet T.
Dumke Foundation, Dr. Ezekiel R. and Edna Wattis
Eccles Charitable Foundation, Willard L.
Eccles Foundation, George S. and Dolores Dore
Eccles Foundation, Marriner S.
First Security Bank of Utah N.A.
First Security Corp. (Salt Lake City, Utah)
Harris Foundation, William H. and Mattie Wattis
Huntsman Foundation, Jon and Karen
Icon Systems & Software
Kennecott Corp.
Longyear Co.
Margolis Charitable Foundation for Medical Research, Ben B. and Iris M.
Michael Foundation, Herbert I. and Elsa B.
Mrs. Fields, Inc.
Northwest Pipeline Corp.
Novell Inc.
Producers Livestock Marketing Association
Questar Corp.
Shaw Charitable Trust, Mary Elizabeth Dee
Smith Food & Drug
Steiner Corp.
Stewart Educational Foundation, Donnell B. and Elizabeth Dee Shaw
Swanson Family Foundation, Dr. W.C.
Swim Foundation, Arthur L.
Utah Power & Light Co.
Zions Bancorp.

Vermont

Ben & Jerry's Homemade
Central Vermont Public Service Corp.
Cherry Hill Cooperative Cannery
Cone-Blanchard Machine Co.
General Educational Fund
Lintilhac Foundation
Merchants Bancshares
National Life of Vermont
Proctor Trust, Mortimer R.
Scott Foundation, Walter
Scott Fund, Olin
Seventh Generation
Union Mutual Fire Insurance Co.

Virginia

Aid Association for the Blind
Airbus Industrie of America
American Filtrona Corp.
Applied Energy Services
Banner Industries, Inc.
Bassett Furniture Industries, Inc.
Batten Foundation
BDM International
Beazley Foundation
Best Products Co.
Bionetics Corp.
Blount Educational Foundation, David S.
Booz Allen & Hamilton
Bristol Steel & Iron Works
British Aerospace Inc.
Bryant Foundation
Burroughs Educational Fund, N. R.
Bustard Charitable Permanent Trust Fund, Elizabeth and James
Cabell III and Maude Morgan Cabell Foundation, Robert G.
Cable & Wireless Communications
Camp Foundation
Campbell Foundation, Ruth and Henry
Carter Foundation, Beirne
Central Fidelity Banks, Inc.
Chesapeake Corp.
Circuit City Stores
Cole Trust, Quincy
Contel Federal Systems
Cooper Wood Products
Crestar Financial Corp.
CSX Corp.
Dan River, Inc.
Dibrell Brothers, Inc.
Durell Foundation, George Edward
DynCorp
Easley Trust, Andrew H. and Anne O.
English Foundation, W. C.
Estes Foundation
Ethyl Corp.
Fairchild Corp.
Farm Fresh Inc. (Norfolk, Virginia)
Federal Home Loan Mortgage Corp. (Freddie Mac)
First Virginia Banks
Fitz-Gibbon Charitable Trust
Flagler Foundation
Fleet Co., Inc., C.B.
Frederick Foundation
Freedom Forum
Funderburke & Associates
Gannett Co.
General Dynamics Corp.
Goodman & Company
Gottwald Foundation
Graphic Arts Show Co. Inc.
Gray Foundation, Garland
Hampton Casting Division
Harrison and Conrad Memorial Trust
Hastings Trust
Hecht's
Heilig-Meyers Co.
Henkel-Harris Co., Inc.
Herndon Foundation
Higher Education Publications
Home Beneficial Corp.
Hopeman Brothers
Hopkins Foundation, John Jay
Houff Transfer, Inc.
Hunter Trust, Emily S. and Coleman A.
Ivakota Association
James River Coal Co.
James River Corp. of Virginia
Jeffress Memorial Trust, Elizabeth G.
Jeffress Memorial Trust, Thomas F. and Kate Miller
Jones Foundation, W. Alton
Kaul Foundation
Kentland Foundation
Kloeckner-Pentaplast of America
Lacy Foundation
Lafarge Corp.
Landmark Communications
Lane Co., Inc.
Lane Foundation, Minnie and Bernard
Lawrence Foundation, Lind
Lawyers Title Foundation
Lincoln-Lane Foundation
Luck Stone
Mars, Inc.
Mars Foundation
Massey Foundation
McCrea Foundation
McDougall Charitable Trust, Ruth Camp
McMahon Charitable Trust Fund, Father John J.
Media General, Inc.
Memorial Foundation for Children
Metropolitan Health Foundation
Mobil Oil Corp.
Mohasco Corp.
Morgan and Samuel Tate Morgan, Jr. Foundation, Marietta McNeil
Newport News Shipbuilding & Dry Dock Co.
Noland Co.
Norfolk Shipbuilding & Drydock Corp.
Norfolk Southern Corp.
North Shore Foundation
Northern Virginia Natural Gas
Ohrstrom Foundation
Old Dominion Box Co.
Olmsted Foundation, George and Carol
Olsson Memorial Foundation, Elis
Omega World Travel
O'Sullivan Corp.
Overnite Transportation Co.
Owens & Minor, Inc.
Pannill Scholarship Foundation, William Letcher
PemCo. Corp.
Pendleton Construction Corp.
Petroleum Marketers
Planning Research Corp.
Portsmouth General Hospital Foundation
Primark Corp.
Rangeley Educational Trust
Reynolds Foundation, Richard S.
Reynolds Metals Co.
Richardson Benevolent Foundation, C. E.
Richfood Holdings
Richmond Newspapers
Robertshaw Controls Co.
Rolls-Royce Inc.
Royston Manufacturing Corp.
Scott Foundation, William R., John G., and Emma
Seay Memorial Trust, George and Effie
Shenandoah Life Insurance Co.
Smith Family Foundation, Charles E.
Tarmac America Inc.
Taylor Foundation
Thalhimer and Family Foundation, Charles G.
Thalhimer Brothers Inc.
Thalhimer, Jr. and Family Foundation, William B.
Thomas Memorial Foundation, Theresa A.
Thurman Charitable Foundation for Children, Edgar A.
Tilghman, Sr., Charitable Trust, Bell and Horace
Titmus Foundation
Treakle Foundation, J. Edwin
Tredegar Industries
Truland Foundation
Truland Systems Corp.
Tultex Corp.
Ukrop's Super Markets, Inc.
United Co.
Universal Leaf Tobacco Co.
Uslico Corp.
Virginia Power Co.
Wareheim Foundation, E. C.
Washington Forrest Foundation
Wheat First Securites
Winkler Foundation, Mark and Catherine

Washington

Airborne Express Co.
Alaska Airlines, Inc.
Aldus Corp.
Allen Foundation for Medical Research, Paul G.
ALPAC Corp.
Anderson Foundation
Archibald Charitable Foundation, Norman
Arise Charitable Trust
Bartell Drug Co.
Bishop Foundation
Bishop Foundation, E. K. and Lillian F.
Bloedel Foundation
Boeing Co.
Bullitt Foundation
Burlington Resources
Cascade Natural Gas Corp.
Cawsey Trust
Cheney Foundation, Ben B.
Cominco American Inc.
Comstock Foundation
Cook Foundation, Louella
Cowles Foundation, Harriet Cheney
Cowles Foundation, William H.
Dudley Foundation
Dupar Foundation
Eldec Corp.
Esterline Technologies Corp.
Fales Foundation Trust
Federated American Insurance
Forest Foundation
Foster Foundation
Fuchs Foundation, Gottfried & Mary
Geneva Foundation
Glaser Foundation
Guse Endowment Trust, Frank J. and Adelaide
Haas Foundation, Saul and Dayee G.
Harder Foundation
Hemingway Foundation, Robert G.
Horizons Foundation
Johnston-Fix Foundation
Johnston-Hanson Foundation
Kawabe Memorial Fund
Kilworth Charitable Foundation, Florence B.
Kilworth Charitable Trust, William
Klingensmith Charitable Foundation, Agnes
Kreielsheimer Foundation Trust
La Croix Water Co.
Lamb-Weston Inc.
Lassen Foundation, Irving A.
Leuthold Foundation
LIN Broadcasting Corp.
Lockwood Foundation, Byron W. and Alice L.
Longview Fibre Co.
Lozier Foundation
Mayne Nickless
McCaw Cellular Communications
McCaw Foundation
McEachern Charitable Trust, D. V. & Ida J.
Medina Foundation
Merrill Foundation, R. D.
Microsoft Corp.
Murdock Charitable Trust, M. J.
Murray Foundation
Nesholm Family Foundation
New Horizon Foundation
Norcliffe Fund
Nordstrom, Inc.
Odessa Trading Co.
Olympia Brewing Co.
PACCAR
Pacific Coca-Cola Bottling Co.
Pegasus Gold Corp.

Petrie Trust, Lorene M.
PGL Building Products
Pickering Industries
Poncin Scholarship Fund
Puget Sound National Bank
Puget Sound Power & Light Co.
Quest for Truth Foundation
Ray Foundation
REI-Recreational Equipment,
Inc.
SAFECO Corp.
Seafirst Corp.
Seattle Times Co.
See Foundation, Charles
Sequoia Foundation
Shemanski Testamentary Trust,
Tillie and Alfred
Sigourney Award Trust, Mary S.
Simpson Investment Co.
Skinner Corp.
Snyder Foundation, Frost and
Margaret
Stewardship Foundation
Stubblefield, Estate of Joseph L.
T & T United Truck Lines
Tamaki Foundation
Thurston Charitable Foundation
Unigard Security Insurance Co.
U.S. Bank of Washington
Univar Corp.
Washington Mutual Savings
Bank
Washington Natural Gas Co.
Washington Trust Bank
Washington Water Power Co.
Wasmer Foundation
Welch Testamentary Trust,
George T.
Wells Foundation, A. Z.
Weyerhaeuser Co.
Wharton Foundation
Wyman Youth Trust

West Virginia

Board of Trustees of the Prichard
School
Bowen Foundation, Ethel N.
Brown Family Foundation, John
Mathew Gay
Carbon Fuel Co.
Carter Family Foundation
Chambers Memorial, James B.
Chesapeake & Potomac
Telephone Co. of West Virginia
Clay Foundation
CNG Transmission Corp.
Daywood Foundation
East Foundation, Sarita Kenedy
Fenton Foundation
First Fidelity Bancorp, Inc.

Hunnicutt Foundation, H. P. and
Anne S.
Inco Alloys International
Jacobson Foundation, Bernard
H. and Blanche E.
Kennedy Memorial Fund, Mark
H.
Laughlin Trust, George A.
Maier Foundation, Sarah Pauline
McDonough Foundation, Bernard
One Valley Bank, N.A.
Price Educational Foundation,
Herschel C.
Ravenswood Aluminum Corp.
Santa Maria Foundation
Schoenbaum Family Foundation
Shott, Jr. Foundation, Hugh I.
Teubert Charitable Trust, James
H. and Alice
U.S. Silica Co.
Weirton Steel Corp.

Wisconsin

Alexander Charitable Foundation
Alexander Foundation, Judd S.
Alexander Foundation, Walter
Andres Charitable Trust, Frank
G.
Appleton Papers
Applied Power, Inc.
Autotrol Corp.
Badger Meter, Inc.
Baird & Co., Robert W.
Banc One Wisconsin Corp.
Banta Corp.
Bassett Foundation, Norman
Bergner Co., P.A.
Birnschein Foundation, Alvin
and Marion
Blue Cross and Blue Shield
United of Wisconsin
Foundation
Bolz Family Foundation,
Eugenie Mayer
Bradley Foundation, Lynde and
Harry
Brady Foundation, W. H.
Brillion Iron Works
Brotz Family Foundation, Frank
G.
Bucyrus-Erie
Case Co., J.I.
Charter Manufacturing Co.
Christensen Charitable and
Religious Foundation, L. C.
Church Mutual Insurance
Clark Family Foundation, Emory
T.
Cleary Foundation
Consolidated Papers

Cornerstone Foundation of
Northeastern Wisconsin
Cremer Foundation
Cudahy Fund, Patrick and Anna
M.
CUNA Mutual Insurance Group
DEC International, Inc.
Demmer Foundation, Edward U.
Earth Care Paper, Inc.
Employers Insurance of Wausau,
A Mutual Co.
Endries Fastener & Supply Co.
Evinrude Foundation, Ralph
Evjue Foundation
First Financial Bank FSB
Firstar Bank Milwaukee NA
Firstar Corp.
Formrite Tube Co.
Fromm Scholarship Trust, Walter
and Mabel
Giddings & Lewis
Godfrey Co.
Goldbach Foundation, Ray and
Marie
Grede Foundries
Greene Manufacturing Co.
Greenheck Fan Corp.
Harley-Davidson, Inc.
Harnischfeger Foundation
Heileman Brewing Co., Inc., G.
Hein-Werner Corp.
Helfaer Foundation, Evan and
Marion
Humphrey Foundation, Glenn &
Gertrude
Janesville Foundation
Jeffris Family Foundation
Jockey International
Johnson Controls
Johnson Foundation
Johnson & Son, S.C.
Journal Communications
Kikkoman Foods, Inc.
Kimball Co., Miles
Klingler Foundation, Helen and
Charles
Kohl Charities, Herbert H.
Kohler Co.
Kohler Foundation
Krause Foundation, Charles A.
Kress Foundation, George
Ladish Co.
Ladish Family Foundation,
Herman W.
Ladish Malting Co.
Lappin Electric Co.
Lindsay Foundation
Madison Gas & Electric Co.
Manitowoc Co.
Manpower, Inc.
Marathon Cheese Corp.

Marcus Corp.
Marinette Marine Corp.
Marquette Electronics
Marshall & Ilsley Bank
Mautz Paint Co.
Mayer Foods Corp., Oscar
Maynard Steel Casting Co.
McBeath Foundation, Faye
Medalist Industries, Inc.
Menasha Corp.
MGIC Investment Corp.
Mielke Family Foundation
Miller Brewing Co.
Miller Foundation, Steve J.
Monaghan Charitable Trust, Rose
Mosinee Paper Corp.
National Presto Industries
Neenah Foundry Co.
Nelson Industries, Inc.
Northern Engraving Corp.
Northwestern National Insurance
Group
Oshkosh B'Gosh
Oshkosh Truck Corp.
Park Bank
Parker Pen USA Ltd.
Peters Foundation, R. D. and
Linda
Peterson Builders
Peterson Foundation, Fred J.
Pfister and Vogel Tanning Co.
Phillips Family Foundation, L. E.
Phipps Foundation, William H.
Pick Charitable Trust, Melitta S.
Pieper Electric
Plastics Engineering Co.
Pollybill Foundation
Prange Co., H. C.
Pukall Lumber
Rahr Malting Co.
Rayovac Corp.
Reinhart Institutional Foods
Reiss Coal Co., C.
Rennebohm Foundation, Oscar
Rite-Hite Corp.
Roddis Foundation, Hamilton
Roehl Foundation
Rolfs Foundation, Robert T.
Rolfs Foundation, Thomas J.
Ross Memorial Foundation, Will
Roundy's Inc.
Rubenstein Foundation, Philip
Rutledge Charity, Edward
Schlegel Foundation, Oscar C.
and Augusta
Schoenleber Foundation
Schreiber Foods, Inc.
Schroeder Foundation, Walter
Sentry Insurance Co.
Shattuck Charitable Trust, S. F.
Siebert Lutheran Foundation

Smith Corp., A.O.
Smith Family Foundation, Theda
Clark
Snap-on Tools Corp.
SNC Manufacturing Co.
Stackner Family Foundation
Steinhauer Charitable Foundation
Stry Foundation, Paul E.
Surgical Science Foundation for
Research and Development
Time Insurance Co.
U.S. Oil/Schmidt Family
Foundation, Inc.
Universal Foods Corp.
Vilter Manufacturing Corp.
Vollrath Co.
Wagner Foundation, Ltd., R. H.
Wagner Manufacturing Co., E. R.
Walter Family Trust, Byron L.
Wausau Insurance Cos.
Wausau Paper Mills Co.
Wauwatosa Savings & Loan
Association
Wehr Foundation, Todd
Western Publishing Co., Inc.
WICOR, Inc.
Wigwam Mills
Wisconsin Bell, Inc.
Wisconsin Centrifugal
Wisconsin Energy Corp.
Wisconsin Power & Light Co.
Wisconsin Public Service Corp.
Wood Foundation, Lester G.
Woodson Foundation,
Aytchmonde
Young Foundation, Irvin L.
Ziegler Foundation
Ziemann Foundation

Wyoming

Bryan Foundation, Dodd and
Dorothy L.
Goodstein Foundation
Kamps Memorial Foundation,
Gertrude
Perkins Foundation, B. F. &
Rose H.
Sargent Foundation, Newell B.
Stock Foundation, Paul
Storer Foundation, George B.
Surrena Memorial Fund, Harry
and Thelma
Tonkin Foundation, Tom and
Helen
True Oil Co.
Ucross Foundation
Weiss Foundation, William E.
Whitney Benefits

International

Canada

Nicol Scholarship Foundation,

Helen Kavanagh

England

Smith Horticultural Trust, Stanley

Lebanon

Hariri Foundation

Index to Corporations and Foundations by Operating Location

Arizona (cont.)

Manufacturers Life Insurance
  Co. of America
Manville Corp.
Marshall Foundation
Marshall Fund
Marshall & Ilsley Bank
Masco Corp.
McDonnell Douglas Corp.
McDonnell Douglas Corp.-West
McGraw-Hill
McKesson Corp.
Mead Corp.
Medtronic
Meredith Corp.
Morris Foundation, Margaret T.
Morrison-Knudsen Corp.
Motorola
Mulcahy Foundation
National Medical Enterprises
New England Business Service
Newmont Mining Corp.
Northern Trust Co.
Norwest Corp.
Nucor Corp.
PacifiCorp
Parker-Hannifin Corp.
Peck Foundation, Milton and
  Lillian
Pendleton Memorial Fund,
  William L. and Ruth T.
Perini Corp.
Phelps Dodge Corp.
Phillips Petroleum Co.
Pioneer Hi-Bred International
Procter & Gamble Co.
Prudential Insurance Co. of
  America
Pulitzer Publishing Co.
Raymond Educational
  Foundation
REI-Recreational Equipment,
  Inc.
Research Corporation
Ringier-America
Robson Foundation, LaNelle
Santa Fe Pacific Corp.
Sara Lee Corp.
Scripps Co., E.W.
Sealy, Inc.
Sky Chefs, Inc.
Smitty's Super Valu, Inc.
Solheim Foundation
State Farm Mutual Automobile
  Insurance Co.
Steele Foundation
Stone Container Corp.
Sundstrand Corp.
Talley Industries, Inc.
Tandem Computers
Target Stores
Tell Foundation
3M Co.
Tomkins Industries, Inc.
Travelers Cos.
TRW Corp.
Tucson Electric Power Co.
Tucson Osteopathic Medical
  Foundation
UDC-Universal Development LP
US WEST
Valley National Bank of Arizona
Van Schaick Scholarship Fund,
  Nellie
Varian Associates
Volkswagen of America, Inc.
Wal-Mart Stores
Walgreen Co.
Washington Post Co.
Webb Foundation, Del E.
Westinghouse Electric Corp.
Whiteman Foundation, Edna
  Rider
Wynn's International, Inc.

Arkansas

AEGON USA, Inc.
Air Products & Chemicals
ALLTEL Corp.
Alumax
AMAX
Amcast Industrial Corp.
Ameron, Inc.
Archer-Daniels-Midland Co.
Arkansas Best Corp.
Arkansas Power & Light Co.
Arkla
Avnet, Inc.
Ball Corp.
Baxter International
Bemis Company
Boatmen's Bancshares
Bodenhamer Foundation
Boise Cascade Corp.
Borg-Warner Corp.
Bridgestone/Firestone
Browning-Ferris Industries
Brunswick Corp.
Campbell Soup Co.
Carrier Corp.
Ceco Corp.
Charter Medical Corp.
Climatic Corp.
Coastal Corp.
Cohn Co., M.M.
Coltec Industries
Commercial Metals Co.
ConAgra
Cooper Industries
Cooper Tire & Rubber Co.
Corke Educational Trust, Hubert
  and Alice
CPC International
CTS Corp.
Dillard Department Stores, Inc.
Dollar General Corp.
Douglas & Lomason Company
Dow Chemical Co.
du Pont de Nemours & Co., E. I.
Ethyl Corp.
Fairfield Communities, Inc.
First Commercial Bank N.A.
FMC Corp.
Foxmeyer Corp.
GenCorp
Georgia-Pacific Corp.
Gerber Products Co.
Hospital Corp. of America
Hudson Foods
Humana
Hunt Transport Services, J.B.
Illinois Tool Works
Inland Container Corp.
Inland Steel Industries
International Paper Co.
ITT Corp.
ITT Rayonier
James River Corp. of Virginia
Jefferson Smurfit Corp.
Johnson Controls
Jones Charitable Trust, Harvey
  and Bernice
Jones Foundation, Harvey and
  Bernice
Kimberly-Clark Corp.
La-Z-Boy Chair Co.
Levi Strauss & Co.
Liberty Corp.
LTV Corp.
Manville Corp.
Mark IV Industries
Mass Merchandisers, Inc.
McKesson Corp.
Mead Corp.
Murphy Foundation
Murphy Oil Corp.
National Medical Enterprises
New York Times Co.
Newmont Mining Corp.
Oklahoma Gas & Electric Co.
Olin Corp.

Oneida Ltd.
Orbit Valve Co.
Paxton Co., Frank
Pioneer Hi-Bred International
Pirelli Armstrong Tire Corp.
Potlatch Corp.
Prudential Insurance Co. of
  America
Quanex Corp.
Rebsamen Companies, Inc.
Reliable Life Insurance Co.
Reynolds Foundation, Donald W.
Riceland Foods, Inc.
Riggs Benevolent Fund
Ringier-America
Rockefeller Foundation,
  Winthrop
Rockefeller Trust, Winthrop
Rohr Inc.
Ross Foundation
Rouse Co.
Sanyo Manufacturing Corp.
Sara Lee Corp.
Schering-Plough Corp.
Scott Paper Co.
Sealy, Inc.
Sequa Corp.
Smith Corp., A.O.
Southwestern Bell Corp.
Stone Container Corp.
Sturgis Charitable and
  Educational Trust, Roy and
  Christine
Tandem Computers
Target Stores
Temple-Inland
3M Co.
Torchmark Corp.
Tracor, Inc.
Travelers Cos.
Trinity Foundation
TRINOVA Corp.
Tyson Foods, Inc.
Union Camp Corp.
Union Pacific Corp.
Wal-Mart Stores
Wal-Mart Stores, Inc.
Walton Family Foundation
Weyerhaeuser Co.
Whirlpool Corp.
White Consolidated Industries
Wolverine World Wide, Inc.
Wrape Family Charitable Trust

California

Abbott Laboratories
Ace Beverage Co.
Acme-Cleveland Corp.
Advanced Micro Devices
AEGON USA, Inc.
Aequus Institute
Aerojet
Aerospace Corp.
Affiliated Publications, Inc.
Agway
Ahmanson & Co., H.F.
Ahmanson Foundation
Air France
Air Products & Chemicals
Akzo America
Albertson's
Alcan Aluminum Corp.
Alco Standard Corp.
Alexander & Baldwin, Inc.
Alfa-Laval, Inc.
Alhambra Foundry Co., Ltd.
Allen Charitable Trust, Phil N.
Allergan, Inc.
Alliant Techsystems
AlliedSignal
Alltel/Western Region
Alpert Foundation, Herb
Alpha Beta Stores, Inc.
Alumax
Aluminum Co. of America
Amado Foundation, Maurice

AMAX
Amcast Industrial Corp.
Amdahl Corp.
America West Airlines
American Building Maintenance
  Industries
American Cyanamid Co.
American Electronics
American Express Co.
American Financial Corp.
American Foundation
American Honda Motor Co.
American International Group,
  Inc.
American Microsystems, Inc.
American President Cos.
American Stores Co.
American Suzuki Motor Corp.
American Telephone &
  Telegraph Co.
American Telephone &
  Telegraph Co./Los Angeles
  Region
American Telephone &
  Telegraph Co./San Francisco
  Region
Amerigas
Ameron, Inc.
AMETEK
Amgen, Inc.
AMR Corp.
Amstar Corp.
Amway Corp.
Analog Devices
Angeles Corp.
Angelica Corp.
Anheuser-Busch Cos.
AON Corp.
Apple Computer, Inc.
ARA Services
Arata Brothers Trust
Aratex Services
Arcata Corp.
Arcata Graphics Co.
ARCO
Arden Group, Inc.
Argonaut Group
Argyros Foundation
Arkelian Foundation, Ben H. and
  Gladys
Armor All Products Corp.
Armstrong World Industries Inc.
Arrillaga Foundation
Arrow Electronics, Inc.
Artevel Foundation
Arvin Industries
Asea Brown Boveri
Associated Foundations
AST Research, Inc.
Atari Corp.
Atkinson Co., Guy F.
Atkinson Foundation
Atkinson Foundation, Myrtle L.
Aura Cacia
Autodesk, Inc.
Automatic Data Processing, Inc.
Autry Foundation
Avery Dennison Corp.
Avery-Fuller Children's Center
Avis Inc.
Avnet, Inc.
Avon Products
AXIA Incorporated
B.H.P. Minerals
Babcock Memorial Endowment,
  William
Backer Spielvogel Bates U.S.
Bairnco Corp.
Baker Commodities
Baker Foundation, R. C.
Baker Foundation, Solomon R.
  and Rebecca D.
Baker Hughes Inc.
Baker International Corp.
Ball Corp.
Banca Commerciale Italiana,
  New York Branch

Bancal Tri-State Corp.
Bancroft-Whitney Co.
Bandag, Inc.
Bank Hapoalim B.M.
Bank Leumi Trust Co. of New
  York
Bank of A. Levy
Bank of America
Bank of America - Giannini
  Foundation
Bank of Boston Corp.
Bank of New York
Bank of San Francisco Co.
Bank of the Orient
BankAmerica Corp.
Bankers Life & Casualty Co.
Bankers Trust Co.
Bannan Foundation, Arline and
  Thomas J.
Bannerman Foundation, William
  C.
Banque Francaise du Commerce
  Exterieur
Banta Corp.
Banyan Tree Foundation
Barbara's Bakery
Barker Foundation, Donald R.
Barnes Group
Baskin-Robbins USA CO.
Baxter Foundation, Donald E.
  and Delia B.
Baxter International
Bayview Federal Bank
Beaver Foundation
Bechtel Group
Bechtel, Jr. Foundation, S. D.
Beckman Foundation, Arnold
  and Mabel
Beckman Instruments
Becton Dickinson & Co.
Bekins Co.
Bekins Foundation, Milo W.
Bel Air Mart
Bell Industries
Bellini Foundation
Belo Corp., A.H.
Bemis Company
Benbough Foundation, Legler
Bergen Brunswig Corp.
Berger Foundation, H.N. and
  Frances C.
Berger Trust II, H. N. and
  Frances C.
Bergstrom Foundation, Erik E.
  and Edith H.
Berkey Foundation, Peter
Berry Foundation, Lowell
Best Products Co.
Bettingen Corporation, Burton G.
Betz Laboratories
Beynon Foundation, Kathryne
BFGoodrich
BHP Utah International
Big Three Industries
Bing Fund
Bird Inc.
Bireley Foundation
Black & Decker Corp.
Blackman Foundation, Aaron
  and Marie
Bloomfield Foundation, Sam and
  Rie
Blount
Blue Diamond Growers
BMW of North America, Inc.
BOC Group
Boeckmann Charitable
  Foundation
Boise Cascade Corp.
Booth Foundation, Otis
Borchard Foundation, Albert and
  Elaine
Borden
Borg-Warner Corp.
Borun Foundation, Anna Borun
  and Harry
Bosack and Bette M. Kruger
  Foundation, Leonard X.

Boswell Foundation, James G.
Bothin Foundation
Bourns, Inc.
Bowles and Robert Bowles Memorial Fund, Ethel Wilson
Bradford Foundation, George and Ruth
Braun Foundation
Bren Foundation, Donald L.
Brenner Foundation, Mervyn
Bright Family Foundation
Broad, Inc.
Broccoli Charitable Foundation, Dana and Albert R.
Brotman Foundation of California
Brown & Sons, Alex
Browning-Ferris Industries
Brunetti Charitable Trust, Dionigi
Brunswick Corp.
Brush Wellman Inc.
Buchalter, Nemer, Fields, & Younger
Bucyrus-Erie
Bull Foundation, Henry W.
Bumble Bee Seafoods Inc.
Burlington Air Express Inc.
Burnand Medical and Educational Foundation, Alphonse A.
Burnham Foundation
Burns Family Foundation
Burns Foundation
Burns Foundation, Fritz B.
Cadbury Beverages Inc.
Caddock Foundation
Cadence Design Systems
Caesar's World, Inc.
Cahill Foundation, John R.
CalComp, Inc.
Calex Manufacturing Co.
CalFed Inc.
California Educational Initiatives Fund
California Foundation for Biochemical Research
California & Hawaiian Sugar Co.
CalMat Co.
Campbell Soup Co.
Capital Cities/ABC
Capital Fund Foundation
Capital Group
Capital Holding Corp.
Care Enterprises
Carpenter Technology Corp.
Carrier Corp.
Carter-Wallace
Castle & Co., A.M.
Castle & Cooke
Castle Industries
Catalina Co.
Caterpillar
CBS Inc.
Ceco Corp.
Cedars-Sinai Medical Center Section D Fund
Chais Family Foundation
Charter Medical Corp.
Chartwell Foundation
Chase Manhattan Bank, N.A.
Chesebrough-Pond's
Chevron Corp.
Chicago Title and Trust Co.
Chiron Corp.
Christie Electric Corp.
Chrysler Corp.
Chubb Corp.
CIBA-GEIGY Corp.
CIGNA Corp.
Cincinnati Milacron
Circuit City Stores
Citibank, F.S.B.
Citicorp
City National Bank
City of Hope 1989 Section E Foundation
Civitas Fund

Clopay Corp.
Clorox Co.
Clougherty Charitable Trust, Francis H.
Coast Federal Bank
Colburn Collection
Colburn Fund
Coltec Industries
Columbia Foundation
Columbia Savings Charitable Foundation
Columbia Savings & Loan Association
Comerica
Commerce Clearing House
Commercial Intertech Corp.
Commerzbank AG, New York
Community Psychiatric Centers
Comprecare Foundation
Compton Foundation
Computer Associates International
Computer Sciences Corp.
ConAgra
Confidence Foundation
Connell Foundation, Michael J.
Conner Peripherals
Consolidated Electrical Distributors
Consolidated Freightways
Continental Airlines
Continental Corp.
Contraves USA
Control Data Corp.
Cook Brothers Educational Fund
Cook Family Trust
Cooper Industries
Copley Press
Cornnuts, Inc.
Courtaulds Fibers Inc.
Cow Hollow Foundation
Cowell Foundation, S. H.
Cox Enterprises
CPC International
Crail-Johnson Foundation
Cramer Foundation
Crane & Co.
Crane Co.
Crean Foundation
Credit Agricole
Credit Suisse
Crocker Trust, Mary A.
Crum and Forster
Crummer Foundation, Roy E.
CTS Corp.
Cubic Corp.
CUNA Mutual Insurance Group
Curtin-Palohermo Charitable Remainder Trust
Dai-Ichi Kangyo Bank of California
Daily News
Dalgety Inc.
Daly Charitable Foundation Trust, Robert and Nancy
Darling Foundation, Hugh and Hazel
Dataproducts Corp.
Davies Charitable Trust
Day Foundation, Willametta K.
Dayton Hudson Corp.
de Dampierre Memorial Foundation, Marie C.
Del Monte Foods
Delta Air Lines
Deluxe Corp.
Deutsch Co.
Deutsche Bank AG
Dexter Corp.
DFS Group Limited
DHL Airways Inc.
Diamond Walnut Growers
Diasonics, Inc.
Diener Foundation, Frank C.
Digital Equipment Corp.
Digital Sciences Corp.

DiRosa Foundation, Rene and Veronica
Disney Family Foundation, Roy
Dixie Yarns, Inc.
Doelger Charitable Trust, Thelma
Doheny Foundation, Carrie Estelle
Dole Food Company, Inc.
Dole Fresh Vegetables
Domino of California
Donaldson, Lufkin & Jenrette
Donnelley & Sons Co., R.R.
Douglas Charitable Foundation
Dover Corp.
Dow Chemical Co.
Dow Jones & Co.
Downey Savings & Loan Association
Downing Foundation, J. C.
Dresser Industries
Dreyer's & Edy's Grand Ice Cream
Drown Foundation, Joseph
Drum Foundation
du Pont de Nemours & Co., E. I.
Ducommun Inc.
Dun & Bradstreet Corp.
Dunning Foundation
Durfee Foundation
Early Medical Research Trust, Margaret E.
Easton Aluminum
Eaton Corp.
Eaton Foundation, Edwin M. and Gertrude S.
Ebell of Los Angeles Rest Cottage Association
Ebell of Los Angeles Scholarship Endowment Fund
Echlin Inc.
EG&G Inc.
Eisenberg Foundation, Ben B. and Joyce E.
Elf Atochem North America
Elixir Industries
Emerson Electric Co.
Emery Worldwide
EMI Records Group
Environment Now
Equitable Life Assurance Society of the U.S.
Ernest & Julio Gallo Winery
Erteszek Foundation
Essick Foundation
Everest & Jennings International
Exchange Bank
Factor Family Foundation, Max
Fairchild Corp.
Fairfield Foundation, Freeman E.
Falk Foundation, Elizabeth M.
Famous Amos Chocolate Chip Cookie Co.
Fantastic Foods
Far West Financial Corp.
Farallon Foundation
Farmers Group, Inc.
Fedco, Inc.
Federal National Mortgage Assn., Fannie Mae
Feintech Foundation
Fellner Memorial Foundation, Leopold and Clara M.
Femino Foundation
Fiat U.S.A., Inc.
Fidelity Federal Savings & Loan
Financial Corp. of Santa Barbara
Fireman's Fund Insurance Co.
First American Financial Corp.
First Fruit
First Interstate Bank of California
First Mississippi Corp.
FKI Holdings Inc.
Fleet Bank
Fleet Financial Group
Fleetwood Enterprises, Inc.
Fleishhacker Foundation
Flintridge Foundation

Floyd Family Foundation
Fluor Corp.
FMC Corp.
Foote, Cone & Belding Communications
Foothills Foundation
Forest City Enterprises
Forest Lawn Foundation
Foster Farms
Fox Inc.
Fox Foundation, John H.
Freedom Newspapers Inc.
Freightliner Corp.
Friedman Bag Co.
Friedman Family Foundation
Fritz Cos.
Frozfruit Corp.
Fujitsu America, Inc.
Fujitsu Systems of America, Inc.
Fuller Co., H.B.
Furth Foundation
Fusenot Charity Foundation, Georges and Germaine
G.A.G. Charitable Corporation
G.P.G. Foundation
Gallo Foundation, Ernest
Gallo Foundation, Julio R.
Gannett Co.
Gap, The
Garland Foundation, John Jewett and H. Chandler
GATX Corp.
Geffen Foundation, David
GEICO Corp.
Gellert Foundation, Carl
Gellert Foundation, Celia Berta
Gellert Foundation, Fred
GenCorp
Genentech
General Dynamics Corp.
General Electric Co.
General Motors Corp.
General Reinsurance Corp.
GenRad
Gensler Jr. & Associates, M. Arthur
Georgia-Pacific Corp.
Gerber Products Co.
Gerbode Foundation, Wallace Alexander
Getty Foundation, Ann and Gordon
Getty Trust, J. Paul
Ghidotti Foundation, William and Marian
Giant Food
Gildred Foundation
Gillette Co.
Gilmore Foundation, Earl B.
Gilmore Foundation, William G.
Girard Foundation
Givenchy, Inc.
Gleason Foundation, James
Gleason Foundation, Katherine
Glendale Federal Bank
Global Van Lines
Gluck Foundation, Maxwell H.
Goel Foundation
Golden Grain Macaroni Co.
Golden State Foods Corp.
Golden West Financial Corp.
Golden West Foundation
Goldman Fund, Richard and Rhoda
Goldman Sachs & Co.
Goldrich Family Foundation
Goldsmith Family Foundation
Goldwyn Foundation, Samuel
Goodman Foundation, Edward and Marion
Goodyear Tire & Rubber Co.
Goulds Pumps
Graco
Grainger, W.W.
Grand Auto, Inc.
Great American First Savings Bank, FSB

Great Western Financial Corp.
Green Foundation, Burton E.
Greenville Foundation
Greiner Trust, Virginia
Gross Charitable Trust, Stella B.
Grousbeck Family Foundation
GTE Corp.
Gumbiner Foundation, Josephine
Haas Fund, Miriam and Peter
Haas Fund, Walter and Elise
Haas, Jr. Fund, Evelyn and Walter
Hafif Family Foundation
Haigh-Scatena Foundation
Hale Foundation, Crescent Porter
Halsell Foundation, O. L.
Hamilton Oil Corp.
Hammer United World College Trust, Armand
Hancock Foundation, Luke B.
Handy & Harman
Hannon Foundation, William H.
Hanson Office Products
Harden Foundation
Harland Co., John H.
Harman Foundation, Reed L. and Nan H.
Harper Group
HarperCollins Publishers
Harris Corp.
Harris Trust & Savings Bank
Harsco Corp.
Harte-Hanks Communications, Inc.
Hayden Foundation, William R. and Virginia
Haynes Foundation, John Randolph and Dora
Hedco Foundation
Heinz Co., H.J.
Heller Financial
Helms Foundation
Hench Foundation, John C.
Herbst Foundation
Hershey Foods Corp.
Hertz Foundation, Fannie and John
Heublein
Hewlett Foundation, William and Flora
Hewlett-Packard Co.
Hexcel Corp.
Hills Fund, Edward E.
Hilton Hotels Corp.
Hitachi
Hoag Family Foundation, George
Hoffman Foundation, H. Leslie Hoffman and Elaine S.
Hofmann Co.
Hogan Foundation, Royal Barney
Holmes & Narver Services Inc.
Holt Foundation, William Knox
Home Depot
Home Savings of America, FA
Homeland Foundation
Homestake Mining Co.
Homestead Financial Corp.
HON Industries
Hoover, Jr. Foundation, Margaret W. and Herbert
Hospital Corp. of America
Household International
Howe and Mitchell B. Howe Foundation, Lucite Horton
Hubbard Broadcasting
Hubbell Inc.
Huck International Inc.
Huffy Corp.
Hughes Aircraft Co.
Humana
Hume Foundation, Jaquelin
Hunt Manufacturing Co.
Hyundai Motor America
I Have A Dream Foundation - Los Angeles
IBM Corp.
Illinois Tool Works

California (cont.)

Imagine Foods
IMO Industries Inc.
Imperial Bancorp
Imperial Corp. of America
In His Name
Ingersoll-Rand Co.
Inland Container Corp.
Inland Steel Industries
Institute for Research on Learning
Intel Corp.
Intermark, Inc.
International Aluminum Corp.
International Multifoods Corp.
International Paper Co.
International Rectifier Corp.
Interpublic Group of Cos.
Ira-Hiti Foundation for Deep Ecology
Irmas Charitable Foundation, Audrey and Sydney
Irvine Foundation, James
Irvine Health Foundation
Irvine Medical Center
Irwin Charity Foundation, William G.
Ishiyama Foundation
Israel Discount Bank of New York
ITT Corp.
ITT Hartford Insurance Group
ITT Rayonier
J.P. Morgan & Co.
Jackson Family Foundation, Ann
Jacobs Engineering Group
Jacoby Foundation, Lela Beren and Norman
Jafra Cosmetics, Inc. (U.S.)
James River Corp. of Virginia
Jameson Foundation, J. W. and Ida M.
Janeway Foundation, Elizabeth Bixby
Jefferson Endowment Fund, John Percival and Mary C.
Jefferson-Pilot
Jefferson-Pilot Communications
Jefferson Smurfit Corp.
Jeffries & Co.
Jerome Foundation
Jewett Foundation, George Frederick
Johnson Inc., Axel
Johnson Controls
Johnson Foundation, Walter S.
Johnson & Higgins
Johnson & Johnson
Johnson & Son, S.C.
Jones Foundation, Fletcher Jorgensen Co., Earle M.
Joslyn Corp.
Joslyn Foundation, Marcellus I.
Jostens
Kaiser Aluminum & Chemical Corp.
Kaiser Cement Corp.
Kaiser Family Foundation, Henry J.
Kaiser Steel Resources
Kaisertech Ltd.
Kal Kan Foods, Inc.
Kasler Corp.
Kaufman & Broad Home Corp.
Kawasaki Motors Corp., U.S.A.
Keck Foundation, W. M.
Keck, Jr. Foundation, William M.
Keebler Co.
Kellogg's
Kemper National Insurance Cos.
Kendall Health Care Products
Kenwood U.S.A. Corp.
Kerr Foundation, A. H.
Kerr Glass Manufacturing Corp.
Kest Family Foundation, Sol and Clara

Kikkoman International, Inc.
Kimball International
Kimberly-Clark Corp.
Kingsley Foundation, Lewis A.
Kirchgessner Foundation, Karl
Kirkhill Rubber Co.
Knight-Ridder, Inc.
Knudsen Foundation, Tom and Valley
Kohl Charitable Foundation, Allen D.
Komes Foundation
Koret Foundation
Korn/Ferry International
Koulaieff Educational Fund, Trustees of Ivan Y.
KPMG Peat Marwick
Kraft Foodservice
Kraft General Foods
Kyocera International Inc.
L. L. W. W. Foundation
L.A. Gear
La-Z-Boy Chair Co.
Lakeside Foundation
Landis & Gyr, Inc.
Landmark Land Co., Inc.
Langendorf Foundation, Stanley S.
Lannan Foundation
Layne Foundation
Leavey Foundation, Thomas and Dorothy
Lebus Trust, Bertha
Ledler Corp.
Lee Enterprises
LEF Foundation
Lennox International, Inc.
Leonardt Foundation
Levi Strauss & Co.
Levine Family Foundation, Hyman
Levinson Foundation, Max and Anna
Levy Foundation, Hyman Jebb
Levy-Markus Foundation
Lewis Homes of California
Life Investors Insurance Company of America
Lilly & Co., Eli
Lincoln National Corp.
Lincy Foundation
Lipton, Thomas J.
Liquid Air Corp.
Little, Arthur D.
Littlefield Foundation, Edmund Wattis
Litton Industries
Livingston Memorial Foundation
Llagas Foundation
Lockheed Corp.
Long Foundation, J.M.
Longs Drug Stores
Louisiana-Pacific Corp.
LSI Logic Corp.
Lucas Cancer Foundation, Richard M.
Lucky Stores
Lund Foundation
Lurie Foundation, Louis R.
Luster Family Foundation
Lux Foundation, Miranda
Lyon Co., William
Lytel Foundation, Bertha Russ
M. E. G. Foundation
M/A-COM, Inc.
MacAndrews & Forbes Holdings
MacKenzie Foundation
Macmillan, Inc.
Macy & Co., R.H.
Magnatek
Magowan Family Foundation
Maguire Thomas Partners
Makita U.S.A., Inc.
Management Compensation Group/Dulworth Inc.
Mann Foundation, Ted

Manufacturers Life Insurance Co. of America
Manville Corp.
Margoes Foundation
Mariani Nut Co.
Maritz Inc.
Mark Controls Corp.
Mark IV Industries
Marley Co.
Marshburn Foundation
Martin-Brower Co., The
Martin Foundation, Della
Masco Corp.
Masserini Charitable Trust, Maurice J.
Matson Navigation Co.
Mattel
Max Charitable Foundation
Maxfield Foundation
Maxicare Health Plans
Maxtor Corp.
May Department Stores Co.
May Foundation, Wilbur
Mayacamas Corp.
Mazda Motors of America (Central), Inc.
Mazda North America
MCA
McAlister Charitable Foundation, Harold
McBean Charitable Trust, Alletta Morris
McBean Family Foundation
McConnell Foundation
McCormick & Co.
McDonnell Douglas Corp.
McDonnell Douglas Corp.-West
McGraw-Hill
MCI Communications Corp.
McKenzie Family Foundation, Richard
McKesson Corp.
Mead Corp.
Mead Foundation, Giles W. and Elise G.
Measurex Corp.
Media General, Inc.
Medtronic
Meland Outreach
Mellon Bank Corp.
Mellon PSFS
Mercedes-Benz of North America, Inc.
Merck & Co.
Meredith Corp.
Mericos Foundation
Mervyn's
Metropolitan Theatres Corp.
Meyer Fund, Milton and Sophie
Microdot, Inc.
MicroSim Corp.
Miles Inc.
Milken Family Medical Foundation
Milken Foundation, L. and S.
Milken Institute for Job and Capital Formation
Miller Brewing Company/California
Miller & Co.
Miller Foundation, Earl B. and Loraine H.
Milliken & Co.
Mitchell Family Foundation, Edward D. and Anna
Mitsubishi Electric America
Mitsubishi Motor Sales of America, Inc.
Mitsui & Co. (U.S.A.)
Mobil Oil Corp.
Modern Maid Food Products, Inc.
Modglin Family Foundation
Monterey Bay Aquarium Foundation
Montgomery Street Foundation
Moore Family Foundation
Morgan Stanley & Co.

Morrison-Knudsen Corp.
Morton International
Mosher Foundation, Samuel B.
Moskowitz Foundation, Irving I.
Moss Foundation
Motorola
Muller Foundation
Munger Foundation, Alfred C.
Murdock Development Co.
Murdy Foundation
Murphey Foundation, Lluella Morey
Murphy Foundation, Dan
Muth Foundation, Peter and Mary
Nakamichi Foundation, E.
Nalco Chemical Co.
Nash-Finch Co.
National Dollar Stores, Ltd.
National Medical Enterprises
National Metal & Steel
National Pro-Am Youth Fund
National Semiconductor Corp.
Natural Heritage Foundation
NCR Corp.
NEC Electronics, Inc.
NEC USA
Nelson Foundation, Florence
Nestle U.S.A. Inc.
Neutrogena Corp.
New York Times Co.
Newhall Foundation, Henry Mayo
Newhall Land & Farming Co.
Newman Charitable Trust, Calvin M. and Raquel H.
News America Publishing Inc.
Nissan Motor Corporation in U.S.A.
NMB (USA) Inc.
Norman Foundation, Andrew
Norman/Nethercutt Foundation, Merle
Norris Foundation, Kenneth T. and Eileen L.
Nortek, Inc.
North American Philips Corp.
North Face, The
Northern Telecom Inc.
Northern Trust Co.
Northrop Corp.
Norton Co.
Norwest Corp.
Oak Foundation U.S.A.
Oak Industries
Obayashi America Corp.
Occidental Petroleum Corp.
Odell and Helen Pfeiffer Odell Fund, Robert Stewart
Ogilvy & Mather Worldwide
Olin Corp.
Olivetti Office USA, Inc.
Oracle Corp.
Orion Capital Corp.
Orleton Trust Fund
Osher Foundation, Bernard
Ostern Foundation
Ottenstein Family Foundation
Owens-Corning Fiberglas Corp.
Oxford Industries, Inc.
Oxnard Foundation
PACCAR
Pacific Enterprises
Pacific Gas & Electric Co.
Pacific Mutual Life Insurance Co.
Pacific Telesis Group
Pacific Western Foundation
PacifiCorp
Packard Foundation, David and Lucile
Packard Humanities Institute
Page Foundation, George B.
Pall Corp.
Paramount Communications Inc.
Pardee Construction Co.
Parker Foundation
Parker-Hannifin Corp.
Parsons Corp.

Parsons Foundation, Ralph M.
Parvin Foundation, Albert
Pasadena Area Residential Aid
Patagonia
Pauley Foundation, Edwin W.
Peck/Jones Construction Corp.
Peery Foundation
Penn Central Corp.
Peppers Foundation, Ann
PepsiCo
Perini Corp.
Perkin-Elmer Corp.
Peters Foundation, Leon S.
Pfaffinger Foundation
Pfeiffer Research Foundation, Gustavus and Louise
Phelps Dodge Corp.
Philibosian Foundation, Stephen
Philip Morris Cos.
Phillipps Foundation
Pic 'N' Save Corp.
Pickford Foundation, Mary
Pioneer Electronics (USA) Inc.
Pioneer Hi-Bred International
Pirelli Armstrong Tire Corp.
Pittston Co.
Plantronics, Inc.
Playboy Enterprises, Inc.
Plitt Southern Theatres
PMC Inc.
Poinsettia Foundation, Paul and Magdalena Ecke
Polaroid Corp.
Polinsky-Rivkin Family Foundation
Pope Family Foundation, Blanche & Edker
Posey Trust, Addison
Potlatch Corp.
Powell Foundation, Charles Lee
PPG Industries
Prairie Foundation
Pratt Memorial Fund
Presley Cos.
Preuss Foundation
Price Company
Prime Computer, Inc.
Procter & Gamble Co.
Progressive Corp.
Provigo Corp. Inc.
Prudential Insurance Co. of America
Pyramid Technology Corp.
Qantas Airways Ltd.
Quaker Chemical Corp.
Quaker Oats Co.
Quantum Chemical Corp.
R. P. Foundation
Radin Foundation
Raley's
Ralston Purina Co.
Rasmussen Foundation
Raychem Corp.
Raytheon Co.
Redlands Federal Bank
REI-Recreational Equipment, Inc.
Reinghardt Foundation, Albert
Reliance Insurance Cos.
Republic New York Corp.
Research-Cottrell Inc.
Revlon
Reynolds & Reynolds Co.
Rhone-Poulenc Rorer
Richley, Inc.
Ricoh Electronics Inc.
Rigler-Deutsch Foundation
Ringier-America
Riordan Foundation
RJR Nabisco Inc.
Roadway Services, Inc.
Roberts Foundation
Robertshaw Controls Co.
Robinson Foundation
Rockwell International Corp.
Rogers Foundation, Mary Stuart
Rohm and Haas Company

Rohr Inc.
Rolm Systems
Roseburg Forest Products Co.
Rosen Foundation, Michael Alan
Rosenberg Foundation
Rosenberg, Jr. Family
 Foundation, Louise and Claude
Roth Family Foundation
Rouse Co.
Royal Group Inc.
Ryan Foundation, David Claude
Ryder System
Rykoff & Co., S.E.
S.G. Foundation
SAFECO Corp.
Safeway, Inc.
Salomon
Salvatori Foundation, Henry
Samsung America Inc.
San Diego Gas & Electric
San Diego Trust & Savings Bank
San Francisco Federal Savings &
 Loan Association
Sandoz Corp.
Sandy Foundation, George H.
Sanguinetti Foundation,
 Annunziata
Santa Fe International Corp.
Santa Fe Pacific Corp.
Sanyo Fisher Service Corp.
Sanyo Manufacturing Corp.
Sara Lee Corp.
Sara Lee Hosiery
Saroyan Foundation, William
Sattler Beneficial Trust, Daniel
 A. and Edna J.
Saturno Foundation
Schering-Plough Corp.
Schieffelin & Somerset Co.
Schlinger Foundation
Schlumberger Ltd.
Schwab & Co., Charles
Schwab Foundation, Charles and
 Helen
Science Applications
 International Corp.
Scientific-Atlanta
Scott Foundation, Virginia Steele
Scripps Co., E.W.
Scripps Foundation, Ellen
 Browning
SDB Foundation
Seagate Technology
Seagram & Sons, Joseph E.
Sealy, Inc.
Sears, Roebuck and Co.
Seascape Senior Housing, Inc.
Seaver Charitable Trust, Richard
 C.
Seaver Institute
SECO
Seebee Trust, Frances
Sefton Foundation, J. W.
Sega of America
Segal Charitable Trust, Barnet
Segerstrom Foundation
Sequa Corp.
Setzer Foundation
Seven Springs Foundation
Shaklee Corp.
Shapell Foundation, Nathan and
 Lilly
Shapell Industries, Inc.
Shaw Industries
Shea Co., John F.
Shea Foundation
Shea Foundation, Edmund and
 Mary
Shea Foundation, John and
 Dorothy
Sheldahl Inc.
Shell Oil Co.
Shenandoah Foundation
Sherwin-Williams Co.
Shoong Foundation, Milton
Shorenstein Foundation, Walter
 H. and Phyllis J.

Shuwa Investments Corp.
Siebe North Inc.
Siemens Medical Systems Inc.
Sierra Health Foundation
Sierra Pacific Industries
Silicon Systems Inc.
Simon Foundation, Jennifer Jones
Simon Foundation, Robert Ellis
Simpson Investment Co.
Simpson Paper Co.
Simpson PSB Foundation
Sizzler International
Skaggs Foundation, L. J. and
 Mary C.
Skandia America Reinsurance
 Corp.
Small Educational and
 Charitable Trust, Rita H.
Smith Corp., A.O.
Smith Foundation, Lon V.
Smith Trust, May and Stanley
Smucker Co., J.M.
Smucker Co., J.M.
Snap-on Tools Corp.
Software Toolworks
Sony Corp. of America
South Coast Foundation
Southdown, Inc.
Southern California Edison Co.
Southern California Gas Co.
Southern Pacific Transportation
 Co.
Southland Corp.
Specialty Restaurants Corp.
Spectra-Physics Analytical
Sprague, Jr. Foundation, Caryll
 M. and Norman F.
Springs Industries
Sprint
Square D Co.
Stamps Foundation, James L.
Standard Brands Paint Co.
Standard Pacific Corp.
Standard Products Co.
Stanford Theater Foundation
Stanley Works
Stans Foundation
State Farm Mutual Automobile
 Insurance Co.
Stauffer Charitable Trust, John
Stauffer Foundation, John and
 Beverly
Steel, Sr. Foundation, Marshall
Steelcase
Steele Foundation, Harry and
 Grace
Stein Foundation, Jules and Doris
Steiner Corp.
Stella D'Oro Biscuit Co.
Stern Memorial Trust, Sidney
Stern Private Charitable
 Foundation Trust, Charles H.
 and Anna S.
Stillwell Charitable Trust, Glen
 and Dorothy
Stone Container Corp.
Strauss Foundation, Leon
Stuart Center Charitable Trust,
 Hugh
Stuart Foundation, Elbridge and
 Evelyn
Stuart Foundations
Stulsaft Foundation, Morris
Sumitomo Bank of California
Sun-Diamond Growers of
 California
Sun Microsystems
Sundstrand Corp.
Sunkist Growers
Swift Memorial Health Care
 Foundation
Swig Charity Foundation, Mae
 and Benjamin
Swig Foundation
Swinerton & Walberg Co.
Swiss American Securities, Inc.
Swiss Bank Corp.
Syntex Corp.

Tandem Computers
Tandon Corp.
Tandy Corp.
Tang Foundation
Taper Foundation, Mark
Taper Foundation, S. Mark
Target Stores
Taube Family Foundation
Teac America, Inc.
Teichert
Tektronix
Teledyne
Teleflex Inc.
Teleklew Productions
Temple-Inland
Tension Envelope Corp.
Teradyne, Inc.
Texaco
Textron
Thagard Foundation
Thomas Medical Foundation,
 Roy E.
Thornton Foundation
Thornton Foundation, Flora L.
Thornton Foundation, John M.
 and Sally B.
3M Co.
Thrifty Corp.
Thrifty Oil Co.
Thums Long Beach Co.
Tidewater, Inc.
Time Warner
Times Mirror Co.
Timken Co.
Timme Revocable Trust, Abigail
 S.
TMZ Corp.
Tomkins Industries, Inc.
Torchmark Corp.
Toro Co.
Tosco Corp. Refining Division
Toshiba America, Inc.
Toyota Motor Sales, U.S.A.
Tracor, Inc.
Transamerica Corp.
Transamerica Occidental Life
 Insurance Co.
Travelers Cos.
Treadwell Foundation, Nora
 Eccles
Treasure Chest Advertising Co.
TRINOVA Corp.
Tropicana Products, Inc.
Trust Funds
TRW Corp.
Tuohy Foundation, Alice Tweed
Turner Construction Co.
Turner Corp.
Twentieth Century-Fox Film
 Corp.
Twentieth Century Insurance Co.
Tyson Foods, Inc.
UGI Corp.
UNC, Inc.
Unilever United States
Union Bank
Union Bank of Switzerland Los
 Angeles Branch
Union Bank of Switzerland New
 York Branch
Union Camp Corp.
Union Carbide Corp.
Union Pacific Corp.
Unisys Corp.
United Airlines
United Artists Theatre Circuits
United Dominion Industries
United States Borax & Chemical
 Corp.
U.S. Leasing International
United States Trust Co. of New
 York
United Technologies Corp.
Universal Foods Corp.
Unocal Corp.
Upjohn California Fund
US Bancorp

USG Corp.
USLIFE Corp.
Uvas Foundation
Valley Foundation
Valley Foundation, Wayne and
 Gladys
Van Camp Foundation
van Loben Sels - Eleanor Slate
 van Lobel Sels Charitable
 Foundation, Ernst D.
Van Nuys Charities, J. B. and
 Emily
Van Nuys Foundation, I. N. and
 Susanna H.
Varian Associates
Viele Scholarship Trust, Frances
 S.
Volkswagen of America, Inc.
Von der Ahe Foundation
Von der Ahe, Jr. Trust, Theodore
 Albert
Vons Cos., Inc.
W. W. W. Foundation
Wade Endowment Fund,
 Elizabeth Firth
Wal-Mart Stores
Walgreen Co.
Walker Foundation, Smith
Walker Foundation, T. B.
Disney Co., Walt
Warsh-Mott Legacy
Washington Post Co.
Wasserman Foundation
Watkins-Johnson Co.
Watt Industry
Webb Educational and
 Charitable Trust, Torrey H.
 and Dorothy K.
Weiler Foundation
Weingart Foundation
Weisman Art Foundation,
 Frederick R.
Weisz Foundation, David and
 Sylvia
Wells Fargo & Co.
Wertheimer Foundation
Western Cardiac Foundation
Westinghouse Electric Corp.
Wetterau
Weyerhaeuser Co.
Whittaker Corp.
Whittell Trust for Disabled
 Veterans of Foreign Wars, Elia
Whittier Foundation, L. K.
WICOR, Inc.
Wilbur-Ellis Co.
Wilbur Foundation, Marguerite
 Eyer
Wilsey Bennet Co.
Wimpey Inc., George
Winchell's Donut Houses
 Operating Company
Witco Corp.
Witter Foundation, Dean
Wollenberg Foundation
Wood-Claeyssens Foundation
World Savings & Loan
 Association
Wrigley Co., Wm. Jr.
Wyle Laboratories
Wyman-Gordon Co.
Wynn's International, Inc.
Xerox Corp.
York International Corp.
Yosemite Asset Management
Young & Rubicam
Zellerbach Family Fund
Ziegler Foundation, Ruth/Allen
Zurn Industries

Colorado

Ackerman Trust, Anna Keesling
Air Products & Chemicals
Akzo America
Albertson's
Alco Standard Corp.
Alumax

Aluminum Co. of America
AMAX
American Natural Resources Co.
American Telephone &
 Telegraph Co.
American Telephone &
 Telegraph Co./Denver Region
Amoco Corp.
Anadarko Petroleum Corp.
Anheuser-Busch Cos.
Animal Assistance Foundation
Anschutz Family Foundation
Apache Corp.
ARA Services
Archer-Daniels-Midland Co.
ARCO
Armco Inc.
Arrow Electronics, Inc.
Avnet, Inc.
Bacon Foundation, E. L. and
 Oma
Ball Corp.
Banc One - Colorado Corp.
Bancroft, Jr. Foundation, Hugh
Baxter International
Bell Industries
Best Products Co.
Boettcher Foundation
Boise Cascade Corp.
Bonfils-Stanton Foundation
Borden
Browning-Ferris Industries
Buell Foundation, Temple Hoyne
Burgess Trust, Ralph L. and
 Florence R.
Burlington Northern Inc.
Burnett Construction Co.
Business Men's Assurance Co. of
 America
Capital Cities/ABC
Charter Medical Corp.
Chevron Corp.
Chrysler Corp.
CIBA-GEIGY Corp.
Citicorp
Coastal Corp.
COBE Laboratories, Inc.
Colorado Interstate Gas Co.
Colorado National Bankshares
Colorado State Bank of Denver
Colorado Trust
Computer Associates
 International
ConAgra
Conoco Inc.
Continental Airlines
Coors Brewing Co.
Coors Foundation, Adolph
Culbro Corp.
Cyprus Minerals Co.
Dayton Hudson Corp.
Dekalb Energy Co.
Delta Air Lines
Deluxe Corp.
Digital Equipment Corp.
Donnelley & Sons Co., R.R.
Dover Corp.
Dow Jones & Co.
du Pont de Nemours & Co., E. I.
Dun & Bradstreet Corp.
Duncan Trust, John G.
Durr-Fillauer Medical
Eastman Kodak Co.
Edmondson Foundation, Joseph
 Henry
EG&G Inc.
El Pomar Foundation
Elf Aquitaine, Inc.
Emerson Electric Co.
EMI Records Group
Equitable Life Assurance Society
 of the U.S.
Evening Post Publishing Co.
Fairfield-Meeker Charitable
 Trust, Freeman E.
First Bank System

Colorado (cont.)

First Colorado Bank & Trust, N.A.
First Interstate Bank of Denver
Fishback Foundation Trust, Harmes C.
FMC Corp.
Forest Oil Corp.
Foxmeyer Corp.
Frontier Oil & Refining Co.
Gannett Co.
Gates Corp.
Gates Foundation
GEICO Corp.
General Electric Co.
General Service Foundation
Georgia-Pacific Corp.
Glidden Co.
Gold Fields Mining Co.
Graco
Great-West Life Assurance Co.
Greeley Gas Co.
Hamilton Oil Corp.
Heginbotham Trust, Will E.
Hewit Family Foundation
Hewlett-Packard Co.
Hill Foundation
Holly Sugar Corp.
Hospital Corp. of America
Huffy Corp.
Hughes Charitable Trust, Mabel Y.
Humana
Hunt Alternatives Fund
Hunter Trust, A. V.
IBM Corp.
IDEX Corp.
Illinois Tool Works
Imperial Holly Corp.
Inco Alloys International
Indiana Insurance Cos.
Ingersoll-Rand Co.
Inland Container Corp.
Inland Steel Industries
International Multifoods Corp.
ITT Corp.
ITT Hartford Insurance Group
ITT Rayonier
Jefferson-Pilot
Jefferson-Pilot Communications
Jeppesen Sanderson
JFM Foundation
Johnson Foundation, Helen K. and Arthur E.
Johnson & Higgins
Joslin-Needham Family Foundation
Kaman Corp.
Keebler Co.
Kemper National Insurance Cos.
Kemper Securities Inc.
Kitzmiller/Bales Trust
KN Energy, Inc.
Knight-Ridder, Inc.
Kraft General Foods
Litton Industries
Louisiana Land & Exploration Co.
Lowe Foundation
M.D.C. Holdings
Manitou Foundation
Manufacturers Life Insurance Co. of America
Manville Corp.
Martin & Deborah Flug Foundation
Martin Marietta Aggregates
Martin Marietta Corp.
May Department Stores Co.
McDonnell Douglas Corp.
McDonnell Douglas Corp.-West
McGraw-Hill
Mead Corp.
Medtronic
Mellon Bank Corp.
Mellon PSFS

Mobil Oil Corp.
Monfort Charitable Foundation
Monfort of Colorado, Inc.
Morrison Charitable Trust, Pauline A. and George R.
Mullen Foundation, J. K.
National Medical Enterprises
Nationale-Nederlanden North America Corp.
NCR Corp.
Needmor Fund
Newhall Land & Farming Co.
Newmont Mining Corp.
Norgren Foundation, Carl A.
Norwest Corp.
Occidental Oil & Gas Corp.
Occidental Petroleum Corp.
O'Fallon Trust, Martin J. and Mary Anne
Oppenheimer & Co., Inc.
Orion Capital Corp.
Outokumpu-American Brass Co.
Owens-Corning Fiberglas Corp.
Parker-Hannifin Corp.
Paxton Co., Frank
Peerless Insurance Co.
Peierls Foundation
Penn Central Corp.
Petteys Memorial Foundation, Jack
Pfizer
Phelps, Inc.
Phelps Dodge Corp.
Philip Morris Cos.
Phillips Petroleum Co.
Pilot Trust
Pioneer Fund
Piton Foundation
Pittsburgh & Midway Coal Mining Co.
Progressive Corp.
Public Service Co. of Colorado
Rabb Foundation, Harry W.
Ralston Purina Co.
Raytheon Engineers & Constructors
REI-Recreational Equipment, Inc.
Rennie Scholarship Fund, Waldo E.
Research-Cottrell Inc.
Rio Grande Railroad
Rouse Co.
Sachs Foundation
SAFECO Corp.
Safeway, Inc.
Saint Paul Cos.
Santa Fe Pacific Corp.
Schramm Foundation
Scripps Co., E.W.
Sealy, Inc.
Security Life of Denver
Shwayder Foundation, Fay
Southland Corp.
Spectra-Physics Analytical
Square D Co.
State Farm Mutual Automobile Insurance Co.
Sterne-Elder Memorial Trust
Stone Container Corp.
Stone Trust, H. Chase
Storage Technology Corp.
Sundstrand Corp.
Super Valu Stores
Syntex Corp.
Tandem Computers
Target Stores
Taylor Foundation, Ruth and Vernon
Tele-Communications, Inc.
Teledyne
Temple-Inland
Texaco
Texas Instruments
Thatcher Foundation
3M Co.
Tidewater, Inc.

Times Mirror Co.
Timken Co.
Travelers Cos.
True North Foundation
TRW Corp.
Turner Construction Co.
Turner Corp.
UNC, Inc.
Union Camp Corp.
Union Pacific Corp.
Unisys Corp.
United Technologies Corp.
US WEST
Valmont Industries
Volkswagen of America, Inc.
Wal-Mart Stores
Walgreen Co.
Weckbaugh Foundation, Eleanore Mullen
Wells Fargo & Co.
Wendy's International, Inc.
Wheeler Trust, Clara
Williams Family Foundation
Wolf Foundation, Melvin and Elaine
Woodward Governor Co.
Xerox Corp.

Connecticut

Acme United Corp.
Advest Group, Inc.
Advo System Inc.
Aetna Life & Casualty Co.
Air Express International Corp.
Alco Standard Corp.
Allegheny Ludlum Corp.
AlliedSignal
Alpert & Co., Inc., Herman
AMAX
American Brands
American Cyanamid Co.
American Greetings Corp.
American Home Products Corp.
American Maize Products
American National Bank
American National Can Co.
American Tobacco Co.
Ames Department Stores
AMETEK
Amoco Corp.
Amstar Corp.
Anchor Fasteners
Arbor Acres Farm, Inc.
Armco Inc.
Arrow Electronics, Inc.
ASARCO
Asea Brown Boveri
Atkinson Co., Guy F.
Auerbach Foundation, Beatrice Fox
Avis Inc.
Avnet, Inc.
Bairnco Corp.
Baker Foundation, Elinor Patterson
Bank of Boston Connecticut
Bank of Boston Corp.
Bank of New York
Bankers Trust Co.
Barclays Bank of New York
Barden Corp.
Barnes Foundation
Barnes Group
Baskin-Robbins USA CO.
Baxter International
BayBanks
Becton Dickinson & Co.
Belding Heminway Co.
Bennett Foundation, Carl and Dorothy
Berbecker Scholarship Fund, Walter J. and Lille
Bergen Brunswig Corp.
Bingham Trust, The
Bissell Foundation, J. Walton
Black & Decker Corp.

Bodine Corp.
Boise Cascade Corp.
Bowater Inc.
Brakeley, John Price Jones Inc.
Bristol-Myers Squibb Co.
Bristol Savings Bank
Brown & Sons, Alex
Browning-Ferris Industries
Brunswick Corp.
Burndy Corp.
Cadbury Beverages Inc.
Campbell Soup Co.
Capital Cities/ABC
Carey Industries
Carstensen Memorial Foundation, Fred R. and Hazel W.
Carter Co., William
Carter-Wallace
Casey Foundation, Annie E.
Chadwick Fund, Dorothy Jordan
Champion International Corp.
Chapin Foundation, Frances
Chapman Foundation, William H.
Chase Manhattan Bank, N.A.
Chase Packaging Corp.
Chesebrough-Pond's
Childs Memorial Fund for Medical Research, Jane Coffin
Chrysler Corp.
CIGNA Corp.
Citicorp
Citizens Utilities Co.
Clabir Corp.
CM Alliance Cos.
Coats & Clark Inc.
Coltec Industries
Commercial Intertech Corp.
Community Cooperative Development Foundation
Computer Associates International
Connecticut General Corp.
Connecticut Natural Gas Corp.
Connecticut Savings Bank
Consolidated Freightways
Control Data Corp.
Cooper Industries
Cowles Media Co.
Cox Enterprises
Crompton & Knowles Corp.
Crystal Brands
Culbro Corp.
Culpeper Foundation, Charles E.
Culpeper Memorial Foundation, Daphne Seybolt
Dana Corp.
Day Foundation, Nancy Sayles
Dell Foundation, Hazel
Deloitte & Touche
Deluxe Corp.
Dennett Foundation, Marie G.
Devon Group
Dexter Corp.
Dibner Fund
Donnelley & Sons Co., R.R.
Dover Corp.
Dow Chemical Co.
Dow Corning Corp.
Dresser Industries
Dreyfus Corp., Louis
du Pont de Nemours & Co., E. I.
Dun & Bradstreet Corp.
Duracell International
Duty Free International
Eagle-Picher Industries
Eaton Corp.
Echlin Inc.
Eder Foundation, Sidney and Arthur
Educational Foundation of America
EIS Foundation
Elf Aquitaine, Inc.
Ellis Fund
Emerson Electric Co.
EMI Records Group

Engelberg Foundation
Ensign-Bickford Industries
Ensworth Charitable Foundation
EnviroSource
Equitable Life Assurance Society of the U.S.
Fairchild Corp.
Fairchild Foundation, Sherman
FIP Corp.
First Brands Corp.
Fisher Brothers
Fisher Foundation
FKI Holdings Inc.
Fleet Bank
Fleet Bank N.A.
Fleet Financial Group
Folsom Foundation, Maud Glover
Foote, Cone & Belding Communications
Forbes
Foster-Davis Foundation
Fox Foundation Trust, Jacob L. and Lewis
Fox Steel Co.
Franks Nursery and Crafts
Fraser Paper Ltd.
Freas Foundation
Gannett Co.
General Dynamics Corp.
General Electric Co.
General Housewares Corp.
General Reinsurance Corp.
General Signal Corp.
Georgia-Pacific Corp.
Glidden Co.
Goodyear Tire & Rubber Co.
Grolier, Inc.
GTE Corp.
Hallmark Cards
Handy & Harman
Harcourt Foundation, Ellen Knowles
Harsco Corp.
Harte-Hanks Communications, Inc.
Hartford Courant Foundation
Hartford Steam Boiler Inspection & Insurance Co.
Heinz Co., H.J.
Heritage Foundation
Hershey Foods Corp.
Herzog Foundation, Carl J.
Heublein
Hoffman Foundation, Maximillian E. and Marion O.
Home Depot
Howmet Corp.
Howmet Corp., Winstead Machining
Hubbell Inc.
Huisking Foundation
Hydraulic Co.
IBM Corp.
Illinois Tool Works
IMO Industries Inc.
Inco Alloys International
Industrial Risk Insurers
Ingersoll-Rand Co.
Inland Steel Industries
ITT Corp.
ITT Hartford Insurance Group
ITT Rayonier
IU International
James River Corp. of Virginia
Johnson Inc., Axel
Johnson & Higgins
Johnson & Johnson
Jones and Bessie D. Phelps Foundation, Cyrus W. and Amy F.
Jones Fund, Paul L.
Jost Foundation, Charles and Mabel P.
Journal Communications
Kaman Corp.
Kimberly-Clark Corp.
Kloeckner-Pentaplast of America

Operating Location Index

District of Columbia (cont.)

Gudelsky Family Foundation, Isadore and Bertha
Gumenick Foundation, Nathan and Sophie
Harris Corp.
Healy Family Foundation, M. A.
Hechinger Co.
Higginson Trust, Corina
Hill-Snowdon Foundation
Himmelfarb Foundation, Paul and Annetta
Hitachi
Hoechst Celanese Corp.
IBM Corp.
Indiana Insurance Cos.
ITT Hartford Insurance Group
Japanese American Agon Friendship League
Jerusalem Fund for Education and Community Development
Johnson & Higgins
Johnston Trust for Charitable and Educational Purposes, James M.
Jones Construction Co., J.A.
Kapiloff Foundation, Leonard
Kaplan Foundation, Charles I. and Mary
Kennedy, Jr. Foundation, Joseph P.
Kiplinger Foundation
Kiplinger Washington Editors
Knight-Ridder, Inc.
Koch Charitable Foundation, Charles G.
KPMG Peat Marwick
Lambe Charitable Foundation, Claude R.
Lea Foundation, Helen Sperry
Lehrman Foundation, Jacob and Charlotte
Lincoln National Corp.
Little, Arthur D.
Loughran Foundation, Mary and Daniel
Loyola Foundation
Manville Corp.
Mapco Inc.
Marpat Foundation
Marriott Foundation, J. Willard
May Department Stores Co.
McGraw-Hill
MCI Communications Corp.
Meyer Foundation, Eugene and Agnes E.
Mitsubishi Electric America
MNC Financial
National Medical Enterprises
Nationale-Nederlanden North America Corp.
NationsBank Corp.
News America Publishing Inc.
Norfolk Southern Corp.
Ogilvy & Mather Worldwide
Olin Corp.
Panhandle Eastern Corp.
Parsons Corp.
Peerless Insurance Co.
Post Foundation of D.C., Marjorie Merriweather
Potomac Electric Power Co.
Prudential Insurance Co. of America
Public Welfare Foundation
Reasoner, Davis & Fox
Replogle Foundation, Luther I.
Riggs National Bank
RJR Nabisco Inc.
Ross Foundation, Walter G.
Rouse Co.
Scripps Co., E.W.
Sea-Land Service
Sears, Roebuck and Co.
Security Life of Denver

Shell Oil Co.
Sprint
Steuart Petroleum Co.
Stewart Trust under the will of Helen S. Devore, Alexander and Margaret
Stewart Trust under the will of Mary E. Stewart, Alexander and Margaret
Stone Foundation, David S.
Strong Foundation, Hattie M.
Student Loan Marketing Association
Syntex Corp.
3M Co.
Times Mirror Co.
TJX Cos.
Travelers Cos.
TRW Corp.
Union Carbide Corp.
Unisys Corp.
United Airlines
United Technologies Corp.
Uslico Corp.
Volkswagen of America, Inc.
Wallace Genetic Foundation
Washington Post Co.
Wasserman Foundation, George
Westinghouse Electric Corp.
Westport Fund
Willard Foundation, Helen Parker
WJLA Inc.
Wouk Foundation, Abe
Xerox Corp.

Florida

Abitibi-Price
Abraham Foundation, Anthony R.
Action Products International
Adams Foundation, Arthur F. and Alice E.
AEGON USA, Inc.
Affiliated Publications, Inc.
Air France
Air Products & Chemicals
Albertson's
Alco Standard Corp.
Aldeen Charity Trust, G. W.
AlliedSignal
Alumax
Aluminum Co. of America
Amaturo Foundation
AMAX
Amcast Industrial Corp.
American Bankers Insurance Group
American Capital Corp.
American Cyanamid Co.
American Express Co.
American Financial Corp.
American Maize Products
American Savings & Loan Association of Florida
American Telephone & Telegraph Co.
AMETEK
Anchor Glass Container Corp.
Anheuser-Busch Cos.
APL Corp.
Applebaum Foundation
Appleman Foundation
ARA Services
Archbold Expeditions
Archer-Daniels-Midland Co.
Armco Inc.
Armstrong World Industries Inc.
Arrow Electronics, Inc.
Aurora Foundation
Avis Inc.
Avnet, Inc.
Bacardi Imports
Bairnco Corp.
Baker Foundation, George T.
Ball Corp.
Bank Hapoalim B.M.
Bank of Boston Connecticut

Bank of Boston Corp.
Bank of New York
BankAmerica Corp.
Bankers Life & Casualty Co.
Bankers Trust Co.
Barnett Banks
Bassett Furniture Industries, Inc.
Bastien Memorial Foundation, John E. and Nellie J.
Batchelor Foundation
Bausch & Lomb
Baxter International
Bay Branch Foundation
BCR Foundation
Bearings, Inc.
Beattie Foundation Trust, Cordelia Lee
BellSouth Corp.
Beneficial Corp.
Best Products Co.
Betz Laboratories
Beveridge Foundation, Frank Stanley
BFGoodrich
Bible Alliance
Bickerton Charitable Trust, Lydia H.
Blair Foundation, John
Blank Family Foundation
Block, H&R
BOC Group
Borden
Bradish Trust, Norman C.
Brennan Foundation Trust
Breyer Foundation
Briggs Family Foundation
Bristol-Myers Squibb Co.
Broad Foundation, Shepard
Brown Brothers Harriman & Co.
Brown Charitable Trust, Peter D. and Dorothy S.
Brown & Sons, Alex
Browning-Ferris Industries
Brunswick Corp.
Burdines
Burger King Corp.
Burlington Northern Inc.
Bush Charitable Foundation, Edyth
Butler Foundation, Alice
Campbell Soup Co.
Carnival Cruise Lines
Catlin Charitable Trust, Kathleen K.
CBS Inc.
Celotex Corp.
Centel Corp.
Champion International Corp.
Charter Medical Corp.
Chase Manhattan Bank, N.A.
Chastain Charitable Foundation, Robert Lee and Thomas M.
Chatlos Foundation
Chevron Corp.
Childress Foundation, Francis and Miranda
Chrysler Corp.
Chubb Corp.
CIGNA Corp.
Circuit City Stores
Citibank, F.S.B.
Citicorp
Citizens & Southern National Bank of Florida
Clopay Corp.
Clorox Co.
Coastal Corp.
Cobb Family Foundation
Cohen Foundation, George M.
Comcast Corp.
Comerica
Commercial Metals Co.
Community Health Association
Computer Associates International
Computer Sciences Corp.
ConAgra

Conn Memorial Foundation
Continental Airlines
Continental Bank N.A.
Continental Corp.
Cottrell Foundation
Coulter Corp.
Cox Enterprises
Crane & Co.
Crane Co.
Crane Foundation, Raymond E. and Ellen F.
Credit Suisse
CSX Corp.
Culbro Corp.
Davis Family - W.D. Charities, James E.
Davis Family - W.D. Charities, Tine W.
Davis Foundations, Arthur Vining
Day Charitable Foundation, Harry M.
Delacorte Fund, George
Delta Air Lines
Deltona Corp.
Deluxe Corp.
Dettman Foundation, Leroy E.
Dial Corp.
Dodge Foundation, P. L.
Dollar General Corp.
Donaldson, Lufkin & Jenrette
Donnelley & Sons Co., R.R.
Dover Corp.
Dow Chemical Co.
Dow Jones & Co.
du Pont de Nemours & Co., E. I.
Dubow Family Foundation
Dun & Bradstreet Corp.
Dunspaugh-Dalton Foundation
duPont Foundation, Alfred I.
duPont Fund, Jessie Ball
Durr-Fillauer Medical
DWG Corp.
Eagles Memorial Foundation
Eastern Air Lines
Eaton Corp.
Ebert Charitable Foundation, Horatio B.
Echlin Inc.
Echlin Foundation
Eckerd Corp., Jack
EG&G Inc.
Einstein Fund, Albert E. and Birdie W.
Ellis Foundation
Enron Corp.
Equimark Corp.
Equitable Life Assurance Society of the U.S.
Exxon Corp.
Fairchild Corp.
Falk Foundation, David
Federated Department Stores and Allied Stores Corp.
Fireman Charitable Foundation, Paul and Phyllis
First Alabama Bancshares
First Union Corp.
First Union National Bank of Florida
Firstar Bank Milwaukee NA
Fish Foundation, Bert
Fleet Bank
Fleet Financial Group
Florida East Coast Industries
Florida Power Corp.
Florida Power & Light Co.
Florida Rock Industries
Florida Steel Corp.
FMC Corp.
Ford III Memorial Foundation, Jefferson Lee
Forest City Enterprises
Fort Pierce Memorial Hospital Scholarship Foundation
Fortin Foundation of Florida
Fortune Bank
Foulds Trust, Claiborne F

Foxmeyer Corp.
Freeport-McMoRan
Friends' Foundation Trust, A.
Frueauff Foundation, Charles A.
Fuller Co., H.B.
Gann Charitable Foundation, Joseph and Rae
Gannett Co.
Garner Charitable Trust, James G.
GATX Corp.
General Development Corp.
General Mills
General Motors Corp.
Genius Foundation, Elizabeth Morse
Georgia-Pacific Corp.
Gerson Trust, B. Milfred
Gillett Foundation, Elesabeth Ingalls
Glendale Federal Bank
Glidden Co.
Goldman Sachs & Co.
Goldstein Foundation, Alfred and Ann
Gooding Charitable Foundation, Luca
Goodwin Foundation, Leo
Goodyear Tire & Rubber Co.
Gore Family Memorial Foundation
Grace & Co., W.R.
Grader Foundation, K. W.
Great Western Financial Corp.
Greater Construction Corp. Charitable Foundation, Inc.
Griffin, Sr., Foundation, C. V.
Grobstein Charitable Trust No. 2, Ethel
Gronewaldt Foundation, Alice Busch
Grumman Corp.
GTE Corp.
Gulf Power Co.
Gulfstream Housing Corp.
Halliburton Co.
Halmos Foundation
Handy & Harman
Hanley Family Foundation
Hanson Office Products
Harcourt Brace Jovanovich
Harris Corp.
Harris Foundation, John H. and Lucille
Harris Trust & Savings Bank
Harsco Corp.
Harte-Hanks Communications, Inc.
Hartford Steam Boiler Inspection & Insurance Co.
Haven Charitable Foundation, Nina
Hayward Foundation Charitable Trust, John T. and Winifred
Hercules Inc.
Holmes Foundation
Home Depot
Honeywell
Hospital Corp. of America
Houck Foundation, May K.
Hovnanian Foundation, Hirair and Anna
Howell Foundation, Eric and Jessie
Hubbard Broadcasting
Hughes Supply, Inc.
Huizenga Family Foundation
Humana
Hyman Construction Co., George
IBM Corp.
ICI Americas
Inland Container Corp.
Inland Steel Industries
International Multifoods Corp.
International Paper Co.
Isaly Klondike Co.
ITT Corp.
ITT Hartford Insurance Group

ITT Rayonier
J.P. Morgan & Co.
Jaharis Family Foundation
Jefferson-Pilot
Jefferson-Pilot Communications
Jefferson Smurfit Corp.
Jenkins Foundation, George W.
Jennings Foundation, Alma
Johnson Inc., Axel
Johnson Controls
Johnson & Higgins
Johnson & Johnson
Johnson & Son, S.C.
Jones Intercable, Inc.
Kaman Corp.
Keating Family Foundation
Kelly Tractor Co.
Kennedy Family Foundation,
   Ethel and W. George
Kirbo Charitable Trust, Thomas
   M. and Irene B.
Kloeckner-Pentaplast of America
Kloster Cruise Ltd.
Knight Foundation, John S. and
   James L.
Knight-Ridder, Inc.
Koch Foundation
Koger Properties
Kohl Foundation, Sidney
Kraft General Foods
Kugelman Foundation
Kysor Industrial Corp.
Lafarge Corp.
Landegger Charitable Foundation
Landis & Gyr, Inc.
Larsh Foundation Charitable
   Trust
Lattner Foundation, Forrest C.
Lauffer Trust, Charles A.
Law Foundation, Robert O.
Lehigh Portland Cement Co.
Lennar Corp.
Leu Foundation, Harry P.
Levi Strauss & Co.
Lewis Foundation, Frank J.
Link Foundation
Lipton Foundation
Lipton, Thomas J.
Litton Industries
Lockheed Corp.
Loren Industries Inc.
Lost Tree Charitable Foundation
Lowe Foundation, Joe and Emily
Luria's
Lynn Foundation, E. M.
MacLeod Stewardship
   Foundation
Magruder Foundation, Chesley
   G.
Mann Foundation, John Jay
Manufacturers Life Insurance
   Co. of America
Manville Corp.
Mark Controls Corp.
Markey Charitable Trust, Lucille
   P.
Marshall & Ilsley Bank
Martin Marietta Aggregates
Martin Marietta Corp.
May Mitchell Royal Foundation
McDonnell Douglas Corp.
McDonnell Douglas Corp.-West
McIntosh Foundation
Mead Corp.
Media General, Inc.
Mellon PSFS
Menasha Corp.
Mercedes-Benz of North
   America, Inc.
Meredith Corp.
Messing Foundation, Morris M.
   and Helen F.
Metal Industries
Meyer Foundation, Baron de
   Hirsch
Meyer Foundation, Bert and
   Mary

Mida Foundation
Midlantic Banks, Inc.
Miller Brewing Co.
Mills Charitable Foundation,
   Henry L. and Kathryn
Mineral Trust
Minnesota Power & Light Co.
Monsanto Co.
Moore Foundation, Martha G.
Morgan Foundation, Louie R.
   and Gertrude
Morrison-Knudsen Corp.
Motorola
National City Corp.
National Medical Enterprises
NationsBank Corp.
Nationwide Insurance Cos.
NBD Bank
NCR Corp.
NEC USA
New York Times Co.
North American Philips Corp.
Northern Trust Co.
Norwest Corp.
NUI Corp.
NVF Co.
Occidental Petroleum Corp.
Olin Corp.
Orion Capital Corp.
Outboard Marine Corp.
Overstreet Foundation
Overstreet Investment Co.
Owens-Corning Fiberglas Corp.
Pall Corp.
Parker-Hannifin Corp.
Parsons - W.D. Charities, Vera
   Davis
Paulucci Family Foundation
Pearce Foundation, Dr. M. Lee
Penn Central Corp.
Phelps Dodge Corp.
Philip Morris Cos.
Phillips Foundation, A. P.
Phillips Foundation, Dr. P.
Picower Foundation, Jeffrey M.
   and Barbara
Pioneer Hi-Bred International
Pittway Corp.
Pope Foundation, Lois B.
Posnack Family Foundation of
   Hollywood
Poynter Fund
Progressive Corp.
Prudential Insurance Co. of
   America
Publix Supermarkets
Pyramid Foundation
Quaker Oats Co.
Quantum Chemical Corp.
Racal-Milgo
Rales and Ruth Rales
   Foundation, Norman R.
Raytheon Engineers &
   Constructors
Reinhold Foundation, Paul E.
   and Ida Klare
Republic New York Corp.
Revlon
Rice Family Foundation, Jacob
   and Sophie
Rinker Materials Corp.
Rinker, Sr. Foundation, M. E.
River Branch Foundation
Rosenberg Family Foundation,
   William
Rosenberg Foundation, William
   J. and Tina
Rouse Co.
Royal Crown Cos., Inc.
Rumbaugh Foundation, J. H. and
   F. H.
Russell Memorial Foundation,
   Robert
Ryder System
SAFECO Corp.
St. Joe Paper Co.
Saint Paul Cos.

Samsung America Inc.
Sara Lee Corp.
Saunders Foundation
Schecter Private Foundation,
   Aaron and Martha
Schering Laboratories
Schering-Plough Corp.
Schultz Foundation
Scotty's, Inc.
Scripps Co., E.W.
Seagram & Sons, Joseph E.
Selby and Marie Selby
   Foundation, William G.
Sentinel Communications Co.
Sequa Corp.
Servico, Inc.
Shapiro Foundation, Carl and
   Ruth
Shell Oil Co.
Siebe North Inc.
Simon Foundation, Sidney,
   Milton and Leoma
Sky Chefs, Inc.
Smith Benevolent Association,
   Buckingham
Society Corp.
Sonesta International Hotels
   Corp.
Sony Corp. of America
Soref Foundation, Samuel M.
   Soref and Helene K.
Southdown, Inc.
Southland Corp.
Southmark Corp.
Southtrust Corp.
Speer Foundation, Roy M.
Sprint
Square D Co.
Stacy Foundation, Festus
Standard Chartered Bank New
   York
State Farm Mutual Automobile
   Insurance Co.
Stauffer Communications
Stone Container Corp.
Storage Technology Corp.
Storer Communications Inc.
Stuart Foundation, Edward C.
Sun Banks Inc.
Sunburst Foundation
Swisher Foundation, Carl S.
Swiss American Securities, Inc.
Swiss Bank Corp.
Sylvester Foundation, Harcourt
   M. and Virginia W.
Synovus Financial Corp.
Tampa Electric
Tandem Computers
Target Stores
Tarmac America Inc.
Taylor Family Foundation, Jack
Teleflex Inc.
Temple-Inland
Terry Foundation, C. Herman
Tetley, Inc.
Texaco
Textron
Thomas Foundation, Dorothy
Thoresen Foundation
3M Co.
TJX Cos.
Travelers Cos.
Tropicana Products, Inc.
Turner Corp.
UNC, Inc.
Unilever United States
Union Camp Corp.
United States Sugar Corp.
United States Trust Co. of New
   York
United Technologies Corp.
United Telephone Co. of Florida
USG Corp.
Valspar Corp.
Vilter Manufacturing Corp.
Volen Charitable Trust, Benjamin
Volkswagen of America, Inc.

Wahlstrom Foundation
Wal-Mart Stores
Walgreen Co.
Disney Co., Walt
Walter Industries
Ware Foundation
Washington Post Co.
Weatherwax Foundation
Weintraub Family Foundation,
   Joseph
Wells Foundation, Lillian S.
Wertheim Foundation, Dr.
   Herbert A.
West Co.
Westinghouse Electric Corp.
Westvaco Corp.
Wetterau
Weyerhaeuser Co.
Whitehall Foundation
Wiggins Memorial Trust, J. J.
Wilder Foundation
Williams Foundation, Edna
   Sproull
Wilson Foundation, Hugh and
   Mary
Winn-Dixie Stores
Wiseheart Foundation
Witco Corp.
Wolfson Family Foundation
Yulman Trust, Morton and Helen
Zurn Industries

Georgia

Abreu Charitable Trust u/w/o
   May P. Abreu, Francis I.
AEC Trust
AEGON USA, Inc.
AFLAC
Agway
Air Products & Chemicals
Akzo America
Albany International Corp.
Alco Standard Corp.
Alexander & Alexander
   Services, Inc.
Alumax
Aluminum Co. of America
AMAX
America West Airlines
American Business Products, Inc.
American Express Co.
American Financial Corp.
American Home Products Corp.
American Security Bank
American Telephone &
   Telegraph Co.
American Telephone &
   Telegraph Co./Atlanta Region
Amoco Corp.
Anderson Foundation, Peyton
APAC Inc.
ARA Services
Archer-Daniels-Midland Co.
Armco Inc.
Armstrong World Industries Inc.
Arnold Fund
Arrow Electronics, Inc.
Atlanta Foundation
Atlanta Gas Light Co.
Atlanta Journal & Constitution
Atlantic Realty Co.
Avery Dennison Corp.
Avis Inc.
Avnet, Inc.
Avon Products
Baker Foundation, Clark and
   Ruby
Bandag, Inc.
Bank South Corp.
Bard, C. R.
Barnes Group
Barnett Banks
Bausch & Lomb
Baxter International
Beck Foundation, Lewis H.
Belk Stores

Bell Industries
BellSouth Corp.
Bellsouth Telecommunications,
   Inc.
Beloco Foundation
Bergen Brunswig Corp.
Bibb Co.
Black & Decker Corp.
Blue Circle Inc.
BMW of North America, Inc.
BOC Group
Boise Cascade Corp.
Borg-Warner Corp.
Bradley-Turner Foundation
Brown & Sons, Alex
Brown & Williamson Tobacco
   Corp.
Browning-Ferris Industries
Bruno's Inc.
Brunswick Corp.
Burke Foundation, Thomas C.
Cabot Corp.
Callaway Foundation
Callaway Foundation, Fuller E.
Camp Younts Foundation
Campbell Foundation, J. Bulow
Campbell Soup Co.
Capital Cities/ABC
Carrier Corp.
Castle & Co., A.M.
CBI Industries
Central Soya Co.
Challenge Foundation
Champion International Corp.
Charter Medical Corp.
Chatham Valley Foundation
Cherokee Foundation
Chevron Corp.
Chick-Fil-A, Inc.
Chrysler Corp.
Churches Homes Foundation
CIBA-GEIGY Corp.
Circuit City Stores
Citicorp
Citizens Union Bank
Clopay Corp.
Clorox Co.
Coachmen Industries
Coats & Clark Inc.
Cobb Educational Fund, Ty
Coca-Cola Co.
Collins & Aikman Corp.
Collins & Aikman Holdings
   Corp.
Colonial Oil Industries, Inc.
Commerzbank AG, New York
Community Enterprises
Computer Associates
   International
ConAgra
Continental Bank N.A.
Cook Batson Foundation
Cooper Industries
Courts Foundation
Cox Enterprises
Cox, Jr. Foundation, James M.
Crawford & Co.
Credit Suisse
Creel Foundation
Crum and Forster
Culbro Corp.
Curtice-Burns Foods
Cyprus Minerals Co.
Day Foundation, Cecil B.
Delta Air Lines
Deluxe Corp.
Digital Communications
   Associates, Inc.
Digital Equipment Corp.
Dixie Yarns, Inc.
Dodson Foundation, James
   Glenwell and Clara May
Dollar General Corp.
Dorminy Foundation, John Henry
Douglas & Lomason Company
Dover Corp.
Dow Chemical Co.

Georgia (cont.)

Dow Jones & Co.
du Pont de Nemours & Co., E. I.
Durr-Fillauer Medical
Eaton Corp.
Eckerd Corp., Jack
Ecolab
Edison Brothers Stores
Eka Nobel
Elf Atochem North America
Elkin Memorial Foundation, Neil
 Warren and William Simpson
Emerson Electric Co.
EMI Records Group
English Memorial Fund,
 Florence C. and H. L.
Eni-Chem America, Inc.
Equifax
Equitable Life Assurance Society
 of the U.S.
Eureka Co.
Evans Foundation, Lettie Pate
Exposition Foundation
Farley Industries
Federal National Mortgage
 Assn., Fannie Mae
Federated Department Stores and
 Allied Stores Corp.
Ferro Corp.
Fieldcrest Cannon
Fireman's Fund Insurance Co.
First National Bank of Atlanta
First Union Corp.
Flagler Co.
Fleet Bank
Fleet Financial Group
Flowers Industries, Inc.
Fortis Inc.
Foundation for Advancement of
 Chiropractic Education
Franklin Foundation, John and
 Mary
Fuller Co., H.B.
Fuqua Foundation, J. B.
Fuqua Industries, Inc.
Gage Foundation, Philip and
 Irene Toll
Gannett Co.
Garden Foundation, Allan C. and
 Lelia J.
GATX Corp.
GEICO Corp.
General American Life Insurance
 Co.
General Electric Co.
General Motors Corp.
General Reinsurance Corp.
General Tire Inc.
Genuine Parts Co.
Georgia Gulf Corp.
Georgia Health Foundation
Georgia-Pacific Corp.
Georgia Pork Producers
 Association
Georgia Power Co.
Georgia Scientific and Technical
 Research Foundation
Gholston Trust, J. K.
Gilbert, Jr. Charitable Trust, Price
Glancy Foundation, Lenora and
 Alfred
Glenmore Distilleries Co.
Glenn Memorial Foundation,
 Wilbur Fisk
Gold Kist, Inc.
Goodyear Tire & Rubber Co.
Graco
Graves Foundation
GTE Corp.
Gulfstream Aerospace Corp.
Haley Foundation, W. B.
Hallmark Cards
Harland Charitable Foundation,
 John and Wilhelmina D.
Harland Co., John H.
Harris Corp.

Hartmarx Corp.
Haverty Furniture Cos., Inc.
Health 1st Foundation
Heileman Brewing Co., Inc., G.
Heller Financial
Hercules Inc.
Herndon Foundation, Alonzo F.
 Herndon and Norris B.
Hewlett-Packard Co.
Hill and Family Foundation,
 Walter Clay
Hitachi
Hodge Foundation
Hollis Foundation
Home Depot
HON Industries
Hospital Corp. of America
Howell Fund
Hubbell Inc.
Humana
Hyundai Motor America
IBM Corp.
Illges Foundation, John P. and
 Dorothy S.
Illges Memorial Foundation, A.
 and M. L.
Imlay Foundation
Indiana Insurance Cos.
Inland Container Corp.
Inland Steel Industries
Interface Inc.
Intermark, Inc.
International Multifoods Corp.
Interpublic Group of Cos.
ITT Hartford Insurance Group
Jefferson-Pilot
Jefferson-Pilot Communications
Jefferson Smurfit Corp.
Jinks Foundation, Ruth T.
Johnson Controls
Johnson & Higgins
Johnson & Johnson
Johnson, Lane, Space, Smith &
 Co., Inc.
Johnson & Son, S.C.
Jones Construction Co., J.A.
Keebler Co.
Kimberly-Clark Corp.
Kloeckner-Pentaplast of America
Knight-Ridder, Inc.
Kuse Foundation, James R.
Kysor Industrial Corp.
Lane Memorial Foundation,
 Mills Bee
Langdale Co.
Lanier Brothers Foundation
Lanier Business Products, Inc.
Law Companies Group
Lee Foundation, Ray M. and
 Mary Elizabeth
Lennox International, Inc.
Levi Strauss & Co.
Life Insurance Co. of Georgia
Life Investors Insurance
 Company of America
Litton Industries
Livingston Foundation
Lockheed Corp.
Loridans Foundation, Charles
Love Foundation, Gay and
 Erskine
Macy & Co., R.H.
Manufacturers Life Insurance
 Co. of America
Manville Corp.
Marion Fabrics
Marshall Foundation, Mattie H.
Marshall Trust in Memory of
 Sanders McDaniel, Harriet
 McDaniel
McCamish Foundation
McCarthy Foundation, John and
 Margaret
McCormick & Co.
McDonnell Douglas Corp.
McGraw-Hill
MCI Communications Corp.

McKesson Corp.
Mead Corp.
Menasha Corp.
Merck & Co.
Miller Brewing Co.
Miller Brewing
 Company/Georgia
Milliken & Co.
Mitsui & Co. (U.S.A.)
Mizuno Corporation of America
Mohasco Corp.
Monsanto Co.
Montana Power Co.
Moore Foundation, Roy C.
Moore Memorial Foundation,
 James Starr
Murata Erie North America
Murphy Foundation, Katherine
 and John
Nalco Chemical Co.
Nash-Finch Co.
National Computer Systems
National Data Corp.
National Distributing Co., Inc.
National Medical Enterprises
National Service Industries
Nationale-Nederlanden North
 America Corp.
NationsBank Corp.
New York Times Co.
Newmont Mining Corp.
Nordson Corp.
Norfolk Southern Corp.
Northern Telecom Inc.
Norton Co.
Norwest Corp.
NutraSweet Co.
Ogilvy & Mather Worldwide
Olin Corp.
Oneida Ltd.
Outboard Marine Corp.
Owens-Corning Fiberglas Corp.
Oxford Foundation
Oxford Industries, Inc.
Parker-Hannifin Corp.
Parker, Jr. Foundation, William
 A.
Patterson-Barclay Memorial
 Foundation
Peerless Insurance Co.
Pet
Phelps Dodge Corp.
Philip Morris Cos.
Pickett and Hatcher Educational
 Fund
Piggly Wiggly Southern
Pioneer Hi-Bred International
Pitts Foundation, William H. and
 Lula E.
Pittulloch Foundation
Polaroid Corp.
Porter Testamentary Trust, James
 Hyde
PPG Industries
Primerica Corp.
Primerica Financial Services
Printpack, Inc.
Procter & Gamble Co.
Prudential Insurance Co. of
 America
Quaker Chemical Corp.
Racetrac Petroleum
Ragan Charitable Foundation,
 Carolyn King
Raleigh Linen Service/National
 Distributing Co.
REI-Recreational Equipment,
 Inc.
Reliance Electric Co.
Rhone-Poulenc Rorer
Rich Foundation
Rich Products Corp.
Robinson Foundation, J. Mack
Rochester Telephone Corp.
Roddenbery Co., Inc., W.B.
Rollins Inc.
Rouse Co.

RTM
Saab Cars USA, Inc.
SAFECO Corp.
Salomon
Samsung America Inc.
Sara Lee Corp.
Savannah Electric & Power Co.
Schering-Plough Corp.
Schlumberger Ltd.
Schwob Foundation, Simon
Scientific-Atlanta
Scripps Co., E.W.
Sealy, Inc.
Security Life of Denver
Senior Citizens Foundation
Sewell Foundation, Warren P.
 and Ava F.
Shaw Industries
Sherwin-Williams Co.
Skandia America Reinsurance
 Corp.
SKF USA, Inc.
Sonat
Sonoco Products Co.
Sony Corp. of America
Southern Bell
Southwire Co.
Spectra-Physics Analytical
Spiegel
Springs Industries
Sprint
Standard Chartered Bank New
 York
Stanley Works
State Farm Mutual Automobile
 Insurance Co.
Steiner Charitable Fund, Albert
Stone Container Corp.
Super Valu Stores
Swiss American Securities, Inc.
Swiss Bank Corp.
Synovus Financial Corp.
Tandem Computers
Target Stores
Taylor Trust, Lydia M.
Temple-Inland
Tetley, Inc.
Textron
Third National Corp.
Thomaston Mills, Inc.
3M Co.
Timken Co.
TJX Cos.
Tomlinson Foundation, Kate and
 Elwyn
Torchmark Corp.
Transco Energy Company
Travelers Cos.
TRINOVA Corp.
Trust Co. Bank
Tull Charitable Foundation
Turner Broadcasting System
Turner Corp.
Turner Foundation
Unilever United States
Union Camp Corp.
Union Carbide Corp.
Union Manufacturing Co.
Unisys Corp.
United Dominion Industries
United Merchants &
 Manufacturers
United Parcel Service of America
United Technologies Corp.
USG Corp.
USX Corp.
Volkswagen of America, Inc.
Vulcan Materials Co.
Wachovia Bank of Georgia, N.A.
Waffle House, Inc.
Wal-Mart Stores
Walton Monroe Mills
Wardlaw Fund, Gertrude and
 William C.
Watkins Associated Industries
Watkins Christian Foundation
Wehadkee Foundation

West Foundation
Wetterau
Weyerhaeuser Co.
White Consolidated Industries
Whitehead Foundation, Joseph B.
Whitehead Foundation, Lettie
 Pate
Williams Family Foundation of
 Georgia
Williams, Jr. Family Foundation,
 A. L.
Wilson Foundation, Frances
 Wood
Winn-Dixie Stores
Winter Construction Co.
Woodruff Foundation, Robert W.
Woodward Fund-Atlanta, David,
 Helen, Marian
Woolley Foundation, Vasser
World Carpets
Wrigley Co., Wm. Jr.
Xerox Corp.
Y.K.K. (U.S.A.) Inc.
Zaban Foundation
Zurn Industries

Hawaii

Alexander & Baldwin, Inc.
ALPAC Corp.
Ameron, Inc.
Amfac/JMB Hawaii
AON Corp.
ARA Services
Armco Inc.
Atherton Family Foundation
Baldwin Memorial Foundation,
 Fred
Bancorp Hawaii
Baxter International
BHP Pacific Resources
Boise Cascade Corp.
Brewer and Co., Ltd., C.
Castle & Cooke
Castle Foundation, Harold K. L.
Castle Foundation, Samuel N.
 and Mary
Castle Trust, George P. and Ida
 Tenney
Chevron Corp.
Computer Associates
 International
Cooke Foundation
Crum and Forster
Dover Corp.
Fireman's Fund Insurance Co.
First Hawaiian
Frear Eleemosynary Trust, Mary
 D. and Walter F.
Gannett Co.
Givenchy, Inc.
Hawaii National Bank
Hawaiian Telephone Co.
HEI Inc.
Hobart Memorial Fund, Marion
 W.
Holy Land Charitable Trust
Hopper Foundation, May
 Templeton
Johnson & Higgins
Lee Enterprises
Manufacturers Life Insurance
 Co. of America
Matsushita Electric Corp. of
 America
McInerny Foundation
Mead Corp.
Moore Foundation, O. L.
Morrison-Knudsen Corp.
NEC USA
Oceanic Cablevision Foundation
Ogilvy & Mather Worldwide
Persis Corp.
Pioneer Hi-Bred International
Reynolds Metals Co.
Saint Paul Cos.
Schieffelin & Somerset Co.
Servco Pacific

Skinner Corp.
Sony Corp. of America
Straub Estate, Gertrude S.
Tandem Computers
3M Co.
Toshiba America, Inc.
Travelers Cos.
United Airlines
Vidinha Charitable Trust, A. and E.
Watumull Fund, J.
Weyerhaeuser Co.
Wilcox General Trust, George N.
Wilcox Trust, S. W.
Zimmerman Foundation, Hans and Clara Davis

Idaho

Albertson's
ALPAC Corp.
Alumax
Amalgamated Sugar Co.
AMAX
American Microsystems, Inc.
Arrow Electronics, Inc.
Beckman Foundation, Leland D.
Bergen Brunswig Corp.
Best Products Co.
Blount
Boise Cascade Corp.
Browning-Ferris Industries
CHC Foundation
Cunningham Foundation, Laura Moore
Cyprus Minerals Co.
Daugherty Foundation
Durr-Fillauer Medical
EG&G Inc.
Equimark Corp.
Evening Post Publishing Co.
First Interstate Bank NW Region
First Security Bank of Idaho N.A.
First Security Corp. (Salt Lake City, Utah)
FMC Corp.
Gannett Co.
Hecla Mining Co.
Heinz Co., H.J.
Hewlett-Packard Co.
Intermountain Gas Industries
Johnson & Higgins
Kasiska Family Foundation
Land O'Lakes
Louisiana-Pacific Corp.
Mead Corp.
Monsanto Co.
Morrison Foundation, Harry W.
Morrison-Knudsen Corp.
National Medical Enterprises
Ore-Ida Foods, Inc.
Pet
Pioneer Hi-Bred International
Potlatch Corp.
Saint Paul Cos.
Sandoz Corp.
Simplot Co., J.R.
Skinner Corp.
Steiner Corp.
Target Stores
Union Pacific Corp.
Universal Foods Corp.
US WEST
Washington Mutual Savings Bank
West One Bancorp
West One Bank Idaho
Whiting Foundation, Macauley and Helen Dow
Whittenberger Foundation, Claude R. and Ethel B.

Illinois

Abbott Laboratories
Ace Hardware Corp.
Acorn Corrugated Box Co.
AEGON USA, Inc.

Aetna Life & Casualty Co.
Aigner
Air France
Air Products & Chemicals
Akzo America
Akzo Chemicals Inc.
Alberto-Culver Co.
Alco Standard Corp.
Alexander & Alexander Services, Inc.
Allegheny Ludlum Corp.
Allen-Heath Memorial Foundation
AlliedSignal
Allstate Insurance Co.
Allyn Foundation
Alsdorf Foundation
Alumax
AMAX
AMCORE Bank, N.A. Rockford
America West Airlines
American Brands
American Decal & Manufacturing Co.
American Express Co.
American Financial Corp.
American Greetings Corp.
American National Bank & Trust Co. of Chicago
American National Can Co.
American Stores Co.
American Telephone & Telegraph Co.
American Telephone & Telegraph Co./Chicago Region
Ameritech Corp.
Ameritech Development
Ameritech Information Systems
Ameritech International
Ameritech Mobile Communications
Ameritech Services
AMETEK
Amoco Corp.
Amsted Industries
Andersen Foundation, Arthur
Anderson Industries
Andersons Management Corp.
Andreas Foundation
Andrew Corp.
Anheuser-Busch Cos.
AON Corp.
APV Crepaco Inc.
ARA Services
Aratex Services
Archer-Daniels-Midland Co.
Armco Inc.
Armstrong World Industries Inc.
Arrow Electronics, Inc.
Asea Brown Boveri
Atwood Foundation
Atwood Industries
Augat, Inc.
Avery Dennison Corp.
Avis Inc.
Avnet, Inc.
Avon Products
AXIA Incorporated
Azteca Foods, Inc.
Balcor Co.
Ball Corp.
Banc One Illinois Corp.
Banca Commerciale Italiana, New York Branch
Bang & Olufsen of America, Inc.
Bank Hapoalim B.M.
Bank Leumi Trust Co. of New York
BankAmerica Corp.
Bankers Life & Casualty Co.
Barber-Colman Co.
Barber-Greene Co.
Barnes Group
Bates Memorial Foundation, George A.
Bauer Foundation, M. R.
Baum Family Fund, Alvin H.

Baxter International
Beidler Charitable Trust, Francis
Bell Federal Savings & Loan Association
Bell Industries
Beloit Foundation
Bemis Company
Benefit Trust Life Insurance Co.
Bere Foundation
Berger Foundation, Albert E.
Bergner Co., P.A.
Bergstrom Manufacturing Co.
Bersted Foundation
Best Foundation, Walter J. and Edith E.
Beverly Bank
BFGoodrich
Binks Manufacturing Co.
Bitco Corp.
Bjorkman Foundation
Black & Decker Corp.
Blair and Co., William
Blount
Blowitz-Ridgeway Foundation
Blum Foundation, Harry and Maribel G.
Blum Foundation, Nathan and Emily S.
Blum-Kovler Foundation
BMW of North America, Inc.
Boatmen's Bancshares
Bock Charitable Trust, George W.
Boise Cascade Corp.
Boler Co.
Boothroyd Foundation, Charles H. and Bertha L.
Boots Pharmaceuticals, Inc.
Borden
Borg-Warner Corp.
Borwell Charitable Foundation
Bosch Corp., Robert
Boulevard Bank, N.A.
Bound to Stay Bound Books Foundation
Bowater Inc.
Bowyer Foundation, Ambrose and Gladys
Brach Foundation, Edwin I.
Brach Foundation, Helen
Brand Cos.
Bridgestone/Firestone
Brown & Associates, Clayton
Browning-Ferris Industries
Brunner Foundation, Fred J.
Brunswick Corp.
Buchanan Family Foundation
Buehler Foundation, A. C.
Burlington Northern Inc.
Butler Family Foundation, George W. and Gladys S.
Butler Manufacturing Co.
Butz Foundation
C.P. Rail Systems
Cabot Corp.
Caestecker Foundation, Charles and Marie
Camp and Bennet Humiston Trust, Apollos
Campbell Soup Co.
Capital Cities/ABC
Carrier Corp.
Carter-Wallace
Carus Corp.
Carylon Foundation
Castle & Co., A.M.
Caterpillar
CBI Industries
CBS Inc.
Ceco Corp.
Centel Corp.
Central Illinois Public Service Co.
Central Soya Co.
Centralia Foundation
Chamberlain Manufacturing Corp.

Chanin Family Foundation, Paul R.
Chapin-May Foundation of Illinois
Charter Medical Corp.
Chase Manhattan Bank, N.A.
Cheney Foundation, Elizabeth F.
Chesebrough-Pond's
Chicago Board of Trade
Chicago City Bank & Trust Co.
Chicago Milwaukee Corp.
Chicago Resource Center
Chicago Sun-Times, Inc.
Chicago Title and Trust Co.
Chicago Tribune Co.
Chicago White Metal Casting
Chiquita Brands Co.
Chrysler Corp.
Chubb Corp.
CIGNA Corp.
Cincinnati Milacron
Circuit City Stores
Citicorp
CLARCOR
Clark Equipment Co.
Clopay Corp.
Clorox Co.
CNA Insurance Cos.
Cohn Family Foundation, Robert and Terri
Cole Taylor Financial Group
Coleman Foundation
Coltec Industries
Combs Foundation, Earle M. and Virginia M.
Comer Foundation
Comerica
Commerce Clearing House
Commerzbank AG, New York
Commonwealth Edison Co.
Commonwealth Industries Corp.
Computer Associates International
ConAgra
Consolidated Papers
Consolidated Rail Corp. (Conrail)
Continental Bank N.A.
Continental Corp.
Cookson America
Cooper Charitable Trust, Richard H.
Cooper Industries
Copley Press
Copperweld Corp.
Corroon & Black of Illinois
Costain Holdings Inc.
Cotter & Co.
Country Cos.
Cox Charitable Trust, A. G.
Cox Enterprises
CPC International
CR Industries
Crane & Co.
Crane Co.
Credit Agricole
Credit Suisse
CRI Charitable Trust
CRL Inc.
Crompton & Knowles Corp.
Crowell Trust, Henry P. and Susan C.
Crown Charitable Fund, Edward A.
Crown Memorial, Arie and Ida
Crum and Forster
CTS Corp.
Cuneo Foundation
Curtice-Burns Foods
Curtis Industries, Helene
Cyprus Minerals Co.
Dalgety Inc.
Dan River, Inc.
Dana Corp.
Dartnell Corp.
Davee Foundation
Dean Foods Co.
Dean Witter Discover

Deere & Co.
DeKalb Genetics Corp.
Delta Air Lines
Deluxe Corp.
Demos Foundation, N.
DeSoto
Deutsche Bank AG
Dexter Corp.
Dial Corp.
Dick Family Foundation
Dickey-John Corp.
Digital Equipment Corp.
Dillon Foundation
Dollar General Corp.
Donaldson Co.
Donaldson, Lufkin & Jenrette
Donnelley Foundation, Elliott and Ann
Donnelley Foundation, Gaylord and Dorothy
Donnelley & Sons Co., R.R.
Douglas & Lomason Company
Dover Corp.
Dow Chemical Co.
Dow Jones & Co.
Dower Foundation, Thomas W.
Driehaus Foundation, Richard H.
du Pont de Nemours & Co., E. I.
Duchossois Industries
Dun & Bradstreet Corp.
Duplex Products, Inc.
Eaton Corp.
Echlin Inc.
Ecolab
Eisenberg Foundation, George M.
Elco Charitable Foundation
Elf Atochem North America
Elgin Sweeper Co.
Emerson Electric Co.
EMI Records Group
Employers Insurance of Wausau, A Mutual Co.
Employers Mutual Casualty Co.
Encyclopaedia Britannica, Inc.
Eni-Chem America, Inc.
Epaphroditus Foundation
Equitable Life Assurance Society of the U.S.
Erickson Charitable Fund, Eben W.
Ethyl Corp.
Eureka Co.
Exxon Corp.
Fabyan Foundation
Fairchild Corp.
Fairview Foundation
Falk Medical Research Foundation, Dr. Ralph and Marian
Fanuc U.S.A. Corp.
Farley Industries
Farmers & Mechanics Bank
Fearn International, Inc.
Federal National Mortgage Assn., Fannie Mae
Feinberg Foundation, Joseph and Bessie
Fel-Pro Incorporated
Fiat U.S.A., Inc.
Field Foundation, Jamee and Marshall
Field Foundation of Illinois
Fireman's Fund Insurance Co.
First Chicago
First National Bank of Evergreen Park
First National Bank & Trust Co. of Rockford
Firstar Bank Milwaukee NA
Fleming Charitable Trust, Joseph F.
Florsheim Shoe Co.
Fluor Corp.
FMC Corp.
Foote, Cone & Belding Communications
Forest Fund

Illinois (cont.)

Foster and Gallagher
Four Wheels, Inc.
Fox Inc.
Foxmeyer Corp.
Fraida Foundation
Frank Fund, Zollie and Elaine
Frankel Foundation
Franklin Life Insurance Co.
Fraser Paper Ltd.
Fruit of the Loom, Inc.
Fry Foundation, Lloyd A.
Fuller Co., H.B.
Fullerton Metals Co.
Galter Foundation
Galvin Foundation, Robert W.
Gannett Co.
GATX Corp.
Gavin Foundation, James and Zita
Gaylord Container Corp.
Geifman Family Foundation
General Dynamics Corp.
General Electric Co.
General Housewares Corp.
General Motors Corp.
General Reinsurance Corp.
General Tire Inc.
Geneseo Foundation
Georgia-Pacific Corp.
Getz Foundation, Emma and Oscar
Gillespie Memorial Fund, Boynton
Goldberg Family Foundation, Milton D. and Madeline L.
Goldenberg Foundation, Max
Goldman Foundation, Morris and Rose
Goldman Sachs & Co.
Goodyear Tire & Rubber Co.
Graco
Graham Foundation for Advanced Studies in the Fine Arts
Grainger Foundation
Grainger, W.W.
Grant Thornton
Grenzebach & Associates, John
Griffith Laboratories Foundation, Inc.
Griswold Trust, Jessie
Growmark, Inc.
GSC Enterprises
H. B. B. Foundation
Haffner Foundation
Hales Charitable Fund
Hales Foundation, William M.
Hallmark Cards
Hammer Foundation, Armand
Hanna Co., M.A.
Hanson Testamentary Charitable Trust, Anna Emery
Harper Foundation, Philip S.
HarperCollins Publishers
Harris Corp.
Harris Family Foundation, Hunt and Diane
Harris Foundation, H. H.
Harris Foundation, J. Ira and Nicki
Harris Trust & Savings Bank
Harrison Foundation, Fred G.
Harsco Corp.
Hartmarx Corp.
Hay Foundation, John I.
Hazeltine Corp.
Heed Ophthalmic Foundation
Heileman Brewing Co., Inc., G.
Heller Financial
Heller Foundation, Walter E.
Henkel Corp.
Henry Foundation
Herald News
Heritage Pullman Bank & Trust
Hermann Foundation, Grover

Hesston Corp.
Hewlett-Packard Co.
Hobbs Foundation
Hoffer Plastics Corp.
Honeywell
Hook Drug
Hoover Foundation, H. Earl
Hopper Memorial Foundation, Bertrand
Hospital Corp. of America
Houghton Mifflin Co.
Household International
Huizenga Foundation, Jennie
Humana
Hyundai Motor America
I and G Charitable Foundation
IBM Corp.
ICI Americas
Ideal Industries
IDEX Corp.
Illinois Bell
Illinois Central Railroad Co.
Illinois Cereal Mills
Illinois Consolidated Telephone Co.
Illinois Power Co.
Illinois Tool Works
IMCERA Group Inc.
Ingersoll Milling Machine Co.
Inland Container Corp.
Inland Steel Industries
Interco
International Multifoods Corp.
International Paper Co.
Interpublic Group of Cos.
Interstate National Corp.
Iowa-Illinois Gas & Electric Co.
ITT Corp.
ITT Hartford Insurance Group
ITT Rayonier
J.P. Morgan & Co.
James & Co., Fred S.
James River Corp. of Virginia
Jefferson Smurfit Corp.
Jim Beam Brands Co.
Johnson Controls
Johnson Foundation, A. D.
Johnson & Higgins
Johnson & Johnson
Joslyn Corp.
Jostens
Joyce Foundation
Jupiter Industries, Inc.
Kaman Corp.
Kaplan Foundation, Mayer and Morris
Kapoor Charitable Foundation
Katten, Muchin, & Zavis
Katy Industries Inc.
Kearney Inc., A.T.
Keebler Co.
Keeney Trust, Hattie Hannah
Kelco Industries, Inc.
Kellstadt Foundation
Kelly Foundation, Donald P. and Byrd M.
Kelly Foundation, T. Lloyd
Kemper Educational and Charitable Fund
Kemper Investors Life Insurance Co.
Kemper National Insurance Cos.
Kendall Foundation, George R.
Kern Foundation Trust
Kirkland & Ellis
Klein Tools
Kline Trust IV, Harry L.
Knowles Foundation
KPMG Peat Marwick
Kraft General Foods
Kysor Industrial Corp.
La-Co. Industries, Inc.
Landis & Gyr, Inc.
Lapham-Hickey Steel Corp.
LaSalle Bank Lake View
LaSalle National Bank
Lasalle National Corp.

Lawson Products, Inc.
Lederer Foundation, Francis L.
Lee Enterprises
Lehmann Foundation, Otto W.
Leo Burnett Co.
Levinson's, Inc.
Levy Circulating Co., Charles
Levy Foundation, Charles and Ruth
Lincoln National Corp.
Linde Foundation, Ronald and Maxine
Litton Industries
Lizzadro Family Foundation, Joseph
Loews Corp.
Logan Foundation, E. J.
Lord Educational Fund
Louis Foundation, Michael W.
LTV Corp.
Lumpkin Foundation
Lurie Family Foundation
MacArthur Foundation, J. Roderick
MacArthur Foundation, John D. and Catherine T.
MacLean-Fogg Co.
Macmillan, Inc.
Magic Chef
Manilow Foundation, Nathan
Mansfield Foundation, Albert and Anne
Manufacturers Life Insurance Co. of America
Manville Corp.
Mapco Inc.
Maritz Inc.
Mark Controls Corp.
Marmon Group, Inc.
Marshall Field's
Martin-Brower Co., The
Martin Foundation, Bert William
Mason Charitable Foundation
Masonite Corp.
Material Service Corp.
Matsushita Electric Corp. of America
Mattel
Mayer Charitable Trust, Oscar G. & Elsa S.
Maytag Corp.
Mazza Foundation
MCA
McCormick & Co.
McCormick Foundation, Chauncey and Marion Deering
McCormick Tribune Foundation, Robert R.
McDonald's Corp.
McFarland Charitable Foundation
McGraw Foundation
McGraw-Hill
MCI Communications Corp.
McIntosh Foundation
McWane Inc.
Mead Corp.
Mellinger Educational Foundation, Edward Arthur
Mellon Bank Corp.
Mellon PSFS
Mercantile Bancorp
Mercedes-Benz of North America, Inc.
Mercer, William M.
Merrion Foundation
Metromail Corp.
Metropolitan Bank & Trust Co.
Miami Corp.
Midas International Corp.
MidCon Corp.
Midway Airlines
Miles Inc.
Millard Charitable Trust, Adah K.
Miller & Co.
Milwaukee Golf Development Co.

Mitchell Family Foundation, Bernard and Marjorie
Mitsui & Co. (U.S.A.)
Mobil Oil Corp.
Modern Maid Food Products, Inc.
Molex, Inc.
Monsanto Co.
Montgomery Elevator Co.
Montgomery Ward & Co.
Monticello College Foundation
Moore Business Forms, Inc.
Moorman Manufacturing Co.
Morgan Stanley & Co.
Morrison-Knudsen Corp.
Morton International
Morton Memorial Fund, Mark
Motorola
Mueller Co.
Nalco Chemical Co.
National Manufacturing Co.
National Medical Enterprises
National Starch & Chemical Corp.
Navistar International Corp.
NBD Bank
Neese Family Foundation
Negaunee Foundation
New Prospect Foundation
New York Times Co.
Newell Co.
News America Publishing Inc.
Nicor, Inc.
Nielsen Co., A.C.
Norris Foundation, Dellora A. and Lester J.
North American Philips Corp.
Northern Illinois Gas Co.
Northern Telecom Inc.
Northern Trust Co.
Northrop Corp.
Northwestern Golf Co.
Northwestern Steel & Wire Co.
Norton Co.
Norton Memorial Corporation, Geraldi
Norwest Corp.
NutraSweet Co.
Nuveen & Co., Inc., John
Oakite Products
Occidental Petroleum Corp.
Offield Family Foundation
Old Republic International Corp.
Olin Corp.
Oppenheimer & Co., Inc.
Oppenheimer Family Foundation
Orion Capital Corp.
Outboard Marine Corp.
Outokumpu-American Brass Co.
Owens-Corning Fiberglas Corp.
Packaging Corporation of America
Pamida, Inc.
Park-Ohio Industries Inc.
Parker-Hannifin Corp.
Parsons Corp.
Paxton Co., Frank
Payne Foundation, Frank E. and Seba B.
Peoples Energy Corp.
Pepper Cos.
Perina Corp
Perkins Foundation, Edwin E.
Pesch Family Foundation
Pet
Petersen Foundation, Esper A.
PHH Corp.
Philip Morris Cos.
Pick, Jr. Fund, Albert
Picker International
Pioneer Hi-Bred International
Pittway Corp.
Playboy Enterprises, Inc.
Polaroid Corp.
Portec, Inc.
PPG Industries
Premark International
Prentice Foundation, Abra

Prince Trust, Abbie Norman
Pritzker Foundation
Prudential-Bache Securities
Prudential Insurance Co. of America
Pullman Educational Foundation, George M.
Quaker Oats Co.
Quality Metal Finishing Foundation
Quantum Chemical Corp.
Quincy Newspapers
R. F. Foundation
Ragen, Jr. Memorial Fund Trust No. 1, James M.
Rand McNally and Co.
Raytheon Engineers & Constructors
RB&W Corp.
Reade Industrial Fund
Reflector Hardware Corp.
Regenstein Foundation
REI-Recreational Equipment, Inc.
Relations Foundation
Reliance Electric Co.
Research-Cottrell Inc.
Retirement Research Foundation
Reynolds Metals Co.
Reynolds & Reynolds Co.
Rhoades Fund, Otto L. and Hazel L.
Rhone-Poulenc Rorer
Rice Foundation
Ringier-America
Robin Family Foundation, Albert A.
Rochester Telephone Corp.
Rockford Acromatics Products Co./Aircraft Gear Corp.
Rockford Products Corp.
Rockwell International Corp.
Rohm and Haas Company
Rosenbaum Foundation, Paul and Gabriella
Rosenthal Foundation, Benjamin J.
Rothschild Foundation, Hulda B. and Maurice L.
Rouse Co.
Royal Group Inc.
Royal Insurance Co. of America
Russell Charitable Foundation, Tom
Rust-Oleum Corp.
Ryan Foundation, Patrick G. and Shirley W.
SAFECO Corp.
Safety-Kleen Corp.
Saint Paul Cos.
St. Paul Federal Bank for Savings
Salomon
Salwil Foundation
Sandoz Corp.
Sang Foundation, Elsie O. and Philip D.
Santa Fe Pacific Corp.
Sara Lee Corp.
Sara Lee Hosiery
Schering-Plough Corp.
Schiff, Hardin & Waite
Schmidt Charitable Foundation, William E.
Schmitt Foundation, Arthur J.
Schneider Foundation, Robert E.
Schnuck Markets
Scholl Foundation, Dr.
Scott, Foresman & Co.
Scrivner, Inc.
Seabury Foundation
Seagram & Sons, Joseph E.
Sealy, Inc.
Searle & Co., G.D.
Sears, Roebuck and Co.
Seeley Foundation
Seid Foundation, Barre
ServiceMaster Co. L.P.
Shaklee Corp.

Shapiro Family Foundation, Soretta and Henry
Shapiro Foundation, Charles and M. R.
Shaw Foundation, Walden W. and Jean Young
Shaw Industries
Shell Oil Co.
Sherwin-Williams Co.
Shirk Foundation, Russell and Betty
Siebe North Inc.
Siemens Medical Systems Inc.
Sigma-Aldrich Corp.
Silver Spring Foundation
Silvestri Corp.
Simpson Foundation, John M.
Siragusa Foundation
Sjostrom & Sons
Skandia America Reinsurance Corp.
Skidmore, Owings & Merrill
Smith Charitable Trust
Smith Corp., A.O.
Smith Oil Corp.
Smysor Memorial Fund, Harry L. and John L.
Snite Foundation, Fred B.
Society Corp.
Soft Sheen Products Co.
Solo Cup Co.
Solomon Foundation, Sarah M.
Sony Corp. of America
Spartus Corp.
Special People In Need
Spencer Foundation
Spiegel
Sprague Memorial Institute, Otho S. A.
Springs Industries
SPX Corp.
Square D Co.
Staley, Jr. Foundation, A. E.
Staley Manufacturing Co., A.E.
Standard Chartered Bank New York
State Farm Mutual Automobile Insurance Co.
Steigerwaldt Foundation, Donna Wolf
Stein Roe & Farnham Investment Council
Steiner Corp.
Stella D'Oro Biscuit Co.
Stepan Co.
Sterling Winthrop
Stern Foundation, Irvin
Stone Container Corp.
Stone Family Foundation, Jerome H.
Stone Family Foundation, Norman H.
Stone Forest Industries
Stone Foundation, W. Clement and Jessie V.
Storage Technology Corp.
Sudix Foundation
Sulzer Family Foundation
Sun Chemical Corp.
Sun Electric Corp.
Sundstrand Corp.
Super Valu Stores
Swift Co. Inc., John S.
Swift-Eckrich Inc.
Swiss American Securities, Inc.
Swiss Bank Corp.
T.T.X. Co.
Talley Industries, Inc.
Tandem Computers
Target Stores
TCF Banking & Savings, FSB
TDK Corp. of America
Teledyne
Temple-Inland
Tenneco
Teradyne, Inc.
Textron

Thompson Family Fund, Lucille S.
Thomson Newspapers Corp.
Thorson Foundation
3M Co.
Thyssen Specialty Steels
Tibstra Charitable Foundation, Thomas and Gertrude
Times Mirror Co.
Timken Co.
TJX Cos.
Tokheim Corp.
Tombstone Pizza Corp.
Tootsie Roll Industries, Inc.
Toshiba America, Inc.
Transamerica Corp.
Travelers Cos.
TRINOVA Corp.
Turner Construction Co.
Turner Corp.
Twentieth Century-Fox Film Corp.
Tyndale House Foundation
Uarco Inc.
Union Bank of Switzerland Los Angeles Branch
Union Bank of Switzerland New York Branch
Union Camp Corp.
Union Carbide Corp.
Union Electric Co.
Union Pacific Corp.
Unisys Corp.
United Airlines
United Conveyor Corp.
United Missouri Bancshares, Inc.
United Stationers Inc.
UNO-VEN Co.
USG Corp.
USLIFE Corp.
UST
USX Corp.
Valmont Industries
Valspar Corp.
Varlen Corp.
Volkswagen of America, Inc.
Vulcan Materials Co.
Wal-Mart Stores
Walgreen Co.
Wallace Computer Services
Ward Foundation, A. Montgomery
Warner Electric Brake & Clutch Co.
Washington National Insurance Co.
Washington Square Health Foundation
Waste Management
Werner Foundation, Clara and Spencer
Western Shade Cloth Charitable Foundation
Weyerhaeuser Co.
White Consolidated Industries
White Foundation, W. P. and H. B.
Whitman Corp.
Wieboldt Foundation
Willmott Foundation, Peter S.
Winona Corporation
Witco Corp.
Woods Charitable Fund
Woodward Governor Co.
World Book Inc.
Wrap-On Co.
Wrigley Co., Wm. Jr.
Wurlitzer Foundation, Farny R.
Wyne Foundation
Xerox Corp.
Young Charity Trust Northern Trust Company
Young & Rubicam
Zurn Industries

Indiana
Abitibi-Price

AGFA Division of Miles Inc.
Agway
Alco Standard Corp.
Allegheny Ludlum Corp.
AlliedSignal
Alumax
Aluminum Co. of America
AMAX
AMAX Coal Industries
Amcast Industrial Corp.
Ameribank
American Brands
American Electric Power
American General Finance
American Home Products Corp.
American Maize Products
American National Can Co.
American Red Ball World Wide Movers
American United Life Insurance Co.
Ameritech Corp.
Ameritech Publishing
Ameritech Services
Amsted Industries
Anacomp, Inc.
Anderson Foundation, John W.
Andersons Management Corp.
AON Corp.
Archer-Daniels-Midland Co.
Armco Inc.
Arrow Electronics, Inc.
Arvin Industries
Avery Dennison Corp.
Avnet, Inc.
Ayres Foundation, Inc.
Backer Spielvogel Bates U.S.
Ball Brothers Foundation
Ball Corp.
Ball Foundation, George and Frances
Ball-InCon Glass Packaging Corp.
Banc One Illinois Corp.
Basic American Medical, Inc.
Baxter International
Bell Industries
Bemis Company
Benefit Trust Life Insurance Co.
Bethlehem Steel Corp.
BFGoodrich
Bierhaus Foundation
Bindley Western Industries
Biomet
Black & Decker Corp.
Blount
Boehringer Mannheim Corp.
Boise Cascade Corp.
Borden
Borg-Warner Corp.
Bowsher-Booher Foundation
Bridgestone/Firestone
Brink Unitrust, Julia H.
Bristol-Myers Squibb Co.
Bronstein Foundation, Sol and Arlene
Browning-Ferris Industries
Brunswick Corp.
C.P. Rail Systems
Cabot Corp.
Campbell Soup Co.
Carrier Corp.
Caterpillar
Central Newspapers, Inc.
Central Soya Co.
Charter Medical Corp.
Chesapeake Corp.
Chrysler Corp.
CIGNA Corp.
Citizens Gas & Coke Utility
CLARCOR
Clark Equipment Co.
Clowes Fund
Coachmen Industries
Cole Foundation, Olive B.
Coleman Scholarship Trust, Lillian R.

Coltec Industries
Computer Associates International
Consolidated Rail Corp. (Conrail)
Cooper Industries
Cooper Tire & Rubber Co.
Cosco, Inc.
Countrymark Cooperative
CPC International
CR Industries
Crescent Plastics
Crown International, Inc.
CSX Corp.
CTS Corp.
Culbro Corp.
Cummins Engine Co.
Curtice-Burns Foods
Dana Corp.
Dayton Hudson Corp.
DCB Corp.
Decio Foundation, Arthur J.
Dekko Foundation
Delco Electronics Corp.
Delta Tau Delta Educational Fund
Deluxe Corp.
Dexter Corp.
Dial Corp.
Dollar General Corp.
Donaldson Co.
Donnelley & Sons Co., R.R.
Dow Chemical Co.
Dow Corning Corp.
Dow Elanco Inc.
Dresser Industries
du Pont de Nemours & Co., E. I.
Duncan Trust, James R.
Eagle-Picher Industries
Eaton Corp.
Echlin Inc.
Emerson Electric Co.
English-Bonter-Mitchell Foundation
Erb Lumber Co.
Eureka Co.
Excel Industries (Elkhart, Indiana)
Federal-Mogul Corp.
Ferro Corp.
Fifth Third Bancorp
First Source Corp.
Foellinger Foundation
Ford Meter Box Co.
Forum Group, Inc.
Franklin Electric Company Inc. (Bluffton, Indiana)
Frisch's Restaurants Inc.
Froderman Foundation
Gannett Co.
GATX Corp.
GenCorp
General Electric Co.
General Housewares Corp.
General Motors Corp.
Georgia-Pacific Corp.
Glick Foundation, Eugene and Marilyn
Globe Valve Corp.
Goodman Jewelers, Inc.
Graphic Printing Co.
Great Lakes Chemical Corp.
Griffith Foundation, W. C.
GTE Corp.
Habig Foundation, Arnold F.
Hand Industries
Handy & Harman
Hanson Office Products
Harris Corp.
Harris Stores, Paul
Harsco Corp.
Hartmarx Corp.
Heileman Brewing Co., Inc., G.
Hercules Inc.
Hillenbrand Industries
Hitachi
Hook Drug
Hubbell Inc.
Huber, Hunt & Nichols

Huntington Bancshares Inc.
Hutzell Foundation
IMCERA Group Inc.
Indiana Bell Telephone Co.
Indiana Desk Co.
Indiana Gas and Chemical Corp.
Indiana Gas Co.
Indiana Insurance Cos.
Indianapolis Newspapers, Inc.
Indianapolis Water Co.
Inland Container Corp.
Inland Steel Industries
International Multifoods Corp.
IPALCO Enterprises
ITT Corp.
ITT Hartford Insurance Group
ITT Rayonier
James River Corp. of Virginia
Jasper Desk Co.
Jasper Seating Co.
Jasper Table Co.
Jasper Wood Products Co.
Jefferson Smurfit Corp.
JOFCo., Inc.
Johnson Controls
Jordan Foundation, Arthur
Journal Gazette Co.
Keebler Co.
Keller-Crescent Co.
Kilbourne Residuary Charitable Trust, E. H.
Kimball International
Kloeckner-Pentaplast of America
Knight-Ridder, Inc.
Koch Sons, George
Kraft General Foods
Kuehn Foundation
Kuhne Foundation Trust, Charles
La Porte Casting Division
Lassus Brothers Oil
Lehigh Portland Cement Co.
Leighton-Oare Foundation
Liberty Corp.
Liberty National Bank
Lilly & Co., Eli
Lilly Endowment
Lincoln National Corp.
LTV Corp.
Manufacturers Life Insurance Co. of America
Manville Corp.
Mapco Inc.
Marathon Oil, Indiana Refining Division
Marley Co.
Marsh Supermarkets, Inc.
Martin Foundation
Maryland Casualty Co.
Masco Corp.
Maxon Charitable Foundation
May Department Stores Co.
Mayflower Group
Maytag Corp.
McCormick & Co.
McGill Manufacturing Co.
McGraw-Hill
McMillen Foundation
Mead Corp.
Mellon Bank Corp.
Mellon PSFS
Menasha Corp.
Meridian Insurance Group Inc.
Metropolitan Health Council of Indianapolis
MidAmerica Radio Co.
Miles Inc.
Minnetrista Cultural Foundation
Moore Foundation
Morrill Charitable Foundation
National City Bank
National City Bank of Evansville
National City Bank of Indiana
National City Corp.
Nationale-Nederlanden North America Corp.
NBD Bank
NBD Bank, N.A.

Indiana (cont.)

Newmont Mining Corp.
NIBCO Inc.
Noll Foundation
Norfolk Southern Corp.
Nortek, Inc.
North American Philips Corp.
Northern Indiana Fuel & Light Co.
Northern Indiana Public Service Co.
Norwest Corp.
Noyes, Jr. Memorial Foundation, Nicholas H.
Oakley Foundation, Hollie and Anna
O'Brien Foundation, Cornelius and Anna Cook
O'Connor Foundation, Magee
Ogle Foundation, Paul
Old National Bank in Evansville
Oliver Memorial Trust Foundation
Ontario Corp.
Owens-Corning Fiberglas Corp.
Parker-Hannifin Corp.
Patrick Industries Inc.
Pechiney Corp.
Peerless Insurance Co.
Peoples Drug Stores Inc.
Pfizer
Phelps Dodge Corp.
Philip Morris Cos.
Pioneer Hi-Bred International
Plumsock Fund
Pott Foundation, Robert and Elaine
PPG Industries
Prudential Insurance Co. of America
PSI Energy
Pulitzer Publishing Co.
Quaker Oats Co.
Quanex Corp.
Raker Foundation, M. E.
Ransburg Corp.
Raper Foundation, Tom
Reilly Industries
Reliance Electric Co.
Reynolds & Reynolds Co.
Rieke Corp.
Rochester Telephone Corp.
Saemann Foundation, Franklin I.
Sara Lee Corp.
Schnuck Markets
Schust Foundation, Clarence L. and Edith B.
Scripps Co., E.W.
Seagram & Sons, Joseph E.
Sealy, Inc.
Security Life of Denver
Shell Oil Co.
Sherman Educational Fund
SKF USA, Inc.
Skyline Corp.
Smock Foundation, Frank and Laura
Society Corp.
Somers Foundation, Byron H.
South Bend Tribune
Southern Indiana Gas & Electric Co.
Sprint
Sprint United Telephone
SPX Corp.
Square D Co.
Standard Register Co.
Star Bank, N.A.
State Farm Mutual Automobile Insurance Co.
Stone Container Corp.
Storer Scholarship Foundation, Oliver W.
Subaru-Isuzu Automotive Inc.
Sundstrand Corp.
Super Valu Stores

Tandem Computers
Target Stores
Tele-Communications, Inc.
Teledyne
Tenneco
Textron
Thirty-Five Twenty, Inc.
3M Co.
Thrush-Thompson Foundation
Tokheim Corp.
Tomkins Industries, Inc.
Travelers Cos.
TRINOVA Corp.
TRW Corp.
Tyson Fund
Ulrich Chemical, Inc.
UNC, Inc.
Unilever United States
Union Camp Cook
Union City Body Co.
United Technologies Corp.
Universal Foods Corp.
USG Corp.
USX Corp.
Vevay-Switzerland County Foundation
Vulcan Materials Co.
Wal-Mart Stores
West Foundation
Westwood Endowment
Wetterau
Whirlpool Corp.
White Consolidated Industries
Willamette Industries, Inc.
Winchester Foundation
Winn-Dixie Stores
Witco Corp.
Xerox Corp.
Zimmer Inc.
Zollner Foundation

Iowa

Adler Foundation Trust, Philip D. and Henrietta B.
AEGON USA, Inc.
AFLAC
Agway
Aluminum Co. of America
AMAX
American Brands
American Home Products Corp.
American Investment Co.
ARA Services
Arbie Mineral Feed Co.
Archer-Daniels-Midland Co.
Armco Inc.
Arrow Electronics, Inc.
Avnet, Inc.
Bandag, Inc.
Baxter International
Bechtel Charitable Remainder Uni-Trust, Harold R.
Bechtel Charitable Remainder Uni-Trust, Marie H.
Bechtel Testamentary Charitable Trust, H. R.
Belding Heminway Co.
Bergen Brunswig Corp.
Blank Fund, Myron and Jacqueline
Blount
Boatmen's Bancshares
Bohen Foundation
Brenton Banks Inc.
Bridgestone/Firestone
Browning-Ferris Industries
Burlington Northern Inc.
C.P. Rail Systems
Carver Charitable Trust, Roy J.
Caterpillar
Central Life Assurance Co.
Central Soya Co.
Century Companies of America
CertainTeed Corp.
Champion Spark Plug Co.
Charter Medical Corp.

Citizens First National Bank
Coachmen Industries
Coltec Industries
ConAgra
Cooper Industries
Cowles Foundation, Gardner and Florence Call
Cox Enterprises
Cummins Engine Co.
Curtice-Burns Foods
Dayton Hudson Corp.
Deere & Co.
Deluxe Corp.
Demco Charitable Foundation
Dexter Co.
Dollar General Corp.
Donaldson Co.
Donnelley & Sons Co., R.R.
Douglas & Lomason Company
Dow Jones & Co.
du Pont de Nemours & Co., E. I.
Dun & Bradstreet Corp.
E and M Charities
Eaton Corp.
Emerson Electric Co.
Employers Mutual Casualty Co.
Equitable Life Assurance Society of the U.S.
Fahrney Education Foundation
FDL Foods/Dubuque Packing Co.
Fireman's Fund Insurance Co.
Firstar Bank Milwaukee NA
Forster Charitable Trust, James W. and Ella B.
Gannett Co.
Gazette Co.
Georgia-Pacific Corp.
Gillette Co.
Glazer Foundation, Madelyn L.
Goodyear Tire & Rubber Co.
Grinnell Mutual Reinsurance Co.
Guaranty Bank & Trust Co.
Hall Foundation
Hanson Foundation
Harper Brush Works
Harsco Corp.
Hawkeye Bancorporation
Hawley Foundation
Heinz Co., H.J.
HON Industries
Hubbard Milling Co.
Hy-Vee Food Stores
IES Industries
IMT Insurance Co.
Inland Steel Industries
Inter-State Assurance Co.
Interstate Power Co.
Iowa-Illinois Gas & Electric Co.
Iowa Savings Bank
Iowa State Bank
JELD-WEN, Inc.
Jensen Construction Co.
K-Products
Kemper National Insurance Cos.
Kinney-Lindstrom Foundation
Kraft General Foods
Kuyper Foundation, Peter H. and E. Lucille Gaass
Lance, Inc.
Land O'Lakes
Lee Enterprises
Lehigh Portland Cement Co.
Lennox International, Inc.
Life Investors Insurance Company of America
Lindstrom Foundation, Kinney
Litton Industries
Mapco Inc.
Masco Corp.
Maytag Corp.
Maytag Family Foundation, Fred
McDonald Industries, Inc., A. Y.
McElroy Trust, R. J.
McWane Inc.
Menasha Corp.
Meredith Corp.
Mid-Iowa Health Foundation

Midwest Gas Co.
Midwest Resources
Monsanto Co.
Motorola
National By-Products
National Computer Systems
National Travelers Life Co.
Norwest Corp.
Olin Corp.
Owen Industries, Inc.
Pamida, Inc.
Paxton Co., Frank
Pella Corp.
Philip Morris Cos.
Pioneer Hi-Bred International
Pirelli Armstrong Tire Corp.
Preferred Risk Mutual Insurance Co.
Principal Financial Group
Procter & Gamble Co.
Quad City Osteopathic Foundation
Quaker Oats Co.
Quantum Chemical Corp.
Ralston Purina Co.
Rouse Co.
Ruan Foundation Trust, John
Sara Lee Corp.
Scrivner, Inc.
Sheaffer Inc.
Sherman Educational Fund, Mabel E.
Simpson Investment Co.
Spahn & Rose Lumber Co.
Square D Co.
Stanley Consultants
Statesman Group, Inc.
Stone Container Corp.
Super Valu Stores
Syntex Corp.
Tandem Computers
Tandy Corp.
Target Stores
Tele-Communications, Inc.
Tension Envelope Corp.
Terra Industries
3M Co.
Travelers Cos.
Tyson Foods, Inc.
Union Camp Corp.
United Dominion Industries
United Fire & Casualty Co.
US WEST
USG Corp.
Van Buren Foundation
Vermeer Charitable Foundation
Vermeer Investment Company Foundation
Vermeer Manufacturing Co.
Vulcan Materials Co.
Wahlert Foundation
Wal-Mart Stores
Waldinger Corp.
Weitz Corp.
Weyerhaeuser Co.
White Consolidated Industries
Wilbur-Ellis Co.
Winnebago Industries, Inc.
Witco Corp.
Witte, Jr. Foundation, John H.
Younkers, Inc.

Kansas

Abell Education Trust, Jennie G. and Pearl
Abitibi-Price
Alco Standard Corp.
Alfa-Laval, Inc.
AlliedSignal
Alumax
AMAX
America West Airlines
Archer-Daniels-Midland Co.
Armco Inc.
Arrow Electronics, Inc.
Avnet, Inc.

AXIA Incorporated
Baehr Foundation, Louis W. and Dolpha
Bank IV
Bard, C. R.
Baughman Foundation
Baxter International
Beech Aircraft Corp.
Bemis Company
Beren Foundation, Robert M.
Best Products Co.
Binney & Smith Inc.
Black & Veatch
Block, H&R
Boeing Co.
Boise Cascade Corp.
Borden
Borg-Warner Corp.
Breidenthal Foundation, Willard J. and Mary G.
Browning-Ferris Industries
Business Men's Assurance Co. of America
C.P. Rail Systems
Castle & Co., A.M.
Cessna Aircraft Co.
Charter Medical Corp.
Clorox Co.
Coastal Corp.
Coleman Co.
CR Industries
Davis Foundation, James A. and Juliet L.
Dayton Hudson Corp.
Deluxe Corp.
DeVore Foundation
Dillons Super Markets
Dollar General Corp.
Dover Corp.
Dreiling and Albina Dreiling Charitable Trust, Leo J.
du Pont de Nemours & Co., E. I.
Duckwall-Alco Stores
Eaton Corp.
Echlin Inc.
EMI Records Group
Excel Corp.
Fink Foundation
First National Bank in Wichita
FMC Corp.
Forster-Powers Charitable Trust
Fourth Financial Corp.
Fuller Co., H.B.
Garvey Fund, Jean and Willard
Garvey Kansas Foundation
Garvey Trust, Olive White
Gault-Hussey Charitable Trust
General Electric Co.
General Reinsurance Corp.
Georgia-Pacific Corp.
Goodyear Tire & Rubber Co.
Graham Charitable Trust, William L.
Hallmark Cards
Hansen Foundation, Dane G.
Hedrick Foundation, Frank E.
Hesston Corp.
Hospital Corp. of America
Humana
Ingersoll-Rand Co.
Inland Container Corp.
Inland Steel Industries
Insurance Management Associates
International Multifoods Corp.
ITT Hartford Insurance Group
Jefferson Smurfit Corp.
Jellison Benevolent Society
Jones Foundation, Walter S. and Evan C.
Jostens
Kansas City Power & Light Co.
Kansas Power & Light/Western Resources
Kauffman Foundation, Muriel McBrien
Kejr Foundation

Kice Industries, Inc.
Knight-Ridder, Inc.
Koch Charitable Trust, David H.
Koch Industries
Law Company, Inc.
Learjet Inc.
Lee Apparel Co.
Lehigh Portland Cement Co.
Litton Industries
Macy & Co., R.H.
Manufacturers Life Insurance
Co. of America
Manville Corp.
Mapco Inc.
Maritz Inc.
Marley Co.
May Department Stores Co.
Mercantile Bancorp
Merck & Co.
Meredith Corp.
Mingenback Foundation, Julia J.
Misco Industries
Morton International
Motorola
Multimedia, Inc.
NCR Corp.
Norwest Corp.
O'Connor Co.
Olin Corp.
Pamida, Inc.
Parker-Hannifin Corp.
PepsiCo
Pioneer Hi-Bred International
Pizza Hut
Powell Family Foundation
PPG Industries
Procter & Gamble Co.
Quaker Oats Co.
Quantum Chemical Corp.
Reliable Life Insurance Co.
Rice Foundation, Ethel and
Raymond F.
Ringier-America
Rochester Telephone Corp.
Ross Foundation
Saint Paul Cos.
Salgo Charitable Trust, Nicholas
M.
Santa Fe Pacific Corp.
Sara Lee Corp.
Schowalter Foundation
Scrivner, Inc.
Scroggins Foundation, Arthur E.
and Cornelia C.
Seaboard Corp.
Sealright Co., Inc.
Sealy, Inc.
Security Benefit Life Insurance
Co.
Security State Bank
Sky Chefs, Inc.
Smith Foundation, Kenneth L.
and Eva S.
Smoot Charitable Foundation
Southwestern Bell Corp.
Sprint
Stanley Works
Stauffer Communications
Sterling Winthrop
Target Stores
Teledyne
Tenneco
Tension Envelope Corp.
Texaco
Timken Co.
Tomkins Industries, Inc.
Toro Co.
Travelers Cos.
Trusler Foundation
Union Carbide Corp.
Union Pacific Corp.
Vulcan Materials Co.
Wal-Mart Stores
Wal-Mart Stores, Inc.
Western Resources
Williams Charitable Trust, Mary
Jo

Williams Cos.
Witco Corp.
Yellow Corp.

Kentucky

Abel Construction Co.
Air Products & Chemicals
Akzo America
Alco Standard Corp.
Alumax
AMAX
American Brands
American Electric Power
AMETEK
ARA Services
Aristech Chemical Corp.
Armco Inc.
Armstrong World Industries Inc.
Ashland Oil
Banc One Illinois Corp.
Bank of Louisville
Barnes Group
Bearings, Inc.
BellSouth Corp.
Bemis Company
Berwind Corp.
BFGoodrich
Bird Inc.
Black & Decker Corp.
Blue Cross & Blue Shield of
Kentucky Foundation
Boise Cascade Corp.
Briggs & Stratton Corp.
Brown-Forman Corp.
Brown Foundation, James
Graham
Brown Foundation, W. L. Lyons
Brown & Williamson Tobacco
Corp.
Browning-Ferris Industries
Brunswick Corp.
Burlington Northern Inc.
C. E. and S. Foundation
Capital Holding Corp.
Centel Corp.
Charter Medical Corp.
Chesapeake Corp.
Circuit City Stores
Clopay Corp.
Clorox Co.
Collins Co.
Commercial Bank
Commercial Intertech Corp.
Commonwealth Life Insurance
Co.
ConAgra
Cooke Foundation Corporation,
V. V.
Cooper Industries
Corning Incorporated
Courier-Journal & Louisville
Times
Cralle Foundation
Cyprus Minerals Co.
Dairymen, Inc.
Dana Corp.
Dayton Hudson Corp.
Deluxe Corp.
Diederich Educational Trust
Fund, John T. and Ada
Dollar General Corp.
Donaldson Co.
Donnelley & Sons Co., R.R.
Dover Corp.
Dow Corning Corp.
du Pont de Nemours & Co., E. I.
Eaton Corp.
Elf Atochem North America
Emerson Electric Co.
Enterprise Coal Co.
Equitable Resources
Farley Industries
Ferre Revocable Trust, Joseph C.
Fifth Third Bancorp
First Mississippi Corp.
Frisch's Restaurants Inc.

Fruit of the Loom, Inc.
Gannett Co.
Gardner Charitable Foundation,
Edith D.
General Electric Co.
General Motors Corp.
General Tire Inc.
Gheens Foundation
Glenmore Distilleries Co.
Goodyear Tire & Rubber Co.
Greenebaum, Doll & McDonald
Hayswood Foundation
Hershey Foods Corp.
Hitachi
HON Industries
Hook Drug
Hope Memorial Fund, Blanche
and Thomas
Hospital Corp. of America
Houchens Foundation, Ervin G.
Humana
Hunt Manufacturing Co.
Huntington Bancshares Inc.
IBM Corp.
ICH Corp.
IMCERA Group Inc.
Ingersoll-Rand Co.
Inland Container Corp.
International Multifoods Corp.
James River Corp. of Virginia
Jefferson Smurfit Corp.
Johnson Controls
Johnson & Higgins
Kentucky Central Life Insurance
Kentucky Foundation for Women
Kentucky Fried Chicken Corp.
Kentucky Utilities Co.
Kimball International
Kloeckner-Pentaplast of America
Knight-Ridder, Inc.
Kuhlman Corp.
LaViers Foundation, Harry and
Maxie
Levi Strauss & Co.
Levy's Lumber & Building
Centers
Liberty Corp.
Litton Industries
Louisville Gas & Electric Co.
Mallinckrodt Specialty
Chemicals Co.
Mapco Inc.
Masco Corp.
Mead Corp.
Michael-Walters Industries
Million Memorial Park Trust, E.
C.
Mills Foundation, Ralph E.
Mosinee Paper Corp.
National City Corp.
National Medical Enterprises
NationsBank Corp.
New York Times Co.
Norton Foundation Inc.
Occidental Petroleum Corp.
Ogden College Fund
Olin Corp.
Parker-Hannifin Corp.
Paxton Co., Frank
PepsiCo
Phelps Dodge Corp.
Philip Morris Cos.
Pinkerton Tobacco Co.
Pittston Co.
PNC Bank
Porter Paint Co.
Procter & Gamble Co.
Quaker Oats Co.
Quantum Chemical Corp.
Ralston Purina Co.
Reed Foundation
Reynolds Metals Co.
Robinson Mountain Fund, E. O.
Rohm and Haas Company
Rosenthal Foundation
Roth Foundation, Louis T.
Rouse Co.

Sara Lee Corp.
Scheirich Co., H.J.
Schneider Foundation Corp., Al
J.
Scott Paper Co.
Scripps Co., E.W.
Seagram & Sons, Joseph E.
Sherwin-Williams Co.
SKF USA, Inc.
Smith Corp., A.O.
SPX Corp.
Square D Co.
Standard Products Co.
Star Bank, N.A.
Stone Container Corp.
Sutherland Foundation
Tandem Computers
Target Stores
Texas Gas Transmission Corp.
Texas Instruments
Thomas Foundation, Joan and
Lee
Thomas Industries
3M Co.
Travelers Cos.
TRINOVA Corp.
TRW Corp.
Union Camp Corp.
Union Carbide Corp.
United Dominion Industries
Valvoline Inc.
Vogt Machine Co., Henry
Vulcan Materials Co.
Wal-Mart Stores
Westmoreland Coal Co.
Wetterau
Weyerhaeuser Co.
Winn-Dixie Stores
Yeager Charitable Trust, Lester
E.
Young Memorial Fund, John B.
and Brownie

Louisiana

Air Products & Chemicals
AMAX
American Cyanamid Co.
Amoco Corp.
AmSouth Bancorporation
Anheuser-Busch Cos.
ARA Services
Archer-Daniels-Midland Co.
ARCO
Arkla
Armco Inc.
Avondale Industries, Inc.
Azby Fund
Babcock & Wilcox Co.
Baker Hughes Inc.
Ball Corp.
Bank of Boston Connecticut
Bank of Boston Corp.
Baxter International
Beaird Foundation, Charles T.
BellSouth Corp.
Big Three Industries
Bird Inc.
Boeing Co.
Boh Brothers Construction Co.
Boise Cascade Corp.
Booth-Bricker Fund
Boots Pharmaceuticals, Inc.
Borden
Borg-Warner Corp.
BP America
Bridgestone/Firestone
Brown Foundation, Joe W. and
Dorothy Dorsett
Browning-Ferris Industries
Brunswick Corp.
Burton Foundation, William T.
and Ethel Lewis
Cabot Corp.
Cahn Family Foundation
CBI Industries
Central & South West Services

Charter Medical Corp.
Chevron Corp.
Circuit City Stores
Commercial Metals Co.
Community Coffee Co.
Computer Associates
International
Conoco Inc.
Consolidated Natural Gas Co.
Cooper Industries
Copolymer Rubber & Chemical
Corp.
Coughlin-Saunders Foundation
Courtaulds Fibers Inc.
Cox Enterprises
Delta Air Lines
Deluxe Corp.
Dollar General Corp.
Dow Chemical Co.
du Pont de Nemours & Co., E. I.
Durr-Fillauer Medical
Eckerd Corp., Jack
Emerson Electric Co.
Entergy Corp.
Entex
Equitable Life Assurance Society
of the U.S.
Ethyl Corp.
Exxon Corp.
Ferro Corp.
FINA, Inc.
Fireman's Fund Insurance Co.
First Commerce Corp.
First Mississippi Corp.
Florida Steel Corp.
Foxmeyer Corp.
Frazier Foundation
Freeman Foundation, Ella West
Freeport-McMoRan
Gannett Co.
GATX Corp.
Georgia-Pacific Corp.
German Protestant Orphan
Asylum Association
Glazer Foundation, Jerome S.
Goldring Family Foundation
Halliburton Co.
Helis Foundation
Heymann Special Account, Mr.
and Mrs. Jimmy
Heymann-Wolf Foundation
Hibernia Corp.
Hospital Corp. of America
Humana
Hurley Foundation, Ed E. and
Gladys
Inland Container Corp.
Inland Steel Industries
International Paper Co.
Interpublic Group of Cos.
ITT Hartford Insurance Group
James River Corp. of Virginia
Johnson & Higgins
Jones Family Foundation,
Eugenie and Joseph
Keller Family Foundation
Kraus Co., Ltd.
Lakeside National Bank
Lamar Corp.
Libby-Dufour Fund, Trustees of
the
Liberty Corp.
Litton Industries
Louisiana Gas Services
Louisiana Land & Exploration
Co.
Louisiana Power & Light
Co./New Orleans Public
Service
Lupin Foundation
Lykes Brothers Steamship Co.
Manufacturers Life Insurance
Co. of America
Manville Corp.
Martin Marietta Aggregates
Martin Marietta Corp.
McDermott

Louisiana (cont.)

McIlhenny and Sons Corp
Mellon Bank Corp.
Middle South Utilities
Mobil Oil Corp.
Monroe Foundation (1976), J. Edgar
Monsanto Co.
Morton International
Murphy Oil Corp.
Nalco Chemical Co.
National Medical Enterprises
New York Times Co.
Offshore Logistics
Olin Corp.
Pan-American Life Insurance Co.
Paxton Co., Frank
Pennington Foundation, Irene W. and C. B.
Pennzoil Co.
Poindexter Foundation
Powers Foundation
PPG Industries
Premier Bank
Premier Bank Lafayette
Premier Bank of South Louisiana
Procter & Gamble Co.
Prudential Insurance Co. of America
Quantum Chemical Corp.
Reily & Co., William B.
RosaMary Foundation
Rouse Co.
Rowan Cos., Inc.
Saint Paul Cos.
Santa Fe International Corp.
Sara Lee Corp.
Schlieder Educational Foundation, Edward G.
Sequa Corp.
Shell Oil Co.
Shreveport Publishing Corp.
Sonat
Sonesta International Hotels Corp.
Southwestern Electric Power Co.
State Farm Mutual Automobile Insurance Co.
Stern Foundation, Percival
Stone Container Corp.
Tandem Computers
Target Stores
Teledyne
Tenneco
Tesoro Petroleum Corp.
Texaco
Texas Industries, Inc.
Textron
Tidewater, Inc.
Transco Energy Company
Travelers Cos.
Union Camp Corp.
Union Carbide Corp.
Union Pacific Corp.
Unocal Corp.
Vulcan Materials Co.
Wal-Mart Stores
Westvaco Corp.
Wheless Foundation
Whitney National Bank
Williams Cos.
Williams Foundation, Kemper and Leila
Winn-Dixie Stores
Winn Educational Trust, Fanny Edith
Wisdom Foundation, Mary F.
Witco Corp.
Woldenberg Foundation
Woolf Foundation, William C.
Xerox Corp.
Young Foundation, H and B
Zapata Corp.
Zemurray Foundation
Zigler Foundation, Fred B. and Ruth B.

Maine

Armco Inc.
Asea Brown Boveri
Bangor Savings Bank
Bank of Boston Connecticut
Bank of Boston Corp.
Bean, L.L.
Boise Cascade Corp.
Borden
Bowater Inc.
Carpenter Technology Corp.
Casco Northern Bank
Central Maine Power Co.
Champion International Corp.
Citicorp
Cooper Industries
Davenport Trust Fund
Dexter Shoe Co.
Eastern Fine Paper, Inc.
Fleet Bank
Fleet Bank of Maine
Fleet Financial Group
Fraser Paper Ltd.
Gannett Publishing Co., Guy
Gardiner Savings Institution FSB
Georgia-Pacific Corp.
International Paper Co.
Israel Discount Bank of New York
James River Corp. of Virginia
Johnson & Higgins
Key Bank of Maine
M/A-COM, Inc.
Manville Corp.
Mearl Corp.
Moosehead Manufacturing Co.
Mulford Trust, Clarence E.
National Starch & Chemical Corp.
New England Telephone Co.
New York Times Co.
North American Philips Corp.
Parker-Hannifin Corp.
Peoples Heritage Savings Bank
Pet
Phillips-Van Heusen Corp.
Quantum Chemical Corp.
Rivers and Trails North East
Scott Paper Co.
Sewall Foundation, Elmina
Shaw's Supermarkets
Tom's of Maine
UNUM Corp.
Webber Oil Co.
Westinghouse Electric Corp.
Wetterau
Weyerhaeuser Co.
Xtra Corp.
Zurn Industries

Maryland

Abell Foundation, Charles S.
Abell Foundation, The
Abramson Family Foundation
AEGON USA, Inc.
Alco Standard Corp.
Allegheny Power System, Inc.
AlliedSignal
Alpha Industries
Alumax
AMAX
America West Airlines
American Cyanamid Co.
American Trading & Production Corp.
Amoco Corp.
Amsted Industries
ARA Services
Arcata Corp.
Arcata Graphics Co.
Armco Inc.
Arrow Electronics, Inc.
Avnet, Inc.
B & O Railroad Museum
Bairnco Corp.

Baker, Jr. Memorial Fund, William G.
Baker Trust, Clayton
Baker, Watts & Co.
Baldwin, Jr. Foundation, Summerfield
Ball Corp.
Baltimore Bancorp.
Baltimore Gas & Electric Co.
Baltimore Life Insurance Co.
Bank Foundation, Helen and Merrill
Banner Life Insurance Co.
Barlow Family Foundation, Milton A. and Gloria G.
Barton-Gillet Co.
Bausch & Lomb
Bechtel Group
Becton Dickinson & Co.
Beitzell & Co.
Bell Atlantic Corp.
Beretta U.S.A. Corp.
Berwind Corp.
Best Products Co.
Bethlehem Steel Corp.
Black & Decker Corp.
Blaustein Foundation, Jacob and Hilda
Blaustein Foundation, Louis and Henrietta
Blaustein Foundation, Morton K. and Jane
Blum Foundation, Lois and Irving
Boise Cascade Corp.
Borden
Brown, Jr. Charitable Trust, Frank D.
Brown & Sons, Alex
Browning-Ferris Industries
Brunswick Corp.
Campbell Foundation
Campbell Soup Co.
Casey Foundation, Eugene B.
Centel Corp.
Chase Manhattan Bank, N.A.
Chesapeake Corp.
Chesapeake & Potomac Telephone Co.
Chevron Corp.
Chevy Chase Savings Bank FSB
CIGNA Corp.
Circuit City Stores
Citicorp
Clark Charitable Foundation
Clark-Winchcole Foundation
Clopay Corp.
Clorox Co.
Cohen Foundation, Naomi and Nehemiah
Commercial Credit Co.
Communications Satellite Corp. (COMSAT)
Computer Associates International
Computer Sciences Corp.
ConAgra
Consolidated Rail Corp. (Conrail)
CPC International
Crane & Co.
Crestar Financial Corp.
Crown Books Foundation, Inc.
Crown Central Petroleum Corp.
CSX Corp.
Dart Group Corp.
Delmarva Power & Light Co.
Deluxe Corp.
Dexter Corp.
Discovery Channel/Cable Education Network
Dollar General Corp.
Douglas & Lomason Company
Dover Corp.
Dow Jones & Co.
Dresser Industries
Dun & Bradstreet Corp.
Eastern Stainless Corp.

EG&G Inc.
Egenton Home
Fairchild Corp.
First Maryland Bancorp
First Union Corp.
Fisher Foundation, Gramma
FMC Corp.
Foundation for Iranian Studies
Fox Inc.
France Foundation, Jacob and Annita
Freeman Foundation, Carl M.
Fuller Co., H.B.
General Electric Co.
General Motors Corp.
Giant Food
Giant Food Stores
Goldseker Foundation of Maryland, Morris
Goodyear Tire & Rubber Co.
Gordon Charitable Trust, Peggy and Yale
Grady Management
Gross Foundation, Louis H.
Grumman Corp.
Gudelsky Family Foundation, Homer and Martha
Halliburton Co.
Handy & Harman
Hanson Office Products
Harte-Hanks Communications, Inc.
Hartmarx Corp.
Hechinger Co.
Hecht-Levi Foundation
Heileman Brewing Co., Inc., G.
Hewlett-Packard Co.
Hirschhorn Foundation, David and Barbara B.
Hobbs Foundation, Emmert
Hoffberger Foundation
Home Depot
Hughes Medical Institute, Howard
Humana
Hyman Construction Co., George
IBM Corp.
Isaacs Foundation, Harry Z.
ITT Hartford Insurance Group
Johnson Inc., Axel
Johnson & Higgins
Kelly, Jr. Memorial Foundation, Ensign C. Markland
Kerr Fund, Grayce B.
Knapp Educational Fund
Knapp Foundation
Knott Foundation, Marion I. and Henry J.
Kraft General Foods
Legg Mason Inc.
Lehigh Portland Cement Co.
Leidy Foundation, John J.
Levitt Foundation, Richard S.
Life Sciences Research Foundation
Lincoln National Corp.
Litton Industries
Loats Foundation
M/A-COM, Inc.
M.E. Foundation
Macht Foundation, Morton and Sophia
Manger and Audrey Cordero Plitt Trust, Clarence
Manor Care
Manville Corp.
Mapco Inc.
Marriott Corp.
Martin Marietta Aggregates
Martin Marietta Corp.
Maryland Casualty Co.
May Department Stores Co.
McCormick & Co.
McDonnell Douglas Corp.-West
McGregor Foundation, Thomas and Frances
Mead Corp.

Mechanic Foundation, Morris A.
Mellon Bank Corp.
Mellon PSFS
Mercantile Bankshares Corp.
Mercedes-Benz of North America, Inc.
Meredith Corp.
Merrick Foundation, Robert G. and Anne M.
Merry-Go-Round Enterprises, Inc.
Meyerhoff Foundation, Lyn P.
Meyerhoff Fund, Joseph
Middendorf Foundation
Mine Safety Appliances Co.
MNC Financial
Moriah Fund
Morrison-Knudsen Corp.
Mulford Foundation, Vincent
Mullan Foundation, Thomas F. and Clementine L.
Myers and Sons, D.
Nathan Foundation
National Medical Enterprises
NationsBank Corp.
Nationwide Insurance Cos.
Norwest Corp.
Number Ten Foundation
OMNI Construction
O'Neil Foundation, W.
Outokumpu-American Brass Co.
Owens-Corning Fiberglas Corp.
Oxford Development Group
PaineWebber
Pearlstone Foundation, Peggy Meyerhoff
Penn Central Corp.
Perdue Farms
Pet
PHH Corp.
Philip Morris Cos.
Pioneer Hi-Bred International
Polinger Foundation, Howard and Geraldine
Poole & Kent Co.
Potomac Edison Co.
Potomac Electric Power Co.
PPG Industries
Preston Trucking Co., Inc.
Price Associates, T. Rowe
Primerica Corp.
Procter & Gamble Co.
Procter & Gamble Cosmetic & Fragrance Products
Quality Inn International
Quantum Chemical Corp.
REI-Recreational Equipment, Inc.
Rohr Inc.
Rollins Luetkemeyer Charitable Foundation
Rosenberg Foundation, Henry and Ruth Blaustein
Rosenbloom Foundation, Ben and Esther
Rosenthal-Statter Foundation
Rouse Co.
Royal Group Inc.
Ryan Family Charitable Foundation
Ryland Group
Sachs Electric Corp.
SCM Chemicals Inc.
Scripps Co., E.W.
Seagram & Sons, Joseph E.
Sealy, Inc.
Sequa Corp.
Shapiro, Inc.
Shapiro Fund, Albert
Shell Oil Co.
Sheridan Foundation, Thomas B. and Elizabeth M.
Sherwin-Williams Co.
Signet Bank/Maryland
Smith Foundation, Gordon V. and Helen C.

State Farm Mutual Automobile Insurance Co.
Stern Family Fund
Stewart Memorial Trust, J. C.
Stone Container Corp.
Straus Foundation, Aaron and Lillie
Tandem Computers
Tauber Foundation
Teledyne
Telinde Trust, Richard W.
Thalheimer Foundation, Alvin and Fanny Blaustein
Thorn, Jr. Foundation, Columbus W.
Three Swallows Foundation
3M Co.
Times Mirror Co.
Town Creek Foundation
Tracor, Inc.
Transco Energy Company
Travelers Cos.
TRINOVA Corp.
Tucker Foundation, Marcia Brady
UNC, Inc.
Unger Foundation, Aber D.
Unilever United States
United Iron & Metal Co.
United Merchants & Manufacturers
USF&G Co.
Valspar Corp.
Volkswagen of America, Inc.
Ward Machinery Co.
Warfield Memorial Fund, Anna Emory
Weinberg Foundation, Harry and Jeanette
Weir Foundation Trust
Westinghouse Electric Corp.
Westvaco Corp.
Wetterau
Weyerhaeuser Co.
White Coffee Pot Family Inns
Widgeon Foundation
Wilson Sanitarium for Children of Baltimore City, Thomas
Zamoiski Co.

Massachusetts

Acushnet Co.
Adams Trust, Charles E. and Caroline J.
Addison-Wesley Publishing Co.
Advest Group, Inc.
Affiliated Publications, Inc.
Agape Foundation
AGFA Division of Miles Inc.
Agway
Air France
Albany International Corp.
Alden Trust, George I.
Alden Trust, John W.
Alden's Inc.
Algonquin Energy, Inc.
Alpha Industries
Alumax
AMAX
Amcast Industrial Corp.
Amdur Braude Riley, Inc.
American Biltrite
American Brands
American Cyanamid Co.
American Express Co.
American International Group, Inc.
American Mutual Insurance Cos.
American Natural Resources Co.
American Optical Corp.
American Saw & Manufacturing Co.
American Stores Co.
American Telephone & Telegraph Co.
Ames Department Stores
AMETEK
Amoskeag Co.

Analog Devices
Analogic Corp.
Anheuser-Busch Cos.
Ansin Private Foundation, Ronald M.
AON Corp.
Apollo Computer Inc.
APV Crepaco Inc.
ARA Services
Arakelian Foundation, Mary Alice
Arcata Corp.
Arcata Graphics Co.
Arkwright-Boston Manufacturers Mutual
Armco Inc.
Armstrong World Industries Inc.
Arrow Electronics, Inc.
Astra Pharmaceutical Products, Inc.
Attleboro Pawtucket Savings Bank
Augat, Inc.
Avery Dennison Corp.
Avis Inc.
Avnet, Inc.
Ayling Scholarship Foundation, Alice S.
Azadoutioun Foundation
Babson Foundation, Paul and Edith
Babson-Webber-Mustard Fund
Bachrach, Inc.
Bacon Trust, Charles F.
Badger Co., Inc.
Bailey Wildlife Foundation
Bairnco Corp.
Baker Hughes Inc.
Balfour Foundation, L. G.
Bank Hapoalim B.M.
Bank of Boston Connecticut
Bank of Boston Corp.
Bard, C. R.
Bausch & Lomb
Baxter International
BayBanks
Beaucourt Foundation
Bemis Company
Benfamil Charitable Trust
Berenson Charitable Foundation, Theodore W. and Evelyn
Berwind Corp.
BFGoodrich
Bird Inc.
Birmingham Foundation
Black & Decker Corp.
Blake Foundation, S. P.
Blanchard Foundation
Blount
Boise Cascade Corp.
Bolten Charitable Foundation, John
Borden
Borg-Warner Corp.
Boston Co., Inc.
Boston Edison Co.
Boston Fatherless and Widows Society
Boston Gas Co.
Boston Mutual Life Insurance Co.
Boynton Fund, John W.
Braitmayer Foundation
Bright Charitable Trust, Alexander H.
Brown Inc., John
Brown & Sons, Alex
Browning-Ferris Industries
Bull HN Information Systems Inc.
Bushee Foundation, Florence Evans
Cabot Corp.
Cabot Family Charitable Trust
Cabot-Saltonstall Charitable Trust
Cabot Stains

Cadence Design Systems
Cambridge Mustard Seed Foundation
Campbell and Adah E. Hall Charity Fund, Bushrod H.
Capital Cities/ABC
Carteh Foundation
Carter-Wallace
Castle & Co., A.M.
Central Maine Power Co.
Charles River Laboratories
Charlesbank Homes
Charlton, Jr. Charitable Trust, Earle P.
Chase Charity Foundation, Alfred E.
Chase Trust, Alice P.
Childs Charitable Foundation, Roberta M.
Chomerics, Inc.
Chrysler Corp.
CIBA-GEIGY Corp.
Circuit City Stores
Citicorp
Clark Charitable Trust
Clark Home for Aged People, Ella
Clipper Ship Foundation
Coastal Corp.
Cole National Corp.
Colgan Scholarship Fund, James W.
Coltec Industries
Commonwealth Energy System
Computer Associates International
Computer Sciences Corp.
ConAgra
Connell LP
Continental Wingate Co., Inc.
Contraves USA
Cooper Industries
Country Curtains, Inc.
Courier Corp.
Cove Charitable Trust
Cowan Foundation Corporation, Lillian L. and Harry A.
Cox Charitable Trust, Jessie B.
Cox Enterprises
Cox Foundation
CPC International
Crane & Co.
Cranston Print Works
Crapo Charitable Foundation, Henry H.
Cumberland Farms
Cummings Properties Management, Inc.
Damon Corp.
Daniels Foundation, Fred Harris
Delta Air Lines
Deluxe Corp.
Demoulas Supermarkets
Dennison Manufacturing Co.
Devereaux Foundation
Devonshire Associates
Dewar, A.W.G.
Dewing Foundation, Frances R.
Dexter Charitable Fund, Eugene A.
Dexter Corp.
Digital Equipment Corp.
Donaldson, Lufkin & Jenrette
Donnelley & Sons Co., R.R.
Dow Jones & Co.
Doyle Charitable Foundation
du Pont de Nemours & Co., E. I.
Dun & Bradstreet Corp.
Dunkin' Donuts
Dunn Foundation, Elizabeth Ordway
Dynatech Corp.
Eastern Bank Foundation
Eastern Enterprises
Eastman Gelatine Corp.
Eaton Corp.

Eaton Memorial Fund, Georgiana Goddard
Edgerton Foundation, Harold E.
Edwards Scholarship Fund
EG&G Inc.
Ellison Foundation
Ellsworth Foundation, Ruth H. and Warren A.
Emerson Electric Co.
EMI Records Group
Enron Corp.
Equitable Life Assurance Society of the U.S.
Erving Paper Mills
Factory Mutual Engineering Corp.
Farley Industries
Farm Credit Banks of Springfield
Farnsworth Trust, Charles A.
Fay Charitable Fund, Aubert J.
Federated Department Stores and Allied Stores Corp.
Feldberg Family Foundation
Fiduciary Trust Co.
Filene Foundation, Lincoln and Therese
Filene's Sons Co., William
First Petroleum Corp.
Fisher Foundation
Flatley Foundation
Fleet Bank
Fleet Financial Group
Fletcher Foundation
FMR Corp.
Foley, Hoag & Eliot
Ford Foundation, Joseph F. and Clara
Foster Foundation, Joseph C. and Esther
Fraser Foundation, Richard M. and Helen T.
French Foundation
Friendly Ice Cream Corp.
Friendship Fund
Fuller Co., H.B.
Fuller Foundation, George F. and Sybil H.
Galileo Electro-Optics Corp.
Gannett Co.
GCA Corp.
Gear Motion
General Dynamics Corp.
General Electric Co.
General Housewares Corp.
General Mills
General Reinsurance Corp.
Genetics Institute
GenRad
Gerondelis Foundation
Gillette Co.
Global Van Lines
Globe Newspaper Co.
Goddard Homestead
Goldberg Family Foundation
Goldberg Family Foundation, Israel and Matilda
Goldman Sachs & Co.
Goodyear Tire & Rubber Co.
Gordon Foundation
Gorin Foundation, Nehemiah
Grass Foundation
Grass Instrument Co.
GTE Corp.
Gulf USA Corp.
Hagler Foundation, Jon L.
Hampden Papers
Handy & Harman
Hanover Insurance Co.
Harcourt General
Harrington Foundation, Francis A. and Jacquelyn H.
Harrington Trust, George
Harte-Hanks Communications, Inc.
Harvard Apparatus Foundation
Harvard Musical Association
Hasbro

Hayden Recreation Center, Josiah Willard
Hazeltine Corp.
Henderson Foundation
Henderson Foundation, George B.
Henkel Corp.
Heritage Travel Inc./Thomas Cook Travel
Hewlett-Packard Co.
Heydt Fund, Nan and Matilda
Higgins Foundation, Aldus C.
Hills Department Stores, Inc.
Hixon Fund for Religion and Education, Alexander & Adelaide
HMK Enterprises
Hoche-Scofield Foundation
Hoffman Foundation, John Ernest
Holyoke Mutual Insurance Co. in Salem
Home Depot
Home for Aged Men
Hood Foundation, Charles H.
Hood Inc., H.P.
Hopedale Foundation
Hornblower Fund, Henry
Horne Trust, Mabel
Houghton Mifflin Co.
Housatonic Curtain Co.
House Educational Trust, Susan Cook
Howard Benevolent Society
Humane Society of the Commonwealth of Massachusetts
Hyams Foundation
Hyde Manufacturing Co.
Hyman Construction Co., George
Iacocca Foundation
ICI Americas
Illinois Tool Works
IMO Industries Inc.
Index Technology Corp.
Ingersoll-Rand Co.
Inland Steel Industries
Instron Corp.
Insurance Systems, Inc.
Interco
International Data Group
International Paper Co.
Island Foundation
Israel Discount Bank of New York
ITT Corp.
ITT Hartford Insurance Group
ITT Rayonier
Jackson Charitable Trust, Marion Gardner
James River Corp. of Virginia
John Hancock Mutual Life Insurance Co.
Johnson Inc., Axel
Johnson Controls
Johnson Foundation, Howard
Johnson Fund, Edward C.
Johnson & Higgins
Johnson & Johnson
Johnson & Son, S.C.
Jostens
Kaman Corp.
Kapor Family Foundation
Kayem Foods, Inc.
Kelley and Elza Kelley Foundation, Edward Bangs
Kendall Foundation, Henry P.
Kendall Health Care Products
Keyport Life Insurance Co.
Killam Trust, Constance
Kilmartin Industries
Kimberly-Clark Corp.
King Trust, Charles A.
Knowles Trust A, Leonora H.
Kraft Foundation
Kraft General Foods
Ladd Charitable Corporation, Helen and George

Massachusetts (cont.)

Lechmere
Levy Foundation, June Rockwell
Liberty Mutual Insurance Group/Boston
Linnell Foundation
Lipsky Foundation, Fred and Sarah
Little, Arthur D.
Little Brown & Co., Inc.
Little Family Foundation
Litton Industries
Litton/Itek Optical Systems
LoJack Corp.
Loomis House
Loomis-Sayles & Co.
Lotus Development Corp.
Lowell Institute, Trustees of the
Luce Charitable Foundation, Stephen C.
M/A-COM, Inc.
Macmillan, Inc.
Macom-Venitz
Malden Mills Industries
Manufacturers Life Insurance Co. of America
Mark IV Industries
Marshalls Inc.
Masco Corp.
Massachusetts Charitable Mechanics Association
Massachusetts Mutual Life Insurance Co.
May Department Stores Co.
McCarthy Memorial Trust Fund, Catherine
McCormick & Co.
McEvoy Foundation, Mildred H.
McGraw-Hill
Mead Corp.
Mechanics Bank
Medtronic
Mellon Bank Corp.
Mellon PSFS
Memorial Foundation for the Blind
Menasha Corp.
Merck Fund, John
Mifflin Memorial Fund, George H. and Jane A.
Millipore Corp.
Milton Bradley Co.
Mitre Corp.
Mobil Oil Corp.
Monsanto Co.
Morgan Construction Co.
Morrison-Knudsen Corp.
Morse Foundation, Richard P. and Claire W.
Morse Shoe, Inc.
Morton International
Motorola
National Forge Co.
Naurison Scholarship Fund, James Z.
NEC Technologies, Inc.
NEC USA
Nellie Mae
New Balance Athletic Shoe
New Cycle Foundation
New England Biolabs Foundation
New England Business Service
New England Electric System
New England Foundation
New England Grocer Supply
New England Mutual Life Insurance Co.
New England Telephone Co.
News America Publishing Inc.
Noonan Memorial Fund under the will of Frank Noonan, Deborah Munroe
North American Philips Corp.
Northeast Utilities
Norton Co.
NRC, Inc.

NYNEX Corp.
Oak Industries
O'Brien Foundation, James W.
Ocean Spray Cranberries
Olin Corp.
Orchard Foundation
Orion Capital Corp.
PaineWebber
Panhandle Eastern Corp.
Pappas Charitable Foundation, Bessie
Pappas Charitable Foundation, Thomas Anthony
Paramount Communications Inc.
Parexel International Corp.
Parker Brothers and Company Inc.
Parker Foundation, Theodore Edson
Parker-Hannifin Corp.
Parsons Corp.
Payless Cashways Inc.
Peabody Charitable Fund, Amelia
Peabody Foundation
Peabody Foundation, Amelia
Pellegrino-Realmuto Charitable Foundation
Perini Corp.
Perini Foundation, Joseph
Perpetual Benevolent Fund
Perpetual Trust for Charitable Giving
Philip Morris Cos.
Phillips Trust, Edwin
Phoenix Home Life Mutual Insurance Co.
Pierce Charitable Trust, Harold Whitworth
Pilgrim Foundation
Pioneer Group
Polaroid Corp.
Poorvu Foundation, William and Lia
PQ Corp.
Prime Computer, Inc.
Procter & Gamble Co.
Property Capital Trust
Prouty Foundation, Olive Higgins
Providence Energy Corp.
Prudential-Bache Securities
Prudential Insurance Co. of America
Putnam Prize Fund for the Promotion of Scholarship, William Lowell
Quabaug Corp.
Quantum Chemical Corp.
Rabb Charitable Foundation, Sidney and Esther
Rabb Charitable Trust, Sidney R.
Ramlose Foundation, George A.
Rand-Whitney Packaging-Delmar Corp.
Ratshesky Foundation, A. C.
Raytheon Co.
Raytheon Engineers & Constructors
Reebok International Ltd.
Reed Publishing USA
REI-Recreational Equipment, Inc.
Reisman Charitable Trust, George C. and Evelyn R.
Rexham Inc.
Rice Charitable Foundation, Albert W.
Riley Foundation, Mabel Louise
Riley Stoker Co.
River Road Charitable Corporation
Rochester Telephone Corp.
Rockwell International Corp.
Rodgers Trust, Elizabeth Killam
Rogers Family Foundation
Rohm and Haas Company
Rouse Co.
Rowland Foundation

Rubenstein Charitable Foundation, Lawrence J. and Anne
Rubin Family Fund, Cele H. and William B.
Russell Trust, Josephine G.
Sacharuna Foundation
Sailors' Snug Harbor of Boston
Saint Johnsbury Trucking Co.
Saint Paul Cos.
Salem News Publishing Co.
Salomon
Saltonstall Charitable Foundation, Richard
Sanders Trust, Charles
Sawyer Charitable Foundation
Schrafft and Bertha E. Schrafft Charitable Trust, William E.
Scott Paper Co.
Seaboard Corp.
Sealy, Inc.
Seiler Corp.
Sequa Corp.
Shapiro Charity Fund, Abraham
Shaw Foundation, Gardiner Howland
Shaw Fund for Mariner's Children
Shawmut Bank of Franklin County
Shawmut National Corp.
Shawmut Needham Bank, N.A.
Shawmut Worcester County Bank, N.A.
Shaw's Supermarkets
Shell Oil Co.
Sherman Family Charitable Trust, George and Beatrice
Simplex Time Recorder Co.
Smith Foundation, Richard and Susan
Smith Fund, Horace
Sonesta International Hotels Corp.
South-Western Publishing Co.
Stanhome Inc.
Star Markets Co.
Stare Fund
Starrett Co., L.S.
State Mutual Life Assurance Co.
State Street Bank & Trust Co.
Stearns Charitable Foundation, Anna B.
Stearns Trust, Artemas W.
Steiger Memorial Fund, Albert
Stevens Foundation, Abbot and Dorothy H.
Stevens Foundation, Nathaniel and Elizabeth P.
Stoddard Charitable Trust
Stone Charitable Foundation
Stone Container Corp.
Stone Fund, Albert H. and Reuben S.
Stoneman Charitable Foundation, Anne and David
Stratford Foundation
Stride Rite Corp.
Sun Life Assurance Co. of Canada (U.S.)
Sun Microsystems
Swank, Inc.
Swasey Fund for Relief of Public School Teachers of Newburyport
Swensrud Charitable Trust, Sidney A.
Tandem Computers
Technical Training Foundation
Teledyne
Teradyne, Inc.
Texas Instruments
Textron
Thermo Electron Corp.
Thompson Trust, Thomas
Thorn Apple Valley, Inc.
3M Co.
Times Mirror Co.

TJX Cos.
Totsy Manufacturing Co.
Towle Manufacturing Co.
Town & Country Corp.
Travelers Cos.
Travelli Fund, Charles Irwin
TRW Corp.
Tupancy-Harris Foundation of 1986
Turner Construction Co.
Turner Corp.
Twentieth Century-Fox Film Corp.
21st Century Foods
Union Camp Corp.
Union Carbide Corp.
United Asset Management Corp.
United Merchants & Manufacturers
United States Trust Co. of New York
United Technologies Corp.
Unitrode Corp.
Urann Foundation
Varian Associates
Victaulic Co. of America
Vingo Trust II
Volkswagen of America, Inc.
Walgreen Co.
Wallace Foundation, George R.
Wallace & Wallace Ltd.
Walsh Charity Trust, Blanche M.
Wang Laboratories, Inc.
Warren Co., S.D.
Waters Foundation
WCVB-TV
Weber Charities Corp., Frederick E.
Webster Charitable Foundation
Webster Co., H. K.
Webster Foundation, Edwin S.
Welch Foods
Wells Trust Fund, Fred W.
Westinghouse Electric Corp.
Weston Associates/R.C.M. Corp.
Westvaco Corp.
Wetterau
Wharton Trust, William P.
Wheelwright Scientific School
White Consolidated Industries
White Construction Co.
Williams Foundation, Arthur Ashley
Winthrop Trust, Clara B.
Wolfson Foundation, Louis E.
Wyman-Gordon Co.
Xerox Corp.
Xtra Corp.
Yawkey Foundation II

Michigan

Abbott Laboratories
Abitibi-Price
Abrams Foundation, Talbert and Leota
Acustar Inc.
Agway
Akzo America
Akzo Chemicals Inc.
Alco Standard Corp.
AlliedSignal
Alma Piston Co.
Alro Steel Corp.
Alumax
AMAX
American Cyanamid Co.
American Electric Power
American Natural Resources Co.
American Standard
Americana Foundation
Ameritech Corp.
Ameritech Publishing
Amway Corp.
Andersons Management Corp.
Archer-Daniels-Midland Co.
Armco Inc.

Arrow Electronics, Inc.
Arvin Industries
ASARCO
Asgrow Seed Co.
Augat, Inc.
Auto Specialties Manufacturing Co.
Avis Inc.
Avnet, Inc.
Awrey Bakeries
Backer Spielvogel Bates U.S.
Baldwin Foundation
Banc One Illinois Corp.
Bank of Alma
Bargman Foundation, Theodore and Mina
Barnes Group
Barstow Foundation
Barton-Malow Co.
Batts Foundation
Bauervic Foundation, Charles M.
Bauervic-Paisley Foundation
Bausch & Lomb
Baxter International
Bechtel Group
Beldon II Fund
Bell Industries
Bentley Foundation, Alvin M.
Bergen Brunswig Corp.
Berwind Corp.
Besser Co.
Besser Foundation
BFGoodrich
Bierlein Family Foundation
Bishop Charitable Trust, A. G.
Black & Decker Corp.
Blount
Blue Cross/Blue Shield of Michigan
Boise Cascade Corp.
Borden
Borg-Warner Corp.
Borman's
Bosch Corp., Robert
Boutell Memorial Fund, Arnold and Gertrude
Bray Charitable Trust, Viola E.
Brown Inc., John
Browning-Ferris Industries
Brunswick Corp.
Budd Co.
C.P. Rail Systems
Cablevision of Michigan
Cadillac Products
Campbell Soup Co.
Capital Cities/ABC
Castle & Co., A.M.
Centel Corp.
CertainTeed Corp.
Chamberlin Foundation, Gerald W.
Champion International Corp.
Chicago Pneumatic Tool Co.
Chrysler Corp.
Cincinnati Milacron
Citizens Commercial & Savings Bank
Clark Equipment Co.
Coachmen Industries
Coastal Corp.
Cold Heading Co.
Coltec Industries
Comerica
Computer Associates International
Computer Sciences Corp.
Consolidated Freightways
Consumers Power Co.
Continental Corp.
Cook Charitable Foundation
Cooper Industries
Cox Enterprises
Crane Co.
CUNA Mutual Insurance Group
Curtice-Burns Foods
Dalton Foundation, Dorothy U.
Dana Corp.

Dart Foundation
Davenport Foundation, M. E.
Dayton Hudson Corp.
Dayton-Walther Corp.
Delano Foundation, Mignon Sherwood
Deluxe Corp.
DeRoy Foundation, Helen L.
DeRoy Testamentary Foundation
Deseranno Educational Foundation
Detroit Edison Co.
DeVlieg Foundation, Charles
DeVos Foundation, Richard and Helen
Dexter Industries
Difco Laboratories
Domino's Pizza
Douglas & Lomason Company
Dover Corp.
Dow Chemical Co.
Dow Corning Corp.
Dow Foundation, Herbert H. and Barbara C.
Dow Foundation, Herbert H. and Grace A.
Dow Fund, Alden and Vada
Dresser Industries
du Pont de Nemours & Co., E. I.
Eagle-Picher Industries
Earhart Foundation
Earl-Beth Foundation
Eaton Corp.
Echlin Inc.
Eddy Family Memorial Fund, C. K.
Eden Foods
EG&G Inc.
Elf Atochem North America
Erb Lumber Co.
Ewald Foundation, H. T.
Fabri-Kal Corp.
Fairchild Corp.
Farwell Foundation, Drusilla
Federal-Mogul Corp.
Federal Screw Works
Fiat U.S.A., Inc.
Fibre Converters
First Federal of Michigan
First Mississippi Corp.
First of America Bank Corp.
Fisher Foundation, Max M. and Marjorie S.
FKI Holdings Inc.
Ford Fund, Benson and Edith
Ford Fund, Eleanor and Edsel
Ford Fund, Walter and Josephine
Ford Fund, William and Martha
Ford II Fund, Henry
Ford Motor Co.
Forest City Enterprises
Franklin Bank
Fruehauf Foundation
Fuller Co., H.B.
Gannett Co.
Gast Manufacturing Corp.
GenCorp
General Dynamics Corp.
General Motors Corp.
Georgia-Pacific Corp.
Gerber Products Co.
Gershenson Foundation, Charles H.
Gerstacker Foundation, Rollin M.
Gilmore Foundation, Irving S.
Glidden Co.
Graco
Grainger, W.W.
Grand Rapids Label Co.
Grand Trunk Corp.
Great Lakes Bancorp, FSB
Great Lakes Casting Corp.
Greater Lansing Foundation
Green Charitable Trust, Leslie H. and Edith C.
Grumman Corp.
Guardian Industries Corp.

Hammond Machinery
Handleman Co.
Handy & Harman
Hanna Co., M.A.
Hanson Office Products
Harding Foundation, Charles Stewart
HarperCollins Publishers
Haworth, Inc.
Hayes Albion Industries
Heileman Brewing Co., Inc., G.
Heinz Co., H.J.
Henkel Corp.
Hercules Inc.
Herman Foundation, John and Rose
Herrick Foundation
Hess Charitable Trust, Myrtle E. and William C.
Heublein
Hexcel Corp.
Hiram Walker & Sons Inc.
Hitachi
Holden Fund, James and Lynelle
Holley Foundation
Holman
Honigman Foundation
Hook Drug
Household International
Hudson-Webber Foundation
Hudson's
Humana
Hunter Foundation, Edward and Irma
Huntington Bancshares Inc.
Hurst Foundation
Illinois Tool Works
Imerman Memorial Foundation, Stanley
India Foundation
Ingersoll-Rand Co.
Inland Steel Industries
Intelligent Controls
International Multifoods Corp.
Interpublic Group of Cos.
Isuzu Motors America Inc.
ITT Corp.
ITT Hartford Insurance Group
ITT Rayonier
Jackson National Life Insurance Co.
Jacobson Stores, Inc.
James River Corp. of Virginia
Jeffers Memorial Fund, Michael
Jefferson Smurfit Corp.
Johnson Inc., Axel
Johnson Controls
Johnson & Higgins
Jostens
Journal Communications
JSJ Corp.
Kantzler Foundation
Karmazin Products Corp.
Kasle Steel Corp.
Kaufman Endowment Fund, Louis G.
Kaufman Memorial Trust, Chaim, Fanny, Louis, Benjamin, and Anne Florence
Keebler Co.
Keeler Fund, Miner S. and Mary Ann
Kellogg Foundation, W. K.
Kellogg's
Kelly Services
Kennametal
Kimberly-Clark Corp.
KitchenAid Inc.
Kloeckner-Pentaplast of America
Kmart Corp.
Knight-Ridder, Inc.
Kolene Corp.
Kowalski Sausage Co.
Kresge Foundation
Kysor Industrial Corp.
La-Z-Boy Chair Co.
Lafarge Corp.

Levy Co., Edward C.
Levy Foundation, Edward C.
Lincoln Health Care Foundation
Lincoln National Corp.
Litton Industries
Loeb Charitable Trust, Stella and Frederick S.
Loutit Foundation
LTV Corp.
Maas Foundation, Benard L.
Manat Foundation
Manoogian Foundation, Alex and Marie
Manufacturers Life Insurance Co. of America
Manufacturers National Bank of Detroit
Manville Corp.
Mardigian Foundation
Maritz Inc.
Mark IV Industries
Masco Corp.
McGregor Fund
McIntyre Foundation, B. D. and Jane E.
McIntyre Foundation, C. S. and Marion F.
McKesson Corp.
McLouth Steel-An Employee Owned Co.
Mead Corp.
Meijer Inc.
Menasha Corp.
Mendel Foundation
Meredith Corp.
Merillat Foundation, Orville D. and Ruth A.
Merkley Charitable Trust
Mette Foundation
Michigan Bell Telephone Co.
Michigan Consolidated Gas Co.
Michigan Gas Utilities
Michigan Mutual Insurance Corp.
Michigan National Corp.
Michigan Wheel Corp.
Miller Charitable Foundation, C. John and Reva
Miller Foundation
Miller Inc., Herman
Mills Fund, Frances Goll
Monroe Auto Equipment Co.
Monroe-Brown Foundation
Monsanto Co.
Moore Foundation, C. F.
Morley Brothers Foundation
Morrison-Knudsen Corp.
Morton International
Mott Foundation, Charles Stewart
Mott Fund, Ruth
National Medical Enterprises
National Standard Co.
NBD Bank
NBD Genesee Bank
Newmont Mining Corp.
News America Publishing Inc.
Northern Telecom Inc.
Norton Co.
NutraSweet Co.
Old Kent Bank & Trust Co.
Oleson Foundation
Outboard Marine Corp.
Padnos Iron & Metal Co., Louis
Pamida, Inc.
Pardee Foundation, Elsa U.
Park-Ohio Industries Inc.
Parker-Hannifin Corp.
Pechiney Corp.
Penske Corp.
Perina Corp
Perini Corp.
Perry Drug Stores
Peterson & Co. Consulting
PHM Corp.
Pioneer Hi-Bred International
PK Lumber Co.
Plante & Moran, CPAs
Plym Foundation

Polk & Co., R.L.
PPG Industries
Prentis Family Foundation, Meyer and Anna
Prince Corp.
Protherapy of America
Prudential Insurance Co. of America
Quaker Chemical Corp.
Quaker Oats Co.
Quanex Corp.
R&B Tool Co.
Ransom Fidelity Company
Ratner Foundation, Milton M.
Robertshaw Controls Co.
Robertson Brothers
Rochester Telephone Corp.
Rockwell International Corp.
Rohlik Foundation, Sigmund and Sophie
Rouge Steel Co.
Rouse Co.
Ryder System
Sage Foundation
Sara Lee Corp.
Scherer Foundation, Karla
Schlumberger Ltd.
Scientific Brake & Equipment Co.
Scott Paper Co.
Scripps Co., E.W.
Sealy, Inc.
Sebastian Foundation
Sehn Foundation
Seidman Family Foundation
Seymour and Troester Foundation
Shapero Foundation, Nate S. and Ruth B.
Sheldahl Inc.
Shelden Fund, Elizabeth, Allan and Warren
Shell Oil Co.
Shiffman Foundation
Silverman Fluxus Collection Foundation, Gilbert and Lila
Simone Foundation
Simpson Foundation
Simpson Industries
Simpson Investment Co.
Skillman Foundation
Smith Corp., A.O.
Society Corp.
Sotheby's
Southland Corp.
Sparton Corp.
Spectra-Physics Analytical
Spring Arbor Distributors
SPX Corp.
Standard Federal Bank
Standard Products Co.
Stanley Works
State Farm Mutual Automobile Insurance Co.
Steelcase
Stone Container Corp.
Stroh Brewery Co.
Strosacker Foundation, Charles J.
Tandem Computers
Target Stores
Taubman Foundation, A. Alfred
Tecumseh Products Co.
Teitel Charitable Trust, Ben N.
Teledyne
Teleflex Inc.
Tenneco
Textron
Thoman Foundation, W. B. and Candace
Thorn Apple Valley, Inc.
3M Co.
Thyssen Specialty Steels
Timken Co.
Timmis Foundation, Michael & Nancy
Tiscornia Foundation
Todd Co., A.M.
Tomkins Industries, Inc.

Torchmark Corp.
Towsley Foundation, Harry A. and Margaret D.
Transamerica Corp.
Travelers Cos.
Trico Foundation
Triford Foundation
TRINOVA Corp.
TRW Corp.
Turner Construction Co.
Turner Corp.
Twentieth Century-Fox Film Corp.
Tyson Foods, Inc.
Union Camp Corp.
Union Carbide Corp.
Unisys Corp.
United Technologies, Automotive
United Technologies Corp.
Upjohn Co.
Upjohn Foundation, Harold and Grace
Upton Foundation, Frederick S.
Van Andel Foundation, Jay and Betty
Vicksburg Foundation
Vlasic Foundation
Volkswagen of America, Inc.
Vollbrecht Foundation, Frederick A.
Voplex Corp.
Vulcan Materials Co.
Wal-Mart Stores
Walbridge Aldinger Co.
Walgreen Co.
Walker Co., Shaw
Walker Foundation, L. C. and Margaret
Warner-Lambert Co.
Washington Post Co.
Wege Foundation
Wenger Foundation, Henry L. and Consuelo S.
Westerman Foundation, Samuel L.
Westinghouse Electric Corp.
Weyerhaeuser Co.
Whirlpool Corp.
White Consolidated Industries
Whiteley Foundation, John and Elizabeth
Whiting Foundation
Whiting Memorial Foundation, Henry and Harriet
Whitney Fund, David M.
Wickes Foundation, Harvey Randall
Wickson-Link Memorial Foundation
Wilson Fund, Matilda R.
Wilson Trust, Lula C.
Winship Memorial Scholarship Foundation
Witco Corp.
Wolverine World Wide, Inc.
Word Investments
Xtra Corp.
Zimmerman Foundation, Mary and George Herbert

Minnesota

ADC Telecommunications
AG Processing Inc.
AHS Foundation
Alco Standard Corp.
Alliant Techsystems
Alliss Educational Foundation, Charles and Ellora
Alworth Memorial Fund, Marshall H. and Nellie
America West Airlines
American Amusement Arcades
American Express Co.
American Linen Supply Co.
American Standard
Andersen Corp.
Andersen Foundation

Minnesota (cont.)

Andersen Foundation, Hugh J.
Apogee Enterprises Inc.
APV Crepaco Inc.
Archer-Daniels-Midland Co.
Arkla
Armco Inc.
Arrow Electronics, Inc.
Ashland Oil
Athwin Foundation
Atkinson Co., Guy F.
Avnet, Inc.
AXIA Incorporated
Baker Hughes Inc.
Banta Corp.
Bauervic Foundation, Peggy
Bausch & Lomb
Baxter International
Beim Foundation
Bell Industries
Bemis Company
Best Products Co.
Bigelow Foundation, F. R.
Bio-Medicus, Inc.
Blandin Foundation
Blue Cross and Blue Shield of
    Minnesota Foundation Inc.
BMC Industries
Boise Cascade Corp.
Borden
Boulevard Foundation
Bremer Foundation, Otto
Browning-Ferris Industries
Brunswick Corp.
Burlington Northern Inc.
Bush Foundation
Business Incentives
Butler Family Foundation,
    Patrick and Aimee
Butler Manufacturing Co.
C.P. Rail Systems
Campbell Soup Co.
Capital Cities/ABC
Cargill
Caring and Sharing Foundation
Carlson Cos.
Carolyn Foundation
Caterpillar
CBI Industries
CENEX
Centel Corp.
Chadwick Foundation
Champion International Corp.
Cherne Foundation, Albert W.
Chrysler Corp.
Chubb Corp.
Citicorp
Cochrane Memorial Trust, 1988
    Irrevocable
Commercial Intertech Corp.
Computer Associates
    International
ConAgra
Control Data Corp.
Cowles Media Co.
Cray Research
CTS Corp.
Cyprus Minerals Co.
Dain Bosworth/Inter-Regional
    Financial Group
Davis Foundation, Edwin W. and
    Catherine M.
Dayton Hudson Corp.
Dayton's
Deere & Co.
Deluxe Corp.
Dial Corp.
Donaldson Co.
Douglas Corp.
Dover Corp.
Dow Chemical Co.
Dow Jones & Co.
Driscoll Foundation
Dun & Bradstreet Corp.
Eastern Enterprises
Eaton Corp.

Ecolab
Eddy Foundation
Edwards Memorial Trust
Ellerbe Becket
Emerson Electric Co.
Faribault Foods
Farmstead Foods
Federal-Mogul Corp.
Federated Life Insurance Co.
Fingerhut Corp.
Fingerhut Family Foundation
First Bank System
Firstar Bank Milwaukee NA
Fiterman Charitable Foundation,
    Miles and Shirley
FMC Corp.
Foldcraft Co.
Forest City Enterprises
Fortis Inc.
Fortis Benefits Insurance
    Company/Fortis Financial
    Group
Fuller Co., H.B.
Gannett Co.
General Housewares Corp.
General Mills
Georgia-Pacific Corp.
Getsch Family Foundation Trust
Gillette Co.
GNB Inc.
Good Value Home, Inc.
Graco
Grainger, W.W.
Gray Charitable Trust, Mary S.
Griggs and Mary Griggs Burke
    Foundation, Mary Livingston
Grossman Foundation, N. Bud
Grotto Foundation
Groves & Sons Co., S.J.
Hallett Charitable Trust
Hallett Charitable Trust, Jessie F.
Harsco Corp.
Hartford Steam Boiler Inspection
    & Insurance Co.
Hartz Foundation
Harvest States Cooperative
Heileman Brewing Co., Inc., G.
Heilicher Foundation, Menahem
Heinz Co., H.J.
Hersey Foundation
Hiawatha Education Foundation
Honeywell
Hormel & Co., George A.
Hotchkiss Foundation, W. R.
Hubbard Broadcasting
Hubbard Milling Co.
Hudson Jewellers, J.B.
Hulings Foundation, Mary
    Andersen
IBM Corp.
ICI Americas
IDS Financial Services
Illinois Tool Works
Independent Financial Corp.
Ingersoll-Rand Co.
Inland Container Corp.
Inland Steel Industries
Intelligent Controls
International Dairy Queen, Inc.
International Multifoods Corp.
ITT Corp.
ITT Hartford Insurance Group
ITT Rayonier
Jerome Foundation
Johnson Co., E. F.
Johnson & Higgins
Johnson & Son, S.C.
Jostens
Kasal Charitable Trust, Father
Knight-Ridder, Inc.
Krelitz Industries
Land O'Lakes
Lee Enterprises
Liberty Diversified Industries
    Inc.
Lieberman Enterprises
Lilly & Co., Eli

Lilly Foundation, Richard Coyle
Litton Industries
LTV Corp.
Lutheran Brotherhood
    Foundation
Mankato Citizens Telephone Co.
Manufacturers Life Insurance
    Co. of America
Manville Corp.
Mapco Inc.
Marbrook Foundation
Mardag Foundation
Maritz Inc.
McGraw-Hill
McKnight Foundation
McKnight Foundation, Sumner T.
McNeely Foundation
McVay Foundation
Mead Corp.
Meadowood Foundation
Medtronic
MEI Diversified, Inc.
Menasha Corp.
Merrill Corp.
Metroquip
Minnegasco
Minnesota Foundation
Minnesota Mutual Life
    Insurance Co.
Minnesota Power & Light Co.
Mitchell, Jr. Trust, Oscar
Moore Business Forms, Inc.
Moore, Costello & Hart
Mortenson Co., M.A.
MSI Insurance
MTS Systems Corp.
Munsingwear, Inc.
Mutual Service Life Insurance
    Cos.
Nash-Finch Co.
Nash Foundation
National Car Rental System, Inc.
National Computer Systems
National Presto Industries
NCR Corp.
Neilson Foundation, George W.
North American Life & Casualty
    Co.
North American Philips Corp.
North Star Research Foundation
North Star Steel Co.
North Star Universal Inc.
Northern Star Foundation
Northern States Power Co.
Northern Telecom Inc.
Northwest Airlines, Inc.
Northwest Area Foundation
Northwestern National Insurance
    Group
Northwestern National Life
    Insurance Co.
Norwest Corp.
Oakleaf Foundation
O'Brien Foundation, Alice M.
Onan Corp.
Onan Family Foundation
O'Neil Foundation, Casey Albert
    T.
Ordean Foundation
O'Shaughnessy Foundation, I. A.
Owens-Corning Fiberglas Corp.
PacifiCorp
Pamida, Inc.
Parker-Hannifin Corp.
Pax Christi Foundation
Payless Cashways Inc.
Pearson Foundation, E. M.
Pentair
Perkin-Elmer Corp.
Pfizer
Phelps Dodge Corp.
Philip Morris Cos.
Phillips Family Foundation, Jay
    and Rose
Pillsbury Co.
Piper Jaffray Cos.
Polaris Industries, LP

Potlatch Corp.
Prudential Insurance Co. of
    America
Quantum Chemical Corp.
Quebecor Printing (USA) Inc.
Quinlan Foundation, Elizabeth C.
Ralston Purina Co.
Red Wing Shoe Co.
Reell Precision Manufacturing
Regis Corp.
REI-Recreational Equipment,
    Inc.
Reliance Electric Co.
Remmele Engineering, Inc.
Rodman Foundation
Rosemount, Inc.
Rouse Co.
Saint Croix Foundation
Saint Paul Cos.
Sandoz Corp.
Sara Lee Corp.
Schering Trust for Arthritis
    Research, Margaret Harvey
Schott Foundation
Schwan's Sales Enterprises
Sealy, Inc.
Security Life Insurance Co. of
    America
Seneca Foods Corp.
Sexton Foundation
Sheily Co., J.L.
Sheldahl Inc.
Sifco Industries Inc.
SIT Investment Associates, Inc.
Southways Foundation
Sprint
SPX Corp.
State Farm Mutual Automobile
    Insurance Co.
Stauffer Communications
Stirtz, Bernards & Co.
Stone Container Corp.
Sundet Foundation
Super Valu Stores
Sweatt Foundation, Harold W.
Tandem Computers
Target Stores
Taylor Corp.
TCF Banking & Savings, FSB
Teledyne
Tennant Co.
Tension Envelope Corp.
Textron
Thorpe Foundation, James R.
3M Co.
Thyssen Specialty Steels
Timken Co.
Toro Co.
Tozer Foundation
Travelers Cos.
Travelers Express Co.
Tyson Foods, Inc.
Union Carbide Corp.
Unisys Corp.
US WEST
USG Corp.
USX Corp.
Valspar Corp.
Van Evera Foundation, Dewitt
    Caroline
Wal-Mart Stores
Walgreen Co.
Walker Foundation, Archie D.
    and Bertha H.
Wallestad Foundation
Wallin Foundation
Warner Foundation, Lee and
    Rose
Washington Post Co.
Wasie Foundation
Wedum Foundation
West Publishing Co.
Westinghouse Electric Corp.
Weyerhaeuser Co.
Weyerhaeuser Family Foundation
Weyerhaeuser Foundation,
    Frederick and Margaret L.

Weyerhaeuser Memorial
    Foundation, Charles A.
White Consolidated Industries
Whiteside Scholarship Fund,
    Robert B. and Sophia

Mississippi

Alco Standard Corp.
Alumax
AMAX
Armco Inc.
Armstrong Foundation
Armstrong World Industries Inc.
Baird Charitable Trust, William
    Robert
Barnes Group
Baxter International
BellSouth Corp.
Black & Decker Corp.
Borg-Warner Corp.
Browning-Ferris Industries
Brunswick Corp.
Bryan Foods
C.P. Rail Systems
Ceco Corp.
Charter Medical Corp.
Community Foundation
ConAgra
Cooper Industries
Cooper Tire & Rubber Co.
Croft Metals
Deluxe Corp.
Deposit Guaranty National Bank
Dollar General Corp.
Douglas & Lomason Company
Dover Corp.
du Pont de Nemours & Co., E. I.
Durr-Fillauer Medical
Eastover Bank for Savings
Eastover Corp.
Eckerd Corp., Jack
Eka Nobel
Emerson Electric Co.
Entex
Feild Co-Operative Association
First Mississippi Corp.
FMC Corp.
Gannett Co.
GenCorp
General Motors Corp.
Georgia-Pacific Corp.
Hanson Office Products
Hardin Foundation, Phil
Heinz Co., H.J.
Hercules Inc.
Humana
Ingalls Shipbuilding
Inland Container Corp.
Interco
International Paper Co.
Irby Construction Co.
James River Corp. of Virginia
Johnson Day Trust, Carl and
    Virginia
Jostens
Kimball International
Kimberly-Clark Corp.
Knight-Ridder, Inc.
Kyle Educational Trust, S. H.
    and D. W.
La-Z-Boy Chair Co.
Lennox International, Inc.
Levi Strauss & Co.
Litton Industries
Luckyday Foundation
Manville Corp.
Masco Corp.
McRae Foundation
Menasha Corp.
Mississippi Chemical Corp.
Mississippi Power Co.
Mississippi Power & Light Co.
Mohasco Corp.
Morton International
Mosinee Paper Corp.
National Medical Enterprises

National Presto Industries
New York Times Co.
Northrop Corp.
Oster/Sunbeam Appliance Co.
Parker-Hannifin Corp.
Phelps Dodge Corp.
Pioneer Hi-Bred International
Prudential Insurance Co. of
America
Quantum Chemical Corp.
Revlon
Ringier-America
Rochester Telephone Corp.
Sara Lee Corp.
Sara Lee Hosiery
Schillig Trust, Ottilie
Scott Paper Co.
Sealy, Inc.
SPX Corp.
Stone Container Corp.
Super Valu Stores
Teledyne
Thomasville Furniture Industries
Toro Co.
Transco Energy Company
Travelers Cos.
TRINOVA Corp.
Trustmark National Bank
TRW Corp.
Union Camp Corp.
Union Planters Corp.
United Dominion Industries
United Technologies Corp.
Vicksburg Hospital Medical
Foundation
Wal-Mart Stores
Walker Foundation, W. E.
Walker Wildlife Conservation
Foundation
Weyerhaeuser Co.
Winn-Dixie Stores
Witco Corp.
Zapata Corp.

Missouri

ACF Industries, Inc.
Affiliated Publications, Inc.
AFLAC
Alco Standard Corp.
AlliedSignal
Alumax
AMAX
America West Airlines
American Cyanamid Co.
American Home Products Corp.
American Investment Co.
American National Insurance
American Standard
Amoco Corp.
Angelica Corp.
Anheuser-Busch Cos.
Apex Oil Co.
ARA Services
Arch Mineral Corp.
Armco Inc.
Arkansas Power & Light Co.
Armco Inc.
Arrow Electronics, Inc.
Arvin Industries
Avery Dennison Corp.
Avnet, Inc.
Bairnco Corp.
Baker Hughes Inc.
Banta Co.
Barrows Foundation, Geraldine
and R. A.
Bartlett & Co.
Baskin-Robbins USA CO.
Bausch & Lomb
Baxter International
Bemis Company
Benefit Trust Life Insurance Co.
Best Products Co.
Black & Decker Corp.
Black & Veatch
Bloch Foundation, Henry W. and
Marion H.

Block Family Charitable Trust,
Ephraim
Block Family Foundation,
Emphraim
Block, H&R
Boatmen's Bancshares
Bohan Foundation, Ruth H.
Boise Cascade Corp.
Borden
Brisley and Noma Brisley
Phillips Scholarship Loan
Fund, Ella Frances
Bromley Residuary Trust, Guy I.
Brown Foundation, George
Warren
Brown Group
Brown Shoe Co.
Browning-Ferris Industries
Burlington Northern Inc.
Bush Family Foundation, Peter
W.
Business Men's Assurance Co. of
America
Butler Manufacturing Co.
Capital Cities/ABC
Capital Holding Corp.
Castle & Co., A.M.
CertainTeed Corp.
Charter Medical Corp.
Chemtech Industries
Chesebrough-Pond's
Chrysler Corp.
Circuit City Stores
Citicorp
Clark Oil & Refining Corp.
Clorox Co.
Columbia Terminals Co.
Commerce Bancshares, Inc.
Commercial Metals Co.
Comprehensive Care Corp.
Computer Associates
International
ConAgra
Cooper Industries
Cowden Foundation, Louetta M.
Cox Enterprises
CPI Corp.
CR Industries
Crane & Co.
Crane Co.
Crum and Forster
CSX Corp.
Cyprus Minerals Co.
Danforth Foundation
Dayton Hudson Corp.
Deer Creek Foundation
Deluxe Corp.
Dennison Manufacturing Co.
Dillard Department Stores, Inc.
Diversified Industries, Inc.
Dollar General Corp.
Donaldson Co.
Douglas & Lomason Company
Dow Chemical Co.
Dow Jones & Co.
Eagle-Picher Industries
Eaton Corp.
Echlin Inc.
Edison Brothers Stores
Edison Foundation, Harry
Edison Foundation, Irving and
Beatrice C.
Edwards & Sons, A.G.
EG&G Inc.
Elf Aquitaine, Inc.
Emerson Electric Co.
Empire District Electric Co.
Enright Foundation
Enterprise Rent-A-Car Co.
Ethyl Corp.
Fabick Tractor Co., John
Farm & Home Savings
Association
Farmland Industries, Inc.
Federal-Mogul Corp.
Ferrell Cos.
Fireman's Fund Insurance Co.

Flarsheim Charitable
Foundation, Louis and
Elizabeth
Food Barn Stores, Inc.
Fortis Benefits Insurance
Company/Fortis Financial
Group
Foxmeyer Corp.
Francis Families Foundation
Fru-Con Construction Corp.
Fulbright and Monroe L. Swyers
Foundation, James H.
Gannett Co.
Garvey Memorial Foundation,
Edward Chase
Gateway Apparel
Gaylord Foundation, Clifford
Willard
GenCorp
General American Life Insurance
Co.
General Dynamics Corp.
Georgia-Pacific Corp.
Goodyear Tire & Rubber Co.
Grant Charitable Trust, Elberth
R. and Gladys F.
Graybar Electric Co.
Green Foundation, Allen P. and
Josephine B.
Green Industries, A. P.
Group Health Plan Inc.
Guth Lighting Co.
Hall Family Foundations
Hallmark Cards
Hamilton Foundation, Florence P.
Hanson Office Products
Harvard Interiors Manufacturing
Co.
Helzberg Foundation, Shirley
and Barnett
Hercules Inc.
Herschend Family Foundation
Hershey Foods Corp.
Hospital Corp. of America
Hubbard Milling Co.
Hubbell Inc.
Humana
IMCERA Group Inc.
Ingram Trust, Joe
Inland Container Corp.
Inland Steel Industries
Interco
International Multifoods Corp.
Interstate Brands Corp.
ITT Corp.
ITT Hartford Insurance Group
ITT Rayonier
James River Corp. of Virginia
Jefferson Smurfit Corp.
Johnson Controls
Johnson & Higgins
Johnson & Son, S.C.
Jordan and Ettie A. Jordan
Charitable Foundation, Mary
Ranken
Jostens
Kahn Memorial Trust
Kansas City Power & Light Co.
Kansas City Southern Industries
Kellwood Co.
Kelty Pack, Inc.
Kemper Charitable Lead Trust,
William T.
Kemper Charitable Trust,
William T.
Kemper Foundation, Enid and
Crosby
Kemper Foundation, William T.
Kemper Memorial Foundation,
David Woods
Korte Construction Co.
La-Z-Boy Chair Co.
Laclede Gas Co.
Laclede Steel Co.
Leader Foundation
Leggett & Platt, Inc.
Lichtenstein Foundation, David
B.

Litton Industries
Loose Trust, Carrie J.
Loose Trust, Harry Wilson
Lopata Foundation, Stanley and
Lucy
Louisiana-Pacific Corp.
Love Charitable Foundation,
John Allan
Lowenstein Brothers Foundation
Magic Chef
Mallinckrodt, Jr. Foundation,
Edward
Mallinckrodt Specialty
Chemicals Co.
Manville Corp.
Mapco Inc.
Marion Merrell Dow
Maritz Inc.
May Department Stores Co.
Maytag Corp.
McBride & Son Associates
McCourtney Trust, Flora S.
McCray Lumber Co.
McDonnell Douglas Corp.
McDonnell Douglas Corp.-West
McDonnell Foundation, James S.
McGee Foundation
Mead Corp.
Mercantile Bancorp
Merck & Co.
Messick Charitable Trust, Harry
F.
Messing Family Charitable
Foundation
Mid-America Dairymen
Miles Inc.
Miller-Mellor Association
Millstone Foundation
Missouri Farmers Association
Missouri Public Service
Monsanto Co.
Moog Automotive, Inc.
Morgan Charitable Residual
Trust, W. and E.
Moss Charitable Trust, Finis M.
National Medical Enterprises
Nationwide Insurance Cos.
New England Business Service
Newmont Mining Corp.
Nichols Co., J.C.
Old American Insurance Co.
Olin Charitable Trust, John M.
Olin Corp.
Olin Foundation, Spencer T. and
Ann W.
Oppenstein Brothers Foundation
Orchard Corp. of America.
Orscheln Co.
Outboard Marine Corp.
Owens-Corning Fiberglas Corp.
PacifiCorp
Pamida, Inc.
Paxton Co., Frank
Payless Cashways Inc.
Peabody Holding Company Inc.
Pendergast-Weyer Foundation
Pet
Petrolite Corp.
Pettus, Jr. Foundation, James T.
Pillsbury Foundation
Pitzman Fund
Plaster Foundation, Robert W.
Pott Foundation, Herman T. and
Phenie R.
PPG Industries
Procter & Gamble Co.
Prudential Insurance Co. of
America
Pulitzer Publishing Co.
Quaker Oats Co.
Quantum Chemical Corp.
Ralston Purina Co.
Reliable Life Insurance Co.
Reynolds Foundation, J. B.
Reynolds Metals Co.
Rhoden Charitable Foundation,
Elmer C.

Roblee Foundation, Joseph H.
and Florence A.
Rouse Co.
Royal Group Inc.
Sachs Fund
SAFECO Corp.
Santa Fe Pacific Corp.
Sara Lee Corp.
Schnuck Markets
Scripps Co., E.W.
Sears, Roebuck and Co.
SECO
Sequa Corp.
Share Foundation
Shaw Foundation, Arch W.
Shell Oil Co.
Shelter Mutual Insurance Co.
Sherwood Medical Co.
Shoenberg Foundation
Shughart, Thomson & Kilroy,
P.C.
Sigma-Aldrich Corp.
Slusher Charitable Foundation,
Roy W.
Sosland Foundation
Souers Charitable Trust, Sidney
W. and Sylvia N.
Southwestern Bell Corp.
Speas Foundation, Victor E.
Speas Memorial Trust, John W.
and Effie E.
Sprint
Square D Co.
Stanley Works
State Farm Mutual Automobile
Insurance Co.
Stauffer Communications
Steadley Memorial Trust, Kent
D. and Mary L.
Stern Foundation for the Arts,
Richard J.
Stone Container Corp.
Storz Instrument Co.
Stowers Foundation
Stride Rite Corp.
Stupp Brothers Bridge & Iron Co.
Stupp Foundation, Norman J.
Sunderland Foundation, Lester T.
Sunmark Capital Corp.
Sunnen Foundation
Swift Co. Inc., John S.
Syntex Corp.
Tamko Asphalt Products
Tandem Computers
Tandy Corp.
Target Stores
Taylor Charitable Trust, Jack
DeLoss
Teledyne
Tension Envelope Corp.
Tetley, Inc.
Thompson Charitable Trust,
Sylvia G.
3M Co.
Tilles Nonsectarian Charity
Fund, Rosalie
Times Mirror Co.
Torchmark Corp.
Trans World Airlines
Travelers Cos.
Turner Charitable Trust,
Courtney S.
UniGroup Inc.
Unilever United States
Union Camp Corp.
Union Carbide Corp.
Union Electric Co.
Union Pacific Corp.
United Dominion Industries
United Missouri Bancshares, Inc.
United Van Lines, Inc.
Universal Foods Corp.
Utilicorp United
Valley Line Co.
Voelkerding Charitable Trust,
Walter and Jean
Wal-Mart Stores

Missouri (cont.)

Walgreen Co.
Ward Foundation, Louis L. and Adelaide C.
Webb Foundation
Western Resources
Westinghouse Electric Corp.
Westlake Scholarship Fund, James L. and Nellie M.
Wetterau
Weyerhaeuser Co.
Whitaker Charitable Foundation, Lyndon C.
Williams Cos.
Wolff Foundation, John M.
Wolff Shoe Co.
Woods Foundation, James H.
Wornall Charitable Trust and Foundation, Kearney
Xerox Corp.
Xtra Corp.

Montana

American Stores Co.
AON Corp.
ARCO
Armco Inc.
Bair Memorial Trust, Charles M.
Best Products Co.
Boise Cascade Corp.
Browning-Ferris Industries
Burlington Northern Inc.
Champion International Corp.
Conoco Inc.
Deluxe Corp.
du Pont de Nemours & Co., E. I.
Equitable Resources
Evening Post Publishing Co.
Exxon Corp.
First Bank System
First Interstate Bancsystem of Montana
First Interstate Bank NW Region
Gallagher Family Foundation, Lewis P.
Gannett Co.
Haynes Foundation
Heisey Foundation
Knowles Charitable Memorial Trust, Gladys E.
Land O'Lakes
Lee Endowment Foundation
Lee Enterprises
Manville Corp.
Mead Corp.
Montana Power Co.
Morrison-Knudsen Corp.
National Medical Enterprises
Norwest Corp.
PacifiCorp
Pamida, Inc.
Saint Paul Cos.
Super Valu Stores
Target Stores
US WEST
Westmoreland Coal Co.

Nebraska

AG Processing Inc.
Albertson's
Ameritas Life Insurance Corp.
Amoco Corp.
Archer-Daniels-Midland Co.
Armco Inc.
Armour Food Co.
Baer Foundation, Alan and Marcia
Bausch & Lomb
Baxter International
Becton Dickinson & Co.
Beef America Inc.
Bemis Company
Berkshire Hathaway
Blount

Borden
Browning-Ferris Industries
Brunswick Corp.
Buckley Trust, Thomas D.
Buffett Foundation
Burlington Northern Inc.
Campbell Soup Co.
Centel Corp.
Central Soya Co.
CLARCOR
Commercial Federal Corp.
Computer Associates International
ConAgra
Cooper Foundation
Cox Enterprises
Cox Foundation, James M.
Criss Memorial Foundation, Dr. C.C. and Mabel L.
Curtice-Burns Foods
Cyprus Minerals Co.
Dayton Hudson Corp.
Deluxe Corp.
Dollar General Corp.
Donnelley & Sons Co., R.R.
Douglas & Lomason Company
Eaton Corp.
Enron Corp.
Faith Charitable Trust
Farley Industries
Farr Trust, Frank M. and Alice M.
FirsTier Bank N.A. Omaha
Giger Foundation, Paul and Oscar
Goodyear Tire & Rubber Co.
Great West Casualty Co.
Hershey Foods Corp.
Hitchcock Foundation, Gilbert M. and Martha H.
IBP, Inc.
Inland Container Corp.
ITT Hartford Insurance Group
Jostens
Keene Trust, Hazel R.
Kellogg's
Kiewit Foundation, Peter
Kiewit Sons, Peter
KN Energy, Inc.
Land O'Lakes
Lane Foundation, Winthrop and Frances
Lee Enterprises
Lincoln Family Foundation
Lincoln Telecommunications Co.
Livingston Foundation, Milton S. and Corinne N.
Manufacturers Life Insurance Co. of America
Mapco Inc.
Metromail Corp.
Minnegasco
Mutual of Omaha Insurance Co.
National Medical Enterprises
Norwest Bank Nebraska
Norwest Corp.
Nucor Corp.
Occidental Petroleum Corp.
Pamida, Inc.
Physicians Mutual Insurance
Pioneer Hi-Bred International
Pitney Bowes
Prudential Insurance Co. of America
Pulitzer Publishing Co.
Quivey-Bay State Foundation
Reynolds Foundation, Edgar
Richardson County Bank and Trust Co.
Rogers Foundation
Saint Paul Cos.
Schering-Plough Corp.
Scott, Jr. Charitable Foundation, Walter
Scoular Co.
Scrivner, Inc.
Sprint
Square D Co.

State Farm Mutual Automobile Insurance Co.
Storz Foundation, Robert Herman
Tandem Computers
Target Stores
3M Co.
Travelers Cos.
TRINOVA Corp.
Union Pacific Corp.
US WEST
Valmont Industries
Wal-Mart Stores
Weller Foundation
West Co.
Witco Corp.

Nevada

Alco Standard Corp.
Alltel/Western Region
America West Airlines
ARCO
Armstrong World Industries Inc.
Bally's - Las Vegas
Bergen Brunswig Corp.
Bing Fund
Boise Cascade Corp.
Buck Foundation, Carol Franc
Caesar's World, Inc.
Centel Corp.
Charter Medical Corp.
Chevron Corp.
Circuit City Stores
Circus Circus Enterprises
Citicorp
Clorox Co.
Cord Foundation, E. L.
Cyprus Minerals Co.
Dayton Hudson Corp.
Deere & Co.
Dial Corp.
Donnelley & Sons Co., R.R.
Eagle-Picher Industries
EG&G Inc.
Federated Department Stores and Allied Stores Corp.
First Mississippi Corp.
FMC Corp.
Gabelli Foundation
Gannett Co.
Great Western Financial Corp.
Harrah's Hotels & Casinos
Hawkins Foundation, Robert Z.
Hexcel Corp.
Hilton Foundation, Conrad N.
Home Depot
Homestake Mining Co.
Humana
ITT Hartford Insurance Group
Johnson & Higgins
Journal Communications
Landmark Communications
Levi Strauss & Co.
Lied Foundation Trust
Magma Copper Co.
Mead Corp.
Meredith Corp.
Mirage Casino-Hotel
National Medical Enterprises
Nevada Power Co.
Newmont Mining Corp.
Pacific Telesis Group
Pechiney Corp.
Porsche Cars North America, Inc.
PriMerit F.S.B.
Promus Cos.
Quanex Corp.
Redfield Foundation, Nell J.
Robertshaw Controls Co.
Rochlin Foundation, Abraham and Sonia
Sara Lee Corp.
Sara Lee Hosiery
Sierra Pacific Resources
SKF USA, Inc.
Sotheby's
Southland Corp.

Southwest Gas Corp.
Spiegel
Springs Industries
Summa Development Corp.
Sundstrand Corp.
Tandem Computers
Target Stores
Thompson Charitable Foundation, Marion G.
Timken Co.
Union Pacific Corp.
Wiegand Foundation, E. L.
Witco Corp.

New Hampshire

Abex Inc.
Alco Standard Corp.
American International Group, Inc.
Anheuser-Busch Cos.
APV Crepaco Inc.
Armco Inc.
Avnet, Inc.
Barker Foundation
Baxter International
Bean Foundation, Norwin S. and Elizabeth N.
Bell Industries
Benz Trust, Doris L.
Browning-Ferris Industries
Burndy Corp.
Chubb Corp.
Chubb Life Insurance Co. of America
Cogswell Benevolent Trust
Dayton Hudson Corp.
Dexter Corp.
Digital Equipment Corp.
Dingman Foundation, Michael D.
Eastman Foundation, Alexander
Emerson Electric Co.
First NH Banks, Inc.
Fitch Trust f/b/o Cheshire Health Foundation, Leon M. and Hazel E.
Fleet Bank
Fleet Bank of Keene
Fleet Financial Group
Forest City Enterprises
Foundation for Seacoast Health
Freygang Foundation, Walter Henry
Fuller Foundation
GenCorp
Greenspan Foundation
Grinnell Corp.
Hewlett-Packard Co.
Home Depot
Hospital Corp. of America
Hubbard Farms
Hunt Foundation, Samuel P.
Indiana Insurance Cos.
Ingersoll-Rand Co.
ITT Hartford Insurance Group
James River Corp. of Virginia
Jameson Trust, Oleonda
Johnson Inc., Axel
Kingsbury Corp.
Kollsman Instrument Co.
Kraft General Foods
Lincolnshire
Lindsay Trust, Agnes M.
Litton Industries
Lockheed Sanders
Lord Scholarship Fund Trust, Henry C.
Lydall, Inc.
M/A-COM, Inc.
Markem Corp.
Mascoma Savings Bank
McGraw-Hill
Merck & Co.
Millipore Corp.
Monadnock Paper Mills
Morton International
MPB Corp.

Nashua Trust Co.
National Medical Enterprises
Nationale-Nederlanden North America Corp.
New England Business Service
New England Telephone Co.
New Hampshire Ball Bearings
Nike Inc.
Northern Telecom Inc.
Norton Co.
Page Belting Co.
Peerless Insurance Co.
Philip Morris Cos.
Phillips Foundation, Ellis L.
Putnam Foundation
Quantum Chemical Corp.
Raytheon Co.
Security Life of Denver
Sequa Corp.
Shaw's Supermarkets
Smith Charitable Foundation, Lou and Lutza
Smyth Trust, Marion C.
Standex International Corp.
Teledyne
Teleflex Inc.
Teradyne, Inc.
Textron
Travelers Cos.
Tyco Laboratories, Inc.
Union Carbide Corp.
Unitrode Corp.
Wagner and George Hosser Scholarship Fund Trust, Edward
Wetterau
Wyman-Gordon Co.

New Jersey

Abitibi-Price
Abraham & Straus
Abrams Foundation
Acme-Cleveland Corp.
AEGON USA, Inc.
Aetna Life & Casualty Co.
AGFA Division of Miles Inc.
Agway
Air Products & Chemicals
Air & Water Technologies Corp.
Akzo America
Akzo Chemicals Inc.
Alexander & Alexander Services, Inc.
Alfa-Laval, Inc.
Allied Educational Foundation Fund
AlliedSignal
Alumax
AMAX
Amerada Hess Corp.
America West Airlines
American Cyanamid Co.
American Home Products Corp.
American International Group, Inc.
American Re-Insurance Co.
American Standard
American Telephone & Telegraph Co.
American Telephone & Telegraph Co./New Jersey Region
American Water Works Co., Inc.
Ames Department Stores
Anderson Foundation
Anheuser-Busch Cos.
AON Corp.
ARA Services
Armco Inc.
Armstrong World Industries Inc.
Arrow Electronics, Inc.
Asea Brown Boveri
Ashland Oil
Athlone Industries, Inc.
Atlantic Foundation
Ausimont, U.S.A.

Automatic Data Processing, Inc.
Avery Dennison Corp.
Avis Inc.
Avnet, Inc.
Ball Corp.
Ballet Makers
Bank of New York
Barbour Foundation, Bernice
Barclays Bank of New York
Bard, C. R.
Barnes Group
BASF Corp.
Baskin-Robbins USA CO.
Bausch & Lomb
Baxter International
Beck Foundation, Elsie E. & Joseph W.
Becton Dickinson & Co.
Beekman Memorial Home
Belding Heminway Co.
Bell Atlantic Corp.
Bell Communications Research
Bell Laboratories
Bemis Company
Beneficial Corp.
Bergen Brunswig Corp.
Bergen Foundation, Frank and Lydia
Bergen Record Corp.
Berlex Laboratories
Berrie Foundation, Russell
Berwind Corp.
Best Products Co.
BFGoodrich
Big Three Industries
Black & Decker Corp.
Block Drug Co.
BMW of North America, Inc.
BOC Group
Boise Cascade Corp.
Bonner Foundation, Corella and Bertram
Borden
Borden Memorial Foundation, Mary Owen
Borg-Warner Corp.
Bosch Corp., Robert
Brady Foundation
Brennan Foundation, Robert E.
Bristol-Myers Squibb Co.
Brody Foundation, Frances
Brooklyn Union Gas Co.
Brother International Corp.
Brown-Forman Corp.
Brown Inc., John
Browning-Ferris Industries
Brundage Charitable, Scientific, and Wildlife Conservation Foundation, Charles E. and Edna T.
Buehler Foundation, Emil
Bunbury Company
Business Men's Assurance Co. of America
Caesar's World, Inc.
Campbell Soup Co.
Cape Branch Foundation
Capita Charitable Trust, Emil
Carter-Wallace
Caspersen Foundation for Aid to Health and Education, O. W.
Chicago Pneumatic Tool Co.
Chubb Corp.
Church & Dwight Co.
CIBA-GEIGY Corp.
Ciba-Geigy Corp. (Pharmaceuticals Division)
CIGNA Corp.
Circuit City Stores
CIT Group Holdings
Citicorp
Clarion Hotel
Clorox Co.
Coastal Corp.
Colonial Stores
Colt Foundation, James J.
Coltec Industries

Commerce Clearing House
Commercial Metals Co.
Computer Associates International
Computer Sciences Corp.
ConAgra
Concord Chemical Co.
Connell Rice & Sugar Co.
Consolidated Freightways
Consolidated Rail Corp. (Conrail)
Continental Can Co.
Continental Corp.
Cooper Industries
Corestates Bank
Corning Incorporated
Cosmair, Inc.
Courtaulds Fibers Inc.
CPC International
Crane Fund for Widows and Children
Crompton & Knowles Corp.
Crum and Forster
CSX Corp.
Cubic Corp.
Curtice-Burns Foods
Curtiss-Wright Corp.
Cyprus Minerals Co.
Darby Foundation
Deluxe Corp.
Dennison Manufacturing Co.
Dexter Corp.
Diabetes Research and Education Foundation
Dixie Yarns, Inc.
Dodge Foundation, Geraldine R.
Dover Corp.
Dow Jones & Co.
Dresser Industries
Dreyfus Corp.
Drueding Foundation
du Pont de Nemours & Co., E. I.
Duke Foundation, Doris
Dun & Bradstreet Corp.
Eaton Corp.
Ecolab
Edison Fund, Charles
EG&G Inc.
Egan Machinery Co.
Elastimold Corp.
Elf Aquitaine, Inc.
Elizabethtown Gas Co.
Elizabethtown Water Co.
Emerson Electric Co.
Emerson Radio Corp.
EMI Records Group
Engelhard Foundation, Charles
Exxon Corp.
Fairchild Corp.
Fanwood Foundation
Fedders Corp.
Federal-Mogul Corp.
Federal Paper Board Co.
Federated Department Stores and Allied Stores Corp.
Fiat U.S.A., Inc.
Fireman's Fund Insurance Co.
First Fidelity Bancorporation
Fischer & Porter Co.
Fluor Corp.
FMC Corp.
Foodarama Supermarkets, Inc.
Formosa Plastics Corp. U.S.A.
Foster Wheeler Corp.
Freightliner Corp.
Frelinghuysen Foundation
Friedland Family Foundation, Samuel
Friedman Brothers Foundation
Fuller Co., H.B.
Fund for New Jersey
GAF Corp.
Gannett Co.
GATX Corp.
GenCorp
General Color Co.
General Public Utilities Corp.
General Reinsurance Corp.

Georgia-Pacific Corp.
Gindi Associates Foundation
Gitano Group
Goodall Rubber Co.
Goodyear Tire & Rubber Co.
Goya Foods
GrandMet Consumer Products, Inc.
Grassmann Trust, E. J.
Great Atlantic & Pacific Tea Co. Inc.
Gucci America Inc.
Gulton Foundation
Gund Foundation
Hackett Foundation
Handy & Harman
Hanna Co., M.A.
Hanson Office Products
Harris Brothers Foundation
Harris Corp.
Harsco Corp.
Harte-Hanks Communications, Inc.
Hartz Mountain Corp.
Harvard Industries
Hasbro
Havens Foundation, O. W.
Hechinger Co.
Henkel Corp.
Hercules Inc.
Hewlett-Packard Co.
Hite Foundation
Hobart Corp.
Hoechst Celanese Corp.
Hoffmann-La Roche
Holzer Memorial Foundation, Richard H.
Homasote Co.
Home Depot
Hovnanian Enterprises Inc., K.
Howard Savings Bank
Howson-Algraphy, Inc.
Huber Corp., J.M.
Huber Foundation
Hunt Chemical Corp., Phillip A.
Hyde and Watson Foundation
Hyundai Motor America
IBM Corp.
ICI Americas
Illinois Tool Works
IMO Industries Inc.
Ingersoll-Rand Co.
Inland Container Corp.
Inland Steel Industries
Innovating Worthy Projects Foundation
International Flavors & Fragrances
International Foundation
International Multifoods Corp.
IPCO Corp.
Ise America
Israel Discount Bank of New York
ITT Corp.
ITT Hartford Insurance Group
ITT Rayonier
James River Corp. of Virginia
Jamesway Corp.
Jaqua Foundation
Jaydor Corp.
Jersey Central Power & Light Co.
Jockey Hollow Foundation
Johnson Inc., Axel
Johnson Foundation, Barbara P.
Johnson Foundation, Robert Wood
Johnson & Higgins
Johnson & Johnson
Jones Fund, Blanche and George
Kajima International, Inc.
Kaplen Foundation
Kellogg Foundation, Peter and Cynthia K.
Kellogg's
Kennedy Foundation, John R.
Kennedy Foundation, Quentin J.

Kerney Foundation, James
Ketchum & Co.
Kimberly-Clark Corp.
Kirby Foundation, F. M.
Klipstein Foundation, Ernest Christian
Knight-Ridder, Inc.
Knistrom Foundation, Fanny and Svante
Koh-I-Noor Rapidograph Inc.
Kraft General Foods
KSM Foundation
L & F Products
Large Foundation
Lasky Co.
Laura Ashley Inc.
Lautenberg Foundation
Lazarus Charitable Trust, Helen and Charles
Lehigh Press, Inc.
Levin Foundation, Philip and Janice
Lionel Corp.
Lipton, Thomas J.
Litton Industries
Liz Claiborne
Lockheed Corp.
Lummus Crest, Inc.
MacAndrews & Forbes Holdings
Macy & Co., R.H.
Mamiye Brothers
Maneely Fund
Manufacturers Life Insurance Co. of America
Manville Corp.
Martin Family Fund
Martini Foundation, Nicholas
Matchbox Toys (USA) Ltd.
Matsushita Electric Corp. of America
Mayfair Super Markets
MCA
McCormick & Co.
McCutchen Foundation
McGraw Foundation, Curtis W.
McGraw-Hill
McMurray-Bennnett Foundation
Melitta North America Inc.
Mellon Bank Corp.
Mellon PSFS
Menasha Corp.
Mennen Co.
Mercedes-Benz of North America, Inc.
Merck & Co.
Meredith Corp.
Metallurg, Inc.
Metromedia Co.
Mettler Instrument Corp.
Meyer Memorial Foundation, Aaron and Rachel
Midlantic Banks, Inc.
Miles Inc.
Miller & Co.
Minolta Corp.
Mobil Oil Corp.
Moore Business Forms, Inc.
Moore & Co., Benjamin
Morton International
Mutual of New York
Nabisco Foods Group
Nalco Chemical Co.
National Medical Enterprises
National Starch & Chemical Corp.
National Westminster Bank New Jersey
NEC USA
New Jersey Bell Telephone Company
New Jersey Manufacturers Insurance Co.
New Jersey National Bank
New Jersey Resources Corp.
New Valley
New York Times Co.

Newcombe Foundation, Charlotte W.
Newhouse Publication Corp.
News America Publishing Inc.
North American Philips Corp.
Northern Telecom Inc.
Norton Co.
Norwest Corp.
NUI Corp.
Oakite Products
Ohl, Jr. Trust, George A.
Oki America Inc.
Okonite Co.
Olin Corp.
Olivetti Office USA, Inc.
Openaka Corp.
Orange Orphan Society
Orange & Rockland Utilities, Inc.
Ortho Diagnostic Systems, Inc.
Ortho-McNeil Pharmaceutical
Outokumpu-American Brass Co.
Owens-Corning Fiberglas Corp.
Paddington Corp.
Pantasote Polymers
Paramount Communications Inc.
Parke-Davis Group
Parthenon Sportswear
Pechiney Corp.
Penn Central Corp.
Peridot Chemicals (NJ)
Pet
Pfizer
Phelps Dodge Corp.
PHH Corp.
Philip Morris Cos.
Phillips-Van Heusen Corp.
Polaroid Corp.
Polychrome Corp.
PQ Corp.
Prince Manufacturing, Inc.
Procter & Gamble Co.
Promus Cos.
Prudential-Bache Securities
Prudential Insurance Co. of America
Public Service Electric & Gas Co.
Quaker Hill Foundation
Read Foundation, Charles L.
Reckitt & Colman
Red Devil
Research-Cottrell Inc.
Reviva Labs
Revlon
Rhone-Poulenc Inc.
Ricoh Corp.
Rippel Foundation, Fannie E.
RJR Nabisco Inc.
Rochester Telephone Corp.
Rosenhaus Peace Foundation, Sarah and Matthew
Rouse Co.
Rukin Philanthropic Foundation, David and Eleanore
Russ Togs
Rutgers Community Health Foundation
Sagamore Foundation
Saint Paul Cos.
Samsung America Inc.
Sandoz Corp.
Sandy Hill Foundation
Sanyo Fisher U.S.A. Corp.
Sara Lee Corp.
Schamach Foundation, Milton
Schenck Fund, L. P.
Schering-Plough Corp.
Schimmel Foundation
Schindler Elevator Corp.
Schultz Foundation
Schumann Foundation, Florence and John
Schumann Fund for New Jersey
Schwab & Co., Charles
Schwartz Foundation, Arnold A.
Sealed Air Corp.
Sequa Corp.

New Jersey (cont.)

Seton Co.
Shaklee Corp.
Sharp Electronics Corp.
Shell Oil Co.
Shepherd Foundation
Sherwin-Williams Co.
Siemens Medical Systems Inc.
Sigma-Aldrich Corp.
Simon Foundation, William E.
and Carol G.
Singer Company
Six Flags Theme Parks Inc.
Snyder Foundation, Harold B.
and Dorothy A.
Somers Corp.
(Mersman/Waldron)
Sony Corp. of America
Soundesign Corp.
South Branch Foundation
South Jersey Industries
Southwestern Bell Corp.
Spectra-Physics Analytical
Sprint
State Farm Mutual Automobile
Insurance Co.
Stern Foundation, Leonard N.
Stern Foundation, Max
Stone Container Corp.
Strauss Foundation, Judy and
Howard E.
Stroehmann Bakeries
Subaru of America Inc.
Sullivan Foundation, Algernon
Sydney
Summit Bancorporation
Sun Chemical Corp.
Sunshine Biscuits
Sutcliffe Foundation, Walter and
Louise
Sutton Foundation
Tandem Computers
Taub Foundation, Henry and
Marilyn
Taub Foundation, Joseph and
Arlene
Teledyne
Tenneco
Tension Envelope Corp.
Terner Foundation
Tetley, Inc.
Thomas & Betts Corp.
3M Co.
TJX Cos.
Tomlinson Family Foundation
Toshiba America, Inc.
Toys "R" Us, Inc.
Transco Energy Company
Travelers Cos.
TRINOVA Corp.
Tropicana Products, Inc.
Turrell Fund
Twentieth Century-Fox Film
Corp.
Tyson Foods, Inc.
UJB Financial Corp.
UNC, Inc.
Unilever United States
Union Camp Corp.
Union Carbide Corp.
Union Foundation
United Merchants &
Manufacturers
Universal Foods Corp.
Upton Charitable Foundation,
Lucy and Eleanor S.
Valley National Bancorp
Van Houten Charitable Trust
Victaulic Co. of America
Victoria Foundation
Video Software Dealers
Association
Visciglia Foundation, Frank
Volkswagen of America, Inc.
Vollmer Foundation
Walgreen Co.

Disney Co., Walt
Warner-Lambert Co.
Webcraft Technologies
Wellman Inc.
Weyerhaeuser Co.
Wheaton Industries
White Consolidated Industries
Wilf Family Foundation
Willits Foundation
Winslow Foundation
Witco Corp.
Xerox Corp.
Zock Endowment Trust
Zurn Industries

New Mexico

AMAX
Arizona Public Service Co.
Avnet, Inc.
Ball Corp.
Bank of America
Bell Industries
Bellamah Foundation, Dale J.
Best Products Co.
Charter Medical Corp.
Chevron Corp.
Citicorp
Continental Divide Electric
Co-op
Culbro Corp.
Dayton Hudson Corp.
Deluxe Corp.
Dial Corp.
Digital Equipment Corp.
du Pont de Nemours & Co., E. I.
EG&G Inc.
Enron Corp.
Frost Foundation
Furr's Supermarkets
Hershey Foods Corp.
Honeywell
Hospital Corp. of America
Hubbard Broadcasting
Intel Corp.
International Multifoods Corp.
Johnson & Johnson
Lea County Electric Co-op
Lee Enterprises
Levi Strauss & Co.
Maddox Foundation, J. F.
Manville Corp.
Mark IV Industries
Motorola
National Medical Enterprises
National Presto Industries
Navajo Refining Co.
Newmont Mining Corp.
Paxton Co., Frank
Phelps Dodge Corp.
Phillips Foundation, Waite and
Genevieve
Phillips Petroleum Co.
Public Service Co. of New
Mexico
Pulitzer Publishing Co.
Raytheon Co.
REI-Recreational Equipment,
Inc.
Sandia National Laboratories
Santa Fe Pacific Corp.
Sara Lee Corp.
Sara Lee Hosiery
Scripps Co., E.W.
Shell Oil Co.
Stone Container Corp.
Sunwest Bank of Albuquerque,
N.A.
Tandem Computers
Target Stores
Texas-New Mexico Power Co.
Tracor, Inc.
Travelers Cos.
Triskelion Ltd.
UNC, Inc.
US WEST
Wal-Mart Stores

New York

Aarque Cos.
Abelard Foundation
Abeles Foundation, Joseph and
Sophia
Abraham Foundation
Abraham & Straus
Abrams Foundation, Benjamin
and Elizabeth
Abrons Foundation, Louis and
Anne
Achelis Foundation
Ada Foundation, Julius
Adams Memorial Fund, Emma J.
Adler Foundation
Advertising Checking Bureau
Aeroflex Foundation
Affiliated Publications, Inc.
AFLAC
AGFA Division of Miles Inc.
Agway
Air France
AKC Fund
Akzo America
Ala Vi Foundation of New York
Albany International Corp.
Alco Standard Corp.
Alexander & Alexander
Services, Inc.
Alexander Foundation, Joseph
Allegheny Ludlum Corp.
Allegheny Power System, Inc.
Allen Brothers Foundation
Allen & Co.
Allen Foundation, Frances
Allen Foundation, Rita
Alliance Capital Management
Corp.
AlliedSignal
Allyn Foundation
Altman Foundation
Altschul Foundation
Alumax
Aluminum Co. of America
AMAX
Amerada Hess Corp.
American Brands
American Cyanamid Co.
American Express Co.
American Financial Corp.
American Greetings Corp.
American Home Products Corp.
American International Group,
Inc.
American Maize Products
American Natural Resources Co.
American Savings & Loan
Association of Florida
American Standard
American Stock Exchange
American Telephone &
Telegraph Co.
American Telephone &
Telegraph Co./New York City
Region
American Telephone &
Telegraph Co./New York
Region
Ames Department Stores
AMETEK
Ampacet Corp.
Andal Corp.
Anderson Foundation
Anheuser-Busch Cos.
AON Corp.
Apple and Eve
Apple Bank for Savings
ARA Services
Arcata Corp.
Arcata Graphics Co.
Archbold Charitable Trust,
Adrian and Jessie
Arell Foundation
Arkell Hall Foundation
Armco Inc.
Armstrong World Industries Inc.
Aron Charitable Foundation, J.

Arrow Electronics, Inc.
Arvin Industries
Asahi Glass America, Inc.
ASARCO
Asea Brown Boveri
Associated Food Stores
Associated Products
Astor Foundation, Vincent
Atalanta/Sosnoff Capital Corp.
Atlantic Foundation of New York
Atlantic Mutual Cos.
Atran Foundation
Augat, Inc.
Avery Dennison Corp.
AVI CHAI - A Philanthropic
Foundation
Avis Inc.
Avnet, Inc.
Avon Products
Axe-Houghton Foundation
Ayco Corp.
Ayer Inc., N.W.
Baccarat Inc.
Bachmann Foundation
Backer Spielvogel Bates U.S.
Badgeley Residuary Charitable
Trust, Rose M.
Bag Bazaar, Ltd.
Baier Foundation, Marie
Baird Foundation
Baird Foundation, Cameron
Baker Trust, George F.
Baldwin Foundation, David M.
and Barbara
Ball Chain Manufacturing Co.
Ball Corp.
Bally Inc.
Banbury Fund
Banca Commerciale Italiana,
New York Branch
Banco Portugues do Atlantico,
New York Branch
Bancorp Hawaii
Banfi Vintners
Bank Hapoalim B.M.
Bank Leumi Trust Co. of New
York
Bank of Boston Connecticut
Bank of New York
Bank of Tokyo Trust Co.
BankAmerica Corp.
Bankers Life & Casualty Co.
Bankers Trust Co.
Banque Francaise du Commerce
Exterieur
Bantam Doubleday Dell
Publishing Group, Inc.
Barclays Bank of New York
BarclaysAmerican Corp.
Bard, C. R.
Barker Foundation, J. M. R.
Barker Welfare Foundation
Barnes Group
Barnett Charitable Foundation,
Lawrence and Isabel
Barth Foundation, Theodore H.
Bartsch Memorial Trust, Ruth
Baskin-Robbins USA CO.
Bass and Edythe and Sol G.
Atlas Fund, Sandra Atlas
Bausch & Lomb
Baxter International
Bay Foundation
Bayne Fund, Howard
BBDO Worldwide
Beck Foundation
Bedford Fund
Bedminster Fund
Beinecke Foundation
Beir Foundation
Belding Heminway Co.
Belfer Foundation
Belmont Metals
Benenson Foundation, Frances
and Benjamin
Benetton

Bennett Memorial Corporation,
James Gordon
Bennett Scholarship Fund,
Margaret A. and Lawrence J.
Bergen Brunswig Corp.
Berkowitz Family Foundation,
Louis
Berlin Charitable Fund, Irving
Bernstein & Co., Sanford C.
Berwind Corp.
Bethlehem Steel Corp.
Biddle Foundation, Margaret T.
Bidermann Industries
Big Three Industries
Big V Supermarkets
Bill Communications
Bingham Second Betterment
Fund, William
Black & Decker Corp.
Blackmer Foundation, Henry M.
Blackstone Group LP
Bleibtreu Foundation, Jacob
Blinken Foundation
Bloomingdale's
Bluhdorn Charitable Trust,
Charles G. and Yvette
Blum Foundation, Edith C.
Blum Foundation, Edna F.
Bobst Foundation, Elmer and
Mamdouha
BOC Group
Bodman Foundation
Boehm Foundation
Boise Cascade Corp.
Boisi Family Foundation
Booth Ferris Foundation
Borden
Borg-Warner Corp.
Bostwick Foundation, Albert C.
Botwinick-Wolfensohn
Foundation
Bowne Foundation, Robert
Bozell, Inc.
BP America
Brace Foundation, Donald C.
Branta Foundation
Bravmann Foundation, Ludwig
Brencanda Foundation
Bristol-Myers Squibb Co.
British Airways
Brody Foundation, Carolyn and
Kenneth D.
Brookdale Foundation
Brooklyn Benevolent Society
Brooklyn Union Gas Co.
Brooks Brothers
Brooks Fashion Stores Inc.
Brooks Foundation, Gladys
Brown Brothers Harriman & Co.
Brown & Sons, Alex
Browning-Ferris Industries
Bruner Foundation
Brunner Foundation, Robert
Buffalo Color Corp.
Buffalo Forge Co.
Bugher Foundation
Buhl Family Foundation
Bulova Fund
Burchfield Foundation, Charles
E.
Burden Foundation, Florence V.
Burlington Industries
Burnham Donor Fund, Alfred G.
Burns Foundation, Jacob
Butler Foundation, J. Homer
Bydale Foundation
C.P. Rail Systems
Cable & Wireless
Communications
Cablevision Systems Corp.
Calder Foundation, Louis
Caldwell Manufacturing Co.
Callanan Industries
Campbell Soup Co.
Canadian Imperial Bank of
Commerce
Candlesticks Inc.

Canon U.S.A., Inc.
Cantor Foundation, Iris and B. Gerald
Capital Cities/ABC
Carlisle Cos.
Carnahan-Jackson Foundation
Carnegie Corporation of New York
Carrier Corp.
Carrols Corp.
Carter-Wallace
Cartier, Inc.
Carvel Foundation, Thomas and Agnes
Cary Charitable Trust, Mary Flagler
Castle & Co., A.M.
CBS Inc.
Center for Educational Programs
Central Hudson Gas & Electric Corp.
Central National-Gottesman
Central Trust Co.
Chait Memorial Foundation, Sara
Champion International Corp.
Champion Products, Inc.
Chapman Charitable Corporation, Howard and Bess
Charina Foundation
Charitable Foundation of the Burns Family
Charles River Laboratories
Chase Lincoln First Bank, N.A.
Chase Manhattan Bank, N.A.
Chazen Foundation
Cheatham Foundation, Owen
Chemical Bank
Chernow Trust for the Benefit of Charity Dated 3/13/75, Michael
Chesapeake Corp.
Chicago Pneumatic Tool Co.
Children's Foundation of Erie County
China Medical Board of New York
China Times Cultural Foundation
Chisholm Foundation
Choice Courier Systems Inc.
Christian Dior New York, Inc.
Christie, Manson & Woods International, Inc.
Christodora
Chrysler Corp.
Chubb Corp.
CIBA-GEIGY Corp.
Ciba-Geigy Corp. (Pharmaceuticals Division)
CIGNA Corp.
Cintas Foundation
CIT Group Holdings
Citicorp
Claiborne Art Ortenberg Foundation, Liz
Clark Charitable Trust, Frank E.
Clark Family Charitable Trust, Andrew L.
Clark Foundation
Clark Foundation, Edna McConnell
Clark Foundation, Robert Sterling
Clover Foundation
Cohen Family Foundation, Saul Z. and Amy Scheuer
Cohen Foundation, Wilfred P.
Cohn Foundation, Herman and Terese
Cohn Foundation, Peter A. and Elizabeth S.
Coleman Foundation
Coleman, Jr. Foundation, George E.
Coles Family Foundation
Colgate-Palmolive Co.
Collins Foundation, Joseph
Coltec Industries
Comcast Corp.
Commerce Clearing House

Commercial Metals Co.
Commerzbank AG, New York
Common Giving Fund
Commonwealth Fund
Community National Bank & Trust Co. of New York
Computer Associates International
Concord Fabrics, Inc.
Conde Nast Publications, Inc.
Consolidated Edison Co. of New York Inc.
Consolidated Papers
Consolidated Rail Corp. (Conrail)
Consumer Farmer Foundation
Contempo Communications
Continental Bank N.A.
Continental Corp.
Continental Grain Co.
Contraves USA
Control Data Corp.
Cook & Co., Frederic W.
Cook Foundation
Cookson America
Cooper Industries
Coopers & Lybrand
CooperVision, Inc.
Coral Reef Foundation
Corestates Bank
Cornell Trust, Peter C.
Corning Incorporated
Corporate Printing Co.
Cosmair, Inc.
Courtaulds Fibers Inc.
Cowles Charitable Trust
Cox Enterprises
Craigmyle Foundation
Crane & Co.
Crane Co.
Cranshaw Corporation
Cranston Print Works
Crary Foundation, Bruce L.
Credit Agricole
Credit Suisse
Creditanstalt-Bankverein, New York
Cross Co., A.T.
Crossland Savings FSB
Crum and Forster
CT Corp. System
Cubic Corp.
Culbro Corp.
Culver Foundation, Constans
Cummings Foundation, James H.
Cummings Foundation, Nathan
Cummings Memorial Fund Trust, Frances L. and Edwin L.
Cummins Engine Co.
Curtice-Burns Foods
Curtiss-Wright Corp.
Dahesh Museum
Dairylea Cooperative Inc.
Daiwa Securities America Inc.
Dalgety Inc.
Dammann Fund
Dan River, Inc.
Dana Charitable Trust, Eleanor Naylor
Dana Foundation, Charles A.
Danforth Co., John W.
Daniel & Co., Gerard
Daniel Foundation, Gerard and Ruth
D'Arcy Masius Benton & Bowles Inc.
Darrah Charitable Trust, Jessie Smith
Davenport-Hatch Foundation
David-Weill Foundation, Michel
Davis Foundation, Shelby Cullom
Davis Foundation, Simon and Annie
Day Family Foundation
DCNY Corp.
DDB Needham Worldwide
de Hirsch Fund, Baron

de Kay Foundation
De Lima Co., Paul
de Rothschild Foundation, Edmond
Dean Witter Discover
DeCamp Foundation, Ira W.
Deer Valley Farm
Delany Charitable Trust, Beatrice P.
Delavan Foundation, Nelson B.
Delaware North Cos.
Dellwood Foods, Inc.
Delta Air Lines
Deluxe Corp.
Dennison Manufacturing Co.
Dent Family Foundation, Harry
Dentsu, Inc., NY
Deutsche Bank AG
Dewar Foundation
Dexter Corp.
Dial Corp.
Diamond Foundation, Aaron
Dickenson Foundation, Harriet Ford
Dime Savings Bank of New York
DNP (America), Inc.
Dobson Foundation
Dodge Foundation, Cleveland H.
Doherty Charitable Foundation, Henry L. and Grace
Dolan Family Foundation
Dollar Dry Dock Bank
Dollard Charitable Trust
Donaldson Charitable Trust, Oliver S. and Jennie R.
Donaldson, Lufkin & Jenrette
Donnelley & Sons Co., R.R.
Donner Foundation, William H.
Donovan, Leisure, Newton & Irvine
Dorot Foundation
Dorr Foundation
Doty Family Foundation
Dover Corp.
Dow Jones & Co.
Doyle Dane Bernback Group
Dreitzer Foundation
Dreyfus Corp.
Dreyfus Foundation, Camille and Henry
Dreyfus Foundation, Jean and Louis
Dreyfus Foundation, Max and Victoria
du Pont de Nemours & Co., E. I.
Dula Educational and Charitable Foundation, Caleb C. and Julia W.
Dun & Bradstreet Corp.
Dunlop Tire Corp.
Durst Foundation
Dyson Foundation
Dyson-Kissner-Moran Corp.
Eastern Star Hall and Home Foundation
Eastman Kodak Co.
Eaton Corp.
Echlin Inc.
Eckman Charitable Foundation, Samuel and Rae
Edmonds Foundation, Dean S.
Edouard Foundation
Edwards Foundation, O. P. and W. E.
EG&G Inc.
Ehrman Foundation, Fred and Susan
Elf Aquitaine, Inc.
Elf Atochem North America
Ellsworth Trust, W. H.
Emerson Electric Co.
Emerson Foundation, Fred L.
Eni-Chem America, Inc.
Entenmann's Inc.
Equitable Life Assurance Society of the U.S.
Equitable Variable Life Insurance Co.

Ernst & Young
Erpf Fund, Armand G.
Essel Foundation
Esselte Pendaflex Corp.
Ettinger Foundation
European American Bank
Evans Foundation, Edward P.
Evans Foundation, T. M.
Evening Post Publishing Co.
Everett Charitable Trust
FAB Industries
Fairchild Corp.
Faith Home Foundation
Falk Foundation, Michael David
Farley Industries
Faulkner Trust, Marianne Gaillard
Fay's Incorporated
Federated Department Stores and Allied Stores Corp.
Feil Foundation, Louis and Gertrude
Fein Foundation
Ferkauf Foundation, Eugene and Estelle
Ferriday Fund Charitable Trust
Ferro Corp.
Fiat U.S.A., Inc.
Fieldcrest Cannon
Fife Foundation, Elias and Bertha
Fink Foundation
First Boston
First Chicago
First Empire State Corp.
First Fidelity Bancorporation
Fischbach Foundation
Fischel Foundation, Harry and Jane
Fish Foundation, Vain and Harry
Fisher Brothers
Fisher-Price
Fishoff Family Foundation
Fisons Corp.
Flagler Co.
Fleet Bank
Fleet Bank of New York
Fleet Financial Group
Flemm Foundation, John J.
Fogel Foundation, Shalom and Rebecca
Food Emporium
Foote, Cone & Belding Communications
Foote Mineral Co.
Forbes
Forbes Charitable Trust, Herman
Forchheimer Foundation
Ford Foundation
Forest City Enterprises
Fortis Inc.
Foundation for Child Development
Foundation for the Needs of Others
Fox Inc.
Frank Foundation, Ernest and Elfriede
Frankel Foundation, George and Elizabeth F.
Frasch Foundation for Chemical Research (under the will of Elizabeth B. Frasch), Herman
Freeman Charitable Trust, Samuel
Freightliner Corp.
Frese Foundation, Arnold D.
Frey Trust f/b/o YMCA, Harry D.
Fribourg Foundation
Friedman Foundation, Stephen and Barbara
Frohlich Charitable Trust, Ludwig W.
Fruchthandler Foundation, Alex and Ruth
Frumkes Foundation, Alana and Lewis
Fuchsberg Family Foundation

Fuchsberg Family Foundation, Abraham
Fuld Health Trust, Helene
Fuller Co., H.B.
Gaisman Foundation, Catherine and Henry J.
Gannett Co.
Garfinkle Family Foundation
GATX Corp.
Gebbie Foundation
GEICO Corp.
Geist Foundation
Gelb Foundation, Lawrence M.
General Atlantic Partners L.P.
General Color Co.
General Electric Co.
General Mills
General Motors Corp.
General Railway Signal Corp.
General Reinsurance Corp.
General Steel Fabricators
Genesco
Georgia-Pacific Corp.
Gerber Products Co.
Gerschel Foundation, Patrick A.
Gifford Charitable Corporation, Rosamond
Gilder Foundation
Gilman Foundation, Howard
Gilman Investment Co.
Gilman Paper Co.
Ginsberg Family Foundation, Moses
Gitano Group
Givenchy, Inc.
Glanville Family Foundation
Gleason Memorial Fund
Gleason Works
Glenn Foundation for Medical Research, Paul F.
Glickenhaus & Co.
Global Van Lines
Gloeckner Foundation, Fred
Goldberger Foundation, Edward and Marjorie
Golden Family Foundation
Goldie-Anna Charitable Trust
Goldman & Brothers, Inc., William P.
Goldman Charitable Trust, Sol
Goldman Foundation, Herman
Goldman Sachs & Co.
Goldome F.S.B
Goldsmith Foundation, Horace W.
Goldsmith Foundation, Nathan and Louise
Goldstein Foundation, Leslie and Roslyn
Golub Corp.
Goode Trust, Mae Stone
Goodman Family Foundation
Goodman Memorial Foundation, Joseph C. and Clare F.
Goodstein Family Foundation, David
Goodyear Foundation, Josephine
Goodyear Tire & Rubber Co.
Gordon/Rousmaniere/Roberts Fund
Gottlieb Foundation, Adolph and Esther
Gould Foundation, Florence J.
Gould Foundation for Children, Edwin
Goulds Pumps
Grant Foundation, Charles M. and Mary D.
Grant Foundation, William T.
Graphic Controls Corp.
Grateful Foundation
Great Lakes Carbon Corp.
Great Western Financial Corp.
Greater New York Savings Bank
Green Fund
Greenberg Foundation, Alan C.
Greene Foundation, David J.
Greene Foundation, Jerome L.

New York (cont.)

Greene Foundation, Robert Z.
Greentree Foundation
Greenwall Foundation
Grenfell Association of America
Greve Foundation, William and Mary
Griffis Foundation
Grigg-Lewis Trust
Grow Group
Gruber Research Foundation, Lila
Grumman Corp.
Gruss Charitable and Educational Foundation, Oscar and Regina
Gruss Charitable Foundation, Emanuel and Riane
Gruss Petroleum Corp.
Guardian Life Insurance Co. of America
Gucci America Inc.
Guggenheim Foundation, Daniel and Florence
Guggenheim Foundation, Harry Frank
Guggenheim Memorial Foundation, John Simon
Gund Foundation, Geoffrey
Gurwin Foundation, J.
Guth Lighting Co.
Gutman Foundation, Edna and Monroe C.
Guttag Foundation, Irwin and Marjorie
Guttman Foundation, Stella and Charles
Hagedorn Fund
Hall & Co. Inc., Frank B.
Halloran Foundation, Mary P. Dolciani
Handy & Harman
Hang Seng Bank
Hansen Memorial Foundation, Irving
Hanson Office Products
Harding Educational and Charitable Foundation
Harkness Ballet Foundation
Harkness Foundation, William Hale
HarperCollins Publishers
Harriman Foundation, Gladys and Roland
Harriman Foundation, Mary W.
Harris Corp.
Harris Trust & Savings Bank
Harrison Foundation Trust, Francena T.
Harsco Corp.
Hartford Foundation, John A.
Hartman Foundation, Jesse and Dorothy
Hartmarx Corp.
Hatch Charitable Trust, Margaret Milliken
Hauser Foundation
Hayden Foundation, Charles
Hazeltine Corp.
Hazen Foundation, Edward W.
Hearst Corp.
Hearst Foundation
Hearst Foundation, William Randolph
Hebrew Technical Institute
Hechinger Co.
Heckscher Foundation for Children
Heffernan & Co.
Heineman Foundation for Research, Educational, Charitable, and Scientific Purposes
Heinz Co., H.J.
Heller Financial
Hendrickson Brothers
Hershey Foods Corp.

Hess Foundation
Hettinger Foundation
Heyward Memorial Fund, DuBose and Dorothy
Hidary Foundation, Jacob
Hilliard Corp.
Hillman Family Foundation, Alex
Hirschl Trust for Charitable Purposes, Irma T.
Hitachi
HKH Foundation
Hobbs Charitable Trust, John H.
Hoechst Celanese Corp.
Hoffman Foundation, Marion O. and Maximilian
Holtzmann Foundation, Jacob L. and Lillian
Home Box Office
Home Depot
Homeland Foundation
HON Industries
Hooper Handling
Hopkins Foundation, Josephine Lawrence
Horncrest Foundation
Horowitz Foundation, Gedale B. and Barbara S.
Houghton Mifflin Co.
House of Gross
Howard and Bush Foundation
Hoyt Foundation, Stewart W. and Willma C.
Huck International Inc.
Hudson Neckwear
Hughes Memorial Foundation, Charles Evans
Hugoton Foundation
Hultquist Foundation
Hunt Alternatives Fund, Helen
Hunt Trust for Episcopal Charitable Institutions, Virginia
Hurford Foundation
Hutchins Foundation, Mary J.
Hyde, Jr. Scholarship Fund, J.R.
I. and L. Association
IBM Corp.
IBM South Africa Projects Fund
Icahn Foundation, Carl C.
ICC Industries
IDEX Corp.
IDS Financial Services
Illinois Tool Works
IMO Industries Inc.
Inco Alloys International
Indiana Insurance Cos.
Industrial Bank of Japan Trust Co.
Inland Steel Industries
Innisfree Foundation
Innovation Packaging
Instrument Systems Corp.
Integrated Resources
Interco
Intercontinental Hotels Corp.
International Flavors & Fragrances
International Fund for Health and Family Planning
International Multifoods Corp.
International Paper Co.
International Standard Electric Corp.
Interpublic Group of Cos.
Iroquois Avenue Foundation
Israel Discount Bank of New York
Israel Foundation, A. Cremieux
ISS International Service System
Itoh (C.) International (America), Inc.
ITT Corp.
ITT Hartford Insurance Group
ITT Rayonier
Ittleson Foundation
Ix & Sons, Frank
J C S Foundation
J.P. Morgan & Co.

Jackson Hole Preserve
Jacobson & Sons, Benjamin
James River Corp. of Virginia
Jefferson Smurfit Corp.
Jephson Educational Trust No. 1
Jephson Educational Trust No. 2
Jesselson Foundation
Jewish Foundation for Education of Women
JJJ Foundation
JM Foundation
Jockey Club Foundation
Johnson Inc., Axel
Johnson Charitable Trust, Keith Wold
Johnson Controls
Johnson Endeavor Foundation, Christian A.
Johnson Foundation, Willard T. C.
Johnson & Higgins
Johnson & Son, S.C.
Jones Construction Co., J.A.
Jones Foundation, Daisy Marquis
Joselow Foundation
Josephson International Inc.
Joukowsky Family Foundation
Joy Family Foundation
Joyce Foundation, John M. and Mary A.
JTB International, Inc.
Julia R. and Estelle L. Foundation
Jurodin Fund
Jurzykowski Foundation, Alfred
Kade Foundation, Max
Kane-Miller Corp.
Kane Paper Corp.
Kanematsu-Gosho U.S.A. Inc.
Kaplan Foundation, Rita J. and Stanley H.
Kaplan Fund, J. M.
Kaplun Foundation, Morris J. and Betty
Katzenberger Foundation
Kaufman Foundation, Henry & Elaine
Kaufmann Foundation, Henry
Kaufmann Foundation, Marion Esser
Kautz Family Foundation
Kawaler Foundation, Morris and Nellie L.
Kaye, Scholer, Fierman, Hays & Handler
Keefe, Bruyette & Woods
Kellogg Foundation, J. C.
Kennedy Foundation, Ethel
Kenworthy - Sarah H. Swift Foundation, Marion E.
Kepco, Inc.
Kern Foundation, Ilma
Ketchum Communications
Kevorkian Fund, Hagop
Key Food Stores Cooperative Inc.
KH Foundation
Kidder, Peabody & Co.
Killough Trust, Walter H. D.
Kimberly-Clark Corp.
Kimmelman Foundation, Helen & Milton
King Kullen Grocery Co., Inc.
Kingspoint Industries
Kingston Foundation
Klau Foundation, David W. and Sadie
Klee Foundation, Conrad and Virginia
Klingenstein Fund, Esther A. and Joseph
Klosk Fund, Louis and Rose
Knight-Ridder, Inc.
Knox Family Foundation
Knox Foundation, Seymour H.
Kopf Foundation
Kopf Foundation, Elizabeth Christy
KPMG Peat Marwick

Kraft General Foods
Kramer Foundation
Kramer Foundation, C. L. C.
Kravis Foundation, Henry R.
Kremer Foundation Trust, George
Kress Foundation, Samuel H.
Krimendahl II Foundation, H. Frederick
Kunstadter Family Foundation, Albert
L and L Foundation
Ladies' Home Journal Magazine
Laerdal Foundation, Asmund S.
Lambda Electronics Inc.
Lambert Memorial Foundation, Gerard B.
Landis & Gyr, Inc.
Lang Foundation, Eugene M.
Langeloth Foundation, Jacob and Valeria
Larsen Fund
Lasdon Foundation
Lastfogel Foundation, Abe and Frances
Lauder Foundation
Laura Ashley Inc.
Lavanburg-Corner House
Lawrence Foundation, Alice
Lawyers Co-operative Publishing Co.
Lazar Foundation
Lazard Freres & Co.
LeaRonal, Inc.
LeBrun Foundation
Ledwith Charitable Trust Bank, Mary B.
Lee Foundation, James T.
Lehigh Portland Cement Co.
Lehman Foundation, Edith and Herbert
Lehman Foundation, Robert
Leibovitz Foundation, Morris P.
Lemberg Foundation
Leonhardt Foundation, Dorothea L.
Leslie Fay Cos., Inc.
Leucadia National Corp.
Levinson Foundation, Morris L.
Leviton Manufacturing Co.
Levy Foundation, Betty and Norman F.
Levy Foundation, Jerome
Liberman Foundation, Bertha & Isaac
Lincoln Fund
Lincoln National Corp.
Lindner Foundation, Fay J.
Lingnan Foundation
Link, Jr. Foundation, George
Linus Foundation
Lipchitz Foundation, Jacques and Yulla
Lipton, Thomas J.
List Foundation, Albert A.
Littauer Foundation, Lucius N.
Little, Arthur D.
Litton Industries
Litwin Foundation
Liz Claiborne
Loeb Foundation, Frances and John L.
Loeb Partners Corp.
Loewenberg Foundation
Loews Corp.
Loewy Family Foundation
Long Island Lighting Co.
Loral Corp.
Lord & Taylor
Lorillard Tobacco Inc.
Lounsbery Foundation, Richard
Lowenstein Foundation, Leon
LTV Corp.
Lubo Fund
Luce Charitable Trust, Theodore
Luce Foundation, Henry
Lurcy Charitable and Educational Trust, Georges

Lydall, Inc.
M/A-COM, Inc.
MacAndrews & Forbes Holdings
MacDonald Foundation, James A.
MacDonald Foundation, Marquis George
MacKall and Evanina Evans Bell MacKall Trust, Paul
Maclellan Foundation, Robert L. and Kathrina H.
Macmillan, Inc.
Macy & Co., R.H.
Macy, Jr. Foundation, Josiah
Madison Mutual Insurance Co.
Mailman Family Foundation, A. L.
Mailman Foundation
Mamiye Brothers
Mandeville Foundation
Manning and Emma Austin Manning Foundation, James Hilton
Manpower, Inc.
Mapplethorpe Foundation, Robert
Marcade Group, Inc.
Marcus Brothers Textiles Inc.
Marine Midland Banks
Maritz Inc.
Mark IV Industries
Markle Foundation, John and Mary R.
Marks Family Foundation
Marsh & McLennan Cos.
Martin-Brower Co., The
Marubeni America Corp.
Marx Foundation, Virginia & Leonard
Maryland Casualty Co.
Masco Corp.
Mastronardi Charitable Foundation, Charles A.
Mather Fund, Richard
Mathers Charitable Foundation, G. Harold and Leila Y.
Mathis-Pfohl Foundation
Mattel
Mattus Foundation, Reuben and Rose
Matz Foundation — Edelman Division
May Department Stores Co.
Mayer Foundation, Louis B.
Mays , Inc., J.W.
MBIA, Inc.
MCA
McCann Foundation
McCarthy Charities
McCarthy Foundation, Michael W.
McConnell Foundation, Neil A.
McCrory Corp.
McDonald Foundation, J. M.
McGonagle Foundation, Dextra Baldwin
McGraw Foundation, Donald C.
McGraw-Hill
MCI Communications Corp.
MCJ Foundation
McKesson Corp.
McKinsey & Co.
Medtronic
Meenan Oil Co., Inc.
Mellam Family Foundation
Mellon Bank Corp.
Mellon Foundation, Andrew W.
Mellon PSFS
Melohn Foundation
Melville Corp.
Memton Fund
Menschel Foundation, Robert and Joyce
Mercantile Stores Co.
Mercedes-Benz of North America, Inc.
Mercury Aircraft
Mercy, Jr. Foundation, Sue and Eugene
Meredith Corp.

Meridien Hotels
Merrill Lynch & Co.
Mertz Foundation, Martha
Mertz-Gilmore Foundation, Joyce
Metallgesellschaft Corp.
Metropolitan Life Insurance Co.
Mex-Am Cultural Foundation
Meyer Foundation
Midland Montagu
Midlantic Banks, Inc.
Milbank Foundation, Dunlevy
Miles Inc.
Miles Inc., Diagnostic Division
Millbrook Tribute Garden
Miller Brewing Company/New York
Miller & Co.
Miller Fund, Kathryn and Gilbert
Milliken & Co.
Milstein Family Foundation
Milton Gordon Foundation
Minnesota Power & Light Co.
Mitrani Family Foundation
Mitsubishi Electric America
Mitsubishi Heavy Industries America
Mitsubishi International Corp.
Mitsubishi Kasei America
Mitsui & Co. (U.S.A.)
Mnuchin Foundation
Mobil Oil Corp.
Model Foundation, Leo
Modern Maid Food Products, Inc.
Monarch Machine Tool Co.
Monell Foundation, Ambrose
Moog, Inc.
Moore Business Forms, Inc.
Morania Foundation
Morgan Stanley & Co.
Morgenstern Foundation, Morris
Morris Foundation, Norman M.
Morris Foundation, William T.
Morrison-Knudsen Corp.
Morse-Diesel International
Morse, Jr. Foundation, Enid and Lester S.
Morton International
Moses Fund, Henry and Lucy
Mostyn Foundation
Motorola
Mott Charitable Trust/Spectemur Agendo, Stewart R.
Mulligan Charitable Trust, Mary S.
Multimedia, Inc.
Murphy Charitable Fund, George E. and Annette Cross
Murray, Jr. Foundation, John P.
Mutual of America Life
Mutual of New York
Nathan Berkman & Co.
National Broadcasting Co., Inc.
National Center for Automated Information Retrieval
National Fuel Gas Co.
National Medical Enterprises
National Spinning Co.
Nationale-Nederlanden North America Corp.
Nationwide Insurance Cos.
NCR Corp.
NEC USA
Nelco Sewing Machine Sales Corp.
Nepera Inc.
Neu Foundation, Hugo and Doris
Neuberger Foundation, Roy R. and Marie S.
New-Land Foundation
New & Sons, Hugo
New Street Capital Corp.
New World Foundation
New York Foundation
New York Life Insurance Co.
New York Marine & General Insurance Co.
New York Mercantile Exchange

New York Post Corp.
New York Racing Association
New York State Electric & Gas Corp.
New York Stock Exchange
New York Telephone Co.
New York Times Co.
The New Yorker Magazine, Inc.
Newbrook Charitable Foundation
Newhouse Foundation, Samuel I.
Newhouse Publication Corp.
Newman Assistance Fund, Jerome A. and Estelle R.
Newmont Mining Corp.
News America Publishing Inc.
Newsweek, Inc.
Niagara Mohawk Power Corp.
Nias Foundation, Henry
Nichimen America, Inc.
Nichols Farmhouse
Nichols Foundation
Nippon Life Insurance Co.
Noble Charitable Trust, John L. and Ethel G.
Noble Foundation, Edward John
Nomura Securities International
Norcross Wildlife Foundation
Norman Foundation
Normandie Foundation
North American Philips Corp.
North American Reinsurance Corp.
Northern Trust Co.
Northwestern National Insurance Group
Northwestern National Life Insurance Co.
Norton Co.
Norton & Co., W.W.
Norwest Corp.
Noyes Foundation, Jessie Smith
N've Shalom Foundation
NYNEX Corp.
Occidental Petroleum Corp.
O'Connor Foundation, A. Lindsay and Olive B.
Odyssey Partners
Oestreicher Foundation, Sylvan and Ann
Ogden Corp.
Ogden Foundation, Ralph E.
Ogilvy & Mather Worldwide
Olin Corp.
Olin Foundation, F. W.
Olin Foundation, John M.
Olive Bridge Fund
Olsten Corp.
Olympus Corp.
Oneida Ltd.
O'Neil Foundation, Cyril F. and Marie E.
Open Society Fund
Oppenheimer and Flora Oppenheimer Haas Trust, Leo
Oppenheimer & Co., Inc.
Oppenheimer Management Corp.
Orange & Rockland Utilities, Inc.
Orion Capital Corp.
Osborn Charitable Trust, Edward B.
Osceola Foundation
Oshkosh B'Gosh
Osram Corp.
O'Sullivan Children Foundation
O'Toole Foundation, Theresa and Edward
Outokumpu-American Brass Co.
Overbrook Foundation
Overseas Shipholding Group
Owens-Corning Fiberglas Corp.
Oxford Industries, Inc.
PacifiCorp
PaineWebber
Paley Foundation, William S.
Palisades Educational Foundation
Palisano Foundation, Vincent and Harriet

Pall Corp.
Palmer Fund, Francis Asbury
Panhandle Eastern Corp.
Paramount Communications Inc.
Park Communications Inc.
Parker-Hannifin Corp.
Parnes Foundation, E. H.
Parshelsky Foundation, Moses L.
Parsons and Whittemore Inc.
Parsons Corp.
Patrina Foundation
Paul and C. Michael Paul Foundation, Josephine Bay
Peerless Insurance Co.
Penguin USA Inc.
Penney Foundation, James C.
Penzance Foundation
PepsiCo
Perini Corp.
Perkin-Elmer Corp.
Perkin Fund
Perkins Memorial Foundation, George W.
Perley Fund, Victor E.
Pettus Crowe Foundation
Pfizer
Pforzheimer Foundation, Carl and Lily
Phelps Dodge Corp.
Philip Morris Cos.
Philippe Foundation
Phillips-Van Heusen Corp.
Phipps Foundation, Howard
Phoenix Home Life Mutual Insurance Co.
Piankova Foundation, Tatiana
Picker International
Pincus Family Fund
Pines Bridge Foundation
Pinewood Foundation
Pinkerton Foundation
Pioneer Fund
Pittway Corp.
Plant Memorial Fund, Henry B.
Playboy Enterprises, Inc.
Pluta Family Foundation
Ply-Gem Industries, Inc.
Pollock-Krasner Foundation
Pope Foundation
Porter Foundation, Mrs. Cheever
Potts Memorial Foundation
Pratt & Lambert, Inc.
Premier Industrial Corp.
Price Foundation, Louis and Harold
Price Waterhouse-U.S.
Primerica Corp.
Pritchard Charitable Trust, William E. and Maude S.
Procter & Gamble Co.
Propp Sons Fund, Morris and Anna
Prospect Hill Foundation
Prudential-Bache Securities
Prudential Insurance Co. of America
Quaker Oats Co.
Quantum Chemical Corp.
Ralston Purina Co.
Ramapo Trust
Randolph Foundation
Random House Inc.
Rankin and Elizabeth Forbes Rankin Trust, William
Raskin Foundation, Hirsch and Braine
Rauch Foundation
Raymond Corp.
Reader's Digest Association
Reed Foundation
Reed Foundation, Philip D.
Reed Publishing USA
REI-Recreational Equipment, Inc.
Reich & Tang L.P.
Reicher Foundation, Anne & Harry J.

Reliance Group Holdings, Inc.
Reliance Insurance Cos.
Republic New York Corp.
Research Institute of America
Resnick Foundation, Jack and Pearl
Restaurant Associates, Inc.
Revlon
Revson Foundation, Charles H.
Reynolds Foundation, Christopher
Reynolds Metals Co.
Rhodebeck Charitable Trust
Rich Products Corp.
Richardson Charitable Trust, Anne S.
Richardson Foundation, Frank E. and Nancy M.
Richardson Foundation, Smith
Richmond Foundation, Frederick W.
Ridgefield Foundation
Ritter Foundation
Ritter Foundation, May Ellen and Gerald
RJR Nabisco Inc.
Robinson Fund, Maurice R.
Robison Foundation, Ellis H. and Doris B.
Roche Relief Foundation, Edward and Ellen
Rochester Community Savings Bank
Rochester Gas & Electric Corp.
Rochester Midland Corp.
Rochester Telephone Corp.
Rockefeller Brothers Fund
Rockefeller Family & Associates
Rockefeller Family Fund
Rockefeller Foundation
Rockefeller Fund, David
Rodgers Foundation, Richard & Dorothy
Rohatyn Foundation, Felix and Elizabeth
Rose Foundation, Billy
Rosen Foundation, Joseph
Rosenberg Foundation, Sunny and Abe
Rosenkranz Foundation
Rosenstiel Foundation
Rosenthal Foundation, Ida and William
Rosenthal Foundation, Richard and Lois
Rosenwald Family Fund, William
Ross Foundation, Arthur
Ross Foundation, Lyn & George M.
Rouse Co.
Rubin Foundation, Rob E. & Judith O.
Rubin Foundation, Samuel
Rubinstein Foundation, Helena
Rudin Foundation
Rudin Foundation, Louis and Rachel
Rudin Foundation, Samuel and May
Ruffin Foundation, Peter B. & Adeline W.
Russ Togs
Ryan Foundation, Nina M.
Ryder System
Sage Foundation, Russell
St. Faith's House Foundation
St. Giles Foundation
Saint Paul Cos.
Saks Fifth Ave.
Salomon
Salomon Foundation, Richard & Edna
Saltz Foundation, Gary
Samsung America Inc.
Samuels Foundation, Fan Fox and Leslie R.
Sandoz Corp.
Sanwa Bank Ltd. New York

Sara Lee Corp.
Sasco Foundation
Saul Foundation, Joseph E. & Norma G.
Schaffer Foundation, H.
Schaffer Foundation, Michael & Helen
Schapiro Fund, M. A.
Schepp Foundation, Leopold
Schering-Plough Corp.
Scherman Foundation
Scheuer Family Foundation, S. H. and Helen R.
Schieffelin Residuary Trust, Sarah I.
Schieffelin & Somerset Co.
Schiff Foundation
Schiff Foundation, Dorothy
Schlegel Corp.
Schloss & Co., Marcus
Schlumberger Ltd.
Schneiderman Foundation, Roberta and Irwin
Scholastic Inc.
Schulman Management Corp.
Schwartz Foundation, David
Schwartz Fund for Education and Health Research, Arnold and Marie
Scott, Foresman & Co.
Scott Paper Co.
Scripps Co., E.W.
Scrivner, Inc.
Seagram & Sons, Joseph E.
Sealy, Inc.
Sears, Roebuck and Co.
Sedgwick James Inc.
Seevak Family Foundation
Seneca Foods Corp.
Sequa Corp.
Sharp Electronics Corp.
Sharp Foundation
Sharp Foundation, Evelyn
Shatford Memorial Trust, J. D.
Shaw's Supermarkets
Sheafer Charitable Trust, Emma A.
Shearson, Lehman & Hutton
Sheinberg Foundation, Eric P.
Sheldon Foundation, Ralph C.
Shell Oil Co.
Shubert Foundation
Silverburgh Foundation, Grace, George & Judith
Silverman Foundation, Marty and Dorothy
Silverweed Foundation
Simon & Schuster Inc.
Simpson Investment Co.
Sinsheimer Fund, Alexandrine and Alexander L.
Skadden, Arps, Slate, Meagher and Flom Fellowship Foundation
Skandia America Reinsurance Corp.
SKF USA, Inc.
Skirball Foundation
Slant/Fin Corp.
Slaughter Foundation, Charles
Slifka Foundation, Alan B.
Slifka Foundation, Joseph and Sylvia
Sloan Foundation, Alfred P.
Smeal Foundation, Mary Jean & Frank P.
Smith Barney, Harris Upham & Co.
Smith Corona Corp.
Smith Fund, George D.
Smithers Foundation, Christopher D.
Snow Foundation, John Ben
Snow Memorial Trust, John Ben
Snyder Fund, Valentine Perry
Society Corp.
Sofia American Schools
Sogem Holding Ltd.

New York (cont.)

Soling Family Foundation
Solow Foundation
Solow Foundation, Sheldon H.
Sony Corp. of America
Soros Foundation-Hungary
Sotheby's
Southland Corp.
Sperry Fund
Spiegel Family Foundation, Jerry and Emily
Spingold Foundation, Nate B. and Frances
Spiritus Gladius Foundation
Spiro Foundation, Donald W.
Sprague Educational and Charitable Foundation, Seth
Springs Industries
Sprint
Spunk Fund
Staley Foundation, Thomas F.
Standard Chartered Bank New York
Standard Motor Products, Inc.
Standard Products Co.
Stanton Fund, Ruth and Frank
Starr Foundation
Starrett Housing Corp.
State Farm Mutual Automobile Insurance Co.
State Street Bank & Trust Co.
Statler Foundation
Statter Foundation, Amy Plant
Steele-Reese Foundation
Stein Foundation, Joseph F.
Steinbach Fund, Ruth and Milton
Steinberg Family Foundation, Meyer and Jean
Steinhardt Foundation, Judy and Michael
Steiniger Charitable Foundation, Edward & Joan
Stella D'Oro Biscuit Co.
Sterling Winthrop
Stern Foundation, Bernice and Milton
Stern Foundation, Gustav and Irene
Stern Foundation, Marjorie and Michael
Stone & Webster, Inc.
Stony Wold Herbert Fund
Stott Foundation, Robert L.
Straus Foundation, Martha Washington Straus and Harry H.
Straus Foundation, Philip A. and Lynn
Stuart Foundation
Suburban Propane
Sullivan Musical Foundation, William Matheus
Sulzberger Foundation
Sulzer Brothers Inc.
Sumitomo Corp. of America
Sumitomo Trust & Banking Co., Ltd.
Summerfield Foundation, Solon E.
Surdna Foundation
Sussman Trust, Otto
Swanson Foundation
Swiss American Securities, Inc.
Swiss Bank Corp.
Switzer Foundation
Taconic Foundation
Tai and Co., J. T.
Talley Industries, Inc.
Tambrands Inc.
Tandem Computers
Taylor Foundation, Fred and Harriett
TBG, Inc.
Teagle Foundation
Teledyne
Tennant Co.
Tetley, Inc.

Texaco
Textron
Thanksgiving Foundation
Thomson Information Publishing Group
Thorne Foundation
3M Co.
Thyssen Specialty Steels
Tiger Foundation
Time Warner
Times Mirror Co.
Tinker Foundation
Tisch Foundation
Titan Industrial Co.
TJX Cos.
Tokai Bank, Ltd.
Tomen America, Inc.
Topps Company
Tops Markets, Inc.
Torchmark Corp.
Tortuga Foundation
Toshiba America, Inc.
Towers Perrin
Transamerica Corp.
Transco Energy Company
Travelers Cos.
Triangle Industries
Trimble Family Foundation, Robert Mize and Isa White
Tripifoods
Tropicana Products, Inc.
Truman Foundation, Mildred Faulkner
Trump Group
Trust for Mutual Understanding
TRW Corp.
Tsai Foundation, Gerald
Tuch Foundation, Michael
Tucker Anthony, Inc.
Turner Construction Co.
Turner Corp.
Turner Fund, Ruth
Twentieth Century-Fox Film Corp.
21 International Holdings
UIS, Inc.
UJB Financial Corp.
UNC, Inc.
Unilever United States
Union Bank of Switzerland Los Angeles Branch
Union Bank of Switzerland New York Branch
Union Carbide Corp.
Unisys Corp.
United Dominion Industries
United Industrial Corp.
United Merchants & Manufacturers
United Missouri Bancshares, Inc.
United States-Japan Foundation
U.S. News & World Report
United States Trust Co. of New York
United Technologies Corp.
United Togs Inc.
Unitrode Corp.
Uris Brothers Foundation
USG Corp.
Ushkow Foundation
USLIFE Corp.
Utica National Insurance Group
van Ameringen Foundation
Vanneck-Bailey Foundation
Vernitron Corp.
Vernon Fund, Miles Hodsdon
Vetlesen Foundation, G. Unger
Viacom International Inc.
Victory Markets, Inc.
Vidda Foundation
Volkswagen of America, Inc.
Volvo North America Corp.
Wachtell, Lipton, Rosen & Katz
Waldbaum, Inc.
Waldbaum Family Foundation, I.
Wallace-Reader's Digest Fund, DeWitt

Wallace Reader's Digest Fund, Lila
Wallach Foundation, Miriam G. and Ira D.
Disney Co., Walt
Warhol Foundation for the Visual Arts, Andy
Warner Fund, Albert and Bessie
Warren and Beatrice W. Blanding Foundation, Riley J. and Lillian N.
Washington Post Co.
Washington Square Fund
Wasily Family Foundation
Waterfowl Research Foundation
WEA Enterprises Co.
Weeden Foundation, Frank
Weezie Foundation
Weight Watchers International
Weil, Gotshal & Manges Foundation
Weiler Foundation, Theodore & Renee
Weinberg Foundation, John L.
Weinberg, Jr. Foundation, Sidney J.
Weininger Foundation, Richard and Gertrude
Weinstein Foundation, Alex J.
Weinstein Foundation, J.
Weiss Foundation, Stephen and Suzanne
Wendt Foundation, Margaret L.
Wenner-Gren Foundation for Anthropological Research
Werblow Charitable Trust, Nina W.
Westchester Health Fund
Western New York Foundation
Westinghouse Broadcasting Co.
Westinghouse Electric Corp.
WestLB New York Branch
Westvaco Corp.
Wheeling-Pittsburgh Corp.
Whitehead Foundation
Whiting Foundation, Mrs. Giles
Whitney Foundation, Helen Hay
Wien Foundation, Lawrence A.
Wiener Foundation, Malcolm Hewitt
Wilber National Bank
Wiley & Sons, Inc., John
Willmott Foundation, Fred & Floy
Wilson Foundation, Elaine P. and Richard U.
Wilson Foundation, H. W.
Wilson Foundation, Marie C. and Joseph C.
Winston Foundation, Norman and Rosita
Winston Research Foundation, Harry
Witco Corp.
Wolverine World Wide, Inc.
Woodland Foundation
Woodner Family Collection, Ian
Woodward Fund
Woolworth Co., F.W.
WSP&R Charitable Trust Fund
Wunsch Foundation
Xerox Corp.
Yamaichi International (America) Inc.
Young & Rubicam
Youth Foundation
Zarkin Memorial Foundation, Charles
Zenkel Foundation
Ziff Communications Co.
Zilkha & Sons
Zimmermann Fund, Marie and John
Zlinkoff Fund for Medical Research and Education, Sergei S.
Zuckerberg Foundation, Roy J.

North Carolina

Abbott Laboratories
Abernethy Testamentary Charitable Trust, Maye Morrison
Abitibi-Price
Acme-McCrary Corp.
Aeroglide Corp.
AFLAC
Air Products & Chemicals
Akzo America
Akzo Chemicals Inc.
Alcatel NA Cable Systems, Inc.
Alco Standard Corp.
AlliedSignal
Alumax
Aluminum Co. of America
AMAX
American Brands
American Cyanamid Co.
American Greetings Corp.
American Home Products Corp.
American International Group, Inc.
American Otological Society
American Schlafhorst Foundation, Inc.
AMETEK
Amoco Corp.
AMP
Analog Devices
Anderson Foundation, Robert C. and Sadie G.
ARA Services
Archer-Daniels-Midland Co.
Armco Inc.
Armstrong World Industries Inc.
Arrow Electronics, Inc.
Arvin Industries
Avery Dennison Corp.
Avis Inc.
Avnet, Inc.
Babcock Foundation, Mary Reynolds
Ball Corp.
Bandag, Inc.
Bank of Boston Corp.
Banta Corp.
Barclays Bank of New York
BarclaysAmerican Corp.
Barnes Group
Bassett Furniture Industries, Inc.
Bausch & Lomb
Baxter International
BB&T Financial Corp.
Becton Dickinson & Co.
Belding Heminway Co.
Belk Stores
BellSouth Corp.
Benetton
Best Products Co.
Biddle Foundation, Mary Duke
Black & Decker Corp.
Blount
Blue Bell, Inc.
Boise Cascade Corp.
Borden
Borg-Warner Corp.
Bosch Corp., Robert
Bossong Hosiery Mills
Brad Ragan, Inc.
Branch Banking & Trust Co.
Brenner Foundation
Bridgestone/Firestone
Bristol-Myers Squibb Co.
Brooke Group Ltd.
Brown Inc., John
Brown & Sons, Alex
Brown & Williamson Tobacco Corp.
Broyhill Family Foundation
Brunswick Corp.
Bryan Family Foundation, Kathleen Price and Joseph M.
Bryan Foundation, James E. and Mary Z.
Burlington Industries

Burress, J.W.
Burroughs Wellcome Co.
Campbell Soup Co.
Cannon Foundation
Capital Cities/ABC
Capital Holding Corp.
Carlyle & Co. Jewelers
Carolina Power & Light Co.
Carolina Steel Corp.
Carolina Telephone & Telegraph Co.
Carter Charitable Trust, Wilbur Lee
Castle & Co., A.M.
CCB Financial Corp.
Centel Corp.
Central Soya Co.
Champion International Corp.
Charter Medical Corp.
Chesapeake Corp.
Chesebrough-Pond's
Christian Training Foundation
Circuit City Stores
Classic Leather
Clorox Co.
Coffey Foundation
Cole Foundation
Collins & Aikman Corp.
Collins & Aikman Holdings Corp.
Coltec Industries
Commercial Intertech Corp.
Computer Associates International
Cone Mills Corp.
Connemara Fund
Consolidated Freightways
Cooper Industries
Corning Incorporated
Covington Foundation, Marion Stedman
Cox Enterprises
CPC International
CR Industries
Crane & Co.
Crane Co.
Cranston Print Works
Croft Metals
Crompton & Knowles Corp.
Culbro Corp.
Cummins Engine Co.
Dalton Foundation, Harry L.
Dana Corp.
Davis Charitable Foundation, Champion McDowell
Davis Hospital Foundation
Deluxe Corp.
Deutsch Co.
Dexter Corp.
Dickson Foundation
Dillard Paper Co.
Dixie Yarns, Inc.
Dollar General Corp.
Donnelley & Sons Co., R.R.
Dove-Knight & Associates, P.A., Architects
Dover Corp.
Dover Foundation
Dow Corning Corp.
Dow Jones & Co.
du Pont de Nemours & Co., E. I.
Duke Endowment
Duke Power Co.
Durham Corp.
Durham Merchants Association Charitable Foundation
Eaton Corp.
Echlin Inc.
Eckerd Corp., Jack
Exxon Corp.
Fairchild Corp.
Farley Industries
Fast Food Merchandisers
Ferebee Endowment, Percy O.
Fieldcrest Cannon
FINA, Inc.
Finch Foundation, Doak

Finch Foundation, Thomas
Austin
Finley Foundation, A. E.
First Citizens Bank and Trust Co.
First Mississippi Corp.
First Union Corp.
Fletcher Foundation, A. J.
FMC Corp.
Food Lion Inc.
Fuller Co., H.B.
Gannett Co.
General Electric Co.
General Tire Inc.
Georgia-Pacific Corp.
Gerber Products Co.
Giles Foundation, Edward C.
Gilmer-Smith Foundation
Ginter Foundation, Karl and
Anna
Glaxo
Glenn Foundation, Carrie C. &
Lena V.
Goodyear Tire & Rubber Co.
Goody's Manufacturing Corp.
Guilford Mills
Halstead Foundation
Hampton Industries
Hanes Foundation, John W. and
Anna H.
Harris Corp.
Harris Foundation, James J. and
Angelia M.
Harris-Teeter Super Markets
Hartmarx Corp.
Harvey Foundation, Felix
Heinz Co., H.J.
Hemby Foundation, Alex
Henkel Corp.
Henredon Furniture Industries
Hillsdale Fund
Hitachi
Hoechst Celanese Corp.
Hoffmann-La Roche
Holding Foundation, Robert P.
Holzman USA, Philipp
Home Depot
HON Industries
Hospital Corp. of America
Humana
Hunt Manufacturing Co.
Hurley Foundation, J. F.
IBM Corp.
Inco Alloys International
Ingersoll-Rand Co.
Inland Steel Industries
Interco
International Multifoods Corp.
ITT Corp.
ITT Hartford Insurance Group
IU International
Janirve Foundation
Jefferson-Pilot
Jefferson-Pilot Communications
Jefferson Smurfit Corp.
JELD-WEN, Inc.
Johnson Inc., Axel
Johnson Controls
Johnson & Higgins
Jones Construction Co., J.A.
Jostens
Keebler Co.
Kellenberger Historical
Foundation, May Gordon
Latham
Kenan Family Foundation
Kenan, Jr. Charitable Trust,
William R.
Kennametal
Kimball International
Kimberly-Clark Corp.
Knight-Ridder, Inc.
La-Z-Boy Chair Co.
Lamb Foundation, Kirkland S.
and Rena B.
Lance, Inc.
Landmark Communications
Lane Charitable Trust, Melvin R.

Laporte Inc.
Levi Strauss & Co.
Liberty Hosiery Mills
Litton Industries
Livingstone Charitable
Foundation, Betty J. and J.
Stanley
Love Foundation, Martha and
Spencer
Lowe's Cos.
Lydall, Inc.
Magee Christian Education
Foundation
Mallinckrodt Specialty
Chemicals Co.
Manufacturers Life Insurance
Co. of America
Manville Corp.
Mark IV Industries
Marsh Furniture Co.
Martin Marietta Aggregates
Masco Corp.
Mast Drug Co.
McClure Educational and
Development Fund, James G.
K.
McDevitt Street Bovis Inc.
Mead Corp.
Mebane Packaging Corp.
Media General, Inc.
Merck & Co.
Miller Brewing Company/North
Carolina
Milliken & Co.
Millis Foundation, James H. and
Jesse E.
Minnesota Power & Light Co.
Mitsubishi Semiconductor
America, Inc. Funds
Mohasco Corp.
Monsanto Co.
Moore & Sons, B.C.
Morehead Foundation, John
Motley
Morgan Trust for Charity,
Religion, and Education
Morris Charitable Foundation, E.
A.
MTS Systems Corp.
Nanney Foundation, Charles and
Irene
Nash-Finch Co.
National Gypsum Co.
National Medical Enterprises
National Service Industries
National Starch & Chemical
Corp.
NationsBank Corp.
Nationwide Insurance Cos.
New York Times Co.
Newport News Shipbuilding &
Dry Dock Co.
News & Observer Publishing Co.
North American Philips Corp.
North Carolina Foam Foundation
Norton Co.
Nucor Corp.
Oakite Products
Outboard Marine Corp.
Owens-Corning Fiberglas Corp.
Palin Foundation
Pepsi-Cola Bottling Co. of
Charlotte
Perkins Memorial Fund, James J.
and Marie Richardson
Perry-Griffin Foundation
Philip Morris Cos.
Piedmont Natural Gas Co., Inc.
Pioneer Hi-Bred International
Pirelli Armstrong Tire Corp.
Poole Equipment Co., Gregory
PPG Industries
Preyer Fund, Mary Norris
Prickett Fund, Lynn R. and Karl
E.
Procter & Gamble Co.
Prudential Insurance Co. of
America

Pulitzer Publishing Co.
Quaker Oats Co.
Quantum Chemical Corp.
R. L. Stowe Mills Inc.
Radiator Specialty Co.
Randleigh Foundation Trust
REI-Recreational Equipment,
Inc.
Reichhold Chemicals, Inc.
Reliance Electric Co.
Research-Cottrell Inc.
Rexham Inc.
Reynolds Charitable Trust, Kate
B.
Reynolds Foundation, Z. Smith
Rhone-Poulenc Inc.
Richardson Fund, Grace
Richardson Fund, Mary Lynn
Ringier-America
Rixson Foundation, Oscar C.
RJR Nabisco Inc.
Rogers Charitable Trust, Florence
Rohm and Haas Company
Rose's Stores, Inc.
Ross, Johnston & Kersting
Rouse Co.
Royal Group Inc.
Rubbermaid
Ruddick Corp.
Sandoz Corp.
Sara Lee Corp.
Sara Lee Hosiery
Scrivner of North Carolina Inc.
SECO
Shelton Cos.
Sherwin-Williams Co.
Siemens Medical Systems Inc.
Smith Corp., A.O.
Sonoco Products Co.
Southern Furniture Co.
Spalding Health Care Trust
Springs Industries
Sprint
Square D Co.
Standard Products Co.
Stanley Works
Steelcase
Sternberger Foundation, Sigmund
Stewards Fund
Stone Container Corp.
Stonecutter Mills Corp.
Stowe, Jr. Foundation, Robert
Lee
Susquehanna Corp.
Talley Industries, Inc.
Tandem Computers
Tanner Cos.
Target Stores
Teledyne
Tenneco
Tension Envelope Corp.
Textron
Thomas Built Buses L.P.
Thomasville Furniture Industries
Thorn Apple Valley, Inc.
3M Co.
Timken Co.
Tracor, Inc.
Transco Energy Company
Travelers Cos.
Trexler Foundation
TRINOVA Corp.
Trion
Turner Corp.
Tyson Foods, Inc.
Unifi, Inc.
Union Camp Corp.
United Dominion Industries
Universal Leaf Tobacco Co.
Valdese Manufacturing Co., Inc.
Van Every Foundation, Philip L.
Virginia Power Co.
Vulcan Materials Co.
Wachovia Bank & Trust Co.,
N.A.
Wal-Mart Stores

Weaver Foundation
Wellons Foundation
West Co.
Westinghouse Electric Corp.
Weyerhaeuser Co.
Whitener Foundation
Winn-Dixie Stores
Yale Security Inc.
Yost Trust, Elizabeth Burns

North Dakota

Archer-Daniels-Midland Co.
Armco Inc.
Best Products Co.
Bucyrus-Erie
Burlington Northern Inc.
C.P. Rail Systems
Clark Equipment Co.
Dayton Hudson Corp.
Dial Corp.
Employers Mutual Casualty Co.
First Bank System
Knight-Ridder, Inc.
Land O'Lakes
Leach Foundation, Tom &
Frances
Lee Enterprises
MDU Resources Group, Inc.
Minnesota Power & Light Co.
Myra Foundation
Northern States Power Co.
Norwest Corp.
Pamida, Inc.
Pioneer Hi-Bred International
Quantum Chemical Corp.
Rochester Telephone Corp.
Saint Paul Cos.
Sara Lee Corp.
Steiger Tractor
Stern Family Foundation, Alex
Super Valu Stores
Target Stores
Tenneco
3M Co.
US WEST
Wal-Mart Stores

Ohio

ABB Process Automation
Abbott Laboratories
Abitibi-Price
Access Energy Corp.
Acme-Cleveland Corp.
AGA Gas, Inc.
Air Products & Chemicals
Airborne Express Co.
Akzo America
Albrecht Grocery Co., Fred W.
Alcan Aluminum Corp.
Alco Standard Corp.
Alexander & Alexander
Services, Inc.
AlliedSignal
ALLTEL Corp.
Alms Trust, Eleanora
Alumax
Aluminum Co. of America
AMAX
Amcast Industrial Corp.
America West Airlines
American Aggregates Corp.
American Brands
American Capital Corp.
American Cyanamid Co.
American Electric Power
American Financial Corp.
American Foundation
Corporation
American Greetings Corp.
American Home Products Corp.
American Honda Motor Co.
American Society of Ephesus
American Standard
American Telephone &
Telegraph Co.

American Welding &
Manufacturing Co.
Ameritech Corp.
Ameritech Publishing
AMETEK
Anchor Fasteners
Anderson Foundation, William P
Andersons Management Corp.
Andrews Foundation
Anheuser-Busch Cos.
AON Corp.
Appleton Papers
ARA Services
Archer-Daniels-Midland Co.
ARCO Chemical
Aristech Chemical Corp.
Armco Inc.
Armco Steel Co.
Armington Fund, Evenor
Arrow Electronics, Inc.
Arvin Industries
Asea Brown Boveri
Ashland Oil
Austin Memorial Foundation
Avery Dennison Corp.
Avis Inc.
Avnet, Inc.
Avon Products
AXIA Incorporated
Baird Brothers Co.
Baker Charitable Foundation,
Jessie Foos
Ball Corp.
Banc One Illinois Corp.
Bank of New York
Bank One, Cambridge, NA
Bank One, Cleveland, NA
Bank One, Columbus, NA
Bank One, Coshocton, NA
Bank One, Dayton, NA
Bank One, Dover, NA
Bank One, Portsmouth, NA
Bank One, Sidney, NA
Bank One, Youngstown, NA
Banner Industries, Inc.
Bardes Corp.
Barnes Group
Barry Corp., R. G.
Battelle
Baumker Charitable Foundation,
Elsie and Harry
Baxter International
Bearings, Inc.
Bechtel Group
Beecher Foundation, Florence
Simon
Beeghly Fund, Leon A.
Beerman Foundation
Belden Brick Co., Inc.
Bell Industries
Bemis Company
Benefit Trust Life Insurance Co.
Benua Foundation
Berkman Co., Louis
Berkman Foundation, Louis and
Sandra
Berry & Co., L.M.
Berry Foundation, Loren M.
Best Products Co.
Bethlehem Steel Corp.
BFGoodrich
Bicknell Fund
Bingham Foundation, William
Black & Decker Corp.
Blade Communications
Block, H&R
Bob Evans Farms
Boise Cascade Corp.
Borden
BP America
BP Exploration
Britton Fund
Brown Inc., John
Browning-Ferris Industries
Browning Masonic Memorial
Fund, Otis Avery

Ohio (cont.)

Bruening Foundation, Eva L. and Joseph M.
Brunswick Corp.
Brush Foundation
Brush Wellman Inc.
Calhoun Charitable Trust, Kenneth
Campbell Soup Co.
Capital Cities/ABC
Care Enterprises
Carrier Corp.
Castle & Co., A.M.
Caterpillar
Cayuga Foundation
Centel Corp.
Centerior Energy Corp.
Central Soya Co.
Cessna Aircraft Co.
Champion International Corp.
Champion Spark Plug Co.
Charities Foundation
Charter Medical Corp.
Chemed Corp.
Chesapeake Corp.
Chiquita Brands Co.
Chrysler Corp.
CIBA-GEIGY Corp.
Cincinnati Bell
Cincinnati Enquirer
Cincinnati Financial Corp.
Cincinnati Foundation for the Aged
Cincinnati Gas & Electric Co.
Cincinnati Milacron
Cincom Systems, Inc.
Circuit City Stores
Clark Equipment Co.
Cleveland-Cliffs
Clopay Corp.
Clorox Co.
Codrington Charitable Foundation, George W.
Cole National Corp.
Collins & Aikman Corp.
Collins & Aikman Holdings Corp.
Columbia Gas Distribution Cos.
Columbus Dispatch Printing Co.
Columbus Life Insurance Co.
Columbus Southern Power Co.
Comerica
Commercial Intertech Corp.
Community Mutual Insurance Co.
Computer Associates International
Consolidated Freightways
Consolidated Natural Gas Co.
Continental Corp.
Contraves USA
Cooper Industries
Cooper Tire & Rubber Co.
Copeland Corp.
Copperweld Corp.
Copperweld Steel Co.
Corbett Foundation
Corbin Foundation, Mary S. and David C.
Corning Incorporated
Cox Enterprises
Crandall Memorial Foundation, J. Ford
Crane & Co.
Crane Co.
Crompton & Knowles Corp.
CSC Industries
Cummins Engine Co.
Curtice-Burns Foods
Dana Corp.
Danis Industries
Dater Foundation, Charles H.
Dauch Foundation, William
Davey Tree Expert Co.
Dayton Foundation Depository
Dayton Hudson Corp.

Dayton Power and Light Co.
Dayton-Walther Corp.
DeBartolo Corp., Edward J.
Debartolo Foundation, Marie P.
Delta Air Lines
Deluxe Corp.
Dentsply International, Inc.
Deuble Foundation, George H.
Dexter Corp.
Didier Taylor Refractories Corp.
Diebold, Inc.
Dillard Department Stores, Inc.
Dively Foundation, George S.
Dollar General Corp.
Donnelley & Sons Co., R.R.
Dover Corp.
Dow Chemical Co.
Dow Jones & Co.
Dresser Industries
du Pont de Nemours & Co., E. I.
Duriron Co., Inc.
Eagle-Picher Industries
Easco Corp.
East Ohio Gas Co.
Eastern Enterprises
Eaton Corp.
Eaton Foundation, Cyrus
Ebco Manufacturing Co.
Echlin Inc.
Edwards Industries
EG&G Inc.
El-An Foundation
Electric Power Equipment Co.
Elf Atochem North America
Emerson Electric Co.
Emery Memorial, Thomas J.
English Foundation, Walter and Marian
Enterprises Inc.
Epp Fund B Charitable Trust, Otto C.
Equitable Life Assurance Society of the U.S.
Erb Lumber Co.
Ernsthausen Charitable Foundation, John F. and Doris E.
Eureka Co.
Evans Foundation, Thomas J.
Exxon Corp.
Eyman Trust, Jesse
Fairchild Corp.
Farley Industries
Federal-Mogul Corp.
Federated Department Stores and Allied Stores Corp.
Ferro Corp.
Fifth Third Bancorp
Figgie International
Finnegan Foundation, John D.
Firan Foundation
Fireman's Fund Insurance Co.
Firestone, Jr. Foundation, Harvey
Flickinger Memorial Trust
Flowers Charitable Trust, Albert W. and Edith V.
FMR Corp.
Ford and Ada Ford Fund, S. N.
Forest City Enterprises
Foss Memorial Employees Trust, Donald J.
Fox Charitable Foundation, Harry K. & Emma R.
Foxmeyer Corp.
Frankino Charitable Foundation, Samuel J. and Connie
French Oil Mill Machinery Co.
Frisch's Restaurants Inc.
Frohman Foundation, Sidney
Frohring Foundation, Paul & Maxine
Frohring Foundation, William O. and Gertrude Lewis
Fuller Co., H.B.
Gannett Co.
GAR Foundation
Gardner Foundation

GATX Corp.
GenCorp
General Electric Co.
General Housewares Corp.
General Motors Corp.
General Reinsurance Corp.
General Tire Inc.
Generation Trust
Georgia-Pacific Corp.
Gerlach Foundation
Gerson Family Foundation, Benjamin J.
Glidden Co.
Goerlich Family Foundation
Goodyear Tire & Rubber Co.
Gould Inc.
Gradison & Co.
Green Acres Foundation
Greif Brothers Corp.
Gries Charity Fund, Lucile and Robert H.
Gries Family Foundation
Grimes Foundation
Griswold Foundation, John C.
Gross Charitable Trust, Walter L. and Nell R.
Grumman Corp.
Gund Foundation, George
H.C.S. Foundation
Handy & Harman
Hankins Foundation
Hanna Co., M.A.
Harris Corp.
Harsco Corp.
Harte-Hanks Communications, Inc.
Hartzell Industries, Inc.
Haskell Fund
Hauserman, Inc.
Hauss-Helms Foundation
Hayfields Foundation
Hechinger Co.
Heinz Co., H.J.
Hershey Foundation
Hexcel Corp.
Hobart Corp.
Homewood Corp.
Honda of America Manufacturing, Inc.
Hook Drug
Hoover Foundation
Hoover Fund-Trust, W. Henry
Hosler Memorial Educational Fund, Dr. R. S.
Hubbell Inc.
Huffy Corp.
Humana
Humphrey Fund, George M. and Pamela S.
Huntington Bancshares Inc.
Huntington Fund for Education, John
Iddings Benevolent Trust
Illinois Tool Works
IMCERA Group Inc.
IMO Industries Inc.
Imperial Electric
Indiana Insurance Cos.
Ingalls Foundation, Louise H. and David S.
Inland Container Corp.
Inland Steel Industries
International Multifoods Corp.
International Paper Co.
Ireland Foundation
Irwin-Sweeney-Miller Foundation
ITT Corp.
ITT Hartford Insurance Group
ITT Rayonier
James River Corp. of Virginia
Jarson-Stanley and Mickey Kaplan Foundation, Isaac & Esther
Jasam Foundation
Jefferson Smurfit Corp.
JELD-WEN, Inc.

Jennings Foundation, Martha Holden
Jergens Foundation, Andrew
Johnson Controls
Johnson & Higgins
Johnson & Johnson
Joslyn Corp.
Kangesser Foundation, Robert E., Harry A., and M. Sylvia
Kaplan Trucking Co.
KDI Corp.
Keebler Co.
Kemper National Insurance Cos.
Kendall Health Care Products
Kenridge Fund
Kettering Family Foundation
Kettering Fund
Kibble Foundation
Kilcawley Fund, William H.
Kimberly-Clark Corp.
Kling Trust, Louise
Knight-Ridder, Inc.
Kobacker Co.
Kramer Foundation, Louise
Kuhns Investment Co.
Kulas Foundation
Lafarge Corp.
Lamson & Sessions Co.
Lancaster Colony
Laub Foundation
LDI Charitable Foundation
Leaseway Transportation Corp.
Lennon Foundation, Fred A.
Lennox International, Inc.
Libbey-Owens Ford Co.
Liberty Corp.
The Limited, Inc.
Lincoln Electric Co.
Lincoln National Corp.
Lippitt Foundation, Katherine Kenyon
Litton Industries
Loctite Corp.
Louisiana-Pacific Corp.
LTV Corp.
Lubrizol Corp.
Lukens
Lyons Physician's Supply Co.
M.T.D. Products
MalCo Products Inc.
Mandel Foundation, Jack N. and Lilyan
Mandel Foundation, Joseph and Florence
Mandel Foundation, Morton and Barbara
Manufacturers Life Insurance Co. of America
Manville Corp.
Mark IV Industries
Markey Charitable Fund, John C.
Marshall Field's
Masco Corp.
Massie Trust, David Meade
Mather and William Gwinn Mather Fund, Elizabeth Ring
Mather Charitable Trust, S. Livingston
Mauger Insurance Co.
May Department Stores Co.
Mayerson Foundation, Manuel D. and Rhoda
Maytag Corp.
McAlonan Trust, John A.
McDermott
McDonald & Co. Securities
McDonnell Douglas Corp.
McFawn Trust No. 2, Lois Sisler
McIntire Educational Fund, John
McMaster Foundation, Harold and Helen
McWane Inc.
Mead Corp.
Mead Fund, Nelson
Mellen Foundation
Mellon Bank Corp.
Mellon PSFS

Menasha Corp.
Messenger Publishing Co.
Midland Co.
Midland Mutual Life Insurance Co.
Midmark Corp.
Mill-Rose Co.
Miller Brewing Company/Ohio
Miller Charitable Trust, Lewis N.
Miller Memorial Trust, George Lee
Milliken & Co.
Miniger Memorial Foundation, Clement O.
Minster Machine Co.
Mirapaul Foundation
Monarch Machine Tool Co.
Monsanto Co.
Montgomery Foundation
Mooney Chemicals
Moores Foundation, Harry C.
Mor-Flo Industries, Inc.
Morgan Foundation, Burton D.
Morrison-Knudsen Corp.
Morton International
Mosinee Paper Corp.
Motch Corp.
Multimedia, Inc.
Murch Foundation
Murphy Foundation, John P.
Musson Charitable Foundation, R. C. and Katharine M.
NACCO Industries
Nason Foundation
National City Bank, Columbus
National City Corp.
National Gypsum Co.
National Machinery Co.
National Medical Enterprises
Nationwide Insurance Cos.
NCR Corp.
New Orphan Asylum Scholarship Foundation
Newmont Mining Corp.
Newport News Shipbuilding & Dry Dock Co.
Nord Family Foundation
Nordson Corp.
North American Coal Corp.
North American Philips Corp.
Norton Co.
Norwest Corp.
NuTone Inc.
O'Bleness Foundation, Charles G.
Oglebay Norton Co.
Ohio Bell Telephone Co.
Ohio Casualty Corp.
Ohio Citizens Bank
Ohio Edison Corp.
Ohio National Life Insurance Co.
Ohio Road Paving Co.
Ohio Savings Bank
Ohio Valley Foundation
Olin Corp.
1525 Foundation
O'Neil Foundation, M. G.
O'Neill Charitable Corporation, F. J.
O'Neill Foundation, William J. and Dorothy K.
Ormet Corp.
Osborn Manufacturing Co.
OsCo. Industries
Outokumpu-American Brass Co.
Owens-Corning Fiberglas Corp.
Owens-Illinois
PACCAR
Palm Beach Co.
Paramount Communications Inc.
Park National Bank
Park-Ohio Industries Inc.
Parker-Hannifin Corp.
Paulstan
Paxton Co., Frank
Penn Central Corp.
Perkins Charitable Foundation

Peterloon Foundation
Philip Morris Cos.
Philips Foundation, Jesse
Picker International
Pioneer Hi-Bred International
Pitney Bowes
Pittway Corp.
PMI Food Equipment Group Inc.
Pollock Company Foundation,
William B.
Ponderosa, Inc.
Powell Co., William
Powers Higher Educational
Fund, Edward W. and Alice R.
PPG Industries
Preformed Line Products Co.
Premier Industrial Corp.
Prentiss Foundation, Elisabeth
Severance
Procter & Gamble Co.
Progressive Corp.
Prudential Insurance Co. of
America
Ralston Purina Co.
Ranco, Inc.
Ranney Foundation, P. K.
Ransburg Corp.
RB&W Corp.
Reeves Foundation
Reinberger Foundation
Reliance Electric Co.
Renner Foundation
Republic Engineered Steels
Rexham Inc.
Reynolds & Reynolds Co.
Rice Foundation, Helen Steiner
Rich Products Corp.
Riser Foods
Ritchie Memorial Foundation,
Charles E. and Mabel M.
Ritter Charitable Trust, George
W. & Mary F.
Roadway Services, Inc.
Robbins & Myers, Inc.
Robertshaw Controls Co.
Rockwell International Corp.
Rolls-Royce Inc.
Rosenthal Foundation, Samuel
Ross Corp.
Ross Laboratories
Rotterman Trust, Helen L. and
Marie F.
Rouse Co.
RPM, Inc.
Rubbermaid
Rupp Foundation, Fran and
Warren
Russell Charitable Trust,
Josephine S.
Ryder System
SAFECO Corp.
Saint Gerard Foundation
Saint Paul Cos.
Sandoz Corp.
Sandusky International Inc.
Sapirstein-Stone-Weiss
Foundation
Sara Lee Corp.
Schermer Charitable Trust,
Frances
Schey Foundation
Schiff Foundation, John J. and
Mary R.
Schlink Foundation, Albert G.
and Olive H.
Schmidlapp Trust No. 1, Jacob G.
Schmidlapp Trust No. 2, Jacob G.
Schottenstein Foundation,
Jerome & Saul
Schottenstein Stores Corp.
Schulman Inc., A.
Scott and Fetzer Co.
Scripps Co., E.W.
Seagram & Sons, Joseph E.
Sealy, Inc.
Sears Family Foundation

Seasongood Good Government
Foundation, Murray and Agnes
Seaway Food Town
Second Foundation
Semple Foundation, Louise Taft
Seton Co.
Shafer Foundation, Richard H.
and Ann
Sheadle Trust, Jasper H.
Shell Oil Co.
Sherwin-Williams Co.
Shinnick Educational Fund,
William M.
Siebe North Inc.
Sifco Industries Inc.
Simpson Industries
SKF USA, Inc.
Sky Chefs, Inc.
Slemp Foundation
Smith Charitable Fund, Eleanor
Armstrong
Smith Corp., A.O.
Smith Foundation, Kelvin and
Eleanor
Smith, Jr. Charitable Trust, Jack
J.
Smith 1980 Charitable Trust,
Kelvin
Smucker Co., J.M.
Smucker Co., J.M.
Society Corp.
South Waite Foundation
South-Western Publishing Co.
Spectra-Physics Analytical
Sprint
Sprint United Telephone
SPX Corp.
Square D Co.
Standard Products Co.
Standard Register Co.
Standard Textile Co., Inc.
Stanley Works
Star Bank, N.A.
State Farm Mutual Automobile
Insurance Co.
Sterkel Trust, Justine
Sterling Inc.
Stocker Foundation
Stone Container Corp.
Stone Foundation, France
Stranahan Foundation
Sudbury Inc.
Sun Chemical Corp.
Sun Co.
Sundstrand Corp.
Super Food Services
Super Valu Stores
Superior's Brand Meats
Switzer Foundation
Tait Foundation, Frank M.
Talley Industries, Inc.
Tamarkin Co.
Tandem Computers
Target Stores
Tele-Communications, Inc.
Teledyne
Teleflex Inc.
Tenneco
Textron
Thendara Foundation
Thor Industries, Inc.
3M Co.
Timken Co.
Timken Foundation of Canton
Tippit Charitable Trust, C.
Carlisle and Margaret M.
Toledo Edison Co.
Tomkins Industries, Inc.
TransOhio Savings Bank
Tranzonic Cos.
Travelers Cos.
Tremco Inc.
Treuhaft Foundation
TRINOVA Corp.
True Trust, Henry A.
Trustcorp, Inc.
TRW Corp.

Turner Charitable Foundation,
Harry and Violet
Turner Corp.
Union Camp Corp.
Union Carbide Corp.
Union Central Life Insurance Co.
United Dominion Industries
US Shoe Corp.
USG Corp.
USX Corp.
V and V Foundation
Value City Furniture
Van Huffel Foundation, I. J.
Van Wert County Foundation
Volkswagen of America, Inc.
W. L. T.
Wagnalls Memorial
Wal-Mart Stores
Walgreen Co.
Watson Foundation, Walter E.
and Caroline H.
Wayne Steel Inc.
Wean Foundation, Raymond John
Weatherhead Foundation
Weiss Fund, Clara
Wellman Foundation, S. K.
Wendy's International, Inc.
Western Southern Life Insurance
Co.
Westinghouse Electric Corp.
Wexner Foundation
Weyerhaeuser Co.
Wheeling-Pittsburgh Corp.
Whirlpool Corp.
White Castle System
White Consolidated Industries
Wildermuth Foundation, E. F.
Wilkof Foundation, Edward and
Ruth
Williamson Co.
Wodecroft Foundation
Women's Project Foundation
Worthington Industries, Inc.
XTEK Inc.
Yale Security Inc.
Yassenoff Foundation, Leo
Young Foundation, Hugo H. and
Mabel B.
Zonas Trust, Steven K.

Oklahoma

Air Products & Chemicals
Akzo America
Allegheny Ludlum Corp.
Altec Lansing Corp.
Amerada Hess Corp.
American Fidelity Corp.
American Financial Corp.
American National Insurance
Anadarko Petroleum Corp.
Anheuser-Busch Cos.
Anthony Co., C.R.
AON Corp.
Apache Corp.
ARA Services
Archer-Daniels-Midland Co.
ARCO
Arkla
Armco Inc.
Arrow Electronics, Inc.
Arvin Industries
Avnet, Inc.
Badger Meter, Inc.
Baker Hughes Inc.
Ball Corp.
Bank of Oklahoma, N.A.
Baxter International
Beatty Trust, Cordelia Lunceford
Belo Corp., A.H.
Bergen Brunswig Corp.
Bernsen Foundation, Grace and
Franklin
Black & Decker Corp.
Blount
Boatmen's Bancshares

Boatmen's First National Bank
of Oklahoma
Borg-Warner Corp.
Bovaird Foundation, Mervin
Brand Foundation, C. Harold and
Constance
Bridgestone/Firestone
Broadhurst Foundation
Brunswick Corp.
Burlington Northern Inc.
Campbell Foundation
Castle & Co., A.M.
CBI Industries
Central & South West Services
Chapman Charitable Trust, H. A.
and Mary K.
Chevron Corp.
Chrysler Corp.
Circuit City Stores
Collins & Aikman Corp.
Collins Foundation, George and
Jennie
Collins, Jr. Foundation, George
Fulton
Cooper Industries
Cox Enterprises
CR Industries
Crum and Forster
Cuesta Foundation
Dayton Hudson Corp.
Deluxe Corp.
Dollar General Corp.
Dover Corp.
du Pont de Nemours & Co., E. I.
Durr-Fillauer Medical
Eagle-Picher Industries
Eaton Corp.
Eckerd Corp., Jack
EG&G Inc.
Elf Atochem North America
First Interstate Bank & Trust Co.
First Mississippi Corp.
Fleming Companies, Inc.
Foxmeyer Corp.
Gannett Co.
Georgia-Pacific Corp.
Goddard Foundation, Charles B.
Goodyear Tire & Rubber Co.
Goulds Pumps
Grace Petroleum Corp.
Grimes Foundation, Otha H.
Gussman Foundation, Herbert
and Roseline
Hadson Corp.
Halliburton Co.
Handy & Harman
Hanson Office Products
Harmon Foundation, Pearl M.
and Julia J.
Harris Foundation
Harsco Corp.
Helmerich Foundation
Helmerich & Payne Inc.
Home Depot
Hospital Corp. of America
Ingersoll-Rand Co.
Inland Steel Industries
ITT Corp.
ITT Hartford Insurance Group
Johnson Controls
Johnson Educational and
Benevolent Trust, Dexter G.
Johnson & Higgins
Jones Foundation, Montfort
Jones and Allie Brown
Kaiser Foundation, Betty E. and
George B.
Kerr Foundation
Kerr Foundation, Robert S. and
Grayce B.
Kerr-McGee Corp.
Kimberly-Clark Corp.
Kirkpatrick Foundation
Kirkpatrick Oil Co.
Liberty Glass Co.
Louisiana Land & Exploration
Co.

Lyon Foundation
Mabee Foundation, J. E. and L.
E.
Manufacturers Life Insurance
Co. of America
Mapco Inc.
Mark Controls Corp.
Mark IV Industries
McCasland Foundation
McDonnell Douglas Corp.
McDonnell Douglas Corp.-West
McGee Foundation
McMahon Foundation
Mead Corp.
Memorex Telex Corp.
Merck & Co.
Merrick Foundation
National Medical Enterprises
Newmont Mining Corp.
Noble Affiliates, Inc.
Noble Foundation, Samuel
Roberts
Noble Foundation, Vivian Bilby
Northrop Corp.
Norwest Corp.
Occidental Oil & Gas Corp.
Oklahoma Gas & Electric Co.
Oklahoman Foundation
ONEOK Inc.
Owens-Corning Fiberglas Corp.
PACCAR
Parker Drilling Co.
Parman Foundation, Robert A.
Paxton Co., Frank
Penn Central Corp.
Pet
Phillips Petroleum Co.
Phoenix Resource Cos.
Prudential Insurance Co. of
America
Public Service Co. of Oklahoma
Puterbaugh Foundation
Quaker Chemical Corp.
Rapp Foundation, Robert Glenn
Revlon
Reynolds & Reynolds Co.
Royal Group Inc.
Santa Fe International Corp.
Santa Fe Pacific Corp.
Sarkeys Foundation
Scripps Co., E.W.
Scrivner, Inc.
SECO
Sequa Corp.
Shaklee Corp.
Share Trust, Charles Morton
Smith International
Sooner Pipe & Supply Corp.
Southwestern Bell Corp.
State Farm Mutual Automobile
Insurance Co.
Stauffer Communications
Stone Container Corp.
Sun Co.
Tandem Computers
Target Stores
Taubman Foundation, Herman P.
and Sophia
Tenneco
Texaco
3M Co.
Titus Foundation, C. W.
Torchmark Corp.
Trans-Apex
Travelers Cos.
28:19
Union Equity Division of
Farmland Industries
Union Pacific Corp.
USG Corp.
Wal-Mart Stores
Warren Charite
Warren Foundation, William K.
Wegener Foundation, Herman
and Mary
Western Resources
WestStar Bank N.A.

Oklahoma (cont.)

Weyerhaeuser Co.
Williams Cos.
Winn-Dixie Stores
Witco Corp.
Wood Charitable Trust, W. P.
Young Foundation, R. A.
Zarrow Foundation, Anne and Henry
Zebco/Motorguide Corp.
Zink Foundation, John Steele

Oregon

Agway
Air Products & Chemicals
Albertson's
Alco Standard Corp.
Alltel/Western Region
ALPAC Corp.
Alumax
Amalgamated Sugar Co.
AMAX
America West Airlines
Ameron, Inc.
AON Corp.
Archer-Daniels-Midland Co.
ARCO
Armco Inc.
Arrow Electronics, Inc.
Autzen Foundation
Avnet, Inc.
Baxter International
Bell Industries
Bend Millwork Systems
Bergen Brunswig Corp.
Berwind Corp.
Best Products Co.
Bird Inc.
Blount
Boeing Co.
Bohemia Inc.
Boise Cascade Corp.
Browning-Ferris Industries
Burlington Northern Inc.
Cadence Design Systems
Capital Cities/ABC
Carpenter Foundation
Caterpillar
Chevron Corp.
Chiles Foundation
Chrysler Corp.
Chubb Corp.
CIBA-GEIGY Corp.
Citicorp
Clark Foundation
Clemens Foundation
Clorox Co.
Coachmen Industries
Collins Foundation
Collins-McDonald Trust Fund
Collins Medical Trust
Commercial Bank
Computer Associates International
Consolidated Freightways
Corroon & Black of Oregon
Corvallis Clinic
Country Cos.
Crestar Food Products, Inc.
Curtice-Burns Foods
Dayton Hudson Corp.
Deluxe Corp.
Donnelley & Sons Co., R.R.
Dow Corning Corp.
Eaton Corp.
Elf Atochem North America
Failing Fund, Henry
First Interstate Bank NW Region
First Interstate Bank of Oregon
Fohs Foundation
Ford Foundation, Kenneth W.
Forest City Enterprises
Frank Family Foundation, A. J.
Frank Lumber Co.
Freightliner Corp.

Friendly Rosenthal Foundation
Fuller Co., H.B.
Gannett Co.
GATX Corp.
General Accident Insurance Co. of America
Georgia-Pacific Corp.
Gunderson Trust, Helen Paulson
Heileman Brewing Co., Inc., G.
Hercules Inc.
Hewlett-Packard Co.
Higgins Charitable Trust, Lorene Sails
Hunt Charitable Trust, C. Giles
Hyster-Yale
Intel Corp.
International Flavors & Fragrances
International Paper Co.
Jackson Foundation
James River Corp. of Virginia
Jantzen, Inc.
Jefferson Smurfit Corp.
JELD-WEN, Inc.
Johnson Controls
Johnson & Higgins
Kelley Family Foundation Trust, Lora L. and Martin N.
Key Bank of Oregon
Land O'Lakes
Lee Enterprises
Litton Industries
Louisiana-Pacific Corp.
Manufacturers Life Insurance Co. of America
Manville Corp.
May Department Stores Co.
Mead Corp.
Medford Corp.
Menasha Corp.
Mentor Graphics
Merlo Foundation, Harry A.
Meyer, Inc., Fred
Meyer Memorial Trust
Miller Brewing Co.
NACCO Industries
Nationwide Insurance Cos.
Nerco, Inc.
Nike Inc.
Nortek, Inc.
Northwest Natural Gas Co.
Northwest Publishing Co. — Portland
OCRI Foundation
Ore-Ida Foods, Inc.
Oregon Cutting Systems
Oregon Mutual Insurance Co.
Orion Capital Corp.
OSF International, Inc.
Owens-Corning Fiberglas Corp.
Pacific Enterprises
PacifiCorp
Parker-Hannifin Corp.
PayLess Drug Stores
Pennsylvania General Insurance Co.
Peterson Memorial Fund, Chris and Mary L.
Philip Morris Cos.
Pioneer Trust Bank, NA
Pope & Talbot, Inc.
Portland Food Products Co.
Portland General Electric Co.
Precision Castparts Corp.
Reebok International Ltd.
REI-Recreational Equipment, Inc.
Reynolds Metals Co.
Rhone-Poulenc Inc.
Roseburg Forest Products Co.
SAFECO Corp.
Saint Paul Cos.
Sara Lee Corp.
Schlumberger Ltd.
Scripps Co., E.W.
Simpson Investment Co.
Skinner Corp.

Smucker Co., J.M.
Southland Corp.
Spectra-Physics Analytical
Sprint
Stanley Works
State Farm Mutual Automobile Insurance Co.
Steiner Corp.
Stone Container Corp.
Sunshine Biscuits
Super Valu Stores
Target Stores
Tektronix
Teledyne
Templeton Foundation, Herbert A.
3M Co.
Times Mirror Co.
Travelers Cos.
TRINOVA Corp.
Tucker Charitable Trust, Rose E.
Union Pacific Corp.
United Grocers, Inc.
US Bancorp
US WEST
Volkswagen of America, Inc.
Washington Mutual Savings Bank
Wessinger Foundation
West One Bancorp
Wetterau
Weyerhaeuser Co.
Wheeler Foundation
Willamette Industries, Inc.
Witco Corp.
Woodard Family Foundation
Wyss Foundation

Pennsylvania

Acme Markets
Action Industries, Inc.
AEGON USA, Inc.
Affiliated Publications, Inc.
AGFA Division of Miles Inc.
Agway
Air France
Air Products & Chemicals
Akzo America
Akzo Chemicals Inc.
Akzo Salt Co.
Alco Standard Corp.
Alexander & Alexander Services, Inc.
Allegheny Foundation
Allegheny Ludlum Corp.
Allegheny Power System, Inc.
AlliedSignal
Alumax
Aluminum Co. of America
AMAX
Amcast Industrial Corp.
American Brands
American Home Products Corp.
American Natural Resources Co.
American Standard
American Stores Co.
American Telephone & Telegraph Co.
Amerigas
Ames Charitable Trust, Harriett
Ames Department Stores
AMETEK
AMP
Amsco International
Annenberg Foundation
AON Corp.
Appleton Papers
ARA Services
Arcadia Foundation
Arcata Corp.
Arcata Graphics Co.
ARCO Chemical
Aristech Chemical Corp.
Armco Inc.
Armstrong World Industries Inc.
Arronson Foundation

Asea Brown Boveri
Asplundh Foundation
Avery Dennison Corp.
Avis Inc.
Avnet, Inc.
Aydin Corp.
Baker Foundation, Dexter F. and Dorothy H.
Ball Corp.
Bank Hapoalim B.M.
Bank Leumi Trust Co. of New York
BankAmerica Corp.
Barnes Group
Barnes & Roche
Barra Foundation
Bartol Foundation, Stockton Rush
Bausch & Lomb
Baxter International
Becton Dickinson & Co.
Bell Atlantic Corp.
Bemis Company
Benedum Foundation, Claude Worthington
Beneficia Foundation
Berkman Charitable Trust, Allen H. and Selma W.
Berry Foundation, Archie W. and Grace
Berwind Corp.
Best Products Co.
Bethlehem Steel Corp.
Betts Industries
Betz Foundation Trust, Theodora B.
Betz Laboratories
Billy Penn Corp
Binney & Smith Inc.
Binswanger Co.
Bishop Foundation, Vernon and Doris
Blair Corp.
Blount
Boeing Co.
Boise Cascade Corp.
Borden
Borg-Warner Corp.
Bozzone Family Foundation
BP America
Brodart Co.
Bronstein Foundation, Soloman and Sylvia
Brown & Sons, Alex
Brown & Williamson Tobacco Corp.
Browning-Ferris Industries
Brush Wellman Inc.
Bryn Mawr Trust Co.
Budd Co.
Buhl Foundation
Burndy Corp.
Burron Medical
C.P. Rail Systems
Cabot Corp.
Caesar's World, Inc.
Calgon Corp.
Campbell Foundation, Charles Talbot
Campbell Soup Co.
Capital Cities/ABC
Capital Holding Corp.
Caplan Charity Foundation, Julius H.
Cardinal Industries
Carpenter Foundation, E. Rhodes and Leona B.
Carpenter Technology Corp.
Carthage Foundation
Cassett Foundation, Louis N.
Castle & Co., A.M.
Caterpillar
Cawsl Corp.
CBS Inc.
CertainTeed Corp.

Chambers Development Co. Charitable Fund
Charter Medical Corp.
Chesapeake Corp.
Chevron Corp.
Chrysler Corp.
CIGNA Corp.
Circuit City Stores
Citicorp
Claneil Foundation
Clapp Charitable and Educational Trust, George H.
CLARCOR
Clorox Co.
Coachmen Industries
Coastal Corp.
Coen Family Foundation, Charles S. and Mary
Colket Foundation, Ethel D.
Colonial Penn Group, Inc.
Coltec Industries
Comcast Corp.
Commodore International Ltd.
Computer Associates International
ConAgra
Conair, Inc.
Connelly Foundation
Consol Energy Inc.
Consolidated Natural Gas Co.
Consolidated Rail Corp. (Conrail)
Conston Corp.
Continental Bancorp, Inc.
Contraves USA
Control Data Corp.
Cookson America
Cooper Industries
Copernicus Society of America
Copperweld Corp.
Corestates Bank
Corning Incorporated
Cowles Media Co.
Cox Enterprises
CPC International
Crane & Co.
Crane Co.
Crawford Estate, E. R.
Crels Foundation
Crompton & Knowles Corp.
Crown Cork & Seal Co., Inc.
Culbro Corp.
Curtice-Burns Foods
Cyprus Minerals Co.
Dalsimer Fund, Craig
Dana Corp.
Dauphin Deposit Corp.
Decision Data Computer Corp.
Deluxe Corp.
DeMoss Foundation, Arthur S.
Dentsply International, Inc.
Development Dimensions International
Diamond State Telephone Co.
Dick Corp.
Dietrich Foundation, William B.
Dollar General Corp.
Donnelley & Sons Co., R.R.
Donnelly Foundation, Mary J.
Douty Foundation
Dow Jones & Co.
Dresser Industries
Driscoll Co., L.F.
du Pont de Nemours & Co., E. I.
Dun & Bradstreet Corp.
Duquesne Light Co.
Dynamet, Inc.
Eagle-Picher Industries
Eastern Foundry Co.
Eberly Foundation
Eccles Foundation, Ralph M. and Ella M.
Eden Hall Foundation
Edgewater Steel Corp.
Educators Mutual Life Insurance Co.
EG&G Inc.
Elf Atochem North America

Ellis Grant and Scholarship Fund, Charles E.
Emergency Aid of Pennsylvania Foundation
Emerson Electric Co.
EMI Records Group
Equimark Corp.
Equitable Resources
Fabri-Kal Corp.
Fair Oaks Foundation, Inc.
Falk Medical Fund, Maurice
Farley Industries
Federal-Mogul Corp.
Federal National Mortgage Assn., Fannie Mae
Federation Foundation of Greater Philadelphia
Feinstein Foundation, Myer and Rosaline
Fels Fund, Samuel S.
Female Association of Philadelphia
Ferranti Tech
Ferro Corp.
Fiat U.S.A., Inc.
Fidelity Bank
Fidelity Mutual Life Insurance Co.
Fieldcrest Cannon
Finley Charitable Trust, J. B.
Firestone Foundation, Roger S.
First Fidelity Bancorporation
First Fidelity Bank
First Maryland Bancorp
First Mississippi Corp.
First Pennsylvania Bank NA
First Valley Bank
Fischer & Porter Co.
FKI Holdings Inc.
FMC Corp.
Foerderer Foundation, Percival E. and Ethel Brown
Foote, Cone & Belding Communications
Forest City Enterprises
Forest Oil Corp.
Foster Charitable Trust
Foster Co., L.B.
Fourjay Foundation
Fox Foundation, Richard J.
Franklin Mint Corp.
Freeport Brick Co.
Frick Educational Commission, Henry C.
Frick Foundation, Helen Clay
Gahagen Charitable Trust, Zella J.
Gannett Co.
Garrigues Trust, Edwin B.
GATX Corp.
GenCorp
General Accident Insurance Co. of America
General Electric Co.
General Machine Works
General Motors Corp.
General Reinsurance Corp.
Genesco
Georgia-Pacific Corp.
Gershman Foundation, Joel
Giant Eagle
Giant Food Stores
Gibson Foundation, Addison H.
Gilbert Associates, Inc.
Glatfelter Co., P.H.
Glencairn Foundation
Glenmede Trust Corp.
Glosser Foundation, David A.
Goldman Foundation, William
Goldman Sachs & Co.
Goodyear Tire & Rubber Co.
Goulds Pumps
Grable Foundation
Grass Family Foundation
Greenfield Foundation, Albert M.
Groome Beatty Trust, Helen D.
Gruen Marketing

Grumbacher Foundation, M. S.
Grumman Corp.
Grundy Foundation
Guardian Life Insurance Co. of America
Hall Charitable Trust, Evelyn A. J.
Hall Foundation
Halliburton Co.
Hallowell Foundation
Hambay Foundation, James T.
Hamilton Bank
Handy & Harman
Hanna Co., M.A.
Hanson Office Products
Harland Co., John H.
Harleysville Mutual Insurance Co.
HarperCollins Publishers
Harris Corp.
Harsco Corp.
Harte-Hanks Communications, Inc.
Hazen Charitable Trust, Lita Annenberg
Hechinger Co.
Heinz Co., H.J.
Heinz Endowment, Howard
Heinz Endowment, Vira I.
Heinz Family Foundation
Heinz Foundation, Drue
Henkel Corp.
Herr Foods
Hershey Entertainment & Resort Co.
Hershey Foods Corp.
Hewlett-Packard Co.
Hexcel Corp.
High Foundation
Hillman Co.
Hillman Foundation
Hillman Foundation, Henry L.
Holdeen Fund 55-10
Holdeen Fund 50-10
Holdeen Fund 45-10
HON Industries
Hooker Charitable Trust, Janet A.
Hooper Foundation, Elizabeth S.
Hopwood Charitable Trust, John M.
Houghton & Co., E.F.
Hoyt Foundation
Huffy Corp.
Hulme Charitable Foundation, Milton G.
Humana
Hunt Foundation
Hunt Foundation, Roy A.
Hunt Manufacturing Co.
Huston Charitable Trust, Stewart
Huston Foundation
ICI Americas
Illinois Tool Works
IMCERA Group Inc.
IMO Industries Inc.
IMS America Ltd.
Inco Alloys International
Independence Foundation
Ingersoll-Rand Co.
Inland Container Corp.
Inland Steel Industries
Institute for Bio-Information Research
Integra Bank
Integra Bank/South
International Paper Co.
ITT Corp.
ITT Hartford Insurance Group
ITT Rayonier
IU International
J. D. B. Fund
J&L Specialty Products Corp.
James River Corp. of Virginia
Janssen Foundation, Henry
JELD-WEN, Inc.
Jennings Foundation, Mary Hillman

Jessop Steel Co.
Jewish Healthcare Foundation of Pittsburgh
Johnson & Higgins
Johnson & Johnson
Johnson Matthey Investments
Jostens
Justus Trust, Edith C.
Kaman Corp.
Kavanagh Foundation, T. James
Keebler Co.
Kelley Foundation, Kate M.
Kellmer Co., Jack
Kellogg's
Kennametal
Ketchum Communications
Keystone Weaving Mills
Klein Charitable Foundation, Raymond
Kline Foundation, Charles and Figa
Kline Foundation, Josiah W. and Bessie H.
Kloeckner-Pentaplast of America
Knight-Ridder, Inc.
Knudsen Charitable Foundation, Earl
Korman Family Foundation, Hyman
Kraft General Foods
Kulicke & Soffa Industries
Kunkel Foundation, John Crain
Kynett Memorial Foundation, Edna G.
Lafarge Corp.
LamCo. Communications
Lamson & Sessions Co.
Lancaster Newspapers
Laros Foundation, R. K.
Laurel Foundation
Lebanon Mutual Insurance Co.
Lebovitz Fund
Lehigh Portland Cement Co.
Lesher Foundation, Margaret and Irvin
Levee Charitable Trust, Polly Annenberg
Levitt Foundation
Lionel Corp.
Lipton, Thomas J.
Litton Industries
Lockhart Iron & Steel Co.
Loews Corp.
Lord Corp.
Love Foundation, George H. and Margaret McClintic
LTV Corp.
Ludwick Institute
Lukens
Mack Foundation, J. S.
Magee Carpet Co.
Mallinckrodt Specialty Chemicals Co.
Mandell Foundation, Samuel P.
Manufacturers Life Insurance Co. of America
Manville Corp.
Maryland Casualty Co.
Masco Corp.
Masland & Sons, C.H.
Massey Charitable Trust
Matthews International Corp.
May Department Stores Co.
McCormick Trust, Anne
McCrory Corp.
McCune Charitable Trust, John R.
McCune Foundation
McDonnell Douglas Corp.-West
McFeely-Rogers Foundation
McGraw-Hill
McKaig Foundation, Lalitta Nash
McKee Poor Fund, Virginia A.
McKenna Foundation, Katherine Mabis
McKenna Foundation, Philip M.
McKesson Corp.

McLean Contributionship
McMannis and A. Haskell McMannis Educational Fund, William J.
McNeil Consumer Products
McNeil, Jr. Charitable Trust, Robert L.
McShain Charities, John
Mead Corp.
Measey Foundation, Benjamin and Mary Siddons
Mellon Bank Corp.
Mellon Foundation, Richard King
Mellon PSFS
Mellon Stuart Construction Inc.
Menasha Corp.
Mengle Foundation, Glenn and Ruth
Merck & Co.
Merck Human Health Division
Meridian Bancorp
Merit Oil Corp.
Meritor Financial Group
Metal Industries
Michaels Scholarship Fund, Frank J.
Miles Inc.
Miller Charitable Foundation, Howard E. and Nell E.
Miller & Co.
Millstein Charitable Foundation
Mine Safety Appliances Co.
MNC Financial
Morris Charitable Trust, Charles M.
Morrison-Knudsen Corp.
Morton International
Motter Printing Press Co.
Muller Foundation, C. John and Josephine
Murphy Co., G.C.
National Computer Systems
National Forge Co.
National Medical Enterprises
National Steel
Nationwide Insurance Cos.
Neville Chemical Co.
New Penn Motor Express
New York Times Co.
Newport News Shipbuilding & Dry Dock Co.
News America Publishing Inc.
Norton Co.
Norton & Co., W.W.
Norwest Corp.
Novotny Charitable Trust, Yetta Deitch
Nutri/System Inc.
Oakite Products
Oberkotter Family Foundation
Oberlaender Foundation, Gustav
Ohio Edison Corp.
Olin Corp.
Olivetti Office USA, Inc.
1957 Charity Trust
Orange & Rockland Utilities, Inc.
Ortho-McNeil Pharmaceutical
Outokumpu-American Brass Co.
Owens-Corning Fiberglas Corp.
Oxford Foundation
Packer Foundation, Horace B.
Paley Foundation, Goldie
Park-Ohio Industries Inc.
Patterson Charitable Fund, W. I.
Penn Foundation, William
Penn Industrial Chemical Corp.
Penn Mutual Life Insurance Co.
Penn Savings Bank, a division of Sovereign Bank Bank of Princeton, a division of Sovereign Bank
Penn Traffic Co.
Pennbank
Pennsylvania Dutch Co.
Pennsylvania General Insurance Co.
Pennsylvania Knitted Outerwear Manufacturing Association

Pennsylvania Power & Light
Pennzoil Co.
Pep Boys
Pet
Peters Foundation, Charles F.
Pew Charitable Trusts
Philadelphia Electric Co.
Philadelphia Industries
Philip Morris Cos.
Phillips Charitable Trust, Dr. and Mrs. Arthur William
Phillips-Van Heusen Corp.
Picker International
Piedmont Health Care Foundation
Pilgrim Industries
Pine Tree Foundation
Pioneer Hi-Bred International
Piper Foundation
Pitt-Des Moines Inc.
Pittsburgh Child Guidance Foundation
Pittsburgh National Bank
Plankenhorn Foundation, Harry
PMA Industries
PNC Bank
PNC Bank
Polk Foundation
Pottstown Mercury
PPG Industries
PQ Corp.
Premier Dental Products Co.
Presser Foundation
Procter & Gamble Co.
Provident Mutual Life Insurance Co. of Philadelphia
Prudential Insurance Co. of America
Pulitzer Publishing Co.
Quaker Chemical Corp.
Quaker Oats Co.
Quaker State Corp.
Ransburg Corp.
Raymark Corp.
Raytheon Engineers & Constructors
RB&W Corp.
Reedman Car-Truck World Center
REI-Recreational Equipment, Inc.
Reidler Foundation
Reliance Insurance Cos.
Rhone-Poulenc Rorer
Rider-Pool Foundation
Rite Aid Corp.
Rittenhouse Foundation
Roadway Services, Inc.
Rochester & Pittsburgh Coal Co.
Rochester Telephone Corp.
Rock Foundation, Milton and Shirley
Rockwell Foundation
Rockwell International Corp.
Rodale Press
Rohm and Haas Company
Rosenberg Foundation, Alexis
Rosenbluth Travel Agency
Roth Foundation
Rouse Co.
Ruddick Corp.
Rudy, Jr. Trust, George B.
Rust International Corp.
Safeguard Scientifics Foundation
St. Mary's Catholic Foundation
Saint Paul Cos.
Sanyo Audio Manufacturing (U.S.A.) Corp.
Sara Lee Corp.
Sargent Electric Co.
Scaife Family Foundation
Scaife Foundation, Sarah
Schautz Foundation, Walter L.
Schlumberger Ltd.
Schmidt & Sons, C.
Scholler Foundation

Pennsylvania (cont.)

Schoonmaker J-Sewkly Valley Hospital Trust
Schwartz and Robert Schwartz Foundation, Bernard
Scott Paper Co.
Scripps Co., E.W.
Sealy, Inc.
SECO
Sequa Corp.
Servistar Corp.
Seton Co.
Seybert Institution for Poor Boys and Girls, Adam and Maria Sarah
Shaffer Family Charitable Trust
Shared Medical Systems Corp.
Sharon Steel Corp.
Sheppard Foundation, Lawrence B.
Shoemaker Co., R.M.
Shoemaker Fund, Thomas H. and Mary Williams
Shoemaker Trust for Shoemaker Scholarship Fund, Ray S.
Shore Fund
Shuster Memorial Trust, Herman
SICO Foundation
Siebe North Inc.
Simmons Family Foundation, R. P.
Simon Charitable Trust, Esther
Simpson Investment Co.
SKF USA, Inc.
Smith Charitable Trust, W. W.
Smith Foundation
Smith Golden Rule Trust Fund, Fred G.
Smith Memorial Fund, Ethel Sergeant Clark
SmithKline Beecham
Smucker Co., J.M.
Snayberger Memorial Foundation, Harry E. and Florence W.
Snee-Reinhardt Charitable Foundation
Snider Foundation
Snyder Charitable Fund, W. P.
Sordoni Enterprises
Sordoni Foundation
Southland Corp.
Spang & Co.
Speyer Foundation, Alexander C. and Tillie S.
Spiegel
Springs Industries
Sprint
SPS Technologies
Stabler Cos., Inc.
Stabler Foundation, Donald B. and Dorothy L.
Stackpole-Hall Foundation
Standard Register Co.
Standard Steel Speciality Co.
Stanley Works
State Farm Mutual Automobile Insurance Co.
Staunton Farm Foundation
Stein Foundation, Louis
Steinman Foundation, James Hale
Steinman Foundation, John Frederick
Steinsapir Family Foundation, Julius L. and Libhie B.
Sterling Winthrop
Stern Family Foundation, Harry
Stewart Alexander Foundation
Stokes Foundation, Lydia B.
Stone Container Corp.
Stott Foundation, Louis L.
Strauss Foundation
Strawbridge & Clothier
Strawbridge Foundation of Pennsylvania I, Margaret Dorrance

Strawbridge Foundation of Pennsylvania II, Margaret Dorrance
Stroehmann Bakeries
Stroud Foundation
Strouse, Greenberg & Co.
Sun Co.
Sunbeam-Oster
Super Valu Stores
Superior Tube Co.
Susquehanna Investment Group
Susquehanna-Pfaltzgraff Co.
Tamarkin Co.
Tandem Computers
Tasty Baking Co.
Teledyne
Teleflex Inc.
Tenneco
Tetley, Inc.
Textron
3M Co.
Thrift Drug, Inc.
Thyssen Specialty Steels
Tidewater, Inc.
Times Mirror Co.
Tippens Foundation
Tokheim Corp.
Tomkins Industries, Inc.
Transco Energy Company
Transtar Inc.
Travelers Cos.
Trees Charitable Trust, Edith L.
Trexler Trust, Harry C.
TRINOVA Corp.
Turner Corp.
Twentieth Century-Fox Film Corp.
UGI Corp.
UJB Financial Corp.
Uniform Tubes, Inc.
Union Camp Corp.
Union Carbide Corp.
Union Pacific Corp.
Unisys Corp.
United Merchants & Manufacturers
United Refining Co
United Service Foundation
U.S. Healthcare, Inc.
United Telephone System (Eastern Group)
Universal Health Services, Inc.
Universal Leaf Tobacco Co.
USLIFE Corp.
USX Corp.
Valley Bancorp
Valspar Corp.
Vanguard Group of Investment Cos.
Vesper Corp.
Vesuvius Charitable Foundation
VF Corp.
Victaulic Co. of America
Vincent Trust, Anna M.
Waldorf Educational Foundation
Walker Educational and Charitable Foundation, Alex C.
Wardle Family Foundation
Warwick Foundation
Washington Post Co.
Waters Charitable Trust, Robert S.
Weisbrod Foundation Trust Dept., Robert and Mary
Wells Foundation, Franklin H. and Ruth L.
West Co.
Westinghouse Electric Corp.
Westmoreland Coal Co.
Westvaco Corp.
Wetterau
Weyerhaeuser Co.
Whalley Charitable Trust
Whitaker Foundation
Whitaker Fund, Helen F.
White Consolidated Industries

Williams Charitable Trust, John C.
Williams Foundation, C. K.
Witco Corp.
Wolf Foundation, Benjamin and Fredora K.
Wolverine World Wide, Inc.
Wood Foundation of Chambersburg, PA
Worthington Industries, Inc.
Wurts Memorial, Henrietta Tower
WWF Paper Corp.
Wyomissing Foundation
Xerox Corp.
York Barbell Co.
York International Corp.
Zippo Manufacturing Co.
Zurn Industries

Puerto Rico

Abbott Laboratories
Acme-Cleveland Corp.
American Bankers Insurance Group
American Home Products Corp.
ARA Services
Arrow Electronics, Inc.
Avon Products
Bacardi Imports
Becton Dickinson & Co.
Bristol-Myers Squibb Co.
Browning-Ferris Industries
Chesebrough-Pond's
CPC International
Cross Co., A.T.
Echlin Inc.
Fairchild Corp.
Foote, Cone & Belding Communications
Gerber Products Co.
Harland Co., John H.
Loctite Corp.
Medtronic
Pall Corp.
Phillips Petroleum Co.
Ransburg Corp.
RJR Nabisco Inc.
Schering-Plough Corp.
Sealy, Inc.
Storage Technology Corp.
Texaco
Unilever United States
Warner-Lambert Co.
Wolverine World Wide, Inc.
Zacharia Foundation, Isaac Herman

Rhode Island

Allendale Mutual Insurance Co.
AlliedSignal
Almac's, Inc.
Alperin/Hirsch Family Foundation
Ann & Hope
Armbrust Chain Co.
Armco Inc.
Attleboro Pawtucket Savings Bank
Avnet, Inc.
Bafflin Foundation
Bairnco Corp.
Ballou & Co., B.A.
Bank of Boston Connecticut
Bank of Boston Corp.
Bard, C. R.
Baxter International
Brown Inc., John
Brown & Sharpe Manufacturing Co.
Capital Cities/ABC
Carol Cable Co.
Champlin Foundations
Citizens Bank
Clarke Trust, John
Cookson America
Cox Enterprises

CPC International
Cranston Print Works
Cross Co., A.T.
DeBlois Oil Co.
Dimeo Construction Co.
Eastland Bank
EG&G Inc.
ETCO Inc.
Fleet Bank
Fleet Financial Group
Ford Foundation, Edward E.
Galkin Charitable Trust, Ira S. and Anna
General Dynamics Corp.
General Housewares Corp.
Genesis Foundation
Gilbane Building Co.
Gilbane Foundation, Thomas and William
Haffenreffer Family Fund
Hanson Office Products
Harris Corp.
Hasbro
Hassenfeld Foundation
Hillenbrand Industries
Hoechst Celanese Corp.
Home Depot
Jaffe Foundation
Johnstone and H. Earle Kimball Foundation, Phyllis Kimball
Kenney Manufacturing Co.
Kimball Foundation, Horace A. Kimball and S. Ella
Koffler Family Foundation
Leesona Corp.
Littlefield Memorial Trust, Ida Ballou
Mark IV Industries
Mine Safety Appliances Co.
New England Telephone Co.
New York Times Co.
Nortek, Inc.
North American Philips Corp.
Penn Central Corp.
Peoples Drug Stores Inc.
Providence Energy Corp.
Providence Journal Company
Quantum Chemical Corp.
Raytheon Co.
Reynolds Metals Co.
Rhode Island Hospital Trust National Bank
Shawmut National Corp.
Shaw's Supermarkets
Siebe North Inc.
Stanley Works
Sunbeam-Oster
Textron
Torchmark Corp.
Travelers Cos.
United Merchants & Manufacturers
Van Beuren Charitable Foundation
Volkswagen of America, Inc.
Watson Foundation, Thomas J.
Wetterau

South Carolina

Abney Foundation
Albany International Corp.
Alco Standard Corp.
Alice Manufacturing Co.
AlliedSignal
Alumax
AMAX
ARA Services
Archer-Daniels-Midland Co.
Arkwright Foundation
Armco Inc.
Armstrong World Industries Inc.
Arvin Industries
Atkinson Co., Guy F.
Avis Inc.
Avnet, Inc.
Bailey Foundation

Bailey & Son, Bankers, M.S.
Baker & Baker
Ball Corp.
Bank of Boston Corp.
Bannon Foundation
Bard, C. R.
Bausch & Lomb
Baxter International
Becton Dickinson & Co.
Belk Stores
Belk Stores
BellSouth Corp.
Bird Inc.
Black & Decker Corp.
Blount
Borden
Bowater Inc.
Brown & Williamson Tobacco Corp.
Brunswick Corp.
Budweiser of Columbia
Builder Marts of America
Campbell Soup Co.
Carolina Power & Light Co.
Carpenter Technology Corp.
CBI Industries
Central Soya Co.
Chapin Foundation of Myrtle Beach, South Carolina
Charter Medical Corp.
Church & Dwight Co.
Cincinnati Milacron
Circuit City Stores
Cline Co.
Close Foundation
Coats & Clark Inc.
Coleman Co.
Colonial Life & Accident Insurance Co.
ConAgra
Cooper Industries
County Bank
Cox Enterprises
Culbro Corp.
Cummins Engine Co.
Curtiss-Wright Corp.
Dan River, Inc.
Dana Corp.
Delta Woodside Industries
Dibrell Brothers, Inc.
Dixie Yarns, Inc.
Dollar General Corp.
Donnelley & Sons Co., R.R.
Dow Chemical Co.
Dresser Industries
du Pont de Nemours & Co., E. I.
Duke Power Co.
Durr-Fillauer Medical
Eastman Kodak Co.
Eaton Corp.
Eckerd Corp., Jack
Emerson Electric Co.
Ethyl Corp.
Evening Post Publishing Co.
Fabri-Kal Corp.
Fairey Educational Fund, Kittie M.
Farley Industries
Federal-Mogul Corp.
Fieldcrest Cannon
First Union Corp.
Fleet Bank
Fleet Financial Group
Florida Steel Corp.
Fluor Corp.
FMC Corp.
Fuller Foundation, C. G.
Fullerton Foundation
General Electric Co.
General Motors Corp.
Georgia-Pacific Corp.
Gerber Products Co.
Goodyear Tire & Rubber Co.
Greenwood Mills
Gregg-Graniteville Foundation
Hanna Co., M.A.

Harte-Hanks Communications,
　Inc.
Hillenbrand Industries
Hitachi
Hoechst Celanese Corp.
Home Depot
Hopewell Foundation
Horne Foundation, Dick
Hospital Corp. of America
Hubbell Inc.
Humana
Inland Container Corp.
Inman Mills
International Paper Co.
ITT Corp.
Jackson Mills
James River Corp. of Virginia
Johnson & Higgins
Jones Construction Co., J.A.
Jostens
Kimberly-Clark Corp.
Kloeckner-Pentaplast of America
Knight-Ridder, Inc.
Kraft General Foods
La-Z-Boy Chair Co.
Liberty Corp.
Litton Industries
Lockheed Corp.
Love Foundation, Lucyle S.
Marley Co.
Maytag Corp.
Mead Corp.
Media General, Inc.
Merck Family Fund
Michelin North America
Milliken & Co.
Mohasco Corp.
Monsanto Co.
Morton International
Mount Vernon Mills
Multimedia, Inc.
National Medical Enterprises
NationsBank Corp.
NCR Corp.
New York Times Co.
Nordson Corp.
Nucor Corp.
Olin Corp.
Owens-Corning Fiberglas Corp.
Parker-Hannifin Corp.
Philip Morris Cos.
Phillips Petroleum Co.
Pioneer Hi-Bred International
Porsche Cars North America, Inc.
Procter & Gamble Co.
Pulitzer Publishing Co.
Quantum Chemical Corp.
Reliance Electric Co.
Rexham Inc.
Rhone-Poulenc Inc.
Roadway Services, Inc.
Rock Hill Telephone Co.
Roe Foundation
Sara Lee Corp.
Sara Lee Hosiery
SCANA Corp.
Scripps Co., E.W.
Scurry Foundation, D. L.
Self Foundation
Sequa Corp.
Shaw Industries
Siebe North Inc.
Simpson Foundation
Smith Charities, John
Smith Corp., A.O.
Sonoco Products Co.
South Carolina Electric & Gas
　Co.
Southtrust Corp.
Springs Foundation
Springs Industries
Sprint
Square D Co.
Standard Products Co.
Steel Heddle Manufacturing Co.
Stevens Foundation, John T.

Stone Container Corp.
Support Systems International
Symmes Foundation, F. W.
Talley Industries, Inc.
Target Stores
Textron
Thomas & Betts Corp.
3M Co.
Timken Co.
Transco Energy Company
Travelers Cos.
Union Camp Corp.
United Merchants &
　Manufacturers
Vulcan Materials Co.
Wal-Mart Stores
Warner-Lambert Co.
Westinghouse Electric Corp.
Westvaco Corp.
Wetterau
White Consolidated Industries
Winn-Dixie Stores

South Dakota

Alumax
AMAX
Armco Inc.
Bemis Company
C.P. Rail Systems
Charter Medical Corp.
Citicorp
CR Industries
Cummins Engine Co.
Dayton Hudson Corp.
First Bank System
Gannett Co.
Graco
Harvest States Cooperative
Hatterscheidt Foundation
Hubbard Milling Co.
Knight-Ridder, Inc.
Land O'Lakes
Masco Corp.
Minnegasco
Northern States Power Co.
Norwest Corp.
Pamida, Inc.
Pioneer Hi-Bred International
Royal Group Inc.
Sheldahl Inc.
Sioux Steel Co.
Stauffer Communications
Target Stores
3M Co.
Toshiba America, Inc.
US WEST
Wal-Mart Stores

Tennessee

Affiliated Publications, Inc.
AFG Industries, Inc.
Akzo America
Akzo Chemicals Inc.
Aladdin Industries, Incorporated
Albany International Corp.
Alco Standard Corp.
AlliedSignal
Aluminum Co. of America
American Electric Power
American General Life &
　Accident Insurance Co.
American Greetings Corp.
American Standard
Ansley Foundation, Dantzler
　Bond
ARA Services
Arcata Corp.
Arcata Graphics Co.
Archer-Daniels-Midland Co.
Armco Inc.
Armstrong World Industries Inc.
Arvin Industries
ASARCO
Atlanta Gas Light Co.

Avery Dennison Corp.
Avis Inc.
Avnet, Inc.
Ball Corp.
Barnes Group
Baxter International
Bechtel Group
Bell Industries
BellSouth Corp.
Belz Foundation
Bemis Company
Benwood Foundation
Berwind Corp.
Black & Decker Corp.
Boatmen's Bancshares
Boeing Co.
Boise Cascade Corp.
Borden
Bowater Inc.
Bradford & Co., J.C.
Bridgestone/Firestone
Briggs Foundation, T. W.
Brinkley Foundation
Brown Charitable Trust, Dora
　Maclellan
Brown-Forman Corp.
Browning-Ferris Industries
Brunswick Corp.
Burlington Northern Inc.
Caldwell Foundation, Hardwick
Carrier Corp.
Cartinhour Foundation
Charter Medical Corp.
Chattem, Inc.
Christy-Houston Foundation
Chrysler Corp.
Chubb Corp.
Circuit City Stores
Citizens Union Bank
Clopay Corp.
Clorox Co.
Cole Foundation, Robert H. and
　Monica H.
ConAgra
Constar International Inc.
Conwood Co. L.P.
Cooper Industries
Copperweld Corp.
Crestar Food Products, Inc.
Cubic Corp.
Culbro Corp.
Cummins Engine Co.
Currey Foundation, Brownlee
Danner Foundation
Davis Foundation, Joe C.
Dayton Hudson Corp.
Dean Foods, Jimmy
Deere & Co.
Deluxe Corp.
Dennison Manufacturing Co.
Dial Corp.
Dixie-Portland Flour Mills
Dixie Yarns, Inc.
Dollar General Corp.
Donnelley & Sons Co., R.R.
Douglas & Lomason Company
Dover Corp.
Dover Elevator Systems Inc.
Dow Corning Corp.
du Pont de Nemours & Co., E. I.
Duriron Co., Inc.
Durr-Fillauer Medical
Eastman Chemical Co.
Eastman Kodak Co.
Eaton Corp.
Echlin Inc.
Eckerd Corp., Jack
Eka Nobel
Emerson Electric Co.
Equitable Resources
Farley Industries
Federal Express Corp.
Federal-Mogul Corp.
Federated Department Stores and
　Allied Stores Corp.
Ferro Corp.

First American Corp. (Nashville,
　Tennessee)
First Mississippi Corp.
First Tennessee Bank
First Union Corp.
Foster Charitable Foundation, M.
　Stratton
Fuller Co., H.B.
Gannett Co.
GenCorp
General Electric Co.
Genesco
Goldman Sachs & Co.
Goldsmith Foundation
Goodyear Tire & Rubber Co.
Gordon Family Foundation, Joel
　C. and Bernice W.
Great Western Financial Corp.
H. R. H. Family Foundation
Handy & Harman
Hanna Co., M.A.
Harsco Corp.
Heil Co.
Helena Chemical Co.
Home Depot
Hospital Corp. of America
Humana
Hurlbut Memorial Fund, Orion
　L. and Emma S.
Hutcheson Foundation, Hazel
　Montague
Hyde Foundation, J. R.
Illinois Tool Works
Ingram Book Co.
Ingram Industries
Inland Container Corp.
Inland Steel Industries
International Multifoods Corp.
International Paper Co.
Interstate Packaging Co.
James River Corp. of Virginia
Jefferson Smurfit Corp.
Jewell Memorial Foundation,
　Daniel Ashley and Irene
　Houston
Johnson & Higgins
Johnson & Son, S.C.
Jostens
Kellogg's
Kimball International
Kimberly-Clark Corp.
Kraft General Foods
La-Z-Boy Chair Co.
Leu Foundation
Levi Strauss & Co.
Lincoln National Corp.
Litton Industries
Lowenstein Foundation, William
　P. and Marie R.
Lyndhurst Foundation
Maclellan Charitable Trust, R. J.
Maclellan Foundation
Magic Chef
Manufacturers Life Insurance
　Co. of America
Manville Corp.
Mapco Inc.
Marley Co.
Martin Marietta Corp.
Masco Corp.
Massengill-DeFriece Foundation
Massey Foundation, Jack C.
Maytag Corp.
Mead Corp.
Memphis Light Gas & Water
　Division
Menasha Corp.
Monsanto Co.
Morristown Casting Support
　Division
Murray Ohio Manufacturing Co.
National Medical Enterprises
NationsBank Corp.
Nationwide Insurance Cos.
New York Times Co.
Newmont Mining Corp.

Newport News Shipbuilding &
　Dry Dock Co.
Nike Inc.
Norfolk Southern Corp.
North American Philips Corp.
North American Royalties
Northern Telecom Inc.
Norton Co.
NYNEX Corp.
Oak Hall, Inc.
Olin Corp.
1939 Foundation
Outboard Marine Corp.
Owens-Corning Fiberglas Corp.
PACCAR
Parsons Corp.
Persis Corp.
Pet
Philip Morris Cos.
Pioneer Hi-Bred International
Pirelli Armstrong Tire Corp.
Plough Foundation
Potter Foundation, Justin and
　Valere
Precision Rubber Products
Procter & Gamble Co.
Promus Cos.
Provident Life & Accident
　Insurance Co.
Prudential Insurance Co. of
　America
Quaker Oats Co.
Quantum Chemical Corp.
Ralston Purina Co.
Raychem Corp.
Raytheon Co.
Red Food Stores, Inc.
Reflection Riding
Reliance Electric Co.
Republic Automotive Parts, Inc.
Revlon
Reynolds Foundation, Eleanor T.
Rhone-Poulenc Inc.
Ringier-America
Robertshaw Controls Co.
Rohm and Haas Company
Russ Togs
SAFECO Corp.
Sara Lee Corp.
Schadt Foundation
Schering-Plough Corp.
Schilling Motors
Scripps Co., E.W.
Scrivner, Inc.
SCT Yarns
Sealy, Inc.
Sedgwick James Inc.
Shaw Industries
Shoney's Inc.
Smith Corp., A.O.
Smucker Co., J.M.
Southtrust Corp.
Springs Industries
Sprint
Square D Co.
Standard Register Co.
Stanley Works
State Farm Mutual Automobile
　Insurance Co.
Steiner Corp.
Stephens Foundation Trust
Stokely, Jr. Foundation, William
　B.
Stone Container Corp.
Tandem Computers
Target Stores
Teledyne
Templeton Foundation, John
Tenneco
Tension Envelope Corp.
Texas Instruments
Textron
Third National Corp.
Thomas & Betts Corp.
Thomasville Furniture Industries
Thompson Charitable Foundation
3M Co.

Tennessee (cont.)

Timken Co.
Tokheim Corp.
Toms Foundation
Tonya Memorial Foundation
Toshiba America, Inc.
Travelers Cos.
TRINOVA Corp.
TRW Corp.
TSC STores, Inc.
Tyson Foods, Inc.
Union Camp Corp.
Union Carbide Corp.
Union Planters Corp.
United Inns, Inc.
United Technologies Corp.
UST
Van Vleet Foundation
Vulcan Materials Co.
Wal-Mart Stores
Walgreen Co.
Walter Industries
Washington Foundation
Werthan Foundation
Werthan Packaging, Inc.
Westend Foundation
Wetterau
Whirlpool Corp.
White Consolidated Industries
Winn-Dixie Stores
Witco Corp.
Woods-Greer Foundation
Wurzburg, Inc.
Wynn's International, Inc.
Zimmerman Family Foundation,
    Raymond

Texas

Abbott Laboratories
Abell-Hanger Foundation
Abercrombie Foundation
Adams Resources & Energy, Inc.
Advanced Micro Devices
AEGON USA, Inc.
Air France
Air Products & Chemicals
Akzo America
Alberto-Culver Co.
Albertson's
Alco Standard Corp.
Alcon Laboratories, Inc.
Alexander Foundation, Robert
    D. and Catherine R.
Alumax
Aluminum Co. of America
AMAX
Amerada Hess Corp.
America West Airlines
American Brands
American Cyanamid Co.
American Financial Corp.
American General Corp.
American Greetings Corp.
American Home Products Corp.
American National Insurance
American Natural Resources Co.
American Savings & Loan
    Association of Florida
American Standard
American Stores Co.
American Telephone &
    Telegraph Co./Dallas Region
Ameron, Inc.
Amoco Corp.
AMR Corp.
Anadarko Petroleum Corp.
Anderson Charitable Trust,
    Josephine
Anderson Foundation, M. D.
Anheuser-Busch Cos.
Apache Corp.
ARA Services
Archer-Daniels-Midland Co.
ARCO
ARCO Chemical

Aristech Chemical Corp.
Arkla
Armco Inc.
Arrow Electronics, Inc.
ASARCO
Associated Milk Producers, Inc.
Atari Corp.
Austin Industries
Avery Dennison Corp.
Aviall, Inc.
Avnet, Inc.
Backer Spielvogel Bates U.S.
Baker Hughes Inc.
Ball Corp.
Banc One Illinois Corp.
Bandag, Inc.
Bank of Boston Corp.
Bank One, Texas-Houston Office
Bank One, Texas, NA
BankAmerica Corp.
Bankers Life & Casualty Co.
Banque Francaise du Commerce
    Exterieur
Barnes Group
Barnes Scholarship Trust, Fay T.
Baroid Corp.
Bass Corporation, Perry and
    Nancy Lee
Bass Foundation
Bass Foundation, Harry
Baumberger Endowment
Bausch & Lomb
Baxter International
Beal Foundation
Beasley Foundation, Theodore
    and Beulah
Bechtel Group
Behmann Brothers Foundation
Bell Helicopter Textron
Bell Trust
Belo Corp., A.H.
Beren Trust D, Harry H.
Bergen Brunswig Corp.
Bertha Foundation
Best Products Co.
Betz Laboratories
BFGoodrich
Big Three Industries
Biological Humanics Foundation
Black & Decker Corp.
Blount
BMW of North America, Inc.
Boeing Co.
Boise Cascade Corp.
Bonner & Moore Associates
Bordeaux Foundation
Borden
Bosque Foundation
Bowers Foundation
BP America
BP Exploration
Brackenridge Foundation,
    George W.
Braniff International Airlines
Bridgestone/Firestone
Bridwell Foundation, J. S.
Brinker Girls' Tennis
    Foundation, Maureen Connolly
Brochsteins Inc.
Brown and C. A. Lupton
    Foundation, T. J.
Brown Foundation
Brown Foundation, M. K.
Brown & Root, Inc.
Brown & Sharpe Manufacturing
    Co.
Brown & Sons, Alex
Brown Inc., Tom
Browning-Ferris Industries
Brunswick Corp.
Bryce Memorial Fund, William
    and Catherine
Burkitt Foundation
Burlington Northern Inc.
Burlington Resources
Business Records Corp.
Butler Manufacturing Co.

C.I.O.S.
Cable & Wireless
    Communications
Cabot Corp.
Cactus Feeders Inc.
Cadbury Beverages Inc.
Cain Foundation, Effie and
    Wofford
Cain Foundation, Gordon and
    Mary
Caleb Brett U.S.A. Inc.
Caltex Petroleum Corp.
Cameron Foundation, Harry S.
    and Isabel C.
Campbell Soup Co.
Campbell Taggart, Inc.
Capital Cities/ABC
Carrier Corp.
Carter Foundation, Amon G.
Castle & Co., A.M.
Caston Foundation, M. C. and
    Mattie
Cauthorn Charitable Trust, John
    and Mildred
CBI Industries
Centel Corp.
Centex Corp.
Central Bank of the South
Central Power & Light Co.
Central & South West Services
CertainTeed Corp.
Champion International Corp.
Charter Medical Corp.
Chase Manhattan Bank, N.A.
Chevron Corp.
Chilton Foundation Trust
Chrysler Corp.
Chubb Corp.
Church's Fried Chicken, Inc.
CIGNA Corp.
Cimarron Foundation
Circuit City Stores
Citicorp
Clarity Holdings Corp.
Clayton Fund
Clements Foundation
Cleveland-Cliffs
Clopay Corp.
Clorox Co.
Coachmen Industries
Coastal Corp.
Coca-Cola Co.
Cockrell Foundation
Coleman Co.
Collins Co.
Collins Foundation, Carr P.
Collins Foundation, James M.
Colorado Interstate Gas Co.
Coltec Industries
Comerica
Commercial Metals Co.
Community Hospital Foundation
Compaq Computer Corp.
Computer Associates
    International
Computer Sciences Corp.
ConAgra
Conoco Inc.
Consolidated Freightways
Constantin Foundation
Continental Airlines
Continental Bank N.A.
Contran Corp.
Cook Foundation, Loring
Cook, Sr. Charitable Foundation,
    Kelly Gene
Cooper Industries
Cooper Oil Tool
Corpus Christi Exploration Co.
Courtaulds Fibers Inc.
Cox Charitable Trust, Opal G.
Cox Enterprises
Craig Foundation, J. Paul
CRC Evans Pipeline
    International, Inc.
Credit Suisse
Crown Central Petroleum Corp.

CRS Sirrine Engineers
Crum and Forster
Crump Fund, Joe and Jessie
CTS Corp.
Cullen Foundation
Cullen/Frost Bankers
Cullum Cos.
Curtice-Burns Foods
Davidson Family Charitable
    Foundation
Davis Foundation, Ken W.
Dayton Hudson Corp.
Delhi Gas Pipeline Co.
Delta Air Lines
Deluxe Corp.
Dexter Corp.
Dial Corp.
Diamond Shamrock
Digicon
Dillard Department Stores, Inc.
Dishman Charitable Foundation
    Trust, H. E. and Kate
Dodge Jones Foundation
Dollar General Corp.
Donaldson, Lufkin & Jenrette
Donnelley & Sons Co., R.R.
Doss Foundation, M. S.
Dougherty, Jr. Foundation, James
    R.
Douglas & Lomason Company
Dover Corp.
Dow Chemical Co.
Dow Jones & Co.
Dresser Industries
DSC Communications Co.
du Pont de Nemours & Co., E. I.
Dues Charitable Foundation,
    Cesle C. and Mamie
Dunagan Foundation
Duncan Foundation, Lillian H.
    and C. W.
Dunn Research Foundation, John
    S.
Durr-Fillauer Medical
E-Systems
Eagle-Picher Industries
Early Foundation
Eastman Kodak Co.
Eaton Corp.
Eckerd Corp., Jack
Ecolab
EDS Corp.
Edwards Foundation, Jes
EG&G Inc.
Electronic Data Systems Corp.
Elf Aquitaine, Inc.
Elf Atochem North America
Elkins Foundation, J. A. and
    Isabel M.
Elkins, Jr. Foundation, Margaret
    and James A.
Ellwood Foundation
Emerson Electric Co.
Enron Corp.
Enserch Corp.
Enterra Corp.
Entex
Equitable Life Assurance Society
    of the U.S.
Ethyl Corp.
Exxon Corp.
Fair Foundation, R. W.
Fairchild Corp.
Farish Fund, William Stamps
Farley Industries
Fashion Bar
Fasken Foundation
Favrot Fund
Federal National Mortgage
    Assn., Fannie Mae
Feldman Foundation
Ferguson Family Foundation,
    Kittie and Rugeley
Fifth Avenue Foundation
Fikes Foundation, Leland
FINA, Inc.
Fireman's Fund Insurance Co.

First Interstate Bank of Texas,
    N.A.
First Mississippi Corp.
First Security Corp. (Salt Lake
    City, Utah)
Fish Foundation, Ray C.
Fleming Foundation
Florence Foundation
Fluor Corp.
FMC Corp.
FMR Corp.
Fondren Foundation
Fort Worth Star Telegram
Fox Inc.
Foxmeyer Corp.
Franklin Charitable Trust, Ershel
Frees Foundation
Friona Industries L.P.
Frito-Lay
Frost National Bank
Fuller Co., H.B.
Fuller Foundation
Gannett Co.
Garvey Texas Foundation
GATX Corp.
General Dynamics Corp.
General Housewares Corp.
General Motors Corp.
General Tire Inc.
George Foundation
Georgia-Pacific Corp.
Gill Foundation, Pauline Allen
Gilman and Gonzalez-Falla
    Theatre Foundation
Gilman, Jr. Foundation, Sondra
    and Charles
Glaze Foundation, Robert and
    Ruth
Global Van Lines
Goldman Sachs & Co.
Goodyear Tire & Rubber Co.
Gordon Foundation, Meyer and
    Ida
Goulds Pumps
Graco
Grant-Norpac, Inc.
Green Foundation
Griffin Foundation, Rosa May
Grocers Supply Co.
GSC Enterprises
GTE Corp.
Haas Foundation, Paul and Mary
Hachar Charitable Trust, D. D.
Hadson Corp.
Haggar Apparel Corp.
Haggar Foundation
Haggerty Foundation
Haghenbeck Foundation,
    Antonio Y. De La Lama
Halff Foundation, G. A. C.
Hall Financial Group
Hallberg Foundation, E. L. and
    R. F.
Halliburton Co.
Hallmark Cards
Halsell Foundation, Ewing
Hamilton Oil Corp.
Hamman Foundation, George
    and Mary Josephine
Hammill Foundation, Donald D.
Handy & Harman
Hankamer Foundation, Curtis
    and Doris K.
Hanna Co., M.A.
Hanson Office Products
Harrington Foundation, Don and
    Sybil
Harris Corp.
Harsco Corp.
Harte-Hanks Communications,
    Inc.
Hartford Steam Boiler Inspection
    & Insurance Co.
Hawn Foundation
HCB Contractors
Heath Foundation, Ed and Mary
Heileman Brewing Co., Inc., G.

Heller Financial
Henry Foundation, Patrick
Hercules Inc.
Hervey Foundation
Herzstein Charitable Foundation, Albert and Ethel
Hexcel Corp.
Hightower Foundation, Walter
Hillcrest Foundation
Hitachi
Hobby Foundation
Hoblitzelle Foundation
Hoechst Celanese Corp.
Hofheinz Foundation, Irene Cafcalas
Hofheinz Fund
Hofstetter Trust, Bessie
Home Depot
HON Industries
Hospital Corp. of America
Houston Endowment
Houston Industries
Houston Post Co.
Howell Corp.
Howmet Corp., Wichita Falls Casting Division
Howmet Corp., Wichita Falls Refurbishment Center
Hubbard Broadcasting
Hubbard Foundation, R. Dee and Joan Dale
Huck International Inc.
Huffington Foundation
Hugg Trust, Leoia W. and Charles H.
Humana
Humphreys Foundation
Hunt Oil Co.
Huthsteiner Fine Arts Trust
Hyman Construction Co., George
IBM Corp.
Illinois Tool Works
IMO Industries Inc.
Imperial Holly Corp.
Independent Bankshares
Indiana Insurance Cos.
Ingersoll-Rand Co.
Inland Container Corp.
Inland Steel Industries
Intercraft Co., Inc.
Intermark, Inc.
International Flavors & Fragrances
International Multifoods Corp.
International Paper Co.
Interpublic Group of Cos.
Iroquois Brands, Ltd.
ITT Hartford Insurance Group
J.P. Morgan & Co.
James River Corp. of Virginia
JCPenney Co.
Jefferson Smurfit Corp.
JMK-A M Micallef Charitable Foundation
Johnson Controls
Johnson Foundation, Burdine
Johnson Foundation, M. G. and Lillie A.
Johnson & Higgins
Johnson & Johnson
Johnson & Son, S.C.
Jones Foundation, Helen
Jonsson Foundation
Jostens
Justin Industries, Inc.
Kahn Dallas Symphony Foundation, Louise W. and Edmund J.
Kaneb Services, Inc.
Kayser Foundation
Keith Co., Ben E.
Keith Foundation Trust, Ben E.
Kellogg Co., M.W.
Kempner Fund, Harris and Eliza
Kenedy Memorial Foundation, John G. and Marie Stella
Kerr-McGee Corp.

Keystone International
Killson Educational Foundation, Winifred and B. A.
Kilroy Foundation, William S. and Lora Jean
Kimball International
Kimberly-Clark Corp.
King Foundation, Carl B. and Florence E.
King Ranch
Kleberg Foundation for Wildlife Conservation, Caesar
Kleberg, Jr. and Helen C. Kleberg Foundation, Robert J.
Klein Fund, Nathan J.
Knox, Sr., and Pearl Wallis Knox Charitable Foundation, Robert W.
Koehler Foundation, Marcia and Otto
KPMG Peat Marwick
Kraft General Foods
Kysor Industrial Corp.
La Quinta Motor Inns
Lafarge Corp.
Lance, Inc.
Lard Trust, Mary Potishman
LBJ Family Foundation
LDB Corp.
Lehigh Portland Cement Co.
Lennox International, Inc.
Levi Strauss & Co.
Levit Family Foundation, Joe
Lewis Foundation, Lillian Kaiser
Libbey-Owens Ford Co.
Lightner Sams Foundation
Lincoln National Corp.
Lincoln Property Co.
Lindsay Student Aid Fund, Franklin
Little, Arthur D.
Litton Industries
Lockheed Corp.
Loews Corp.
Lomas Financial Corp.
Lone Star Gas Co.
Los Trigos Fund
Louisiana Land & Exploration Co.
Louisiana-Pacific Corp.
Lowe Foundation
LTV Corp.
Lubrizol Corp.
Luby's Cafeterias
Luchsinger Family Foundation
Luse Foundation, W. P. and Bulah
Luttrell Trust
Lux Trust, Dr. Konrad and Clara
Lyondell Petrochemical Co.
Lyons Foundation
M/A/R/C Inc.
Maddox Trust, Web
Maguire Oil Co.
Manufacturers Life Insurance Co. of America
Manville Corp.
Mapco Inc.
Maritz Inc.
Mark IV Industries
Marley Co.
Marshall Field's
Mary Kay Cosmetics
Mary Kay Foundation
Mattel
Maxus Energy Corp.
May Department Stores Co.
Mayborn Foundation, Frank W.
Mayer Foundation, James and Eva
Mayor Foundation, Oliver Dewey
McAshan Foundation
McCormick & Co.
McCullough Foundation, Ralph H. and Ruth J.
McDermott
McDermott Foundation, Eugene

McDonald Foundation, Tillie and Tom
McDonnell Douglas Corp.
McDonnell Douglas Corp.-West
McGovern Foundation, John P.
McGovern Fund for the Behavioral Sciences
McKee Foundation, Robert E. and Evelyn
McMillan, Jr. Foundation, Bruce
McNutt Charitable Trust, Amy Shelton
Mead Corp.
Meadows Foundation
Mellon Bank Corp.
Mellon PSFS
Memorex Telex Corp.
Menil Foundation
Meredith Foundation
Mesa Inc.
Meyer Family Foundation, Paul J.
Meyer Foundation, Alice Kleberg Reynolds
Mid-Continent Supply Co.
Miller Brewing Company/Texas
Millhollon Educational Trust Estate, Nettie
Mitchell Energy & Development Corp.
Mitsui & Co. (U.S.A.)
Mobil Oil Corp.
Mobility Foundation
Moncrief Foundation, William A. and Elizabeth B.
Monsanto Co.
Moody Foundation
Moore Business Forms, Inc.
Moores Foundation
MorningStar Foods
Morris Foundation
Morrison-Knudsen Corp.
Morrison Trust, Louise L.
Morton International
Moss Foundation, Harry S.
Moss Heart Trust, Harry S.
Motorola
Munson Foundation, W. B.
Murfee Endowment, Kathryn
Nalco Chemical Co.
National Convenience Stores, Inc.
National Gypsum Co.
National Medical Enterprises
NationsBank Corp.
NationsBank Texas
Navarro County Educational Foundation
NCH Corp.
NEC USA
Neiman Marcus
New York Life Insurance Co.
Newmont Mining Corp.
News America Publishing Inc.
Norman Foundation, Summers A.
North American Philips Corp.
Northen, Mary Moody
Northern Telecom Inc.
Northern Trust Co.
NorthPark National Bank
Northrop Corp.
Norton Co.
Norwest Corp.
Nucor Corp.
Occidental Oil & Gas Corp.
Occidental Petroleum Corp.
O'Connor Foundation, Kathryn
O'Donnell Foundation
Ogilvy & Mather Worldwide
Oldham Little Church Foundation
Olin Corp.
O'Quinn Foundation, John M. and Nancy C.
Orion Capital Corp.
Orleans Trust, Carrie S.
Oshman's Sporting Goods, Inc.
Overlake Foundation

Owen Trust, B. B.
Owens-Corning Fiberglas Corp.
Owsley Foundation, Alvin and Lucy
Oxford Industries, Inc.
Oxy Petrochemicals Inc.
PACCAR
Pacific Enterprises
PaineWebber
Pangburn Foundation
Panhandle Eastern Corp.
Parsons Corp.
Paxton Co., Frank
Pay 'N Save Inc.
Pearle Vision
Pechiney Corp.
Penn Central Corp.
Pennzoil Co.
PepsiCo
Perkins Foundation, Joe and Lois
Perkins-Prothro Foundation
Permian Corp.
Perot Foundation
Pet
Phelps Dodge Corp.
PHH Corp.
Philip Morris Cos.
Phillips Petroleum Co.
Picker International
Piedmont Natural Gas Co., Inc.
Pier 1 Imports, Inc.
Pilgrim's Pride Corp.
Pineywoods Foundation
Pioneer Concrete of America Inc.
Pioneer Hi-Bred International
Piper Foundation, Minnie Stevens
Pittston Co.
Placid Oil Co.
Pogo Producing Co.
Pool Energy Services Co.
Potts and Sibley Foundation
PPG Industries
Priddy Foundation
Primerica Corp.
Pro-line Corp.
Procter & Gamble Co.
Progressive Corp.
Promus Cos.
Prudential Insurance Co. of America
Puett Foundation, Nelson
Quaker Chemical Corp.
Quaker Oats Co.
Quanex Corp.
Quantum Chemical Corp.
Rachal Foundation, Ed
Rainwater Charitable Foundation
Reading & Bates Corp.
Recognition Equipment
Redman Foundation
Redman Industries
REI-Recreational Equipment, Inc.
Reliable Life Insurance Co.
Reliance Electric Co.
Republic Financial Services, Inc.
Republic New York Corp.
Rexene Products Co.
Reynolds Metals Co.
RGK Foundation
Rhone-Poulenc Inc.
Richardson Foundation, Sid W.
Rienzi Foundation
River Blindness Foundation
Riviana Foods
Roberts Foundation, Dora
Roberts Foundation, Summerfield G.
Robinson Foundation
Rockwell Fund
Rockwell International Corp.
Rogers Foundation
Rohm and Haas Company
Rohr Inc.
Rouse Co.
Rowan Cos., Inc.

RSR Corp.
Ryder System
SAFECO Corp.
Saint Paul Cos.
Salomon
Sammons Enterprises
Sams Foundation, Earl C.
Santa Fe International Corp.
Santa Fe Pacific Corp.
Sara Lee Corp.
Sarofim Foundation
Scaler Foundation
Schering-Plough Corp.
Schlumberger Ltd.
Scott Foundation, William E.
Scott Paper Co.
Scripps Co., E.W.
Scrivner, Inc.
Scurlock Foundation
Sealy, Inc.
Seay Charitable Trust, Sarah M. and Charles E.
Security Capital Corp.
Sedco Inc.
Seibel Foundation, Abe and Annie
Semmes Foundation
Sequa Corp.
Service Corp. International
Seymour Foundation, W. L. and Louise E.
SGS-Thomson Microelectronics Inc.
Sharp Foundation, Charles S. and Ruth C.
Shaw Industries
Shell Oil Co.
Sherwin-Williams Co.
Simpson Investment Co.
Six Flags Theme Parks Inc.
Skaggs Alpha Beta Co.
Sky Chefs, Inc.
Smith and W. Aubrey Smith Charitable Foundation, Clara Blackford
Smith Corp., A.O.
Smith Foundation, Bob and Vivian
Smith Foundation, Julia and Albert
Smith International
Snyder General Corp.
Society Corp.
Sonat
Sonat Exploration
Sonat Offshore Drilling
Sony Corp. of America
South Plains Foundation
South Texas Charitable Foundation
Southdown, Inc.
Southland Corp.
Southmark Corp.
Southwest Airlines Co.
Southwestern Bell Corp.
Southwestern Life Insurance Co.
Southwestern Public Service Co.
Sprint
Square D Co.
Standard Register Co.
Stanley Works
Star Enterprise
Stark Foundation, Nelda C. and H. J. Lutcher
Starling Foundation, Dorothy Richard
State Farm Mutual Automobile Insurance Co.
Steinhagen Benevolent Trust, B. A. and Elinor
Stemmons Foundation
Sterling Chemicals Inc.
Sterling Software Inc.
Stewart & Stevenson Services
Stieren Foundation, Arthur T. and Jane J.
Stone Container Corp.

Texas (cont.)

Stonestreet Trust, Eusebia S.
Storage Technology Corp.
Strake Foundation
Summerlee Foundation
Sumners Foundation, Hatton W.
Swalm Foundation
Swiss American Securities, Inc.
Swiss Bank Corp.
Sysco Corp.
Tandem Computers
Tandy Corp.
Tandy Foundation, Anne Burnett
and Charles
Tandy Foundation, David L.
Target Stores
Tartt Scholarship Fund, Hope
Pierce
Taub Foundation
Tauber Oil Co.
Team Banchares Inc.
Team Bank Houston
Technical Foundation of America
Tele-Communications, Inc.
Telecom Corp.
Teledyne
Teleflex Inc.
Temple Foundation, T. L. L.
Temple-Inland
Tenneco
Tension Envelope Corp.
Terry Foundation
Tesoro Petroleum Corp.
Texaco
Texas Commerce Bank Houston,
N.A.
Texas Energy Museum
Texas Industries, Inc.
Texas Instruments
Texas-New Mexico Power Co.
Texas Olefins Co.
Textron
3M Co.
Tidewater, Inc.
Tigon Corp.
Times Mirror Co.
Timken Co.
Tobin Foundation
Tokheim Corp.
Tomkins Industries, Inc.
Torchmark Corp.
Toshiba America, Inc.
Tracor, Inc.
Transco Energy Company
Tranzonic Cos.
Travelers Cos.
Trinity Industries, Inc.
TRINOVA Corp.
Trull Foundation
TRW Corp.
TU Electric Co.
Turner Charitable Foundation
Turner Corp.
Twentieth Century-Fox Film
Corp.
Tyler Corp.
Tyson Foods, Inc.
Union Camp Corp.
Union Carbide Corp.
Union Pacific Corp.
Union Texas Petroleum
Unisys Inc.
United Dominion Industries
United Gas Pipe Line Co.
United Savings Association of
Texas
United Services Automobile
Association
United States Trust Co. of New
York
Unocal Corp.
Unocal-Union Oil of California
USG Corp.
USLIFE Corp.
USX Corp.
Vale-Asche Foundation

Valero Energy Corp.
Vaughan Foundation, Rachael
and Ben
Vaughn Foundation
Vaughn, Jr. Foundation Fund,
James M.
Veritas Foundation
Vista Chemical Company
Volkswagen of America, Inc.
Vulcan Materials Co.
Waggoner Charitable Trust,
Crystelle
Waggoner Foundation, E. Paul
and Helen Buck
Wal-Mart Stores
Wal-Mart Stores, Inc.
Walgreen Co.
Walsh Foundation
Walthall Perpetual Charitable
Trust, Marjorie T.
Ward Co., Joe L.
Ward Heritage Foundation,
Mamie McFaddin
Weatherford International, Inc.
Weaver Foundation, Gil and
Dody
Weiner Foundation
Weiner's Stores
Welch Foundation, Robert A.
Wells Fargo & Co.
Wendy's International, Inc.
West Foundation
West Foundation, Neva and
Wesley
West Texas Corp., J. M.
West Texas Utilities Co.
Westinghouse Electric Corp.
Weyerhaeuser Co.
White Foundation, Erle and
Emma
White Trust, G. R.
Wilbur-Ellis Co.
Willard Helping Fund, Cecilia
Young
Wills Foundation
Wilson Foundation, John and
Nevils
Wilson Public Trust, Ralph
Winn-Dixie Stores
Wise Foundation and Charitable
Trust, Watson W.
Witco Corp.
Wolens Foundation, Kalman and
Ida
Wolff Memorial Foundation,
Pauline Sterne
Woltman Foundation, B. M.
Wortham Foundation
Worthing Scholarship Fund
Wright Foundation, Lola
Wynn's International, Inc.
Xerox Corp.
York International Corp.
Zachry Co., H. B.
Zachry Co., H.B.
Zale Corp.
Zale Foundation
Zale Foundation, William and
Sylvia
Zapata Corp.

Utah

Abbott Laboratories
Air Products & Chemicals
Albertson's
Alco Standard Corp.
Amalgamated Sugar Co.
AMAX
American Express Co.
American Stores Co.
ARCO
Armco Inc.
Arrow Electronics, Inc.
Avis Inc.
Avnet, Inc.
Baker Hughes Inc.

Bamberger and John Ernest
Bamberger Memorial
Foundation, Ruth Eleanor
Baxter International
Becton Dickinson & Co.
Bell Industries
Bergen Brunswig Corp.
Best Products Co.
Boise Cascade Corp.
Borden
Browning
Browning Charitable
Foundation, Val A.
Browning-Ferris Industries
Caine Charitable Foundation,
Marie Eccles
Callister Foundation, Paul Q.
Castle & Co., A.M.
Charter Medical Corp.
Chevron Corp.
Coleman Co.
Computer Associates
International
Cyprus Minerals Co.
Dayton Hudson Corp.
Dee Foundation, Annie Taylor
Dee Foundation, Lawrence T.
and Janet T.
Delta Air Lines
Deluxe Corp.
Donnelley & Sons Co., R.R.
Dumke Foundation, Dr. Ezekiel
R. and Edna Wattis
Duriron Co., Inc.
Durr-Fillauer Medical
Eaton Corp.
Eccles Charitable Foundation,
Willard L.
Eccles Foundation, George S.
and Dolores Dore
Eccles Foundation, Marriner S.
EG&G Inc.
First Security Bank of Utah N.A.
First Security Corp. (Salt Lake
City, Utah)
FMR Corp.
GATX Corp.
Georgia-Pacific Corp.
Harris Foundation, William H.
and Mattie Wattis
Hercules Inc.
Hospital Corp. of America
Humana
Huntsman Foundation, Jon and
Karen
Icon Systems & Software
IDS Financial Services
Jefferson Smurfit Corp.
Johnson & Higgins
Kennecott Corp.
Kimberly-Clark Corp.
La-Z-Boy Chair Co.
Land O'Lakes
Litton Industries
Lockheed Corp.
Longyear Co.
Manufacturers Life Insurance
Co. of America
Margolis Charitable Foundation
for Medical Research, Ben B.
and Iris M.
Mark IV Industries
McDonnell Douglas Corp.
McDonnell Douglas Corp.-West
Mead Corp.
Michael Foundation, Herbert I.
and Elsa B.
Milliken & Co.
Morton International
Mrs. Fields, Inc.
National Medical Enterprises
Northwest Pipeline Corp.
Norwest Corp.
Novell Inc.
Nucor Corp.
Owens-Corning Fiberglas Corp.
PacifiCorp
Parker-Hannifin Corp.

Producers Livestock Marketing
Association
Questar Corp.
REI-Recreational Equipment,
Inc.
Shaw Charitable Trust, Mary
Elizabeth Dee
Smith Food & Drug
Steiner Corp.
Stewart Educational Foundation,
Donnell B. and Elizabeth Dee
Shaw
Stone Container Corp.
Swanson Family Foundation, Dr.
W.C.
Swim Foundation, Arthur L.
Tandem Computers
Teleflex Inc.
Thorn Apple Valley, Inc.
3M Co.
Travelers Cos.
TRW Corp.
Union Pacific Corp.
Unisys Corp.
US WEST
Utah Power & Light Co.
Varian Associates
West One Bancorp
Williams Cos.
Zions Bancorp.

Vermont

Armco Inc.
Bank of Boston Connecticut
Bank of Boston Corp.
Ben & Jerry's Homemade
Browning-Ferris Industries
Central Vermont Public Service
Corp.
Cherry Hill Cooperative Cannery
ConAgra
Cone-Blanchard Machine Co.
Cooper Industries
Crown Central Petroleum Corp.
Cyprus Minerals Co.
Gannett Co.
General Educational Fund
Georgia-Pacific Corp.
Grand Trunk Corp.
IBM Corp.
Johnson Controls
Lintilhac Foundation
Merchants Bancshares
National Life of Vermont
National Medical Enterprises
New England Telephone Co.
Olin Corp.
Proctor Trust, Mortimer R.
Quaker Oats Co.
Quantum Chemical Corp.
Rochester Telephone Corp.
Scott Foundation, Walter
Scott Fund, Olin
Seventh Generation
Simpson Investment Co.
Standard Register Co.
Stanley Works
Textron
Union Mutual Fire Insurance Co.

Virgin Islands

Brown-Forman Corp.
Grumman Corp.
Raymond Corp.

Virginia

Abbott Laboratories
AFLAC
Aid Association for the Blind
Airborne Express Co.
Airbus Industrie of America
Alco Standard Corp.
AlliedSignal
Alumax
AMAX

American Brands
American Electric Power
American Express Co.
American Filtrona Corp.
American Home Products Corp.
American Natural Resources Co.
AMP
Anheuser-Busch Cos.
AON Corp.
Applied Energy Services
Archer-Daniels-Midland Co.
Armco Inc.
Armstrong World Industries Inc.
Avis Inc.
Avnet, Inc.
Ball Corp.
Banner Industries, Inc.
BASF Corp.
Bassett Furniture Industries, Inc.
Batten Foundation
Baxter International
BDM International
Beazley Foundation
Belk Stores
Bell Atlantic Corp.
Belo Corp., A.H.
Bergen Brunswig Corp.
Best Products Co.
Bionetics Corp.
Blount Educational Foundation,
David S.
BMW of North America, Inc.
Boeing Co.
Booz Allen & Hamilton
Borden
Bridgestone/Firestone
Bristol Steel & Iron Works
British Aerospace Inc.
Brown & Sons, Alex
Browning-Ferris Industries
Brunswick Corp.
Bryant Foundation
Burroughs Educational Fund, N.
R.
Bustard Charitable Permanent
Trust Fund, Elizabeth and
James
Cabell III and Maude Morgan
Cabell Foundation, Robert G.
Cable & Wireless
Communications
Camp Foundation
Campbell Foundation, Ruth and
Henry
Carter Foundation, Beirne
Centel Corp.
Central Fidelity Banks, Inc.
Charter Medical Corp.
Chesapeake Corp.
Chesapeake & Potomac
Telephone Co.
Chrysler Corp.
Circuit City Stores
Citicorp
Coastal Corp.
Cole Trust, Quincy
Commercial Metals Co.
Computer Associates
International
Computer Sciences Corp.
Consolidated Natural Gas Co.
Contel Federal Systems
Cooper Industries
Cooper Wood Products
Coors Brewing Co.
Corning Incorporated
Cox Enterprises
Crestar Financial Corp.
CSX Corp.
Dan River, Inc.
Delmarva Power & Light Co.
Deluxe Corp.
Dibrell Brothers, Inc.
Dollar General Corp.
Donnelley & Sons Co., R.R.
Dow Jones & Co.
du Pont de Nemours & Co., E. I.

Durell Foundation, George
Edward
DynCorp
Easley Trust, Andrew H. and
Anne O.
Echlin Inc.
EG&G Inc.
English Foundation, W. C.
Estes Foundation
Ethyl Corp.
Fairchild Corp.
Farm Fresh Inc. (Norfolk,
Virginia)
Federal Home Loan Mortgage
Corp. (Freddie Mac)
Federal-Mogul Corp.
Fieldcrest Cannon
First Union Corp.
First Virginia Banks
Fitz-Gibbon Charitable Trust
Flagler Foundation
Fleet Co., Inc., C.B.
Forest City Enterprises
Frederick Foundation
Freedom Forum
Funderburke & Associates
Gannett Co.
General Dynamics Corp.
General Electric Co.
Georgia-Pacific Corp.
Giant Food
Giant Food Stores
Global Van Lines
Goodman & Company
Goodyear Tire & Rubber Co.
Gottwald Foundation
Graphic Arts Show Co. Inc.
Gray Foundation, Garland
Grumman Corp.
Hampton Casting Division
Harrison and Conrad Memorial
Trust
Hastings Trust
Hechinger Co.
Hecht's
Heilig-Meyers Co.
Heinz Co., H.J.
Henkel-Harris Co., Inc.
Hercules Inc.
Herndon Foundation
Hershey Foods Corp.
Higher Education Publications
Hillenbrand Industries
Hoechst Celanese Corp.
Home Beneficial Corp.
Home Depot
HON Industries
Hopeman Brothers
Hopkins Foundation, John Jay
Hospital Corp. of America
Houff Transfer, Inc.
Household International
Hubbell Inc.
Humana
Hunter Trust, Emily S. and
Coleman A.
IBM Corp.
Illinois Tool Works
Ingersoll-Rand Co.
Inland Container Corp.
Inland Steel Industries
Interco
ITT Corp.
ITT Hartford Insurance Group
ITT Rayonier
Ivakota Association
Ix & Sons, Frank
James River Coal Co.
James River Corp. of Virginia
Jefferson-Pilot
Jefferson-Pilot Communications
Jeffress Memorial Trust,
Elizabeth G.
Jeffress Memorial Trust, Thomas
F. and Kate Miller
Johnson Inc., Axel
Johnson & Higgins

Jones Construction Co., J.A.
Jones Foundation, W. Alton
Kaul Foundation
Kentland Foundation
Kloeckner-Pentaplast of America
Kraft General Foods
Lacy Foundation
Lafarge Corp.
Lane Co., Inc.
Lane Foundation, Minnie and
Bernard
Lawrence Foundation, Lind
Lawyers Title Foundation
Levi Strauss & Co.
Lincoln-Lane Foundation
Lincoln National Corp.
Litton Industries
Luck Stone
Lydall, Inc.
M/A-COM, Inc.
MacAndrews & Forbes Holdings
Manufacturers Life Insurance
Co. of America
Manville Corp.
Mapco Inc.
Mars, Inc.
Mars Foundation
Masco Corp.
Massey Foundation
May Department Stores Co.
McCormick & Co.
McCrea Foundation
McDermott
McDougall Charitable Trust,
Ruth Camp
McMahon Charitable Trust
Fund, Father John J.
Mead Corp.
Media General, Inc.
Memorial Foundation for
Children
Menasha Corp.
Merck & Co.
Metropolitan Health Foundation
MNC Financial
Mobil Oil Corp.
Mohasco Corp.
Morgan and Samuel Tate
Morgan, Jr. Foundation,
Marietta McNeil
Morton International
Nash-Finch Co.
National Medical Enterprises
NationsBank Corp.
Nationwide Insurance Cos.
NBD Bank
Newport News Shipbuilding &
Dry Dock Co.
Noland Co.
Norfolk Shipbuilding & Drydock
Corp.
Norfolk Southern Corp.
North Shore Foundation
Northern Virginia Natural Gas
Ohrstrom Foundation
Old Dominion Box Co.
Olmsted Foundation, George and
Carol
Olsson Memorial Foundation,
Elis
Omega World Travel
O'Sullivan Corp.
Overnite Transportation Co.
Owens & Minor, Inc.
PacifiCorp
Pannill Scholarship Foundation,
William Letcher
Paxton Co., Frank
Pechiney Corp.
PemCo. Corp.
Pendleton Construction Corp.
Penn Central Corp.
Petroleum Marketers
Philip Morris Cos.
Picker International
Pittston Co.

Planning Research Corp.
Portsmouth General Hospital
Foundation
Primark Corp.
Progressive Corp.
Provigo Corp. Inc.
Prudential Insurance Co. of
America
Quantum Chemical Corp.
Rangeley Educational Trust
REI-Recreational Equipment,
Inc.
Revlon
Reynolds Foundation, Richard S.
Reynolds Metals Co.
Rich Products Corp.
Richardson Benevolent
Foundation, C. E.
Richfood Holdings
Richmond Newspapers
Robertshaw Controls Co.
Rolls-Royce Inc.
Rouse Co.
Royston Manufacturing Corp.
Rubbermaid
Ryland Group
SAFECO Corp.
Safeway, Inc.
Sara Lee Corp.
Sara Lee Hosiery
Science Applications
International Corp.
Scott Foundation, William R.,
John G., and Emma
Scripps Co., E.W.
Sealy, Inc.
Seay Memorial Trust, George
and Effie
Sequa Corp.
Shenandoah Life Insurance Co.
Siebe North Inc.
Smith Family Foundation,
Charles E.
Southland Corp.
Sprint
Stanley Works
State Farm Mutual Automobile
Insurance Co.
Stone Container Corp.
Stroehmann Bakeries
Tandem Computers
Tarmac America Inc.
Taylor Foundation
Teledyne
Tenneco
Thalhimer and Family
Foundation, Charles G.
Thalhimer Brothers Inc.
Thalhimer, Jr. and Family
Foundation, William B.
Thomas Memorial Foundation,
Theresa A.
3M Co.
Thurman Charitable Foundation
for Children, Edgar A.
Tilghman, Sr., Charitable Trust,
Bell and Horace
Time Warner
Titmus Foundation
Transco Energy Company
Travelers Cos.
Treakle Foundation, J. Edwin
Tredegar Industries
TRINOVA Corp.
Truland Foundation
Truland Systems Corp.
TRW Corp.
Tultex Corp.
Turner Construction Co.
Turner Corp.
Ukrop's Super Markets, Inc.
Union Camp Corp.
Unisys Corp.
United Co.
United Technologies Corp.
Universal Leaf Tobacco Co.
Uslico Corp.

Virginia Power Co.
Vulcan Materials Co.
Wal-Mart Stores
Wareheim Foundation, E. C.
Washington Forrest Foundation
Washington Post Co.
Westinghouse Electric Corp.
Westmoreland Coal Co.
Westvaco Corp.
Weyerhaeuser Co.
Wheat First Securites
Winkler Foundation, Mark and
Catherine
Winn-Dixie Stores
Wynn's International, Inc.
Xerox Corp.
York International Corp.
Zapata Corp.

Washington

Agway
Airborne Express Co.
Alaska Airlines, Inc.
Albany International Corp.
Albertson's
Alco Standard Corp.
Aldus Corp.
Allen Foundation for Medical
Research, Paul G.
ALPAC Corp.
Alumax
Aluminum Co. of America
AMAX
America West Airlines
American Express Co.
American Home Products Corp.
Anderson Foundation
Archer-Daniels-Midland Co.
Archibald Charitable
Foundation, Norman
ARCO
Arise Charitable Trust
Armco Inc.
Arrow Electronics, Inc.
Augat, Inc.
Avnet, Inc.
Ball Corp.
BankAmerica Corp.
Barnes Group
Bartell Drug Co.
Battelle
Baxter International
Bell Industries
Bemis Company
Bergen Brunswig Corp.
Best Products Co.
BFGoodrich
Bishop Foundation
Bishop Foundation, E. K. and
Lillian F.
Bloedel Foundation
Boeing Co.
Boise Cascade Corp.
Borden
BP America
Bristol-Myers Squibb Co.
Brunswick Corp.
Budd Co.
Bullitt Foundation
Burlington Northern Inc.
Burlington Resources
Campbell Soup Co.
Capital Cities/ABC
Cascade Natural Gas Corp.
Cawsey Trust
Champion International Corp.
Cheney Foundation, Ben B.
Chevron Corp.
CIBA-GEIGY Corp.
Citicorp
Cominco American Inc.
Computer Associates
International
Comstock Foundation
ConAgra
Cook Foundation, Louella

Cooper Industries
Cowles Foundation, Harriet
Cheney
Cowles Foundation, William H.
Cox Enterprises
CPC International
Crum and Forster
Curtice-Burns Foods
Dayton Hudson Corp.
Deluxe Corp.
Dover Corp.
Dow Jones & Co.
Dudley Foundation
Dupar Foundation
Durr-Fillauer Medical
Eldec Corp.
Elf Atochem North America
Esterline Technologies Corp.
Fales Foundation Trust
Federated American Insurance
Federated Department Stores and
Allied Stores Corp.
First Bank System
First Interstate Bank NW Region
Forest Foundation
Foster Foundation
Fuchs Foundation, Gottfried &
Mary
Fuller Co., H.B.
Gannett Co.
GATX Corp.
General Reinsurance Corp.
Geneva Foundation
Georgia-Pacific Corp.
Glaser Foundation
Great Western Financial Corp.
Guardian Life Insurance Co. of
America
Guse Endowment Trust, Frank J.
and Adelaide
Haas Foundation, Saul and
Dayee G.
Hamilton Oil Corp.
Hanna Co., M.A.
Hanson Office Products
Harder Foundation
Hemingway Foundation, Robert
G.
Hewlett-Packard Co.
Home Depot
HON Industries
Horizons Foundation
Hubbard Broadcasting
Humana
Inland Steel Industries
Interpublic Group of Cos.
ITT Corp.
ITT Hartford Insurance Group
ITT Rayonier
James River Corp. of Virginia
Johnson & Higgins
Johnston-Fix Foundation
Johnston-Hanson Foundation
Kawabe Memorial Fund
Kilworth Charitable Foundation,
Florence B.
Kilworth Charitable Trust,
William
Klingensmith Charitable
Foundation, Agnes
Kreielsheimer Foundation Trust
La Croix Water Co.
Lamb-Weston Inc.
Land O'Lakes
Lassen Foundation, Irving A.
Lehigh Portland Cement Co.
Leuthold Foundation
Leviton Manufacturing Co.
Lilly & Co., Eli
LIN Broadcasting Corp.
Lockwood Foundation, Byron
W. and Alice L.
Longview Fibre Co.
Lozier Foundation
Manufacturers Life Insurance
Co. of America
Manville Corp.

Washington (cont.)

Mayne Nickless
McCaw Cellular
  Communications
McCaw Foundation
McEachern Charitable Trust, D.
  V. & Ida J.
McGraw-Hill
McKesson Corp.
Mead Corp.
Medina Foundation
Menasha Corp.
Merrill Foundation, R. D.
Microsoft Corp.
Miller Brewing Co.
Mitsui & Co. (U.S.A.)
Mobil Oil Corp.
Motorola
Murdock Charitable Trust, M. J.
Murray Foundation
National Medical Enterprises
Nesholm Family Foundation
New Horizon Foundation
Newport News Shipbuilding &
  Dry Dock Co.
News America Publishing Inc.
Norcliffe Fund
Nordstrom, Inc.
Northwestern National Insurance
  Group
Northwestern National Life
  Insurance Co.
Odessa Trading Co.
Ogilvy & Mather Worldwide
Olin Corp.
Olympia Brewing Co.
PACCAR
Pacific Coca-Cola Bottling Co.
Pacific Enterprises
PacifiCorp
Pegasus Gold Corp.
PemCo. Corp.
Persis Corp.
Petrie Trust, Lorene M.
PGL Building Products
Phelps Dodge Corp.
Philip Morris Cos.
Phillips Petroleum Co.
Pickering Industries
Pioneer Hi-Bred International
Poncin Scholarship Fund
PPG Industries
Prudential Insurance Co. of
  America
Puget Sound National Bank
Puget Sound Power & Light Co.
Quaker Oats Co.
Quantum Chemical Corp.
Quest for Truth Foundation
Ray Foundation
REI-Recreational Equipment,
  Inc.
Rhone-Poulenc Inc.
Rohr Inc.
Rouse Co.
SAFECO Corp.
Saint Paul Cos.
Sara Lee Corp.
Scott Paper Co.
Scripps Co., E.W.
Scrivner, Inc.
Seafirst Corp.
Seattle Times Co.
See Foundation, Charles
Sequoia Foundation
Shell Oil Co.
Shemanski Testamentary Trust,
  Tillie and Alfred
Sigourney Award Trust, Mary S.
Simpson Investment Co.
Skinner Corp.
Sky Chefs, Inc.
Smith Corp., A.O.
Smucker Co., J.M.
Snyder Foundation, Frost and
  Margaret

Spectra-Physics Analytical
Spiegel
Sprint
Standard Chartered Bank New
  York
Stewardship Foundation
Stubblefield, Estate of Joseph L.
Sundstrand Corp.
Super Valu Stores
T & T United Truck Lines
Tamaki Foundation
Tandem Computers
Target Stores
Tenneco
3M Co.
Thurston Charitable Foundation
Timken Co.
Travelers Cos.
Turner Corp.
Twentieth Century-Fox Film
  Corp.
Tyson Foods, Inc.
Unigard Security Insurance Co.
Union Carbide Corp.
Union Pacific Corp.
United Airlines
U.S. Bank of Washington
Univar Corp
US Bancorp
US WEST
Uslico Corp.
UST
Volkswagen of America, Inc.
Washington Mutual Savings
  Bank
Washington Natural Gas Co.
Washington Post Co.
Washington Trust Bank
Washington Water Power Co.
Wasmer Foundation
Welch Testamentary Trust,
  George T.
Wells Foundation, A. Z.
West One Bancorp
Westinghouse Electric Corp.
Weyerhaeuser Co.
Wharton Foundation
Witco Corp.
Wyman Youth Trust
Zurn Industries

West Virginia

Allegheny Power System, Inc.
American Electric Power
American Natural Resources Co.
ARCO Chemical
Aristech Chemical Corp.
Armco Inc.
Asea Brown Boveri
Bell Atlantic Corp.
Berwind Corp.
BFGoodrich
Board of Trustees of the Prichard
  School
Borden
Borg-Warner Corp.
Bowen Foundation, Ethel N.
Brown Family Foundation, John
  Mathew Gay
Browning-Ferris Industries
Butler Manufacturing Co.
Carbon Fuel Co.
Carter Family Foundation
Chambers Memorial, James B.
Chesapeake & Potomac
  Telephone Co.
Chesapeake & Potomac
  Telephone Co. of West Virginia
Circuit City Stores
Clay Foundation
Clorox Co.
CNG Transmission Corp.
Coastal Corp.
Consolidated Natural Gas Co.
Corning Incorporated
CSX Corp.

Cyprus Minerals Co.
Daywood Foundation
Dollar General Corp.
du Pont de Nemours & Co., E. I.
East Foundation, Sarita Kenedy
EG&G Inc.
Exxon Corp.
Fenton Foundation
First Fidelity Bancorp, Inc.
FMC Corp.
Gannett Co.
Georgia-Pacific Corp.
Giant Food Stores
Goodyear Tire & Rubber Co.
Hanson Office Products
Heinz Co., H.J.
Hercules Inc.
Hospital Corp. of America
Humana
Hunnicutt Foundation, H. P. and
  Anne S.
IMO Industries Inc.
Inco Alloys International
Jacobson Foundation, Bernard
  H. and Blanche E.
Kennedy Memorial Fund, Mark
  H.
Laughlin Trust, George A.
Lee Enterprises
Lockheed Corp.
LTV Corp.
Maier Foundation, Sarah Pauline
Manville Corp.
McDonough Foundation, Bernard
Monsanto Co.
Olin Corp.
One Valley Bank, N.A.
PacifiCorp
Pittston Co.
PPG Industries
Price Educational Foundation,
  Herschel C.
Quantum Chemical Corp.
Ravenswood Aluminum Corp.
Santa Maria Foundation
Schoenbaum Family Foundation
Scripps Co., E.W.
Shell Oil Co.
Shott, Jr. Foundation, Hugh I.
Teubert Charitable Trust, James
  H. and Alice
3M Co.
Travelers Cos.
Union Carbide Corp.
United States Borax & Chemical
  Corp.
U.S. Silica Co.
USX Corp.
Virginia Power Co.
Wal-Mart Stores
Weirton Steel Corp.
Westmoreland Coal Co.
Wetterau
Wheeling-Pittsburgh Corp.

Wisconsin

Akzo America
Albany International Corp.
Alco Standard Corp.
Alexander Charitable Foundation
Alexander Foundation, Judd S.
Alexander Foundation, Walter
Alfa-Laval, Inc.
Alumax
AMAX
Amcast Industrial Corp.
America West Airlines
American Brands
American Express Co.
American Home Products Corp.
American Standard
Ameritech Corp.
Ameritech Publishing
AMETEK
Amstar Corp.
Amsted Industries

Andersen Corp.
Andres Charitable Trust, Frank
  G.
Appleton Papers
Applied Power, Inc.
APV Crepaco Inc.
Archer-Daniels-Midland Co.
Armco Inc.
Arrow Electronics, Inc.
Autotrol Corp.
Avnet, Inc.
Backer Spielvogel Bates U.S.
Badger Meter, Inc.
Baird & Co., Robert W.
Banc One Illinois Corp.
Banc One Wisconsin Corp.
Bank of Boston Connecticut
Banta Corp.
Barnes Group
Bassett Foundation, Norman
Baxter International
Bell Industries
Bemis Company
Bergner Co., P.A.
Birnschein Foundation, Alvin
  and Marion
Black & Decker Corp.
Blue Cross and Blue Shield
  United of Wisconsin
  Foundation
BOC Group
Boise Cascade Corp.
Bolz Family Foundation,
  Eugenie Mayer
Borden
Bosch Corp., Robert
Bradley Foundation, Lynde and
  Harry
Brady Foundation, W. H.
Briggs & Stratton Corp.
Brillion Iron Works
Brotz Family Foundation, Frank
  G.
Brown Group
Browning-Ferris Industries
Brunswick Corp.
Bucyrus-Erie
Budd Co.
C.P. Rail Systems
Cadence Design Systems
Campbell Soup Co.
Case Co., J.I.
Castle & Co., A.M.
Castle Industries
Charter Manufacturing Co.
Charter Medical Corp.
Chesapeake Corp.
Christensen Charitable and
  Religious Foundation, L. C.
Chrysler Corp.
Church Mutual Insurance
Clark Family Foundation, Emory
  T.
Cleary Foundation
Clorox Co.
Coltec Industries
Computer Associates
  International
ConAgra
Consolidated Papers
Cooper Industries
Cornerstone Foundation of
  Northeastern Wisconsin
Corning Incorporated
Cox Enterprises
CPC International
Cray Research
Cremer Foundation
CTS Corp.
Cudahy Fund, Patrick and Anna
  M.
CUNA Mutual Insurance Group
Dayton Hudson Corp.
DEC International, Inc.
Deere & Co.
Deluxe Corp.
Demmer Foundation, Edward U.

Dial Corp.
Donaldson Co.
Dover Corp.
Dresser Industries
Earth Care Paper, Inc.
Eaton Corp.
Ecolab
Emerson Electric Co.
Employers Insurance of Wausau,
  A Mutual Co.
Endries Fastener & Supply Co.
Evinrude Foundation, Ralph
Evjue Foundation
Fairchild Corp.
Fireman's Fund Insurance Co.
First Bank System
First Financial Bank FSB
Firstar Bank Milwaukee NA
Firstar Corp.
Fleet Financial Group
FMC Corp.
Formrite Tube Co.
Fortis Inc.
Foxmeyer Corp.
Fromm Scholarship Trust, Walter
  and Mabel
Fuller Co., H.B.
Gannett Co.
General Electric Co.
General Motors Corp.
Georgia-Pacific Corp.
Giddings & Lewis
Godfrey Co.
Goldbach Foundation, Ray and
  Marie
Goodyear Tire & Rubber Co.
Grainger, W.W.
Grand Trunk Corp.
Grede Foundries
Greene Manufacturing Co.
Greenheck Fan Corp.
Guardian Life Insurance Co. of
  America
Handy & Harman
Harley-Davidson, Inc.
Harnischfeger Foundation
Heileman Brewing Co., Inc., G.
Hein-Werner Corp.
Helfaer Foundation, Evan and
  Marion
Henkel Corp.
Hercules Inc.
Huffy Corp.
Humphrey Foundation, Glenn &
  Gertrude
IDEX Corp.
IDS Financial Services
Illinois Tool Works
Indiana Insurance Cos.
Inland Container Corp.
Inland Steel Industries
International Multifoods Corp.
International Paper Co.
James River Corp. of Virginia
Janesville Foundation
Jefferson Smurfit Corp.
Jeffris Family Foundation
Jockey International
Johnson Controls
Johnson Foundation
Johnson & Son, S.C.
Journal Communications
Kemper National Insurance Cos.
Kikkoman Foods, Inc.
Kimball Co., Miles
Kimberly-Clark Corp.
Klingler Foundation, Helen and
  Charles
Kloeckner-Pentaplast of America
Kohl Charities, Herbert H.
Kohler Co.
Kohler Foundation
Kraft General Foods
Krause Foundation, Charles A.
Kress Foundation, George
La Croix Water Co.
Ladish Co.

Ladish Family Foundation,
Herman W.
Ladish Malting Co.
Land O'Lakes
Lappin Electric Co.
Lee Enterprises
Lincoln National Corp.
Lindsay Foundation
Madison Gas & Electric Co.
Manitowoc Co.
Manpower, Inc.
Manufacturers Life Insurance
Co. of America
Manville Corp.
Mapco Inc.
Marathon Cheese Corp.
Marcus Corp.
Marinette Marine Corp.
Marquette Electronics
Marshall Field's
Marshall & Ilsley Bank
Mautz Paint Co.
Mayer Foods Corp., Oscar
Maynard Steel Casting Co.
McBeath Foundation, Faye
Mead Corp.
Medalist Industries, Inc.
Menasha Corp.
MGIC Investment Corp.
Mielke Family Foundation
Miller Brewing Co.
Miller Foundation, Steve J.
Minnesota Power & Light Co.
Monaghan Charitable Trust, Rose
Mosinee Paper Corp.
Nash-Finch Co.
National Presto Industries
National Starch & Chemical
Corp.
NCR Corp.
Neenah Foundry Co.
Nelson Industries, Inc.
New England Business Service
Nordson Corp.
Northern Engraving Corp.
Northwestern National Insurance
Group

Norwest Corp.
Olin Corp.
Ore-Ida Foods, Inc.
Oshkosh B'Gosh
Oshkosh Truck Corp.
Oster/Sunbeam Appliance Co.
Outboard Marine Corp.
Outokumpu-American Brass Co.
Owens-Corning Fiberglas Corp.
Pamida, Inc.
Park Bank
Parker-Hannifin Corp.
Parker Pen USA Ltd.
Pet
Peters Foundation, R. D. and
Linda
Peterson Builders
Peterson Foundation, Fred J.
Pfister and Vogel Tanning Co.
Philip Morris Cos.
Phillips Family Foundation, L. E.
Phipps Foundation, William H.
Pick Charitable Trust, Melitta S.
Pieper Electric
Pioneer Hi-Bred International
Pittway Corp.
Plastics Engineering Co.
Pollybill Foundation
PPG Industries
Prange Co., H. C.
Procter & Gamble Co.
Pukall Lumber
Quantum Chemical Corp.
Rahr Malting Co.
Rayovac Corp.
Reinhart Institutional Foods
Reiss Coal Co., C.
Rennebohm Foundation, Oscar
Ringier-America
Rite-Hite Corp.
RJR Nabisco Inc.
Rochester Telephone Corp.
Rockwell International Corp.
Roddis Foundation, Hamilton
Roehl Foundation
Rolfs Foundation, Robert T.
Rolfs Foundation, Thomas J.

Ross Memorial Foundation, Will
Roundy's Inc.
Rouse Co.
Rubenstein Foundation, Philip
Rutledge Charity, Edward
Ryder System
Saint Paul Cos.
Sara Lee Corp.
Schlegel Foundation, Oscar C.
and Augusta
Schoenleber Foundation
Schreiber Foods, Inc.
Schroeder Foundation, Walter
Scott Paper Co.
Sentry Insurance Co.
Shattuck Charitable Trust, S. F.
Siebe North Inc.
Siebert Lutheran Foundation
Siemens Medical Systems Inc.
Sigma-Aldrich Corp.
Smith Corp., A.O.
Smith Family Foundation, Theda
Clark
Smucker Co., J.M.
Snap-on Tools Corp.
SNC Manufacturing Co.
Springs Industries
SPX Corp.
Square D Co.
Stackner Family Foundation
Steinhauer Charitable Foundation
Stry Foundation, Paul E.
Sundstrand Corp.
Super Valu Stores
Surgical Science Foundation for
Research and Development
Tandem Computers
Target Stores
Teledyne
Tenneco
Textron
3M Co.
Time Insurance Co.
Timken Co.
Toro Co.
Travelers Cos.
TRINOVA Corp.

Union Camp Corp.
Union Carbide Corp.
United Dominion Industries
U.S. Oil/Schmidt Family
Foundation, Inc.
Universal Foods Corp.
USG Corp.
USLIFE Corp.
Valspar Corp.
Vilter Manufacturing Corp.
Vollrath Co.
Vulcan Materials Co.
Wagner Foundation, Ltd., R. H.
Wagner Manufacturing Co., E. R.
Wal-Mart Stores
Walgreen Co.
Walter Family Trust, Byron L.
Wausau Insurance Cos.
Wausau Paper Mills Co.
Wauwatosa Savings & Loan
Association
Wehr Foundation, Todd
Western Publishing Co., Inc.
Weyerhaeuser Co.
WICOR, Inc.
Wigwam Mills
Wisconsin Bell, Inc.
Wisconsin Centrifugal
Wisconsin Energy Corp.
Wisconsin Power & Light Co.
Wisconsin Public Service Corp.
Wood Foundation, Lester G.
Woodson Foundation,
Aytchmonde
Young Foundation, Irvin L.
Ziegler Foundation
Ziemann Foundation

Wyoming

AMAX
Archer-Daniels-Midland Co.
ARCO
Armco Inc.
Best Products Co.
Browning-Ferris Industries
Bryan Foundation, Dodd and
Dorothy L.

Burlington Northern Inc.
Central & South West Services
Chevron Corp.
Cyprus Minerals Co.
Eaton Corp.
Exxon Corp.
First Security Corp. (Salt Lake
City, Utah)
Georgia-Pacific Corp.
Goodstein Foundation
Kamps Memorial Foundation,
Gertrude
KN Energy, Inc.
Land O'Lakes
Litton Industries
Mobil Oil Corp.
National Medical Enterprises
Norwest Corp.
Pamida, Inc.
Perkins Foundation, B. F. &
Rose H.
Phelps Dodge Corp.
Prudential Insurance Co. of
America
Public Service Co. of Colorado
Public Service Co. of Oklahoma
Sargent Foundation, Newell B.
Sprint
Stock Foundation, Paul
Storer Foundation, George B.
Surrena Memorial Fund, Harry
and Thelma
Target Stores
Tonkin Foundation, Tom and
Helen
True Oil Co.
Ucross Foundation
US WEST
Wal-Mart Stores
Weiss Foundation, William E.
Whitney Benefits
Williams Cos.

Operating Location Index

3023

Index to Corporations and Foundations by Grant Type

Capital (cont.)

Cabell III and Maude Morgan
 Cabell Foundation, Robert G.
Cablevision of Michigan
Cabot Corp.
Cabot Family Charitable Trust
Cain Foundation, Effie and
 Wofford
Cain Foundation, Gordon and
 Mary
Caldwell Foundation, Hardwick
Callaway Foundation
Callaway Foundation, Fuller E.
Camp and Bennet Humiston
 Trust, Apollos
Camp Foundation
Campbell and Adah E. Hall
 Charity Fund, Bushrod H.
Campbell Foundation
Campbell Foundation, J. Bulow
Campbell Soup Co.
Cannon Foundation
Cape Branch Foundation
Capital Holding Corp.
Cargill
Carnahan-Jackson Foundation
Carolina Power & Light Co.
Carolyn Foundation
Carpenter Foundation, E. Rhodes
 and Leona B.
Carpenter Technology Corp.
Carrier Corp.
Carter Foundation, Amon G.
Carver Charitable Trust, Roy J.
Cascade Natural Gas Corp.
Caspersen Foundation for Aid to
 Health and Education, O. W.
Cassett Foundation, Louis N.
Castle Foundation, Harold K. L.
Castle Foundation, Samuel N.
 and Mary
Caterpillar
Catlin Charitable Trust, Kathleen
 K.
Cayuga Foundation
Center for Educational Programs
Centerior Energy Corp.
Central Bank of the South
Central Fidelity Banks, Inc.
Central Hudson Gas & Electric
 Corp.
Central Life Assurance Co.
Central Maine Power Co.
Central Soya Co.
Cessna Aircraft Co.
Champion International Corp.
Champlin Foundations
Chandler Foundation
Chapman Charitable
 Corporation, Howard and Bess
Charitable Foundation of the
 Burns Family
Charlesbank Homes
Chase Charity Foundation,
 Alfred E.
Chase Lincoln First Bank, N.A.
Chase Manhattan Bank, N.A.
Chase Trust, Alice P.
Chatham Valley Foundation
Chatlos Foundation
Chazen Foundation
Cheney Foundation, Ben B.
Chesapeake Corp.
Chesebrough-Pond's
Chiles Foundation
Christy-Houston Foundation
Ciba-Geigy Corp.
 (Pharmaceuticals Division)
Cincinnati Bell
Cincinnati Gas & Electric Co.
Cincinnati Milacron
Citizens Commercial & Savings
 Bank
Citizens First National Bank
Clark Charitable Trust
Clark Equipment Co.

Clark Family Foundation, Emory
 T.
Clark Foundation
Clay Foundation
Cleveland-Cliffs
Clipper Ship Foundation
Clorox Co.
Close Foundation
Clowes Fund
CM Alliance Cos.
CNG Transmission Corp.
Coastal Corp.
Cobb Family Foundation
Coca-Cola Co.
Cockrell Foundation
Cohen Foundation, George M.
Cole Foundation, Olive B.
Coleman Co.
Coleman Foundation
Collins Foundation
Collins Foundation, George and
 Jennie
Collins, Jr. Foundation, George
 Fulton
Collins-McDonald Trust Fund
Colorado State Bank of Denver
Coltec Industries
Columbia Foundation
Columbus Dispatch Printing Co.
Columbus Southern Power Co.
Comer Foundation
Comerica
Commerce Clearing House
Commercial Intertech Corp.
Commercial Metals Co.
Commonwealth Edison Co.
Community Cooperative
 Development Foundation
Community Hospital Foundation
Computer Sciences Corp.
Comstock Foundation
Cone Mills Corp.
Conn Memorial Foundation
Connelly Foundation
Consolidated Natural Gas Co.
Consolidated Papers
Constantin Foundation
Consumers Power Co.
Contran Corp.
Cooke Foundation
Cooper Industries
Coors Foundation, Adolph
Copley Press
Corbett Foundation
Cornell Trust, Peter C.
Cornerstone Foundation of
 Northeastern Wisconsin
Corpus Christi Exploration Co.
Cosmair, Inc.
Coughlin-Saunders Foundation
Country Curtains, Inc.
Courts Foundation
Cove Charitable Trust
Covington Foundation, Marion
 Stedman
Cowan Foundation Corporation,
 Lillian L. and Harry A.
Cowden Foundation, Louetta M.
Cowell Foundation, S. H.
Cowles Charitable Trust
Cowles Foundation, Harriet
 Cheney
Cowles Media Co.
Cox Enterprises
Cox Foundation
Cox, Jr. Foundation, James M.
CPI Corp.
CR Industries
Craig Foundation, J. Paul
Crandall Memorial Foundation,
 J. Ford
Credit Agricole
Crestar Financial Corp.
Crestlea Foundation
Crocker Trust, Mary A.
Crown Memorial, Arie and Ida
Crystal Trust

Cuesta Foundation
Cullen Foundation
Cullen/Frost Bankers
Cummings Foundation, James H.
Cummins Engine Co.
Cuneo Foundation
Cunningham Foundation, Laura
 Moore
Curtice-Burns Foods
Dain Bosworth/Inter-Regional
 Financial Group
Dalton Foundation, Dorothy U.
Daly Charitable Foundation
 Trust, Robert and Nancy
Dana Corp.
Danforth Foundation
Daniels Foundation, Fred Harris
Danis Industries
Darling Foundation, Hugh and
 Hazel
Dart Group Corp.
Dater Foundation, Charles H.
Davenport Foundation, M. E.
Davenport-Hatch Foundation
Davidson Family Charitable
 Foundation
Davis Foundations, Arthur Vining
Day Foundation, Cecil B.
Dayton Hudson Corp.
Dayton Power and Light Co.
Daywood Foundation
DeCamp Foundation, Ira W.
Dee Foundation, Lawrence T.
 and Janet T.
Deere & Co.
DeKalb Genetics Corp.
Delaware North Cos.
Delta Air Lines
Deluxe Corp.
DeRoy Foundation, Helen L.
Detroit Edison Co.
Deuble Foundation, George H.
Devereaux Foundation
DeVore Foundation
DeVos Foundation, Richard and
 Helen
Dexter Charitable Fund, Eugene
 A.
Dietrich Foundation, William B.
Dillon Foundation
Dodge Foundation, Cleveland H.
Dodge Foundation, P. L.
Dodson Foundation, James
 Glenwell and Clara May
Doheny Foundation, Carrie
 Estelle
Dolan Family Foundation
Dollar General Corp.
Donaldson Co.
Donnelley & Sons Co., R.R.
Donnelly Foundation, Mary J.
Dorr Foundation
Doss Foundation, M. S.
Dougherty, Jr. Foundation, James
 R.
Douglas & Lomason Company
Dover Foundation
Dow Foundation, Herbert H. and
 Grace A.
Doyle Charitable Foundation
Dreiling and Albina Dreiling
 Charitable Trust, Leo J.
Dresser Industries
Drum Foundation
du Pont de Nemours & Co., E. I.
Dubow Family Foundation
Duchossois Industries
Duke Endowment
Duke Power Co.
Dumke Foundation, Dr. Ezekiel
 R. and Edna Wattis
Duncan Trust, John G.
Dunspaugh-Dalton Foundation
Dupar Foundation
duPont Foundation, Chichester
duPont Fund, Jessie Ball
Durham Corp.

Duriron Co., Inc.
Durr-Fillauer Medical
Dyson Foundation
East Ohio Gas Co.
Eastern Enterprises
Eastman Kodak Co.
Eaton Corp.
Ebert Charitable Foundation,
 Horatio B.
Eccles Foundation, Marriner S.
Eccles Foundation, Ralph M. and
 Ella M.
Eckerd Corp., Jack
Eden Hall Foundation
Eder Foundation, Sidney and
 Arthur
Edison Foundation, Harry
EIS Foundation
El Pomar Foundation
Elf Atochem North America
Elgin Sweeper Co.
Elkin Memorial Foundation, Neil
 Warren and William Simpson
Ellsworth Foundation, Ruth H.
 and Warren A.
Emergency Aid of Pennsylvania
 Foundation
Emerson Foundation, Fred L.
Ensign-Bickford Industries
Equifax
Ethyl Corp.
Evans Foundation, Lettie Pate
Evans Foundation, T. M.
Evans Foundation, Thomas J.
Evening Post Publishing Co.
Evinrude Foundation, Ralph
Exchange Bank
Exposition Foundation
Fabri-Kal Corp.
Factor Family Foundation, Max
Fair Play Foundation
Fairchild Foundation, Sherman
Falk Foundation, David
Farish Fund, William Stamps
Farmland Industries, Inc.
Farnsworth Trust, Charles A.
Farr Trust, Frank M. and Alice
 M.
Favrot Fund
Fay's Incorporated
Federal Express Corp.
Federal Home Loan Mortgage
 Corp. (Freddie Mac)
Federal-Mogul Corp.
Federal National Mortgage
 Assn., Fannie Mae
Federated Department Stores and
 Allied Stores Corp.
Feinstein Foundation, Myer and
 Rosaline
Ferebee Endowment, Percy O.
Fidelity Bank
Field Foundation of Illinois
Fieldcrest Cannon
Fifth Avenue Foundation
Fifth Third Bancorp
Fikes Foundation, Leland
FINA, Inc.
Finch Foundation, Thomas
 Austin
Fink Foundation
Finley Charitable Trust, J. B.
Finnegan Foundation, John D.
First Chicago
First Fidelity Bancorporation
First Financial Bank FSB
First Hawaiian
First Interstate Bank NW Region
First Interstate Bank of Arizona
First Interstate Bank of California
First Interstate Bank of Denver
First Interstate Bank of Oregon
First Interstate Bank of Texas,
 N.A.
First Maryland Bancorp
First Mississippi Corp.
First of America Bank Corp.

First Tennessee Bank
First Union Corp.
Firstar Bank Milwaukee NA
FirsTier Bank N.A. Omaha
Fish Foundation, Bert
Fish Foundation, Ray C.
Fleet Financial Group
Fleishhacker Foundation
Fleming Companies, Inc.
Florence Foundation
Florida Power Corp.
Fluor Corp.
FMR Corp.
Foellinger Foundation
Fondren Foundation
Foothills Foundation
Forbes
Ford and Ada Ford Fund, S. N.
Ford Motor Co.
Forest Foundation
Forest Oil Corp.
Foster Foundation
Foster Foundation, Joseph C. and
 Esther
Foulds Trust, Claiborne F
Fourth Financial Corp.
France Foundation, Jacob and
 Annita
Franklin Foundation, John and
 Mary
Franklin Mint Corp.
Fraser Paper Ltd.
Frear Eleemosynary Trust, Mary
 D. and Walter F.
Frederick Foundation
Freedom Forum
Freeman Foundation, Ella West
Freeport-McMoRan
Frees Foundation
Frick Foundation, Helen Clay
Friends' Foundation Trust, A.
Friendship Fund
Froderman Foundation
Frohring Foundation, William O.
 and Gertrude Lewis
Frueauff Foundation, Charles A.
Fuchs Foundation, Gottfried &
 Mary
Fuld Health Trust, Helene
Fuller Foundation, C. G.
Fuller Foundation, George F. and
 Sybil H.
Funderburke & Associates
Fusenot Charity Foundation,
 Georges and Germaine
Gallagher Family Foundation,
 Lewis P.
Gap, The
GAR Foundation
Garvey Kansas Foundation
Garvey Texas Foundation
Gates Foundation
Gault-Hussey Charitable Trust
Gazette Co.
Gebbie Foundation
Gellert Foundation, Carl
Gellert Foundation, Celia Berta
Gellert Foundation, Fred
General Accident Insurance Co.
 of America
General American Life Insurance
 Co.
General Dynamics Corp.
General Machine Works
General Mills
General Motors Corp.
General Railway Signal Corp.
General Reinsurance Corp.
General Signal Corp.
GenRad
George Foundation
Georgia-Pacific Corp.
Georgia Power Co.
Gerber Products Co.
Gerstacker Foundation, Rollin M.
Gheens Foundation
Giant Food Stores

Gifford Charitable Corporation, Rosamond
Gillette Co.
Gilmore Foundation, Irving S.
Ginter Foundation, Karl and Anna
Gleason Memorial Fund
Glencoe Foundation
Glenmore Distilleries Co.
Glenn Memorial Foundation, Wilbur Fisk
Glick Foundation, Eugene and Marilyn
Goddard Foundation, Charles B.
Golden Family Foundation
Goldman Foundation, Herman
Goldome F.S.B
Goldsmith Family Foundation
Goodstein Family Foundation, David
Goodyear Foundation, Josephine
Goodyear Tire & Rubber Co.
Gottwald Foundation
Grable Foundation
Grace & Co., W.R.
Graco
Graham Charitable Trust, William L.
Graham Fund, Philip L.
Grainger Foundation
Grand Rapids Label Co.
Grant Charitable Trust, Elberth R. and Gladys F.
Grant Foundation, Charles M. and Mary D.
Graphic Controls Corp.
Grassmann Trust, E. J.
Gray Foundation, Garland
Great Western Financial Corp.
Greater Lansing Foundation
Greeley Gas Co.
Green Foundation, Allen P. and Josephine B.
Greene Manufacturing Co.
Gregg-Graniteville Foundation
Gries Charity Fund, Lucile and Robert H.
Griffin Foundation, Rosa May
Griffith Foundation, W. C.
Griggs and Mary Griggs Burke Foundation, Mary Livingston
Grimes Foundation
Groome Beatty Trust, Helen D.
Grumbacher Foundation, M. S.
Grundy Foundation
Gulf Power Co.
Gulfstream Aerospace Corp.
Guttman Foundation, Stella and Charles
H.C.S. Foundation
Haas Foundation, Paul and Mary
Haas Fund, Miriam and Peter
Haas Fund, Walter and Elise
Haas, Jr. Fund, Evelyn and Walter
Haffner Foundation
Hagedorn Fund
Hale Foundation, Crescent Porter
Hales Charitable Fund
Hall Family Foundations
Hall Foundation
Hallmark Cards
Hallowell Foundation
Halsell Foundation, Ewing
Hamilton Bank
Hamilton Oil Corp.
Hamman Foundation, George and Mary Josephine
Hammer Foundation, Armand
Hanes Foundation, John W. and Anna H.
Harcourt General
Harden Foundation
Hardin Foundation, Phil
Harland Charitable Foundation, John and Wilhelmina D.
Harrington Foundation, Don and Sybil

Harrington Foundation, Francis A. and Jacquelyn H.
Harris Foundation
Harris Trust & Savings Bank
Harsco Corp.
Hartford Courant Foundation
Hartmarx Corp.
Haskell Fund
Hayden Foundation, Charles
Hayden Foundation, William R. and Virginia
Hazen Foundation, Edward W.
Hechinger Co.
Heckscher Foundation for Children
Hecla Mining Co.
Hedco Foundation
Heginbotham Trust, Will E.
HEI Inc.
Heinz Co., H.J.
Heinz Endowment, Howard
Heinz Endowment, Vira I.
Helfaer Foundation, Evan and Marion
Helmerich Foundation
Hemby Foundation, Alex
Henderson Foundation, George B.
Herbst Foundation
Hermann Foundation, Grover
Herrick Foundation
Hershey Foods Corp.
Hershey Foundation
Hervey Foundation
Hess Foundation
Heublein
Heydt Fund, Nan and Matilda
Higgins Charitable Trust, Lorene Sails
Hightower Foundation, Walter
Hill and Family Foundation, Walter Clay
Hill Crest Foundation
Hillcrest Foundation
Hillman Foundation
Hillman Foundation, Henry L.
Hilton Foundation, Conrad N.
Hitchcock Foundation, Gilbert M. and Martha H.
Hobbs Foundation
Hoblitzelle Foundation
Hoche-Scofield Foundation
Hoechst Celanese Corp.
Hoffberger Foundation
Hoffman Foundation, Maximillian E. and Marion O.
Holden Fund, James and Lynelle
Holt Foundation, William Knox
Home Depot
HON Industries
Honeywell
Hooper Foundation, Elizabeth S.
Hoover Foundation
Hopedale Foundation
Hopewell Foundation
Hopkins Foundation, John Jay
Horizons Foundation
Hospital Corp. of America
Houghton Mifflin Co.
Houston Endowment
Houston Industries
Hoyt Foundation
Hoyt Foundation, Stewart W. and Willma C.
Hubbard Broadcasting
Hubbard Foundation, R. Dee and Joan Dale
Hubbard Milling Co.
Hubbell Inc.
Hudson-Webber Foundation
Huffy Corp.
Hughes Charitable Trust, Mabel Y.
Hulings Foundation, Mary Andersen
Humana

Humphrey Fund, George M. and Pamela S.
Hunt Alternatives Fund
Hunt Charitable Trust, C. Giles
Hunt Foundation
Hunt Foundation, Roy A.
Hunt Foundation, Samuel P.
Hunt Manufacturing Co.
Hunter Foundation, Edward and Irma
Huntington Fund for Education, John
Hurst Foundation
Huston Foundation
Hyams Foundation
Hyde and Watson Foundation
Hyde Manufacturing Co.
Hyster-Yale
IBM Corp.
Iddings Benevolent Trust
IES Industries
Illges Foundation, John P. and Dorothy S.
Illinois Bell
Illinois Tool Works
Imerman Memorial Foundation, Stanley
Imperial Bancorp
Indiana Bell Telephone Co.
Indiana Insurance Cos.
Ingalls Foundation, Louise H. and David S.
Inland Container Corp.
Inland Steel Industries
Interco
International Foundation
International Multifoods Corp.
International Paper Co.
Iowa-Illinois Gas & Electric Co.
Irvine Foundation, James
Irwin Charity Foundation, William G.
Israel Discount Bank of New York
ITT Hartford Insurance Group
ITT Rayonier
J. D. B. Fund
J.P. Morgan & Co.
Jackson Foundation
Jacobs Engineering Group
James River Corp. of Virginia
Janesville Foundation
Janirve Foundation
Jaydor Corp.
JELD-WEN, Inc.
Jergens Foundation, Andrew
Jesselson Foundation
Jewell Memorial Foundation, Daniel Ashley and Irene Houston
Jewett Foundation, George Frederick
John Hancock Mutual Life Insurance Co.
Johnson Controls
Johnson Foundation, Helen K. and Arthur E.
Johnson Foundation, M. G. and Lillie A.
Johnson Fund, Edward C.
Johnson & Higgins
Johnston-Hanson Foundation
Jones Construction Co., J.A.
Jones Family Foundation, Eugenie and Joseph
Jones Foundation, Daisy Marquis
Jonsson Foundation
Jordan and Ettie A. Jordan Charitable Foundation, Mary Ranken
Jordan Foundation, Arthur
Jostens
Joukowsky Family Foundation
Journal Gazette Co.
Joy Family Foundation
Joyce Foundation, John M. and Mary A.

Kangesser Foundation, Robert E., Harry A., and M. Sylvia
Kantzler Foundation
Kaplan Foundation, Rita J. and Stanley H.
Kaufman Memorial Trust, Chaim, Fanny, Louis, Benjamin, and Anne Florence
Kaul Foundation Trust, Hugh
Kavanagh Foundation, T. James
Kawabe Memorial Fund
Keck Foundation, W. M.
Keith Foundation Trust, Ben E.
Kellenberger Historical Foundation, May Gordon Latham
Keller-Crescent Co.
Kelley and Elza Kelley Foundation, Edward Bangs
Kellwood Co.
Kelly, Jr. Memorial Foundation, Ensign C. Markland
Kemper Charitable Lead Trust, William T.
Kempner Fund, Harris and Eliza
Kenedy Memorial Foundation, John G. and Marie Stella
Kennecott Corp.
Kennedy Memorial Fund, Mark H.
Kent-Lucas Foundation
Kerney Foundation, James
Kerr Foundation
Kerr Foundation, A. H.
Kerr Fund, Grayce B.
Kettering Family Foundation
Kettering Fund
Kieckhefer Foundation, J. W.
Kiewit Foundation, Peter
Kiewit Sons, Peter
Kilbourne Residuary Charitable Trust, E. H.
Kilcawley Fund, William H.
Killough Trust, Walter H. D.
Kilworth Charitable Foundation, Florence B.
Kilworth Charitable Trust, William
Kimball International
Kimberly-Clark Corp.
Kimmelman Foundation, Helen & Milton
Kinney-Lindstrom Foundation
Kiplinger Foundation
Kirby Foundation, F. M.
Kirkpatrick Foundation
Kitzmiller/Bales Trust
Klau Foundation, David W. and Sadie
Kleberg Foundation for Wildlife Conservation, Caesar
Klein Fund, Nathan J.
Knight Foundation, John S. and James L.
Knott Foundation, Marion I. and Henry J.
Koch Charitable Trust, David H.
Koch Foundation
Koehler Foundation, Marcia and Otto
Kohler Co.
Kohler Foundation
Komes Foundation
Koopman Fund
Koret Foundation
Kramer Foundation, Louise
Krause Foundation, Charles A.
Kreielsheimer Foundation Trust
Kresge Foundation
Kuhne Foundation Trust, Charles
Kulas Foundation
Kutz Foundation, Milton and Hattie
Laclede Gas Co.
Laffey-McHugh Foundation
Lakeside Foundation
Land O'Lakes
Landmark Communications

Larsen Fund
Lassen Foundation, Irving A.
Laub Foundation
Laurel Foundation
LaViers Foundation, Harry and Maxie
Leavey Foundation, Thomas and Dorothy
Lee Enterprises
Lemberg Foundation
Leo Burnett Co.
Leuthold Foundation
Levinson Foundation, Max and Anna
Levy Foundation, June Rockwell
Lewis Foundation, Lillian Kaiser
Library Association of Warehouse Point
Lightner Sams Foundation
Lilly & Co., Eli
Lilly Foundation, Richard Coyle
Lincoln Electric Co.
Lincoln National Corp.
Lincoln Telecommunications Co.
Lindsay Trust, Agnes M.
Lindstrom Foundation, Kinney
Link, Jr. Foundation, George
Lintilhac Foundation
Little Family Foundation
Littlefield Memorial Trust, Ida Ballou
Livingston Foundation, Milton S. and Corinne N.
Lockheed Corp.
Lockheed Sanders
Longwood Foundation
Loridans Foundation, Charles
Louisiana Land & Exploration Co.
Louisiana-Pacific Corp.
Louisiana Power & Light Co./New Orleans Public Service
Loutit Foundation
Love Foundation, George H. and Margaret McClintic
Lowe Foundation
Loyola Foundation
LTV Corp.
Lubrizol Corp.
Luce Foundation, Henry
Luck Stone
Lydall, Inc.
Lyons Foundation
Lytel Foundation, Bertha Russ
M. E. G. Foundation
Mabee Foundation, J. E. and L. E.
MacDonald Foundation, James A.
Macht Foundation, Morton and Sophia
Maclellan Charitable Trust, R. J.
Maclellan Foundation
Maddox Foundation, J. F.
Maier Foundation, Sarah Pauline
Manoogian Foundation, Alex and Marie
Manville Corp.
Mapco Inc.
Marbrook Foundation
Mardag Foundation
Maritz Inc.
Marmot Foundation
Marpat Foundation
Marriott Foundation, J. Willard
Mars Foundation
Marshall & Ilsley Bank
Martin Foundation
Martin Foundation, Bert William
Masco Corp.
Mascoma Savings Bank
Massachusetts Mutual Life Insurance Co.
Massengill-DeFriece Foundation
Massey Foundation
Material Service Corp.

Grant Type Index

Capital (cont.)

Mather and William Gwinn
  Mather Fund, Elizabeth Ring
Maxus Energy Corp.
May Department Stores Co.
May Foundation, Wilbur
Mayerson Foundation, Manuel
  D. and Rhoda
Maytag Corp.
Maytag Family Foundation, Fred
MBIA, Inc.
McBeath Foundation, Faye
McCann Foundation
McCasland Foundation
McCormick & Co.
McCormick Foundation,
  Chauncey and Marion Deering
McCormick Tribune Foundation,
  Robert R.
McCullough Foundation, Ralph
  H. and Ruth J.
McCune Foundation
McDermott Foundation, Eugene
McDonald & Co. Securities
McDonald Foundation, J. M.
McDonnell Douglas Corp.
McDonnell Douglas Corp.-West
McDonnell Foundation, James S.
McDonough Foundation, Bernard
McEachern Charitable Trust, D.
  V. & Ida J.
McElroy Trust, R. J.
McFawn Trust No. 2, Lois Sisler
McFeely-Rogers Foundation
McGee Foundation
McGonagle Foundation, Dextra
  Baldwin
McGovern Fund for the
  Behavioral Sciences
McGraw Foundation
McGregor Fund
MCI Communications Corp.
McInerny Foundation
McKee Foundation, Robert E.
  and Evelyn
McKenna Foundation, Katherine
  Mabis
McKenna Foundation, Philip M.
McKnight Foundation
McLean Contributionship
McMahon Foundation
McWane Inc.
Mead Corp.
Meadowood Foundation
Meadows Foundation
Medina Foundation
Mellon Bank Corp.
Mellon Foundation, Richard King
Memton Fund
Mercantile Bancorp
Mercury Aircraft
Meredith Corp.
Merillat Foundation, Orville D.
  and Ruth A.
Merrick Foundation
Merrick Foundation, Robert G.
  and Anne M.
Merrill Lynch & Co.
Meyer Foundation, Alice
  Kleberg Reynolds
Meyer Foundation, Baron de
  Hirsch
Meyer Foundation, Eugene and
  Agnes E.
Meyer Foundation, Robert R.
Meyer Memorial Trust
Meyerhoff Fund, Joseph
Michigan Bell Telephone Co.
Michigan Gas Utilities
Mid-Iowa Health Foundation
Midwest Resources
Milbank Foundation, Dunlevy
Miles Inc.
Milken Foundation, L. and S.
Millard Charitable Trust, Adah K.
Millbrook Tribute Garden

Miller Foundation
Milliken & Co.
Mills Charitable Foundation,
  Henry L. and Kathryn
Mills Fund, Frances Goll
Millstein Charitable Foundation
Mine Safety Appliances Co.
Mingenback Foundation, Julia J.
Minnesota Mutual Life
  Insurance Co.
Mitchell Energy & Development
  Corp.
Mobil Oil Corp.
Monell Foundation, Ambrose
Monroe-Brown Foundation
Monroe Foundation (1976), J.
  Edgar
Montana Power Co.
Montgomery Street Foundation
Moody Foundation
Moog Automotive, Inc.
Moore Charitable Foundation,
  Marjorie
Moore Foundation, Roy C.
Moores Foundation, Harry C.
Morgan and Samuel Tate
  Morgan, Jr. Foundation,
  Marietta McNeil
Morgan Foundation, Burton D.
Morgan Trust for Charity,
  Religion, and Education
Morley Brothers Foundation
Morris Charitable Foundation, E.
  A.
Morris Foundation, Margaret T.
Morrison Charitable Trust,
  Pauline A. and George R.
Morrison Foundation, Harry W.
Morton International
Moses Fund, Henry and Lucy
Mosher Foundation, Samuel B.
Moss Charitable Trust, Finis M.
Moss Heart Trust, Harry S.
Motorola
MTS Systems Corp.
Mulcahy Foundation
Muller Foundation, C. John and
  Josephine
Mulligan Charitable Trust, Mary
  S.
Munson Foundation, W. B.
Murch Foundation
Murdock Charitable Trust, M. J.
Murphey Foundation, Lluella
  Morey
Murphy Foundation
Murphy Foundation, John P.
Murphy Oil Corp.
Murray Foundation
Nabisco Foods Group
Nalco Chemical Co.
Nash Foundation
National City Bank, Columbus
National City Corp.
National Computer Systems
National Fuel Gas Co.
National Gypsum Co.
National Life of Vermont
National Pro-Am Youth Fund
National Starch & Chemical
  Corp.
National Westminster Bank New
  Jersey
NationsBank Corp.
Nationwide Insurance Cos.
NBD Bank
NBD Bank, N.A.
NBD Genesee Bank
Neese Family Foundation
New England Business Service
New England Mutual Life
  Insurance Co.
New York Life Insurance Co.
New York Mercantile Exchange
New York Telephone Co.
Newhouse Foundation, Samuel I.
News & Observer Publishing Co.
Nichols Co., J.C.

Nichols Foundation
Noble Foundation, Edward John
Noble Foundation, Samuel
  Roberts
Noble Foundation, Vivian Bilby
Norcliffe Fund
Nord Family Foundation
Nordson Corp.
Norfolk Shipbuilding & Drydock
  Corp.
Norfolk Southern Corp.
Norgren Foundation, Carl A.
Norman Foundation, Andrew
North American Life & Casualty
  Co.
North American Reinsurance
  Corp.
Northeast Utilities
Northern Indiana Public Service
  Co.
Northern States Power Co.
Northern Trust Co.
Northrop Corp.
Northwest Natural Gas Co.
Norwest Corp.
Noyes, Jr. Memorial Foundation,
  Nicholas H.
NuTone Inc.
O'Brien Foundation, Alice M.
Occidental Petroleum Corp.
O'Connor Foundation, A.
  Lindsay and Olive B.
O'Connor Foundation, Kathryn
O'Donnell Foundation
O'Fallon Trust, Martin J. and
  Mary Anne
Oglebay Norton Co.
Ohio Bell Telephone Co.
Ohio National Life Insurance Co.
Ohio Valley Foundation
Ohl, Jr. Trust, George A.
Ohrstrom Foundation
Oki America Inc.
Oklahoma Gas & Electric Co.
Old National Bank in Evansville
Oldham Little Church Foundation
Olin Corp.
Olin Foundation, F. W.
Oliver Memorial Trust
  Foundation
1525 Foundation
1957 Charity Trust
O'Neill Charitable Corporation,
  F. J.
Ontario Corp.
Ordean Foundation
Ore-Ida Foods, Inc.
Ortho Diagnostic Systems, Inc.
O'Shaughnessy Foundation, I. A.
O'Sullivan Children Foundation
O'Toole Foundation, Theresa
  and Edward
Owen Trust, B. B.
Owsley Foundation, Alvin and
  Lucy
Oxford Industries, Inc.
PACCAR
Pacific Enterprises
Pacific Gas & Electric Co.
Pacific Mutual Life Insurance Co.
PacifiCorp
Packard Foundation, David and
  Lucile
Padnos Iron & Metal Co., Louis
Palin Foundation
Palmer Fund, Frank Loomis
Pan-American Life Insurance Co.
Panhandle Eastern Corp.
Pappas Charitable Foundation,
  Thomas Anthony
Parker Foundation
Parker Foundation, Theodore
  Edson
Parker-Hannifin Corp.
Parsons Foundation, Ralph M.
Patterson Charitable Fund, W. I.
Pauley Foundation, Edwin W.

Payne Foundation, Frank E. and
  Seba B.
Peabody Charitable Fund, Amelia
Pearlstone Foundation, Peggy
  Meyerhoff
Pella Corp.
Penn Foundation, William
Penn Savings Bank, a division of
  Sovereign Bank Bank of
  Princeton, a division of
  Sovereign Bank
Pentair
People's Bank
Peoples Energy Corp.
Perkin-Elmer Corp.
Perkins Foundation, Joe and Lois
Persis Corp.
Pet
Peters Foundation, Leon S.
Petersen Foundation, Esper A.
Peterson Foundation, Fred J.
Pfizer
Phelps Dodge Corp.
PHH Corp.
Philadelphia Electric Co.
Philibosian Foundation, Stephen
Phillips Family Foundation, Jay
  and Rose
Phillips Family Foundation, L. E.
Phillips Foundation, Dr. P.
Phipps Foundation, William H.
Pick, Jr. Fund, Albert
Pineywoods Foundation
Pitney Bowes
Pitts Foundation, William H. and
  Lula E.
Pittsburgh National Bank
Plough Foundation
Poindexter Foundation
Polaroid Corp.
Polk Foundation
Pollybill Foundation
Porter Testamentary Trust, James
  Hyde
Portland General Electric Co.
Post Foundation of D.C.,
  Marjorie Merriweather
Potomac Electric Power Co.
Potter Foundation, Justin and
  Valere
Potts Memorial Foundation
Powell Family Foundation
PPG Industries
Pratt Memorial Fund
Premier Industrial Corp.
Prentiss Foundation, Elisabeth
  Severance
Presser Foundation
Price Associates, T. Rowe
Prince Trust, Abbie Norman
Principal Financial Group
Pritzker Foundation
Procter & Gamble Co.
Procter & Gamble Cosmetic &
  Fragrance Products
Promus Cos.
Prospect Hill Foundation
Prouty Foundation, Olive Higgins
Providence Energy Corp.
Providence Journal Company
Provident Life & Accident
  Insurance Co.
Provigo Corp. Inc.
Public Service Co. of New
  Mexico
Public Service Electric & Gas
  Co.
Puett Foundation, Nelson
Pulitzer Publishing Co.
Puterbaugh Foundation
Putnam Foundation
Quaker Oats Co.
Quantum Chemical Corp.
Questar Corp.
Rabb Charitable Trust, Sidney R.
Radiator Specialty Co.
Ralston Purina Co.

Rapp Foundation, Robert Glenn
Raskob Foundation for Catholic
  Activities
Ratner Foundation, Milton M.
Ratshesky Foundation, A. C.
Ray Foundation
Raymond Corp.
Raymond Educational
  Foundation
Raytheon Co.
Reasoner, Davis & Fox
Red Wing Shoe Co.
Redfield Foundation, Nell J.
Redman Foundation
Reeves Foundation
Regenstein Foundation
Reily & Co., William B.
Reinberger Foundation
Reinhold Foundation, Paul E.
  and Ida Klare
Reliance Electric Co.
Rennebohm Foundation, Oscar
Rexham Inc.
Reynolds Charitable Trust, Kate
  B.
Reynolds Foundation, Donald W.
Reynolds Foundation, Edgar
Reynolds Foundation, J. B.
Reynolds Foundation, Richard S.
Reynolds Metals Co.
Rhoden Charitable Foundation,
  Elmer C.
Rhone-Poulenc Rorer
Rich Foundation
Rider-Pool Foundation
Riley Foundation, Mabel Louise
Rippel Foundation, Fannie E.
Ritchie Memorial Foundation,
  Charles E. and Mabel M.
RJR Nabisco Inc.
Robertshaw Controls Co.
Roblee Foundation, Joseph H.
  and Florence A.
Rochester Midland Corp.
Rockwell Foundation
Rockwell Fund
Rockwell International Corp.
Rodman Foundation
Roe Foundation
Rogers Foundation
Rohm and Haas Company
Rohr Inc.
Rolfs Foundation, Robert T.
RosaMary Foundation
Roseburg Forest Products Co.
Rosenthal Foundation, Richard
  and Hinda
Ross Foundation
Ross Foundation, Walter G.
Ross Laboratories
Rouse Co.
Royal Group Inc.
Rubbermaid
Rubenstein Charitable
  Foundation, Lawrence J. and
  Anne
Russell Charitable Trust,
  Josephine S.
Russell Trust, Josephine G.
SAFECO Corp.
Sage Foundation
Saint Paul Cos.
Sams Foundation, Earl C.
San Diego Gas & Electric
Sandusky International Inc.
Sandy Hill Foundation
Santa Fe Pacific Corp.
Sara Lee Hosiery
Sarkeys Foundation
Saunders Foundation
Scaife Family Foundation
Scaife Foundation, Sarah
Schenck Fund, L. P.
Schering-Plough Corp.
Scheuer Family Foundation, S.
  H. and Helen R.
Schey Foundation

Schieffelin & Somerset Co.
Schiff Foundation
Schlieder Educational
   Foundation, Edward G.
Schlumberger Ltd.
Schmidlapp Trust No. 1, Jacob G.
Schmidlapp Trust No. 2, Jacob G.
Schottenstein Foundation,
   Jerome & Saul
Schowalter Foundation
Schroeder Foundation, Walter
Schultz Foundation
Schwab & Co., Charles
Scott Foundation, Walter
Scott Foundation, William E.
Scott Foundation, William R.,
   John G., and Emma
Scrivner, Inc.
Scurlock Foundation
Sealright Co., Inc.
Sears Family Foundation
Seay Memorial Trust, George
   and Effie
Security Life of Denver
Seidman Family Foundation
Selby and Marie Selby
   Foundation, William G.
Self Foundation
Semmes Foundation
Semple Foundation, Louise Taft
Sentinel Communications Co.
Sequoia Foundation
Sewell Foundation, Warren P.
   and Ava F.
Shawmut National Corp.
Shawmut Worcester County
   Bank, N.A.
Shaw's Supermarkets
Sheaffer Inc.
Shelden Fund, Elizabeth, Allan
   and Warren
Sheldon Foundation, Ralph C.
Shell Oil Co.
Shelton Cos.
Shenandoah Life Insurance Co.
Sheppard Foundation, Lawrence
   B.
Sheridan Foundation, Thomas B.
   and Elizabeth M.
Sherwin-Williams Co.
Shirk Foundation, Russell and
   Betty
Shoemaker Fund, Thomas H.
   and Mary Williams
Shoenberg Foundation
Shoong Foundation, Milton
Shott, Jr. Foundation, Hugh I.
Siebert Lutheran Foundation
Signet Bank/Maryland
Silverman Foundation, Marty
   and Dorothy
Simon Foundation, William E.
   and Carol G.
Simpson Foundation
Simpson Investment Co.
Skillman Foundation
Skinner Corp.
Slemp Foundation
Smith and W. Aubrey Smith
   Charitable Foundation, Clara
   Blackford
Smith Charitable Foundation,
   Lou and Lutza
Smith Charitable Trust
Smith Charitable Trust, W. W.
Smith Charities, John
Smith Corp., A.O.
Smith Foundation
Smith Foundation, Kelvin and
   Eleanor
Smith Foundation, Richard and
   Susan
Smith Horticultural Trust, Stanley
Smith, Jr. Charitable Trust, Jack
   J.
Smith, Jr. Foundation, M. W.
Smith Memorial Fund, Ethel
   Sergeant Clark

SNET
Snow Foundation, John Ben
Snyder Fund, Valentine Perry
Society Corp.
Solo Cup Co.
Somers Foundation, Byron H.
Sordoni Foundation
Soref Foundation, Samuel M.
   Soref and Helene K.
South Waite Foundation
Southern Bell
Southern California Edison Co.
Southways Foundation
Speas Foundation, Victor E.
Speas Memorial Trust, John W.
   and Effie E.
Springs Foundation
Sprint
Square D Co.
Stabler Foundation, Donald B.
   and Dorothy L.
Stackner Family Foundation
Stackpole-Hall Foundation
Stamps Foundation, James L.
Stanley Charitable Foundation,
   A. W.
Stanley Works
Stans Foundation
Star Bank, N.A.
Starr Foundation
State Farm Mutual Automobile
   Insurance Co.
State Street Bank & Trust Co.
Statler Foundation
Stauffer Foundation, John and
   Beverly
Steadley Memorial Trust, Kent
   D. and Mary L.
Stearns Trust, Artemas W.
Steelcase
Steele Foundation
Steele Foundation, Harry and
   Grace
Steiger Memorial Fund, Albert
Steigerwaldt Foundation, Donna
   Wolf
Stein Foundation, Jules and Doris
Steinhagen Benevolent Trust, B.
   A. and Elinor
Steinman Foundation, James
   Hale
Steinman Foundation, John
   Frederick
Sterling Inc.
Stern Memorial Trust, Sidney
Sternberger Foundation, Sigmund
Stevens Foundation, Abbot and
   Dorothy H.
Stevens Foundation, Nathaniel
   and Elizabeth P.
Stewardship Foundation
Stewart Educational Foundation,
   Donnell B. and Elizabeth Dee
   Shaw
Stocker Foundation
Stockham Valves & Fittings
Stone Charitable Foundation
Stone Container Corp.
Stone Foundation
Stone Foundation, France
Storer Foundation, George B.
Strake Foundation
Stranahan Foundation
Straus Foundation, Aaron and
   Lillie
Stride Rite Corp.
Stroud Foundation
Stulsaft Foundation, Morris
Stupp Foundation, Norman J.
Sturgis Charitable and
   Educational Trust, Roy and
   Christine
Subaru-Isuzu Automotive Inc.
Sulzberger Foundation
Sunderland Foundation, Lester T.
Sundstrand Corp.
Swalm Foundation
Swisher Foundation, Carl S.

Symmes Foundation, F. W.
Tandy Foundation, Anne Burnett
   and Charles
Tanner Cos.
Taper Foundation, Mark
Tauber Foundation
Taubman Foundation, Herman P.
   and Sophia
Teledyne
Teleklew Productions
Temple Foundation, T. L. L.
Tennant Co.
Tenneco
Texas Commerce Bank Houston,
   N.A.
Texas Instruments
Textron
Thermo Electron Corp.
Thomas & Betts Corp.
Thomas Industries
Thompson Trust, Thomas
Thorpe Foundation, James R.
Thorson Foundation
Time Warner
Times Mirror Co.
Timken Co.
Timken Foundation of Canton
Tisch Foundation
Tiscornia Foundation
TJX Cos.
Tokheim Corp.
Toms Foundation
Tonya Memorial Foundation
Torchmark Corp.
Totsy Manufacturing Co.
Transco Energy Company
Travelers Cos.
Treadwell Foundation, Nora
   Eccles
Treakle Foundation, J. Edwin
Treuhaft Foundation
Trexler Trust, Harry C.
TRINOVA Corp.
Tropicana Products, Inc.
True North Foundation
Trust Co. Bank
TRW Corp.
Tucker Charitable Trust, Rose E.
Tucker Foundation, Marcia Brady
Tucson Electric Power Co.
Tull Charitable Foundation
Tuohy Foundation, Alice Tweed
Turner Charitable Foundation
Turner Charitable Trust,
   Courtney S.
Turrell Fund
Union Bank
Union Camp Corp.
Union Central Life Insurance Co.
Union Electric Co.
Union Foundation
Union Pacific Corp.
United Dominion Industries
U.S. Bank of Washington
United States Borax & Chemical
   Corp.
United States Sugar Corp.
United States Trust Co. of New
   York
United Technologies Corp.
United Telephone System
   (Eastern Group)
Univar Corp.
Universal Foods Corp.
Upjohn Co.
Upjohn Foundation, Harold and
   Grace
Uris Brothers Foundation
US Bancorp
USF&G Co.
USG Corp.
UST
USX Corp.
Valero Energy Corp.
Valley Foundation
Valley Foundation, Wayne and
   Gladys

Valley National Bank of Arizona
Van Buren Foundation
Van Evera Foundation, Dewitt
   Caroline
Van Houten Charitable Trust
Vanderbilt Trust, R. T.
Vaughan Foundation, Rachael
   and Ben
Vermeer Manufacturing Co.
Victoria Foundation
Vidda Foundation
Vingo Trust II
Virginia Power Co.
Vogt Machine Co., Henry
Vollrath Co.
Vulcan Materials Co.
W. W. W. Foundation
Wachovia Bank of Georgia, N.A.
Wachovia Bank & Trust Co.,
   N.A.
Waggoner Charitable Trust,
   Crystelle
Waggoner Foundation, E. Paul
   and Helen Buck
Wahlstrom Foundation
Wal-Mart Stores
Walker Foundation, Archie D.
   and Bertha H.
Wallace Foundation, George R.
Walsh Charity Trust, Blanche M.
Disney Co., Walt
Walter Family Trust, Byron L.
Ward Foundation, A.
   Montgomery
Ward Foundation, Louis L. and
   Adelaide C.
Warner-Lambert Co.
Washington Forrest Foundation
Washington Mutual Savings
   Bank
Watumull Fund, J.
Wean Foundation, Raymond John
Webb Charitable Trust, Susan
   Mott
Webb Foundation
Webb Foundation, Del E.
Webster Foundation, Edwin S.
Wegener Foundation, Herman
   and Mary
Weinberg Foundation, Harry and
   Jeanette
Weingart Foundation
Weir Foundation Trust
Weisbrod Foundation Trust
   Dept., Robert and Mary
Weiss Foundation, William E.
Welfare Foundation
Wells Foundation, Franklin H.
   and Ruth L.
Wendt Foundation, Margaret L.
Werner Foundation, Clara and
   Spencer
West Co.
West Foundation, Neva and
   Wesley
West One Bancorp
Western New York Foundation
Westinghouse Electric Corp.
Westport Fund
Westvaco Corp.
Wetterau
Weyerhaeuser Co.
Weyerhaeuser Foundation,
   Frederick and Margaret L.
Wheat First Securites
Whirlpool Corp.
Whitaker Foundation
White Foundation, W. P. and H.
   B.
White Trust, G. R.
Whitehead Foundation
Whitehead Foundation, Joseph B.
Whiteman Foundation, Edna
   Rider
Whitman Corp.
Wickes Foundation, Harvey
   Randall
WICOR, Inc.

Wiegand Foundation, E. L.
Wiggins Memorial Trust, J. J.
Wigwam Mills
Wilcox General Trust, George N.
Wilcox Trust, S. W.
Wilder Foundation
Willard Foundation, Helen Parker
Williams Charitable Trust, John
   C.
Williams Cos.
Wilson Foundation, Hugh and
   Mary
Wilson Foundation, John and
   Nevils
Wilson Foundation, Marie C.
   and Joseph C.
Wilson Fund, Matilda R.
Wilson Trust, Lula C.
Wisconsin Bell, Inc.
Wisconsin Energy Corp.
Wisconsin Power & Light Co.
Wisconsin Public Service Corp.
Witte, Jr. Foundation, John H.
Witter Foundation, Dean
Wolfson Family Foundation
Wood Charitable Trust, W. P.
Woodland Foundation
Woodruff Foundation, Robert W.
Woods Foundation, James H.
Woods-Greer Foundation
Woodward Fund-Atlanta, David,
   Helen, Marian
Woodward Fund-Watertown,
   David, Helen, and Marian
Woodward Governor Co.
Wortham Foundation
Wright Foundation, Lola
Wurlitzer Foundation, Farny R.
Wurts Memorial, Henrietta Tower
Wyman-Gordon Co.
Wyomissing Foundation
Xerox Corp.
Yassenoff Foundation, Leo
Yellow Corp.
Yost Trust, Elizabeth Burns
Young Foundation, Hugo H. and
   Mabel B.
Young Foundation, Irvin L.
Zachry Co., H. B.
Zenkel Foundation
Ziemann Foundation
Zigler Foundation, Fred B. and
   Ruth B.
Zurn Industries

Challenge

Abell-Hanger Foundation
Ahmanson Foundation
Alabama Power Co.
Aladdin Industries, Incorporated
Alden Trust, George I.
ALPAC Corp.
Aluminum Co. of America
Amdahl Corp.
American Honda Motor Co.
American Natural Resources Co.
American Telephone &
   Telegraph Co./New York City
   Region
Ameritech Publishing
Anschutz Family Foundation
AON Corp.
Apache Corp.
Arkla
Armco Inc.
Armco Steel Co.
Arvin Industries
Atkinson Foundation, Myrtle L.
Ball Brothers Foundation
Bank of Boston Corp.
Bank of Louisville
Bankers Trust Co.
Battelle
Bechtel, Jr. Foundation, S. D.
Becton Dickinson & Co.
Beech Aircraft Corp.

Challenge (cont.)

Benwood Foundation
Best Products Co.
Beveridge Foundation, Frank Stanley
Bingham Foundation, William
Binney & Smith Inc.
Birch Foundation, Stephen and Mary
Block, H&R
Boehringer Mannheim Corp.
Boeing Co.
Boettcher Foundation
Booz Allen & Hamilton
Borden
Borg-Warner Corp.
BP America
Bradley Foundation, Lynde and Harry
Bridgestone/Firestone
Brillion Iron Works
British Airways
Brown Foundation
Brown Foundation, James Graham
Browning-Ferris Industries
Brunswick Corp.
Bryan Family Foundation, Kathleen Price and Joseph M.
Burdines
Bush Charitable Foundation, Edyth
Bush Foundation
C.P. Rail Systems
Cablevision of Michigan
Cabot Corp.
Cafritz Foundation, Morris and Gwendolyn
Calder Foundation, Louis
Cameron Foundation, Harry S. and Isabel C.
Campbell Foundation, J. Bulow
Campbell Soup Co.
Cannon Foundation
Carter Foundation, Amon G.
Cary Charitable Trust, Mary Flagler
Casey Foundation, Annie E.
Central Maine Power Co.
Century Companies of America
Chase Manhattan Bank, N.A.
Chatlos Foundation
Chesebrough-Pond's
Cincinnati Gas & Electric Co.
Circuit City Stores
Citizens Commercial & Savings Bank
Clay Foundation
CNG Transmission Corp.
Coca-Cola Co.
Coleman Foundation
Collins Foundation
Constantin Foundation
Contran Corp.
Cooper Industries
Cowell Foundation, S. H.
Cox Charitable Trust, Jessie B.
CR Industries
Cummings Memorial Fund Trust, Frances L. and Edwin L.
Cummins Engine Co.
Davidson Family Charitable Foundation
Davis Foundations, Arthur Vining
DeCamp Foundation, Ira W.
Delaware North Cos.
Detroit Edison Co.
Digital Equipment Corp.
Dodge Foundation, Geraldine R.
Doheny Foundation, Carrie Estelle
du Pont de Nemours & Co., E. I.
Duke Endowment
Duke Power Co.
duPont Fund, Jessie Ball
Duriron Co., Inc.

East Ohio Gas Co.
Eastman Kodak Co.
Eccles Foundation, George S. and Dolores Dore
Educational Foundation of America
Emerson Foundation, Fred L.
Ethyl Corp.
Evening Post Publishing Co.
Farish Fund, William Stamps
Federal Express Corp.
Federated Department Stores and Allied Stores Corp.
Fidelity Bank
First Interstate Bank of Denver
First Mississippi Corp.
First of America Bank Corp.
First Tennessee Bank
Fleet Financial Group
Fleming Companies, Inc.
Foellinger Foundation
Foley, Hoag & Eliot
Freeport-McMoRan
Frost Foundation
Fuller Foundation, George F. and Sybil H.
Funderburke & Associates
GAR Foundation
Gates Foundation
GATX Corp.
General Motors Corp.
General Signal Corp.
GenRad
Georgia Power Co.
Gheens Foundation
Gillette Co.
Globe Newspaper Co.
Goldsmith Foundation, Horace W.
Graham Foundation for Advanced Studies in the Fine Arts
Great Western Financial Corp.
Griggs and Mary Griggs Burke Foundation, Mary Livingston
Haas, Jr. Fund, Evelyn and Walter
Hall Foundation
Hallmark Cards
Heinz Co., H.J.
Hemby Foundation, Alex
Hermann Foundation, Grover
Hewlett Foundation, William and Flora
Hillcrest Foundation
Hoblitzelle Foundation
Hofmann Co.
Home Depot
Howard and Bush Foundation
Irvine Foundation, James
ITT Hartford Insurance Group
JELD-WEN, Inc.
Jennings Foundation, Martha Holden
JM Foundation
Johnson Controls
Johnson Endeavor Foundation, Christian A.
Johnson Foundation, M. G. and Lillie A.
Johnson & Higgins
Jones Foundation, Daisy Marquis
Kettering Fund
King Ranch
Knight Foundation, John S. and James L.
Koret Foundation
Kresge Foundation
Kulas Foundation
Lilly & Co., Eli
Lilly Endowment
Lincoln National Corp.
Littauer Foundation, Lucius N.
Liz Claiborne
Longwood Foundation
Louisiana Power & Light Co./New Orleans Public Service

LTV Corp.
Luce Foundation, Henry
Mabee Foundation, J. E. and L. E.
MacArthur Foundation, John D. and Catherine T.
Maclellan Foundation
Mardag Foundation
Massachusetts Mutual Life Insurance Co.
Mayer Foundation, Louis B.
Maytag Family Foundation, Fred
McBeath Foundation, Faye
McCormick & Co.
McCormick Tribune Foundation, Robert R.
McCune Foundation
McDermott Foundation, Eugene
McDonnell Douglas Corp.
McDonnell Douglas Corp.-West
McInerny Foundation
MCJ Foundation
McKnight Foundation
Meadows Foundation
Mellon Bank Corp.
Mellon Foundation, Andrew W.
Mercantile Bancorp
Meyer Memorial Trust
Michigan Gas Utilities
Miles Inc.
Millipore Corp.
Mississippi Power Co.
Moody Foundation
Mott Foundation, Charles Stewart
Murdock Charitable Trust, M. J.
Murphy Foundation, John P.
Nalco Chemical Co.
National City Bank, Columbus
National Computer Systems
National Gypsum Co.
National Westminster Bank New Jersey
New England Telephone Co.
New York Telephone Co.
News & Observer Publishing Co.
Noble Foundation, Samuel Roberts
Norman Foundation, Andrew
Northern Trust Co.
Oki America Inc.
Olin Corp.
Ontario Corp.
Ortho Diagnostic Systems, Inc.
Pacific Enterprises
Padnos Iron & Metal Co., Louis
Pamida, Inc.
Pan-American Life Insurance Co.
Parsons Foundation, Ralph M.
Perkin-Elmer Corp.
Pew Charitable Trusts
Pioneer Trust Bank, NA
Plough Foundation
Powell Family Foundation
Prentiss Foundation, Elisabeth Severance
Procter & Gamble Cosmetic & Fragrance Products
Promus Cos.
Prospect Hill Foundation
Prudential Insurance Co. of America
Public Service Co. of New Mexico
Public Service Electric & Gas Co.
Quaker Oats Co.
Raytheon Co.
Reinberger Foundation
Retirement Research Foundation
Rexham Inc.
Reynolds Charitable Trust, Kate B.
Riley Foundation, Mabel Louise
RJR Nabisco Inc.
Rockefeller Brothers Fund
Rockefeller Family Fund
Rogers Charitable Trust, Florence

Rohm and Haas Company
Rohr Inc.
RosaMary Foundation
Roseburg Forest Products Co.
Ross Corp.
Rouse Co.
Ryder System
SAFECO Corp.
Sandusky International Inc.
Sarkeys Foundation
Scherman Foundation
Schmidlapp Trust No. 1, Jacob G.
Seafirst Corp.
Seagram & Sons, Joseph E.
Self Foundation
Shaw's Supermarkets
Signet Bank/Maryland
Smith Charitable Trust, W. W.
SNET
Southern California Edison Co.
Speas Foundation, Victor E.
Speas Memorial Trust, John W. and Effie E.
Sprague Educational and Charitable Foundation, Seth
Springs Foundation
Stanley Works
State Street Bank & Trust Co.
Steelcase
Steele Foundation, Harry and Grace
Stewardship Foundation
Stockham Valves & Fittings
Swift Co. Inc., John S.
Tandy Foundation, Anne Burnett and Charles
Teagle Foundation
Teleklew Productions
Tenneco
Texaco
Thermo Electron Corp.
3M Co.
Timken Foundation of Canton
TJX Cos.
Trexler Trust, Harry C.
Turrell Fund
Union Pacific Corp.
United States-Japan Foundation
Universal Foods Corp.
Unocal Corp.
UNUM Corp.
US Bancorp
UST
Valero Energy Corp.
Varian Associates
Vollrath Co.
Wachovia Bank & Trust Co., N.A.
Disney Co., Walt
Washington Mutual Savings Bank
Weingart Foundation
Wells Fargo & Co.
Wendt Foundation, Margaret L.
West One Bancorp
Westvaco Corp.
Zale Foundation
Zurn Industries

Conference/Seminar

Abell Foundation, Charles S.
Aequus Institute
Alcon Laboratories, Inc.
Alexander Foundation, Joseph
Amado Foundation, Maurice
American Financial Corp.
American Microsystems, Inc.
American Telephone & Telegraph Co./New York City Region
Ameritech Corp.
Arca Foundation
Archbold Charitable Trust, Adrian and Jessie
Archibald Charitable Foundation, Norman

Arkla
Armstrong Foundation
Atlanta Gas Light Co.
Atran Foundation
AVI CHAI - A Philanthropic Foundation
Axe-Houghton Foundation
Baird & Co., Robert W.
Bank of New York
Bank One, Youngstown, NA
Barnes Foundation
Battelle
Bean Foundation, Norwin S. and Elizabeth N.
BellSouth Corp.
Benton Foundation
Bergen Foundation, Frank and Lydia
Berry Foundation, Lowell
Beveridge Foundation, Frank Stanley
Bingham Foundation, William
Booz Allen & Hamilton
Bradley Foundation, Lynde and Harry
Brady Foundation, W. H.
Brencanda Foundation
Brookdale Foundation
Brown Charitable Trust, Dora Maclellan
Browning-Ferris Industries
Brush Foundation
Burkitt Foundation
Burroughs Wellcome Co.
Bydale Foundation
Campbell and Adah E. Hall Charity Fund, Bushrod H.
Carnegie Corporation of New York
Cascade Natural Gas Corp.
Casey Foundation, Annie E.
Castle Foundation, Samuel N. and Mary
Chevron Corp.
China Medical Board of New York
Ciba-Geigy Corp. (Pharmaceuticals Division)
Close Foundation
Cockrell Foundation
Coleman Co.
Columbus Dispatch Printing Co.
Coors Brewing Co.
Copernicus Society of America
Credit Suisse
Cullen/Frost Bankers
Cummins Engine Co.
Danforth Foundation
DeCamp Foundation, Ira W.
DeKalb Genetics Corp.
Deloitte & Touche
Dentsu, Inc., NY
Deuble Foundation, George H.
Dexter Charitable Fund, Eugene A.
Dodge Foundation, Geraldine R.
Drum Foundation
du Pont de Nemours & Co., E. I.
Duke Endowment
Duke Power Co.
Eastman Foundation, Alexander
Ensign-Bickford Industries
Exxon Corp.
Falk Medical Fund, Maurice
Fifth Third Bancorp
Fleishhacker Foundation
Ford Foundation
Foundation for Child Development
Freedom Forum
Frick Educational Commission, Henry C.
Fry Foundation, Lloyd A.
Fund for New Jersey
Funderburke & Associates
Gates Foundation
General Mills

General Motors Corp.
Georgia Power Co.
German Marshall Fund of the
United States
Gillette Co.
Gould Foundation, Florence J.
Gould Foundation for Children,
Edwin
Graham Foundation for
Advanced Studies in the Fine
Arts
Greater Lansing Foundation
Green Foundation, Allen P. and
Josephine B.
Greve Foundation, William and
Mary
Gulf Power Co.
Haigh-Scatena Foundation
Hardin Foundation, Phil
Heinz Co., H.J.
Hershey Foods Corp.
Humana
Hunt Foundation, Samuel P.
International Foundation
Irwin-Sweeney-Miller
Foundation
Israel Discount Bank of New
York
Janesville Foundation
Jennings Foundation, Martha
Holden
Johnson Foundation, Barbara P.
Kenedy Memorial Foundation,
John G. and Marie Stella
Kentucky Foundation for Women
Kerr Foundation, Robert S. and
Grayce B.
Klingenstein Fund, Esther A. and
Joseph
Koch Charitable Trust, David H.
Koh-I-Noor Rapidograph Inc.
Kohler Foundation
Koret Foundation
Kress Foundation, Samuel H.
Kynett Memorial Foundation,
Edna G.
Larsen Fund
Laurel Foundation
Lingnan Foundation
Littauer Foundation, Lucius N.
Littlefield Memorial Trust, Ida
Ballou
Lowell Institute, Trustees of the
Luce Foundation, Henry
Lutheran Brotherhood
Foundation
Lyndhurst Foundation
Macy, Jr. Foundation, Josiah
Mallinckrodt Specialty
Chemicals Co.
Marbrook Foundation
Mardag Foundation
Marion Merrell Dow
McConnell Foundation, Neil A.
McLean Contributionship
Meadows Foundation
Merrill Lynch & Co.
Meserve Memorial Fund, Albert
and Helen
Midwest Resources
Milken Foundation, L. and S.
Mine Safety Appliances Co.
Mitsubishi International Corp.
Mitsui & Co. (U.S.A.)
Mobility Foundation
Moore Foundation
Morris Charitable Foundation, E.
A.
Mott Fund, Ruth
National City Bank, Columbus
National Computer Systems
National Westminster Bank New
Jersey
New York Telephone Co.
Norcliffe Fund
Northern Indiana Public Service
Co.
Olin Foundation, John M.

1957 Charity Trust
Oppenstein Brothers Foundation
Ortho Diagnostic Systems, Inc.
Palmer Fund, Frank Loomis
Pamida, Inc.
Pan-American Life Insurance Co.
Peppers Foundation, Ann
Perkin-Elmer Corp.
Phillips Foundation, Ellis L.
Post Foundation of D.C.,
Marjorie Merriweather
Presser Foundation
Prudential Insurance Co. of
America
PSI Energy
Radiator Specialty Co.
Rauch Foundation
Revson Foundation, Charles H.
Reynolds Foundation,
Christopher
Reynolds Foundation, J. B.
Reynolds Foundation, Richard S.
Reynolds Foundation, Z. Smith
RGK Foundation
Rockefeller Foundation
Rockefeller Trust, Winthrop
Sage Foundation, Russell
Salvatori Foundation, Henry
San Diego Gas & Electric
Scaife Family Foundation
Scaife Foundation, Sarah
Science Applications
International Corp.
Semmes Foundation
Siebert Lutheran Foundation
Sierra Health Foundation
Sloan Foundation, Alfred P.
Smithers Foundation,
Christopher D.
Southland Corp.
Spingold Foundation, Nate B.
and Frances
Square D Co.
Stackner Family Foundation
Stans Foundation
Stern Foundation, Irvin
Stevens Foundation, Nathaniel
and Elizabeth P.
Stony Wold Herbert Fund
Sulzberger Foundation
Tinker Foundation
Treuhaft Foundation
Trull Foundation
Trust Funds
Turner Charitable Foundation
van Loben Sels - Eleanor Slate
van Lobel Sels Charitable
Foundation, Ernst D.
Vollrath Co.
Walker Foundation, Archie D.
and Bertha H.
Wedum Foundation
Weight Watchers International
Welch Foundation, Robert A.
Wenner-Gren Foundation for
Anthropological Research
Western New York Foundation
Wiley & Sons, Inc., John
Wilson Foundation, Hugh and
Mary
Wilson Foundation, Marie C.
and Joseph C.
Witco Corp.

Department

AlliedSignal
Aluminum Co. of America
Amoco Corp.
AON Corp.
Applebaum Foundation
ARCO
ARCO Chemical
Auerbach Foundation, Beatrice
Fox
Baker, Jr. Memorial Fund,
William G.
Banbury Fund

Batten Foundation
BFGoodrich
Blount
Booz Allen & Hamilton
Borden
Brach Foundation, Helen
Burdines
Cain Foundation, Effie and
Wofford
Carnegie Corporation of New
York
Caterpillar
Chase Manhattan Bank, N.A.
Chevron Corp.
Cullen Foundation
DeKalb Genetics Corp.
Delany Charitable Trust,
Beatrice P.
Dingman Foundation, Michael D.
Doheny Foundation, Carrie
Estelle
Dresser Industries
du Pont de Nemours & Co., E. I.
Eccles Foundation, George S.
and Dolores Dore
Eccles Foundation, Marriner S.
English-Bonter-Mitchell
Foundation
Equitable Life Assurance Society
of the U.S.
Exxon Corp.
Fidelity Bank
First Interstate Bank of Oregon
Fish Foundation, Bert
Forster Charitable Trust, James
W. and Ella B.
Franklin Foundation, John and
Mary
GAR Foundation
General Motors Corp.
Getty Foundation, Ann and
Gordon
Gheens Foundation
Gillette Co.
Gould Foundation, Florence J.
Graham Foundation for
Advanced Studies in the Fine
Arts
Griggs and Mary Griggs Burke
Foundation, Mary Livingston
Halliburton Co.
Harriman Foundation, Mary W.
Harsco Corp.
Hillman Foundation
Hoechst Celanese Corp.
Humana
Inland Steel Industries
Israel Discount Bank of New
York
Joy Family Foundation
Kerr Foundation
Mardag Foundation
Massey Foundation
Maxus Energy Corp.
Mayer Foundation, James and
Eva
McCasland Foundation
Meadows Foundation
Merck & Co.
Meredith Corp.
Mobil Oil Corp.
Morgan Charitable Residual
Trust, W. and E.
Morris Foundation, William T.
NBD Bank
Newhouse Foundation, Samuel I.
Newmont Mining Corp.
Oki America Inc.
Olin Corp.
O'Neill Charitable Corporation,
F. J.
PACCAR
Packard Foundation, David and
Lucile
Phillips Petroleum Co.
Plough Foundation
Post Foundation of D.C.,
Marjorie Merriweather

PPG Industries
Price Waterhouse-U.S.
Pritzker Foundation
Prospect Hill Foundation
Prudential Insurance Co. of
America
Reinberger Foundation
RJR Nabisco Inc.
Rohm and Haas Company
Rouse Co.
Rutgers Community Health
Foundation
Sandoz Corp.
Scaife Family Foundation
Scaife Foundation, Sarah
Schlinger Foundation
Shell Oil Co.
Sloan Foundation, Alfred P.
Square D Co.
Stone & Webster, Inc.
Storer Foundation, George B.
Sumitomo Bank of California
Tenneco
Texaco
Texas Instruments
Thompson Charitable Foundation
Tisch Foundation
TRW Corp.
Union Carbide Corp.
Unocal Corp.
Vulcan Materials Co.
Wean Foundation, Raymond John
Westinghouse Electric Corp.
Whirlpool Corp.
Woolley Foundation, Vasser
Xerox Corp.
Yost Trust, Elizabeth Burns

Emergency

Abney Foundation
Acushnet Co.
Adams Memorial Fund, Emma J.
Agway
Aladdin Industries, Incorporated
Alexander Foundation, Walter
Alltel/Western Region
Alumax
Alyeska Pipeline Service Co.
American Brands
American Saw & Manufacturing
Co.
Armington Fund, Evenor
Atlanta Foundation
Atran Foundation
Avis Inc.
Babcock Foundation, Mary
Reynolds
Ball Corp.
Bank of A. Levy
Bank of America Arizona
Barstow Foundation
Bassett Foundation, Norman
Bean Foundation, Norwin S. and
Elizabeth N.
Beazley Foundation
Beeghly Fund, Leon A.
Bel Air Mart
Benenson Foundation, Frances
and Benjamin
Berkman Charitable Trust, Allen
H. and Selma W.
Beveridge Foundation, Frank
Stanley
Bishop Charitable Trust, A. G.
Blanchard Foundation
Boehm Foundation
Booz Allen & Hamilton
Braun Foundation
Bray Charitable Trust, Viola E.
Brencanda Foundation
Brewer and Co., Ltd., C.
Britton Fund
Brown Foundation, George
Warren
Brush Foundation

Buchalter, Nemer, Fields, &
Younger
Bush Charitable Foundation,
Edyth
Butler Foundation, J. Homer
Camp Foundation
Carpenter Foundation, E. Rhodes
and Leona B.
Caspersen Foundation for Aid to
Health and Education, O. W.
CBI Industries
Central Maine Power Co.
Central Vermont Public Service
Corp.
Charlton, Jr. Charitable Trust,
Earle P.
Ciba-Geigy Corp.
(Pharmaceuticals Division)
Coastal Corp.
Cooper Foundation
Cornell Trust, Peter C.
Cosmair, Inc.
Cowden Foundation, Louetta M.
Cowles Charitable Trust
Crane Co.
Crocker Trust, Mary A.
Dalton Foundation, Dorothy U.
Daniels Foundation, Fred Harris
Daywood Foundation
de Hirsch Fund, Baron
Dee Foundation, Lawrence T.
and Janet T.
Delaware North Cos.
DeRoy Foundation, Helen L.
Deuble Foundation, George H.
Dillon Foundation
Dorr Foundation
Douglas & Lomason Company
Drum Foundation
du Pont de Nemours & Co., E. I.
Duke Endowment
Duncan Trust, John G.
Dupar Foundation
duPont Foundation, Alfred I.
Eccles Foundation, Ralph M. and
Ella M.
Eder Foundation, Sidney and
Arthur
Edwards Foundation, O. P. and
W. E.
EIS Foundation
Ellsworth Foundation, Ruth H.
and Warren A.
Emergency Aid of Pennsylvania
Foundation
English-Bonter-Mitchell
Foundation
Ensworth Charitable Foundation
Evans Foundation, T. M.
Evjue Foundation
Falk Foundation, David
Ferebee Endowment, Percy O.
Ferro Corp.
Fidelity Bank
Fifth Avenue Foundation
Filene Foundation, Lincoln and
Therese
Fingerhut Family Foundation
First Mississippi Corp.
Foellinger Foundation
Frederick Foundation
Friendly Rosenthal Foundation
Friends' Foundation Trust, A.
Frohring Foundation, William O.
and Gertrude Lewis
Fuchs Foundation, Gottfried &
Mary
Georgia Power Co.
Gerson Family Foundation,
Benjamin J.
Gilmore Foundation, Irving S.
Glencoe Foundation
Glenn Foundation, Carrie C. &
Lena V.
Glickenhaus & Co.
Goddard Foundation, Charles B.
Goodstein Family Foundation,
David

Emergency (cont.)

Goodyear Foundation, Josephine
Greater Lansing Foundation
Green Foundation, Allen P. and Josephine B.
Greene Manufacturing Co.
Gries Charity Fund, Lucile and Robert H.
Griffin Foundation, Rosa May
Gruber Research Foundation, Lila
Haas Foundation, Paul and Mary
Haas Foundation, Saul and Dayee G.
Haffner Foundation
Hales Charitable Fund
Hancock Foundation, Luke B.
Hanes Foundation, John W. and Anna H.
Harden Foundation
Hatch Charitable Trust, Margaret Milliken
Heublein
Higginson Trust, Corina
Hillman Foundation, Henry L.
Himmelfarb Foundation, Paul and Annetta
Hofmann Co.
Hughes Charitable Trust, Mabel Y.
Humphrey Fund, George M. and Pamela S.
Hunt Foundation, Samuel P.
Hunter Foundation, Edward and Irma
Huthsteiner Fine Arts Trust
Iddings Benevolent Trust
Irwin-Sweeney-Miller Foundation
ITT Rayonier
Ivakota Association
Jerusalem Fund for Education and Community Development
Joselow Foundation
Joyce Foundation, John M. and Mary A.
Kaufman Endowment Fund, Louis G.
Kavanagh Foundation, T. James
Kawabe Memorial Fund
Keith Foundation Trust, Ben E.
Kelley and Elza Kelley Foundation, Edward Bangs
Kennecott Corp.
Kerr Foundation, A. H.
Kerr Foundation, Robert S. and Grayce B.
Kieckhefer Foundation, J. W.
Kimball Foundation, Horace A. Kimball and S. Ella
Kimmelman Foundation, Helen & Milton
Kirkpatrick Foundation
Koch Charitable Trust, David H.
Koopman Fund
Kutz Foundation, Milton and Hattie
Langendorf Foundation, Stanley S.
Lassen Foundation, Irving A.
Lewis Foundation, Lillian Kaiser
Liquid Air Corp.
Louisiana-Pacific Corp.
Loutit Foundation
MacDonald Foundation, James A.
Macht Foundation, Morton and Sophia
Marbrook Foundation
Mardag Foundation
Massachusetts Mutual Life Insurance Co.
Massengill-DeFriece Foundation
Maxfield Foundation
Mayerson Foundation, Manuel D. and Rhoda
MBIA, Inc.
McBride & Son Associates

McDonough Foundation, Bernard
McEachern Charitable Trust, D. V. & Ida J.
McFeely-Rogers Foundation
MCI Communications Corp.
McKee Foundation, Robert E. and Evelyn
McKee Poor Fund, Virginia A.
McMillan Foundation, D. W.
Meyerhoff Fund, Joseph
Midwest Resources
Milbank Foundation, Dunlevy
Milken Family Medical Foundation
Miller Foundation
Mills Charitable Foundation, Henry L. and Kathryn
Millstein Charitable Foundation
Millstone Foundation
Monroe Foundation (1976), J. Edgar
Montgomery Street Foundation
Moore Foundation, Roy C.
Morley Brothers Foundation
Morton Memorial Fund, Mark
Mulcahy Foundation
Murphy Foundation, John P.
National Computer Systems
National Gypsum Co.
National Pro-Am Youth Fund
NBD Bank
New Prospect Foundation
New York Mercantile Exchange
Norcliffe Fund
Oak Foundation U.S.A.
O'Connor Foundation, Kathryn
OCRI Foundation
Oki America Inc.
Onan Family Foundation
1957 Charity Trust
O'Neil Foundation, Casey Albert T.
Oppenstein Brothers Foundation
Ormet Corp.
Owsley Foundation, Alvin and Lucy
Oxford Industries, Inc.
Page Foundation, George B.
Pamida, Inc.
Parker Foundation
Patterson Charitable Fund, W. I.
Pearlstone Foundation, Peggy Meyerhoff
Pendergast-Weyer Foundation
Perkin-Elmer Corp.
Pioneer Trust Bank, NA
Pratt Memorial Fund
Presser Foundation
Proctor Trust, Mortimer R.
Prudential-Bache Securities
Prudential Insurance Co. of America
Questar Corp.
Quinlan Foundation, Elizabeth C.
R. F. Foundation
R. P. Foundation
Ratshesky Foundation, A. C.
Ray Foundation
Reynolds Foundation, J. B.
Rice Foundation, Helen Steiner
Richardson Fund, Mary Lynn
Rider-Pool Foundation
Roblee Foundation, Joseph H. and Florence A.
Roe Foundation
Rogers Charitable Trust, Florence
Roseburg Forest Products Co.
Ross Laboratories
Rubenstein Charitable Foundation, Lawrence J. and Anne
Russell Trust, Josephine G.
St. Faith's House Foundation
San Diego Gas & Electric
Sara Lee Hosiery
Scurlock Foundation
Sears Family Foundation

Semmes Foundation
Seybert Institution for Poor Boys and Girls, Adam and Maria Sarah
Shaw Foundation, Gardiner Howland
Sheldon Foundation, Ralph C.
Shenandoah Life Insurance Co.
Sheridan Foundation, Thomas B. and Elizabeth M.
Simpson Foundation
Slemp Foundation
Smith Benevolent Association, Buckingham
Smith Charitable Trust, W. W.
Smith Charities, John
Smith, Jr. Foundation, M. W.
Smith Memorial Fund, Ethel Sergeant Clark
Snyder Fund, Valentine Perry
Sonoco Products Co.
Southland Corp.
Spectra-Physics Analytical
Stamps Foundation, James L.
Stanley Charitable Foundation, A. W.
Starr Foundation
Stearns Trust, Artemas W.
Steel, Sr. Foundation, Marshall
Stern Foundation, Irvin
Stern Memorial Trust, Sidney
Stevens Foundation, Nathaniel and Elizabeth P.
Stocker Foundation
Stockham Valves & Fittings
Straus Foundation, Martha Washington Straus and Harry H.
Stroud Foundation
Sulzberger Foundation
Sunderland Foundation, Lester T.
Swalm Foundation
Swig Charity Foundation, Mae and Benjamin
Templeton Foundation, Herbert A.
Thompson Trust, Thomas
Time Insurance Co.
Timken Co.
Tiscornia Foundation
Toms Foundation
Tonkin Foundation, Tom and Helen
Towsley Foundation, Harry A. and Margaret D.
Treuhaft Foundation
True North Foundation
Truman Foundation, Mildred Faulkner
Trust Funds
Tucker Foundation, Marcia Brady
Turner Charitable Foundation
Unilever United States
Union Bank of Switzerland Los Angeles Branch
United Dominion Industries
United States Sugar Corp.
Valero Energy Corp.
van Loben Sels - Eleanor Slate van Lobel Sels Charitable Foundation, Ernst D.
Vaughan Foundation, Rachael and Ben
Vilter Manufacturing Corp.
Vulcan Materials Co.
Waggoner Charitable Trust, Crystelle
Washington Forrest Foundation
Weber Charities Corp., Frederick E.
Wells Foundation, Franklin H. and Ruth L.
West Co.
Western New York Foundation
Weyerhaeuser Family Foundation
White Foundation, W. P. and H. B.

Whiteman Foundation, Edna Rider
Williams Charitable Trust, Mary Jo
Wilson Foundation, Marie C. and Joseph C.
Wilson Trust, Lula C.
Wisconsin Public Service Corp.
Woodward Governor Co.
Wunsch Foundation
Wurlitzer Foundation, Farny R.
Wurts Memorial, Henrietta Tower
Wyomissing Foundation
Yassenoff Foundation, Leo
Zarrow Foundation, Anne and Henry
Zurn Industries

Employee Matching Gifts

Abbott Laboratories
Advanced Micro Devices
Aerospace Corp.
Aetna Life & Casualty Co.
Air Products & Chemicals
Alabama Power Co.
Albany International Corp.
Alexander & Baldwin, Inc.
Allegheny Ludlum Corp.
Allendale Mutual Insurance Co.
AlliedSignal
Allstate Insurance Co.
Alltel/Western Region
ALPAC Corp.
Aluminum Co. of America
Alyeska Pipeline Service Co.
AMAX
American Brands
American Cyanamid Co.
American Electric Power
American Express Co.
American Home Products Corp.
American President Cos.
American Standard
American Stock Exchange
American Telephone & Telegraph Co.
American Telephone & Telegraph Co./Dallas Region
American Telephone & Telegraph Co./New York City Region
American United Life Insurance Co.
Ameritech Corp.
Ameritech Publishing
Ameritech Services
Amfac/JMB Hawaii
Amoco Corp.
Analog Devices
Anheuser-Busch Cos.
AON Corp.
Appleton Papers
Archer-Daniels-Midland Co.
ARCO
ARCO Chemical
Argonaut Group
Aristech Chemical Corp.
Arizona Public Service Co.
Arkla
Armco Inc.
Armco Steel Co.
Asea Brown Boveri
Ashland Oil
Augat, Inc.
Avon Products
Ball Corp.
Baltimore Gas & Electric Co.
Banc One Illinois Corp.
Banc One Wisconsin Corp.
Bank of America Arizona
Bank of Boston Connecticut
Bank of Boston Corp.
Bank of New York
Bank One, Texas-Houston Office
Bankers Trust Co.

Banner Life Insurance Co.
Baxter International
BayBanks
Bechtel Group
Bell Helicopter Textron
Bemis Company
Benefit Trust Life Insurance Co.
Best Products Co.
BFGoodrich
BHP Pacific Resources
Binney & Smith Inc.
Block, H&R
Bloomingdale's
Blount
Boeing Co.
Boise Cascade Corp.
Borden
Borg-Warner Corp.
Boston Edison Co.
Bowater Inc.
BP America
Bridgestone/Firestone
Bristol-Myers Squibb Co.
Brown Group
Brown & Williamson Tobacco Corp.
Brunswick Corp.
Bucyrus-Erie
Burlington Industries
Burlington Northern Inc.
Burlington Resources
Burroughs Wellcome Co.
Butler Manufacturing Co.
Cabot Corp.
Campbell Soup Co.
Capital Holding Corp.
Carolina Power & Light Co.
Carrier Corp.
Castle & Co., A.M.
Caterpillar
CBI Industries
Centerior Energy Corp.
Central Life Assurance Co.
Central Maine Power Co.
Central & South West Services
Cessna Aircraft Co.
Champion International Corp.
Chase Manhattan Bank, N.A.
Chemical Bank
Chesapeake Corp.
Chesebrough-Pond's
Chevron Corp.
Chrysler Corp.
CIGNA Corp.
Cincinnati Bell
Circuit City Stores
Citicorp
CLARCOR
Clorox Co.
CM Alliance Cos.
CNA Insurance Cos.
CNG Transmission Corp.
Coca-Cola Co.
Coleman Co.
Colorado National Bankshares
Comerica
Commercial Intertech Corp.
Compaq Computer Corp.
Conoco Inc.
Consolidated Freightways
Consolidated Natural Gas Co.
Consolidated Papers
Consolidated Rail Corp. (Conrail)
Consumers Power Co.
Continental Bank N.A.
Continental Corp.
Contran Corp.
Cooper Industries
Cooper Tire & Rubber Co.
Copley Press
Corning Incorporated
Cowles Media Co.
CPC International
CPI Corp.
Cray Research
Credit Agricole

Crestar Financial Corp.
Crum and Forster
Cummins Engine Co.
Dana Corp.
Deloitte & Touche
Delta Air Lines
Deluxe Corp.
Deposit Guaranty National Bank
Detroit Edison Co.
Dexter Corp.
Digital Equipment Corp.
Donaldson Co.
Donaldson, Lufkin & Jenrette
Donnelley & Sons Co., R.R.
Dow Corning Corp.
Dresser Industries
du Pont de Nemours & Co., E. I.
Duke Power Co.
Dun & Bradstreet Corp.
Duquesne Light Co.
Eastern Enterprises
Eaton Corp.
Eckerd Corp., Jack
Ecolab
Elf Atochem North America
Emerson Electric Co.
Enron Corp.
Equifax
Equitable Life Assurance Society
    of the U.S.
Ernst & Young
Ethyl Corp.
Exxon Corp.
Federal Express Corp.
Federal-Mogul Corp.
Federated Department Stores and
    Allied Stores Corp.
Fel-Pro Incorporated
Fidelity Bank
Fifth Third Bancorp
Fireman's Fund Insurance Co.
First Bank System
First Boston
First Chicago
First Fidelity Bancorporation
First Financial Bank FSB
First Interstate Bank NW Region
First Interstate Bank of California
First Interstate Bank of Denver
First Interstate Bank of Oregon
First Maryland Bancorp
First of America Bank Corp.
First Union Corp.
First Union National Bank of
    Florida
Fisher-Price
Fleet Bank
Fleet Financial Group
Fleming Companies, Inc.
Fluor Corp.
FMC Corp.
FMR Corp.
Ford Motor Co.
Fox Inc.
Freeport-McMoRan
Fuller Co., H.B.
Gap, The
GATX Corp.
GEICO Corp.
GenCorp
General Dynamics Corp.
General Electric Co.
General Mills
General Reinsurance Corp.
General Signal Corp.
General Tire Inc.
Georgia Power Co.
Gerber Products Co.
Gillette Co.
Glatfelter Co., P.H.
Globe Corp.
Globe Newspaper Co.
Gould Inc.
Grace & Co., W.R.
Graco
Grant Thornton

Graphic Controls Corp.
Great Western Financial Corp.
Grinnell Mutual Reinsurance Co.
GTE Corp.
Guardian Life Insurance Co. of
    America
Halliburton Co.
Hallmark Cards
Harcourt General
HarperCollins Publishers
Harris Corp.
Harris Trust & Savings Bank
Harsco Corp.
Hartford Steam Boiler Inspection
    & Insurance Co.
Hartmarx Corp.
HEI Inc.
Heinz Co., H.J.
Heller Financial
Hershey Foods Corp.
Heublein
Hewlett-Packard Co.
Hitachi
Hoechst Celanese Corp.
Hoffmann-La Roche
Home Depot
Honeywell
Hospital Corp. of America
Houghton Mifflin Co.
Household International
Huffy Corp.
Hunt Manufacturing Co.
ICI Americas
IDS Financial Services
IES Industries
Illinois Bell
Illinois Tool Works
IMCERA Group Inc.
Intel Corp.
International Flavors &
    Fragrances
International Multifoods Corp.
International Paper Co.
Iowa-Illinois Gas & Electric Co.
ITT Hartford Insurance Group
J.P. Morgan & Co.
James River Corp. of Virginia
JCPenney Co.
John Hancock Mutual Life
    Insurance Co.
Johnson Co., E. F.
Johnson Controls
Johnson & Higgins
Johnson & Johnson
Johnson & Son, S.C.
Jones Construction Co., J.A.
Jostens
Kajima International, Inc.
Keebler Co.
Kellwood Co.
Kennecott Corp.
Kerr-McGee Corp.
Kidder, Peabody & Co.
Kingsbury Corp.
Kirkland & Ellis
Kmart Corp.
KPMG Peat Marwick
Laclede Gas Co.
Lafarge Corp.
Land O'Lakes
Leo Burnett Co.
Levi Strauss & Co.
Lilly & Co., Eli
Lincoln National Corp.
Lipton, Thomas J.
Liz Claiborne
Loews Corp.
Lotus Development Corp.
Louisiana Land & Exploration
    Co.
Lubrizol Corp.
Lydall, Inc.
Macy & Co., R.H.
Maguire Oil Co.
Mallinckrodt Specialty
    Chemicals Co.

Manufacturers Life Insurance
    Co. of America
Manville Corp.
Mapco Inc.
Marinette Marine Corp.
Maritz Inc.
Marsh & McLennan Cos.
Martin Marietta Corp.
Massachusetts Mutual Life
    Insurance Co.
Mattel
May Department Stores Co.
Mayer Foods Corp., Oscar
Maytag Corp.
MBIA, Inc.
McCormick & Co.
McDonald's Corp.
McDonnell Douglas Corp.
McGraw-Hill
McKesson Corp.
Mead Corp.
Medtronic
Melitta North America Inc.
Mellon Bank Corp.
Mercedes-Benz of North
    America, Inc.
Merck & Co.
Meredith Corp.
Meridian Bancorp
Merit Oil Corp.
Merrill Lynch & Co.
Metropolitan Life Insurance Co.
Mettler Instrument Corp.
MGIC Investment Corp.
Michigan Bell Telephone Co.
Michigan Consolidated Gas Co.
Midwest Resources
Millipore Corp.
Minnegasco
Mitsubishi Electric America
Mitsui & Co. (U.S.A.)
Mobil Oil Corp.
Monsanto Co.
Montgomery Ward & Co.
Morgan Stanley & Co.
Morton International
Motorola
MSI Insurance
MTS Systems Corp.
Murphy Oil Corp.
Mutual of New York
Nabisco Foods Group
National City Bank, Columbus
National City Corp.
National Computer Systems
National Medical Enterprises
National Starch & Chemical
    Corp.
National Steel
National Westminster Bank New
    Jersey
NationsBank Corp.
Nationwide Insurance Cos.
NBD Bank
NBD Bank, N.A.
NCR Corp.
New England Telephone Co.
New York State Electric & Gas
    Corp.
New York Telephone Co.
The New Yorker Magazine, Inc.
Nike Inc.
Nissan Motor Corporation in
    U.S.A.
Nordson Corp.
Norfolk Southern Corp.
Northern Indiana Public Service
    Co.
Northern States Power Co.
Northern Trust Co.
Northwestern National Life
    Insurance Co.
Norton Co.
Norwest Corp.
NYNEX Corp.
Occidental Oil & Gas Corp.
Occidental Petroleum Corp.

Ohio Bell Telephone Co.
Ohio Citizens Bank
Ohio National Life Insurance Co.
Oki America Inc.
Oklahoma Gas & Electric Co.
Olin Corp.
Ontario Corp.
Ore-Ida Foods, Inc.
Ormet Corp.
Outboard Marine Corp.
Owens-Corning Fiberglas Corp.
Oxford Industries, Inc.
PACCAR
Pacific Mutual Life Insurance Co.
Pacific Telesis Group
Packaging Corporation of
    America
Padnos Iron & Metal Co., Louis
Pan-American Life Insurance Co.
Panhandle Eastern Corp.
Paramount Communications Inc.
Parke-Davis Group
Parker-Hannifin Corp.
Patagonia
Pella Corp.
Pennsylvania Power & Light
Pennzoil Co.
Pentair
People's Bank
Peoples Energy Corp.
PepsiCo
Pfizer
Phelps Dodge Corp.
PHH Corp.
Philip Morris Cos.
Phillips Petroleum Co.
Phoenix Home Life Mutual
    Insurance Co.
Piper Jaffray Cos.
Pitney Bowes
Pittsburgh National Bank
Pittway Corp.
PMA Industries
Polaroid Corp.
Potlatch Corp.
PPG Industries
Price Associates, T. Rowe
Price Waterhouse-U.S.
Principal Financial Group
Procter & Gamble Co.
Procter & Gamble Cosmetic &
    Fragrance Products
Promus Cos.
Providence Energy Corp.
Provident Life & Accident
    Insurance Co.
Prudential Insurance Co. of
    America
Public Service Co. of Colorado
Public Service Electric & Gas
    Co.
Puget Sound Power & Light Co.
Quaker Oats Co.
Quantum Chemical Corp.
Reader's Digest Association
Reebok International Ltd.
Reichhold Chemicals, Inc.
Reliable Life Insurance Co.
Reliance Electric Co.
Republic New York Corp.
Revlon
Reynolds Metals Co.
Rhone-Poulenc Rorer
RJR Nabisco Inc.
Rockwell International Corp.
Rohm and Haas Company
Rohr Inc.
Ross, Johnston & Kersting
Ross Laboratories
Royal Group Inc.
Rubbermaid
Ryder System
SAFECO Corp.
Saint Paul Cos.
Salomon
Santa Fe Pacific Corp.
Sara Lee Corp.

Sara Lee Hosiery
Schering-Plough Corp.
Science Applications
    International Corp.
Sealright Co., Inc.
Searle & Co., G.D.
Security Life of Denver
Sentinel Communications Co.
Shaklee Corp.
Shawmut National Corp.
Shell Oil Co.
Shenandoah Life Insurance Co.
Sherwin-Williams Co.
Skinner Corp.
Smith Corp., A.O.
SmithKline Beecham
SNET
Society Corp.
Sonat
Sonoco Products Co.
Sony Corp. of America
Southern Co. Services
Southwestern Bell Corp.
Springs Industries
Sprint
Sprint United Telephone
Square D Co.
Stanley Works
State Farm Mutual Automobile
    Insurance Co.
State Street Bank & Trust Co.
Sterling Winthrop
Stride Rite Corp.
Subaru of America Inc.
Sumitomo Bank of California
Sun Co.
Sun Microsystems
Sundstrand Corp.
Syntex Corp.
Tandy Corp.
TCF Banking & Savings, FSB
Tektronix
Teledyne
Teleflex Inc.
Temple-Inland
Texaco
Texas Commerce Bank Houston,
    N.A.
Texas Instruments
Textron
Thomas & Betts Corp.
3M Co.
Time Insurance Co.
Times Mirror Co.
Toyota Motor Sales, U.S.A.
Tracor, Inc.
Transamerica Corp.
Transco Energy Company
Travelers Cos.
Travelers Express Co.
TRINOVA Corp.
Triskelion Ltd.
Trust Co. Bank
TRW Corp.
Union Camp Corp.
Union Electric Co.
Union Pacific Corp.
United Parcel Service of America
U.S. Leasing International
United States Trust Co. of New
    York
United Technologies Corp.
United Telephone System
    (Eastern Group)
Universal Foods Corp.
Unocal Corp.
UNUM Corp.
Upjohn Co.
US Bancorp
US WEST
USF&G Co.
USG Corp.
UST
USX Corp.
Utilicorp United
Valley National Bank of Arizona
Varian Associates

Employee Matching Gifts (cont.)

Virginia Power Co.
Vulcan Materials Co.
Wachovia Bank of Georgia, N.A.
Wachovia Bank & Trust Co., N.A.
Warner-Lambert Co.
Washington Mutual Savings Bank
Washington Post Co.
Waste Management
Wells Fargo & Co.
West Co.
West One Bancorp
Westinghouse Electric Corp.
Westvaco Corp.
Weyerhaeuser Co.
Whirlpool Corp.
White Consolidated Industries
Wiley & Sons, Inc., John
Williams Cos.
Winn-Dixie Stores
Wisconsin Energy Corp.
Wisconsin Power & Light Co.
Wyman-Gordon Co.
Xerox Corp.
Yellow Corp.

Endowment

Abell Foundation, Charles S.
Abell Foundation, The
Abney Foundation
Abrams Foundation, Talbert and Leota
Achelis Foundation
Ackerman Trust, Anna Keesling
Agway
Ahmanson Foundation
Ala Vi Foundation of New York
Alabama Power Co.
Alden Trust, George I.
Alexander Foundation, Joseph
ALPAC Corp.
Amado Foundation, Maurice
American Financial Corp.
American Foundation
American Home Products Corp.
Anderson Foundation, Robert C. and Sadie G.
Andrews Foundation
AON Corp.
Arkla
Armco Steel Co.
Arronson Foundation
Astor Foundation, Vincent
Atherton Family Foundation
Atkinson Foundation, Myrtle L.
Atran Foundation
Baehr Foundation, Louis W. and Dolpha
Bailey Foundation
Baird & Co., Robert W.
Baker Foundation, Clark and Ruby
Baker Trust, George F.
Bancorp Hawaii
Bank of Boston Corp.
Bank of New York
Barker Foundation, J. M. R.
Barnett Banks
Barrows Foundation, Geraldine and R. A.
Barstow Foundation
Battelle
Baughman Foundation
Baumker Charitable Foundation, Elsie and Harry
Bayne Fund, Howard
Beazley Foundation
Beeghly Fund, Leon A.
Belden Brick Co., Inc.
Belk Stores
Belo Corp., A.H.

Berger Foundation, H.N. and Frances C.
Berkman Charitable Trust, Allen H. and Selma W.
Berry Foundation, Lowell
Bettingen Corporation, Burton G.
Beynon Foundation, Kathryne
Birch Foundation, Stephen and Mary
Blair and Co., William
Blount
Bodman Foundation
Boehringer Mannheim Corp.
Booth-Bricker Fund
Booz Allen & Hamilton
Borg-Warner Corp.
Bound to Stay Bound Books Foundation
Bourns, Inc.
Brach Foundation, Helen
Brackenridge Foundation, George W.
Bren Foundation, Donald L.
Britton Fund
Brooks Foundation, Gladys
Brown Foundation
Brown Foundation, James Graham
Browning Charitable Foundation, Val A.
Bryan Family Foundation, Kathleen Price and Joseph M.
Buck Foundation, Carol Franc
Buell Foundation, Temple Hoyne
Burkitt Foundation
Burns Foundation, Fritz B.
Butler Family Foundation, Patrick and Aimee
C. E. and S. Foundation
Cablevision of Michigan
Cabot Family Charitable Trust
Cain Foundation, Effie and Wofford
California Foundation for Biochemical Research
Campbell Foundation
Campbell Foundation, J. Bulow
Capital Holding Corp.
Central Fidelity Banks, Inc.
Central Vermont Public Service Corp.
CertainTeed Corp.
Charina Foundation
Chase Lincoln First Bank, N.A.
Cherne Foundation, Albert W.
China Medical Board of New York
Clark Charitable Trust
Cleary Foundation
Cleveland-Cliffs
Clorox Co.
Clowes Fund
Coca-Cola Co.
Cockrell Foundation
Cogswell Benevolent Trust
Columbia Foundation
Columbus Dispatch Printing Co.
Compton Foundation
Consolidated Papers
Coors Foundation, Adolph
Copernicus Society of America
Copley Press
Cowles Charitable Trust
Cowles Foundation, Gardner and Florence Call
Cowles Foundation, Harriet Cheney
Cowles Foundation, William H.
Cowles Media Co.
Cox, Jr. Foundation, James M.
CR Industries
Crandall Memorial Foundation, J. Ford
Crown Memorial, Arie and Ida
Cuesta Foundation
Cullen Foundation
Cullen/Frost Bankers
Cummins Engine Co.

Cunningham Foundation, Laura Moore
Daniels Foundation, Fred Harris
Danis Industries
Darling Foundation, Hugh and Hazel
Davidson Family Charitable Foundation
Davis Foundation, Shelby Cullom
Davis Foundations, Arthur Vining
Day Family Foundation
DeCamp Foundation, Ira W.
DeKalb Genetics Corp.
Delaware North Cos.
Demoulas Supermarkets
Detroit Edison Co.
Dettman Foundation, Leroy E.
Deuble Foundation, George H.
DeVore Foundation
Dodge Foundation, Cleveland H.
Donaldson Co.
Dow Foundation, Herbert H. and Barbara C.
Dreiling and Albina Dreiling Charitable Trust, Leo J.
Duchossois Industries
Duke Endowment
Duke Power Co.
Dunspaugh-Dalton Foundation
duPont Foundation, Chichester
Dyson Foundation
E and M Charities
Eaton Foundation, Cyrus
Eden Hall Foundation
Emerson Foundation, Fred L.
Ethyl Corp.
Evjue Foundation
Exposition Foundation
Fairchild Foundation, Sherman
Falk Medical Fund, Maurice
Fanwood Foundation
Federation Foundation of Greater Philadelphia
Fikes Foundation, Leland
FINA, Inc.
First Chicago
First Interstate Bank of California
First Mississippi Corp.
First Union Corp.
Firstar Bank Milwaukee NA
Fish Foundation, Vain and Harry
Fishback Foundation Trust, Harmes C.
Fleishhacker Foundation
Fluor Corp.
FMR Corp.
Fohs Foundation
Fondren Foundation
Foothills Foundation
Forbes
Ford Foundation
Ford Foundation, Edward E.
Forest Oil Corp.
Fourth Financial Corp.
Franklin Foundation, John and Mary
Franklin Mint Corp.
Freeman Foundation, Ella West
Freeport-McMoRan
Frick Foundation, Helen Clay
Frueauff Foundation, Charles A.
Funderburke & Associates
GAR Foundation
Gates Foundation
Gault-Hussey Charitable Trust
Geifman Family Foundation
Gellert Foundation, Carl
Gellert Foundation, Celia Berta
Gellert Foundation, Fred
General Reinsurance Corp.
GenRad
George Foundation
Georgia-Pacific Corp.
Georgia Power Co.
Gerber Products Co.
Gheens Foundation

Gifford Charitable Corporation, Rosamond
Gillette Co.
Glenmore Distilleries Co.
Glickenhaus & Co.
Gloeckner Foundation, Fred
Goldie-Anna Charitable Trust
Goldsmith Family Foundation
Goldsmith Foundation, Horace W.
Gottlieb Foundation, Adolph and Esther
Gould Foundation, Florence J.
Graham Fund, Philip L.
Grainger Foundation
Graphic Controls Corp.
Grassmann Trust, E. J.
Gray Foundation, Garland
Green Foundation, Allen P. and Josephine B.
Gries Charity Fund, Lucile and Robert H.
Griggs and Mary Griggs Burke Foundation, Mary Livingston
Haffner Foundation
Hales Charitable Fund
Hanes Foundation, John W. and Anna H.
Harder Foundation
Hardin Foundation, Phil
Hargis Charitable Foundation, Estes H. and Florence Parker
Harland Charitable Foundation, John and Wilhelmina D.
Haskell Fund
Hearst Foundation
Hearst Foundation, William Randolph
Hechinger Co.
Heinz Co., H.J.
Heinz Endowment, Howard
Heinz Endowment, Vira I.
Hermann Foundation, Grover
Herndon Foundation
Herrick Foundation
Hershey Foods Corp.
Hewlett Foundation, William and Flora
Hightower Foundation, Walter
Hillman Foundation
Hillman Foundation, Henry L.
Hilton Foundation, Conrad N.
Hitchcock Foundation, Gilbert M. and Martha H.
Hoffberger Foundation
Hoffman Foundation, Maximillian E. and Marion O.
Hofmann Co.
Holt Foundation, William Knox
Hopwood Charitable Trust, John M.
Hubbard Foundation, R. Dee and Joan Dale
Huffington Foundation
Hughes Charitable Trust, Mabel Y.
Hulings Foundation, Mary Andersen
Humana
Humane Society of the Commonwealth of Massachusetts
Humphrey Fund, George M. and Pamela S.
Hunt Alternatives Fund
Hunt Foundation
Huthsteiner Fine Arts Trust
Iacocca Foundation
IBM South Africa Projects Fund
Illges Foundation, John P. and Dorothy S.
Illges Memorial Foundation, A. and M. L.
Independence Foundation
Ingalls Foundation, Louise H. and David S.
ITT Hartford Insurance Group
ITT Rayonier

Jackson Foundation
James River Corp. of Virginia
Jennings Foundation, Mary Hillman
Jewett Foundation, George Frederick
JFM Foundation
Johnson Co., E. F.
Johnson Endeavor Foundation, Christian A.
Johnson Fund, Edward C.
Johnston-Fix Foundation
Johnston-Hanson Foundation
Jones Family Foundation, Eugenie and Joseph
Joukowsky Family Foundation
Keith Foundation Trust, Ben E.
Kellstadt Foundation
Kelly, Jr. Memorial Foundation, Ensign C. Markland
Kempner Fund, Harris and Eliza
Kenan, Jr. Charitable Trust, William R.
Kern Foundation, Ilma
Kerr Foundation
Kerr Foundation, Robert S. and Grayce B.
Kerr Fund, Grayce B.
Kettering Family Foundation
Kettering Fund
Kieckhefer Foundation, J. W.
Kiplinger Foundation
Kirchgessner Foundation, Karl
Kirkpatrick Foundation
Kline Foundation, Josiah W. and Bessie H.
Knight Foundation, John S. and James L.
Knott Foundation, Marion I. and Henry J.
Koch Charitable Trust, David H.
Kohler Foundation
Komes Foundation
Koopman Fund
KPMG Peat Marwick
Larsen Fund
Lastfogel Foundation, Abe and Frances
Leavey Foundation, Thomas and Dorothy
Lee Enterprises
Lemberg Foundation
Leuthold Foundation
Lewis Foundation, Lillian Kaiser
Lilly Foundation, Richard Coyle
Lincoln National Corp.
Link, Jr. Foundation, George
Little Family Foundation
Litton Industries
Loridans Foundation, Charles
Louisiana Land & Exploration Co.
Louisiana Power & Light Co./New Orleans Public Service
Loutit Foundation
Lowenstein Foundation, William P. and Marie R.
MacDonald Foundation, James A.
Macht Foundation, Morton and Sophia
Maddox Foundation, J. F.
Maier Foundation, Sarah Pauline
Mapco Inc.
Marbrook Foundation
Mardag Foundation
Margoes Foundation
Martin Foundation, Della
Massengill-DeFriece Foundation
Mather and William Gwinn Mather Fund, Elizabeth Ring
Mather Fund, Richard
Maytag Family Foundation, Fred
McCasland Foundation
McCormick & Co.
McCormick Foundation, Chauncey and Marion Deering

McCullough Foundation, Ralph
H. and Ruth J.
McCune Foundation
McDermott Foundation, Eugene
McElroy Trust, R. J.
McFeely-Rogers Foundation
McGonagle Foundation, Dextra
Baldwin
McGregor Fund
McKenna Foundation, Katherine
Mabis
Mead Corp.
Meadows Foundation
Mellon Foundation, Andrew W.
Memton Fund
Menil Foundation
Mericos Foundation
Meyerhoff Fund, Joseph
Middendorf Foundation
Milbank Foundation, Dunlevy
Miller Foundation
Mitchell Energy & Development
Corp.
Monell Foundation, Ambrose
Moore Charitable Foundation,
Marjorie
Moore Foundation, Roy C.
Moses Fund, Henry and Lucy
Mulcahy Foundation
Mulligan Charitable Trust, Mary
S.
Munson Foundation, W. B.
Murch Foundation
Murphy Foundation
Murray Foundation
Nationwide Insurance Cos.
New England Mutual Life
Insurance Co.
Newhouse Foundation, Samuel I.
News & Observer Publishing Co.
Nichols Co., J.C.
Nichols Foundation
Noble Foundation, Vivian Bilby
Norcliffe Fund
Norfolk Southern Corp.
Noyes, Jr. Memorial Foundation,
Nicholas H.
Oaklawn Foundation
Obernauer Foundation
O'Connor Foundation, A.
Lindsay and Olive B.
O'Connor Foundation, Kathryn
O'Donnell Foundation
Oglebay Norton Co.
Ohio Citizens Bank
Ohrstrom Foundation
Oliver Memorial Trust
Foundation
1525 Foundation
1957 Charity Trust
O'Neill Charitable Corporation,
F. J.
O'Neill Foundation, William J.
and Dorothy K.
Ontario Corp.
Orleton Trust Fund
O'Sullivan Children Foundation
O'Toole Foundation, Theresa
and Edward
Overbrook Foundation
Overseas Shipholding Group
Pamida, Inc.
Panhandle Eastern Corp.
Pappas Charitable Foundation,
Thomas Anthony
Parvin Foundation, Albert
Pearlstone Foundation, Peggy
Meyerhoff
Pentair
Pepsi-Cola Bottling Co. of
Charlotte
Philibosian Foundation, Stephen
Philippe Foundation
Phillips Foundation, Ellis L.
Pickford Foundation, Mary
Plough Foundation
Plumsock Fund

Post Foundation of D.C.,
Marjorie Merriweather
Potts Memorial Foundation
Poynter Fund
Prentice Foundation, Abra
Price Foundation, Louis and
Harold
Procter & Gamble Cosmetic &
Fragrance Products
Promus Cos.
Public Service Co. of New
Mexico
Pulitzer Publishing Co.
Puterbaugh Foundation
Quinlan Foundation, Elizabeth C.
Radiator Specialty Co.
Raleigh Linen Service/National
Distributing Co.
Ralston Purina Co.
Ranney Foundation, P. K.
Ratner Foundation, Milton M.
Redman Foundation
Regenstein Foundation
REI-Recreational Equipment,
Inc.
Reinberger Foundation
Rexham Inc.
Reynolds Foundation, Donald W.
Reynolds Foundation, Richard S.
Rider-Pool Foundation
Rigler-Deutsch Foundation
Robertshaw Controls Co.
Roblee Foundation, Joseph H.
and Florence A.
Rockwell Foundation
RosaMary Foundation
Rosenberg Family Foundation,
William
Ross Foundation
Rouse Co.
Rubenstein Charitable
Foundation, Lawrence J. and
Anne
Ruffin Foundation, Peter B. &
Adeline W.
S.G. Foundation
Sage Foundation
Saunders Charitable Foundation,
Helen M.
Sawyer Charitable Foundation
Schlieder Educational
Foundation, Edward G.
Schmitt Foundation, Arthur J.
Schrafft and Bertha E. Schrafft
Charitable Trust, William E.
Scott Foundation, Walter
Scrivner, Inc.
Scurlock Foundation
Scurry Foundation, D. L.
Seaway Food Town
Second Foundation
Security State Bank
Seeley Foundation
Seidman Family Foundation
Semple Foundation, Louise Taft
Seymour Foundation, W. L. and
Louise E.
Shaw Fund for Mariner's
Children
Sheafer Charitable Trust, Emma
A.
Shelden Fund, Elizabeth, Allan
and Warren
Sheridan Foundation, Thomas B.
and Elizabeth M.
Shoemaker Fund, Thomas H.
and Mary Williams
Shughart, Thomson & Kilroy,
P.C.
Signet Bank/Maryland
Simmons Family Foundation, R.
P.
Simon Foundation, William E.
and Carol G.
Simpson Foundation
Simpson Investment Co.
Skillman Foundation
Slemp Foundation

Smith Charities, John
Smith, Jr. Foundation, M. W.
Snyder Fund, Valentine Perry
Sonoco Products Co.
Sordoni Foundation
Southern California Edison Co.
Southways Foundation
Speer Foundation, Roy M.
Springs Foundation
Stabler Foundation, Donald B.
and Dorothy L.
Star Bank, N.A.
Starling Foundation, Dorothy
Richard
Starr Foundation
Stauffer Charitable Trust, John
Steele Foundation, Harry and
Grace
Stein Foundation, Jules and Doris
Steinhagen Benevolent Trust, B.
A. and Elinor
Stern Memorial Trust, Sidney
Stevens Foundation, Abbot and
Dorothy H.
Stevens Foundation, Nathaniel
and Elizabeth P.
Stocker Foundation
Stone Charitable Foundation
Stone Foundation
Strauss Foundation, Leon
Stroud Foundation
Stupp Foundation, Norman J.
Sturgis Charitable and
Educational Trust, Roy and
Christine
Sulzberger Foundation
Summerfield Foundation, Solon
E.
Sumners Foundation, Hatton W.
Sunderland Foundation, Lester T.
Swalm Foundation
Switzer Foundation
Sylvester Foundation, Harcourt
M. and Virginia W.
Tandy Foundation, Anne Burnett
and Charles
Texas Instruments
Titan Industrial Co.
TJX Cos.
Tokheim Corp.
Totsy Manufacturing Co.
Transco Energy Company
Trees Charitable Trust, Edith L.
Treuhaft Foundation
Tull Charitable Foundation
Turner Charitable Foundation
Union Bank of Switzerland Los
Angeles Branch
Union Camp Corp.
Union Foundation
USF&G Co.
Uvas Foundation
Valero Energy Corp.
Van Evera Foundation, Dewitt
Caroline
Vanderbilt Trust, R. T.
Varian Associates
Vaughan Foundation, Rachael
and Ben
Vicksburg Hospital Medical
Foundation
Vidda Foundation
Vulcan Materials Co.
Wachovia Bank & Trust Co.,
N.A.
Waggoner Charitable Trust,
Crystelle
Wahlstrom Foundation
Wallace Foundation, George R.
Ward Foundation, Louis L. and
Adelaide C.
Wasie Foundation
Wasmer Foundation
Wean Foundation, Raymond John
Weatherhead Foundation
Webb Educational and
Charitable Trust, Torrey H.
and Dorothy K.

Weber Charities Corp., Frederick
E.
Webster Foundation, Edwin S.
Weinberg Foundation, Harry and
Jeanette
Weinstein Foundation, J.
Weir Foundation Trust
Wells Foundation, Lillian S.
Werner Foundation, Clara and
Spencer
Western New York Foundation
Westport Fund
Westvaco Corp.
Whitaker Charitable Foundation,
Lyndon C.
White Consolidated Industries
Whitehead Charitable Foundation
Whiteman Foundation, Edna
Rider
Whittier Foundation, L. K.
Wilbur Foundation, Marguerite
Eyer
Wilder Foundation
Willard Foundation, Helen Parker
Williams Charitable Trust, Mary
Jo
Williams Cos.
Wills Foundation
Wilson Foundation, Marie C.
and Joseph C.
Witco Corp.
Witte, Jr. Foundation, John H.
Wolens Foundation, Kalman and
Ida
Wolfson Foundation, Louis E.
Wollenberg Foundation
Woodland Foundation
Woods Foundation, James H.
Woodward Fund-Watertown,
David, Helen, and Marian
Wright Foundation, Lola
Wurlitzer Foundation, Farny R.
Wyss Foundation
Zachry Co., H. B.
Zamoiski Co.
Zigler Foundation, Fred B. and
Ruth B.
Zurn Industries

Fellowship

Abney Foundation
Aequus Institute
Akzo America
AlliedSignal
Allyn Foundation
Aluminum Co. of America
AMAX
American Honda Motor Co.
Amoco Corp.
Andersen Corp.
Arkla
ASARCO
Bank of America - Giannini
Foundation
Baxter Foundation, Donald E.
and Delia B.
Benton Foundation
Berger Foundation, H.N. and
Frances C.
BFGoodrich
Blount
Booz Allen & Hamilton
Boswell Foundation, James G.
Bradley Foundation, Lynde and
Harry
Broadhurst Foundation
Brookdale Foundation
Brown Charitable Trust, Dora
Maclellan
Bruner Foundation
Burkitt Foundation
Burns Foundation, Fritz B.
Burroughs Wellcome Co.
Bush Foundation
Cabot Corp.
Caddock Foundation

Cain Foundation, Effie and
Wofford
Campbell and Adah E. Hall
Charity Fund, Bushrod H.
Chase Manhattan Bank, N.A.
Chevron Corp.
Childs Memorial Fund for
Medical Research, Jane Coffin
China Medical Board of New
York
Cintas Foundation
Citicorp
Clayton Fund
Coca-Cola Co.
Collins Foundation, Joseph
Commonwealth Fund
Compton Foundation
Connell Foundation, Michael J.
Cook Brothers Educational Fund
Cook Inlet Region
Coughlin-Saunders Foundation
Danforth Foundation
Daniels Foundation, Fred Harris
Davis Foundation, Edwin W. and
Catherine M.
DeKalb Genetics Corp.
Deloitte & Touche
Detroit Edison Co.
DeVlieg Foundation, Charles
Dodge Foundation, Geraldine R.
Donner Foundation, William H.
Dow Chemical Co.
Drum Foundation
du Pont de Nemours & Co., E. I.
Duke Endowment
Durr-Fillauer Medical
Earhart Foundation
Eastman Kodak Co.
Eccles Foundation, George S.
and Dolores Dore
Equitable Life Assurance Society
of the U.S.
Ernst & Young
Exxon Corp.
Fairchild Foundation, Sherman
Finley Foundation, A. E.
First Chicago
Fisher Foundation
Fleishhacker Foundation
Flinn Foundation
Foerderer Foundation, Percival
E. and Ethel Brown
Ford Foundation
Foundation for Child
Development
Francis Families Foundation
Franklin Foundation, John and
Mary
Freedom Forum
Funderburke & Associates
Gates Foundation
General Atlantic Partners L.P.
General Electric Co.
General Motors Corp.
Georgia Power Co.
German Marshall Fund of the
United States
Getty Trust, J. Paul
Glenn Foundation for Medical
Research, Paul F.
Goodyear Tire & Rubber Co.
Grace & Co., W.R.
Graham Foundation for
Advanced Studies in the Fine
Arts
Grass Foundation
Green Foundation, Allen P. and
Josephine B.
GTE Corp.
Guggenheim Memorial
Foundation, John Simon
Hardin Foundation, Phil
Haynes Foundation, John
Randolph and Dora
Heed Ophthalmic Foundation
Heinz Co., H.J.
Hermann Foundation, Grover
Herrick Foundation

Fellowship *(cont.)*

Hillman Foundation
Hoffberger Foundation
Hoffmann-La Roche
Holden Fund, James and Lynelle
Houston Endowment
Hughes Medical Institute, Howard
Iacocca Foundation
IBM Corp.
Inland Steel Industries
Intel Corp.
Jerome Foundation
Johnson Foundation, Barbara P.
Johnson Foundation, Robert Wood
Johnson & Johnson
Johnson & Son, S.C.
Joukowsky Family Foundation
Kaiser Family Foundation, Henry J.
Keck Foundation, W. M.
Kellogg Foundation, W. K.
Kempner Fund, Harris and Eliza
Kentucky Foundation for Women
Kevorkian Fund, Hagop
King Trust, Charles A.
Klingenstein Fund, Esther A. and Joseph
Koch Charitable Trust, David H.
KPMG Peat Marwick
Kress Foundation, Samuel H.
Kynett Memorial Foundation, Edna G.
Lalor Foundation
Lambe Charitable Foundation, Claude R.
Larsen Fund
Lemberg Foundation
Life Sciences Research Foundation
Lilly & Co., Eli
Lilly Endowment
Link Foundation
Link, Jr. Foundation, George
Little, Arthur D.
Little Family Foundation
Lockheed Corp.
Luce Foundation, Henry
Lurcy Charitable and Educational Trust, Georges
Lux Foundation, Miranda
MacArthur Foundation, John D. and Catherine T.
MacDonald Foundation, James A.
Mallinckrodt Specialty Chemicals Co.
Marion Merrell Dow
Markey Charitable Trust, Lucille P.
Marpat Foundation
Maxus Energy Corp.
Maytag Family Foundation, Fred
McCann Foundation
McElroy Trust, R. J.
McKnight Foundation
Meadows Foundation
Measey Foundation, Benjamin and Mary Siddons
Mellen Foundation
Mellon Bank Corp.
Mellon Foundation, Andrew W.
Menil Foundation
Mercantile Bancorp
Merck & Co.
Mericos Foundation
Millipore Corp.
Mobility Foundation
Monticello College Foundation
Moriah Fund
Morris Foundation, William T.
Moses Fund, Henry and Lucy
MTS Systems Corp.
New York Times Co.
Newcombe Foundation, Charlotte W.

Nichols Foundation
Olin Corp.
Olin Foundation, John M.
Olin Foundation, Spencer T. and Ann W.
Olsson Memorial Foundation, Elis
1957 Charity Trust
O'Neill Charitable Corporation, F. J.
Open Society Fund
Osher Foundation, Bernard
Pacific Mutual Life Insurance Co.
Panhandle Eastern Corp.
Pappas Charitable Foundation, Thomas Anthony
Parsons Foundation, Ralph M.
Perkin-Elmer Corp.
Phillips Petroleum Co.
Piper Foundation, Minnie Stevens
Plough Foundation
Potlatch Corp.
Presser Foundation
Price Waterhouse-U.S.
Prudential Insurance Co. of America
Puett Foundation, Nelson
Quaker Oats Co.
Revson Foundation, Charles H.
Rhode Island Hospital Trust National Bank
Richmond Foundation, Frederick W.
Rider-Pool Foundation
RJR Nabisco Inc.
Rockefeller Foundation
Rohm and Haas Company
Rubinstein Foundation, Helena
Rudin Foundation, Louis and Rachel
Sage Foundation
Sandoz Corp.
Sara Lee Hosiery
Scaife Foundation, Sarah
Schepp Foundation, Leopold
Schering-Plough Corp.
Schlumberger Ltd.
Schmitt Foundation, Arthur J.
Seagram & Sons, Joseph E.
Skidmore, Owings & Merrill
Sloan Foundation, Alfred P.
Smith Charitable Trust, W. W.
Smith Foundation, Richard and Susan
Smith Fund, Horace
Snow Foundation, John Ben
Snow Memorial Trust, John Ben
South Branch Foundation
South Plains Foundation
Spingold Foundation, Nate B. and Frances
Square D Co.
Stauffer Charitable Trust, John
Steinman Foundation, John Frederick
Stewardship Foundation
Stony Wold Herbert Fund
Sulzberger Foundation
Syntex Corp.
Tenneco
Texaco
Thorson Foundation
Three Swallows Foundation
3M Co.
TRW Corp.
Tuch Foundation, Michael
Turner Charitable Foundation
Union Camp Corp.
United States Sugar Corp.
Unocal Corp.
Upton Charitable Foundation, Lucy and Eleanor S.
Valero Energy Corp.
Varian Associates
Vaughn, Jr. Foundation Fund, James M.

Vulcan Materials Co.
Wagnalls Memorial
Watson Foundation, Thomas J.
Webb Foundation
Welch Foundation, Robert A.
Wenner-Gren Foundation for Anthropological Research
Wexner Foundation
Whirlpool Corp.
Whitaker Fund, Helen F.
Whiting Foundation, Mrs. Giles
Whitney Foundation, Helen Hay
Wilson Foundation, Marie C. and Joseph C.
Winston Foundation, Norman and Rosita
Wisconsin Public Service Corp.
Witco Corp.
Wyman-Gordon Co.
Xerox Corp.

General Support

ABB Process Automation
Abbott Laboratories
Abel Construction Co.
Abelard Foundation
Abeles Foundation, Joseph and Sophia
Abell Foundation, Charles S.
Abell-Hanger Foundation
Abercrombie Foundation
Abernethy Testamentary Charitable Trust, Maye Morrison
Abitibi-Price
Abney Foundation
Abraham Foundation
Abraham Foundation, Anthony R.
Abraham & Straus
Abrams Foundation
Abrams Foundation, Benjamin and Elizabeth
Abramson Family Foundation
Abroms Charitable Foundation
Abrons Foundation, Louis and Anne
Ace Beverage Co.
ACF Industries, Inc.
Achelis Foundation
Ackerman Trust, Anna Keesling
Acme-Cleveland Corp.
Acme-McCrary Corp.
Acme United Corp.
Acorn Corrugated Box Co.
Action Industries, Inc.
Acushnet Co.
Ada Foundation, Julius
Adams Foundation, Arthur F. and Alice E.
Adams Memorial Fund, Emma J.
Adams Trust, Charles E. and Caroline J.
Addison-Wesley Publishing Co.
Adler Foundation Trust, Philip D. and Henrietta B.
Advanced Micro Devices
AEC Trust
AEGON USA, Inc.
Aequus Institute
Aeroflex Foundation
Aerospace Corp.
Aetna Life & Casualty Co.
AFG Industries, Inc.
AFLAC
AGA Gas, Inc.
Agape Foundation
AGFA Division of Miles Inc.
Ahmanson Foundation
AHS Foundation
Aid Association for the Blind
Aigner
Air Products & Chemicals
Airborne Express Co.
AKC Fund
Akzo Chemicals Inc.
Alabama Gas Corp. (An Energen Co.)

Alabama Power Co.
Alaska Airlines, Inc.
Alcan Aluminum Corp.
Alco Standard Corp.
Aldeen Charity Trust, G. W.
Alexander & Baldwin, Inc.
Alexander Charitable Foundation
Alexander Foundation, Joseph
Alexander Foundation, Judd S.
Alexander Foundation, Robert D. and Catherine R.
Alhambra Foundry Co., Ltd.
Alice Manufacturing Co.
Allegheny Foundation
Allegheny Ludlum Corp.
Allen Brothers Foundation
Allen Foundation for Medical Research, Paul G.
Allen Foundation, Frances
Allen Foundation, Rita
Allen-Heath Memorial Foundation
Allergan, Inc.
AlliedSignal
Allstate Insurance Co.
Alltel/Western Region
Allyn Foundation
Alma Piston Co.
Alms Trust, Eleanora
ALPAC Corp.
Alperin/Hirsch Family Foundation
Alpert Foundation, Herb
Alro Steel Corp.
Alsdorf Foundation
Altschul Foundation
Alumax
Aluminum Co. of America
Alyeska Pipeline Service Co.
Amado Foundation, Maurice
Amaturo Foundation
AMAX
Amcast Industrial Corp.
AMCORE Bank, N.A. Rockford
Amdahl Corp.
Amdur Braude Riley, Inc.
Ameribank
America West Airlines
American Aggregates Corp.
American Brands
American Cyanamid Co.
American Electric Power
American Fidelity Corp.
American Filtrona Corp.
American Financial Corp.
American Foundation
American General Corp.
American General Finance
American Home Products Corp.
American Honda Motor Co.
American Microsystems, Inc.
American National Bank & Trust Co. of Chicago
American National Can Co.
American Natural Resources Co.
American Saw & Manufacturing Co.
American Schlafhorst Foundation, Inc.
American Society of Ephesus
American Standard
American Stock Exchange
American Telephone & Telegraph Co.
American Telephone & Telegraph Co./New York City Region
American United Life Insurance Co.
American Welding & Manufacturing Co.
Americana Foundation
Ameritas Life Insurance Corp.
Ames Charitable Trust, Harriett
Ames Department Stores
AMETEK
Amfac/JMB Hawaii

Amoco Corp.
AMP
Ampacet Corp.
Amsterdam Foundation, Jack and Mimi Leviton
Anacomp, Inc.
Analog Devices
Andersen Corp.
Andersen Foundation
Andersen Foundation, Arthur
Andersen Foundation, Hugh J.
Anderson Foundation
Anderson Foundation
Anderson Foundation, John W.
Anderson Foundation, M. D.
Anderson Foundation, Peyton
Anderson Foundation, Robert C. and Sadie G.
Anderson Foundation, William P.
Anderson Industries
Andersons Management Corp.
Andreas Foundation
Andres Charitable Trust, Frank G.
Andrews Foundation
Anheuser-Busch Cos.
Animal Assistance Foundation
Anschutz Family Foundation
Ansin Private Foundation, Ronald M.
Ansley Foundation, Dantzler Bond
AON Corp.
Apache Corp.
Apple Computer, Inc.
Applebaum Foundation
Appleby Foundation
Appleby Trust, Scott B. and Annie P.
Appleman Foundation
APV Crepaco Inc.
Arakelian Foundation, Mary Alice
Arata Brothers Trust
Arbie Mineral Feed Co.
Arca Foundation
Arcadia Foundation
Arcana Foundation
Arcata Corp.
Archbold Charitable Trust, Adrian and Jessie
Archer-Daniels-Midland Co.
Archibald Charitable Foundation, Norman
ARCO
ARCO Chemical
Arell Foundation
Aristech Chemical Corp.
Arizona Public Service Co.
Arkansas Best Corp.
Arkansas Power & Light Co.
Arkelian Foundation, Ben H. and Gladys
Arkla
Arkwright-Boston Manufacturers Mutual
Arkwright Foundation
Armbrust Chain Co.
Armco Inc.
Armco Steel Co.
Armington Fund, Evenor
Armstrong Foundation
Armstrong World Industries Inc.
Arnold Fund
Aron Charitable Foundation, J.
Arrillaga Foundation
Arronson Foundation
Artevel Foundation
Arvin Industries
ASARCO
Asea Brown Boveri
Ashland Oil
Asplundh Foundation
Associated Food Stores
Associated Foundations
Astor Foundation, Vincent
Atalanta/Sosnoff Capital Corp.

Atherton Family Foundation
Atkinson Foundation
Atkinson Foundation, Myrtle L.
Atlanta Foundation
Atlanta Journal & Constitution
Atlantic Foundation of New York
Atran Foundation
Attleboro Pawtucket Savings Bank
Auerbach Foundation, Beatrice Fox
Aurora Foundation
Austin Memorial Foundation
Autotrol Corp.
Autry Foundation
Avery Dennison Corp.
Avis Inc.
Awrey Bakeries
AXIA Incorporated
Ayres Foundation, Inc.
Azadoutioun Foundation
Azby Fund
Babcock Foundation, Mary Reynolds
Babcock & Wilcox Co.
Babson Foundation, Paul and Edith
Bacardi Imports
Bachmann Foundation
Backer Spielvogel Bates U.S.
Bacon Foundation, E. L. and Oma
Bacon Trust, Charles F.
Badgeley Residuary Charitable Trust, Rose M.
Badger Meter, Inc.
Baer Foundation, Alan and Marcia
Bafflin Foundation
Bag Bazaar, Ltd.
Baier Foundation, Marie
Bailey Wildlife Foundation
Bair Memorial Trust, Charles M.
Baird Charitable Trust, William Robert
Baird & Co., Robert W.
Baird Foundation, Cameron
Baker & Baker
Baker Foundation, Clark and Ruby
Baker Foundation, Dexter F. and Dorothy H.
Baker Foundation, Elinor Patterson
Baker Foundation, George T.
Baker Foundation, R. C.
Baker Foundation, Solomon R. and Rebecca D.
Baker Trust, Clayton
Baker Trust, George F.
Baker, Watts & Co.
Baldwin Foundation
Baldwin Foundation, David M. and Barbara
Baldwin, Jr. Foundation, Summerfield
Baldwin Memorial Foundation, Fred
Balfour Foundation, L. G.
Ball Brothers Foundation
Ball Corp.
Ballet Makers
Bally's - Las Vegas
Baltimore Gas & Electric Co.
Baltimore Life Insurance Co.
Banbury Fund
Banc One Illinois Corp.
Banc One Wisconsin Corp.
Banco Portugues do Atlantico, New York Branch
Bancorp Hawaii
Banfi Vintners
Bang & Olufsen of America, Inc.
Bank Foundation, Helen and Merrill
Bank Hapoalim B.M.
Bank IV

Bank Leumi Trust Co. of New York
Bank of A. Levy
Bank of America Arizona
Bank of Boston Connecticut
Bank of Louisville
Bank of New York
Bank of Oklahoma, N.A.
Bank of San Francisco Co.
Bank of Tokyo Trust Co.
Bank One, Texas-Houston Office
Bank One, Texas, NA
Bank One, Youngstown, NA
Bank South Corp.
BankAmerica Corp.
Bankers Trust Co.
Bannan Foundation, Arline and Thomas J.
Bannerman Foundation, William C.
Bannon Foundation
Banta Corp.
Bantam Doubleday Dell Publishing Group, Inc.
Banyan Tree Foundation
Barbour Foundation, Bernice
Barclays Bank of New York
BarclaysAmerican Corp.
Bard, C. R.
Barden Corp.
Bardes Corp.
Bargman Foundation, Theodore and Mina
Barker Foundation
Barker Foundation, Donald R.
Barker Foundation, J. M. R.
Barker Welfare Foundation
Barlow Family Foundation, Milton A. and Gloria G.
Barnes Group
Barnett Charitable Foundation, Lawrence and Isabel
Barrows Foundation, Geraldine and R. A.
Barry Corp., R. G.
Barth Foundation, Theodore H.
Bartlett & Co.
Bartol Foundation, Stockton Rush
Barton-Malow Co.
Bartsch Memorial Trust, Ruth
Bashinsky Foundation
Bass and Edythe and Sol G. Atlas Fund, Sandra Atlas
Bass Corporation, Perry and Nancy Lee
Bass Foundation
Bass Foundation, Harry
Bassett Foundation, Norman
Bastien Memorial Foundation, John E. and Nellie J.
Batchelor Foundation
Battelle
Batten Foundation
Batts Foundation
Bauer Foundation, M. R.
Bauervic Foundation, Charles M.
Bauervic Foundation, Peggy
Baum Family Fund, Alvin H.
Bausch & Lomb
Bay Branch Foundation
Bay Foundation
BayBanks
Bayne Fund, Howard
BCR Foundation
BDM International
Beach Foundation Trust A for Brunswick Hospital, Thomas N. and Mildred V.
Beach Foundation Trust D for Baptist Village, Thomas N. and Mildred V.
Beach Foundation Trust for First Baptist Church, Thomas N. and Mildred V.
Beach Foundation Trust for the University of Alabama-Birmingham

Diabetes Hospital, Thomas N. and Mildred V.
Beal Foundation
Bean Foundation, Norwin S. and Elizabeth N.
Beasley Foundation, Theodore and Beulah
Beaucourt Foundation
Beaver Foundation
Beazley Foundation
Bechtel Charitable Remainder Uni-Trust, Harold R.
Bechtel Charitable Remainder Uni-Trust, Marie H.
Bechtel Group
Bechtel, Jr. Foundation, S. D.
Beck Foundation
Bedford Fund
Bedminster Fund
Beech Aircraft Corp.
Beecher Foundation, Florence Simon
Beeghly Fund, Leon A.
Beerman Foundation
Beeson Charitable Trust, Dwight M.
Behmann Brothers Foundation
Beinecke Foundation
Beir Foundation
Beitzell & Co.
Bekins Foundation, Milo W.
Bel Air Mart
Belden Brick Co., Inc.
Belding Heminway Co.
Beldon Fund
Beldon II Fund
Belfer Foundation
Belk Stores
Belk Stores
Bell Communications Research
Bell Helicopter Textron
Bell Trust
Bellamah Foundation, Dale J.
Belmont Metals
Beloco Foundation
Beloit Foundation
Belz Foundation
Bemis Company
Ben & Jerry's Homemade
Benbough Foundation, Legler
Bend Millwork Systems
Bender Foundation
Beneficia Foundation
Benefit Trust Life Insurance Co.
Benenson Foundation, Frances and Benjamin
Benetton
Benfamil Charitable Trust
Bennett Foundation, Carl and Dorothy
Benua Foundation
Benwood Foundation
Benz Trust, Doris L.
Bere Foundation
Beren Foundation, Robert M.
Berenson Charitable Foundation, Theodore W. and Evelyn
Beretta U.S.A. Corp.
Berger Foundation, Albert E.
Berger Foundation, H.N. and Frances C.
Bergstrom Foundation, Erik E. and Edith H.
Bergstrom Manufacturing Co.
Berkey Foundation, Peter
Berkman Charitable Trust, Allen H. and Selma W.
Berkman Foundation, Louis and Sandra
Berlin Charitable Fund, Irving
Bernstein & Co., Sanford C.
Bernstein Foundation, Diane and Norman
Berrie Foundation, Russell
Berry Foundation, Archie W. and Grace
Berry Foundation, Loren M.
Berry Foundation, Lowell

Bersted Foundation
Bertha Foundation
Berwind Corp.
Besser Foundation
Best Foundation, Walter J. and Edith E.
Best Products Co.
Bethlehem Steel Corp.
Bettingen Corporation, Burton G.
Betts Industries
Betz Foundation Trust, Theodora B.
Beveridge Foundation, Frank Stanley
Beynon Foundation, Kathryne
BFGoodrich
Bibb Co.
Bickerton Charitable Trust, Lydia H.
Bicknell Fund
Biddle Foundation, Margaret T.
Bierhaus Foundation
Bierlein Family Foundation
Big Three Industries
Big V Supermarkets
Bing Fund
Bing Fund
Bingham Foundation, William
Bingham Second Betterment Fund, William
Binney & Smith Inc.
Binswanger Co.
Biomet
Bionetics Corp.
Birch Foundation, Stephen and Mary
Bird Inc.
Bireley Foundation
Birnschein Foundation, Alvin and Marion
Bishop Foundation, E. K. and Lillian F.
Bishop Foundation, Vernon and Doris
Bishop Trust for the SPCA of Manatee County, Florida, Lillian H.
Bismarck Charitable Trust, Mona
Bissell Foundation, J. Walton
Bjorkman Foundation
Black & Decker Corp.
Blackman Foundation, Aaron and Marie
Blackmer Foundation, Henry M.
Blade Communications
Blair and Co., William
Blair Foundation, John
Blake Foundation, S. P.
Blanchard Foundation
Blank Family Foundation
Blank Fund, Myron and Jacqueline
Blaustein Foundation, Jacob and Hilda
Blaustein Foundation, Louis and Henrietta
Blaustein Foundation, Morton K. and Jane
Bleibtreu Foundation, Jacob
Blinken Foundation
Block Family Charitable Trust, Ephraim
Block Family Foundation, Emphraim
Block, H&R
Bloedel Foundation
Bloedorn Foundation, Walter A.
Bloomfield Foundation, Sam and Rie
Bloomingdale's
Blount
Blount Educational and Charitable Foundation, Mildred Weedon
Blue Bell, Inc.
Blue Cross and Blue Shield of Minnesota Foundation Inc.

Blue Cross and Blue Shield United of Wisconsin Foundation
Bluhdorn Charitable Trust, Charles G. and Yvette
Blum Foundation, Edith C.
Blum Foundation, Edna F.
Blum Foundation, Harry and Maribel G.
Blum Foundation, Lois and Irving
Blum Foundation, Nathan and Emily S.
Blum-Kovler Foundation
BMC Industries
BMW of North America, Inc.
Board of Trustees of the Prichard School
Boatmen's Bancshares
Boatmen's First National Bank of Oklahoma
Bob Evans Farms
Bobst Foundation, Elmer and Mamdouha
Bock Charitable Trust, George W.
Bodenhamer Foundation
Bodine Corp.
Bodman Foundation
Boeckmann Charitable Foundation
Boettcher Foundation
Boh Brothers Construction Co.
Bohan Foundation, Ruth H.
Boisi Family Foundation
Boler Co.
Bolten Charitable Foundation, John
Bolz Family Foundation, Eugenie Mayer
Bonfils-Stanton Foundation
Bonner Foundation, Corella and Bertram
Booth Foundation, Otis
Booz Allen & Hamilton
Bordeaux Foundation
Borden
Borden Memorial Foundation, Mary Owen
Borg-Warner Corp.
Borkee Hagley Foundation
Borman's
Borun Foundation, Anna Borun and Harry
Borwell Charitable Foundation
Bosch Corp., Robert
Bossong Hosiery Mills
Boston Edison Co.
Boston Fatherless and Widows Society
Boston Gas Co.
Boswell Foundation, James G.
Botwinick-Wolfensohn Foundation
Boulevard Bank, N.A.
Boulevard Foundation
Bound to Stay Bound Books Foundation
Boutell Memorial Fund, Arnold and Gertrude
Bovaird Foundation, Mervin
Bowater Inc.
Bowers Foundation
Bowne Foundation, Robert
Bowsher-Booher Foundation
Bowyer Foundation, Ambrose and Gladys
Boynton Fund, John W.
Bozzone Family Foundation
BP America
Brace Foundation, Donald C.
Brach Foundation, Edwin I.
Brach Foundation, Helen
Bradford & Co., J.C.
Bradley Foundation, Lynde and Harry
Bradley-Turner Foundation
Brady Foundation
Branch Banking & Trust Co.

General Support (cont.)

Brand Cos.
Brand Foundation, C. Harold and Constance
Branta Foundation
Braun Foundation
Bravmann Foundation, Ludwig
Breidenthal Foundation, Willard J. and Mary G.
Bremer Foundation, Otto
Bren Foundation, Donald L.
Brennan Foundation, Robert E.
Brenner Foundation
Brenton Banks Inc.
Brewer and Co., Ltd., C.
Breyer Foundation
Bridgestone/Firestone
Briggs Family Foundation
Briggs Foundation, T. W.
Briggs & Stratton Corp.
Bright Charitable Trust, Alexander H.
Brillion Iron Works
Brink Unitrust, Julia H.
Brinkley Foundation
Bristol-Myers Squibb Co.
Bristol Savings Bank
British Airways
Britton Fund
Broad Foundation, Shepard
Broccoli Charitable Foundation, Dana and Albert R.
Brochsteins Inc.
Brody Foundation, Carolyn and Kenneth D.
Brody Foundation, Frances
Bronstein Foundation, Sol and Arlene
Bronstein Foundation, Soloman and Sylvia
Brooklyn Benevolent Society
Brooklyn Union Gas Co.
Brooks Brothers
Brotman Foundation of California
Brown and C. A. Lupton Foundation, T. J.
Brown Charitable Trust, Dora Maclellan
Brown Charitable Trust, Peter D. and Dorothy S.
Brown Family Foundation, John Mathew Gay
Brown Foundation
Brown Foundation, George Warren
Brown Foundation, M. K.
Brown Foundation, W. L. Lyons
Brown Group
Brown, Jr. Charitable Trust, Frank D.
Brown & Sharpe Manufacturing Co.
Brown & Sons, Alex
Brown & Williamson Tobacco Corp.
Browning Charitable Foundation, Val A.
Browning-Ferris Industries
Brownley Trust, Walter
Broyhill Family Foundation
Bruening Foundation, Eva L. and Joseph M.
Brundage Charitable, Scientific, and Wildlife Conservation Foundation, Charles E. and Edna T.
Brunetti Charitable Trust, Dionigi
Brunner Foundation, Robert
Bruno Foundation, Angelo
Brunswick Corp.
Brush Foundation
Bryant Foundation
Bryce Memorial Fund, William and Catherine
Buchanan Family Foundation

Buck Foundation, Carol Franc
Buckley Trust, Thomas D.
Bucyrus-Erie
Budweiser of Columbia
Buehler Foundation, A. C.
Buffalo Forge Co.
Buffett Foundation
Buhl Family Foundation
Builder Marts of America
Bull Foundation, Henry W.
Bull HN Information Systems Inc.
Bullitt Foundation
Bunbury Company
Burdines
Burger King Corp.
Burgess Trust, Ralph L. and Florence R.
Burkitt Foundation
Burlington Industries
Burlington Resources
Burnand Medical and Educational Foundation, Alphonse A.
Burnham Donor Fund, Alfred G.
Burnham Foundation
Burns Family Foundation
Burns Foundation
Burns Foundation, Fritz B.
Burns International
Burress, J.W.
Burroughs Wellcome Co.
Business Incentives
Business Men's Assurance Co. of America
Bustard Charitable Permanent Trust Fund, Elizabeth and James
Butler Family Foundation, George W. and Gladys S.
Butler Family Foundation, Patrick and Aimee
Butler Foundation, J. Homer
Butler Manufacturing Co.
Bydale Foundation
C. E. and S. Foundation
C.P. Rail Systems
Cable & Wireless Communications
Cablevision of Michigan
Cabot Corp.
Cabot Family Charitable Trust
Cabot-Saltonstall Charitable Trust
Cadbury Beverages Inc.
Caddock Foundation
Cadence Design Systems
Cadillac Products
Caesar's World, Inc.
Cafritz Foundation, Morris and Gwendolyn
Cahill Foundation, John R.
Cahn Family Foundation
Cain Foundation, Gordon and Mary
Caine Charitable Foundation, Marie Eccles
CalComp, Inc.
Calder Foundation, Louis
Calhoun Charitable Trust, Kenneth
California & Hawaiian Sugar Co.
Callaway Foundation
Callaway Foundation, Fuller E.
Callister Foundation, Paul Q.
Cambridge Mustard Seed Foundation
Cameron Foundation, Harry S. and Isabel C.
Cameron Memorial Fund, Alpin J. and Alpin W.
Camp Foundation
Camp Younts Foundation
Campbell Foundation
Campbell Foundation, Charles Talbot
Campbell Foundation, Ruth and Henry

Campbell Soup Co.
Candlesticks Inc.
Cantor Foundation, Iris and B. Gerald
Cape Branch Foundation
Capital Cities/ABC
Capital Fund Foundation
Capital Holding Corp.
Caplan Charity Foundation, Julius H.
Carbon Fuel Co.
Cargill
Carlson Cos.
Carlyle & Co. Jewelers
Carnahan-Jackson Foundation
Carnegie Corporation of New York
Carnival Cruise Lines
Carolina Power & Light Co.
Carolina Telephone & Telegraph Co.
Carpenter Foundation
Carpenter Foundation, E. Rhodes and Leona B.
Carpenter Technology Corp.
Carr Real Estate Services
Carrier Corp.
Carstensen Memorial Foundation, Fred R. and Hazel W.
Carteh Foundation
Carter Charitable Trust, Wilbur Lee
Carter Foundation, Amon G.
Carter Foundation, Beirne
Carter-Wallace
Carthage Foundation
Cartier, Inc.
Carvel Foundation, Thomas and Agnes
Cary Charitable Trust, Mary Flagler
Carylon Foundation
Cascade Natural Gas Corp.
Casco Northern Bank
Casey Foundation, Eugene B.
Cassett Foundation, Louis N.
Castle & Co., A.M.
Castle & Cooke
Castle Foundation, Harold K. L.
Castle Foundation, Samuel N. and Mary
Castle Industries
Caterpillar
Catlin Charitable Trust, Kathleen K.
Cauthorn Charitable Trust, John and Mildred
Cawsey Trust
Cayuga Foundation
CBI Industries
CBS Inc.
CCB Financial Corp.
Ceco Corp.
Cedars-Sinai Medical Center Section D Fund
CENEX
Centel Corp.
Center for Educational Programs
Centex Corp.
Central Bank of the South
Central Life Assurance Co.
Central Maine Power Co.
Central National-Gottesman
Central Newspapers, Inc.
Central & South West Services
Central Soya Co.
Central Trust Co.
Central Vermont Public Service Corp.
Century Companies of America
CertainTeed Corp.
Cessna Aircraft Co.
Chadwick Fund, Dorothy Jordan
Chais Family Foundation
Chait Memorial Foundation, Sara
Challenge Foundation

Chamberlin Foundation, Gerald W.
Chambers Memorial, James B.
Champion International Corp.
Chandler Foundation
Chanin Family Foundation, Paul R.
Chapin Foundation, Frances
Chapin-May Foundation of Illinois
Chapman Charitable Corporation, Howard and Bess
Chapman Charitable Trust, H. A. and Mary K.
Charina Foundation
Charities Foundation
Charles River Laboratories
Charlton, Jr. Charitable Trust, Earle P.
Charter Manufacturing Co.
Charter Medical Corp.
Chartwell Foundation
Chase Charity Foundation, Alfred E.
Chase Lincoln First Bank, N.A.
Chase Manhattan Bank, N.A.
Chase Trust, Alice P.
Chastain Charitable Foundation, Robert Lee and Thomas M.
Chatham Valley Foundation
Chatlos Foundation
CHC Foundation
Chemical Bank
Cheney Foundation, Ben B.
Cheney Foundation, Elizabeth F.
Cherne Foundation, Albert W.
Chernow Trust for the Benefit of Charity Dated 3/13/75, Michael
Cherokee Foundation
Chesapeake & Potomac Telephone Co.
Chesebrough-Pond's
Chevron Corp.
Chicago Board of Trade
Chicago Sun-Times, Inc.
Chicago Tribune Co.
Children's Foundation of Erie County
Childress Foundation, Francis and Miranda
Childs Charitable Foundation, Roberta M.
Chilton Foundation Trust
China Times Cultural Foundation
Chiquita Brands Co.
Chisholm Foundation
Christensen Charitable and Religious Foundation, L. C.
Christian Dior New York, Inc.
Christian Training Foundation
Christian Workers Foundation
Christie, Manson & Woods International, Inc.
Christodora
Christy-Houston Foundation
Chrysler Corp.
Churches Homes Foundation
CIBA-GEIGY Corp.
Cimarron Foundation
Cincinnati Bell
Cincinnati Enquirer
Cincinnati Foundation for the Aged
Cincinnati Gas & Electric Co.
Cincinnati Milacron
Circuit City Stores
CIT Group Holdings
Citicorp
Citizens Bank
Citizens Commercial & Savings Bank
Citizens First National Bank
City of Hope 1989 Section E Foundation
Civitas Fund
Clabir Corp.
Claiborne Art Ortenberg Foundation, Liz

Claneil Foundation
Clapp Charitable and Educational Trust, George H.
CLARCOR
Clark Charitable Foundation
Clark Charitable Trust, Frank E.
Clark Equipment Co.
Clark Family Charitable Trust, Andrew L.
Clark Foundation
Clark Foundation
Clark Foundation, Edna McConnell
Clark-Winchcole Foundation
Clarke Trust, John
Classic Leather
Clay Foundation
Clayton Fund
Cleary Foundation
Clements Foundation
Cleveland-Cliffs
Cline Co.
Clipper Ship Foundation
Clorox Co.
Close Foundation
Clougherty Charitable Trust, Francis H.
Clover Foundation
Clowes Fund
CM Alliance Cos.
CNA Insurance Cos.
CNG Transmission Corp.
Coachmen Industries
Coastal Corp.
Coats & Clark Inc.
Cobb Family Foundation
Coca-Cola Co.
Cockrell Foundation
Codrington Charitable Foundation, George W.
Coen Family Foundation, Charles S. and Mary
Cogswell Benevolent Trust
Cohen Family Foundation, Saul Z. and Amy Scheuer
Cohen Foundation, George M.
Cohen Foundation, Manny and Ruthy
Cohen Foundation, Naomi and Nehemiah
Cohen Foundation, Wilfred P.
Cohn Co., M.M.
Cohn Family Foundation, Robert and Terri
Cohn Foundation, Herman and Terese
Cohn Foundation, Peter A. and Elizabeth S.
Colburn Fund
Cole Foundation
Cole Foundation, Olive B.
Cole Foundation, Robert H. and Monica H.
Cole National Corp.
Cole Taylor Financial Group
Cole Trust, Quincy
Coleman Co.
Coleman Foundation
Coleman Foundation
Coleman, Jr. Foundation, George E.
Coles Family Foundation
Colgate-Palmolive Co.
Colket Foundation, Ethel D.
Collins & Aikman Holdings Corp.
Collins Co.
Collins Foundation
Collins Foundation, Carr P.
Collins Foundation, James M.
Colonial Life & Accident Insurance Co.
Colonial Oil Industries, Inc.
Colonial Stores
Colorado National Bankshares
Colorado State Bank of Denver
Colt Foundation, James J.
Columbia Foundation

Columbia Savings Charitable
Foundation
Columbia Savings & Loan
Association
Columbus Dispatch Printing Co.
Comer Foundation
Comer Foundation
Comerica
Cominco American Inc.
Commerce Bancshares, Inc.
Commerce Clearing House
Commercial Federal Corp.
Commercial Intertech Corp.
Commercial Metals Co.
Commerzbank AG, New York
Common Giving Fund
Common Wealth Trust
Commonwealth Edison Co.
Community Enterprises
Community Foundation
Comprecare Foundation
Compton Foundation
Computer Sciences Corp.
ConAgra
Concord Chemical Co.
Cone Mills Corp.
Confidence Foundation
Connelly Foundation
Connemara Fund
Conoco Inc.
Consolidated Freightways
Consolidated Natural Gas Co.
Consolidated Papers
Consolidated Rail Corp. (Conrail)
Conston Corp.
Consumer Farmer Foundation
Consumers Power Co.
Contempo Communications
Continental Airlines
Continental Divide Electric
Co-op
Continental Grain Co.
Contraves USA
Conwood Co. L.P.
Cook Charitable Foundation
Cook Family Trust
Cook Foundation
Cook Foundation, Loring
Cooke Foundation
Cooke Foundation Corporation,
V. V.
Cookson America
Cooper Charitable Trust, Richard
H.
Cooper Foundation
Cooper Industries
Cooper Oil Tool
Cooper Tire & Rubber Co.
Coors Brewing Co.
Coors Foundation, Adolph
Copolymer Rubber & Chemical
Corp.
Copperweld Corp.
Copperweld Steel Co.
Coral Reef Foundation
Corbin Foundation, Mary S. and
David C.
Cord Foundation, E. L.
Corestates Bank
Cornell Trust, Peter C.
Cornerstone Foundation of
Northeastern Wisconsin
Corpus Christi Exploration Co.
Corvallis Clinic
Cosmair, Inc.
Cottrell Foundation
Country Cos.
Country Curtains, Inc.
Countrymark Cooperative
County Bank
Courier-Journal & Louisville
Times
Courts Foundation
Cove Charitable Trust
Covington and Burling
Covington Foundation, Marion
Stedman

Cow Hollow Foundation
Cowles Charitable Trust
Cowles Foundation, Gardner and
Florence Call
Cowles Media Co.
Cox Charitable Trust, A. G.
Cox Foundation
Cox, Jr. Foundation, James M.
CPC International
CR Industries
Craig Foundation, J. Paul
Craigmyle Foundation
Crail-Johnson Foundation
Cramer Foundation
Crane Co.
Crane Foundation, Raymond E.
and Ellen F.
Crane Fund for Widows and
Children
Cranshaw Corporation
Cranston Print Works
Crapo Charitable Foundation,
Henry H.
Crary Foundation, Bruce L.
Crawford & Co.
Credit Agricole
Credit Suisse
Creditanstalt-Bankverein, New
York
Creel Foundation
Crels Foundation
Cremer Foundation
Crescent Plastics
Crestar Financial Corp.
Crestlea Foundation
CRI Charitable Trust
CRL Inc.
Crocker Trust, Mary A.
Crowell Trust, Henry P. and
Susan C.
Crown Books Foundation, Inc.
Crown Central Petroleum Corp.
Crown Charitable Fund, Edward
A.
Crown Cork & Seal Co., Inc.
Crown Memorial, Arie and Ida
Crum and Forster
Crummer Foundation, Roy E.
CT Corp. System
CTS Corp.
Cubic Corp.
Cudahy Fund, Patrick and Anna
M.
Culbro Corp.
Cullen Foundation
Cullen/Frost Bankers
Culpeper Memorial Foundation,
Daphne Seybolt
Culver Foundation, Constans
Cummings Foundation, Nathan
Cummings Memorial Fund
Trust, Frances L. and Edwin L.
Cummins Engine Co.
CUNA Mutual Insurance Group
Cuneo Foundation
Curran Foundation
Curtice-Burns Foods
Curtis Industries, Helene
Cyprus Minerals Co.
Dahesh Museum
Dai-Ichi Kangyo Bank of
California
Daily News
Dain Bosworth/Inter-Regional
Financial Group
Daiwa Securities America Inc.
Dalgety Inc.
Dalton Foundation, Dorothy U.
Dalton Foundation, Harry L.
Daly Charitable Foundation
Trust, Robert and Nancy
Dammann Fund
Dan River, Inc.
Dana Charitable Trust, Eleanor
Naylor
Dana Corp.
Danforth Co., John W.

Danforth Foundation
Daniel Foundation, Gerard and
Ruth
Daniel Foundation of Alabama
Daniels Foundation, Fred Harris
Danis Industries
Danner Foundation
Darby Foundation
Darrah Charitable Trust, Jessie
Smith
Dart Foundation
Dart Group Corp.
Dater Foundation, Charles H.
Dauch Foundation, William
Daugherty Foundation
Davee Foundation
Davey Tree Expert Co.
David-Weill Foundation, Michel
Davies Charitable Trust
Davis Charitable Foundation,
Champion McDowell
Davis Family - W.D. Charities,
James E.
Davis Family - W.D. Charities,
Tine W.
Davis Foundation, Edwin W. and
Catherine M.
Davis Foundation, James A. and
Juliet L.
Davis Foundation, Ken W.
Davis Foundation, Shelby
Cullom
Davis Foundation, Simon and
Annie
Davis Foundations, Arthur Vining
Davis Hospital Foundation
Day Family Foundation
Day Foundation, Cecil B.
Day Foundation, Nancy Sayles
Day Foundation, Willametta K.
Dayton Hudson Corp.
Dayton Power and Light Co.
Dayton's
Daywood Foundation
DCB Corp.
DCNY Corp.
de Dampierre Memorial
Foundation, Marie C.
De Lima Co., Paul
Dean Witter Discover
Debartolo Foundation, Marie P.
DEC International, Inc.
DeCamp Foundation, Ira W.
Decio Foundation, Arthur J.
Dee Foundation, Annie Taylor
Dee Foundation, Lawrence T.
and Janet T.
Deere & Co.
Dekalb Energy Co.
DeKalb Genetics Corp.
Dekko Foundation
Delacorte Fund, George
Delano Foundation, Mignon
Sherwood
Delany Charitable Trust,
Beatrice P.
Delaware North Cos.
Dell Foundation, Hazel
Delta Air Lines
Deluxe Corp.
Demco Charitable Foundation
DeMoss Foundation, Arthur S.
Demoulas Supermarkets
Dennett Foundation, Marie G.
Dennison Manufacturing Co.
Dent Family Foundation, Harry
Dentsply International, Inc.
Dentsu, Inc., NY
Deposit Guaranty National Bank
DeRoy Foundation, Helen L.
DeRoy Testamentary Foundation
Deseranno Educational
Foundation
DeSoto
Detroit Edison Co.
Deutsch Co.
Devereaux Foundation

DeVlieg Foundation, Charles
Devonshire Associates
Devonwood Foundation
DeVore Foundation
DeVos Foundation, Richard and
Helen
Dewar Foundation
Dexter Corp.
Dexter Industries
Dexter Shoe Co.
Dial Corp.
Diamond Foundation, Aaron
Diamond State Telephone Co.
Diamond Walnut Growers
Dick Family Foundation
Dickenson Foundation, Harriet
Ford
Dickson Foundation
Diebold, Inc.
Diener Foundation, Frank C.
Digicon
Digital Equipment Corp.
Dillard Paper Co.
Dillon Foundation
Dime Savings Bank of New York
Dimeo Construction Co.
Dimick Foundation
Dingman Foundation, Michael D.
DiRosa Foundation, Rene and
Veronica
Dishman Charitable Foundation
Trust, H. E. and Kate
Disney Family Foundation, Roy
Dively Foundation, George S.
Dixie Yarns, Inc.
Dobson Foundation
Dodge Foundation, Cleveland H.
Dodge Foundation, Geraldine R.
Dodge Foundation, P. L.
Dodge Jones Foundation
Dodson Foundation, James
Glenwell and Clara May
Doelger Charitable Trust, Thelma
Doheny Foundation, Carrie
Estelle
Dolan Family Foundation
Dollar General Corp.
Domino of California
Donaldson Charitable Trust,
Oliver S. and Jennie R.
Donaldson Co.
Donnelley Foundation, Gaylord
and Dorothy
Donnelley & Sons Co., R.R.
Donnelly Foundation, Mary J.
Donovan, Leisure, Newton &
Irvine
Dorminy Foundation, John Henry
Dorot Foundation
Doty Family Foundation
Dougherty, Jr. Foundation, James
R.
Douglas Charitable Foundation
Douglas Corp.
Douglas & Lomason Company
Douty Foundation
Dover Corp.
Dow Chemical Co.
Dow Corning Corp.
Dow Foundation, Herbert H. and
Barbara C.
Dow Foundation, Herbert H. and
Grace A.
Dow Fund, Alden and Vada
Dow Jones & Co.
Dower Foundation, Thomas W.
Downs Perpetual Charitable
Trust, Ellason
Doyle Dane Bernback Group
Dreitzer Foundation
Dresser Industries
Dreyer's & Edy's Grand Ice
Cream
Dreyfus Foundation, Jean and
Louis
Dreyfus Foundation, Max and
Victoria
Driehaus Foundation, Richard H.

Driscoll Foundation
Drown Foundation, Joseph
Drueding Foundation
Drum Foundation
du Pont de Nemours & Co., E. I.
Duchossois Industries
Dues Charitable Foundation,
Cesle C. and Mamie
Duke Endowment
Duke Foundation, Doris
Duke Power Co.
Dumke Foundation, Dr. Ezekiel
R. and Edna Wattis
Dun & Bradstreet Corp.
Duncan Foundation, Lillian H.
and C. W.
Duncan Trust, James R.
Dunn Research Foundation, John
S.
Dunning Foundation
Dunspaugh-Dalton Foundation
duPont Foundation, Alfred I.
duPont Foundation, Chichester
Duquesne Light Co.
Durell Foundation, George
Edward
Durham Corp.
Durham Merchants Association
Charitable Foundation
Duriron Co., Inc.
Durst Foundation
Dweck Foundation, Samuel R.
Dynamet, Inc.
Dyson Foundation
Eagle-Picher Industries
Early Foundation
Easley Trust, Andrew H. and
Anne O.
East Foundation, Sarita Kenedy
East Ohio Gas Co.
Eastern Bank Foundation
Eastern Fine Paper, Inc.
Eastern Star Hall and Home
Foundation
Eastover Corp.
Eaton Corp.
Eaton Foundation, Cyrus
Eaton Foundation, Edwin M. and
Gertrude S.
Eaton Memorial Fund,
Georgiana Goddard
Ebell of Los Angeles Rest
Cottage Association
Eberly Foundation
Ebsco Industries
Eccles Charitable Foundation,
Willard L.
Eccles Foundation, George S.
and Dolores Dore
Eccles Foundation, Marriner S.
Eccles Foundation, Ralph M. and
Ella M.
Echlin Inc.
Echlin Foundation
Eckerd Corp., Jack
Eckman Charitable Foundation,
Samuel and Rae
Ecolab
Edgewater Steel Corp.
Edison Brothers Stores
Edison Foundation, Harry
Edison Foundation, Irving and
Beatrice C.
Edison Fund, Charles
Edmonds Foundation, Dean S.
Edmondson Foundation, Joseph
Henry
Edouard Foundation
Edwards Foundation, O. P. and
W. E.
Edwards Industries
Edwards Memorial Trust
Edwards & Sons, A.G.
EG&G Inc.
Egenton Home
Ehrman Foundation, Fred and
Susan

General Support (cont.)

Einstein Fund, Albert E. and Birdie W.
Eisenberg Foundation, Ben B. and Joyce E.
Eisenberg Foundation, George M.
Eka Nobel
El-An Foundation
El Pomar Foundation
Elco Charitable Foundation
Electric Power Equipment Co.
Elf Aquitaine, Inc.
Elf Atochem North America
Elgin Sweeper Co.
Elizabethtown Gas Co.
Elkin Memorial Foundation, Neil Warren and William Simpson
Elkins Foundation, J. A. and Isabel M.
Elkins, Jr. Foundation, Margaret and James A.
Ellis Foundation
Ellis Fund
Ellison Foundation
Ellsworth Foundation, Ruth H. and Warren A.
Ellsworth Trust, W. H.
Emerson Electric Co.
Emerson Foundation, Fred L.
Emery Memorial, Thomas J.
EMI Records Group
Employers Mutual Casualty Co.
Endries Fastener & Supply Co.
Engelhard Foundation, Charles
English-Bonter-Mitchell Foundation
English Foundation, W. C.
English Foundation, Walter and Marian
Eni-Chem America, Inc.
Enright Foundation
Enron Corp.
Ensign-Bickford Industries
Enterprise Rent-A-Car Co.
Entex
Environment Now
Epaphroditus Foundation
Epp Fund B Charitable Trust, Otto C.
Equifax
Equitable Life Assurance Society of the U.S.
Equitable Resources
Erb Lumber Co.
Erickson Charitable Fund, Eben W.
Ernest & Julio Gallo Winery
Ernst & Young
Ernsthausen Charitable Foundation, John F. and Doris E.
Erpf Fund, Armand G.
Erving Paper Mills
Essick Foundation
Estes Foundation
Ethyl Corp.
Eureka Co.
European American Bank
Evans Foundation, Edward P.
Evans Foundation, T. M.
Evans Foundation, Thomas J.
Evening Post Publishing Co.
Everett Charitable Trust
Evinrude Foundation, Ralph
Evjue Foundation
Ewald Foundation, H. T.
Excel Industries (Elkhart, Indiana)
Exchange Bank
Exxon Corp.
Eyman Trust, Jesse
FAB Industries
Fabick Tractor Co., John
Fabri-Kal Corp.
Factor Family Foundation, Max

Failing Fund, Henry
Fair Foundation, R. W.
Fair Oaks Foundation, Inc.
Fair Play Foundation
Fairchild Foundation, Sherman
Fairfield Foundation, Freeman E.
Faith Charitable Trust
Faith Home Foundation
Falcon Foundation
Falk Foundation, David
Falk Foundation, Elizabeth M.
Falk Foundation, Michael David
Falk Medical Research Foundation, Dr. Ralph and Marian
Fanwood Foundation
Far West Financial Corp.
Farallon Foundation
Farley Industries
Farmers Group, Inc.
Farmland Industries, Inc.
Farnsworth Trust, Charles A.
Farr Trust, Frank M. and Alice M.
Farwell Foundation, Drusilla
Faulkner Trust, Marianne Gaillard
Favrot Fund
Fay Charitable Fund, Aubert J.
Fay's Incorporated
Federal Express Corp.
Federal Home Loan Mortgage Corp. (Freddie Mac)
Federal-Mogul Corp.
Federal National Mortgage Assn., Fannie Mae
Federal Screw Works
Federated Life Insurance Co.
Federation Foundation of Greater Philadelphia
Feil Foundation, Louis and Gertrude
Feild Co-Operative Association
Fein Foundation
Feinberg Foundation, Joseph and Bessie
Feinstein Foundation, Myer and Rosaline
Fel-Pro Incorporated
Felburn Foundation
Feldberg Family Foundation
Feldman Foundation
Fellner Memorial Foundation, Leopold and Clara M.
Fels Fund, Samuel S.
Fenton Foundation
Ferguson Family Foundation, Kittie and Rugeley
Ferre Revocable Trust, Joseph C.
Ferriday Fund Charitable Trust
Ferro Corp.
Fiat U.S.A., Inc.
Fibre Converters
Fidelity Bank
Field Foundation, Jamee and Marshall
Fife Foundation, Elias and Bertha
Fifth Third Bancorp
Fig Tree Foundation
Fikes Foundation, Leland
FINA, Inc.
Finch Foundation, Doak
Finch Foundation, Thomas Austin
Fingerhut Family Foundation
Fink Foundation
Finley Charitable Trust, J. B.
Firan Foundation
Fireman Charitable Foundation, Paul and Phyllis
Firestone Foundation, Roger S.
Firestone, Jr. Foundation, Harvey
First Boston
First Brands Corp.
First Chicago
First Commercial Bank N.A.
First Financial Bank FSB

First Fruit
First Interstate Bancsystem of Montana
First Interstate Bank of Arizona
First Interstate Bank of California
First Interstate Bank of Denver
First Interstate Bank of Oregon
First Interstate Bank of Texas, N.A.
First Maryland Bancorp
First Mississippi Corp.
First National Bank in Wichita
First National Bank of Evergreen Park
First National Bank & Trust Co. of Rockford
First NH Banks, Inc.
First of America Bank Corp.
First Petroleum Corp.
First Security Bank of Idaho N.A.
First Security Corp. (Salt Lake City, Utah)
First Tennessee Bank
First Union Corp.
First Union National Bank of Florida
Firstar Bank Milwaukee NA
FirsTier Bank N.A. Omaha
Fischbach Foundation
Fischel Foundation, Harry and Jane
Fischer & Porter Co.
Fish Foundation, Bert
Fish Foundation, Ray C.
Fish Foundation, Vain and Harry
Fisher Brothers
Fisher Foundation
Fisher Foundation
Fisher Foundation, Gramma
Fisher Foundation, Max M. and Marjorie S.
Fisher-Price
Fishoff Family Foundation
Fitch Trust f/b/o Cheshire Health Foundation, Leon M. and Hazel E.
FKI Holdings Inc.
Flagler Co.
Flagler Foundation
Flatley Foundation
Fleet Bank
Fleet Bank of New York
Fleishhacker Foundation
Fleming Companies, Inc.
Fleming Foundation
Flemm Foundation, John J.
Fletcher Foundation
Flickinger Memorial Trust
Florence Foundation
Florence Foundation
Florida Power Corp.
Florida Rock Industries
Florida Steel Corp.
Florsheim Shoe Co.
Flowers Charitable Trust, Albert W. and Edith V.
Floyd Family Foundation
Fluor Corp.
FMC Corp.
Fogel Foundation, Shalom and Rebecca
Folger Fund
Fondren Foundation
Foote, Cone & Belding Communications
Foote Mineral Co.
Forbes
Forbes Charitable Trust, Herman
Forchheimer Foundation
Forchheimer Memorial Foundation Trust, Louise and Josie
Ford Foundation
Ford Foundation, Joseph F. and Clara
Ford Foundation, Kenneth W.
Ford Fund, Eleanor and Edsel
Ford Fund, Walter and Josephine

Ford Fund, William and Martha
Ford II Fund, Henry
Ford III Memorial Foundation, Jefferson Lee
Ford Meter Box Co.
Ford Motor Co.
Forest City Enterprises
Forest Fund
Forest Lawn Foundation
Forest Oil Corp.
Formrite Tube Co.
Forster Charitable Trust, James W. and Ella B.
Forster-Powers Charitable Trust
Fort Worth Star Telegram
Fortin Foundation of Florida
Fortis Inc.
Fortis Benefits Insurance Company/Fortis Financial Group
Foster and Gallagher
Foster Charitable Foundation, M. Stratton
Foster Charitable Trust
Foster Co., L.B.
Foster-Davis Foundation
Foster Wheeler Corp.
Foundation for Advancement of Chiropractic Education
Foundation for Child Development
Foundation for Iranian Studies
Foundation for Middle East Peace
Foundation for the Needs of Others
Fourjay Foundation
Fourth Financial Corp.
Fowler Memorial Foundation, John Edward
Fox Inc.
Fox Charitable Foundation, Harry K. & Emma R.
Fox Foundation, John H.
Fox Foundation, Richard J.
Fox Steel Co.
Fraida Foundation
France Foundation, Jacob and Annita
Francis Families Foundation
Frank Family Foundation, A. J.
Frank Foundation, Ernest and Elfriede
Frank Fund, Zollie and Elaine
Frankel Foundation
Frankel Foundation, George and Elizabeth F.
Frankino Charitable Foundation, Samuel J. and Connie
Franklin Charitable Trust, Ershel
Franklin Foundation, John and Mary
Franklin Mint Corp.
Fraser Paper Ltd.
Frear Eleemosynary Trust, Mary D. and Walter F.
Freas Foundation
Frederick Foundation
Freed Foundation
Freedom Forum
Freeman Charitable Trust, Samuel
Freeman Foundation, Ella West
Freeport Brick Co.
Freeport-McMoRan
Freightliner Corp.
Frelinghuysen Foundation
French Foundation
French Oil Mill Machinery Co.
Frese Foundation, Arnold D.
Frey Trust f/b/o YMCA, Harry D.
Freygang Foundation, Walter Henry
Fribourg Foundation
Frick Foundation, Helen Clay
Friedland Family Foundation, Samuel
Friedman Brothers Foundation

Friedman Family Foundation
Friedman Foundation, Stephen and Barbara
Friends' Foundation Trust, A.
Frisch's Restaurants Inc.
Frito-Lay
Frohlich Charitable Trust, Ludwig W.
Frohring Foundation, Paul & Maxine
Frohring Foundation, William O. and Gertrude Lewis
Frost Foundation
Fruchthandler Foundation, Alex and Ruth
Frueauff Foundation, Charles A.
Fruehauf Foundation
Frumkes Foundation, Alana and Lewis
Fuchs Foundation, Gottfried & Mary
Fuchsberg Family Foundation
Fuchsberg Family Foundation, Abraham
Fujitsu America, Inc.
Fujitsu Systems of America, Inc.
Fuller Co., H.B.
Fuller Foundation
Fuller Foundation, George F. and Sybil H.
Fullerton Metals Co.
Fund for New Jersey
Funderburke & Associates
Fuqua Foundation, J. B.
Furth Foundation
Fusenot Charity Foundation, Georges and Germaine
G.P.G. Foundation
Gage Foundation, Philip and Irene Toll
Gahagen Charitable Trust, Zella J.
Galkin Charitable Trust, Ira S. and Anna
Gallagher Family Foundation, Lewis P.
Gallo Foundation, Ernest
Gallo Foundation, Julio R.
Galter Foundation
Galvin Foundation, Robert W.
Gann Charitable Foundation, Joseph and Rae
Gannett Co.
Gap, The
Gardner Charitable Foundation, Edith D.
Garfinkle Family Foundation
Garland Foundation, John Jewett and H. Chandler
Garner Charitable Trust, James G.
Garvey Fund, Jean and Willard
Garvey Memorial Foundation, Edward Chase
Garvey Trust, Olive White
Gates Corp.
Gates Foundation
Gateway Apparel
GATX Corp.
Gavin Foundation, James and Zita
Gaylord Foundation, Clifford Willard
Gazette Co.
Gear Motion
Gebbie Foundation
Geffen Foundation, David
GEICO Corp.
Geifman Family Foundation
Geist Foundation
Gelb Foundation, Lawrence M.
Gellert Foundation, Carl
Gellert Foundation, Celia Berta
Gellert Foundation, Fred
Gelman Foundation, Melvin and Estelle
GenCorp

General Accident Insurance Co. of America
General American Life Insurance Co.
General Atlantic Partners L.P.
General Development Corp.
General Dynamics Corp.
General Machine Works
General Mills
General Motors Corp.
General Public Utilities Corp.
General Railway Signal Corp.
General Reinsurance Corp.
General Service Foundation
General Signal Corp.
General Tire Inc.
Generation Trust
Geneseo Foundation
Genesis Foundation
Geneva Foundation
Genius Foundation, Elizabeth Morse
GenRad
George Foundation
Georgia Health Foundation
Georgia-Pacific Corp.
Georgia Power Co.
Gerard Foundation, Sumner
Gerber Products Co.
Gerlach Foundation
German Protestant Orphan Asylum Association
Gerondelis Foundation
Gershman Foundation, Joel
Gerson Family Foundation, Benjamin J.
Gerson Trust, B. Milfred
Gerstacker Foundation, Rollin M.
Getsch Family Foundation Trust
Getty Foundation, Ann and Gordon
Getz Foundation, Emma and Oscar
Ghidotti Foundation, William and Marian
Giant Eagle
Giant Food
Giant Food Stores
Gibson Foundation, E. L.
Giddings & Lewis
Giger Foundation, Paul and Oscar
Gilbane Foundation, Thomas and William
Gilbert, Jr. Charitable Trust, Price
Gilder Foundation
Giles Foundation, Edward C.
Gill Foundation, Pauline Allen
Gillett Foundation, Elesabeth Ingalls
Gillette Co.
Gilman and Gonzalez-Falla Theatre Foundation
Gilman Foundation, Howard
Gilman, Jr. Foundation, Sondra and Charles
Gilman Paper Co.
Gilmer-Smith Foundation
Gilmore Foundation, Earl B.
Gilmore Foundation, William G.
Gindi Associates Foundation
Ginsberg Family Foundation, Moses
Gitano Group
Givenchy, Inc.
Glancy Foundation, Lenora and Alfred
Glanville Family Foundation
Glaze Foundation, Robert and Ruth
Glazer Foundation, Jerome S.
Glazer Foundation, Madelyn L.
Gleason Foundation, James
Gleason Foundation, Katherine
Gleason Memorial Fund
Gleason Works
Glen Eagles Foundation
Glencairn Foundation

Glencoe Foundation
Glenmore Distilleries Co.
Glenn Foundation, Carrie C. & Lena V.
Glick Foundation, Eugene and Marilyn
Glidden Co.
Globe Corp.
Globe Newspaper Co.
Glosser Foundation, David A.
Gluck Foundation, Maxwell H.
Goddard Foundation, Charles B.
Goerlich Family Foundation
Goldbach Foundation, Ray and Marie
Goldberg Family Foundation
Goldberg Family Foundation, Israel and Matilda
Goldberg Family Foundation, Milton D. and Madeline L.
Goldberger Foundation, Edward and Marjorie
Golden Family Foundation
Goldenberg Foundation, Max
Goldman Charitable Trust, Sol
Goldman Foundation, Aaron and Cecile
Goldman Foundation, Herman
Goldman Foundation, Morris and Rose
Goldman Fund, Richard and Rhoda
Goldring Family Foundation
Goldsmith Foundation
Goldsmith Foundation, Horace W.
Goldstein Foundation, Alfred and Ann
Goldstein Foundation, Leslie and Roslyn
Golub Corp.
Good Samaritan
Goodall Rubber Co.
Goodman & Company
Goodman Family Foundation
Goodman Foundation, Edward and Marion
Goodman Memorial Foundation, Joseph C. and Clare F.
Goodstein Family Foundation, David
Goodstein Foundation
Goodwin Foundation, Leo
Goodyear Tire & Rubber Co.
Goody's Manufacturing Corp.
Gordon Foundation
Gordon Foundation, Meyer and Ida
Gordon/Rousmaniere/Roberts Fund
Gorin Foundation, Nehemiah
Gottesman Fund
Gould Inc.
Gould Foundation, Florence J.
Gould Foundation for Children, Edwin
Grable Foundation
Grace & Co., W.R.
Graco
Grader Foundation, K. W.
Gradison & Co.
Grainger Foundation
Grainger, W.W.
Grand Rapids Label Co.
Grand Trunk Corp.
Grant Foundation, Charles M. and Mary D.
Graphic Arts Show Co. Inc.
Graphic Controls Corp.
Grass Family Foundation
Gray Charitable Trust, Mary S.
Gray Foundation, Garland
Graybar Electric Co.
Great Atlantic & Pacific Tea Co. Inc.
Great Lakes Bancorp, FSB
Great Lakes Casting Corp.
Great-West Life Assurance Co.

Great Western Financial Corp.
Greater Construction Corp. Charitable Foundation, Inc.
Grede Foundries
Greeley Gas Co.
Green Charitable Trust, Leslie H. and Edith C.
Green Foundation
Green Foundation, Burton E.
Green Fund
Greenberg Foundation, Alan C.
Greene Foundation, David J.
Greene Foundation, Jerome L.
Greene Foundation, Robert Z.
Greene Manufacturing Co.
Greenebaum, Doll & McDonald
Greenfield Foundation, Albert M.
Greenheck Fan Corp.
Greenspan Foundation
Greenville Foundation
Greiner Trust, Virginia
Greve Foundation, William and Mary
Griffin Foundation, Rosa May
Griffin, Sr., Foundation, C. V.
Griffis Foundation
Griffith Laboratories Foundation, Inc.
Grigg-Lewis Trust
Griggs and Mary Griggs Burke Foundation, Mary Livingston
Grimes Foundation
Grimes Foundation, Otha H.
Grinnell Mutual Reinsurance Co.
Griswold Foundation, John C.
Grobstein Charitable Trust No. 2, Ethel
Gross Charitable Trust, Stella B.
Gross Charitable Trust, Walter L. and Nell R.
Grossman Foundation, N. Bud
Grotto Foundation
Group Health Plan Inc.
Groves & Sons Co., S.J.
Gruber Research Foundation, Lila
Grumman Corp.
Gruss Charitable and Educational Foundation, Oscar and Regina
Gruss Charitable Foundation, Emanuel and Riane
Gruss Petroleum Corp.
GSC Enterprises
GTE Corp.
Guaranty Bank & Trust Co.
Guardian Life Insurance Co. of America
Gucci America Inc.
Gudelsky Family Foundation, Isadore and Bertha
Gulf Power Co.
Gulfstream Aerospace Corp.
Gumenick Foundation, Nathan and Sophie
Gund Foundation
Gund Foundation, George
Gunderson Trust, Helen Paulson
Gurwin Foundation, J.
Guse Endowment Trust, Frank J. and Adelaide
Gussman Foundation, Herbert and Roseline
Guth Lighting Co.
Gutman Foundation, Edna and Monroe C.
Guttag Foundation, Irwin and Marjorie
Guttman Foundation, Stella and Charles
H. B. B. Foundation
Haas Foundation, Paul and Mary
Haas Foundation, Saul and Dayee G.
Haas Fund, Walter and Elise
Haas, Jr. Fund, Evelyn and Walter
Habig Foundation, Arnold F.

Hachar Charitable Trust, D. D.
Hackett Foundation
Haffenreffer Family Fund
Haffner Foundation
Hafif Family Foundation
Hagedorn Fund
Haggar Foundation
Haggerty Foundation
Haghenbeck Foundation, Antonio Y. De La Lama
Hagler Foundation, Jon L.
Haley Foundation, W. B.
Halff Foundation, G. A. C.
Hall Charitable Trust, Evelyn A. J.
Hall Foundation
Hallett Charitable Trust
Halliburton Co.
Hallmark Cards
Halloran Foundation, Mary P. Dolciani
Hallowell Foundation
Halmos Foundation
Halsell Foundation, O. L.
Halstead Foundation
Hambay Foundation, James T.
Hamel Family Charitable Trust, D. A.
Hamilton Bank
Hamilton Foundation, Florence P.
Hamilton Oil Corp.
Hammer Foundation, Armand
Hammer United World College Trust, Armand
Hammond Machinery
Hampden Papers
Hand Industries
Handleman Co.
Hankamer Foundation, Curtis and Doris K.
Hankins Foundation
Hannon Foundation, William H.
Hansen Foundation, Dane G.
Hanson Foundation
Hanson Testamentary Charitable Trust, Anna Emery
HarCo. Drug
Harcourt Foundation, Ellen Knowles
Harcourt General
Harden Foundation
Harder Foundation
Harding Educational and Charitable Foundation
Harding Foundation, Charles Stewart
Hargis Charitable Foundation, Estes H. and Florence Parker
Harkness Ballet Foundation
Harkness Foundation, William Hale
Harland Charitable Foundation, John and Wilhelmina D.
Harland Co., John H.
Harper Brush Works
Harper Foundation, Philip S.
HarperCollins Publishers
Harriman Foundation, Gladys and Roland
Harriman Foundation, Mary W.
Harrington Foundation, Don and Sybil
Harrington Foundation, Francis A. and Jacquelyn H.
Harris Brothers Foundation
Harris Corp.
Harris Foundation, J. Ira and Nicki
Harris Foundation, John H. and Lucille
Harris Foundation, William H. and Mattie Wattis
Harris Stores, Paul
Harris Trust & Savings Bank
Harrison Foundation, Fred G.
Harrison Foundation Trust, Francena T.
Harsco Corp.

Hartford Courant Foundation
Hartford Steam Boiler Inspection & Insurance Co.
Hartman Foundation, Jesse and Dorothy
Hartmarx Corp.
Hartz Foundation
Hartzell Industries, Inc.
Harvest States Cooperative
Harvey Foundation, Felix
Haskell Fund
Hassenfeld Foundation
Hastings Trust
Hatch Charitable Trust, Margaret Milliken
Hatterscheidt Foundation
Hauserman, Inc.
Havens Foundation, O. W.
Hawaii National Bank
Hawn Foundation
Hay Foundation, John I.
Hayfields Foundation
Hayswood Foundation
Hazen Charitable Trust, Lita Annenberg
Hazen Foundation, Edward W.
Healy Family Foundation, M. A.
Hearst Foundation
Hearst Foundation, William Randolph
Heath Foundation, Ed and Mary
Hebrew Technical Institute
Hechinger Co.
Hecht-Levi Foundation
Hecht's
Heckscher Foundation for Children
Hecla Mining Co.
Hedrick Foundation, Frank E.
Heginbotham Trust, Will E.
HEI Inc.
Heileman Brewing Co., Inc., G.
Heilicher Foundation, Menahem
Heineman Foundation for Research, Educational, Charitable, and Scientific Purposes
Heinz Co., H.J.
Heinz Endowment, Howard
Heinz Endowment, Vira I.
Heinz Family Foundation
Heinz Foundation, Drue
Helfaer Foundation, Evan and Marion
Helis Foundation
Heller Financial
Heller Foundation, Walter E.
Helms Foundation
Helzberg Foundation, Shirley and Barnett
Hemby Foundation, Alex
Henderson Foundation
Henderson Foundation, George B.
Hendrickson Brothers
Henkel Corp.
Henry Foundation, Patrick
Herald News
Hercules Inc.
Heritage Foundation
Herman Foundation, John and Rose
Hermann Foundation, Grover
Herndon Foundation
Herndon Foundation, Alonzo F. Herndon and Norris B.
Herrick Foundation
Herschend Family Foundation
Hersey Foundation
Hershey Foods Corp.
Hershey Foundation
Hervey Foundation
Herzog Foundation, Carl J.
Herzstein Charitable Foundation, Albert and Ethel
Hess Charitable Foundation, Ronne and Donald

General Support (cont.)

Hess Charitable Trust, Myrtle E. and William C.
Hess Foundation
Hesston Corp.
Hettinger Foundation
Heublein
Hewit Family Foundation
Hewlett Foundation, William and Flora
Hexcel Corp.
Heymann Special Account, Mr. and Mrs. Jimmy
Heymann-Wolf Foundation
Heyward Memorial Fund, DuBose and Dorothy
Hiawatha Education Foundation
Higgins Charitable Trust, Lorene Sails
Higgins Foundation, Aldus C.
Higginson Trust, Corina
High Foundation
Hightower Foundation, Walter
Hill and Family Foundation, Walter Clay
Hill Foundation
Hill-Snowdon Foundation
Hillcrest Foundation
Hilliard Corp.
Hillman Foundation
Hillman Foundation, Henry L.
Hills Department Stores, Inc.
Hills Fund, Edward E.
Hillsdale Fund
Hilton Foundation, Conrad N.
Himmelfarb Foundation, Paul and Annetta
Hiram Walker & Sons Inc.
Hirschhorn Foundation, David and Barbara B.
Hirschl Trust for Charitable Purposes, Irma T.
Hitchcock Foundation, Gilbert M. and Martha H.
HKH Foundation
Hoag Family Foundation, George
Hobart Memorial Fund, Marion W.
Hobbs Charitable Trust, John H.
Hobbs Foundation, Emmert
Hobby Foundation
Hoechst Celanese Corp.
Hoffberger Foundation
Hoffer Plastics Corp.
Hoffman Foundation, H. Leslie Hoffman and Elaine S.
Hoffman Foundation, John Ernest
Hoffman Foundation, Marion O. and Maximilian
Hoffman Foundation, Maximillian E. and Marion O.
Hofheinz Foundation, Irene Cafcalas
Hofheinz Fund
Hofstetter Trust, Bessie
Hogan Foundation, Royal Barney
Holden Fund, James and Lynelle
Holding Foundation, Robert P.
Holley Foundation
Hollis Foundation
Holmes Foundation
Holtzmann Foundation, Jacob L. and Lillian
Holzer Memorial Foundation, Richard H.
Homasote Co.
Home Depot
Home for Aged Men
Homeland Foundation
Homeland Foundation
HON Industries
Honda of America Manufacturing, Inc.
Honeywell
Honigman Foundation
Hook Drug

Hooker Charitable Trust, Janet A.
Hooper Foundation, Elizabeth S.
Hooper Handling
Hoover Foundation
Hoover Foundation, H. Earl
Hoover Fund-Trust, W. Henry
Hopedale Foundation
Hopeman Brothers
Hopewell Foundation
Hopkins Foundation, John Jay
Hopkins Foundation, Josephine Lawrence
Hopper Memorial Foundation, Bertrand
Hornblower Fund, Henry
Horncrest Foundation
Horne Trust, Mabel
Horowitz Foundation, Gedale B. and Barbara S.
Hospital Corp. of America
Houchens Foundation, Ervin G.
Houck Foundation, May K.
House of Gross
Household International
Houston Endowment
Houston Industries
Hovnanian Foundation, Hirair and Anna
Howe and Mitchell B. Howe Foundation, Lucite Horton
Howell Foundation, Eric and Jessie
Howmet Corp.
Hoyt Foundation
Hoyt Foundation, Stewart W. and Willma C.
Hubbard Milling Co.
Hubbell Inc.
Huber Foundation
Huber, Hunt & Nichols
Hudson Neckwear
Hudson-Webber Foundation
Hudson's
Huffington Foundation
Huffy Corp.
Hughes Aircraft Co.
Hughes Memorial Foundation, Charles Evans
Huizenga Family Foundation
Huizenga Foundation, Jennie
Hulings Foundation, Mary Andersen
Hulme Charitable Foundation, Milton G.
Hultquist Foundation
Humana
Hume Foundation, Jaquelin
Humphrey Foundation, Glenn & Gertrude
Humphrey Fund, George M. and Pamela S.
Hunt Alternatives Fund
Hunt Alternatives Fund, Helen
Hunt Foundation
Hunt Foundation, Roy A.
Hunt Foundation, Samuel P.
Hunt Manufacturing Co.
Hunt Oil Co.
Hunt Trust for Episcopal Charitable Institutions, Virginia
Hunter Trust, A. V.
Hunter Trust, Emily S. and Coleman A.
Huntington Bancshares Inc.
Huntington Fund for Education, John
Huntsman Foundation, Jon and Karen
Hurford Foundation
Hurley Foundation, J. F.
Huston Foundation
Hutcheson Foundation, Hazel Montague
Hutchins Foundation, Mary J.
Huthsteiner Fine Arts Trust
Hyde Foundation, J. R.
Hyde Manufacturing Co.
Hyundai Motor America

I. and L. Association
I and G Charitable Foundation
IBP, Inc.
Icahn Foundation, Carl C.
ICI Americas
Iddings Benevolent Trust
Ideal Industries
IDS Financial Services
IES Industries
Illges Foundation, John P. and Dorothy S.
Illinois Bell
Illinois Power Co.
Illinois Tool Works
IMCERA Group Inc.
Imerman Memorial Foundation, Stanley
Imlay Foundation
Imperial Bancorp
Imperial Electric
IMT Insurance Co.
In His Name
Inco Alloys International
Independence Foundation
Independent Financial Corp.
Index Technology Corp.
India Foundation
Indiana Desk Co.
Indiana Gas and Chemical Corp.
Indiana Insurance Cos.
Industrial Bank of Japan Trust Co.
Ingersoll Milling Machine Co.
Ingram Industries
Inland Container Corp.
Inland Steel Industries
Inman Mills
Insurance Management Associates
Interco
Intercontinental Hotels Corp.
International Flavors & Fragrances
International Fund for Health and Family Planning
International Multifoods Corp.
Interpublic Group of Cos.
Interstate Packaging Co.
Interstate Power Co.
Iowa-Illinois Gas & Electric Co.
Iowa Savings Bank
Iowa State Bank
Ira-Hiti Foundation for Deep Ecology
Ireland Foundation
Irmas Charitable Foundation, Audrey and Sydney
Iroquois Avenue Foundation
Irwin Charity Foundation, William G.
Irwin-Sweeney-Miller Foundation
Isaly Klondike Co.
Ishiyama Foundation
Island Foundation
Israel Discount Bank of New York
Israel Foundation, A. Cremieux
ITT Corp.
ITT Hartford Insurance Group
ITT Rayonier
Ix & Sons, Frank
J. D. B. Fund
J C S Foundation
J.P. Morgan & Co.
Jackson Charitable Trust, Marion Gardner
Jackson Family Foundation, Ann
Jackson Mills
Jacobs Engineering Group
Jacobson Foundation, Bernard H. and Blanche E.
Jacobson & Sons, Benjamin
Jacoby Foundation, Lela Beren and Norman
Jaffe Foundation
Jaharis Family Foundation

James River Corp. of Virginia
Jameson Foundation, J. W. and Ida M.
Jameson Trust, Oleonda
Janeway Foundation, Elizabeth Bixby
Janssen Foundation, Henry
Japanese American Agon Friendship League
Jaqua Foundation
Jarson-Stanley and Mickey Kaplan Foundation, Isaac & Esther
Jasper Desk Co.
Jasper Seating Co.
Jasper Table Co.
Jasper Wood Products Co.
Jaydor Corp.
Jefferson Endowment Fund, John Percival and Mary C.
Jeffress Memorial Trust, Elizabeth G.
Jeffris Family Foundation
JELD-WEN, Inc.
Jennings Foundation, Alma
Jennings Foundation, Mary Hillman
Jensen Construction Co.
Jerome Foundation
Jerome Foundation
Jersey Central Power & Light Co.
Jerusalem Fund for Education and Community Development
Jesselson Foundation
Jewett Foundation, George Frederick
JFM Foundation
Jinks Foundation, Ruth T.
JJJ Foundation
JMK-A M Micallef Charitable Foundation
Jockey Hollow Foundation
JOFCo., Inc.
John Hancock Mutual Life Insurance Co.
Johnson Charitable Trust, Keith Wold
Johnson Controls
Johnson Endeavor Foundation, Christian A.
Johnson Foundation, A. D.
Johnson Foundation, Burdine
Johnson Foundation, Helen K. and Arthur E.
Johnson Foundation, Howard
Johnson Foundation, Walter S.
Johnson Foundation, Willard T. C.
Johnson & Higgins
Johnson & Son, S.C.
Johnston-Fix Foundation
Johnston Trust for Charitable and Educational Purposes, James M.
Johnstone and H. Earle Kimball Foundation, Phyllis Kimball
Jones Charitable Trust, Harvey and Bernice
Jones Construction Co., J.A.
Jones Family Foundation, Eugenie and Joseph
Jones Foundation, Daisy Marquis
Jones Foundation, Harvey and Bernice
Jones Foundation, Montfort Jones and Allie Brown
Jones Fund, Blanche and George
Jones Intercable, Inc.
Jonsson Foundation
Jordan Foundation, Arthur
Joselow Foundation
Joslin-Needham Family Foundation
Joslyn Corp.
Jostens
Joukowsky Family Foundation
Journal Communications
Joy Family Foundation

Joyce Foundation
JSJ Corp.
Julia R. and Estelle L. Foundation
Jurodin Fund
Jurzykowski Foundation, Alfred
Justus Trust, Edith C.
Kahn Dallas Symphony Foundation, Louise W. and Edmund J.
Kaiser Cement Corp.
Kaiser Foundation, Betty E. and George B.
Kaman Corp.
Kamps Memorial Foundation, Gertrude
Kane Paper Corp.
Kangesser Foundation, Robert E., Harry A., and M. Sylvia
Kao Corp. of America (DE)
Kapiloff Foundation, Leonard
Kaplan Foundation, Charles I. and Mary
Kaplan Foundation, Rita J. and Stanley H.
Kaplan Fund, J. M.
Kaplen Foundation
Kaplun Foundation, Morris J. and Betty
Kapoor Charitable Foundation
Kapor Family Foundation
Kasal Charitable Trust, Father
Kasle Steel Corp.
Katten, Muchin, & Zavis
Katzenberger Foundation
Kauffman Foundation, Muriel McBrien
Kaufman & Broad Home Corp.
Kaufman Foundation, Henry & Elaine
Kaufman Memorial Trust, Chaim, Fanny, Louis, Benjamin, and Anne Florence
Kaufmann Foundation, Henry
Kaul Foundation Trust, Hugh
Kautz Family Foundation
Kavanagh Foundation, T. James
Kawaler Foundation, Morris and Nellie L.
Kawasaki Motors Corp., U.S.A.
Kaye, Scholer, Fierman, Hays & Handler
Kayser Foundation
Kearney Inc., A.T.
Keating Family Foundation
Keck, Jr. Foundation, William M.
Keebler Co.
Keeler Fund, Miner S. and Mary Ann
Keene Trust, Hazel R.
Keeney Trust, Hattie Hannah
Keith Foundation Trust, Ben E.
Kejr Foundation
Kellenberger Historical Foundation, May Gordon Latham
Keller Family Foundation
Kelley Foundation, Kate M.
Kellogg Co., M.W.
Kellogg Foundation, J. C.
Kellogg Foundation, Peter and Cynthia K.
Kellogg's
Kellwood Co.
Kelly Foundation, T. Lloyd
Kelly, Jr. Memorial Foundation, Ensign C. Markland
Kelly Tractor Co.
Kemper Charitable Lead Trust, William T.
Kemper Charitable Trust, William T.
Kemper Educational and Charitable Fund
Kemper Foundation, Enid and Crosby
Kemper Foundation, William T.

Kemper Memorial Foundation, David Woods
Kenan Family Foundation
Kenan, Jr. Charitable Trust, William R.
Kendall Foundation, George R.
Kendall Foundation, Henry P.
Kendall Health Care Products
Kenedy Memorial Foundation, John G. and Marie Stella
Kennametal
Kennedy Family Foundation, Ethel and W. George
Kennedy Foundation, Ethel
Kennedy Foundation, John R.
Kennedy Foundation, Quentin J.
Kennedy Memorial Fund, Mark H.
Kenridge Fund
Kent Foundation, Ada Howe
Kent-Lucas Foundation
Kenwood U.S.A. Corp.
Kenworthy - Sarah H. Swift Foundation, Marion E.
Kepco, Inc.
Kern Foundation, Ilma
Kerr Foundation, Robert S. and Grayce B.
Kerr Fund, Grayce B.
Kerr-McGee Corp.
Kest Family Foundation, Sol and Clara
Ketchum & Co.
Kettering Family Foundation
Kettering Fund
Kevorkian Fund, Hagop
Key Bank of Maine
Key Food Stores Cooperative Inc.
Kidder, Peabody & Co.
Kieckhefer Foundation, J. W.
Kiewit Sons, Peter
Kikkoman International, Inc.
Kilbourne Residuary Charitable Trust, E. H.
Kilcawley Fund, William H.
Killough Trust, Walter H. D.
Killson Educational Foundation, Winifred and B. A.
Kilmartin Industries
Kilworth Charitable Foundation, Florence B.
Kimball Co., Miles
Kimball Foundation, Horace A.
Kimball and S. Ella
Kimball International
Kimberly-Clark Corp.
Kimmelman Foundation, Helen & Milton
King Kullen Grocery Co., Inc.
Kingsbury Corp.
Kingsley Foundation
Kingston Foundation
Kinney-Lindstrom Foundation
Kiplinger Foundation
Kirbo Charitable Trust, Thomas M. and Irene B.
Kirby Foundation, F. M.
Kirchgessner Foundation, Karl
Kirkhill Rubber Co.
Kirkland & Ellis
Klau Foundation, David W. and Sadie
Kleberg, Jr. and Helen C. Kleberg Foundation, Robert J.
Klee Foundation, Conrad and Virginia
Klein Charitable Foundation, Raymond
Klein Fund, Nathan J.
Kline Foundation, Charles and Figa
Kline Foundation, Josiah W. and Bessie H.
Kling Trust, Louise
Klingenstein Fund, Esther A. and Joseph
Klingler Foundation, Helen & Charles

Klipstein Foundation, Ernest Christian
Kloeckner-Pentaplast of America
Klosk Fund, Louis and Rose
Kmart Corp.
KN Energy, Inc.
Knight-Ridder, Inc.
Knistrom Foundation, Fanny and Svante
Knott Foundation, Marion I. and Henry J.
Knowles Charitable Memorial Trust, Gladys E.
Knox Family Foundation
Knox Foundation, Seymour H.
Knox, Sr., and Pearl Wallis Knox Charitable Foundation, Robert W.
Knudsen Charitable Foundation, Earl
Knudsen Foundation, Tom and Valley
Kobacker Co.
Koch Charitable Foundation, Charles G.
Koch Charitable Trust, David H.
Koch Foundation
Koch Industries
Koch Sons, George
Koffler Family Foundation
Koh-I-Noor Rapidograph Inc.
Kohl Charitable Foundation, Allen D.
Kohl Foundation, Sidney
Kohler Co.
Kohn-Joseloff Fund
Komes Foundation
Koopman Fund
Kopf Foundation
Kopf Foundation, Elizabeth Christy
Koret Foundation
Korman Family Foundation, Hyman
Kowalski Sausage Co.
Kraft Foundation
Kramer Foundation
Kramer Foundation, C. L. C.
Krause Foundation, Charles A.
Kravis Foundation, Henry R.
Kreielsheimer Foundation Trust
Kremer Foundation Trust, George
Kress Foundation, George
Krieble Foundation, Vernon K.
Krimendahl II Foundation, H. Frederick
KSM Foundation
Kugelman Foundation
Kuhne Foundation Trust, Charles
Kuhns Investment Co.
Kulas Foundation
Kulicke & Soffa Industries
Kunkel Foundation, John Crain
Kuse Foundation, James R.
Kutz Foundation, Milton and Hattie
Kuyper Foundation, Peter H. and E. Lucille Gaass
Kyocera International Inc.
Kysor Industrial Corp.
L and L Foundation
La-Z-Boy Chair Co.
Laclede Gas Co.
Lacy Foundation
Ladd Charitable Corporation, Helen and George
Ladish Co.
Ladish Family Foundation, Herman W.
Laerdal Foundation, Asmund S.
Laffey-McHugh Foundation
Lakeside Foundation
Lakeside National Bank
Lamb Foundation, Kirkland S. and Rena B.
Lambda Electronics Inc.
Lambe Charitable Foundation, Claude R.

Lambert Memorial Foundation, Gerard B.
LamCo. Communications
Lamson & Sessions Co.
Lancaster Colony
Lance, Inc.
Land O'Lakes
Landegger Charitable Foundation
Landmark Communications
Lane Charitable Trust, Melvin R.
Lane Co., Inc.
Lane Foundation, Minnie and Bernard
Lane Memorial Foundation, Mills Bee
Lang Foundation, Eugene M.
Langdale Co.
Langendorf Foundation, Stanley S.
Lannan Foundation
Lapham-Hickey Steel Corp.
Lard Trust, Mary Potishman
Large Foundation
Laros Foundation, R. K.
Larsen Fund
Larsh Foundation Charitable Trust
LaSalle Bank Lake View
Lasalle National Corp.
Lasdon Foundation
Lasky Co.
Lassus Brothers Oil
Lastfogel Foundation, Abe and Frances
Lattner Foundation, Forrest C.
Lauder Foundation
Lauffer Trust, Charles A.
Laurel Foundation
Lautenberg Foundation
LaViers Foundation, Harry and Maxie
Law Foundation, Robert O.
Lawrence Foundation, Alice
Lawyers Title Foundation
Lazar Foundation
Lazarus Charitable Trust, Helen and Charles
LBJ Family Foundation
LDI Charitable Foundation
Lea Foundation, Helen Sperry
Leach Foundation, Tom & Frances
Leaseway Transportation Corp.
Leavey Foundation, Thomas and Dorothy
Lebanon Mutual Insurance Co.
Lebovitz Fund
Lebus Trust, Bertha
Lechmere
Lederer Foundation, Francis L.
Lee Endowment Foundation
Lee Enterprises
Lee Foundation, Ray M. and Mary Elizabeth
Leesona Corp.
LEF Foundation
Legg Mason Inc.
Lehigh Portland Cement Co.
Lehman Foundation, Edith and Herbert
Lehman Foundation, Robert
Lehmann Foundation, Otto W.
Lehrman Foundation, Jacob and Charlotte
Leibovitz Foundation, Morris P.
Leighton-Oare Foundation
Lender Family Foundation
Lennon Foundation, Fred A.
Lennox International, Inc.
Leo Burnett Co.
Leonardt Foundation
Leonhardt Foundation, Dorothea L.
Leonhardt Foundation, Frederick H.
Leu Foundation
Leucadia National Corp.

Leuthold Foundation
Levee Charitable Trust, Polly Annenberg
Levin Foundation, Philip and Janice
Levine Family Foundation, Hyman
Levinson Foundation, Max and Anna
Levinson Foundation, Morris L.
Levit Family Foundation, Joe
Leviton Manufacturing Co.
Levitt Foundation
Levitt Foundation, Richard S.
Levy Foundation, Betty and Norman F.
Levy Foundation, Charles and Ruth
Levy Foundation, Edward C.
Levy Foundation, Hyman Jebb
Levy Foundation, Jerome
Levy Foundation, June Rockwell
Levy's Lumber & Building Centers
Lewis Foundation, Frank J.
Libby-Dufour Fund, Trustees of the
Liberman Foundation, Bertha & Isaac
Liberty Corp.
Liberty Diversified Industries Inc.
Liberty Hosiery Mills
Liberty Mutual Insurance Group/Boston
Lichtenstein Foundation, David B.
Lieberman Enterprises
Lied Foundation Trust
Life Insurance Co. of Georgia
Life Investors Insurance Company of America
Lilly & Co., Eli
Lilly Endowment
Lilly Foundation, Richard Coyle
LIN Broadcasting Corp.
Lincoln Electric Co.
Lincoln Family Foundation
Lincoln Health Care Foundation
Lincoln National Corp.
Lincoln Telecommunications Co.
Lincolnshire
Lincy Foundation
Linde Foundation, Ronald and Maxine
Lindner Foundation, Fay J.
Lindstrom Foundation, Kinney
Link, Jr. Foundation, George
Linn-Henley Charitable Trust
Linnell Foundation
Lintilhac Foundation
Linus Foundation
Lippitt Foundation, Katherine Kenyon
Lipsky Foundation, Fred and Sarah
Lipton Foundation
Lipton, Thomas J.
Liquid Air Corp.
List Foundation, Albert A.
Littauer Foundation, Lucius N.
Little, Arthur D.
Little Family Foundation
Littlefield Foundation, Edmund Wattis
Littlefield Memorial Trust, Ida Ballou
Litton Industries
Litton/Itek Optical Systems
Litwin Foundation
Livingston Foundation
Livingston Foundation, Milton S. and Corinne N.
Livingston Memorial Foundation
Liz Claiborne
Lizzadro Family Foundation, Joseph
Llagas Foundation

Loats Foundation
Lockhart Iron & Steel Co.
Lockheed Corp.
Lockwood Foundation, Byron W. and Alice L.
Loctite Corp.
Loeb Partners Corp.
Loewenberg Foundation
Loews Corp.
Loewy Family Foundation
Logan Foundation, E. J.
Lomas Financial Corp.
Long Foundation, J.M.
Longs Drug Stores
Longview Fibre Co.
Lopata Foundation, Stanley and Lucy
Lord Corp.
Loridans Foundation, Charles
Lost Tree Charitable Foundation
Loughran Foundation, Mary and Daniel
Louis Foundation, Michael W.
Louisiana Land & Exploration Co.
Louisiana-Pacific Corp.
Louisiana Power & Light Co./New Orleans Public Service
Louisville Gas & Electric Co.
Loutit Foundation
Love Charitable Foundation, John Allan
Love Foundation, Gay and Erskine
Love Foundation, George H. and Margaret McClintic
Love Foundation, Lucyle S.
Love Foundation, Martha and Spencer
Lovett Foundation
Lowe Foundation
Lowe Foundation
Lowe Foundation, Joe and Emily
Lowell Institute, Trustees of the
Lowenstein Brothers Foundation
Lowenstein Foundation, Leon
Lowe's Cos.
Lozier Foundation
LTV Corp.
Lubo Fund
Lubrizol Corp.
Luce Charitable Foundation, Stephen C.
Luce Charitable Trust, Theodore
Luce Foundation, Henry
Luchsinger Family Foundation
Luck Stone
Luckyday Foundation
Lumpkin Foundation
Lund Foundation
Lupin Foundation
Lurie Family Foundation
Lurie Foundation, Louis R.
Luse Foundation, W. P. and Bulah
Luster Family Foundation
Lutheran Brotherhood Foundation
Luttrell Trust
Lux Trust, Dr. Konrad and Clara
Lykes Brothers Steamship Co.
Lynn Foundation, E. M.
Lyon Foundation
Lyondell Petrochemical Co.
M. E. G. Foundation
M/A-COM, Inc.
M.E. Foundation
M.T.D. Products
Maas Foundation, Benard L.
MacAndrews & Forbes Holdings
MacArthur Foundation, John D. and Catherine T.
MacCurdy Salisbury Educational Foundation
MacDonald Foundation, James A.
Macht Foundation, Morton and Sophia

General Support (cont.)

Mack Foundation, J. S.
MacKall and Evanina Evans Bell MacKall Trust, Paul
MacKenzie Foundation
Maclellan Foundation
Maclellan Foundation, Robert L. and Kathrina H.
MacLeod Stewardship Foundation
Macmillan, Inc.
Macy & Co., R.H.
Maddox Foundation, J. F.
Maddox Trust, Web
Madison Gas & Electric Co.
Magma Copper Co.
Magowan Family Foundation
Magruder Foundation, Chesley G.
Mailman Foundation
Makita U.S.A., Inc.
MalCo Products Inc.
Mallinckrodt Specialty Chemicals Co.
Mamiye Brothers
Manat Foundation
Mandel Foundation, Jack N. and Lilyan
Mandel Foundation, Joseph and Florence
Mandel Foundation, Morton and Barbara
Mandell Foundation, Samuel P.
Mandeville Foundation
Maneely Fund
Manilow Foundation, Nathan
Manitou Foundation
Manitowoc Co.
Mankato Citizens Telephone Co.
Mann Foundation, John Jay
Mann Foundation, Ted
Manoogian Foundation, Alex and Marie
Mansfield Foundation, Albert and Anne
Manufacturers Life Insurance Co. of America
Manufacturers National Bank of Detroit
Manville Corp.
Mapco Inc.
Marathon Oil, Indiana Refining Division
Marbrook Foundation
Marcus Brothers Textiles Inc.
Marcus Corp.
Mardag Foundation
Mardigian Foundation
Margolis Charitable Foundation for Medical Research, Ben B. and Iris M.
Marine Midland Banks
Marinette Marine Corp.
Marion Merrell Dow
Markey Charitable Fund, John C.
Markey Charitable Trust, Lucille P.
Marley Co.
Marpat Foundation
Marquette Electronics
Marriott Corp.
Marriott Foundation, J. Willard
Mars Foundation
Marsh & McLennan Cos.
Marshall Field's
Marshall Foundation
Marshall Fund
Marshall & Ilsley Bank
Marshburn Foundation
Martin & Deborah Flug Foundation
Martin Family Fund
Martin Foundation
Martin Foundation, Bert William
Martin Marietta Aggregates

Martin Marietta Corp.
Martini Foundation, Nicholas
Marubeni America Corp.
Marx Foundation, Virginia & Leonard
Masco Corp.
Mascoma Savings Bank
Mason Charitable Foundation
Mass Merchandisers, Inc.
Massachusetts Mutual Life Insurance Co.
Massengill-DeFriece Foundation
Massey Charitable Trust
Massey Foundation
Massie Trust, David Meade
Mastronardi Charitable Foundation, Charles A.
Material Service Corp.
Mather and William Gwinn Mather Fund, Elizabeth Ring
Mather Charitable Trust, S. Livingston
Mather Fund, Richard
Mathis-Pfohl Foundation
Mattel
Matthews International Corp.
Mattus Foundation, Reuben and Rose
Matz Foundation — Edelman Division
Mautz Paint Co.
Max Charitable Foundation
Maxon Charitable Foundation
Maxus Energy Corp.
May Charitable Trust, Ben
May Foundation, Wilbur
Mayborn Foundation, Frank W.
Mayer Charitable Trust, Oscar G. & Elsa S.
Mayer Foods Corp., Oscar
Mayer Foundation, James and Eva
Mayor Foundation, Oliver Dewey
Maytag Corp.
Maytag Family Foundation, Fred
Mazda Motors of America (Central), Inc.
Mazda North America
Mazer Foundation, Jacob and Ruth
Mazza Foundation
MBIA, Inc.
MCA
McAlister Charitable Foundation, Harold
McAlonan Trust, John A.
McBean Charitable Trust, Alletta Morris
McBean Family Foundation
McBeath Foundation, Faye
McCamish Foundation
McCann Foundation
McCarthy Charities
McCarthy Foundation, John and Margaret
McCarthy Foundation, Michael W.
McCarthy Memorial Trust Fund, Catherine
McCasland Foundation
McCaw Cellular Communications
McCaw Foundation
McConnell Foundation, Neil A.
McCormick Foundation, Chauncey and Marion Deering
McCormick Tribune Foundation, Robert R.
McCormick Trust, Anne
McCray Lumber Co.
McCrea Foundation
McCullough Foundation, Ralph H. and Ruth J.
McCune Charitable Trust, John R.
McCutchen Foundation
McDermott
McDermott Foundation, Eugene

McDonald Foundation, J. M.
McDonald Industries, Inc., A. Y.
McDonnell Douglas Corp.
McDonnell Douglas Corp.-West
McDonough Foundation, Bernard
McDougall Charitable Trust, Ruth Camp
McElroy Trust, R. J.
McEvoy Foundation, Mildred H.
McFawn Trust No. 2, Lois Sisler
McFeely-Rogers Foundation
McGee Foundation
McGonagle Foundation, Dextra Baldwin
McGovern Foundation, John P.
McGovern Fund for the Behavioral Sciences
McGraw Foundation, Curtis W.
McGraw Foundation, Donald C.
McGraw-Hill
McGregor Foundation, Thomas and Frances
McGregor Fund
MCI Communications Corp.
McInerny Foundation
McIntosh Foundation
McIntosh Foundation
McIntyre Foundation, C. S. and Marion F.
MCJ Foundation
McKee Foundation, Robert E. and Evelyn
McKenna Foundation, Katherine Mabis
McKesson Corp.
McKnight Foundation
McKnight Foundation, Sumner T.
McLendon Educational Fund, Violet H.
McMahon Foundation
McMaster Foundation, Harold and Helen
McMillan Foundation, D. W.
McMillan, Jr. Foundation, Bruce
McMillen Foundation
McMurray-Bennnett Foundation
McNeely Foundation
McNeil, Jr. Charitable Trust, Robert L.
McNutt Charitable Trust, Amy Shelton
McRae Foundation
McShain Charities, John
McVay Foundation
McWane Inc.
MDU Resources Group, Inc.
Mead Corp.
Mead Fund, Nelson
Meadowood Foundation
Meadows Foundation
Mechanic Foundation, Morris A.
Mechanics Bank
Media General, Inc.
Medina Foundation
Medtronic
Meek Foundation
Meenan Oil Co., Inc.
Meland Outreach
Melitta North America Inc.
Mellam Family Foundation
Mellon Bank Corp.
Mellon Foundation, Andrew W.
Mellon Foundation, Richard King
Mellon PSFS
Melohn Foundation
Memorial Foundation for the Blind
Memphis Light Gas & Water Division
Memton Fund
Menasha Corp.
Mendel Foundation
Mengle Foundation, Glenn and Ruth
Menil Foundation
Menschel Foundation, Robert and Joyce

Mentor Graphics
Mercantile Bankshares Corp.
Mercedes-Benz of North America, Inc.
Merchants Bancshares
Merck Fund, John
Merck Human Health Division
Mercury Aircraft
Mercy, Jr. Foundation, Sue and Eugene
Meredith Corp.
Meredith Foundation
Mericos Foundation
Merillat Foundation, Orville D. and Ruth A.
Merit Oil Corp.
Meritor Financial Group
Merkley Charitable Trust
Merrick Foundation, Robert G. and Anne M.
Merrill Foundation, R. D.
Merrill Lynch & Co.
Merrion Foundation
Merry-Go-Round Enterprises, Inc.
Mertz Foundation, Martha
Mertz-Gilmore Foundation, Joyce
Mervyn's
Mesa Inc.
Messing Foundation, Morris M. and Helen F.
Metal Industries
Metallgesellschaft Corp.
Metropolitan Health Foundation
Metropolitan Life Insurance Co.
Metropolitan Theatres Corp.
Mex-Am Cultural Foundation
Meyer Family Foundation, Paul J.
Meyer Foundation, Alice Kleberg Reynolds
Meyer Foundation, Eugene and Agnes E.
Meyer Foundation, George C.
Meyer Foundation, Robert R.
Meyer Fund, Milton and Sophie
Meyer Memorial Foundation, Aaron and Rachel
Meyer Memorial Trust
Meyerhoff Foundation, Lyn P.
MGIC Investment Corp.
Michael Foundation, Herbert I. and Elsa B.
Michael-Walters Industries
Michigan Bell Telephone Co.
Michigan Gas Utilities
Michigan National Corp.
Microsoft Corp.
Mid-Iowa Health Foundation
MidCon Corp.
Middendorf Foundation
Midland Co.
Midland Mutual Life Insurance Co.
Midmark Corp.
Midwest Resources
Mielke Family Foundation
Milbank Foundation, Dunlevy
Miles Inc.
Milken Family Medical Foundation
Milken Foundation, L. and S.
Mill-Rose Co.
Millard Charitable Trust, Adah K.
Millbrook Tribute Garden
Miller Charitable Foundation, C. John and Reva
Miller Charitable Foundation, Howard E. and Nell E.
Miller Charitable Trust, Lewis N.
Miller Foundation
Miller Foundation, Earl B. and Loraine H.
Miller Foundation, Steve J.
Miller-Mellor Association
Miller Memorial Trust, George Lee
Milliken & Co.

Milliken Foundation, Agnes G.
Millipore Corp.
Mills Foundation, Ralph E.
Millstone Foundation
Milstein Family Foundation
Mine Safety Appliances Co.
Mineral Trust
Miniger Memorial Foundation, Clement O.
Minnegasco
Minnesota Mutual Life Insurance Co.
Minnesota Power & Light Co.
Minolta Corp.
Minster Machine Co.
Mirage Casino-Hotel
Mirapaul Foundation
Misco Industries
Mississippi Chemical Corp.
Mississippi Power & Light Co.
Missouri Farmers Association
Missouri Public Service
Mitchell Family Foundation, Bernard and Marjorie
Mitchell Family Foundation, Edward D. and Anna
Mitrani Family Foundation
Mitre Corp.
Mitsubishi Electric America
Mitsubishi Heavy Industries America
Mitsubishi International Corp.
Mnuchin Foundation
Mobil Oil Corp.
Model Foundation, Leo
Mohasco Corp.
Monadnock Paper Mills
Monaghan Charitable Trust, Rose
Monarch Machine Tool Co.
Moncrief Foundation, William A. and Elizabeth B.
Monell Foundation, Ambrose
Monfort Charitable Foundation
Monfort of Colorado, Inc.
Monroe Auto Equipment Co.
Monroe-Brown Foundation
Monroe Foundation (1976), J. Edgar
Montana Power Co.
Montgomery Elevator Co.
Montgomery Foundation
Montgomery Street Foundation
Montgomery Ward & Co.
Moog Automotive, Inc.
Moore Business Forms, Inc.
Moore, Costello & Hart
Moore Family Foundation
Moore Foundation, C. F.
Moore Foundation, Edward S.
Moore Foundation, Martha G.
Moore Foundation, O. L.
Moore Foundation, Roy C.
Moore Memorial Foundation, James Starr
Moore & Sons, B.C.
Moores Foundation
Moores Foundation, Harry C.
Moorman Manufacturing Co.
Moosehead Manufacturing Co.
Morania Foundation
Morgan Charitable Residual Trust, W. and E.
Morgan Construction Co.
Morgan Foundation, Burton D.
Morgan Foundation, Louie R. and Gertrude
Morgan Stanley & Co.
Morgan Trust for Charity, Religion, and Education
Morgenstern Foundation, Morris
Moriah Fund
Morley Brothers Foundation
Morrill Charitable Foundation
Morris Charitable Foundation, E. A.
Morris Charitable Trust, Charles M.

Morris Foundation
Morris Foundation, Margaret T.
Morris Foundation, Norman M.
Morris Foundation, William T.
Morrison Charitable Trust, Pauline A. and George R.
Morrison Foundation, Harry W.
Morrison Trust, Louise L.
Morse Foundation, Richard P. and Claire W.
Morse, Jr. Foundation, Enid and Lester S.
Morse Shoe, Inc.
Morton International
Mosbacher, Jr. Foundation, Emil
Moses Fund, Henry and Lucy
Mosher Foundation, Samuel B.
Mosinee Paper Corp.
Moss Foundation, Harry S.
Motch Corp.
Motorola
Mott Charitable Trust/Spectemur Agendo, Stewart R.
Mott Foundation, Charles Stewart
Mott Fund, Ruth
Motter Printing Press Co.
Mount Vernon Mills
MSI Insurance
MTS Systems Corp.
Mulcahy Foundation
Mulford Foundation, Vincent
Mulford Trust, Clarence E.
Mullan Foundation, Thomas F. and Clementine L.
Mullen Foundation, J. K.
Muller Foundation
Muller Foundation, C. John and Josephine
Multimedia, Inc.
Munger Foundation, Alfred C.
Murch Foundation
Murdy Foundation
Murfee Endowment, Kathryn
Murphey Foundation, Lluella Morey
Murphy Charitable Fund, George E. and Annette Cross
Murphy Co., G.C.
Murphy Foundation
Murphy Foundation, Dan
Murphy Foundation, John P.
Musson Charitable Foundation, R. C. and Katharine M.
Muth Foundation, Peter and Mary
Mutual of America Life
Myers and Sons, D.
Myra Foundation
Nabisco Foods Group
Nakamichi Foundation, E.
Nalco Chemical Co.
Nash Foundation
Nashua Trust Co.
Nason Foundation
Nathan Berkman & Co.
Nathan Foundation
National Center for Automated Information Retrieval
National City Bank, Columbus
National City Bank of Evansville
National City Bank of Indiana
National City Corp.
National Computer Systems
National Convenience Stores, Inc.
National Data Corp.
National Forge Co.
National Gypsum Co.
National Life of Vermont
National Machinery Co.
National Medical Enterprises
National Presto Industries
National Service Industries
National Standard Co.
National Starch & Chemical Corp.
National Steel

National Westminster Bank New Jersey
Nationale-Nederlanden North America Corp.
Nationwide Insurance Cos.
Natural Heritage Foundation
Navistar International Corp.
NBD Bank
NBD Bank, N.A.
NBD Genesee Bank
NCR Corp.
NEC Technologies, Inc.
NEC USA
Needmor Fund
Neenah Foundry Co.
Neese Family Foundation
Negaunee Foundation
Neilson Foundation, George W.
Nelco Sewing Machine Sales Corp.
Nelson Foundation, Florence
Nelson Industries, Inc.
Nestle U.S.A. Inc.
Neu Foundation, Hugo and Doris
Neuberger Foundation, Roy R. and Marie S.
New Cycle Foundation
New England Business Service
New England Foundation
New England Mutual Life Insurance Co.
New Hampshire Ball Bearings
New Horizon Foundation
New Jersey Bell Telephone Company
New Jersey Resources Corp.
New-Land Foundation
New Prospect Foundation
New Street Capital Corp.
New York Foundation
New York Life Insurance Co.
New York Mercantile Exchange
New York State Electric & Gas Corp.
New York Stock Exchange
New York Telephone Co.
New York Times Co.
The New Yorker Magazine, Inc.
Newbrook Charitable Foundation
Newhall Foundation, Henry Mayo
Newhouse Foundation, Samuel I.
Newman Assistance Fund, Jerome A. and Estelle R.
Newman's Own
Newmil Bancorp
Newmont Mining Corp.
News America Publishing Inc.
News & Observer Publishing Co.
Niagara Mohawk Power Corp.
NIBCO Inc.
Nichimen America, Inc.
Nichols Co., J.C.
Nichols Foundation
Nike Inc.
Nissan Motor Corporation in U.S.A.
Noble Charitable Trust, John L. and Ethel G.
Noble Foundation, Edward John
Noble Foundation, Vivian Bilby
Norcliffe Fund
Norcross Wildlife Foundation
Nord Family Foundation
Nordson Corp.
Norfolk Shipbuilding & Drydock Corp.
Norgren Foundation, Carl A.
Norman Foundation
Norman/Nethercutt Foundation, Merle
Normandie Foundation
Norris Foundation, Dellora A. and Lester J.
Norris Foundation, Kenneth T. and Eileen L.
Nortek, Inc.

North American Coal Corp.
North American Life & Casualty Co.
North American Philips Corp.
North American Reinsurance Corp.
North Carolina Foam Foundation
North Shore Foundation
Northeast Utilities
Northen, Mary Moody
Northern Indiana Public Service Co.
Northern Star Foundation
Northern States Power Co.
Northern Telecom Inc.
Northern Trust Co.
NorthPark National Bank
Northrop Corp.
Northwest Natural Gas Co.
Northwestern National Insurance Group
Northwestern National Life Insurance Co.
Norton Co.
Norton Memorial Corporation, Geraldi
Norwest Bank Nebraska
Norwest Corp.
Novotny Charitable Trust, Yetta Deitch
Nucor Corp.
Number Ten Foundation
NuTone Inc.
NutraSweet Co.
N've Shalom Foundation
Oak Foundation U.S.A.
Oak Industries
Oakleaf Foundation
Oakley Foundation, Hollie and Anna
Obayashi America Corp.
Oberkotter Family Foundation
Oberlaender Foundation, Gustav
O'Bleness Foundation, Charles G.
O'Brien Foundation, Cornelius and Anna Cook
Occidental Oil & Gas Corp.
Occidental Petroleum Corp.
Oceanic Cablevision Foundation
O'Connor Co.
O'Connor Foundation, A. Lindsay and Olive B.
O'Connor Foundation, Kathryn
O'Connor Foundation, Magee
OCRI Foundation
Odell and Helen Pfeiffer Odell Fund, Robert Stewart
O'Donnell Foundation
Odyssey Partners
Oestreicher Foundation, Sylvan and Ann
Offield Family Foundation
Ogden Foundation, Ralph E.
Ogilvy & Mather Worldwide
Ogle Foundation, Paul
Oglebay Norton Co.
Ohio Casualty Corp.
Ohio Edison Corp.
Ohio National Life Insurance Co.
Ohio Savings Bank
Ohio Valley Foundation
Oki America Inc.
Oklahoma Gas & Electric Co.
Oklahoman Foundation
Old Dominion Box Co.
Old Kent Bank & Trust Co.
Old National Bank in Evansville
Old Republic International Corp.
Oldham Little Church Foundation
Oleson Foundation
Olin Charitable Trust, John M.
Olin Corp.
Olin Foundation, F. W.
Olin Foundation, Spencer T. and Ann W.
Olive Bridge Fund

Olivetti Office USA, Inc.
Olmsted Foundation, George and Carol
Olsson Memorial Foundation, Elis
Olympia Brewing Co.
Onan Family Foundation
1525 Foundation
1957 Charity Trust
One Valley Bank, N.A.
O'Neil Foundation, Casey Albert T.
O'Neil Foundation, Cyril F. and Marie E.
O'Neil Foundation, M. G.
O'Neil Foundation, W.
O'Neill Foundation, William J. and Dorothy K.
Ontario Corp.
Oppenheimer and Flora Oppenheimer Haas Trust, Leo
Oppenheimer Family Foundation
Oppenstein Brothers Foundation
O'Quinn Foundation, John M. and Nancy C.
Orange & Rockland Utilities, Inc.
Orbit Valve Co.
Orchard Corp. of America.
Orchard Foundation
Ordean Foundation
Orion Capital Corp.
Orleans Trust, Carrie S.
Orleton Trust Fund
Orscheln Co.
Ortho Diagnostic Systems, Inc.
Osborn Charitable Trust, Edward B.
Osborn Manufacturing Co.
Osceola Foundation
OsCo. Industries
O'Shaughnessy Foundation, I. A.
Osher Foundation, Bernard
Oshkosh B'Gosh
Oshkosh Truck Corp.
Oster/Sunbeam Appliance Co.
Ostern Foundation
O'Toole Foundation, Theresa and Edward
Ottenstein Family Foundation
Outokumpu-American Brass Co.
Overbrook Foundation
Overlake Foundation
Overnite Transportation Co.
Overseas Shipholding Group
Overstreet Foundation
Owen Industries, Inc.
Owen Trust, B. B.
Owens-Corning Fiberglas Corp.
Owens-Illinois
Owsley Foundation, Alvin and Lucy
Oxford Foundation
Oxford Industries, Inc.
Oxnard Foundation
PACCAR
Pacific Enterprises
Pacific Gas & Electric Co.
Pacific Mutual Life Insurance Co.
Pacific Western Foundation
Packaging Corporation of America
Packard Foundation, David and Lucile
Packard Humanities Institute
Packer Foundation, Horace B.
Page Belting Co.
Page Foundation, George B.
Paley Foundation, Goldie
Paley Foundation, William S.
Palin Foundation
Palmer-Fry Memorial Trust, Lily
Palmer Fund, Francis Asbury
Pamida, Inc.
Pan-American Life Insurance Co.
Pangburn Foundation
Panhandle Eastern Corp.

Pappas Charitable Foundation, Bessie
Park Bank
Park National Bank
Park-Ohio Industries Inc.
Parke-Davis Group
Parker Drilling Co.
Parker Foundation
Parker-Hannifin Corp.
Parker, Jr. Foundation, William A.
Parman Foundation, Robert A.
Parnes Foundation, E. H.
Parshelsky Foundation, Moses L.
Parsons Foundation, Ralph M.
Parsons - W.D. Charities, Vera Davis
Parthenon Sportswear
Parvin Foundation, Albert
Pasadena Area Residential Aid
Patagonia
Patrick Industries Inc.
Patterson-Barclay Memorial Foundation
Patterson Charitable Fund, W. I.
Paul and C. Michael Paul Foundation, Josephine Bay
Pauley Foundation, Edwin W.
Paulstan
Paulucci Family Foundation
Pax Christi Foundation
Paxton Co., Frank
PayLess Drug Stores
Payne Foundation, Frank E. and Seba B.
Peabody Foundation
Peabody Foundation, Amelia
Pearce Foundation, Dr. M. Lee
Pearson Foundation, E. M.
Peck Foundation, Milton and Lillian
Peerless Insurance Co.
Pellegrino-Realmuto Charitable Foundation
PemCo. Corp.
Pendergast-Weyer Foundation
Pendleton Construction Corp.
Penn Savings Bank, a division of Sovereign Bank Bank of Princeton, a division of Sovereign Bank
Pennington Foundation, Irene W. and C. B.
Pennsylvania Dutch Co.
Pennsylvania General Insurance Co.
Pennsylvania Knitted Outerwear Manufacturing Association
Pennsylvania Power & Light
Pennzoil Co.
Pentair
Penzance Foundation
Peoples Energy Corp.
Pepsi-Cola Bottling Co. of Charlotte
PepsiCo
Perini Corp.
Perini Foundation, Joseph
Perkin-Elmer Corp.
Perkin Fund
Perkins Charitable Foundation
Perkins Foundation, Edwin E.
Perkins Memorial Foundation, George W.
Perkins Memorial Fund, James J. and Marie Richardson
Perkins-Prothro Foundation
Perley Fund, Victor E.
Perot Foundation
Perpetual Benevolent Fund
Perry Drug Stores
Pesch Family Foundation
Pet
Peterloon Foundation
Peters Foundation, Charles F.
Peters Foundation, R. D. and Linda
Petersen Foundation, Esper A.

General Support (cont.)

Peterson Foundation, Fred J.
Peterson Memorial Fund, Chris and Mary L.
Petrie Trust, Lorene M.
Petteys Memorial Foundation, Jack
Pettus Crowe Foundation
Pettus, Jr. Foundation, James T.
Pew Charitable Trusts
Pfaffinger Foundation
Pfeiffer Research Foundation, Gustavus and Louise
Pfister and Vogel Tanning Co.
Pfizer
Pforzheimer Foundation, Carl and Lily
Phelps, Inc.
Phelps Dodge Corp.
PHH Corp.
Philadelphia Industries
Philip Morris Cos.
Philips Foundation, Jesse
Phillipps Foundation
Phillips Family Foundation, Jay and Rose
Phillips Family Foundation, L. E.
Phillips Foundation, A. P.
Phillips Foundation, Ellis L.
Phillips Foundation, Waite and Genevieve
Phillips Petroleum Co.
Phillips Trust, Edwin
Phillips-Van Heusen Corp.
Phipps Foundation, Howard
Phipps Foundation, William H.
Phoenix Home Life Mutual Insurance Co.
Phoenix Resource Cos.
Physicians Mutual Insurance
Piankova Foundation, Tatiana
Pick Charitable Trust, Melitta S.
Pick, Jr. Fund, Albert
Pickford Foundation, Mary
Picower Foundation, Jeffrey M. and Barbara
Piedmont Health Care Foundation
Pieper Electric
Pierce Charitable Trust, Harold Whitworth
Pillsbury Co.
Pillsbury Foundation
Pilot Trust
Pincus Family Fund
Pine Tree Foundation
Pines Bridge Foundation
Pinewood Foundation
Pineywoods Foundation
Pioneer Electronics (USA) Inc.
Pioneer Fund
Pioneer Fund
Pioneer Hi-Bred International
Pioneer Trust Bank, NA
Piper Foundation
Piper Jaffray Cos.
Pirelli Armstrong Tire Corp.
Pitney Bowes
Pitt-Des Moines Inc.
Pitts Foundation, William H. and Lula E.
Pittsburgh National Bank
Pittulloch Foundation
Pittway Corp.
Pitzman Fund
Plankenhorn Foundation, Harry
Plant Memorial Fund, Henry B.
Plantronics, Inc.
Plaster Foundation, Robert W.
Plitt Southern Theatres
Plough Foundation
Plumsock Fund
PMA Industries
PMI Food Equipment Group Inc.
PNC Bank

Poindexter Foundation
Poinsettia Foundation, Paul and Magdalena Ecke
Polaroid Corp.
Polinger Foundation, Howard and Geraldine
Polinsky-Rivkin Family Foundation
Pollock Company Foundation, William B.
Pollybill Foundation
Polychrome Corp.
Ponderosa, Inc.
Poole & Kent Co.
Poorvu Foundation, William and Lia
Pope Foundation
Pope Foundation, Lois B.
Porter Foundation, Mrs. Cheever
Porter Paint Co.
Porter Testamentary Trust, James Hyde
Portland Food Products Co.
Portland General Electric Co.
Posnack Family Foundation of Hollywood
Post Foundation of D.C., Marjorie Merriweather
Potlatch Corp.
Potter Foundation, Justin and Valere
Potts and Sibley Foundation
Pottstown Mercury
Powell Co., William
Powell Family Foundation
Powell Foundation, Charles Lee
Powers Foundation
Powers Higher Educational Fund, Edward W. and Alice R.
Poynter Fund
PPG Industries
PQ Corp.
Prairie Foundation
Prange Co., H. C.
Pratt Memorial Fund
Premark International
Premier Bank
Premier Dental Products Co.
Premier Industrial Corp.
Prentis Family Foundation, Meyer and Anna
Preston Trust, Evelyn W.
Preyer Fund, Mary Norris
Price Associates, T. Rowe
Price Foundation, Lucien B. and Katherine E.
Prickett Fund, Lynn R. and Karl E.
Primark Corp.
Prime Computer, Inc.
Primerica Corp.
Prince Corp.
Prince Manufacturing, Inc.
Prince Trust, Abbie Norman
Principal Financial Group
Pritzker Foundation
Procter & Gamble Co.
Procter & Gamble Cosmetic & Fragrance Products
Producers Livestock Marketing Association
Promus Cos.
Propp Sons Fund, Morris and Anna
Prospect Hill Foundation
Prouty Foundation, Olive Higgins
Providence Energy Corp.
Providence Journal Company
Provident Life & Accident Insurance Co.
Provigo Corp. Inc.
Prudential-Bache Securities
Prudential Insurance Co. of America
Psychists
Public Service Co. of Colorado
Public Service Electric & Gas Co.

Public Welfare Foundation
Puett Foundation, Nelson
Pukall Lumber
Pulitzer Publishing Co.
Puterbaugh Foundation
Putnam Foundation
Pyramid Foundation
Pyramid Technology Corp.
Quabaug Corp.
Quaker Chemical Corp.
Quaker Hill Foundation
Quaker Oats Co.
Quaker State Corp.
Quality Metal Finishing Foundation
Quanex Corp.
Quantum Chemical Corp.
Questar Corp.
Quincy Newspapers
Quinlan Foundation, Elizabeth C.
Quivey-Bay State Foundation
R. P. Foundation
R&B Tool Co.
Rabb Charitable Foundation, Sidney and Esther
Rabb Foundation, Harry W.
Rachal Foundation, Ed
Radin Foundation
Ragan Charitable Foundation, Carolyn King
Ragen, Jr. Memorial Fund Trust No. 1, James M.
Rahr Malting Co.
Raker Foundation, M. E.
Raleigh Linen Service/National Distributing Co.
Rales and Ruth Rales Foundation, Norman R.
Raley's
Ralston Purina Co.
Ramlose Foundation, George A.
Ranco, Inc.
Randa
Randleigh Foundation Trust
Rankin and Elizabeth Forbes Rankin Trust, William
Ranney Foundation, P. K.
Ransburg Corp.
Ransom Fidelity Company
Rapp Foundation, Robert Glenn
Raskin Foundation, Hirsch and Braine
Raskob Foundation for Catholic Activities
Rasmussen Foundation
Ratner Foundation, Milton M.
Ratshesky Foundation, A. C.
Ray Foundation
Read Foundation, Charles L.
Reading & Bates Corp.
Reasoner, Davis & Fox
Rebsamen Companies, Inc.
Red Devil
Red Wing Shoe Co.
Reed Foundation
Reed Foundation, Philip D.
Reedman Car-Truck World Center
Regenstein Foundation
Regis Corp.
Reicher Foundation, Anne & Harry J.
Reichhold Chemicals, Inc.
Reidler Foundation
Reilly Industries
Reily & Co., William B.
Reinberger Foundation
Reinhart Institutional Foods
Reinhold Foundation, Paul E. and Ida Klare
Reisman Charitable Trust, George C. and Evelyn R.
Relations Foundation
Reliance Electric Co.
Reliance Group Holdings, Inc.
Rennebohm Foundation, Oscar
Renner Foundation

Replogle Foundation, Luther I.
Republic Automotive Parts, Inc.
Republic New York Corp.
Resnick Foundation, Jack and Pearl
Revlon
Rexham Inc.
Reynolds Charitable Trust, Kate B.
Reynolds Foundation, Donald W.
Reynolds Foundation, Eleanor T.
Reynolds Foundation, J. B.
Reynolds Foundation, Richard S.
Reynolds Foundation, Z. Smith
Reynolds Metals Co.
Reynolds & Reynolds Co.
Rhoades Fund, Otto L. and Hazel E.
Rhode Island Hospital Trust National Bank
Rhodebeck Charitable Trust
Rhone-Poulenc Inc.
Rhone-Poulenc Rorer
Rice Charitable Foundation, Albert W.
Rice Family Foundation, Jacob and Sophie
Rice Foundation
Rice Foundation, Ethel and Raymond F.
Rice Foundation, Helen Steiner
Rich Co., F.D.
Rich Foundation
Rich Products Corp.
Richardson Benevolent Foundation, C. E.
Richardson Charitable Trust, Anne S.
Richardson Foundation, Frank E. and Nancy M.
Richardson Foundation, Sid W.
Richardson Fund, Grace
Richardson Fund, Mary Lynn
Ricoh Corp.
Rider-Pool Foundation
Ridgefield Foundation
Rieke Corp.
Rienzi Foundation
Riggs Benevolent Fund
Riggs National Bank
Rigler-Deutsch Foundation
Ringier-America
Rinker Materials Corp.
Riordan Foundation
Rippel Foundation, Fannie E.
Risdon Corp.
Ritchie Memorial Foundation, Charles E. and Mabel M.
Rite-Hite Corp.
Ritter Charitable Trust, George W. and Mary F.
Ritter Foundation
Ritter Foundation, May Ellen and Gerald
River Blindness Foundation
River Branch Foundation
River Road Charitable Corporation
RJR Nabisco Inc.
Robbins & Myers, Inc.
Roberts Foundation
Roberts Foundation, Dora
Roberts Foundation, Summerfield G.
Robertshaw Controls Co.
Robertson Brothers
Robin Family Foundation, Albert A.
Robinson Foundation
Robinson Foundation
Robinson Foundation, J. Mack
Robinson Fund, Charles Nelson
Robinson Fund, Maurice R.
Robinson Mountain Fund, E. O.
Robison Foundation, Ellis H. and Doris B.
Robson Foundation, LaNelle

Roche Relief Foundation, Edward and Ellen
Rochester Midland Corp.
Rochester Telephone Corp.
Rochlin Foundation, Abraham and Sonia
Rock Foundation, Milton and Shirley
Rockefeller Brothers Fund
Rockefeller Family Fund
Rockfall Foundation
Rockford Acromatics Products Co./Aircraft Gear Corp.
Rockford Products Corp.
Rockwell Foundation
Rockwell International Corp.
Roddenbery Co., Inc., W.B.
Roddis Foundation, Hamilton
Rodgers Foundation, Richard & Dorothy
Rodgers Trust, Elizabeth Killam
Roe Foundation
Roehl Foundation
Rogers Charitable Trust, Florence
Rogers Family Foundation
Rogers Foundation
Rogers Foundation
Rogers Foundation, Mary Stuart
Rogow Birken Foundation
Rohatyn Foundation, Felix and Elizabeth
Rohlik Foundation, Sigmund and Sophie
Rohm and Haas Company
Rohr Inc.
Rolfs Foundation, Robert T.
Rollins Luetkemeyer Charitable Foundation
Romill Foundation
RosaMary Foundation
Rose Foundation, Billy
Roseburg Forest Products Co.
Rosen Foundation, Joseph
Rosenbaum Foundation, Paul and Gabriella
Rosenberg Foundation, Alexis
Rosenberg Foundation, Henry and Ruth Blaustein
Rosenberg Foundation, Sunny and Abe
Rosenberg Foundation, William J. and Tina
Rosenberg, Jr. Family Foundation, Louise and Claude
Rosenbloom Foundation, Ben and Esther
Rosenhaus Peace Foundation, Sarah and Matthew
Rosenstiel Foundation
Rosenthal Foundation, Benjamin J.
Rosenthal Foundation, Richard and Hinda
Rosenthal Foundation, Richard and Lois
Rosenthal Foundation, Samuel
Rosenthal-Statter Foundation
Rosenwald Family Fund, William
Ross Foundation
Ross Foundation
Ross Foundation, Arthur
Ross Foundation, Lyn & George M.
Ross Foundation, Walter G.
Ross Laboratories
Ross Memorial Foundation, Will
Roth Family Foundation
Roth Foundation, Louis T.
Rotterman Trust, Helen L. and Marie F.
Rouse Co.
Rowland Foundation
Royal Group Inc.
RTM
Ruan Foundation Trust, John
Rubenstein Charitable Foundation, Lawrence J. and Anne

Rubenstein Foundation, Philip
Rubin Family Fund, Cele H. and William B.
Rubin Foundation, Rob E. & Judith O.
Rubin Foundation, Samuel
Rubinstein Foundation, Helena
Ruddick Corp.
Rudin Foundation
Rudin Foundation, Louis and Rachel
Rudin Foundation, Samuel and May
Rukin Philanthropic Foundation, David and Eleanore
Rumbaugh Foundation, J. H. and F. H.
Rupp Foundation, Fran and Warren
Russ Togs
Russell Charitable Foundation, Tom
Russell Educational Foundation, Benjamin and Roberta
Russell Memorial Foundation, Robert
Russell Trust, Josephine G.
Ryan Family Charitable Foundation
Ryan Foundation, Nina M.
Ryan Foundation, Patrick G. and Shirley W.
Ryder System
Ryland Group
Sacharuna Foundation
Sachs Fund
Saemann Foundation, Franklin I.
SAFECO Corp.
Safeguard Scientifics Foundation
Sagamore Foundation
Sage Foundation
Sailors' Snug Harbor of Boston
Saint Croix Foundation
Saint Gerard Foundation
St. Giles Foundation
St. Mary's Catholic Foundation
Saint Paul Cos.
Salgo Charitable Trust, Nicholas M.
Salomon
Salomon Foundation, Richard & Edna
Saltonstall Charitable Foundation, Richard
Salvatori Foundation, Henry
Salwil Foundation
San Diego Gas & Electric
San Diego Trust & Savings Bank
Sanders Trust, Charles
Sandoz Corp.
Sandusky International Inc.
Sandy Hill Foundation
Sang Foundation, Elsie O. and Philip D.
Sanguinetti Foundation, Annunziata
Santa Fe Pacific Corp.
Santa Maria Foundation
Sapirstein-Stone-Weiss Foundation
Sara Lee Corp.
Sara Lee Hosiery
Sargent Foundation, Newell B.
Sarofim Foundation
Saroyan Foundation, William
Sasco Foundation
Sattler Beneficial Trust, Daniel A. and Edna J.
Saturno Foundation
Saul Foundation, Joseph E. & Norma G.
Saunders Charitable Foundation, Helen M.
Sawyer Charitable Foundation
Scaife Family Foundation
Scaife Foundation, Sarah
Scaler Foundation
SCANA Corp.

Schadt Foundation
Schaffer Foundation, H.
Schaffer Foundation, Michael & Helen
Schamach Foundation, Milton
Schapiro Fund, M. A.
Schautz Foundation, Walter L.
Schecter Private Foundation, Aaron and Martha
Scheirich Co., H.J.
Schenck Fund, L. P.
Scherer Foundation, Karla
Schering-Plough Corp.
Schering Trust for Arthritis Research, Margaret Harvey
Scherman Foundation
Schermer Charitable Trust, Frances
Schey Foundation
Schieffelin & Somerset Co.
Schiff Foundation
Schiff Foundation, Dorothy
Schiff Foundation, John J. and Mary R.
Schiff, Hardin & Waite
Schillig Trust, Ottilie
Schilling Motors
Schimmel Foundation
Schiro Fund
Schlinger Foundation
Schlink Foundation, Albert G. and Olive H.
Schlumberger Ltd.
Schmidlapp Trust No. 2, Jacob G.
Schmidt Charitable Foundation, William E.
Schmidt & Sons, C.
Schmitt Foundation, Arthur J.
Schneider Foundation Corp., Al J.
Schneider Foundation, Robert E.
Schneiderman Foundation, Roberta and Irwin
Schoenbaum Family Foundation
Schoenleber Foundation
Scholler Foundation
Schoonmaker J-Sewkly Valley Hospital Trust
Schott Foundation
Schrafft and Bertha E. Schrafft Charitable Trust, William E.
Schramm Foundation
Schreiber Foods, Inc.
Schroeder Foundation, Walter
Schultz Foundation
Schultz Foundation
Schumann Foundation, Florence and John
Schust Foundation, Clarence L. and Edith B.
Schwab & Co., Charles
Schwab Foundation, Charles and Helen
Schwartz and Robert Schwartz Foundation, Bernard
Schwartz Foundation, Arnold A.
Schwartz Foundation, Bernard Lee
Schwartz Foundation, David
Schwartz Fund for Education and Health Research, Arnold and Marie
Schwob Foundation, Simon
Science Applications International Corp.
Scientific-Atlanta
Scott and Fetzer Co.
Scott, Foresman & Co.
Scott Foundation, Virginia Steele
Scott Foundation, William E.
Scott Foundation, William R., John G., and Emma
Scott, Jr. Charitable Foundation, Walter
Scott Paper Co.
Scotty's, Inc.
Scoular Co.

Scripps Foundation, Ellen Browning
Scrivner, Inc.
Scrivner of North Carolina Inc.
SCT Yarns
Scurlock Foundation
Seabury Foundation
Seafirst Corp.
Seagram & Sons, Joseph E.
Sealaska Corp.
Sealright Co., Inc.
Searle & Co., G.D.
Sears Family Foundation
Seasongood Good Government Foundation, Murray and Agnes
Seaver Charitable Trust, Richard C.
Seaway Food Town
Seay Charitable Trust, Sarah M. and Charles E.
Seay Memorial Trust, George and Effie
Sebastian Foundation
Second Foundation
Security Benefit Life Insurance Co.
Security Life of Denver
Security State Bank
See Foundation, Charles
Seevak Family Foundation
Sefton Foundation, J. W.
Sega of America
Segal Charitable Trust, Barnet
Segerstrom Foundation
Sehn Foundation
Seid Foundation, Barre
Seidman Family Foundation
Selby and Marie Selby Foundation, William G.
Semmes Foundation
Seneca Foods Corp.
Senior Citizens Foundation
Sentry Insurance Co.
Sequoia Foundation
Servco Pacific
ServiceMaster Co. L.P.
Setzer Foundation
Sewall Foundation, Elmina
Sexton Foundation
Seymour and Troester Foundation
Seymour Foundation, W. L. and Louise E.
Shafer Foundation, Richard H. and Ann
Shaffer Family Charitable Trust
Shaklee Corp.
Shapell Foundation, Nathan and Lilly
Shapero Foundation, Nate S. and Ruth B.
Shapiro, Inc.
Shapiro Charity Fund, Abraham
Shapiro Foundation, Carl and Ruth
Shapiro Foundation, Charles and M. R.
Shapiro Fund, Albert
Share Foundation
Sharon Steel Corp.
Sharp Foundation, Charles S. and Ruth C.
Sharp Foundation, Evelyn
Shattuck Charitable Trust, S. F.
Shaw Charitable Trust, Mary Elizabeth Dee
Shaw Foundation, Arch W.
Shaw Foundation, Walden W. and Jean Young
Shaw Industries
Shawmut Bank of Franklin County
Shawmut National Corp.
Shawmut Worcester County Bank, N.A.
Shaw's Supermarkets
Shea Co., John F.
Shea Foundation, Edmund and Mary

Shea Foundation, John and Dorothy
Sheafer Charitable Trust, Emma A.
Sheaffer Inc.
Sheinberg Foundation, Eric P.
Shelden Fund, Elizabeth, Allan and Warren
Sheldon Foundation, Ralph C.
Shell Oil Co.
Shelter Mutual Insurance Co.
Shelton Cos.
Shemanski Testamentary Trust, Tillie and Alfred
Shenandoah Foundation
Shenandoah Life Insurance Co.
Shepherd Foundation
Sheppard Foundation, Lawrence B.
Sheridan Foundation, Thomas B. and Elizabeth M.
Sherman Family Charitable Trust, George and Beatrice
Sherwin-Williams Co.
Shiffman Foundation
Shoemaker Fund, Thomas H. and Mary Williams
Shoenberg Foundation
Shoney's Inc.
Shore Fund
Shorenstein Foundation, Walter H. and Phyllis J.
Shott, Jr. Foundation, Hugh I.
Shubert Foundation
Shughart, Thomson & Kilroy, P.C.
Shuster Memorial Trust, Herman
Shuwa Investments Corp.
Shwayder Foundation, Fay
Siebe North Inc.
Sierra Pacific Industries
Sierra Pacific Resources
Sifco Industries Inc.
Signet Bank/Maryland
Silver Spring Foundation
Silverman Foundation, Marty and Dorothy
Silverweed Foundation
Simkins Industries, Inc.
Simmons Family Foundation, R. P.
Simon Charitable Trust, Esther
Simon Foundation, Jennifer Jones
Simon Foundation, William E. and Carol G.
Simone Foundation
Simpson Foundation
Simpson Foundation, John M.
Simpson Industries
Simpson Investment Co.
Simpson PSB Foundation
Sinsheimer Fund, Alexandrine and Alexander L.
Sioux Steel Co.
SIT Investment Associates, Inc.
Sizzler International
Sjostrom & Sons
Skandia America Reinsurance Corp.
SKF USA, Inc.
Skillman Foundation
Skinner Corp.
Skirball Foundation
Slant/Fin Corp.
Slaughter, Jr. Foundation, William E.
Slifka Foundation, Alan B.
Slifka Foundation, Joseph and Sylvia
Slusher Charitable Foundation, Roy W.
Smeal Foundation, Mary Jean & Frank P.
Smith and W. Aubrey Smith Charitable Foundation, Clara Blackford
Smith Charitable Fund, Eleanor Armstrong

Smith Charitable Trust
Smith Charitable Trust, W. W.
Smith Charities, John
Smith Corp., A.O.
Smith Family Foundation, Charles E.
Smith Family Foundation, Theda Clark
Smith Foundation
Smith Foundation, Bob and Vivian
Smith Foundation, Gordon V. and Helen C.
Smith Foundation, Julia and Albert
Smith Foundation, Kelvin and Eleanor
Smith Foundation, Kenneth L. and Eva S.
Smith Foundation, Lon V.
Smith Foundation, Richard and Susan
Smith Golden Rule Trust Fund, Fred G.
Smith, Jr. Foundation, M. W.
Smith Memorial Fund, Ethel Sergeant Clark
Smith 1963 Charitable Trust, Don McQueen
Smock Foundation, Frank and Laura
Smoot Charitable Foundation
Smucker Co., J.M.
Smucker Co., J.M.
SNC Manufacturing Co.
Snee-Reinhardt Charitable Foundation
SNET
Snider Foundation
Snite Foundation, Fred B.
Snyder Charitable Fund, W. P.
Snyder Foundation, Frost and Margaret
Snyder Foundation, Harold B. and Dorothy A.
Snyder Fund, Valentine Perry
Society Corp.
Society for Savings
Sofia American Schools
Solheim Foundation
Soling Family Foundation
Solo Cup Co.
Solomon Foundation, Sarah M.
Solow Foundation
Solow Foundation, Sheldon H.
Sonat
Sonoco Products Co.
Sony Corp. of America
Sooner Pipe & Supply Corp.
Sordoni Foundation
Sosland Foundation
Souers Charitable Trust, Sidney W. and Sylvia N.
South Bend Tribune
South Carolina Electric & Gas Co.
South Texas Charitable Foundation
Southern Bell
Southern California Edison Co.
Southern California Gas Co.
Southern Co. Services
Southern Furniture Co.
Southern Indiana Gas & Electric Co.
Southland Corp.
Southtrust Corp.
Southways Foundation
Southwest Gas Corp.
Southwestern Public Service Co.
Spahn & Rose Lumber Co.
Spalding Health Care Trust
Spang & Co.
Speas Foundation, Victor E.
Speas Memorial Trust, John W. and Effie E.
Special People In Need
Spectra-Physics Analytical

General Support (cont.)

Speer Foundation, Roy M.
Speyer Foundation, Alexander C. and Tillie S.
Spiegel
Spiegel Family Foundation, Jerry and Emily
Spiritus Gladius Foundation
Spiro Foundation, Donald W.
Sprague Educational and Charitable Foundation, Seth
Sprague, Jr. Foundation, Caryll M. and Norman F.
Sprint
Sprint United Telephone
SPS Technologies
Spunk Fund
SPX Corp.
Square D Co.
Stabler Foundation, Donald B. and Dorothy L.
Stackner Family Foundation
Stackpole-Hall Foundation
Stacy Foundation, Festus
Staley, Jr. Foundation, A. E.
Staley Manufacturing Co., A.E.
Standard Brands Paint Co.
Standard Chartered Bank New York
Standard Products Co.
Standard Register Co.
Standard Steel Speciality Co.
Stanley Works
Stans Foundation
Star Bank, N.A.
Stare Fund
Stark Foundation, Nelda C. and H. J. Lutcher
Starling Foundation, Dorothy Richard
Starr Foundation
Starrett Co., L.S.
State Mutual Life Assurance Co.
State Street Bank & Trust Co.
Statter Foundation, Amy Plant
Stauffer Charitable Trust, John
Stauffer Communications
Stauffer Foundation, John and Beverly
Staunton Farm Foundation
Steadley Memorial Trust, Kent D. and Mary L.
Stearns Charitable Foundation, Anna B.
Stearns Trust, Artemas W.
Steel, Sr. Foundation, Marshall
Steelcase
Steele Foundation
Steele Foundation, Harry and Grace
Steele-Reese Foundation
Stein Foundation, Joseph F.
Stein Foundation, Jules and Doris
Stein Foundation, Louis
Stein Roe & Farnham Investment Council
Steinbach Fund, Ruth and Milton
Steinberg Family Foundation, Meyer and Jean
Steiner Charitable Fund, Albert
Steiner Corp.
Steinhardt Foundation, Judy and Michael
Steinhauer Charitable Foundation
Steinman Foundation, James Hale
Steinman Foundation, John Frederick
Steinsapir Family Foundation, Julius L. and Libhie B.
Stella D'Oro Biscuit Co.
Stemmons Foundation
Stephens Foundation Trust
Sterkel Trust, Justine
Sterling Inc.
Sterling Winthrop

Stern Family Foundation, Alex
Stern Family Foundation, Harry
Stern Family Fund
Stern Foundation, Bernice and Milton
Stern Foundation for the Arts, Richard J.
Stern Foundation, Gustav and Irene
Stern Foundation, Leonard N.
Stern Private Charitable Foundation Trust, Charles H. and Anna S.
Sternberger Foundation, Sigmund
Sterne-Elder Memorial Trust
Steuart Petroleum Co.
Stevens Foundation, John T.
Stevens Foundation, Nathaniel and Elizabeth P.
Stewards Fund
Stewardship Foundation
Stewart & Stevenson Services
Stewart Trust under the will of Helen S. Devore, Alexander and Margaret
Stewart Trust under the will of Mary E. Stewart, Alexander and Margaret
Stieren Foundation, Arthur T. and Jane J.
Stillwell Charitable Trust, Glen and Dorothy
Stirtz, Bernards & Co.
Stock Foundation, Paul
Stoddard Charitable Trust
Stokely, Jr. Foundation, William B.
Stone Charitable Foundation
Stone Container Corp.
Stone Family Foundation, Jerome H.
Stone Family Foundation, Norman H.
Stone Foundation
Stone Foundation, David S.
Stone Foundation, France
Stone Foundation, W. Clement and Jessie V.
Stone Trust, H. Chase
Stonecutter Mills Corp.
Stoneman Charitable Foundation, Anne and David
Stonestreet Trust, Eusebia S.
Storage Technology Corp.
Storer Communications Inc.
Storer Foundation, George B.
Storz Foundation, Robert Herman
Stott Foundation, Louis L.
Stott Foundation, Robert L.
Stowe, Jr. Foundation, Robert Lee
Stowers Foundation
Strake Foundation
Stranahan Foundation
Stratford Foundation
Straus Foundation, Aaron and Lillie
Straus Foundation, Martha Washington Straus and Harry H.
Straus Foundation, Philip A. and Lynn
Strauss Foundation
Strauss Foundation, Judy and Howard E.
Strauss Foundation, Leon
Strawbridge & Clothier
Strawbridge Foundation of Pennsylvania I, Margaret Dorrance
Strawbridge Foundation of Pennsylvania II, Margaret Dorrance
Stroh Brewery Co.
Strosacker Foundation, Charles J.
Stroud Foundation
Strouse, Greenberg & Co.
Stry Foundation, Paul E.

Stuart Center Charitable Trust, Hugh
Stuart Foundation
Stuart Foundation, Edward C.
Stuart Foundations
Stulsaft Foundation, Morris
Stupp Brothers Bridge & Iron Co.
Sturgis Charitable and Educational Trust, Roy and Christine
Subaru-Isuzu Automotive Inc.
Subaru of America Inc.
Sudix Foundation
Sullivan Foundation, Ray H. and Pauline
Sulzberger Foundation
Sumitomo Bank of California
Sumitomo Corp. of America
Summerfield Foundation, Solon E.
Summerlee Foundation
Sumners Foundation, Hatton W.
Sun Banks Inc.
Sun Co.
Sundstrand Corp.
Sunmark Capital Corp.
Super Valu Stores
Superior Tube Co.
Surdna Foundation
Surgical Science Foundation for Research and Development
Surrena Memorial Fund, Harry and Thelma
Susquehanna-Pfaltzgraff Co.
Sussman Fund, Edna Bailey
Sutcliffe Foundation, Walter and Louise
Sutton Foundation
Swalm Foundation
Swanson Family Foundation, Dr. W.C.
Swanson Foundation
Sweatt Foundation, Harold W.
Sweet Life Foods
Swensrud Charitable Trust, Sidney A.
Swift Co. Inc., John S.
Swift Memorial Health Care Foundation
Swig Charity Foundation, Mae and Benjamin
Swig Foundation
Swim Foundation, Arthur L.
Swisher Foundation, Carl S.
Swiss American Securities, Inc.
Swiss Bank Corp.
Synovus Financial Corp.
Syntex Corp.
Taconic Foundation
Tai and Co., J. T.
Tait Foundation, Frank M.
Talley Industries, Inc.
Tamarkin Co.
Tampa Electric
Tandem Computers
Tandy Corp.
Tandy Foundation, Anne Burnett and Charles
Tandy Foundation, David L.
Tang Foundation
Tanner Cos.
Taper Foundation, Mark
Taper Foundation, S. Mark
Tarmac America Inc.
Tasty Baking Co.
Taub Foundation
Taub Foundation, Henry and Marilyn
Taub Foundation, Joseph and Arlene
Taube Family Foundation
Tauber Foundation
Taubman Foundation, Herman P. and Sophia
Taylor Charitable Trust, Jack DeLoss
Taylor Family Foundation, Jack
Taylor Foundation

Taylor Foundation, Fred and Harriett
Taylor Foundation, Ruth and Vernon
Taylor Trust, Lydia M.
TCF Banking & Savings, FSB
Teagle Foundation
Teichert
Tektronix
Teledyne
Teleklew Productions
Tell Foundation
Temple Foundation, T. L. L.
Temple-Inland
Templeton Foundation, Herbert A.
Templeton Foundation, John
Tennant Co.
Tension Envelope Corp.
Terner Foundation
Terry Foundation, C. Herman
Tesoro Petroleum Corp.
Tetley, Inc.
Teubert Charitable Trust, James H. and Alice
Texaco
Texas Commerce Bank Houston, N.A.
Texas Gas Transmission Corp.
Texas Industries, Inc.
Texas Instruments
Textron
Thagard Foundation
Thalheimer Foundation, Alvin and Fanny Blaustein
Thalhimer and Family Foundation, Charles G.
Thalhimer Brothers Inc.
Thalhimer, Jr. and Family Foundation, William B.
Thanksgiving Foundation
Thatcher Foundation
Thendara Foundation
Thermo Electron Corp.
Thirty-Five Twenty, Inc.
Thomas & Betts Corp.
Thomas Built Buses L.P.
Thomas Foundation, Dorothy
Thomas Foundation, Joan and Lee
Thomas Industries
Thomas Medical Foundation, Roy E.
Thomasville Furniture Industries
Thompson Charitable Foundation
Thompson Charitable Foundation, Marion G.
Thompson Trust, Thomas
Thomson Information Publishing Group
Thoresen Foundation
Thorne Foundation
Thornton Foundation, Flora L.
Thorpe Foundation, James R.
Three Swallows Foundation
3M Co.
Thrush-Thompson Foundation
Thurman Charitable Foundation for Children, Edgar A.
Thurston Charitable Foundation
Thyssen Specialty Steels
Tibstra Charitable Foundation, Thomas and Gertrude
Tiger Foundation
Time Warner
Times Mirror Co.
Timken Co.
Timken Foundation of Canton
Timme Revocable Trust, Abigail S.
Timmis Foundation, Michael & Nancy
Tippens Foundation
Tippit Charitable Trust, C. Carlisle and Margaret M.
Tisch Foundation
Tiscornia Foundation
Titan Industrial Co.

Titmus Foundation
Titus Foundation, C. W.
TJX Cos.
Tobin Foundation
Todd Co., A.M.
Tokheim Corp.
Tomkins Industries, Inc.
Tomlinson Foundation, Kate and Elwyn
Torchmark Corp.
Tortuga Foundation
Totsy Manufacturing Co.
Towle Manufacturing Co.
Town & Country Corp.
Towsley Foundation, Harry A. and Margaret D.
Toyota Motor Sales, U.S.A.
Tozer Foundation
Tracor, Inc.
Tractor & Equipment Co.
Transamerica Corp.
Transco Energy Company
Tranzonic Cos.
Travelers Cos.
Travelers Express Co.
Treadwell Foundation, Nora Eccles
Treakle Foundation, J. Edwin
Trees Charitable Trust, Edith L.
Tremco Inc.
Treuhaft Foundation
Trexler Trust, Harry C.
Triangle Industries
Triford Foundation
Trimble Family Foundation, Robert Mize and Isa White
TRINOVA Corp.
Trion
Tripifoods
Tropicana Products, Inc.
True North Foundation
True Oil Co.
True Trust, Henry A.
Truland Foundation
Trull Foundation
Truman Foundation, Mildred Faulkner
Trusler Foundation
Trust Funds
Trustmark National Bank
TRW Corp.
TU Electric Co.
Tucker Charitable Trust, Rose E.
Tucson Electric Power Co.
Tupancy-Harris Foundation of 1986
Turner Charitable Foundation
Turrell Fund
21 International Holdings
28:19
Tyndale House Foundation
Tyson Foods, Inc.
Tyson Fund
Ukrop's Super Markets, Inc.
Unger Foundation, Aber D.
Unigard Security Insurance Co.
Unilever United States
Union Bank
Union Bank of Switzerland Los Angeles Branch
Union Bank of Switzerland New York Branch
Union Camp Corp.
Union Carbide Corp.
Union Central Life Insurance Co.
Union Electric Co.
Union Equity Division of Farmland Industries
Union Manufacturing Co.
Union Pacific Corp.
Unisys Corp.
United Airlines
United Co.
United Conveyor Corp.
United Dominion Industries
United Gas Pipe Line Co.
United Illuminating Co.

United Merchants & Manufacturers
United Service Foundation
United Services Automobile Association
U.S. Bank of Washington
United States Borax & Chemical Corp.
U.S. Leasing International
U.S. Oil/Schmidt Family Foundation, Inc.
U.S. Silica Co.
United States Sugar Corp.
United States Trust Co. of New York
United Stationers Inc.
United Technologies, Automotive
United Telephone Co. of Florida
United Telephone System (Eastern Group)
United Togs Inc.
Unitrode Corp.
Universal Foods Corp.
Universal Leaf Tobacco Co.
Unocal Corp.
Upjohn California Fund
Upjohn Co.
Upton Charitable Foundation, Lucy and Eleanor S.
Upton Foundation, Frederick S.
Uris Brothers Foundation
US Bancorp
US WEST
USF&G Co.
USG Corp.
Ushkow Foundation
Uslico Corp.
UST
USX Corp.
Utica National Insurance Group
Utilicorp United
Uvas Foundation
V and V Foundation
Valdese Manufacturing Co., Inc.
Vale Foundation, Ruby R.
Valencia Charitable Trust
Valentine Foundation, Lawson
Valero Energy Corp.
Valley Foundation, Wayne and Gladys
Valley National Bancorp
Valley National Bank of Arizona
Valmont Industries
Valspar Corp.
van Ameringen Foundation
Van Andel Foundation, Jay and Betty
Van Buren Foundation
Van Camp Foundation
Van Evera Foundation, Dewitt Caroline
Van Every Foundation, Philip L.
Van Houten Charitable Trust
Van Huffel Foundation, I. J.
Van Nuys Charities, J. B. and Emily
Van Nuys Foundation, I. N. and Susanna H.
Van Wert County Foundation
Vance Charitable Foundation, Robert C.
Varian Associates
Vaughan Foundation, Rachael and Ben
Vaughn Foundation
Veritas Foundation
Vermeer Charitable Foundation
Vermeer Investment Company Foundation
Vermeer Manufacturing Co.
Vesper Corp.
Vesuvius Charitable Foundation
Vetlesen Foundation, G. Unger
Victoria Foundation
Vidda Foundation
Vidinha Charitable Trust, A. and E.
Vilter Manufacturing Corp.

Virginia Power Co.
Visciglia Foundation, Frank
Vlasic Foundation
Voelkerding Charitable Trust, Walter and Jean
Volen Charitable Trust, Benjamin
Volkswagen of America, Inc.
Vollbrecht Foundation, Frederick A.
Vollmer Foundation
Von der Ahe Foundation
Von der Ahe, Jr. Trust, Theodore Albert
Von Rebay Foundation, Hilla
Vulcan Materials Co.
Wachovia Bank & Trust Co., N.A.
Wachtell, Lipton, Rosen & Katz
Wade Endowment Fund, Elizabeth Firth
Waggoner Charitable Trust, Crystelle
Wagner Manufacturing Co., E. R.
Wahlert Foundation
Wal-Mart Stores
Waldbaum, Inc.
Waldbaum Family Foundation, I.
Waldinger Corp.
Waldorf Educational Foundation
Walgreen Co.
Walker Educational and Charitable Foundation, Alex C.
Walker Foundation, Archie D. and Bertha H.
Walker Foundation, L. C. and Margaret
Walker Foundation, Smith
Walker Foundation, W. E.
Walker Wildlife Conservation Foundation
Wallace Computer Services
Wallace Genetic Foundation
Wallace-Reader's Digest Fund, DeWitt
Wallace Reader's Digest Fund, Lila
Wallach Foundation, Miriam G. and Ira D.
Wallin Foundation
Walsh Foundation
Disney Co., Walt
Walter Industries
Walthall Perpetual Charitable Trust, Marjorie T.
Walton Family Foundation
Ward Co., Joe L.
Ward Foundation, Louis L. and Adelaide C.
Ward Heritage Foundation, Mamie McFaddin
Wardle Family Foundation
Ware Foundation
Wareheim Foundation, E. C.
Warhol Foundation for the Visual Arts, Andy
Warner Electric Brake & Clutch Co.
Warner Foundation, Lee and Rose
Warner Fund, Albert and Bessie
Warner-Lambert Co.
Warren and Beatrice W. Blanding Foundation, Riley J. and Lillian N.
Warren Charite
Warren Foundation, William K.
Warsh-Mott Legacy
Washington Forrest Foundation
Washington Mutual Savings Bank
Washington Natural Gas Co.
Washington Post Co.
Washington Square Fund
Washington Trust Bank
Washington Water Power Co.
Wasie Foundation
Wasily Family Foundation
Wasserman Foundation

Wasserman Foundation, George
Waste Management
Waterfowl Research Foundation
Waters Charitable Trust, Robert S.
Waters Foundation
Watkins Christian Foundation
Watson Foundation, Walter E. and Caroline H.
Watumull Fund, J.
Wausau Insurance Cos.
Wausau Paper Mills Co.
Wauwatosa Savings & Loan Association
Wean Foundation, Raymond John
Weatherwax Foundation
Weaver Foundation
Webb Charitable Trust, Susan Mott
Webb Foundation
Webb Foundation, Del E.
Webster Charitable Foundation
Weckbaugh Foundation, Eleanore Mullen
Weeden Foundation, Frank
Weezie Foundation
Wege Foundation
Wehadkee Foundation
Weil, Gotshal & Manges Foundation
Weiler Foundation
Weiler Foundation, Theodore & Renee
Weinberg Foundation, John L.
Weinberg, Jr. Foundation, Sidney J.
Weiner Foundation
Weininger Foundation, Richard and Gertrude
Weinstein Foundation, Alex J.
Weinstein Foundation, J.
Weintraub Family Foundation, Joseph
Weir Foundation Trust
Weisman Art Foundation, Frederick R.
Weiss Foundation, Stephen and Suzanne
Weiss Foundation, William E.
Weiss Fund, Clara
Weisz Foundation, David and Sylvia
Wellman Foundation, S. K.
Wells Fargo & Co.
Wells Foundation, A. Z.
Wells Foundation, Lillian S.
Wendt Foundation, Margaret L.
Wenger Foundation, Henry L. and Consuelo S.
Werblow Charitable Trust, Nina W.
Werner Foundation, Clara and Spencer
Werthan Foundation
Wessinger Foundation
West Co.
West Foundation
West Foundation
West Foundation, Neva and Wesley
West One Bancorp
West Texas Corp., J. M.
Westend Foundation
Westerman Foundation, Samuel L.
Western Shade Cloth Charitable Foundation
Western Southern Life Insurance Co.
Westinghouse Broadcasting Co.
Westinghouse Electric Corp.
WestLB New York Branch
Weston Associates/R.C.M. Corp.
Westport Fund
Westvaco Corp.
Westwood Endowment
Wetterau
Weyerhaeuser Co.

Weyerhaeuser Memorial Foundation, Charles A.
Whalley Charitable Trust
Wharton Foundation
Wheat First Securites
Wheeler Foundation
Wheeler Foundation, Wilmot
Wheless Foundation
Whitaker Charitable Foundation, Lyndon C.
White Coffee Pot Family Inns
White Construction Co.
White Foundation, Erle and Emma
White Foundation, W. P. and H. B.
White Trust, G. R.
Whitehead Foundation
Whitehead Foundation, Lettie Pate
Whiteley Foundation, John and Elizabeth
Whiteman Foundation, Edna Rider
Whitener Foundation
Whiting Foundation
Whiting Foundation, Macauley and Helen Dow
Whiting Memorial Foundation, Henry and Harriet
Whitman Corp.
Whitney Fund, David M.
Whittaker Corp.
Whittenberger Foundation, Claude R. and Ethel B.
Wickson-Link Memorial Foundation
WICOR, Inc.
Widgeon Foundation
Wieboldt Foundation
Wien Foundation, Lawrence A.
Wiener Foundation, Malcolm Hewitt
Wigwam Mills
Wilber National Bank
Wilbur-Ellis Co.
Wilcox General Trust, George N.
Wilcox Trust, S. W.
Wilder Foundation
Wildermuth Foundation, E. F.
Wiley & Sons, Inc., John
Wilf Family Foundation
Wilkof Foundation, Edward and Ruth
Williams Charitable Trust, John C.
Williams Charitable Trust, Mary Jo
Williams Cos.
Williams Family Foundation
Williams Family Foundation of Georgia
Williams Foundation, Arthur Ashley
Williams Foundation, C. K.
Williams Foundation, Edna Sproull
Willits Foundation
Willmott Foundation, Peter S.
Wilmington Trust Co.
Wilsey Bennet Co.
Wilson Foundation, Elaine P. and Richard U.
Wilson Foundation, Frances Wood
Wilson Foundation, Hugh and Mary
Wilson Foundation, John and Nevils
Wilson Foundation, Marie C. and Joseph C.
Wilson Public Trust, Ralph
Wilson Sanitarium for Children of Baltimore City, Thomas
Wimpey Inc., George
Winchester Foundation
Winkler Foundation, Mark and Catherine

Winn-Dixie Stores
Winnebago Industries, Inc.
Winona Corporation
Winslow Foundation
Winston Foundation, Norman and Rosita
Winter Construction Co.
Winthrop Trust, Clara B.
Wiremold Co.
Wisconsin Bell, Inc.
Wisconsin Centrifugal
Wisconsin Energy Corp.
Wisconsin Power & Light Co.
Wisconsin Public Service Corp.
Wisdom Foundation, Mary F.
Wise Foundation and Charitable Trust, Watson W.
Wiseheart Foundation
Witco Corp.
Witte, Jr. Foundation, John H.
Wodecroft Foundation
Woldenberg Foundation
Wolf Foundation, Melvin and Elaine
Wolff Memorial Foundation, Pauline Sterne
Wolff Shoe Co.
Wollenberg Foundation
Wolverine World Wide, Inc.
Women's Project Foundation
Wood-Claeyssens Foundation
Wood Foundation, Lester G.
Wood Foundation of Chambersburg, PA
Woodard Family Foundation
Woodland Foundation
Woods Charitable Fund
Woods Foundation, James H.
Woodson Foundation, Aytchmonde
Woodward Fund
Woodward Fund-Atlanta, David, Helen, Marian
Woolf Foundation, William C.
Woolley Foundation, Vasser
Word Investments
Wornall Charitable Trust and Foundation, Kearney
Wortham Foundation
Wouk Foundation, Abe
Wrigley Co., Wm. Jr.
WSP&R Charitable Trust Fund
Wunsch Foundation
Wurlitzer Foundation, Farny R.
Wurts Memorial, Henrietta Tower
Wurzburg, Inc.
WWF Paper Corp.
Wyman-Gordon Co.
Wyman Youth Trust
Wyne Foundation
Wyss Foundation
Xerox Corp.
XTEK Inc.
Xtra Corp.
Y.K.K. (U.S.A.) Inc.
Yawkey Foundation II
Yeager Charitable Trust, Lester E.
Yellow Corp.
York Barbell Co.
Yost Trust, Elizabeth Burns
Young Charity Trust Northern Trust Company
Young Foundation, H and B
Young Foundation, Irvin L.
Young Foundation, R. A.
Young Foundation, Robert R.
Young & Rubicam
Younkers, Inc.
Yulman Trust, Morton and Helen
Zaban Foundation
Zacharia Foundation, Isaac Herman
Zachry Co., H. B.
Zale Foundation, William and Sylvia
Zamoiski Co.

General Support
(cont.)

Zapata Corp.
Zarkin Memorial Foundation, Charles
Zarrow Foundation, Anne and Henry
Zellerbach Family Fund
Zemurray Foundation
Zenkel Foundation
Ziegler Foundation
Ziegler Foundation for the Blind, E. Matilda
Ziegler Foundation, Ruth/Allen
Zigler Foundation, Fred B. and Ruth B.
Zilkha & Sons
Zimmerman Family Foundation, Raymond
Zimmerman Foundation, Mary and George Herbert
Zimmermann Fund, Marie and John
Zink Foundation, John Steele
Zlinkoff Fund for Medical Research and Education, Sergei S.
Zock Endowment Trust
Zollner Foundation
Zonas Trust, Steven K.
Zuckerberg Foundation, Roy J.
Zurn Industries

Loan

Amoco Corp.
Babcock Foundation, Mary Reynolds
Bailey Foundation
Bamberger and John Ernest Bamberger Memorial Foundation, Ruth Eleanor
Bean Foundation, Norwin S. and Elizabeth N.
Birch Foundation, Stephen and Mary
Bremer Foundation, Otto
Broadhurst Foundation
Bryan Foundation, Dodd and Dorothy L.
Burroughs Educational Fund, N. R.
Close Foundation
Coffey Foundation
Cole Foundation, Olive B.
Colgan Scholarship Fund, James W.
Collins Foundation, James M.
Consumer Farmer Foundation
Cooper Wood Products
Coughlin-Saunders Foundation
Crump Fund, Joe and Jessie
CTS Corp.
Davenport Trust Fund
Davis Foundation, Joe C.
Delta Tau Delta Educational Fund
Deuble Foundation, George H.
Dougherty Foundation
Drown Foundation, Joseph
Edwards Foundation, O. P. and W. E.
Edwards Scholarship Fund
Feild Co-Operative Association
Fidelity Bank
Flickinger Memorial Trust
Ford Foundation
Gibson Foundation, Addison H.
Griswold Trust, Jessie
Hachar Charitable Trust, D. D.
Haigh-Scatena Foundation
Hamilton Bank
Harmon Foundation, Pearl M. and Julia J.
Heinz Endowment, Howard
Hitachi
Hopedale Foundation

Hurley Foundation, Ed E. and Gladys
Ingram Trust, Joe
Irvine Foundation, James
Jeffers Memorial Fund, Michael
Johnson Day Trust, Carl and Virginia
Johnson Educational and Benevolent Trust, Dexter G.
Kempner Fund, Harris and Eliza
Klein Fund, Nathan J.
Koulaieff Educational Fund, Trustees of Ivan Y.
Laughlin Trust, George A.
Layne Foundation
Lindsay Student Aid Fund, Franklin
Lord Educational Fund
Manger and Audrey Cordero Plitt Trust, Clarence
Marshburn Foundation
Mellinger Educational Foundation, Edward Arthur
Meyer Foundation, Eugene and Agnes E.
Miller Foundation
Millhollon Educational Trust Estate, Nettie
North Star Research Foundation
Ontario Corp.
Ordean Foundation
People's Bank
Perkin-Elmer Corp.
Perkins Foundation, B. F. & Rose H.
Pickett and Hatcher Educational Fund
Piton Foundation
Plitt Southern Theatres
Puett Foundation, Nelson
Rangeley Educational Trust
Raskob Foundation, Bill
Regenstein Foundation
Rutledge Charity, Edward
Scott Fund, Olin
Seibel Foundation, Abe and Annie
Sherman Educational Fund, Mabel E.
Shinnick Educational Fund, William M.
Sierra Health Foundation
Smith Fund, Horace
Snyder Foundation, Harold B. and Dorothy A.
Stewart Memorial Trust, J. C.
Straus Foundation, Aaron and Lillie
Strong Foundation, Hattie M.
Swift Memorial Health Care Foundation
Thorn, Jr. Foundation, Columbus W.
Uris Brothers Foundation
Washington Mutual Savings Bank
Wellons Foundation
Western New York Foundation
Whitney Benefits

Matching

Access Energy Corp.
AEGON USA, Inc.
Aeroglide Corp.
Ahmanson Foundation
Akzo America
Akzo Chemicals Inc.
Alabama Power Co.
Albertson's
Alcan Aluminum Corp.
Alexander Foundation, Judd S.
ALPAC Corp.
Alpha Industries
American General Finance
American International Group, Inc.
American Microsystems, Inc.

American Mutual Insurance Cos.
American National Bank
American National Can Co.
American Optical Corp.
AMP
Amsco International
Amstar Corp.
Amsted Industries
Anchor Fasteners
Apache Corp.
ARA Services
ASARCO
Atlanta Gas Light Co.
Atran Foundation
AXIA Incorporated
B.H.P. Minerals
Bailey Foundation
Baker Hughes Inc.
Baltimore Bancorp.
Bancroft-Whitney Co.
Bank of A. Levy
BarclaysAmerican Corp.
Barnes & Roche
Barton-Gillet Co.
Beech Aircraft Corp.
Bell Communications Research
Bell Federal Savings & Loan Association
Bergen Record Corp.
Bernsen Foundation, Grace and Franklin
Berry & Co., L.M.
Bill Communications
Bingham Foundation, William
Biomet
Bishop Foundation, E. K. and Lillian F.
Blair and Co., William
BMC Industries
Boots Pharmaceuticals, Inc.
Booz Allen & Hamilton
Boston Mutual Life Insurance Co.
Brakeley, John Price Jones Inc.
Bristol Savings Bank
Brown-Forman Corp.
Brown Foundation
Brown Inc., John
Buffalo Color Corp.
Burdines
Business Men's Assurance Co. of America
C.P. Rail Systems
Cablevision of Michigan
Cabot Stains
Cadbury Beverages Inc.
Calex Manufacturing Co.
California & Hawaiian Sugar Co.
Callanan Industries
Callaway Foundation
Callaway Foundation, Fuller E.
Carpenter Technology Corp.
Carr Real Estate Services
CBS Inc.
CCB Financial Corp.
Ceco Corp.
Centel Corp.
Central Hudson Gas & Electric Corp.
Central Life Assurance Co.
Central Soya Co.
Central Vermont Public Service Corp.
Century Companies of America
Chamberlain Manufacturing Corp.
Charities Foundation
Chase Lincoln First Bank, N.A.
Chemtech Industries
Chesapeake & Potomac Telephone Co.
Chicago Title and Trust Co.
Chubb Life Insurance Co. of America
Church & Dwight Co.
Church Mutual Insurance
Cincinnati Gas & Electric Co.

Citibank, F.S.B.
Citizens Commercial & Savings Bank
Cleveland-Cliffs
Clopay Corp.
CNG Transmission Corp.
Coats & Clark Inc.
Cockrell Foundation
Collins & Aikman Corp.
Colonial Parking
Commercial Intertech Corp.
Commonwealth Energy System
Commonwealth Life Insurance Co.
Communications Satellite Corp. (COMSAT)
Community Mutual Insurance Co.
Computer Associates International
Connecticut Savings Bank
Cook & Co., Frederic W.
Cooke Foundation
Corbett Foundation
Crown Central Petroleum Corp.
CSX Corp.
Cuneo Foundation
Dain Bosworth/Inter-Regional Financial Group
Dalton Foundation, Dorothy U.
Danforth Foundation
DeKalb Genetics Corp.
DeSoto
Deuble Foundation, George H.
Dewar, A.W.G.
Diamond Shamrock
Didier Taylor Refractories Corp.
Diebold, Inc.
Difco Laboratories
Digital Sciences Corp.
Dillon Foundation
Dodge Foundation, Cleveland H.
Dole Food Company, Inc.
Dollar Dry Dock Bank
Dove-Knight & Associates, P.A., Architects
Dover Corp.
Dow Foundation, Herbert H. and Grace A.
Durham Corp.
East Ohio Gas Co.
Eastland Bank
Educators Mutual Life Insurance Co.
Egan Machinery Co.
Elf Aquitaine, Inc.
Elizabethtown Gas Co.
Elizabethtown Water Co.
Enserch Corp.
Ensign-Bickford Industries
Enterprises Inc.
Equifax
Ernest & Julio Gallo Winery
European American Bank
Factory Mutual Engineering Corp.
Far West Financial Corp.
Farm Credit Banks of Springfield
Ferranti Tech
Ferro Corp.
Fiduciary Trust Co.
FINA, Inc.
Fingerhut Corp.
First Fidelity Bancorp, Inc.
First Mississippi Corp.
First Valley Bank
First Virginia Banks
Fleet Bank N.A.
Flintridge Foundation
Foellinger Foundation
Ford Foundation, Edward E.
Fortis Inc.
Fortis Benefits Insurance Company/Fortis Financial Group
Foster Foundation
Foster Wheeler Corp.

Foundation for Seacoast Health
Fowler Memorial Foundation, John Edward
Fraser Paper Ltd.
Freedom Forum
Freeman Charitable Trust, Samuel
Freightliner Corp.
Fullerton Foundation
Funderburke & Associates
Galileo Electro-Optics Corp.
Gast Manufacturing Corp.
Gates Corp.
Gebbie Foundation
General Accident Insurance Co. of America
General Color Co.
General Housewares Corp.
General Signal Corp.
Gensler Jr. & Associates, M. Arthur
Georgia Pork Producers Association
Getty Trust, J. Paul
Gilbane Building Co.
Glatfelter Co., P.H.
Glendale Federal Bank
Glenmede Trust Corp.
Glidden Co.
Goldome F.S.B
Good Value Home, Inc.
Goulds Pumps
Graphic Printing Co.
Great Lakes Carbon Corp.
Great West Casualty Co.
Greenwood Mills
Grenzebach & Associates, John
Grumman Corp.
Hamilton Bank
Hamman Foundation, George and Mary Josephine
Hancock Foundation, Luke B.
Hanes Foundation, John W. and Anna H.
Harden Foundation
Hardin Foundation, Phil
Harleysville Mutual Insurance Co.
Haworth, Inc.
Heileman Brewing Co., Inc., G.
Hercules Inc.
Hershey Entertainment & Resort Co.
Higher Education Publications
Holmes & Narver Services Inc.
Home Depot
Hoover, Jr. Foundation, Margaret W. and Herbert
Hopwood Charitable Trust, John M.
Hormel & Co., George A.
Howmet Corp.
Hoyt Foundation, Stewart W. and Willma C.
Hubbard Foundation, R. Dee and Joan Dale
Hubbard Milling Co.
Hubbell Inc.
Huck International Inc.
Hughes Aircraft Co.
Hunt Alternatives Fund
Hydraulic Co.
Hyster-Yale
Indiana Bell Telephone Co.
Industrial Risk Insurers
Innovation Packaging
Instron Corp.
Integra Bank/South
Intelligent Controls
International Student Exchange Cards
Ira-Hiti Foundation for Deep Ecology
ITT Rayonier
IU International
Jackson Foundation
Jackson Hole Preserve

JM Foundation
Johnson Co., E. F.
Johnson Foundation, Robert Wood
Jones Foundation, Daisy Marquis
Joukowsky Family Foundation
JSJ Corp.
Jurzykowski Foundation, Alfred
Kansas City Southern Industries
Karmazin Products Corp.
Keefe, Bruyette & Woods
Kempner Fund, Harris and Eliza
Kerr Foundation, Robert S. and Grayce B.
Kerr Fund, Grayce B.
King Ranch
Kiplinger Foundation
Kirkpatrick Foundation
Kline Foundation, Josiah W. and Bessie H.
Knott Foundation, Marion I. and Henry I.
Kohler Foundation
Korte Construction Co.
LaSalle National Bank
Law Companies Group
Law Company, Inc.
Lawyers Co-operative Publishing Co.
Libbey-Owens Ford Co.
Liquid Air Corp.
LoJack Corp.
Loughran Foundation, Mary and Daniel
Loyola Foundation
Lucky Stores
Lummus Crest, Inc.
Lutheran Brotherhood Foundation
M/A/R/C Inc.
MacArthur Foundation, John D. and Catherine T.
MacLean-Fogg Co.
Maclellan Charitable Trust, R. J.
Madison Mutual Insurance Co.
Maier Foundation, Sarah Pauline
Mailman Family Foundation, A. L.
Mallinckrodt Specialty Chemicals Co.
Management Compensation Group/Dulworth Inc.
Manufacturers National Bank of Detroit
Marion Fabrics
Mark IV Industries
Marley Co.
Marmot Foundation
Martin Foundation
Mast Drug Co.
Maxus Energy Corp.
Mayer Foundation, James and Eva
McDonnell Foundation, James S.
Mebane Packaging Corp.
Menasha Corp.
Mericos Foundation
Meridian Insurance Group Inc.
Meritor Financial Group
Mettler Instrument Corp.
Meyer Foundation, Eugene and Agnes E.
Meyerhoff Fund, Joseph
Michigan Mutual Insurance Corp.
Middendorf Foundation
Middlesex Mutual Assurance Co.
Midland Montagu
Milton Bradley Co.
Minnesota Mutual Life Insurance Co.
Mitchell Energy & Development Corp.
Monroe Auto Equipment Co.
Montana Power Co.
Moore McCormack Resources
Morley Brothers Foundation
Morse Shoe, Inc.
Mutual of America Life

NACCO Industries
National City Bank, Columbus
National Forge Co.
National Gypsum Co.
Nationale-Nederlanden North America Corp.
Nellie Mae
Nepera Inc.
New England Electric System
New Jersey National Bank
Newmont Mining Corp.
News America Publishing Inc.
Noble Foundation, Samuel Roberts
North American Life & Casualty Co.
North American Philips Corp.
North American Reinsurance Corp.
Northern Illinois Gas Co.
Northern Indiana Public Service Co.
Northern Virginia Natural Gas
Norton & Co., W.W.
Noyes, Jr. Memorial Foundation, Nicholas H.
NRC, Inc.
Nuveen & Co., Inc., John
Oakite Products
Oglebay Norton Co.
Ohio Edison Corp.
Ohrstrom Foundation
OMNI Construction
Ontario Corp.
Openaka Corp.
Oppenstein Brothers Foundation
Ortho Diagnostic Systems, Inc.
O'Toole Foundation, Theresa and Edward
Owens-Illinois
Pacific Enterprises
Palmer Fund, Frank Loomis
Peabody Charitable Fund, Amelia
Pearle Vision
Penn Central Corp.
Pennbank
Pentair
Perkin-Elmer Corp.
Perry Drug Stores
Peterson & Co. Consulting
Phillips Foundation, Dr. P.
Pinkerton Tobacco Co.
Pioneer Group
Pirelli Armstrong Tire Corp.
Plante & Moran, CPAs
Plantronics, Inc.
Pogo Producing Co.
Poole Equipment Co., Gregory
Pope & Talbot, Inc.
Preferred Risk Mutual Insurance Co.
Preformed Line Products Co.
Prospect Hill Foundation
Provident Mutual Life Insurance Co. of Philadelphia
Public Service Co. of New Mexico
Quaker State Corp.
Ramapo Trust
Raymond Corp.
Raytheon Engineers & Constructors
Redlands Federal Bank
Reeves Foundation
Reliance Insurance Cos.
Research-Cottrell Inc.
Research Institute of America
Rexham Inc.
Rivers and Trails North East
Riviana Foods
Rockefeller Brothers Fund
Rockefeller Family & Associates
Rockefeller Trust, Winthrop
Rolm Systems
Ross Foundation
Royal Insurance Co. of America
Rust International Corp.

San Diego Gas & Electric
Schiff, Hardin & Waite
Schulman Management Corp.
Schwab & Co., Charles
Scientific Brake & Equipment Co.
Scrivner, Inc.
Sealed Air Corp.
Second Foundation
Security Benefit Life Insurance Co.
Sedgwick James Inc.
Semple Foundation, Louise Taft
Seton Co.
Shearson, Lehman & Hutton
Sheldahl Inc.
Shott, Jr. Foundation, Hugh I.
Silvestri Corp.
Skandia America Reinsurance Corp.
Skillman Foundation
Smith International
Snow Memorial Trust, John Ben
Somers Corp. (Mersman/Waldron)
Sonat Exploration
South-Western Publishing Co.
Southern Bell
Spectra-Physics Analytical
Spring Arbor Distributors
SPX Corp.
Stamps Foundation, James L.
Standex International Corp.
Stanhome Inc.
Star Enterprise
Steel Heddle Manufacturing Co.
Steiger Tractor
Stein Roe & Farnham Investment Council
Stern Memorial Trust, Sidney
Stevens Foundation, Abbot and Dorothy H.
Stone & Webster, Inc.
Student Loan Marketing Association
Super Valu Stores
Susquehanna Investment Group
Swalm Foundation
Swank, Inc.
Swiss American Securities, Inc.
T.T.X. Co.
Tambrands Inc.
Tennant Co.
Tesoro Petroleum Corp.
Tetley, Inc.
Texas Gas Transmission Corp.
Time Warner Cable
Torrington Co.
Towers Perrin
Trans-Apex
Transtar Inc.
Travelers Express Co.
Tremco Inc.
Turner Charitable Foundation
Turner Charitable Trust, Courtney S.
Turner Corp.
Twentieth Century-Fox Film Corp.
Twentieth Century Insurance Co.
UGI Corp.
UJB Financial Corp.
Unilever United States
Union Central Life Insurance Co.
Union Mutual Fire Insurance Co.
United Fire & Casualty Co.
United Services Automobile Association
U.S. Bank of Washington
USLIFE Corp.
Utica National Insurance Group
Valley Foundation
Valley Foundation, Wayne and Gladys
Victoria Foundation
Vollrath Co.
Wagnalls Memorial

Waldbaum, Inc.
Wallace & Wallace Ltd.
Watkins-Johnson Co.
Wausau Insurance Cos.
Welch Foods
Werner Foundation, Clara and Spencer
Western Publishing Co., Inc.
WestStar Bank N.A.
Whittaker Corp.
Wiley & Sons, Inc., John
Wiremold Co.
Wisconsin Bell, Inc.
Wyomissing Foundation
Yosemite Asset Management
Young & Rubicam
Zurn Industries

Multiyear/ Continuing Support

Abel Construction Co.
Achelis Foundation
Acushnet Co.
Agway
Air Products & Chemicals
AKC Fund
Ala Vi Foundation of New York
Alabama Power Co.
Albany International Corp.
Alltel/Western Region
Amado Foundation, Maurice
American Brands
American Foundation Corporation
American General Finance
American Honda Motor Co.
American Microsystems, Inc.
American Saw & Manufacturing Co.
American Telephone & Telegraph Co./Dallas Region
American Telephone & Telegraph Co./New York City Region
American United Life Insurance Co.
Ameritas Life Insurance Corp.
Amfac/JMB Hawaii
Amoco Corp.
Amsted Industries
Andreas Foundation
Apache Corp.
Archbold Charitable Trust, Adrian and Jessie
ARCO Chemical
Arkla
Armington Fund, Evenor
Arvin Industries
ASARCO
Atran Foundation
Autzen Foundation
Babcock Foundation, Mary Reynolds
Babcock & Wilcox Co.
Ball Corp.
Ballet Makers
Bamberger and John Ernest Bamberger Memorial Foundation, Ruth Eleanor
Banc One Illinois Corp.
Bank of Louisville
Banner Life Insurance Co.
Bargman Foundation, Theodore and Mina
Barker Foundation, J. M. R.
Bartol Foundation, Stockton Rush
Bass Foundation, Harry
Batten Foundation
BayBanks
Bean, L.L.
Bechtel Group
Beech Aircraft Corp.
Beeghly Fund, Leon A.
Beidler Charitable Trust, Francis

Bell Communications Research
Benefit Trust Life Insurance Co.
Benton Foundation
Bergen Foundation, Frank and Lydia
Bergner Co., P.A.
Berkman Charitable Trust, Allen H. and Selma W.
Bernsen Foundation, Grace and Franklin
Berry Foundation, Lowell
Besser Foundation
Bethlehem Steel Corp.
Beveridge Foundation, Frank Stanley
Binney & Smith Inc.
Biomet
Bishop Charitable Trust, A. G.
Bjorkman Foundation
Blair and Co., William
Blandin Foundation
Block, H&R
Blowitz-Ridgeway Foundation
Bodman Foundation
Boehringer Mannheim Corp.
Booz Allen & Hamilton
Botwinick-Wolfensohn Foundation
Boulevard Foundation
Bourns, Inc.
Bowles and Robert Bowles Memorial Fund, Ethel Wilson
Bowne Foundation, Robert
Brady Foundation, W. H.
Bray Charitable Trust, Viola E.
Brencanda Foundation
Britton Fund
Broadhurst Foundation
Brown Charitable Trust, Dora Maclellan
Brown Foundation, George Warren
Brown & Sons, Alex
Brown & Williamson Tobacco Corp.
Browning Charitable Foundation, Val A.
Bruening Foundation, Eva L. and Joseph M.
Brunner Foundation, Fred J.
Brush Foundation
Buck Foundation, Carol Franc
Buehler Foundation, Emil
Buell Foundation, Temple Hoyne
Burchfield Foundation, Charles E.
Burkitt Foundation
Bush Foundation
Butler Family Foundation, Patrick and Aimee
Butler Foundation, J. Homer
Butler Manufacturing Co.
Butz Foundation
Bydale Foundation
Cabot Family Charitable Trust
Cain Foundation, Gordon and Mary
Campbell and Adah E. Hall Charity Fund, Bushrod H.
Capital Holding Corp.
Cary Charitable Trust, Mary Flagler
Caspersen Foundation for Aid to Health and Education, O. W.
CBS Inc.
Ceco Corp.
Centerior Energy Corp.
Central Maine Power Co.
Central Vermont Public Service Corp.
Century Companies of America
Cessna Aircraft Co.
Champion International Corp.
Chandler Foundation
Chase Lincoln First Bank, N.A.

Multiyear/Continuing Support (cont.)

Chase Manhattan Bank, N.A.
Chemical Bank
Cherne Foundation, Albert W.
Chicago Resource Center
Chicago Title and Trust Co.
Cincinnati Bell
Cincinnati Enquirer
Citizens Commercial & Savings Bank
Clark Charitable Trust
Cleveland-Cliffs
CNA Insurance Cos.
CNG Transmission Corp.
Coleman Co.
Coleman Foundation
Columbia Foundation
Commerce Clearing House
Commercial Metals Co.
Community Enterprises
Connemara Fund
Cooke Foundation
Copernicus Society of America
Cornell Trust, Peter C.
Courts Foundation
Cove Charitable Trust
Covington Foundation, Marion Stedman
Cowan Foundation Corporation, Lillian L. and Harry A.
Cox Foundation
Cuesta Foundation
Cullen/Frost Bankers
Culpeper Foundation, Charles E.
Culpeper Memorial Foundation, Daphne Seybolt
Culver Foundation, Constans
Dalton Foundation, Dorothy U.
Daniels Foundation, Fred Harris
Dater Foundation, Charles H.
Davenport-Hatch Foundation
Davis Foundation, Ken W.
Davis Foundation, Shelby Cullom
Day Foundation, Nancy Sayles
Dayton Power and Light Co.
de Kay Foundation
de Rothschild Foundation, Edmond
DeKalb Genetics Corp.
DelMar Foundation, Charles
Dentsu, Inc., NY
Deposit Guaranty National Bank
DeVore Foundation
Dillon Foundation
Dixie Yarns, Inc.
Dodge Foundation, Cleveland H.
Dollar General Corp.
Donaldson Co.
Donnelley Foundation, Elliott and Ann
Douglas & Lomason Company
Dover Foundation
Dow Foundation, Herbert H. and Barbara C.
Drum Foundation
du Pont de Nemours & Co., E. I.
Duke Endowment
Duke Foundation, Doris
duPont Fund, Jessie Ball
Dyson Foundation
East Ohio Gas Co.
Eaton Corp.
Eccles Foundation, George S. and Dolores Dore
Eccles Foundation, Ralph M. and Ella M.
Eddy Foundation
Eder Foundation, Sidney and Arthur
Edwards Foundation, O. P. and W. E.
EIS Foundation
Ellsworth Foundation, Ruth H. and Warren A.

English-Bonter-Mitchell Foundation
English Memorial Fund, Florence C. and H. L.
Ensign-Bickford Industries
Ensworth Charitable Foundation
Enterprise Rent-A-Car Co.
Equifax
Evans Foundation, T. M.
Evjue Foundation
Exposition Foundation
Falk Medical Fund, Maurice
Fay's Incorporated
Federal-Mogul Corp.
Ferkauf Foundation, Eugene and Estelle
Ferro Corp.
Fidelity Bank
Fifth Avenue Foundation
Fikes Foundation, Leland
Filene Foundation, Lincoln and Therese
Finch Foundation, Thomas Austin
Fingerhut Family Foundation
Fink Foundation
Fireman Charitable Foundation, Paul and Phyllis
First Mississippi Corp.
First of America Bank Corp.
First Union Corp.
Firstar Bank Milwaukee NA
Fishback Foundation Trust, Harmes C.
Fleming Companies, Inc.
Flinn Foundation
Flintridge Foundation
Foothills Foundation
Franklin Foundation, John and Mary
Franklin Mint Corp.
Frear Eleemosynary Trust, Mary D. and Walter F.
Freed Foundation
Freeman Charitable Trust, Samuel
Freeport-McMoRan
Frees Foundation
Friendly Rosenthal Foundation
Frisch's Restaurants Inc.
Frohring Foundation, William O. and Gertrude Lewis
Fry Foundation, Lloyd A.
Fuchs Foundation, Gottfried & Mary
Fullerton Metals Co.
Fund for New Jersey
Funderburke & Associates
Fusenot Charity Foundation, Georges and Germaine
G.A.G. Charitable Corporation
Gardner Foundation
Gebbie Foundation
Gellert Foundation, Carl
Gellert Foundation, Celia Berta
Gellert Foundation, Fred
General Reinsurance Corp.
General Tire Inc.
GenRad
Georgia Power Co.
German Marshall Fund of the United States
Gerson Family Foundation, Benjamin J.
Getty Trust, J. Paul
Gillette Co.
Glaxo
Glencoe Foundation
Globe Newspaper Co.
Goddard Foundation, Charles B.
Goldman Foundation, William
Goldome F.S.B
Goldseker Foundation of Maryland, Morris
Goldsmith Family Foundation
Goldsmith Foundation, Horace W.

Goodstein Family Foundation, David
Gordon Charitable Trust, Peggy and Yale
Gould Foundation for Children, Edwin
Grable Foundation
Graco
Grant Foundation, Charles M. and Mary D.
Gray Charitable Trust, Mary S.
Gray Foundation, Garland
Greene Manufacturing Co.
Gries Charity Fund, Lucile and Robert H.
Griffin Foundation, Rosa May
Griffith Foundation, W. C.
Gross Charitable Trust, Stella B.
Gulfstream Aerospace Corp.
Haas Fund, Miriam and Peter
Haas Fund, Walter and Elise
Haas, Jr. Fund, Evelyn and Walter
Haggar Foundation
Hales Charitable Fund
Hamilton Bank
Hamman Foundation, George and Mary Josephine
Hammer Foundation, Armand
Harden Foundation
Hardin Foundation, Phil
Harding Foundation, Charles Stewart
Haskell Fund
Hay Foundation, John I.
Hayden Foundation, William R. and Virginia
Health 1st Foundation
Hechinger Co.
Heinz Endowment, Howard
Henderson Foundation
Hervey Foundation
Hesston Corp.
Hewlett Foundation, William and Flora
Higginson Trust, Corina
Hightower Foundation, Walter
Hillcrest Foundation
Hilton Foundation, Conrad N.
Hitachi
Hoche-Scofield Foundation
Hoechst Celanese Corp.
Holden Fund, James and Lynelle
Home Depot
Hopkins Foundation, John Jay
Household International
Hoyt Foundation
Hughes Charitable Trust, Mabel Y.
Hughes Memorial Foundation, Charles Evans
Humphrey Fund, George M. and Pamela S.
Hunt Alternatives Fund
Hunt Foundation, Samuel P.
Huthsteiner Fine Arts Trust
ICI Americas
Iddings Benevolent Trust
Illinois Power Co.
Imerman Memorial Foundation, Stanley
Indiana Bell Telephone Co.
Inland Steel Industries
Irwin-Sweeney-Miller Foundation
ITT Rayonier
Jackson Foundation
James River Corp. of Virginia
Janesville Foundation
JCPenney Co.
Jennings Foundation, Martha Holden
Jewell Memorial Foundation, Daniel Ashley and Irene Houston
Johnson Foundation, Walter S.
Johnston-Hanson Foundation

Jones Charitable Trust, Harvey and Bernice
Jordan Foundation, Arthur
Joselow Foundation
Joslyn Foundation, Marcellus I.
Joyce Foundation
Joyce Foundation, John M. and Mary A.
Jurzykowski Foundation, Alfred
Kaiser Family Foundation, Henry J.
Kangesser Foundation, Robert E., Harry A., and M. Sylvia
Kaplan Foundation, Mayer and Morris
Kaplan Foundation, Rita J. and Stanley H.
Kavanagh Foundation, T. James
Kawabe Memorial Fund
Keith Foundation Trust, Ben E.
Kellogg Foundation, W. K.
Kemper Educational and Charitable Fund
Kemper National Insurance Cos.
Kempner Fund, Harris and Eliza
Kennecott Corp.
Kent-Lucas Foundation
Kentucky Foundation for Women
Kerr Foundation, A. H.
Kettering Family Foundation
Kieckhefer Foundation, J. W.
Killam Trust, Constance
Kilroy Foundation, William S. and Lora Jean
Kilworth Charitable Trust, William
Kingsbury Corp.
Kiplinger Foundation
Kirchgessner Foundation, Karl
Kirkland & Ellis
Kirkpatrick Foundation
Kleberg, Jr. and Helen C. Kleberg Foundation, Robert J.
Klingenstein Fund, Esther A. and Joseph
Koch Charitable Trust, David H.
Komes Foundation
Koopman Fund
Koret Foundation
KPMG Peat Marwick
Krause Foundation, Charles A.
Kreielsheimer Foundation Trust
Laclede Gas Co.
Lafarge Corp.
Lakeside Foundation
Landegger Charitable Foundation
Langeloth Foundation, Jacob and Valeria
Lasdon Foundation
Lassen Foundation, Irving A.
Laub Foundation
LBJ Family Foundation
Lee Foundation, James T.
Lehman Foundation, Robert
Leuthold Foundation
Lewis Foundation, Lillian Kaiser
Lilly Endowment
Lilly Foundation, Richard Coyle
Lincoln Fund
Lindsay Foundation
Lindsay Trust, Agnes M.
Link Foundation
Little, Arthur D.
Livingston Foundation, Milton S. and Corinne N.
Lockheed Sanders
Loughran Foundation, Mary and Daniel
Louisiana Land & Exploration Co.
Louisiana Power & Light Co./New Orleans Public Service
LTV Corp.
Lubrizol Corp.
Luck Stone
Lupin Foundation
Lux Foundation, Miranda

Lydall, Inc.
Lyndhurst Foundation
Lytel Foundation, Bertha Russ
M. E. G. Foundation
MacArthur Foundation, John D. and Catherine T.
MacDonald Foundation, James A.
Macht Foundation, Morton and Sophia
Maclellan Charitable Trust, R. J.
Magruder Foundation, Chesley G.
Mallinckrodt Specialty Chemicals Co.
Marbrook Foundation
Mardag Foundation
Margoes Foundation
Maritz Inc.
Mark IV Industries
Marley Co.
Martin Foundation
Martin Foundation, Bert William
Massachusetts Mutual Life Insurance Co.
Massengill-DeFriece Foundation
Material Service Corp.
Maytag Family Foundation, Fred
McBride & Son Associates
McCann Foundation
McCasland Foundation
McDonnell Foundation, James S.
McDonough Foundation, Bernard
McFeely-Rogers Foundation
McGee Foundation
McGovern Fund for the Behavioral Sciences
McGraw Foundation
McGraw Foundation, Curtis W.
MCI Communications Corp.
McKee Foundation, Robert E. and Evelyn
Mellon Foundation, Andrew W.
Melville Corp.
Memorial Foundation for Children
Menasha Corp.
Meyer Foundation, Eugene and Agnes E.
Meyerhoff Fund, Joseph
Michigan Gas Utilities
Midwest Resources
Millard Charitable Trust, Adah K.
Mills Fund, Frances Goll
Millstone Foundation
Minnegasco
Minnesota Foundation
Missouri Farmers Association
Monell Foundation, Ambrose
Montana Power Co.
Montgomery Street Foundation
Moore Charitable Foundation, Marjorie
Moore Foundation
Moore Foundation, O. L.
Moore Foundation, Roy C.
Morley Brothers Foundation
Motorola
Mott Fund, Ruth
MTS Systems Corp.
Mulcahy Foundation
Mulligan Charitable Trust, Mary S.
Murphy Foundation, John P.
Nash Foundation
National City Bank, Columbus
National Computer Systems
National Life of Vermont
National Medical Enterprises
National Starch & Chemical Corp.
NBD Bank
Neese Family Foundation
Nestle U.S.A. Inc.
New England Mutual Life Insurance Co.
New Prospect Foundation
The New Yorker Magazine, Inc.

News & Observer Publishing Co.
Nias Foundation, Henry
Nichols Foundation
Nike Inc.
Noble Foundation, Vivian Bilby
Norcliffe Fund
Norfolk Shipbuilding & Drydock Corp.
Northeast Utilities
Northern Indiana Public Service Co.
Northwest Natural Gas Co.
Norwest Corp.
Noyes Foundation, Jessie Smith
O'Brien Foundation, Alice M.
O'Connor Foundation, Kathryn
Oglebay Norton Co.
Ohio Bell Telephone Co.
Ohrstrom Foundation
Olin Corp.
Oliver Memorial Trust Foundation
Onan Family Foundation
1525 Foundation
1957 Charity Trust
O'Neil Foundation, Casey Albert T.
Ontario Corp.
O'Toole Foundation, Theresa and Edward
Overbrook Foundation
Owens-Corning Fiberglas Corp.
Owsley Foundation, Alvin and Lucy
Page Foundation, George B.
Paley Foundation, William S.
Palisades Educational Foundation
Pan-American Life Insurance Co.
Pappas Charitable Foundation, Thomas Anthony
Parker Foundation
Patterson Charitable Fund, W. I.
Paul and C. Michael Paul Foundation, Josephine Bay
Pauley Foundation, Edwin W.
Pearlstone Foundation, Peggy Meyerhoff
Peery Foundation
Pendergast-Weyer Foundation
Pendleton Memorial Fund, William L. and Ruth T.
Penn Foundation, William
People's Bank
Peoples Energy Corp.
Perkin-Elmer Corp.
Peterson Foundation, Fred J.
Pfizer
Phelps Dodge Corp.
Philibosian Foundation, Stephen
Phillips Foundation, Ellis L.
Pick, Jr. Fund, Albert
Pitts Foundation, William H. and Lula E.
Pittsburgh National Bank
Pitzman Fund
Portland General Electric Co.
Pott Foundation, Herman T. and Phenie R.
Pratt Memorial Fund
Prentice Foundation, Abra
Prince Trust, Abbie Norman
Principal Financial Group
Providence Journal Company
Quaker Oats Co.
Questar Corp.
Quinlan Foundation, Elizabeth C.
R. F. Foundation
Ranney Foundation, P. K.
Ray Foundation
Raymond Educational Foundation
Regenstein Foundation
Reliance Electric Co.
Republic New York Corp.
Retirement Research Foundation
Reynolds Foundation, Christopher

Reynolds Foundation, J. B.
Reynolds Foundation, Richard S.
Rice Foundation, Helen Steiner
Richardson Foundation, Sid W.
Rittenhouse Foundation
Rockefeller Brothers Fund
Rockefeller Foundation
Rockwell Foundation
Roe Foundation
Rohr Inc.
Roseburg Forest Products Co.
Rosenberg Family Foundation, William
Rouse Co.
Rubinstein Foundation, Helena
Ryan Foundation, David Claude
St. Faith's House Foundation
St. Mary's Catholic Foundation
Saint Paul Cos.
Samuels Foundation, Fan Fox and Leslie R.
Sandy Foundation, George H.
Sandy Hill Foundation
Sara Lee Corp.
Scaler Foundation
Scherman Foundation
Schieffelin Residuary Trust, Sarah I.
Schrafft and Bertha E. Schrafft Charitable Trust, William E.
Schumann Fund for New Jersey
Schwab & Co., Charles
Science Applications International Corp.
Scott Foundation, Walter
Sears Family Foundation
Seaway Food Town
Second Foundation
Security Life of Denver
Seidman Family Foundation
Semmes Foundation
Shaklee Corp.
Shaw Foundation, Gardiner Howland
Sheafer Charitable Trust, Emma A.
Shelden Fund, Elizabeth, Allan and Warren
Shelton Cos.
Sheridan Foundation, Thomas B. and Elizabeth M.
Shoemaker Fund, Thomas H. and Mary Williams
Shoenberg Foundation
Sierra Health Foundation
Signet Bank/Maryland
Skillman Foundation
Sloan Foundation, Alfred P.
Smith Charitable Trust, W. W.
Smith Foundation, Kenneth L. and Eva S.
Smith, Jr. Foundation, M. W.
Smith Memorial Fund, Ethel Sergeant Clark
Smyth Trust, Marion C.
Snyder Foundation, Harold B. and Dorothy A.
Snyder Fund, Valentine Perry
Soling Family Foundation
Somers Foundation, Byron H.
Sonoco Products Co.
Sordoni Foundation
South Branch Foundation
South Waite Foundation
Southern Bell
Southland Corp.
Spectra-Physics Analytical
Springs Industries
Stabler Foundation, Donald B. and Dorothy L.
Stackner Family Foundation
Stanley Charitable Foundation, A. W.
Stans Foundation
Starr Foundation
Stauffer Foundation, John and Beverly

Steele Foundation, Harry and Grace
Steigerwaldt Foundation, Donna Wolf
Steiner Charitable Fund, Albert
Stern Foundation, Irvin
Stern Foundation, Leonard N.
Stern Foundation, Max
Stevens Foundation, Abbot and Dorothy H.
Stevens Foundation, Nathaniel and Elizabeth P.
Stewards Fund
Stewart Trust under the will of Helen S. Devore, Alexander and Margaret
Stocker Foundation
Stockham Valves & Fittings
Stone Foundation, France
Stone & Webster, Inc.
Stony Wold Herbert Fund
Straus Foundation, Aaron and Lillie
Strawbridge Foundation of Pennsylvania II, Margaret Dorrance
Stride Rite Corp.
Stroud Foundation
Stuart Foundation, Edward C.
Sulzer Family Foundation
Target Stores
Teagle Foundation
Teleklew Productions
Templeton Foundation, Herbert A.
Tetley, Inc.
Texas Gas Transmission Corp.
Thomas Foundation, Dorothy
Thorson Foundation
3M Co.
Times Mirror Co.
Timken Co.
Tiscornia Foundation
Tonya Memorial Foundation
Tosco Corp. Refining Division
Town Creek Foundation
Towsley Foundation, Harry A. and Margaret D.
Travelers Cos.
Treakle Foundation, J. Edwin
Triford Foundation
Trull Foundation
Turner Charitable Foundation
Union Camp Corp.
Union Carbide Corp.
Universal Foods Corp.
UNUM Corp.
Uris Brothers Foundation
Valero Energy Corp.
van Ameringen Foundation
Vanneck-Bailey Foundation
Varian Associates
Vaughan Foundation, Rachael and Ben
Vevay-Switzerland County Foundation
Vogt Machine Co., Henry
Vollmer Foundation
Vollrath Co.
Vulcan Materials Co.
Waggoner Charitable Trust, Crystelle
Wahlstrom Foundation
Walker Foundation, T. B.
Wallace-Reader's Digest Fund, DeWitt
Walsh Foundation
Warsh-Mott Legacy
Washington Forrest Foundation
Washington Mutual Savings Bank
Washington Post Co.
Watkins Christian Foundation
Watumull Fund, J.
Weaver Foundation, Gil and Dody
Webb Charitable Trust, Susan Mott

Webb Foundation
Weinstein Foundation, J.
Weir Foundation Trust
Weiss Foundation, William E.
West Co.
West One Bancorp
Westinghouse Broadcasting Co.
Westport Fund
Westvaco Corp.
Weyerhaeuser Foundation, Frederick and Margaret L.
Weyerhaeuser Memorial Foundation, Charles A.
White Foundation, W. P. and H. B.
Whiteman Foundation, Edna Rider
Whitman Corp.
Whittell Trust for Disabled Veterans of Foreign Wars, Elia
Wilcox General Trust, George N.
Wilcox Trust, S. W.
Wilson Foundation, Marie C. and Joseph C.
Wilson Trust, Lula C.
Woods Charitable Fund
Woods-Greer Foundation
Woodward Governor Co.
Woolley Foundation, Vasser
Wright Foundation, Lola
Wurlitzer Foundation, Farny R.
Wurts Memorial, Henrietta Tower
Wyomissing Foundation
Yellow Corp.
Zachry Co., H. B.
Ziegler Foundation for the Blind, E. Matilda
Ziemann Foundation

Operating Expenses
Abreu Charitable Trust u/w/o May P. Abreu, Francis I.
Achelis Foundation
AHS Foundation
Air Products & Chemicals
Aladdin Industries, Incorporated
ALPAC Corp.
Alyeska Pipeline Service Co.
Amado Foundation, Maurice
AMAX
American Brands
American Electric Power
American General Finance
American Microsystems, Inc.
American Saw & Manufacturing Co.
American Telephone & Telegraph Co./New York City Region
American United Life Insurance Co.
Americana Foundation
Amoco Corp.
AMP
Amsted Industries
Andalusia Health Services
Andersen Foundation, Hugh J.
Anderson Foundation
AON Corp.
Apache Corp.
Arcana Foundation
Armco Steel Co.
Armington Fund, Evenor
Arvin Industries
Astor Foundation, Vincent
Athwin Foundation
Awrey Bakeries
Ayres Foundation, Inc.
Babcock Foundation, Mary Reynolds
Baker Charitable Foundation, Jessie Foos
Baker Foundation, R. C.
Baker Trust, Clayton
Ball Brothers Foundation
Ballet Makers
Baltimore Gas & Electric Co.

Bamberger and John Ernest Bamberger Memorial Foundation, Ruth Eleanor
Banfi Vintners
Bank of A. Levy
Bank of America Arizona
Bank of Louisville
Bankers Trust Co.
Bannerman Foundation, William C.
Barker Foundation, Donald R.
Barker Foundation, J. M. R.
Barstow Foundation
Bartol Foundation, Stockton Rush
Bauer Foundation, M. R.
Bauervic Foundation, Charles M.
Bauervic-Paisley Foundation
Baughman Foundation
Beaird Foundation, Charles T.
Beazley Foundation
Bechtel Group
Bechtel, Jr. Foundation, S. D.
Beckman Foundation, Leland D.
Bedsole Foundation, J. L.
Beeghly Fund, Leon A.
Beidler Charitable Trust, Francis
Belden Brick Co., Inc.
BellSouth Corp.
Berkman Charitable Trust, Allen H. and Selma W.
Berry Foundation, Lowell
Bertha Foundation
Berwind Corp.
Besser Foundation
Bethlehem Steel Corp.
Bigelow Foundation, F. R.
Bishop Charitable Trust, A. G.
Block, H&R
Bloedel Foundation
Blue Cross and Blue Shield United of Wisconsin Foundation
Boatmen's First National Bank of Oklahoma
Boehm Foundation
Boehringer Mannheim Corp.
Bohen Foundation
Bolten Charitable Foundation, John
Booz Allen & Hamilton
Borden Memorial Foundation, Mary Owen
Borg-Warner Corp.
Bosque Foundation
Boulevard Foundation
Bowne Foundation, Robert
Boynton Fund, John W.
Brach Foundation, Helen
Bradley Foundation, Lynde and Harry
Brencanda Foundation
Brenner Foundation, Mervyn
Bridgestone/Firestone
Bridwell Foundation, J. S.
Briggs & Stratton Corp.
Bright Charitable Trust, Alexander H.
Bright Family Foundation
Brillion Iron Works
Britton Fund
Brown Charitable Trust, Dora Maclellan
Brown Foundation
Brown Foundation, George Warren
Brown Foundation, Joe W. and Dorothy Dorsett
Brown & Williamson Tobacco Corp.
Brownley Trust, Walter
Bruening Foundation, Eva L. and Joseph M.
Brush Foundation
Bryan Family Foundation, Kathleen Price and Joseph M.
Buehler Foundation, Emil
Buell Foundation, Temple Hoyne

Operating Expenses (cont.)

Bullitt Foundation
Burchfield Foundation, Charles E.
Burkitt Foundation
Butler Manufacturing Co.
Butz Foundation
Bydale Foundation
C.P. Rail Systems
Caestecker Foundation, Charles and Marie
Cain Foundation, Effie and Wofford
Cain Foundation, Gordon and Mary
Caine Charitable Foundation, Marie Eccles
Callaway Foundation
Callaway Foundation, Fuller E.
Camp and Bennet Humiston Trust, Apollos
Campbell and Adah E. Hall Charity Fund, Bushrod H.
Campbell Soup Co.
Capital Holding Corp.
Cargill
Carpenter Foundation
Carteh Foundation
Cartinhour Foundation
Cary Charitable Trust, Mary Flagler
Caspersen Foundation for Aid to Health and Education, O. W.
Caterpillar
Cauthorn Charitable Trust, John and Mildred
CBI Industries
CBS Inc.
Centerior Energy Corp.
Central Soya Co.
Chapin Foundation of Myrtle Beach, South Carolina Charitable Fund
Chase Charity Foundation, Alfred E.
Chase Manhattan Bank, N.A.
Cheatham Foundation, Owen
Chicago Resource Center
Chicago Sun-Times, Inc.
Childs Charitable Foundation, Roberta M.
Chiles Foundation
Ciba-Geigy Corp. (Pharmaceuticals Division)
CIGNA Corp.
Circuit City Stores
Clark Charitable Trust
Cleveland-Cliffs
Clipper Ship Foundation
Clorox Co.
Clowes Fund
CNA Insurance Cos.
Cogswell Benevolent Trust
Cole Foundation
Coleman Co.
Colorado State Bank of Denver
Coltec Industries
Comer Foundation
Commerce Clearing House
Commercial Intertech Corp.
Commercial Metals Co.
Common Giving Fund
Compaq Computer Corp.
Confidence Foundation
Consolidated Natural Gas Co.
Consumers Power Co.
Contran Corp.
Cook Foundation, Louella
Cooke Foundation
Coors Foundation, Adolph
Cornell Trust, Peter C.
Corvallis Clinic
Courts Foundation
Cove Charitable Trust
Cowles Charitable Trust

Cowles Foundation, Gardner and Florence Call
Cox Foundation
Crawford Estate, E. R.
Crels Foundation
Crum and Forster
CTS Corp.
Cudahy Fund, Patrick and Anna M.
Cullen/Frost Bankers
Curtice-Burns Foods
Dain Bosworth/Inter-Regional Financial Group
Daniels Foundation, Fred Harris
Dart Foundation
Dauch Foundation, William
Davidson Family Charitable Foundation
Davis Foundation, Edwin W. and Catherine M.
Davis Foundation, Shelby Cullom
de Hirsch Fund, Baron
Delavan Foundation, Nelson B.
Delaware North Cos.
Deluxe Corp.
Deposit Guaranty National Bank
DeRoy Foundation, Helen L.
DeVore Foundation
Dietrich Foundation, William B.
Dodge Foundation, Cleveland H.
Dodge Foundation, Geraldine R.
Dollar General Corp.
Donaldson Co.
Donnelley Foundation, Gaylord and Dorothy
Donnelley & Sons Co., R.R.
Dorr Foundation
Dougherty, Jr. Foundation, James R.
Douglas & Lomason Company
Dover Foundation
Dow Foundation, Herbert H. and Grace A.
Doyle Charitable Foundation
Dresser Industries
Drum Foundation
du Bois Foundation, E. Blois
Duke Endowment
Dula Educational and Charitable Foundation, Caleb C. and Julia W.
Duncan Trust, John G.
duPont Foundation, Chichester
East Foundation, Sarita Kenedy
Eastman Foundation, Alexander
Eastman Kodak Co.
Eccles Foundation, George S. and Dolores Dore
Eccles Foundation, Marriner S.
Eccles Foundation, Ralph M. and Ella M.
Eder Foundation, Sidney and Arthur
Edwards Foundation, Jes
Edwards Foundation, O. P. and W. E.
Elizabethtown Gas Co.
Ellsworth Foundation, Ruth H. and Warren A.
Ellwood Foundation
English-Bonter-Mitchell Foundation
Enron Corp.
Enterprise Rent-A-Car Co.
Evans Foundation, T. M.
Evans Foundation, Thomas J.
Evening Post Publishing Co.
Evinrude Foundation, Ralph
Fairfield Foundation, Freeman E.
Fales Foundation Trust
Falk Foundation, David
Fanwood Foundation
Farnsworth Trust, Charles A.
Farr Trust, Frank M. and Alice M.
Faulkner Trust, Marianne Gaillard

Favrot Fund
Federal Home Loan Mortgage Corp. (Freddie Mac)
Federal-Mogul Corp.
Fel-Pro Incorporated
Ferro Corp.
Fidelity Bank
Field Foundation of Illinois
Fieldcrest Cannon
Fikes Foundation, Leland
Filene Foundation, Lincoln and Therese
Finch Foundation, Thomas Austin
Fingerhut Family Foundation
Fink Foundation
Finley Foundation, A. E.
First Bank System
First Chicago
First Interstate Bank of Arizona
First Interstate Bank of California
First Interstate Bank of Denver
First Interstate Bank of Texas, N.A.
First Mississippi Corp.
First Union Corp.
Firstar Bank Milwaukee NA
Fish Foundation, Bert
Fish Foundation, Ray C.
Fleishhacker Foundation
Fleming Companies, Inc.
Flintridge Foundation
Fluor Corp.
Foellinger Foundation
Folger Fund
Forest Foundation
Fourth Financial Corp.
Fowler Memorial Foundation, John Edward
Franklin Foundation, John and Mary
Franklin Mint Corp.
Frazier Foundation
Frear Eleemosynary Trust, Mary D. and Walter F.
Frederick Foundation
Freed Foundation
Freeman Charitable Trust, Samuel
Freeman Foundation, Carl M.
Freeport-McMoRan
Frisch's Restaurants Inc.
Froderman Foundation
Frohring Foundation, William O. and Gertrude Lewis
Frueauff Foundation, Charles A.
Fuchs Foundation, Gottfried & Mary
Fuller Co., H.B.
Funderburke & Associates
Fuqua Foundation, J. B.
Fusenot Charity Foundation, Georges and Germaine
Gallagher Family Foundation, Lewis P.
Garvey Kansas Foundation
GATX Corp.
Gault-Hussey Charitable Trust
Gebbie Foundation
Gellert Foundation, Carl
Gellert Foundation, Celia Berta
Gellert Foundation, Fred
General Dynamics Corp.
General Mills
Generation Trust
Genesis Foundation
Genius Foundation, Elizabeth Morse
GenRad
Georgia Power Co.
German Protestant Orphan Asylum Association
Gerson Family Foundation, Benjamin J.
Gholston Trust, J. K.
Gifford Charitable Corporation, Rosamond
Gill Foundation, Pauline Allen

Gillette Co.
Gilmore Foundation, Irving S.
Ginter Foundation, Karl and Anna
Glancy Foundation, Lenora and Alfred
Glaxo
Gleason Works
Glencoe Foundation
Glenn Memorial Foundation, Wilbur Fisk
Glick Foundation, Eugene and Marilyn
Globe Newspaper Co.
Goddard Foundation, Charles B.
Goldman Foundation, William
Goldome F.S.B
Gottwald Foundation
Gould Foundation for Children, Edwin
Grable Foundation
Graco
Grant Foundation, Charles M. and Mary D.
Gray Foundation, Garland
Great Western Financial Corp.
Green Foundation
Gries Charity Fund, Lucile and Robert H.
Griffin Foundation, Rosa May
Gutman Foundation, Edna and Monroe C.
Guttman Foundation, Stella and Charles
H.C.S. Foundation
Haas Foundation, Paul and Mary
Haas Fund, Miriam and Peter
Haas, Jr. Fund, Evelyn and Walter
Hagedorn Fund
Hale Foundation, Crescent Porter
Hales Charitable Fund
Hallowell Foundation
Hamilton Bank
Harden Foundation
Harding Foundation, Charles Stewart
Harrington Foundation, Don and Sybil
Harris Family Foundation, Hunt and Diane
Harris Foundation
Hartford Courant Foundation
Harvard Musical Association
Haskell Fund
Hazen Foundation, Edward W.
Health 1st Foundation
Hechinger Co.
Heginbotham Trust, Will E.
Heinz Endowment, Howard
Heinz Endowment, Vira I.
Heritage Foundation
Herndon Foundation
Herndon Foundation, Alonzo F. Herndon and Norris B.
Hershey Foods Corp.
Hervey Foundation
Hesston Corp.
Hewlett Foundation, William and Flora
Higginson Trust, Corina
Hightower Foundation, Walter
Hill and Family Foundation, Walter Clay
Hill Crest Foundation
Hill Foundation
Hillman Family Foundation, Alex
Hillman Foundation, Henry L.
Hilton Foundation, Conrad N.
Hofheinz Fund
Holden Fund, James and Lynelle
Home Depot
Home for Aged Men
Homeland Foundation
Honeywell
Hooper Foundation, Elizabeth S.
Hoover Foundation
Houghton Mifflin Co.

Household International
Houston Endowment
Hovnanian Foundation, Hirair and Anna
Howell Fund
Hoyt Foundation, Stewart W. and Willma C.
Hubbard Broadcasting
Hudson-Webber Foundation
Hughes Charitable Trust, Mabel Y.
Huisking Foundation
Hulings Foundation, Mary Andersen
Hume Foundation, Jaquelin
Humphrey Fund, George M. and Pamela S.
Hunt Foundation, Roy A.
Hunter Trust, A. V.
Huntington Fund for Education, John
Hurst Foundation
Huston Foundation
Huthsteiner Fine Arts Trust
Hyams Foundation
ICI Americas
Iddings Benevolent Trust
Illges Foundation, John P. and Dorothy S.
Illges Memorial Foundation, A. and M. L.
Illinois Power Co.
IMCERA Group Inc.
Indiana Bell Telephone Co.
Inland Container Corp.
International Multifoods Corp.
Irwin-Sweeney-Miller Foundation
Island Foundation
ITT Rayonier
J.P. Morgan & Co.
James River Corp. of Virginia
Jellison Benevolent Society
Jenkins Foundation, George W.
Jerusalem Fund for Education and Community Development
Jewell Memorial Foundation, Daniel Ashley and Irene Houston
Jinks Foundation, Ruth T.
Johnson Co., E. F.
Johnson Controls
Johnson Fund, Edward C.
Jones and Bessie D. Phelps Foundation, Cyrus W. and Amy F.
Jones Foundation, Helen
Jordan Foundation, Arthur
Joslyn Foundation, Marcellus I.
Jost Foundation, Charles and Mabel P.
Journal Gazette Co.
Joyce Foundation
Jurzykowski Foundation, Alfred
Kaiser Cement Corp.
Kangesser Foundation, Robert E., Harry A., and M. Sylvia
Kantzler Foundation
Kaplan Foundation, Mayer and Morris
Kaplan Fund, J. M.
Kaufman Endowment Fund, Louis G.
Kavanagh Foundation, T. James
Kawabe Memorial Fund
Keith Foundation Trust, Ben E.
Kelley and Elza Kelley Foundation, Edward Bangs
Kemper Educational and Charitable Fund
Kempner Fund, Harris and Eliza
Kenan Family Foundation
Kent-Lucas Foundation
Kerr Foundation
Kerr Foundation, A. H.
Kettering Family Foundation
Kettering Fund
Killough Trust, Walter H. D.

Kilroy Foundation, William S.
and Lora Jean
Kilworth Charitable Trust,
William
Kimball International
Kimberly-Clark Corp.
Kingsbury Corp.
Kiplinger Foundation
Kirchgessner Foundation, Karl
Kirkpatrick Foundation
Kitzmiller/Bales Trust
Klee Foundation, Conrad and
Virginia
Kline Foundation, Josiah W. and
Bessie H.
Klingenstein Fund, Esther A. and
Joseph
Knott Foundation, Marion I. and
Henry J.
Koehler Foundation, Marcia and
Otto
Komes Foundation
Koret Foundation
Kramer Foundation, Louise
Kunstadter Family Foundation,
Albert
Kutz Foundation, Milton and
Hattie
L. L. W. W. Foundation
Laclede Gas Co.
Lakeside Foundation
Lanier Brothers Foundation
Laub Foundation
Leach Foundation, Tom &
Frances
Lechmere
Lee Foundation, Ray M. and
Mary Elizabeth
Leo Burnett Co.
Leu Foundation, Harry P.
Leuthold Foundation
Lewis Foundation, Lillian Kaiser
Life Insurance Co. of Georgia
Lightner Sams Foundation
Lilly & Co., Eli
Lilly Endowment
Lincoln Electric Co.
Lindstrom Foundation, Kinney
Lingnan Foundation
Lockheed Corp.
Lockheed Sanders
Lowe Foundation
Lowenstein Foundation, William
P. and Marie R.
LTV Corp.
Lubrizol Corp.
Lund Foundation
Lux Foundation, Miranda
Lyndhurst Foundation
Lyons Foundation
Lytel Foundation, Bertha Russ
MacDonald Foundation, James A.
Macht Foundation, Morton and
Sophia
Maclellan Foundation
Maddox Foundation, J. F.
Maier Foundation, Sarah Pauline
Manoogian Foundation, Alex
and Marie
Marbrook Foundation
Margoes Foundation
Maritz Inc.
Marley Co.
Marpat Foundation
Marriott Corp.
Marshall Foundation, Mattie H.
Marshall Trust in Memory of
Sanders McDaniel, Harriet
McDaniel
Massachusetts Charitable
Mechanics Association
Massachusetts Mutual Life
Insurance Co.
Massengill-DeFriece Foundation
Material Service Corp.
May Department Stores Co.
May Foundation, Wilbur
Maytag Family Foundation, Fred

MBIA, Inc.
McCasland Foundation
McCormick Tribune Foundation,
Robert R.
McDermott Foundation, Eugene
McDonough Foundation, Bernard
McFeely-Rogers Foundation
McGee Foundation
McGraw Foundation
MCI Communications Corp.
McKee Foundation, Robert E.
and Evelyn
McKee Poor Fund, Virginia A.
McKenna Foundation, Philip M.
McKesson Corp.
McNutt Charitable Trust, Amy
Shelton
Meadows Foundation
Melville Corp.
Memorial Foundation for
Children
Mercantile Bancorp
Meredith Corp.
Mericos Foundation
Merit Oil Corp.
Merrion Foundation
Meyer Foundation, Eugene and
Agnes E.
Mid-Iowa Health Foundation
Midwest Resources
Mills Fund, Frances Goll
Mingenback Foundation, Julia J.
Minnesota Foundation
Minnesota Mutual Life
Insurance Co.
Moncrief Foundation, William
A. and Elizabeth B.
Montgomery Street Foundation
Moore Charitable Foundation,
Marjorie
Moore Foundation
Moore Foundation, Roy C.
Morley Brothers Foundation
Morris Foundation, Margaret T.
Moses Fund, Henry and Lucy
Mosher Foundation, Samuel B.
Moss Charitable Trust, Finis M.
Mott Fund, Ruth
Mulcahy Foundation
Muller Foundation
Munson Foundation, W. B.
Murphy Foundation
Murphy Foundation, John P.
Murphy Foundation, Katherine
and John
Nalco Chemical Co.
National City Bank, Columbus
National Computer Systems
National Forge Co.
National Life of Vermont
National Starch & Chemical
Corp.
NBD Bank
NBD Bank, N.A.
NEC USA
Needmor Fund
Nellie Mae
Nestle U.S.A. Inc.
New England Business Service
New England Mutual Life
Insurance Co.
New Horizon Foundation
New Prospect Foundation
New Street Capital Corp.
New York Foundation
Noble Foundation, Vivian Bilby
Nomura Securities International
Norcliffe Fund
Norfolk Southern Corp.
Northeast Utilities
Northern Indiana Public Service
Co.
Northern States Power Co.
Northwest Natural Gas Co.
Northwestern National Life
Insurance Co.
Norton Foundation Inc.

Norwest Corp.
Noyes, Jr. Memorial Foundation,
Nicholas H.
N've Shalom Foundation
O'Brien Foundation, Alice M.
O'Connor Foundation, A.
Lindsay and Olive B.
O'Connor Foundation, Kathryn
Oglebay Norton Co.
Ohio Bell Telephone Co.
Ohio National Life Insurance Co.
Ohrstrom Foundation
Onan Family Foundation
1525 Foundation
1957 Charity Trust
O'Neil Foundation, Casey Albert
T.
Ontario Corp.
Oppenstein Brothers Foundation
Orange Orphan Society
Ordean Foundation
Ortho Diagnostic Systems, Inc.
Owen Trust, B. B.
Owens-Corning Fiberglas Corp.
Owsley Foundation, Alvin and
Lucy
Oxford Foundation
Pacific Enterprises
Page Foundation, George B.
Palisades Educational Foundation
Palmer-Fry Memorial Trust, Lily
Parker Foundation
Patterson Charitable Fund, W. I.
Paul and C. Michael Paul
Foundation, Josephine Bay
Pax Christi Foundation
Payne Foundation, Frank E. and
Seba B.
Peabody Charitable Fund, Amelia
Pendergast-Weyer Foundation
Penney Foundation, James C.
Perkin-Elmer Corp.
Perkins Foundation, Joe and Lois
Perley Fund, Victor E.
Peters Foundation, Leon S.
Pew Charitable Trusts
Pfizer
Philadelphia Electric Co.
Phillips Family Foundation, L. E.
Phillips Foundation, Dr. P.
Phillips Trust, Edwin
Pilot Trust
Pioneer Trust Bank, NA
Piper Foundation
Polaroid Corp.
Post Foundation of D.C.,
Marjorie Merriweather
Pott Foundation, Herman T. and
Phenie R.
Potter Foundation, Justin and
Valere
Powell Family Foundation
PPG Industries
Pratt Memorial Fund
Price Foundation, Louis and
Harold
Priddy Foundation
Prince Corp.
Proctor Trust, Mortimer R.
Prouty Foundation, Olive Higgins
Providence Energy Corp.
Provident Life & Accident
Insurance Co.
Prudential Insurance Co. of
America
Public Welfare Foundation
Puget Sound Power & Light Co.
Quinlan Foundation, Elizabeth C.
R. F. Foundation
Radiator Specialty Co.
Ramlose Foundation, George A.
Ratshesky Foundation, A. C.
Ray Foundation
Redman Foundation
Reeves Foundation
Reflection Riding
Relations Foundation

Reynolds Charitable Trust, Kate
B.
Reynolds Foundation, Richard S.
Reynolds Foundation, Z. Smith
Rice Foundation, Helen Steiner
Richardson Foundation, Sid W.
Richardson Fund, Mary Lynn
Ritchie Memorial Foundation,
Charies E. and Mabel M.
Ritter Charitable Trust, George
W. & Mary F.
RJR Nabisco Inc.
Robinson Foundation
Rockwell Foundation
Rockwell Fund
Rodman Foundation
Roe Foundation
Rogers Charitable Trust, Florence
Rohr Inc.
Rouse Co.
Royal Group Inc.
Rudy, Jr. Trust, George B.
Rutledge Charity, Edward
SAFECO Corp.
St. Mary's Catholic Foundation
Saint Paul Cos.
Salomon
Sams Foundation, Earl C.
San Diego Gas & Electric
Sandy Foundation, George H.
Sandy Hill Foundation
Santa Fe Pacific Corp.
Santa Maria Foundation
Sara Lee Corp.
Sara Lee Hosiery
Saturno Foundation
Saunders Foundation
Scaife Family Foundation
Scaler Foundation
Schenck Fund, L. P.
Scherman Foundation
Schiff, Hardin & Waite
Schlieder Educational
Foundation, Edward G.
Schrafft and Bertha E. Schrafft
Charitable Trust, William E.
Schramm Foundation
Schultz Foundation
Schwab & Co., Charles
Science Applications
International Corp.
Scott Foundation, Walter
Sears Family Foundation
Seay Memorial Trust, George
and Effie
Second Foundation
Sega of America
Semmes Foundation
Sharp Foundation, Charles S.
and Ruth C.
Shaw Foundation, Gardiner
Howland
Shaw Fund for Mariner's
Children
Shawmut National Corp.
Sheafer Charitable Trust, Emma
A.
Shell Oil Co.
Shenandoah Life Insurance Co.
Sheridan Foundation, Thomas B.
and Elizabeth M.
Shirk Foundation, Russell and
Betty
Shoemaker Fund, Thomas H.
and Mary Williams
Shoong Foundation, Milton
Simon Foundation, William E.
and Carol G.
Siragusa Foundation
Smith Charitable Trust, W. W.
Smith Corp., A.O.
Smith Foundation
Smith Horticultural Trust, Stanley
Smith, Jr. Foundation, M. W.
Smith Memorial Fund, Ethel
Sergeant Clark
Smith 1980 Charitable Trust,
Kelvin

Smithers Foundation,
Christopher D.
Snyder Foundation, Harold B.
and Dorothy A.
Snyder Fund, Valentine Perry
Society Corp.
Solo Cup Co.
Sooner Pipe & Supply Corp.
Soref Foundation, Samuel M.
Soref and Helene K.
South Waite Foundation
Sprague Educational and
Charitable Foundation, Seth
Sprint
Stabler Foundation, Donald B.
and Dorothy L.
Stackner Family Foundation
Stamps Foundation, James L.
Star Bank, N.A.
State Street Bank & Trust Co.
Stern Family Foundation, Alex
Stern Foundation, Irvin
Stern Foundation, Leonard N.
Stern Memorial Trust, Sidney
Stevens Foundation, Abbot and
Dorothy H.
Stevens Foundation, Nathaniel
and Elizabeth P.
Stewards Fund
Stewardship Foundation
Stewart Trust under the will of
Helen S. Devore, Alexander
and Margaret
Stewart Trust under the will of
Mary E. Stewart, Alexander
and Margaret
Stock Foundation, Paul
Stocker Foundation
Strawbridge Foundation of
Pennsylvania II, Margaret
Dorrance
Stride Rite Corp.
Stulsaft Foundation, Morris
Stupp Foundation, Norman J.
Subaru of America Inc.
Sulzberger Foundation
Sulzer Family Foundation
Sunderland Foundation, Lester T.
Swalm Foundation
Swim Foundation, Arthur L.
Taubman Foundation, A. Alfred
TCF Banking & Savings, FSB
Teleklew Productions
Templeton Foundation, Herbert
A.
Texas Gas Transmission Corp.
Thomas Memorial Foundation,
Theresa A.
Thornton Foundation
Thornton Foundation, John M.
and Sally B.
Thorpe Foundation, James R.
3M Co.
Thurman Charitable Foundation
for Children, Edgar A.
Time Insurance Co.
Tisch Foundation
Tonkin Foundation, Tom and
Helen
Town Creek Foundation
Towsley Foundation, Harry A.
and Margaret D.
Treuhaft Foundation
TRINOVA Corp.
True North Foundation
Trull Foundation
TRW Corp.
Tucker Charitable Trust, Rose E.
Turner Charitable Foundation
United Service Foundation
Unitrode Corp.
Universal Foods Corp.
US Bancorp
USF&G Co.
Vale-Asche Foundation
Valley Foundation
Van Evera Foundation, Dewitt
Caroline

Blue Cross/Blue Shield of Michigan
Bluhdorn Charitable Trust, Charles G. and Yvette
Blum Foundation, Edna F.
Boatmen's First National Bank of Oklahoma
Boehm Foundation
Bohen Foundation
Boise Cascade Corp.
Booth-Bricker Fund
Booth Ferris Foundation
Booz Allen & Hamilton
Borden Memorial Foundation, Mary Owen
Borg-Warner Corp.
Borman's
Boswell Foundation, James G.
Botwinick-Wolfensohn Foundation
Boulevard Foundation
Bowles and Robert Bowles Memorial Fund, Ethel Wilson
Bowne Foundation, Robert
BP America
Brach Foundation, Helen
Brackenridge Foundation, George W.
Bradley Foundation, Lynde and Harry
Brady Foundation, W. H.
Bremer Foundation, Otto
Brencanda Foundation
Bridgestone/Firestone
Bristol-Myers Squibb Co.
Bromley Residuary Trust, Guy I.
Brookdale Foundation
Brother International Corp.
Brown Charitable Trust, Dora Maclellan
Brown Foundation
Brown Foundation, James Graham
Browning Charitable Foundation, Val A.
Browning-Ferris Industries
Bruening Foundation, Eva L. and Joseph M.
Bruner Foundation
Brunswick Corp.
Brush Foundation
Buck Foundation, Carol Franc
Bucyrus-Erie
Buhl Foundation
Bullitt Foundation
Burden Foundation, Florence V.
Burkitt Foundation
Burlington Industries
Bush Charitable Foundation, Edyth
Bush Foundation
Butler Family Foundation, Patrick and Aimee
Butler Foundation, J. Homer
Bydale Foundation
C.I.O.S.
Cabell III and Maude Morgan Cabell Foundation, Robert G.
Cablevision of Michigan
Cabot Corp.
Cabot Family Charitable Trust
Cafritz Foundation, Morris and Gwendolyn
Cain Foundation, Effie and Wofford
Caine Charitable Foundation, Marie Eccles
Calder Foundation, Louis
California Educational Initiatives Fund
Campbell and Adah E. Hall Charity Fund, Bushrod H.
Campbell Soup Co.
Cannon Foundation
Capital Holding Corp.
Cargill
Carnahan-Jackson Foundation

Carnegie Corporation of New York
Carolyn Foundation
Carpenter Foundation, E. Rhodes and Leona B.
Carrier Corp.
Carteh Foundation
Carter Family Foundation
Carter Foundation, Amon G.
Carver Charitable Trust, Roy J.
Cary Charitable Trust, Mary Flagler
Cascade Natural Gas Corp.
Casey Foundation, Annie E.
Castle Foundation, Harold K. L.
Castle Foundation, Samuel N. and Mary
Castle Trust, George P. and Ida Tenney
Caterpillar
CBS Inc.
Centel Corp.
Central Maine Power Co.
CertainTeed Corp.
Cessna Aircraft Co.
Challenge Foundation
Champion International Corp.
Chase Charity Foundation, Alfred E.
Chase Lincoln First Bank, N.A.
Chase Manhattan Bank, N.A.
Chase Trust, Alice P.
Chatlos Foundation
Cheatham Foundation, Owen
Chemical Bank
Cheney Foundation, Ben B.
Chesebrough-Pond's
Chevron Corp.
Chicago Title and Trust Co.
Chicago Tribune Co.
Chiles Foundation
China Medical Board of New York
Christodora
Chrysler Corp.
Ciba-Geigy Corp. (Pharmaceuticals Division)
CIGNA Corp.
Cincinnati Bell
Citicorp
Citizens Commercial & Savings Bank
CLARCOR
Clark Foundation, Edna McConnell
Clorox Co.
CM Alliance Cos.
Coca-Cola Co.
Cockrell Foundation
Cole Foundation, Olive B.
Coleman Co.
Coleman Foundation
Collins Foundation
Colorado Trust
Columbia Foundation
Columbus Dispatch Printing Co.
Comerica
Commerce Clearing House
Commonwealth Fund
Compton Foundation
Comstock Foundation
ConAgra
Conn Memorial Foundation
Connecticut Natural Gas Corp.
Connell Foundation, Michael J.
Conoco Inc.
Consolidated Papers
Constantin Foundation
Consumers Power Co.
Continental Bank N.A.
Continental Corp.
Contran Corp.
Control Data Corp.
Cook Inlet Region
Cooke Foundation
Cooper Industries
Coors Brewing Co.

Coors Foundation, Adolph
Copley Press
Copperweld Steel Co.
Corbett Foundation
Cornerstone Foundation of Northeastern Wisconsin
Corning Incorporated
Cosmair, Inc.
Cove Charitable Trust
Cow Hollow Foundation
Cowden Foundation, Louetta M.
Cowell Foundation, S. H.
Cowles Charitable Trust
Cox Charitable Trust, Jessie B.
Cox Enterprises
Cox Foundation
Cox, Jr. Foundation, James M.
CPC International
CR Industries
Cray Research
CRI Charitable Trust
Crocker Trust, Mary A.
Crowell Trust, Henry P. and Susan C.
Crown Central Petroleum Corp.
Cudahy Fund, Patrick and Anna M.
Cullen Foundation
Cullen/Frost Bankers
Culpeper Foundation, Charles E.
Cummings Foundation, James H.
Cummings Foundation, Nathan
Cummings Memorial Fund Trust, Frances L. and Edwin L.
Cummins Engine Co.
Curtice-Burns Foods
Dalton Foundation, Dorothy U.
Dammann Fund
Dana Charitable Trust, Eleanor Naylor
Dana Foundation, Charles A.
Danforth Foundation
Daniels Foundation, Fred Harris
Dater Foundation, Charles H.
Davenport-Hatch Foundation
Davidson Family Charitable Foundation
Davis Foundation, Edwin W. and Catherine M.
Davis Foundation, Joe C.
Davis Foundations, Arthur Vining
Dayton Hudson Corp.
Dayton Power and Light Co.
de Hirsch Fund, Baron
DeCamp Foundation, Ira W.
Deer Creek Foundation
Deere & Co.
DeKalb Genetics Corp.
Deluxe Corp.
DeMoss Foundation, Arthur S.
DeRoy Testamentary Foundation
Detroit Edison Co.
Devereaux Foundation
DeVore Foundation
DeVos Foundation, Richard and Helen
Dewing Foundation, Frances R.
Dexter Corp.
Diamond Foundation, Aaron
Diamond Walnut Growers
Dibner Fund
Dietrich Foundation, William B.
Digital Equipment Corp.
Dixie Yarns, Inc.
Dodge Foundation, Cleveland H.
Dodge Foundation, Geraldine R.
Dodson Foundation, James Glenwell and Clara May
Doheny Foundation, Carrie Estelle
Domino's Pizza
Donaldson Co.
Donnelley Foundation, Gaylord and Dorothy
Donnelley & Sons Co., R.R.
Donnelly Foundation, Mary J.
Donner Foundation, William H.

Dorr Foundation
Doss Foundation, M. S.
Dougherty, Jr. Foundation, James R.
Douglas & Lomason Company
Dover Foundation
Dow Chemical Co.
Dresser Industries
Dreyfus Foundation, Camille and Henry
Dreyfus Foundation, Max and Victoria
Drown Foundation, Joseph
Drum Foundation
du Pont de Nemours & Co., E. I.
Duchossois Industries
Duke Endowment
Duke Power Co.
Dunagan Foundation
Duncan Trust, John G.
Dunn Foundation, Elizabeth Ordway
Dunspaugh-Dalton Foundation
Dupar Foundation
duPont Fund, Jessie Ball
Durfee Foundation
Dyson Foundation
Earl-Beth Foundation
Eastern Enterprises
Eastman Kodak Co.
Eaton Foundation, Cyrus
Eccles Foundation, George S. and Dolores Dore
Eccles Foundation, Marriner S.
Echlin Inc.
Eckerd Corp., Jack
Eddy Family Memorial Fund, C. K.
Eden Hall Foundation
Edison Fund, Charles
Educational Foundation of America
Edwards Foundation, O. P. and W. E.
El Pomar Foundation
Electronic Data Systems Corp.
Emergency Aid of Pennsylvania Foundation
Emerson Electric Co.
Emerson Foundation, Fred L.
Enron Corp.
Ensign-Bickford Industries
Enterprise Rent-A-Car Co.
Equitable Life Assurance Society of the U.S.
Evans Foundation, Lettie Pate
Evjue Foundation
Exxon Corp.
Factor Family Foundation, Max
Fairchild Foundation, Sherman
Falk Foundation, David
Falk Medical Fund, Maurice
Farish Fund, William Stamps
Farmers Group, Inc.
Federal Express Corp.
Federal Home Loan Mortgage Corp. (Freddie Mac)
Federal National Mortgage Assn., Fannie Mae
Federated Department Stores and Allied Stores Corp.
Federated Life Insurance Co.
Feinstein Foundation, Myer and Rosaline
Fel-Pro Incorporated
Feldman Foundation
Fels Fund, Samuel S.
Fidelity Bank
Field Foundation of Illinois
Fieldcrest Cannon
Fifth Third Bancorp
Fikes Foundation, Leland
Filene Foundation, Lincoln and Therese
FINA, Inc.
Fingerhut Family Foundation
Finley Charitable Trust, J. B.

Fireman's Fund Insurance Co.
First Bank System
First Chicago
First Fidelity Bancorporation
First Fruit
First Hawaiian
First Interstate Bank NW Region
First Interstate Bank of Arizona
First Interstate Bank of California
First Interstate Bank of Oregon
First Interstate Bank of Texas, N.A.
First Mississippi Corp.
First of America Bank Corp.
First Tennessee Bank
First Union Corp.
Flarsheim Charitable Foundation, Louis and Elizabeth
Fleet Financial Group
Fleishhacker Foundation
Flinn Foundation
Florence Foundation
Fluor Corp.
Foellinger Foundation
Foley, Hoag & Eliot
Fondren Foundation
Ford Foundation
Ford Foundation, Edward E.
Ford Fund, Benson and Edith
Ford Fund, Walter and Josephine
Ford Motor Co.
Forest Foundation
Foster Foundation
Foundation for Child Development
Foundation for Seacoast Health
Fourth Financial Corp.
Fowler Memorial Foundation, John Edward
France Foundation, Jacob and Annita
Franklin Foundation, John and Mary
Fraser Paper Ltd.
Frederick Foundation
Freed Foundation
Freedom Forum
Freeman Foundation, Carl M.
Freeport-McMoRan
Frees Foundation
Freightliner Corp.
Frick Educational Commission, Henry C.
Friendship Fund
Frueauff Foundation, Charles A.
Fry Foundation, Lloyd A.
Fuchs Foundation, Gottfried & Mary
Fuller Co., H.B.
Fullerton Foundation
Fund for New Jersey
Funderburke & Associates
Fusenot Charity Foundation, Georges and Germaine
Gannett Co.
Gannett Publishing Co., Guy
Gap, The
GAR Foundation
Garvey Trust, Olive White
GATX Corp.
Gault-Hussey Charitable Trust
Gebbie Foundation
Geffen Foundation, David
GEICO Corp.
Gellert Foundation, Carl
Gellert Foundation, Celia Berta
Gellert Foundation, Fred
General American Life Insurance Co.
General Electric Co.
General Mills
General Motors Corp.
General Railway Signal Corp.
General Service Foundation
George Foundation
Georgia Health Foundation

Project (cont.)

Bechtel Group
Beck Foundation
Beckman Foundation, Arnold and Mabel
Beeson Charitable Trust, Dwight M.
Bell Communications Research
Bellamah Foundation, Dale J.
Bellini Foundation
Benbough Foundation, Legler
Benedum Foundation, Claude Worthington
Benefit Trust Life Insurance Co.
Benton Foundation
Berkowitz Family Foundation, Louis
Berry Foundation, Archie W. and Grace
Bethlehem Steel Corp.
Bettingen Corporation, Burton G.
Biddle Foundation, Margaret T.
Biological Humanics Foundation
Birch Foundation, Stephen and Mary
Bishop Foundation
Black & Veatch
Blount
Blowitz-Ridgeway Foundation
Blue Cross/Blue Shield of Michigan
Bluhdorn Charitable Trust, Charles G. and Yvette
Bobst Foundation, Elmer and Mamdouha
Boehringer Mannheim Corp.
Bonfils-Stanton Foundation
Booth-Bricker Fund
Boothroyd Foundation, Charles H. and Bertha L.
Booz Allen & Hamilton
Bosque Foundation
Bostwick Foundation, Albert C.
Botwinick-Wolfensohn Foundation
Bovaird Foundation, Mervin
Bozzone Family Foundation
Brackenridge Foundation, George W.
Bradley Foundation, Lynde and Harry
Brady Foundation, W. H.
Bristol-Myers Squibb Co.
Broadhurst Foundation
Brookdale Foundation
Brown Foundation
Brown Foundation, Joe W. and Dorothy Dorsett
Brown & Williamson Tobacco Corp.
Browning-Ferris Industries
Bruner Foundation
Bruno Charitable Foundation, Joseph S.
Brunswick Corp.
Brush Foundation
Buehler Foundation, A. C.
Buehler Foundation, Emil
Bugher Foundation
Buhl Foundation
Burden Foundation, Florence V.
Burkitt Foundation
Burnham Donor Fund, Alfred G.
Burns Foundation, Jacob
Burroughs Wellcome Co.
Butz Foundation
Bydale Foundation
Cabot Corp.
Cain Foundation, Gordon and Mary
California Foundation for Biochemical Research
Camp Foundation
Campbell Foundation, Charles Talbot
Cape Branch Foundation
Capita Charitable Trust, Emil
Capital Holding Corp.

Carnegie Corporation of New York
Carpenter Foundation
Carteh Foundation
Carthage Foundation
Carver Charitable Trust, Roy J.
Casey Foundation, Annie E.
Caspersen Foundation for Aid to Health and Education, O. W.
CBI Industries
Central Maine Power Co.
Central Soya Co.
Chadwick Foundation
Chait Memorial Foundation, Sara
Charles River Laboratories
Chernow Trust for the Benefit of Charity Dated 3/13/75, Michael
Chevron Corp.
Chiles Foundation
Church & Dwight Co.
Ciba-Geigy Corp. (Pharmaceuticals Division)
Cincinnati Enquirer
Citicorp
Clark Family Charitable Trust, Andrew L.
Clark Foundation, Edna McConnell
Clark Foundation, Robert Sterling
Cleveland-Cliffs
Clowes Fund
Coastal Corp.
Cole Foundation, Robert H. and Monica H.
Coleman Co.
Coleman, Jr. Foundation, George E.
Collins Foundation, James M.
Collins Medical Trust
Colorado National Bankshares
Columbia Savings Charitable Foundation
Comer Foundation
Cominco American Inc.
Commerce Clearing House
Commonwealth Fund
Compton Foundation
Conoco Inc.
Cook Inlet Region
Cooper Foundation
Cosmair, Inc.
Cox Foundation
CPC International
CR Industries
Crail-Johnson Foundation
Crump Fund, Joe and Jessie
Culpeper Foundation, Charles E.
Cummings Foundation, James H.
Currey Foundation, Brownlee
Cyprus Minerals Co.
Dalsimer Fund, Craig
Dalton Foundation, Dorothy U.
Dammann Fund
Dana Corp.
Davis Foundation, Edwin W. and Catherine M.
Davis Foundation, Joe C.
de Hirsch Fund, Baron
Debartolo Foundation, Marie P.
DeCamp Foundation, Ira W.
Dee Foundation, Lawrence T. and Janet T.
DeKalb Genetics Corp.
Delaware North Cos.
Dexter Corp.
Diabetes Research and Education Foundation
Diamond Foundation, Aaron
Dietrich Foundation, William B.
Digital Equipment Corp.
Dillon Foundation
Dimick Foundation
Dodge Foundation, Geraldine R.
Dodson Foundation, James Glenwell and Clara May

Doheny Foundation, Carrie Estelle
Doherty Charitable Foundation, Henry L. and Grace
Donaldson Charitable Trust, Oliver S. and Jennie R.
Donner Foundation, William H.
Dorr Foundation
Dougherty, Jr. Foundation, James R.
Douglas & Lomason Company
Dow Chemical Co.
Dow Foundation, Herbert H. and Grace A.
Dresser Industries
Dreyfus Foundation, Jean and Louis
Dreyfus Foundation, Max and Victoria
Driscoll Foundation
Drum Foundation
du Pont de Nemours & Co., E. I.
Duke Endowment
Dumke Foundation, Dr. Ezekiel R. and Edna Wattis
Duncan Trust, John G.
Dunn Research Foundation, John S.
Dunspaugh-Dalton Foundation
Dupar Foundation
Duriron Co., Inc.
Earhart Foundation
Early Medical Research Trust, Margaret E.
Eastman Kodak Co.
Eccles Charitable Foundation, Willard L.
Eckman Charitable Foundation, Samuel and Rae
Eddy Foundation
Eden Hall Foundation
Edgerton Foundation, Harold E.
Edison Foundation, Harry
Edison Fund, Charles
Educational Foundation of America
Ellwood Foundation
Emerson Foundation, Fred L.
English-Bonter-Mitchell Foundation
Enron Corp.
Ensign-Bickford Industries
Equitable Life Assurance Society of the U.S.
Ernest & Julio Gallo Winery
Erteszek Foundation
Essel Foundation
Evans Foundation, T. M.
Evinrude Foundation, Ralph
Exxon Corp.
Factor Family Foundation, Max
Fairchild Foundation, Sherman
Falcon Foundation
Falk Foundation, David
Falk Medical Research Foundation, Dr. Ralph and Marian
Farish Fund, William Stamps
Farnsworth Trust, Charles A.
Favrot Fund
Federal-Mogul Corp.
Femino Foundation
Ferkauf Foundation, Eugene and Estelle
Fikes Foundation, Leland
Fingerhut Family Foundation
Finley Foundation, A. E.
Firan Foundation
First Mississippi Corp.
Fish Foundation, Ray C.
Flinn Foundation
Foerderer Foundation, Percival E. and Ethel Brown
Fondren Foundation
Forchheimer Memorial Foundation Trust, Louise and Josie
Ford Foundation

Ford II Fund, Henry
Ford III Memorial Foundation, Jefferson Lee
Ford Motor Co.
Forest Oil Corp.
Foster Foundation
Foster Foundation, Joseph C. and Esther
Foundation for Advancement of Chiropractic Education
Foundation for Child Development
Foundation for Middle East Peace
Fourth Financial Corp.
Fox Foundation, Richard J.
Francis Families Foundation
Franklin Electric Company Inc. (Bluffton, Indiana)
Franklin Foundation, John and Mary
Frasch Foundation for Chemical Research (under the will of Elizabeth B. Frasch), Herman
Freedom Forum
Freeport-McMoRan
Freightliner Corp.
Frick Educational Commission, Henry C.
Frohman Foundation, Sidney
Frost Foundation
Frueauff Foundation, Charles A.
Fry Foundation, Lloyd A.
Fuchs Foundation, Gottfried & Mary
Fund for New Jersey
Funderburke & Associates
Fusenot Charity Foundation, Georges and Germaine
Gaisman Foundation, Catherine and Henry J.
Gardner Charitable Foundation, Edith D.
Garner Charitable Trust, James G.
Garvey Texas Foundation
GEICO Corp.
Geist Foundation
Gellert Foundation, Carl
Gellert Foundation, Celia Berta
Gellert Foundation, Fred
Gelman Foundation, Melvin and Estelle
Genentech
General American Life Insurance Co.
General Development Corp.
General Electric Co.
General Motors Corp.
Georgia Health Foundation
Georgia Power Co.
Gerard Foundation, Sumner
German Marshall Fund of the United States
Gerschel Foundation, Patrick A.
Getty Trust, J. Paul
Gheens Foundation
Giant Eagle
Gifford Charitable Corporation, Rosamond
Gillette Co.
Gilmer-Smith Foundation
Gleason Memorial Fund
Glenn Foundation for Medical Research, Paul F.
Glickenhaus & Co.
Goddard Foundation, Charles B.
Goldman Foundation, William
Goldwyn Foundation, Samuel
Goode Trust, Mae Stone
Goodman & Company
Goodyear Foundation, Josephine
Gould Inc.
Gould Foundation, Florence J.
Graham Foundation for Advanced Studies in the Fine Arts
Grainger Foundation

Grant Foundation, William T.
Graphic Arts Show Co. Inc.
Graphic Controls Corp.
Grass Foundation
Great-West Life Assurance Co.
Greater Lansing Foundation
Greenwall Foundation
Greve Foundation, William and Mary
Gries Charity Fund, Lucile and Robert H.
Gross Foundation, Louis H.
Grotto Foundation
Gruber Research Foundation, Lila
Gudelsky Family Foundation, Isadore and Bertha
Guggenheim Foundation, Daniel and Florence
Guggenheim Foundation, Harry Frank
Gulton Foundation
Gumenick Foundation, Nathan and Sophie
Gund Foundation, Geoffrey
Haas Foundation, Paul and Mary
Haigh-Scatena Foundation
Hales Charitable Fund
Halff Foundation, G. A. C.
Halsell Foundation, Ewing
Hamman Foundation, George and Mary Josephine
Hammer Foundation, Armand
Hanes Foundation, John W. and Anna H.
Hankamer Foundation, Curtis and Doris K.
Hansen Memorial Foundation, Irving
Hardin Foundation, Phil
Harriman Foundation, Mary W.
Harris Foundation, John H. and Lucille
Harsco Corp.
Hartmarx Corp.
Hawn Foundation
Haynes Foundation, John Randolph and Dora
Hayward Foundation Charitable Trust, John T. and Winifred
Hearst Foundation
Hearst Foundation, William Randolph
Heinz Endowment, Vira I.
Helfaer Foundation, Evan and Marion
Hemingway Foundation, Robert G.
Hermann Foundation, Grover
Herrick Foundation
Hershey Foods Corp.
Hervey Foundation
Herzog Foundation, Carl J.
Higginson Trust, Corina
Hill Crest Foundation
Hill Foundation
Hillcrest Foundation
Hilton Foundation, Conrad N.
Himmelfarb Foundation, Paul and Annetta
Hoag Family Foundation, George
Hoechst Celanese Corp.
Hoffman Foundation, John Ernest
Hoffmann-La Roche
Hofmann Co.
Holden Fund, James and Lynelle
Holt Foundation, William Knox
Homeland Foundation
Honda of America Manufacturing, Inc.
Hood Foundation, Charles H.
Hooper Foundation, Elizabeth S.
Hoover, Jr. Foundation, Margaret W. and Herbert
Hornblower Fund, Henry
Horne Trust, Mabel
Houston Industries

Research (cont.)

Hughes Charitable Trust, Mabel Y.
Hughes Medical Institute, Howard
Hughes Memorial Foundation, Charles Evans
Hugoton Foundation
Huisking Foundation
Hulings Foundation, Mary Andersen
Humana
Humane Society of the Commonwealth of Massachusetts
Humphrey Fund, George M. and Pamela S.
Hunt Foundation, Roy A.
Hunt Foundation, Samuel P.
Hyde and Watson Foundation
Iacocca Foundation
IBM Corp.
IMCERA Group Inc.
Ingalls Foundation, Louise H. and David S.
Ira-Hiti Foundation for Deep Ecology
Iroquois Avenue Foundation
Irwin Charity Foundation, William G.
Island Foundation
Israel Discount Bank of New York
ITT Hartford Insurance Group
ITT Rayonier
Jackson Foundation
Jameson Foundation, J. W. and Ida M.
Jeffress Memorial Trust, Thomas F. and Kate Miller
Jesselson Foundation
JM Foundation
Johnson Co., E. F.
Johnson Foundation, A. D.
Johnson Foundation, Barbara P.
Johnson Foundation, Walter S.
Johnson & Johnson
Julia R. and Estelle L. Foundation
Kade Foundation, Max
Kaiser Family Foundation, Henry J.
Kaplan Foundation, Rita J. and Stanley H.
Kaplun Foundation, Morris J. and Betty
Kaufmann Foundation, Marion Esser
Kavanagh Foundation, T. James
Kayser Foundation
Keck Foundation, W. M.
Kelley and Elza Kelley Foundation, Edward Bangs
Kemper Foundation, William T.
Kemper National Insurance Cos.
Kempner Fund, Harris and Eliza
Kenridge Fund
Kentucky Foundation for Women
Kerr Foundation
Kettering Family Foundation
Kettering Fund
Kevorkian Fund, Hagop
Kidder, Peabody & Co.
Kieckhefer Foundation, J. W.
Killough Trust, Walter H. D.
Kilworth Charitable Foundation, Florence B.
Kimmelman Foundation, Helen & Milton
King Ranch
King Trust, Charles A.
Kirchgessner Foundation, Karl
Kleberg, Jr. and Helen C. Kleberg Foundation, Robert J.
Kline Foundation, Josiah W. and Bessie H.

Klingenstein Fund, Esther A. and Joseph
Klingler Foundation, Helen and Charles
Knowles Foundation
Koehler Foundation, Marcia and Otto
Kohl Charities, Herbert H.
Komes Foundation
KPMG Peat Marwick
Kress Foundation, Samuel H.
Kulas Foundation
Kynett Memorial Foundation, Edna G.
Laerdal Foundation, Asmund S.
Lalor Foundation
Lane Foundation, Winthrop and Frances
Lard Trust, Mary Potishman
Larsen Fund
Lasdon Foundation
Lawrence Foundation, Lind
Leavey Foundation, Thomas and Dorothy
LeBrun Foundation
Lee Foundation, James T.
Lemberg Foundation
Leonhardt Foundation, Dorothea L.
Levee Charitable Trust, Polly Annenberg
Levy Foundation, June Rockwell
Life Sciences Research Foundation
Lightner Sams Foundation
Lilly Endowment
Lilly Foundation, Richard Coyle
Lincoln National Corp.
Lingnan Foundation
Littauer Foundation, Lucius N.
Litton/Itek Optical Systems
Lockheed Corp.
Loose Trust, Carrie J.
Loose Trust, Harry Wilson
Lounsbery Foundation, Richard
Love Charitable Foundation, John Allan
LTV Corp.
Lucas Cancer Foundation, Richard M.
Luce Foundation, Henry
Lydall, Inc.
M. E. G. Foundation
MacArthur Foundation, J. Roderick
MacArthur Foundation, John D. and Catherine T.
MacDonald Foundation, James A.
Macht Foundation, Morton and Sophia
MacKall and Evanina Evans Bell MacKall Trust, Paul
Maclellan Foundation
Mailman Family Foundation, A. L.
Mallinckrodt, Jr. Foundation, Edward
Mallinckrodt Specialty Chemicals Co.
Manning and Emma Austin Manning Foundation, James Hilton
Mapplethorpe Foundation, Robert
Marbrook Foundation
Mardag Foundation
Margoes Foundation
Marion Merrell Dow
Markey Charitable Trust, Lucille P.
Markle Foundation, John and Mary R.
Marmot Foundation
Marpat Foundation
Mars Foundation
Martin Foundation, Della
Mary Kay Foundation
Masserini Charitable Trust, Maurice J.

Massey Charitable Trust
Massey Foundation, Jack C.
Mathers Charitable Foundation, G. Harold and Leila Y.
Maxfield Foundation
May Foundation, Wilbur
May Mitchell Royal Foundation
Mayer Foundation, Louis B.
Maytag Family Foundation, Fred
McConnell Foundation, Neil A.
McDermott Foundation, Eugene
McDonnell Douglas Corp.-West
McDonnell Foundation, James S.
McFawn Trust No. 2, Lois Sisler
McGonagle Foundation, Dextra Baldwin
McGovern Foundation, John P.
McGraw Foundation
MCI Communications Corp.
McKee Foundation, Robert E. and Evelyn
McKenna Foundation, Philip M.
McKnight Foundation
Mead Foundation, Giles W. and Elise G.
Meadows Foundation
Mellon Bank Corp.
Mellon Foundation, Andrew W.
Menil Foundation
Merck Family Fund
Merck Fund, John
Merrill Foundation, R. D.
Messing Family Charitable Foundation
Metropolitan Life Insurance Co.
Meyer Foundation
Meyer Foundation, Baron de Hirsch
Meyer Foundation, Eugene and Agnes E.
Meyer Foundation, Robert R.
Midwest Resources
Milken Family Medical Foundation
Milken Foundation, L. and S.
Miller Fund, Kathryn and Gilbert
Millipore Corp.
Mills Charitable Foundation, Henry L. and Kathryn
Millstein Charitable Foundation
Millstone Foundation
Mitchell Energy & Development Corp.
Mitchell Family Foundation, Bernard and Marjorie
Mitsubishi International Corp.
Mobil Oil Corp.
Mobility Foundation
Monell Foundation, Ambrose
Monroe Foundation (1976), J. Edgar
Moody Foundation
Moore Foundation, Roy C.
Moriah Fund
Morley Brothers Foundation
Morris Foundation
Morris Foundation, William T.
Moss Heart Trust, Harry S.
Mulcahy Foundation
Mulligan Charitable Trust, Mary S.
Murdock Charitable Trust, M. J.
Murfee Endowment, Kathryn
Murphey Foundation, Lluella Morey
Murphy Foundation, John P.
National Center for Automated Information Retrieval
National Starch & Chemical Corp.
National Westminster Bank New Jersey
NEC USA
New England Biolabs Foundation
New England Foundation
New England Mutual Life Insurance Co.
New York Mercantile Exchange

New York Times Co.
Newhouse Foundation, Samuel I.
Newmont Mining Corp.
News & Observer Publishing Co.
Nichols Foundation
Noble Charitable Trust, John L. and Ethel G.
Noble Foundation, Samuel Roberts
Nordson Corp.
Norfolk Southern Corp.
Norris Foundation, Kenneth T. and Eileen L.
Northern Telecom Inc.
Northwest Area Foundation
Northwest Natural Gas Co.
Northwestern National Life Insurance Co.
Obernauer Foundation
O'Brien Foundation, Alice M.
O'Donnell Foundation
Ohio National Life Insurance Co.
Ohl, Jr. Trust, George A.
Oki America Inc.
Olin Charitable Trust, John M.
Olin Foundation, John M.
Olin Foundation, Spencer T. and Ann W.
1957 Charity Trust
O'Neil Foundation, Casey Albert T.
Open Society Fund
Ortho Diagnostic Systems, Inc.
O'Shaughnessy Foundation, I. A.
O'Toole Foundation, Theresa and Edward
Oxnard Foundation
Pacific Mutual Life Insurance Co.
Packard Foundation, David and Lucile
PaineWebber
Palmer Fund, Frank Loomis
Pan-American Life Insurance Co.
Panhandle Eastern Corp.
Pappas Charitable Foundation, Thomas Anthony
Pardee Foundation, Elsa U.
Parke-Davis Group
Parker Foundation
Parker, Jr. Foundation, William A.
Parsons - W.D. Charities, Vera Davis
Patterson and Clara Guthrie Patterson Trust, Robert Leet
Patterson Charitable Fund, W. I.
Pearce Foundation, Dr. M. Lee
Peierls Foundation
Pennzoil Co.
Perkin-Elmer Corp.
Peters Foundation, R. D. and Linda
Petersen Foundation, Esper A.
Pew Charitable Trusts
Pfeiffer Research Foundation, Gustavus and Louise
Pfizer
Phelps Dodge Corp.
Philippe Foundation
Phillips Family Foundation, Jay and Rose
Phillips Family Foundation, L. E.
Phillips Petroleum Co.
Pines Bridge Foundation
Pioneer Fund
Pioneer Trust Bank, NA
Pittsburgh Child Guidance Foundation
Plitt Southern Theatres
Poncin Scholarship Fund
Pope Foundation
Potts Memorial Foundation
Powell Foundation, Charles Lee
PPG Industries
Pratt Memorial Fund
Prentiss Foundation, Elisabeth Severance
Preuss Foundation

Price Waterhouse-U.S.
Prince Trust, Abbie Norman
Pritzker Foundation
Procter & Gamble Cosmetic & Fragrance Products
Psychists
Puett Foundation, Nelson
Quantum Chemical Corp.
Quest for Truth Foundation
Quinlan Foundation, Elizabeth C.
Ramapo Trust
Ramlose Foundation, George A.
Ranney Foundation, P. K.
Rasmussen Foundation
Ratner Foundation, Milton M.
Rauch Foundation
Ray Foundation
Rennebohm Foundation, Oscar
Research Corporation
Retirement Research Foundation
Revson Foundation, Charles H.
Reynolds Foundation, Christopher
Reynolds Foundation, Edgar
Reynolds Foundation, J. B.
Reynolds Foundation, Richard S.
RGK Foundation
Rhone-Poulenc Rorer
Richardson Foundation, Sid W.
Richardson Foundation, Smith
Richardson Fund, Grace
Richmond Foundation, Frederick W.
Rider-Pool Foundation
Rippel Foundation, Fannie E.
RJR Nabisco Inc.
Roberts Foundation, Summerfield G.
Robertshaw Controls Co.
Robinson Foundation
Robinson Foundation, J. Mack
Rockefeller Foundation
Rockwell Fund
Roehl Foundation
RosaMary Foundation
Rosenberg Family Foundation, William
Rosenberg, Jr. Family Foundation, Louise and Claude
Rosenthal Foundation, Richard and Hinda
Rosenthal Foundation, Samuel
Rosenthal-Statter Foundation
Ross Foundation
Ross Laboratories
Roth Foundation
Rowland Foundation
Rubenstein Foundation, Philip
Rubinstein Foundation, Helena
Rudin Foundation, Louis and Rachel
Ryland Group
Sagamore Foundation
Sage Foundation
Sage Foundation, Russell
St. Giles Foundation
St. Mary's Catholic Foundation
Saltonstall Charitable Foundation, Richard
Saltz Foundation, Gary
San Diego Gas & Electric
Sandoz Corp.
Sarkeys Foundation
Scaife Foundation, Sarah
Schamach Foundation, Milton
Schepp Foundation, Leopold
Schering-Plough Corp.
Scheuer Family Foundation, S. H. and Helen R.
Schiff Foundation
Schlieder Educational Foundation, Edward G.
Schlink Foundation, Albert G. and Olive H.
Schlumberger Ltd.
Scholler Foundation

Schottenstein Foundation, Jerome & Saul
Schroeder Foundation, Walter
Schultz Foundation
Schwartz Foundation, Bernard Lee
Science Applications International Corp.
Scott Foundation, Walter
Scurlock Foundation
Seagram & Sons, Joseph E.
Sealright Co., Inc.
Sears Family Foundation
Seaver Institute
Seebee Trust, Frances
Seeley Foundation
Seidman Family Foundation
Semmes Foundation
Seybert Institution for Poor Boys and Girls, Adam and Maria Sarah
Shapiro Family Foundation, Soretta and Henry
Shaw Fund for Mariner's Children
Shelden Fund, Elizabeth, Allan and Warren
Shell Oil Co.
Shelter Mutual Insurance Co.
Shoenberg Foundation
Shook Foundation, Barbara Ingalls
Shoong Foundation, Milton
Simon Charitable Trust, Esther
Simon Foundation, Jennifer Jones
Simon Foundation, Sidney, Milton and Leoma
Sinsheimer Fund, Alexandrine and Alexander L.
Siragusa Foundation
Skaggs Foundation, L. J. and Mary C.
Skillman Foundation
Slaughter Foundation, Charles
Slifka Foundation, Joseph and Sylvia
Sloan Foundation, Alfred P.
Smart Family Foundation
Smith Charitable Trust, W. W.
Smith Foundation, Julia and Albert
Smith Fund, George D.
Smith Horticultural Trust, Stanley
Smith, Jr. Foundation, M. W.
Smith Memorial Fund, Ethel Sergeant Clark
Smith 1980 Charitable Trust, Kelvin
Smithers Foundation, Christopher D.
Snow Memorial Trust, John Ben
Solo Cup Co.
Sonoco Products Co.
Soref Foundation, Samuel M. Soref and Helene K.
Soros Foundation-Hungary
South Branch Foundation
South Plains Foundation
Southland Corp.
Speas Memorial Trust, John W. and Effie E.
Speer Foundation, Roy M.
Spencer Foundation
Spingold Foundation, Nate B. and Frances
Sprague Memorial Institute, Otho S. A.
Spunk Fund
Square D Co.
Stackner Family Foundation
Stans Foundation
Stein Foundation, Joseph F.
Stein Foundation, Jules and Doris
Stein Roe & Farnham Investment Council
Steinbach Fund, Ruth and Milton
Steiner Charitable Fund, Albert

Steinhagen Benevolent Trust, B. A. and Elinor
Stern Memorial Trust, Sidney
Stocker Foundation
Stone Foundation, France
Stony Wold Herbert Fund
Stowers Foundation
Straus Foundation, Martha Washington Straus and Harry H.
Strauss Foundation
Strawbridge Foundation of Pennsylvania II, Margaret Dorrance
Stroud Foundation
Stupp Foundation, Norman J.
Sturgis Charitable and Educational Trust, Roy and Christine
Swanson Foundation
Swim Foundation, Arthur L.
Switzer Foundation
Tamko Asphalt Products
Tandem Computers
Tanner Cos.
Taubman Foundation, A. Alfred
Taubman Foundation, Herman P. and Sophia
Taylor Foundation, Fred and Harriett
Taylor Trust, Lydia M.
Technical Foundation of America
Technical Training Foundation
Tektronix
Teledyne
Tenneco
Texaco
Texas Instruments
Thagard Foundation
Thorpe Foundation, James R.
Timken Co.
Tinker Foundation
Tisch Foundation
Toms Foundation
Towsley Foundation, Harry A. and Margaret D.
Transamerica Corp.
Travelers Cos.
Treadwell Foundation, Nora Eccles
Treakle Foundation, J. Edwin
Treuhaft Foundation
Trimble Family Foundation, Robert Mize and Isa White
Trust Funds
TRW Corp.
Turner Charitable Foundation
Turner Fund, Ruth
Union Camp Corp.
United Dominion Industries
United Parcel Service of America
Universal Foods Corp.
Unocal Corp.
Upton Charitable Foundation, Lucy and Eleanor S.
V and V Foundation
Vale-Asche Foundation
Valero Energy Corp.
Valley Foundation, Wayne and Gladys
Valley National Bancorp
van Ameringen Foundation
Van Every Foundation, Philip L.
van Loben Sels - Eleanor Slate van Lobel Sels Charitable Foundation, Ernst D.
Vanneck-Bailey Foundation
Varian Associates
Vaughan Foundation, Rachael and Ben
Vaughn Foundation
Vaughn, Jr. Foundation Fund, James M.
Vernon Fund, Miles Hodsdon
Vicksburg Hospital Medical Foundation
Victoria Foundation
Vidda Foundation

Vollbrecht Foundation, Frederick A.
Vollrath Co.
Waggoner Charitable Trust, Crystelle
Waggoner Foundation, E. Paul and Helen Buck
Wahlstrom Foundation
Wal-Mart Stores
Walker Educational and Charitable Foundation, Alex C.
Walker Foundation, Archie D. and Bertha H.
Walker Foundation, T. B.
Wallace Genetic Foundation
Disney Co., Walt
Ware Foundation
Warsh-Mott Legacy
Washington Square Fund
Washington Square Health Foundation
Wasie Foundation
Wean Foundation, Raymond John
Weatherhead Foundation
Weaver Foundation, Gil and Dody
Webb Foundation
Webb Foundation, Del E.
Webster Foundation, Edwin S.
Weight Watchers International
Weisman Art Foundation, Frederick R.
Weiss Foundation, Stephen and Suzanne
Welch Foundation, Robert A.
Wells Foundation, Lillian S.
Wendt Foundation, Margaret L.
Wenner-Gren Foundation for Anthropological Research
Wertheim Foundation, Dr. Herbert A.
West Foundation
West Foundation, Neva and Wesley
Western Cardiac Foundation
Westport Fund
Weyerhaeuser Co.
Wharton Trust, William P.
Wheeler Trust, Clara
Whitaker Charitable Foundation, Lyndon C.
Whitaker Foundation
Whitaker Fund, Helen F.
White Foundation, W. P. and H. B.
Whitehall Foundation
Whitehead Charitable Foundation
Whiteman Foundation, Edna Rider
Whiting Foundation
Whitney Foundation, Helen Hay
Wilbur Foundation, Marguerite Eyer
Wilder Foundation
Willard Foundation, Helen Parker
Williams Family Foundation
Wills Foundation
Wilson Foundation, H. W.
Wilson Foundation, Marie C. and Joseph C.
Wilson Sanitarium for Children of Baltimore City, Thomas
Winston Foundation, Norman and Rosita
Winston Research Foundation, Harry
Wisconsin Energy Corp.
Witco Corp.
Wolens Foundation, Kalman and Ida
Wolff Foundation, John M.
Woman's Seamen's Friend Society of Connecticut
Wood Charitable Trust, W. P.
Woodner Family Collection, Ian
Woodward Fund
Wright Foundation, Lola
Wurlitzer Foundation, Farny R.

Wyman-Gordon Co.
Young Foundation, Robert R.
Zachry Co., H. B.

Scholarship

Abeles Foundation, Joseph and Sophia
Abell Education Trust, Jennie G. and Pearl
Abell Foundation, Charles S.
Abney Foundation
Achelis Foundation
Acushnet Co.
Adams Foundation, Arthur F. and Alice E.
AEGON USA, Inc.
Aequus Institute
AGFA Division of Miles Inc.
Ahmanson Foundation
Akzo America
Ala Vi Foundation of New York
Alabama Power Co.
Aladdin Industries, Incorporated
Alden Trust, George I.
Alexander Foundation, Joseph
Alexander Foundation, Judd S.
Alexander Foundation, Walter
Alhambra Foundry Co., Ltd.
Allied Educational Foundation Fund
AlliedSignal
Alliss Educational Foundation, Charles and Ellora
Alltel/Western Region
Allyn Foundation
ALPAC Corp.
Aluminum Co. of America
Alworth Memorial Fund, Marshall H. and Nellie
AMAX
American Cyanamid Co.
American Financial Corp.
American General Finance
American Honda Motor Co.
American Microsystems, Inc.
American Natural Resources Co.
American Optical Corp.
American Standard
American United Life Insurance Co.
Ameritech Publishing
Amoco Corp.
Andalusia Health Services
Anderson Foundation
Anderson Foundation
Ann & Hope
AON Corp.
Appleby Foundation
Appleton Papers
Arcana Foundation
Archer-Daniels-Midland Co.
Arise Charitable Trust
Arkansas Power & Light Co.
Arkell Hall Foundation
Arkla
Armco Inc.
Armco Steel Co.
Armstrong World Industries Inc.
Arrillaga Foundation
Arronson Foundation
ASARCO
Associated Foundations
Atherton Family Foundation
Atkinson Foundation, Myrtle L.
Atlanta Gas Light Co.
Atran Foundation
Attleboro Pawtucket Savings Bank
Auerbach Foundation, Beatrice Fox
Avon Products
AXIA Incorporated
Ayer Inc., N.W.
Ayling Scholarship Foundation, Alice S.
Babcock & Wilcox Co.

Backer Spielvogel Bates U.S.
Bailey Foundation
Bair Memorial Trust, Charles M.
Baker Foundation, Clark and Ruby
Baker Foundation, R. C.
Baker Trust, George F.
Balfour Foundation, L. G.
Bamberger and John Ernest Bamberger Memorial Foundation, Ruth Eleanor
Banc One Illinois Corp.
Bank of A. Levy
Bank of America Arizona
Bannerman Foundation, William C.
Barden Corp.
Barker Foundation
Barnes Foundation
Barnes Scholarship Trust, Fay T.
Barnett Banks
Bashinsky Foundation
Bass Foundation, Harry
Bastien Memorial Foundation, John E. and Nellie J.
Baughman Foundation
Baumberger Endowment
Baumker Charitable Foundation, Elsie and Harry
Baxter Foundation, Donald E. and Delia B.
Bean Foundation, Norwin S. and Elizabeth N.
Beattie Foundation Trust, Cordelia Lee
Beatty Trust, Cordelia Lunceford
Beazley Foundation
Bechtel Charitable Remainder Uni-Trust, Harold R.
Bechtel Charitable Remainder Uni-Trust, Marie H.
Bechtel Group
Bechtel, Jr. Foundation, S. D.
Beck Foundation, Elsie E. & Joseph W.
Beck Foundation, Lewis H.
Becton Dickinson & Co.
Bedsole Foundation, J. L.
Beech Aircraft Corp.
Beeghly Fund, Leon A.
Belden Brick Co., Inc.
Bell Communications Research
Bellamah Foundation, Dale J.
Beneficial Corp.
Bennett Memorial Corporation, James Gordon
Bennett Scholarship Fund, Margaret A. and Lawrence J.
Bentley Foundation, Alvin M.
Benz Trust, Doris L.
Berbecker Scholarship Fund, Walter J. and Lille
Bergen Foundation, Frank and Lydia
Berger Foundation, H.N. and Frances C.
Bergner Co., P.A.
Berkman Charitable Trust, Allen H. and Selma W.
Berry Foundation, Lowell
Bertha Foundation
Besser Foundation
Best Products Co.
Bethlehem Steel Corp.
BFGoodrich
Bibb Co.
Bicknell Fund
Biddle Foundation, Mary Duke
Bingham Second Betterment Fund, William
Biological Humanics Foundation
Birmingham Foundation
Bishop Foundation, E. K. and Lillian F.
Black & Veatch
Blade Communications
Blandin Foundation

Scholarship (cont.)

Blaustein Foundation, Morton K. and Jane
Blinken Foundation
Block, H&R
Blount
Blount Educational and Charitable Foundation, Mildred Weedon
Blount Educational Foundation, David S.
Blue Cross and Blue Shield of Minnesota Foundation Inc.
Blue Cross and Blue Shield United of Wisconsin Foundation
Blue Cross & Blue Shield of Kentucky Foundation
Bluhdorn Charitable Trust, Charles G. and Yvette
Board of Trustees of the Prichard School
Boatmen's First National Bank of Oklahoma
Bodman Foundation
Boehringer Mannheim Corp.
Boeing Co.
Boettcher Foundation
Bohemia Inc.
Bonfils-Stanton Foundation
Booth-Bricker Fund
Boothroyd Foundation, Charles H. and Bertha L.
Booz Allen & Hamilton
Borchard Foundation, Albert and Elaine
Borg-Warner Corp.
Bosch Corp., Robert
Boston Edison Co.
Boswell Foundation, James G.
Botwinick-Wolfensohn Foundation
Bourns, Inc.
Bovaird Foundation, Mervin
Bowen Foundation, Ethel N.
Bowyer Foundation, Ambrose and Gladys
Brach Foundation, Helen
Brackenridge Foundation, George W.
Bradford Foundation, George and Ruth
Bradish Trust, Norman C.
Brennan Foundation, Robert E.
Brenton Banks Inc.
Bridgestone/Firestone
Briggs & Stratton Corp.
Brillion Iron Works
Brisley and Noma Brisley Phillips Scholarship Loan Fund, Ella Frances
Britton Fund
Broadhurst Foundation
Brookdale Foundation
Brooks Foundation, Gladys
Brown Brothers Harriman & Co.
Brown Charitable Trust, Dora Maclellan
Brown Foundation, George Warren
Brown Foundation, James Graham
Brown Foundation, Joe W. and Dorothy Dorsett
Brown & Williamson Tobacco Corp.
Broyhill Family Foundation
Bruening Foundation, Eva L. and Joseph M.
Bryan Foundation, James E. and Mary Z.
Buehler Foundation, Emil
Buell Foundation, Temple Hoyne
Buffett Foundation
Burchfield Foundation, Charles E.
Burger King Corp.

Burkitt Foundation
Burnham Donor Fund, Alfred G.
Burns Foundation, Fritz B.
Burroughs Wellcome Co.
Burton Foundation, William T. and Ethel Lewis
Bushee Foundation, Florence Evans
Butler Foundation, Alice
Butler Foundation, J. Homer
Butler Manufacturing Co.
C.P. Rail Systems
Cablevision of Michigan
Cabot Corp.
Caestecker Foundation, Charles and Marie
Cafritz Foundation, Morris and Gwendolyn
Cain Foundation, Gordon and Mary
Callaway Foundation
Callaway Foundation, Fuller E.
Cameron Foundation, Harry S. and Isabel C.
Camp Foundation
Capital Holding Corp.
Cargill
Caring and Sharing Foundation
Carnahan-Jackson Foundation
Carolina Power & Light Co.
Carpenter Foundation
Carpenter Technology Corp.
Carrier Corp.
Carter Family Foundation
Cartinhour Foundation
Carver Charitable Trust, Roy J.
Caston Foundation, M. C. and Mattie
Cayuga Foundation
CBS Inc.
Ceco Corp.
CENEX
Central Bank of the South
Central Maine Power Co.
Central National-Gottesman
Central Newspapers, Inc.
Central Soya Co.
Chandler Foundation
Chapin-May Foundation of Illinois
Chapman Charitable Corporation, Howard and Bess
Chapman Foundation, William H.
Charina Foundation
Chase Lincoln First Bank, N.A.
Chase Manhattan Bank, N.A.
Chatlos Foundation
Cheatham Foundation, Owen
Cheney Foundation, Ben B.
Chesapeake Corp.
Chesebrough-Pond's
Chevron Corp.
Chiles Foundation
China Medical Board of New York
China Times Cultural Foundation
Chrysler Corp.
Churches Homes Foundation
CIGNA Corp.
Cincinnati Milacron
Circuit City Stores
Citicorp
Citizens Union Bank
City National Bank
Clark Charitable Trust
Clark Foundation
Clay Foundation
Clayton Fund
Clemens Foundation
Clements Foundation
Cleveland-Cliffs
Clorox Co.
CNA Insurance Cos.
Coastal Corp.
Cobb Educational Fund, Ty
Coca-Cola Co.
Cockrell Foundation

Coffey Foundation
Cohen Foundation, Naomi and Nehemiah
Cole Foundation, Olive B.
Coleman Co.
Coleman Foundation
Coleman Scholarship Trust, Lillian R.
Coles Family Foundation
Colgate-Palmolive Co.
Collins Foundation, George and Jennie
Collins Foundation, Joseph
Collins, Jr. Foundation, George Fulton
Collins-McDonald Trust Fund
Collins Medical Trust
Colt Foundation, James J.
Columbus Dispatch Printing Co.
Commercial Bank
Commercial Intertech Corp.
Community Enterprises
Community Hospital Foundation
Cone-Blanchard Machine Co.
Confidence Foundation
Conn Memorial Foundation
Consolidated Papers
Continental Can Co.
Continental Corp.
Continental Grain Co.
Cook Foundation, Loring
Cook, Sr. Charitable Foundation, Kelly Gene
Cooper Foundation
Cooper Wood Products
Coors Foundation, Adolph
Copley Press
Copolymer Rubber & Chemical Corp.
Cosmair, Inc.
Coughlin-Saunders Foundation
Cox Charitable Trust, Opal G.
Cox Foundation, James M.
CPC International
Crandall Memorial Foundation, J. Ford
Crary Foundation, Bruce L.
Crawford Estate, E. R.
Creel Foundation
Cremer Foundation
Croft Metals
Crowell Trust, Henry P. and Susan C.
Crown Central Petroleum Corp.
Crump Fund, Joe and Jessie
CSC Industries
Cullen/Frost Bankers
Cunningham Foundation, Laura Moore
Curtice-Burns Foods
Danforth Foundation
Danis Industries
Darling Foundation, Hugh and Hazel
Dart Group Corp.
Dater Foundation, Charles H.
Davenport-Hatch Foundation
Davenport Trust Fund
Davey Tree Expert Co.
Davis Charitable Foundation, Champion McDowell
Davis Foundation, Edwin W. and Catherine M.
Davis Foundation, James A. and Juliet L.
Davis Hospital Foundation
Day Family Foundation
Dean Witter Discover
DeCamp Foundation, Ira W.
Dee Foundation, Lawrence T. and Janet T.
DeKalb Genetics Corp.
Delaware North Cos.
DelMar Foundation, Charles
Delta Tau Delta Educational Fund
Demos Foundation, N.
Deposit Guaranty National Bank

DeRoy Foundation, Helen L.
Deseranno Educational Foundation
Dettman Foundation, Leroy E.
Deuble Foundation, George H.
Devereaux Foundation
DeVlieg Foundation, Charles
Diamond Shamrock
Dickson Foundation
Diederich Educational Trust Fund, John T. and Ada
Dillon Foundation
Donaldson Co.
Dorr Foundation
Dougherty Foundation
Dougherty, Jr. Foundation, James R.
Douglas & Lomason Company
Dow Chemical Co.
Doyle Dane Bernback Group
Dreiling and Albina Dreiling Charitable Trust, Leo J.
Drown Foundation, Joseph
Drum Foundation
du Bois Foundation, E. Blois
du Pont de Nemours & Co., E. I.
Duke Endowment
Duke Power Co.
Dunagan Foundation
Dupar Foundation
Duriron Co., Inc.
Durr-Fillauer Medical
Dyson Foundation
Eastman Foundation, Alexander
Eastman Kodak Co.
Ebell of Los Angeles Scholarship Endowment Fund
Eccles Foundation, George S. and Dolores Dore
Echlin Foundation
Eckerd Corp., Jack
Eddy Foundation
Eden Hall Foundation
Edwards Foundation, O. P. and W. E.
EIS Foundation
El Pomar Foundation
Elf Atochem North America
Elgin Sweeper Co.
Elizabethtown Gas Co.
Elkin Memorial Foundation, Neil Warren and William Simpson
Ellis Grant and Scholarship Fund, Charles E.
Ellison Foundation
Ellwood Foundation
Emerson Foundation, Fred L.
English-Bonter-Mitchell Foundation
Eni-Chem America, Inc.
Ensign-Bickford Industries
Equitable Life Assurance Society of the U.S.
Ernest & Julio Gallo Winery
Erving Paper Mills
Ethyl Corp.
Ettinger Foundation
Evans Foundation, Thomas J.
Everett Charitable Trust
Evinrude Foundation, Ralph
Evjue Foundation
Ewald Foundation, H. T.
Exxon Corp.
Factor Family Foundation, Max
Fahrney Education Foundation
Fairchild Foundation, Sherman
Fairey Educational Fund, Kittie M.
Fairfield-Meeker Charitable Trust, Freeman E.
Farmers Group, Inc.
Federated Department Stores and Allied Stores Corp.
Federation Foundation of Greater Philadelphia
Feinstein Foundation, Myer and Rosaline
Femino Foundation

Fieldcrest Cannon
Fink Foundation
First Fidelity Bancorporation
First Interstate Bank NW Region
First Interstate Bank of Arizona
First Interstate Bank of California
First Interstate Bank of Oregon
First Interstate Bank of Texas, N.A.
First Mississippi Corp.
First of America Bank Corp.
First Union Corp.
Fish Foundation, Ray C.
Fishback Foundation Trust, Harmes C.
Fisher Foundation
Fisher-Price
Fisons Corp.
Fitz-Gibbon Charitable Trust
Fleet Financial Group
Fletcher Foundation, A. J.
Flinn Foundation
Fluor Corp.
Fohs Foundation
Ford and Ada Ford Fund, S. N.
Ford Foundation, Edward E.
Ford Fund, William and Martha
Ford II Fund, Henry
Forest City Enterprises
Fort Pierce Memorial Hospital Scholarship Foundation
Fortis Inc.
Foster Foundation
Foundation for Seacoast Health
Fourth Financial Corp.
Fox Foundation Trust, Jacob L. and Lewis
Franklin Foundation, John and Mary
Fraser Paper Ltd.
Frederick Foundation
Freedom Forum
Friendship Fund
Froderman Foundation
Frohring Foundation, William O. and Gertrude Lewis
Fromm Scholarship Trust, Walter and Mabel
Frueauff Foundation, Charles A.
Fry Foundation, Lloyd A.
Fuchs Foundation, Gottfried & Mary
Fulbright and Monroe L. Swyers Foundation, James H.
Fuller Foundation, C. G.
Fullerton Foundation
Funderburke & Associates
Gabelli Foundation
Gallagher Family Foundation, Lewis P.
GAR Foundation
Gardiner Savings Institution FSB
Gardner Foundation
Garner Charitable Trust, James G.
Garrigues Trust, Edwin B.
Garvey Kansas Foundation
GEICO Corp.
Gellert Foundation, Carl
Gellert Foundation, Celia Berta
GenCorp
Genentech
General American Life Insurance Co.
General Educational Fund
General Motors Corp.
General Reinsurance Corp.
General Signal Corp.
General Steel Fabricators
Geneseo Foundation
George Foundation
Georgia Health Foundation
Georgia-Pacific Corp.
Georgia Power Co.
Gerber Products Co.
Gerondelis Foundation

Gershenson Foundation, Charles
H.
Getty Trust, J. Paul
Ghidotti Foundation, William
and Marian
Gholston Trust, J. K.
Gibson Foundation, Addison H.
Gibson Foundation, E. L.
Gilder Foundation
Giles Foundation, Edward C.
Gillespie Memorial Fund,
Boynton
Gillette Co.
Gilmore Foundation, Irving S.
Ginter Foundation, Karl and
Anna
Gleason Foundation, Katherine
Gleason Memorial Fund
Goldie-Anna Charitable Trust
Goldman Foundation, Herman
Goldman Foundation, William
Goldman Sachs & Co.
Goldwyn Foundation, Samuel
Golub Corp.
Goodstein Family Foundation,
David
Goodyear Tire & Rubber Co.
Gordy Family Educational Trust
Fund, George E.
Gore Family Memorial
Foundation
Gottwald Foundation
Gould Inc.
Gould Foundation for Children,
Edwin
Grace & Co., W.R.
Graco
Graham Charitable Trust,
William L.
Graphic Controls Corp.
Grassmann Trust, E. J.
Gray Foundation, Garland
Great-West Life Assurance Co.
Greater Lansing Foundation
Green Foundation, Allen P. and
Josephine B.
Green Industries, A. P.
Greene Foundation, Robert Z.
Gregg-Graniteville Foundation
Grimes Foundation
Grotto Foundation
Groves & Sons Co., S.J.
Grundy Foundation
GTE Corp.
Guardian Industries Corp.
Gulf Power Co.
H.C.S. Foundation
Hachar Charitable Trust, D. D.
Hadson Corp.
Hagedorn Fund
Haggar Foundation
Hale Foundation, Crescent Porter
Hales Charitable Fund
Hall Foundation
Halsell Foundation, Ewing
Hamilton Bank
Hamman Foundation, George
and Mary Josephine
Handleman Co.
Hankins Foundation
Hansen Foundation, Dane G.
Harden Foundation
Hardin Foundation, Phil
Harding Foundation, Charles
Stewart
Hariri Foundation
Harkness Foundation, William
Hale
Harper Brush Works
Harris Foundation, H. H.
Harris Foundation, James J. and
Angelia M.
Harrison Foundation, Fred G.
Harsco Corp.
Hartford Courant Foundation
Hartmarx Corp.
Harvard Musical Association

Haskell Fund
Hatterscheidt Foundation
Hauss-Helms Foundation
Haven Charitable Foundation,
Nina
Hayden Recreation Center,
Josiah Willard
Haynes Foundation
Haynes Foundation, John
Randolph and Dora
Hearst Foundation
Hearst Foundation, William
Randolph
Hechinger Co.
Hedco Foundation
HEI Inc.
Heileman Brewing Co., Inc., G.
Heinz Co., H.J.
Heinz Endowment, Vira I.
Heisey Foundation
Heller Financial
Helmerich & Payne Inc.
Hemingway Foundation, Robert
G.
Hermann Foundation, Grover
Herrick Foundation
Hertz Foundation, Fannie and
John
Hervey Foundation
Hettinger Foundation
Heublein
Hexcel Corp.
Hill Crest Foundation
Hillman Foundation
Hilton Foundation, Conrad N.
Hitchcock Foundation, Gilbert
M. and Martha H.
Hobbs Foundation, Emmert
Hodge Foundation
Hoffberger Foundation
Hoffman Foundation,
Maximillian E. and Marion O.
Hofmann Co.
Holden Fund, James and Lynelle
Holding Foundation, Robert P.
Holt Foundation, William Knox
Homeland Foundation
HON Industries
Honda of America
Manufacturing, Inc.
Hook Drug
Hoover Foundation
Hope Memorial Fund, Blanche
and Thomas
Horncrest Foundation
Horne Foundation, Dick
Horowitz Foundation, Gedale B.
and Barbara S.
Hosler Memorial Educational
Fund, Dr. R. S.
Hospital Corp. of America
Hotchkiss Foundation, W. R.
House Educational Trust, Susan
Cook
Houston Endowment
Hubbard Farms
Hubbard Foundation, R. Dee and
Joan Dale
Hubbard Milling Co.
Hugg Trust, Leoia W. and
Charles H.
Hughes Memorial Foundation,
Charles Evans
Humana
Humphreys Foundation
Hunt Alternatives Fund
Huntington Fund for Education,
John
Hyde Foundation, J. R.
Hyde, Jr. Scholarship Fund, J.R.
Hyster-Yale
Iddings Benevolent Trust
Illges Foundation, John P. and
Dorothy S.
Illinois Power Co.
Illinois Tool Works
IMCERA Group Inc.
Imlay Foundation

Inco Alloys International
Independence Foundation
Independent Financial Corp.
Inland Container Corp.
Inland Steel Industries
Intel Corp.
ITT Hartford Insurance Group
ITT Rayonier
Ivakota Association
Jackson Mills
Jafra Cosmetics, Inc. (U.S.)
Jameson Foundation, J. W. and
Ida M.
Janesville Foundation
Jaqua Foundation
JELD-WEN, Inc.
Jellison Benevolent Society
Jephson Educational Trust No. 1
Jephson Educational Trust No. 2
Jerusalem Fund for Education
and Community Development
Jesselson Foundation
Jewell Memorial Foundation,
Daniel Ashley and Irene
Houston
Jewish Foundation for Education
of Women
Jockey Hollow Foundation
Johnson Controls
Johnson Endeavor Foundation,
Christian A.
Johnson Foundation, Helen K.
and Arthur E.
Johnson Foundation, M. G. and
Lillie A.
Johnson & Son, S.C.
Johnston-Hanson Foundation
Johnston Trust for Charitable
and Educational Purposes,
James M.
Jones Family Foundation,
Eugenie and Joseph
Jones Foundation, Fletcher
Jones Foundation, Harvey and
Bernice
Jones Foundation, Helen
Jones Fund, Paul L.
Jordan Charitable Trust, Martha
Annie
Joslyn Foundation, Marcellus I.
Jostens
Joukowsky Family Foundation
Kaplan Foundation, Mayer and
Morris
Kasal Charitable Trust, Father
Kasiska Family Foundation
Kaufman Endowment Fund,
Louis G.
Kaufman Foundation, Henry &
Elaine
Kaufmann Foundation, Marion
Esser
Keck Foundation, W. M.
Kelley and Elza Kelley
Foundation, Edward Bangs
Kelly, Jr. Memorial Foundation,
Ensign C. Markland
Kelly Tractor Co.
Kempner Fund, Harris and Eliza
Kennecott Corp.
Kern Foundation, Ilma
Kerney Foundation, James
Kerr Foundation, Robert S. and
Grayce B.
Kerr Fund, Grayce B.
Kerr-McGee Corp.
Kibble Foundation
Kiewit Foundation, Peter
Kiewit Sons, Peter
Kikkoman International, Inc.
Kilbourne Residuary Charitable
Trust, E. H.
Killam Trust, Constance
Kilworth Charitable Foundation,
Florence D.
Kilworth Charitable Trust,
William
Kimball Co., Miles

Kimball International
Kimberly-Clark Corp.
King Foundation, Carl B. and
Florence E.
Kingsbury Corp.
Kingsley Foundation, Lewis A.
Kirchgessner Foundation, Karl
Kline Foundation, Josiah W. and
Bessie H.
Kmart Corp.
Knapp Educational Fund
Knudsen Foundation, Tom and
Valley
Koch Charitable Trust, David H.
Koch Foundation
Koch Industries
Koch Sons, George
Koh-I-Noor Rapidograph Inc.
Kohler Co.
Kohler Foundation
Komes Foundation
Koopman Fund
Koret Foundation
Koulaieff Educational Fund,
Trustees of Ivan Y.
KPMG Peat Marwick
Kreielsheimer Foundation Trust
Kress Foundation, George
Kutz Foundation, Milton and
Hattie
Kyle Educational Trust, S. H.
and D. W.
Kyocera International Inc.
Lafarge Corp.
Laffey-McHugh Foundation
Lamb Foundation, Kirkland S.
and Rena B.
Lang Foundation, Eugene M.
Larsen Fund
Lassen Foundation, Irving A.
Laub Foundation
Lavanburg-Corner House
Law Foundation, Robert O.
LBJ Family Foundation
Lea County Electric Co-op
Leach Foundation, Tom &
Frances
Leavey Foundation, Thomas and
Dorothy
Lee Endowment Foundation
Lee Foundation, James T.
Leidy Foundation, John J.
Lemberg Foundation
Lender Family Foundation
Lennox International, Inc.
Lesher Foundation, Margaret and
Irvin
Leu Foundation
Leucadia National Corp.
Leuthold Foundation
Levy Foundation, Charles and
Ruth
Levy Foundation, June Rockwell
Liberty Corp.
Life Investors Insurance
Company of America
Lilly Endowment
Lincoln Fund
Lincoln Health Care Foundation
Lincoln-Lane Foundation
Lincoln National Corp.
Lindsay Trust, Agnes M.
Link, Jr. Foundation, George
Littlefield Memorial Trust, Ida
Ballou
Litton Industries
Loats Foundation
Lockheed Corp.
Loews Corp.
Long Foundation, George A. and
Grace
Lord Educational Fund
Lord Scholarship Fund Trust,
Henry C.
Loughran Foundation, Mary and
Daniel
Louisiana Land & Exploration
Co.

Louisiana-Pacific Corp.
Love Foundation, Gay and
Erskine
Love Foundation, Lucyle S.
Lowenstein Foundation, William
P. and Marie R.
LTV Corp.
Lubrizol Corp.
Lucky Stores
Ludwick Institute
Lupin Foundation
Lutheran Brotherhood
Foundation
Lux Foundation, Miranda
Lydall, Inc.
Lynch Scholarship Foundation,
John B.
Lytel Foundation, Bertha Russ
M/A-COM, Inc.
MacDonald Foundation, James A.
Macht Foundation, Morton and
Sophia
Maddox Foundation, J. F.
Magee Christian Education
Foundation
Maier Foundation, Sarah Pauline
Mallinckrodt Specialty
Chemicals Co.
Manville Corp.
Mapco Inc.
Mardag Foundation
Margoes Foundation
Mariani Nut Co.
Marinette Marine Corp.
Marley Co.
Marriott Foundation, J. Willard
Marshall & Ilsley Bank
Martin Marietta Corp.
Marubeni America Corp.
Masserini Charitable Trust,
Maurice J.
Mathis-Pfohl Foundation
Mattel
Mauger Insurance Co.
Maxus Energy Corp.
May Mitchell Royal Foundation
Mayer Foundation, James and
Eva
Maytag Corp.
Maytag Family Foundation, Fred
MBIA, Inc.
McAshan Foundation
McCann Foundation
McCarthy Charities
McCasland Foundation
McClure Educational and
Development Fund, James G.
K.
McConnell Foundation
McCormick & Co.
McCormick Foundation,
Chauncey and Marion Deering
McCourtney Trust, Flora S.
McCullough Foundation, Ralph
H. and Ruth J.
McDermott
McDermott Foundation, Eugene
McDonnell Douglas Corp.
McElroy Trust, R. J.
McFarland Charitable Foundation
McFeely-Rogers Foundation
McGee Foundation
McGovern Foundation, John P.
McGraw Foundation
MCI Communications Corp.
McInerny Foundation
McIntire Educational Fund, John
McIntyre Foundation, B. D. and
Jane E.
McKaig Foundation, Lalitta Nash
McKee Foundation, Robert E.
and Evelyn
McKenna Foundation, Katherine
Mabis
McKenna Foundation, Philip M.
McLendon Educational Fund,
Violet H.

Scholarship (cont.)

McMahon Charitable Trust Fund, Father John J.
McMahon Foundation
McMannis and A. Haskell McMannis Educational Fund, William J.
McMillan, Jr. Foundation, Bruce
McMurray-Bennnett Foundation
McShain Charities, John
McWane Inc.
Mead Foundation, Giles W. and Elise G.
Meadows Foundation
Measey Foundation, Benjamin and Mary Siddons
Melitta North America Inc.
Mellinger Educational Foundation, Edward Arthur
Mellon Bank Corp.
Memton Fund
Menasha Corp.
Mengle Foundation, Glenn and Ruth
Mercantile Bancorp
Merrill Lynch & Co.
Meserve Memorial Fund, Albert and Helen
Messing Family Charitable Foundation
Metropolitan Health Foundation
Metropolitan Life Insurance Co.
Mette Foundation
Meyer Foundation, Eugene and Agnes E.
Meyer Foundation, Robert R.
Meyerhoff Fund, Joseph
Michaels Scholarship Fund, Frank J.
Mid-Iowa Health Foundation
Midmark Corp.
Mifflin Memorial Fund, George H. and Jane A.
Milbank Foundation, Dunlevy
Milken Foundation, L. and S.
Miller Foundation
Mills Charitable Foundation, Henry L. and Kathryn
Minnegasco
Minnesota Foundation
Missouri Farmers Association
Mitchell Energy & Development Corp.
Mitchell, Jr. Trust, Oscar
Mitsui & Co. (U.S.A.)
Mobil Oil Corp.
Mobility Foundation
Monsanto Co.
Montana Power Co.
Monticello College Foundation
Moore & Co., Benjamin
Moore Foundation, Roy C.
Moores Foundation, Harry C.
Moorman Manufacturing Co.
Moosehead Manufacturing Co.
Morehead Foundation, John Motley
Morgan Foundation, Burton D.
Moriah Fund
Morley Brothers Foundation
Morris Foundation, Margaret T.
Morris Foundation, William T.
Moses Fund, Henry and Lucy
Mosher Foundation, Samuel B.
Motorola
Muller Foundation, C. John and Josephine
Mulligan Charitable Trust, Mary S.
Munson Foundation, W. B.
Murphey Foundation, Lluella Morey
Murphy Foundation
Murray Foundation
Myra Foundation
Nabisco Foods Group

Nalco Chemical Co.
National City Bank, Columbus
National Computer Systems
National Fuel Gas Co.
National Presto Industries
National Pro-Am Youth Fund
National Standard Co.
National Starch & Chemical Corp.
National Westminster Bank New Jersey
Naurison Scholarship Fund, James Z.
NBD Bank
Neese Family Foundation
New England Mutual Life Insurance Co.
New Orphan Asylum Scholarship Foundation
New Penn Motor Express
New York Life Insurance Co.
New York Mercantile Exchange
New York Telephone Co.
New York Times Co.
The New Yorker Magazine, Inc.
Newcombe Foundation, Charlotte W.
Newmont Mining Corp.
News & Observer Publishing Co.
Nichols Foundation
Nicol Scholarship Foundation, Helen Kavanagh
Nike Inc.
Noll Foundation
Norfolk Southern Corp.
Norris Foundation, Kenneth T. and Eileen L.
Northern Indiana Fuel & Light Co.
Northern Indiana Public Service Co.
Northern Star Foundation
Northwest Natural Gas Co.
Northwestern National Life Insurance Co.
Noyes, Jr. Memorial Foundation, Nicholas H.
Oaklawn Foundation
Obernauer Foundation
O'Brien Foundation, Cornelius and Anna Cook
O'Brien Foundation, James W.
O'Connor Foundation, A. Lindsay and Olive B.
Odessa Trading Co.
Ogden College Fund
Oglebay Norton Co.
Ohl, Jr. Trust, George A.
Oki America Inc.
Oklahoma Gas & Electric Co.
Olin Corp.
Olin Foundation, John M.
Olmsted Foundation, George and Carol
1957 Charity Trust
1939 Foundation
O'Neill Charitable Corporation, F. J.
Ontario Corp.
Ordean Foundation
Ore-Ida Foods, Inc.
Ormet Corp.
Orscheln Co.
Ortho Diagnostic Systems, Inc.
Osher Foundation, Bernard
Outboard Marine Corp.
Overbrook Foundation
Owsley Foundation, Alvin and Lucy
Pacific Mutual Life Insurance Co.
Pacific Telesis Group
Packaging Corporation of America
Packer Foundation, Horace B.
Padnos Iron & Metal Co., Louis
Paley Foundation, William S.
Palisades Educational Foundation

Palisano Foundation, Vincent and Harriet
Palmer Fund, Frank Loomis
Pan-American Life Insurance Co.
Pannill Scholarship Foundation, William Letcher
Pappas Charitable Foundation, Thomas Anthony
Parker-Hannifin Corp.
Parsons Foundation, Ralph M.
Pauley Foundation, Edwin W.
Pearlstone Foundation, Peggy Meyerhoff
Penn Industrial Chemical Corp.
Peppers Foundation, Ann
Pepsi-Cola Bottling Co. of Charlotte
Perina Corp
Perini Corp.
Perini Foundation, Joseph
Perkin-Elmer Corp.
Perkins Foundation, B. F. & Rose H.
Peters Foundation, Leon S.
Peters Foundation, R. D. and Linda
Petteys Memorial Foundation, Jack
Pfizer
Phelps Dodge Corp.
Philibosian Foundation, Stephen
Philips Foundation, Jesse
Phillips Family Foundation, Jay and Rose
Phillips Family Foundation, L. E.
Phillips Petroleum Co.
Phipps Foundation, William H.
Pickford Foundation, Mary
Pilgrim Foundation
Piper Foundation
Piper Foundation, Minnie Stevens
Plumsock Fund
Pluta Family Foundation
Plym Foundation
Polychrome Corp.
Pope Foundation
Portland General Electric Co.
Post Foundation of D.C., Marjorie Merriweather
Potlatch Corp.
Pott Foundation, Robert and Elaine
Potter Foundation, Justin and Valere
Potts Memorial Foundation
Powell Family Foundation
Poynter Fund
PPG Industries
Premier Industrial Corp.
Presser Foundation
Price Educational Foundation, Herschel C.
Price Foundation, Louis and Harold
Price Waterhouse-U.S.
Procter & Gamble Cosmetic & Fragrance Products
Promus Cos.
Prospect Hill Foundation
Protheray of America
Providence Journal Company
Prudential Insurance Co. of America
PSI Energy
Public Service Electric & Gas Co.
Puett Foundation, Nelson
Pulitzer Publishing Co.
Pullman Educational Foundation, George M.
Puterbaugh Foundation
Quaker Oats Co.
Quantum Chemical Corp.
Questar Corp.
Quinlan Foundation, Elizabeth C.
Raskin Foundation, Hirsch and Braine

Ratner Foundation, Milton M.
Ratshesky Foundation, A. C.
Raymond Educational Foundation
Reader's Digest Association
Rebsamen Companies, Inc.
Red Devil
Redfield Foundation, Nell J.
Redman Foundation
Regis Corp.
REI- Recreational Equipment, Inc.
Reilly Industries
Reiss Coal Co., C.
Reliable Life Insurance Co.
Reliance Electric Co.
Rennie Scholarship Fund, Waldo E.
Rexham Inc.
Reynolds Foundation, Donald W.
Reynolds Foundation, Edgar
Reynolds Foundation, Richard S.
RGK Foundation
Rhoden Charitable Foundation, Elmer C.
Rhone-Poulenc Rorer
Rice Foundation, Ethel and Raymond F.
Richardson County Bank and Trust Co.
Richfood Holdings
Riggs Benevolent Fund
Rinker Materials Corp.
RJR Nabisco Inc.
Roberts Foundation, Summerfield G.
Robertshaw Controls Co.
Robertson Brothers
Robison Foundation, Ellis H. and Doris B.
Roblee Foundation, Joseph H. and Florence A.
Rockwell Foundation
Rockwell Fund
Rockwell International Corp.
Rodman Foundation
Rogers Charitable Trust, Florence
Rogers Foundation
Rohm and Haas Company
Rohr Inc.
Rolfs Foundation, Robert T.
Rolfs Foundation, Thomas J.
Romill Foundation
RosaMary Foundation
Rosenthal Foundation, Ida and William
Ross Foundation, Arthur
Roth Foundation
Rotterman Trust, Helen L. and Marie F.
Rouse Co.
Rowland Foundation
Royal Group Inc.
Rubinstein Foundation, Helena
Rudin Foundation, Louis and Rachel
Russell Educational Foundation, Benjamin and Roberta
Russell Trust, Josephine G.
Rutledge Charity, Edward
Ryder System
Sachs Foundation
Sage Foundation
San Diego Gas & Electric
Sandoz Corp.
Sandy Hill Foundation
Santa Fe Pacific Corp.
Sargent Foundation, Newell B.
Saunders Foundation
Scaife Family Foundation
Scaife Foundation, Sarah
Scherer Foundation, Karla
Schering-Plough Corp.
Scheuer Family Foundation, S. H. and Helen R.
Schieffelin & Somerset Co.
Schiff, Hardin & Waite

Schlinger Foundation
Schlumberger Ltd.
Schmitt Foundation, Arthur J.
Schowalter Foundation
Schrafft and Bertha E. Schrafft Charitable Trust, William E.
Schultz Foundation
Schwab & Co., Charles
Science Applications International Corp.
Scott Fund, Olin
Scripps Co., E.W.
Scroggins Foundation, Arthur E. and Cornelia C.
SCT Yarns
Scurry Foundation, D. L.
SDB Foundation
Seabury Foundation
Selby and Marie Selby Foundation, William G.
Semple Foundation, Louise Taft
Servistar Corp.
Seybert Institution for Poor Boys and Girls, Adam and Maria Sarah
Shaklee Corp.
Share Trust, Charles Morton
Sharp Foundation
Shatford Memorial Trust, J. D.
Shaw Fund for Mariner's Children
Shea Foundation
Shelter Mutual Insurance Co.
Shenandoah Life Insurance Co.
Sheridan Foundation, Thomas B. and Elizabeth M.
Sherman Educational Fund
Shinnick Educational Fund, William M.
Shirk Foundation, Russell and Betty
Shoemaker Fund, Thomas H. and Mary Williams
Shoemaker Trust for Shoemaker Scholarship Fund, Ray S.
Shoney's Inc.
Shoong Foundation, Milton
SICO Foundation
Sierra Pacific Industries
Simmons Family Foundation, R. P.
Simon Foundation, William E. and Carol G.
Simpson Foundation
Siragusa Foundation
Skillman Foundation
Slemp Foundation
Smeal Foundation, Mary Jean & Frank P.
Smith Charitable Trust, W. W.
Smith Charities, John
Smith Corp., A.O.
Smith Foundation, Kelvin and Eleanor
Smith Fund, Horace
Smith, Jr. Foundation, M. W.
Smith Memorial Fund, Ethel Sergeant Clark
Smysor Memorial Fund, Harry L. and John L.
Smyth Trust, Marion C.
Snayberger Memorial Foundation, Harry E. and Florence W.
Snow Foundation, John Ben
Snow Memorial Trust, John Ben
Society for the Increase of the Ministry
Sofia American Schools
Solo Cup Co.
Sonoco Products Co.
Sony Corp. of America
Sotheby's
South Branch Foundation
South Plains Foundation
Southern Bell
Southern California Edison Co.
Southland Corp.

Special People In Need
Sperry Fund
Spingold Foundation, Nate B. and Frances
Springs Foundation
Square D Co.
Stabler Foundation, Donald B. and Dorothy L.
Stackner Family Foundation
Star Bank, N.A.
Stark Foundation, Nelda C. and H. J. Lutcher
Starling Foundation, Dorothy Richard
Starr Foundation
Starrett Co., L.S.
State Farm Mutual Automobile Insurance Co.
Statler Foundation
Stauffer Foundation, John and Beverly
Stearns Trust, Artemas W.
Steele Foundation, Harry and Grace
Steele-Reese Foundation
Steigerwaldt Foundation, Donna Wolf
Stein Foundation, Joseph F.
Steinman Foundation, James Hale
Stemmons Foundation
Stern Foundation, Gustav and Irene
Stern Foundation, Irvin
Stern Memorial Trust, Sidney
Sternberger Foundation, Sigmund
Stewart Alexander Foundation
Stewart Educational Foundation, Donnell B. and Elizabeth Dee Shaw
Stewart Memorial Trust, J. C.
Stocker Foundation
Stockham Valves & Fittings
Stone Foundation, France
Stone Fund, Albert H. and Reuben S.
Stone & Webster, Inc.
Storer Foundation, George B.
Storer Scholarship Foundation, Oliver W.
Straub Estate, Gertrude S.
Stride Rite Corp.
Stroud Foundation
Stuart Foundation, Edward C.
Stubblefield, Estate of Joseph L.
Stupp Foundation, Norman J.
Sullivan Foundation, Algernon Sydney
Sullivan Foundation, Ray H. and Pauline
Sulzberger Foundation
Sulzer Family Foundation
Summerfield Foundation, Solon E.
Sun Co.
Sunburst Foundation
Sundet Foundation
Sunkist Growers
Swalm Foundation
Swim Foundation, Arthur L.
Swisher Foundation, Carl S.
Switzer Foundation
Switzer Foundation
Talley Industries, Inc.
Tartt Scholarship Fund, Hope Pierce
Taubman Foundation, Herman P. and Sophia
Taylor Family Foundation, Jack
Technical Training Foundation
Tektronix
Teledyne
Temple Foundation, T. L. L.
Temple-Inland
Templeton Foundation, Herbert A.
Tennant Co.
Tenneco

Terry Foundation
Tesoro Petroleum Corp.
Texaco
Texas Industries, Inc.
Texas Instruments
Textron
Thatcher Foundation
Thermo Electron Corp.
Thoman Foundation, W. B. and Candace
Thomas Memorial Foundation, Theresa A.
Thomson Information Publishing Group
Thorpe Foundation, James R.
Thorson Foundation
3M Co.
Tilles Nonsectarian Charity Fund, Rosalie
Times Mirror Co.
Tiscornia Foundation
TJX Cos.
Tonkin Foundation, Tom and Helen
Tosco Corp. Refining Division
Totsy Manufacturing Co.
Toyota Motor Sales, U.S.A.
Tozer Foundation
Tractor & Equipment Co.
Transamerica Corp.
Transco Energy Company
Travelli Fund, Charles Irwin
Treakle Foundation, J. Edwin
Trinity Foundation
Tropicana Products, Inc.
Trull Foundation
Trust Funds
TRW Corp.
Tuch Foundation, Michael
Tucker Charitable Trust, Rose E.
Tucker Foundation, Marcia Brady
Tull Charitable Foundation
Tuohy Foundation, Alice Tweed
Turner Charitable Foundation
Turner Fund, Ruth
Turrell Fund
Ukrop's Super Markets, Inc.
Union Camp Corp.
Union City Body Co.
Union Electric Co.
Union Manufacturing Co.
United Conveyor Corp.
United Parcel Service of America
Unitrode Corp.
Universal Foods Corp.
Unocal Corp.
Upjohn Co.
Upton Foundation, Frederick S.
Urann Foundation
USF&G Co.
USG Corp.
UST
USX Corp.
Van Buren Foundation
Van Evera Foundation, Dewitt Caroline
Van Every Foundation, Philip L.
Van Schaick Scholarship Fund, Nellie
Van Vleet Foundation
Varian Associates
Vermeer Manufacturing Co.
Vernon Fund, Miles Hodsdon
Vicksburg Hospital Medical Foundation
Vidinha Charitable Trust, A. and E.
Viele Scholarship Trust, Frances S.
Vincent Trust, Anna M.
Vollrath Co.
Vulcan Materials Co.
Waffle House, Inc.
Waggoner Charitable Trust, Crystelle
Waggoner Foundation, E. Paul and Helen Buck

Wagnalls Memorial
Wagner and George Hosser Scholarship Fund Trust, Edward
Wagner Foundation, Ltd., R. H.
Wahlert Foundation
Wahlstrom Foundation
Wal-Mart Stores
Wal-Mart Stores, Inc.
Waldbaum, Inc.
Walker Foundation, W. E.
Wallace-Reader's Digest Fund, DeWitt
Walsh Charity Trust, Blanche M.
Disney Co., Walt
Ward Foundation, A. Montgomery
Ward Foundation, Louis L. and Adelaide C.
Warwick Foundation
Washington Forrest Foundation
Washington Post Co.
Washington Square Fund
Washington Square Health Foundation
Wasie Foundation
Waste Management
Watumull Fund, J.
Wean Foundation, Raymond John
Weber Charities Corp., Frederick E.
Weiler Foundation, Theodore & Renee
Weiss Foundation, William E.
Welch Testamentary Trust, George T.
Weller Foundation
Wells Trust Fund, Fred W.
Werner Foundation, Clara and Spencer
West Co.
West Foundation
Westend Foundation
Westinghouse Electric Corp.
Westlake Scholarship Fund, James L. and Nellie M.
Westport Fund
Wheelwright Scientific School
Whirlpool Corp.
White Foundation, W. P. and H. B.
White Trust, G. R.
Whitehead Foundation, Lettie Pate
Whiteley Foundation, John and Elizabeth
Whiteside Scholarship Fund, Robert B. and Sophia
Whittenberger Foundation, Claude R. and Ethel B.
Wickes Foundation, Harvey Randall
Wiggins Memorial Trust, J. J.
Wilder Foundation
Willard Foundation, Helen Parker
Williams Charitable Trust, Mary Jo
Williams Family Foundation
Williams Foundation, Arthur Ashley
Williams Foundation, Kemper and Leila
Willits Foundation
Wilson Foundation, Frances Wood
Wilson Foundation, H. W.
Wilson Foundation, Hugh and Mary
Wilson Foundation, Marie C. and Joseph C.
Winchester Foundation
Winn-Dixie Stores
Winship Memorial Scholarship Foundation
Winston Foundation, Norman and Rosita
Wisconsin Power & Light Co.
Wisconsin Public Service Corp.

Witco Corp.
Witte, Jr. Foundation, John H.
Wolens Foundation, Kalman and Ida
Wolf Foundation, Benjamin and Fredora K.
Wolfson Foundation, Louis E.
Woltman Foundation, B. M.
Woman's Seamen's Friend Society of Connecticut
Wood Charitable Trust, W. P.
Woods Foundation, James H.
Woods-Greer Foundation
Woodward Fund-Watertown, David, Helen, and Marian
Wornall Charitable Trust and Foundation, Kearney
Worthing Scholarship Fund
Wyman-Gordon Co.
Xerox Corp.
Young Foundation, H and B
Young Foundation, Hugo H. and Mabel B.
Young Foundation, Irvin L.
Young Memorial Fund, John B. and Brownie
Youth Foundation
Zachry Co., H. B.
Zenkel Foundation
Ziegler Foundation
Ziemann Foundation
Zigler Foundation, Fred B. and Ruth B.
Zimmerman Foundation, Hans and Clara Davis

Seed Money

Abell Foundation, Charles S.
Abell Foundation, The
Abell-Hanger Foundation
Abney Foundation
Acushnet Co.
Agway
Ahmanson Foundation
Alabama Power Co.
Aladdin Industries, Incorporated
Alden Trust, John W.
Alexander & Baldwin, Inc.
Alexander Foundation, Judd S.
Alms Trust, Eleanora
ALPAC Corp.
Aluminum Co. of America
American Honda Motor Co.
American Saw & Manufacturing Co.
Amoco Corp.
Andersons Management Corp.
Archibald Charitable Foundation, Norman
ARCO
Arkla
Armco Inc.
Armco Steel Co.
Arronson Foundation
Atlanta Foundation
Atlanta Gas Light Co.
Atran Foundation
Autzen Foundation
Axe-Houghton Foundation
Babcock Foundation, Mary Reynolds
Bacon Trust, Charles F.
Baehr Foundation, Louis W. and Dolpha
Baker Trust, Clayton
Bank of Boston Corp.
Bank One, Youngstown, NA
BankAmerica Corp.
Barnes Foundation
Bartol Foundation, Stockton Rush
Baxter International
Bayne Fund, Howard
Bean Foundation, Norwin S. and Elizabeth N.
Becton Dickinson & Co.
Beech Aircraft Corp.

Beim Foundation
Bell Communications Research
BellSouth Corp.
Benedum Foundation, Claude Worthington
Best Products Co.
Beveridge Foundation, Frank Stanley
Biddle Foundation, Mary Duke
Bigelow Foundation, F. R.
Bishop Foundation, E. K. and Lillian F.
Blandin Foundation
Boehm Foundation
Boeing Co.
Borden Memorial Foundation, Mary Owen
Borg-Warner Corp.
Boston Gas Co.
Botwinick-Wolfensohn Foundation
Bowne Foundation, Robert
Bray Charitable Trust, Viola E.
Bremer Foundation, Otto
Brencanda Foundation
Bridgestone/Firestone
Broadhurst Foundation
Brookdale Foundation
Bruening Foundation, Eva L. and Joseph M.
Brush Foundation
Bryan Family Foundation, Kathleen Price and Joseph M.
Buell Foundation, Temple Hoyne
Buhl Foundation
Burden Foundation, Florence V.
Burkitt Foundation
Bush Charitable Foundation, Edyth
Bydale Foundation
Cablevision of Michigan
Cabot Corp.
Cafritz Foundation, Morris and Gwendolyn
Camp Foundation
Campbell and Adah E. Hall Charity Fund, Bushrod H.
Carnahan-Jackson Foundation
Carnegie Corporation of New York
Carpenter Foundation
Carter Foundation, Amon G.
Carver Charitable Trust, Roy J.
Cascade Natural Gas Corp.
Casey Foundation, Annie E.
Central Maine Power Co.
Chase Lincoln First Bank, N.A.
Chevron Corp.
Chicago Resource Center
Chicago Sun-Times, Inc.
Close Foundation
CNG Transmission Corp.
Colorado Trust
Columbia Foundation
Cooper Foundation
Cooper Industries
Cornell Trust, Peter C.
Corning Incorporated
Cove Charitable Trust
Cowden Foundation, Louetta M.
CPC International
CR Industries
Cremer Foundation
Crocker Trust, Mary A.
Cummins Engine Co.
Dain Bosworth/Inter-Regional Financial Group
Dalton Foundation, Dorothy U.
Dana Corp.
Danforth Foundation
Dater Foundation, Charles H.
Davis Foundation, Joe C.
Daywood Foundation
de Hirsch Fund, Baron
Dean Witter Discover
DeKalb Genetics Corp.
DelMar Foundation, Charles

Seed Money (cont.)

Dewing Foundation, Frances R.
Dexter Charitable Fund, Eugene A.
Dillon Foundation
Doheny Foundation, Carrie Estelle
Dollar General Corp.
Donnelley & Sons Co., R.R.
Dorr Foundation
Dougherty, Jr. Foundation, James R.
Douty Foundation
Dow Corning Corp.
Dow Foundation, Herbert H. and Grace A.
Drum Foundation
du Pont de Nemours & Co., E. I.
Duchossois Industries
Duke Endowment
Duncan Trust, John G.
Earl-Beth Foundation
Eaton Foundation, Cyrus
Edison Fund, Charles
Educational Foundation of America
Edwards Foundation, O. P. and W. E.
Ensign-Bickford Industries
Ensworth Charitable Foundation
Evans Foundation, Thomas J.
Evjue Foundation
Falk Foundation, David
Falk Medical Fund, Maurice
Farish Fund, William Stamps
Farnsworth Trust, Charles A.
Federal Express Corp.
Federated Department Stores and Allied Stores Corp.
Fel-Pro Incorporated
Ferebee Endowment, Percy O.
Fidelity Bank
Fikes Foundation, Leland
First of America Bank Corp.
First Union Corp.
Fisher Foundation
Fleishhacker Foundation
Fletcher Foundation, A. J.
Flinn Foundation
Foley, Hoag & Eliot
Ford Foundation
Foster Foundation
Foundation for Seacoast Health
Fowler Memorial Foundation, John Edward
Franklin Foundation, John and Mary
Freedom Forum
Freeman Foundation, Carl M.
Freightliner Corp.
Frick Educational Commission, Henry C.
Friendly Rosenthal Foundation
Frohring Foundation, William O. and Gertrude Lewis
Frost Foundation
Fry Foundation, Lloyd A.
Fullerton Foundation
Fund for New Jersey
Funderburke & Associates
Fusenot Charity Foundation, Georges and Germaine
GAR Foundation
GATX Corp.
General Atlantic Partners L.P.
General Signal Corp.
GenRad
George Foundation
Georgia Health Foundation
Giant Food Stores
Gifford Charitable Corporation, Rosamond
Ginter Foundation, Karl and Anna
Glaser Foundation
Glaxo

Glen Eagles Foundation
Globe Newspaper Co.
Goddard Foundation, Charles B.
Goldman Fund, Richard and Rhoda
Goldseker Foundation of Maryland, Morris
Goldwyn Foundation, Samuel
Gould Foundation for Children, Edwin
Grant Foundation, Charles M. and Mary D.
Gray Foundation, Garland
Greater Lansing Foundation
Green Foundation, Allen P. and Josephine B.
Greene Manufacturing Co.
Greenville Foundation
Greve Foundation, William and Mary
Gross Charitable Trust, Stella B.
Grotto Foundation
Guggenheim Foundation, Daniel and Florence
Gund Foundation, George
Haas Foundation, Paul and Mary
Haffner Foundation
Haigh-Scatena Foundation
Hall Family Foundations
Hall Foundation
Hallmark Cards
Hancock Foundation, Luke B.
Hartford Courant Foundation
Hazen Foundation, Edward W.
Heinz Endowment, Vira I.
Heller Financial
Hesston Corp.
Hewlett Foundation, William and Flora
Heydt Fund, Nan and Matilda
Higginson Trust, Corina
Hightower Foundation, Walter
Hill and Family Foundation, Walter Clay
Hillman Foundation
Hitachi
Hoche-Scofield Foundation
Hoffmann-La Roche
Home Depot
Honeywell
Hood Foundation, Charles H.
Hoover, Jr. Foundation, Margaret W. and Herbert
Hopwood Charitable Trust, John M.
Horizons Foundation
Houston Industries
Hoyt Foundation
Hoyt Foundation, Stewart W. and Willma C.
Hudson-Webber Foundation
Hughes Charitable Trust, Mabel Y.
Hughes Memorial Foundation, Charles Evans
Hulings Foundation, Mary Andersen
Hunt Foundation, Samuel P.
Hunt Manufacturing Co.
Illges Foundation, John P. and Dorothy S.
Illinois Power Co.
Inco Alloys International
Innovating Worthy Projects Foundation
International Foundation
Irvine Foundation, James
ITT Rayonier
Ittleson Foundation
Janesville Foundation
Jasam Foundation
JELD-WEN, Inc.
Jennings Foundation, Martha Holden
Jennings Foundation, Mary Hillman
Jergens Foundation, Andrew
Jerome Foundation

JM Foundation
Johnson Foundation, Walter S.
Johnson & Son, S.C.
Jones Foundation, Daisy Marquis
Joukowsky Family Foundation
Kaiser Family Foundation, Henry J.
Kantzler Foundation
Kaplan Foundation, Rita J. and Stanley H.
Kaplan Fund, J. M.
Kaufman Endowment Fund, Louis G.
Kawabe Memorial Fund
Keith Foundation Trust, Ben E.
Kellogg Foundation, W. K.
Kempner Fund, Harris and Eliza
Kennedy, Jr. Foundation, Joseph P.
Kerr Foundation, Robert S. and Grayce B.
Kerr Fund, Grayce B.
Kettering Family Foundation
Kieckhefer Foundation, J. W.
Kiewit Foundation, Peter
Kimball Foundation, Horace A. Kimball and S. Ella
Kingsbury Corp.
Kirchgessner Foundation, Karl
Kirkpatrick Foundation
Klingenstein Fund, Esther A. and Joseph
Knott Foundation, Marion I. and Henry J.
Koch Charitable Trust, David H.
Komes Foundation
Koret Foundation
Kutz Foundation, Milton and Hattie
Lavanburg-Corner House
LEF Foundation
Levy Foundation, June Rockwell
Lilly & Co., Eli
Lilly Foundation, Richard Coyle
Lincoln Electric Co.
Lincoln Fund
Lincoln National Corp.
Lindsay Trust, Agnes M.
Lingnan Foundation
Litton/Itek Optical Systems
Lotus Development Corp.
Lounsbery Foundation, Richard
Loutit Foundation
Lux Foundation, Miranda
Lyndhurst Foundation
Lytel Foundation, Bertha Russ
M. E. G. Foundation
MacArthur Foundation, J. Roderick
MacDonald Foundation, James A.
Macht Foundation, Morton and Sophia
Maclellan Charitable Trust, R. J.
Maclellan Foundation
Mailman Family Foundation, A. L.
Marbrook Foundation
Mardag Foundation
Martin Foundation
Material Service Corp.
Maxfield Foundation
Mayerson Foundation, Manuel D. and Rhoda
MBIA, Inc.
McBeath Foundation, Faye
McCune Foundation
McDonnell Douglas Corp.-West
McGonagle Foundation, Dextra Baldwin
McGraw Foundation
McInerny Foundation
McKee Foundation, Robert E. and Evelyn
McKenna Foundation, Katherine Mabis
McKenna Foundation, Philip M.
McLean Contributionship

Mead Foundation, Giles W. and Elise G.
Meadows Foundation
Medtronic
Mellon Bank Corp.
Merck Family Fund
Merrick Foundation
Meserve Memorial Fund, Albert and Helen
Metropolitan Life Insurance Co.
Meyer Foundation, Eugene and Agnes E.
Meyer Memorial Trust
Meyerhoff Fund, Joseph
Michigan Consolidated Gas Co.
Midwest Resources
Milbank Foundation, Dunlevy
Miles Inc.
Miller Foundation
Mills Fund, Frances Goll
Minnesota Mutual Life Insurance Co.
Mobility Foundation
Montgomery Foundation
Moore Charitable Foundation, Marjorie
Moores Foundation, Harry C.
Morgan Foundation, Burton D.
Morley Brothers Foundation
Mott Foundation, Charles Stewart
Mott Fund, Ruth
MTS Systems Corp.
Murdock Charitable Trust, M. J.
Murphy Foundation, John P.
National City Bank, Columbus
Nationwide Insurance Cos.
NBD Bank
NEC USA
Needmor Fund
Nellie Mae
New World Foundation
New York Mercantile Exchange
News & Observer Publishing Co.
Noble Foundation, Samuel Roberts
Norcliffe Fund
Norman Foundation
Norman Foundation, Andrew
Northern Trust Co.
Northwest Area Foundation
Northwest Natural Gas Co.
Noyes Foundation, Jessie Smith
O'Brien Foundation, Alice M.
O'Connor Foundation, Kathryn
OCRI Foundation
Ohl, Jr. Trust, George A.
Ohrstrom Foundation
Olin Corp.
Oliver Memorial Trust Foundation
Onan Family Foundation
1525 Foundation
1957 Charity Trust
O'Neil Foundation, Casey Albert T.
Ontario Corp.
Oppenstein Brothers Foundation
Owsley Foundation, Alvin and Lucy
Packard Foundation, David and Lucile
Palmer Fund, Frank Loomis
Pardee Foundation, Elsa U.
Parker Foundation
Parsons Foundation, Ralph M.
Patterson and Clara Guthrie Patterson Trust, Robert Leet
Paul and C. Michael Paul Foundation, Josephine Bay
Penn Savings Bank, a division of Sovereign Bank Bank of Princeton, a division of Sovereign Bank
Penney Foundation, James C.
Perkin-Elmer Corp.
Pew Charitable Trusts
Phillips Foundation, Ellis L.

Pineywoods Foundation
Pinkerton Foundation
Pioneer Trust Bank, NA
Plough Foundation
Polaroid Corp.
Polk Foundation
Presser Foundation
Preyer Fund, Mary Norris
Prince Trust, Abbie Norman
Promus Cos.
Providence Journal Company
Prudential Insurance Co. of America
PSI Energy
Public Service Co. of New Mexico
Public Service Electric & Gas Co.
Public Welfare Foundation
Quaker Oats Co.
Quinlan Foundation, Elizabeth C.
Radiator Specialty Co.
Ramapo Trust
Raskob Foundation for Catholic Activities
Rauch Foundation
Ray Foundation
Retirement Research Foundation
Reynolds Charitable Trust, Kate B.
Reynolds Foundation, J. B.
Reynolds Foundation, Z. Smith
Rice Foundation, Helen Steiner
Richmond Foundation, Frederick W.
Riley Foundation, Mabel Louise
Rittenhouse Foundation
Roblee Foundation, Joseph H. and Florence A.
Roche Relief Foundation, Edward and Ellen
Rockefeller Foundation, Winthrop
Rockefeller Trust, Winthrop
Roe Foundation
Rohm and Haas Company
RosaMary Foundation
Rosenberg Family Foundation, William
Rosenstiel Foundation
Rosenthal Foundation, Ida and William
Ross Foundation
Rothschild Foundation, Hulda B. and Maurice L.
Rouse Co.
Russell Charitable Trust, Josephine S.
Ryan Family Charitable Foundation
St. Faith's House Foundation
St. Mary's Catholic Foundation
Saint Paul Cos.
Samuels Foundation, Fan Fox and Leslie R.
Sara Lee Corp.
Sara Lee Hosiery
Schering-Plough Corp.
Schmidlapp Trust No. 1, Jacob G.
Schultz Foundation
Schumann Foundation, Florence and John
Scott Foundation, Walter
SDB Foundation
Seafirst Corp.
Second Foundation
Semmes Foundation
Seybert Institution for Poor Boys and Girls, Adam and Maria Sarah
Sheafer Charitable Trust, Emma A.
Sheridan Foundation, Thomas B. and Elizabeth M.
Shoemaker Fund, Thomas H. and Mary Williams
Shoong Foundation, Milton
Siebert Lutheran Foundation

Simon Foundation, Robert Ellis
Simpson Investment Co.
Skillman Foundation
Slemp Foundation
Smith Charitable Trust, W. W.
Smith, Jr. Charitable Trust, Jack J.
Smith, Jr. Foundation, M. W.
Smith Memorial Fund, Ethel Sergeant Clark
SNET
Snow Memorial Trust, John Ben
Snyder Foundation, Harold B. and Dorothy A.
Snyder Fund, Valentine Perry
Sonat
Sordoni Foundation
South Plains Foundation
Speas Foundation, Victor E.
Speas Memorial Trust, John W. and Effie E.
Sprague Educational and Charitable Foundation, Seth
Springs Foundation
Stackner Family Foundation
Stackpole-Hall Foundation
Stanley Works

Steelcase
Steinhagen Benevolent Trust, B. A. and Elinor
Sterling Inc.
Stern Foundation, Leonard N.
Stern Memorial Trust, Sidney
Stevens Foundation, Abbot and Dorothy H.
Stewart Trust under the will of Helen S. Devore, Alexander and Margaret
Stewart Trust under the will of Mary E. Stewart, Alexander and Margaret
Stocker Foundation
Straus Foundation, Aaron and Lillie
Stroud Foundation
Stuart Foundation, Edward C.
Subaru of America Inc.
Sulzberger Foundation
Sunderland Foundation, Lester T.
Tandy Foundation, Anne Burnett and Charles
Teagle Foundation
Technical Foundation of America
Teleklew Productions

Templeton Foundation, Herbert A.
Thoman Foundation, W. B. and Candace
Thorpe Foundation, James R.
Time Insurance Co.
Tiscornia Foundation
Toms Foundation
Toshiba America, Inc.
Town Creek Foundation
Transamerica Corp.
Treuhaft Foundation
Trull Foundation
Trust Co. Bank
Trust Funds
Tucker Foundation, Marcia Brady
Tull Charitable Foundation
Tuohy Foundation, Alice Tweed
Turner Charitable Foundation
Turner Charitable Trust, Courtney S.
Turrell Fund
UNUM Corp.
Upjohn Foundation, Harold and Grace
UST
Valero Energy Corp.

van Ameringen Foundation
Van Houten Charitable Trust
van Loben Sels - Eleanor Slate van Lobel Sels Charitable Foundation, Ernst D.
Varian Associates
Vermeer Charitable Foundation
Vermeer Manufacturing Co.
Virginia Power Co.
Vollrath Co.
Vulcan Materials Co.
Waggoner Charitable Trust, Crystelle
Wahlstrom Foundation
Wallace-Reader's Digest Fund, DeWitt
Walsh Charity Trust, Blanche M.
Ward Heritage Foundation, Mamie McFaddin
Washington Forrest Foundation
Washington Mutual Savings Bank
Webb Foundation
Wedum Foundation
Weingart Foundation
Wells Foundation, Franklin H. and Ruth L.

Wendt Foundation, Margaret L.
Werner Foundation, Clara and Spencer
Western New York Foundation
Weyerhaeuser Family Foundation
Whitaker Foundation
Whitaker Fund, Helen F.
Whiteman Foundation, Edna Rider
Whittier Foundation, L. K.
Wilbur Foundation, Marguerite Eyer
Wilson Foundation, Marie C. and Joseph C.
Wilson Trust, Lula C.
Wisconsin Power & Light Co.
Woods Charitable Fund
Woods Foundation, James H.
Woodward Governor Co.
Wyomissing Foundation
Yassenoff Foundation, Leo
Zale Foundation
Zurn Industries

Index to Corporations by Nonmonetary Support Type

Cause-related Marketing & Promotion

Action Products International
Alcan Aluminum Corp.
American Cyanamid Co.
American Electric Power
Atlanta Gas Light Co.
Backer Spielvogel Bates U.S.
Bally's - Las Vegas
Banc One Illinois Corp.
Banc One Wisconsin Corp.
Bank of Louisville
BankAmerica Corp.
Bayview Federal Bank
Bean, L.L.
Bel Air Mart
Benefit Trust Life Insurance Co.
Bloomingdale's
Boatmen's Bancshares
Boehringer Mannheim Corp.
Booz Allen & Hamilton
Bridgestone/Firestone
British Airways
Brown & Williamson Tobacco Corp.
Browning-Ferris Industries
Bryn Mawr Trust Co.
Butler Manufacturing Co.
Carrols Corp.
Cartier, Inc.
Central Trust Co.
CertainTeed Corp.
Charter Medical Corp.
Citibank, F.S.B.
Citizens Bank
Citizens Commercial & Savings Bank
City National Bank
Coast Federal Bank
Coleman Co.
Columbus Southern Power Co.
Continental Corp.
Coors Brewing Co.
Courier-Journal & Louisville Times
CPI Corp.
Cullen/Frost Bankers
Curtis Industries, Helene
Dai-Ichi Kangyo Bank of California
Delmarva Power & Light Co.
Deposit Guaranty National Bank
Donaldson, Lufkin & Jenrette
Dreyer's & Edy's Grand Ice Cream
Echlin Inc.
Eckerd Corp., Jack
Equitable Resources
Fay's Incorporated
Ferro Corp.
Fidelity Bank
First Alabama Bancshares
First of America Bank Corp.
First Union National Bank of Florida
Fleet Financial Group
Fox Inc.
Franklin Mint Corp.
Freightliner Corp.
Frisch's Restaurants Inc.
GenCorp
Giant Food
Gillette Co.
Globe Newspaper Co.
Great Western Financial Corp.
Grumman Corp.

Gucci America Inc.
Heller Financial
Hershey Foods Corp.
Household International
Ingram Industries
Jefferson-Pilot Communications
Kao Corp. of America (DE)
Kellogg Co., M.W.
King Kullen Grocery Co., Inc.
Kloeckner-Pentaplast of America
Kmart Corp.
Liberty National Bank
Lykes Brothers Steamship Co.
Marion Merrell Dow
Marsh Supermarkets, Inc.
Mattel
Mazda Motors of America (Central), Inc.
Mazda North America
MBIA, Inc.
McDonald & Co. Securities
Melitta North America Inc.
Michigan Gas Utilities
Minnegasco
Minnesota Power & Light Co.
Mississippi Power Co.
National City Bank, Columbus
National Data Corp.
National Fuel Gas Co.
NBD Bank, N.A.
New England Grocer Supply
News & Observer Publishing Co.
North American Reinsurance Corp.
Northern Indiana Public Service Co.
Northern Trust Co.
Northwest Airlines, Inc.
Norwest Bank Nebraska
Ogilvy & Mather Worldwide
Ohio Casualty Corp.
Ohio Citizens Bank
Old Kent Bank & Trust Co.
Parsons Corp.
Penn Savings Bank, a division of Sovereign Bank Bank of Princeton, a division of Sovereign Bank
People's Bank
PHH Corp.
Philip Morris Cos.
Phoenix Home Life Mutual Insurance Co.
Pillsbury Co.
PSI Energy
Publix Supermarkets
Raley's
Ralston Purina Co.
Royal Group Inc.
Scott Paper Co.
Seaway Food Town
Servistar Corp.
Shoney's Inc.
Signet Bank/Maryland
SKF USA, Inc.
Smith Food & Drug
Smucker Co., J.M.
Sotheby's
Southern Indiana Gas & Electric Co.
Southland Corp.
Southtrust Corp.
Sprint
Star Bank, N.A.
State Street Bank & Trust Co.
Stirtz, Bernards & Co.
Storer Communications Inc.
Tenneco

Texas-New Mexico Power Co.
TJX Cos.
Torchmark Corp.
Toro Co.
Tosco Corp. Refining Division
Towle Manufacturing Co.
Trustmark National Bank
Unilever United States
Union Equity Division of Farmland Industries
US Bancorp
Washington Natural Gas Co.
Washington Post Co.
Wells Fargo & Co.
Wetterau

Donated Equipment

Advanced Micro Devices
Aetna Life & Casualty Co.
AFLAC
AGFA Division of Miles Inc.
Agway
Air Products & Chemicals
Akzo Chemicals Inc.
AlliedSignal
Alltel/Western Region
Almac's, Inc.
ALPAC Corp.
Alyeska Pipeline Service Co.
AMAX Coal Industries
American Cyanamid Co.
American Electric Power
American General Corp.
American Microsystems, Inc.
American Natural Resources Co.
American Telephone & Telegraph Co.
American Telephone & Telegraph Co./Dallas Region
Ameritech Publishing
Ameritech Services
Amfac/JMB Hawaii
Amoco Corp.
Analog Devices
Apple Computer, Inc.
Appleton Papers
Archer-Daniels-Midland Co.
ARCO
Arkla
ASARCO
Atlanta Gas Light Co.
Avon Products
Bally's - Las Vegas
Banc One Wisconsin Corp.
Bank of A. Levy
Bank of America Arizona
Bank of Boston Corp.
Bank of Louisville
Bank of Oklahoma, N.A.
Bank One, Texas-Houston Office
BankAmerica Corp.
Barber-Colman Co.
Baskin-Robbins USA CO.
Battelle
Bausch & Lomb
Baxter International
Bean, L.L.
Becton Dickinson & Co.
Bell Atlantic Corp.
Bell Communications Research
Bell Helicopter Textron
Bell Industries
Bellsouth Telecommunications, Inc.
Benefit Trust Life Insurance Co.
Best Products Co.
Bethlehem Steel Corp.

BFGoodrich
Big Three Industries
Boeing Co.
Boise Cascade Corp.
Booz Allen & Hamilton
Boston Edison Co.
Bourns, Inc.
Branch Banking & Trust Co.
Brodart Co.
Brown & Williamson Tobacco Corp.
Bruno's Inc.
Burdines
Burlington Industries
Burlington Northern Inc.
Burndy Corp.
Burroughs Wellcome Co.
C.P. Rail Systems
Cablevision of Michigan
Cabot Corp.
Caesar's World, Inc.
Canon U.S.A., Inc.
Capital Holding Corp.
Cargill
Carr Real Estate Services
Carrols Corp.
Cascade Natural Gas Corp.
Caterpillar
Centel Corp.
Centerior Energy Corp.
Central Fidelity Banks, Inc.
Central Hudson Gas & Electric Corp.
Central Maine Power Co.
Central Trust Co.
Century Companies of America
CertainTeed Corp.
Champion International Corp.
Chase Manhattan Bank, N.A.
Chemical Bank
Chesapeake & Potomac Telephone Co.
Chesebrough-Pond's
Chevron Corp.
Chrysler Corp.
Church & Dwight Co.
Church's Fried Chicken, Inc.
CIBA-GEIGY Corp.
Ciba-Geigy Corp. (Pharmaceuticals Division)
CIGNA Corp.
Cincinnati Bell
Cincinnati Milacron
Citibank, F.S.B.
Citizens Bank
Citizens Commercial & Savings Bank
Citizens & Southern National Bank of Florida
Clark Equipment Co.
Clorox Co.
CNA Insurance Cos.
Coachmen Industries
Coca-Cola Co.
Coleman Co.
Colonial Life & Accident Insurance Co.
Colorado Interstate Gas Co.
Columbus Southern Power Co.
Comerica
Cominco American Inc.
Commerce Clearing House
Commercial Federal Corp.
Commonwealth Edison Co.
Compaq Computer Corp.
Computer Associates International
Computer Sciences Corp.

Cone Mills Corp.
Conoco Inc.
Consolidated Natural Gas Co.
Consolidated Papers
Consolidated Rail Corp. (Conrail)
Cooper Industries
Cooper Tire & Rubber Co.
Coors Brewing Co.
Cotter & Co.
Cox Enterprises
CPC International
CPI Corp.
CR Industries
Cubic Corp.
Cullen/Frost Bankers
CUNA Mutual Insurance Group
Curtiss-Wright Corp.
Dana Corp.
Dayton Power and Light Co.
Dean Witter Discover
DeKalb Genetics Corp.
Delaware North Cos.
Delmarva Power & Light Co.
Dentsply International, Inc.
Detroit Edison Co.
Dexter Co.
Diamond Shamrock
Digital Equipment Corp.
Dow Chemical Co.
Dow Jones & Co.
Dreyer's & Edy's Grand Ice Cream
du Pont de Nemours & Co., E. I.
Duke Power Co.
Duquesne Light Co.
DynCorp
East Ohio Gas Co.
Eastman Kodak Co.
Eaton Corp.
Echlin Inc.
Edwards & Sons, A.G.
Electronic Data Systems Corp.
Elizabethtown Gas Co.
Employers Mutual Casualty Co.
Enserch Corp.
Entex
Equitable Life Assurance Society of the U.S.
Ethyl Corp.
Eureka Co.
European American Bank
Exxon Corp.
FAB Industries
Farm Fresh Inc. (Norfolk, Virginia)
Farmland Industries, Inc.
Federal Home Loan Mortgage Corp. (Freddie Mac)
Fidelity Bank
Figgie International
Fireman's Fund Insurance Co.
First Alabama Bancshares
First Bank System
First Boston
First Chicago
First Fidelity Bancorporation
First Interstate Bank NW Region
First Interstate Bank of Arizona
First Interstate Bank of Denver
First Interstate Bank of Oregon
First Maryland Bancorp
First Mississippi Corp.
First Tennessee Bank
First Union Corp.
First Union National Bank of Florida
Fisher Brothers
Fleet Bank

Donated Equipment (cont.)

Fleet Financial Group
Florida Power Corp.
Flowers Industries, Inc.
Fluor Corp.
Ford Motor Co.
Forest Oil Corp.
Fortis Benefits Insurance Company/Fortis Financial Group
Foster Wheeler Corp.
Fox Inc.
Franklin Electric Company Inc. (Bluffton, Indiana)
Franklin Mint Corp.
Fraser Paper Ltd.
Freeport-McMoRan
Freightliner Corp.
Frisch's Restaurants Inc.
Fuller Co., H.B.
Funderburke & Associates
GATX Corp.
GEICO Corp.
GenCorp
General Electric Co.
General Motors Corp.
General Reinsurance Corp.
General Signal Corp.
Georgia-Pacific Corp.
Georgia Power Co.
Giant Food
Giant Food Stores
Gillette Co.
Glaxo
Graphic Controls Corp.
Great American First Savings Bank, FSB
Great-West Life Assurance Co.
Great Western Financial Corp.
GTE Corp.
Gulfstream Aerospace Corp.
Hadson Corp.
Hamilton Oil Corp.
Harris Corp.
Harris Trust & Savings Bank
Hecla Mining Co.
Hein-Werner Corp.
Heller Financial
Helmerich & Payne Inc.
Hercules Inc.
Hesston Corp.
Hitachi
Hoechst Celanese Corp.
Hoffmann-La Roche
Holly Sugar Corp.
Holyoke Mutual Insurance Co. in Salem
Honeywell
Houston Industries
Howell Corp.
Hunt Oil Co.
Huntington Bancshares Inc.
IBM Corp.
ICI Americas
Illinois Bell
Illinois Power Co.
IMCERA Group Inc.
Inco Alloys International
Inland Steel Industries
Intermountain Gas Industries
International Paper Co.
Interstate Power Co.
ITT Hartford Insurance Group
J.P. Morgan & Co.
Jefferson-Pilot Communications
Johnson Controls
Johnson & Higgins
Jones Construction Co., J.A.
Journal Communications
Kansas Power & Light/Western Resources
Kellogg Co., M.W.
Kennecott Corp.
Kerr-McGee Corp.

Kingsbury Corp.
Kohler Co.
KPMG Peat Marwick
Laclede Gas Co.
Lafarge Corp.
Land O'Lakes
Leaseway Transportation Corp.
Leggett & Platt, Inc.
Lilly & Co., Eli
Lincoln National Corp.
Lincoln Telecommunications Co.
Litton/Itek Optical Systems
Lockheed Corp.
Lockheed Sanders
Loctite Corp.
Long Island Lighting Co.
Lord Corp.
Louisiana-Pacific Corp.
Louisiana Power & Light Co./New Orleans Public Service
LTV Corp.
Lydall, Inc.
Lykes Brothers Steamship Co.
Mallinckrodt Specialty Chemicals Co.
Marion Merrell Dow
Maritz Inc.
Marley Co.
Marsh & McLennan Cos.
Mascoma Savings Bank
Masland & Sons, C.H.
Masonite Corp.
Massachusetts Mutual Life Insurance Co.
Maxus Energy Corp.
Mazda Motors of America (Central), Inc.
Mazda North America
MBIA, Inc.
McCaw Cellular Communications
McCormick & Co.
McDonnell Douglas Corp.
MCI Communications Corp.
Mead Corp.
Measurex Corp.
Mellon Bank Corp.
Mercedes-Benz of North America, Inc.
Merck Human Health Division
Meridian Bancorp
Meritor Financial Group
Merrill Lynch & Co.
Mervyn's
Mesa Inc.
Metropolitan Life Insurance Co.
Metroquip
Meyer, Inc., Fred
Michigan Consolidated Gas Co.
Midlantic Banks, Inc.
Midwest Resources
Miller Inc., Herman
Millipore Corp.
Minnegasco
Minnesota Mutual Life Insurance Co.
Mississippi Chemical Corp.
Mississippi Power Co.
Mitchell Energy & Development Corp.
Mitre Corp.
Mitsui & Co. (U.S.A.)
Monsanto Co.
Montana Power Co.
Moorman Manufacturing Co.
Morgan Stanley & Co.
Morrison-Knudsen Corp.
Morton International
MTS Systems Corp.
Nabisco Foods Group
Nalco Chemical Co.
National City Bank, Columbus
National City Corp.
National Computer Systems
National Convenience Stores, Inc.

National Fuel Gas Co.
National Life of Vermont
National Medical Enterprises
National Steel
NationsBank Corp.
Nationwide Insurance Cos.
Navajo Refining Co.
NBD Bank
NBD Bank, N.A.
NCR Corp.
New England Grocer Supply
New England Mutual Life Insurance Co.
New England Telephone Co.
New Jersey Bell Telephone Company
New Jersey Manufacturers Insurance Co.
New Jersey Resources Corp.
New York State Electric & Gas Corp.
New York Telephone Co.
The New Yorker Magazine, Inc.
Niagara Mohawk Power Corp.
Noland Co.
Nordson Corp.
Norfolk Southern Corp.
Northern Illinois Gas Co.
Northern Indiana Public Service Co.
Northern States Power Co.
Northern Trust Co.
Northern Virginia Natural Gas
Northrop Corp.
Northwest Natural Gas Co.
Northwestern National Life Insurance Co.
Norton Co.
Norwest Bank Nebraska
Nucor Corp.
NuTone Inc.
NutraSweet Co.
Occidental Oil & Gas Corp.
Ohio Bell Telephone Co.
Ohio National Life Insurance Co.
Olin Corp.
Olivetti Office USA, Inc.
Orange & Rockland Utilities, Inc.
Ormet Corp.
Ortho Diagnostic Systems, Inc.
Oshman's Sporting Goods, Inc.
Overnite Transportation Co.
Owens-Corning Fiberglas Corp.
Owens-Illinois
Pacific Mutual Life Insurance Co.
PacifiCorp
Pan-American Life Insurance Co.
Panhandle Eastern Corp.
Parke-Davis Group
Patagonia
Paxton Co., Frank
Pentair
People's Bank
Peoples Drug Stores Inc.
Perkin-Elmer Corp.
Pfizer
Philadelphia Electric Co.
Philip Morris Cos.
Phillips Petroleum Co.
Pillsbury Co.
Plantronics, Inc.
Playboy Enterprises, Inc.
PNC Bank
Polychrome Corp.
Ponderosa, Inc.
Portland General Electric Co.
Premark International
Price Associates, T. Rowe
Prime Computer, Inc.
PriMerit F.S.B.
Principal Financial Group
Promus Cos.
Providence Energy Corp.
Providence Journal Company
Provident Life & Accident Insurance Co.

Prudential Insurance Co. of America
PSI Energy
Public Service Co. of Colorado
Public Service Co. of Oklahoma
Public Service Electric & Gas Co.
Publix Supermarkets
Pyramid Technology Corp.
Quaker Oats Co.
Quantum Chemical Corp.
Questar Corp.
Racal-Milgo
Ralston Purina Co.
Raychem Corp.
RB&W Corp.
Reading & Bates Corp.
Recognition Equipment
REI-Recreational Equipment, Inc.
Reliable Life Insurance Co.
Republic New York Corp.
Restaurant Associates, Inc.
Reynolds Metals Co.
Reynolds & Reynolds Co.
Rhone-Poulenc Rorer
Riggs National Bank
RJR Nabisco Inc.
Robbins & Myers, Inc.
Rockwell International Corp.
Rohm and Haas Company
Rohr Inc.
Rouse Co.
Royal Group Inc.
Ryder System
SAFECO Corp.
Saint Paul Cos.
San Diego Gas & Electric
Santa Fe Pacific Corp.
Sanyo Manufacturing Corp.
Sara Lee Corp.
SCANA Corp.
Schering-Plough Corp.
Science Applications International Corp.
Scientific-Atlanta
Scripps Co., E.W.
Seafirst Corp.
Sealright Co., Inc.
Seaway Food Town
Security Benefit Life Insurance Co.
Security Life of Denver
Servistar Corp.
Shaklee Corp.
Shaw Industries
Shenandoah Life Insurance Co.
Signet Bank/Maryland
SKF USA, Inc.
Smith Corp., A.O.
Smith Food & Drug
SNET
Sonat
Sonoco Products Co.
Sony Corp. of America
Southern California Edison Co.
Southern Co. Services
Southland Corp.
Southwestern Public Service Co.
Southwire Co.
Sprint
Square D Co.
Standard Chartered Bank New York
Stanley Works
Star Bank, N.A.
State Farm Mutual Automobile Insurance Co.
State Mutual Life Assurance Co.
State Street Bank & Trust Co.
Sterling Inc.
Storage Technology Corp.
Stride Rite Corp.
Swinerton & Walberg Co.
Tandem Computers
Tarmac America Inc.
Tektronix

Teledyne
Teleklew Productions
Tenneco
Tesoro Petroleum Corp.
Texas Gas Transmission Corp.
Texas Instruments
3M Co.
Time Insurance Co.
Time Warner Cable
TJX Cos.
Torchmark Corp.
Toro Co.
Tosco Corp. Refining Division
Tracor, Inc.
TRINOVA Corp.
Triskelion Ltd.
Tropicana Products, Inc.
Trustmark National Bank
Tucson Electric Power Co.
Unilever United States
Union Bank
Union Carbide Corp.
Union Central Life Insurance Co.
Union Electric Co.
Union Equity Division of Farmland Industries
Unisys Corp.
U.S. Leasing International
United States Trust Co. of New York
United Telephone System (Eastern Group)
Unitrode Corp.
UNUM Corp.
Upjohn Co.
US Bancorp
US WEST
Valero Energy Corp.
Valley National Bank of Arizona
Varian Associates
Virginia Power Co.
Vogt Machine Co., Henry
Vollrath Co.
Vulcan Materials Co.
Wachovia Bank of Georgia, N.A.
Wallace Computer Services
Washington Mutual Savings Bank
Washington Natural Gas Co.
Washington Post Co.
Washington Water Power Co.
Wells Fargo & Co.
Wendy's International, Inc.
West One Bancorp
Westinghouse Electric Corp.
Whirlpool Corp.
WICOR, Inc.
Winter Construction Co.
Wisconsin Bell, Inc.
Wisconsin Energy Corp.
Wisconsin Power & Light Co.
Wisconsin Public Service Corp.
Wyman-Gordon Co.

Donated Products

Abbott Laboratories
Abitibi-Price
Addison-Wesley Publishing Co.
Advanced Micro Devices
Aetna Life & Casualty Co.
AFLAC
Air France
Akzo Chemicals Inc.
Albany International Corp.
Albertson's
Alcan Aluminum Corp.
Alcon Laboratories, Inc.
Alltel/Western Region
ALPAC Corp.
America West Airlines
American Cyanamid Co.
American Electric Power
American Home Products Corp.
American Microsystems, Inc.
American Suzuki Motor Corp.

American Telephone &
Telegraph Co./Dallas Region
Amfac/JMB Hawaii
Amoco Corp.
Ampacet Corp.
AMR Corp.
Analog Devices
Anheuser-Busch Cos.
Appleton Papers
Asgrow Seed Co.
Atari Corp.
Avery Dennison Corp.
Avon Products
Bacardi Imports
Baccarat Inc.
Bally's - Las Vegas
Bang & Olufsen of America, Inc.
Bantam Doubleday Dell
Publishing Group, Inc.
Bard, C. R.
Barry Corp., R. G.
Baskin-Robbins USA CO.
Bausch & Lomb
Baxter International
Bean, L.L.
Becton Dickinson & Co.
Bel Air Mart
Bell Industries
Bellsouth Telecommunications,
Inc.
Benetton
Bergen Brunswig Corp.
Besser Co.
Best Products Co.
Best Western International
Bethlehem Steel Corp.
BHP Pacific Resources
Big Three Industries
Big V Supermarkets
Binney & Smith Inc.
Black & Decker Corp.
Bloomingdale's
BMW of North America, Inc.
Boatmen's Bancshares
Bob Evans Farms
Boehringer Mannheim Corp.
Boise Cascade Corp.
Boots Pharmaceuticals, Inc.
Borden
Bowater Inc.
Briggs & Stratton Corp.
Bristol-Myers Squibb Co.
British Airways
Brodart Co.
Brooks Brothers
Brother International Corp.
Brown Group
Brown & Williamson Tobacco
Corp.
Bruno's Inc.
Brunswick Corp.
Budd Co.
Burdines
Burger King Corp.
Burroughs Wellcome Co.
Butler Manufacturing Co.
Cabot Corp.
Cadence Design Systems
Caesar's World, Inc.
Campbell Soup Co.
Canon U.S.A., Inc.
Carrols Corp.
Castle & Cooke
Centex Corp.
Central Maine Power Co.
CertainTeed Corp.
Champion International Corp.
Chesapeake & Potomac
Telephone Co.
Chesebrough-Pond's
Christian Dior New York, Inc.
Christie, Manson & Woods
International, Inc.
Chrysler Corp.
Church & Dwight Co.
Church's Fried Chicken, Inc.
CIBA-GEIGY Corp.

Ciba-Geigy Corp.
(Pharmaceuticals Division)
Cincinnati Gas & Electric Co.
Circuit City Stores
Citizens & Southern National
Bank of Florida
Clark Equipment Co.
Clorox Co.
Coachmen Industries
Coast Federal Bank
Coats & Clark Inc.
Coca-Cola Co.
Coleman Co.
Colgate-Palmolive Co.
Compaq Computer Corp.
Continental Airlines
Contraves USA
Cooper Industries
Cooper Tire & Rubber Co.
Coors Brewing Co.
Cornnuts, Inc.
Cosmair, Inc.
Cotter & Co.
CPC International
CPI Corp.
Cubic Corp.
Cullen/Frost Bankers
Curtice-Burns Foods
Curtis Industries, Helene
Curtiss-Wright Corp.
Dairylea Cooperative Inc.
Dean Foods Co.
DeKalb Genetics Corp.
Delaware North Cos.
Deluxe Corp.
Dentsply International, Inc.
Diamond Shamrock
Dollar General Corp.
Dow Chemical Co.
Dreyer's & Edy's Grand Ice
Cream
du Pont de Nemours & Co., E. I.
Dunlop Tire Corp.
Duplex Products, Inc.
Eastern Fine Paper, Inc.
Eastman Kodak Co.
Ebsco Industries
Echlin Inc.
Eckerd Corp., Jack
Ecolab
Elizabethtown Gas Co.
EMI Records Group
Esselte Pendaflex Corp.
Eureka Co.
FAB Industries
Farm Fresh Inc. (Norfolk,
Virginia)
Farmland Industries, Inc.
Fay's Incorporated
Federal Express Corp.
Figgie International
First Brands Corp.
First Interstate Bank of Denver
First Tennessee Bank
Fisher-Price
Fleming Companies, Inc.
Flowers Industries, Inc.
Food Lion Inc.
Ford Motor Co.
Foster Wheeler Corp.
Fox Inc.
Franklin Electric Company Inc.
(Bluffton, Indiana)
Franklin Mint Corp.
Freightliner Corp.
Frisch's Restaurants Inc.
Frito-Lay
Fuller Co., H.B.
Gap, The
GenCorp
General Electric Co.
General Mills
General Motors Corp.
General Tire Inc.
Genesco
Georgia-Pacific Corp.
Georgia Power Co.

Gerber Products Co.
Giant Food
Giant Food Stores
Gillette Co.
Givenchy, Inc.
Glaxo
Glenmore Distilleries Co.
Glidden Co.
Graphic Controls Corp.
Great Atlantic & Pacific Tea Co.
Inc.
Grocers Supply Co.
Gucci America Inc.
Hallmark Cards
Harcourt Brace Jovanovich
Harcourt General
HarperCollins Publishers
Hasbro
Haverty Furniture Cos., Inc.
Hawkeye Bancorporation
Hein-Werner Corp.
Heller Financial
Hercules Inc.
Hershey Foods Corp.
Hewlett-Packard Co.
Hoffmann-La Roche
Holly Sugar Corp.
Home Depot
Houghton Mifflin Co.
Hunt Manufacturing Co.
Hy-Vee Food Stores
Hyster-Yale
IBM Corp.
Inland Steel Industries
Intel Corp.
International Multifoods Corp.
International Paper Co.
Iroquois Brands, Ltd.
JCPenney Co.
Johnson Controls
Johnson & Johnson
Kansas Power & Light/Western
Resources
Kao Corp. of America (DE)
Katy Industries Inc.
Kawasaki Motors Corp., U.S.A.
Keebler Co.
Kendall Health Care Products
Kenwood U.S.A. Corp.
Kikkoman International, Inc.
King Kullen Grocery Co., Inc.
Kingsbury Corp.
Kmart Corp.
Koh-I-Noor Rapidograph Inc.
Kohler Co.
Kraft General Foods
Kyocera International Inc.
L.A. Gear
Lafarge Corp.
Land O'Lakes
Leaseway Transportation Corp.
Leggett & Platt, Inc.
Lennar Corp.
Levi Strauss & Co.
Liberty National Bank
Lilly & Co., Eli
Liquid Air Corp.
Loctite Corp.
Loews Corp.
Longview Fibre Co.
Lord Corp.
Lotus Development Corp.
Louisiana-Pacific Corp.
Lucky Stores
Lukens
Luria's
Lykes Brothers Steamship Co.
Macmillan, Inc.
Magic Chef
Makita U.S.A., Inc.
Mallinckrodt Specialty
Chemicals Co.
Marion Merrell Dow
Marriott Corp.
Marsh Supermarkets, Inc.
Masland & Sons, C.H.

Mass Merchandisers, Inc.
Matchbox Toys (USA) Ltd.
Matsushita Electric Corp. of
America
Mattel
Mayer Foods Corp., Oscar
Maytag Corp.
Mazda Motors of America
(Central), Inc.
Mazda North America
McCaw Cellular
Communications
McCormick & Co.
McGraw-Hill
McKesson Corp.
Mead Corp.
Medalist Industries, Inc.
Medtronic
Melitta North America Inc.
Melville Corp.
Mennen Co.
Mercantile Stores Co.
Merck & Co.
Merck Human Health Division
Merry-Go-Round Enterprises,
Inc.
Mervyn's
Michigan Bell Telephone Co.
Microsoft Corp.
Midlantic Banks, Inc.
Miles Inc.
Miller Brewing Co.
Miller Inc., Herman
Millipore Corp.
Minnegasco
Mitsubishi International Corp.
Mizuno Corporation of America
Molex, Inc.
Moore Medical Corp.
Nabisco Foods Group
Nash-Finch Co.
National Computer Systems
National Convenience Stores,
Inc.
National Distributing Co., Inc.
National Fuel Gas Co.
National Gypsum Co.
Navajo Refining Co.
Nestle U.S.A. Inc.
New England Electric System
New England Grocer Supply
New Jersey Bell Telephone
Company
Newell Co.
News America Publishing Inc.
Niagara Mohawk Power Corp.
Nike Inc.
Noland Co.
Nordson Corp.
North American Philips Corp.
Northern Telecom Inc.
Northern Virginia Natural Gas
Northwest Natural Gas Co.
Norton Co.
Nucor Corp.
NuTone Inc.
NutraSweet Co.
Ocean Spray Cranberries
Oki America Inc.
Old Kent Bank & Trust Co.
Oneida Ltd.
Ore-Ida Foods, Inc.
Ortho Diagnostic Systems, Inc.
Oshman's Sporting Goods, Inc.
Oster/Sunbeam Appliance Co.
Owens & Minor, Inc.
Packaging Corporation of
America
Palm Beach Co.
Parisian Inc.
Parke-Davis Group
Patagonia
Paxton Co., Frank
Penn Mutual Life Insurance Co.
Penn Savings Bank, a division of
Sovereign Bank Bank of

Princeton, a division of
Sovereign Bank
Pentair
Peoples Drug Stores Inc.
Pepsi-Cola Bottling Co. of
Charlotte
PepsiCo
Perkin-Elmer Corp.
Perry Drug Stores
Pet
Pfizer
Phelps Dodge Corp.
Philip Morris Cos.
Pillsbury Co.
Pioneer Electronics (USA) Inc.
PNC Bank
Polaroid Corp.
Ponderosa, Inc.
Pope & Talbot, Inc.
Portland General Electric Co.
Premark International
Procter & Gamble Co.
Promus Cos.
Provigo Corp. Inc.
Public Service Electric & Gas
Co.
Publix Supermarkets
Quaker Oats Co.
Questar Corp.
Racal-Milgo
Raley's
Ralston Purina Co.
Raychem Corp.
Raytheon Co.
RB&W Corp.
Recognition Equipment
Red Wing Shoe Co.
Reebok International Ltd.
REI-Recreational Equipment,
Inc.
Restaurant Associates, Inc.
Rhone-Poulenc Rorer
Ricoh Corp.
Ricoh Electronics Inc.
Risdon Corp.
RJR Nabisco Inc.
Robbins & Myers, Inc.
Rohm and Haas Company
Ross Laboratories
Rubbermaid
Rust-Oleum Corp.
Safeway, Inc.
Saks Fifth Ave.
Sanyo Manufacturing Corp.
Sara Lee Corp.
Schering-Plough Corp.
Schieffelin & Somerset Co.
Scott, Foresman & Co.
Scott Paper Co.
Scrivner, Inc.
Scrivner of North Carolina Inc.
Seagram & Sons, Joseph E.
Searle & Co., G.D.
Seaway Food Town
ServiceMaster Co. L.P.
Servistar Corp.
Shaw's Supermarkets
Sheaffer Inc.
Shoney's Inc.
Simpson Investment Co.
SKF USA, Inc.
Smith Corp., A.O.
Smith Food & Drug
Smucker Co., J.M.
Sonoco Products Co.
Southland Corp.
Southwire Co.
Spiegel
Springs Industries
Standard Brands Paint Co.
Steelcase
Sterling Inc.
Sterling Winthrop
Steuart Petroleum Co.
Storer Communications Inc.
Subaru of America Inc.
Sun Microsystems

Donated Products (cont.)

Swank, Inc.
Syntex Corp.
Talley Industries, Inc.
Tasty Baking Co.
Tektronix
Tenneco
Texas Gas Transmission Corp.
Texas Instruments
Thomasville Furniture Industries
Thomson Information Publishing Group
3M Co.
Timex Corp.
TJX Cos.
Tops Markets, Inc.
Toro Co.
Tosco Corp. Refining Division
Toshiba America, Inc.
Towle Manufacturing Co.
Toyota Motor Sales, U.S.A.
TRINOVA Corp.
Tropicana Products, Inc.
Tultex Corp.
Unilever United States
Union Bank of Switzerland Los Angeles Branch
Union Camp Corp.
United States Borax & Chemical Corp.
Universal Foods Corp.
Upjohn Co.
US Shoe Corp.
Valley National Bancorp
VF Corp.
Virginia Power Co.
Vulcan Materials Co.
Waldbaum, Inc.
Wallace Computer Services
Warner-Lambert Co.
Washington Mutual Savings Bank
Washington Natural Gas Co.
Washington Post Co.
Wells Fargo & Co.
Wendy's International, Inc.
Whirlpool Corp.
White Consolidated Industries
Wiley & Sons, Inc., John
World Savings & Loan Association
WWF Paper Corp.

In-kind Services

Abitibi-Price
Action Products International
Advanced Micro Devices
AEGON USA, Inc.
Aetna Life & Casualty Co.
Air Products & Chemicals
Alabama Gas Corp. (An Energen Co.)
Alabama Power Co.
Alaska Airlines, Inc.
Alcan Aluminum Corp.
Alexander & Baldwin, Inc.
AlliedSignal
ALPAC Corp.
Alyeska Pipeline Service Co.
America West Airlines
American Brands
American Cyanamid Co.
American General Corp.
American Natural Resources Co.
American President Cos.
American Stock Exchange
American Telephone & Telegraph Co./Dallas Region
American United Life Insurance Co.
Ameritech Publishing
Ameritech Services
Amfac/JMB Hawaii

Apache Corp.
ARCO
Arizona Public Service Co.
Arkla
ASARCO
Ashland Oil
Atkinson Co., Guy F.
Atlanta Gas Light Co.
Avon Products
Babcock & Wilcox Co.
Ball Corp.
Bally's - Las Vegas
Baltimore Gas & Electric Co.
Banc One Wisconsin Corp.
Bank of America Arizona
Bank of Boston Connecticut
Bank of Boston Corp.
Bank of Oklahoma, N.A.
Bank One, Texas-Houston Office
Bank One, Youngstown, NA
Baskin-Robbins USA CO.
Bausch & Lomb
Baxter International
BayBanks
Bean, L.L.
Becton Dickinson & Co.
Bell Communications Research
Bellsouth Telecommunications, Inc.
Benefit Trust Life Insurance Co.
Best Products Co.
Bethlehem Steel Corp.
Big V Supermarkets
Binney & Smith Inc.
Bird Inc.
Bloomingdale's
Bob Evans Farms
Boehringer Mannheim Corp.
Boeing Co.
Booz Allen & Hamilton
Borden
Boston Edison Co.
Bridgestone/Firestone
Brooklyn Union Gas Co.
Brown Group
Brown & Williamson Tobacco Corp.
Browning-Ferris Industries
Burdines
Butler Manufacturing Co.
Cablevision of Michigan
Cabot Corp.
Capital Holding Corp.
Cascade Natural Gas Corp.
Caterpillar
CBS Inc.
Centel Corp.
Centerior Energy Corp.
Central Maine Power Co.
Central Trust Co.
Century Companies of America
CertainTeed Corp.
Chase Lincoln First Bank, N.A.
Chemical Bank
Chesebrough-Pond's
Christie, Manson & Woods International, Inc.
Church & Dwight Co.
CIBA-GEIGY Corp.
Ciba-Geigy Corp. (Pharmaceuticals Division)
CIGNA Corp.
Cincinnati Bell
Cincinnati Gas & Electric Co.
Citibank, F.S.B.
Citizens Commercial & Savings Bank
Clorox Co.
CNA Insurance Cos.
CNG Transmission Corp.
Coastal Corp.
Coca-Cola Co.
Coleman Co.
Colgate-Palmolive Co.
Colonial Life & Accident Insurance Co.
Colorado Interstate Gas Co.

Columbus Dispatch Printing Co.
Columbus Southern Power Co.
Comerica
Commercial Federal Corp.
Conoco Inc.
Consolidated Rail Corp. (Conrail)
Consumers Power Co.
Continental Airlines
Continental Bank N.A.
Contraves USA
Control Data Corp.
Coors Brewing Co.
Corestates Bank
Cox Enterprises
CPC International
CPI Corp.
Crum and Forster
Cullen/Frost Bankers
Dana Corp.
Dayton Hudson Corp.
Dayton Power and Light Co.
DeKalb Genetics Corp.
Delaware North Cos.
Delmarva Power & Light Co.
Detroit Edison Co.
Dime Savings Bank of New York
Dimeo Construction Co.
Donnelley & Sons Co., R.R.
Dow Chemical Co.
Dreyer's & Edy's Grand Ice Cream
du Pont de Nemours & Co., E. I.
Duquesne Light Co.
Durham Corp.
East Ohio Gas Co.
Eaton Corp.
Echlin Inc.
Edwards & Sons, A.G.
Elizabethtown Gas Co.
Enserch Corp.
Entex
Equitable Life Assurance Society of the U.S.
European American Bank
Fairfield Communities, Inc.
Fay's Incorporated
Federal Express Corp.
Ferro Corp.
Fidelity Bank
Financial Corp. of Santa Barbara
Fireman's Fund Insurance Co.
First Alabama Bancshares
First Chicago
First Commercial Bank N.A.
First Fidelity Bancorporation
First Interstate Bank of Denver
First of America Bank Corp.
First Tennessee Bank
Fleet Bank
Fleming Companies, Inc.
Florida Power Corp.
Fluor Corp.
Fortis Benefits Insurance Company/Fortis Financial Group
Fox Inc.
Franklin Mint Corp.
Fraser Paper Ltd.
Freightliner Corp.
Fuller Co., H.B.
Gannett Co.
Gates Corp.
GATX Corp.
GEICO Corp.
GenCorp
General Electric Co.
General Motors Corp.
General Signal Corp.
General Tire Inc.
Georgia Power Co.
Giant Food
Gillette Co.
Glatfelter Co., P.H.
Graco
Graphic Controls Corp.
Great American First Savings Bank, FSB

Great-West Life Assurance Co.
Great Western Financial Corp.
Grocers Supply Co.
Grumman Corp.
Gulfstream Aerospace Corp.
HEI Inc.
Hoffmann-La Roche
Hospital Corp. of America
Household International
Houston Industries
Hunt Oil Co.
Huntington Bancshares Inc.
Hyster-Yale
ICI Americas
Illinois Bell
Illinois Power Co.
IMCERA Group Inc.
Inco Alloys International
Indiana Insurance Cos.
Inland Steel Industries
Intermountain Gas Industries
ITT Hartford Insurance Group
JCPenney Co.
Jefferson-Pilot Communications
John Hancock Mutual Life Insurance Co.
Johnson Co., E. F.
Johnson Controls
Jostens
Journal Communications
Keller-Crescent Co.
Kellogg Co., M.W.
Kemper National Insurance Cos.
Kerr-McGee Corp.
King Kullen Grocery Co., Inc.
Kingsbury Corp.
Kohler Co.
Leo Burnett Co.
Life Insurance Co. of Georgia
Lilly & Co., Eli
Lincoln Telecommunications Co.
Little, Arthur D.
Lockheed Corp.
Long Island Lighting Co.
Lord Corp.
Lotus Development Corp.
LTV Corp.
Lykes Brothers Steamship Co.
Makita U.S.A., Inc.
Mallinckrodt Specialty Chemicals Co.
Marion Merrell Dow
Maritz Inc.
Marriott Corp.
Marsh & McLennan Cos.
Marsh Supermarkets, Inc.
Massachusetts Mutual Life Insurance Co.
MBIA, Inc.
McBride & Son Associates
McCaw Cellular Communications
McDonald & Co. Securities
McDonald's Corp.
McDonnell Douglas Corp.
McKesson Corp.
Mead Corp.
Melitta North America Inc.
Mellon Bank Corp.
Mercedes-Benz of North America, Inc.
Merck Human Health Division
Meridian Bancorp
Meritor Financial Group
Metropolitan Life Insurance Co.
Meyer, Inc., Fred
Michigan Bell Telephone Co.
Michigan Consolidated Gas Co.
Midwest Resources
Minnesota Mutual Life Insurance Co.
Minnesota Power & Light Co.
Mississippi Chemical Corp.
Mississippi Power Co.
Mississippi Power & Light Co.
Mitchell Energy & Development Corp.

Morrison-Knudsen Corp.
MTS Systems Corp.
Multimedia, Inc.
National City Bank, Columbus
National City Bank of Indiana
National Fuel Gas Co.
National Life of Vermont
NationsBank Corp.
NBD Bank
New England Grocer Supply
New England Mutual Life Insurance Co.
New Street Capital Corp.
New York State Electric & Gas Corp.
New York Telephone Co.
News & Observer Publishing Co.
Northeast Utilities
Northern Illinois Gas Co.
Northern Trust Co.
Northern Virginia Natural Gas
Northwest Airlines, Inc.
Northwest Natural Gas Co.
Northwestern National Life Insurance Co.
Norton Co.
Norwest Bank Nebraska
Nucor Corp.
Ohio Citizens Bank
Oki America Inc.
Olin Corp.
Ontario Corp.
Orange & Rockland Utilities, Inc.
Ormet Corp.
Owens-Corning Fiberglas Corp.
Owens-Illinois
Pacific Enterprises
Pacific Gas & Electric Co.
Pacific Mutual Life Insurance Co.
Panhandle Eastern Corp.
Parke-Davis Group
Parsons Corp.
Patagonia
Penn Savings Bank, a division of Sovereign Bank Bank of Princeton, a division of Sovereign Bank
People's Bank
Pfizer
Phelps, Inc.
Phelps Dodge Corp.
Philadelphia Electric Co.
Philip Morris Cos.
Pioneer Hi-Bred International
Plantronics, Inc.
PNC Bank
Ponderosa, Inc.
Portland General Electric Co.
Pratt & Lambert, Inc.
Primerica Corp.
Principal Financial Group
Producers Livestock Marketing Association
Promus Cos.
Providence Energy Corp.
Providence Journal Company
Provident Life & Accident Insurance Co.
Provident Mutual Life Insurance Co. of Philadelphia
Prudential Insurance Co. of America
PSI Energy
Public Service Co. of Colorado
Public Service Co. of Oklahoma
Public Service Electric & Gas Co.
Publix Supermarkets
Puget Sound Power & Light Co.
Quaker Oats Co.
Questar Corp.
Raley's
Ralston Purina Co.
Raychem Corp.
Republic New York Corp.
Reynolds & Reynolds Co.
Rhone-Poulenc Rorer

Ricoh Corp.
Ricoh Electronics Inc.
Riggs National Bank
RJR Nabisco Inc.
Rochester Community Savings Bank
Rohm and Haas Company
Rohr Inc.
Ross Laboratories
Rouse Co.
Royal Group Inc.
Ryder System
SAFECO Corp.
San Diego Gas & Electric
Santa Fe Pacific Corp.
Sara Lee Corp.
Schering-Plough Corp.
Schwab & Co., Charles
Seafirst Corp.
Seaway Food Town
Security Benefit Life Insurance Co.
Security Life of Denver
Shaklee Corp.
Shenandoah Life Insurance Co.
Shoney's Inc.
Smith Corp., A.O.
Smith Food & Drug
SNET
Society Corp.
Sonat
Sooner Pipe & Supply Corp.
Sotheby's
Southern Bell
Southern California Edison Co.
Southern Co. Services
Southland Corp.
Sprint
Standard Brands Paint Co.
Stanley Works
Star Bank, N.A.
State Farm Mutual Automobile Insurance Co.
State Mutual Life Assurance Co.
State Street Bank & Trust Co.
Steelcase
Storage Technology Corp.
Storer Communications Inc.
Sun Co.
Sun Microsystems
Super Valu Stores
Syntex Corp.
Tandem Computers
Teledyne
Tenneco
Tesoro Petroleum Corp.
Texas Commerce Bank Houston, N.A.
Texas-New Mexico Power Co.
3M Co.
Time Insurance Co.
Time Warner Cable
Times Mirror Co.
Torchmark Corp.
Toro Co.
Tosco Corp. Refining Division
Tracor, Inc.
Transamerica Corp.
Travelers Cos.
Tropicana Products, Inc.
Trustmark National Bank
Unigard Security Insurance Co.
Union Carbide Corp.
Union Central Life Insurance Co.
Union Equity Division of Farmland Industries
Union Planters Corp.
Unisys Corp.
United Airlines
United Illuminating Co.
U.S. Bank of Washington
United States Trust Co. of New York
United Technologies Corp.
UNUM Corp.
US Bancorp
Valero Energy Corp.

Valley National Bank of Arizona
Varian Associates
Virginia Power Co.
Vulcan Materials Co.
Washington Mutual Savings Bank
Washington Natural Gas Co.
Washington Post Co.
Washington Water Power Co.
Waste Management
Wausau Insurance Cos.
Wells Fargo & Co.
West One Bancorp
Westinghouse Electric Corp.
Wetterau
Weyerhaeuser Co.
Williams Cos.
Winter Construction Co.
Xerox Corp.
Yellow Corp.

Loaned Employees

Abitibi-Price
AEGON USA, Inc.
Aerospace Corp.
AFLAC
Air Products & Chemicals
Alabama Gas Corp. (An Energen Co.)
Alabama Power Co.
ALPAC Corp.
American Electric Power
American General Corp.
American Microsystems, Inc.
American Telephone & Telegraph Co./Dallas Region
American United Life Insurance Co.
Amfac/JMB Hawaii
Apache Corp.
Archer-Daniels-Midland Co.
ARCO
Arkla
Atlanta Gas Light Co.
Babcock & Wilcox Co.
Backer Spielvogel Bates U.S.
Banc One Illinois Corp.
Banc One Wisconsin Corp.
Bank Hapoalim B.M.
Bank of Boston Connecticut
Bank One, Texas, NA
Bank One, Youngstown, NA
BankAmerica Corp.
Barber-Colman Co.
Barnett Banks
Battelle
Baxter International
Bean, L.L.
Bell Helicopter Textron
Bellsouth Telecommunications, Inc.
Beretta U.S.A. Corp.
Bird Inc.
Boeing Co.
Boots Pharmaceuticals, Inc.
Booz Allen & Hamilton
Brooklyn Union Gas Co.
Brown & Williamson Tobacco Corp.
Browning-Ferris Industries
Bryn Mawr Trust Co.
Burdines
Burlington Industries
Burndy Corp.
C.P. Rail Systems
Cabot Corp.
Capital Holding Corp.
Carrols Corp.
Cascade Natural Gas Corp.
Centel Corp.
Centex Corp.
Central Hudson Gas & Electric Corp.
Central Life Assurance Co.
Central Maine Power Co.
Central & South West Services

Central Trust Co.
CertainTeed Corp.
Christie, Manson & Woods International, Inc.
Church & Dwight Co.
Ciba-Geigy Corp. (Pharmaceuticals Division)
Cincinnati Gas & Electric Co.
Citizens Bank
Citizens & Southern National Bank of Florida
CLARCOR
CNG Transmission Corp.
Coastal Corp.
Colonial Life & Accident Insurance Co.
Columbus Southern Power Co.
Contraves USA
Cray Research
Cullen/Frost Bankers
Curtis Industries, Helene
Dan River, Inc.
Dana Corp.
Delaware North Cos.
Delmarva Power & Light Co.
Dexter Corp.
Dollar General Corp.
Dow Chemical Co.
Dreyer's & Edy's Grand Ice Cream
du Pont de Nemours & Co., E. I.
Duquesne Light Co.
Duriron Co., Inc.
DynCorp
Eaton Corp.
Echlin Inc.
Edwards & Sons, A.G.
Elizabethtown Gas Co.
Enserch Corp.
Entex
Equifax
Equitable Life Assurance Society of the U.S.
Equitable Resources
Ethyl Corp.
Federal National Mortgage Assn., Fannie Mae
Ferro Corp.
Fidelity Bank
First Alabama Bancshares
First Interstate Bank NW Region
First Interstate Bank of Oregon
First of America Bank Corp.
First Tennessee Bank
First Union National Bank of Florida
Fleet Bank
Florida Power Corp.
Florida Power & Light Co.
Forest City Enterprises
Freeport-McMoRan
Freightliner Corp.
GATX Corp.
GenCorp
General Electric Co.
General Mills
General Tire Inc.
Genesco
Gillette Co.
Graphic Controls Corp.
Great-West Life Assurance Co.
Great Western Financial Corp.
Grumman Corp.
Gulfstream Aerospace Corp.
Hecla Mining Co.
Helmerich & Payne Inc.
Holly Sugar Corp.
Holyoke Mutual Insurance Co. in Salem
Houston Industries
Huntington Bancshares Inc.
IBM Corp.
Illinois Power Co.
Inco Alloys International
Intermountain Gas Industries
Interstate Power Co.
IPALCO Enterprises

Iroquois Brands, Ltd.
Jefferson-Pilot Communications
John Hancock Mutual Life Insurance Co.
Johnson Controls
Journal Communications
Kellogg Co., M.W.
Kennecott Corp.
Kiewit Sons, Peter
Kingsbury Corp.
Kloeckner-Pentaplast of America
Leaseway Transportation Corp.
Liberty National Bank
Lilly & Co., Eli
Lincoln Telecommunications Co.
Lockheed Sanders
Long Island Lighting Co.
LTV Corp.
Lykes Brothers Steamship Co.
Mallinckrodt Specialty Chemicals Co.
Maritz Inc.
Marsh Supermarkets, Inc.
Mass Merchandisers, Inc.
Massachusetts Mutual Life Insurance Co.
Matsushita Electric Corp. of America
Mattel
MBIA, Inc.
McCaw Cellular Communications
McCormick & Co.
McDermott
McDonald & Co. Securities
McDonnell Douglas Corp.
MDU Resources Group, Inc.
Mead Corp.
Melitta North America Inc.
Mercantile Bancorp
Meritor Financial Group
Mesa Inc.
Metropolitan Life Insurance Co.
Michigan Consolidated Gas Co.
Michigan Gas Utilities
Midlantic Banks, Inc.
Midwest Resources
Minnegasco
Minnesota Mutual Life Insurance Co.
Minnesota Power & Light Co.
Mississippi Power Co.
Mississippi Power & Light Co.
Mitchell Energy & Development Corp.
Morrison-Knudsen Corp.
Multimedia, Inc.
Mutual of New York
National City Bank, Columbus
National City Bank of Indiana
National Computer Systems
National Convenience Stores, Inc.
National Data Corp.
National Fuel Gas Co.
National Life of Vermont
National Steel
NationsBank Corp.
NBD Bank
New England Grocer Supply
New England Mutual Life Insurance Co.
New Jersey Manufacturers Insurance Co.
New Jersey Resources Corp.
News & Observer Publishing Co.
Niagara Mohawk Power Corp.
Nordson Corp.
North American Life & Casualty Co.
Northeast Utilities
Northern Illinois Gas Co.
Northern Indiana Public Service Co.
NorthPark National Bank
Northwest Natural Gas Co.

Northwestern National Life Insurance Co.
Norwest Bank Nebraska
NYNEX Corp.
Oglebay Norton Co.
Ohio Citizens Bank
Oki America Inc.
Oklahoma Gas & Electric Co.
Ontario Corp.
Orion Capital Corp.
Owens-Corning Fiberglas Corp.
Owens & Minor, Inc.
PACCAR
Pacific Gas & Electric Co.
Palm Beach Co.
Pan-American Life Insurance Co.
Panhandle Eastern Corp.
Parsons Corp.
Patagonia
Peerless Insurance Co.
Pentair
People's Bank
Pfizer
Phelps, Inc.
Philadelphia Electric Co.
PNC Bank
Polychrome Corp.
PriMerit F.S.B.
Principal Financial Group
Producers Livestock Marketing Association
Promus Cos.
Prudential Insurance Co. of America
Public Service Co. of Oklahoma
Puget Sound Power & Light Co.
Quaker Chemical Corp.
Questar Corp.
Ralston Purina Co.
Raychem Corp.
Reading & Bates Corp.
Rhone-Poulenc Rorer
Riggs National Bank
Risdon Corp.
Robbins & Myers, Inc.
Rochester Community Savings Bank
Rohm and Haas Company
Rohr Inc.
Royal Group Inc.
Ryder System
Safeway, Inc.
San Diego Gas & Electric
Sara Lee Corp.
SCANA Corp.
Schering-Plough Corp.
Scrivner, Inc.
Shawmut Bank of Franklin County
Shell Oil Co.
Shenandoah Life Insurance Co.
Signet Bank/Maryland
Simpson Investment Co.
Smith Corp., A.O.
Smith Food & Drug
Sooner Pipe & Supply Corp.
Southern Co. Services
Southtrust Corp.
Spectra-Physics Analytical
Spiegel
Star Bank, N.A.
State Street Bank & Trust Co.
Subaru-Isuzu Automotive Inc.
Swinerton & Walberg Co.
Tandem Computers
Tenneco
Tesoro Petroleum Corp.
Tetley, Inc.
Texas Gas Transmission Corp.
Texas Instruments
3M Co.
Time Insurance Co.
Toro Co.
Tracor, Inc.
Transco Energy Company
Triskelion Ltd.
Tropicana Products, Inc.

Loaned Employees (cont.)

Trustmark National Bank
Union Camp Corp.
UNUM Corp.
US Bancorp
US WEST
Valley National Bancorp
Valley National Bank of Arizona
Varian Associates
Virginia Power Co.
Vulcan Materials Co.
Washington Mutual Savings Bank
Washington Natural Gas Co.
West One Bancorp
Wetterau
Weyerhaeuser Co.
Winter Construction Co.
Wisconsin Bell, Inc.
Wisconsin Energy Corp.
Wisconsin Power & Light Co.
Wisconsin Public Service Corp.
WWF Paper Corp.
Wyman-Gordon Co.
Xerox Corp.

Loaned Executives

AEGON USA, Inc.
AFLAC
Albany International Corp.
Alexander & Baldwin, Inc.
ALPAC Corp.
Alyeska Pipeline Service Co.
Amdahl Corp.
American Electric Power
American General Corp.
American Microsystems, Inc.
American President Cos.
American Telephone & Telegraph Co./Dallas Region
American United Life Insurance Co.
Ameritech Publishing
Ameritech Services
Amfac/JMB Hawaii
ARCO
Arkla
Atlanta Gas Light Co.
Backer Spielvogel Bates U.S.
Ball Corp.
Banc One Illinois Corp.
Banc One Wisconsin Corp.
Bank of America Arizona
Bank One, Dayton, NA
Bank One, Texas, NA
Barber-Colman Co.
Barnett Banks
Battelle
Bean, L.L.
Bell Atlantic Corp.
BellSouth Corp.
Benefit Trust Life Insurance Co.
Beretta U.S.A. Corp.
Binney & Smith Inc.
Bird Inc.
Boeing Co.
Branch Banking & Trust Co.
Brooklyn Union Gas Co.
Brown Group
Brown & Williamson Tobacco Corp.
Browning-Ferris Industries
Burdines
Burlington Industries
C.P. Rail Systems
Cabot Corp.
Capital Holding Corp.
Cargill
Carrier Corp.
Carrols Corp.
Cascade Natural Gas Corp.
Caterpillar
Centel Corp.

Centerior Energy Corp.
Central Fidelity Banks, Inc.
Central Hudson Gas & Electric Corp.
Central Life Assurance Co.
Central Maine Power Co.
Central & South West Services
Central Trust Co.
Church & Dwight Co.
CIBA-GEIGY Corp.
Citizens Commercial & Savings Bank
Citizens & Southern National Bank of Florida
City National Bank
CLARCOR
Cleveland-Cliffs
CNG Transmission Corp.
Colonial Life & Accident Insurance Co.
Columbus Southern Power Co.
Commercial Federal Corp.
Commercial Intertech Corp.
Commonwealth Edison Co.
Contraves USA
Cooper Oil Tool
Corning Incorporated
Country Cos.
Courier-Journal & Louisville Times
CPI Corp.
CR Industries
Cullen/Frost Bankers
Dan River, Inc.
Dana Corp.
D'Arcy Masius Benton & Bowles Inc.
Dayton Hudson Corp.
Deere & Co.
Delmarva Power & Light Co.
Detroit Edison Co.
Dexter Corp.
Diamond Shamrock
Dimeo Construction Co.
Donnelley & Sons Co., R.R.
Dow Chemical Co.
Dreyer's & Edy's Grand Ice Cream
du Pont de Nemours & Co., E. I.
Duke Power Co.
Duquesne Light Co.
DynCorp
East Ohio Gas Co.
Eaton Corp.
Edwards & Sons, A.G.
Electronic Data Systems Corp.
Elizabethtown Gas Co.
Employers Mutual Casualty Co.
Enron Corp.
Entex
Exxon Corp.
Fabri-Kal Corp.
Fairfield Communities, Inc.
Federal Express Corp.
Ferro Corp.
Fidelity Bank
First Alabama Bancshares
First Chicago
First Interstate Bank & Trust Co.
First NH Banks, Inc.
First of America Bank Corp.
First Tennessee Bank
First Union National Bank of Florida
Fleet Bank
Florida Power Corp.
Florida Power & Light Co.
Forest City Enterprises
Freeport-McMoRan
GenCorp
General Accident Insurance Co. of America
General Electric Co.
General Mills
General Signal Corp.
Genesco
Gillette Co.

Glaxo
Graco
Graphic Controls Corp.
Great-West Life Assurance Co.
Great Western Financial Corp.
Grumman Corp.
Gulfstream Aerospace Corp.
Harris Trust & Savings Bank
Hazeltine Corp.
Hecla Mining Co.
HEI Inc.
Hein-Werner Corp.
Hershey Foods Corp.
Hoechst Celanese Corp.
Holyoke Mutual Insurance Co. in Salem
Houston Industries
Howmet Corp.
IBM Corp.
ICI Americas
IDS Financial Services
Illinois Bell
Inco Alloys International
Indiana Bell Telephone Co.
Indiana Insurance Cos.
Inland Steel Industries
Intermountain Gas Industries
Iroquois Brands, Ltd.
ITT Hartford Insurance Group
Jantzen, Inc.
Jefferson-Pilot Communications
John Hancock Mutual Life Insurance Co.
Johnson Controls
Jostens
Journal Communications
Kellogg Co., M.W.
Kennecott Corp.
Kiewit Sons, Peter
King Kullen Grocery Co., Inc.
Kmart Corp.
Knight-Ridder, Inc.
Land O'Lakes
Lane Co., Inc.
Leaseway Transportation Corp.
Liberty National Bank
Life Insurance Co. of Georgia
Lilly & Co., Eli
Lincoln Telecommunications Co.
Lockheed Sanders
Loctite Corp.
Long Island Lighting Co.
Lord Corp.
Louisiana Power & Light Co./New Orleans Public Service
LTV Corp.
Lydall, Inc.
Lykes Brothers Steamship Co.
Mallinckrodt Specialty Chemicals Co.
Marion Merrell Dow
Marsh Supermarkets, Inc.
Mass Merchandisers, Inc.
McCaw Cellular Communications
McCormick & Co.
McDonald & Co. Securities
McDonnell Douglas Corp.
MDU Resources Group, Inc.
Mead Corp.
Melitta North America Inc.
Mellon Bank Corp.
Mercantile Bancorp
Metropolitan Life Insurance Co.
Michigan Bell Telephone Co.
Michigan Consolidated Gas Co.
Michigan Gas Utilities
Midlantic Banks, Inc.
Midwest Resources
Minnegasco
Mississippi Power Co.
Mississippi Power & Light Co.
Mitre Corp.
Morrison-Knudsen Corp.
Multimedia, Inc.

Murphy Oil Corp.
Nalco Chemical Co.
National City Bank, Columbus
National Computer Systems
National Convenience Stores, Inc.
National Data Corp.
National Fuel Gas Co.
National Steel
NationsBank Corp.
NBD Bank
NBD Bank, N.A.
New England Grocer Supply
New Jersey Manufacturers Insurance Co.
New York Telephone Co.
News & Observer Publishing Co.
Northern Illinois Gas Co.
Northern Indiana Public Service Co.
Northern States Power Co.
Northern Trust Co.
Northwest Natural Gas Co.
Northwestern National Life Insurance Co.
Norwest Bank Nebraska
Norwest Corp.
Nucor Corp.
Ogilvy & Mather Worldwide
Oklahoma Gas & Electric Co.
Ontario Corp.
Owens-Corning Fiberglas Corp.
PacifiCorp
Palm Beach Co.
Pan-American Life Insurance Co.
Panhandle Eastern Corp.
Parisian Inc.
Parsons Corp.
Patagonia
Peerless Insurance Co.
Penn Mutual Life Insurance Co.
Pentair
People's Bank
Peoples Energy Corp.
Pfizer
Phelps, Inc.
Philadelphia Electric Co.
Pitney Bowes
Plantronics, Inc.
Portland General Electric Co.
PriMerit F.S.B.
Procter & Gamble Co.
Promus Cos.
Providence Energy Corp.
Provident Life & Accident Insurance Co.
Prudential Insurance Co. of America
Public Service Co. of Oklahoma
Public Service Electric & Gas Co.
Puget Sound Power & Light Co.
Quaker Chemical Corp.
Quaker Oats Co.
Questar Corp.
Ralston Purina Co.
Reading & Bates Corp.
Reynolds & Reynolds Co.
Rhone-Poulenc Rorer
Riggs National Bank
Risdon Corp.
Rochester Community Savings Bank
Rochester Gas & Electric Corp.
Rohm and Haas Company
Ryder System
Sara Lee Corp.
SCANA Corp.
Seafirst Corp.
Shawmut Bank of Franklin County
Shell Oil Co.
Shenandoah Life Insurance Co.
Signet Bank/Maryland
Simpson Investment Co.
Smith Corp., A.O.
Smith Food & Drug

SNET
Sonat
Southern Bell
Southern California Edison Co.
Southern Indiana Gas & Electric Co.
Southtrust Corp.
Southwestern Public Service Co.
Spectra-Physics Analytical
Spiegel
Sprint
Standard Brands Paint Co.
Star Bank, N.A.
State Farm Mutual Automobile Insurance Co.
State Mutual Life Assurance Co.
State Street Bank & Trust Co.
Stone & Webster, Inc.
Subaru of America Inc.
Sumitomo Trust & Banking Co., Ltd.
Swinerton & Walberg Co.
Tenneco
Tesoro Petroleum Corp.
Texas Instruments
Texas-New Mexico Power Co.
3M Co.
Time Insurance Co.
Tracor, Inc.
Triskelion Ltd.
Tropicana Products, Inc.
Trustmark National Bank
Union Electric Co.
United Parcel Service of America
Universal Foods Corp.
US Bancorp
US WEST
Valero Energy Corp.
Valley National Bank of Arizona
Varian Associates
Vulcan Materials Co.
Wachovia Bank & Trust Co., N.A.
Washington Mutual Savings Bank
Washington Natural Gas Co.
Washington Post Co.
Washington Water Power Co.
West One Bancorp
Westinghouse Electric Corp.
Wetterau
Weyerhaeuser Co.
Williams Cos.
Winter Construction Co.
Wisconsin Bell, Inc.
Wisconsin Power & Light Co.
Wyman-Gordon Co.

Workplace Solicitation

Akzo Chemicals Inc.
Alabama Gas Corp. (An Energen Co.)
Alabama Power Co.
Alltel/Western Region
ALPAC Corp.
American Cyanamid Co.
American Microsystems, Inc.
American Telephone & Telegraph Co.
American United Life Insurance Co.
Asea Brown Boveri
Atkinson Co., Guy F.
Atlanta Gas Light Co.
Babcock & Wilcox Co.
Backer Spielvogel Bates U.S.
Bally's - Las Vegas
Banc One Wisconsin Corp.
Banner Life Insurance Co.
Bean, L.L.
Bel Air Mart
Bethlehem Steel Corp.
Brooks Brothers
Brown & Williamson Tobacco Corp.

Burndy Corp.
C.P. Rail Systems
Cargill
Carrols Corp.
Centel Corp.
CertainTeed Corp.
CIBA-GEIGY Corp.
City National Bank
CLARCOR
Cleveland-Cliffs
Clorox Co.
Columbus Southern Power Co.
Cubic Corp.
Cullen/Frost Bankers
Dan River, Inc.
DeKalb Genetics Corp.
Delaware North Cos.
Delmarva Power & Light Co.
Deltona Corp.
Detroit Edison Co.
Diamond Shamrock
Dimeo Construction Co.
du Pont de Nemours & Co., E. I.
Duke Power Co.
Duriron Co., Inc.
DynCorp
Ebsco Industries
Enron Corp.
Entex
Equitable Life Assurance Society
  of the U.S.
Equitable Resources
Exxon Corp.
FAB Industries

Fel-Pro Incorporated
First Alabama Bancshares
First Boston
First Tennessee Bank
Forest Oil Corp.
Freeport-McMoRan
Frisch's Restaurants Inc.
GATX Corp.
GenCorp
General Electric Co.
General Tire Inc.
Gillette Co.
Glenmore Distilleries Co.
Graco
Grand Trunk Corp.
Great Western Financial Corp.
Hadson Corp.
HarperCollins Publishers
Hazeltine Corp.
HEI Inc.
Hiram Walker & Sons Inc.
Holly Sugar Corp.
Hospital Corp. of America
Howell Corp.
Howmet Corp.
Inco Alloys International
International Paper Co.
JCPenney Co.
Jefferson-Pilot Communications
Johnson Controls
Kawasaki Motors Corp., U.S.A.
Keller-Crescent Co.
Kellogg Co., M.W.
Kiewit Sons, Peter

Kikkoman International, Inc.
King Kullen Grocery Co., Inc.
Koh-I-Noor Rapidograph Inc.
Leaseway Transportation Corp.
Liberty National Bank
Lincoln National Corp.
Liquid Air Corp.
Long Island Lighting Co.
Louisiana Power & Light
  Co./New Orleans Public
  Service
LTV Corp.
Marion Merrell Dow
Marriott Corp.
MBIA, Inc.
Medtronic
Mellon Bank Corp.
Merry-Go-Round Enterprises,
  Inc.
Midwest Resources
Minnegasco
Mississippi Power & Light Co.
MTS Systems Corp.
Mutual of New York
National City Bank, Columbus
National Computer Systems
National Convenience Stores,
  Inc.
National Data Corp.
National Fuel Gas Co.
National Life of Vermont
National Standard Co.
NBD Bank, N.A.
New England Grocer Supply

New England Mutual Life
  Insurance Co.
News America Publishing Inc.
Nike Inc.
North American Life & Casualty
  Co.
Northeast Utilities
Northern Illinois Gas Co.
NorthPark National Bank
Ohio National Life Insurance Co.
Ontario Corp.
Owens & Minor, Inc.
PACCAR
Pfizer
Pratt & Lambert, Inc.
Price Associates, T. Rowe
Primerica Corp.
Promus Cos.
Providence Energy Corp.
Provident Life & Accident
  Insurance Co.
PSI Energy
Public Service Co. of Oklahoma
Raley's
Ralston Purina Co.
Rhone-Poulenc Rorer
RJR Nabisco Inc.
Rochester Community Savings
  Bank
Royal Group Inc.
Ryder System
Saint Paul Cos.
Sara Lee Corp.
Scott, Foresman & Co.
Scrivner, Inc.

Seaway Food Town
Security Life of Denver
Sheaffer Inc.
Shenandoah Life Insurance Co.
Signet Bank/Maryland
Smith Food & Drug
Southern Bell
Southland Corp.
Southtrust Corp.
Spiegel
State Mutual Life Assurance Co.
Storer Communications Inc.
Swinerton & Walberg Co.
Texas Gas Transmission Corp.
3M Co.
Time Warner Cable
TJX Cos.
Transco Energy Company
Tropicana Products, Inc.
Union Carbide Corp.
Union Planters Corp.
United Parcel Service of America
Unitrode Corp.
Universal Foods Corp.
Valley National Bancorp
Vulcan Materials Co.
Warner-Lambert Co.
Washington Mutual Savings

  Bank
Westinghouse Electric Corp.
Wiley & Sons, Inc., John
Williams Cos.
Wisconsin Energy Corp.
Yellow Corp.

Nonmonetary Support Type Index

Index to Corporations and Foundations by Recipient Type

Arts & Humanities

Arts Appreciation

Ahmanson Foundation
Albertson's
Alltel/Western Region
ALPAC Corp.
American Natural Resources Co.
Ameritech Services
Amfac/JMB Hawaii
Anderson Foundation, William P.
Annenberg Foundation
Arcana Foundation
Armco Inc.
Attleboro Pawtucket Savings Bank
Augat, Inc.
Bank of New York
BankAmerica Corp.
Bemis Company
Bingham Foundation, William
Binney & Smith Inc.
Blair and Co., William
Blandin Foundation
Block, H&R
Cabot Corp.
Cain Foundation, Effie and Wofford
Centerior Energy Corp.
Central Maine Power Co.
Central Soya Co.
Century Companies of America
Chase Manhattan Bank, N.A.
Chicago Sun-Times, Inc.
Chicago Title and Trust Co.
Ciba-Geigy Corp. (Pharmaceuticals Division)
Citicorp
Clorox Co.
CNA Insurance Cos.
Colonial Life & Accident Insurance Co.
Cowles Charitable Trust
Cullen/Frost Bankers
Cummins Engine Co.
Dayton Hudson Corp.
Deluxe Corp.
Dentsu, Inc., NY
Deposit Guaranty National Bank
Diamond Foundation, Aaron
Dimeo Construction Co.
DiRosa Foundation, Rene and Veronica
Dixie Yarns, Inc.
Dodge Foundation, Geraldine R.
Dorot Foundation
du Pont de Nemours & Co., E. I.
Emerson Electric Co.
Ensworth Charitable Foundation
Fidelity Bank
First Interstate Bank NW Region
First Interstate Bank of Oregon
Fleishhacker Foundation
Foellinger Foundation
Franklin Mint Corp.
Freedom Forum
Freeport-McMoRan
Fry Foundation, Lloyd A.
Gilman Foundation, Howard
Gray Foundation, Garland
Graybar Electric Co.
Haas Fund, Walter and Elise
Hechinger Co.
Hospital Corp. of America
Hunt Manufacturing Co.
Indiana Bell Telephone Co.
J.P. Morgan & Co.

Jameson Trust, Oleonda
Jerome Foundation
John Hancock Mutual Life Insurance Co.
Johnson & Higgins
Kennecott Corp.
Kennedy, Jr. Foundation, Joseph P.
Kimberly-Clark Corp.
Kingsbury Corp.
Liberty National Bank
Lowe Foundation, Joe and Emily
Mallinckrodt Specialty Chemicals Co.
Martin Foundation
McEvoy Foundation, Mildred H.
McKesson Corp.
Meadows Foundation
MNC Financial
National Computer Systems
The New Yorker Magazine, Inc.
News & Observer Publishing Co.
Norman Foundation, Andrew
Northern Indiana Public Service Co.
Northwest Natural Gas Co.
Norton Co.
Ogden Foundation, Ralph E.
Ortho Diagnostic Systems, Inc.
Owen Industries, Inc.
Pacific Telesis Group
Persis Corp.
Philip Morris Cos.
Providence Energy Corp.
Providence Journal Company
Provident Life & Accident Insurance Co.
Pulitzer Publishing Co.
Reliable Life Insurance Co.
Rohm and Haas Company
Roseburg Forest Products Co.
Royal Group Inc.
Russell Memorial Foundation, Robert
Sara Lee Hosiery
Schrafft and Bertha E. Schrafft Charitable Trust, William E.
Seaway Food Town
Security Life of Denver
Sedgwick James Inc.
Sentinel Communications Co.
Shelton Cos.
Shenandoah Life Insurance Co.
Shott, Jr. Foundation, Hugh I.
Skirball Foundation
Southwestern Bell Corp.
Steinman Foundation, John Frederick
Storage Technology Corp.
Stulsaft Foundation, Morris
Textron
Time Warner Cable
Tisch Foundation
Toyota Motor Sales, U.S.A.
Trust Co. Bank
Tyler Corp.
Union Bank of Switzerland Los Angeles Branch
United Technologies Corp.
Valero Energy Corp.
Varian Associates
Vevay-Switzerland County Foundation
Volkswagen of America, Inc.
Wallace Reader's Digest Fund, Lila
Weisman Art Foundation, Frederick R.
Wertheim Foundation, Dr. Herbert A.
West Co.

Winter Construction Co.
Wunsch Foundation

Arts Associations

Abell-Hanger Foundation
Acushnet Co.
Alabama Power Co.
Alco Standard Corp.
Alcon Laboratories, Inc.
AlliedSignal
Alltel/Western Region
ALPAC Corp.
Altman Foundation
Alumax
Aluminum Co. of America
AMAX
AMCORE Bank, N.A. Rockford
American Cyanamid Co.
American Electric Power
American Fidelity Corp.
American Foundation Corporation
American National Bank & Trust Co. of Chicago
American Natural Resources Co.
American President Cos.
American Saw & Manufacturing Co.
American Schlafhorst Foundation, Inc.
American Telephone & Telegraph Co.
American United Life Insurance Co.
Ameritas Life Insurance Corp.
Ameritech Corp.
Ameritech Services
Ames Department Stores
Amfac/JMB Hawaii
Amoco Corp.
AMR Corp.
Amsted Industries
Anderson Foundation, M. D.
Andersons Management Corp.
AON Corp.
Appleton Papers
Archer-Daniels-Midland Co.
ARCO Chemical
Aristech Chemical Corp.
Arkansas Power & Light Co.
Armco Inc.
Arrillaga Foundation
Arvin Industries
Atlanta Gas Light Co.
Attleboro Pawtucket Savings Bank
Avon Products
Azby Fund
Backer Spielvogel Bates U.S.
Baker Foundation, George T.
Ballet Makers
Banc One Illinois Corp.
Banc One Wisconsin Corp.
Bank of Boston Corp.
Bank of Louisville
Bank of New York
Bank One, Texas-Houston Office
Bank South Corp.
BankAmerica Corp.
Bankers Trust Co.
Banner Life Insurance Co.
BarclaysAmerican Corp.
Barnes Group
Barra Foundation
Bartlett & Co.
Battelle
Bauer Foundation, M. R.
Baughman Foundation
Beattie Foundation Trust, Cordelia Lee

Bedsole Foundation, J. L.
Beech Aircraft Corp.
Beeghly Fund, Leon A.
Belk Stores
Bell Communications Research
Bell Industries
Belz Foundation
Bemis Company
Beneficial Corp.
Benwood Foundation
Bergner Co., P.A.
Bethlehem Steel Corp.
Beveridge Foundation, Frank Stanley
Biddle Foundation, Mary Duke
Bingham Foundation, William
Bingham Second Betterment Fund, William
Binney & Smith Inc.
Binswanger Co.
Blanchard Foundation
Blandin Foundation
Blaustein Foundation, Jacob and Hilda
Block, H&R
Blount
Blue Bell, Inc.
Blue Cross and Blue Shield of Minnesota Foundation Inc.
Boatmen's Bancshares
Boatmen's First National Bank of Oklahoma
Boh Brothers Construction Co.
Boots Pharmaceuticals, Inc.
Booz Allen & Hamilton
Borden
Borman's
Bothin Foundation
Botwinick-Wolfensohn Foundation
Bowater Inc.
BP America
Bridgestone/Firestone
Briggs Foundation, T. W.
Brown & Williamson Tobacco Corp.
Browning-Ferris Industries
Buckley Trust, Thomas D.
Bucyrus-Erie
Burdines
Burlington Industries
Burlington Northern Inc.
Burlington Resources
Burroughs Wellcome Co.
C.P. Rail Systems
Cable & Wireless Communications
Cablevision of Michigan
Cabot Corp.
Cafritz Foundation, Morris and Gwendolyn
California Educational Initiatives Fund
Callaway Foundation
Cameron Foundation, Harry S. and Isabel C.
Capital Cities/ABC
Capital Holding Corp.
Carnival Cruise Lines
Carolina Power & Light Co.
Carpenter Foundation, E. Rhodes and Leona B.
Carter Foundation, Amon G.
Casey Foundation, Eugene B.
Caspersen Foundation for Aid to Health and Education, O. W.
CBI Industries
Cedars-Sinai Medical Center Section D Fund
Centerior Energy Corp.
Central Bank of the South

Central Hudson Gas & Electric Corp.
Central Life Assurance Co.
Central Maine Power Co.
Central Soya Co.
CertainTeed Corp.
Cessna Aircraft Co.
Chapman Charitable Trust, H. A. and Mary K.
Charities Foundation
Chase Manhattan Bank, N.A.
Cheney Foundation, Ben B.
Chesapeake Corp.
Chevron Corp.
Chicago Sun-Times, Inc.
Chrysler Corp.
CIBA-GEIGY Corp.
Ciba-Geigy Corp. (Pharmaceuticals Division)
Circuit City Stores
Citicorp
Clark Foundation, Robert Sterling
Clark-Winchcole Foundation
Cleveland-Cliffs
Clipper Ship Foundation
Clorox Co.
Clowes Fund
CM Alliance Cos.
CNA Insurance Cos.
Coffey Foundation
Coleman Co.
Collins & Aikman Holdings Corp.
Collins Foundation
Collins Foundation, Carr P.
Colonial Life & Accident Insurance Co.
Columbia Foundation
Columbus Dispatch Printing Co.
Commerce Clearing House
Compaq Computer Corp.
ConAgra
Consolidated Papers
Consumer Farmer Foundation
Continental Corp.
Cooke Foundation
Cooper Industries
Coors Brewing Co.
Cord Foundation, E. L.
Country Curtains, Inc.
Cowles Charitable Trust
Cowles Media Co.
Cox Enterprises
CPC International
CPI Corp.
CR Industries
Credit Suisse
Crown Books Foundation, Inc.
Crown Central Petroleum Corp.
Crum and Forster
CT Corp. System
Cullen/Frost Bankers
Cummings Foundation, Nathan
Cummins Engine Co.
Curtice-Burns Foods
Dain Bosworth/Inter-Regional Financial Group
Daly Charitable Foundation Trust, Robert and Nancy
Dammann Fund
Dana Charitable Trust, Eleanor Naylor
Davis Foundation, Edwin W. and Catherine M.
Dayton Hudson Corp.
Delaware North Cos.
Deluxe Corp.
Demoulas Supermarkets
Deposit Guaranty National Bank

Arts Associations (cont.)

Detroit Edison Co.
Devonwood Foundation
Devonwood Foundation
DeVos Foundation, Richard and Helen
Dexter Corp.
Dietrich Foundation, William B.
Dietrich Foundation, William B.
Dimeo Construction Co.
Dimick Foundation
DiRosa Foundation, Rene and Veronica
Dixie Yarns, Inc.
Dodge Foundation, Cleveland H.
Dodge Foundation, Geraldine R.
Dodge Jones Foundation
Donaldson Charitable Trust, Oliver S. and Jennie R.
Donnelley Foundation, Gaylord and Dorothy
Dougherty, Jr. Foundation, James R.
Douglas & Lomason Company
Dow Corning Corp.
Dresser Industries
Dreyfus Foundation, Max and Victoria
du Pont de Nemours & Co., E. I.
Duke Power Co.
Dumke Foundation, Dr. Ezekiel R. and Edna Wattis
Dunspaugh-Dalton Foundation
duPont Foundation, Chichester
Dyson Foundation
E and M Charities
Eaton Corp.
Eaton Foundation, Cyrus
Eccles Foundation, George S. and Dolores Dore
Emerson Electric Co.
Emerson Foundation, Fred L.
Emery Memorial, Thomas J.
Engelhard Foundation, Charles
English-Bonter-Mitchell Foundation
Ensign-Bickford Industries
Equifax
Equimark Corp.
Equitable Life Assurance Society of the U.S.
Ethyl Corp.
Exxon Corp.
Falk Foundation, David
Faulkner Trust, Marianne Gaillard
Federal Express Corp.
Federal National Mortgage Assn., Fannie Mae
Fidelity Bank
Filene Foundation, Lincoln and Therese
First Boston
First Fidelity Bancorporation
First Interstate Bank of Arizona
First Interstate Bank of Oregon
First Mississippi Corp.
First Tennessee Bank
First Union Corp.
First Union National Bank of Florida
FirsTier Bank N.A. Omaha
Fish Foundation, Ray C.
Fleet Bank of New York
Fleishhacker Foundation
Fleming Foundation
Florida Power Corp.
Florida Power & Light Co.
Fluor Corp.
Folger Fund
Forbes
Ford Foundation
Ford Fund, Walter and Josephine
Ford Meter Box Co.

Ford Motor Co.
Forest City Enterprises
Fort Worth Star Telegram
Foundation for the Needs of Others
Fourth Financial Corp.
Francis Families Foundation
Frankino Charitable Foundation, Samuel J. and Connie
Franklin Mint Corp.
Fraser Paper Ltd.
Freedom Forum
Freeman Foundation, Carl M.
Freeport-McMoRan
Frisch's Restaurants Inc.
Frohlich Charitable Trust, Ludwig W.
Fuchsberg Family Foundation
Fuller Foundation
Gannett Co.
Garrigues Trust, Edwin B.
Garvey Trust, Olive White
Gateway Apparel
Gazette Co.
GEICO Corp.
General Dynamics Corp.
General Mills
General Motors Corp.
General Reinsurance Corp.
Geneseo Foundation
Genius Foundation, Elizabeth Morse
Georgia-Pacific Corp.
Georgia Power Co.
Gerbode Foundation, Wallace Alexander
Getty Foundation, Ann and Gordon
Giant Food Stores
Glaser Foundation
Glaxo
Glenmore Distilleries Co.
Goldberger Foundation, Edward and Marjorie
Goldome F.S.B
Goldwyn Foundation, Samuel
Grass Family Foundation
Grassmann Trust, E. J.
Graybar Electric Co.
Great-West Life Assurance Co.
Green Fund
Greentree Foundation
Gregg-Graniteville Foundation
Greve Foundation, William and Mary
Griffis Foundation
Griggs and Mary Griggs Burke Foundation, Mary Livingston
Grinnell Mutual Reinsurance Co.
Gross Charitable Trust, Walter L. and Nell R.
Gucci America Inc.
Gudelsky Family Foundation, Homer and Martha
Gund Foundation, Geoffrey
Haas Fund, Walter and Elise
Hall Charitable Trust, Evelyn A. J.
Hallmark Cards
Halsell Foundation, Ewing
Hamilton Bank
Hamilton Foundation, Florence O.
Hancock Foundation, Luke B.
Hankins Foundation
Hansen Foundation, Dane G.
Harmon Foundation, Pearl M. and Julia J.
Harriman Foundation, Mary W.
Harris Foundation, John H. and Lucille
Harsco Corp.
Hartford Courant Foundation
Hawn Foundation
Hechinger Co.
Hecla Mining Co.
Heginbotham Trust, Will E.
Heileman Brewing Co., Inc., G.

Heineman Foundation for Research, Educational, Charitable, and Scientific Purposes
Heinz Co., H.J.
Heinz Foundation, Drue
Herndon Foundation
Hershey Foods Corp.
Heublein
Hewlett Foundation, William and Flora
Heyward Memorial Fund, DuBose and Dorothy
Hillman Foundation, Henry L.
Hoche-Scofield Foundation
Holzer Memorial Foundation, Richard H.
HON Industries
Hook Drug
Hooker Charitable Trust, Janet A.
Horne Foundation, Dick
Hospital Corp. of America
Houston Industries
Hubbard Broadcasting
Huffy Corp.
Hultquist Foundation
Hunt Alternatives Fund, Helen
Huthsteiner Fine Arts Trust
IBM Corp.
Icahn Foundation, Carl C.
ICI Americas
IES Industries
Illinois Tool Works
Inco Alloys International
Index Technology Corp.
Indiana Bell Telephone Co.
Indiana Desk Co.
Indiana Insurance Cos.
Inland Container Corp.
Inman Mills
Interco
International Paper Co.
Ireland Foundation
Irvine Foundation, James
Isaly Klondike Co.
ITT Corp.
ITT Hartford Insurance Group
ITT Rayonier
Jackson Charitable Trust, Marion Gardner
Jackson Foundation
James River Corp. of Virginia
Janirve Foundation
JCPenney Co.
Jenkins Foundation, George W.
Jennings Foundation, Martha Holden
Jerome Foundation
John Hancock Mutual Life Insurance Co.
Johnson Co., E. F.
Johnson Controls
Johnson Fund, Edward C.
Johnson & Higgins
Johnson & Son, S.C.
Jonsson Foundation
Jordan and Ettie A. Jordan Charitable Foundation, Mary Ranken
Jostens
Journal Gazette Co.
JSJ Corp.
Kahn Memorial Trust
Kantzler Foundation
Keene Trust, Hazel R.
Keller-Crescent Co.
Kellogg's
Kellwood Co.
Kenedy Memorial Foundation, John G. and Marie Stella
Kennecott Corp.
Kepco, Inc.
Kern Foundation, Ilma
Kerr Foundation, Robert S. and Grayce B.
Kerr Fund, Grayce B.
Kerr-McGee Corp.

Kiewit Foundation, Peter
Kiewit Sons, Peter
Kimball International
Kimberly-Clark Corp.
Kingsbury Corp.
Kiplinger Foundation
Klee Foundation, Conrad and Virginia
Kline Foundation, Josiah W. and Bessie H.
Koch Industries
Koehler Foundation, Marcia and Otto
Koh-I-Noor Rapidograph Inc.
Kohler Foundation
Kreielsheimer Foundation Trust
Kress Foundation, Samuel H.
Kulas Foundation
Kunkel Foundation, John Crain
Kunstadter Family Foundation, Albert
Kyocera International Inc.
Lance, Inc.
Langdale Co.
Lard Trust, Mary Potishman
Lard Trust, Mary Potishman
Lauder Foundation
Lawrence Foundation, Alice
LEF Foundation
Leuthold Foundation
Levitt Foundation, Richard S.
Lieberman Enterprises
Life Insurance Co. of Georgia
Lightner Sams Foundation
Lilly & Co., Eli
Lilly Foundation, Richard Coyle
Link, Jr. Foundation, George
Lipton, Thomas J.
Little, Arthur D.
Livingston Foundation
Loewy Family Foundation
Long Island Lighting Co.
Louisiana Land & Exploration Co.
Lowe Foundation, Joe and Emily
LTV Corp.
Lubrizol Corp.
Lurcy Charitable and Educational Trust, Georges
Lydall, Inc.
Lynn Foundation, E. M.
Lytel Foundation, Bertha Russ
MacArthur Foundation, John D. and Catherine T.
Macy & Co., R.H.
Magma Copper Co.
Magruder Foundation, Chesley G.
Manoogian Foundation, Alex and Marie
Maritz Inc.
Marpat Foundation
Marquette Electronics
Marriott Corp.
Marriott Foundation, J. Willard
Marsh & McLennan Cos.
Marshall Field's
Marshall & Ilsley Bank
Martin Foundation
Martin Marietta Corp.
Massey Charitable Trust
Mather and William Gwinn Mather Fund, Elizabeth Ring
May Department Stores Co.
MBIA, Inc.
MCA
McAlister Charitable Foundation, Harold
McCarthy Foundation, Michael W.
McCasland Foundation
McCormick Trust, Anne
McCune Charitable Trust, John R.
McDermott Foundation, Eugene
McDonnell Douglas Corp.
McDonnell Douglas Corp.-West

McDonough Foundation, Bernard
McEvoy Foundation, Mildred H.
McFawn Trust No. 2, Lois Sisler
McGraw Foundation, Donald C.
McGraw-Hill
McGregor Fund
McLean Contributionship
McNutt Charitable Trust, Amy Shelton
McWane Inc.
MDU Resources Group, Inc.
Mead Corp.
Meadows Foundation
Mechanic Foundation, Morris A.
Mellen Foundation
Mellon Bank Corp.
Mendel Foundation
Menschel Foundation, Robert and Joyce
Meridian Bancorp
Merrick Foundation
Mertz-Gilmore Foundation, Joyce
Mervyn's
Metropolitan Life Insurance Co.
Michigan Bell Telephone Co.
Microsoft Corp.
Midwest Resources
Miles Inc.
Milliken & Co.
Mingenback Foundation, Julia J.
Misco Industries
Mnuchin Foundation
Mobil Oil Corp.
Monell Foundation, Ambrose
Monsanto Co.
Montgomery Street Foundation
Moody Foundation
Moorman Manufacturing Co.
Morgan Trust for Charity, Religion, and Education
Morrison Foundation, Harry W.
Moses Fund, Henry and Lucy
Moss Foundation, Harry S.
Motorola
Mott Fund, Ruth
Mueller Co.
Nash Foundation
National Fuel Gas Co.
National Life of Vermont
National Westminster Bank New Jersey
Nationwide Insurance Cos.
NBD Bank
NBD Bank, N.A.
New England Mutual Life Insurance Co.
New York Life Insurance Co.
New York Telephone Co.
The New Yorker Magazine, Inc.
Newhouse Foundation, Samuel I.
News & Observer Publishing Co.
Nike Inc.
Norfolk Shipbuilding & Drydock Corp.
Norfolk Southern Corp.
Northern Indiana Public Service Co.
Northwest Natural Gas Co.
Norwest Bank Nebraska
Noyes, Jr. Memorial Foundation, Nicholas H.
O'Brien Foundation, Cornelius and Anna Cook
O'Connor Co.
O'Connor Foundation, A. Lindsay and Olive B.
OCRI Foundation
Odyssey Partners
Ogilvy & Mather Worldwide
Oglebay Norton Co.
Oklahoman Foundation
Olin Corp.
Ontario Corp.
Overbrook Foundation
Overseas Shipholding Group
Owen Industries, Inc.
Pacific Enterprises

PacifiCorp
Packard Foundation, David and Lucile
Paley Foundation, William S.
Pangburn Foundation
Panhandle Eastern Corp.
Paramount Communications Inc.
Parker Foundation, Theodore Edson
Penn Foundation, William
Pennzoil Co.
Peoples Energy Corp.
Pepsi-Cola Bottling Co. of Charlotte
Perry Drug Stores
Persis Corp.
Pet
Peterloon Foundation
Petrie Trust, Lorene M.
Pfizer
Pforzheimer Foundation, Carl and Lily
Philip Morris Cos.
Philips Foundation, Jesse
Phillips Family Foundation, Jay and Rose
Phillips Petroleum Co.
Pick, Jr. Fund, Albert
Pittsburgh National Bank
Pittway Corp.
Plitt Southern Theatres
Polaroid Corp.
Polychrome Corp.
Porsche Cars North America, Inc.
Potomac Electric Power Co.
PPG Industries
Premier Bank
Premier Industrial Corp.
Price Foundation, Louis and Harold
Primerica Corp.
Prince Manufacturing, Inc.
Pritzker Foundation
Procter & Gamble Co.
Providence Energy Corp.
Provident Life & Accident Insurance Co.
Prudential Insurance Co. of America
Public Service Co. of Colorado
Puget Sound Power & Light Co.
Pulitzer Publishing Co.
Quaker Oats Co.
Radin Foundation
Ralston Purina Co.
Randleigh Foundation Trust
Regis Corp.
Reily & Co., William B.
Reinberger Foundation
Reliable Life Insurance Co.
Reliance Electric Co.
Reynolds Foundation, Donald W.
Reynolds Foundation, Richard S.
Reynolds Metals Co.
Rice Foundation
Rich Products Corp.
Richardson Foundation, Sid W.
RJR Nabisco Inc.
Robertshaw Controls Co.
Rockefeller Foundation
Rockwell Fund
Rockwell International Corp.
Rohm and Haas Company
Rohr Inc.
Romill Foundation
RosaMary Foundation
Rose Foundation, Billy
Roseburg Forest Products Co.
Rosenstiel Foundation
Ross Foundation
Ross Foundation, Lyn & George M.
Rouse Co.
Rowland Foundation
Royal Group Inc.
Rubbermaid
Rubin Foundation, Samuel

Russell Educational Foundation, Benjamin and Roberta
Ryan Foundation, Nina M.
Safeguard Scientifics Foundation
Sage Foundation
Santa Fe Pacific Corp.
Sara Lee Corp.
Sara Lee Hosiery
Saunders Charitable Foundation, Helen M.
Schering-Plough Corp.
Schieffelin & Somerset Co.
Schloss & Co., Marcus
Schwab & Co., Charles
Scott Foundation, Virginia Steele
Scott Foundation, William E.
Scrivner, Inc.
Scrivner of North Carolina Inc.
Scurlock Foundation
Searle & Co., G.D.
Seaver Institute
Seaway Food Town
Security Life of Denver
Sedgwick James Inc.
Seeley Foundation
Sentinel Communications Co.
Shawmut National Corp.
Sheafer Charitable Trust, Emma A.
Sheaffer Inc.
Shenandoah Life Insurance Co.
Shott, Jr. Foundation, Hugh I.
Shubert Foundation
Simon Charitable Trust, Esther
Simon Foundation, William E. and Carol G.
Simpson Investment Co.
Skinner Corp.
Skirball Foundation
Slant/Fin Corp.
Smith Foundation, Kelvin and Eleanor
SNET
Somers Foundation, Byron H.
Sonat
Sooner Pipe & Supply Corp.
Sosland Foundation
Sotheby's
South Waite Foundation
Southern California Edison Co.
Southwestern Bell Corp.
Speyer Foundation, Alexander C. and Tillie S.
Springs Foundation
Springs Industries
Square D Co.
Stackpole-Hall Foundation
Staley Manufacturing Co., A.E.
Stark Foundation, Nelda C. and H. J. Lutcher
Starr Foundation
State Street Bank & Trust Co.
Steiger Memorial Fund, Albert
Steinhagen Benevolent Trust, B. A. and Elinor
Sterling Inc.
Stevens Foundation, John T.
Storer Foundation, George B.
Strake Foundation
Stratford Foundation
Strawbridge Foundation of Pennsylvania II, Margaret Dorrance
Stride Rite Corp.
Sulzberger Foundation
Summerfield Foundation, Solon E.
Sun Co.
Swig Charity Foundation, Mae and Benjamin
Swig Foundation
Tandy Foundation, Anne Burnett and Charles
Tanner Cos.
Taylor Foundation, Ruth and Vernon
TCF Banking & Savings, FSB

Teledyne
Teleflex Inc.
Tenneco
Tesoro Petroleum Corp.
Texas Commerce Bank Houston, N.A.
Texas Gas Transmission Corp.
Textron
Thomas & Betts Corp.
Thyssen Specialty Steels
Times Mirror Co.
Timken Co.
Tokheim Corp.
Tomkins Industries, Inc.
Towsley Foundation, Harry A. and Margaret D.
Toyota Motor Sales, U.S.A.
Tozer Foundation
Trexler Trust, Harry C.
TRINOVA Corp.
True Trust, Henry A.
Truman Foundation, Mildred Faulkner
Trusler Foundation
Trust Co. Bank
Trust for Mutual Understanding
Union Bank of Switzerland Los Angeles Branch
Union Camp Corp.
Union Electric Co.
United Airlines
United States Sugar Corp.
Universal Leaf Tobacco Co.
US Bancorp
US WEST
USX Corp.
Valley National Bank of Arizona
Valmont Industries
Van Every Foundation, Philip L.
Virginia Power Co.
Volkswagen of America, Inc.
Vulcan Materials Co.
Wachovia Bank & Trust Co., N.A.
Waggoner Charitable Trust, Crystelle
Waldbaum, Inc.
Wallace Reader's Digest Fund, Lila
Wallach Foundation, Miriam G. and Ira D.
Warhol Foundation for the Visual Arts, Andy
Warren Foundation, William K.
Washington Mutual Savings Bank
Waste Management
Wean Foundation, Raymond John
Weaver Foundation
Weeden Foundation, Frank
Weiler Foundation, Theodore & Renee
Weisman Art Foundation, Frederick R.
Wells Foundation, Franklin H. and Ruth L.
Western New York Foundation
Weyerhaeuser Co.
Whirlpool Corp.
Whitaker Foundation
Whitaker Fund, Helen F.
Whitehead Foundation
Wilbur-Ellis Co.
Williams Cos.
Winchester Foundation
Winter Construction Co.
Wisconsin Energy Corp.
Witte, Jr. Foundation, John H.
Wolens Foundation, Kalman and Ida
Woods Charitable Fund
Wortham Foundation
Wyomissing Foundation
Xerox Corp.
Yost Trust, Elizabeth Burns
Zachry Co., H. B.
Zellerbach Family Fund

Arts Centers

Abrams Foundation, Benjamin and Elizabeth
Ace Beverage Co.
Alabama Power Co.
Albertson's
Alexander Foundation, Joseph
Alexander Foundation, Walter
Allendale Mutual Insurance Co.
AlliedSignal
Alltel/Western Region
ALPAC Corp.
Alumax
Aluminum Co. of America
AMAX
American Aggregates Corp.
American Brands
American Cyanamid Co.
American Electric Power
American Express Co.
American Foundation Corporation
American National Bank & Trust Co. of Chicago
American Natural Resources Co.
American Telephone & Telegraph Co.
American United Life Insurance Co.
Ameritech Services
Amfac/JMB Hawaii
Amoco Corp.
Anacomp, Inc.
Andersen Corp.
Andersons Management Corp.
Archer-Daniels-Midland Co.
ARCO
Argyros Foundation
Aristech Chemical Corp.
Arkansas Power & Light Co.
Arkell Hall Foundation
Armbrust Chain Co.
Armco Inc.
Armco Steel Co.
Ashland Oil
Atalanta/Sosnoff Capital Corp.
Atherton Family Foundation
Atlanta Foundation
Atlanta Gas Light Co.
Attleboro Pawtucket Savings Bank
Auerbach Foundation, Beatrice Fox
Avis Inc.
Avon Products
Babcock & Wilcox Co.
Backer Spielvogel Bates U.S.
Baier Foundation, Marie
Bancorp Hawaii
Bank of Boston Corp.
Bank of Louisville
Bank of New York
Bank South Corp.
BankAmerica Corp.
Bankers Trust Co.
Banner Life Insurance Co.
BarclaysAmerican Corp.
Barnett Banks
Barra Foundation
Barry Corp., R. G.
Barstow Foundation
Bassett Foundation, Norman
Batten Foundation
Bean Foundation, Norwin S. and Elizabeth N.
Beerman Foundation
Belden Brick Co., Inc.
Belk Stores
Bemis Company
Bender Foundation
Beneficia Foundation
Benenson Foundation, Frances and Benjamin
Berger Foundation, Albert E.
Berlin Charitable Fund, Irving

Bernsen Foundation, Grace and Franklin
BFGoodrich
Bickerton Charitable Trust, Lydia H.
Biddle Foundation, Mary Duke
Bierlein Family Foundation
Bingham Foundation, William
Binney & Smith Inc.
Bishop Foundation
Bishop Foundation, E. K. and Lillian F.
Blair and Co., William
Blair Foundation, John
Blake Foundation, S. P.
Blandin Foundation
Blank Fund, Myron and Jacqueline
Blaustein Foundation, Jacob and Hilda
Blinken Foundation
Block, H&R
Blount
Blum Foundation, Harry and Maribel G.
Blum-Kovler Foundation
Boatmen's First National Bank of Oklahoma
Boeing Co.
Boettcher Foundation
Bolz Family Foundation, Eugenie Mayer
Bonfils-Stanton Foundation
Booz Allen & Hamilton
Borman's
Boswell Foundation, James G.
Botwinick-Wolfensohn Foundation
Bowater Inc.
BP America
Brace Foundation, Donald C.
Brach Foundation, Helen
Bray Charitable Trust, Viola E.
Brennan Foundation, Robert E.
Brenton Banks Inc.
Brewer and Co., Ltd., C.
Breyer Foundation
Bridwell Foundation, J. S.
Briggs Foundation, T. W.
Bristol-Myers Squibb Co.
British Airways
Broadhurst Foundation
Brown Foundation
Brown & Williamson Tobacco Corp.
Browning Charitable Foundation, Val A.
Buell Foundation, Temple Hoyne
Buhl Family Foundation
Bull Foundation, Henry W.
Burdines
Bush Foundation
Butler Family Foundation, Patrick and Aimee
Bydale Foundation
Cabot Corp.
Cafritz Foundation, Morris and Gwendolyn
California & Hawaiian Sugar Co.
Camp Foundation
Camp Younts Foundation
Canon U.S.A., Inc.
Cantor Foundation, Iris and B. Gerald
Capital Holding Corp.
Cargill
Carpenter Foundation, E. Rhodes and Leona B.
Carrier Corp.
Carvel Foundation, Thomas and Agnes
Cassett Foundation, Louis N.
Castle Foundation, Harold K. L.
Castle Foundation, Samuel N. and Mary
Caterpillar
CBI Industries

Arts Centers (cont.)

Cedars-Sinai Medical Center Section D Fund
Centerior Energy Corp.
Central Life Assurance Co.
Central Maine Power Co.
Chadwick Fund, Dorothy Jordan
Chamberlin Foundation, Gerald W.
Chambers Development Co.
Chapman Charitable Trust, H. A. and Mary K.
Charina Foundation
Charities Foundation
Chase Manhattan Bank, N.A.
Chastain Charitable Foundation, Robert Lee and Thomas M.
Chemical Bank
Cheney Foundation, Ben B.
Cheney Foundation, Elizabeth F.
Cherokee Foundation
Chesebrough-Pond's
Chevron Corp.
Chicago Sun-Times, Inc.
Chrysler Corp.
CIBA-GEIGY Corp.
Ciba-Geigy Corp. (Pharmaceuticals Division)
Citicorp
Citizens Bank
Citizens Commercial & Savings Bank
Clark Foundation, Robert Sterling
Clorox Co.
CNA Insurance Cos.
Cobb Family Foundation
Cohen Foundation, Manny and Ruthy
Cohen Foundation, Naomi and Nehemiah
Colonial Life & Accident Insurance Co.
Coltec Industries
Columbia Foundation
Comstock Foundation
Connell Foundation, Michael J.
Connell Foundation, Michael J.
Connelly Foundation
Consolidated Natural Gas Co.
Contempo Communications
Continental Corp.
Cooke Foundation
Cooke Foundation Corporation, V. V.
Cooper Foundation
Coors Brewing Co.
Coors Foundation, Adolph
Copley Press
Cord Foundation, E. L.
Country Curtains, Inc.
Courts Foundation
Cowles Charitable Trust
Cowles Foundation, Gardner and Florence Call
Cowles Media Co.
Cox, Jr. Foundation, James M.
CPC International
CR Industries
Crane Foundation, Raymond E. and Ellen F.
Crary Foundation, Bruce L.
Crawford & Co.
Credit Suisse
Crestar Financial Corp.
Crum and Forster
CT Corp. System
Cuesta Foundation
Culver Foundation, Constans
CUNA Mutual Insurance Group
Curtice-Burns Foods
Daily News
Dain Bosworth/Inter-Regional Financial Group
Dalton Foundation, Dorothy U.
Dammann Fund

Dana Charitable Trust, Eleanor Naylor
Danis Industries
Dart Group Corp.
Day Foundation, Nancy Sayles
Dayton Hudson Corp.
DEC International, Inc.
Deere & Co.
Dekalb Energy Co.
Delaware North Cos.
Deluxe Corp.
Demoulas Supermarkets
Deposit Guaranty National Bank
DeRoy Testamentary Foundation
Detroit Edison Co.
Deuble Foundation, George H.
DeVos Foundation, Richard and Helen
Dewing Foundation, Frances R.
Dexter Industries
Dial Corp.
Dickson Foundation
Dillard Paper Co.
Dimeo Construction Co.
DNP (America), Inc.
Dobson Foundation
Dodge Foundation, Geraldine R.
Donaldson Co.
Donovan, Leisure, Newton & Irvine
Douglas Charitable Foundation
Douty Foundation
Dow Corning Corp.
Dow Foundation, Herbert H. and Barbara C.
Dow Foundation, Herbert H. and Grace A.
Dow Fund, Alden and Vada
Dower Foundation, Thomas W.
Downs Perpetual Charitable Trust, Ellason
Dresser Industries
du Pont de Nemours & Co., E. I.
Duke Power Co.
Dun & Bradstreet Corp.
Dunagan Foundation
Durst Foundation
Easley Trust, Andrew H. and Anne O.
Eaton Corp.
Eaton Foundation, Cyrus
Eccles Foundation, George S. and Dolores Dore
Eccles Foundation, Marriner S.
Eden Hall Foundation
El Pomar Foundation
Elf Atochem North America
Elizabethtown Gas Co.
Ellis Foundation
Emerson Electric Co.
Emerson Foundation, Fred L.
Emery Memorial, Thomas J.
Engelhard Foundation, Charles
English-Bonter-Mitchell Foundation
Enterprise Rent-A-Car Co.
Equifax
Equitable Life Assurance Society of the U.S.
Erb Lumber Co.
Erpf Fund, Armand G.
Ethyl Corp.
Evans Foundation, Lettie Pate
Evjue Foundation
Exxon Corp.
Fairchild Foundation, Sherman
Falcon Foundation
Fanwood Foundation
Farallon Foundation
Farish Fund, William Stamps
Federal Express Corp.
Federal-Mogul Corp.
Federal Screw Works
Federated Life Insurance Co.
Federation Foundation of Greater Philadelphia

Feil Foundation, Louis and Gertrude
Feintech Foundation
Fels Fund, Samuel S.
Femino Foundation
Fidelity Bank
Fifth Third Bancorp
Filene Foundation, Lincoln and Therese
Finley Foundation, A. E.
Fireman's Fund Insurance Co.
Firestone Foundation, Roger S.
First Boston
First Fidelity Bancorporation
First Hawaiian
First Interstate Bank of Arizona
First Interstate Bank of California
First Interstate Bank of Oregon
First Maryland Bancorp
First National Bank & Trust Co. of Rockford
First NH Banks, Inc.
First Tennessee Bank
First Union Corp.
Firstar Bank Milwaukee NA
Fish Foundation, Vain and Harry
Fishback Foundation Trust, Harmes C.
Fisher Foundation, Gramma
Fleet Financial Group
Fleishhacker Foundation
Flintridge Foundation
Florida Power & Light Co.
Fluor Corp.
Foellinger Foundation
Folger Fund
Foothills Foundation
Forbes
Ford Foundation
Ford Fund, Benson and Edith
Ford Fund, Walter and Josephine
Ford Motor Co.
Frankel Foundation, George and Elizabeth F.
Franklin Mint Corp.
Freedom Forum
Freeman Foundation, Ella West
Freeport-McMoRan
Frelinghuysen Foundation
Frohlich Charitable Trust, Ludwig W.
Fry Foundation, Lloyd A.
Fuller Co., H.B.
Fuller Foundation, George F. and Sybil H.
Fuqua Foundation, J. B.
Furth Foundation
Garvey Kansas Foundation
Gates Foundation
Gault-Hussey Charitable Trust
Gelb Foundation, Lawrence M.
General Electric Co.
General Mills
General Motors Corp.
General Railway Signal Corp.
General Reinsurance Corp.
Georgia-Pacific Corp.
Georgia Power Co.
Gerlach Foundation
Gerstacker Foundation, Rollin M.
Getty Foundation, Ann and Gordon
Gheens Foundation
Giant Eagle
Giant Food
Giddings & Lewis
Gilbert, Jr. Charitable Trust, Price
Gillette Co.
Gilman and Gonzalez-Falla Theatre Foundation
Gilmore Foundation, Irving S.
Glaxo
Glazer Foundation, Madelyn L.
Gleason Foundation, Katherine
Glen Eagles Foundation
Glickenhaus & Co.
Glosser Foundation, David A.

Goldberg Family Foundation
Goldman Foundation, Herman
Goldome F.S.B
Goldstein Foundation, Leslie and Roslyn
Goodman Family Foundation
Goodwin Foundation, Leo
Gradison & Co.
Grainger Foundation
Graphic Controls Corp.
Graybar Electric Co.
Great-West Life Assurance Co.
Greater Lansing Foundation
Green Fund
Greene Foundation, Jerome L.
Greenebaum, Doll & McDonald
Greenfield Foundation, Albert M.
Greve Foundation, William and Mary
Griffis Foundation
Griggs and Mary Griggs Burke Foundation, Mary Livingston
Grossman Foundation, N. Bud
Grumbacher Foundation, M. S.
Gruss Charitable Foundation, Emanuel and Riane
Gruss Petroleum Corp.
GTE Corp.
Guardian Life Insurance Co. of America
Gucci America Inc.
Gulfstream Aerospace Corp.
Gussman Foundation, Herbert and Roseline
H. B. B. Foundation
Haas Foundation, Paul and Mary
Haas Fund, Walter and Elise
Hall Charitable Trust, Evelyn A. J.
Halliburton Co.
Hallmark Cards
Halsell Foundation, Ewing
Hammer Foundation, Armand
Hansen Foundation, Dane G.
Hanson Foundation
Harden Foundation
Harland Co., John H.
Harriman Foundation, Mary W.
Harrington Foundation, Francis A. and Jacquelyn H.
Harris Corp.
Harris Foundation, James J. and Angelia M.
Harsco Corp.
Hawkins Foundation, Robert Z.
Hayfields Foundation
Hazen Charitable Trust, Lita Annenberg
Hearst Foundation, William Randolph
Hechinger Co.
Heckscher Foundation for Children
Heinz Co., H.J.
Heller Foundation, Walter E.
Helmerich Foundation
Henderson Foundation, George B.
Henkel Corp.
Herndon Foundation
Hershey Foundation
Hess Foundation
Heymann Special Account, Mr. and Mrs. Jimmy
Heymann-Wolf Foundation
Higgins Charitable Trust, Lorene Sails
Higginson Trust, Corina
Hill and Family Foundation, Walter Clay
Hilliard Corp.
Hillman Foundation
Hofmann Co.
Holmes Foundation
Holzer Memorial Foundation, Richard H.
Hooker Charitable Trust, Janet A.
Hoover Foundation

Hoover Fund-Trust, W. Henry
Hopkins Foundation, Josephine Lawrence
Hopwood Charitable Trust, John M.
Hospital Corp. of America
Howard and Bush Foundation
Howe and Mitchell B. Howe Foundation, Lucite Horton
Howell Foundation, Eric and Jessie
Howell Fund
Hubbard Broadcasting
Hudson-Webber Foundation
Huffy Corp.
Hulings Foundation, Mary Andersen
Humana
Hunt Manufacturing Co.
IBM Corp.
IDS Financial Services
Illges Foundation, John P. and Dorothy S.
Imlay Foundation
Inco Alloys International
Indiana Bell Telephone Co.
Indiana Insurance Cos.
Inland Container Corp.
Interco
International Paper Co.
Irvine Foundation, James
Isaly Klondike Co.
ITT Corp.
ITT Hartford Insurance Group
ITT Rayonier
Ix & Sons, Frank
J.P. Morgan & Co.
Jaffe Foundation
James River Corp. of Virginia
Janirve Foundation
Jeffress Memorial Trust, Elizabeth G.
Jenkins Foundation, George W.
Jennings Foundation, Mary Hillman
John Hancock Mutual Life Insurance Co.
Johnson Co., E. F.
Johnson Controls
Johnson Endeavor Foundation, Christian A.
Johnson & Higgins
Johnson & Johnson
Johnson & Son, S.C.
Jones Foundation, Harvey and Bernice
Jonsson Foundation
Jost Foundation, Charles and Mabel P.
Kangesser Foundation, Robert E., Harry A., and M. Sylvia
Kapiloff Foundation, Leonard
Kaplan Foundation, Rita J. and Stanley H.
Kaufmann Foundation, Henry
Kearney Inc., A.T.
Keck, Jr. Foundation, William M.
Kemper Educational and Charitable Fund
Kempner Fund, Harris and Eliza
Kennametal
Kennecott Corp.
Kerr Foundation
Kerr Foundation, Robert S. and Grayce B.
Kettering Fund
Kieckhefer Foundation, J. W.
Kilcawley Fund, William H.
Kimberly-Clark Corp.
Kimmelman Foundation, Helen & Milton
Kingsbury Corp.
Kingsley Foundation, Lewis A.
Kiplinger Foundation
Kirbo Charitable Trust, Thomas M. and Irene B.
Kirkpatrick Foundation

Klau Foundation, David W. and Sadie
Klee Foundation, Conrad and Virginia
Knox Foundation, Seymour H.
Knox, Sr., and Pearl Wallis Knox Charitable Foundation, Robert W.
Knudsen Foundation, Tom and Valley
Koch Industries
Koehler Foundation, Marcia and Otto
Kohler Foundation
Kramer Foundation
Kramer Foundation, Louise
Kresge Foundation
Kress Foundation, George
Krimendahl II Foundation, H. Frederick
Kuyper Foundation, Peter H. and E. Lucille Gaass
Kysor Industrial Corp.
Lafarge Corp.
LamCo. Communications
Landmark Communications
Lanier Brothers Foundation
Lannan Foundation
Large Foundation
Lastfogel Foundation, Abe and Frances
Lauder Foundation
Lawrence Foundation, Alice
Lee Foundation, Ray M. and Mary Elizabeth
LEF Foundation
Leibovitz Foundation, Morris P.
Lemberg Foundation
Leo Burnett Co.
Liberty Corp.
Liberty National Bank
Life Insurance Co. of Georgia
Lightner Sams Foundation
Lilly Foundation, Richard Coyle
Link, Jr. Foundation, George
Lipton, Thomas J.
Little Family Foundation
Litton Industries
Loewenberg Foundation
Long Island Lighting Co.
Loughran Foundation, Mary and Daniel
Louisiana Land & Exploration Co.
Louisiana Power & Light Co./New Orleans Public Service
Lowe Foundation, Joe and Emily
LTV Corp.
Lubo Fund
Lund Foundation
Lupin Foundation
Lurie Foundation, Louis R.
Lyndhurst Foundation
M/A-COM, Inc.
MacAndrews & Forbes Holdings
MacArthur Foundation, John D. and Catherine T.
Macy & Co., R.H.
Madison Gas & Electric Co.
Mailman Foundation
Manoogian Foundation, Alex and Marie
Marley Co.
Mars Foundation
Marsh & McLennan Cos.
Marshall Field's
Martin Foundation
Martin Marietta Corp.
Marubeni America Corp.
Masco Corp.
Massey Charitable Trust
Massey Foundation, Jack C.
Material Service Corp.
Mather Charitable Trust, S. Livingston
Matz Foundation — Edelman Division

May Department Stores Co.
Mayborn Foundation, Frank W.
Maytag Corp.
Maytag Family Foundation, Fred
MCA
McCarthy Foundation, Michael W.
McDonnell Douglas Corp.
McElroy Trust, R. J.
McGraw-Hill
McGregor Fund
MCI Communications Corp.
McIntosh Foundation
McIntyre Foundation, B. D. and Jane E.
McIntyre Foundation, C. S. and Marion F.
MCJ Foundation
McKenna Foundation, Philip M.
McMurray-Bennnett Foundation
Mead Corp.
Meadows Foundation
Medtronic
Menschel Foundation, Robert and Joyce
Merck & Co.
Mercy, Jr. Foundation, Sue and Eugene
Meredith Corp.
Meredith Foundation
Meridian Bancorp
Mervyn's
Metropolitan Life Insurance Co.
Metropolitan Theatres Corp.
Meyer Foundation, Eugene and Agnes E.
Meyer Memorial Foundation, Aaron and Rachel
Meyer Memorial Trust
Michael Foundation, Herbert I. and Elsa B.
Michigan Bell Telephone Co.
Middendorf Foundation
Midmark Corp.
Midwest Resources
Milbank Foundation, Dunlevy
Miles Inc.
Miller Fund, Kathryn and Gilbert
Milliken & Co.
Mine Safety Appliances Co.
Minnegasco
Mitchell Family Foundation, Edward D. and Anna
MNC Financial
Mobil Oil Corp.
Monadnock Paper Mills
Monell Foundation, Ambrose
Monsanto Co.
Moore Foundation, O. L.
Moore & Sons, B.C.
Morgan and Samuel Tate Morgan, Jr. Foundation, Marietta McNeil
Morgan Construction Co.
Morris Foundation, William F.
Morrison-Knudsen Corp.
Morse Foundation, Richard P. and Claire W.
Morse, Jr. Foundation, Enid and Lester S.
Moses Fund, Henry and Lucy
Mott Fund, Ruth
Muller Foundation
Murdy Foundation
Murphy Foundation
Murphy Foundation, Katherine and John
Murphy Oil Corp.
Nash Foundation
National Computer Systems
National Fuel Gas Co.
National Life of Vermont
National Service Industries
National Starch & Chemical Corp.
National Westminster Bank New Jersey

Nationale-Nederlanden North America Corp.
NationsBank Corp.
Nationwide Insurance Cos.
NBD Bank
Nestle U.S.A. Inc.
New England Mutual Life Insurance Co.
New York Life Insurance Co.
New York Stock Exchange
New York Telephone Co.
The New Yorker Magazine, Inc.
Newhouse Foundation, Samuel I.
News & Observer Publishing Co.
Noble Foundation, Edward John
Noble Foundation, Samuel Roberts
Nordson Corp.
Norfolk Shipbuilding & Drydock Corp.
Norfolk Southern Corp.
Norris Foundation, Dellora A. and Lester J.
Norris Foundation, Kenneth T. and Eileen L.
North Shore Foundation
Northern Indiana Public Service Co.
Northern States Power Co.
Northern Telecom Inc.
Northwest Area Foundation
Northwest Natural Gas Co.
Norton Co.
Norton Memorial Corporation, Geraldi
O'Connor Co.
O'Connor Foundation, A. Lindsay and Olive B.
Ogden Foundation, Ralph E.
Ohio National Life Insurance Co.
Ohrstrom Foundation
Old Dominion Box Co.
Olin Corp.
Olsson Memorial Foundation, Elis
Orleton Trust Fund
Osborn Charitable Trust, Edward B.
Osher Foundation, Bernard
Oshkosh B'Gosh
Overbrook Foundation
Overseas Shipholding Group
Pacific Enterprises
Pacific Gas & Electric Co.
Pacific Mutual Life Insurance Co.
Palmer Fund, Frank Loomis
Panhandle Eastern Corp.
Pappas Charitable Foundation, Thomas Anthony
Paramount Communications Inc.
Parker-Hannifin Corp.
Parsons Foundation, Ralph M.
Pasadena Area Residential Aid
Peabody Foundation, Amelia
Pearlstone Foundation, Peggy Meyerhoff
Penn Foundation, William
Pennzoil Co.
Peppers Foundation, Ann
Pepsi-Cola Bottling Co. of Charlotte
Peterloon Foundation
Pfizer
Pforzheimer Foundation, Carl and Lily
Phelps Dodge Corp.
Philip Morris Cos.
Philips Foundation, Jesse
Phillips Family Foundation, Jay and Rose
Phillips Foundation, Dr. P.
Phillips Petroleum Co.
Phipps Foundation, William H.
Pines Bridge Foundation
Pinkerton Foundation
Piper Foundation, Minnie Stevens
Piper Jaffray Cos.

Pitney Bowes
Pittsburgh National Bank
Pittway Corp.
Plumsock Fund
PNC Bank
Polaroid Corp.
Porter Foundation, Mrs. Cheever
Post Foundation of D.C., Marjorie Merriweather
Potomac Electric Power Co.
Powell Family Foundation
Prange Co., H. C.
Premier Industrial Corp.
Prentis Family Foundation, Meyer and Anna
Priddy Foundation
Primerica Corp.
Procter & Gamble Co.
Procter & Gamble Cosmetic & Fragrance Products
Providence Journal Company
Prudential Insurance Co. of America
Public Service Co. of Colorado
Public Service Electric & Gas Co.
Puget Sound Power & Light Co.
Pyramid Foundation
Quaker Oats Co.
Quivey-Bay State Foundation
Ralston Purina Co.
Rebsamen Companies, Inc.
Recognition Equipment
Red Wing Shoe Co.
Reed Foundation
Regis Corp.
Reily & Co., William B.
Reinberger Foundation
Reliable Life Insurance Co.
Rennebohm Foundation, Oscar
Revlon
Reynolds Foundation, Donald W.
Reynolds Metals Co.
Reynolds & Reynolds Co.
Rhone-Poulenc Rorer
Rice Charitable Foundation, Albert W.
Rice Foundation, Ethel and Raymond F.
Rich Co., F.D.
Rich Foundation
Rich Products Corp.
Richardson Benevolent Foundation, C. E.
Richardson Foundation, Smith
Rider-Pool Foundation
Rigler-Deutsch Foundation
Riley Foundation, Mabel Louise
RJR Nabisco Inc.
Rochester Gas & Electric Corp.
Rockefeller Foundation
Rockwell International Corp.
Rodgers Foundation, Richard & Dorothy
Rohatyn Foundation, Felix and Elizabeth
RosaMary Foundation
Rose Foundation, Billy
Roseburg Forest Products Co.
Rosenberg Foundation, William J. and Tina
Rosenthal Foundation, Richard and Hinda
Rosenwald Family Fund, William
Ross Foundation
Rouse Co.
Royal Group Inc.
RTM
Rubbermaid
Rubin Foundation, Samuel
Rudin Foundation, Samuel and May
Russell Charitable Trust, Josephine S.
Salomon Foundation, Richard & Edna
San Diego Gas & Electric

Santa Fe Pacific Corp.
Sara Lee Corp.
Saunders Foundation
Schapiro Fund, M. A.
Schering-Plough Corp.
Schieffelin Residuary Trust, Sarah I.
Schlumberger Ltd.
Schroeder Foundation, Walter
Schultz Foundation
Schwartz Foundation, David
Scott and Fetzer Co.
Scott Foundation, Virginia Steele
Scrivner, Inc.
Seafirst Corp.
Seagram & Sons, Joseph E.
Seaver Charitable Trust, Richard C.
Seaway Food Town
Security Life of Denver
Sedgwick James Inc.
Segerstrom Foundation
Semmes Foundation
Sentinel Communications Co.
Seymour and Troester Foundation
Shapiro, Inc.
Sharp Foundation
Shawmut National Corp.
Sheafer Charitable Trust, Emma A.
Sheaffer Inc.
Shelton Cos.
Shenandoah Foundation
Shenandoah Life Insurance Co.
Shirk Foundation, Russell and Betty
Signet Bank/Maryland
Simmons Family Foundation, R. P.
Skinner Corp.
Slifka Foundation, Alan B.
Smith Charitable Foundation, Lou and Lutza
Smith Family Foundation, Theda Clark
Smith Foundation
Smith Memorial Fund, Ethel Sergeant Clark
SmithKline Beecham
SNET
Snider Foundation
Snow Memorial Trust, John Ben
Snyder Charitable Fund, W. P.
Snyder Fund, Valentine Perry
Solow Foundation
Solow Foundation, Sheldon H.
Sonat
Sonoco Products Co.
South Branch Foundation
Southern California Edison Co.
Southways Foundation
Southwestern Bell Corp.
Spingold Foundation, Nate B. and Frances
Spiritus Gladius Foundation
Sprague, Jr. Foundation, Caryll M. and Norman F.
SPS Technologies
Square D Co.
Starr Foundation
State Street Bank & Trust Co.
Steadley Memorial Trust, Kent D. and Mary L.
Steelcase
Steinhardt Foundation, Judy and Michael
Steinhauer Charitable Foundation
Sterling Inc.
Sterling Winthrop
Stevens Foundation, John T.
Stoddard Charitable Trust
Stone Container Corp.
Stone Trust, H. Chase
Stone & Webster, Inc.
Strawbridge Foundation of Pennsylvania I, Margaret Dorrance

Recipient Type Index

Arts Centers (cont.)

Stride Rite Corp.
Strosacker Foundation, Charles J.
Subaru of America Inc.
Sumitomo Corp. of America
Sun Co.
Sunderland Foundation, Lester T.
Swig Foundation
Swiss Bank Corp.
Symmes Foundation, F. W.
Synovus Financial Corp.
Syntex Corp.
Tamarkin Co.
Taub Foundation, Henry and
   Marilyn
TCF Banking & Savings, FSB
Teledyne
Teleflex Inc.
Tennant Co.
Tenneco
Tetley, Inc.
Texaco
Texas Commerce Bank Houston,
   N.A.
Texas Gas Transmission Corp.
Texas Instruments
Textron
Thatcher Foundation
Thendara Foundation
Thermo Electron Corp.
Thomas & Betts Corp.
Thomas Foundation, Joan and
   Lee
Thornton Foundation, John M.
   and Sally B.
3M Co.
Times Mirror Co.
Timken Foundation of Canton
Tisch Foundation
Titan Industrial Co.
TJX Cos.
Tobin Foundation
Tosco Corp. Refining Division
Toyota Motor Sales, U.S.A.
Transco Energy Company
Treadwell Foundation, Nora
   Eccles
Trinity Foundation
Truland Foundation
Trust Co. Bank
Tull Charitable Foundation
Tyson Foods, Inc.
Unilever United States
Union Bank
Union Bank of Switzerland Los
   Angeles Branch
Union Electric Co.
United Dominion Industries
United States Trust Co. of New
   York
United Technologies Corp.
Universal Leaf Tobacco Co.
Unocal Corp.
Upton Foundation, Frederick S.
Uris Brothers Foundation
USX Corp.
Valley National Bank of Arizona
Van Wert County Foundation
Vaughn, Jr. Foundation Fund,
   James M.
Vidda Foundation
Virginia Power Co.
Von der Ahe Foundation
Vulcan Materials Co.
Wachovia Bank of Georgia, N.A.
Wachovia Bank & Trust Co.,
   N.A.
Wahlstrom Foundation
Walker Foundation, L. C. and
   Margaret
Walker Foundation, T. B.
Wallace Reader's Digest Fund,
   Lila
Disney Co., Walt
Walter Industries
Ward Co., Joe L.

Wardlaw Fund, Gertrude and
   William C.
Warhol Foundation for the Visual
   Arts, Andy
Warner-Lambert Co.
Warwick Foundation
Washington Mutual Savings
   Bank
Wasmer Foundation
Wasserman Foundation
Waters Charitable Trust, Robert
   S.
Watumull Fund, J.
Wean Foundation, Raymond John
Webster Foundation, Edwin S.
Wege Foundation
Weil, Gotshal & Manges
   Foundation
Weiler Foundation
Weiler Foundation, Theodore &
   Renee
Weingart Foundation
Weininger Foundation, Richard
   and Gertrude
Weir Foundation Trust
Weisman Art Foundation,
   Frederick R.
Weiss Foundation, Stephen and
   Suzanne
Welch Testamentary Trust,
   George T.
Wendt Foundation, Margaret L.
West Co.
West Foundation
Westerman Foundation, Samuel
   L.
Westinghouse Electric Corp.
Westvaco Corp.
Weyerhaeuser Memorial
   Foundation, Charles A.
Whirlpool Corp.
Whitehead Foundation
Whitehead Foundation, Joseph B.
Whitney Fund, David M.
Widgeon Foundation
Wiegand Foundation, E. L.
Wien Foundation, Lawrence A.
Wigwam Mills
Wilkof Foundation, Edward and
   Ruth
Williams Cos.
Williams Foundation, C. K.
Wilson Fund, Matilda R.
Winnebago Industries, Inc.
Winston Foundation, Norman
   and Rosita
Winter Construction Co.
Wisconsin Bell, Inc.
Witco Corp.
Woodruff Foundation, Robert W.
Woods Charitable Fund
Woodward Fund-Atlanta, David,
   Helen, Marian
Wurlitzer Foundation, Farny R.
Wyman Youth Trust
Xerox Corp.
Y.K.K. (U.S.A.) Inc.
Yellow Corp.
Young & Rubicam
Younkers, Inc.
Zellerbach Family Fund
Zemurray Foundation

Arts Festivals

Abell Foundation, The
Air Products & Chemicals
Alabama Power Co.
Allegheny Ludlum Corp.
Alltel/Western Region
ALPAC Corp.
Alsdorf Foundation
Alumax
Aluminum Co. of America
American Express Co.
American Financial Corp.
American Saw & Manufacturing
   Co.

American Telephone &
   Telegraph Co.
Amoco Corp.
Amsted Industries
Andersen Foundation, Arthur
AON Corp.
Archer-Daniels-Midland Co.
ARCO Chemical
Armco Inc.
Armstrong World Industries Inc.
Atlanta Gas Light Co.
Atlantic Foundation
Attleboro Pawtucket Savings
   Bank
Avon Products
Ballet Makers
Baltimore Gas & Electric Co.
Banc One Illinois Corp.
Bank South Corp.
Bauer Foundation, M. R.
Bel Air Mart
Benedum Foundation, Claude
   Worthington
Beneficial Corp.
Benton Foundation
Bethlehem Steel Corp.
Biddle Foundation, Mary Duke
Binney & Smith Inc.
Block, H&R
Blount
Blue Bell, Inc.
Blue Cross and Blue Shield
   United of Wisconsin
   Foundation
Blum-Kovler Foundation
Booz Allen & Hamilton
Briggs & Stratton Corp.
Buchanan Family Foundation
Burlington Resources
Carpenter Technology Corp.
Centerior Energy Corp.
Central Bank of the South
Central Maine Power Co.
Chambers Development Co.
Chase Manhattan Bank, N.A.
Chastain Charitable Foundation,
   Robert Lee and Thomas M.
Cheney Foundation, Elizabeth F.
Chevron Corp.
Chicago Sun-Times, Inc.
Chiles Foundation
Cincinnati Bell
Citicorp
Clorox Co.
CNA Insurance Cos.
Cohen Foundation, Naomi and
   Nehemiah
Collins Foundation
Colonial Life & Accident
   Insurance Co.
Commerce Clearing House
Compaq Computer Corp.
Connelly Foundation
Consolidated Natural Gas Co.
County Bank
Cowles Media Co.
CPC International
Crestlea Foundation
Crown Central Petroleum Corp.
Cullen/Frost Bankers
Cummins Engine Co.
CUNA Mutual Insurance Group
Dalton Foundation, Dorothy U.
Dana Charitable Trust, Eleanor
   Naylor
Daniel Foundation of Alabama
Delaware North Cos.
Dell Foundation, Hazel
Deposit Guaranty National Bank
Devonwood Foundation
Dimeo Construction Co.
Dodge Foundation, Geraldine R.
Donnelley Foundation, Elliott
   and Ann
Donnelley Foundation, Gaylord
   and Dorothy
Dow Corning Corp.

Dresser Industries
Dreyfus Foundation, Max and
   Victoria
Driscoll Foundation
du Pont de Nemours & Co., E. I.
Duke Power Co.
Eagle-Picher Industries
Eastover Corp.
Eaton Foundation, Cyrus
Eccles Foundation, George S.
   and Dolores Dore
Eccles Foundation, Marriner S.
Enron Corp.
Exxon Corp.
Fair Play Foundation
Farallon Foundation
Federal-Mogul Corp.
Fieldcrest Cannon
Fifth Avenue Foundation
First Interstate Bank of Arizona
First Interstate Bank of Oregon
First Tennessee Bank
First Union Corp.
FirsTier Bank N.A. Omaha
Fleishhacker Foundation
Florida Power & Light Co.
Ford Fund, Walter and Josephine
Forest Oil Corp.
Frankel Foundation
Franklin Mint Corp.
Freedom Forum
Freeport-McMoRan
Frelinghuysen Foundation
Friedman Family Foundation
Garvey Kansas Foundation
Garvey Texas Foundation
General Motors Corp.
Georgia-Pacific Corp.
Georgia Power Co.
Getty Foundation, Ann and
   Gordon
Gilmore Foundation, Irving S.
Globe Newspaper Co.
Godfrey Co.
Goodman Family Foundation
Grainger Foundation
Greene Foundation, Jerome L.
Greve Foundation, William and
   Mary
Gulf Power Co.
Haas Fund, Walter and Elise
Haffenreffer Family Fund
Hales Charitable Fund
Halsell Foundation, Ewing
Hechinger Co.
Hecla Mining Co.
Heinz Co., H.J.
Heinz Endowment, Vira I.
Helfaer Foundation, Evan and
   Marion
Heller Foundation, Walter E.
Heymann Special Account, Mr.
   and Mrs. Jimmy
Hillsdale Fund
Holding Foundation, Robert P.
Hooker Charitable Trust, Janet A.
Horne Foundation, Dick
Hulings Foundation, Mary
   Andersen
Hunt Alternatives Fund
Hunt Foundation, Roy A.
Indiana Bell Telephone Co.
Inland Container Corp.
Inman Mills
International Paper Co.
Irmas Charitable Foundation,
   Audrey and Sydney
Janssen Foundation, Henry
Jennings Foundation, Mary
   Hillman
Johnson Controls
Johnson Foundation, A. D.
Johnson & Higgins
Keebler Co.
Keller-Crescent Co.
Kennecott Corp.
Kentucky Foundation for Women

Kerr Foundation
Kerr Foundation, Robert S. and
   Grayce B.
Kettering Fund
Kingsbury Corp.
Kohl Charitable Foundation,
   Allen D.
Kohl Charitable Foundation,
   Allen D.
Lafarge Corp.
Lightner Sams Foundation
Lincoln National Corp.
Lipton, Thomas J.
Littlefield Foundation, Edmund
   Wattis
Long Island Lighting Co.
Lowe Foundation, Joe and Emily
LTV Corp.
Lyndhurst Foundation
Lyon Foundation
MacArthur Foundation, John D.
   and Catherine T.
Macht Foundation, Morton and
   Sophia
Macy & Co., R.H.
Marcus Corp.
Marquette Electronics
Marshall & Ilsley Bank
Martin Marietta Corp.
McDermott Foundation, Eugene
McDonnell Douglas Corp.-West
Mead Corp.
Meadows Foundation
Mellon Bank Corp.
Mervyn's
Miles Inc.
Mine Safety Appliances Co.
MNC Financial
Mobil Oil Corp.
Monsanto Co.
Morrison-Knudsen Corp.
Mosher Foundation, Samuel B.
Nashua Trust Co.
National Life of Vermont
National Machinery Co.
National Westminster Bank New
   Jersey
NBD Bank
New York Telephone Co.
The New Yorker Magazine, Inc.
Newhouse Foundation, Samuel I.
Newman Assistance Fund,
   Jerome A. and Estelle R.
News & Observer Publishing Co.
Noble Foundation, Edward John
Nordson Corp.
Norfolk Southern Corp.
Northern Indiana Public Service
   Co.
Northwest Natural Gas Co.
Norton Memorial Corporation,
   Geraldi
Norwest Bank Nebraska
Odell and Helen Pfeiffer Odell
   Fund, Robert Stewart
1957 Charity Trust
O'Neil Foundation, Casey Albert
   T.
Ontario Corp.
O'Shaughnessy Foundation, I. A.
Overbrook Foundation
Oxford Industries, Inc.
Pacific Enterprises
Pacific Mutual Life Insurance Co.
Palmer Fund, Frank Loomis
Paul and C. Michael Paul
   Foundation, Josephine Bay
Paulucci Family Foundation
Penn Foundation, William
Pennzoil Co.
People's Bank
Pepsi-Cola Bottling Co. of
   Charlotte
Pew Charitable Trusts
Phillips Foundation, Dr. P.
Phillips Foundation, Ellis L.
Pick, Jr. Fund, Albert

Piper Jaffray Cos.
Pittsburgh National Bank
Portland General Electric Co.
PPG Industries
Price Associates, T. Rowe
Pritzker Foundation
Procter & Gamble Cosmetic &
Fragrance Products
Providence Energy Corp.
Provident Life & Accident
Insurance Co.
Public Service Co. of Colorado
Quaker Oats Co.
Questar Corp.
R. P. Foundation
Rales and Ruth Rales
Foundation, Norman R.
Recognition Equipment
Reed Foundation
Reinberger Foundation
Rich Co., F.D.
Rite-Hite Corp.
Rockefeller Foundation
Rockwell Foundation
Rockwell International Corp.
Rohm and Haas Company
Rose Foundation, Billy
Rudin Foundation, Samuel and
May
San Diego Gas & Electric
Sara Lee Corp.
Sargent Foundation, Newell B.
Schering-Plough Corp.
Schneider Foundation Corp., Al
J.
Schneiderman Foundation,
Roberta and Irwin
Schrafft and Bertha E. Schrafft
Charitable Trust, William E.
Schroeder Foundation, Walter
Schwartz Foundation, David
Science Applications
International Corp.
Seaway Food Town
Security Life of Denver
Sedgwick James Inc.
Semmes Foundation
Shapiro Family Foundation,
Soretta and Henry
Shell Oil Co.
Shoney's Inc.
Signet Bank/Maryland
Silverweed Foundation
SNET
Snyder Charitable Fund, W. P.
Soling Family Foundation
Sonat
Southern Bell
Southwestern Bell Corp.
Springs Industries
Square D Co.
Star Bank, N.A.
Starling Foundation, Dorothy
Richard
Starr Foundation
Steinhauer Charitable Foundation
Sternberger Foundation, Sigmund
Stokely, Jr. Foundation, William
B.
Stone Family Foundation,
Jerome H.
Summerfield Foundation, Solon
E.
Target Stores
Taub Foundation, Henry and
Marilyn
Tenneco
Texaco
Texas Gas Transmission Corp.
Thirty-Five Twenty, Inc.
Trexler Trust, Harry C.
Trust Co. Bank
Trust for Mutual Understanding
Tucker Charitable Trust, Rose E.
Union Camp Corp.
Union Electric Co.
Universal Leaf Tobacco Co.

USX Corp.
Varian Associates
Virginia Power Co.
Vulcan Materials Co.
Wachovia Bank & Trust Co.,
N.A.
Wal-Mart Stores
Wallace Reader's Digest Fund,
Lila
Waste Management
Wean Foundation, Raymond John
Williams Foundation, Arthur
Ashley
Winnebago Industries, Inc.
Winston Foundation, Norman
and Rosita
Winter Construction Co.
Wisconsin Power & Light Co.
Wisconsin Public Service Corp.
Wood Foundation, Lester G.
Wyomissing Foundation
Zamoiski Co.

Arts Funds
Abrons Foundation, Louis and
Anne
Aeroflex Foundation
Ahmanson Foundation
Air Products & Chemicals
Alden Trust, John W.
Allendale Mutual Insurance Co.
ALPAC Corp.
Alpert Foundation, Herb
Alumax
Aluminum Co. of America
Amcast Industrial Corp.
American Electric Power
American National Bank & Trust
Co. of Chicago
Ameritech Services
Amfac/JMB Hawaii
Amoco Corp.
AMP
Anheuser-Busch Cos.
Arakelian Foundation, Mary
Alice
Archer-Daniels-Midland Co.
Armco Inc.
Arvin Industries
Ashland Oil
Atherton Family Foundation
Avis Inc.
Avon Products
Baird Foundation
Ballet Makers
Banc One Wisconsin Corp.
Bank of Boston Corp.
Bank of Louisville
BankAmerica Corp.
Bankers Trust Co.
Bardes Corp.
Barry Corp., R. G.
Bartol Foundation, Stockton
Rush
Bass Foundation
Bauer Foundation, M. R.
Belden Brick Co., Inc.
Belding Heminway Co.
Bend Millwork Systems
Benedum Foundation, Claude
Worthington
Beveridge Foundation, Frank
Stanley
Binney & Smith Inc.
Block, H&R
Blue Bell, Inc.
Blue Cross and Blue Shield of
Minnesota Foundation Inc.
Blue Cross & Blue Shield of
Kentucky Foundation
Blum Foundation, Harry and
Maribel G.
Boatmen's Bancshares
Boeing Co.
Boh Brothers Construction Co.
Boler Co.
Booz Allen & Hamilton

Boynton Fund, John W.
Braun Foundation
Breidenthal Foundation, Willard
J. and Mary G.
Briggs & Stratton Corp.
Bristol-Myers Squibb Co.
Brown and C. A. Lupton
Foundation, T. J.
Brown & Williamson Tobacco
Corp.
Brunswick Corp.
Buck Foundation, Carol Franc
Bucyrus-Erie
Burdines
Burlington Industries
Burlington Resources
Burndy Corp.
Bush Foundation
C.I.O.S.
C.P. Rail Systems
Cabot Corp.
Cabot Family Charitable Trust
Camp Foundation
Campbell Foundation, Ruth and
Henry
Capital Cities/ABC
Capital Holding Corp.
Carolyn Foundation
Cawsey Trust
Central Hudson Gas & Electric
Corp.
Central Maine Power Co.
Central Soya Co.
Charter Manufacturing Co.
Chase Manhattan Bank, N.A.
Chastain Charitable Foundation,
Robert Lee and Thomas M.
Chevron Corp.
Cincinnati Bell
Cincinnati Gas & Electric Co.
Cincinnati Milacron
Cintas Foundation
CIT Group Holdings
Citicorp
Citizens Bank
Clay Foundation
CM Alliance Cos.
CNA Insurance Cos.
Cohen Family Foundation, Saul
Z. and Amy Scheuer
Columbia Foundation
Columbus Dispatch Printing Co.
Cone Mills Corp.
Continental Corp.
Cook Charitable Foundation
Cooper Industries
Copolymer Rubber & Chemical
Corp.
Courier-Journal & Louisville
Times
Cowles Media Co.
CPC International
Cramer Foundation
Crown Books Foundation, Inc.
Cudahy Fund, Patrick and Anna
M.
Cullen/Frost Bankers
Cummins Engine Co.
Daily News
Dain Bosworth/Inter-Regional
Financial Group
Danis Industries
Dayton Hudson Corp.
Dayton Power and Light Co.
DCB Corp.
Delano Foundation, Mignon
Sherwood
DelMar Foundation, Charles
Deposit Guaranty National Bank
Dexter Industries
Donaldson Co.
Dresser Industries
du Pont de Nemours & Co., E. I.
Duke Power Co.
Dula Educational and Charitable
Foundation, Caleb C. and Julia
W.

Durst Foundation
Eagle-Picher Industries
Eaton Corp.
Enron Corp.
Ethyl Corp.
Factor Family Foundation, Max
Federal Express Corp.
Federal-Mogul Corp.
Federated Department Stores and
Allied Stores Corp.
Federated Life Insurance Co.
Ferkauf Foundation, Eugene and
Estelle
Fifth Third Bancorp
First Boston
First Interstate Bank of Arizona
First Interstate Bank of Oregon
First Tennessee Bank
First Union Corp.
First Union National Bank of
Florida
Fleming Companies, Inc.
Florida Power Corp.
Foellinger Foundation
Forbes
Frank Foundation, Ernest and
Elfriede
Frear Eleemosynary Trust, Mary
D. and Walter F.
Freedom Forum
Freeport-McMoRan
Frisch's Restaurants Inc.
Fuller Co., H.B.
Fuller Foundation
Funderburke & Associates
General American Life Insurance
Co.
General Motors Corp.
Georgia Power Co.
Gerbode Foundation, Wallace
Alexander
Gill Foundation, Pauline Allen
Glaxo
Glen Eagles Foundation
Glenmore Distilleries Co.
Goodman Family Foundation
Gradison & Co.
Green Fund
Greenebaum, Doll & McDonald
Gucci America Inc.
Gutman Foundation, Edna and
Monroe C.
H. B. B. Foundation
Hall Charitable Trust, Evelyn A.
J.
Hawkins Foundation, Robert Z.
Hayfields Foundation
Hazen Foundation, Edward W.
Healy Family Foundation, M. A.
Hecht-Levi Foundation
Heileman Brewing Co., Inc., G.
Heinz Endowment, Vira I.
Heinz Foundation, Drue
Hershey Foods Corp.
Heymann Special Account, Mr.
and Mrs. Jimmy
Hooper Handling
Hospital Corp. of America
Houchens Foundation, Ervin G.
Houck Foundation, May K.
Houston Industries
Hubbard Broadcasting
Huffy Corp.
Hultquist Foundation
Humana
Hunt Alternatives Fund
Huthsteiner Fine Arts Trust
IBM Corp.
Indiana Bell Telephone Co.
Indiana Desk Co.
Inland Container Corp.
Inman Mills
Interco
International Paper Co.
Irvine Foundation, James
ITT Corp.
ITT Hartford Insurance Group

J.P. Morgan & Co.
James River Corp. of Virginia
Jarson-Stanley and Mickey
Kaplan Foundation, Isaac &
Esther
JOFCo., Inc.
Johnson Controls
Johnson Endeavor Foundation,
Christian A.
Johnson Foundation, Barbara P.
Johnson & Higgins
Johnson & Son, S.C.
Katzenberger Foundation
Kentucky Foundation for Women
Kerr Foundation
Kerr Fund, Grayce B.
Kerr-McGee Corp.
Kettering Fund
Kimberly-Clark Corp.
Kingsbury Corp.
Kramer Foundation, C. L. C.
Kuhne Foundation Trust, Charles
Kunkel Foundation, John Crain
Lambe Charitable Foundation,
Claude R.
LEF Foundation
Levy's Lumber & Building
Centers
Liberty Corp.
Liberty National Bank
Lilly & Co., Eli
Lincoln National Corp.
Long Island Lighting Co.
Louisiana Power & Light
Co./New Orleans Public
Service
LTV Corp.
Lydall, Inc.
Lyndhurst Foundation
Macy & Co., R.H.
Maier Foundation, Sarah Pauline
Manoogian Foundation, Alex
and Marie
Maritz Inc.
Mark IV Industries
Marley Co.
Marshall Field's
Marshall & Ilsley Bank
Martin Marietta Corp.
Masco Corp.
May Department Stores Co.
MCA
McCasland Foundation
McCaw Cellular
Communications
McDonnell Douglas Corp.
McGraw-Hill
Meadows Foundation
Merck Family Fund
Mericos Foundation
Merrick Foundation, Robert G.
and Anne M.
Meyer Foundation, Baron de
Hirsch
Milliken & Co.
Minnegasco
Minnesota Mutual Life
Insurance Co.
Mobil Oil Corp.
Monadnock Paper Mills
Moog Automotive, Inc.
Morris Foundation, Margaret T.
Motorola
MTS Systems Corp.
Nabisco Foods Group
Nalco Chemical Co.
NBD Bank
NCR Corp.
Nesholm Family Foundation
The New Yorker Magazine, Inc.
Newhouse Foundation, Samuel I.
Newman Charitable Trust,
Calvin M. and Raquel H.
News & Observer Publishing Co.
Norfolk Southern Corp.
North Shore Foundation
Northeast Utilities

Arts Funds (cont.)

Northern States Power Co.
Northwest Natural Gas Co.
Norton Co.
Norton Foundation Inc.
Norwest Bank Nebraska
Norwest Corp.
NuTone Inc.
Ogilvy & Mather Worldwide
Ohio National Life Insurance Co.
Ohio Valley Foundation
Ohl, Jr. Trust, George A.
Oklahoma Gas & Electric Co.
Oppenstein Brothers Foundation
Ore-Ida Foods, Inc.
Orleton Trust Fund
OsCo. Industries
O'Shaughnessy Foundation, I. A.
PACCAR
Pacific Enterprises
Pacific Mutual Life Insurance Co.
Pamida, Inc.
Park Bank
Pepsi-Cola Bottling Co. of
  Charlotte
Peterloon Foundation
Pfizer
Phelps Dodge Corp.
Philadelphia Electric Co.
Philibosian Foundation, Stephen
Philips Foundation, Jesse
Phillips Foundation, Dr. P.
Phillips Petroleum Co.
Pick Charitable Trust, Melitta S.
Piper Foundation, Minnie
  Stevens
PNC Bank
Polaroid Corp.
Powell Co., William
Preyer Fund, Mary Norris
Price Associates, T. Rowe
Promus Cos.
Prudential Insurance Co. of
  America
Public Service Electric & Gas
  Co.
Puget Sound Power & Light Co.
Pulitzer Publishing Co.
Quaker Oats Co.
Quincy Newspapers
Reichhold Chemicals, Inc.
Reliable Life Insurance Co.
Reynolds & Reynolds Co.
Riley Foundation, Mabel Louise
Rockwell International Corp.
Rohm and Haas Company
Rosenbaum Foundation, Paul
  and Gabriella
Roth Family Foundation
Roth Foundation, Louis T.
Rouse Co.
Rubin Foundation, Rob E. &
  Judith O.
Rupp Foundation, Fran and
  Warren
Russell Memorial Foundation,
  Robert
SAFECO Corp.
Saint Paul Cos.
San Diego Gas & Electric
Santa Fe Pacific Corp.
Sara Lee Hosiery
Scheirich Co., H.J.
Schmidlapp Trust No. 1, Jacob G.
Schroeder Foundation, Walter
Scrivner, Inc.
Searle & Co., G.D.
Seaver Institute
Sedgwick James Inc.
Semple Foundation, Louise Taft
Sentinel Communications Co.
Shawmut National Corp.
Shaw's Supermarkets
Shott, Jr. Foundation, Hugh I.
Simon Foundation, William E.
  and Carol G.

Skinner Corp.
Smith Corp., A.O.
SNET
Solow Foundation, Sheldon H.
Somers Foundation, Byron H.
Southwestern Bell Corp.
Special People In Need
Sprague Educational and
  Charitable Foundation, Seth
Square D Co.
Standard Register Co.
Star Bank, N.A.
Starr Foundation
Steiger Memorial Fund, Albert
Sterling Inc.
Sulzberger Foundation
Swiss Bank Corp.
Teledyne
Teleflex Inc.
Tenneco
Texaco
Texas Commerce Bank Houston,
  N.A.
Texas Gas Transmission Corp.
Texas Instruments
Textron
Thendara Foundation
Thornton Foundation, John M.
  and Sally B.
Times Mirror Co.
Timken Co.
Tisch Foundation
TJX Cos.
Tokheim Corp.
Torchmark Corp.
Towsley Foundation, Harry A.
  and Margaret D.
Travelers Cos.
TRINOVA Corp.
Trust Co. Bank
Ukrop's Super Markets, Inc.
Union Bank
Union Camp Corp.
Union Electric Co.
Upton Foundation, Frederick S.
Valspar Corp.
Van Andel Foundation, Jay and
  Betty
Vogt Machine Co., Henry
Vulcan Materials Co.
Wachovia Bank & Trust Co.,
  N.A.
Wasserman Foundation
Waste Management
Wean Foundation, Raymond John
West Co.
Westend Foundation
Wetterau
Weyerhaeuser Co.
Wheat First Securites
Whirlpool Corp.
Whitaker Charitable Foundation,
  Lyndon C.
Whitaker Fund, Helen F.
Wiener Foundation, Malcolm
  Hewitt
Winter Construction Co.
Wisconsin Energy Corp.
Woldenberg Foundation
Woodward Fund
Xerox Corp.
XTEK Inc.
Ziegler Foundation

Arts Institutes

Abbott Laboratories
Abeles Foundation, Joseph and
  Sophia
Abell Foundation, The
Abramson Family Foundation
Abroms Charitable Foundation
Ahmanson Foundation
Alco Standard Corp.
Alexander Foundation, Joseph
Alexander Foundation, Judd S.
Algonquin Energy, Inc.

Allendale Mutual Insurance Co.
AlliedSignal
Alltel/Western Region
Alsdorf Foundation
Aluminum Co. of America
Amcast Industrial Corp.
American Electric Power
American Foundation
  Corporation
American National Bank & Trust
  Co. of Chicago
American Natural Resources Co.
Ameritech Services
Amfac/JMB Hawaii
Amoco Corp.
Amsted Industries
Andersen Corp.
Anderson Foundation, William P.
AON Corp.
Archer-Daniels-Midland Co.
Aristech Chemical Corp.
Armco Inc.
Armco Steel Co.
Athwin Foundation
Atlanta Gas Light Co.
Attleboro Pawtucket Savings
  Bank
Augat, Inc.
Autzen Foundation
Avon Products
Ayres Foundation, Inc.
Baird Foundation, Cameron
Baker, Jr. Memorial Fund,
  William G.
Ball Corp.
Bank of Boston Corp.
Bankers Trust Co.
Barra Foundation
Barrows Foundation, Geraldine
  and R. A.
Barry Corp., R. G.
Bauer Foundation, M. R.
Baxter International
Bayne Fund, Howard
Beecher Foundation, Florence
  Simon
Belding Heminway Co.
Belz Foundation
Bender Foundation
Benton Foundation
Bergen Foundation, Frank and
  Lydia
Berger Foundation, Albert E.
Berkman Charitable Trust, Allen
  H. and Selma W.
Berlin Charitable Fund, Irving
Bernstein & Co., Sanford C.
Berwind Corp.
Binney & Smith Inc.
Bishop Charitable Trust, A. G.
Blair and Co., William
Block, H&R
Blount
Bluhdorn Charitable Trust,
  Charles G. and Yvette
Blum Foundation, Lois and
  Irving
Boehringer Mannheim Corp.
Booz Allen & Hamilton
Borden
Borden Memorial Foundation,
  Mary Owen
Borman's
Boston Edison Co.
Boulevard Foundation
BP America
Brach Foundation, Helen
Brackenridge Foundation,
  George W.
Bray Charitable Trust, Viola E.
Bridgestone/Firestone
Briggs & Stratton Corp.
Brody Foundation, Carolyn and
  Kenneth D.
Brown Foundation
Brunswick Corp.
Buchanan Family Foundation

Buck Foundation, Carol Franc
Burgess Trust, Ralph L. and
  Florence R.
Butler Family Foundation,
  Patrick and Aimee
Butler Manufacturing Co.
Cabot Corp.
Cafritz Foundation, Morris and
  Gwendolyn
Cameron Memorial Fund, Alpin
  J. and Alpin W.
Camp Foundation
Capital Holding Corp.
Cargill
Carter-Wallace
Cassett Foundation, Louis N.
CBI Industries
Centel Corp.
Centerior Energy Corp.
Central Maine Power Co.
Central & South West Services
CertainTeed Corp.
Chamberlin Foundation, Gerald
  W.
Chambers Development Co.
Chastain Charitable Foundation,
  Robert Lee and Thomas M.
Cheatham Foundation, Owen
Chesebrough-Pond's
Chicago Sun-Times, Inc.
Chrysler Corp.
Citicorp
Citizens Bank
Claneil Foundation
Clark Charitable Foundation
CNA Insurance Cos.
Codrington Charitable
  Foundation, George W.
Cohen Family Foundation, Saul
  Z. and Amy Scheuer
Cohn Family Foundation, Robert
  and Terri
Collins Foundation, Carr P.
Colonial Life & Accident
  Insurance Co.
Columbia Foundation
Columbus Dispatch Printing Co.
Comerica
Commerce Clearing House
Commonwealth Edison Co.
Compton Foundation
Consolidated Freightways
Consolidated Natural Gas Co.
Consumers Power Co.
Continental Corp.
Cook Foundation
Cooper Charitable Trust, Richard
  H.
Cow Hollow Foundation
Cowles Charitable Trust
Cowles Media Co.
Credit Agricole
Crestlea Foundation
CRI Charitable Trust
Criss Memorial Foundation, Dr.
  C.C. and Mabel L.
Crum and Forster
CT Corp. System
Cudahy Fund, Patrick and Anna
  M.
Cullen/Frost Bankers
Currey Foundation, Brownlee
Cyprus Minerals Co.
Dana Corp.
Danis Industries
Davee Foundation
Day Foundation, Willametta K.
Dayton Hudson Corp.
Dayton Power and Light Co.
Delavan Foundation, Nelson B.
Delaware North Cos.
Deluxe Corp.
Deposit Guaranty National Bank
DeRoy Foundation, Helen L.
DeRoy Testamentary Foundation
Dewing Foundation, Frances R.
Dick Family Foundation

DiRosa Foundation, Rene and
  Veronica
Disney Family Foundation, Roy
Donaldson Co.
Donnelley Foundation, Elliott
  and Ann
Donnelley & Sons Co., R.R.
Douglas & Lomason Company
Dow Corning Corp.
Dreyfus Foundation, Jean and
  Louis
Driscoll Foundation
du Pont de Nemours & Co., E. I.
Duchossois Industries
Dynamet, Inc.
Earl-Beth Foundation
East Foundation, Sarita Kenedy
Eaton Foundation, Cyrus
Educational Foundation of
  America
EG&G Inc.
Emerson Electric Co.
Emerson Foundation, Fred L.
Emery Memorial, Thomas J.
Engelhard Foundation, Charles
Equitable Life Assurance Society
  of the U.S.
Erb Lumber Co.
Erpf Fund, Armand G.
Exposition Foundation
Exxon Corp.
Failing Fund, Henry
Fairchild Foundation, Sherman
Farwell Foundation, Drusilla
Federal-Mogul Corp.
Federal National Mortgage
  Assn., Fannie Mae
Federal Screw Works
Federated Department Stores and
  Allied Stores Corp.
Fel-Pro Incorporated
Fidelity Bank
Field Foundation, Jamee and
  Marshall
Field Foundation of Illinois
Fig Tree Foundation
Fireman's Fund Insurance Co.
First Boston
First Interstate Bank NW Region
First Interstate Bank of Oregon
First Tennessee Bank
First Union Corp.
Fisher Foundation, Gramma
Fisher Foundation, Max M. and
  Marjorie S.
Fleet Bank of New York
Florida Power Corp.
Florida Power & Light Co.
FMC Corp.
Foote, Cone & Belding
  Communications
Ford Fund, Benson and Edith
Ford Fund, Eleanor and Edsel
Ford Fund, Walter and Josephine
Ford II Fund, Henry
Ford Motor Co.
Forest City Enterprises
Francis Families Foundation
Freeport-McMoRan
Freygang Foundation, Walter
  Henry
Frohring Foundation, William O.
  and Gertrude Lewis
Fruehauf Foundation
Fry Foundation, Lloyd A.
Funderburke & Associates
GAR Foundation
Garrigues Trust, Edwin B.
GATX Corp.
GenCorp
General Mills
General Motors Corp.
General Tire Inc.
Georgia Power Co.
Gershman Foundation, Joel
Getty Foundation, Ann and
  Gordon

Getty Trust, J. Paul
Giant Eagle
Gilder Foundation
Gill Foundation, Pauline Allen
Glaze Foundation, Robert and Ruth
Gluck Foundation, Maxwell H.
Goldman Foundation, Morris and Rose
Goldman Fund, Richard and Rhoda
Goldsmith Foundation, Horace W.
Graham Foundation for Advanced Studies in the Fine Arts
Grainger Foundation
Graybar Electric Co.
Green Fund
Greene Foundation, Jerome L.
Greenfield Foundation, Albert M.
Greenspan Foundation
Gudelsky Family Foundation, Homer and Martha
Hale Foundation, Crescent Porter
Hales Charitable Fund
Halff Foundation, G. A. C.
Hall Charitable Trust, Evelyn A. J.
Hallmark Cards
Handleman Co.
Hanes Foundation, John W. and Anna H.
Hankins Foundation
Hardin Foundation, Phil
Harding Educational and Charitable Foundation
Harriman Foundation, Mary W.
Harris Trust & Savings Bank
Hartman Foundation, Jesse and Dorothy
Hartmarx Corp.
Healy Family Foundation, M. A.
Heckscher Foundation for Children
Heinz Endowment, Howard
Heller Foundation, Walter E.
Hess Charitable Foundation, Ronne and Donald
Hill and Family Foundation, Walter Clay
Hobbs Foundation, Emmert
Honeywell
Hoover Foundation
Hopeman Brothers
Horne Foundation, Dick
Hospital Corp. of America
Hoyt Foundation
Hubbard Broadcasting
Hudson-Webber Foundation
Huffy Corp.
Hunt Foundation, Samuel P.
Huntington Fund for Education, John
Huston Foundation
IBM Corp.
IDS Financial Services
Illinois Power Co.
Illinois Tool Works
IMCERA Group Inc.
Indiana Bell Telephone Co.
Ingalls Foundation, Louise H. and David S.
International Multifoods Corp.
J.P. Morgan & Co.
Jackson Foundation
Janssen Foundation, Henry
Jasam Foundation
Jefferson Endowment Fund, John Percival and Mary C.
Jeffress Memorial Trust, Elizabeth G.
Jennings Foundation, Martha Holden
Jergens Foundation, Andrew
Jerome Foundation
Jesselson Foundation

John Hancock Mutual Life Insurance Co.
Johnson Controls
Johnson Endeavor Foundation, Christian A.
Johnson & Higgins
Jones Foundation, Fletcher
Jordan Foundation, Arthur
Jostens
JSJ Corp.
Kauffman Foundation, Muriel McBrien
Kaufman Memorial Trust, Chaim, Fanny, Louis, Benjamin, and Anne Florence
Keating Family Foundation
Kelly Foundation, T. Lloyd
Kemper Charitable Trust, William T.
Kemper Educational and Charitable Fund
Kemper Foundation, Enid and Crosby
Kemper Foundation, William T.
Kerr Foundation
Kerr Fund, Grayce B.
Kettering Fund
Kevorkian Fund, Hagop
Kilcawley Fund, William H.
Kiplinger Foundation
Klein Charitable Foundation, Raymond
Kmart Corp.
Knowles Foundation
Koehler Foundation, Marcia and Otto
Kohler Foundation
Kresge Foundation
Kress Foundation, Samuel H.
Krieble Foundation, Vernon K.
Kulas Foundation
Kysor Industrial Corp.
Lane Memorial Foundation, Mills Bee
Lannan Foundation
Larsen Fund
Lederer Foundation, Francis L.
Lehman Foundation, Robert
Leidy Foundation, John J.
Leo Burnett Co.
Levitt Foundation, Richard S.
Lieberman Enterprises
Lied Foundation Trust
Lincoln Fund
List Foundation, Albert A.
Lockheed Sanders
Love Foundation, Martha and Spencer
Lubrizol Corp.
Lund Foundation
Lupin Foundation
Lyndhurst Foundation
MacArthur Foundation, John D. and Catherine T.
MacDonald Foundation, James A.
Macy & Co., R.H.
Mailman Foundation
Mandell Foundation, Samuel P.
Manger and Audrey Cordero Plitt Trust, Clarence
Manilow Foundation, Nathan
Manoogian Foundation, Alex and Marie
Maritz Inc.
Marriott Corp.
Marsh & McLennan Cos.
Marshall Field's
Marshall & Ilsley Bank
Masco Corp.
Mather and William Gwinn Mather Fund, Elizabeth Ring
Mather Charitable Trust, S. Livingston
Mayer Charitable Trust, Oscar G. & Elsa S.
MCA
McBean Family Foundation

McCormick Foundation, Chauncey and Marion Deering
McGraw-Hill
Mead Corp.
Meadows Foundation
Mellon Foundation, Richard King
Memorial Foundation for Children
Mericos Foundation
Metropolitan Life Insurance Co.
Meyer Foundation, Alice Kleberg Reynolds
Michigan Consolidated Gas Co.
Midmark Corp.
Minnegasco
Mobil Oil Corp.
Model Foundation, Leo
Monsanto Co.
Morgan Construction Co.
Morris Foundation, Margaret T.
Morse, Jr. Foundation, Enid and Lester S.
Morton International
Motorola
MTS Systems Corp.
Mueller Co.
Murch Foundation
Murphy Foundation, John P.
Nalco Chemical Co.
National Computer Systems
National Gypsum Co.
NBD Bank
NCR Corp.
New England Mutual Life Insurance Co.
New-Land Foundation
New Prospect Foundation
New York Telephone Co.
New York Times Co.
The New Yorker Magazine, Inc.
Newhall Foundation, Henry Mayo
Norman Foundation, Andrew
Northern States Power Co.
Northern Trust Co.
Northwest Natural Gas Co.
O'Connor Foundation, A. Lindsay and Olive B.
Offield Family Foundation
Ogilvy & Mather Worldwide
Oglebay Norton Co.
Ohio Bell Telephone Co.
Ohio National Life Insurance Co.
Olin Corp.
Olsson Memorial Foundation, Elis
Ontario Corp.
Open Society Fund
Orleton Trust Fund
Outboard Marine Corp.
Overbrook Foundation
Paley Foundation, Goldie
Paramount Communications Inc.
Parker Foundation
Parshelsky Foundation, Moses L.
Paul and C. Michael Paul Foundation, Josephine Bay
Penn Foundation, William
Peoples Energy Corp.
Perkins Foundation, Edwin E.
Persis Corp.
Peterloon Foundation
Pforzheimer Foundation, Carl and Lily
Philibosian Foundation, Stephen
Philip Morris Cos.
Piankova Foundation, Tatiana
Pick Charitable Trust, Melitta S.
Pittway Corp.
Pollybill Foundation
Porter Testamentary Trust, James Hyde
Portland General Electric Co.
Price Associates, T. Rowe
Pritzker Foundation
Prudential Insurance Co. of America

Puget Sound Power & Light Co.
Pulitzer Publishing Co.
Quaker Oats Co.
Randa
Recognition Equipment
Regenstein Foundation
Reinberger Foundation
Reliable Life Insurance Co.
Reliance Electric Co.
Replogle Foundation, Luther I.
Reynolds & Reynolds Co.
Rhoades Fund, Otto L. and Hazel E.
Rice Foundation
Richmond Foundation, Frederick W.
Rittenhouse Foundation
Robin Family Foundation, Albert A.
Rockefeller Foundation
Rockwell International Corp.
Rohm and Haas Company
Rose Foundation, Billy
Rosen Foundation, Joseph
Ross Memorial Foundation, Will
Rothschild Foundation, Hulda B. and Maurice L.
Ryan Foundation, Nina M.
Sachs Fund
Sage Foundation
Saint Paul Cos.
San Diego Gas & Electric
Santa Fe Pacific Corp.
Sara Lee Corp.
Sarkeys Foundation
Scherer Foundation, Karla
Schroeder Foundation, Walter
Schwartz Fund for Education and Health Research, Arnold and Marie
Scott Foundation, Virginia Steele
Searle & Co., G.D.
Sears Family Foundation
Sedgwick James Inc.
Segerstrom Foundation
Seid Foundation, Barre
Shapero Foundation, Nate S. and Ruth B.
Shapiro Family Foundation, Soretta and Henry
Shawmut National Corp.
Shoney's Inc.
Shwayder Foundation, Fay
Silver Spring Foundation
Simpson Industries
Simpson Investment Co.
Siragusa Foundation
SIT Investment Associates, Inc.
Skillman Foundation
Smith Foundation
Smith Foundation, Lon V.
Snider Foundation
Solomon Foundation, Sarah M.
Sonoco Products Co.
Southern California Edison Co.
Southways Foundation
Southwestern Bell Corp.
Speyer Foundation, Alexander C. and Tillie S.
Sprague Educational and Charitable Foundation, Seth
SPS Technologies
Square D Co.
Stackner Family Foundation
Starling Foundation, Dorothy Richard
Starr Foundation
State Street Bank & Trust Co.
Steelcase
Steele Foundation, Harry and Grace
Stein Foundation, Jules and Doris
Stern Foundation for the Arts, Richard J.
Stone Container Corp.
Strauss Foundation
Tait Foundation, Frank M.

Tamarkin Co.
Taylor Foundation, Ruth and Vernon
TCF Banking & Savings, FSB
Tektronix
Teleflex Inc.
Tension Envelope Corp.
Textron
Thalhimer and Family Foundation, Charles G.
Thoresen Foundation
3M Co.
Times Mirror Co.
TJX Cos.
Towsley Foundation, Harry A. and Margaret D.
Toyota Motor Sales, U.S.A.
Tucker Charitable Trust, Rose E.
21 International Holdings
Union Electric Co.
Universal Foods Corp.
Unocal Corp.
Upton Foundation, Frederick S.
US Bancorp
USG Corp.
Van Camp Foundation
Van Wert County Foundation
Vlasic Foundation
Vulcan Materials Co.
Walgreen Co.
Walker Foundation, T. B.
Wallace Reader's Digest Fund, Lila
Wallin Foundation
Walsh Foundation
Disney Co., Walt
Warhol Foundation for the Visual Arts, Andy
Warner Foundation, Lee and Rose
Wasserman Foundation
Waste Management
Wean Foundation, Raymond John
Webb Charitable Trust, Susan Mott
Webster Foundation, Edwin S.
Weinberg Foundation, John L.
Weisman Art Foundation, Frederick R.
Wellman Foundation, S. K.
Wenger Foundation, Henry L. and Consuelo S.
Wessinger Foundation
West Co.
Weyerhaeuser Co.
Weyerhaeuser Foundation, Frederick and Margaret L.
Whirlpool Corp.
White Consolidated Industries
Whiting Foundation
Wiegand Foundation, E. L.
Wilcox General Trust, George N.
Wiley & Sons, Inc., John
Willard Helping Fund, Cecilia Young
Williams Cos.
Wilson Public Trust, Ralph
Winona Corporation
Women's Project Foundation
Wood Foundation, Lester G.
Wunsch Foundation
Wurlitzer Foundation, Farny R.
Wyne Foundation
Xerox Corp.
Yellow Corp.

Cinema

Amfac/JMB Hawaii
Argyros Foundation
Atherton Family Foundation
BHP Pacific Resources
Bingham Foundation, William
Blum-Kovler Foundation
Bohen Foundation
Bridgestone/Firestone
Broadhurst Foundation

Recipient Type Index

Cinema (cont.)

Broccoli Charitable Foundation, Dana and Albert R.
Burchfield Foundation, Charles E.
Bush Foundation
Carpenter Foundation, E. Rhodes and Leona B.
Cedars-Sinai Medical Center Section D Fund
Central Maine Power Co.
Chartwell Foundation
Chase Manhattan Bank, N.A.
Chicago Resource Center
Chicago Sun-Times, Inc.
CNA Insurance Cos.
Columbia Foundation
Commerce Clearing House
Continental Corp.
Cooke Foundation
Coors Brewing Co.
Crocker Trust, Mary A.
Cummings Foundation, Nathan
Daly Charitable Foundation Trust, Robert and Nancy
Durst Foundation
Fleishhacker Foundation
Forbes
Ford Foundation
Fribourg Foundation
Getz Foundation, Emma and Oscar
Glickenhaus & Co.
Greene Foundation, Jerome L.
Griggs and Mary Griggs Burke Foundation, Mary Livingston
Gund Foundation, George
Hiawatha Education Foundation
Hillman Family Foundation, Alex
Ittleson Foundation
Jerome Foundation
Kaplan Foundation, Rita J. and Stanley H.
Katten, Muchin, & Zavis
Kennecott Corp.
Kresge Foundation
Lastfogel Foundation, Abe and Frances
Laurel Foundation
LEF Foundation
Levinson Foundation, Max and Anna
Lincoln National Corp.
Long Island Lighting Co.
Lowe Foundation, Joe and Emily
MacArthur Foundation, John D. and Catherine T.
Macy & Co., R.H.
Mann Foundation, Ted
Marsh & McLennan Cos.
Martin Family Fund
Mayer Foundation, Louis B.
MCA
McGraw-Hill
Meadows Foundation
Metropolitan Theatres Corp.
Meyer Foundation, Eugene and Agnes E.
Middendorf Foundation
Morris Foundation, Margaret T.
Mosher Foundation, Samuel B.
The New Yorker Magazine, Inc.
Newhouse Foundation, Samuel I.
Nias Foundation, Henry
O'Sullivan Children Foundation
Pacific Enterprises
Packard Foundation, David and Lucile
Paramount Communications Inc.
Parsons Foundation, Ralph M.
Phillips Petroleum Co.
Pickford Foundation, Mary
Playboy Enterprises, Inc.
Plitt Southern Theatres
Rockefeller Foundation
Rose Foundation, Billy

Rosenstiel Foundation
Rosenthal Foundation, Richard and Hinda
Rubin Foundation, Samuel
Salomon Foundation, Richard & Edna
Sara Lee Corp.
Seidman Family Foundation
Shoong Foundation, Milton
Simon Foundation, Jennifer Jones
Simon Foundation, William E. and Carol G.
Southwestern Bell Corp.
Sprague Educational and Charitable Foundation, Seth
Strauss Foundation
Taylor Foundation, Ruth and Vernon
Terner Foundation
Titan Industrial Co.
Wallace Genetic Foundation
Disney Co., Walt
Ware Foundation
Weiler Foundation, Theodore & Renee
Weyerhaeuser Family Foundation
Zellerbach Family Fund

Community Arts

Abbott Laboratories
Abeles Foundation, Joseph and Sophia
Abramson Family Foundation
Abreu Charitable Trust u/w/o May P. Abreu, Francis I.
Ace Beverage Co.
Action Industries, Inc.
Acushnet Co.
Adler Foundation Trust, Philip D. and Henrietta B.
AEGON USA, Inc.
Aeroflex Foundation
AFLAC
AHS Foundation
Air Products & Chemicals
Akzo America
Alabama Power Co.
Albany International Corp.
Albertson's
Alexander Charitable Foundation
Alexander Foundation, Judd S.
Alexander Foundation, Robert D. and Catherine R.
Alexander Foundation, Walter
Algonquin Energy, Inc.
Allen-Heath Memorial Foundation
AlliedSignal
Alltel/Western Region
ALPAC Corp.
Alsdorf Foundation
Altschul Foundation
Alumax
Aluminum Co. of America
America West Airlines
American Aggregates Corp.
American Brands
American Foundation Corporation
American National Bank & Trust Co. of Chicago
American Natural Resources Co.
Ameritech Services
Ames Department Stores
Amfac/JMB Hawaii
Amoco Corp.
AMR Corp.
Andersen Foundation, Arthur
Anderson Charitable Trust, Josephine
Anderson Foundation
Anderson Foundation
Andrews Foundation
Angelica Corp.
Anheuser-Busch Cos.
Ansin Private Foundation, Ronald M.

Apache Corp.
Apple Computer, Inc.
Appleby Trust, Scott B. and Annie P.
Arakelian Foundation, Mary Alice
ARCO
Arkansas Power & Light Co.
Arkwright-Boston Manufacturers Mutual
Arkwright Foundation
Armstrong Foundation
Arnold Fund
Ashland Oil
Atalanta/Sosnoff Capital Corp.
Atherton Family Foundation
Athwin Foundation
Atlanta Foundation
Atlanta Gas Light Co.
Atlantic Foundation
Attleboro Pawtucket Savings Bank
Atwood Foundation
Autzen Foundation
Avis Inc.
Avon Products
Axe-Houghton Foundation
Bachmann Foundation
Backer Spielvogel Bates U.S.
Baer Foundation, Alan and Marcia
Bailey Foundation
Ballet Makers
Bank of America Arizona
Bank of Boston Corp.
Bank of Tokyo Trust Co.
BankAmerica Corp.
Bannerman Foundation, William C.
Bardes Corp.
Barker Foundation, J. M. R.
Barnes Group
Barry Corp., R. G.
Bassett Foundation, Norman
Battelle
Baumker Charitable Foundation, Elsie and Harry
BCR Foundation
Bean Foundation, Norwin S. and Elizabeth N.
Beasley Foundation, Theodore and Beulah
Beattie Foundation Trust, Cordelia Lee
Beckman Foundation, Leland D.
Beerman Foundation
Beim Foundation
Belz Foundation
Benbough Foundation, Legler
Bend Millwork Systems
Benefit Trust Life Insurance Co.
Benua Foundation
Benz Trust, Doris L.
Berger Foundation, Albert E.
Berkman Charitable Trust, Allen H. and Selma W.
Berlin Charitable Fund, Irving
Bernsen Foundation, Grace and Franklin
Bernstein & Co., Sanford C.
Berrie Foundation, Russell
Berry Foundation, Loren M.
Bethlehem Steel Corp.
BFGoodrich
Big V Supermarkets
Binney & Smith Inc.
Birnschein Foundation, Alvin and Marion
Bishop Charitable Trust, A. G.
Bishop Foundation, E. K. and Lillian F.
Blade Communications
Blanchard Foundation
Blaustein Foundation, Louis and Henrietta
Block, H&R
Bloomfield Foundation, Sam and Rie

Blount Educational and Charitable Foundation, Mildred Weedon
Blue Bell, Inc.
Blue Cross and Blue Shield United of Wisconsin Foundation
Blum Foundation, Edith C.
Boatmen's Bancshares
Bohen Foundation
Boise Cascade Corp.
Borden
Borman's
Borwell Charitable Foundation
Botwinick-Wolfensohn Foundation
Boulevard Foundation
Boutell Memorial Fund, Arnold and Gertrude
Bowater Inc.
BP America
Brach Foundation, Helen
Bray Charitable Trust, Viola E.
Bridgestone/Firestone
Briggs Foundation, T. W.
Briggs & Stratton Corp.
Brinkley Foundation
Bristol Savings Bank
Broccoli Charitable Foundation, Dana and Albert R.
Brochsteins Inc.
Brody Foundation, Carolyn and Kenneth D.
Brotman Foundation of California
Brotz Family Foundation, Frank G.
Brown Foundation, W. L. Lyons
Brown & Williamson Tobacco Corp.
Broyhill Family Foundation
Brundage Charitable, Scientific, and Wildlife Conservation Foundation, Charles E. and Edna T.
Brunswick Corp.
Bryce Memorial Fund, William and Catherine
Bull Foundation, Henry W.
Burdines
Burgess Trust, Ralph L. and Florence R.
Burlington Resources
Burndy Corp.
Burnham Foundation
Bushee Foundation, Florence Evans
Butler Family Foundation, Patrick and Aimee
Butler Manufacturing Co.
Butz Foundation
C. E. and S. Foundation
Cable & Wireless Communications
Cablevision of Michigan
Cabot Corp.
Cafritz Foundation, Morris and Gwendolyn
Caine Charitable Foundation, Marie Eccles
Callaway Foundation
Cameron Memorial Fund, Alpin J. and Alpin W.
Camp Younts Foundation
Campbell Foundation
Campbell Foundation
Campbell Foundation, Charles Talbot
Campbell Soup Co.
Capital Holding Corp.
Carbon Fuel Co.
Carlson Cos.
Carolyn Foundation
Carpenter Foundation, E. Rhodes and Leona B.
Carpenter Technology Corp.
Carr Real Estate Services
Carrier Corp.

Carstensen Memorial Foundation, Fred R. and Hazel W.
Carter Foundation, Amon G.
Cassett Foundation, Louis N.
Caterpillar
Cawsey Trust
Cayuga Foundation
Cedars-Sinai Medical Center Section D Fund
Central Fidelity Banks, Inc.
Central Life Assurance Co.
Central Maine Power Co.
Central Vermont Public Service Corp.
Century Companies of America
Chadwick Foundation
Chambers Development Co.
Charitable Foundation of the Burns Family
Charities Foundation
Charter Manufacturing Co.
Chase Manhattan Bank, N.A.
Chase Trust, Alice P.
Chastain Charitable Foundation, Robert Lee and Thomas M.
Chatham Valley Foundation
Chazen Foundation
Cheatham Foundation, Owen
Chemical Bank
Cheney Foundation, Elizabeth F.
Cherne Foundation, Albert W.
Cherokee Foundation
Chesapeake Corp.
Chevron Corp.
Chicago Board of Trade
Chicago Sun-Times, Inc.
Chicago Title and Trust Co.
Christensen Charitable and Religious Foundation, L. C.
Church & Dwight Co.
Ciba-Geigy Corp. (Pharmaceuticals Division)
CIT Group Holdings
Citibank, F.S.B.
Clabir Corp.
Clark Charitable Trust
Clark Foundation
Cleary Foundation
Clorox Co.
CM Alliance Cos.
CNA Insurance Cos.
CNG Transmission Corp.
Codrington Charitable Foundation, George W.
Cogswell Benevolent Trust
Cohen Foundation, George M.
Cohen Foundation, Naomi and Nehemiah
Cohn Family Foundation, Robert and Terri
Colburn Fund
Cole Foundation, Robert H. and Monica H.
Cole Trust, Quincy
Coleman Co.
Collins Foundation, George and Jennie
Collins, Jr. Foundation, George Fulton
Colonial Life & Accident Insurance Co.
Columbia Foundation
Columbia Savings Charitable Foundation
Comer Foundation
Commerce Bancshares, Inc.
Commerce Clearing House
Commonwealth Edison Co.
Connell Foundation, Michael J.
Consolidated Papers
Consumer Farmer Foundation
Continental Corp.
Cooper Charitable Trust, Richard H.
Cooper Foundation
Coors Brewing Co.

Copolymer Rubber & Chemical Corp.
Corestates Bank
Corning Incorporated
County Bank
Covington Foundation, Marion Stedman
Cow Hollow Foundation
Cowles Charitable Trust
Cowles Media Co.
CPC International
Crandall Memorial Foundation, J. Ford
Crapo Charitable Foundation, Henry H.
Crescent Plastics
Crestar Financial Corp.
Crocker Trust, Mary A.
Crown Memorial, Arie and Ida
CT Corp. System
Cuesta Foundation
Cullen/Frost Bankers
Culver Foundation, Constans
Cummins Engine Co.
CUNA Mutual Insurance Group
Curtice-Burns Foods
Dai-Ichi Kangyo Bank of California
Daily News
Dalton Foundation, Harry L.
Dan River, Inc.
Dana Charitable Trust, Eleanor Naylor
Danis Industries
Davee Foundation
Davies Charitable Trust
Davis Family - W.D. Charities, Tine W.
Davis Foundation, James A. and Juliet L.
Davis Foundation, Ken W.
Day Foundation, Nancy Sayles
Day Foundation, Willametta K.
Dayton Hudson Corp.
Daywood Foundation
DCB Corp.
DEC International, Inc.
Dee Foundation, Annie Taylor
Dee Foundation, Lawrence T. and Janet T.
Delano Foundation, Mignon Sherwood
Delaware North Cos.
DelMar Foundation, Charles
Deposit Guaranty National Bank
DeRoy Foundation, Helen L.
Deuble Foundation, George H.
DeVlieg Foundation, Charles
Devonwood Foundation
Dewing Foundation, Frances R.
Dexter Charitable Fund, Eugene A.
Dick Family Foundation
Dietrich Foundation, William B.
Digital Equipment Corp.
Dillard Paper Co.
Dimeo Construction Co.
DiRosa Foundation, Rene and Veronica
Dixie Yarns, Inc.
Dodge Foundation, Geraldine R.
Donaldson Co.
Donnelley Foundation, Elliott and Ann
Dow Corning Corp.
Dow Foundation, Herbert H. and Barbara C.
Dreyfus Foundation, Max and Victoria
Driscoll Foundation
du Pont de Nemours & Co., E. I.
Duchossois Industries
Duke Power Co.
Dunspaugh-Dalton Foundation
duPont Foundation, Chichester
Durfee Foundation
Easley Trust, Andrew H. and Anne O.

East Ohio Gas Co.
Eaton Corp.
Eaton Foundation, Cyrus
Eccles Foundation, George S. and Dolores Dore
Eccles Foundation, Marriner S.
Eckerd Corp., Jack
Edgewater Steel Corp.
Edwards Industries
El Pomar Foundation
Elkins, Jr. Foundation, Margaret and James A.
Ellsworth Foundation, Ruth H. and Warren A.
Emerson Electric Co.
English-Bonter-Mitchell Foundation
English Foundation, Walter and Marian
Enright Foundation
Ensworth Charitable Foundation
Erb Lumber Co.
Erpf Fund, Armand G.
Ethyl Corp.
Evinrude Foundation, Ralph
Evjue Foundation
Exposition Foundation
Exxon Corp.
Fair Oaks Foundation, Inc.
Fairfield-Meeker Charitable Trust, Freeman E.
Fales Foundation Trust
Falk Foundation, David
Falk Medical Fund, Maurice
Farwell Foundation, Drusilla
Federal-Mogul Corp.
Federal Screw Works
Federated Life Insurance Co.
Feild Co-Operative Association
Feintech Foundation
Fidelity Bank
Fifth Avenue Foundation
Fifth Third Bancorp
Fig Tree Foundation
Fingerhut Family Foundation
Finley Charitable Trust, J. B.
Fireman's Fund Insurance Co.
Firestone Foundation, Roger S.
First Chicago
First Interstate Bank of Oregon
First Tennessee Bank
First Union Corp.
Fishback Foundation Trust, Harmes C.
Fisher Foundation
Flarsheim Charitable Foundation, Louis and Elizabeth
Fleet Financial Group
Fleishhacker Foundation
Fletcher Foundation
Flintridge Foundation
Florida Power Corp.
FMC Corp.
Foothills Foundation
Ford Meter Box Co.
Ford Motor Co.
Forest Fund
Foster Charitable Foundation, M. Stratton
Foster Co., L.B.
Foster Foundation, Joseph C. and Esther
Foundation for the Needs of Others
Fox Inc.
Fox Charitable Foundation, Harry K. & Emma R.
Fox Foundation, John H.
Frank Foundation, Ernest and Elfriede
Frank Fund, Zollie and Elaine
Franklin Mint Corp.
Fraser Paper Ltd.
Frear Eleemosynary Trust, Mary D. and Walter F.
Freeport-McMoRan

Freightliner Corp.
Frelinghuysen Foundation
French Foundation
French Oil Mill Machinery Co.
Fribourg Foundation
Frick Educational Commission, Henry C.
Friedman Family Foundation
Fuchs Foundation, Gottfried & Mary
Fuller Foundation
Furth Foundation
Fusenot Charity Foundation, Georges and Germaine
G.A.G. Charitable Corporation
Gage Foundation, Philip and Irene Toll
Gallo Foundation, Ernest
Garvey Kansas Foundation
Garvey Memorial Foundation, Edward Chase
Garvey Trust, Olive White
GATX Corp.
Gaylord Foundation, Clifford Willard
GEICO Corp.
Geifman Family Foundation
Gellert Foundation, Carl
Gellert Foundation, Fred
General American Life Insurance Co.
General Signal Corp.
General Tire Inc.
Geneseo Foundation
GenRad
Georgia Power Co.
Gerber Products Co.
Gerbode Foundation, Wallace Alexander
Gerlach Foundation
Gerondelis Foundation
Gerschel Foundation, Patrick A.
Gershman Foundation, Joel
Getz Foundation, Emma and Oscar
Giant Eagle
Giant Food
Giddings & Lewis
Giger Foundation, Paul and Oscar
Gilman, Jr. Foundation, Sondra and Charles
Ginter Foundation, Karl and Anna
Glaser Foundation
Glaxo
Glaze Foundation, Robert and Ruth
Glazer Foundation, Madelyn L.
Glick Foundation, Eugene and Marilyn
Glosser Foundation, David A.
Goerlich Family Foundation
Goldberg Family Foundation
Goldman Foundation, Herman
Goldring Family Foundation
Goldsmith Family Foundation
Goldsmith Foundation
Goldsmith Foundation, Horace W.
Goodman Family Foundation
Goodstein Foundation
Gordon Charitable Trust, Peggy and Yale
Gould Inc.
Grace & Co., W.R.
Gradison & Co.
Graybar Electric Co.
Great-West Life Assurance Co.
Green Foundation
Greene Foundation, David J.
Greenfield Foundation, Albert M.
Griffith Foundation, W. C.
Groome Beatty Trust, Helen D.
Gross Charitable Trust, Stella B.
Grossman Foundation, N. Bud
Gruss Charitable Foundation, Emanuel and Riane
Gruss Petroleum Corp.

GSC Enterprises
Guaranty Bank & Trust Co.
Guardian Life Insurance Co. of America
Gucci America Inc.
Gulton Foundation
Gund Foundation, George
Gussman Foundation, Herbert and Roseline
Gutman Foundation, Edna and Monroe C.
Haas Foundation, Paul and Mary
Haas Fund, Miriam and Peter
Haffner Foundation
Haley Foundation, W. B.
Hall Charitable Trust, Evelyn A. J.
Hamilton Oil Corp.
Hanes Foundation, John W. and Anna H.
Hankins Foundation
Hansen Foundation, Dane G.
Hanson Foundation
Harding Foundation, Charles Stewart
Harris Corp.
Harris Family Foundation, Hunt and Diane
Harris Foundation, James J. and Angelia M.
Harris Foundation, William H. and Mattie Wattis
Harsco Corp.
Hartman Foundation, Jesse and Dorothy
Harvest States Cooperative
Hauserman, Inc.
Hawn Foundation
Hayfields Foundation
Healy Family Foundation, M. A.
HEI Inc.
Heilicher Foundation, Menaham
Heinz Endowment, Vira I.
Heinz Foundation, Drue
Helfaer Foundation, Evan and Marion
Helis Foundation
Heller Foundation, Walter E.
Heymann Special Account, Mr. and Mrs. Jimmy
Heymann-Wolf Foundation
Higgins Charitable Trust, Lorene Sails
Higgins Foundation, Aldus C.
Higginson Trust, Corina
High Foundation
Hill and Family Foundation, Walter Clay
Hill-Snowdon Foundation
Hilliard Corp.
Hillman Family Foundation, Alex
Hills Fund, Edward E.
Hitchcock Foundation, Gilbert M. and Martha H.
Hitchcock Foundation, Gilbert M. and Martha H.
Hoblitzelle Foundation
Hoffman Foundation, Marion O. and Maximilian
Hofheinz Foundation, Irene Cafcalas
Holden Fund, James and Lynelle
Holley Foundation
Hollis Foundation
Holmes Foundation
Holzer Memorial Foundation, Richard H.
Honda of America Manufacturing, Inc.
Honeywell
Hooper Handling
Hoover Foundation
Hoover Foundation, H. Earl
Hopkins Foundation, Josephine Lawrence

Hornblower Fund, Henry
Horncrest Foundation
House Educational Trust, Susan Cook
Houston Industries
Howell Foundation, Eric and Jessie
Howell Fund
Hoyt Foundation
Hoyt Foundation, Stewart W. and Willma C.
Hubbard Broadcasting
Huffy Corp.
Hulme Charitable Foundation, Milton G.
Humana
Hume Foundation, Jaquelin
Humphreys Foundation
Hunt Charitable Trust, C. Giles
Hunt Foundation
Hunt Foundation, Samuel P.
Hunt Manufacturing Co.
Huthsteiner Fine Arts Trust
IBM Corp.
Icahn Foundation, Carl C.
ICI Americas
Iddings Benevolent Trust
Illges Memorial Foundation, A. and M. L.
Illinois Bell
Illinois Power Co.
Indiana Bell Telephone Co.
Inman Mills
Intel Corp.
International Multifoods Corp.
Interstate Packaging Co.
Iowa-Illinois Gas & Electric Co.
Ireland Foundation
Irvine Foundation, James
Irwin-Sweeney-Miller Foundation
ITT Hartford Insurance Group
Ix & Sons, Frank
J.P. Morgan & Co.
Jacobson Foundation, Bernard H. and Blanche E.
James River Corp. of Virginia
Jameson Foundation, J. W. and Ida M.
Janeway Foundation, Elizabeth Bixby
Jarson-Stanley and Mickey Kaplan Foundation, Isaac & Esther
Jarson-Stanley and Mickey Kaplan Foundation, Isaac & Esther
Jenkins Foundation, George W.
JFM Foundation
JOFCo., Inc.
John Hancock Mutual Life Insurance Co.
Johnson Foundation, A. D.
Johnson & Higgins
Johnson & Johnson
Johnson & Son, S.C.
Johnston-Hanson Foundation
Jones and Bessie D. Phelps Foundation, Cyrus W. and Amy F.
Jones Construction Co., J.A.
Jones Family Foundation, Eugenie and Joseph
Jordan Foundation, Arthur
Joyce Foundation
JSJ Corp.
Kantzler Foundation
Katzenberger Foundation
Kaufman Memorial Trust, Chaim, Fanny, Louis, Benjamin, and Anne Florence
Kearney Inc., A.T.
Keating Family Foundation
Keene Trust, Hazel R.
Keith Foundation Trust, Ben E.
Keller-Crescent Co.
Keller Family Foundation

Community Arts (cont.)

Kelley and Elza Kelley
  Foundation, Edward Bangs
Kemper Educational and
  Charitable Fund
Kennametal
Kennecott Corp.
Kennedy, Jr. Foundation, Joseph
  P.
Kerr Fund, Grayce B.
Kilroy Foundation, William S.
  and Lora Jean
Kilworth Charitable Foundation,
  Florence B.
Kimball International
Kimberly-Clark Corp.
King Ranch
Kingsbury Corp.
Kingsley Foundation, Lewis A.
Kirby Foundation, F. M.
Klipstein Foundation, Ernest
  Christian
Knox Family Foundation
Knox, Sr., and Pearl Wallis Knox
  Charitable Foundation, Robert
  W.
Knudsen Charitable Foundation,
  Earl
Kobacker Co.
Koehler Foundation, Marcia and
  Otto
Kohler Foundation
Komes Foundation
Koopman Fund
Kowalski Sausage Co.
Kraft Foundation
Kramer Foundation
Kramer Foundation, Louise
Kress Foundation, George
Krimendahl II Foundation, H.
  Frederick
Kuehn Foundation
Kulas Foundation
Kysor Industrial Corp.
La-Z-Boy Chair Co.
Ladd Charitable Corporation,
  Helen and George
Ladish Family Foundation,
  Herman W.
Lafarge Corp.
Lakeside Foundation
Lamson & Sessions Co.
Land O'Lakes
Lane Memorial Foundation,
  Mills Bee
Langendorf Foundation, Stanley
  S.
Lassus Brothers Oil
Laurel Foundation
Lautenberg Foundation
Lawrence Foundation, Alice
Lazarus Charitable Trust, Helen
  and Charles
Leach Foundation, Tom &
  Frances
Lebovitz Fund
Lee Endowment Foundation
Lee Foundation, Ray M. and
  Mary Elizabeth
Legg Mason Inc.
Leidy Foundation, John J.
Lemberg Foundation
Lennon Foundation, Fred A.
Leonhardt Foundation, Dorothea
  L.
Leu Foundation, Harry P.
Leuthold Foundation
Lewis Foundation, Lillian Kaiser
Liberty Corp.
Liberty Hosiery Mills
Lilly & Co., Eli
Lilly Endowment
Lilly Foundation, Richard Coyle
Lincoln National Corp.
Linn-Henley Charitable Trust
Liquid Air Corp.
Liz Claiborne

Lockheed Sanders
Lockwood Foundation, Byron
  W. and Alice L.
Long Foundation, George A. and
  Grace
Long Island Lighting Co.
Louisiana Land & Exploration
  Co.
Lounsbery Foundation, Richard
Love Foundation, George H. and
  Margaret McClintic
Love Foundation, Martha and
  Spencer
Lowe Foundation, Joe and Emily
Lozier Foundation
LTV Corp.
Lubo Fund
Lubo Fund
Lukens
Lupin Foundation
Lurie Foundation, Louis R.
Lydall, Inc.
Lyndhurst Foundation
Lyon Foundation
Maas Foundation, Benard L.
MacArthur Foundation, John D.
  and Catherine T.
MacCurdy Salisbury Educational
  Foundation
MacDonald Foundation, James A.
Macht Foundation, Morton and
  Sophia
Macy & Co., R.H.
Maddox Trust, Web
Madison Gas & Electric Co.
Magma Copper Co.
Magowan Family Foundation
Maier Foundation, Sarah Pauline
Mailman Family Foundation, A.
  L.
Mandel Foundation, Morton and
  Barbara
Mandell Foundation, Samuel P.
Mandeville Foundation
Manilow Foundation, Nathan
Marcus Corp.
Maritz Inc.
Markey Charitable Fund, John C.
Marquette Electronics
Marshall Fund
Martin Marietta Aggregates
Masserini Charitable Trust,
  Maurice J.
Mather and William Gwinn
  Mather Fund, Elizabeth Ring
Mather Fund, Richard
Mathis-Pfohl Foundation
Matthews International Corp.
Mayer Foods Corp., Oscar
Mayer Foundation, James and
  Eva
Mayor Foundation, Oliver Dewey
McBean Family Foundation
McCarthy Charities
McConnell Foundation, Neil A.
McDonald & Co. Securities
McDonald Industries, Inc., A. Y.
McDonnell Douglas Corp.-West
McFawn Trust No. 2, Lois Sisler
McGonagle Foundation, Dextra
  Baldwin
McGraw-Hill
McMahon Foundation
McNeely Foundation
McRae Foundation
McVay Foundation
Meadows Foundation
Media General, Inc.
Mellon Bank Corp.
Mellon Foundation, Richard King
Memton Fund
Menasha Corp.
Mendel Foundation
Menschel Foundation, Robert
  and Joyce
Mentor Graphics
Merck Human Health Division

Mercy, Jr. Foundation, Sue and
  Eugene
Meredith Foundation
Merrill Foundation, R. D.
Meyer Foundation, Alice
  Kleberg Reynolds
Meyer Foundation, Baron de
  Hirsch
Meyer Foundation, Eugene and
  Agnes E.
Michigan Bell Telephone Co.
Mielke Family Foundation
Miles Inc.
Mill-Rose Co.
Miller Charitable Foundation,
  Howard E. and Nell E.
Miller Foundation, Steve J.
Miller Fund, Kathryn and Gilbert
Miller-Mellor Association
Milstein Family Foundation
Mingenback Foundation, Julia J.
Miniger Memorial Foundation,
  Clement O.
Minnegasco
Minnesota Power & Light Co.
Minolta Corp.
Minster Machine Co.
Mitchell Family Foundation,
  Bernard and Marjorie
Mitchell Family Foundation,
  Edward D. and Anna
Mitsubishi International Corp.
Mnuchin Foundation
Mobil Oil Corp.
Monadnock Paper Mills
Monfort Charitable Foundation
Monroe Auto Equipment Co.
Montgomery Street Foundation
Moore Foundation, O. L.
Morgan and Samuel Tate
  Morgan, Jr. Foundation,
  Marietta McNeil
Morgan Construction Co.
Morrill Charitable Foundation
Morris Foundation, Norman M.
Morrison-Knudsen Corp.
Morse, Jr. Foundation, Enid and
  Lester S.
Mosinee Paper Corp.
Mott Fund, Ruth
Mulcahy Foundation
Mulford Foundation, Vincent
Mulligan Charitable Trust, Mary
  S.
Munson Foundation, W. B.
Murfee Endowment, Kathryn
Murray Foundation
Myra Foundation
Nabisco Foods Group
Nalco Chemical Co.
Nanney Foundation, Charles and
  Irene
Nash Foundation
National City Bank of Evansville
National Computer Systems
National Gypsum Co.
National Pro-Am Youth Fund
National Westminster Bank New
  Jersey
NEC Technologies, Inc.
Neilson Foundation, George W.
Nesholm Family Foundation
New England Business Service
New England Mutual Life
  Insurance Co.
New Horizon Foundation
New York Mercantile Exchange
New York Stock Exchange
New York Telephone Co.
New York Times Co.
The New Yorker Magazine, Inc.
Newman Assistance Fund,
  Jerome A. and Estelle R.
Newman's Own
News & Observer Publishing Co.
Nias Foundation, Henry
Nichols Foundation
Nordson Corp.

Normandie Foundation
Norris Foundation, Kenneth T.
  and Eileen L.
Nortek, Inc.
Northern Star Foundation
Northern States Power Co.
Northern Telecom Inc.
Northwest Area Foundation
Northwest Natural Gas Co.
Northwestern National Insurance
  Group
Norton Co.
Norton Foundation Inc.
Norwest Bank Nebraska
Oaklawn Foundation
Occidental Oil & Gas Corp.
OCRI Foundation
O'Fallon Trust, Martin J. and
  Mary Anne
Oglebay Norton Co.
Ohio Valley Foundation
Oki America Inc.
Olin Corp.
Oliver Memorial Trust
  Foundation
1957 Charity Trust
O'Neil Foundation, Casey Albert
  T.
Ontario Corp.
OsCo. Industries
Oshkosh B'Gosh
Oshkosh Truck Corp.
Ottenstein Family Foundation
Owen Industries, Inc.
Owens-Corning Fiberglas Corp.
Owsley Foundation, Alvin and
  Lucy
Pacific Enterprises
Pacific Telesis Group
Packaging Corporation of
  America
Packard Foundation, David and
  Lucile
Pangburn Foundation
Pappas Charitable Foundation,
  Bessie
Park National Bank
Park National Bank
Parker Drilling Co.
Parker Foundation
Parker Foundation, Theodore
  Edson
Parker Foundation, Theodore
  Edson
Pasadena Area Residential Aid
Peabody Foundation, Amelia
Pearlstone Foundation, Peggy
  Meyerhoff
Pendleton Memorial Fund,
  William L. and Ruth T.
Penn Foundation, William
Penn Savings Bank, a division of
  Sovereign Bank Bank of
  Princeton, a division of
  Sovereign Bank
Pennzoil Co.
People's Bank
Pepsi-Cola Bottling Co. of
  Charlotte
Perkin-Elmer Corp.
Perry Drug Stores
Pesch Family Foundation
Peterloon Foundation
Petrie Trust, Lorene M.
Pforzheimer Foundation, Carl
  and Lily
Phelps Dodge Corp.
PHH Corp.
Philadelphia Industries
Philip Morris Cos.
Philips Foundation, Jesse
Phillips Foundation, A. P.
Phillips Foundation, Dr. P.
Phillips Foundation, Ellis L.
Phillips Petroleum Co.
Physicians Mutual Insurance
Piankova Foundation, Tatiana
Pillsbury Co.

Pineywoods Foundation
Pineywoods Foundation
Pioneer Hi-Bred International
Piper Foundation, Minnie
  Stevens
Pitney Bowes
Pitt-Des Moines Inc.
Pittsburgh National Bank
Pittulloch Foundation
Playboy Enterprises, Inc.
Poindexter Foundation
Polaroid Corp.
Polinger Foundation, Howard
  and Geraldine
Pollock Company Foundation,
  William B.
Pollybill Foundation
Poorvu Foundation, William and
  Lia
Post Foundation of D.C.,
  Marjorie Merriweather
Potts and Sibley Foundation
PPG Industries
Prairie Foundation
Pratt Memorial Fund
Prentis Family Foundation,
  Meyer and Anna
Preston Trust, Evelyn W.
Preyer Fund, Mary Norris
Price Associates, T. Rowe
Priddy Foundation
Primerica Corp.
Prince Corp.
Principal Financial Group
Pritzker Foundation
Prudential Insurance Co. of
  America
PSI Energy
Public Service Co. of Colorado
Putnam Foundation
Pyramid Foundation
Quaker Chemical Corp.
Quaker Hill Foundation
Quaker Oats Co.
Quincy Newspapers
Quinlan Foundation, Elizabeth C.
R. P. Foundation
Rabb Charitable Trust, Sidney R.
Rabb Foundation, Harry W.
Radin Foundation
Rahr Malting Co.
Raleigh Linen Service/National
  Distributing Co.
Ramlose Foundation, George A.
Randa
Raymond Educational
  Foundation
Rebsamen Companies, Inc.
Recognition Equipment
Reed Foundation
Reliable Life Insurance Co.
Reynolds Foundation, Donald W.
Reynolds Foundation, J. B.
Reynolds & Reynolds Co.
Rhoades Fund, Otto L. and
  Hazel E.
Rice Charitable Foundation,
  Albert W.
Rice Foundation, Helen Steiner
Richmond Foundation, Frederick
  W.
Rienzi Foundation
Rigler-Deutsch Foundation
Ritchie Memorial Foundation,
  Charles E. and Mabel M.
Rite-Hite Corp.
Rittenhouse Foundation
River Branch Foundation
RJR Nabisco Inc.
Robbins & Myers, Inc.
Roberts Foundation
Robinson Foundation
Robinson Fund, Charles Nelson
Robison Foundation, Ellis H. and
  Doris B.
Robson Foundation, LaNelle

Rock Foundation, Milton and
Shirley
Rockefeller Foundation
Rockford Products Corp.
Rockwell Foundation
Rockwell International Corp.
Rodman Foundation
Rogers Charitable Trust, Florence
Rogers Family Foundation
Rogers Foundation
Rogers Foundation
Rohatyn Foundation, Felix and
Elizabeth
Rohm and Haas Company
Rolfs Foundation, Robert T.
Rollins Luetkemeyer Charitable
Foundation
Roseburg Forest Products Co.
Rosen Foundation, Joseph
Rosenbaum Foundation, Paul
and Gabriella
Rosenberg Foundation, Alexis
Rosenberg Foundation, Henry
and Ruth Blaustein
Rosenthal Foundation, Samuel
Ross Foundation
Ross Foundation, Arthur
Ross Memorial Foundation, Will
Roth Family Foundation
Rouse Co.
Royal Group Inc.
Ruan Foundation Trust, John
Ruddick Corp.
Rupp Foundation, Fran and
Warren
Russell Charitable Trust,
Josephine S.
Sachs Fund
Saemann Foundation, Franklin I.
SAFECO Corp.
Saint Croix Foundation
San Diego Gas & Electric
Sandusky International Inc.
Santa Fe Pacific Corp.
Sara Lee Corp.
Sara Lee Hosiery
Sargent Foundation, Newell B.
Saunders Foundation
Schecter Private Foundation,
Aaron and Martha
Scheirich Co., H.J.
Schenck Fund, L. P.
Schering-Plough Corp.
Schey Foundation
Schiff Foundation
Schilling Motors
Schmitt Foundation, Arthur J.
Schneider Foundation Corp., Al
J.
Schoenleber Foundation
Schultz Foundation
Schwab & Co., Charles
Schwob Foundation, Simon
Scott and Fetzer Co.
Scott Foundation, Virginia Steele
Scott Foundation, William E.
Scrivner, Inc.
Seafirst Corp.
Sealright Co., Inc.
Sears Family Foundation
Seaway Food Town
Seay Charitable Trust, Sarah M.
and Charles E.
Sebastian Foundation
Security Life of Denver
Sedgwick James Inc.
See Foundation, Charles
Segal Charitable Trust, Barnet
Segerstrom Foundation
Seid Foundation, Barre
Seidman Family Foundation
Selby and Marie Selby
Foundation, William G.
Sentry Insurance Co.
Setzer Foundation
Shapero Foundation, Nate S. and
Ruth B.

Shapiro Family Foundation,
Soretta and Henry
Sharon Steel Corp.
Shawmut National Corp.
Sheafer Charitable Trust, Emma
A.
Sheaffer Inc.
Sheinberg Foundation, Eric P.
Sheldon Foundation, Ralph C.
Shoney's Inc.
Shott, Jr. Foundation, Hugh I.
Shwayder Foundation, Fay
Sierra Pacific Resources
Silverweed Foundation
Simmons Family Foundation, R.
P.
Simpson Industries
Simpson Investment Co.
SIT Investment Associates, Inc.
Skinner Corp.
Slaughter, Jr. Foundation,
William E.
Slemp Foundation
Slifka Foundation, Alan B.
Smith, Jr. Foundation, M. W.
Smith Memorial Fund, Ethel
Sergeant Clark
Smoot Charitable Foundation
Smucker Co., J.M.
Smyth Trust, Marion C.
Snee-Reinhardt Charitable
Foundation
SNET
Snyder Charitable Fund, W. P.
Solheim Foundation
Soling Family Foundation
Solow Foundation
Somers Foundation, Byron H.
Sonoco Products Co.
Sordoni Foundation
South Branch Foundation
Southern California Edison Co.
Southways Foundation
Southwest Gas Corp.
Southwestern Bell Corp.
Spectra-Physics Analytical
Speyer Foundation, Alexander C.
and Tillie S.
Springs Foundation
Springs Industries
Stackner Family Foundation
Standard Register Co.
Stanley Charitable Foundation,
A. W.
Stanley Works
Stare Fund
State Street Bank & Trust Co.
Statter Foundation, Amy Plant
Stauffer Communications
Steigerwaldt Foundation, Donna
Wolf
Steiner Corp.
Steinhagen Benevolent Trust, B.
A. and Elinor
Steinman Foundation, James
Hale
Steinman Foundation, John
Frederick
Stemmons Foundation
Sterkel Trust, Justine
Sterling Winthrop
Stern Foundation for the Arts,
Richard J.
Stern Foundation, Leonard N.
Sternberger Foundation, Sigmund
Stokely, Jr. Foundation, William
B.
Stone Foundation, France
Stoneman Charitable
Foundation, Anne and David
Storz Foundation, Robert Herman
Stowe, Jr. Foundation, Robert
Lee
Strauss Foundation
Strawbridge Foundation of
Pennsylvania II, Margaret
Dorrance
Stride Rite Corp.

Stuart Center Charitable Trust,
Hugh
Subaru-Isuzu Automotive Inc.
Subaru of America Inc.
Sumitomo Bank of California
Sun Banks Inc.
Sunderland Foundation, Lester T.
Super Valu Stores
Superior Tube Co.
Swig Charity Foundation, Mae
and Benjamin
Swig Foundation
Tait Foundation, Frank M.
Talley Industries, Inc.
Tamarkin Co.
Tandy Foundation, David L.
Target Stores
Taub Foundation
TDK Corp. of America
Teledyne
Teleflex Inc.
Templeton Foundation, Herbert
A.
Tenneco
Tension Envelope Corp.
Tetley, Inc.
Texaco
Texas Commerce Bank Houston,
N.A.
Texas Gas Transmission Corp.
Textron
Thalheimer Foundation, Alvin
and Fanny Blaustein
Thalhimer and Family
Foundation, Charles G.
Thalhimer Brothers Inc.
Thalhimer, Jr. and Family
Foundation, William B.
Thirty-Five Twenty, Inc.
Thoman Foundation, W. B. and
Candace
Thomasville Furniture Industries
Thompson Trust, Thomas
Thornton Foundation, John M.
and Sally B.
Thorpe Foundation, James R.
Thorson Foundation
3M Co.
Tisch Foundation
TJX Cos.
Tobin Foundation
Todd Co., A.M.
Toms Foundation
Torchmark Corp.
Tosco Corp. Refining Division
Tozer Foundation
Transco Energy Company
Tranzonic Cos.
Tropicana Products, Inc.
Truland Foundation
Truman Foundation, Mildred
Faulkner
Trusler Foundation
Trust Co. Bank
TRW Corp.
TU Electric Co.
Tuch Foundation, Michael
Tucker Foundation, Marcia Brady
Twentieth Century-Fox Film
Corp.
Tyson Foods, Inc.
Ukrop's Super Markets, Inc.
Unger Foundation, Aber D.
Union Camp Corp.
Union Central Life Insurance Co.
United States Borax & Chemical
Corp.
United States Trust Co. of New
York
United Technologies Corp.
Unitrode Corp.
Univar Corp.
Universal Foods Corp.
Universal Leaf Tobacco Co.
Unocal Corp.
Upjohn California Fund
Upjohn Co.

Upton Charitable Foundation,
Lucy and Eleanor S.
V and V Foundation
Valdese Manufacturing Co., Inc.
Valspar Corp.
Van Andel Foundation, Jay and
Betty
Vance Charitable Foundation,
Robert C.
Vesuvius Charitable Foundation
Vilter Manufacturing Corp.
Virginia Power Co.
Vlasic Foundation
Vulcan Materials Co.
Wachovia Bank & Trust Co.,
N.A.
Wagner Manufacturing Co., E. R.
Wahlstrom Foundation
Wal-Mart Stores
Waldbaum, Inc.
Walker Foundation, Archie D.
and Bertha H.
Walsh Foundation
Walthall Perpetual Charitable
Trust, Marjorie T.
Wardlaw Fund, Gertrude and
William C.
Warren Charite
Washington Forrest Foundation
Washington Mutual Savings
Bank
Washington Trust Bank
Washington Water Power Co.
Wasmer Foundation
Waters Charitable Trust, Robert
S.
Watson Foundation, Walter E.
and Caroline H.
Wausau Paper Mills Co.
Weaver Foundation
Webster Charitable Foundation
Wege Foundation
Weiner Foundation
Weir Foundation Trust
Weisbrod Foundation Trust
Dept., Robert and Mary
Welch Testamentary Trust,
George T.
Wellman Foundation, S. K.
Wells Foundation, Franklin H.
and Ruth L.
Wenger Foundation, Henry L.
and Consuelo S.
Werthan Foundation
Wertheim Foundation, Dr.
Herbert A.
West Co.
West One Bancorp
Western New York Foundation
Weyerhaeuser Co.
Weyerhaeuser Memorial
Foundation, Charles A.
Wheeler Foundation, Wilmot
Wheless Foundation
Whirlpool Corp.
Whitaker Charitable Foundation,
Lyndon C.
Whitaker Foundation
Whiteman Foundation, Edna
Rider
Whitney Fund, David M.
Whittenberger Foundation,
Claude R. and Ethel B.
Wilder Foundation
Willard Helping Fund, Cecilia
Young
Williams Family Foundation of
Georgia
Williams Foundation, Arthur
Ashley
Wilmington Trust Co.
Wilson Foundation, Hugh and
Mary
Wilson Public Trust, Ralph
Wilson Trust, Lula C.
Winchester Foundation
Winnebago Industries, Inc.
Winter Construction Co.

Winthrop Trust, Clara B.
Wisconsin Energy Corp.
Wisconsin Power & Light Co.
Wisdom Foundation, Mary F.
Wiseheart Foundation
Witte, Jr. Foundation, John H.
Wolff Foundation, John M.
Wolff Shoe Co.
Wolverine World Wide, Inc.
Wood Charitable Trust, W. P.
Wood-Claeyssens Foundation
Wood Foundation, Lester G.
Woodruff Foundation, Robert W.
Woods Charitable Fund
Woods-Greer Foundation
Woolley Foundation, Vasser
Wornall Charitable Trust and
Foundation, Kearney
Wright Foundation, Lola
Wurlitzer Foundation, Farny R.
Wurzburg, Inc.
Wyman Youth Trust
Wyne Foundation
Wyomissing Foundation
Xtra Corp.
Yassenoff Foundation, Leo
Yawkey Foundation II
Yellow Corp.
Yost Trust, Elizabeth Burns
Young Foundation, Hugo H. and
Mabel B.
Young Foundation, R. A.
Zamoiski Co.
Zarrow Foundation, Anne and
Henry
Zellerbach Family Fund
Zemurray Foundation
Zimmerman Family Foundation,
Raymond

Dance

Abbott Laboratories
Abeles Foundation, Joseph and
Sophia
Abell Foundation, The
Abell-Hanger Foundation
Achelis Foundation
Action Industries, Inc.
Adams Foundation, Arthur F. and
Alice E.
AEGON USA, Inc.
Air France
Air Products & Chemicals
Alabama Power Co.
Albany International Corp.
Alcon Laboratories, Inc.
Alexander Foundation, Robert
D. and Catherine R.
Allegheny Ludlum Corp.
AlliedSignal
Alms Trust, Eleanora
ALPAC Corp.
Alumax
Aluminum Co. of America
AMAX
AMCORE Bank, N.A. Rockford
American Cyanamid Co.
American Cyanamid Co.
American Electric Power
American Express Co.
American Foundation
Corporation
American National Bank & Trust
Co. of Chicago
American President Cos.
American Stock Exchange
American Telephone &
Telegraph Co.
Ameritas Life Insurance Corp.
AMETEK
Amfac/JMB Hawaii
Amoco Corp.
Amsterdam Foundation, Jack
and Mimi Leviton
Anderson Charitable Trust,
Josephine
AON Corp.

Dance (cont.)

Apache Corp.
Apple Computer, Inc.
Arcana Foundation
Archibald Charitable
 Foundation, Norman
ARCO
Aristech Chemical Corp.
Arizona Public Service Co.
Arkansas Power & Light Co.
Armco Steel Co.
Arrillaga Foundation
Atherton Family Foundation
Attleboro Pawtucket Savings
 Bank
Atwood Foundation
Bachmann Foundation
Backer Spielvogel Bates U.S.
Baker Foundation, Dexter F. and
 Dorothy H.
Baker, Jr. Memorial Fund,
 William G.
Ballet Makers
Baltimore Gas & Electric Co.
Bank of Louisville
Bank of San Francisco Co.
Bankers Trust Co.
BarclaysAmerican Corp.
Barnes Group
Barry Corp., R. G.
Barstow Foundation
Barth Foundation, Theodore H.
Bartol Foundation, Stockton
 Rush
Battelle
Bauer Foundation, M. R.
BCR Foundation
Beattie Foundation Trust,
 Cordelia Lee
Beinecke Foundation
Belding Heminway Co.
Belfer Foundation
Benedum Foundation, Claude
 Worthington
Benetton
Benua Foundation
Berger Foundation, Albert E.
Bernsen Foundation, Grace and
 Franklin
Berwind Corp.
Beveridge Foundation, Frank
 Stanley
BFGoodrich
Biddle Foundation, Mary Duke
Bingham Foundation, William
Binney & Smith Inc.
Birch Foundation, Stephen and
 Mary
Birnschein Foundation, Alvin
 and Marion
Bishop Foundation, E. K. and
 Lillian F.
Bissell Foundation, J. Walton
Blair and Co., William
Blanchard Foundation
Bloch Foundation, Henry W. and
 Marion H.
Block, H&R
Blount
Blowitz-Ridgeway Foundation
Blum-Kovler Foundation
Boatmen's Bancshares
Bodman Foundation
Boeing Co.
Boh Brothers Construction Co.
Boise Cascade Corp.
Boler Co.
Booth Ferris Foundation
Borden
Borman's
Boston Edison Co.
Bovaird Foundation, Mervin
Bowater Inc.
BP America
Bradford & Co., J.C.

Bradley Foundation, Lynde and
 Harry
Brady Foundation
Bren Foundation, Donald L.
Bridgestone/Firestone
Briggs & Stratton Corp.
Brody Foundation, Carolyn and
 Kenneth D.
Brooks Brothers
Brown and C. A. Lupton
 Foundation, T. J.
Brown Foundation
Brown Foundation, M. K.
Brown & Williamson Tobacco
 Corp.
Browning Charitable
 Foundation, Val A.
Brunswick Corp.
Bryan Family Foundation,
 Kathleen Price and Joseph M.
Bryce Memorial Fund, William
 and Catherine
Buck Foundation, Carol Franc
Bucyrus-Erie
Bull Foundation, Henry W.
Bunbury Company
Burdines
Burlington Resources
Bush Foundation
Butler Manufacturing Co.
Cabot Corp.
Cafritz Foundation, Morris and
 Gwendolyn
Cain Foundation, Gordon and
 Mary
Caine Charitable Foundation,
 Marie Eccles
Cameron Foundation, Harry S.
 and Isabel C.
Camp Foundation
Campbell Foundation
Capital Cities/ABC
Carpenter Foundation, E. Rhodes
 and Leona B.
CBI Industries
Centerior Energy Corp.
Central Maine Power Co.
Chanin Family Foundation, Paul
 R.
Chapman Charitable Trust, H. A.
 and Mary K.
Chase Manhattan Bank, N.A.
Chastain Charitable Foundation,
 Robert Lee and Thomas M.
Cheatham Foundation, Owen
Chemical Bank
Cheney Foundation, Ben B.
Cheney Foundation, Elizabeth F.
Cherokee Foundation
Chevron Corp.
Chicago Sun-Times, Inc.
Citicorp
CLARCOR
Clark Foundation, Robert
 Sterling
Clark-Winchcole Foundation
Clorox Co.
Clowes Fund
CNA Insurance Cos.
CNG Transmission Corp.
Cockrell Foundation
Codrington Charitable
 Foundation, George W.
Cole Foundation, Robert H. and
 Monica H.
Cole Trust, Quincy
Coleman Co.
Collins Foundation
Colonial Life & Accident
 Insurance Co.
Columbia Foundation
Columbus Dispatch Printing Co.
Commonwealth Edison Co.
Compton Foundation
Comstock Foundation
ConAgra
Consolidated Natural Gas Co.
Continental Corp.

Contran Corp.
Cooper Charitable Trust, Richard
 H.
Cooper Industries
Coors Brewing Co.
Copley Press
Coral Reef Foundation
Corbett Foundation
Cord Foundation, E. L.
Cosmair, Inc.
Country Curtains, Inc.
Courts Foundation
Cowles Charitable Trust
Cowles Media Co.
CPC International
CPI Corp.
Credit Agricole
Crum and Forster
Cudahy Fund, Patrick and Anna
 M.
Cullen Foundation
Culpeper Foundation, Charles E.
Cummins Engine Co.
Dana Charitable Trust, Eleanor
 Naylor
Danis Industries
Dayton Hudson Corp.
Dayton Power and Light Co.
Dean Witter Discover
Dee Foundation, Annie Taylor
Dee Foundation, Lawrence T.
 and Janet T.
Deluxe Corp.
Demoulas Supermarkets
Dennison Manufacturing Co.
Deposit Guaranty National Bank
Devonwood Foundation
Dexter Corp.
Dial Corp.
Diamond Foundation, Aaron
Digital Equipment Corp.
Dobson Foundation
Dodge Foundation, Geraldine R.
Donaldson Co.
Dougherty, Jr. Foundation, James
 R.
Douty Foundation
Dow Corning Corp.
Dresser Industries
Dreyfus Foundation, Max and
 Victoria
du Pont de Nemours & Co., E. I.
Duchossois Industries
Duke Power Co.
Dyson Foundation
Eastover Corp.
Eaton Corp.
Eccles Charitable Foundation,
 Willard L.
Eccles Foundation, George S.
 and Dolores Dore
Eccles Foundation, Marriner S.
Eckman Charitable Foundation,
 Samuel and Rae
Educational Foundation of
 America
Elf Atochem North America
Elkins, Jr. Foundation, Margaret
 and James A.
Emerson Electric Co.
EMI Records Group
Encyclopaedia Britannica, Inc.
Engelhard Foundation, Charles
English Foundation, Walter and
 Marian
English Memorial Fund,
 Florence C. and H. L.
Enron Corp.
Enterprise Rent-A-Car Co.
Equitable Life Assurance Society
 of the U.S.
Erpf Fund, Armand G.
Evans Foundation, Edward P.
Exxon Corp.
Fales Foundation Trust
Farish Fund, William Stamps

Federal National Mortgage
 Assn., Fannie Mae
Federation Foundation of
 Greater Philadelphia
Feild Co-Operative Association
Feintech Foundation
Fels Fund, Samuel S.
Fidelity Bank
Fig Tree Foundation
FINA, Inc.
Finley Foundation, A. E.
Fireman's Fund Insurance Co.
Firestone Foundation, Roger S.
First Boston
First Chicago
First Interstate Bank NW Region
First Interstate Bank of Arizona
First Interstate Bank of California
First Interstate Bank of Oregon
First Maryland Bancorp
First Mississippi Corp.
First Tennessee Bank
First Union Corp.
Firstar Bank Milwaukee NA
Fischbach Foundation
Fish Foundation, Ray C.
Fisher Foundation
Flagler Foundation
Fleet Financial Group
Fleishhacker Foundation
Fleming Foundation
Fletcher Foundation, A. J.
Florida Power & Light Co.
Fluor Corp.
Fondren Foundation
Foote, Cone & Belding
 Communications
Forbes
Ford Foundation
Ford Fund, Benson and Edith
Forest Foundation
Forest Fund
Forest Oil Corp.
Foundation for the Needs of
 Others
Francis Families Foundation
Frank Foundation, Ernest and
 Elfriede
Frankel Foundation
Freedom Forum
Freeman Charitable Trust,
 Samuel
Freeport-McMoRan
Frisch's Restaurants Inc.
Fry Foundation, Lloyd A.
Fuchs Foundation, Gottfried &
 Mary
Fuller Co., H.B.
Funderburke & Associates
G.A.G. Charitable Corporation
Galvin Foundation, Robert W.
Garfinkle Family Foundation
Garvey Texas Foundation
Gates Foundation
GATX Corp.
Gelman Foundation, Melvin and
 Estelle
GenCorp
General Accident Insurance Co.
 of America
General American Life Insurance
 Co.
General Electric Co.
General Mills
General Motors Corp.
Georgia-Pacific Corp.
Georgia Power Co.
Getty Foundation, Ann and
 Gordon
Giant Eagle
Giant Food
Gilbert, Jr. Charitable Trust, Price
Gilder Foundation
Gillette Co.
Gilman Foundation, Howard
Gilmore Foundation, Irving S.

Glancy Foundation, Lenora and
 Alfred
Glenmore Distilleries Co.
Glidden Co.
Globe Corp.
Globe Newspaper Co.
Goldberger Foundation, Edward
 and Marjorie
Goldman Foundation, Herman
Goldman Foundation, Morris
 and Rose
Goldman Fund, Richard and
 Rhoda
Goldsmith Foundation, Horace
 W.
Goodman Family Foundation
Goodwin Foundation, Leo
Gould Foundation, Florence J.
Gradison & Co.
Great-West Life Assurance Co.
Green Fund
Greenberg Foundation, Alan C.
Greene Foundation, Jerome L.
Greenfield Foundation, Albert M.
Greentree Foundation
Greenwall Foundation
Gregg-Graniteville Foundation
Gries Charity Fund, Lucile and
 Robert H.
Griffis Foundation
Griggs and Mary Griggs Burke
 Foundation, Mary Livingston
Gross Charitable Trust, Stella B.
Gucci America Inc.
Guggenheim Foundation, Daniel
 and Florence
Gulf Power Co.
Gund Foundation, George
Guttman Foundation, Stella and
 Charles
Haas Foundation, Paul and Mary
Haas Fund, Miriam and Peter
Haas Fund, Walter and Elise
Hagler Foundation, Jon L.
Hallmark Cards
Hamilton Oil Corp.
Hamman Foundation, George
 and Mary Josephine
Harding Foundation, Charles
 Stewart
Harkness Ballet Foundation
Harkness Foundation, William
 Hale
Harmon Foundation, Pearl M.
 and Julia J.
Harriman Foundation, Gladys
 and Roland
Harriman Foundation, Mary W.
Harrington Foundation, Don and
 Sybil
Harris Foundation, J. Ira and
 Nicki
Harrison Foundation Trust,
 Francena T.
Harsco Corp.
Hartford Courant Foundation
Hechinger Co.
Heckscher Foundation for
 Children
Heinz Co., H.J.
Heinz Endowment, Vira I.
Heinz Foundation, Drue
Helfaer Foundation, Evan and
 Marion
Helmerich Foundation
Henderson Foundation
Henkel Corp.
Hervey Foundation
Hess Charitable Foundation,
 Ronne and Donald
Hess Foundation
Hewlett Foundation, William and
 Flora
Heyward Memorial Fund,
 DuBose and Dorothy
Hiawatha Education Foundation
Higgins Charitable Trust, Lorene
 Sails

Higginson Trust, Corina
Hillman Foundation
Hills Fund, Edward E.
Hofheinz Foundation, Irene Cafcalas
Hogan Foundation, Royal Barney
Holzer Memorial Foundation, Richard H.
Homeland Foundation
Honeywell
Hooker Charitable Trust, Janet A.
Hopwood Charitable Trust, John M.
Hospital Corp. of America
Houston Industries
Howard and Bush Foundation
Howell Fund
Hoyt Foundation
Humana
Humphreys Foundation
Hunt Alternatives Fund
Hunt Foundation, Roy A.
Hunt Manufacturing Co.
Huthsteiner Fine Arts Trust
Hyde Foundation, J. R.
IBM Corp.
IDS Financial Services
Illinois Bell
Illinois Tool Works
IMCERA Group Inc.
Index Technology Corp.
Indiana Bell Telephone Co.
Interco
International Flavors & Fragrances
International Paper Co.
Irvine Foundation, James
Irwin Charity Foundation, William G.
ITT Corp.
ITT Hartford Insurance Group
J.P. Morgan & Co.
Jackson Foundation
Jarson-Stanley and Mickey Kaplan Foundation, Isaac & Esther
Jasam Foundation
JCPenney Co.
Jeffress Memorial Trust, Elizabeth G.
Jennings Foundation, Martha Holden
Jerome Foundation
Jewett Foundation, George Frederick
John Hancock Mutual Life Insurance Co.
Johnson Controls
Johnson Endeavor Foundation, Christian A.
Johnson & Higgins
Johnson & Johnson
Jones Construction Co., J.A.
Kaiser Cement Corp.
Kaplan Foundation, Rita J. and Stanley H.
Katten, Muchin, & Zavis
Kauffman Foundation, Muriel McBrien
Kaul Foundation Trust, Hugh
Kautz Family Foundation
Keating Family Foundation
Keith Foundation Trust, Ben E.
Keller-Crescent Co.
Kemper Memorial Foundation, David Woods
Kennecott Corp.
Kentucky Foundation for Women
Kerr Foundation
Kerr Fund, Grayce B.
Kiewit Sons, Peter
Kilroy Foundation, William S. and Lora Jean
Kimberly-Clark Corp.
Kingsbury Corp.
Kingsley Foundation
Kirkpatrick Foundation

Knight Foundation, John S. and James L.
Koch Charitable Trust, David H.
Koch Industries
Kohler Foundation
Koopman Fund
Koret Foundation
Kraft General Foods
Kreielsheimer Foundation Trust
Krimendahl II Foundation, H. Frederick
Kulas Foundation
Kunstadter Family Foundation, Albert
L. L. W. W. Foundation
L and L Foundation
Laclede Gas Co.
Lakeside Foundation
Lamson & Sessions Co.
Langendorf Foundation, Stanley S.
Lard Trust, Mary Potishman
Lastfogel Foundation, Abe and Frances
Lauder Foundation
Laurel Foundation
Lazarus Charitable Trust, Helen and Charles
Lea Foundation, Helen Sperry
Lechmere
Lehrman Foundation, Jacob and Charlotte
Lemberg Foundation
Levin Foundation, Philip and Janice
Levy Foundation, Charles and Ruth
Life Insurance Co. of Georgia
Lilly & Co., Eli
Lincoln Electric Co.
Lincoln National Corp.
Lipton, Thomas J.
Little Family Foundation
Long Foundation, George A. and Grace
Loughran Foundation, Mary and Daniel
Louisiana Land & Exploration Co.
Love Foundation, Martha and Spencer
Lowe Foundation, Joe and Emily
LTV Corp.
Lubrizol Corp.
M/A-COM, Inc.
MacArthur Foundation, John D. and Catherine T.
MacDonald Foundation, Marquis George
Macy & Co., R.H.
Maddox Trust, Web
Magowan Family Foundation
Magruder Foundation, Chesley G.
Mailman Foundation
MalCo Products Inc.
Mandel Foundation, Jack N. and Lilyan
Mapco Inc.
Mardigian Foundation
Maritz Inc.
Marquette Electronics
Mars Foundation
Marsh & McLennan Cos.
Marshall Field's
Marshall Trust in Memory of Sanders McDaniel, Harriet McDaniel
Martin Marietta Corp.
Marubeni America Corp.
Massey Foundation
Max Charitable Foundation
May Foundation, Wilbur
Maytag Co.
Maytag Family Foundation, Fred
MCA
McDonnell Douglas Corp.-West
McFawn Trust No. 2, Lois Sisler

McGraw Foundation, Curtis W.
McGraw-Hill
McInerny Foundation
McKesson Corp.
McKnight Foundation
McLean Contributionship
McRae Foundation
Mead Corp.
Meadows Foundation
Mellon Bank Corp.
Mellon Foundation, Andrew W.
Mellon Foundation, Richard King
Memton Fund
Mendel Foundation
Menschel Foundation, Robert and Joyce
Mentor Graphics
Mercantile Bancorp
Mertz-Gilmore Foundation, Joyce
Mervyn's
Metropolitan Life Insurance Co.
Meyer Foundation, Eugene and Agnes E.
Meyer Foundation, Robert R.
Meyer Memorial Trust
Middendorf Foundation
Miller Foundation, Steve J.
Mine Safety Appliances Co.
Minnegasco
Mirapaul Foundation
MNC Financial
Mobil Oil Corp.
Monell Foundation, Ambrose
Monsanto Co.
Montgomery Street Foundation
Monticello College Foundation
Morgan and Samuel Tate Morgan, Jr. Foundation, Marietta McNeil
Morgan Foundation, Burton D.
Morgan Stanley & Co.
Morris Foundation, Margaret T.
Morris Foundation, William T.
Morse, Jr. Foundation, Enid and Lester S.
Moses Fund, Henry and Lucy
Motorola
Murphy Foundation, John P.
Murphy Foundation, Katherine and John
Myra Foundation
Nalco Chemical Co.
National City Corp.
National Gypsum Co.
National Starch & Chemical Corp.
National Steel
National Westminster Bank New Jersey
Nationale-Nederlanden North America Corp.
NationsBank Corp.
NBD Bank, N.A.
Neuberger Foundation, Roy R. and Marie S.
New England Biolabs Foundation
New England Mutual Life Insurance Co.
New York Telephone Co.
New York Times Co.
The New Yorker Magazine, Inc.
Newhouse Foundation, Samuel I.
News & Observer Publishing Co.
Norfolk Southern Corp.
Northwest Area Foundation
Northwest Natural Gas Co.
Norton Co.
Norwest Bank Nebraska
Noyes, Jr. Memorial Foundation, Nicholas H.
Ogilvy & Mather Worldwide
Oglebay Norton Co.
Olin Corp.
Ore-Ida Foods, Inc.
Osborn Charitable Trust, Edward B.
Overbrook Foundation

Owsley Foundation, Alvin and Lucy
Oxford Foundation
Pacific Enterprises
Pacific Gas & Electric Co.
Pacific Mutual Life Insurance Co.
Pacific Telesis Group
Packard Foundation, David and Lucile
Paley Foundation, William S.
Pangburn Foundation
Pappas Charitable Foundation, Thomas Anthony
Paramount Communications Inc.
Parker Drilling Co.
Parshelsky Foundation, Moses L.
Peabody Foundation, Amelia
Pearlstone Foundation, Peggy Meyerhoff
Penn Foundation, William
Pennsylvania General Insurance Co.
Pennzoil Co.
People's Bank
Peoples Energy Corp.
Pepsi-Cola Bottling Co. of Charlotte
Pew Charitable Trusts
Pfizer
Pforzheimer Foundation, Carl and Lily
Phelps Dodge Corp.
Philadelphia Electric Co.
Philadelphia Industries
Philip Morris Cos.
Philips Foundation, Jesse
Phillips Petroleum Co.
Piankova Foundation, Tatiana
Pick, Jr. Fund, Albert
Picower Foundation, Jeffrey M. and Barbara
Pincus Family Fund
Pines Bridge Foundation
Pioneer Hi-Bred International
Plumsock Fund
Polaroid Corp.
Portland General Electric Co.
Post Foundation of D.C., Marjorie Merriweather
Potlatch Corp.
Potomac Electric Power Co.
Powell Family Foundation
PPG Industries
Premier Industrial Corp.
Prince Trust, Abbie Norman
Principal Financial Group
Pritzker Foundation
Procter & Gamble Cosmetic & Fragrance Products
Public Service Co. of Colorado
Puget Sound Power & Light Co.
Pulitzer Publishing Co.
Quaker Oats Co.
Questar Corp.
Randleigh Foundation Trust
Ratshesky Foundation, A. C.
Reliable Life Insurance Co.
Reliance Electric Co.
Republic New York Corp.
Revson Foundation, Charles H.
Reynolds Foundation, Richard S.
Reynolds & Reynolds Co.
Rhone-Poulenc Inc.
Rice Foundation
Rich Foundation
Richmond Foundation, Frederick W.
Rigler-Deutsch Foundation
RJR Nabisco Inc.
Robbins & Myers, Inc.
Roberts Foundation
Robinson Fund, Charles Nelson
Robison Foundation, Ellis H. and Doris B.
Rock Foundation, Milton and Shirley
Rockefeller Foundation

Rockwell Foundation
Rockwell Fund
Rockwell International Corp.
Rohatyn Foundation, Felix and Elizabeth
Rohm and Haas Company
RosaMary Foundation
Rose Foundation, Billy
Rosenberg, Jr. Family Foundation, Louise and Claude
Rosenstiel Foundation
Rosenthal Foundation, Ida and William
Roth Family Foundation
Rothschild Foundation, Hulda B. and Maurice L.
Rouse Co.
Royal Group Inc.
Rubenstein Charitable Foundation, Lawrence J. and Anne
Rubin Foundation, Rob E. & Judith O.
Rubinstein Foundation, Helena
Rudin Foundation, Samuel and May
Ryder System
SAFECO Corp.
Saint Paul Cos.
Samuels Foundation, Fan Fox and Leslie R.
San Diego Gas & Electric
Santa Fe Pacific Corp.
Sara Lee Corp.
Sarkeys Foundation
Schadt Foundation
Schering-Plough Corp.
Scherman Foundation
Scheuer Family Foundation, S. H. and Helen R.
Schey Foundation
Schieffelin & Somerset Co.
Schiro Fund
Schlumberger Ltd.
Schrafft and Bertha E. Schrafft Charitable Trust, William E.
Schultz Foundation
Schwartz Foundation, Bernard Lee
Scott Foundation, William E.
Scrivner, Inc.
Scurlock Foundation
Seafirst Corp.
Searle & Co., G.D.
Sears Family Foundation
Security Benefit Life Insurance Co.
Security Life of Denver
Sedgwick James Inc.
Segerstrom Foundation
Sharp Foundation
Sharp Foundation, Evelyn
Shawmut National Corp.
Sheafer Charitable Trust, Emma A.
Sheaffer Inc.
Shell Oil Co.
Shenandoah Life Insurance Co.
Shubert Foundation
Shughart, Thomson & Kilroy, P.C.
Shwayder Foundation, Fay
Simon Charitable Trust, Esther
Simon Foundation, William E. and Carol G.
Simpson Investment Co.
Skinner Corp.
Smith Corp., A.O.
Smith Foundation, Kelvin and Eleanor
Smith, Jr. Foundation, M. W.
SmithKline Beecham
SNET
Sonoco Products Co.
Sosland Foundation
South Branch Foundation
Southern California Edison Co.
Southwestern Bell Corp.

Dance (cont.)

Spiegel Family Foundation, Jerry
and Emily
Sprague Educational and
Charitable Foundation, Seth
Spunk Fund
Square D Co.
Stanley Works
Starr Foundation
State Street Bank & Trust Co.
Steelcase
Stein Foundation, Jules and Doris
Steiner Corp.
Stemmons Foundation
Sterling Winthrop
Stern Foundation, Gustav and
Irene
Stevens Foundation, Abbot and
Dorothy H.
Stewart Educational Foundation,
Donnell B. and Elizabeth Dee
Shaw
Stocker Foundation
Storz Foundation, Robert Herman
Stowe, Jr. Foundation, Robert
Lee
Strake Foundation
Stranahan Foundation
Stride Rite Corp.
Stulsaft Foundation, Morris
Subaru of America Inc.
Sun Co.
Swig Charity Foundation, Mae
and Benjamin
Swig Foundation
Swiss Bank Corp.
Talley Industries, Inc.
Tandy Foundation, Anne Burnett
and Charles
Target Stores
Tasty Baking Co.
Taylor Foundation, Ruth and
Vernon
Teleflex Inc.
Tenneco
Tetley, Inc.
Texaco
Texas Gas Transmission Corp.
Textron
Thermo Electron Corp.
Thoman Foundation, W. B. and
Candace
3M Co.
Thurston Charitable Foundation
Times Mirror Co.
Tisch Foundation
Titus Foundation, C. W.
TJX Cos.
Tomkins Industries, Inc.
Tomlinson Foundation, Kate and
Elwyn
Torchmark Corp.
Transco Energy Company
Travelers Cos.
Trexler Trust, Harry C.
TRINOVA Corp.
Triskelion Ltd.
Truland Foundation
Trust Co. Bank
Trust for Mutual Understanding
Tucker Charitable Trust, Rose E.
Tucker Foundation, Marcia Brady
Turner Charitable Foundation
21 International Holdings
Union Bank
Union Electric Co.
Union Pacific Corp.
United Airlines
United States Trust Co. of New
York
Universal Leaf Tobacco Co.
Unocal Corp.
UNUM Corp.
Upjohn California Fund
Upton Foundation, Frederick S.
USX Corp.

Virginia Power Co.
Vulcan Materials Co.
Wachovia Bank & Trust Co.,
N.A.
Wade Endowment Fund,
Elizabeth Firth
Wal-Mart Stores
Walker Foundation, W. E.
Wallace Foundation, George R.
Wallace Reader's Digest Fund,
Lila
Wallach Foundation, Miriam G.
and Ira D.
Walsh Foundation
Warner Fund, Albert and Bessie
Washington Forrest Foundation
Wasmer Foundation
Wean Foundation, Raymond John
Weil, Gotshal & Manges
Foundation
Weiler Foundation, Theodore &
Renee
Weinberg, Jr. Foundation, Sidney
J.
Weiss Foundation, Stephen and
Suzanne
Welch Testamentary Trust,
George T.
Wendt Foundation, Margaret L.
Werblow Charitable Trust, Nina
W.
Wertheim Foundation, Dr.
Herbert A.
West One Bancorp
Westinghouse Electric Corp.
Weyerhaeuser Co.
Whirlpool Corp.
White Consolidated Industries
Whitehead Foundation
Whiting Foundation, Macauley
and Helen Dow
Whittenberger Foundation,
Claude R. and Ethel B.
Wickes Foundation, Harvey
Randall
Wiegand Foundation, E. L.
Wildermuth Foundation, E. F.
Wiley & Sons, Inc., John
Williams Cos.
Winston Foundation, Norman
and Rosita
Winston Research Foundation,
Harry
Winter Construction Co.
Wisdom Foundation, Mary F.
Wiseheart Foundation
Woods Charitable Fund
Wyman Youth Trust
Wyomissing Foundation
Xerox Corp.
Yellow Corp.
Young & Rubicam
Zellerbach Family Fund
Zemurray Foundation
Zenkel Foundation
Zilkha & Sons
Zink Foundation, John Steele

Ethnic Arts

Alltel/Western Region
ALPAC Corp.
Alumax
Ameritech Services
AMETEK
Apache Corp.
Apple Computer, Inc.
Archer-Daniels-Midland Co.
ARCO
ARCO Chemical
Arizona Public Service Co.
Atlanta Gas Light Co.
Attleboro Pawtucket Savings
Bank
Avon Products
Backer Spielvogel Bates U.S.
Banco Portugues do Atlantico,
New York Branch

Bank of America Arizona
Bank of Boston Corp.
Bank One, Texas-Houston Office
Bankers Trust Co.
Barry Corp., R. G.
Bartol Foundation, Stockton
Rush
Baughman Foundation
Belo Corp., A.H.
Benenson Foundation, Frances
and Benjamin
Block, H&R
Boeing Co.
Borman's
Brotman Foundation of
California
Brown & Williamson Tobacco
Corp.
Bush Foundation
Cabot Corp.
Capital Cities/ABC
Carter Foundation, Amon G.
CBS Inc.
Central Maine Power Co.
Chase Manhattan Bank, N.A.
Chicago Sun-Times, Inc.
Cintas Foundation
Citicorp
Clark Foundation, Robert
Sterling
Clorox Co.
CNA Insurance Cos.
Coleman Co.
Colonial Life & Accident
Insurance Co.
Columbia Foundation
Commonwealth Edison Co.
Cook Inlet Region
Coors Brewing Co.
Cosmair, Inc.
Cowles Media Co.
CPC International
Cullen/Frost Bankers
Cummings Foundation, Nathan
Dayton Hudson Corp.
Dayton Power and Light Co.
du Pont de Nemours & Co., E. I.
Duchossois Industries
Duke Power Co.
Duncan Foundation, Lillian H.
and C. W.
Enron Corp.
Equifax
Equitable Life Assurance Society
of the U.S.
Federated Department Stores and
Allied Stores Corp.
Fidelity Bank
Fireman's Fund Insurance Co.
First Chicago
First Fidelity Bancorporation
First Tennessee Bank
First Union Corp.
Flagler Co.
Fleet Financial Group
Fleishhacker Foundation
Flintridge Foundation
Foellinger Foundation
Forbes
Ford Foundation
Foundation for Iranian Studies
Freedom Forum
Freeport-McMoRan
Fry Foundation, Lloyd A.
Funderburke & Associates
Furth Foundation
G.P.G. Foundation
GATX Corp.
General Electric Co.
Georgia Power Co.
Getty Foundation, Ann and
Gordon
Getty Trust, J. Paul
Grace & Co., W.R.
Graybar Electric Co.
Gucci America Inc.
Haas Fund, Walter and Elise

Hall Charitable Trust, Evelyn A.
J.
Hallmark Cards
Harkness Foundation, William
Hale
Heckscher Foundation for
Children
Higginson Trust, Corina
Homeland Foundation
Honeywell
Houston Industries
IBM Corp.
Indiana Bell Telephone Co.
Indiana Insurance Cos.
International Multifoods Corp.
Irvine Foundation, James
Ishiyama Foundation
J.P. Morgan & Co.
John Hancock Mutual Life
Insurance Co.
Johnson Endeavor Foundation,
Christian A.
Johnson Foundation, Barbara P.
Johnson & Higgins
Jones Foundation, Helen
Jordan and Ettie A. Jordan
Charitable Foundation, Mary
Ranken
Jostens
Kaiser Cement Corp.
Kennecott Corp.
Kettering Family Foundation
Kevorkian Fund, Hagop
Kingsbury Corp.
Lannan Foundation
Lard Trust, Mary Potishman
Life Insurance Co. of Georgia
Littauer Foundation, Lucius N.
Long Island Lighting Co.
Louisiana Land & Exploration
Co.
Lurie Foundation, Louis R.
MacArthur Foundation, John D.
and Catherine T.
Magma Copper Co.
Mandeville Foundation
Manoogian Foundation, Alex
and Marie
Mardigian Foundation
Maritz Inc.
Marshall Field's
Mayer Foods Corp., Oscar
Mazda Motors of America
(Central), Inc.
Mazda North America
McCasland Foundation
McDermott Foundation, Eugene
McDonald & Co. Securities
Meadows Foundation
Mervyn's
Metropolitan Life Insurance Co.
Mex-Am Cultural Foundation
Meyer Foundation, Eugene and
Agnes E.
Meyer Memorial Trust
Mitsubishi International Corp.
Mobil Oil Corp.
Monsanto Co.
Motorola
National Westminster Bank New
Jersey
New England Mutual Life
Insurance Co.
New York Telephone Co.
New York Times Co.
The New Yorker Magazine, Inc.
Nordson Corp.
Northeast Utilities
Northern Indiana Public Service
Co.
Northern States Power Co.
Northwest Natural Gas Co.
Norton Co.
Ogden Foundation, Ralph E.
Osher Foundation, Bernard
Overseas Shipholding Group
Pacific Enterprises

Pacific Gas & Electric Co.
Pacific Mutual Life Insurance Co.
Pacific Telesis Group
Paulucci Family Foundation
Penn Foundation, William
Penn Savings Bank, a division of
Sovereign Bank Bank of
Princeton, a division of
Sovereign Bank
Peoples Energy Corp.
Pew Charitable Trusts
Philadelphia Electric Co.
Philip Morris Cos.
Playboy Enterprises, Inc.
Portland General Electric Co.
Post Foundation of D.C.,
Marjorie Merriweather
Public Service Co. of Colorado
Quaker Oats Co.
Rasmussen Foundation
Recognition Equipment
Revson Foundation, Charles H.
Rockefeller Foundation
Rohm and Haas Company
Rouse Co.
Royal Group Inc.
Saint Paul Cos.
San Diego Gas & Electric
Sara Lee Corp.
Schieffelin & Somerset Co.
Scrivner, Inc.
Sealaska Corp.
Seaway Food Town
Security Life of Denver
Sedgwick James Inc.
Seven Springs Foundation
Shawmut National Corp.
Shenandoah Life Insurance Co.
Shoney's Inc.
Shoong Foundation, Milton
Skirball Foundation
SNET
Solow Foundation
Sony Corp. of America
Southern California Edison Co.
Southwestern Bell Co.
Sprague Educational and
Charitable Foundation, Seth
Starr Foundation
State Street Bank & Trust Co.
Steelcase
Swiss Bank Corp.
Target Stores
Teleflex Inc.
Texaco
3M Co.
Tisch Foundation
Transco Energy Company
True Trust, Henry A.
Trull Foundation
Trust Co. Bank
21 International Holdings
Union Camp Corp.
U.S. Leasing International
Vulcan Materials Co.
Wallace Reader's Digest Fund,
Lila
Warhol Foundation for the Visual
Arts, Andy
Whirlpool Corp.
Winter Construction Co.
Zellerbach Family Fund

General

ABB Process Automation
Acorn Corrugated Box Co.
Addison-Wesley Publishing Co.
Aeroglide Corp.
AFG Industries, Inc.
Ahmanson & Co., H.F.
Airborne Express Co.
Alabama Gas Corp. (An Energen
Co.)
Aladdin Industries, Incorporated
Alaska Airlines, Inc.
Alyeska Pipeline Service Co.

AMCORE Bank, N.A. Rockford
Amdahl Corp.
American Filtrona Corp.
American General Corp.
American General Life & Accident Insurance Co.
American Mutual Insurance Cos.
American National Bank
American National Can Co.
American Re-Insurance Co.
American Stock Exchange
American Stores Co.
American Telephone & Telegraph Co./New York City Region
Ameritech Publishing
Amoskeag Co.
Ampacet Corp.
Anacomp, Inc.
ARA Services
Arcata Corp.
Aristech Chemical Corp.
Arkansas Best Corp.
Arkla
Armco Steel Co.
Asahi Glass America, Inc.
Atlanta Journal & Constitution
Attleboro Pawtucket Savings Bank
Autodesk, Inc.
Avery Dennison Corp.
Awrey Bakeries
AXIA Incorporated
Baird & Co., Robert W.
Baker, Watts & Co.
Ball Corp.
Bally's - Las Vegas
Baltimore Life Insurance Co.
Bank of America Arizona
Bank of Boston Connecticut
Bank of Louisville
Bank of Oklahoma, N.A.
Bank One, Texas-Houston Office
Bank One, Texas, NA
Barry Corp., R. G.
Barton-Gillet Co.
BASF Corp.
Bayview Federal Bank
BDM International
Belden Brick Co., Inc.
Bell Helicopter Textron
Benefit Trust Life Insurance Co.
Bergen Record Corp.
Berwind Corp.
Betz Laboratories
Bill Communications
Binney & Smith Inc.
Bionetics Corp.
Birmingham News Co.
Black & Decker Corp.
Blair and Co., William
Bloomingdale's
Bob Evans Farms
Boston Gas Co.
Boston Mutual Life Insurance Co.
Boulevard Bank, N.A.
Bourns, Inc.
Bradford & Co., J.C.
Brakeley, John Price Jones Inc.
Branch Banking & Trust Co.
Brewer and Co., Ltd., C.
Briggs & Stratton Corp.
Brooklyn Union Gas Co.
Bryn Mawr Trust Co.
Buffalo Forge Co.
Bull HN Information Systems Inc.
Business Men's Assurance Co. of America
Cadence Design Systems
Caesar's World, Inc.
Caldwell Manufacturing Co.
Capital Group
Capital Holding Corp.
Carolina Telephone & Telegraph Co.

Carr Real Estate Services
Casco Northern Bank
Castle & Cooke
CCB Financial Corp.
Centex Corp.
Central Life Assurance Co.
Central Maine Power Co.
Central Trust Co.
Charter Medical Corp.
Chase Lincoln First Bank, N.A.
Chemtech Industries
Chicago Sun-Times, Inc.
Chicago Title and Trust Co.
Chubb Life Insurance Co. of America
Citizens Gas & Coke Utility
Clark Equipment Co.
CNA Insurance Cos.
Coachmen Industries
Coastal Corp.
Coleman Co.
Colgate-Palmolive Co.
Colonial Parking
Colonial Penn Group, Inc.
Colorado Interstate Gas Co.
Colorado National Bankshares
Commerce Clearing House
Commercial Federal Corp.
Commercial Intertech Corp.
Commonwealth Life Insurance Co.
Community Mutual Insurance Co.
Computer Associates International
Computer Sciences Corp.
Consolidated Rail Corp. (Conrail)
Continental Airlines
Control Data Corp.
Conwood Co. L.P.
Cooper Oil Tool
Cooper Tire & Rubber Co.
Corvallis Clinic
Credit Agricole
Creditanstalt-Bankverein, New York
CSX Corp.
CT Corp. System
Cubic Corp.
Culbro Corp.
Curtis Industries, Helene
Danforth Co., John W.
Dayton's
Dean Witter Discover
DEC International, Inc.
Delmarva Power & Light Co.
Diamond Shamrock
Diamond State Telephone Co.
Dibrell Brothers, Inc.
Didier Taylor Refractories Corp.
Diebold, Inc.
Dime Savings Bank of New York
Dover Corp.
Dreyer's & Edy's Grand Ice Cream
Drown Foundation, Joseph
Durham Corp.
Duriron Co., Inc.
Dynatech Corp.
Eastland Bank
Ebsco Industries
Educators Mutual Life Insurance Co.
Edwards & Sons, A.G.
Electronic Data Systems Corp.
Employers Insurance of Wausau, A Mutual Co.
Employers Mutual Casualty Co.
Encyclopaedia Britannica, Inc.
Ensearch Corp.
Entex
Equimark Corp.
Equitable Resources
Evening Post Publishing Co.
Excel Industries (Elkhart, Indiana)
Fabri-Kal Corp.

Fairfield Communities, Inc.
Farmers Group, Inc.
Federated Life Insurance Co.
Ferranti Tech
Ferrell Cos.
Ferro Corp.
Filene's Sons Co., William
First Alabama Bancshares
First Brands Corp.
First Commercial Bank N.A.
First Interstate Bank of Denver
First Interstate Bank & Trust Co.
First National Bank in Wichita
First NH Banks, Inc.
First of America Bank Corp.
First Security Bank of Idaho N.A.
First Security Bank of Utah N.A.
First Union National Bank of Florida
Fischer & Porter Co.
Fisher-Price
Fleet Bank
Fleet Bank N.A.
Florida Power & Light Co.
Fortis Benefits Insurance Company/Fortis Financial Group
Foxmeyer Corp.
Frito-Lay
Fullerton Metals Co.
Galileo Electro-Optics Corp.
Gast Manufacturing Corp.
Gates Corp.
General Color Co.
General Housewares Corp.
General Railway Signal Corp.
General Signal Corp.
General Tire Inc.
Genesco
GenRad
Glatfelter Co., P.H.
Glendale Federal Bank
Grainger, W.W.
Grand Rapids Label Co.
Grand Trunk Corp.
Graphic Controls Corp.
Great Lakes Bancorp, FSB
Great Lakes Carbon Corp.
Grinnell Mutual Reinsurance Co.
Hand Industries
Handy & Harman
Harbert Corp.
Harcourt General
Harleysville Mutual Insurance Co.
Harnischfeger Foundation
Harris Stores, Paul
Hartford Steam Boiler Inspection & Insurance Co.
Haworth, Inc.
Hecla Mining Co.
Heil Co.
Herald News
Hercules Inc.
Hiram Walker & Sons Inc.
Hobart Corp.
Holly Sugar Corp.
Holyoke Mutual Insurance Co. in Salem
Home Savings of America, FA
Howell Corp.
Howmet Corp.
Huber, Hunt & Nichols
Huck International Inc.
Hudson Jewellers, J.B.
Hudson's
Huffy Corp.
Hughes Aircraft Co.
Hunt Oil Co.
Huntington Bancshares Inc.
ICH Corp.
Illinois Power Co.
Industrial Risk Insurers
Ingram Industries
Integra Bank/South
Intermark, Inc.
Interpublic Group of Cos.

Isaly Klondike Co.
Itoh (C.) International (America), Inc.
IU International
Jefferson-Pilot
Jefferson-Pilot Communications
Jefferson Smurfit Corp.
Jersey Central Power & Light Co.
Johnson Inc., Axel
Jones Construction Co., J.A.
Journal Communications
Kaiser Aluminum & Chemical Corp.
Kaman Corp.
Kaneb Services, Inc.
Karmazin Products Corp.
Kaufman & Broad Home Corp.
Kaye, Scholer, Fierman, Hays & Handler
Keefe, Bruyette & Woods
Kellogg Co., M.W.
Kellwood Co.
Kendall Health Care Products
Kennecott Corp.
Ketchum & Co.
Kimball International
Kinder-Care Learning Centers
King Kullen Grocery Co., Inc.
KN Energy, Inc.
Kulicke & Soffa Industries
L.A. Gear
Lafarge Corp.
Lambda Electronics Inc.
LaSalle Bank Lake View
Law Companies Group
Law Company, Inc.
Leaseway Transportation Corp.
Libbey-Owens Ford Co.
Liberty Mutual Insurance Group/Boston
LIN Broadcasting Corp.
Lincoln Telecommunications Co.
Loctite Corp.
Lomas Financial Corp.
Longs Drug Stores
Lord Corp.
Louisville Gas & Electric Co.
Lowe's Co.
MacLean-Fogg Co.
Maguire Oil Co.
Manitowoc Co.
Manufacturers Life Insurance Co. of America
Marine Midland Banks
Marion Fabrics
Marion Merrell Dow
Mascoma Savings Bank
Massachusetts Mutual Life Insurance Co.
MBIA, Inc.
Measurex Corp.
Meenan Oil Co., Inc.
Mennen Co.
Mercantile Bankshares Corp.
Meridian Insurance Group Inc.
Merit Oil Corp.
Mesa Inc.
Mettler Instrument Corp.
Meyer, Inc., Fred
Michigan Mutual Insurance Corp.
Michigan National Corp.
MidCon Corp.
Midland Co.
Midland Mutual Life Insurance Co.
Minnesota Power & Light Co.
Mississippi Chemical Corp.
Mississippi Power & Light Co.
Missouri Public Service
Mitre Corp.
Monfort of Colorado, Inc.
Monsanto Co.
Moore, Costello & Hart
Morse Shoe, Inc.
Mount Vernon Mills
MTS Systems Corp.
Mutual of America Life

Nash-Finch Co.
National Car Rental System, Inc.
National City Bank, Columbus
National City Bank of Indiana
National Computer Systems
National Convenience Stores, Inc.
National Data Corp.
National Forge Co.
National Fuel Gas Co.
NationsBank Texas
Navajo Refining Co.
New Jersey National Bank
New Jersey Resources Corp.
New York Mercantile Exchange
New York State Electric & Gas Corp.
The New Yorker Magazine, Inc.
Niagara Mohawk Power Corp.
NIBCO Inc.
Nike Inc.
Nomura Securities International
Nordstrom, Inc.
Norfolk Shipbuilding & Drydock Corp.
Nortek, Inc.
North American Coal Corp.
Northern Virginia Natural Gas
NorthPark National Bank
Northrop Corp.
Northwest Natural Gas Co.
Norton & Co., W.W.
NRC, Inc.
Oakite Products
Ogilvy & Mather Worldwide
Ohio Casualty Corp.
Ohio Citizens Bank
Ohio Edison Corp.
Old Kent Bank & Trust Co.
Old Republic International Corp.
One Valley Bank, N.A.
Orange & Rockland Utilities, Inc.
Orion Capital Corp.
Ormet Corp.
Oster/Sunbeam Appliance Co.
Owens-Illinois
Packaging Corporation of America
Padnos Iron & Metal Co., Louis
Pamida, Inc.
Park-Ohio Industries Inc.
Patrick Industries Inc.
Paxton Co., Frank
PayLess Drug Stores
Pennsylvania Power & Light
Pentair
People's Bank
Persis Corp.
PHH Corp.
Phoenix Resource Cos.
Pioneer Trust Bank, NA
Plante & Moran, CPAs
Plantronics, Inc.
PMI Food Equipment Group Inc.
PNC Bank
Ponderosa, Inc.
Primark Corp.
Prime Computer, Inc.
PriMerit F.S.B.
Producers Livestock Marketing Association
Providence Energy Corp.
Provident Mutual Life Insurance Co. of Philadelphia
PSI Energy
Public Service Co. of Oklahoma
Quaker State Corp.
Questar Corp.
Raley's
Ranco, Inc.
Ransburg Corp.
Raytheon Engineers & Constructors
RB&W Corp.
Reading & Bates Corp.
Reasoner, Davis & Fox
Reliable Life Insurance Co.

General (cont.)

Reliance Group Holdings, Inc.
Reliance Insurance Cos.
Republic Automotive Parts, Inc.
Research-Cottrell Inc.
Riggs National Bank
Risdon Corp.
Riviana Foods
Rochester Community Savings Bank
Rochester Gas & Electric Corp.
Rochester Telephone Corp.
Ross Laboratories
Royal Group Inc.
Santa Fe International Corp.
Sara Lee Hosiery
Sargent Electric Co.
SCANA Corp.
Scientific-Atlanta
Scientific Brake & Equipment Co.
Scott, Foresman & Co.
Scotty's, Inc.
Sea-Land Service
Sealed Air Corp.
Sealright Co., Inc.
SECO
Security Life of Denver
Seneca Foods Corp.
ServiceMaster Co. L.P.
Seton Co.
Shaw Industries
Shawmut Bank of Franklin County
Sheldahl Inc.
Simkins Industries, Inc.
Smith Barney, Harris Upham & Co.
SNC Manufacturing Co.
Society for Savings
Somers Corp. (Mersman/Waldron)
Sonoco Products Co.
Southern Indiana Gas & Electric Co.
Southland Corp.
Southtrust Corp.
Southwestern Public Service Co.
Sprint United Telephone
Standard Brands Paint Co.
State Mutual Life Assurance Co.
Steel Heddle Manufacturing Co.
Steuart Petroleum Co.
Stewart & Stevenson Services
Stirtz, Bernards & Co.
Storage Technology Corp.
Storer Communications Inc.
Strawbridge & Clothier
Stroh Brewery Co.
Student Loan Marketing Association
Sumitomo Trust & Banking Co., Ltd.
Susquehanna-Pfaltzgraff Co.
T.T.X. Co.
Tasty Baking Co.
TCF Banking & Savings, FSB
Time Warner
Torrington Co.
Towle Manufacturing Co.
Town & Country Corp.
Trans-Apex
Transtar Inc.
Travelers Express Co.
Tremco Inc.
Triskelion Ltd.
Trustmark National Bank
Tucson Electric Power Co.
Turner Corp.
Twentieth Century Insurance Co.
UJB Financial Corp.
Unigard Security Insurance Co.
Union Equity Division of Farmland Industries
United Gas Pipe Line Co.
United Illuminating Co.

U.S. Bank of Washington
United Stationers Inc.
United Telephone Co. of Florida
United Telephone System (Eastern Group)
US Bancorp
Valero Energy Corp.
Valley National Bancorp
Vons Cos., Inc.
Wang Laboratories, Inc.
Washington National Insurance Co.
Washington Natural Gas Co.
Washington Water Power Co.
Wausau Insurance Cos.
Welch Foods
West One Bancorp
Wilbur-Ellis Co.
Wimpey Inc., George
Wiremold Co.
Wisconsin Bell, Inc.
Wisconsin Public Service Corp.
Wyman-Gordon Co.
Wynn's International, Inc.
Y.K.K. (U.S.A.) Inc.
Zapata Corp.
Zurn Industries

History/Historic Preservation

Abbott Laboratories
Abell-Hanger Foundation
Abreu Charitable Trust u/w/o May P. Abreu, Francis I.
Acushnet Co.
Adler Foundation Trust, Philip D. and Henrietta B.
AEGON USA, Inc.
Aequus Institute
AFLAC
Ahmanson Foundation
AHS Foundation
Air France
Air Products & Chemicals
Akzo Chemicals Inc.
Albertson's
Alexander Charitable Foundation
Alexander Foundation, Joseph
Alexander Foundation, Judd S.
Allegheny Foundation
Allegheny Ludlum Corp.
Allendale Mutual Insurance Co.
AlliedSignal
Alms Trust, Eleanora
ALPAC Corp.
Alumax
Aluminum Co. of America
AMAX
AMCORE Bank, N.A. Rockford
American Brands
American Express Co.
American Financial Corp.
American Foundation Corporation
American Natural Resources Co.
American Saw & Manufacturing Co.
American Society of Ephesus
Ameritech Services
AMETEK
Amfac/JMB Hawaii
AMR Corp.
Amsted Industries
Andersen Corp.
Andersen Foundation
Anderson Charitable Trust, Josephine
Anderson Foundation, Peyton
Andersons Management Corp.
Andreas Foundation
Anheuser-Busch Cos.
AON Corp.
Arakelian Foundation, Mary Alice
Arata Brothers Trust
Arcadia Foundation

Archbold Charitable Trust, Adrian and Jessie
Argyros Foundation
Archer-Daniels-Midland Co.
Arkansas Power & Light Co.
Armco Inc.
Armington Fund, Evenor
Armstrong World Industries Inc.
Aron Charitable Foundation, J.
Ashland Oil
Asplundh Foundation
Associated Foundations
Astor Foundation, Vincent
Atalanta/Sosnoff Capital Corp.
Atlanta Gas Light Co.
Atran Foundation
Attleboro Pawtucket Savings Bank
Autry Foundation
AVI CHAI - A Philanthropic Foundation
Azadoutioun Foundation
Azby Fund
Babcock & Wilcox Co.
Backer Spielvogel Bates U.S.
Bacon Trust, Charles F.
Baehr Foundation, Louis W. and Dolpha
Baer Foundation, Alan and Marcia
Baird Foundation
Baker & Baker
Baker Foundation, Dexter F. and Dorothy H.
Baker Hughes Inc.
Baldwin, Jr. Foundation, Summerfield
Ball Brothers Foundation
Baltimore Gas & Electric Co.
Banc One Illinois Corp.
Banc One Wisconsin Corp.
Bancorp Hawaii
Banfi Vintners
Bank of Boston Corp.
Bank of New York
Bank South Corp.
Bankers Trust Co.
Bardes Corp.
Barker Foundation
Barker Welfare Foundation
Barnes Group
Barra Foundation
Baughman Foundation
Bausch & Lomb
Bay Foundation
Beaird Foundation, Charles T.
Beasley Foundation, Theodore and Beulah
Bedsole Foundation, J. L.
Beech Aircraft Corp.
Beecher Foundation, Florence Simon
Behmann Brothers Foundation
Beinecke Foundation
Belding Heminway Co.
Belo Corp., A.H.
Beloit Foundation
Benbough Foundation, Legler
Bender Foundation
Benedum Foundation, Claude Worthington
Benetton
Bentley Foundation, Alvin M.
Bernsen Foundation, Grace and Franklin
Bethlehem Steel Corp.
Beveridge Foundation, Frank Stanley
Beynon Foundation, Kathryne
BFGoodrich
Binney & Smith Inc.
Bishop Foundation, Vernon and Doris
Blackmer Foundation, Henry M.
Blake Foundation, S. P.
Blandin Foundation
Bloedel Foundation

Bloedorn Foundation, Walter A.
Blount
Blue Bell, Inc.
Blue Cross & Blue Shield of Alabama
Blum Foundation, Harry and Maribel G.
Blum Foundation, Lois and Irving
Blum-Kovler Foundation
Boatmen's Bancshares
Boettcher Foundation
Bonfils-Stanton Foundation
Booth-Bricker Fund
Borden
Borg-Warner Corp.
Borman's
Borwell Charitable Foundation
Bostwick Foundation, Albert C.
Bowsher-Booher Foundation
Bozzone Family Foundation
BP America
Brach Foundation, Helen
Bradley-Turner Foundation
Brady Foundation, W. H.
Braun Foundation
Brewer and Co., Ltd., C.
Bridgestone/Firestone
Briggs & Stratton Corp.
Brillion Iron Works
Bristol-Myers Squibb Co.
Bronstein Foundation, Sol and Arlene
Bronstein Foundation, Soloman and Sylvia
Brotz Family Foundation, Frank G.
Brown Foundation
Brown Foundation, James Graham
Brown Foundation, M. K.
Brown & Williamson Tobacco Corp.
Browning Charitable Foundation, Val A.
Bruening Foundation, Eva L. and Joseph M.
Brunswick Corp.
Bryan Family Foundation, Kathleen Price and Joseph M.
Buchanan Family Foundation
Bucyrus-Erie
Buehler Foundation, Emil
Buell Foundation, Temple Hoyne
Buell Foundation, Temple Hoyne
Buhl Family Foundation
Burdines
Burlington Industries
Burns Foundation, Fritz B.
Bushee Foundation, Florence Evans
Butler Family Foundation, Patrick and Aimee
C.P. Rail Systems
Cabell III and Maude Morgan Cabell Foundation, Robert G.
Cablevision of Michigan
Cabot Corp.
Cabot Family Charitable Trust
Cabot-Saltonstall Charitable Trust
Caestecker Foundation, Charles and Marie
Cafritz Foundation, Morris and Gwendolyn
Caldwell Foundation, Hardwick
Calhoun Charitable Trust, Kenneth
California Educational Initiatives Fund
Callaway Foundation
Cameron Foundation, Harry S. and Isabel C.
Camp and Bennet Humiston Trust, Apollos
Camp Foundation
Campbell Foundation, Charles Talbot

Campbell Foundation, J. Bulow
Campbell Foundation, Ruth and Henry
Canon U.S.A., Inc.
Capital Holding Corp.
Cargill
Carolina Power & Light Co.
Carolyn Foundation
Carrier Corp.
Carter Foundation, Amon G.
Carter Foundation, Beirne
Carter-Wallace
Cartier, Inc.
Cassett Foundation, Louis N.
Caterpillar
Cauthorn Charitable Trust, John and Mildred
CBI Industries
Centel Corp.
Centerior Energy Corp.
Central Fidelity Banks, Inc.
Central Hudson Gas & Electric Corp.
Central Maine Power Co.
Century Companies of America
CertainTeed Corp.
Chadwick Foundation
Champlin Foundations
Chapin Foundation, Frances
Charina Foundation
Chatham Valley Foundation
Cheney Foundation, Ben B.
Cheney Foundation, Elizabeth F.
Cherokee Foundation
Chesapeake Corp.
Chevron Corp.
Chicago Sun-Times, Inc.
Childs Charitable Foundation, Roberta M.
Chilton Foundation Trust
Christensen Charitable and Religious Foundation, L. C.
Church & Dwight Co.
Citicorp
Claneil Foundation
Clark Charitable Foundation
Clark Foundation
Clark-Winchole Foundation
Clements Foundation
Cleveland-Cliffs
Clorox Co.
Close Foundation
CM Alliance Cos.
CNA Insurance Cos.
Cockrell Foundation
Codrington Charitable Foundation, George W.
Cohn Foundation, Herman and Terese
Cole Taylor Financial Group
Cole Trust, Quincy
Coleman, Jr. Foundation, George E.
Collins Foundation
Collins Foundation, James M.
Colonial Life & Accident Insurance Co.
Colonial Oil Industries, Inc.
Colt Foundation, James J.
Coltec Industries
Columbia Foundation
Commerce Bancshares, Inc.
Commerce Clearing House
Common Wealth Trust
Comstock Foundation
Confidence Foundation
Connelly Foundation
Consolidated Natural Gas Co.
Consolidated Papers
Consumers Power Co.
Continental Corp.
Continental Grain Co.
Contran Corp.
Cook Foundation, Loring
Cooper Industries
Coors Brewing Co.
Coors Foundation, Adolph

Copley Press
Cord Foundation, E. L.
Corestates Bank
Corning Incorporated
Cosmair, Inc.
Country Curtains, Inc.
Courts Foundation
Covington and Burling
Covington Foundation, Marion Stedman
Cowden Foundation, Louetta M.
Cowles Charitable Trust
Cowles Media Co.
Cox, Jr. Foundation, James M.
CPC International
CR Industries
Crandall Memorial Foundation, J. Ford
Cranston Print Works
Crapo Charitable Foundation, Henry H.
Crary Foundation, Bruce L.
Crawford Estate, E. R.
Crels Foundation
Crestar Financial Corp.
Crestlea Foundation
Crum and Forster
Crummer Foundation, Roy E.
Crystal Trust
Cudahy Fund, Patrick and Anna M.
Cullen/Frost Bankers
Culpeper Foundation, Charles E.
Culpeper Memorial Foundation, Daphne Seybolt
Cummins Engine Co.
CUNA Mutual Insurance Group
Dalton Foundation, Harry L.
Dana Charitable Trust, Eleanor Naylor
Dana Corp.
Daniels Foundation, Fred Harris
Darby Foundation
Dater Foundation, Charles H.
Dauphin Deposit Corp.
Davenport-Hatch Foundation
Davis Foundation, Edwin W. and Catherine M.
Davis Foundation, Shelby Cullom
Day Family Foundation
Day Foundation, Nancy Sayles
Dee Foundation, Annie Taylor
Dee Foundation, Lawrence T. and Janet T.
Delavan Foundation, Nelson B.
Delaware North Cos.
Deluxe Corp.
Demoulas Supermarkets
Deposit Guaranty National Bank
DeSoto
Detroit Edison Co.
Devonshire Associates
Dexter Corp.
Dick Family Foundation
Dickson Foundation
Dietrich Foundation, William B.
Dimeo Construction Co.
DiRosa Foundation, Rene and Veronica
Dixie Yarns, Inc.
Dobson Foundation
Dodge Jones Foundation
Donaldson Charitable Trust, Oliver S. and Jennie R.
Donaldson Co.
Donnelley Foundation, Elliott and Ann
Donnelley Foundation, Gaylord and Dorothy
Donnelley & Sons Co., R.R.
Donovan, Leisure, Newton & Irvine
Dougherty, Jr. Foundation, James R.
Douglas & Lomason Company
Dow Corning Corp.

Dresser Industries
Dreyfus Foundation, Max and Victoria
du Pont de Nemours & Co., E. I.
Duke Power Co.
Dula Educational and Charitable Foundation, Caleb C. and Julia W.
Dun & Bradstreet Corp.
Dunagan Foundation
Duncan Foundation, Lillian H. and C. W.
Dunn Foundation, Elizabeth Ordway
Dunspaugh-Dalton Foundation
duPont Foundation, Alfred I.
duPont Foundation, Chichester
duPont Fund, Jessie Ball
Durst Foundation
Easley Trust, Andrew H. and Anne O.
Eastern Bank Foundation
Eastern Enterprises
Eaton Corp.
Eaton Foundation, Cyrus
Eddy Family Memorial Fund, C. K.
Edison Fund, Charles
Edmonds Foundation, Dean S.
EG&G Inc.
EIS Foundation
El Pomar Foundation
Elco Charitable Foundation
Elf Atochem North America
Ellis Grant and Scholarship Fund, Charles E.
Ellsworth Foundation, Ruth H. and Warren A.
Emergency Aid of Pennsylvania Foundation
Emerson Electric Co.
Emerson Foundation, Fred L.
Emery Memorial, Thomas J.
Engelhard Foundation, Charles
English-Bonter-Mitchell Foundation
English Memorial Fund, Florence C. and H. L.
Enron Corp.
Ensign-Bickford Industries
Ensworth Charitable Foundation
Equifax
Ernsthausen Charitable Foundation, John F. and Doris E.
Erpf Fund, Armand G.
Ethyl Corp.
Evans Foundation, Lettie Pate
Evans Foundation, T. M.
Exposition Foundation
Exxon Corp.
Fabri-Kal Corp.
Failing Fund, Henry
Fair Foundation, R. W.
Fair Play Foundation
Falcon Foundation
Falk Medical Fund, Maurice
Fanwood Foundation
Farr Trust, Frank M. and Alice M.
Favrot Fund
Federal-Mogul Corp.
Fein Foundation
Feinstein Foundation, Myer and Rosaline
Fellner Memorial Foundation, Leopold and Clara M.
Femino Foundation
Ferriday Fund Charitable Trust
Fibre Converters
Field Foundation, Jamee and Marshall
Fifth Avenue Foundation
Fifth Third Bancorp
Fikes Foundation, Leland
FINA, Inc.
Fireman's Fund Insurance Co.
Firestone, Jr. Foundation, Harvey

First Hawaiian
First Interstate Bank of Arizona
First Interstate Bank of California
First Maryland Bancorp
First National Bank in Wichita
First Tennessee Bank
First Union Corp.
Firstar Bank Milwaukee NA
Fish Foundation, Ray C.
Fishback Foundation Trust, Harmes C.
Fisher Foundation
Fisher Foundation, Max M. and Marjorie S.
Fitz-Gibbon Charitable Trust
Flagler Foundation
Flatley Foundation
Fleet Bank of New York
Fleet Financial Group
Fleishhacker Foundation
Fletcher Foundation
Florida Power & Light Co.
Florida Rock Industries
Flowers Charitable Trust, Albert W. and Edith V.
FMR Corp.
Foellinger Foundation
Fondren Foundation
Forbes
Ford Foundation
Ford Fund, Benson and Edith
Ford Fund, Walter and Josephine
Ford Motor Co.
Forest Foundation
Forest Oil Corp.
Forster Charitable Trust, James W. and Ella B.
Fort Worth Star Telegram
Fortin Foundation of Florida
Foster Foundation, Joseph C. and Esther
Foundation for Middle East Peace
France Foundation, Jacob and Annita
Francis Families Foundation
Frank Foundation, Ernest and Elfriede
Franklin Foundation, John and Mary
Fraser Paper Ltd.
Freas Foundation
Freedom Forum
Freeport Brick Co.
Freeport-McMoRan
French Foundation
Fribourg Foundation
Frick Educational Commission, Henry C.
Frick Foundation, Helen Clay
Friends' Foundation Trust, A.
Frohring Foundation, William O. and Gertrude Lewis
Fry Foundation, Lloyd A.
Fuchs Foundation, Gottfried & Mary
Fuller Foundation
Fuller Foundation, George F. and Sybil H.
Funderburke & Associates
Fuqua Foundation, J. B.
Gage Foundation, Philip and Irene Toll
Garland Foundation, John Jewett and H. Chandler
Gates Foundation
GATX Corp.
Gavin Foundation, James and Zita
Gebbie Foundation
GEICO Corp.
Gelman Foundation, Melvin and Estelle
GenCorp
General Electric Co.
General Machine Works
General Mills
General Motors Corp.

Genius Foundation, Elizabeth Morse
GenRad
Georgia-Pacific Corp.
Georgia Power Co.
Gershman Foundation, Joel
Getty Trust, J. Paul
Giant Food Stores
Gilder Foundation
Gill Foundation, Pauline Allen
Gilmer-Smith Foundation
Glancy Foundation, Lenora and Alfred
Glaxo
Gleason Foundation, Katherine
Gleason Memorial Fund
Goddard Foundation, Charles B.
Goldberg Family Foundation, Milton D. and Madeline L.
Goldman Fund, Richard and Rhoda
Goldsmith Family Foundation
Goldsmith Foundation
Golub Corp.
Goodman Foundation, Edward and Marion
Gottwald Foundation
Gould Foundation, Florence J.
Graham Foundation for Advanced Studies in the Fine Arts
Grainger Foundation
Graphic Controls Corp.
Grassmann Trust, E. J.
Gray Charitable Trust, Mary S.
Graybar Electric Co.
Great Lakes Casting Corp.
Green Foundation
Green Foundation, Allen P. and Josephine B.
Green Fund
Greenebaum, Doll & McDonald
Greenheck Fan Corp.
Greve Foundation, William and Mary
Griffith Foundation, W. C.
Grigg-Lewis Trust
Griggs and Mary Griggs Burke Foundation, Mary Livingston
Groome Beatty Trust, Helen D.
Gross Charitable Trust, Stella B.
Grumbacher Foundation, M. S.
Grundy Foundation
Gruss Petroleum Corp.
Guaranty Bank & Trust Co.
Guardian Life Insurance Co. of America
Gulf Power Co.
Gulfstream Aerospace Corp.
H. B. B. Foundation
Haas Fund, Walter and Elise
Haffenreffer Family Fund
Hales Charitable Fund
Hall Charitable Trust, Evelyn A. J.
Hallmark Cards
Halmos Foundation
Hamilton Bank
Hamilton Foundation, Florence P.
Hammer Foundation, Armand
Hampden Papers
Hanes Foundation, John W. and Anna H.
Hankins Foundation
Harding Educational and Charitable Foundation
Harding Foundation, Charles Stewart
Harriman Foundation, Gladys and Roland
Harriman Foundation, Mary W.
Harrington Foundation, Don and Sybil
Harris Foundation, J. Ira and Nicki
Harris Foundation, William H. and Mattie Wattis
Harris Trust & Savings Bank

Harsco Corp.
Hartford Courant Foundation
Hartford Steam Boiler Inspection & Insurance Co.
Hartmarx Corp.
Hassenfeld Foundation
Hastings Trust
Hay Foundation, John I.
Haynes Foundation, John Randolph and Dora
Hazen Charitable Trust, Lita Annenberg
Hechinger Co.
Hecht-Levi Foundation
Heckscher Foundation for Children
Hecla Mining Co.
Heginbotham Trust, Will E.
HEI Inc.
Heileman Brewing Co., Inc., G.
Heinz Co., H.J.
Heinz Foundation, Drue
Heller Foundation, Walter E.
Helmerich Foundation
Henderson Foundation
Henderson Foundation, George B.
Henkel Corp.
Herndon Foundation
Herndon Foundation, Alonzo F. Herndon and Norris B.
Hersey Foundation
Herzstein Charitable Foundation, Albert and Ethel
Hess Foundation
Hewit Family Foundation
Heymann Special Account, Mr. and Mrs. Jimmy
Higgins Charitable Trust, Lorene Sails
High Foundation
Hill and Family Foundation, Walter Clay
Hillcrest Foundation
Hilliard Corp.
Hillman Foundation, Henry L.
Hillsdale Fund
Hitchcock Foundation, Gilbert M. and Martha H.
HKH Foundation
Hobbs Charitable Trust, John H.
Hobbs Foundation
Hobby Foundation
Hoblitzelle Foundation
Hofheinz Foundation, Irene Cafcalas
Homasote Co.
Homeland Foundation
Honigman Foundation
Hooker Charitable Trust, Janet A.
Hooper Foundation, Elizabeth S.
Hoover Foundation
Hoover Fund-Trust, W. Henry
Hopedale Foundation
Hopkins Foundation, John Jay
Hornblower Fund, Henry
Hospital Corp. of America
Houston Endowment
Houston Industries
Howard and Bush Foundation
Howe and Mitchell B. Howe Foundation, Lucite Horton
Howell Fund
Hoyt Foundation
Hubbard Broadcasting
Hubbell Inc.
Hudson-Webber Foundation
Huffy Corp.
Hulings Foundation, Mary Andersen
Hultquist Foundation
Humana
Humane Society of the Commonwealth of Massachusetts
Hunt Charitable Trust, C. Giles
Hunt Foundation, Roy A.
Hunt Foundation, Samuel P.

History/Historic Preservation (cont.)

Hurley Foundation, J. F.
Hyde and Watson Foundation
Hyde Manufacturing Co.
IBM Corp.
IES Industries
Illinois Tool Works
IMCERA Group Inc.
Imerman Memorial Foundation, Stanley
Indiana Bell Telephone Co.
Indiana Insurance Cos.
Inland Container Corp.
Insurance Management Associates
Interco
International Paper Co.
Ireland Foundation
Irwin-Sweeney-Miller Foundation
ITT Rayonier
J.P. Morgan & Co.
Jackson Family Foundation, Ann
Jackson Foundation
Jackson Hole Preserve
Jacobson Foundation, Bernard H. and Blanche E.
Janesville Foundation
Janssen Foundation, Henry
Jaqua Foundation
Jasam Foundation
Jeffress Memorial Trust, Elizabeth G.
Jennings Foundation, Martha Holden
Jennings Foundation, Mary Hillman
Jensen Construction Co.
Jergens Foundation, Andrew
Jewett Foundation, George Frederick
Jinks Foundation, Ruth T.
JMK-A M Micallef Charitable Foundation
Jockey Hollow Foundation
John Hancock Mutual Life Insurance Co.
Johnson Co., E. F.
Johnson Controls
Johnson Fund, Edward C.
Johnson & Higgins
Johnson & Son, S.C.
Johnston-Hanson Foundation
Jones Family Foundation, Eugenie and Joseph
Jordan and Ettie A. Jordan Charitable Foundation, Mary Ranken
Jordan Foundation, Arthur
Joukowsky Family Foundation
Kaiser Cement Corp.
Kantzler Foundation
Kapiloff Foundation, Leonard
Kaplan Foundation, Charles I. and Mary
Kaplan Foundation, Mayer and Morris
Keating Family Foundation
Keebler Co.
Keene Trust, Hazel R.
Keith Foundation Trust, Ben E.
Kellenberger Historical Foundation, May Gordon Latham
Keller-Crescent Co.
Kelly Foundation, T. Lloyd
Kelly, Jr. Memorial Foundation, Ensign C. Markland
Kemper Educational and Charitable Fund
Kempner Fund, Harris and Eliza
Kennecott Corp.
Kent-Lucas Foundation
Kepco, Inc.
Kerr Foundation

Kerr Foundation, Robert S. and Grayce B.
Kerr-McGee Corp.
Kettering Family Foundation
Kettering Fund
Kiewit Foundation, Peter
Kiewit Sons, Peter
Kilroy Foundation, William S. and Lora Jean
Kimberly-Clark Corp.
King Foundation, Carl B. and Florence E.
Kingsbury Corp.
Kingsley Foundation
Kinney-Lindstrom Foundation
Kiplinger Foundation
Kirkpatrick Foundation
Klee Foundation, Conrad and Virginia
Klein Charitable Foundation, Raymond
Kline Foundation, Josiah W. and Bessie H.
Kloeckner-Pentaplast of America
Knapp Foundation
Knight Foundation, John S. and James L.
Knox Foundation, Seymour H.
Knox, Sr., and Pearl Wallis Knox Charitable Foundation, Robert W.
Knudsen Charitable Foundation, Earl
Kobacker Co.
Koch Industries
Koh-I-Noor Rapidograph Inc.
Kohl Charitable Foundation, Allen D.
Kohler Foundation
Koopman Fund
Kraft Foundation
Krause Foundation, Charles A.
Kress Foundation, Samuel H.
Krieble Foundation, Vernon K.
KSM Foundation
Kunstadter Family Foundation, Albert
Kuyper Foundation, Peter H. and E. Lucille Gaass
L. L. W. W. Foundation
La-Z-Boy Chair Co.
Laclede Gas Co.
Landegger Charitable Foundation
Lane Memorial Foundation, Mills Bee
Lanier Brothers Foundation
Large Foundation
Large Foundation
Laros Foundation, R. K.
Laurel Foundation
Lautenberg Foundation
LBJ Family Foundation
Lea Foundation, Helen Sperry
Lebanon Mutual Insurance Co.
Lebus Trust, Bertha
Lederer Foundation, Francis L.
Lee Enterprises
Lee Foundation, Ray M. and Mary Elizabeth
Legg Mason Inc.
Lehrman Foundation, Jacob and Charlotte
Leighton-Oare Foundation
Lemberg Foundation
Lennon Foundation, Fred A.
Leo Burnett Co.
Leu Foundation
Levy Foundation, Jerome
Life Insurance Co. of Georgia
Lightner Sams Foundation
Lilly & Co., Eli
Lincoln Electric Co.
Lincoln National Corp.
Linde Foundation, Ronald and Maxine
Lindstrom Foundation, Kinney
Linn-Henley Charitable Trust
Lipton, Thomas J.

Littauer Foundation, Lucius N.
Little Family Foundation
Livingston Foundation
Llagas Foundation
Loeb Foundation, Frances and John L.
Loews Corp.
Long Island Lighting Co.
Longwood Foundation
Loridans Foundation, Charles
Louisiana Land & Exploration Co.
Louisiana Power & Light Co./New Orleans Public Service
Lounsbery Foundation, Richard
Lovett Foundation
Lowe Foundation, Joe and Emily
Lowenstein Foundation, Leon
LTV Corp.
Lubo Fund
Lubrizol Corp.
Luce Foundation, Henry
Luck Stone
Ludwick Institute
Lyndhurst Foundation
Lynn Foundation, E. M.
Lyon Foundation
Maas Foundation, Benard L.
MacArthur Foundation, John D. and Catherine T.
MacDonald Foundation, James A.
Mack Foundation, J. S.
Macy & Co., R.H.
Maddox Trust, Web
Magowan Family Foundation
Magruder Foundation, Chesley G.
Mallinckrodt Specialty Chemicals Co.
Mandeville Foundation
Mankato Citizens Telephone Co.
Manville Corp.
Marcus Corp.
Mardag Foundation
Maritz Inc.
Marmot Foundation
Marpat Foundation
Marquette Electronics
Marsh & McLennan Cos.
Marshall Foundation
Marshall & Ilsley Bank
Marshall Trust in Memory of Sanders McDaniel, Harriet McDaniel
Martin Marietta Corp.
Marx Foundation, Virginia & Leonard
Massengill-DeFriece Foundation
Masserini Charitable Trust, Maurice J.
Massey Charitable Trust
Massey Foundation
Massie Trust, David Meade
Material Service Corp.
Mather and William Gwinn Mather Fund, Elizabeth Ring
Mather Charitable Trust, S. Livingston
Mathis-Pfohl Foundation
Mattus Foundation, Reuben and Rose
Mayborn Foundation, Frank W.
Mayer Charitable Trust, Oscar G. & Elsa S.
Mayor Foundation, Oliver Dewey
Maytag Family Foundation, Fred
MBIA, Inc.
MCA
McBean Charitable Trust, Alletta Morris
McCann Foundation
McCasland Foundation
McCormick & Co.
McCormick Tribune Foundation, Robert R.
McCune Foundation
McDermott Foundation, Eugene

McDonald & Co. Securities
McDonald Foundation, J. M.
McDonald Industries, Inc., A. Y.
McDonnell Douglas Corp.-West
McDougall Charitable Trust, Ruth Camp
McEachern Charitable Trust, D. V. & Ida J.
McElroy Trust, R. J.
McEvoy Foundation, Mildred H.
McFawn Trust No. 2, Lois Sisler
McGraw Foundation, Donald C.
McGraw-Hill
McGregor Fund
McInerny Foundation
McKenna Foundation, Katherine Mabis
McKnight Foundation, Sumner T.
McLean Contributionship
McMahon Foundation
MDU Resources Group, Inc.
Mead Corp.
Meadows Foundation
Media General, Inc.
Mellon Bank Corp.
Mellon Foundation, Andrew W.
Mellon Foundation, Richard King
Memorial Foundation for Children
Menasha Corp.
Menschel Foundation, Robert and Joyce
Meredith Corp.
Merrick Foundation
Merrick Foundation, Robert G. and Anne M.
Metropolitan Life Insurance Co.
Meyer Memorial Trust
Michigan Bell Telephone Co.
Middendorf Foundation
Midwest Resources
Mifflin Memorial Fund, George H. and Jane A.
Mill-Rose Co.
Miller Charitable Trust, Lewis N.
Miller Memorial Trust, George Lee
Milliken Foundation, Agnes G.
Millstein Charitable Foundation
Misco Industries
Mitchell Energy & Development Corp.
MNC Financial
Mobil Oil Corp.
Model Foundation, Leo
Monfort Charitable Foundation
Monroe Auto Equipment Co.
Monroe Foundation (1976), J. Edgar
Monsanto Co.
Montana Power Co.
Montgomery Foundation
Montgomery Street Foundation
Moore Foundation, Edward S.
Moore Foundation, O. L.
Moore Memorial Foundation, James Starr
Moores Foundation, Harry C.
Morgan and Samuel Tate Morgan, Jr. Foundation, Marietta McNeil
Morgan Construction Co.
Morgan Foundation, Burton D.
Morgan Trust for Charity, Religion, and Education
Morley Brothers Foundation
Morris Foundation, Margaret T.
Morris Foundation, Norman M.
Morris Foundation, William T.
Morrison Charitable Trust, Pauline A. and George R.
Moses Fund, Henry and Lucy
Moss Charitable Trust, Finis M.
Mott Fund, Ruth
Mulford Trust, Clarence E.
Mulligan Charitable Trust, Mary S.
Munson Foundation, W. B.

Murch Foundation
Murdy Foundation
Murphey Foundation, Lluella Morey
Murphy Foundation
Murphy Foundation, Katherine and John
Muth Foundation, Peter and Mary
Myra Foundation
Nalco Chemical Co.
Nash Foundation
Nason Foundation
National By-Products
National City Bank of Evansville
National City Corp.
National Computer Systems
National Fuel Gas Co.
National Gypsum Co.
National Life of Vermont
National Service Industries
National Steel
National Westminster Bank New Jersey
Nationale-Nederlanden North America Corp.
Nationwide Insurance Cos.
NBD Bank
NBD Bank, N.A.
Neese Family Foundation
Nelson Industries, Inc.
Neuberger Foundation, Roy R. and Marie S.
New England Foundation
New York Life Insurance Co.
New York Mercantile Exchange
New York Telephone Co.
New York Times Co.
The New Yorker Magazine, Inc.
Newhall Foundation, Henry Mayo
Newhouse Foundation, Samuel I.
News & Observer Publishing Co.
Noble Foundation, Samuel Roberts
Nord Family Foundation
Nordson Corp.
Norfolk Shipbuilding & Drydock Corp.
Norfolk Southern Corp.
Norgren Foundation, Carl A.
Norman Foundation, Andrew
North American Royalties
Northern Indiana Public Service Co.
Northwest Natural Gas Co.
Northwestern National Insurance Group
Norton Co.
Norton Memorial Corporation, Geraldi
Number Ten Foundation
O'Brien Foundation, Alice M.
O'Brien Foundation, Cornelius and Anna Cook
Oceanic Cablevision Foundation
O'Connor Foundation, A. Lindsay and Olive B.
O'Fallon Trust, Martin J. and Mary Anne
Offield Family Foundation
Ogle Foundation, Paul
Oglebay Norton Co.
Ohio Valley Foundation
Oklahoma Gas & Electric Co.
Old Dominion Box Co.
Oleson Foundation
Olin Corp.
Oliver Memorial Trust Foundation
Olsson Memorial Foundation, Elis
Onan Family Foundation
O'Neil Foundation, Casey Albert T.
O'Neill Charitable Corporation, F. J.
Ontario Corp.
Ormet Corp.

Osceola Foundation
Ottenstein Family Foundation
Overbrook Foundation
Overlake Foundation
Overseas Shipholding Group
Owsley Foundation, Alvin and Lucy
Oxford Foundation
Oxford Foundation
PACCAR
Pacific Enterprises
PacifiCorp
Packard Foundation, David and Lucile
Page Belting Co.
Page Foundation, George B.
Palin Foundation
Palmer Fund, Frank Loomis
Paramount Communications Inc.
Park National Bank
Parker Foundation
Parker-Hannifin Corp.
Parker, Jr. Foundation, William A.
Parsons Foundation, Ralph M.
Pasadena Area Residential Aid
Patterson-Barclay Memorial Foundation
Paul and C. Michael Paul Foundation, Josephine Bay
Payne Foundation, Frank E. and Seba B.
Pearce Foundation, Dr. M. Lee
Peery Foundation
Pella Corp.
Penn Foundation, William
Pennzoil Co.
Peoples Energy Corp.
Pepsi-Cola Bottling Co. of Charlotte
Perkins Charitable Foundation
Perkins Memorial Foundation, George W.
Persis Corp.
Petersen Foundation, Esper A.
Pew Charitable Trusts
Pfizer
Pforzheimer Foundation, Carl and Lily
Phelps Dodge Corp.
Phillipps Foundation
Phillips Family Foundation, Jay and Rose
Phillips Foundation, Dr. P.
Phillips Foundation, Waite and Genevieve
Phillips Petroleum Co.
Phipps Foundation, Howard
Phipps Foundation, William H.
Pickford Foundation, Mary
Pieper Electric
Pittsburgh National Bank
Pittulloch Foundation
Pittway Corp.
Plaster Foundation, Robert W.
Plumsock Fund
Pollock Company Foundation, William B.
Poorvu Foundation, William and Lia
Porter Testamentary Trust, James Hyde
Post Foundation of D.C., Marjorie Merriweather
Potomac Electric Power Co.
Pott Foundation, Herman T. and Phenie R.
Potter Foundation, Justin and Valere
Powell Co., William
Powell Family Foundation
PPG Industries
Pratt Memorial Fund
Premier Dental Products Co.
Premier Industrial Corp.
Prentice Foundation, Abra
Price Associates, T. Rowe
Priddy Foundation

Prince Trust, Abbie Norman
Pritzker Foundation
Procter & Gamble Co.
Procter & Gamble Cosmetic & Fragrance Products
Providence Journal Company
Prudential Insurance Co. of America
Public Service Co. of Colorado
Public Service Electric & Gas Co.
Pulitzer Publishing Co.
Putnam Foundation
Quaker Chemical Corp.
Quaker Oats Co.
Questar Corp.
Quincy Newspapers
Quivey-Bay State Foundation
R. P. Foundation
Ralston Purina Co.
Ranney Foundation, P. K.
Ray Foundation
Raymond Corp.
Raymond Educational Foundation
Recognition Equipment
Red Wing Shoe Co.
Reed Foundation, Philip D.
Reeves Foundation
Regenstein Foundation
Reily & Co., William B.
Reinberger Foundation
Reinhart Institutional Foods
Reliance Electric Co.
Rennebohm Foundation, Oscar
Reynolds Foundation, Richard S.
Rice Charitable Foundation, Albert W.
Rice Foundation
Rice Foundation, Ethel and Raymond F.
Rich Products Corp.
Richardson Charitable Trust, Anne S.
Richardson Foundation, Frank E. and Nancy M.
Rieke Corp.
Ritchie Memorial Foundation, Charles E. and Mabel M.
RJR Nabisco Inc.
Robbins & Myers, Inc.
Roberts Foundation, Dora
Robinson Foundation
Robinson Foundation, J. Mack
Robison Foundation, Ellis H. and Doris B.
Rockefeller Trust, Winthrop
Rockfall Foundation
Rockwell Fund
Rockwell International Corp.
Roddis Foundation, Hamilton
Rodman Foundation
Rogers Charitable Trust, Florence
Rogers Family Foundation
Rogers Foundation
Rohm and Haas Company
Rose Foundation, Billy
Rosenbloom Foundation, Ben and Esther
Ross Foundation
Ross Foundation, Arthur
Ross Foundation, Lyn & George M.
Royal Group Inc.
Ruan Foundation Trust, John
Rubbermaid
Rudin Foundation, Samuel and May
Russell Charitable Foundation, Tom
Russell Charitable Trust, Josephine S.
Russell Memorial Foundation, Robert
Ryan Foundation, Patrick G. and Shirley W.
SAFECO Corp.
Saint Croix Foundation

Salvatori Foundation, Henry
San Diego Gas & Electric
San Diego Trust & Savings Bank
Sang Foundation, Elsie O. and Philip D.
Santa Fe Pacific Corp.
Sara Lee Corp.
Sara Lee Hosiery
Sasco Foundation
Saunders Foundation
Sawyer Charitable Foundation
Scaife Family Foundation
Schering-Plough Corp.
Schieffelin Residuary Trust, Sarah I.
Schiff Foundation
Schmidlapp Trust No. 1, Jacob G.
Schmidlapp Trust No. 2, Jacob G.
Schoenleber Foundation
Schottenstein Foundation, Jerome & Saul
Schreiber Foods, Inc.
Schultz Foundation
Schwartz Foundation, David
Schwartz Fund for Education and Health Research, Arnold and Marie
Scott Foundation, William E.
Scott, Jr. Charitable Foundation, Walter
Scripps Foundation, Ellen Browning
Scrivner, Inc.
Scurlock Foundation
Seaver Charitable Trust, Richard C.
Security Life of Denver
Sedgwick James Inc.
Sefton Foundation, J. W.
Sentinel Communications Co.
Sewall Foundation, Elmina
Shapiro Foundation, Charles and M. R.
Shaw Foundation, Arch W.
Shawmut National Corp.
Sheafer Charitable Trust, Emma A.
Sheaffer Inc.
Shelden Fund, Elizabeth, Allan and Warren
Shell Oil Co.
Shelton Cos.
Shenandoah Life Insurance Co.
Sheridan Foundation, Thomas B. and Elizabeth M.
Sherwin-Williams Co.
Shoenberg Foundation
Signet Bank/Maryland
Simon Charitable Trust, Esther
Simon Foundation, William E. and Carol G.
Simpson Foundation
Simpson Industries
Simpson Investment Co.
Sizzler International
Skaggs Foundation, L. J. and Mary C.
Slant/Fin Corp.
Smeal Foundation, Mary Jean & Frank P.
Smith and W. Aubrey Smith Charitable Foundation, Clara Blackford
Smith Charitable Foundation, Lou and Lutza
Smith Corp., A.O.
Smith Family Foundation, Charles E.
Smith Family Foundation, Theda Clark
Smith Foundation, Richard and Susan
Smith, Jr. Foundation, M. W.
Smith Memorial Fund, Ethel Sergeant Clark
SmithKline Beecham
SNET
Snider Foundation

Snow Foundation, John Ben
Snow Memorial Trust, John Ben
Snyder Charitable Fund, W. P.
Somers Foundation, Byron H.
Sonat
Sonoco Products Co.
South Bend Tribune
South Branch Foundation
South Waite Foundation
Southern California Edison Co.
Southwestern Bell Corp.
Sprague Educational and Charitable Foundation, Seth
Springs Industries
Stackpole-Hall Foundation
Stans Foundation
Star Bank, N.A.
Stark Foundation, Nelda C. and H. J. Lutcher
Starr Foundation
State Street Bank & Trust Co.
Steelcase
Steele-Reese Foundation
Stein Foundation, Joseph F.
Steinberg Family Foundation, Meyer and Jean
Steiner Corp.
Steinhagen Benevolent Trust, B. A. and Elinor
Steinman Foundation, James Hale
Stemmons Foundation
Sterling Inc.
Stern Family Foundation, Alex
Sternberger Foundation, Sigmund
Stevens Foundation, Abbot and Dorothy H.
Stevens Foundation, Nathaniel and Elizabeth P.
Stock Foundation, Paul
Stoddard Charitable Trust
Stone Charitable Foundation
Stone Container Corp.
Stone Foundation, David S.
Stott Foundation, Robert L.
Strake Foundation
Stratford Foundation
Strawbridge Foundation of Pennsylvania II, Margaret Dorrance
Stupp Foundation, Norman J.
Sulzberger Foundation
Sulzer Family Foundation
Summerlee Foundation
Susquehanna Investment Group
Swanson Family Foundation, Dr. W.C.
Sweatt Foundation, Harold W.
Swiss Bank Corp.
Symmes Foundation, F. W.
Tait Foundation, Frank M.
Tandy Foundation, Anne Burnett and Charles
Tandy Foundation, David L.
Tauber Foundation
Taubman Foundation, A. Alfred
Taylor Foundation, Ruth and Vernon
Taylor Trust, Lydia M.
Teledyne
Teleflex Inc.
Tenneco
Tetley, Inc.
Texaco
Texas Commerce Bank Houston, N.A.
Textron
Thalhimer, Jr. and Family Foundation, William B.
Thanksgiving Foundation
Thendara Foundation
Thompson Trust, Thomas
Thorne Foundation
Thorpe Foundation, James R.
Thorson Foundation
3M Co.
Times Mirror Co.

Timken Foundation of Canton
Tisch Foundation
Titmus Foundation
Titus Foundation, C. W.
TJX Cos.
Tomlinson Foundation, Kate and Elwyn
Tonkin Foundation, Tom and Helen
Torchmark Corp.
Tozer Foundation
Tranzonic Cos.
Treakle Foundation, J. Edwin
Treuhaft Foundation
Trexler Trust, Harry C.
Triford Foundation
Triskelion Ltd.
True Oil Co.
True Trust, Henry A.
Trull Foundation
Truman Foundation, Mildred Faulkner
Trust Co. Bank
Tucker Foundation, Marcia Brady
Tuohy Foundation, Alice Tweed
Tupancy-Harris Foundation of 1986
Turner Charitable Foundation
21 International Holdings
Tyson Fund
Union Bank
Union Camp Corp.
Union Electric Co.
Union Foundation
Union Pacific Corp.
United Technologies Corp.
Universal Foods Corp.
Universal Leaf Tobacco Co.
Unocal Corp.
Upton Foundation, Frederick S.
US WEST
USG Corp.
USX Corp.
Utica National Insurance Group
Uvas Foundation
V and V Foundation
Van Every Foundation, Philip L.
Van Nuys Foundation, I. N. and Susanna H.
Van Wert County Foundation
Vanderbilt Trust, R. T.
Varian Associates
Vidda Foundation
Vilter Manufacturing Corp.
Vingo Trust II
Volkswagen of America, Inc.
Vulcan Materials Co.
Wachovia Bank & Trust Co., N.A.
Waggoner Foundation, E. Paul and Helen Buck
Wagner Foundation, Ltd., R. H.
Wahlert Foundation
Wal-Mart Stores
Walker Foundation, Smith
Wallace Foundation, George R.
Walter Family Trust, Byron L.
Ward Co., Joe L.
Ware Foundation
Warhol Foundation for the Visual Arts, Andy
Warren Charite
Warwick Foundation
Wasmer Foundation
Wasserman Foundation, George
Waste Management
Waters Charitable Trust, Robert S.
Wean Foundation, Raymond John
Weaver Foundation
Webb Charitable Trust, Susan Mott
Webb Foundation, Del E.
Weiler Foundation
Weir Foundation Trust
Weiss Foundation, William E.

History/Historic Preservation (cont.)

Welch Testamentary Trust, George T.
Wellman Foundation, S. K.
Wendt Foundation, Margaret L.
Wenger Foundation, Henry L. and Consuelo S.
Werblow Charitable Trust, Nina W.
Wessinger Foundation
West Co.
West Foundation
West Texas Corp., J. M.
Western New York Foundation
Westvaco Corp.
Weyerhaeuser Co.
Weyerhaeuser Family Foundation
Whalley Charitable Trust
Wharton Foundation
Wheat First Securites
Wheeler Foundation
Whirlpool Corp.
Whitehead Foundation
Wickson-Link Memorial Foundation
Wien Foundation, Lawrence A.
Wiener Foundation, Malcolm Hewitt
Wilcox Trust, S. W.
Wilder Foundation
Wilf Family Foundation
Williams Cos.
Williams Family Foundation
Williams Family Foundation of Georgia
Williams Foundation, Arthur Ashley
Wilson Foundation, H. W.
Wilson Fund, Matilda R.
Wimpey Inc., George
Winona Corporation
Winston Foundation, Norman and Rosita
Winter Construction Co.
Winthrop Trust, Clara B.
Wisconsin Bell, Inc.
Wisconsin Energy Corp.
Wisconsin Power & Light Co.
Wiseheart Foundation
Witte, Jr. Foundation, John H.
Witter Foundation, Dean
Woman's Seamen's Friend Society of Connecticut
Wood Charitable Trust, W. P.
Woodruff Foundation, Robert W.
Woods Charitable Fund
Woods Foundation, James H.
Woodward Fund-Atlanta, David, Helen, Marian
Woodward Governor Co.
Woolley Foundation, Vasser
Wornall Charitable Trust and Foundation, Kearney
Wunsch Foundation
Wyman-Gordon Co.
Wyman Youth Trust
Wyomissing Foundation
Xerox Corp.
Yellow Corp.
Young Foundation, H and B
Young Foundation, R. A.
Zaban Foundation
Zacharia Foundation, Isaac Herman
Zemurray Foundation
Ziegler Foundation, Ruth/Allen
Zilkha & Sons
Zuckerberg Foundation, Roy J.

Libraries

Abbott Laboratories
Abell-Hanger Foundation
Abrams Foundation, Talbert and Leota
Abrons Foundation, Louis and Anne
ACF Industries, Inc.
Achelis Foundation
Acushnet Co.
Adams Foundation, Arthur F. and Alice E.
Adler Foundation
Adler Foundation Trust, Philip D. and Henrietta B.
AEGON USA, Inc.
Aeroflex Foundation
Ahmanson Foundation
Air France
Air Products & Chemicals
Akzo America
Akzo Chemicals Inc.
Ala Vi Foundation of New York
Alabama Power Co.
Albertson's
Alcon Laboratories, Inc.
Alexander Foundation, Joseph
Allegheny Foundation
Allegheny Ludlum Corp.
Allen Brothers Foundation
Allen-Heath Memorial Foundation
Allendale Mutual Insurance Co.
AlliedSignal
Alltel/Western Region
Allyn Foundation
Alma Piston Co.
ALPAC Corp.
Alsdorf Foundation
Altman Foundation
Alumax
Aluminum Co. of America
Amado Foundation, Maurice
AMAX
American Brands
American National Bank & Trust Co. of Chicago
American Natural Resources Co.
American United Life Insurance Co.
Ameritas Life Insurance Corp.
Ameritech Services
Ames Charitable Trust, Harriett
AMETEK
Amfac/JMB Hawaii
Amoco Corp.
Andersen Corp.
Andersen Foundation
Anderson Foundation
Anderson Foundation, John W.
Anderson Foundation, M. D.
Andersons Management Corp.
Andreas Foundation
Andres Charitable Trust, Frank G.
Anheuser-Busch Cos.
Ansin Private Foundation, Ronald M.
AON Corp.
Appleby Trust, Scott B. and Annie P.
Appleton Papers
Arcadia Foundation
Arcana Foundation
Archer-Daniels-Midland Co.
Aristech Chemical Corp.
Arkansas Power & Light Co.
Arkelian Foundation, Ben H. and Gladys
Arkell Hall Foundation
Arkwright Foundation
Armbrust Chain Co.
Armco Inc.
Armstrong World Industries Inc.
Arrillaga Foundation
Astor Foundation, Vincent
Atran Foundation
Avon Products
Ayres Foundation, Inc.
Babcock & Wilcox Co.
Babson Foundation, Paul and Edith

Bacon Foundation, E. L. and Oma
Badgeley Residuary Charitable Trust, Rose M.
Baehr Foundation, Louis W. and Dolpha
Baker Hughes Inc.
Baker Trust, George F.
Balfour Foundation, L. G.
Ball Foundation, George and Frances
Banc One Wisconsin Corp.
Bank of America Arizona
Bank of Boston Corp.
Bank of New York
Bank One, Texas-Houston Office
BankAmerica Corp.
Bankers Trust Co.
Bannon Foundation
Barker Welfare Foundation
Barra Foundation
Battelle
Baughman Foundation
Bayne Fund, Howard
Beaucourt Foundation
Bechtel Charitable Remainder Uni-Trust, Marie H.
Bechtel, Jr. Foundation, S. D.
Beck Foundation
Bedford Fund
Bedsole Foundation, J. L.
Bekins Foundation, Milo W.
Beloit Foundation
Bemis Company
Benedum Foundation, Claude Worthington
Benenson Foundation, Frances and Benjamin
Benetton
Benwood Foundation
Berger Foundation, H.N. and Frances C.
Bernstein & Co., Sanford C.
Berwind Corp.
Bethlehem Steel Corp.
Betts Industries
Beveridge Foundation, Frank Stanley
BFGoodrich
Bigelow Foundation, F. R.
Binney & Smith Inc.
Bismarck Charitable Trust, Mona
Bissell Foundation, J. Walton
Blackmer Foundation, Henry M.
Blair and Co., William
Blake Foundation, S. P.
Blandin Foundation
Blaustein Foundation, Louis and Henrietta
Blinken Foundation
Block, H&R
Bloedorn Foundation, Walter A.
Blount
Blount Educational and Charitable Foundation, Mildred Weedon
Blum Foundation, Edna F.
Blum Foundation, Harry and Maribel G.
Blum-Kovler Foundation
Boatmen's Bancshares
Bodman Foundation
Boeckmann Charitable Foundation
Boeing Co.
Boise Cascade Corp.
Boothroyd Foundation, Charles H. and Bertha L.
Borden
Borman's
Botwinick-Wolfensohn Foundation
Bound to Stay Bound Books Foundation
Bowater Inc.
Bozzone Family Foundation
BP America

Brackenridge Foundation, George W.
Brady Foundation
Braun Foundation
Brenner Foundation, Mervyn
Breyer Foundation
Bridgestone/Firestone
Brillion Iron Works
Bristol-Myers Squibb Co.
Brooks Foundation, Gladys
Brown Foundation, M. K.
Brown & Williamson Tobacco Corp.
Brunswick Corp.
Bryant Foundation
Buchanan Family Foundation
Bucyrus-Erie
Buhl Family Foundation
Buhl Foundation
Bunbury Company
Burchfield Foundation, Charles E.
Burdines
Burns Foundation
Bush Foundation
Butz Foundation
Cabell III and Maude Morgan Cabell Foundation, Robert G.
Cable & Wireless Communications
Cabot Corp.
Cain Foundation, Gordon and Mary
Calhoun Charitable Trust, Kenneth
California Educational Initiatives Fund
Cameron Foundation, Harry S. and Isabel C.
Canon U.S.A., Inc.
Capital Holding Corp.
Cargill
Carnahan-Jackson Foundation
Carpenter Foundation
Carpenter Foundation, E. Rhodes and Leona B.
Carpenter Technology Corp.
Carter Foundation, Amon G.
Cassett Foundation, Louis N.
Cawsey Trust
Cayuga Foundation
CBI Industries
CBS Inc.
Centerior Energy Corp.
Central Hudson Gas & Electric Corp.
Central Maine Power Co.
Central Vermont Public Service Corp.
Century Companies of America
Chadwick Fund, Dorothy Jordan
Champion International Corp.
Champlin Foundations
Chapin Foundation, Frances
Chapin Foundation of Myrtle Beach, South Carolina
Charina Foundation
Chase Manhattan Bank, N.A.
Chastain Charitable Foundation, Robert Lee and Thomas M.
Cheatham Foundation, Owen
Cherokee Foundation
Chesapeake Corp.
Chesebrough-Pond's
Chevron Corp.
Chicago Sun-Times, Inc.
Chicago Tribune Co.
Christensen Charitable and Religious Foundation, L. C.
Christian Dior New York, Inc.
Chrysler Corp.
Church & Dwight Co.
Citibank, F.S.B.
Citicorp
Citizens Bank
Clark Foundation
Clay Foundation

Clayton Fund
Clements Foundation
Clorox Co.
Close Foundation
Clowes Fund
CM Alliance Cos.
CNA Insurance Cos.
CNG Transmission Corp.
Cockrell Foundation
Cohen Family Foundation, Saul Z. and Amy Scheuer
Cohn Foundation, Peter A. and Elizabeth S.
Cole Foundation
Collins Foundation
Collins Foundation, George and Jennie
Collins, Jr. Foundation, George Fulton
Colonial Life & Accident Insurance Co.
Coltec Industries
Columbia Foundation
Comerica
Commerce Bancshares, Inc.
Commerce Clearing House
Commonwealth Edison Co.
Comprecare Foundation
Cone-Blanchard Machine Co.
Cone Mills Corp.
Connemara Fund
Consolidated Natural Gas Co.
Consolidated Papers
Consumers Power Co.
Continental Corp.
Cooke Foundation Corporation, V. V.
Cooper Charitable Trust, Richard H.
Cooper Industries
Copley Press
Cord Foundation, E. L.
Cornell Trust, Peter C.
Corning Incorporated
Cosmair, Inc.
Cowles Charitable Trust
Cowles Foundation, Gardner and Florence Call
Cowles Media Co.
CPC International
CR Industries
Cranston Print Works
Crawford Estate, E. R.
Crawford Estate, E. R.
Crestlea Foundation
Crum and Forster
CT Corp. System
Cullen/Frost Bankers
Culpeper Foundation, Charles E.
Cummings Foundation, James H.
Cummins Engine Co.
Cuneo Foundation
Curtice-Burns Foods
Daily News
Dalton Foundation, Harry L.
Dana Charitable Trust, Eleanor Naylor
Daniel Foundation of Alabama
Darby Foundation
Darrah Charitable Trust, Jessie Smith
Dater Foundation, Charles H.
Davis Foundation, Shelby Cullom
Daywood Foundation
DEC International, Inc.
Deere & Co.
Dekko Foundation
Delaware North Cos.
Dell Foundation, Hazel
Demos Foundation, N.
Demoulas Supermarkets
Dennison Manufacturing Co.
Deposit Guaranty National Bank
Detroit Edison Co.
Deuble Foundation, George H.
DeVore Foundation

Dexter Corp.
Dial Corp.
Diamond Foundation, Aaron
Diamond Shamrock
Dibner Fund
Digital Equipment Corp.
Dillon Foundation
Dimeo Construction Co.
Dishman Charitable Foundation Trust, H. E. and Kate
Dixie Yarns, Inc.
Dodge Foundation, Cleveland H.
Dodge Foundation, Geraldine R.
Doherty Charitable Foundation, Henry L. and Grace
Donaldson Charitable Trust, Oliver S. and Jennie R.
Donaldson Co.
Donnelley Foundation, Gaylord and Dorothy
Donnelley & Sons Co., R.R.
Doss Foundation, M. S.
Douglas & Lomason Company
Dover Foundation
Dow Corning Corp.
Dow Jones & Co.
Downs Perpetual Charitable Trust, Ellason
Dresser Industries
Dreyfus Foundation, Max and Victoria
du Pont de Nemours & Co., E. I.
Duchossois Industries
Duke Foundation, Doris
Duke Power Co.
Dula Educational and Charitable Foundation, Caleb C. and Julia W.
Dun & Bradstreet Corp.
Dunagan Foundation
Durfee Foundation
Dyson Foundation
Eastman Kodak Co.
Eaton Corp.
Ebsco Industries
Eccles Foundation, Ralph M. and Ella M.
Eddy Family Memorial Fund, C. K.
Eden Hall Foundation
Edmonds Foundation, Dean S.
Einstein Fund, Albert E. and Birdie W.
El Pomar Foundation
Elf Atochem North America
Ellis Fund
Emerson Foundation, Fred L.
Encyclopaedia Britannica, Inc.
Engelhard Foundation, Charles
English-Bonter-Mitchell Foundation
Enron Corp.
Erpf Fund, Armand G.
Essick Foundation
Ethyl Corp.
Ettinger Foundation
Eureka Co.
Evans Foundation, Thomas J.
Exxon Corp.
Fabri-Kal Corp.
Failing Fund, Henry
Fair Foundation, R. W.
Fair Play Foundation
Fairchild Foundation, Sherman
Fanwood Foundation
Farr Trust, Frank M. and Alice M.
Federal-Mogul Corp.
Federated Life Insurance Co.
Feild Co-Operative Association
Felburn Foundation
Femino Foundation
Ferebee Endowment, Percy O.
Fidelity Bank
Fieldcrest Cannon
Fikes Foundation, Leland
FINA, Inc.

Finch Foundation, Doak
Finch Foundation, Thomas Austin
Fireman's Fund Insurance Co.
Firestone, Jr. Foundation, Harvey
First Boston
First Chicago
First Fidelity Bancorporation
First Fidelity Bancorporation
First Hawaiian
First Interstate Bank of Arizona
First Interstate Bank of California
First Interstate Bank of Oregon
First Tennessee Bank
First Union Corp.
First Union National Bank of Florida
Firstar Bank Milwaukee NA
FirsTier Bank N.A. Omaha
Fischbach Foundation
Fish Foundation, Vain and Harry
Fishback Foundation Trust, Harmes C.
Fleet Bank of New York
Fleet Financial Group
Fleming Companies, Inc.
Florida Power & Light Co.
Fohs Foundation
Folger Fund
Forbes
Ford Foundation
Ford Fund, Walter and Josephine
Ford Motor Co.
Forest Foundation
Forest Lawn Foundation
Forest Oil Corp.
France Foundation, Jacob and Annita
Freas Foundation
Freedom Forum
Freeport Brick Co.
Freeport-McMoRan
Frelinghuysen Foundation
Frick Educational Commission, Henry C.
Frohman Foundation, Sidney
Frohring Foundation, William O. and Gertrude Lewis
Fry Foundation, Lloyd A.
Fujitsu America, Inc.
Fuller Foundation, C. G.
Fuller Foundation, C. G.
Funderburke & Associates
Fuqua Foundation, J. B.
Galter Foundation
Gannett Publishing Co., Guy
Gap, The
Garland Foundation, John Jewett and H. Chandler
Garvey Trust, Olive White
Gates Foundation
GATX Corp.
Gebbie Foundation
GenCorp
General Electric Co.
General Mills
General Motors Corp.
General Reinsurance Corp.
Genius Foundation, Elizabeth Morse
GenRad
Georgia-Pacific Corp.
Georgia Power Co.
Gerber Products Co.
Getty Foundation, Ann and Gordon
Gheens Foundation
Ghidotti Foundation, William and Marian
Giant Eagle
Giant Food
Giant Food Stores
Gifford Charitable Corporation, Rosamond
Gilder Foundation
Giles Foundation, Edward C.
Gillette Co.

Gilman Foundation, Howard
Gilmer-Smith Foundation
Gilmore Foundation, William G.
Glanville Family Foundation
Glen Eagles Foundation
Glencoe Foundation
Glenn Foundation, Carrie C. & Lena V.
Goddard Foundation, Charles B.
Goldberg Family Foundation
Goldberg Family Foundation, Milton D. and Madeline L.
Golden Family Foundation
Goldsmith Foundation, Horace W.
Goldwyn Foundation, Samuel
Goodman & Company
Gordon/Rousmaniere/Roberts Fund
Gould Inc.
Graham Foundation for Advanced Studies in the Fine Arts
Grainger Foundation
Great-West Life Assurance Co.
Green Foundation, Allen P. and Josephine B.
Green Fund
Greenwall Foundation
Gregg-Graniteville Foundation
Griffis Foundation
Griffith Foundation, W. C.
Grigg-Lewis Trust
Griggs and Mary Griggs Burke Foundation, Mary Livingston
Griswold Foundation, John C.
Grumbacher Foundation, M. S.
Grundy Foundation
Guaranty Bank & Trust Co.
Guardian Life Insurance Co. of America
Gulf Power Co.
Haas Fund, Walter and Elise
Hachar Charitable Trust, D. D.
Haffenreffer Family Fund
Haffner Foundation
Hagedorn Fund
Haggar Foundation
Haley Foundation, W. B.
Hall Charitable Trust, Evelyn A. J.
Hallett Charitable Trust
Halsell Foundation, Ewing
Halstead Foundation
Hamel Family Charitable Trust, D. A.
Hamilton Bank
Hamilton Foundation, Florence P.
Hammer Foundation, Armand
Hanes Foundation, John W. and Anna H.
Hansen Foundation, Dane G.
Hardin Foundation, Phil
HarperCollins Publishers
Harriman Foundation, Gladys and Roland
Harriman Foundation, Mary W.
Harrington Foundation, Francis A. and Jacquelyn H.
Harris Foundation, John H. and Lucille
Harsco Corp.
Hartford Courant Foundation
Hartford Steam Boiler Inspection & Insurance Co.
Hartman Foundation, Jesse and Dorothy
Hartmarx Corp.
Hartz Foundation
Harvey Foundation, Felix
Hatch Charitable Trust, Margaret Milliken
Hayden Foundation, Charles
Haynes Foundation, John Randolph and Dora
Hazen Foundation, Edward W.
Hebrew Technical Institute
Hechinger Co.

Hecht-Levi Foundation
Heckscher Foundation for Children
Hecla Mining Co.
Hedco Foundation
Heginbotham Trust, Will E.
Heileman Brewing Co., Inc., G.
Heineman Foundation for Research, Educational, Charitable, and Scientific Purposes
Heinz Co., H.J.
Heinz Endowment, Vira I.
Heinz Foundation, Drue
Heller Financial
Helms Foundation
Henkel Corp.
Henry Foundation, Patrick
Hermann Foundation, Grover
Hershey Foods Corp.
Heublein
Hewit Family Foundation
Hiawatha Education Foundation
Higginson Trust, Corina
Hillcrest Foundation
Himmelfarb Foundation, Paul and Annetta
HKH Foundation
Hoag Family Foundation, George
Hobby Foundation
Hoffman Foundation, Marion O. and Maximilian
Holzer Memorial Foundation, Richard H.
HON Industries
Hooper Foundation, Elizabeth S.
Hoover Foundation
Hoover, Jr. Foundation, Margaret W. and Herbert
Hopwood Charitable Trust, John M.
Hospital Corp. of America
Houston Endowment
Houston Industries
Howell Foundation, Eric and Jessie
Howell Fund
Hugoton Foundation
Hultquist Foundation
Humana
Humphrey Fund, George M. and Pamela S.
Hunt Charitable Trust, C. Giles
Hunt Foundation
Hunt Foundation, Roy A.
Hunt Foundation, Samuel P.
Huthsteiner Fine Arts Trust
IBM Corp.
ICI Americas
IES Industries
Illinois Tool Works
Inland Container Corp.
International Flavors & Fragrances
International Foundation
International Paper Co.
Iowa-Illinois Gas & Electric Co.
Irwin Charity Foundation, William G.
ITT Hartford Insurance Group
J.P. Morgan & Co.
Jackson Foundation
James River Corp. of Virginia
Janirve Foundation
Janssen Foundation, Henry
JELD-WEN, Inc.
Jennings Foundation, Mary Hillman
Jesselson Foundation
Jewell Memorial Foundation, Daniel Ashley and Irene Houston
Jewett Foundation, George Frederick
Jockey Hollow Foundation
John Hancock Mutual Life Insurance Co.
Johnson Controls

Johnson Foundation, Burdine
Johnson & Higgins
Johnson & Son, S.C.
Jones Foundation, Harvey and Bernice
Jones Foundation, Helen
Jones Foundation, Montfort Jones and Allie Brown
Jordan and Ettie A. Jordan Charitable Foundation, Mary Ranken
Joslin-Needham Family Foundation
Journal Gazette Co.
Justus Trust, Edith C.
Kaplan Foundation, Rita J. and Stanley H.
Kaplan Fund, J. M.
Kaplun Foundation, Morris J. and Betty
Kaul Foundation Trust, Hugh
Kaye, Scholer, Fierman, Hays & Handler
Kayser Foundation
Keating Family Foundation
Kelley and Elza Kelley Foundation, Edward Bangs
Kelley Foundation, Kate M.
Kellogg Foundation, W. K.
Kemper Educational and Charitable Fund
Kemper Memorial Foundation, David Woods
Kempner Fund, Harris and Eliza
Kennametal
Kennecott Corp.
Kennedy Foundation, John R.
Kern Foundation Trust
Kerr Foundation
Kerr Foundation, Robert S. and Grayce B.
Kevorkian Fund, Hagop
Kiewit Foundation, Peter
Kilroy Foundation, William S. and Lora Jean
Kimball Foundation, Horace A. Kimball and S. Ella
Kimball International
Kimberly-Clark Corp.
Kingsbury Corp.
Kinney-Lindstrom Foundation
Kiplinger Foundation
Kirbo Charitable Trust, Thomas M. and Irene B.
Kirkpatrick Foundation
Kitzmiller/Bales Trust
Kline Foundation, Josiah W. and Bessie H.
Klosk Fund, Louis and Rose
Kmart Corp.
Knott Foundation, Marion I. and Henry J.
Knox, Sr., and Pearl Wallis Knox Charitable Foundation, Robert W.
Koehler Foundation, Marcia and Otto
Kohn-Joseloff Fund
Koopman Fund
Kress Foundation, Samuel H.
Krieble Foundation, Vernon K.
Kutz Foundation, Milton and Hattie
Kuyper Foundation, Peter H. and E. Lucille Gaass
La-Z-Boy Chair Co.
Laffey-McHugh Foundation
Landegger Charitable Foundation
Lane Foundation, Minnie and Bernard
Lang Foundation, Eugene M.
Langendorf Foundation, Stanley S.
Larsen Fund
Lattner Foundation, Forrest C.
Laurel Foundation
LBJ Family Foundation
Lea Foundation, Helen Sperry

Libraries (cont.)

Lebanon Mutual Insurance Co.
Lebus Trust, Bertha
Lederer Foundation, Francis L.
Lee Enterprises
Lehman Foundation, Robert
Leidy Foundation, John J.
Leighton-Oare Foundation
Lennon Foundation, Fred A.
Levy Foundation, June Rockwell
Liberman Foundation, Bertha &
 Isaac
Life Insurance Co. of Georgia
Lindstrom Foundation, Kinney
Linn-Henley Charitable Trust
Lipton, Thomas J.
Littauer Foundation, Lucius N.
Little, Arthur D.
Loews Corp.
Long Island Lighting Co.
Longwood Foundation
Lovett Foundation
Lowe Foundation, Joe and Emily
Lowenstein Foundation, Leon
Lozier Foundation
Luce Charitable Foundation,
 Stephen C.
Lukens
Lumpkin Foundation
Lurcy Charitable and
 Educational Trust, Georges
Lydall, Inc.
M.E. Foundation
M.T.D. Products
MacArthur Foundation, John D.
 and Catherine T.
MacCurdy Salisbury Educational
 Foundation
MacDonald Foundation, James A.
MacDonald Foundation, Marquis
 George
MacLeod Stewardship
 Foundation
Macmillan, Inc.
Macy & Co., R.H.
Madison Gas & Electric Co.
Magma Copper Co.
Magowan Family Foundation
Magruder Foundation, Chesley
 G.
Mailman Foundation
Manoogian Foundation, Alex
 and Marie
Marbrook Foundation
Mardag Foundation
Maritz Inc.
Markey Charitable Fund, John C.
Marpat Foundation
Marquette Electronics
Marriott Foundation, J. Willard
Marsh & McLennan Cos.
Marshall Foundation, Mattie H.
Martin Marietta Corp.
Martini Foundation, Nicholas
Marx Foundation, Virginia &
 Leonard
Massengill-DeFriece Foundation
Massey Foundation, Jack C.
Mathis-Pfohl Foundation
May Foundation, Wilbur
Mayor Foundation, Oliver Dewey
MBIA, Inc.
MCA
McCormick & Co.
McCormick Foundation,
 Chauncey and Marion Deering
McCune Charitable Trust, John
 R.
McDonald & Co. Securities
McDonnell Douglas Corp.-West
McEachern Charitable Trust, D.
 V. & Ida J.
McElroy Trust, R. J.
McFeely-Rogers Foundation
McGraw-Hill

McKenna Foundation, Katherine
 Mabis
McKenna Foundation, Philip M.
McLean Contributionship
McMurray-Bennnett Foundation
MDU Resources Group, Inc.
Mead Corp.
Mead Foundation, Giles W. and
 Elise G.
Meadows Foundation
Mellam Family Foundation
Mellen Foundation
Mellinger Educational
 Foundation, Edward Arthur
Mellon Bank Corp.
Mellon Foundation, Andrew W.
Mellon Foundation, Richard King
Memorial Foundation for the
 Blind
Mengle Foundation, Glenn and
 Ruth
Menschel Foundation, Robert
 and Joyce
Merck & Co.
Merck Human Health Division
Meredith Foundation
Metropolitan Life Insurance Co.
Meyer Fund, Milton and Sophie
Meyer Memorial Trust
Meyerhoff Fund, Joseph
Mid-Iowa Health Foundation
Middendorf Foundation
Mielke Family Foundation
Mifflin Memorial Fund, George
 H. and Jane A.
Millbrook Tribute Garden
Miller Charitable Trust, Lewis N.
Miller Fund, Kathryn and Gilbert
Milliken & Co.
Milstein Family Foundation
Mine Safety Appliances Co.
Mitchell Energy & Development
 Corp.
Mitsubishi International Corp.
MNC Financial
Mnuchin Foundation
Mobil Oil Corp.
Model Foundation, Leo
Mohasco Corp.
Monarch Machine Tool Co.
Monell Foundation, Ambrose
Monroe-Brown Foundation
Monsanto Co.
Montana Power Co.
Monticello College Foundation
Moore Charitable Foundation,
 Marjorie
Moore Foundation, Edward S.
Morgan and Samuel Tate
 Morgan, Jr. Foundation,
 Marietta McNeil
Morgan Charitable Residual
 Trust, W. and E.
Morgan Stanley & Co.
Morris Foundation, Margaret T.
Morrison Charitable Trust,
 Pauline A. and George R.
Morrison-Knudsen Corp.
Morse, Jr. Foundation, Enid and
 Lester S.
Moses Fund, Henry and Lucy
Mott Fund, Ruth
MTS Systems Corp.
Mulcahy Foundation
Mulford Trust, Clarence E.
Mullen Foundation, J. K.
Muller Foundation
Munger Foundation, Alfred C.
Munson Foundation, W. B.
Murch Foundation
Murphy Foundation
Musson Charitable Foundation,
 R. C. and Katharine M.
Myra Foundation
Nabisco Foods Group
Nalco Chemical Co.
National Gypsum Co.

National Life of Vermont
National Steel
National Westminster Bank New
 Jersey
NBD Bank
NBD Bank, N.A.
Nestle U.S.A. Inc.
New England Business Service
New-Land Foundation
New York Life Insurance Co.
New York Telephone Co.
New York Times Co.
The New Yorker Magazine, Inc.
Newhouse Foundation, Samuel I.
Newman's Own
Noble Foundation, Edward John
Northwest Natural Gas Co.
Norton Co.
Norton Foundation Inc.
Norwest Bank Nebraska
Norwest Corp.
Oaklawn Foundation
Occidental Oil & Gas Corp.
O'Connor Foundation, A.
 Lindsay and Olive B.
O'Connor Foundation, Kathryn
Oestreicher Foundation, Sylvan
 and Ann
Offield Family Foundation
Ogilvy & Mather Worldwide
Oglebay Norton Co.
Ohrstrom Foundation
Old Dominion Box Co.
Old National Bank in Evansville
Olin Corp.
O'Neil Foundation, Cyril F. and
 Marie E.
Orchard Corp. of America.
Ore-Ida Foods, Inc.
Osceola Foundation
Outboard Marine Corp.
Overbrook Foundation
Owen Industries, Inc.
Owsley Foundation, Alvin and
 Lucy
Pacific Enterprises
Pacific Mutual Life Insurance Co.
Pacific Telesis Group
Packaging Corporation of
 America
Packard Foundation, David and
 Lucile
Packer Foundation, Horace B.
PaineWebber
Paley Foundation, William S.
Palisades Educational Foundation
Palisano Foundation, Vincent
 and Harriet
Pamida, Inc.
Panhandle Eastern Corp.
Parker Foundation
Parker-Hannifin Corp.
Patterson-Barclay Memorial
 Foundation
Payne Foundation, Frank E. and
 Seba B.
Pella Corp.
Penn Foundation, William
Pennsylvania Dutch Co.
Pennzoil Co.
Peoples Energy Corp.
Pepsi-Cola Bottling Co. of
 Charlotte
Perkin-Elmer Corp.
Petrie Trust, Lorene M.
Petteys Memorial Foundation,
 Jack
Pettus Crowe Foundation
Pfizer
Pforzheimer Foundation, Carl
 and Lily
Phelps Dodge Corp.
PHH Corp.
Philadelphia Electric Co.
Philibosian Foundation, Stephen
Phillips Family Foundation, Jay
 and Rose

Phillips Family Foundation, L. E.
Phipps Foundation, Howard
Pickford Foundation, Mary
Pioneer Fund
Piper Foundation
Piper Foundation
Piper Foundation, Minnie
 Stevens
Pittsburgh Child Guidance
 Foundation
Pittsburgh National Bank
Polinsky-Rivkin Family
 Foundation
Potomac Electric Power Co.
Pott Foundation, Herman T. and
 Phenie R.
Potter Foundation, Justin and
 Valere
PPG Industries
Premier Industrial Corp.
Price Associates, T. Rowe
Price Foundation, Louis and
 Harold
Priddy Foundation
Prince Trust, Abbie Norman
Pritzker Foundation
Procter & Gamble Cosmetic &
 Fragrance Products
Proctor Trust, Mortimer R.
Providence Energy Corp.
Providence Journal Company
Provident Life & Accident
 Insurance Co.
Provigo Corp. Inc.
Prudential-Bache Securities
Public Service Electric & Gas
 Co.
Pulitzer Publishing Co.
Quaker Hill Foundation
Quaker Oats Co.
Quantum Chemical Corp.
R&B Tool Co.
Rachal Foundation, Ed
Ralston Purina Co.
Ratner Foundation, Milton M.
Read Foundation, Charles L.
Regenstein Foundation
Reichhold Chemicals, Inc.
Reidler Foundation
Reinberger Foundation
Republic New York Corp.
Reynolds Foundation, Donald W.
Rhone-Poulenc Inc.
Richardson Charitable Trust,
 Anne S.
Richardson Foundation, Frank E.
 and Nancy M.
Rieke Corp.
Ringier-America
Rittenhouse Foundation
Ritter Charitable Trust, George
 W. & Mary F.
RJR Nabisco Inc.
Robinson Fund, Maurice R.
Robison Foundation, Ellis H. and
 Doris B.
Rochlin Foundation, Abraham
 and Sonia
Rockwell Fund
Rockwell International Corp.
Rodgers Foundation, Richard &
 Dorothy
Rogers Family Foundation
Rohatyn Foundation, Felix and
 Elizabeth
Rohm and Haas Company
Romill Foundation
Rose Foundation, Billy
Roseburg Forest Products Co.
Ross Corp.
Ross Laboratories
Rouse Co.
Rowland Foundation
Royal Group Inc.
Rubin Family Fund, Cele H. and
 William B.
Rubinstein Foundation, Helena

Russell Charitable Foundation,
 Tom
Russell Educational Foundation,
 Benjamin and Roberta
Russell Trust, Josephine G.
SAFECO Corp.
Salomon
Salomon Foundation, Richard &
 Edna
San Diego Gas & Electric
Sandusky International Inc.
Santa Fe Pacific Corp.
Sara Lee Corp.
Sara Lee Hosiery
Sarkeys Foundation
Saroyan Foundation, William
Sasco Foundation
Scaife Family Foundation
Scaler Foundation
Schenck Fund, L. P.
Scherer Foundation, Karla
Schering-Plough Corp.
Scherman Foundation
Schieffelin Residuary Trust,
 Sarah I.
Schiff Foundation, Dorothy
Schiro Fund
Schloss & Co., Marcus
Schlumberger Ltd.
Scholl Foundation, Dr.
Schowalter Foundation
Schwab & Co., Charles
Schwartz Foundation, Arnold A.
Schwob Foundation, Simon
Scott and Fetzer Co.
Scott Foundation, Virginia Steele
Scrivner, Inc.
Scroggins Foundation, Arthur E.
 and Cornelia C.
Scurlock Foundation
Seabury Foundation
Searle & Co., G.D.
Seaway Food Town
Second Foundation
Security Life of Denver
Sedgwick James Inc.
Segal Charitable Trust, Barnet
Self Foundation
Semmes Foundation
Sentry Insurance Co.
Share Trust, Charles Morton
Sharp Foundation
Shaw Foundation, Arch W.
Shawmut National Corp.
Shaw's Supermarkets
Shea Foundation, Edmund and
 Mary
Sheaffer Inc.
Sheinberg Foundation, Eric P.
Shell Oil Co.
Shenandoah Life Insurance Co.
Sheppard Foundation, Lawrence
 B.
Sifco Industries Inc.
Signet Bank/Maryland
Simon Foundation, William E.
 and Carol G.
Simpson Investment Co.
Simpson PSB Foundation
Slant/Fin Corp.
Slemp Foundation
Smeal Foundation, Mary Jean &
 Frank P.
Smith and W. Aubrey Smith
 Charitable Foundation, Clara
 Blackford
Smith Charitable Fund, Eleanor
 Armstrong
Smith Corp., A.O.
Smith Foundation, Kelvin and
 Eleanor
Smith Foundation, Lon V.
Smith, Jr. Foundation, M. W.
Smith Memorial Fund, Ethel
 Sergeant Clark
Snee-Reinhardt Charitable
 Foundation

SNET
Snow Foundation, John Ben
Snow Memorial Trust, John Ben
Snyder Charitable Fund, W. P.
Solow Foundation
Sonat
Sonoco Products Co.
Sordoni Foundation
South Bend Tribune
South Branch Foundation
Southern California Edison Co.
Southwestern Bell Corp.
Speer Foundation, Roy M.
Speyer Foundation, Alexander C.
and Tillie S.
Sprague Educational and
Charitable Foundation, Seth
Springs Foundation
Square D Co.
Stabler Foundation, Donald B.
and Dorothy L.
Stackpole-Hall Foundation
Stanley Works
Stare Fund
Starr Foundation
Steadley Memorial Trust, Kent
D. and Mary L.
Steele-Reese Foundation
Stein Foundation, Jules and Doris
Steinbach Fund, Ruth and Milton
Steinhagen Benevolent Trust, B.
A. and Elinor
Sterling Winthrop
Stern Foundation, Leonard N.
Sternberger Foundation, Sigmund
Stevens Foundation, Abbot and
Dorothy H.
Stevens Foundation, John T.
Stevens Foundation, Nathaniel
and Elizabeth P.
Stokely, Jr. Foundation, William
B.
Stone Charitable Foundation
Stott Foundation, Robert L.
Stroud Foundation
Stuart Foundation
Sulzberger Foundation
Sulzer Family Foundation
Sumitomo Bank of California
Summerfield Foundation, Solon
E.
Swalm Foundation
Swift Co. Inc., John S.
Swig Charity Foundation, Mae
and Benjamin
Swiss Bank Corp.
Symmes Foundation, F. W.
Taub Foundation
Taub Foundation, Joseph and
Arlene
Taubman Foundation, A. Alfred
Taylor Foundation, Ruth and
Vernon
TCF Banking & Savings, FSB
Teichert
Teledyne
Teleflex Inc.
Temple Foundation, T. L. L.
Temple-Inland
Tenneco
Tetley, Inc.
Teubert Charitable Trust, James
H. and Alice
Texaco
Texas Commerce Bank Houston,
N.A.
Textron
Thomasville Furniture Industries
Thomson Information Publishing
Group
Thorne Foundation
Thornton Foundation
3M Co.
Times Mirror Co.
Timken Foundation of Canton
Tisch Foundation
Tiscornia Foundation

Tobin Foundation
Todd Co., A.M.
Tonya Memorial Foundation
Transamerica Corp.
Transco Energy Company
Travelers Cos.
Treakle Foundation, J. Edwin
Trexler Trust, Harry C.
TRINOVA Corp.
Triskelion Ltd.
Trull Foundation
Trust Co. Bank
Tull Charitable Foundation
Tyson Fund
Unilever United States
Union Bank
Union Camp Corp.
Union Electric Co.
United Dominion Industries
U.S. Leasing International
Unitrode Corp.
Unocal Corp.
Upjohn Foundation, Harold and
Grace
Upton Foundation, Frederick S.
Uris Brothers Foundation
USG Corp.
Valmont Industries
Van Evera Foundation, Dewitt
Caroline
Van Every Foundation, Philip L.
Van Nuys Foundation, I. N. and
Susanna H.
Vanderbilt Trust, R. T.
Vanneck-Bailey Foundation
Vaughn, Jr. Foundation Fund,
James M.
Vesper Corp.
Vetlesen Foundation, G. Unger
Vevay-Switzerland County
Foundation
Vicksburg Foundation
Vilter Manufacturing Corp.
Virginia Power Co.
Vulcan Materials Co.
Wachovia Bank & Trust Co.,
N.A.
Wal-Mart Stores
Wallace Foundation, George R.
Wallace-Reader's Digest Fund,
DeWitt
Wallach Foundation, Miriam G.
and Ira D.
Wardle Family Foundation
Warren and Beatrice W.
Blanding Foundation, Riley J.
and Lillian N.
Washington Water Power Co.
Wean Foundation, Raymond John
Webber Oil Co.
Weckbaugh Foundation,
Eleanore Mullen
Weil, Gotshal & Manges
Foundation
Weiler Foundation, Theodore &
Renee
Weinberg Foundation, John L.
Weingart Foundation
Welch Testamentary Trust,
George T.
Welfare Foundation
Wells Foundation, Franklin H.
and Ruth L.
West One Bancorp
Western New York Foundation
WestLB New York Branch
Westvaco Corp.
Weyerhaeuser Co.
Weyerhaeuser Foundation,
Frederick and Margaret L.
Weyerhaeuser Memorial
Foundation, Charles A.
Wharton Foundation
Wheat First Securites
Whirlpool Corp.
Whiting Foundation, Macauley
and Helen Dow
Whitney Fund, David M.

Whittier Foundation, L. K.
Wickes Foundation, Harvey
Randall
Wickson-Link Memorial
Foundation
WICOR, Inc.
Wiener Foundation, Malcolm
Hewitt
Wiley & Sons, Inc., John
Willard Helping Fund, Cecilia
Young
Williams Charitable Trust, John
C.
Williams Cos.
Wilmington Trust Co.
Wilson Foundation, H. W.
Winchester Foundation
Winston Foundation, Norman
and Rosita
Winter Construction Co.
Wisconsin Power & Light Co.
Wisconsin Public Service Corp.
Witco Corp.
Wolverine World Wide, Inc.
Wright Foundation, Lola
Wyman Youth Trust
Wyomissing Foundation
Xerox Corp.
Young Foundation, H and B
Young Foundation, Irvin L.
Young Foundation, Robert R.
Zachry Co., H. B.
Zenkel Foundation
Zlinkoff Fund for Medical
Research and Education,
Sergei S.
Zock Endowment Trust
Zollner Foundation

Literary Arts

Abell Foundation, The
Abrons Foundation, Louis and
Anne
Ahmanson Foundation
Alltel/Western Region
ALPAC Corp.
Aluminum Co. of America
AMCORE Bank, N.A. Rockford
Ameritech Services
Anacomp, Inc.
Attleboro Pawtucket Savings
Bank
Bank of New York
Bankers Trust Co.
Banyan Tree Foundation
Barker Foundation, J. M. R.
Biddle Foundation, Mary Duke
Binney & Smith Inc.
Blandin Foundation
Block, H&R
Blount
Borman's
Brace Foundation, Donald C.
Bush Foundation
Butler Family Foundation,
Patrick and Aimee
Bydale Foundation
Cabot Corp.
Cafritz Foundation, Morris and
Gwendolyn
Carpenter Foundation
Central Maine Power Co.
Chambers Development Co.
Chase Manhattan Bank, N.A.
Chicago Sun-Times, Inc.
Clark Foundation, Robert
Sterling
Clipper Ship Foundation
Clorox Co.
CNA Insurance Cos.
CNG Transmission Corp.
Collins Foundation
Columbus Dispatch Printing Co.
Copernicus Society of America
Cosmair, Inc.
Cowden Foundation, Louetta M.
Crown Books Foundation, Inc.

Dart Group Corp.
Davee Foundation
Deluxe Corp.
Dewing Foundation, Frances R.
Dodge Foundation, Geraldine R.
Donnelley Foundation, Gaylord
and Dorothy
Donnelley & Sons Co., R.R.
du Pont de Nemours & Co., E. I.
Duchossois Industries
Durham Merchants Association
Charitable Foundation
Eccles Foundation, George S.
and Dolores Dore
Electric Power Equipment Co.
Evans Foundation, T. M.
Feild Co-Operative Association
Fidelity Bank
First Mississippi Corp.
First Union Corp.
Fleishhacker Foundation
Forbes
Ford Motor Co.
Garvey Memorial Foundation,
Edward Chase
Gelman Foundation, Melvin and
Estelle
General Mills
Goodman Family Foundation
Grotto Foundation
Haas Fund, Walter and Elise
Halsell Foundation, Ewing
Hankins Foundation
Hardin Foundation, Phil
HarperCollins Publishers
Hartman Foundation, Jesse and
Dorothy
Hartzell Industries, Inc.
Hechinger Co.
Heinz Co., H.J.
Heinz Foundation, Drue
Heymann Special Account, Mr.
and Mrs. Jimmy
Hilliard Corp.
Hodge Foundation
Honeywell
Houston Endowment
Huthsteiner Fine Arts Trust
Indiana Bell Telephone Co.
ITT Hartford Insurance Group
J.P. Morgan & Co.
Jerome Foundation
Johnson Foundation, Barbara P.
Johnson & Higgins
Kaplun Foundation, Morris J.
and Betty
Knowles Foundation
Kohn-Joseloff Fund
Lannan Foundation
Laurel Foundation
Levinson Foundation, Max and
Anna
Littauer Foundation, Lucius N.
Long Island Lighting Co.
Louisiana Power & Light
Co./New Orleans Public
Service
Ludwick Institute
Lurie Foundation, Louis R.
Macmillan, Inc.
Macy & Co., R.H.
Magowan Family Foundation
Maritz Inc.
Marquette Electronics
Marshall Field's
Marshall Fund
McGraw-Hill
McKnight Foundation
Meadows Foundation
Mellon Foundation, Andrew W.
Merck Family Fund
Meyer Foundation, Eugene and
Agnes E.
Mobil Oil Corp.
New Cycle Foundation
New England Mutual Life
Insurance Co.

New York Telephone Co.
New York Times Co.
The New Yorker Magazine, Inc.
Newhouse Foundation, Samuel I.
News & Observer Publishing Co.
Norfolk Southern Corp.
Northwest Area Foundation
Norton Co.
OCRI Foundation
Oestreicher Foundation, Sylvan
and Ann
Packard Foundation, David and
Lucile
Penn Foundation, William
Pittsburgh National Bank
PPG Industries
Prince Trust, Abbie Norman
Pritzker Foundation
Quaker Oats Co.
Rockefeller Foundation
Ross Foundation, Arthur
Rouse Co.
Rubin Foundation, Samuel
Russell Charitable Trust,
Josephine S.
Saint Paul Cos.
Sara Lee Hosiery
Scherman Foundation
Security Life of Denver
Sedgwick James Inc.
Shea Foundation
Shenandoah Life Insurance Co.
Slant/Fin Corp.
Sprague Educational and
Charitable Foundation, Seth
Spunk Fund
Steelcase
Stein Foundation, Jules and Doris
Teleflex Inc.
Truland Foundation
Union Camp Corp.
Virginia Power Co.
Vulcan Materials Co.
Wallace Reader's Digest Fund,
Lila
Whiting Foundation, Mrs. Giles
Wiener Foundation, Malcolm
Hewitt
Williams Foundation, Arthur
Ashley
Winter Construction Co.

Museums/Galleries

Abbott Laboratories
Abeles Foundation, Joseph and
Sophia
Abell-Hanger Foundation
Abraham Foundation
Abraham & Straus
Abramson Family Foundation
Abrons Foundation, Louis and
Anne
Achelis Foundation
Acme United Corp.
Acushnet Co.
Adams Foundation, Arthur F. and
Alice E.
Adams Trust, Charles E. and
Caroline J.
AEGON USA, Inc.
AFLAC
Ahmanson Foundation
Air France
Air Products & Chemicals
Airbus Industrie of America
Akzo Chemicals Inc.
Albany International Corp.
Alberto-Culver Co.
Alco Standard Corp.
Alcon Laboratories, Inc.
Alden Trust, George I.
Alexander & Baldwin, Inc.
Alexander Charitable Foundation
Alexander Foundation, Joseph
Alexander Foundation, Judd S.
Algonquin Energy, Inc.
Allegheny Foundation

Museums/Galleries (cont.)

Allendale Mutual Insurance Co.
Alliant Techsystems
AlliedSignal
ALPAC Corp.
Alsdorf Foundation
Altman Foundation
Alumax
Aluminum Co. of America
Amado Foundation, Maurice
AMAX
AMCORE Bank, N.A. Rockford
American Brands
American Cyanamid Co.
American Electric Power
American Express Co.
American Fidelity Corp.
American Financial Corp.
American Foundation Corporation
American General Finance
American Home Products Corp.
American National Bank & Trust Co. of Chicago
American Natural Resources Co.
American President Cos.
American Saw & Manufacturing Co.
American Stock Exchange
American Telephone & Telegraph Co.
American United Life Insurance Co.
Ameritech Corp.
Ameritech Services
AMETEK
Amfac/JMB Hawaii
Amoco Corp.
AMP
Amsted Industries
Amsterdam Foundation, Jack and Mimi Leviton
Anacomp, Inc.
Analog Devices
Andersen Corp.
Anderson Foundation, M. D.
Andersons Management Corp.
Angelica Corp.
Anheuser-Busch Cos.
Annenberg Foundation
Ansin Private Foundation, Ronald M.
AON Corp.
Apache Corp.
Apple Computer, Inc.
Appleby Foundation
Appleby Trust, Scott B. and Annie P.
Appleton Papers
Arakelian Foundation, Mary Alice
Arcadia Foundation
Archer-Daniels-Midland Co.
Archibald Charitable Foundation, Norman
ARCO Chemical
Argyros Foundation
Arizona Public Service Co.
Arkansas Power & Light Co.
Arkell Hall Foundation
Armco Inc.
Armco Steel Co.
Aron Charitable Foundation, J.
Arvin Industries
Ashland Oil
Asplundh Foundation
Astor Foundation, Vincent
Atalanta/Sosnoff Capital Corp.
Atherton Family Foundation
Athwin Foundation
Atkinson Foundation
Atlanta Foundation
Atlanta Gas Light Co.
Atran Foundation

Attleboro Pawtucket Savings Bank
Auerbach Foundation, Beatrice Fox
Austin Memorial Foundation
Autry Foundation
Autzen Foundation
Avis Inc.
Avon Products
Azby Fund
Babcock & Wilcox Co.
Babson Foundation, Paul and Edith
Bachmann Foundation
Backer Spielvogel Bates U.S.
Badger Meter, Inc.
Baer Foundation, Alan and Marcia
Bafflin Foundation
Bailey Foundation
Baird Brothers Co.
Baird & Co., Robert W.
Baker & Baker
Baker Foundation, Dexter F. and Dorothy H.
Baker Foundation, R. C.
Baker Foundation, Solomon R. and Rebecca D.
Baker Hughes Inc.
Baker, Jr. Memorial Fund, William G.
Baker Trust, Clayton
Baldwin, Jr. Foundation, Summerfield
Baldwin Memorial Foundation, Fred
Ball Brothers Foundation
Ball Corp.
Ball Foundation, George and Frances
Baltimore Gas & Electric Co.
Bamberger and John Ernest Bamberger Memorial Foundation, Ruth Eleanor
Banc One Illinois Corp.
Banco Portugues do Atlantico, New York Branch
Bancorp Hawaii
Bang & Olufsen of America, Inc.
Bank Hapoalim B.M.
Bank Leumi Trust Co. of New York
Bank of A. Levy
Bank of America Arizona
Bank of Boston Corp.
Bank of Louisville
Bank of New York
Bank One, Texas-Houston Office
Bank One, Youngstown, NA
Bank South Corp.
BankAmerica Corp.
Bankers Trust Co.
Bannerman Foundation, William C.
Barclays Bank of New York
Bard, C. R.
Bardes Corp.
Bargman Foundation, Theodore and Mina
Barker Foundation, J. M. R.
Barker Welfare Foundation
Barra Foundation
Barry Corp., R. G.
Barstow Foundation
Bartlett & Co.
Bartol Foundation, Stockton Rush
Bass Foundation
Bass Foundation, Harry
Battelle
Batts Foundation
Bauer Foundation, M. R.
Bauervic Foundation, Charles M.
Baumker Charitable Foundation, Elsie and Harry
Bausch & Lomb
Baxter International
Bay Foundation

BayBanks
Bayne Fund, Howard
Beaird Foundation, Charles T.
Beal Foundation
Bean, L.L.
Bechtel Group
Bechtel, Jr. Foundation, S. D.
Bedsole Foundation, J. L.
Beech Aircraft Corp.
Beerman Foundation
Behmann Brothers Foundation
Beinecke Foundation
Bekins Foundation, Milo W.
Belden Brick Co., Inc.
Belding Heminway Co.
Belfer Foundation
Belk Stores
Belo Corp., A.H.
Belz Foundation
Bemis Company
Benedum Foundation, Claude Worthington
Beneficia Foundation
Beneficial Corp.
Benenson Foundation, Frances and Benjamin
Benetton
Beretta U.S.A. Corp.
Berger Foundation, Albert E.
Bergner Co., P.A.
Berlin Charitable Fund, Irving
Bernsen Foundation, Grace and Franklin
Bernstein & Co., Sanford C.
Berrie Foundation, Russell
Berry Foundation, Loren M.
Berwind Corp.
Best Products Co.
Bethlehem Steel Corp.
Beveridge Foundation, Frank Stanley
BFGoodrich
BHP Pacific Resources
Bibb Co.
Bicknell Fund
Biddle Foundation, Mary Duke
Bigelow Foundation, F. R.
Bingham Foundation, William
Binney & Smith Inc.
Binswanger Co.
Bionetics Corp.
Birch Foundation, Stephen and Mary
Bird Inc.
Bishop Foundation, E. K. and Lillian F.
Blade Communications
Blair Foundation, John
Blake Foundation, S. P.
Blanchard Foundation
Blandin Foundation
Blaustein Foundation, Jacob and Hilda
Blaustein Foundation, Louis and Henrietta
Blinken Foundation
Bloch Foundation, Henry W. and Marion H.
Block, H&R
Bloedel Foundation
Bloomfield Foundation, Sam and Rie
Blount
Blount Educational and Charitable Foundation, Mildred Weedon
Blue Bell, Inc.
Bluhdorn Charitable Trust, Charles G. and Yvette
Blum Foundation, Edith C.
Blum Foundation, Lois and Irving
Blum-Kovler Foundation
BMW of North America, Inc.
Board of Trustees of the Prichard School
Boatmen's Bancshares

Bodenhamer Foundation
Bodman Foundation
Boehringer Mannheim Corp.
Boeing Co.
Boettcher Foundation
Boh Brothers Construction Co.
Bohen Foundation
Boise Cascade Corp.
Bolz Family Foundation, Eugenie Mayer
Bonfils-Stanton Foundation
Booth-Bricker Fund
Borden
Borman's
Boston Edison Co.
Bostwick Foundation, Albert C.
Bostwick Foundation, Albert C.
Bothin Foundation
Boulevard Foundation
Bourns, Inc.
Bovaird Foundation, Mervin
Bowater Inc.
BP America
Brach Foundation, Helen
Brackenridge Foundation, George W.
Bradley Foundation, Lynde and Harry
Bradley-Turner Foundation
Braun Foundation
Braun Foundation
Bravmann Foundation, Ludwig
Bray Charitable Trust, Viola E.
Bren Foundation, Donald L.
Brenner Foundation
Brewer and Co., Ltd., C.
Breyer Foundation
Bridgestone/Firestone
Bridwell Foundation, J. S.
Briggs & Stratton Co.
Bright Charitable Trust, Alexander H.
Brinkley Foundation
Bristol-Myers Squibb Co.
Bristol Savings Bank
British Airways
Britton Fund
Broccoli Charitable Foundation, Dana and Albert R.
Brochsteins Inc.
Bronstein Foundation, Soloman and Sylvia
Brooks Brothers
Brother International Corp.
Brotman Foundation of California
Brown and C. A. Lupton Foundation, T. J.
Brown Foundation
Brown Foundation, M. K.
Brown Group
Brown, Jr. Charitable Trust, Frank D.
Brown & Sons, Alex
Brown & Williamson Tobacco Corp.
Browning-Ferris Industries
Brundage Charitable, Scientific, and Wildlife Conservation Foundation, Charles E. and Edna T.
Brunswick Corp.
Bryan Family Foundation, Kathleen Price and Joseph M.
Bryant Foundation
Buchalter, Nemer, Fields, & Younger
Bucyrus-Erie
Buehler Foundation, Emil
Buell Foundation, Temple Hoyne
Buhl Family Foundation
Builder Marts of America
Bull HN Information Systems Inc.
Bunbury Company
Burchfield Foundation, Charles E.
Burdines

Burgess Trust, Ralph L. and Florence R.
Burlington Industries
Burlington Resources
Bush Foundation
Bushee Foundation, Florence Evans
Butler Manufacturing Co.
C.P. Rail Systems
Cabell III and Maude Morgan Cabell Foundation, Robert G.
Cabot Corp.
Cafritz Foundation, Morris and Gwendolyn
Cahn Family Foundation
Cain Foundation, Gordon and Mary
Caine Charitable Foundation, Marie Eccles
Caldwell Foundation, Hardwick
Calhoun Charitable Trust, Kenneth
California Educational Initiatives Fund
Callaway Foundation
Cameron Foundation, Harry S. and Isabel C.
Camp Foundation
Camp Younts Foundation
Campbell Foundation
Campbell Foundation, J. Bulow
Cannon Foundation
Canon U.S.A., Inc.
Cape Branch Foundation
Capital Cities/ABC
Capital Fund Foundation
Capital Holding Corp.
Cargill
Carnival Cruise Lines
Carolina Power & Light Co.
Carolyn Foundation
Carpenter Foundation
Carpenter Foundation, E. Rhodes and Leona B.
Carpenter Technology Corp.
Carrier Corp.
Carstensen Memorial Foundation, Fred R. and Hazel W.
Carter Foundation, Amon G.
Carter-Wallace
Carylon Foundation
Cascade Natural Gas Corp.
Castle Foundation, Harold K. L.
Castle Foundation, Samuel N. and Mary
Caterpillar
CBI Industries
CBS Inc.
Ceco Corp.
Centel Corp.
Centerior Energy Corp.
Central Maine Power Co.
Central Vermont Public Service Corp.
Century Companies of America
CertainTeed Corp.
Cessna Aircraft Co.
Chadwick Fund, Dorothy Jordan
Chambers Development Co.
Champion International Corp.
Chapin Foundation, Frances
Chapman Charitable Trust, H. A. and Mary K.
Charina Foundation
Charities Foundation
Charter Manufacturing Co.
Chartwell Foundation
Chase Manhattan Bank, N.A.
Chatham Valley Foundation
Chazen Foundation
Cheatham Foundation, Owen
Chemical Bank
Cheney Foundation, Ben B.
Cheney Foundation, Elizabeth F.
Chesapeake Corp.
Chevron Corp.

Museums/Galleries (cont.)

Francis Families Foundation
Franklin Foundation, John and Mary
Franklin Mint Corp.
Frear Eleemosynary Trust, Mary D. and Walter F.
Freas Foundation
Freed Foundation
Freedom Forum
Freeman Charitable Trust, Samuel
Freeman Foundation, Carl M.
Freeman Foundation, Ella West
Freeport-McMoRan
Frelinghuysen Foundation
French Foundation
Frese Foundation, Arnold D.
Fribourg Foundation
Frick Educational Commission, Henry C.
Frick Foundation, Helen Clay
Friedman Family Foundation
Friedman Foundation, Stephen and Barbara
Friends' Foundation Trust, A.
Friendship Fund
Frisch's Restaurants Inc.
Frohlich Charitable Trust, Ludwig W.
Frohman Foundation, Sidney
Frohring Foundation, Paul & Maxine
Fry Foundation, Lloyd A.
Fujitsu America, Inc.
Fujitsu Systems of America, Inc.
Fuller Co., H.B.
Fuller Foundation
Fuller Foundation
Fuller Foundation, George F. and Sybil H.
Funderburke & Associates
Fusenot Charity Foundation, Georges and Germaine
G.P.G. Foundation
Gabelli Foundation
Gage Foundation, Philip and Irene Toll
Galkin Charitable Trust, Ira S. and Anna
Gallo Foundation, Ernest
Gannett Publishing Co., Guy
GAR Foundation
Gardner Charitable Foundation, Edith D.
Garvey Texas Foundation
Gates Foundation
GATX Corp.
Geffen Foundation, David
GEICO Corp.
Geifman Family Foundation
Gellert Foundation, Fred
Gelman Foundation, Melvin and Estelle
GenCorp
General Accident Insurance Co. of America
General Atlantic Partners L.P.
General Machine Works
General Mills
General Motors Corp.
General Reinsurance Corp.
Genius Foundation, Elizabeth Morse
GenRad
George Foundation
Georgia-Pacific Corp.
Georgia Power Co.
Gerber Products Co.
Gerlach Foundation
Gerschel Foundation, Patrick A.
Gershman Foundation, Joel
Gerson Trust, B. Milfred
Getty Foundation, Ann and Gordon

Getty Trust, J. Paul
Getz Foundation, Emma and Oscar
Gheens Foundation
Giant Food
Gifford Charitable Corporation, Rosamond
Gillett Foundation, Elesabeth Ingalls
Gillette Co.
Gilman, Jr. Foundation, Sondra and Charles
Gilmore Foundation, Earl B.
Gilmore Foundation, Irving S.
Gilmore Foundation, William G.
Ginter Foundation, Karl and Anna
Givenchy, Inc.
Glancy Foundation, Lenora and Alfred
Glanville Family Foundation
Glaxo
Gleason Foundation, Katherine
Gleason Memorial Fund
Glencairn Foundation
Glencoe Foundation
Glenmore Distilleries Co.
Glick Foundation, Eugene and Marilyn
Glickenhaus & Co.
Glidden Co.
Globe Corp.
Globe Newspaper Co.
Glosser Foundation, David A.
Gluck Foundation, Maxwell H.
Goerlich Family Foundation
Goldberg Family Foundation
Goldberg Family Foundation, Milton D. and Madeline L.
Goldberger Foundation, Edward and Marjorie
Golden Family Foundation
Goldman Foundation, Aaron and Cecile
Goldman Foundation, Morris and Rose
Goldman Fund, Richard and Rhoda
Goldome F.S.B
Goldring Family Foundation
Goldseker Foundation of Maryland, Morris
Goldsmith Family Foundation
Goldsmith Foundation, Horace W.
Goldwyn Foundation, Samuel
Goodman & Company
Gordon/Rousmaniere/Roberts Fund
Gorin Foundation, Nehemiah
Gottesman Fund
Gottwald Foundation
Gould Inc.
Gould Foundation, Florence J.
Gradison & Co.
Graham Foundation for Advanced Studies in the Fine Arts
Graham Fund, Philip L.
Graphic Controls Corp.
Grassmann Trust, E. J.
Gray Foundation, Garland
Graybar Electric Co.
Great-West Life Assurance Co.
Greeley Gas Co.
Green Foundation
Green Fund
Greene Foundation, David J.
Greene Foundation, Jerome L.
Greene Foundation, Robert Z.
Greenfield Foundation, Albert M.
Greenheck Fan Corp.
Greentree Foundation
Greenwall Foundation
Gregg-Graniteville Foundation
Greve Foundation, William and Mary

Gries Charity Fund, Lucile and Robert H.
Griffis Foundation
Griffith Foundation, W. C.
Griggs and Mary Griggs Burke Foundation, Mary Livingston
Gross Charitable Trust, Stella B.
Groves & Sons Co., S.J.
GTE Corp.
Guardian Life Insurance Co. of America
Gucci America Inc.
Gudelsky Family Foundation, Homer and Martha
Gudelsky Family Foundation, Isadore and Bertha
Guggenheim Foundation, Daniel and Florence
Gund Foundation, George
Gutman Foundation, Edna and Monroe C.
Guttman Foundation, Stella and Charles
H. B. B. Foundation
Haas Foundation, Paul and Mary
Haas Foundation, Saul and Dayee G.
Haas Fund, Miriam and Peter
Haas Fund, Walter and Elise
Haas, Jr. Fund, Evelyn and Walter
Haffner Foundation
Haggar Foundation
Haggerty Foundation
Hagler Foundation, Jon L.
Haley Foundation, W. B.
Halff Foundation, G. A. C.
Hall Charitable Trust, Evelyn A. J.
Hall Family Foundations
Hall Foundation
Hallmark Cards
Halsell Foundation, Ewing
Hamilton Bank
Hamilton Oil Corp.
Hamman Foundation, George and Mary Josephine
Hammer Foundation, Armand
Hanes Foundation, John W. and Anna H.
Hankins Foundation
Hansen Foundation, Dane G.
Harden Foundation
Hardin Foundation, Phil
Harland Charitable Foundation, John and Wilhelmina D.
Harriman Foundation, Gladys and Roland
Harriman Foundation, Mary W.
Harrington Foundation, Don and Sybil
Harrington Foundation, Francis A. and Jacquelyn H.
Harris Corp.
Harris Foundation, J. Ira and Nicki
Harris Foundation, William H. and Mattie Wattis
Harsco Corp.
Hartford Steam Boiler Inspection & Insurance Co.
Hartmarx Corp.
Hassenfeld Foundation
Hastings Trust
Hatterscheidt Foundation
Hawn Foundation
Hayden Foundation, Charles
Haynes Foundation, John Randolph and Dora
Hazen Charitable Trust, Lita Annenberg
Healy Family Foundation, M. A.
Hearst Foundation
Hearst Foundation, William Randolph
Heath Foundation, Ed and Mary
Hechinger Co.
Hecht-Levi Foundation

Heckscher Foundation for Children
Heginbotham Trust, Will E.
Heileman Brewing Co., Inc., G.
Heinz Co., H.J.
Heinz Endowment, Vira I.
Heinz Foundation, Drue
Helfaer Foundation, Evan and Marion
Heller Foundation, Walter E.
Helmerich Foundation
Hench Foundation, John C.
Henkel Corp.
Herndon Foundation
Herndon Foundation, Alonzo F. Herndon and Norris B.
Hershey Foods Corp.
Hershey Foundation
Hervey Foundation
Hess Charitable Foundation, Ronne and Donald
Hess Foundation
Heublein
Hewit Family Foundation
Hewlett-Packard Co.
Hexcel Corp.
Heymann Special Account, Mr. and Mrs. Jimmy
Heymann-Wolf Foundation
Hiawatha Education Foundation
Higgins Charitable Trust, Lorene Sails
Higginson Trust, Corina
Hill and Family Foundation, Walter Clay
Hill Foundation
Hilliard Corp.
Hillman Family Foundation, Alex
Hillman Foundation
Hillman Foundation, Henry L.
Hills Fund, Edward E.
Himmelfarb Foundation, Paul and Annetta
Hitchcock Foundation, Gilbert M. and Martha H.
HKH Foundation
Hobbs Foundation
Hobby Foundation
Hoblitzelle Foundation
Hoche-Scofield Foundation
Hodge Foundation
Hoechst Celanese Corp.
Hoffberger Foundation
Hoffer Plastics Corp.
Hofheinz Foundation, Irene Cafcalas
Hogan Foundation, Royal Barney
Hollis Foundation
Holt Foundation, William Knox
Holzer Memorial Foundation, Richard H.
Homeland Foundation
Homeland Foundation
HON Industries
Honeywell
Honigman Foundation
Hooker Charitable Trust, Janet A.
Hooper Foundation, Elizabeth S.
Hoover Foundation, H. Earl
Hopedale Foundation
Hopkins Foundation, John Jay
Hopwood Charitable Trust, John M.
Hornblower Fund, Henry
Horowitz Foundation, Gedale B. and Barbara S.
Hospital Corp. of America
Household International
Houston Endowment
Houston Industries
Hubbard Broadcasting
Hubbard Foundation, R. Dee and Joan Dale
Hubbell Inc.
Hudson-Webber Foundation
Huffy Corp.

Hughes Charitable Trust, Mabel Y.
Huizenga Family Foundation
Humana
Humane Society of the Commonwealth of Massachusetts
Hume Foundation, Jaquelin
Hunt Foundation, Roy A.
Hunt Manufacturing Co.
Hurford Foundation
Huston Foundation
Huthsteiner Fine Arts Trust
Hyams Foundation
Hyde and Watson Foundation
I. and L. Association
IBM Corp.
Icahn Foundation, Carl C.
ICI Americas
Iddings Benevolent Trust
IDS Financial Services
Illinois Bell
Illinois Tool Works
IMCERA Group Inc.
Inco Alloys International
Indiana Bell Telephone Co.
Indiana Gas and Chemical Corp.
Indiana Insurance Cos.
Ingalls Foundation, Louise H. and David S.
Inland Container Corp.
Insurance Management Associates
Interco
International Flavors & Fragrances
International Paper Co.
Ireland Foundation
Irmas Charitable Foundation, Audrey and Sydney
Irwin Charity Foundation, William G.
Irwin-Sweeney-Miller Foundation
Isaly Klondike Co.
Ishiyama Foundation
ITT Corp.
ITT Hartford Insurance Group
ITT Rayonier
J.P. Morgan & Co.
Jackson Charitable Trust, Marion Gardner
Jackson Family Foundation, Ann
Jackson Foundation
Jacobson Foundation, Bernard H. and Blanche E.
Jacobson & Sons, Benjamin
Jaharis Family Foundation
James River Corp. of Virginia
Janeway Foundation, Elizabeth Bixby
Janirve Foundation
Janssen Foundation, Henry
JCPenney Co.
JELD-WEN, Inc.
Jenkins Foundation, George W.
Jennings Foundation, Martha Holden
Jensen Construction Co.
Jergens Foundation, Andrew
Jerome Foundation
Jerome Foundation
Jesselson Foundation
Jewett Foundation, George Frederick
JFM Foundation
JMK-A M Micallef Charitable Foundation
John Hancock Mutual Life Insurance Co.
Johnson Co., E. F.
Johnson Controls
Johnson Endeavor Foundation, Christian A.
Johnson Foundation, Burdine
Johnson Foundation, Howard
Johnson Fund, Edward C.
Johnson & Higgins

Johnson & Johnson
Johnson & Son, S.C.
Jones and Bessie D. Phelps Foundation, Cyrus W. and Amy F.
Jones Family Foundation, Eugenie and Joseph
Jones Foundation, Helen
Jones Fund, Blanche and George
Jones Intercable, Inc.
Jonsson Foundation
Jordan Foundation, Arthur
Jostens
Joukowsky Family Foundation
Journal Gazette Co.
Joyce Foundation
JSJ Corp.
Jurodin Fund
Jurzykowski Foundation, Alfred
Kahn Memorial Trust
Kangesser Foundation, Robert E., Harry A., and M. Sylvia
Kapiloff Foundation, Leonard
Kaplan Foundation, Charles I. and Mary
Kaplan Foundation, Mayer and Morris
Kaplan Foundation, Rita J. and Stanley H.
Kaplan Fund, J. M.
Kapor Family Foundation
Kasle Steel Corp.
Kaufman Foundation, Henry & Elaine
Kaufman Foundation, Henry & Elaine
Kaufmann Foundation, Henry
Kawabe Memorial Fund
Kearney Inc., A.T.
Keating Family Foundation
Keck Foundation, W. M.
Keebler Co.
Keeler Fund, Miner S. and Mary Ann
Keene Trust, Hazel R.
Keller-Crescent Co.
Keller Family Foundation
Kellogg Foundation, W. K.
Kellwood Co.
Kelly, Jr. Memorial Foundation, Ensign C. Markland
Kemper Charitable Trust, William T.
Kemper Educational and Charitable Fund
Kemper Foundation, Enid and Crosby
Kemper Foundation, William T.
Kemper Memorial Foundation, David Woods
Kemper National Insurance Cos.
Kempner Fund, Harris and Eliza
Kendall Foundation, Henry P.
Kenedy Memorial Foundation, John G. and Marie Stella
Kennametal
Kennecott Corp.
Kent-Lucas Foundation
Kern Foundation Trust
Kerney Foundation, James
Kerr Foundation
Kerr Foundation, Robert S. and Grayce B.
Kerr Fund, Grayce B.
Kerr-McGee Corp.
Kettering Family Foundation
Kettering Fund
Kevorkian Fund, Hagop
Key Bank of Maine
Kieckhefer Foundation, J. W.
Kiewit Foundation, Peter
Kiewit Sons, Peter
Kilroy Foundation, William S. and Lora Jean
Kimball Co., Miles
Kimball International
Kimberly-Clark Corp.

Kimmelman Foundation, Helen & Milton
King Foundation, Carl B. and Florence E.
King Ranch
Kingsbury Corp.
Kingsley Foundation
Kinney-Lindstrom Foundation
Kiplinger Foundation
Kirby Foundation, F. M.
Kirkland & Ellis
Kirkpatrick Foundation
Klau Foundation, David W. and Sadie
Kleberg, Jr. and Helen C. Kleberg Foundation, Robert J.
Klee Foundation, Conrad and Virginia
Klein Charitable Foundation, Raymond
Kmart Corp.
Knapp Foundation
Knight Foundation, John S. and James L.
Knistrom Foundation, Fanny and Svante
Knox Family Foundation
Knox Foundation, Seymour H.
Knudsen Foundation, Tom and Valley
Koch Charitable Trust, David H.
Koch Sons, George
Koehler Foundation, Marcia and Otto
Kohl Charitable Foundation, Allen D.
Kohl Charities, Herbert H.
Kohl Foundation, Sidney
Kohler Foundation
Kopf Foundation
Koret Foundation
Krause Foundation, Charles A.
Kravis Foundation, Henry R.
Kreielsheimer Foundation Trust
Kresge Foundation
Kress Foundation, Samuel H.
Krimendahl II Foundation, H. Frederick
Kuehn Foundation
Kugelman Foundation
Kuhne Foundation Trust, Charles
Kuyper Foundation, Peter H. and E. Lucille Gaass
L. L. W. W. Foundation
L and L Foundation
La-Z-Boy Chair Co.
Laclede Gas Co.
Lafarge Corp.
Lakeside Foundation
Lakeside National Bank
Lance, Inc.
Landmark Communications
Langendorf Foundation, Stanley S.
Lannan Foundation
Lard Trust, Mary Potishman
Large Foundation
Laros Foundation, R. K.
LaSalle National Bank
Lasky Co.
Lastfogel Foundation, Abe and Frances
Lattner Foundation, Forrest C.
Lauder Foundation
Laurel Foundation
Lautenberg Foundation
Lawrence Foundation, Alice
Lawrence Foundation, Lind
Leach Foundation, Tom & Frances
Lebovitz Fund
Lebus Trust, Bertha
Lechmere
Lee Endowment Foundation
Lee Foundation, Ray M. and Mary Elizabeth
LEF Foundation
Legg Mason Inc.

Lehman Foundation, Robert
Lehman Foundation, Jacob and Charlotte
Leighton-Oare Foundation
Lemberg Foundation
Lennon Foundation, Fred A.
Leo Burnett Co.
Leonhardt Foundation, Dorothea L.
Leonhardt Foundation, Frederick H.
Leu Foundation
Levee Charitable Trust, Polly Annenberg
Levin Foundation, Philip and Janice
Levitt Foundation
Levy Foundation, Betty and Norman F.
Levy Foundation, Edward C.
Levy Foundation, Jerome
Liberman Foundation, Bertha & Isaac
Liberty Corp.
Lieberman Enterprises
Life Insurance Co. of Georgia
Lightner Sams Foundation
Lilly & Co., Eli
Lilly Endowment
Lilly Foundation, Richard Coyle
Lincoln Electric Co.
Lincoln National Corp.
Lindstrom Foundation, Kinney
Link, Jr. Foundation, George
Linn-Henley Charitable Trust
Linnell Foundation
Lipton Foundation
Lipton, Thomas J.
Littauer Foundation, Lucius N.
Little, Arthur D.
Little Family Foundation
Litton Industries
Livingston Foundation
Liz Claiborne
Lizzadro Family Foundation, Joseph
Lockheed Sanders
Lockwood Foundation, Byron W. and Alice L.
Loews Corp.
Long Foundation, George A. and Grace
Long Island Lighting Co.
Longwood Foundation
Lotus Development Corp.
Loughran Foundation, Mary and Daniel
Louisiana Land & Exploration Co.
Louisiana Power & Light Co./New Orleans Public Service
Lounsbery Foundation, Richard
Loutit Foundation
Love Charitable Foundation, John Allan
Love Foundation, Martha and Spencer
Lovett Foundation
Lowe Foundation, Joe and Emily
Lowenstein Foundation, Leon
Lowenstein Foundation, William P. and Marie R.
Loyola Foundation
Lozier Foundation
Lubo Fund
Lubrizol Corp.
Luce Foundation, Henry
Luck Stone
Luckyday Foundation
Ludwick Institute
Lukens
Lurcy Charitable and Educational Trust, Georges
Lurie Foundation, Louis R.
Lydall, Inc.
Lyndhurst Foundation
Lynn Foundation, E. M.

Lyon Foundation
Lytel Foundation, Bertha Russ
M/A-COM, Inc.
Mabee Foundation, J. E. and L. E.
MacArthur Foundation, John D. and Catherine T.
MacCurdy Salisbury Educational Foundation
MacDonald Foundation, James A.
Maclellan Foundation
Macmillan, Inc.
Macy & Co., R.H.
Maddox Trust, Web
Magowan Family Foundation
Magruder Foundation, Chesley G.
Mailman Family Foundation, A. L.
Mailman Foundation
Makita U.S.A., Inc.
Mandel Foundation, Joseph and Florence
Mandel Foundation, Morton and Barbara
Mandell Foundation, Samuel P.
Mandeville Foundation
Manilow Foundation, Nathan
Manoogian Foundation, Alex and Marie
Mapco Inc.
Mapplethorpe Foundation, Robert
Marathon Oil, Indiana Refining Division
Marbrook Foundation
Mardag Foundation
Maritz Inc.
Mark IV Industries
Markey Charitable Fund, John C.
Marmot Foundation
Marpat Foundation
Marquette Electronics
Marriott Corp.
Marriott Foundation, J. Willard
Mars Foundation
Marsh & McLennan Cos.
Marshall Field's
Marshall & Ilsley Bank
Martin Foundation
Martin Marietta Corp.
Marx Foundation, Virginia & Leonard
Marx Foundation, Virginia & Leonard
Masco Corp.
Massachusetts Charitable Mechanics Association
Massengill-DeFriece Foundation
Masserini Charitable Trust, Maurice J.
Massey Foundation
Mather and William Gwinn Mather Fund, Elizabeth Ring
Mather Fund, Richard
Mathis-Pfohl Foundation
Mattus Foundation, Reuben and Rose
Matz Foundation — Edelman Division
Mautz Paint Co.
Max Charitable Foundation
Maxon Charitable Foundation
May Department Stores Co.
Mayborn Foundation, Frank W.
Mayer Charitable Trust, Oscar G. & Elsa S.
Mayer Foundation, Louis B.
Maytag Corp.
Maytag Family Foundation, Fred
Mazer Foundation, Jacob and Ruth
MBIA, Inc.
MCA
McAlister Charitable Foundation, Harold
McBean Charitable Trust, Alletta Morris
McBean Family Foundation

McCasland Foundation
McCaw Foundation
McConnell Foundation, Neil A.
McCormick & Co.
McCrea Foundation
McCune Foundation
McDermott Foundation, Eugene
McDonald & Co. Securities
McDonald Foundation, J. M.
McDonald Industries, Inc., A. Y.
McDonald's Corp.
McDonnell Douglas Corp.
McDonnell Douglas Corp.-West
McDougall Charitable Trust, Ruth Camp
McEachern Charitable Trust, D. V. & Ida J.
McElroy Trust, R. J.
McEvoy Foundation, Mildred H.
McGonagle Foundation, Dextra Baldwin
McGovern Foundation, John P.
McGovern Fund for the Behavioral Sciences
McGraw-Hill
McGregor Foundation, Thomas and Frances
MCI Communications Corp.
McInerny Foundation
McIntosh Foundation
McKenna Foundation, Katherine Mabis
McKesson Corp.
McKnight Foundation, Sumner T.
McLean Contributionship
McMaster Foundation, Harold and Helen
McShain Charities, John
McVay Foundation
Mead Corp.
Mead Foundation, Giles W. and Elise G.
Meadows Foundation
Media General, Inc.
Medtronic
Mellon Bank Corp.
Mellon Foundation, Andrew W.
Mellon Foundation, Richard King
Menasha Corp.
Menil Foundation
Menschel Foundation, Robert and Joyce
Mercantile Bancorp
Merck Family Fund
Merck Human Health Division
Mercury Aircraft
Mercy, Jr. Foundation, Sue and Eugene
Meredith Corp.
Mericos Foundation
Merit Oil Corp.
Merrick Foundation, Robert G. and Anne M.
Merrill Foundation, R. D.
Merrill Lynch & Co.
Mervyn's
Metropolitan Life Insurance Co.
Metropolitan Theatres Corp.
Mex-Am Cultural Foundation
Meyer Foundation
Meyer Foundation, Alice Kleberg Reynolds
Meyer Foundation, Robert R.
Meyer Fund, Milton and Sophie
Meyer Memorial Trust
Michigan Bell Telephone Co.
Mifflin Memorial Fund, George H. and Jane A.
Milbank Foundation, Dunlevy
Miles Inc.
Milken Foundation, L. and S.
Millard Charitable Trust, Adah K.
Miller Foundation, Earl B. and Loraine H.
Milliken & Co.
Millipore Corp.
Mills Foundation, Ralph E.

Recipient Type Index

Museums/Galleries (cont.)

Milstein Family Foundation
Mine Safety Appliances Co.
Mineral Trust
Mingenback Foundation, Julia J.
Miniger Memorial Foundation, Clement O.
Minnesota Mutual Life Insurance Co.
Mirapaul Foundation
Mitchell Energy & Development Corp.
Mitchell Family Foundation, Bernard and Marjorie
Mitchell Family Foundation, Edward D. and Anna
Mitsubishi International Corp.
MNC Financial
Mnuchin Foundation
Mobil Oil Corp.
Model Foundation, Leo
Monell Foundation, Ambrose
Monfort Charitable Foundation
Monroe Auto Equipment Co.
Monsanto Co.
Montana Power Co.
Montgomery Foundation
Montgomery Street Foundation
Monticello College Foundation
Moore Business Forms, Inc.
Moore Foundation, Edward S.
Moore Memorial Foundation, James Starr
Moores Foundation, Harry C.
Morgan Construction Co.
Morgan Stanley & Co.
Morrill Charitable Foundation
Morris Foundation, Margaret T.
Morris Foundation, William T.
Morrison Charitable Trust, Pauline A. and George R.
Morrison-Knudsen Corp.
Morse Foundation, Richard P. and Claire W.
Morse, Jr. Foundation, Enid and Lester S.
Morton International
Moses Fund, Henry and Lucy
Mosher Foundation, Samuel B.
Moss Foundation, Harry S.
Motorola
Mott Fund, Ruth
MTS Systems Corp.
Mulcahy Foundation
Mullen Foundation, J. K.
Muller Foundation, C. John and Josephine
Mulligan Charitable Trust, Mary S.
Multimedia, Inc.
Munger Foundation, Alfred C.
Munson Foundation, W. B.
Murch Foundation
Murdock Charitable Trust, M. J.
Murfee Endowment, Kathryn
Murphy Foundation, Katherine and John
Murray Foundation
Myers and Sons, D.
Nabisco Foods Group
Nalco Chemical Co.
National By-Products
National City Bank of Evansville
National City Corp.
National Computer Systems
National Fuel Gas Co.
National Gypsum Co.
National Life of Vermont
National Presto Industries
National Starch & Chemical Corp.
National Steel
National Westminster Bank New Jersey

Nationale-Nederlanden North America Corp.
NationsBank Corp.
Nationwide Insurance Cos.
Natural Heritage Foundation
NBD Bank
NBD Bank, N.A.
Nestle U.S.A. Inc.
Neu Foundation, Hugo and Doris
Neuberger Foundation, Roy R. and Marie S.
New England Biolabs Foundation
New England Foundation
New England Mutual Life Insurance Co.
New England Telephone Co.
New-Land Foundation
New Prospect Foundation
New York Life Insurance Co.
New York Stock Exchange
New York Telephone Co.
New York Times Co.
The New Yorker Magazine, Inc.
Newhouse Foundation, Samuel I.
Newman's Own
Newmont Mining Corp.
News & Observer Publishing Co.
Nichimen America, Inc.
Nichols Co., J.C.
Nichols Foundation
Noble Foundation, Edward John
Noble Foundation, Samuel Roberts
Norcliffe Fund
Nordson Corp.
Norfolk Shipbuilding & Drydock Corp.
Norfolk Southern Corp.
Norgren Foundation, Carl A.
Norman Foundation, Andrew
Norris Foundation, Dellora A. and Lester J.
Nortek, Inc.
North American Life & Casualty Co.
North American Philips Corp.
North American Reinsurance Corp.
Northern Indiana Public Service Co.
Northern Star Foundation
Northern States Power Co.
Northern Telecom Inc.
Northern Trust Co.
Northwest Area Foundation
Northwest Natural Gas Co.
Northwestern National Life Insurance Co.
Norton Co.
Norton Memorial Corporation, Geraldi
Norwest Corp.
Noyes, Jr. Memorial Foundation, Nicholas H.
Oberlaender Foundation, Gustav
O'Brien Foundation, Cornelius and Anna Cook
Occidental Oil & Gas Corp.
Occidental Petroleum Corp.
O'Connor Foundation, A. Lindsay and Olive B.
OCRI Foundation
Odell and Helen Pfeiffer Odell Fund, Robert Stewart
Oestreicher Foundation, Sylvan and Ann
Offield Family Foundation
Ogden Foundation, Ralph E.
Ogilvy & Mather Worldwide
Oglebay Norton Co.
Ohio Bell Telephone Co.
Ohio National Life Insurance Co.
Ohio Valley Foundation
Ohl, Jr. Trust, George A.
Ohrstrom Foundation
Oklahoma Gas & Electric Co.
Old National Bank in Evansville
Olin Corp.

Olin Foundation, John M.
Olin Foundation, Spencer T. and Ann W.
Oliver Memorial Trust Foundation
Olivetti Office USA, Inc.
Olmsted Foundation, George and Carol
Olsson Memorial Foundation, Elis
1525 Foundation
O'Neil Foundation, Casey Albert T.
O'Neil Foundation, M. G.
O'Neill Charitable Corporation, F. J.
Ontario Corp.
Open Society Fund
Oppenstein Brothers Foundation
Orchard Corp. of America.
Ore-Ida Foods, Inc.
Orleton Trust Fund
Osborn Charitable Trust, Edward B.
Osceola Foundation
OsCo. Industries
O'Shaughnessy Foundation, I. A.
Osher Foundation, Bernard
Oshkosh B'Gosh
Oshkosh Truck Corp.
Outboard Marine Corp.
Overbrook Foundation
Overlake Foundation
Overnite Transportation Co.
Overseas Shipholding Group
Owen Industries, Inc.
Owen Trust, B. B.
Owens-Corning Fiberglas Corp.
Owsley Foundation, Alvin and Lucy
Oxford Industries, Inc.
PACCAR
Pacific Enterprises
Pacific Gas & Electric Co.
Pacific Mutual Life Insurance Co.
Pacific Telesis Group
PacifiCorp
Packaging Corporation of America
Packard Foundation, David and Lucile
PaineWebber
Paley Foundation, Goldie
Paley Foundation, William S.
Palin Foundation
Palmer Fund, Frank Loomis
Pamida, Inc.
Pan-American Life Insurance Co.
Panhandle Eastern Corp.
Pappas Charitable Foundation, Bessie
Paramount Communications Inc.
Parke-Davis Group
Parker Drilling Co.
Parker Foundation
Parker-Hannifin Corp.
Parshelsky Foundation, Moses L.
Parsons Foundation, Ralph M.
Pasadena Area Residential Aid
Patterson-Barclay Memorial Foundation
Pauley Foundation, Edwin W.
Payne Foundation, Frank E. and Seba B.
Peabody Foundation, Amelia
Pearson Foundation, E. M.
Pella Corp.
Pellegrino-Realmuto Charitable Foundation
Penn Foundation, William
Pennsylvania General Insurance Co.
Pennzoil Co.
People's Bank
Peoples Energy Corp.
Pepsi-Cola Bottling Co. of Charlotte
Perkin-Elmer Corp.

Perkins Charitable Foundation
Perkins Foundation, Joe and Lois
Perkins Memorial Fund, James J. and Marie Richardson
Perot Foundation
Persis Corp.
Peters Foundation, Leon S.
Petrie Trust, Lorene M.
Pew Charitable Trusts
Pfizer
Pforzheimer Foundation, Carl and Lily
Phelps, Inc.
Phelps Dodge Corp.
PHH Corp.
Philibosian Foundation, Stephen
Philip Morris Cos.
Phillips Foundation, Jesse
Phillips Family Foundation, Jay and Rose
Phillips Foundation, Dr. P.
Phillips Foundation, Waite and Genevieve
Phillips Petroleum Co.
Phipps Foundation, Howard
Pick Charitable Trust, Melitta S.
Pick, Jr. Fund, Albert
Picker International
Pickford Foundation, Mary
Pierce Charitable Trust, Harold Whitworth
Pines Bridge Foundation
Pinewood Foundation
Pioneer Trust Bank, NA
Pittsburgh National Bank
Pittulloch Foundation
Pittway Corp.
Plant Memorial Fund, Henry B.
Plough Foundation
PNC Bank
Polaroid Corp.
Polk Foundation
Pollybill Foundation
Polychrome Corp.
Poorvu Foundation, William and Lia
Porsche Cars North America, Inc.
Porter Testamentary Trust, James Hyde
Portland Food Products Co.
Post Foundation of D.C., Marjorie Merriweather
Potlatch Corp.
Potomac Electric Power Co.
Pott Foundation, Herman T. and Phenie R.
Potter Foundation, Justin and Valere
Potts and Sibley Foundation
Powell Family Foundation
Poynter Fund
PPG Industries
Pratt Memorial Fund
Premier Dental Products Co.
Premier Industrial Corp.
Price Associates, T. Rowe
Primerica Corp.
Prince Trust, Abbie Norman
Pritzker Foundation
Procter & Gamble Co.
Procter & Gamble Cosmetic & Fragrance Products
Promus Cos.
Propp Sons Fund, Morris and Anna
Prospect Hill Foundation
Prouty Foundation, Olive Higgins
Providence Energy Corp.
Providence Journal Company
Provident Life & Accident Insurance Co.
Prudential-Bache Securities
Prudential Insurance Co. of America
Public Service Co. of Colorado
Public Service Co. of New Mexico

Public Service Electric & Gas Co.
Puget Sound Power & Light Co.
Pulitzer Publishing Co.
Pyramid Foundation
Quaker Chemical Corp.
Quaker Oats Co.
Quantum Chemical Corp.
Questar Corp.
Quinlan Foundation, Elizabeth C.
Rabb Charitable Foundation, Sidney and Esther
Rabb Charitable Trust, Sidney R.
Radin Foundation
Raleigh Linen Service/National Distributing Co.
Ralston Purina Co.
Randa
Ranney Foundation, P. K.
Rasmussen Foundation
Rauch Foundation
Ray Foundation
Raytheon Co.
Recognition Equipment
Reed Foundation, Philip D.
Regenstein Foundation
Regis Corp.
Reichhold Chemicals, Inc.
Reilly Industries
Reinberger Foundation
Reinhold Foundation, Paul E. and Ida Klare
Reliance Electric Co.
Replogle Foundation, Luther I.
Republic New York Corp.
Revlon
Reynolds Foundation, Donald W.
Reynolds Foundation, J. B.
Reynolds Foundation, Richard S.
Reynolds Metals Co.
Rhone-Poulenc Inc.
Rhone-Poulenc Rorer
Rice Charitable Foundation, Albert W.
Rice Foundation
Rice Foundation, Ethel and Raymond F.
Rice Foundation, Helen Steiner
Rich Co., F.D.
Rich Foundation
Rich Products Corp.
Richardson Charitable Trust, Anne S.
Richardson Foundation, Frank E. and Nancy M.
Richmond Foundation, Frederick W.
Ridgefield Foundation
Rieke Corp.
Rienzi Foundation
Rigler-Deutsch Foundation
Riley Foundation, Mabel Louise
Ringier-America
Ritchie Memorial Foundation, Charles E. and Mabel M.
Rite-Hite Corp.
Ritter Charitable Trust, George W. & Mary F.
River Branch Foundation
RJR Nabisco Inc.
Robbins & Myers, Inc.
Roberts Foundation
Roberts Foundation, Dora
Robertshaw Controls Co.
Robin Family Foundation, Albert A.
Robinson Foundation
Robinson Foundation, J. Mack
Robinson Fund, Maurice R.
Robison Foundation, Ellis H. and Doris B.
Roblee Foundation, Joseph H. and Florence A.
Rochester Gas & Electric Corp.
Rochlin Foundation, Abraham and Sonia
Rockefeller Brothers Fund

Rockefeller Foundation
Rockford Products Corp.
Rockwell Fund
Rockwell International Corp.
Roddis Foundation, Hamilton
Rodgers Foundation, Richard & Dorothy
Rodgers Trust, Elizabeth Killam
Rodman Foundation
Rogers Charitable Trust, Florence
Rogers Family Foundation
Rogers Foundation
Rohm and Haas Company
RosaMary Foundation
Rose Foundation, Billy
Rosen Foundation, Joseph
Rosenberg Foundation, Henry and Ruth Blaustein
Rosenstiel Foundation
Rosenthal Foundation, Ida and William
Rosenthal Foundation, Richard and Hinda
Ross Foundation, Arthur
Ross Foundation, Lyn & George M.
Roth Foundation, Louis T.
Rothschild Foundation, Hulda B. and Maurice L.
Rowland Foundation
Royal Group Inc.
Rubbermaid
Rubenstein Charitable Foundation, Lawrence J. and Anne
Rubin Foundation, Samuel
Rubinstein Foundation, Helena
Rudin Foundation, Samuel and May
Ruffin Foundation, Peter B. & Adeline W.
Russell Memorial Foundation, Robert
Ryder System
SAFECO Corp.
Saint Paul Cos.
Salgo Charitable Trust, Nicholas M.
Salomon
Salomon Foundation, Richard & Edna
Saltonstall Charitable Foundation, Richard
Sams Foundation, Earl C.
San Diego Gas & Electric
San Diego Trust & Savings Bank
Sandusky International Inc.
Santa Fe Pacific Corp.
Sara Lee Cos.
Sara Lee Hosiery
Sarkeys Foundation
Saul Foundation, Joseph E. & Norma G.
Saunders Foundation
Scaler Foundation
Schadt Foundation
Schapiro Fund, M. A.
Scherer Foundation, Karla
Schering-Plough Corp.
Scherman Foundation
Scheuer Family Foundation, S. H. and Helen R.
Schieffelin Residuary Trust, Sarah I.
Schieffelin & Somerset Co.
Schiff Foundation
Schiff Foundation, Dorothy
Schiff Foundation, John J. and Mary R.
Schlumberger Ltd.
Schmidlapp Trust No. 1, Jacob G.
Schmitt Foundation, Arthur J.
Scholl Foundation, Dr.
Schott Foundation
Schrafft and Bertha E. Schrafft Charitable Trust, William E.
Schroeder Foundation, Walter
Schwab & Co., Charles

Schwab Foundation, Charles and Helen
Schwartz and Robert Schwartz Foundation, Bernard
Schwartz Foundation, Bernard Lee
Schwartz Foundation, David
Schwartz Fund for Education and Health Research, Arnold and Marie
Schwob Foundation, Simon
Scott Foundation, William E.
Scoular Co.
Scripps Foundation, Ellen Browning
Scrivner, Inc.
Scurlock Foundation
Seabury Foundation
Seafirst Corp.
Seagram & Sons, Joseph E.
Sealright Co., Inc.
Seasongood Good Government Foundation, Murray and Agnes
Seaver Charitable Trust, Richard C.
Seaver Institute
Seaway Food Town
Seay Charitable Trust, Sarah M. and Charles E.
Seay Memorial Trust, George and Effie
Sebastian Foundation
Second Foundation
Security Life of Denver
Security State Bank
Sedgwick James Inc.
Seevak Family Foundation
Sefton Foundation, J. W.
Seidman Family Foundation
Self Foundation
Semmes Foundation
Semple Foundation, Louise Taft
Sentinel Communications Co.
Sequa Corp.
Servco Pacific
Setzer Foundation
Seven Springs Foundation
Shaklee Corp.
Shapell Foundation, Nathan and Lilly
Shapiro Fund, Albert
Share Trust, Charles Morton
Sharp Foundation
Sharp Foundation, Evelyn
Shaw Foundation, Arch W.
Shawmut National Corp.
Shaw's Supermarkets
Shea Foundation
Sheaffer Inc.
Sheinberg Foundation, Eric P.
Shelden Fund, Elizabeth, Allan and Warren
Shell Oil Co.
Shenandoah Foundation
Shenandoah Life Insurance Co.
Sheridan Foundation, Thomas B. and Elizabeth M.
Sherman Family Charitable Trust, George and Beatrice
Sherwin-Williams Co.
Shiffman Foundation
Shoenberg Foundation
Shorenstein Foundation, Walter H. and Phyllis J.
Shughart, Thomson & Kilroy, P.C.
Shuwa Investments Corp.
Sierra Pacific Industries
Signet Bank/Maryland
Silverman Fluxus Collection Foundation, Gilbert and Lila
Simon Charitable Trust, Esther
Simon Foundation, William E. and Carol G.
Simpson Foundation, John M.
Simpson Investment Co.
Simpson PSB Foundation
Siragusa Foundation

Skaggs Foundation, L. J. and Mary C.
Skandia America Reinsurance Corp.
Skinner Corp.
Skirball Foundation
Slant/Fin Corp.
Slifka Foundation, Joseph and Sylvia
Sloan Foundation, Alfred P.
Smart Family Foundation
Smeal Foundation, Mary Jean & Frank P.
Smith and W. Aubrey Smith Charitable Foundation, Clara Blackford
Smith Charitable Fund, Eleanor Armstrong
Smith Corp., A.O.
Smith Family Foundation, Charles E.
Smith Family Foundation, Theda Clark
Smith Foundation, Bob and Vivian
Smith Foundation, Kelvin and Eleanor
Smith Foundation, Lon V.
Smith Foundation, Richard and Susan
Smith Horticultural Trust, Stanley
Smith, Jr. Foundation, M. W.
SmithKline Beecham
SNET
Snider Foundation
Snow Foundation, John Ben
Snow Memorial Trust, John Ben
Soling Family Foundation
Solow Foundation
Somers Foundation, Byron H.
Sonat
Sooner Pipe & Supply Corp.
Sordoni Foundation
Sosland Foundation
South Waite Foundation
Southern California Edison Co.
Southwest Gas Corp.
Southwestern Bell Corp.
Speyer Foundation, Alexander C. and Tillie S.
Spiegel Family Foundation, Jerry and Emily
Spingold Foundation, Nate B. and Frances
Spiritus Gladius Foundation
Sprague Educational and Charitable Foundation, Seth
Sprague, Jr. Foundation, Caryll M. and Norman F.
Springs Industries
Spunk Fund
Square D Co.
Stackner Family Foundation
Staley, Jr. Foundation, A. E.
Staley Manufacturing Co., A.E.
Standard Chartered Bank New York
Stanley Charitable Foundation, A. W.
Stanley Works
Stans Foundation
Star Bank, N.A.
Stark Foundation, Nelda C. and H. J. Lutcher
Starr Foundation
State Street Bank & Trust Co.
Statter Foundation, Amy Plant
Stauffer Foundation, John and Beverly
Steel, Sr. Foundation, Marshall
Steelcase
Steele Foundation, Harry and Grace
Steigerwaldt Foundation, Donna Wolf
Stein Foundation, Joseph F.
Stein Foundation, Jules and Doris

Steinberg Family Foundation, Meyer and Jean
Steiner Corp.
Steinhagen Benevolent Trust, B. A. and Elinor
Steinhardt Foundation, Judy and Michael
Sterling Winthrop
Stern Foundation, Bernice and Milton
Stern Foundation for the Arts, Richard J.
Stern Foundation, Leonard N.
Stern Memorial Trust, Sidney
Sterne-Elder Memorial Trust
Stevens Foundation, Abbot and Dorothy H.
Stevens Foundation, Nathaniel and Elizabeth P.
Stock Foundation, Paul
Stocker Foundation
Stockham Valves & Fittings
Stoddard Charitable Trust
Stokely, Jr. Foundation, William B.
Stone Charitable Foundation
Stone Container Corp.
Stone Family Foundation, Jerome H.
Stone Foundation, David S.
Stone Foundation, France
Stone Trust, H. Chase
Storz Foundation, Robert Herman
Strake Foundation
Stranahan Foundation
Stratford Foundation
Straus Foundation, Aaron and Lillie
Straus Foundation, Philip A. and Lynn
Strauss Foundation
Strawbridge Foundation of Pennsylvania I, Margaret Dorrance
Stride Rite Corp.
Stuart Center Charitable Trust, Hugh
Stulsaft Foundation, Morris
Stupp Foundation, Norman J.
Subaru of America Inc.
Sudix Foundation
Sulzberger Foundation
Sumitomo Bank of California
Summerfield Foundation, Solon E.
Summerlee Foundation
Sumners Foundation, Hatton W.
Sun Co.
Sundstrand Corp.
Swalm Foundation
Swift Co. Inc., John S.
Swig Charity Foundation, Mae and Benjamin
Swig Foundation
Swiss American Securities, Inc.
Swiss Bank Corp.
Synovus Financial Corp.
Tait Foundation, Frank M.
Talley Industries, Inc.
Tandy Foundation, Anne Burnett and Charles
Tandy Foundation, David L.
Taper Foundation, S. Mark
Target Stores
Tasty Baking Co.
Taub Foundation
Taub Foundation, Henry and Marilyn
Taub Foundation, Joseph and Arlene
Taube Family Foundation
Tauber Foundation
Taylor Foundation, Ruth and Vernon
TCF Banking & Savings, FSB
Teledyne
Teleflex Inc.
Temple-Inland

Templeton Foundation, Herbert A.
Tennant Co.
Tenneco
Terner Foundation
Tetley, Inc.
Texaco
Texas Commerce Bank Houston, N.A.
Texas Gas Transmission Corp.
Texas Instruments
Textron
Thalheimer Foundation, Alvin and Fanny Blaustein
Thanksgiving Foundation
Thatcher Foundation
Thendara Foundation
Thermo Electron Corp.
Thomas & Betts Corp.
Thomasville Furniture Industries
Thorne Foundation
Thornton Foundation
Thornton Foundation, Flora L.
Thornton Foundation, John M. and Sally B.
Thorson Foundation
3M Co.
Thurston Charitable Foundation
Times Mirror Co.
Timken Co.
Timken Foundation of Canton
Tisch Foundation
Titan Industrial Co.
Titus Foundation, C. W.
TJX Cos.
Tobin Foundation
Torchmark Corp.
Tosco Corp. Refining Division
Totsy Manufacturing Co.
Towsley Foundation, Harry A. and Margaret D.
Toyota Motor Sales, U.S.A.
Tozer Foundation
Tracor, Inc.
Transamerica Corp.
Transco Energy Company
Travelers Cos.
Trexler Trust, Harry C.
TRINOVA Corp.
Tropicana Products, Inc.
True Oil Co.
True Trust, Henry A.
Truland Foundation
Trull Foundation
Trust Co. Bank
TRW Corp.
TU Electric Co.
Tucker Charitable Trust, Rose E.
Tucker Foundation, Marcia Brady
Tull Charitable Foundation
Tuohy Foundation, Alice Tweed
Turner Charitable Foundation
Turner Charitable Trust, Courtney S.
21 International Holdings
Tyler Corp.
Tyson Foods, Inc.
Unilever United States
Union Bank
Union Bank of Switzerland Los Angeles Branch
Union Bank of Switzerland New York Branch
Union Camp Corp.
Union Electric Co.
Union Pacific Corp.
Unisys Corp.
United Airlines
United Dominion Industries
U.S. Leasing International
U.S. Silica Co.
United States Trust Co. of New York
United Technologies Corp.
Unitrode Corp.
Univar Corp.
Universal Foods Corp.

Museums/Galleries (cont.)

Universal Leaf Tobacco Co.
Unocal Corp.
UNUM Corp.
Upjohn California Fund
Upjohn Co.
Uris Brothers Foundation
US Bancorp
US WEST
USG Corp.
Ushkow Foundation
USX Corp.
Vale-Asche Foundation
Valley Foundation
Valley National Bank of Arizona
Valmont Industries
Van Andel Foundation, Jay and Betty
Van Every Foundation, Philip L.
Van Nuys Charities, J. B. and Emily
Van Nuys Foundation, I. N. and Susanna H.
Van Vleet Foundation
Van Wert County Foundation
Vance Charitable Foundation, Robert C.
Vanneck-Bailey Foundation
Varian Associates
Vaughn, Jr. Foundation Fund, James M.
Vesper Corp.
Vidda Foundation
Vilter Manufacturing Corp.
Vingo Trust II
Virginia Power Co.
Volkswagen of America, Inc.
Von der Ahe Foundation
Von Rebay Foundation, Hilla
Vulcan Materials Co.
W. W. W. Foundation
Wachovia Bank & Trust Co., N.A.
Waggoner Foundation, E. Paul and Helen Buck
Wahlstrom Foundation
Wal-Mart Stores
Waldbaum, Inc.
Walgreen Co.
Walker Foundation, Archie D. and Bertha H.
Walker Foundation, L. C. and Margaret
Walker Foundation, Smith
Walker Foundation, T. B.
Wallace Foundation, George R.
Wallace Genetic Foundation
Wallace Reader's Digest Fund, Lila
Wallach Foundation, Miriam G. and Ira D.
Disney Co., Walt
Walter Family Trust, Byron L.
Walthall Perpetual Charitable Trust, Marjorie T.
Warhol Foundation for the Visual Arts, Andy
Warner Electric Brake & Clutch Co.
Warner Foundation, Lee and Rose
Warner Fund, Albert and Bessie
Warren Charite
Washington Post Co.
Washington Water Power Co.
Wasserman Foundation
Wasserman Foundation, George
Waste Management
Watumull Fund, J.
Wean Foundation, Raymond John
Weatherhead Foundation
Weatherwax Foundation
Weaver Foundation
Webb Charitable Trust, Susan Mott

Webber Oil Co.
Webster Foundation, Edwin S.
Weeden Foundation, Frank
Wege Foundation
Weil, Gotshal & Manges Foundation
Weiler Foundation
Weiler Foundation, Theodore & Renee
Weinberg Foundation, John L.
Weingart Foundation
Weininger Foundation, Richard and Gertrude
Weinstein Foundation, J.
Weir Foundation Trust
Weisman Art Foundation, Frederick R.
Weiss Foundation, Stephen and Suzanne
Weiss Foundation, William E.
Weisz Foundation, David and Sylvia
Welfare Foundation
Wellman Foundation, S. K.
Wells Foundation, Franklin H. and Ruth L.
Wendt Foundation, Margaret L.
Wenger Foundation, Henry L. and Consuelo S.
Werblow Charitable Trust, Nina W.
West Co.
West Foundation
West One Bancorp
West Texas Corp., J. M.
Western Southern Life Insurance Co.
WestLB New York Branch
Westport Fund
Westvaco Corp.
Wetterau
Weyerhaeuser Co.
Whalley Charitable Trust
Wheat First Securites
Wheeler Foundation
Whirlpool Corp.
Whitaker Foundation
White Consolidated Industries
Whitehead Charitable Foundation
Whitehead Foundation
Whiteman Foundation, Edna Rider
Whittier Foundation, L. K.
Wickes Foundation, Harvey Randall
Wickson-Link Memorial Foundation
WICOR, Inc.
Wiegand Foundation, E. L.
Wiener Foundation, Malcolm Hewitt
Wilbur-Ellis Co.
Wilcox Trust, S. W.
Wilder Foundation
Wiley & Sons, Inc., John
Wilf Family Foundation
Williams Cos.
Wilmington Trust Co.
Wilson Foundation, Elaine P. and Richard U.
Wilson Foundation, Frances Wood
Wilson Foundation, H. W.
Wilson Foundation, Marie C. and Joseph C.
Wilson Fund, Matilda R.
Winona Corporation
Winston Foundation, Norman and Rosita
Winston Research Foundation, Harry
Winter Construction Co.
Winthrop Trust, Clara B.
Wisconsin Energy Corp.
Wisconsin Power & Light Co.
Wisconsin Public Service Corp.
Wisdom Foundation, Mary F.
Wiseheart Foundation

Witco Corp.
Witter Foundation, Dean
Wodecroft Foundation
Wolf Foundation, Melvin and Elaine
Wollenberg Foundation
Wolverine World Wide, Inc.
Wood Foundation of Chambersburg, PA
Woodard Family Foundation
Woodruff Foundation, Robert W.
Woods Charitable Fund
Woodson Foundation, Aytchmonde
Woodward Fund
Woodward Governor Co.
Woolley Foundation, Vasser
Wornall Charitable Trust and Foundation, Kearney
Wright Foundation, Lola
Wunsch Foundation
Wyman-Gordon Co.
Wyman Youth Trust
Wyomissing Foundation
Xerox Corp.
Xtra Corp.
Yawkey Foundation II
Yeager Charitable Trust, Lester E.
Yellow Corp.
Young Foundation, R. A.
Young & Rubicam
Zale Foundation
Zamoiski Co.
Zemurray Foundation
Zenkel Foundation
Ziegler Foundation for the Blind, E. Matilda
Zigler Foundation, Fred B. and Ruth B.
Zilkha & Sons
Zink Foundation, John Steele
Zuckerberg Foundation, Roy J.

Music

Abbott Laboratories
Abell Foundation, The
Abell-Hanger Foundation
Abraham & Straus
Abrams Foundation, Benjamin and Elizabeth
Abreu Charitable Trust u/w/o May P. Abreu, Francis I.
Abrons Foundation, Louis and Anne
Ace Beverage Co.
Action Industries, Inc.
Acushnet Co.
Adams Foundation, Arthur F. and Alice E.
Adler Foundation Trust, Philip D. and Henrietta B.
AEGON USA, Inc.
Agway
Ahmanson Foundation
AHS Foundation
Air France
Air Products & Chemicals
Akzo Chemicals Inc.
Alabama Power Co.
Albany International Corp.
Alberto-Culver Co.
Albertson's
Alco Standard Corp.
Alcon Laboratories, Inc.
Alexander Foundation, Judd S.
Alexander Foundation, Robert D. and Catherine R.
Allegheny Ludlum Corp.
Allendale Mutual Insurance Co.
AlliedSignal
Alltel/Western Region
Allyn Foundation
ALPAC Corp.
Alpert Foundation, Herb
Altman Foundation
Altschul Foundation

Alumax
Aluminum Co. of America
AMAX
American Brands
American Electric Power
American Express Co.
American Fidelity Corp.
American Foundation Corporation
American General Finance
American National Bank & Trust Co. of Chicago
American Natural Resources Co.
American President Cos.
American Telephone & Telegraph Co.
American United Life Insurance Co.
Ameritas Life Insurance Corp.
Ameritech Corp.
Ameritech Services
Ames Charitable Trust, Harriett
AMETEK
Amfac/JMB Hawaii
Amoco Corp.
AMP
AMR Corp.
Amsted Industries
Anacomp, Inc.
Andersen Corp.
Andersen Foundation, Arthur
Anderson Charitable Trust, Josephine
Anderson Foundation, M. D.
Anderson Foundation, William P.
Andersons Management Corp.
Annenberg Foundation
Ansin Private Foundation, Ronald M.
AON Corp.
Apache Corp.
Apple Computer, Inc.
Appleby Trust, Scott B. and Annie P.
Appleton Papers
Arcadia Foundation
Archer-Daniels-Midland Co.
Archibald Charitable Foundation, Norman
ARCO Chemical
Argyros Foundation
Aristech Chemical Corp.
Arizona Public Service Co.
Arkansas Power & Light Co.
Armbrust Chain Co.
Armco Inc.
Arnold Fund
Aron Charitable Foundation, J.
Arvin Industries
Ashland Oil
Atherton Family Foundation
Athwin Foundation
Atlanta Gas Light Co.
Attleboro Pawtucket Savings Bank
Atwood Foundation
Auerbach Foundation, Beatrice Fox
Avis Inc.
Avon Products
Awrey Bakeries
Babcock & Wilcox Co.
Babson Foundation, Paul and Edith
Backer Spielvogel Bates U.S.
Badgeley Residuary Charitable Trust, Rose M.
Baier Foundation, Marie
Baird Foundation, Cameron
Baker Foundation, Dexter F. and Dorothy H.
Baker Foundation, R. C.
Baldwin Memorial Foundation, Fred
Ball Corp.
Ball Foundation, George and Frances

Baltimore Gas & Electric Co.
Banc One Wisconsin Corp.
Bancroft, Jr. Foundation, Hugh
Bank Hapoalim B.M.
Bank of A. Levy
Bank of America Arizona
Bank of Boston Corp.
Bank of New York
Bank of San Francisco Co.
Bank of Tokyo Trust Co.
Bank One, Youngstown, NA
BankAmerica Corp.
Bankers Trust Co.
Barclays Bank of New York
BarclaysAmerican Corp.
Bard, C. R.
Bardes Corp.
Barker Foundation
Barker Foundation, J. M. R.
Barker Welfare Foundation
Barry Corp., R. G.
Barth Foundation, Theodore H.
Bartol Foundation, Stockton Rush
Bass Foundation
Bassett Foundation, Norman
Battelle
Batten Foundation
Batts Foundation
Bauer Foundation, M. R.
Bauervic Foundation, Peggy
Baumker Charitable Foundation, Elsie and Harry
Bausch & Lomb
Baxter International
Bayne Fund, Howard
Beattie Foundation Trust, Cordelia Lee
Bechtel, Jr. Foundation, S. D.
Beckman Foundation, Leland D.
Beech Aircraft Corp.
Beecher Foundation, Florence Simon
Beerman Foundation
Bekins Foundation, Milo W.
Belding Heminway Co.
Belfer Foundation
Bell Atlantic Corp.
Belz Foundation
Bemis Company
Benbough Foundation, Legler
Bender Foundation
Benedum Foundation, Claude Worthington
Beneficia Foundation
Benefit Trust Life Insurance Co.
Bere Foundation
Bergen Foundation, Frank and Lydia
Bergner Co., P.A.
Berkman Charitable Trust, Allen H. and Selma W.
Berlin Charitable Fund, Irving
Bernsen Foundation, Grace and Franklin
Bernstein & Co., Sanford C.
Berry Foundation, Loren M.
Berwind Corp.
Best Products Co.
Beveridge Foundation, Frank Stanley
BFGoodrich
Bibb Co.
Biddle Foundation, Mary Duke
Bigelow Foundation, F. R.
Binney & Smith Inc.
Birch Foundation, Stephen and Mary
Bissell Foundation, J. Walton
Blade Communications
Blake Foundation, S. P.
Blandin Foundation
Blaustein Foundation, Jacob and Hilda
Blaustein Foundation, Louis and Henrietta
Blinken Foundation

Block, H&R
Bloomfield Foundation, Sam and Rie
Blount
Blue Bell, Inc.
Blue Cross & Blue Shield of Alabama
Blum Foundation, Edna F.
Blum-Kovler Foundation
Boatmen's Bancshares
Boatmen's First National Bank of Oklahoma
Bodman Foundation
Boeckmann Charitable Foundation
Boehringer Mannheim Corp.
Boeing Co.
Boh Brothers Construction Co.
Boise Cascade Corp.
Bolz Family Foundation, Eugenie Mayer
Bonfils-Stanton Foundation
Booz Allen & Hamilton
Borden
Borden Memorial Foundation, Mary Owen
Borg-Warner Corp.
Borman's
Boston Edison Co.
Botwinick-Wolfensohn Foundation
Boulevard Foundation
Boutell Memorial Fund, Arnold and Gertrude
Bovaird Foundation, Mervin
Bowater Inc.
Bozzone Family Foundation
BP America
Brach Foundation, Helen
Brackenridge Foundation, George W.
Bradford & Co., J.C.
Bradley Foundation, Lynde and Harry
Bradley-Turner Foundation
Brady Foundation
Branta Foundation
Brenner Foundation, Mervyn
Brewer and Co., Ltd., C.
Bridgestone/Firestone
Brillion Iron Works
Brinkley Foundation
Bristol Savings Bank
British Airways
Brochsteins Inc.
Brooks Brothers
Brotz Family Foundation, Frank G.
Brown and C. A. Lupton Foundation, T. J.
Brown Foundation
Brown Foundation, W. L. Lyons
Brown Group
Brown & Sons, Alex
Brown & Williamson Tobacco Corp.
Browning Charitable Foundation, Val A.
Browning-Ferris Industries
Brundage Charitable, Scientific, and Wildlife Conservation Foundation, Charles E. and Edna T.
Bruno Foundation, Angelo
Brunswick Corp.
Bryan Family Foundation, Kathleen Price and Joseph M.
Bryce Memorial Fund, William and Catherine
Buchanan Family Foundation
Buck Foundation, Carol Franc
Bucyrus-Erie
Buhl Foundation
Builder Marts of America
Burchfield Foundation, Charles E.
Burdines

Burgess Trust, Ralph L. and Florence R.
Burlington Northern Inc.
Burlington Resources
Burnham Foundation
Burroughs Wellcome Co.
Bush Charitable Foundation, Edyth
Bush Foundation
Butler Family Foundation, George W. and Gladys S.
Butler Family Foundation, Patrick and Aimee
Butler Manufacturing Co.
C.P. Rail Systems
Cabell III and Maude Morgan Cabell Foundation, Robert G.
Cable & Wireless Communications
Cabot Corp.
Cabot Family Charitable Trust
Cafritz Foundation, Morris and Gwendolyn
Cain Foundation, Gordon and Mary
Caine Charitable Foundation, Marie Eccles
Calhoun Charitable Trust, Kenneth
California Educational Initiatives Fund
California & Hawaiian Sugar Co.
Campbell Foundation
Campbell Foundation
Campbell Foundation, Charles Talbot
Cantor Foundation, Iris and B. Gerald
Capital Holding Corp.
Cargill
Carlson Cos.
Carnival Cruise Lines
Carolina Power & Light Co.
Carpenter Foundation, E. Rhodes and Leona B.
Carpenter Technology Corp.
Carrier Corp.
Carstensen Memorial Foundation, Fred R. and Hazel W.
Carter Foundation, Amon G.
Carter-Wallace
Cary Charitable Trust, Mary Flagler
Carylon Foundation
Cassett Foundation, Louis N.
Castle Foundation, Samuel N. and Mary
CBI Industries
Ceco Corp.
Centerior Energy Corp.
Central Life Assurance Co.
Central Maine Power Co.
Central Vermont Public Service Corp.
CertainTeed Corp.
Cessna Aircraft Co.
Chadwick Fund, Dorothy Jordan
Chamberlin Foundation, Gerald W.
Chambers Development Co.
Chambers Memorial, James B.
Chapin Foundation, Frances
Chapman Charitable Trust, H. A. and Mary K.
Charities Foundation
Charter Manufacturing Co.
Chartwell Foundation
Chase Manhattan Bank, N.A.
Chase Trust, Alice P.
Chastain Charitable Foundation, Robert Lee and Thomas M.
Chatham Valley Foundation
Chazen Foundation
Cheatham Foundation, Owen
Chemical Bank
Cheney Foundation, Ben B.
Cheney Foundation, Elizabeth F.

Cherokee Foundation
Chesapeake Corp.
Chesebrough-Pond's
Chevron Corp.
Chicago Board of Trade
Chicago Sun-Times, Inc.
Chicago Title and Trust Co.
Chicago Tribune Co.
Chiles Foundation
Christensen Charitable and Religious Foundation, L. C.
Chrysler Corp.
Church & Dwight Co.
Ciba-Geigy Corp. (Pharmaceuticals Division)
Cincinnati Bell
Circuit City Stores
Citicorp
CLARCOR
Clark Charitable Trust
Clark Foundation
Clark Foundation
Clark Foundation, Robert Sterling
Clark-Winchcole Foundation
Clay Foundation
Cleveland-Cliffs
Clipper Ship Foundation
Clorox Co.
Clowes Fund
CNA Insurance Cos.
CNG Transmission Corp.
Coats & Clark Inc.
Cobb Family Foundation
Codrington Charitable Foundation, George W.
Cogswell Benevolent Trust
Cohen Family Foundation, Saul Z. and Amy Scheuer
Cohen Foundation, George M.
Cohen Foundation, Naomi and Nehemiah
Colburn Fund
Cole Foundation, Olive B.
Cole Foundation, Robert H. and Monica H.
Cole Trust, Quincy
Coleman Co.
Coleman, Jr. Foundation, George E.
Collins & Aikman Holdings Corp.
Collins Foundation
Collins Foundation, Carr P.
Colonial Life & Accident Insurance Co.
Colonial Oil Industries, Inc.
Columbus Dispatch Printing Co.
Comer Foundation
Comerica
Commerce Bancshares, Inc.
Commerce Clearing House
Community Health Association
Compaq Computer Corp.
Compton Foundation
Comstock Foundation
ConAgra
Connell Foundation, Michael J.
Connelly Foundation
Consolidated Natural Gas Co.
Consolidated Papers
Consumers Power Co.
Continental Corp.
Contran Corp.
Cook Foundation
Cooke Foundation
Cooper Charitable Trust, Richard H.
Cooper Foundation
Cooper Industries
Coors Brewing Co.
Coors Foundation, Adolph
Copley Press
Copolymer Rubber & Chemical Corp.
Corbett Foundation
Cord Foundation, E. L.

Cornell Trust, Peter C.
Cosmair, Inc.
Country Curtains, Inc.
Covington Foundation, Marion Stedman
Cowles Charitable Trust
Cowles Foundation, Gardner and Florence Call
Cowles Media Co.
CPC International
CPI Corp.
CR Industries
Crandall Memorial Foundation, J. Ford
Crane & Co.
Credit Suisse
Crescent Plastics
Crestlea Foundation
CRL Inc.
Crown Books Foundation, Inc.
Crown Memorial, Arie and Ida
Crum and Forster
Crystal Trust
CTS Corp.
Cuesta Foundation
Cullen Foundation
Cullen/Frost Bankers
Culpeper Foundation, Charles E.
Culver Foundation, Constans
Cummings Foundation, Nathan
Cummins Engine Co.
CUNA Mutual Insurance Group
Cuneo Foundation
Cunningham Foundation, Laura Moore
Curtice-Burns Foods
Dai-Ichi Kangyo Bank of California
Dain Bosworth/Inter-Regional Financial Group
Dalton Foundation, Harry L.
Daly Charitable Foundation Trust, Robert and Nancy
Dammann Fund
Dana Charitable Trust, Eleanor Naylor
Dana Corp.
Daniel Foundation of Alabama
Danis Industries
Danner Foundation
Davidson Family Charitable Foundation
Davies Charitable Trust
Davis Family - W.D. Charities, Tine W.
Davis Foundation, Edwin W. and Catherine M.
Davis Foundation, Shelby Cullom
Day Family Foundation
Day Foundation, Nancy Sayles
Dayton Hudson Corp.
Daywood Foundation
Dean Witter Discover
Dee Foundation, Lawrence T. and Janet T.
Deere & Co.
Delany Charitable Trust, Beatrice P.
Delaware North Cos.
Deluxe Corp.
Demoulas Supermarkets
Dennett Foundation, Marie G.
Dennison Manufacturing Co.
Deposit Guaranty National Bank
DeRoy Foundation, Helen L.
DeSoto
Detroit Edison Co.
Deuble Foundation, George H.
Deutsch Co.
DeVlieg Foundation, Charles
DeVos Foundation, Richard and Helen
Dewar Foundation
Dewing Foundation, Frances R.
Dexter Corp.
Dexter Industries

Dial Corp.
Diamond Foundation, Aaron
Dick Family Foundation
Dillon Foundation
Dimeo Construction Co.
Dimick Foundation
DiRosa Foundation, Rene and Veronica
Dixie Yarns, Inc.
Dodge Foundation, Geraldine R.
Donaldson Co.
Dorminy Foundation, John Henry
Doty Family Foundation
Douglas Charitable Foundation
Douglas & Lomason Company
Dow Corning Corp.
Dow Fund, Alden and Vada
Dresser Industries
Dreyfus Foundation, Jean and Louis
Dreyfus Foundation, Max and Victoria
du Pont de Nemours & Co., E. I.
Dubow Family Foundation
Duchossois Industries
Duke Power Co.
Dula Educational and Charitable Foundation, Caleb C. and Julia W.
Duncan Foundation, Lillian H. and C. W.
Dunspaugh-Dalton Foundation
Dupar Foundation
duPont Foundation, Chichester
Dynamet, Inc.
Dyson Foundation
Earl-Beth Foundation
Eastern Enterprises
Eastman Kodak Co.
Eastover Corp.
Eaton Corp.
Eaton Foundation, Cyrus
Eaton Foundation, Edwin M. and Gertrude S.
Eberly Foundation
Eccles Foundation, George S. and Dolores Dore
Eccles Foundation, Marriner S.
Eckerd Corp., Jack
Eden Hall Foundation
Eder Foundation, Sidney and Arthur
Edgewater Steel Corp.
Educational Foundation of America
Edwards Industries
EG&G Inc.
El-An Foundation
El Pomar Foundation
Elf Atochem North America
Emerson Electric Co.
Emerson Foundation, Fred L.
Emery Memorial, Thomas J.
EMI Records Group
Encyclopaedia Britannica, Inc.
Engelhard Foundation, Charles
English-Bonter-Mitchell Foundation
English Foundation, Walter and Marian
Enron Corp.
Ensign-Bickford Industries
Ensworth Charitable Foundation
Enterprise Rent-A-Car Co.
Equimark Corp.
Equitable Life Assurance Society of the U.S.
Erb Lumber Co.
Ernest & Julio Gallo Winery
Erpf Fund, Armand G.
Ethyl Corp.
Ettinger Foundation
Evjue Foundation
Exxon Corp.
Factor Family Foundation, Max
Fair Oaks Foundation, Inc.

Recipient Type Index

Music (cont.)

Fairfield-Meeker Charitable Trust, Freeman E.
Falcon Foundation
Fales Foundation Trust
Falk Foundation, David
Fanwood Foundation
Farish Fund, William Stamps
Farley Industries
Farnsworth Trust, Charles A.
Farr Trust, Frank M. and Alice M.
Farwell Foundation, Drusilla
Federal-Mogul Corp.
Federal National Mortgage Assn., Fannie Mae
Federated Department Stores and Allied Stores Corp.
Federated Life Insurance Co.
Feintech Foundation
Fels Fund, Samuel S.
Femino Foundation
Ferguson Family Foundation, Kittie and Rugeley
Ferkauf Foundation, Eugene and Estelle
Fiat U.S.A., Inc.
Fidelity Bank
Field Foundation of Illinois
Fieldcrest Cannon
Fifth Avenue Foundation
Fifth Third Bancorp
Fig Tree Foundation
Fikes Foundation, Leland
Filene Foundation, Lincoln and Therese
FINA, Inc.
Fingerhut Family Foundation
Finnegan Foundation, John D.
Firan Foundation
Fireman's Fund Insurance Co.
Firestone Foundation, Roger S.
Firestone, Jr. Foundation, Harvey
First Bank System
First Boston
First Chicago
First Fidelity Bancorporation
First Interstate Bank NW Region
First Interstate Bank of Arizona
First Interstate Bank of California
First Interstate Bank of Denver
First Interstate Bank of Oregon
First Interstate Bank of Texas, N.A.
First Maryland Bancorp
First National Bank & Trust Co. of Rockford
First NH Banks, Inc.
First Tennessee Bank
First Union Corp.
Firstar Bank Milwaukee NA
Fischbach Foundation
Fish Foundation, Ray C.
Fishback Foundation Trust, Harmes C.
Fisher Foundation
Fisher Foundation
Flagler Foundation
Fleet Bank of New York
Fleet Financial Group
Fleishhacker Foundation
Fleming Companies, Inc.
Fleming Foundation
Fletcher Foundation, A. J.
Florida Power Corp.
Florida Rock Industries
Fluor Corp.
FMC Corp.
Fondren Foundation
Foote, Cone & Belding Communications
Foothills Foundation
Forbes
Ford Foundation
Ford Fund, Benson and Edith
Ford Fund, Eleanor and Edsel

Ford Fund, Walter and Josephine
Ford Meter Box Co.
Ford Motor Co.
Forest City Enterprises
Forest Foundation
Forest Fund
Forest Lawn Foundation
Forest Oil Corp.
Fort Worth Star Telegram
Foster and Gallagher
Foster Charitable Foundation, M. Stratton
Foster Charitable Trust
Foster Co., L.B.
Foster Foundation
Foundation for the Needs of Others
Fourth Financial Corp.
France Foundation, Jacob and Annita
Frank Foundation, Ernest and Elfriede
Frank Fund, Zollie and Elaine
Frankel Foundation
Franklin Foundation, John and Mary
Franklin Mint Corp.
Frear Eleemosynary Trust, Mary D. and Walter F.
Freedom Forum
Freeman Charitable Trust, Samuel
Freeman Foundation, Carl M.
Freeport-McMoRan
Frelinghuysen Foundation
Frese Foundation, Arnold D.
Fribourg Foundation
Frick Educational Commission, Henry C.
Friedman Family Foundation
Friendship Fund
Frisch's Restaurants Inc.
Frohring Foundation, William O. and Gertrude Lewis
Fry Foundation, Lloyd A.
Fuchs Foundation, Gottfried & Mary
Fuchsberg Family Foundation, Abraham
Fujitsu Systems of America, Inc.
Fuller Co., H.B.
Fuller Foundation, George F. and Sybil H.
Funderburke & Associates
Fuqua Foundation, J. B.
Furth Foundation
Fusenot Charity Foundation, Georges and Germaine
G.P.G. Foundation
Galter Foundation
Gannett Publishing Co., Guy Gap, The
GAR Foundation
Garrigues Trust, Edwin B.
Garvey Kansas Foundation
Garvey Memorial Foundation, Edward Chase
Garvey Texas Foundation
Garvey Trust, Olive White
Gates Foundation
Gateway Apparel
GATX Corp.
Gazette Co.
GEICO Corp.
General Accident Insurance Co. of America
General American Life Insurance Co.
General Electric Co.
General Mills
General Motors Corp.
General Railway Signal Corp.
General Reinsurance Corp.
General Signal Corp.
General Tire Inc.
Genius Foundation, Elizabeth Morse
GenRad

Georgia-Pacific Corp.
Georgia Power Co.
Gerber Products Co.
Gerbode Foundation, Wallace Alexander
Gerlach Foundation
Gerondelis Foundation
Getty Foundation, Ann and Gordon
Getz Foundation, Emma and Oscar
Gheens Foundation
Ghidotti Foundation, William and Marian
Giant Eagle
Giant Food
Giger Foundation, Paul and Oscar
Gill Foundation, Pauline Allen
Gillett Foundation, Elesabeth Ingalls
Gillette Co.
Gilman Foundation, Howard
Gilmore Foundation, William G.
Ginter Foundation, Karl and Anna
Glancy Foundation, Lenora and Alfred
Glaser Foundation
Glaxo
Glaze Foundation, Robert and Ruth
Glazer Foundation, Madelyn L.
Gleason Memorial Fund
Glenmore Distilleries Co.
Glick Foundation, Eugene and Marilyn
Glickenhaus & Co.
Glidden Co.
Globe Corp.
Globe Newspaper Co.
Glosser Foundation, David A.
Gluck Foundation, Maxwell H.
Goldberg Family Foundation
Goldberger Foundation, Edward and Marjorie
Goldie-Anna Charitable Trust
Goldman Foundation, Herman
Goldman Fund, Richard and Rhoda
Goldome F.S.B
Goldsmith Family Foundation
Goldsmith Foundation, Horace W.
Goldstein Foundation, Leslie and Roslyn
Golub Corp.
Goodman Family Foundation
Gordon Charitable Trust, Peggy and Yale
Gordon/Rousmaniere/Roberts Fund
Gould Inc.
Gould Foundation, Florence J.
Graco
Gradison & Co.
Grainger Foundation
Grassmann Trust, E. J.
Graybar Electric Co.
Great-West Life Assurance Co.
Green Foundation
Green Fund
Greene Foundation, David J.
Greene Foundation, Jerome L.
Greene Foundation, Robert Z.
Greenfield Foundation, Albert M.
Greenspan Foundation
Greenwall Foundation
Gregg-Graniteville Foundation
Greve Foundation, William and Mary
Gries Charity Fund, Lucile and Robert H.
Griffis Foundation
Griggs and Mary Griggs Burke Foundation, Mary Livingston
Gross Charitable Trust, Stella B.
Grossman Foundation, N. Bud
Groves & Sons Co., S.J.

Grundy Foundation
Gruss Charitable Foundation, Emanuel and Riane
GSC Enterprises
Guaranty Bank & Trust Co.
Guardian Life Insurance Co. of America
Gund Foundation, George
Gussman Foundation, Herbert and Roseline
Haas Foundation, Paul and Mary
Haas Fund, Miriam and Peter
Haas Fund, Walter and Elise
Haas, Jr. Fund, Evelyn and Walter
Hachar Charitable Trust, D. D.
Haffenreffer Family Fund
Hafif Family Foundation
Hale Foundation, Crescent Porter
Halff Foundation, G. A. C.
Hall Family Foundations
Hall Foundation
Hall Foundation
Hallmark Cards
Halsell Foundation, Ewing
Hamilton Bank
Hamilton Oil Corp.
Hamman Foundation, George and Mary Josephine
Hammer Foundation, Armand
Hancock Foundation, Luke B.
Hand Industries
Handleman Co.
Hanes Foundation, John W. and Anna H.
Hankins Foundation
HarCo. Drug
Harding Foundation, Charles Stewart
Harkness Ballet Foundation
Harkness Foundation, William Hale
Harper Foundation, Philip S.
Harrington Foundation, Don and Sybil
Harris Family Foundation, Hunt and Diane
Harris Foundation
Harris Foundation, John H. and Lucille
Harris Foundation, William H. and Mattie Wattis
Harrison Foundation Trust, Francena T.
Harsco Corp.
Hartford Courant Foundation
Hartman Foundation, Jesse and Dorothy
Hartmarx Corp.
Harvard Musical Association
Hawkins Foundation, Robert Z.
Hayfields Foundation
Hazen Foundation, Edward W.
Healy Family Foundation, M. A.
Hearst Foundation
Hearst Foundation, William Randolph
Hechinger Co.
Hecht-Levi Foundation
Heckscher Foundation for Children
HEI Inc.
Heilicher Foundation, Menahem
Heineman Foundation for Research, Educational, Charitable, and Scientific Purposes
Heinz Co., H.J.
Heinz Endowment, Vira I.
Heinz Family Foundation
Heinz Foundation, Drue
Helfaer Foundation, Evan and Marion
Helis Foundation
Heller Financial
Heller Foundation, Walter E.
Helmerich Foundation
Henderson Foundation

Henkel Corp.
Hermann Foundation, Grover
Herndon Foundation
Herrick Foundation
Hershey Foods Corp.
Hess Charitable Foundation, Ronne and Donald
Hesston Corp.
Hewlett Foundation, William and Flora
Hewlett-Packard Co.
Heymann Special Account, Mr. and Mrs. Jimmy
Heyward Memorial Fund, DuBose and Dorothy
Hiawatha Education Foundation
Higgins Charitable Trust, Lorene Sails
Higginson Trust, Corina
Hill Crest Foundation
Hill-Snowdon Foundation
Hillman Family Foundation, Alex
Hillman Foundation, Henry L.
Hillsdale Fund
Himmelfarb Foundation, Paul and Annetta
Hitchcock Foundation, Gilbert M. and Martha H.
Hoag Family Foundation, George
Hoche-Scofield Foundation
Hoffberger Foundation
Hoffer Plastics Corp.
Hoffman Foundation, H. Leslie Hoffman and Elaine S.
Hogan Foundation, Royal Barney
Holden Fund, James and Lynelle
Holley Foundation
Hollis Foundation
Holt Foundation, William Knox
Holzer Memorial Foundation, Richard H.
Honeywell
Honigman Foundation
Hooker Charitable Trust, Janet A.
Hooper Foundation, Elizabeth S.
Hooper Handling
Hoover Foundation
Hopkins Foundation, Josephine Lawrence
Hopwood Charitable Trust, John M.
Hospital Corp. of America
House Educational Trust, Susan Cook
Household International
Houston Endowment
Houston Industries
Howard and Bush Foundation
Howe and Mitchell B. Howe Foundation, Lucite Horton
Howell Foundation, Eric and Jessie
Hubbard Broadcasting
Hubbard Milling Co.
Hudson-Webber Foundation
Huffy Corp.
Hughes Charitable Trust, Mabel Y.
Huizenga Family Foundation
Huizenga Foundation, Jennie
Hulings Foundation, Mary Andersen
Hulme Charitable Foundation, Milton G.
Hultquist Foundation
Humana
Hume Foundation, Jaquelin
Hunt Alternatives Fund
Hunt Foundation
Hunt Foundation, Roy A.
Hunt Manufacturing Co.
Huston Foundation
Huthsteiner Fine Arts Trust
Hyde and Watson Foundation
IBM Corp.
ICI Americas
IDS Financial Services
IES Industries

Illinois Bell
Illinois Tool Works
IMCERA Group Inc.
Imperial Bancorp
Indiana Bell Telephone Co.
Indiana Desk Co.
Indiana Insurance Cos.
Ingalls Foundation, Louise H. and David S.
Inland Container Corp.
Inman Mills
Innovating Worthy Projects Foundation
Interco
International Flavors & Fragrances
International Multifoods Corp.
International Paper Co.
Interstate Packaging Co.
Iowa-Illinois Gas & Electric Co.
Iowa State Bank
Ireland Foundation
Irmas Charitable Foundation, Audrey and Sydney
Irvine Foundation, James
Irwin Charity Foundation, William G.
Israel Foundation, A. Cremieux
ITT Corp.
ITT Hartford Insurance Group
J.P. Morgan & Co.
Jacobs Engineering Group
Jacobson Foundation, Bernard H. and Blanche E.
Jacobson & Sons, Benjamin
Jaffe Foundation
Jameson Foundation, J. W. and Ida M.
Jameson Trust, Oleonda
Janssen Foundation, Henry
JCPenney Co.
Jefferson Endowment Fund, John Percival and Mary C.
Jeffress Memorial Trust, Elizabeth G.
Jellison Benevolent Society
Jennings Foundation, Martha Holden
Jephson Educational Trust No. 1
Jerome Foundation
Jewett Foundation, George Frederick
JFM Foundation
Jockey Hollow Foundation
John Hancock Mutual Life Insurance Co.
Johnson Controls
Johnson Endeavor Foundation, Christian A.
Johnson Foundation, Helen K. and Arthur E.
Johnson Foundation, Howard
Johnson Fund, Edward C.
Johnson & Higgins
Johnson & Johnson
Johnson & Son, S.C.
Johnston-Fix Foundation
Johnston-Hanson Foundation
Jones Family Foundation, Eugenie and Joseph
Jonsson Foundation
Jordan and Ettie A. Jordan Charitable Foundation, Mary Ranken
Jordan Foundation, Arthur
Joukowsky Family Foundation
Joyce Foundation
JSJ Corp.
Julia R. and Estelle L. Foundation
Jurodin Fund
Jurzykowski Foundation, Alfred
Kahn Dallas Symphony Foundation, Louise W. and Edmund J.
Kahn Memorial Trust
Kaiser Cement Corp.

Kaplan Foundation, Mayer and Morris
Kaplan Foundation, Rita J. and Stanley H.
Kasle Steel Corp.
Kauffman Foundation, Muriel McBrien
Kearney Inc., A.T.
Keck, Jr. Foundation, William M.
Keebler Co.
Keeler Fund, Miner S. and Mary Ann
Keith Foundation Trust, Ben E.
Keller-Crescent Co.
Keller Family Foundation
Kelly, Jr. Memorial Foundation, Ensign C. Markland
Kemper Charitable Lead Trust, William T.
Kemper Educational and Charitable Fund
Kemper Foundation, Enid and Crosby
Kemper Memorial Foundation, David Woods
Kempner Fund, Harris and Eliza
Kenedy Memorial Foundation, John G. and Marie Stella
Kennametal
Kennecott Corp.
Kerr-McGee Corp.
Kettering Family Foundation
Kieckhefer Foundation, J. W.
Kiewit Sons, Peter
Kilcawley Fund, William H.
Killam Trust, Constance
Kilworth Charitable Foundation, Florence B.
Kimball International
Kimberly-Clark Corp.
Kimmelman Foundation, Helen & Milton
Kingsbury Corp.
Kingsley Foundation, Lewis A.
Kiplinger Foundation
Kirbo Charitable Trust, Thomas M. and Irene B.
Kirkland & Ellis
Klau Foundation, David W. and Sadie
Klee Foundation, Conrad and Virginia
Kline Foundation, Josiah W. and Bessie H.
Klipstein Foundation, Ernest Christian
Kmart Corp.
Knight Foundation, John S. and James L.
Knott Foundation, Marion I. and Henry J.
Knox Foundation, Seymour H.
Knudsen Foundation, Tom and Valley
Koehler Foundation, Marcia and Otto
Kohl Charitable Foundation, Allen D.
Kohler Foundation
Komes Foundation
Koret Foundation
Koulaieff Educational Fund, Trustees of Ivan Y.
Kowalski Sausage Co.
Kraft General Foods
Kramer Foundation, C. L. C.
Krause Foundation, Charles A.
Kreielsheimer Foundation Trust
Kress Foundation, George
Krimendahl II Foundation, H. Frederick
Kugelman Foundation
Kuhne Foundation Trust, Charles
Kulas Foundation
La-Z-Boy Chair Co.
Laclede Gas Co.
Lance, Inc.

Langendorf Foundation, Stanley S.
Lard Trust, Mary Potishman
Lasky Co.
Lauder Foundation
Laurel Foundation
Lea Foundation, Helen Sperry
Leavey Foundation, Thomas and Dorothy
Lechmere
Lederer Foundation, Francis L.
Lee Foundation, Ray M. and Mary Elizabeth
Legg Mason Inc.
Lehrman Foundation, Jacob and Charlotte
Leidy Foundation, John J.
Leighton-Oare Foundation
Lemberg Foundation
Leo Burnett Co.
Leonhardt Foundation, Dorothea L.
Leuthold Foundation
Levin Foundation, Philip and Janice
Levy Foundation, June Rockwell
Liberty Diversified Industries Inc.
Liberty National Bank
Lieberman Enterprises
Life Insurance Co. of Georgia
Lightner Sams Foundation
Lilly & Co., Eli
Lincoln Electric Co.
Lincoln National Corp.
Lipton, Thomas J.
Little, Arthur D.
Little Family Foundation
Littlefield Foundation, Edmund Wattis
Litton Industries
Lockheed Sanders
Lockwood Foundation, Byron W. and Alice L.
Long Island Lighting Co.
Louisiana Land & Exploration Co.
Lounsbery Foundation, Richard
Love Foundation, George H. and Margaret McClintic
Lovett Foundation
Lowe Foundation, Joe and Emily
LTV Corp.
Lubrizol Corp.
Lupin Foundation
Lurie Foundation, Louis R.
Lydall, Inc.
Lyndhurst Foundation
Lynn Foundation, E. M.
M/A-COM, Inc.
Maas Foundation, Benard L.
MacArthur Foundation, John D. and Catherine T.
MacCurdy Salisbury Educational Foundation
Maclellan Foundation, Robert L. and Kathrina H.
Macy & Co., R.H.
Maddox Trust, Web
Madison Gas & Electric Co.
Magma Copper Co.
Magowan Family Foundation
Maier Foundation, Sarah Pauline
Mallinckrodt Specialty Chemicals Co.
Mandell Foundation, Samuel P.
Mandeville Foundation
Maneely Fund
Mankato Citizens Telephone Co.
Mann Foundation, Ted
Manoogian Foundation, Alex and Marie
Marbrook Foundation
Marcus Corp.
Maritz Inc.
Mark IV Industries
Marpat Foundation
Marquette Electronics

Marriott Foundation, J. Willard
Mars Foundation
Marsh & McLennan Cos.
Marshall Field's
Marshall & Ilsley Bank
Martin & Deborah Flug Foundation
Martin Foundation
Martin Marietta Aggregates
Martin Marietta Corp.
Marubeni America Corp.
Masco Corp.
Massey Charitable Trust
Massey Foundation
Massey Foundation, Jack C.
Mastronardi Charitable Foundation, Charles A.
Material Service Corp.
Mather and William Gwinn Mather Fund, Elizabeth Ring
Mather Fund, Richard
Matz Foundation — Edelman Division
Mautz Paint Co.
Maxon Charitable Foundation
May Department Stores Co.
Mayer Charitable Trust, Oscar G. & Elsa S.
Mayer Foundation, James and Eva
Mayerson Foundation, Manuel D. and Rhoda
Maytag Corp.
Maytag Family Foundation, Fred
MCA
McAlister Charitable Foundation, Harold
McBean Family Foundation
McCann Foundation
McCarthy Charities
McConnell Foundation
McCormick & Co.
McCormick Foundation, Chauncey and Marion Deering
McCormick Tribune Foundation, Robert R.
McCormick Trust, Anne
McCutchen Foundation
McDonald & Co. Securities
McDonald Industries, Inc., A. Y.
McDonnell Douglas Corp.
McDonnell Douglas Corp.-West
McElroy Trust, R. J.
McFawn Trust No. 2, Lois Sisler
McGraw Foundation, Curtis W.
McGraw-Hill
McGregor Foundation, Thomas and Frances
McGregor Fund
MCI Communications Corp.
McInerny Foundation
McKee Foundation, Robert E. and Evelyn
McKenna Foundation, Katherine Mabis
McKesson Corp.
McKnight Foundation
McLean Contributionship
McMahon Foundation
McNeely Foundation
McRae Foundation
McWane Inc.
MDU Resources Group, Inc.
Mead Corp.
Mead Fund, Nelson
Meadows Foundation
Medtronic
Melitta North America Inc.
Mellen Foundation
Mellon Bank Corp.
Mellon Foundation, Andrew W.
Mellon Foundation, Richard King
Memorial Foundation for Children
Memton Fund
Menasha Corp.

Menschel Foundation, Robert and Joyce
Mentor Graphics
Mercantile Bancorp
Merck & Co.
Mercy, Jr. Foundation, Sue and Eugene
Mericos Foundation
Meridian Bancorp
Merrick Foundation, Robert G. and Anne M.
Merrill Foundation, R. D.
Mertz-Gilmore Foundation, Joyce
Mervyn's
Metropolitan Life Insurance Co.
Meyer Foundation
Meyer Foundation, Baron de Hirsch
Meyer Foundation, Eugene and Agnes E.
Meyer Foundation, Robert R.
Meyer Memorial Trust
Meyerhoff Fund, Joseph
Michigan Bell Telephone Co.
Michigan Consolidated Gas Co.
Midwest Resources
Miles Inc.
Mill-Rose Co.
Miller Charitable Foundation, Howard E. and Nell E.
Miller Foundation, Steve J.
Miller Fund, Kathryn and Gilbert
Miller-Mellor Association
Mine Safety Appliances Co.
Miniger Memorial Foundation, Clement O.
Minnegasco
Minnesota Mutual Life Insurance Co.
Minolta Corp.
Misco Industries
Mitchell Family Foundation, Edward D. and Anna
MNC Financial
Mobil Oil Corp.
Monell Foundation, Ambrose
Monfort Charitable Foundation
Monsanto Co.
Montana Power Co.
Montgomery Street Foundation
Moore Foundation
Moore Foundation, Edward S.
Moores Foundation, Harry C.
Moorman Manufacturing Co.
Morgan Foundation, Burton D.
Morgan Trust for Charity, Religion, and Education
Morrill Charitable Foundation
Morris Foundation, William T.
Morrison-Knudsen Corp.
Morse Foundation, Richard P. and Claire W.
Morse, Jr. Foundation, Enid and Lester S.
Moses Fund, Henry and Lucy
Mosher Foundation, Samuel B.
Motorola
Mulford Foundation, Vincent
Mullen Foundation, J. K.
Muller Foundation
Munson Foundation, W. B.
Murdock Charitable Trust, M. J.
Murdy Foundation
Murphy Foundation
Murphy Foundation, John P.
Murphy Foundation, Katherine and John
Murray Foundation
Myra Foundation
Nakamichi Foundation, E.
Nalco Chemical Co.
Nash Foundation
National City Bank of Evansville
National City Corp.
National Computer Systems
National Fuel Gas Co.
National Gypsum Co.

Music (cont.)

National Life of Vermont
National Pro-Am Youth Fund
National Service Industries
National Steel
National Westminster Bank New
  Jersey
Nationale-Nederlanden North
  America Corp.
NationsBank Corp.
Nationwide Insurance Cos.
NBD Bank
NBD Bank, N.A.
Negaunee Foundation
Nesholm Family Foundation
Nestle U.S.A. Inc.
Neuberger Foundation, Roy R.
  and Marie S.
New England Business Service
New England Foundation
New England Mutual Life
  Insurance Co.
New Horizon Foundation
New-Land Foundation
New York Life Insurance Co.
New York Telephone Co.
New York Times Co.
The New Yorker Magazine, Inc.
Newhouse Foundation, Samuel I.
Newmont Mining Corp.
News & Observer Publishing Co.
Nichimen America, Inc.
Nichols Co., J.C.
Nichols Foundation
Noble Foundation, Edward John
Nordson Corp.
Norfolk Southern Corp.
Norgren Foundation, Carl A.
Norman Foundation, Andrew
Norris Foundation, Dellora A.
  and Lester J.
Norris Foundation, Kenneth T.
  and Eileen L.
Nortek, Inc.
North American Life & Casualty
  Co.
Northern Indiana Public Service
  Co.
Northern States Power Co.
Northern Telecom Inc.
Northern Trust Co.
Northwest Area Foundation
Northwest Natural Gas Co.
Northwestern National Insurance
  Group
Northwestern National Life
  Insurance Co.
Norton Co.
Norton Memorial Corporation,
  Geraldi
Norwest Bank Nebraska
Norwest Corp.
Noyes, Jr. Memorial Foundation,
  Nicholas H.
Oaklawn Foundation
Occidental Oil & Gas Corp.
Occidental Petroleum Corp.
O'Connor Foundation, A.
  Lindsay and Olive B.
OCRI Foundation
Odyssey Partners
Offield Family Foundation
Ogden Foundation, Ralph E.
Ogilvy & Mather Worldwide
Oglebay Norton Co.
Ohio Valley Foundation
Oklahoma Gas & Electric Co.
Old National Bank in Evansville
Olin Corp.
Olin Foundation, Spencer T. and
  Ann W.
Onan Family Foundation
1957 Charity Trust
O'Neil Foundation, Casey Albert
  T.

O'Neil Foundation, Cyril F. and
  Marie E.
Ontario Corp.
Oppenstein Brothers Foundation
Orchard Corp. of America.
Ore-Ida Foods, Inc.
Osborn Charitable Trust, Edward
  B.
O'Shaughnessy Foundation, I. A.
Oshkosh B'Gosh
Oshkosh Truck Corp.
Overseas Shipholding Group
Owsley Foundation, Alvin and
  Lucy
PACCAR
Pacific Enterprises
Pacific Gas & Electric Co.
Pacific Mutual Life Insurance Co.
Pacific Telesis Group
PacifiCorp
Packard Foundation, David and
  Lucile
Palmer Fund, Frank Loomis
Pangburn Foundation
Panhandle Eastern Corp.
Pappas Charitable Foundation,
  Bessie
Parke-Davis Group
Parker-Hannifin Corp.
Parsons Foundation, Ralph M.
Patterson-Barclay Memorial
  Foundation
Paul and C. Michael Paul
  Foundation, Josephine Bay
Peabody Charitable Fund, Amelia
Peabody Foundation, Amelia
Pearlstone Foundation, Peggy
  Meyerhoff
Pendleton Memorial Fund,
  William L. and Ruth T.
Penn Foundation, William
Pennsylvania General Insurance
  Co.
Pennzoil Co.
People's Bank
Peppers Foundation, Ann
Pepsi-Cola Bottling Co. of
  Charlotte
Perini Corp.
Perkin Fund
Perot Foundation
Perry Drug Stores
Persis Corp.
Pet
Pew Charitable Trusts
Pfister and Vogel Tanning Co.
Pfizer
Phelps Dodge Corp.
PHH Corp.
Philadelphia Electric Co.
Philadelphia Industries
Philibosian Foundation, Stephen
Philip Morris Cos.
Philips Foundation, Jesse
Phillips Family Foundation, Jay
  and Rose
Phillips Foundation, A. P.
Phillips Foundation, Dr. P.
Phillips Foundation, Ellis L.
Phillips Petroleum Co.
Pick Charitable Trust, Melitta S.
Pick, Jr. Fund, Albert
Picker International
Pickford Foundation, Mary
Pierce Charitable Trust, Harold
  Whitworth
Pillsbury Foundation
Pines Bridge Foundation
Pinewood Foundation
Piper Foundation, Minnie
  Stevens
Piper Jaffray Cos.
Pittsburgh National Bank
Pittulloch Foundation
Pittway Corp.
Plitt Southern Theatres
Plough Foundation

Plym Foundation
Poindexter Foundation
Polaroid Corp.
Polinger Foundation, Howard
  and Geraldine
Pollock Company Foundation,
  William B.
Pollybill Foundation
Poorvu Foundation, William and
  Lia
Porter Testamentary Trust, James
  Hyde
Portland General Electric Co.
Post Foundation of D.C.,
  Marjorie Merriweather
Potlatch Corp.
Potomac Electric Power Co.
Potter Foundation, Justin and
  Valere
Potts and Sibley Foundation
Pottstown Mercury
Powers Foundation
PPG Industries
Premier Bank
Premier Industrial Corp.
Preston Trust, Evelyn W.
Preyer Fund, Mary Norris
Price Associates, T. Rowe
Prickett Fund, Lynn R. and Karl
  E.
Primerica Corp.
Prince Trust, Abbie Norman
Principal Financial Group
Pritzker Foundation
Procter & Gamble Co.
Procter & Gamble Cosmetic &
  Fragrance Products
Promus Cos.
Prospect Hill Foundation
Providence Energy Corp.
Providence Journal Company
Provident Life & Accident
  Insurance Co.
Prudential-Bache Securities
Prudential Insurance Co. of
  America
Public Service Co. of Colorado
Puget Sound Power & Light Co.
Pulitzer Publishing Co.
Putnam Foundation
Quaker Hill Foundation
Quaker Oats Co.
Quantum Chemical Corp.
Questar Corp.
Rabb Charitable Foundation,
  Sidney and Esther
Rabb Charitable Trust, Sidney R.
Radin Foundation
Ralston Purina Co.
Ramlose Foundation, George A.
Ratner Foundation, Milton M.
Ratshesky Foundation, A. C.
Rauch Foundation
Ray Foundation
Raymond Educational
  Foundation
Recognition Equipment
Red Wing Shoe Co.
Reed Foundation
Regenstein Foundation
Regis Corp.
Reichhold Chemicals, Inc.
Reidler Foundation
Reilly Industries
Reinberger Foundation
Relations Foundation
Reliable Life Insurance Co.
Reliance Electric Co.
Replogle Foundation, Luther I.
Republic New York Corp.
Resnick Foundation, Jack and
  Pearl
Revlon
Reynolds Foundation, Donald W.
Reynolds Foundation, J. B.
Reynolds Foundation, Richard S.
Reynolds Metals Co.

Reynolds & Reynolds Co.
Rhone-Poulenc Inc.
Rhone-Poulenc Rorer
Rice Foundation, Ethel and
  Raymond F.
Rich Co., F.D.
Rich Products Corp.
Richardson Foundation, Sid W.
Richmond Foundation, Frederick
  W.
Rienzi Foundation
Rigler-Deutsch Foundation
Ritchie Memorial Foundation,
  Charles E. and Mabel M.
Rittenhouse Foundation
RJR Nabisco Inc.
Roberts Foundation
Roberts Foundation, Dora
Robin Family Foundation, Albert
  A.
Robinson Foundation
Robinson Fund, Charles Nelson
Robison Foundation, Ellis H. and
  Doris B.
Robson Foundation, LaNelle
Rochester Gas & Electric Corp.
Rock Foundation, Milton and
  Shirley
Rockefeller Foundation
Rockwell Foundation
Rockwell Fund
Rockwell International Corp.
Rodgers Foundation, Richard &
  Dorothy
Rodman Foundation
Rogers Charitable Trust, Florence
Rogers Family Foundation
Rogers Foundation
Rohlik Foundation, Sigmund and
  Sophie
Rohm and Haas Company
Rohr Inc.
Rolfs Foundation, Robert T.
RosaMary Foundation
Rose Foundation, Billy
Roseburg Forest Products Co.
Rosenberg Foundation, Henry
  and Ruth Blaustein
Rosenberg Foundation, William
  J. and Tina
Rosenberg, Jr. Family
  Foundation, Louise and Claude
Rosenbloom Foundation, Ben
  and Esther
Rosenstiel Foundation
Rosenthal Foundation, Ida and
  William
Rosenthal Foundation, Richard
  and Hinda
Rosenthal Foundation, Samuel
Ross Foundation, Lyn & George
  M.
Roth Family Foundation
Rothschild Foundation, Hulda B.
  and Maurice L.
Rouse Co.
Rowland Foundation
Royal Group Inc.
RTM
Rubinstein Foundation, Helena
Rudin Foundation
Rudin Foundation, Samuel and
  May
Rupp Foundation, Fran and
  Warren
Russell Charitable Trust,
  Josephine S.
Ryan Foundation, Nina M.
Ryan Foundation, Patrick G. and
  Shirley W.
Ryder System
Sachs Fund
Sage Foundation
Sailors' Snug Harbor of Boston
Saint Croix Foundation
Saint Paul Cos.
Salomon

Saltonstall Charitable
  Foundation, Richard
Samuels Foundation, Fan Fox
  and Leslie R.
San Diego Gas & Electric
Sang Foundation, Elsie O. and
  Philip D.
Santa Fe Pacific Corp.
Sara Lee Corp.
Sara Lee Hosiery
Sargent Foundation, Newell B.
Sarkeys Foundation
Saunders Charitable Foundation,
  Helen M.
Scheirich Co., H.J.
Schenck Fund, L. P.
Scherer Foundation, Karla
Schering-Plough Corp.
Scherman Foundation
Scheuer Family Foundation, S.
  H. and Helen R.
Schey Foundation
Schieffelin & Somerset Co.
Schiff Foundation
Schilling Motors
Schimmel Foundation
Schmitt Foundation, Arthur J.
Scholl Foundation, Dr.
Schrafft and Bertha E. Schrafft
  Charitable Trust, William E.
Schroeder Foundation, Walter
Schultz Foundation
Schwab & Co., Charles
Schwab Foundation, Charles and
  Helen
Schwartz Foundation, David
Schwartz Fund for Education
  and Health Research, Arnold
  and Marie
Schwob Foundation, Simon
Scott and Fetzer Co.
Scott Foundation, Virginia Steele
Scott, Jr. Charitable Foundation,
  Walter
Scrivner, Inc.
Seabury Foundation
Seafirst Corp.
Sealright Co., Inc.
Searle & Co., G.D.
Sears Family Foundation
Seaver Charitable Trust, Richard
  C.
Seay Charitable Trust, Sarah M.
  and Charles E.
Security Benefit Life Insurance
  Co.
Security Life of Denver
Security State Bank
Sedgwick James Inc.
See Foundation, Charles
Segal Charitable Trust, Barnet
Segerstrom Foundation
Seid Foundation, Barre
Semple Foundation, Louise Taft
Sentinel Communications Co.
Servco Pacific
Shaklee Corp.
Shapero Foundation, Nate S. and
  Ruth B.
Shapiro Family Foundation,
  Soretta and Henry
Shapiro Foundation, Charles and
  M. R.
Shapiro Fund, Albert
Sharon Steel Corp.
Sharp Foundation
Shawmut National Corp.
Shawmut Worcester County
  Bank, N.A.
Shaw's Supermarkets
Shea Co., John F.
Sheafer Charitable Trust, Emma
  A.
Sheaffer Inc.
Shelden Fund, Elizabeth, Allan
  and Warren
Shell Oil Co.
Shelter Mutual Insurance Co.

Shenandoah Life Insurance Co.
Sheridan Foundation, Thomas B. and Elizabeth M.
Shoney's Inc.
Shorenstein Foundation, Walter H. and Phyllis J.
Shughart, Thomson & Kilroy, P.C.
Shwayder Foundation, Fay
Sierra Pacific Industries
Signet Bank/Maryland
Simmons Family Foundation, R. P.
Simon Charitable Trust, Esther
Simon Foundation, William E. and Carol G.
Simpson Industries
Simpson Investment Co.
Sjostrom & Sons
Skaggs Foundation, L. J. and Mary C.
Skillman Foundation
Skinner Corp.
Skirball Foundation
Slant/Fin Corp.
Smith Charitable Fund, Eleanor Armstrong
Smith Charities, John
Smith Corp., A.O.
Smith Foundation, Lon V.
Smith Memorial Fund, Ethel Sergeant Clark
SmithKline Beecham
Smoot Charitable Foundation
Smucker Co., J.M.
Smyth Trust, Marion C.
SNET
Snider Foundation
Solheim Foundation
Somers Foundation, Byron H.
Sonat
Sonoco Products Co.
Sordoni Foundation
Sosland Foundation
South Branch Foundation
Southern California Edison Co.
Southways Foundation
Southwestern Bell Corp.
Spiegel Family Foundation, Jerry and Emily
Sprague Educational and Charitable Foundation, Seth
SPS Technologies
SPX Corp.
Square D Co.
Stabler Foundation, Donald B. and Dorothy L.
Standard Chartered Bank New York
Stanley Charitable Foundation, A. W.
Stanley Works
Star Bank, N.A.
Stare Fund
Starling Foundation, Dorothy Richard
Starr Foundation
State Street Bank & Trust Co.
Stauffer Foundation, John and Beverly
Steel, Sr. Foundation, Marshall
Steelcase
Steele Foundation
Steele Foundation, Harry and Grace
Steigerwaldt Foundation, Donna Wolf
Stein Foundation, Jules and Doris
Steinberg Family Foundation, Meyer and Jean
Steiner Corp.
Steinman Foundation, James Hale
Stemmons Foundation
Sterkel Trust, Justine
Sterling Inc.
Sterling Winthrop

Stern Foundation for the Arts, Richard J.
Sterne-Elder Memorial Trust
Stevens Foundation, Abbot and Dorothy H.
Stevens Foundation, Nathaniel and Elizabeth P.
Stewart Educational Foundation, Donnell B. and Elizabeth Dee Shaw
Stocker Foundation
Stoddard Charitable Trust
Stokely, Jr. Foundation, William B.
Stone Charitable Foundation
Stone Container Corp.
Stone Foundation, France
Stone Trust, H. Chase
Stoneman Charitable Foundation, Anne and David
Strake Foundation
Stranahan Foundation
Straus Foundation, Aaron and Lillie
Strauss Foundation
Strawbridge Foundation of Pennsylvania II, Margaret Dorrance
Stride Rite Corp.
Stroud Foundation
Stuart Center Charitable Trust, Hugh
Stubblefield, Estate of Joseph L.
Stulsaft Foundation, Morris
Sturgis Charitable and Educational Trust, Roy and Christine
Subaru-Isuzu Automotive Inc.
Subaru of America Inc.
Sulzberger Foundation
Sumitomo Bank of California
Sumitomo Corp. of America
Summerfield Foundation, Solon E.
Sun Co.
Superior Tube Co.
Surdna Foundation
Swig Foundation
Swiss Bank Corp.
Tait Foundation, Frank M.
Talley Industries, Inc.
Tamarkin Co.
Tamko Asphalt Products
Tandy Foundation, Anne Burnett and Charles
Tandy Foundation, David L.
Target Stores
Tasty Baking Co.
Taub Foundation
TCF Banking & Savings, FSB
Teichert
Tektronix
Teledyne
Teleflex Inc.
Templeton Foundation, Herbert A.
Tennant Co.
Tenneco
Tetley, Inc.
Texaco
Texas Commerce Bank Houston, N.A.
Texas Gas Transmission Corp.
Texas Instruments
Textron
Thalheimer Foundation, Alvin and Fanny Blaustein
Thalhimer and Family Foundation, Charles G.
Thalhimer Brothers Inc.
Thalhimer, Jr. and Family Foundation, William B.
Thanksgiving Foundation
Thatcher Foundation
Thirty-Five Twenty, Inc.
Thompson Charitable Foundation
3M Co.
Time Insurance Co.

Times Mirror Co.
Tisch Foundation
Tiscornia Foundation
Titus Foundation, C. W.
Tobin Foundation
Todd Co., A.M.
Tomkins Industries, Inc.
Torchmark Corp.
Towsley Foundation, Harry A. and Margaret D.
Tozer Foundation
Transamerica Corp.
Transco Energy Company
Travelers Cos.
Travelli Fund, Charles Irwin
Treakle Foundation, J. Edwin
Trexler Trust, Harry C.
TRINOVA Corp.
True Oil Co.
Trull Foundation
Truman Foundation, Mildred Faulkner
Trust Co. Bank
Trust for Mutual Understanding
TRW Corp.
Tuch Foundation, Michael
Tucker Charitable Trust, Rose E.
Tupancy-Harris Foundation of 1986
Turner Charitable Trust, Courtney S.
Turrell Fund
Unger Foundation, Aber D.
Unilever United States
Union Bank
Union Bank of Switzerland New York Branch
Union Camp Corp.
Union Electric Co.
Union Pacific Corp.
Unisys Corp.
United Airlines
United Conveyor Corp.
U.S. Leasing International
United States Trust Co. of New York
United Technologies Corp.
Universal Foods Corp.
Universal Leaf Tobacco Co.
Unocal Corp.
UNUM Corp.
Upjohn California Fund
Upjohn Co.
Upjohn Foundation, Harold and Grace
Upton Charitable Foundation, Lucy and Eleanor S.
Upton Foundation, Frederick S.
Uris Brothers Foundation
US Bancorp
US WEST
USX Corp.
Valmont Industries
Valspar Corp.
Van Nuys Charities, J. B. and Emily
Van Wert County Foundation
Vance Charitable Foundation, Robert C.
Vaughn Foundation
Vernon Fund, Miles Hodsdon
Vesuvius Charitable Foundation
Vevay-Switzerland County Foundation
Vidda Foundation
Vingo Trust II
Virginia Power Co.
Vlasic Foundation
Vulcan Materials Co.
W. W. W. Foundation
Waggoner Charitable Trust, Crystelle
Wal-Mart Stores
Waldbaum, Inc.
Walker Foundation, T. B.
Wallace Reader's Digest Fund, Lila

Walsh Foundation
Disney Co., Walt
Ward Foundation, A. Montgomery
Ward Foundation, Louis L. and Adelaide C.
Warner Electric Brake & Clutch Co.
Warner Foundation, Lee and Rose
Warwick Foundation
Washington Post Co.
Washington Trust Bank
Washington Water Power Co.
Wasmer Foundation
Waste Management
Waters Charitable Trust, Robert S.
Watson Foundation, Walter E. and Caroline H.
Wean Foundation, Raymond John
Webb Charitable Trust, Susan Mott
Webster Charitable Foundation
Webster Foundation, Edwin S.
Wege Foundation
Weiler Foundation, Theodore & Renee
Weisbrod Foundation Trust Dept., Robert and Mary
Weiss Foundation, William E.
Weisz Foundation, David and Sylvia
Wells Foundation, Franklin H. and Ruth L.
Werthan Foundation
West One Bancorp
West Texas Corp., J. M.
Westinghouse Electric Corp.
WestLB New York Branch
Weston Associates/R.C.M. Corp.
Wetterau
Weyerhaeuser Co.
Weyerhaeuser Foundation, Frederick and Margaret L.
Weyerhaeuser Memorial Foundation, Charles A.
Wheeler Foundation
Wheeler Foundation, Wilmot
Wheless Foundation
Whirlpool Corp.
Whitaker Charitable Foundation, Lyndon C.
Whitaker Foundation
Whitaker Fund, Helen F.
White Consolidated Industries
Whiteman Foundation, Edna Rider
Whiting Foundation
Whiting Foundation, Macauley and Helen Dow
Whitman Corp.
Whitney Fund, David M.
Whittenberger Foundation, Claude R. and Ethel B.
Wickes Foundation, Harvey Randall
Wickson-Link Memorial Foundation
WICOR, Inc.
Wiegand Foundation, E. L.
Wien Foundation, Lawrence A.
Wilbur Foundation, Marguerite Eyer
Wilkof Foundation, Edward and Ruth
Willard Helping Fund, Cecilia Young
Williams Cos.
Williams Foundation, Arthur Ashley
Willmott Foundation, Peter S.
Wilmington Trust Co.
Wilson Foundation, Elaine P. and Richard U.
Winchester Foundation
Winston Foundation, Norman and Rosita

Winter Construction Co.
Winthrop Trust, Clara B.
Wisconsin Energy Corp.
Wisconsin Power & Light Co.
Wisdom Foundation, Mary F.
Witco Corp.
Wodecroft Foundation
Wolff Shoe Co.
Wollenberg Foundation
Wolverine World Wide, Inc.
Wood-Claeyssens Foundation
Wood Foundation, Lester G.
Woods Charitable Fund
Woods-Greer Foundation
Woolf Foundation, William C.
Woolley Foundation, Vasser
Wortham Foundation
Wright Foundation, Lola
Wurlitzer Foundation, Farny R.
Wurzburg, Inc.
Wyne Foundation
Wyomissing Foundation
Xerox Corp.
Xtra Corp.
Yeager Charitable Trust, Lester E.
Yellow Corp.
Young Foundation, H and B
Young Foundation, Hugo H. and Mabel B.
Young Foundation, Robert R.
Young & Rubicam
Younkers, Inc.
Zachry Co., H. B.
Zamoiski Co.
Zellerbach Family Fund
Ziegler Foundation, Ruth/Allen
Zimmerman Family Foundation, Raymond

Opera

Abeles Foundation, Joseph and Sophia
Abell Foundation, The
Abrams Foundation, Benjamin and Elizabeth
Abrons Foundation, Louis and Anne
Achelis Foundation
Adams Foundation, Arthur F. and Alice E.
Air Products & Chemicals
Albertson's
Alcon Laboratories, Inc.
Allegheny Ludlum Corp.
Allen Foundation, Rita
AlliedSignal
Alltel/Western Region
Alltel/Western Region
ALPAC Corp.
Alumax
Aluminum Co. of America
American Brands
American Electric Power
American Express Co.
American Home Products Corp.
American National Bank & Trust Co. of Chicago
American Natural Resources Co.
American Saw & Manufacturing Co.
American Telephone & Telegraph Co.
American United Life Insurance Co.
Ameritech Corp.
Ameritech Services
Amfac/JMB Hawaii
Amoco Corp.
Andersen Foundation
Anderson Foundation, M. D.
Andersons Management Corp.
Angelica Corp.
Annenberg Foundation
AON Corp.
Archbold Charitable Trust, Adrian and Jessie

Opera (cont.)

Archer-Daniels-Midland Co.
Archibald Charitable Foundation, Norman
Arizona Public Service Co.
Arkansas Power & Light Co.
Armco Inc.
Ashland Oil
Atherton Family Foundation
Atlanta Gas Light Co.
Attleboro Pawtucket Savings Bank
Avon Products
Badgeley Residuary Charitable Trust, Rose M.
Baier Foundation, Marie
Baker Foundation, Dexter F. and Dorothy H.
Baker, Jr. Memorial Fund, William G.
Baker Trust, Clayton
Bank of America Arizona
Bank of New York
Bank of San Francisco Co.
Bankers Trust Co.
Barry Corp., R. G.
Bass Foundation
Battelle
Bauer Foundation, M. R.
Bauervic Foundation, Peggy
Baxter International
Bechtel, Jr. Foundation, S. D.
Beckman Foundation, Leland D.
Bedminster Fund
Beir Foundation
Belz Foundation
Bemis Company
Benedum Foundation, Claude Worthington
Beneficia Foundation
Benua Foundation
Benwood Foundation
Bergen Foundation, Frank and Lydia
Berlin Charitable Fund, Irving
Bernsen Foundation, Grace and Franklin
Bernstein & Co., Sanford C.
BFGoodrich
Biddle Foundation, Mary Duke
Binney & Smith Inc.
Blade Communications
Blair and Co., William
Block, H&R
Blount
Blue Cross & Blue Shield of Kentucky Foundation
Bluhdorn Charitable Trust, Charles G. and Yvette
Blum Foundation, Edith C.
Blum-Kovler Foundation
Bobst Foundation, Elmer and Mamdouha
Bodman Foundation
Boehringer Mannheim Corp.
Boeing Co.
Boettcher Foundation
Bohen Foundation
Boise Cascade Corp.
Boler Co.
Bonfils-Stanton Foundation
Booz Allen & Hamilton
Borden
Borwell Charitable Foundation
Botwinick-Wolfensohn Foundation
Bowater Inc.
BP America
Bradley Foundation, Lynde and Harry
Bradley-Turner Foundation
Bravmann Foundation, Ludwig
Breyer Foundation
Broadhurst Foundation
Brochsteins Inc.
Brown Foundation

Brundage Charitable, Scientific, and Wildlife Conservation Foundation, Charles E. and Edna T.
Buchanan Family Foundation
Buck Foundation, Carol Franc
Bucyrus-Erie
Buhl Foundation
Burdines
Burgess Trust, Ralph L. and Florence R.
Burlington Northern Inc.
Burnham Foundation
Burns Foundation, Jacob
Bush Foundation
Butler Family Foundation, Patrick and Aimee
Cabot Corp.
Cafritz Foundation, Morris and Gwendolyn
Caine Charitable Foundation, Marie Eccles
Campbell Foundation
Capital Holding Corp.
Cargill
Carolina Power & Light Co.
Carpenter Foundation
Carpenter Foundation, E. Rhodes and Leona B.
Carrier Corp.
Carter-Wallace
Casey Foundation, Eugene B.
CBI Industries
Centel Corp.
Centerior Energy Corp.
Central Life Assurance Co.
Central Maine Power Co.
Central Soya Co.
Chambers Development Co.
Chapman Charitable Trust, H. A. and Mary K.
Chartwell Foundation
Chase Manhattan Bank, N.A.
Cheatham Foundation, Owen
Chemical Bank
Cheney Foundation, Ben B.
Chernow Trust for the Benefit of Charity Dated 3/13/75, Michael
Chevron Corp.
Chicago Board of Trade
Chicago Sun-Times, Inc.
Chiles Foundation
Chrysler Corp.
Ciba-Geigy Corp. (Pharmaceuticals Division)
Cincinnati Bell
Citicorp
Clark Foundation
Clark Foundation, Robert Sterling
Clark-Winchcole Foundation
Cleveland-Cliffs
Clorox Co.
Clowes Fund
CNA Insurance Cos.
Colburn Fund
Cole Foundation, Robert H. and Monica H.
Collins Foundation
Colonial Life & Accident Insurance Co.
Columbia Foundation
Columbus Dispatch Printing Co.
Comerica
Commerce Clearing House
Commonwealth Edison Co.
ConAgra
Consolidated Natural Gas Co.
Consumers Power Co.
Cooke Foundation
Cooper Industries
Coors Brewing Co.
Copley Press
Corestates Bank
Cosmair, Inc.
Country Curtains, Inc.
Cowles Charitable Trust

Cowles Foundation, Gardner and Florence Call
Cowles Media Co.
Crane Foundation, Raymond E. and Ellen F.
Cranshaw Corporation
Crawford & Co.
Crestar Financial Corp.
Crown Books Foundation, Inc.
Crown Memorial, Arie and Ida
Crum and Forster
Cullen Foundation
Culpeper Foundation, Charles E.
Culver Foundation, Constans
Dain Bosworth/Inter-Regional Financial Group
Dana Charitable Trust, Eleanor Naylor
Daniel Foundation, Gerard and Ruth
Dart Group Corp.
Davis Foundation, Edwin W. and Catherine M.
Davis Foundation, Simon and Annie
Day Foundation, Nancy Sayles
Dayton Hudson Corp.
Dayton Power and Light Co.
Dean Witter Discover
Dee Foundation, Annie Taylor
Delany Charitable Trust, Beatrice P.
Delaware North Cos.
Deluxe Corp.
Demoulas Supermarkets
Dentsu, Inc., NY
Deposit Guaranty National Bank
DeRoy Testamentary Foundation
Detroit Edison Co.
Dewar Foundation
Dewing Foundation, Frances R.
Dexter Corp.
Dial Corp.
Diamond Foundation, Aaron
Dillon Foundation
Dimeo Construction Co.
Dimick Foundation
Dobson Foundation
Dodge Foundation, Geraldine R.
Donaldson Co.
Douglas & Lomason Company
Dresser Industries
Dreyfus Foundation, Jean and Louis
Dreyfus Foundation, Max and Victoria
Driscoll Foundation
du Pont de Nemours & Co., E. I.
Duchossois Industries
Duke Power Co.
Dula Educational and Charitable Foundation, Caleb C. and Julia W.
Dynamet, Inc.
Dyson Foundation
Early Foundation
Eaton Corp.
Eaton Foundation, Cyrus
Eccles Foundation, George S. and Dolores Dore
Eccles Foundation, Marriner S.
Eckman Charitable Foundation, Samuel and Rae
Edgewater Steel Corp.
Edmonds Foundation, Dean S.
El Pomar Foundation
Elf Atochem North America
Emerson Electric Co.
Emery Memorial, Thomas J.
Encyclopaedia Britannica, Inc.
Engelhard Foundation, Charles
Enron Corp.
Equitable Life Assurance Society of the U.S.
Ernest & Julio Gallo Winery
Ethyl Corp.
Evans Foundation, T. M.

Exxon Corp.
Fairchild Corp.
Fales Foundation Trust
Farley Industries
Farwell Foundation, Drusilla
Federal-Mogul Corp.
Federal National Mortgage Assn., Fannie Mae
Federated Department Stores and Allied Stores Corp.
Feild Co-Operative Association
Feinberg Foundation, Joseph and Bessie
Fels Fund, Samuel S.
Fidelity Bank
Fifth Avenue Foundation
FINA, Inc.
Fireman's Fund Insurance Co.
First Bank System
First Boston
First Chicago
First Interstate Bank of Arizona
First Interstate Bank of California
First Interstate Bank of Oregon
First Maryland Bancorp
First Tennessee Bank
First Union Corp.
Firstar Bank Milwaukee NA
Fischbach Foundation
Fishback Foundation Trust, Harmes C.
Fisher Foundation, Gramma
Fleming Foundation
Flinn Foundation
Florida Power & Light Co.
Fluor Corp.
FMC Corp.
Fohs Foundation
Folger Fund
Forbes
Ford Fund, Benson and Edith
Ford Fund, Walter and Josephine
Ford Meter Box Co.
Ford Motor Co.
Forest Foundation
Forest Oil Corp.
Foster Co., L.B.
Foster Foundation
Foster Foundation, Joseph C. and Esther
Foundation for the Needs of Others
Fox Foundation, John H.
Francis Families Foundation
Frank Foundation, Ernest and Elfriede
Frank Fund, Zollie and Elaine
Frankel Foundation
Frear Eleemosynary Trust, Mary D. and Walter F.
Freeman Charitable Trust, Samuel
Freeman Foundation, Carl M.
Freeport-McMoRan
Frohlich Charitable Trust, Ludwig W.
Fry Foundation, Lloyd A.
Fuller Co., H.B.
Funderburke & Associates
Galvin Foundation, Robert W.
Gannett Publishing Co., Guy
Garvey Memorial Foundation, Edward Chase
Gates Foundation
GATX Corp.
GEICO Corp.
Gelman Foundation, Melvin and Estelle
General American Life Insurance Co.
General Electric Co.
General Mills
General Motors Corp.
General Reinsurance Corp.
Georgia-Pacific Corp.
Gerlach Foundation
Gerson Trust, B. Milfred

Getty Foundation, Ann and Gordon
Getz Foundation, Emma and Oscar
Giant Eagle
Giant Food
Giger Foundation, Paul and Oscar
Gilder Foundation
Gilman Foundation, Howard
Gilmore Foundation, William G.
Glenmore Distilleries Co.
Glickenhaus & Co.
Gluck Foundation, Maxwell H.
Goldman Foundation, Morris and Rose
Goldman Fund, Richard and Rhoda
Goldsmith Foundation
Goodstein Foundation
Grainger Foundation
Graphic Controls Corp.
Grassmann Trust, E. J.
Graybar Electric Co.
Greater Lansing Foundation
Green Fund
Greenwall Foundation
Gregg-Graniteville Foundation
Griggs and Mary Griggs Burke Foundation, Mary Livingston
Gruss Charitable Foundation, Emanuel and Riane
Guardian Life Insurance Co. of America
H. B. B. Foundation
Haas Foundation, Paul and Mary
Haas Fund, Walter and Elise
Haas, Jr. Fund, Evelyn and Walter
Hale Foundation, Crescent Porter
Hallmark Cards
Halsell Foundation, Ewing
Handleman Co.
Harkness Foundation, William Hale
Harmon Foundation, Pearl M. and Julia J.
Harrison Foundation Trust, Francena T.
Harsco Corp.
Hartmarx Corp.
Hawkins Foundation, Robert Z.
Hawn Foundation
Hearst Foundation
Hearst Foundation, William Randolph
Hechinger Co.
Heckscher Foundation for Children
Heinz Co., H.J.
Heinz Endowment, Howard
Heinz Endowment, Vira I.
Helfaer Foundation, Evan and Marion
Heller Foundation, Walter E.
Helmerich Foundation
Herman Foundation, John and Rose
Hewlett Foundation, William and Flora
Heyward Memorial Fund, DuBose and Dorothy
Hill Foundation
Hills Fund, Edward E.
Hillsdale Fund
Himmelfarb Foundation, Paul and Annetta
Hitchcock Foundation, Gilbert M. and Martha H.
Hobby Foundation
Hogan Foundation, Royal Barney
Holzer Memorial Foundation, Richard H.
Homeland Foundation
Honeywell
Hooker Charitable Trust, Janet A.
Hoover Foundation
Hopwood Charitable Trust, John M.

Horowitz Foundation, Gedale B.
and Barbara S.
Hospital Corp. of America
Household International
Houston Endowment
Howell Foundation, Eric and
Jessie
Hoyt Foundation, Stewart W. and
Willma C.
Hubbard Broadcasting
Hudson-Webber Foundation
Huffy Corp.
Hulings Foundation, Mary
Andersen
Hulme Charitable Foundation,
Milton G.
Hume Foundation, Jaquelin
Humphreys Foundation
Hunt Foundation
Hunt Foundation, Samuel P.
Hunt Manufacturing Co.
IBM Corp.
Icahn Foundation, Carl C.
ICI Americas
IES Industries
Illges Memorial Foundation, A.
and M. L.
Illinois Bell
Illinois Tool Works
IMCERA Group Inc.
IMT Insurance Co.
Indiana Bell Telephone Co.
Interco
International Flavors &
Fragrances
International Paper Co.
Iowa State Bank
Ireland Foundation
Irvine Foundation, James
Irwin Charity Foundation,
William G.
ITT Corp.
ITT Hartford Insurance Group
J C S Foundation
J.P. Morgan & Co.
Jackson Foundation
Jaffe Foundation
JCPenney Co.
Jennings Foundation, Martha
Holden
Jerome Foundation
John Hancock Mutual Life
Insurance Co.
Johnson Controls
Johnson Endeavor Foundation,
Christian A.
Johnson Foundation, Helen K.
and Arthur E.
Johnson Foundation, Willard T.
C.
Johnson & Higgins
Jones and Bessie D. Phelps
Foundation, Cyrus W. and
Amy F.
Jones Construction Co., J.A.
Joselow Foundation
Jostens
JSJ Corp.
Kaplan Foundation, Rita J. and
Stanley H.
Kauffman Foundation, Muriel
McBrien
Kearney Inc., A.T.
Keating Family Foundation
Kelly Foundation, T. Lloyd
Kelly, Jr. Memorial Foundation,
Ensign C. Markland
Kemper Educational and
Charitable Fund
Kemper Foundation, Enid and
Crosby
Kemper National Insurance Cos.
Kennecott Corp.
Kennedy Family Foundation,
Ethel and W. George
Kern Foundation, Ilma
Kiewit Foundation, Peter
Kiewit Sons, Peter

Kimberly-Clark Corp.
Kimmelman Foundation, Helen
& Milton
Kingsbury Corp.
Kingsley Foundation
Kingsley Foundation, Lewis A.
Kirkland & Ellis
Klau Foundation, David W. and
Sadie
Kline Foundation, Josiah W. and
Bessie H.
Klipstein Foundation, Ernest
Christian
Kmart Corp.
Knight Foundation, John S. and
James L.
Knowles Foundation
Knox, Sr., and Pearl Wallis Knox
Charitable Foundation, Robert
W.
Koch Industries
Kohn-Joseloff Fund
Koret Foundation
Kreielsheimer Foundation Trust
Kulas Foundation
Kuyper Foundation, Peter H. and
E. Lucille Gaass
L and L Foundation
Laclede Gas Co.
Landmark Communications
Lang Foundation, Eugene M.
Langendorf Foundation, Stanley
S.
Lard Trust, Mary Potishman
Lastfogel Foundation, Abe and
Frances
Lechmere
Lehrman Foundation, Jacob and
Charlotte
Leidy Foundation, John J.
Leo Burnett Co.
Leonhardt Foundation, Dorothea
L.
Lewis Foundation, Lillian Kaiser
Lilly & Co., Eli
Lincoln Electric Co.
Lincolnshire
Lippitt Foundation, Katherine
Kenyon
Litwin Foundation
Loewenberg Foundation
Long Island Lighting Co.
Louisiana Land & Exploration
Co.
Louisiana-Pacific Corp.
Lowe Foundation, Joe and Emily
Lubrizol Corp.
Lurcy Charitable and
Educational Trust, Georges
Lurie Foundation, Louis R.
Lydall, Inc.
MacArthur Foundation, John D.
and Catherine T.
Macy & Co., R.H.
Magruder Foundation, Chesley
G.
Mallinckrodt Specialty
Chemicals Co.
Mandell Foundation, Samuel P.
Maneely Fund
Maritz Inc.
Marley Co.
Marquette Electronics
Mars Foundation
Marsh & McLennan Cos.
Marshall Field's
Martin Family Fund
Martin Marietta Corp.
Mary Kay Foundation
Massey Charitable Trust
Massey Foundation
Mastronardi Charitable
Foundation, Charles A.
Mather Fund, Richard
Mathis-Pfohl Foundation
Matthews International Corp.
Mayer Charitable Trust, Oscar
G. & Elsa S.

Maytag Corp.
Maytag Family Foundation, Fred
McBean Family Foundation
McCaw Foundation
McCormick Tribune Foundation,
Robert R.
McDonald & Co. Securities
McDonnell Douglas Corp.
McDonnell Douglas Corp.-West
McDougall Charitable Trust,
Ruth Camp
McGraw Foundation, Donald C.
McGraw-Hill
McGregor Fund
McKesson Corp.
McMurray-Bennnett Foundation
Mead Corp.
Meadows Foundation
Mechanic Foundation, Morris A.
Medtronic
Mellon Bank Corp.
Mellon Foundation, Andrew W.
Mentor Graphics
Mervyn's
Metropolitan Life Insurance Co.
Meyer Memorial Trust
Michigan Bell Telephone Co.
Michigan Consolidated Gas Co.
Middendorf Foundation
Miles Inc.
Miller Charitable Foundation,
Howard E. and Nell E.
Miller Foundation, Steve J.
Miller Fund, Kathryn and Gilbert
Milstein Family Foundation
Mine Safety Appliances Co.
Miniger Memorial Foundation,
Clement O.
Minnegasco
Minnesota Mutual Life
Insurance Co.
Minster Machine Co.
Mitchell Energy & Development
Corp.
Mitchell Family Foundation,
Bernard and Marjorie
MNC Financial
Mnuchin Foundation
Mobil Oil Corp.
Monell Foundation, Ambrose
Monsanto Co.
Montgomery Street Foundation
Moody Foundation
Moore Foundation, Edward S.
Moores Foundation, Harry C.
Morris Foundation, Margaret T.
Morris Foundation, William T.
Morse, Jr. Foundation, Enid and
Lester S.
Morton International
Moses Fund, Henry and Lucy
Moss Foundation, Harry S.
Motorola
MTS Systems Corp.
Mulcahy Foundation
Mulford Foundation, Vincent
Murdy Foundation
Murphy Foundation, John P.
Nakamichi Foundation, E.
Nalco Chemical Co.
National City Corp.
National Computer Systems
National Gypsum Co.
National Life of Vermont
National Starch & Chemical
Corp.
Nationwide Insurance Cos.
NBD Bank
NBD Bank, N.A.
Nesholm Family Foundation
New England Mutual Life
Insurance Co.
New York Telephone Co.
New York Times Co.
The New Yorker Magazine, Inc.
Newhouse Foundation, Samuel I.
Nord Family Foundation

Nordson Corp.
Norfolk Shipbuilding & Drydock
Corp.
Norfolk Southern Corp.
Norman/Nethercutt Foundation,
Merle
Norris Foundation, Dellora A.
and Lester J.
North Shore Foundation
Northern Star Foundation
Northern States Power Co.
Northern Telecom Inc.
Northern Trust Co.
Northwest Area Foundation
Northwest Natural Gas Co.
Norton Co.
Norwest Corp.
Noyes, Jr. Memorial Foundation,
Nicholas H.
Oaklawn Foundation
O'Brien Foundation, Cornelius
and Anna Cook
O'Donnell Foundation
Ogden Foundation, Ralph E.
Oglebay Norton Co.
Ohio Bell Telephone Co.
Olin Corp.
Orchard Corp. of America
Osher Foundation, Bernard
Oshkosh B'Gosh
Overbrook Foundation
Owsley Foundation, Alvin and
Lucy
PACCAR
Pacific Gas & Electric Co.
Pacific Mutual Life Insurance Co.
Pacific Telesis Group
PacifiCorp
Packard Foundation, David and
Lucile
Pangburn Foundation
Panhandle Eastern Corp.
Paramount Communications Inc.
Parker Foundation
Parker-Hannifin Corp.
Peabody Charitable Fund, Amelia
Peabody Foundation, Amelia
Pearce Foundation, Dr. M. Lee
Penn Foundation, William
Pennzoil Co.
Peoples Energy Corp.
Perot Foundation
Petersen Foundation, Esper A.
Pew Charitable Trusts
Pfizer
Pforzheimer Foundation, Carl
and Lily
Phelps Dodge Corp.
PHH Corp.
Philadelphia Electric Co.
Phillipps Foundation
Phillips Petroleum Co.
Piankova Foundation, Tatiana
Pick, Jr. Fund, Albert
Pines Bridge Foundation
Pinewood Foundation
Pioneer Hi-Bred International
Pitt-Des Moines Inc.
Pittsburgh National Bank
Pittway Corp.
Polaroid Corp.
Porsche Cars North America, Inc.
Portland General Electric Co.
Post Foundation of D.C.,
Marjorie Merriweather
Potlatch Corp.
Potomac Electric Power Co.
Pott Foundation, Herman T. and
Phenie R.
PPG Industries
Prairie Foundation
Premier Bank
Premier Industrial Corp.
Prentis Family Foundation,
Meyer and Anna
Price Associates, T. Rowe

Primerica Corp.
Principal Financial Group
Pritzker Foundation
Procter & Gamble Co.
Procter & Gamble Cosmetic &
Fragrance Products
Promus Cos.
Providence Energy Corp.
Provident Life & Accident
Insurance Co.
Prudential Insurance Co. of
America
Public Service Co. of Colorado
Pulitzer Publishing Co.
Pyramid Foundation
Quaker Oats Co.
Questar Corp.
Rabb Foundation, Harry W.
Radin Foundation
Recognition Equipment
Regenstein Foundation
Reinberger Foundation
Reliable Life Insurance Co.
Republic New York Corp.
Reynolds Foundation, J. B.
Reynolds Foundation, Richard S.
Reynolds & Reynolds Co.
Rich Co., F.D.
Rich Foundation
Richardson Charitable Trust,
Anne S.
Richardson Foundation, Frank E.
and Nancy M.
Rigler-Deutsch Foundation
Roberts Foundation
Rockwell Foundation
Rockwell Fund
Rockwell International Corp.
Rohatyn Foundation, Felix and
Elizabeth
Rohm and Haas Company
Rose Foundation, Billy
Rosenstiel Foundation
Ross Laboratories
Royal Group Inc.
Ryan Foundation, Patrick G. and
Shirley W.
Ryder System
SAFECO Corp.
Saint Croix Foundation
Salomon
Samuels Foundation, Fan Fox
and Leslie R.
San Diego Gas & Electric
Santa Fe Pacific Corp.
Sara Lee Corp.
Scheirich Co., H.J.
Scherman Foundation
Scheuer Family Foundation, S.
H. and Helen R.
Schey Foundation
Schieffelin Residuary Trust,
Sarah I.
Schiro Fund
Scholl Foundation, Dr.
Schwab & Co., Charles
Schwartz Foundation, David
Schwartz Fund for Education
and Health Research, Arnold
and Marie
Scott, Jr. Charitable Foundation,
Walter
Scurlock Foundation
Seabury Foundation
Seafirst Corp.
Searle & Co., G.D.
Seaver Charitable Trust, Richard
C.
Seaway Food Town
Security Life of Denver
Sedgwick James Inc.
Segerstrom Foundation
Seid Foundation, Barre
Semple Foundation, Louise Taft
Setzer Foundation
Shaklee Corp.

Opera (cont.)

Shapiro Family Foundation, Soretta and Henry
Sharon Steel Corp.
Sharp Foundation
Sharp Foundation, Evelyn
Shawmut National Corp.
Sheafer Charitable Trust, Emma A.
Shell Oil Co.
Shenandoah Life Insurance Co.
Sherwin-Williams Co.
Shoney's Inc.
Shorenstein Foundation, Walter H. and Phyllis J.
Sierra Pacific Resources
Signet Bank/Maryland
Silver Spring Foundation
Simmons Family Foundation, R. P.
Simpson Investment Co.
Siragusa Foundation
Skaggs Foundation, L. J. and Mary C.
Skillman Foundation
Skinner Corp.
Slant/Fin Corp.
Slaughter, Jr. Foundation, William E.
Smith Foundation, Kelvin and Eleanor
SNC Manufacturing Co.
Snite Foundation, Fred B.
Sonat
Sonoco Products Co.
Sooner Pipe & Supply Corp.
Sosland Foundation
Southern California Edison Co.
Southwestern Bell Corp.
Spiegel Family Foundation, Jerry and Emily
Spingold Foundation, Nate B. and Frances
Sprague Educational and Charitable Foundation, Seth
Square D Co.
Stanley Works
Starr Foundation
State Street Bank & Trust Co.
Steel, Sr. Foundation, Marshall
Steelcase
Steele Foundation, Harry and Grace
Steigerwaldt Foundation, Donna Wolf
Stein Foundation, Jules and Doris
Steinman Foundation, James Hale
Steinman Foundation, John Frederick
Stemmons Foundation
Stern Family Foundation, Alex
Stern Foundation for the Arts, Richard J.
Sterne-Elder Memorial Trust
Stevens Foundation, Abbot and Dorothy H.
Stieren Foundation, Arthur T. and Jane J.
Stone Container Corp.
Stone Family Foundation, Jerome H.
Stone Foundation, France
Stone Trust, H. Chase
Storz Foundation, Robert Herman
Stowe, Jr. Foundation, Robert Lee
Stranahan Foundation
Straus Foundation, Aaron and Lillie
Strauss Foundation
Stride Rite Corp.
Stuart Foundation
Stulsaft Foundation, Morris
Sullivan Musical Foundation, William Matheus

Sulzberger Foundation
Sunderland Foundation, Lester T.
Swig Charity Foundation, Mae and Benjamin
Swig Foundation
Syntex Corp.
Tait Foundation, Frank M.
Target Stores
Taub Foundation, Henry and Marilyn
Taylor Foundation, Ruth and Vernon
TCF Banking & Savings, FSB
Teledyne
Teleflex Inc.
Templeton Foundation, Herbert A.
Tennant Co.
Tenneco
Texaco
Texas Commerce Bank Houston, N.A.
Textron
Thoresen Foundation
Thornton Foundation, Flora L.
Thornton Foundation, John M. and Sally B.
3M Co.
Times Mirror Co.
Tobin Foundation
Toms Foundation
Torchmark Corp.
Toyota Motor Sales, U.S.A.
Tozer Foundation
Tracor, Inc.
Transamerica Corp.
Transco Energy Company
Tranzonic Cos.
Treuhaft Foundation
Trexler Trust, Harry C.
True North Foundation
Trull Foundation
Trust Co. Bank
Trust for Mutual Understanding
TRW Corp.
Tuch Foundation, Michael
Tucker Charitable Trust, Rose E.
Turner Charitable Foundation
Ukrop's Super Markets, Inc.
Union Bank
Union Pacific Corp.
United Airlines
U.S. Leasing International
United States Trust Co. of New York
United Technologies Corp.
Universal Foods Corp.
Unocal Corp.
Uris Brothers Foundation
US Bancorp
US WEST
USG Corp.
USX Corp.
Valentine Foundation, Lawson
Valley Foundation
Valspar Corp.
Van Andel Foundation, Jay and Betty
Vermeer Manufacturing Co.
Vidda Foundation
Virginia Power Co.
Vulcan Materials Co.
Wachovia Bank & Trust Co., N.A.
Waggoner Charitable Trust, Crystelle
Walgreen Co.
Wallace Reader's Digest Fund, Lila
Wallach Foundation, Miriam G. and Ira D.
Walsh Foundation
Walter Family Trust, Byron L.
Warren Charite
Washington Post Co.
Waste Management
Wean Foundation, Raymond John

Weaver Foundation
Weiler Foundation, Theodore & Renee
Weiner Foundation
Weisbrod Foundation Trust Dept., Robert and Mary
Weiss Foundation, Stephen and Suzanne
Wendt Foundation, Margaret L.
Werblow Charitable Trust, Nina W.
Wessinger Foundation
West One Bancorp
West Texas Corp., J. M.
Westerman Foundation, Samuel L.
Westinghouse Electric Corp.
Wetterau
Weyerhaeuser Co.
Wheeler Foundation, Wilmot
Whirlpool Corp.
Whitaker Charitable Foundation, Lyndon C.
Whitaker Fund, Helen F.
White Consolidated Industries
Whitehead Foundation
Whitman Corp.
Whitney Fund, David M.
WICOR, Inc.
Wiley & Sons, Inc., John
Williams Cos.
Wilmington Trust Co.
Winston Foundation, Norman and Rosita
Winston Research Foundation, Harry
Winter Construction Co.
Wiseheart Foundation
Woldenberg Foundation
Woods Charitable Fund
Woodward Fund-Atlanta, David, Helen, Marian
Wortham Foundation
Wurlitzer Foundation, Farny R.
Xerox Corp.
Xtra Corp.
Yellow Corp.
Zale Foundation
Zellerbach Family Fund
Zemurray Foundation
Zilkha & Sons

Performing Arts

Abbott Laboratories
Abraham & Straus
Abramson Family Foundation
Abrons Foundation, Louis and Anne
Ahmanson Foundation
AHS Foundation
Air France
Air Products & Chemicals
Alabama Power Co.
Albany International Corp.
Alberto-Culver Co.
Albertson's
Alexander & Baldwin, Inc.
Alexander Foundation, Judd S.
Alexander Foundation, Walter
Allendale Mutual Insurance Co.
AlliedSignal
Alltel/Western Region
Alms Trust, Eleanora
ALPAC Corp.
Alumax
Aluminum Co. of America
Amaturo Foundation
AMAX
AMCORE Bank, N.A. Rockford
America West Airlines
American Brands
American Electric Power
American Express Co.
American Foundation Corporation
American Microsystems, Inc.
American Natural Resources Co.

American President Cos.
American Stock Exchange
American Telephone & Telegraph Co.
American United Life Insurance Co.
Ameritech Corp.
Ameritech Services
Ames Department Stores
Amfac/JMB Hawaii
Amoco Corp.
AMR Corp.
Amsterdam Foundation, Jack and Mimi Leviton
Anderson Foundation, M. D.
Andrews Foundation
Angelica Corp.
AON Corp.
Apache Corp.
Apple Computer, Inc.
Appleton Papers
Archer-Daniels-Midland Co.
ARCO
ARCO Chemical
Argyros Foundation
Arizona Public Service Co.
Arkansas Power & Light Co.
Armco Inc.
Armco Steel Co.
Aron Charitable Foundation, J.
Arronson Foundation
ASARCO
Atalanta/Sosnoff Capital Corp.
Atherton Family Foundation
Atkinson Foundation
Atlanta Gas Light Co.
Attleboro Pawtucket Savings Bank
Auerbach Foundation, Beatrice Fox
Autzen Foundation
Avis Inc.
Avon Products
Awrey Bakeries
Backer Spielvogel Bates U.S.
Badgeley Residuary Charitable Trust, Rose M.
Badger Meter, Inc.
Baier Foundation, Marie
Baird & Co., Robert W.
Baird Foundation, Cameron
Baker & Baker
Baker Foundation, Dexter F. and Dorothy H.
Baker Foundation, R. C.
Baker Hughes Inc.
Baker Trust, George F.
Ball Corp.
Bancorp Hawaii
Bank Hapoalim B.M.
Bank of Boston Corp.
Bank of New York
Bank of San Francisco Co.
Bank One, Texas-Houston Office
BankAmerica Corp.
Bankers Trust Co.
Banner Life Insurance Co.
BarclaysAmerican Corp.
Barrows Foundation, Geraldine and R. A.
Barry Corp., R. G.
Bartlett & Co.
Bartlett & Co.
Bass Foundation
Battelle
Batts Foundation
Bauer Foundation, M. R.
Bausch & Lomb
BayBanks
Bean Foundation, Norwin S. and Elizabeth N.
Bean, L.L.
Beasley Foundation, Theodore and Beulah
Beattie Foundation Trust, Cordelia Lee
Bemis Company

Bend Millwork Systems
Benefit Trust Life Insurance Co.
Benenson Foundation, Frances and Benjamin
Benetton
Benwood Foundation
Beretta U.S.A. Corp.
Bergen Foundation, Frank and Lydia
Berlin Charitable Fund, Irving
Berwind Corp.
Bethlehem Steel Corp.
Beveridge Foundation, Frank Stanley
BFGoodrich
BHP Pacific Resources
Bickerton Charitable Trust, Lydia H.
Bigelow Foundation, F. R.
Binney & Smith Inc.
Birch Foundation, Stephen and Mary
Bishop Foundation
Bishop Foundation, E. K. and Lillian F.
Bissell Foundation, J. Walton
Blair and Co., William
Blandin Foundation
Blinken Foundation
Block, H&R
Bloedel Foundation
Blount
Blue Cross and Blue Shield United of Wisconsin Foundation
Blum Foundation, Edith C.
BMW of North America, Inc.
Boatmen's Bancshares
Boehringer Mannheim Corp.
Boeing Co.
Boettcher Foundation
Boise Cascade Corp.
Bolz Family Foundation, Eugenie Mayer
Booth Ferris Foundation
Booz Allen & Hamilton
Borg-Warner Corp.
Borman's
Bowater Inc.
BP America
Bradford & Co., J.C.
Bradley Foundation, Lynde and Harry
Branta Foundation
Brenner Foundation, Mervyn
Briggs & Stratton Corp.
Bristol-Myers Squibb Co.
Broccoli Charitable Foundation, Dana and Albert R.
Brochsteins Inc.
Brown Foundation
Brown Group
Brown & Sons, Alex
Brown & Williamson Tobacco Corp.
Browning-Ferris Industries
Bruening Foundation, Eva L. and Joseph M.
Buck Foundation, Carol Franc
Buell Foundation, Temple Hoyne
Buhl Family Foundation
Burdines
Burgess Trust, Ralph L. and Florence R.
Burlington Northern Inc.
Butler Manufacturing Co.
C.P. Rail Systems
Cable & Wireless Communications
Cabot Corp.
Cafritz Foundation, Morris and Gwendolyn
Callaway Foundation
Cameron Foundation, Harry S. and Isabel C.
Camp Younts Foundation
Campbell Foundation
Campbell Foundation

Campbell Soup Co.
Canon U.S.A., Inc.
Capital Cities/ABC
Capital Holding Corp.
Carpenter Foundation, E. Rhodes and Leona B.
Carpenter Technology Corp.
Carrier Corp.
Carter-Wallace
Cartier, Inc.
Cascade Natural Gas Corp.
Cassett Foundation, Louis N.
Caterpillar
CBI Industries
CBS Inc.
Centerior Energy Corp.
Central Bank of the South
Central Hudson Gas & Electric Corp.
Central Life Assurance Co.
Central Maine Power Co.
Chadwick Fund, Dorothy Jordan
Chambers Development Co.
Charina Foundation
Charitable Foundation of the Burns Family
Charter Manufacturing Co.
Chase Manhattan Bank, N.A.
Chastain Charitable Foundation, Robert Lee and Thomas M.
Chazen Foundation
Chemical Bank
Cheney Foundation, Elizabeth F.
Cherokee Foundation
Chesebrough-Pond's
Chevron Corp.
Chicago Sun-Times, Inc.
Chicago Tribune Co.
Chrysler Corp.
Ciba-Geigy Corp. (Pharmaceuticals Division)
CIT Group Holdings
Citicorp
Clark Foundation
Clark Foundation, Robert Sterling
Cleveland-Cliffs
Clorox Co.
Close Foundation
CM Alliance Cos.
CNA Insurance Cos.
CNG Transmission Corp.
Cohen Foundation, Manny and Ruthy
Cohen Foundation, Naomi and Nehemiah
Coleman Co.
Coles Family Foundation
Collins Foundation
Colonial Life & Accident Insurance Co.
Columbus Dispatch Printing Co.
Commerce Clearing House
Commerzbank AG, New York
Commonwealth Edison Co.
Compton Foundation
Comstock Foundation
Connelly Foundation
Consolidated Freightways
Consolidated Papers
Contempo Communications
Cooper Industries
Coors Brewing Co.
Copley Press
Cord Foundation, E. L.
Corning Incorporated
Corpus Christi Exploration Co.
Cosmair, Inc.
Country Curtains, Inc.
Cowles Charitable Trust
Cowles Media Co.
Cox Enterprises
CPC International
CPI Corp.
CR Industries
Crapo Charitable Foundation, Henry H.

Credit Suisse
CRL Inc.
Crum and Forster
CT Corp. System
Cudahy Fund, Patrick and Anna M.
Cullen/Frost Bankers
Cummins Engine Co.
CUNA Mutual Insurance Group
Currey Foundation, Brownlee
Daily News
Dalton Foundation, Harry L.
Dana Charitable Trust, Eleanor Naylor
Danis Industries
Darby Foundation
Dayton Hudson Corp.
Dayton Power and Light Co.
De Lima Co., Paul
Dean Witter Discover
DEC International, Inc.
Deere & Co.
Dekalb Energy Co.
Delacorte Fund, George
Delaware North Cos.
Deluxe Corp.
Dennett Foundation, Marie G.
Dentsu, Inc., NY
Deposit Guaranty National Bank
Detroit Edison Co.
Deuble Foundation, George H.
DeVlieg Foundation, Charles
Dewing Foundation, Frances R.
Dial Corp.
Diamond Foundation, Aaron
Dickson Foundation
Digital Equipment Corp.
Dillard Paper Co.
Dimeo Construction Co.
Dimick Foundation
Dimick Foundation
Dobson Foundation
Dodge Foundation, Geraldine R.
Donaldson Co.
Donnelley & Sons Co., R.R.
Dorot Foundation
Dow Corning Corp.
Dreitzer Foundation
Dresser Industries
Dreyfus Foundation, Max and Victoria
du Pont de Nemours & Co., E. I.
Duchossois Industries
Duke Power Co.
Dun & Bradstreet Corp.
Dupar Foundation
Durr-Fillauer Medical
Dynamet, Inc.
Dyson Foundation
Easley Trust, Andrew H. and Anne O.
Eastman Kodak Co.
Eastover Corp.
Eaton Corp.
Eaton Foundation, Cyrus
Eccles Foundation, George S. and Dolores Dore
Eccles Foundation, Marriner S.
Eckerd Corp., Jack
Eckman Charitable Foundation, Samuel and Rae
Ecolab
Eder Foundation, Sidney and Arthur
Educational Foundation of America
Edwards Industries
Einstein Fund, Albert E. and Birdie W.
Eisenberg Foundation, Ben B. and Joyce E.
Elf Atochem North America
Emerson Electric Co.
EMI Records Group
Encyclopaedia Britannica, Inc.
English-Bonter-Mitchell Foundation

Enron Corp.
Ensworth Charitable Foundation
Equitable Life Assurance Society of the U.S.
Ethyl Corp.
Eureka Co.
Evinrude Foundation, Ralph
Exxon Corp.
Fairchild Corp.
Falk Foundation, David
Fanwood Foundation
Farish Fund, William Stamps
Farley Industries
Farnsworth Trust, Charles A.
Farwell Foundation, Drusilla
Fay's Incorporated
Federal-Mogul Corp.
Federal National Mortgage Assn., Fannie Mae
Federated Department Stores and Allied Stores Corp.
Fels Fund, Samuel S.
Ferkauf Foundation, Eugene and Estelle
Fidelity Bank
Fifth Avenue Foundation
Fifth Third Bancorp
Fig Tree Foundation
FINA, Inc.
Fireman's Fund Insurance Co.
First Bank System
First Boston
First Chicago
First Interstate Bank NW Region
First Interstate Bank of Arizona
First Interstate Bank of California
First Interstate Bank of Denver
First Interstate Bank of Oregon
First Interstate Bank of Texas, N.A.
First Tennessee Bank
First Union Corp.
First Union National Bank of Florida
Firstar Bank Milwaukee NA
Fish Foundation, Ray C.
Fishback Foundation Trust, Harmes C.
Fisher Brothers
Fisher Foundation
Fleet Bank of New York
Fleet Financial Group
Fleishhacker Foundation
Fleming Companies, Inc.
Fleming Foundation
Florida Power & Light Co.
Fluor Corp.
FMR Corp.
Foothills Foundation
Ford Foundation
Ford Meter Box Co.
Ford Motor Co.
Forest Foundation
Forest Oil Corp.
Foster Foundation
Foundation for the Needs of Others
Fox Foundation, John H.
Foxmeyer Corp.
Francis Families Foundation
Fraser Paper Ltd.
Freas Foundation
Freed Foundation
Freedom Forum
Freeman Charitable Trust, Samuel
Freeport-McMoRan
Frese Foundation, Arnold D.
Fribourg Foundation
Frisch's Restaurants Inc.
Frohring Foundation, William O. and Gertrude Lewis
Fry Foundation, Lloyd A.
Fuchsberg Family Foundation, Abraham
Fuller Foundation, George F. and Sybil H.

Funderburke & Associates
Fusenot Charity Foundation, Georges and Germaine
Gannett Co.
Gannett Publishing Co., Guy
GAR Foundation
Garvey Kansas Foundation
Garvey Memorial Foundation, Edward Chase
Garvey Texas Foundation
Gates Foundation
GATX Corp.
Gaylord Foundation, Clifford Willard
Gazette Co.
Gebbie Foundation
GEICO Corp.
Gelb Foundation, Lawrence M.
Gelman Foundation, Melvin and Estelle
GenCorp
General American Life Insurance Co.
General Dynamics Corp.
General Electric Co.
General Machine Works
General Mills
General Motors Corp.
General Railway Signal Corp.
General Reinsurance Corp.
General Signal Corp.
GenRad
Georgia Power Co.
Gerlach Foundation
Gerschel Foundation, Patrick A.
Getty Foundation, Ann and Gordon
Giant Eagle
Giant Food
Giger Foundation, Paul and Oscar
Gilman and Gonzalez-Falla Theatre Foundation
Gilman Foundation, Howard
Gilman, Jr. Foundation, Sondra and Charles
Gilmore Foundation, Irving S.
Gitano Group
Glaxo
Gleason Memorial Fund
Glenmore Distilleries Co.
Glosser Foundation, David A.
Goldman Foundation, Herman
Goldsmith Foundation, Horace W.
Goldstein Foundation, Leslie and Roslyn
Golub Corp.
Goodman Family Foundation
Goodwin Foundation, Leo
Goodyear Tire & Rubber Co.
Gould Foundation, Florence J.
Grace & Co., W.R.
Gradison & Co.
Graphic Controls Corp.
Graybar Electric Co.
Great-West Life Assurance Co.
Great Western Financial Corp.
Green Foundation, Allen P. and Josephine B.
Green Fund
Greene Foundation, Jerome L.
Greenspan Foundation
Greenwall Foundation
Gregg-Graniteville Foundation
Grossman Foundation, N. Bud
Grumbacher Foundation, M. S.
Gruss Petroleum Corp.
GTE Corp.
Guardian Life Insurance Co. of America
Gucci America Inc.
Gutman Foundation, Edna and Monroe C.
Haas Fund, Walter and Elise
Haas, Jr. Fund, Evelyn and Walter
Hachar Charitable Trust, D. D.

Hafif Family Foundation
Hale Foundation, Crescent Porter
Hall Charitable Trust, Evelyn A. J.
Hall Family Foundations
Halliburton Co.
Hallmark Cards
Halmos Foundation
Hamilton Bank
Hamilton Oil Corp.
Hamman Foundation, George and Mary Josephine
Hanes Foundation, John W. and Anna H.
Hankins Foundation
Harkness Ballet Foundation
Harland Charitable Foundation, John and Wilhelmina D.
Harmon Foundation, Pearl M. and Julia J.
Harrington Foundation, Francis A. and Jacquelyn H.
Harris Corp.
Harris Foundation
Harris Foundation, James J. and Angelia M.
Harsco Corp.
Hartford Courant Foundation
Hartford Steam Boiler Inspection & Insurance Co.
Hartman Foundation, Jesse and Dorothy
Hauserman, Inc.
Hawn Foundation
Hazen Charitable Trust, Lita Annenberg
Healy Family Foundation, M. A.
Hearst Foundation
Hearst Foundation, William Randolph
Hechinger Co.
Hecla Mining Co.
HEI Inc.
Heilicher Foundation, Menahem
Heinz Co., H.J.
Heinz Endowment, Howard
Heinz Endowment, Vira I.
Helfaer Foundation, Evan and Marion
Herndon Foundation
Herrick Foundation
Hershey Foods Corp.
Herzstein Charitable Foundation, Albert and Ethel
Hewlett Foundation, William and Flora
Heyward Memorial Fund, DuBose and Dorothy
Higgins Foundation, Aldus C.
Higginson Trust, Corina
High Foundation
Hill-Snowdon Foundation
Hilliard Corp.
Hillman Foundation, Henry L.
Hillsdale Fund
Hoechst Celanese Corp.
Hoffberger Foundation
Hoffer Plastics Corp.
Hoffman Foundation, Marion O. and Maximilian
Hofheinz Foundation, Irene Cafcalas
Holzer Memorial Foundation, Richard H.
Honeywell
Hooker Charitable Trust, Janet A.
Hopkins Foundation, Josephine Lawrence
Horizons Foundation
Hospital Corp. of America
Houston Industries
Howard and Bush Foundation
Howell Foundation, Eric and Jessie
Hubbard Broadcasting
Hubbell Inc.
Hudson-Webber Foundation
Huizenga Family Foundation

Performing Arts (cont.)

Hulme Charitable Foundation, Milton G.
Hunt Alternatives Fund
Hunt Foundation
Hunt Manufacturing Co.
Huston Foundation
Huthsteiner Fine Arts Trust
Hyde Foundation, J. R.
IBM Corp.
Icahn Foundation, Carl C.
ICI Americas
IDS Financial Services
Illinois Power Co.
Illinois Tool Works
IMCERA Group Inc.
IMT Insurance Co.
Indiana Insurance Cos.
Inland Container Corp.
Interco
Intercontinental Hotels Corp.
Interstate Packaging Co.
Irvine Foundation, James
Irwin Charity Foundation, William G.
ITT Hartford Insurance Group
J C S Foundation
J.P. Morgan & Co.
Jackson Foundation
Jacobson & Sons, Benjamin
James River Corp. of Virginia
JCPenney Co.
Jennings Foundation, Alma
Jennings Foundation, Martha Holden
Jerome Foundation
Jewett Foundation, George Frederick
John Hancock Mutual Life Insurance Co.
Johnson Controls
Johnson Endeavor Foundation, Christian A.
Johnson Foundation, Burdine
Johnson & Higgins
Johnson & Johnson
Johnson & Son, S.C.
Jones Construction Co., J.A.
Jordan and Ettie A. Jordan Charitable Foundation, Mary Ranken
Jost Foundation, Charles and Mabel P.
Jostens
Journal Gazette Co.
Joyce Foundation
JSJ Corp.
Jurzykowski Foundation, Alfred
Kapiloff Foundation, Leonard
Kaplan Foundation, Charles I. and Mary
Keating Family Foundation
Keck Foundation, W. M.
Kelley and Elza Kelley Foundation, Edward Bangs
Kellwood Co.
Kemper Foundation, Enid and Crosby
Kennecott Corp.
Kennedy, Jr. Foundation, Joseph P.
Kenworthy - Sarah H. Swift Foundation, Marion E.
Kerr-McGee Corp.
Kettering Fund
Kiewit Foundation, Peter
Kilworth Charitable Foundation, Florence S.
Kimberly-Clark Corp.
Kimmelman Foundation, Helen & Milton
Kingsbury Corp.
Kirbo Charitable Trust, Thomas M. and Irene B.
Kirby Foundation, F. M.

Kirkpatrick Foundation
Kline Foundation, Josiah W. and Bessie H.
Kmart Corp.
Kobacker Co.
Kohl Foundation, Sidney
Kohn-Joseloff Fund
Koret Foundation
Kraft Foundation
Kraft General Foods
Kramer Foundation, Louise
Kresge Foundation
Kress Foundation, George
Krimendahl II Foundation, H. Frederick
Kuehn Foundation
Kulas Foundation
Laclede Gas Co.
Ladd Charitable Corporation, Helen and George
Ladish Co.
Lafarge Corp.
Lamson & Sessions Co.
Lance, Inc.
Land O'Lakes
Lang Foundation, Eugene M.
Lannan Foundation
Larsen Fund
Lassus Brothers Oil
Lechmere
Lee Endowment Foundation
Lehrman Foundation, Jacob and Charlotte
Leighton-Oare Foundation
Lemberg Foundation
Levinson Foundation, Morris L.
Levy Foundation, Jerome
Lewis Foundation, Lillian Kaiser
Liberty Corp.
Liberty National Bank
Lightner Sams Foundation
Lilly & Co., Eli
Lilly Endowment
Lincoln National Corp.
Lipton, Thomas J.
Little, Arthur D.
Loews Corp.
Loewy Family Foundation
Long Foundation, George A. and Grace
Long Island Lighting Co.
Loughran Foundation, Mary and Daniel
Louisiana-Pacific Corp.
Lowe Foundation, Joe and Emily
Lowenstein Foundation, Leon
LTV Corp.
Lubrizol Corp.
Luck Stone
Lydall, Inc.
Lyndhurst Foundation
MacArthur Foundation, John D. and Catherine T.
MacDonald Foundation, Marquis George
Macy & Co., R.H.
Magowan Family Foundation
Maier Foundation, Sarah Pauline
Mailman Family Foundation, A. L.
Mallinckrodt Specialty Chemicals Co.
Mandel Foundation, Jack N. and Lilyan
Mandell Foundation, Samuel P.
Manilow Foundation, Nathan
Mapco Inc.
Marcus Corp.
Maritz Inc.
Marriott Corp.
Marriott Foundation, J. Willard
Mars Foundation
Marsh & McLennan Cos.
Marshall Field's
Marshall & Ilsley Bank
Martin Foundation
Marubeni America Corp.

Masserini Charitable Trust, Maurice J.
Massey Charitable Trust
Massey Foundation, Jack C.
Matz Foundation — Edelman Division
Mautz Paint Co.
May Department Stores Co.
Mayer Foods Corp., Oscar
Mayor Foundation, Oliver Dewey
Maytag Family Foundation, Fred
Mazda Motors of America (Central), Inc.
Mazda North America
MBIA, Inc.
MCA
McCune Foundation
McDonald & Co. Securities
McDonald Industries, Inc., A. Y.
McDonnell Douglas Corp.
McDonnell Douglas Corp.-West
McDougall Charitable Trust, Ruth Camp
McElroy Trust, R. J.
McGonagle Foundation, Dextra Baldwin
McGraw Foundation, Donald C.
McGraw-Hill
MCI Communications Corp.
MCJ Foundation
McKesson Corp.
McKnight Foundation
McLean Contributionship
Mead Corp.
Mead Fund, Nelson
Meadows Foundation
Medtronic
Mellon Bank Corp.
Mellon Foundation, Andrew W.
Mellon Foundation, Richard King
Memton Fund
Mendel Foundation
Menil Foundation
Menschel Foundation, Robert and Joyce
Mentor Graphics
Mercantile Bancorp
Merck & Co.
Merck Human Health Division
Mercy, Jr. Foundation, Sue and Eugene
Meredith Corp.
Meridian Bancorp
Mertz-Gilmore Foundation, Joyce
Mervyn's
Messing Foundation, Morris M. and Helen F.
Metropolitan Life Insurance Co.
Mettler Instrument Corp.
Meyer Foundation, Eugene and Agnes E.
Meyer Memorial Trust
MGIC Investment Corp.
Michigan Bell Telephone Co.
Michigan Consolidated Gas Co.
Midwest Resources
Miles Inc.
Miller Fund, Kathryn and Gilbert
Millipore Corp.
Mine Safety Appliances Co.
Miniger Memorial Foundation, Clement O.
Minnegasco
Mitchell Energy & Development Corp.
Mitsubishi Heavy Industries America
Mitsubishi International Corp.
MNC Financial
Mnuchin Foundation
Mobil Oil Corp.
Monfort Charitable Foundation
Monroe Auto Equipment Co.
Monroe Foundation (1976), J. Edgar
Monsanto Co.
Montgomery Street Foundation

Moore Memorial Foundation, James Starr
Moore & Sons, B.C.
Morgan Construction Co.
Morrill Charitable Foundation
Morrison-Knudsen Corp.
Morse Foundation, Richard P. and Claire W.
Morse, Jr. Foundation, Enid and Lester S.
Morton International
Mosinee Paper Corp.
Mott Fund, Ruth
MTS Systems Corp.
Mulford Foundation, Vincent
Muller Foundation
Mulligan Charitable Trust, Mary S.
Munson Foundation, W. B.
Murch Foundation
Murdy Foundation
Murphy Foundation, John P.
Murray Foundation
Myers and Sons, D.
Myra Foundation
Nabisco Foods Group
Nalco Chemical Co.
National City Bank of Evansville
National Computer Systems
National Forge Co.
National Gypsum Co.
National Life of Vermont
National Machinery Co.
National Presto Industries
National Westminster Bank New Jersey
Nationale-Nederlanden North America Corp.
NationsBank Corp.
NBD Bank
NBD Bank, N.A.
NCR Corp.
Nesholm Family Foundation
Neuberger Foundation, Roy R. and Marie S.
New England Business Service
New England Mutual Life Insurance Co.
New England Telephone Co.
New Horizon Foundation
New York Mercantile Exchange
New York Stock Exchange
New York Telephone Co.
New York Times Co.
The New Yorker Magazine, Inc.
Newhouse Foundation, Samuel I.
Newman Assistance Fund, Jerome A. and Estelle R.
News & Observer Publishing Co.
Nias Foundation, Henry
Nordson Corp.
Norfolk Southern Corp.
Normandie Foundation
Nortek, Inc.
North Shore Foundation
Northern Indiana Public Service Co.
Northern States Power Co.
Northern Telecom Inc.
Northern Trust Co.
Northwest Area Foundation
Northwest Natural Gas Co.
Northwestern National Insurance Group
Northwestern National Life Insurance Co.
Norton Co.
Norwest Bank Nebraska
Noyes, Jr. Memorial Foundation, Nicholas H.
NYNEX Corp.
O'Bleness Foundation, Charles G.
Occidental Petroleum Corp.
Ogilvy & Mather Worldwide
Oglebay Norton Co.
Ohio Bell Telephone Co.

Olin Corp.
Olive Bridge Fund
Olsson Memorial Foundation, Elis
1957 Charity Trust
Ontario Corp.
Ore-Ida Foods, Inc.
Orleton Trust Fund
Ormet Corp.
Osborn Charitable Trust, Edward B.
Osceola Foundation
O'Shaughnessy Foundation, I. A.
Osher Foundation, Bernard
Oshkosh B'Gosh
Ottenstein Family Foundation
Outboard Marine Corp.
Overnite Transportation Co.
Oxford Industries, Inc.
PACCAR
Pacific Enterprises
Pacific Gas & Electric Co.
Pacific Mutual Life Insurance Co.
Pacific Telesis Group
PacifiCorp
Packard Foundation, David and Lucile
Panhandle Eastern Corp.
Pappas Charitable Foundation, Bessie
Park Bank
Park National Bank
Parshelsky Foundation, Moses L.
Paul and C. Michael Paul Foundation, Josephine Bay
Peabody Foundation, Amelia
Pearlstone Foundation, Peggy Meyerhoff
Peery Foundation
Penn Foundation, William
Pennzoil Co.
People's Bank
Peoples Energy Corp.
Pepsi-Cola Bottling Co. of Charlotte
Pepsi-Cola Bottling Co. of Charlotte
PepsiCo
Perkin-Elmer Corp.
Persis Corp.
Pew Charitable Trusts
Pfister and Vogel Tanning Co.
Pfizer
PHH Corp.
Philip Morris Cos.
Philips Foundation, Jesse
Phillips Foundation, Dr. P.
Phillips Petroleum Co.
Physicians Mutual Insurance
Pick Charitable Trust, Melitta S.
Picker International
Pieper Electric
Pillsbury Foundation
Pincus Family Fund
Pines Bridge Foundation
Pioneer Hi-Bred International
Piper Foundation, Minnie Stevens
Pittsburgh National Bank
Pittway Corp.
Polaroid Corp.
Pollybill Foundation
Portland General Electric Co.
Post Foundation of D.C., Marjorie Merriweather
Potlatch Corp.
Potomac Electric Power Co.
Powell Family Foundation
PPG Industries
Prange Co., H. C.
Pratt Memorial Fund
Preston Trust, Evelyn W.
Primerica Corp.
Principal Financial Group
Prouty Foundation, Olive Higgins
Providence Energy Corp.
Providence Journal Company

Provident Life & Accident Insurance Co.
Prudential-Bache Securities
Prudential Insurance Co. of America
PSI Energy
Public Service Co. of Colorado
Public Service Electric & Gas Co.
Pukall Lumber
Pyramid Foundation
Quaker Chemical Corp.
Quaker Oats Co.
Questar Corp.
Ralston Purina Co.
Ramlose Foundation, George A.
Recognition Equipment
Red Wing Shoe Co.
Reichhold Chemicals, Inc.
Reliable Life Insurance Co.
Reliance Electric Co.
Republic New York Corp.
Rexham Inc.
Reynolds Foundation, J. B.
Reynolds Metals Co.
Reynolds & Reynolds Co.
Rhone-Poulenc Inc.
Rice Charitable Foundation, Albert W.
Rienzi Foundation
Riley Foundation, Mabel Louise
Rite-Hite Corp.
Rittenhouse Foundation
RJR Nabisco Inc.
Robbins & Myers, Inc.
Robertshaw Controls Co.
Robson Foundation, LaNelle
Rockefeller Foundation
Rockford Products Corp.
Rockwell Foundation
Rockwell Fund
Rockwell International Corp.
Rodgers Foundation, Richard & Dorothy
Rodman Foundation
Rohm and Haas Company
Rohr Inc.
Rolfs Foundation, Robert T.
RosaMary Foundation
Roseburg Forest Products Co.
Rosen Foundation, Joseph
Rosenberg Foundation, Alexis
Rosenberg Foundation, William J. and Tina
Rosenstiel Foundation
Ross Foundation
Ross Memorial Foundation, Will
Rouse Co.
Royal Group Inc.
Rubin Foundation, Samuel
Rubinstein Foundation, Helena
Ruddick Corp.
SAFECO Corp.
Saint Croix Foundation
Saint Paul Cos.
Samuels Foundation, Fan Fox and Leslie R.
San Diego Gas & Electric
Sandusky International Inc.
Santa Fe Pacific Corp.
Sara Lee Corp.
Sara Lee Hosiery
Saunders Charitable Foundation, Helen M.
Saunders Foundation
Schecter Private Foundation, Aaron and Martha
Scherman Foundation
Schey Foundation
Schieffelin Residuary Trust, Sarah I.
Schreiber Foods, Inc.
Schroeder Foundation, Walter
Schwab & Co., Charles
Schwartz Foundation, David
Scott and Fetzer Co.
Scrivner, Inc.

Scurlock Foundation
Seafirst Corp.
Sealright Co., Inc.
Searle & Co., G.D.
Seaway Food Town
Security Life of Denver
Sedgwick James Inc.
Segerstrom Foundation
Shaklee Corp.
Shapero Foundation, Nate S. and Ruth B.
Shapiro Fund, Albert
Sharon Steel Corp.
Sharp Foundation
Sharp Foundation, Evelyn
Shawmut National Corp.
Sheaffer Inc.
Shell Oil Co.
Shenandoah Life Insurance Co.
Sherwin-Williams Co.
Shoney's Inc.
Shubert Foundation
Shwayder Foundation, Fay
Signet Bank/Maryland
Simon Foundation, Sidney, Milton and Leoma
Simpson Investment Co.
SIT Investment Associates, Inc.
Skaggs Foundation, L. J. and Mary C.
Slifka Foundation, Alan B.
Smith Charitable Fund, Eleanor Armstrong
Smith Corp., A.O.
Smith Foundation, Kelvin and Eleanor
SmithKline Beecham
Smucker Co., J.M.
SNET
Society Corp.
Soling Family Foundation
Solow Foundation
Sonat
Sonoco Products Co.
Sooner Pipe & Supply Corp.
Southern California Edison Co.
Southwest Gas Corp.
Southwestern Bell Corp.
Special People In Need
Spectra-Physics Analytical
Spiritus Gladius Foundation
Sprague Educational and Charitable Foundation, Seth
Sprint
SPX Corp.
Stanley Charitable Foundation, A. W.
Stanley Works
State Street Bank & Trust Co.
Steelcase
Steele Foundation
Steele Foundation, Harry and Grace
Stein Foundation, Jules and Doris
Steinhauer Charitable Foundation
Sterling Inc.
Sterling Winthrop
Stern Family Fund
Stern Foundation for the Arts, Richard J.
Stoddard Charitable Trust
Storage Technology Corp.
Stranahan Foundation
Straus Foundation, Aaron and Lillie
Strauss Foundation
Stride Rite Corp.
Strong Foundation, Hattie M.
Stuart Center Charitable Trust, Hugh
Stulsaft Foundation, Morris
Sturgis Charitable and Educational Trust, Roy and Christine
Subaru of America Inc.
Summerfield Foundation, Solon E.

Sun Co.
Sunderland Foundation, Lester T.
Sundstrand Corp.
Susquehanna Investment Group
Swiss Bank Corp.
Symmes Foundation, F. W.
Syntex Corp.
Tait Foundation, Frank M.
Tandy Corp.
Target Stores
Taub Foundation
TCF Banking & Savings, FSB
Tektronix
Teledyne
Teleflex Inc.
Tenneco
Tetley, Inc.
Texaco
Texas Commerce Bank Houston, N.A.
Textron
Thalheimer Foundation, Alvin and Fanny Blaustein
Thalhimer, Jr. and Family Foundation, William B.
Thermo Electron Corp.
Thoman Foundation, W. B. and Candace
Thomasville Furniture Industries
Thornton Foundation, John M. and Sally B.
3M Co.
Time Insurance Co.
Times Mirror Co.
Tisch Foundation
Titus Foundation, C. W.
TJX Cos.
Torchmark Corp.
Toyota Motor Sales, U.S.A.
Tozer Foundation
Tracor, Inc.
Transamerica Corp.
Transco Energy Company
Tranzonic Cos.
Travelers Cos.
TRINOVA Corp.
Tropicana Products, Inc.
Truland Foundation
Trull Foundation
Trust Co. Bank
Trust for Mutual Understanding
TRW Corp.
TU Electric Co.
Unilever United States
Union Bank
Union Bank of Switzerland New York Branch
Union Electric Co.
Union Pacific Co.
U.S. Leasing International
United States Trust Co. of New York
United Technologies Corp.
Unitrode Corp.
Universal Foods Corp.
Universal Leaf Tobacco Co.
Unocal Corp.
UNUM Corp.
Upjohn Co.
Uris Brothers Foundation
US Bancorp
USX Corp.
V and V Foundation
Valdese Manufacturing Co., Inc.
Valley National Bank of Arizona
Valspar Corp.
Van Wert County Foundation
Vaughan Foundation, Rachael and Ben
Veritas Foundation
Vidda Foundation
Virginia Power Co.
Vlasic Foundation
Vulcan Materials Co.
Wachovia Bank & Trust Co., N.A.

Wade Endowment Fund, Elizabeth Firth
Walker Foundation, T. B.
Wallace Reader's Digest Fund, Lila
Walsh Foundation
Disney Co., Walt
Walter Family Trust, Byron L.
Ward Foundation, A. Montgomery
Warner-Lambert Co.
Washington Mutual Savings Bank
Washington Post Co.
Washington Trust Bank
Washington Water Power Co.
Wasmer Foundation
Waste Management
Wausau Paper Mills Co.
Webster Foundation, Edwin S.
Weiler Foundation, Theodore & Renee
Weininger Foundation, Richard and Gertrude
Weinstein Foundation, Alex J.
Wells Fargo & Co.
Werthan Foundation
West Co.
West One Bancorp
Westinghouse Electric Corp.
Westvaco Corp.
Wetterau
Weyerhaeuser Memorial Foundation, Charles A.
Wharton Foundation
Whirlpool Corp.
Whitaker Charitable Foundation, Lyndon C.
Whitaker Fund, Helen F.
Whitehead Foundation
WICOR, Inc.
Wiegand Foundation, E. L.
Wien Foundation, Lawrence A.
Wiley & Sons, Inc., John
Williams Cos.
Wilmington Trust Co.
Wilson Foundation, Marie C. and Joseph C.
Winter Construction Co.
Wisconsin Energy Corp.
Wisconsin Power & Light Co.
Wisconsin Public Service Corp.
Wisdom Foundation, Mary F.
Witco Corp.
Wolff Foundation, John M.
Wolverine World Wide, Inc.
Woods Charitable Fund
Woodward Fund-Atlanta, David, Helen, Marian
Woodward Governor Co.
Wortham Foundation
Wright Foundation, Lola
Wyomissing Foundation
Yellow Corp.
Zellerbach Family Fund
Zemurray Foundation
Zimmerman Family Foundation, Raymond

Public Broadcasting

Abbott Laboratories
Abrons Foundation, Louis and Anne
AEGON USA, Inc.
Ahmanson Foundation
AHS Foundation
Air France
Air Products & Chemicals
Akzo America
Akzo Chemicals Inc.
Albertson's
Alcan Aluminum Corp.
Alcon Laboratories, Inc.
Alexander & Baldwin, Inc.
Alexander Foundation, Joseph
Alexander Foundation, Walter
Algonquin Energy, Inc.

Allegheny Ludlum Corp.
Allen-Heath Memorial Foundation
Allendale Mutual Insurance Co.
Alliant Techsystems
AlliedSignal
Allyn Foundation
Alms Trust, Eleanora
ALPAC Corp.
Alumax
Aluminum Co. of America
AMAX
American Brands
American Electric Power
American General Finance
American Home Products Corp.
American Natural Resources Co.
American Saw & Manufacturing Co.
American Schlafhorst Foundation, Inc.
American United Life Insurance Co.
Ameritas Life Insurance Corp.
Ameritech Services
Amfac/JMB Hawaii
Amoco Corp.
AMP
Amsted Industries
Analog Devices
Andersen Corp.
Andersen Foundation, Hugh J.
Anderson Foundation, John W.
Andersons Management Corp.
Angelica Corp.
Annenberg Foundation
AON Corp.
Apache Corp.
Appleman Foundation
Arakelian Foundation, Mary Alice
Arata Brothers Trust
Arcadia Foundation
Archer-Daniels-Midland Co.
ARCO Chemical
Aristech Chemical Corp.
Arizona Public Service Co.
Armco Inc.
Armco Steel Co.
Asea Brown Boveri
Ashland Oil
Atherton Family Foundation
Atlanta Gas Light Co.
Attleboro Pawtucket Savings Bank
Auerbach Foundation, Beatrice Fox
Avon Products
Axe-Houghton Foundation
Babcock Foundation, Mary Reynolds
Babson Foundation, Paul and Edith
Baird Foundation, Cameron
Baker Foundation, Dexter F. and Dorothy H.
Baker Trust, Clayton
Baldwin Memorial Foundation, Fred
Ball Corp.
Banc One Illinois Corp.
Bancorp Hawaii
Banfi Vintners
Bang & Olufsen of America, Inc.
Bank of America Arizona
Bank of Boston Corp.
Bank of Louisville
Bank of New York
Bank One, Texas-Houston Office
BankAmerica Corp.
Bankers Trust Co.
Barclays Bank of New York
Bard, C. R.
Barra Foundation
Barth Foundation, Theodore H.
Bass and Edythe and Sol G. Atlas Fund, Sandra Atlas

Public Broadcasting (cont.)

Battelle
Bauer Foundation, M. R.
Bay Foundation
Bayne Fund, Howard
Bean, L.L.
Beck Foundation
Beech Aircraft Corp.
Beerman Foundation
Behmann Brothers Foundation
Beim Foundation
Beir Foundation
Belding Heminway Co.
Beloco Foundation
Beneficia Foundation
Benton Foundation
Bergner Co., P.A.
Bernstein & Co., Sanford C.
Berry Foundation, Loren M.
Berwind Corp.
Best Products Co.
Bethlehem Steel Corp.
Bettingen Corporation, Burton G.
Beveridge Foundation, Frank Stanley
BFGoodrich
BHP Pacific Resources
Bigelow Foundation, F. R.
Bingham Foundation, William
Binney & Smith Inc.
Bionetics Corp.
Blade Communications
Blake Foundation, S. P.
Blandin Foundation
Blinken Foundation
Bloedorn Foundation, Walter A.
Bloomfield Foundation, Sam and Rie
Blount
Blowitz-Ridgeway Foundation
Blum-Kovler Foundation
BMW of North America, Inc.
Boatmen's First National Bank of Oklahoma
Boehringer Mannheim Corp.
Boettcher Foundation
Bolten Charitable Foundation, John
Bonfils-Stanton Foundation
Booth-Bricker Fund
Booz Allen & Hamilton
Borwell Charitable Foundation
Boswell Foundation, James G.
Bowater Inc.
Bozzone Family Foundation
BP America
Brackenridge Foundation, George W.
Bradford Foundation, George and Ruth
Brady Foundation
Braun Foundation
Brenner Foundation, Mervyn
Breyer Foundation
Bridgestone/Firestone
Briggs Family Foundation
Briggs & Stratton Corp.
Bright Family Foundation
Brillion Iron Works
Bristol-Myers Squibb Co.
British Airways
Brown Group
Brown & Sons, Alex
Brown & Williamson Tobacco Corp.
Bruening Foundation, Eva L. and Joseph M.
Bryan Family Foundation, Kathleen Price and Joseph M.
Buchalter, Nemer, Fields, & Younger
Buchanan Family Foundation
Buck Foundation, Carol Franc
Bucyrus-Erie

Buehler Foundation, A. C.
Bull Foundation, Henry W.
Bunbury Company
Burden Foundation, Florence V.
Burdines
Burlington Northern Inc.
Burlington Resources
Burnham Donor Fund, Alfred G.
Burns Foundation, Fritz B.
Burroughs Wellcome Co.
Bush Foundation
Butler Family Foundation, Patrick and Aimee
Bydale Foundation
C.P. Rail Systems
Cabot-Saltonstall Charitable Trust
Cafritz Foundation, Morris and Gwendolyn
Cain Foundation, Gordon and Mary
Caine Charitable Foundation, Marie Eccles
Calhoun Charitable Trust, Kenneth
California Educational Initiatives Fund
Cameron Foundation, Harry S. and Isabel C.
Camp Foundation
Canon U.S.A., Inc.
Capital Cities/ABC
Capital Fund Foundation
Capital Holding Corp.
Caplan Charity Foundation, Julius H.
Cargill
Carnegie Corporation of New York
Carolyn Foundation
Carpenter Foundation
Carpenter Foundation, E. Rhodes and Leona B.
Carrier Corp.
Carter Foundation, Amon G.
Carter-Wallace
Carvel Foundation, Thomas and Agnes
Cascade Natural Gas Corp.
Cassett Foundation, Louis N.
Castle & Co., A.M.
Castle Foundation, Harold K. L.
Castle Foundation, Samuel N. and Mary
Caterpillar
Cedars-Sinai Medical Center Section D Fund
Central Maine Power Co.
Central Soya Co.
Central Vermont Public Service Corp.
Century Companies of America
Chadwick Foundation
Chadwick Fund, Dorothy Jordan
Chais Family Foundation
Charities Foundation
Chase Manhattan Bank, N.A.
Chastain Charitable Foundation, Robert Lee and Thomas M.
Cheatham Foundation, Owen
Chemical Bank
Chicago Board of Trade
Chicago Title and Trust Co.
Christian Training Foundation
Christie, Manson & Woods International, Inc.
Chrysler Corp.
Church & Dwight Co.
CIBA-GEIGY Corp.
Circuit City Stores
Citicorp
Claneil Foundation
Clark Foundation
Clark-Winchcole Foundation
Cleary Foundation
Clorox Co.
Close Foundation
CM Alliance Cos.

CNA Insurance Cos.
CNG Transmission Corp.
Coast Federal Bank
Codrington Charitable Foundation, George W.
Cogswell Benevolent Trust
Cohen Foundation, Naomi and Nehemiah
Cohen Foundation, Wilfred P.
Cohn Foundation, Herman and Terese
Coles Family Foundation
Collins Foundation
Collins Foundation, Carr P.
Collins Foundation, James M.
Colonial Oil Industries, Inc.
Columbia Foundation
Columbus Southern Power Co.
Comerica
Commerce Clearing House
Commerzbank AG, New York
Commonwealth Edison Co.
Commonwealth Fund
Compaq Computer Corp.
Comstock Foundation
Cone-Blanchard Machine Co.
Connell Foundation, Michael J.
Connemara Fund
Consolidated Freightways
Consolidated Natural Gas Co.
Consolidated Papers
Consumers Power Co.
Contempo Communications
Continental Corp.
Contran Corp.
Cooper Foundation
Cooper Industries
Coors Brewing Co.
Coors Foundation, Adolph
Copolymer Rubber & Chemical Corp.
Copperweld Corp.
Corbett Foundation
Cord Foundation, E. L.
Cornell Trust, Peter C.
Corning Incorporated
Corpus Christi Exploration Co.
Cosmair, Inc.
Country Curtains, Inc.
Cowles Charitable Trust
Cowles Media Co.
CPC International
Crown Central Petroleum Corp.
Crum and Forster
Crummer Foundation, Roy E.
CT Corp. System
CTS Corp.
Cudahy Fund, Patrick and Anna M.
Cullen Foundation
Cullen/Frost Bankers
Culpeper Foundation, Charles E.
Cummings Foundation, Nathan
Cummins Engine Co.
Cunningham Foundation, Laura Moore
Curtice-Burns Foods
Dai-Ichi Kangyo Bank of California
Dain Bosworth/Inter-Regional Financial Group
Daly Charitable Foundation Trust, Robert and Nancy
Dammann Fund
Dana Charitable Trust, Eleanor Naylor
Dana Corp.
Danis Industries
Dater Foundation, Charles H.
Davee Foundation
Davis Foundation, Edwin W. and Catherine M.
Davis Foundation, James A. and Juliet L.
Davis Foundation, Joe C.
Davis Foundation, Shelby Cullom

Davis Foundations, Arthur Vining
Dayton Hudson Corp.
De Lima Co., Paul
DEC International, Inc.
Decio Foundation, Arthur J.
Deer Creek Foundation
Deere & Co.
Dekalb Energy Co.
Delaware North Cos.
Deluxe Corp.
Dennett Foundation, Marie G.
Dennison Manufacturing Co.
Deposit Guaranty National Bank
DeSoto
Detroit Edison Co.
Deutsch Co.
Dexter Corp.
Dial Corp.
Dial Corp.
Diamond Foundation, Aaron
Dick Family Foundation
Dickson Foundation
Digital Equipment Corp.
Disney Family Foundation, Roy
Dixie Yarns, Inc.
Dodge Foundation, Geraldine R.
Donaldson Co.
Donnelley Foundation, Elliott and Ann
Donner Foundation, William H.
Dorr Foundation
Dougherty, Jr. Foundation, James R.
Douglas & Lomason Company
Dow Corning Corp.
Dresser Industries
Dreyfus Foundation, Max and Victoria
du Pont de Nemours & Co., E. I.
Dubow Family Foundation
Duchossois Industries
Dumke Foundation, Dr. Ezekiel R. and Edna Wattis
Dunn Foundation, Elizabeth Ordway
Durfee Foundation
Dweck Foundation, Samuel R.
Dyson Foundation
Earl-Beth Foundation
Eastern Enterprises
Eastern Fine Paper, Inc.
Eaton Corp.
Ecolab
Edison Fund, Charles
Electric Power Equipment Co.
Elf Atochem North America
Emerson Electric Co.
Emery Memorial, Thomas J.
Encyclopaedia Britannica, Inc.
Endries Fastener & Supply Co.
Engelhard Foundation, Charles
English-Bonter-Mitchell Foundation
Enright Foundation
Enron Corp.
Enterprise Rent-A-Car Co.
Ernest & Julio Gallo Winery
Ethyl Corp.
Evjue Foundation
Exxon Corp.
Fair Foundation, R. W.
Fair Oaks Foundation, Inc.
Falk Foundation, David
Falk Medical Fund, Maurice
Farish Fund, William Stamps
Farwell Foundation, Drusilla
Fay's Incorporated
Federal Express Corp.
Federal-Mogul Corp.
Federal National Mortgage Assn., Fannie Mae
Federated Department Stores and Allied Stores Corp.
Federated Life Insurance Co.
Feild Co-Operative Association
Fein Foundation

Feinstein Foundation, Myer and Rosaline
Fel-Pro Incorporated
Ferebee Endowment, Percy O.
Ferguson Family Foundation, Kittie and Rugeley
Ferkauf Foundation, Eugene and Estelle
Fibre Converters
Fidelity Bank
Field Foundation of Illinois
Fifth Avenue Foundation
Fig Tree Foundation
Filene Foundation, Lincoln and Therese
FINA, Inc.
Finley Charitable Trust, J. B.
Fireman's Fund Insurance Co.
Firestone, Jr. Foundation, Harvey
First Bank System
First Boston
First Chicago
First Fruit
First Hawaiian
First Interstate Bank NW Region
First Interstate Bank of Arizona
First Interstate Bank of Denver
First Interstate Bank of Oregon
First Tennessee Bank
First Union Corp.
First Union National Bank of Florida
Fish Foundation, Ray C.
Fleishhacker Foundation
Flemm Foundation, John J.
Fletcher Foundation, A. J.
Florida Power & Light Co.
Fluor Corp.
Forbes
Ford Foundation
Ford II Fund, Henry
Forest Fund
Foster and Gallagher
Foundation for Middle East Peace
Fourth Financial Corp.
Fowler Memorial Foundation, John Edward
Fox Charitable Foundation, Harry K. & Emma R.
Francis Families Foundation
Frankel Foundation, George and Elizabeth F.
Frear Eleemosynary Trust, Mary D. and Walter F.
Freas Foundation
Freedom Forum
Freeport-McMoRan
Freygang Foundation, Walter Henry
Friends' Foundation Trust, A.
Frisch's Restaurants Inc.
Fruehauf Foundation
Fruehauf Foundation
Fry Foundation, Lloyd A.
Fuller Co., H.B.
Fuller Foundation, George F. and Sybil H.
Funderburke & Associates
Fuqua Foundation, J. B.
Gage Foundation, Philip and Irene Toll
Garland Foundation, John Jewett and H. Chandler
Garvey Texas Foundation
Garvey Trust, Olive White
Gates Foundation
GATX Corp.
GEICO Corp.
Gellert Foundation, Fred
GenCorp
General Electric Co.
General Mills
General Motors Corp.
General Reinsurance Corp.
Generation Trust
Georgia-Pacific Corp.

Gerber Products Co.
Gerbode Foundation, Wallace Alexander
German Marshall Fund of the United States
Getty Foundation, Ann and Gordon
Giant Food
Giant Food Stores
Gifford Charitable Corporation, Rosamond
Gill Foundation, Pauline Allen
Gillette Co.
Glaxo
Gleason Foundation, Katherine
Glen Eagles Foundation
Glenmore Distilleries Co.
Glenn Foundation, Carrie C. & Lena V.
Glidden Co.
Globe Newspaper Co.
Goldberg Family Foundation
Goldman Foundation, Morris and Rose
Goldman Foundation, William
Goldring Family Foundation
Goldstein Foundation, Alfred and Ann
Gordon Charitable Trust, Peggy and Yale
Gould Inc.
Grace & Co., W.R.
Graco
Grader Foundation, K. W.
Grainger Foundation
Grant Foundation, William T.
Graphic Controls Corp.
Greater Lansing Foundation
Green Foundation, Burton E.
Greene Foundation, Jerome L.
Gries Charity Fund, Lucile and Robert H.
Griffin, Sr., Foundation, C. V.
Griggs and Mary Griggs Burke Foundation, Mary Livingston
Grossman Foundation, N. Bud
Grotto Foundation
Gruss Charitable Foundation, Emanuel and Riane
GTE Corp.
Guardian Life Insurance Co. of America
Gucci America Inc.
Gudelsky Family Foundation, Homer and Martha
Gulton Foundation
Gund Foundation, George
H. B. B. Foundation
H.C.S. Foundation
Haas Foundation, Paul and Mary
Haas Fund, Miriam and Peter
Haas Fund, Walter and Elise
Hagedorn Fund
Haggar Foundation
Hagler Foundation, Jon L.
Hallmark Cards
Halsell Foundation, Ewing
Hamilton Oil Corp.
Hansen Foundation, Dane G.
Harcourt Foundation, Ellen Knowles
Hardin Foundation, Phil
Harper Foundation, Philip S.
Harriman Foundation, Gladys and Roland
Harriman Foundation, Mary W.
Harsco Corp.
Hartford Courant Foundation
Hartford Steam Boiler Inspection & Insurance Co.
Hartmarx Corp.
Hartz Foundation
Hartz Foundation
Harvest States Cooperative
Hawkins Foundation, Robert Z.
Hawley Foundation
Hayfields Foundation

Haynes Foundation, John Randolph and Dora
Hazen Foundation, Edward W.
Hechinger Co.
Heckscher Foundation for Children
Hecla Mining Co.
HEI Inc.
Heileman Brewing Co., Inc., G.
Heinz Co., H.J.
Heinz Endowment, Vira I.
Heinz Foundation, Drue
Heller Financial
Heller Foundation, Walter E.
Henkel Corp.
Herbst Foundation
Herndon Foundation
Herrick Foundation
Hershey Foods Corp.
Hesston Corp.
Hettinger Foundation
Heublein
Heyward Memorial Fund, DuBose and Dorothy
Higgins Charitable Trust, Lorene Sails
Higgins Foundation, Aldus C.
Hill Foundation
Hillman Family Foundation, Alex
Hillsdale Fund
Himmelfarb Foundation, Paul and Annetta
HKH Foundation
Hobbs Foundation
Hoechst Celanese Corp.
Hoffman Foundation, Marion O. and Maximilian
Hoffman Foundation, Maximillian E. and Marion O.
Honeywell
Honigman Foundation
Hooker Charitable Trust, Janet A.
Hopedale Foundation
Hopwood Charitable Trust, John M.
Horizons Foundation
Hospital Corp. of America
Houck Foundation, May K.
Houston Industries
Huffy Corp.
Hulings Foundation, Mary Andersen
Hulme Charitable Foundation, Milton G.
Humana
Hunt Foundation, Roy A.
Hunt Manufacturing Co.
Huthsteiner Fine Arts Trust
IBM Corp.
Icahn Foundation, Carl C.
ICI Americas
Ideal Industries
IES Industries
Illges Memorial Foundation, A. and M. L.
Illinois Power Co.
Illinois Tool Works
Index Technology Corp.
Inland Container Corp.
Insurance Management Associates
International Paper Co.
Interstate National Corp.
Interstate Packaging Co.
Iowa Savings Bank
ITT Corp.
ITT Hartford Insurance Group
ITT Rayonier
Ittleson Foundation
J.P. Morgan & Co.
Jackson Foundation
Jacobson & Sons, Benjamin
James River Corp. of Virginia
Jameson Foundation, J. W. and Ida M.
Jameson Trust, Oleonda
Janirve Foundation

Janssen Foundation, Henry
Jarson-Stanley and Mickey Kaplan Foundation, Isaac & Esther
JCPenney Co.
Jennings Foundation, Mary Hillman
Jerome Foundation
Jewett Foundation, George Frederick
John Hancock Mutual Life Insurance Co.
Johnson Controls
Johnson & Higgins
Johnson & Johnson
Johnston-Hanson Foundation
Jones Foundation, Helen
Joselow Foundation
Jostens
Journal Gazette Co.
JSJ Corp.
Jurodin Fund
Kaplan Foundation, Rita J. and Stanley H.
Kaplen Foundation
Keebler Co.
Keith Foundation Trust, Ben E.
Keller-Crescent Co.
Kemper Charitable Lead Trust, William T.
Kempner Fund, Harris and Eliza
Kenan, Jr. Charitable Trust, William R.
Kenedy Memorial Foundation, John G. and Marie Stella
Kennametal
Kennecott Corp.
Kennedy Foundation, Ethel
Kern Foundation, Ilma
Kettering Fund
Key Food Stores Cooperative Inc.
Kimball International
Kimberly-Clark Corp.
Kimmelman Foundation, Helen & Milton
King Foundation, Carl B. and Florence E.
King Ranch
Kingsbury Corp.
Kingsley Foundation, Lewis A.
Kinney-Lindstrom Foundation
Kirby Foundation, F. M.
Klau Foundation, David W. and Sadie
Kline Foundation, Josiah W. and Bessie H.
Kmart Corp.
Knox Foundation, Seymour H.
Koch Foundation
Koch Sons, George
Koffler Family Foundation
Kohn-Joseloff Fund
Koopman Fund
Koret Foundation
Kramer Foundation, C. L. C.
Kresge Foundation
Krieble Foundation, Vernon K.
Kugelman Foundation
Kuhne Foundation Trust, Charles
Kuhns Investment Co.
Kulas Foundation
Kunkel Foundation, John Crain
Kuyper Foundation, Peter H. and E. Lucille Gaass
Kysor Industrial Corp.
Ladd Charitable Corporation, Helen and George
Ladish Co.
Lafarge Corp.
Laffey-McHugh Foundation
Lance, Inc.
Lassus Brothers Oil
Lattner Foundation, Forrest C.
Laurel Foundation
Lautenberg Foundation
Lawrence Foundation, Alice
Lea Foundation, Helen Sperry

Leavey Foundation, Thomas and Dorothy
Lederer Foundation, Francis L.
Lee Enterprises
Lehigh Portland Cement Co.
Lehrman Foundation, Jacob and Charlotte
Leighton-Oare Foundation
Lemberg Foundation
Lennon Foundation, Fred A.
Leo Burnett Co.
Leuthold Foundation
Levin Foundation, Philip and Janice
Lilly & Co., Eli
Lincoln Family Foundation
Lincoln National Corp.
Lindstrom Foundation, Kinney
Linn-Henley Charitable Trust
Lintilhac Foundation
Lipton, Thomas J.
Little Family Foundation
Litton/Itek Optical Systems
Lockhart Iron & Steel Co.
Lockheed Sanders
Loeb Foundation, Frances and John L.
Loeb Partners Corp.
Loewy Family Foundation
Long Island Lighting Co.
Louisiana Land & Exploration Co.
Lounsbery Foundation, Richard
Love Charitable Foundation, John Allan
Lowe Foundation, Joe and Emily
Lowell Institute, Trustees of the
Lowenstein Foundation, Leon
Lowenstein Foundation, William P. and Marie R.
Lubrizol Corp.
Ludwick Institute
Lurcy Charitable and Educational Trust, Georges
Lurie Foundation, Louis R.
Luttrell Trust
Lux Foundation, Miranda
Lydall, Inc.
Lyons Foundation
Maas Foundation, Benard L.
MacArthur Foundation, J. Roderick
MacArthur Foundation, John D. and Catherine T.
MacDonald Foundation, James A.
Macy & Co., R.H.
Magowan Family Foundation
Mandel Foundation, Morton and Barbara
Mandell Foundation, Samuel P.
Marine Midland Banks
Maritz Inc.
Mark IV Industries
Markey Charitable Fund, John C.
Markle Foundation, John and Mary R.
Marley Co.
Marpat Foundation
Marquette Electronics
Marriott Corp.
Marsh & McLennan Cos.
Marshburn Foundation
Martin Foundation
Martin Marietta Corp.
Marubeni America Corp.
Marx Foundation, Virginia & Leonard
Mary Kay Foundation
Masco Corp.
Mason Charitable Foundation
Massey Charitable Trust
Massey Foundation, Jack C.
Mastronardi Charitable Foundation, Charles A.
Mather and William Gwinn Mather Fund, Elizabeth Ring
Maxon Charitable Foundation

May Department Stores Co.
Maytag Corp.
Maytag Family Foundation, Fred
McCormick & Co.
McCormick Foundation, Chauncey and Marion Deering
McCune Charitable Trust, John R.
McDermott
McDonald & Co. Securities
McDonald Foundation, J. M.
McDonnell Douglas Corp.
McDonnell Douglas Corp.-West
McElroy Trust, R. J.
McEvoy Foundation, Mildred H.
McGraw-Hill
McGregor Foundation, Thomas and Frances
McInerny Foundation
McKee Foundation, Robert E. and Evelyn
McKenna Foundation, Katherine Mabis
McKenna Foundation, Philip M.
McKnight Foundation
McMaster Foundation, Harold and Helen
MDU Resources Group, Inc.
Mead Corp.
Mead Fund, Nelson
Meadows Foundation
Mechanic Foundation, Morris A.
Media General, Inc.
Medtronic
Mellon Bank Corp.
Memorial Foundation for the Blind
Memton Fund
Menasha Corp.
Mentor Graphics
Merck & Co.
Mericos Foundation
Metropolitan Life Insurance Co.
Meyer Memorial Trust
Michigan Bell Telephone Co.
Middendorf Foundation
Mielke Family Foundation
Milbank Foundation, Dunlevy
Miles Inc.
Miller Fund, Kathryn and Gilbert
Mills Charitable Foundation, Henry L. and Kathryn
Mine Safety Appliances Co.
Minnegasco
Minnesota Mutual Life Insurance Co.
Misco Industries
Mitchell Family Foundation, Edward D. and Anna
Mitsubishi Heavy Industries America
Mitsubishi International Corp.
MNC Financial
Mobil Oil Corp.
Monell Foundation, Ambrose
Monfort Charitable Foundation
Monroe Foundation (1976), J. Edgar
Monsanto Co.
Montgomery Ward & Co.
Moore Foundation, O. L.
Moores Foundation, Harry C.
Morgan Trust for Charity, Religion, and Education
Morrill Charitable Foundation
Morris Foundation
Morrison-Knudsen Corp.
Morse Foundation, Richard P. and Claire W.
Morton International
Moses Fund, Henry and Lucy
Motorola
Mott Fund, Ruth
MTS Systems Corp.
Murphy Foundation
Murphy Foundation, Dan
Murray Foundation

Public Broadcasting (cont.)

Nabisco Foods Group
Nakamichi Foundation, E.
Nalco Chemical Co.
Nash Foundation
National Computer Systems
National Fuel Gas Co.
National Gypsum Co.
National Life of Vermont
National Machinery Co.
National Presto Industries
National Westminster Bank New Jersey
NBD Bank
NBD Bank, N.A.
NCR Corp.
Negaunee Foundation
New England Foundation
New York Life Insurance Co.
New York Telephone Co.
New York Times Co.
The New Yorker Magazine, Inc.
Newhouse Foundation, Samuel I.
Newman Assistance Fund, Jerome A. and Estelle R.
Newman's Own
News & Observer Publishing Co.
Nias Foundation, Henry
Nordson Corp.
Norfolk Shipbuilding & Drydock Corp.
Norfolk Southern Corp.
Norris Foundation, Kenneth T. and Eileen L.
North American Reinsurance Corp.
North American Royalties
Northern Indiana Public Service Co.
Northern States Power Co.
Northern Telecom Inc.
Northern Trust Co.
Northwest Area Foundation
Northwest Natural Gas Co.
Northwestern National Life Insurance Co.
Norton Co.
Norton Foundation Inc.
Norwest Corp.
NYNEX Corp.
Oaklawn Foundation
Oberlaender Foundation, Gustav
Oceanic Cablevision Foundation
OCRI Foundation
Oestreicher Foundation, Sylvan and Ann
Offield Family Foundation
Ogilvy & Mather Worldwide
Oglebay Norton Co.
Ohio Valley Foundation
Olin Corp.
Olin Foundation, John M.
Onan Family Foundation
O'Neill Charitable Corporation, F. J.
Ontario Corp.
Oppenheimer Family Foundation
Orchard Foundation
Ore-Ida Foods, Inc.
Oshkosh B'Gosh
Outboard Marine Corp.
Overbrook Foundation
Overlake Foundation
Overseas Shipholding Group
Owen Trust, B. B.
Oxford Foundation
Pacific Enterprises
Pacific Mutual Life Insurance Co.
Packaging Corporation of America
Page Belting Co.
Page Foundation, George B.
Palin Foundation

Palisano Foundation, Vincent and Harriet
Pan-American Life Insurance Co.
Pangburn Foundation
Paramount Communications Inc.
Parsons Foundation, Ralph M.
Patterson Charitable Fund, W. I.
Payne Foundation, Frank E. and Seba B.
Pearce Foundation, Dr. M. Lee
Pearlstone Foundation, Peggy Meyerhoff
Pearson Foundation, E. M.
Pella Corp.
Penn Foundation, William
Pennzoil Co.
People's Bank
Peoples Energy Corp.
Pepsi-Cola Bottling Co. of Charlotte
Perini Corp.
Perkin-Elmer Corp.
Persis Corp.
Peterloon Foundation
Peterson Foundation, Fred J.
Petrie Trust, Lorene M.
Petteys Memorial Foundation, Jack
Pfizer
Phelps Dodge Corp.
Phillips Family Foundation, Jay and Rose
Phillips Foundation, Waite and Genevieve
Phillips Petroleum Co.
Pick, Jr. Fund, Albert
Pickford Foundation, Mary
Pillsbury Foundation
Pines Bridge Foundation
Pinewood Foundation
Pioneer Trust Bank, NA
Piper Foundation, Minnie Stevens
Pittsburgh National Bank
Playboy Enterprises, Inc.
Polinger Foundation, Howard and Geraldine
Polinsky-Rivkin Family Foundation
Porsche Cars North America, Inc.
Portland General Electric Co.
Post Foundation of D.C., Marjorie Merriweather
Potomac Electric Power Co.
PPG Industries
Premier Industrial Corp.
Price Associates, T. Rowe
Principal Financial Group
Pritzker Foundation
Procter & Gamble Cosmetic & Fragrance Products
Promus Cos.
Prudential Insurance Co. of America
Public Service Co. of Colorado
Public Service Electric & Gas Co.
Pulitzer Publishing Co.
Putnam Foundation
Quaker Oats Co.
Quinlan Foundation, Elizabeth C.
R. P. Foundation
Rabb Foundation, Harry W.
Radin Foundation
Ralston Purina Co.
Rasmussen Foundation
Raymond Corp.
Rebsamen Companies, Inc.
Red Wing Shoe Co.
Redman Foundation
Reed Foundation, Philip D.
Reinberger Foundation
Republic New York Corp.
Reynolds Foundation, Z. Smith
Reynolds Metals Co.
Reynolds & Reynolds Co.

Rhoades Fund, Otto L. and Hazel E.
Rich Co., F.D.
Richardson Foundation, Smith
Richmond Foundation, Frederick W.
Rigler-Deutsch Foundation
Ritter Foundation, May Ellen and Gerald
Roberts Foundation
Robison Foundation, Ellis H. and Doris B.
Rochester Gas & Electric Corp.
Rochlin Foundation, Abraham and Sonia
Rockefeller Foundation
Rockwell Fund
Rockwell International Corp.
Rodgers Foundation, Richard & Dorothy
Rohatyn Foundation, Felix and Elizabeth
Rohm and Haas Company
Rohr Inc.
Rose Foundation, Billy
Rosenberg Family Foundation, William
Rosenstiel Foundation
Rosenthal Foundation, Benjamin J.
Rosenthal Foundation, Richard and Hinda
Roth Family Foundation
Rouse Co.
Rowland Foundation
Royal Group Inc.
Rubin Foundation, Rob E. & Judith O.
Rubin Foundation, Samuel
Rubinstein Foundation, Helena
Rudin Foundation, Samuel and May
Russell Educational Foundation, Benjamin and Roberta
Sachs Fund
Saemann Foundation, Franklin I.
SAFECO Corp.
Saint Paul Cos.
Salomon
Saltonstall Charitable Foundation, Richard
Sams Foundation, Earl C.
Sara Lee Hosiery
Saunders Charitable Foundation, Helen M.
Saunders Foundation
Scaife Foundation, Sarah
Schadt Foundation
Schaffer Foundation, H.
Schaffer Foundation, Michael & Helen
Scherman Foundation
Schiff Foundation, Dorothy
Schiro Fund
Schlumberger Ltd.
Schmidlapp Trust No. 2, Jacob G.
Schott Foundation
Schramm Foundation
Schultz Foundation
Schumann Foundation, Florence and John
Schumann Fund for New Jersey
Schwab & Co., Charles
Schwartz Fund for Education and Health Research, Arnold and Marie
Schwob Foundation, Simon
Science Applications International Corp.
Scott Paper Co.
Scrivner, Inc.
Seabury Foundation
Seaway Food Town
Security Life of Denver
Sedgwick James Inc.
Semmes Foundation
Setzer Foundation

Shafer Foundation, Richard H. and Ann
Shapiro, Inc.
Sharon Steel Corp.
Sharp Foundation
Sharp Foundation, Charles S. and Ruth C.
Sharp Foundation, Evelyn
Shawmut National Corp.
Shaw's Supermarkets
Shenandoah Life Insurance Co.
Shoney's Inc.
Shorenstein Foundation, Walter H. and Phyllis J.
Sierra Pacific Industries
Signet Bank/Maryland
Simon Foundation, Sidney, Milton and Leoma
Simpson Investment Co.
Skinner Corp.
Slifka Foundation, Joseph and Sylvia
Sloan Foundation, Alfred P.
Smart Family Foundation
Smith Family Foundation, Charles E.
Smith Foundation
Smith Foundation, Kelvin and Eleanor
Smith Fund, George D.
Smucker Co., J.M.
Smyth Trust, Marion C.
SNET
Solow Foundation, Sheldon H.
Sonat
Sonoco Products Co.
Sony Corp. of America
Sordoni Foundation
Soref Foundation, Samuel M. Soref and Helene K.
Sosland Foundation
South Branch Foundation
Southern California Edison Co.
Southwestern Bell Corp.
Sprague Educational and Charitable Foundation, Seth
Sprint
Spunk Fund
SPX Corp.
Square D Co.
Stabler Foundation, Donald B. and Dorothy L.
Stacy Foundation, Festus
Stanley Charitable Foundation, A. W.
Stanley Works
Star Bank, N.A.
Stare Fund
Starr Foundation
Stauffer Communications
Steel, Sr. Foundation, Marshall
Steelcase
Steele Foundation, Harry and Grace
Steiger Memorial Fund, Albert
Stemmons Foundation
Stern Family Foundation, Alex
Stern Family Fund
Stern Memorial Trust, Sidney
Sterne-Elder Memorial Trust
Stoddard Charitable Trust
Stone Container Corp.
Storage Technology Corp.
Stranahan Foundation
Stratford Foundation
Straus Foundation, Philip A. and Lynn
Strauss Foundation
Strong Foundation, Hattie M.
Stuart Foundation
Stulsaft Foundation, Morris
Stupp Foundation, Norman J.
Subaru-Isuzu Automotive Inc.
Sulzberger Foundation
Sumitomo Bank of California
Summerfield Foundation, Solon E.

Sumners Foundation, Hatton W.
Sunmark Capital Corp.
Surdna Foundation
Swift Co. Inc., John S.
Swig Charity Foundation, Mae and Benjamin
Swig Foundation
Tait Foundation, Frank M.
Tandy Foundation, David L.
Target Stores
Taylor Foundation, Ruth and Vernon
TCF Banking & Savings, FSB
Tektronix
Teledyne
Tennant Co.
Tenneco
Tetley, Inc.
Texaco
Texas Commerce Bank Houston, N.A.
Texas Instruments
Textron
Thermo Electron Corp.
Thorne Foundation
Thornton Foundation
Thornton Foundation, Flora L.
Thornton Foundation, John M. and Sally B.
Thorpe Foundation, James R.
3M Co.
Thurston Charitable Foundation
Times Mirror Co.
Timmis Foundation, Michael & Nancy
Tisch Foundation
Titus Foundation, C. W.
Tobin Foundation
Tomkins Industries, Inc.
Tonya Memorial Foundation
Tosco Corp. Refining Division
Town Creek Foundation
Toyota Motor Sales, U.S.A.
Tozer Foundation
Transamerica Corp.
Transco Energy Company
Tranzonic Cos.
Travelers Cos.
TRINOVA Corp.
Triskelion Ltd.
Trull Foundation
Trust Co. Bank
TU Electric Co.
Tucker Charitable Trust, Rose E.
Tuohy Foundation, Alice Tweed
Turner Charitable Foundation
Turner Charitable Trust, Courtney S.
Unilever United States
Union Camp Corp.
Union Pacific Corp.
United Conveyor Corp.
United Dominion Industries
U.S. Leasing International
United States Trust Co. of New York
Universal Foods Corp.
Universal Leaf Tobacco Co.
Upjohn California Fund
Uris Brothers Foundation
US Bancorp
US WEST
USG Corp.
UST
Utica National Insurance Group
Utilicorp United
Valmont Industries
Van Evera Foundation, Dewitt Caroline
Van Nuys Charities, J. B. and Emily
Vaughan Foundation, Rachael and Ben
Vaughn Foundation
Vernon Fund, Miles Hodsdon
Virginia Power Co.
Volkswagen of America, Inc.

Vulcan Materials Co.
Wachovia Bank of Georgia, N.A.
Wachovia Bank & Trust Co., N.A.
Wagner Foundation, Ltd., R. H.
Wal-Mart Stores
Walker Foundation, L. C. and Margaret
Walker Foundation, T. B.
Wallach Foundation, Miriam G. and Ira D.
Disney Co., Walt
Walter Family Trust, Byron L.
Walton Family Foundation
Ward Foundation, A. Montgomery
Ware Foundation
Washington Post Co.
Washington Water Power Co.
Wasserman Foundation
Wasserman Foundation, George
Waste Management
Wauwatosa Savings & Loan Association
Wean Foundation, Raymond John
Webster Charitable Foundation
Weckbaugh Foundation, Eleanore Mullen
Weeden Foundation, Frank
Weiler Foundation
Weinberg Foundation, John L.
Weinberg, Jr. Foundation, Sidney J.
Weingart Foundation
Weisz Foundation, David and Sylvia
Werblow Charitable Trust, Nina W.
Wessinger Foundation
West One Bancorp
Western Shade Cloth Charitable Foundation
Westinghouse Electric Corp.
Weyerhaeuser Co.
Weyerhaeuser Memorial Foundation, Charles A.
Wharton Foundation
Wheeler Foundation, Wilmot
Whirlpool Corp.
Whitaker Fund, Helen F.
Whiting Foundation, Macauley and Helen Dow
Whittier Foundation, L. K.
Wilcox General Trust, George N.
Wiley & Sons, Inc., John
Williams Family Foundation
Williams Family Foundation of Georgia
Williams Foundation, C. K.
Wilmington Trust Co.
Wilson Fund, Matilda R.
Winn-Dixie Stores
Winthrop Trust, Clara B.
Wisconsin Bell, Inc.
Wisconsin Energy Corp.
Wiseheart Foundation
Wood-Claeyssens Foundation
Woodruff Foundation, Robert W.
Woodward Fund-Atlanta, David, Helen, Marian
Woodward Governor Co.
Wurlitzer Foundation, Farny R.
WWF Paper Corp.
Wyss Foundation
Yellow Corp.
Young & Rubicam
Younkers, Inc.
Zachry Co., H. B.
Zale Foundation
Zenkel Foundation
Ziegler Foundation, Ruth/Allen
Zilkha & Sons
Zollner Foundation

Theater

Abbott Laboratories
Abell-Hanger Foundation

Abraham & Straus
Abreu Charitable Trust u/w/o May P. Abreu, Francis I.
Acushnet Co.
Adams Foundation, Arthur F. and Alice E.
Adler Foundation Trust, Philip D. and Henrietta B.
Ahmanson Foundation
AHS Foundation
Air France
Air Products & Chemicals
Alabama Power Co.
Albany International Corp.
Alco Standard Corp.
Alcon Laboratories, Inc.
Alexander Foundation, Walter
Allegheny Ludlum Corp.
Allen-Heath Memorial Foundation
Allendale Mutual Insurance Co.
AlliedSignal
Alltel/Western Region
Allyn Foundation
ALPAC Corp.
Alumax
Aluminum Co. of America
AMAX
AMCORE Bank, N.A. Rockford
American Brands
American Cyanamid Co.
American Cyanamid Co.
American Electric Power
American Express Co.
American National Bank & Trust Co. of Chicago
American Natural Resources Co.
American President Cos.
American Saw & Manufacturing Co.
American Telephone & Telegraph Co.
American United Life Insurance Co.
Ameritech Services
Amfac/JMB Hawaii
Amoco Corp.
AMP
Amsterdam Foundation, Jack and Mimi Leviton
Anacomp, Inc.
Andersen Corp.
Andersen Foundation
Andersen Foundation, Hugh J.
Andrews Foundation
Annenberg Foundation
AON Corp.
Apache Corp.
Apple Computer, Inc.
Appleby Trust, Scott B. and Annie P.
Arcadia Foundation
Arcana Foundation
Archer-Daniels-Midland Co.
Archibald Charitable Foundation, Norman
ARCO Chemical
Arizona Public Service Co.
Arkwright Foundation
Armco Inc.
Armco Steel Co.
Ashland Oil
Atlanta Gas Light Co.
Attleboro Pawtucket Savings Bank
Auerbach Foundation, Beatrice Fox
Autzen Foundation
Avis Inc.
Avon Products
Axe-Houghton Foundation
Backer Spielvogel Bates U.S.
Badger Meter, Inc.
Baird Foundation, Cameron
Baker Foundation, Dexter F. and Dorothy H.
Baker Foundation, R. C.

Baker, Jr. Memorial Fund, William G.
Baldwin Memorial Foundation, Fred
Ball Corp.
Ballet Makers
Baltimore Gas & Electric Co.
Banc One Wisconsin Corp.
Bancorp Hawaii
Bang & Olufsen of America, Inc.
Bank of America Arizona
Bank of Boston Corp.
Bank of Tokyo Trust Co.
Bank One, Youngstown, NA
BankAmerica Corp.
Bankers Trust Co.
Bannerman Foundation, William C.
Barclays Bank of New York
Barker Welfare Foundation
Barra Foundation
Barry Corp., R. G.
Bartol Foundation, Stockton Rush
Bass Foundation
Bassett Foundation, Norman
Battelle
Bauer Foundation, M. R.
Bausch & Lomb
BayBanks
Bean, L.L.
Beasley Foundation, Theodore and Beulah
Beattie Foundation Trust, Cordelia Lee
Beech Aircraft Corp.
Beinecke Foundation
Belding Heminway Co.
Bemis Company
Bend Millwork Systems
Benedum Foundation, Claude Worthington
Benefit Trust Life Insurance Co.
Benwood Foundation
Berlin Charitable Fund, Irving
Bernsen Foundation, Grace and Franklin
Berwind Corp.
Best Products Co.
BHP Pacific Resources
Biddle Foundation, Mary Duke
Bigelow Foundation, F. R.
Binney & Smith Inc.
Birch Foundation, Stephen and Mary
Blair and Co., William
Blandin Foundation
Blank Fund, Myron and Jacqueline
Blinken Foundation
Block, H&R
Blue Cross and Blue Shield United of Wisconsin Foundation
Blum Foundation, Edith C.
Blum-Kovler Foundation
BMW of North America, Inc.
Boatmen's First National Bank of Oklahoma
Bodine Corp.
Boehringer Mannheim Corp.
Boeing Co.
Boise Cascade Corp.
Bolz Family Foundation, Eugenie Mayer
Booth-Bricker Fund
Booth Ferris Foundation
Booz Allen & Hamilton
Borden
Borg-Warner Corp.
Borman's
Bovaird Foundation, Mervin
Bowater Inc.
Bozzone Family Foundation
BP America
Brenner Foundation, Mervyn
Bridgestone/Firestone

Britton Fund
Brochsteins Inc.
Brown Foundation
Brown Group
Brown & Williamson Tobacco Corp.
Bryan Family Foundation, Kathleen Price and Joseph M.
Bryce Memorial Fund, William and Catherine
Buchanan Family Foundation
Buck Foundation, Carol Franc
Bucyrus-Erie
Bunbury Company
Burdines
Burlington Resources
Burnham Foundation
Bush Foundation
Butler Manufacturing Co.
C.P. Rail Systems
Cabell III and Maude Morgan Cabell Foundation, Robert G.
Cabot Corp.
Cabot Family Charitable Trust
Cabot-Saltonstall Charitable Trust
Cafritz Foundation, Morris and Gwendolyn
Cain Foundation, Gordon and Mary
Caine Charitable Foundation, Marie Eccles
Calhoun Charitable Trust, Kenneth
Camp Younts Foundation
Campbell Foundation
Capital Cities/ABC
Capital Holding Corp.
Cargill
Carolina Power & Light Co.
Carolyn Foundation
Carpenter Foundation
Carpenter Foundation, E. Rhodes and Leona B.
Carrier Corp.
Carter-Wallace
Casey Foundation, Eugene B.
Cassett Foundation, Louis N.
Caterpillar
CBI Industries
CBS Inc.
Centel Corp.
Centerior Energy Corp.
Central Life Assurance Co.
Central Maine Power Co.
Central Soya Co.
Century Companies of America
Cessna Aircraft Co.
Chadwick Fund, Dorothy Jordan
Charitable Foundation of the Burns Family
Charter Manufacturing Co.
Chase Manhattan Bank, N.A.
Chastain Charitable Foundation, Robert Lee and Thomas M.
Chatham Valley Foundation
Chazen Foundation
Cheatham Foundation, Owen
Chemical Bank
Cheney Foundation, Elizabeth F.
Chesapeake Corp.
Chevron Corp.
Chicago Resource Center
Chicago Sun-Times, Inc.
Chicago Title and Trust Co.
Chicago Tribune Co.
Christian Dior New York, Inc.
Christie, Manson & Woods International, Inc.
Ciba-Geigy Corp. (Pharmaceuticals Division)
Cincinnati Bell
CIT Group Holdings
Citicorp
CLARCOR
Clark Foundation, Robert Sterling

Clark-Winchcole Foundation
Clay Foundation
Cleveland-Cliffs
Clorox Co.
CNA Insurance Cos.
CNG Transmission Corp.
Coats & Clark Inc.
Codrington Charitable Foundation, George W.
Cohen Foundation, Manny and Ruthy
Cohen Foundation, Naomi and Nehemiah
Cohn Co., M.M.
Coleman Co.
Coles Family Foundation
Collins Foundation
Collins Foundation, Carr P.
Colonial Life & Accident Insurance Co.
Colonial Oil Industries, Inc.
Columbia Foundation
Columbus Dispatch Printing Co.
Commerce Clearing House
Commonwealth Edison Co.
Compaq Computer Corp.
Comstock Foundation
Confidence Foundation
Consolidated Natural Gas Co.
Consolidated Papers
Consumers Power Co.
Contempo Communications
Continental Corp.
Contran Corp.
Cooper Industries
Coors Brewing Co.
Coors Foundation, Adolph
Copley Press
Copperweld Corp.
Cord Foundation, E. L.
Cosmair, Inc.
Country Curtains, Inc.
County Bank
Cowles Foundation, Gardner and Florence Call
Cowles Media Co.
CPC International
CPI Corp.
Cramer Foundation
Crane Co.
Crapo Charitable Foundation, Henry H.
Credit Agricole
Crestlea Foundation
Crum and Forster
CT Corp. System
Cuesta Foundation
Cullen Foundation
Cullen/Frost Bankers
Culpeper Foundation, Charles E.
Cummings Foundation, Nathan
CUNA Mutual Insurance Group
Currey Foundation, Brownlee
Curtice-Burns Foods
Daily News
Dain Bosworth/Inter-Regional Financial Group
Dalton Foundation, Harry L.
Dana Charitable Trust, Eleanor Naylor
Danis Industries
Danner Foundation
Darby Foundation
Dart Group Corp.
Davee Foundation
Davenport-Hatch Foundation
Davies Charitable Trust
Dayton Hudson Corp.
Dayton Power and Light Co.
DEC International, Inc.
Delacorte Fund, George
Delaware North Cos.
Deluxe Corp.
Deposit Guaranty National Bank
DeRoy Testamentary Foundation
Detroit Edison Co.
Deuble Foundation, George H.

Theater (cont.)

Deutsch Co.
Dexter Charitable Fund, Eugene A.
Dexter Corp.
Dexter Industries
Dial Corp.
Dillard Paper Co.
Dimeo Construction Co.
Dimick Foundation
Dodge Foundation, Geraldine R.
Dodge Jones Foundation
Donaldson Co.
Donnelley & Sons Co., R.R.
Douglas & Lomason Company
Dow Corning Corp.
Dresser Industries
Dreyfus Foundation, Max and Victoria
Driscoll Foundation
du Pont de Nemours & Co., E. I.
Duchossois Industries
Duke Power Co.
Dula Educational and Charitable Foundation, Caleb C. and Julia W.
Dumke Foundation, Dr. Ezekiel R. and Edna Wattis
Dunagan Foundation
Duncan Foundation, Lillian H. and C. W.
Dunspaugh-Dalton Foundation
duPont Foundation, Alfred I.
Durst Foundation
Dynamet, Inc.
Easley Trust, Andrew H. and Anne O.
Eastern Enterprises
Eaton Corp.
Eaton Foundation, Cyrus
Eccles Foundation, George S. and Dolores Dore
Eccles Foundation, Marriner S.
Educational Foundation of America
Edwards Industries
Elf Atochem North America
Ellsworth Foundation, Ruth H. and Warren A.
Emerson Electric Co.
Encyclopaedia Britannica, Inc.
Engelhard Foundation, Charles
English-Bonter-Mitchell Foundation
Ensworth Charitable Foundation
Equitable Life Assurance Society of the U.S.
Erving Paper Mills
Ettinger Foundation
Evans Foundation, Lettie Pate
Evans Foundation, Thomas J.
Evinrude Foundation, Ralph
Exxon Corp.
Fales Foundation Trust
Fales Foundation Trust
Falk Foundation, David
Falk Medical Fund, Maurice
Falk Medical Fund, Maurice
Farwell Foundation, Drusilla
Favrot Fund
Federal-Mogul Corp.
Federal National Mortgage Assn., Fannie Mae
Fel-Pro Incorporated
Fels Fund, Samuel S.
Fiat U.S.A., Inc.
Fidelity Bank
Field Foundation of Illinois
Fifth Avenue Foundation
Fifth Third Bancorp
Fig Tree Foundation
Fikes Foundation, Leland
FINA, Inc.
Finnegan Foundation, John D.
Fireman's Fund Insurance Co.
First Bank System

First Chicago
First Fidelity Bancorporation
First Interstate Bank NW Region
First Interstate Bank of Arizona
First Interstate Bank of California
First Interstate Bank of Oregon
First Interstate Bank of Texas, N.A.
First Maryland Bancorp
First Mississippi Corp.
First NH Banks, Inc.
First Tennessee Bank
First Union Corp.
Firstar Bank Milwaukee NA
FirsTier Bank N.A. Omaha
Fish Foundation, Ray C.
Fisher Brothers
Flarsheim Charitable Foundation, Louis and Elizabeth
Fleet Financial Group
Fleishhacker Foundation
Fleming Companies, Inc.
Fleming Foundation
Flinn Foundation
Flintridge Foundation
Florida Power & Light Co.
Flowers Charitable Trust, Albert W. and Edith V.
Fluor Corp.
Fondren Foundation
Foote, Cone & Belding Communications
Forbes
Ford Foundation
Ford Foundation, Kenneth W.
Ford Fund, Walter and Josephine
Ford Motor Co.
Forest Fund
Forest Oil Corp.
Fort Worth Star Telegram
Fourth Financial Corp.
Fox Foundation, John H.
France Foundation, Jacob and Annita
Francis Families Foundation
Frankel Foundation
Frankel Foundation, George and Elizabeth F.
Frear Eleemosynary Trust, Mary D. and Walter F.
Freed Foundation
Freedom Forum
Freeport-McMoRan
Frelinghuysen Foundation
French Foundation
Frick Educational Commission, Henry C.
Frohring Foundation, William O. and Gertrude Lewis
Fry Foundation, Lloyd A.
Fuller Co., H.B.
Fuller Foundation, George F. and Sybil H.
Funderburke & Associates
Galter Foundation
Gannett Publishing Co., Guy
GAR Foundation
Garfinkle Family Foundation
Garvey Memorial Foundation, Edward Chase
Gates Foundation
GATX Corp.
Geffen Foundation, David
GEICO Corp.
General American Life Insurance Co.
General Dynamics Corp.
General Electric Co.
General Mills
General Motors Corp.
General Reinsurance Corp.
General Tire Inc.
GenRad
Georgia-Pacific Corp.
Georgia Power Co.
Gerber Products Co.

Gerschel Foundation, Patrick A.
Gerson Family Foundation, Benjamin J.
Giant Eagle
Giant Food
Giger Foundation, Paul and Oscar
Giger Foundation, Paul and Oscar
Gilder Foundation
Gilman and Gonzalez-Falla Theatre Foundation
Gilman Foundation, Howard
Gilman, Jr. Foundation, Sondra and Charles
Gilmore Foundation, Irving S.
Glancy Foundation, Lenora and Alfred
Glaxo
Gleason Foundation, Katherine
Glenmore Distilleries Co.
Glickenhaus & Co.
Glidden Co.
Globe Newspaper Co.
Goldberg Family Foundation
Golden Family Foundation
Goldman Foundation, Herman
Goldman Fund, Richard and Rhoda
Goldsmith Foundation, Horace W.
Goldwyn Foundation, Samuel
Golub Corp.
Gordon Foundation, Meyer and Ida
Gould Inc.
Gould Foundation, Florence J.
Grace & Co., W.R.
Graham Fund, Philip L.
Graphic Controls Corp.
Graybar Electric Co.
Greene Foundation, Jerome L.
Greenwall Foundation
Greve Foundation, William and Mary
Griffith Foundation, W. C.
Griggs and Mary Griggs Burke Foundation, Mary Livingston
Groome Beatty Trust, Helen D.
Grossman Foundation, N. Bud
Grundy Foundation
Gruss Petroleum Corp.
GTE Corp.
Guardian Life Insurance Co. of America
Gucci America Inc.
Gudelsky Family Foundation, Isadore and Bertha
Gulf Power Co.
Gutman Foundation, Edna and Monroe C.
Haas Fund, Walter and Elise
Hale Foundation, Crescent Porter
Hall Foundation
Hallmark Cards
Hamilton Bank
Hamman Foundation, George and Mary Josephine
Handleman Co.
Hanes Foundation, John W. and Anna H.
Hankins Foundation
Harding Foundation, Charles Stewart
Harkness Foundation, William Hale
Harrington Foundation, Don and Sybil
Harrington Foundation, Francis A. and Jacquelyn H.
Harsco Corp.
Hartford Courant Foundation
Hartman Foundation, Jesse and Dorothy
Hartmarx Corp.
Hauserman, Inc.
Hawn Foundation
Hechinger Co.
Hecht-Levi Foundation

Heckscher Foundation for Children
Hecla Mining Co.
HEI Inc.
Heinz Co., H.J.
Heinz Endowment, Howard
Heinz Endowment, Vira I.
Heinz Foundation, Drue
Helfaer Foundation, Evan and Marion
Henkel Corp.
Hershey Foods Corp.
Hess Foundation
Hewlett Foundation, William and Flora
Heymann-Wolf Foundation
Heyward Memorial Fund, DuBose and Dorothy
Higgins Charitable Trust, Lorene Sails
Higgins Foundation, Aldus C.
Higginson Trust, Corina
High Foundation
Hill-Snowdon Foundation
Hilliard Corp.
Hillman Family Foundation, Alex
Himmelfarb Foundation, Paul and Annetta
Hobby Foundation
Hoechst Celanese Corp.
Hoffman Foundation, Marion O. and Maximilian
Holmes Foundation
Honeywell
Hopwood Charitable Trust, John M.
Horncrest Foundation
Hospital Corp. of America
Houchens Foundation, Ervin G.
Houck Foundation, May K.
Houston Industries
Howell Foundation, Eric and Jessie
Hubbard Broadcasting
Hudson-Webber Foundation
Huffy Corp.
Hulings Foundation, Mary Andersen
Humana
Humphreys Foundation
Hunt Alternatives Fund
Hunt Foundation, Roy A.
Hunt Manufacturing Co.
Huthsteiner Fine Arts Trust
Hyde and Watson Foundation
I. and L. Association
IBM Corp.
ICI Americas
IDS Financial Services
IES Industries
Illinois Bell
Illinois Power Co.
Illinois Tool Works
IMCERA Group Inc.
IMT Insurance Co.
Indiana Bell Telephone Co.
Indiana Insurance Cos.
Ingalls Foundation, Louise H. and David S.
Inland Container Corp.
Insurance Management Associates
Interco
International Multifoods Corp.
International Paper Co.
Interstate Packaging Co.
Iowa-Illinois Gas & Electric Co.
Ireland Foundation
Irmas Charitable Foundation, Audrey and Sydney
Irvine Foundation, James
ITT Hartford Insurance Group
J.P. Morgan & Co.
Jackson Charitable Trust, Marion Gardner
Jackson Foundation
James River Corp. of Virginia

Jarson-Stanley and Mickey Kaplan Foundation, Isaac & Esther
JCPenney Co.
Jenkins Foundation, George W.
Jennings Foundation, Martha Holden
Jennings Foundation, Mary Hillman
Jerome Foundation
John Hancock Mutual Life Insurance Co.
Johnson Foundation, Burdine
Johnson & Higgins
Johnson & Son, S.C.
Johnston-Fix Foundation
Johnston-Hanson Foundation
Jordan and Ettie A. Jordan Charitable Foundation, Mary Ranken
Jordan Foundation, Arthur
Jostens
Journal Gazette Co.
JSJ Corp.
Julia R. and Estelle L. Foundation
Jurzykowski Foundation, Alfred
Kaplan Foundation, Charles I. and Mary
Kaplan Foundation, Mayer and Morris
Kaplan Foundation, Rita J. and Stanley H.
Kaplen Foundation
Kaplun Foundation, Morris J. and Betty
Katten, Muchin, & Zavis
Kauffman Foundation, Muriel McBrien
Kaufman Memorial Trust, Chaim, Fanny, Louis, Benjamin, and Anne Florence
Kaufmann Foundation, Henry
Keating Family Foundation
Keck, Jr. Foundation, William M.
Keith Foundation Trust, Ben E.
Kemper Charitable Lead Trust, William T.
Kemper Charitable Trust, William T.
Kemper Educational and Charitable Fund
Kemper Foundation, Enid and Crosby
Kemper Memorial Foundation, David Woods
Kennametal
Kennecott Corp.
Kennedy Foundation, Ethel
Kentucky Foundation for Women
Kenworthy - Sarah H. Swift Foundation, Marion E.
Kerr Foundation, Robert S. and Grayce B.
Kerr Fund, Grayce B.
Kerr-McGee Corp.
Kiewit Foundation, Peter
Kiewit Sons, Peter
Kilworth Charitable Foundation, Florence B.
Kimball International
Kimberly-Clark Corp.
Kingsbury Corp.
Kinney-Lindstrom Foundation
Kiplinger Foundation
Kline Foundation, Josiah W. and Bessie H.
Kmart Corp.
Knight Foundation, John S. and James L.
Knott Foundation, Marion I. and Henry J.
Knowles Foundation
Knox Foundation, Seymour H.
Knox, Sr., and Pearl Wallis Knox Charitable Foundation, Robert W.
Kobacker Co.
Koch Sons, George

Kohler Foundation
Kohn-Joseloff Fund
Koopman Fund
Koret Foundation
Kraft Foundation
Kraft General Foods
Krieble Foundation, Vernon K.
Kuehn Foundation
Kulas Foundation
L and L Foundation
Ladd Charitable Corporation, Helen and George
Lafarge Corp.
Lamson & Sessions Co.
Landmark Communications
Larsen Fund
LaSalle National Bank
Lassus Brothers Oil
Lastfogel Foundation, Abe and Frances
Laurel Foundation
Lea Foundation, Helen Sperry
Lechmere
Lederer Foundation, Francis L.
Lee Endowment Foundation
Lee Enterprises
Lee Foundation, Ray M. and Mary Elizabeth
LEF Foundation
Lehrman Foundation, Jacob and Charlotte
Leo Burnett Co.
Leonhardt Foundation, Dorothea L.
Levin Foundation, Philip and Janice
Leviton Manufacturing Co.
Levy Foundation, Betty and Norman F.
Levy Foundation, Charles and Ruth
Lewis Foundation, Lillian Kaiser
Liberty Corp.
Lieberman Enterprises
Life Insurance Co. of Georgia
Lilly & Co., Eli
Lilly Endowment
Lilly Foundation, Richard Coyle
Lincoln Electric Co.
Lincoln National Corp.
Link, Jr. Foundation, George
Lintilhac Foundation
Lipton, Thomas J.
Little, Arthur D.
Little Family Foundation
Litton Industries
Loeb Foundation, Frances and John L.
Long Foundation, George A. and Grace
Long Island Lighting Co.
Loridans Foundation, Charles
Loughran Foundation, Mary and Daniel
Louisiana Land & Exploration Co.
Louisiana Power & Light Co./New Orleans Public Service
Love Foundation, Martha and Spencer
Lowe Foundation, Joe and Emily
LTV Corp.
Lubo Fund
Lubrizol Corp.
Lurie Foundation, Louis R.
Lydall, Inc.
Lyndhurst Foundation
MacAndrews & Forbes Holdings
MacArthur Foundation, John D. and Catherine T.
Macmillan, Inc.
Magma Copper Co.
Magowan Family Foundation
Magruder Foundation, Chesley G.
MalCo Products Inc.

Mallinckrodt Specialty Chemicals Co.
Mandel Foundation, Jack N. and Lilyan
Manilow Foundation, Nathan
Marbrook Foundation
Marcus Corp.
Mardag Foundation
Maritz Inc.
Mark IV Industries
Marley Co.
Marpat Foundation
Marquette Electronics
Marriott Corp.
Marriott Foundation, J. Willard
Mars Foundation
Marsh & McLennan Cos.
Marshall Field's
Marshall & Ilsley Bank
Marshall Trust in Memory of Sanders McDaniel, Harriet McDaniel
Martin Foundation
Martin Marietta Corp.
Marubeni America Corp.
Marx Foundation, Virginia & Leonard
Massey Charitable Trust
Massey Foundation, Jack C.
Massie Trust, David Meade
Matz Foundation — Edelman Division
May Department Stores Co.
Mayor Foundation, Oliver Dewey
Maytag Family Foundation, Fred
MCA
McCarthy Charities
McCaw Foundation
McCormick & Co.
McCray Lumber Co.
McCune Foundation
McDonald & Co. Securities
McDonald Industries, Inc., A. Y.
McDonnell Douglas Corp.
McDonnell Douglas Corp.-West
McDonough Foundation, Bernard
McElroy Trust, R. J.
McGraw-Hill
McGregor Foundation, Thomas and Frances
McGregor Fund
McInerny Foundation
MCJ Foundation
McKenna Foundation, Philip M.
McKesson Corp.
McKnight Foundation
McNutt Charitable Trust, Amy Shelton
MDU Resources Group, Inc.
Mead Corp.
Mead Foundation, Giles W. and Elise G.
Meadows Foundation
Mebane Packaging Corp.
Medtronic
Mellon Bank Corp.
Memorial Foundation for Children
Memton Fund
Mendel Foundation
Mentor Graphics
Merck Family Fund
Merrill Foundation, R. D.
Mertz-Gilmore Foundation, Joyce
Mervyn's
Metallgesellschaft Corp.
Metropolitan Life Insurance Co.
Mettler Instrument Corp.
Meyer Foundation, Eugene and Agnes E.
Meyer Memorial Trust
Michigan Bell Telephone Co.
Midwest Resources
Miller Charitable Foundation, Howard E. and Nell E.
Miller Fund, Kathryn and Gilbert
Milliken & Co.

Mine Safety Appliances Co.
Minnegasco
Minnesota Mutual Life Insurance Co.
Mitchell Family Foundation, Edward D. and Anna
Mitsubishi International Corp.
MNC Financial
Mobil Oil Corp.
Monfort Charitable Foundation
Monroe Auto Equipment Co.
Monsanto Co.
Montgomery Street Foundation
Moody Foundation
Moore Memorial Foundation, James Starr
Moore & Sons, B.C.
Mosinee Paper Corp.
Motorola
Mott Fund, Ruth
Mulligan Charitable Trust, Mary S.
Murdock Charitable Trust, M. J.
Murdy Foundation
Murfee Endowment, Kathryn
Murphy Foundation, John P.
Murray Foundation
Myra Foundation
Nabisco Foods Group
National City Corp.
National Computer Systems
National Forge Co.
National Fuel Gas Co.
National Gypsum Co.
National Life of Vermont
National Machinery Co.
National Starch & Chemical Corp.
National Steel
National Westminster Bank New Jersey
Nationale-Nederlanden North America Corp.
NationsBank Corp.
Nationwide Insurance Cos.
NBD Bank
NBD Bank, N.A.
Nesholm Family Foundation
New England Biolabs Foundation
New England Mutual Life Insurance Co.
New York Stock Exchange
New York Telephone Co.
New York Times Co.
The New Yorker Magazine, Inc.
Newman Assistance Fund, Jerome A. and Estelle R.
Newman's Own
News & Observer Publishing Co.
Nord Family Foundation
Nordson Corp.
Norfolk Southern Corp.
Norris Foundation, Kenneth T. and Eileen L.
Northern Indiana Public Service Co.
Northern States Power Co.
Northern Telecom Inc.
Northwest Area Foundation
Northwest Natural Gas Co.
Northwestern National Insurance Group
Northwestern National Life Insurance Co.
Norton Co.
Norton Foundation Inc.
Norton Memorial Corporation, Geraldi
Norwest Bank Nebraska
Norwest Corp.
Noyes, Jr. Memorial Foundation, Nicholas H.
Oak Foundation U.S.A.
O'Bleness Foundation, Charles G.
Occidental Oil & Gas Corp.
Oceanic Cablevision Foundation

O'Connor Foundation, A. Lindsay and Olive B.
OCRI Foundation
Ogilvy & Mather Worldwide
Oglebay Norton Co.
Oklahoma Gas & Electric Co.
Oklahoman Foundation
Olin Corp.
Olive Bridge Fund
Olsson Memorial Foundation, Elis
O'Neill Charitable Corporation, F. J.
Ontario Corp.
Orchard Corp. of America.
Orleton Trust Fund
O'Shaughnessy Foundation, I. A.
Osher Foundation, Bernard
Ottenstein Family Foundation
Overbrook Foundation
Overlake Foundation
Overnite Transportation Co.
Overseas Shipholding Group
Owen Industries, Inc.
Owsley Foundation, Alvin and Lucy
Oxford Industries, Inc.
PACCAR
Pacific Enterprises
Pacific Gas & Electric Co.
Pacific Mutual Life Insurance Co.
Pacific Telesis Group
PacifiCorp
Packard Foundation, David and Lucile
Palmer Fund, Frank Loomis
Pappas Charitable Foundation, Bessie
Paramount Communications Inc.
Park National Bank
Parker Foundation
Parker Foundation, Theodore Edson
Parker-Hannifin Corp.
Parsons Foundation, Ralph M.
Payne Foundation, Frank E. and Seba B.
Peabody Foundation, Amelia
Pearlstone Foundation, Peggy Meyerhoff
Pella Corp.
Penn Foundation, William
Pennzoil Co.
People's Bank
Peoples Energy Corp.
Persis Corp.
Petrie Trust, Lorene M.
Pew Charitable Trusts
Pfister and Vogel Tanning Co.
Pfizer
Pforzheimer Foundation, Carl and Lily
Phelps Dodge Corp.
PHH Corp.
Philips Foundation, Jesse
Phillips Foundation, Dr. P.
Phillips Petroleum Co.
Physicians Mutual Insurance
Pickford Foundation, Mary
Pincus Family Fund
Pines Bridge Foundation
Pineywoods Foundation
Piper Foundation
Piper Jaffray Cos.
Pittsburgh National Bank
Pittway Corp.
Plumsock Fund
PMA Industries
Poinsettia Foundation, Paul and Magdalena Ecke
Polaroid Corp.
Pollybill Foundation
Potomac Electric Power Co.
Powell Family Foundation
Prange Co., H. C.
Pratt Memorial Fund
Premier Bank

Premier Industrial Corp.
Price Associates, T. Rowe
Primerica Corp.
Principal Financial Group
Pritzker Foundation
Procter & Gamble Co.
Procter & Gamble Cosmetic & Fragrance Products
Promus Cos.
Prudential-Bache Securities
Public Service Electric & Gas Co.
Puget Sound Power & Light Co.
Pulitzer Publishing Co.
Quaker Oats Co.
Questar Corp.
Recognition Equipment
Red Devil
Red Wing Shoe Co.
Reed Foundation
Regis Corp.
Reinberger Foundation
Reliance Electric Co.
Replogle Foundation, Luther I.
Republic New York Corp.
Reynolds Foundation, Richard S.
Reynolds Metals Co.
Reynolds & Reynolds Co.
Rienzi Foundation
Rigler-Deutsch Foundation
Riley Foundation, Mabel Louise
Rite-Hite Corp.
Rittenhouse Foundation
Robbins & Myers, Inc.
Robertshaw Controls Co.
Robinson Fund, Charles Nelson
Rochester Gas & Electric Corp.
Rockefeller Foundation
Rockford Products Corp.
Rockwell Fund
Rockwell International Corp.
Rodgers Foundation, Richard & Dorothy
Rodman Foundation
Rogers Charitable Trust, Florence
Rohm and Haas Company
Rohr Inc.
Rolfs Foundation, Robert T.
Rollins Luetkemeyer Charitable Foundation
Rose Foundation, Billy
Rosen Foundation, Joseph
Rosenberg Foundation, Alexis
Rosenberg Foundation, William J. and Tina
Rosenstiel Foundation
Rosenwald Family Fund, William
Ross Laboratories
Ross Memorial Foundation, Will
Rouse Co.
Royal Group Inc.
Rubin Foundation, Rob E. & Judith O.
Rubinstein Foundation, Helena
Ruddick Corp.
Rudin Foundation, Samuel and May
Rupp Foundation, Fran and Warren
Russell Charitable Trust, Josephine S.
Ryan Foundation, Patrick G. and Shirley W.
Ryder System
Saint Croix Foundation
Saint Paul Cos.
Salomon
Samuels Foundation, Fan Fox and Leslie R.
San Diego Gas & Electric
Sandusky International Inc.
Santa Fe Pacific Corp.
Sara Lee Corp.
Sarkeys Foundation
Schecter Private Foundation, Aaron and Martha

Theater (cont.)

Schering-Plough Corp.
Scherman Foundation
Schey Foundation
Schoenleber Foundation
Schreiber Foods, Inc.
Schroeder Foundation, Walter
Schultz Foundation
Schwartz Foundation, David
Scott and Fetzer Co.
Scott Paper Co.
Scrivner, Inc.
Seafirst Corp.
Sealright Co., Inc.
Searle & Co., G.D.
Sears Family Foundation
Seaway Food Town
Security Life of Denver
Security State Bank
Sedgwick James Inc.
Segal Charitable Trust, Barnet
Segerstrom Foundation
Self Foundation
Sentinel Communications Co.
Sharon Steel Corp.
Sharp Foundation, Evelyn
Shawmut National Corp.
Shawmut Worcester County
  Bank, N.A.
Shaw's Supermarkets
Sheafer Charitable Trust, Emma
  A.
Sheaffer Inc.
Shell Oil Co.
Shenandoah Life Insurance Co.
Shoney's Inc.
Shubert Foundation
Signet Bank/Maryland
Simon Charitable Trust, Esther
Simpson Investment Co.
Skaggs Foundation, L. J. and
  Mary C.
Skinner Corp.
Smart Family Foundation
Smeal Foundation, Mary Jean &
  Frank P.
Snee-Reinhardt Charitable
  Foundation
SNET
Snider Foundation
Snow Memorial Trust, John Ben
Soling Family Foundation
Sonat
Sonoco Products Co.
Sordoni Foundation
Sosland Foundation
Southern California Edison Co.
Southways Foundation
Southwest Gas Corp.
Southwestern Bell Corp.
Special People In Need
Spiritus Gladius Foundation
Sprague Educational and
  Charitable Foundation, Seth
SPX Corp.
Square D Co.
Stackner Family Foundation
Stanley Works
Star Bank, N.A.
Starr Foundation
State Street Bank & Trust Co.
Steelcase
Steele Foundation
Steiger Memorial Fund, Albert
Steigerwaldt Foundation, Donna
  Wolf
Stein Foundation, Jules and Doris
Steinhauer Charitable Foundation
Sterling Inc.
Sterling Winthrop
Stoddard Charitable Trust
Stone Container Corp.
Stone Family Foundation,
  Jerome H.
Storz Foundation, Robert Herman

Strake Foundation
Stride Rite Corp.
Stroud Foundation
Stuart Center Charitable Trust,
  Hugh
Subaru of America Inc.
Summerfield Foundation, Solon
  E.
Swiss Bank Corp.
Tait Foundation, Frank M.
Target Stores
Teledyne
Teleflex Inc.
Templeton Foundation, Herbert
  A.
Tennant Co.
Tenneco
Texas Commerce Bank Houston,
  N.A.
Texas Gas Transmission Corp.
Textron
Thalhimer and Family
  Foundation, Charles G.
Thalhimer, Jr. and Family
  Foundation, William B.
Thoman Foundation, W. B. and
  Candace
Thomasville Furniture Industries
Thorpe Foundation, James R.
3M Co.
Times Mirror Co.
Timken Foundation of Canton
Titan Industrial Co.
TJX Cos.
Tokheim Corp.
Tosco Corp. Refining Division
Toyota Motor Sales, U.S.A.
Tozer Foundation
Tracor, Inc.
Transco Energy Company
Tranzonic Cos.
Travelers Cos.
Trexler Trust, Harry C.
TRINOVA Corp.
Triskelion Ltd.
Tropicana Products, Inc.
True North Foundation
Trull Foundation
Trust Co. Bank
Trust for Mutual Understanding
TRW Corp.
TU Electric Co.
Tuch Foundation, Michael
Tull Charitable Foundation
Tuohy Foundation, Alice Tweed
Tupancy-Harris Foundation of
  1986
Turner Charitable Foundation
Turner Charitable Trust,
  Courtney S.
Unger Foundation, Aber D.
Unilever United States
Union Bank
Union Bank of Switzerland New
  York Branch
Union Electric Co.
Union Pacific Corp.
U.S. Leasing International
United States Trust Co. of New
  York
Unitrode Corp.
Universal Foods Corp.
Universal Leaf Tobacco Co.
Unocal Corp.
Upjohn Co.
US Bancorp
US WEST
USG Corp.
UST
USX Corp.
Utilicorp United
V and V Foundation
Valdese Manufacturing Co., Inc.
Valentine Foundation, Lawson
Valley Foundation
Valley National Bank of Arizona
Valspar Corp.

Van Nuys Charities, J. B. and
  Emily
Van Wert County Foundation
Veritas Foundation
Vidda Foundation
Virginia Power Co.
Volkswagen of America, Inc.
Vulcan Materials Co.
Wahlstrom Foundation
Wal-Mart Stores
Walker Foundation, T. B.
Wallace Reader's Digest Fund,
  Lila
Walsh Foundation
Walter Family Trust, Byron L.
Washington Mutual Savings
  Bank
Washington Water Power Co.
Wasmer Foundation
Wasserman Foundation
Waste Management
Watson Foundation, Walter E.
  and Caroline H.
Watumull Fund, J.
Wausau Paper Mills Co.
Wean Foundation, Raymond John
Webster Foundation, Edwin S.
Weeden Foundation, Frank
Weisbrod Foundation Trust
  Dept., Robert and Mary
Wells Foundation, Franklin H.
  and Ruth L.
Wendt Foundation, Margaret L.
West Co.
West One Bancorp
Westerman Foundation, Samuel
  L.
Westinghouse Electric Corp.
Westvaco Corp.
Weyerhaeuser Co.
Weyerhaeuser Foundation,
  Frederick and Margaret L.
Wheeler Foundation
Whirlpool Corp.
Whitaker Charitable Foundation,
  Lyndon C.
Whitaker Foundation
White Consolidated Industries
White Foundation, Erle and
  Emma
Whitehead Foundation
Whitener Foundation
Wiegand Foundation, E. L.
Wilcox General Trust, George N.
Wilcox Trust, S. W.
Williams Cos.
Williams Foundation, Arthur
  Ashley
Williamson Co.
Wilmington Trust Co.
Wilson Fund, Matilda R.
Wilson Public Trust, Ralph
Winston Foundation, Norman
  and Rosita
Winter Construction Co.
Wisconsin Energy Corp.
Wisconsin Power & Light Co.
Wolverine World Wide, Inc.
Woods Charitable Fund
Woodward Fund-Atlanta, David,
  Helen, Marian
Woolley Foundation, Vasser
Wornall Charitable Trust and
  Foundation, Kearney
Wortham Foundation
Wyman Youth Trust
Wyne Foundation
Yellow Corp.
Younkers, Inc.
Zellerbach Family Fund
Zenkel Foundation
Zimmerman Family Foundation,
  Raymond

Visual Arts

Abell Foundation, The
Ahmanson Foundation

Alabama Power Co.
ALPAC Corp.
Aluminum Co. of America
American Express Co.
American National Bank & Trust
  Co. of Chicago
American Natural Resources Co.
American Telephone &
  Telegraph Co.
American United Life Insurance
  Co.
Ameritech Services
Ames Department Stores
Apache Corp.
Appleton Papers
Attleboro Pawtucket Savings
  Bank
Baldwin Memorial Foundation,
  Fred
Bank of Boston Corp.
Bankers Trust Co.
Beldon II Fund
Bemis Company
Bethlehem Steel Corp.
BFGoodrich
Binney & Smith Inc.
Block, H&R
Blount
Boehringer Mannheim Corp.
Bradley Foundation, Lynde and
  Harry
Brown Foundation, James
  Graham
Buck Foundation, Carol Franc
Burdines
Bush Foundation
Central Maine Power Co.
Central Soya Co.
Champion International Corp.
Chase Manhattan Bank, N.A.
Chicago Sun-Times, Inc.
Clark Foundation, Robert
  Sterling
Clorox Co.
CNA Insurance Cos.
CNG Transmission Corp.
Cohn Foundation, Herman and
  Terese
Colonial Life & Accident
  Insurance Co.
Columbia Foundation
Consolidated Freightways
Cosmair, Inc.
Cowles Charitable Trust
Cowles Media Co.
Dayton Hudson Corp.
Dayton Power and Light Co.
Dekalb Energy Co.
Deposit Guaranty National Bank
Dodge Foundation, Geraldine R.
Douglas Charitable Foundation
Dow Corning Corp.
Dreyfus Foundation, Max and
  Victoria
du Pont de Nemours & Co., E. I.
Duchossois Industries
Eaton Corp.
Edgerton Foundation, Harold E.
EIS Foundation
Encyclopaedia Britannica, Inc.
Equitable Life Assurance Society
  of the U.S.
Falk Medical Fund, Maurice
Federated Life Insurance Co.
Finley Charitable Trust, J. B.
Fireman's Fund Insurance Co.
First Interstate Bank NW Region
First Interstate Bank of Arizona
First Interstate Bank of Texas,
  N.A.
First Maryland Bancorp
First Tennessee Bank
First Union Corp.
Fleet Bank of New York
Fleet Financial Group
Francis Families Foundation
Franklin Mint Corp.

Funderburke & Associates
Gannett Co.
Gates Foundation
GATX Corp.
Geffen Foundation, David
General Electric Co.
General Motors Corp.
General Reinsurance Corp.
Gerbode Foundation, Wallace
  Alexander
Getty Trust, J. Paul
Glaxo
Glenmore Distilleries Co.
Globe Newspaper Co.
Goldman Foundation, Herman
Goldwyn Foundation, Samuel
Gottlieb Foundation, Adolph and
  Esther
Gould Foundation, Florence J.
Graham Fund, Philip L.
Griggs and Mary Griggs Burke
  Foundation, Mary Livingston
GTE Corp.
Hall Family Foundations
Hallmark Cards
Hechinger Co.
HEI Inc.
Heineman Foundation for
  Research, Educational,
  Charitable, and Scientific
  Purposes
Heublein
Hillman Family Foundation, Alex
Horizons Foundation
Hospital Corp. of America
Hubbard Broadcasting
Huffy Corp.
Huizenga Family Foundation
Hunt Alternatives Fund
Hunt Manufacturing Co.
I. and L. Association
IBM Corp.
Indiana Bell Telephone Co.
J.P. Morgan & Co.
James River Corp. of Virginia
Jerome Foundation
Johnson & Higgins
Jones Fund, Blanche and George
Kennecott Corp.
Kingsbury Corp.
Koret Foundation
Kraft General Foods
Kreielsheimer Foundation Trust
Lannan Foundation
Lastfogel Foundation, Abe and
  Frances
Lechmere
Levy Foundation, Edward C.
Long Island Lighting Co.
Louisiana Power & Light
  Co./New Orleans Public
  Service
Lubo Fund
Luce Foundation, Henry
Ludwick Institute
Lyndhurst Foundation
MacArthur Foundation, John D.
  and Catherine T.
Macy & Co., R.H.
Maritz Inc.
Marshall Field's
Marshall & Ilsley Bank
May Foundation, Wilbur
Mayer Foods Corp., Oscar
Meadows Foundation
Medtronic
Menil Foundation
Menschel Foundation, Robert
  and Joyce
Mercantile Bancorp
Meredith Corp.
Mervyn's
Meyer Memorial Trust
National Computer Systems
National Life of Vermont
New England Mutual Life
  Insurance Co.

New York Telephone Co.
The New Yorker Magazine, Inc.
News & Observer Publishing Co.
Nord Family Foundation
Northern Indiana Public Service Co.
Northern Telecom Inc.
Northwest Area Foundation
Northwest Natural Gas Co.
Norton Co.
Norwest Bank Nebraska
Occidental Petroleum Corp.
Oglebay Norton Co.
Olin Corp.
Overseas Shipholding Group
PACCAR
Pacific Enterprises
Pacific Telesis Group
Penn Foundation, William
Persis Corp.
Pew Charitable Trusts
Philip Morris Cos.
Pinewood Foundation
Pittway Corp.
Polaroid Corp.
Pollock-Krasner Foundation
Primerica Corp.
Procter & Gamble Cosmetic & Fragrance Products
Providence Energy Corp.
Provident Life & Accident Insurance Co.
Pulitzer Publishing Co.
Rose Foundation, Billy
Rosenwald Family Fund, William
Rouse Co.
Royal Group Inc.
Rubinstein Foundation, Helena
Rudin Foundation, Samuel and May
SAFECO Corp.
Salomon
San Diego Gas & Electric
Sara Lee Corp.
Sara Lee Hosiery
Scherman Foundation
Schrafft and Bertha E. Schrafft Charitable Trust, William E.
Schwartz Foundation, Bernard Lee
Seaway Food Town
Security Life of Denver
Sedgwick James Inc.
Sentinel Communications Co.
Shawmut National Corp.
Shenandoah Life Insurance Co.
Slifka Foundation, Alan B.
Springs Industries
Syntex Corp.
Tandy Foundation, Anne Burnett and Charles
Target Stores
Teledyne
Tenneco
Tracor, Inc.
Transco Energy Company
Trull Foundation
Tull Charitable Foundation
Union Camp Corp.
Union Electric Co.
United States Trust Co. of New York
Upjohn Co.
Upton Foundation, Frederick S.
US Bancorp
Virginia Power Co.
Vulcan Materials Co.
Wallace Reader's Digest Fund, Lila
Warhol Foundation for the Visual Arts, Andy
Washington Water Power Co.
Weisman Art Foundation, Frederick R.
West One Bancorp
Whirlpool Corp.

Wilson Foundation, Elaine P. and Richard U.
Winston Foundation, Norman and Rosita
Winter Construction Co.
Yellow Corp.
Zenkel Foundation

Civic & Public Affairs

Better Government

Acushnet Co.
AFLAC
Alberto-Culver Co.
Alcan Aluminum Corp.
Allendale Mutual Insurance Co.
Aluminum Co. of America
AMAX
American Natural Resources Co.
American Standard
Ameritech Corp.
Amoco Corp.
AMR Corp.
Andersons Management Corp.
Ansin Private Foundation, Ronald M.
AON Corp.
Appleby Trust, Scott B. and Annie P.
Arca Foundation
Archer-Daniels-Midland Co.
Armco Inc.
Armstrong Foundation
Armstrong World Industries Inc.
Atlanta Gas Light Co.
Attleboro Pawtucket Savings Bank
Babcock Foundation, Mary Reynolds
Babcock & Wilcox Co.
Backer Spielvogel Bates U.S.
Ball Corp.
Banbury Fund
Banc One Illinois Corp.
Bank of New York
Bank One, Texas-Houston Office
Barnes Group
Bausch & Lomb
Beidler Charitable Trust, Francis
Ben & Jerry's Homemade
Benton Foundation
Bethlehem Steel Corp.
Bierlein Family Foundation
Binney & Smith Inc.
Biomet
Blair and Co., William
Blum-Kovler Foundation
Boatmen's Bancshares
Boehringer Mannheim Corp.
Bridgestone/Firestone
Brown & Williamson Tobacco Corp.
Buchanan Family Foundation
Burdines
C.P. Rail Systems
Canon U.S.A., Inc.
Carolina Power & Light Co.
Ceco Corp.
Central Bank of the South
Central Life Assurance Co.
Central Maine Power Co.
Central Vermont Public Service Corp.
Chambers Development Co.
Chase Manhattan Bank, N.A.
Chevron Corp.
Cincinnati Bell
Cleveland-Cliffs
CM Alliance Cos.
Cohen Foundation, Naomi and Nehemiah
Colonial Life & Accident Insurance Co.
Columbia Foundation

Cook Charitable Foundation
CPC International
CR Industries
Crestar Financial Corp.
Crum and Forster
CT Corp. System
Cullen/Frost Bankers
Cummins Engine Co.
de Rothschild Foundation, Edmond
Dean Witter Discover
Deer Creek Foundation
Deposit Guaranty National Bank
Dimeo Construction Co.
Dow Fund, Alden and Vada
Dresser Industries
du Pont de Nemours & Co., E. I.
Durell Foundation, George Edward
E and M Charities
East Ohio Gas Co.
Eaton Corp.
Eccles Charitable Foundation, Willard L.
Eccles Foundation, Ralph M. and Ella M.
Elf Atochem North America
Emerson Electric Co.
Emery Memorial, Thomas J.
Encyclopaedia Britannica, Inc.
Enron Corp.
Equitable Life Assurance Society of the U.S.
Ethyl Corp.
Fairchild Corp.
Federal-Mogul Corp.
Federated Life Insurance Co.
Fel-Pro Incorporated
Fidelity Bank
First Chicago
First Fidelity Bancorporation
Firstar Bank Milwaukee NA
Fleet Financial Group
FMC Corp.
Folger Fund
Forbes
Ford Foundation
Forest Foundation
Foster and Gallagher
Foundation for Advancement of Chiropractic Education
Frank Foundation, Ernest and Elfriede
Freedom Forum
Freeport-McMoRan
Friedman Family Foundation
Fruehauf Foundation
Fry Foundation, Lloyd A.
Fund for New Jersey
Funderburke & Associates
Furth Foundation
GEICO Corp.
General Mills
General Motors Corp.
Gerschel Foundation, Patrick A.
Giant Food Stores
Glaxo
Glidden Co.
Great-West Life Assurance Co.
Greater Construction Corp. Charitable Foundation, Inc.
Greenebaum, Doll & McDonald
Guardian Life Insurance Co. of America
Gund Foundation
Haas Fund, Walter and Elise
Harsco Corp.
Hartford Steam Boiler Inspection & Insurance Co.
Hartmarx Corp.
Hastings Trust
Heinz Co., H.J.
Heller Financial
Henkel Corp.
Henry Foundation, Patrick
Higginson Trust, Corina
Hopeman Brothers

Hopkins Foundation, John Jay
Hospital Corp. of America
Household International
Houston Industries
Hunt Alternatives Fund
I. and L. Association
ICI Americas
Illinois Bell
Illinois Power Co.
Illinois Tool Works
Indiana Insurance Cos.
Ingersoll Milling Machine Co.
Inland Steel Industries
ITT Hartford Insurance Group
John Hancock Mutual Life Insurance Co.
Johnson Foundation, Willard T. C.
Johnson & Higgins
Jones Foundation, W. Alton
Kaplan Fund, J. M.
Katten, Muchin, & Zavis
Kellstadt Foundation
Kendall Foundation, Henry P.
Kerr Foundation
Kimball International
Koch Charitable Trust, David H.
Kyocera International Inc.
Lambert Memorial Foundation, Gerard B.
Legg Mason Inc.
Lightner Sams Foundation
Luce Foundation, Henry
MacArthur Foundation, John D. and Catherine T.
Manilow Foundation, Nathan
Maritz Inc.
Massey Charitable Trust
Material Service Corp.
MCA
McBeath Foundation, Faye
McCasland Foundation
McCormick Tribune Foundation, Robert R.
McDermott
McDonald & Co. Securities
McDonnell Douglas Corp.
McGovern Fund for the Behavioral Sciences
McKenna Foundation, Philip M.
McNutt Charitable Trust, Amy Shelton
Mead Corp.
Mellon Bank Corp.
Mellon Foundation, Richard King
Merck Fund, John
Merck Human Health Division
Metropolitan Life Insurance Co.
Meyer Foundation, Alice Kleberg Reynolds
Meyerhoff Fund, Joseph
Midwest Resources
Miller Charitable Foundation, Howard E. and Nell E.
Milliken & Co.
Morrison-Knudsen Corp.
Morton International
Motorola
Mott Charitable Trust/Spectemur Agendo, Stewart R.
Nalco Chemical Co.
National Computer Systems
National Fuel Gas Co.
National Steel
National Westminster Bank New Jersey
NBD Bank
New-Land Foundation
New York Telephone Co.
Nichols Co., J.C.
Noble Foundation, Samuel Roberts
Norman Foundation
Northern Trust Co.
Northwest Area Foundation
Norton Co.
Norwest Bank Nebraska

NuTone Inc.
OCRI Foundation
Oglebay Norton Co.
Orchard Foundation
Ortho Diagnostic Systems, Inc.
Pacific Enterprises
Pacific Mutual Life Insurance Co.
Pan-American Life Insurance Co.
Paramount Communications Inc.
Peoples Energy Corp.
Pepsi-Cola Bottling Co. of Charlotte
Pfizer
Philips Foundation, Jesse
Pittway Corp.
Pritzker Foundation
Provigo Corp. Inc.
Puget Sound Power & Light Co.
Questar Corp.
Randolph Foundation
Reed Foundation
Reily & Co., William B.
Revson Foundation, Charles H.
Reynolds Foundation, Z. Smith
Rich Co., F.D.
Richardson Foundation, Smith
Rigler-Deutsch Foundation
RJR Nabisco Inc.
Rochester Gas & Electric Corp.
Rochester Midland Corp.
Rockefeller Family Fund
Roe Foundation
Rohm and Haas Company
Ross Laboratories
Royal Group Inc.
Ruan Foundation Trust, John
Santa Fe Pacific Corp.
Sara Lee Corp.
Sara Lee Hosiery
Scholl Foundation, Dr.
Schultz Foundation
Schumann Foundation, Florence and John
Scrivner, Inc.
Scrivner of North Carolina Inc.
Seasongood Good Government Foundation, Murray and Agnes
Shaklee Corp.
Shelton Cos.
Shenandoah Life Insurance Co.
Shoemaker Fund, Thomas H. and Mary Williams
Simon Foundation, William E. and Carol G.
SNET
Sonoco Products Co.
Sooner Pipe & Supply Corp.
Southern California Edison Co.
Star Bank, N.A.
Sterling Winthrop
Stern Family Fund
Stern Memorial Trust, Sidney
Stockham Valves & Fittings
Strake Foundation
Sunmark Capital Corp.
Synovus Financial Corp.
Taconic Foundation
Tamko Asphalt Products
Taubman Foundation, A. Alfred
Taylor Foundation, Ruth and Vernon
Teledyne
Tension Envelope Corp.
Tetley, Inc.
Texas Gas Transmission Corp.
Thermo Electron Corp.
Timken Foundation of Canton
Town Creek Foundation
Transco Energy Company
TRW Corp.
Unilever United States
Union Camp Corp.
United States Sugar Corp.
United Technologies Corp.
Valero Energy Corp.
Wachovia Bank & Trust Co., N.A.

Better Government (cont.)

Disney Co., Walt
Warner Fund, Albert and Bessie
Weinberg, Jr. Foundation, Sidney J.
Weingart Foundation
Westinghouse Electric Corp.
Westvaco Corp.
Whitehead Foundation
Woods Charitable Fund
Xerox Corp.

Business/Free Enterprise

Abell-Hanger Foundation
Air Products & Chemicals
Airbus Industrie of America
Alabama Power Co.
Alcon Laboratories, Inc.
Allegheny Ludlum Corp.
Alliant Techsystems
Alumax
Aluminum Co. of America
AMAX
AMCORE Bank, N.A. Rockford
America West Airlines
American Cyanamid Co.
American Electric Power
American Natural Resources Co.
American Telephone & Telegraph Co.
American United Life Insurance Co.
Ameritech Corp.
Ameritech Publishing
Ameritech Services
Amfac/JMB Hawaii
Amoco Corp.
AMP
AMR Corp.
Amsted Industries
Andersen Corp.
AON Corp.
Appleton Papers
Archer-Daniels-Midland Co.
Arkansas Power & Light Co.
Armco Inc.
Armstrong World Industries Inc.
Ashland Oil
Attleboro Pawtucket Savings Bank
Avon Products
Babcock & Wilcox Co.
Baird & Co., Robert W.
Baker Foundation, R. C.
Ball Corp.
Baltimore Gas & Electric Co.
Banc One Illinois Corp.
Bang & Olufsen of America, Inc.
Bank Hapoalim B.M.
Bank of New York
Bank of Tokyo Trust Co.
Bank One, Texas-Houston Office
Bank South Corp.
Bankers Trust Co.
Battelle
Bausch & Lomb
Bedsole Foundation, J. L.
Belden Brick Co., Inc.
Belding Heminway Co.
Belk Stores
Bemis Company
Beretta U.S.A. Corp.
Bernstein & Co., Sanford C.
Bethlehem Steel Corp.
BFGoodrich
Binney & Smith Inc.
Block, H&R
Blue Cross & Blue Shield of Alabama
Blum-Kovler Foundation
Boatmen's Bancshares

Boatmen's First National Bank of Oklahoma
Boehringer Mannheim Corp.
Boise Cascade Corp.
Booz Allen & Hamilton
Borden
Borg-Warner Corp.
Boswell Foundation, James G.
Bradley-Turner Foundation
Bridgestone/Firestone
Bristol-Myers Squibb Co.
British Airways
Brooks Brothers
Brown & Williamson Tobacco Corp.
Broyhill Family Foundation
Bucyrus-Erie
Cablevision of Michigan
Cabot Corp.
Callaway Foundation
Campbell Soup Co.
Capital Cities/ABC
Carolina Power & Light Co.
Carrier Corp.
Cascade Natural Gas Corp.
Centel Corp.
Centerior Energy Corp.
Central Bank of the South
Central Life Assurance Co.
Central Maine Power Co.
Chapman Charitable Trust, H. A. and Mary K.
Chase Manhattan Bank, N.A.
Chesebrough-Pond's
Chevron Corp.
Cincinnati Bell
CIT Group Holdings
Citicorp
CM Alliance Cos.
CNA Insurance Cos.
Coleman Foundation
Collins Foundation, Carr P.
Colonial Life & Accident Insurance Co.
Colonial Oil Industries, Inc.
Colorado National Bankshares
Coltec Industries
Comerica
Common Giving Fund
Comstock Foundation
Cone Mills Corp.
Consolidated Natural Gas Co.
Continental Corp.
Cook, Sr. Charitable Foundation, Kelly Gene
Cooper Industries
Coors Brewing Co.
Coors Foundation, Adolph
Country Curtains, Inc.
CPC International
CR Industries
Crestar Financial Corp.
Cullen/Frost Bankers
Curtice-Burns Foods
Dana Corp.
Davis Foundation, Edwin W. and Catherine M.
Delaware North Cos.
Deposit Guaranty National Bank
Detroit Edison Co.
Dial Corp.
Dodge Jones Foundation
Douglas & Lomason Company
Dow Foundation, Herbert H. and Barbara C.
Dresser Industries
du Pont de Nemours & Co., E. I.
Duke Power Co.
Dun & Bradstreet Corp.
Durst Foundation
E and M Charities
Eka Nobel
Emerson Electric Co.
English Foundation, W. C.
Enron Corp.
Equifax

Equitable Life Assurance Society of the U.S.
Ethyl Corp.
Eureka Co.
European American Bank
Farish Fund, William Stamps
Federal Express Corp.
Federal-Mogul Corp.
Federated Department Stores and Allied Stores Corp.
Fidelity Bank
Fifth Third Bancorp
FINA, Inc.
First Boston
First Brands Corp.
First Interstate Bank of California
First Interstate Bank of Oregon
First Interstate Bank of Texas, N.A.
First Maryland Bancorp
First Mississippi Corp.
First Tennessee Bank
First Union Corp.
Firstar Bank Milwaukee NA
FirsTier Bank N.A. Omaha
Fleet Bank of New York
Fleming Companies, Inc.
FMC Corp.
Ford Meter Box Co.
Ford Motor Co.
Forest City Enterprises
Forest Oil Corp.
Freedom Forum
Freeman Charitable Trust, Samuel
Freeport-McMoRan
Funderburke & Associates
GAR Foundation
Gates Foundation
General Electric Co.
General Mills
General Motors Corp.
General Railway Signal Corp.
Georgia-Pacific Corp.
Gheens Foundation
Giant Food Stores
Glaxo
Gleason Memorial Fund
Glidden Co.
Gould Inc.
Gould Foundation for Children, Edwin
Grace & Co., W.R.
Grossman Foundation, N. Bud
Guardian Life Insurance Co. of America
Gulf Power Co.
Hall Foundation
Halliburton Co.
Hallmark Cards
Hamilton Oil Corp.
Harland Co., John H.
Harris Corp.
Harrison Foundation, Fred G.
Harsco Corp.
Hartmarx Corp.
Hechinger Co.
Hecla Mining Co.
Heileman Brewing Co., Inc., G.
Heinz Co., H.J.
Heinz Endowment, Vira I.
Heller Financial
Henkel Co.
Hershey Foods Corp.
Hoechst Celanese Corp.
HON Industries
Hopeman Brothers
Hospital Corp. of America
Household International
Houston Industries
Huizenga Family Foundation
Humana
Hunt Alternatives Fund
Hyde Manufacturing Co.
ICI Americas
Illinois Tool Works
Indiana Bell Telephone Co.

Indiana Desk Co.
Indiana Insurance Cos.
Inland Container Corp.
Inland Steel Industries
Inman Mills
Interco
Irwin-Sweeney-Miller Foundation
ITT Corp.
ITT Hartford Insurance Group
ITT Rayonier
J.P. Morgan & Co.
James River Corp. of Virginia
JELD-WEN, Inc.
JMK-A M Micallef Charitable Foundation
John Hancock Mutual Life Insurance Co.
Johnson Controls
Johnson Foundation, Willard T. C.
Johnson & Higgins
Johnson & Son, S.C.
Joyce Foundation
Keebler Co.
Keller-Crescent Co.
Kellwood Co.
Kennametal
Kennecott Corp.
Kiewit Sons, Peter
Kimball International
Kimberly-Clark Corp.
Koh-I-Noor Rapidograph Inc.
Krieble Foundation, Vernon K.
Ladish Co.
Lambe Charitable Foundation, Claude R.
Lard Trust, Mary Potishman
Lassus Brothers Oil
Leo Burnett Co.
Liberty Diversified Industries Inc.
Life Insurance Co. of Georgia
Lightner Sams Foundation
Lilly & Co., Eli
Linn-Henley Charitable Trust
Lipton, Thomas J.
LTV Corp.
Lubrizol Corp.
MacArthur Foundation, John D. and Catherine T.
Macy & Co., R.H.
Makita U.S.A., Inc.
Mankato Citizens Telephone Co.
Manville Corp.
Mardag Foundation
Maritz Inc.
Marsh & McLennan Cos.
Martin Marietta Corp.
Maytag Corp.
MCA
McCasland Foundation
McCormick & Co.
McCune Charitable Trust, John R.
McCune Foundation
McDermott
McDonald & Co. Securities
McDonnell Douglas Corp.
McDonnell Douglas Corp.-West
McDonough Foundation, Bernard
McFawn Trust No. 2, Lois Sisler
MCI Communications Corp.
McKenna Foundation, Philip M.
McLean Contributionship
McMillen Foundation
Mead Corp.
Meadows Foundation
Media General, Inc.
Medina Foundation
Mellon Bank Corp.
Mellon Foundation, Richard King
Memton Fund
Merck Human Health Division
Merrill Lynch & Co.
Metropolitan Life Insurance Co.

Meyer Foundation, Bert and Mary
Michigan Bell Telephone Co.
Michigan Consolidated Gas Co.
Midwest Resources
Mitchell Energy & Development Corp.
Mitchell Family Foundation, Edward D. and Anna
Mobil Oil Corp.
Montgomery Street Foundation
Moog Automotive, Inc.
Morrison-Knudsen Corp.
Motorola
Motter Printing Press Co.
Nalco Chemical Co.
Nathan Foundation
National Service Industries
National Steel
National Westminster Bank New Jersey
NBD Bank
New York Life Insurance Co.
New York Telephone Co.
News & Observer Publishing Co.
Nichols Co., J.C.
Noble Foundation, Samuel Roberts
Norfolk Shipbuilding & Drydock Corp.
Norfolk Southern Corp.
Norton Co.
NuTone Inc.
NYNEX Corp.
Ogilvy & Mather Worldwide
Oglebay Norton Co.
Ohrstrom Foundation
Olin Corp.
Olin Foundation, John M.
Ontario Corp.
Orscheln Co.
Outboard Marine Corp.
PACCAR
Pan-American Life Insurance Co.
Paramount Communications Inc.
Pennsylvania General Insurance Co.
Pet
Pew Charitable Trusts
Pfizer
Phelps Dodge Corp.
Philips Foundation, Jesse
Phillips Petroleum Co.
Picker International
Piton Foundation
Pittsburgh National Bank
Potomac Electric Power Co.
PPG Industries
Premier Bank
Pritzker Foundation
Procter & Gamble Co.
Provigo Corp. Inc.
Prudential-Bache Securities
Prudential Insurance Co. of America
Public Service Co. of New Mexico
Pulitzer Publishing Co.
Quaker Oats Co.
Questar Corp.
Ralston Purina Co.
Red Wing Shoe Co.
Reliance Electric Co.
Resnick Foundation, Jack and Pearl
Reynolds Foundation, Donald W.
Reynolds Foundation, Z. Smith
Rhone-Poulenc Rorer
Richardson Foundation, Smith
RJR Nabisco Inc.
Rockwell International Corp.
Rohm and Haas Company
Royal Group Inc.
Rubbermaid
Rubin Foundation, Samuel
Rudin Foundation
Sara Lee Hosiery

Scheuer Family Foundation, S.
H. and Helen R.
Schroeder Foundation, Walter
Science Applications
International Corp.
Scrivner, Inc.
Scrivner of North Carolina Inc.
Seagram & Sons, Joseph E.
Sealright Co., Inc.
Searle & Co., G.D.
Shawmut National Corp.
Shell Oil Co.
Shore Fund
Shott, Jr. Foundation, Hugh I.
Shughart, Thomson & Kilroy,
P.C.
Sierra Pacific Industries
Signet Bank/Maryland
Simpson Investment Co.
Smith Corp., A.O.
SNET
Snider Foundation
Society Corp.
Sonat
Southern California Edison Co.
Spiegel
Sprague Educational and
Charitable Foundation, Seth
Springs Industries
Sprint
Square D Co.
Stanley Works
Star Bank, N.A.
Sterling Winthrop
Stevens Foundation, Abbot and
Dorothy H.
Stockham Valves & Fittings
Stoddard Charitable Trust
Stone Container Corp.
Stone & Webster, Inc.
Strake Foundation
Sun Co.
Sun Microsystems
Sunmark Capital Corp.
Teledyne
Tenneco
Texaco
Texas Instruments
Textron
Thermo Electron Corp.
Timken Co.
Timken Foundation of Canton
TJX Cos.
Tokheim Corp.
Torchmark Corp.
Tozer Foundation
Tracor, Inc.
Transco Energy Company
Trust Co. Bank
Trust for Mutual Understanding
TRW Corp.
TU Electric Co.
Tyson Foods, Inc.
Unilever United States
Union Bank of Switzerland New
York Branch
Union Camp Corp.
Union Carbide Corp.
Unisys Corp.
United Airlines
United Merchants &
Manufacturers
United Parcel Service of America
U.S. Leasing International
United States Sugar Corp.
United States Trust Co. of New
York
United Technologies Corp.
Universal Foods Corp.
Unocal Corp.
Upjohn Co.
US WEST
USX Corp.
Valmont Industries
Van Every Foundation, Philip L.
Vollrath Co.
Vulcan Materials Co.

Wachovia Bank & Trust Co.,
N.A.
Wal-Mart Stores
Walgreen Co.
Walker Educational and
Charitable Foundation, Alex C.
Disney Co., Walt
Walter Industries
Warren Charite
Wenger Foundation, Henry L.
and Consuelo S.
West Co.
Western Southern Life Insurance
Co.
Westvaco Corp.
Weyerhaeuser Co.
Whirlpool Corp.
Whitehead Foundation
Williams Cos.
Wilson Fund, Matilda R.
Wisconsin Energy Corp.
Wisconsin Power & Light Co.
Wurzburg, Inc.
Xerox Corp.

Civil Rights

Abelard Foundation
Abraham & Straus
Abrams Foundation
Acushnet Co.
Ahmanson Foundation
Air Products & Chemicals
Alco Standard Corp.
ALPAC Corp.
Aluminum Co. of America
AMAX
American Brands
American Cyanamid Co.
American Electric Power
American Express Co.
American Telephone &
Telegraph Co.
Ameritech Corp.
Amfac/JMB Hawaii
Amoco Corp.
AMP
AMR Corp.
Andersen Corp.
Andreas Foundation
Anheuser-Busch Cos.
Ansin Private Foundation,
Ronald M.
AON Corp.
Apple Computer, Inc.
Arca Foundation
Archer-Daniels-Midland Co.
ARCO
Aristech Chemical Corp.
Arkansas Power & Light Co.
Arkla
Armco Inc.
Armington Fund, Evenor
Atlanta Gas Light Co.
Attleboro Pawtucket Savings
Bank
Auerbach Foundation, Beatrice
Fox
Augat, Inc.
Avon Products
Babcock Foundation, Mary
Reynolds
Baker & Baker
Bank of New York
Bank One, Texas-Houston Office
BankAmerica Corp.
BarclaysAmerican Corp.
Barden Corp.
Barra Foundation
Bauer Foundation, M. R.
Bell Industries
Ben & Jerry's Homemade
Bernstein & Co., Sanford C.
Bethlehem Steel Corp.
Binney & Smith Inc.
Blair Foundation, John

Blaustein Foundation, Jacob and
Hilda
Block, H&R
Blum-Kovler Foundation
Boehm Foundation
Boise Cascade Corp.
Booz Allen & Hamilton
Borden
Borman's
Boulevard Foundation
Bremer Foundation, Otto
Brenner Foundation
Bridgestone/Firestone
Brown Charitable Trust, Peter D.
and Dorothy S.
Browning-Ferris Industries
Brunswick Corp.
Brush Foundation
Burdines
Burns Foundation, Jacob
Burress, J.W.
Bydale Foundation
C.P. Rail Systems
Cabot Family Charitable Trust
Candlesticks Inc.
Carnival Cruise Lines
Carrier Corp.
Carteh Foundation
Cassett Foundation, Louis N.
Caterpillar
Center for Educational Programs
Centerior Energy Corp.
Central Maine Power Co.
Chais Family Foundation
Chase Manhattan Bank, N.A.
Chazen Foundation
Chemical Bank
Chesebrough-Pond's
Ciba-Geigy Corp.
(Pharmaceuticals Division)
Citicorp
Citizens Commercial & Savings
Bank
Clark Foundation
Clark Foundation, Edna
McConnell
Clark Foundation, Robert
Sterling
Clorox Co.
CM Alliance Cos.
Cohen Foundation, Naomi and
Nehemiah
Columbia Foundation
Commonwealth Edison Co.
Connelly Foundation
Connemara Fund
Conston Corp.
Coors Brewing Co.
Covington and Burling
Cow Hollow Foundation
Cowles Charitable Trust
Cowles Media Co.
CPC International
Crown Memorial, Arie and Ida
Cudahy Fund, Patrick and Anna
M.
Cummings Foundation, Nathan
Cummins Engine Co.
Curtice-Burns Foods
Dana Corp.
Danner Foundation
Davis Foundation, Edwin W. and
Catherine M.
Dayton Hudson Corp.
Deer Creek Foundation
Delaware North Cos.
DelMar Foundation, Charles
Deposit Guaranty National Bank
Detroit Edison Co.
Deutsch Co.
Dial Corp.
Diamond Foundation, Aaron
Donnelley Foundation, Gaylord
and Dorothy
Dorot Foundation
Dorr Foundation

Dow Foundation, Herbert H. and
Barbara C.
Dresser Industries
du Pont de Nemours & Co., E. I.
Duke Power Co.
Dun & Bradstreet Corp.
Durham Merchants Association
Charitable Foundation
Durst Foundation
Eder Foundation, Sidney and
Arthur
EG&G Inc.
Emerson Electric Co.
Equifax
Equitable Life Assurance Society
of the U.S.
Ernest & Julio Gallo Winery
European American Bank
Fair Oaks Foundation, Inc.
Falcon Foundation
Falk Foundation, Michael David
Federal Express Corp.
Federal-Mogul Corp.
Federated Department Stores and
Allied Stores Corp.
Federation Foundation of
Greater Philadelphia
Feil Foundation, Louis and
Gertrude
Fel-Pro Incorporated
Fels Fund, Samuel S.
Ferkauf Foundation, Eugene and
Estelle
Fibre Converters
Fidelity Bank
Fifth Third Bancorp
Fingerhut Family Foundation
Fireman Charitable Foundation,
Paul and Phyllis
First Boston
First Brands Corp.
First Chicago
First Fidelity Bancorporation
First Maryland Bancorp
First Petroleum Corp.
First Tennessee Bank
Firstar Bank Milwaukee NA
Fleet Financial Group
Flemm Foundation, John J.
Florida Steel Corp.
Foley, Hoag & Eliot
Forbes
Ford Foundation
Ford Motor Co.
Forest Foundation
Foster Foundation, Joseph C. and
Esther
Foundation for Child
Development
Foundation for Middle East
Peace
Fowler Memorial Foundation,
John Edward
Fox Inc.
Fraida Foundation
Frankel Foundation, George and
Elizabeth F.
Freedom Forum
Fuchsberg Family Foundation,
Abraham
Funderburke & Associates
Furth Foundation
Geffen Foundation, David
General Electric Co.
General Mills
General Motors Corp.
General Signal Corp.
Georgia-Pacific Corp.
Georgia Power Co.
Gerson Family Foundation,
Benjamin J.
Giant Food Stores
Ginsberg Family Foundation,
Moses
Gleason Foundation, Katherine
Glen Eagles Foundation
Glidden Co.

Goldberger Foundation, Edward
and Marjorie
Goldman Foundation, Aaron and
Cecile
Goldring Family Foundation
Goldsmith Foundation, Horace
W.
Goldstein Foundation, Leslie and
Roslyn
Goldwyn Foundation, Samuel
Gould Inc.
Grace & Co., W.R.
Graybar Electric Co.
Green Fund
Gumenick Foundation, Nathan
and Sophie
Hamilton Bank
Hancock Foundation, Luke B.
Handleman Co.
Harsco Corp.
Hartford Steam Boiler Inspection
& Insurance Co.
Hechinger Co.
Hecla Mining Co.
Heileman Brewing Co., Inc., G.
Heilicher Foundation, Menahem
Heinz Co., H.J.
Hendrickson Brothers
Henkel Corp.
Henry Foundation, Patrick
Henry Foundation, Patrick
Hershey Foods Corp.
Hess Charitable Foundation,
Ronne and Donald
Hillman Foundation, Henry L.
Homeland Foundation
Hospital Corp. of America
Household International
Huber Foundation
Hughes Memorial Foundation,
Charles Evans
Humana
Hunt Alternatives Fund
Hunt Foundation
IBM Corp.
Icahn Foundation, Carl C.
ICI Americas
IES Industries
Illinois Bell
Illinois Tool Works
Imerman Memorial Foundation,
Stanley
Inco Alloys International
Indiana Insurance Cos.
Inland Container Corp.
Inland Steel Industries
Interco
Interstate Packaging Co.
Ireland Foundation
ITT Corp.
ITT Hartford Insurance Group
Ittleson Foundation
Ix & Sons, Frank
J.P. Morgan & Co.
Jameson Trust, Oleonda
JCPenney Co.
John Hancock Mutual Life
Insurance Co.
Johnson Controls
Johnson & Higgins
Johnson & Son, S.C.
Jones Foundation, Daisy Marquis
Kaplan Fund, J. M.
Kaplun Foundation, Morris J.
and Betty
Katten, Muchin, & Zavis
Kaye, Scholer, Fierman, Hays &
Handler
Keebler Co.
Kennecott Corp.
Kenworthy - Sarah H. Swift
Foundation, Marion E.
Kimberly-Clark Corp.
Kimmelman Foundation, Helen
& Milton
Kirkland & Ellis

Civil Rights (cont.)

Kline Foundation, Charles and
  Figa
Knistrom Foundation, Fanny and
  Svante
Koffler Family Foundation
Koh-I-Noor Rapidograph Inc.
Kohl Charitable Foundation,
  Allen D.
Kohl Foundation, Sidney
Koopman Fund
KSM Foundation
Kunstadter Family Foundation,
  Albert
Lasdon Foundation
Lasky Co.
Laurel Foundation
Lautenberg Foundation
Lehrman Foundation, Jacob and
  Charlotte
Lennon Foundation, Fred A.
Leo Burnett Co.
Levi Strauss & Co.
Levinson Foundation, Max and
  Anna
Levy Foundation, Charles and
  Ruth
Levy Foundation, Edward C.
Levy Foundation, Jerome
Lieberman Enterprises
Lilly & Co., Eli
Lipton, Thomas J.
Liquid Air Corp.
List Foundation, Albert A.
Lotus Development Corp.
Lowe Foundation
Lowenstein Foundation, Leon
Lozier Foundation
Maas Foundation, Benard L.
MacArthur Foundation, J.
  Roderick
MacArthur Foundation, John D.
  and Catherine T.
Macmillan, Inc.
Macy & Co., R.H.
Mailman Family Foundation, A.
  L.
MalCo Products Inc.
Manat Foundation
Mandel Foundation, Jack N. and
  Lilyan
Manilow Foundation, Nathan
Maritz Inc.
Marsh & McLennan Cos.
Martin Marietta Corp.
Matthews International Corp.
May Department Stores Co.
Mayerson Foundation, Manuel
  D. and Rhoda
Mazda Motors of America
  (Central), Inc.
Mazda North America
MCA
McConnell Foundation, Neil A.
McDonald & Co. Securities
McGraw-Hill
Mellon Bank Corp.
Merck Fund, John
Merrill Lynch & Co.
Mertz-Gilmore Foundation, Joyce
Metropolitan Life Insurance Co.
Meyer Foundation, Bert and
  Mary
Meyer Foundation, Eugene and
  Agnes E.
Michigan Bell Telephone Co.
MNC Financial
Morrison-Knudsen Corp.
Mosbacher, Jr. Foundation, Emil
Moses Fund, Henry and Lucy
Motorola
Mott Charitable Trust/Spectemur
  Agendo, Stewart R.
National Fuel Gas Co.
National Steel

National Westminster Bank New
  Jersey
NBD Bank
Needmor Fund
New England Mutual Life
  Insurance Co.
New-Land Foundation
New World Foundation
New York Foundation
New York Life Insurance Co.
New York Telephone Co.
The New Yorker Magazine, Inc.
Newhouse Foundation, Samuel I.
Nordson Corp.
Norfolk Southern Corp.
Norman Foundation
Norman Foundation, Andrew
Normandie Foundation
North Carolina Foam Foundation
North Shore Foundation
Norton Co.
NuTone Inc.
Oak Foundation U.S.A.
Olin Corp.
Olin Foundation, John M.
Olive Bridge Fund
Ottenstein Family Foundation
Overbrook Foundation
Pacific Mutual Life Insurance Co.
Paramount Communications Inc.
Pasadena Area Residential Aid
Penn Savings Bank, a division of
  Sovereign Bank Bank of
  Princeton, a division of
  Sovereign Bank
Pennsylvania General Insurance
  Co.
Peoples Energy Corp.
Pettus Crowe Foundation
Pfizer
Phelps Dodge Corp.
Philadelphia Industries
Philip Morris Cos.
Phillips Family Foundation, Jay
  and Rose
Phillips Petroleum Co.
Phillips-Van Heusen Corp.
Picker International
Pincus Family Fund
Pines Bridge Foundation
Pitney Bowes
Pitt-Des Moines Inc.
Pittway Corp.
Playboy Enterprises, Inc.
Polaroid Corp.
Polinger Foundation, Howard
  and Geraldine
Potomac Electric Power Co.
PPG Industries
Preyer Fund, Mary Norris
Price Foundation, Louis and
  Harold
Principal Financial Group
Pritzker Foundation
Procter & Gamble Cosmetic &
  Fragrance Products
Providence Energy Corp.
Provident Life & Accident
  Insurance Co.
Prudential-Bache Securities
Prudential Insurance Co. of
  America
Pulitzer Publishing Co.
Quaker Oats Co.
Ralston Purina Co.
Ratshesky Foundation, A. C.
Reed Foundation
Reliance Electric Co.
Reynolds Foundation, Z. Smith
Rigler-Deutsch Foundation
Riley Foundation, Mabel Louise
Ritter Foundation
Robinson Fund, Maurice R.
Rochester Gas & Electric Corp.
Rockefeller Foundation
Rockwell International Corp.
Roddis Foundation, Hamilton

Rohm and Haas Company
Rosenberg Foundation
Rosenthal Foundation, Ida and
  William
Rosenthal Foundation, Richard
  and Hinda
Ross Laboratories
Roth Family Foundation
Royal Group Inc.
Saint Gerard Foundation
Sara Lee Corp.
Sara Lee Hosiery
Schapiro Fund, M. A.
Schecter Private Foundation,
  Aaron and Martha
Schering-Plough Corp.
Scherman Foundation
Schiff, Hardin & Waite
Schiro Fund
Schwob Foundation, Simon
Scrivner, Inc.
Scrivner of North Carolina Inc.
Seagram & Sons, Joseph E.
Shawmut National Corp.
Sheinberg Foundation, Eric P.
Shell Oil Co.
Shenandoah Life Insurance Co.
Shwayder Foundation, Fay
Simon Foundation, William E.
  and Carol G.
Skirball Foundation
Smith Corp., A.O.
SNET
Snyder Fund, Valentine Perry
South Branch Foundation
Southern Bell
Southern California Edison Co.
Spectra-Physics Analytical
Spiegel
Starr Foundation
State Street Bank & Trust Co.
Stein Foundation, Jules and Doris
Sterling Winthrop
Stern Family Fund
Stern Memorial Trust, Sidney
Stewardship Foundation
Stonecutter Mills Corp.
Stoneman Charitable
  Foundation, Anne and David
Strake Foundation
Straus Foundation, Philip A. and
  Lynn
Sunmark Capital Corp.
Swim Foundation, Arthur L.
Taconic Foundation
Tamko Asphalt Products
Tang Foundation
Taub Foundation
TDK Corp. of America
Texaco
Texas Instruments
Textron
Thermo Electron Corp.
Times Mirror Co.
Tisch Foundation
TJX Cos.
Torchmark Corp.
Tortuga Foundation
Tropicana Products, Inc.
Trust Co. Bank
Twentieth Century-Fox Film
  Corp.
21 International Holdings
Unilever United States
United Airlines
Unocal Corp.
US WEST
UST
van Loben Sels - Eleanor Slate
  van Lobel Sels Charitable
  Foundation, Ernst D.
Von der Ahe Foundation
Von der Ahe, Jr. Trust, Theodore
  Albert
Wachovia Bank & Trust Co.,
  N.A.
Waldbaum Family Foundation, I.

Warner Fund, Albert and Bessie
Warsh-Mott Legacy
Weiner Foundation
Western Southern Life Insurance
  Co.
Westinghouse Electric Corp.
Westvaco Corp.
Whirlpool Corp.
White Consolidated Industries
Wiley & Sons, Inc., John
Winston Foundation, Norman
  and Rosita
Wisconsin Energy Corp.
Witco Corp.
Wolfson Family Foundation
Wollenberg Foundation
Woods Charitable Fund
Wrigley Co., Wm. Jr.
Xerox Corp.
Zale Foundation

Consumer Affairs

American Express Co.
American United Life Insurance
  Co.
Ames Department Stores
AMR Corp.
Apple Computer, Inc.
Atlanta Gas Light Co.
Attleboro Pawtucket Savings
  Bank
Bel Air Mart
Benton Foundation
Binney & Smith Inc.
Blue Cross & Blue Shield of
  Alabama
Borman's
Bridgestone/Firestone
Centel Corp.
Central Maine Power Co.
Comstock Foundation
Crum and Forster
Dresser Industries
Emerson Electric Co.
Equifax
Federated Department Stores and
  Allied Stores Corp.
First Brands Corp.
Forbes
Ford Motor Co.
Funderburke & Associates
Funderburke & Associates
Halliburton Co.
Household International
Hunt Alternatives Fund
Illinois Bell
John Hancock Mutual Life
  Insurance Co.
Johnson & Higgins
LaSalle National Bank
Long Island Lighting Co.
Macy & Co., R.H.
McKenna Foundation, Philip M.
Meyer Foundation, Bert and
  Mary
Michigan Bell Telephone Co.
Millipore Corp.
National Fuel Gas Co.
New England Mutual Life
  Insurance Co.
New York Life Insurance Co.
New York Telephone Co.
The New Yorker Magazine, Inc.
Newhouse Foundation, Samuel I.
Norcliffe Fund
Ogilvy & Mather Worldwide
Oglebay Norton Co.
Pacific Mutual Life Insurance Co.
Peabody Foundation, Amelia
Peoples Energy Corp.
Pfaffinger Foundation
Philadelphia Electric Co.
Philip Morris Cos.
Portland General Electric Co.
Principal Financial Group

Prudential Insurance Co. of
  America
Rochester Gas & Electric Corp.
Sara Lee Hosiery
Searle & Co., G.D.
Seaway Food Town
Security Life of Denver
Shawmut National Corp.
SNET
Southern California Edison Co.
Sterling Winthrop
Teledyne
Torchmark Corp.
Tracor, Inc.
Trust Co. Bank
Trust for Mutual Understanding
TRW Corp.
Union Camp Corp.
Valley National Bank of Arizona
Volkswagen of America, Inc.
Wallace Genetic Foundation
Westvaco Corp.
Whirlpool Corp.

Economic Development

Abell Foundation, The
AFLAC
Air Products & Chemicals
Akzo America
Akzo Chemicals Inc.
Alco Standard Corp.
Alexander Foundation, Judd S.
Allegheny Foundation
Allegheny Ludlum Corp.
Alliant Techsystems
Allyn Foundation
ALPAC Corp.
Altman Foundation
Alumax
Aluminum Co. of America
Alyeska Pipeline Service Co.
AMAX
AMCORE Bank, N.A. Rockford
America West Airlines
American Brands
American Electric Power
American Financial Corp.
American Microsystems, Inc.
American National Bank & Trust
  Co. of Chicago
American Natural Resources Co.
American Stock Exchange
American Telephone &
  Telegraph Co.
American United Life Insurance
  Co.
Ameritech Corp.
Ameritech Publishing
Ameritech Services
Amfac/JMB Hawaii
Amoco Corp.
AON Corp.
Apache Corp.
Arca Foundation
Archer-Daniels-Midland Co.
ARCO
Aristech Chemical Corp.
Arizona Public Service Co.
Arkansas Power & Light Co.
Arvin Industries
Ashland Oil
Atlanta Gas Light Co.
Atlantic Foundation of New York
Attleboro Pawtucket Savings
  Bank
Auerbach Foundation, Beatrice
  Fox
Avon Products
Babcock Foundation, Mary
  Reynolds
Babcock & Wilcox Co.
Baird & Co., Robert W.
Baird Foundation, Cameron
Baker & Baker
Ball Brothers Foundation

Ball Corp.
Ball Foundation, George and Frances
Bally Inc.
Baltimore Gas & Electric Co.
Banc One Wisconsin Corp.
Banfi Vintners
Bank of America Arizona
Bank of Boston Corp.
Bank of New York
Bank of Tokyo Trust Co.
Bank One, Texas-Houston Office
Bank One, Youngstown, NA
Bank South Corp.
BankAmerica Corp.
Barry Corp., R. G.
Battelle
Batten Foundation
Baughman Foundation
Bausch & Lomb
Baxter International
Bechtel Group
Bedsole Foundation, J. L.
Bemis Company
Ben & Jerry's Homemade
Benedum Foundation, Claude Worthington
Benefit Trust Life Insurance Co.
Benwood Foundation
Best Products Co.
Bethlehem Steel Corp.
Binney & Smith Inc.
Blair and Co., William
Blandin Foundation
Blank Family Foundation
Block, H&R
Blount
Boatmen's First National Bank of Oklahoma
Boeing Co.
Boettcher Foundation
Boise Cascade Corp.
Booth Ferris Foundation
Booz Allen & Hamilton
Borden
Boston Edison Co.
Bowater Inc.
BP America
Bradley-Turner Foundation
Bridgestone/Firestone
Briggs & Stratton Corp.
Bristol-Myers Squibb Co.
Brooks Brothers
Brown Foundation, James Graham
Brown Foundation, M. K.
Brown & Williamson Tobacco Corp.
Bucyrus-Erie
Burndy Corp.
Bush Foundation
C.P. Rail Systems
Cabot Corp.
Callaway Foundation, Fuller E.
Camp and Bennet Humiston Trust, Apollos
Campbell Soup Co.
Canadian Imperial Bank of Commerce
Candlesticks Inc.
Capital Holding Corp.
Carnegie Corporation of New York
Carolina Power & Light Co.
Carolina Telephone & Telegraph Co.
Carpenter Technology Corp.
Carr Real Estate Services
Cascade Natural Gas Corp.
Caterpillar
Centerior Energy Corp.
Central Bank of the South
Central Fidelity Banks, Inc.
Central Hudson Gas & Electric Corp.
Central Life Assurance Co.
Central Maine Power Co.

Central Soya Co.
Central Vermont Public Service Corp.
CertainTeed Corp.
Chambers Development Co.
Chase Manhattan Bank, N.A.
CHC Foundation
Chemical Bank
Chesapeake Corp.
Chevron Corp.
Chicago Resource Center
Chicago Title and Trust Co.
Chicago Tribune Co.
Chrysler Corp.
CIT Group Holdings
Citibank, F.S.B.
Citicorp
Clark Foundation, Robert Sterling
Cleveland-Cliffs
Clorox Co.
CM Alliance Cos.
CNG Transmission Corp.
Coachmen Industries
Collins Foundation
Colonial Life & Accident Insurance Co.
Colorado National Bankshares
Coltec Industries
Comerica
Commonwealth Edison Co.
ConAgra
Conoco Inc.
Consolidated Natural Gas Co.
Consumers Power Co.
Continental Bank N.A.
Continental Corp.
Control Data Corp.
Cooper Industries
Coors Foundation, Adolph
Corbin Foundation, Mary S. and David C.
Corning Incorporated
Country Curtains, Inc.
Cowles Media Co.
Cox Enterprises
CPC International
CR Industries
Crestar Financial Corp.
Crown Central Petroleum Corp.
CTS Corp.
Cullen/Frost Bankers
Cummins Engine Co.
CUNA Mutual Insurance Group
Curtice-Burns Foods
Dai-Ichi Kangyo Bank of California
Dain Bosworth/Inter-Regional Financial Group
Daiwa Securities America Inc.
Dalton Foundation, Dorothy U.
Danis Industries
Dayton Hudson Corp.
DEC International, Inc.
Deere & Co.
Delaware North Cos.
Deposit Guaranty National Bank
Detroit Edison Co.
Dexter Corp.
Dial Corp.
Diamond Shamrock
Diamond Walnut Growers
Dimeo Construction Co.
Dixie Yarns, Inc.
Dodge Foundation, Geraldine R.
Donaldson Co.
Donner Foundation, William H.
Douglas & Lomason Company
Dow Corning Corp.
du Pont de Nemours & Co., E. I.
Duke Power Co.
Durr-Fillauer Medical
Eaton Corp.
Eccles Foundation, Ralph M. and Ella M.
Edgewater Steel Corp.
Edwards Industries

El Pomar Foundation
Elf Atochem North America
Emerson Electric Co.
Enron Corp.
Ensworth Charitable Foundation
Equifax
Equitable Life Assurance Society of the U.S.
Ernest & Julio Gallo Winery
Erpf Fund, Armand G.
Ethyl Corp.
European American Bank
Exxon Corp.
Federal-Mogul Corp.
Federal National Mortgage Assn., Fannie Mae
Federal Screw Works
Federated Department Stores and Allied Stores Corp.
Federated Life Insurance Co.
Fidelity Bank
Field Foundation of Illinois
First Bank System
First Boston
First Brands Corp.
First Chicago
First Fidelity Bancorporation
First Interstate Bank NW Region
First Interstate Bank of California
First Maryland Bancorp
First National Bank & Trust Co. of Rockford
First Tennessee Bank
First Union Corp.
Firstar Bank Milwaukee NA
Fishback Foundation Trust, Harmes C.
Fleet Bank
Fleet Bank of New York
Fleet Financial Group
Florida Power & Light Co.
Flowers Charitable Trust, Albert W. and Edith V.
Fluor Corp.
Forbes
Ford Foundation
Forest City Enterprises
Forest Oil Corp.
Forster Charitable Trust, James W. and Ella B.
Fox Charitable Foundation, Harry K. & Emma R.
Fox Steel Co.
Freedom Forum
Freeport-McMoRan
French Oil Mill Machinery Co.
Frisch's Restaurants Inc.
Fry Foundation, Lloyd A.
Fund for New Jersey
Funderburke & Associates
Funderburke & Associates
Gannett Co.
GATX Corp.
GenCorp
General Accident Insurance Co. of America
General Atlantic Partners L.P.
General Electric Co.
General Mills
General Motors Corp.
General Railway Signal Corp.
General Reinsurance Corp.
General Signal Corp.
Georgia-Pacific Corp.
Georgia Power Co.
Gerbode Foundation, Wallace Alexander
German Marshall Fund of the United States
Gheens Foundation
Giant Eagle
Giant Food Stores
Gilmer-Smith Foundation
Glaxo
Glenmore Distilleries Co.
Glickenhaus & Co.
Glidden Co.

Globe Newspaper Co.
Goldome F.S.B
Goldseker Foundation of Maryland, Morris
Gould Inc.
Grace & Co., W.R.
Graco
Grant Foundation, Charles M. and Mary D.
Great Western Financial Corp.
Grimes Foundation
Grotto Foundation
Grundy Foundation
Guardian Life Insurance Co. of America
Gund Foundation, George
Hall Family Foundations
Hall Foundation
Hallmark Cards
Hamilton Bank
Hamilton Oil Corp.
Harden Foundation
Harris Corp.
Harris Trust & Savings Bank
Harsco Corp.
Hartford Steam Boiler Inspection & Insurance Co.
Hartmarx Corp.
Hechinger Co.
Hecla Mining Co.
Heinz Co., H.J.
Heinz Endowment, Howard
Heinz Endowment, Vira I.
Henderson Foundation, George B.
Heritage Pullman Bank & Trust
Hershey Foods Corp.
Herzog Foundation, Carl J.
Herzstein Charitable Foundation, Albert and Ethel
Heublein
Hewlett Foundation, William and Flora
Hillman Foundation
Home Depot
Homeland Foundation
Honeywell
Hopeman Brothers
Horizons Foundation
Hospital Corp. of America
Household International
Houston Industries
Howard and Bush Foundation
Hubbard Broadcasting
Hudson-Webber Foundation
Hudson's
Humana
Hunt Alternatives Fund
Hunt Manufacturing Co.
Hunter Foundation, Edward and Irma
Hyams Foundation
Ideal Industries
Illinois Bell
Illinois Power Co.
Illinois Tool Works
Inco Alloys International
Indiana Bell Telephone Co.
Indiana Insurance Cos.
Industrial Bank of Japan Trust Co.
Inland Container Corp.
Inland Steel Industries
Interco
Iowa-Illinois Gas & Electric Co.
Irvine Foundation, James
ITT Hartford Insurance Group
ITT Rayonier
J.P. Morgan & Co.
James River Corp. of Virginia
JCPenney Co.
John Hancock Mutual Life Insurance Co.
Johnson Controls
Johnson & Higgins
Johnson & Son, S.C.
Jones Foundation, W. Alton

Joyce Foundation
Justus Trust, Edith C.
Kaplan Fund, J. M.
Katten, Muchin, & Zavis
Keebler Co.
Keller-Crescent Co.
Kellogg Foundation, W. K.
Kennametal
Kennecott Corp.
Kerr Foundation
Kerr Foundation, Robert S. and Grayce B.
Kerr-McGee Corp.
Kettering Fund
Kiewit Foundation, Peter
Kiewit Sons, Peter
Kimball International
Kingsbury Corp.
Kiplinger Foundation
Kulas Foundation
La-Z-Boy Chair Co.
Laclede Gas Co.
Lance, Inc.
Laurel Foundation
LBJ Family Foundation
Lee Endowment Foundation
Lee Foundation, Ray M. and Mary Elizabeth
Levi Strauss & Co.
Levinson Foundation, Max and Anna
Liberty National Bank
Lilly & Co., Eli
Lilly Endowment
Lincoln Electric Co.
Lincoln National Corp.
Lipton, Thomas J.
Little, Arthur D.
Loews Corp.
Long Island Lighting Co.
Lotus Development Corp.
Louisiana Power & Light Co./New Orleans Public Service
LTV Corp.
Lydall, Inc.
Lyndhurst Foundation
MacArthur Foundation, John D. and Catherine T.
Maclellan Charitable Trust, R. J.
Maclellan Foundation
Mardag Foundation
Marion Merrell Dow
Maritz Inc.
Mark IV Industries
Marsh & McLennan Cos.
Marshall & Ilsley Bank
Martin Marietta Corp.
Marubeni America Corp.
Material Service Corp.
May Department Stores Co.
MCA
McCormick & Co.
McCormick Tribune Foundation, Robert R.
McDonald & Co. Securities
McDonnell Douglas Corp.
McGregor Fund
MCI Communications Corp.
McKenna Foundation, Katherine Mabis
McLean Contributionship
Mead Corp.
Meadows Foundation
Mellon Bank Corp.
Mellon Foundation, Richard King
Menasha Corp.
Mercantile Bancorp
Merchants Bancshares
Merck Family Fund
Merck Fund, John
Merck Human Health Division
Meridian Bancorp
Meritor Financial Group
Metropolitan Life Insurance Co.
Meyer Foundation, Bert and Mary

Recipient Type Index

Economic Development (cont.)

Meyer Foundation, Eugene and Agnes E.
Meyer Memorial Trust
Michigan Bell Telephone Co.
Michigan Consolidated Gas Co.
Michigan Gas Utilities
Middendorf Foundation
Midwest Resources
Milken Institute for Job and Capital Formation
Mine Safety Appliances Co.
Minnegasco
Mitsubishi International Corp.
MNC Financial
Mobil Oil Corp.
Montana Power Co.
Montgomery Ward & Co.
Moody Foundation
Moore Family Foundation
Morgan Stanley & Co.
Morrison-Knudsen Corp.
Moss Charitable Trust, Finis M.
Motorola
Mott Foundation, Charles Stewart
MTS Systems Corp.
Murphy Foundation
National City Corp.
National Computer Systems
National Forge Co.
National Fuel Gas Co.
National Gypsum Co.
National Starch & Chemical Corp.
National Steel
National Westminster Bank New Jersey
NationsBank Corp.
Nationwide Insurance Cos.
NBD Bank
NBD Bank, N.A.
Nestle U.S.A. Inc.
New York Foundation
New York Life Insurance Co.
New York Telephone Co.
Newhouse Foundation, Samuel I.
News & Observer Publishing Co.
Noble Foundation, Samuel Roberts
Nordson Corp.
Norfolk Southern Corp.
North American Life & Casualty Co.
North American Philips Corp.
North American Reinsurance Corp.
Northeast Utilities
Northern Indiana Public Service Co.
Northwest Area Foundation
Northwest Natural Gas Co.
Northwestern National Life Insurance Co.
Norton Co.
Norwest Bank Nebraska
NYNEX Corp.
O'Connor Foundation, A. Lindsay and Olive B.
Ogilvy & Mather Worldwide
Oglebay Norton Co.
Ohio National Life Insurance Co.
Oklahoman Foundation
Ontario Corp.
Orbit Valve Co.
Ormet Corp.
Overnite Transportation Co.
Oxford Industries, Inc.
Pacific Gas & Electric Co.
Pacific Mutual Life Insurance Co.
PacifiCorp
Pan-American Life Insurance Co.
Pappas Charitable Foundation, Thomas Anthony
Paramount Communications Inc.

Parker-Hannifin Corp.
Pennsylvania General Insurance Co.
People's Bank
Peoples Energy Corp.
Perkin-Elmer Corp.
Pet
Peterson Foundation, Fred J.
Pew Charitable Trusts
Pfizer
Phelps Dodge Corp.
Philip Morris Cos.
Phillips Family Foundation, Jay and Rose
Phillips Petroleum Co.
Phoenix Home Life Mutual Insurance Co.
Physicians Mutual Insurance
Pick, Jr. Fund, Albert
Pillsbury Co.
Pioneer Hi-Bred International
Piton Foundation
Pitts Foundation, William H. and Lula E.
Pittsburgh National Bank
Pittway Corp.
Plough Foundation
PNC Bank
Pollock Company Foundation, William B.
Portland General Electric Co.
Potlatch Corp.
PPG Industries
Premier Industrial Corp.
Primerica Corp.
Principal Financial Group
Procter & Gamble Co.
Procter & Gamble Cosmetic & Fragrance Products
Promus Cos.
Providence Energy Corp.
Providence Journal Company
Provident Life & Accident Insurance Co.
Prudential Insurance Co. of America
PSI Energy
Public Service Co. of Colorado
Public Service Electric & Gas Co.
Puget Sound Power & Light Co.
Pulitzer Publishing Co.
Puterbaugh Foundation
Quaker Oats Co.
Questar Corp.
Red Wing Shoe Co.
Reliable Life Insurance Co.
Reliance Electric Co.
Republic New York Corp.
Reynolds Foundation, Donald W.
Reynolds Foundation, Z. Smith
Reynolds & Reynolds Co.
Rich Products Corp.
Richardson Foundation, Smith
Riley Foundation, Mabel Louise
Robertshaw Controls Co.
Rochester Gas & Electric Corp.
Rochester Telephone Corp.
Rockefeller Brothers Fund
Rockefeller Foundation
Rockefeller Foundation, Winthrop
Rockefeller Trust, Winthrop
Rockwell International Corp.
Rohm and Haas Company
Rohr Inc.
RosaMary Foundation
Royal Group Inc.
Rubbermaid
Ryder System
SAFECO Corp.
Saint Paul Cos.
Salomon
San Diego Gas & Electric
Sandusky International Inc.
Sara Lee Corp.
Sara Lee Hosiery

Sargent Foundation, Newell B.
Scaife Foundation, Sarah
Schapiro Fund, M. A.
Scherman Foundation
Scheuer Family Foundation, S. H. and Helen R.
Schlumberger Ltd.
Science Applications International Corp.
Scrivner, Inc.
Scrivner of North Carolina Inc.
Searle & Co., G.D.
Security Life of Denver
Security State Bank
Shawmut National Corp.
Shell Oil Co.
Shenandoah Life Insurance Co.
Sherwin-Williams Co.
Sierra Pacific Resources
Signet Bank/Maryland
Simpson Investment Co.
Skinner Corp.
Smith Corp., A.O.
SmithKline Beecham
SNET
Society Corp.
Sonat
Sonoco Products Co.
Sordoni Foundation
Sosland Foundation
Southern California Edison Co.
Southwestern Bell Corp.
Sprague Educational and Charitable Foundation, Seth
Sprague Memorial Institute, Otho S. A.
Springs Foundation
Springs Industries
Sprint
SPX Corp.
Stackpole-Hall Foundation
State Street Bank & Trust Co.
Steelcase
Sterling Inc.
Stone Container Corp.
Strake Foundation
Stride Rite Corp.
Stupp Brothers Bridge & Iron Co.
Sulzberger Foundation
Sumitomo Bank of California
Sun Co.
Sun Microsystems
Synovus Financial Corp.
Taconic Foundation
Teledyne
Teleklew Productions
Tesoro Petroleum Corp.
Tetley, Inc.
Texas Commerce Bank Houston, N.A.
Texas Gas Transmission Corp.
Textron
Thermo Electron Corp.
Thomas & Betts Corp.
Thomas Industries
3M Co.
Time Insurance Co.
Times Mirror Co.
Tinker Foundation
Tonkin Foundation, Tom and Helen
Tosco Corp. Refining Division
Transco Energy Company
Tropicana Products, Inc.
Trust Co. Bank
TU Electric Co.
Tucker Charitable Trust, Rose E.
Tyson Foods, Inc.
Unilever United States
Union Bank
Union Camp Corp.
Union Central Life Insurance Co.
Union Electric Co.
Unisys Corp.
United Airlines
United States Trust Co. of New York

Unitrode Corp.
Universal Foods Corp.
Unocal Corp.
UNUM Corp.
US Bancorp
US WEST
USG Corp.
Utica National Insurance Group
Van Buren Foundation
Victoria Foundation
Vulcan Materials Co.
Wachovia Bank of Georgia, N.A.
Wachovia Bank & Trust Co., N.A.
Wal-Mart Stores
Wallace Genetic Foundation
Walter Industries
Washington Water Power Co.
Wauwatosa Savings & Loan Association
Wean Foundation, Raymond John
Weinberg, Jr. Foundation, Sidney J.
Wells Fargo & Co.
Wendt Foundation, Margaret L.
Westinghouse Electric Corp.
Westvaco Corp.
Wetterau
Weyerhaeuser Co.
Wheat First Securites
Whirlpool Corp.
Whitehead Foundation
Wieboldt Foundation
Wilkof Foundation, Edward and Ruth
Williams Cos.
Willmott Foundation, Peter S.
Wilson Fund, Matilda R.
Wisconsin Energy Corp.
Wisconsin Power & Light Co.
Witte, Jr. Foundation, John H.
Woods Charitable Fund
Wyomissing Foundation
Xerox Corp.
Yellow Corp.
Zale Foundation

Economics

Abbott Laboratories
Ahmanson Foundation
Air Products & Chemicals
Alliant Techsystems
Aluminum Co. of America
AMAX
American Cyanamid Co.
American Telephone & Telegraph Co.
Ameritech Corp.
Amoco Corp.
AON Corp.
Arca Foundation
Arcana Foundation
Arkansas Power & Light Co.
Armco Inc.
Armstrong Foundation
Armstrong World Industries Inc.
Atran Foundation
Attleboro Pawtucket Savings Bank
Avon Products
Ball Corp.
Bankers Trust Co.
BFGoodrich
Binney & Smith Inc.
Boise Cascade Corp.
Borden
Burlington Resources
Bydale Foundation
Cabot Corp.
Cain Foundation, Gordon and Mary
Carthage Foundation
Central Maine Power Co.
Charitable Fund
Chase Manhattan Bank, N.A.
Chevron Corp.

CIT Group Holdings
Citicorp
CM Alliance Cos.
Colonial Life & Accident Insurance Co.
Coltec Industries
Consolidated Papers
Continental Corp.
Cooper Industries
Coors Brewing Co.
Coors Foundation, Adolph
Daniel Foundation of Alabama
Dean Witter Discover
Delaware North Cos.
Detroit Edison Co.
Dial Corp.
Donner Foundation, William H.
Dresser Industries
du Pont de Nemours & Co., E. I.
Dun & Bradstreet Corp.
E and M Charities
Eaton Corp.
Eccles Foundation, George S. and Dolores Dore
Edgewater Steel Corp.
Emerson Electric Co.
Equifax
Equitable Life Assurance Society of the U.S.
Exxon Corp.
Federal-Mogul Corp.
First Boston
First Interstate Bank of Oregon
First Maryland Bancorp
Ford Foundation
Ford Motor Co.
Funderburke & Associates
Funderburke & Associates
GenCorp
General Accident Insurance Co. of America
General Electric Co.
General Motors Corp.
Georgia Power Co.
German Marshall Fund of the United States
Gillette Co.
Grace & Co., W.R.
Grainger Foundation
Greenfield Foundation, Albert M.
Gregg-Graniteville Foundation
Guardian Life Insurance Co. of America
Handleman Co.
Hardin Foundation, Phil
Harsco Corp.
Heinz Co., H.J.
Hershey Foods Corp.
Hopeman Brothers
Hospital Corp. of America
Hunt Alternatives Fund
Indiana Bell Telephone Co.
Indiana Desk Co.
Inland Container Corp.
ITT Corp.
Jewett Foundation, George Frederick
John Hancock Mutual Life Insurance Co.
Johnson & Higgins
Kaufman Foundation, Henry & Elaine
Keck, Jr. Foundation, William M.
Keebler Co.
Kennametal
Kerr-McGee Corp.
Kimberly-Clark Corp.
Koch Charitable Foundation, Charles G.
Koch Charitable Trust, David H.
Lambe Charitable Foundation, Claude R.
Lance, Inc.
Lane Co., Inc.
Liberty National Bank
Lilly & Co., Eli
Litton Industries

Louisiana Land & Exploration Co.
MacArthur Foundation, John D. and Catherine T.
Macy & Co., R.H.
Marsh & McLennan Cos.
Maxfield Foundation
McCormick Tribune Foundation, Robert R.
McDonnell Douglas Corp.
McKenna Foundation, Philip M.
Media General, Inc.
Mellon Foundation, Andrew W.
Mellon Foundation, Richard King
Merchants Bancshares
Merck Fund, John
Metropolitan Life Insurance Co.
Monroe Auto Equipment Co.
Montgomery Street Foundation
Motorola
Mott Fund, Ruth
Multimedia, Inc.
National Computer Systems
Natural Heritage Foundation
NBD Bank
NBD Bank, N.A.
New World Foundation
New York Life Insurance Co.
New York Stock Exchange
New York Telephone Co.
Noble Foundation, Samuel Roberts
Norton Co.
Noyes Foundation, Jessie Smith
Olin Foundation, John M.
PACCAR
Pacific Mutual Life Insurance Co.
PacifiCorp
Panhandle Eastern Corp.
Paramount Communications Inc.
Peoples Energy Corp.
Perini Corp.
Perkin-Elmer Corp.
Pfizer
Phelps Dodge Corp.
PHH Corp.
Phillipps Foundation
Phillips Petroleum Co.
Pitt-Des Moines Inc.
PPG Industries
Procter & Gamble Co.
Promus Cos.
Prudential Insurance Co. of America
Quaker Oats Co.
Randolph Foundation
Reynolds Metals Co.
Richardson Foundation, Smith
Rockefeller Foundation
Rockefeller Trust, Winthrop
Rockwell International Corp.
Rohr Inc.
Sage Foundation, Russell
Saint Paul Cos.
Santa Fe Pacific Corp.
Scaife Foundation, Sarah
Shawmut National Corp.
Shell Oil Co.
Shenandoah Life Insurance Co.
Sloan Foundation, Alfred P.
Smeal Foundation, Mary Jean & Frank P.
Sonat
Southern California Edison Co.
Spang & Co.
Staley Manufacturing Co., A.E.
Stanley Works
Starr Foundation
State Farm Mutual Automobile Insurance Co.
State Street Bank & Trust Co.
Stern Family Fund
Stranahan Foundation
Sun Banks Inc.
Sunmark Capital Corp.
Sunnen Foundation
Tamko Asphalt Products

Tektronix
Texaco
Texas Commerce Bank Houston, N.A.
Texas Gas Transmission Corp.
Texas Instruments
Textron
Thermo Electron Corp.
Thirty-Five Twenty, Inc.
Transco Energy Company
Trust Co. Bank
Tyson Foods, Inc.
Union Camp Corp.
Unocal Corp.
Vulcan Materials Co.
Wal-Mart Stores
Walker Educational and Charitable Foundation, Alex C.
Wallace Genetic Foundation
Warner-Lambert Co.
Weinberg, Jr. Foundation, Sidney J.
West One Bancorp
Westvaco Corp.
Weyerhaeuser Co.
Whirlpool Corp.
Wiener Foundation, Malcolm Hewitt
Wyomissing Foundation
Xerox Corp.

Environmental Affairs

Abbott Laboratories
Abelard Foundation
Abell Foundation, Charles S.
Abell Foundation, The
Abell-Hanger Foundation
Abrams Foundation, Benjamin and Elizabeth
Abrons Foundation, Louis and Anne
Acushnet Co.
Adams Memorial Fund, Emma J.
Agape Foundation
Agway
Ahmanson Foundation
AHS Foundation
Air Products & Chemicals
AKC Fund
Alabama Power Co.
Alexander Foundation, Judd S.
Algonquin Energy, Inc.
Allegheny Foundation
Allendale Mutual Insurance Co.
AlliedSignal
Alms Trust, Eleanora
ALPAC Corp.
Aluminum Co. of America
Alyeska Pipeline Service Co.
AMAX
Amdahl Corp.
America West Airlines
American Brands
American Building Maintenance Industries
American Cyanamid Co.
American Electric Power
American Foundation Corporation
American Natural Resources Co.
American Telephone & Telegraph Co.
Americana Foundation
Ameritech Services
Amfac/JMB Hawaii
Amoco Corp.
Analog Devices
Andersen Corp.
Andersons Management Corp.
Andreas Foundation
Andres Charitable Trust, Frank G.
Anheuser-Busch Cos.
AON Corp.
Apache Corp.

Apple Computer, Inc.
Appleman Foundation
Appleton Papers
Arcadia Foundation
Archer-Daniels-Midland Co.
Archibald Charitable Foundation, Norman
ARCO
ARCO Chemical
Aristech Chemical Corp.
Arizona Public Service Co.
Arkansas Power & Light Co.
Arkla
Armco Inc.
Armington Fund, Evenor
Aron Charitable Foundation, J.
ASARCO
Ashland Oil
Atherton Family Foundation
Atlanta Gas Light Co.
Atran Foundation
Attleboro Pawtucket Savings Bank
Auerbach Foundation, Beatrice Fox
Austin Memorial Foundation
Autry Foundation
Autzen Foundation
Avis Inc.
Avon Products
Azadoutioun Foundation
Babcock Foundation, Mary Reynolds
Babcock & Wilcox Co.
Babson Foundation, Paul and Edith
Bailey Wildlife Foundation
Baker Trust, Clayton
Baker Trust, George F.
Baldwin, Jr. Foundation, Summerfield
Ball Brothers Foundation
Baltimore Gas & Electric Co.
Banbury Fund
Banc One Illinois Corp.
Bancorp Hawaii
Bancorp Hawaii
Bank of America Arizona
Bank of Boston Connecticut
Bank of New York
Bank One, Texas-Houston Office
Bankers Trust Co.
Bannerman Foundation, William C.
Barbour Foundation, Bernice
Bard, C. R.
Barker Foundation, Donald R.
Barker Foundation, J. M. R.
Barnes Group
Barth Foundation, Theodore H.
Bass Corporation, Perry and Nancy Lee
Bass Foundation
Batten Foundation
Bauer Foundation, M. R.
Bausch & Lomb
Bay Foundation
Bayne Fund, Howard
BCR Foundation
BCR Foundation
Bean, L.L.
Bechtel Charitable Remainder Uni-Trust, Harold R.
Bechtel Charitable Remainder Uni-Trust, Marie H.
Beckman Foundation, Leland D.
Bedford Fund
Bedminster Fund
Beech Aircraft Corp.
Beidler Charitable Trust, Francis
Beim Foundation
Beinecke Foundation
Beir Foundation
Belden Brick Co., Inc.
Beldon Fund
Beldon II Fund
Belfer Foundation

Belk Stores
Beloco Foundation
Belz Foundation
Bemis Company
Ben & Jerry's Homemade
Bend Millwork Systems
Benedum Foundation, Claude Worthington
Beneficia Foundation
Beneficial Corp.
Benua Foundation
Benwood Foundation
Berger Foundation, H.N. and Frances C.
Bersted Foundation
Berwind Corp.
Best Products Co.
Bethlehem Steel Corp.
Beveridge Foundation, Frank Stanley
Bicknell Fund
Biddle Foundation, Mary Duke
Bierlein Family Foundation
Bigelow Foundation, F. R.
Bing Fund
Bing Fund
Bingham Foundation, William
Bingham Second Betterment Fund, William
Binney & Smith Inc.
Bionetics Corp.
Birch Foundation, Stephen and Mary
Bishop Foundation
Blackmer Foundation, Henry M.
Blandin Foundation
Blank Fund, Myron and Jacqueline
Blaustein Foundation, Louis and Henrietta
Bleibtreu Foundation, Jacob
Blinken Foundation
Bloedel Foundation
Blount
Blowitz-Ridgeway Foundation
Bluhdorn Charitable Trust, Charles G. and Yvette
Blum-Kovler Foundation
Boatmen's First National Bank of Oklahoma
Bob Evans Farms
Bodenhamer Foundation
Bodman Foundation
Boeing Co.
Bohen Foundation
Boise Cascade Corp.
Bolz Family Foundation, Eugenie Mayer
Booth-Bricker Fund
Booth Ferris Foundation
Booz Allen & Hamilton
Borden
Borg-Warner Corp.
Borkee Hagley Foundation
Borman's
Borun Foundation, Anna Borun and Harry
Bostwick Foundation, Albert C.
Boswell Foundation, James G.
Botwinick-Wolfensohn Foundation
Bovaird Foundation, Mervin
Bowater Inc.
BP America
Bradford Foundation, George and Ruth
Brady Foundation
Brady Foundation, W. H.
Bremer Foundation, Otto
Brewer and Co., Ltd., C.
Breyer Foundation
Bridgestone/Firestone
Bright Charitable Trust, Alexander H.
Bristol-Myers Squibb Co.
Brooklyn Union Gas Co.
Brooks Foundation, Gladys

Brown Foundation
Brown Foundation, M. K.
Brown Foundation, W. L. Lyons
Brown & Williamson Tobacco Corp.
Browning-Ferris Industries
Brundage Charitable, Scientific, and Wildlife Conservation Foundation, Charles E. and Edna T.
Brunswick Corp.
Bryan Family Foundation, Kathleen Price and Joseph M.
Bryant Foundation
Buchanan Family Foundation
Buhl Family Foundation
Bull HN Information Systems Inc.
Bullitt Foundation
Bunbury Company
Burdines
Burlington Resources
Burnham Donor Fund, Alfred G.
Burns Foundation, Fritz B.
Bush Foundation
Bydale Foundation
C.P. Rail Systems
Cabell III and Maude Morgan Cabell Foundation, Robert G.
Cabot Corp.
Cabot Family Charitable Trust
Cabot-Saltonstall Charitable Trust
Cafritz Foundation, Morris and Gwendolyn
Cain Foundation, Gordon and Mary
California Educational Initiatives Fund
Camp and Bennet Humiston Trust, Apollos
Camp Younts Foundation
Campbell Foundation
Campbell Foundation, Ruth and Henry
Cape Branch Foundation
Cargill
Carnahan-Jackson Foundation
Carnegie Corporation of New York
Carolina Power & Light Co.
Carolyn Foundation
Carpenter Foundation
Carpenter Foundation, E. Rhodes and Leona B.
Carpenter Technology Corp.
Carter Foundation, Amon G.
Carter Foundation, Beirne
Carter-Wallace
Carthage Foundation
Cary Charitable Trust, Mary Flagler
Cascade Natural Gas Corp.
Castle Foundation, Harold K. L.
Castle Foundation, Samuel N. and Mary
Caterpillar
Centerior Energy Corp.
Central Maine Power Co.
Central & South West Services
Central Vermont Public Service Corp.
CertainTeed Corp.
Chadwick Foundation
Chadwick Fund, Dorothy Jordan
Champion International Corp.
Champlin Foundations
Charina Foundation
Charities Foundation
Chase Charity Foundation, Alfred E.
Chase Manhattan Bank, N.A.
Chatham Valley Foundation
CHC Foundation
Cheatham Foundation, Owen
Chevron Corp.

Environmental Affairs (cont.)

Childs Charitable Foundation, Roberta M.
Chiles Foundation
China Medical Board of New York
Christodora
Church & Dwight Co.
Ciba-Geigy Corp. (Pharmaceuticals Division)
Circuit City Stores
Citicorp
Claiborne Art Ortenberg Foundation, Liz
Claneil Foundation
Clark Charitable Trust
Clark Foundation
Clark Foundation
Clark Foundation, Robert Sterling
Clorox Co.
Close Foundation
CM Alliance Cos.
Cobb Family Foundation
Codrington Charitable Foundation, George W.
Cogswell Benevolent Trust
Cohen Family Foundation, Saul Z. and Amy Scheuer
Cohen Foundation, Naomi and Nehemiah
Cohn Foundation, Herman and Terese
Colburn Fund
Cole Foundation
Cole Foundation, Olive B.
Cole Foundation, Robert H. and Monica H.
Coleman Co.
Coleman Co.
Coleman, Jr. Foundation, George E.
Coles Family Foundation
Collins & Aikman Holdings Corp.
Collins Foundation
Collins Foundation, Carr P.
Colonial Life & Accident Insurance Co.
Colorado State Bank of Denver
Columbia Foundation
Cominco American Inc.
Commerce Clearing House
Commonwealth Fund
Compton Foundation
ConAgra
Cone Mills Corp.
Confidence Foundation
Connell Foundation, Michael J.
Connemara Fund
Conoco Inc.
Consolidated Natural Gas Co.
Consolidated Papers
Consumers Power Co.
Continental Corp.
Control Data Corp.
Cook Batson Foundation
Cook Brothers Educational Fund
Cook Foundation
Cooke Foundation
Cooper Industries
Coors Brewing Co.
Coors Foundation, Adolph
Coral Reef Foundation
Corbin Foundation, Mary S. and David C.
Corpus Christi Exploration Co.
Covington and Burling
Cowles Charitable Trust
Cox Charitable Trust, Jessie B.
Cox Foundation
Cox, Jr. Foundation, James M.
CPC International
Craigmyle Foundation
Crane & Co.

Crane Co.
Crary Foundation, Bruce L.
Crestlea Foundation
CRI Charitable Trust
CRL Inc. .
Crocker Trust, Mary A.
Crown Central Petroleum Corp.
Crum and Forster
Crummer Foundation, Roy E.
Crystal Trust
CT Corp. System
Cudahy Fund, Patrick and Anna M.
Cullen/Frost Bankers
Culver Foundation, Constans
Cummings Foundation, Nathan
Cummins Engine Co.
Curtice-Burns Foods
Cyprus Minerals Co.
Dalton Foundation, Harry L.
Daly Charitable Foundation Trust, Robert and Nancy
Dammann Fund
Dana Corp.
Daniel Foundation of Alabama
Daniels Foundation, Fred Harris
Darby Foundation
Darrah Charitable Trust, Jessie Smith
Dart Foundation
Davey Tree Expert Co.
Davies Charitable Trust
Davis Family - W.D. Charities, James E.
Davis Foundation, Edwin W. and Catherine M.
Davis Foundation, James A. and Juliet L.
Davis Foundation, Shelby Cullom
Day Family Foundation
Day Foundation, Nancy Sayles
DEC International, Inc.
Dee Foundation, Annie Taylor
Deer Creek Foundation
Deere & Co.
Dekalb Energy Co.
Delavan Foundation, Nelson B.
Delaware North Cos.
Demoulas Supermarkets
Deposit Guaranty National Bank
DeVlieg Foundation, Charles
Devonshire Associates
Dewing Foundation, Frances R.
Dexter Charitable Fund, Eugene A.
Dexter Corp.
Dick Family Foundation
Digital Equipment Corp.
Dillon Foundation
DiRosa Foundation, Rene and Veronica
Disney Family Foundation, Roy
Dobson Foundation
Dodge Foundation, Cleveland H.
Dodge Foundation, Geraldine R.
Donaldson Charitable Trust, Oliver S. and Jennie R.
Donaldson Co.
Donnelley Foundation, Elliott and Ann
Donnelley Foundation, Gaylord and Dorothy
Donner Foundation, William H.
Dorr Foundation
Dougherty, Jr. Foundation, James R.
Douglas Charitable Foundation
Dow Corning Corp.
Downs Perpetual Charitable Trust, Ellason
Dreyfus Foundation, Max and Victoria
Driscoll Foundation
du Pont de Nemours & Co., E. I.
Duchossois Industries
Duke Power Co.

Dumke Foundation, Dr. Ezekiel R. and Edna Wattis
Dunn Foundation, Elizabeth Ordway
Dunspaugh-Dalton Foundation
duPont Foundation, Chichester
Durfee Foundation
Dyson Foundation
Earl-Beth Foundation
Earth Care Paper, Inc.
Easley Trust, Andrew H. and Anne O.
Eastman Kodak Co.
Eaton Corp.
Eberly Foundation
Edison Foundation, Harry
Educational Foundation of America
EG&G Inc.
El Pomar Foundation
Elf Atochem North America
Elkins, Jr. Foundation, Margaret and James A.
Emerson Electric Co.
Engelhard Foundation, Charles
English-Bonter-Mitchell Foundation
English Memorial Fund, Florence C. and H. L.
Enright Foundation
Enron Corp.
Ensign-Bickford Industries
Ensworth Charitable Foundation
Environment Now
Erpf Fund, Armand G.
Estes Foundation
Ethyl Corp.
Ettinger Foundation
Evans Foundation, Edward P.
Evans Foundation, T. M.
Exxon Corp.
Fabri-Kal Corp.
Fair Play Foundation
Falcon Foundation
Fanwood Foundation
Farallon Foundation
Farish Fund, William Stamps
Faulkner Trust, Marianne Gaillard
Favrot Fund
Federal Express Corp.
Federal Screw Works
Fein Foundation
Felburn Foundation
Fels Fund, Samuel S.
Fibre Converters
Field Foundation, Jamee and Marshall
Field Foundation of Illinois
Fieldcrest Cannon
Fikes Foundation, Leland
FINA, Inc.
Fireman's Fund Insurance Co.
First Brands Corp.
First Chicago
First Fidelity Bancorporation
First Hawaiian
First Interstate Bank of California
First Interstate Bank of Texas, N.A.
First Maryland Bancorp
First Mississippi Corp.
First Tennessee Bank
First Union Corp.
First Union National Bank of Florida
Firstar Bank Milwaukee NA
Fish Foundation, Ray C.
Fish Foundation, Vain and Harry
Fishback Foundation Trust, Harmes C.
Fisher Foundation
Flagler Foundation
Fleet Bank of New York
Flemm Foundation, John J.
Flintridge Foundation
Florida Power & Light Co.

Florida Power & Light Co.
Florida Rock Industries
Fluor Corp.
FMC Corp.
FMR Corp.
Foerderer Foundation, Percival E. and Ethel Brown
Fohs Foundation
Fondren Foundation
Foote, Cone & Belding Communications
Forbes
Forbes Charitable Trust, Herman
Ford Foundation
Ford Fund, Benson and Edith
Ford Fund, Walter and Josephine
Ford Motor Co.
Forest Foundation
Formrite Tube Co.
Fortin Foundation of Florida
Foster-Davis Foundation
Foster Foundation
Foundation for the Needs of Others
Fowler Memorial Foundation, John Edward
Fox Charitable Foundation, Harry K. & Emma R.
France Foundation, Jacob and Annita
Frank Foundation, Ernest and Elfriede
Franklin Mint Corp.
Frear Eleemosynary Trust, Mary D. and Walter F.
Freed Foundation
Freedom Forum
Freeport-McMoRan
Frelinghuysen Foundation
French Foundation
Frese Foundation, Arnold D.
Frick Educational Commission, Henry C.
Friendship Fund
Frost Foundation
Fry Foundation, Lloyd A.
Fund for New Jersey
Funderburke & Associates
Funderburke & Associates
Furth Foundation
Fusenot Charity Foundation, Georges and Germaine
Galvin Foundation, Robert W.
Gap, The
Garland Foundation, John Jewett and H. Chandler
Gateway Apparel
Gebbie Foundation
GEICO Corp.
GenCorp
General Atlantic Partners L.P.
General Electric Co.
General Mills
General Motors Corp.
General Reinsurance Corp.
General Service Foundation
Generation Trust
Genius Foundation, Elizabeth Morse
Georgia-Pacific Corp.
Gerard Foundation, Sumner
Gerber Products Co.
Gerbode Foundation, Wallace Alexander
German Marshall Fund of the United States
Gerstacker Foundation, Rollin M.
Gheens Foundation
Giant Eagle
Giant Food Stores
Giger Foundation, Paul and Oscar
Gilder Foundation
Gill Foundation, Pauline Allen
Gilman Foundation, Howard
Gilman, Jr. Foundation, Sondra and Charles
Gilmer-Smith Foundation

Gilmore Foundation, Earl B.
Glanville Family Foundation
Gleason Foundation, James
Gleason Foundation, Katherine
Glen Eagles Foundation
Globe Corp.
Goldberg Family Foundation
Golden Family Foundation
Goldman Charitable Trust, Sol
Goldman Foundation, Aaron and Cecile
Goldman Fund, Richard and Rhoda
Goldsmith Foundation
Goldsmith Foundation, Horace W.
Goldstein Foundation, Alfred and Ann
Goldwyn Foundation, Samuel
Good Samaritan
Gordon/Rousmaniere/Roberts Fund
Gould Foundation for Children, Edwin
Grace & Co., W.R.
Grainger Foundation
Grassmann Trust, E. J.
Gray Foundation, Garland
Greater Lansing Foundation
Green Foundation, Allen P. and Josephine B.
Green Fund
Greene Manufacturing Co.
Greenheck Fan Corp.
Greentree Foundation
Greenville Foundation
Gregg-Graniteville Foundation
Greve Foundation, William and Mary
Griffith Foundation, W. C.
Griffith Laboratories Foundation, Inc.
Griggs and Mary Griggs Burke Foundation, Mary Livingston
Grimes Foundation
Griswold Foundation, John C.
Gronewaldt Foundation, Alice Busch
Groome Beatty Trust, Helen D.
Grumbacher Foundation, M. S.
Gulf Power Co.
Gulfstream Aerospace Corp.
Gund Foundation
Gund Foundation, George
Guttman Foundation, Stella and Charles
H. B. B. Foundation
Haas Fund, Walter and Elise
Haffenreffer Family Fund
Haffner Foundation
Hall Charitable Trust, Evelyn A. J.
Hall Foundation
Halliburton Co.
Hamel Family Charitable Trust, D. A.
Hamilton Bank
Hamman Foundation, George and Mary Josephine
Hampden Papers
Hanes Foundation, John W. and Anna H.
Harden Foundation
Harder Foundation
Harding Educational and Charitable Foundation
Harding Foundation, Charles Stewart
Harper Foundation, Philip S.
Harriman Foundation, Gladys and Roland
Harriman Foundation, Mary W.
Harris Corp.
Harris Foundation, William H. and Mattie Wattis
Harrison Foundation, Fred G.
Hartford Steam Boiler Inspection & Insurance Co.

Hartz Foundation
Haskell Fund
Hastings Trust
Haynes Foundation, John Randolph and Dora
Hazen Charitable Trust, Lita Annenberg
Hazen Foundation, Edward W.
Healy Family Foundation, M. A.
Hebrew Technical Institute
Hechinger Co.
Heckscher Foundation for Children
Hecla Mining Co.
HEI Inc.
Heileman Brewing Co., Inc., G.
Heineman Foundation for Research, Educational, Charitable, and Scientific Purposes
Heinz Co., H.J.
Heinz Family Foundation
Heinz Foundation, Drue
Helfaer Foundation, Evan and Marion
Helms Foundation
Henderson Foundation, George B.
Hendrickson Brothers
Hermann Foundation, Grover
Hershey Foods Corp.
Hewlett Foundation, William and Flora
Hewlett-Packard Co.
Heymann Special Account, Mr. and Mrs. Jimmy
Higginson Trust, Corina
Hill and Family Foundation, Walter Clay
Hillsdale Fund
Hitachi
Hoche-Scofield Foundation
Hoechst Celanese Corp.
Hoffer Plastics Corp.
Hoffman Foundation, Maximillian E. and Marion O.
Hoffmann-La Roche
Hofmann Co.
Holley Foundation
Holmes Foundation
Holtzmann Foundation, Jacob L. and Lillian
Homeland Foundation
Honeywell
Hooker Charitable Trust, Janet A.
Hoover Foundation
Hoover Foundation, H. Earl
Hopkins Foundation, John Jay
Hopkins Foundation, Josephine Lawrence
Hopwood Charitable Trust, John M.
Horizons Foundation
Horne Foundation, Dick
Hospital Corp. of America
House Educational Trust, Susan Cook
Houston Industries
Hubbard Broadcasting
Hubbell Inc.
Huber Foundation
Hughes Memorial Foundation, Charles Evans
Huizenga Family Foundation
Hulings Foundation, Mary Andersen
Humana
Humphrey Foundation, Glenn & Gertrude
Hunt Foundation
Hunt Foundation, Roy A.
Hunter Foundation, Edward and Irma
Huston Foundation
Hutchins Foundation, Mary J.
Hyde and Watson Foundation
I. and L. Association
IBM Corp.

Icahn Foundation, Carl C.
ICI Americas
Iddings Benevolent Trust
IES Industries
Illges Foundation, John P. and Dorothy S.
Illinois Power Co.
Indiana Insurance Cos.
Ingersoll Milling Machine Co.
Inland Container Corp.
Inland Steel Industries
Insurance Management Associates
International Flavors & Fragrances
International Foundation
International Paper Co.
Iowa-Illinois Gas & Electric Co.
Ira-Hiti Foundation for Deep Ecology
Ireland Foundation
Isaly Klondike Co.
Island Foundation
ITT Corp.
ITT Rayonier
Ittleson Foundation
Ix & Sons, Frank
J. D. B. Fund
J.P. Morgan & Co.
Jackson Charitable Trust, Marion Gardner
Jackson Family Foundation, Ann
Jackson Foundation
Jackson Hole Preserve
Jacobson Foundation, Bernard H. and Blanche E.
Jaffe Foundation
James River Corp. of Virginia
Jameson Trust, Oleonda
Janirve Foundation
Jeffress Memorial Trust, Elizabeth G.
Jenkins Foundation, George W.
Jennings Foundation, Mary Hillman
Jewell Memorial Foundation, Daniel Ashley and Irene Houston
Jewett Foundation, George Frederick
Jockey Hollow Foundation
John Hancock Mutual Life Insurance Co.
Johnson Controls
Johnson Foundation, Burdine
Johnson Foundation, Howard
Johnson & Higgins
Johnson & Son, S.C.
Jones and Bessie D. Phelps Foundation, Cyrus W. and Amy F.
Jones Foundation, Montfort Jones and Allie Brown
Jones Foundation, W. Alton
Joselow Foundation
Jost Foundation, Charles and Mabel P.
Joukowsky Family Foundation
Joyce Foundation
Jurodin Fund
Jurzykowski Foundation, Alfred
Kantzler Foundation
Kaplan Fund, J. M.
Kaplen Foundation
Kaufmann Foundation, Henry
Kautz Family Foundation
Keck, Jr. Foundation, William M.
Keeler Fund, Miner S. and Mary Ann
Keller Family Foundation
Kellogg Foundation, J. C.
Kempner Fund, Harris and Eliza
Kendall Foundation, George R.
Kendall Foundation, Henry P.
Kennametal
Kennecott Corp.
Kennedy Foundation, Ethel

Kennedy Memorial Fund, Mark H.
Kent-Lucas Foundation
Kentland Foundation
Kerr Foundation, Robert S. and Grayce B.
Kerr Fund, Grayce B.
Kettering Family Foundation
Kettering Fund
Key Bank of Maine
Kiewit Foundation, Peter
Killam Trust, Constance
Kimball Foundation, Horace A. Kimball and S. Ella
Kimball International
Kimberly-Clark Corp.
Kimmelman Foundation, Helen & Milton
King Foundation, Carl B. and Florence E.
Kingsbury Corp.
Kingsley Foundation
Kinney-Lindstrom Foundation
Kiplinger Foundation
Kirbo Charitable Trust, Thomas M. and Irene B.
Kirby Foundation, F. M.
Klau Foundation, David W. and Sadie
Kleberg Foundation for Wildlife Conservation, Caesar Kleberg, Jr. and Helen C.
Kleberg Foundation, Robert J.
Klingenstein Fund, Esther A. and Joseph
Knapp Educational Fund
Knapp Foundation
Knox Family Foundation
Knox Foundation, Seymour H.
Koch Charitable Trust, David H.
Koffler Family Foundation
Kopf Foundation, Elizabeth Christy
Kraft Foundation
Kraft General Foods
Kramer Foundation, C. L. C.
Krause Foundation, Charles A.
Kresge Foundation
Kress Foundation, George
Krieble Foundation, Vernon K.
Krimendahl II Foundation, H. Frederick
Kuehn Foundation
Ladd Charitable Corporation, Helen and George
Lafarge Corp.
Lakeside Foundation
Lamson & Sessions Co.
Land O'Lakes
Lane Co., Inc.
Lane Memorial Foundation, Mills Bee
Larsen Fund
Lattner Foundation, Forrest C.
Lauder Foundation
Laurel Foundation
Lavanburg-Corner House
Lazar Foundation
Lazarus Charitable Trust, Helen and Charles
LBJ Family Foundation
Lebanon Mutual Insurance Co.
Lebovitz Fund
LEF Foundation
Lehigh Portland Cement Co.
Lennox International, Inc.
Leonhardt Foundation, Frederick H.
Levinson Foundation, Max and Anna
Levy Foundation, Jerome
Liberman Foundation, Bertha & Isaac
Liberty Corp.
Lightner Sams Foundation
Lilly & Co., Eli
Lilly Foundation, Richard Coyle
Lincoln Electric Co.

Lincoln National Corp.
Lincy Foundation
Linn-Henley Charitable Trust
Linnell Foundation
Lintilhac Foundation
Lipton, Thomas J.
Littauer Foundation, Lucius N.
Little, Arthur D.
Little Family Foundation
Littlefield Foundation, Edmund Wattis
Litwin Foundation
Liz Claiborne
Lizzadro Family Foundation, Joseph
Llagas Foundation
Long Island Lighting Co.
Longwood Foundation
Loomis House
Louisiana Land & Exploration Co.
Louisiana-Pacific Corp.
Louisiana Power & Light Co./New Orleans Public Service
Lowenstein Foundation, Leon
LTV Corp.
Lubrizol Corp.
Luce Charitable Trust, Theodore
Lurie Foundation, Louis R.
Luse Foundation, W. P. and Bulah
Lyndhurst Foundation
Lytel Foundation, Bertha Russ
Maas Foundation, Benard L.
MacArthur Foundation, John D. and Catherine T.
MacDonald Foundation, James A.
MacDonald Foundation, Marquis George
Maclellan Charitable Trust, R. J.
Maddox Trust, Web
Madison Gas & Electric Co.
Magma Copper Co.
Magowan Family Foundation
Mallinckrodt Specialty Chemicals Co.
Mandel Foundation, Morton and Barbara
Mandell Foundation, Samuel P.
Mandeville Foundation
Mardag Foundation
Marine Midland Banks
Maritz Inc.
Marmot Foundation
Marpat Foundation
Mars Foundation
Marsh & McLennan Cos.
Marshall Fund
Marshall & Ilsley Bank
Martin Foundation
Martin Foundation, Bert William
Martin Marietta Corp.
Marubeni America Corp.
Mary Kay Foundation
Masco Corp.
Massachusetts Charitable Mechanics Association
Massengill-DeFriece Foundation
Mather and William Gwinn Mather Fund, Elizabeth Ring
May Department Stores Co.
Mayer Foods Corp., Oscar
Maytag Corp.
Maytag Family Foundation, Fred
MBIA, Inc.
MCA
McAlister Charitable Foundation, Harold
McAlonan Trust, John A.
McBean Charitable Trust, Alletta Morris
McCamish Foundation
McCaw Cellular Communications
McConnell Foundation
McConnell Foundation, Neil A.
McCormick & Co.

McCormick Foundation, Chauncey and Marion Deering
McCune Foundation
McDonald Foundation, J. M.
McDonnell Douglas Corp.-West
McDonough Foundation, Bernard
McElroy Trust, R. J.
McEvoy Foundation, Mildred H.
McFeely-Rogers Foundation
McGraw Foundation
McGraw-Hill
McGregor Foundation, Thomas and Frances
McGregor Fund
MCI Communications Corp.
McInerny Foundation
McIntosh Foundation
McKenna Foundation, Katherine Mabis
McKnight Foundation
McKnight Foundation, Sumner T.
McLean Contributionship
McMillan, Jr. Foundation, Bruce
MDU Resources Group, Inc.
Mead Corp.
Mead Foundation, Giles W. and Elise G.
Mead Fund, Nelson
Meadowood Foundation
Mebane Packaging Corp.
Media General, Inc.
Mellon Foundation, Andrew W.
Mellon Foundation, Richard King
Memton Fund
Menasha Corp.
Merck & Co.
Merck Family Fund
Merck Fund, John
Mercy, Jr. Foundation, Sue and Eugene
Meredith Corp.
Mericos Foundation
Merkley Charitable Trust
Merrick Foundation, Robert G. and Anne M.
Mertz-Gilmore Foundation, Joyce
Metropolitan Life Insurance Co.
Meyer Foundation, Alice Kleberg Reynolds
Meyer Foundation, Baron de Hirsch
Meyer Memorial Trust
Michigan Bell Telephone Co.
Michigan Consolidated Gas Co.
Michigan Gas Utilities
Midwest Resources
Mielke Family Foundation
Mifflin Memorial Fund, George H. and Jane A.
Milken Foundation, L. and S.
Miller Brewing Co.
Miller Foundation, Steve J.
Milliken & Co.
Mine Safety Appliances Co.
MNC Financial
Mobil Oil Corp.
Model Foundation, Leo
Monadnock Paper Mills
Monell Foundation, Ambrose
Monfort Charitable Foundation
Moody Foundation
Moore Family Foundation
Moore Foundation, C. F.
Moore Foundation, Edward S.
Moore Foundation, Roy C.
Moores Foundation
Morgan Foundation, Burton D.
Moriah Fund
Morris Foundation, Margaret T.
Morris Foundation, William T.
Morrison Charitable Trust, Pauline A. and George R.
Morrison-Knudsen Corp.
Morse, Jr. Foundation, Enid and Lester S.
Moses Fund, Henry and Lucy
Moss Charitable Trust, Finis M.

Environmental Affairs (cont.)

Motorola
Mott Charitable Trust/Spectemur Agendo, Stewart R.
Mott Foundation, Charles Stewart
Mott Fund, Ruth
MTS Systems Corp.
Mueller Co.
Mullan Foundation, Thomas F. and Clementine L.
Murdy Foundation
Murphy Charitable Fund, George E. and Annette Cross
Nalco Chemical Co.
Nason Foundation
Nathan Berkman & Co.
National Computer Systems
National Fuel Gas Co.
National Life of Vermont
National Presto Industries
National Starch & Chemical Corp.
National Westminster Bank New Jersey
Natural Heritage Foundation
NBD Bank
Needmor Fund
Neu Foundation, Hugo and Doris
New England Biolabs Foundation
New England Mutual Life Insurance Co.
New Horizon Foundation
New-Land Foundation
New World Foundation
New York Foundation
New York Mercantile Exchange
New York Telephone Co.
Newhouse Foundation, Samuel I.
Newman's Own
News & Observer Publishing Co.
Nichols Foundation
Nike Inc.
Nippon Life Insurance Co.
Noble Foundation, Edward John
Norcross Wildlife Foundation
Nordson Corp.
Norfolk Southern Corp.
Norman Foundation
Norman Foundation, Andrew
North Shore Foundation
Northeast Utilities
Northen, Mary Moody
Northern Star Foundation
Northwest Area Foundation
Norton Co.
Norton Foundation Inc.
Noyes Foundation, Jessie Smith
Noyes, Jr. Memorial Foundation, Nicholas H.
Oaklawn Foundation
O'Brien Foundation, Alice M.
Occidental Oil & Gas Corp.
Occidental Petroleum Corp.
O'Connor Foundation, A. Lindsay and Olive B.
OCRI Foundation
Odell and Helen Pfeiffer Odell Fund, Robert Stewart
Odyssey Partners
O'Fallon Trust, Martin J. and Mary Anne
Ogden Foundation, Ralph E.
Ogilvy & Mather Worldwide
Oglebay Norton Co.
Ohrstrom Foundation
Oki America Inc.
Oleson Foundation
Olin Corp.
Olin Foundation, John M.
Olin Foundation, Spencer T. and Ann W.
Olive Bridge Fund
Olsson Memorial Foundation, Elis

1525 Foundation
Osborn Charitable Trust, Edward B.
Osceola Foundation
O'Shaughnessy Foundation, I. A.
Oshkosh B'Gosh
Overbrook Foundation
Overnite Transportation Co.
Overseas Shipholding Group
Oxford Foundation
Pacific Gas & Electric Co.
Pacific Mutual Life Insurance Co.
PacifiCorp
Packard Foundation, David and Lucile
Page Foundation, George B.
PaineWebber
Palmer-Fry Memorial Trust, Lily
Paramount Communications Inc.
Parsons Foundation, Ralph M.
Pasadena Area Residential Aid
Patagonia
Peabody Charitable Fund, Amelia
Peabody Foundation, Amelia
Peierls Foundation
Pella Corp.
Penn Foundation, William
Penney Foundation, James C.
Pennington Foundation, Irene W. and C. B.
Perkin-Elmer Corp.
Perkins Charitable Foundation
Perkins Memorial Foundation, George W.
Persis Corp.
Peters Foundation, R. D. and Linda
Petrie Trust, Lorene M.
Pew Charitable Trusts
Pfizer
Phelps Dodge Corp.
Philadelphia Electric Co.
Philip Morris Cos.
Philips Foundation, Jesse
Phillips Foundation, Ellis L.
Phillips Petroleum Co.
Phipps Foundation, Howard
Piedmont Health Care Foundation
Pierce Charitable Trust, Harold Whitworth
Pilot Trust
Pincus Family Fund
Pines Bridge Foundation
Pinewood Foundation
Pineywoods Foundation
Piton Foundation
Pitt-Des Moines Inc.
Plant Memorial Fund, Henry B.
Plaster Foundation, Robert W.
Plumsock Fund
Plym Foundation
Poinsettia Foundation, Paul and Magdalena Ecke
Polaroid Corp.
Pollybill Foundation
Portland General Electric Co.
Post Foundation of D.C., Marjorie Merriweather
Potlatch Corp.
Potomac Electric Power Co.
Pott Foundation, Herman T. and Phenie R.
Potts and Sibley Foundation
Powell Co., William
PPG Industries
Prairie Foundation
Preyer Fund, Mary Norris
Price Associates, T. Rowe
Price Foundation, Louis and Harold
Prickett Fund, Lynn R. and Karl E.
Prince Trust, Abbie Norman
Principal Financial Group
Pritzker Foundation
Procter & Gamble Co.

Procter & Gamble Cosmetic & Fragrance Products
Promus Cos.
Prospect Hill Foundation
Providence Energy Corp.
Providence Journal Company
Provident Life & Accident Insurance Co.
Prudential-Bache Securities
Prudential Insurance Co. of America
PSI Energy
Public Service Co. of Colorado
Public Service Electric & Gas Co.
Public Welfare Foundation
Puget Sound Power & Light Co.
Pulitzer Publishing Co.
Putnam Foundation
Quaker Chemical Corp.
Quaker Hill Foundation
Questar Corp.
Radiator Specialty Co.
Rahr Malting Co.
Raker Foundation, M. E.
Ralston Purina Co.
Ransom Fidelity Company
Raytheon Co.
Red Wing Shoe Co.
Reed Foundation, Philip D.
Reedman Car-Truck World Center
REI-Recreational Equipment, Inc.
Reily & Co., William B.
Reliable Life Insurance Co.
Reynolds Foundation, Donald W.
Reynolds Foundation, Richard S.
Reynolds Foundation, Z. Smith
Reynolds Metals Co.
Rhone-Poulenc Rorer
Rice Foundation
Richardson Charitable Trust, Anne S.
Ricoh Corp.
Rigler-Deutsch Foundation
Riordan Foundation
Roberts Foundation
Robinson Foundation
Robison Foundation, Ellis H. and Doris B.
Robson Foundation, LaNelle
Rochester Gas & Electric Corp.
Rockefeller Brothers Fund
Rockefeller Family Fund
Rockefeller Foundation
Rockfall Foundation
Rockwell Foundation
Rockwell Fund
Rockwell International Corp.
Roddenbery Co., Inc., W.B.
Rodgers Trust, Elizabeth Killam
Rogers Charitable Trust, Florence
Rohlik Foundation, Sigmund and Sophie
Rohm and Haas Company
Rohr Inc.
Romill Foundation
RosaMary Foundation
Rose Foundation, Billy
Rosen Foundation, Joseph
Rosenberg Foundation, Sunny and Abe
Rosenberg, Jr. Family Foundation, Louise and Claude
Rosenthal Foundation, Benjamin J.
Rosenthal Foundation, Richard and Hinda
Ross Foundation
Ross Foundation, Arthur
Ross Memorial Foundation, Will
Rowland Foundation
Royal Group Inc.
Ruddick Corp.
Rukin Philanthropic Foundation, David and Eleanore

Rupp Foundation, Fran and Warren
Ryan Family Charitable Foundation
Ryan Foundation, Nina M.
Sacharuna Foundation
Sachs Fund
SAFECO Corp.
Salwil Foundation
San Diego Gas & Electric
Santa Fe Pacific Corp.
Sara Lee Hosiery
Sarkeys Foundation
Sasco Foundation
Scaife Foundation, Sarah
Schapiro Fund, M. A.
Scherer Foundation, Karla
Scherman Foundation
Scheuer Family Foundation, S. H. and Helen R.
Schieffelin Residuary Trust, Sarah I.
Schiff Foundation
Schiff Foundation, Dorothy
Schlinger Foundation
Schloss & Co., Marcus
Schlumberger Ltd.
Schneider Foundation, Robert E.
Schoenbaum Family Foundation
Scholler Foundation
Schott Foundation
Schroeder Foundation, Walter
Schultz Foundation
Schultz Foundation
Schumann Foundation, Florence and John
Schumann Fund for New Jersey
Schust Foundation, Clarence L. and Edith B.
Schwab & Co., Charles
Schwartz Foundation, David
Schwartz Fund for Education and Health Research, Arnold and Marie
Science Applications International Corp.
Scott, Jr. Charitable Foundation, Walter
Scripps Foundation, Ellen Browning
Scrivner, Inc.
Scurry Foundation, D. L.
Sealaska Corp.
Sears Family Foundation
Seasongood Good Government Foundation, Murray and Agnes
Seay Memorial Trust, George and Effie
Security Life of Denver
Security State Bank
Sedgwick James Inc.
Seebee Trust, Frances
Seeley Foundation
Seidman Family Foundation
Sentinel Communications Co.
Sequoia Foundation
Setzer Foundation
Seven Springs Foundation
Sewall Foundation, Elmina
Sexton Foundation
Shaklee Corp.
Shaw Foundation, Arch W.
Shawmut National Corp.
Shawmut Worcester County Bank, N.A.
Sheinberg Foundation, Eric P.
Sheldon Foundation, Ralph C.
Shell Oil Co.
Shelton Cos.
Shenandoah Life Insurance Co.
Shoenberg Foundation
Shook Foundation, Barbara Ingalls
Shore Fund
Sierra Pacific Resources
Signet Bank/Maryland
Simon Charitable Trust, Esther

Simon Foundation, Sidney, Milton and Leoma
Simpson Foundation, John M.
Simpson Investment Co.
Skaggs Foundation, L. J. and Mary C.
Skinner Corp.
Slant/Fin Corp.
Slemp Foundation
Smith Charitable Foundation, Lou and Lutza
Smith Charitable Fund, Eleanor Armstrong
Smith Corp., A.O.
Smith Foundation, Kelvin and Eleanor
Smith Memorial Fund, Ethel Sergeant Clark
Smith 1980 Charitable Trust, Kelvin
Smith 1963 Charitable Trust, Don McQueen
Snee-Reinhardt Charitable Foundation
SNET
Snider Foundation
Snow Foundation, John Ben
Snow Memorial Trust, John Ben
Snyder Fund, Valentine Perry
Society for Savings
Sonoco Products Co.
Sosland Foundation
South Branch Foundation
South Carolina Electric & Gas Co.
South Waite Foundation
Southern California Edison Co.
Southern California Gas Co.
Special People In Need
Speyer Foundation, Alexander C. and Tillie S.
Sprague Educational and Charitable Foundation, Seth
Sprague, Jr. Foundation, Caryll M. and Norman F.
Springs Foundation
Springs Industries
SPS Technologies
Square D Co.
Stackpole-Hall Foundation
Staley, Jr. Foundation, A. E.
Standard Products Co.
Stanley Works
Starr Foundation
Stearns Charitable Foundation, Anna B.
Steel, Sr. Foundation, Marshall
Steele Foundation, Harry and Grace
Stein Foundation, Jules and Doris
Stern Family Fund
Stern Memorial Trust, Sidney
Stevens Foundation, Abbot and Dorothy H.
Stewardship Foundation
Stewart Educational Foundation, Donnell B. and Elizabeth Dee Shaw
Stocker Foundation
Stoddard Charitable Trust
Stokely, Jr. Foundation, William B.
Stone Container Corp.
Storer Foundation, George B.
Stott Foundation, Robert L.
Strake Foundation
Stranahan Foundation
Strawbridge Foundation of Pennsylvania I, Margaret Dorrance
Strawbridge Foundation of Pennsylvania II, Margaret Dorrance
Stroud Foundation
Stry Foundation, Paul E.
Subaru of America Inc.
Sudix Foundation
Sulzberger Foundation

Summerfield Foundation, Solon E.
Summerlee Foundation
Super Valu Stores
Surdna Foundation
Sussman Fund, Edna Bailey
Sweatt Foundation, Harold W.
Swensrud Charitable Trust, Sidney A.
Switzer Foundation
Symmes Foundation, F. W.
Tandem Computers
Taub Foundation
Taubman Foundation, A. Alfred
Taylor Foundation, Ruth and Vernon
Teichert
Teledyne
Templeton Foundation, Herbert A.
Tennant Co.
Tenneco
Tension Envelope Corp.
Texaco
Textron
Thanksgiving Foundation
Thendara Foundation
Thermo Electron Corp.
Thorson Foundation
3M Co.
Times Mirror Co.
Tinker Foundation
Tisch Foundation
Todd Co., A.M.
Tomlinson Foundation, Kate and Elwyn
Tortuga Foundation
Tosco Corp. Refining Division
Town Creek Foundation
Tracor, Inc.
Transco Energy Company
Treakle Foundation, J. Edwin
Trexler Trust, Harry C.
Triford Foundation
TRINOVA Corp.
True North Foundation
True Oil Co.
Truland Foundation
Trull Foundation
Truman Foundation, Mildred Faulkner
Trust Co. Bank
Trust for Mutual Understanding
TU Electric Co.
Tuch Foundation, Michael
Tucker Charitable Trust, Rose E.
Tupancy-Harris Foundation of 1986
Tyson Foods, Inc.
Ukrop's Super Markets, Inc.
Union Bank
Union Camp Corp.
Union Carbide Corp.
Union Electric Co.
Union Foundation
United States Sugar Corp.
United States Trust Co. of New York
United Technologies Corp.
Universal Leaf Tobacco Co.
Unocal Corp.
Upjohn Foundation, Harold and Grace
Upton Foundation, Frederick S.
US Bancorp
US WEST
USX Corp.
Uvas Foundation
Vale-Asche Foundation
Valero Energy Corp.
Van Every Foundation, Philip L.
Vanderbilt Trust, R. T.
Vanneck-Bailey Foundation
Varian Associates
Vaughan Foundation, Rachael and Ben
Veritas Foundation

Vesuvius Charitable Foundation
Vetlesen Foundation, G. Unger
Victoria Foundation
Vidda Foundation
Vingo Trust II
Virginia Power Co.
Vollrath Co.
Vulcan Materials Co.
Wachovia Bank & Trust Co., N.A.
Waggoner Foundation, E. Paul and Helen Buck
Wal-Mart Stores
Walker Educational and Charitable Foundation, Alex C.
Walker Foundation, Archie D. and Bertha H.
Walker Foundation, L. C. and Margaret
Walker Foundation, T. B.
Walker Wildlife Conservation Foundation
Wallace Genetic Foundation
Wallach Foundation, Miriam G. and Ira D.
Disney Co., Walt
Walter Family Trust, Byron L.
Walter Industries
Warner Fund, Albert and Bessie
Warsh-Mott Legacy
Warwick Foundation
Washington Water Power Co.
Waste Management
Waterfowl Research Foundation
Waters Charitable Trust, Robert S.
Waters Foundation
Wausau Paper Mills Co.
Wean Foundation, Raymond John
Webster Foundation, Edwin S.
Wedum Foundation
Weeden Foundation, Frank
Weezie Foundation
Wege Foundation
Weil, Gotshal & Manges Foundation
Weiler Foundation, Theodore & Renee
Weinberg Foundation, John L.
Weinberg, Jr. Foundation, Sidney J.
Weiss Foundation, William E.
Welfare Foundation
Wellman Foundation, S. K.
Wendt Foundation, Margaret L.
Wenger Foundation, Henry L. and Consuelo S.
Wessinger Foundation
Westerman Foundation, Samuel L.
Western Resources
Westinghouse Electric Corp.
Westvaco Corp.
Westwood Endowment
Weyerhaeuser Co.
Weyerhaeuser Family Foundation
Weyerhaeuser Foundation, Frederick and Margaret L.
Wharton Trust, William P.
Wheeler Foundation
Whirlpool Corp.
Whitaker Charitable Foundation, Lyndon C.
Whitehead Foundation
Whiteman Foundation, Edna Rider
Whiting Foundation
Whiting Foundation, Macauley and Helen Dow
WICOR, Inc.
Wieboldt Foundation
Wiener Foundation, Malcolm Hewitt
Wilbur-Ellis Co.
Wilcox Trust, S. W.
Wilder Foundation
Williams Cos.

Williams Family Foundation of Georgia
Wilmington Trust Co.
Wilson Foundation, H. W.
Wilson Foundation, Hugh and Mary
Winkler Foundation, Mark and Catherine
Winona Corporation
Winter Construction Co.
Wisconsin Energy Corp.
Wisconsin Power & Light Co.
Wisdom Foundation, Mary F.
Wiseheart Foundation
Witte, Jr. Foundation, John H.
Witter Foundation, Dean
Wodecroft Foundation
Wood Foundation of Chambersburg, PA
Woodruff Foundation, Robert W.
Woods Foundation, James H.
Woodward Fund-Atlanta, David, Helen, Marian
Woodward Governor Co.
Wrigley Co., Wm. Jr.
Wyne Foundation
Wyomissing Foundation
Xerox Corp.
Zamoiski Co.
Zemurray Foundation
Zenkel Foundation
Ziegler Foundation

Ethnic/Minority Organizations

Abelard Foundation
Abrams Foundation
Abramson Family Foundation
Abrons Foundation, Louis and Anne
Adams Trust, Charles E. and Caroline J.
AFLAC
Air Products & Chemicals
Ala Vi Foundation of New York
Alco Standard Corp.
Alliant Techsystems
AlliedSignal
Allyn Foundation
ALPAC Corp.
Alyeska Pipeline Service Co.
Amado Foundation, Maurice
AMAX
American Brands
American Electric Power
American Express Co.
American Financial Corp.
American National Bank & Trust Co. of Chicago
American Telephone & Telegraph Co.
Ameritech Services
Amway Corp.
Andersen Corp.
Apple Computer, Inc.
Archer-Daniels-Midland Co.
ARCO
Arizona Public Service Co.
Armstrong Foundation
Armstrong World Industries Inc.
Atkinson Foundation
Atlanta Gas Light Co.
Atran Foundation
Attleboro Pawtucket Savings Bank
Avon Products
Bacardi Imports
Bag Bazaar, Ltd.
Baier Foundation, Marie
Baird Foundation, Cameron
Baker & Baker
Baltimore Gas & Electric Co.
Banbury Fund
Bancorp Hawaii
Banfi Vintners
Bank of America Arizona

Bank of Boston Connecticut
Bank of Tokyo Trust Co.
Bard, C. R.
Barnett Charitable Foundation, Lawrence and Isabel
Bechtel Group
Beir Foundation
Belding Heminway Co.
Belfer Foundation
Ben & Jerry's Homemade
Beren Foundation, Robert M.
Berlin Charitable Fund, Irving
Bernstein & Co., Sanford C.
Bethlehem Steel Corp.
Binney & Smith Inc.
Blair Foundation, John
Blanchard Foundation
Bleibtreu Foundation, Jacob
Block, H&R
Blum Foundation, Lois and Irving
Boehm Foundation
Boeing Co.
Booz Allen & Hamilton
Borden
Borman's
Boston Edison Co.
Botwinick-Wolfensohn Foundation
Boulevard Foundation
Brady Foundation, W. H.
Brenner Foundation
Brody Foundation, Carolyn and Kenneth D.
Bronstein Foundation, Sol and Arlene
Brown Charitable Trust, Peter D. and Dorothy S.
Bruening Foundation, Eva L. and Joseph M.
Buchalter, Nemer, Fields, & Younger
Buhl Family Foundation
Burdines
Burns International
Burress, J.W.
Bush Foundation
Cain Foundation, Gordon and Mary
Callister Foundation, Paul Q.
Campbell Soup Co.
Candlesticks Inc.
Capital Fund Foundation
Capital Holding Corp.
Carnegie Corporation of New York
Carpenter Foundation, E. Rhodes and Leona B.
Carteh Foundation
Ceco Corp.
Central Maine Power Co.
Cessna Aircraft Co.
Chais Family Foundation
Chazen Foundation
Chemical Bank
Circuit City Stores
CIT Group Holdings
Citizens Bank
Clark Charitable Trust
Clorox Co.
CM Alliance Cos.
Collins & Aikman Holdings Corp.
Collins Foundation, Carr P.
Colonial Life & Accident Insurance Co.
Columbia Foundation
Conoco Inc.
Consolidated Freightways
Continental Corp.
Copernicus Society of America
Cornell Trust, Peter C.
Covington and Burling
Cowles Foundation, Harriet Cheney
Cranston Print Works
Crown Central Petroleum Corp.

Crown Memorial, Arie and Ida
Cullen/Frost Bankers
Cummins Engine Co.
Daily News
Dain Bosworth/Inter-Regional Financial Group
Dayton Hudson Corp.
de Hirsch Fund, Baron
de Rothschild Foundation, Edmond
Deer Creek Foundation
DelMar Foundation, Charles
Deposit Guaranty National Bank
Detroit Edison Co.
Deutsch Co.
Devonshire Associates
Dial Corp.
Diamond Foundation, Aaron
Diamond Walnut Growers
Dibner Fund
Digital Equipment Corp.
Dodge Jones Foundation
Donaldson Charitable Trust, Oliver S. and Jennie R.
Dorot Foundation
Douty Foundation
du Pont de Nemours & Co., E. I.
Duchossois Industries
Dula Educational and Charitable Foundation, Caleb C. and Julia W.
EG&G Inc.
Eisenberg Foundation, Ben B. and Joyce E.
Elf Atochem North America
Emery Memorial, Thomas J.
Encyclopaedia Britannica, Inc.
Enron Corp.
Fair Oaks Foundation, Inc.
Fairchild Corp.
Falk Foundation, Michael David
Falk Medical Fund, Maurice
Farley Industries
Farnsworth Trust, Charles A.
Federal Express Corp.
Federation Foundation of Greater Philadelphia
Feil Foundation, Louis and Gertrude
Feinberg Foundation, Joseph and Bessie
Feinstein Foundation, Myer and Rosaline
Fel-Pro Incorporated
Fellner Memorial Foundation, Leopold and Clara M.
Ferkauf Foundation, Eugene and Estelle
Fidelity Bank
Field Foundation of Illinois
Fig Tree Foundation
Fingerhut Family Foundation
Finnegan Foundation, John D.
Fireman Charitable Foundation, Paul and Phyllis
First Fidelity Bancorporation
First Interstate Bank of California
First Maryland Bancorp
First Petroleum Corp.
First Tennessee Bank
First Union Corp.
Firstar Bank Milwaukee NA
Fischbach Foundation
Fischel Foundation, Harry and Jane
Fisher Foundation
Fiterman Charitable Foundation, Miles and Shirley
Flagler Co.
Fleet Financial Group
Flemm Foundation, John J.
Florida Power & Light Co.
Florida Steel Corp.
Foellinger Foundation
Fohs Foundation
Foley, Hoag & Eliot
Forbes

Ethnic/Minority Organizations (cont.)

Forchheimer Foundation
Ford Foundation
Forest Foundation
Foster Charitable Trust
Foster Foundation, Joseph C. and Esther
Fox Charitable Foundation, Harry K. & Emma R.
Fox Charitable Foundation, Harry K. & Emma R.
Fox Foundation, Richard J.
Fraida Foundation
Frankel Foundation
Frankel Foundation, George and Elizabeth F.
Freedom Forum
Freeman Foundation, Carl M.
Friedman Brothers Foundation
Friedman Foundation, Stephen and Barbara
Friendly Rosenthal Foundation
Frost Foundation
Fry Foundation, Lloyd A.
Fuchsberg Family Foundation, Abraham
Fund for New Jersey
Funderburke & Associates
Funderburke & Associates
Furth Foundation
Galkin Charitable Trust, Ira S. and Anna
Galter Foundation
Garfinkle Family Foundation
Geifman Family Foundation
Gelman Foundation, Melvin and Estelle
General American Life Insurance Co.
General Dynamics Corp.
Georgia Power Co.
Gerber Products Co.
German Marshall Fund of the United States
German Protestant Orphan Asylum Association
Gerson Trust, B. Milfred
Giant Eagle
Gillette Co.
Gilman Foundation, Howard
Ginsberg Family Foundation, Moses
Gitano Group
Gleason Foundation, James
Gleason Foundation, Katherine
Glenmore Distilleries Co.
Glickenhaus & Co.
Globe Newspaper Co.
Glosser Foundation, David A.
Goldberg Family Foundation
Goldberg Family Foundation, Israel and Matilda
Goldberger Foundation, Edward and Marjorie
Goldman Foundation, Morris and Rose
Goldman Foundation, William
Goldring Family Foundation
Goldsmith Family Foundation
Goldsmith Foundation, Horace W.
Goldstein Foundation, Leslie and Roslyn
Golub Corp.
Goodman Foundation, Edward and Marion
Goodstein Family Foundation, David
Gordon Foundation, Meyer and Ida
Gorin Foundation, Nehemiah
Grass Family Foundation
Graybar Electric Co.
Greene Foundation, Jerome L.
Greenfield Foundation, Albert M.

Greenspan Foundation
Gries Charity Fund, Lucile and Robert H.
Grotto Foundation
Gruber Research Foundation, Lila
Gruss Charitable and Educational Foundation, Oscar and Regina
Gruss Charitable Foundation, Emanuel and Riane
Gudelsky Family Foundation, Isadore and Bertha
Guggenheim Foundation, Daniel and Florence
Gurwin Foundation, J.
Gussman Foundation, Herbert and Roseline
Guttag Foundation, Irwin and Marjorie
Hall Family Foundations
Hallmark Cards
Hamilton Bank
Handleman Co.
Harris Foundation, J. Ira and Nicki
Hartford Courant Foundation
Hartman Foundation, Jesse and Dorothy
Hassenfeld Foundation
Haynes Foundation, John Randolph and Dora
Hazen Foundation, Edward W.
Hebrew Technical Institute
Hechinger Co.
Hecht-Levi Foundation
Heilicher Foundation, Menahem
Helis Foundation
Henry Foundation, Patrick
Henry Foundation, Patrick
Hersey Foundation
Hershey Foods Corp.
Hershey Foundation
Hess Charitable Foundation, Ronne and Donald
Heublein
High Foundation
Hillsdale Fund
Himmelfarb Foundation, Paul and Annetta
Hitachi
Hobby Foundation
Hoechst Celanese Corp.
Hofheinz Foundation, Irene Cafcalas
Hogan Foundation, Royal Barney
Holtzmann Foundation, Jacob L. and Lillian
Holzer Memorial Foundation, Richard H.
Honeywell
Honigman Foundation
Horowitz Foundation, Gedale B. and Barbara S.
Houghton Mifflin Co.
Household International
Hovnanian Foundation, Hirair and Anna
Hovnanian Foundation, Hirair and Anna
Hubbard Broadcasting
Huber Foundation
Hudson Neckwear
Hughes Charitable Trust, Mabel Y.
Hughes Memorial Foundation, Charles Evans
Humana
Hunt Alternatives Fund
Hyams Foundation
I. and L. Association
I and G Charitable Foundation
IBM South Africa Projects Fund
IBP, Inc.
Illinois Power Co.
Imerman Memorial Foundation, Stanley
Indiana Bell Telephone Co.

Inland Container Corp.
Inland Steel Industries
Intel Corp.
Interco
Irmas Charitable Foundation, Audrey and Sydney
Irvine Foundation, James
ITT Corp.
ITT Rayonier
J.P. Morgan & Co.
Jackson Foundation
Jacobson & Sons, Benjamin
Jaffe Foundation
Jarson-Stanley and Mickey Kaplan Foundation, Isaac & Esther
Jaydor Corp.
JCPenney Co.
Jensen Construction Co.
Johnson Charitable Trust, Keith Wold
Johnson Foundation, Barbara P.
Johnson & Higgins
Jones Foundation, Daisy Marquis
Joselow Foundation
Journal Gazette Co.
Jurodin Fund
Jurzykowski Foundation, Alfred
Kapiloff Foundation, Leonard
Kaplan Foundation, Charles I. and Mary
Kaplen Foundation
Kaufman Foundation, Henry & Elaine
Kaufman Memorial Trust, Chaim, Fanny, Louis, Benjamin, and Anne Florence
Kaufmann Foundation, Henry
Kawabe Memorial Fund
Keating Family Foundation
Kenedy Memorial Foundation, John G. and Marie Stella
Kennecott Corp.
Kenworthy - Sarah H. Swift Foundation, Marion E.
Kest Family Foundation, Sol and Clara
Kevorkian Fund, Hagop
Kiewit Foundation, Peter
Kimberly-Clark Corp.
King Foundation, Carl B. and Florence E.
Kingsbury Corp.
Kirkland & Ellis
Klau Foundation, David W. and Sadie
Klein Fund, Nathan J.
Kline Foundation, Charles and Figa
Klingenstein Fund, Esther A. and Joseph
Klosk Fund, Louis and Rose
Kmart Corp.
Knistrom Foundation, Fanny and Svante
Koffler Family Foundation
Kohl Charitable Foundation, Allen D.
Kohl Foundation, Sidney
Kohn-Joseloff Fund
Koopman Fund
Korman Family Foundation, Hyman
Kowalski Sausage Co.
Kraft Foundation
Kugelman Foundation
Lamb Foundation, Kirkland S. and Rena B.
Langendorf Foundation, Stanley S.
Laros Foundation, R. K.
Lasdon Foundation
Lasdon Foundation
Lasky Co.
Laurel Foundation
Lautenberg Foundation
Lavanburg-Corner House
Lawrence Foundation, Alice

Lazar Foundation
LeBrun Foundation
Lee Foundation, James T.
Lehrman Foundation, Jacob and Charlotte
Leidy Foundation, John J.
Lemberg Foundation
Lender Family Foundation
Levi Strauss & Co.
Levinson Foundation, Max and Anna
Levinson Foundation, Max and Anna
Levinson Foundation, Morris L.
Leviton Manufacturing Co.
Levitt Foundation, Richard S.
Levy Foundation, Betty and Norman F.
Levy Foundation, Edward C.
Levy Foundation, Edward C.
Levy Foundation, Hyman Jebb
Lewis Foundation, Lillian Kaiser
Liberman Foundation, Bertha & Isaac
Liberty Corp.
Liberty Diversified Industries Inc.
Lieberman Enterprises
Lincy Foundation
Litton Industries
Loeb Foundation, Frances and John L.
Long Island Lighting Co.
Lotus Development Corp.
Lowenstein Brothers Foundation
Lowenstein Foundation, William P. and Marie R.
Lubo Fund
Lurie Foundation, Louis R.
Maas Foundation, Benard L.
MacArthur Foundation, J. Roderick
Mailman Foundation
MalCo Products Inc.
Manat Foundation
Mandel Foundation, Jack N. and Lilyan
Mandel Foundation, Joseph and Florence
Mandel Foundation, Morton and Barbara
Manilow Foundation, Nathan
Marcus Brothers Textiles Inc.
Mardigian Foundation
Maritz Inc.
Marmot Foundation
Marriott Corp.
Marx Foundation, Virginia & Leonard
Material Service Corp.
Mayerson Foundation, Manuel D. and Rhoda
Mazer Foundation, Jacob and Ruth
MBIA, Inc.
MCA
McConnell Foundation, Neil A.
McCormick Tribune Foundation, Robert R.
McFawn Trust No. 2, Lois Sisler
McGraw-Hill
McGregor Foundation, Thomas and Frances
MCI Communications Corp.
MCJ Foundation
McKnight Foundation
Mead Corp.
Meadows Foundation
Media General, Inc.
Medina Foundation
Mellon Bank Corp.
Melohn Foundation
Merck & Co.
Meridian Bancorp
Mertz-Gilmore Foundation, Joyce
Mex-Am Cultural Foundation
Meyer Foundation, Bert and Mary

Meyer Memorial Trust
Meyerhoff Fund, Joseph
Michigan Gas Utilities
Middendorf Foundation
Midwest Resources
Miles Inc.
Milken Foundation, L. and S.
Milliken & Co.
Mitchell Family Foundation, Edward D. and Anna
Morris Foundation, Norman M.
Morrison-Knudsen Corp.
Morse Foundation, Richard P. and Claire W.
Moses Fund, Henry and Lucy
Motorola
Mott Charitable Trust/Spectemur Agendo, Stewart R.
MTS Systems Corp.
National Forge Co.
National Fuel Gas Co.
Navistar International Corp.
NBD Bank
Needmor Fund
Nesholm Family Foundation
Nestle U.S.A. Inc.
New England Mutual Life Insurance Co.
New World Foundation
New York Foundation
New York Telephone Co.
The New Yorker Magazine, Inc.
Newhouse Foundation, Samuel I.
Newman Assistance Fund, Jerome A. and Estelle R.
Norfolk Southern Corp.
Norman Foundation
Normandie Foundation
Northeast Utilities
Northern Star Foundation
Northern States Power Co.
N've Shalom Foundation
Odyssey Partners
Oestreicher Foundation, Sylvan and Ann
Ogden Foundation, Ralph E.
Ogilvy & Mather Worldwide
Ohio National Life Insurance Co.
Oki America Inc.
Olin Corp.
Olive Bridge Fund
Osceola Foundation
Osher Foundation, Bernard
Ottenstein Family Foundation
Pacific Gas & Electric Co.
Pacific Telesis Group
Parthenon Sportswear
Parvin Foundation, Albert
Paulucci Family Foundation
Penn Foundation, William
Perkin-Elmer Corp.
Perry Drug Stores
Pettus Crowe Foundation
Philibosian Foundation, Stephen
Pick, Jr. Fund, Albert
Pincus Family Fund
Pincus Family Fund
Pitney Bowes
Pittsburgh National Bank
Pittway Corp.
Plumsock Fund
Polinger Foundation, Howard and Geraldine
Pope Foundation
Posnack Family Foundation of Hollywood
PPG Industries
Premier Industrial Corp.
Prentis Family Foundation, Meyer and Anna
Preyer Fund, Mary Norris
Price Foundation, Louis and Harold
Prickett Fund, Lynn R. and Karl E.
Principal Financial Group
Pritzker Foundation

Procter & Gamble Cosmetic & Fragrance Products
Propp Sons Fund, Morris and Anna
Providence Energy Corp.
Providence Journal Company
Prudential Insurance Co. of America
Public Service Co. of New Mexico
Public Service Electric & Gas Co.
Quaker Oats Co.
Raleigh Linen Service/National Distributing Co.
Rales and Ruth Rales Foundation, Norman R.
Raskin Foundation, Hirsch and Braine
Ratshesky Foundation, A. C.
Reliable Life Insurance Co.
Republic New York Corp.
Retirement Research Foundation
Revlon
Reynolds Foundation, Z. Smith
Reynolds Metals Co.
Richmond Foundation, Frederick W.
Ridgefield Foundation
Riley Foundation, Mabel Louise
Ritter Foundation
Robin Family Foundation, Albert A.
Rochlin Foundation, Abraham and Sonia
Rockefeller Foundation
Rockefeller Foundation, Winthrop
Rodgers Foundation, Richard & Dorothy
Rogow Birken Foundation
Rohlik Foundation, Sigmund and Sophie
Rohr Inc.
Rosen Foundation, Joseph
Rosenberg Foundation
Rosenberg Foundation, Sunny and Abe
Rosenbloom Foundation, Ben and Esther
Rosenstiel Foundation
Rosenthal Foundation, Richard and Hinda
Ross Foundation, Lyn & George M.
Roth Foundation, Louis T.
Royal Group Inc.
Rubbermaid
Rubenstein Foundation, Philip
Ruddick Corp.
Rudin Foundation
Rukin Philanthropic Foundation, David and Eleanore
Ryder System
SAFECO Corp.
Sailors' Snug Harbor of Boston
Salomon
San Diego Gas & Electric
Sang Foundation, Elsie O. and Philip D.
Santa Fe Pacific Corp.
Sara Lee Corp.
Sara Lee Hosiery
Schaffer Foundation, H.
Schamach Foundation, Milton
Schapiro Fund, M. A.
Schecter Private Foundation, Aaron and Martha
Scherman Foundation
Schermer Charitable Trust, Frances
Schiff, Hardin & Waite
Schiro Fund
Schlumberger Ltd.
Schultz Foundation
Schumann Fund for New Jersey
Schwartz Foundation, David
Schwob Foundation, Simon

Science Applications International Corp.
Seabury Foundation
Seagram & Sons, Joseph E.
Security Life of Denver
See Foundation, Charles
Seevak Family Foundation
Seid Foundation, Barre
Sentinel Communications Co.
Sequa Corp.
Seven Springs Foundation
Seybert Institution for Poor Boys and Girls, Adam and Maria Sarah
Shapell Foundation, Nathan and Lilly
Shapiro, Inc.
Shapiro Charity Fund, Abraham
Shapiro Family Foundation, Soretta and Henry
Shapiro Foundation, Charles and M. R.
Shapiro Fund, Albert
Shawmut National Corp.
Shell Oil Co.
Shenandoah Life Insurance Co.
Sherman Family Charitable Trust, George and Beatrice
Shiffman Foundation
Shoong Foundation, Milton
Shwayder Foundation, Fay
Silver Spring Foundation
Simon Foundation, Sidney, Milton and Leoma
Simon Foundation, William E. and Carol G.
Simone Foundation
Skirball Foundation
Slant/Fin Corp.
Slifka Foundation, Alan B.
Slifka Foundation, Joseph and Sylvia
Smith Family Foundation, Charles E.
Smith Foundation, Bob and Vivian
Snider Foundation
Snyder Fund, Valentine Perry
Society for Savings
Sonoco Products Co.
Sony Corp. of America
Southern California Gas Co.
Speyer Foundation, Alexander C. and Tillie S.
Spiegel Family Foundation, Jerry and Emily
Spingold Foundation, Nate B. and Frances
Star Bank, N.A.
State Farm Mutual Automobile Insurance Co.
Stein Foundation, Joseph F.
Steinbach Fund, Ruth and Milton
Steinberg Family Foundation, Meyer and Jean
Steinhardt Foundation, Judy and Michael
Steinsapir Family Foundation, Julius L. and Libhie B.
Sterling Winthrop
Stern Family Foundation, Harry
Stern Family Fund
Stern Foundation, Bernice and Milton
Stern Foundation, Gustav and Irene
Stern Foundation, Irvin
Stern Memorial Trust, Sidney
Stone Charitable Foundation
Stone Container Corp.
Stone Family Foundation, Norman H.
Stone Foundation, David S.
Stoneman Charitable Foundation, Anne and David
Strake Foundation

Straus Foundation, Martha Washington Straus and Harry H.
Summerfield Foundation, Solon E.
Sutton Foundation
Swensrud Charitable Trust, Sidney A.
Swig Charity Foundation, Mae and Benjamin
Tamarkin Co.
Tandy Foundation, David L.
Tang Foundation
Taper Foundation, Mark
Taub Foundation
Taub Foundation, Henry and Marilyn
Taube Family Foundation
Tauber Foundation
Taubman Foundation, Herman P. and Sophia
Taylor Foundation, Ruth and Vernon
Teledyne
Tenneco
Texas Commerce Bank Houston, N.A.
Texas Gas Transmission Corp.
Thalheimer Foundation, Alvin and Fanny Blaustein
Three Swallows Foundation
Time Insurance Co.
Times Mirror Co.
TJX Cos.
Tosco Corp. Refining Division
Tracor, Inc.
Transco Energy Company
Tranzonic Cos.
Trexler Trust, Harry C.
Trust Co. Bank
Tucker Charitable Trust, Rose E.
Tucker Foundation, Marcia Brady
21 International Holdings
Unilever United States
Union Bank
Union Camp Corp.
Union Electric Co.
United Airlines
United Parcel Service of America
United Technologies Corp.
Universal Foods Corp.
Universal Leaf Tobacco Co.
Upjohn Co.
US Bancorp
Valmont Industries
van Loben Sels - Eleanor Slate van Lobel Sels Charitable Foundation, Ernst D.
Varian Associates
Vetlesen Foundation, G. Unger
Vingo Trust II
Virginia Power Co.
Volkswagen of America, Inc.
Wachtell, Lipton, Rosen & Katz
Walgreen Co.
Warner-Lambert Co.
Disney Co., Walt
Washington Water Power Co.
Waste Management
Weiner Foundation
Wendt Foundation, Margaret L.
Weston Associates/R.C.M. Corp.
Weyerhaeuser Family Foundation
Whitman Corp.
WICOR, Inc.
Wiener Foundation, Malcolm Hewitt
Wilf Family Foundation
Wilkof Foundation, Edward and Ruth
Williams Cos.
Wilmington Trust Co.
Winn-Dixie Stores
Winston Foundation, Norman and Rosita
Winter Construction Co.
Wisconsin Bell, Inc.

Wisconsin Power & Light Co.
Witco Corp.
Wolf Foundation, Melvin and Elaine
Wolfson Family Foundation
Woods Charitable Fund
Woodward Governor Co.
WWF Paper Corp.
Yulman Trust, Morton and Helen
Zale Foundation
Zellerbach Family Fund

First Amendment issues

Arca Foundation
Babcock Foundation, Mary Reynolds
Bannan Foundation, Arline and Thomas J.
Binney & Smith Inc.
Boehm Foundation
Brody Foundation, Carolyn and Kenneth D.
Capital Cities/ABC
Carthage Foundation
Central Maine Power Co.
Chicago Tribune Co.
Columbia Foundation
Coors Foundation, Adolph
Courier-Journal & Louisville Times
Cowles Media Co.
Deer Creek Foundation
Diamond Foundation, Aaron
Donnelley Foundation, Gaylord and Dorothy
Dorr Foundation
Dow Foundation, Herbert H. and Barbara C.
Dow Jones & Co.
Dula Educational and Charitable Foundation, Caleb C. and Julia W.
Encyclopaedia Britannica, Inc.
Ford Foundation
Freedom Forum
Funderburke & Associates
Funderburke & Associates
General Motors Corp.
HarperCollins Publishers
Jurodin Fund
Kaplan Foundation, Rita J. and Stanley H.
Kaplan Fund, J. M.
Klau Foundation, David W. and Sadie
Klingenstein Fund, Esther A. and Joseph
Knight Foundation, John S. and James L.
Knight-Ridder, Inc.
Landmark Communications
MacArthur Foundation, J. Roderick
McCormick Tribune Foundation, Robert R.
McGraw-Hill
Medina Foundation
Merck Fund, John
Mertz-Gilmore Foundation, Joyce
National Computer Systems
New York Times Co.
The New Yorker Magazine, Inc.
Newhouse Foundation, Samuel I.
News & Observer Publishing Co.
Norman Foundation
Offield Family Foundation
Overbrook Foundation
Persis Corp.
Pew Charitable Trusts
Playboy Enterprises, Inc.
Price Foundation, Louis and Harold
Pulitzer Publishing Co.
Reynolds Foundation, Donald W.
Reynolds Foundation, Z. Smith
Scripps Co., E.W.

Sentinel Communications Co.
Simon Foundation, William E. and Carol G.
Stern Memorial Trust, Sidney
Strake Foundation
Sunnen Foundation
Thomas Foundation, Joan and Lee
Times Mirror Co.
Triskelion Ltd.
Whirlpool Corp.
Wiener Foundation, Malcolm Hewitt
Wiley & Sons, Inc., John

General

ABB Process Automation
Addison-Wesley Publishing Co.
Advanced Micro Devices
Aeroglide Corp.
AFG Industries, Inc.
AGA Gas, Inc.
Ahmanson & Co., H.F.
Airborne Express Co.
Alabama Gas Corp. (An Energen Co.)
Aladdin Industries, Incorporated
Alaska Airlines, Inc.
Alyeska Pipeline Service Co.
AMCORE Bank, N.A. Rockford
Amdahl Corp.
American Filtrona Corp.
American General Corp.
American General Life & Accident Insurance Co.
American Mutual Insurance Cos.
American National Bank
American Re-Insurance Co.
American Stock Exchange
American Stores Co.
American Telephone & Telegraph Co./New York City Region
Ameritech Publishing
Amoskeag Co.
Ampacet Corp.
Anacomp, Inc.
Andrew Corp.
ARA Services
Arcata Co.
Aristech Chemical Corp.
Arkansas Best Corp.
Arkla
Armco Steel Co.
Asahi Glass America, Inc.
Atlanta Journal & Constitution
Attleboro Pawtucket Savings Bank
Autodesk, Inc.
Autotrol Corp.
Avery Dennison Corp.
AXIA Incorporated
Baird Brothers Co.
Baird & Co., Robert W.
Baker, Watts & Co.
Ball Corp.
Bally's - Las Vegas
Baltimore Life Insurance Co.
Bank of America Arizona
Bank of Boston Connecticut
Bank of Louisville
Bank of Oklahoma, N.A.
Bank One, Texas-Houston Office
Bank One, Texas, NA
Barry Corp., R. G.
Barton-Gillet Co.
Bayview Federal Bank
BDM International
Belden Brick Co., Inc.
Benefit Trust Life Insurance Co.
Bergen Record Corp.
Berwind Corp.
Betz Laboratories
Bill Communications
Binney & Smith Inc.

General (cont.)

Bionetics Corp.
Birmingham News Co.
Black & Decker Corp.
Blair and Co., William
Bloomingdale's
Boston Gas Co.
Boston Mutual Life Insurance Co.
Bound to Stay Bound Books Foundation
Bourns, Inc.
Brakeley, John Price Jones Inc.
Branch Banking & Trust Co.
Brewer and Co., Ltd., C.
Briggs & Stratton Corp.
Brooklyn Union Gas Co.
Bryn Mawr Trust Co.
Buffalo Forge Co.
Business Men's Assurance Co. of America
Cadence Design Systems
Caesar's World, Inc.
Caldwell Manufacturing Co.
Capital Holding Corp.
Carolina Telephone & Telegraph Co.
Carr Real Estate Services
Casco Northern Bank
Castle & Cooke
Castle Industries
CCB Financial Corp.
Centex Corp.
Central Life Assurance Co.
Central Maine Power Co.
Central Trust Co.
Charter Medical Corp.
Chase Lincoln First Bank, N.A.
Chemtech Industries
Chicago Sun-Times, Inc.
Chubb Life Insurance Co. of America
CIBA-GEIGY Corp.
Citizens Gas & Coke Utility
Clark Equipment Co.
CNA Insurance Cos.
Coachmen Industries
Coastal Corp.
Coleman Co.
Colgate-Palmolive Co.
Colonial Parking
Colonial Penn Group, Inc.
Colorado Interstate Gas Co.
Colorado National Bankshares
Colorado State Bank of Denver
Commerce Clearing House
Commercial Federal Corp.
Commercial Intertech Corp.
Commonwealth Life Insurance Co.
Community Mutual Insurance Co.
Computer Associates International
Computer Sciences Corp.
Consolidated Rail Corp. (Conrail)
Continental Airlines
Conwood Co. L.P.
Cooper Oil Tool
Cooper Tire & Rubber Co.
Corvallis Clinic
Credit Agricole
Creditanstalt-Bankverein, New York
CSX Corp.
CT Corp. System
Cubic Corp.
Culbro Corp.
Curtis Industries, Helene
Danforth Co., John W.
Dayton's
Dean Witter Discover
DEC International, Inc.
Delmarva Power & Light Co.
Diamond Shamrock
Diamond State Telephone Co.

Dibrell Brothers, Inc.
Didier Taylor Refractories Corp.
Diebold, Inc.
Dime Savings Bank of New York
Dover Corp.
Dreyer's & Edy's Grand Ice Cream
Durham Corp.
Duriron Co., Inc.
Eastland Bank
Ebsco Industries
Echlin Inc.
Educators Mutual Life Insurance Co.
Edwards & Sons, A.G.
Electronic Data Systems Corp.
Employers Insurance of Wausau, A Mutual Co.
Employers Mutual Casualty Co.
Encyclopaedia Britannica, Inc.
Enserch Corp.
Entex
Equimark Corp.
Equitable Resources
Evening Post Publishing Co.
Fabri-Kal Corp.
Fairfield Communities, Inc.
Farmers Group, Inc.
Farmland Industries, Inc.
Federated Life Insurance Co.
Ferranti Tech
Ferrell Cos.
Ferro Corp.
Filene's Sons Co., William
First Alabama Bancshares
First Brands Corp.
First Commercial Bank N.A.
First Interstate Bank of Denver
First Interstate Bank & Trust Co.
First National Bank in Wichita
First NH Banks, Inc.
First of America Bank Corp.
First Security Bank of Idaho N.A.
First Security Bank of Utah N.A.
First Union National Bank of Florida
Fischer & Porter Co.
Fisher-Price
Fleet Bank
Fleet Bank N.A.
Florida Power & Light Co.
Fortis Benefits Insurance Company/Fortis Financial Group
Foxmeyer Corp.
Frito-Lay
Galileo Electro-Optics Corp.
Gast Manufacturing Corp.
Gates Corp.
General Color Co.
General Housewares Corp.
General Railway Signal Corp.
General Signal Corp.
General Tire Inc.
Genesco
GenRad
Glatfelter Co., P.H.
Glendale Federal Bank
Grainger, W.W.
Grand Rapids Label Co.
Grand Trunk Corp.
Graphic Controls Corp.
Great Lakes Bancorp, FSB
Great Lakes Carbon Corp.
Grinnell Mutual Reinsurance Co.
Handy & Harman
Harbert Corp.
Harleysville Mutual Insurance Co.
Harnischfeger Foundation
Harris Stores, Paul
Hartford Steam Boiler Inspection & Insurance Co.
Haworth, Inc.
Hecla Mining Co.
Heil Co.
Hercules Inc.

Hiram Walker & Sons Inc.
Hobart Corp.
Holly Sugar Corp.
Holyoke Mutual Insurance Co. in Salem
Homasote Co.
Home Savings of America, FA
Howell Corp.
Howmet Corp.
Huber, Hunt & Nichols
Huck International Inc.
Hudson Jewellers, J.B.
Hudson's
Huffy Corp.
Hughes Aircraft Co.
Hunt Oil Co.
Huntington Bancshares Inc.
ICH Corp.
Illinois Power Co.
Industrial Risk Insurers
Ingram Industries
Integra Bank/South
Intermark, Inc.
International Flavors & Fragrances
Interpublic Group of Cos.
Isaly Klondike Co.
IU International
Jefferson-Pilot
Jefferson-Pilot Communications
Jefferson Smurfit Corp.
Jersey Central Power & Light Co.
Jones Construction Co., J.A.
Journal Communications
Kaiser Aluminum & Chemical Corp.
Kaman Corp.
Karmazin Products Corp.
Kaufman & Broad Home Corp.
Kaye, Scholer, Fierman, Hays & Handler
Keefe, Bruyette & Woods
Kellogg Co., M.W.
Kellwood Co.
Kendall Health Care Products
Kennecott Corp.
Ketchum & Co.
Kimball International
King Kullen Grocery Co., Inc.
KN Energy, Inc.
Kulicke & Soffa Industries
L.A. Gear
Lafarge Corp.
Lambda Electronics Inc.
Langdale Co.
LaSalle Bank Lake View
Law Companies Group
Law Company, Inc.
Leaseway Transportation Corp.
Libbey-Owens Ford Co.
Liberty Mutual Insurance Group/Boston
LIN Broadcasting Corp.
Lincoln Telecommunications Co.
Lockheed Sanders
Loctite Corp.
Lomas Financial Corp.
Longs Drug Stores
Longview Fibre Co.
Louisville Gas & Electric Co.
Lowe's Cos.
Lykes Brothers Steamship Co.
MacLean-Fogg Co.
Maguire Oil Co.
Manitowoc Co.
Manufacturers Life Insurance Co. of America
Marine Midland Banks
Marion Fabrics
Mascoma Savings Bank
Mass Merchandisers, Inc.
Massachusetts Mutual Life Insurance Co.
MBIA, Inc.
Measurex Corp.
Meenan Oil Co., Inc.
Mellon PSFS

Memphis Light Gas & Water Division
Mennen Co.
Mercantile Bankshares Corp.
Meridian Insurance Group Inc.
Merit Oil Corp.
Mesa Inc.
Mettler Instrument Corp.
Meyer, Inc., Fred
Michigan Mutual Insurance Corp.
Michigan National Corp.
MidCon Corp.
Midland Co.
Midland Mutual Life Insurance Co.
Midmark Corp.
Minnesota Power & Light Co.
Minolta Corp.
Mississippi Chemical Corp.
Mississippi Power & Light Co.
Missouri Public Service
Mitre Corp.
Monfort of Colorado, Inc.
Moore, Costello & Hart
Morse Shoe, Inc.
MTS Systems Corp.
Mutual of America Life
Nash-Finch Co.
National Car Rental System, Inc.
National City Bank, Columbus
National City Bank of Indiana
National Computer Systems
National Convenience Stores, Inc.
National Data Corp.
National Forge Co.
National Fuel Gas Co.
National Standard Co.
NationsBank Texas
Navajo Refining Co.
New Jersey National Bank
New Jersey Resources Corp.
New York Mercantile Exchange
New York State Electric & Gas Corp.
The New Yorker Magazine, Inc.
Niagara Mohawk Power Corp.
NIBCO Inc.
Nike Inc.
Nomura Securities International
Norfolk Shipbuilding & Drydock Corp.
Nortek, Inc.
North American Coal Corp.
Northern Telecom Inc.
Northern Virginia Natural Gas
NorthPark National Bank
Northrop Corp.
Northwest Natural Gas Co.
Norton & Co., W.W.
NRC, Inc.
Oak Industries
Oakite Products
Ohio Casualty Corp.
Ohio Citizens Bank
Ohio Edison Corp.
Old Kent Bank & Trust Co.
Old Republic International Corp.
One Valley Bank, N.A.
Orange & Rockland Utilities, Inc.
Orion Capital Corp.
Ormet Corp.
Oster/Sunbeam Appliance Co.
Owens-Illinois
Packaging Corporation of America
Padnos Iron & Metal Co., Louis
Pamida, Inc.
Patrick Industries Inc.
Paxton Co., Frank
PayLess Drug Stores
Pendleton Construction Corp.
Pennsylvania Power & Light
Pentair
People's Bank
Perry Drug Stores
Persis Corp.

PHH Corp.
Phoenix Resource Cos.
Pioneer Trust Bank, NA
Piper Jaffray Cos.
Plante & Moran, CPAs
Plantronics, Inc.
PMI Food Equipment Group Inc.
PNC Bank
Ponderosa, Inc.
Primark Corp.
Prime Computer, Inc.
PriMerit F.S.B.
Producers Livestock Marketing Association
Providence Energy Corp.
Provident Mutual Life Insurance Co. of Philadelphia
PSI Energy
Public Service Co. of Oklahoma
Quaker State Corp.
Questar Corp.
Raley's
Ranco, Inc.
Ransburg Corp.
Raychem Corp.
Raytheon Engineers & Constructors
RB&W Corp.
Reading & Bates Corp.
Reasoner, Davis & Fox
Reliable Life Insurance Co.
Reliance Group Holdings, Inc.
Reliance Insurance Cos.
Republic Automotive Parts, Inc.
Research-Cottrell Inc.
Riggs National Bank
Risdon Corp.
Riviana Foods
Rochester Community Savings Bank
Rochester Gas & Electric Corp.
Rochester Telephone Corp.
Rollins Inc.
Roseburg Forest Products Co.
Ross Laboratories
Royal Group Inc.
Santa Fe International Corp.
Sanyo Manufacturing Corp.
Sara Lee Hosiery
Sargent Electric Co.
SCANA Corp.
Scientific-Atlanta
Scientific Brake & Equipment Co.
Scott, Foresman & Co.
Scotty's, Inc.
Sea-Land Service
Sealed Air Corp.
Sealright Co., Inc.
SECO
Security Life of Denver
Seneca Foods Corp.
ServiceMaster Co. L.P.
Seton Co.
Shaw Industries
Shawmut Bank of Franklin County
Sheldahl Inc.
Simkins Industries, Inc.
SKF USA, Inc.
SNC Manufacturing Co.
Society Corp.
Society for Savings (Mersman/Waldron)
Sonoco Products Co.
Southern Co. Services
Southern Indiana Gas & Electric Co.
Southland Corp.
Southwestern Public Service Co.
Sprint United Telephone
Standard Brands Paint Co.
State Mutual Life Assurance Co.
Steel Heddle Manufacturing Co.
Steuart Petroleum Co.
Stewart & Stevenson Services

Stirtz, Bernards & Co.
Storage Technology Corp.
Storer Communications Inc.
Stroh Brewery Co.
Student Loan Marketing
    Association
T.T.X. Co.
Tampa Electric
TCF Banking & Savings, FSB
Terra Industries
Time Warner
Torrington Co.
Towle Manufacturing Co.
Town & Country Corp.
Trans-Apex
Transtar Inc.
Travelers Express Co.
Tremco Inc.
Triskelion Ltd.
Trustmark National Bank
Tucson Electric Power Co.
Turner Corp.
Twentieth Century Insurance Co.
UJB Financial Corp.
Unigard Security Insurance Co.
Union Equity Division of
    Farmland Industries
United Gas Pipe Line Co.
United Illuminating Co.
United Stationers Inc.
United Telephone Co. of Florida
United Telephone System
    (Eastern Group)
US Bancorp
Valley National Bancorp
Vons Cos., Inc.
Washington National Insurance
    Co.
Washington Natural Gas Co.
Washington Water Power Co.
Wausau Insurance Cos.
Webber Oil Co.
Welch Foods
West One Bancorp
Westinghouse Broadcasting Co.
Whittaker Corp.
Wilbur-Ellis Co.
Wimpey Inc., George
Wiremold Co.
Wisconsin Bell, Inc.
Wisconsin Public Service Corp.
Wyman-Gordon Co.
Wynn's International, Inc.
Y.K.K. (U.S.A.) Inc.
Zapata Corp.
Zurn Industries

Housing

Abraham Foundation
Achelis Foundation
Ackerman Trust, Anna Keesling
Air Products & Chemicals
AlliedSignal
Allstate Insurance Co.
ALPAC Corp.
Altman Foundation
Aluminum Co. of America
American Electric Power
American Financial Corp.
American National Bank & Trust
    Co. of Chicago
American Saw & Manufacturing
    Co.
Americana Foundation
Amfac/JMB Hawaii
Amoco Corp.
Apache Corp.
Apple Computer, Inc.
Arcadia Foundation
ARCO
Arizona Public Service Co.
Astor Foundation, Vincent
Atlanta Gas Light Co.
Attleboro Pawtucket Savings
    Bank

Babcock Foundation, Mary
    Reynolds
Badgeley Residuary Charitable
    Trust, Rose M.
Badger Meter, Inc.
Baird Foundation, Cameron
Baltimore Gas & Electric Co.
Banc One Illinois Corp.
Bank of America Arizona
Bank of Boston Connecticut
Bank of Boston Corp.
Bank of New York
Bank of Tokyo Trust Co.
Bank One, Texas-Houston Office
Bank One, Youngstown, NA
BankAmerica Corp.
Barnes Group
Batten Foundation
Batts Foundation
Bausch & Lomb
Bean Foundation, Norwin S. and
    Elizabeth N.
Beazley Foundation
Belding Heminway Co.
Benedum Foundation, Claude
    Worthington
Berry Foundation, Archie W. and
    Grace
Bethlehem Steel Corp.
Beveridge Foundation, Frank
    Stanley
Bigelow Foundation, F. R.
Bingham Second Betterment
    Fund, William
Blank Family Foundation
Block, H&R
Blum Foundation, Edna F.
Bodman Foundation
Boeing Co.
Boettcher Foundation
Booth Ferris Foundation
Borkee Hagley Foundation
Brach Foundation, Helen
Bucyrus-Erie
Bush Foundation
Cafritz Foundation, Morris and
    Gwendolyn
Campbell Soup Co.
Canadian Imperial Bank of
    Commerce
Capital Holding Corp.
Cargill
Carter Foundation, Amon G.
Carter Foundation, Beirne
Caterpillar
Central Hudson Gas & Electric
    Corp.
Central Life Assurance Co.
Central Maine Power Co.
CertainTeed Corp.
Challenge Foundation
Charlesbank Homes
Chase Manhattan Bank, N.A.
Chemical Bank
Chevron Corp.
Chicago Title and Trust Co.
Citibank, F.S.B.
Clark Foundation, Robert
    Sterling
Clark-Winchcole Foundation
CM Alliance Cos.
CNA Insurance Cos.
Coast Federal Bank
Coffey Foundation
Collins Foundation
Colonial Life & Accident
    Insurance Co.
Columbus Southern Power Co.
Commerce Bancshares, Inc.
Commonwealth Edison Co.
Community Cooperative
    Development Foundation
Connecticut Natural Gas Corp.
Consolidated Natural Gas Co.
Consumer Farmer Foundation
Continental Bank N.A.
Continental Corp.

Cooke Foundation
Cosmair, Inc.
Cowell Foundation, S. H.
Cowles Media Co.
Crum and Forster
Crystal Trust
Cummins Engine Co.
Curtice-Burns Foods
Dai-Ichi Kangyo Bank of
    California
Demco Charitable Foundation
Deposit Guaranty National Bank
Digital Equipment Corp.
Dimeo Construction Co.
Dodge Foundation, Geraldine R.
Donaldson Co.
Donovan, Leisure, Newton &
    Irvine
du Pont de Nemours & Co., E. I.
Duke Power Co.
Dyson Foundation
Easley Trust, Andrew H. and
    Anne O.
Eaton Corp.
Eccles Foundation, Marriner S.
Ecolab
Eden Hall Foundation
Edwards Foundation, O. P. and
    W. E.
Emergency Aid of Pennsylvania
    Foundation
Emery Memorial, Thomas J.
English Memorial Fund,
    Florence C. and H. L.
Ensworth Charitable Foundation
Ernsthausen Charitable
    Foundation, John F. and Doris
    E.
Erteszek Foundation
Estes Foundation
Exxon Corp.
Fabri-Kal Corp.
Fales Foundation Trust
Falk Foundation, David
Federal-Mogul Corp.
Federal-Mogul Corp.
Federal National Mortgage
    Assn., Fannie Mae
Fidelity Bank
Fifth Third Bancorp
Fikes Foundation, Leland
FINA, Inc.
Fireman's Fund Insurance Co.
First Bank System
First Chicago
First Fidelity Bancorporation
First Financial Bank FSB
First Interstate Bank NW Region
First Interstate Bank of Arizona
First Interstate Bank of California
First Maryland Bancorp
First Union Corp.
First Union National Bank of
    Florida
Fleet Financial Group
Florida Power & Light Co.
FMR Corp.
Fondren Foundation
Forbes
Ford Foundation
Ford Meter Box Co.
Franklin Foundation, John and
    Mary
Frederick Foundation
Freed Foundation
Freedom Forum
Freeport-McMoRan
Fry Foundation, Lloyd A.
Fuchs Foundation, Gottfried &
    Mary
Fund for New Jersey
Funderburke & Associates
Funderburke & Associates
Garner Charitable Trust, James
    G.
GATX Corp.
GEICO Corp.

General Mills
General Motors Corp.
General Railway Signal Corp.
General Reinsurance Corp.
Georgia Health Foundation
Georgia Power Co.
Gerson Family Foundation,
    Benjamin J.
Gerstacker Foundation, Rollin M.
Gilmore Foundation, Irving S.
Ginter Foundation, Karl and
    Anna
Glenmore Distilleries Co.
Globe Newspaper Co.
Goldseker Foundation of
    Maryland, Morris
Goldsmith Family Foundation
Goodyear Foundation, Josephine
Grace & Co., W.R.
Graco
Graham Fund, Philip L.
Grassmann Trust, E. J.
Graybar Electric Co.
Great Western Financial Corp.
Green Fund
Griffin Foundation, Rosa May
Grundy Foundation
Gund Foundation, George
Haas Fund, Walter and Elise
Haas, Jr. Fund, Evelyn and
    Walter
Hall Family Foundations
Hallmark Cards
Hamilton Bank
Harden Foundation
Harriman Foundation, Mary W.
Hartford Courant Foundation
Hartford Steam Boiler Inspection
    & Insurance Co.
Hartmarx Corp.
Hartzell Industries, Inc.
Harvey Foundation, Felix
Haynes Foundation, John
    Randolph and Dora
Hazen Foundation, Edward W.
Hebrew Technical Institute
Hechinger Co.
Heckscher Foundation for
    Children
Hedrick Foundation, Frank E.
HEI Inc.
Heinz Endowment, Howard
Heinz Endowment, Vira I.
Heublein
Hewlett Foundation, William and
    Flora
Heydt Fund, Nan and Matilda
Hillcrest Foundation
Hilliard Corp.
Hillman Foundation
Himmelfarb Foundation, Paul
    and Annetta
HKH Foundation
Hoblitzelle Foundation
Hoffer Plastics Corp.
Home Depot
Home Savings of America, FA
Honeywell
Hopper Memorial Foundation,
    Bertrand
Hospital Corp. of America
Houck Foundation, May K.
Household International
Howard and Bush Foundation
Hudson-Webber Foundation
Hunt Alternatives Fund
Hyams Foundation
IBM South Africa Projects Fund
IDS Financial Services
Illinois Bell
Illinois Tool Works
Inland Steel Industries
Insurance Management
    Associates
Interco
Irvine Foundation, James
ITT Corp.

ITT Hartford Insurance Group
J.P. Morgan & Co.
Jackson Foundation
Jacobson & Sons, Benjamin
James River Corp. of Virginia
Janirve Foundation
JELD-WEN, Inc.
Jennings Foundation, Mary
    Hillman
Johnson Controls
Johnson & Son, S.C.
Johnston-Hanson Foundation
Jones Foundation, Daisy Marquis
Jones Foundation, Helen
Jones Foundation, Helen
Jones Intercable, Inc.
Joy Family Foundation
Kaufmann Foundation, Henry
Kennecott Corp.
Kennedy Foundation, John R.
Kentland Foundation
Kenworthy - Sarah H. Swift
    Foundation, Marion E.
Kimball International
Knight Foundation, John S. and
    James L.
Koch Sons, George
Kunkel Foundation, John Crain
Lafarge Corp.
Lance, Inc.
LDI Charitable Foundation
Lehman Foundation, Edith and
    Herbert
Lennox International, Inc.
Liberty Corp.
Liberty National Bank
Lilly & Co., Eli
Lincoln National Corp.
Lindsay Trust, Agnes M.
Little, Arthur D.
Little Family Foundation
Longwood Foundation
Loughran Foundation, Mary and
    Daniel
Louisiana Power & Light
    Co./New Orleans Public
    Service
Love Foundation, Lucyle S.
Lowenstein Brothers Foundation
Lukens
Lurie Foundation, Louis R.
Lydall, Inc.
Lyndhurst Foundation
M. E. G. Foundation
MacArthur Foundation, John D.
    and Catherine T.
Maclellan Foundation, Robert L.
    and Kathrina H.
Macmillan, Inc.
Magruder Foundation, Chesley
    G.
Manville Corp.
Mardag Foundation
Marshall & Ilsley Bank
Martin Foundation
Martin Marietta Corp.
MBIA, Inc.
McAlonan Trust, John A.
McCasland Foundation
McCormick Tribune Foundation,
    Robert R.
McCune Foundation
McDonnell Douglas Corp.
McDonnell Douglas Corp.-West
McGregor Fund
MCJ Foundation
McKnight Foundation
Meadows Foundation
Medina Foundation
Mellon Bank Corp.
Mellon Foundation, Richard King
Merck Human Health Division
Meridian Bancorp
Metropolitan Life Insurance Co.
Meyer Foundation, Eugene and
    Agnes E.
Meyer Memorial Trust

Housing (cont.)

Michigan Gas Utilities
Midwest Resources
Miller Charitable Foundation, Howard E. and Nell E.
MNC Financial
Mobil Oil Corp.
Morgan Stanley & Co.
Morris Charitable Foundation, E. A.
Moses Fund, Henry and Lucy
Motorola
Murphy Foundation, John P.
National Fuel Gas Co.
National Gypsum Co.
National Life of Vermont
National Machinery Co.
NationsBank Corp.
NBD Bank
NBD Bank, N.A.
Needmor Fund
Nestle U.S.A. Inc.
Neu Foundation, Hugo and Doris
New England Mutual Life Insurance Co.
New Street Capital Corp.
New York Foundation
New York Telephone Co.
Newman's Own
Newmil Bancorp
News & Observer Publishing Co.
Nordson Corp.
Northeast Utilities
Northern States Power Co.
Northern Trust Co.
Northwest Area Foundation
Northwest Natural Gas Co.
Norwest Bank Nebraska
Norwest Corp.
Ogilvy & Mather Worldwide
Ohio National Life Insurance Co.
O'Neill Charitable Corporation, F. J.
Ontario Corp.
Oppenstein Brothers Foundation
O'Shaughnessy Foundation, I. A.
Owen Trust, B. B.
Pacific Mutual Life Insurance Co.
Pacific Telesis Group
PacifiCorp
Packard Foundation, David and Lucile
Park Bank
Parker Foundation, Theodore Edson
Pax Christi Foundation
Peabody Charitable Fund, Amelia
Penn Foundation, William
Penney Foundation, James C.
People's Bank
Peoples Energy Corp.
Peppers Foundation, Ann
Pepsi-Cola Bottling Co. of Charlotte
Perkin-Elmer Corp.
Pettus, Jr. Foundation, James T.
Pew Charitable Trusts
Philadelphia Electric Co.
Philip Morris Cos.
Phillips Family Foundation, Jay and Rose
Phoenix Home Life Mutual Insurance Co.
Pitney Bowes
Piton Foundation
Pittsburgh National Bank
Pittway Corp.
Polaroid Corp.
Portland General Electric Co.
PPG Industries
Price Foundation, Louis and Harold
Primerica Corp.
Principal Financial Group
Pritzker Foundation

Procter & Gamble Co.
Procter & Gamble Cosmetic & Fragrance Products
Providence Energy Corp.
Providence Journal Company
Provident Life & Accident Insurance Co.
Prudential-Bache Securities
Public Service Electric & Gas Co.
Public Welfare Foundation
Puett Foundation, Nelson
Quaker Oats Co.
Redman Foundation
Reily & Co., William B.
Rennebohm Foundation, Oscar
Republic New York Corp.
Retirement Research Foundation
Revson Foundation, Charles H.
Reynolds Foundation, Z. Smith
Reynolds Metals Co.
Riggs National Bank
Riggs National Bank
Riley Foundation, Mabel Louise
Roberts Foundation
Robertson Brothers
Rochester Community Savings Bank
Rockefeller Foundation
Rockefeller Foundation, Winthrop
Rockwell International Corp.
Rohm and Haas Company
Rosenberg Foundation
Royal Group Inc.
Ryan Family Charitable Foundation
Ryder System
SAFECO Corp.
St. Faith's House Foundation
Saint Paul Cos.
Sara Lee Corp.
Sarkeys Foundation
Scaife Family Foundation
Scherman Foundation
Schmidlapp Trust No. 1, Jacob G.
Schmitt Foundation, Arthur J.
Scott Foundation, William R., John G., and Emma
Seafirst Corp.
Senior Services of Stamford
Sentinel Communications Co.
Shawmut National Corp.
Shawmut Worcester County Bank, N.A.
Signet Bank/Maryland
SIT Investment Associates, Inc.
Skinner Corp.
Smith Memorial Fund, Ethel Sergeant Clark
Snee-Reinhardt Charitable Foundation
Society for Savings
Southern California Edison Co.
Stanley Charitable Foundation, A. W.
Stanley Works
Star Bank, N.A.
State Street Bank & Trust Co.
Steelcase
Stoddard Charitable Trust
Straus Foundation, Aaron and Lillie
Strosacker Foundation, Charles J.
Sumitomo Bank of California
Taconic Foundation
Tamko Asphalt Products
Tandy Foundation, Anne Burnett and Charles
Taylor Family Foundation, Jack
TCF Banking & Savings, FSB
Teleklew Productions
Tenneco
Texas Commerce Bank Houston, N.A.
Texas Gas Transmission Corp.
Thompson Charitable Foundation

3M Co.
Time Insurance Co.
Todd Co., A.M.
Transco Energy Company
Trion
True Oil Co.
Truland Foundation
Trull Foundation
Trust Co. Bank
Unger Foundation, Aber D.
Union Bank
Union Electric Co.
U.S. Leasing International
United States Trust Co. of New York
Universal Leaf Tobacco Co.
Upjohn Co.
Upjohn Foundation, Harold and Grace
Uris Brothers Foundation
US Bancorp
Uslico Corp.
Valley National Bancorp
Van Every Foundation, Philip L.
Victoria Foundation
Virginia Power Co.
Wachovia Bank of Georgia, N.A.
Waldinger Corp.
Washington Mutual Savings Bank
Washington Water Power Co.
Wasserman Foundation
Wauwatosa Savings & Loan Association
Webster Charitable Foundation
Wells Fargo & Co.
West One Bancorp
Westinghouse Electric Corp.
Wetterau
Weyerhaeuser Co.
Whirlpool Corp.
White Consolidated Industries
Whitehead Foundation
Whiteman Foundation, Edna Rider
WICOR, Inc.
Wieboldt Foundation
Williams Charitable Trust, Mary Jo
Williams Cos.
Williams Foundation, C. K.
Wilson Foundation, Frances Wood
Woods Charitable Fund
Woodward Fund-Atlanta, David, Helen, Marian
Woodward Governor Co.
Xerox Corp.
Ziemann Foundation

International Affairs

Abelard Foundation
Aequus Institute
Air France
Airbus Industrie of America
Alexander Foundation, Joseph
Allegheny Ludlum Corp.
AlliedSignal
Aluminum Co. of America
AMAX
American Brands
American Express Co.
American Financial Corp.
American National Bank & Trust Co. of Chicago
American Natural Resources Co.
American Stock Exchange
American Telephone & Telegraph Co.
Amfac/JMB Hawaii
Amoco Corp.
AON Corp.
Arca Foundation
Archer-Daniels-Midland Co.
ARCO Chemical
Armco Inc.

Armington Fund, Evenor
Armstrong World Industries Inc.
Aron Charitable Foundation, J.
Atlanta Foundation
Auerbach Foundation, Beatrice Fox
Baehr Foundation, Louis W. and Dolpha
Baird Foundation, Cameron
Bank Hapoalim B.M.
Bank of New York
Bankers Trust Co.
Banyan Tree Foundation
Barra Foundation
Battelle
Batten Foundation
Bausch & Lomb
BDM International
Beck Foundation
Benenson Foundation, Frances and Benjamin
Bernstein & Co., Sanford C.
Binney & Smith Inc.
Bishop Foundation
Block, H&R
Blum-Kovler Foundation
Boeckmann Charitable Foundation
Boehm Foundation
Booz Allen & Hamilton
Borden
Botwinick-Wolfensohn Foundation
Bradley Foundation, Lynde and Harry
Brady Foundation, W. H.
Branta Foundation
Bravmann Foundation, Ludwig
Briggs & Stratton Corp.
British Airways
Brown & Williamson Tobacco Corp.
Bull HN Information Systems Inc.
Burns Foundation
Bydale Foundation
Cabot Corp.
Candlesticks Inc.
Carlson Cos.
Carnegie Corporation of New York
Carnival Cruise Lines
Carteh Foundation
Carthage Foundation
Cayuga Foundation
Central National-Gottesman
CertainTeed Corp.
Chais Family Foundation
Chambers Development Co.
Chase Manhattan Bank, N.A.
Chazen Foundation
Chevron Corp.
China Times Cultural Foundation
CIT Group Holdings
Citicorp
Clark Charitable Trust
Clover Foundation
Cohen Foundation, Wilfred P.
Coleman, Jr. Foundation, George E.
Coles Family Foundation
Columbia Foundation
Columbus Dispatch Printing Co.
Commerzbank AG, New York
Compton Foundation
Continental Corp.
Cow Hollow Foundation
CPC International
CRL Inc.
Crown Central Petroleum Corp.
Cudahy Fund, Patrick and Anna M.
Cullen/Frost Bankers
Cummins Engine Co.
Davee Foundation
Davis Foundation, Edwin W. and Catherine M.

Davis Foundation, Shelby Cullom
de Hirsch Fund, Baron
Delany Charitable Trust, Beatrice P.
Delaware North Cos.
DelMar Foundation, Charles
Demco Charitable Foundation
Dettman Foundation, Leroy E.
Deutsch Co.
Dial Corp.
Diamond Foundation, Aaron
Donner Foundation, William H.
Dougherty, Jr. Foundation, James R.
Dresser Industries
du Pont de Nemours & Co., E. I.
Duke Power Co.
Dynamet, Inc.
Earhart Foundation
Early Foundation
Eaton Corp.
Edouard Foundation
Ehrman Foundation, Fred and Susan
Elgin Sweeper Co.
Emergency Aid of Pennsylvania Foundation
Emerson Electric Co.
Engelhard Foundation, Charles
Epaphroditus Foundation
Equitable Life Assurance Society of the U.S.
Erpf Fund, Armand G.
Ettinger Foundation
Exxon Corp.
Falk Medical Fund, Maurice
Farley Industries
Ferebee Endowment, Percy O.
Fidelity Bank
First Boston
First Maryland Bancorp
Flagler Co.
Flatley Foundation
Flintridge Foundation
Fohs Foundation
Foote, Cone & Belding Communications
Forbes
Ford Foundation
Fortis Inc.
Foundation for Iranian Studies
Foundation for Middle East Peace
Fox Foundation, Richard J.
Fraida Foundation
Frank Fund, Zollie and Elaine
Freedom Forum
Freeman Charitable Trust, Samuel
Fribourg Foundation
Friedman Foundation, Stephen and Barbara
Frohlich Charitable Trust, Ludwig W.
Funderburke & Associates
Funderburke & Associates
Gallagher Family Foundation, Lewis P.
Garfinkle Family Foundation
Geist Foundation
General Dynamics Corp.
General Electric Co.
General Mills
General Motors Corp.
General Service Foundation
Generation Trust
Genesis Foundation
German Marshall Fund of the United States
Gerschel Foundation, Patrick A.
Gilbane Foundation, Thomas and William
Gitano Group
Glickenhaus & Co.
Golden Family Foundation
Goldring Family Foundation

Goodman Family Foundation
Gordon/Rousmaniere/Roberts Fund
Gould Foundation, Florence J.
Grass Family Foundation
Grass Family Foundation
Green Fund
Greenville Foundation
Greve Foundation, William and Mary
Grotto Foundation
Gruber Research Foundation, Lila
Gruss Charitable Foundation, Emanuel and Riane
Gruss Petroleum Corp.
Gudelsky Family Foundation, Isadore and Bertha
Gurwin Foundation, J.
Gussman Foundation, Herbert and Roseline
Guttman Foundation, Stella and Charles
Haas Fund, Walter and Elise
Hagler Foundation, Jon L.
Harriman Foundation, Mary W.
Harris Foundation, William H. and Mattie Wattis
Hazen Foundation, Edward W.
Hedco Foundation
Heinz Co., H.J.
Henkel Corp.
Henry Foundation, Patrick
Hermann Foundation, Grover
Hewlett Foundation, William and Flora
HKH Foundation
Hobbs Charitable Trust, John H.
Hoffberger Foundation
Hoffmann-La Roche
Homeland Foundation
Honda of America Manufacturing, Inc.
Hooper Foundation, Elizabeth S.
Hooper Foundation, Elizabeth S.
Hoover Fund-Trust, W. Henry
Hopkins Foundation, John Jay
Hopwood Charitable Trust, John M.
Horncrest Foundation
Hovnanian Foundation, Hirair and Anna
Hubbard Broadcasting
Huizenga Foundation, Jennie
Hunt Foundation
Hunt Foundation, Roy A.
I and G Charitable Foundation
India Foundation
Inland Steel Industries
Intercontinental Hotels Corp.
International Fund for Health and Family Planning
Ira-Hiti Foundation for Deep Ecology
Ishiyama Foundation
Jacobs Engineering Group
Jesselson Foundation
Jewett Foundation, George Frederick
Johnson Controls
Johnson Foundation, Barbara P.
Johnson & Son, S.C.
Jones Foundation, Helen
Jones Foundation, W. Alton
Jordan and Ettie A. Jordan Charitable Foundation, Mary Ranken
Joselow Foundation
Joukowsky Family Foundation
Jurzykowski Foundation, Alfred
Kapiloff Foundation, Leonard
Kaplen Foundation
Kaplun Foundation, Morris J. and Betty
Kautz Family Foundation
Kawabe Memorial Fund
Keck, Jr. Foundation, William M.
Kejr Foundation

Kemper Foundation, Enid and Crosby
Kendall Foundation, Henry P.
Kennametal
Kennedy Foundation, John R.
Kentland Foundation
Kepco, Inc.
Kerr-McGee Corp.
Kest Family Foundation, Sol and Clara
Kimberly-Clark Corp.
Klosk Fund, Louis and Rose
Knowles Charitable Memorial Trust, Gladys E.
Knox Family Foundation
Knox, Sr., and Pearl Wallis Knox Charitable Foundation, Robert W.
Kohl Charitable Foundation, Allen D.
Kohl Foundation, Sidney
Krieble Foundation, Vernon K.
Krieble Foundation, Vernon K.
Kunstadter Family Foundation, Albert
Kyocera International Inc.
L. L. W. W. Foundation
Lakeside Foundation
Lamb Foundation, Kirkland S. and Rena B.
Lambert Memorial Foundation, Gerard B.
Lane Foundation, Minnie and Bernard
Lasdon Foundation
Lasky Co.
Lautenberg Foundation
Law Foundation, Robert O.
Lazar Foundation
Lea Foundation, Helen Sperry
LeBrun Foundation
Lender Family Foundation
Lennon Foundation, Fred A.
Levinson Foundation, Morris L.
Levy Foundation, Edward C.
Levy Foundation, Edward C.
Liberty Corp.
Lincoln Electric Co.
Lipton, Thomas J.
Littauer Foundation, Lucius N.
Lounsbery Foundation, Richard
Lowenstein Foundation, William P. and Marie R.
Luce Foundation, Henry
M. E. G. Foundation
M.E. Foundation
MacArthur Foundation, J. Roderick
MacArthur Foundation, John D. and Catherine T.
Maclellan Charitable Trust, R. J.
Macmillan, Inc.
Makita U.S.A., Inc.
Mandel Foundation, Joseph and Florence
Mandel Foundation, Morton and Barbara
Mandeville Foundation
Mann Foundation, John Jay
Manoogian Foundation, Alex and Marie
Marshall & Ilsley Bank
Martin Foundation
Martin Marietta Corp.
Marubeni America Corp.
Material Service Corp.
Matthews International Corp.
Mayerson Foundation, Manuel D. and Rhoda
Maytag Family Foundation, Fred
McCune Charitable Trust, John R.
McCutchen Foundation
McDonnell Douglas Corp.
McDonnell Foundation, James S.
McIntosh Foundation
McKenna Foundation, Philip M.
McKnight Foundation

Melohn Foundation
Menschel Foundation, Robert and Joyce
Merck & Co.
Merck Fund, John
Mertz-Gilmore Foundation, Joyce
Milliken & Co.
Mitchell Family Foundation, Edward D. and Anna
Mitsubishi International Corp.
Mitsui & Co. (U.S.A.)
Mobil Oil Corp.
Moriah Fund
Morrison-Knudsen Corp.
Moskowitz Foundation, Irving I.
Mott Charitable Trust/Spectemur Agendo, Stewart R.
Mott Foundation, Charles Stewart
National Pro-Am Youth Fund
National Westminster Bank New Jersey
Nationale-Nederlanden North America Corp.
NBD Bank
Neu Foundation, Hugo and Doris
New Cycle Foundation
New-Land Foundation
New Prospect Foundation
New World Foundation
Newman's Own
Nichimen America, Inc.
Noble Foundation, Edward John
Nordson Corp.
Norman Foundation
Normandie Foundation
North Shore Foundation
O'Donnell Foundation
Ogden Foundation, Ralph E.
Olin Foundation, John M.
Open Society Fund
Overbrook Foundation
Overseas Shipholding Group
PACCAR
Paramount Communications Inc.
Perini Corp.
Pfizer
Phelps Dodge Corp.
Phillipps Foundation
Phillips Petroleum Co.
Phillips-Van Heusen Corp.
Pioneer Hi-Bred International
Pittway Corp.
PPG Industries
Prickett Fund, Lynn R. and Karl E.
Procter & Gamble Cosmetic & Fragrance Products
Prospect Hill Foundation
Pulitzer Publishing Co.
Ralston Purina Co.
Randolph Foundation
Reed Foundation, Philip D.
Reynolds Foundation, Christopher
Richardson Foundation, Frank E. and Nancy M.
Richardson Foundation, Smith
Ridgefield Foundation
Rockefeller Brothers Fund
Rockefeller Foundation
Rockefeller Trust, Winthrop
Rockwell International Corp.
Rosenhaus Peace Foundation, Sarah and Matthew
Rosenthal Foundation, Benjamin J.
Rosenwald Family Fund, William
Rubin Foundation, Samuel
Sacharuna Foundation
Salgo Charitable Trust, Nicholas M.
Salomon Foundation, Richard & Edna
Salvatori Foundation, Henry
Scaife Foundation, Sarah
Schecter Private Foundation, Aaron and Martha

Scheuer Family Foundation, S. H. and Helen R.
Schumann Foundation, Florence and John
Schwartz Foundation, David
Scrivner, Inc.
Seagram & Sons, Joseph E.
Searle & Co., G.D.
Sebastian Foundation
See Foundation, Charles
Segal Charitable Trust, Barnet
Sequoia Foundation
Shawmut Worcester County Bank, N.A.
Shell Oil Co.
Shiffman Foundation
Shoemaker Fund, Thomas H. and Mary Williams
Signet Bank/Maryland
Skirball Foundation
Slant/Fin Corp.
Sloan Foundation, Alfred P.
Soros Foundation-Hungary
Sosland Foundation
Starr Foundation
Steinhardt Foundation, Judy and Michael
Stern Family Fund
Stern Memorial Trust, Sidney
Stone Container Corp.
Sumitomo Trust & Banking Co., Ltd.
Sunmark Capital Corp.
Tamko Asphalt Products
Taub Foundation, Joseph and Arlene
Taubman Foundation, A. Alfred
Taylor Foundation, Ruth and Vernon
TDK Corp. of America
Teledyne
Texaco
Texas Instruments
Textron
Thirty-Five Twenty, Inc.
Thomas & Betts Corp.
Thomas Foundation, Joan and Lee
Timmis Foundation, Michael & Nancy
Tinker Foundation
Tisch Foundation
Trust for Mutual Understanding
21 International Holdings
Union Bank of Switzerland Los Angeles Branch
United Merchants & Manufacturers
United States-Japan Foundation
Unocal Corp.
Ushkow Foundation
Uslico Corp.
Vetlesen Foundation, G. Unger
Von der Ahe Foundation
Von der Ahe, Jr. Trust, Theodore Albert
Wallace Genetic Foundation
Wallach Foundation, Miriam G. and Ira D.
Disney Co., Walt
Warsh-Mott Legacy
Wasserman Foundation
Wean Foundation, Raymond John
Weeden Foundation, Frank
Weinberg Foundation, John L.
West Foundation
Westvaco Corp.
Westwood Endowment
Weyerhaeuser Family Foundation
Weyerhaeuser Foundation, Frederick and Margaret L.
Whitehead Foundation
Wiener Foundation, Malcolm Hewitt
Williams Cos.
Wolf Foundation, Melvin and Elaine
Wyomissing Foundation

Xerox Corp.
Young Foundation, Irvin L.
Young & Rubicam
Zachry Co., H. B.
Zilkha & Sons

Law & Justice

Abbott Laboratories
Abell-Hanger Foundation
Acushnet Co.
Ahmanson Foundation
Alice Manufacturing Co.
Allegheny Ludlum Corp.
Allendale Mutual Insurance Co.
AlliedSignal
Allstate Insurance Co.
Altschul Foundation
Aluminum Co. of America
Amaturo Foundation
AMAX
American Cyanamid Co.
American Financial Corp.
American National Bank & Trust Co. of Chicago
Amoco Corp.
Amsted Industries
Anderson Foundation, John W.
Andrews Foundation
Ansley Foundation, Dantzler Bond
AON Corp.
Apple Computer, Inc.
Archer-Daniels-Midland Co.
Armco Inc.
Arrillaga Foundation
Ashland Oil
Associated Foundations
Atlanta Gas Light Co.
Atran Foundation
Attleboro Pawtucket Savings Bank
Avon Products
Azby Fund
Babcock Foundation, Mary Reynolds
Baker Trust, Clayton
Baltimore Gas & Electric Co.
Banc One Illinois Corp.
Bank One, Texas-Houston Office
Bankers Trust Co.
Bauer Foundation, M. R.
Baughman Foundation
Beaird Foundation, Charles T.
Beech Aircraft Corp.
Belding Heminway Co.
Ben & Jerry's Homemade
Bentley Foundation, Alvin M.
Berwind Corp.
Bethlehem Steel Corp.
Bettingen Corporation, Burton G.
BFGoodrich
Bicknell Fund
Bionetics Corp.
Birch Foundation, Stephen and Mary
Blair and Co., William
Block, H&R
Booth-Bricker Fund
Borden
Borun Foundation, Anna Borun and Harry
Bostwick Foundation, Albert C.
Boswell Foundation, James G.
Botwinick-Wolfensohn Foundation
Bradley-Turner Foundation
Bridgestone/Firestone
Bristol-Myers Squibb Co.
Brooks Brothers
Brown & Williamson Tobacco Corp.
Bryan Family Foundation, Kathleen Price and Joseph M.
Burden Foundation, Florence V.
Burlington Industries
Burndy Corp.

Law & Justice
(cont.)

Burns Foundation, Fritz B.
Burns Foundation, Jacob
Bush Foundation
Cablevision of Michigan
Cabot Corp.
Cabot-Saltonstall Charitable
  Trust
Cain Foundation, Gordon and
  Mary
Campbell Soup Co.
Carnegie Corporation of New
  York
Carter Foundation, Amon G.
Carthage Foundation
Caterpillar
Centel Corp.
Centerior Energy Corp.
Chase Manhattan Bank, N.A.
Chevron Corp.
Childs Charitable Foundation,
  Roberta M.
Clark Foundation, Edna
  McConnell
Clipper Ship Foundation
Clorox Co.
Clowes Fund
CM Alliance Cos.
CNA Insurance Cos.
Cohen Foundation, Naomi and
  Nehemiah
Coleman Co.
Collins Foundation, Carr P.
Colonial Life & Accident
  Insurance Co.
Columbia Foundation
Columbus Dispatch Printing Co.
Commerce Clearing House
Comprecare Foundation
Continental Corp.
Cooper Industries
Coors Foundation, Adolph
Cord Foundation, E. L.
Cow Hollow Foundation
Cowan Foundation Corporation,
  Lillian L. and Harry A.
CPC International
CR Industries
Crestlea Foundation
Crum and Forster
CT Corp. System
Culpeper Foundation, Charles E.
de Rothschild Foundation,
  Edmond
Deere & Co.
Deposit Guaranty National Bank
Deutsch Co.
DeVos Foundation, Richard and
  Helen
Diamond Foundation, Aaron
DiRosa Foundation, Rene and
  Veronica
Donovan, Leisure, Newton &
  Irvine
Douty Foundation
Dow Foundation, Herbert H. and
  Barbara C.
Dresser Industries
du Pont de Nemours & Co., E. I.
Dun & Bradstreet Corp.
Dupar Foundation
Dyson Foundation
Earhart Foundation
Eaton Corp.
Eccles Foundation, Marriner S.
EG&G Inc.
Elf Atochem North America
Emerson Electric Co.
Erteszek Foundation
Exxon Corp.
Federal-Mogul Corp.
Federal National Mortgage
  Assn., Fannie Mae
Federated Life Insurance Co.

Fidelity Bank
Fieldcrest Cannon
Fifth Third Bancorp
FINA, Inc.
Fireman Charitable Foundation,
  Paul and Phyllis
First Chicago
First Fidelity Bancorporation
First Hawaiian
First Interstate Bank of Arizona
First Interstate Bank of California
First Interstate Bank of Texas,
  N.A.
First Mississippi Corp.
Fletcher Foundation
Florida Power & Light Co.
FMC Corp.
Ford Foundation
Ford Motor Co.
Fort Worth Star Telegram
Foundation for Child
  Development
Foundation for Middle East
  Peace
Frear Eleemosynary Trust, Mary
  D. and Walter F.
Freeport Brick Co.
Friedland Family Foundation,
  Samuel
Friedman Foundation, Stephen
  and Barbara
Fry Foundation, Lloyd A.
Fuchsberg Family Foundation
Fuchsberg Family Foundation,
  Abraham
Furth Foundation
Fusenot Charity Foundation,
  Georges and Germaine
General Electric Co.
General Mills
General Motors Corp.
General Reinsurance Corp.
Georgia-Pacific Corp.
Gheens Foundation
Giant Eagle
Giant Food
Giant Food Stores
Gillette Co.
Gilmore Foundation, Earl B.
Gleason Foundation, Katherine
Gleason Works
Glen Eagles Foundation
Glickenhaus & Co.
Goldman Foundation, Herman
Goldsmith Foundation, Horace
  W.
Goldwyn Foundation, Samuel
Good Samaritan
Gould Foundation, Florence J.
Grace & Co., W.R.
GTE Corp.
Guardian Life Insurance Co. of
  America
Guggenheim Foundation, Daniel
  and Florence
Gulfstream Aerospace Corp.
Halloran Foundation, Mary P.
  Dolciani
Harper Foundation, Philip S.
Harsco Corp.
Hartmarx Corp.
Hartz Foundation
Hastings Trust
Haynes Foundation, John
  Randolph and Dora
Hazen Foundation, Edward W.
Hechinger Co.
Heginbotham Trust, Will E.
Heinz Co., H.J.
Henkel Corp.
Hess Charitable Foundation,
  Ronne and Donald
Heymann-Wolf Foundation
Hill Foundation

Hoag Family Foundation, George
Hofheinz Foundation, Irene
  Cafcalas
Homeland Foundation
Hospital Corp. of America
Houston Industries
Hudson-Webber Foundation
Hunter Trust, A. V.
Huston Foundation
Hyams Foundation
Illinois Bell
Illinois Tool Works
Indiana Insurance Cos.
Inland Steel Industries
Irwin Charity Foundation,
  William G.
ITT Hartford Insurance Group
Ittleson Foundation
Janirve Foundation
JMK-A M Micallef Charitable
  Foundation
John Hancock Mutual Life
  Insurance Co.
Johnson & Higgins
Johnson & Son, S.C.
Jones Foundation, Daisy Marquis
Jones Foundation, Fletcher
Jones Foundation, W. Alton
Jurodin Fund
Kaplan Foundation, Rita J. and
  Stanley H.
Kaye, Scholer, Fierman, Hays &
  Handler
Kayser Foundation
Kennecott Corp.
Kerney Foundation, James
Kerr Foundation
Kerr-McGee Corp.
Kettering Fund
Kimball International
Kirkland & Ellis
Lassus Brothers Oil
Leo Burnett Co.
Lightner Sams Foundation
Lincoln Electric Co.
Link, Jr. Foundation, George
Lipton, Thomas J.
Litton Industries
Litton/Itek Optical Systems
Loridans Foundation, Charles
Louisiana Land & Exploration
  Co.
LTV Corp.
Lurie Foundation, Louis R.
MacAndrews & Forbes Holdings
MacArthur Foundation, J.
  Roderick
MacArthur Foundation, John D.
  and Catherine T.
Maclellan Charitable Trust, R. J.
Macy & Co., R.H.
Mailman Family Foundation, A.
  L.
Marshall Foundation
Martin Marietta Corp.
Mason Charitable Foundation
Massie Trust, David Meade
May Foundation, Wilbur
Maytag Family Foundation, Fred
MCA
McConnell Foundation
McCormick & Co.
McCormick Tribune Foundation,
  Robert R.
McDonnell Douglas Corp.
McGraw-Hill
McKenna Foundation, Philip M.
McMahon Foundation
MDU Resources Group, Inc.
Mead Corp.
Meadows Foundation
Media General, Inc.
Merck Fund, John
Mertz-Gilmore Foundation, Joyce
Metropolitan Life Insurance Co.
Meyer Foundation, Bert and
  Mary

Meyer Foundation, Eugene and
  Agnes E.
Meyer Memorial Trust
Michael Foundation, Herbert I.
  and Elsa B.
Michigan Bell Telephone Co.
Milbank Foundation, Dunlevy
Miller Fund, Kathryn and Gilbert
Milliken & Co.
Mitchell Family Foundation,
  Edward D. and Anna
MNC Financial
Mobil Oil Corp.
Montgomery Street Foundation
Moody Foundation
Moore Charitable Foundation,
  Marjorie
Morris Foundation, Margaret T.
Moskowitz Foundation, Irving I.
Motorola
Nalco Chemical Co.
National Computer Systems
National Gypsum Co.
National Machinery Co.
National Westminster Bank New
  Jersey
Nationwide Insurance Cos.
NBD Bank
New-Land Foundation
New Prospect Foundation
New York Foundation
New York Life Insurance Co.
New York Telephone Co.
The New Yorker Magazine, Inc.
Newman Assistance Fund,
  Jerome A. and Estelle R.
Nichols Co., J.C.
Noble Foundation, Samuel
  Roberts
Norfolk Southern Corp.
Norman Foundation
Norman Foundation, Andrew
Norris Foundation, Kenneth T.
  and Eileen L.
Nortek, Inc.
North American Reinsurance
  Corp.
Northeast Utilities
Northern Trust Co.
Ogilvy & Mather Worldwide
Olin Foundation, John M.
Oppenheimer Family Foundation
Overbrook Foundation
Overseas Shipholding Group
Owen Trust, B. B.
PACCAR
Pacific Mutual Life Insurance Co.
Pacific Telesis Group
Pappas Charitable Foundation,
  Thomas Anthony
Parker Foundation, Theodore
  Edson
Peabody Charitable Fund, Amelia
Penn Savings Bank, a division of
  Sovereign Bank Bank of
  Princeton, a division of
  Sovereign Bank
Peoples Energy Corp.
Perkin-Elmer Corp.
Pettus Crowe Foundation
Pfizer
Phelps Dodge Corp.
Philadelphia Electric Co.
Phillips Foundation, Dr. P.
Phillips Petroleum Co.
Pillsbury Foundation
Pineywoods Foundation
Pittway Corp.
Playboy Enterprises, Inc.
Plitt Southern Theatres
Polaroid Corp.
Poorvu Foundation, William and
  Lia
Powell Family Foundation
PPG Industries
Price Foundation, Louis and
  Harold

Procter & Gamble Cosmetic &
  Fragrance Products
Prudential-Bache Securities
Prudential Insurance Co. of
  America
Public Service Electric & Gas
  Co.
Public Welfare Foundation
Puget Sound Power & Light Co.
Quantum Chemical Corp.
Randolph Foundation
Ratshesky Foundation, A. C.
Red Wing Shoe Co.
Reynolds Foundation, Z. Smith
Rhodebeck Charitable Trust
Richardson Foundation, Smith
Ritter Charitable Trust, George
  W. & Mary F.
Rock Foundation, Milton and
  Shirley
Rockefeller Foundation
Rockwell International Corp.
Rohm and Haas Company
Rohr Inc.
Rosenberg Foundation
Rubbermaid
Rudin Foundation
Salomon
Santa Fe Pacific Corp.
Sara Lee Corp.
Sargent Foundation, Newell B.
Scaife Family Foundation
Scaife Foundation, Sarah
Scherman Foundation
Schiff, Hardin & Waite
Schumann Foundation, Florence
  and John
Scrivner, Inc.
Scrivner of North Carolina Inc.
Searle & Co., G.D.
Seasongood Good Government
  Foundation, Murray and Agnes
Sefton Foundation, J. W.
Segal Charitable Trust, Barnet
Shawmut National Corp.
Shell Oil Co.
Silverweed Foundation
Slant/Fin Corp.
SmithKline Beecham
SNET
Southern California Edison Co.
Sprague Educational and
  Charitable Foundation, Seth
Springs Foundation
SPS Technologies
Starr Foundation
State Farm Mutual Automobile
  Insurance Co.
State Street Bank & Trust Co.
Stauffer Communications
Sterling Inc.
Stern Family Fund
Stern Memorial Trust, Sidney
Stewardship Foundation
Stillwell Charitable Trust, Glen
  and Dorothy
Stockham Valves & Fittings
Stranahan Foundation
Stride Rite Corp.
Summerfield Foundation, Solon
  E.
Sumners Foundation, Hatton W.
Sunmark Capital Corp.
Super Valu Stores
Taconic Foundation
Tamko Asphalt Products
Tarmac America Inc.
Teledyne
Tenneco
Texaco
Texas Instruments
Textron
Thalheimer Foundation, Alvin
  and Fanny Blaustein
Thomas Foundation, Joan and
  Lee
3M Co.

Timken Co.
TJX Cos.
Transco Energy Company
TRINOVA Corp.
Tropicana Products, Inc.
True Oil Co.
Trull Foundation
Trust Co. Bank
Trust for Mutual Understanding
Union Camp Corp.
Union Carbide Corp.
United Technologies Corp.
Unocal Corp.
US WEST
USG Corp.
UST
van Loben Sels - Eleanor Slate
  van Lobel Sels Charitable
  Foundation, Ernst D.
Von der Ahe, Jr. Trust, Theodore
  Albert
Wal-Mart Stores
Disney Co., Walt
Wareheim Foundation, E. C.
Weil, Gotshal & Manges
  Foundation
Weingart Foundation
West One Bancorp
Western Shade Cloth Charitable
  Foundation
Whirlpool Corp.
White Consolidated Industries
Whitehead Foundation
Wieboldt Foundation
Wiggins Memorial Trust, J. J.
Wilbur Foundation, Marguerite
  Eyer
Williams Cos.
Williams Foundation, Kemper
  and Leila
Witco Corp.
Wollenberg Foundation
Woods Charitable Fund
Woodward Governor Co.
Woolley Foundation, Vasser
WSP&R Charitable Trust Fund
Xerox Corp.
Zarrow Foundation, Anne and
  Henry

Municipalities

Abell-Hanger Foundation
Abitibi-Price
Abney Foundation
Abraham & Straus
Alexander Foundation, Judd S.
Altman Foundation
Aluminum Co. of America
American General Finance
American Optical Corp.
American President Cos.
American Welding &
  Manufacturing Co.
Andalusia Health Services
Andersen Corp.
Andersen Foundation, Hugh J.
Andersons Management Corp.
Andres Charitable Trust, Frank
  G.
Animal Assistance Foundation
Appleman Foundation
Arakelian Foundation, Mary
  Alice
ARCO Chemical
Arkell Hall Foundation
Armco Inc.
Arronson Foundation
Attleboro Pawtucket Savings
  Bank
Auerbach Foundation, Beatrice
  Fox
Azby Fund
Bacon Foundation, E. L. and
  Oma
Badger Meter, Inc.
Baird Brothers Co.
Baird & Co., Robert W.

Banbury Fund
Banc One Illinois Corp.
Bang & Olufsen of America, Inc.
Bank of A. Levy
Bank One, Texas-Houston Office
Bank South Corp.
Barker Foundation
Barnes Group
Bartlett & Co.
Batts Foundation
Baughman Foundation
Beatty Trust, Cordelia Lunceford
Beazley Foundation
Bechtel Charitable Remainder
  Uni-Trust, Marie H.
Bend Millwork Systems
Benenson Foundation, Frances
  and Benjamin
Beretta U.S.A. Corp.
Berger Foundation, H.N. and
  Frances C.
Bethlehem Steel Corp.
Betts Industries
Bigelow Foundation, F. R.
Bionetics Corp.
Bloedorn Foundation, Walter A.
Bloomfield Foundation, Sam and
  Rie
Blount
Blount Educational and
  Charitable Foundation,
  Mildred Weedon
Blowitz-Ridgeway Foundation
Blue Bell, Inc.
Boatmen's First National Bank
  of Oklahoma
Bolz Family Foundation,
  Eugenie Mayer
Booth-Bricker Fund
Borden
Borg-Warner Corp.
Boswell Foundation, James G.
Boutell Memorial Fund, Arnold
  and Gertrude
Bovaird Foundation, Mervin
Brady Foundation
Bremer Foundation, Otto
Brenton Banks Inc.
Bridwell Foundation, J. S.
Brillion Iron Works
Brown Foundation, James
  Graham
Brown Foundation, M. K.
Browning-Ferris Industries
Bryant Foundation
Buckley Trust, Thomas D.
Bucyrus-Erie
Buehler Foundation, Emil
Buhl Family Foundation
Bunbury Company
C.P. Rail Systems
Cabot Corp.
Cain Foundation, Effie and
  Wofford
Callaway Foundation
Callaway Foundation, Fuller E.
Camp Foundation
Camp Younts Foundation
Campbell Foundation, J. Bulow
Campbell Foundation, Ruth and
  Henry
Canon U.S.A., Inc.
Capital Cities/ABC
Carey Industries
Carnahan-Jackson Foundation
Carnival Cruise Lines
Carpenter Foundation
Cascade Natural Gas Corp.
Casey Foundation, Annie E.
Cayuga Foundation
Centel Corp.
Central Bank of the South
Central Maine Power Co.
Central Soya Co.
Chambers Memorial, James B.
Chandler Foundation

Chanin Family Foundation, Paul
  R.
Charitable Fund
Chase Manhattan Bank, N.A.
Chase Trust, Alice P.
CHC Foundation
Cheney Foundation, Ben B.
Chiles Foundation
Christensen Charitable and
  Religious Foundation, L. C.
Christie, Manson & Woods
  International, Inc.
Christodora
Churches Homes Foundation
CIT Group Holdings
Clark Foundation, Edna
  McConnell
Clarke Trust, John
Clorox Co.
Cobb Family Foundation
Coffey Foundation
Cohen Foundation, George M.
Colburn Fund
Cole Foundation, Olive B.
Cole Trust, Quincy
Coles Family Foundation
Colt Foundation, James J.
Coltec Industries
Columbia Foundation
Columbus Dispatch Printing Co.
Common Wealth Trust
Commonwealth Fund
Community Enterprises
Cone Mills Corp.
Consumer Farmer Foundation
Cornell Trust, Peter C.
CPC International
CRL Inc.
Crown Central Petroleum Corp.
Cullen Foundation
CUNA Mutual Insurance Group
Dai-Ichi Kangyo Bank of
  California
Davis Foundation, Ken W.
Delano Foundation, Mignon
  Sherwood
Dell Foundation, Hazel
Deuble Foundation, George H.
Devonshire Associates
DeVore Foundation
Dewar Foundation
Dexter Charitable Fund, Eugene
  A.
Dibner Fund
Dietrich Foundation, William B.
Dillon Foundation
Dimeo Construction Co.
Dodge Jones Foundation
Donovan, Leisure, Newton &
  Irvine
Downs Perpetual Charitable
  Trust, Ellason
Dreyfus Foundation, Max and
  Victoria
du Pont de Nemours & Co., E. I.
Duke Power Co.
Dunning Foundation
duPont Foundation, Chichester
Durst Foundation
E and M Charities
Eagle-Picher Industries
Eastern Bank Foundation
Eaton Foundation, Cyrus
Eaton Foundation, Cyrus
Eccles Foundation, Ralph M. and
  Ella M.
Eckman Charitable Foundation,
  Samuel and Rae
Eddy Family Memorial Fund, C.
  K.
Edgewater Steel Corp.
Edouard Foundation
Edwards Foundation, O. P. and
  W. E.
Einstein Fund, Albert E. and
  Birdie W.
Elkins, Jr. Foundation, Margaret
  and James A.

Ellis Grant and Scholarship
  Fund, Charles E.
Emergency Aid of Pennsylvania
  Foundation
Emerson Foundation, Fred L.
English Foundation, Walter and
  Marian
English Foundation, Walter and
  Marian
English Memorial Fund,
  Florence C. and H. L.
Ensign-Bickford Industries
Evans Foundation, Thomas J.
Eyman Trust, Jesse
Fair Foundation, R. W.
Fairfield-Meeker Charitable
  Trust, Freeman E.
Farr Trust, Frank M. and Alice
  M.
Faulkner Trust, Marianne
  Gaillard
Feild Co-Operative Association
Ferebee Endowment, Percy O.
Finch Foundation, Thomas
  Austin
First Boston
First Fidelity Bancorporation
First Interstate Bank of Oregon
First Union Corp.
Fish Foundation, Ray C.
Fisher Foundation
Fleishhacker Foundation
Fletcher Foundation
Flintridge Foundation
Florida Power & Light Co.
Flowers Charitable Trust, Albert
  W. and Edith V.
Ford Foundation
Ford Fund, William and Martha
Ford Meter Box Co.
Forest Foundation
Foster-Davis Foundation
Freeman Charitable Trust,
  Samuel
Freeport Brick Co.
Freeport-McMoRan
Friends' Foundation Trust, A.
Frohman Foundation, Sidney
Fuchs Foundation, Gottfried &
  Mary
Fund for New Jersey
Funderburke & Associates
Funderburke & Associates
Galvin Foundation, Robert W.
Gebbie Foundation
Gellert Foundation, Fred
General American Life Insurance
  Co.
General Mills
Geneseo Foundation
George Foundation
Georgia-Pacific Corp.
Giant Eagle
Giant Food Stores
Gibson Foundation, E. L.
Gifford Charitable Corporation,
  Rosamond
Gillett Foundation, Elesabeth
  Ingalls
Gilman Foundation, Howard
Gilmer-Smith Foundation
Glazer Foundation, Jerome S.
Goldman Charitable Trust, Sol
Goodman & Company
Goodyear Foundation, Josephine
Gould Foundation for Children,
  Edwin
Gray Foundation, Garland
Green Foundation, Burton E.
Greenebaum, Doll & McDonald
Gries Charity Fund, Lucile and
  Robert H.
Grimes Foundation
Grimes Foundation
Grundy Foundation
Guggenheim Foundation, Daniel
  and Florence
Gund Foundation

Hagler Foundation, Jon L.
Hale Foundation, Crescent Porter
Halloran Foundation, Mary P.
  Dolciani
Handy & Harman
Hanes Foundation, John W. and
  Anna H.
Hansen Foundation, Dane G.
Harrington Foundation, Don and
  Sybil
Harrison Foundation, Fred G.
Hartzell Industries, Inc.
Hauserman, Inc.
Hawkins Foundation, Robert Z.
Hayfields Foundation
Hechinger Co.
Heginbotham Trust, Will E.
Heileman Brewing Co., Inc., G.
Heinz Endowment, Howard
Helfaer Foundation, Evan and
  Marion
Helmerich Foundation
Henderson Foundation, George
  B.
Henkel Corp.
Herrick Foundation
Hersey Foundation
Hess Charitable Trust, Myrtle E.
  and William C.
Hesston Corp.
Heyward Memorial Fund,
  DuBose and Dorothy
Hobby Foundation
Hoche-Scofield Foundation
Hoover Foundation
Hopedale Foundation
Horne Foundation, Dick
Horowitz Foundation, Gedale B.
  and Barbara S.
Houston Endowment
Houston Industries
Howell Foundation, Eric and
  Jessie
Hoyt Foundation, Stewart W. and
  Willma C.
Huffy Corp.
Huizenga Family Foundation
Hulings Foundation, Mary
  Andersen
Hunt Charitable Trust, C. Giles
Hunt Charitable Trust, C. Giles
Hunter Foundation, Edward and
  Irma
Hurst Foundation
Huston Foundation
Iddings Benevolent Trust
Indiana Desk Co.
Inland Container Corp.
Iowa Savings Bank
Irwin-Sweeney-Miller
  Foundation
Jacobson & Sons, Benjamin
Janesville Foundation
Jenkins Foundation, George W.
Johnson Foundation, Burdine
Johnson & Son, S.C.
Jones Foundation, Daisy Marquis
Jones Foundation, Montfort
  Jones and Allie Brown
Joslin-Needham Family
  Foundation
Justus Trust, Edith C.
Kantzler Foundation
Kapiloff Foundation, Leonard
Kaufman Endowment Fund,
  Louis G.
Kellogg Foundation, W. K.
Kellogg's
Kemper Foundation, Enid and
  Crosby
Kempner Fund, Harris and Eliza
Kentland Foundation
Kettering Fund
Kiewit Foundation, Peter
Kilroy Foundation, William S.
  and Lora Jean
Kimberly-Clark Corp.
Kinney-Lindstrom Foundation

Recipient Type Index

Municipalities (cont.)

Kirbo Charitable Trust, Thomas M. and Irene B.
Kirkhill Rubber Co.
Kitzmiller/Bales Trust
Knapp Foundation
Knox, Sr., and Pearl Wallis Knox Charitable Foundation, Robert W.
Koehler Foundation, Marcia and Otto
Kunkel Foundation, John Crain
L. L. W. W. Foundation
La-Z-Boy Chair Co.
Ladd Charitable Corporation, Helen and George
Laerdal Foundation, Asmund S.
Lancaster Colony
Lance, Inc.
Lane Co., Inc.
Laros Foundation, R. K.
Lasky Co.
Lassen Foundation, Irving A.
Lassus Brothers Oil
Lee Endowment Foundation
Lennox International, Inc.
Levy Foundation, June Rockwell
Liberty Corp.
Lightner Sams Foundation
Lincoln Family Foundation
Lindstrom Foundation, Kinney
Litton/Itek Optical Systems
Loutit Foundation
LTV Corp.
Lubo Fund
Lyon Foundation
MacCurdy Salisbury Educational Foundation
Maclellan Charitable Trust, R. J.
Maddox Trust, Web
Mallinckrodt Specialty Chemicals Co.
Marcus Corp.
Maritz Inc.
Marquette Electronics
Marshall Fund
Martin Marietta Corp.
Massengill-DeFriece Foundation
Massie Trust, David Meade
Massie Trust, David Meade
Maxon Charitable Foundation
May Foundation, Wilbur
Mayor Foundation, Oliver Dewey
Mazza Foundation
MBIA, Inc.
McCann Foundation
McCarthy Memorial Trust Fund, Catherine
McConnell Foundation
McDermott Foundation, Eugene
McDonough Foundation, Bernard
McElroy Trust, R. J.
McFeely-Rogers Foundation
McGovern Fund for the Behavioral Sciences
McKenna Foundation, Katherine Mabis
McKnight Foundation
McMahon Foundation
McMillan, Jr. Foundation, Bruce
MDU Resources Group, Inc.
Mead Corp.
Meadows Foundation
Medina Foundation
Melitta North America Inc.
Menschel Foundation, Robert and Joyce
Merchants Bancshares
Meredith Foundation
Mettler Instrument Corp.
Meyer Memorial Foundation, Aaron and Rachel
Michigan Gas Utilities
Millbrook Tribute Garden
Miller Foundation
Milliken Foundation, Agnes G.

Mobil Oil Corp.
Mohasco Corp.
Moncrief Foundation, William A. and Elizabeth B.
Monfort Charitable Foundation
Montgomery Foundation
Moody Foundation
Moore Foundation, C. F.
Moorman Manufacturing Co.
Morgan Foundation, Louie R. and Gertrude
Morris Foundation, Margaret T.
Morrison Foundation, Harry W.
Moss Charitable Trust, Finis M.
Mott Charitable Trust/Spectemur Agendo, Stewart R.
Mueller Co.
Mulford Trust, Clarence E.
Multimedia, Inc.
Murphy Co., G.C.
Murray Foundation
Nashua Trust Co.
Nathan Foundation
National Machinery Co.
Neenah Foundry Co.
Neese Family Foundation
Nelson Industries, Inc.
Newman Assistance Fund, Jerome A. and Estelle R.
News & Observer Publishing Co.
Norcross Wildlife Foundation
Nord Family Foundation
Northern Star Foundation
O'Connor Foundation, A. Lindsay and Olive B.
O'Connor Foundation, Kathryn
Ogle Foundation, Paul
Ohrstrom Foundation
Olsson Memorial Foundation, Elis
O'Neil Foundation, Casey Albert T.
O'Neill Charitable Corporation, F. J.
Orbit Valve Co.
Owen Trust, B. B.
Owsley Foundation, Alvin and Lucy
Oxford Foundation
PACCAR
Pacific Mutual Life Insurance Co.
Packaging Corporation of America
Packard Foundation, David and Lucile
Packer Foundation, Horace B.
Palmer Fund, Frank Loomis
Pappas Charitable Foundation, Bessie
Park Bank
Pasadena Area Residential Aid
Penney Foundation, James C.
Perkins Memorial Foundation, George W.
Peterson Foundation, Fred J.
Petrie Trust, Lorene M.
Petteys Memorial Foundation, Jack
PHH Corp.
Philips Foundation, Jesse
Phillips Foundation, Dr. P.
Phillips Petroleum Co.
Phipps Foundation, William H.
Physicians Mutual Insurance
Pineywoods Foundation
Pinkerton Foundation
Piton Foundation
PMA Industries
Porter Foundation, Mrs. Cheever
Potomac Electric Power Co.
PPG Industries
Preston Trust, Evelyn W.
Proctor Trust, Mortimer R.
Provigo Corp. Inc.
Pukall Lumber
Quaker Oats Co.

Quality Metal Finishing Foundation
Quanex Corp.
R. P. Foundation
R&B Tool Co.
Ranney Foundation, P. K.
Ratner Foundation, Milton M.
Reily & Co., William B.
Rennebohm Foundation, Oscar
Reynolds Foundation, Donald W.
Richardson Benevolent Foundation, C. E.
Rider-Pool Foundation
Rieke Corp.
Riggs Benevolent Fund
Riordan Foundation
Robbins & Myers, Inc.
Roberts Foundation, Dora
Rogers Foundation
Romill Foundation
Rosenbaum Foundation, Paul and Gabriella
Ross Foundation
Ross Foundation, Arthur
Rudin Foundation
Sage Foundation
Sargent Foundation, Newell B.
Scaife Family Foundation
Scott and Fetzer Co.
Scrivner, Inc.
Seaver Charitable Trust, Richard C.
Seay Memorial Trust, George and Effie
Second Foundation
Security State Bank
Sefton Foundation, J. W.
Segal Charitable Trust, Barnet
Selby and Marie Selby Foundation, William G.
Servco Pacific
Shapero Foundation, Nate S. and Ruth B.
Share Trust, Charles Morton
Shattuck Charitable Trust, S. F.
Sheinberg Foundation, Eric P.
Shoemaker Fund, Thomas H. and Mary Williams
Shott, Jr. Foundation, Hugh I.
Shuwa Investments Corp.
Simon Foundation, William E. and Carol G.
Simpson Foundation
Simpson Investment Co.
Slemp Foundation
Smith and W. Aubrey Smith Charitable Foundation, Clara Blackford
Smoot Charitable Foundation
Snow Memorial Trust, John Ben
Snyder Charitable Fund, W. P.
Soling Family Foundation
Sordoni Foundation
South Carolina Electric & Gas Co.
South Texas Charitable Foundation
Springs Foundation
SPX Corp.
Stackpole-Hall Foundation
Stamps Foundation, James L.
Standard Products Co.
Star Bank, N.A.
Starrett Co., L.S.
Stauffer Communications
Steadley Memorial Trust, Kent D. and Mary L.
Stearns Charitable Foundation, Anna B.
Stearns Trust, Artemas W.
Steel, Sr. Foundation, Marshall
Stein Foundation, Louis
Steinman Foundation, James Hale
Sterling Winthrop
Stern Foundation, Irvin
Stevens Foundation, Abbot and Dorothy H.

Stevens Foundation, John T.
Stewart Educational Foundation, Donnell B. and Elizabeth Dee Shaw
Stone Trust, H. Chase
Stoneman Charitable Foundation, Anne and David
Stuart Foundation
Stupp Brothers Bridge & Iron Co.
Stupp Foundation, Norman J.
Sulzberger Foundation
Sumitomo Bank of California
Sumners Foundation, Hatton W.
Swanson Family Foundation, Dr. W.C.
Swig Charity Foundation, Mae and Benjamin
Swig Foundation
Switzer Foundation
Symmes Foundation, F. W.
Tait Foundation, Frank M.
Taub Foundation, Henry and Marilyn
Temple-Inland
Terner Foundation
Texas Instruments
Textron
Thalheimer Foundation, Alvin and Fanny Blaustein
Thalhimer and Family Foundation, Charles G.
Thatcher Foundation
Thirty-Five Twenty, Inc.
Thrush-Thompson Foundation
Timken Foundation of Canton
Tippens Foundation
Tonkin Foundation, Tom and Helen
Tonya Memorial Foundation
Trexler Trust, Harry C.
Triangle Industries
Truman Foundation, Mildred Faulkner
Trust Co. Bank
Tucker Charitable Trust, Rose E.
28:19
Tyson Foods, Inc.
Tyson Fund
Ukrop's Super Markets, Inc.
Unilever United States
Union Camp Corp.
U.S. Oil/Schmidt Family Foundation, Inc.
United States Sugar Corp.
Universal Leaf Tobacco Co.
Upjohn Foundation, Harold and Grace
Utica National Insurance Group
Valdese Manufacturing Co., Inc.
Valentine Foundation, Lawson
Van Buren Foundation
Van Every Foundation, Philip L.
Van Wert County Foundation
Vesper Corp.
Vevay-Switzerland County Foundation
Vicksburg Foundation
Vulcan Materials Co.
Waggoner Foundation, E. Paul and Helen Buck
Wahlstrom Foundation
Wal-Mart Stores
Walgreen Co.
Wallace Computer Services
Ward Co., Joe L.
Warsh-Mott Legacy
Waste Management
Wean Foundation, Raymond John
Webber Oil Co.
Weinberg, Jr. Foundation, Sidney J.
Wellons Foundation
Weyerhaeuser Co.
Whalley Charitable Trust
Wheat First Securites
Wheeler Foundation, Wilmot
Whirlpool Corp.

White Trust, G. R.
Whiting Foundation, Macauley and Helen Dow
Whiting Memorial Foundation, Henry and Harriet
Whittenberger Foundation, Claude R. and Ethel B.
Wickson-Link Memorial Foundation
Wiggins Memorial Trust, J. J.
Wilbur Foundation, Marguerite Eyer
Willard Helping Fund, Cecilia Young
Williams Charitable Trust, John C.
Williams Foundation, Kemper and Leila
Wilsey Bennet Co.
Winkler Foundation, Mark and Catherine
Winnebago Industries, Inc.
Winthrop Trust, Clara B.
Wood Charitable Trust, W. P.
Wood Foundation of Chambersburg, PA
Woodard Family Foundation
Woods Charitable Fund
Wurts Memorial, Henrietta Tower
Wyne Foundation
Wyomissing Foundation
Yeager Charitable Trust, Lester E.
York Barbell Co.
Young Foundation, H and B
Youth Foundation
Zarrow Foundation, Anne and Henry
Zemurray Foundation
Ziegler Foundation, Ruth/Allen

National Security

Arca Foundation
Archer-Daniels-Midland Co.
Babcock & Wilcox Co.
Batchelor Foundation
Bingham Foundation, William
Booz Allen & Hamilton
Briggs & Stratton Corp.
Carnegie Corporation of New York
Carthage Foundation
CHC Foundation
Cohen Foundation, Naomi and Nehemiah
Colonial Life & Accident Insurance Co.
Community Health Association
Coors Foundation, Adolph
CPC International
Davis Foundation, Edwin W. and Catherine M.
Dorot Foundation
Duke Power Co.
Earhart Foundation
Erving Paper Mills
Forbes
Funderburke & Associates
Funderburke & Associates
General Dynamics Corp.
Gillett Foundation, Elesabeth Ingalls
Glickenhaus & Co.
Henry Foundation, Patrick
Hewlett Foundation, William and Flora
HKH Foundation
Ingersoll Milling Machine Co.
Jones Foundation, W. Alton
Kautz Family Foundation
MacArthur Foundation, John D. and Catherine T.
McDonnell Douglas Corp.
McKenna Foundation, Philip M.
Mertz-Gilmore Foundation, Joyce
Morrison Trust, Louise L.
Moskowitz Foundation, Irving I.

Philanthropic Organizations (cont.)

Callaway Foundation, Fuller E.
Campbell Foundation, J. Bulow
Cannon Foundation
Capital Fund Foundation
Capital Holding Corp.
Carnegie Corporation of New York
Carpenter Foundation, E. Rhodes and Leona B.
Carpenter Technology Corp.
Carter Foundation, Beirne
Casey Foundation, Eugene B.
Centel Corp.
Central Hudson Gas & Electric Corp.
Central Maine Power Co.
Central & South West Services
Century Companies of America
Chandler Foundation
Chapman Charitable Trust, H. A. and Mary K.
Charina Foundation
Chase Charity Foundation, Alfred E.
Chase Manhattan Bank, N.A.
Cheney Foundation, Ben B.
Chesapeake Corp.
CIT Group Holdings
CIT Group Holdings
Citizens Bank
Clark-Winchcole Foundation
Cleveland-Cliffs
Clipper Ship Foundation
Close Foundation
Clowes Fund
Cole Foundation, Olive B.
Colonial Life & Accident Insurance Co.
Columbia Foundation
Columbus Dispatch Printing Co.
Commonwealth Fund
Concord Chemical Co.
Cone Mills Corp.
Conn Memorial Foundation
Cook Charitable Foundation
Copperweld Corp.
Cosmair, Inc.
County Bank
Cox Charitable Trust, Jessie B.
Cox, Jr. Foundation, James M.
CRL Inc.
Crown Books Foundation, Inc.
Cullen Foundation
CUNA Mutual Insurance Group
Daly Charitable Foundation Trust, Robert and Nancy
Dammann Fund
Danforth Foundation
Danner Foundation
Davis Foundation, Edwin W. and Catherine M.
Davis Foundation, Shelby Cullom
De Lima Co., Paul
Dekko Foundation
Delany Charitable Trust, Beatrice P.
DeMoss Foundation, Arthur S.
Demoulas Supermarkets
Deutsch Co.
DeVlieg Foundation, Charles
DeVos Foundation, Richard and Helen
Dexter Shoe Co.
Dibner Fund
Diener Foundation, Frank C.
Dishman Charitable Foundation Trust, H. E. and Kate
Dixie Yarns, Inc.
Dobson Foundation
Dodge Foundation, Cleveland H.
Dodge Foundation, P. L.
Doelger Charitable Trust, Thelma

Donovan, Leisure, Newton & Irvine
Dorminy Foundation, John Henry
Dougherty, Jr. Foundation, James R.
Dow Foundation, Herbert H. and Grace A.
du Pont de Nemours & Co., E. I.
Durfee Foundation
Dynamet, Inc.
Eden Hall Foundation
Edison Fund, Charles
Edwards Foundation, O. P. and W. E.
Eisenberg Foundation, Ben B. and Joyce E.
Ellison Foundation
English-Bonter-Mitchell Foundation
Erb Lumber Co.
Essel Foundation
Essick Foundation
Estes Foundation
Factor Family Foundation, Max
Fair Play Foundation
Farnsworth Trust, Charles A.
Federated Life Insurance Co.
Feintech Foundation
Feldberg Family Foundation
Field Foundation of Illinois
Fig Tree Foundation
Filene Foundation, Lincoln and Therese
Finley Foundation, A. E.
Fireman's Fund Insurance Co.
Firestone Foundation, Roger S.
First Maryland Bancorp
First Mississippi Corp.
First Petroleum Corp.
First Union Corp.
Fish Foundation, Ray C.
Flagler Foundation
Flintridge Foundation
Florida Power & Light Co.
Foote Mineral Co.
Ford Foundation
Ford Meter Box Co.
Forest Lawn Foundation
Forest Oil Corp.
Fortis Inc.
Foster Charitable Trust
Foster Foundation, Joseph C. and Esther
Foundation for Child Development
Foundation for the Needs of Others
Fowler Memorial Foundation, John Edward
France Foundation, Jacob and Annita
Franklin Mint Corp.
Frederick Foundation
Freed Foundation
Freedom Forum
Freeman Charitable Trust, Samuel
Freeman Foundation, Carl M.
Frisch's Restaurants Inc.
Frohlich Charitable Trust, Ludwig W.
Fruehauf Foundation
Fund for New Jersey
Funderburke & Associates
Funderburke & Associates
G.P.G. Foundation
Gabelli Foundation
Gaisman Foundation, Catherine and Henry J.
Galkin Charitable Trust, Ira S. and Anna
Gannett Publishing Co., Guy
Gateway Apparel
Gazette Co.
GEICO Corp.
General Accident Insurance Co. of America

General American Life Insurance Co.
Generation Trust
Genius Foundation, Elizabeth Morse
Georgia Power Co.
Gerstacker Foundation, Rollin M.
Giant Eagle
Giger Foundation, Paul and Oscar
Gill Foundation, Pauline Allen
Gilman Paper Co.
Gilmore Foundation, Irving S.
Gitano Group
Globe Corp.
Goldberg Family Foundation
Goldman Foundation, Herman
Goldman Fund, Richard and Rhoda
Goldseker Foundation of Maryland, Morris
Goodwin Foundation, Leo
Gorin Foundation, Nehemiah
Gottesman Fund
Gould Foundation, Florence J.
Grassmann Trust, E. J.
Graybar Electric Co.
Greater Construction Corp. Charitable Foundation, Inc.
Greenheck Fan Corp.
Greenspan Foundation
Gross Charitable Trust, Walter L. and Nell R.
Grotto Foundation
Gulfstream Aerospace Corp.
Gund Foundation
Haas Fund, Walter and Elise
Haas, Jr. Fund, Evelyn and Walter
Habig Foundation, Arnold F.
Haggar Foundation
Hall Family Foundations
Hallmark Cards
Hamilton Foundation, Florence P.
Hampden Papers
Hand Industries
Handleman Co.
Hankamer Foundation, Curtis and Doris K.
Harden Foundation
Harding Educational and Charitable Foundation
Hargis Charitable Foundation, Estes H. and Florence Parker
Harriman Foundation, Gladys and Roland
Harrington Foundation, Don and Sybil
Harris Foundation
Hassenfeld Foundation
Hatterscheidt Foundation
Hazen Foundation, Edward W.
Hecht-Levi Foundation
Hecla Mining Co.
Heinz Endowment, Howard
Heinz Endowment, Vira I.
Heinz Foundation, Drue
Helms Foundation
Hench Foundation, John C.
Herbst Foundation
Herzog Foundation, Carl J.
Heymann-Wolf Foundation
Heymann-Wolf Foundation
Higgins Charitable Trust, Lorene Sails
Higginson Trust, Corina
Hightower Foundation, Walter
Hillman Foundation
Hobby Foundation
Hoffer Plastics Corp.
Hoffman Foundation, H. Leslie Hoffman and Elaine S.
Hoffmann-La Roche
Holley Foundation
Holtzmann Foundation, Jacob L. and Lillian
Homeland Foundation
Honeywell

Hoover Foundation
Hoover, Jr. Foundation, Margaret W. and Herbert
Hopwood Charitable Trust, John M.
Houck Foundation, May K.
Household International
Hoyt Foundation, Stewart W. and Willma C.
Hubbard Broadcasting
Hubbell Inc.
Huber Foundation
Hudson-Webber Foundation
Hughes Charitable Trust, Mabel Y.
Huizenga Family Foundation
Hulings Foundation, Mary Andersen
Humana
Hunt Alternatives Fund
Hunt Alternatives Fund, Helen
Hunt Foundation, Roy A.
Hunter Trust, A. V.
Hurford Foundation
Hurst Foundation
Huston Foundation
Hyde and Watson Foundation
Icahn Foundation, Carl C.
Illinois Power Co.
Imlay Foundation
Indiana Bell Telephone Co.
Ingalls Foundation, Louise H. and David S.
Interco
International Foundation
Irmas Charitable Foundation, Audrey and Sydney
Irvine Foundation, James
Irvine Health Foundation
Isaly Klondike Co.
Island Foundation
ITT Rayonier
Jacobson Foundation, Bernard H. and Blanche E.
Jacobson & Sons, Benjamin
Jarson-Stanley and Mickey Kaplan Foundation, Isaac & Esther
Jerome Foundation
Jewett Foundation, George Frederick
Johnson Fund, Edward C.
Jones Foundation, Daisy Marquis
Jones Fund, Blanche and George
Joslyn Foundation, Marcellus I.
Joukowsky Family Foundation
Joyce Foundation, John M. and Mary A.
Jurzykowski Foundation, Alfred
Kahn Memorial Trust
Kaiser Family Foundation, Henry J.
Kaplan Foundation, Mayer and Morris
Keene Trust, Hazel R.
Kellmer Co., Jack
Kellogg Foundation, J. C.
Kennametal
Kerr Foundation, Robert S. and Grayce B.
Kieckhefer Foundation, J. W.
Kiewit Foundation, Peter
King Foundation, Carl B. and Florence E.
Kiplinger Foundation
Kirby Foundation, F. M.
Klau Foundation, David W. and Sadie
Klein Charitable Foundation, Raymond
Klein Fund, Nathan J.
Knox Family Foundation
Knox Foundation, Seymour H.
Koch Industries
Kohl Charitable Foundation, Allen D.
Koopman Fund
Kopf Foundation

Kraft Foundation
Kugelman Foundation
Kunstadter Family Foundation, Albert
L. L. W. W. Foundation
Lancaster Colony
Lance, Inc.
Lane Foundation, Minnie and Bernard
Lang Foundation, Eugene M.
Lasky Co.
Lattner Foundation, Forrest C.
Laurel Foundation
Law Foundation, Robert O.
Lazar Foundation
LBJ Family Foundation
LDI Charitable Foundation
Leavey Foundation, Thomas and Dorothy
Lebanon Mutual Insurance Co.
Leidy Foundation, John J.
Levinson Foundation, Morris L.
Levitt Foundation, Richard S.
Levy Foundation, Betty and Norman F.
Levy Foundation, Charles and Ruth
Levy Foundation, Hyman Jebb
Lightner Sams Foundation
Lilly Endowment
Lincy Foundation
Lipton, Thomas J.
List Foundation, Albert A.
Littauer Foundation, Lucius N.
Little, Arthur D.
Little Family Foundation
Livingston Foundation, Milton S. and Corinne N.
Lockwood Foundation, Byron W. and Alice L.
Loeb Foundation, Frances and John L.
Loeb Partners Corp.
Louis Foundation, Michael W.
Lounsbery Foundation, Richard
Loutit Foundation
Lovett Foundation
Lowe Foundation, Joe and Emily
Lowenstein Foundation, Leon
Luce Charitable Foundation, Stephen C.
Lydall, Inc.
Lyndhurst Foundation
Lynn Foundation, E. M.
MacArthur Foundation, John D. and Catherine T.
MacLeod Stewardship Foundation
Maddox Trust, Web
Mailman Foundation
Mallinckrodt Specialty Chemicals Co.
Manoogian Foundation, Alex and Marie
Marcus Corp.
Mardag Foundation
Margoes Foundation
Maritz Inc.
Marmot Foundation
Marshall Foundation
Marshburn Foundation
Martin Marietta Corp.
Marx Foundation, Virginia & Leonard
Mary Kay Foundation
Mason Charitable Foundation
Masserini Charitable Trust, Maurice J.
Max Charitable Foundation
McBean Family Foundation
McCasland Foundation
McCormick Foundation, Chauncey and Marion Deering
McCormick Tribune Foundation, Robert R.
McCune Charitable Trust, John R.
McDonald & Co. Securities

McDonnell Foundation, James S.
McEachern Charitable Trust, D. V. & Ida J.
McElroy Trust, R. J.
McFeely-Rogers Foundation
McGonagle Foundation, Dextra Baldwin
McGovern Fund for the Behavioral Sciences
McGraw Foundation, Donald C.
McGregor Fund
MCJ Foundation
McKenna Foundation, Katherine Mabis
McNutt Charitable Trust, Amy Shelton
McRae Foundation
Mead Corp.
Mead Fund, Nelson
Media General, Inc.
Medina Foundation
Mellen Foundation
Memton Fund
Merck Family Fund
Mericos Foundation
Merrick Foundation, Robert G. and Anne M.
Mertz-Gilmore Foundation, Joyce
Meyer Foundation, Eugene and Agnes E.
Meyer Memorial Trust
Meyerhoff Fund, Joseph
Michigan Consolidated Gas Co.
Middendorf Foundation
Midwest Resources
Milken Family Medical Foundation
Miller Foundation
Miniger Memorial Foundation, Clement O.
Misco Industries
Mnuchin Foundation
Mohasco Corp.
Monell Foundation, Ambrose
Montgomery Street Foundation
Moore Foundation, Edward S.
Moores Foundation, Harry C.
Morgan Foundation, Burton D.
Morrison-Knudsen Corp.
Morse Foundation, Richard P. and Claire W.
Moses Fund, Henry and Lucy
Motorola
Mott Foundation, Charles Stewart
Murdock Charitable Trust, M. J.
Myers and Sons, D.
Nason Foundation
Nathan Berkman & Co.
National Computer Systems
National Starch & Chemical Corp.
Neese Family Foundation
Neu Foundation, Hugo and Doris
New England Foundation
New York Life Insurance Co.
Newhouse Foundation, Samuel I.
Newman Assistance Fund, Jerome A. and Estelle R.
Noble Foundation, Edward John
Nord Family Foundation
Norgren Foundation, Carl A.
Normandie Foundation
Norris Foundation, Dellora A. and Lester J.
Norris Foundation, Kenneth T. and Eileen L.
Northern Star Foundation
Northwest Area Foundation
Norwest Bank Nebraska
Oak Foundation U.S.A.
O'Connor Foundation, A. Lindsay and Olive B.
Offield Family Foundation
Ogle Foundation, Paul
Ohrstrom Foundation
Olin Foundation, Spencer T. and Ann W.
Olive Bridge Fund

Olsson Memorial Foundation, Elis
Oppenheimer and Flora Oppenheimer Haas Trust, Leo
Oppenstein Brothers Foundation
Ore-Ida Foods, Inc.
Oshkosh B'Gosh
Overbrook Foundation
Overseas Shipholding Group
Owen Trust, B. B.
Oxford Industries, Inc.
Packard Foundation, David and Lucile
Pappas Charitable Foundation, Thomas Anthony
Parshelsky Foundation, Moses L.
Parsons Foundation, Ralph M.
Parsons - W.D. Charities, Vera Davis
Peery Foundation
Perot Foundation
PHH Corp.
Philip Morris Cos.
Philips Foundation, Jesse
Phillips Family Foundation, Jay and Rose
Phillips Family Foundation, L. E.
Phillips Foundation, Dr. P.
Pillsbury Foundation
Pines Bridge Foundation
Pinewood Foundation
Piper Foundation, Minnie Stevens
Piton Foundation
Pittsburgh National Bank
Pittway Corp.
Playboy Enterprises, Inc.
PMA Industries
Pott Foundation, Herman T. and Phenie R.
Powell Family Foundation
Premier Industrial Corp.
Price Foundation, Louis and Harold
Prickett Fund, Lynn R. and Karl E.
Pritzker Foundation
Procter & Gamble Cosmetic & Fragrance Products
Putnam Foundation
Questar Corp.
R. P. Foundation
Rabb Charitable Trust, Sidney R.
Ramapo Trust
Ratshesky Foundation, A. C.
Reed Foundation
Regenstein Foundation
Reinberger Foundation
Reisman Charitable Trust, George C. and Evelyn R.
Reliable Life Insurance Co.
Revson Foundation, Charles H.
Reynolds Foundation, Christopher
Reynolds Foundation, Edgar
Reynolds Metals Co.
Reynolds & Reynolds Co.
Rich Foundation
Ritter Foundation
Roche Relief Foundation, Edward and Ellen
Rochlin Foundation, Abraham and Sonia
Rockefeller Foundation
Rockefeller Trust, Winthrop
Rogers Corp.
RosaMary Foundation
Rose Foundation, Billy
Rosenberg Foundation
Rosenstiel Foundation
Rosenwald Family Fund, William
Rubbermaid
Rubenstein Charitable Foundation, Lawrence J. and Anne
Rubin Family Fund, Cele H. and William B.
Rubin Foundation, Samuel

Ruddick Corp.
Rudin Foundation
Ryan Foundation, Nina M.
Safeguard Scientifics Foundation
Sagamore Foundation
Sage Foundation
Sandy Foundation, George H.
Sandy Hill Foundation
Sapirstein-Stone-Weiss Foundation
Sara Lee Corp.
Sara Lee Hosiery
Sarkeys Foundation
Sattler Beneficial Trust, Daniel A. and Edna J.
Scaife Family Foundation
Schautz Foundation, Walter L.
Schering-Plough Corp.
Scheuer Family Foundation, S. H. and Helen R.
Schiro Fund
Schmidlapp Trust No. 1, Jacob G.
Schrafft and Bertha E. Schrafft Charitable Trust, William E.
Schultz Foundation
Schwab & Co., Charles
Seaway Food Town
Second Foundation
Security Life of Denver
Sehn Foundation
Semmes Foundation
Sequoia Foundation
Shaffer Family Charitable Trust
Shapiro Charity Fund, Abraham
Shapiro Family Foundation, Soretta and Henry
Shapiro Fund, Albert
Simon Foundation, William E. and Carol G.
SIT Investment Associates, Inc.
Skillman Foundation
Slant/Fin Corp.
Slifka Foundation, Alan B.
Sloan Foundation, Alfred P.
Smeal Foundation, Mary Jean & Frank P.
Smith Charities, John
Smith Family Foundation, Theda Clark
Smith Foundation, Bob and Vivian
Smith Foundation, Lon V.
Smith Foundation, Richard and Susan
Snow Memorial Trust, John Ben
Solo Cup Co.
Sonat
Sooner Pipe & Supply Corp.
Soref Foundation, Samuel M. Soref and Helene K.
Sosland Foundation
Star Bank, N.A.
Starr Foundation
Stauffer Foundation, John and Beverly
Stearns Charitable Foundation, Anna B.
Steele Foundation
Steele-Reese Foundation
Steinman Foundation, James Hale
Stern Foundation, Bernice and Milton
Stevens Foundation, Abbot and Dorothy H.
Stockham Valves & Fittings
Stone Charitable Foundation
Stone Container Corp.
Stone Foundation
Stoneman Charitable Foundation, Anne and David
Strake Foundation
Stranahan Foundation
Straus Foundation, Aaron and Lillie
Strauss Foundation
Strong Foundation, Hattie M.
Sulzberger Foundation

Summerfield Foundation, Solon E.
Swanson Family Foundation, Dr. W.C.
Swig Foundation
Synovus Financial Corp.
Taconic Foundation
Taper Foundation, Mark
Taub Foundation, Henry and Marilyn
Taylor Foundation, Ruth and Vernon
TCF Banking & Savings, FSB
Tiger Foundation
Time Insurance Co.
Timken Co.
Timken Foundation of Canton
TJX Cos.
Tomkins Industries, Inc.
Totsy Manufacturing Co.
Towsley Foundation, Harry A. and Margaret D.
Tozer Foundation
Trees Charitable Trust, Edith L.
Treuhaft Foundation
Tull Charitable Foundation
Turner Charitable Foundation
United States Sugar Corp.
Universal Leaf Tobacco Co.
Upjohn Foundation, Harold and Grace
Upton Foundation, Frederick S.
US Bancorp
Uvas Foundation
Valley Foundation
Valley Foundation, Wayne and Gladys
Van Andel Foundation, Jay and Betty
Van Every Foundation, Philip L.
Van Houten Charitable Trust
Vanneck-Bailey Foundation
Vesper Corp.
Von Rebay Foundation, Hilla
Wachtell, Lipton, Rosen & Katz
Walker Educational and Charitable Foundation, Alex C.
Wallace Genetic Foundation
Disney Co., Walt
Ward Heritage Foundation, Mamie McFaddin
Warfield Memorial Fund, Anna Emory
Warren Foundation, William K.
Washington Forrest Foundation
Washington Water Power Co.
Wasserman Foundation
Weber Charities Corp., Frederick E.
Weinberg Foundation, John L.
Weir Foundation Trust
Weisman Art Foundation, Frederick R.
Weiss Foundation, Stephen and Suzanne
Whitaker Charitable Foundation, Lyndon C.
White Construction Co.
Whitehead Foundation, Joseph B.
Wilf Family Foundation
Wilkof Foundation, Edward and Ruth
Williams Cos.
Wilsey Bennet Co.
Wilson Fund, Matilda R.
Wilson Trust, Lula C.
Winter Construction Co.
Women's Project Foundation
Woodward Governor Co.
Zale Foundation
Zink Foundation, John Steele

Professional & Trade Associations

Abbott Laboratories
Abell-Hanger Foundation
AFLAC

Air France
Algonquin Energy, Inc.
Allegheny Ludlum Corp.
Allendale Mutual Insurance Co.
Alliant Techsystems
AlliedSignal
ALPAC Corp.
Aluminum Co. of America
AMAX
America West Airlines
American President Cos.
American United Life Insurance Co.
Ameritas Life Insurance Corp.
Ames Department Stores
Amfac/JMB Hawaii
Amoco Corp.
AMP
AMR Corp.
Angelica Corp.
Aristech Chemical Corp.
Arkansas Power & Light Co.
Armco Inc.
Armstrong World Industries Inc.
Atlanta Gas Light Co.
Auerbach Foundation, Beatrice Fox
Babcock & Wilcox Co.
Backer Spielvogel Bates U.S.
Ball Corp.
Baltimore Gas & Electric Co.
Banc One Illinois Corp.
Banc One Wisconsin Corp.
Banfi Vintners
Bankers Trust Co.
Bass Foundation, Harry
Battelle
Batten Foundation
Bauer Foundation, M. R.
Bechtel Group
Bechtel, Jr. Foundation, S. D.
Beech Aircraft Corp.
Bell Communications Research
Benton Foundation
Berger Foundation, H.N. and Frances C.
Blade Communications
BMW of North America, Inc.
Boehringer Mannheim Corp.
Booz Allen & Hamilton
Borden
Brady Foundation, W. H.
Bristol-Myers Squibb Co.
British Airways
Brooks Brothers
Bucyrus-Erie
Bunbury Company
Burns Foundation
Burns Foundation, Fritz B.
Burroughs Wellcome Co.
Butler Manufacturing Co.
Capital Cities/ABC
Carnegie Corporation of New York
Carolina Power & Light Co.
Cartier, Inc.
Centel Corp.
Centerior Energy Corp.
Central Bank of the South
Central Hudson Gas & Electric Corp.
Central Maine Power Co.
Central Soya Co.
CertainTeed Corp.
Chase Manhattan Bank, N.A.
Chesapeake Corp.
Chevron Corp.
Cincinnati Bell
Collins & Aikman Holdings Corp.
Colonial Life & Accident Insurance Co.
Columbia Foundation
Cominco American Inc.
Commerce Clearing House
Cone Mills Corp.
Continental Corp.

Professional & Trade Associations (cont.)

Country Curtains, Inc.
Covington and Burling
Cowles Media Co.
CPC International
CR Industries
Cullen/Frost Bankers
Dai-Ichi Kangyo Bank of California
Danforth Foundation
Dean Witter Discover
Delaware North Cos.
Detroit Edison Co.
Dodge Foundation, Geraldine R.
Donnelley Foundation, Gaylord and Dorothy
Doty Family Foundation
Douglas Charitable Foundation
Douglas & Lomason Company
Dresser Industries
du Pont de Nemours & Co., E. I.
Duke Power Co.
Eaton Corp.
Eckerd Corp., Jack
Edwards Industries
Electric Power Equipment Co.
Ellison Foundation
Emerson Electric Co.
Encyclopaedia Britannica, Inc.
Equitable Life Assurance Society of the U.S.
Exxon Corp.
Farwell Foundation, Drusilla
Fein Foundation
Fieldcrest Cannon
FINA, Inc.
Finley Charitable Trust, J. B.
First Brands Corp.
First Fidelity Bancorporation
First Tennessee Bank
Fitz-Gibbon Charitable Trust
Florida Power & Light Co.
Forbes
Ford Meter Box Co.
Forest Lawn Foundation
Fox Inc.
Franklin Mint Corp.
Friedman Family Foundation
Frisch's Restaurants Inc.
Frohlich Charitable Trust, Ludwig W.
Fuller Foundation, George F. and Sybil H.
Funderburke & Associates
Funderburke & Associates
Furth Foundation
GEICO Corp.
General American Life Insurance Co.
General Mills
General Motors Corp.
General Tire Inc.
Georgia Power Co.
Gerber Products Co.
Gheens Foundation
Gilman Foundation, Howard
Gleason Foundation, James
Glenmore Distilleries Co.
Goldman Foundation, Herman
Goldseker Foundation of Maryland, Morris
Goldwyn Foundation, Samuel
Golub Corp.
Goodstein Family Foundation, David
Graphic Arts Show Co. Inc.
Grass Foundation
Graybar Electric Co.
Grede Foundries
Gulf Power Co.
Guth Lighting Co.
Haffner Foundation
Haggar Foundation

Hansen Memorial Foundation, Irving
Harmon Foundation, Pearl M. and Julia J.
Harris Corp.
Harris Family Foundation, Hunt and Diane
Harsco Corp.
Hartmarx Corp.
Hastings Trust
Hazen Foundation, Edward W.
Healy Family Foundation, M. A.
Hechinger Co.
Heinz Co., H.J.
Heller Financial
Herbst Foundation
Hess Charitable Foundation, Ronne and Donald
Higginson Trust, Corina
High Foundation
HKH Foundation
Hofheinz Foundation, Irene Cafcalas
Hopkins Foundation, Josephine Lawrence
Houston Endowment
Houston Industries
Hulings Foundation, Mary Andersen
Humana
Huntsman Foundation, Jon and Karen
Huthsteiner Fine Arts Trust
I. and L. Association
Ideal Industries
Illinois Power Co.
Illinois Tool Works
Indiana Desk Co.
Indiana Insurance Cos.
Inland Steel Industries
Inman Mills
Interco
Island Foundation
ITT Hartford Insurance Group
Jackson Hole Preserve
James River Corp. of Virginia
JMK-A M Micallef Charitable Foundation
John Hancock Mutual Life Insurance Co.
Johnson Controls
Johnson & Higgins
Johnson & Son, S.C.
Kapoor Charitable Foundation
Kaufman Memorial Trust, Chaim, Fanny, Louis, Benjamin, and Anne Florence
Kaye, Scholer, Fierman, Hays & Handler
Keebler Co.
Keller-Crescent Co.
Kellmer Co., Jack
Kennecott Corp.
Kerr-McGee Corp.
Kiplinger Foundation
Knight-Ridder, Inc.
Koh-I-Noor Rapidograph Inc.
Kyocera International Inc.
Ladish Co.
Lancaster Colony
Landmark Communications
Lane Foundation, Winthrop and Frances
Leavey Foundation, Thomas and Dorothy
Lee Enterprises
Lehman Foundation, Edith and Herbert
Leo Burnett Co.
Levy Foundation, Betty and Norman F.
Liberty Corp.
Life Insurance Co. of Georgia
Lincoln Electric Co.
Lincy Foundation
Little, Arthur D.
Litton Industries
Loews Corp.

Long Island Lighting Co.
Louisiana Land & Exploration Co.
Lounsbery Foundation, Richard
Lubo Fund
Maclellan Foundation
Macy & Co., R.H.
Magma Copper Co.
Mailman Family Foundation, A. L.
Mailman Foundation
Manoogian Foundation, Alex and Marie
Marpat Foundation
Marriott Foundation, J. Willard
Marshall & Ilsley Bank
Martin Marietta Corp.
Marubeni America Corp.
Material Service Corp.
MCA
McCarthy Foundation, Michael W.
McCormick & Co.
McCormick Tribune Foundation, Robert R.
McDermott
McDonald & Co. Securities
McGraw Foundation, Donald C.
MCI Communications Corp.
Mead Corp.
Mebane Packaging Corp.
Media General, Inc.
Medina Foundation
Mellen Foundation
Mellon Bank Corp.
Memton Fund
Meredith Corp.
Meyer Foundation, Bert and Mary
Middendorf Foundation
Milliken & Co.
Mine Safety Appliances Co.
Mitchell Energy & Development Corp.
Mobil Oil Corp.
Monsanto Co.
Moog Automotive, Inc.
Moorman Manufacturing Co.
Morrison-Knudsen Corp.
National Computer Systems
National Westminster Bank New Jersey
Nationale-Nederlanden North America Corp.
NBD Bank
Needmor Fund
New England Mutual Life Insurance Co.
New York Life Insurance Co.
Newhouse Foundation, Samuel I.
News & Observer Publishing Co.
Nordson Corp.
Norfolk Southern Corp.
Northwest Natural Gas Co.
Norton Co.
O'Connor Foundation, A. Lindsay and Olive B.
Ogilvy & Mather Worldwide
Oglebay Norton Co.
O'Neill Charitable Corporation, F. J.
Ontario Corp.
Ore-Ida Foods, Inc.
Ormet Corp.
Overbrook Foundation
Oxford Industries, Inc.
PacifiCorp
Paley Foundation, William S.
Palmer Fund, Frank Loomis
Pappas Charitable Foundation, Thomas Anthony
Paramount Communications Inc.
Parsons Foundation, Ralph M.
Peoples Energy Corp.
Peterson Foundation, Fred J.
Pfizer

Pforzheimer Foundation, Carl and Lily
PHH Corp.
Phillips Petroleum Co.
Pinkerton Foundation
Pittsburgh National Bank
Pittway Corp.
Playboy Enterprises, Inc.
Pope Foundation, Lois B.
Portland General Electric Co.
Premier Industrial Corp.
Procter & Gamble Cosmetic & Fragrance Products
Providence Journal Company
Public Service Electric & Gas Co.
Pulitzer Publishing Co.
Quaker Oats Co.
Questar Corp.
Ralston Purina Co.
Retirement Research Foundation
Reynolds Foundation, Donald W.
Reynolds Foundation, Richard S.
Reynolds Metals Co.
Robinson Fund, Maurice R.
Rockwell International Corp.
Rosenwald Family Fund, William
San Diego Gas & Electric
Sandoz Corp.
Schieffelin & Somerset Co.
Schlumberger Ltd.
Schmitt Foundation, Arthur J.
Scholl Foundation, Dr.
Schust Foundation, Clarence L. and Edith B.
Science Applications International Corp.
Scripps Co., E.W.
Scrivner, Inc.
Scrivner of North Carolina Inc.
Shenandoah Life Insurance Co.
Signet Bank/Maryland
Simon Foundation, William E. and Carol G.
Skillman Foundation
Slant/Fin Corp.
Sloan Foundation, Alfred P.
Smith Foundation, Kelvin and Eleanor
SNET
Snow Memorial Trust, John Ben
Sonat
Sooner Pipe & Supply Corp.
Southern California Edison Co.
Spectra-Physics Analytical
Sprague Educational and Charitable Foundation, Seth
Sprague Memorial Institute, Otho S. A.
Springs Industries
Square D Co.
Standard Chartered Bank New York
Star Bank, N.A.
State Farm Mutual Automobile Insurance Co.
Statler Foundation
Sterling Winthrop
Stockham Valves & Fittings
Stoddard Charitable Trust
Sulzberger Foundation
Summerfield Foundation, Solon E.
Tanner Cos.
Taub Foundation, Henry and Marilyn
Teledyne
Tenneco
Textron
Thermo Electron Corp.
Thomas & Betts Corp.
Times Mirror Co.
Tosco Corp. Refining Division
Tracor, Inc.
Tropicana Products, Inc.
TU Electric Co.

Twentieth Century-Fox Film Corp.
Tyson Foods, Inc.
Unilever United States
Union Camp Corp.
United States Sugar Corp.
Universal Leaf Tobacco Co.
Unocal Corp.
Uris Brothers Foundation
US WEST
Valley Foundation, Wayne and Gladys
Valmont Industries
Wachovia Bank & Trust Co., N.A.
Wagner Foundation, Ltd., R. H.
Wal-Mart Stores
Warner-Lambert Co.
Warren Foundation, William K.
Waste Management
Wean Foundation, Raymond John
Weeden Foundation, Frank
West Co.
WestLB New York Branch
Westvaco Corp.
Whirlpool Corp.
Whitaker Charitable Foundation, Lyndon C.
Williams Charitable Trust, Mary Jo
Williams Cos.
Wisconsin Centrifugal
Wollenberg Foundation
Woodward Fund-Atlanta, David, Helen, Marian
Xerox Corp.
Young & Rubicam

Public Policy

Abell-Hanger Foundation
Aequus Institute
AFLAC
Ahmanson Foundation
Air Products & Chemicals
Allegheny Foundation
Allendale Mutual Insurance Co.
Alliant Techsystems
AlliedSignal
Allstate Insurance Co.
Alma Piston Co.
ALPAC Corp.
Altschul Foundation
Alumax
Aluminum Co. of America
AMAX
American Cyanamid Co.
American Express Co.
American Natural Resources Co.
American Saw & Manufacturing Co.
American Stock Exchange
American Telephone & Telegraph Co.
Ameritech Corp.
Ames Charitable Trust, Harriett
Amoco Corp.
Andersen Corp.
Andersons Management Corp.
Anheuser-Busch Cos.
Anschutz Family Foundation
Ansin Private Foundation, Ronald M.
AON Corp.
Apple Computer, Inc.
Arca Foundation
Archer-Daniels-Midland Co.
Armco Inc.
Armington Fund, Evenor
Armstrong Foundation
ASARCO
Ashland Oil
Atherton Family Foundation
Auerbach Foundation, Beatrice Fox
Avon Products
Babcock Foundation, Mary Reynolds

Baker Foundation, Clark and
Ruby
Ball Corp.
Banbury Fund
Bancorp Hawaii
Bank of Boston Corp.
Bank South Corp.
BankAmerica Corp.
Bankers Trust Co.
Banyan Tree Foundation
Barker Foundation, J. M. R.
Batten Foundation
Bauer Foundation, M. R.
Bausch & Lomb
Beal Foundation
Bechtel Group
Becton Dickinson & Co.
Beech Aircraft Corp.
Beldon II Fund
Bemis Company
Benbough Foundation, Legler
Benedum Foundation, Claude
Worthington
Benton Foundation
Beretta U.S.A. Corp.
Bethlehem Steel Corp.
Bettingen Corporation, Burton G.
BFGoodrich
Birnschein Foundation, Alvin
and Marion
Blair Foundation, John
Blaustein Foundation, Jacob and
Hilda
Blinken Foundation
Block, H&R
Blue Bell, Inc.
Blue Cross and Blue Shield of
Minnesota Foundation Inc.
Blum-Kovler Foundation
Boeckmann Charitable
Foundation
Boehm Foundation
Boise Cascade Corp.
Booz Allen & Hamilton
Borden
Borman's
BP America
Bradley Foundation, Lynde and
Harry
Brady Foundation, W. H.
Branta Foundation
Bridgestone/Firestone
Bristol-Myers Squibb Co.
Brody Foundation, Carolyn and
Kenneth D.
Brown Charitable Trust, Dora
Maclellan
Brown & Williamson Tobacco
Corp.
Browning-Ferris Industries
Broyhill Family Foundation
Bryan Family Foundation,
Kathleen Price and Joseph M.
Buffett Foundation
Buhl Foundation
Burden Foundation, Florence V.
Burroughs Wellcome Co.
Bydale Foundation
C.P. Rail Systems
Cain Foundation, Gordon and
Mary
Capital Cities/ABC
Capital Fund Foundation
Carnegie Corporation of New
York
Carnival Cruise Lines
Carolina Power & Light Co.
Carolyn Foundation
Carpenter Technology Corp.
Carteh Foundation
Carthage Foundation
Cartier, Inc.
Casey Foundation, Annie E.
Castle Foundation, Harold K. L.
Caterpillar
Centerior Energy Corp.
Central Bank of the South

Central Life Assurance Co.
Central Maine Power Co.
CertainTeed Corp.
Chase Manhattan Bank, N.A.
Chevron Corp.
Chicago Resource Center
Chicago Tribune Co.
Chrysler Corp.
CIGNA Corp.
Cincinnati Bell
Citicorp
Clark Foundation, Edna
McConnell
Clark Foundation, Robert
Sterling
Clay Foundation
Clayton Fund
Clowes Fund
CM Alliance Cos.
CNA Insurance Cos.
Coast Federal Bank
Coleman, Jr. Foundation, George
E.
Colorado Trust
Columbia Foundation
Columbia Savings Charitable
Foundation
Common Giving Fund
Commonwealth Fund
Compton Foundation
Consolidated Natural Gas Co.
Continental Corp.
Cooper Industries
Coors Foundation, Adolph
Corning Incorporated
Country Curtains, Inc.
Covington and Burling
Cow Hollow Foundation
Cowell Foundation, S. H.
Cox, Jr. Foundation, James M.
CPC International
CR Industries
Crown Memorial, Arie and Ida
Cummins Engine Co.
Curran Foundation
Danforth Foundation
Davis Foundation, Edwin W. and
Catherine M.
Davis Foundation, Ken W.
Davis Foundation, Shelby
Cullom
Dayton Hudson Corp.
Deer Creek Foundation
Delavan Foundation, Nelson B.
DelMar Foundation, Charles
DeMoss Foundation, Arthur S.
Deposit Guaranty National Bank
Dettman Foundation, Leroy E.
Deutsch Co.
DeVos Foundation, Richard and
Helen
Diamond Foundation, Aaron
Dick Family Foundation
Dodge Foundation, Cleveland H.
Dodge Foundation, Geraldine R.
Dodge Jones Foundation
Donnelley & Sons Co., R.R.
Donner Foundation, William H.
Donovan, Leisure, Newton &
Irvine
Dorot Foundation
Dorr Foundation
Dow Foundation, Herbert H. and
Barbara C.
du Pont de Nemours & Co., E. I.
Duke Power Co.
Dun & Bradstreet Corp.
Durell Foundation, George
Edward
Durst Foundation
Dyson Foundation
Earhart Foundation
Eaton Corp.
Eaton Foundation, Cyrus
Eberly Foundation
Edouard Foundation

Educational Foundation of
America
Einstein Fund, Albert E. and
Birdie W.
Elf Atochem North America
Emerson Electric Co.
EMI Records Group
Engelhard Foundation, Charles
English Memorial Fund,
Florence C. and H. L.
Enron Corp.
Ensign-Bickford Industries
Ensworth Charitable Foundation
Equitable Life Assurance Society
of the U.S.
Erteszek Foundation
European American Bank
Exxon Corp.
Factor Family Foundation, Max
Fales Foundation Trust
Federal-Mogul Corp.
Federal National Mortgage
Assn., Fannie Mae
Fel-Pro Incorporated
Feldberg Family Foundation
Fels Fund, Samuel S.
Field Foundation, Jamee and
Marshall
Fife Foundation, Elias and Bertha
Fikes Foundation, Leland
FINA, Inc.
Finley Foundation, A. E.
First Boston
First Interstate Bank of California
First Interstate Bank of Denver
First Interstate Bank of Denver
First Interstate Bank of Texas,
N.A.
First Maryland Bancorp
First Tennessee Bank
Firstar Bank Milwaukee NA
Fish Foundation, Ray C.
Fisher Foundation, Max M. and
Marjorie S.
Fluor Corp.
FMC Corp.
Fondren Foundation
Forbes
Ford Foundation
Ford Motor Co.
Foster Foundation
Foundation for Child
Development
Foundation for Middle East
Peace
Fox Foundation, Richard J.
Freeman Charitable Trust,
Samuel
Freeport-McMoRan
Friedman Family Foundation
Friedman Foundation, Stephen
and Barbara
Friendship Fund
Fruehauf Foundation
Fruehauf Foundation
Fry Foundation, Lloyd A.
Fuchsberg Family Foundation
Fund for New Jersey
Funderburke & Associates
Funderburke & Associates
Furth Foundation
Gates Foundation
Gelb Foundation, Lawrence M.
GenCorp
General American Life Insurance
Co.
General Electric Co.
General Mills
General Motors Corp.
General Reinsurance Corp.
General Service Foundation
Gerbode Foundation, Wallace
Alexander
German Marshall Fund of the
United States
Gleason Memorial Fund
Globe Corp.

Gordon/Rousmaniere/Roberts
Fund
Gottesman Fund
Grace & Co., W.R.
Grant Foundation, William T.
Green Fund
Greve Foundation, William and
Mary
Griswold Foundation, John C.
Gross Charitable Trust, Walter L.
and Nell R.
Gruss Petroleum Corp.
GTE Corp.
Gulf Power Co.
Gund Foundation, George
Guttman Foundation, Stella and
Charles
Haas Foundation, Paul and Mary
Haas, Jr. Fund, Evelyn and
Walter
Haffner Foundation
Halliburton Co.
Harriman Foundation, Gladys
and Roland
Harriman Foundation, Mary W.
Harsco Corp.
Hartmarx Corp.
Hartzell Industries, Inc.
Hastings Trust
Haynes Foundation, John
Randolph and Dora
Hechinger Co.
Heinz Co., H.J.
Heller Financial
Henry Foundation, Patrick
Hermann Foundation, Grover
Hershey Foods Corp.
Hess Foundation
Hewlett Foundation, William and
Flora
Higginson Trust, Corina
Hill-Snowdon Foundation
Hillman Foundation, Henry L.
Hillsdale Fund
HKH Foundation
Hoechst Celanese Corp.
Hoffman Foundation,
Maximillian E. and Marion O.
Homeland Foundation
Homeland Foundation
HON Industries
Hooper Foundation, Elizabeth S.
Hopeman Brothers
Horncrest Foundation
Hospital Corp. of America
Household International
Houston Endowment
Houston Industries
Hubbell Inc.
Huber Foundation
Hughes Memorial Foundation,
Charles Evans
Hume Foundation, Jaquelin
Hunt Alternatives Fund
Hurford Foundation
Huston Foundation
Hyams Foundation
IBM Corp.
ICI Americas
Iddings Benevolent Trust
IES Industries
Illinois Bell
Illinois Power Co.
Illinois Tool Works
Independence Foundation
Ingersoll Milling Machine Co.
Inland Container Corp.
Inland Steel Industries
Intercontinental Hotels Corp.
Ira-Hiti Foundation for Deep
Ecology
Irvine Foundation, James
Island Foundation
ITT Hartford Insurance Group
Ittleson Foundation
J.P. Morgan & Co.
Jasper Wood Products Co.

JCPenney Co.
Jewett Foundation, George
Frederick
JM Foundation
John Hancock Mutual Life
Insurance Co.
Johnson & Higgins
Johnson & Son, S.C.
Jones Foundation, Daisy Marquis
Jones Foundation, W. Alton
Jordan Foundation, Arthur
Joukowsky Family Foundation
Joyce Foundation
Kaiser Family Foundation,
Henry J.
Kaplan Foundation, Rita J. and
Stanley H.
Kaye, Scholer, Fierman, Hays &
Handler
Keller Family Foundation
Kellogg Foundation, J. C.
Kellogg Foundation, W. K.
Kellogg's
Kendall Foundation, Henry P.
Kennametal
Kennedy, Jr. Foundation, Joseph
P.
Kerr Fund, Grayce B.
Kerr-McGee Corp.
Kieckhefer Foundation, J. W.
Kimball International
Kiplinger Foundation
Kirby Foundation, F. M.
Klingenstein Fund, Esther A. and
Joseph
Kmart Corp.
Koch Charitable Trust, David H.
Koch Charitable Trust, David H.
Kresge Foundation
Krieble Foundation, Vernon K.
Kunstadter Family Foundation,
Albert
Laclede Gas Co.
Ladd Charitable Corporation,
Helen and George
Ladish Co.
Laerdal Foundation, Asmund S.
Lambe Charitable Foundation,
Claude R.
Lauder Foundation
Laurel Foundation
Lautenberg Foundation
Lazar Foundation
LBJ Family Foundation
Lea Foundation, Helen Sperry
Lennon Foundation, Fred A.
Levinson Foundation, Max and
Anna
Levy Foundation, Edward C.
Lightner Sams Foundation
Lilly & Co., Eli
Lilly Endowment
Lincoln National Corp.
Lincy Foundation
Lipton, Thomas J.
Lipton, Thomas J.
Liquid Air Corp.
Llagas Foundation
Long Foundation, George A. and
Grace
Louisiana Land & Exploration
Co.
Lowe Foundation, Joe and Emily
Luce Foundation, Henry
MacArthur Foundation, John D.
and Catherine T.
Maclellan Charitable Trust, R. J.
Maclellan Foundation
Macmillan, Inc.
Macy & Co., R.H.
Mailman Family Foundation, A.
L.
MalCo Products Inc.
Manilow Foundation, Nathan
Manville Corp.
Mapco Inc.
Marine Midland Banks

Public Policy (cont.)

Maritz Inc.
Markle Foundation, John and Mary R.
Marriott Foundation, J. Willard
Marsh & McLennan Cos.
Martin Marietta Corp.
Mary Kay Foundation
Masserini Charitable Trust, Maurice J.
Material Service Corp.
May Department Stores Co.
May Foundation, Wilbur
Mayborn Foundation, Frank W.
Mayer Foods Corp., Oscar
MCA
McConnell Foundation, Neil A.
McCormick Tribune Foundation, Robert R.
McCune Charitable Trust, John R.
McDonnell Douglas Corp.
McGonagle Foundation, Dextra Baldwin
McIntyre Foundation, C. S. and Marion F.
McKenna Foundation, Philip M.
McKesson Corp.
Mead Foundation, Giles W. and Elise G.
Medina Foundation
Meek Foundation
Mellon Bank Corp.
Mellon Foundation, Andrew W.
Merck & Co.
Merrill Lynch & Co.
Mertz-Gilmore Foundation, Joyce
Metropolitan Life Insurance Co.
Meyer Family Foundation, Paul J.
Meyer Memorial Trust
Meyerhoff Fund, Joseph
Milbank Foundation, Dunlevy
Miles Inc.
Milliken & Co.
Millipore Corp.
Mine Safety Appliances Co.
Mitsubishi Heavy Industries America
Mitsubishi International Corp.
Mobil Oil Corp.
Monell Foundation, Ambrose
Monsanto Co.
Montgomery Street Foundation
Moore Foundation, O. L.
Moriah Fund
Morrison-Knudsen Corp.
Moskowitz Foundation, Irving I.
Motorola
Mott Foundation, Charles Stewart
Mott Fund, Ruth
Murdock Charitable Trust, M. J.
Murphy Foundation
National Computer Systems
National Steel
National Westminster Bank New Jersey
Natural Heritage Foundation
NBD Bank
Needmor Fund
New England Biolabs Foundation
New England Foundation
New-Land Foundation
New Prospect Foundation
New World Foundation
New York Foundation
New York Stock Exchange
New York Telephone Co.
Newhouse Foundation, Samuel I.
Newman's Own
News & Observer Publishing Co.
Noble Foundation, Samuel Roberts
Noble Foundation, Vivian Bilby
Norfolk Southern Corp.
Norman Foundation

Northwest Area Foundation
Norton Co.
Noyes Foundation, Jessie Smith
Oakleaf Foundation
Odell and Helen Pfeiffer Odell Fund, Robert Stewart
O'Donnell Foundation
Odyssey Partners
Ogilvy & Mather Worldwide
Oglebay Norton Co.
Olin Corp.
Olin Foundation, John M.
O'Neil Foundation, W.
Open Society Fund
Oppenheimer Family Foundation
Outboard Marine Corp.
Overbrook Foundation
PACCAR
Pacific Enterprises
Pacific Mutual Life Insurance Co.
Packard Foundation, David and Lucile
Paley Foundation, William S.
Paramount Communications Inc.
Parsons Foundation, Ralph M.
Parvin Foundation, Albert
PayLess Drug Stores
Peabody Foundation, Amelia
Penney Foundation, James C.
Pennzoil Co.
Petersen Foundation, Esper A.
Pew Charitable Trusts
Pfizer
Pforzheimer Foundation, Carl and Lily
Phelps Dodge Corp.
Philip Morris Cos.
Phillipps Foundation
Phillips Family Foundation, Jay and Rose
Phillips Family Foundation, L. E.
Phillips Foundation, Ellis L.
Phillips Petroleum Co.
Picker International
Pincus Family Fund
Pines Bridge Foundation
Pioneer Fund
Piton Foundation
Pitt-Des Moines Inc.
Pittway Corp.
Playboy Enterprises, Inc.
Post Foundation of D.C., Marjorie Merriweather
PPG Industries
Price Associates, T. Rowe
Procter & Gamble Co.
Prospect Hill Foundation
Prudential Insurance Co. of America
Public Service Electric & Gas Co.
Puett Foundation, Nelson
Quaker Oats Co.
Ralston Purina Co.
Ramapo Trust
Randolph Foundation
Ratshesky Foundation, A. C.
Raymond Corp.
Regenstein Foundation
Reliance Electric Co.
Rennebohm Foundation, Oscar
Republic New York Corp.
Retirement Research Foundation
Revson Foundation, Charles H.
Reynolds Foundation, Christopher
Reynolds Metals Co.
Richardson Foundation, Smith
RJR Nabisco Inc.
Robinson Fund, Maurice R.
Rockefeller Family Fund
Rockefeller Foundation
Rockefeller Foundation, Winthrop
Rockwell International Corp.
Roe Foundation
RosaMary Foundation

Rose Foundation, Billy
Rosenbloom Foundation, Ben and Esther
Rosenthal Foundation, Benjamin J.
Roth Family Foundation
Rubin Foundation, Rob E. & Judith O.
Rubin Foundation, Samuel
Sacharuna Foundation
SAFECO Corp.
Sage Foundation, Russell
Santa Fe Pacific Corp.
Scaife Family Foundation
Scaife Foundation, Sarah
Schecter Private Foundation, Aaron and Martha
Schering-Plough Corp.
Scherman Foundation
Scheuer Family Foundation, S. H. and Helen R.
Schultz Foundation
Schumann Foundation, Florence and John
Schumann Fund for New Jersey
Schwartz Foundation, David
Scrivner, Inc.
Seagram & Sons, Joseph E.
Searle & Co., G.D.
Seasongood Good Government Foundation, Murray and Agnes
Security Life of Denver
Sequoia Foundation
Seven Springs Foundation
Shell Oil Co.
Shiffman Foundation
Shoemaker Fund, Thomas H. and Mary Williams
Shorenstein Foundation, Walter H. and Phyllis J.
Simon Foundation, William E. and Carol G.
Simpson Investment Co.
Skillman Foundation
Skirball Foundation
Slant/Fin Corp.
Sloan Foundation, Alfred P.
Smith Foundation, Kelvin and Eleanor
SmithKline Beecham
SNET
Sordoni Foundation
Southern California Edison Co.
Southern Furniture Co.
Southwestern Bell Corp.
Sprague Educational and Charitable Foundation, Seth
Springs Industries
Stamps Foundation, James L.
Starr Foundation
Steele Foundation, Harry and Grace
Steinhardt Foundation, Judy and Michael
Sterling Winthrop
Stern Family Fund
Stern Memorial Trust, Sidney
Strake Foundation
Stranahan Foundation
Straus Foundation, Aaron and Lillie
Stuart Foundations
Summerfield Foundation, Solon E.
Sun Co.
Sunmark Capital Corp.
Sunmark Capital Corp.
Sunnen Foundation
Swensrud Charitable Trust, Sidney A.
Swig Foundation
Syntex Corp.
Tamko Asphalt Products
Taubman Foundation, A. Alfred
Taylor Foundation, Ruth and Vernon
Teledyne
Templeton Foundation, John

Tenneco
Texaco
Textron
Thermo Electron Corp.
Thirty-Five Twenty, Inc.
Time Insurance Co.
Times Mirror Co.
Tinker Foundation
Tisch Foundation
Tortuga Foundation
Town Creek Foundation
Transco Energy Company
Triford Foundation
Tropicana Products, Inc.
Trust Co. Bank
TRW Corp.
Unilever United States
Union Camp Corp.
Unisys Corp.
United Parcel Service of America
United States-Japan Foundation
U.S. Leasing International
United States Sugar Corp.
United States Trust Co. of New York
United Technologies Corp.
Unocal Corp.
US WEST
USG Corp.
USX Corp.
Van Andel Foundation, Jay and Betty
Varian Associates
Vaughan Foundation, Rachael and Ben
Vollrath Co.
Von der Ahe, Jr. Trust, Theodore Albert
Wal-Mart Stores
Walgreen Co.
Walker Educational and Charitable Foundation, Alex C.
Wallace Genetic Foundation
Wallach Foundation, Miriam G. and Ira D.
Disney Co., Walt
Walton Family Foundation
Ware Foundation
Warner Fund, Albert and Bessie
Washington Forrest Foundation
Washington Post Co.
Wean Foundation, Raymond John
Weeden Foundation, Frank
Weil, Gotshal & Manges Foundation
Weinberg, Jr. Foundation, Sidney J.
Weingart Foundation
Wellons Foundation
Westinghouse Electric Corp.
Westport Fund
Westvaco Corp.
Westwood Endowment
Weyerhaeuser Co.
Whirlpool Corp.
Wieboldt Foundation
Wiegand Foundation, E. L.
Wiener Foundation, Malcolm Hewitt
Williams Cos.
Wilson Foundation, H. W.
Wilson Public Trust, Ralph
Witter Foundation, Dean
Wollenberg Foundation
Woods Charitable Fund
Xerox Corp.
Zellerbach Family Fund
Zilkha & Sons

Rural Affairs

Agway
ALPAC Corp.
Alyeska Pipeline Service Co.
Anheuser-Busch Cos.
Apple Computer, Inc.
Arkla

Atlanta Gas Light Co.
Babcock Foundation, Mary Reynolds
Ben & Jerry's Homemade
Bicknell Fund
Blandin Foundation
Blank Family Foundation
Boettcher Foundation
Bremer Foundation, Otto
Brunswick Corp.
Bush Foundation
Carolyn Foundation
Cascade Natural Gas Corp.
CENEX
Central Bank of the South
Central Maine Power Co.
Central Soya Co.
Challenge Foundation
Chase Manhattan Bank, N.A.
Chevron Corp.
Clayton Fund
Corbin Foundation, Mary S. and David C.
Crels Foundation
Cudahy Fund, Patrick and Anna M.
Cummins Engine Co.
Curtice-Burns Foods
Dick Family Foundation
Duke Power Co.
Eaton Corp.
Farr Trust, Frank M. and Alice M.
Federal-Mogul Corp.
First Interstate Bank of Oregon
Ford Foundation
Foxmeyer Corp.
Fund for New Jersey
Funderburke & Associates
Funderburke & Associates
General Motors Corp.
Georgia Power Co.
Gulf Power Co.
Haas Foundation, Paul and Mary
Haffner Foundation
Haffner Foundation
Hansen Foundation, Dane G.
Heinz Co., H.J.
Hospital Corp. of America
Journal Gazette Co.
Kaplan Fund, J. M.
Kellogg Foundation, W. K.
Kettering Fund
Land O'Lakes
Laurel Foundation
Levinson Foundation, Max and Anna
MacArthur Foundation, J. Roderick
Mardag Foundation
Marion Merrell Dow
McCormick Foundation, Chauncey and Marion Deering
McElroy Trust, R. J.
McKnight Foundation
Meadows Foundation
Meyer Foundation, Bert and Mary
Moorman Manufacturing Co.
Mott Foundation, Charles Stewart
NBD Bank
Needmor Fund
New World Foundation
Newhouse Foundation, Samuel I.
News & Observer Publishing Co.
Noble Foundation, Samuel Roberts
Norman Foundation
Northwest Area Foundation
Norton Co.
Noyes Foundation, Jessie Smith
Parker Foundation, Theodore Edson
Penn Savings Bank, a division of Sovereign Bank Bank of Princeton, a division of Sovereign Bank

Pioneer Hi-Bred International
Public Welfare Foundation
Quanex Corp.
Raymond Corp.
Reynolds Foundation, Z. Smith
Rice Charitable Foundation,
Albert W.
RJR Nabisco Inc.
Rockefeller Foundation,
Winthrop
Rosenberg Foundation
Sacharuna Foundation
Saltonstall Charitable
Foundation, Richard
Schneider Foundation Corp., Al
J.
Scott Foundation, William R.,
John G., and Emma
Spahn & Rose Lumber Co.
Square D Co.
Starr Foundation
Sunmark Capital Corp.
Susquehanna Investment Group
Swim Foundation, Arthur L.
Tamko Asphalt Products
Trust Funds
US Bancorp
Van Schaick Scholarship Fund,
Nellie
Wallace Genetic Foundation
Wellman Foundation, S. K.
Westwood Endowment
Weyerhaeuser Co.
Wilbur Foundation, Marguerite
Eyer
Williams Cos.
Woods Charitable Fund
Young Foundation, Hugo H. and
Mabel B.

Safety

Abbott Laboratories
Abell-Hanger Foundation
Abitibi-Price
AGFA Division of Miles Inc.
Air Products & Chemicals
Akzo America
Akzo Chemicals Inc.
Ala Vi Foundation of New York
Alcon Laboratories, Inc.
Algonquin Energy, Inc.
AlliedSignal
Allstate Insurance Co.
ALPAC Corp.
Aluminum Co. of America
AMAX
American Saw & Manufacturing
Co.
Amfac/JMB Hawaii
Amoco Corp.
AMP
Amsted Industries
AON Corp.
Archer-Daniels-Midland Co.
Arkansas Power & Light Co.
Armco Inc.
Atlanta Gas Light Co.
Aurora Foundation
Babcock Foundation, Mary
Reynolds
Baldwin, Jr. Foundation,
Summerfield
Ball Corp.
Banbury Fund
Bank Hapoalim B.M.
Bankers Trust Co.
BASF Corp.
Batten Foundation
Beazley Foundation
Beech Aircraft Corp.
Bemis Company
Berwind Corp.
Bethlehem Steel Corp.
Blair and Co., William
Blount
Blue Cross & Blue Shield of
Alabama

Boehringer Mannheim Corp.
Bovaird Foundation, Mervin
Bridwell Foundation, J. S.
Briggs & Stratton Corp.
Bucyrus-Erie
Burlington Northern Inc.
Bustard Charitable Permanent
Trust Fund, Elizabeth and
James
Butler Manufacturing Co.
Cabot Corp.
Capital Cities/ABC
Capital Holding Corp.
Carey Industries
Carter Foundation, Amon G.
Central Maine Power Co.
Central Soya Co.
Century Companies of America
Chase Manhattan Bank, N.A.
Chevron Corp.
Chrysler Corp.
CIGNA Corp.
Clorox Co.
CNA Insurance Cos.
CNG Transmission Corp.
Cole Foundation, Olive B.
Colonial Life & Accident
Insurance Co.
Columbus Southern Power Co.
Commonwealth Fund
Conoco Inc.
Continental Corp.
Cooper Industries
CPC International
Craigmyle Foundation
Cranshaw Corporation
Crown Central Petroleum Corp.
Crum and Forster
Curtice-Burns Foods
Danner Foundation
Davis Foundation, Shelby
Cullom
Deere & Co.
Demoulas Supermarkets
Detroit Edison Co.
Dietrich Foundation, William B.
Dimeo Construction Co.
Dingman Foundation, Michael D.
Douglas & Lomason Company
Douty Foundation
Downs Perpetual Charitable
Trust, Ellason
Dresser Industries
Dreyfus Foundation, Max and
Victoria
du Pont de Nemours & Co., E. I.
Duchossois Industries
Duke Power Co.
Eccles Foundation, Ralph M. and
Ella M.
Eckman Charitable Foundation,
Samuel and Rae
Elizabethtown Gas Co.
Emerson Foundation, Fred L.
Ensign-Bickford Industries
Erving Paper Mills
Exxon Corp.
Federal-Mogul Corp.
Federated Life Insurance Co.
Felburn Foundation
Fieldcrest Cannon
First Fidelity Bancorporation
First Interstate Bank of Oregon
First Union Corp.
Fish Foundation, Ray C.
Fleet Financial Group
Florida Power & Light Co.
Forbes
Ford Motor Co.
Forster Charitable Trust, James
W. and Ella B.
Fort Worth Star Telegram
Fraser Paper Ltd.
Freeport Brick Co.
Freeport-McMoRan
Frohring Foundation, William O.
and Gertrude Lewis

Fujitsu Systems of America, Inc.
Funderburke & Associates
Funderburke & Associates
Fusenot Charity Foundation,
Georges and Germaine
Gaisman Foundation, Catherine
and Henry J.
Garfinkle Family Foundation
Gazette Co.
GEICO Corp.
General Motors Corp.
General Reinsurance Corp.
George Foundation
Gheens Foundation
Giant Food Stores
Givenchy, Inc.
Glaxo
Gleason Works
Grainger Foundation
Grassmann Trust, E. J.
Grinnell Mutual Reinsurance Co.
Guardian Life Insurance Co. of
America
Guggenheim Foundation, Daniel
and Florence
Gulf Power Co.
Halloran Foundation, Mary P.
Dolciani
Harsco Corp.
Hartmarx Corp.
Hechinger Co.
Hecla Mining Co.
Heileman Brewing Co., Inc., G.
Heinz Co., H.J.
Henkel Corp.
Herrick Foundation
Hershey Foods Corp.
Hess Charitable Foundation,
Ronne and Donald
Heymann-Wolf Foundation
Hillsdale Fund
Hospital Corp. of America
Houston Industries
Hubbard Milling Co.
Hubbell Inc.
Hyde Manufacturing Co.
IBP, Inc.
Index Technology Corp.
Indiana Gas and Chemical Corp.
Indiana Insurance Cos.
Inland Container Corp.
International Flavors &
Fragrances
ITT Hartford Insurance Group
James River Corp. of Virginia
Japanese American Agon
Friendship League
JELD-WEN, Inc.
Johnson & Higgins
Johnson & Johnson
Johnson & Son, S.C.
Jones Foundation, Daisy Marquis
Kennecott Corp.
Kerr-McGee Corp.
Kiewit Foundation, Peter
Kimball International
Kimberly-Clark Corp.
Kiplinger Foundation
Kmart Corp.
Lancaster Colony
Life Insurance Co. of Georgia
Lincoln Electric Co.
Lincy Foundation
Link, Jr. Foundation, George
Lipton Foundation
Lipton, Thomas J.
Liquid Air Corp.
Long Island Lighting Co.
Louisiana Land & Exploration
Co.
Lowe Foundation, Joe and Emily
Lowenstein Foundation, Leon
Lynn Foundation, E. M.
Macy & Co., R.H.
Makita U.S.A., Inc.
Mallinckrodt Specialty
Chemicals Co.

Maneely Fund
Manville Corp.
Martin Marietta Corp.
Material Service Corp.
May Department Stores Co.
Mazza Foundation
McCann Foundation
McConnell Foundation
McDermott
McIntosh Foundation
MDU Resources Group, Inc.
Mead Corp.
Meadows Foundation
Merck & Co.
Merck Human Health Division
Metropolitan Life Insurance Co.
Michigan Bell Telephone Co.
Michigan Gas Utilities
Midwest Resources
Milliken & Co.
Mine Safety Appliances Co.
Mobil Oil Corp.
Moog Automotive, Inc.
Moore & Sons, B.C.
Moosehead Manufacturing Co.
Morgan Charitable Residual
Trust, W. and E.
Morrison-Knudsen Corp.
Moskowitz Foundation, Irving I.
Motch Corp.
Motorola
National City Corp.
National Fuel Gas Co.
National Machinery Co.
National Steel
National Westminster Bank New
Jersey
Nationale-Nederlanden North
America Corp.
NBD Bank
New York Mercantile Exchange
New York Telephone Co.
Nissan Motor Corporation in
U.S.A.
Norfolk Southern Corp.
Northeast Utilities
Norton Co.
NuTone Inc.
O'Connor Foundation, A.
Lindsay and Olive B.
Oglebay Norton Co.
Oki America Inc.
Old Dominion Box Co.
Ormet Corp.
Overbrook Foundation
Overseas Shipholding Group
PACCAR
Pacific Mutual Life Insurance Co.
Pennzoil Co.
Pfizer
Phelps Dodge Corp.
PHH Corp.
Phillips Family Foundation, L. E.
Phillips Petroleum Co.
Pittsburgh National Bank
Pittway Corp.
Powell Family Foundation
PPG Industries
Premier Industrial Corp.
Procter & Gamble Co.
Provigo Corp. Inc.
Prudential Insurance Co. of
America
Public Service Electric & Gas
Co.
Pukall Lumber
Quaker Oats Co.
Quanex Corp.
Quantum Chemical Corp.
Recognition Equipment
Reily & Co., William B.
Reynolds Metals Co.
Ricoh Corp.
Robertshaw Controls Co.
Rochester Gas & Electric Corp.
Rockwell International Corp.
Rogers Charitable Trust, Florence

Rogers Foundation
Rollins Luetkemeyer Charitable
Foundation
Roseburg Forest Products Co.
Royal Group Inc.
Rubin Foundation, Samuel
SAFECO Corp.
San Diego Gas & Electric
Scaife Family Foundation
Scrivner, Inc.
Scrivner of North Carolina Inc.
Seaver Charitable Trust, Richard
C.
Security State Bank
Sedgwick James Inc.
Shell Oil Co.
Shenandoah Life Insurance Co.
Sierra Pacific Industries
Sierra Pacific Resources
Simon Foundation, William E.
and Carol G.
Simpson Investment Co.
Slant/Fin Corp.
Smith Corp., A.O.
SNET
Sonoco Products Co.
South Texas Charitable
Foundation
Southern California Edison Co.
SPS Technologies
Square D Co.
State Farm Mutual Automobile
Insurance Co.
State Street Bank & Trust Co.
Sterling Inc.
Stevens Foundation, Abbot and
Dorothy H.
Subaru of America Inc.
Taylor Foundation
Teichert
Teledyne
Temple Foundation, T. L. L.
Tenneco
Tetley, Inc.
Texaco
Textron
Thomas & Betts Corp.
3M Co.
Tomkins Industries, Inc.
Torchmark Corp.
Treakle Foundation, J. Edwin
Tropicana Products, Inc.
Trust Co. Bank
TU Electric Co.
Tyson Foods, Inc.
Tyson Fund
Unilever United States
Union Camp Corp.
Union Carbide Corp.
United Airlines
U.S. Silica Co.
Van Every Foundation, Philip L.
Vermeer Manufacturing Co.
Vevay-Switzerland County
Foundation
Virginia Power Co.
Wal-Mart Stores
Wallace Genetic Foundation
Washington Water Power Co.
Waste Management
Wean Foundation, Raymond John
Westvaco Corp.
Whirlpool Corp.
White Trust, G. R.
Wiggins Memorial Trust, J. J.
Williams Cos.
Winter Construction Co.
Wisconsin Centrifugal
Wisconsin Power & Light Co.
Woodward Governor Co.
Yost Trust, Elizabeth Burns
Young Foundation, Hugo H. and
Mabel B.

Urban & Community Affairs

Abbott Laboratories
Abrons Foundation, Louis and Anne
Acushnet Co.
Ahmanson Foundation
Air Products & Chemicals
Alabama Power Co.
Alco Standard Corp.
Alcon Laboratories, Inc.
Alexander Foundation, Judd S.
Algonquin Energy, Inc.
Alice Manufacturing Co.
Allegheny Foundation
Allegheny Ludlum Corp.
Allendale Mutual Insurance Co.
AlliedSignal
Allstate Insurance Co.
ALPAC Corp.
Aluminum Co. of America
Alyeska Pipeline Service Co.
AMAX
AMAX Coal Industries
AMCORE Bank, N.A. Rockford
America West Airlines
American Brands
American Cyanamid Co.
American Express Co.
American Financial Corp.
American National Bank & Trust Co. of Chicago
American Natural Resources Co.
American President Cos.
American Saw & Manufacturing Co.
American Stock Exchange
American Telephone & Telegraph Co.
American United Life Insurance Co.
American Welding & Manufacturing Co.
Ameritech Corp.
Ames Department Stores
AMETEK
Amfac/JMB Hawaii
Amoco Corp.
AMP
AMR Corp.
Amsted Industries
Andersen Corp.
Andersons Management Corp.
Andres Charitable Trust, Frank G.
Angelica Corp.
Anheuser-Busch Cos.
AON Corp.
Apple Computer, Inc.
Archer-Daniels-Midland Co.
ARCO
ARCO Chemical
Aristech Chemical Corp.
Arkansas Power & Light Co.
Arkla
Arkwright-Boston Manufacturers Mutual
Armco Inc.
Armco Steel Co.
Aron Charitable Foundation, J.
Arronson Foundation
Arvin Industries
Ashland Oil
Astor Foundation, Vincent
Atherton Family Foundation
Athwin Foundation
Atkinson Foundation
Atlantic Foundation of New York
Avon Products
Badger Meter, Inc.
Baehr Foundation, Louis W. and Dolpha
Bag Bazaar, Ltd.
Baird Foundation, Cameron
Baker, Jr. Memorial Fund, William G.

Bally Inc.
Baltimore Gas & Electric Co.
Banc One Illinois Corp.
Banc One Wisconsin Corp.
Bancorp Hawaii
Bancorp Hawaii
Bank of America Arizona
Bank of Boston Corp.
Bank One, Texas-Houston Office
Bank One, Youngstown, NA
BankAmerica Corp.
Bankers Trust Co.
Banyan Tree Foundation
BarclaysAmerican Corp.
Bard, C. R.
Barnes Group
Bass Foundation
Bausch & Lomb
Baxter International
BayBanks
Bechtel Group
Bedsole Foundation, J. L.
Beidler Charitable Trust, Francis
Beitzell & Co.
Belding Heminway Co.
Belk Stores
Bemis Company
Bend Millwork Systems
Benedum Foundation, Claude Worthington
Benefit Trust Life Insurance Co.
Best Products Co.
Bethlehem Steel Corp.
Betts Industries
Beveridge Foundation, Frank Stanley
BFGoodrich
Big V Supermarkets
Block, H&R
Blount
Blue Bell, Inc.
Blum-Kovler Foundation
Boatmen's Bancshares
Boatmen's First National Bank of Oklahoma
Boehm Foundation
Boehringer Mannheim Corp.
Booth-Bricker Fund
Boots Pharmaceuticals, Inc.
Booz Allen & Hamilton
Borden
Borman's
Boston Edison Co.
Boutell Memorial Fund, Arnold and Gertrude
Bovaird Foundation, Mervin
Bowater Inc.
BP America
Brach Foundation, Helen
Bradley-Turner Foundation
Brady Foundation, W. H.
Bridgestone/Firestone
Briggs & Stratton Corp.
Bristol-Myers Squibb Co.
Brookdale Foundation
Brown Group
Brown & Williamson Tobacco Corp.
Bucyrus-Erie
Budweiser of Columbia
Burlington Industries
Burlington Northern Inc.
Burndy Corp.
Bush Foundation
C.P. Rail Systems
Cable & Wireless Communications
Cain Foundation, Gordon and Mary
Campbell Foundation, Ruth and Henry
Candlesticks Inc.
Canon U.S.A., Inc.
Capital Cities/ABC
Capital Fund Foundation
Capital Holding Corp.

Carnegie Corporation of New York
Carnival Cruise Lines
Carolina Power & Light Co.
Carteh Foundation
Carter Foundation, Amon G.
Cartier, Inc.
Cary Charitable Trust, Mary Flagler
Cascade Natural Gas Corp.
Caterpillar
Cayuga Foundation
CBS Inc.
Ceco Corp.
Centerior Energy Corp.
Central Bank of the South
Central Fidelity Banks, Inc.
Central Maine Power Co.
Central & South West Services
Central Soya Co.
Century Companies of America
CertainTeed Corp.
Chadwick Foundation
Chambers Development Co.
Champion International Corp.
Chandler Foundation
Charina Foundation
Charitable Fund
Chase Manhattan Bank, N.A.
Chemical Bank
Chesebrough-Pond's
Chevron Corp.
Chicago Title and Trust Co.
Christensen Charitable and Religious Foundation, L. C.
Chrysler Corp.
Church & Dwight Co.
Churches Homes Foundation
CIGNA Corp.
Cincinnati Bell
Cincinnati Gas & Electric Co.
Cincinnati Milacron
Circuit City Stores
CIT Group Holdings
Citibank, F.S.B.
Citicorp
Citizens Bank
Clark Foundation
Clark Foundation, Edna McConnell
Cleveland-Cliffs
Clipper Ship Foundation
Clorox Co.
CM Alliance Cos.
CNA Insurance Cos.
Coast Federal Bank
Codrington Charitable Foundation, George W.
Coffey Foundation
Cole Foundation, Olive B.
Coleman Co.
Coles Family Foundation
Collins & Aikman Holdings Corp.
Collins Foundation
Columbia Foundation
Comerica
Commerce Clearing House
Commerzbank AG, New York
Common Wealth Trust
Commonwealth Edison Co.
Commonwealth Fund
Comstock Foundation
Connell Foundation, Michael J.
Connelly Foundation
Conoco Inc.
Consolidated Natural Gas Co.
Constantin Foundation
Consumers Power Co.
Continental Bank N.A.
Continental Corp.
Control Data Corp.
Coors Brewing Co.
Copley Press
Corbin Foundation, Mary S. and David C.
Cosmair, Inc.

Cowell Foundation, S. H.
Cowles Charitable Trust
Cowles Media Co.
Cox Enterprises
CPC International
CR Industries
CRL Inc.
Crocker Trust, Mary A.
Crum and Forster
Crystal Trust
CT Corp. System
Cudahy Fund, Patrick and Anna M.
CUNA Mutual Insurance Group
Curtice-Burns Foods
Dai-Ichi Kangyo Bank of California
Dain Bosworth/Inter-Regional Financial Group
Dana Corp.
Danforth Foundation
Daniel Foundation of Alabama
Dayton Hudson Corp.
Dayton Power and Light Co.
Dean Witter Discover
Deere & Co.
Delano Foundation, Mignon Sherwood
Delany Charitable Trust, Beatrice P.
Delaware North Cos.
Demoulas Supermarkets
Dennison Manufacturing Co.
Deposit Guaranty National Bank
Deuble Foundation, George H.
Dexter Corp.
Dickson Foundation
Digital Equipment Corp.
Dillon Foundation
Dodge Foundation, Cleveland H.
Dodge Foundation, Geraldine R.
Dodge Foundation, P. L.
Dodson Foundation, James Glenwell and Clara May
Donnelley & Sons Co., R.R.
Donovan, Leisure, Newton & Irvine
Doss Foundation, M. S.
Douglas & Lomason Company
Douty Foundation
Dover Corp.
Dow Corning Corp.
Downs Perpetual Charitable Trust, Ellason
Dresser Industries
Dreyfus Foundation, Jean and Louis
Dreyfus Foundation, Max and Victoria
du Pont de Nemours & Co., E. I.
Duke Power Co.
Dula Educational and Charitable Foundation, Caleb C. and Julia W.
Dun & Bradstreet Corp.
Durr-Fillauer Medical
Dweck Foundation, Samuel R.
Dynamet, Inc.
Eagle-Picher Industries
Eaton Corp.
Eccles Charitable Foundation, Willard L.
Eccles Foundation, Marriner S.
Eckerd Corp., Jack
Edgewater Steel Corp.
Edouard Foundation
Edwards & Sons, A.G.
Eisenberg Foundation, Ben B. and Joyce E.
Electronic Data Systems Corp.
Elf Atochem North America
Ellsworth Foundation, Ruth H. and Warren A.
Emergency Aid of Pennsylvania Foundation
Emerson Electric Co.
Endries Fastener & Supply Co.

English-Bonter-Mitchell Foundation
Enron Corp.
Equitable Life Assurance Society of the U.S.
Ernest & Julio Gallo Winery
Erteszek Foundation
Ethyl Corp.
European American Bank
Exxon Corp.
Fairchild Corp.
Fairfield Foundation, Freeman E.
Fairfield-Meeker Charitable Trust, Freeman E.
Falcon Foundation
Fales Foundation Trust
Falk Foundation, David
Falk Medical Fund, Maurice
Farnsworth Trust, Charles A.
Farr Trust, Frank M. and Alice M.
Federal Express Corp.
Federal-Mogul Corp.
Federal National Mortgage Assn., Fannie Mae
Federated Life Insurance Co.
Fels Fund, Samuel S.
Ferebee Endowment, Percy O.
Fiat U.S.A., Inc.
Fibre Converters
Fidelity Bank
Field Foundation of Illinois
First Boston
First Chicago
First Fidelity Bancorporation
First Hawaiian
First Interstate Bank of Arizona
First Interstate Bank of California
First Interstate Bank of Oregon
First Interstate Bank of Texas, N.A.
First Maryland Bancorp
First National Bank & Trust Co. of Rockford
First Tennessee Bank
First Union Corp.
Firstar Bank Milwaukee NA
Fisher Brothers
Fisher Foundation
Flarsheim Charitable Foundation, Louis and Elizabeth
Fleet Bank
Fleet Financial Group
Fleishhacker Foundation
Fletcher Foundation
Florida Power Corp.
Florida Power & Light Co.
Fluor Corp.
Forbes
Ford Foundation
Ford Fund, William and Martha
Ford II Fund, Henry
Ford Meter Box Co.
Ford Motor Co.
Forest City Enterprises
Formrite Tube Co.
Foster and Gallagher
Foundation for Child Development
Foundation for Middle East Peace
Fox Charitable Foundation, Harry K. & Emma R.
Fox Foundation, John H.
Frankel Foundation
Franklin Charitable Trust, Ershel
Franklin Foundation, John and Mary
Fraser Paper Ltd.
Freedom Forum
Freeman Foundation, Ella West
Freeport Brick Co.
Freightliner Corp.
Frick Educational Commission, Henry C.
Frisch's Restaurants Inc.

Recipient Type Index

Urban & Community Affairs (cont.)

Parker-Hannifin Corp.
Parsons Foundation, Ralph M.
Paulstan
Pax Christi Foundation
Peabody Charitable Fund, Amelia
Penn Foundation, William
Penn Savings Bank, a division of Sovereign Bank Bank of Princeton, a division of Sovereign Bank
Penney Foundation, James C.
Pennsylvania General Insurance Co.
Pennzoil Co.
Peoples Energy Corp.
PepsiCo
Perkin-Elmer Corp.
Perley Fund, Victor E.
Peterson Foundation, Fred J.
Pew Charitable Trusts
Pfizer
Pforzheimer Foundation, Carl and Lily
Phelps Dodge Corp.
PHH Corp.
Philadelphia Electric Co.
Phillipps Foundation
Phillips Charitable Trust, Dr. and Mrs. Arthur William
Phillips Family Foundation, Jay and Rose
Phillips Petroleum Co.
Pieper Electric
Pines Bridge Foundation
Pineywoods Foundation
Pinkerton Foundation
Pioneer Trust Bank, NA
Pitney Bowes
Piton Foundation
Pitt-Des Moines Inc.
Pittsburgh National Bank
Pittway Corp.
PNC Bank
Polaroid Corp.
Porsche Cars North America, Inc.
Porter Foundation, Mrs. Cheever
Portland General Electric Co.
Potomac Electric Power Co.
Pottstown Mercury
Powell Family Foundation
PPG Industries
Premier Industrial Corp.
Preston Trust, Evelyn W.
Price Associates, T. Rowe
Prickett Fund, Lynn R. and Karl E.
Priddy Foundation
Prince Manufacturing, Inc.
Prince Trust, Abbie Norman
Principal Financial Group
Pritzker Foundation
Procter & Gamble Co.
Procter & Gamble Cosmetic & Fragrance Products
Proctor Trust, Mortimer R.
Promus Cos.
Providence Energy Corp.
Provident Life & Accident Insurance Co.
Provigo Corp. Inc.
Prudential Insurance Co. of America
PSI Energy
Public Service Electric & Gas Co.
Public Welfare Foundation
Quaker Oats Co.
Quanex Corp.
Ralston Purina Co.
Randolph Foundation
Ratshesky Foundation, A. C.
Raytheon Co.
Reeves Foundation
Reily & Co., William B.

Relations Foundation
Reliable Life Insurance Co.
Reliance Electric Co.
Revlon
Revson Foundation, Charles H.
Reynolds Foundation, Z. Smith
Reynolds Metals Co.
Rhodebeck Charitable Trust
Rhone-Poulenc Rorer
Riggs Benevolent Fund
Riley Foundation, Mabel Louise
RJR Nabisco Inc.
Robbins & Myers, Inc.
Rochester Gas & Electric Corp.
Rochester Midland Corp.
Rockefeller Brothers Fund
Rockefeller Foundation
Rockwell International Corp.
Rogers Foundation
Rohatyn Foundation, Felix and Elizabeth
Rohm and Haas Company
Rollins Luetkemeyer Charitable Foundation
Rosenbaum Foundation, Paul and Gabriella
Rosenberg Foundation
Ruddick Corp.
Rudin Foundation
Russell Trust, Josephine G.
Sacharuna Foundation
SAFECO Corp.
St. Mary's Catholic Foundation
San Diego Trust & Savings Bank
Sandy Hill Foundation
Santa Fe Pacific Corp.
Sara Lee Corp.
Sara Lee Hosiery
Sargent Foundation, Newell B.
Saunders Foundation
Scaife Family Foundation
Scheirich Co., H.J.
Scherman Foundation
Scheuer Family Foundation, S. H. and Helen R.
Schmitt Foundation, Arthur J.
Schwab & Co., Charles
Scott and Fetzer Co.
Scrivner, Inc.
Seafirst Corp.
Security Life of Denver
Sentinel Communications Co.
Seven Springs Foundation
Shapiro, Inc.
Shawmut National Corp.
Shell Oil Co.
Shenandoah Life Insurance Co.
Sherwin-Williams Co.
Shott, Jr. Foundation, Hugh I.
Shughart, Thomson & Kilroy, P.C.
Sierra Pacific Industries
Signet Bank/Maryland
Silverweed Foundation
Simon Foundation, William E. and Carol G.
Simpson Foundation
Skinner Corp.
Slant/Fin Corp.
Smith Barney, Harris Upham & Co.
Smith Charitable Fund, Eleanor Armstrong
Smith Corp., A.O.
SmithKline Beecham
Smucker Co., J.M.
SNET
Snyder Charitable Fund, W. P.
Snyder Foundation, Harold B. and Dorothy A.
Society Corp.
Sonat
Sonoco Products Co.
Sony Corp. of America
Sooner Pipe & Supply Corp.
Sordoni Foundation
Sosland Foundation

South Carolina Electric & Gas Co.
Southern California Edison Co.
Southern California Gas Co.
Southways Foundation
Southwestern Bell Corp.
Spiegel
Sprague Educational and Charitable Foundation, Seth
Sprague Memorial Institute, Otho S. A.
Stackpole-Hall Foundation
Standex International Corp.
Stanley Works
State Street Bank & Trust Co.
Stauffer Communications
Steadley Memorial Trust, Kent D. and Mary L.
Steele-Reese Foundation
Stein Foundation, Jules and Doris
Steinhauer Charitable Foundation
Sterling Winthrop
Stewardship Foundation
Stocker Foundation
Stone Container Corp.
Strake Foundation
Stranahan Foundation
Straus Foundation, Aaron and Lillie
Strawbridge & Clothier
Stride Rite Corp.
Subaru of America Inc.
Sumitomo Bank of California
Sun Co.
Sun Microsystems
Sunnen Foundation
Swalm Foundation
Synovus Financial Corp.
Tamko Asphalt Products
Tandem Computers
TCF Banking & Savings, FSB
Teledyne
Teleflex Inc.
Temple Foundation, T. L. L.
Tenneco
Texaco
Texas Gas Transmission Corp.
Texas Instruments
Textron
Thomas Foundation, Joan and Lee
3M Co.
Thyssen Specialty Steels
Times Mirror Co.
Tonkin Foundation, Tom and Helen
Tonya Memorial Foundation
Tosco Corp. Refining Division
Transamerica Corp.
Transco Energy Company
Tranzonic Cos.
Triford Foundation
TRINOVA Corp.
Tropicana Products, Inc.
True Trust, Henry A.
Trust Co. Bank
TU Electric Co.
Tyson Foods, Inc.
Tyson Fund
Ukrop's Super Markets, Inc.
Unilever United States
Union Bank
Union Bank of Switzerland Los Angeles Branch
Union Camp Corp.
United Airlines
United Parcel Service of America
United States Borax & Chemical Corp.
United States Trust Co. of New York
United Technologies Corp.
Universal Foods Corp.
Universal Leaf Tobacco Co.
Unocal Corp.
Upjohn Co.

Upjohn Foundation, Harold and Grace
Upton Foundation, Frederick S.
Uris Brothers Foundation
US WEST
USG Corp.
UST
USX Corp.
Utica National Insurance Group
Valdese Manufacturing Co., Inc.
Valley National Bank of Arizona
Van Buren Foundation
Vanneck-Bailey Foundation
Vevay-Switzerland County Foundation
Vicksburg Foundation
Virginia Power Co.
Volkswagen of America, Inc.
Von der Ahe, Jr. Trust, Theodore Albert
Wachovia Bank & Trust Co., N.A.
Waggoner Charitable Trust, Crystelle
Wagnalls Memorial
Wal-Mart Stores
Walgreen Co.
Wallace Computer Services
Disney Co., Walt
Warhol Foundation for the Visual Arts, Andy
Warner Fund, Albert and Bessie
Warner-Lambert Co.
Warren Foundation, William K.
Washington Forrest Foundation
Washington Water Power Co.
Waste Management
Wean Foundation, Raymond John
Webb Charitable Trust, Susan Mott
Webster Foundation, Edwin S.
Weinberg Foundation, John L.
Weinstein Foundation, J.
Wells Fargo & Co.
West Co.
West Foundation
Westvaco Corp.
Wetterau
Whirlpool Corp.
White Consolidated Industries
Whitehead Foundation
Whitehead Foundation, Joseph B.
Whitman Corp.
Wickes Foundation, Harvey Randall
WICOR, Inc.
Widgeon Foundation
Wieboldt Foundation
Wigwam Mills
Wilcox General Trust, George N.
Wilkof Foundation, Edward and Ruth
Williams Cos.
Wilson Foundation, Marie C. and Joseph C.
Winnebago Industries, Inc.
Winston Foundation, Norman and Rosita
Winter Construction Co.
Winthrop Trust, Clara B.
Wisconsin Energy Corp.
Wisconsin Power & Light Co.
Women's Project Foundation
Woods Charitable Fund
Woodward Governor Co.
Xerox Corp.
Yeager Charitable Trust, Lester E.
Yellow Corp.
York Barbell Co.
Young & Rubicam
Zale Foundation, William and Sylvia
Zamoiski Co.

Women's Affairs

Abbott Laboratories

Abrams Foundation, Benjamin and Elizabeth
Air Products & Chemicals
Alberto-Culver Co.
Alco Standard Corp.
Allegheny Ludlum Corp.
Allendale Mutual Insurance Co.
Alliant Techsystems
AlliedSignal
ALPAC Corp.
Alumax
Aluminum Co. of America
AMAX
American Brands
American Cyanamid Co.
American Electric Power
American Express Co.
American National Bank & Trust Co. of Chicago
American Stock Exchange
American Telephone & Telegraph Co.
Ameritech Corp.
Ameritech Services
Ames Department Stores
Amfac/JMB Hawaii
Amoco Corp.
Apple Computer, Inc.
Appleby Trust, Scott B. and Annie P.
Archer-Daniels-Midland Co.
ARCO
ARCO Chemical
Arizona Public Service Co.
Arkansas Power & Light Co.
Armco Inc.
Arronson Foundation
Atlanta Gas Light Co.
Atran Foundation
Attleboro Pawtucket Savings Bank
Avon Products
Azadoutioun Foundation
Bacardi Imports
Baird Foundation, Cameron
Baldwin Memorial Foundation, Fred
Bally Inc.
Bank of America Arizona
Bank of Boston Corp.
Bankers Trust Co.
Barra Foundation
Bausch & Lomb
Beaird Foundation, Charles T.
Bechtel, Jr. Foundation, S. D.
Belfer Foundation
Bemis Company
Ben & Jerry's Homemade
Berwind Corp.
Betts Industries
BFGoodrich
Bingham Second Betterment Fund, William
Bireley Foundation
Block, H&R
Blount
Blowitz-Ridgeway Foundation
Boatmen's Bancshares
Boehm Foundation
Boise Cascade Corp.
Bonfils-Stanton Foundation
Booz Allen & Hamilton
Borden
Boston Edison Co.
Boston Fatherless and Widows Society
Bowne Foundation, Robert
BP America
Brach Foundation, Helen
Bremer Foundation, Otto
Bridwell Foundation, J. S.
Briggs Family Foundation
Brown Charitable Trust, Dora Maclellan
Brown & Williamson Tobacco Corp.
Brunswick Corp.

Buehler Foundation, Emil
Buhl Family Foundation
Burlington Northern Inc.
Burnand Medical and
  Educational Foundation,
  Alphonse A.
Bush Foundation
Cabot Corp.
Cahn Family Foundation
Campbell and Adah E. Hall
  Charity Fund, Bushrod H.
Canon U.S.A., Inc.
Capital Cities/ABC
Capital Holding Corp.
Carnegie Corporation of New
  York
Carolyn Foundation
Carter Family Foundation
Central Maine Power Co.
Central Soya Co.
Chait Memorial Foundation, Sara
Charlesbank Homes
Chase Manhattan Bank, N.A.
Cherne Foundation, Albert W.
Chernow Trust for the Benefit of
  Charity Dated 3/13/75, Michael
Chevron Corp.
Chicago Resource Center
Chicago Sun-Times, Inc.
Chicago Title and Trust Co.
Chiles Foundation
Chrysler Corp.
Churches Homes Foundation
Citicorp
Clark Foundation, Robert
  Sterling
Clorox Co.
CM Alliance Cos.
CNA Insurance Cos.
Cohen Family Foundation, Saul
  Z. and Amy Scheuer
Collins, Jr. Foundation, George
  Fulton
Coltec Industries
Commerce Clearing House
Consolidated Natural Gas Co.
Consumer Farmer Foundation
Cooper Industries
Coors Brewing Co.
Coors Foundation, Adolph
Copperweld Corp.
Cord Foundation, E. L.
Corning Incorporated
Country Curtains, Inc.
Courts Foundation
Cowan Foundation Corporation,
  Lillian L. and Harry A.
Cowan Foundation Corporation,
  Lillian L. and Harry A.
Cowles Charitable Trust
Cowles Media Co.
CRL Inc.
CT Corp. System
Cummins Engine Co.
Curtice-Burns Foods
Dain Bosworth/Inter-Regional
  Financial Group
Daly Charitable Foundation
  Trust, Robert and Nancy
Danner Foundation
Dayton Hudson Corp.
Dean Witter Discover
Deer Creek Foundation
Delano Foundation, Mignon
  Sherwood
DeRoy Foundation, Helen L.
DeRoy Testamentary Foundation
Detroit Edison Co.
Dexter Corp.
Diamond Foundation, Aaron
Dick Family Foundation
Dimeo Construction Co.
Dodge Foundation, Geraldine R.
Dougherty, Jr. Foundation, James
  R.
Douty Foundation
Dresser Industries

du Pont de Nemours & Co., E. I.
Duchossois Industries
Duke Power Co.
Duncan Trust, John G.
Duncan Trust, John G.
Durfee Foundation
Easley Trust, Andrew H. and
  Anne O.
Egenton Home
Emergency Aid of Pennsylvania
  Foundation
Emery Memorial, Thomas J.
Encyclopaedia Britannica, Inc.
Enron Corp.
Equifax
Equitable Life Assurance Society
  of the U.S.
Exxon Corp.
Eyman Trust, Jesse
FAB Industries
Fair Oaks Foundation, Inc.
Falk Medical Fund, Maurice
Falk Medical Research
  Foundation, Dr. Ralph and
  Marian
Fanwood Foundation
Farnsworth Trust, Charles A.
Federal-Mogul Corp.
Federated Department Stores and
  Allied Stores Corp.
Fel-Pro Incorporated
Fels Fund, Samuel S.
Fidelity Bank
Field Foundation of Illinois
Fikes Foundation, Leland
FINA, Inc.
Finley Foundation, A. E.
Fireman's Fund Insurance Co.
First Fidelity Bancorporation
First Interstate Bank of California
Firstar Bank Milwaukee NA
Fischel Foundation, Harry and
  Jane
Fisher Foundation, Max M. and
  Marjorie S.
Fleet Financial Group
Flemm Foundation, John J.
Florida Power & Light Co.
Ford Foundation
Forest City Enterprises
Forest Fund
Fort Worth Star Telegram
Foster Co., L.B.
Foundation for Seacoast Health
Frank Foundation, Ernest and
  Elfriede
Freedom Forum
Freeport-McMoRan
Frees Foundation
Frese Foundation, Arnold D.
Friedman Family Foundation
Frohring Foundation, William O.
  and Gertrude Lewis
Frohring Foundation, William O.
  and Gertrude Lewis
Frost Foundation
Fuchs Foundation, Gottfried &
  Mary
Funderburke & Associates
Gardner Charitable Foundation,
  Edith D.
General Electric Co.
General Mills
General Motors Corp.
General Railway Signal Corp.
General Reinsurance Corp.
General Service Foundation
Genesis Foundation
Genius Foundation, Elizabeth
  Morse
Georgia Power Co.
Gerbode Foundation, Wallace
  Alexander
German Protestant Orphan
  Asylum Association
Gerson Family Foundation,
  Benjamin J.
Gerson Trust, B. Milfred

Getz Foundation, Emma and
  Oscar
Giant Eagle
Giant Food Stores
Gilmore Foundation, Earl B.
Glaxo
Glenmore Distilleries Co.
Glickenhaus & Co.
Globe Corp.
Golden Family Foundation
Goldman Foundation, William
Goldstein Foundation, Alfred
  and Ann
Gould Inc.
Grace & Co., W.R.
Grant Foundation, Charles M.
  and Mary D.
Great-West Life Assurance Co.
Green Fund
Greene Foundation, Robert Z.
Greenville Foundation
Grossman Foundation, N. Bud
Guggenheim Foundation, Daniel
  and Florence
Gulf Power Co.
Gund Foundation, George
Hampden Papers
Harper Foundation, Philip S.
Harris Trust & Savings Bank
Hartmarx Corp.
Hebrew Technical Institute
Hechinger Co.
Hecla Mining Co.
Heileman Brewing Co., Inc., G.
Heinz Co., H.J.
Heinz Foundation, Drue
Henkel Corp.
Henry Foundation, Patrick
Herndon Foundation
Hershey Foods Corp.
Heymann Special Account, Mr.
  and Mrs. Jimmy
Hitachi
Hogan Foundation, Royal Barney
Holtzmann Foundation, Jacob L.
  and Lillian
Homeland Foundation
Horizons Foundation
Horne Trust, Mabel
Hospital Corp. of America
Household International
Houston Industries
Huber Foundation
Huffy Corp.
Humana
Hunt Alternatives Fund
I. and L. Association
IBM Corp.
Illinois Power Co.
Illinois Tool Works
Indiana Bell Telephone Co.
Indiana Insurance Cos.
Inland Steel Industries
Interco
International Flavors &
  Fragrances
Irmas Charitable Foundation,
  Audrey and Sydney
Irvine Foundation, James
ITT Corp.
ITT Hartford Insurance Group
J.P. Morgan & Co.
Jackson Foundation
Jacobson Foundation, Bernard
  H. and Blanche E.
JCPenney Co.
Jerusalem Fund for Education
  and Community Development
JFM Foundation
John Hancock Mutual Life
  Insurance Co.
Johnson Controls
Johnson & Johnson
Joselow Foundation
Kangesser Foundation, Robert
  E., Harry A., and M. Sylvia
Kellogg Foundation, W. K.

Kennametal
Kennecott Corp.
Kennedy Foundation, Ethel
Kimball Foundation, Horace A.
  Kimball and S. Ella
King Foundation, Carl B. and
  Florence E.
Kiplinger Foundation
Klosk Fund, Louis and Rose
Kmart Corp.
Knox, Sr., and Pearl Wallis Knox
  Charitable Foundation, Robert
  W.
Kohl Foundation, Sidney
Koopman Fund
Kraft General Foods
Kramer Foundation, Louise
Ladd Charitable Corporation,
  Helen and George
Lafarge Corp.
Lakeside Foundation
Lakeside Foundation
Lance, Inc.
Large Foundation
Lautenberg Foundation
Lawrence Foundation, Alice
Levi Strauss & Co.
Levinson Foundation, Max and
  Anna
Leviton Manufacturing Co.
Levy Foundation, Charles and
  Ruth
Levy's Lumber & Building
  Centers
Liberty Corp.
Lincoln National Corp.
Lipton, Thomas J.
Little, Arthur D.
Livingston Memorial Foundation
Long Island Lighting Co.
Lowe Foundation, Joe and Emily
LTV Corp.
Lydall, Inc.
MacArthur Foundation, J.
  Roderick
MacArthur Foundation, John D.
  and Catherine T.
Macht Foundation, Morton and
  Sophia
Macy & Co., R.H.
MalCo Products Inc.
Mallinckrodt Specialty
  Chemicals Co.
Mandel Foundation, Jack N. and
  Lilyan
Mandel Foundation, Morton and
  Barbara
Maritz Inc.
Marriott Corp.
Marsh & McLennan Cos.
Martin Marietta Corp.
Material Service Corp.
MBIA, Inc.
McCormick Tribune Foundation,
  Robert R.
McDonald & Co. Securities
McElroy Trust, R. J.
McGraw-Hill
McIntosh Foundation
McKee Foundation, Robert E.
  and Evelyn
McKesson Corp.
McKnight Foundation
Mead Corp.
Medina Foundation
Melitta North America Inc.
Mellon Bank Corp.
Melohn Foundation
Merck & Co.
Merrill Lynch & Co.
Messing Family Charitable
  Foundation
Metropolitan Life Insurance Co.
Meyer Foundation, Eugene and
  Agnes E.
Meyer Memorial Foundation,
  Aaron and Rachel
Midwest Resources

Mitchell Foundation
Mobil Oil Corp.
Model Foundation, Leo
Monadnock Paper Mills
Monroe-Brown Foundation
Monticello College Foundation
Moog Automotive, Inc.
Morgan Foundation, Burton D.
Morris Foundation
Morton International
Motorola
Mulford Trust, Clarence E.
Nalco Chemical Co.
National City Corp.
National Computer Systems
National Gypsum Co.
National Westminster Bank New
  Jersey
NBD Bank
Needmor Fund
New England Mutual Life
  Insurance Co.
New-Land Foundation
New Prospect Foundation
New World Foundation
New York Foundation
New York Life Insurance Co.
New York Mercantile Exchange
New York Telephone Co.
New York Times Co.
The New Yorker Magazine, Inc.
News & Observer Publishing Co.
Noble Foundation, Vivian Bilby
Norman Foundation
Norman Foundation, Andrew
Norris Foundation, Dellora A.
  and Lester J.
Northern States Power Co.
Northern Trust Co.
Northwest Natural Gas Co.
Northwestern National Life
  Insurance Co.
Norton Co.
Norton Foundation Inc.
Noyes Foundation, Jessie Smith
NuTone Inc.
Offield Family Foundation
Ogden Foundation, Ralph E.
Ogilvy & Mather Worldwide
Oglebay Norton Co.
Ohio Savings Bank
Old Dominion Box Co.
Orleans Trust, Carrie S.
Overlake Foundation
Overseas Shipholding Group
Oxford Industries, Inc.
Pacific Gas & Electric Co.
Pacific Mutual Life Insurance Co.
Pacific Telesis Group
Packard Foundation, David and
  Lucile
Paramount Communications Inc.
Paul and C. Michael Paul
  Foundation, Josephine Bay
Peabody Foundation, Amelia
Penn Savings Bank, a division of
  Sovereign Bank Bank of
  Princeton, a division of
  Sovereign Bank
Pennington Foundation, Irene W.
  and C. B.
Peoples Energy Corp.
Pepsi-Cola Bottling Co. of
  Charlotte
Perkin-Elmer Corp.
Pettus Crowe Foundation
Pfizer
Philip Morris Cos.
Phillips Family Foundation, Jay
  and Rose
Piedmont Health Care
  Foundation
Pincus Family Fund
Pitney Bowes
Piton Foundation
Pittway Corp.
Playboy Enterprises, Inc.

Women's Affairs (cont.)

Polaroid Corp.
Potomac Electric Power Co.
PPG Industries
Premier Industrial Corp.
Prince Corp.
Principal Financial Group
Pritzker Foundation
Providence Journal Company
Prudential Insurance Co. of America
Public Service Co. of Colorado
Public Service Electric & Gas Co.
Quaker Oats Co.
Raskin Foundation, Hirsch and Braine
Reisman Charitable Trust, George C. and Evelyn R.
Relations Foundation
Revson Foundation, Charles H.
Reynolds Foundation, Donald W.
Reynolds Foundation, Z. Smith
Richardson Charitable Trust, Anne S.
RJR Nabisco Inc.
Rockefeller Family Fund
Rockefeller Foundation
Rockford Acromatics Products Co./Aircraft Gear Corp.
Rockwell International Corp.
Rogers Corp.
Rosenberg Foundation
Rosenberg Foundation, Sunny and Abe
Rosenthal Foundation, Ida and William
Roth Foundation, Louis T.
Rubenstein Charitable Foundation, Lawrence J. and Anne
Rubin Family Fund, Cele H. and William B.
Russ Togs
Salomon
Saltonstall Charitable Foundation, Richard
Santa Fe Pacific Corp.
Sara Lee Corp.
Scaife Family Foundation
Scherer Foundation, Karla
Schoonmaker J-Sewkly Valley Hospital Trust
Science Applications International Corp.
Scripps Foundation, Ellen Browning
Scrivner, Inc.
Scurlock Foundation
Searle & Co., G.D.
Security Life of Denver
Seevak Family Foundation
Seven Springs Foundation
Seybert Institution for Poor Boys and Girls, Adam and Maria Sarah
Shawmut National Corp.
Shell Oil Co.
Signet Bank/Maryland
Silverburgh Foundation, Grace, George & Judith
Simon Foundation, William E. and Carol G.
SIT Investment Associates, Inc.
Skinner Corp.
Smith Horticultural Trust, Stanley
SNET
Snow Memorial Trust, John Ben
Sonoco Products Co.
Southern California Edison Co.
Southern California Gas Co.
Spectra-Physics Analytical
Spiegel
Sprague Educational and Charitable Foundation, Seth
Standard Register Co.

Starr Foundation
State Street Bank & Trust Co.
Steelcase
Stern Family Fund
Stern Foundation, Leonard N.
Stone Container Corp.
Stride Rite Corp.
Strong Foundation, Hattie M.
Subaru of America Inc.
Sunnen Foundation
Tandem Computers
Tandy Foundation, David L.
Tandy Foundation, David L.
Taubman Foundation, A. Alfred
TCF Banking & Savings, FSB
Teledyne
Teleflex Inc.
Teleklew Productions
Tennant Co.
Tenneco
Texaco
Texas Commerce Bank Houston, N.A.
Textron
3M Co.
Times Mirror Co.
TJX Cos.
Town Creek Foundation
Tracor, Inc.
Transco Energy Company
Trust Co. Bank
Union Bank of Switzerland Los Angeles Branch
Union Camp Corp.
United Airlines
United Parcel Service of America
U.S. Leasing International
United Technologies Corp.
Unocal Corp.
US Bancorp
US WEST
Valley National Bank of Arizona
Valmont Industries
Varian Associates
Vaughan Foundation, Rachael and Ben
Virginia Power Co.
Wachovia Bank & Trust Co., N.A.
Wal-Mart Stores
Walgreen Co.
Walthall Perpetual Charitable Trust, Marjorie T.
Washington Water Power Co.
Wean Foundation, Raymond John
Weber Charities Corp., Frederick E.
Weeden Foundation, Frank
Weinstein Foundation, Alex J.
Wenger Foundation, Henry L. and Consuelo S.
West One Bancorp
Westinghouse Electric Corp.
Westport Fund
Westvaco Corp.
Whirlpool Corp.
White Foundation, Erle and Emma
Whitehead Foundation
WICOR, Inc.
Wieboldt Foundation
Williams Cos.
Winn-Dixie Stores
Wolf Foundation, Melvin and Elaine
Women's Project Foundation
Woods Charitable Fund
Woodward Fund
Wright Foundation, Lola
Wurts Memorial, Henrietta Tower
Xerox Corp.
Young Foundation, Robert R.

Zoos/Botanical Gardens

Abbott Laboratories

Abeles Foundation, Joseph and Sophia
Abraham Foundation, Anthony R.
Abraham & Straus
Abrons Foundation, Louis and Anne
Achelis Foundation
Acme-McCrary Corp.
Adams Foundation, Arthur F. and Alice E.
Ahmanson Foundation
AHS Foundation
Alabama Power Co.
Alco Standard Corp.
Allegheny Ludlum Corp.
Allendale Mutual Insurance Co.
AlliedSignal
ALPAC Corp.
Altman Foundation
Alumax
AMAX
America West Airlines
American Brands
American Electric Power
American Express Co.
American Financial Corp.
American Foundation Corporation
American National Bank & Trust Co. of Chicago
American Natural Resources Co.
American United Life Insurance Co.
Ameritech Services
AMETEK
Amoco Corp.
Amsted Industries
Anacomp, Inc.
Analog Devices
Andersen Corp.
Anderson Foundation, William P.
Andersons Management Corp.
Angelica Corp.
Anheuser-Busch Cos.
AON Corp.
Arcadia Foundation
Archer-Daniels-Midland Co.
ARCO
Armbrust Chain Co.
Aron Charitable Foundation, J.
Arronson Foundation
Asplundh Foundation
Associated Foundations
Astor Foundation, Vincent
Atlantic Foundation
Atran Foundation
Autry Foundation
Autzen Foundation
Avis Inc.
Avon Products
Ayres Foundation, Inc.
Bacon Foundation, E. L. and Oma
Badger Meter, Inc.
Bailey Wildlife Foundation
Baird & Co., Robert W.
Baird Foundation
Baker Foundation, Elinor Patterson
Baker, Jr. Memorial Fund, William G.
Baltimore Gas & Electric Co.
Banbury Fund
Banc One Illinois Corp.
Banc One Wisconsin Corp.
Bank Foundation, Helen and Merrill
Bank IV
Bank of America Arizona
Bank of New York
Bannerman Foundation, William C.
BarclaysAmerican Corp.
Bardes Corp.
Barker Welfare Foundation
Barnes Group
Barra Foundation

Barth Foundation, Theodore H.
Bartlett & Co.
Bass Foundation
Bassett Foundation, Norman
Battelle
Bay Foundation
Bayne Fund, Howard
Beattie Foundation Trust, Cordelia Lee
Bechtel, Jr. Foundation, S. D.
Beck Foundation
Beech Aircraft Corp.
Beidler Charitable Trust, Francis
Beinecke Foundation
Belding Heminway Co.
Beloco Foundation
Bemis Company
Benbough Foundation, Legler
Bend Millwork Systems
Beneficia Foundation
Benefit Trust Life Insurance Co.
Bere Foundation
Berger Foundation, H.N. and Frances C.
Bernsen Foundation, Grace and Franklin
Berwind Corp.
Beveridge Foundation, Frank Stanley
Biddle Foundation, Margaret T.
Bingham Second Betterment Fund, William
Binswanger Co.
Bionetics Corp.
Birch Foundation, Stephen and Mary
Bird Inc.
Blackmer Foundation, Henry M.
Blair and Co., William
Blanchard Foundation
Blaustein Foundation, Jacob and Hilda
Block, H&R
Blowitz-Ridgeway Foundation
Blue Cross & Blue Shield of Alabama
Blum-Kovler Foundation
Boatmen's Bancshares
Bodman Foundation
Boehringer Mannheim Corp.
Boeing Co.
Boettcher Foundation
Boh Brothers Construction Co.
Boise Cascade Corp.
Bonfils-Stanton Foundation
Booth-Bricker Fund
Borman's
Borwell Charitable Foundation
Boston Edison Co.
Bostwick Foundation, Albert C.
Boutell Memorial Fund, Arnold and Gertrude
Bovaird Foundation, Mervin
Bowater Inc.
Brackenridge Foundation, George W.
Brewer and Co., Ltd., C.
Bridgestone/Firestone
Briggs Foundation, T. W.
Brink Unitrust, Julia H.
Bristol-Myers Squibb Co.
Brooks Foundation, Gladys
Brown and C. A. Lupton Foundation, T. J.
Brown Foundation
Brown Group
Brown & Sons, Alex
Brown & Williamson Tobacco Corp.
Bryant Foundation
Bryce Memorial Fund, William and Catherine
Buchanan Family Foundation
Bucyrus-Erie
Buffett Foundation
Builder Marts of America
Burkitt Foundation

Burnand Medical and Educational Foundation, Alphonse A.
Burnham Foundation
Butler Family Foundation, Patrick and Aimee
Butz Foundation
Cabell III and Maude Morgan Cabell Foundation, Robert G.
Cain Foundation, Gordon and Mary
Caldwell Foundation, Hardwick
Callaway Foundation, Fuller E.
Camp and Bennet Humiston Trust, Apollos
Capital Holding Corp.
Carolina Power & Light Co.
Carter Foundation, Amon G.
Cary Charitable Trust, Mary Flagler
Cassett Foundation, Louis N.
Castle Foundation, Harold K. L.
Centel Corp.
Central Bank of the South
Central & South West Services
Central Soya Co.
Cessna Aircraft Co.
Chadwick Foundation
Chadwick Fund, Dorothy Jordan
Champlin Foundations
Charities Foundation
Chastain Charitable Foundation, Robert Lee and Thomas M.
Chemical Bank
Chevron Corp.
Chicago Board of Trade
Chiles Foundation
Christodora
Chrysler Corp.
Cincinnati Bell
Cincinnati Milacron
Citibank, F.S.B.
Citicorp
Citizens Bank
Claneil Foundation
Clark Charitable Trust
Clark Foundation
Clark Foundation
Clark-Winchcole Foundation
Clements Foundation
Cleveland-Cliffs
Clorox Co.
CNA Insurance Cos.
Cobb Family Foundation
Cockrell Foundation
Cohen Family Foundation, Saul Z. and Amy Scheuer
Cole Foundation, Robert H. and Monica H.
Coleman Co.
Coleman, Jr. Foundation, George E.
Collins & Aikman Holdings Corp.
Collins Foundation, Carr P.
Collins Foundation, James M.
Collins, Jr. Foundation, George Fulton
Colonial Life & Accident Insurance Co.
Columbia Terminals Co.
Columbus Dispatch Printing Co.
Columbus Southern Power Co.
Commerce Bancshares, Inc.
Commerce Clearing House
Commonwealth Edison Co.
ConAgra
Connemara Fund
Consolidated Natural Gas Co.
Consolidated Papers
Consumers Power Co.
Continental Corp.
Contran Corp.
Cook Foundation
Cooke Foundation
Cooper Charitable Trust, Richard H.

Cooper Foundation
Cooper Industries
Coors Foundation, Adolph
Copley Press
Corestates Bank
Cornell Trust, Peter C.
Corpus Christi Exploration Co.
Cosmair, Inc.
Country Curtains, Inc.
County Bank
Courts Foundation
Covington Foundation, Marion Stedman
Cowles Charitable Trust
Cowles Media Co.
Cox Enterprises
CPC International
CPI Corp.
CR Industries
Crane Foundation, Raymond E. and Ellen F.
Credit Agricole
Crestlea Foundation
Crown Central Petroleum Corp.
Crum and Forster
CT Corp. System
Cullen/Frost Bankers
Culver Foundation, Constans
CUNA Mutual Insurance Group
Cunningham Foundation, Laura Moore
Cyprus Minerals Co.
Dalton Foundation, Harry L.
Dana Corp.
Darby Foundation
Darrah Charitable Trust, Jessie Smith
Dater Foundation, Charles H.
Davies Charitable Trust
Davis Foundation, Edwin W. and Catherine M.
DEC International, Inc.
Delany Charitable Trust, Beatrice P.
Delaware North Cos.
Deposit Guaranty National Bank
DeRoy Foundation, Helen L.
DeSoto
Detroit Edison Co.
DeVore Foundation
Dial Corp.
Diamond Foundation, Aaron
Dick Family Foundation
Dickson Foundation
Dietrich Foundation, William B.
Dillon Foundation
Dimeo Construction Co.
Dingman Foundation, Michael D.
Dixie Yarns, Inc.
Dobson Foundation
Dodge Foundation, Cleveland H.
Dodge Foundation, Geraldine R.
Doelger Charitable Trust, Thelma
Donaldson Charitable Trust, Oliver S. and Jennie R.
Donaldson Co.
Donnelley & Sons Co., R.R.
Douglas & Lomason Company
Dow Corning Corp.
Dow Foundation, Herbert H. and Grace A.
Downs Perpetual Charitable Trust, Ellason
Dresser Industries
Dreyfus Foundation, Max and Victoria
du Pont de Nemours & Co., E. I.
Duchossois Industries
Duke Foundation, Doris
Duke Power Co.
Dula Educational and Charitable Foundation, Caleb C. and Julia W.
Dumke Foundation, Dr. Ezekiel R. and Edna Wattis
Dunspaugh-Dalton Foundation
Durst Foundation

Dyson Foundation
Eastern Enterprises
Eccles Foundation, George S. and Dolores Dore
Eccles Foundation, Marriner S.
Edgerton Foundation, Harold E.
El Pomar Foundation
Elf Atochem North America
Emerson Electric Co.
Emery Memorial, Thomas J.
Engelhard Foundation, Charles
English Foundation, Walter and Marian
English Memorial Fund, Florence C. and H. L.
Enron Corp.
Enterprise Rent-A-Car Co.
Equifax
Erpf Fund, Armand G.
Essick Foundation
Eureka Co.
Evans Foundation, Edward P.
Evans Foundation, T. M.
Evjue Foundation
Ewald Foundation, H. T.
Exposition Foundation
Exxon Corp.
Fabick Tractor Co., John
Fair Oaks Foundation, Inc.
Fair Play Foundation
Falk Foundation, David
Farallon Foundation
Favrot Fund
Federal-Mogul Corp.
Fein Foundation
Fein Foundation
Fel-Pro Incorporated
Ferguson Family Foundation, Kittie and Rugeley
Fidelity Bank
Field Foundation, Jamee and Marshall
Field Foundation of Illinois
Fieldcrest Cannon
Fifth Third Bancorp
Fikes Foundation, Leland
FINA, Inc.
Fireman's Fund Insurance Co.
First Chicago
First Fidelity Bancorporation
First Interstate Bank of Arizona
First Interstate Bank of California
First Maryland Bancorp
First Tennessee Bank
First Union Corp.
Firstar Bank Milwaukee NA
Fish Foundation, Ray C.
Fishback Foundation Trust, Harmes C.
Flarsheim Charitable Foundation, Louis and Elizabeth
Fleet Financial Group
Florida Power & Light Co.
FMC Corp.
Foellinger Foundation
Foote, Cone & Belding Communications
Forbes
Ford Fund, Benson and Edith
Forest Oil Corp.
Fortin Foundation of Florida
Foster-Davis Foundation
Fourth Financial Corp.
Fox Foundation, John H.
France Foundation, Jacob and Annita
Franklin Foundation, John and Mary
Freed Foundation
Freedom Forum
Freeport Brick Co.
Freeport-McMoRan
Frelinghuysen Foundation
French Foundation
Frick Foundation, Helen Clay
Frisch's Restaurants Inc.

Frohring Foundation, Paul & Maxine
Fry Foundation, Lloyd A.
Fuller Foundation
Funderburke & Associates
Fuqua Foundation, J. B.
Furth Foundation
Gage Foundation, Philip and Irene Toll
Galvin Foundation, Robert W.
GAR Foundation
Garvey Memorial Foundation, Edward Chase
Garvey Texas Foundation
Gelman Foundation, Melvin and Estelle
General American Life Insurance Co.
General Electric Co.
General Mills
General Motors Corp.
General Railway Signal Corp.
General Tire Inc.
Geneseo Foundation
GenRad
Georgia-Pacific Corp.
Georgia Power Co.
Gerschel Foundation, Patrick A.
Giant Eagle
Giant Food
Gill Foundation, Pauline Allen
Gillett Foundation, Elesabeth Ingalls
Gillette Co.
Gilman, Jr. Foundation, Sondra and Charles
Gilmer-Smith Foundation
Gilmore Foundation, William G.
Glancy Foundation, Lenora and Alfred
Glaxo
Globe Corp.
Goldberg Family Foundation, Milton D. and Madeline L.
Golden Family Foundation
Goldome F.S.B
Goldsmith Foundation
Goodman & Company
Goodman Foundation, Edward and Marion
Grace & Co., W.R.
Gradison & Co.
Grant Charitable Trust, Elberth R. and Gladys F.
Graybar Electric Co.
Green Fund
Greenberg Foundation, Alan C.
Greenfield Foundation, Albert M.
Greentree Foundation
Griffis Foundation
Griffith Foundation, W. C.
Griggs and Mary Griggs Burke Foundation, Mary Livingston
Guardian Life Insurance Co. of America
H. B. B. Foundation
Haffenreffer Family Fund
Haffner Foundation
Hagedorn Fund
Haggar Foundation
Hall Charitable Trust, Evelyn A. J.
Hallmark Cards
Halsell Foundation, Ewing
Hamman Foundation, George and Mary Josephine
Handleman Co.
Hanes Foundation, John W. and Anna H.
Hanson Foundation
HarCo. Drug
Hargis Charitable Foundation, Estes H. and Florence Parker
Harper Foundation, Philip S.
Harriman Foundation, Mary W.
Harris Foundation
Harris Foundation, William H. and Mattie Wattis

Harrison Foundation, Fred G.
Hastings Trust
Hatch Charitable Trust, Margaret Milliken
Hayden Foundation, Charles
Hazen Charitable Trust, Lita Annenberg
Hazen Foundation, Edward W.
Hechinger Co.
Hecht-Levi Foundation
Hedrick Foundation, Frank E.
Heinz Co., H.J.
Heinz Family Foundation
Heinz Foundation, Drue
Helfaer Foundation, Evan and Marion
Helmerich Foundation
Henderson Foundation, George B.
Henkel Corp.
Herrick Foundation
Hewit Family Foundation
Hiawatha Education Foundation
Hill and Family Foundation, Walter Clay
Hillman Foundation
HKH Foundation
Hoffmann-La Roche
Homeland Foundation
Hook Drug
Hopkins Foundation, John Jay
Hopkins Foundation, Josephine Lawrence
Horizons Foundation
Hospital Corp. of America
Houston Industries
Howell Fund
Hoyt Foundation
Hubbard Broadcasting
Hudson-Webber Foundation
Humana
Hunt Alternatives Fund, Helen
Hunt Foundation, Roy A.
Hutcheson Foundation, Hazel Montague
IBM Corp.
Illinois Bell
Illinois Tool Works
IMCERA Group Inc.
Indiana Bell Telephone Co.
Indiana Insurance Cos.
Inland Container Corp.
Inland Steel Industries
Insurance Management Associates
Intel Corp.
Interco
International Flavors & Fragrances
International Paper Co.
Iroquois Avenue Foundation
ITT Corp.
J.P. Morgan & Co.
Jackson Foundation
Jackson Hole Preserve
Jacobson & Sons, Benjamin
Jameson Foundation, J. W. and Ida M.
Jameson Trust, Oleonda
JCPenney Co.
Jeffress Memorial Trust, Elizabeth G.
Johnson Charitable Trust, Keith Wold
Johnson Controls
Johnson Foundation, Burdine
Johnson Foundation, Helen K. and Arthur E.
Johnson Foundation, Howard
Johnson & Higgins
Johnson & Son, S.C.
Jones Family Foundation, Eugenie and Joseph
Jones Foundation, Montfort Jones and Allie Brown
Jones Foundation, W. Alton
Jonsson Foundation

Jordan and Ettie A. Jordan Charitable Foundation, Mary Ranken
Jordan Foundation, Arthur
Joukowsky Family Foundation
Jurodin Fund
Jurzykowski Foundation, Alfred
Kaplan Foundation, Mayer and Morris
Keating Family Foundation
Keck, Jr. Foundation, William M.
Keller Family Foundation
Kellogg Foundation, J. C.
Kellwood Co.
Kelly Tractor Co.
Kemper Memorial Foundation, David Woods
Kennecott Corp.
Kerr Foundation, Robert S. and Grayce B.
Kerr-McGee Corp.
Kettering Fund
Kiewit Sons, Peter
Killam Trust, Constance
Kimball International
Kimberly-Clark Corp.
King Foundation, Carl B. and Florence E.
Kingsley Foundation
Kirkpatrick Foundation
Klau Foundation, David W. and Sadie
Kleberg Foundation for Wildlife Conservation, Caesar
Kleberg, Jr. and Helen C. Kleberg Foundation, Robert J.
Klee Foundation, Conrad and Virginia
Kmart Corp.
Knapp Foundation
Knox, Sr., and Pearl Wallis Knox Charitable Foundation, Robert W.
Koehler Foundation, Marcia and Otto
Koopman Fund
Kowalski Sausage Co.
Kraft Foundation
Kraft General Foods
Krause Foundation, Charles A.
Kresge Foundation
Krimendahl II Foundation, H. Frederick
Kuehn Foundation
Kunkel Foundation, John Crain
Laclede Gas Co.
Laffey-McHugh Foundation
Lancaster Colony
Lance, Inc.
Lane Memorial Foundation, Mills Bee
Langendorf Foundation, Stanley S.
Lanier Brothers Foundation
Lattner Foundation, Forrest C.
Lauder Foundation
Laurel Foundation
LBJ Family Foundation
Leach Foundation, Tom & Frances
Lee Enterprises
Lee Foundation, Ray M. and Mary Elizabeth
Lehmann Foundation, Otto W.
Lennon Foundation, Fred A.
Lennox International, Inc.
Liberty Diversified Industries Inc.
Lied Foundation Trust
Life Insurance Co. of Georgia
Lightner Sams Foundation
Lilly Endowment
Lincoln Electric Co.
Lincoln National Corp.
Lincolnshire
Linn-Henley Charitable Trust
Lipton, Thomas J.
Little, Arthur D.

Zoos/Botanical Gardens (cont.)

Little Family Foundation
Lockwood Foundation, Byron W. and Alice L.
Loews Corp.
Long Island Lighting Co.
Longwood Foundation
Lopata Foundation, Stanley and Lucy
Louisiana Land & Exploration Co.
Louisiana-Pacific Corp.
Louisiana Power & Light Co./New Orleans Public Service
Lounsbery Foundation, Richard
Love Charitable Foundation, John Allan
Love Foundation, Gay and Erskine
Lowe Foundation
Lowe Foundation, Joe and Emily
Lowenstein Foundation, Leon
LTV Corp.
Lubrizol Corp.
Ludwick Institute
Lurie Foundation, Louis R.
Luse Foundation, W. P. and Bulah
Lux Trust, Dr. Konrad and Clara
MacArthur Foundation, John D. and Catherine T.
Macy & Co., R.H.
Maddox Trust, Web
Madison Gas & Electric Co.
Magowan Family Foundation
Mailman Family Foundation, A. L.
Mallinckrodt Specialty Chemicals Co.
Mandell Foundation, Samuel P.
Marathon Oil, Indiana Refining Division
Maritz Inc.
Mark IV Industries
Marmot Foundation
Marquette Electronics
Mars Foundation
Marsh & McLennan Cos.
Marshall Fund
Marshall & Ilsley Bank
Marshall Trust in Memory of Sanders McDaniel, Harriet McDaniel
Martin Marietta Corp.
Mason Charitable Foundation
Massey Foundation
Massey Foundation, Jack C.
Mather and William Gwinn Mather Fund, Elizabeth Ring
Mathis-Pfohl Foundation
Maytag Corp.
McAlonan Trust, John A.
McBean Family Foundation
McCann Foundation
McCormick Foundation, Chauncey and Marion Deering
McCormick Tribune Foundation, Robert R.
McDermott Foundation, Eugene
McDonald & Co. Securities
McDonald & Co. Securities
McDonnell Douglas Corp.
McDonnell Douglas Corp.-West
McDonnell Foundation, James S.
McDonough Foundation, Bernard
McFeely-Rogers Foundation
McGonagle Foundation, Dextra Baldwin
McGraw-Hill
McGregor Fund
McIntosh Foundation
McKee Foundation, Robert E. and Evelyn
McKnight Foundation, Sumner T.
McLean Contributionship

McNutt Charitable Trust, Amy Shelton
Mead Corp.
Meadows Foundation
Media General, Inc.
Melitta North America Inc.
Mellon Foundation, Andrew W.
Memton Fund
Mentor Graphics
Merck Family Fund
Merck Human Health Division
Mericos Foundation
Merrill Lynch & Co.
Metropolitan Life Insurance Co.
Meyer Foundation, Alice Kleberg Reynolds
Meyer Foundation, George C.
Meyer Foundation, Robert R.
Meyer Memorial Trust
Michigan Bell Telephone Co.
Middendorf Foundation
Midwest Resources
Mifflin Memorial Fund, George H. and Jane A.
Milbank Foundation, Dunlevy
Miller Foundation
Mine Safety Appliances Co.
Mobil Oil Corp.
Model Foundation, Leo
Monfort Charitable Foundation
Monsanto Co.
Montana Power Co.
Montgomery Foundation
Moody Foundation
Moores Foundation
Moores Foundation, Harry C.
Moorman Manufacturing Co.
Morgan and Samuel Tate Morgan, Jr. Foundation, Marietta McNeil
Morgan Construction Co.
Morgan Foundation, Burton D.
Morley Brothers Foundation
Morris Foundation, Margaret T.
Morris Foundation, William T.
Morrison Charitable Trust, Pauline A. and George R.
Morrison-Knudsen Corp.
Morse, Jr. Foundation, Enid and Lester S.
Morton International
Moses Fund, Henry and Lucy
Mosher Foundation, Samuel B.
Moskowitz Foundation, Irving I.
Moss Foundation, Harry S.
Motorola
Mott Fund, Ruth
Mullen Foundation, J. K.
Murfee Endowment, Kathryn
Murphy Foundation, Katherine and John
Murray Foundation
Nalco Chemical Co.
Nash Foundation
National City Corp.
National Computer Systems
National Fuel Gas Co.
National Gypsum Co.
National Service Industries
National Steel
Nationwide Insurance Cos.
NBD Bank
NBD Bank, N.A.
Neilson Foundation, George W.
Nestle U.S.A. Inc.
New England Biolabs Foundation
New England Business Service
New Horizon Foundation
New York Foundation
New York Life Insurance Co.
New York Telephone Co.
The New Yorker Magazine, Inc.
Newhouse Foundation, Samuel I.
News & Observer Publishing Co.
Nichols Foundation
Noble Foundation, Edward John
Norcross Wildlife Foundation

Nordson Corp.
Norfolk Southern Corp.
Norgren Foundation, Carl A.
Norris Foundation, Dellora A. and Lester J.
North American Reinsurance Corp.
North American Royalties
Northern Star Foundation
Northern States Power Co.
Northern Trust Co.
Northwest Natural Gas Co.
Norton Co.
Norton Memorial Corporation, Geraldi
Norwest Bank Nebraska
Noyes, Jr. Memorial Foundation, Nicholas H.
Oaklawn Foundation
Occidental Oil & Gas Corp.
O'Connor Co.
O'Connor Foundation, A. Lindsay and Olive B.
O'Connor Foundation, Magee
Odell and Helen Pfeiffer Odell Fund, Robert Stewart
Odyssey Partners
O'Fallon Trust, Martin J. and Mary Anne
Offield Family Foundation
Ogilvy & Mather Worldwide
Oglebay Norton Co.
Ohio Bell Telephone Co.
Ohio National Life Insurance Co.
Ohio Valley Foundation
Ohrstrom Foundation
Oklahoma Gas & Electric Co.
Old National Bank in Evansville
Olin Foundation, Spencer T. and Ann W.
Oliver Memorial Trust Foundation
Olsson Memorial Foundation, Elis
Onan Family Foundation
Ontario Corp.
Oppenheimer Family Foundation
Ore-Ida Foods, Inc.
Osborn Charitable Trust, Edward B.
Oshkosh B'Gosh
Outboard Marine Corp.
Overbrook Foundation
Owen Industries, Inc.
Oxford Foundation
Oxford Foundation
Oxford Industries, Inc.
Pacific Mutual Life Insurance Co.
Packard Foundation, David and Lucile
Page Foundation, George B.
Paley Foundation, William S.
Palmer-Fry Memorial Trust, Lily
Pangburn Foundation
Panhandle Eastern Corp.
Pappas Charitable Foundation, Thomas Anthony
Paramount Communications Inc.
Parker Drilling Co.
Parker Foundation
Parker-Hannifin Corp.
Pasadena Area Residential Aid
Peabody Foundation, Amelia
Peck Foundation, Milton and Lillian
Peery Foundation
Penn Foundation, William
Pennzoil Co.
Peoples Energy Corp.
Perkin-Elmer Corp.
Perkin Fund
Perkins Charitable Foundation
Perkins Memorial Foundation, George W.
Perry Drug Stores
Peterloon Foundation
Pfizer

PHH Corp.
Philip Morris Cos.
Philips Foundation, Jesse
Phillips Foundation, Waite and Genevieve
Phipps Foundation, Howard
Pieper Electric
Pines Bridge Foundation
Pittsburgh National Bank
Pittulloch Foundation
Pittway Corp.
Pitzman Fund
Poinsettia Foundation, Paul and Magdalena Ecke
Pott Foundation, Herman T. and Phenie R.
Potts and Sibley Foundation
Powell Co., William
Powell Family Foundation
Prairie Foundation
Premier Industrial Corp.
Prentice Foundation, Abra
Preston Trust, Evelyn W.
Price Associates, T. Rowe
Prickett Fund, Lynn R. and Karl E.
Pritzker Foundation
Procter & Gamble Co.
Procter & Gamble Cosmetic & Fragrance Products
Prospect Hill Foundation
Prudential-Bache Securities
Public Service Co. of Colorado
Puett Foundation, Nelson
Quaker Chemical Corp.
Quaker Oats Co.
Questar Corp.
Quivey-Bay State Foundation
Radin Foundation
Randa
Ransom Fidelity Company
Recognition Equipment
Reflection Riding
Regenstein Foundation
Reidler Foundation
Reinberger Foundation
Rennebohm Foundation, Oscar
Republic New York Corp.
Reynolds Foundation, Richard S.
Reynolds Metals Co.
Rhone-Poulenc Rorer
Rice Foundation
Rich Foundation
Rich Products Corp.
Robinson Foundation
Rochester Gas & Electric Corp.
Rockfall Foundation
Rockford Products Corp.
Rockwell Foundation
Rockwell Fund
Rockwell International Corp.
Rogers Charitable Trust, Florence
Rohm and Haas Company
Rohr Inc.
RosaMary Foundation
Rosenstiel Foundation
Rosenthal Foundation, Benjamin J.
Ross Foundation, Arthur
Ross Laboratories
Rouse Co.
Rudin Foundation
Russell Charitable Trust, Josephine S.
Ryan Foundation, David Claude
Ryan Foundation, Patrick G. and Shirley W.
Sacharuna Foundation
Sachs Fund
SAFECO Corp.
Salomon
Saltonstall Charitable Foundation, Richard
Sams Foundation, Earl C.
San Diego Gas & Electric
Sara Lee Corp.
Sarkeys Foundation

Saunders Foundation
Scherman Foundation
Schey Foundation
Schieffelin Residuary Trust, Sarah I.
Schiff Foundation
Schiff, Hardin & Waite
Schilling Motors
Schlinger Foundation
Scholl Foundation, Dr.
Schrafft and Bertha E. Schrafft Charitable Trust, William E.
Schroeder Foundation, Walter
Schwab & Co., Charles
Schwartz Foundation, David
Schwartz Fund for Education and Health Research, Arnold and Marie
Scott Foundation, William E.
Scott, Jr. Charitable Foundation, Walter
Scripps Foundation, Ellen Browning
Scrivner, Inc.
Scurlock Foundation
Seafirst Corp.
Sears Family Foundation
Seaway Food Town
Security Life of Denver
Sedgwick James Inc.
See Foundation, Charles
Seebee Trust, Frances
Sefton Foundation, J. W.
Setzer Foundation
Shaklee Corp.
Shattuck Charitable Trust, S. F.
Shaw Foundation, Arch W.
Shawmut National Corp.
Sheinberg Foundation, Eric P.
Sheldon Foundation, Ralph C.
Shell Oil Co.
Shelton Cos.
Shenandoah Life Insurance Co.
Shoenberg Foundation
Shook Foundation, Barbara Ingalls
Shoong Foundation, Milton
Shwayder Foundation, Fay
Simon Foundation, Sidney, Milton and Leoma
Simpson Foundation, John M.
Simpson Investment Co.
Siragusa Foundation
Skinner Corp.
Skirball Foundation
Slant/Fin Corp.
Slifka Foundation, Alan B.
Smith Charitable Fund, Eleanor Armstrong
Smith Horticultural Trust, Stanley
Smith, Jr. Foundation, M. W.
Snee-Reinhardt Charitable Foundation
SNET
Snyder Fund, Valentine Perry
Sonat
Sosland Foundation
Souers Charitable Trust, Sidney W. and Sylvia N.
South Branch Foundation
Southern California Edison Co.
Southwestern Bell Corp.
Sprague Educational and Charitable Foundation, Seth
Stackner Family Foundation
Staley, Jr. Foundation, A. E.
Star Bank, N.A.
Starr Foundation
State Street Bank & Trust Co.
Stauffer Foundation, John and Beverly
Steel, Sr. Foundation, Marshall
Steelcase
Steele Foundation, Harry and Grace
Stein Foundation, Jules and Doris
Steiner Corp.

Steinhardt Foundation, Judy and Michael
Steinhauer Charitable Foundation
Sterling Winthrop
Stern Foundation, Leonard N.
Sterne-Elder Memorial Trust
Stevens Foundation, Abbot and Dorothy H.
Stocker Foundation
Stone Container Corp.
Stone Foundation
Stott Foundation, Robert L.
Strake Foundation
Strauss Foundation
Strawbridge Foundation of Pennsylvania II, Margaret Dorrance
Stride Rite Corp.
Stulsaft Foundation, Morris
Stupp Brothers Bridge & Iron Co.
Stupp Foundation, Norman J.
Subaru of America Inc.
Sulzberger Foundation
Sunderland Foundation, Lester T.
Sweatt Foundation, Harold W.
Swensrud Charitable Trust, Sidney A.
Swig Foundation
Swiss Bank Corp.
Synovus Financial Corp.
Talley Industries, Inc.
Tandy Foundation, Anne Burnett and Charles
Tasty Baking Co.
Taylor Foundation, Ruth and Vernon
Teleflex Inc.
Tennant Co.
Tenneco
Texas Commerce Bank Houston, N.A.
Textron
Thanksgiving Foundation
Thatcher Foundation
Thorne Foundation
Thornton Foundation, John M. and Sally B.
Thorson Foundation
3M Co.
Time Insurance Co.
Times Mirror Co.
Timken Co.
Todd Co., A.M.
Tomlinson Foundation, Kate and Elwyn
Tonya Memorial Foundation
Tortuga Foundation
Transamerica Corp.
Transco Energy Company
Trion
Triskelion Ltd.
Truland Foundation
Truman Foundation, Mildred Faulkner
Trusler Foundation
Trust Co. Bank
Trust for Mutual Understanding
TU Electric Co.
Tuch Foundation, Michael
Tucker Charitable Trust, Rose E.
Tucker Foundation, Marcia Brady
Tull Charitable Foundation
Turner Charitable Foundation
Ukrop's Super Markets, Inc.
Unilever United States
Union Bank of Switzerland Los Angeles Branch
Union Camp Corp.
Union Foundation
United Parcel Service of America
United States Trust Co. of New York
Universal Foods Corp.
Universal Leaf Tobacco Co.
Uris Brothers Foundation
USG Corp.
Uvas Foundation

V and V Foundation
Vale-Asche Foundation
Valley National Bank of Arizona
Van Every Foundation, Philip L.
Vanderbilt Trust, R. T.
Vanneck-Bailey Foundation
Vaughan Foundation, Rachael and Ben
Vetlesen Foundation, G. Unger
Vidda Foundation
Vingo Trust II
Vulcan Materials Co.
Wachovia Bank & Trust Co., N.A.
Wade Endowment Fund, Elizabeth Firth
Wal-Mart Stores
Walgreen Co.
Walker Wildlife Conservation Foundation
Wallace Reader's Digest Fund, Lila
Wallach Foundation, Miriam G. and Ira D.
Disney Co., Walt
Walthall Perpetual Charitable Trust, Marjorie T.
Wardlaw Fund, Gertrude and William C.
Warwick Foundation
Washington Water Power Co.
Wasserman Foundation
Waste Management
Wean Foundation, Raymond John
Weatherwax Foundation
Webster Foundation, Edwin S.
Weeden Foundation, Frank
Wehr Foundation, Todd
Weiler Foundation, Theodore & Renee
Wenger Foundation, Henry L. and Consuelo S.
West Co.
West Foundation
West One Bancorp
Western New York Foundation
Western Southern Life Insurance Co.
Westvaco Corp.
Wetterau
Weyerhaeuser Co.
Weyerhaeuser Memorial Foundation, Charles A.
Wharton Trust, William P.
Whirlpool Corp.
Whitaker Charitable Foundation, Lyndon C.
White Consolidated Industries
Whiting Foundation, Macauley and Helen Dow
Whitney Fund, David M.
Whittier Foundation, L. K.
Wickes Foundation, Harvey Randall
Wickson-Link Memorial Foundation
WICOR, Inc.
Widgeon Foundation
Wien Foundation, Lawrence A.
Wiener Foundation, Malcolm Hewitt
Wiley & Sons, Inc., John
Williams Cos.
Wilmington Trust Co.
Wilson Foundation, Elaine P. and Richard U.
Wilson Foundation, Frances Wood
Wilson Foundation, H. W.
Winkler Foundation, Mark and Catherine
Winter Construction Co.
Wisconsin Bell, Inc.
Wisconsin Energy Corp.
Wisconsin Public Service Corp.
Wisdom Foundation, Mary F.
Witter Foundation, Dean

Wolf Foundation, Melvin and Elaine
Woodland Foundation
Woodward Fund
Wortham Foundation
Wouk Foundation, Abe
Wurzburg, Inc.
Wyne Foundation
Wyomissing Foundation
Yeager Charitable Trust, Lester E.
Young Foundation, H and B
Younkers, Inc.
Zaban Foundation
Zachry Co., H. B.
Zarkin Memorial Foundation, Charles
Zemurray Foundation
Zink Foundation, John Steele

Education

Agricultural Education

Agway
ALPAC Corp.
American Electric Power
American Natural Resources Co.
American Saw & Manufacturing Co.
Americana Foundation
Amfac/JMB Hawaii
Andersons Management Corp.
Anheuser-Busch Cos.
Archer-Daniels-Midland Co.
Atlanta Gas Light Co.
Auerbach Foundation, Beatrice Fox
Banc One Illinois Corp.
Bankers Trust Co.
Behmann Brothers Foundation
Boatmen's First National Bank of Oklahoma
Boswell Foundation, James G.
Breidenthal Foundation, Willard J. and Mary G.
Bremer Foundation, Otto
Briggs & Stratton Corp.
Butler Manufacturing Co.
Camp Foundation
Carvel Foundation, Thomas and Agnes
CENEX
Centel Corp.
Central Maine Power Co.
Central Soya Co.
Chesapeake Corp.
Church & Dwight Co.
Clougherty Charitable Trust, Francis H.
Colonial Life & Accident Insurance Co.
ConAgra
Country Curtains, Inc.
Countrymark Cooperative
Cox Charitable Trust, Jessie B.
Cullen/Frost Bankers
Curtice-Burns Foods
Dana Corp.
de Hirsch Fund, Baron
DEC International, Inc.
Deere & Co.
DeKalb Genetics Corp.
Delano Foundation, Mignon Sherwood
Diamond Walnut Growers
Dixie Yarns, Inc.
Donaldson Co.
Dreyfus Foundation, Max and Victoria
du Pont de Nemours & Co., E. I.
Duke Power Co.
Dula Educational and Charitable Foundation, Caleb C. and Julia W.

Educational Foundation of America
Endries Fastener & Supply Co.
Farmland Industries, Inc.
First Interstate Bank of Oregon
First Union Corp.
Flickinger Memorial Trust
Fohs Foundation
Ford Foundation
Ford Meter Box Co.
Foster-Davis Foundation
Foster-Davis Foundation
Frasch Foundation for Chemical Research (under the will of Elizabeth B. Frasch), Herman
Freeport-McMoRan
Funderburke & Associates
Garvey Kansas Foundation
Garvey Texas Foundation
General Mills
General Tire Inc.
Georgia Power Co.
Gerber Products Co.
Ghidotti Foundation, William and Marian
Grace & Co., W.R.
Gray Foundation, Garland
Grinnell Mutual Reinsurance Co.
Habig Foundation, Arnold F.
Haffner Foundation
Halliburton Co.
Hand Industries
Hansen Foundation, Dane G.
Harden Foundation
Harvest States Cooperative
Hatterscheidt Foundation
Hershey Foods Corp.
Homeland Foundation
IES Industries
International Multifoods Corp.
International Student Exchange Cards
ITT Hartford Insurance Group
Jerome Foundation
Johnson Co., E. F.
Johnson Controls
Keene Trust, Hazel R.
Kellogg Foundation, W. K.
Land O'Lakes
Lazar Foundation
Levinson Foundation, Max and Anna
Liberty National Bank
Lytel Foundation, Bertha Russ
May Foundation, Wilbur
McDougall Charitable Trust, Ruth Camp
McIntyre Foundation, C. S. and Marion F.
McLean Contributionship
Mead Corp.
Meadows Foundation
Mellon Foundation, Richard King
Midwest Resources
Missouri Farmers Association
Mobil Oil Corp.
Moorman Manufacturing Co.
Motorola
National Machinery Co.
Nestle U.S.A. Inc.
Newhall Foundation, Henry Mayo
Noble Foundation, Samuel Roberts
Northern Indiana Public Service Co.
Norwest Bank Nebraska
O'Connor Foundation, A. Lindsay and Olive B.
Ohrstrom Foundation
Ore-Ida Foods, Inc.
Parsons - W.D. Charities, Vera Davis
Paul and C. Michael Paul Foundation, Josephine Bay
Phillips Petroleum Co.
Pioneer Hi-Bred International

Powell Family Foundation
Prouty Foundation, Olive Higgins
Quaker Oats Co.
Quanex Corp.
RJR Nabisco Inc.
Rockefeller Foundation
Rockefeller Trust, Winthrop
Rohm and Haas Company
Rubbermaid
Ryan Family Charitable Foundation
Sage Foundation
Sanders Trust, Charles
Santa Fe Pacific Corp.
Sarkeys Foundation
Seafirst Corp.
Sedgwick James Inc.
Sierra Pacific Resources
Smucker Co., J.M.
Sofia American Schools
Strawbridge Foundation of Pennsylvania II, Margaret Dorrance
Stuart Foundation, Elbridge and Evelyn
Sunkist Growers
Temple Foundation, T. L. L.
Terry Foundation
Time Warner Cable
Tyson Foods, Inc.
Unilever United States
Union Camp Corp.
United States Sugar Corp.
Unocal Corp.
Valero Energy Corp.
Wachovia Bank & Trust Co., N.A.
Waggoner Foundation, E. Paul and Helen Buck
Wal-Mart Stores
Wallace Genetic Foundation
Wells Trust Fund, Fred W.
West One Bancorp
White Trust, G. R.
Williams Foundation, Arthur Ashley
Winona Corporation
Wisconsin Public Service Corp.
Zemurray Foundation

Arts Education

Abell Foundation, The
Abrons Foundation, Louis and Anne
Ahmanson Foundation
Alden Trust, George I.
Alice Manufacturing Co.
ALPAC Corp.
Alpert Foundation, Herb
Altman Foundation
American Brands
American Electric Power
American Express Co.
American Financial Corp.
American Natural Resources Co.
Ameritech Services
Ames Charitable Trust, Harriett
Ames Department Stores
AMP
AMR Corp.
Andersen Corp.
Andersen Foundation, Hugh J.
Anheuser-Busch Cos.
Annenberg Foundation
AON Corp.
Apache Corp.
Arcana Foundation
ARCO Chemical
Atherton Family Foundation
Avon Products
Bacardi Imports
Baker Foundation, Dexter F. and Dorothy H.
Bankers Trust Co.
Barra Foundation
Belding Heminway Co.

Arts Education (cont.)

Belfer Foundation
Bell Atlantic Corp.
Bell Industries
Beneficia Foundation
Berger Foundation, H.N. and Frances C.
Biddle Foundation, Mary Duke
Bingham Foundation, William
Binney & Smith Inc.
Blandin Foundation
Block, H&R
Blum-Kovler Foundation
Boatmen's First National Bank of Oklahoma
Bodman Foundation
Booth Ferris Foundation
Booz Allen & Hamilton
Boston Edison Co.
BP America
Brach Foundation, Helen
Bradley-Turner Foundation
Brown Foundation
Bull Foundation, Henry W.
Burdines
Burlington Northern Inc.
Burlington Resources
Burns Foundation, Fritz B.
Cafritz Foundation, Morris and Gwendolyn
Calder Foundation, Louis
Carpenter Foundation, E. Rhodes and Leona B.
Carter Foundation, Amon G.
Cary Charitable Trust, Mary Flagler
Casey Foundation, Eugene B.
CBI Industries
Centerior Energy Corp.
Central Bank of the South
Central Maine Power Co.
Chase Trust, Alice P.
Chemical Bank
Chesebrough-Pond's
Chevron Corp.
Chicago Sun-Times, Inc.
Chicago Tribune Co.
Children's Foundation of Erie County
Church & Dwight Co.
Citicorp
Claneil Foundation
Clark Foundation
Clorox Co.
CM Alliance Cos.
CNA Insurance Cos.
CNG Transmission Corp.
Coca-Cola Co.
Cohen Family Foundation, Saul Z. and Amy Scheuer
Collins Foundation
Colonial Life & Accident Insurance Co.
Commerce Clearing House
Conn Memorial Foundation
Connelly Foundation
Consolidated Papers
Continental Corp.
Corbett Foundation
Country Curtains, Inc.
Cowles Charitable Trust
Cowles Media Co.
Cox Charitable Trust, Jessie B.
Cramer Foundation
Cullen/Frost Bankers
Cummings Foundation, Nathan
Cummins Engine Co.
Daniel Foundation of Alabama
Danner Foundation
Deutsch Co.
Dexter Industries
Diamond Foundation, Aaron
Dimeo Construction Co.

DiRosa Foundation, Rene and Veronica
Dixie Yarns, Inc.
Dodge Foundation, Cleveland H.
Dodge Foundation, Geraldine R.
Dreyfus Foundation, Max and Victoria
Duke Power Co.
duPont Fund, Jessie Ball
Eaton Foundation, Cyrus
Eccles Foundation, Marriner S.
Educational Foundation of America
Edwards Industries
Elf Atochem North America
Emerson Electric Co.
Engelhard Foundation, Charles
English-Bonter-Mitchell Foundation
Equifax
Exxon Corp.
Fairchild Foundation, Sherman
Farallon Foundation
Farish Fund, William Stamps
Federated Department Stores and Allied Stores Corp.
Federation Foundation of Greater Philadelphia
Feinberg Foundation, Joseph and Bessie
Fidelity Bank
Fifth Third Bancorp
Fig Tree Foundation
Firestone Foundation, Roger S.
Firestone, Jr. Foundation, Harvey
First Fidelity Bancorporation
First Maryland Bancorp
First National Bank & Trust Co. of Rockford
First Union Corp.
Fiterman Charitable Foundation, Miles and Shirley
Fletcher Foundation, A. J.
Foote, Cone & Belding Communications
Ford Foundation
Ford Fund, Eleanor and Edsel
Ford Fund, Walter and Josephine
France Foundation, Jacob and Annita
Francis Families Foundation
Franklin Mint Corp.
Frisch's Restaurants Inc.
Fry Foundation, Lloyd A.
Fuller Foundation, George F. and Sybil H.
Funderburke & Associates
Gannett Co.
GAR Foundation
GATX Corp.
General Electric Co.
General Mills
General Motors Corp.
Georgia Power Co.
Gerber Products Co.
Gershman Foundation, Joel
Getty Foundation, Ann and Gordon
Ginter Foundation, Karl and Anna
Ginter Foundation, Karl and Anna
Gitano Group
Gluck Foundation, Maxwell H.
Goldsmith Foundation, Horace W.
Goodman Family Foundation
Gordon/Rousmaniere/Roberts Fund
Gould Foundation, Florence J.
Grace & Co., W.R.
Graham Foundation for Advanced Studies in the Fine Arts
Green Fund
Greene Foundation, Jerome L.
Greenfield Foundation, Albert M.

Greve Foundation, William and Mary
Gries Charity Fund, Lucile and Robert H.
Griggs and Mary Griggs Burke Foundation, Mary Livingston
Guardian Life Insurance Co. of America
Gudelsky Family Foundation, Homer and Martha
Gulfstream Aerospace Corp.
Haas Fund, Walter and Elise
Haggar Foundation
Hall Charitable Trust, Evelyn A. J.
Hall Family Foundations
Hallmark Cards
Hancock Foundation, Luke B.
Hand Industries
Hanes Foundation, John W. and Anna H.
Hansen Foundation, Dane G.
Harden Foundation
Hardin Foundation, Phil
Harkness Ballet Foundation
Harriman Foundation, Mary W.
Harris Foundation, J. Ira and Nicki
Harsco Corp.
Hayden Foundation, Charles
Healy Family Foundation, M. A.
Hechinger Co.
Heckscher Foundation for Children
Heineman Foundation for Research, Educational, Charitable, and Scientific Purposes
Heinz Co., H.J.
Heinz Endowment, Vira I.
Hershey Foods Corp.
Hess Charitable Foundation, Ronne and Donald
Hess Foundation
Heyward Memorial Fund, DuBose and Dorothy
Hiawatha Education Foundation
Higginson Trust, Corina
High Foundation
Hoffberger Foundation
Horne Foundation, Dick
Hospital Corp. of America
Howard and Bush Foundation
Hoyt Foundation, Stewart W. and Willma C.
Huffy Corp.
Hulings Foundation, Mary Andersen
Hunt Manufacturing Co.
Hyde and Watson Foundation
I. and L. Association
Indiana Bell Telephone Co.
Interco
ITT Corp.
Ittleson Foundation
J.P. Morgan & Co.
Jellison Benevolent Society
Jennings Foundation, Martha Holden
Jephson Educational Trust No. 1
Jerome Foundation
Johnson Endeavor Foundation, Christian A.
Johnson & Higgins
Jones Foundation, Daisy Marquis
Jordan Foundation, Arthur
Joyce Foundation
Julia R. and Estelle L. Foundation
Katzenberger Foundation
Kaul Foundation Trust, Hugh
Keating Family Foundation
Kellogg Foundation, W. K.
Kennedy, Jr. Foundation, Joseph P.
Kimberly-Clark Corp.
Kingsbury Corp.
Kiplinger Foundation

Knight Foundation, John S. and James L.
Knox Foundation, Seymour H.
Komes Foundation
Kraft General Foods
Kreielsheimer Foundation Trust
Kress Foundation, Samuel H.
Krieble Foundation, Vernon K.
Kulas Foundation
Kysor Industrial Corp.
L. L. W. W. Foundation
L and L Foundation
Lang Foundation, Eugene M.
Lehman Foundation, Robert
Leviton Manufacturing Co.
Lewis Foundation, Lillian Kaiser
Link, Jr. Foundation, George
List Foundation, Albert A.
Little Family Foundation
Littlefield Memorial Trust, Ida Ballou
Liz Claiborne
Loeb Partners Corp.
Long Foundation, George A. and Grace
Loughran Foundation, Mary and Daniel
Love Foundation, Martha and Spencer
Lowe Foundation, Joe and Emily
Lowenstein Foundation, Leon
Luce Foundation, Henry
Lukens
Lyndhurst Foundation
Manilow Foundation, Nathan
Mann Foundation, Ted
Manoogian Foundation, Alex and Marie
Mark IV Industries
Marquette Electronics
Marshall Field's
Marshall & Ilsley Bank
Mayer Foundation, Louis B.
MCA
McCaw Cellular Communications
McCormick Tribune Foundation, Robert R.
McCune Charitable Trust, John R.
McDermott Foundation, Eugene
McDonald's Corp.
McElroy Trust, R. J.
McIntosh Foundation
MCJ Foundation
McShain Charities, John
Mead Corp.
Meadows Foundation
Mellon Foundation, Andrew W.
Mellon Foundation, Richard King
Meredith Corp.
Merrick Foundation, Robert G. and Anne M.
Mervyn's
Metropolitan Life Insurance Co.
Meyer Foundation, Eugene and Agnes E.
Meyer Foundation, Robert R.
Meyer Memorial Trust
Michigan Bell Telephone Co.
Middendorf Foundation
Mitsubishi Electric America
Mobil Oil Corp.
Monell Foundation, Ambrose
Morgan Stanley & Co.
Morris Foundation, William T.
Morrison-Knudsen Corp.
Moses Fund, Henry and Lucy
Murphy Foundation
National Computer Systems
NBD Bank
New England Mutual Life Insurance Co.
New Street Capital Corp.
New York Life Insurance Co.
New York Telephone Co.
The New Yorker Magazine, Inc.

Newhouse Foundation, Samuel I.
Noble Foundation, Edward John
Nordson Corp.
Norfolk Southern Corp.
Northern Indiana Public Service Co.
Norton Co.
Ogden Foundation, Ralph E.
Ogilvy & Mather Worldwide
Oklahoman Foundation
Orchard Corp. of America.
Osceola Foundation
Osher Foundation, Bernard
Overbrook Foundation
PACCAR
Pacific Enterprises
Pacific Telesis Group
PacifiCorp
Packaging Corporation of America
Packard Foundation, David and Lucile
Parsons Foundation, Ralph M.
Peabody Charitable Fund, Amelia
Peery Foundation
Penn Foundation, William
Penzance Foundation
Perkins Memorial Foundation, George W.
Perot Foundation
Persis Corp.
Pew Charitable Trusts
Philibosian Foundation, Stephen
Philip Morris Cos.
Philips Foundation, Jesse
Picower Foundation, Jeffrey M. and Barbara
Pines Bridge Foundation
Pinkerton Foundation
Pittway Corp.
Plough Foundation
Polaroid Corp.
Poorvu Foundation, William and Lia
Porter Testamentary Trust, James Hyde
Price Associates, T. Rowe
Pritzker Foundation
Procter & Gamble Cosmetic & Fragrance Products
Providence Journal Company
Prudential Insurance Co. of America
Putnam Foundation
Ralston Purina Co.
Ramlose Foundation, George A.
Raymond Educational Foundation
Reinberger Foundation
Reliable Life Insurance Co.
Reliance Electric Co.
Rice Foundation
Richardson Foundation, Smith
RJR Nabisco Inc.
Robinson Fund, Maurice R.
Rockefeller Foundation
Rohm and Haas Company
Rose Foundation, Billy
Rosenstiel Foundation
Rouse Co.
Rowland Foundation
Rubinstein Foundation, Helena
SAFECO Corp.
Safeguard Scientifics Foundation
Sage Foundation
Salomon
San Diego Gas & Electric
Sara Lee Corp.
Scherer Foundation, Karla
Schering-Plough Corp.
Scherman Foundation
Schlumberger Ltd.
Scholl Foundation, Dr.
Schroeder Foundation, Walter
Seafirst Corp.
Searle & Co., G.D.
Sears Family Foundation

Seaway Food Town
Security Life of Denver
Sedgwick James Inc.
Seid Foundation, Barre
Selby and Marie Selby
  Foundation, William G.
Self Foundation
Sharp Foundation, Evelyn
Shawmut National Corp.
Shelton Cos.
Simon Charitable Trust, Esther
Simon Foundation, William E.
  and Carol G.
Simpson PSB Foundation
Skinner Corp.
Smith Foundation, Kelvin and
  Eleanor
Smyth Trust, Marion C.
Sony Corp. of America
Sosland Foundation
Sotheby's
South Branch Foundation
Southwestern Bell Corp.
Speyer Foundation, Alexander C.
  and Tillie S.
Sprague Educational and
  Charitable Foundation, Seth
Springs Industries
Square D Co.
Star Bank, N.A.
Starling Foundation, Dorothy
  Richard
Starr Foundation
State Street Bank & Trust Co.
Steelcase
Steinman Foundation, John
  Frederick
Stoddard Charitable Trust
Stone Container Corp.
Stride Rite Corp.
Stulsaft Foundation, Morris
Summerfield Foundation, Solon
  E.
Taylor Foundation, Ruth and
  Vernon
Tektronix
Textron
3M Co.
Times Mirror Co.
Transco Energy Company
Trexler Trust, Harry C.
Trust Co. Bank
Union Bank
Union Bank of Switzerland Los
  Angeles Branch
United Airlines
U.S. Leasing International
Unitrode Corp.
Unocal Corp.
Upton Foundation, Frederick S.
Uris Brothers Foundation
USF&G Co.
USX Corp.
Wallace Reader's Digest Fund,
  Lila
Disney Co., Walt
Warhol Foundation for the Visual
  Arts, Andy
Wasmer Foundation
Wasserman Foundation
Wean Foundation, Raymond John
Weezie Foundation
Weinberg, Jr. Foundation, Sidney
  J.
Weingart Foundation
Wendt Foundation, Margaret L.
West Foundation
West One Bancorp
Whirlpool Corp.
Wiegand Foundation, E. L.
Williams Charitable Trust, Mary
  Jo
Wilson Fund, Matilda R.
Winter Construction Co.
Wisconsin Energy Corp.
Woodner Family Collection, Ian

Woods Charitable Fund
Xerox Corp.
XTEK Inc.
Yassenoff Foundation, Leo
Yellow Corp.
Zilkha & Sons

Business Education

Abbott Laboratories
AFLAC
Air Products & Chemicals
Alberto-Culver Co.
Albertson's
Algonquin Energy, Inc.
Allegheny Ludlum Corp.
Allendale Mutual Insurance Co.
Alliant Techsystems
Allstate Insurance Co.
Alltel/Western Region
ALPAC Corp.
Alumax
Aluminum Co. of America
AMAX
AMCORE Bank, N.A. Rockford
America West Airlines
American Brands
American Cyanamid Co.
American Express Co.
American Financial Corp.
American General Finance
American Microsystems, Inc.
American Natural Resources Co.
American Stock Exchange
American Telephone &
  Telegraph Co.
Ameritas Life Insurance Corp.
Ameritech Publishing
Ames Department Stores
Amfac/JMB Hawaii
Amoco Corp.
AMP
Anderson Foundation, M. D.
Angelica Corp.
Archer-Daniels-Midland Co.
Arizona Public Service Co.
Armco Steel Co.
Atlanta Gas Light Co.
Attleboro Pawtucket Savings
  Bank
Avon Products
Babcock & Wilcox Co.
Baird & Co., Robert W.
Bally Inc.
Banc One Wisconsin Corp.
Bank IV
Bank of Boston Corp.
Bank of Louisville
Bank One, Youngstown, NA
BankAmerica Corp.
Bankers Trust Co.
BarclaysAmerican Corp.
Barden Corp.
Barnes Group
Battelle
Batten Foundation
Belden Brick Co., Inc.
Benefit Trust Life Insurance Co.
Bergner Co., P.A.
Berwind Corp.
Bethlehem Steel Corp.
BFGoodrich
Binney & Smith Inc.
Biomet
Bloch Foundation, Henry W. and
  Marion H.
Block, H&R
Blount
Blue Bell, Inc.
Blue Cross & Blue Shield of
  Kentucky Foundation
Boatmen's Bancshares
Boatmen's First National Bank
  of Oklahoma
Boeing Co.
Boh Brothers Construction Co.
Boise Cascade Corp.

Booz Allen & Hamilton
Borden
Bosch Corp., Robert
Boston Edison Co.
Botwinick-Wolfensohn
  Foundation
Bowater Inc.
Bozzone Family Foundation
Bradford & Co., J.C.
Bridgestone/Firestone
Bristol-Myers Squibb Co.
Brooks Brothers
Brooks Foundation, Gladys
Brown & Sons, Alex
Browning-Ferris Industries
Brunswick Corp.
Bucyrus-Erie
Burdines
Burlington Northern Inc.
Burns Family Foundation
Burns Foundation, Jacob
Butler Family Foundation,
  George W. and Gladys S.
Cabot Corp.
California & Hawaiian Sugar Co.
Campbell Soup Co.
Capital Cities/ABC
Capital Holding Corp.
Cascade Natural Gas Corp.
Caterpillar
CBI Industries
Ceco Corp.
Centel Corp.
Central Maine Power Co.
Central & South West Services
Central Soya Co.
Charina Foundation
Chase Manhattan Bank, N.A.
Chevron Corp.
Chiles Foundation
Chrysler Corp.
Church & Dwight Co.
Citicorp
Cleveland-Cliffs
Clorox Co.
CM Alliance Cos.
CNA Insurance Cos.
CNG Transmission Corp.
Coca-Cola Co.
Coleman Co.
Coleman Foundation
Coles Family Foundation
Colonial Life & Accident
  Insurance Co.
Colonial Oil Industries, Inc.
Coltec Industries
Columbia Foundation
Columbus Dispatch Printing Co.
ConAgra
Cone Mills Corp.
Conoco Inc.
Consolidated Natural Gas Co.
Consolidated Papers
Consolidated Rail Corp. (Conrail)
Continental Corp.
Continental Grain Co.
Contraves USA
Control Data Corp.
Cook Foundation
Cooper Industries
Coors Brewing Co.
Coors Foundation, Adolph
Cowles Media Co.
CPC International
CR Industries
Crestar Financial Corp.
CRL Inc.
Crum and Forster
CTS Corp.
Cullen/Frost Bankers
Cummins Engine Co.
CUNA Mutual Insurance Group
Cyprus Minerals Co.
Dai-Ichi Kangyo Bank of
  California
Dain Bosworth/Inter-Regional
  Financial Group

Dana Corp.
Davenport-Hatch Foundation
Dean Witter Discover
DEC International, Inc.
Dekko Foundation
Delaware North Cos.
Demoulas Supermarkets
Dennison Manufacturing Co.
Detroit Edison Co.
Devereaux Foundation
Diamond Shamrock
Dickson Foundation
Dimeo Construction Co.
Dingman Foundation, Michael D.
Dively Foundation, George S.
Donaldson Co.
Donaldson, Lufkin & Jenrette
du Pont de Nemours & Co., E. I.
Duke Power Co.
Dun & Bradstreet Corp.
Duriron Co., Inc.
East Ohio Gas Co.
Eaton Corp.
Eccles Foundation, George S.
  and Dolores Dore
Ecolab
EG&G Inc.
Elf Atochem North America
Ellis Fund
Emerson Electric Co.
Encyclopaedia Britannica, Inc.
Enron Corp.
Equifax
Equitable Life Assurance Society
  of the U.S.
Ernest & Julio Gallo Winery
Ernst & Young
Exxon Corp.
Fair Oaks Foundation, Inc.
Federal-Mogul Corp.
Federated Department Stores and
  Allied Stores Corp.
Federated Life Insurance Co.
Fidelity Bank
Fieldcrest Cannon
Fireman's Fund Insurance Co.
First Bank System
First Boston
First Chicago
First Hawaiian
First Interstate Bank of Arizona
First Interstate Bank of California
First Interstate Bank of Oregon
First Interstate Bank of Texas,
  N.A.
First Maryland Bancorp
First Mississippi Corp.
First Petroleum Corp.
First Union Corp.
Firstar Bank Milwaukee NA
FirsTier Bank N.A. Omaha
Florida Power & Light Co.
FMC Corp.
Fondren Foundation
Foote, Cone & Belding
  Communications
Ford Motor Co.
Fortis Benefits Insurance
  Company/Fortis Financial
  Group
Franklin Foundation, John and
  Mary
Fraser Paper Ltd.
Freeport-McMoRan
Funderburke & Associates
Fuqua Foundation, J. B.
Gabelli Foundation
Gear Motion
GEICO Corp.
GenCorp
General Accident Insurance Co.
  of America
General American Life Insurance
  Co.
General Electric Co.
General Mills
General Motors Corp.

General Signal Corp.
Georgia-Pacific Corp.
Georgia Power Co.
Gerber Products Co.
Gillette Co.
Glaxo
Goldsmith Foundation, Horace
  W.
Golub Corp.
Goodyear Tire & Rubber Co.
Gordon Foundation, Meyer and
  Ida
Gould Inc.
Grace & Co., W.R.
Graco
Graphic Controls Corp.
Great-West Life Assurance Co.
Great Western Financial Corp.
Gregg-Graniteville Foundation
GTE Corp.
Guardian Life Insurance Co. of
  America
Haas, Jr. Fund, Evelyn and
  Walter
Hagler Foundation, Jon L.
Halliburton Co.
Hallmark Cards
Hamel Family Charitable Trust,
  D. A.
HarCo. Drug
Harsco Corp.
Hartmarx Corp.
Harvey Foundation, Felix
Hawkins Foundation, Robert Z.
Hechinger Co.
Hecla Mining Co.
HEI Inc.
Heinz Co., H.J.
Hershey Foods Corp.
Herzstein Charitable Foundation,
  Albert and Ethel
Hess Foundation
Hewlett-Packard Co.
Hillcrest Foundation
Hobbs Charitable Trust, John H.
HON Industries
Honeywell
Hopper Memorial Foundation,
  Bertrand
Hospital Corp. of America
Household International
Hubbard Broadcasting
Huffy Corp.
Humana
Hurford Foundation
Illinois Power Co.
Illinois Tool Works
IMCERA Group Inc.
IMT Insurance Co.
Inco Alloys International
Indiana Bell Telephone Co.
Indiana Insurance Cos.
Inland Container Corp.
Inland Steel Industries
International Flavors &
  Fragrances
International Multifoods Corp.
International Student Exchange
  Cards
Itoh (C.) International
  (America), Inc.
ITT Corp.
ITT Hartford Insurance Group
J.P. Morgan & Co.
JCPenney Co.
Jennings Foundation, Alma
John Hancock Mutual Life
  Insurance Co.
Johnson Co., E. F.
Johnson Controls
Johnson & Higgins
Johnson & Son, S.C.
Jostens
JSJ Corp.
Kautz Family Foundation
Kearney Inc., A.T.
Kellogg Foundation, W. K.

Business Education (cont.)

Kellstadt Foundation
Kemper National Insurance Cos.
Kennecott Corp.
Kidder, Peabody & Co.
Kimberly-Clark Corp.
King Ranch
KPMG Peat Marwick
Krimendahl II Foundation, H.
  Frederick
Ladish Co.
Land O'Lakes
Landmark Communications
Lautenberg Foundation
Liberty Hosiery Mills
Liberty National Bank
Life Insurance Co. of Georgia
Lincoln Electric Co.
Lipton Foundation
Lipton, Thomas J.
Little Family Foundation
Llagas Foundation
Long Foundation, J.M.
Long Island Lighting Co.
Lowe Foundation, Joe and Emily
Lowenstein Foundation, Leon
LTV Corp.
Lubrizol Corp.
Lydall, Inc.
Macy & Co., R.H.
Magma Copper Co.
Magruder Foundation, Chesley
  G.
Mankato Citizens Telephone Co.
Manville Corp.
Marathon Oil, Indiana Refining
  Division
Marinette Marine Corp.
Marion Merrell Dow
Marion Merrell Dow
Marley Co.
Mars Foundation
Marsh & McLennan Cos.
Marshall & Ilsley Bank
Martin Marietta Corp.
Marubeni America Corp.
Massey Foundation
May Department Stores Co.
Maytag Corp.
MBIA, Inc.
MCA
McCasland Foundation
McCormick & Co.
McCormick Tribune Foundation,
  Robert R.
McDonald & Co. Securities
McDonnell Douglas Corp.
McGraw-Hill
MCI Communications Corp.
MCJ Foundation
McKenna Foundation, Philip M.
McWane Inc.
Mead Corp.
Meadows Foundation
Mechanics Bank
Media General, Inc.
Melitta North America Inc.
Mellon Bank Corp.
Mellon Foundation, Richard King
Melville Corp.
Menasha Corp.
Merrill Lynch & Co.
Metropolitan Life Insurance Co.
Michigan Bell Telephone Co.
Milliken & Co.
Mills Foundation, Ralph E.
Mine Safety Appliances Co.
Minnesota Mutual Life
  Insurance Co.
Mitsubishi International Corp.
MNC Financial
Mobil Oil Corp.
Monroe-Brown Foundation
Moore Foundation, Edward S.

Motch Corp.
Motorola
Multimedia, Inc.
Nalco Chemical Co.
Nathan Berkman & Co.
National City Corp.
National Computer Systems
National Westminster Bank New
  Jersey
NationsBank Corp.
Navistar International Corp.
NBD Bank
New England Mutual Life
  Insurance Co.
New York Life Insurance Co.
New York Telephone Co.
Nissan Motor Corporation in
  U.S.A.
Noble Foundation, Samuel
  Roberts
Nomura Securities International
Nordson Corp.
Norfolk Southern Corp.
Northern Indiana Public Service
  Co.
Northern States Power Co.
Northwest Natural Gas Co.
Northwestern National Life
  Insurance Co.
Norton Co.
NYNEX Corp.
Ogilvy & Mather Worldwide
Oglebay Norton Co.
Olin Charitable Trust, John M.
Olin Corp.
Olin Foundation, John M.
O'Neill Charitable Corporation,
  F. J.
Ontario Corp.
Overnite Transportation Co.
PACCAR
Pacific Enterprises
Pacific Mutual Life Insurance Co.
Pacific Telesis Group
Packaging Corporation of
  America
Palisades Educational Foundation
Pan-American Life Insurance Co.
Panhandle Eastern Corp.
Paramount Communications Inc.
Parker-Hannifin Corp.
Peierls Foundation
Pennzoil Co.
Perini Corp.
Perkin-Elmer Corp.
Pet
Pfizer
Phelps Dodge Corp.
PHH Corp.
Philadelphia Electric Co.
Philip Morris Cos.
Phillips Petroleum Co.
Pillsbury Co.
Pincus Family Fund
Pinkerton Foundation
Piper Jaffray Cos.
Pittway Corp.
Polaroid Corp.
Poorvu Foundation, William and
  Lia
Portland General Electric Co.
Powell Family Foundation
PPG Industries
Premier Bank
Premier Industrial Corp.
Price Associates, T. Rowe
Price Foundation, Louis and
  Harold
Price Waterhouse-U.S.
Principal Financial Group
Procter & Gamble Cosmetic &
  Fragrance Products
Prudential Insurance Co. of
  America
Public Service Co. of Colorado
Public Service Electric & Gas
  Co.

Puget Sound Power & Light Co.
Pulitzer Publishing Co.
Quaker Oats Co.
Questar Corp.
Raymond Corp.
Red Wing Shoe Co.
Regis Corp.
Reichhold Chemicals, Inc.
Reliance Electric Co.
Reynolds Foundation, Donald W.
Reynolds Foundation, Richard S.
RGK Foundation
Rhone-Poulenc Rorer
Rich Products Corp.
Richardson Foundation, Smith
Rinker Materials Corp.
RJR Nabisco Inc.
Roberts Foundation,
  Summerfield G.
Robertshaw Controls Co.
Rockwell International Corp.
Rohm and Haas Company
Rohr Inc.
Rosenberg, Jr. Family
  Foundation, Louise and Claude
Rosenbloom Foundation, Ben
  and Esther
Rouse Co.
Royal Group Inc.
Ruan Foundation Trust, John
Rubbermaid
Rubin Family Fund, Cele H. and
  William B.
Ruddick Corp.
Ryder System
SAFECO Corp.
Salomon
San Diego Gas & Electric
Santa Fe Pacific Corp.
Sara Lee Corp.
Sara Lee Hosiery
Schering-Plough Corp.
Schiff Foundation
Schwab & Co., Charles
Science Applications
  International Corp.
Scrivner, Inc.
Seafirst Corp.
Seagram & Sons, Joseph E.
Sealright Co., Inc.
Sears, Roebuck and Co.
Security Life of Denver
Sedgwick James Inc.
Servco Pacific
Shawmut National Corp.
Shawmut Worcester County
  Bank, N.A.
Shell Oil Co.
Shelter Mutual Insurance Co.
Shenandoah Life Insurance Co.
Sherwin-Williams Co.
Shoney's Inc.
Signet Bank/Maryland
Simon Foundation, William E.
  and Carol G.
Simpson Investment Co.
Simpson PSB Foundation
SIT Investment Associates, Inc.
Skandia America Reinsurance
  Corp.
Skinner Corp.
Smith Corp., A.O.
Smith Foundation, Kelvin and
  Eleanor
SNET
Snow Memorial Trust, John Ben
Society Corp.
Sonat
Sonoco Products Co.
South Bend Tribune
Southern California Edison Co.
Southwestern Bell Corp.
Springs Industries
Sprint
SPX Corp.
Square D Co.
Stanley Works

Star Bank, N.A.
Starr Foundation
State Farm Mutual Automobile
  Insurance Co.
Steinbach Fund, Ruth and Milton
Stone Container Corp.
Stone Family Foundation,
  Jerome H.
Stone & Webster, Inc.
Storage Technology Corp.
Stott Foundation, Robert L.
Strake Foundation
Stranahan Foundation
Stuart Foundation, Elbridge and
  Evelyn
Subaru of America Inc.
Sumitomo Bank of California
Summerfield Foundation, Solon
  E.
Sun Co.
Sun Microsystems
Sunmark Capital Corp.
Swim Foundation, Arthur L.
Tandem Computers
TCF Banking & Savings, FSB
Teledyne
Tenneco
Tesoro Petroleum Corp.
Texaco
Texas Commerce Bank Houston,
  N.A.
Texas Gas Transmission Corp.
Texas Instruments
Textron
Thermo Electron Corp.
3M Co.
Times Mirror Co.
Timken Co.
Tisch Foundation
Titan Industrial Co.
TJX Cos.
Tokheim Corp.
Tomkins Industries, Inc.
Transco Energy Company
TRINOVA Corp.
Tropicana Products, Inc.
Trust Co. Bank
Tyler Corp.
Tyson Foods, Inc.
Unilever United States
Union Bank
Union Camp Corp.
United Airlines
United Merchants &
  Manufacturers
United Parcel Service of America
United Technologies Corp.
Unitrode Corp.
Univar Corp.
Universal Foods Corp.
Unocal Corp.
US Bancorp
US WEST
USF&G Co.
USX Corp.
Valley Foundation
Valley National Bank of Arizona
Valmont Industries
Valspar Corp.
Varian Associates
Vogt Machine Co., Henry
Volkswagen of America, Inc.
Vollbrecht Foundation, Frederick
  A.
Wachovia Bank & Trust Co.,
  N.A.
Wachtell, Lipton, Rosen & Katz
Wal-Mart Stores
Waldorf Educational Foundation
Disney Co., Walt
Walter Industries
Washington Water Power Co.
Webb Foundation
Wedum Foundation
Weinberg Foundation, John L.
Weinberg, Jr. Foundation, Sidney
  J.

Wells Fargo & Co.
West One Bancorp
Westvaco Corp.
Weyerhaeuser Co.
Whirlpool Corp.
Whitehead Foundation
WICOR, Inc.
Wiegand Foundation, E. L.
Williams Cos.
Winter Construction Co.
Wisconsin Energy Corp.
Wisconsin Public Service Corp.
Witco Corp.
Witter Foundation, Dean
Wollenberg Foundation
Xerox Corp.
Yellow Corp.
Young & Rubicam
Younkers, Inc.

Career/Vocational Education

Abraham & Straus
Achelis Foundation
Air France
Air Products & Chemicals
Albany International Corp.
Alcon Laboratories, Inc.
Allegheny Ludlum Corp.
Allendale Mutual Insurance Co.
Allstate Insurance Co.
Alltel/Western Region
ALPAC Corp.
Altman Foundation
Alumax
AMCORE Bank, N.A. Rockford
America West Airlines
American Brands
American Express Co.
American Natural Resources Co.
American Saw & Manufacturing
  Co.
Amfac/JMB Hawaii
AMP
Andersen Corp.
Anderson Foundation, John W.
Anheuser-Busch Cos.
Annenberg Foundation
Ashland Oil
Atlanta Gas Light Co.
Attleboro Pawtucket Savings
  Bank
Avon Products
Banc One Wisconsin Corp.
Bankers Trust Co.
Barth Foundation, Theodore H.
Batten Foundation
Bechtel Charitable Remainder
  Uni-Trust, Marie H.
Beckman Foundation, Leland D.
Beech Aircraft Corp.
Bemis Company
Benefit Trust Life Insurance Co.
Bethlehem Steel Corp.
Binney & Smith Inc.
Block, H&R
Blue Cross and Blue Shield
  United of Wisconsin
  Foundation
BMW of North America, Inc.
Boatmen's First National Bank
  of Oklahoma
Bodman Foundation
Boeing Co.
Boise Cascade Corp.
Bonfils-Stanton Foundation
Borg-Warner Corp.
Boston Edison Co.
Bovaird Foundation, Mervin
Bozzone Family Foundation
BP America
Brach Foundation, Helen
Bremer Foundation, Otto
Bridgestone/Firestone
Brunswick Corp.

Bryan Foundation, James E. and Mary Z.
Bucyrus-Erie
Buhl Foundation
Burden Foundation, Florence V.
Burlington Resources
Burndy Corp.
Burroughs Wellcome Co.
Cablevision of Michigan
Cabot Corp.
Cahill Foundation, John R.
Calder Foundation, Louis
Cameron Foundation, Harry S. and Isabel C.
Capital Holding Corp.
Carbon Fuel Co.
Carpenter Technology Corp.
Carr Real Estate Services
CBI Industries
Centerior Energy Corp.
Central Maine Power Co.
Central Vermont Public Service Corp.
Century Companies of America
Chevron Corp.
Chicago Tribune Co.
Christian Dior New York, Inc.
Chrysler Corp.
Cincinnati Bell
Citicorp
Clark Foundation
Clay Foundation
Clemens Foundation
Clorox Co.
CM Alliance Cos.
CNA Insurance Cos.
CNG Transmission Corp.
Cole Foundation
Collins & Aikman Holdings Corp.
Commonwealth Fund
Consolidated Natural Gas Co.
Consolidated Papers
Cooper Industries
Coors Brewing Co.
Country Curtains, Inc.
Countrymark Cooperative
Cowell Foundation, S. H.
Cowles Media Co.
CPC International
CR Industries
Crum and Forster
CT Corp. System
Cullen/Frost Bankers
Dana Corp.
Dayton Hudson Corp.
Delaware North Cos.
Detroit Edison Co.
Dolan Family Foundation
Donaldson Co.
Douglas & Lomason Company
Dresser Industries
Dreyfus Foundation, Max and Victoria
du Pont de Nemours & Co., E. I.
Duke Power Co.
Eaton Corp.
Eccles Foundation, Marriner S.
Elf Atochem North America
Elizabethtown Gas Co.
English-Bonter-Mitchell Foundation
Enron Corp.
Enterprise Rent-A-Car Co.
Equitable Life Assurance Society of the U.S.
Exxon Corp.
Federal-Mogul Corp.
Federated Life Insurance Co.
Fel-Pro Incorporated
Fidelity Bank
Fieldcrest Cannon
First Interstate Bank of Oregon
First Maryland Bancorp
First Union Corp.
Flickinger Memorial Trust
Ford Foundation

Formrite Tube Co.
Fox Inc.
Freedom Forum
Frisch's Restaurants Inc.
Fry Foundation, Lloyd A.
Funderburke & Associates
Gannett Co.
GATX Corp.
General American Life Insurance Co.
General Mills
General Motors Corp.
German Marshall Fund of the United States
Giant Food Stores
Gitano Group
Grace & Co., W.R.
Graco
Graphic Controls Corp.
Great-West Life Assurance Co.
Gregg-Graniteville Foundation
Gries Charity Fund, Lucile and Robert H.
Grimes Foundation, Otha H.
Hancock Foundation, Luke B.
Hankins Foundation
Hansen Foundation, Dane G.
Hartmarx Corp.
Hayden Foundation, Charles
Hebrew Technical Institute
Hechinger Co.
HEI Inc.
Heydt Fund, Nan and Matilda
Higgins Foundation, Aldus C.
Hillcrest Foundation
Home Depot
Honeywell
Hospital Corp. of America
Hubbard Broadcasting
Humana
Humphrey Foundation, Glenn & Gertrude
Humphrey Fund, George M. and Pamela S.
IBM South Africa Projects Fund
ICI Americas
IES Industries
Illinois Power Co.
Inland Container Corp.
Interco
Intercontinental Hotels Corp.
International Student Exchange Cards
ITT Corp.
Janesville Foundation
JCPenney Co.
JFM Foundation
John Hancock Mutual Life Insurance Co.
Johnson Controls
Johnson & Higgins
Jostens
JSJ Corp.
Justus Trust, Edith C.
Kellogg Foundation, W. K.
Kennecott Corp.
Kidder, Peabody & Co.
Kilmartin Industries
Kingsbury Corp.
Laclede Gas Co.
Laffey-McHugh Foundation
Lee Endowment Foundation
Leo Burnett Co.
Levi Strauss & Co.
Liberty National Bank
Lincoln Electric Co.
Lincoln Fund
Little, Arthur D.
Long Island Lighting Co.
Louisiana Land & Exploration Co.
Lowenstein Brothers Foundation
Ludwick Institute
Lux Foundation, Miranda
Macy & Co., R.H.
Makita U.S.A., Inc.
Marion Merrell Dow

Marshall Field's
Martin Marietta Corp.
Massachusetts Charitable Mechanics Association
McCasland Foundation
McCune Foundation
McDonald's Corp.
McDonnell Douglas Corp.
MCI Communications Corp.
McInerny Foundation
McMahon Foundation
McShain Charities, John
Mead Corp.
Meadows Foundation
Mellon Bank Corp.
Melville Corp.
Mercedes-Benz of North America, Inc.
Metropolitan Life Insurance Co.
Michigan Consolidated Gas Co.
Michigan Gas Utilities
Midwest Resources
Miller Foundation, Earl B. and Loraine H.
Milliken & Co.
Minnegasco
MNC Financial
Mobil Oil Corp.
Morgan Stanley & Co.
Motorola
MTS Systems Corp.
Nalco Chemical Co.
National Computer Systems
National Gypsum Co.
National Life of Vermont
National Presto Industries
National Westminster Bank New Jersey
NBD Bank
Nestle U.S.A. Inc.
New World Foundation
New York Foundation
New York Mercantile Exchange
New York Telephone Co.
New York Times Co.
Nias Foundation, Henry
Nissan Motor Corporation in U.S.A.
Noble Foundation, Samuel Roberts
North American Reinsurance Corp.
Northern States Power Co.
Northwestern National Life Insurance Co.
Norton Co.
NuTone Inc.
NYNEX Corp.
Oglebay Norton Co.
1525 Foundation
Ontario Corp.
Ormet Corp.
Oxford Industries, Inc.
Pacific Gas & Electric Co.
Pacific Mutual Life Insurance Co.
Packaging Corporation of America
Padnos Iron & Metal Co., Louis
Panhandle Eastern Corp.
Paramount Communications Inc.
Penn Foundation, William
Pet
Pettus, Jr. Foundation, James T.
Pew Charitable Trusts
Pfizer
Phillips Family Foundation, L. E.
Pillsbury Co.
Piton Foundation
Polaroid Corp.
Portland General Electric Co.
Principal Financial Group
Pritzker Foundation
Procter & Gamble Cosmetic & Fragrance Products
Providence Journal Company
Prudential Insurance Co. of America

Public Service Electric & Gas Co.
Quaker Oats Co.
Questar Corp.
Ralston Purina Co.
Republic New York Corp.
Reynolds Metals Co.
Riley Foundation, Mabel Louise
Rockwell International Corp.
Rohm and Haas Company
Roseburg Forest Products Co.
Royal Group Inc.
Rubin Foundation, Samuel
Saint Paul Cos.
San Diego Gas & Electric
Sandoz Corp.
Sara Lee Corp.
Sara Lee Hosiery
Scaife Family Foundation
Schieffelin & Somerset Co.
Science Applications International Corp.
Scrivner, Inc.
Seafirst Corp.
Searle & Co., G.D.
Sears, Roebuck and Co.
Sedgwick James Inc.
Selby and Marie Selby Foundation, William G.
Servistar Corp.
Shawmut National Corp.
Shell Oil Co.
Signet Bank/Maryland
Simon Foundation, William E. and Carol G.
Simpson Investment Co.
Slemp Foundation
Smith Foundation, Kelvin and Eleanor
Sony Corp. of America
Southern Bell
Southern California Edison Co.
Southern California Gas Co.
Southwestern Bell Corp.
Spiegel
Springs Industries
Star Bank, N.A.
Statler Foundation
Sterling Winthrop
Stockham Valves & Fittings
Stone Container Corp.
Stulsaft Foundation, Morris
Sun Microsystems
Technical Foundation of America
Technical Training Foundation
Teledyne
Tenneco
Texaco
Textron
Thermo Electron Corp.
3M Co.
Times Mirror Co.
Tippit Charitable Trust, C. Carlisle and Margaret M.
TJX Cos.
Torchmark Corp.
Tropicana Products, Inc.
Turrell Fund
Twentieth Century-Fox Film Corp.
Unilever United States
Union Camp Corp.
United Airlines
United Parcel Service of America
United Technologies Corp.
Unitrode Corp.
Universal Foods Corp.
Unocal Corp.
USX Corp.
Vesper Corp.
Vogt Machine Co., Henry
Volkswagen of America, Inc.
Vollbrecht Foundation, Frederick A.
Wachovia Bank & Trust Co., N.A.
Wal-Mart Stores

Wallace Genetic Foundation
Wallace-Reader's Digest Fund, DeWitt
Wedum Foundation
Weller Foundation
Wells Fargo & Co.
Whirlpool Corp.
Williams Cos.
Wilson Fund, Matilda R.
Winter Construction Co.
Wisconsin Public Service Corp.
Xerox Corp.
Yeager Charitable Trust, Lester E.
Zollner Foundation

Colleges & Universities

Abbott Laboratories
Abel Construction Co.
Abeles Foundation, Joseph and Sophia
Abell-Hanger Foundation
Abercrombie Foundation
Abernethy Testamentary Charitable Trust, Maye Morrison
Abitibi-Price
Abney Foundation
Abraham Foundation
Abraham Foundation, Anthony R.
Abraham & Straus
Abrams Foundation
Abrams Foundation, Benjamin and Elizabeth
Abrams Foundation, Talbert and Leota
Abramson Family Foundation
Abreu Charitable Trust u/w/o May P. Abreu, Francis I.
Abroms Charitable Foundation
Abrons Foundation, Louis and Anne
Ace Beverage Co.
ACF Industries, Inc.
Acme-Cleveland Corp.
Acme United Corp.
Acushnet Co.
Acushnet Co.
Ada Foundation, Julius
Adams Foundation, Arthur F. and Alice E.
Adams Trust, Charles E. and Caroline J.
Adler Foundation
Adler Foundation Trust, Philip D. and Henrietta B.
Advanced Micro Devices
AEC Trust
AEGON USA, Inc.
Aequus Institute
Aeroflex Foundation
Aetna Life & Casualty Co.
AFLAC
AGFA Division of Miles Inc.
Agway
Ahmanson Foundation
Air Products & Chemicals
AKC Fund
Akzo America
Akzo Chemicals Inc.
Ala Vi Foundation of New York
Alabama Power Co.
Alberto-Culver Co.
Albertson's
Alco Standard Corp.
Alcon Laboratories, Inc.
Aldeen Charity Trust, G. W.
Alden Trust, George I.
Alexander & Baldwin, Inc.
Alexander Charitable Foundation
Alexander Foundation, Joseph
Alexander Foundation, Judd S.
Alexander Foundation, Walter
Algonquin Energy, Inc.
Alice Manufacturing Co.

Colleges & Universities (cont.)

Allegheny Foundation
Allegheny Ludlum Corp.
Allen Foundation for Medical Research, Paul G.
Allen Foundation, Frances
Allen Foundation, Rita
Allendale Mutual Insurance Co.
Allergan, Inc.
Alliant Techsystems
AlliedSignal
Alliss Educational Foundation, Charles and Ellora
Allstate Insurance Co.
Alltel/Western Region
Allyn Foundation
Allyn Foundation
Alma Piston Co.
ALPAC Corp.
Alperin/Hirsch Family Foundation
Alro Steel Corp.
Alsdorf Foundation
Altman Foundation
Altschul Foundation
Alumax
Aluminum Co. of America
AMAX
Amcast Industrial Corp.
AMCORE Bank, N.A. Rockford
America West Airlines
American Aggregates Corp.
American Brands
American Building Maintenance Industries
American Cyanamid Co.
American Electric Power
American Express Co.
American Financial Corp.
American Foundation Corporation
American General Finance
American Home Products Corp.
American Honda Motor Co.
American National Bank & Trust Co. of Chicago
American Natural Resources Co.
American Optical Corp.
American President Cos.
American Saw & Manufacturing Co.
American Standard
American Stock Exchange
American Telephone & Telegraph Co.
American United Life Insurance Co.
Americana Foundation
Ameritas Life Insurance Corp.
Ameritech Corp.
Ameritech Publishing
Ameritech Services
Ameritech Services
Ames Charitable Trust, Harriett
Ames Department Stores
AMETEK
Amfac/JMB Hawaii
Amoco Corp.
AMP
AMR Corp.
Amsted Industries
Amsterdam Foundation, Jack and Mimi Leviton
Analog Devices
Andersen Corp.
Andersen Foundation
Andersen Foundation, Arthur
Anderson Foundation
Anderson Foundation
Anderson Foundation, John W.
Anderson Foundation, M. D.
Anderson Foundation, Robert C. and Sadie G.
Anderson Foundation, William P.

Anderson Industries
Andersons Management Corp.
Andreas Foundation
Andrews Foundation
Anheuser-Busch Cos.
Animal Assistance Foundation
Annenberg Foundation
Ansley Foundation, Dantzler Bond
AON Corp.
Applebaum Foundation
Appleby Foundation
Appleby Trust, Scott B. and Annie P.
Appleton Papers
Arata Brothers Trust
Arbie Mineral Feed Co.
Arca Foundation
Arcadia Foundation
Archbold Charitable Trust, Adrian and Jessie
Archer-Daniels-Midland Co.
Archibald Charitable Foundation, Norman
ARCO
ARCO Chemical
Arell Foundation
Argyros Foundation
Aristech Chemical Corp.
Arizona Public Service Co.
Arkansas Power & Light Co.
Arkelian Foundation, Ben H. and Gladys
Arkell Hall Foundation
Arkla
Arkwright-Boston Manufacturers Mutual
Arkwright Foundation
Armbrust Chain Co.
Armco Inc.
Armco Steel Co.
Armington Fund, Evenor
Armstrong Foundation
Armstrong World Industries Inc.
Arnold Fund
Aron Charitable Foundation, J.
Arrillaga Foundation
Arronson Foundation
Arvin Industries
ASARCO
Asea Brown Boveri
Ashland Oil
Asplundh Foundation
Associated Foundations
Atalanta/Sosnoff Capital Corp.
Atherton Family Foundation
Athwin Foundation
Atkinson Foundation
Atkinson Foundation, Myrtle L.
Atlanta Gas Light Co.
Atlantic Foundation of New York
Atran Foundation
Atwood Foundation
Auerbach Foundation, Beatrice Fox
Aurora Foundation
Austin Memorial Foundation
Autry Foundation
Autzen Foundation
Avon Products
Ayres Foundation, Inc.
Azadoutioun Foundation
Azby Fund
Babcock & Wilcox Co.
Babson Foundation, Paul and Edith
Bachmann Foundation
Backer Spielvogel Bates U.S.
Badgeley Residuary Charitable Trust, Rose M.
Badger Meter, Inc.
Baehr Foundation, Louis W. and Dolpha
Baer Foundation, Alan and Marcia
Bag Bazaar, Ltd.
Baier Foundation, Marie

Bailey Foundation
Bailey Wildlife Foundation
Baird & Co., Robert W.
Baird Foundation
Baird Foundation, Cameron
Baker & Baker
Baker Foundation, Clark and Ruby
Baker Foundation, Dexter F. and Dorothy H.
Baker Foundation, George T.
Baker Foundation, R. C.
Baker, Jr. Memorial Fund, William G.
Baker Trust, Clayton
Baker Trust, George F.
Baldwin Foundation
Baldwin Foundation, David M. and Barbara
Baldwin, Jr. Foundation, Summerfield
Balfour Foundation, L. G.
Ball Brothers Foundation
Ball Corp.
Ball Foundation, George and Frances
Bally Inc.
Baltimore Gas & Electric Co.
Bamberger and John Ernest Bamberger Memorial Foundation, Ruth Eleanor
Banbury Fund
Banc One Illinois Corp.
Banc One Wisconsin Corp.
Bancorp Hawaii
Bancorp Hawaii
Banfi Vintners
Bang & Olufsen of America, Inc.
Bank Foundation, Helen and Merrill
Bank IV
Bank of A. Levy
Bank of America Arizona
Bank of America - Giannini Foundation
Bank of Boston Connecticut
Bank of Boston Corp.
Bank of Tokyo Trust Co.
Bank One, Texas-Houston Office
Bank One, Texas, NA
Bank One, Youngstown, NA
Bank South Corp.
BankAmerica Corp.
Bankers Trust Co.
Bannan Foundation, Arline and Thomas J.
Banner Life Insurance Co.
Bannerman Foundation, William C.
Bannon Foundation
Banta Corp.
Banyan Tree Foundation
Barbour Foundation, Bernice
Barclays Bank of New York
BarclaysAmerican Corp.
Bard, C. R.
Barden Corp.
Bargman Foundation, Theodore and Mina
Barker Foundation
Barker Foundation, Donald R.
Barker Foundation, J. M. R.
Barlow Family Foundation, Milton A. and Gloria G.
Barnes Foundation
Barnes Group
Barnett Banks
Barnett Charitable Foundation, Lawrence and Isabel
Barra Foundation
Barry Corp., R. G.
Barstow Foundation
Barth Foundation, Theodore H.
Bartlett & Co.
Bass and Edythe and Sol G. Atlas Fund, Sandra Atlas
Bass Corporation, Perry and Nancy Lee

Bass Foundation
Bass Foundation, Harry
Bassett Foundation, Norman
Bastien Memorial Foundation, John E. and Nellie J.
Battelle
Batten Foundation
Batts Foundation
Bauervic Foundation, Charles M.
Bauervic Foundation, Peggy
Bauervic-Paisley Foundation
Baughman Foundation
Baum Family Fund, Alvin H.
Baumberger Endowment
Baumker Charitable Foundation, Elsie and Harry
Bausch & Lomb
Baxter Foundation, Donald E. and Delia B.
Baxter International
Bay Branch Foundation
Bay Foundation
BayBanks
Bayne Fund, Howard
BCR Foundation
Beaird Foundation, Charles T.
Beal Foundation
Bean Foundation, Norwin S. and Elizabeth N.
Beasley Foundation, Theodore and Beulah
Beatty Trust, Cordelia Lunceford
Beazley Foundation
Bechtel Charitable Remainder Uni-Trust, Harold R.
Bechtel Charitable Remainder Uni-Trust, Marie H.
Bechtel Group
Bechtel, Jr. Foundation, S. D.
Beck Foundation
Beck Foundation, Elsie E. & Joseph W.
Beck Foundation, Lewis H.
Beckman Foundation, Arnold and Mabel
Beckman Foundation, Leland D.
Becton Dickinson & Co.
Bedminster Fund
Bedsole Foundation, J. L.
Beech Aircraft Corp.
Beeghly Fund, Leon A.
Beerman Foundation
Behmann Brothers Foundation
Beidler Charitable Trust, Francis
Beim Foundation
Beinecke Foundation
Beir Foundation
Beitzell & Co.
Bekins Foundation, Milo W.
Bel Air Mart
Belden Brick Co., Inc.
Belding Heminway Co.
Belfer Foundation
Belk Stores
Bell Atlantic Corp.
Bell Communications Research
Bellamah Foundation, Dale J.
BellSouth Corp.
Belmont Metals
Beloco Foundation
Beloit Foundation
Belz Foundation
Bemis Company
Benbough Foundation, Legler
Bender Foundation
Benedum Foundation, Claude Worthington
Beneficial Corp.
Benefit Trust Life Insurance Co.
Benenson Foundation, Frances and Benjamin
Benetton
Benfamil Charitable Trust
Bennett Foundation, Carl and Dorothy
Bentley Foundation, Alvin M.
Benton Foundation

Benua Foundation
Benz Trust, Doris L.
Berbecker Scholarship Fund, Walter J. and Lille
Bere Foundation
Beren Foundation, Robert M.
Berenson Charitable Foundation, Theodore W. and Evelyn
Bergen Foundation, Frank and Lydia
Berger Foundation, Albert E.
Berger Foundation, H.N. and Frances C.
Bergner Co., P.A.
Bergstrom Manufacturing Co.
Berkey Foundation, Peter
Berkman Charitable Trust, Allen H. and Selma W.
Berkman Foundation, Louis and Sandra
Berkowitz Family Foundation, Louis
Berlin Charitable Fund, Irving
Bernsen Foundation, Grace and Franklin
Bernstein & Co., Sanford C.
Berrie Foundation, Russell
Berry Foundation, Loren M.
Berry Foundation, Lowell
Berwind Corp.
Besser Foundation
Best Products Co.
Bethlehem Steel Corp.
Bettingen Corporation, Burton G.
Betts Industries
Beveridge Foundation, Frank Stanley
Beynon Foundation, Kathryne
BFGoodrich
BHP Pacific Resources
Bibb Co.
Bickerton Charitable Trust, Lydia H.
Bicknell Fund
Biddle Foundation, Margaret T.
Biddle Foundation, Mary Duke
Bierhaus Foundation
Bigelow Foundation, F. R.
Bing Fund
Bing Fund
Bingham Foundation, William
Bingham Second Betterment Fund, William
Binney & Smith Inc.
Binswanger Co.
Bionetics Corp.
Birch Foundation, Stephen and Mary
Bird Inc.
Bireley Foundation
Birmingham Foundation
Birnschein Foundation, Alvin and Marion
Bishop Charitable Trust, A. G.
Bishop Foundation, E. K. and Lillian F.
Bishop Foundation, Vernon and Doris
Bismarck Charitable Trust, Mona
Bissell Foundation, J. Walton
Blackmer Foundation, Henry M.
Blade Communications
Blair Foundation, John
Blake Foundation, S. P.
Blanchard Foundation
Blank Fund, Myron and Jacqueline
Blaustein Foundation, Jacob and Hilda
Blaustein Foundation, Morton K. and Jane
Bleibtreu Foundation, Jacob
Bloch Foundation, Henry W. and Marion H.
Block, H&R
Bloedorn Foundation, Walter A.
Bloomfield Foundation, Sam and Rie

Blount
Blount Educational and Charitable Foundation, Mildred Weedon
Blowitz-Ridgeway Foundation
Blue Bell, Inc.
Blue Cross and Blue Shield United of Wisconsin Foundation
Blue Cross & Blue Shield of Alabama
Blum Foundation, Edith C.
Blum Foundation, Harry and Maribel G.
Blum Foundation, Lois and Irving
Blum-Kovler Foundation
BMC Industries
Board of Trustees of the Prichard School
Boatmen's Bancshares
Boatmen's First National Bank of Oklahoma
Bobst Foundation, Elmer and Mamdouha
Bodenhamer Foundation
Bodine Corp.
Boeckmann Charitable Foundation
Boehm Foundation
Boehringer Mannheim Corp.
Boeing Co.
Boettcher Foundation
Boh Brothers Construction Co.
Bohan Foundation, Ruth H.
Bohemia Inc.
Bohen Foundation
Boise Cascade Corp.
Boisi Family Foundation
Boler Co.
Bonner Foundation, Corella and Bertram
Booth-Bricker Fund
Booth Ferris Foundation
Booth Foundation, Otis
Boothroyd Foundation, Charles H. and Bertha L.
Boots Pharmaceuticals, Inc.
Booz Allen & Hamilton
Borden
Borden Memorial Foundation, Mary Owen
Borg-Warner Corp.
Borman's
Borun Foundation, Anna Borun and Harry
Borwell Charitable Foundation
Bosch Corp., Robert
Bosque Foundation
Bossong Hosiery Mills
Boston Edison Co.
Bostwick Foundation, Albert C.
Botwinick-Wolfensohn Foundation
Boulevard Foundation
Bourns, Inc.
Boutell Memorial Fund, Arnold and Gertrude
Bovaird Foundation, Mervin
Bowater Inc.
Bowers Foundation
Bowles and Robert Bowles Memorial Fund, Ethel Wilson
Bowne Foundation, Robert
Bowyer Foundation, Ambrose and Gladys
Bozzone Family Foundation
BP America
Brach Foundation, Helen
Brackenridge Foundation, George W.
Bradford & Co., J.C.
Bradford Foundation, George and Ruth
Bradish Trust, Norman C.
Bradley Foundation, Lynde and Harry
Bradley-Turner Foundation

Braitmayer Foundation
Branta Foundation
Bravmann Foundation, Ludwig
Bray Charitable Trust, Viola E.
Breidenthal Foundation, Willard J. and Mary G.
Bremer Foundation, Otto
Bren Foundation, Donald L.
Brennan Foundation, Robert E.
Brenner Foundation
Brenner Foundation, Mervyn
Brewer and Co., Ltd., C.
Bridgestone/Firestone
Bridwell Foundation, J. S.
Briggs Family Foundation
Briggs Foundation, T. W.
Briggs & Stratton Corp.
Bright Charitable Trust, Alexander H.
Bright Family Foundation
Brillion Iron Works
Brinkley Foundation
Bristol-Myers Squibb Co.
Bristol Savings Bank
British Airways
Britton Fund
Broad Foundation, Shepard
Broadhurst Foundation
Broccoli Charitable Foundation, Dana and Albert R.
Brody Foundation, Carolyn and Kenneth D.
Brody Foundation, Frances
Bromley Residuary Trust, Guy I.
Bronstein Foundation, Sol and Arlene
Bronstein Foundation, Soloman and Sylvia
Brookdale Foundation
Brooklyn Benevolent Society
Brooks Foundation, Gladys
Brother International Corp.
Brotz Family Foundation, Frank G.
Brown and C. A. Lupton Foundation, T. J.
Brown Charitable Trust, Dora Maclellan
Brown Family Foundation, John Mathew Gay
Brown Foundation
Brown Foundation, George Warren
Brown Foundation, James Graham
Brown Foundation, Joe W. and Dorothy Dorsett
Brown Foundation, W. L. Lyons
Brown Group
Brown, Jr. Charitable Trust, Frank D.
Brown & Sharpe Manufacturing Co.
Brown & Sons, Alex
Brown & Williamson Tobacco Corp.
Browning Charitable Foundation, Val A.
Browning Charitable Foundation, Val A.
Browning-Ferris Industries
Broyhill Family Foundation
Bruening Foundation, Eva L. and Joseph M.
Bruner Foundation
Bruno Charitable Foundation, Joseph S.
Bruno Foundation, Angelo
Brunswick Corp.
Brush Foundation
Bryan Family Foundation, Kathleen Price and Joseph M.
Bryan Foundation, James E. and Mary Z.
Bryant Foundation
Bryce Memorial Fund, William and Catherine
Buchanan Family Foundation

Bucyrus-Erie
Budweiser of Columbia
Buehler Foundation, Emil
Buell Foundation, Temple Hoyne
Buell Foundation, Temple Hoyne
Bugher Foundation
Buhl Foundation
Bull Foundation, Henry W.
Bull HN Information Systems Inc.
Bunbury Company
Burchfield Foundation, Charles E.
Burden Foundation, Florence V.
Burdines
Burgess Trust, Ralph L. and Florence R.
Burkitt Foundation
Burlington Industries
Burlington Northern Inc.
Burlington Resources
Burnand Medical and Educational Foundation, Alphonse A.
Burndy Corp.
Burnham Donor Fund, Alfred G.
Burnham Foundation
Burns Foundation, Fritz B.
Burns Foundation, Jacob
Burress, J.W.
Burroughs Wellcome Co.
Bush Charitable Foundation, Edyth
Bush Foundation
Business Incentives
Bustard Charitable Permanent Trust Fund, Elizabeth and James
Butler Family Foundation, George W. and Gladys S.
Butler Family Foundation, Patrick and Aimee
Butler Manufacturing Co.
Butz Foundation
Bydale Foundation
C. E. and S. Foundation
C.I.O.S.
C.P. Rail Systems
Cabell III and Maude Morgan Cabell Foundation, Robert G.
Cablevision of Michigan
Cabot Corp.
Cabot Family Charitable Trust
Cabot-Saltonstall Charitable Trust
Cadbury Beverages Inc.
Cadence Design Systems
Caestecker Foundation, Charles and Marie
Cafritz Foundation, Morris and Gwendolyn
Cain Foundation, Effie and Wofford
Cain Foundation, Gordon and Mary
Caine Charitable Foundation, Marie Eccles
CalComp, Inc.
Calder Foundation, Louis
Calhoun Charitable Trust, Kenneth
California Foundation for Biochemical Research
Callaway Foundation
Callaway Foundation, Fuller E.
Callister Foundation, Paul Q.
Cambridge Mustard Seed Foundation
Cameron Foundation, Harry S. and Isabel C.
Cameron Memorial Fund, Alpin J. and Alpin W.
Camp Foundation
Camp Younts Foundation
Campbell Foundation
Campbell Foundation, Charles Talbot
Campbell Foundation, J. Bulow

Campbell Foundation, Ruth and Henry
Campbell Soup Co.
Cannon Foundation
Canon U.S.A., Inc.
Cantor Foundation, Iris and B. Gerald
Cape Branch Foundation
Capita Charitable Trust, Emil
Capital Cities/ABC
Capital Fund Foundation
Capital Holding Corp.
Caplan Charity Foundation, Julius H.
Carbon Fuel Co.
Cargill
Carlson Cos.
Carlyle & Co. Jewelers
Carnahan-Jackson Foundation
Carnegie Corporation of New York
Carolina Power & Light Co.
Carpenter Foundation
Carpenter Foundation
Carpenter Foundation, E. Rhodes and Leona B.
Carpenter Technology Corp.
Carrier Corp.
Carstensen Memorial Foundation, Fred R. and Hazel W.
Carter Family Foundation
Carter Foundation, Amon G.
Carter-Wallace
Carthage Foundation
Cartinhour Foundation
Carvel Foundation, Thomas and Agnes
Carver Charitable Trust, Roy J.
Cascade Natural Gas Corp.
Casey Foundation, Eugene B.
Caspersen Foundation for Aid to Health and Education, O. W.
Cassett Foundation, Louis N.
Castle & Co., A.M.
Castle Foundation, Harold K. L.
Castle Foundation, Samuel N. and Mary
Castle Industries
Castle Trust, George P. and Ida Tenney
Caterpillar
CBI Industries
CBS Inc.
Ceco Corp.
Cedars-Sinai Medical Center Section D Fund
CENEX
Centel Corp.
Centerior Energy Corp.
Central Fidelity Banks, Inc.
Central Hudson Gas & Electric Corp.
Central Maine Power Co.
Central Newspapers, Inc.
Central & South West Services
Central Soya Co.
Central Vermont Public Service Corp.
Century Companies of America
CertainTeed Corp.
Cessna Aircraft Co.
Chadwick Foundation
Chadwick Fund, Dorothy Jordan
Chait Memorial Foundation, Sara
Challenge Foundation
Chamberlin Foundation, Gerald W.
Chambers Development Co.
Chambers Memorial, James B.
Champion International Corp.
Champlin Foundations
Chandler Foundation
Chapin Foundation, Frances
Chapin-May Foundation of Illinois
Chapman Charitable Corporation, Howard and Bess

Chapman Charitable Trust, H. A. and Mary K.
Charina Foundation
Charitable Foundation of the Burns Family
Charities Foundation
Charlton, Jr. Charitable Trust, Earle P.
Charter Manufacturing Co.
Chase Manhattan Bank, N.A.
Chase Trust, Alice P.
Chastain Charitable Foundation, Robert Lee and Thomas M.
Chatham Valley Foundation
Chatlos Foundation
Chazen Foundation
Cheney Foundation, Ben B.
Cheney Foundation, Elizabeth F.
Cherne Foundation, Albert W.
Chernow Trust for the Benefit of Charity Dated 3/13/75, Michael
Cherokee Foundation
Chesapeake Corp.
Chesebrough-Pond's
Chevron Corp.
Chicago Title and Trust Co.
Childress Foundation, Francis and Miranda
Childs Charitable Foundation, Roberta M.
Chiles Foundation
Chilton Foundation Trust
China Medical Board of New York
China Times Cultural Foundation
Chiquita Brands Co.
Chisholm Foundation
Christian Dior New York, Inc.
Christian Workers Foundation
Christodora
Christy-Houston Foundation
Chrysler Corp.
Chubb Corp.
Church & Dwight Co.
Churches Homes Foundation
CIBA-GEIGY Corp.
Ciba-Geigy Corp. (Pharmaceuticals Division)
CIGNA Corp.
Cincinnati Bell
Cincinnati Gas & Electric Co.
Cincinnati Milacron
CIT Group Holdings
Citicorp
Citizens Bank
Citizens Commercial & Savings Bank
Citizens First National Bank
Claneil Foundation
Clapp Charitable and Educational Trust, George H.
CLARCOR
Clark Charitable Foundation
Clark Charitable Trust
Clark Family Charitable Trust, Andrew L.
Clark Family Foundation, Emory T.
Clark Foundation
Clark Foundation
Clark-Winchcole Foundation
Clarke Trust, John
Classic Leather
Clay Foundation
Clayton Fund
Cleary Foundation
Clemens Foundation
Clements Foundation
Cleveland-Cliffs
Cline Co.
Clorox Co.
Close Foundation
Clougherty Charitable Trust, Francis H.
Clover Foundation
Clowes Fund
CM Alliance Cos.

Colleges & Universities (cont.)

CNG Transmission Corp.
Cobb Family Foundation
Coca-Cola Co.
Cockrell Foundation
Codrington Charitable Foundation, George W.
Coen Family Foundation, Charles S. and Mary
Coffey Foundation
Cogswell Benevolent Trust
Cohen Family Foundation, Saul Z. and Amy Scheuer
Cohen Foundation, George M.
Cohen Foundation, Manny and Ruthy
Cohen Foundation, Naomi and Nehemiah
Cohen Foundation, Wilfred P.
Cohn Family Foundation, Robert and Terri
Cohn Foundation, Herman and Terese
Cohn Foundation, Peter A. and Elizabeth S.
Cole Foundation, Olive B.
Cole Foundation, Robert H. and Monica H.
Cole National Corp.
Cole Trust, Quincy
Coleman Co.
Coleman Foundation
Coles Family Foundation
Colket Foundation, Ethel D.
Collins & Aikman Holdings Corp.
Collins Foundation
Collins Foundation, Carr P.
Collins Foundation, George and Jennie
Collins Foundation, James M.
Collins, Jr. Foundation, George Fulton
Colonial Life & Accident Insurance Co.
Colonial Oil Industries, Inc.
Colonial Penn Group, Inc.
Colorado Trust
Colt Foundation, James J.
Coltec Industries
Columbia Foundation
Columbus Dispatch Printing Co.
Columbus Southern Power Co.
Comer Foundation
Comerica
Cominco American Inc.
Commerce Clearing House
Commerzbank AG, New York
Common Giving Fund
Common Wealth Trust
Commonwealth Edison Co.
Commonwealth Fund
Community Coffee Co.
Community Enterprises
Community Foundation
Community Hospital Foundation
Comstock Foundation
ConAgra
Cone Mills Corp.
Confidence Foundation
Conn Memorial Foundation
Connell Foundation, Michael J.
Connelly Foundation
Connemara Fund
Conoco Inc.
Consolidated Freightways
Consolidated Natural Gas Co.
Consolidated Papers
Constantin Foundation
Consumers Power Co.
Continental Corp.
Continental Grain Co.
Contran Corp.
Contraves USA

Cook Batson Foundation
Cook Charitable Foundation
Cook Foundation, Louella
Cook, Sr. Charitable Foundation, Kelly Gene
Cooke Foundation
Cooper Foundation
Cooper Industries
Coopers & Lybrand
Coors Brewing Co.
Coors Foundation, Adolph
Copernicus Society of America
Copley Press
Copolymer Rubber & Chemical Corp.
Copperweld Corp.
Corbett Foundation
Corbin Foundation, Mary S. and David C.
Cord Foundation, E. L.
Cornell Trust, Peter C.
Corning Incorporated
Corpus Christi Exploration Co.
Cosden Trust f/b/o the University of Arizona College of Medicine, Curtis C.
Cottrell Foundation
Coughlin-Saunders Foundation
Country Curtains, Inc.
County Bank
Courts Foundation
Cove Charitable Trust
Covington and Burling
Cow Hollow Foundation
Cowles Charitable Trust
Cowles Foundation, Gardner and Florence Call
Cowles Foundation, Harriet Cheney
Cowles Foundation, William H.
Cowles Media Co.
Cox Charitable Trust, Jessie B.
Cox Enterprises
CPC International
CPI Corp.
CR Industries
Craigmyle Foundation
Crail-Johnson Foundation
Cramer Foundation
Crandall Memorial Foundation, J. Ford
Crane Foundation, Raymond E. and Ellen F.
Crane Fund for Widows and Children
Cranshaw Corporation
Cranston Print Works
Crapo Charitable Foundation, Henry H.
Crawford & Co.
Crawford Estate, E. R.
Cray Research
Credit Agricole
Credit Suisse
Creel Foundation
Crels Foundation
Crescent Plastics
Crestar Financial Corp.
Crestlea Foundation
Criss Memorial Foundation, Dr. C.C. and Mabel L.
CRL Inc.
Crocker Trust, Mary A.
Crowell Trust, Henry P. and Susan C.
Crown Books Foundation, Inc.
Crown Central Petroleum Corp.
Crown Charitable Fund, Edward A.
Crown Cork & Seal Co., Inc.
Crum and Forster
Crummer Foundation, Roy E.
Crystal Trust
CT Corp. System
CTS Corp.
Cuesta Foundation
Cullen Foundation

Cullen/Frost Bankers
Culpeper Foundation, Charles E.
Culpeper Memorial Foundation, Daphne Seybolt
Culver Foundation, Constans
Cummings Foundation, James H.
Cummings Memorial Fund Trust, Frances L. and Edwin L.
Cummins Engine Co.
CUNA Mutual Insurance Group
Cuneo Foundation
Cunningham Foundation, Laura Moore
Curran Foundation
Currey Foundation, Brownlee
Curtice-Burns Foods
Cyprus Minerals Co.
Daily News
Dain Bosworth/Inter-Regional Financial Group
Dalsimer Fund, Craig
Dalton Foundation, Dorothy U.
Dalton Foundation, Harry L.
Daly Charitable Foundation Trust, Robert and Nancy
Dammann Fund
Dan River, Inc.
Dana Corp.
Dana Foundation, Charles A.
Danforth Foundation
Daniel Foundation, Gerard and Ruth
Daniel Foundation of Alabama
Daniels Foundation, Fred Harris
Danis Industries
Danner Foundation
Darby Foundation
Darling Foundation, Hugh and Hazel
Dart Group Corp.
Davee Foundation
Davenport Foundation, M. E.
Davenport-Hatch Foundation
Davey Tree Expert Co.
David-Weill Foundation, Michel
Davies Charitable Trust
Davis Charitable Foundation, Champion McDowell
Davis Family - W.D. Charities, James E.
Davis Family - W.D. Charities, Tine W.
Davis Foundation, Edwin W. and Catherine M.
Davis Foundation, James A. and Juliet A.
Davis Foundation, Joe C.
Davis Foundation, Shelby Cullom
Davis Foundation, Simon and Annie
Davis Foundations, Arthur Vining
Day Family Foundation
Day Foundation, Cecil B.
Day Foundation, Nancy Sayles
Day Foundation, Willametta K.
Dayton Power and Light Co.
Daywood Foundation
DCB Corp.
de Hirsch Fund, Baron
De Lima Co., Paul
de Rothschild Foundation, Edmond
Dean Witter Discover
DeCamp Foundation, Ira W.
Decio Foundation, Arthur J.
Dee Foundation, Annie Taylor
Dee Foundation, Lawrence T. and Janet T.
Deere & Co.
Dekalb Energy Co.
DeKalb Genetics Corp.
Delany Charitable Trust, Beatrice P.
Delavan Foundation, Nelson B.
Delaware North Cos.
Dell Foundation, Hazel
DelMar Foundation, Charles

Deloitte & Touche
Delta Air Lines
Deluxe Corp.
Demco Charitable Foundation
Demos Foundation, N.
Demoulas Supermarkets
Dennison Manufacturing Co.
Dentsply International, Inc.
Deposit Guaranty National Bank
DeRoy Foundation, Helen L.
DeRoy Testamentary Foundation
Deseranno Educational Foundation
DeSoto
Detroit Edison Co.
Dettman Foundation, Leroy E.
Deuble Foundation, George H.
Deutsch Co.
DeVlieg Foundation, Charles
Devonshire Associates
Devonwood Foundation
DeVore Foundation
DeVos Foundation, Richard and Helen
Dewar Foundation
Dewing Foundation, Frances R.
Dexter Corp.
Dexter Industries
Dexter Shoe Co.
Dial Corp.
Diamond Foundation, Aaron
Dibner Fund
Dick Family Foundation
Dickson Foundation
Dietrich Foundation, William B.
Digital Equipment Corp.
Dillon Foundation
Dimeo Construction Co.
Dingman Foundation, Michael D.
Dishman Charitable Foundation Trust, H. E. and Kate
Disney Family Foundation, Roy
Dively Foundation, George S.
Dixie Yarns, Inc.
Dobson Foundation
Dodge Foundation, Cleveland H.
Dodge Foundation, Geraldine R.
Dodge Foundation, P. L.
Dodge Jones Foundation
Dodson Foundation, James Glenwell and Clara May
Doheny Foundation, Carrie Estelle
Doherty Charitable Foundation, Henry L. and Grace
Dollar General Corp.
Domino of California
Domino's Pizza
Donaldson Charitable Trust, Oliver S. and Jennie R.
Donaldson Co.
Donaldson, Lufkin & Jenrette
Donnelley Foundation, Elliott and Ann
Donnelley Foundation, Gaylord and Dorothy
Donnelley & Sons Co., R.R.
Donnelly Foundation, Mary J.
Donner Foundation, William H.
Donovan, Leisure, Newton & Irvine
Dorminy Foundation, John Henry
Dorot Foundation
Dorr Foundation
Doty Family Foundation
Dougherty, Jr. Foundation, James R.
Douglas Charitable Foundation
Douglas Corp.
Douglas & Lomason Company
Douty Foundation
Dover Foundation
Dow Chemical Co.
Dow Corning Corp.
Dow Foundation, Herbert H. and Barbara C.

Dow Foundation, Herbert H. and Grace A.
Dow Fund, Alden and Vada
Dow Jones & Co.
Dower Foundation, Thomas W.
Downs Perpetual Charitable Trust, Ellason
Dreiling and Albina Dreiling Charitable Trust, Leo J.
Dreitzer Foundation
Dresser Industries
Dreyfus Foundation, Camille and Henry
Dreyfus Foundation, Jean and Louis
Dreyfus Foundation, Max and Victoria
Driscoll Foundation
Drown Foundation, Joseph
Drum Foundation
du Bois Foundation, E. Blois
du Pont de Nemours & Co., E. I.
Dubow Family Foundation
Duke Endowment
Duke Foundation, Doris
Duke Power Co.
Dula Educational and Charitable Foundation, Caleb C. and Julia W.
Dumke Foundation, Dr. Ezekiel R. and Edna Wattis
Dun & Bradstreet Corp.
Dunagan Foundation
Duncan Foundation, Lillian H. and C. W.
Duncan Trust, James R.
Duncan Trust, John G.
Dunn Foundation, Elizabeth Ordway
Dunn Research Foundation, John S.
Dunning Foundation
Dunspaugh-Dalton Foundation
Dupar Foundation
duPont Foundation, Alfred I.
duPont Fund, Jessie Ball
Durell Foundation, George Edward
Durfee Foundation
Durr-Fillauer Medical
Durst Foundation
Durst Foundation
Dynamet, Inc.
Dyson Foundation
Eagle-Picher Industries
Earl-Beth Foundation
Easley Trust, Andrew H. and Anne O.
East Foundation, Sarita Kenedy
Eastern Enterprises
Eastern Fine Paper, Inc.
Eastern Foundry Co.
Eastman Kodak Co.
Eastover Corp.
Eaton Corp.
Eaton Foundation, Cyrus
Eaton Foundation, Edwin M. and Gertrude S.
Eberly Foundation
Ebert Charitable Foundation, Horatio B.
Eccles Foundation, George S. and Dolores Dore
Eccles Foundation, Marriner S.
Eccles Foundation, Ralph M. and Ella M.
Echlin Foundation
Eckerd Corp., Jack
Eckman Charitable Foundation, Samuel and Rae
Ecolab
Eddy Foundation
Eden Hall Foundation
Eder Foundation, Sidney and Arthur
Edgerton Foundation, Harold E.
Edison Foundation, Harry

Edison Foundation, Irving and Beatrice C.
Edison Fund, Charles
Edmonds Foundation, Dean S.
Educational Foundation of America
Edwards Foundation, O. P. and W. E.
Edwards Industries
EG&G Inc.
Ehrman Foundation, Fred and Susan
Einstein Fund, Albert E. and Birdie W.
EIS Foundation
Eisenberg Foundation, Ben B. and Joyce E.
Eisenberg Foundation, George M.
Eka Nobel
El-An Foundation
El Pomar Foundation
Elco Charitable Foundation
Electric Power Equipment Co.
Elf Aquitaine, Inc.
Elf Atochem North America
Elkin Memorial Foundation, Neil Warren and William Simpson
Elkins, Jr. Foundation, Margaret and James A.
Ellis Foundation
Ellis Fund
Ellison Foundation
Ellsworth Foundation, Ruth H. and Warren A.
Ellsworth Trust, W. H.
Emergency Aid of Pennsylvania Foundation
Emerson Electric Co.
Emerson Foundation, Fred L.
Emery Memorial, Thomas J.
Engelhard Foundation, Charles
English-Bonter-Mitchell Foundation
English Foundation, W. C.
English Foundation, Walter and Marian
English Memorial Fund, Florence C. and H. L.
Enron Corp.
Ensworth Charitable Foundation
Enterprise Rent-A-Car Co.
Equifax
Equimark Corp.
Equitable Life Assurance Society of the U.S.
Erickson Charitable Fund, Eben W.
Ernest & Julio Gallo Winery
Ernst & Young
Ernsthausen Charitable Foundation, John F. and Doris E.
Erpf Fund, Armand G.
Essel Foundation
Essick Foundation
Estes Foundation
Ethyl Corp.
Ettinger Foundation
Eureka Co.
European American Bank
Evans Foundation, Lettie Pate
Evans Foundation, T. M.
Everett Charitable Trust
Evinrude Foundation, Ralph
Evjue Foundation
Ewald Foundation, H. T.
Excel Industries (Elkhart, Indiana)
Exposition Foundation
Exxon Corp.
Eyman Trust, Jesse
FAB Industries
Fabick Tractor Co., John
Fabri-Kal Corp.
Factor Family Foundation, Max
Failing Fund, Henry
Fair Foundation, R. W.
Fair Oaks Foundation, Inc.

Fair Play Foundation
Fairchild Corp.
Fairchild Foundation, Sherman
Falk Foundation, David
Falk Foundation, Michael David
Falk Medical Fund, Maurice
Fanwood Foundation
Farallon Foundation
Farish Fund, William Stamps
Farley Industries
Farmers Group, Inc.
Farwell Foundation, Drusilla
Farwell Foundation, Drusilla
Faulkner Trust, Marianne Gaillard
Favrot Fund
Federal Express Corp.
Federal-Mogul Corp.
Federal National Mortgage Assn., Fannie Mae
Federal Screw Works
Federated Department Stores and Allied Stores Corp.
Federated Life Insurance Co.
Federated Life Insurance Co.
Federated Life Insurance Co.
Federation Foundation of Greater Philadelphia
Feil Foundation, Louis and Gertrude
Fein Foundation
Feinberg Foundation, Joseph and Bessie
Feinstein Foundation, Myer and Rosaline
Feintech Foundation
Feldberg Family Foundation
Feldman Foundation
Fellner Memorial Foundation, Leopold and Clara M.
Femino Foundation
Femino Foundation
Fenton Foundation
Ferkauf Foundation, Eugene and Estelle
Fidelity Bank
Field Foundation, Jamee and Marshall
Field Foundation of Illinois
Fieldcrest Cannon
Fife Foundation, Elias and Bertha
Fifth Avenue Foundation
Fifth Third Bancorp
Fig Tree Foundation
Fikes Foundation, Leland
Filene Foundation, Lincoln and Therese
FINA, Inc.
Finch Foundation, Thomas Austin
Fink Foundation
Fink Foundation
Finley Foundation, A. E.
Finnegan Foundation, John D.
Firan Foundation
Fireman Charitable Foundation, Paul and Phyllis
Fireman's Fund Insurance Co.
Firestone Foundation, Roger S.
First Bank System
First Boston
First Brands Corp.
First Chicago
First Financial Bank FSB
First Hawaiian
First Interstate Bank NW Region
First Interstate Bank of Arizona
First Interstate Bank of California
First Interstate Bank of Oregon
First Interstate Bank of Texas, N.A.
First Maryland Bancorp
First Mississippi Corp.
First National Bank in Wichita
First National Bank of Evergreen Park
First National Bank & Trust Co. of Rockford

First NH Banks, Inc.
First Petroleum Corp.
First Security Corp. (Salt Lake City, Utah)
First Tennessee Bank
First Union Corp.
First Union National Bank of Florida
Firstar Bank Milwaukee NA
FirsTier Bank N.A. Omaha
Fish Foundation, Ray C.
Fish Foundation, Vain and Harry
Fishback Foundation Trust, Harmes C.
Fisher Brothers
Fisher Foundation
Fitz-Gibbon Charitable Trust
FKI Holdings Inc.
Flagler Foundation
Flarsheim Charitable Foundation, Louis and Elizabeth
Flatley Foundation
Fleet Bank
Fleet Bank of New York
Fleet Financial Group
Fleming Foundation
Flemm Foundation, John J.
Fletcher Foundation, A. J.
Flickinger Memorial Trust
Flintridge Foundation
Florence Foundation
Florence Foundation
Florida Power Corp.
Florida Power & Light Co.
Florida Rock Industries
Florida Steel Corp.
Flowers Charitable Trust, Albert W. and Edith V.
Floyd Family Foundation
Fluor Corp.
FMC Corp.
Foellinger Foundation
Foerderer Foundation, Percival E. and Ethel Brown
Fohs Foundation
Fondren Foundation
Foote, Cone & Belding Communications
Foothills Foundation
Forbes
Forchheimer Foundation
Ford Foundation
Ford Foundation, Joseph F. and Clara
Ford Foundation, Kenneth W.
Ford Fund, Benson and Edith
Ford Fund, Walter and Josephine
Ford Fund, William and Martha
Ford II Fund, Henry
Ford III Memorial Foundation, Jefferson Lee
Ford Meter Box Co.
Ford Motor Co.
Forest City Enterprises
Forest Foundation
Forest Fund
Forest Lawn Foundation
Forest Oil Corp.
Fort Worth Star Telegram
Fortin Foundation of Florida
Foster-Davis Foundation
Foster Foundation
Foster Foundation, Joseph C. and Esther
Foulds Trust, Claiborne F
Foundation for Advancement of Chiropractic Education
Foundation for Child Development
Foundation for Iranian Studies
Foundation for the Needs of Others
Fourjay Foundation
Fourth Financial Corp.
Fowler Memorial Foundation, John Edward

Fox Inc.
Fox Charitable Foundation, Harry K. & Emma R.
Fox Foundation, Richard J.
Fox Steel Co.
Fraida Foundation
France Foundation, Jacob and Annita
Francis Families Foundation
Frank Family Foundation, A. J.
Frank Foundation, Ernest and Elfriede
Frank Fund, Zollie and Elaine
Frankel Foundation
Frankel Foundation, George and Elizabeth F.
Franklin Charitable Trust, Ershel
Franklin Foundation, John and Mary
Frasch Foundation for Chemical Research (under the will of Elizabeth B. Frasch), Herman
Fraser Paper Ltd.
Frazier Foundation
Frear Eleemosynary Trust, Mary D. and Walter F.
Freas Foundation
Frederick Foundation
Freed Foundation
Freedom Forum
Freeman Charitable Trust, Samuel
Freeman Foundation, Carl M.
Freeman Foundation, Ella West
Freeport-McMoRan
Frees Foundation
Frelinghuysen Foundation
French Oil Mill Machinery Co.
Frese Foundation, Arnold D.
Freygang Foundation, Walter Henry
Fribourg Foundation
Frick Educational Commission, Henry C.
Friedman Foundation, Stephen and Barbara
Friends' Foundation Trust, A.
Friendship Fund
Frisch's Restaurants Inc.
Froderman Foundation
Frohman Foundation, Sidney
Frohring Foundation, Paul & Maxine
Frohring Foundation, William O. and Gertrude Lewis
Frost Foundation
Frueauff Foundation, Charles A.
Fruehauf Foundation
Frumkes Foundation, Alana and Lewis
Fry Foundation, Lloyd A.
Fuchs Foundation, Gottfried & Mary
Fuchsberg Family Foundation
Fujitsu America, Inc.
Fujitsu Systems of America, Inc.
Fuld Health Trust, Helene
Fuller Co., H.B.
Fuller Foundation
Fuller Foundation, C. G.
Fuller Foundation, George F. and Sybil H.
Fullerton Foundation
Funderburke & Associates
Fuqua Foundation, J. B.
Furth Foundation
Fusenot Charity Foundation, Georges and Germaine
G.A.G. Charitable Corporation
Gabelli Foundation
Gage Foundation, Philip and Irene Toll
Gaisman Foundation, Catherine and Henry J.
Galkin Charitable Trust, Ira S. and Anna
Gallagher Family Foundation, Lewis P.

Gallo Foundation, Ernest
Gallo Foundation, Julio R.
GAR Foundation
Gardner Charitable Foundation, Edith D.
Garfinkle Family Foundation
Garland Foundation, John Jewett and H. Chandler
Garner Charitable Trust, James G.
Garrigues Trust, Edwin B.
Garvey Fund, Jean and Willard
Garvey Kansas Foundation
Garvey Memorial Foundation, Edward Chase
Garvey Texas Foundation
Garvey Trust, Olive White
Gates Foundation
Gateway Apparel
GATX Corp.
Gault-Hussey Charitable Trust
Gavin Foundation, James and Zita
Gaylord Foundation, Clifford Willard
Gazette Co.
Gebbie Foundation
GEICO Corp.
Geist Foundation
Gelb Foundation, Lawrence M.
Gellert Foundation, Carl
Gellert Foundation, Celia Berta
Gellert Foundation, Fred
Gelman Foundation, Melvin and Estelle
GenCorp
Genentech
General Accident Insurance Co. of America
General American Life Insurance Co.
General Atlantic Partners L.P.
General Development Corp.
General Dynamics Corp.
General Electric Co.
General Mills
General Motors Corp.
General Railway Signal Corp.
General Reinsurance Corp.
General Signal Corp.
General Tire Inc.
Generation Trust
Genesis Foundation
Genius Foundation, Elizabeth Morse
Genius Foundation, Elizabeth Morse
GenRad
George Foundation
Georgia Health Foundation
Georgia-Pacific Corp.
Georgia Power Co.
Gerard Foundation, Sumner
Gerber Products Co.
Gerbode Foundation, Wallace Alexander
Gerlach Foundation
Gerondelis Foundation
Gerschel Foundation, Patrick A.
Gershenson Foundation, Charles H.
Gershman Foundation, Joel
Gerson Trust, B. Milfred
Gerstacker Foundation, Rollin M.
Getsch Family Foundation Trust
Getty Foundation, Ann and Gordon
Getty Trust, J. Paul
Getz Foundation, Emma and Oscar
Gheens Foundation
Gholston Trust, J. K.
Giant Eagle
Giant Food
Giant Food Stores
Gibson Foundation, Addison H.
Gibson Foundation, E. L.

Colleges & Universities (cont.)

Giddings & Lewis
Gifford Charitable Corporation, Rosamond
Giger Foundation, Paul and Oscar
Gilbane Foundation, Thomas and William
Gilbert, Jr. Charitable Trust, Price
Gilder Foundation
Gill Foundation, Pauline Allen
Gillette Co.
Gilman, Jr. Foundation, Sondra and Charles
Gilman Paper Co.
Gilmer-Smith Foundation
Gilmore Foundation, Earl B.
Gilmore Foundation, Irving S.
Gilmore Foundation, William G.
Ginter Foundation, Karl and Anna
Givenchy, Inc.
Glancy Foundation, Lenora and Alfred
Glanville Family Foundation
Glaxo
Glaze Foundation, Robert and Ruth
Glazer Foundation, Jerome S.
Glazer Foundation, Madelyn L.
Gleason Foundation, James
Gleason Foundation, Katherine
Gleason Memorial Fund
Glenmore Distilleries Co.
Glenn Foundation, Carrie C. & Lena V.
Glenn Foundation for Medical Research, Paul F.
Glickenhaus & Co.
Globe Corp.
Goerlich Family Foundation
Goldberg Family Foundation
Goldberg Family Foundation, Israel and Matilda
Goldberg Family Foundation, Milton D. and Madeline L.
Goldberger Foundation, Edward and Marjorie
Golden Family Foundation
Goldenberg Foundation, Max
Goldie-Anna Charitable Trust
Goldman Foundation, Aaron and Cecile
Goldman Foundation, Herman
Goldman Foundation, William
Goldman Fund, Richard and Rhoda
Goldman Sachs & Co.
Goldome F.S.B
Goldring Family Foundation
Goldseker Foundation of Maryland, Morris
Goldsmith Family Foundation
Goldsmith Foundation
Goldsmith Foundation, Horace W.
Goldstein Foundation, Alfred and Ann
Goldwyn Foundation, Samuel
Golub Corp.
Good Samaritan
Goode Trust, Mae Stone
Goodman Family Foundation
Goodman Memorial Foundation, Joseph C. and Clare F.
Goodstein Family Foundation, David
Goodstein Foundation
Goodwin Foundation, Leo
Goodyear Tire & Rubber Co.
Goody's Manufacturing Corp.
Gordon Charitable Trust, Peggy and Yale
Gordon Foundation
Gordon/Rousmaniere/Roberts Fund

Gore Family Memorial Foundation
Gorin Foundation, Nehemiah
Gottesman Fund
Gottwald Foundation
Gould Foundation, Florence J.
Gould Foundation for Children, Edwin
Goulds Pumps
Grace & Co., W.R.
Graco
Grader Foundation, K. W.
Gradison & Co.
Graham Charitable Trust, William L.
Graham Foundation for Advanced Studies in the Fine Arts
Grainger Foundation
Grant Charitable Trust, Elberth R. and Gladys F.
Grant Foundation, Charles M. and Mary D.
Grant Foundation, William T.
Graphic Arts Show Co. Inc.
Graphic Controls Corp.
Grass Family Foundation
Grass Foundation
Grassmann Trust, E. J.
Gray Charitable Trust, Mary S.
Gray Foundation, Garland
Great Atlantic & Pacific Tea Co. Inc.
Great-West Life Assurance Co.
Great Western Financial Corp.
Greater Lansing Foundation
Grede Foundries
Greeley Gas Co.
Green Foundation
Green Foundation, Allen P. and Josephine B.
Green Foundation, Burton E.
Green Fund
Greenberg Foundation, Alan C.
Greene Foundation, David J.
Greene Foundation, Jerome L.
Greene Foundation, Robert Z.
Greenebaum, Doll & McDonald
Greenfield Foundation, Albert M.
Greenspan Foundation
Greentree Foundation
Greenville Foundation
Greenwall Foundation
Greenwood Mills
Gregg-Graniteville Foundation
Greve Foundation, William and Mary
Gries Charity Fund, Lucile and Robert H.
Griffin Foundation, Rosa May
Griffin, Sr., Foundation, C. V.
Griffis Foundation
Griffith Foundation, W. C.
Griggs and Mary Griggs Burke Foundation, Mary Livingston
Grimes Foundation
Grimes Foundation, Otha H.
Grinnell Mutual Reinsurance Co.
Griswold Foundation, John C.
Grobstein Charitable Trust No. 2, Ethel
Groome Beatty Trust, Helen D.
Gross Charitable Trust, Walter L. and Nell R.
Gross Foundation, Louis H.
Grossman Foundation, N. Bud
Grotto Foundation
Group Health Plan Inc.
Groves & Sons Co., S.J.
Gruber Research Foundation, Lila
Grumbacher Foundation, M. S.
Gruss Charitable Foundation, Emanuel and Riane
Gruss Petroleum Corp.
GTE Corp.
Guaranty Bank & Trust Co.

Guardian Life Insurance Co. of America
Gudelsky Family Foundation, Homer and Martha
Gudelsky Family Foundation, Isadore and Bertha
Guggenheim Foundation, Daniel and Florence
Guggenheim Foundation, Harry Frank
Gulf Power Co.
Gulfstream Aerospace Corp.
Gulton Foundation
Gumenick Foundation, Nathan and Sophie
Gund Foundation, Geoffrey
Gund Foundation, George
Gurwin Foundation, J.
Gussman Foundation, Herbert and Roseline
Gutman Foundation, Edna and Monroe C.
Guttag Foundation, Irwin and Marjorie
Guttman Foundation, Stella and Charles
H. B. B. Foundation
H.C.S. Foundation
Haas Foundation, Paul and Mary
Haas Foundation, Saul and Dayee G.
Haas Fund, Miriam and Peter
Haas Fund, Walter and Elise
Haas, Jr. Fund, Evelyn and Walter
Habig Foundation, Arnold F.
Haffenreffer Family Fund
Haffner Foundation
Hafif Family Foundation
Hagedorn Fund
Haggar Foundation
Haggerty Foundation
Hagler Foundation, Jon L.
Hale Foundation, Crescent Porter
Hales Charitable Fund
Halff Foundation, G. A. C.
Hall Charitable Trust, Evelyn A. J.
Hall Family Foundations
Hall Foundation
Hall Foundation
Hallett Charitable Trust
Hallett Charitable Trust, Jessie F.
Halliburton Co.
Hallmark Cards
Halloran Foundation, Mary P. Dolciani
Halmos Foundation
Halsell Foundation, Ewing
Halsell Foundation, O. L.
Hamel Family Charitable Trust, D. A.
Hamilton Bank
Hamilton Oil Corp.
Hamman Foundation, George and Mary Josephine
Hammer Foundation, Armand
Hancock Foundation, Luke B.
Hand Industries
Handleman Co.
Handy & Harman
Hanes Foundation, John W. and Anna H.
Hankamer Foundation, Curtis and Doris K.
Hankins Foundation
Hannon Foundation, William H.
Hansen Foundation, Dane G.
Hansen Memorial Foundation, Irving
Hanson Foundation
Hanson Testamentary Charitable Trust, Anna Emery
HarCo. Drug
Harcourt Foundation, Ellen Knowles
Harden Foundation
Hardin Foundation, Phil

Harding Educational and Charitable Foundation
Harding Foundation, Charles Stewart
Hargis Charitable Foundation, Estes H. and Florence Parker
Harkness Ballet Foundation
Harkness Foundation, William Hale
Harland Charitable Foundation, John and Wilhelmina D.
Harland Co., John H.
Harper Brush Works
Harper Foundation, Philip S.
Harriman Foundation, Gladys and Roland
Harriman Foundation, Mary W.
Harrington Foundation, Don and Sybil
Harrington Foundation, Francis A. and Jacquelyn H.
Harris Brothers Foundation
Harris Corp.
Harris Family Foundation, Hunt and Diane
Harris Foundation
Harris Foundation, H. H.
Harris Foundation, J. Ira and Nicki
Harris Foundation, James J. and Angelia M.
Harris Foundation, John H. and Lucille
Harris Foundation, William H. and Mattie Wattis
Harris Trust & Savings Bank
Harrison Foundation Trust, Francena T.
Harsco Corp.
Hartford Courant Foundation
Hartford Foundation, John A.
Hartford Steam Boiler Inspection & Insurance Co.
Hartman Foundation, Jesse and Dorothy
Hartmarx Corp.
Hartzell Industries, Inc.
Harvard Apparatus Foundation
Harvest States Cooperative
Harvey Foundation, Felix
Haskell Fund
Hassenfeld Foundation
Hastings Trust
Hatch Charitable Trust, Margaret Milliken
Hatterscheidt Foundation
Hauserman, Inc.
Hawkins Foundation, Robert Z.
Hawley Foundation
Hawn Foundation
Hayden Foundation, Charles
Hayden Foundation, William R. and Virginia
Haynes Foundation
Haynes Foundation, John Randolph and Dora
Hazen Charitable Trust, Lita Annenberg
Healy Family Foundation, M. A.
Hearst Foundation
Hearst Foundation, William Randolph
Heath Foundation, Ed and Mary
Hebrew Technical Institute
Hechinger Co.
Hecht-Levi Foundation
Heckscher Foundation for Children
Hecla Mining Co.
Hedco Foundation
HEI Inc.
Heileman Brewing Co., Inc., G.
Heineman Foundation for Research, Educational, Charitable, and Scientific Purposes
Heinz Co., H.J.
Heinz Endowment, Howard

Heinz Endowment, Vira I.
Heinz Foundation, Drue
Helfaer Foundation, Evan and Marion
Helis Foundation
Heller Financial
Helms Foundation
Helzberg Foundation, Shirley and Barnett
Hemby Foundation, Alex
Hemingway Foundation, Robert G.
Henderson Foundation
Henderson Foundation, George B.
Hendrickson Brothers
Henkel Corp.
Henry Foundation, Patrick
Hermann Foundation, Grover
Herndon Foundation
Herndon Foundation, Alonzo F. Herndon and Norris B.
Herrick Foundation
Hersey Foundation
Hershey Foods Corp.
Hervey Foundation
Herzog Foundation, Carl J.
Herzstein Charitable Foundation, Albert and Ethel
Hess Charitable Foundation, Ronne and Donald
Hess Charitable Trust, Myrtle E. and William C.
Hess Foundation
Heublein
Hewlett Foundation, William and Flora
Hewlett-Packard Co.
Hexcel Corp.
Heydt Fund, Nan and Matilda
Heymann Special Account, Mr. and Mrs. Jimmy
Heymann-Wolf Foundation
Heyward Memorial Fund, DuBose and Dorothy
Hiawatha Education Foundation
Higgins Charitable Trust, Lorene Sails
Higgins Foundation, Aldus C.
High Foundation
Hill and Family Foundation, Walter Clay
Hill Crest Foundation
Hill Foundation
Hill-Snowdon Foundation
Hillcrest Foundation
Hillman Family Foundation, Alex
Hillman Foundation
Hillman Foundation, Henry L.
Hills Fund, Edward E.
Hillsdale Fund
Hilton Foundation, Conrad N.
Himmelfarb Foundation, Paul and Annetta
Hirschl Trust for Charitable Purposes, Irma T.
Hitchcock Foundation, Gilbert M. and Martha H.
Hobbs Charitable Trust, John H.
Hobbs Foundation
Hobby Foundation
Hoblitzelle Foundation
Hoche-Scofield Foundation
Hodge Foundation
Hoechst Celanese Corp.
Hoffberger Foundation
Hoffman Foundation, H. Leslie Hoffman and Elaine S.
Hoffman Foundation, Marion O. and Maximilian
Hoffman Foundation, Maximillian E. and Marion O.
Hoffmann-La Roche
Hofheinz Foundation, Irene Cafcalas
Hofheinz Fund
Hofstetter Trust, Bessie
Hogan Foundation, Royal Barney

Holden Fund, James and Lynelle
Holding Foundation, Robert P.
Holley Foundation
Hollis Foundation
Holmes Foundation
Holt Foundation, William Knox
Holtzmann Foundation, Jacob L. and Lillian
Holzer Memorial Foundation, Richard H.
Home for Aged Men
Homeland Foundation
HON Industries
Honda of America Manufacturing, Inc.
Honeywell
Honigman Foundation
Hood Foundation, Charles H.
Hook Drug
Hooker Charitable Trust, Janet A.
Hooper Foundation, Elizabeth S.
Hoover Foundation
Hoover Fund-Trust, W. Henry
Hoover, Jr. Foundation, Margaret W. and Herbert
Hopedale Foundation
Hopeman Brothers
Hopewell Foundation
Hopkins Foundation, John Jay
Hopper Memorial Foundation, Bertrand
Hopwood Charitable Trust, John M.
Hornblower Fund, Henry
Horncrest Foundation
Horne Trust, Mabel
Horowitz Foundation, Gedale B. and Barbara S.
Hospital Corp. of America
Houchens Foundation, Ervin G.
House Educational Trust, Susan Cook
Household International
Houston Endowment
Houston Industries
Hovnanian Foundation, Hirair and Anna
Howe and Mitchell B. Howe Foundation, Lucite Horton
Howell Foundation, Eric and Jessie
Howell Fund
Hoyt Foundation
Hubbard Broadcasting
Hubbard Foundation, R. Dee and Joan Dale
Hubbard Milling Co.
Hubbell Inc.
Huber Foundation
Hudson-Webber Foundation
Huffy Corp.
Hugg Trust, Leoia W. and Charles H.
Hughes Medical Institute, Howard
Hughes Memorial Foundation, Charles Evans
Hugoton Foundation
Huisking Foundation
Huizenga Family Foundation
Huizenga Foundation, Jennie
Hulings Foundation, Mary Andersen
Hulme Charitable Foundation, Milton G.
Hultquist Foundation
Humana
Hume Foundation, Jaquelin
Humphrey Foundation, Glenn & Gertrude
Humphrey Fund, George M. and Pamela S.
Humphreys Foundation
Hunt Foundation
Hunt Foundation, Roy A.
Hunt Foundation, Samuel P.
Hunt Manufacturing Co.

Huntington Fund for Education, John
Huntsman Foundation, Jon and Karen
Hurford Foundation
Hurley Foundation, J. F.
Hurst Foundation
Huston Foundation
Hutcheson Foundation, Hazel Montague
Huthsteiner Fine Arts Trust
Hyde and Watson Foundation
Hyde Foundation, J. R.
Hyde Manufacturing Co.
I. and L. Association
I and G Charitable Foundation
Iacocca Foundation
IBM Corp.
Icahn Foundation, Carl C.
Icahn Foundation, Carl C.
ICI Americas
Iddings Benevolent Trust
IDS Financial Services
IES Industries
Illges Foundation, John P. and Dorothy S.
Illges Memorial Foundation, A. and M. L.
Illinois Bell
Illinois Power Co.
Illinois Tool Works
IMCERA Group Inc.
Imerman Memorial Foundation, Stanley
Imlay Foundation
Imperial Bancorp
Inco Alloys International
Independence Foundation
Independent Financial Corp.
Indiana Bell Telephone Co.
Indiana Desk Co.
Indiana Gas and Chemical Corp.
Indiana Insurance Cos.
Industrial Bank of Japan Trust Co.
Ingalls Foundation, Louise H. and David S.
Ingersoll Milling Machine Co.
Inland Container Corp.
Inland Steel Industries
Inman Mills
Innovating Worthy Projects Foundation
Insurance Management Associates
Intel Corp.
Interco
International Flavors & Fragrances
International Foundation
International Multifoods Corp.
International Paper Co.
International Student Exchange Cards
Interstate Packaging Co.
Iowa Savings Bank
Iowa State Bank
Ireland Foundation
Irmas Charitable Foundation, Audrey and Sydney
Irvine Foundation, James
Irvine Health Foundation
Irwin Charity Foundation, William G.
Irwin-Sweeney-Miller Foundation
Isaly Klondike Co.
Ishiyama Foundation
Island Foundation
Israel Foundation, A. Cremieux
ITT Corp.
ITT Hartford Insurance Group
ITT Rayonier
Ittleson Foundation
Ix & Sons, Frank
J C S Foundation
J.P. Morgan & Co.

Jackson Charitable Trust, Marion Gardner
Jackson Family Foundation, Ann
Jackson Foundation
Jackson Hole Preserve
Jackson Mills
Jacobs Engineering Group
Jacobson Foundation, Bernard H. and Blanche E.
Jacobson & Sons, Benjamin
Jaffe Foundation
Jaharis Family Foundation
James River Corp. of Virginia
Jameson Foundation, J. W. and Ida M.
Janesville Foundation
Janirve Foundation
Janssen Foundation, Henry
Jaqua Foundation
Jarson-Stanley and Mickey Kaplan Foundation, Isaac & Esther
Jasam Foundation
Jasper Desk Co.
Jasper Seating Co.
Jasper Table Co.
Jasper Wood Products Co.
Jaydor Corp.
JCPenney Co.
Jeffress Memorial Trust, Elizabeth G.
Jeffress Memorial Trust, Thomas F. and Kate Miller
JELD-WEN, Inc.
Jellison Benevolent Society
Jenkins Foundation, George W.
Jennings Foundation, Alma
Jennings Foundation, Martha Holden
Jennings Foundation, Mary Hillman
Jephson Educational Trust No. 1
Jesselson Foundation
Jewell Memorial Foundation, Daniel Ashley and Irene Houston
Jewett Foundation, George Frederick
JFM Foundation
Jinks Foundation, Ruth T.
JJJ Foundation
JMK-A M Micallef Charitable Foundation
JOFCo., Inc.
Johnson Charitable Trust, Keith Wold
Johnson Co., E. F.
Johnson Controls
Johnson Endeavor Foundation, Christian A.
Johnson Foundation, Barbara P.
Johnson Foundation, Burdine
Johnson Foundation, Helen K. and Arthur E.
Johnson Foundation, Howard
Johnson Foundation, M. G. and Lillie A.
Johnson Foundation, Walter S.
Johnson Fund, Edward C.
Johnson & Higgins
Johnson & Johnson
Johnson & Son, S.C.
Johnston-Fix Foundation
Johnston-Hanson Foundation
Johnston Trust for Charitable and Educational Purposes, James M.
Jones and Bessie D. Phelps Foundation, Cyrus W. and Amy F.
Jones Charitable Trust, Harvey and Bernice
Jones Construction Co., J.A.
Jones Family Foundation, Eugenie and Joseph
Jones Foundation, Daisy Marquis
Jones Foundation, Fletcher

Jones Foundation, Harvey and Bernice
Jones Foundation, Helen
Jones Foundation, Montfort Jones and Allie Brown
Jones Foundation, W. Alton
Jones Fund, Blanche and George
Jones Fund, Paul L.
Jonsson Foundation
Jordan and Ettie A. Jordan Charitable Foundation, Mary Ranken
Jordan Foundation, Arthur
Joselow Foundation
Joslyn Foundation, Marcellus I.
Jost Foundation, Charles and Mabel P.
Joukowsky Family Foundation
Journal Gazette Co.
Joyce Foundation
Joyce Foundation, John M. and Mary A.
JSJ Corp.
Julia R. and Estelle L. Foundation
Jurodin Fund
Jurzykowski Foundation, Alfred
Kade Foundation, Max
Kahn Memorial Trust
Kaiser Cement Corp.
Kaiser Family Foundation, Henry J.
Kangesser Foundation, Robert E., Harry A., and M. Sylvia
Kantzler Foundation
Kapiloff Foundation, Leonard
Kaplan Foundation, Mayer and Morris
Kaplan Foundation, Rita J. and Stanley H.
Kaplen Foundation
Kaplun Foundation, Morris J. and Betty
Kapoor Charitable Foundation
Kapor Family Foundation
Kasiska Family Foundation
Kasle Steel Corp.
Katten, Muchin, & Zavis
Katzenberger Foundation
Kaufman Foundation, Henry & Elaine
Kaufmann Foundation, Henry
Kaufmann Foundation, Marion Esser
Kaul Foundation Trust, Hugh
Kautz Family Foundation
Kavanagh Foundation, T. James
Kearney Inc., A.T.
Keating Family Foundation
Keck Foundation, W. M.
Keck, Jr. Foundation, William M.
Keebler Co.
Keeler Fund, Miner S. and Mary Ann
Keene Trust, Hazel R.
Keith Foundation Trust, Ben E.
Kellenberger Historical Foundation, May Gordon Latham
Keller-Crescent Co.
Keller Family Foundation
Kelley and Elza Kelley Foundation, Edward Bangs
Kellmer Co., Jack
Kellogg Foundation, J. C.
Kellogg Foundation, W. K.
Kellstadt Foundation
Kellwood Co.
Kelly Foundation, T. Lloyd
Kelly Tractor Co.
Kemper Charitable Trust, William T.
Kemper Educational and Charitable Fund
Kemper Foundation, Enid and Crosby
Kemper Foundation, William T.

Kemper Memorial Foundation, David Woods
Kemper National Insurance Cos.
Kempner Fund, Harris and Eliza
Kenan Family Foundation
Kenan, Jr. Charitable Trust, William R.
Kendall Foundation, George R.
Kendall Foundation, Henry P.
Kennametal
Kennecott Corp.
Kennedy Family Foundation, Ethel and W. George
Kennedy Foundation, Ethel
Kennedy Foundation, John R.
Kennedy Foundation, Quentin J.
Kennedy, Jr. Foundation, Joseph P.
Kennedy Memorial Fund, Mark H.
Kent Foundation, Ada Howe
Kent-Lucas Foundation
Kentland Foundation
Kenworthy - Sarah H. Swift Foundation, Marion E.
Kepco, Inc.
Kern Foundation Trust
Kerney Foundation, James
Kerr Foundation
Kerr Foundation, A. H.
Kerr Fund, Grayce B.
Kerr-McGee Corp.
Kettering Family Foundation
Kettering Fund
Kevorkian Fund, Hagop
Key Bank of Maine
Kidder, Peabody & Co.
Kiewit Foundation, Peter
Kiewit Sons, Peter
Kilcawley Fund, William H.
Killam Trust, Constance
Killough Trust, Walter H. D.
Killson Educational Foundation, Winifred and B. A.
Kilmartin Industries
Kilroy Foundation, William S. and Lora Jean
Kilworth Charitable Foundation, Florence B.
Kilworth Charitable Trust, William
Kimball Co., Miles
Kimball Foundation, Horace A. Kimball and S. Ella
Kimball International
Kimberly-Clark Corp.
King Foundation, Carl B. and Florence E.
King Ranch
Kingsbury Corp.
Kingsley Foundation, Lewis A.
Kiplinger Foundation
Kirbo Charitable Trust, Thomas M. and Irene B.
Kirby Foundation, F. M.
Kirchgessner Foundation, Karl
Kirkhill Rubber Co.
Kirkpatrick Foundation
Klau Foundation, David W. and Sadie
Kleberg Foundation for Wildlife Conservation, Caesar
Kleberg, Jr. and Helen C. Kleberg Foundation, Robert J.
Klee Foundation, Conrad and Virginia
Klein Fund, Nathan J.
Kline Foundation, Charles and Figa
Kline Foundation, Josiah W. and Bessie H.
Klingenstein Fund, Esther A. and Joseph
Klingler Foundation, Helen and Charles
Klipstein Foundation, Ernest Christian
Klosk Fund, Louis and Rose

Colleges & Universities (cont.)

Kmart Corp.
Knapp Educational Fund
Knapp Foundation
Knight Foundation, John S. and James L.
Knistrom Foundation, Fanny and Svante
Knott Foundation, Marion I. and Henry J.
Knowles Charitable Memorial Trust, Gladys E.
Knowles Foundation
Knox Family Foundation
Knox Foundation, Seymour H.
Knox, Sr., and Pearl Wallis Knox Charitable Foundation, Robert W.
Knudsen Charitable Foundation, Earl
Knudsen Foundation, Tom and Valley
Koch Charitable Trust, David H.
Koch Industries
Koch Sons, George
Koehler Foundation, Marcia and Otto
Koffler Family Foundation
Koh-I-Noor Rapidograph Inc.
Kohl Charitable Foundation, Allen D.
Kohl Charities, Herbert H.
Kohl Foundation, Sidney
Kohler Foundation
Kohn-Joseloff Fund
Komes Foundation
Koopman Fund
Kopf Foundation
Kopf Foundation, Elizabeth Christy
Koret Foundation
Koulaieff Educational Fund, Trustees of Ivan Y.
Kowalski Sausage Co.
KPMG Peat Marwick
Kraft Foundation
Kramer Foundation
Kramer Foundation, Louise
Krause Foundation, Charles A.
Kresge Foundation
Kress Foundation, George
Kress Foundation, Samuel H.
Krieble Foundation, Vernon K.
Krimendahl II Foundation, H. Frederick
KSM Foundation
Kuehn Foundation
Kugelman Foundation
Kuhns Investment Co.
Kulas Foundation
Kunkel Foundation, John Crain
Kunstadter Family Foundation, Albert
Kuse Foundation, James R.
Kutz Foundation, Milton and Hattie
Kuyper Foundation, Peter H. and E. Lucille Gaass
Kyle Educational Trust, S. H. and D. W.
Kynett Memorial Foundation, Edna G.
Kyocera International Inc.
Kysor Industrial Corp.
L and L Foundation
La-Z-Boy Chair Co.
Laclede Gas Co.
Ladd Charitable Corporation, Helen and George
Ladish Co.
Ladish Family Foundation, Herman W.
Laerdal Foundation, Asmund S.
Lafarge Corp.
Laffey-McHugh Foundation

Lakeside Foundation
Lalor Foundation
Lamb Foundation, Kirkland S. and Rena B.
Lambe Charitable Foundation, Claude R.
LamCo. Communications
Lamson & Sessions Co.
Lance, Inc.
Land O'Lakes
Landegger Charitable Foundation
Landmark Communications
Lane Memorial Foundation, Mills Bee
Lang Foundation, Eugene M.
Langdale Co.
Lanier Brothers Foundation
Lapham-Hickey Steel Corp.
Lard Trust, Mary Potishman
Laros Foundation, R. K.
Larsen Fund
LaSalle National Bank
Lasdon Foundation
Lasky Co.
Lassus Brothers Oil
Lastfogel Foundation, Abe and Frances
Laub Foundation
Lauder Foundation
Laurel Foundation
Lautenberg Foundation
Law Foundation, Robert O.
Lawrence Foundation, Alice
Lawrence Foundation, Lind
Lawyers Title Foundation
Lazar Foundation
Lazarus Charitable Trust, Helen and Charles
LBJ Family Foundation
Lea Foundation, Helen Sperry
Leach Foundation, Tom & Frances
Leavey Foundation, Thomas and Dorothy
Lebanon Mutual Insurance Co.
Lebovitz Fund
LeBrun Foundation
Lebus Trust, Bertha
Lee Endowment Foundation
Lee Enterprises
Lee Foundation, James T.
Lee Foundation, Ray M. and Mary Elizabeth
Leesona Corp.
Legg Mason Inc.
Lehigh Portland Cement Co.
Lehman Foundation, Edith and Herbert
Lehman Foundation, Robert
Lehmann Foundation, Otto W.
Lehrman Foundation, Jacob and Charlotte
Leidy Foundation, John J.
Leighton-Oare Foundation
Lemberg Foundation
Lender Family Foundation
Lennon Foundation, Fred A.
Lennox International, Inc.
Leo Burnett Co.
Leonardt Foundation
Leonhardt Foundation
Leonhardt Foundation, Frederick H.
Leu Foundation
Leuthold Foundation
Levin Foundation, Philip and Janice
Levine Family Foundation, Hyman
Levinson Foundation, Max and Anna
Levinson Foundation, Morris L.
Leviton Manufacturing Co.
Levitt Foundation
Levitt Foundation, Richard S.
Levy Foundation, Betty and Norman F.
Levy Foundation, Charles and Ruth

Levy Foundation, Charles and Ruth
Levy Foundation, Edward C.
Levy Foundation, Hyman Jebb
Levy Foundation, Jerome
Levy Foundation, June Rockwell
Lewis Foundation, Frank J.
Lewis Foundation, Lillian Kaiser
Liberman Foundation, Bertha & Isaac
Liberty Corp.
Liberty Diversified Industries Inc.
Liberty Hosiery Mills
Lichtenstein Foundation, David B.
Lieberman Enterprises
Lied Foundation Trust
Life Insurance Co. of Georgia
Life Investors Insurance Company of America
Lightner Sams Foundation
Lilly & Co., Eli
Lilly Endowment
Lilly Foundation, Richard Coyle
Lincoln Electric Co.
Lincoln Family Foundation
Lincoln Fund
Lincoln Health Care Foundation
Lincoln National Corp.
Lincy Foundation
Linde Foundation, Ronald and Maxine
Lindner Foundation, Fay J.
Lindsay Trust, Agnes M.
Lindstrom Foundation, Kinney
Lingnan Foundation
Link Foundation
Link, Jr. Foundation, George
Linn-Henley Charitable Trust
Linnell Foundation
Lintilhac Foundation
Linus Foundation
Lippitt Foundation, Katherine Kenyon
Lipton, Thomas J.
Liquid Air Corp.
List Foundation, Albert A.
Littauer Foundation, Lucius N.
Little, Arthur D.
Little Family Foundation
Littlefield Foundation, Edmund Wattis
Litton Industries
Litton/Itek Optical Systems
Livingston Foundation
Livingston Foundation, Milton S. and Corinne N.
Livingstone Charitable Foundation, Betty J. and J. Stanley
Lizzadro Family Foundation, Joseph
Llagas Foundation
Lockheed Corp.
Lockheed Sanders
Lockwood Foundation, Byron W. and Alice L.
Loeb Foundation, Frances and John L.
Loeb Partners Corp.
Loewenberg Foundation
Loews Corp.
Loewy Family Foundation
Long Foundation, J.M.
Long Island Lighting Co.
Longwood Foundation
Loridans Foundation, Charles
Loughran Foundation, Mary and Daniel
Louis Foundation, Michael W.
Louisiana Land & Exploration Co.
Louisiana-Pacific Corp.
Louisiana Power & Light Co./New Orleans Public Service
Lounsbery Foundation, Richard

Loutit Foundation
Love Charitable Foundation, John Allan
Love Foundation, Gay and Erskine
Love Foundation, George H. and Margaret McClintic
Love Foundation, Martha and Spencer
Lovett Foundation
Lowe Foundation, Joe and Emily
Lowell Institute, Trustees of the
Lowenstein Foundation, Leon
Lowenstein Foundation, William P. and Marie R.
Loyola Foundation
Lozier Foundation
LTV Corp.
Lubrizol Corp.
Lucas Cancer Foundation, Richard M.
Luce Foundation, Henry
Luck Stone
Luckyday Foundation
Ludwick Institute
Lukens
Lumpkin Foundation
Lupin Foundation
Lurcy Charitable and Educational Trust, Georges
Lurie Family Foundation
Lurie Foundation, Louis R.
Luse Foundation, W. P. and Bulah
Lutheran Brotherhood Foundation
Luttrell Trust
Lux Trust, Dr. Konrad and Clara
Lydall, Inc.
Lynn Foundation, E. M.
Lyons Foundation
Lytel Foundation, Bertha Russ
M. E. G. Foundation
M.E. Foundation
M.T.D. Products
Maas Foundation, Benard L.
Mabee Foundation, J. E. and L. E.
MacAndrews & Forbes Holdings
MacArthur Foundation, John D. and Catherine T.
MacDonald Foundation, James A.
MacDonald Foundation, Marquis George
Macht Foundation, Morton and Sophia
Mack Foundation, J. S.
MacKall and Evanina Evans Bell MacKall Trust, Paul
MacKenzie Foundation
Maclellan Charitable Trust, R. J.
Maclellan Foundation
Maclellan Foundation, Robert L. and Kathrina H.
Macmillan, Inc.
Macy & Co., R.H.
Macy, Jr. Foundation, Josiah
Maddox Foundation, J. F.
Madison Gas & Electric Co.
Madison Mutual Insurance Co.
Magee Christian Education Foundation
Magma Copper Co.
Magowan Family Foundation
Magruder Foundation, Chesley G.
Maier Foundation, Sarah Pauline
Mailman Family Foundation, A. L.
Mailman Foundation
Makita U.S.A., Inc.
Mallinckrodt, Jr. Foundation, Edward
Mallinckrodt Specialty Chemicals Co.
Mandel Foundation, Jack N. and Lilyan
Mandel Foundation, Joseph and Florence

Mandel Foundation, Morton and Barbara
Mandell Foundation, Samuel P.
Mandeville Foundation
Maneely Fund
Manger and Audrey Cordero Plitt Trust, Clarence
Manitou Foundation
Mankato Citizens Telephone Co.
Mann Foundation, John Jay
Mann Foundation, Ted
Manning and Emma Austin Manning Foundation, James Hilton
Manoogian Foundation, Alex and Marie
Mansfield Foundation, Albert and Anne
Manufacturers Life Insurance Co. of America
Manville Corp.
Mapco Inc.
Marathon Oil, Indiana Refining Division
Marcus Corp.
Mardag Foundation
Mardigian Foundation
Margoes Foundation
Margolis Charitable Foundation for Medical Research, Ben B. and Iris M.
Marine Midland Banks
Marion Merrell Dow
Maritz Inc.
Mark IV Industries
Markey Charitable Fund, John C.
Markey Charitable Trust, Lucille P.
Markle Foundation, John and Mary R.
Marley Co.
Marmot Foundation
Marpat Foundation
Marriott Corp.
Marriott Foundation, J. Willard
Mars Foundation
Marshall Foundation
Marshall Foundation, Mattie H.
Marshall & Ilsley Bank
Marshall Trust in Memory of Sanders McDaniel, Harriet McDaniel
Martin & Deborah Flug Foundation
Martin Family Fund
Martin Foundation
Martin Foundation, Bert William
Martin Marietta Aggregates
Martin Marietta Corp.
Martini Foundation, Nicholas
Marubeni America Corp.
Marx Foundation, Virginia & Leonard
Mary Kay Foundation
Masco Corp.
Massachusetts Mutual Life Insurance Co.
Massengill-DeFriece Foundation
Masserini Charitable Trust, Maurice J.
Massey Charitable Trust
Massey Foundation
Massey Foundation, Jack C.
Mastronardi Charitable Foundation, Charles A.
Material Service Corp.
Mather and William Gwinn Mather Fund, Elizabeth Ring
Mather Fund, Richard
Mathers Charitable Foundation, G. Harold and Leila Y.
Mathis-Pfohl Foundation
Matthews International Corp.
Mattus Foundation, Reuben and Rose
Matz Foundation — Edelman Division
Maxfield Foundation

Maxus Energy Corp.
May Charitable Trust, Ben
May Department Stores Co.
May Foundation, Wilbur
May Mitchell Royal Foundation
Mayborn Foundation, Frank W.
Mayer Charitable Trust, Oscar G. & Elsa S.
Mayer Foundation, James and Eva
Mayer Foundation, Louis B.
Mayerson Foundation, Manuel D. and Rhoda
Mayor Foundation, Oliver Dewey
Maytag Corp.
Maytag Family Foundation, Fred
Mazer Foundation, Jacob and Ruth
Mazza Foundation
MBIA, Inc.
MCA
McAlister Charitable Foundation, Harold
McBeath Foundation, Faye
McCann Foundation
McCarthy Foundation, Michael W.
McCarthy Memorial Trust Fund, Catherine
McCasland Foundation
McCormick & Co.
McCormick Foundation, Chauncey and Marion Deering
McCormick Tribune Foundation, Robert R.
McCrea Foundation
McCullough Foundation, Ralph H. and Ruth J.
McCune Charitable Trust, John R.
McCune Foundation
McCutchen Foundation
McDermott
McDermott Foundation, Eugene
McDonald & Co. Securities
McDonald & Co. Securities
McDonald Foundation, J. M.
McDonald Industries, Inc., A. Y.
McDonald's Corp.
McDonnell Douglas Corp.
McDonnell Foundation, James S.
McDonough Foundation, Bernard
McDougall Charitable Trust, Ruth Camp
McEachern Charitable Trust, D. V. & Ida J.
McElroy Trust, R. J.
McEvoy Foundation, Mildred H.
McFawn Trust No. 2, Lois Sisler
McFeely-Rogers Foundation
McGee Foundation
McGee Foundation
McGraw Foundation
McGraw Foundation, Curtis W.
McGraw Foundation, Donald C.
McGraw-Hill
McGregor Foundation, Thomas and Frances
McGregor Fund
MCI Communications Corp.
McInerny Foundation
McIntosh Foundation
McIntosh Foundation
McIntyre Foundation, B. D. and Jane E.
McIntyre Foundation, C. S. and Marion F.
MCJ Foundation
McKee Foundation, Robert E. and Evelyn
McKenna Foundation, Katherine Mabis
McKenna Foundation, Philip M.
McKesson Corp.
McKnight Foundation
McLean Contributionship
McLendon Educational Fund, Violet H.

McMahon Charitable Trust Fund, Father John J.
McMahon Foundation
McMillan, Jr. Foundation, Bruce
McMurray-Bennnett Foundation
McNeely Foundation
McNeil, Jr. Charitable Trust, Robert L.
McNutt Charitable Trust, Amy Shelton
McRae Foundation
McShain Charities, John
McVay Foundation
McWane Inc.
MDU Resources Group, Inc.
Mead Corp.
Mead Foundation, Giles W. and Elise G.
Meadowood Foundation
Meadows Foundation
Measey Foundation, Benjamin and Mary Siddons
Mechanic Foundation, Morris A.
Mechanics Bank
Medtronic
Meek Foundation
Melitta North America Inc.
Mellam Family Foundation
Mellen Foundation
Mellon Bank Corp.
Mellon Foundation, Andrew W.
Mellon Foundation, Richard King
Melville Corp.
Memorial Foundation for the Blind
Memton Fund
Menasha Corp.
Mendel Foundation
Mengle Foundation, Glenn and Ruth
Menil Foundation
Menschel Foundation, Robert and Joyce
Mentor Graphics
Mercantile Bancorp
Merchants Bancshares
Merck & Co.
Merck Family Fund
Merck Fund, John
Merck Human Health Division
Mercury Aircraft
Mercy, Jr. Foundation, Sue and Eugene
Meredith Corp.
Mericos Foundation
Meridian Bancorp
Merillat Foundation, Orville D. and Ruth A.
Merit Oil Corp.
Merrick Foundation
Merrick Foundation, Robert G. and Anne M.
Merrill Lynch & Co.
Messick Charitable Trust, Harry F.
Messing Foundation, Morris M. and Helen F.
Metal Industries
Metallgesellschaft Corp.
Metropolitan Health Foundation
Metropolitan Life Insurance Co.
Metropolitan Theatres Corp.
Mette Foundation
Mettler Instrument Corp.
Meyer Family Foundation, Paul J.
Meyer Foundation
Meyer Foundation, Alice Kleberg Reynolds
Meyer Foundation, Baron de Hirsch
Meyer Foundation, Robert R.
Meyer Memorial Foundation, Aaron and Rachel
Meyer Memorial Trust
Meyerhoff Fund, Joseph
MGIC Investment Corp.

Michael Foundation, Herbert I. and Elsa B.
Michigan Bell Telephone Co.
Michigan Consolidated Gas Co.
Michigan Gas Utilities
Microsoft Corp.
Mid-Iowa Health Foundation
Middendorf Foundation
Midwest Resources
Mielke Family Foundation
Mifflin Memorial Fund, George H. and Jane A.
Milbank Foundation, Dunlevy
Miles Inc.
Milken Family Medical Foundation
Milken Foundation, L. and S.
Milken Institute for Job and Capital Formation
Miller Charitable Foundation, C. John and Reva
Miller Charitable Trust, Lewis N.
Miller Foundation
Miller Foundation, Earl B. and Loraine H.
Miller Foundation, Steve J.
Miller Fund, Kathryn and Gilbert
Miller-Mellor Association
Miller Memorial Trust, George Lee
Milliken & Co.
Milliken Foundation, Agnes G.
Millipore Corp.
Mills Charitable Foundation, Henry L. and Kathryn
Mills Foundation, Ralph E.
Mills Fund, Frances Goll
Millstein Charitable Foundation
Millstone Foundation
Milstein Family Foundation
Mine Safety Appliances Co.
Mingenback Foundation, Julia J.
Miniger Memorial Foundation, Clement O.
Minnegasco
Minnesota Mutual Life Insurance Co.
Minster Machine Co.
Mirapaul Foundation
Misco Industries
Missouri Farmers Association
Mitchell Energy & Development Corp.
Mitchell Family Foundation, Bernard and Marjorie
Mitchell Family Foundation, Edward D. and Anna
Mitchell Foundation
Mitrani Family Foundation
Mitsui & Co. (U.S.A.)
MNC Financial
Mnuchin Foundation
Mobil Oil Corp.
Mobility Foundation
Model Foundation, Leo
Mohasco Corp.
Monaghan Charitable Trust, Rose
Moncrief Foundation, William A. and Elizabeth B.
Monell Foundation, Ambrose
Monfort Charitable Foundation
Monroe Auto Equipment Co.
Monroe-Brown Foundation
Monroe Foundation (1976), J. Edgar
Monsanto Co.
Montana Power Co.
Montgomery Elevator Co.
Montgomery Foundation
Montgomery Street Foundation
Monticello College Foundation
Moody Foundation
Moog Automotive, Inc.
Moore Family Foundation
Moore Foundation
Moore Foundation, C. F.
Moore Foundation, Edward S.

Moore Foundation, Martha G.
Moore Foundation, O. L.
Moore Foundation, O. L.
Moore Foundation, Roy C.
Moore Memorial Foundation, James Starr
Moore & Sons, B.C.
Moores Foundation
Moores Foundation, Harry C.
Moorman Manufacturing Co.
Morgan and Samuel Tate Morgan, Jr. Foundation, Marietta McNeil
Morgan Construction Co.
Morgan Foundation, Burton D.
Morgan Stanley & Co.
Morgan Trust for Charity, Religion, and Education
Moriah Fund
Morley Brothers Foundation
Morris Charitable Foundation, E. A.
Morris Foundation, Margaret T.
Morris Foundation, Norman M.
Morris Foundation, William T.
Morrison Foundation, Harry W.
Morrison-Knudsen Corp.
Morrison Trust, Louise L.
Morse Foundation, Richard P. and Claire W.
Morse, Jr. Foundation, Enid and Lester S.
Morton International
Mosbacher, Jr. Foundation, Emil
Moses Fund, Henry and Lucy
Mosher Foundation, Samuel B.
Mosinee Paper Corp.
Moskowitz Foundation, Irving I.
Moss Charitable Trust, Finis M.
Moss Heart Trust, Harry S.
Mostyn Foundation
Motorola
Mott Fund, Ruth
Motter Printing Press Co.
MTS Systems Corp.
Mueller Co.
Mulcahy Foundation
Mulford Trust, Clarence E.
Mullan Foundation, Thomas F. and Clementine L.
Mullen Foundation, J. K.
Muller Foundation
Multimedia, Inc.
Munger Foundation, Alfred C.
Murch Foundation
Murdock Charitable Trust, M. J.
Murdy Foundation
Murfee Endowment, Kathryn
Murphy Co., G.C.
Murphy Foundation
Murphy Foundation, Dan
Murphy Foundation, John P.
Murphy Foundation, Katherine and John
Murphy Oil Corp.
Murray Foundation
Muth Foundation, Peter and Mary
Mutual of New York
Myra Foundation
Nabisco Foods Group
Nalco Chemical Co.
Nanney Foundation, Charles and Irene
Nashua Trust Co.
Nason Foundation
Nathan Foundation
National By-Products
National City Bank of Evansville
National City Corp.
National Computer Systems
National Forge Co.
National Fuel Gas Co.
National Gypsum Co.
National Life of Vermont
National Machinery Co.
National Medical Enterprises
National Presto Industries

National Pro-Am Youth Fund
National Service Industries
National Steel
National Westminster Bank New Jersey
NationsBank Corp.
Nationwide Insurance Cos.
Natural Heritage Foundation
Navistar International Corp.
NBD Bank
NBD Bank, N.A.
NCR Corp.
NEC Technologies, Inc.
Neenah Foundry Co.
Neese Family Foundation
Nelco Sewing Machine Sales Corp.
Nellie Mae
Nelson Industries, Inc.
Nesholm Family Foundation
Nestle U.S.A. Inc.
Neu Foundation, Hugo and Doris
Neuberger Foundation, Roy R. and Marie S.
New Cycle Foundation
New England Business Service
New England Foundation
New England Mutual Life Insurance Co.
New Horizon Foundation
New Jersey Bell Telephone Company
New-Land Foundation
New Street Capital Corp.
New York Life Insurance Co.
New York Mercantile Exchange
New York Stock Exchange
New York Telephone Co.
New York Times Co.
The New Yorker Magazine, Inc.
Newcombe Foundation, Charlotte W.
Newhall Foundation, Henry Mayo
Newhouse Foundation, Samuel I.
Newman Assistance Fund, Jerome A. and Estelle R.
Newman Charitable Trust, Calvin M. and Raquel H.
Newmont Mining Corp.
News & Observer Publishing Co.
Nias Foundation, Henry
Nichols Co., J.C.
Nichols Foundation
Nike Inc.
Nissan Motor Corporation in U.S.A.
Noble Foundation, Edward John
Noble Foundation, Samuel Roberts
Nomura Securities International
Norcliffe Fund
Nord Family Foundation
Nordson Corp.
Norfolk Shipbuilding & Drydock Corp.
Norfolk Southern Corp.
Norgren Foundation, Carl A.
Norman Foundation, Andrew
Normandie Foundation
Norris Foundation, Dellora A. and Lester J.
Norris Foundation, Kenneth T. and Eileen L.
Nortek, Inc.
North American Life & Casualty Co.
North American Philips Corp.
North Shore Foundation
Northeast Utilities
Northen, Mary Moody
Northern Indiana Public Service Co.
Northern Star Foundation
Northern States Power Co.
Northern Telecom Inc.
Northern Trust Co.
Northwest Natural Gas Co.

Colleges & Universities (cont.)

Northwestern National Insurance Group
Northwestern National Life Insurance Co.
Norton Co.
Norton Memorial Corporation, Geraldi
Norwest Bank Nebraska
Norwest Corp.
Noyes, Jr. Memorial Foundation, Nicholas H.
NuTone Inc.
NutraSweet Co.
NYNEX Corp.
Oak Foundation U.S.A.
Oaklawn Foundation
Oakley Foundation, Hollie and Anna
Oberkotter Family Foundation
Oberlaender Foundation, Gustav
Obernauer Foundation
O'Bleness Foundation, Charles G.
O'Brien Foundation, Cornelius and Anna Cook
O'Brien Foundation, James W.
Occidental Oil & Gas Corp.
Occidental Petroleum Corp.
OCRI Foundation
Odell and Helen Pfeiffer Odell Fund, Robert Stewart
O'Donnell Foundation
Odyssey Partners
Oestreicher Foundation, Sylvan and Ann
Offield Family Foundation
Ogden Foundation, Ralph E.
Ogilvy & Mather Worldwide
Oglebay Norton Co.
Ohio Bell Telephone Co.
Ohio Citizens Bank
Ohio National Life Insurance Co.
Ohrstrom Foundation
Oklahoma Gas & Electric Co.
Old Dominion Box Co.
Old National Bank in Evansville
Oleson Foundation
Olin Charitable Trust, John M.
Olin Corp.
Olin Foundation, F. W.
Olin Foundation, John M.
Olin Foundation, Spencer T. and Ann W.
Olive Bridge Fund
Oliver Memorial Trust Foundation
Olivetti Office USA, Inc.
Olmsted Foundation, George and Carol
Olsson Memorial Foundation, Elis
1525 Foundation
1957 Charity Trust
O'Neil Foundation, Cyril F. and Marie E.
O'Neil Foundation, W.
O'Neill Charitable Corporation, F. J.
O'Neill Foundation, William J. and Dorothy K.
Ontario Corp.
Open Society Fund
Oppenstein Brothers Foundation
O'Quinn Foundation, John M. and Nancy C.
Orbit Valve Co.
Orchard Corp. of America.
Ordean Foundation
Ore-Ida Foods, Inc.
Orleton Trust Fund
Orscheln Co.
Ortho Diagnostic Systems, Inc.
Osborn Charitable Trust, Edward B.

Osborn Manufacturing Co.
Osceola Foundation
O'Shaughnessy Foundation, I. A.
Osher Foundation, Bernard
Oshkosh B'Gosh
Oshkosh Truck Corp.
O'Toole Foundation, Theresa and Edward
Ottenstein Family Foundation
Outboard Marine Corp.
Overbrook Foundation
Overseas Shipholding Group
Overstreet Foundation
Owen Industries, Inc.
Owen Trust, B. B.
Owens-Corning Fiberglas Corp.
Owsley Foundation, Alvin and Lucy
Oxford Foundation
Oxford Foundation
Oxford Industries, Inc.
Oxnard Foundation
PACCAR
Pacific Enterprises
Pacific Gas & Electric Co.
Pacific Mutual Life Insurance Co.
Pacific Telesis Group
Pacific Western Foundation
PacifiCorp
Packaging Corporation of America
Packard Foundation, David and Lucile
Packard Humanities Institute
Packer Foundation, Horace B.
Padnos Iron & Metal Co., Louis
PaineWebber
Paley Foundation, William S.
Palin Foundation
Palisades Educational Foundation
Palisano Foundation, Vincent and Harriet
Palmer Fund, Francis Asbury
Palmer Fund, Frank Loomis
Pamida, Inc.
Pan-American Life Insurance Co.
Panhandle Eastern Corp.
Pappas Charitable Foundation, Thomas Anthony
Paramount Communications Inc.
Park National Bank
Parke-Davis Group
Parker Drilling Co.
Parker Foundation
Parker-Hannifin Corp.
Parker, Jr. Foundation, William A.
Parman Foundation, Robert A.
Parsons Foundation, Ralph M.
Parsons - W.D. Charities, Vera Davis
Parvin Foundation, Albert
Pasadena Area Residential Aid
Patterson and Clara Guthrie Patterson Trust, Robert Leet
Patterson-Barclay Memorial Foundation
Patterson Charitable Fund, W. I.
Pauley Foundation, Edwin W.
Paulucci Family Foundation
Payne Foundation, Frank E. and Seba B.
Peabody Charitable Fund, Amelia
Peabody Foundation, Amelia
Pearce Foundation, Dr. M. Lee
Pearson Foundation, E. M.
Peerless Insurance Co.
Peierls Foundation
Pella Corp.
Pellegrino-Realmuto Charitable Foundation
PemCo. Corp.
Pendergast-Weyer Foundation
Penn Foundation, William
Penney Foundation, James C.
Pennsylvania Knitted Outerwear Manufacturing Association

Pennzoil Co.
Penzance Foundation
People's Bank
Peoples Energy Corp.
Peppers Foundation, Ann
Pepsi-Cola Bottling Co. of Charlotte
Pepsi-Cola Bottling Co. of Charlotte
PepsiCo
Perini Corp.
Perini Foundation, Joseph
Perkin-Elmer Corp.
Perkin Fund
Perkins Charitable Foundation
Perkins Foundation, Edwin E.
Perkins Foundation, Joe and Lois
Perkins Memorial Foundation, George W.
Perkins Memorial Fund, James J. and Marie Richardson
Perkins-Prothro Foundation
Perot Foundation
Perpetual Benevolent Fund
Perry Drug Stores
Persis Corp.
Pet
Peters Foundation, Charles F.
Peters Foundation, Leon S.
Peters Foundation, R. D. and Linda
Petersen Foundation, Esper A.
Petrie Trust, Lorene M.
Petteys Memorial Foundation, Jack
Pew Charitable Trusts
Pfaffinger Foundation
Pfeiffer Research Foundation, Gustavus and Louise
Pfizer
Pforzheimer Foundation, Carl and Lily
Pfriem Foundation, Norma F.
Phelps, Inc.
Phelps Dodge Corp.
PHH Corp.
Philadelphia Electric Co.
Philadelphia Industries
Philip Morris Cos.
Philips Foundation, Jesse
Phillipps Foundation
Phillips Charitable Trust, Dr. and Mrs. Arthur William
Phillips Family Foundation, Jay and Rose
Phillips Family Foundation, L. E.
Phillips Foundation, A. P.
Phillips Foundation, Dr. P.
Phillips Foundation, Ellis L.
Phillips Foundation, Waite and Genevieve
Phillips Petroleum Co.
Phipps Foundation, Howard
Physicians Mutual Insurance
Pick Charitable Trust, Melitta S.
Pick, Jr. Fund, Albert
Picker International
Pickett and Hatcher Educational Fund
Pickford Foundation, Mary
Picower Foundation, Jeffrey M. and Barbara
Piedmont Health Care Foundation
Pierce Charitable Trust, Harold Whitworth
Pillsbury Foundation
Pincus Family Fund
Pines Bridge Foundation
Pinkerton Foundation
Pioneer Fund
Pioneer Fund
Pioneer Hi-Bred International
Piper Foundation, Minnie Stevens
Piper Jaffray Cos.
Pitney Bowes
Piton Foundation

Pitt-Des Moines Inc.
Pitts Foundation, William H. and Lula E.
Pittsburgh National Bank
Pittulloch Foundation
Pittway Corp.
Pitzman Fund
Plant Memorial Fund, Henry B.
Plaster Foundation, Robert W.
Plitt Southern Theatres
Plough Foundation
Plumsock Fund
Plym Foundation
PMA Industries
Poindexter Foundation
Poinsettia Foundation, Paul and Magdalena Ecke
Polaroid Corp.
Polinger Foundation, Howard and Geraldine
Pollock Company Foundation, William B.
Pollybill Foundation
Polychrome Corp.
Poole & Kent Co.
Poorvu Foundation, William and Lia
Pope Foundation
Pope Foundation, Lois B.
Porsche Cars North America, Inc.
Porter Foundation, Mrs. Cheever
Porter Testamentary Trust, James Hyde
Portland General Electric Co.
Posnack Family Foundation of Hollywood
Post Foundation of D.C., Marjorie Merriweather
Potlatch Corp.
Potomac Electric Power Co.
Pott Foundation, Herman T. and Phenie R.
Pott Foundation, Robert and Elaine
Potter Foundation, Justin and Valere
Potts and Sibley Foundation
Potts Memorial Foundation
Powell Co., William
Powell Family Foundation
Powell Foundation, Charles Lee
Powers Foundation
Powers Higher Educational Fund, Edward W. and Alice R.
Poynter Fund
PPG Industries
Precision Rubber Products
Preferred Risk Mutual Insurance Co.
Premier Bank
Premier Industrial Corp.
Prentice Foundation, Abra
Prentis Family Foundation, Meyer and Anna
Preuss Foundation
Preyer Fund, Mary Norris
Price Associates, T. Rowe
Price Foundation, Louis and Harold
Price Foundation, Lucien B. and Katherine E.
Price Waterhouse-U.S.
Prickett Fund, Lynn R. and Karl E.
Prince Corp.
Prince Manufacturing, Inc.
Prince Trust, Abbie Norman
Principal Financial Group
Pritzker Foundation
Procter & Gamble Co.
Procter & Gamble Cosmetic & Fragrance Products
Promus Cos.
Propp Sons Fund, Morris and Anna
Prospect Hill Foundation
Prouty Foundation, Olive Higgins
Providence Energy Corp.

Providence Journal Company
Provident Life & Accident Insurance Co.
Provigo Corp. Inc.
Prudential-Bache Securities
Prudential Insurance Co. of America
PSI Energy
Psychists
Public Service Co. of Colorado
Public Service Co. of New Mexico
Public Service Electric & Gas Co.
Puget Sound Power & Light Co.
Pukall Lumber
Pulitzer Publishing Co.
Puterbaugh Foundation
Putnam Foundation
Pyramid Technology Corp.
Quabaug Corp.
Quaker Chemical Corp.
Quaker Oats Co.
Quantum Chemical Corp.
Quest for Truth Foundation
Questar Corp.
Quincy Newspapers
Quinlan Foundation, Elizabeth C.
R. F. Foundation
R. P. Foundation
Rabb Charitable Foundation, Sidney and Esther
Rabb Charitable Trust, Sidney R.
Rachal Foundation, Ed
Radiator Specialty Co.
Radin Foundation
Ragen, Jr. Memorial Fund Trust No. 1, James M.
Rahr Malting Co.
Raker Foundation, M. E.
Raleigh Linen Service/National Distributing Co.
Ralston Purina Co.
Ramapo Trust
Ramlose Foundation, George A.
Randa
Randleigh Foundation Trust
Randolph Foundation
Ranney Foundation, P. K.
Ransom Fidelity Company
Rapp Foundation, Robert Glenn
Raskin Foundation, Hirsch and Braine
Raskob Foundation for Catholic Activities
Rasmussen Foundation
Ratner Foundation, Milton M.
Rauch Foundation
Ray Foundation
Raymond Corp.
Raymond Educational Foundation
Raytheon Co.
Read Foundation, Charles L.
Reader's Digest Association
Rebsamen Companies, Inc.
Recognition Equipment
Red Devil
Red Wing Shoe Co.
Redfield Foundation, Nell J.
Redman Foundation
Reed Foundation
Reed Foundation, Philip D.
Reedman Car-Truck World Center
Reeves Foundation
Regenstein Foundation
Regis Corp.
Reichhold Chemicals, Inc.
Reidler Foundation
Reilly Industries
Reily & Co., William B.
Reinberger Foundation
Reinhart Institutional Foods
Reinhold Foundation, Paul E. and Ida Klare
Relations Foundation

Reliable Life Insurance Co.
Reliance Electric Co.
Rennebohm Foundation, Oscar
Renner Foundation
Replogle Foundation, Luther I.
Republic New York Corp.
Research Corporation
Resnick Foundation, Jack and Pearl
Revlon
Rexham Inc.
Reynolds Foundation, Christopher
Reynolds Foundation, Donald W.
Reynolds Foundation, Edgar
Reynolds Foundation, J. B.
Reynolds Foundation, Richard S.
Reynolds Metals Co.
RGK Foundation
Rhoden Charitable Foundation, Elmer C.
Rhone-Poulenc Rorer
Rice Family Foundation, Jacob and Sophie
Rice Foundation, Ethel and Raymond F.
Rich Foundation
Rich Products Corp.
Richardson Benevolent Foundation, C. E.
Richardson Charitable Trust, Anne S.
Richardson Foundation, Frank E. and Nancy M.
Richardson Foundation, Sid W.
Richardson Foundation, Smith
Richmond Foundation, Frederick W.
Ricoh Corp.
Rider-Pool Foundation
Ridgefield Foundation
Rienzi Foundation
Riggs Benevolent Fund
Riley Foundation, Mabel Louise
Ringier-America
Rinker Materials Corp.
Ritchie Memorial Foundation, Charles E. and Mabel M.
Rittenhouse Foundation
Ritter Charitable Trust, George W. & Mary F.
Ritter Foundation
Ritter Foundation, May Ellen and Gerald
River Branch Foundation
River Road Charitable Corporation
RJR Nabisco Inc.
Robbins & Myers, Inc.
Roberts Foundation
Robertshaw Controls Co.
Robertson Brothers
Robin Family Foundation, Albert A.
Robinson Foundation
Robinson Foundation
Robinson Foundation, J. Mack
Robinson Fund, Maurice R.
Robinson Mountain Fund, E. O.
Robison Foundation, Ellis H. and Doris B.
Roblee Foundation, Joseph H. and Florence A.
Robson Foundation, LaNelle
Roche Relief Foundation, Edward and Ellen
Rochester Gas & Electric Corp.
Rochester Midland Corp.
Rochester Telephone Corp.
Rockefeller Brothers Fund
Rockefeller Foundation
Rockefeller Foundation, Winthrop
Rockefeller Trust, Winthrop
Rockfall Foundation
Rockford Acromatics Products Co./Aircraft Gear Corp.
Rockford Products Corp.

Rockwell Foundation
Rockwell Fund
Rockwell International Corp.
Roddenbery Co., Inc., W.B.
Rodgers Foundation, Richard & Dorothy
Rodgers Trust, Elizabeth Killam
Rodman Foundation
Rogers Charitable Trust, Florence
Rogers Corp.
Rogers Family Foundation
Rogers Foundation
Rogers Foundation, Mary Stuart
Rogow Birken Foundation
Rohlik Foundation, Sigmund and Sophie
Rohm and Haas Company
Rohr Inc.
Rolfs Foundation, Thomas J.
Rollins Luetkemeyer Charitable Foundation
Romill Foundation
RosaMary Foundation
Rose Foundation, Billy
Roseburg Forest Products Co.
Rosen Foundation, Joseph
Rosenbaum Foundation, Paul and Gabriella
Rosenberg Foundation, Alexis
Rosenberg Foundation, Henry and Ruth Blaustein
Rosenberg Foundation, Sunny and Abe
Rosenbloom Foundation, Ben and Esther
Rosenstiel Foundation
Rosenthal Foundation, Ida and William
Rosenthal Foundation, Richard and Hinda
Rosenthal Foundation, Samuel
Rosenwald Family Fund, William
Ross Foundation
Ross Foundation
Ross Foundation, Arthur
Ross Foundation, Lyn & George M.
Ross Foundation, Walter G.
Ross Laboratories
Ross Memorial Foundation, Will
Roth Family Foundation
Rothschild Foundation, Hulda B. and Maurice L.
Rotterman Trust, Helen L. and Marie F.
Rouse Co.
Rowland Foundation
Royal Group Inc.
RTM
Ruan Foundation Trust, John
Rubbermaid
Rubenstein Charitable Foundation, Lawrence J. and Anne
Rubin Family Fund, Cele H. and William B.
Rubin Foundation, Rob E. & Judith O.
Rubin Foundation, Samuel
Rubinstein Foundation, Helena
Ruddick Corp.
Rudin Foundation
Rudin Foundation, Louis and Rachel
Rudin Foundation, Samuel and May
Rudy, Jr. Trust, George B.
Ruffin Foundation, Peter B. & Adeline W.
Rukin Philanthropic Foundation, David and Eleanore
Rumbaugh Foundation, J. H. and F. H.
Russell Charitable Foundation, Tom
Russell Charitable Trust, Josephine S.

Russell Educational Foundation, Benjamin and Roberta
Russell Memorial Foundation, Robert
Ryan Foundation, Nina M.
Ryan Foundation, Patrick G. and Shirley W.
Ryder System
Sachs Fund
Saemann Foundation, Franklin I.
SAFECO Corp.
Sage Foundation
Sage Foundation, Russell
Saint Gerard Foundation
St. Giles Foundation
St. Mary's Catholic Foundation
Saint Paul Cos.
Salgo Charitable Trust, Nicholas M.
Salomon Foundation, Richard & Edna
Salvatori Foundation, Henry
Salwil Foundation
San Diego Gas & Electric
San Diego Trust & Savings Bank
Sandoz Corp.
Sandusky International Inc.
Sandy Foundation, George H.
Sandy Hill Foundation
Sang Foundation, Elsie O. and Philip D.
Santa Fe Pacific Corp.
Santa Maria Foundation
Sapirstein-Stone-Weiss Foundation
Sara Lee Corp.
Sargent Foundation, Newell B.
Sarkeys Foundation
Sasco Foundation
Saul Foundation, Joseph E. & Norma G.
Saunders Charitable Foundation, Helen M.
Saunders Foundation
Scaife Family Foundation
Scaife Foundation, Sarah
Scaler Foundation
Schadt Foundation
Schaffer Foundation, H.
Schaffer Foundation, Michael & Helen
Schamach Foundation, Milton
Schapiro Fund, M. A.
Schautz Foundation, Walter L.
Schecter Private Foundation, Aaron and Martha
Scherer Foundation, Karla
Schering-Plough Corp.
Schermer Charitable Trust, Frances
Scheuer Family Foundation, S. H. and Helen R.
Schey Foundation
Schiff Foundation
Schiff Foundation, Dorothy
Schiff Foundation, John J. and Mary R.
Schiff, Hardin & Waite
Schillig Trust, Ottilie
Schilling Motors
Schiro Fund
Schlieder Educational Foundation, Edward G.
Schlink Foundation, Albert G. and Olive H.
Schloss & Co., Marcus
Schlumberger Ltd.
Schmidt Charitable Foundation, William E.
Schmitt Foundation, Arthur J.
Schneider Foundation Corp., Al J.
Schneider Foundation, Robert E.
Schoenbaum Family Foundation
Schoenleber Foundation
Scholl Foundation, Dr.
Scholler Foundation

Schoonmaker J-Sewkly Valley Hospital Trust
Schott Foundation
Schowalter Foundation
Schramm Foundation
Schreiber Foods, Inc.
Schroeder Foundation, Walter
Schultz Foundation
Schumann Foundation, Florence and John
Schwartz Foundation, Bernard Lee
Schwartz Foundation, David
Schwartz Fund for Education and Health Research, Arnold and Marie
Schwob Foundation, Simon
Science Applications International Corp.
Scott and Fetzer Co.
Scott Foundation, William R., John G., and Emma
Scott Fund, Olin
Scott, Jr. Charitable Foundation, Walter
Scoular Co.
Scripps Co., E.W.
Scripps Foundation, Ellen Browning
Scrivner, Inc.
Scrivner of North Carolina Inc.
Scroggins Foundation, Arthur E. and Cornelia C.
Scurlock Foundation
Scurry Foundation, D. L.
SDB Foundation
Seabury Foundation
Seafirst Corp.
Seagram & Sons, Joseph E.
Searle & Co., G.D.
Sears Family Foundation
Seasongood Good Government Foundation, Murray and Agnes
Seaver Charitable Trust, Richard C.
Seaver Institute
Seaway Food Town
Seay Charitable Trust, Sarah M. and Charles E.
Sebastian Foundation
Second Foundation
Security Benefit Life Insurance Co.
Security Life of Denver
Security State Bank
Sedgwick James Inc.
See Foundation, Charles
Seebee Trust, Frances
Seevak Family Foundation
Segerstrom Foundation
Sehn Foundation
Seid Foundation, Barre
Seidman Family Foundation
Selby and Marie Selby Foundation, William G.
Self Foundation
Semmes Foundation
Semple Foundation, Louise Taft
Sentinel Communications Co.
Sequoia Foundation
Servco Pacific
Sexton Foundation
Seybert Institution for Poor Boys and Girls, Adam and Maria Sarah
Seymour and Troester Foundation
Seymour Foundation, W. L. and Louise E.
Shafer Foundation, Richard H. and Ann
Shaffer Family Charitable Trust
Shaklee Corp.
Shapell Foundation, Nathan and Lilly
Shapero Foundation, Nate S. and Ruth B.
Shapiro Charity Fund, Abraham

Shapiro Family Foundation, Soretta and Henry
Shapiro Foundation, Carl and Ruth
Shapiro Foundation, Charles and M. R.
Share Foundation
Share Trust, Charles Morton
Sharon Steel Corp.
Sharp Electronics Corp.
Sharp Foundation, Charles S. and Ruth C.
Shattuck Charitable Trust, S. F.
Shaw Charitable Trust, Mary Elizabeth Dee
Shaw Foundation, Arch W.
Shaw Foundation, Walden W. and Jean Young
Shawmut National Corp.
Shawmut Worcester County Bank, N.A.
Shaw's Supermarkets
Shea Foundation
Shea Foundation, John and Dorothy
Sheaffer Inc.
Shell Oil Co.
Shelter Mutual Insurance Co.
Shelton Cos.
Shemanski Testamentary Trust, Tillie and Alfred
Shenandoah Foundation
Shenandoah Life Insurance Co.
Sheridan Foundation, Thomas B. and Elizabeth M.
Sherman Educational Fund, Mabel E.
Sherman Family Charitable Trust, George and Beatrice
Sherwin-Williams Co.
Shirk Foundation, Russell and Betty
Shoney's Inc.
Shook Foundation, Barbara Ingalls
Shoong Foundation, Milton
Shorenstein Foundation, Walter H. and Phyllis J.
Shott, Jr. Foundation, Hugh I.
Shughart, Thomson & Kilroy, P.C.
Shughart, Thomson & Kilroy, P.C.
Shwayder Foundation, Fay
SICO Foundation
Siebert Lutheran Foundation
Sifco Industries Inc.
Signet Bank/Maryland
Silver Spring Foundation
Simmons Family Foundation, R. P.
Simon Charitable Trust, Esther
Simon Foundation, William E. and Carol G.
Simpson Foundation
Simpson Foundation
Simpson Foundation
Simpson Industries
Simpson Investment Co.
Simpson Paper Co.
Simpson PSB Foundation
Sinsheimer Fund, Alexandrine and Alexander L.
Siragusa Foundation
Sizzler International
Skillman Foundation
Skinner Corp.
Skirball Foundation
Slant/Fin Corp.
Slaughter, Jr. Foundation, William E.
Slemp Foundation
Slifka Foundation, Alan B.
Slifka Foundation, Joseph and Sylvia
Sloan Foundation, Alfred P.
Smart Family Foundation

Colleges & Universities (cont.)

Smeal Foundation, Mary Jean & Frank P.
Smith and W. Aubrey Smith Charitable Foundation, Clara Blackford
Smith Charitable Fund, Eleanor Armstrong
Smith Charitable Trust
Smith Charitable Trust, W. W.
Smith Charities, John
Smith Corp., A.O.
Smith Family Foundation, Charles E.
Smith Family Foundation, Theda Clark
Smith Foundation
Smith Foundation, Bob and Vivian
Smith Foundation, Gordon V. and Helen C.
Smith Foundation, Kelvin and Eleanor
Smith Foundation, Richard and Susan
Smith Fund, George D.
Smith Golden Rule Trust Fund, Fred G.
Smith Horticultural Trust, Stanley
Smith Memorial Fund, Ethel Sergeant Clark
Smith 1963 Charitable Trust, Don McQueen
Smithers Foundation, Christopher D.
SmithKline Beecham
Smock Foundation, Frank and Laura
Smoot Charitable Foundation
Smucker Co., J.M.
Smucker Co., J.M.
Smyth Trust, Marion C.
SNET
Snider Foundation
Snite Foundation, Fred B.
Snow Foundation, John Ben
Snow Memorial Trust, John Ben
Snyder Charitable Fund, W. P.
Snyder Foundation, Frost and Margaret
Society Corp.
Society for the Increase of the Ministry
Sofia American Schools
Solheim Foundation
Soling Family Foundation
Solomon Foundation, Sarah M.
Solow Foundation
Solow Foundation, Sheldon H.
Sonat
Sonoco Products Co.
Sony Corp. of America
Sooner Pipe & Supply Corp.
Sordoni Foundation
Soref Foundation, Samuel M.
Soref and Helene K.
Sosland Foundation
Souers Charitable Trust, Sidney W. and Sylvia N.
South Bend Tribune
South Branch Foundation
South Carolina Electric & Gas Co.
South Plains Foundation
South Texas Charitable Foundation
Southern California Edison Co.
Southways Foundation
Southwest Gas Corp.
Southwestern Bell Corp.
Spahn & Rose Lumber Co.
Spang & Co.
Speas Foundation, Victor E.
Spectra-Physics Analytical
Speer Foundation, Roy M.

Spencer Foundation
Sperry Fund
Speyer Foundation, Alexander C. and Tillie S.
Spiegel Family Foundation, Jerry and Emily
Spingold Foundation, Nate B. and Frances
Spiritus Gladius Foundation
Sprague Educational and Charitable Foundation, Seth
Sprague, Jr. Foundation, Caryll M. and Norman F.
Springs Foundation
Springs Industries
Sprint
SPS Technologies
Spunk Fund
SPX Corp.
Square D Co.
Stabler Foundation, Donald B. and Dorothy L.
Stackner Family Foundation
Stackpole-Hall Foundation
Staley Foundation, Thomas F.
Staley, Jr. Foundation, A. E.
Staley Manufacturing Co., A.E.
Stamps Foundation, James L.
Standard Products Co.
Stanley Charitable Foundation, A. W.
Stanley Consultants
Stanley Works
Stans Foundation
Star Bank, N.A.
Stare Fund
Starling Foundation, Dorothy Richard
Starr Foundation
Starrett Co., L.S.
State Farm Mutual Automobile Insurance Co.
State Street Bank & Trust Co.
Statler Foundation
Statter Foundation, Amy Plant
Stauffer Charitable Trust, John
Stauffer Communications
Stauffer Foundation, John and Beverly
Staunton Farm Foundation
Steel, Sr. Foundation, Marshall
Steelcase
Steele Foundation
Steele-Reese Foundation
Steiger Memorial Fund, Albert
Steigerwaldt Foundation, Donna Wolf
Stein Foundation, Joseph F.
Stein Foundation, Jules and Doris
Stein Foundation, Louis
Steinbach Fund, Ruth and Milton
Steinberg Family Foundation, Meyer and Jean
Steiner Charitable Fund, Albert
Steinhardt Foundation, Judy and Michael
Steinhauer Charitable Foundation
Steinman Foundation, James Hale
Steinman Foundation, John Frederick
Steinsapir Family Foundation, Julius L. and Libhie B.
Stemmons Foundation
Stephens Foundation Trust
Sterling Winthrop
Stern Family Foundation, Alex
Stern Family Foundation, Harry
Stern Foundation, Irvin
Stern Foundation, Leonard N.
Stern Foundation, Max
Stern Memorial Trust, Sidney
Stern Private Charitable Foundation Trust, Charles H. and Anna S.
Sternberger Foundation, Sigmund
Stevens Foundation, Abbot and Dorothy H.

Stewardship Foundation
Stewart Educational Foundation, Donnell B. and Elizabeth Dee Shaw
Stewart Trust under the will of Helen S. Devore, Alexander and Margaret
Stock Foundation, Paul
Stockham Valves & Fittings
Stoddard Charitable Trust
Stokely, Jr. Foundation, William B.
Stone Charitable Foundation
Stone Container Corp.
Stone Family Foundation, Jerome H.
Stone Foundation
Stone Foundation, France
Stone Trust, H. Chase
Stonecutter Mills Corp.
Stoneman Charitable Foundation, Anne and David
Stony Wold Herbert Fund
Storage Technology Corp.
Storer Foundation, George B.
Storz Foundation, Robert Herman
Stott Foundation, Louis L.
Stott Foundation, Robert L.
Stowe, Jr. Foundation, Robert Lee
Strake Foundation
Stranahan Foundation
Stratford Foundation
Straus Foundation, Martha Washington Straus and Harry H.
Straus Foundation, Philip A. and Lynn
Strauss Foundation
Strawbridge Foundation of Pennsylvania I, Margaret Dorrance
Strawbridge Foundation of Pennsylvania II, Margaret Dorrance
Stride Rite Corp.
Strosacker Foundation, Charles J.
Stroud Foundation
Strouse, Greenberg & Co.
Stry Foundation, Paul E.
Stuart Center Charitable Trust, Hugh
Stuart Foundation
Stuart Foundation, Edward C.
Stuart Foundation, Elbridge and Evelyn
Stubblefield, Estate of Joseph L.
Stupp Brothers Bridge & Iron Co.
Stupp Foundation, Norman J.
Sturgis Charitable and Educational Trust, Roy and Christine
Subaru-Isuzu Automotive Inc.
Subaru of America Inc.
Sullivan Foundation, Algernon Sydney
Sulzberger Foundation
Sulzer Family Foundation
Sumitomo Bank of California
Sumitomo Corp. of America
Summerfield Foundation, Solon E.
Sumners Foundation, Hatton W.
Sun Banks Inc.
Sun Co.
Sunderland Foundation, Lester T.
Sundstrand Corp.
Sunmark Capital Corp.
Sunnen Foundation
Super Valu Stores
Superior Tube Co.
Surdna Foundation
Sussman Fund, Edna Bailey
Sutcliffe Foundation, Walter and Louise
Sutton Foundation
Swalm Foundation
Sweatt Foundation, Harold W.

Swift Co. Inc., John S.
Swig Charity Foundation, Mae and Benjamin
Swig Foundation
Swim Foundation, Arthur L.
Swisher Foundation, Carl S.
Swiss Bank Corp.
Switzer Foundation
Switzer Foundation
Symmes Foundation, F. W.
Synovus Financial Corp.
Syntex Corp.
Taconic Foundation
Tai and Co., J. T.
Tait Foundation, Frank M.
Tamarkin Co.
Tamko Asphalt Products
Tandem Computers
Tandy Foundation, Anne Burnett and Charles
Tandy Foundation, David L.
Tang Foundation
Taper Foundation, Mark
Taper Foundation, S. Mark
Tasty Baking Co.
Taub Foundation
Taub Foundation, Henry and Marilyn
Taub Foundation, Joseph and Arlene
Taube Family Foundation
Tauber Foundation
Taubman Foundation, Herman P. and Sophia
Taylor Family Foundation, Jack
Taylor Foundation
Taylor Foundation, Ruth and Vernon
TCF Banking & Savings, FSB
Teagle Foundation
Technical Foundation of America
Technical Training Foundation
Teichert
Tektronix
Teledyne
Tell Foundation
Temple Foundation, T. L. L.
Temple-Inland
Templeton Foundation, Herbert A.
Templeton Foundation, John
Tennant Co.
Tenneco
Tension Envelope Corp.
Terry Foundation
Tetley, Inc.
Teubert Charitable Trust, James H. and Alice
Texaco
Texas Commerce Bank Houston, N.A.
Texas Gas Transmission Corp.
Texas Instruments
Textron
Thagard Foundation
Thalheimer Foundation, Alvin and Fanny Blaustein
Thalhimer and Family Foundation, Charles G.
Thalhimer Brothers Inc.
Thalhimer, Jr. and Family Foundation, William B.
Thanksgiving Foundation
Thatcher Foundation
Thermo Electron Corp.
Thoman Foundation, W. B. and Candace
Thomas & Betts Corp.
Thomas Built Buses L.P.
Thomas Foundation, Dorothy
Thomas Foundation, Joan and Lee
Thomas Memorial Foundation, Theresa A.
Thomasville Furniture Industries
Thompson Charitable Foundation
Thompson Charitable Foundation, Marion G.

Thomson Information Publishing Group
Thoresen Foundation
Thorne Foundation
Thornton Foundation
Thornton Foundation, Flora L.
Thornton Foundation, John M. and Sally B.
Thorpe Foundation, James R.
Thorson Foundation
Three Swallows Foundation
3M Co.
Thrush-Thompson Foundation
Thurston Charitable Foundation
Times Mirror Co.
Timken Co.
Timme Revocable Trust, Abigail S.
Tinker Foundation
Tippens Foundation
Tippit Charitable Trust, C. Carlisle and Margaret M.
Tisch Foundation
Tiscornia Foundation
Titan Industrial Co.
Titmus Foundation
TJX Cos.
Todd Co., A.M.
Tokai Bank, Ltd.
Tokheim Corp.
Tomkins Industries, Inc.
Tomlinson Foundation, Kate and Elwyn
Toms Foundation
Tonya Memorial Foundation
Torchmark Corp.
Towsley Foundation, Harry A. and Margaret D.
Toyota Motor Sales, U.S.A.
Tozer Foundation
Tracor, Inc.
Tractor & Equipment Co.
Transco Energy Company
Tranzonic Cos.
Travelers Cos.
Travelli Fund, Charles Irwin
Treadwell Foundation, Nora Eccles
Treakle Foundation, J. Edwin
Treuhaft Foundation
Trexler Trust, Harry C.
Triford Foundation
Trinity Foundation
TRINOVA Corp.
Tropicana Products, Inc.
True Oil Co.
Truland Foundation
Trull Foundation
Trusler Foundation
Trust Co. Bank
Trust for Mutual Understanding
TRW Corp.
TU Electric Co.
Tuch Foundation, Michael
Tucker Charitable Trust, Rose E.
Tull Charitable Foundation
Tuohy Foundation, Alice Tweed
Tupancy-Harris Foundation of 1986
Turner Charitable Foundation
Turner Charitable Trust, Courtney S.
Turrell Fund
Twentieth Century-Fox Film Corp.
21 International Holdings
Tyler Corp.
Tyson Foods, Inc.
Ukrop's Super Markets, Inc.
Unger Foundation, Aber D.
Unilever United States
Union Bank
Union Camp Corp.
Union Carbide Corp.
Union Central Life Insurance Co.
Union Electric Co.
Union Foundation

Union Manufacturing Co.
Union Pacific Corp.
United Conveyor Corp.
United Dominion Industries
United Merchants &
  Manufacturers
United Parcel Service of America
U.S. Leasing International
United States Sugar Corp.
United States Trust Co. of New
  York
United Technologies, Automotive
United Technologies Corp.
United Togs Inc.
Univar Corp.
Universal Foods Corp.
Universal Leaf Tobacco Co.
Universal Leaf Tobacco Co.
Unocal Corp.
Upjohn California Fund
Upjohn Co.
Upjohn Foundation, Harold and
  Grace
Upton Charitable Foundation,
  Lucy and Eleanor S.
Upton Foundation, Frederick S.
US Bancorp
US WEST
USF&G Co.
USG Corp.
Ushkow Foundation
Uslico Corp.
UST
USX Corp.
Utilicorp United
Uvas Foundation
V and V Foundation
Vale Foundation, Ruby R.
Valentine Foundation, Lawson
Valley Foundation
Valley Foundation, Wayne and
  Gladys
Valley National Bank of Arizona
Valmont Industries
Valspar Corp.
van Ameringen Foundation
Van Andel Foundation, Jay and
  Betty
Van Evera Foundation, Dewitt
  Caroline
Van Every Foundation, Philip L.
Van Houten Charitable Trust
Van Huffel Foundation, I. J.
Van Nuys Foundation, I. N. and
  Susanna H.
Van Schaick Scholarship Fund,
  Nellie
Van Vleet Foundation
Vanderbilt Trust, R. T.
Vanneck-Bailey Foundation
Varian Associates
Vaughn Foundation
Vaughn, Jr. Foundation Fund,
  James M.
Veritas Foundation
Vermeer Investment Company
  Foundation
Vermeer Manufacturing Co.
Vernon Fund, Miles Hodsdon
Vesuvius Charitable Foundation
Vetlesen Foundation, G. Unger
Vicksburg Foundation
Vicksburg Hospital Medical
  Foundation
Vidda Foundation
Vidinha Charitable Trust, A. and
  E.
Vingo Trust II
Virginia Power Co.
Visciglia Foundation, Frank
Vogt Machine Co., Henry
Volen Charitable Trust, Benjamin
Volkswagen of America, Inc.
Vollbrecht Foundation, Frederick
  A.
Von der Ahe Foundation
Vulcan Materials Co.

Wachovia Bank of Georgia, N.A.
Wachovia Bank & Trust Co.,
  N.A.
Wachtell, Lipton, Rosen & Katz
Waggoner Charitable Trust,
  Crystelle
Waggoner Foundation, E. Paul
  and Helen Buck
Wagner Manufacturing Co., E. R.
Wahlert Foundation
Wahlstrom Foundation
Wal-Mart Stores
Waldbaum, Inc.
Waldorf Educational Foundation
Walgreen Co.
Walker Educational and
  Charitable Foundation, Alex C.
Walker Foundation, Archie D.
  and Bertha H.
Walker Foundation, L. C. and
  Margaret
Walker Foundation, T. B.
Walker Foundation, W. E.
Wallace Computer Services
Wallace Foundation, George R.
Wallace Genetic Foundation
Wallach Foundation, Miriam G.
  and Ira D.
Wallin Foundation
Walsh Foundation
Disney Co., Walt
Walter Family Trust, Byron L.
Walter Industries
Walton Family Foundation
Ward Foundation, A.
  Montgomery
Wardlaw Fund, Gertrude and
  William C.
Wardle Family Foundation
Ware Foundation
Warner Electric Brake & Clutch
  Co.
Warner Foundation, Lee and
  Rose
Warner-Lambert Co.
Warren and Beatrice W.
  Blanding Foundation, Riley J.
  and Lillian N.
Warren Charite
Warren Foundation, William K.
Warwick Foundation
Washington Forrest Foundation
Washington Mutual Savings
  Bank
Washington Trust Bank
Washington Water Power Co.
Wasie Foundation
Wasserman Foundation
Wasserman Foundation, George
Waste Management
Waters Charitable Trust, Robert
  S.
Waters Foundation
Watson Foundation, Thomas J.
Watson Foundation, Walter E.
  and Caroline H.
Watumull Fund, J.
Wausau Paper Mills Co.
Wauwatosa Savings & Loan
  Association
Wean Foundation, Raymond John
Weatherhead Foundation
Weaver Foundation
Weaver Foundation, Gil and
  Dody
Webb Charitable Trust, Susan
  Mott
Webb Educational and
  Charitable Trust, Torrey H.
  and Dorothy K.
Webb Foundation
Webb Foundation, Del E.
Webster Foundation, Edwin S.
Weckbaugh Foundation,
  Eleanore Mullen
Weeden Foundation, Frank
Weezie Foundation
Wege Foundation

Wegener Foundation, Herman
  and Mary
Wehadkee Foundation
Wehr Foundation, Todd
Weight Watchers International
Weil, Gotshal & Manges
  Foundation
Weiler Foundation
Weinberg Foundation, John L.
Weinberg, Jr. Foundation, Sidney
  J.
Weingart Foundation
Weininger Foundation, Richard
  and Gertrude
Weinstein Foundation, Alex J.
Weinstein Foundation, J.
Weintraub Family Foundation,
  Joseph
Weir Foundation Trust
Weiss Foundation, Stephen and
  Suzanne
Weiss Foundation, William E.
Weiss Fund, Clara
Weisz Foundation, David and
  Sylvia
Welch Testamentary Trust,
  George T.
Welfare Foundation
Wellman Foundation, S. K.
Wellons Foundation
Wells Foundation, Franklin H.
  and Ruth L.
Wells Foundation, Lillian S.
Wendt Foundation, Margaret L.
Wenger Foundation, Henry L.
  and Consuelo S.
Wenner-Gren Foundation for
  Anthropological Research
Werblow Charitable Trust, Nina
  W.
Werblow Charitable Trust, Nina
  W.
Werthan Foundation
West Co.
West Foundation
West Foundation
West Foundation, Neva and
  Wesley
West Texas Corp., J. M.
Westend Foundation
Westerman Foundation, Samuel
  L.
Western Cardiac Foundation
Western Shade Cloth Charitable
  Foundation
Western Southern Life Insurance
  Co.
Westinghouse Electric Corp.
Westport Fund
WestStar Bank N.A.
Westvaco Corp.
Wetterau
Weyerhaeuser Co.
Weyerhaeuser Family Foundation
Weyerhaeuser Foundation,
  Frederick and Margaret L.
Weyerhaeuser Memorial
  Foundation, Charles A.
Whalley Charitable Trust
Wharton Foundation
Wheat First Securites
Wheeler Foundation
Wheeler Foundation, Wilmot
Wheeler Trust, Clara
Wheless Foundation
Whirlpool Corp.
Whitaker Charitable Foundation,
  Lyndon C.
Whitaker Foundation
White Consolidated Industries
White Construction Co.
White Foundation, Erle and
  Emma
White Foundation, W. P. and H.
  B.
White Trust, G. R.
Whitehall Foundation
Whitehead Charitable Foundation

Whitehead Foundation
Whitehead Foundation, Joseph B.
Whitehead Foundation, Lettie
  Pate
Whitener Foundation
Whiting Foundation
Whiting Foundation, Macauley
  and Helen Dow
Whiting Foundation, Mrs. Giles
Whitman Corp.
Whitney Foundation, Helen Hay
Whitney Fund, David M.
Whittenberger Foundation,
  Claude R. and Ethel B.
Whittier Foundation, L. K.
Wickes Foundation, Harvey
  Randall
Wickson-Link Memorial
  Foundation
WICOR, Inc.
Widgeon Foundation
Wiegand Foundation, E. L.
Wien Foundation, Lawrence A.
Wiener Foundation, Malcolm
  Hewitt
Wiggins Memorial Trust, J. J.
Wigwam Mills
Wilber National Bank
Wilbur-Ellis Co.
Wilbur Foundation, Marguerite
  Eyer
Wilcox Trust, S. W.
Wilder Foundation
Wildermuth Foundation, E. F.
Wiley & Sons, Inc., John
Wilf Family Foundation
Wilkof Foundation, Edward and
  Ruth
Willard Foundation, Helen Parker
Willard Helping Fund, Cecilia
  Young
Williams Charitable Trust, John
  C.
Williams Cos.
Williams Family Foundation
Williams Family Foundation of
  Georgia
Williams Foundation, C. K.
Williams Foundation, Edna
  Sproull
Williams, Jr. Family Foundation,
  A. L.
Williamson Co.
Willits Foundation
Willmott Foundation, Fred &
  Floy
Willmott Foundation, Peter S.
Wilmington Trust Co.
Wilsey Bennet Co.
Wilson Foundation, Elaine P. and
  Richard U.
Wilson Foundation, Frances
  Wood
Wilson Foundation, H. W.
Wilson Foundation, Hugh and
  Mary
Wilson Foundation, John and
  Nevils
Wilson Foundation, Marie C.
  and Joseph C.
Wilson Fund, Matilda R.
Wilson Sanitarium for Children
  of Baltimore City, Thomas
Wilson Trust, Lula C.
Winchester Foundation
Winkler Foundation, Mark and
  Catherine
Winn-Dixie Stores
Winona Corporation
Winston Foundation, Norman
  and Rosita
Winston Research Foundation,
  Harry
Winthrop Trust, Clara B.
Wisconsin Bell, Inc.
Wisconsin Energy Corp.
Wisconsin Power & Light Co.
Wisconsin Public Service Corp.

Wisdom Foundation, Mary F.
Wiseheart Foundation
Witco Corp.
Witte, Jr. Foundation, John H.
Witter Foundation, Dean
Wodecroft Foundation
Woldenberg Foundation
Wolens Foundation, Kalman and
  Ida
Wolf Foundation, Melvin and
  Elaine
Wolff Foundation, John M.
Wolfson Family Foundation
Wollenberg Foundation
Wolverine World Wide, Inc.
Wood Charitable Trust, W. P.
Wood Foundation, Lester G.
Wood Foundation of
  Chambersburg, PA
Woodard Family Foundation
Woodland Foundation
Woodner Family Collection, Ian
Woodruff Foundation, Robert W.
Woods Charitable Fund
Woods Foundation, James H.
Woods-Greer Foundation
Woodward Fund
Woodward Fund-Atlanta, David,
  Helen, Marian
Woodward Fund-Watertown,
  David, Helen, and Marian
Woodward Governor Co.
Woolf Foundation, William C.
Woolley Foundation, Vasser
Wornall Charitable Trust and
  Foundation, Kearney
Wrape Family Charitable Trust
Wright Foundation, Lola
Wunsch Foundation
Wurlitzer Foundation, Farny R.
Wurzburg, Inc.
Wyman-Gordon Co.
Wyman Youth Trust
Wyne Foundation
Wyomissing Foundation
Wyss Foundation
Xerox Corp.
XTEK Inc.
Xtra Corp.
Yassenoff Foundation, Leo
Yeager Charitable Trust, Lester
  E.
Yellow Corp.
York Barbell Co.
Yosemite Asset Management
Young Foundation, Irvin L.
Young Foundation, R. A.
Young Foundation, Robert R.
Young & Rubicam
Younkers, Inc.
Youth Foundation
Yulman Trust, Morton and Helen
Zachry Co., H. B.
Zale Foundation
Zemurray Foundation
Zenkel Foundation
Ziegler Foundation
Ziegler Foundation for the Blind,
  E. Matilda
Ziegler Foundation, Ruth/Allen
Ziemann Foundation
Zigler Foundation, Fred B. and
  Ruth B.
Zilkha & Sons
Zimmerman Family Foundation,
  Raymond
Zimmerman Foundation, Mary
  and George Herbert
Zimmermann Fund, Marie and
  John
Zink Foundation, John Steele
Zlinkoff Fund for Medical
  Research and Education,
  Sergei S.
Zollner Foundation
Zuckerberg Foundation, Roy J.

Community & Junior Colleges

Abbott Laboratories
Abeles Foundation, Joseph and Sophia
Abrams Foundation, Talbert and Leota
AFLAC
Akzo America
Ala Vi Foundation of New York
Alabama Power Co.
Albertson's
Alden Trust, George I.
Algonquin Energy, Inc.
Allendale Mutual Insurance Co.
AlliedSignal
Allstate Insurance Co.
Alltel/Western Region
ALPAC Corp.
Alumax
Aluminum Co. of America
AMCORE Bank, N.A. Rockford
American Brands
American Electric Power
American Express Co.
Ameritech Services
Ameritech Services
Amoco Corp.
Amsted Industries
Andalusia Health Services
Andersen Foundation
Arcadia Foundation
Archer-Daniels-Midland Co.
Archibald Charitable Foundation, Norman
ARCO Chemical
Armco Inc.
Arvin Industries
Asea Brown Boveri
Ashland Oil
Atkinson Foundation
Atlanta Gas Light Co.
Atlantic Foundation
Auerbach Foundation, Beatrice Fox
Baehr Foundation, Louis W. and Dolpha
Ball Corp.
Bamberger and John Ernest Bamberger Memorial Foundation, Ruth Eleanor
Bank of America Arizona
Bank of Boston Corp.
Bankers Trust Co.
Barker Foundation, Donald R.
Barry Corp., R. G.
Battelle
BCR Foundation
Beal Foundation
Bedsole Foundation, J. L.
Beech Aircraft Corp.
Benefit Trust Life Insurance Co.
Benz Trust, Doris L.
Besser Foundation
Betts Industries
BFGoodrich
Binney & Smith Inc.
Blank Family Foundation
Block, H&R
Boeing Co.
Boise Cascade Corp.
Bovaird Foundation, Mervin
Bowater Inc.
Bray Charitable Trust, Viola E.
Bremer Foundation, Otto
Brewer and Co., Ltd., C.
Bristol Savings Bank
Brunswick Corp.
Bryan Foundation, Dodd and Dorothy L.
Buehler Foundation, Emil
Burden Foundation, Florence V.
Burdines
Burndy Corp.
Bush Foundation

Bustard Charitable Permanent Trust Fund, Elizabeth and James
Cablevision of Michigan
Cabot Corp.
Callister Foundation, Paul Q.
Campbell Soup Co.
Capital Holding Corp.
Carolina Power & Light Co.
Carpenter Foundation
Carter Foundation, Amon G.
Cascade Natural Gas Corp.
Ceco Corp.
Centerior Energy Corp.
Central Life Assurance Co.
Central Maine Power Co.
Century Companies of America
Chait Memorial Foundation, Sara
Chastain Charitable Foundation, Robert Lee and Thomas M.
Cheney Foundation, Ben B.
Chesapeake Corp.
Ciba-Geigy Corp. (Pharmaceuticals Division)
Citicorp
Clorox Co.
Close Foundation
CM Alliance Cos.
Coffey Foundation
Cohen Foundation, Naomi and Nehemiah
Cole Foundation
Collins Foundation, Carr P.
Colonial Life & Accident Insurance Co.
Columbus Southern Power Co.
ConAgra
Connelly Foundation
Consolidated Natural Gas Co.
Coors Brewing Co.
Country Curtains, Inc.
Cowles Foundation, Harriet Cheney
Cowles Media Co.
Cox Charitable Trust, Jessie B.
CPC International
Cranston Print Works
Crary Foundation, Bruce L.
Crawford Estate, E. R.
Crown Central Petroleum Corp.
CTS Corp.
Culpeper Memorial Foundation, Daphne Seybolt
Cummins Engine Co.
Curtice-Burns Foods
Dain Bosworth/Inter-Regional Financial Group
Dalton Foundation, Dorothy U.
Dana Corp.
Davenport Foundation, M. E.
Davenport-Hatch Foundation
Davis Foundation, James A. and Juliet L.
DeKalb Genetics Corp.
Delaware North Cos.
Delta Air Lines
Deposit Guaranty National Bank
Detroit Edison Co.
Dettman Foundation, Leroy E.
Dexter Corp.
Dickenson Foundation, Harriet Ford
Dillon Foundation
Dimeo Construction Co.
Dixie Yarns, Inc.
Donaldson Co.
Douglas & Lomason Company
Dow Corning Corp.
Dow Fund, Alden and Vada
du Bois Foundation, E. Blois
du Pont de Nemours & Co., E. I.
duPont Foundation, Alfred I.
Durfee Foundation
E and M Charities
Eagle-Picher Industries
Eagle-Picher Industries
Early Foundation

Eaton Corp.
Eccles Foundation, George S. and Dolores Dore
Eccles Foundation, Marriner S.
Educational Foundation of America
Einstein Fund, Albert E. and Birdie W.
Elf Atochem North America
Elgin Sweeper Co.
Emerson Electric Co.
Ensworth Charitable Foundation
Everett Charitable Trust
Fair Foundation, R. W.
Fairfield-Meeker Charitable Trust, Freeman E.
Falk Foundation, Elizabeth M.
Fidelity Bank
Fieldcrest Cannon
Finch Foundation, Thomas Austin
Fireman's Fund Insurance Co.
First Interstate Bank NW Region
First Interstate Bank of Arizona
First Interstate Bank of Oregon
First Maryland Bancorp
First Union Corp.
Fish Foundation, Bert
Flarsheim Charitable Foundation, Louis and Elizabeth
Fleet Bank of New York
Fleet Financial Group
Florida Power & Light Co.
FMC Corp.
Ford Foundation
Ford II Fund, Henry
Forest Foundation
Franklin Foundation, John and Mary
Frederick Foundation
Fuller Foundation, George F. and Sybil H.
Funderburke & Associates
Gazette Co.
Gear Motion
GenCorp
Genentech
General Mills
General Motors Corp.
General Reinsurance Corp.
General Signal Corp.
George Foundation
Georgia Power Co.
Gerber Products Co.
Gerstacker Foundation, Rollin M.
Giant Food
Goldman Foundation, William
Grainger Foundation
Great Lakes Casting Corp.
Greater Lansing Foundation
Greenfield Foundation, Albert M.
Gregg-Graniteville Foundation
Griffin, Sr., Foundation, C. V.
Grigg-Lewis Trust
Grundy Foundation
GTE Corp.
Guardian Life Insurance Co. of America
Gulf Power Co.
Hachar Charitable Trust, D. D.
Hagedorn Fund
Hall Foundation
Hall Foundation
Halliburton Co.
Hansen Foundation, Dane G.
Hardin Foundation, Phil
Harrington Foundation, Don and Sybil
Harris Corp.
Harris Family Foundation, Hunt and Diane
Harsco Corp.
Hartz Foundation
Hartz Foundation
Havens Foundation, O. W.
Hechinger Co.

Hecla Mining Co.
Heinz Co., H.J.
Herrick Foundation
Hershey Foods Corp.
Hewlett-Packard Co.
Hexcel Corp.
HON Industries
Horne Trust, Mabel
Hospital Corp. of America
Houston Industries
Howe and Mitchell B. Howe Foundation, Lucite Horton
Hubbard Foundation, R. Dee and Joan Dale
Hugg Trust, Leoia W. and Charles H.
Hultquist Foundation
Hunt Charitable Trust, C. Giles
Hunt Foundation
Hyde Foundation, J. R.
IBM Corp.
ICI Americas
Iddings Benevolent Trust
IES Industries
Illinois Tool Works
Independent Financial Corp.
Intel Corp.
Interco
International Student Exchange Cards
ITT Hartford Insurance Group
Jackson Family Foundation, Ann
Jackson Foundation
Jameson Foundation, J. W. and Ida M.
Jasam Foundation
JCPenney Co.
JELD-WEN, Inc.
Jennings Foundation, Alma
Johnson Co., E. F.
Johnson Controls
Johnson Foundation, M. G. and Lillie A.
Johnson & Higgins
Jones Construction Co., J.A.
Jones Foundation, Daisy Marquis
Jones Fund, Paul L.
Jonsson Foundation
JSJ Corp.
Keith Foundation Trust, Ben E.
Kelley and Elza Kelley Foundation, Edward Bangs
Kellogg Foundation, W. K.
Kennecott Corp.
Kerney Foundation, James
Kettering Family Foundation
Kidder, Peabody & Co.
Kilworth Charitable Trust, William
Kingsbury Corp.
Kiplinger Foundation
Kline Foundation, Josiah W. and Bessie H.
Knox Family Foundation
Koch Sons, George
Kysor Industrial Corp.
La-Z-Boy Chair Co.
Landegger Charitable Foundation
Lane Co., Inc.
Lane Foundation, Minnie and Bernard
Laros Foundation, R. K.
Lassus Brothers Oil
Lee Endowment Foundation
Leuthold Foundation
Leviton Manufacturing Co.
Lincoln Fund
Lincoln National Corp.
Lipton, Thomas J.
Lockheed Corp.
Lockheed Sanders
Long Island Lighting Co.
Loose Trust, Carrie J.
LTV Corp.
Lubrizol Corp.
Lydall, Inc.

Macht Foundation, Morton and Sophia
Macmillan, Inc.
Macy & Co., R.H.
Maritz Inc.
Marshall Foundation
Martin Foundation
Marx Foundation, Virginia & Leonard
Massachusetts Mutual Life Insurance Co.
Massey Foundation
Mayor Foundation, Oliver Dewey
McCann Foundation
McCasland Foundation
McLendon Educational Fund, Violet H.
McRae Foundation
Mead Corp.
Meadows Foundation
Medtronic
Metropolitan Health Foundation
Metropolitan Life Insurance Co.
Mettler Instrument Corp.
Meyer Foundation, Bert and Mary
Meyer Foundation, Eugene and Agnes E.
Meyer Memorial Trust
Michigan Gas Utilities
Midwest Resources
Mills Charitable Foundation, Henry L. and Kathryn
Mine Safety Appliances Co.
Minnegasco
Minolta Corp.
MNC Financial
Mohasco Corp.
Monsanto Co.
Montana Power Co.
Moorman Manufacturing Co.
Motorola
MTS Systems Corp.
Mueller Co.
Mulcahy Foundation
Nathan Foundation
National Computer Systems
National Gypsum Co.
National Life of Vermont
National Presto Industries
National Westminster Bank New Jersey
NationsBank Corp.
Navistar International Corp.
NBD Bank
Nellie Mae
Nestle U.S.A. Inc.
New England Business Service
New England Mutual Life Insurance Co.
New York Life Insurance Co.
New York Telephone Co.
Newhouse Foundation, Samuel I.
News & Observer Publishing Co.
Nord Family Foundation
Norfolk Shipbuilding & Drydock Corp.
Northeast Utilities
Northern States Power Co.
Northwestern National Life Insurance Co.
Norton Co.
Norwest Bank Nebraska
Norwest Corp.
Occidental Oil & Gas Corp.
Occidental Petroleum Corp.
O'Connor Foundation, A. Lindsay and Olive B.
Oglebay Norton Co.
Olin Corp.
Olin Foundation, Spencer T. and Ann W.
Ontario Corp.
Outboard Marine Corp.
Overstreet Foundation
Owens-Corning Fiberglas Corp.
Pacific Telesis Group

Palisades Educational Foundation
Parke-Davis Group
Parker Foundation, Theodore
   Edson
Parker-Hannifin Corp.
Peabody Charitable Fund, Amelia
Penn Foundation, William
Pennsylvania Knitted Outerwear
   Manufacturing Association
Peoples Energy Corp.
Pepsi-Cola Bottling Co. of
   Charlotte
Perkin-Elmer Corp.
Petteys Memorial Foundation,
   Jack
Pfizer
Phelps, Inc.
Phelps Dodge Corp.
Philadelphia Electric Co.
Philip Morris Cos.
Phillips Foundation, A. P.
Phillips Petroleum Co.
Portland General Electric Co.
Principal Financial Group
Promus Cos.
Providence Energy Corp.
Provident Life & Accident
   Insurance Co.
Prudential Insurance Co. of
   America
Public Service Electric & Gas
   Co.
Quaker Oats Co.
Questar Corp.
Radiator Specialty Co.
Raskob Foundation for Catholic
   Activities
Ray Foundation
Recognition Equipment
Redfield Foundation, Nell J.
Redman Foundation
Retirement Research Foundation
Reynolds Charitable Trust, Kate
   B.
Reynolds Foundation, Z. Smith
Reynolds Metals Co.
Rice Foundation, Helen Steiner
Richardson Benevolent
   Foundation, C. E.
Rittenhouse Foundation
Roberts Foundation, Dora
Roblee Foundation, Joseph H.
   and Florence A.
Rockwell International Corp.
Rohm and Haas Company
Rohr Inc.
Roseburg Forest Products Co.
Rosenberg Foundation, William
   J. and Tina
Rouse Co.
Ruddick Corp.
Russell Educational Foundation,
   Benjamin and Roberta
Russell Memorial Foundation,
   Robert
Sara Lee Hosiery
Sargent Foundation, Newell B.
Science Applications
   International Corp.
Scott Fund, Olin
Scroggins Foundation, Arthur E.
   and Cornelia C.
Scurry Foundation, D. L.
Searle & Co., G.D.
Security State Bank
Sedgwick James Inc.
Selby and Marie Selby
   Foundation, William G.
Sentinel Communications Co.
Shawmut National Corp.
Sheldon Foundation, Ralph C.
Shenandoah Life Insurance Co.
Shoney's Inc.
Shott, Jr. Foundation, Hugh I.
Signet Bank/Maryland
Simpson Industries
Simpson Investment Co.

Smith and W. Aubrey Smith
   Charitable Foundation, Clara
   Blackford
Smith Corp., A.O.
SNET
Sonoco Products Co.
Speas Memorial Trust, John W.
   and Effie E.
Springs Industries
Sprint
Square D Co.
Stabler Foundation, Donald B.
   and Dorothy L.
Staley, Jr. Foundation, A. E.
Staley Manufacturing Co., A.E.
Steelcase
Stevens Foundation, Abbot and
   Dorothy H.
Stocker Foundation
Stockham Valves & Fittings
Stonecutter Mills Corp.
Stupp Foundation, Norman J.
Sumitomo Bank of California
Summerfield Foundation, Solon
   E.
Sundstrand Corp.
Talley Industries, Inc.
Tandem Computers
Taub Foundation
TCF Banking & Savings, FSB
Teledyne
Tenneco
Texas Gas Transmission Corp.
Texas Instruments
Textron
Thermo Electron Corp.
Thomas & Betts Corp.
Thomas Industries
Thompson Charitable
   Foundation, Marion G.
3M Co.
Timken Foundation of Canton
Towsley Foundation, Harry A.
   and Margaret D.
Toyota Motor Sales, U.S.A.
Tracor, Inc.
Transco Energy Company
Trexler Trust, Harry C.
TRINOVA Corp.
Trion
True Oil Co.
Trull Foundation
Truman Foundation, Mildred
   Faulkner
TU Electric Co.
Tupancy-Harris Foundation of
   1986
Union Camp Corp.
Union Electric Co.
United Parcel Service of America
United Technologies Corp.
Universal Leaf Tobacco Co.
Vicksburg Hospital Medical
   Foundation
Visciglia Foundation, Frank
Volkswagen of America, Inc.
Vollbrecht Foundation, Frederick
   A.
Wachovia Bank of Georgia, N.A.
Wachovia Bank & Trust Co.,
   N.A.
Wareheim Foundation, E. C.
Washington Mutual Savings
   Bank
Washington Trust Bank
Washington Water Power Co.
Wasmer Foundation
Webb Foundation
Weezie Foundation
Wege Foundation
Weinberg Foundation, John L.
Welch Testamentary Trust,
   George T.
Wells Foundation, A. Z.
West Co.
Westvaco Corp.
Weyerhaeuser Co.

Wheat First Securites
Whirlpool Corp.
Whitaker Foundation
White Foundation, Erle and
   Emma
Wiggins Memorial Trust, J. J.
Williams Charitable Trust, Mary
   Jo
Williams Cos.
Witte, Jr. Foundation, John H.
Wrigley Co., Wm. Jr.
Wyman-Gordon Co.
Xerox Corp.
Yellow Corp.

Continuing Education

Abbott Laboratories
AlliedSignal
American Brands
American Express Co.
Amoco Corp.
Anderson Foundation, John W.
Anheuser-Busch Cos.
Apache Corp.
Atlanta Gas Light Co.
Bank of America Arizona
Bank of Boston Connecticut
Bank One, Texas-Houston Office
Benefit Trust Life Insurance Co.
Binney & Smith Inc.
Block, H&R
Blue Cross and Blue Shield
   United of Wisconsin
   Foundation
Boatmen's First National Bank
   of Oklahoma
Boeing Co.
Borden
Bowater Inc.
Capital Holding Corp.
Central Maine Power Co.
CIT Group Holdings
Citicorp
Citizens Union Bank
Cleveland-Cliffs
Clorox Co.
Cone-Blanchard Machine Co.
Dimeo Construction Co.
Dollar General Corp.
Dorminy Foundation, John Henry
Dupar Foundation
duPont Foundation, Alfred I.
Federal Express Corp.
Federated Department Stores and
   Allied Stores Corp.
Fels Fund, Samuel S.
Fireman's Fund Insurance Co.
First NH Banks, Inc.
First Union Corp.
First Union National Bank of
   Florida
Florida Power & Light Co.
Florida Rock Industries
Forest Foundation
Funderburke & Associates
General Mills
General Motors Corp.
Glaze Foundation, Robert and
   Ruth
Graphic Controls Corp.
Grotto Foundation
Haigh-Scatena Foundation
Hallmark Cards
Hansen Foundation, Dane G.
Harland Co., John H.
Harris Corp.
Hartford Courant Foundation
Hill Foundation
Hunt Alternatives Fund
Illinois Power Co.
Indiana Bell Telephone Co.
Inland Steel Industries
International Student Exchange
   Cards
J.P. Morgan & Co.

John Hancock Mutual Life
   Insurance Co.
Johnson Controls
Johnson & Higgins
JSJ Corp.
Kellogg Foundation, W. K.
King Ranch
Kingsbury Corp.
Kowalski Sausage Co.
Lavanburg-Corner House
Liberty National Bank
Lightner Sams Foundation
Lincoln Fund
Lindsay Trust, Agnes M.
Little, Arthur D.
Long Island Lighting Co.
Louisiana Land & Exploration
   Co.
Lydall, Inc.
Macy & Co., R.H.
Martin Foundation
Massey Charitable Trust
McKenna Foundation, Philip M.
Mead Corp.
Meadows Foundation
Mitchell Energy & Development
   Corp.
Mobil Oil Corp.
Morris Foundation
Motorola
MTS Systems Corp.
National Computer Systems
New England Mutual Life
   Insurance Co.
Nissan Motor Corporation in
   U.S.A.
Noble Foundation, Samuel
   Roberts
Northern Indiana Public Service
   Co.
Ormet Corp.
Overseas Shipholding Group
Perkin-Elmer Corp.
Polaroid Corp.
Portland General Electric Co.
Prudential Insurance Co. of
   America
Reliable Life Insurance Co.
Reliance Electric Co.
Retirement Research Foundation
Rockwell International Corp.
Rohr Inc.
Royal Group Inc.
SAFECO Corp.
Santa Fe Pacific Corp.
Science Applications
   International Corp.
Searle & Co., G.D.
Sedgwick James Inc.
Sentinel Communications Co.
Shawmut National Corp.
Siebert Lutheran Foundation
Signet Bank/Maryland
Simpson Investment Co.
SNET
Sonat
Springs Industries
State Street Bank & Trust Co.
Sterling Winthrop
Storage Technology Corp.
Sylvester Foundation, Harcourt
   M. and Virginia W.
3M Co.
Times Mirror Co.
Union Camp Corp.
United Parcel Service of America
Universal Foods Corp.
Unocal Corp.
Valley National Bank of Arizona
Volkswagen of America, Inc.
Wal-Mart Stores
Westvaco Corp.
Winter Construction Co.
Wyman-Gordon Co.
Xerox Corp.

Economic Education

Acushnet Co.
Acushnet Co.
Air Products & Chemicals
Akzo Chemicals Inc.
Albany International Corp.
Albertson's
Alcan Aluminum Corp.
Allegheny Foundation
Allegheny Ludlum Corp.
Alliant Techsystems
Allstate Insurance Co.
ALPAC Corp.
Alumax
Aluminum Co. of America
AMAX
AMCORE Bank, N.A. Rockford
America West Airlines
American Brands
American Cyanamid Co.
American Express Co.
American Financial Corp.
American Saw & Manufacturing
   Co.
American United Life Insurance
   Co.
Ameritas Life Insurance Corp.
Ameritech Corp.
Amfac/JMB Hawaii
Amoco Corp.
Andersen Corp.
Appleton Papers
Archer-Daniels-Midland Co.
ARCO
Arkansas Power & Light Co.
Armco Inc.
Arvin Industries
Ashland Oil
Atlanta Gas Light Co.
Attleboro Pawtucket Savings
   Bank
Avon Products
AXIA Incorporated
Ball Brothers Foundation
Ball Corp.
Banc One Illinois Corp.
BankAmerica Corp.
Bankers Trust Co.
BarclaysAmerican Corp.
Bard, C. R.
Barra Foundation
Battelle
Baughman Foundation
Bedsole Foundation, J. L.
Beech Aircraft Corp.
Belden Brick Co., Inc.
Belk Stores
Best Products Co.
Bethlehem Steel Corp.
BFGoodrich
BHP Pacific Resources
Bibb Co.
Binney & Smith Inc.
Blair and Co., William
Block, H&R
Blount
Blum-Kovler Foundation
Boatmen's Bancshares
Boeing Co.
Boettcher Foundation
Boise Cascade Corp.
Bowater Inc.
Bradley Foundation, Lynde and
   Harry
Bridgestone/Firestone
Brown Foundation, James
   Graham
Brown Group
Bucyrus-Erie
Business Incentives
C.P. Rail Systems
Cabot Corp.
Callaway Foundation
Capital Holding Corp.
Cargill
Carolina Power & Light Co.

Economic Education (cont.)

Carrier Corp.
Carter Foundation, Amon G.
Caterpillar
Ceco Corp.
Centerior Energy Corp.
Central Maine Power Co.
Central National-Gottesman
Chase Manhattan Bank, N.A.
Chesebrough-Pond's
Chevron Corp.
Chicago Title and Trust Co.
Chrysler Corp.
Cincinnati Bell
Citicorp
Citizens Bank
Cleveland-Cliffs
Clorox Co.
CM Alliance Cos.
CNA Insurance Cos.
Coachmen Industries
Cockrell Foundation
Colonial Life & Accident
  Insurance Co.
Colonial Oil Industries, Inc.
Columbus Dispatch Printing Co.
Cone Mills Corp.
Conn Memorial Foundation
Conoco Inc.
Consolidated Freightways
Consolidated Natural Gas Co.
Consolidated Papers
Consumers Power Co.
Continental Corp.
Cooper Industries
Coors Brewing Co.
Cowles Media Co.
CPC International
CR Industries
Crestar Financial Corp.
Crown Central Petroleum Corp.
Crum and Forster
Curran Foundation
Dain Bosworth/Inter-Regional
  Financial Group
Dana Corp.
Davis Foundation, Shelby
  Cullom
Dean Witter Discover
DEC International, Inc.
Deere & Co.
Delaware North Cos.
Deluxe Corp.
Deposit Guaranty National Bank
Detroit Edison Co.
Dimeo Construction Co.
Dively Foundation, George S.
Dively Foundation, George S.
Donaldson Co.
Dresser Industries
du Pont de Nemours & Co., E. I.
Duke Power Co.
Durst Foundation
Eaton Corp.
Eckerd Corp., Jack
Edwards & Sons, A.G.
Elf Atochem North America
Emerson Electric Co.
Endries Fastener & Supply Co.
English-Bonter-Mitchell
  Foundation
English Memorial Fund,
  Florence C. and H. L.
Enron Corp.
Equifax
Ethyl Corp.
Exxon Corp.
Federal-Mogul Corp.
Federated Department Stores and
  Allied Stores Corp.
Fidelity Bank
First Bank System
First Boston
First Chicago
First Hawaiian

First Interstate Bank of Arizona
First Interstate Bank of California
First Interstate Bank of Oregon
First Interstate Bank of Texas,
  N.A.
First Maryland Bancorp
First Tennessee Bank
First Union Corp.
Firstar Bank Milwaukee NA
Fleet Bank of New York
Fleet Financial Group
Fleming Companies, Inc.
Florida Power Corp.
Florida Power & Light Co.
Florida Steel Corp.
FMC Corp.
Ford Foundation
Ford Motor Co.
Formrite Tube Co.
Fortis Benefits Insurance
  Company/Fortis Financial
  Group
Fourth Financial Corp.
France Foundation, Jacob and
  Annita
Fraser Paper Ltd.
Freedom Forum
Freeport-McMoRan
Frisch's Restaurants Inc.
Funderburke & Associates
Gates Foundation
General American Life Insurance
  Co.
General Electric Co.
General Mills
General Motors Corp.
General Tire Inc.
Georgia-Pacific Corp.
Georgia Power Co.
Gheens Foundation
Goodyear Tire & Rubber Co.
Grace & Co., W.R.
Graco
Great-West Life Assurance Co.
Gregg-Graniteville Foundation
GTE Corp.
Guardian Life Insurance Co. of
  America
Harsco Corp.
Hartmarx Corp.
Hechinger Co.
HEI Inc.
Heileman Brewing Co., Inc., G.
Heinz Co., H.J.
Hershey Foods Corp.
Honeywell
Hospital Corp. of America
Household International
Houston Industries
Hubbard Broadcasting
IDS Financial Services
Illinois Bell
Illinois Tool Works
Indiana Bell Telephone Co.
Inland Container Corp.
Inland Steel Industries
Interco
International Paper Co.
International Student Exchange
  Cards
ITT Corp.
ITT Rayonier
James River Corp. of Virginia
JCPenney Co.
Jewett Foundation, George
  Frederick
John Hancock Mutual Life
  Insurance Co.
Johnson Co., E. F.
Johnson Controls
Johnson Endeavor Foundation,
  Christian A.
Johnson Foundation, Helen K.
  and Arthur E.
Johnson & Higgins
Johnson & Son, S.C.
Jostens

Keebler Co.
Kellogg Foundation, J. C.
Kellogg Foundation, W. K.
Kellstadt Foundation
Kennecott Corp.
Kerr Foundation, Robert S. and
  Grayce B.
Kerr-McGee Corp.
Kidder, Peabody & Co.
Kiewit Sons, Peter
Kimberly-Clark Corp.
Koch Charitable Trust, David H.
Krieble Foundation, Vernon K.
Laclede Gas Co.
Lance, Inc.
Liberty National Bank
Life Insurance Co. of Georgia
Lilly Endowment
Lincoln National Corp.
Lipton, Thomas J.
Lockheed Corp.
Longview Fibre Co.
Love Foundation, Gay and
  Erskine
LTV Corp.
Lubrizol Corp.
Lydall, Inc.
Macy & Co., R.H.
Marbrook Foundation
Maritz Inc.
Martin Marietta Corp.
Mason Charitable Foundation
Material Service Corp.
Maxon Charitable Foundation
McCormick & Co.
McCormick Tribune Foundation,
  Robert R.
McDonnell Douglas Corp.
McElroy Trust, R. J.
MCI Communications Corp.
McInerny Foundation
McKenna Foundation, Philip M.
MDU Resources Group, Inc.
Mead Corp.
Meadows Foundation
Mellon Foundation, Richard King
Merrill Lynch & Co.
Metropolitan Life Insurance Co.
Milliken & Co.
Mine Safety Appliances Co.
Minnegasco
Minnesota Mutual Life
  Insurance Co.
Mitsubishi International Corp.
MNC Financial
Mobil Oil Corp.
Monell Foundation, Ambrose
Monsanto Co.
Montgomery Street Foundation
Moore Family Foundation
Moore Foundation, Edward S.
Motorola
MTS Systems Corp.
Multimedia, Inc.
Nalco Chemical Co.
National City Corp.
National Computer Systems
National Service Industries
National Westminster Bank New
  Jersey
NationsBank Corp.
NBD Bank
NBD Bank, N.A.
New York Telephone Co.
Newhouse Foundation, Samuel I.
Noble Foundation, Samuel
  Roberts
Norfolk Shipbuilding & Drydock
  Corp.
Norfolk Southern Corp.
North American Life & Casualty
  Co.
Northeast Utilities
Northwestern National Life
  Insurance Co.
Norton Co.
Norton Foundation Inc.

NYNEX Corp.
Ogilvy & Mather Worldwide
Oglebay Norton Co.
Ohio National Life Insurance Co.
Olin Foundation, John M.
Olin Foundation, Spencer T. and
  Ann W.
Ontario Corp.
O'Shaughnessy Foundation, I. A.
Overnite Transportation Co.
PACCAR
Pacific Mutual Life Insurance Co.
Pacific Telesis Group
Packaging Corporation of
  America
Panhandle Eastern Corp.
Paramount Communications Inc.
Parsons Foundation, Ralph M.
Perkin-Elmer Corp.
Pfizer
Phelps Dodge Corp.
Phillipps Foundation
Phillips Foundation, Dr. P.
Phillips Petroleum Co.
Pittway Corp.
PPG Industries
Procter & Gamble Co.
Procter & Gamble Cosmetic &
  Fragrance Products
Providence Energy Corp.
Provident Life & Accident
  Insurance Co.
Prudential Insurance Co. of
  America
Public Service Co. of Colorado
Quaker Oats Co.
Questar Corp.
Red Wing Shoe Co.
Reichhold Chemicals, Inc.
Reynolds Metals Co.
Richardson Foundation, Smith
Rockwell International Corp.
Rohm and Haas Company
Ross Foundation
Rubbermaid
SAFECO Corp.
Safeguard Scientifics Foundation
Sage Foundation, Russell
Salomon
San Diego Gas & Electric
Santa Fe Pacific Corp.
Scaife Family Foundation
Scaife Foundation, Sarah
Schwab & Co., Charles
Scrivner, Inc.
Seafirst Corp.
Sealright Co., Inc.
Searle & Co., G.D.
Security Benefit Life Insurance
  Co.
Security Life of Denver
Sedgwick James Inc.
Shawmut National Corp.
Shell Oil Co.
Shenandoah Life Insurance Co.
Sherwin-Williams Co.
Signet Bank/Maryland
Simpson Investment Co.
Sloan Foundation, Alfred P.
Smith Corp., A.O.
Sonat
Sonoco Products Co.
Southern California Edison Co.
Springs Industries
Sprint
Square D Co.
Stanley Works
Star Bank, N.A.
Starr Foundation
State Farm Mutual Automobile
  Insurance Co.
Stone Container Corp.
Stranahan Foundation
Sumners Foundation, Hatton W.
Sundstrand Corp.
Sunmark Capital Corp.
Synovus Financial Corp.

Tamko Asphalt Products
Tektronix
Teledyne
Tenneco
Texaco
Texas Instruments
Textron
Thermo Electron Corp.
Thomas Industries
3M Co.
Times Mirror Co.
Tozer Foundation
Transamerica Corp.
Transco Energy Company
TRINOVA Corp.
Tropicana Products, Inc.
Trust Co. Bank
Tyson Foods, Inc.
Unilever United States
Union Bank
Union Camp Corp.
Union Carbide Corp.
Union Electric Co.
Union Pacific Corp.
United Parcel Service of America
United States Sugar Corp.
Univar Corp.
Universal Leaf Tobacco Co.
Unocal Corp.
US WEST
USX Corp.
Valley National Bank of Arizona
Valmont Industries
Virginia Power Co.
Vogt Machine Co., Henry
Volkswagen of America, Inc.
Vollrath Co.
Vulcan Materials Co.
Wachovia Bank & Trust Co.,
  N.A.
Wal-Mart Stores
Walgreen Co.
Washington Water Power Co.
Wells Fargo & Co.
Weyerhaeuser Co.
Whirlpool Corp.
White Consolidated Industries
Whitehead Foundation
Whiting Foundation, Macauley
  and Helen Dow
WICOR, Inc.
Williams Cos.
Wisconsin Energy Corp.
Wyman-Gordon Co.
Xerox Corp.
XTEK Inc.
Yellow Corp.

Education Administration

Abell Foundation, The
Amoco Corp.
Armco Inc.
Belden Brick Co., Inc.
Bigelow Foundation, F. R.
Binney & Smith Inc.
Block, H&R
Boeing Co.
Borg-Warner Corp.
Burdines
Burns Foundation, Fritz B.
Bush Foundation
Campbell Soup Co.
Central Maine Power Co.
Citicorp
Cleveland-Cliffs
Colorado Trust
Danforth Foundation
Dodge Foundation, Geraldine R.
du Pont de Nemours & Co., E. I.
Duke Power Co.
Equitable Life Assurance Society
  of the U.S.
Ford Foundation
Fox Foundation, Richard J.
Funderburke & Associates

Gluck Foundation, Maxwell H.
Grossman Foundation, N. Bud
Hall Family Foundations
Heinz Endowment, Howard
Illinois Power Co.
International Student Exchange
   Cards
ITT Hartford Insurance Group
Jennings Foundation, Martha
   Holden
Johnson Foundation, Walter S.
Johnson & Higgins
Kellogg Foundation, W. K.
Lilly Endowment
Mayer Foods Corp., Oscar
McDonnell Douglas Corp.
Meadows Foundation
Mellon Foundation, Richard King
National Computer Systems
Nordson Corp.
NYNEX Corp.
O'Neill Charitable Corporation,
   F. J.
Paramount Communications Inc.
Petrie Trust, Lorene M.
Premier Industrial Corp.
Pritzker Foundation
Prudential Insurance Co. of
   America
Regis Corp.
Rockefeller Foundation,
   Winthrop
Rohm and Haas Company
Rosenberg Family Foundation,
   William
Sedgwick James Inc.
Selby and Marie Selby
   Foundation, William G.
Taylor Foundation, Ruth and
   Vernon
TCF Banking & Savings, FSB
Union Camp Corp.
United States Sugar Corp.
Wal-Mart Stores
Wieboldt Foundation
Woods Charitable Fund

Education
Associations

Abbott Laboratories
Abell-Hanger Foundation
Abrons Foundation, Louis and
   Anne
Adams Foundation, Arthur F. and
   Alice E.
Ahmanson Foundation
Air Products & Chemicals
Alden Trust, George I.
Allegheny Foundation
Allegheny Ludlum Corp.
Alliant Techsystems
Altman Foundation
Aluminum Co. of America
AMAX
American Brands
American Financial Corp.
American Natural Resources Co.
American President Cos.
American Saw & Manufacturing
   Co.
American Telephone &
   Telegraph Co.
AMETEK
Amoco Corp.
Andersen Corp.
Anderson Foundation, John W.
Andersons Management Corp.
Annenberg Foundation
Anschutz Family Foundation
Archer-Daniels-Midland Co.
Arkansas Power & Light Co.
Armco Inc.
Aron Charitable Foundation, J.
Arvin Industries
Ashland Oil
Atherton Family Foundation

Atlanta Gas Light Co.
Balfour Foundation, L. G.
Banbury Fund
Banc One Illinois Corp.
Banfi Vintners
Bank of Louisville
Bank of New York
Bankers Trust Co.
Barnett Charitable Foundation,
   Lawrence and Isabel
Barra Foundation
Barry Corp., R. G.
Batten Foundation
Bauer Foundation, M. R.
Becton Dickinson & Co.
Bedsole Foundation, J. L.
BellSouth Corp.
Beveridge Foundation, Frank
   Stanley
BFGoodrich
Big V Supermarkets
Bigelow Foundation, F. R.
Binney & Smith Inc.
Blaustein Foundation, Jacob and
   Hilda
Blount
Blum-Kovler Foundation
Boatmen's First National Bank
   of Oklahoma
Boehringer Mannheim Corp.
Boler Co.
Borden
Boston Edison Co.
Brach Foundation, Helen
Bradley-Turner Foundation
Brown & Williamson Tobacco
   Corp.
Brunswick Corp.
Buhl Foundation
Burlington Industries
Burlington Resources
Burns Foundation, Fritz B.
Burroughs Wellcome Co.
Butler Manufacturing Co.
C.P. Rail Systems
Cable & Wireless
   Communications
Cafritz Foundation, Morris and
   Gwendolyn
Callaway Foundation
Cameron Foundation, Harry S.
   and Isabel C.
Capital Fund Foundation
Capital Holding Corp.
Carnegie Corporation of New
   York
Carnival Cruise Lines
Carolyn Foundation
Carpenter Technology Corp.
Carrier Corp.
Carter-Wallace
CBI Industries
CBS Inc.
Centel Corp.
Centerior Energy Corp.
Central Maine Power Co.
Central & South West Services
Central Soya Co.
Chase Manhattan Bank, N.A.
Chesapeake Corp.
Chesebrough-Pond's
Chevron Corp.
Chicago Tribune Co.
Chrysler Corp.
Citibank, F.S.B.
Citicorp
Citizens Bank
Cleveland-Cliffs
Clipper Ship Foundation
Clorox Co.
Clowes Fund
CNG Transmission Corp.
Cole Foundation, Olive B.
Collins Foundation
Collins Foundation, Carr P.
Columbus Dispatch Printing Co.
Commerce Clearing House

Cone Mills Corp.
Consumers Power Co.
Cooper Industries
Coors Foundation, Adolph
Country Curtains, Inc.
County Bank
Cowles Media Co.
CPC International
CUNA Mutual Insurance Group
Daiwa Securities America Inc.
Daly Charitable Foundation
   Trust, Robert and Nancy
Danforth Foundation
Deloitte & Touche
Delta Air Lines
Deluxe Corp.
Detroit Edison Co.
Deutsch Co.
Dixie Yarns, Inc.
Dodge Foundation, Geraldine R.
Doheny Foundation, Carrie
   Estelle
Donnelley & Sons Co., R.R.
Donner Foundation, William H.
Douglas & Lomason Company
Dover Foundation
Dow Chemical Co.
Dow Jones & Co.
Dreyfus Foundation, Max and
   Victoria
du Pont de Nemours & Co., E. I.
Duke Power Co.
Dun & Bradstreet Corp.
Eaton Corp.
Eccles Foundation, George S.
   and Dolores Dore
Eden Hall Foundation
Edison Fund, Charles
Emerson Electric Co.
Endries Fastener & Supply Co.
Engelhard Foundation, Charles
English-Bonter-Mitchell
   Foundation
Enron Corp.
Equifax
Equitable Life Assurance Society
   of the U.S.
Ernst & Young
Ernsthausen Charitable
   Foundation, John F. and Doris
   E.
Exxon Corp.
Fairchild Corp.
Farish Fund, William Stamps
Farnsworth Trust, Charles A.
Federal Home Loan Mortgage
   Corp. (Freddie Mac)
Federal-Mogul Corp.
Federated Department Stores and
   Allied Stores Corp.
Federated Life Insurance Co.
First Chicago
First Mississippi Corp.
Fish Foundation, Ray C.
Foellinger Foundation
Forbes
Ford Foundation
Ford Fund, Walter and Josephine
Ford II Fund, Henry
Ford Meter Box Co.
Ford Motor Co.
Foundation for Advancement of
   Chiropractic Education
Foundation for Child
   Development
Freedom Forum
Freeman Charitable Trust,
   Samuel
Freightliner Corp.
French Oil Mill Machinery Co.
Frueauff Foundation, Charles A.
Fry Foundation, Lloyd A.
Fund for New Jersey
Funderburke & Associates
Funderburke & Associates
GAR Foundation
GEICO Corp.

General Electric Co.
General Mills
General Motors Corp.
General Signal Corp.
General Tire Inc.
George Foundation
Georgia-Pacific Corp.
Georgia Power Co.
Gheens Foundation
Gitano Group
Glaxo
Glickenhaus & Co.
Goodyear Tire & Rubber Co.
Gorin Foundation, Nehemiah
Grainger Foundation
Grant Foundation, William T.
Grassmann Trust, E. J.
Green Fund
Greve Foundation, William and
   Mary
Groves & Sons Co., S.J.
Gulf Power Co.
Guttag Foundation, Irwin and
   Marjorie
Hall Charitable Trust, Evelyn A.
   J.
Hamilton Bank
Hamilton Oil Corp.
Hancock Foundation, Luke B.
Hankins Foundation
Harcourt General
Harriman Foundation, Mary W.
Harsco Corp.
Hechinger Co.
Heckscher Foundation for
   Children
Heinz Co., H.J.
Heinz Endowment, Howard
Herrick Foundation
Homeland Foundation
Hooker Charitable Trust, Janet A.
Hospital Corp. of America
Household International
Houston Endowment
Hoyt Foundation, Stewart W. and
   Willma C.
Humana
Hunt Alternatives Fund
IBM Corp.
Ideal Industries
Imperial Bancorp
Inland Container Corp.
Inland Steel Industries
Interco
International Flavors &
   Fragrances
International Student Exchange
   Cards
Iowa Savings Bank
Irvine Foundation, James
ITT Rayonier
Ittleson Foundation
Jacobson & Sons, Benjamin
Janirve Foundation
Johnson Co., E. F.
Johnson Controls
Johnson Foundation, Walter S.
Johnson & Higgins
Johnston Trust for Charitable
   and Educational Purposes,
   James M.
Jostens
Journal Gazette Co.
Julia R. and Estelle L.
   Foundation
Kade Foundation, Max
Kaufmann Foundation, Henry
Kellogg Foundation, W. K.
Kemper Charitable Trust,
   William T.
Kennametal
Kerr-McGee Corp.
Kettering Fund
Kimball International
Kimberly-Clark Corp.
Koch Sons, George
Koret Foundation

Krieble Foundation, Vernon K.
Ladish Co.
Laffey-McHugh Foundation
Lamson & Sessions Co.
Lance, Inc.
Large Foundation
Laurel Foundation
Lawyers Title Foundation
Leavey Foundation, Thomas and
   Dorothy
Lebanon Mutual Insurance Co.
Lee Foundation, James T.
Lee Foundation, Ray M. and
   Mary Elizabeth
Lennox International, Inc.
Levy Foundation, Charles and
   Ruth
Lewis Foundation, Frank J.
Liberty Corp.
Life Insurance Co. of Georgia
Lilly & Co., Eli
Lilly Endowment
Lincoln National Corp.
Lipton, Thomas J.
Liquid Air Corp.
Litton Industries
Lockheed Corp.
Long Foundation, George A. and
   Grace
Loutit Foundation
Lowe Foundation, Joe and Emily
Lowenstein Foundation, Leon
Luce Foundation, Henry
Lurie Foundation, Louis R.
Lydall, Inc.
Maclellan Foundation
Marcus Corp.
Marine Midland Banks
Marriott Foundation, J. Willard
Marshall & Ilsley Bank
Masco Corp.
May Department Stores Co.
Maytag Corp.
MCA
McBean Family Foundation
McCasland Foundation
McConnell Foundation, Neil A.
McCormick Tribune Foundation,
   Robert R.
McDonnell Douglas Corp.
McGee Foundation
McGraw-Hill
MCI Communications Corp.
McKenna Foundation, Katherine
   Mabis
McMahon Foundation
Mead Corp.
Meadows Foundation
Medina Foundation
Mellon Bank Corp.
Mellon Foundation, Andrew W.
Mellon Foundation, Richard King
Merck Fund, John
Merrick Foundation
Michigan Bell Telephone Co.
Michigan Consolidated Gas Co.
Milliken & Co.
Mine Safety Appliances Co.
Mitsubishi International Corp.
Mobil Oil Corp.
Monell Foundation, Ambrose
Monroe-Brown Foundation
Moorman Manufacturing Co.
Moriah Fund
Morris Foundation
Moses Fund, Henry and Lucy
Motorola
Mott Foundation, Charles Stewart
Multimedia, Inc.
Nalco Chemical Co.
National By-Products
National Computer Systems
National Fuel Gas Co.
National Starch & Chemical
   Corp.
National Westminster Bank New
   Jersey

Education Associations (cont.)

NBD Bank
Nellie Mae
New-Land Foundation
New World Foundation
New York Life Insurance Co.
New York Telephone Co.
The New Yorker Magazine, Inc.
Newhouse Foundation, Samuel I.
News & Observer Publishing Co.
Noble Foundation, Edward John
Noble Foundation, Vivian Bilby
Nordson Corp.
Norfolk Shipbuilding & Drydock Corp.
Norfolk Southern Corp.
Northern Indiana Public Service Co.
Norton Co.
NuTone Inc.
Oakley Foundation, Hollie and Anna
O'Brien Foundation, Cornelius and Anna Cook
Occidental Petroleum Corp.
O'Donnell Foundation
Oglebay Norton Co.
Oglebay Norton Co.
Ohl, Jr. Trust, George A.
Olin Foundation, John M.
Olin Foundation, Spencer T. and Ann W.
O'Neill Charitable Corporation, F. J.
Overbrook Foundation
PACCAR
Packard Foundation, David and Lucile
PaineWebber
Palisades Educational Foundation
Paramount Communications Inc.
Parman Foundation, Robert A.
Parsons Foundation, Ralph M.
Payne Foundation, Frank E. and Seba B.
Peabody Charitable Fund, Amelia
Pearlstone Foundation, Peggy Meyerhoff
Pennsylvania Dutch Co.
Pennsylvania General Insurance Co.
PepsiCo
Perkin-Elmer Corp.
Perley Fund, Victor E.
Perot Foundation
Pew Charitable Trusts
Pfizer
Pforzheimer Foundation, Carl and Lily
Phelps, Inc.
Phelps Dodge Corp.
Philip Morris Cos.
Phillipps Foundation
Phillips Charitable Trust, Dr. and Mrs. Arthur William
Phillips Family Foundation, Jay and Rose
Phillips Petroleum Co.
Pick, Jr. Fund, Albert
Pierce Charitable Trust, Harold Whitworth
Pineywoods Foundation
Pinkerton Foundation
Pitt-Des Moines Inc.
Pittsburgh National Bank
Pittway Corp.
Plaster Foundation, Robert W.
Pollock Company Foundation, William B.
Porter Paint Co.
Posnack Family Foundation of Hollywood
Potlatch Corp.
Potomac Electric Power Co.
Powell Family Foundation
PPG Industries

Premier Industrial Corp.
Price Waterhouse-U.S.
Procter & Gamble Cosmetic & Fragrance Products
Prouty Foundation, Olive Higgins
Prudential-Bache Securities
Prudential Insurance Co. of America
Quaker Oats Co.
Quality Metal Finishing Foundation
Raymond Corp.
Raymond Educational Foundation
Red Wing Shoe Co.
Reed Foundation, Philip D.
Reily & Co., William B.
Relations Foundation
Reynolds Foundation, Donald W.
Reynolds Foundation, Richard S.
Reynolds Metals Co.
Richmond Foundation, Frederick W.
Ringier-America
Robertshaw Controls Co.
Rockefeller Brothers Fund
Rockwell International Corp.
Roe Foundation
Rogers Charitable Trust, Florence
Rohm and Haas Company
Rolfs Foundation, Thomas J.
Romill Foundation
Rose Foundation, Billy
Rosenberg Family Foundation, William
Ross Foundation
Ross Foundation
Roth Family Foundation
Rubbermaid
Rubin Foundation, Samuel
Ryan Foundation, Patrick G. and Shirley W.
SAFECO Corp.
Sandy Hill Foundation
Santa Fe Pacific Corp.
Saunders Charitable Foundation, Helen M.
Scaife Foundation, Sarah
Scherer Foundation, Karla
Schering-Plough Corp.
Scherman Foundation
Schiff, Hardin & Waite
Schlumberger Ltd.
Scholl Foundation, Dr.
Schramm Foundation
Schumann Fund for New Jersey
Schwartz Foundation, Bernard Lee
Science Applications International Corp.
Scott and Fetzer Co.
Scrivner, Inc.
Searle & Co., G.D.
Seasongood Good Government Foundation, Murray and Agnes
Sedgwick James Inc.
Sega of America
Shawmut National Corp.
Shawmut Worcester County Bank, N.A.
Shell Oil Co.
Shelter Mutual Insurance Co.
Shenandoah Life Insurance Co.
Shoong Foundation, Milton
Shorenstein Foundation, Walter H. and Phyllis J.
Signet Bank/Maryland
Simon Foundation, Jennifer Jones
Simon Foundation, William E. and Carol G.
Sjostrom & Sons
Sloan Foundation, Alfred P.
Smithers Foundation, Christopher D.
SmithKline Beecham
SNET
Solow Foundation

Solow Foundation, Sheldon H.
Sonat
Sooner Pipe & Supply Corp.
Sprague Educational and Charitable Foundation, Seth
Springs Industries
Sprint
Stackpole-Hall Foundation
Star Bank, N.A.
Starr Foundation
State Farm Mutual Automobile Insurance Co.
Steele-Reese Foundation
Steigerwaldt Foundation, Donna Wolf
Steinberg Family Foundation, Meyer and Jean
Steinman Foundation, James Hale
Sterling Winthrop
Stevens Foundation, Abbot and Dorothy H.
Stone Charitable Foundation
Stone Container Corp.
Stonecutter Mills Corp.
Strake Foundation
Stranahan Foundation
Stuart Foundations
Stulsaft Foundation, Morris
Subaru of America Inc.
Sudix Foundation
Summerfield Foundation, Solon E.
Sun Co.
Sussman Fund, Edna Bailey
Synovus Financial Corp.
Taconic Foundation
Tandy Foundation, Anne Burnett and Charles
Taube Family Foundation
TCF Banking & Savings, FSB
Teledyne
Tenneco
Texaco
Texas Instruments
Textron
Thirty-Five Twenty, Inc.
Thomas & Betts Corp.
3M Co.
Thrush-Thompson Foundation
Thyssen Specialty Steels
Times Mirror Co.
Timken Co.
Tisch Foundation
TJX Cos.
Tomkins Industries, Inc.
Transamerica Corp.
Tremco Inc.
Trinity Foundation
TRINOVA Corp.
Tropicana Products, Inc.
Tull Charitable Foundation
Turrell Fund
28:19
Unilever United States
Union Camp Corp.
United Merchants & Manufacturers
United Parcel Service of America
United States Sugar Corp.
Unocal Corp.
Upjohn Foundation, Harold and Grace
USX Corp.
Uvas Foundation
Valley Foundation, Wayne and Gladys
Van Every Foundation, Philip L.
Virginia Power Co.
Wal-Mart Stores
Wallace-Reader's Digest Fund, DeWitt
Warner-Lambert Co.
Warren Foundation, William K.
Wean Foundation, Raymond John
Weatherwax Foundation

Webb Educational and Charitable Trust, Torrey H. and Dorothy K.
Weezie Foundation
Wehadkee Foundation
Wenger Foundation, Henry L. and Consuelo S.
Westvaco Corp.
Weyerhaeuser Co.
Wheat First Securites
Whirlpool Corp.
White Consolidated Industries
Wieboldt Foundation
Wilbur Foundation, Marguerite Eyer
Wilkof Foundation, Edward and Ruth
Williams Cos.
Willmott Foundation, Peter S.
Winthrop Trust, Clara B.
Wisconsin Energy Corp.
Woods Charitable Fund
Woodward Fund-Atlanta, David, Helen, Marian
Wyman-Gordon Co.
Xerox Corp.
Yeager Charitable Trust, Lester E.
Young Foundation, R. A.

Education Funds

Abercrombie Foundation
Achelis Foundation
Ackerman Trust, Anna Keesling
Acme-McCrary Corp.
Acushnet Co.
Agape Foundation
Ahmanson Foundation
Air Products & Chemicals
Alco Standard Corp.
Alcon Laboratories, Inc.
Alexander Foundation, Joseph
Alhambra Foundry Co., Ltd.
Allegheny Ludlum Corp.
Alliss Educational Foundation, Charles and Ellora
ALPAC Corp.
Aluminum Co. of America
Amaturo Foundation
AMAX
Amcast Industrial Corp.
American Cyanamid Co.
American Electric Power
American Express Co.
American Financial Corp.
American National Bank & Trust Co. of Chicago
American Optical Corp.
American Standard
American Telephone & Telegraph Co.
American Welding & Manufacturing Co.
Ames Department Stores
AMETEK
Amfac/JMB Hawaii
Amsted Industries
Andalusia Health Services
Andersen Corp.
Andersen Foundation
Anderson Foundation, John W.
Andres Charitable Trust, Frank G.
Anheuser-Busch Cos.
Annenberg Foundation
AON Corp.
Archer-Daniels-Midland Co.
ARCO Chemical
Aristech Chemical Corp.
Arkansas Power & Light Co.
Armco Inc.
Armstrong Foundation
Armstrong World Industries Inc.
Arrillaga Foundation
Arvin Industries
Ashland Oil
Atherton Family Foundation

Atlanta Gas Light Co.
Atwood Foundation
Auerbach Foundation, Beatrice Fox
Austin Memorial Foundation
Avon Products
Azadoutioun Foundation
Azby Fund
Badger Meter, Inc.
Baker, Jr. Memorial Fund, William G.
Baker Trust, Clayton
Balfour Foundation, L. G.
Ball Foundation, George and Frances
Baltimore Gas & Electric Co.
Banc One Wisconsin Corp.
Banfi Vintners
Bank of Boston Connecticut
Bank of Boston Corp.
Bank of Louisville
Bank South Corp.
Bard, C. R.
Bardes Corp.
Barker Foundation
Barnes Foundation
Barnes Group
Bashinsky Foundation
Batten Foundation
Bauervic-Paisley Foundation
Baughman Foundation
Bausch & Lomb
Beazley Foundation
Bechtel Group
Bedford Fund
Bedsole Foundation, J. L.
Beech Aircraft Corp.
Beidler Charitable Trust, Francis
Beinecke Foundation
Belding Heminway Co.
Beldon Fund
Belk Stores
Belo Corp., A.H.
Bemis Company
Bender Foundation
Benedum Foundation, Claude Worthington
Beneficia Foundation
Beneficial Corp.
Benwood Foundation
Berger Foundation, H.N. and Frances C.
Bergner Co., P.A.
Bernsen Foundation, Grace and Franklin
Bernstein & Co., Sanford C.
Bertha Foundation
Beveridge Foundation, Frank Stanley
BFGoodrich
Bickerton Charitable Trust, Lydia H.
Bierhaus Foundation
Bigelow Foundation, F. R.
Bingham Second Betterment Fund, William
Bingham Trust, The
Binney & Smith Inc.
Bird Inc.
Bishop Foundation, E. K. and Lillian F.
Blake Foundation, S. P.
Blaustein Foundation, Morton K. and Jane
Block, H&R
Blount
Blue Bell, Inc.
Blue Cross and Blue Shield of Minnesota Foundation Inc.
Blue Cross and Blue Shield United of Wisconsin Foundation
Blum-Kovler Foundation
BMC Industries
Bodenhamer Foundation
Boeing Co.
Borden

Borden Memorial Foundation, Mary Owen
Boston Edison Co.
Bound to Stay Bound Books Foundation
Bozzone Family Foundation
Brach Foundation, Helen
Bradley-Turner Foundation
Brady Foundation, W. H.
Branta Foundation
Bravmann Foundation, Ludwig
Bray Charitable Trust, Viola E.
Brenner Foundation
Brenton Banks Inc.
Bridgestone/Firestone
Britton Fund
Broccoli Charitable Foundation, Dana and Albert R.
Brooklyn Union Gas Co.
Brown Foundation
Brown, Jr. Charitable Trust, Frank D.
Browning Charitable Foundation, Val A.
Brundage Charitable, Scientific, and Wildlife Conservation Foundation, Charles E. and Edna T.
Bruner Foundation
Bryant Foundation
Bucyrus-Erie
Buell Foundation, Temple Hoyne
Buffett Foundation
Burchfield Foundation, Charles E.
Burdines
Burlington Industries
Burlington Resources
Burnand Medical and Educational Foundation, Alphonse A.
Burroughs Wellcome Co.
Butler Foundation, Alice
Cabot Corp.
Cafritz Foundation, Morris and Gwendolyn
Cain Foundation, Gordon and Mary
Caldwell Foundation, Hardwick
Cameron Memorial Fund, Alpin J. and Alpin W.
Camp Foundation
Capital Fund Foundation
Capital Holding Corp.
Carnival Cruise Lines
Carolina Power & Light Co.
Carpenter Foundation, E. Rhodes and Leona B.
Carpenter Technology Corp.
Carter-Wallace
Cascade Natural Gas Corp.
Castle Trust, George P. and Ida Tenney
Caterpillar
Ceco Corp.
Centel Corp.
Central Bank of the South
Central Maine Power Co.
Central & South West Services
Central Soya Co.
Chamberlin Foundation, Gerald W.
Chandler Foundation
Chapin-May Foundation of Illinois
Charities Foundation
Chase Manhattan Bank, N.A.
Chesapeake Corp.
Chesebrough-Pond's
Chevron Corp.
Christensen Charitable and Religious Foundation, L. C.
Christodora
Cincinnati Bell
CIT Group Holdings
Citicorp
Citizens Bank
Claneil Foundation

Clark Foundation
Clark-Winchcole Foundation
Clarke Trust, John
Classic Leather
Clements Foundation
Cleveland-Cliffs
Clorox Co.
Clover Foundation
CNG Transmission Corp.
Coffey Foundation
Cohen Foundation, Naomi and Nehemiah
Cohn Foundation, Herman and Terese
Coleman Co.
Coles Family Foundation
Collins Foundation
Collins Foundation, George and Jennie
Collins Medical Trust
Colonial Oil Industries, Inc.
Columbus Dispatch Printing Co.
Conn Memorial Foundation
Continental Corp.
Continental Grain Co.
Cook Foundation, Loring
Cooper Industries
Copolymer Rubber & Chemical Corp.
Corbin Foundation, Mary S. and David C.
Corestates Bank
Cornell Trust, Peter C.
Corpus Christi Exploration Co.
Country Curtains, Inc.
County Bank
Cowles Media Co.
Cox Charitable Trust, Jessie B.
Crane & Co.
Crane Co.
Cranston Print Works
Crawford & Co.
Creel Foundation
Crescent Plastics
CRL Inc.
Crocker Trust, Mary A.
Crown Central Petroleum Corp.
Crum and Forster
Cullen/Frost Bankers
Cummins Engine Co.
Daily News
Dain Bosworth/Inter-Regional Financial Group
Dalton Foundation, Dorothy U.
Dana Corp.
Danforth Foundation
Daniel Foundation of Alabama
Darling Foundation, Hugh and Hazel
Davies Charitable Trust
Day Foundation, Cecil B.
De Lima Co., Paul
Delany Charitable Trust, Beatrice P.
Delta Air Lines
Demoulas Supermarkets
Dennison Manufacturing Co.
Deposit Guaranty National Bank
DeSoto
Detroit Edison Co.
Deuble Foundation, George H.
DeVos Foundation, Richard and Helen
Dibner Fund
Dillon Foundation
Dixie Yarns, Inc.
Dodge Foundation, P. L.
Dodge Jones Foundation
Donaldson Co.
Dorminy Foundation, John Henry
Doty Family Foundation
Dougherty, Jr. Foundation, James R.
Douty Foundation
Dower Foundation, Thomas W.
Dresser Industries
du Pont de Nemours & Co., E. I.

Dubow Family Foundation
Duchossois Industries
Duke Power Co.
Dun & Bradstreet Corp.
Dunagan Foundation
Dunspaugh-Dalton Foundation
Dweck Foundation, Samuel R.
Eastover Corp.
Eaton Corp.
Eccles Foundation, Ralph M. and Ella M.
Echlin Foundation
Edwards Industries
Ehrman Foundation, Fred and Susan
Einstein Fund, Albert E. and Birdie W.
Electric Power Equipment Co.
Ellis Grant and Scholarship Fund, Charles E.
Emerson Electric Co.
Endries Fastener & Supply Co.
Enron Corp.
Equifax
Ernest & Julio Gallo Winery
Ernsthausen Charitable Foundation, John F. and Doris E.
Essick Foundation
Exposition Foundation
Exxon Corp.
Fair Oaks Foundation, Inc.
Fair Play Foundation
Fairfield-Meeker Charitable Trust, Freeman E.
Faith Home Foundation
Falcon Foundation
Falk Foundation, David
Falk Medical Fund, Maurice
Farish Fund, William Stamps
Farley Industries
Federal-Mogul Corp.
Federal National Mortgage Assn., Fannie Mae
Federal Screw Works
Federated Department Stores and Allied Stores Corp.
Federated Life Insurance Co.
Feil Foundation, Louis and Gertrude
Fenton Foundation
Fieldcrest Cannon
Fifth Third Bancorp
Finley Foundation, A. E.
Firestone Foundation, Roger S.
First Boston
First Brands Corp.
First Chicago
First Fidelity Bancorporation
First Interstate Bank of Oregon
First Maryland Bancorp
First Mississippi Corp.
First Petroleum Corp.
First Union Corp.
Fish Foundation, Ray C.
Fish Foundation, Vain and Harry
Fitz-Gibbon Charitable Trust
Fleming Companies, Inc.
Fletcher Foundation
Fletcher Foundation, A. J.
Florida Power Corp.
Florida Steel Corp.
Foellinger Foundation
Fohs Foundation
Foote Mineral Co.
Ford Foundation
Ford Fund, Benson and Edith
Ford Meter Box Co.
Foundation for Middle East Peace
Foundation for Seacoast Health
Fourth Financial Corp.
Foxmeyer Corp.
France Foundation, Jacob and Annita
Franklin Foundation, John and Mary

Frederick Foundation
Freedom Forum
Freeman Foundation, Ella West
French Oil Mill Machinery Co.
Frick Educational Commission, Henry C.
Frohman Foundation, Sidney
Frueauff Foundation, Charles A.
Fry Foundation, Lloyd A.
Funderburke & Associates
Funderburke & Associates
G.A.G. Charitable Corporation
Gaisman Foundation, Catherine and Henry J.
Galkin Charitable Trust, Ira S. and Anna
Gallo Foundation, Ernest
GAR Foundation
Gault-Hussey Charitable Trust
Gear Motion
Gebbie Foundation
GEICO Corp.
General Accident Insurance Co. of America
General American Life Insurance Co.
General Mills
General Motors Corp.
General Tire Inc.
Genesis Foundation
Georgia-Pacific Corp.
Georgia Power Co.
Gerber Products Co.
Gerson Family Foundation, Benjamin J.
Gheens Foundation
Gholston Trust, J. K.
Giant Eagle
Giant Food
Gifford Charitable Corporation, Rosamond
Gill Foundation, Pauline Allen
Gillette Co.
Gilman Paper Co.
Gilmore Foundation, Irving S.
Gitano Group
Gleason Memorial Fund
Gleason Works
Glenmore Distilleries Co.
Glick Foundation, Eugene and Marilyn
Glosser Foundation, David A.
Gluck Foundation, Maxwell H.
Goddard Foundation, Charles B.
Goerlich Family Foundation
Goldberg Family Foundation
Goldseker Foundation of Maryland, Morris
Goldsmith Foundation, Horace W.
Goldwyn Foundation, Samuel
Good Samaritan
Goodman Memorial Foundation, Joseph C. and Clare F.
Goodyear Tire & Rubber Co.
Goody's Manufacturing Corp.
Gordon Foundation, Meyer and Ida
Gottesman Fund
Gould Foundation for Children, Edwin
Grace & Co., W.R.
Grassmann Trust, E. J.
Graybar Electric Co.
Green Fund
Greenville Foundation
Grundy Foundation
Guaranty Bank & Trust Co.
Guardian Life Insurance Co. of America
Gulf Power Co.
Gulton Foundation
Gund Foundation, George
Guttman Foundation, Stella and Charles
Haas Foundation, Paul and Mary
Haas Fund, Walter and Elise

Hadson Corp.
Haggar Foundation
Hall Charitable Trust, Evelyn A. J.
Hallett Charitable Trust
Hamel Family Charitable Trust, D. A.
Hancock Foundation, Luke B.
Handy & Harman
Hankins Foundation
HarCo. Drug
Harden Foundation
Hardin Foundation, Phil
Harding Foundation, Charles Stewart
Harper Brush Works
Harper Foundation, Philip S.
Harris Foundation, James J. and Angelia M.
Harsco Corp.
Hartford Courant Foundation
Hartford Steam Boiler Inspection & Insurance Co.
Hartmarx Corp.
Hartz Foundation
Harvey Foundation, Felix
Haskell Fund
Hatch Charitable Trust, Margaret Milliken
Hayfields Foundation
Hazen Foundation, Edward W.
Hecht-Levi Foundation
Heinz Co., H.J.
Heinz Endowment, Howard
Heinz Endowment, Vira I.
Heinz Family Foundation
Helfaer Foundation, Evan and Marion
Henderson Foundation, George B.
Hermann Foundation, Grover
Herndon Foundation
Hershey Foundation
Hettinger Foundation
Hewit Family Foundation
Hiawatha Education Foundation
Higgins Foundation, Aldus C.
High Foundation
Hill Foundation
Hobbs Charitable Trust, John H.
Hobbs Foundation
Hodge Foundation
Hoffman Foundation, Maximillian E. and Marion O.
Hoffmann-La Roche
Holding Foundation, Robert P.
Hollis Foundation
Holmes Foundation
Holt Foundation, William Knox
Homeland Foundation
Honigman Foundation
Hoover Foundation
Hoover, Jr. Foundation, Margaret W. and Herbert
Hopedale Foundation
Hopper Memorial Foundation, Bertrand
Horncrest Foundation
Horowitz Foundation, Gedale B. and Barbara S.
Hospital Corp. of America
Houck Foundation, May K.
Houghton Mifflin Co.
House Educational Trust, Susan Cook
Hovnanian Foundation, Hirair and Anna
Hubbard Broadcasting
Hubbell Inc.
Huffy Corp.
Huisking Foundation
Hultquist Foundation
Humana
Hunt Alternatives Fund
Hunter Trust, Emily S. and Coleman A.
Huntington Fund for Education, John

Education Funds (cont.)

I. and L. Association
Iacocca Foundation
IES Industries
Illges Foundation, John P. and Dorothy S.
Illinois Tool Works
IMT Insurance Co.
Independent Financial Corp.
Inland Container Corp.
Inland Steel Industries
Inman Mills
Interco
International Multifoods Corp.
Iowa Savings Bank
Isaly Klondike Co.
ITT Hartford Insurance Group
ITT Rayonier
Ix & Sons, Frank
Jacobson Foundation, Bernard H. and Blanche E.
Janssen Foundation, Henry
Jasper Seating Co.
Jefferson Endowment Fund, John Percival and Mary C.
Jergens Foundation, Andrew
Jockey Hollow Foundation
John Hancock Mutual Life Insurance Co.
Johnson Co., E. F.
Johnson Controls
Johnson Foundation, Helen K. and Arthur E.
Johnson & Higgins
Johnson & Son, S.C.
Jonsson Foundation
Jonsson Foundation
Journal Gazette Co.
Joyce Foundation
Julia R. and Estelle L. Foundation
Jurzykowski Foundation, Alfred
Kaiser Cement Corp.
Kaplun Foundation, Morris J. and Betty
Kasiska Family Foundation
Kautz Family Foundation
Kearney Inc., A.T.
Keck, Jr. Foundation, William M.
Kellogg Foundation, J. C.
Kellogg Foundation, Peter and Cynthia K.
Kellogg Foundation, W. K.
Kenan, Jr. Charitable Trust, William R.
Kendall Foundation, George R.
Kennametal
Kennedy Foundation, Ethel
Kerr Foundation
Kerr Fund, Grayce B.
Kettering Family Foundation
Kimberly-Clark Corp.
Kingsbury Corp.
Kingsley Foundation, Lewis A.
Kirby Foundation, F. M.
Kirkhill Rubber Co.
Kirkpatrick Foundation
Knapp Educational Fund
Knox Foundation, Seymour H.
Kohl Charities, Herbert H.
Koret Foundation
Koulaieff Educational Fund, Trustees of Ivan Y.
Kuhns Investment Co.
Kulas Foundation
Kunstadter Family Foundation, Albert
La-Z-Boy Chair Co.
Lacy Foundation
Ladish Co.
Laffey-McHugh Foundation
Lalor Foundation
Lance, Inc.
Lang Foundation, Eugene M.

Langdale Co.
Lassus Brothers Oil
Lavanburg-Corner House
Law Foundation, Robert O.
Lawyers Title Foundation
Leavey Foundation, Thomas and Dorothy
Lebus Trust, Bertha
Lederer Foundation, Francis L.
Lee Enterprises
Lee Foundation, James T.
Legg Mason Inc.
Lehigh Portland Cement Co.
Lehman Foundation, Robert
Lemberg Foundation
Lennon Foundation, Fred A.
Lennox International, Inc.
Leo Burnett Co.
Leu Foundation, Harry P.
Leucadia National Corp.
Levinson Foundation, Morris L.
Levy's Lumber & Building Centers
Liberty Corp.
Liberty Hosiery Mills
Lied Foundation Trust
Lilly & Co., Eli
Lincoln Electric Co.
Lincoln Fund
Lincoln National Corp.
Lindstrom Foundation, Kinney
Link, Jr. Foundation, George
Lipton, Thomas J.
Littauer Foundation, Lucius N.
Little, Arthur D.
Lockheed Corp.
Lockwood Foundation, Byron W. and Alice L.
Loeb Partners Corp.
Loewy Family Foundation
Loewy Family Foundation
Long Foundation, J.M.
Loose Trust, Carrie J.
Loose Trust, Harry Wilson
Lost Tree Charitable Foundation
Louisiana Land & Exploration Co.
Love Charitable Foundation, John Allan
Love Foundation, Lucyle S.
Lowe Foundation, Joe and Emily
Lowenstein Foundation, Leon
Luck Stone
Lund Foundation
Lutheran Brotherhood Foundation
Lux Foundation, Miranda
Lynn Foundation, E. M.
Macht Foundation, Morton and Sophia
Maclellan Charitable Trust, R. J.
Macmillan, Inc.
Macy & Co., R.H.
Maier Foundation, Sarah Pauline
Maneely Fund
Marcus Corp.
Mars Foundation
Marshall Foundation
Marshall & Ilsley Bank
Martin Marietta Aggregates
Martin Marietta Corp.
Massachusetts Mutual Life Insurance Co.
Massey Foundation
Mathis-Pfohl Foundation
Mautz Paint Co.
Max Charitable Foundation
May Department Stores Co.
Maytag Corp.
MCA
McAshan Foundation
McCamish Foundation
McCann Foundation
McCarthy Charities
McCasland Foundation
McConnell Foundation

McCormick Foundation, Chauncey and Marion Deering
McCormick Tribune Foundation, Robert R.
McDonnell Douglas Corp.
McDougall Charitable Trust, Ruth Camp
McElroy Trust, R. J.
MCI Communications Corp.
McMurray-Bennnett Foundation
McNeely Foundation
McShain Charities, John
Mead Corp.
Meadows Foundation
Mebane Packaging Corp.
Media General, Inc.
Mellam Family Foundation
Mellon Bank Corp.
Mellon Foundation, Richard King
Memorial Foundation for Children
Mengle Foundation, Glenn and Ruth
Mentor Graphics
Mericos Foundation
Merrick Foundation, Robert G. and Anne M.
Metropolitan Theatres Corp.
Meyer Foundation, Eugene and Agnes E.
Michael Foundation, Herbert I. and Elsa B.
Michigan Bell Telephone Co.
Midmark Corp.
Midwest Resources
Milken Family Medical Foundation
Milken Foundation, L. and S.
Millard Charitable Trust, Adah K.
Milliken & Co.
Mine Safety Appliances Co.
Minnegasco
Minnesota Mutual Life Insurance Co.
MNC Financial
Mobil Oil Corp.
Monarch Machine Tool Co.
Monell Foundation, Ambrose
Monroe-Brown Foundation
Montgomery Foundation
Montgomery Ward & Co.
Moore & Sons, B.C.
Moorman Manufacturing Co.
Morehead Foundation, John Motley
Morgan Construction Co.
Morris Foundation
Morris Foundation, William T.
Morrison-Knudsen Corp.
Morse, Jr. Foundation, Enid and Lester S.
Mosinee Paper Corp.
Motorola
Mott Charitable Trust/Spectemur Agendo, Stewart R.
Mulford Foundation, Vincent
Myers and Sons, D.
Nabisco Foods Group
National Computer Systems
National Starch & Chemical Corp.
NBD Bank
Neilson Foundation, George W.
New-Land Foundation
New Prospect Foundation
New World Foundation
New York Foundation
New York Life Insurance Co.
New York Telephone Co.
The New Yorker Magazine, Inc.
Newcombe Foundation, Charlotte W.
Newhouse Foundation, Samuel I.
News & Observer Publishing Co.
Nike Inc.
Noble Foundation, Samuel Roberts
Nordson Corp.

Norfolk Southern Corp.
Normandie Foundation
North Shore Foundation
Northern Indiana Public Service Co.
Northern Telecom Inc.
Norton Co.
Norton Memorial Corporation, Geraldi
Norwest Bank Nebraska
Norwest Corp.
Number Ten Foundation
Oaklawn Foundation
Oberkotter Family Foundation
O'Brien Foundation, James W.
Occidental Oil & Gas Corp.
O'Connor Foundation, A. Lindsay and Olive B.
Ohio Valley Foundation
Ohl, Jr. Trust, George A.
Ohrstrom Foundation
Old Dominion Box Co.
Olin Charitable Trust, John M.
Olsson Memorial Foundation, Elis
O'Neill Charitable Corporation, F. J.
Oppenstein Brothers Foundation
Orchard Foundation
Osborn Manufacturing Co.
O'Shaughnessy Foundation, I. A.
Overbrook Foundation
Overlake Foundation
Owen Trust, B. B.
Oxford Foundation
PACCAR
Pacific Mutual Life Insurance Co.
PacifiCorp
Panhandle Eastern Corp.
Paramount Communications Inc.
Park National Bank
Parker-Hannifin Corp.
Pearlstone Foundation, Peggy Meyerhoff
Peierls Foundation
Pellegrino-Realmuto Charitable Foundation
Penney Foundation, James C.
Pennsylvania Dutch Co.
Peppers Foundation, Ann
Perini Foundation, Joseph
Perkin-Elmer Corp.
Perkins Memorial Foundation, George W.
Perley Fund, Victor E.
Peters Foundation, Leon S.
Peterson Foundation, Fred J.
Peterson Foundation, Fred J.
Pfizer
Phelps Dodge Corp.
PHH Corp.
Philadelphia Electric Co.
Philip Morris Cos.
Philips Foundation, Jesse
Phillips Charitable Trust, Dr. and Mrs. Arthur William
Phillips Family Foundation, Jay and Rose
Phillips Foundation, Dr. P.
Phillips Petroleum Co.
Phillips-Van Heusen Corp.
Pierce Charitable Trust, Harold Whitworth
Pillsbury Foundation
Pine Tree Foundation
Pines Bridge Foundation
Pinkerton Foundation
Piper Foundation, Minnie Stevens
Pitney Bowes
Pittsburgh National Bank
Pittway Corp.
Plym Foundation
Poole & Kent Co.
Porter Paint Co.
Portland General Electric Co.
Potomac Electric Power Co.

Pott Foundation, Herman T. and Phenie R.
Powell Co., William
Powell Family Foundation
Powers Foundation
Premier Industrial Corp.
Prickett Fund, Lynn R. and Karl E.
Pritzker Foundation
Procter & Gamble Cosmetic & Fragrance Products
Prudential Insurance Co. of America
Puett Foundation, Nelson
Pulitzer Publishing Co.
Putnam Foundation
Quaker Oats Co.
Quanex Corp.
Quincy Newspapers
Quinlan Foundation, Elizabeth C.
Quivey-Bay State Foundation
Rachal Foundation, Ed
Rahr Malting Co.
Ralston Purina Co.
Ranney Foundation, P. K.
Ratner Foundation, Milton M.
Raymond Educational Foundation
Read Foundation, Charles L.
Rebsamen Companies, Inc.
Red Wing Shoe Co.
Reeves Foundation
Reidler Foundation
Reilly Industries
Reily & Co., William B.
Reinberger Foundation
Reliable Life Insurance Co.
Rennebohm Foundation, Oscar
Revlon
Reynolds Foundation, Donald W.
Reynolds Foundation, Richard S.
Reynolds Foundation, Z. Smith
Reynolds Metals Co.
Reynolds & Reynolds Co.
Rice Foundation, Ethel and Raymond F.
Rice Foundation, Helen Steiner
Rider-Pool Foundation
Ridgefield Foundation
Riggs Benevolent Fund
Riordan Foundation
Ritchie Memorial Foundation, Charles E. and Mabel M.
RJR Nabisco Inc.
Robbins & Myers, Inc.
Roberts Foundation, Dora
Robertshaw Controls Co.
Robinson Fund, Maurice R.
Robison Foundation, Ellis H. and Doris B.
Rockwell International Corp.
Rodgers Trust, Elizabeth Killam
Rohatyn Foundation, Felix and Elizabeth
Rohm and Haas Company
Rosenberg Foundation, Sunny and Abe
Rosenthal Foundation, Ida and William
Royal Group Inc.
Rubbermaid
Rubin Family Fund, Cele H. and William B.
Rubin Foundation, Samuel
Russell Educational Foundation, Benjamin and Roberta
Ryder System
Saint Croix Foundation
Saint Paul Cos.
Salgo Charitable Trust, Nicholas M.
San Diego Gas & Electric
Sandy Hill Foundation
Sara Lee Hosiery
Saunders Charitable Foundation, Helen M.
Saunders Foundation

Scaife Family Foundation
Schecter Private Foundation, Aaron and Martha
Schering-Plough Corp.
Schey Foundation
Schroeder Foundation, Walter
Schwartz and Robert Schwartz Foundation, Bernard
Scoular Co.
SCT Yarns
Searle & Co., G.D.
Security Benefit Life Insurance Co.
Security Life of Denver
Sedgwick James Inc.
Sentry Insurance Co.
Share Trust, Charles Morton
Shenandoah Foundation
Shenandoah Life Insurance Co.
Shoney's Inc.
Shore Fund
Sifco Industries Inc.
Simon Foundation, William E. and Carol G.
Simpson Foundation
Sizzler International
Skillman Foundation
Slant/Fin Corp.
Smith Corp., A.O.
Smith Foundation, Kelvin and Eleanor
Sonat
Sordoni Foundation
Sosland Foundation
South Bend Tribune
Southwestern Bell Corp.
Special People In Need
Speyer Foundation, Alexander C. and Tillie S.
Sprague Educational and Charitable Foundation, Seth
Square D Co.
Stabler Foundation, Donald B. and Dorothy L.
Staley, Jr. Foundation, A. E.
Standard Products Co.
Star Bank, N.A.
Starrett Co., L.S.
State Street Bank & Trust Co.
Steelcase
Steiger Memorial Fund, Albert
Stein Foundation, Jules and Doris
Stemmons Foundation
Sterling Winthrop
Stern Family Foundation, Alex
Stern Foundation, Leonard N.
Sternberger Foundation, Sigmund
Stevens Foundation, Abbot and Dorothy H.
Stone Container Corp.
Stonecutter Mills Corp.
Stott Foundation, Robert L.
Strake Foundation
Stranahan Foundation
Strong Foundation, Hattie M.
Sulzberger Foundation
Summerfield Foundation, Solon E.
Sunmark Capital Corp.
Sylvester Foundation, Harcourt M. and Virginia W.
Synovus Financial Corp.
Talley Industries, Inc.
Tanner Cos.
Taub Foundation, Henry and Marilyn
Taylor Foundation
Taylor Foundation, Fred and Harriett
Taylor Foundation, Ruth and Vernon
Teledyne
Tennant Co.
Tenneco
Texaco
Texas Commerce Bank Houston, N.A.

Texas Instruments
Textron
Thalhimer Brothers Inc.
Thirty-Five Twenty, Inc.
Thoman Foundation, W. B. and Candace
Thomas & Betts Corp.
Thomas Industries
Thorpe Foundation, James R.
3M Co.
Times Mirror Co.
Timken Foundation of Canton
Tinker Foundation
Tippens Foundation
TJX Cos.
Tomkins Industries, Inc.
Tosco Corp. Refining Division
Toyota Motor Sales, U.S.A.
Tozer Foundation
Transamerica Corp.
Trion
Trust Co. Bank
Tuohy Foundation, Alice Tweed
Turrell Fund
Tyson Foods, Inc.
Ukrop's Super Markets, Inc.
Union Bank
Union Bank of Switzerland Los Angeles Branch
Union Camp Corp.
Union Electric Co.
Union Foundation
Union Manufacturing Co.
Union Pacific Corp.
United Merchants & Manufacturers
United Parcel Service of America
U.S. Leasing International
United States Sugar Corp.
Universal Leaf Tobacco Co.
Unocal Corp.
Upjohn Co.
Upton Foundation, Frederick S.
US WEST
USF&G Co.
Utilicorp United
Van Camp Foundation
Van Every Foundation, Philip L.
Van Houten Charitable Trust
Vetlesen Foundation, G. Unger
Vicksburg Foundation
Virginia Power Co.
Visciglia Foundation, Frank
Vogt Machine Co., Henry
Vulcan Materials Co.
W. W. W. Foundation
Wachovia Bank & Trust Co., N.A.
Wahlert Foundation
Wal-Mart Stores
Wallace Genetic Foundation
Disney Co., Walt
Warner-Lambert Co.
Washington Forrest Foundation
Waste Management
Wauwatosa Savings & Loan Association
Webster Charitable Foundation
Wedum Foundation
Wege Foundation
Wehadkee Foundation
Weiler Foundation, Theodore & Renee
Weinberg Foundation, John L.
Wells Fargo & Co.
Wells Foundation, Franklin H. and Ruth L.
West Co.
Westend Foundation
Westport Fund
Westvaco Corp.
Wetterau
Weyerhaeuser Co.
Whirlpool Corp.
Whitehead Foundation
Whiting Foundation
Whiting Foundation, Mrs. Giles

Whittenberger Foundation, Claude R. and Ethel B.
Wickes Foundation, Harvey Randall
Wiener Foundation, Malcolm Hewitt
Williams Charitable Trust, Mary Jo
Williams Cos.
Williams Foundation, Arthur Ashley
Williams Foundation, Edna Sproull
Winchester Foundation
Wisconsin Centrifugal
Wisconsin Energy Corp.
Wollenberg Foundation
Wood Foundation, Lester G.
Wornall Charitable Trust and Foundation, Kearney
Wrigley Co., Wm. Jr.
Wunsch Foundation
Xerox Corp.
Yeager Charitable Trust, Lester E.
Young & Rubicam
Zemurray Foundation

Elementary Education

Abell Foundation, Charles S.
Abell Foundation, The
Abercrombie Foundation
Achelis Foundation
AFLAC
Ahmanson Foundation
Alabama Power Co.
Albertson's
Alexander & Baldwin, Inc.
Algonquin Energy, Inc.
Allendale Mutual Insurance Co.
AlliedSignal
Alltel/Western Region
ALPAC Corp.
Altman Foundation
America West Airlines
American Brands
American Electric Power
American Honda Motor Co.
American Saw & Manufacturing Co.
American Telephone & Telegraph Co.
Ameritech Services
Ameritech Services
Ames Department Stores
AMETEK
Andersen Corp.
Andersen Foundation
Anschutz Family Foundation
AON Corp.
Apache Corp.
Apple Computer, Inc.
ARCO Chemical
Arkla
Arvin Industries
Astor Foundation, Vincent
Atherton Family Foundation
Atlanta Gas Light Co.
Babcock Foundation, Mary Reynolds
Babcock & Wilcox Co.
Bank of Boston Corp.
Bank of New York
Bank One, Texas-Houston Office
BankAmerica Corp.
Bankers Trust Co.
Bannon Foundation
BarclaysAmerican Corp.
Bartlett & Co.
Battelle
BellSouth Corp.
Benwood Foundation
Binney & Smith Inc.
Blair and Co., William

Blaustein Foundation, Jacob and Hilda
Bodman Foundation
Boeing Co.
Boler Co.
Booth-Bricker Fund
Booz Allen & Hamilton
Bovaird Foundation, Mervin
Brackenridge Foundation, George W.
Bradford & Co., J.C.
Brown Foundation
Bucyrus-Erie
Buhl Foundation
Burns Foundation, Fritz B.
Cable & Wireless Communications
Cablevision of Michigan
Cabot Corp.
Calder Foundation, Louis
California Educational Initiatives Fund
Cameron Foundation, Harry S. and Isabel C.
Canon U.S.A., Inc.
Capital Holding Corp.
Carpenter Foundation, E. Rhodes and Leona B.
Carpenter Technology Corp.
Carter Foundation, Amon G.
Carver Charitable Trust, Roy J.
Castle Foundation, Samuel N. and Mary
Central Maine Power Co.
Chase Manhattan Bank, N.A.
Cheney Foundation, Ben B.
Chevron Corp.
Ciba-Geigy Corp. (Pharmaceuticals Division)
CIGNA Corp.
Cincinnati Bell
Citibank, F.S.B.
Citicorp
Clark Foundation
Classic Leather
Clorox Co.
CM Alliance Cos.
CNA Insurance Cos.
Coca-Cola Co.
Colonial Stores
Colorado National Bankshares
Columbus Southern Power Co.
Commerce Clearing House
Connelly Foundation
Consolidated Natural Gas Co.
Continental Bank N.A.
Cowell Foundation, S. H.
Cowles Media Co.
Cox Charitable Trust, Jessie B.
Cummings Memorial Fund Trust, Frances L. and Edwin L.
Cummins Engine Co.
Danforth Foundation
DeKalb Genetics Corp.
Delaware North Cos.
Digital Equipment Corp.
Dodge Foundation, Geraldine R.
Dodge Jones Foundation
Duchossois Industries
Duke Power Co.
duPont Fund, Jessie Ball
Eastern Enterprises
Encyclopaedia Britannica, Inc.
Enron Corp.
Evans Foundation, Edward P.
Exxon Corp.
Fanwood Foundation
Farmers Group, Inc.
Federal-Mogul Corp.
Federated Life Insurance Co.
Fidelity Bank
Fieldcrest Cannon
Fikes Foundation, Leland
Fireman's Fund Insurance Co.
First Bank System
First Interstate Bank NW Region
First Tennessee Bank

First Union Corp.
First Union National Bank of Florida
Fleming Companies, Inc.
Florida Power & Light Co.
Foundation for the Needs of Others
Foxmeyer Corp.
Francis Families Foundation
Freeport-McMoRan
Fry Foundation, Lloyd A.
Fuller Co., H.B.
Gear Motion
GenCorp
Genentech
General Motors Corp.
General Railway Signal Corp.
George Foundation
Georgia Power Co.
Ghidotti Foundation, William and Marian
Giant Eagle
Glaxo
Globe Newspaper Co.
Goddard Foundation, Charles B.
Gregg-Graniteville Foundation
Grimes Foundation
Gulf Power Co.
Haas Fund, Walter and Elise
Hallmark Cards
Halloran Foundation, Mary P. Dolciani
Halstead Foundation
Hand Industries
Hardin Foundation, Phil
Hartford Steam Boiler Inspection & Insurance Co.
Hayden Foundation, Charles
Heckscher Foundation for Children
Hecla Mining Co.
Heinz Endowment, Howard
Heinz Foundation, Drue
Heller Financial
Herrick Foundation
Hershey Foundation
Hewlett-Packard Co.
Hillsdale Fund
Hitachi
Home Depot
Honeywell
Hubbell Inc.
Humana
Hunt Manufacturing Co.
Illinois Power Co.
IMCERA Group Inc.
Indiana Bell Telephone Co.
Industrial Bank of Japan Trust Co.
Inland Container Corp.
Inland Steel Industries
Intel Corp.
International Paper Co.
International Student Exchange Cards
J.P. Morgan & Co.
JCPenney Co.
Johnson Co., E. F.
Johnson Controls
Johnson Foundation, Walter S.
Johnson & Higgins
Joyce Foundation
Julia R. and Estelle L. Foundation
Kellogg Foundation, W. K.
Kenedy Memorial Foundation, John G. and Marie Stella
Kennecott Corp.
Kilworth Charitable Trust, William
King Ranch
Kirby Foundation, F. M.
Knapp Educational Fund
Kulas Foundation
Lilly Endowment
Lockheed Sanders
Long Island Lighting Co.

Recipient Type Index

Elementary Education (cont.)

Louisiana Power & Light Co./New Orleans Public Service
LTV Corp.
Lydall, Inc.
Lyndhurst Foundation
Maclellan Foundation
Manville Corp.
Mardag Foundation
Marion Merrell Dow
Maritz Inc.
Mars Foundation
Marsh & McLennan Cos.
Marshall & Ilsley Bank
Marshalls Inc.
Martin Marietta Corp.
Massie Trust, David Meade
Matsushita Electric Corp. of America
Mattel
Maxon Charitable Foundation
Maxus Energy Corp.
Mayer Foods Corp., Oscar
MBIA, Inc.
McDonnell Douglas Corp.
McElroy Trust, R. J.
McInerny Foundation
Meadows Foundation
Medtronic
Merck Human Health Division
Meyer Foundation, Eugene and Agnes E.
Meyer Memorial Trust
Midwest Resources
Mississippi Power Co.
Monsanto Co.
Moore Foundation, Edward S.
MTS Systems Corp.
Murphy Foundation
Murphy Foundation, Dan
Nabisco Foods Group
National Computer Systems
National Fuel Gas Co.
National Starch & Chemical Corp.
National Westminster Bank New Jersey
NBD Bank
Nellie Mae
New England Foundation
New England Mutual Life Insurance Co.
New Street Capital Corp.
New York Mercantile Exchange
The New Yorker Magazine, Inc.
Newhall Foundation, Henry Mayo
Northeast Utilities
Northern Telecom Inc.
Northwest Natural Gas Co.
Northwestern National Life Insurance Co.
Norwest Bank Nebraska
Noyes, Jr. Memorial Foundation, Nicholas H.
O'Connor Foundation, A. Lindsay and Olive B.
Ohrstrom Foundation
Ore-Ida Foods, Inc.
Osceola Foundation
OsCo. Industries
O'Shaughnessy Foundation, I. A.
Oshkosh B'Gosh
Pacific Telesis Group
Packaging Corporation of America
Packard Foundation, David and Lucile
Padnos Iron & Metal Co., Louis
Panhandle Eastern Corp.
Paramount Communications Inc.
Parsons Foundation, Ralph M.

Parsons - W.D. Charities, Vera Davis
Penn Foundation, William
Penzance Foundation
People's Bank
Peoples Energy Corp.
Persis Corp.
Pew Charitable Trusts
Phillips Foundation, Dr. P.
Phillips Petroleum Co.
Pillsbury Co.
Pinkerton Foundation
Piper Jaffray Cos.
Pitney Bowes
Pittway Corp.
Plough Foundation
Polaroid Corp.
Price Associates, T. Rowe
Proctor Trust, Mortimer R.
Prudential Insurance Co. of America
PSI Energy
Public Service Electric & Gas Co.
Quaker Oats Co.
Quantum Chemical Corp.
Randleigh Foundation Trust
Reliable Life Insurance Co.
Reynolds Foundation, Z. Smith
Reynolds Metals Co.
Richardson Foundation, Sid W.
Ricoh Corp.
Ricoh Electronics Inc.
RJR Nabisco Inc.
Rochester Telephone Corp.
Rockefeller Foundation, Winthrop
Rockwell Fund
Rogers Foundation
Rohatyn Foundation, Felix and Elizabeth
Rohr Inc.
Roseburg Forest Products Co.
Royal Group Inc.
SAFECO Corp.
Salomon
San Diego Gas & Electric
Sandusky International Inc.
Sara Lee Hosiery
Schmidlapp Trust No. 2, Jacob G.
Scholl Foundation, Dr.
Scrivner, Inc.
Seaver Charitable Trust, Richard C.
Seaway Food Town
Security Life of Denver
Sedgwick James Inc.
Seybert Institution for Poor Boys and Girls, Adam and Maria Sarah
Shell Oil Co.
Shoney's Inc.
Siebert Lutheran Foundation
Signet Bank/Maryland
Smart Family Foundation
Smucker Co., J.M.
SNET
Snow Foundation, John Ben
Sonoco Products Co.
Sosland Foundation
Springs Industries
Stackner Family Foundation
Stanley Works
State Street Bank & Trust Co.
Sterling Winthrop
Stern Foundation, Gustav and Irene
Stonecutter Mills Corp.
Storage Technology Corp.
Stuart Foundations
Stulsaft Foundation, Morris
Sturgis Charitable and Educational Trust, Roy and Christine
Swalm Foundation
Syntex Corp.
Tandem Computers

Tanner Cos.
Temple Foundation, T. L. L.
Temple-Inland
Texas Instruments
TJX Cos.
Tosco Corp. Refining Division
Toyota Motor Sales, U.S.A.
Tozer Foundation
Tracor, Inc.
Transco Energy Company
Travelers Cos.
Tropicana Products, Inc.
Turrell Fund
Unilever United States
Union Camp Corp.
Union Electric Co.
U.S. Leasing International
United States Sugar Corp.
Unitrode Corp.
Universal Leaf Tobacco Co.
Valley National Bancorp
Varian Associates
Vulcan Materials Co.
Wachovia Bank & Trust Co., N.A.
Wal-Mart Stores
Washington Mutual Savings Bank
Washington Post Co.
Washington Water Power Co.
Waste Management
Weingart Foundation
Wells Fargo & Co.
West Foundation
West One Bancorp
Western New York Foundation
Westvaco Corp.
Wetterau
Weyerhaeuser Co.
Weyerhaeuser Memorial Foundation, Charles A.
Whirlpool Corp.
White Consolidated Industries
Whitehead Foundation, Joseph B.
Whittier Foundation, L. K.
WICOR, Inc.
Wiegand Foundation, E. L.
Wiggins Memorial Trust, J. J.
Williams Cos.
Xerox Corp.
Yost Trust, Elizabeth Burns

Engineering Education

Abbott Laboratories
Air Products & Chemicals
Alabama Power Co.
Alliant Techsystems
AlliedSignal
Alumax
Aluminum Co. of America
AMAX
American Cyanamid Co.
American Electric Power
American Natural Resources Co.
American Telephone & Telegraph Co.
Ameritech Services
AMETEK
Amoco Corp.
AMP
Appleton Papers
ARCO
Arkansas Power & Light Co.
Armco Inc.
Ashland Oil
Atlanta Gas Light Co.
Babcock & Wilcox Co.
Badger Meter, Inc.
Baker Hughes Inc.
Ball Corp.
Bankers Trust Co.
Battelle
Bechtel Group
Bechtel, Jr. Foundation, S. D.
Becton Dickinson & Co.

Berwind Corp.
Bethlehem Steel Corp.
BFGoodrich
Black & Veatch
Boatmen's First National Bank of Oklahoma
Boeing Co.
Boise Cascade Corp.
Booz Allen & Hamilton
Bosch Corp., Robert
Bowater Inc.
BP America
Brady Foundation, W. H.
Bridgestone/Firestone
Briggs & Stratton Corp.
Brown Foundation
Brunswick Corp.
Bucyrus-Erie
Burndy Corp.
Cabot Corp.
Capital Cities/ABC
Carolina Power & Light Co.
Carrier Corp.
Caterpillar
CBI Industries
Central Maine Power Co.
Champion International Corp.
Chevron Corp.
Chrysler Corp.
Ciba-Geigy Corp.
  (Pharmaceuticals Division)
Cincinnati Milacron
Coca-Cola Co.
Cockrell Foundation
Columbus Southern Power Co.
Conoco Inc.
Consolidated Natural Gas Co.
Consolidated Papers
Consolidated Rail Corp. (Conrail)
Consumers Power Co.
Contraves USA
Control Data Corp.
Cowles Media Co.
Cox Charitable Trust, Jessie B.
CR Industries
Cray Research
Cullen/Frost Bankers
Cummins Engine Co.
Cyprus Minerals Co.
Daniel Foundation of Alabama
Deere & Co.
DeSoto
Detroit Edison Co.
DeVlieg Foundation, Charles
Digital Equipment Corp.
Donaldson Co.
Douglas & Lomason Company
Dow Chemical Co.
Dow Corning Corp.
Dresser Industries
du Pont de Nemours & Co., E. I.
Duke Power Co.
Eastman Kodak Co.
Eaton Corp.
Edmonds Foundation, Dean S.
Eka Nobel
Emerson Electric Co.
Enron Corp.
Ensworth Charitable Foundation
Exxon Corp.
Federal-Mogul Corp.
FINA, Inc.
Florida Power & Light Co.
Fluor Corp.
FMC Corp.
Ford Motor Co.
Freeport-McMoRan
Funderburke & Associates
Funderburke & Associates
General Electric Co.
General Mills
General Motors Corp.
GenRad
Georgia Power Co.
Gleason Foundation, Katherine
Gleason Memorial Fund

Goodyear Tire & Rubber Co.
Gould Inc.
Grace & Co., W.R.
Graphic Controls Corp.
Grassmann Trust, E. J.
Grede Foundries
Greenheck Fan Corp.
GTE Corp.
Gulfstream Aerospace Corp.
Harris Corp.
Hatterscheidt Foundation
Hecla Mining Co.
HEI Inc.
Helfaer Foundation, Evan and Marion
Hershey Foods Corp.
Hewlett-Packard Co.
Hoechst Celanese Corp.
Honeywell
IBM Corp.
Illinois Bell
Illinois Power Co.
Illinois Tool Works
Inco Alloys International
Indiana Bell Telephone Co.
Ingersoll Milling Machine Co.
Inland Steel Industries
Intel Corp.
International Paper Co.
International Student Exchange Cards
ITT Corp.
Johnson Co., E. F.
Johnson Controls
Johnson & Higgins
Keck Foundation, W. M.
Kellogg Foundation, W. K.
Kennametal
Kennecott Corp.
Kerr-McGee Corp.
Kiewit Sons, Peter
Kimberly-Clark Corp.
Kingsbury Corp.
Ladish Co.
Liberty National Bank
Little, Arthur D.
Livingston Memorial Foundation
Long Island Lighting Co.
Louisiana Power & Light Co./New Orleans Public Service
LTV Corp.
Lubrizol Corp.
Magma Copper Co.
Mallinckrodt Specialty Chemicals Co.
Marquette Electronics
Martin Marietta Corp.
Massey Foundation
Maxus Energy Corp.
Maytag Corp.
McCormick Tribune Foundation, Robert R.
McDonnell Douglas Corp.
McWane Inc.
Mead Corp.
Medtronic
Menasha Corp.
Merck & Co.
Michigan Bell Telephone Co.
Michigan Consolidated Gas Co.
Midwest Resources
Mine Safety Appliances Co.
Minnegasco
Mobil Oil Corp.
Monroe-Brown Foundation
Monsanto Co.
Montana Power Co.
Motorola
MTS Systems Corp.
Nalco Chemical Co.
National Computer Systems
National Fuel Gas Co.
National Presto Industries
National Westminster Bank New Jersey
Navistar International Corp.

Northeast Utilities
Northern Indiana Public Service Co.
Norton Co.
NYNEX Corp.
Occidental Petroleum Corp.
Oglebay Norton Co.
Olin Corp.
Outboard Marine Corp.
Overseas Shipholding Group
PACCAR
Pacific Gas & Electric Co.
Pacific Telesis Group
Packaging Corporation of America
Padnos Iron & Metal Co., Louis
Panhandle Eastern Corp.
Parker-Hannifin Corp.
Parsons Foundation, Ralph M.
Penn Foundation, William
Pennzoil Co.
Pfizer
Philip Morris Cos.
Phillips Petroleum Co.
Polaroid Corp.
Powell Foundation, Charles Lee
PPG Industries
Public Service Electric & Gas Co.
Pyramid Technology Corp.
Quaker Oats Co.
Questar Corp.
Raytheon Co.
Reliance Electric Co.
Roberts Foundation, Summerfield G.
Rockwell International Corp.
Rohm and Haas Company
Rohr Inc.
Rolfs Foundation, Robert T.
San Diego Gas & Electric
Santa Fe Pacific Corp.
Schlieder Educational Foundation, Edward G.
Science Applications International Corp.
Scrivner, Inc.
Sedgwick James Inc.
Shawmut National Corp.
Shell Oil Co.
Sloan Foundation, Alfred P.
Smith Corp., A.O.
SNET
Sonat
Sonoco Products Co.
Southern California Edison Co.
Southern California Gas Co.
Southwestern Bell Corp.
Sprint
Square D Co.
Storage Technology Corp.
Stratford Foundation
Sun Co.
Sundstrand Corp.
Tandem Computers
Teagle Foundation
Tektronix
Tenneco
Texaco
Texas Instruments
Textron
3M Co.
Tosco Corp. Refining Division
Toshiba America, Inc.
Toyota Motor Sales, U.S.A.
Tracor, Inc.
Transco Energy Company
TRINOVA Corp.
Tropicana Products, Inc.
Union Camp Corp.
Union Carbide Corp.
Union Electric Co.
United Conveyor Corp.
United Parcel Service of America
United Technologies Corp.
Universal Foods Corp.
US WEST

USX Corp.
Varian Associates
Virginia Power Co.
Volkswagen of America, Inc.
Vulcan Materials Co.
Washington Water Power Co.
Waste Management
Westinghouse Electric Corp.
Weyerhaeuser Co.
Whirlpool Corp.
WICOR, Inc.
Wilson Fund, Matilda R.
Wisconsin Energy Corp.
Wisconsin Public Service Corp.
Witco Corp.
Xerox Corp.

Faculty Development

Abell-Hanger Foundation
Alden Trust, George I.
AlliedSignal
Aluminum Co. of America
AMAX
America West Airlines
American Natural Resources Co.
American Telephone & Telegraph Co.
Ameritech Services
Amoco Corp.
Appleton Papers
Archer-Daniels-Midland Co.
Atherton Family Foundation
Bankers Trust Co.
Battelle
BellSouth Corp.
Bettingen Corporation, Burton G.
Boehringer Mannheim Corp.
Boeing Co.
Boler Co.
Booth Ferris Foundation
Brown Foundation
Bryan Family Foundation, Kathleen Price and Joseph M.
Burger King Corp.
Burlington Industries
Burroughs Wellcome Co.
Bush Foundation
Cabot Corp.
Caterpillar
Central Maine Power Co.
Chase Manhattan Bank, N.A.
Chevron Corp.
CIGNA Corp.
Cohn Foundation, Herman and Terese
Commonwealth Fund
Community Coffee Co.
Cowles Charitable Trust
Cowles Media Co.
CPC International
Cray Research
Cullen/Frost Bankers
Danforth Foundation
DeRoy Testamentary Foundation
Diamond Foundation, Aaron
Digital Equipment Corp.
Dodge Foundation, Geraldine R.
Donaldson Co.
du Pont de Nemours & Co., E. I.
Duke Endowment
Educational Foundation of America
Exxon Corp.
Fairchild Foundation, Sherman
Federated Department Stores and Allied Stores Corp.
First Tennessee Bank
First Union Corp.
Ford Foundation
Ford Foundation, Edward E.
Francis Families Foundation
Franklin Foundation, John and Mary
Fry Foundation, Lloyd A.
Funderburke & Associates
Funderburke & Associates

General Electric Co.
General Mills
General Signal Corp.
Georgia Power Co.
Gheens Foundation
GTE Corp.
Halliburton Co.
Hardin Foundation, Phil
Haynes Foundation, John Randolph and Dora
Hearst Foundation, William Randolph
Heinz Endowment, Howard
Heinz Endowment, Vira I.
Hermann Foundation, Grover
Hewlett Foundation, William and Flora
Hunt Alternatives Fund
IBM Corp.
Illinois Power Co.
Indiana Bell Telephone Co.
Inland Steel Industries
International Student Exchange Cards
Irvine Foundation, James
Ittleson Foundation
J.P. Morgan & Co.
Jackson Family Foundation, Ann
Janeway Foundation, Elizabeth Bixby
Jennings Foundation, Martha Holden
Johnson Co., E. F.
Johnson Foundation, Walter S.
Johnson & Higgins
Johnston Trust for Charitable and Educational Purposes, James M.
Joyce Foundation
Kade Foundation, Max
Kellogg Foundation, W. K.
Kemper National Insurance Cos.
Kerr Foundation
King Ranch
Klingenstein Fund, Esther A. and Joseph
KPMG Peat Marwick
Lilly Endowment
Long Island Lighting Co.
LTV Corp.
Luce Foundation, Henry
Mallinckrodt Specialty Chemicals Co.
Mayer Foods Corp., Oscar
McElroy Trust, R. J.
Meadows Foundation
Melitta North America Inc.
Mellon Bank Corp.
Meyer Foundation, Eugene and Agnes E.
Mississippi Power Co.
National Computer Systems
National Forge Co.
National Westminster Bank New Jersey
Noble Foundation, Edward John
Noble Foundation, Samuel Roberts
Nomura Securities International
Norton Co.
Pacific Telesis Group
Perkin-Elmer Corp.
Pew Charitable Trusts
Pfizer
Phillips Petroleum Co.
Pilot Trust
Powell Family Foundation
Prudential Insurance Co. of America
PSI Energy
Public Service Co. of New Mexico
Raskob Foundation for Catholic Activities
Recognition Equipment
Reed Foundation, Philip D.
Republic New York Corp.
Richardson Foundation, Sid W.

RJR Nabisco Inc.
Rockwell International Corp.
Rohm and Haas Company
Schering-Plough Corp.
Schlumberger Ltd.
Scholl Foundation, Dr.
Sedgwick James Inc.
Shell Oil Co.
Shenandoah Life Insurance Co.
Siebert Lutheran Foundation
Signet Bank/Maryland
Sloan Foundation, Alfred P.
Sonoco Products Co.
Southern California Edison Co.
Southwestern Bell Corp.
Springs Industries
Sterling Winthrop
Stulsaft Foundation, Morris
TCF Banking & Savings, FSB
Teagle Foundation
Tenneco
Towsley Foundation, Harry A. and Margaret D.
Union Camp Corp.
Union Pacific Corp.
Unocal Corp.
Uris Brothers Foundation
US Bancorp
Varian Associates
Waldorf Educational Foundation
Wallace-Reader's Digest Fund, DeWitt
Washington Post Co.
Washington Water Power Co.
Westinghouse Electric Corp.
Xerox Corp.

General

ABB Process Automation
Action Products International
Addison-Wesley Publishing Co.
Aeroglide Corp.
AFG Industries, Inc.
AGA Gas, Inc.
Ahmanson & Co., H.F.
Airborne Express Co.
Alabama Gas Corp. (An Energen Co.)
Aladdin Industries, Incorporated
Alaska Airlines, Inc.
Allegheny Power System, Inc.
Alyeska Pipeline Service Co.
AMAX Coal Industries
AMCORE Bank, N.A. Rockford
American Filtrona Corp.
American General Corp.
American General Life & Accident Insurance Co.
American Mutual Insurance Cos.
American National Bank
American National Can Co.
American Re-Insurance Co.
American Stock Exchange
American Stores Co.
American Telephone & Telegraph Co./New York City Region
Ameritech Publishing
Ameritech Services
Amoskeag Co.
Ampacet Corp.
Anacomp, Inc.
Andrew Corp.
ARA Services
Arcata Corp.
Aristech Chemical Corp.
Arkansas Best Corp.
Arkla
Armco Steel Co.
Asahi Glass America, Inc.
Atlanta Journal & Constitution
Attleboro Pawtucket Savings Bank
Autodesk, Inc.
Avery Dennison Corp.
AXIA Incorporated

Baird & Co., Robert W.
Baker, Watts & Co.
Ball Corp.
Bally's - Las Vegas
Baltimore Life Insurance Co.
Bank of Boston Connecticut
Bank of Louisville
Bank of Oklahoma, N.A.
Bank One, Texas-Houston Office
Barry Corp., R. G.
Barton-Gillet Co.
BASF Corp.
Bayview Federal Bank
BDM International
Bean, L.L.
Belden Brick Co., Inc.
Bell Helicopter Textron
Benefit Trust Life Insurance Co.
Bergen Record Corp.
Bergstrom Manufacturing Co.
Berwind Corp.
Betz Laboratories
Bill Communications
Binney & Smith Inc.
Birmingham News Co.
Black & Decker Corp.
Blair and Co., William
Bloomingdale's
Bob Evans Farms
Boler Co.
Boston Gas Co.
Boston Mutual Life Insurance Co.
Boulevard Bank, N.A.
Bourns, Inc.
Bradford & Co., J.C.
Brakeley, John Price Jones Inc.
Branch Banking & Trust Co.
Brewer and Co., Ltd., C.
Briggs & Stratton Corp.
Brooklyn Union Gas Co.
Bryn Mawr Trust Co.
Buffalo Forge Co.
Burns International
Burress, J.W.
Business Men's Assurance Co. of America
Cadence Design Systems
Cadillac Products
Caesar's World, Inc.
Caldwell Manufacturing Co.
Capital Holding Corp.
Carolina Telephone & Telegraph Co.
Carr Real Estate Services
Casco Northern Bank
Castle & Cooke
CCB Financial Corp.
Centex Corp.
Central Life Assurance Co.
Central Maine Power Co.
Central Trust Co.
Charter Medical Corp.
Chase Lincoln First Bank, N.A.
Chemtech Industries
Chesapeake & Potomac Telephone Co.
Chicago Sun-Times, Inc.
Chicago Title and Trust Co.
Chubb Life Insurance Co. of America
Cincinnati Enquirer
Citizens Gas & Coke Utility
Citizens Union Bank
Clark Equipment Co.
CNA Insurance Cos.
Coachmen Industries
Coastal Corp.
Coleman Co.
Colgate-Palmolive Co.
Colonial Parking
Colonial Stores
Colorado Interstate Gas Co.
Colorado National Bankshares
Commercial Federal Corp.
Commercial Intertech Corp.

General (cont.)

Commonwealth Life Insurance Co.
Community Mutual Insurance Co.
Computer Associates International
Computer Sciences Corp.
Consolidated Rail Corp. (Conrail)
Continental Airlines
Control Data Corp.
Conwood Co. L.P.
Cooper Oil Tool
Cooper Tire & Rubber Co.
Corpus Christi Exploration Co.
Corvallis Clinic
Countrymark Cooperative
County Bank
Credit Agricole
Creditanstalt-Bankverein, New York
CSX Corp.
CT Corp. System
Cubic Corp.
Culbro Corp.
Curtis Industries, Helene
Cyprus Minerals Co.
Danforth Co., John W.
Dean Witter Discover
DEC International, Inc.
Delmarva Power & Light Co.
Diamond Shamrock
Diamond State Telephone Co.
Dibrell Brothers, Inc.
Didier Taylor Refractories Corp.
Diebold, Inc.
Dime Savings Bank of New York
Dollar General Corp.
Dover Corp.
Dreyer's & Edy's Grand Ice Cream
Duquesne Light Co.
Durham Corp.
Duriron Co., Inc.
Dynatech Corp.
Eastland Bank
Ebsco Industries
Echlin Inc.
Educators Mutual Life Insurance Co.
Electronic Data Systems Corp.
Employers Insurance of Wausau, A Mutual Co.
Employers Mutual Casualty Co.
Encyclopaedia Britannica, Inc.
Ensersch Corp.
Entex
Equimark Corp.
Equitable Resources
Evening Post Publishing Co.
Fabri-Kal Corp.
Fairfield Communities, Inc.
Farmers Group, Inc.
Federal Paper Board Co.
Federated Life Insurance Co.
Ferranti Tech
Ferrell Cos.
Ferro Corp.
Filene's Sons Co., William
First Alabama Bancshares
First Brands Corp.
First Commercial Bank N.A.
First Interstate Bank of Denver
First Interstate Bank & Trust Co.
First National Bank in Wichita
First NH Banks, Inc.
First of America Bank Corp.
First Security Bank of Idaho N.A.
First Security Bank of Utah N.A.
First Union National Bank of Florida
Fischer & Porter Co.
Fisher-Price
Fleet Bank N.A.
Florida Power & Light Co.
Foxmeyer Corp.

Frito-Lay
Galileo Electro-Optics Corp.
Gast Manufacturing Corp.
Gates Corp.
General Color Co.
General Development Corp.
General Housewares Corp.
General Railway Signal Corp.
General Signal Corp.
General Tire Inc.
Genesco
GenRad
Glatfelter Co., P.H.
Glendale Federal Bank
Grainger, W.W.
Grand Rapids Label Co.
Graphic Controls Corp.
Graybar Electric Co.
Great Lakes Bancorp, FSB
Great Lakes Carbon Corp.
Grinnell Mutual Reinsurance Co.
Grumman Corp.
Hammond Machinery
Hand Industries
Handy & Harman
Harbert Corp.
Harcourt General
Harleysville Mutual Insurance Co.
Harnischfeger Foundation
Harris Stores, Paul
Hartford Steam Boiler Inspection & Insurance Co.
Haworth, Inc.
Hecla Mining Co.
Heil Co.
Herald News
Hercules Inc.
Hertz Foundation, Fannie and John
Hiram Walker & Sons Inc.
Hobart Corp.
Holly Sugar Corp.
Holyoke Mutual Insurance Co. in Salem
Homasote Co.
Home Savings of America, FA
Howell Corp.
Howmet Corp.
Huber Corp., J.M.
Huber, Hunt & Nichols
Huck International Inc.
Hudson Jewellers, J.B.
Huffy Corp.
Hughes Aircraft Co.
Hunt Oil Co.
Huntington Bancshares Inc.
ICH Corp.
Illinois Power Co.
Industrial Risk Insurers
Ingram Industries
Integra Bank/South
Intermark, Inc.
Interpublic Group of Cos.
Interstate Power Co.
Iowa-Illinois Gas & Electric Co.
Isaly Klondike Co.
Itoh (C.) International (America), Inc.
IU International
Jefferson-Pilot
Jefferson-Pilot Communications
Jefferson Smurfit Corp.
Jersey Central Power & Light Co.
Johnson Inc., Axel
Jones Construction Co., J.A.
Journal Communications
Kaiser Aluminum & Chemical Corp.
Kaman Corp.
Kaneb Services, Inc.
Karmazin Products Corp.
Kaufman & Broad Home Corp.
Kaye, Scholer, Fierman, Hays & Handler
Keefe, Bruyette & Woods
Kellogg Co., M.W.

Kellwood Co.
Kendall Health Care Products
Kennecott Corp.
Ketchum & Co.
Kimball International
King Kullen Grocery Co., Inc.
KN Energy, Inc.
Knight-Ridder, Inc.
Kulicke & Soffa Industries
L.A. Gear
Lafarge Corp.
Lambda Electronics Inc.
Langdale Co.
LaSalle Bank Lake View
Law Companies Group
Law Company, Inc.
Leaseway Transportation Corp.
Libbey-Owens Ford Co.
Liberty Mutual Insurance Group/Boston
LIN Broadcasting Corp.
Lincoln Telecommunications Co.
Loctite Corp.
Lomas Financial Corp.
Longs Drug Stores
Lord Corp.
Louisville Gas & Electric Co.
Lowe's Cos.
Lykes Brothers Steamship Co.
MacLean-Fogg Co.
Maguire Oil Co.
Manitowoc Co.
Marine Midland Banks
Marion Fabrics
Marubeni America Corp.
Mascoma Savings Bank
Mass Merchandisers, Inc.
Massachusetts Mutual Life Insurance Co.
MBIA, Inc.
McDonald & Co. Securities
Measurex Corp.
Meenan Oil Co., Inc.
Mellon PSFS
Memphis Light Gas & Water Division
Mennen Co.
Mercantile Bankshares Corp.
Meridian Insurance Group Inc.
Merit Oil Corp.
Mesa Inc.
Metroquip
Mettler Instrument Corp.
Meyer, Inc., Fred
Michigan Mutual Insurance Corp.
Michigan National Corp.
MidAmerica Radio Co.
MidCon Corp.
Midland Co.
Midland Mutual Life Insurance Co.
Midmark Corp.
Milton Bradley Co.
Minnesota Power & Light Co.
Mississippi Chemical Corp.
Mississippi Power & Light Co.
Missouri Public Service
Mitre Corp.
Monfort of Colorado, Inc.
Moore, Costello & Hart
Morse Shoe, Inc.
MTS Systems Corp.
Mutual of America Life
Nash-Finch Co.
National Car Rental System, Inc.
National City Bank, Columbus
National City Bank of Indiana
National Computer Systems
National Convenience Stores, Inc.
National Data Corp.
National Forge Co.
National Fuel Gas Co.
National Standard Co.
NationsBank Texas
Navajo Refining Co.
New Balance Athletic Shoe

New Jersey National Bank
New Jersey Resources Corp.
New York Mercantile Exchange
New York State Electric & Gas Corp.
The New Yorker Magazine, Inc.
Niagara Mohawk Power Corp.
NIBCO Inc.
Nortek, Inc.
North American Coal Corp.
Northern Telecom Inc.
Northern Virginia Natural Gas
NorthPark National Bank
Northrop Corp.
Northwest Natural Gas Co.
Norton & Co., W.W.
NRC, Inc.
NUI Corp.
Oak Industries
Oakite Products
Ogilvy & Mather Worldwide
Ohio Casualty Corp.
Ohio Citizens Bank
Ohio Edison Co.
Oki America Inc.
Old Kent Bank & Trust Co.
Old Republic International Corp.
One Valley Bank, N.A.
Orange & Rockland Utilities, Inc.
Orion Capital Corp.
Ormet Corp.
Oster/Sunbeam Appliance Co.
Owens-Illinois
Packaging Corporation of America
Padnos Iron & Metal Co., Louis
Pamida, Inc.
Pan-American Life Insurance Co.
Patrick Industries Inc.
Paxton Co., Frank
PayLess Drug Stores
Pennsylvania Power & Light
Pentair
People's Bank
Perry Drug Stores
Persis Corp.
PHH Corp.
Philadelphia Electric Co.
Phoenix Home Life Mutual Insurance Co.
Phoenix Resource Cos.
Pioneer Trust Bank, NA
Plante & Moran, CPAs
Plantronics, Inc.
PMI Food Equipment Group Inc.
PNC Bank
Ponderosa, Inc.
Porter Paint Co.
Primark Corp.
Prime Computer, Inc.
PriMerit F.S.B.
Producers Livestock Marketing Association
Providence Energy Corp.
Provident Mutual Life Insurance Co. of Philadelphia
PSI Energy
Public Service Co. of Oklahoma
Quaker State Corp.
Questar Corp.
Raley's
Ranco, Inc.
Ransburg Corp.
Raychem Corp.
Raytheon Engineers & Constructors
RB&W Corp.
Reading & Bates Corp.
Reasoner, Davis & Fox
Redlands Federal Bank
Reliable Life Insurance Co.
Reliance Group Holdings, Inc.
Reliance Insurance Cos.
Republic Automotive Parts, Inc.
Research-Cottrell Inc.
Riggs National Bank
Risdon Corp.

Riviana Foods
Rochester Community Savings Bank
Rochester Gas & Electric Corp.
Rochester Telephone Corp.
Rollins Inc.
Roseburg Forest Products Co.
Ross Corp.
Ross Laboratories
Royal Group Inc.
Santa Fe International Corp.
Sanyo Manufacturing Corp.
Sara Lee Hosiery
Sargent Electric Co.
SCANA Corp.
Scientific-Atlanta
Scientific Brake & Equipment Co.
Scott, Foresman & Co.
Scotty's, Inc.
Sea-Land Service
Sealed Air Corp.
Sealright Co., Inc.
SECO
Security Life of Denver
Seneca Foods Corp.
ServiceMaster Co. L.P.
Seton Co.
Shaw Industries
Shawmut Bank of Franklin County
Sheldahl Inc.
Simkins Industries, Inc.
SKF USA, Inc.
Smith Barney, Harris Upham & Co.
SNC Manufacturing Co.
Society for Savings
Somers Corp. (Mersman/Waldron)
Southern Co. Services
Southern Indiana Gas & Electric Co.
Southland Corp.
Southwestern Public Service Co.
Sprint United Telephone
Standard Brands Paint Co.
Standard Steel Speciality Co.
Standex International Corp.
State Mutual Life Assurance Co.
Steel Heddle Manufacturing Co.
Stein Roe & Farnham Investment Council
Steuart Petroleum Co.
Stewart & Stevenson Services
Stirtz, Bernards & Co.
Storage Technology Corp.
Storer Communications Inc.
Strawbridge & Clothier
Stroh Brewery Co.
Student Loan Marketing Association
T.T.X. Co.
Tampa Electric
Tandy Corp.
TCF Banking & Savings, FSB
Time Warner
Torrington Co.
Towle Manufacturing Co.
Town & Country Corp.
Trans-Apex
Transtar Inc.
Travelers Express Co.
Tremco Inc.
Tripifoods
Triskelion Ltd.
Trustmark National Bank
Tucson Electric Power Co.
Turner Corp.
Twentieth Century Insurance Co.
Tyler Corp.
UJB Financial Corp.
Unigard Security Insurance Co.
Union Equity Division of Farmland Industries
United Gas Pipe Line Co.
United Illuminating Co.

United Stationers Inc.
United Telephone Co. of Florida
United Telephone System
  (Eastern Group)
US Bancorp
Vermeer Charitable Foundation
Vons Cos., Inc.
Wang Laboratories, Inc.
Washington National Insurance
  Co.
Washington Natural Gas Co.
Wausau Insurance Cos.
Welch Foods
West One Bancorp
Whittaker Corp.
Wimpey Inc., George
Wiremold Co.
Wisconsin Bell, Inc.
Wyman-Gordon Co.
Wynn's International, Inc.
Y.K.K. (U.S.A.) Inc.
Zapata Corp.
Zurn Industries

Health & Physical Education

Abbott Laboratories
Abel Construction Co.
AFLAC
AMCORE Bank, N.A. Rockford
American Financial Corp.
American National Bank & Trust
  Co. of Chicago
Ameritas Life Insurance Corp.
Amoco Corp.
AMP
Anheuser-Busch Cos.
AON Corp.
Bemis Company
Boatmen's Bancshares
Brackenridge Foundation,
  George W.
Cablevision of Michigan
Cabot Corp.
Callaway Foundation, Fuller E.
Carnegie Corporation of New
  York
Central Maine Power Co.
Chase Manhattan Bank, N.A.
Chrysler Corp.
Coors Foundation, Adolph
Crestlea Foundation
Cullen/Frost Bankers
Dana Corp.
DeCamp Foundation, Ira W.
Educational Foundation of
  America
English-Bonter-Mitchell
  Foundation
Fay's Incorporated
Federated Life Insurance Co.
Fibre Converters
Fibre Converters
First Interstate Bank of Oregon
First Maryland Bancorp
First Union Corp.
Foothills Foundation
Forest Foundation
Foster Charitable Trust
Foundation for Advancement of
  Chiropractic Education
Funderburke & Associates
Funderburke & Associates
General Motors Corp.
Georgia Power Co.
Giger Foundation, Paul and Oscar
Gregg-Graniteville Foundation
Guttman Foundation, Stella and
  Charles
Hamman Foundation, George
  and Mary Josephine
Hankins Foundation
Hayden Foundation, Charles
Heinz Co., H.J.
Hermann Foundation, Grover
Herrick Foundation

Higgins Charitable Trust, Lorene
  Sails
Hospital Corp. of America
Inland Container Corp.
International Student Exchange
  Cards
ITT Hartford Insurance Group
Jackson Hole Preserve
Johnson & Higgins
Joyce Foundation
Kellogg Foundation, W. K.
Kerr Foundation
Kerr Foundation, Robert S. and
  Grayce B.
Killam Trust, Constance
Lance, Inc.
Lilly & Co., Eli
Lincoln National Corp.
Lipton, Thomas J.
Long Foundation, J.M.
Lounsbery Foundation, Richard
Lurie Foundation, Louis R.
MacArthur Foundation, John D.
  and Catherine T.
Marmot Foundation
Massengill-DeFriece Foundation
Mayer Charitable Trust, Oscar
  G. & Elsa S.
McAlonan Trust, John A.
McCormick Tribune Foundation,
  Robert R.
McDermott Foundation, Eugene
McDonald's Corp.
McMillen Foundation
Meadows Foundation
Metropolitan Life Insurance Co.
Mid-Iowa Health Foundation
Murphy Foundation, John P.
National Computer Systems
National Fuel Gas Co.
New England Mutual Life
  Insurance Co.
New York Life Insurance Co.
New York Mercantile Exchange
Noble Foundation, Edward John
Norton Co.
Pacific Mutual Life Insurance Co.
Palin Foundation
Phelps Dodge Corp.
Phillips Petroleum Co.
Procter & Gamble Cosmetic &
  Fragrance Products
Providence Energy Corp.
Provident Life & Accident
  Insurance Co.
Prudential Insurance Co. of
  America
Ranney Foundation, P. K.
Rubin Foundation, Samuel
San Diego Gas & Electric
Santa Fe Pacific Corp.
Schering-Plough Corp.
Schwartz Fund for Education
  and Health Research, Arnold
  and Marie
Security Life of Denver
Sedgwick James Inc.
Shaklee Corp.
Shawmut National Corp.
Shenandoah Life Insurance Co.
Simpson Industries
Sonoco Products Co.
South Waite Foundation
Speas Foundation, Victor E.
Stare Fund
Starr Foundation
Sterling Winthrop
Strong Foundation, Hattie M.
Texaco
Time Insurance Co.
Upjohn Co.
Vanneck-Bailey Foundation
Disney Co., Walt

International Exchange

AlliedSignal
Aluminum Co. of America
BankAmerica Corp.
Berry Foundation, Lowell
BMW of North America, Inc.
Bosch Corp., Robert
British Airways
Brown & Williamson Tobacco
  Corp.
Bunbury Company
Cabot Corp.
CertainTeed Corp.
Citicorp
Clover Foundation
Colonial Life & Accident
  Insurance Co.
Commerzbank AG, New York
CPC International
Credit Agricole
Cullen/Frost Bankers
Cummins Engine Co.
Davis Foundation, Shelby
  Cullom
Dodge Foundation, Cleveland H.
Dorr Foundation
du Pont de Nemours & Co., E. I.
Educational Foundation of
  America
Emerson Electric Co.
Fidelity Bank
First Fruit
Frohlich Charitable Trust,
  Ludwig W.
Fry Foundation, Lloyd A.
Funderburke & Associates
Funderburke & Associates
General Electric Co.
General Mills
General Motors Corp.
German Marshall Fund of the
  United States
Goodyear Tire & Rubber Co.
Gould Foundation, Florence J.
Graco
Great Atlantic & Pacific Tea Co.
  Inc.
Honda of America
  Manufacturing, Inc.
Honeywell
Intercontinental Hotels Corp.
International Student Exchange
  Cards
Johnson & Son, S.C.
JTB International, Inc.
Kade Foundation, Max
Kellogg Foundation, W. K.
Kiplinger Foundation
Kirby Foundation, F. M.
Liquid Air Corp.
Luce Foundation, Henry
Lurcy Charitable and
  Educational Trust, Georges
Lydall, Inc.
MacArthur Foundation, John D.
  and Catherine T.
Maclellan Foundation
Marubeni America Corp.
McElroy Trust, R. J.
McIntosh Foundation
McMillen Foundation
Meyer Memorial Trust
Mitchell Family Foundation,
  Edward D. and Anna
Mitsubishi International Corp.
Mitsui & Co. (U.S.A.)
Mobil Oil Corp.
Model Foundation, Leo
National Computer Systems
National Westminster Bank New
  Jersey
Nichimen America, Inc.
Osher Foundation, Bernard
Phelps Dodge Corp.
Phillips Petroleum Co.
Pulitzer Publishing Co.

Reed Foundation
Rockefeller Brothers Fund
Rockefeller Foundation
Salgo Charitable Trust, Nicholas
  M.
Sara Lee Corp.
Scrivner, Inc.
Seabury Foundation
Sedgwick James Inc.
Sofia American Schools
Starr Foundation
Stewardship Foundation
Subaru of America Inc.
Sumitomo Corp. of America
TDK Corp. of America
Tinker Foundation
Trust Co. Bank
Trust for Mutual Understanding
Union Bank of Switzerland New
  York Branch
Unocal Corp.
Volkswagen of America, Inc.
Ware Foundation
Xerox Corp.

International Studies

Air France
Alumax
Aluminum Co. of America
American Express Co.
Annenberg Foundation
Arca Foundation
Archer-Daniels-Midland Co.
ARCO Chemical
Atran Foundation
Banbury Fund
BankAmerica Corp.
Bechtel, Jr. Foundation, S. D.
Bender Foundation
Blank Family Foundation
Blum-Kovler Foundation
Bosch Corp., Robert
Bradley Foundation, Lynde and
  Harry
Cabot Corp.
Carnegie Corporation of New
  York
Carnival Cruise Lines
Chase Manhattan Bank, N.A.
Citicorp
Clover Foundation
Coca-Cola Co.
Coleman, Jr. Foundation, George
  E.
Coles Family Foundation
Colonial Life & Accident
  Insurance Co.
Columbia Foundation
Commerzbank AG, New York
Compton Foundation
Country Curtains, Inc.
CPC International
Dentsu, Inc., NY
Deposit Guaranty National Bank
Deutsch Co.
Dial Corp.
Donner Foundation, William H.
Dresser Industries
du Pont de Nemours & Co., E. I.
Exxon Corp.
FINA, Inc.
First Hawaiian
Ford Foundation
Foundation for Iranian Studies
Franklin Foundation, John and
  Mary
Funderburke & Associates
Funderburke & Associates
General Electric Co.
General Mills
General Motors Corp.
General Reinsurance Corp.
German Marshall Fund of the
  United States
Goodyear Tire & Rubber Co.

Greve Foundation, William and
  Mary
Gruss Petroleum Corp.
Harriman Foundation, Mary W.
Heinz Co., H.J.
Herzstein Charitable Foundation,
  Albert and Ethel
Hewlett Foundation, William and
  Flora
Industrial Bank of Japan Trust
  Co.
Ingalls Foundation, Louise H.
  and David S.
Intercontinental Hotels Corp.
International Flavors &
  Fragrances
International Student Exchange
  Cards
Ishiyama Foundation
ITT Hartford Insurance Group
Jaffe Foundation
Joukowsky Family Foundation
Kaufman Foundation, Henry &
  Elaine
Kawasaki Motors Corp., U.S.A.
Kellogg Foundation, W. K.
Kent Foundation, Ada Howe
Kent-Lucas Foundation
Kerr-McGee Corp.
Kirby Foundation, F. M.
Kline Foundation, Charles and
  Figa
Kress Foundation, Samuel H.
Kunstadter Family Foundation,
  Albert
Lanier Brothers Foundation
LBJ Family Foundation
Lieberman Enterprises
Littauer Foundation, Lucius N.
Littlefield Foundation, Edmund
  Wattis
Livingston Foundation
Luce Foundation, Henry
Lurcy Charitable and
  Educational Trust, Georges
MacArthur Foundation, John D.
  and Catherine T.
Mandel Foundation, Jack N. and
  Lilyan
Marcus Brothers Textiles Inc.
Mardigian Foundation
Marubeni America Corp.
McDonnell Douglas Corp.
Melitta North America Inc.
Mex-Am Cultural Foundation
Meyer Foundation, Eugene and
  Agnes E.
Meyer Memorial Trust
Milstein Family Foundation
Mitchell Family Foundation,
  Edward D. and Anna
Mitsubishi International Corp.
Mitsui & Co. (U.S.A.)
Mobil Oil Corp.
Montgomery Street Foundation
National Computer Systems
National Pro-Am Youth Fund
National Westminster Bank New
  Jersey
Nomura Securities International
Olin Foundation, John M.
O'Neill Charitable Corporation,
  F. J.
Open Society Fund
Osher Foundation, Bernard
Overseas Shipholding Group
Paley Foundation, William S.
Pepsi-Cola Bottling Co. of
  Charlotte
Phillips Petroleum Co.
Piper Foundation, Minnie
  Stevens
Pittway Corp.
Pritzker Foundation
Proctor Trust, Mortimer R.
Reed Foundation, Philip D.
Reynolds Foundation,
  Christopher

International Studies (cont.)

Richardson Foundation, Smith
Ridgefield Foundation
Rigler-Deutsch Foundation
Rockefeller Brothers Fund
Russell Memorial Foundation, Robert
Salgo Charitable Trust, Nicholas M.
Scaife Foundation, Sarah
Schlumberger Ltd.
Scrivner, Inc.
Sedgwick James Inc.
Shell Oil Co.
Sifco Industries Inc.
Sloan Foundation, Alfred P.
Sulzberger Foundation
Sumitomo Corp. of America
Taylor Foundation, Ruth and Vernon
Texaco
Textron
Times Mirror Co.
Times Mirror Co.
Tinker Foundation
Trust Co. Bank
Unocal Corp.
Van Schaick Scholarship Fund, Nellie
Volkswagen of America, Inc.
Walker Educational and Charitable Foundation, Alex C.
Wallace Genetic Foundation
Ware Foundation
Weinberg, Jr. Foundation, Sidney J.
Westvaco Corp.
Whirlpool Corp.
Whitehead Foundation
Woodward Fund-Atlanta, David, Helen, Marian
Xerox Corp.

Journalism Education

Aluminum Co. of America
Ameritech Services
Amfac/JMB Hawaii
Annenberg Foundation
Atlanta Gas Light Co.
Ball Corp.
Benton Foundation
Blank Family Foundation
Cabot Family Charitable Trust
Capital Cities/ABC
Central Newspapers, Inc.
Chevron Corp.
Chicago Title and Trust Co.
Chicago Tribune Co.
Clorox Co.
CNG Transmission Corp.
Cook, Sr. Charitable Foundation, Kelly Gene
Copley Press
Cowles Media Co.
Cox Enterprises
Cox, Jr. Foundation, James M.
Dow Jones & Co.
du Pont de Nemours & Co., E. I.
Exxon Corp.
Ford Motor Co.
Freedom Forum
Funderburke & Associates
Funderburke & Associates
Georgia Power Co.
Globe Newspaper Co.
Graham Fund, Philip L.
Heinz Co., H.J.
Illinois Power Co.
Indiana Bell Telephone Co.
International Student Exchange Cards
ITT Hartford Insurance Group
Journal Gazette Co.
Kellogg Foundation, W. K.

Kiewit Foundation, Peter
Kiplinger Foundation
Knight Foundation, John S. and James L.
Landmark Communications
Liberty National Bank
McCormick Tribune Foundation, Robert R.
McElroy Trust, R. J.
McKenna Foundation, Philip M.
McMahon Foundation
Meadows Foundation
Media General, Inc.
Merck & Co.
Meredith Corp.
New York Times Co.
The New Yorker Magazine, Inc.
Newhouse Foundation, Samuel I.
News & Observer Publishing Co.
Noble Foundation, Samuel Roberts
Olin Foundation, John M.
Playboy Enterprises, Inc.
Plumsock Fund
Poynter Fund
Pulitzer Publishing Co.
Reader's Digest Association
Robinson Fund, Maurice R.
Rogers Corp.
Scripps Co., E.W.
Sedgwick James Inc.
Sentinel Communications Co.
Shell Oil Co.
Snow Memorial Trust, John Ben
Sprague Educational and Charitable Foundation, Seth
Starr Foundation
Sunmark Capital Corp.
Texaco
3M Co.
Times Mirror Co.
Westinghouse Broadcasting Co.

Legal Education

Abbott Laboratories
Ahmanson Foundation
Alexander Foundation, Joseph
AlliedSignal
Aluminum Co. of America
AMAX
American Natural Resources Co.
American United Life Insurance Co.
Ames Charitable Trust, Harriett
AMP
Anderson Foundation, M. D.
Ansley Foundation, Dantzler Bond
AON Corp.
Archbold Charitable Trust, Adrian and Jessie
Archer-Daniels-Midland Co.
Bankers Trust Co.
Banyan Tree Foundation
Bargman Foundation, Theodore and Mina
Barker Foundation, J. M. R.
Barlow Family Foundation, Milton A. and Gloria G.
Bauer Foundation, M. R.
Bechtel Group
Bechtel, Jr. Foundation, S. D.
Beinecke Foundation
Belding Heminway Co.
Bemis Company
Beneficial Corp.
Benua Foundation
Berkman Charitable Trust, Allen H. and Selma W.
Berwind Corp.
Bethlehem Steel Corp.
Block, H&R
Blum Foundation, Edith C.
Blum Foundation, Lois and Irving
Blum Foundation, Nathan and Emily S.

Boehm Foundation
Borg-Warner Corp.
Brackenridge Foundation, George W.
Brown and C. A. Lupton Foundation, T. J.
Bryant Foundation
Buchalter, Nemer, Fields, & Younger
Burns Foundation
Burns Foundation, Fritz B.
Burns Foundation, Jacob
Business Incentives
C. E. and S. Foundation
Cabot Family Charitable Trust
Cameron Memorial Fund, Alpin J. and Alpin W.
Capital Cities/ABC
Carnegie Corporation of New York
Carolina Power & Light Co.
Carstensen Memorial Foundation, Fred R. and Hazel W.
Cassett Foundation, Louis N.
Central & South West Services
Chicago Title and Trust Co.
CIT Group Holdings
Clark Family Charitable Trust, Andrew L.
Connelly Foundation
Cord Foundation, E. L.
Country Curtains, Inc.
Covington and Burling
Cowles Foundation, William H.
Cox Charitable Trust, Jessie B.
Culpeper Memorial Foundation, Daphne Seybolt
Darling Foundation, Hugh and Hazel
Davis Foundation, Simon and Annie
Dekalb Energy Co.
Delany Charitable Trust, Beatrice P.
Dewar Foundation
Donaldson Charitable Trust, Oliver S. and Jennie R.
Donaldson Co.
Donovan, Leisure, Newton & Irvine
du Pont de Nemours & Co., E. I.
Eccles Foundation, George S. and Dolores Dore
Emerson Electric Co.
Exxon Corp.
Fair Oaks Foundation, Inc.
Fair Play Foundation
Federal-Mogul Corp.
First Union Corp.
Fleet Bank of New York
Florida Power Corp.
Florida Power & Light Co.
Foster Charitable Trust
Foundation for Middle East Peace
Fox Charitable Foundation, Harry K. & Emma R.
Franklin Foundation, John and Mary
Frederick Foundation
Frueauff Foundation, Charles A.
Fuchsberg Family Foundation
Fuchsberg Family Foundation, Abraham
Funderburke & Associates
Funderburke & Associates
Galvin Foundation, Robert W.
Gaylord Foundation, Clifford Willard
General Electric Co.
General Mills
General Motors Corp.
Gheens Foundation
Goodyear Tire & Rubber Co.
Gore Family Memorial Foundation
Gorin Foundation, Nehemiah

Grassmann Trust, E. J.
Green Fund
Greene Foundation, Jerome L.
Grinnell Mutual Reinsurance Co.
Gross Charitable Trust, Stella B.
Grotto Foundation
Gruss Petroleum Corp.
Hagedorn Fund
Halliburton Co.
Harding Educational and Charitable Foundation
Heinz Co., H.J.
Hermann Foundation, Grover
Hess Foundation
Hoffberger Foundation
Holt Foundation, William Knox
Holtzmann Foundation, Jacob L. and Lillian
Horowitz Foundation, Gedale B. and Barbara S.
Houston Endowment
Hughes Memorial Foundation, Charles Evans
I. and L. Association
Imerman Memorial Foundation, Stanley
Indiana Bell Telephone Co.
International Student Exchange Cards
ITT Hartford Insurance Group
Jameson Foundation, J. W. and Ida M.
Jameson Foundation, J. W. and Ida M.
Jones and Bessie D. Phelps Foundation, Cyrus W. and Amy F.
Jones Family Foundation, Eugenie and Joseph
Jost Foundation, Charles and Mabel P.
Jurodin Fund
Katten, Muchin, & Zavis
Kayser Foundation
Kellogg Foundation, W. K.
Kerr Foundation
Kerr-McGee Corp.
Killson Educational Foundation, Winifred and B. A.
Kirbo Charitable Trust, Thomas M. and Irene B.
Kirkland & Ellis
Kline Foundation, Josiah W. and Bessie H.
Kowalski Sausage Co.
Lane Foundation, Winthrop and Frances
Lea Foundation, Helen Sperry
LeBrun Foundation
Leidy Foundation, John J.
Levinson Foundation, Morris L.
Levy Foundation, Charles and Ruth
Link, Jr. Foundation, George
Linn-Henley Charitable Trust
Lipton, Thomas J.
Littauer Foundation, Lucius N.
Loridans Foundation, Charles
Loughran Foundation, Mary and Daniel
Loyola Foundation
Luce Foundation, Henry
Macy & Co., R.H.
Maier Foundation, Sarah Pauline
Maneely Fund
Mansfield Foundation, Albert and Anne
Martin & Deborah Flug Foundation
Massey Foundation, Jack C.
Mathis-Pfohl Foundation
Mayer Foundation, James and Eva
MBIA, Inc.
MCA
McCann Foundation
McDonnell Douglas Corp.
McDonough Foundation, Bernard

McGonagle Foundation, Dextra Baldwin
MCI Communications Corp.
McIntosh Foundation
McKenna Foundation, Philip M.
Meadows Foundation
Mellen Foundation
Mellon Foundation, Andrew W.
Memton Fund
Merck Fund, John
Milbank Foundation, Dunlevy
Mobil Oil Corp.
Munger Foundation, Alfred C.
Nanney Foundation, Charles and Irene
New-Land Foundation
New World Foundation
New York Life Insurance Co.
Newhouse Foundation, Samuel I.
Norfolk Southern Corp.
Obernauer Foundation
O'Connor Foundation, A. Lindsay and Olive B.
Oglebay Norton Co.
Olin Foundation, John M.
Overbrook Foundation
Overseas Shipholding Group
Patterson Charitable Fund, W. I.
Pfizer
Pines Bridge Foundation
Piper Foundation, Minnie Stevens
PMA Industries
Pulitzer Publishing Co.
Quaker Oats Co.
Reed Foundation
Reed Foundation, Philip D.
Revson Foundation, Charles H.
Rich Products Corp.
Richardson Foundation, Smith
Rockwell Fund
Rosenthal Foundation, Ida and William
Rouse Co.
Rubin Foundation, Samuel
Sage Foundation
Scaife Foundation, Sarah
Scholl Foundation, Dr.
Schwartz Foundation, David
Scott Foundation, Walter
Seasongood Good Government Foundation, Murray and Agnes
Sedgwick James Inc.
Seevak Family Foundation
Semple Foundation, Louise Taft
Shell Oil Co.
Sierra Pacific Resources
Slifka Foundation, Alan B.
Snow Foundation, John Ben
Snow Memorial Trust, John Ben
Sonat
Southways Foundation
Southwest Gas Corp.
Spiegel Family Foundation, Jerry and Emily
Sprague Educational and Charitable Foundation, Seth
Starr Foundation
Stein Foundation, Joseph F.
Stone Container Corp.
Strauss Foundation
Summerfield Foundation, Solon E.
Sumners Foundation, Hatton W.
Taper Foundation, Mark
Taper Foundation, S. Mark
Texaco
Textron
3M Co.
Times Mirror Co.
TJX Cos.
Tracor, Inc.
Treuhaft Foundation
Trust Co. Bank
Union Camp Corp.
Unocal Corp.
US WEST

Vale Foundation, Ruby R.
van Loben Sels - Eleanor Slate
   van Lobel Sels Charitable
   Foundation, Ernst D.
Vaughn Foundation
Walker Educational and
   Charitable Foundation, Alex C.
Disney Co., Walt
Warwick Foundation
Wean Foundation, Raymond John
Weil, Gotshal & Manges
   Foundation
Weinstein Foundation, Alex J.
Weintraub Family Foundation,
   Joseph
White Trust, G. R.
Wiegand Foundation, E. L.
Winston Foundation, Norman
   and Rosita
Wollenberg Foundation
Woolley Foundation, Vasser
Xtra Corp.
Young Foundation, Robert R.

Liberal Arts Education

Ahmanson Foundation
Allendale Mutual Insurance Co.
Aluminum Co. of America
American Electric Power
American Telephone &
   Telegraph Co.
Ameritech Services
Amfac/JMB Hawaii
Annenberg Foundation
Arcadia Foundation
Arvin Industries
Ayres Foundation, Inc.
Balfour Foundation, L. G.
Ball Corp.
Bank of New York
BellSouth Corp.
Block, H&R
Brown Foundation
Brown Foundation, James
   Graham
Brunswick Corp.
Carter Foundation, Amon G.
Chase Manhattan Bank, N.A.
Chatlos Foundation
Chrysler Corp.
Columbus Dispatch Printing Co.
Consolidated Natural Gas Co.
Cooper Industries
Dana Foundation, Charles A.
Davis Foundations, Arthur Vining
Donaldson Co.
Duke Endowment
Duke Power Co.
duPont Fund, Jessie Ball
Eccles Foundation, George S.
   and Dolores Dore
First Union Corp.
Ford Foundation
Funderburke & Associates
Funderburke & Associates
General Reinsurance Corp.
Georgia-Pacific Corp.
Georgia Power Co.
Grace & Co., W.R.
Graphic Controls Corp.
Hall Family Foundations
Hearst Foundation, William
   Randolph
Hewlett Foundation, William and
   Flora
Homeland Foundation
Honeywell
Indiana Bell Telephone Co.
Inland Steel Industries
International Student Exchange
   Cards
J.P. Morgan & Co.
Johnson Endeavor Foundation,
   Christian A.
Johnson & Higgins

Kade Foundation, Max
Keck Foundation, W. M.
Kellogg Foundation, W. K.
Lilly Endowment
Luce Foundation, Henry
McCormick Tribune Foundation,
   Robert R.
Mead Corp.
Mellon Foundation, Andrew W.
Meyer Memorial Trust
Mobil Oil Corp.
National Computer Systems
The New Yorker Magazine, Inc.
Northern Indiana Public Service
   Co.
Oglebay Norton Co.
Penn Foundation, William
Pew Charitable Trusts
Pickett and Hatcher Educational
   Fund
Providence Energy Corp.
Provident Life & Accident
   Insurance Co.
Rockwell Fund
Rohm and Haas Company
Sara Lee Hosiery
Scott, Jr. Charitable Foundation,
   Walter
Sedgwick James Inc.
Shawmut National Corp.
Siebert Lutheran Foundation
Sonat
Springs Industries
Sterling Winthrop
Teagle Foundation
3M Co.
Times Mirror Co.
Union Camp Corp.
Weingart Foundation
Whirlpool Corp.
Wisconsin Energy Corp.
Xerox Corp.

Literacy

Abell Foundation, The
Abell-Hanger Foundation
Abitibi-Price
Achelis Foundation
Ahmanson Foundation
Air Products & Chemicals
Alabama Power Co.
Allen Foundation, Frances
Allendale Mutual Insurance Co.
AlliedSignal
Alltel/Western Region
ALPAC Corp.
Altman Foundation
Alumax
Aluminum Co. of America
America West Airlines
American Brands
American Express Co.
Ameritech Corp.
Ameritech Services
AMETEK
Amoco Corp.
AMP
Amsted Industries
Andersons Management Corp.
Anschutz Family Foundation
Apache Corp.
Apple Computer, Inc.
Arcadia Foundation
ARCO
ARCO Chemical
Arkla
Armco Inc.
Ashland Oil
Astor Foundation, Vincent
Atalanta/Sosnoff Capital Corp.
Atlanta Gas Light Co.
Atlantic Foundation of New York
Atwood Foundation
Auerbach Foundation, Beatrice
   Fox
Avon Products

Babcock Foundation, Mary
   Reynolds
Bacardi Imports
Badger Meter, Inc.
Baker, Jr. Memorial Fund,
   William G.
Ball Corp.
Bancorp Hawaii
Bank of A. Levy
Bank of America Arizona
Bank of Boston Connecticut
Bank of Boston Corp.
Bannon Foundation
Bantam Doubleday Dell
   Publishing Group, Inc.
Barclays Bank of New York
Battelle
BCR Foundation
Beatty Trust, Cordelia Lunceford
Beitzell & Co.
Bell Atlantic Corp.
Bentley Foundation, Alvin M.
Bibb Co.
Bigelow Foundation, F. R.
Binney & Smith Inc.
Birch Foundation, Stephen and
   Mary
Blair and Co., William
Block, H&R
Blue Cross & Blue Shield of
   Alabama
Blum Foundation, Nathan and
   Emily S.
Boatmen's First National Bank
   of Oklahoma
Boeing Co.
Boise Cascade Corp.
Borden
Bowne Foundation, Robert
Bradley-Turner Foundation
Brady Foundation, W. H.
Bremer Foundation, Otto
Brewer and Co., Ltd., C.
Browning-Ferris Industries
Brunswick Corp.
Bucyrus-Erie
Buhl Foundation
Bull Foundation, Henry W.
Burden Foundation, Florence V.
Burlington Resources
Cabell III and Maude Morgan
   Cabell Foundation, Robert G.
Cadbury Beverages Inc.
Capital Cities/ABC
Capital Holding Corp.
Carnegie Corporation of New
   York
Carolina Power & Light Co.
Carolyn Foundation
Carrier Corp.
Cartier, Inc.
Castle Foundation, Samuel N.
   and Mary
Centel Corp.
Central Maine Power Co.
Champion International Corp.
Chase Manhattan Bank, N.A.
Chatham Valley Foundation
Chemical Bank
Cherne Foundation, Albert W.
Chevron Corp.
Chicago Sun-Times, Inc.
Chicago Title and Trust Co.
Chicago Tribune Co.
CIGNA Corp.
Cincinnati Bell
Citicorp
Clorox Co.
CM Alliance Cos.
CNA Insurance Cos.
Columbus Southern Power Co.
Commerce Clearing House
Cone Mills Corp.
Consolidated Natural Gas Co.
Consolidated Papers
Cook Foundation
Cook Foundation, Louella

Coors Foundation, Adolph
Copley Press
Copperweld Corp.
Cornell Trust, Peter C.
Cowden Foundation, Louetta M.
Cowles Charitable Trust
Cowles Media Co.
Cox Charitable Trust, Jessie B.
Cox Enterprises
CPC International
Crocker Trust, Mary A.
Crown Books Foundation, Inc.
Crown Central Petroleum Corp.
Crown Memorial, Arie and Ida
Cudahy Fund, Patrick and Anna
   M.
Cullen/Frost Bankers
Cummings Memorial Fund
   Trust, Frances L. and Edwin L.
Curtice-Burns Foods
Daniels Foundation, Fred Harris
Davenport-Hatch Foundation
Day Foundation, Cecil B.
Deposit Guaranty National Bank
Detroit Edison Co.
Dewing Foundation, Frances R.
Diamond Foundation, Aaron
Digital Equipment Corp.
Dollar General Corp.
Donaldson Co.
Donnelley & Sons Co., R.R.
Donner Foundation, William H.
Dreyfus Foundation, Jean and
   Louis
Drown Foundation, Joseph
du Pont de Nemours & Co., E. I.
Duke Power Co.
duPont Foundation, Chichester
Dyson Foundation
Emergency Aid of Pennsylvania
   Foundation
Emerson Electric Co.
Encyclopaedia Britannica, Inc.
Ensworth Charitable Foundation
Equifax
Equitable Life Assurance Society
   of the U.S.
Ettinger Foundation
Fales Foundation Trust
Federated Department Stores and
   Allied Stores Corp.
Fel-Pro Incorporated
Fidelity Bank
Field Foundation of Illinois
Fikes Foundation, Leland
First Brands Corp.
First Fidelity Bancorporation
First Interstate Bank of Arizona
First Interstate Bank of Texas,
   N.A.
First Mississippi Corp.
First Union Corp.
First Union National Bank of
   Florida
Firstar Bank Milwaukee NA
Fish Foundation, Ray C.
Fleet Financial Group
Fleming Companies, Inc.
Ford Foundation
Forest Oil Corp.
Foster Foundation
Franklin Foundation, John and
   Mary
Franklin Mint Corp.
Frederick Foundation
Freed Foundation
Freedom Forum
Fry Foundation, Lloyd A.
Funderburke & Associates
Funderburke & Associates
Gage Foundation, Philip and
   Irene Toll
Gannett Co.
Gates Foundation
GATX Corp.
General Dynamics Corp.
General Electric Co.

General Mills
General Motors Corp.
General Reinsurance Corp.
General Tire Inc.
Genesis Foundation
George Foundation
Georgia-Pacific Corp.
Georgia Power Co.
Giant Food Stores
Glenn Foundation, Carrie C. &
   Lena V.
Globe Newspaper Co.
Goddard Foundation, Charles B.
Goldman Foundation, Herman
Goldseker Foundation of
   Maryland, Morris
Graco
Gradison & Co.
Grant Foundation, Charles M.
   and Mary D.
Graphic Controls Corp.
Greene Manufacturing Co.
Greentree Foundation
Griggs and Mary Griggs Burke
   Foundation, Mary Livingston
GTE Corp.
Guardian Life Insurance Co. of
   America
Gulf Power Co.
Gulfstream Aerospace Corp.
Haas Fund, Walter and Elise
Haggar Foundation
Hallmark Cards
Hamman Foundation, George
   and Mary Josephine
Hancock Foundation, Luke B.
Harmon Foundation, Pearl M.
   and Julia J.
HarperCollins Publishers
Hasbro
Hearst Foundation
Hearst Foundation, William
   Randolph
Heinz Foundation, Drue
Heller Financial
Hershey Foods Corp.
Heublein
Hewlett Foundation, William and
   Flora
Hillcrest Foundation
Hilliard Corp.
Hilliard Corp.
Hillman Foundation
Hillsdale Fund
Hoblitzelle Foundation
Hospital Corp. of America
Household International
Houston Industries
Howard and Bush Foundation
Hunt Alternatives Fund
Hunt Charitable Trust, C. Giles
Hunt Manufacturing Co.
Hunter Trust, A. V.
Hyams Foundation
IBM Corp.
IBM South Africa Projects Fund
ICI Americas
Illinois Power Co.
Illinois Tool Works
Imlay Foundation
Indiana Bell Telephone Co.
Inland Steel Industries
International Paper Co.
International Student Exchange
   Cards
ITT Corp.
ITT Hartford Insurance Group
J.P. Morgan & Co.
Janssen Foundation, Henry
JCPenney Co.
Jennings Foundation, Mary
   Hillman
Johnson Controls
Johnson Foundation, Walter S.
Johnson & Higgins
Jones Foundation, Daisy Marquis
Jostens

Clarke Trust, John
Clayton Fund
Clowes Fund
Cohen Foundation, Naomi and Nehemiah
Coleman Co.
Collins Foundation
Collins Foundation, James M.
Collins Foundation, Joseph
Collins Medical Trust
Colorado Trust
Commonwealth Fund
Community Hospital Foundation
Compaq Computer Corp.
Cosden Trust f/b/o the University of Arizona College of Medicine, Curtis C.
Cox, Jr. Foundation, James M.
Crestlea Foundation
Cullen Foundation
Cullen/Frost Bankers
Culpeper Foundation, Charles E.
Cuneo Foundation
Dalsimer Fund, Craig
Dammann Fund
Dana Corp.
Dana Foundation, Charles A.
Danner Foundation
Davee Foundation
Davenport-Hatch Foundation
Davis Foundation, Edwin W. and Catherine M.
Davis Foundations, Arthur Vining
Davis Hospital Foundation
DeCamp Foundation, Ira W.
Delany Charitable Trust, Beatrice P.
Delta Air Lines
Demoulas Supermarkets
Dennison Manufacturing Co.
Devonwood Foundation
Dickson Foundation
Dorminy Foundation, John Henry
Dorot Foundation
Doyle Charitable Foundation
Dresser Industries
Dreyfus Foundation, Jean and Louis
Dreyfus Foundation, Max and Victoria
Dula Educational and Charitable Foundation, Caleb C. and Julia W.
Duncan Foundation, Lillian H. and C. W.
Duncan Trust, James R.
Dunn Research Foundation, John S.
Dunspaugh-Dalton Foundation
duPont Foundation, Alfred I.
Durr-Fillauer Medical
Eccles Foundation, George S. and Dolores Dore
Eddy Foundation
Edison Fund, Charles
Educational Foundation of America
Einstein Fund, Albert E. and Birdie W.
Elkins, Jr. Foundation, Margaret and James A.
Emerson Electric Co.
Engelhard Foundation, Charles
English-Bonter-Mitchell Foundation
Enron Corp.
Equitable Life Assurance Society of the U.S.
Evans Foundation, T. M.
Exxon Corp.
Falk Foundation, Michael David
Falk Medical Fund, Maurice
Farish Fund, William Stamps
Federated Department Stores and Allied Stores Corp.
Feil Foundation, Louis and Gertrude
Feintech Foundation

Femino Foundation
Fifth Third Bancorp
Fikes Foundation, Leland
Finley Foundation, A. E.
First Maryland Bancorp
First Mississippi Corp.
Firstar Bank Milwaukee NA
Fish Foundation, Bert
Fish Foundation, Vain and Harry
Florence Foundation
Foerderer Foundation, Percival E. and Ethel Brown
Forbes
Forchheimer Foundation
Ford Foundation, Joseph F. and Clara
Ford III Memorial Foundation, Jefferson Lee
Fraida Foundation
France Foundation, Jacob and Annita
Francis Families Foundation
Frankel Foundation, George and Elizabeth F.
Franklin Charitable Trust, Ershel
Franklin Foundation, John and Mary
Frederick Foundation
Frohlich Charitable Trust, Ludwig W.
Frohman Foundation, Sidney
Frueauff Foundation, Charles A.
Fuller Foundation, George F. and Sybil H.
Fullerton Foundation
Funderburke & Associates
Gaisman Foundation, Catherine and Henry J.
Galvin Foundation, Robert W.
General American Life Insurance Co.
General Development Corp.
General Dynamics Corp.
General Mills
Gerber Products Co.
Gerson Family Foundation, Benjamin J.
Gibson Foundation, Addison H.
Glenn Foundation, Carrie C. & Lena V.
Glenn Foundation for Medical Research, Paul F.
Globe Corp.
Goldenberg Foundation, Max
Goldman Foundation, Herman
Goldsmith Family Foundation
Goode Trust, Mae Stone
Goodstein Family Foundation, David
Goodyear Tire & Rubber Co.
Goody's Manufacturing Corp.
Gordon/Rousmaniere/Roberts Fund
Gottesman Fund
Grace & Co., W.R.
Grainger Foundation
Graphic Controls Corp.
Grass Foundation
Grassmann Trust, E. J.
Gray Foundation, Garland
Green Fund
Greenspan Foundation
Griswold Foundation, John C.
Group Health Plan Inc.
Gulton Foundation
Hachar Charitable Trust, D. D.
Halliburton Co.
Hammer Foundation, Armand
Hankamer Foundation, Curtis and Doris K.
Hansen Foundation, Dane G.
Hansen Memorial Foundation, Irving
Harding Foundation, Charles Stewart
Harriman Foundation, Gladys and Roland

Harrington Foundation, Don and Sybil
Harris Foundation, William H. and Mattie Wattis
Harsco Corp.
Hartford Foundation, John A.
Hatch Charitable Trust, Margaret Milliken
Hazen Charitable Trust, Lita Annenberg
Health 1st Foundation
Hearst Foundation
Hearst Foundation, William Randolph
Hechinger Co.
Heckscher Foundation for Children
Heinz Co., H.J.
Heinz Endowment, Howard
Heinz Endowment, Vira I.
Helfaer Foundation, Evan and Marion
Herndon Foundation
Herrick Foundation
Herzog Foundation, Carl J.
Herzstein Charitable Foundation, Albert and Ethel
Hess Foundation
Hewlett-Packard Co.
Higgins Charitable Trust, Lorene Sails
Hillcrest Foundation
Hillman Family Foundation, Alex
Hirschl Trust for Charitable Purposes, Irma T.
Hoblitzelle Foundation
Hoffmann-La Roche
Holden Fund, James and Lynelle
Holtzmann Foundation, Jacob L. and Lillian
Hook Drug
Hoover, Jr. Foundation, Margaret W. and Herbert
Hopedale Foundation
Horncrest Foundation
Horne Trust, Mabel
Hospital Corp. of America
Houston Endowment
Hubbell Inc.
Hughes Medical Institute, Howard
Hughes Memorial Foundation, Charles Evans
Hugoton Foundation
Humana
Humane Society of the Commonwealth of Massachusetts
Humphrey Foundation, Glenn & Gertrude
Huntington Fund for Education, John
Huston Foundation
Hyde and Watson Foundation
I. and L. Association
IBM South Africa Projects Fund
Independence Foundation
Index Technology Corp.
India Foundation
Innovating Worthy Projects Foundation
International Student Exchange Cards
ITT Hartford Insurance Group
Jaharis Family Foundation
Jaqua Foundation
Jeffress Memorial Trust, Thomas F. and Kate Miller
Jennings Foundation, Alma
Jewett Foundation, George Frederick
Jockey Hollow Foundation
John Hancock Mutual Life Insurance Co.
Johnson Controls
Johnson Foundation, Robert Wood
Johnson & Higgins

Johnson & Son, S.C.
Johnston Trust for Charitable and Educational Purposes, James M.
Jones Charitable Trust, Harvey and Bernice
Jones Foundation, Daisy Marquis
Jones Fund, Paul L.
Joyce Foundation, John M. and Mary A.
Joyce Foundation, John M. and Mary A.
Kade Foundation, Max
Kapiloff Foundation, Leonard
Kaufmann Foundation, Henry
Keck Foundation, W. M.
Kellogg Foundation, W. K.
Kempner Fund, Harris and Eliza
Kennedy, Jr. Foundation, Joseph P.
Kern Foundation, Ilma
Kerr Foundation
Kettering Family Foundation
Key Bank of Maine
Killson Educational Foundation, Winifred and B. A.
Kilmartin Industries
Kimberly-Clark Corp.
King Foundation, Carl B. and Florence E.
Kirbo Charitable Trust, Thomas M. and Irene B.
Kirby Foundation, F. M.
Kirchgessner Foundation, Karl
Kleberg, Jr. and Helen C. Kleberg Foundation, Robert J.
Klosk Fund, Louis and Rose
Knapp Foundation
Knox Family Foundation
Kohl Foundation, Sidney
Kramer Foundation
Kunkel Foundation, John Crain
Kynett Memorial Foundation, Edna G.
Kysor Industrial Corp.
L and L Foundation
Ladish Family Foundation, Herman W.
Lasdon Foundation
Lasky Co.
Lazar Foundation
Lightner Sams Foundation
Lilly & Co., Eli
Lincoln Fund
Lincoln Health Care Foundation
Link, Jr. Foundation, George
Lipton, Thomas J.
Livingston Memorial Foundation
Long Foundation, J.M.
Lowe Foundation, Joe and Emily
Lowenstein Foundation, Leon
MacArthur Foundation, John D. and Catherine T.
MacKall and Evanina Evans Bell MacKall Trust, Paul
MacKenzie Foundation
Macy & Co., R.H.
Macy, Jr. Foundation, Josiah
Maier Foundation, Sarah Pauline
Mailman Family Foundation, A. L.
Mallinckrodt, Jr. Foundation, Edward
Manning and Emma Austin Manning Foundation, James Hilton
Manoogian Foundation, Alex and Marie
Manville Corp.
Margoes Foundation
Marion Merrell Dow
Markey Charitable Trust, Lucille P.
Marquette Electronics
Mars Foundation
Marshall & Ilsley Bank
Masco Corp.
Massey Foundation

Mather and William Gwinn Mather Fund, Elizabeth Ring
May Department Stores Co.
Mayer Charitable Trust, Oscar G. & Elsa S.
Mayor Foundation, Oliver Dewey
Maytag Family Foundation, Fred
Mazer Foundation, Jacob and Ruth
MCA
McBeath Foundation, Faye
McCormick Tribune Foundation, Robert R.
McDermott Foundation, Eugene
McGonagle Foundation, Dextra Baldwin
McGovern Fund for the Behavioral Sciences
MCI Communications Corp.
Meadows Foundation
Measey Foundation, Benjamin and Mary Siddons
Medtronic
Mellen Foundation
Mellon Foundation, Richard King
Merck & Co.
Merck Fund, John
Merrick Foundation, Robert G. and Anne M.
Metropolitan Health Foundation
Mette Foundation
Michael Foundation, Herbert I. and Elsa B.
Middendorf Foundation
Milliken & Co.
Mitrani Family Foundation
Mobil Oil Corp.
Monell Foundation, Ambrose
Montgomery Street Foundation
Moore Foundation, Edward S.
Morris Foundation, Margaret T.
Morris Foundation, William T.
Mosbacher, Jr. Foundation, Emil
Moses Fund, Henry and Lucy
Moss Heart Trust, Harry S.
Mulcahy Foundation
Mulligan Charitable Trust, Mary S.
Murphy Foundation, John P.
Nalco Chemical Co.
National Medical Enterprises
New England Foundation
New-Land Foundation
New York Life Insurance Co.
New York Mercantile Exchange
The New Yorker Magazine, Inc.
Newhouse Foundation, Samuel I.
Nias Foundation, Henry
Norman Foundation, Andrew
NYNEX Corp.
Oberkotter Family Foundation
Occidental Petroleum Corp.
O'Connor Foundation, A. Lindsay and Olive B.
O'Connor Foundation, Kathryn
Offield Family Foundation
Ogden Foundation, Ralph E.
Oglebay Norton Co.
Ohl, Jr. Trust, George A.
Olsson Memorial Foundation, Elis
Orchard Corp. of America.
Ordean Foundation
Oshkosh B'Gosh
Overseas Shipholding Group
Oxford Foundation
Oxnard Foundation
Pacific Mutual Life Insurance Co.
Paley Foundation, William S.
Pappas Charitable Foundation, Thomas Anthony
Paramount Communications Inc.
Park Bank
Parke-Davis Group
Patterson and Clara Guthrie Patterson Trust, Robert Leet

Medical Education (cont.)

Pennsylvania Knitted Outerwear Manufacturing Association
Perkin Fund
Perkins Charitable Foundation
Perot Foundation
Peters Foundation, R. D. and Linda
Pew Charitable Trusts
Pfeiffer Research Foundation, Gustavus and Louise
Pfizer
Phelps Dodge Corp.
Philip Morris Cos.
Phillips Family Foundation, Jay and Rose
Pines Bridge Foundation
Pioneer Fund
Pittway Corp.
Plough Foundation
Polaroid Corp.
Pope Foundation
Porter Foundation, Mrs. Cheever
Porter Testamentary Trust, James Hyde
Potter Foundation, Justin and Valere
Potts Memorial Foundation
Prentice Foundation, Abra
Prentiss Foundation, Elisabeth Severance
Pritzker Foundation
Procter & Gamble Cosmetic & Fragrance Products
Prudential Insurance Co. of America
Pulitzer Publishing Co.
Quaker Oats Co.
Rabb Charitable Trust, Sidney R.
Raleigh Linen Service/National Distributing Co.
Ralston Purina Co.
Ramapo Trust
Rapp Foundation, Robert Glenn
Raymond Educational Foundation
Redman Foundation
Reinberger Foundation
Reynolds Charitable Trust, Kate B.
Reynolds Foundation, Richard S.
RGK Foundation
Rhone-Poulenc Rorer
Rice Foundation, Ethel and Raymond F.
Rienzi Foundation
Ritter Foundation
Robison Foundation, Ellis H. and Doris B.
Rockefeller Foundation
Roddis Foundation, Hamilton
Rodgers Foundation, Richard & Dorothy
Rogers Foundation
Rosenberg Foundation, Alexis
Rosenberg Foundation, Sunny and Abe
Rosenstiel Foundation
Rosenthal Foundation, Richard and Hinda
Rosenthal Foundation, Samuel
Rosenwald Family Fund, William
Rowland Foundation
Rubin Family Fund, Cele H. and William B.
Ruddick Corp.
Rudin Foundation, Louis and Rachel
Russell Memorial Foundation, Robert
St. Giles Foundation
San Diego Gas & Electric
Santa Fe Pacific Corp.
Sarkeys Foundation
Saunders Foundation

Scaife Family Foundation
Schaffer Foundation, Michael & Helen
Schering-Plough Corp.
Schlieder Educational Foundation, Edward G.
Schlinger Foundation
Schlumberger Ltd.
Scholl Foundation, Dr.
Schreiber Foods, Inc.
Schultz Foundation
Schwartz Foundation, David
Schwartz Fund for Education and Health Research, Arnold and Marie
Scott Foundation, Walter
Scurry Foundation, D. L.
Sedgwick James Inc.
Segerstrom Foundation
Sharp Foundation, Charles S. and Ruth C.
Shattuck Charitable Trust, S. F.
Shelden Fund, Elizabeth, Allan and Warren
Shelton Cos.
Shenandoah Life Insurance Co.
Sherman Family Charitable Trust, George and Beatrice
Silverweed Foundation
Sinsheimer Fund, Alexandrine and Alexander L.
Slant/Fin Corp.
Slaughter Foundation, Charles Smith and W. Aubrey Smith
Smith Charitable Foundation, Clara Blackford
Smith Corp., A.O.
Smith Fund, George D.
Smithers Foundation, Christopher D.
SmithKline Beecham
Snyder Foundation, Frost and Margaret
Sofia American Schools
Solomon Foundation, Sarah M.
Sonat
Soros Foundation-Hungary
Sosland Foundation
South Plains Foundation
Spang & Co.
Speas Foundation, Victor E.
Speas Memorial Trust, John W. and Effie E.
Sprague Educational and Charitable Foundation, Seth
Sprague, Jr. Foundation, Caryll M. and Norman F.
Sprague Memorial Institute, Otho S. A.
Star Bank, N.A.
Starr Foundation
Steiner Charitable Fund, Albert
Sterling Winthrop
Stern Memorial Trust, Sidney
Stern Private Charitable Foundation Trust, Charles H. and Anna S.
Stewart Trust under the will of Helen S. Devore, Alexander and Margaret
Stone Foundation
Stone Foundation, France
Strake Foundation
Stranahan Foundation
Straus Foundation, Martha Washington Straus and Harry H.
Stupp Foundation, Norman J.
Sulzberger Foundation
Summerfield Foundation, Solon E.
Surgical Science Foundation for Research and Development
Swift Co. Inc., John S.
Swim Foundation, Arthur L.
Swisher Foundation, Carl S.
Switzer Foundation

Sylvester Foundation, Harcourt M. and Virginia W.
Tai and Co., J. T.
Taub Foundation
Tauber Foundation
Taylor Family Foundation, Jack
Telinde Trust, Richard W.
Texaco
Texas Instruments
Textron
Thomas Memorial Foundation, Theresa A.
3M Co.
Times Mirror Co.
TJX Cos.
Towsley Foundation, Harry A. and Margaret D.
Treadwell Foundation, Nora Eccles
Trull Foundation
Trust Co. Bank
Tyson Foods, Inc.
Union Camp Corp.
Union Foundation
Universal Foods Corp.
Unocal Corp.
Upjohn Co.
Uvas Foundation
Valley Foundation
van Ameringen Foundation
Van Houten Charitable Trust
Veritas Foundation
Vicksburg Hospital Medical Foundation
Vingo Trust II
Wal-Mart Stores
Waldinger Corp.
Walthall Perpetual Charitable Trust, Marjorie T.
Ware Foundation
Warren Charite
Washington Square Health Foundation
Wean Foundation, Raymond John
Webb Foundation, Del E.
Weight Watchers International
Weiler Foundation, Theodore & Renee
Weintraub Family Foundation, Joseph
Weller Foundation
Wertheim Foundation, Dr. Herbert A.
West Co.
West Foundation, Neva and Wesley
West Texas Corp., J. M.
Westchester Health Fund
Western Cardiac Foundation
Westvaco Corp.
Whirlpool Corp.
Whitaker Charitable Foundation, Lyndon C.
Whitaker Foundation
Whitehead Charitable Foundation
Whitehead Foundation, Lettie Pate
Whitney Foundation, Helen Hay
Wiegand Foundation, E. L.
Wildermuth Foundation, E. F.
Wilf Family Foundation
Willits Foundation
Winn-Dixie Stores
Winston Foundation, Norman and Rosita
Witco Corp.
Wolff Memorial Foundation, Pauline Sterne
Wolfson Foundation, Louis E.
Wollenberg Foundation
Wood Foundation, Lester G.
Woodruff Foundation, Robert W.
Zenkel Foundation
Zimmermann Fund, Marie and John
Zlinkoff Fund for Medical Research and Education, Sergei S.

Minority Education

Abbott Laboratories
Abell Foundation, The
Abell-Hanger Foundation
Achelis Foundation
Acushnet Co.
Aetna Life & Casualty Co.
Ahmanson Foundation
Air Products & Chemicals
Akzo Chemicals Inc.
Alabama Power Co.
Albertson's
Alcon Laboratories, Inc.
Allegheny Ludlum Corp.
Allendale Mutual Insurance Co.
Alliant Techsystems
AlliedSignal
Allstate Insurance Co.
Allyn Foundation
Alma Piston Co.
ALPAC Corp.
Altman Foundation
Alumax
Aluminum Co. of America
AMAX
AMCORE Bank, N.A. Rockford
Amdahl Corp.
America West Airlines
American Brands
American Electric Power
American Express Co.
American Financial Corp.
American Honda Motor Co.
American National Bank & Trust Co. of Chicago
American Natural Resources Co.
American Saw & Manufacturing Co.
American Telephone & Telegraph Co.
American United Life Insurance Co.
Ameritech Corp.
Amoco Corp.
AMP
AMR Corp.
Amsterdam Foundation, Jack and Mimi Leviton
Analog Devices
Andersen Corp.
Andersen Foundation
Andersons Management Corp.
Anheuser-Busch Cos.
Apache Corp.
Apple Computer, Inc.
Appleton Papers
Archer-Daniels-Midland Co.
ARCO
Arkansas Power & Light Co.
Armco Inc.
Armstrong World Industries Inc.
Arvin Industries
Atkinson Foundation
Atlanta Gas Light Co.
Avon Products
Bacardi Imports
Baird & Co., Robert W.
Balfour Foundation, L. G.
Ball Corp.
Ball Foundation, George and Frances
Banc One Illinois Corp.
Bank of America Arizona
Bank of Boston Corp.
Bank of Louisville
Bank of New York
BankAmerica Corp.
Bankers Trust Co.
Barnes Group
Barnett Banks
Battelle
Bauer Foundation, M. R.
Bausch & Lomb
Bechtel Group
Belding Heminway Co.
Belk Stores

Bell Atlantic Corp.
BellSouth Corp.
Bemis Company
Bergner Co., P.A.
Berwind Corp.
Bernstein & Co., Sanford C.
Bethlehem Steel Corp.
Bethlehem Steel Corp.
Bettingen Corporation, Burton G.
Betz Laboratories
BFGoodrich
Bigelow Foundation, F. R.
Blandin Foundation
Block, H&R
Blount
Blum-Kovler Foundation
Boatmen's Bancshares
Bodine Corp.
Bodman Foundation
Boehringer Mannheim Corp.
Boeing Co.
Boise Cascade Corp.
Borden
Borg-Warner Corp.
Borman's
Bosch Corp., Robert
Boston Edison Co.
Bowater Inc.
Bowyer Foundation, Ambrose and Gladys
BP America
Brach Foundation, Helen
Bremer Foundation, Otto
Bridgestone/Firestone
Briggs & Stratton Corp.
Britton Fund
Brown, Jr. Charitable Trust, Frank D.
Brown & Williamson Tobacco Corp.
Brunswick Corp.
Bryan Family Foundation, Kathleen Price and Joseph M.
Bucyrus-Erie
Buhl Foundation
Burlington Industries
Burlington Resources
Bush Foundation
Butler Manufacturing Co.
C.P. Rail Systems
Cabot Corp.
Calhoun Charitable Trust, Kenneth
Campbell Soup Co.
Capital Cities/ABC
Capital Holding Corp.
Carnegie Corporation of New York
Carolina Telephone & Telegraph Co.
Carrier Corp.
Carter Foundation, Amon G.
Carter-Wallace
Caterpillar
Cayuga Foundation
CBS Inc.
Centel Corp.
Center for Educational Programs
Centerior Energy Corp.
Central Maine Power Co.
Central Newspapers, Inc.
Central Soya Co.
CertainTeed Corp.
Champion International Corp.
Chase Manhattan Bank, N.A.
Chemical Bank
Chesebrough-Pond's
Chevron Corp.
Chicago Sun-Times, Inc.
Chicago Title and Trust Co.
Chilton Foundation Trust
China Times Cultural Foundation
Chrysler Corp.
Cincinnati Bell
Circuit City Stores
Citicorp
Clark Foundation

Clark Foundation, Edna McConnell
Cleveland-Cliffs
Clorox Co.
CM Alliance Cos.
CNA Insurance Cos.
Coca-Cola Co.
Coen Family Foundation, Charles S. and Mary
Coleman Foundation
Coltec Industries
Comerica
Compton Foundation
ConAgra
Connelly Foundation
Conoco Inc.
Consolidated Natural Gas Co.
Consolidated Papers
Consolidated Rail Corp. (Conrail)
Continental Bank N.A.
Cook Inlet Region
Coors Brewing Co.
Copperweld Corp.
Cornell Trust, Peter C.
Corning Incorporated
Country Curtains, Inc.
Cowles Charitable Trust
Cowles Media Co.
Cox Charitable Trust, Jessie B.
CPC International
CPI Corp.
Crane Fund for Widows and Children
Crawford & Co.
Crestar Financial Corp.
CT Corp. System
Cudahy Fund, Patrick and Anna M.
Cummings Memorial Fund Trust, Frances L. and Edwin L.
Cummins Engine Co.
CUNA Mutual Insurance Group
Curtice-Burns Foods
Cyprus Minerals Co.
Dain Bosworth/Inter-Regional Financial Group
Dana Corp.
Dana Foundation, Charles A.
Danforth Foundation
Davey Tree Expert Co.
Davis Foundation, Edwin W. and Catherine M.
de Hirsch Fund, Baron
de Rothschild Foundation, Edmond
Dean Witter Discover
Deere & Co.
Delaware North Cos.
Delta Air Lines
Dennison Manufacturing Co.
Dentsply International, Inc.
DeSoto
Detroit Edison Co.
Devereaux Foundation
DeVlieg Foundation, Charles
Dexter Corp.
Dial Corp.
Diamond Foundation, Aaron
Digital Equipment Corp.
Dodge Foundation, Geraldine R.
Donaldson Co.
Donaldson Co.
Douglas & Lomason Company
Douty Foundation
Dow Chemical Co.
Dow Corning Corp.
Dow Jones & Co.
Dresser Industries
Dreyfus Foundation, Max and Victoria
Drown Foundation, Joseph
du Pont de Nemours & Co., E. I.
Duchossois Industries
Duke Endowment
Duke Power Co.
Dun & Bradstreet Corp.
Duncan Trust, John G.

duPont Fund, Jessie Ball
Durfee Foundation
E and M Charities
Eastman Kodak Co.
Eaton Corp.
Ecolab
Eden Hall Foundation
Edison Foundation, Irving and Beatrice C.
Educational Foundation of America
Egenton Home
Elf Atochem North America
Emerson Electric Co.
English-Bonter-Mitchell Foundation
Enron Corp.
Equifax
Equitable Life Assurance Society of the U.S.
Ernest & Julio Gallo Winery
Ernst & Young
European American Bank
Exposition Foundation
Exxon Corp.
Fair Oaks Foundation, Inc.
Fairchild Corp.
Faith Home Foundation
Fanwood Foundation
Farish Fund, William Stamps
Federal Express Corp.
Federal-Mogul Corp.
Federal National Mortgage Assn., Fannie Mae
Federal Screw Works
Federal Screw Works
Federated Department Stores and Allied Stores Corp.
Fels Fund, Samuel S.
Fidelity Bank
FINA, Inc.
Fink Foundation
Fireman Charitable Foundation, Paul and Phyllis
Firestone Foundation, Roger S.
First Bank System
First Boston
First Brands Corp.
First Chicago
First Interstate Bank NW Region
First Interstate Bank of California
First Interstate Bank of Oregon
First Union Corp.
Firstar Bank Milwaukee NA
Fish Foundation, Ray C.
Flagler Foundation
Fleet Financial Group
Fleming Companies, Inc.
Flinn Foundation
Florida Power Corp.
Florida Power & Light Co.
Fluor Corp.
FMC Corp.
Fohs Foundation
Forbes
Ford Foundation
Ford Fund, Walter and Josephine
Ford II Fund, Henry
Ford Motor Co.
Forest Fund
Franklin Foundation, John and Mary
Freedom Forum
Freeport-McMoRan
Friedman Foundation, Stephen and Barbara
Frueauff Foundation, Charles A.
Fry Foundation, Lloyd A.
Fujitsu America, Inc.
Funderburke & Associates
Gap, The
Garvey Texas Foundation
GATX Corp.
GenCorp
General Electric Co.
General Mills
General Motors Corp.

General Railway Signal Corp.
Georgia-Pacific Corp.
Georgia Power Co.
Gerber Products Co.
Gerbode Foundation, Wallace Alexander
Gheens Foundation
Giant Eagle
Giant Food
Giant Food Stores
Gitano Group
Glazer Foundation, Jerome S.
Glickenhaus & Co.
Goodman Family Foundation
Goodyear Tire & Rubber Co.
Gordon Foundation, Meyer and Ida
Grace & Co., W.R.
Graco
Grant Foundation, Charles M. and Mary D.
Graphic Controls Corp.
Great-West Life Assurance Co.
Great Western Financial Corp.
Greentree Foundation
Greenwall Foundation
Griggs and Mary Griggs Burke Foundation, Mary Livingston
GTE Corp.
Gulfstream Aerospace Corp.
Hagedorn Fund
Hall Foundation
Hallmark Cards
Hamilton Bank
Hancock Foundation, Luke B.
Handleman Co.
HarperCollins Publishers
Harriman Foundation, Mary W.
Hartmarx Corp.
Hatch Charitable Trust, Margaret Milliken
Hawn Foundation
Hearst Foundation
Hearst Foundation, William Randolph
Hechinger Co.
Heinz Co., H.J.
Heller Financial
Hershey Foods Corp.
Hershey Foundation
Hess Charitable Foundation, Ronne and Donald
Heublein
Hewlett Foundation, William and Flora
Hewlett-Packard Co.
Higginson Trust, Corina
Hill Foundation
Hill-Snowdon Foundation
Hitachi
Hobitzelle Foundation
Hoechst Celanese Corp.
Hoffmann-La Roche
Hofheinz Foundation, Irene Cafcalas
Holmes Foundation
Holzer Memorial Foundation, Richard H.
Homeland Foundation
Honeywell
Hospital Corp. of America
Household International
Houston Industries
Howard and Bush Foundation
Hubbard Broadcasting
Huffy Corp.
Humana
IBM Corp.
ICI Americas
IDS Financial Services
Illinois Power Co.
Illinois Tool Works
IMCERA Group Inc.
Inco Alloys International
Indiana Bell Telephone Co.
Indiana Insurance Cos.
Inland Container Corp.

Inland Steel Industries
Intel Corp.
Interco
International Multifoods Corp.
International Paper Co.
Irvine Foundation, James
ITT Corp.
ITT Hartford Insurance Group
ITT Rayonier
J.P. Morgan & Co.
Jarson-Stanley and Mickey Kaplan Foundation, Isaac & Esther
JCPenney Co.
Jennings Foundation, Martha Holden
Jennings Foundation, Mary Hillman
Jergens Foundation, Andrew
Jewett Foundation, George Frederick
John Hancock Mutual Life Insurance Co.
Johnson Controls
Johnson Foundation, Walter S.
Johnson & Higgins
Johnson & Johnson
Johnson & Son, S.C.
Jostens
Joukowsky Family Foundation
Julia R. and Estelle L. Foundation
Jurodin Fund
Jurzykowski Foundation, Alfred
Kaiser Family Foundation, Henry J.
Katzenberger Foundation
Keck, Jr. Foundation, William M.
Keebler Co.
Kellogg Foundation, W. K.
Kendall Foundation, George R.
Kennecott Corp.
Kennedy Foundation, Ethel
Kerr-McGee Corp.
Kidder, Peabody & Co.
Kiewit Foundation, Peter
Kiewit Sons, Peter
Kimball International
Kimberly-Clark Corp.
Kiplinger Foundation
Klau Foundation, David W. and Sadie
Kmart Corp.
Knight Foundation, John S. and James L.
Koulaieff Educational Fund, Trustees of Ivan Y.
KPMG Peat Marwick
Kraft General Foods
Lacy Foundation
Laffey-McHugh Foundation
Lance, Inc.
Land O'Lakes
Landmark Communications
Lautenberg Foundation
Lennon Foundation, Fred A.
Levy Foundation, Hyman Jebb
Lichtenstein Foundation, David B.
Life Insurance Co. of Georgia
Lilly & Co., Eli
Lilly Endowment
Lincoln National Corp.
Lingnan Foundation
Lipton, Thomas J.
Liquid Air Corp.
Little, Arthur D.
Litton Industries
Lockheed Corp.
Long Island Lighting Co.
Lotus Development Corp.
Louisiana Power & Light Co./New Orleans Public Service
Lowe Foundation, Joe and Emily
Lowenstein Brothers Foundation
Lowenstein Foundation, Leon

LTV Corp.
Lubrizol Corp.
Luce Foundation, Henry
Luchsinger Family Foundation
Lukens
Lurcy Charitable and Educational Trust, Georges
Lurie Foundation, Louis R.
Lynn Foundation, E. M.
Maas Foundation, Benard L.
MacArthur Foundation, John D. and Catherine T.
Macy & Co., R.H.
Macy, Jr. Foundation, Josiah
Mallinckrodt Specialty Chemicals Co.
Mandel Foundation, Morton and Barbara
Manoogian Foundation, Alex and Marie
Maritz Inc.
Marmot Foundation
Mars Foundation
Marsh & McLennan Cos.
Mary Kay Foundation
Masco Corp.
Massey Foundation
Matthews International Corp.
Maxus Energy Corp.
May Department Stores Co.
Mayer Foods Corp., Oscar
Maytag Corp.
Maytag Family Foundation, Fred
MCA
McBeath Foundation, Faye
McBride & Son Associates
McConnell Foundation
McCormick & Co.
McCormick Tribune Foundation, Robert R.
McDonald & Co. Securities
McDonald's Corp.
McDonnell Douglas Corp.
McDonough Foundation, Bernard
McElroy Trust, R. J.
McGraw-Hill
MCJ Foundation
McKnight Foundation
McLean Contributionship
Mead Corp.
Meadows Foundation
Medtronic
Mellam Family Foundation
Mellon Bank Corp.
Mellon Foundation, Andrew W.
Mellon Foundation, Richard King
Melville Corp.
Merck & Co.
Meridian Bancorp
Merrill Lynch & Co.
Metropolitan Life Insurance Co.
Michigan Consolidated Gas Co.
Michigan Gas Utilities
Millipore Corp.
Millstone Foundation
Mine Safety Appliances Co.
Minnesota Mutual Life Insurance Co.
Mobil Oil Corp.
Monell Foundation, Ambrose
Monsanto Co.
Moore & Sons, B.C.
Moores Foundation, Harry C.
Moorman Manufacturing Co.
Morgan Stanley & Co.
Morton International
Moses Fund, Henry and Lucy
Motorola
Mott Foundation, Charles Stewart
MTS Systems Corp.
Nalco Chemical Co.
National City Corp.
National Computer Systems
National Fuel Gas Co.
National Medical Enterprises
National Westminster Bank New Jersey

Minority Education
(cont.)
Navistar International Corp.
NBD Bank
NBD Bank, N.A.
Neilson Foundation, George W.
Nellie Mae
Nestle U.S.A. Inc.
New England Mutual Life
 Insurance Co.
New-Land Foundation
New Prospect Foundation
New York Foundation
New York Life Insurance Co.
New York Mercantile Exchange
New York Times Co.
The New Yorker Magazine, Inc.
Newman Charitable Trust,
 Calvin M. and Raquel H.
News & Observer Publishing Co.
Nike Inc.
Nissan Motor Corporation in
 U.S.A.
Nordson Corp.
Northeast Utilities
Northern States Power Co.
Northern Telecom Inc.
Northwest Natural Gas Co.
Northwestern National Life
 Insurance Co.
Noyes, Jr. Memorial Foundation,
 Nicholas H.
NuTone Inc.
NYNEX Corp.
Oglebay Norton Co.
Ohio National Life Insurance Co.
Ohl, Jr. Trust, George A.
Olin Corp.
Olin Foundation, Spencer T. and
 Ann W.
Olsson Memorial Foundation,
 Elis
Overbrook Foundation
Owens-Corning Fiberglas Corp.
Owens-Illinois
Oxford Foundation
Oxford Industries, Inc.
PACCAR
Pacific Gas & Electric Co.
Pacific Mutual Life Insurance Co.
Pacific Telesis Group
Packaging Corporation of
 America
Panhandle Eastern Corp.
Pappas Charitable Foundation,
 Bessie
Paramount Communications Inc.
Parke-Davis Group
Parker-Hannifin Corp.
Parsons Foundation, Ralph M.
Parsons - W.D. Charities, Vera
 Davis
Payne Foundation, Frank E. and
 Seba B.
Peierls Foundation
Penn Foundation, William
Pennsylvania General Insurance
 Co.
Perini Corp.
Perkin-Elmer Corp.
Pew Charitable Trusts
Pfeiffer Research Foundation,
 Gustavus and Louise
Pfizer
Phelps Dodge Corp.
PHH Corp.
Philip Morris Cos.
Phillips Petroleum Co.
Pick, Jr. Fund, Albert
Pierce Charitable Trust, Harold
 Whitworth
Pillsbury Co.
Pillsbury Foundation
Pitney Bowes
Pitt-Des Moines Inc.
Pittway Corp.
PNC Bank

Polaroid Corp.
Pope Foundation
Potomac Electric Power Co.
Powell Family Foundation
PPG Industries
Price Associates, T. Rowe
Principal Financial Group
Procter & Gamble Co.
Procter & Gamble Cosmetic &
 Fragrance Products
Promus Cos.
Prudential Insurance Co. of
 America
Public Service Co. of Colorado
Public Service Electric & Gas
 Co.
Pulitzer Publishing Co.
Quaker Oats Co.
R. F. Foundation
Ralston Purina Co.
Raskin Foundation, Hirsch and
 Braine
Raytheon Co.
Reily & Co., William B.
Reliable Life Insurance Co.
Reliance Electric Co.
Republic New York Corp.
Revlon
Reynolds Foundation, Z. Smith
Reynolds Metals Co.
Riley Foundation, Mabel Louise
RJR Nabisco Inc.
Rochester Telephone Corp.
Rockefeller Foundation
Rockefeller Foundation,
 Winthrop
Rockwell International Corp.
Rohlik Foundation, Sigmund and
 Sophie
Rohm and Haas Company
Rohr Inc.
Rolfs Foundation, Robert T.
Rosenberg Foundation
Rosenthal Foundation, Ida and
 William
Rowland Foundation
Royal Group Inc.
Rubinstein Foundation, Helena
Ryder System
SAFECO Corp.
Saint Paul Cos.
Salomon
San Diego Gas & Electric
Santa Fe Pacific Corp.
Sara Lee Corp.
Sara Lee Hosiery
Schapiro Fund, M. A.
Schering-Plough Corp.
Schieffelin & Somerset Co.
Schiff Foundation, Dorothy
Schlumberger Ltd.
Scholl Foundation, Dr.
Schrafft and Bertha E. Schrafft
 Charitable Trust, William E.
Schultz Foundation
Science Applications
 International Corp.
Scripps Co., E.W.
Scrivner, Inc.
Seafirst Corp.
Seagram & Sons, Joseph E.
Sealaska Corp.
Sears, Roebuck and Co.
Sebastian Foundation
Security Life of Denver
Sedgwick James Inc.
Sega of America
Selby and Marie Selby
 Foundation, William G.
Sentinel Communications Co.
Shawmut National Corp.
Shea Foundation
Shell Oil Co.
Shenandoah Life Insurance Co.
Signet Bank/Maryland
Slant/Fin Corp.
Sloan Foundation, Alfred P.

Smith Corp., A.O.
Smith Family Foundation,
 Charles E.
SNET
Snyder Charitable Fund, W. P.
Sonat
Sonoco Products Co.
Sony Corp. of America
Sosland Foundation
Southern California Edison Co.
Southern California Gas Co.
Southwestern Bell Corp.
Sprague Educational and
 Charitable Foundation, Seth
Springs Industries
Sprint
SPX Corp.
Square D Co.
Stanley Works
Starr Foundation
State Farm Mutual Automobile
 Insurance Co.
State Street Bank & Trust Co.
Steinhauer Charitable Foundation
Sterling Winthrop
Stone Container Corp.
Storage Technology Corp.
Strake Foundation
Strong Foundation, Hattie M.
Stulsaft Foundation, Morris
Summerfield Foundation, Solon
 E.
Sun Co.
Sun Microsystems
Sundstrand Corp.
Tandem Computers
TCF Banking & Savings, FSB
Tektronix
Teledyne
Temple Foundation, T. L. L.
Tenneco
Texaco
Texas Commerce Bank Houston,
 N.A.
Texas Instruments
Textron
Thomas & Betts Corp.
3M Co.
Time Insurance Co.
Times Mirror Co.
Tinker Foundation
TJX Cos.
Tosco Corp. Refining Division
Towsley Foundation, Harry A.
 and Margaret D.
Toyota Motor Sales, U.S.A.
Tozer Foundation
Transco Energy Company
Tropicana Products, Inc.
Trull Foundation
Trust Co. Bank
Turrell Fund
Unilever United States
Union Camp Corp.
Union Pacific Corp.
Unisys Corp.
United Airlines
United Parcel Service of America
U.S. Leasing International
United Technologies Corp.
Universal Leaf Tobacco Co.
Unocal Corp.
Upjohn Co.
Upton Foundation, Frederick S.
US WEST
UST
USX Corp.
Varian Associates
Victoria Foundation
Vulcan Materials Co.
Wal-Mart Stores
Wallace-Reader's Digest Fund,
 DeWitt
Washington Water Power Co.
Waste Management
Wean Foundation, Raymond John
Webster Foundation, Edwin S.

Weingart Foundation
Wells Fargo & Co.
West Co.
Westinghouse Electric Corp.
Westvaco Corp.
Weyerhaeuser Co.
Whirlpool Corp.
White Consolidated Industries
Whitman Corp.
Whitney Fund, David M.
Wickes Foundation, Harvey
 Randall
WICOR, Inc.
Wien Foundation, Lawrence A.
Winn-Dixie Stores
Wisconsin Energy Corp.
Wodecroft Foundation
Wollenberg Foundation
Woodland Foundation
Wrigley Co., Wm. Jr.
Wurlitzer Foundation, Farny R.
Xerox Corp.
Young Foundation, Robert R.
Zarrow Foundation, Anne and
 Henry

Preschool Education
Ahmanson Foundation
ALPAC Corp.
Aluminum Co. of America
AMAX
AMCORE Bank, N.A. Rockford
America West Airlines
American Express Co.
Andersen Corp.
Annenberg Foundation
Apache Corp.
ARCO
Atherton Family Foundation
Babcock Foundation, Mary
 Reynolds
Bank of Boston Corp.
Belk Stores
Beveridge Foundation, Frank
 Stanley
Binney & Smith Inc.
Block, H&R
Boeing Co.
Bremer Foundation, Otto
Buhl Foundation
Burns Foundation, Fritz B.
Cabot Corp.
Cafritz Foundation, Morris and
 Gwendolyn
Capital Holding Corp.
Carnegie Corporation of New
 York
Castle Foundation, Samuel N.
 and Mary
Cayuga Foundation
Central Maine Power Co.
Chase Manhattan Bank, N.A.
Clorox Co.
CNA Insurance Cos.
Coleman Foundation
Colonial Stores
Colorado National Bankshares
Cowell Foundation, S. H.
Cullen/Frost Bankers
DeRoy Testamentary Foundation
Dial Corp.
Diamond Foundation, Aaron
du Pont de Nemours & Co., E. I.
Emery Memorial, Thomas J.
Fidelity Bank
Fifth Avenue Foundation
Fikes Foundation, Leland
Fireman Charitable Foundation,
 Paul and Phyllis
First Boston
First Interstate Bank of Texas,
 N.A.
First Tennessee Bank
First Union Corp.
Fischel Foundation, Harry and
 Jane

Fisher-Price
Fleming Companies, Inc.
Foothills Foundation
Ford Fund, Walter and Josephine
Foundation for Child
 Development
Francis Families Foundation
Frederick Foundation
Frohring Foundation, William O.
 and Gertrude Lewis
Fry Foundation, Lloyd A.
General Mills
Globe Newspaper Co.
Graham Fund, Philip L.
Gudelsky Family Foundation,
 Homer and Martha
Gund Foundation, George
Hachar Charitable Trust, D. D.
Hall Family Foundations
Hallmark Cards
Halstead Foundation
Harris Foundation, James J. and
 Angelia M.
Hayden Foundation, Charles
Heckscher Foundation for
 Children
Heginbotham Trust, Will E.
Hiawatha Education Foundation
Home Depot
Honeywell
Hospital Corp. of America
Humana
Hunt Alternatives Fund
Industrial Bank of Japan Trust
 Co.
International Student Exchange
 Cards
Irwin-Sweeney-Miller
 Foundation
Island Foundation
Jackson Foundation
JCPenney Co.
Jennings Foundation, Martha
 Holden
Johnson Foundation, Walter S.
Johnson Fund, Edward C.
Johnson & Higgins
Jones Foundation, Daisy Marquis
Jones Intercable, Inc.
Julia R. and Estelle L.
 Foundation
Kaiser Cement Corp.
Kellogg Foundation, W. K.
Kemper Foundation, Enid and
 Crosby
Kennedy, Jr. Foundation, Joseph
 P.
Kieckhefer Foundation, J. W.
Kugelman Foundation
Lincoln National Corp.
Longwood Foundation
Louisiana Land & Exploration
 Co.
Lutheran Brotherhood
 Foundation
Lyndhurst Foundation
Magruder Foundation, Chesley
 G.
Mardag Foundation
Maritz Inc.
McElroy Trust, R. J.
McInerny Foundation
Meadows Foundation
Meredith Corp.
Meyer Memorial Trust
National Computer Systems
National Machinery Co.
New Street Capital Corp.
New York Mercantile Exchange
The New Yorker Magazine, Inc.
Nordson Corp.
Norton Co.
NYNEX Corp.
Odell and Helen Pfeiffer Odell
 Fund, Robert Stewart
O'Neill Charitable Corporation,
 F. J.
Ore-Ida Foods, Inc.

Pacific Telesis Group
Penn Foundation, William
People's Bank
Pepsi-Cola Bottling Co. of Charlotte
PHH Corp.
Pillsbury Co.
Plough Foundation
Polaroid Corp.
Primerica Corp.
Principal Financial Group
Quaker Oats Co.
Reliable Life Insurance Co.
Reynolds Foundation, Z. Smith
Rohm and Haas Company
Roseburg Forest Products Co.
Royal Group Inc.
Rubinstein Foundation, Helena
San Diego Gas & Electric
Sara Lee Hosiery
Scherer Foundation, Karla
Scott Paper Co.
Sedgwick James Inc.
Selby and Marie Selby Foundation, William G.
Sentinel Communications Co.
Shoney's Inc.
Siebert Lutheran Foundation
Simon Charitable Trust, Esther
Sosland Foundation
Springs Industries
Straus Foundation, Aaron and Lillie
Stuart Foundations
Taylor Foundation, Ruth and Vernon
Towsley Foundation, Harry A. and Margaret D.
Transco Energy Company
TRW Corp.
Turrell Fund
Union Camp Corp.
United States Sugar Corp.
Uris Brothers Foundation
Wal-Mart Stores
Weingart Foundation
Woods Charitable Fund
Xerox Corp.

Private Education (precollege)

Abel Construction Co.
Abercrombie Foundation
Abitibi-Price
Abreu Charitable Trust u/w/o May P. Abreu, Francis I.
Abrons Foundation, Louis and Anne
Adams Foundation, Arthur F. and Alice E.
Advanced Micro Devices
AEGON USA, Inc.
AGFA Division of Miles Inc.
Ahmanson Foundation
AKC Fund
Alcan Aluminum Corp.
Alco Standard Corp.
Alcon Laboratories, Inc.
Alden Trust, George I.
Alden Trust, John W.
Alexander Foundation, Joseph
Alexander Foundation, Walter
Alhambra Foundry Co., Ltd.
Allendale Mutual Insurance Co.
Alliant Techsystems
AlliedSignal
Alltel/Western Region
Allyn Foundation
Alma Piston Co.
ALPAC Corp.
Alperin/Hirsch Family Foundation
AMCORE Bank, N.A. Rockford
Ameribank
America West Airlines
American Brands

American Financial Corp.
American Foundation Corporation
American Honda Motor Co.
American National Bank & Trust Co. of Chicago
American Optical Corp.
American President Cos.
American Standard
Ameritech Services
Ameritech Services
AMETEK
Amfac/JMB Hawaii
AMP
Andersen Corp.
Anderson Charitable Trust, Josephine
Anderson Foundation
Anderson Foundation
Anderson Foundation, M. D.
Anderson Foundation, William P.
Andersons Management Corp.
Andreas Foundation
Andrews Foundation
Annenberg Foundation
Ansin Private Foundation, Ronald M.
Applebaum Foundation
Appleman Foundation
Arata Brothers Trust
Arbie Mineral Feed Co.
Archbold Charitable Trust, Adrian and Jessie
Arkwright Foundation
Armstrong Foundation
Aron Charitable Foundation, J.
Arrillaga Foundation
ASARCO
Atherton Family Foundation
Atlantic Foundation
Atwood Foundation
Auerbach Foundation, Beatrice Fox
Autzen Foundation
AVI CHAI - A Philanthropic Foundation
Avis Inc.
Ayres Foundation, Inc.
Azby Fund
Babson Foundation, Paul and Edith
Badger Meter, Inc.
Bag Bazaar, Ltd.
Baier Foundation, Marie
Baird & Co., Robert W.
Baird Foundation, Cameron
Baker Foundation, R. C.
Baker, Jr. Memorial Fund, William G.
Baker Trust, George F.
Baldwin Foundation
Baldwin Foundation, David M. and Barbara
Baldwin, Jr. Foundation, Summerfield
Baldwin Memorial Foundation, Fred
Ball Brothers Foundation
Banbury Fund
Banc One Illinois Corp.
Banc One Illinois Corp.
Bancorp Hawaii
Banfi Vintners
Bank Leumi Trust Co. of New York
Bank of A. Levy
Bank of New York
Bank One, Texas-Houston Office
Bannan Foundation, Arline and Thomas J.
Bannon Foundation
Barclays Bank of New York
Barker Foundation, Donald R.
Barker Foundation, J. M. R.
Barlow Family Foundation, Milton A. and Gloria G.
Barnes Foundation

Barnes Group
Barnett Charitable Foundation, Lawrence and Isabel
Barra Foundation
Barton-Malow Co.
Bartsch Memorial Trust, Ruth
Bass Foundation
Batten Foundation
Bauer Foundation, M. R.
Bauervic Foundation, Charles M.
Bauervic Foundation, Peggy
Bauervic-Paisley Foundation
Bausch & Lomb
Bay Branch Foundation
Bay Foundation
Bayne Fund, Howard
Beal Foundation
Beatty Trust, Cordelia Lunceford
Beaver Foundation
Bechtel Charitable Remainder Uni-Trust, Marie H.
Bechtel, Jr. Foundation, S. D.
Beck Foundation, Elsie E. & Joseph W.
Bedminster Fund
Beinecke Foundation
Beir Foundation
Beitzell & Co.
Beloit Foundation
Bemis Company
Beneficia Foundation
Benetton
Benz Trust, Doris L.
Bergstrom Manufacturing Co.
Bernsen Foundation, Grace and Franklin
Bernstein & Co., Sanford C.
Best Foundation, Walter J. and Edith E.
Bethlehem Steel Corp.
Beveridge Foundation, Frank Stanley
Bickerton Charitable Trust, Lydia H.
Bicknell Fund
Biddle Foundation, Margaret T.
Biddle Foundation, Mary Duke
Bingham Foundation, William
Bingham Second Betterment Fund, William
Binney & Smith Inc.
Binswanger Co.
Bird Inc.
Birmingham Foundation
Bishop Foundation, Vernon and Doris
Blackmer Foundation, Henry M.
Blake Foundation, S. P.
Blaustein Foundation, Jacob and Hilda
Blaustein Foundation, Louis and Henrietta
Block, H&R
Blount
Blowitz-Ridgeway Foundation
Blum-Kovler Foundation
Board of Trustees of the Prichard School
Bodenhamer Foundation
Boeing Co.
Boettcher Foundation
Booth-Bricker Fund
Borkee Hagley Foundation
Bostwick Foundation, Albert C.
Bovaird Foundation, Mervin
Bowers Foundation
Bowyer Foundation, Ambrose and Gladys
Brach Foundation, Helen
Bradley-Turner Foundation
Bren Foundation, Donald L.
Brenner Foundation, Mervyn
Brewer and Co., Ltd., C.
Briggs Family Foundation
Bright Charitable Trust, Alexander H.
Bright Family Foundation

Brinkley Foundation
Bristol Savings Bank
Broadhurst Foundation
Brody Foundation, Frances
Brooklyn Benevolent Society
Brooks Foundation, Gladys
Brown Charitable Trust, Dora Maclellan
Brown Foundation
Brown Foundation, Joe W. and Dorothy Dorsett
Brown, Jr. Charitable Trust, Frank D.
Brown & Williamson Tobacco Corp.
Browning Charitable Foundation, Val A.
Broyhill Family Foundation
Bruening Foundation, Eva L. and Joseph M.
Brunner Foundation, Robert
Bryant Foundation
Buchanan Family Foundation
Buckley Trust, Thomas D.
Bucyrus-Erie
Bulova Fund
Bunbury Company
Burchfield Foundation, Charles E.
Burden Foundation, Florence V.
Burdines
Burke Foundation, Thomas C.
Burkitt Foundation
Burns Family Foundation
Burns Foundation
Burns Foundation, Fritz B.
Burress, J.W.
Bustard Charitable Permanent Trust Fund, Elizabeth and James
Butz Foundation
C.I.O.S.
C.P. Rail Systems
Cablevision of Michigan
Cabot Corp.
Cabot Family Charitable Trust
Cabot-Saltonstall Charitable Trust
Cadbury Beverages Inc.
Caddock Foundation
Cafritz Foundation, Morris and Gwendolyn
Cain Foundation, Gordon and Mary
Caldwell Foundation, Hardwick
Calhoun Charitable Trust, Kenneth
Cameron Foundation, Harry S. and Isabel C.
Cameron Memorial Fund, Alpin J. and Alpin W.
Camp Foundation
Camp Younts Foundation
Campbell Foundation
Campbell Foundation, J. Bulow
Campbell Foundation, Ruth and Henry
Cannon Foundation
Cape Branch Foundation
Capital Cities/ABC
Capital Holding Corp.
Carlson Cos.
Carter Foundation, Amon G.
Cartinhour Foundation
Carvel Foundation, Thomas and Agnes
Carylon Foundation
Caspersen Foundation for Aid to Health and Education, O. W.
Castle Foundation, Harold K. L.
Castle Foundation, Samuel N. and Mary
CBS Inc.
Cedars-Sinai Medical Center Section D Fund
Center for Educational Programs
Centerior Energy Corp.
Central Bank of the South

CertainTeed Corp.
Chamberlin Foundation, Gerald W.
Chambers Memorial, James B.
Champlin Foundations
Chandler Foundation
Chapin Foundation, Frances
Chapman Charitable Trust, H. A. and Mary K.
Charina Foundation
Charitable Foundation of the Burns Family
Charities Foundation
Chartwell Foundation
Chase Manhattan Bank, N.A.
Chatham Valley Foundation
Cheney Foundation, Ben B.
Cherne Foundation, Albert W.
Cherokee Foundation
Childress Foundation, Francis and Miranda
Chiles Foundation
Chiquita Brands Co.
Chisholm Foundation
Christensen Charitable and Religious Foundation, L. C.
Christodora
Churches Homes Foundation
Cimarron Foundation
Cincinnati Bell
CIT Group Holdings
Citicorp
Citizens Bank
Claneil Foundation
Clapp Charitable and Educational Trust, George H.
Clark Charitable Trust
Clark Family Charitable Trust, Andrew L.
Clark Foundation
Clark-Winchcole Foundation
Clarke Trust, John
Clay Foundation
Clayton Fund
Clements Foundation
Cleveland-Cliffs
Cline Co.
Clorox Co.
Clougherty Charitable Trust, Francis H.
Clowes Fund
CM Alliance Cos.
CNA Insurance Cos.
Coca-Cola Co.
Cogswell Benevolent Trust
Colburn Fund
Cole National Corp.
Cole Trust, Quincy
Coleman, Jr. Foundation, George E.
Coles Family Foundation
Collins Foundation, Carr P.
Collins Foundation, James M.
Collins, Jr. Foundation, George Fulton
Colonial Life & Accident Insurance Co.
Colonial Oil Industries, Inc.
Colonial Stores
Columbia Foundation
Columbia Terminals Co.
Comer Foundation
Commerce Clearing House
Community Enterprises
Community Foundation
Community Health Association
Conn Memorial Foundation
Connelly Foundation
Connemara Fund
Constantin Foundation
Cooke Foundation
Cooper Charitable Trust, Richard H.
Coors Foundation, Adolph
Copley Press
Coral Reef Foundation
Country Curtains, Inc.

Private Education (precollege) (cont.)

Courts Foundation
Cowan Foundation Corporation, Lillian L. and Harry A.
Cowles Charitable Trust
Cowles Foundation, Gardner and Florence Call
Cowles Foundation, Harriet Cheney
Cowles Foundation, William H.
Cowles Media Co.
Cox Charitable Trust, Jessie B.
Cox Foundation
CPC International
Craigmyle Foundation
Crane Foundation, Raymond E. and Ellen F.
Crane Fund for Widows and Children
Cranshaw Corporation
Crapo Charitable Foundation, Henry H.
Creel Foundation
Crels Foundation
Crestlea Foundation
Criss Memorial Foundation, Dr. C.C. and Mabel L.
CRL Inc.
CRL Inc.
Crocker Trust, Mary A.
Crummer Foundation, Roy E.
Crystal Trust
Cullen Foundation
Cullen/Frost Bankers
Culpeper Memorial Foundation, Daphne Seybolt
Cummins Engine Co.
Cuneo Foundation
Dalton Foundation, Harry L.
Daly Charitable Foundation Trust, Robert and Nancy
Dana Corp.
Danner Foundation
Darby Foundation
Dart Foundation
Dart Group Corp.
Davenport Foundation, M. E.
Davenport-Hatch Foundation
Davies Charitable Trust
Davis Family - W.D. Charities, James E.
Davis Family - W.D. Charities, Tine W.
Davis Foundation, Edwin W. and Catherine M.
Davis Foundation, Shelby Cullom
Day Family Foundation
Day Foundation, Willametta K.
DCB Corp.
de Dampierre Memorial Foundation, Marie C.
Decio Foundation, Arthur J.
Delany Charitable Trust, Beatrice P.
Delaware North Cos.
DelMar Foundation, Charles
Demoulas Supermarkets
Dennett Foundation, Marie G.
Deseranno Educational Foundation
Detroit Edison Co.
Deuble Foundation, George H.
Deutsch Co.
Devonshire Associates
Devonwood Foundation
DeVore Foundation
DeVos Foundation, Richard and Helen
Dewar Foundation
Dewing Foundation, Frances R.
Dibner Fund
Dickson Foundation
Diener Foundation, Frank C.
Dietrich Foundation, William B.

Dillon Foundation
Disney Family Foundation, Roy
Dobson Foundation
Dodge Foundation, Cleveland H.
Dodge Foundation, Geraldine R.
Doheny Foundation, Carrie Estelle
Doherty Charitable Foundation, Henry L. and Grace
Dolan Family Foundation
Domino's Pizza
Donaldson Charitable Trust, Oliver S. and Jennie R.
Donaldson Co.
Donaldson Co.
Donnelley Foundation, Elliott and Ann
Donnelly Foundation, Mary J.
Dorminy Foundation, John Henry
Doty Family Foundation
Dow Fund, Alden and Vada
Dower Foundation, Thomas W.
Downs Perpetual Charitable Trust, Ellason
Dreiling and Albina Dreiling Charitable Trust, Leo J.
Dreyfus Foundation, Jean and Louis
Dreyfus Foundation, Max and Victoria
Driscoll Foundation
Drum Foundation
du Pont de Nemours & Co., E. I.
Duchossois Industries
Duke Power Co.
Dula Educational and Charitable Foundation, Caleb C. and Julia W.
Dunagan Foundation
Duncan Trust, John G.
Dunspaugh-Dalton Foundation
Dupar Foundation
duPont Foundation, Chichester
duPont Fund, Jessie Ball
Earl-Beth Foundation
Easley Trust, Andrew H. and Anne O.
East Foundation, Sarita Kenedy
Eastman Foundation, Alexander
Eaton Corp.
Eaton Foundation, Cyrus
Eccles Foundation, Marriner S.
Eden Hall Foundation
Eder Foundation, Sidney and Arthur
Educational Foundation of America
Edwards Foundation, O. P. and W. E.
Egenton Home
Ehrman Foundation, Fred and Susan
El Pomar Foundation
Elco Charitable Foundation
Electric Power Equipment Co.
Elf Atochem North America
Elkin Memorial Foundation, Neil Warren and William Simpson
Elkins Foundation, J. A. and Isabel M.
Ellis Fund
Ellis Grant and Scholarship Fund, Charles E.
Emerson Electric Co.
Emery Memorial, Thomas J.
EMI Records Group
Engelhard Foundation, Charles
English Foundation, W. C.
Enron Corp.
Ensign-Bickford Industries
Ensworth Charitable Foundation
Equimark Corp.
Ernsthausen Charitable Foundation, John F. and Doris E.
Erpf Fund, Armand G.
Erteszek Foundation
Estes Foundation

Ettinger Foundation
Evans Foundation, Lettie Pate
Ewald Foundation, H. T.
Exposition Foundation
Failing Fund, Henry
Fairchild Foundation, Sherman
Farish Fund, William Stamps
Farley Industries
Farm & Home Savings Association
Federated Department Stores and Allied Stores Corp.
Feild Co-Operative Association
Feinstein Foundation, Myer and Rosaline
Femino Foundation
Fenton Foundation
Ferebee Endowment, Percy O.
Ferkauf Foundation, Eugene and Estelle
Field Foundation, Jamee and Marshall
Fikes Foundation, Leland
Finch Foundation, Thomas Austin
Fink Foundation
Finley Charitable Trust, J. B.
Finley Foundation, A. E.
Fireman Charitable Foundation, Paul and Phyllis
Firestone Foundation, Roger S.
Firestone, Jr. Foundation, Harvey
First Boston
First Fidelity Bancorporation
First Hawaiian
First Mississippi Corp.
First Petroleum Corp.
FirsTier Bank N.A. Omaha
Fischbach Foundation
Fischel Foundation, Harry and Jane
Fish Foundation, Ray C.
Fish Foundation, Vain and Harry
Fishback Foundation Trust, Harmes C.
Fitz-Gibbon Charitable Trust
Flagler Foundation
Flatley Foundation
Fleet Financial Group
Fleishhacker Foundation
Fleming Companies, Inc.
Fleming Foundation
Flemm Foundation, John J.
Florence Foundation
Florida Power & Light Co.
Florida Steel Corp.
Foerderer Foundation, Percival E. and Ethel Brown
Fogel Foundation, Shalom and Rebecca
Fohs Foundation
Folger Fund
Fondren Foundation
Foothills Foundation
Forbes
Forbes Charitable Trust, Herman
Ford Foundation, Edward E.
Ford Fund, Benson and Edith
Ford Fund, Eleanor and Edsel
Ford Fund, Walter and Josephine
Ford Fund, William and Martha
Ford II Fund, Henry
Forest Oil Corp.
Forster-Powers Charitable Trust
Foster Charitable Foundation, M. Stratton
Foster-Davis Foundation
Foster Foundation, Joseph C. and Esther
Foundation for the Needs of Others
France Foundation, Jacob and Annita
Francis Families Foundation
Frank Family Foundation, A. J.
Frank Foundation, Ernest and Elfriede
Frankel Foundation

Frankel Foundation, George and Elizabeth F.
Franklin Charitable Trust, Ershel
Franklin Foundation, John and Mary
Frear Eleemosynary Trust, Mary D. and Walter F.
Freas Foundation
Frederick Foundation
Freeman Foundation, Carl M.
Frelinghuysen Foundation
Frese Foundation, Arnold D.
Friedman Brothers Foundation
Friedman Family Foundation
Friedman Foundation, Stephen and Barbara
Friendship Fund
Frohlich Charitable Trust, Ludwig W.
Frohring Foundation, Paul & Maxine
Frohring Foundation, William O. and Gertrude Lewis
Frost Foundation
Fruehauf Foundation
Fry Foundation, Lloyd A.
Fuchsberg Family Foundation
Fuller Foundation
Funderburke & Associates
Fuqua Foundation, J. B.
Fusenot Charity Foundation, Georges and Germaine
Gabelli Foundation
Gage Foundation, Philip and Irene Toll
Gallagher Family Foundation, Lewis P.
Gallo Foundation, Ernest
Gallo Foundation, Julio R.
Galter Foundation
Galvin Foundation, Robert W.
GAR Foundation
Garland Foundation, John Jewett and H. Chandler
Garner Charitable Trust, James G.
Garvey Memorial Foundation, Edward Chase
Garvey Texas Foundation
Gates Foundation
Gavin Foundation, James and Zita
Gazette Co.
Gebbie Foundation
Gelb Foundation, Lawrence M.
Gellert Foundation, Carl
Gellert Foundation, Celia Berta
Gellert Foundation, Fred
Gelman Foundation, Melvin and Estelle
GenCorp
General Accident Insurance Co. of America
General Mills
General Reinsurance Corp.
General Signal Corp.
Generation Trust
Genesis Foundation
Georgia Power Co.
Gerard Foundation, Sumner
Gerlach Foundation
Gerschel Foundation, Patrick A.
Gerson Family Foundation, Benjamin J.
Getsch Family Foundation Trust
Getty Foundation, Ann and Gordon
Gheens Foundation
Ghidotti Foundation, William and Marian
Gilbert, Jr. Charitable Trust, Price
Gilder Foundation
Gill Foundation, Pauline Allen
Gillette Co.
Gilman and Gonzalez-Falla Theatre Foundation
Gilman, Jr. Foundation, Sondra and Charles

Gilmer-Smith Foundation
Gilmore Foundation, Earl B.
Gilmore Foundation, William G.
Gitano Group
Glancy Foundation, Lenora and Alfred
Glaxo
Glazer Foundation, Jerome S.
Glazer Foundation, Madelyn L.
Glen Eagles Foundation
Glencairn Foundation
Glencoe Foundation
Glenn Foundation, Carrie C. & Lena V.
Goerlich Family Foundation
Goldbach Foundation, Ray and Marie
Goldberg Family Foundation
Goldberg Family Foundation, Israel and Matilda
Goldberger Foundation, Edward and Marjorie
Goldie-Anna Charitable Trust
Goldman Foundation, Herman
Goldman Sachs & Co.
Goldring Family Foundation
Goldseker Foundation of Maryland, Morris
Goldsmith Family Foundation
Goldstein Foundation, Leslie and Roslyn
Goldwyn Foundation, Samuel
Good Samaritan
Goodman Foundation, Edward and Marion
Gordon/Rousmaniere/Roberts Fund
Gore Family Memorial Foundation
Gottwald Foundation
Gould Foundation for Children, Edwin
Graco
Grainger Foundation
Grass Family Foundation
Grassmann Trust, E. J.
Gray Foundation, Garland
Grede Foundries
Green Foundation
Green Fund
Greenfield Foundation, Albert M.
Greentree Foundation
Gries Charity Fund, Lucile and Robert H.
Griffith Foundation, W. C.
Griggs and Mary Griggs Burke Foundation, Mary Livingston
Grimes Foundation
Griswold Foundation, John C.
Gross Charitable Trust, Stella B.
Gross Charitable Trust, Walter L. and Nell R.
Gross Foundation, Louis H.
Gruss Charitable and Educational Foundation, Oscar and Regina
Gruss Charitable Foundation, Emanuel and Riane
Gruss Petroleum Corp.
GSC Enterprises
GTE Corp.
Gund Foundation
Gund Foundation, Geoffrey
Gunderson Trust, Helen Paulson
Gurwin Foundation, J.
Gutman Foundation, Edna and Monroe C.
H.C.S. Foundation
Haas Foundation, Saul and Dayee G.
Haas Fund, Miriam and Peter
Haas, Jr. Fund, Evelyn and Walter
Habig Foundation, Arnold F.
Hachar Charitable Trust, D. D.
Hackett Foundation
Haffenreffer Family Fund
Haffner Foundation

Haggar Foundation
Haggerty Foundation
Hale Foundation, Crescent Porter
Hales Charitable Fund
Hall Charitable Trust, Evelyn A. J.
Halloran Foundation, Mary P. Dolciani
Halmos Foundation
Halsell Foundation, Ewing
Hamilton Bank
Hamilton Foundation, Florence P.
Hamman Foundation, George and Mary Josephine
Hanes Foundation, John W. and Anna H.
Hankins Foundation
Hannon Foundation, William H.
Hanson Testamentary Charitable Trust, Anna Emery
Hardin Foundation, Phil
Hargis Charitable Foundation, Estes H. and Florence Parker
Harmon Foundation, Pearl M. and Julia J.
Harper Brush Works
Harriman Foundation, Gladys and Roland
Harriman Foundation, Mary W.
Harrington Foundation, Francis A. and Jacquelyn H.
Harris Brothers Foundation
Harris Foundation, James J. and Angelia M.
Harris Foundation, John H. and Lucille
Harris Foundation, William H. and Mattie Wattis
Hartford Steam Boiler Inspection & Insurance Co.
Hartzell Industries, Inc.
Hastings Trust
Havens Foundation, O. W.
Hawkins Foundation, Robert Z.
Hawn Foundation
Hay Foundation, John I.
Hayden Foundation, Charles
Hayswood Foundation
Hazen Foundation, Edward W.
Hearst Foundation
Hearst Foundation, William Randolph
Hechinger Co.
Hecht-Levi Foundation
Hedco Foundation
Hedrick Foundation, Frank E.
Heinz Co., H.J.
Heinz Endowment, Howard
Heinz Endowment, Vira I.
Heinz Family Foundation
Helfaer Foundation, Evan and Marion
Heller Financial
Helms Foundation
Hemby Foundation, Alex
Henderson Foundation
Henry Foundation, Patrick
Herbst Foundation
Heritage Foundation
Hermann Foundation, Grover
Herndon Foundation
Hersey Foundation
Hershey Foundation
Hervey Foundation
Herzstein Charitable Foundation, Albert and Ethel
Hess Charitable Foundation, Ronne and Donald
Hess Charitable Trust, Myrtle E. and William C.
Hess Foundation
Hettinger Foundation
Heymann Special Account, Mr. and Mrs. Jimmy
Hiawatha Education Foundation
Higgins Foundation, Aldus C.
High Foundation
Hill-Snowdon Foundation

Hillcrest Foundation
Hillman Foundation
Hillman Foundation, Henry L.
Hills Fund, Edward E.
Hillsdale Fund
Hitchcock Foundation, Gilbert M. and Martha H.
Hobbs Charitable Trust, John H.
Hobbs Foundation
Hobbs Foundation, Emmert
Hoblitzelle Foundation
Hoffman Foundation, Maximillian E. and Marion O.
Hofheinz Foundation, Irene Cafcalas
Hogan Foundation, Royal Barney
Holley Foundation
Hollis Foundation
Holmes Foundation
Holt Foundation, William Knox
Holtzmann Foundation, Jacob L. and Lillian
Holzer Memorial Foundation, Richard H.
Homeland Foundation
Honigman Foundation
Hoover Foundation
Hoover Fund-Trust, W. Henry
Hopewell Foundation
Hopkins Foundation, John Jay
Hopwood Charitable Trust, John M.
Hornblower Fund, Henry
Horncrest Foundation
Houston Endowment
Howe and Mitchell B. Howe Foundation, Lucite Horton
Howell Fund
Hudson Neckwear
Hugoton Foundation
Huisking Foundation
Huizenga Foundation, Jennie
Hulings Foundation, Mary Andersen
Hulme Charitable Foundation, Milton G.
Humana
Hume Foundation, Jaquelin
Humphrey Foundation, Glenn & Gertrude
Humphrey Fund, George M. and Pamela S.
Hunt Charitable Trust, C. Giles
Hunt Foundation
Hunt Foundation, Roy A.
Hunter Trust, Emily S. and Coleman A.
Hutcheson Foundation, Hazel Montague
Hyde and Watson Foundation
Iacocca Foundation
IBM Corp.
Illges Foundation, John P. and Dorothy S.
Illges Memorial Foundation, A. and M. L.
Imerman Memorial Foundation, Stanley
Imlay Foundation
Indiana Bell Telephone Co.
Indiana Gas and Chemical Corp.
Ingalls Foundation, Louise H. and David S.
Ingersoll Milling Machine Co.
Inman Mills
Innovating Worthy Projects Foundation
International Student Exchange Cards
Interstate Packaging Co.
Ireland Foundation
Irwin Charity Foundation, William G.
Israel Foundation, A. Cremieux
ITT Hartford Insurance Group
Ivakota Association
Ix & Sons, Frank
Jackson Family Foundation, Ann

Jackson Mills
Jameson Trust, Oleonda
Janesville Foundation
Janeway Foundation, Elizabeth Bixby
Janssen Foundation, Henry
Jasam Foundation
Jasper Desk Co.
Jasper Table Co.
Jasper Wood Products Co.
Jeffress Memorial Trust, Elizabeth G.
JELD-WEN, Inc.
Jennings Foundation, Martha Holden
Jergens Foundation, Andrew
Jesselson Foundation
Jewell Memorial Foundation, Daniel Ashley and Irene Houston
JFM Foundation
Jinks Foundation, Ruth T.
JMK-A M Micallef Charitable Foundation
Jockey Hollow Foundation
Johnson Co., E. F.
Johnson Endeavor Foundation, Christian A.
Johnson Foundation, A. D.
Johnson Foundation, Burdine
Johnson Foundation, Helen K. and Arthur E.
Johnson Foundation, Howard
Johnson Fund, Edward C.
Johnson & Higgins
Johnson & Son, S.C.
Johnston-Fix Foundation
Johnston-Hanson Foundation
Johnstone and H. Earle Kimball Foundation, Phyllis Kimball
Jones Family Foundation, Eugenie and Joseph
Jones Foundation, Harvey and Bernice
Jones Fund, Blanche and George
Jones Intercable, Inc.
Jonsson Foundation
Jordan and Ettie A. Jordan Charitable Foundation, Mary Ranken
Joselow Foundation
Joukowsky Family Foundation
Journal Gazette Co.
Joyce Foundation, John M. and Mary A.
JSJ Corp.
Julia R. and Estelle L. Foundation
Kangesser Foundation, Robert E., Harry A., and M. Sylvia
Kaplun Foundation, Morris J. and Betty
Kaufman Endowment Fund, Louis G.
Kaufman Memorial Trust, Chaim, Fanny, Louis, Benjamin, and Anne Florence
Kavanagh Foundation, T. James
Keck Foundation, W. M.
Keebler Co.
Keith Foundation Trust, Ben E.
Keller Family Foundation
Kelley Foundation, Kate M.
Kellogg Foundation, J. C.
Kellogg Foundation, Peter and Cynthia K.
Kellogg Foundation, W. K.
Kelly Foundation, T. Lloyd
Kelly, Jr. Memorial Foundation, Ensign C. Markland
Kemper Charitable Trust, William T.
Kemper Foundation, Enid and Crosby
Kemper Memorial Foundation, David Woods
Kenan, Jr. Charitable Trust, William R.

Kennecott Corp.
Kennedy Foundation, Ethel
Kennedy Foundation, John R.
Kenridge Fund
Kentland Foundation
Kerr Foundation, Robert S. and Grayce B.
Kettering Family Foundation
Key Bank of Maine
Killson Educational Foundation, Winifred and B. A.
Kilroy Foundation, William S. and Lora Jean
Kimball Foundation, Horace A. Kimball and S. Ella
Kimball International
King Foundation, Carl B. and Florence E.
King Ranch
Kiplinger Foundation
Kirby Foundation, F. M.
Kline Foundation, Charles and Figa
Klingenstein Fund, Esther A. and Joseph
Klipstein Foundation, Ernest Christian
Knapp Foundation
Knistrom Foundation, Fanny and Svante
Knott Foundation, Marion I. and Henry J.
Knox Foundation, Seymour H.
Kobacker Co.
Koch Charitable Foundation, Charles G.
Koch Sons, George
Koehler Foundation, Marcia and Otto
Koffler Family Foundation
Kohl Charitable Foundation, Allen D.
Kohn-Joseloff Fund
Komes Foundation
Koopman Fund
Kopf Foundation, Elizabeth Christy
Kraft Foundation
Kramer Foundation
Kramer Foundation, Louise
Krause Foundation, Charles A.
Kunkel Foundation, John Crain
Kuyper Foundation, Peter H. and E. Lucille Gaass
Kysor Industrial Corp.
L. L. W. W. Foundation
Ladd Charitable Corporation, Helen and George
Ladish Co.
Ladish Family Foundation, Herman W.
Laffey-McHugh Foundation
Lakeside National Bank
Lane Foundation, Minnie and Bernard
Lane Memorial Foundation, Mills Bee
Lang Foundation, Eugene M.
Langendorf Foundation, Stanley S.
Lanier Brothers Foundation
Lapham-Hickey Steel Corp.
Larsen Fund
LaSalle National Bank
Lattner Foundation, Forrest C.
Laub Foundation
Laurel Foundation
Law Foundation, Robert O.
Lawrence Foundation, Alice
Lazarus Charitable Trust, Helen and Charles
Lea Foundation, Helen Sperry
Leavey Foundation, Thomas and Dorothy
Lederer Foundation, Francis L.
Lehigh Portland Cement Co.
Lehman Foundation, Edith and Herbert

Lehman Foundation, Robert
Lehrman Foundation, Jacob and Charlotte
Leighton-Oare Foundation
Lender Family Foundation
Lennon Foundation, Fred A.
Lennox International, Inc.
Leonardt Foundation
Leonhardt Foundation, Frederick H.
Leu Foundation
Leuthold Foundation
Levine Family Foundation, Hyman
Levinson Foundation, Max and Anna
Levy Foundation, Charles and Ruth
Levy Foundation, June Rockwell
Levy's Lumber & Building Centers
Lewis Foundation, Frank J.
Lewis Foundation, Lillian Kaiser
Liberman Foundation, Bertha & Isaac
Lieberman Enterprises
Lightner Sams Foundation
Lilly Foundation, Richard Coyle
Lindsay Trust, Agnes M.
Link, Jr. Foundation, George
Linnell Foundation
Lipsky Foundation, Fred and Sarah
Littauer Foundation, Lucius N.
Little Family Foundation
Littlefield Foundation, Edmund Wattis
Littlefield Memorial Trust, Ida Ballou
Livingston Memorial Foundation
Llagas Foundation
Lockheed Corp.
Loeb Foundation, Frances and John L.
Loewy Family Foundation
Long Foundation, George A. and Grace
Longwood Foundation
Loridans Foundation, Charles
Loughran Foundation, Mary and Daniel
Louisiana Land & Exploration Co.
Love Charitable Foundation, John Allan
Love Foundation, George H. and Margaret McClintic
Lovett Foundation
Lowe Foundation, Joe and Emily
Lowenstein Brothers Foundation
Lowenstein Foundation, Leon
Loyola Foundation
LTV Corp.
Lubrizol Corp.
Luck Stone
Ludwick Institute
Lumpkin Foundation
Lund Foundation
Lurcy Charitable and Educational Trust, Georges
Lurie Foundation, Louis R.
Luse Foundation, W. P. and Bulah
Lutheran Brotherhood Foundation
Lux Foundation, Miranda
Lydall, Inc.
Lyons Foundation
Lytel Foundation, Bertha Russ
M.T.D. Products
MacAndrews & Forbes Holdings
MacCurdy Salisbury Educational Foundation
Mack Foundation, J. S.
Maclellan Charitable Trust, R. J.
Maclellan Foundation
Maclellan Foundation, Robert L. and Kathrina H.

Private Education (precollege) (cont.)

MacLeod Stewardship Foundation
Macy & Co., R.H.
Maddox Trust, Web
Magowan Family Foundation
Magruder Foundation, Chesley G.
Makita U.S.A., Inc.
MalCo Products Inc.
Mamiye Brothers
Mandeville Foundation
Maneely Fund
Manger and Audrey Cordero Plitt Trust, Clarence
Manoogian Foundation, Alex and Marie
Marbrook Foundation
Mardag Foundation
Margoes Foundation
Marine Midland Banks
Marinette Marine Corp.
Markey Charitable Fund, John C.
Marmot Foundation
Marquette Electronics
Mars Foundation
Marsh & McLennan Cos.
Marshall & Ilsley Bank
Marshall Trust in Memory of Sanders McDaniel, Harriet McDaniel
Martin & Deborah Flug Foundation
Martin Marietta Aggregates
Martini Foundation, Nicholas
Marubeni America Corp.
Mason Charitable Foundation
Massachusetts Charitable Mechanics Association
Massey Charitable Trust
Massey Foundation
Massey Foundation, Jack C.
Massie Trust, David Meade
Mather and William Gwinn Mather Fund, Elizabeth Ring
Mather Charitable Trust, S. Livingston
Mathis-Pfohl Foundation
Matz Foundation — Edelman Division
Mautz Paint Co.
Maxfield Foundation
Maytag Family Foundation, Fred
Mazer Foundation, Jacob and Ruth
Mazza Foundation
McAlister Charitable Foundation, Harold
McAlonan Trust, John A.
McBean Family Foundation
McCamish Foundation
McCarthy Charities
McConnell Foundation, Neil A.
McCormick Tribune Foundation, Robert R.
McCray Lumber Co.
McCrea Foundation
McCune Charitable Trust, John R.
McCutchen Foundation
McDougall Charitable Trust, Ruth Camp
McElroy Trust, R. J.
McEvoy Foundation, Mildred H.
McFawn Trust No. 2, Lois Sisler
McFeely-Rogers Foundation
McGee Foundation
McGee Foundation
McGraw Foundation
McGraw Foundation, Curtis W.
McGraw Foundation, Donald C.
McGregor Foundation, Thomas and Frances
McGregor Fund

McInerny Foundation
McIntosh Foundation
McIntyre Foundation, C. S. and Marion F.
McKee Foundation, Robert E. and Evelyn
McKenna Foundation, Katherine Mabis
McKnight Foundation, Sumner T.
McLean Contributionship
McMahon Charitable Trust Fund, Father John J.
McNutt Charitable Trust, Amy Shelton
McShain Charities, John
McWane Inc.
Mead Foundation, Giles W. and Elise G.
Mead Fund, Nelson
Meadowood Foundation
Meadows Foundation
Medina Foundation
Medtronic
Meland Outreach
Mellon Foundation, Richard King
Melohn Foundation
Memorial Foundation for Children
Memton Fund
Merchants Bancshares
Mercy, Jr. Foundation, Sue and Eugene
Merillat Foundation, Orville D. and Ruth A.
Merrick Foundation, Robert G. and Anne M.
Merrill Foundation, R. D.
Merrion Foundation
Meserve Memorial Fund, Albert and Helen
Messing Foundation, Morris M. and Helen F.
Meyer Family Foundation, Paul J.
Meyer Foundation
Meyer Foundation, Alice Kleberg Reynolds
Meyerhoff Foundation, Lyn P.
Meyerhoff Fund, Joseph
Middendorf Foundation
Mifflin Memorial Fund, George H. and Jane A.
Milbank Foundation, Dunlevy
Milken Foundation, L. and S.
Mill-Rose Co.
Millbrook Tribute Garden
Miller-Mellor Association
Milliken & Co.
Milliken Foundation, Agnes G.
Mills Charitable Foundation, Henry L. and Kathryn
Mingenback Foundation, Julia J.
Mitchell Foundation
Mitrani Family Foundation
Model Foundation, Leo
Mohasco Corp.
Monaghan Charitable Trust, Rose
Monell Foundation, Ambrose
Monfort Charitable Foundation
Monroe-Brown Foundation
Monroe Foundation (1976), J. Edgar
Moore Foundation, Edward S.
Moore Foundation, O. L.
Moore Foundation, Roy C.
Moosehead Manufacturing Co.
Morgan and Samuel Tate Morgan, Jr. Foundation, Marietta McNeil
Morgan Construction Co.
Morgenstern Foundation, Morris
Morrison-Knudsen Foundation
Morrison-Knudsen Corp.
Morse, Jr. Foundation, Enid and Lester S.
Mosher Foundation, Samuel B.
Moskowitz Foundation, Irving I.
Motorola

Mueller Co.
Mulford Foundation, Vincent
Mulford Trust, Clarence E.
Mullan Foundation, Thomas F. and Clementine L.
Mullen Foundation, J. K.
Muller Foundation
Muller Foundation, C. John and Josephine
Mulligan Charitable Trust, Mary S.
Munger Foundation, Alfred C.
Murch Foundation
Murdock Charitable Trust, M. J.
Murphy Foundation, Dan
Murphy Foundation, Katherine and John
Nabisco Foods Group
National City Bank of Evansville
National Computer Systems
National Machinery Co.
National Westminster Bank New Jersey
NBD Bank
Neenah Foundry Co.
Neu Foundation, Hugo and Doris
New England Business Service
New England Foundation
New Horizon Foundation
New World Foundation
New York Times Co.
Newbrook Charitable Foundation
Newman Charitable Trust, Calvin M. and Raquel H.
Nichols Foundation
Noble Foundation, Samuel Roberts
Norcliffe Fund
Norgren Foundation, Carl A.
Norris Foundation, Dellora A. and Lester J.
Norris Foundation, Kenneth T. and Eileen L.
North American Royalties
North Shore Foundation
Norton Co.
Noyes, Jr. Memorial Foundation, Nicholas H.
Oaklawn Foundation
O'Brien Foundation, Cornelius and Anna Cook
O'Brien Foundation, James W.
Occidental Petroleum Corp.
O'Connor Foundation, Kathryn
Odell and Helen Pfeiffer Odell Fund, Robert Stewart
Odyssey Partners
Oestreicher Foundation, Sylvan and Ann
O'Fallon Trust, Martin J. and Mary Anne
Offield Family Foundation
Ogden Foundation, Ralph E.
Oglebay Norton Co.
Ohio Bell Telephone Co.
Ohio Savings Bank
Ohl, Jr. Trust, George A.
Ohrstrom Foundation
Olin Corp.
Olin Foundation, Spencer T. and Ann W.
Olivetti Office USA, Inc.
Olsson Memorial Foundation, Elis
1957 Charity Trust
O'Neil Foundation, Casey Albert T.
O'Neil Foundation, M. G.
O'Neil Foundation, W.
O'Neill Charitable Corporation, F. J.
O'Neill Foundation, William J. and Dorothy K.
Ontario Corp.
Open Society Fund
Oppenheimer and Flora Oppenheimer Haas Trust, Leo
Oppenstein Brothers Foundation

Orchard Corp. of America.
Orchard Foundation
Ore-Ida Foods, Inc.
Osceola Foundation
O'Shaughnessy Foundation, I. A.
Oshkosh B'Gosh
Oshkosh Truck Corp.
O'Sullivan Children Foundation
O'Toole Foundation, Theresa and Edward
Ottenstein Family Foundation
Overbrook Foundation
Oxford Foundation
PACCAR
Page Belting Co.
Palisano Foundation, Vincent and Harriet
Pamida, Inc.
Panhandle Eastern Corp.
Pappas Charitable Foundation, Bessie
Pappas Charitable Foundation, Thomas Anthony
Paramount Communications Inc.
Pasadena Area Residential Aid
Patterson-Barclay Memorial Foundation
Payne Foundation, Frank E. and Seba B.
Peabody Charitable Fund, Amelia
Peabody Foundation, Amelia
Pearlstone Foundation, Peggy Meyerhoff
Pella Corp.
Pendergast-Weyer Foundation
Pennington Foundation, Irene W. and C. B.
Pennsylvania Knitted Outerwear Manufacturing Association
Penzance Foundation
Peoples Energy Corp.
Perini Corp.
Perkin-Elmer Corp.
Perkins Charitable Foundation
Perkins Memorial Foundation, George W.
Perot Foundation
Persis Corp.
Peterloon Foundation
Peterson Foundation, Fred J.
Pfizer
PHH Corp.
Philibosian Foundation, Stephen
Phillips Foundation, Waite and Genevieve
Phipps Foundation, Howard
Physicians Mutual Insurance
Picower Foundation, Jeffrey M. and Barbara
Pillsbury Foundation
Pincus Family Fund
Pinkerton Foundation
Pitts Foundation, William H. and Lula E.
Pittsburgh National Bank
Pittway Corp.
Pitzman Fund
Plant Memorial Fund, Henry B.
Plaster Foundation, Robert W.
Plym Foundation
Poindexter Foundation
Poinsettia Foundation, Paul and Magdalena Ecke
Polaroid Corp.
Pope Foundation
Porter Testamentary Trust, James Hyde
Posnack Family Foundation of Hollywood
Powell Family Foundation
PPG Industries
Prairie Foundation
Premier Dental Products Co.
Prentice Foundation, Abra
Prentis Family Foundation, Meyer and Anna
Price Associates, T. Rowe

Price Foundation, Lucien B. and Katherine E.
Prickett Fund, Lynn R. and Karl E.
Prince Manufacturing, Inc.
Prince Trust, Abbie Norman
Pritzker Foundation
Propp Sons Fund, Morris and Anna
Providence Energy Corp.
Provident Life & Accident Insurance Co.
Prudential Insurance Co. of America
Psychists
Public Service Electric & Gas Co.
Pulitzer Publishing Co.
Quaker Chemical Corp.
Quaker Hill Foundation
Quaker Oats Co.
Quality Metal Finishing Foundation
Quantum Chemical Corp.
Quincy Newspapers
Quinlan Foundation, Elizabeth C.
Ragen, Jr. Memorial Fund Trust No. 1, James M.
Raker Foundation, M. E.
Rales and Ruth Rales Foundation, Norman R.
Ralston Purina Co.
Randleigh Foundation Trust
Rapp Foundation, Robert Glenn
Raskob Foundation for Catholic Activities
Ratner Foundation, Milton M.
Rauch Foundation
Ray Foundation
Regenstein Foundation
Reinhart Institutional Foods
Reinhold Foundation, Paul E. and Ida Klare
Reisman Charitable Trust, George C. and Evelyn R.
Revlon
Reynolds Foundation, Richard S.
Reynolds Metals Co.
Rice Foundation
Rice Foundation, Helen Steiner
Richardson Foundation, Sid W.
Ringier-America
Rinker Materials Corp.
Rite-Hite Corp.
Ritter Foundation, May Ellen and Gerald
Roberts Foundation
Robinson Foundation
Robinson Foundation
Robinson Foundation, J. Mack
Rochlin Foundation, Abraham and Sonia
Rockford Acromatics Products Co./Aircraft Gear Corp.
Rockwell Fund
Roehl Foundation
Rohlik Foundation, Sigmund and Sophie
Rohm and Haas Company
Rollins Luetkemeyer Charitable Foundation
Romill Foundation
RosaMary Foundation
Rosenbaum Foundation, Paul and Gabriella
Rosenberg Foundation, Henry and Ruth Blaustein
Rosenberg Foundation, Sunny and Abe
Rosenthal Foundation, Ida and William
Rosenwald Family Fund, William
Royal Group Inc.
Rubbermaid
Rubenstein Foundation, Philip
Rudin Foundation
Ruffin Foundation, Peter B. & Adeline W.

Recipient Type Index

Public Education (precollege) (cont.)

Acushnet Co.
Advanced Micro Devices
AEC Trust
AEGON USA, Inc.
AGFA Division of Miles Inc.
Ahmanson Foundation
Akzo Chemicals Inc.
Alabama Power Co.
Alcan Aluminum Corp.
Alcon Laboratories, Inc.
Alexander & Baldwin, Inc.
Alexander Foundation, Judd S.
Alhambra Foundry Co., Ltd.
Allendale Mutual Insurance Co.
Alliant Techsystems
AlliedSignal
Alltel/Western Region
ALPAC Corp.
Alpert Foundation, Herb
Amdahl Corp.
America West Airlines
American Brands
American Express Co.
American Financial Corp.
American General Finance
American Honda Motor Co.
American Natural Resources Co.
American President Cos.
American Saw & Manufacturing Co.
American Standard
American Stock Exchange
American Telephone & Telegraph Co.
Ameritech Services
Ameritech Services
Ames Department Stores
Amfac/JMB Hawaii
AMP
Andalusia Health Services
Andersen Corp.
Anderson Foundation
Andres Charitable Trust, Frank G.
Andrews Foundation
Annenberg Foundation
AON Corp.
Apple Computer, Inc.
ARCO
ARCO Chemical
ARCO Chemical
Arkansas Power & Light Co.
Armco Steel Co.
Armstrong World Industries Inc.
Arnold Fund
Arvin Industries
Ashland Oil
Atkinson Foundation
Atwood Foundation
Axe-Houghton Foundation
Babcock Foundation, Mary Reynolds
Babcock & Wilcox Co.
Balfour Foundation, L. G.
Ball Brothers Foundation
Bamberger and John Ernest Bamberger Memorial Foundation, Ruth Eleanor
Banc One Illinois Corp.
Banc One Wisconsin Corp.
Bancorp Hawaii
Bank Hapoalim B.M.
Bank of Boston Connecticut
Bank of Boston Corp.
Bank One, Texas-Houston Office
Bankers Trust Co.
Bannon Foundation
Barclays Bank of New York
Barker Foundation
Barnes Foundation
Bashinsky Foundation
Bassett Foundation, Norman
Battelle

Bauer Foundation, M. R.
Bauervic-Paisley Foundation
Baughman Foundation
Bay Foundation
Beattie Foundation Trust, Cordelia Lee
Beatty Trust, Cordelia Lunceford
Bechtel Group
Beckman Foundation, Leland D.
Bedford Fund
Bedsole Foundation, J. L.
Beidler Charitable Trust, Francis
Belk Stores
Bell Atlantic Corp.
BellSouth Corp.
Bemis Company
Bend Millwork Systems
Benetton
Benwood Foundation
Bernstein & Co., Sanford C.
Bertha Foundation
Besser Foundation
Bethlehem Steel Corp.
Betts Industries
Bibb Co.
Binney & Smith Inc.
Bird Inc.
Bishop Foundation
Bissell Foundation, J. Walton
Block, H&R
Bloedel Foundation
Blount
Blount Educational and Charitable Foundation, Mildred Weedon
Blue Bell, Inc.
BMC Industries
BMW of North America, Inc.
Boatmen's First National Bank of Oklahoma
Bodenhamer Foundation
Boeing Co.
Bonfils-Stanton Foundation
Boots Pharmaceuticals, Inc.
Booz Allen & Hamilton
Borwell Charitable Foundation
Bound to Stay Bound Books Foundation
BP America
Brach Foundation, Helen
Brackenridge Foundation, George W.
Brenner Foundation, Mervyn
Briggs & Stratton Corp.
Bristol Savings Bank
Brown Foundation
Brown & Williamson Tobacco Corp.
Bruner Foundation
Brush Foundation
Bryan Foundation, James E. and Mary Z.
Bucyrus-Erie
Buhl Foundation
Burdines
Burger King Corp.
Burns International
Cablevision of Michigan
Cabot Corp.
Cadbury Beverages Inc.
Cafritz Foundation, Morris and Gwendolyn
Cahill Foundation, John R.
Caldwell Foundation, Hardwick
California Educational Initiatives Fund
Cameron Foundation, Harry S. and Isabel C.
Camp Younts Foundation
Cannon Foundation
Capital Cities/ABC
Capital Holding Corp.
Carnahan-Jackson Foundation
Carnegie Corporation of New York
Carpenter Foundation, E. Rhodes and Leona B.

Carter Foundation, Amon G.
Carver Charitable Trust, Roy J.
Casey Foundation, Annie E.
Castle & Co., A.M.
Catlin Charitable Trust, Kathleen K.
Cauthorn Charitable Trust, John and Mildred
Center for Educational Programs
Central Fidelity Banks, Inc.
Central Life Assurance Co.
Central Maine Power Co.
Chambers Memorial, James B.
Champion International Corp.
Champlin Foundations
Chase Manhattan Bank, N.A.
CHC Foundation
Chemical Bank
Cheney Foundation, Ben B.
Chesapeake Corp.
Chevron Corp.
Chiles Foundation
Christensen Charitable and Religious Foundation, L. C.
CIGNA Corp.
Cincinnati Bell
Circuit City Stores
CIT Group Holdings
Citicorp
Clark Foundation, Edna McConnell
Classic Leather
Clay Foundation
Clorox Co.
CM Alliance Cos.
CNA Insurance Cos.
CNG Transmission Corp.
Coats & Clark Inc.
Coca-Cola Co.
Coleman Co.
Collins-McDonald Trust Fund
Colonial Life & Accident Insurance Co.
Colonial Stores
Colorado National Bankshares
Colorado Trust
Comerica
Cominco American Inc.
Commercial Bank
Community Enterprises
Community Health Association
Cone Mills Corp.
Conoco Inc.
Consolidated Natural Gas Co.
Consumer Farmer Foundation
Contran Corp.
Coors Brewing Co.
Country Curtains, Inc.
Cowell Foundation, S. H.
Cowles Media Co.
Cox Charitable Trust, Jessie B.
CPC International
Crane Co.
CRL Inc.
Cudahy Fund, Patrick and Anna M.
Cullen/Frost Bankers
Cummings Memorial Fund Trust, Frances L. and Edwin L.
Cummins Engine Co.
CUNA Mutual Insurance Group
Cuneo Foundation
Dana Corp.
Dana Foundation, Charles A.
Danforth Foundation
Dart Foundation
Daugherty Foundation
Davidson Family Charitable Foundation
DeKalb Genetics Corp.
Dekko Foundation
DeRoy Testamentary Foundation
Detroit Edison Co.
Dewing Foundation, Frances R.
Dexter Corp.
Diamond Foundation, Aaron
Diener Foundation, Frank C.

Dillon Foundation
DiRosa Foundation, Rene and Veronica
Dively Foundation, George S.
Dixie Yarns, Inc.
Dodge Foundation, Geraldine R.
Dodge Foundation, P. L.
Dodge Jones Foundation
Donaldson Co.
Dorr Foundation
Dow Chemical Co.
Dow Foundation, Herbert H. and Grace A.
Dow Fund, Alden and Vada
du Pont de Nemours & Co., E. I.
Duchossois Industries
Duke Power Co.
duPont Foundation, Chichester
duPont Fund, Jessie Ball
E and M Charities
Eastern Fine Paper, Inc.
Eastman Kodak Co.
Eastover Corp.
Eaton Corp.
Eccles Foundation, George S. and Dolores Dore
Eccles Foundation, Ralph M. and Ella M.
Edwards Foundation, O. P. and W. E.
Edwards & Sons, A.G.
Elgin Sweeper Co.
Emerson Electric Co.
EMI Records Group
Enron Corp.
Equitable Life Assurance Society of the U.S.
Ernsthausen Charitable Foundation, John F. and Doris E.
Evans Foundation, Edward P.
Evans Foundation, Thomas J.
Evjue Foundation
Exxon Corp.
Fairfield-Meeker Charitable Trust, Freeman E.
Farmers Group, Inc.
Federal-Mogul Corp.
Federated Department Stores and Allied Stores Corp.
Federated Life Insurance Co.
Felburn Foundation
Fieldcrest Cannon
Fifth Third Bancorp
FINA, Inc.
Finch Foundation, Doak
First Fidelity Bancorporation
First Hawaiian
First Interstate Bank NW Region
First Interstate Bank of Arizona
First Mississippi Corp.
First Tennessee Bank
First Union Corp.
First Union National Bank of Florida
FirsTier Bank N.A. Omaha
Fleet Financial Group
Fleming Companies, Inc.
Flintridge Foundation
Florida Power & Light Co.
Foote Mineral Co.
Ford Foundation
Ford Meter Box Co.
Ford Motor Co.
Forest Foundation
Foster-Davis Foundation
Foundation for Seacoast Health
French Oil Mill Machinery Co.
Frick Educational Commission, Henry C.
Frohman Foundation, Sidney
Fry Foundation, Lloyd A.
Fuller Foundation, George F. and Sybil H.
Funderburke & Associates
Gallagher Family Foundation, Lewis P.

Gap, The
GAR Foundation
Garland Foundation, John Jewett and H. Chandler
Gault-Hussey Charitable Trust
Gellert Foundation, Celia Berta
Gellert Foundation, Fred
Genentech
General Accident Insurance Co. of America
General American Life Insurance Co.
General Electric Co.
General Mills
General Motors Corp.
GenRad
George Foundation
Georgia Power Co.
Gerber Products Co.
Gerbode Foundation, Wallace Alexander
Gerson Family Foundation, Benjamin J.
Gheens Foundation
Ghidotti Foundation, William and Marian
Gholston Trust, J. K.
Gifford Charitable Corporation, Rosamond
Gilder Foundation
Gill Foundation, Pauline Allen
Gilman Paper Co.
Glaxo
Glaze Foundation, Robert and Ruth
Glenn Foundation, Carrie C. & Lena V.
Globe Newspaper Co.
Glosser Foundation, David A.
Goddard Foundation, Charles B.
Goldbach Foundation, Ray and Marie
Goldman Sachs & Co.
Golub Corp.
Good Samaritan
Grace & Co., W.R.
Grader Foundation, K. W.
Graham Fund, Philip L.
Grainger Foundation
Grant Foundation, Charles M. and Mary D.
Gray Foundation, Garland
Great Western Financial Corp.
Greenfield Foundation, Albert M.
Griffin Foundation, Rosa May
Grimes Foundation
Groome Beatty Trust, Helen D.
Grundy Foundation
GTE Corp.
Gudelsky Family Foundation, Homer and Martha
Gulfstream Aerospace Corp.
Gund Foundation, George
Haas Foundation, Paul and Mary
Haas Fund, Miriam and Peter
Haas Fund, Walter and Elise
Hall Family Foundations
Hallmark Cards
Halloran Foundation, Mary P. Dolciani
Hancock Foundation, Luke B.
Hand Industries
Hannon Foundation, William H.
Hardin Foundation, Phil
Harper Brush Works
Harper Foundation, Philip S.
Harrington Foundation, Don and Sybil
Harrison Foundation, Fred G.
Harsco Corp.
Hartmarx Corp.
Hartzell Industries, Inc.
Hawkins Foundation, Robert Z.
Hayden Foundation, Charles
Hayden Foundation, William R. and Virginia
Hechinger Co.

Heckscher Foundation for Children
Heginbotham Trust, Will E.
Heileman Brewing Co., Inc., G.
Heinz Co., H.J.
Heinz Endowment, Howard
Heinz Endowment, Vira I.
Heller Financial
Herrick Foundation
Hershey Foods Corp.
Hiawatha Education Foundation
Higgins Foundation, Aldus C.
Hillcrest Foundation
Hillman Foundation
Hillsdale Fund
Hitachi
Hodge Foundation
Hoffman Foundation, Marion O. and Maximilian
Hofstetter Trust, Bessie
Holden Fund, James and Lynelle
Holt Foundation, William Knox
Honda of America Manufacturing, Inc.
Honeywell
Hoover Foundation
Hopper Memorial Foundation, Bertrand
Horne Foundation, Dick
Hospital Corp. of America
Houston Endowment
Howard and Bush Foundation
Howe and Mitchell B. Howe Foundation, Lucile Horton
Hubbard Broadcasting
Hubbard Foundation, R. Dee and Joan Dale
Huffy Corp.
Hugoton Foundation
Humana
Hunt Alternatives Fund
Hunt Charitable Trust, C. Giles
Hunt Manufacturing Co.
Hunter Foundation, Edward and Irma
Hurley Foundation, J. F.
Hurst Foundation
Iacocca Foundation
IBM Corp.
IBP, Inc.
IES Industries
Illinois Power Co.
Indiana Bell Telephone Co.
Industrial Bank of Japan Trust Co.
Inland Container Corp.
Inland Steel Industries
Innovating Worthy Projects Foundation
Intel Corp.
International Flavors & Fragrances
International Paper Co.
International Student Exchange Cards
Ishiyama Foundation
Island Foundation
ITT Hartford Insurance Group
J.P. Morgan & Co.
Jackson Foundation
Jacobson Foundation, Bernard H. and Blanche E.
JCPenney Co.
Jenkins Foundation, George W.
Jennings Foundation, Martha Holden
Jewell Memorial Foundation, Daniel Ashley and Irene Houston
Johnson Co., E. F.
Johnson Foundation, Walter S.
Johnson & Higgins
Johnson & Son, S.C.
Jones Foundation, Montfort Jones and Allie Brown
Joslin-Needham Family Foundation
Journal Gazette Co.

Joyce Foundation
Kantzler Foundation
Kapiloff Foundation, Leonard
Kaufman Endowment Fund, Louis G.
Kellogg Foundation, W. K.
Kemper Educational and Charitable Fund
Kempner Fund, Harris and Eliza
Kenan Family Foundation
Kenedy Memorial Foundation, John G. and Marie Stella
Kennecott Corp.
Kern Foundation Trust
Kerr Foundation
Kerr Foundation, Robert S. and Grayce B.
Kettering Family Foundation
Kidder, Peabody & Co.
Kimball International
King Ranch
Kingsley Foundation, Lewis A.
Kiplinger Foundation
Kirbo Charitable Trust, Thomas M. and Irene B.
Kitzmiller/Bales Trust
Klein Fund, Nathan J.
Knapp Educational Fund
Knapp Foundation
Knudsen Foundation, Tom and Valley
Kraft General Foods
Krause Foundation, Charles A.
Kysor Industrial Corp.
Laffey-McHugh Foundation
Lance, Inc.
Lane Co., Inc.
Lang Foundation, Eugene M.
Lassen Foundation, Irving A.
Lavanburg-Corner House
Leavey Foundation, Thomas and Dorothy
Leighton-Oare Foundation
Leo Burnett Co.
Liberty Corp.
Lightner Sams Foundation
Lilly Endowment
Lindstrom Foundation, Kinney
Linn-Henley Charitable Trust
Little, Arthur D.
Littlefield Foundation, Edmund Wattis
Liz Claiborne
Long Island Lighting Co.
Loose Trust, Carrie J.
Loose Trust, Harry Wilson
Louisiana Power & Light Co./New Orleans Public Service
Love Foundation, George H. and Margaret McClintic
Lowenstein Foundation, Leon
LTV Corp.
Ludwick Institute
Lux Foundation, Miranda
Lydall, Inc.
Lyndhurst Foundation
Lyon Foundation
Lyondell Petrochemical Co.
Lytel Foundation, Bertha Russ
Maddox Foundation, J. F.
Maier Foundation, Sarah Pauline
Mailman Family Foundation, A. L.
Makita U.S.A., Inc.
Mankato Citizens Telephone Co.
Mardag Foundation
Marine Midland Banks
Marinette Marine Corp.
Marion Merrell Dow
Maritz Inc.
Marley Co.
Marshall Foundation
Martin Marietta Corp.
Massachusetts Mutual Life Insurance Co.
Massey Charitable Trust

Massie Trust, David Meade
Matsushita Electric Corp. of America
Mayer Foods Corp., Oscar
Maytag Corp.
McCasland Foundation
McConnell Foundation
McDermott Foundation, Eugene
McDonnell Douglas Corp.
McElroy Trust, R. J.
McEvoy Foundation, Mildred H.
McFeely-Rogers Foundation
McGraw Foundation, Curtis W.
McGregor Fund
MCI Communications Corp.
McIntosh Foundation
McMahon Foundation
McMillan, Jr. Foundation, Bruce
Mead Corp.
Mead Foundation, Giles W. and Elise G.
Meadows Foundation
Medtronic
Mellon Bank Corp.
Mellon Foundation, Richard King
Melville Corp.
Merck & Co.
Merck Human Health Division
Mericos Foundation
Merrick Foundation
Messick Charitable Trust, Harry F.
Meyer Foundation, Eugene and Agnes E.
Meyer Memorial Trust
Michigan Consolidated Gas Co.
Michigan Gas Utilities
Mielke Family Foundation
Miller Foundation
Miller Foundation, Steve J.
Milliken & Co.
Milliken Foundation, Agnes G.
Mills Charitable Foundation, Henry L. and Kathryn
Minnegasco
Minnesota Power & Light Co.
Mobil Oil Corp.
Monfort Charitable Foundation
Moore Foundation
Moore Foundation, O. L.
Moore Memorial Foundation, James Starr
Morgan and Samuel Tate Morgan, Jr. Foundation, Marietta McNeil
Morrison-Knudsen Corp.
Moskowitz Foundation, Irving I.
Motorola
Mulcahy Foundation
Mulford Trust, Clarence E.
Murphy Foundation
Myra Foundation
Nabisco Foods Group
Nason Foundation
National Computer Systems
National Machinery Co.
National Presto Industries
National Pro-Am Youth Fund
NEC Technologies, Inc.
Nellie Mae
New England Business Service
New Horizon Foundation
New Street Capital Corp.
New York Times Co.
The New Yorker Magazine, Inc.
Newhall Foundation, Henry Mayo
Newman's Own
News & Observer Publishing Co.
Nissan Motor Corporation in U.S.A.
Noble Foundation, Samuel Roberts
Nord Family Foundation
Nordson Corp.
North American Royalties
Northeast Utilities

Northern Telecom Inc.
Northwestern National Life Insurance Co.
Norton Co.
Norton Foundation Inc.
Norwest Bank Nebraska
Noyes, Jr. Memorial Foundation, Nicholas H.
Oakley Foundation, Hollie and Anna
O'Connor Foundation, A. Lindsay and Olive B.
O'Donnell Foundation
Ohio Valley Foundation
Ohrstrom Foundation
Olin Corp.
O'Neill Foundation, William J. and Dorothy K.
Ontario Corp.
Ore-Ida Foods, Inc.
Owens-Corning Fiberglas Corp.
Pacific Mutual Life Insurance Co.
Pacific Telesis Group
Packaging Corporation of America
Padnos Iron & Metal Co., Louis
Palin Foundation
Panhandle Eastern Corp.
Parker Foundation
Parsons Foundation, Ralph M.
Peery Foundation
Pella Corp.
Penn Foundation, William
Pennsylvania Dutch Co.
People's Bank
Peoples Energy Corp.
Peppers Foundation, Ann
Perkin-Elmer Corp.
Perot Foundation
Persis Corp.
Peters Foundation, R. D. and Linda
Pfizer
PHH Corp.
Philadelphia Electric Co.
Phillips Foundation, Dr. P.
Phillips Trust, Edwin
Phipps Foundation, William H.
Pick, Jr. Fund, Albert
Pieper Electric
Pillsbury Foundation
Pilot Trust
Pinkerton Foundation
Pioneer Electronics (USA) Inc.
Piper Foundation, Minnie Stevens
Piton Foundation
Plough Foundation
PNC Bank
Polaroid Corp.
Potomac Electric Power Co.
Powell Family Foundation
PPG Industries
Price Associates, T. Rowe
Primerica Corp.
Procter & Gamble Co.
Proctor Trust, Mortimer R.
Providence Energy Corp.
Providence Journal Company
Provident Life & Accident Insurance Co.
Provigo Corp. Inc.
Prudential Insurance Co. of America
PSI Energy
Public Service Co. of New Mexico
Public Service Electric & Gas Co.
Puett Foundation, Nelson
Quaker Oats Co.
Randolph Foundation
Red Wing Shoe Co.
Reeves Foundation
Reichhold Chemicals, Inc.
Reliance Electric Co.
Reynolds Foundation, Z. Smith

Reynolds Metals Co.
Reynolds & Reynolds Co.
Rhone-Poulenc Inc.
Richardson Foundation, Sid W.
Rider-Pool Foundation
Ringier-America
Ritchie Memorial Foundation, Charles E. and Mabel M.
RJR Nabisco Inc.
Roberts Foundation, Dora
Robinson Fund, Maurice R.
Rochester Telephone Corp.
Rockefeller Brothers Fund
Rockefeller Foundation, Winthrop
Rockfall Foundation
Rockford Products Corp.
Rogers Charitable Trust, Florence
Rohatyn Foundation, Felix and Elizabeth
Rohm and Haas Company
Ross Foundation
Royal Group Inc.
Rubbermaid
Russell Memorial Foundation, Robert
Ryder System
SAFECO Corp.
Sage Foundation
Salomon
Sandusky International Inc.
Santa Fe Pacific Corp.
Sarkeys Foundation
Schenck Fund, L. P.
Schmidlapp Trust No. 1, Jacob G.
Schroeder Foundation, Walter
Schwab & Co., Charles
Scrivner, Inc.
Scrivner of North Carolina Inc.
Seabury Foundation
Searle & Co., G.D.
Security Life of Denver
Sedgwick James Inc.
Sega of America
Semmes Foundation
Semple Foundation, Louise Taft
Sentinel Communications Co.
Share Trust, Charles Morton
Shatford Memorial Trust, J. D.
Shawmut National Corp.
Shea Foundation
Shea Foundation, John and Dorothy
Shell Oil Co.
Shiffman Foundation
Shoney's Inc.
Shott, Jr. Foundation, Hugh I.
Sierra Pacific Resources
Sifco Industries Inc.
Signet Bank/Maryland
Simpson Foundation
Simpson Investment Co.
Sjostrom & Sons
Skinner Corp.
Slemp Foundation
Smith and W. Aubrey Smith Charitable Foundation, Clara Blackford
Smith Fund, George D.
Smith, Jr. Charitable Trust, Jack J.
Snow Foundation, John Ben
Snyder Foundation, Frost and Margaret
Sony Corp. of America
Southern California Gas Co.
Southwestern Bell Corp.
Spahn & Rose Lumber Co.
Sprague Educational and Charitable Foundation, Seth
Springs Foundation
Springs Industries
Sprint
SPX Corp.
Stackner Family Foundation
Stanley Works
Star Bank, N.A.

Public Education (precollege) (cont.)

Starrett Co., L.S.
State Street Bank & Trust Co.
Stemmons Foundation
Stern Family Foundation, Alex
Stern Foundation, Leonard N.
Stevens Foundation, John T.
Stevens Foundation, Nathaniel and Elizabeth P.
Stock Foundation, Paul
Stocker Foundation
Straus Foundation, Aaron and Lillie
Stride Rite Corp.
Strong Foundation, Hattie M.
Stuart Foundations
Sumitomo Bank of California
Sun Co.
Sun Microsystems
Swanson Family Foundation, Dr. W.C.
Tamko Asphalt Products
Tandy Corp.
Tandy Foundation, Anne Burnett and Charles
Tang Foundation
TCF Banking & Savings, FSB
Tektronix
Teledyne
Temple-Inland
Templeton Foundation, Herbert A.
Tenneco
Teubert Charitable Trust, James H. and Alice
Textron
Thoman Foundation, W. B. and Candace
Thomasville Furniture Industries
Thornton Foundation, Flora L.
Timken Foundation of Canton
TJX Cos.
Tomkins Industries, Inc.
Toshiba America, Inc.
Tozer Foundation
Tracor, Inc.
Transco Energy Company
Travelers Cos.
Trinity Foundation
Tropicana Products, Inc.
Trull Foundation
Trust Co. Bank
TRW Corp.
Tull Charitable Foundation
Tuohy Foundation, Alice Tweed
Union Camp Corp.
Union Carbide Corp.
United Airlines
United Dominion Industries
United States-Japan Foundation
U.S. Silica Co.
United States Sugar Corp.
United Technologies Corp.
Universal Leaf Tobacco Co.
Unocal Corp.
UNUM Corp.
Upjohn Foundation, Harold and Grace
Van Buren Foundation
Van Every Foundation, Philip L.
Van Huffel Foundation, I. J.
Van Nuys Foundation, I. N. and Susanna H.
Van Wert County Foundation
Varian Associates
Vaughn Foundation
Vermeer Manufacturing Co.
Vicksburg Foundation
Vlasic Foundation
Vulcan Materials Co.
W. W. W. Foundation
Wahlert Foundation
Wal-Mart Stores

Wallace-Reader's Digest Fund, DeWitt
Ware Foundation
Washington Mutual Savings Bank
Washington Post Co.
Washington Water Power Co.
Wasserman Foundation, George
Waste Management
Wausau Paper Mills Co.
Wean Foundation, Raymond John
Weckbaugh Foundation, Eleanore Mullen
Wegener Foundation, Herman and Mary
Weinberg, Jr. Foundation, Sidney J.
Weiss Foundation, William E.
Wells Fargo & Co.
West Foundation
Western New York Foundation
Western Shade Cloth Charitable Foundation
Westinghouse Electric Corp.
Wetterau
Weyerhaeuser Co.
Whirlpool Corp.
Whitehead Foundation, Joseph B.
Whiting Foundation
Whittenberger Foundation, Claude R. and Ethel B.
WICOR, Inc.
Wiggins Memorial Trust, J. J.
Wilbur-Ellis Co.
Williams Cos.
Williams Family Foundation
Williams Family Foundation of Georgia
Willmott Foundation, Fred & Floy
Wisconsin Energy Corp.
Wolens Foundation, Kalman and Ida
Wollenberg Foundation
Woods Charitable Fund
Woodward Fund-Atlanta, David, Helen, Marian
Xerox Corp.
Yost Trust, Elizabeth Burns
Young Foundation, H and B
Young Foundation, Hugo H. and Mabel B.

Religious Education

Abrams Foundation
Abrams Foundation, Benjamin and Elizabeth
ACF Industries, Inc.
Acme-Cleveland Corp.
Acme United Corp.
Ala Vi Foundation of New York
Aldeen Charity Trust, G. W.
Alden Trust, George I.
Allendale Mutual Insurance Co.
Alperin/Hirsch Family Foundation
Altman Foundation
Amado Foundation, Maurice
Amoco Corp.
Amsted Industries
Andersen Corp.
Andersen Foundation
Anderson Foundation, Robert C. and Sadie G.
Andreas Foundation
Annenberg Foundation
AON Corp.
Applebaum Foundation
Appleman Foundation
Arbie Mineral Feed Co.
Archer-Daniels-Midland Co.
Archibald Charitable Foundation, Norman
Arkansas Power & Light Co.
Arkell Hall Foundation
Arkwright Foundation
Arronson Foundation

Artevel Foundation
ASARCO
Atalanta/Sosnoff Capital Corp.
Atherton Family Foundation
Atkinson Foundation, Myrtle L.
Atran Foundation
Aurora Foundation
AVI CHAI - A Philanthropic Foundation
Bag Bazaar, Ltd.
Baird Foundation, Cameron
Baldwin Foundation
Banc One Illinois Corp.
Bancorp Hawaii
Bannan Foundation, Arline and Thomas J.
Barlow Family Foundation, Milton A. and Gloria G.
Barnes Group
Barra Foundation
Barry Corp., R. G.
Bauer Foundation, M. R.
Bauervic Foundation, Charles M.
Baughman Foundation
Beatty Trust, Cordelia Lunceford
Bedminster Fund
Bedsole Foundation, J. L.
Beeghly Fund, Leon A.
Beerman Foundation
Beinecke Foundation
Belfer Foundation
Belz Foundation
Bemis Company
Bemis Company
Benfamil Charitable Trust
Bere Foundation
Beren Foundation, Robert M.
Bergstrom Manufacturing Co.
Berkman Charitable Trust, Allen H. and Selma W.
Bernstein & Co., Sanford C.
Bernstein Foundation, Diane and Norman
Berry Foundation, Lowell
Bettingen Corporation, Burton G.
Bierhaus Foundation
Birmingham Foundation
Bishop Foundation, Vernon and Doris
Blaustein Foundation, Jacob and Hilda
Blaustein Foundation, Louis and Henrietta
Blount
Blum Foundation, Edith C.
Board of Trustees of the Prichard School
Boh Brothers Construction Co.
Booth-Bricker Fund
Borg-Warner Corp.
Borman's
Bourns, Inc.
Bowers Foundation
Bozzone Family Foundation
Brach Foundation, Helen
Bridgestone/Firestone
Broadhurst Foundation
Brody Foundation, Carolyn and Kenneth D.
Brooks Foundation, Gladys
Brotz Family Foundation, Frank G.
Brown Charitable Trust, Dora Maclellan
Bruening Foundation, Eva L. and Joseph M.
Bruner Foundation
Brunner Foundation, Robert
Bryan Foundation, James E. and Mary Z.
Bryant Foundation
Bucyrus-Erie
Burchfield Foundation, Charles E.
Burgess Trust, Ralph L. and Florence R.
Burns Foundation, Jacob
Burress, J.W.

Bustard Charitable Permanent Trust Fund, Elizabeth and James
C. E. and S. Foundation
C.I.O.S.
Caddock Foundation
Caestecker Foundation, Charles and Marie
Callister Foundation, Paul Q.
Cameron Foundation, Harry S. and Isabel C.
Campbell Foundation
Capital Fund Foundation
Caplan Charity Foundation, Julius H.
Carnival Cruise Lines
Carpenter Foundation, E. Rhodes and Leona B.
Carter Charitable Trust, Wilbur Lee
Cartinhour Foundation
Carvel Foundation, Thomas and Agnes
Central Bank of the South
Central National-Gottesman
Central & South West Services
Central Soya Co.
Chamberlin Foundation, Gerald W.
Chapin-May Foundation of Illinois
Chartwell Foundation
Chatlos Foundation
Chiles Foundation
Chiquita Brands Co.
Chisholm Foundation
Christian Training Foundation
Christian Workers Foundation
Clark Charitable Trust
Clarke Trust, John
Collins Foundation
Columbus Dispatch Printing Co.
Commercial Metals Co.
Community Foundation
Conn Memorial Foundation
Conston Corp.
Coors Foundation, Adolph
Cottrell Foundation
Cranston Print Works
CRL Inc.
Crowell Trust, Henry P. and Susan C.
Cudahy Fund, Patrick and Anna M.
CUNA Mutual Insurance Group
Cuneo Foundation
Danner Foundation
Davis Foundation, Edwin W. and Catherine M.
Davis Foundation, Simon and Annie
Davis Foundations, Arthur Vining
Day Foundation, Cecil B.
Daywood Foundation
de Dampierre Memorial Foundation, Marie C.
De Lima Co., Paul
de Rothschild Foundation, Edmond
Demoulas Supermarkets
Deseranno Educational Foundation
DeVos Foundation, Richard and Helen
Dexter Corp.
Dietrich Foundation, William B.
Dodge Foundation, P. L.
Doheny Foundation, Carrie Estelle
Domino of California
Domino's Pizza
Donnelly Foundation, Mary J.
Dorot Foundation
Doty Family Foundation
Dougherty, Jr. Foundation, James R.
Douglas Corp.
Dower Foundation, Thomas W.

Driscoll Foundation
Drum Foundation
Duke Endowment
Duke Power Co.
Duncan Trust, James R.
Duncan Trust, James R.
duPont Foundation, Alfred I.
E and M Charities
Early Foundation
East Foundation, Sarita Kenedy
Eaton Corp.
Edison Foundation, Irving and Beatrice C.
Ehrman Foundation, Fred and Susan
El-An Foundation
Ellis Grant and Scholarship Fund, Charles E.
Emerson Electric Co.
English-Bonter-Mitchell Foundation
English Foundation, W. C.
Equimark Corp.
Erickson Charitable Fund, Eben W.
Ernest & Julio Gallo Winery
Estes Foundation
FAB Industries
Failing Fund, Henry
Fairchild Corp.
Farish Fund, William Stamps
Federated Department Stores and Allied Stores Corp.
Feil Foundation, Louis and Gertrude
Feinberg Foundation, Joseph and Bessie
Feintech Foundation
Feldman Foundation
Fellner Memorial Foundation, Leopold and Clara M.
Fifth Third Bancorp
Finley Charitable Trust, J. B.
Fireman Charitable Foundation, Paul and Phyllis
Firestone Foundation, Roger S.
First Fruit
First Interstate Bank of Texas, N.A.
First Maryland Bancorp
First Mississippi Corp.
First Petroleum Corp.
Fischbach Foundation
Fischel Foundation, Harry and Jane
Fishoff Family Foundation
Flickinger Memorial Trust
Fogel Foundation, Shalom and Rebecca
Fohs Foundation
Forchheimer Foundation
Ford Foundation, Joseph F. and Clara
Forest City Enterprises
Forest Foundation
Forest Lawn Foundation
Fortin Foundation of Florida
Franklin Charitable Trust, Ershel
Franklin Foundation, John and Mary
Frazier Foundation
Freas Foundation
Frederick Foundation
Friedland Family Foundation, Samuel
Friedman Brothers Foundation
Friedman Foundation, Stephen and Barbara
Friends' Foundation Trust, A.
Fruehauf Foundation
Fuchs Foundation, Gottfried & Mary
Funderburke & Associates
Gabelli Foundation
Gavin Foundation, James and Zita
GEICO Corp.
Gellert Foundation, Celia Berta

General Accident Insurance Co.
of America
General Mills
Gerson Trust, B. Milfred
Gerstacker Foundation, Rollin M.
Getsch Family Foundation Trust
Gheens Foundation
Giant Eagle
Gibson Foundation, E. L.
Gillette Co.
Gilmore Foundation, Earl B.
Gilmore Foundation, William G.
Gindi Associates Foundation
Gitano Group
Glanville Family Foundation
Glaze Foundation, Robert and
Ruth
Goldberg Family Foundation,
Israel and Matilda
Goldberger Foundation, Edward
and Marjorie
Goldman Foundation, Aaron and
Cecile
Goldman Foundation, Herman
Goldstein Foundation, Leslie and
Roslyn
Gordon Foundation
Grader Foundation, K. W.
Greeley Gas Co.
Green Fund
Greene Foundation, David J.
Greenspan Foundation
Greenville Foundation
Gross Charitable Trust, Walter L.
and Nell R.
Grousbeck Family Foundation
Gruber Research Foundation,
Lila
Guttag Foundation, Irwin and
Marjorie
Guttman Foundation, Stella and
Charles
Haas Foundation, Paul and Mary
Habig Foundation, Arnold F.
Haffenreffer Family Fund
Hagedorn Fund
Haggar Foundation
Haggerty Foundation
Hale Foundation, Crescent Porter
Hallett Charitable Trust
Hallett Charitable Trust, Jessie F.
Halliburton Co.
Hamilton Bank
Hamman Foundation, George
and Mary Josephine
Hanes Foundation, John W. and
Anna H.
Hansen Foundation, Dane G.
Hardin Foundation, Phil
Harding Foundation, Charles
Stewart
Harsco Corp.
Hawkins Foundation, Robert Z.
Hawn Foundation
Hayden Foundation, William R.
and Virginia
Heath Foundation, Ed and Mary
Hechinger Co.
Heilicher Foundation, Menahem
Heinz Co., H.J.
Helms Foundation
Herrick Foundation
Herzstein Charitable Foundation,
Albert and Ethel
Hess Foundation
Hexcel Corp.
Hiawatha Education Foundation
Hidary Foundation, Jacob
High Foundation
Hillsdale Fund
Hoffberger Foundation
Holtzmann Foundation, Jacob L.
and Lillian
Homeland Foundation
Homeland Foundation
Hoover Foundation, H. Earl
Hopewell Foundation

Horowitz Foundation, Gedale B.
and Barbara S.
House of Gross
Houston Endowment
Hudson Neckwear
Hudson-Webber Foundation
Hugg Trust, Leoia W. and
Charles H.
Hugoton Foundation
Huizenga Family Foundation
Huizenga Foundation, Jennie
Hunt Trust for Episcopal
Charitable Institutions, Virginia
Huston Foundation
Hyde and Watson Foundation
Hyde Foundation, J. R.
Iddings Benevolent Trust
Illges Memorial Foundation, A.
and M. L.
Imerman Memorial Foundation,
Stanley
Indiana Desk Co.
Inland Container Corp.
International Student Exchange
Cards
Irwin-Sweeney-Miller
Foundation
ITT Hartford Insurance Group
Ivakota Association
Jackson Hole Preserve
Jacobson & Sons, Benjamin
Jaharis Family Foundation
Jameson Foundation, J. W. and
Ida M.
Jasper Desk Co.
Jasper Table Co.
Jasper Wood Products Co.
Jeffress Memorial Trust,
Elizabeth G.
Jesselson Foundation
Jewett Foundation, George
Frederick
Jinks Foundation, Ruth T.
JMK-A M Micallef Charitable
Foundation
JOFCo., Inc.
Johnston-Hanson Foundation
Jones Charitable Trust, Harvey
and Bernice
Jones Foundation, Harvey and
Bernice
Jonsson Foundation
Joselow Foundation
Joyce Foundation, John M. and
Mary A.
Julia R. and Estelle L.
Foundation
Kangesser Foundation, Robert
E., Harry A., and M. Sylvia
Kapiloff Foundation, Leonard
Kaplun Foundation, Morris J.
and Betty
Kasal Charitable Trust, Father
Kavanagh Foundation, T. James
Kelley Foundation, Kate M.
Kelly Tractor Co.
Kemper Foundation, Enid and
Crosby
Kenedy Memorial Foundation,
John G. and Marie Stella
Kennametal
Kennedy Foundation, Quentin J.
Kent Foundation, Ada Howe
Kentland Foundation
Kerr Foundation, A. H.
Key Food Stores Cooperative Inc.
Kilworth Charitable Foundation,
Florence B.
Kimball International
Kirby Foundation, F. M.
Klau Foundation, David W. and
Sadie
Knapp Foundation
Knott Foundation, Marion I. and
Henry J.
Koch Foundation
Koch Sons, George
Komes Foundation

Koret Foundation
Korman Family Foundation,
Hyman
Koulaieff Educational Fund,
Trustees of Ivan Y.
Kraft Foundation
Kuyper Foundation, Peter H. and
E. Lucille Gaass
Kysor Industrial Corp.
La-Z-Boy Chair Co.
Lamb Foundation, Kirkland S.
and Rena B.
Lance, Inc.
Law Foundation, Robert O.
Leavey Foundation, Thomas and
Dorothy
Lee Foundation, Ray M. and
Mary Elizabeth
Leighton-Oare Foundation
Lemberg Foundation
Lennon Foundation, Fred A.
Leuthold Foundation
Levine Family Foundation,
Hyman
Levy Foundation, Betty and
Norman F.
Lewis Foundation, Frank J.
Libby-Dufour Fund, Trustees of
the
Lightner Sams Foundation
Lilly Endowment
Link, Jr. Foundation, George
Littauer Foundation, Lucius N.
Lizzadro Family Foundation,
Joseph
Louis Foundation, Michael W.
Louisiana Land & Exploration
Co.
Lounsbery Foundation, Richard
Love Foundation, George H. and
Margaret McClintic
Lowe Foundation, Joe and Emily
Lowenstein Brothers Foundation
Loyola Foundation
Luce Foundation, Henry
Lupin Foundation
Lutheran Brotherhood
Foundation
Lyons Foundation
M.E. Foundation
MacDonald Foundation, James A.
Maclellan Charitable Trust, R. J.
Maclellan Foundation
Maclellan Foundation, Robert L.
and Kathrina H.
Magee Christian Education
Foundation
Maier Foundation, Sarah Pauline
Mamiye Brothers
Mandell Foundation, Samuel P.
Maneely Fund
Mankato Citizens Telephone Co.
Marcus Brothers Textiles Inc.
Marshall Foundation, Mattie H.
Marshall Trust in Memory of
Sanders McDaniel, Harriet
McDaniel
Martin Marietta Corp.
Masco Corp.
Massey Foundation
Maxfield Foundation
Mayerson Foundation, Manuel
D. and Rhoda
McAlonan Trust, John A.
McBean Family Foundation
McCasland Foundation
McCune Charitable Trust, John
R.
McGraw Foundation, Donald C.
McKenna Foundation, Philip M.
McMahon Charitable Trust
Fund, Father John J.
McMaster Foundation, Harold
and Helen
McMillan, Jr. Foundation, Bruce
McMillen Foundation
McShain Charities, John
Melohn Foundation

Menil Foundation
Merillat Foundation, Orville D.
and Ruth A.
Merrick Foundation, Robert G.
and Anne M.
Meyer Family Foundation, Paul
J.
Meyerhoff Fund, Joseph
Miller Charitable Foundation, C.
John and Reva
Mills Foundation, Ralph E.
Millstone Foundation
Mitrani Family Foundation
Moore & Sons, B.C.
Moores Foundation, Harry C.
Morgan Foundation, Burton D.
Morgan Trust for Charity,
Religion, and Education
Morgenstern Foundation, Morris
Morris Charitable Foundation, E.
A.
Morris Foundation, Norman M.
Moskowitz Foundation, Irving I.
Mostyn Foundation
Mullen Foundation, J. K.
Murdock Charitable Trust, M. J.
Murfee Endowment, Kathryn
Murphy Foundation, Dan
Murphy Foundation, Katherine
and John
Musson Charitable Foundation,
R. C. and Katharine M.
National City Bank of Evansville
National Machinery Co.
Nelco Sewing Machine Sales
Corp.
New York Life Insurance Co.
Newhouse Foundation, Samuel I.
Newman Charitable Trust,
Calvin M. and Raquel H.
Norcliffe Fund
Norwest Bank Nebraska
N've Shalom Foundation
Occidental Petroleum Corp.
O'Connor Foundation, Kathryn
Ohio Savings Bank
Ohrstrom Foundation
Old National Bank in Evansville
Olive Bridge Fund
Olsson Memorial Foundation,
Elis
O'Neill Charitable Corporation,
F. J.
O'Neill Foundation, William J.
and Dorothy K.
Orscheln Co.
Osher Foundation, Bernard
O'Toole Foundation, Theresa
and Edward
Overseas Shipholding Group
Overstreet Foundation
Pacific Western Foundation
Palmer Fund, Francis Asbury
Parnes Foundation, E. H.
Parsons - W.D. Charities, Vera
Davis
Paulstan
Paulucci Family Foundation
Pendergast-Weyer Foundation
Pennington Foundation, Irene W.
and C. B.
Perkins Memorial Foundation,
George W.
Perpetual Benevolent Fund
Pew Charitable Trusts
Phillips Family Foundation, Jay
and Rose
Phillips Foundation, Ellis L.
Phillips-Van Heusen Corp.
Pillsbury Foundation
Pine Tree Foundation
Piper Foundation, Minnie
Stevens
Pitts Foundation, William H. and
Lula E.
Pittulloch Foundation
Premier Dental Products Co.

Price Foundation, Louis and
Harold
Price Foundation, Lucien B. and
Katherine E.
Procter & Gamble Cosmetic &
Fragrance Products
Proctor Trust, Mortimer R.
Propp Sons Fund, Morris and
Anna
Pyramid Foundation
Quabaug Corp.
Quinlan Foundation, Elizabeth C.
Radiator Specialty Co.
Ragan Charitable Foundation,
Carolyn King
Raker Foundation, M. E.
Raleigh Linen Service/National
Distributing Co.
Rapp Foundation, Robert Glenn
Raskob Foundation for Catholic
Activities
Ratner Foundation, Milton M.
Reily & Co., William B.
Relations Foundation
Replogle Foundation, Luther I.
Republic New York Corp.
Resnick Foundation, Jack and
Pearl
Revlon
Richardson Benevolent
Foundation, C. E.
Richardson Fund, Mary Lynn
Roblee Foundation, Joseph H.
and Florence A.
Rockwell Fund
Rogers Charitable Trust, Florence
Rogers Foundation
Rosenbaum Foundation, Paul
and Gabriella
Rosenbaum Foundation, Paul
and Gabriella
Rosenbloom Foundation, Ben
and Esther
Rosenhaus Peace Foundation,
Sarah and Matthew
Rosenthal Foundation, Benjamin
J.
Rosenthal Foundation, Richard
and Hinda
Rosenthal Foundation, Samuel
Rotterman Trust, Helen L. and
Marie F.
RTM
Russell Memorial Foundation,
Robert
Saint Gerard Foundation
St. Mary's Catholic Foundation
Santa Maria Foundation
Sapirstein-Stone-Weiss
Foundation
Schautz Foundation, Walter L.
Scheuer Family Foundation, S.
H. and Helen R.
Schlieder Educational
Foundation, Edward G.
Schmitt Foundation, Arthur J.
Schneider Foundation Corp., Al
J.
Scholler Foundation
Schottenstein Foundation,
Jerome & Saul
Schowalter Foundation
Schust Foundation, Clarence L.
and Edith B.
Schwartz Foundation, David
Seabury Foundation
Seagram & Sons, Joseph E.
Seaver Charitable Trust, Richard
C.
Sequoia Foundation
Sexton Foundation
Seymour and Troester Foundation
Shapell Foundation, Nathan and
Lilly
Shapero Foundation, Nate S. and
Ruth B.
Shapiro Family Foundation,
Soretta and Henry

Religious Education (cont.)

Shapiro Foundation, Charles and M. R.
Share Foundation
Shattuck Charitable Trust, S. F.
Shea Foundation, Edmund and Mary
Shoemaker Fund, Thomas H. and Mary Williams
Siebert Lutheran Foundation
Simon Foundation, William E. and Carol G.
Simone Foundation
Simpson Foundation
Simpson Paper Co.
Sioux Steel Co.
Slant/Fin Corp.
Smith Charitable Trust
Smith Charities, John
Smith Family Foundation, Charles E.
Smith Foundation, Gordon V. and Helen C.
Snite Foundation, Fred B.
Snyder Foundation, Frost and Margaret
Snyder Foundation, Harold B. and Dorothy A.
Society for the Increase of the Ministry
Solheim Foundation
Solo Cup Co.
Solow Foundation
Sony Corp. of America
Sooner Pipe & Supply Corp.
Soref Foundation, Samuel M. Soref and Helene K.
Special People In Need
Speer Foundation, Roy M.
Sprague Educational and Charitable Foundation, Seth
Staley Foundation, Thomas F.
Stamps Foundation, James L.
Starr Foundation
Stauffer Communications
Stearns Trust, Artemas W.
Steinhardt Foundation, Judy and Michael
Steinman Foundation, John Frederick
Steinsapir Family Foundation, Julius L. and Libhie B.
Stephens Foundation Trust
Sterkel Trust, Justine
Stern Family Foundation, Harry
Stern Foundation, Max
Stern Memorial Trust, Sidney
Stewardship Foundation
Stonecutter Mills Corp.
Stowe, Jr. Foundation, Robert Lee
Strake Foundation
Stranahan Foundation
Stratford Foundation
Strawbridge Foundation of Pennsylvania I, Margaret Dorrance
Stuart Foundation, Elbridge and Evelyn
Sullivan Foundation, Ray H. and Pauline
Sumners Foundation, Hatton W.
Sutton Foundation
Swig Charity Foundation, Mae and Benjamin
Tandy Foundation, David L.
Taub Foundation, Henry and Marilyn
Taube Family Foundation
Taubman Foundation, Herman P. and Sophia
Taylor Foundation
Taylor Foundation, Ruth and Vernon
Teagle Foundation

Tell Foundation
Templeton Foundation, John
Terner Foundation
Tibstra Charitable Foundation, Thomas and Gertrude
Tippit Charitable Trust, C. Carlisle and Margaret M.
Tisch Foundation
Tozer Foundation
Trees Charitable Trust, Edith L.
Trull Foundation
Trust Co. Bank
Trust Funds
Tucker Foundation, Marcia Brady
21 International Holdings
Union Camp Corp.
United Service Foundation
U.S. Oil/Schmidt Family Foundation, Inc.
United Togs Inc.
Universal Leaf Tobacco Co.
Upton Foundation, Frederick S.
Valley Foundation, Wayne and Gladys
Van Andel Foundation, Jay and Betty
Van Huffel Foundation, I. J.
Vermeer Investment Company Foundation
Vermeer Manufacturing Co.
Vingo Trust II
Visciglia Foundation, Frank
Von der Ahe Foundation
Waggoner Foundation, E. Paul and Helen Buck
Wahlert Foundation
Wal-Mart Stores
Walker Foundation, W. E.
Ware Foundation
Warren and Beatrice W. Blanding Foundation, Riley J. and Lillian N.
Warwick Foundation
Washington Forrest Foundation
Washington Foundation
Wasserman Foundation, George
Wean Foundation, Raymond John
Webb Charitable Trust, Susan Mott
Wedum Foundation
Weezie Foundation
Wegener Foundation, Herman and Mary
Weiler Foundation
Weinberg, Jr. Foundation, Sidney J.
Weininger Foundation, Richard and Gertrude
Weisz Foundation, David and Sylvia
Wellons Foundation
Werner Foundation, Clara and Spencer
Westvaco Corp.
Wexner Foundation
Weyerhaeuser Foundation, Frederick and Margaret L.
Wharton Foundation
White Trust, G. R.
Wiegand Foundation, E. L.
Wilder Foundation
Wilf Family Foundation
Wilkof Foundation, Edward and Ruth
Willits Foundation
Wilsey Bennet Co.
Wolens Foundation, Kalman and Ida
Wolff Shoe Co.
Woltman Foundation, B. M.
Wood Charitable Trust, W. P.
Woods-Greer Foundation
Woodward Fund-Atlanta, David, Helen, Marian
Wouk Foundation, Abe
Wrape Family Charitable Trust
Wurzburg, Inc.
XTEK Inc.

Young Foundation, Irvin L.
Youth Foundation
Yulman Trust, Morton and Helen
Zacharia Foundation, Isaac Herman
Zachry Co., H. B.
Ziegler Foundation, Ruth/Allen
Zimmerman Foundation, Mary and George Herbert

Science/Technology Education

Abbott Laboratories
Abell Foundation, The
Abell-Hanger Foundation
Abney Foundation
Abroms Charitable Foundation
Acushnet Co.
Acushnet Co.
Adams Trust, Charles E. and Caroline J.
Advanced Micro Devices
Aerospace Corp.
Ahmanson Foundation
Air Products & Chemicals
Akzo America
Alabama Power Co.
Alcon Laboratories, Inc.
Alden Trust, George I.
Alexander Foundation, Joseph
Allegheny Ludlum Corp.
Allen Foundation, Rita
Alliant Techsystems
AlliedSignal
ALPAC Corp.
Alperin/Hirsch Family Foundation
Aluminum Co. of America
AMAX
American Cyanamid Co.
American Electric Power
American Fidelity Corp.
American Foundation Corporation
American Honda Motor Co.
American National Bank & Trust Co. of Chicago
American Natural Resources Co.
American Optical Corp.
American Telephone & Telegraph Co.
Ameritech Services
AMETEK
Amfac/JMB Hawaii
Amoco Corp.
AMP
AMR Corp.
Amsted Industries
Amsted Industries
Analog Devices
Andersen Corp.
Anheuser-Busch Cos.
AON Corp.
Apple Computer, Inc.
Appleton Papers
Archer-Daniels-Midland Co.
ARCO
Arell Foundation
Aristech Chemical Corp.
Arizona Public Service Co.
Arkansas Power & Light Co.
Arkell Hall Foundation
Arkwright Foundation
Armco Inc.
Armstrong World Industries Inc.
Arvin Industries
ASARCO
Asea Brown Boveri
Axe-Houghton Foundation
Badger Meter, Inc.
Baker Hughes Inc.
Ball Corp.
Baltimore Gas & Electric Co.
Banbury Fund
Bank of Boston Corp.
Bankers Trust Co.

Bannon Foundation
Barker Foundation
Barnes Group
Barra Foundation
Barth Foundation, Theodore H.
Battelle
Bauervic Foundation, Charles M.
Bauervic Foundation, Peggy
Bausch & Lomb
Baxter Foundation, Donald E. and Delia B.
Bay Foundation
Bechtel Group
Bechtel, Jr. Foundation, S. D.
Beckman Foundation, Leland D.
Becton Dickinson & Co.
Bedminster Fund
Beech Aircraft Corp.
Beinecke Foundation
Beldon Fund
Belk Stores
Bell Atlantic Corp.
Belz Foundation
Beneficia Foundation
Bennett Foundation, Carl and Dorothy
Besser Foundation
Bethlehem Steel Corp.
Betz Laboratories
BFGoodrich
Bireley Foundation
Block, H&R
Blount
Blum-Kovler Foundation
Boatmen's First National Bank of Oklahoma
Boehringer Mannheim Corp.
Boeing Co.
Booz Allen & Hamilton
Borden
Borg-Warner Corp.
Borman's
Bosch Corp., Robert
Boston Edison Co.
Bowles and Robert Bowles Memorial Fund, Ethel Wilson
Bowne Foundation, Robert
BP America
Brackenridge Foundation, George W.
Bradley-Turner Foundation
Bren Foundation, Donald L.
Brenner Foundation
Bridgestone/Firestone
Brown & Williamson Tobacco Corp.
Browning Charitable Foundation, Val A.
Brunswick Corp.
Buckley Trust, Thomas D.
Bucyrus-Erie
Buell Foundation, Temple Hoyne
Builder Marts of America
Bull HN Information Systems Inc.
Burlington Resources
Burndy Corp.
Burns Foundation, Fritz B.
Bush Charitable Foundation, Edyth
Bush Foundation
Butler Manufacturing Co.
Cabot Corp.
Cabot Family Charitable Trust
Cadence Design Systems
Caestecker Foundation, Charles and Marie
Cafritz Foundation, Morris and Gwendolyn
California Foundation for Biochemical Research
Campbell Soup Co.
Carnegie Corporation of New York
Carrier Corp.
Carter Foundation, Amon G.
Carver Charitable Trust, Roy J.

Cary Charitable Trust, Mary Flagler
Cascade Natural Gas Corp.
Central Hudson Gas & Electric Corp.
Central Maine Power Co.
Central National-Gottesman
Central & South West Services
Chapin-May Foundation of Illinois
Chase Manhattan Bank, N.A.
Chesapeake Corp.
Chevron Corp.
Chiles Foundation
Chrysler Corp.
CIBA-GEIGY Corp.
Ciba-Geigy Corp. (Pharmaceuticals Division)
Cincinnati Milacron
Citicorp
Clark Family Foundation, Emory T.
Cleveland-Cliffs
Clorox Co.
Close Foundation
Coca-Cola Co.
Cole Taylor Financial Group
Collins Foundation
Collins Foundation, Carr P.
Columbus Southern Power Co.
Community Coffee Co.
Connell Foundation, Michael J.
Conoco Inc.
Consolidated Natural Gas Co.
Consolidated Papers
Consumers Power Co.
Contraves USA
Cook Foundation, Loring
Cooper Industries
Coors Brewing Co.
Coors Foundation, Adolph
Corning Incorporated
County Bank
Cox Charitable Trust, Jessie B.
CPC International
Cranston Print Works
Cray Research
Cullen Foundation
Cullen/Frost Bankers
Cummins Engine Co.
Dan River, Inc.
Dana Corp.
DeCamp Foundation, Ira W.
Deere & Co.
DeKalb Genetics Corp.
Delany Charitable Trust, Beatrice P.
Delta Air Lines
DeSoto
Detroit Edison Co.
DeVlieg Foundation, Charles
Dewar Foundation
Dibner Fund
Digital Equipment Corp.
Dodge Foundation, Geraldine R.
Donaldson Co.
Dorr Foundation
Dow Chemical Co.
Dow Corning Corp.
Dow Foundation, Herbert H. and Barbara C.
Dow Foundation, Herbert H. and Grace A.
Dresser Industries
Dreyfus Foundation, Max and Victoria
du Pont de Nemours & Co., E. I.
Duke Endowment
Duke Power Co.
Duncan Trust, John G.
Durfee Foundation
Eastman Kodak Co.
Eaton Corp.
Edgerton Foundation, Harold E.
Edison Fund, Charles
Edmonds Foundation, Dean S.

Educational Foundation of
America
EG&G Inc.
Elf Atochem North America
Ellsworth Foundation, Ruth H.
and Warren A.
Emerson Electric Co.
English-Bonter-Mitchell
Foundation
English Memorial Fund,
Florence C. and H. L.
Enron Corp.
Equimark Corp.
Essick Foundation
Ethyl Corp.
Exxon Corp.
Fairchild Foundation, Sherman
Farallon Foundation
Federal-Mogul Corp.
Federated Department Stores and
Allied Stores Corp.
Fikes Foundation, Leland
First Fidelity Bancorporation
First Hawaiian
First Interstate Bank of Oregon
First Maryland Bancorp
First Mississippi Corp.
First National Bank & Trust Co.
of Rockford
First Union Corp.
Fischbach Foundation
Fish Foundation, Vain and Harry
Fleet Financial Group
Flickinger Memorial Trust
Florida Power & Light Co.
Fluor Corp.
Forbes
Ford Foundation
Ford Fund, Walter and Josephine
Ford Fund, William and Martha
Ford III Memorial Foundation,
Jefferson Lee
Ford Motor Co.
Foster-Davis Foundation
Fox Foundation, Richard J.
Foxmeyer Corp.
Francis Families Foundation
Frankel Foundation
Franklin Foundation, John and
Mary
Freeport-McMoRan
Freygang Foundation, Walter
Henry
Friendship Fund
Frueauff Foundation, Charles A.
Fry Foundation, Lloyd A.
Fuller Foundation, George F. and
Sybil H.
Funderburke & Associates
Fusenot Charity Foundation,
Georges and Germaine
Galvin Foundation, Robert W.
Gannett Publishing Co., Guy
Garvey Memorial Foundation,
Edward Chase
GEICO Corp.
Genentech
General Electric Co.
General Mills
General Motors Corp.
GenRad
George Foundation
Georgia-Pacific Corp.
Georgia Power Co.
Gerber Products Co.
Getty Foundation, Ann and
Gordon
Gilmore Foundation, William G.
Glanville Family Foundation
Glaxo
Glenn Foundation for Medical
Research, Paul F.
Goldberg Family Foundation,
Israel and Matilda
Golden Family Foundation
Goldenberg Foundation, Max
Golub Corp.

Good Samaritan
Goodyear Tire & Rubber Co.
Gould Inc.
Grace & Co., W.R.
Graphic Arts Show Co. Inc.
Grass Foundation
Grassmann Trust, E. J.
Grede Foundries
Greenwall Foundation
Grimes Foundation
GTE Corp.
Gudelsky Family Foundation,
Isadore and Bertha
Gulfstream Aerospace Corp.
Gulton Foundation
Hall Family Foundations
Halliburton Co.
Hamilton Oil Corp.
Handy & Harman
Hankamer Foundation, Curtis
and Doris K.
Hansen Foundation, Dane G.
Harrington Foundation, Francis
A. and Jacquelyn H.
Harris Family Foundation, Hunt
and Diane
Harris Foundation, H. H.
Harsco Corp.
Hartmarx Corp.
Haynes Foundation
Hearst Foundation
Hearst Foundation, William
Randolph
Hecla Mining Co.
Hedco Foundation
Heileman Brewing Co., Inc., G.
Heinz Co., H.J.
Heinz Endowment, Vira I.
Herrick Foundation
Hershey Foods Corp.
Hess Foundation
Hewlett-Packard Co.
Hill-Snowdon Foundation
Hillcrest Foundation
Himmelfarb Foundation, Paul
and Annetta
Hitachi
Hoche-Scofield Foundation
Hoechst Celanese Corp.
Hoffmann-La Roche
Hofheinz Foundation, Irene
Cafcalas
Holt Foundation, William Knox
Honeywell
Hooper Foundation, Elizabeth S.
Hoover Foundation
Hughes Medical Institute,
Howard
Humane Society of the
Commonwealth of
Massachusetts
Humphrey Foundation, Glenn &
Gertrude
Hyde Manufacturing Co.
IBM Corp.
ICI Americas
Illinois Bell
Illinois Power Co.
Illinois Tool Works
IMCERA Group Inc.
Inco Alloys International
Indiana Bell Telephone Co.
Indiana Gas and Chemical Corp.
Inland Container Corp.
Inland Steel Industries
Intel Corp.
Interco
International Paper Co.
International Student Exchange
Cards
Irwin Charity Foundation,
William G.
Ishiyama Foundation
ITT Corp.
ITT Hartford Insurance Group
ITT Rayonier
Jackson Hole Preserve

Jacobs Engineering Group
Jaqua Foundation
Jeffress Memorial Trust, Thomas
F. and Kate Miller
JELD-WEN, Inc.
Jennings Foundation, Martha
Holden
Jephson Educational Trust No. 1
John Hancock Mutual Life
Insurance Co.
Johnson Co., E. F.
Johnson Controls
Johnson Foundation, Walter S.
Johnson & Higgins
Johnson & Son, S.C.
Johnston Trust for Charitable
and Educational Purposes,
James M.
Jones Foundation, Daisy Marquis
Jones Foundation, Helen
Jurzykowski Foundation, Alfred
Kade Foundation, Max
Kaiser Cement Corp.
Kapor Family Foundation
Keck Foundation, W. M.
Kellogg Foundation, W. K.
Kennecott Corp.
Kerr Foundation
Kerr Foundation, Robert S. and
Grayce B.
Kerr Fund, Grayce B.
Kerr-McGee Corp.
Killam Trust, Constance
Kimball Co., Miles
Kimberly-Clark Corp.
Kingsbury Corp.
Kingsley Foundation, Lewis A.
Kiplinger Foundation
Kirchgessner Foundation, Karl
Klingler Foundation, Helen and
Charles
Knudsen Foundation, Tom and
Valley
Koch Charitable Trust, David H.
Kresge Foundation
Krieble Foundation, Vernon K.
Kuhne Foundation Trust, Charles
Kunstadter Family Foundation,
Albert
Kyocera International Inc.
Ladish Co.
Lafarge Corp.
Lakeside Foundation
Lalor Foundation
Leesona Corp.
Lemberg Foundation
Lennox International, Inc.
Leo Burnett Co.
Levinson Foundation, Max and
Anna
Leviton Manufacturing Co.
Life Insurance Co. of Georgia
Lightner Sams Foundation
Lilly & Co., Eli
Link Foundation
Lipton, Thomas J.
List Foundation, Albert A.
Little, Arthur D.
Littlefield Foundation, Edmund
Wattis
Litton Industries
Litton/Itek Optical Systems
Livingston Memorial Foundation
Lockheed Corp.
Loeb Partners Corp.
Long Island Lighting Co.
Louisiana Land & Exploration
Co.
Louisiana-Pacific Corp.
Louisiana Power & Light
Co./New Orleans Public
Service
Lounsbery Foundation, Richard
Lowell Institute, Trustees of the
LTV Corp.
Lubrizol Corp.
Ludwick Institute

Lurcy Charitable and
Educational Trust, Georges
Lyons Foundation
Lytel Foundation, Bertha Russ
M/A-COM, Inc.
Magma Copper Co.
Mallinckrodt Specialty
Chemicals Co.
Manville Corp.
Margoes Foundation
Marion Merrell Dow
Mark IV Industries
Martin Marietta Corp.
Marubeni America Corp.
Massey Foundation
Maxus Energy Corp.
May Department Stores Co.
Mayborn Foundation, Frank W.
Maytag Family Foundation, Fred
McAlister Charitable
Foundation, Harold
McBeath Foundation, Faye
McCormick & Co.
McDonnell Douglas Corp.
McDonnell Foundation, James S.
McElroy Trust, R. J.
McFawn Trust No. 2, Lois Sisler
McGonagle Foundation, Dextra
Baldwin
McGraw Foundation
McGregor Fund
MCI Communications Corp.
McKee Foundation, Robert E.
and Evelyn
McKenna Foundation, Philip M.
McLean Contributionship
Mead Corp.
Mead Foundation, Giles W. and
Elise G.
Medina Foundation
Medtronic
Mellon Bank Corp.
Mellon Foundation, Andrew W.
Mercantile Bancorp
Merck & Co.
Merck Family Fund
Merck Human Health Division
Metallgesellschaft Corp.
Metropolitan Life Insurance Co.
Mettler Instrument Corp.
Meyer Foundation, Eugene and
Agnes E.
Meyer Memorial Trust
Michael Foundation, Herbert I.
and Elsa B.
Michigan Bell Telephone Co.
Michigan Gas Utilities
Miles Inc.
Miller Foundation, Earl B. and
Loraine H.
Miller Memorial Trust, George
Lee
Milliken & Co.
Millipore Corp.
Mills Fund, Frances Goll
Mine Safety Appliances Co.
Minnesota Mutual Life
Insurance Co.
Mitchell Energy & Development
Corp.
Mitsubishi Electric America
Mobil Oil Corp.
Monsanto Co.
Moore Family Foundation
Moorman Manufacturing Co.
Motorola
MTS Systems Corp.
Munger Foundation, Alfred C.
Murdock Charitable Trust, M. J.
Murphy Foundation
Murphy Foundation, Dan
Nalco Chemical Co.
Nason Foundation
National Computer Systems
National Presto Industries
National Westminster Bank New
Jersey

NationsBank Corp.
NBD Bank
NEC Technologies, Inc.
NEC USA
New England Biolabs Foundation
New England Telephone Co.
New York Mercantile Exchange
New York Times Co.
The New Yorker Magazine, Inc.
Newmont Mining Corp.
Noble Foundation, Samuel
Roberts
Nordson Corp.
Northeast Utilities
Northern Indiana Public Service
Co.
Norton Co.
NYNEX Corp.
Occidental Petroleum Corp.
Oglebay Norton Co.
Ohio Bell Telephone Co.
Ohrstrom Foundation
Oklahoman Foundation
Olin Corp.
Orchard Foundation
Osher Foundation, Bernard
Oxford Industries, Inc.
PACCAR
Pacific Gas & Electric Co.
Pacific Telesis Group
PacifiCorp
Packaging Corporation of
America
Packard Foundation, David and
Lucile
Packer Foundation, Horace B.
Panhandle Eastern Corp.
Pappas Charitable Foundation,
Thomas Anthony
Parke-Davis Group
Parsons Foundation, Ralph M.
Pasadena Area Residential Aid
Pauley Foundation, Edwin W.
Peabody Foundation, Amelia
Pella Corp.
Penn Foundation, William
Pennzoil Co.
Penzance Foundation
Peppers Foundation, Ann
Perkin-Elmer Corp.
Peters Foundation, R. D. and
Linda
Pfeiffer Research Foundation,
Gustavus and Louise
Pfizer
Phelps Dodge Corp.
Phillips Petroleum Co.
Pick, Jr. Fund, Albert
Pierce Charitable Trust, Harold
Whitworth
Pioneer Hi-Bred International
Pitney Bowes
Pittway Corp.
Plitt Southern Theatres
Polaroid Corp.
Poole & Kent Co.
Portland General Electric Co.
Potomac Electric Power Co.
Pott Foundation, Herman T. and
Phenie R.
Pott Foundation, Robert and
Elaine
Potts Memorial Foundation
Powell Foundation, Charles Lee
PPG Industries
Premier Industrial Corp.
Preuss Foundation
Principal Financial Group
Procter & Gamble Cosmetic &
Fragrance Products
Promus Cos.
Providence Energy Corp.
Provident Life & Accident
Insurance Co.
Public Service Co. of Colorado
Public Service Electric & Gas
Co.

Science/Technology Education (cont.)

Pulitzer Publishing Co.
Quabaug Corp.
Quaker Oats Co.
Ralston Purina Co.
Raytheon Co.
Reliance Electric Co.
Revlon
Revson Foundation, Charles H.
Reynolds Metals Co.
RGK Foundation
Rice Foundation
Ricoh Electronics Inc.
Riggs Benevolent Fund
Rigler-Deutsch Foundation
River Branch Foundation
River Road Charitable
    Corporation
RJR Nabisco Inc.
Robinson Foundation
Rochester Telephone Corp.
Rockefeller Foundation
Rockefeller Foundation,
    Winthrop
Rockwell International Corp.
Rodgers Trust, Elizabeth Killam
Rodman Foundation
Rohm and Haas Company
Rolfs Foundation, Robert T.
Roseburg Forest Products Co.
Rosenstiel Foundation
Ross Foundation
Rubin Foundation, Samuel
Rubinstein Foundation, Helena
Russell Educational Foundation,
    Benjamin and Roberta
San Diego Gas & Electric
Sandoz Corp.
Sandusky International Inc.
Santa Fe Pacific Corp.
Scaife Family Foundation
Schautz Foundation, Walter L.
Schering-Plough Corp.
Schlieder Educational
    Foundation, Edward G.
Schlinger Foundation
Scholl Foundation, Dr.
Schott Foundation
Schrafft and Bertha E. Schrafft
    Charitable Trust, William E.
Science Applications
    International Corp.
Scott Foundation, William R.,
    John G., and Emma
Scrivner, Inc.
Searle & Co., G.D.
Sedgwick James Inc.
Sega of America
Selby and Marie Selby
    Foundation, William G.
Self Foundation
Shea Foundation, Edmund and
    Mary
Shell Oil Co.
Shelton Cos.
Sifco Industries Inc.
Simmons Family Foundation, R.
    P.
Simpson Investment Co.
Slant/Fin Corp.
Sloan Foundation, Alfred P.
SNET
Snyder Foundation, Harold B.
    and Dorothy A.
Sonat
Sonoco Products Co.
Sony Corp. of America
South Carolina Electric & Gas
    Co.
Southern California Edison Co.
Southern California Gas Co.
Southwestern Bell Corp.
Speas Foundation, Victor E.
Sprint

SPX Corp.
Stanley Works
Starr Foundation
Starrett Co., L.S.
State Street Bank & Trust Co.
Statler Foundation
Stauffer Charitable Trust, John
Sterling Winthrop
Stern Memorial Trust, Sidney
Stoddard Charitable Trust
Stone Container Corp.
Storage Technology Corp.
Stratford Foundation
Stuart Foundation, Edward C.
Sudix Foundation
Sun Co.
Sussman Fund, Edna Bailey
Sylvester Foundation, Harcourt
    M. and Virginia W.
Syntex Corp.
Tandem Computers
Tang Foundation
Taylor Foundation, Ruth and
    Vernon
Teagle Foundation
Technical Foundation of America
Technical Training Foundation
Tektronix
Teledyne
Tenneco
Texaco
Texas Instruments
Textron
Thermo Electron Corp.
Thomas & Betts Corp.
Thornton Foundation
3M Co.
Times Mirror Co.
Toshiba America, Inc.
Towsley Foundation, Harry A.
    and Margaret D.
Toyota Motor Sales, U.S.A.
Tracor, Inc.
Transco Energy Company
Trinity Foundation
Tropicana Products, Inc.
Trust Co. Bank
TRW Corp.
Tyson Foods, Inc.
Unilever United States
Union Camp Corp.
Union Carbide Corp.
Union Electric Co.
Unisys Corp.
United Airlines
United States Sugar Corp.
United Technologies Corp.
United Togs Inc.
Universal Foods Corp.
Unocal Corp.
Upjohn Co.
US WEST
USX Corp.
Van Evera Foundation, Dewitt
    Caroline
Varian Associates
Vetlesen Foundation, G. Unger
Vulcan Materials Co.
Wagner Foundation, Ltd., R. H.
Wal-Mart Stores
Walker Foundation, L. C. and
    Margaret
Disney Co., Walt
Warner Electric Brake & Clutch
    Co.
Warner-Lambert Co.
Waste Management
Wean Foundation, Raymond John
Weaver Foundation
Webb Educational and
    Charitable Trust, Torrey H.
    and Dorothy K.
Webb Foundation, Del E.
Webster Foundation, Edwin S.
Wedum Foundation
Wehr Foundation, Todd
Weiler Foundation

Weiss Foundation, William E.
Welch Foundation, Robert A.
West Foundation, Neva and
    Wesley
West Texas Corp., J. M.
Westinghouse Electric Corp.
Westvaco Corp.
Weyerhaeuser Co.
Wheeler Foundation
Wheelwright Scientific School
Wheless Foundation
Whirlpool Corp.
Whitaker Foundation
White Construction Co.
Whittier Foundation, L. K.
Wilcox General Trust, George N.
Williams Cos.
Wilson Foundation, Marie C.
    and Joseph C.
Wilson Fund, Matilda R.
Wisconsin Energy Corp.
Wolverine World Wide, Inc.
Wyomissing Foundation
Xerox Corp.
Young Foundation, R. A.

Social Sciences Education

Ahmanson Foundation
AlliedSignal
American Express Co.
American National Bank & Trust
    Co. of Chicago
Ameritech Services
Apple Computer, Inc.
Atran Foundation
Block, H&R
Bovaird Foundation, Mervin
Bradley Foundation, Lynde and
    Harry
Central Bank of the South
Central Maine Power Co.
Coca-Cola Co.
Cowles Charitable Trust
du Pont de Nemours & Co., E. I.
Duke Power Co.
Durell Foundation, George
    Edward
Educational Foundation of
    America
Ehrman Foundation, Fred and
    Susan
Exxon Corp.
First Union Corp.
Ford Foundation
Foundation for Child
    Development
Frank Foundation, Ernest and
    Elfriede
Funderburke & Associates
Garvey Kansas Foundation
Goldberg Family Foundation
Golden Family Foundation
Green Fund
Haynes Foundation, John
    Randolph and Dora
Henry Foundation, Patrick
Indiana Bell Telephone Co.
International Student Exchange
    Cards
Ittleson Foundation
JFM Foundation
Johnson Foundation, Walter S.
Johnson & Higgins
Kellogg Foundation, W. K.
Kenworthy - Sarah H. Swift
    Foundation, Marion E.
Koch Charitable Trust, David H.
Lance, Inc.
LBJ Family Foundation
Levinson Foundation, Morris L.
Long Island Lighting Co.
Luce Foundation, Henry
Macy & Co., R.H.
Martin Marietta Corp.
Model Foundation, Leo

Nalco Chemical Co.
Nordson Corp.
Olin Foundation, John M.
People's Bank
Pittway Corp.
Red Wing Shoe Co.
Reynolds Foundation,
    Christopher
Rhoden Charitable Foundation,
    Elmer C.
Richardson Foundation, Smith
Sage Foundation, Russell
Salvatori Foundation, Henry
Santa Fe Pacific Corp.
Schapiro Fund, M. A.
Schiff Foundation, Dorothy
Sedgwick James Inc.
Shawmut National Corp.
Sloan Foundation, Alfred P.
Sumners Foundation, Hatton W.
Sunmark Capital Corp.
Tamko Asphalt Products
Texaco
Town Creek Foundation
Union Camp Corp.
Unocal Corp.
Whirlpool Corp.
Wiener Foundation, Malcolm
    Hewitt
Winston Foundation, Norman
    and Rosita
Wisconsin Energy Corp.
Zellerbach Family Fund

Special Education

Achelis Foundation
Acushnet Co.
AFLAC
Akzo America
Alden Trust, John W.
ALPAC Corp.
Altman Foundation
AMCORE Bank, N.A. Rockford
American Brands
American National Bank & Trust
    Co. of Chicago
American Saw & Manufacturing
    Co.
Ameritech Services
Amfac/JMB Hawaii
Amoco Corp.
Andersen Corp.
Anderson Foundation, Hugh J.
Anderson Foundation, M. D.
Anheuser-Busch Cos.
Apple Computer, Inc.
Appleby Trust, Scott B. and
    Annie P.
Arakelian Foundation, Mary
    Alice
Armbrust Chain Co.
Atherton Family Foundation
Atlanta Gas Light Co.
Avon Products
Bacardi Imports
Baker Foundation, R. C.
Ball Brothers Foundation
Baltimore Gas & Electric Co.
Bedsole Foundation, J. L.
Berger Foundation, H.N. and
    Frances C.
Beveridge Foundation, Frank
    Stanley
Bingham Foundation, William
Binney & Smith Inc.
Block, H&R
Blue Cross & Blue Shield of
    Kentucky Foundation
Boeing Co.
Boise Cascade Corp.
Borden
Bothin Foundation
Bradley-Turner Foundation
Bridgestone/Firestone
Brown Foundation, James
    Graham
Buhl Foundation

Burns Foundation, Fritz B.
Cabot Corp.
Cafritz Foundation, Morris and
    Gwendolyn
Cameron Foundation, Harry S.
    and Isabel C.
Capital Holding Corp.
Carter Foundation, Amon G.
Carvel Foundation, Thomas and
    Agnes
Cascade Natural Gas Corp.
Casey Foundation, Eugene B.
Castle Foundation, Samuel N.
    and Mary
Central Bank of the South
Central National-Gottesman
Cessna Aircraft Co.
Chanin Family Foundation, Paul
    R.
Chase Manhattan Bank, N.A.
Chatlos Foundation
Cheney Foundation, Ben B.
Ciba-Geigy Corp.
    (Pharmaceuticals Division)
CIT Group Holdings
Citibank, F.S.B.
Citicorp
Clark-Winchcole Foundation
Clayton Fund
Clipper Ship Foundation
Clorox Co.
CM Alliance Cos.
CNG Transmission Corp.
Cockrell Foundation
Collins Foundation
Colonial Stores
Commerce Clearing House
Constantin Foundation
Cox Charitable Trust, Jessie B.
Cox Enterprises
Cox, Jr. Foundation, James M.
Creel Foundation
Cummings Memorial Fund
    Trust, Frances L. and Edwin L.
Curtice-Burns Foods
Dana Corp.
DeCamp Foundation, Ira W.
Dentsu, Inc., NY
Dodge Foundation, P. L.
Donaldson Co.
Dorr Foundation
Douty Foundation
Dreyfus Foundation, Max and
    Victoria
Duchossois Industries
Dula Educational and Charitable
    Foundation, Caleb C. and Julia
    W.
Dupar Foundation
Eccles Charitable Foundation,
    Willard L.
Edison Fund, Charles
Educational Foundation of
    America
Egenton Home
Emergency Aid of Pennsylvania
    Foundation
Equifax
Factor Family Foundation, Max
Fanwood Foundation
Farish Fund, William Stamps
Federated Department Stores and
    Allied Stores Corp.
Feild Co-Operative Association
Ferkauf Foundation, Eugene and
    Estelle
Finnegan Foundation, John D.
Firestone, Jr. Foundation, Harvey
First Interstate Bank of Oregon
First Maryland Bancorp
First Union Corp.
Fish Foundation, Ray C.
Ford Fund, Walter and Josephine
Forest Foundation
Forest Oil Corp.
Franklin Foundation, John and
    Mary

Freygang Foundation, Walter Henry
Frohring Foundation, William O. and Gertrude Lewis
Frueauff Foundation, Charles A.
Fry Foundation, Lloyd A.
Funderburke & Associates
Fusenot Charity Foundation, Georges and Germaine
Garvey Kansas Foundation
Gellert Foundation, Carl
General Mills
General Signal Corp.
GenRad
Georgia-Pacific Corp.
Giant Food
Globe Newspaper Co.
Gottesman Fund
Grace & Co., W.R.
Grainger Foundation
Grassmann Trust, E. J.
Green Fund
Gudelsky Family Foundation, Isadore and Bertha
Guttman Foundation, Stella and Charles
H.C.S. Foundation
Hallmark Cards
Hamman Foundation, George and Mary Josephine
Hardin Foundation, Phil
Harland Charitable Foundation, John and Wilhelmina D.
Hawn Foundation
Hayden Foundation, Charles
Hearst Foundation
Hearst Foundation, William Randolph
Heinz Co., H.J.
Hermann Foundation, Grover
Heydt Fund, Nan and Matilda
Hillcrest Foundation
Hillman Foundation
Hillman Foundation, Henry L.
Hoblitzelle Foundation
Hornblower Fund, Henry
Hubbard Broadcasting
Humana
Hyde and Watson Foundation
IBM Corp.
Inland Steel Industries
International Student Exchange Cards
Irvine Health Foundation
ITT Hartford Insurance Group
Jackson Hole Preserve
Jennings Foundation, Martha Holden
Jennings Foundation, Mary Hillman
John Hancock Mutual Life Insurance Co.
Johnson & Higgins
Johnson & Son, S.C.
Johnston Trust for Charitable and Educational Purposes, James M.
Julia R. and Estelle L. Foundation
Kellogg Foundation, W. K.
Kemper Foundation, Enid and Crosby
Kennecott Corp.
Kennedy, Jr. Foundation, Joseph P.
Kidder, Peabody & Co.
Kiewit Foundation, Peter
Kilworth Charitable Foundation, Florence B.
Kinney-Lindstrom Foundation
Kirby Foundation, F. M.
Kirchgessner Foundation, Karl
Knapp Foundation
Knott Foundation, Marion I. and Henry J.
Kohl Charities, Herbert H.
Kulas Foundation
Lawrence Foundation, Alice

Leavey Foundation, Thomas and Dorothy
Legg Mason Inc.
Lewis Foundation, Frank J.
Lightner Sams Foundation
Lindsay Trust, Agnes M.
Link, Jr. Foundation, George
Linn-Henley Charitable Trust
Little, Arthur D.
Littlefield Memorial Trust, Ida Ballou
Long Foundation, George A. and Grace
Long Island Lighting Co.
Loughran Foundation, Mary and Daniel
Lounsbery Foundation, Richard
Lowe Foundation, Joe and Emily
Lowenstein Foundation, Leon
Lund Foundation
Lydall, Inc.
Macy & Co., R.H.
Mardag Foundation
Marpat Foundation
Martin Marietta Corp.
Massachusetts Charitable Mechanics Association
Massey Charitable Trust
Mattel
Maxus Energy Corp.
Mazza Foundation
McBeath Foundation, Faye
McBride & Son Associates
McCasland Foundation
McCormick Tribune Foundation, Robert R.
McCune Charitable Trust, John R.
McCune Foundation
McDonald Foundation, J. M.
McDonald's Corp.
McGraw Foundation
McInerny Foundation
McMahon Foundation
Mead Corp.
Medina Foundation
Mellon Bank Corp.
Mellon Foundation, Richard King
Memorial Foundation for the Blind
Merrick Foundation, Robert G. and Anne M.
Mitsubishi Electric America
Mobil Oil Corp.
Murdock Charitable Trust, M. J.
Murphy Foundation, Katherine and John
Nalco Chemical Co.
Nashua Trust Co.
National Computer Systems
New England Mutual Life Insurance Co.
New-Land Foundation
New York Telephone Co.
New York Times Co.
The New Yorker Magazine, Inc.
Newhouse Foundation, Samuel I.
News & Observer Publishing Co.
Oaklawn Foundation
Oberkotter Family Foundation
Oceanic Cablevision Foundation
O'Neill Charitable Corporation, F. J.
Ordean Foundation
Owen Trust, B. B.
Packaging Corporation of America
Palisano Foundation, Vincent and Harriet
Pappas Charitable Foundation, Bessie
Parsons Foundation, Ralph M.
Peabody Foundation
Peabody Foundation, Amelia
Phillips Petroleum Co.
Pinkerton Foundation
Polaroid Corp.

Polk Foundation
Powell Family Foundation
Pritzker Foundation
Prudential Insurance Co. of America
Randleigh Foundation Trust
Raskob Foundation for Catholic Activities
Reynolds Charitable Trust, Kate B.
Reynolds Foundation, Richard S.
Riley Foundation, Mabel Louise
Rockwell Fund
Rockwell International Corp.
Rohm and Haas Company
Rowland Foundation
Sage Foundation
Santa Fe Pacific Corp.
Schlumberger Ltd.
Schmidlapp Trust No. 1, Jacob G.
Scholl Foundation, Dr.
Schwartz Foundation, Arnold A.
Scott Foundation, Walter
Scroggins Foundation, Arthur E. and Cornelia C.
Seabury Foundation
Seafirst Corp.
Sedgwick James Inc.
Shenandoah Life Insurance Co.
Signet Bank/Maryland
Simon Foundation, William E. and Carol G.
Skinner Corp.
Smith Foundation, Kelvin and Eleanor
Sosland Foundation
Southern California Edison Co.
Southwestern Bell Corp.
Spang & Co.
Sprague Educational and Charitable Foundation, Seth
Star Bank, N.A.
Starr Foundation
Steele Foundation, Harry and Grace
Steinbach Fund, Ruth and Milton
Stewart Trust under the will of Helen S. Devore, Alexander and Margaret
Strake Foundation
Stulsaft Foundation, Morris
Sunnen Foundation
Swalm Foundation
Temple Foundation, T. L. L.
Teubert Charitable Trust, James H. and Alice
Texaco
3M Co.
Todd Co., A.M.
Trexler Trust, Harry C.
Trust Co. Bank
Turrell Fund
Union Bank of Switzerland Los Angeles Branch
Union Camp Corp.
Uris Brothers Foundation
van Ameringen Foundation
Victoria Foundation
Vulcan Materials Co.
Wal-Mart Stores
Webb Charitable Trust, Susan Mott
Weingart Foundation
Weisbrod Foundation Trust Dept., Robert and Mary
Wendt Foundation, Margaret L.
Whitehead Foundation, Joseph B.
Wilson Fund, Matilda R.
Wyomissing Foundation
Xerox Corp.

Student Aid

Abell Foundation, The
Abell-Hanger Foundation
Abercrombie Foundation
Acme-McCrary Corp.
Acushnet Co.

Adams Foundation, Arthur F. and Alice E.
AGFA Division of Miles Inc.
Ahmanson Foundation
Akzo Chemicals Inc.
Alco Standard Corp.
Alden Trust, George I.
Allendale Mutual Insurance Co.
Alliant Techsystems
Alliss Educational Foundation, Charles and Ellora
Alltel/Western Region
ALPAC Corp.
Altman Foundation
Aluminum Co. of America
AMAX
American Cyanamid Co.
American General Finance
American Natural Resources Co.
American Standard
AMETEK
Amfac/JMB Hawaii
Amoco Corp.
Andersen Corp.
Appleton Papers
Archer-Daniels-Midland Co.
ARCO Chemical
Arkansas Power & Light Co.
Armco Inc.
Armstrong World Industries Inc.
Atherton Family Foundation
Atkinson Foundation
Atkinson Foundation, Myrtle L.
Auerbach Foundation, Beatrice Fox
Avon Products
Badger Meter, Inc.
Baker Trust, George F.
Balfour Foundation, L. G.
Banbury Fund
Banfi Vintners
Bank of Boston Corp.
Bank One, Texas-Houston Office
BankAmerica Corp.
Barclays Bank of New York
Barden Corp.
Barden Corp.
Barnes Group
Bashinsky Foundation
Bauer Foundation, M. R.
Baughman Foundation
Baumberger Endowment
Baxter International
Bechtel Group
Bedsole Foundation, J. L.
Beech Aircraft Corp.
Belding Heminway Co.
Bemis Company
Beneficial Corp.
Benefit Trust Life Insurance Co.
Bennett Scholarship Fund, Margaret A. and Lawrence J.
Berger Foundation, H.N. and Frances C.
BFGoodrich
Bibb Co.
Binney & Smith Inc.
Blandin Foundation
Blount
Blue Bell, Inc.
Blue Cross and Blue Shield of Minnesota Foundation Inc.
Blue Cross & Blue Shield of Alabama
Blue Cross & Blue Shield of Kentucky Foundation
Blum-Kovler Foundation
Boeing Co.
Boettcher Foundation
Borden
Bosch Corp., Robert
Boswell Foundation, James G.
Bovaird Foundation, Mervin
Bradley Foundation, Lynde and Harry
Bridgestone/Firestone

Brown & Williamson Tobacco Corp.
Bryan Family Foundation, Kathleen Price and Joseph M.
Bucyrus-Erie
Burger King Corp.
Butler Foundation, Alice
Cablevision of Michigan
Cabot Corp.
Cafritz Foundation, Morris and Gwendolyn
Cain Foundation, Effie and Wofford
Calder Foundation, Louis
Callaway Foundation, Fuller E.
Capital Cities/ABC
Cargill
Carter-Wallace
Carver Charitable Trust, Roy J.
Caterpillar
Ceco Corp.
CENEX
Central Bank of the South
Central Maine Power Co.
Central National-Gottesman
Central Soya Co.
Chapman Charitable Corporation, Howard and Bess
Cheney Foundation, Ben B.
Chesapeake Corp.
Chevron Corp.
Chubb Corp.
Circuit City Stores
CIT Group Holdings
Citizens Bank
Clemens Foundation
CM Alliance Cos.
CNG Transmission Corp.
Coca-Cola Co.
Cockrell Foundation
Coleman Co.
Colonial Life & Accident Insurance Co.
Cone-Blanchard Machine Co.
Cone Mills Corp.
Connelly Foundation
Consolidated Freightways
Continental Can Co.
Continental Corp.
Cook, Sr. Charitable Foundation, Kelly Gene
Cooper Industries
Country Curtains, Inc.
Cox, Jr. Foundation, James M.
CPC International
Cray Research
Creel Foundation
Crowell Trust, Henry P. and Susan C.
Crown Central Petroleum Corp.
Crum and Forster
CTS Corp.
CUNA Mutual Insurance Group
Dana Foundation, Charles A.
Danis Industries
Dart Group Corp.
DeCamp Foundation, Ira W.
Deloitte & Touche
Detroit Edison Co.
Deuble Foundation, George H.
DeVlieg Foundation, Charles
Dibner Fund
Dixie Yarns, Inc.
Dodge Foundation, Geraldine R.
Donaldson Co.
Donovan, Leisure, Newton & Irvine
Dougherty Foundation
Dougherty, Jr. Foundation, James R.
Dow Chemical Co.
Doyle Dane Bernback Group
Dresser Industries
Dreyfus Foundation, Max and Victoria
Drown Foundation, Joseph
du Bois Foundation, E. Blois

Student Aid (cont.)

du Pont de Nemours & Co., E. I.
Duchossois Industries
Duke Endowment
Duke Power Co.
Dunagan Foundation
Eaton Corp.
Educational Foundation of
America
Egenton Home
Ehrman Foundation, Fred and
Susan
El Pomar Foundation
Elgin Sweeper Co.
Ellis Grant and Scholarship
Fund, Charles E.
Ellison Foundation
Emerson Electric Co.
Emerson Foundation, Fred L.
Engelhard Foundation, Charles
English-Bonter-Mitchell
Foundation
Ensign-Bickford Industries
Equitable Life Assurance Society
of the U.S.
Ernst & Young
Erteszek Foundation
Erving Paper Mills
Factor Family Foundation, Max
Fairchild Foundation, Sherman
Federated Department Stores and
Allied Stores Corp.
Feil Foundation, Louis and
Gertrude
Fellner Memorial Foundation,
Leopold and Clara M.
Fig Tree Foundation
Firestone Foundation, Roger S.
First Interstate Bank of Oregon
First Interstate Bank of Texas,
N.A.
First Maryland Bancorp
First Mississippi Corp.
FirsTier Bank N.A. Omaha
Fish Foundation, Ray C.
Fish Foundation, Vain and Harry
Fleet Financial Group
Florida Power & Light Co.
Fohs Foundation
Forbes Charitable Trust, Herman
Ford Foundation, Edward E.
Ford Fund, Walter and Josephine
Franklin Charitable Trust, Ershel
Franklin Foundation, John and
Mary
Freedom Forum
Froderman Foundation
Frohring Foundation, William O.
and Gertrude Lewis
Fry Foundation, Lloyd A.
Fuchs Foundation, Gottfried &
Mary
Funderburke & Associates
Galkin Charitable Trust, Ira S.
and Anna
Gallagher Family Foundation,
Lewis P.
General American Life Insurance
Co.
General Educational Fund
General Electric Co.
General Mills
General Motors Corp.
George Foundation
Georgia-Pacific Corp.
Gheens Foundation
Giant Eagle
Giant Food Stores
Gibson Foundation, Addison H.
Gillespie Memorial Fund,
Boynton
Gilmore Foundation, Irving S.
Gleason Memorial Fund
Glenmore Distilleries Co.
Glosser Foundation, David A.
Goldman Foundation, Herman

Golub Corp.
Good Samaritan
Goodman Family Foundation
Goodyear Tire & Rubber Co.
Gordon Foundation, Meyer and
Ida
Gradison & Co.
Grassmann Trust, E. J.
Great-West Life Assurance Co.
Great Western Financial Corp.
Greater Lansing Foundation
Green Industries, A. P.
Griggs and Mary Griggs Burke
Foundation, Mary Livingston
Groves & Sons Co., S.J.
Haggar Foundation
Hamman Foundation, George
and Mary Josephine
Hancock Foundation, Luke B.
Handleman Co.
Hansen Foundation, Dane G.
Hardin Foundation, Phil
Harriman Foundation, Mary W.
Harris Foundation, James J. and
Angelia M.
Haskell Fund
Hastings Trust
Hatch Charitable Trust, Margaret
Milliken
Haynes Foundation, John
Randolph and Dora
Hechinger Co.
Heckscher Foundation for
Children
Heileman Brewing Co., Inc., G.
Heinz Co., H.J.
Heinz Endowment, Vira I.
Hermann Foundation, Grover
Herrick Foundation
Herzog Foundation, Carl J.
Hess Foundation
Hexcel Corp.
Hodge Foundation
Hoffman Foundation,
Maximillian E. and Marion O.
Holt Foundation, William Knox
HON Industries
Honda of America
Manufacturing, Inc.
Hook Drug
Hospital Corp. of America
Houston Endowment
Hoyt Foundation
Hubbard Foundation, R. Dee and
Joan Dale
Hubbard Milling Co.
Hubbell Inc.
Huffy Corp.
Humana
Hunt Alternatives Fund
Hunt Manufacturing Co.
Hyde, Jr. Scholarship Fund, J.R.
Illinois Tool Works
Inland Steel Industries
Interco
International Student Exchange
Cards
Irwin-Sweeney-Miller
Foundation
ITT Corp.
ITT Hartford Insurance Group
ITT Rayonier
Jennings Foundation, Martha
Holden
Jewish Foundation for Education
of Women
Jockey Hollow Foundation
Johnson Controls
Johnson Foundation, Helen K.
and Arthur E.
Johnson & Higgins
Johnson & Son, S.C.
Johnston Trust for Charitable
and Educational Purposes,
James M.
Jones Intercable, Inc.
Journal Gazette Co.
Kawabe Memorial Fund

Kejr Foundation
Kellmer Co., Jack
Kellogg Foundation, W. K.
Kemper Foundation, Enid and
Crosby
Kennametal
Kennedy Foundation, Ethel
Kerr-McGee Corp.
Kidder, Peabody & Co.
Kiewit Foundation, Peter
Kimberly-Clark Corp.
King Foundation, Carl B. and
Florence E.
Kingsley Foundation, Lewis A.
Kirby Foundation, F. M.
Kohler Foundation
Koopman Fund
KPMG Peat Marwick
Krieble Foundation, Vernon K.
Ladish Co.
Lance, Inc.
Lang Foundation, Eugene M.
Law Foundation, Robert O.
Lemberg Foundation
Lennox International, Inc.
Levi Strauss & Co.
Liberty Corp.
Liberty National Bank
Life Investors Insurance
Company of America
Lilly Endowment
Lincoln Electric Co.
Link, Jr. Foundation, George
Little, Arthur D.
Lockheed Corp.
Loews Corp.
Louis Foundation, Michael W.
Louisiana Land & Exploration
Co.
Love Foundation, Lucyle S.
Lowe Foundation, Joe and Emily
Lowenstein Foundation, Leon
Lukens
Lurie Foundation, Louis R.
Lutheran Brotherhood
Foundation
M/A-COM, Inc.
Mandeville Foundation
Mankato Citizens Telephone Co.
Manoogian Foundation, Alex
and Marie
Marinette Marine Corp.
Marion Merrell Dow
Marley Co.
Marquette Electronics
Marriott Foundation, J. Willard
Mars Foundation
Marshall & Ilsley Bank
Martin Marietta Aggregates
Martin Marietta Corp.
Mary Kay Foundation
Mayborn Foundation, Frank W.
Mayor Foundation, Oliver Dewey
Maytag Family Foundation, Fred
MBIA, Inc.
MCA
McConnell Foundation
McCormick & Co.
McCormick Tribune Foundation,
Robert R.
McCray Lumber Co.
McCullough Foundation, Ralph
H. and Ruth J.
McDermott Foundation, Eugene
McDonnell Douglas Corp.-West
McGovern Foundation, John P.
McGraw Foundation
McGraw-Hill
MCI Communications Corp.
McLendon Educational Fund,
Violet H.
McMillan, Jr. Foundation, Bruce
McShain Charities, John
MDU Resources Group, Inc.
Mead Corp.
Mellon Bank Corp.
Mellon Foundation, Richard King

Merrick Foundation
Meyer Foundation, Alice
Kleberg Reynolds
Meyerhoff Fund, Joseph
Michael Foundation, Herbert I.
and Elsa B.
Michigan Gas Utilities
Mifflin Memorial Fund, George
H. and Jane A.
Milbank Foundation, Dunlevy
Minster Machine Co.
Mirage Casino-Hotel
Missouri Farmers Association
Mobil Oil Corp.
Mohasco Corp.
Monarch Machine Tool Co.
Monfort Charitable Foundation
Montana Power Co.
Monticello College Foundation
Moody Foundation
Morehead Foundation, John
Motley
Morris Foundation, Margaret T.
Morrison Foundation, Harry W.
Morrison-Knudsen Corp.
Moses Fund, Henry and Lucy
Mostyn Foundation
Murphy Foundation
Nabisco Foods Group
Nason Foundation
National City Bank of Evansville
National Computer Systems
National Starch & Chemical
Corp.
National Westminster Bank New
Jersey
Navistar International Corp.
NBD Bank
New England Mutual Life
Insurance Co.
New York Mercantile Exchange
New York Telephone Co.
Newcombe Foundation,
Charlotte W.
Newhouse Foundation, Samuel I.
Newmont Mining Corp.
News America Publishing Inc.
News & Observer Publishing Co.
Norfolk Southern Corp.
Northern Indiana Public Service
Co.
Northern States Power Co.
Norton Co.
Norton Memorial Corporation,
Geraldi
O'Brien Foundation, James W.
O'Connor Foundation, A.
Lindsay and Olive B.
Odell and Helen Pfeiffer Odell
Fund, Robert Stewart
O'Donnell Foundation
Old National Bank in Evansville
Olin Corp.
Olin Foundation, Spencer T. and
Ann W.
O'Neill Charitable Corporation,
F. J.
Ontario Corp.
O'Shaughnessy Foundation, I. A.
Osher Foundation, Bernard
Oxford Foundation
Pacific Mutual Life Insurance Co.
Pacific Telesis Group
Palisades Educational Foundation
Paramount Communications Inc.
Parsons Foundation, Ralph M.
Payne Foundation, Frank E. and
Seba B.
Peery Foundation
Peierls Foundation
Pella Corp.
Pennzoil Co.
Perini Foundation, Joseph
Peterson Foundation, Fred J.
Petteys Memorial Foundation,
Jack
Phelps Dodge Corp.
PHH Corp.

Philips Foundation, Jesse
Phillips Family Foundation, Jay
and Rose
Phillips Petroleum Co.
Phipps Foundation, William H.
Pickett and Hatcher Educational
Fund
Pierce Charitable Trust, Harold
Whitworth
Pinkerton Foundation
Pioneer Hi-Bred International
Piper Foundation
Piper Foundation, Minnie
Stevens
Pittway Corp.
Plym Foundation
Pope Foundation
Portland General Electric Co.
Potomac Electric Power Co.
Potter Foundation, Justin and
Valere
Powell Family Foundation
PPG Industries
Pritzker Foundation
Procter & Gamble Co.
Prospect Hill Foundation
Protherapy of America
Pulitzer Publishing Co.
Pullman Educational
Foundation, George M.
Quaker Oats Co.
Raymond Educational
Foundation
Rebsamen Companies, Inc.
Red Devil
Reed Foundation, Philip D.
Reilly Industries
Reliable Life Insurance Co.
Reynolds Foundation, Donald W.
Reynolds Foundation, Richard S.
Rice Foundation, Ethel and
Raymond F.
Rice Foundation, Ethel and
Raymond F.
Rich Products Corp.
Richardson Benevolent
Foundation, C. E.
Rinker Materials Corp.
Ritchie Memorial Foundation,
Charles E. and Mabel M.
RJR Nabisco Inc.
Robbins & Myers, Inc.
Robertson Brothers
Rockefeller Foundation
Rockwell Fund
Rockwell International Corp.
Rogers Family Foundation
Rohlik Foundation, Sigmund and
Sophie
Rohm and Haas Company
Rolfs Foundation, Robert T.
Rowland Foundation
Rubinstein Foundation, Helena
Sandoz Corp.
Sandy Foundation, George H.
Sandy Hill Foundation
Santa Fe Pacific Corp.
Sarkeys Foundation
Scaife Family Foundation
Schecter Private Foundation,
Aaron and Martha
Schering-Plough Corp.
Scheuer Family Foundation, S.
H. and Helen R.
Schlumberger Ltd.
Scholl Foundation, Dr.
Scripps Co., E.W.
Scrivner, Inc.
Seagram & Sons, Joseph E.
Sedgwick James Inc.
Seibel Foundation, Abe and
Annie
Selby and Marie Selby
Foundation, William G.
Seybert Institution for Poor Boys
and Girls, Adam and Maria
Sarah
Shawmut National Corp.

Shell Oil Co.
Shelter Mutual Insurance Co.
Shelter Mutual Insurance Co.
Shenandoah Life Insurance Co.
Shoney's Inc.
Shuwa Investments Corp.
Sierra Pacific Industries
Signet Bank/Maryland
Skidmore, Owings & Merrill
Skillman Foundation
Slusher Charitable Foundation,
Roy W.
Smith Charitable Trust, W. W.
Smith Corp., A.O.
Smith Foundation, Kelvin and
Eleanor
South Carolina Electric & Gas
Co.
Sprague Educational and
Charitable Foundation, Seth
Springs Foundation
Square D Co.
Stabler Foundation, Donald B.
and Dorothy L.
Stark Foundation, Nelda C. and
H. J. Lutcher
Starr Foundation
State Farm Mutual Automobile
Insurance Co.
State Street Bank & Trust Co.
Statler Foundation
Steele Foundation, Harry and
Grace
Steele-Reese Foundation
Sternberger Foundation, Sigmund
Stockham Valves & Fittings
Stone Container Corp.
Storer Foundation, George B.
Stulsaft Foundation, Morris
Summerfield Foundation, Solon
E.
Sun Co.
Surdna Foundation
Swalm Foundation
Synovus Financial Corp.
Taylor Foundation
Taylor Foundation, Ruth and
Vernon
Tektronix
Teledyne
Tennant Co.
Tenneco
Texaco
Texas Industries, Inc.
Texas Instruments
Textron
Thirty-Five Twenty, Inc.
Thomas & Betts Corp.
3M Co.
Times Mirror Co.
Timken Foundation of Canton
Totsy Manufacturing Co.
Tozer Foundation
Tractor & Equipment Co.
Tropicana Products, Inc.
Trull Foundation
Tuohy Foundation, Alice Tweed
Turrell Fund
Tyson Foods, Inc.
Union Camp Corp.
Union Manufacturing Co.
United Conveyor Corp.
United Parcel Service of America
Unocal Corp.
US WEST
Valley National Bancorp
Valmont Industries
Van Houten Charitable Trust
Van Nuys Foundation, I. N. and
Susanna H.
Varian Associates
Vermeer Manufacturing Co.
Wagnalls Memorial
Wal-Mart Stores
Wal-Mart Stores, Inc.
Waldbaum, Inc.
Washington Square Fund

Wean Foundation, Raymond John
Webster Foundation, Edwin S.
Weezie Foundation
Weingart Foundation
West Co.
Westlake Scholarship Fund,
James L. and Nellie M.
Whirlpool Corp.
White Trust, G. R.
Whitehead Foundation, Lettie
Pate
Wickes Foundation, Harvey
Randall
Williams Family Foundation
Winn-Dixie Stores
Witco Corp.
Wolf Foundation, Benjamin and
Fredora K.
Wolfson Foundation, Louis E.
WWF Paper Corp.
Young Foundation, Hugo H. and
Mabel B.
Young & Rubicam

Health

Emergency/
Ambulance
Services

Air Products & Chemicals
Albertson's
Allendale Mutual Insurance Co.
Alliant Techsystems
Alltel/Western Region
Aluminum Co. of America
AMAX
American Brands
American Natural Resources Co.
Amfac/JMB Hawaii
AMP
Arkell Hall Foundation
Armco Inc.
Baldwin, Jr. Foundation,
Summerfield
Bankers Trust Co.
Bard, C. R.
Barnes Group
Beitzell & Co.
Bell Communications Research
Bemis Company
Bethlehem Steel Corp.
BFGoodrich
Binney & Smith Inc.
Blount Educational and
Charitable Foundation,
Mildred Weedon
Blum Foundation, Edna F.
Boehringer Mannheim Corp.
Boettcher Foundation
Boise Cascade Corp.
Brady Foundation
Bremer Foundation, Otto
Brenner Foundation
Bryant Foundation
Burns Foundation, Fritz B.
Carpenter Foundation, E. Rhodes
and Leona B.
Casey Foundation, Eugene B.
Caspersen Foundation for Aid to
Health and Education, O. W.
Central Maine Power Co.
Century Companies of America
CHC Foundation
Church & Dwight Co.
Ciba-Geigy Corp.
(Pharmaceuticals Division)
Circuit City Stores
Citicorp
Citizens Bank
CNG Transmission Corp.
Collins-McDonald Trust Fund
Colonial Life & Accident
Insurance Co.
Colt Foundation, James J.

Continental Corp.
Coors Brewing Co.
Country Curtains, Inc.
Crum and Forster
Curtice-Burns Foods
Cyprus Minerals Co.
DeCamp Foundation, Ira W.
DeKalb Genetics Corp.
Deuble Foundation, George H.
Diamond Shamrock
Dietrich Foundation, William B.
Dixie Yarns, Inc.
Dreyfus Foundation, Max and
Victoria
du Pont de Nemours & Co., E. I.
Duke Power Co.
Dula Educational and Charitable
Foundation, Caleb C. and Julia
W.
Eastman Foundation, Alexander
Eckman Charitable Foundation,
Samuel and Rae
Eden Hall Foundation
Elizabethtown Gas Co.
Ellsworth Trust, W. H.
Emerson Foundation, Fred L.
Essick Foundation
Ethyl Corp.
Fair Oaks Foundation, Inc.
Fairchild Corp.
Falcon Foundation
First Union Corp.
Florence Foundation
FMC Corp.
Foote Mineral Co.
Formrite Tube Co.
Foster Foundation
Freeport Brick Co.
Freeport Brick Co.
French Oil Mill Machinery Co.
Frueauff Foundation, Charles A.
Funderburke & Associates
General American Life Insurance
Co.
General Mills
General Motors Corp.
General Reinsurance Corp.
General Signal Corp.
Gitano Group
Gould Inc.
Grimes Foundation
Grimes Foundation
Gulf Power Co.
Habig Foundation, Arnold F.
Hachar Charitable Trust, D. D.
Hall Foundation
Halloran Foundation, Mary P.
Dolciani
Hargis Charitable Foundation,
Estes H. and Florence Parker
Harriman Foundation, Mary W.
Harris Brothers Foundation
Harris Corp.
Harsco Corp.
Hartz Foundation
Havens Foundation, O. W.
Hechinger Co.
Heckscher Foundation for
Children
Hecla Mining Co.
Hershey Foods Corp.
Homasote Co.
Hoover, Jr. Foundation, Margaret
W. and Herbert
Hubbell Inc.
Hutchins Foundation, Mary J.
Indiana Desk Co.
Inland Container Corp.
International Flavors &
Fragrances
International Paper Co.
James River Corp. of Virginia
Jasper Desk Co.
Jasper Table Co.
Jasper Wood Products Co.
Jeffris Family Foundation

Jewell Memorial Foundation,
Daniel Ashley and Irene
Houston
Johnson Foundation, M. G. and
Lillie A.
Johnson & Higgins
Johnston Trust for Charitable
and Educational Purposes,
James M.
Jones Foundation, Daisy Marquis
Joslin-Needham Family
Foundation
Jurodin Fund
Kellogg Foundation, W. K.
Kennedy Foundation, John R.
Kentland Foundation
Kimberly-Clark Corp.
King Ranch
Kinney-Lindstrom Foundation
Kiplinger Foundation
Kitzmiller/Bales Trust
Kline Foundation, Josiah W. and
Bessie H.
Klipstein Foundation, Ernest
Christian
Knapp Foundation
Knox Family Foundation
Laerdal Foundation, Asmund S.
Lane Co., Inc.
Large Foundation
Lowe Foundation, Joe and Emily
Macy & Co., R.H.
Manville Corp.
Martin Marietta Corp.
Massie Trust, David Meade
McCasland Foundation
McCaw Cellular
Communications
MDU Resources Group, Inc.
Meadows Foundation
Merit Oil Corp.
Merrick Foundation
Mettler Instrument Corp.
Meyer Foundation, Alice
Kleberg Reynolds
Milliken & Co.
Mobil Oil Corp.
Montgomery Foundation
Moody Foundation
Moosehead Manufacturing Co.
Morgan and Samuel Tate
Morgan, Jr. Foundation,
Marietta McNeil
Morris Charitable Foundation, E.
A.
Morrison-Knudsen Corp.
Moss Charitable Trust, Finis M.
Nalco Chemical Co.
National Starch & Chemical
Corp.
New York Life Insurance Co.
The New Yorker Magazine, Inc.
Northeast Utilities
Norton Co.
Olin Corp.
Ormet Corp.
Ortho Diagnostic Systems, Inc.
Overbrook Foundation
Packaging Corporation of
America
Pennzoil Co.
Pfizer
PHH Corp.
Prudential Insurance Co. of
America
Public Service Electric & Gas
Co.
Quabaug Corp.
Quanex Corp.
Quantum Chemical Corp.
R&B Tool Co.
Rachal Foundation, Ed
Ranney Foundation, P. K.
Recognition Equipment
Richardson Foundation, Sid W.
Rohm and Haas Company
Roseburg Forest Products Co.
Royal Group Inc.

Ryan Foundation, David Claude
Sara Lee Hosiery
Seay Memorial Trust, George
and Effie
Shenandoah Life Insurance Co.
Simpson Investment Co.
Smith Corp., A.O.
Sonoco Products Co.
Speas Foundation, Victor E.
Sprague Educational and
Charitable Foundation, Seth
Square D Co.
Stackpole-Hall Foundation
Taylor Foundation
Taylor Foundation, Ruth and
Vernon
Tenneco
Thomas & Betts Corp.
Thomas Memorial Foundation,
Theresa A.
Time Warner Cable
Tisch Foundation
Tosco Corp. Refining Division
Treakle Foundation, J. Edwin
Tyson Foods, Inc.
Tyson Fund
Union Camp Corp.
United States Sugar Corp.
Valero Energy Corp.
Vevay-Switzerland County
Foundation
Virginia Power Co.
Wal-Mart Stores
Weinberg Foundation, John L.
Wendt Foundation, Margaret L.
West Foundation, Neva and
Wesley
West One Bancorp
Weyerhaeuser Co.
Wheeler Foundation, Wilmot
Whitaker Foundation
WICOR, Inc.
Williams Charitable Trust, John
C.
Winnebago Industries, Inc.
Wolverine World Wide, Inc.
Woodward Governor Co.
WWF Paper Corp.
Yost Trust, Elizabeth Burns

General

ABB Process Automation
Addison-Wesley Publishing Co.
Aeroglide Corp.
AFG Industries, Inc.
AGA Gas, Inc.
Ahmanson & Co., H.F.
Airborne Express Co.
Alabama Gas Corp. (An Energen
Co.)
Aladdin Industries, Incorporated
AMCORE Bank, N.A. Rockford
American Filtrona Corp.
American General Corp.
American General Life &
Accident Insurance Co.
American Mutual Insurance Cos.
American National Bank
American National Can Co.
American Stock Exchange
American Stores Co.
American Telephone &
Telegraph Co./New York City
Region
Ameritech Publishing
Ampacet Corp.
Anacomp, Inc.
ARA Services
Arkansas Best Corp.
Arkla
Atlanta Journal & Constitution
Attleboro Pawtucket Savings
Bank
Avery Dennison Corp.
Baird & Co., Robert W.
Baker, Watts & Co.
Ball Corp.

Recipient Type Index

General *(cont.)*

Bally's - Las Vegas
Baltimore Life Insurance Co.
Bank of America Arizona
Bank of Boston Connecticut
Bank of Louisville
Bank of Oklahoma, N.A.
Bank One, Texas-Houston Office
Barry Corp., R. G.
Barton-Gillet Co.
BASF Corp.
Bayview Federal Bank
Beitzel & Co.
Belden Brick Co., Inc.
Bell Helicopter Textron
Belmont Metals
Benefit Trust Life Insurance Co.
Bergen Record Corp.
Berwind Corp.
Betz Laboratories
Bill Communications
Binney & Smith Inc.
Black & Decker Corp.
Blair and Co., William
Bloomingdale's
Boston Gas Co.
Boston Mutual Life Insurance
  Co.
Bourns, Inc.
Brakeley, John Price Jones Inc.
Branch Banking & Trust Co.
Brewer and Co., Ltd., C.
Briggs & Stratton Corp.
Brooklyn Union Gas Co.
Business Men's Assurance Co. of
  America
Caesar's World, Inc.
Capital Holding Corp.
Carolina Telephone & Telegraph
  Co.
Carr Real Estate Services
Casco Northern Bank
Castle & Cooke
CBS Inc.
CCB Financial Corp.
Centex Corp.
Central Life Assurance Co.
Central Maine Power Co.
Charter Medical Corp.
Chemtech Industries
Chubb Life Insurance Co. of
  America
Cincinnati Gas & Electric Co.
CNA Insurance Cos.
Coachmen Industries
Coastal Corp.
Coleman Co.
Colgate-Palmolive Co.
Colonial Parking
Colorado National Bankshares
Colorado State Bank of Denver
Commercial Intertech Corp.
Commonwealth Life Insurance
  Co.
Community Mutual Insurance
  Co.
Computer Associates
  International
Consolidated Rail Corp. (Conrail)
Continental Airlines
Conwood Co. L.P.
Cooper Oil Tool
Cooper Tire & Rubber Co.
Corvallis Clinic
Credit Agricole
Creditanstalt-Bankverein, New
  York
CSX Corp.
CT Corp. System
Cubic Corp.
Culbro Corp.
Curtis Industries, Helene
Cyprus Minerals Co.
Dean Witter Discover
DEC International, Inc.

Delmarva Power & Light Co.
Diamond Shamrock
Diamond State Telephone Co.
Didier Taylor Refractories Corp.
Diebold, Inc.
Dime Savings Bank of New York
Dover Corp.
Dreyer's & Edy's Grand Ice
  Cream
Duquesne Light Co.
Durham Corp.
Duriron Co., Inc.
Eastland Bank
Ebsco Industries
Educators Mutual Life Insurance
  Co.
Employers Insurance of Wausau,
  A Mutual Co.
Employers Mutual Casualty Co.
Encyclopaedia Britannica, Inc.
Enserch Corp.
Entex
Evening Post Publishing Co.
Fabri-Kal Corp.
Fairfield Communities, Inc.
Farmers Group, Inc.
Federal Paper Board Co.
Federated Life Insurance Co.
Ferranti Tech
Ferrell Cos.
Ferro Corp.
First Alabama Bancshares
First Brands Corp.
First Commercial Bank N.A.
First Interstate Bank of Denver
First National Bank in Wichita
First NH Banks, Inc.
First of America Bank Corp.
First Union National Bank of
  Florida
Fisher-Price
Fleet Bank N.A.
Florida Power & Light Co.
Fox Inc.
Foxmeyer Corp.
Frito-Lay
Galileo Electro-Optics Corp.
Gast Manufacturing Corp.
Gates Corp.
General Color Co.
General Housewares Corp.
General Railway Signal Corp.
General Signal Corp.
General Tire Inc.
GenRad
Glatfelter Co., P.H.
Glendale Federal Bank
Goulds Pumps
Grand Rapids Label Co.
Graphic Controls Corp.
Graybar Electric Co.
Great Lakes Carbon Corp.
Grinnell Mutual Reinsurance Co.
Grumman Corp.
Handy & Harman
Harleysville Mutual Insurance
  Co.
Harnischfeger Foundation
Harris Stores, Paul
Haworth, Inc.
Hecla Mining Co.
Hercules Inc.
Hobart Corp.
Home Savings of America, FA
Howmet Corp.
Huber, Hunt & Nichols
Huck International Inc.
Huffy Corp.
Hughes Aircraft Co.
Hunt Oil Co.
ICH Corp.
Illinois Power Co.
Industrial Risk Insurers
Ingram Industries
Integra Bank/South
Interstate National Corp.
Iowa-Illinois Gas & Electric Co.

Isaly Klondike Co.
IU International
Jefferson-Pilot
Jones Construction Co., J.A.
Kaiser Aluminum & Chemical
  Corp.
Kaman Corp.
Karmazin Products Corp.
Kaufman & Broad Home Corp.
Kaye, Scholer, Fierman, Hays &
  Handler
Keefe, Bruyette & Woods
Kellwood Co.
Kendall Health Care Products
Kennecott Corp.
Ketchum & Co.
Kimball International
King Kullen Grocery Co., Inc.
KN Energy, Inc.
Kulicke & Soffa Industries
L.A. Gear
Lafarge Corp.
Lambda Electronics Inc.
LaSalle Bank Lake View
Law Companies Group
Law Company, Inc.
Leaseway Transportation Corp.
Libbey-Owens Ford Co.
Liberty Mutual Insurance
  Group/Boston
LIN Broadcasting Corp.
Lincoln Telecommunications Co.
Lomas Financial Corp.
Longs Drug Stores
Lord Corp.
Louisville Gas & Electric Co.
Lowe's Cos.
Lykes Brothers Steamship Co.
MacLean-Fogg Co.
Maguire Oil Co.
Manitowoc Co.
Manufacturers Life Insurance
  Co. of America
Marine Midland Banks
Marion Fabrics
Maritz Inc.
Marubeni America Corp.
Mascoma Savings Bank
Mass Merchandisers, Inc.
Massachusetts Mutual Life
  Insurance Co.
Mayer Foods Corp., Oscar
MBIA, Inc.
McDonald & Co. Securities
Measurex Corp.
Meenan Oil Co., Inc.
Mellon PSFS
Mercantile Bankshares Corp.
Meridian Insurance Group Inc.
Merit Oil Corp.
Mesa Inc.
Mettler Instrument Corp.
Meyer, Inc., Fred
Michigan Mutual Insurance Corp.
Michigan National Corp.
Midland Mutual Life Insurance
  Co.
Minnesota Power & Light Co.
Mississippi Chemical Corp.
Mississippi Power & Light Co.
Monfort of Colorado, Inc.
Moore, Costello & Hart
Morse Shoe, Inc.
Motter Printing Press Co.
MTS Systems Corp.
Mutual of America Life
National City Bank, Columbus
National City Bank of Indiana
National Computer Systems
National Convenience Stores,
  Inc.
National Data Corp.
National Forge Co.
National Fuel Gas Co.
National Standard Co.
NationsBank Texas
New Jersey National Bank

New Jersey Resources Corp.
New York Mercantile Exchange
New York State Electric & Gas
  Corp.
The New Yorker Magazine, Inc.
Niagara Mohawk Power Corp.
NIBCO Inc.
Norfolk Shipbuilding & Drydock
  Corp.
North American Coal Corp.
Northrop Corp.
Northwest Natural Gas Co.
Norton & Co., W.W.
NRC, Inc.
Oakite Products
Ogilvy & Mather Worldwide
Ohio Casualty Corp.
Ohio Citizens Bank
Ohio Edison Corp.
Oki America Inc.
Old Republic International Corp.
One Valley Bank, N.A.
Ontario Corp.
Orange & Rockland Utilities, Inc.
Orion Capital Corp.
Ormet Corp.
Oster/Sunbeam Appliance Co.
Owens-Illinois
Packaging Corporation of
  America
Padnos Iron & Metal Co., Louis
Pamida, Inc.
Pan-American Life Insurance Co.
Patrick Industries Inc.
PayLess Drug Stores
Pennsylvania Power & Light
Pentair
Perry Drug Stores
Persis Corp.
PHH Corp.
Phoenix Home Life Mutual
  Insurance Co.
Phoenix Resource Cos.
Pioneer Trust Bank, NA
Plante & Moran, CPAs
Plantronics, Inc.
PMI Food Equipment Group Inc.
Ponderosa, Inc.
Preferred Risk Mutual Insurance
  Co.
Primark Corp.
Prime Computer, Inc.
PriMerit F.S.B.
Producers Livestock Marketing
  Association
Providence Energy Corp.
Provident Mutual Life Insurance
  Co. of Philadelphia
PSI Energy
Public Service Co. of Oklahoma
Quaker State Corp.
Questar Corp.
Raley's
Ranco, Inc.
Ransburg Corp.
Raytheon Engineers &
  Constructors
Reading & Bates Corp.
Reasoner, Davis & Fox
Reliable Life Insurance Co.
Reliance Group Holdings, Inc.
Reliance Insurance Cos.
Republic Automotive Parts, Inc.
Research-Cottrell Inc.
Risdon Corp.
Riviana Foods
Roseburg Forest Products Co.
Ross Laboratories
Royal Group Inc.
Santa Fe International Corp.
Sara Lee Hosiery
SCANA Corp.
Scientific-Atlanta
Scientific Brake & Equipment
  Co.
Scotty's, Inc.
Sea-Land Service

Sealed Air Corp.
Sealright Co., Inc.
SECO
Security Life of Denver
Seneca Foods Corp.
ServiceMaster Co. L.P.
Seton Co.
Shaw Industries
Sheldahl Inc.
Simkins Industries, Inc.
SNC Manufacturing Co.
Society for Savings
Somers Corp.
  (Mersman/Waldron)
Sonoco Products Co.
Southern Co. Services
Southland Corp.
Sprint United Telephone
Staley Manufacturing Co., A.E.
State Mutual Life Assurance Co.
Steel Heddle Manufacturing Co.
Stewart & Stevenson Services
Storage Technology Corp.
Storer Communications Inc.
Strawbridge & Clothier
Stroh Brewery Co.
T.T.X. Co.
Tampa Electric
TCF Banking & Savings, FSB
Texas Gas Transmission Corp.
Time Warner
Torrington Co.
Towle Manufacturing Co.
Town & Country Corp.
Trans-Apex
Travelers Express Co.
Tremco Inc.
Triskelion Ltd.
Trustmark National Bank
Tucson Electric Power Co.
Turner Corp.
Twentieth Century Insurance Co.
Tyler Corp.
UJB Financial Corp.
Unigard Security Insurance Co.
U.S. Bank of Washington
United Stationers Inc.
United Telephone System
  (Eastern Group)
US Bancorp
Wang Laboratories, Inc.
Washington Natural Gas Co.
Washington Water Power Co.
Wausau Insurance Cos.
Welch Foods
West One Bancorp
Whittaker Corp.
WICOR, Inc.
Wimpey Inc., George
Wiremold Co.
Wisconsin Bell, Inc.
Wyman-Gordon Co.
Y.K.K. (U.S.A.) Inc.
Zurn Industries

Geriatric Health

Albertson's
Alexander Foundation, Joseph
Aluminum Co. of America
American Home Products Corp.
Appleman Foundation
Atherton Family Foundation
Atran Foundation
Attleboro Pawtucket Savings
  Bank
Battelle
Bell Industries
Bernstein & Co., Sanford C.
Berwind Corp.
Bethlehem Steel Corp.
Beveridge Foundation, Frank
  Stanley
BFGoodrich
Block, H&R
Borchard Foundation, Albert and
  Elaine

Borman's
Brach Foundation, Helen
Bremer Foundation, Otto
Brochsteins Inc.
Brookdale Foundation
Brookdale Foundation
Bruening Foundation, Eva L. and
  Joseph M.
Burden Foundation, Florence V.
Burndy Corp.
Bush Foundation
Cablevision of Michigan
Cafritz Foundation, Morris and
  Gwendolyn
Capital Holding Corp.
Carnival Cruise Lines
Central Maine Power Co.
Chase Manhattan Bank, N.A.
Ciba-Geigy Corp.
  (Pharmaceuticals Division)
Clorox Co.
Coast Federal Bank
Colonial Life & Accident
  Insurance Co.
Colonial Penn Group, Inc.
Colorado Trust
Commonwealth Fund
Comprecare Foundation
Corvallis Clinic
Cox Charitable Trust, Jessie B.
Crum and Forster
CT Corp. System
CTS Corp.
Curtice-Burns Foods
Dana Foundation, Charles A.
Davis Charitable Foundation,
  Champion McDowell
Davis Hospital Foundation
DeCamp Foundation, Ira W.
Deutsch Co.
Doyle Charitable Foundation
du Pont de Nemours & Co., E. I.
Duke Endowment
Duncan Trust, James R.
Durr-Fillauer Medical
East Ohio Gas Co.
Eccles Foundation, Marriner S.
Eder Foundation, Sidney and
  Arthur
Educational Foundation of
  America
Enron Corp.
Factor Family Foundation, Max
Fay's Incorporated
Fels Fund, Samuel S.
Fidelity Bank
First Union Corp.
Flinn Foundation
Florida Power & Light Co.
Florida Rock Industries
Ford III Memorial Foundation,
  Jefferson Lee
Foundation for Seacoast Health
Frank Foundation, Ernest and
  Elfriede
Frankel Foundation, George and
  Elizabeth F.
Frederick Foundation
Freedom Forum
Friendly Rosenthal Foundation
Frohring Foundation, William O.
  and Gertrude Lewis
Fuchs Foundation, Gottfried &
  Mary
Fullerton Foundation
Funderburke & Associates
GATX Corp.
General Mills
GenRad
Georgia Health Foundation
Georgia Power Co.
Gershman Foundation, Joel
Gerson Trust, B. Milfred
Ginter Foundation, Karl and
  Anna
Glenn Foundation for Medical
  Research, Paul F.

Glickenhaus & Co.
Goldberg Family Foundation
Goldstein Foundation, Leslie and
  Roslyn
Goodman Foundation, Edward
  and Marion
Gorin Foundation, Nehemiah
Greene Foundation, Robert Z.
Gregg-Graniteville Foundation
Griffin Foundation, Rosa May
Gruber Research Foundation,
  Lila
GTE Corp.
Gurwin Foundation, J.
Habig Foundation, Arnold F.
Hagedorn Fund
Hall Foundation
Halsell Foundation, Ewing
Harper Foundation, Philip S.
Harriman Foundation, Gladys
  and Roland
Harrington Foundation, Don and
  Sybil
Hartford Foundation, John A.
Hearst Foundation, William
  Randolph
Hechinger Co.
Heinz Endowment, Vira I.
Helfaer Foundation, Evan and
  Marion
Herbst Foundation
Heymann Special Account, Mr.
  and Mrs. Jimmy
Hill Foundation
Hoag Family Foundation, George
Hopkins Foundation, Josephine
  Lawrence
ICI Americas
Imperial Bancorp
ITT Corp.
Ittleson Foundation
J.P. Morgan & Co.
Janirve Foundation
Jenkins Foundation, George W.
Jewish Healthcare Foundation of
  Pittsburgh
Johnson Foundation, Robert
  Wood
Johnson & Higgins
Johnson & Johnson
Jones Foundation, Daisy Marquis
Kawabe Memorial Fund
Kellogg Foundation, W. K.
Kennecott Corp.
Kimberly-Clark Corp.
Klosk Fund, Louis and Rose
Koehler Foundation, Marcia and
  Otto
Kohl Charitable Foundation,
  Allen D.
Kohl Foundation, Sidney
Kramer Foundation
Lazar Foundation
Lee Enterprises
Leighton-Oare Foundation
Lender Family Foundation
Lindner Foundation, Fay J.
Loeb Foundation, Frances and
  John L.
Long Island Lighting Co.
Lowe Foundation, Joe and Emily
Lowenstein Brothers Foundation
Lowenstein Foundation, William
  P. and Marie R.
Lurie Foundation, Louis R.
Maas Foundation, Benard L.
Mamiye Brothers
Mardag Foundation
Margolis Charitable Foundation
  for Medical Research, Ben B.
  and Iris M.
Marion Merrell Dow
MBIA, Inc.
McAlister Charitable
  Foundation, Harold
McCune Foundation
McGregor Fund
McLean Contributionship

McMillen Foundation
McNutt Charitable Trust, Amy
  Shelton
Meadows Foundation
Medtronic
Memorial Foundation for
  Children
Merck & Co.
Merrill Lynch & Co.
Metropolitan Life Insurance Co.
Meyer Memorial Trust
Michigan Bell Telephone Co.
Mid-Iowa Health Foundation
Middendorf Foundation
Mobil Oil Corp.
Moody Foundation
National City Corp.
National Fuel Gas Co.
National Machinery Co.
New England Mutual Life
  Insurance Co.
New York Foundation
New York Life Insurance Co.
New York Mercantile Exchange
New York Telephone Co.
The New Yorker Magazine, Inc.
Nias Foundation, Henry
Norton Co.
Novotny Charitable Trust, Yetta
  Deitch
Ogilvy & Mather Worldwide
O'Neil Foundation, W.
Pacific Mutual Life Insurance Co.
Parshelsky Foundation, Moses L.
Penn Foundation, William
Pew Charitable Trusts
Pfizer
Prudential Insurance Co. of
  America
Public Welfare Foundation
Ramapo Trust
Raytheon Co.
Recognition Equipment
Reicher Foundation, Anne &
  Harry J.
Retirement Research Foundation
Reynolds Charitable Trust, Kate
  B.
Rice Foundation
Rieke Corp.
Robison Foundation, Ellis H. and
  Doris B.
Rohm and Haas Company
Rosenberg Foundation, Sunny
  and Abe
Royal Group Inc.
Samuels Foundation, Fan Fox
  and Leslie R.
San Diego Gas & Electric
Saunders Foundation
Schamach Foundation, Milton
Scheuer Family Foundation, S.
  H. and Helen R.
Schmidlapp Trust No. 1, Jacob G.
Schwartz and Robert Schwartz
  Foundation, Bernard
Schwob Foundation, Simon
Seaway Food Town
Senior Services of Stamford
Shapiro Fund, Albert
Siebert Lutheran Foundation
Simpson Foundation
Smith Charitable Trust, W. W.
Smock Foundation, Frank and
  Laura
Snee-Reinhardt Charitable
  Foundation
Snider Foundation
Sooner Pipe & Supply Corp.
Southern Bell
Southern California Edison Co.
Speas Foundation, Victor E.
Sprague Educational and
  Charitable Foundation, Seth
Steinhagen Benevolent Trust, B.
  A. and Elinor
Sterkel Trust, Justine
Stranahan Foundation

Strauss Foundation
Summerfield Foundation, Solon
  E.
Synovus Financial Corp.
Tamarkin Co.
Taper Foundation, Mark
Terner Foundation
3M Co.
Time Insurance Co.
Travelers Cos.
Trust Co. Bank
Tull Charitable Foundation
Union Camp Corp.
United States Trust Co. of New
  York
van Ameringen Foundation
Wal-Mart Stores
Whirlpool Corp.
Whiting Foundation
Wolff Memorial Foundation,
  Pauline Sterne
Woodward Governor Co.

Health Care Cost Containment

Allstate Insurance Co.
Altman Foundation
Aluminum Co. of America
American Electric Power
American Microsystems, Inc.
American Natural Resources Co.
Ball Corp.
Battelle
Baxter International
Bemis Company
Bethlehem Steel Corp.
Boettcher Foundation
Bovaird Foundation, Mervin
Carter Foundation, Amon G.
Chevron Corp.
Chrysler Corp.
CIGNA Corp.
Citicorp
CM Alliance Cos.
Colonial Life & Accident
  Insurance Co.
Cox Charitable Trust, Jessie B.
CPC International
DeKalb Genetics Corp.
Digital Equipment Corp.
du Pont de Nemours & Co., E. I.
Duke Endowment
Duke Power Co.
Federated Life Insurance Co.
Fibre Converters
First Union Corp.
Flinn Foundation
FMC Corp.
Ford Motor Co.
Friedman Family Foundation
Gallagher Family Foundation,
  Lewis P.
Gallagher Family Foundation,
  Lewis P.
Gates Foundation
General Mills
General Reinsurance Corp.
Gilmore Foundation, Earl B.
Glaxo
Great-West Life Assurance Co.
GTE Corp.
Guardian Life Insurance Co. of
  America
Hartford Foundation, John A.
Hoche-Scofield Foundation
Hospital Corp. of America
IBM Corp.
Illinois Bell
Indiana Bell Telephone Co.
ITT Hartford Insurance Group
J.P. Morgan & Co.
JM Foundation
John Hancock Mutual Life
  Insurance Co.
Johnson Foundation, Robert
  Wood

Johnson & Higgins
Keller-Crescent Co.
Kellogg Foundation, W. K.
Kilworth Charitable Foundation,
  Florence B.
Life Insurance Co. of Georgia
Lilly & Co., Eli
LTV Corp.
Lydall, Inc.
Meadows Foundation
Merck & Co.
Merck Human Health Division
Metropolitan Life Insurance Co.
Meyer Memorial Trust
Nalco Chemical Co.
National Computer Systems
National Fuel Gas Co.
The New Yorker Magazine, Inc.
Noble Foundation, Samuel
  Roberts
Northwest Area Foundation
Norton Co.
NYNEX Corp.
Ohio Bell Telephone Co.
Pacific Mutual Life Insurance Co.
Perkins-Prothro Foundation
Pew Charitable Trusts
PPG Industries
Prentiss Foundation, Elisabeth
  Severance
Principal Financial Group
Prudential Insurance Co. of
  America
Quaker Oats Co.
Ralston Purina Co.
Raytheon Co.
Reliance Electric Co.
Retirement Research Foundation
Rockwell International Corp.
Rohm and Haas Company
SAFECO Corp.
Scrivner, Inc.
Seaway Food Town
Security Life of Denver
Sheaffer Inc.
Shenandoah Life Insurance Co.
SNET
Sonat
Springs Industries
State Street Bank & Trust Co.
Steelcase
Sterling Winthrop
Tennant Co.
Textron
3M Co.
Time Insurance Co.
Tropicana Products, Inc.
TRW Corp.
United States Trust Co. of New
  York
United Technologies Corp.
UST
Vollrath Co.
West One Bancorp
Whirlpool Corp.
WICOR, Inc.
Wimpey Inc., George
Xerox Corp.

Health Funds

Abell-Hanger Foundation
Ace Beverage Co.
ACF Industries, Inc.
Achelis Foundation
Alcon Laboratories, Inc.
Algonquin Energy, Inc.
Alltel/Western Region
Altman Foundation
Aluminum Co. of America
AMAX
American Foundation
American National Bank & Trust
  Co. of Chicago
American Schlafhorst
  Foundation, Inc.
AMETEK

Health Funds (cont.)

AMR Corp.
Annenberg Foundation
AON Corp.
Arata Brothers Trust
Archbold Charitable Trust,
Adrian and Jessie
Arizona Public Service Co.
Armco Inc.
Arrillaga Foundation
Atherton Family Foundation
Auerbach Foundation, Beatrice
Fox
Avon Products
Awrey Bakeries
Azadoutioun Foundation
Baird Foundation
Baker Foundation, Dexter F. and
Dorothy H.
Baker, Jr. Memorial Fund,
William G.
Bard, C. R.
Barker Foundation, J. M. R.
Barry Corp., R. G.
Batts Foundation
Baumker Charitable Foundation,
Elsie and Harry
Beasley Foundation, Theodore
and Beulah
Bedminster Fund
Bellini Foundation
Bemis Company
Beneficial Corp.
Bicknell Fund
Bierlein Family Foundation
Bingham Second Betterment
Fund, William
Bionetics Corp.
Bishop Foundation, E. K. and
Lillian F.
Block, H&R
BMC Industries
Boh Brothers Construction Co.
Bonner Foundation, Corella and
Bertram
Brach Foundation, Helen
Bray Charitable Trust, Viola E.
Breidenthal Foundation, Willard
J. and Mary G.
Briggs & Stratton Corp.
Brooks Brothers
Browning-Ferris Industries
Brundage Charitable, Scientific,
and Wildlife Conservation
Foundation, Charles E. and
Edna T.
Burke Foundation, Thomas C.
C.P. Rail Systems
Cabot-Saltonstall Charitable
Trust
Campbell and Adah E. Hall
Charity Fund, Bushrod H.
Carpenter Technology Corp.
Cauthorn Charitable Trust, John
and Mildred
Centel Corp.
Central Bank of the South
Cessna Aircraft Co.
Chambers Memorial, James B.
Chernow Trust for the Benefit of
Charity Dated 3/13/75, Michael
Chevron Corp.
Church & Dwight Co.
Clark Foundation
Cleary Foundation
Clorox Co.
Clowes Fund
CM Alliance Cos.
Cole Foundation
Collins, Jr. Foundation, George
Fulton
Colorado State Bank of Denver
Columbia Foundation
Columbus Dispatch Printing Co.
Commerzbank AG, New York
Commonwealth Fund

ConAgra
Continental Corp.
Cooper Industries
Coors Brewing Co.
Copperweld Steel Co.
Corvallis Clinic
County Bank
Courts Foundation
CPC International
Crane & Co.
Crestar Financial Corp.
Cuesta Foundation
Dalton Foundation, Dorothy U.
Davis Foundation, Edwin W. and
Catherine M.
Delany Charitable Trust,
Beatrice P.
Detroit Edison Co.
DeVos Foundation, Richard and
Helen
Dexter Corp.
Dimeo Construction Co.
Donaldson Co.
Douglas Charitable Foundation
Dover Foundation
Dreyfus Foundation, Jean and
Louis
Duchossois Industries
Dunagan Foundation
Dunn Research Foundation, John
S.
Eastman Foundation, Alexander
Eaton Corp.
Eckerd Corp., Jack
Eyman Trust, Jesse
Falk Medical Fund, Maurice
Federal-Mogul Corp.
Federated Department Stores and
Allied Stores Corp.
Ferguson Family Foundation,
Kittie and Rugeley
Fifth Third Bancorp
First Financial Bank FSB
First Interstate Bank of Oregon
First Union Corp.
Fitz-Gibbon Charitable Trust
FMC Corp.
Frederick Foundation
Frelinghuysen Foundation
Funderburke & Associates
GAR Foundation
Georgia-Pacific Corp.
Giant Food Stores
Gibson Foundation, Addison H.
Goldman Foundation, Herman
Goldsmith Family Foundation
Grace & Co., W.R.
Green Fund
Groves & Sons Co., S.J.
Gulf Power Co.
Hall Charitable Trust, Evelyn A.
J.
Hampden Papers
Hanes Foundation, John W. and
Anna H.
Harden Foundation
Harris Brothers Foundation
Hawkins Foundation, Robert Z.
Hawn Foundation
Hechinger Co.
Hecht's
Herzog Foundation, Carl J.
Heublein
Heydt Fund, Nan and Matilda
Hiawatha Education Foundation
Hobby Foundation
Hubbard Broadcasting
Hughes Charitable Trust, Mabel
Y.
Inland Container Corp.
Inland Steel Industries
Jones Fund, Blanche and George
Joslyn Foundation, Marcellus I.
Joukowsky Family Foundation
Julia R. and Estelle L.
Foundation
Keller-Crescent Co.

Kellogg Foundation, W. K.
Kepco, Inc.
Kerr-McGee Corp.
Kieckhefer Foundation, J. W.
King Foundation, Carl B. and
Florence E.
Knott Foundation, Marion I. and
Henry J.
Knox Foundation, Seymour H.
Kuhne Foundation Trust, Charles
Lattner Foundation, Forrest C.
Lauder Foundation
Laurel Foundation
LDI Charitable Foundation
Leavey Foundation, Thomas and
Dorothy
Leonhardt Foundation, Frederick
H.
Life Investors Insurance
Company of America
Link, Jr. Foundation, George
Lipton, Thomas J.
Long Foundation, J.M.
LTV Corp.
Lydall, Inc.
Macy & Co., R.H.
Marriott Corp.
Mars Foundation
Martin Marietta Corp.
May Department Stores Co.
McCune Charitable Trust, John
R.
McGovern Foundation, John P.
Mead Corp.
Meadows Foundation
Measey Foundation, Benjamin
and Mary Siddons
Metropolitan Life Insurance Co.
Midmark Corp.
Miller Memorial Trust, George
Lee
Mine Safety Appliances Co.
Mobil Oil Corp.
Montgomery Foundation
Morris Foundation, William T.
National Presto Industries
National Starch & Chemical
Corp.
National Westminster Bank New
Jersey
New England Foundation
The New Yorker Magazine, Inc.
Newman's Own
Newmil Bancorp
Norcliffe Fund
North Carolina Foam Foundation
North Shore Foundation
Northwestern National Life
Insurance Co.
Oakley Foundation, Hollie and
Anna
Oberlaender Foundation, Gustav
O'Neil Foundation, W.
Orchard Foundation
Osborn Manufacturing Co.
Overlake Foundation
Pamida, Inc.
Parker-Hannifin Corp.
Parsons - W.D. Charities, Vera
Davis
Phelps Dodge Corp.
Phillips Foundation, Dr. P.
Phillips Foundation, Ellis L.
Pittway Corp.
Reliable Life Insurance Co.
Reynolds Foundation, Donald W.
Reynolds Foundation, Richard S.
Richardson Fund, Mary Lynn
Rodgers Trust, Elizabeth Killam
Royal Group Inc.
RTM
Sailors' Snug Harbor of Boston
Scaife Family Foundation
Schmidlapp Trust No. 1, Jacob G.
Schmitt Foundation, Arthur J.
Schott Foundation
Scott and Fetzer Co.

Scrivner, Inc.
Second Foundation
Seybert Institution for Poor Boys
and Girls, Adam and Maria
Sarah
Shaffer Family Charitable Trust
Shawmut National Corp.
Shell Oil Co.
Shenandoah Life Insurance Co.
Shenandoah Life Insurance Co.
Shoney's Inc.
Signet Bank/Maryland
Smith and W. Aubrey Smith
Charitable Foundation, Clara
Blackford
Smith Benevolent Association,
Buckingham
Smith Fund, George D.
SmithKline Beecham
Snow Memorial Trust, John Ben
Sonat
Sooner Pipe & Supply Corp.
Southern California Gas Co.
Speas Foundation, Victor E.
Sprague Educational and
Charitable Foundation, Seth
Square D Co.
Sterling Inc.
Sterling Winthrop
Stratford Foundation
Summerfield Foundation, Solon
E.
Swig Foundation
Tasty Baking Co.
Taylor Foundation, Ruth and
Vernon
Texas Instruments
Thomas & Betts Corp.
Thomas Industries
Thompson Trust, Thomas
Times Mirror Co.
Tisch Foundation
Tiscornia Foundation
Transamerica Corp.
Treadwell Foundation, Nora
Eccles
Treuhaft Foundation
Tucker Charitable Trust, Rose E.
Union Camp Corp.
Union Foundation
U.S. Oil/Schmidt Family
Foundation, Inc.
United States Trust Co. of New
York
Univar Corp.
Universal Leaf Tobacco Co.
Valley Foundation
Valley National Bank of Arizona
Van Houten Charitable Trust
Vlasic Foundation
Wachovia Bank & Trust Co.,
N.A.
Wahlert Foundation
Wal-Mart Stores
Waldbaum Family Foundation, I.
Warner-Lambert Co.
Waste Management
Webster Charitable Foundation
Webster Foundation, Edwin S.
Weeden Foundation, Frank
Weinberg Foundation, John L.
Weinberg, Jr. Foundation, Sidney
J.
Wendt Foundation, Margaret L.
Westchester Health Fund
Westvaco Corp.
Whirlpool Corp.
Williams Cos.
Williams Foundation, Edna
Sproull
Wilson Foundation, John and
Nevils
Wrigley Co., Wm. Jr.
Wyomissing Foundation

Health Organizations

Abbott Laboratories

Abel Construction Co.
Abell-Hanger Foundation
Abrams Foundation, Benjamin
and Elizabeth
Acushnet Co.
Adler Foundation
AFLAC
Ahmanson Foundation
AKC Fund
Akzo America
Akzo Chemicals Inc.
Alabama Power Co.
Alden Trust, John W.
Alexander & Baldwin, Inc.
Alexander Foundation, Joseph
Alexander Foundation, Robert
D. and Catherine R.
Allen-Heath Memorial
Foundation
Allendale Mutual Insurance Co.
AlliedSignal
Allstate Insurance Co.
ALPAC Corp.
Altman Foundation
Altschul Foundation
Alumax
Aluminum Co. of America
Amado Foundation, Maurice
AMAX
America West Airlines
American Aggregates Corp.
American Brands
American Natural Resources Co.
American United Life Insurance
Co.
AMETEK
AMP
Amsted Industries
Andalusia Health Services
Andersen Corp.
Andersen Foundation
Andersen Foundation, Hugh J.
Anderson Charitable Trust,
Josephine
Anderson Foundation, John W.
Anderson Foundation, M. D.
Anheuser-Busch Cos.
Annenberg Foundation
Anschutz Family Foundation
Apache Corp.
Apple Computer, Inc.
Arcadia Foundation
Archibald Charitable
Foundation, Norman
Arkansas Power & Light Co.
Armbrust Chain Co.
Armco Inc.
Ashland Oil
Atherton Family Foundation
Atkinson Foundation, Myrtle L.
Atlanta Gas Light Co.
Autry Foundation
Avis Inc.
Avon Products
Awrey Bakeries
Bacardi Imports
Backer Spielvogel Bates U.S.
Badgeley Residuary Charitable
Trust, Rose M.
Baehr Foundation, Louis W. and
Dolpha
Baird Charitable Trust, William
Robert
Baird & Co., Robert W.
Baker & Baker
Baker & Baker
Baker Foundation, R. C.
Baldwin Foundation, David M.
and Barbara
Ball Foundation, George and
Frances
Banbury Fund
Bancorp Hawaii
Banfi Vintners
Bank of A. Levy
Bank of America - Giannini
Foundation

Bank of Boston Corp.
Bank of New York
Bank One, Texas-Houston Office
BankAmerica Corp.
Bankers Trust Co.
Bannan Foundation, Arline and Thomas J.
Bannerman Foundation, William C.
Bard, C. R.
Barnett Charitable Foundation, Lawrence and Isabel
Barra Foundation
Barrows Foundation, Geraldine and R. A.
Barry Corp., R. G.
Barton-Malow Co.
Bartsch Memorial Trust, Ruth
Batts Foundation
Bauer Foundation, M. R.
Baxter International
Bean Foundation, Norwin S. and Elizabeth N.
Beasley Foundation, Theodore and Beulah
Beazley Foundation
Bedford Fund
Bedsole Foundation, J. L.
Beecher Foundation, Florence Simon
Bel Air Mart
Belk Stores
Bellini Foundation
Belo Corp., A.H.
Benbough Foundation, Legler
Benedum Foundation, Claude Worthington
Beneficial Corp.
Benenson Foundation, Frances and Benjamin
Benwood Foundation
Berrie Foundation, Russell
Berry Foundation, Archie W. and Grace
Bersted Foundation
Bertha Foundation
Besser Foundation
Bethlehem Steel Corp.
Bettingen Corporation, Burton G.
Beveridge Foundation, Frank Stanley
BFGoodrich
Bickerton Charitable Trust, Lydia H.
Bierhaus Foundation
Big V Supermarkets
Bingham Second Betterment Fund, William
Birnschein Foundation, Alvin and Marion
Bissell Foundation, J. Walton
Bjorkman Foundation
Blank Family Foundation
Blaustein Foundation, Jacob and Hilda
Blaustein Foundation, Louis and Henrietta
Block, H&R
Blount
Blue Cross and Blue Shield of Minnesota Foundation Inc.
Blue Cross & Blue Shield of Alabama
Blum Foundation, Lois and Irving
Boatmen's Bancshares
Boatmen's First National Bank of Oklahoma
Bobst Foundation, Elmer and Mamdouha
Bodman Foundation
Boehringer Mannheim Corp.
Booth-Bricker Fund
Boothroyd Foundation, Charles H. and Bertha L.
Boots Pharmaceuticals, Inc.
Booz Allen & Hamilton
Borman's

Boston Edison Co.
Boswell Foundation, James G.
Bothin Foundation
Botwinick-Wolfensohn Foundation
Bovaird Foundation, Mervin
Bowater Inc.
Bowsher-Booher Foundation
Boynton Fund, John W.
BP America
Brach Foundation, Edwin I.
Brach Foundation, Helen
Bradley-Turner Foundation
Brady Foundation
Brennan Foundation, Robert E.
Bridgestone/Firestone
Briggs & Stratton Corp.
Brillion Iron Works
Bristol-Myers Squibb Co.
Bristol Savings Bank
British Airways
Brochsteins Inc.
Brooks Brothers
Brown Family Foundation, John Mathew Gay
Brown Foundation
Brown Foundation, James Graham
Browning-Ferris Industries
Brundage Charitable, Scientific, and Wildlife Conservation Foundation, Charles E. and Edna T.
Brunner Foundation, Robert
Brunswick Corp.
Bryan Family Foundation, Kathleen Price and Joseph M.
Buchanan Family Foundation
Bucyrus-Erie
Burlington Industries
Burndy Corp.
Burnham Donor Fund, Alfred G.
Burns Foundation, Fritz B.
Burns International
Burroughs Wellcome Co.
Butler Manufacturing Co.
Cabell III and Maude Morgan Cabell Foundation, Robert G.
Cabot Corp.
Cafritz Foundation, Morris and Gwendolyn
Cameron Foundation, Harry S. and Isabel C.
Campbell Foundation, Charles Talbot
Campbell Foundation, Ruth and Henry
Cannon Foundation
Canon U.S.A., Inc.
Cantor Foundation, Iris and B. Gerald
Carnegie Corporation of New York
Carnival Cruise Lines
Carolina Power & Light Co.
Carolyn Foundation
Carpenter Technology Corp.
Carrier Corp.
Carter Family Foundation
Carter Foundation, Amon G.
Carter-Wallace
Cartier, Inc.
Carvel Foundation, Thomas and Agnes
Caspersen Foundation for Aid to Health and Education, O. W.
Castle Foundation, Harold K. L.
Castle Foundation, Samuel N. and Mary
Caterpillar
CBI Industries
Centerior Energy Corp.
Central Bank of the South
Central Fidelity Banks, Inc.
Central Maine Power Co.
Central Soya Co.
Century Companies of America
CertainTeed Corp.

Chambers Development Co.
Champlin Foundations
Charles River Laboratories
Charter Manufacturing Co.
Chase Manhattan Bank, N.A.
Chatlos Foundation
CHC Foundation
Chernow Trust for the Benefit of Charity Dated 3/13/75, Michael
Chevron Corp.
Childress Foundation, Francis and Miranda
China Medical Board of New York
Church & Dwight Co.
Churches Homes Foundation
Ciba-Geigy Corp. (Pharmaceuticals Division)
Cincinnati Milacron
CIT Group Holdings
Citicorp
City of Hope 1989 Section E Foundation
Claneil Foundation
CLARCOR
Clark Foundation
Clark-Winchcole Foundation
Clayton Fund
Cleveland-Cliffs
Clorox Co.
Clowes Fund
CM Alliance Cos.
CNA Insurance Cos.
Cockrell Foundation
Cohen Family Foundation, Saul Z. and Amy Scheuer
Cole Foundation
Coleman Co.
Coles Family Foundation
Collins Foundation
Collins, Jr. Foundation, George Fulton
Collins Medical Trust
Colonial Oil Industries, Inc.
Colorado Trust
Commerzbank AG, New York
Commonwealth Edison Co.
Commonwealth Fund
Community Hospital Foundation
Comstock Foundation
Concord Chemical Co.
Cone-Blanchard Machine Co.
Cone Mills Corp.
Connelly Foundation
Consolidated Papers
Constantin Foundation
Continental Corp.
Cook Foundation, Loring
Cooke Foundation
Cooper Industries
Coors Brewing Co.
Coors Foundation, Adolph
Copperweld Steel Co.
Corbett Foundation
Corpus Christi Exploration Co.
Corvallis Clinic
Cove Charitable Trust
Cowles Charitable Trust
Cox Charitable Trust, A. G.
Cox Charitable Trust, Jessie B.
CPC International
Crane Co.
Credit Agricole
Crestar Financial Corp.
Crown Central Petroleum Corp.
Crown Cork & Seal Co., Inc.
Crum and Forster
Crystal Trust
Cudahy Fund, Patrick and Anna M.
Culpeper Memorial Foundation, Daphne Seybolt
Cummings Memorial Fund Trust, Frances L. and Edwin L.
CUNA Mutual Insurance Group
Curtice-Burns Foods

Dain Bosworth/Inter-Regional Financial Group
Dammann Fund
Dana Corp.
Daniel Foundation of Alabama
Davis Foundation, Joe C.
DCNY Corp.
DEC International, Inc.
DeCamp Foundation, Ira W.
Deere & Co.
Delacorte Fund, George
Delavan Foundation, Nelson B.
Dentsply International, Inc.
Deposit Guaranty National Bank
DeRoy Testamentary Foundation
DeVos Foundation, Richard and Helen
Dewing Foundation, Frances R.
Dexter Corp.
Dexter Shoe Co.
Diamond Foundation, Aaron
Diamond Walnut Growers
Diener Foundation, Frank C.
Digital Equipment Corp.
Dimeo Construction Co.
Dodge Foundation, Cleveland H.
Dodge Foundation, P. L.
Dodge Jones Foundation
Doheny Foundation, Carrie Estelle
Donaldson Charitable Trust, Oliver S. and Jennie R.
Dougherty, Jr. Foundation, James R.
Dresser Industries
du Pont de Nemours & Co., E. I.
Duke Endowment
Duke Power Co.
Dun & Bradstreet Corp.
Duncan Trust, James R.
Dunspaugh-Dalton Foundation
duPont Foundation, Alfred I.
duPont Foundation, Chichester
duPont Fund, Jessie Ball
Durfee Foundation
Durr-Fillauer Medical
Dynamet, Inc.
Eastern Enterprises
Eastman Foundation, Alexander
Eastman Kodak Co.
Eaton Corp.
Ebell of Los Angeles Rest Cottage Association
Eccles Foundation, George S. and Dolores Dore
Eckerd Corp., Jack
Eden Hall Foundation
Edwards Memorial Trust
Ellsworth Trust, W. H.
Emerson Foundation, Fred L.
Encyclopaedia Britannica, Inc.
Engelhard Foundation, Charles
English-Bonter-Mitchell Foundation
English Memorial Fund, Florence C. and H. L.
Enron Corp.
Ensign-Bickford Industries
Ensworth Charitable Foundation
Equifax
Ernsthausen Charitable Foundation, John F. and Doris E.
Erteszek Foundation
Essick Foundation
Ethyl Corp.
Exxon Corp.
Fabick Tractor Co., John
Falcon Foundation
Falk Medical Fund, Maurice
Farallon Foundation
Farish Fund, William Stamps
Farwell Foundation, Drusilla
Faulkner Trust, Marianne Gaillard
Federal Express Corp.
Federal-Mogul Corp.

Federation Foundation of Greater Philadelphia
Feinberg Foundation, Joseph and Bessie
Feintech Foundation
Fibre Converters
Field Foundation of Illinois
Fieldcrest Cannon
Fife Foundation, Elias and Bertha
Fikes Foundation, Leland
FINA, Inc.
Fink Foundation
Firestone, Jr. Foundation, Harvey
First Fidelity Bancorporation
First Interstate Bank of California
First Interstate Bank of Oregon
First Union Corp.
First Union National Bank of Florida
Fish Foundation, Ray C.
Fish Foundation, Vain and Harry
Fisher Foundation
Fitch Trust f/b/o Cheshire Health Foundation, Leon M. and Hazel E.
Fiterman Charitable Foundation, Miles and Shirley
Fleet Bank of New York
Flemm Foundation, John J.
Florence Foundation
Florida Power Corp.
Florida Power & Light Co.
FMC Corp.
FMR Corp.
Foerderer Foundation, Percival E. and Ethel Brown
Fohs Foundation
Forbes
Ford Foundation
Ford III Memorial Foundation, Jefferson Lee
Ford Motor Co.
Forest City Enterprises
Forest Foundation
Fortis Benefits Insurance Company/Fortis Financial Group
Foster Foundation
Foundation for Seacoast Health
Foundation for the Needs of Others
Fourth Financial Corp.
Fox Foundation, John H.
Fraida Foundation
Frank Foundation, Ernest and Elfriede
Frankel Foundation, George and Elizabeth F.
Fraser Paper Ltd.
Freeman Foundation, Carl M.
Frees Foundation
Friedman Family Foundation
Friendship Fund
Frisch's Restaurants Inc.
Froderman Foundation
Frohman Foundation, Sidney
Frueauff Foundation, Charles A.
Fry Foundation, Lloyd A.
Fuller Foundation, George F. and Sybil H.
Fund for New Jersey
Funderburke & Associates
Gannett Publishing Co., Guy
Gateway Apparel
GATX Corp.
Gault-Hussey Charitable Trust
Gavin Foundation, James and Zita
Gavin Foundation, James and Zita
Gaylord Foundation, Clifford Willard
Gazette Co.
Gear Motion
General Mills
General Motors Corp.
General Reinsurance Corp.
General Tire Inc.

Health Organizations (cont.)

Genius Foundation, Elizabeth Morse
Georgia-Pacific Corp.
Georgia Power Co.
Gerber Products Co.
German Protestant Orphan Asylum Association
Giant Eagle
Giant Food Stores
Gibson Foundation, E. L.
Giger Foundation, Paul and Oscar
Giles Foundation, Edward C.
Gillette Co.
Gilman, Jr. Foundation, Sondra and Charles
Ginter Foundation, Karl and Anna
Glaxo
Gleason Foundation, Katherine
Glenmore Distilleries Co.
Glenn Foundation, Carrie C. & Lena V.
Glick Foundation, Eugene and Marilyn
Glickenhaus & Co.
Goddard Foundation, Charles B.
Godfrey Co.
Goerlich Family Foundation
Goldman Foundation, Herman
Goldman Foundation, William
Goldsmith Foundation
Goldwyn Foundation, Samuel
Golub Corp.
Goodyear Tire & Rubber Co.
Gould Inc.
Grace & Co., W.R.
Grader Foundation, K. W.
Grainger Foundation
Graphic Controls Corp.
Grassmann Trust, E. J.
Green Foundation
Green Foundation, Burton E.
Green Fund
Greene Manufacturing Co.
Greenspan Foundation
Gregg-Graniteville Foundation
Grigg-Lewis Trust
Grimes Foundation
Gross Foundation, Louis H.
Group Health Plan Inc.
Groves & Sons Co., S.J.
Gruber Research Foundation, Lila
Grumbacher Foundation, M. S.
Guaranty Bank & Trust Co.
Gulf Power Co.
Gulton Foundation
Gussman Foundation, Herbert and Roseline
Haas Foundation, Paul and Mary
Hachar Charitable Trust, D. D.
Hackett Foundation
Hafif Family Foundation
Haggerty Foundation
Hagler Foundation, Jon L.
Hall Charitable Trust, Evelyn A. J.
Hall Foundation
Hambay Foundation, James T.
Hammer Foundation, Armand
Hancock Foundation, Luke B.
Hankins Foundation
Hanson Foundation
Hargis Charitable Foundation, Estes H. and Florence Parker
Harriman Foundation, Gladys and Roland
Harriman Foundation, Mary W.
Harris Corp.
Harris Foundation
Harsco Corp.
Hartford Courant Foundation

Hartford Steam Boiler Inspection & Insurance Co.
Hartmarx Corp.
Hartzell Industries, Inc.
Hawn Foundation
Hayfields Foundation
Hayswood Foundation
Hearst Foundation, William Randolph
Hechinger Co.
Hecht's
Hedrick Foundation, Frank E.
HEI Inc.
Heinz Co., H.J.
Helzberg Foundation, Shirley and Barnett
Henderson Foundation, George B.
Hermann Foundation, Grover
Herrick Foundation
Hess Foundation
Heublein
Hewit Family Foundation
Heymann Special Account, Mr. and Mrs. Jimmy
Higgins Charitable Trust, Lorene Sails
Hilton Foundation, Conrad N.
Hirschhorn Foundation, David and Barbara B.
Hobby Foundation
Hoblitzelle Foundation
Hoffberger Foundation
Hoffmann-La Roche
Hofmann Co.
Hofstetter Trust, Bessie
Hogan Foundation, Royal Barney
Holley Foundation
Holmes Foundation
Homeland Foundation
Hooper Foundation, Elizabeth S.
Hopkins Foundation, Josephine Lawrence
Hopwood Charitable Trust, John M.
Hospital Corp. of America
Household International
Houston Endowment
Houston Industries
Howard and Bush Foundation
Hubbard Broadcasting
Hubbard Milling Co.
Hubbell Inc.
Huber Foundation
Huffy Corp.
Hughes Charitable Trust, Mabel Y.
Hugoton Foundation
Hunt Alternatives Fund
Hunt Foundation
Hurlbut Memorial Fund, Orion L. and Emma S.
Huston Foundation
Hyams Foundation
Hyde and Watson Foundation
Hyundai Motor America
I. and L. Association
IBM Corp.
IBP, Inc.
Iddings Benevolent Trust
Illinois Bell
Imperial Bancorp
Index Technology Corp.
Indiana Insurance Cos.
Ingalls Foundation, Louise H. and David S.
Inland Container Corp.
Inman Mills
Innovating Worthy Projects Foundation
International Paper Co.
Ireland Foundation
Irvine Foundation, James
Irwin Charity Foundation, William G.
ITT Hartford Insurance Group
Ittleson Foundation

J.P. Morgan & Co.
Jackson Foundation
Jacobson & Sons, Benjamin
Janirve Foundation
Janssen Foundation, Henry
Jarson-Stanley and Mickey Kaplan Foundation, Isaac & Esther
Jasper Seating Co.
Jaydor Corp.
JCPenney Co.
JELD-WEN, Inc.
Jennings Foundation, Alma
Jennings Foundation, Mary Hillman
Jewish Healthcare Foundation of Pittsburgh
Jockey Hollow Foundation
Johnson Charitable Trust, Keith Wold
Johnson Foundation, Robert Wood
Johnson & Higgins
Johnson & Johnson
Johnstone and H. Earle Kimball Foundation, Phyllis Kimball
Jones Foundation, Daisy Marquis
Jonsson Foundation
Joslin-Needham Family Foundation
Jost Foundation, Charles and Mabel P.
Journal Gazette Co.
Julia R. and Estelle L. Foundation
Kaiser Family Foundation, Henry J.
Kangesser Foundation, Robert E., Harry A., and M. Sylvia
Kantzler Foundation
Kasle Steel Corp.
Kauffman Foundation, Muriel McBrien
Kaufman Endowment Fund, Louis G.
Kavanagh Foundation, T. James
Kawabe Memorial Fund
Kayser Foundation
Keebler Co.
Keith Foundation Trust, Ben E.
Kelley Foundation, Kate M.
Kellogg Foundation, W. K.
Kellogg's
Kelly Tractor Co.
Kempner Fund, Harris and Eliza
Kennametal
Kennedy Foundation, Ethel
Kerr-McGee Corp.
Kettering Fund
Kiewit Foundation, Peter
Kiewit Sons, Peter
Kilworth Charitable Trust, William
Kimmelman Foundation, Helen & Milton
King Ranch
Kiplinger Foundation
Kirchgessner Foundation, Karl
Klee Foundation, Conrad and Virginia
Kline Foundation, Josiah W. and Bessie H.
Knowles Foundation
Knowles Foundation
Koehler Foundation, Marcia and Otto
Koopman Fund
Koret Foundation
Kowalski Sausage Co.
Kramer Foundation
Kresge Foundation
Kress Foundation, George
Kuhns Investment Co.
Kynett Memorial Foundation, Edna G.
Kysor Industrial Corp.
Lacy Foundation
Ladish Co.

Lambert Memorial Foundation, Gerard B.
LamCo. Communications
Lance, Inc.
Lane Co., Inc.
Lane Foundation, Minnie and Bernard
Lang Foundation, Eugene M.
Langdale Co.
Lard Trust, Mary Potishman
Large Foundation
Laros Foundation, R. K.
Larsen Fund
Law Foundation, Robert O.
Lazarus Charitable Trust, Helen and Charles
LDI Charitable Foundation
Leavey Foundation, Thomas and Dorothy
LeBrun Foundation
Lee Endowment Foundation
Lehigh Portland Cement Co.
Lehman Foundation, Edith and Herbert
Lehrman Foundation, Jacob and Charlotte
Leidy Foundation, John J.
Leighton-Oare Foundation
Lennox International, Inc.
Leo Burnett Co.
Leonardt Foundation
Levee Charitable Trust, Polly Annenberg
Levy Foundation, Betty and Norman F.
Levy Foundation, June Rockwell
Levy's Lumber & Building Centers
Lewis Foundation, Frank J.
Liberty Corp.
Life Insurance Co. of Georgia
Lilly & Co., Eli
Lincoln Electric Co.
Lindsay Trust, Agnes M.
Lindstrom Foundation, Kinney
Lipsky Foundation, Fred and Sarah
Lipton, Thomas J.
Littauer Foundation, Lucius N.
Littlefield Memorial Trust, Ida Ballou
Logan Foundation, E. J.
Lost Tree Charitable Foundation
Lotus Development Corp.
Louisiana Land & Exploration Co.
Lowenstein Foundation, Leon
LTV Corp.
Lubrizol Corp.
Luce Charitable Trust, Theodore
Luchsinger Family Foundation
Lumpkin Foundation
Lurie Family Foundation
Lurie Foundation, Louis R.
Luse Foundation, W. P. and Bulah
Lutheran Brotherhood Foundation
Lydall, Inc.
Lynn Foundation, E. M.
Lyon Foundation
Lytel Foundation, Bertha Russ
MacAndrews & Forbes Holdings
MacArthur Foundation, John D. and Catherine T.
MacLeod Stewardship Foundation
Macy & Co., R.H.
Macy, Jr. Foundation, Josiah
Madison Gas & Electric Co.
Magowan Family Foundation
Mailman Family Foundation, A. L.
Mamiye Brothers
Manufacturers Life Insurance Co. of America
Manufacturers Life Insurance Co. of America
Manville Corp.

Mardag Foundation
Marriott Corp.
Marriott Foundation, J. Willard
Marshall & Ilsley Bank
Martin Marietta Corp.
Martini Foundation, Nicholas
Massey Charitable Trust
Mather and William Gwinn Mather Fund, Elizabeth Ring
Mathis-Pfohl Foundation
Maxfield Foundation
May Department Stores Co.
May Foundation, Wilbur
May Mitchell Royal Foundation
Mayer Foundation, James and Eva
Maytag Family Foundation, Fred
MBIA, Inc.
McBean Family Foundation
McBeath Foundation, Faye
McBride & Son Associates
McCasland Foundation
McCormick & Co.
McCormick Foundation, Chauncey and Marion Deering
McCullough Foundation, Ralph H. and Ruth J.
McCune Foundation
McCutchen Foundation
McDonnell Douglas Corp.-West
McEachern Charitable Trust, D. V. & Ida J.
McFeely-Rogers Foundation
McGraw-Hill
MCI Communications Corp.
McInerny Foundation
McMillan, Jr. Foundation, Bruce
McNutt Charitable Trust, Amy Shelton
McShain Charities, John
MDU Resources Group, Inc.
Mead Fund, Nelson
Meadows Foundation
Mechanics Bank
Mellen Foundation
Mellon Bank Corp.
Mellon Foundation, Richard King
Memorial Foundation for the Blind
Mendel Foundation
Menschel Foundation, Robert and Joyce
Mercury Aircraft
Mercy, Jr. Foundation, Sue and Eugene
Meridian Bancorp
Merrill Lynch & Co.
Metal Industries
Metropolitan Health Foundation
Metropolitan Life Insurance Co.
Mettler Instrument Corp.
Meyer Foundation, Alice Kleberg Reynolds
Meyer Foundation, Baron de Hirsch
Meyer Foundation, Robert R.
Meyer Memorial Trust
Middendorf Foundation
Milbank Foundation, Dunlevy
Miller Foundation, Steve J.
Miller-Mellor Association
Milstein Family Foundation
Mine Safety Appliances Co.
Miniger Memorial Foundation, Clement O.
Minolta Corp.
Missouri Farmers Association
Mitchell Family Foundation, Edward D. and Anna
Mitrani Family Foundation
Mobil Oil Corp.
Moncrief Foundation, William A. and Elizabeth B.
Monell Foundation, Ambrose
Montgomery Street Foundation
Moog Automotive, Inc.
Moore Family Foundation

Moore Foundation, Edward S.
Moore Foundation, Martha G.
Moore Foundation, O. L.
Moorman Manufacturing Co.
Morrill Charitable Foundation
Morris Foundation
Morrison-Knudsen Corp.
Morrison Trust, Louise L.
Moses Fund, Henry and Lucy
Motter Printing Press Co.
Mulligan Charitable Trust, Mary S.
Munson Foundation, W. B.
Murphy Foundation, John P.
Murray Foundation
Nalco Chemical Co.
Nashua Trust Co.
Nathan Foundation
National City Bank, Columbus
National City Bank of Evansville
National Forge Co.
National Gypsum Co.
National Life of Vermont
National Machinery Co.
National Medical Enterprises
National Pro-Am Youth Fund
National Steel
Nationwide Insurance Cos.
Navistar International Corp.
NBD Bank
NCR Corp.
Nelson Foundation, Florence
Nelson Industries, Inc.
Nesholm Family Foundation
Neuberger Foundation, Roy R. and Marie S.
New Cycle Foundation
New England Mutual Life Insurance Co.
New Horizon Foundation
New World Foundation
New York Foundation
New York Life Insurance Co.
New York Telephone Co.
The New Yorker Magazine, Inc.
Newhouse Foundation, Samuel I.
Noble Charitable Trust, John L. and Ethel G.
Noble Foundation, Samuel Roberts
Noonan Memorial Fund under the will of Frank Noonan, Deborah Munroe
Norfolk Shipbuilding & Drydock Corp.
Norfolk Southern Corp.
North American Life & Casualty Co.
Northern Trust Co.
Northwest Natural Gas Co.
Norton Co.
Norwest Bank Nebraska
NuTone Inc.
Occidental Petroleum Corp.
Oceanic Cablevision Foundation
Odyssey Partners
Ogden Foundation, Ralph E.
Ogilvy & Mather Worldwide
Ogle Foundation, Paul
Oglebay Norton Co.
Ohio Savings Bank
Ohl, Jr. Trust, George A.
Oleson Foundation
Olin Corp.
Olive Bridge Fund
Olympia Brewing Co.
1957 Charity Trust
Oppenheimer Family Foundation
Orscheln Co.
Osborn Manufacturing Co.
Oshkosh B'Gosh
O'Sullivan Children Foundation
O'Toole Foundation, Theresa and Edward
Overbrook Foundation
PACCAR
Pacific Mutual Life Insurance Co.

Packard Foundation, David and Lucile
Packer Foundation, Horace B.
Pappas Charitable Foundation, Bessie
Parker-Hannifin Corp.
Parsons Foundation, Ralph M.
Parsons - W.D. Charities, Vera Davis
Parvin Foundation, Albert
Pasadena Area Residential Aid
Patterson-Barclay Memorial Foundation
Peabody Charitable Fund, Amelia
Penn Foundation, William
Pennzoil Co.
Penzance Foundation
Peoples Energy Corp.
PepsiCo
Perkin-Elmer Corp.
Perkin Fund
Perkins Foundation, Edwin E.
Perot Foundation
Persis Corp.
Petersen Foundation, Esper A.
Petteys Memorial Foundation, Jack
Pettus Crowe Foundation
Pfizer
Phelps Dodge Corp.
PHH Corp.
Phillips Charitable Trust, Dr. and Mrs. Arthur William
Phillips Family Foundation, Jay and Rose
Phillips Petroleum Co.
Phillips-Van Heusen Corp.
Piankova Foundation, Tatiana
Piedmont Health Care Foundation
Pierce Charitable Trust, Harold Whitworth
Pineywoods Foundation
Pioneer Trust Bank, NA
Pitzman Fund
Plant Memorial Fund, Henry B.
Plitt Southern Theatres
Pollock Company Foundation, William B.
Potomac Electric Power Co.
Pott Foundation, Herman T. and Phenie R.
Potts Memorial Foundation
PPG Industries
Premier Industrial Corp.
Prentis Family Foundation, Meyer and Anna
Prentiss Foundation, Elisabeth Severance
Preuss Foundation
Preyer Fund, Mary Norris
Price Associates, T. Rowe
Priddy Foundation
Principal Financial Group
Pritzker Foundation
Procter & Gamble Co.
Procter & Gamble Cosmetic & Fragrance Products
Propp Sons Fund, Morris and Anna
Providence Journal Company
Prudential-Bache Securities
Prudential Insurance Co. of America
Public Welfare Foundation
Putnam Foundation
Quaker Chemical Corp.
Quaker Oats Co.
Quest for Truth Foundation
Questar Corp.
R. F. Foundation
R&B Tool Co.
Ramapo Trust
Ramlose Foundation, George A.
Rankin and Elizabeth Forbes Rankin Trust, William
Ranney Foundation, P. K.
Ransom Fidelity Company

Raskob Foundation for Catholic Activities
Rasmussen Foundation
Raymond Corp.
Recognition Equipment
Reichhold Chemicals, Inc.
Reily & Co., William B.
Reinberger Foundation
Reliable Life Insurance Co.
Reliance Electric Co.
Rennebohm Foundation, Oscar
Retirement Research Foundation
Reynolds Charitable Trust, Kate B.
Reynolds Foundation, Donald W.
Reynolds Foundation, J. B.
RGK Foundation
Rhoden Charitable Foundation, Elmer C.
Rhone-Poulenc Rorer
Rice Foundation
Rice Foundation, Helen Steiner
Rich Products Corp.
Richardson Fund, Grace
Rieke Corp.
Rienzi Foundation
Robison Foundation, Ellis H. and Doris B.
Roblee Foundation, Joseph H. and Florence A.
Robson Foundation, LaNelle
Rockefeller Foundation
Rockford Acromatics Products Co./Aircraft Gear Corp.
Rockford Products Corp.
Rockwell Fund
Rockwell International Corp.
Rodgers Foundation, Richard & Dorothy
Rogers Foundation
Rogers Foundation
Rohm and Haas Company
Rohr Inc.
Rolfs Foundation, Thomas J.
RosaMary Foundation
Rose Foundation, Billy
Roseburg Forest Products Co.
Rosenberg Foundation, Henry and Ruth Blaustein
Rosenstiel Foundation
Rosenthal Foundation, Benjamin J.
Rosenthal-Statter Foundation
Ross Foundation, Walter G.
Ross Laboratories
Roth Foundation
Rowland Foundation
Royal Group Inc.
Ruan Foundation Trust, John
Rubbermaid
Rubenstein Foundation, Philip
Rubinstein Foundation, Helena
Ruddick Corp.
Rudin Foundation
Rudin Foundation, Samuel and May
Rudy, Jr. Trust, George B.
Ruffin Foundation, Peter B. & Adeline W.
Rukin Philanthropic Foundation, David and Eleanore
Russell Charitable Trust, Josephine S.
Ryland Group
SAFECO Corp.
Safeguard Scientifics Foundation
Sage Foundation
Saint Croix Foundation
Saint Gerard Foundation
Salgo Charitable Trust, Nicholas M.
Salomon Foundation, Richard & Edna
San Diego Gas & Electric
San Diego Trust & Savings Bank
Sandoz Corp.
Sandy Hill Foundation

Sara Lee Corp.
Sara Lee Hosiery
Sawyer Charitable Foundation
Scaife Family Foundation
Schaffer Foundation, Michael & Helen
Schamach Foundation, Milton
Schiff Foundation
Schmidlapp Trust No. 1, Jacob G.
Scholl Foundation, Dr.
Scholler Foundation
Schoonmaker J-Sewkly Valley Hospital Trust
Schroeder Foundation, Walter
Schultz Foundation
Schust Foundation, Clarence L. and Edith B.
Schwartz Foundation, Arnold A.
Schwartz Foundation, Bernard Lee
Science Applications International Corp.
Scott and Fetzer Co.
Scott Foundation, William E.
Scrivner, Inc.
Scroggins Foundation, Arthur E. and Cornelia C.
Seafirst Corp.
Sealaska Corp.
Sealright Co., Inc.
Searle & Co., G.D.
Seaway Food Town
Seay Memorial Trust, George and Effie
Security Benefit Life Insurance Co.
Security Life of Denver
Senior Services of Stamford
Sentinel Communications Co.
Sentry Insurance Co.
Sequoia Foundation
Shawmut National Corp.
Shea Foundation
Sheaffer Inc.
Shell Oil Co.
Shenandoah Life Insurance Co.
Sheppard Foundation, Lawrence B.
Shoney's Inc.
Shwayder Foundation, Fay
Sierra Pacific Industries
Sifco Industries Inc.
Simmons Family Foundation, R. P.
Simon Foundation, William E. and Carol G.
Simpson Industries
SIT Investment Associates, Inc.
Skirball Foundation
Smeal Foundation, Mary Jean & Frank P.
Smith Charitable Fund, Eleanor Armstrong
Smith Charitable Trust, W. W.
Smith Family Foundation, Theda Clark
Smith Foundation, Bob and Vivian
Smith Foundation, Gordon V. and Helen C.
Smith Foundation, Richard and Susan
Smith Memorial Fund, Ethel Sergeant Clark
Smithers Foundation, Christopher D.
SmithKline Beecham
Smucker Co., J.M.
SNC Manufacturing Co.
Snee-Reinhardt Charitable Foundation
SNET
Snyder Foundation, Harold B. and Dorothy A.
Society for Savings
Soling Family Foundation
Somers Foundation, Byron H.
Sonat

Sonoco Products Co.
Sony Corp. of America
Sooner Pipe & Supply Corp.
Sordoni Foundation
Souers Charitable Trust, Sidney W. and Sylvia N.
South Waite Foundation
Southern California Edison Co.
Speas Foundation, Victor E.
Speas Memorial Trust, John W. and Effie E.
Spiegel Family Foundation, Jerry and Emily
Sprague Educational and Charitable Foundation, Seth
Springs Foundation
SPS Technologies
Spunk Fund
Stackner Family Foundation
Stacy Foundation, Festus
Staley, Jr. Foundation, A. E.
Standard Products Co.
Star Bank, N.A.
Stare Fund
State Street Bank & Trust Co.
Stauffer Communications
Stauffer Foundation, John and Beverly
Steelcase
Steele Foundation
Steiger Memorial Fund, Albert
Stein Foundation, Joseph F.
Stein Foundation, Louis
Steiner Charitable Fund, Albert
Sterkel Trust, Justine
Sterling Inc.
Sterling Winthrop
Stern Family Foundation, Harry
Stern Family Fund
Stern Foundation, Bernice and Milton
Stern Foundation, Leonard N.
Sterne-Elder Memorial Trust
Stewart Educational Foundation, Donnell B. and Elizabeth Dee Shaw
Stillwell Charitable Trust, Glen and Dorothy
Stocker Foundation
Stone Charitable Foundation
Stone Foundation, France
Stone Trust, H. Chase
Stone & Webster, Inc.
Stony Wold Herbert Fund
Strake Foundation
Strauss Foundation, Leon
Stupp Brothers Bridge & Iron Co.
Sturgis Charitable and Educational Trust, Roy and Christine
Subaru of America Inc.
Sumitomo Bank of California
Swanson Foundation
Sweatt Foundation, Harold W.
Sweet Life Foods
Swift Memorial Health Care Foundation
Synovus Financial Corp.
Tai and Co., J. T.
Talley Industries, Inc.
Taper Foundation, Mark
Tarmac America Inc.
Taub Foundation
Taubman Foundation, A. Alfred
Taylor Foundation, Fred and Harriett
Taylor Foundation, Ruth and Vernon
Teledyne
Templeton Foundation, John
Tenneco
Terner Foundation
Tesoro Petroleum Corp.
Texaco
Texas Commerce Bank Houston, N.A.
Textron

Health Organizations (cont.)

Thomas & Betts Corp.
Thoresen Foundation
3M Co.
Thurston Charitable Foundation
Times Mirror Co.
Timken Co.
Tippens Foundation
Tiscornia Foundation
TJX Cos.
Todd Co., A.M.
Tokheim Corp.
Tomkins Industries, Inc.
Torchmark Corp.
Tozer Foundation
Tracor, Inc.
Treadwell Foundation, Nora Eccles
TRINOVA Corp.
Trion
Tropicana Products, Inc.
Trust Co. Bank
Tull Charitable Foundation
Turner Fund, Ruth
Tyler Corp.
Tyson Foods, Inc.
Tyson Fund
Unger Foundation, Aber D.
Unilever United States
Union Camp Corp.
Union Electric Co.
Unisys Corp.
United Parcel Service of America
United States Borax & Chemical Corp.
U.S. Oil/Schmidt Family Foundation, Inc.
United States Sugar Corp.
United States Trust Co. of New York
United Technologies Corp.
Universal Leaf Tobacco Co.
Unocal Corp.
Upjohn California Fund
Upjohn Co.
USG Corp.
Ushkow Foundation
UST
USX Corp.
Vale-Asche Foundation
van Ameringen Foundation
Van Buren Foundation
Van Nuys Charities, J. B. and Emily
Varian Associates
Veritas Foundation
Vicksburg Hospital Medical Foundation
Vidda Foundation
Virginia Power Co.
Vollbrecht Foundation, Frederick A.
Vulcan Materials Co.
Wachovia Bank & Trust Co., N.A.
Waggoner Charitable Trust, Crystelle
Wal-Mart Stores
Waldinger Corp.
Walker Foundation, L. C. and Margaret
Walker Foundation, W. E.
Wallace Computer Services
Walter Industries
Warner-Lambert Co.
Warren Foundation, William K.
Washington Forrest Foundation
Washington Square Fund
Washington Square Health Foundation
Wasily Family Foundation
Watson Foundation, Walter E. and Caroline H.
Wausau Paper Mills Co.
Wean Foundation, Raymond John

Weaver Foundation, Gil and Dody
Wege Foundation
Weisz Foundation, David and Sylvia
Wellman Foundation, S. K.
Wells Foundation, A. Z.
Wells Foundation, Franklin H. and Ruth L.
Wells Trust Fund, Fred W.
Wendt Foundation, Margaret L.
Wenger Foundation, Henry L. and Consuelo S.
Westchester Health Fund
Western Cardiac Foundation
Westvaco Corp.
Weyerhaeuser Co.
Wheless Foundation
Whirlpool Corp.
Whitehead Charitable Foundation
Whiting Memorial Foundation, Henry and Harriet
Whittell Trust for Disabled Veterans of Foreign Wars, Elia
Wickes Foundation, Harvey Randall
Wigwam Mills
Wilbur-Ellis Co.
Wilder Foundation
Wildermuth Foundation, E. F.
Williams Cos.
Willits Foundation
Wilson Foundation, Marie C. and Joseph C.
Wisconsin Centrifugal
Wisconsin Energy Corp.
Wisconsin Power & Light Co.
Wodecroft Foundation
Wolfson Family Foundation
Woman's Seamen's Friend Society of Connecticut
Wood-Claeyssens Foundation
Woodward Fund-Atlanta, David, Helen. Marian
Woodward Fund-Watertown, David, Helen, and Marian
Wrigley Co., Wm. Jr.
Wurts Memorial, Henrietta Tower
Wyman-Gordon Co.
Wyomissing Foundation
Yost Trust, Elizabeth Burns
Young Foundation, Hugo H. and Mabel B.
Zamoiski Co.
Zock Endowment Trust

Hospices

Abell-Hanger Foundation
Abney Foundation
AFLAC
Aigner
Albany International Corp.
Allen-Heath Memorial Foundation
Allendale Mutual Insurance Co.
AlliedSignal
ALPAC Corp.
Alumax
Aluminum Co. of America
American Aggregates Corp.
American Cyanamid Co.
American Financial Corp.
American General Finance
American National Bank & Trust Co. of Chicago
American Natural Resources Co.
Ames Department Stores
Amfac/JMB Hawaii
Amoco Corp.
AMP
Anderson Foundation, John W.
Anschutz Family Foundation
Apple Computer, Inc.
Appleby Trust, Scott B. and Annie P.
Arcadia Foundation
Aristech Chemical Corp.

Arizona Public Service Co.
Armco Inc.
Arvin Industries
ASARCO
Atherton Family Foundation
Atlanta Gas Light Co.
Attleboro Pawtucket Savings Bank
Atwood Foundation
Auerbach Foundation, Beatrice Fox
Avon Products
Bacon Trust, Charles F.
Baltimore Gas & Electric Co.
Bank of America Arizona
Bank One, Youngstown, NA
Banner Life Insurance Co.
Barden Corp.
Barra Foundation
Bay Branch Foundation
Beal Foundation
Bedford Fund
Beech Aircraft Corp.
Benbough Foundation, Legler
Benefit Trust Life Insurance Co.
Betts Industries
Beveridge Foundation, Frank Stanley
BHP Pacific Resources
Bickerton Charitable Trust, Lydia H.
Birmingham Foundation
Blair Foundation, John
Block, H&R
Bloomfield Foundation, Sam and Rie
Blue Bell, Inc.
Blum-Kovler Foundation
Bobst Foundation, Elmer and Mamdouha
Bock Charitable Trust, George W.
Boeing Co.
Boettcher Foundation
Bonfils-Stanton Foundation
Borman's
Bourns, Inc.
Bowater Inc.
Brach Foundation, Helen
Braun Foundation
Bremer Foundation, Otto
Bridwell Foundation, J. S.
Brooks Foundation, Gladys
Brown Foundation
Browning-Ferris Industries
Brownley Trust, Walter
Brunswick Corp.
Buchalter, Nemer, Fields, & Younger
Bull Foundation, Henry W.
Burden Foundation, Florence V.
Burndy Corp.
Cafritz Foundation, Morris and Gwendolyn
Cahn Family Foundation
Cain Foundation, Gordon and Mary
Cameron Foundation, Harry S. and Isabel C.
Campbell and Adah E. Hall Charity Fund, Bushrod H.
Campbell Foundation
Campbell Foundation, Ruth and Henry
Carnival Cruise Lines
Carpenter Foundation, E. Rhodes and Leona B.
Casey Foundation, Eugene B.
Castle Foundation, Samuel N. and Mary
CBI Industries
Ceco Corp.
Central Hudson Gas & Electric Corp.
Central Life Assurance Co.
Central Maine Power Co.
Century Companies of America
Chapin Foundation, Frances

Chatham Valley Foundation
Cheatham Foundation, Owen
Chevron Corp.
Christy-Houston Foundation
Ciba-Geigy Corp. (Pharmaceuticals Division)
Citicorp
Clipper Ship Foundation
Clorox Co.
Cockrell Foundation
Collins Foundation
Collins Medical Trust
Colonial Life & Accident Insurance Co.
Colorado Trust
Coltec Industries
Columbia Foundation
Confidence Foundation
Connelly Foundation
Consolidated Papers
Cooke Foundation
Coors Brewing Co.
Copley Press
Copperweld Steel Co.
Corvallis Clinic
Country Curtains, Inc.
Cox Enterprises
Crels Foundation
Crum and Forster
CT Corp. System
CTS Corp.
Cullen/Frost Bankers
Culpeper Memorial Foundation, Daphne Seybolt
Cummins Engine Co.
Cuneo Foundation
Curtice-Burns Foods
Danis Industries
Davis Foundation, Joe C.
Davis Foundations, Arthur Vining
DeKalb Genetics Corp.
Delano Foundation, Mignon Sherwood
Dennett Foundation, Marie G.
Dial Corp.
Dibner Fund
Dickson Foundation
Digital Equipment Corp.
Dodge Jones Foundation
Donaldson Co.
Doss Foundation, M. S.
Douglas & Lomason Company
Dover Foundation
Dresser Industries
Dreyfus Foundation, Max and Victoria
du Pont de Nemours & Co., E. I.
Duke Endowment
Duke Power Co.
Dunn Research Foundation, John S.
Dunspaugh-Dalton Foundation
Dynamet, Inc.
Eastman Foundation, Alexander
Eaton Corp.
Eccles Charitable Foundation, Willard L.
Eccles Foundation, Marriner S.
Echlin Foundation
Eckerd Corp., Jack
Edison Foundation, Harry
Elkins, Jr. Foundation, Margaret and James A.
Ellsworth Foundation, Ruth H. and Warren A.
Emery Memorial, Thomas J.
Engelhard Foundation, Charles
Equifax
Ernest & Julio Gallo Winery
Ettinger Foundation
Farley Industries
Fay's Incorporated
Federal-Mogul Corp.
Federated Department Stores and Allied Stores Corp.
Fidelity Bank
Fifth Third Bancorp

Fink Foundation
Finley Foundation, A. E.
Finnegan Foundation, John D.
First Interstate Bank of Arizona
First Interstate Bank of California
First Interstate Bank of Oregon
First Maryland Bancorp
First Union Corp.
Fishback Foundation Trust, Harmes C.
Fleet Bank of New York
Florida Power & Light Co.
Forbes
Ford Fund, Walter and Josephine
Forest Lawn Foundation
Forest Oil Corp.
Fowler Memorial Foundation, John Edward
Fox Foundation, John H.
Frankel Foundation
Freas Foundation
Freedom Forum
Frost Foundation
Frueauff Foundation, Charles A.
Funderburke & Associates
Gallo Foundation, Julio R.
GATX Corp.
GEICO Corp.
Gelman Foundation, Melvin and Estelle
General Motors Corp.
General Railway Signal Corp.
General Reinsurance Corp.
General Signal Corp.
Georgia Power Co.
Gerber Products Co.
Gibson Foundation, E. L.
Gifford Charitable Corporation, Rosamond
Gilmer-Smith Foundation
Gilmore Foundation, William G.
Ginter Foundation, Karl and Anna
Glenn Foundation, Carrie C. & Lena V.
Goldman Fund, Richard and Rhoda
Goldome F.S.B
Golub Corp.
Goodstein Foundation
Goodyear Foundation, Josephine
Gore Family Memorial Foundation
Grace & Co., W.R.
Graphic Controls Corp.
Grassmann Trust, E. J.
Greeley Gas Co.
Green Fund
Griffin, Sr., Foundation, C. V.
Gronewaldt Foundation, Alice Busch
Guardian Life Insurance Co. of America
Gulfstream Aerospace Corp.
Haas Fund, Walter and Elise
Haas, Jr. Fund, Evelyn and Walter
Hall Charitable Trust, Evelyn A. J.
Halloran Foundation, Mary P. Dolciani
Hamilton Bank
Hansen Foundation, Dane G.
Hanson Foundation
Harden Foundation
Harriman Foundation, Mary W.
Harrington Foundation, Don and Sybil
Hartz Foundation
Hatterscheidt Foundation
Hechinger Co.
Hecla Mining Co.
HEI Inc.
Heinz Co., H.J.
Helis Foundation
Hemby Foundation, Alex
Hermann Foundation, Grover

Hershey Foods Corp.
Herzstein Charitable Foundation, Albert and Ethel
Hill Foundation
Hillsdale Fund
Hopwood Charitable Trust, John M.
Howell Foundation, Eric and Jessie
Huffy Corp.
Humphrey Foundation, Glenn & Gertrude
Hunter Trust, A. V.
Hurley Foundation, J. F.
Hutchins Foundation, Mary J.
ICI Americas
Ideal Industries
Illges Memorial Foundation, A. and M. L.
IMT Insurance Co.
Inland Steel Industries
Innovating Worthy Projects Foundation
Interco
Iowa Savings Bank
Iowa State Bank
ITT Hartford Insurance Group
ITT Rayonier
Jackson Foundation
JELD-WEN, Inc.
Jenkins Foundation, George W.
JFM Foundation
Johnson Foundation, A. D.
Johnson & Higgins
Johnston Trust for Charitable and Educational Purposes, James M.
Jurzykowski Foundation, Alfred
Kavanagh Foundation, T. James
Keebler Co.
Keeler Fund, Miner S. and Mary Ann
Keller-Crescent Co.
Kellogg Foundation, W. K.
Kelly Foundation, T. Lloyd
Kennecott Corp.
Kentland Foundation
Kerr Foundation, Robert S. and Grayce B.
Kerr-McGee Corp.
Kimball International
Kingston Foundation
Kirby Foundation, F. M.
Kline Foundation, Josiah W. and Bessie H.
Knox Family Foundation
Knox Foundation, Seymour H.
Kopf Foundation, Elizabeth Christy
Kowalski Sausage Co.
Kramer Foundation, Louise
Kugelman Foundation
Kysor Industrial Corp.
Laffey-McHugh Foundation
Lapham-Hickey Steel Corp.
Large Foundation
Lattner Foundation, Forrest C.
Law Foundation, Robert O.
Leach Foundation, Tom & Frances
Lee Foundation, James T.
Lennon Foundation, Fred A.
Leo Burnett Co.
Levy's Lumber & Building Centers
Liberty National Bank
Lintilhac Foundation
Lipton, Thomas J.
Livingston Memorial Foundation
Lizzadro Family Foundation, Joseph
Logan Foundation, E. J.
Louisiana Land & Exploration Co.
Louisiana-Pacific Corp.
Love Foundation, George H. and Margaret McClintic
Lubrizol Corp.

Luchsinger Family Foundation
Lydall, Inc.
Lyons Foundation
MacDonald Foundation, Marquis George
Mack Foundation, J. S.
MacLeod Stewardship Foundation
Maddox Foundation, J. F.
Magowan Family Foundation
Maneely Fund
Mansfield Foundation, Albert and Anne
Mardag Foundation
Marion Merrell Dow
Marmot Foundation
Mars Foundation
Martin Foundation
Martin Marietta Corp.
Masserini Charitable Trust, Maurice J.
May Mitchell Royal Foundation
Mayer Foundation, James and Eva
Maytag Family Foundation, Fred
McBean Charitable Trust, Alletta Morris
McBean Family Foundation
McCarthy Foundation, Michael W.
McCasland Foundation
McDonald & Co. Securities
McDonald & Co. Securities
McDonnell Douglas Corp.-West
McGraw-Hill
McInerny Foundation
McKee Foundation, Robert E. and Evelyn
McKnight Foundation, Sumner T.
McMahon Foundation
Mead Corp.
Mead Fund, Nelson
Meadows Foundation
Mellon Foundation, Richard King
Memton Fund
Mericos Foundation
Meyer Foundation, Eugene and Agnes E.
Meyer Memorial Trust
Mid-Iowa Health Foundation
Miller Foundation, Earl B. and Loraine H.
Mitchell Energy & Development Corp.
Mobil Oil Corp.
Monroe Foundation (1976), J. Edgar
Montana Power Co.
Moore Foundation, C. F.
Morris Foundation, Margaret T.
Motorola
Mulford Trust, Clarence E.
Mullen Foundation, J. K.
Murphy Foundation, Dan
Nalco Chemical Co.
Nashua Trust Co.
Nathan Foundation
National Computer Systems
National Forge Co.
National Fuel Gas Co.
National Life of Vermont
National Machinery Co.
New York Telephone Co.
The New Yorker Magazine, Inc.
News & Observer Publishing Co.
Noble Foundation, Samuel Roberts
North Carolina Foam Foundation
Northern Indiana Public Service Co.
Northern Trust Co.
Northwest Natural Gas Co.
Norton Co.
O'Bleness Foundation, Charles G.
Occidental Oil & Gas Corp.
O'Connor Foundation, A. Lindsay and Olive B.

O'Connor Foundation, Kathryn
OCRI Foundation
O'Fallon Trust, Martin J. and Mary Anne
Offield Family Foundation
Ogden Foundation, Ralph E.
Oglebay Norton Co.
Ohrstrom Foundation
Olin Corp.
Olive Bridge Fund
Olympia Brewing Co.
Oppenstein Brothers Foundation
Ormet Corp.
Osborn Charitable Trust, Edward B.
O'Shaughnessy Foundation, I. A.
Osher Foundation, Bernard
Overbrook Foundation
Oxford Foundation
Oxford Industries, Inc.
Pacific Mutual Life Insurance Co.
Packaging Corporation of America
Padnos Iron & Metal Co., Louis
Paley Foundation, William S.
Palin Foundation
Paramount Communications Inc.
Patterson-Barclay Memorial Foundation
Pennzoil Co.
Pepsi-Cola Bottling Co. of Charlotte
Perini Foundation, Joseph
Perkin-Elmer Corp.
Perkins-Prothro Foundation
Pfizer
Phillips Foundation, Dr. P.
Piankova Foundation, Tatiana
Pittsburgh National Bank
Pittway Corp.
Playboy Enterprises, Inc.
Polaroid Corp.
Posnack Family Foundation of Hollywood
Potomac Electric Power Co.
Potts Memorial Foundation
Pratt Memorial Fund
Premier Industrial Corp.
Providence Journal Company
Public Welfare Foundation
Pulitzer Publishing Co.
Quaker Oats Co.
Rapp Foundation, Robert Glenn
Raskob Foundation for Catholic Activities
Raymond Educational Foundation
Reynolds Charitable Trust, Kate B.
Rhoades Fund, Otto L. and Hazel E.
Rice Charitable Foundation, Albert W.
Rice Foundation, Helen Steiner
Richardson Charitable Trust, Anne S.
Roberts Foundation, Dora
Rochlin Foundation, Abraham and Sonia
Rockwell Fund
Rockwell International Corp.
Rohm and Haas Company
Rohr Inc.
Rosenberg Family Foundation, William
Rosenthal Foundation, Benjamin J.
Ross Foundation, Walter G.
Rouse Co.
Royal Group Inc.
Ruddick Corp.
Sage Foundation
San Diego Gas & Electric
Sandy Hill Foundation
Sara Lee Hosiery
Saunders Foundation
Sawyer Charitable Foundation

Scaife Family Foundation
Schaffer Foundation, H.
Schmidlapp Trust No. 1, Jacob G.
Schultz Foundation
Science Applications International Corp.
Scripps Foundation, Ellen Browning
Seay Memorial Trust, George and Effie
Sentinel Communications Co.
Shapiro Foundation, Charles and M. R.
Shawmut National Corp.
Sheldon Foundation, Ralph C.
Shell Oil Co.
Sierra Pacific Industries
Silver Spring Foundation
Simon Foundation, William E. and Carol G.
Simpson Foundation, John M.
Simpson Investment Co.
SIT Investment Associates, Inc.
Skinner Corp.
Slant/Fin Corp.
Smock Foundation, Frank and Laura
Snider Foundation
Sooner Pipe & Supply Corp.
South Bend Tribune
Southern California Edison Co.
Southern Furniture Co.
Special People In Need
Spiro Foundation, Donald W.
Sprague Educational and Charitable Foundation, Seth
Springs Industries
Stabler Foundation, Donald B. and Dorothy L.
Stans Foundation
Starr Foundation
Steelcase
Steele-Reese Foundation
Steinman Foundation, John Frederick
Sterling Winthrop
Sterne-Elder Memorial Trust
Stewards Fund
Stewart Trust under the will of Mary E. Stewart, Alexander and Margaret
Stocker Foundation
Storage Technology Corp.
Strake Foundation
Strauss Foundation
Strawbridge Foundation of Pennsylvania II, Margaret Dorrance
Stubblefield, Estate of Joseph L.
Sulzer Family Foundation
Swalm Foundation
Synovus Financial Corp.
Tandem Computers
Tarmac America Inc.
Teleflex Inc.
Temple Foundation, T. L. L.
Tenneco
Texaco
Texas Commerce Bank Houston, N.A.
Textron
Thermo Electron Corp.
Thomas & Betts Corp.
Thomas Built Buses L.P.
Thornton Foundation, John M. and Sally B.
Times Mirror Co.
Tiscornia Foundation
TJX Cos.
Tracor, Inc.
Transamerica Corp.
Transco Energy Company
Tupancy-Harris Foundation of 1986
Turner Charitable Foundation
Union Camp Corp.
Union Carbide Corp.
Union Pacific Corp.

U.S. Leasing International
United States Sugar Corp.
Upjohn California Fund
US Bancorp
USG Corp.
Valley Foundation
Van Every Foundation, Philip L.
Vermeer Manufacturing Co.
Vesuvius Charitable Foundation
Virginia Power Co.
Vogt Machine Co., Henry
Wachovia Bank & Trust Co., N.A.
Wal-Mart Stores
Walthall Perpetual Charitable Trust, Marjorie T.
Ware Foundation
Warner Foundation, Lee and Rose
Washington Square Fund
Wean Foundation, Raymond John
Weaver Foundation
Weinberg, Jr. Foundation, Sidney J.
Weingart Foundation
Weiss Fund, Clara
Wells Trust Fund, Fred W.
Western Southern Life Insurance Co.
Wetterau
Weyerhaeuser Co.
Whirlpool Corp.
Whitaker Charitable Foundation, Lyndon C.
Whitaker Foundation
White Foundation, Erle and Emma
Wilcox General Trust, George N.
Wimpey Inc., George
Winn-Dixie Stores
Wodecroft Foundation
Wolf Foundation, Melvin and Elaine
Wollenberg Foundation
Woodward Fund
Woodward Governor Co.
Xerox Corp.
Yeager Charitable Trust, Lester E.

Hospitals

Abbott Laboratories
Abel Construction Co.
Abeles Foundation, Joseph and Sophia
Abell-Hanger Foundation
Abitibi-Price
Abney Foundation
Abraham Foundation
Abraham Foundation, Anthony R.
Abraham & Straus
Abrams Foundation, Benjamin and Elizabeth
Abramson Family Foundation
Abrons Foundation, Louis and Anne
Achelis Foundation
Acme-McCrary Corp.
Acme United Corp.
Acorn Corrugated Box Co.
Acushnet Co.
Ada Foundation, Julius
Adams Foundation, Arthur F. and Alice E.
Adams Memorial Fund, Emma J.
Adler Foundation
Advanced Micro Devices
AEGON USA, Inc.
Aeroflex Foundation
Agway
Ahmanson Foundation
Aid Association for the Blind
Aigner
Air France
AKC Fund
Akzo America
Akzo Chemicals Inc.

Hospitals (cont.)

Ala Vi Foundation of New York
Alberto-Culver Co.
Albertson's
Alcan Aluminum Corp.
Alcon Laboratories, Inc.
Aldeen Charity Trust, G. W.
Alden Trust, John W.
Alexander & Baldwin, Inc.
Alexander Charitable Foundation
Alexander Foundation, Joseph
Alexander Foundation, Judd S.
Alexander Foundation, Robert D. and Catherine R.
Allegheny Ludlum Corp.
Allen Foundation, Frances
Allen-Heath Memorial Foundation
Allendale Mutual Insurance Co.
AlliedSignal
Alltel/Western Region
Allyn Foundation
Alma Piston Co.
ALPAC Corp.
Altman Foundation
Altschul Foundation
Alumax
Aluminum Co. of America
Amado Foundation, Maurice
Amaturo Foundation
AMAX
AMCORE Bank, N.A. Rockford
America West Airlines
American Brands
American Cyanamid Co.
American Electric Power
American Financial Corp.
American Foundation Corporation
American Home Products Corp.
American National Bank & Trust Co. of Chicago
American Natural Resources Co.
American President Cos.
American Saw & Manufacturing Co.
American Schlafhorst Foundation, Inc.
American Telephone & Telegraph Co.
American United Life Insurance Co.
Ameritas Life Insurance Corp.
Ames Charitable Trust, Harriett
Ames Department Stores
AMETEK
Amfac/JMB Hawaii
Amoco Corp.
AMP
AMR Corp.
Amsterdam Foundation, Jack and Mimi Leviton
Analog Devices
Andalusia Health Services
Andersen Corp.
Andersen Foundation
Andersen Foundation, Arthur
Anderson Charitable Trust, Josephine
Anderson Foundation
Anderson Foundation, M. D.
Anderson Foundation, William P.
Andres Charitable Trust, Frank G.
Angelica Corp.
Anheuser-Busch Cos.
Annenberg Foundation
Anschutz Family Foundation
AON Corp.
Applebaum Foundation
Appleby Foundation
Arakelian Foundation, Mary Alice
Arata Brothers Trust
Arcadia Foundation

Archbold Charitable Trust, Adrian and Jessie
Archer-Daniels-Midland Co.
Archibald Charitable Foundation, Norman
ARCO Chemical
Arizona Public Service Co.
Arkansas Power & Light Co.
Arkelian Foundation, Ben H. and Gladys
Arkell Hall Foundation
Arkla
Armbrust Chain Co.
Armco Inc.
Armstrong World Industries Inc.
Aron Charitable Foundation, J.
Arronson Foundation
Asea Brown Boveri
Ashland Oil
Asplundh Foundation
Associated Food Stores
Associated Foundations
Atherton Family Foundation
Atlanta Foundation
Atran Foundation
Attleboro Pawtucket Savings Bank
Atwood Foundation
Auerbach Foundation, Beatrice Fox
Austin Memorial Foundation
Autzen Foundation
Avis Inc.
Avon Products
Awrey Bakeries
Ayres Foundation, Inc.
Azby Fund
Babcock & Wilcox Co.
Babson Foundation, Paul and Edith
Bacardi Imports
Bachmann Foundation
Backer Spielvogel Bates U.S.
Bacon Foundation, E. L. and Oma
Badgeley Residuary Charitable Trust, Rose M.
Badger Meter, Inc.
Baehr Foundation, Louis W. and Dolpha
Bair Memorial Trust, Charles M.
Baird Brothers Co.
Baird & Co., Robert W.
Baird Foundation, Cameron
Baker & Baker
Baker Foundation, George T.
Baker Foundation, R. C.
Baker Foundation, Solomon R. and Rebecca D.
Baker, Jr. Memorial Fund, William G.
Baker Trust, George F.
Baldwin Foundation, David M. and Barbara
Baldwin, Jr. Foundation, Summerfield
Balfour Foundation, L. G.
Ball Brothers Foundation
Ball Foundation, George and Frances
Bally Inc.
Baltimore Gas & Electric Co.
Bamberger and John Ernest Bamberger Memorial Foundation, Ruth Eleanor
Banbury Fund
Banc One Illinois Corp.
Banc One Wisconsin Corp.
Bancorp Hawaii
Bancroft, Jr. Foundation, Hugh
Banfi Vintners
Bank Foundation, Helen and Merrill
Bank Leumi Trust Co. of New York
Bank of America Arizona
Bank of Boston Connecticut
Bank of Boston Corp.

Bank of New York
Bank One, Texas-Houston Office
Bank One, Youngstown, NA
BankAmerica Corp.
Bankers Trust Co.
Bannan Foundation, Arline and Thomas J.
Banner Life Insurance Co.
Bannerman Foundation, William C.
Bantam Doubleday Dell Publishing Group, Inc.
Barbour Foundation, Bernice
Barclays Bank of New York
Bard, C. R.
Barden Corp.
Bardes Corp.
Barker Foundation, Donald R.
Barker Foundation, J. M. R.
Barnes Group
Barnett Charitable Foundation, Lawrence and Isabel
Barra Foundation
Barrows Foundation, Geraldine and R. A.
Barth Foundation, Theodore H.
Barton-Malow Co.
Bartsch Memorial Trust, Ruth
Bass and Edythe and Sol G. Atlas Fund, Sandra Atlas
Bass Foundation
Bass Foundation, Harry
Battelle
Batts Foundation
Bauer Foundation, M. R.
Bauervic Foundation, Peggy
Bauervic-Paisley Foundation
Baughman Foundation
Bay Branch Foundation
BayBanks
Bayne Fund, Howard
Beach Foundation Trust A for Brunswick Hospital, Thomas N. and Mildred V.
Beach Foundation Trust for the University of Alabama-Birmingham Diabetes Hospital, Thomas N. and Mildred V.
Beal Foundation
Bean, L.L.
Beasley Foundation, Theodore and Beulah
Beazley Foundation
Beck Foundation
Becton Dickinson & Co.
Bedford Fund
Bedminster Fund
Bedsole Foundation, J. L.
Beech Aircraft Corp.
Beecher Foundation, Florence Simon
Beerman Foundation
Beeson Charitable Trust, Dwight M.
Behmann Brothers Foundation
Beir Foundation
Bekins Foundation, Milo W.
Belding Heminway Co.
Belfer Foundation
Belk Stores
Belk Stores
Bell Communications Research
Bellamah Foundation, Dale J.
Bellini Foundation
Belmont Metals
Belo Corp., A.H.
Beloco Foundation
Belz Foundation
Bemis Company
Bender Foundation
Benedum Foundation, Claude Worthington
Benetton
Benfamil Charitable Trust
Bennett Foundation, Carl and Dorothy
Benua Foundation

Benz Trust, Doris L.
Bere Foundation
Berenson Charitable Foundation, Theodore W. and Evelyn
Beretta U.S.A. Corp.
Berger Foundation, Albert E.
Berger Foundation, H.N. and Frances C.
Bergner Co., P.A.
Berkey Foundation, Peter
Berkman Foundation, Louis and Sandra
Berkowitz Family Foundation, Louis
Berlin Charitable Fund, Irving
Bernsen Foundation, Grace and Franklin
Bernstein & Co., Sanford C.
Bernstein Foundation, Diane and Norman
Berrie Foundation, Russell
Berry Foundation, Archie W. and Grace
Berry Foundation, Loren M.
Bersted Foundation
Bertha Foundation
Berwind Corp.
Best Foundation, Walter J. and Edith E.
Betz Foundation Trust, Theodora B.
Beveridge Foundation, Frank Stanley
Beynon Foundation, Kathryne
BFGoodrich
BHP Pacific Resources
Bickerton Charitable Trust, Lydia H.
Biddle Foundation, Margaret T.
Bierhaus Foundation
Bierlein Family Foundation
Bingham Foundation, William
Bingham Second Betterment Fund, William
Binswanger Co.
Biological Humanics Foundation
Birch Foundation, Stephen and Mary
Bireley Foundation
Birmingham Foundation
Birnschein Foundation, Alvin and Marion
Bishop Foundation, E. K. and Lillian F.
Bjorkman Foundation
Blackmer Foundation, Henry M.
Blair and Co., William
Blair Foundation, John
Blanchard Foundation
Blank Family Foundation
Blaustein Foundation, Jacob and Hilda
Blaustein Foundation, Louis and Henrietta
Bleibtreu Foundation, Jacob
Blinken Foundation
Bloch Foundation, Henry W. and Marion H.
Block, H&R
Bloomfield Foundation, Sam and Rie
Blount
Blount Educational and Charitable Foundation, Mildred Weedon
Blowitz-Ridgeway Foundation
Blue Bell, Inc.
Blue Cross & Blue Shield of Alabama
Bluhdorn Charitable Trust, Charles G. and Yvette
Blum Foundation, Harry and Maribel G.
Blum Foundation, Nathan and Emily S.
Blum-Kovler Foundation
BMW of North America, Inc.
Boatmen's Bancshares

Boatmen's First National Bank of Oklahoma
Bob Evans Farms
Bobst Foundation, Elmer and Mamdouha
Bodman Foundation
Boehm Foundation
Boh Brothers Construction Co.
Boise Cascade Corp.
Boisi Family Foundation
Bonfils-Stanton Foundation
Booth-Bricker Fund
Boothroyd Foundation, Charles H. and Bertha L.
Booz Allen & Hamilton
Bordeaux Foundation
Borden
Borg-Warner Corp.
Borkee Hagley Foundation
Borman's
Borun Foundation, Anna Borun and Harry
Borwell Charitable Foundation
Bosque Foundation
Boston Edison Co.
Bostwick Foundation, Albert C.
Boswell Foundation, James G.
Bothin Foundation
Bourns, Inc.
Boutell Memorial Fund, Arnold and Gertrude
Bovaird Foundation, Mervin
Bowater Inc.
Bowles and Robert Bowles Memorial Fund, Ethel Wilson
Bowyer Foundation, Ambrose and Gladys
Bozzone Family Foundation
BP America
Brace Foundation, Donald C.
Brach Foundation, Edwin I.
Brach Foundation, Helen
Brackenridge Foundation, George W.
Bradish Trust, Norman C.
Bradley Foundation, Lynde and Harry
Bradley-Turner Foundation
Brady Foundation
Brand Foundation, C. Harold and Constance
Branta Foundation
Braun Foundation
Breidenthal Foundation, Willard J. and Mary G.
Bremer Foundation, Otto
Brenner Foundation
Brenner Foundation, Mervyn
Brewer and Co., Ltd., C.
Breyer Foundation
Bridgestone/Firestone
Briggs Family Foundation
Brink Unitrust, Julia H.
Brinkley Foundation
Bristol-Myers Squibb Co.
Bristol Savings Bank
Broad Foundation, Shepard
Broccoli Charitable Foundation, Dana and Albert R.
Brochsteins Inc.
Brody Foundation, Carolyn and Kenneth D.
Bronstein Foundation, Sol and Arlene
Brooks Brothers
Brooks Foundation, Gladys
Brotz Family Foundation, Frank G.
Brown Family Foundation, John Mathew Gay
Brown Foundation
Brown Foundation, Joe W. and Dorothy Dorsett
Brown Foundation, W. L. Lyons
Brown Group
Brown, Jr. Charitable Trust, Frank D.

Brown & Sharpe Manufacturing Co.
Brown & Sons, Alex
Browning Charitable Foundation, Val A.
Brownley Trust, Walter
Broyhill Family Foundation
Bruening Foundation, Eva L. and Joseph M.
Brunetti Charitable Trust, Dionigi
Bruno Charitable Foundation, Joseph S.
Brunswick Corp.
Bryant Foundation
Bryce Memorial Fund, William and Catherine
Buchalter, Nemer, Fields, & Younger
Buchanan Family Foundation
Buckley Trust, Thomas D.
Bucyrus-Erie
Buehler Foundation, A. C.
Buehler Foundation, Emil
Buhl Family Foundation
Bunbury Company
Burden Foundation, Florence V.
Burlington Industries
Burnand Medical and Educational Foundation, Alphonse A.
Burndy Corp.
Burnham Donor Fund, Alfred G.
Burnham Foundation
Burns Foundation, Fritz B.
Burns Foundation, Jacob
Burroughs Wellcome Co.
Bush Charitable Foundation, Edyth
Bush Foundation
Bushee Foundation, Florence Evans
Business Incentives
Butz Foundation
C.P. Rail Systems
Cable & Wireless Communications
Cablevision of Michigan
Cabot Corp.
Cabot-Saltonstall Charitable Trust
Cadbury Beverages Inc.
Caestecker Foundation, Charles and Marie
Cafritz Foundation, Morris and Gwendolyn
Cahn Family Foundation
Cain Foundation, Gordon and Mary
Calhoun Charitable Trust, Kenneth
California & Hawaiian Sugar Co.
Callaway Foundation
Callaway Foundation, Fuller E.
Callister Foundation, Paul Q.
Callister Foundation, Paul Q.
Cameron Foundation, Harry S. and Isabel C.
Cameron Memorial Fund, Alpin J. and Alpin W.
Camp Younts Foundation
Campbell and Adah E. Hall Charity Fund, Bushrod H.
Campbell Foundation
Campbell Foundation, Charles Talbot
Campbell Foundation, J. Bulow
Campbell Foundation, Ruth and Henry
Campbell Soup Co.
Cannon Foundation
Cantor Foundation, Iris and B. Gerald
Capital Fund Foundation
Caplan Charity Foundation, Julius H.
Cargill
Carlson Cos.
Carnahan-Jackson Foundation

Carolina Power & Light Co.
Carpenter Foundation
Carpenter Foundation
Carpenter Foundation, E. Rhodes and Leona B.
Carpenter Technology Corp.
Carrier Corp.
Carstensen Memorial Foundation, Fred R. and Hazel W.
Carter Family Foundation
Carter Foundation, Amon G.
Carter-Wallace
Carvel Foundation, Thomas and Agnes
Caspersen Foundation for Aid to Health and Education, O. W.
Cassett Foundation, Louis N.
Castle Foundation, Harold K. L.
Castle Foundation, Samuel N. and Mary
Caterpillar
Cawsey Trust
Cayuga Foundation
CBI Industries
Ceco Corp.
Cedars-Sinai Medical Center Section D Fund
Centel Corp.
Centerior Energy Corp.
Central Fidelity Banks, Inc.
Central Hudson Gas & Electric Corp.
Central Maine Power Co.
Central National-Gottesman
Central Soya Co.
CertainTeed Corp.
Cessna Aircraft Co.
Chadwick Foundation
Chait Memorial Foundation, Sara
Chambers Development Co.
Chambers Memorial, James B.
Champion International Corp.
Champlin Foundations
Chanin Family Foundation, Paul R.
Chapin Foundation, Frances
Chapin-May Foundation of Illinois
Chapman Charitable Corporation, Howard and Bess
Chapman Charitable Trust, H. A. and Mary K.
Charina Foundation
Charlton, Jr. Charitable Trust, Earle P.
Chartwell Foundation
Chase Charity Foundation, Alfred E.
Chase Manhattan Bank, N.A.
Chase Trust, Alice P.
Chatham Valley Foundation
Chatlos Foundation
Chazen Foundation
CHC Foundation
Cheney Foundation, Ben B.
Chernow Trust for the Benefit of Charity Dated 3/13/75, Michael
Chesapeake Corp.
Chevron Corp.
Chicago Title and Trust Co.
Childress Foundation, Francis and Miranda
Chilton Foundation Trust
Christy-Houston Foundation
Church & Dwight Co.
Ciba-Geigy Corp. (Pharmaceuticals Division)
Cimarron Foundation
Cincinnati Bell
CIT Group Holdings
Citicorp
Citizens Bank
City National Bank
City of Hope 1989 Section E Foundation
Claneil Foundation

Clapp Charitable and Educational Trust, George H.
CLARCOR
Clark Charitable Foundation
Clark Family Foundation, Emory T.
Clark Foundation
Clark-Winchcole Foundation
Clay Foundation
Cleary Foundation
Cleveland-Cliffs
Clorox Co.
Close Foundation
Clougherty Charitable Trust, Francis H.
Clowes Fund
CM Alliance Cos.
CNA Insurance Cos.
CNG Transmission Corp.
Cockrell Foundation
Codrington Charitable Foundation, George W.
Coen Family Foundation, Charles S. and Mary
Coffey Foundation
Cogswell Benevolent Trust
Cohen Foundation, George M.
Cohen Foundation, Manny and Ruthy
Cohen Foundation, Naomi and Nehemiah
Cohen Foundation, Wilfred P.
Cohn Foundation, Herman and Terese
Cohn Foundation, Peter A. and Elizabeth S.
Cole Foundation
Cole National Corp.
Cole Taylor Financial Group
Coleman Co.
Coleman Foundation
Coles Family Foundation
Colket Foundation, Ethel D.
Collins & Aikman Holdings Corp.
Collins Foundation, Carr P.
Collins Foundation, George and Jennie
Collins Foundation, James M.
Collins-McDonald Trust Fund
Collins Medical Trust
Colonial Life & Accident Insurance Co.
Colorado Trust
Colt Foundation, James J.
Coltec Industries
Columbus Dispatch Printing Co.
Comer Foundation
Comerica
Common Giving Fund
Commonwealth Edison Co.
Commonwealth Fund
Community Enterprises
Community Hospital Foundation
Comstock Foundation
Cone-Blanchard Machine Co.
Confidence Foundation
Connelly Foundation
Connemara Fund
Consolidated Natural Gas Co.
Consolidated Papers
Constantin Foundation
Continental Corp.
Contraves USA
Cook Batson Foundation
Cook Foundation, Loring
Cooke Foundation
Cooper Charitable Trust, Richard H.
Cooper Industries
Coors Brewing Co.
Copley Press
Copperweld Corp.
Corbin Foundation, Mary S. and David C.
Cord Foundation, E. L.
Cornell Trust, Peter C.

Corvallis Clinic
Cosmair, Inc.
Cottrell Foundation
Coughlin-Saunders Foundation
Country Curtains, Inc.
County Bank
Cove Charitable Trust
Cowan Foundation Corporation, Lillian L. and Harry A.
Cowden Foundation, Louetta M.
Cowles Charitable Trust
Cox Charitable Trust, A. G.
Cox Charitable Trust, Jessie B.
Cox Enterprises
Cox Foundation
Cox, Jr. Foundation, James M.
CPC International
CPI Corp.
CR Industries
Craigmyle Foundation
Crail-Johnson Foundation
Crandall Memorial Foundation, J. Ford
Crane Co.
Crane Foundation, Raymond E. and Ellen F.
Crane Fund for Widows and Children
Cranshaw Corporation
Cranston Print Works
Crary Foundation, Bruce L.
Crawford Estate, E. R.
Crels Foundation
Crescent Plastics
Crestar Financial Corp.
Crestlea Foundation
CRI Charitable Trust
Criss Memorial Foundation, Dr. C.C. and Mabel L.
CRL Inc.
Crown Books Foundation, Inc.
Crown Charitable Fund, Edward A.
Crown Cork & Seal Co., Inc.
Crum and Forster
Crummer Foundation, Roy E.
Crump Fund, Joe and Jessie
Crystal Trust
CT Corp. System
Cuesta Foundation
Cullen Foundation
Cullen/Frost Bankers
Culpeper Foundation, Charles E.
Culpeper Memorial Foundation, Daphne Seybolt
Cummings Foundation, James H.
Cummings Memorial Fund Trust, Frances L. and Edwin L.
Cuneo Foundation
Cunningham Foundation, Laura Moore
Curtice-Burns Foods
Cyprus Minerals Co.
Dammann Fund
Dana Corp.
Dana Foundation, Charles A.
Danis Industries
Darby Foundation
Dater Foundation, Charles H.
Daugherty Foundation
Davenport-Hatch Foundation
David-Weill Foundation, Michel
Davidson Family Charitable Foundation
Davis Family - W.D. Charities, James E.
Davis Foundation, Edwin W. and Catherine M.
Davis Foundation, Joe C.
Davis Foundation, Ken W.
Davis Foundation, Shelby Cullom
Davis Foundation, Simon and Annie
Davis Foundations, Arthur Vining
Davis Hospital Foundation
Day Family Foundation

Day Foundation, Willametta K.
DCNY Corp.
de Dampierre Memorial Foundation, Marie C.
de Kay Foundation
de Rothschild Foundation, Edmond
DEC International, Inc.
DeCamp Foundation, Ira W.
Decio Foundation, Arthur J.
Dee Foundation, Annie Taylor
Dee Foundation, Lawrence T. and Janet T.
DeKalb Genetics Corp.
Delacorte Fund, George
Delany Charitable Trust, Beatrice P.
Delavan Foundation, Nelson B.
Delaware North Cos.
Dell Foundation, Hazel
Demoulas Supermarkets
Dennett Foundation, Marie G.
Dennison Manufacturing Co.
Dent Family Foundation, Harry
Deposit Guaranty National Bank
DeRoy Testamentary Foundation
DeSoto
Detroit Edison Co.
Dettman Foundation, Leroy E.
Deuble Foundation, George H.
Deutsch Co.
Devonshire Associates
DeVore Foundation
DeVos Foundation, Richard and Helen
Dewar Foundation
Dexter Charitable Fund, Eugene A.
Dexter Corp.
Dexter Shoe Co.
Dibner Fund
Dick Family Foundation
Dickenson Foundation, Harriet Ford
Dickson Foundation
Dillard Paper Co.
Dillon Foundation
Dimeo Construction Co.
Dingman Foundation, Michael D.
Dishman Charitable Foundation Trust, H. E. and Kate
Dively Foundation, George S.
Dixie Yarns, Inc.
Dobson Foundation
Dodge Jones Foundation
Dodson Foundation, James Glenwell and Clara May
Doelger Charitable Trust, Thelma
Doheny Foundation, Carrie Estelle
Doherty Charitable Foundation, Henry L. and Grace
Dolan Family Foundation
Domino of California
Donaldson Charitable Trust, Oliver S. and Jennie R.
Donaldson Co.
Donnelley Foundation, Elliott and Ann
Donnelley & Sons Co., R.R.
Donnelly Foundation, Mary J.
Dorminy Foundation, John Henry
Doss Foundation, M. S.
Doty Family Foundation
Dougherty, Jr. Foundation, James R.
Douglas Charitable Foundation
Douglas & Lomason Company
Dow Foundation, Herbert H. and Grace A.
Dow Jones & Co.
Dower Foundation, Thomas W.
Doyle Charitable Foundation
Dreiling and Albina Dreiling Charitable Trust, Leo J.
Dresser Industries
Dreyfus Foundation, Jean and Louis

Hospitals (cont.)

Dreyfus Foundation, Max and Victoria
Driscoll Foundation
du Pont de Nemours & Co., E. I.
Duchossois Industries
Duke Endowment
Duke Foundation, Doris
Duke Power Co.
Dula Educational and Charitable Foundation, Caleb C. and Julia W.
Dumke Foundation, Dr. Ezekiel R. and Edna Wattis
Dun & Bradstreet Corp.
Dunagan Foundation
Duncan Foundation, Lillian H. and C. W.
Duncan Trust, James R.
Duncan Trust, John G.
Dunn Research Foundation, John S.
Dunspaugh-Dalton Foundation
duPont Foundation, Chichester
duPont Fund, Jessie Ball
Duquesne Light Co.
Durr-Fillauer Medical
Dyson Foundation
Earl-Beth Foundation
Eastern Bank Foundation
Eastern Fine Paper, Inc.
Eastman Foundation, Alexander
Eastover Corp.
Eaton Corp.
Ebell of Los Angeles Rest Cottage Association
Ebell of Los Angeles Scholarship Endowment Fund
Ebert Charitable Foundation, Horatio B.
Eccles Foundation, George S. and Dolores Dore
Eccles Foundation, Marriner S.
Eccles Foundation, Ralph M. and Ella M.
Echlin Inc.
Echlin Foundation
Eckerd Corp., Jack
Eddy Family Memorial Fund, C. K.
Eden Hall Foundation
Eder Foundation, Sidney and Arthur
Edgerton Foundation, Harold E.
Edgewater Steel Corp.
Edison Foundation, Harry
Edison Foundation, Irving and Beatrice C.
Edison Fund, Charles
Edouard Foundation
Edwards Industries
Edwards Memorial Trust
EG&G Inc.
Einstein Fund, Albert E. and Birdie W.
EIS Foundation
Eisenberg Foundation, Ben B. and Joyce E.
Eisenberg Foundation, George M.
El Pomar Foundation
Electric Power Equipment Co.
Elf Aquitaine, Inc.
Elf Atochem North America
Elkin Memorial Foundation, Neil Warren and William Simpson
Elkins, Jr. Foundation, Margaret and James A.
Ellis Foundation
Ellison Foundation
Ellsworth Foundation, Ruth H. and Warren A.
Ellsworth Trust, W. H.
Emerson Electric Co.
Emerson Foundation, Fred L.
Emery Memorial, Thomas J.
EMI Records Group

Encyclopaedia Britannica, Inc.
Engelhard Foundation, Charles
English-Bonter-Mitchell Foundation
Enright Foundation
Enron Corp.
Ensign-Bickford Industries
Enterprise Rent-A-Car Co.
Epp Fund B Charitable Trust, Otto C.
Equitable Life Assurance Society of the U.S.
Ernest & Julio Gallo Winery
Ernsthausen Charitable Foundation, John F. and Doris E.
Erteszek Foundation
Erving Paper Mills
Essick Foundation
Ethyl Corp.
European American Bank
Everett Charitable Trust
Evinrude Foundation, Ralph
Evjue Foundation
Ewald Foundation, H. T.
Exxon Corp.
FAB Industries
Fabick Tractor Co., John
Factor Family Foundation, Max
Failing Fund, Henry
Fairchild Corp.
Fairchild Foundation, Sherman
Fairfield-Meeker Charitable Trust, Freeman E.
Faith Charitable Trust
Falk Foundation, David
Falk Foundation, Michael David
Falk Medical Research Foundation, Dr. Ralph and Marian
Fanwood Foundation
Farallon Foundation
Farley Industries
Farmers Group, Inc.
Farwell Foundation, Drusilla
Fay Charitable Fund, Aubert J.
Fay's Incorporated
Federal-Mogul Corp.
Federal National Mortgage Assn., Fannie Mae
Federal Screw Works
Feil Foundation, Louis and Gertrude
Feinberg Foundation, Joseph and Bessie
Feintech Foundation
Feldberg Family Foundation
Femino Foundation
Fenton Foundation
Ferebee Endowment, Percy O.
Ferguson Family Foundation, Kittie and Rugeley
Fiat U.S.A., Inc.
Field Foundation, Jamee and Marshall
Field Foundation of Illinois
Fieldcrest Cannon
Fifth Avenue Foundation
Fifth Third Bancorp
Fikes Foundation, Leland
FINA, Inc.
Finch Foundation, Doak
Fingerhut Family Foundation
Fink Foundation
Finley Charitable Trust, J. B.
Finley Foundation, A. E.
Finnegan Foundation, John D.
Firan Foundation
Fireman Charitable Foundation, Paul and Phyllis
Firestone Foundation, Roger S.
Firestone, Jr. Foundation, Harvey
First Fidelity Bancorporation
First Financial Bank FSB
First Hawaiian
First Interstate Bank of Arizona
First Interstate Bank of California

First Interstate Bank of Oregon
First Interstate Bank of Texas, N.A.
First Maryland Bancorp
First National Bank in Wichita
First National Bank of Evergreen Park
First National Bank & Trust Co. of Rockford
First NH Banks, Inc.
First Petroleum Corp.
First Tennessee Bank
First Union Corp.
First Union National Bank of Florida
Firstar Bank Milwaukee NA
FirsTier Bank N.A. Omaha
Fish Foundation, Ray C.
Fish Foundation, Vain and Harry
Fisher Brothers
Fisher Foundation
Fitz-Gibbon Charitable Trust
FKI Holdings Inc.
Flagler Foundation
Flatley Foundation
Fleet Bank of New York
Fleet Financial Group
Fleming Foundation
Flemm Foundation, John J.
Flinn Foundation
Florence Foundation
Florence Foundation
Florida Power Corp.
FMC Corp.
FMR Corp.
Foerderer Foundation, Percival E. and Ethel Brown
Folger Fund
Fondren Foundation
Foothills Foundation
Forbes
Forbes Charitable Trust, Herman
Forchheimer Foundation
Ford Foundation, Joseph F. and Clara
Ford Fund, Benson and Edith
Ford Fund, Eleanor and Edsel
Ford Fund, Walter and Josephine
Ford Fund, William and Martha
Ford II Fund, Henry
Ford III Memorial Foundation, Jefferson Lee
Ford Motor Co.
Forest City Enterprises
Forest Fund
Forest Lawn Foundation
Forest Oil Corp.
Forster Charitable Trust, James W. and Ella B.
Fort Worth Star Telegram
Fortin Foundation of Florida
Fortis Inc.
Foster Charitable Trust
Foster Co., L.B.
Foster Foundation
Foster Foundation, Joseph C. and Esther
Foundation for Seacoast Health
Fourjay Foundation
Fourth Financial Corp.
Fox Inc.
Fox Foundation, John H.
Fox Steel Co.
France Foundation, Jacob and Annita
Frank Foundation, Ernest and Elfriede
Frank Fund, Zollie and Elaine
Frankel Foundation
Frankel Foundation, George and Elizabeth F.
Franklin Charitable Trust, Ershel
Franklin Foundation, John and Mary
Franklin Mint Corp.
Fraser Paper Ltd.

Frear Eleemosynary Trust, Mary D. and Walter F.
Freas Foundation
Frederick Foundation
Freed Foundation
Freedom Forum
Freeman Foundation, Carl M.
Freeport Brick Co.
Freeport-McMoRan
Frees Foundation
Frelinghuysen Foundation
French Foundation
Frese Foundation, Arnold D.
Freygang Foundation, Walter Henry
Fribourg Foundation
Friedland Family Foundation, Samuel
Friedman Family Foundation
Friends' Foundation Trust, A.
Friendship Fund
Froderman Foundation
Frohlich Charitable Trust, Ludwig W.
Frohman Foundation, Sidney
Frohring Foundation, Paul & Maxine
Frost Foundation
Frueauff Foundation, Charles A.
Fry Foundation, Lloyd A.
Fuchs Foundation, Gottfried & Mary
Fuchsberg Family Foundation, Abraham
Fujitsu America, Inc.
Fuller Foundation
Fuller Foundation, George F. and Sybil H.
Fullerton Foundation
Funderburke & Associates
Fuqua Foundation, J. B.
Fusenot Charity Foundation, Georges and Germaine
Gabelli Foundation
Gage Foundation, Philip and Irene Toll
Gaisman Foundation, Catherine and Henry J.
Galkin Charitable Trust, Ira S. and Anna
Gallagher Family Foundation, Lewis P.
Gallo Foundation, Ernest
Gallo Foundation, Julio R.
Galter Foundation
Galvin Foundation, Robert W.
Gannett Publishing Co., Guy
GAR Foundation
Garland Foundation, John Jewett and H. Chandler
Garner Charitable Trust, James G.
Garvey Texas Foundation
GATX Corp.
Gault-Hussey Charitable Trust
Gavin Foundation, James and Zita
Gaylord Foundation, Clifford Willard
Gebbie Foundation
GEICO Corp.
Gelb Foundation, Lawrence M.
Gellert Foundation, Carl
Gellert Foundation, Celia Berta
Gellert Foundation, Fred
General Accident Insurance Co. of America
General American Life Insurance Co.
General Machine Works
General Mills
General Motors Corp.
General Reinsurance Corp.
General Signal Corp.
General Tire Inc.
Geneseo Foundation
GenRad
George Foundation

Georgia Health Foundation
Georgia-Pacific Corp.
Georgia Power Co.
Gerard Foundation, Sumner
Gerber Products Co.
German Protestant Orphan Asylum Association
Gerondelis Foundation
Gershenson Foundation, Charles H.
Gerson Trust, B. Milfred
Gerson Trust, B. Milfred
Getz Foundation, Emma and Oscar
Ghidotti Foundation, William and Marian
Ghidotti Foundation, William and Marian
Giant Eagle
Giant Food
Giant Food Stores
Gibson Foundation, E. L.
Gifford Charitable Corporation, Rosamond
Gilbert, Jr. Charitable Trust, Price
Gill Foundation, Pauline Allen
Gillett Foundation, Elesabeth Ingalls
Gillette Co.
Gilman, Jr. Foundation, Sondra and Charles
Gilmer-Smith Foundation
Gilmore Foundation, Earl B.
Gilmore Foundation, William G.
Ginsberg Family Foundation, Moses
Ginter Foundation, Karl and Anna
Gitano Group
Glaser Foundation
Glaxo
Glencoe Foundation
Glenn Memorial Foundation, Wilbur Fisk
Glickenhaus & Co.
Glidden Co.
Globe Corp.
Gluck Foundation, Maxwell H.
Goddard Foundation, Charles B.
Goerlich Family Foundation
Goldberg Family Foundation, Israel and Matilda
Goldberg Family Foundation, Milton D. and Madeline L.
Golden Family Foundation
Goldenberg Foundation, Max
Goldie-Anna Charitable Trust
Goldman Charitable Trust, Sol
Goldman Foundation, Herman
Goldman Foundation, Morris and Rose
Goldman Foundation, William
Goldome F.S.B
Goldsmith Family Foundation
Goldsmith Foundation
Goldsmith Foundation, Horace W.
Goldwyn Foundation, Samuel
Golub Corp.
Good Samaritan
Goode Trust, Mae Stone
Goodman & Company
Goodman Family Foundation
Goodman Memorial Foundation, Joseph C. and Clare F.
Goodstein Family Foundation, David
Goodstein Foundation
Goodwin Foundation, Leo
Goodyear Foundation, Josephine
Goodyear Tire & Rubber Co.
Goody's Manufacturing Corp.
Gordon Foundation, Meyer and Ida
Gordon/Rousmaniere/Roberts Fund
Gore Family Memorial Foundation

Gorin Foundation, Nehemiah
Gottesman Fund
Gottwald Foundation
Grace & Co., W.R.
Grader Foundation, K. W.
Gradison & Co.
Grainger Foundation
Grant Foundation, Charles M. and Mary D.
Graphic Controls Corp.
Grass Family Foundation
Grass Foundation
Grassmann Trust, E. J.
Gray Foundation, Garland
Great Atlantic & Pacific Tea Co. Inc.
Great-West Life Assurance Co.
Grede Foundries
Greeley Gas Co.
Green Foundation
Green Foundation, Burton E.
Green Fund
Greenberg Foundation, Alan C.
Greene Foundation, David J.
Greene Foundation, Jerome L.
Greene Foundation, Robert Z.
Greenspan Foundation
Gregg-Graniteville Foundation
Griffin Foundation, Rosa May
Griffin, Sr., Foundation, C. V.
Griffis Foundation
Griffith Foundation, W. C.
Grigg-Lewis Trust
Grimes Foundation
Griswold Foundation, John C.
Gronewaldt Foundation, Alice Busch
Groome Beatty Trust, Helen D.
Gross Charitable Trust, Stella B.
Gross Charitable Trust, Walter L. and Nell R.
Gross Foundation, Louis H.
Grossman Foundation, N. Bud
Grotto Foundation
Group Health Plan Inc.
Gruber Research Foundation, Lila
Grumbacher Foundation, M. S.
Grundy Foundation
Gruss Charitable Foundation, Emanuel and Riane
GTE Corp.
Gucci America Inc.
Gudelsky Family Foundation, Homer and Martha
Gudelsky Family Foundation, Isadore and Bertha
Gulf Power Co.
Gunderson Trust, Helen Paulson
Gurwin Foundation, J.
Gussman Foundation, Herbert and Roseline
Gutman Foundation, Edna and Monroe C.
Guttman Foundation, Stella and Charles
H. B. B. Foundation
Haas Fund, Walter and Elise
Haas, Jr. Fund, Evelyn and Walter
Haffenreffer Family Fund
Hagedorn Fund
Haggar Foundation
Haggerty Foundation
Hales Charitable Fund
Haley Foundation, W. B.
Halff Foundation, G. A. C.
Hall Charitable Trust, Evelyn A. J.
Hall Foundation
Hallett Charitable Trust
Halliburton Co.
Halmos Foundation
Halsell Foundation, O. L.
Hambay Foundation, James T.
Hamilton Foundation, Florence P.
Hamilton Oil Corp.

Hamman Foundation, George and Mary Josephine
Handleman Co.
Handy & Harman
Hanes Foundation, John W. and Anna H.
Hankamer Foundation, Curtis and Doris K.
Hankins Foundation
Hannon Foundation, William H.
Hansen Foundation, Dane G.
Hansen Memorial Foundation, Irving
Hanson Foundation
HarCo. Drug
Harcourt Foundation, Ellen Knowles
Harding Educational and Charitable Foundation
Harkness Ballet Foundation
Harland Charitable Foundation, John and Wilhelmina D.
Harmon Foundation, Pearl M. and Julia J.
Harper Foundation, Philip S.
Harriman Foundation, Gladys and Roland
Harriman Foundation, Mary W.
Harrington Foundation, Don and Sybil
Harrington Trust, George
Harris Brothers Foundation
Harris Corp.
Harris Foundation, J. Ira and Nicki
Harris Foundation, James J. and Angelia M.
Harris Foundation, John H. and Lucille
Harrison Foundation Trust, Francena T.
Harsco Corp.
Hartford Courant Foundation
Hartford Steam Boiler Inspection & Insurance Co.
Hartmarx Corp.
Hartzell Industries, Inc.
Haskell Fund
Hatch Charitable Trust, Margaret Milliken
Havens Foundation, O. W.
Hawkins Foundation, Robert Z.
Hawn Foundation
Hayden Foundation, William R. and Virginia
Hayfields Foundation
Hayward Foundation Charitable Trust, John T. and Winifred
Hazen Charitable Trust, Lita Annenberg
Health 1st Foundation
Hearst Foundation
Hearst Foundation, William Randolph
Hechinger Co.
Heckscher Foundation for Children
Hecla Mining Co.
Hedco Foundation
Hedrick Foundation, Frank E.
Heginbotham Trust, Will E.
HEI Inc.
Heileman Brewing Co., Inc., G.
Heilicher Foundation, Menahem
Heineman Foundation for Research, Educational, Charitable, and Scientific Purposes
Heinz Co., H.J.
Heinz Endowment, Howard
Heinz Endowment, Vira I.
Heinz Family Foundation
Heinz Foundation, Drue
Helfaer Foundation, Evan and Marion
Helis Foundation
Heller Foundation, Walter E.
Helmerich Foundation

Helms Foundation
Helzberg Foundation, Shirley and Barnett
Hemby Foundation, Alex
Hench Foundation, John C.
Henderson Foundation
Hendrickson Brothers
Henkel Corp.
Herman Foundation, John and Rose
Hermann Foundation, Grover
Herrick Foundation
Hersey Foundation
Herzog Foundation, Carl J.
Herzstein Charitable Foundation, Albert and Ethel
Hess Charitable Trust, Myrtle E. and William C.
Hess Foundation
Hettinger Foundation
Heublein
Hewit Family Foundation
Hewlett-Packard Co.
Heydt Fund, Nan and Matilda
Heymann Special Account, Mr. and Mrs. Jimmy
Heymann-Wolf Foundation
Heyward Memorial Fund, DuBose and Dorothy
High Foundation
Hill Crest Foundation
Hill Foundation
Hillcrest Foundation
Hilliard Corp.
Hillman Family Foundation, Alex
Hillman Foundation, Henry L.
Hills Fund, Edward E.
Hillsdale Fund
Hilton Foundation, Conrad N.
Himmelfarb Foundation, Paul and Annetta
Hirschl Trust for Charitable Purposes, Irma T.
Hoag Family Foundation, George
Hobbs Charitable Trust, John H.
Hobbs Foundation
Hobbs Foundation, Emmert
Hobby Foundation
Hoblitzelle Foundation
Hoche-Scofield Foundation
Hoechst Celanese Corp.
Hoffman Foundation, John Ernest
Hoffman Foundation, Marion O. and Maximilian
Hoffman Foundation, Maximillian E. and Marion O.
Hoffmann-La Roche
Hofmann Co.
Holden Fund, James and Lynelle
Holley Foundation
Hollis Foundation
Holmes Foundation
Holzer Memorial Foundation, Richard H.
Home for Aged Men
Homeland Foundation
HON Industries
Honigman Foundation
Hood Foundation, Charles H.
Hook Drug
Hooper Foundation, Elizabeth S.
Hoover Foundation
Hoover Foundation, H. Earl
Hoover, Jr. Foundation, Margaret W. and Herbert
Hopedale Foundation
Hopkins Foundation, Josephine Lawrence
Hopwood Charitable Trust, John M.
Hornblower Fund, Henry
Horne Trust, Mabel
Horowitz Foundation, Gedale B. and Barbara S.
House Educational Trust, Susan Cook
Houston Endowment
Houston Industries

Hovnanian Foundation, Hirair and Anna
Howe and Mitchell B. Howe Foundation, Lucite Horton
Howell Foundation, Eric and Jessie
Hubbard Broadcasting
Hubbell Inc.
Huber Foundation
Hudson-Webber Foundation
Huffy Corp.
Hughes Charitable Trust, Mabel Y.
Hugoton Foundation
Huisking Foundation
Hulme Charitable Foundation, Milton G.
Hultquist Foundation
Humana
Humane Society of the Commonwealth of Massachusetts
Humphrey Foundation, Glenn & Gertrude
Humphrey Fund, George M. and Pamela S.
Hunt Foundation
Hunt Foundation, Roy A.
Hunt Foundation, Samuel P.
Hunt Trust for Episcopal Charitable Institutions, Virginia
Hunter Trust, A. V.
Hunter Trust, Emily S. and Coleman A.
Hurford Foundation
Hurlbut Memorial Fund, Orion L. and Emma S.
Huston Foundation
Hutchins Foundation, Mary J.
Huthsteiner Fine Arts Trust
Hutzell Foundation
Hyde and Watson Foundation
I. and L. Association
Iacocca Foundation
IBM Corp.
Icahn Foundation, Carl C.
ICI Americas
IES Industries
Illges Memorial Foundation, A. and M. L.
Illinois Tool Works
Imerman Memorial Foundation, Stanley
Imperial Bancorp
Indiana Desk Co.
Ingalls Foundation, Louise H. and David S.
Inland Container Corp.
Inland Steel Industries
Innovating Worthy Projects Foundation
Interco
International Flavors & Fragrances
International Paper Co.
Ireland Foundation
Irmas Charitable Foundation, Audrey and Sydney
Iroquois Avenue Foundation
Irwin Charity Foundation, William G.
Ishiyama Foundation
Israel Foundation, A. Cremieux
ITT Corp.
ITT Hartford Insurance Group
Ittleson Foundation
Ix & Sons, Frank
J. D. B. Fund
J. D. B. Fund
J.P. Morgan & Co.
Jackson Charitable Trust, Marion Gardner
Jackson Family Foundation, Ann
Jackson Foundation
Jackson Hole Preserve
Jacobson & Sons, Benjamin
Jaffe Foundation
Jaharis Family Foundation

Jameson Foundation, J. W. and Ida M.
Janirve Foundation
Janssen Foundation, Henry
Jaqua Foundation
Jarson-Stanley and Mickey Kaplan Foundation, Isaac & Esther
Jasper Desk Co.
Jasper Seating Co.
Jasper Table Co.
JCPenney Co.
Jenkins Foundation, George W.
Jennings Foundation, Alma
Jennings Foundation, Mary Hillman
Jerome Foundation
Jersey Central Power & Light Co.
Jerusalem Fund for Education and Community Development
Jesselson Foundation
Jewell Memorial Foundation, Daniel Ashley and Irene Houston
Jewett Foundation, George Frederick
Jinks Foundation, Ruth T.
JJJ Foundation
JMK-A M Micallef Charitable Foundation
Jockey Hollow Foundation
John Hancock Mutual Life Insurance Co.
Johnson Controls
Johnson Foundation, A. D.
Johnson Foundation, Helen K. and Arthur E.
Johnson Foundation, Howard
Johnson Foundation, M. G. and Lillie A.
Johnson Foundation, Robert Wood
Johnson & Higgins
Johnson & Johnson
Johnson & Son, S.C.
Johnston Trust for Charitable and Educational Purposes, James M.
Johnstone and H. Earle Kimball Foundation, Phyllis Kimball
Jones and Bessie D. Phelps Foundation, Cyrus W. and Amy F.
Jones Charitable Trust, Harvey and Bernice
Jones Family Foundation, Eugenie and Joseph
Jones Foundation, Daisy Marquis
Jones Foundation, Daisy Marquis
Jones Foundation, Fletcher
Jones Foundation, Montfort Jones and Allie Brown
Jones Fund, Blanche and George
Jones Fund, Paul L.
Jonsson Foundation
Jordan and Ettie A. Jordan Charitable Foundation, Mary Ranken
Jordan Foundation, Arthur
Joslin-Needham Family Foundation
Joslyn Foundation, Marcellus I.
Jost Foundation, Charles and Mabel P.
Joy Family Foundation
Joyce Foundation, John M. and Mary A.
Julia R. and Estelle L. Foundation
Jurzykowski Foundation, Alfred
Kade Foundation, Max
Kaiser Foundation, Betty E. and George B.
Kangesser Foundation, Robert E., Harry A., and M. Sylvia
Kapiloff Foundation, Leonard
Kaplan Foundation, Mayer and Morris

Hospitals (cont.)

Kaplan Foundation, Rita J. and Stanley H.
Kaplen Foundation
Kaplun Foundation, Morris J. and Betty
Kapoor Charitable Foundation
Katten, Muchin, & Zavis
Kaufmann Foundation, Henry
Kaufmann Foundation, Marion Esser
Kautz Family Foundation
Keebler Co.
Keeler Fund, Miner S. and Mary Ann
Keene Trust, Hazel R.
Keeney Trust, Hattie Hannah
Keith Foundation Trust, Ben E.
Keller-Crescent Co.
Keller Family Foundation
Kelley and Elza Kelley Foundation, Edward Bangs
Kelley Foundation, Kate M.
Kellogg Foundation, J. C.
Kellogg Foundation, W. K.
Kellogg's
Kelly Foundation, T. Lloyd
Kelly Tractor Co.
Kemper Charitable Trust, William T.
Kemper Educational and Charitable Fund
Kemper Foundation, Enid and Crosby
Kenedy Memorial Foundation, John G. and Marie Stella
Kennametal
Kennecott Corp.
Kennedy Family Foundation, Ethel and W. George
Kennedy Foundation, Ethel
Kennedy Foundation, John R.
Kennedy Foundation, Quentin J.
Kennedy, Jr. Foundation, Joseph P.
Kenridge Fund
Kent-Lucas Foundation
Kentland Foundation
Kenworthy - Sarah H. Swift Foundation, Marion E.
Kepco, Inc.
Kerney Foundation, James
Kerr Foundation, Robert S. and Grayce B.
Kerr Fund, Grayce B.
Kerr-McGee Corp.
Kettering Family Foundation
Kettering Fund
Key Bank of Maine
Key Food Stores Cooperative Inc.
Kieckhefer Foundation, J. W.
Kiewit Foundation, Peter
Kiewit Sons, Peter
Killough Trust, Walter H. D.
Kilworth Charitable Foundation, Florence B.
Kilworth Charitable Trust, William
Kimball Co., Miles
Kimball International
Kimberly-Clark Corp.
King Foundation, Carl B. and Florence E.
King Ranch
Kingsley Foundation
Kingsley Foundation, Lewis A.
Kingston Foundation
Kiplinger Foundation
Kirbo Charitable Trust, Thomas M. and Irene B.
Kirby Foundation, F. M.
Kirchgessner Foundation, Karl
Kitzmiller/Bales Trust
Klau Foundation, David W. and Sadie
Kleberg, Jr. and Helen C. Kleberg Foundation, Robert J.

Klee Foundation, Conrad and Virginia
Klein Fund, Nathan J.
Kline Foundation, Josiah W. and Bessie H.
Klingler Foundation, Helen and Charles
Klosk Fund, Louis and Rose
Knapp Foundation
Knight Foundation, John S. and James L.
Knowles Charitable Memorial Trust, Gladys E.
Knowles Foundation
Knox Family Foundation
Knox Foundation, Seymour H.
Kobacker Co.
Koch Charitable Trust, David H.
Koch Sons, George
Koehler Foundation, Marcia and Otto
Koffler Family Foundation
Koh-I-Noor Rapidograph Inc.
Kohl Foundation, Sidney
Kohn-Joseloff Fund
Komes Foundation
Koopman Fund
Kopf Foundation
Kopf Foundation, Elizabeth Christy
Korman Family Foundation, Hyman
Kowalski Sausage Co.
Kraft Foundation
Kramer Foundation
Kramer Foundation, C. L. C.
Kresge Foundation
Kress Foundation, George
Krieble Foundation, Vernon K.
Krimendahl II Foundation, H. Frederick
KSM Foundation
Kuehn Foundation
Kugelman Foundation
Kuhns Investment Co.
Kuyper Foundation, Peter H. and E. Lucille Gaass
Kynett Memorial Foundation, Edna G.
L. L. W. W. Foundation
L and L Foundation
La-Z-Boy Chair Co.
Laclede Gas Co.
Lacy Foundation
Ladish Co.
Ladish Family Foundation, Herman W.
Ladish Malting Co.
Laerdal Foundation, Asmund S.
Laffey-McHugh Foundation
Lakeside Foundation
Lambert Memorial Foundation, Gerard B.
LamCo. Communications
Landegger Charitable Foundation
Lane Foundation, Minnie and Bernard
Lang Foundation, Eugene M.
Langeloth Foundation, Jacob and Valeria
Lanier Brothers Foundation
Lard Trust, Mary Potishman
Large Foundation
Laros Foundation, R. K.
Lasdon Foundation
Lasky Co.
Lastfogel Foundation, Abe and Frances
Lattner Foundation, Forrest C.
Lauder Foundation
Lautenberg Foundation
Law Foundation, Robert O.
Lawrence Foundation, Alice
Lawrence Foundation, Lind
Lazar Foundation
Lazarus Charitable Trust, Helen and Charles
LBJ Family Foundation

Leavey Foundation, Thomas and Dorothy
Lebovitz Fund
Lebus Trust, Bertha
Lee Endowment Foundation
Lee Enterprises
Lee Foundation, James T.
Lee Foundation, Ray M. and Mary Elizabeth
Lehmann Foundation, Otto W.
Lehrman Foundation, Jacob and Charlotte
Leidy Foundation, John J.
Lennon Foundation, Fred A.
Leo Burnett Co.
Leonardt Foundation
Leonhardt Foundation, Dorothea L.
Leonhardt Foundation, Frederick H.
Leuthold Foundation
Levee Charitable Trust, Polly Annenberg
Levin Foundation, Philip and Janice
Levinson Foundation, Morris L.
Leviton Manufacturing Co.
Levy Foundation, Betty and Norman F.
Levy Foundation, Edward C.
Levy Foundation, June Rockwell
Levy's Lumber & Building Centers
Lewis Foundation, Frank J.
Lewis Foundation, Lillian Kaiser
Liberman Foundation, Bertha & Isaac
Liberty Corp.
Lichtenstein Foundation, David B.
Lightner Sams Foundation
Lincoln Electric Co.
Lincoln Health Care Foundation
Lincy Foundation
Lindner Foundation, Fay J.
Lindsay Foundation
Lindsay Trust, Agnes M.
Link, Jr. Foundation, George
Linn-Henley Charitable Trust
Linnell Foundation
Lipton, Thomas J.
Liquid Air Corp.
Littauer Foundation, Lucius N.
Little, Arthur D.
Little Family Foundation
Littlefield Foundation, Edmund Wattis
Littlefield Memorial Trust, Ida Ballou
Litton Industries
Livingston Foundation
Livingston Memorial Foundation
Liz Claiborne
Llagas Foundation
Lockheed Sanders
Lockwood Foundation, Byron W. and Alice L.
Loeb Partners Corp.
Loews Corp.
Loewy Family Foundation
Long Foundation, George A. and Grace
Longwood Foundation
Loose Trust, Harry Wilson
Lopata Foundation, Stanley and Lucy
Lost Tree Charitable Foundation
Louisiana-Pacific Corp.
Lounsbery Foundation, Richard
Loutit Foundation
Love Charitable Foundation, John Allan
Love Foundation, George H. and Margaret McClintic
Lovett Foundation
Lowe Foundation, Joe and Emily
Lowenstein Foundation, Leon

Lowenstein Foundation, William P. and Marie R.
Lozier Foundation
LTV Corp.
Lubrizol Corp.
Luce Charitable Foundation, Stephen C.
Lumpkin Foundation
Lund Foundation
Lurie Family Foundation
Lurie Foundation, Louis R.
Luttrell Trust
Lux Trust, Dr. Konrad and Clara
Lydall, Inc.
Lynn Foundation, E. M.
Lyons Foundation
Lytel Foundation, Bertha Russ
M/A-COM, Inc.
M.T.D. Products
Maas Foundation, Benard L.
Mabee Foundation, J. E. and L. E.
MacAndrews & Forbes Holdings
MacDonald Foundation, James A.
MacDonald Foundation, Marquis George
MacKall and Evanina Evans Bell MacKall Trust, Paul
Macmillan, Inc.
Macy & Co., R.H.
Maddox Trust, Web
Madison Gas & Electric Co.
Magowan Family Foundation
Magruder Foundation, Chesley G.
Mailman Family Foundation, A. L.
Mailman Foundation
Makita U.S.A., Inc.
Mallinckrodt, Jr. Foundation, Edward
Mallinckrodt Specialty Chemicals Co.
Mamiye Brothers
Mandel Foundation, Joseph and Florence
Mandel Foundation, Morton and Barbara
Mandell Foundation, Samuel P.
Mandeville Foundation
Manilow Foundation, Nathan
Mann Foundation, John Jay
Mann Foundation, Ted
Manning and Emma Austin Manning Foundation, James Hilton
Manoogian Foundation, Alex and Marie
Mapco Inc.
Mapplethorpe Foundation, Robert
Marbrook Foundation
Marcus Brothers Textiles Inc.
Marcus Corp.
Mardag Foundation
Margoes Foundation
Margolis Charitable Foundation for Medical Research, Ben B. and Iris M.
Maritz Inc.
Mark IV Industries
Markey Charitable Fund, John C.
Marley Co.
Marmot Foundation
Marriott Foundation, J. Willard
Marshall Foundation
Marshall Foundation, Mattie H.
Marshall & Ilsley Bank
Marshall Trust in Memory of Sanders McDaniel, Harriet McDaniel
Martin Foundation, Bert William
Martin Marietta Aggregates
Martin Marietta Corp.
Mary Kay Foundation
Masco Corp.
Massachusetts Mutual Life Insurance Co.

Masserini Charitable Trust, Maurice J.
Massey Charitable Trust
Massey Foundation
Massie Trust, David Meade
Mastronardi Charitable Foundation, Charles A.
Material Service Corp.
Mather and William Gwinn Mather Fund, Elizabeth Ring
Mathers Charitable Foundation, G. Harold and Leila Y.
Max Charitable Foundation
Maxon Charitable Foundation
May Department Stores Co.
May Foundation, Wilbur
May Mitchell Royal Foundation
Mayer Charitable Trust, Oscar G. & Elsa S.
Mayer Foundation, James and Eva
Mayor Foundation, Oliver Dewey
Maytag Family Foundation, Fred
Mazza Foundation
MCA
McAlister Charitable Foundation, Harold
McAlonan Trust, John A.
McBean Family Foundation
McCann Foundation
McCarthy Charities
McCarthy Foundation, Michael W.
McCarthy Memorial Trust Fund, Catherine
McCasland Foundation
McCormick Tribune Foundation, Robert R.
McCormick Trust, Anne
McCray Lumber Co.
McCrea Foundation
McCullough Foundation, Ralph H. and Ruth J.
McCune Charitable Trust, John R.
McCune Foundation
McDermott
McDermott Foundation, Eugene
McDonald & Co. Securities
McDonald & Co. Securities
McDonald Foundation, J. M.
McDonald's Corp.
McDonnell Douglas Corp.
McDonnell Douglas Corp.-West
McDonough Foundation, Bernard
McEvoy Foundation, Mildred H.
McFawn Trust No. 2, Lois Sisler
McFeely-Rogers Foundation
McGee Foundation
McGonagle Foundation, Dextra Baldwin
McGraw Foundation
McGraw Foundation, Curtis W.
McGraw Foundation, Donald C.
McGraw-Hill
McGregor Foundation, Thomas and Frances
McGregor Fund
MCI Communications Corp.
McInerny Foundation
McIntosh Foundation
McIntosh Foundation
McKee Foundation, Robert E. and Evelyn
McKenna Foundation, Katherine Mabis
McKenna Foundation, Philip M.
McKnight Foundation
McLean Contributionship
McMurray-Bennnett Foundation
McNutt Charitable Trust, Amy Shelton
MDU Resources Group, Inc.
Mead Corp.
Mead Foundation, Giles W. and Elise G.
Mead Fund, Nelson
Meadowood Foundation

Meadows Foundation
Measey Foundation, Benjamin and Mary Siddons
Mebane Packaging Corp.
Mechanic Foundation, Morris A.
Medina Foundation
Meek Foundation
Mellam Family Foundation
Mellen Foundation
Mellon Bank Corp.
Mellon Foundation, Richard King
Memorial Foundation for the Blind
Memton Fund
Menasha Corp.
Mengle Foundation, Glenn and Ruth
Mengle Foundation, Glenn and Ruth
Menschel Foundation, Robert and Joyce
Mercantile Bancorp
Merck & Co.
Merck Family Fund
Merck Human Health Division
Mercury Aircraft
Mercy, Jr. Foundation, Sue and Eugene
Meridian Bancorp
Merrick Foundation
Merrick Foundation, Robert G. and Anne M.
Merrill Foundation, R. D.
Merrill Lynch & Co.
Messing Family Charitable Foundation
Messing Foundation, Morris M. and Helen F.
Metal Industries
Metropolitan Life Insurance Co.
Metropolitan Theatres Corp.
Mettler Instrument Corp.
Meyer Foundation
Meyer Foundation, Baron de Hirsch
Meyer Foundation, Robert R.
Meyer Memorial Foundation, Aaron and Rachel
Meyer Memorial Trust
Meyerhoff Fund, Joseph
MGIC Investment Corp.
Michael Foundation, Herbert I. and Elsa B.
Michigan Bell Telephone Co.
Michigan Consolidated Gas Co.
Michigan Gas Utilities
Middendorf Foundation
Midwest Resources
Milbank Foundation, Dunlevy
Miles Inc.
Milken Family Medical Foundation
Milken Foundation, L. and S.
Mill-Rose Co.
Millbrook Tribute Garden
Miller Charitable Trust, Lewis N.
Miller Foundation, Steve J.
Miller Fund, Kathryn and Gilbert
Miller Memorial Trust, George Lee
Milliken & Co.
Milliken Foundation, Agnes G.
Mills Charitable Foundation, Henry L. and Kathryn
Mills Foundation, Ralph E.
Millstein Charitable Foundation
Milstein Family Foundation
Mine Safety Appliances Co.
Miniger Memorial Foundation, Clement O.
Minolta Corp.
Mitchell Family Foundation, Edward D. and Anna
Mitchell Foundation
MNC Financial
Mnuchin Foundation
Mobil Oil Corp.
Mobility Foundation

Mohasco Corp.
Monarch Machine Tool Co.
Moncrief Foundation, William A. and Elizabeth B.
Monell Foundation, Ambrose
Monfort Charitable Foundation
Monroe Auto Equipment Co.
Monroe Foundation (1976), J. Edgar
Monsanto Co.
Montana Power Co.
Montgomery Foundation
Montgomery Street Foundation
Moody Foundation
Moog Automotive, Inc.
Moore Business Forms, Inc.
Moore Family Foundation
Moore Foundation
Moore Foundation, C. F.
Moore Foundation, Edward S.
Moore Foundation, Martha G.
Moore Memorial Foundation, James Starr
Moores Foundation, Harry C.
Moorman Manufacturing Co.
Morania Foundation
Morgan and Samuel Tate Morgan, Jr. Foundation, Marietta McNeil
Morgan Foundation, Louie R. and Gertrude
Morgan Stanley & Co.
Morgenstern Foundation, Morris
Morley Brothers Foundation
Morris Foundation
Morris Foundation, Margaret T.
Morris Foundation, Norman M.
Morris Foundation, William T.
Morrison Foundation, Harry W.
Morse Foundation, Richard P. and Claire W.
Morse, Jr. Foundation, Enid and Lester S.
Morton International
Mosbacher, Jr. Foundation, Emil
Moses Fund, Henry and Lucy
Mosher Foundation, Samuel B.
Mosinee Paper Corp.
Moss Charitable Trust, Finis M.
Moss Heart Trust, Harry S.
Motorola
Mulford Trust, Clarence E.
Mullan Foundation, Thomas F. and Clementine L.
Mullen Foundation, J. K.
Muller Foundation
Muller Foundation, C. John and Josephine
Mulligan Charitable Trust, Mary S.
Munger Foundation, Alfred C.
Munson Foundation, W. B.
Murch Foundation
Murdy Foundation
Murfee Endowment, Kathryn
Murphey Foundation, Lluella Morey
Murphy Foundation, Dan
Murphy Foundation, John P.
Murphy Foundation, Katherine and John
Murphy Oil Corp.
Murray Foundation
Myers and Sons, D.
Nalco Chemical Co.
Nason Foundation
Nathan Berkman & Co.
Nathan Foundation
National City Bank, Columbus
National City Bank of Evansville
National City Corp.
National Computer Systems
National Forge Co.
National Fuel Gas Co.
National Gypsum Co.
National Life of Vermont
National Machinery Co.

National Presto Industries
National Pro-Am Youth Fund
National Service Industries
National Starch & Chemical Corp.
National Westminster Bank New Jersey
Nationwide Insurance Cos.
Navistar International Corp.
NBD Bank
NBD Bank, N.A.
Neenah Foundry Co.
Neese Family Foundation
Nelco Sewing Machine Sales Corp.
Nelson Industries, Inc.
Nestle U.S.A. Inc.
Neu Foundation, Hugo and Doris
New England Business Service
New England Foundation
New England Mutual Life Insurance Co.
New Horizon Foundation
New Jersey Bell Telephone Company
New-Land Foundation
New York Foundation
New York Life Insurance Co.
New York Mercantile Exchange
New York Telephone Co.
The New Yorker Magazine, Inc.
Newbrook Charitable Foundation
Newhouse Foundation, Samuel I.
Newman Assistance Fund, Jerome A. and Estelle R.
Newman's Own
Newmil Bancorp
News & Observer Publishing Co.
Nias Foundation, Henry
Nichols Co., J.C.
Nichols Foundation
Noble Charitable Trust, John L. and Ethel G.
Noble Foundation, Edward John
Noble Foundation, Samuel Roberts
Noble Foundation, Vivian Bilby
Noonan Memorial Fund under the will of Frank Noonan, Deborah Munroe
Norcliffe Fund
Norfolk Shipbuilding & Drydock Corp.
Norfolk Shipbuilding & Drydock Corp.
Norfolk Southern Corp.
Norgren Foundation, Carl A.
Norman Foundation, Andrew
Norman/Nethercutt Foundation, Merle
Norris Foundation, Dellora A. and Lester J.
Norris Foundation, Kenneth T. and Eileen L.
North American Life & Casualty Co.
North American Philips Corp.
North American Reinsurance Corp.
North Carolina Foam Foundation
Northeast Utilities
Northern Indiana Public Service Co.
Northern Star Foundation
Northern Trust Co.
Northwest Natural Gas Co.
Northwestern National Insurance Group
Norton Co.
Norton Memorial Corporation, Geraldi
Noyes, Jr. Memorial Foundation, Nicholas H.
NuTone Inc.
NutraSweet Co.
Oakley Foundation, Hollie and Anna
Oberlaender Foundation, Gustav

Obernauer Foundation
O'Bleness Foundation, Charles G.
Occidental Oil & Gas Corp.
Occidental Petroleum Corp.
Oceanic Cablevision Foundation
O'Connor Foundation, A. Lindsay and Olive B.
O'Donnell Foundation
Odyssey Partners
Oestreicher Foundation, Sylvan and Ann
Offield Family Foundation
Ogden Foundation, Ralph E.
Ogilvy & Mather Worldwide
Oglebay Norton Co.
Ohio National Life Insurance Co.
Ohl, Jr. Trust, George A.
Ohrstrom Foundation
Oklahoma Gas & Electric Co.
Old National Bank in Evansville
Olin Charitable Trust, John M.
Olin Corp.
Olin Foundation, Spencer T. and Ann W.
Olive Bridge Fund
Oliver Memorial Trust Foundation
Olivetti Office USA, Inc.
Olsson Memorial Foundation, Elis
1957 Charity Trust
O'Neil Foundation, Casey Albert T.
O'Neil Foundation, M. G.
O'Neill Charitable Corporation, F. J.
Ontario Corp.
Oppenheimer and Flora Oppenheimer Haas Trust, Leo
Oppenstein Brothers Foundation
O'Quinn Foundation, John M. and Nancy C.
Orange Orphan Society
Ore-Ida Foods, Inc.
Orscheln Co.
Osborn Charitable Trust, Edward B.
Osborn Manufacturing Co.
Osceola Foundation
O'Shaughnessy Foundation, I. A.
O'Sullivan Children Foundation
O'Toole Foundation, Theresa and Edward
Outboard Marine Corp.
Overbrook Foundation
Overlake Foundation
Overseas Shipholding Group
Owen Trust, B. B.
Owsley Foundation, Alvin and Lucy
Oxford Foundation
Oxford Industries, Inc.
Oxnard Foundation
PACCAR
Pacific Mutual Life Insurance Co.
Pacific Western Foundation
PacifiCorp
Packaging Corporation of America
Packard Foundation, David and Lucile
Packer Foundation, Horace B.
Paley Foundation, William S.
Palisades Educational Foundation
Palmer Fund, Frank Loomis
Panhandle Eastern Corp.
Pappas Charitable Foundation, Bessie
Pappas Charitable Foundation, Thomas Anthony
Pardee Foundation, Elsa U.
Park Bank
Park National Bank
Parke-Davis Group
Parker Foundation
Parker Foundation, Theodore Edson

Parker-Hannifin Corp.
Parker, Jr. Foundation, William A.
Parman Foundation, Robert A.
Parshelsky Foundation, Moses L.
Parsons Foundation, Ralph M.
Parsons - W.D. Charities, Vera Davis
Parthenon Sportswear
Pasadena Area Residential Aid
Patterson and Clara Guthrie Patterson Trust, Robert Leet
Patterson Charitable Fund, W. I.
Paulucci Family Foundation
Payne Foundation, Frank E. and Seba B.
Peabody Charitable Fund, Amelia
Peabody Foundation
Peabody Foundation, Amelia
Pearlstone Foundation, Peggy Meyerhoff
Pella Corp.
Pellegrino-Realmuto Charitable Foundation
PemCo. Corp.
Penn Savings Bank, a division of Sovereign Bank Bank of Princeton, a division of Sovereign Bank
Pennington Foundation, Irene W. and C. B.
Pennsylvania Dutch Co.
Pennzoil Co.
Penzance Foundation
Peoples Energy Corp.
Perini Corp.
Perkin-Elmer Corp.
Perkin Fund
Perkins Charitable Foundation
Perkins Foundation, Edwin E.
Perkins Memorial Foundation, George W.
Perkins Memorial Fund, James J. and Marie Richardson
Persis Corp.
Peters Foundation, Charles F.
Peters Foundation, Leon S.
Petersen Foundation, Esper A.
Peterson Foundation, Fred J.
Peterson Memorial Fund, Chris and Mary L.
Petrie Trust, Lorene M.
Petteys Memorial Foundation, Jack
Pfaffinger Foundation
Pfizer
Pforzheimer Foundation, Carl and Lily
Pfriem Foundation, Norma F.
Phelps, Inc.
Phelps Dodge Corp.
PHH Corp.
Philadelphia Electric Co.
Philadelphia Industries
Philibosian Foundation, Stephen
Philips Foundation, Jesse
Phillips Charitable Trust, Dr. and Mrs. Arthur William
Phillips Family Foundation, Jay and Rose
Phillips Family Foundation, L. E.
Phillips Foundation, A. P.
Phillips Foundation, Dr. P.
Phillips Foundation, Waite and Genevieve
Phillips Petroleum Co.
Phillips-Van Heusen Corp.
Phipps Foundation, William H.
Pick, Jr. Fund, Albert
Picker International
Pickford Foundation, Mary
Piedmont Health Care Foundation
Pierce Charitable Trust, Harold Whitworth
Pincus Family Fund
Pinewood Foundation
Pineywoods Foundation

Hospitals (cont.)

Pioneer Electronics (USA) Inc.
Pitney Bowes
Pittsburgh National Bank
Pittway Corp.
Pitzman Fund
Plant Memorial Fund, Henry B.
Plitt Southern Theatres
Pluta Family Foundation
Poinsettia Foundation, Paul and
    Magdalena Ecke
Polaroid Corp.
Polinsky-Rivkin Family
    Foundation
Polk Foundation
Pollybill Foundation
Polychrome Corp.
Poorvu Foundation, William and
    Lia
Pope Foundation
Pope Foundation, Lois B.
Post Foundation of D.C.,
    Marjorie Merriweather
Potlatch Corp.
Potomac Electric Power Co.
Pott Foundation, Herman T. and
    Phenie R.
Potts and Sibley Foundation
Potts Memorial Foundation
PPG Industries
Prairie Foundation
Prange Co., H. C.
Pratt Memorial Fund
Precision Rubber Products
Prentis Family Foundation,
    Meyer and Anna
Prentiss Foundation, Elisabeth
    Severance
Preuss Foundation
Preyer Fund, Mary Norris
Price Associates, T. Rowe
Price Foundation. Louis and
    Harold
Price Foundation, Lucien B. and
    Katherine E.
Priddy Foundation
Pritzker Foundation
Procter & Gamble Cosmetic &
    Fragrance Products
Propp Sons Fund, Morris and
    Anna
Prouty Foundation, Olive Higgins
Providence Journal Company
Provigo Corp. Inc.
Prudential-Bache Securities
Prudential Insurance Co. of
    America
Psychists
Public Service Co. of New
    Mexico
Public Service Electric & Gas
    Co.
Pukall Lumber
Pulitzer Publishing Co.
Puterbaugh Foundation
Putnam Foundation
Pyramid Foundation
Quabaug Corp.
Quaker Chemical Corp.
Quaker Hill Foundation
Quaker Oats Co.
Quality Metal Finishing
    Foundation
Quantum Chemical Corp.
Questar Corp.
Quincy Newspapers
R. F. Foundation
R&B Tool Co.
Rabb Charitable Foundation,
    Sidney and Esther
Rabb Charitable Trust, Sidney R.
Radin Foundation
Ragen, Jr. Memorial Fund Trust
    No. 1, James M.
Rahr Malting Co.
Raker Foundation, M. E.

Rales and Ruth Rales
    Foundation, Norman R.
Ralston Purina Co.
Ramapo Trust
Ranney Foundation, P. K.
Ransom Fidelity Company
Rapp Foundation, Robert Glenn
Raskin Foundation, Hirsch and
    Braine
Raskob Foundation for Catholic
    Activities
Ratner Foundation, Milton M.
Ratshesky Foundation, A. C.
Rauch Foundation
Read Foundation, Charles L.
Recognition Equipment
Red Devil
Redfield Foundation, Nell J.
Reed Foundation, Philip D.
Reedman Car-Truck World
    Center
Regenstein Foundation
Reicher Foundation, Anne &
    Harry J.
Reichhold Chemicals, Inc.
Reidler Foundation
Reilly Industries
Reinhart Institutional Foods
Reinhold Foundation, Paul E.
    and Ida Klare
Reisman Charitable Trust,
    George C. and Evelyn R.
Reliance Electric Co.
Rennebohm Foundation, Oscar
Replogle Foundation, Luther I.
Resnick Foundation, Jack and
    Pearl
Retirement Research Foundation
Revlon
Reynolds Charitable Trust, Kate
    B.
Reynolds Foundation, Edgar
Reynolds Foundation, J. B.
Reynolds Foundation, Richard S.
Reynolds Metals Co.
Rhoades Fund, Otto L. and
    Hazel E.
Rhone-Poulenc Inc.
Rhone-Poulenc Rorer
Rice Family Foundation, Jacob
    and Sophie
Rice Foundation
Rice Foundation, Helen Steiner
Rich Co., F.D.
Rich Foundation
Rich Products Corp.
Richardson Charitable Trust,
    Anne S.
Richardson Foundation, Sid W.
Richardson Fund, Grace
Ridgefield Foundation
Rieke Corp.
Rienzi Foundation
Riggs Benevolent Fund
Ringier-America
Rinker Materials Corp.
Rippel Foundation, Fannie E.
Ritter Charitable Trust, George
    W. & Mary F.
Ritter Foundation
Ritter Foundation, May Ellen
    and Gerald
RJR Nabisco Inc.
Roberts Foundation, Dora
Robertshaw Controls Co.
Robinson Foundation
Robinson Mountain Fund, E. O.
Robison Foundation, Ellis H. and
    Doris B.
Rochester Gas & Electric Corp.
Rockwell Foundation
Rockwell Fund
Rockwell International Corp.
Rodgers Foundation, Richard &
    Dorothy
Rodman Foundation
Roehl Foundation
Rogers Family Foundation

Rogers Foundation
Rogers Foundation, Mary Stuart
Rohatyn Foundation, Felix and
    Elizabeth
Rohlik Foundation, Sigmund and
    Sophie
Rohm and Haas Company
Rohr Inc.
Rolfs Foundation, Robert T.
Rollins Luetkemeyer Charitable
    Foundation
RosaMary Foundation
Rose Foundation, Billy
Rosen Foundation, Joseph
Rosenberg Foundation, Alexis
Rosenberg Foundation, Henry
    and Ruth Blaustein
Rosenberg Foundation, Sunny
    and Abe
Rosenbloom Foundation, Ben
    and Esther
Rosenstiel Foundation
Rosenthal Foundation, Ida and
    William
Rosenthal Foundation, Richard
    and Hinda
Rosenthal Foundation, Samuel
Rosenwald Family Fund, William
Ross Foundation
Ross Foundation, Arthur
Ross Foundation, Walter G.
Ross Laboratories
Roth Foundation
Rothschild Foundation, Hulda B.
    and Maurice L.
Rouse Co.
Rowland Foundation
Royal Group Inc.
Rubbermaid
Rubenstein Charitable
    Foundation, Lawrence J. and
    Anne
Rubenstein Foundation, Philip
Rubin Foundation, Rob E. &
    Judith O.
Rubinstein Foundation, Helena
Ruddick Corp.
Rudin Foundation
Rudin Foundation, Samuel and
    May
Rukin Philanthropic Foundation,
    David and Eleanore
Russell Memorial Foundation,
    Robert
Russell Trust, Josephine G.
Rutgers Community Health
    Foundation
Ryan Family Charitable
    Foundation
Ryan Foundation, Nina M.
Ryland Group
Sachs Fund
Sagamore Foundation
Sage Foundation
Sailors' Snug Harbor of Boston
Saint Croix Foundation
St. Faith's House Foundation
Saint Gerard Foundation
St. Giles Foundation
Salomon
Salomon Foundation, Richard &
    Edna
Saltonstall Charitable
    Foundation, Richard
Salwil Foundation
Samuels Foundation, Fan Fox
    and Leslie R.
San Diego Gas & Electric
San Diego Trust & Savings Bank
Sanders Trust, Charles
Sandy Hill Foundation
Sang Foundation, Elsie O. and
    Philip D.
Sanguinetti Foundation,
    Annunziata
Santa Maria Foundation
Sapirstein-Stone-Weiss
    Foundation

Sara Lee Hosiery
Sargent Foundation, Newell B.
Sarkeys Foundation
Sasco Foundation
Saunders Charitable Foundation,
    Helen M.
Sawyer Charitable Foundation
Scaife Family Foundation
Scaler Foundation
Schaffer Foundation, H.
Schaffer Foundation, Michael &
    Helen
Schamach Foundation, Milton
Schapiro Fund, M. A.
Schenck Fund, L. P.
Scherer Foundation, Karla
Schering-Plough Corp.
Schey Foundation
Schiff Foundation
Schiff Foundation, Dorothy
Schiff Foundation, John J. and
    Mary R.
Schilling Motors
Schlink Foundation, Albert G.
    and Olive H.
Schlumberger Ltd.
Schmidlapp Trust No. 1, Jacob G.
Schmidt Charitable Foundation,
    William E.
Schneider Foundation, Robert E.
Schoenleber Foundation
Scholl Foundation, Dr.
Scholler Foundation
Schoonmaker J-Sewkly Valley
    Hospital Trust
Schrafft and Bertha E. Schrafft
    Charitable Trust, William E.
Schramm Foundation
Schroeder Foundation, Walter
Schultz Foundation
Schust Foundation, Clarence L.
    and Edith B.
Schwartz Foundation, Arnold A.
Schwartz Foundation, Bernard
    Lee
Schwartz Foundation, David
Schwartz Fund for Education
    and Health Research, Arnold
    and Marie
Schwob Foundation, Simon
Scott and Fetzer Co.
Scott Foundation, Walter
Scripps Foundation, Ellen
    Browning
Scrivner, Inc.
Scrivner of North Carolina Inc.
Scurlock Foundation
Seabury Foundation
Seafirst Corp.
Sealright Co., Inc.
Searle & Co., G.D.
Sears Family Foundation
Seaver Charitable Trust, Richard
    C.
Seaway Food Town
Seay Charitable Trust, Sarah M.
    and Charles E.
Seay Memorial Trust, George
    and Effie
Second Foundation
Security State Bank
See Foundation, Charles
Seevak Family Foundation
Sefton Foundation, J. W.
Seidman Family Foundation
Self Foundation
Sentry Insurance Co.
Sequoia Foundation
Servco Pacific
Setzer Foundation
Shafer Foundation, Richard H.
    and Ann
Shapell Foundation, Nathan and
    Lilly
Shapiro, Inc.
Shapiro Charity Fund, Abraham
Shapiro Family Foundation,
    Soretta and Henry

Shapiro Foundation, Carl and
    Ruth
Shapiro Fund, Albert
Share Trust, Charles Morton
Sharon Steel Corp.
Sharp Foundation, Charles S.
    and Ruth C.
Shattuck Charitable Trust, S. F.
Shaw Foundation, Arch W.
Shaw Foundation, Walden W.
    and Jean Young
Shawmut National Corp.
Shawmut Worcester County
    Bank, N.A.
Shaw's Supermarkets
Shea Co., John F.
Shea Foundation
Shea Foundation, Edmund and
    Mary
Sheaffer Inc.
Sheinberg Foundation, Eric P.
Shelden Fund, Elizabeth, Allan
    and Warren
Sheldon Foundation, Ralph C.
Shell Oil Co.
Shelton Cos.
Shemanski Testamentary Trust,
    Tillie and Alfred
Sheppard Foundation, Lawrence
    B.
Sherman Family Charitable
    Trust, George and Beatrice
Shirk Foundation, Russell and
    Betty
Shoenberg Foundation
Shoney's Inc.
Shook Foundation, Barbara
    Ingalls
Shore Fund
Shorenstein Foundation, Walter
    H. and Phyllis J.
Shughart, Thomson & Kilroy,
    P.C.
Siebert Lutheran Foundation
Sierra Pacific Resources
Signet Bank/Maryland
Silver Spring Foundation
Silverman Foundation, Marty
    and Dorothy
Simmons Family Foundation, R.
    P.
Simon Charitable Trust, Esther
Simon Foundation, Sidney,
    Milton and Leoma
Simon Foundation, William E.
    and Carol G.
Simpson Foundation
Simpson Foundation, John M.
Simpson Investment Co.
Simpson Paper Co.
Siragusa Foundation
Skinner Corp.
Skirball Foundation
Slant/Fin Corp.
Slaughter Foundation, Charles
Slifka Foundation, Joseph and
    Sylvia
Slusher Charitable Foundation,
    Roy W.
Smith and W. Aubrey Smith
    Charitable Foundation, Clara
    Blackford
Smith Benevolent Association,
    Buckingham
Smith Charitable Foundation,
    Lou and Lutza
Smith Charitable Fund, Eleanor
    Armstrong
Smith Charitable Trust
Smith Charitable Trust, W. W.
Smith Charities, John
Smith Corp., A.O.
Smith Foundation
Smith Foundation, Bob and
    Vivian
Smith Foundation, Kenneth L.
    and Eva S.
Smith Foundation, Lon V.

Smith Foundation, Richard and Susan

Smith, Jr. Charitable Trust, Jack J.

Smith 1963 Charitable Trust, Don McQueen

Smucker Co., J.M.

Snee-Reinhardt Charitable Foundation

SNET

Snite Foundation, Fred B.

Snow Foundation, John Ben

Snyder Charitable Fund, W. P.

Snyder Foundation, Harold B. and Dorothy A.

Society Corp.

Solo Cup Co.

Sonat

Sonoco Products Co.

Sony Corp. of America

Sooner Pipe & Supply Corp.

Soros Foundation-Hungary

Sosland Foundation

Souers Charitable Trust, Sidney W. and Sylvia N.

South Plains Foundation

South Texas Charitable Foundation

South Waite Foundation

Southern California Edison Co.

Spahn & Rose Lumber Co.

Spalding Health Care Trust

Spang & Co.

Speas Foundation, Victor E.

Speas Memorial Trust, John W. and Effie E.

Speer Foundation, Roy M.

Spiegel Family Foundation, Jerry and Emily

Spingold Foundation, Nate B. and Frances

Spiritus Gladius Foundation

Spiro Foundation, Donald W.

Sprague Educational and Charitable Foundation, Seth

Sprague, Jr. Foundation, Caryll M. and Norman F.

Sprague Memorial Institute, Otho S. A.

Springs Foundation

Springs Industries

SPS Technologies

SPX Corp.

Square D Co.

Stabler Foundation, Donald B. and Dorothy L.

Stackpole-Hall Foundation

Staley, Jr. Foundation, A. E.

Standard Chartered Bank New York

Standard Products Co.

Standard Register Co.

Standex International Corp.

Stanley Charitable Foundation, A. W.

Stanley Works

Stans Foundation

Star Bank, N.A.

Starr Foundation

Starrett Co., L.S.

State Farm Mutual Automobile Insurance Co.

State Street Bank & Trust Co.

Statler Foundation

Statter Foundation, Amy Plant

Stauffer Charitable Trust, John

Stauffer Foundation, John and Beverly

Staunton Farm Foundation

Stearns Trust, Artemas W.

Steel, Sr. Foundation, Marshall

Steele Foundation, Harry and Grace

Steele-Reese Foundation

Steiger Memorial Fund, Albert

Steigerwaldt Foundation, Donna Wolf

Stein Foundation, Louis

Steinbach Fund, Ruth and Milton

Steinberg Family Foundation, Meyer and Jean

Steiner Charitable Fund, Albert

Steinman Foundation, James Hale

Steinman Foundation, John Frederick

Stella D'Oro Biscuit Co.

Stemmons Foundation

Sterling Inc.

Sterling Winthrop

Stern Family Foundation, Harry

Stern Foundation, Bernice and Milton

Stern Foundation, Leonard N.

Stern Memorial Trust, Sidney

Sterne-Elder Memorial Trust

Stevens Foundation, Abbot and Dorothy H.

Stevens Foundation, Nathaniel and Elizabeth P.

Stewart Trust under the will of Helen S. Devore, Alexander and Margaret

Stewart Trust under the will of Mary E. Stewart, Alexander and Margaret

Stokely, Jr. Foundation, William B.

Stone Charitable Foundation

Stone Container Corp.

Stoneman Charitable Foundation, Anne and David

Stony Wold Herbert Fund

Storer Foundation, George B.

Storz Foundation, Robert Herman

Stott Foundation, Louis L.

Stott Foundation, Robert L.

Strake Foundation

Stranahan Foundation

Stratford Foundation

Straus Foundation, Aaron and Lillie

Straus Foundation, Martha Washington Straus and Harry H.

Strauss Foundation

Strawbridge Foundation of Pennsylvania I, Margaret Dorrance

Strawbridge Foundation of Pennsylvania II, Margaret Dorrance

Stride Rite Corp.

Stuart Center Charitable Trust, Hugh

Stuart Foundation

Stuart Foundation, Elbridge and Evelyn

Stulsaft Foundation, Morris

Stupp Brothers Bridge & Iron Co.

Stupp Foundation, Norman J.

Subaru of America Inc.

Sudix Foundation

Sullivan Foundation, Ray H. and Pauline

Sulzberger Foundation

Summerfield Foundation, Solon E.

Sun Co.

Sunderland Foundation, Lester T.

Sundstrand Corp.

Sunshine Biscuits

Superior Tube Co.

Susquehanna Investment Group

Swalm Foundation

Swanson Foundation

Sweatt Foundation, Harold W.

Swensrud Charitable Trust, Sidney A.

Swift Co. Inc., John S.

Swift Memorial Health Care Foundation

Swig Charity Foundation, Mae and Benjamin

Swim Foundation, Arthur L.

Swisher Foundation, Carl S.

Swiss American Securities, Inc.

Swiss Bank Corp.

Switzer Foundation

Symmes Foundation, F. W.

Synovus Financial Corp.

Tai and Co., J. T.

Tamarkin Co.

Tamko Asphalt Products

Tandy Foundation, Anne Burnett and Charles

Taub Foundation

Taub Foundation, Henry and Marilyn

Taubman Foundation, A. Alfred

Taubman Foundation, Herman P. and Sophia

Taylor Family Foundation, Jack

Taylor Foundation

Taylor Foundation, Fred and Harriet

Taylor Foundation, Ruth and Vernon

Taylor Trust, Lydia M.

Teledyne

Teleflex Inc.

Temple Foundation, T. L. L.

Tenneco

Terner Foundation

Tetley, Inc.

Teubert Charitable Trust, James H. and Alice

Texaco

Texas Commerce Bank Houston, N.A.

Texas Instruments

Textron

Thagard Foundation

Thalheimer Foundation, Alvin and Fanny Blaustein

Thermo Electron Corp.

Thomas & Betts Corp.

Thomas Medical Foundation, Roy E.

Thompson Charitable Foundation

Thompson Trust, Thomas

Thornton Foundation

Thornton Foundation, Flora L.

Thornton Foundation, John M. and Sally B.

Thorson Foundation

3M Co.

Thurston Charitable Foundation

Tibstra Charitable Foundation, Thomas and Gertrude

Times Mirror Co.

Timken Foundation of Canton

Tippit Charitable Trust, C. Carlisle and Margaret M.

Tisch Foundation

Titan Industrial Co.

Titus Foundation, C. W.

TJX Cos.

Tomkins Industries, Inc.

Tomlinson Foundation, Kate and Elwyn

Torchmark Corp.

Tosco Corp. Refining Division

Totsy Manufacturing Co.

Tozer Foundation

Tracor, Inc.

Tractor & Equipment Co.

Transamerica Corp.

Transco Energy Company

Tranzonic Cos.

Travelli Fund, Charles Irwin

Treadwell Foundation, Nora Eccles

Treuhaft Foundation

Triford Foundation

Trimble Family Foundation, Robert Mize and Isa White

TRINOVA Corp.

True Oil Co.

Trust Co. Bank

TRW Corp.

TU Electric Co.

Tucker Charitable Trust, Rose E.

Tupancy-Harris Foundation of 1986

Turner Charitable Foundation

Turner Fund, Ruth

Twentieth Century-Fox Film Corp.

21 International Holdings

Unilever United States

Union Bank

Union Camp Corp.

Union Central Life Insurance Co.

Union Foundation

Union Pacific Corp.

United Airlines

United Conveyor Corp.

United Dominion Industries

United Merchants & Manufacturers

U.S. Oil/Schmidt Family Foundation, Inc.

U.S. Silica Co.

United States Sugar Corp.

United States Trust Co. of New York

United Technologies Corp.

United Togs Inc.

Universal Foods Corp.

Unocal Corp.

Upjohn California Fund

Upjohn Co.

Upton Charitable Foundation, Lucy and Eleanor S.

USF&G Co.

USG Corp.

Ushkow Foundation

Uslico Corp.

V and V Foundation

Valley Foundation

Valley Foundation, Wayne and Gladys

Valley National Bancorp

Valley National Bank of Arizona

Valspar Corp.

van Ameringen Foundation

Van Andel Foundation, Jay and Betty

Van Buren Foundation

Van Every Foundation, Philip L.

Van Houten Charitable Trust

Van Huffel Foundation, I. J.

Van Nuys Charities, J. B. and Emily

Van Nuys Foundation, I. N. and Susanna H.

Vance Charitable Foundation, Robert C.

Vanderbilt Trust, R. T.

Vanneck-Bailey Foundation

Vaughn Foundation

Vermeer Investment Company Foundation

Vernon Fund, Miles Hodsdon

Vesuvius Charitable Foundation

Vidda Foundation

Vidinha Charitable Trust, A. and E.

Vilter Manufacturing Corp.

Virginia Power Co.

Visciglia Foundation, Frank

Volen Charitable Trust, Benjamin

Volkswagen of America, Inc.

Vollbrecht Foundation, Frederick A.

Von der Ahe Foundation

W. W. W. Foundation

Wachovia Bank of Georgia, N.A.

Wachovia Bank & Trust Co., N.A.

Waggoner Charitable Trust, Crystelle

Wagner Foundation, Ltd., R. H.

Wagner Manufacturing Co., E. R.

Wahlstrom Foundation

Wal-Mart Stores

Waldbaum Family Foundation, I.

Walgreen Co.

Walker Foundation, W. E.

Wallace Computer Services

Wallace Foundation, George R.

Wallach Foundation, Miriam G. and Ira D.

Walsh Charity Trust, Blanche M.

Disney Co., Walt

Walter Family Trust, Byron L.

Walter Industries

Walter Industries

Walthall Perpetual Charitable Trust, Marjorie T.

Ward Foundation, A. Montgomery

Ward Foundation, Louis L. and Adelaide C.

Wardlaw Fund, Gertrude and William C.

Ware Foundation

Wareheim Foundation, E. C.

Warner Electric Brake & Clutch Co.

Warner Fund, Albert and Bessie

Warner-Lambert Co.

Warren and Beatrice W. Blanding Foundation, Riley J. and Lillian N.

Warren Charite

Warren Foundation, William K.

Warwick Foundation

Washington Square Health Foundation

Washington Trust Bank

Wasserman Foundation

Waste Management

Waters Charitable Trust, Robert S.

Watkins Christian Foundation

Watson Foundation, Walter E. and Caroline H.

Wausau Paper Mills Co.

Wauwatosa Savings & Loan Association

Wean Foundation, Raymond John

Weaver Foundation

Weaver Foundation. Gil and Dody

Webb Educational and Charitable Trust, Torrey H. and Dorothy K.

Webb Foundation

Webb Foundation, Del E.

Weber Charities Corp., Frederick E.

Webster Charitable Foundation

Webster Foundation, Edwin S.

Weckbaugh Foundation, Eleanore Mullen

Weezie Foundation

Wege Foundation

Wegener Foundation, Herman and Mary

Weight Watchers International

Weiler Foundation

Weiler Foundation, Theodore & Renee

Weinberg Foundation, John L.

Weinberg, Jr. Foundation, Sidney J.

Weingart Foundation

Weininger Foundation, Richard and Gertrude

Weinstein Foundation, Alex J.

Weinstein Foundation, J.

Weintraub Family Foundation, Joseph

Weisbrod Foundation Trust Dept., Robert and Mary

Weiss Foundation, Stephen and Suzanne

Weiss Fund, Clara

Weisz Foundation, David and Sylvia

Wells Foundation, A. Z.

Wells Foundation, Franklin H. and Ruth L.

Wells Foundation, Lillian S.

Wells Trust Fund, Fred W.

Wendt Foundation, Margaret L.

Wenger Foundation, Henry L. and Consuelo S.

Hospitals (cont.)

Werblow Charitable Trust, Nina W.
Wertheim Foundation, Dr. Herbert A.
West Co.
West Foundation, Neva and Wesley
West One Bancorp
Westchester Health Fund
Westerman Foundation, Samuel L.
Western Cardiac Foundation
Western Southern Life Insurance Co.
Westvaco Corp.
Wetterau
Wexner Foundation
Weyerhaeuser Co.
Weyerhaeuser Foundation, Frederick and Margaret L.
Wheeler Foundation
Wheeler Trust, Clara
Whirlpool Corp.
Whitaker Charitable Foundation, Lyndon C.
Whitaker Foundation
White Consolidated Industries
White Foundation, Erle and Emma
White Foundation, W. P. and H. B.
White Trust, G. R.
Whitehead Foundation, Joseph B.
Whiting Foundation
Whiting Foundation, Macauley and Helen Dow
Whitney Fund, David M.
Wickes Foundation, Harvey Randall
Wickson-Link Memorial Foundation
Wiegand Foundation, E. L.
Wien Foundation, Lawrence A.
Wiener Foundation, Malcolm Hewitt
Wilcox General Trust, George N.
Wilcox Trust, S. W.
Wilder Foundation
Wildermuth Foundation, E. F.
Willard Foundation, Helen Parker
Williams Charitable Trust, John C.
Williams Cos.
Williams Family Foundation
Williams Foundation, Arthur Ashley
Williams Foundation, C. K.
Willits Foundation
Wilson Foundation, Frances Wood
Wilson Foundation, H. W.
Wilson Foundation, Marie C. and Joseph C.
Wilson Sanitarium for Children of Baltimore City, Thomas
Wilson Trust, Lula C.
Winn-Dixie Stores
Winona Corporation
Winston Foundation, Norman and Rosita
Winston Research Foundation, Harry
Winthrop Trust, Clara B.
Wisconsin Centrifugal
Wisconsin Energy Corp.
Wisconsin Power & Light Co.
Wisconsin Public Service Corp.
Witco Corp.
Witte, Jr. Foundation, John H.
Wodecroft Foundation
Woldenberg Foundation
Wolf Foundation, Melvin and Elaine
Wolff Foundation, John M.
Wolff Foundation, John M.

Wolff Memorial Foundation, Pauline Sterne
Wolverine World Wide, Inc.
Wood-Claeyssens Foundation
Wood Foundation of Chambersburg, PA
Woodland Foundation
Woodward Fund
Woodward Fund-Atlanta, David, Helen, Marian
Woodward Fund-Watertown, David, Helen, and Marian
Woodward Governor Co.
Woolley Foundation, Vasser
Wornall Charitable Trust and Foundation, Kearney
Wright Foundation, Lola
Wunsch Foundation
Wurzburg, Inc.
Wyman-Gordon Co.
Wyman Youth Trust
Wyomissing Foundation
Xerox Corp.
Xtra Corp.
Yassenoff Foundation, Leo
Yawkey Foundation II
Yeager Charitable Trust, Lester E.
Yost Trust, Elizabeth Burns
Young Foundation, Hugo H. and Mabel B.
Young Foundation, R. A.
Young Foundation, Robert R.
Yulman Trust, Morton and Helen
Zale Foundation
Zale Foundation, William and Sylvia
Zamoiski Co.
Zarkin Memorial Foundation, Charles
Zemurray Foundation
Ziegler Foundation
Zilkha & Sons
Zlinkoff Fund for Medical Research and Education, Sergei S.
Zuckerberg Foundation, Roy J.

Medical Rehabilitation

Abbott Laboratories
Achelis Foundation
Acushnet Co.
Adams Foundation, Arthur F. and Alice E.
Albertson's
Alcon Laboratories, Inc.
Alexander Foundation, Joseph
Allegheny Ludlum Corp.
ALPAC Corp.
Altman Foundation
Aluminum Co. of America
AMAX
American National Bank & Trust Co. of Chicago
American Natural Resources Co.
AMETEK
Amfac/JMB Hawaii
AON Corp.
Apple Computer, Inc.
Armco Inc.
Atherton Family Foundation
Attleboro Pawtucket Savings Bank
Avon Products
Baird & Co., Robert W.
Baker Foundation, R. C.
Barra Foundation
Bauer Foundation, M. R.
Beech Aircraft Corp.
Beneficial Corp.
Besser Foundation
Biomet
Blackmer Foundation, Henry M.
Block, H&R
Blowitz-Ridgeway Foundation
Blum-Kovler Foundation

Bodman Foundation
Bothin Foundation
Bovaird Foundation, Mervin
Brink Unitrust, Julia H.
Buchanan Family Foundation
Bucyrus-Erie
Burlington Northern Inc.
Cafritz Foundation, Morris and Gwendolyn
Callaway Foundation
Cameron Foundation, Harry S. and Isabel C.
Campbell Foundation, J. Bulow
Caplan Charity Foundation, Julius H.
Carrier Corp.
Carter Foundation, Amon G.
CBI Industries
Central Maine Power Co.
Century Companies of America
Chambers Development Co.
Chase Manhattan Bank, N.A.
Chevron Corp.
Ciba-Geigy Corp. (Pharmaceuticals Division)
Citizens Bank
Clark-Winchcole Foundation
Coleman Foundation
Comer Foundation
Compaq Computer Corp.
Comstock Foundation
Conn Memorial Foundation
Connelly Foundation
Coors Brewing Co.
Coors Foundation, Adolph
Corvallis Clinic
Crum and Forster
Cullen/Frost Bankers
Curtice-Burns Foods
DeCamp Foundation, Ira W.
Demoulas Supermarkets
DeSoto
Deutsch Co.
Dial Corp.
Dick Family Foundation
Digital Equipment Corp.
Dixie Yarns, Inc.
Dodge Jones Foundation
Dodson Foundation, James Glenwell and Clara May
Dougherty, Jr. Foundation, James R.
Dreyfus Foundation, Max and Victoria
du Pont de Nemours & Co., E. I.
Dumke Foundation, Dr. Ezekiel R. and Edna Wattis
Duncan Trust, James R.
Dunn Research Foundation, John S.
Dynamet, Inc.
Edgewater Steel Corp.
El Pomar Foundation
Elf Atochem North America
Ellison Foundation
Equifax
Exxon Corp.
Field Foundation of Illinois
Fifth Third Bancorp
First Interstate Bank of California
First Petroleum Corp.
First Union Corp.
Fleet Bank of New York
Ford II Fund, Henry
Foster Co., L.B.
Frankel Foundation
Frear Eleemosynary Trust, Mary D. and Walter F.
French Oil Mill Machinery Co.
Froderman Foundation
Frueauff Foundation, Charles A.
Funderburke & Associates
Galter Foundation
Galvin Foundation, Robert W.
GATX Corp.
GEICO Corp.

General American Life Insurance Co.
General Mills
General Motors Corp.
General Reinsurance Corp.
Georgia-Pacific Corp.
Georgia Power Co.
Gerber Products Co.
Giant Eagle
Gillette Co.
Glenn Foundation for Medical Research, Paul F.
Goldberg Family Foundation
Goldsmith Foundation, Horace W.
Gorin Foundation, Nehemiah
Grace & Co., W.R.
Graham Charitable Trust, William L.
Green Fund
Griffith Foundation, W. C.
Griffith Foundation, W. C.
H. B. B. Foundation
Hagedorn Fund
Hall Charitable Trust, Evelyn A. J.
Hallett Charitable Trust
Hamman Foundation, George and Mary Josephine
Hardin Foundation, Phil
Harriman Foundation, Mary W.
Harrington Foundation, Don and Sybil
Hawn Foundation
Hearst Foundation
Hearst Foundation, William Randolph
Hechinger Co.
HEI Inc.
Heinz Co., H.J.
Heinz Endowment, Howard
Heinz Foundation, Drue
Hiawatha Education Foundation
Hillman Foundation, Henry L.
Hoag Family Foundation, George
Household International
Hubbard Broadcasting
Hubbell Inc.
Hunter Trust, Emily S. and Coleman A.
Illinois Tool Works
Inland Container Corp.
Inland Steel Industries
International Foundation
Interstate National Corp.
Irvine Health Foundation
Irwin Charity Foundation, William G.
Ishiyama Foundation
ITT Hartford Insurance Group
Jasper Desk Co.
Jasper Wood Products Co.
Jennings Foundation, Mary Hillman
JM Foundation
Johnson & Higgins
Jones Foundation, Daisy Marquis
Jost Foundation, Charles and Mabel P.
Kayser Foundation
Keck Foundation, W. M.
Keebler Co.
Keeler Fund, Miner S. and Mary Ann
Kellogg Foundation, W. K.
Kiewit Sons, Peter
King Ranch
Kirby Foundation, F. M.
Kitzmiller/Bales Trust
Knox Foundation, Seymour H.
Knudsen Charitable Foundation, Earl
Koch Sons, George
Koopman Fund
Kowalski Sausage Co.
Kysor Industrial Corp.
Lang Foundation, Eugene M.

Langeloth Foundation, Jacob and Valeria
Lee Foundation, James T.
Lehmann Foundation, Otto W.
Lipton, Thomas J.
Lockheed Sanders
Lydall, Inc.
Lyon Foundation
Lyons Foundation
Macy & Co., R.H.
Marley Co.
Massengill-DeFriece Foundation
Massey Charitable Trust
May Foundation, Wilbur
Mayor Foundation, Oliver Dewey
Mazza Foundation
McCormick Tribune Foundation, Robert R.
McCune Foundation
McDonnell Douglas Corp.-West
McInerny Foundation
McKee Foundation, Robert E. and Evelyn
McLean Contributionship
Meadows Foundation
Medina Foundation
Meyer Foundation, Baron de Hirsch
Meyer Memorial Trust
Mine Safety Appliances Co.
Mobil Oil Corp.
Mobility Foundation
Monell Foundation, Ambrose
Monfort Charitable Foundation
Moody Foundation
Morrison-Knudsen Corp.
Mostyn Foundation
Murphy Foundation, Katherine and John
Nalco Chemical Co.
National City Bank of Evansville
National Machinery Co.
NBD Bank
New England Mutual Life Insurance Co.
New York Life Insurance Co.
New York Mercantile Exchange
New York Telephone Co.
The New Yorker Magazine, Inc.
Noble Foundation, Samuel Roberts
Northwest Natural Gas Co.
Norton Co.
Occidental Oil & Gas Corp.
Olin Corp.
1957 Charity Trust
Ordean Foundation
Pan-American Life Insurance Co.
Pennzoil Co.
Perkin-Elmer Corp.
Persis Corp.
Pfizer
Phillips Petroleum Co.
Pittsburgh National Bank
Pope Foundation
PPG Industries
Price Foundation, Louis and Harold
Procter & Gamble Cosmetic & Fragrance Products
Prudential Insurance Co. of America
Pukall Lumber
Quaker Oats Co.
Questar Corp.
Regenstein Foundation
Rennebohm Foundation, Oscar
Reynolds Metals Co.
Roberts Foundation, Dora
Rockford Acromatics Products Co./Aircraft Gear Corp.
Rockwell Fund
Rockwell International Corp.
Rohm and Haas Company
Rubinstein Foundation, Helena
Santa Fe Pacific Corp.
Sarkeys Foundation

Seabury Foundation
Shawmut National Corp.
Shell Oil Co.
Shore Fund
Signet Bank/Maryland
Sjostrom & Sons
Smith Corp., A.O.
Sonoco Products Co.
Speas Foundation, Victor E.
Sprague Educational and
 Charitable Foundation, Seth
Steelcase
Stein Foundation, Jules and Doris
Steiner Charitable Fund, Albert
Stewart Trust under the will of
 Helen S. Devore, Alexander
 and Margaret
Stone Container Corp.
Strake Foundation
Taylor Foundation, Ruth and
 Vernon
Temple Foundation, T. L. L.
Texaco
3M Co.
Tippens Foundation
TJX Cos.
Torchmark Corp.
Towsley Foundation, Harry A.
 and Margaret D.
Trust Co. Bank
Union Bank
Union Camp Corp.
Union Pacific Corp.
United States Trust Co. of New
 York
Unocal Corp.
USX Corp.
Veritas Foundation
Virginia Power Co.
Wal-Mart Stores
Disney Co., Walt
Warner-Lambert Co.
Wean Foundation, Raymond John
Westvaco Corp.
Weyerhaeuser Co.
Whirlpool Corp.
Wickes Foundation, Harvey
 Randall
Wimpey Inc., George
Wisconsin Energy Corp.
Woodward Governor Co.
Wyomissing Foundation

Medical Research

Abbott Laboratories
Abell-Hanger Foundation
Abraham Foundation
Abraham Foundation, Anthony R.
Abrams Foundation, Benjamin
 and Elizabeth
Abrams Foundation, Talbert and
 Leota
Abramson Family Foundation
Abrons Foundation, Louis and
 Anne
Action Industries, Inc.
Ada Foundation, Julius
Adler Foundation
Aeroflex Foundation
AFLAC
Ahmanson Foundation
Aid Association for the Blind
Air France
AKC Fund
Akzo Chemicals Inc.
Alcon Laboratories, Inc.
Alexander Charitable Foundation
Alexander Foundation, Joseph
Alexander Foundation, Judd S.
Alexander Foundation, Robert
 D. and Catherine R.
Allen Brothers Foundation
Allen Charitable Trust, Phil N.
Allen Foundation, Frances
Allen Foundation, Rita
Allendale Mutual Insurance Co.
Alliant Techsystems

Alltel/Western Region
Allyn Foundation
ALPAC Corp.
Alro Steel Corp.
Alsdorf Foundation
Altschul Foundation
Alumax
Aluminum Co. of America
AMAX
AMAX Coal Industries
Amdur Braude Riley, Inc.
American Brands
American Financial Corp.
American Home Products Corp.
American National Bank & Trust
 Co. of Chicago
American Natural Resources Co.
American Otological Society
American United Life Insurance
 Co.
American Welding &
 Manufacturing Co.
Ameritas Life Insurance Corp.
Ames Charitable Trust, Harriett
AMETEK
Amoco Corp.
Amsterdam Foundation, Jack
 and Mimi Leviton
Andersen Corp.
Andersen Foundation
Andersen Foundation, Arthur
Anderson Charitable Trust,
 Josephine
Anderson Foundation
Anderson Foundation, M. D.
Andersons Management Corp.
Andreas Foundation
Anheuser-Busch Cos.
Ansley Foundation, Dantzler
 Bond
AON Corp.
Applebaum Foundation
Arata Brothers Trust
Arcadia Foundation
Archbold Charitable Trust,
 Adrian and Jessie
Arell Foundation
Argyros Foundation
Aron Charitable Foundation, J.
Arronson Foundation
Atherton Family Foundation
Athwin Foundation
Atkinson Foundation, Myrtle L.
Atlanta Foundation
Atlanta Gas Light Co.
Atran Foundation
Attleboro Pawtucket Savings
 Bank
Augat, Inc.
Avis Inc.
Avon Products
Awrey Bakeries
Babcock & Wilcox Co.
Bacardi Imports
Bachmann Foundation
Backer Spielvogel Bates U.S.
Badgeley Residuary Charitable
 Trust, Rose M.
Badger Meter, Inc.
Baird Foundation
Baker Foundation, R. C.
Baker Foundation, Solomon R.
 and Rebecca D.
Baker Hughes Inc.
Baker Trust, George F.
Baldwin Foundation, David M.
 and Barbara
Banbury Fund
Banfi Vintners
Bank One, Texas-Houston Office
Bankers Trust Co.
Bannan Foundation, Arline and
 Thomas J.
Banner Life Insurance Co.
Bannerman Foundation, William
 C.
Barbour Foundation, Bernice

Bard, C. R.
Bardes Corp.
Barker Foundation
Barker Foundation, Donald R.
Barnes Group
Barnett Charitable Foundation,
 Lawrence and Isabel
Barra Foundation
Barrows Foundation, Geraldine
 and R. A.
Barry Corp., R. G.
Bartsch Memorial Trust, Ruth
Bass and Edythe and Sol G.
 Atlas Fund, Sandra Atlas
Battelle
Batten Foundation
Bauer Foundation, M. R.
Bauervic Foundation, Charles M.
Bauervic Foundation, Peggy
Baxter Foundation, Donald E.
 and Delia B.
Baxter International
Bay Branch Foundation
Bayne Fund, Howard
BCR Foundation
Beaird Foundation, Charles T.
Beal Foundation
Bechtel, Jr. Foundation, S. D.
Beckman Foundation, Arnold
 and Mabel
Becton Dickinson & Co.
Bedford Fund
Bedminster Fund
Beeson Charitable Trust, Dwight
 M.
Behmann Brothers Foundation
Beim Foundation
Bekins Foundation, Milo W.
Belding Heminway Co.
Belfer Foundation
Belk Stores
Bellini Foundation
Beloco Foundation
Belz Foundation
Benbough Foundation, Legler
Beneficial Corp.
Benetton
Bennett Foundation, Carl and
 Dorothy
Benua Foundation
Berger Foundation, H.N. and
 Frances C.
Berkman Foundation, Louis and
 Sandra
Bernsen Foundation, Grace and
 Franklin
Bernstein & Co., Sanford C.
Bernstein Foundation, Diane and
 Norman
Berry Foundation, Archie W. and
 Grace
Berry Foundation, Loren M.
Bettingen Corporation, Burton G.
Bickerton Charitable Trust,
 Lydia H.
Bicknell Fund
Biddle Foundation, Margaret T.
Bierhaus Foundation
Bingham Second Betterment
 Fund, William
Binswanger Co.
Biological Humanics Foundation
Bireley Foundation
Bishop Charitable Trust, A. G.
Bishop Foundation
Bishop Foundation, E. K. and
 Lillian F.
Blackmer Foundation, Henry M.
Blair and Co., William
Blanchard Foundation
Blaustein Foundation, Louis and
 Henrietta
Bleibtreu Foundation, Jacob
Blinken Foundation
Blue Bell, Inc.
Blue Cross/Blue Shield of
 Michigan

Bluhdorn Charitable Trust,
 Charles G. and Yvette
Blum Foundation, Edith C.
Blum Foundation, Harry and
 Maribel G.
Blum-Kovler Foundation
Boatmen's First National Bank
 of Oklahoma
Bodman Foundation
Boehringer Mannheim Corp.
Boisi Family Foundation
Bonfils-Stanton Foundation
Bonner Foundation, Corella and
 Bertram
Boothroyd Foundation, Charles
 H. and Bertha L.
Booz Allen & Hamilton
Borchard Foundation, Albert and
 Elaine
Bosque Foundation
Boston Edison Co.
Bostwick Foundation, Albert C.
Boswell Foundation, James G.
Botwinick-Wolfensohn
 Foundation
Bovaird Foundation, Mervin
Bowers Foundation
Bowles and Robert Bowles
 Memorial Fund, Ethel Wilson
Bowyer Foundation, Ambrose
 and Gladys
Bozzone Family Foundation
Brace Foundation, Donald C.
Brach Foundation, Edwin I.
Brady Foundation
Brand Foundation, C. Harold and
 Constance
Branta Foundation
Braun Foundation
Breyer Foundation
Bridgestone/Firestone
Bridwell Foundation, J. S.
Brink Unitrust, Julia H.
Bristol-Myers Squibb Co.
Britton Fund
Broad Foundation, Shepard
Broadhurst Foundation
Broccoli Charitable Foundation,
 Dana and Albert R.
Brochsteins Inc.
Brody Foundation, Carolyn and
 Kenneth D.
Brooks Brothers
Brooks Foundation, Gladys
Brotman Foundation of
 California
Brotz Family Foundation, Frank
 G.
Brown Charitable Trust, Peter D.
 and Dorothy S.
Brown Foundation, Joe W. and
 Dorothy Dorsett
Broyhill Family Foundation
Bruno Charitable Foundation,
 Joseph S.
Bryant Foundation
Buchanan Family Foundation
Bucyrus-Erie
Buehler Foundation, A. C.
Buehler Foundation, Emil
Bugher Foundation
Bull Foundation, Henry W.
Bunbury Company
Burchfield Foundation, Charles
 E.
Burnand Medical and
 Educational Foundation,
 Alphonse A.
Burnham Donor Fund, Alfred G.
Burnham Foundation
Burns Foundation, Fritz B.
Burns Foundation, Jacob
Burroughs Wellcome Co.
Butz Foundation
Cable & Wireless
 Communications
Cain Foundation, Effie and
 Wofford

Cain Foundation, Gordon and
 Mary
California Foundation for
 Biochemical Research
Campbell and Adah E. Hall
 Charity Fund, Bushrod H.
Campbell Foundation
Campbell Foundation, Charles
 Talbot
Campbell Soup Co.
Canon U.S.A., Inc.
Cantor Foundation, Iris and B.
 Gerald
Capital Cities/ABC
Capital Fund Foundation
Capital Holding Corp.
Cargill
Carlson Cos.
Carnegie Corporation of New
 York
Carnival Cruise Lines
Carstensen Memorial
 Foundation, Fred R. and Hazel
 W.
Carter Family Foundation
Carter-Wallace
Cartier, Inc.
Carvel Foundation, Thomas and
 Agnes
Carylon Foundation
Cassett Foundation, Louis N.
CBI Industries
Ceco Corp.
Cedars-Sinai Medical Center
 Section D Fund
Centel Corp.
Central Life Assurance Co.
Central Maine Power Co.
Central & South West Services
Chadwick Foundation
Chait Memorial Foundation, Sara
Chapman Charitable Trust, H. A.
 and Mary K.
Charina Foundation
Charitable Foundation of the
 Burns Family
Charities Foundation
Charles River Laboratories
Charter Manufacturing Co.
Chartwell Foundation
Chartwell Foundation
Chatham Valley Foundation
Cheatham Foundation, Owen
Cherne Foundation, Albert W.
Chernow Trust for the Benefit of
 Charity Dated 3/13/75, Michael
Chicago Resource Center
Childs Charitable Foundation,
 Roberta M.
Childs Memorial Fund for
 Medical Research, Jane Coffin
Chiles Foundation
China Medical Board of New
 York
Church & Dwight Co.
CIT Group Holdings
Citicorp
Citizens Bank
Clapp Charitable and
 Educational Trust, George H.
Clark Charitable Foundation
Clark Family Charitable Trust,
 Andrew L.
Clark Foundation
Clark Foundation, Edna
 McConnell
Cockrell Foundation
Codrington Charitable
 Foundation, George W.
Coen Family Foundation,
 Charles S. and Mary
Cohen Foundation, Wilfred P.
Cohn Co., M.M.
Cohn Foundation, Herman and
 Terese
Cohn Foundation, Peter A. and
 Elizabeth S.

Medical Research (cont.)

Cole Foundation, Robert H. and Monica H.
Cole National Corp.
Cole Taylor Financial Group
Coleman Co.
Coleman Foundation
Coleman Foundation
Coles Family Foundation
Collins & Aikman Holdings Corp.
Collins Foundation, James M.
Collins Medical Trust
Colonial Life & Accident Insurance Co.
Colt Foundation, James J.
Coltec Industries
Columbia Foundation
Columbia Savings Charitable Foundation
Comer Foundation
Comer Foundation
Compaq Computer Corp.
Confidence Foundation
Connelly Foundation
Continental Corp.
Contran Corp.
Cook Foundation, Loring
Cooke Foundation Corporation, V. V.
Cooper Charitable Trust, Richard H.
Copolymer Rubber & Chemical Corp.
Copperweld Steel Co.
Corestates Bank
Corvallis Clinic
Cosmair, Inc.
Cowles Charitable Trust
Cox Charitable Trust, A. G.
Cox Charitable Trust, Jessie B.
Cox Foundation
CPC International
Craigmyle Foundation
Crail-Johnson Foundation
Crane Co.
Crawford Estate, E. R.
Crestlea Foundation
Crown Charitable Fund, Edward A.
Crummer Foundation, Roy E.
Crump Fund, Joe and Jessie
Cullen Foundation
Cullen/Frost Bankers
Culpeper Foundation, Charles E.
Culpeper Memorial Foundation, Daphne Seybolt
Cummings Foundation, James H.
CUNA Mutual Insurance Group
Cuneo Foundation
Cyprus Minerals Co.
Dain Bosworth/Inter-Regional Financial Group
Dalsimer Fund, Craig
Dammann Fund
Dana Charitable Trust, Eleanor Naylor
Dana Foundation, Charles A.
Daniel Foundation of Alabama
Daniels Foundation, Fred Harris
Danis Industries
Darby Foundation
Dart Group Corp.
Davis Family - W.D. Charities, James E.
Davis Foundation, Edwin W. and Catherine M.
Davis Foundation, Joe C.
Davis Foundation, Joe C.
Davis Foundation, Ken W.
Davis Foundation, Shelby Cullom
DCNY Corp.

de Rothschild Foundation, Edmond
Debartolo Foundation, Marie P.
DeCamp Foundation, Ira W.
Dee Foundation, Annie Taylor
Delacorte Fund, George
Delaware North Cos.
Dentsply International, Inc.
DeRoy Foundation, Helen L.
DeSoto
Dettman Foundation, Leroy E.
Deuble Foundation, George H.
Deutsch Co.
DeVore Foundation
Dewar Foundation
Diabetes Research and Education Foundation
Diamond Foundation, Aaron
Dickson Foundation
Digital Equipment Corp.
Dillard Paper Co.
Dillon Foundation
Dimick Foundation
Dishman Charitable Foundation Trust, H. E. and Kate
Dively Foundation, George S.
Dodson Foundation, James Glenwell and Clara May
Doheny Foundation, Carrie Estelle
Doherty Charitable Foundation, Henry L. and Grace
Dolan Family Foundation
Domino of California
Donaldson Charitable Trust, Oliver S. and Jennie R.
Donnelley Foundation, Elliott and Ann
Dorr Foundation
Doty Family Foundation
Dougherty, Jr. Foundation, James R.
Douglas & Lomason Company
Dreitzer Foundation
Dresser Industries
Dreyfus Foundation, Max and Victoria
Drown Foundation, Joseph
du Pont de Nemours & Co., E. I.
Duchossois Industries
Duke Endowment
Duncan Foundation, Lillian H. and C. W.
Duncan Trust, James R.
Duncan Trust, John G.
Dunn Research Foundation, John S.
duPont Foundation, Chichester
Durst Foundation
Dweck Foundation, Samuel R.
Dynamet, Inc.
Dyson Foundation
Earl-Beth Foundation
Early Medical Research Trust, Margaret E.
East Foundation, Sarita Kenedy
Eastman Foundation, Alexander
Eaton Foundation, Cyrus
Eccles Charitable Foundation, Willard L.
Eccles Foundation, George S. and Dolores Dore
Echlin Foundation
Eckman Charitable Foundation, Samuel and Rae
Eddy Foundation
Edison Foundation, Harry
Edison Foundation, Irving and Beatrice C.
Edison Fund, Charles
Edouard Foundation
Educational Foundation of America
Edwards Foundation, Jes
EG&G Inc.
EIS Foundation
Eisenberg Foundation, Ben B. and Joyce E.

Electric Power Equipment Co.
Elf Aquitaine, Inc.
Elf Atochem North America
Elkin Memorial Foundation, Neil Warren and William Simpson
Elkins Foundation, J. A. and Isabel M.
Ellwood Foundation
Emergency Aid of Pennsylvania Foundation
Emerson Foundation, Fred L.
EMI Records Group
Engelhard Foundation, Charles
Enron Corp.
Equitable Life Assurance Society of the U.S.
Ernest & Julio Gallo Winery
Essel Foundation
Ettinger Foundation
Evans Foundation, T. M.
Exxon Corp.
Factor Family Foundation, Max
Fair Play Foundation
Fairchild Foundation, Sherman
Fanwood Foundation
Farish Fund, William Stamps
Farley Industries
Farwell Foundation, Drusilla
Favrot Fund
Federal-Mogul Corp.
Feil Foundation, Louis and Gertrude
Feild Co-Operative Association
Feinberg Foundation, Joseph and Bessie
Feintech Foundation
Femino Foundation
Ferguson Family Foundation, Kittie and Rugeley
Ferkauf Foundation, Eugene and Estelle
Fiat U.S.A., Inc.
Fife Foundation, Elias and Bertha
Fifth Avenue Foundation
Fig Tree Foundation
Fikes Foundation, Leland
Fingerhut Family Foundation
Firan Foundation
Fireman Charitable Foundation, Paul and Phyllis
First Boston
First Interstate Bank of Oregon
Fish Foundation, Ray C.
Fish Foundation, Vain and Harry
Fishback Foundation Trust, Harmes C.
Fleet Financial Group
Flinn Foundation
Florence Foundation
Florence Foundation
Florida Rock Industries
FMR Corp.
Foerderer Foundation, Percival E. and Ethel Brown
Fondren Foundation
Forbes
Ford Fund, Walter and Josephine
Ford Fund, William and Martha
Ford II Fund, Henry
Ford III Memorial Foundation, Jefferson Lee
Ford III Memorial Foundation, Jefferson Lee
Ford Meter Box Co.
Forest Foundation
Forest Oil Corp.
Fortis Inc.
Foster Co., L.B.
Foster Foundation, Joseph C. and Esther
Foulds Trust, Claiborne F
Fourth Financial Corp.
Fox Charitable Foundation, Harry K. & Emma R.
Fox Foundation, Richard J.
Fox Steel Co.
Francis Families Foundation

Frank Family Foundation, A. J.
Frank Fund, Zollie and Elaine
Frankel Foundation, George and Elizabeth F.
Franklin Foundation, John and Mary
Frear Eleemosynary Trust, Mary D. and Walter F.
Freeman Foundation, Carl M.
Freeport Brick Co.
Freeport-McMoRan
Frelinghuysen Foundation
French Oil Mill Machinery Co.
Freygang Foundation, Walter Henry
Fribourg Foundation
Friedland Family Foundation, Samuel
Friedman Family Foundation
Frohlich Charitable Trust, Ludwig W.
Frohman Foundation, Sidney
Frohring Foundation, William O. and Gertrude Lewis
Frost Foundation
Frueauff Foundation, Charles A.
Fruehauf Foundation
Fuchsberg Family Foundation, Abraham
Fuller Foundation
Fuller Foundation, C. G.
Fuller Foundation, George F. and Sybil H.
Fullerton Foundation
Funderburke & Associates
Fuqua Foundation, J. B.
Furth Foundation
Fusenot Charity Foundation, Georges and Germaine
G.A.G. Charitable Corporation
Gaisman Foundation, Catherine and Henry J.
Gallo Foundation, Ernest
Gallo Foundation, Julio R.
Galter Foundation
Gannett Publishing Co., Guy
Gap, The
Garvey Texas Foundation
Gaylord Foundation, Clifford Willard
Gebbie Foundation
GEICO Corp.
Geist Foundation
Gelb Foundation, Lawrence M.
Gellert Foundation, Carl
Gellert Foundation, Fred
General American Life Insurance Co.
General Development Corp.
General Mills
General Reinsurance Corp.
Georgia Health Foundation
Georgia-Pacific Corp.
Georgia Power Co.
Gerlach Foundation
Gerschel Foundation, Patrick A.
Getz Foundation, Emma and Oscar
Gheens Foundation
Giant Eagle
Giant Food Stores
Gifford Charitable Corporation, Rosamond
Gill Foundation, Pauline Allen
Gillett Foundation, Elesabeth Ingalls
Gillette Co.
Gilman, Jr. Foundation, Sondra and Charles
Gilmer-Smith Foundation
Gilmore Foundation, Earl B.
Gilmore Foundation, William G.
Ginsberg Family Foundation, Moses
Glanville Family Foundation
Glaxo
Glazer Foundation, Jerome S.

Glenn Foundation for Medical Research, Paul F.
Glick Foundation, Eugene and Marilyn
Globe Corp.
Goddard Foundation, Charles B.
Goerlich Family Foundation
Goldberg Family Foundation
Goldberg Family Foundation, Israel and Matilda
Golden Family Foundation
Goldenberg Foundation, Max
Goldie-Anna Charitable Trust
Goldman Foundation, Aaron and Cecile
Goldman Foundation, Herman
Goldsmith Foundation
Goldsmith Foundation, Horace W.
Goldstein Foundation, Leslie and Roslyn
Goldwyn Foundation, Samuel
Goode Trust, Mae Stone
Goodman & Company
Goodman Foundation, Edward and Marion
Goodman Memorial Foundation, Joseph C. and Clare F.
Goodstein Family Foundation, David
Goodstein Foundation
Goodwin Foundation, Leo
Gorin Foundation, Nehemiah
Grace & Co., W.R.
Grader Foundation, K. W.
Grainger Foundation
Graphic Controls Corp.
Grass Foundation
Grassmann Trust, E. J.
Gray Foundation, Garland
Great Atlantic & Pacific Tea Co. Inc.
Great-West Life Assurance Co.
Great Western Financial Corp.
Green Foundation, Burton E.
Green Fund
Greenberg Foundation, Alan C.
Greene Foundation, David J.
Greene Foundation, Robert Z.
Greenville Foundation
Greenwall Foundation
Greve Foundation, William and Mary
Griffin Foundation, Rosa May
Griffin, Sr., Foundation, C. V.
Griffis Foundation
Griggs and Mary Griggs Burke Foundation, Mary Livingston
Gross Charitable Trust, Stella B.
Gross Foundation, Louis H.
Group Health Plan Inc.
Gruber Research Foundation, Lila
GSC Enterprises
Guardian Life Insurance Co. of America
Gucci America Inc.
Gudelsky Family Foundation, Homer and Martha
Gulton Foundation
Gund Foundation, Geoffrey
Gunderson Trust, Helen Paulson
Gurwin Foundation, J.
Gussman Foundation, Herbert and Roseline
Guttman Foundation, Stella and Charles
Haas Foundation, Paul and Mary
Haas Fund, Miriam and Peter
Hagedorn Fund
Haley Foundation, W. B.
Halff Foundation, G. A. C.
Hall Charitable Trust, Evelyn A. J.
Halmos Foundation
Hambay Foundation, James T.
Hamilton Bank

Medical Research (cont.)

Mazer Foundation, Jacob and Ruth
MBIA, Inc.
MCA
McAlister Charitable Foundation, Harold
McCarthy Foundation, Michael W.
McCasland Foundation
McCormick & Co.
McCormick Foundation, Chauncey and Marion Deering
McCormick Tribune Foundation, Robert R.
McCrea Foundation
McCutchen Foundation
McDonald & Co. Securities
McDonald & Co. Securities
McDonnell Douglas Corp.-West
McDonnell Foundation, James S.
McEvoy Foundation, Mildred H.
McGonagle Foundation, Dextra Baldwin
McGovern Foundation, John P.
McGraw Foundation
McGraw Foundation, Donald C.
McGregor Foundation, Thomas and Frances
MCJ Foundation
McKee Foundation, Robert E. and Evelyn
McKnight Foundation
McLean Contributionship
McMillan, Jr. Foundation, Bruce
McNutt Charitable Trust, Amy Shelton
MDU Resources Group, Inc.
Mead Corp.
Mead Foundation, Giles W. and Elise G.
Meadows Foundation
Measey Foundation, Benjamin and Mary Siddons
Mebane Packaging Corp.
Meek Foundation
Mellam Family Foundation
Mellon Bank Corp.
Mellon Foundation, Richard King
Mendel Foundation
Menschel Foundation, Robert and Joyce
Merck & Co.
Merck Fund, John
Mercy, Jr. Foundation, Sue and Eugene
Merrick Foundation
Messing Family Charitable Foundation
Messing Foundation, Morris M. and Helen F.
Metal Industries
Metropolitan Health Foundation
Metropolitan Life Insurance Co.
Meyer Foundation
Meyer Fund, Milton and Sophie
Meyer Memorial Foundation, Aaron and Rachel
Meyer Memorial Trust
Milbank Foundation, Dunlevy
Milken Family Medical Foundation
Milken Foundation, L. and S.
Miller Charitable Trust, Lewis N.
Mills Charitable Foundation, Henry L. and Kathryn
Mills Foundation, Ralph E.
Milstein Family Foundation
Minnesota Mutual Life Insurance Co.
Minster Machine Co.
Mitchell Energy & Development Corp.
Mitchell Family Foundation, Bernard and Marjorie

Mitchell Family Foundation, Edward D. and Anna
Mitsubishi International Corp.
Mnuchin Foundation
Mobil Oil Corp.
Mobility Foundation
Moncrief Foundation, William A. and Elizabeth B.
Monell Foundation, Ambrose
Montgomery Street Foundation
Moody Foundation
Moog Automotive, Inc.
Moore Charitable Foundation, Marjorie
Moore Foundation, C. F.
Moore Foundation, Edward S.
Moore Foundation, Martha G.
Moore Memorial Foundation, James Starr
Morania Foundation
Morris Charitable Foundation, E. A.
Morris Foundation, Norman M.
Morris Foundation, William T.
Morrison Foundation, Harry W.
Morse Foundation, Richard P. and Claire W.
Morse, Jr. Foundation, Enid and Lester S.
Mosbacher, Jr. Foundation, Emil
Moses Fund, Henry and Lucy
Moss Heart Trust, Harry S.
Mott Fund, Ruth
Muller Foundation
Muller Foundation, C. John and Josephine
Munger Foundation, Alfred C.
Murch Foundation
Murdy Foundation
Murfee Endowment, Kathryn
Murphey Foundation, Lluella Morey
Murphy Foundation, Dan
Murphy Foundation, John P.
Murphy Foundation, Katherine and John
Murray Foundation
National Fuel Gas Co.
National Gypsum Co.
National Life of Vermont
National Presto Industries
National Westminster Bank New Jersey
Neu Foundation, Hugo and Doris
Neuberger Foundation, Roy R. and Marie S.
New England Foundation
New England Mutual Life Insurance Co.
New Horizon Foundation
New-Land Foundation
New York Life Insurance Co.
New York Mercantile Exchange
The New Yorker Magazine, Inc.
Newhouse Foundation, Samuel I.
Noble Charitable Trust, John L. and Ethel G.
Noble Foundation, Samuel Roberts
Noble Foundation, Vivian Bilby
Noonan Memorial Fund under the will of Frank Noonan, Deborah Munroe
Norfolk Southern Corp.
Norgren Foundation, Carl A.
Norris Foundation, Kenneth T. and Eileen L.
Nortek, Inc.
North Shore Foundation
Norton Co.
Norton Memorial Corporation, Geraldi
Noyes, Jr. Memorial Foundation, Nicholas H.
NuTone Inc.
Oak Foundation U.S.A.
Oberkotter Family Foundation
Obernauer Foundation

O'Connor Co.
Oestreicher Foundation, Sylvan and Ann
Offield Family Foundation
Ogilvy & Mather Worldwide
Oglebay Norton Co.
Ohio National Life Insurance Co.
Ohrstrom Foundation
Oklahoman Foundation
Olin Charitable Trust, John M.
Olsson Memorial Foundation, Elis
O'Neil Foundation, Casey Albert T.
O'Neil Foundation, M. G.
O'Neill Charitable Corporation, F. J.
Osborn Charitable Trust, Edward B.
OsCo. Industries
Osher Foundation, Bernard
Oshkosh Truck Corp.
O'Sullivan Children Foundation
Ottenstein Family Foundation
Overbrook Foundation
Overlake Foundation
Overseas Shipholding Group
Owen Trust, B. B.
Owsley Foundation, Alvin and Lucy
Oxford Foundation
Oxford Foundation
Oxford Industries, Inc.
Oxnard Foundation
Pacific Western Foundation
Page Foundation, George B.
PaineWebber
Palisades Educational Foundation
Pan-American Life Insurance Co.
Panhandle Eastern Corp.
Pardee Foundation, Elsa U.
Parke-Davis Group
Parker Drilling Co.
Parker Foundation
Parker-Hannifin Corp.
Parker, Jr. Foundation, William A.
Parman Foundation, Robert A.
Parshelsky Foundation, Moses L.
Parsons Foundation, Ralph M.
Parvin Foundation, Albert
Pasadena Area Residential Aid
Patterson and Clara Guthrie Patterson Trust, Robert Leet
Patterson Charitable Fund, W. I.
Pauley Foundation, Edwin W.
Paulucci Family Foundation
Peabody Charitable Fund, Amelia
Peabody Foundation
Pearce Foundation, Dr. M. Lee
Pearlstone Foundation, Peggy Meyerhoff
Peierls Foundation
Pendleton Memorial Fund, William L. and Ruth T.
Pennington Foundation, Irene W. and C. B.
Pennzoil Co.
Penzance Foundation
Perini Foundation, Joseph
Perkin-Elmer Corp.
Perkin Fund
Perkins Foundation, Edwin E.
Perkins Memorial Foundation, George W.
Petersen Foundation, Esper A.
Pfeiffer Research Foundation, Gustavus and Louise
Pfister and Vogel Tanning Co.
Pfizer
PHH Corp.
Philips Foundation, Jesse
Phillips Family Foundation, Jay and Rose
Phillips Foundation, Dr. P.
Phillips Petroleum Co.
Phillips-Van Heusen Corp.

Physicians Mutual Insurance
Piankova Foundation, Tatiana
Pickford Foundation, Mary
Piedmont Health Care Foundation
Pierce Charitable Trust, Harold Whitworth
Pillsbury Foundation
Pines Bridge Foundation
Pioneer Fund
Pioneer Fund
Pittway Corp.
Playboy Enterprises, Inc.
Plym Foundation
Poindexter Foundation
Pollybill Foundation
Poncin Scholarship Fund
Poorvu Foundation, William and Lia
Pope Foundation
Potomac Electric Power Co.
Pott Foundation, Herman T. and Phenie R.
Potts Memorial Foundation
Pottstown Mercury
Powers Foundation
Pratt Memorial Fund
Premier Bank
Prentis Family Foundation, Meyer and Anna
Prentiss Foundation, Elisabeth Severance
Preuss Foundation
Price Foundation, Louis and Harold
Prince Corp.
Principal Financial Group
Pritzker Foundation
Propp Sons Fund, Morris and Anna
Psychists
Puett Foundation, Nelson
Puterbaugh Foundation
Pyramid Foundation
Quaker Chemical Corp.
Quaker Oats Co.
Quanex Corp.
Rachal Foundation, Ed
Rahr Malting Co.
Rales and Ruth Rales Foundation, Norman R.
Ralston Purina Co.
Ramlose Foundation, George A.
Rankin and Elizabeth Forbes Rankin Trust, William
Rapp Foundation, Robert Glenn
Ratner Foundation, Milton M.
Rauch Foundation
Read Foundation, Charles L.
Rebsamen Companies, Inc.
Recognition Equipment
Redfield Foundation, Nell J.
Reed Foundation
Reedman Car-Truck World Center
Reicher Foundation, Anne & Harry J.
Reinhart Institutional Foods
Relations Foundation
Retirement Research Foundation
Reynolds Foundation, J. B.
Reynolds Foundation, Richard S.
Reynolds Metals Co.
Rhoades Fund, Otto L. and Hazel E.
Rice Family Foundation, Jacob and Sophie
Rich Foundation
Richardson Foundation, Sid W.
Richardson Fund, Grace
Richmond Foundation, Frederick W.
Rigler-Deutsch Foundation
Rippel Foundation, Fannie E.
Rite-Hite Corp.
Ritter Foundation
Ritter Foundation, May Ellen and Gerald

RJR Nabisco Inc.
Roberts Foundation, Summerfield G.
Robinson Foundation, J. Mack
Robinson Mountain Fund, E. O.
Robison Foundation, Ellis H. and Doris B.
Roblee Foundation, Joseph H. and Florence A.
Rockefeller Foundation
Rockwell Foundation
Rockwell Fund
Roddis Foundation, Hamilton
Rodgers Foundation, Richard & Dorothy
Rodman Foundation
Rogers Foundation
Rogers Foundation, Mary Stuart
Rohatyn Foundation, Felix and Elizabeth
Rohm and Haas Company
Rollins Luetkemeyer Charitable Foundation
Rose Foundation, Billy
Rosen Foundation, Joseph
Rosenberg Family Foundation, William
Rosenberg, Jr. Family Foundation, Louise and Claude
Rosenhaus Peace Foundation, Sarah and Matthew
Rosenstiel Foundation
Rosenthal Foundation, Richard and Hinda
Rosenthal Foundation, Samuel
Rosenthal-Statter Foundation
Rowland Foundation
Rubenstein Charitable Foundation, Lawrence J. and Anne
Rubenstein Foundation, Philip
Rubinstein Foundation, Helena
Ruddick Corp.
Rudin Foundation
Ruffin Foundation, Peter B. & Adeline W.
Rupp Foundation, Fran and Warren
Russ Togs
Russell Charitable Foundation, Tom
Russell Trust, Josephine G.
Ryan Foundation, Nina M.
Ryan Foundation, Patrick G. and Shirley W.
Ryland Group
Sage Foundation
Saint Gerard Foundation
St. Giles Foundation
Salomon
Saltz Foundation, Gary
San Diego Gas & Electric
Sandoz Corp.
Sandy Foundation, George H.
Sang Foundation, Elsie O. and Philip D.
Sasco Foundation
Sattler Beneficial Trust, Daniel A. and Edna J.
Saunders Foundation
Sawyer Charitable Foundation
Scaife Family Foundation
Schaffer Foundation, Michael & Helen
Schamach Foundation, Milton
Schapiro Fund, M. A.
Schering-Plough Corp.
Schiff Foundation
Schiff Foundation, Dorothy
Schilling Motors
Schiro Fund
Schlink Foundation, Albert G. and Olive H.
Schlumberger Ltd.
Schneider Foundation Corp., Al J.
Schneider Foundation, Robert E.
Scholler Foundation

Schottenstein Foundation, Jerome & Saul
Schramm Foundation
Schroeder Foundation, Walter
Schultz Foundation
Schultz Foundation
Schust Foundation, Clarence L. and Edith B.
Schwartz Foundation, Bernard Lee
Schwartz Foundation, David
Scott and Fetzer Co.
Scott Foundation, Walter
Scott Foundation, William E.
Scripps Foundation, Ellen Browning
Scrivner, Inc.
Scurlock Foundation
Seabury Foundation
Seagram & Sons, Joseph E.
Sealright Co., Inc.
Searle & Co., G.D.
Seaver Institute
Seay Charitable Trust, Sarah M. and Charles E.
Security Life of Denver
See Foundation, Charles
Seebee Trust, Frances
Seevak Family Foundation
Sehn Foundation
Sentry Insurance Co.
Setzer Foundation
Sewall Foundation, Elmina
Shafer Foundation, Richard H. and Ann
Shapiro Foundation, Carl and Ruth
Share Foundation
Share Trust, Charles Morton
Sharon Steel Corp.
Sharp Foundation, Charles S. and Ruth C.
Sharp Foundation, Evelyn
Shea Foundation
Sheinberg Foundation, Eric P.
Shelden Fund, Elizabeth, Allan and Warren
Shell Oil Co.
Shelter Mutual Insurance Co.
Shemanski Testamentary Trust, Tillie and Alfred
Shenandoah Foundation
Shenandoah Life Insurance Co.
Sheppard Foundation, Lawrence B.
Sherman Family Charitable Trust, George and Beatrice
Shirk Foundation, Russell and Betty
Shoenberg Foundation
Shoong Foundation, Milton
Sierra Pacific Industries
Sierra Pacific Resources
Simon Foundation, Jennifer Jones
Simon Foundation, Sidney, Milton and Leoma
Simpson Paper Co.
Siragusa Foundation
Skirball Foundation
Slant/Fin Corp.
Slaughter Foundation, Charles
Slifka Foundation, Joseph and Sylvia
Smith and W. Aubrey Smith Charitable Foundation, Clara Blackford
Smith Charitable Fund, Eleanor Armstrong
Smith Charitable Trust, W. W.
Smith Foundation
Smith Foundation, Bob and Vivian
Smith Foundation, Julia and Albert
Smith Foundation, Lon V.
Smith Foundation, Richard and Susan

Smith 1963 Charitable Trust, Don McQueen
Smithers Foundation, Christopher D.
Snee-Reinhardt Charitable Foundation
Snyder Foundation, Frost and Margaret
Solow Foundation, Sheldon H.
Sonoco Products Co.
Sooner Pipe & Supply Corp.
Sordoni Foundation
Soros Foundation-Hungary
Souers Charitable Trust, Sidney W. and Sylvia N.
South Plains Foundation
South Waite Foundation
Spang & Co.
Speas Memorial Trust, John W. and Effie E.
Spiegel Family Foundation, Jerry and Emily
Spingold Foundation, Nate B. and Frances
Spiritus Gladius Foundation
Sprague, Jr. Foundation, Caryll M. and Norman F.
SPS Technologies
Spunk Fund
Square D Co.
Stackner Family Foundation
Staley, Jr. Foundation, A. E.
Standard Products Co.
Stans Foundation
Stare Fund
Starr Foundation
Starrett Co., L.S.
Statter Foundation, Amy Plant
Stauffer Foundation, John and Beverly
Stein Foundation, Joseph F.
Stein Foundation, Jules and Doris
Stein Foundation, Louis
Steinbach Fund, Ruth and Milton
Steinberg Family Foundation, Meyer and Jean
Steiner Charitable Fund, Albert
Steinhagen Benevolent Trust, B. A. and Elinor
Steinman Foundation, James Hale
Steinman Foundation, John Frederick
Stemmons Foundation
Sterkel Trust, Justine
Sterling Inc.
Sterling Winthrop
Stern Family Foundation, Harry
Stern Foundation, Bernice and Milton
Stern Foundation, Leonard N.
Stern Memorial Trust, Sidney
Stevens Foundation, Abbot and Dorothy H.
Stillwell Charitable Trust, Glen and Dorothy
Stocker Foundation
Stokely, Jr. Foundation, William B.
Stone Container Corp.
Stone Family Foundation, Jerome H.
Stone Trust, H. Chase
Stony Wold Herbert Fund
Stott Foundation, Robert L.
Stowers Foundation
Stratford Foundation
Straus Foundation, Martha Washington Straus and Harry H.
Strauss Foundation
Strauss Foundation, Leon
Strawbridge Foundation of Pennsylvania I, Margaret Dorrance
Strawbridge Foundation of Pennsylvania II, Margaret Dorrance

Stuart Foundation
Stulsaft Foundation, Morris
Stupp Brothers Bridge & Iron Co.
Stupp Foundation, Norman J.
Sudix Foundation
Sulzberger Foundation
Summerfield Foundation, Solon E.
Sumners Foundation, Hatton W.
Swanson Foundation
Sweet Life Foods
Swift Co. Inc., John S.
Swift Memorial Health Care Foundation
Swig Foundation
Swim Foundation, Arthur L.
Swisher Foundation, Carl S.
Tai and Co., J. T.
Talley Industries, Inc.
Tamarkin Co.
Tamko Asphalt Products
Taper Foundation, Mark
Tarmac America Inc.
Taub Foundation
Taub Foundation, Joseph and Arlene
Tauber Foundation
Taubman Foundation, A. Alfred
Taubman Foundation, Herman P. and Sophia
Taylor Family Foundation, Jack
Taylor Foundation, Fred and Harriett
Taylor Foundation, Ruth and Vernon
Teledyne
Temple Foundation, T. L. L.
Tenneco
Terner Foundation
Tetley, Inc.
Texaco
Texas Commerce Bank Houston, N.A.
Texas Instruments
Thagard Foundation
Thorne Foundation
Thornton Foundation, Flora L.
Thornton Foundation, John M. and Sally B.
Thorpe Foundation, James R.
Thrush-Thompson Foundation
Tibstra Charitable Foundation, Thomas and Gertrude
Times Mirror Co.
Tisch Foundation
Titmus Foundation
Titus Foundation, C. W.
Tobin Foundation
Tomlinson Foundation, Kate and Elwyn
Toms Foundation
Tortuga Foundation
Towsley Foundation, Harry A. and Margaret D.
Transco Energy Company
Travelers Cos.
Treadwell Foundation, Nora Eccles
Treakle Foundation, J. Edwin
Treuhaft Foundation
Trimble Family Foundation, Robert Mize and Isa White
Truland Foundation
Tull Charitable Foundation
Tuohy Foundation, Alice Tweed
Turner Charitable Foundation
Turner Fund, Ruth
21 International Holdings
Ukrop's Super Markets, Inc.
Union Bank
Union Camp Corp.
Union Foundation
United Dominion Industries
Universal Foods Corp.
Unocal Corp.
Upjohn California Fund
Upjohn Co.

Upton Charitable Foundation, Lucy and Eleanor S.
USG Corp.
Ushkow Foundation
UST
Vale-Asche Foundation
Valley Foundation, Wayne and Gladys
Valley National Bancorp
Valspar Corp.
van Ameringen Foundation
Van Every Foundation, Philip L.
van Loben Sels - Eleanor Slate van Lobel Sels Charitable Foundation, Ernst D.
Van Nuys Charities, J. B. and Emily
Vance Charitable Foundation, Robert C.
Vanderbilt Trust, R. T.
Vanneck-Bailey Foundation
Vaughn Foundation
Vernon Fund, Miles Hodsdon
Vesuvius Charitable Foundation
Vicksburg Hospital Medical Foundation
Vidinha Charitable Trust, A. and E.
Volkswagen of America, Inc.
Vollbrecht Foundation, Frederick A.
Waggoner Charitable Trust, Crystelle
Waggoner Foundation, E. Paul and Helen Buck
Wagner Manufacturing Co., E. R.
Wal-Mart Stores
Walker Foundation, T. B.
Walker Foundation, W. E.
Walter Family Trust, Byron L.
Walthall Perpetual Charitable Trust, Marjorie T.
Ward Foundation, Louis L. and Adelaide C.
Ward Foundation, Louis L. and Adelaide C.
Ware Foundation
Wareheim Foundation, E. C.
Warren Charite
Warren Foundation, William K.
Washington Square Fund
Washington Square Health Foundation
Wasserman Foundation
Waste Management
Watson Foundation, Walter E. and Caroline H.
Wauwatosa Savings & Loan Association
Webb Foundation
Webb Foundation, Del E.
Weber Charities Corp., Frederick E.
Webster Foundation, Edwin S.
Wegener Foundation, Herman and Mary
Weight Watchers International
Weil, Gotshal & Manges Foundation
Weiler Foundation
Weiler Foundation, Theodore & Renee
Weinberg Foundation, John L.
Weinberg, Jr. Foundation, Sidney J.
Weininger Foundation, Richard and Gertrude
Weiss Foundation, Stephen and Suzanne
Weiss Fund, Clara
Weisz Foundation, David and Sylvia
Wellman Foundation, S. K.
Wells Foundation, Franklin H. and Ruth L.
Wells Foundation, Lillian S.
Wendt Foundation, Margaret L.
Wertheim Foundation, Dr. Herbert A.

West Co.
West Foundation
West Foundation, Neva and Wesley
West Texas Corp., J. M.
Westend Foundation
Westerman Foundation, Samuel L.
Western Cardiac Foundation
Westvaco Corp.
Wetterau
Wheat First Securites
Wheeler Trust, Clara
Wheless Foundation
Whirlpool Corp.
Whitaker Charitable Foundation, Lyndon C.
Whitaker Foundation
Whitehead Charitable Foundation
Whitehead Foundation
Whitener Foundation
Whiting Foundation
Whitney Foundation, Helen Hay
Whittier Foundation, L. K.
Wiegand Foundation, E. L.
Wien Foundation, Lawrence A.
Willard Foundation, Helen Parker
Williams Foundation, Arthur Ashley
Wills Foundation
Wilson Foundation, Marie C. and Joseph C.
Wilson Sanitarium for Children of Baltimore City, Thomas
Winona Corporation
Winston Foundation, Norman and Rosita
Winston Research Foundation, Harry
Wisconsin Energy Corp.
Wodecroft Foundation
Wolff Shoe Co.
Wolfson Family Foundation
Wood-Claeyssens Foundation
Woodward Fund
Woodward Governor Co.
Xerox Corp.
Xtra Corp.
Yassenoff Foundation, Leo
Young Foundation, Robert R.
Zaban Foundation
Zemurray Foundation
Zenkel Foundation
Ziegler Foundation
Zock Endowment Trust

Medical Training

Abbott Laboratories
Abell-Hanger Foundation
Achelis Foundation
Aluminum Co. of America
American Home Products Corp.
American United Life Insurance Co.
Amoco Corp.
Armco Inc.
Atherton Family Foundation
Becton Dickinson & Co.
Beneficial Corp.
Boehringer Mannheim Corp.
Brackenridge Foundation, George W.
Bristol-Myers Squibb Co.
Bush Foundation
Capital Cities/ABC
Centerior Energy Corp.
Clark Foundation
Colonial Life & Accident Insurance Co.
Comer Foundation
Commercial Metals Co.
Commonwealth Fund
Corvallis Clinic
Cummings Foundation, James H.
Dana Foundation, Charles A.
DeCamp Foundation, Ira W.
Devonwood Foundation

Medical Training (cont.)

Doheny Foundation, Carrie Estelle
Dorot Foundation
du Pont de Nemours & Co., E. I.
Eccles Charitable Foundation, Willard L.
Edison Fund, Charles
Exxon Corp.
Foxmeyer Corp.
Franklin Foundation, John and Mary
Funderburke & Associates
General Motors Corp.
General Reinsurance Corp.
Gerber Products Co.
Hearst Foundation, William Randolph
Hoblitzelle Foundation
Hoffmann-La Roche
Hood Foundation, Charles H.
Hospital Corp. of America
Houston Endowment
Hubbard Foundation, R. Dee and Joan Dale
Johnson Foundation, Robert Wood
Johnson & Higgins
Johnson & Son, S.C.
Johnston Trust for Charitable and Educational Purposes, James M.
Kade Foundation, Max
Kellogg Foundation, W. K.
Kerr-McGee Corp.
Lipton, Thomas J.
Lowenstein Foundation, Leon
Macy & Co., R.H.
Macy, Jr. Foundation, Josiah
Manville Corp.
Marion Merrell Dow
Marshall & Ilsley Bank
McElroy Trust, R. J.
MCI Communications Corp.
McKnight Foundation
Meadows Foundation
Mellon Foundation, Richard King
Mercantile Bancorp
Merck & Co.
Metropolitan Life Insurance Co.
Meyer Memorial Trust
Millipore Corp.
Mitchell Family Foundation, Edward D. and Anna
National Medical Enterprises
National Starch & Chemical Corp.
New York Life Insurance Co.
The New Yorker Magazine, Inc.
Pacific Mutual Life Insurance Co.
Perkins Charitable Foundation
Phelps Dodge Corp.
Prentiss Foundation, Elisabeth Severance
Prudential Insurance Co. of America
Revson Foundation, Charles H.
Rockefeller Foundation
Rubinstein Foundation, Helena
Russell Memorial Foundation, Robert
Santa Fe Pacific Corp.
Schering-Plough Corp.
Shawmut National Corp.
Shenandoah Life Insurance Co.
Speas Memorial Trust, John W. and Effie E.
Sprague Educational and Charitable Foundation, Seth
Starr Foundation
Sterling Winthrop
Texaco
Texas Commerce Bank Houston, N.A.
Trust Co. Bank

Union Camp Corp.
Unocal Corp.
van Ameringen Foundation
Washington Square Fund

Mental Health

Abell Foundation, The
Achelis Foundation
Agape Foundation
Ahmanson Foundation
Akzo Chemicals Inc.
Alabama Power Co.
Albertson's
Alexander Foundation, Joseph
Allegheny Ludlum Corp.
Allendale Mutual Insurance Co.
ALPAC Corp.
Aluminum Co. of America
AMAX
American Foundation
American Home Products Corp.
American United Life Insurance Co.
Anderson Foundation, John W.
Andersons Management Corp.
Anschutz Family Foundation
Ansley Foundation, Dantzler Bond
Apple Computer, Inc.
Arcana Foundation
Archbold Charitable Trust, Adrian and Jessie
Aron Charitable Foundation, J.
Atherton Family Foundation
Atkinson Foundation
Atlanta Gas Light Co.
Attleboro Pawtucket Savings Bank
Avon Products
Bacardi Imports
Backer Spielvogel Bates U.S.
Baker Foundation, R. C.
Bank IV
Barker Welfare Foundation
Bass Foundation, Harry
Bauervic-Paisley Foundation
Beidler Charitable Trust, Francis
Ben & Jerry's Homemade
Benwood Foundation
Besser Foundation
Beveridge Foundation, Frank Stanley
Bingham Second Betterment Fund, William
Bingham Trust, The
Block, H&R
Blum-Kovler Foundation
Boatmen's First National Bank of Oklahoma
Boehm Foundation
Boeing Co.
Borden
Borden Memorial Foundation, Mary Owen
Borman's
Bothin Foundation
Bovaird Foundation, Mervin
Bowyer Foundation, Ambrose and Gladys
Bradford Foundation, George and Ruth
Brand Foundation, C. Harold and Constance
Bremer Foundation, Otto
Briggs Family Foundation
Bristol-Myers Squibb Co.
Britton Fund
Brooks Brothers
Brooks Foundation, Gladys
Brown Foundation
Brown Foundation, James Graham
Brunswick Corp.
Burlington Northern Inc.
Bush Foundation
Cafritz Foundation, Morris and Gwendolyn

Cameron Foundation, Harry S. and Isabel C.
Capital Fund Foundation
Carrier Corp.
Carter Foundation, Amon G.
Carter-Wallace
Casey Foundation, Eugene B.
Centerior Energy Corp.
Central Bank of the South
Central Hudson Gas & Electric Corp.
Central Maine Power Co.
Central Vermont Public Service Corp.
Chait Memorial Foundation, Sara
Chambers Memorial, James B.
Chastain Charitable Foundation, Robert Lee and Thomas M.
Cheney Foundation, Ben B.
Chevron Corp.
Church & Dwight Co.
Ciba-Geigy Corp. (Pharmaceuticals Division)
Clark-Winchcole Foundation
Clay Foundation
Clipper Ship Foundation
Clorox Co.
Close Foundation
Cohen Family Foundation, Saul Z. and Amy Scheuer
Collins Foundation
Collins Foundation, Carr P.
Collins Foundation, James M.
Colonial Life & Accident Insurance Co.
Comerica
Comprecare Foundation
Cooper Industries
Coors Brewing Co.
Copperweld Steel Co.
Corvallis Clinic
Cowles Charitable Trust
Cox Charitable Trust, Jessie B.
Cox, Jr. Foundation, James M.
CPC International
CPI Corp.
Crary Foundation, Bruce L.
Crestar Financial Corp.
Crown Central Petroleum Corp.
Cullen/Frost Bankers
Cummins Engine Co.
Curtice-Burns Foods
Daniel Foundation of Alabama
Davis Foundation, Edwin W. and Catherine M.
Day Family Foundation
DeCamp Foundation, Ira W.
DeKalb Genetics Corp.
DeRoy Testamentary Foundation
Detroit Edison Co.
Deutsch Co.
Dexter Corp.
Digital Equipment Corp.
Dimeo Construction Co.
Donaldson Co.
Donnelley & Sons Co., R.R.
Donner Foundation, William H.
Dorot Foundation
Dougherty, Jr. Foundation, James R.
Douglas & Lomason Company
Dover Foundation
Dresser Industries
Dreyfus Foundation, Max and Victoria
du Pont de Nemours & Co., E. I.
Duchossois Industries
Duke Power Co.
Dun & Bradstreet Corp.
Eastern Bank Foundation
Eccles Foundation, Marriner S.
Eden Hall Foundation
Edison Foundation, Harry
El Pomar Foundation
Enron Corp.
Equitable Life Assurance Society of the U.S.

Essel Foundation
Estes Foundation
Factor Family Foundation, Max
Falk Medical Fund, Maurice
Federal National Mortgage Assn., Fannie Mae
Femino Foundation
Ferkauf Foundation, Eugene and Estelle
Field Foundation, Jamee and Marshall
Fikes Foundation, Leland
First Boston
First Interstate Bank of Oregon
First Interstate Bank of Texas, N.A.
First Maryland Bancorp
First Petroleum Corp.
First Union Corp.
Florence Foundation
Florida Power & Light Co.
Forbes
Ford III Memorial Foundation, Jefferson Lee
Foster-Davis Foundation
Foundation for Seacoast Health
Franklin Charitable Trust, Ershel
Franklin Mint Corp.
Freed Foundation
Freedom Forum
Frueauff Foundation, Charles A.
Fry Foundation, Lloyd A.
Fuchsberg Family Foundation, Abraham
Funderburke & Associates
Gallo Foundation, Julio R.
Gannett Co.
GATX Corp.
GEICO Corp.
General Mills
General Motors Corp.
General Reinsurance Corp.
GenRad
George Foundation
Georgia Power Co.
Gerstacker Foundation, Rollin M.
Gheens Foundation
Giant Food
Giant Food Stores
Gillette Co.
Glencoe Foundation
Glenmore Distilleries Co.
Glickenhaus & Co.
Globe Newspaper Co.
Goldman Foundation, Herman
Goldseker Foundation of Maryland, Morris
Grant Foundation, William T.
Grassmann Trust, E. J.
Great Atlantic & Pacific Tea Co. Inc.
Great-West Life Assurance Co.
Green Foundation, Allen P. and Josephine B.
Gregg-Graniteville Foundation
Griffith Foundation, W. C.
Grigg-Lewis Trust
Gudelsky Family Foundation, Homer and Martha
Gulton Foundation
Guttag Foundation, Irwin and Marjorie
Haas Fund, Walter and Elise
Hagedorn Fund
Hamilton Bank
Harden Foundation
Harmon Foundation, Pearl M. and Julia J.
Harriman Foundation, Mary W.
Harrington Trust, George
Harsco Corp.
Hazen Foundation, Edward W.
Hechinger Co.
Heckscher Foundation for Children
HEI Inc.
Heller Financial

Hermann Foundation, Grover
Heydt Fund, Nan and Matilda
Hill Crest Foundation
Hillcrest Foundation
Hobbs Foundation, Emmert
Hobby Foundation
Hodge Foundation
Homeland Foundation
Hooper Foundation, Elizabeth S.
Hospital Corp. of America
Household International
Houston Endowment
Houston Industries
Hubbard Broadcasting
Hubbell Inc.
Humana
Hunt Alternatives Fund
Hutchins Foundation, Mary J.
IBM Corp.
ICI Americas
Illinois Tool Works
Indiana Insurance Cos.
Inland Container Corp.
Inland Steel Industries
Interco
Iowa-Illinois Gas & Electric Co.
Ittleson Foundation
Jackson Charitable Trust, Marion Gardner
Jacobson Foundation, Bernard H. and Blanche E.
Jarson-Stanley and Mickey Kaplan Foundation, Isaac & Esther
Jerusalem Fund for Education and Community Development
Jewish Healthcare Foundation of Pittsburgh
Johnson Foundation, Robert Wood
Johnson & Higgins
Johnston Trust for Charitable and Educational Purposes, James M.
Katten, Muchin, & Zavis
Kellogg Foundation, W. K.
Kennecott Corp.
Kenworthy - Sarah H. Swift Foundation, Marion E.
Kepco, Inc.
Kerr Fund, Grayce B.
Key Bank of Maine
Kimball International
King Ranch
Kingston Foundation
Kiplinger Foundation
Knistrom Foundation, Fanny and Svante
Knott Foundation, Marion I. and Henry J.
Koch Sons, George
Koret Foundation
Kunkel Foundation, John Crain
Laclede Gas Co.
Lang Foundation, Eugene M.
Lattner Foundation, Forrest C.
Levy Foundation, Betty and Norman F.
Lichtenstein Foundation, David B.
Life Insurance Co. of Georgia
Lightner Sams Foundation
Lincoln National Corp.
Lindsay Trust, Agnes M.
Lipsky Foundation, Fred and Sarah
Lipton, Thomas J.
Lockheed Sanders
Lowenstein Foundation, Leon
LTV Corp.
Lydall, Inc.
Lyon Foundation
M. E. G. Foundation
MacArthur Foundation, John D. and Catherine T.
Maclellan Charitable Trust, R. J.
Macy & Co., R.H.

Mailman Family Foundation, A. L.
Mailman Foundation
Manning and Emma Austin Manning Foundation, James Hilton
Mardag Foundation
Margoes Foundation
Maritz Inc.
Marshall & Ilsley Bank
Martin Foundation, Della
Mason Charitable Foundation
Massengill-DeFriece Foundation
Massey Foundation
Mather Charitable Trust, S. Livingston
Maytag Family Foundation, Fred
MCA
McBride & Son Associates
McCormick Tribune Foundation, Robert R.
McDonald & Co. Securities
McDonald & Co. Securities
McDonnell Douglas Corp.-West
McGraw-Hill
McInerny Foundation
McKnight Foundation
McNutt Charitable Trust, Amy Shelton
McWane Inc.
MDU Resources Group, Inc.
Mead Corp.
Meadows Foundation
Meyer Foundation, Eugene and Agnes E.
Meyer Memorial Trust
Michigan Consolidated Gas Co.
Mid-Iowa Health Foundation
Mine Safety Appliances Co.
Mitchell Energy & Development Corp.
Monell Foundation, Ambrose
Moody Foundation
Moog Automotive, Inc.
Moore Business Forms, Inc.
Moore Charitable Foundation, Marjorie
Moore Foundation, C. F.
Moore Foundation, Edward S.
Moore Memorial Foundation, James Starr
Moskowitz Foundation, Irving I.
Mullen Foundation, J. K.
Nalco Chemical Co.
National City Corp.
National Fuel Gas Co.
National Life of Vermont
National Westminster Bank New Jersey
Nationwide Insurance Cos.
New England Mutual Life Insurance Co.
New-Land Foundation
New York Life Insurance Co.
New York Mercantile Exchange
New York Telephone Co.
The New Yorker Magazine, Inc.
Newhouse Foundation, Samuel I.
Norfolk Southern Corp.
Northeast Utilities
Northern States Power Co.
Northern Trust Co.
Northwest Natural Gas Co.
Norton Co.
Norwest Bank Nebraska
NuTone Inc.
Occidental Oil & Gas Corp.
Oglebay Norton Co.
Ohl, Jr. Trust, George A.
Olin Corp.
O'Neil Foundation, W.
Ontario Corp.
Oppenheimer and Flora Oppenheimer Haas Trust, Leo
Ordean Foundation
Osher Foundation, Bernard
Oshkosh B'Gosh

Overseas Shipholding Group
Oxford Foundation
Pacific Mutual Life Insurance Co.
Pan-American Life Insurance Co.
Paramount Communications Inc.
Parker Foundation
Parker Foundation, Theodore Edson
Parker-Hannifin Corp.
Peabody Charitable Fund, Amelia
Peabody Foundation, Amelia
Perkin-Elmer Corp.
Peters Foundation, Leon S.
Pew Charitable Trusts
Pfizer
Phillips Petroleum Co.
Pittway Corp.
Pitzman Fund
Plankenhorn Foundation, Harry
Polaroid Corp.
Poorvu Foundation, William and Lia
Pott Foundation, Herman T. and Phenie R.
PPG Industries
Price Foundation, Louis and Harold
Procter & Gamble Cosmetic & Fragrance Products
Prudential-Bache Securities
Prudential Insurance Co. of America
Puget Sound Power & Light Co.
Pulitzer Publishing Co.
Quaker Oats Co.
Radiator Specialty Co.
Ray Foundation
Read Foundation, Charles L.
Retirement Research Foundation
Reynolds Charitable Trust, Kate B.
Rice Foundation, Ethel and Raymond F.
Robinson Foundation
Roblee Foundation, Joseph H. and Florence A.
Rockwell Fund
Rockwell International Corp.
Rohm and Haas Company
Russ Togs
SAFECO Corp.
San Diego Gas & Electric
Sanguinetti Foundation, Annunziata
Santa Fe Pacific Corp.
Schamach Foundation, Milton
Schenck Fund, L. P.
Schlinger Foundation
Schmidlapp Trust No. 1, Jacob G.
Schneider Foundation, Robert E.
Scrivner, Inc.
See Foundation, Charles
Seeley Foundation
Selby and Marie Selby Foundation, William G.
Share Foundation
Shawmut National Corp.
Sheaffer Inc.
Shell Oil Co.
Shenandoah Life Insurance Co.
Shoong Foundation, Milton
Sierra Health Foundation
Simon Foundation, Jennifer Jones
Simon Foundation, Robert Ellis
Skinner Corp.
Smeal Foundation, Mary Jean & Frank P.
Smith Corp., A.O.
Smith Foundation, Bob and Vivian
SNET
Sonoco Products Co.
Sooner Pipe & Supply Corp.
Sosland Foundation
South Plains Foundation
Speas Foundation, Victor E.

Speas Memorial Trust, John W. and Effie E.
Sprague Educational and Charitable Foundation, Seth
Springs Foundation
Spunk Fund
Square D Co.
Stackpole-Hall Foundation
Stacy Foundation, Festus
State Street Bank & Trust Co.
Steelcase
Steinhagen Benevolent Trust, B. A. and Elinor
Steinman Foundation, John Frederick
Stewart Trust under the will of Helen S. Devore, Alexander and Margaret
Stocker Foundation
Stone Container Corp.
Stone Family Foundation, Jerome H.
Stone Family Foundation, Norman H.
Strake Foundation
Strouse, Greenberg & Co.
Stulsaft Foundation, Morris
Swalm Foundation
Synovus Financial Corp.
Tandy Foundation, Anne Burnett and Charles
Temple Foundation, T. L. L.
Tennant Co.
Tenneco
Terner Foundation
Tetley, Inc.
Texas Commerce Bank Houston, N.A.
Thomas Built Buses L.P.
Thompson Trust, Thomas
3M Co.
Time Insurance Co.
Times Mirror Co.
TJX Cos.
Tracor, Inc.
Tractor & Equipment Co.
Transamerica Corp.
Transco Energy Company
Treadwell Foundation, Nora Eccles
Treuhaft Foundation
Trull Foundation
Trust Co. Bank
Turner Charitable Foundation
Union Camp Corp.
Union Foundation
United Conveyor Corp.
Universal Foods Corp.
Unocal Corp.
USG Corp.
USX Corp.
Utica National Insurance Group
Valley Foundation
van Ameringen Foundation
van Loben Sels - Eleanor Slate van Lobel Sels Charitable Foundation, Ernst D.
Varian Associates
Veritas Foundation
Virginia Power Co.
Vulcan Materials Co.
Wal-Mart Stores
Walgreen Co.
Warren Foundation, William K.
Wasie Foundation
Waste Management
Wean Foundation, Raymond John
Weaver Foundation, Gil and Dody
Webb Charitable Trust, Susan Mott
Weinberg, Jr. Foundation, Sidney J.
Weir Foundation Trust
Weiss Foundation, William E.
Wells Foundation, Franklin H. and Ruth L.
Wendt Foundation, Margaret L.

West Foundation, Neva and Wesley
Western Southern Life Insurance Co.
Whirlpool Corp.
Whiting Memorial Foundation, Henry and Harriet
Wisconsin Energy Corp.
Woodward Governor Co.
Young Foundation, Robert R.
Zarrow Foundation, Anne and Henry
Zellerbach Family Fund
Zuckerberg Foundation, Roy J.

Nursing Services

Achelis Foundation
Ahmanson Foundation
Allen-Heath Memorial Foundation
Allendale Mutual Insurance Co.
Altman Foundation
American Home Products Corp.
American United Life Insurance Co.
Anderson Foundation, John W.
Anderson Foundation, M. D.
Archibald Charitable Foundation, Norman
Armco Inc.
Baier Foundation, Marie
Baker Foundation, R. C.
Bamberger and John Ernest Bamberger Memorial Foundation, Ruth Eleanor
Bank of New York
Battelle
Beasley Foundation, Theodore and Beulah
Becton Dickinson & Co.
Bedsole Foundation, J. L.
Benz Trust, Doris L.
Bethlehem Steel Corp.
Bicknell Fund
Blue Cross & Blue Shield of Kentucky Foundation
Bodine Corp.
Boothroyd Foundation, Charles H. and Bertha L.
Bordeaux Foundation
Borden Memorial Foundation, Mary Owen
Boston Fatherless and Widows Society
Bostwick Foundation, Albert C.
Boynton Fund, John W.
Brach Foundation, Helen
Bremer Foundation, Otto
Bright Charitable Trust, Alexander H.
Britton Fund
Brunswick Corp.
Buchanan Family Foundation
Bush Charitable Foundation, Edyth
Calhoun Charitable Trust, Kenneth
Cameron Foundation, Harry S. and Isabel C.
Camp Younts Foundation
Campbell and Adah E. Hall Charity Fund, Bushrod H.
Carylon Foundation
Central & South West Services
Chatlos Foundation
Chiles Foundation
Chilton Foundation Trust
Ciba-Geigy Corp. (Pharmaceuticals Division)
Clark-Winchcole Foundation
Clarke Trust, John
Codrington Charitable Foundation, George W.
Collins & Aikman Holdings Corp.
Collins Medical Trust
Colonial Life & Accident Insurance Co.

Colorado Trust
Commerce Clearing House
Commonwealth Fund
Comstock Foundation
Concord Chemical Co.
Corbin Foundation, Mary S. and David C.
Corvallis Clinic
Cosmair, Inc.
Cox Charitable Trust, Jessie B.
CPC International
Craigmyle Foundation
Cranshaw Corporation
CT Corp. System
Curtice-Burns Foods
David-Weill Foundation, Michel
Davis Foundation, Edwin W. and Catherine M.
Davis Hospital Foundation
DeCamp Foundation, Ira W.
Dexter Corp.
Dodge Foundation, Cleveland H.
Douty Foundation
Dresser Industries
Dreyfus Foundation, Jean and Louis
Duke Endowment
Dula Educational and Charitable Foundation, Caleb C. and Julia W.
Duncan Trust, James R.
duPont Foundation, Alfred I.
Eastern Bank Foundation
Eastman Foundation, Alexander
Eccles Foundation, George S. and Dolores Dore
Eccles Foundation, Marriner S.
Eddy Family Memorial Fund, C. K.
Eden Hall Foundation
Ellison Foundation
Enron Corp.
Exxon Corp.
Fairfield Foundation, Freeman E.
Fanwood Foundation
Finnegan Foundation, John D.
Firestone, Jr. Foundation, Harvey
First Fidelity Bancorporation
Firstar Bank Milwaukee NA
Flagler Foundation
Ford Fund, Walter and Josephine
Foundation for Seacoast Health
Frank Foundation, Ernest and Elfriede
Frelinghuysen Foundation
Frueauff Foundation, Charles A.
Fry Foundation, Lloyd A.
Fullerton Foundation
Funderburke & Associates
GAR Foundation
Georgia Health Foundation
Gerber Products Co.
Giger Foundation, Paul and Oscar
Gillette Co.
Gilmore Foundation, Irving S.
Grassmann Trust, E. J.
Green Fund
Greenberg Foundation, Alan C.
Group Health Plan Inc.
Hachar Charitable Trust, D. D.
Hagedorn Fund
Haggerty Foundation
Hales Charitable Fund
Hamilton Bank
Harden Foundation
Harding Foundation, Charles Stewart
Harriman Foundation, Gladys and Roland
Harriman Foundation, Mary W.
Hartford Courant Foundation
Hawn Foundation
Hearst Foundation
Hechinger Co.
Heckscher Foundation for Children
Heinz Endowment, Howard

Nursing Services (cont.)

Helfaer Foundation, Evan and Marion
Hillman Family Foundation, Alex
Hirschl Trust for Charitable Purposes, Irma T.
Hoblitzelle Foundation
Hoover Foundation
Hopedale Foundation
Horne Trust, Mabel
Hospital Corp. of America
Hubbell Inc.
Hugoton Foundation
Humana
Hunt Foundation, Samuel P.
Hutchins Foundation, Mary J.
ICI Americas
Iddings Benevolent Trust
Illinois Tool Works
Independence Foundation
Ireland Foundation
Jaffe Foundation
Jockey Hollow Foundation
Johnson Foundation, Helen K. and Arthur E.
Johnson Foundation, Robert Wood
Johnson & Higgins
Jones Charitable Trust, Harvey and Bernice
Jones Foundation, Daisy Marquis
Jones Fund, Paul L.
Julia R. and Estelle L. Foundation
Kawabe Memorial Fund
Kellogg Foundation, W. K.
Kenridge Fund
Kimberly-Clark Corp.
Kiplinger Foundation
Kirbo Charitable Trust, Thomas M. and Irene B.
Knistrom Foundation, Fanny and Svante
Kohler Foundation
Kowalski Sausage Co.
Lakeside Foundation
Lard Trust, Mary Potishman
Lehrman Foundation, Jacob and Charlotte
Lennon Foundation, Fred A.
Lincoln Fund
Lintilhac Foundation
Livingston Memorial Foundation
Loeb Foundation, Frances and John L.
Love Foundation, Martha and Spencer
Lowe Foundation, Joe and Emily
Lubrizol Corp.
Lumpkin Foundation
Lydall, Inc.
Lytel Foundation, Bertha Russ
Macy, Jr. Foundation, Josiah
Marquette Electronics
Mars Foundation
Marshall & Ilsley Bank
Martin Marietta Corp.
Mather and William Gwinn Mather Fund, Elizabeth Ring
Mayor Foundation, Oliver Dewey
McCarthy Foundation, John and Margaret
McDonald & Co. Securities
McDougall Charitable Trust, Ruth Camp
McGraw Foundation, Donald C.
McKee Foundation, Robert E. and Evelyn
Meadows Foundation
Mellam Family Foundation
Mellen Foundation
Memton Fund
Metropolitan Health Foundation
Meyer Memorial Trust

Michigan Consolidated Gas Co.
Milken Family Medical Foundation
Miller Foundation
Mobil Oil Corp.
Moore Charitable Foundation, Marjorie
Morley Brothers Foundation
Morris Foundation, Norman M.
Moses Fund, Henry and Lucy
Moss Heart Trust, Harry S.
Nashua Trust Co.
National Machinery Co.
National Medical Enterprises
National Starch & Chemical Corp.
Neuberger Foundation, Roy R. and Marie S.
New York Life Insurance Co.
The New Yorker Magazine, Inc.
Newman Assistance Fund, Jerome A. and Estelle R.
Northern Indiana Public Service Co.
Norton Co.
Noyes, Jr. Memorial Foundation, Nicholas H.
Oaklawn Foundation
Oglebay Norton Co.
Olin Foundation, Spencer T. and Ann W.
Olive Bridge Fund
1525 Foundation
Orleans Trust, Carrie S.
Osborn Charitable Trust, Edward B.
Overbrook Foundation
Oxford Foundation
Oxford Industries, Inc.
Packaging Corporation of America
Packard Foundation, David and Lucile
Paramount Communications Inc.
Peabody Charitable Fund, Amelia
Peabody Foundation, Amelia
Perkin-Elmer Corp.
Perkins Charitable Foundation
Peterson Memorial Fund, Chris and Mary L.
Pforzheimer Foundation, Carl and Lily
Phillips Foundation, Dr. P.
Pioneer Fund
Piper Foundation
Pittway Corp.
Polaroid Corp.
Pollybill Foundation
Procter & Gamble Cosmetic & Fragrance Products
Psychists
Quaker Hill Foundation
Ralston Purina Co.
Ramlose Foundation, George A.
Regenstein Foundation
Retirement Research Foundation
Rice Foundation, Ethel and Raymond F.
Riggs Benevolent Fund
Ritchie Memorial Foundation, Charles E. and Mabel M.
Rockwell Fund
Rohm and Haas Company
Rose Foundation, Billy
Rosenthal Foundation, Samuel
Rubenstein Charitable Foundation, Lawrence J. and Anne
Rubinstein Foundation, Helena
Ruffin Foundation, Peter B. & Adeline W.
Rutgers Community Health Foundation
Sasco Foundation
Schiff Foundation
Schreiber Foods, Inc.
Seabury Foundation
Searle & Co., G.D.

Seaway Food Town
Sharp Foundation, Charles S. and Ruth C.
Sheppard Foundation, Lawrence B.
Simon Foundation, William E. and Carol G.
Simpson Investment Co.
Smith and W. Aubrey Smith Charitable Foundation, Clara Blackford
Smith Benevolent Association, Buckingham
Smith Charitable Fund, Eleanor Armstrong
Smith Charitable Trust, W. W.
Smith Family Foundation, Theda Clark
Smith Foundation, Bob and Vivian
Smithers Foundation, Christopher D.
Southern California Edison Co.
Speas Foundation, Victor E.
Speas Memorial Trust, John W. and Effie E.
Sprague Educational and Charitable Foundation, Seth
Stackpole-Hall Foundation
Starr Foundation
Sterling Winthrop
Stewart Trust under the will of Mary E. Stewart, Alexander and Margaret
Stone Foundation
Stride Rite Corp.
Stulsaft Foundation, Morris
Summerfield Foundation, Solon E.
Switzer Foundation
Thanksgiving Foundation
Thomas & Betts Corp.
Treakle Foundation, J. Edwin
Trexler Trust, Harry C.
Trust Co. Bank
Turner Fund, Ruth
28:19
Union Camp Corp.
Union Foundation
United States Trust Co. of New York
Upjohn California Fund
Uvas Foundation
Veritas Foundation
Vicksburg Hospital Medical Foundation
Wahlstrom Foundation
Ware Foundation
Warner Foundation, Lee and Rose
Wean Foundation, Raymond John
Weingart Foundation
Wendt Foundation, Margaret L.
Wickson-Link Memorial Foundation
Williams, Jr. Family Foundation, A. L.
Winkler Foundation, Mark and Catherine
Wisconsin Power & Light Co.
Wrigley Co., Wm. Jr.

Nutrition & Health Maintenance

Air Products & Chemicals
Alltel/Western Region
AMCORE Bank, N.A. Rockford
American Home Products Corp.
Apple Computer, Inc.
Atlanta Gas Light Co.
Battelle
Bethlehem Steel Corp.
BHP Pacific Resources
Brach Foundation, Helen
Bristol-Myers Squibb Co.
Brown Family Foundation, John Mathew Gay

Burns Foundation, Fritz B.
Campbell Soup Co.
Cannon Foundation
Carvel Foundation, Thomas and Agnes
Casey Foundation, Eugene B.
Central Maine Power Co.
Colorado Trust
ConAgra
Conoco Inc.
Corvallis Clinic
Cox Charitable Trust, Jessie B.
Dimeo Construction Co.
Duke Endowment
Duke Power Co.
Educational Foundation of America
Exxon Corp.
Federated Life Insurance Co.
First Union Corp.
Ford Foundation
Fullerton Foundation
Funderburke & Associates
GATX Corp.
General Mills
Gerber Products Co.
Hechinger Co.
Heinz Co., H.J.
Hershey Foods Corp.
HKH Foundation
ITT Corp.
John Hancock Mutual Life Insurance Co.
Johnson & Higgins
Johnson & Son, S.C.
Keller-Crescent Co.
Kellogg Foundation, W. K.
Kentland Foundation
Kenworthy - Sarah H. Swift Foundation, Marion E.
Kiewit Foundation, Peter
King Ranch
Lipton, Thomas J.
Long Island Lighting Co.
Lydall, Inc.
Lyon Foundation
Manufacturers Life Insurance Co. of America
Maritz Inc.
Mayor Foundation, Oliver Dewey
McAlister Charitable Foundation, Harold
McCormick & Co.
McCune Foundation
McDonald's Corp.
Metropolitan Life Insurance Co.
National Computer Systems
New England Mutual Life Insurance Co.
New York Foundation
The New Yorker Magazine, Inc.
Northeast Utilities
Northern Trust Co.
Norton Co.
NutraSweet Co.
Ore-Ida Foods, Inc.
Pacific Mutual Life Insurance Co.
Perkin-Elmer Corp.
Pew Charitable Trusts
Philip Morris Cos.
Phillips Petroleum Co.
Pillsbury Co.
Quaker Chemical Corp.
Quaker Oats Co.
Reliable Life Insurance Co.
SAFECO Corp.
Searle & Co., G.D.
Seaway Food Town
Sentinel Communications Co.
Shaklee Corp.
Shawmut National Corp.
Sierra Pacific Industries
Speas Foundation, Victor E.
Stare Fund
Steelcase
Sterling Winthrop
Storage Technology Corp.

Tenneco
Time Insurance Co.
Tonkin Foundation, Tom and Helen
Toyota Motor Sales, U.S.A.
United States Trust Co. of New York
Wal-Mart Stores
White Consolidated Industries
Yost Trust, Elizabeth Burns

Outpatient Health Care Delivery

Abbott Laboratories
ALPAC Corp.
Altman Foundation
American Express Co.
AMP
Andersen Foundation, Hugh J.
AON Corp.
Arizona Public Service Co.
Atherton Family Foundation
Banbury Fund
Barra Foundation
Bemis Company
Bridgestone/Firestone
Bush Foundation
Cafritz Foundation, Morris and Gwendolyn
Casey Foundation, Eugene B.
Centerior Energy Corp.
Chase Manhattan Bank, N.A.
Citicorp
Clark Foundation
Clay Foundation
Clorox Co.
CM Alliance Cos.
Cockrell Foundation
Collins Foundation
Colonial Life & Accident Insurance Co.
Colorado Trust
Commonwealth Fund
Comstock Foundation
Corvallis Clinic
Country Curtains, Inc.
DeCamp Foundation, Ira W.
Deutsch Co.
Donaldson Co.
Dreyfus Foundation, Max and Victoria
Duke Endowment
Duke Power Co.
Dunn Research Foundation, John S.
Easley Trust, Andrew H. and Anne O.
Eccles Foundation, George S. and Dolores Dore
Farish Fund, William Stamps
Farnsworth Trust, Charles A.
Federal Express Corp.
Fifth Third Bancorp
First Interstate Bank of Oregon
First Union Corp.
Fondren Foundation
Fry Foundation, Lloyd A.
Funderburke & Associates
Gannett Co.
GATX Corp.
General American Life Insurance Co.
George Foundation
Green Fund
GTE Corp.
Halsell Foundation, Ewing
Hansen Foundation, Dane G.
Hechinger Co.
Helmerich Foundation
Hyams Foundation
Ittleson Foundation
J.P. Morgan & Co.
JELD-WEN, Inc.
John Hancock Mutual Life Insurance Co.

Pediatric Health (cont.)

Frueauff Foundation, Charles A.
Fruehauf Foundation
Fuchs Foundation, Gottfried & Mary
Fuller Foundation, C. G.
Funderburke & Associates
Fusenot Charity Foundation, Georges and Germaine
Gallo Foundation, Julio R.
Galter Foundation
Gannett Co.
Garvey Texas Foundation
Gaylord Foundation, Clifford Willard
General Mills
General Motors Corp.
Georgia Health Foundation
Gerber Products Co.
Gerlach Foundation
Giant Eagle
Gillette Co.
Gitano Group
Glanville Family Foundation
Glaxo
Glazer Foundation, Jerome S.
Glickenhaus & Co.
Globe Newspaper Co.
Goddard Foundation, Charles B.
Goerlich Family Foundation
Goldman Foundation, Aaron and Cecile
Goldman Foundation, Morris and Rose
Goldome F.S.B
Goldsmith Foundation
Goodman & Company
Goodyear Foundation, Josephine
Goody's Manufacturing Corp.
Gorin Foundation, Nehemiah
Gottwald Foundation
Grant Foundation, William T.
Graphic Controls Corp.
Green Fund
Greene Foundation, David J.
Greene Foundation, Robert Z.
Greenspan Foundation
Grigg-Lewis Trust
Griswold Foundation, John C.
Gross Foundation, Louis H.
Gucci America Inc.
Gulf Power Co.
Gurwin Foundation, J.
H. B. B. Foundation
Haas Foundation, Paul and Mary
Haas Fund, Walter and Elise
Habig Foundation, Arnold F.
Halff Foundation, G. A. C.
Hall Family Foundations
Halsell Foundation, O. L.
Hambay Foundation, James T.
Hamilton Bank
Hamilton Oil Corp.
Harmon Foundation, Pearl M. and Julia J.
Harriman Foundation, Gladys and Roland
Harrington Foundation, Don and Sybil
Harrington Foundation, Francis A. and Jacquelyn H.
Harrington Trust, George
Harsco Corp.
Hasbro
Havens Foundation, O. W.
Hawn Foundation
Hearst Foundation
Hearst Foundation, William Randolph
Hechinger Co.
Heckscher Foundation for Children
Heinz Co., H.J.
Heinz Endowment, Howard

Helis Foundation
Herndon Foundation
Hewit Family Foundation
Hightower Foundation, Walter
Hill Crest Foundation
Hillman Foundation, Henry L.
Hirschl Trust for Charitable Purposes, Irma T.
Hoblitzelle Foundation
Hoffman Foundation, John Ernest
Honda of America Manufacturing, Inc.
Hood Foundation, Charles H.
Hopedale Foundation
Hopkins Foundation, Josephine Lawrence
Hornblower Fund, Henry
Horne Trust, Mabel
Howe and Mitchell B. Howe Foundation, Lucite Horton
Howell Fund
Hubbard Broadcasting
Hubbard Foundation, R. Dee and Joan Dale
Huffy Corp.
Hugoton Foundation
Huisking Foundation
Humphrey Foundation, Glenn & Gertrude
Humphrey Fund, George M. and Pamela S.
Hunt Foundation
Hunt Foundation, Roy A.
Hunt Trust for Episcopal Charitable Institutions, Virginia
Hunter Trust, Emily S. and Coleman A.
Hyams Foundation
Hyde and Watson Foundation
I. and L. Association
Illinois Tool Works
Imerman Memorial Foundation, Stanley
Indiana Insurance Cos.
Inland Container Corp.
Innovating Worthy Projects Foundation
Interco
International Foundation
Interstate Packaging Co.
Irvine Foundation, James
Irwin Charity Foundation, William G.
Irwin-Sweeney-Miller Foundation
Ishiyama Foundation
ITT Hartford Insurance Group
J.P. Morgan & Co.
Jacobson & Sons, Benjamin
Jameson Foundation, J. W. and Ida M.
Jarson-Stanley and Mickey Kaplan Foundation, Isaac & Esther
Jergens Foundation, Andrew
Jerome Foundation
Jewish Healthcare Foundation of Pittsburgh
JMK-A M Micallef Charitable Foundation
Jockey Hollow Foundation
John Hancock Mutual Life Insurance Co.
Johnson Controls
Johnson Foundation, Willard T. C.
Johnson & Higgins
Johnson & Son, S.C.
Johnston Trust for Charitable and Educational Purposes, James M.
Jones Charitable Trust, Harvey and Bernice
Jones Family Foundation, Eugenie and Joseph
Jones Foundation, Daisy Marquis
Jonsson Foundation

Jordan and Ettie A. Jordan Charitable Foundation, Mary Ranken
Jost Foundation, Charles and Mabel P.
Julia R. and Estelle L. Foundation
Kahn Memorial Trust
Kaiser Foundation, Betty E. and George B.
Kapiloff Foundation, Leonard
Kaufmann Foundation, Marion Esser
Kaul Foundation Trust, Hugh
Keith Foundation Trust, Ben E.
Kellogg Foundation, W. K.
Kemper Charitable Trust, William T.
Kemper Educational and Charitable Fund
Kemper Foundation, Enid and Crosby
Kennedy Family Foundation, Ethel and W. George
Kennedy Memorial Fund, Mark H.
Kettering Family Foundation
Kinder-Care Learning Centers
King Ranch
Kiplinger Foundation
Kirkland & Ellis
Kirkpatrick Foundation
Klau Foundation, David W. and Sadie
Klee Foundation, Conrad and Virginia
Klein Fund, Nathan J.
Kloeckner-Pentaplast of America
Knistrom Foundation, Fanny and Svante
Knox Foundation, Seymour H.
Koffler Family Foundation
Kohn-Joseloff Fund
Koopman Fund
Kraft Foundation
Kramer Foundation
Krimendahl II Foundation, H. Frederick
Kuehn Foundation
Laclede Gas Co.
Ladish Co.
Ladish Family Foundation, Herman W.
Lance, Inc.
Lane Foundation, Minnie and Bernard
Lang Foundation, Eugene M.
Lastfogel Foundation, Abe and Frances
Lattner Foundation, Forrest C.
Lavanburg-Corner House
Law Foundation, Robert O.
Lebovitz Fund
Lee Foundation, James T.
Lehmann Foundation, Otto W.
Lender Family Foundation
Levy Foundation, Charles and Ruth
Life Insurance Co. of Georgia
Life Investors Insurance Company of America
Lincoln Electric Co.
Lincoln Health Care Foundation
Lincoln National Corp.
Lindner Foundation, Fay J.
Lindsay Trust, Agnes M.
Livingston Foundation
Logan Foundation, E. J.
Loughran Foundation, Mary and Daniel
Louisiana Land & Exploration Co.
Lovett Foundation
Lowe Foundation
Lowenstein Foundation, Leon
Lozier Foundation
Lukens
Lurie Family Foundation

Lurie Foundation, Louis R.
Luse Foundation, W. P. and Bulah
Luttrell Trust
Lydall, Inc.
MacDonald Foundation, James A.
Macy & Co., R.H.
Magowan Family Foundation
Mailman Family Foundation, A. L.
Mailman Foundation
Mallinckrodt, Jr. Foundation, Edward
Mandel Foundation, Joseph and Florence
Mann Foundation, Ted
Manoogian Foundation, Alex and Marie
Marbrook Foundation
Mardag Foundation
Margolis Charitable Foundation for Medical Research, Ben B. and Iris M.
Mark IV Industries
Marley Co.
Marshall & Ilsley Bank
Marshalls Inc.
Martin Foundation, Bert William
Martin Marietta Aggregates
Masco Corp.
Masserini Charitable Trust, Maurice J.
Massey Foundation, Jack C.
Mastronardi Charitable Foundation, Charles A.
Max Charitable Foundation
Maxfield Foundation
May Department Stores Co.
May Mitchell Royal Foundation
Mayborn Foundation, Frank W.
Mayerson Foundation, Manuel D. and Rhoda
Maytag Family Foundation, Fred
McBeath Foundation, Faye
McCormick Tribune Foundation, Robert R.
McCray Lumber Co.
McCrea Foundation
McCune Charitable Trust, John R.
McDonald's Corp.
McDonnell Douglas Corp.-West
McEachern Charitable Trust, D. V. & Ida J.
McFawn Trust No. 2, Lois Sisler McGregor Fund
MCI Communications Corp.
McKee Foundation, Robert E. and Evelyn
McKnight Foundation
McLean Contributionship
Mead Corp.
Mead Foundation, Giles W. and Elise G.
Meadows Foundation
Mebane Packaging Corp.
Medina Foundation
Merck & Co.
Merck Family Fund
Merrick Foundation, Robert G. and Anne M.
Merrill Foundation, R. D.
Meserve Memorial Fund, Albert and Helen
Messing Family Charitable Foundation
Messing Foundation, Morris M. and Helen F.
Metropolitan Life Insurance Co.
Meyer Foundation, Eugene and Agnes E.
Meyer Memorial Trust
Milken Family Medical Foundation
Milken Foundation, L. and S.
Mill-Rose Co.
Mine Safety Appliances Co.
Mitchell Family Foundation, Edward D. and Anna

Mitrani Family Foundation
Mnuchin Foundation
Mobil Oil Corp.
Moncrief Foundation, William A. and Elizabeth B.
Moody Foundation
Moore Charitable Foundation, Marjorie
Moores Foundation, Harry C.
Moorman Manufacturing Co.
Morgan Foundation, Burton D.
Morris Foundation, Norman M.
Morris Foundation, William T.
Moses Fund, Henry and Lucy
Moss Heart Trust, Harry S.
Mott Fund, Ruth
Mrs. Fields, Inc.
Muller Foundation, C. John and Josephine
Munger Foundation, Alfred C.
Murch Foundation
Murray Foundation
Nalco Chemical Co.
National City Corp.
National Gypsum Co.
Neenah Foundry Co.
New England Mutual Life Insurance Co.
New-Land Foundation
New York Mercantile Exchange
The New Yorker Magazine, Inc.
Newhouse Foundation, Samuel I.
Newman's Own
Nike Inc.
Noonan Memorial Fund under the will of Frank Noonan, Deborah Munroe
Norfolk Southern Corp.
Norris Foundation, Dellora A. and Lester J.
Nortek, Inc.
Northen, Mary Moody
Northwestern National Insurance Group
Norton Memorial Corporation, Geraldi
Norwest Bank Nebraska
Noyes, Jr. Memorial Foundation, Nicholas H.
Oestreicher Foundation, Sylvan and Ann
Ohl, Jr. Trust, George A.
Oklahoman Foundation
Olsson Memorial Foundation, Elis
1957 Charity Trust
O'Neil Foundation, Casey Albert T.
O'Neill Charitable Corporation, F. J.
Oppenheimer and Flora Oppenheimer Haas Trust, Leo
Ore-Ida Foods, Inc.
Orleans Trust, Carrie S.
O'Sullivan Children Foundation
Overbrook Foundation
Overseas Shipholding Group
Oxford Foundation
Oxford Industries, Inc.
PACCAR
Pacific Mutual Life Insurance Co.
Packard Foundation, David and Lucile
Pappas Charitable Foundation, Bessie
Pappas Charitable Foundation, Thomas Anthony
Parsons Foundation, Ralph M.
Parsons - W.D. Charities, Vera Davis
Pasadena Area Residential Aid
Peabody Foundation
Peabody Foundation, Amelia
Pearlstone Foundation, Peggy Meyerhoff
Penn Foundation, William
Pennzoil Co.
Persis Corp.

Peters Foundation, Leon S.
Pew Charitable Trusts
Phelps Dodge Corp.
PHH Corp.
Phillips Charitable Trust, Dr. and
   Mrs. Arthur William
Phillips Petroleum Co.
Physicians Mutual Insurance
Pick, Jr. Fund, Albert
Pickford Foundation, Mary
Picower Foundation, Jeffrey M.
   and Barbara
Pioneer Electronics (USA) Inc.
Pittway Corp.
Pitzman Fund
Polk Foundation
Poorvu Foundation, William and
   Lia
Porsche Cars North America, Inc.
Potomac Electric Power Co.
Prentiss Foundation, Elisabeth
   Severance
Price Associates, T. Rowe
Public Service Co. of Colorado
Public Welfare Foundation
Pulitzer Publishing Co.
Pyramid Foundation
Rabb Charitable Trust, Sidney R.
Radin Foundation
Ralston Purina Co.
Ratner Foundation, Milton M.
Ratshesky Foundation, A. C.
Recognition Equipment
Redfield Foundation, Nell J.
Regis Corp.
Reicher Foundation, Anne &
   Harry J.
Rexham Inc.
Reynolds Charitable Trust, Kate
   B.
Reynolds Metals Co.
Rich Products Corp.
Richardson Fund, Grace
Riggs Benevolent Fund
Ritter Charitable Trust, George
   W. & Mary F.
Robertshaw Controls Co.
Robison Foundation, Ellis H. and
   Doris B.
Robson Foundation, LaNelle
Rockefeller Foundation
Rockwell International Corp.
Rodgers Foundation, Richard &
   Dorothy
Rogers Foundation, Mary Stuart
Rohm and Haas Company
Rosenberg Foundation, Henry
   and Ruth Blaustein
Rosenthal Foundation, Richard
   and Hinda
Rosenthal Foundation, Samuel
Rosenthal-Statter Foundation
Ross Foundation, Walter G.
Rowland Foundation
Rubenstein Charitable
   Foundation, Lawrence J. and
   Anne
Rubinstein Foundation, Helena
Russell Charitable Trust,
   Josephine S.
Russell Trust, Josephine G.
Rutgers Community Health
   Foundation
Saint Croix Foundation
St. Faith's House Foundation
St. Giles Foundation
Salwil Foundation
Samuels Foundation, Fan Fox
   and Leslie R.
San Diego Trust & Savings Bank
Sandy Foundation, George H.
Sanguinetti Foundation,
   Annunziata
Santa Fe Pacific Corp.
Sargent Foundation, Newell B.
Schamach Foundation, Milton
Schey Foundation
Schmidlapp Trust No. 1, Jacob G.

Schoenleber Foundation
Scholler Foundation
Schrafft and Bertha E. Schrafft
   Charitable Trust, William E.
Schroeder Foundation, Walter
Scrivner, Inc.
Scurlock Foundation
Seabury Foundation
Sealright Co., Inc.
Seaway Food Town
Seay Charitable Trust, Sarah M.
   and Charles E.
Security Benefit Life Insurance
   Co.
See Foundation, Charles
Sega of America
Sentinel Communications Co.
Sentry Insurance Co.
Sewall Foundation, Elmina
Shafer Foundation, Richard H.
   and Ann
Shapiro, Inc.
Shapiro Charity Fund, Abraham
Shapiro Foundation, Carl and
   Ruth
Shaw Foundation, Walden W.
   and Jean Young
Shawmut National Corp.
Shea Foundation, Edmund and
   Mary
Shelden Fund, Elizabeth, Allan
   and Warren
Shoenberg Foundation
Shook Foundation, Barbara
   Ingalls
Signet Bank/Maryland
Silverburgh Foundation, Grace,
   George & Judith
Simon Charitable Trust, Esther
   Slant/Fin Corp.
Slusher Charitable Foundation,
   Roy W.
Smeal Foundation, Mary Jean &
   Frank P.
Smith Charitable Foundation,
   Lou and Lutza
Smith Foundation
Smith Foundation, Bob and
   Vivian
Smith Foundation, Kenneth L.
   and Eva S.
Smith Foundation, Lon V.
Smith Foundation, Richard and
   Susan
Smith, Jr. Charitable Trust, Jack
   J.
Snee-Reinhardt Charitable
   Foundation
Snider Foundation
Spang & Co.
Speas Foundation, Victor E.
Speer Foundation, Roy M.
Sprague Educational and
   Charitable Foundation, Seth
Sprague, Jr. Foundation, Caryll
   M. and Norman F.
SPS Technologies
SPX Corp.
Starr Foundation
Stauffer Charitable Trust, John
Steele Foundation, Harry and
   Grace
Stein Foundation, Louis
Steinberg Family Foundation,
   Meyer and Jean
Stemmons Foundation
Sterkel Trust, Justine
Sterling Winthrop
Stern Foundation, Leonard N.
Sterne-Elder Memorial Trust
Stewart Trust under the will of
   Helen S. Devore, Alexander
   and Margaret
Stillwell Charitable Trust, Glen
   and Dorothy
Stocker Foundation
Stokely, Jr. Foundation, William
   B.

Stone Container Corp.
Stone Foundation, David S.
Stranahan Foundation
Stratford Foundation
Straus Foundation, Aaron and
   Lillie
Straus Foundation, Martha
   Washington Straus and Harry
   H.
Strauss Foundation
Strawbridge Foundation of
   Pennsylvania II, Margaret
   Dorrance
Stroud Foundation
Stuart Foundation, Elbridge and
   Evelyn
Stulsaft Foundation, Morris
Sturgis Charitable and
   Educational Trust, Roy and
   Christine
Subaru of America Inc.
Sunshine Biscuits
Swanson Foundation
Synovus Financial Corp.
Tandy Foundation, Anne Burnett
   and Charles
Tasty Baking Co.
Taub Foundation
Taub Foundation, Joseph and
   Arlene
Taylor Foundation, Ruth and
   Vernon
Teledyne
Tetley, Inc.
Texas Commerce Bank Houston,
   N.A.
Texas Instruments
Textron
Thagard Foundation
Thompson Charitable
   Foundation, Marion G.
Thornton Foundation, Flora L.
Thorpe Foundation, James R.
Thurman Charitable Foundation
   for Children, Edgar A.
Time Insurance Co.
Tisch Foundation
Titmus Foundation
Titus Foundation, C. W.
TJX Cos.
Totsy Manufacturing Co.
Transco Energy Company
Travelers Cos.
Trinity Foundation
Truland Foundation
Trull Foundation
Trust Co. Bank
Trust Funds
Tull Charitable Foundation
Turner Fund, Ruth
Tyson Foods, Inc.
Unger Foundation, Aber D.
Unilever United States
Union Pacific Corp.
U.S. Oil/Schmidt Family
   Foundation, Inc.
United States Trust Co. of New
   York
Universal Leaf Tobacco Co.
Unocal Corp.
USF&G Co.
Valley Foundation
Van Houten Charitable Trust
Van Nuys Charities, J. B. and
   Emily
Vanderbilt Trust, R. T.
Vesuvius Charitable Foundation
Vidda Foundation
Vollbrecht Foundation, Frederick
   A.
Waggoner Foundation, E. Paul
   and Helen Buck
Wagner Foundation, Ltd., R. H.
Wal-Mart Stores
Walker Foundation, W. E.
Wareheim Foundation, E. C.
Washington Square Fund

Watson Foundation, Walter E.
   and Caroline H.
Weaver Foundation, Gil and
   Dody
Webb Charitable Trust, Susan
   Mott
Weber Charities Corp., Frederick
   E.
Wegener Foundation, Herman
   and Mary
Weiler Foundation
Weiler Foundation, Theodore &
   Renee
Weinberg, Jr. Foundation, Sidney
   J.
Weingart Foundation
Weir Foundation Trust
Wellman Foundation, S. K.
Wells Foundation, Franklin H.
   and Ruth L.
West Foundation, Neva and
   Wesley
Westerman Foundation, Samuel
   L.
Wexner Foundation
Weyerhaeuser Co.
Whirlpool Corp.
White Consolidated Industries
White Foundation, Erle and
   Emma
White Trust, G. R.
Whitener Foundation
Wildermuth Foundation, E. F.
Williams Family Foundation
Wolf Foundation, Melvin and
   Elaine
Wolff Memorial Foundation,
   Pauline Sterne
Woodward Fund-Atlanta, David,
   Helen, Marian
Woodward Fund-Watertown,
   David, Helen, and Marian
Wornall Charitable Trust and
   Foundation, Kearney
Wunsch Foundation
Wurts Memorial, Henrietta Tower
Wyman Youth Trust
Xtra Corp.
Zale Foundation
Zale Foundation, William and
   Sylvia
Zarrow Foundation, Anne and
   Henry

Public Health

Abbott Laboratories
Abell-Hanger Foundation
Adams Foundation, Arthur F. and
   Alice E.
Albertson's
Allstate Insurance Co.
Alltel/Western Region
ALPAC Corp.
Altman Foundation
AMCORE Bank, N.A. Rockford
American Brands
American Natural Resources Co.
Ames Department Stores
AMR Corp.
Anheuser-Busch Cos.
Apache Corp.
Apple Computer, Inc.
Arnnco Inc.
Armstrong World Industries Inc.
Atlanta Gas Light Co.
Auerbach Foundation, Beatrice
   Fox
Bank of Boston Connecticut
Bank of Boston Corp.
Bank One, Youngstown, NA
Bankers Trust Co.
Ben & Jerry's Homemade
Benedum Foundation, Claude
   Worthington
Beneficial Corp.
Bethlehem Steel Corp.
Block, H&R

Blue Cross and Blue Shield of
   Minnesota Foundation Inc.
Boatmen's First National Bank
   of Oklahoma
Bonner Foundation, Corella and
   Bertram
Brach Foundation, Helen
Burlington Resources
Burroughs Wellcome Co.
Cablevision of Michigan
Carnegie Corporation of New
   York
Carter Foundation, Amon G.
Central Maine Power Co.
Chase Manhattan Bank, N.A.
Chevron Corp.
CM Alliance Cos.
Colonial Life & Accident
   Insurance Co.
Colorado State Bank of Denver
Commonwealth Fund
Cone-Blanchard Machine Co.
Contran Corp.
Corvallis Clinic
Country Curtains, Inc.
CRI Charitable Trust
Cullen/Frost Bankers
Cummins Engine Co.
CUNA Mutual Insurance Group
Curtice-Burns Foods
Deutsch Co.
Diamond Foundation, Aaron
Dively Foundation, George S.
Dunagan Foundation
duPont Foundation, Alfred I.
duPont Foundation, Chichester
Eagle-Picher Industries
Easley Trust, Andrew H. and
   Anne O.
Eastman Foundation, Alexander
Eccles Foundation, George S.
   and Dolores Dore
Eckman Charitable Foundation,
   Samuel and Rae
Ecolab
Ellsworth Trust, W. H.
Engelhard Foundation, Charles
Enron Corp.
Erteszek Foundation
Exxon Corp.
Fairfield Foundation, Freeman E.
Fales Foundation Trust
Falk Medical Fund, Maurice
Federated Life Insurance Co.
Feild Co-Operative Association
Femino Foundation
Fikes Foundation, Leland
First Union Corp.
Fish Foundation, Bert
Florence Foundation
Ford Foundation
Ford Fund, Walter and Josephine
Foster Foundation
Fowler Memorial Foundation,
   John Edward
Friedman Family Foundation
Frueauff Foundation, Charles A.
Fry Foundation, Lloyd A.
Funderburke & Associates
Gallagher Family Foundation,
   Lewis P.
General Motors Corp.
General Reinsurance Corp.
Gilmore Foundation, Earl B.
Gleason Foundation, Katherine
Goldman Fund, Richard and
   Rhoda
Goldwyn Foundation, Samuel
Graphic Controls Corp.
Greenville Foundation
Griffin Foundation, Rosa May
Guttman Foundation, Stella and
   Charles
Haas Foundation, Paul and Mary
Haas Fund, Walter and Elise
Haggar Foundation
Hampden Papers

Public Health (cont.)

Haskell Fund
Hechinger Co.
HEI Inc.
Hiawatha Education Foundation
Hillsdale Fund
Hofstetter Trust, Bessie
Homeland Foundation
Horne Trust, Mabel
Hospital Corp. of America
Hughes Charitable Trust, Mabel Y.
Humane Society of the Commonwealth of Massachusetts
Hunt Alternatives Fund
Hyundai Motor America
Iddings Benevolent Trust
Index Technology Corp.
Irmas Charitable Foundation, Audrey and Sydney
Irvine Foundation, James
Irvine Health Foundation
ITT Hartford Insurance Group
Ittleson Foundation
Jackson Foundation
JM Foundation
John Hancock Mutual Life Insurance Co.
Johnson Controls
Johnson Foundation, Robert Wood
Johnson & Higgins
Kaiser Family Foundation, Henry J.
Kayser Foundation
Keck, Jr. Foundation, William M.
Kellogg Foundation, W. K.
Kennecott Corp.
Kimball Foundation, Horace A. Kimball and S. Ella
King Ranch
Kiplinger Foundation
Kirchgessner Foundation, Karl
Kline Foundation, Josiah W. and Bessie H.
Knistrom Foundation, Fanny and Svante
Kysor Industrial Corp.
Leidy Foundation, John J.
Lennon Foundation, Fred A.
Levi Strauss & Co.
Levy Foundation, Edward C.
Lincy Foundation
Lindsay Trust, Agnes M.
Lockheed Sanders
LTV Corp.
Lydall, Inc.
Lytel Foundation, Bertha Russ
Macy & Co., R.H.
Mandel Foundation, Jack N. and Lilyan
Markey Charitable Fund, John C.
Martin Foundation
May Mitchell Royal Foundation
Mayer Charitable Trust, Oscar G. & Elsa S.
Mayer Foundation, James and Eva
McBeath Foundation, Faye
McCormick Tribune Foundation, Robert R.
McCune Charitable Trust, John R.
McLean Contributionship
McMillen Foundation
Meadows Foundation
Medtronic
Merck Human Health Division
Merrick Foundation, Robert G. and Anne M.
Meyer Foundation, Eugene and Agnes E.
Meyer Memorial Trust
Mid-Iowa Health Foundation

Mills Charitable Foundation, Henry L. and Kathryn
Montgomery Street Foundation
Murch Foundation
National Computer Systems
National Forge Co.
New England Mutual Life Insurance Co.
The New Yorker Magazine, Inc.
Northern Trust Co.
Norton Co.
Norwest Bank Nebraska
Pacific Mutual Life Insurance Co.
Packard Foundation, David and Lucile
Parsons - W.D. Charities, Vera Davis
Peabody Foundation, Amelia
Pearce Foundation, Dr. M. Lee
Penn Foundation, William
Perkin-Elmer Corp.
Pew Charitable Trusts
Philips Foundation, Jesse
Pick, Jr. Fund, Albert
Pinkerton Foundation
Playboy Enterprises, Inc.
Portland General Electric Co.
Premier Industrial Corp.
Pritzker Foundation
Procter & Gamble Cosmetic & Fragrance Products
Public Welfare Foundation
Ratshesky Foundation, A. C.
Raytheon Co.
Recognition Equipment
Reynolds Charitable Trust, Kate B.
Rockefeller Family Fund
Rockefeller Foundation
Rohm and Haas Company
Rosenstiel Foundation
Rubinstein Foundation, Helena
SAFECO Corp.
Saint Paul Cos.
Sara Lee Hosiery
Schering-Plough Corp.
Searle & Co., G.D.
Security Life of Denver
Sentinel Communications Co.
Shawmut National Corp.
Shoney's Inc.
Shore Fund
Simon Foundation, William E. and Carol G.
Skinner Corp.
Smith Corp., A.O.
SNC Manufacturing Co.
Snow Foundation, John Ben
South Carolina Electric & Gas Co.
Speas Foundation, Victor E.
Stamps Foundation, James L.
Steiner Charitable Fund, Albert
Sterling Winthrop
Stern Memorial Trust, Sidney
Straus Foundation, Aaron and Lillie
Sun Co.
Surdna Foundation
Swim Foundation, Arthur L.
Texaco
Time Insurance Co.
Tippit Charitable Trust, C. Carlisle and Margaret M.
TJX Cos.
Towsley Foundation, Harry A. and Margaret D.
Tucker Charitable Trust, Rose E.
Turner Charitable Trust, Courtney S.
Valley Foundation
van Loben Sels - Eleanor Slate van Lobel Sels Charitable Foundation, Ernst D.
Varian Associates
Vidinha Charitable Trust, A. and E.

Virginia Power Co.
Wal-Mart Stores
Washington Square Fund
Waters Foundation
Wausau Paper Mills Co.
Weiler Foundation
Western Resources
Weyerhaeuser Co.
Woodward Fund-Atlanta, David, Helen, Marian
Xerox Corp.
Yost Trust, Elizabeth Burns

Single-Disease Health Associations

Abbott Laboratories
Abell-Hanger Foundation
Abitibi-Price
Abraham Foundation
Abraham Foundation, Anthony R.
Abrams Foundation, Talbert and Leota
Abramson Family Foundation
Ackerman Trust, Anna Keesling
Action Industries, Inc.
Ada Foundation, Julius
Adler Foundation
AEGON USA, Inc.
Aeroflex Foundation
AFLAC
Agway
Ahmanson Foundation
Aigner
Air France
Air Products & Chemicals
Airbus Industrie of America
AKC Fund
Akzo America
Akzo Chemicals Inc.
Ala Vi Foundation of New York
Alabama Power Co.
Alco Standard Corp.
Alexander & Baldwin, Inc.
Alexander Charitable Foundation
Alexander Foundation, Joseph
Alexander Foundation, Judd S.
Algonquin Energy, Inc.
Allegheny Ludlum Corp.
Allen Foundation for Medical Research, Paul G.
Allen Foundation, Frances
Allen Foundation, Rita
Allendale Mutual Insurance Co.
Alliant Techsystems
Alltel/Western Region
Allyn Foundation
ALPAC Corp.
Alro Steel Corp.
Alsdorf Foundation
Altman Foundation
Altschul Foundation
Alumax
Aluminum Co. of America
Amaturo Foundation
AMAX
Amdur Braude Riley, Inc.
America West Airlines
American Brands
American Express Co.
American Financial Corp.
American General Finance
American Home Products Corp.
American National Bank & Trust Co. of Chicago
American Natural Resources Co.
American President Cos.
American Saw & Manufacturing Co.
American Telephone & Telegraph Co.
American United Life Insurance Co.
American Welding & Manufacturing Co.
Ames Charitable Trust, Harriett

Amfac/JMB Hawaii
Amoco Corp.
AMP
AMR Corp.
Amsterdam Foundation, Jack and Mimi Leviton
Anacomp, Inc.
Andersen Corp.
Andersen Foundation
Andersen Foundation, Arthur
Anderson Charitable Trust, Josephine
Anderson Foundation
Anderson Foundation, John W.
Anderson Foundation, M. D.
Andersons Management Corp.
Andreas Foundation
Anheuser-Busch Cos.
Ansin Private Foundation, Ronald M.
AON Corp.
Apple Computer, Inc.
Applebaum Foundation
Appleton Papers
Arata Brothers Trust
Archbold Charitable Trust, Adrian and Jessie
Archibald Charitable Foundation, Norman
Argyros Foundation
Aristech Chemical Corp.
Arkansas Power & Light Co.
Arkell Hall Foundation
Armco Inc.
Armstrong World Industries Inc.
Aron Charitable Foundation, J.
Arronson Foundation
Ashland Oil
Athwin Foundation
Atkinson Foundation, Myrtle L.
Auerbach Foundation, Beatrice Fox
Avis Inc.
Avon Products
Awrey Bakeries
Ayres Foundation, Inc.
Bacardi Imports
Backer Spielvogel Bates U.S.
Badgeley Residuary Charitable Trust, Rose M.
Badger Meter, Inc.
Baird Foundation, Cameron
Baker Foundation, George T.
Baker Foundation, R. C.
Baker Foundation, Solomon R. and Rebecca D.
Baldwin Foundation, David M. and Barbara
Banbury Fund
Banc One Wisconsin Corp.
Banfi Vintners
Bank Hapoalim B.M.
Bank Leumi Trust Co. of New York
Bank of America Arizona
Bank of Boston Corp.
Bank of New York
Banner Life Insurance Co.
Bannerman Foundation, William C.
Barclays Bank of New York
BarclaysAmerican Corp.
Barden Corp.
Bardes Corp.
Barker Foundation
Barnes Group
Barnett Charitable Foundation, Lawrence and Isabel
Barra Foundation
Barrows Foundation, Geraldine and R. A.
Barry Corp., R. G.
Bartsch Memorial Trust, Ruth
Bass and Edythe and Sol G. Atlas Fund, Sandra Atlas
Bastien Memorial Foundation, John E. and Nellie J.

Battelle
Batten Foundation
Bauer Foundation, M. R.
Baughman Foundation
Bay Branch Foundation
BCR Foundation
Beal Foundation
Beattie Foundation Trust, Cordelia Lee
Beazley Foundation
Bechtel, Jr. Foundation, S. D.
Bedford Fund
Beech Aircraft Corp.
Beerman Foundation
Beeson Charitable Trust, Dwight M.
Behmann Brothers Foundation
Bekins Foundation, Milo W.
Belding Heminway Co.
Belfer Foundation
Belk Stores
Bellamah Foundation, Dale J.
Bellini Foundation
Beloco Foundation
Belz Foundation
Bemis Company
Benbough Foundation, Legler
Benefit Trust Life Insurance Co.
Benetton
Bennett Foundation, Carl and Dorothy
Beretta U.S.A. Corp.
Berger Foundation, Albert E.
Berger Foundation, H.N. and Frances C.
Berkey Foundation, Peter
Berkman Foundation, Louis and Sandra
Berkowitz Family Foundation, Louis
Bernsen Foundation, Grace and Franklin
Bernstein & Co., Sanford C.
Bernstein Foundation, Diane and Norman
Berry Foundation, Archie W. and Grace
Berry Foundation, Loren M.
Best Foundation, Walter J. and Edith E.
Bettingen Corporation, Burton G.
Beveridge Foundation, Frank Stanley
Bicknell Fund
Biddle Foundation, Margaret T.
Bierhaus Foundation
Bierlein Family Foundation
Bigelow Foundation, F. R.
Binswanger Co.
Birch Foundation, Stephen and Mary
Bireley Foundation
Birmingham Foundation
Bishop Charitable Trust, A. G.
Bishop Foundation, E. K. and Lillian F.
Blackmer Foundation, Henry M.
Blair and Co., William
Blanchard Foundation
Blank Family Foundation
Blaustein Foundation, Jacob and Hilda
Blinken Foundation
Bloch Foundation, Henry W. and Marion H.
Blount
Blowitz-Ridgeway Foundation
Blue Bell, Inc.
Blue Cross and Blue Shield of Minnesota Foundation Inc.
Blue Cross and Blue Shield United of Wisconsin Foundation
Blue Cross & Blue Shield of Alabama
Blue Cross & Blue Shield of Kentucky Foundation

Bluhdorn Charitable Trust, Charles G. and Yvette
Blum Foundation, Edith C.
Blum Foundation, Harry and Maribel G.
Blum-Kovler Foundation
BMW of North America, Inc.
Boatmen's First National Bank of Oklahoma
Bobst Foundation, Elmer and Mamdouha
Boehringer Mannheim Corp.
Boisi Family Foundation
Boothroyd Foundation, Charles H. and Bertha L.
Borchard Foundation, Albert and Elaine
Bordeaux Foundation
Borden
Borg-Warner Corp.
Borman's
Borwell Charitable Foundation
Boston Edison Co.
Bostwick Foundation, Albert C.
Botwinick-Wolfensohn Foundation
Bovaird Foundation, Mervin
Bowers Foundation
Bowles and Robert Bowles Memorial Fund, Ethel Wilson
Bozzone Family Foundation
Brach Foundation, Edwin I.
Bradford & Co., J.C.
Brady Foundation
Branta Foundation
Braun Foundation
Bray Charitable Trust, Viola E.
Bremer Foundation, Otto
Brennan Foundation, Robert E.
Brewer and Co., Ltd., C.
Bridgestone/Firestone
Bridwell Foundation, J. S.
Briggs Family Foundation
Britton Fund
Broad Foundation, Shepard
Broadhurst Foundation
Broccoli Charitable Foundation, Dana and Albert R.
Brochsteins Inc.
Brooks Foundation, Gladys
Brotman Foundation of California
Brotz Family Foundation, Frank G.
Brown Charitable Trust, Dora Maclellan
Brown Charitable Trust, Peter D. and Dorothy S.
Brown Foundation
Brown Foundation, Joe W. and Dorothy Dorsett
Brown Foundation, M. K.
Browning-Ferris Industries
Brunetti Charitable Trust, Dionigi
Brunner Foundation, Fred J.
Bryan Family Foundation, Kathleen Price and Joseph M.
Bryant Foundation
Buchalter, Nemer, Fields, & Younger
Buchanan Family Foundation
Bucyrus-Erie
Buehler Foundation, Emil
Buell Foundation, Temple Hoyne
Buffett Foundation
Buhl Family Foundation
Burchfield Foundation, Charles E.
Burden Foundation, Florence V.
Burlington Industries
Burnand Medical and Educational Foundation, Alphonse A.
Burnham Donor Fund, Alfred G.
Burnham Foundation
Burns Foundation, Fritz B.
Burns International
Burroughs Wellcome Co.

Burton Foundation, William T. and Ethel Lewis
Business Incentives
Cable & Wireless Communications
Cadbury Beverages Inc.
Cafritz Foundation, Morris and Gwendolyn
Cain Foundation, Effie and Wofford
Cain Foundation, Gordon and Mary
Callaway Foundation
Callaway Foundation, Fuller E.
Cameron Foundation, Harry S. and Isabel C.
Camp Younts Foundation
Campbell Foundation
Campbell Soup Co.
Cantor Foundation, Iris and B. Gerald
Capital Cities/ABC
Capital Holding Corp.
Carlson Cos.
Carnival Cruise Lines
Carolina Power & Light Co.
Carpenter Foundation, E. Rhodes and Leona B.
Carstensen Memorial Foundation, Fred R. and Hazel W.
Carter Family Foundation
Carter Foundation, Amon G.
Carter-Wallace
Cartier, Inc.
Carvel Foundation, Thomas and Agnes
Caspersen Foundation for Aid to Health and Education, O. W.
Cassett Foundation, Louis N.
Castle Foundation, Harold K. L.
Caterpillar
Catlin Charitable Trust, Kathleen K.
CBI Industries
Ceco Corp.
Cedars-Sinai Medical Center Section D Fund
Centel Corp.
Central Fidelity Banks, Inc.
Central Maine Power Co.
Central National-Gottesman
CertainTeed Corp.
Cessna Aircraft Co.
Chait Memorial Foundation, Sara
Chambers Development Co.
Chapman Charitable Trust, H. A. and Mary K.
Charina Foundation
Charitable Foundation of the Burns Family
Charities Foundation
Charles River Laboratories
Chartwell Foundation
Chatham Valley Foundation
Cheatham Foundation, Owen
Cheney Foundation, Ben B.
Cherne Foundation, Albert W.
Chernow Trust for the Benefit of Charity Dated 3/13/75, Michael
Chevron Corp.
Chicago Resource Center
Chicago Title and Trust Co.
Childress Foundation, Francis and Miranda
Chiles Foundation
Chisholm Foundation
Christian Dior New York, Inc.
Ciba-Geigy Corp. (Pharmaceuticals Division)
Cincinnati Bell
Circuit City Stores
CIT Group Holdings
Citicorp
Citizens Bank
Claneil Foundation
Clapp Charitable and Educational Trust, George H.

Clark Charitable Foundation
Clark Foundation
Clark-Winchcole Foundation
Clayton Fund
Clorox Co.
CM Alliance Cos.
Cockrell Foundation
Coen Family Foundation, Charles S. and Mary
Cohen Foundation, Naomi and Nehemiah
Cohen Foundation, Wilfred P.
Cohn Foundation, Peter A. and Elizabeth S.
Cole National Corp.
Cole Taylor Financial Group
Coleman Foundation
Coleman Foundation
Collins & Aikman Holdings Corp.
Collins Foundation
Collins Foundation, James M.
Collins Medical Trust
Colonial Life & Accident Insurance Co.
Colorado Trust
Colt Foundation, James J.
Coltec Industries
Columbia Savings Charitable Foundation
Columbus Dispatch Printing Co.
Comerica
Commerce Clearing House
Commerzbank AG, New York
Commonwealth Edison Co.
Community Health Association
Compaq Computer Corp.
Comprecare Foundation
Comstock Foundation
ConAgra
Connemara Fund
Conston Corp.
Contempo Communications
Continental Corp.
Contraves USA
Cook Foundation, Loring
Cooke Foundation
Cooke Foundation Corporation, V. V.
Cooper Charitable Trust, Richard H.
Cooper Industries
Coors Brewing Co.
Copley Press
Copolymer Rubber & Chemical Corp.
Copperweld Corp.
Cord Foundation, E. L.
Corestates Bank
Cornell Trust, Peter C.
Corpus Christi Exploration Co.
Corvallis Clinic
Cosmair, Inc.
Cox Charitable Trust, A. G.
Cox Foundation
CPC International
CPI Corp.
Craigmyle Foundation
Crane Foundation, Raymond E. and Ellen F.
Crawford & Co.
Crawford Estate, E. R.
Creel Foundation
Crestlea Foundation
CRI Charitable Trust
Crown Central Petroleum Corp.
Crown Central Petroleum Corp.
Crown Charitable Fund, Edward A.
Crown Memorial, Arie and Ida
Crum and Forster
Crummer Foundation, Roy E.
Crump Fund, Joe and Jessie
CT Corp. System
Cullen/Frost Bankers
Culpeper Memorial Foundation, Daphne Seybolt

Cummings Memorial Fund Trust, Frances L. and Edwin L.
Cuneo Foundation
Cunningham Foundation, Laura Moore
Curtice-Burns Foods
Cyprus Minerals Co.
Dai-Ichi Kangyo Bank of California
Dain Bosworth/Inter-Regional Financial Group
Daly Charitable Foundation Trust, Robert and Nancy
Dammann Fund
Dana Corp.
Danis Industries
Danner Foundation
Darby Foundation
Dart Group Corp.
Davenport-Hatch Foundation
Davidson Family Charitable Foundation
Davis Family - W.D. Charities, James E.
Davis Family - W.D. Charities, Tine W.
Davis Foundation, Edwin W. and Catherine M.
Davis Foundation, Ken W.
Davis Foundation, Shelby Cullom
DCNY Corp.
de Rothschild Foundation, Edmond
DeCamp Foundation, Ira W.
Dee Foundation, Lawrence T. and Janet T.
Delacorte Fund, George
Delany Charitable Trust, Beatrice P.
Delaware North Cos.
Demoulas Supermarkets
Dennison Manufacturing Co.
Deposit Guaranty National Bank
DeRoy Foundation, Helen L.
DeSoto
Detroit Edison Co.
Dettman Foundation, Leroy E.
Deuble Foundation, George H.
Deutsch Co.
DeVore Foundation
DeVos Foundation, Richard and Helen
Dewar Foundation
Dexter Corp.
Dial Corp.
Dibner Fund
Dickson Foundation
Dillard Paper Co.
Dillon Foundation
Dimeo Construction Co.
Dimick Foundation
Dishman Charitable Foundation Trust, H. E. and Kate
Disney Family Foundation, Roy
Dively Foundation, George S.
Dodson Foundation, James Glenwell and Clara May
Doheny Foundation, Carrie Estelle
Doherty Charitable Foundation, Henry L. and Grace
Domino of California
Donaldson Charitable Trust, Oliver S. and Jennie R.
Donnelley Foundation, Elliott and Ann
Donnelley Foundation, Gaylord and Dorothy
Doty Family Foundation
Dougherty, Jr. Foundation, James R.
Douglas Charitable Foundation
Douglas & Lomason Company
Dover Corp.
Dower Foundation, Thomas W.
Dresser Industries
du Pont de Nemours & Co., E. I.

Dubow Family Foundation
Duchossois Industries
Duke Power Co.
Dunagan Foundation
Duncan Trust, James R.
Duncan Trust, John G.
Dupar Foundation
duPont Foundation, Alfred I.
duPont Fund, Jessie Ball
Durst Foundation
Durst Foundation
Dweck Foundation, Samuel R.
Dynamet, Inc.
Earl-Beth Foundation
Early Medical Research Trust, Margaret E.
Easley Trust, Andrew H. and Anne O.
Eaton Corp.
Eaton Foundation, Cyrus
Eccles Charitable Foundation, Willard L.
Eccles Foundation, George S. and Dolores Dore
Eccles Foundation, Marriner S.
Echlin Foundation
Eckman Charitable Foundation, Samuel and Rae
Eddy Foundation
Eden Hall Foundation
Eder Foundation, Sidney and Arthur
Edwards Foundation, Jes
EG&G Inc.
Einstein Fund, Albert E. and Birdie W.
EIS Foundation
Eisenberg Foundation, Ben B. and Joyce E.
Electric Power Equipment Co.
Elf Aquitaine, Inc.
Elkin Memorial Foundation, Neil Warren and William Simpson
Elkins Foundation, J. A. and Isabel M.
Emergency Aid of Pennsylvania Foundation
Emerson Electric Co.
Emerson Foundation, Fred L.
Endries Fastener & Supply Co.
Engelhard Foundation, Charles
English-Bonter-Mitchell Foundation
English Memorial Fund, Florence C. and H. L.
Enron Corp.
Ensworth Charitable Foundation
Enterprise Rent-A-Car Co.
Equifax
Equitable Life Assurance Society of the U.S.
Ernest & Julio Gallo Winery
Erteszek Foundation
Essick Foundation
Ettinger Foundation
European American Bank
Evans Foundation, T. M.
Factor Family Foundation, Max
Fair Play Foundation
Fairchild Corp.
Fairfield Foundation, Freeman E.
Falcon Foundation
Falk Foundation, David
Falk Foundation, Michael David
Falk Medical Fund, Maurice
Fanwood Foundation
Farley Industries
Farwell Foundation, Drusilla
Favrot Fund
Fay's Incorporated
Federal Express Corp.
Federal-Mogul Corp.
Federal National Mortgage Assn., Fannie Mae
Federated Department Stores and Allied Stores Corp.
Federation Foundation of Greater Philadelphia

Janssen Foundation, Henry
Jaqua Foundation
Jarson-Stanley and Mickey
 Kaplan Foundation, Isaac &
 Esther
Jasper Seating Co.
Jasper Wood Products Co.
Jaydor Corp.
Jenkins Foundation, George W.
Jergens Foundation, Andrew
Jerome Foundation
John Hancock Mutual Life
 Insurance Co.
Johnson Controls
Johnson Foundation, A. D.
Johnson Foundation, Burdine
Johnson Foundation, Helen K.
 and Arthur E.
Johnson Foundation, Howard
Johnson Foundation, Robert
 Wood
Johnson & Higgins
Johnson & Johnson
Johnson & Son, S.C.
Johnston Trust for Charitable
 and Educational Purposes,
 James M.
Jones and Bessie D. Phelps
 Foundation, Cyrus W. and
 Amy F.
Jones Foundation, Daisy Marquis
Jones Fund, Blanche and George
Jonsson Foundation
Journal Gazette Co.
Julia R. and Estelle L.
 Foundation
Jurodin Fund
Kanematsu-Gosho U.S.A. Inc.
Kaplan Foundation, Rita J. and
 Stanley H.
Kaplen Foundation
Kaplun Foundation, Morris J.
 and Betty
Kapoor Charitable Foundation
Kasle Steel Corp.
Katten, Muchin, & Zavis
Kaufman Memorial Trust,
 Chaim, Fanny, Louis,
 Benjamin, and Anne Florence
Kaufmann Foundation, Marion
 Esser
Kaul Foundation Trust, Hugh
Kavanagh Foundation, T. James
Kayser Foundation
Kearney Inc., A.T.
Keebler Co.
Keith Foundation Trust, Ben E.
Kelley and Elza Kelley
 Foundation, Edward Bangs
Kelley Foundation, Kate M.
Kellmer Co., Jack
Kellogg Foundation, W. K.
Kellwood Co.
Kelly, Jr. Memorial Foundation,
 Ensign C. Markland
Kemper Charitable Trust,
 William T.
Kemper Foundation, Enid and
 Crosby
Kemper Memorial Foundation,
 David Woods
Kempner Fund, Harris and Eliza
Kennametal
Kennedy Family Foundation,
 Ethel and W. George
Kennedy Foundation, Ethel
Kenridge Fund
Kerr Fund, Grayce B.
Kerr-McGee Corp.
Kettering Family Foundation
Key Bank of Maine
Key Food Stores Cooperative Inc.
Kieckhefer Foundation, J. W.
Kiewit Sons, Peter
Kilmartin Industries
Kimball Foundation, Horace A.
 Kimball and S. Ella
Kimberly-Clark Corp.

Kimmelman Foundation, Helen
 & Milton
Kingsley Foundation
Kirby Foundation, F. M.
Kirkhill Rubber Co.
Kirkpatrick Foundation
Klau Foundation, David W. and
 Sadie
Kline Foundation, Josiah W. and
 Bessie H.
Klosk Fund, Louis and Rose
Knapp Foundation
Knistrom Foundation, Fanny and
 Svante
Knowles Foundation
Kobacker Co.
Koffler Family Foundation
Kohl Foundation, Sidney
Kohn-Joseloff Fund
Komes Foundation
Koopman Fund
Koret Foundation
Korman Family Foundation,
 Hyman
Kowalski Sausage Co.
Kramer Foundation
Kramer Foundation, C. L. C.
Krause Foundation, Charles A.
KSM Foundation
Kuhne Foundation Trust, Charles
Kuhns Investment Co.
Kuyper Foundation, Peter H. and
 E. Lucille Gaass
Kysor Industrial Corp.
La-Z-Boy Chair Co.
Lacy Foundation
Ladish Co.
Ladish Family Foundation,
 Herman W.
Laerdal Foundation, Asmund S.
Laffey-McHugh Foundation
Lakeside Foundation
Lamson & Sessions Co.
Lancaster Colony
Lance, Inc.
Lane Charitable Trust, Melvin R.
Lane Foundation, Minnie and
 Bernard
Lanier Brothers Foundation
Lard Trust, Mary Potishman
Large Foundation
Larsen Fund
Lasdon Foundation
Lasky Co.
Lassen Foundation, Irving A.
Lassus Brothers Oil
Lastfogel Foundation, Abe and
 Frances
Lattner Foundation, Forrest C.
Lawrence Foundation, Alice
Lawyers Title Foundation
Lazar Foundation
Lazarus Charitable Trust, Helen
 and Charles
LDI Charitable Foundation
Lebovitz Fund
Lederer Foundation, Francis L.
Lee Enterprises
Lee Foundation, James T.
Lee Foundation, Ray M. and
 Mary Elizabeth
Lehmann Foundation, Otto W.
Leibovitz Foundation, Morris P.
Leidy Foundation, John J.
Leighton-Oare Foundation
Lender Family Foundation
Lennon Foundation, Fred A.
Leo Burnett Co.
Leucadia National Corp.
Leuthold Foundation
Levee Charitable Trust, Polly
 Annenberg
Levi Strauss & Co.
Levy Foundation, Betty and
 Norman F.
Levy Foundation, Edward C.
Levy Foundation, June Rockwell

Liberty Corp.
Lieberman Enterprises
Lied Foundation Trust
Life Insurance Co. of Georgia
Life Investors Insurance
 Company of America
Lilly & Co., Eli
Lincoln Electric Co.
Lincoln National Corp.
Lindner Foundation, Fay J.
Link, Jr. Foundation, George
Linnell Foundation
Linus Foundation
Lipsky Foundation, Fred and
 Sarah
Lipton, Thomas J.
Liquid Air Corp.
Little Family Foundation
Litton Industries
Livingston Foundation
Livingston Memorial Foundation
Liz Claiborne
Llagas Foundation
Lockwood Foundation, Byron
 W. and Alice L.
Loeb Partners Corp.
Loews Corp.
Long Foundation, George A. and
 Grace
Long Island Lighting Co.
Lopata Foundation, Stanley and
 Lucy
Lost Tree Charitable Foundation
Louisiana Land & Exploration
 Co.
Louisiana-Pacific Corp.
Lounsbery Foundation, Richard
Love Charitable Foundation,
 John Allan
Love Foundation, George H. and
 Margaret McClintic
Lowe Foundation
Lowenstein Foundation, Leon
LTV Corp.
Lubrizol Corp.
Lurcy Charitable and
 Educational Trust, Georges
Lurie Family Foundation
Lurie Foundation, Louis R.
Luse Foundation, W. P. and Bulah
Luttrell Trust
Lydall, Inc.
Lynn Foundation, E. M.
Maas Foundation, Benard L.
MacAndrews & Forbes Holdings
MacDonald Foundation, James A.
MacDonald Foundation, Marquis
 George
Mack Foundation, J. S.
Madison Gas & Electric Co.
Magowan Family Foundation
Magruder Foundation, Chesley
 G.
Mailman Family Foundation, A.
 L.
Makita U.S.A., Inc.
Mamiye Brothers
Mandel Foundation, Jack N. and
 Lilyan
Mandel Foundation, Joseph and
 Florence
Mandeville Foundation
Manilow Foundation, Nathan
Mann Foundation, Ted
Manning and Emma Austin
 Manning Foundation, James
 Hilton
Manoogian Foundation, Alex
 and Marie
Manville Corp.
Marcus Brothers Textiles Inc.
Marcus Corp.
Mardag Foundation
Margolis Charitable Foundation
 for Medical Research, Ben B.
 and Iris M.
Marion Merrell Dow
Marley Co.

Marmot Foundation
Marquette Electronics
Marriott Corp.
Mars Foundation
Marshall & Ilsley Bank
Marshall Trust in Memory of
 Sanders McDaniel, Harriet
 McDaniel
Martin Foundation
Martin Foundation, Bert William
Martin Marietta Corp.
Mary Kay Foundation
Massachusetts Charitable
 Mechanics Association
Massey Charitable Trust
Massey Foundation
Massey Foundation, Jack C.
Massie Trust, David Meade
Mastronardi Charitable
 Foundation, Charles A.
Mattus Foundation, Reuben and
 Rose
Maxfield Foundation
May Foundation, Wilbur
May Mitchell Royal Foundation
Mayer Foundation, James and
 Eva
Mayer Foundation, Louis B.
Maytag Family Foundation, Fred
Mazer Foundation, Jacob and
 Ruth
Mazza Foundation
MBIA, Inc.
MCA
McAlister Charitable
 Foundation, Harold
McAlonan Trust, John A.
McCamish Foundation
McCasland Foundation
McCormick Foundation,
 Chauncey and Marion Deering
McCormick Tribune Foundation,
 Robert R.
McCrea Foundation
McCune Charitable Trust, John
 R.
McCutchen Foundation
McDonald & Co. Securities
McDonald Foundation, J. M.
McDonald's Corp.
McDonnell Douglas Corp.-West
McEvoy Foundation, Mildred H.
McGonagle Foundation, Dextra
 Baldwin
McGraw Foundation
McGraw Foundation, Donald C.
McGregor Foundation, Thomas
 and Frances
McGregor Fund
MCI Communications Corp.
McInerny Foundation
McIntosh Foundation
McKee Foundation, Robert E.
 and Evelyn
McKenna Foundation, Katherine
 Mabis
McLean Contributionship
McMillan, Jr. Foundation, Bruce
McNutt Charitable Trust, Amy
 Shelton
McRae Foundation
Mead Corp.
Mead Foundation, Giles W. and
 Elise G.
Meadows Foundation
Medina Foundation
Mellam Family Foundation
Mellen Foundation
Mellon Bank Corp.
Mellon Foundation, Richard King
Memorial Foundation for the
 Blind
Mendel Foundation
Menschel Foundation, Robert
 and Joyce
Mercy, Jr. Foundation, Sue and
 Eugene
Merrill Foundation, R. D.

Merrill Lynch & Co.
Messick Charitable Trust, Harry
 F.
Messing Family Charitable
 Foundation
Messing Foundation, Morris M.
 and Helen F.
Metropolitan Health Foundation
Metropolitan Theatres Corp.
Meyer Foundation
Meyer Memorial Foundation,
 Aaron and Rachel
MGIC Investment Corp.
Michael Foundation, Herbert I.
 and Elsa B.
Middendorf Foundation
Milbank Foundation, Dunlevy
Miles Inc.
Milken Family Medical
 Foundation
Milken Foundation, L. and S.
Miller Charitable Trust, Lewis N.
Miller Fund, Kathryn and Gilbert
Milliken & Co.
Mills Charitable Foundation,
 Henry L. and Kathryn
Mills Foundation, Ralph E.
Millstein Charitable Foundation
Milstein Family Foundation
Mine Safety Appliances Co.
Minster Machine Co.
Mirapaul Foundation
Misco Industries
Mitchell Family Foundation,
 Bernard and Marjorie
Mitchell Family Foundation,
 Edward D. and Anna
Mitrani Family Foundation
Mnuchin Foundation
Moncrief Foundation, William
 A. and Elizabeth B.
Monell Foundation, Ambrose
Monfort Charitable Foundation
Monroe Foundation (1976), J.
 Edgar
Montgomery Street Foundation
Moody Foundation
Moog Automotive, Inc.
Moore Charitable Foundation,
 Marjorie
Moore Foundation, C. F.
Moore Memorial Foundation,
 James Starr
Moores Foundation, Harry C.
Morris Charitable Foundation, E.
 A.
Morris Foundation, Margaret T.
Morris Foundation, Norman M.
Morrison Foundation, Harry W.
Morrison-Knudsen Corp.
Morse Foundation, Richard P.
 and Claire W.
Morse, Jr. Foundation, Enid and
 Lester S.
Mosbacher, Jr. Foundation, Emil
Moskowitz Foundation, Irving I.
Moss Heart Trust, Harry S.
Motch Corp.
Motorola
Mott Fund, Ruth
Mullan Foundation, Thomas F.
 and Clementine L.
Mullen Foundation, J. K.
Muller Foundation
Munger Foundation, Alfred C.
Murch Foundation
Murdy Foundation
Murfee Endowment, Kathryn
Murphy Co., G.C.
Murphy Foundation, Katherine
 and John
Murray Foundation
Nalco Chemical Co.
Nason Foundation
Nathan Berkman & Co.
National City Corp.
National Computer Systems
National Fuel Gas Co.

Single-Disease Health Associations (cont.)

National Gypsum Co.
National Life of Vermont
National Machinery Co.
National Presto Industries
National Westminster Bank New Jersey
Nationwide Insurance Cos.
NBD Bank
Neu Foundation, Hugo and Doris
Neuberger Foundation, Roy R. and Marie S.
New Horizon Foundation
New York Life Insurance Co.
New York Mercantile Exchange
The New Yorker Magazine, Inc.
Newhouse Foundation, Samuel I.
Newman's Own
Nichols Foundation
Noble Charitable Trust, John L. and Ethel G.
Noble Foundation, Samuel Roberts
Noonan Memorial Fund under the will of Frank Noonan, Deborah Munroe
Norfolk Southern Corp.
Norgren Foundation, Carl A.
Norris Foundation, Dellora A. and Lester J.
Norris Foundation, Kenneth T. and Eileen L.
Northern Indiana Public Service Co.
Northwest Natural Gas Co.
Norton Memorial Corporation, Geraldi
Norwest Bank Nebraska
Noyes, Jr. Memorial Foundation, Nicholas H.
NutraSweet Co.
Oak Foundation U.S.A.
Oberkotter Family Foundation
Obernauer Foundation
Occidental Oil & Gas Corp.
Occidental Petroleum Corp.
Oceanic Cablevision Foundation
O'Connor Co.
O'Connor Foundation, A. Lindsay and Olive B.
Oestreicher Foundation, Sylvan and Ann
Offield Family Foundation
Ogilvy & Mather Worldwide
Ohio National Life Insurance Co.
Ohl, Jr. Trust, George A.
Ohrstrom Foundation
Olin Charitable Trust, John M.
Olin Corp.
Olivetti Office USA, Inc.
Olsson Memorial Foundation, Elis
O'Neil Foundation, Casey Albert T.
O'Neil Foundation, M. G.
O'Neill Charitable Corporation, F. J.
Ordean Foundation
Ormet Corp.
Orscheln Co.
Osborn Charitable Trust, Edward B.
Osborn Charitable Trust, Edward B.
OsCo. Industries
Osher Foundation, Bernard
Oshkosh B'Gosh
Oshkosh Truck Corp.
Ostern Foundation
O'Sullivan Children Foundation
Ottenstein Family Foundation
Overbrook Foundation
Overlake Foundation
Overseas Shipholding Group

Owsley Foundation, Alvin and Lucy
Oxford Foundation
Oxford Industries, Inc.
Oxnard Foundation
Pacific Mutual Life Insurance Co.
Packaging Corporation of America
Page Foundation, George B.
PaineWebber
Palin Foundation
Palisades Educational Foundation
Pappas Charitable Foundation, Bessie
Pappas Charitable Foundation, Thomas Anthony
Paramount Communications Inc.
Parker Drilling Co.
Parker Foundation
Parshelsky Foundation, Moses L.
Pasadena Area Residential Aid
Patterson and Clara Guthrie Patterson Trust, Robert Leet
Patterson Charitable Fund, W. I.
Pauley Foundation, Edwin W.
Paulucci Family Foundation
Pax Christi Foundation
Peabody Charitable Fund, Amelia
Peabody Foundation
Peabody Foundation, Amelia
Pearlstone Foundation, Peggy Meyerhoff
Peerless Insurance Co.
Pendleton Memorial Fund, William L. and Ruth T.
Pennsylvania Knitted Outerwear Manufacturing Association
Pennzoil Co.
Pepsi-Cola Bottling Co. of Charlotte
Perini Corp.
Perini Foundation, Joseph
Perkin Fund
Perot Foundation
Peters Foundation, Leon S.
Petersen Foundation, Esper A.
Pettus Crowe Foundation
Pettus, Jr. Foundation, James T.
Pfeiffer Research Foundation, Gustavus and Louise
Pfister and Vogel Tanning Co.
Pfizer
Philips Foundation, Jesse
Phillips Charitable Trust, Dr. and Mrs. Arthur William
Phillips Family Foundation, Jay and Rose
Phillips Foundation, Dr. P.
Phillips Foundation, Waite and Genevieve
Physicians Mutual Insurance
Pick, Jr. Fund, Albert
Picker International
Pickford Foundation, Mary
Picower Foundation, Jeffrey M. and Barbara
Piedmont Health Care Foundation
Pillsbury Foundation
Pincus Family Fund
Pines Bridge Foundation
Pioneer Electronics (USA) Inc.
Pioneer Fund
Pittsburgh National Bank
Pittway Corp.
Plankenhorn Foundation, Harry
Playboy Enterprises, Inc.
Plitt Southern Theatres
PMA Industries
Pollybill Foundation
Poorvu Foundation, William and Lia
Porsche Cars North America, Inc.
Post Foundation of D.C., Marjorie Merriweather
Potomac Electric Power Co.
Potts Memorial Foundation
Pottstown Mercury

PPG Industries
Pratt Memorial Fund
Prentis Family Foundation, Meyer and Anna
Prentiss Foundation, Elisabeth Severance
Preuss Foundation
Preyer Fund, Mary Norris
Price Associates, T. Rowe
Price Foundation, Louis and Harold
Prickett Fund, Lynn R. and Karl E.
Prince Corp.
Principal Financial Group
Pritzker Foundation
Procter & Gamble Cosmetic & Fragrance Products
Propp Sons Fund, Morris and Anna
Prouty Foundation, Olive Higgins
Providence Journal Company
Prudential-Bache Securities
Psychists
Public Welfare Foundation
Puget Sound Power & Light Co.
Pulitzer Publishing Co.
Pyramid Foundation
Quaker Chemical Corp.
Quaker Oats Co.
Quanex Corp.
Questar Corp.
Rachal Foundation, Ed
Radiator Specialty Co.
Radin Foundation
Rales and Ruth Rales Foundation, Norman R.
Ramlose Foundation, George A.
Rankin and Elizabeth Forbes Rankin Trust, William
Rasmussen Foundation
Ratner Foundation, Milton M.
Raymond Corp.
Recognition Equipment
Red Wing Shoe Co.
Reedman Car-Truck World Center
Reicher Foundation, Anne & Harry J.
Reichhold Chemicals, Inc.
Reily & Co., William B.
Reinhart Institutional Foods
Reinhold Foundation, Paul E. and Ida Klare
Reisman Charitable Trust, George C. and Evelyn R.
Relations Foundation
Reliable Life Insurance Co.
Reliance Electric Co.
Revlon
Rexham Inc.
Reynolds Charitable Trust, Kate B.
Reynolds Foundation, Donald W.
Reynolds Foundation, J. B.
Reynolds Metals Co.
RGK Foundation
Rhoades Fund, Otto L. and Hazel E.
Rhone-Poulenc Inc.
Rice Family Foundation, Jacob and Sophie
Rice Foundation
Rich Foundation
Richardson Fund, Grace
Richmond Foundation, Frederick W.
Rigler-Deutsch Foundation
Ringier-America
Rite-Hite Corp.
Ritter Foundation
Ritter Foundation, May Ellen and Gerald
River Branch Foundation
Robertshaw Controls Co.
Robertson Brothers
Robin Family Foundation, Albert A.

Robinson Mountain Fund, E. O.
Roblee Foundation, Joseph H. and Florence A.
Robson Foundation, LaNelle
Rochlin Foundation, Abraham and Sonia
Rockwell Foundation
Rockwell Fund
Rockwell International Corp.
Rogers Charitable Trust, Florence
Rogers Foundation, Mary Stuart
Rohatyn Foundation, Felix and Elizabeth
Rohr Inc.
Rose Foundation, Billy
Rosen Foundation, Joseph
Rosenberg Family Foundation, William
Rosenbloom Foundation, Ben and Esther
Rosenstiel Foundation
Rosenthal Foundation, Richard and Hinda
Rosenthal-Statter Foundation
Ross Foundation, Walter G.
Roth Foundation
Rowland Foundation
RTM
Rubinstein Foundation, Helena
Ruddick Corp.
Rudin Foundation
Ruffin Foundation, Peter B. & Adeline W.
Russ Togs
Russell Charitable Foundation, Tom
Russell Educational Foundation, Benjamin and Roberta
Rutgers Community Health Foundation
Ryan Foundation, Nina M.
Ryan Foundation, Patrick G. and Shirley W.
Ryland Group
Saemann Foundation, Franklin I.
SAFECO Corp.
Safeguard Scientifics Foundation
Sage Foundation
Saint Gerard Foundation
Salomon
Saltz Foundation, Gary
San Diego Gas & Electric
Sandy Foundation, George H.
Sandy Hill Foundation
Sarkeys Foundation
Sattler Beneficial Trust, Daniel A. and Edna J.
Sawyer Charitable Foundation
Scaife Family Foundation
Schaffer Foundation, Michael & Helen
Schapiro Fund, M. A.
Schering-Plough Corp.
Schering Trust for Arthritis Research, Margaret Harvey
Schey Foundation
Schiff Foundation, Dorothy
Schilling Motors
Schiro Fund
Schlink Foundation, Albert G. and Olive H.
Schloss & Co., Marcus
Schmidlapp Trust No. 1, Jacob G.
Schneider Foundation Corp., Al J.
Schneider Foundation, Robert E.
Scholl Foundation, Dr.
Schrafft and Bertha E. Schrafft Charitable Trust, William E.
Schramm Foundation
Schroeder Foundation, Walter
Schultz Foundation
Schwab & Co., Charles
Schwartz Foundation, David
Scott and Fetzer Co.
Scott Foundation, William E.
Scrivner, Inc.
Scurlock Foundation

Seabury Foundation
Sealright Co., Inc.
Searle & Co., G.D.
Seaver Institute
Security Benefit Life Insurance Co.
See Foundation, Charles
Seebee Trust, Frances
Seevak Family Foundation
Selby and Marie Selby Foundation, William G.
Setzer Foundation
Sewall Foundation, Elmina
Shapiro Charity Fund, Abraham
Share Foundation
Sharon Steel Corp.
Sharp Foundation, Charles S. and Ruth C.
Shaw Foundation, Walden W. and Jean Young
Shaw's Supermarkets
Shea Co., John F.
Shea Foundation
Sheaffer Inc.
Sheinberg Foundation, Eric P.
Shell Oil Co.
Shelter Mutual Insurance Co.
Shelton Cos.
Shemanski Testamentary Trust, Tillie and Alfred
Shenandoah Foundation
Shenandoah Life Insurance Co.
Sheppard Foundation, Lawrence B.
Shoenberg Foundation
Shoong Foundation, Milton
Shughart, Thomson & Kilroy, P.C.
Sierra Health Foundation
Sierra Pacific Industries
Sierra Pacific Resources
Signet Bank/Maryland
Simon Foundation, Sidney, Milton and Leoma
Simon Foundation, William E. and Carol G.
Simpson Foundation
Simpson Paper Co.
Siragusa Foundation
SIT Investment Associates, Inc.
Skandia America Reinsurance Corp.
Skirball Foundation
Slant/Fin Corp.
Slaughter Foundation, Charles
Slusher Charitable Foundation, Roy W.
Smith Charitable Fund, Eleanor Armstrong
Smith Charities, John
Smith Foundation
Smith Foundation, Lon V.
Smith Foundation, Richard and Susan
Smith Golden Rule Trust Fund, Fred G.
Smith 1963 Charitable Trust, Don McQueen
Smithers Foundation, Christopher D.
SmithKline Beecham
Snee-Reinhardt Charitable Foundation
SNET
Snite Foundation, Fred B.
Snyder Foundation, Harold B. and Dorothy A.
Solo Cup Co.
Sonat
Sonoco Products Co.
Sooner Pipe & Supply Corp.
Souers Charitable Trust, Sidney W. and Sylvia N.
South Texas Charitable Foundation
Southways Foundation
Spang & Co.
Speas Foundation, Victor E.

Spectra-Physics Analytical
Speer Foundation, Roy M.
Spiegel Family Foundation, Jerry and Emily
Spiritus Gladius Foundation
Spiro Foundation, Donald W.
Sprague Educational and Charitable Foundation, Seth
Springs Industries
SPS Technologies
Square D Co.
Stackner Family Foundation
Stacy Foundation, Festus
Staley, Jr. Foundation, A. E.
Standard Products Co.
Stans Foundation
Star Bank, N.A.
Stark Foundation, Nelda C. and H. J. Lutcher
Starr Foundation
Starrett Co., L.S.
Statter Foundation, Amy Plant
Stauffer Foundation, John and Beverly
Stearns Charitable Foundation, Anna B.
Steelcase
Steele Foundation
Steele-Reese Foundation
Steele-Reese Foundation
Stein Foundation, Joseph F.
Stein Foundation, Louis
Steinbach Fund, Ruth and Milton
Steinberg Family Foundation, Meyer and Jean
Steiner Charitable Fund, Albert
Steinhagen Benevolent Trust, B. A. and Elinor
Steinman Foundation, James Hale
Steinman Foundation, John Frederick
Stemmons Foundation
Stern Family Foundation, Alex
Stern Foundation, Bernice and Milton
Stern Foundation, Gustav and Irene
Stern Foundation, Leonard N.
Stern Memorial Trust, Sidney
Sterne-Elder Memorial Trust
Stewart Educational Foundation, Donnell B. and Elizabeth Dee Shaw
Stewart Trust under the will of Mary E. Stewart, Alexander and Margaret
Stillwell Charitable Trust, Glen and Dorothy
Stocker Foundation
Stokely, Jr. Foundation, William B.
Stone Container Corp.
Stone Family Foundation, Jerome H.
Stone Trust, H. Chase
Storer Foundation, George B.
Stott Foundation, Robert L.
Stowe, Jr. Foundation, Robert Lee
Strake Foundation
Stratford Foundation
Straus Foundation, Martha Washington Straus and Harry H.
Strauss Foundation
Strauss Foundation, Leon
Strawbridge Foundation of Pennsylvania II, Margaret Dorrance
Stulsaft Foundation, Morris
Stupp Brothers Bridge & Iron Co.
Subaru of America Inc.
Sumitomo Corp. of America
Summerfield Foundation, Solon E.
Swanson Foundation

Swift Memorial Health Care Foundation
Swiss American Securities, Inc.
Swiss Bank Corp.
Synovus Financial Corp.
Talley Industries, Inc.
Tamarkin Co.
Tamko Asphalt Products
Tandy Foundation, Anne Burnett and Charles
Taper Foundation, Mark
Tarmac America Inc.
Tasty Baking Co.
Taub Foundation
Taub Foundation, Joseph and Arlene
Taubman Foundation, A. Alfred
Taubman Foundation, Herman P. and Sophia
Taylor Family Foundation, Jack
Taylor Foundation, Fred and Harriett
Taylor Foundation, Ruth and Vernon
Teledyne
Tennant Co.
Tenneco
Terner Foundation
Tetley, Inc.
Texas Commerce Bank Houston, N.A.
Texas Instruments
Textron
Thagard Foundation
Thalhimer Brothers Inc.
Thendara Foundation
Thoman Foundation, W. B. and Candace
Thomas Medical Foundation, Roy E.
Thornton Foundation, John M. and Sally B.
Thorpe Foundation, James R.
3M Co.
Thrush-Thompson Foundation
Thyssen Specialty Steels
Time Insurance Co.
Times Mirror Co.
Tisch Foundation
Titmus Foundation
Titus Foundation, C. W.
TJX Cos.
Tobin Foundation
Tomkins Industries, Inc.
Tomlinson Foundation, Kate and Elwyn
Toms Foundation
Torchmark Corp.
Tortuga Foundation
Towsley Foundation, Harry A. and Margaret D.
Tracor, Inc.
Tractor & Equipment Co.
Transamerica Corp.
Treadwell Foundation, Nora Eccles
Treakle Foundation, J. Edwin
Treuhaft Foundation
Trimble Family Foundation, Robert Mize and Isa White
Tropicana Products, Inc.
Truland Foundation
Trust Co. Bank
Tucker Charitable Trust, Rose E.
Tull Charitable Foundation
Tuohy Foundation, Alice Tweed
Tupancy-Harris Foundation of 1986
Turner Charitable Foundation
Twentieth Century-Fox Film Corp.
21 International Holdings
Tyson Foods, Inc.
Ukrop's Super Markets, Inc.
Unilever United States
Union Bank
Union Bank of Switzerland Los Angeles Branch

Union Camp Corp.
Union Manufacturing Co.
United Airlines
United Dominion Industries
U.S. Leasing International
United States Sugar Corp.
Universal Foods Corp.
Universal Leaf Tobacco Co.
Unocal Corp.
Upjohn California Fund
USF&G Co.
Ushkow Foundation
USX Corp.
Valley Foundation
Valley National Bank of Arizona
Valmont Industries
Valspar Corp.
van Ameringen Foundation
Van Every Foundation, Philip L.
Van Houten Charitable Trust
van Loben Sels - Eleanor Slate van Lobel Sels Charitable Foundation, Ernst D.
Van Nuys Charities, J. B. and Emily
Vanderbilt Trust, R. T.
Vernon Fund, Miles Hodsdon
Vidinha Charitable Trust, A. and E.
Waggoner Charitable Trust, Crystelle
Waggoner Foundation, E. Paul and Helen Buck
Wagner Manufacturing Co., E. R.
Wal-Mart Stores
Walgreen Co.
Walker Foundation, L. C. and Margaret
Walker Foundation, Smith
Walker Foundation, W. E.
Wallace Genetic Foundation
Disney Co., Walt
Walter Family Trust, Byron L.
Walter Industries
Ward Foundation, Louis L. and Adelaide C.
Wardlaw Fund, Gertrude and William C.
Wareheim Foundation, E. C.
Warren Foundation, William K.
Wasserman Foundation
Waste Management
Wauwatosa Savings & Loan Association
Wean Foundation, Raymond John
Weaver Foundation
Webb Foundation
Webb Foundation, Del E.
Webster Foundation, Edwin S.
Wegener Foundation, Herman and Mary
Weil, Gotshal & Manges Foundation
Weiler Foundation
Weiler Foundation, Theodore and Renee
Weinberg Foundation, John L.
Weinberg, Jr. Foundation, Sidney J.
Weinstein Foundation, J.
Weintraub Family Foundation, Joseph
Weisbrod Foundation Trust Dept., Robert and Mary
Weiss Foundation, Stephen and Suzanne
Weiss Fund, Clara
Weisz Foundation, David and Sylvia
Wellman Foundation, S. K.
Wells Fargo & Co.
Wendt Foundation, Margaret L.
West Foundation
West Texas Corp., J. M.
Westerman Foundation, Samuel L.
Western Cardiac Foundation

Western Southern Life Insurance Co.
Westvaco Corp.
Wetterau
Wheat First Securites
Whirlpool Corp.
Whitaker Charitable Foundation, Lyndon C.
White Foundation, Erle and Emma
Whitehead Charitable Foundation
Whitehead Foundation
Whitener Foundation
Whiting Foundation
Whitney Fund, David M.
Wiener Foundation, Malcolm Hewitt
Wilcox General Trust, George N.
Wiley & Sons, Inc., John
Willard Foundation, Helen Parker
Williams Cos.
Williams Family Foundation
Williams Foundation, Arthur Ashley
Williams Foundation, Edna Sproull
Wills Foundation
Wilson Foundation, Frances Wood
Wilson Foundation, Hugh and Mary
Wilson Foundation, Marie C. and Joseph C.
Wilson Sanitarium for Children of Baltimore City, Thomas
Winn-Dixie Stores
Winston Research Foundation, Harry
Wisconsin Energy Corp.
Wisconsin Power & Light Co.
Wisconsin Public Service Corp.
Witco Corp.
Wodecroft Foundation
Wolf Foundation. Melvin and Elaine
Wolff Shoe Co.
Wolfson Family Foundation
Wollenberg Foundation
Wood-Claeyssens Foundation
Woodward Fund
Woodward Fund-Atlanta, David, Helen, Marian
Woodward Fund-Watertown, David, Helen, and Marian
Woodward Governor Co.
Wrigley Co., Wm. Jr.
Xtra Corp.
Yassenoff Foundation, Leo
Young & Rubicam
Younkers, Inc.
Zaban Foundation
Zenkel Foundation
Zock Endowment Trust
Zuckerberg Foundation, Roy J.

International

Foreign Educational Institutions

Aetna Life & Casualty Co.
Ala Vi Foundation of New York
Amado Foundation, Maurice
American Express Co.
Amoco Corp.
Annenberg Foundation
ARCO Chemical
Atlantic Foundation of New York
Bechtel Group
Belding Heminway Co.
Belfer Foundation
Blaustein Foundation, Jacob and Hilda
Blum-Kovler Foundation
Bobst Foundation, Elmer and Mamdouha

Borman's
Buell Foundation, Temple Hoyne
Capital Fund Foundation
Carnegie Corporation of New York
Carnival Cruise Lines
Chase Manhattan Bank, N.A.
Chevron Corp.
China Medical Board of New York
Citicorp
Cummins Engine Co.
Deutsch Co.
Dibner Fund
Digital Equipment Corp.
Dodge Foundation, Cleveland H.
Dorot Foundation
Dougherty, Jr. Foundation, James R.
du Pont de Nemours & Co., E. I.
duPont Foundation, Alfred I.
Duriron Co., Inc.
Engelhard Foundation, Charles
Exxon Corp.
Factor Family Foundation, Max
Farley Industries
Feinberg Foundation, Joseph and Bessie
Feldman Foundation
Fellner Memorial Foundation, Leopold and Clara M.
Fink Foundation
First Fruit
Forbes
Ford Foundation
Foundation for Middle East Peace
Funderburke & Associates
Garfinkle Family Foundation
General Electric Co.
Getty Trust, J. Paul
Gillette Co.
Glenn Foundation for Medical Research, Paul F.
Goldman Foundation, Herman
Gould Foundation, Florence J.
Grant Foundation, William T.
Guggenheim Foundation, Harry Frank
Hammer Foundation, Armand
Herzstein Charitable Foundation, Albert and Ethel
Hess Charitable Foundation, Ronne and Donald
Hewlett-Packard Co.
Humana
IBM Corp.
IBM South Africa Projects Fund
International Foundation
International Student Exchange Cards
J.P. Morgan & Co.
Jaqua Foundation
Johnson Fund, Edward C.
Kaplun Foundation, Morris J. and Betty
Kellogg Foundation, W. K.
Kennecott Corp.
Koch Foundation
Koret Foundation
Kress Foundation, Samuel H.
KSM Foundation
Lakeside Foundation
Lehman Foundation, Robert
Lieberman Enterprises
Lingnan Foundation
Lockheed Corp.
Loeb Foundation, Frances and John L.
Loyola Foundation
Luce Foundation, Henry
Lurcy Charitable and Educational Trust, Georges
MacArthur Foundation, John D. and Catherine T.
Maclellan Charitable Trust, R. J.
Macy, Jr. Foundation, Josiah

Foreign Educational Institutions (cont.)

Mann Foundation, Ted
Marubeni America Corp.
McCasland Foundation
McKnight Foundation
Mellon Foundation, Andrew W.
Menil Foundation
Merck & Co.
Meyerhoff Fund, Joseph
Milbank Foundation, Dunlevy
Mitchell Family Foundation,
  Edward D. and Anna
Morris Charitable Foundation, E. A.
Newhouse Foundation, Samuel I.
Newman's Own
Nomura Securities International
Olin Corp.
Open Society Fund
Osher Foundation, Bernard
Overseas Shipholding Group
Paley Foundation, William S.
Pfizer
Pincus Family Fund
Pinewood Foundation
Raskob Foundation for Catholic
  Activities
Replogle Foundation, Luther I.
Resnick Foundation, Jack and
  Pearl
Revson Foundation, Charles H.
RGK Foundation
Richardson Foundation, Frank E.
  and Nancy M.
Rochlin Foundation, Abraham
  and Sonia
Rockefeller Foundation
Rosenbloom Foundation, Ben
  and Esther
Russ Togs
Russell Memorial Foundation,
  Robert
Sarofim Foundation
Schamach Foundation, Milton
Scheuer Family Foundation, S.
  H. and Helen R.
Schoenbaum Family Foundation
Seabury Foundation
Seagram & Sons, Joseph E.
Shapiro Foundation, Charles and
  M. R.
Slant/Fin Corp.
Sofia American Schools
Spencer Foundation
Starr Foundation
Stein Foundation, Louis
Stevens Foundation, Abbot and
  Dorothy H.
Taub Foundation
Texaco
Tinker Foundation
Van Schaick Scholarship Fund,
  Nellie
Volkswagen of America, Inc.
Vollmer Foundation
Wasserman Foundation
Westinghouse Electric Corp.
Weyerhaeuser Foundation,
  Frederick and Margaret L.
Wilf Family Foundation
Woodner Family Collection, Ian
Xerox Corp.
Ziegler Foundation, Ruth/Allen

General

Asahi Glass America, Inc.
International Flavors &
  Fragrances
Minolta Corp.
Oki America Inc.

International Development/ Relief

Ala Vi Foundation of New York
Aluminum Co. of America
American Brands
American Cyanamid Co.
American Express Co.
AON Corp.
Apache Corp.
Atkinson Foundation
Atkinson Foundation, Myrtle L.
Banyan Tree Foundation
Bard, C. R.
Becton Dickinson & Co.
Bergstrom Foundation, Erik E.
  and Edith H.
Best Western International
Bettingen Corporation, Burton G.
Boeckmann Charitable
  Foundation
Buffett Foundation
Bunbury Company
Carnegie Corporation of New
  York
Caterpillar
Chase Manhattan Bank, N.A.
Chatlos Foundation
Chevron Corp.
Citicorp
Clipper Ship Foundation
Collins & Aikman Holdings
  Corp.
Columbia Foundation
Contran Corp.
Crane Co.
Cudahy Fund, Patrick and Anna
  M.
Cummins Engine Co.
Davee Foundation
Davis Foundation, Edwin W. and
  Catherine M.
de Rothschild Foundation,
  Edmond
Digital Equipment Corp.
Dorr Foundation
du Pont de Nemours & Co., E. I.
Eaton Corp.
Edwards Foundation, Jes
Erteszek Foundation
Exxon Corp.
Falcon Foundation
Feldman Foundation
First Fruit
Fohs Foundation
Ford Foundation
Ford Motor Co.
Frees Foundation
Friedman Family Foundation
Fry Foundation, Lloyd A.
Funderburke & Associates
Gallagher Family Foundation,
  Lewis P.
General Atlantic Partners L.P.
General Dynamics Corp.
General Electric Co.
General Service Foundation
Gerard Foundation, Sumner
Gottesman Fund
Greenville Foundation
Greenville Foundation
Greve Foundation, William and
  Mary
Gruss Charitable Foundation,
  Emanuel and Riane
Gruss Petroleum Corp.
Hancock Foundation, Luke B.
Heinz Co., H.J.
Hermann Foundation, Grover
Hershey Foods Corp.
Hess Foundation
Hoffman Foundation,
  Maximillian E. and Marion O.
Homeland Foundation
Huizenga Foundation, Jennie
IBM Corp.

IBM South Africa Projects Fund
International Foundation
Irmas Charitable Foundation,
  Audrey and Sydney
J.P. Morgan & Co.
Jewett Foundation, George
  Frederick
Johnson & Johnson
Kaplun Foundation, Morris J.
  and Betty
Kellogg Foundation, W. K.
Kempner Fund, Harris and Eliza
Koch Foundation
Kunstadter Family Foundation,
  Albert
Levy Foundation, Edward C.
Lilly Endowment
Lincy Foundation
Lipton, Thomas J.
M. E. G. Foundation
MacArthur Foundation, John D.
  and Catherine T.
Maclellan Charitable Trust, R. J.
Manat Foundation
Mandel Foundation, Morton and
  Barbara
Marion Merrell Dow
Martin Foundation
Matthews International Corp.
McKnight Foundation
Merck & Co.
Mertz-Gilmore Foundation, Joyce
Middendorf Foundation
Miller Charitable Trust, Lewis N.
Millipore Corp.
Mitchell Family Foundation,
  Edward D. and Anna
Mobil Oil Corp.
Moskowitz Foundation, Irving I.
National Computer Systems
Nationwide Insurance Cos.
NBD Bank
The New Yorker Magazine, Inc.
Newman's Own
Ogden Foundation, Ralph E.
O'Neil Foundation, W.
Open Society Fund
Overbrook Foundation
Peierls Foundation
Penzance Foundation
Pfizer
Phelps Dodge Corp.
Phillips Petroleum Co.
Phillips-Van Heusen Corp.
Pillsbury Foundation
Price Foundation, Louis and
  Harold
Raskob Foundation for Catholic
  Activities
Relations Foundation
Reynolds Foundation,
  Christopher
Ridgefield Foundation
Rochlin Foundation, Abraham
  and Sonia
Rockefeller Foundation
Rockefeller Trust, Winthrop
Rosenberg Foundation, Sunny
  and Abe
Rubenstein Charitable
  Foundation, Lawrence J. and
  Anne
Ruffin Foundation, Peter B. &
  Adeline W.
Sacharuna Foundation
Schering-Plough Corp.
Scherman Foundation
Shapiro Fund, Albert
Share Foundation
Shawmut Worcester County
  Bank, N.A.
Shell Oil Co.
Spingold Foundation, Nate B.
  and Frances
Spiro Foundation, Donald W.
SPS Technologies
Stratford Foundation
Sunshine Biscuits

Taylor Charitable Trust, Jack
  DeLoss
Texaco
Textron
Thermo Electron Corp.
3M Co.
Timmis Foundation, Michael &
  Nancy
Tinker Foundation
Trull Foundation
Von der Ahe, Jr. Trust, Theodore
  Albert
Wagner Foundation, Ltd., R. H.
West Foundation
Western Shade Cloth Charitable
  Foundation
Westwood Endowment
Weyerhaeuser Family Foundation
Whitehead Foundation
Wilf Family Foundation
Wunsch Foundation
Xerox Corp.
Young Foundation, Irvin L.

International Health Care

Adams Foundation, Arthur F. and
  Alice E.
Aetna Life & Casualty Co.
Allendale Mutual Insurance Co.
Aluminum Co. of America
American Brands
American Express Co.
Amoco Corp.
Apache Corp.
Atalanta/Sosnoff Capital Corp.
Becton Dickinson & Co.
Belfer Foundation
Blinken Foundation
Bobst Foundation, Elmer and
  Mamdouha
Boehringer Mannheim Corp.
Carnegie Corporation of New
  York
Chase Manhattan Bank, N.A.
Chevron Corp.
China Medical Board of New
  York
Citicorp
Clark Foundation, Edna
  McConnell
Cowell Foundation, S. H.
Crane Co.
du Pont de Nemours & Co., E. I.
Edmondson Foundation, Joseph
  Henry
Exxon Corp.
Ford Foundation
Foundation for the Needs of
  Others
Funderburke & Associates
General Electric Co.
General Service Foundation
Gerard Foundation, Sumner
Gruss Petroleum Corp.
Heinz Co., H.J.
Hermann Foundation, Grover
Herzog Foundation, Carl J.
Homeland Foundation
IBM Corp.
Innovating Worthy Projects
  Foundation
International Foundation
J.P. Morgan & Co.
Kellogg Foundation, W. K.
Koch Foundation
Lacy Foundation
LeBrun Foundation
LeBrun Foundation
Levy Foundation, Edward C.
Lincy Foundation
Lowe Foundation, Joe and Emily
MacArthur Foundation, John D.
  and Catherine T.
Macy, Jr. Foundation, Josiah
Maytag Family Foundation, Fred

McDonnell Foundation, James S.
McGregor Foundation, Thomas
  and Frances
Merck & Co.
Michigan Bell Telephone Co.
Mitchell Family Foundation,
  Edward D. and Anna
Mobil Oil Corp.
The New Yorker Magazine, Inc.
Newman's Own
Phelps Dodge Corp.
Pritzker Foundation
Public Welfare Foundation
Raskob Foundation for Catholic
  Activities
Ridgefield Foundation
Rockefeller Foundation
Russ Togs
Sacharuna Foundation
Scaler Foundation
Schering-Plough Corp.
Scherman Foundation
Scholl Foundation, Dr.
Sofia American Schools
Starr Foundation
Steinhardt Foundation, Judy and
  Michael
Taylor Charitable Trust, Jack
  DeLoss
Texaco
Trull Foundation
Wagner Foundation, Ltd., R. H.
Whitehead Foundation
Williams, Jr. Family Foundation,
  A. L.
Zale Foundation
Ziegler Foundation, Ruth/Allen

International Organizations

Aequus Institute
Ahmanson Foundation
Ala Vi Foundation of New York
Alexander Foundation, Joseph
Allendale Mutual Insurance Co.
Aluminum Co. of America
American Brands
American Cyanamid Co.
American Express Co.
American Society of Ephesus
American Telephone &
  Telegraph Co.
Amway Corp.
Applebaum Foundation
Arca Foundation
Archer-Daniels-Midland Co.
ARCO Chemical
ASARCO
Asgrow Seed Co.
Atlantic Foundation of New York
Atran Foundation
Baier Foundation, Marie
Bass and Edythe and Sol G.
  Atlas Fund, Sandra Atlas
Bay Foundation
Belding Heminway Co.
Bellini Foundation
Bender Foundation
Bismarck Charitable Trust, Mona
Booz Allen & Hamilton
Bradley Foundation, Lynde and
  Harry
Brennan Foundation, Robert E.
Brunner Foundation, Robert
Brush Foundation
Bydale Foundation
Cabot Family Charitable Trust
Caddock Foundation
Candlesticks Inc.
Capital Fund Foundation
Caplan Charity Foundation,
  Julius H.
Carnegie Corporation of New
  York
Carter Family Foundation
Caterpillar

Chadwick Fund, Dorothy Jordan
Charles River Laboratories
Chase Manhattan Bank, N.A.
Chastain Charitable Foundation,
 Robert Lee and Thomas M.
Chevron Corp.
China Medical Board of New
 York
China Times Cultural Foundation
Citicorp
Claiborne Art Ortenberg
 Foundation, Liz
Clark Charitable Trust
Clover Foundation
Cobb Family Foundation
Cohen Foundation, Naomi and
 Nehemiah
Cohen Foundation, Wilfred P.
Columbia Foundation
Cow Hollow Foundation
CPC International
Crane Co.
CRI Charitable Trust
CRL Inc.
Cummins Engine Co.
Davenport-Hatch Foundation
David-Weill Foundation, Michel
de Hirsch Fund, Baron
de Rothschild Foundation,
 Edmond
Deere & Co.
Delaware North Cos.
Demos Foundation, N.
DeMoss Foundation, Arthur S.
Digital Equipment Corp.
Dimeo Construction Co.
Dodge Foundation, Cleveland H.
Dorot Foundation
Doty Family Foundation
Dougherty, Jr. Foundation, James
 R.
Downs Perpetual Charitable
 Trust, Ellason
Dresser Industries
du Pont de Nemours & Co., E. I.
Duke Power Co.
Dunagan Foundation
Eaton Foundation, Edwin M. and
 Gertrude S.
Eisenberg Foundation, Ben B.
 and Joyce E.
Engelhard Foundation, Charles
English Memorial Fund,
 Florence C. and H. L.
Equifax
Equitable Life Assurance Society
 of the U.S.
Erpf Fund, Armand G.
Falk Medical Fund, Maurice
Federal-Mogul Corp.
Feinberg Foundation, Joseph and
 Bessie
Feinstein Foundation, Myer and
 Rosaline
Firan Foundation
Fireman Charitable Foundation,
 Paul and Phyllis
First Fruit
Fiterman Charitable Foundation,
 Miles and Shirley
Flatley Foundation
Flemm Foundation, John J.
Flintridge Foundation
Fohs Foundation
Forbes
Forchheimer Foundation
Ford Foundation
Ford Motor Co.
Foundation for Middle East
 Peace
Freeman Foundation, Carl M.
Frees Foundation
Fribourg Foundation
Frohring Foundation, William O.
 and Gertrude Lewis
Funderburke & Associates
General Atlantic Partners L.P.
General Electric Co.

Generation Trust
Genesis Foundation
Gerard Foundation, Sumner
German Marshall Fund of the
 United States
Gerschel Foundation, Patrick A.
Getty Trust, J. Paul
Gilman Foundation, Howard
Ginter Foundation, Karl and
 Anna
Glencoe Foundation
Gottesman Fund
Gould Foundation, Florence J.
Grass Family Foundation
Greenberg Foundation, Alan C.
Greve Foundation, William and
 Mary
Gruss Petroleum Corp.
Gudelsky Family Foundation,
 Homer and Martha
Gudelsky Family Foundation,
 Isadore and Bertha
Gulton Foundation
Hammer Foundation, Armand
Heinz Co., H.J.
Heinz Foundation, Drue
Herzstein Charitable Foundation,
 Albert and Ethel
Hewlett Foundation, William and
 Flora
Hillman Family Foundation, Alex
HKH Foundation
Homeland Foundation
Homeland Foundation
Hudson Neckwear
Iacocca Foundation
IBM Corp.
IBM South Africa Projects Fund
 In His Name
Irmas Charitable Foundation,
 Audrey and Sydney
Ishiyama Foundation
ITT Corp.
J.P. Morgan & Co.
Jaffe Foundation
Jerome Foundation
Jerusalem Fund for Education
 and Community Development
Jesselson Foundation
Johnson Foundation, Barbara P.
Jones Foundation, W. Alton
Joselow Foundation
Kapoor Charitable Foundation
Kejr Foundation
Kellogg Foundation, W. K.
Key Food Stores Cooperative Inc.
Koret Foundation
Krause Foundation, Charles A.
Kress Foundation, Samuel H.
Krieble Foundation, Vernon K.
Lambert Memorial Foundation,
 Gerard B.
Lastfogel Foundation, Abe and
 Frances
Lauder Foundation
Lautenberg Foundation
Lazar Foundation
LeBrun Foundation
Levin Foundation, Philip and
 Janice
Lieberman Enterprises
Lincy Foundation
Lingnan Foundation
Lipton Foundation
Loeb Foundation, Frances and
 John L.
Lotus Development Corp.
Loyola Foundation
Luce Charitable Trust, Theodore
Luce Foundation, Henry
Lurcy Charitable and
 Educational Trust, Georges
MacArthur Foundation, John D.
 and Catherine T.
Maclellan Foundation
Mandel Foundation, Morton and
 Barbara
Manilow Foundation, Nathan

Mann Foundation, John Jay
Mann Foundation, Ted
Mardigian Foundation
Marpat Foundation
Martin Foundation
Marubeni America Corp.
Mather Charitable Trust, S.
 Livingston
McDonnell Douglas Corp.-West
McKnight Foundation
Merck Fund, John
Mettler Instrument Corp.
Meyerhoff Fund, Joseph
Mobil Oil Corp.
Mott Foundation, Charles Stewart
Nelco Sewing Machine Sales
 Corp.
New England Biolabs Foundation
New-Land Foundation
Newman's Own
Nias Foundation, Henry
Noyes Foundation, Jessie Smith
Oak Foundation U.S.A.
Ogden Foundation, Ralph E.
Ogilvy & Mather Worldwide
Ohrstrom Foundation
Open Society Fund
Overbrook Foundation
Packard Foundation, David and
 Lucile
Pfizer
Phelps Dodge Corp.
Philips Foundation, Jesse
Phillips Petroleum Co.
Phillips-Van Heusen Corp.
Pines Bridge Foundation
Pitt-Des Moines Inc.
Plitt Southern Theatres
Plumsack Fund
Posnack Family Foundation of
 Hollywood
Potomac Electric Power Co.
Potts Memorial Foundation
Preuss Foundation
Price Foundation, Louis and
 Harold
Propp Sons Fund, Morris and
 Anna
Prospect Hill Foundation
Prudential-Bache Securities
Raleigh Linen Service/National
 Distributing Co.
Raskob Foundation for Catholic
 Activities
Reidler Foundation
Relations Foundation
Richmond Foundation, Frederick
 W.
Ridgefield Foundation
Rockefeller Brothers Fund
Rockefeller Foundation
Rosenwald Family Fund, William
Rubin Foundation, Samuel
Rukin Philanthropic Foundation,
 David and Eleanore
Sacharuna Foundation
Salgo Charitable Trust, Nicholas
 M.
Sang Foundation, Elsie O. and
 Philip D.
Sara Lee Corp.
Saturno Foundation
Scaler Foundation
Schapiro Fund, M. A.
Schering-Plough Corp.
Scheuer Family Foundation, S.
 H. and Helen R.
Schimmel Foundation
Scholl Foundation, Dr.
Seabury Foundation
Seagram & Sons, Joseph E.
Shoong Foundation, Milton
Simon Foundation, William E.
 and Carol G.
Skirball Foundation
Slant/Fin Corp.
SmithKline Beecham

Soros Foundation-Hungary
Starr Foundation
Steele Foundation, Harry and
 Grace
Steinhardt Foundation, Judy and
 Michael
Stern Family Foundation, Harry
Stone Foundation, David S.
Sweatt Foundation, Harold W.
Taub Foundation, Henry and
 Marilyn
Three Swallows Foundation
Timken Foundation of Canton
Timmis Foundation, Michael &
 Nancy
Tinker Foundation
Tisch Foundation
Titan Industrial Co.
Trull Foundation
Trust Funds
Tyndale House Foundation
Union Bank of Switzerland Los
 Angeles Branch
Van Camp Foundation
Van Schaick Scholarship Fund,
 Nellie
Vetlesen Foundation, G. Unger
Volkswagen of America, Inc.
Vollmer Foundation
Von der Ahe, Jr. Trust, Theodore
 Albert
Wachovia Bank & Trust Co.,
 N.A.
Wagner Foundation, Ltd., R. H.
Wallace Genetic Foundation
Wallach Foundation, Miriam G.
 and Ira D.
Weinstein Foundation, J.
Werthan Foundation
Western Southern Life Insurance
 Co.
Westport Fund
Weyerhaeuser Family Foundation
Whittell Trust for Disabled
 Veterans of Foreign Wars, Elia
Wiener Foundation, Malcolm
 Hewitt
Wilbur-Ellis Co.
Wilkof Foundation, Edward and
 Ruth
Wolens Foundation, Kalman and
 Ida
Wunsch Foundation
Young Foundation, Irvin L.
Zemurray Foundation
Ziegler Foundation, Ruth/Allen
Zonas Trust, Steven K.

Religion

Churches
Abel Construction Co.
Abell Foundation, Charles S.
Abernethy Testamentary
 Charitable Trust, Maye
 Morrison
Abney Foundation
Abraham Foundation, Anthony R.
Ackerman Trust, Anna Keesling
Adams Memorial Fund, Emma J.
Aequus Institute
Ahmanson Foundation
Alexander Charitable Foundation
Alexander Foundation, Robert
 D. and Catherine R.
Alma Piston Co.
Alms Trust, Eleanora
Alpert Foundation, Herb
Ameribank
American Financial Corp.
American Foundation
 Corporation
American Saw & Manufacturing
 Co.
American Society of Ephesus

Amfac/JMB Hawaii
Andersen Corp.
Andersen Foundation
Anderson Charitable Trust,
 Josephine
Anderson Foundation
Anderson Foundation
Anderson Foundation, John W.
Anderson Foundation, Peyton
Anderson Foundation, Robert C.
 and Sadie G.
Andersons Management Corp.
Andreas Foundation
Annenberg Foundation
Ansley Foundation, Dantzler
 Bond
AON Corp.
Appleby Foundation
Arakelian Foundation, Mary
 Alice
Arata Brothers Trust
Arbie Mineral Feed Co.
Arcadia Foundation
Archer-Daniels-Midland Co.
Archibald Charitable
 Foundation, Norman
Argyros Foundation
Arkell Hall Foundation
Arkwright Foundation
Aron Charitable Foundation, J.
Arronson Foundation
Artevel Foundation
Asgrow Seed Co.
Asplundh Foundation
Atherton Family Foundation
Athwin Foundation
Atkinson Foundation
Atkinson Foundation, Myrtle L.
Aurora Foundation
Austin Memorial Foundation
Autzen Foundation
Azby Fund
Bailey Foundation
Bair Memorial Trust, Charles M.
Baird Brothers Co.
Baker Foundation, George T.
Baker Foundation, R. C.
Baker, Jr. Memorial Fund,
 William G.
Baker Trust, George F.
Baldwin Foundation, David M.
 and Barbara
Baldwin, Jr. Foundation,
 Summerfield
Baldwin Memorial Foundation,
 Fred
Bamberger and John Ernest
 Bamberger Memorial
 Foundation, Ruth Eleanor
Banbury Fund
Bancorp Hawaii
Banfi Vintners
Bank of Louisville
Bannan Foundation, Arline and
 Thomas J.
Bannon Foundation
Bardes Corp.
Barker Foundation, Donald R.
Barlow Family Foundation,
 Milton A. and Gloria G.
Barnett Charitable Foundation,
 Lawrence and Isabel
Barra Foundation
Barrows Foundation, Geraldine
 and R. A.
Barry Corp., R. G.
Barth Foundation, Theodore H.
Barton-Malow Co.
Bass Foundation
Bass Foundation, Harry
Bastien Memorial Foundation,
 John E. and Nellie J.
Bauer Foundation, M. R.
Baum Family Fund, Alvin H.
Bay Branch Foundation
Bayne Fund, Howard
BCR Foundation

Churches (cont.)

Beach Foundation Trust for First Baptist Church, Thomas N. and Mildred V.
Beasley Foundation, Theodore and Beulah
Beazley Foundation
Bechtel, Jr. Foundation, S. D.
Beck Foundation
Beck Foundation, Elsie E. & Joseph W.
Bedford Fund
Beeghly Fund, Leon A.
Behmann Brothers Foundation
Beinecke Foundation
Beitzell & Co.
Belk Stores
Bell Trust
Belmont Metals
Beloco Foundation
Benfamil Charitable Trust
Benua Foundation
Bere Foundation
Berger Foundation, H.N. and Frances C.
Berkey Foundation, Peter
Berkman Foundation, Louis and Sandra
Bernsen Foundation, Grace and Franklin
Berry Foundation, Lowell
Betts Industries
Beveridge Foundation, Frank Stanley
Beynon Foundation, Kathryne
Bickerton Charitable Trust, Lydia H.
Bicknell Fund
Biddle Foundation, Mary Duke
Bierhaus Foundation
Birch Foundation, Stephen and Mary
Birnschein Foundation, Alvin and Marion
Bishop Charitable Trust, A. G.
Bishop Foundation, Vernon and Doris
Bjorkman Foundation
Blackmer Foundation, Henry M.
Blanchard Foundation
Bloedel Foundation
Blount Educational and Charitable Foundation, Mildred Weedon
Bluhdorn Charitable Trust, Charles G. and Yvette
Bodine Corp.
Boeckmann Charitable Foundation
Boisi Family Foundation
Bolten Charitable Foundation, John
Bolz Family Foundation, Eugenie Mayer
Booth-Bricker Fund
Bordeaux Foundation
Borden
Borden Memorial Foundation, Mary Owen
Borman's
Borwell Charitable Foundation
Bostwick Foundation, Albert C.
Bowers Foundation
Bozzone Family Foundation
Brach Foundation, Helen
Bradley-Turner Foundation
Braun Foundation
Brencanda Foundation
Brennan Foundation, Robert E.
Breyer Foundation
Bright Charitable Trust, Alexander H.
Bright Family Foundation
Brillion Iron Works
Broadhurst Foundation

Brody Foundation, Carolyn and Kenneth D.
Bromley Residuary Trust, Guy I.
Brooklyn Benevolent Society
Brown Charitable Trust, Dora Maclellan
Brown Foundation, M. K.
Broyhill Family Foundation
Bruening Foundation, Eva L. and Joseph M.
Brunner Foundation, Fred J.
Bruno Foundation, Angelo
Bryant Foundation
Bryce Memorial Fund, William and Catherine
Buckley Trust, Thomas D.
Buell Foundation, Temple Hoyne
Buffett Foundation
Buhl Family Foundation
Burke Foundation, Thomas C.
Burkitt Foundation
Burns Foundation
Burns Foundation, Fritz B.
Burress, J.W.
Burton Foundation, William T. and Ethel Lewis
Bushee Foundation, Florence Evans
Bustard Charitable Permanent Trust Fund, Elizabeth and James
Butler Family Foundation, George W. and Gladys S.
Butler Family Foundation, Patrick and Aimee
Butler Foundation, J. Homer
Butler Manufacturing Co.
C. E. and S. Foundation
C.I.O.S.
Caddock Foundation
Caestecker Foundation, Charles and Marie
Cain Foundation, Effie and Wofford
Cain Foundation, Gordon and Mary
Calhoun Charitable Trust, Kenneth
Callaway Foundation
Callaway Foundation, Fuller E.
Callister Foundation, Paul Q.
Cameron Foundation, Harry S. and Isabel C.
Camp Younts Foundation
Campbell and Adah E. Hall Charity Fund, Bushrod H.
Campbell Foundation
Campbell Foundation
Campbell Foundation, Ruth and Henry
Candlesticks Inc.
Cannon Foundation
Carlson Cos.
Carnahan-Jackson Foundation
Carpenter Foundation, E. Rhodes and Leona B.
Carstensen Memorial Foundation, Fred R. and Hazel W.
Carter Charitable Trust, Wilbur Lee
Carter Family Foundation
Carter Foundation, Beirne
Cartinhour Foundation
Carvel Foundation, Thomas and Agnes
Cassett Foundation, Louis N.
Castle Foundation, Samuel N. and Mary
Castle Trust, George P. and Ida Tenney
Cauthorn Charitable Trust, John and Mildred
Cawsey Trust
Cayuga Foundation
Chadwick Foundation
Chadwick Fund, Dorothy Jordan
Chais Family Foundation

Chamberlin Foundation, Gerald W.
Chapin Foundation of Myrtle Beach, South Carolina
Chapman Charitable Corporation, Howard and Bess
Charitable Foundation of the Burns Family
Chase Trust, Alice P.
Childress Foundation, Francis and Miranda
Chiles Foundation
Chilton Foundation Trust
Christensen Charitable and Religious Foundation, L. C.
Christian Training Foundation
Citizens First National Bank
Clark Charitable Trust, Frank E.
Clark Family Foundation, Emory T.
Clark Foundation
Clark-Winchcole Foundation
Clarke Trust, John
Clay Foundation
Clements Foundation
Clougherty Charitable Trust, Francis H.
Cobb Family Foundation
Coen Charitable Foundation, Charles S. and Mary
Cogswell Benevolent Trust
Cohn Foundation, Herman and Terese
Cole Foundation
Coleman, Jr. Foundation, George E.
Coles Family Foundation
Collins Co.
Collins Foundation
Collins Foundation, Carr P.
Collins Foundation, George and Jennie
Collins Foundation, James M.
Collins, Jr. Foundation, George Fulton
Colonial Oil Industries, Inc.
Colt Foundation, James J.
Columbus Dispatch Printing Co.
Community Enterprises
Community Foundation
Community Hospital Foundation
Confidence Foundation
Connecticut Natural Gas Corp.
Connelly Foundation
Cook Charitable Foundation
Cook Foundation, Loring
Cook, Sr. Charitable Foundation, Kelly Gene
Cooke Foundation
Cooke Foundation Corporation, V. V.
Cord Foundation, E. L.
Cornell Trust, Peter C.
Cosmair, Inc.
Cottrell Foundation
Coughlin-Saunders Foundation
Country Curtains, Inc.
Courts Foundation
Cox Charitable Trust, A. G.
Cox Foundation
Craig Foundation, J. Paul
Craigmyle Foundation
Crail-Johnson Foundation
Crandall Memorial Foundation, J. Ford
Crane Foundation, Raymond E. and Ellen F.
Crawford Estate, E. R.
Crels Foundation
Crestlea Foundation
Crown Books Foundation, Inc.
Crown Cork & Seal Co., Inc.
Cudahy Fund, Patrick and Anna M.
Cullen/Frost Bankers
Culpeper Memorial Foundation, Daphne Seybolt
Culver Foundation, Constans

Cuneo Foundation
Dalton Foundation, Harry L.
Daly Charitable Foundation Trust, Robert and Nancy
Danis Industries
Danner Foundation
Darrah Charitable Trust, Jessie Smith
Dauch Foundation, William
Davenport-Hatch Foundation
Davidson Family Charitable Foundation
Davis Charitable Foundation, Champion McDowell
Davis Family - W.D. Charities, James E.
Davis Foundation, Edwin W. and Catherine M.
Davis Foundation, Joe C.
Davis Foundation, Ken W.
Day Foundation, Cecil B.
Debartolo Foundation, Marie P.
Dee Charitable Foundation, Lawrence T. and Janet T.
Delany Charitable Trust, Beatrice P.
Delavan Foundation, Nelson B.
Dell Foundation, Hazel
Demco Charitable Foundation
Demoulas Supermarkets
Dennett Foundation, Marie G.
Dent Family Foundation, Harry
DeRoy Foundation, Helen L.
DeRoy Testamentary Foundation
Deseranno Educational Foundation
Dettman Foundation, Leroy E.
Deuble Foundation, George H.
Devonwood Foundation
DeVore Foundation
DeVos Foundation, Richard and Helen
Dewar Foundation
Dexter Charitable Fund, Eugene A.
Dickson Foundation
Diener Foundation, Frank C.
Dillon Foundation
Dimeo Construction Co.
Dimick Foundation
Dively Foundation, George S.
Dobson Foundation
Dodge Foundation, Cleveland H.
Dodge Foundation, P. L.
Doheny Foundation, Carrie Estelle
Doherty Charitable Foundation, Henry L. and Grace
Dolan Family Foundation
Domino's Pizza
Donaldson Charitable Trust, Oliver S. and Jennie R.
Donaldson Co.
Donnelley Foundation, Elliott and Ann
Donnelley Foundation, Gaylord and Dorothy
Donnelly Foundation, Mary J.
Dorot Foundation
Doty Family Foundation
Dougherty, Jr. Foundation, James R.
Douglas Corp.
Dover Foundation
Dow Foundation, Herbert H. and Barbara C.
Downs Perpetual Charitable Trust, Ellason
Doyle Charitable Foundation
Dreyfus Foundation, Max and Victoria
Drum Foundation
Dubow Family Foundation
Duke Endowment
Duke Foundation, Doris
Dunspaugh-Dalton Foundation
duPont Foundation, Alfred I.
duPont Foundation, Chichester

duPont Fund, Jessie Ball
Dyson Foundation
Earl-Beth Foundation
Early Foundation
East Foundation, Sarita Kenedy
Eaton Foundation, Edwin M. and Gertrude S.
Ebell of Los Angeles Rest Cottage Association
Ebert Charitable Foundation, Horatio B.
Eccles Foundation, George S. and Dolores Dore
Eccles Foundation, Ralph M. and Ella M.
Edwards Foundation, Jes
Edwards Foundation, O. P. and W. E.
Einstein Fund, Albert E. and Birdie W.
Elkin Memorial Foundation, Neil Warren and William Simpson
Elkins, Jr. Foundation, Margaret and James A.
Ellis Foundation
Ellsworth Foundation, Ruth H. and Warren A.
Ellsworth Trust, W. H.
Emerson Foundation, Fred L.
Emery Memorial, Thomas J.
Engelhard Foundation, Charles
English-Bonter-Mitchell Foundation
English Foundation, W. C.
English Foundation, Walter and Marian
Enright Foundation
Ensign-Bickford Industries
Epaphroditus Foundation
Erb Lumber Co.
Erickson Charitable Fund, Eben W.
Ernest & Julio Gallo Winery
Ernsthausen Charitable Foundation, John F. and Doris E.
Erteszek Foundation
Essick Foundation
Estes Foundation
Ettinger Foundation
Evans Foundation, T. M.
Evans Foundation, Thomas J.
Everett Charitable Trust
Evjue Foundation
Ewald Foundation, H. T.
Eyman Trust, Jesse
Fabick Tractor Co., John
Fair Foundation, R. W.
Fairfield-Meeker Charitable Trust, Freeman F.
Faith Charitable Trust
Falcon Foundation
Falk Medical Research Foundation, Dr. Ralph and Marian
Fanwood Foundation
Farallon Foundation
Farish Fund, William Stamps
Farley Industries
Farwell Foundation, Drusilla
Farwell Foundation, Drusilla
Fay Charitable Fund, Aubert J.
Fenton Foundation
Ferguson Family Foundation, Kittie and Rugeley
Finch Foundation, Doak
Finch Foundation, Thomas Austin
Fingerhut Family Foundation
Finley Charitable Trust, J. B.
Finley Foundation, A. E.
Finnegan Foundation, John D.
Firan Foundation
First Fruit
Fish Foundation, Vain and Harry
Fitz-Gibbon Charitable Trust
Flatley Foundation
Florence Foundation

Flowers Charitable Trust, Albert W. and Edith V.
Foerderer Foundation, Percival E. and Ethel Brown
Fondren Foundation
Forbes
Ford Fund, Benson and Edith
Ford Fund, Eleanor and Edsel
Ford Fund, Walter and Josephine
Ford Fund, William and Martha
Ford III Memorial Foundation, Jefferson Lee
Forest Foundation
Forster-Powers Charitable Trust
Fortin Foundation of Florida
Foster Charitable Foundation, M. Stratton
Foster-Davis Foundation
Foster Foundation
Foundation for the Needs of Others
Fowler Memorial Foundation, John Edward
Fox Charitable Foundation, Harry K. & Emma R.
France Foundation, Jacob and Annita
Frank Family Foundation, A. J.
Frankino Charitable Foundation, Samuel J. and Connie
Franklin Charitable Trust, Ershel
Frazier Foundation
Frear Eleemosynary Trust, Mary D. and Walter F.
Freas Foundation
Freed Foundation
Freeman Charitable Trust, Samuel
Friends' Foundation Trust, A.
Friendship Fund
Froderman Foundation
Frohring Foundation, William O. and Gertrude Lewis
Fry Foundation, Lloyd A.
Fuchs Foundation, Gottfried & Mary
Fuchsberg Family Foundation, Abraham
Fuller Foundation
Fuller Foundation, C. G.
Fuller Foundation, George F. and Sybil H.
Funderburke & Associates
Fuqua Foundation, J. B.
Fusenot Charity Foundation, Georges and Germaine
G.A.G. Charitable Corporation
Gahagen Charitable Trust, Zella J.
Gaisman Foundation, Catherine and Henry J.
Gallagher Family Foundation, Lewis P.
Gallo Foundation, Julio R.
Garner Charitable Trust, James G.
Garvey Fund, Jean and Willard
Garvey Kansas Foundation
Garvey Texas Foundation
Garvey Trust, Olive White
Gavin Foundation, James and Zita
Gebbie Foundation
Gellert Foundation, Carl
Gellert Foundation, Celia Berta
Generation Trust
Geneseo Foundation
Genesis Foundation
Geneva Foundation
German Protestant Orphan Asylum Association
Gerstacker Foundation, Rollin M.
Getsch Family Foundation Trust
Gholston Trust, J. K.
Gibson Foundation, E. L.
Giger Foundation, Paul and Oscar
Gilbane Foundation, Thomas and William

Giles Foundation, Edward C.
Gill Foundation, Pauline Allen
Gillespie Memorial Fund, Boynton
Glancy Foundation, Lenora and Alfred
Glanville Family Foundation
Glaze Foundation, Robert and Ruth
Gleason Foundation, James
Gleason Foundation, Katherine
Gleason Works
Glencairn Foundation
Glenn Foundation, Carrie C. & Lena V.
Glenn Memorial Foundation, Wilbur Fisk
Glickenhaus & Co.
Goerlich Family Foundation
Goldbach Foundation, Ray and Marie
Goldsmith Foundation
Goodman Foundation, Edward and Marion
Goodwin Foundation, Leo
Gordon/Rousmaniere/Roberts Fund
Gore Family Memorial Foundation
Grader Foundation, K. W.
Grassmann Trust, E. J.
Gray Foundation, Garland
Greater Construction Corp. Charitable Foundation, Inc.
Greater Lansing Foundation
Green Charitable Trust, Leslie H. and Edith C.
Gregg-Graniteville Foundation
Greiner Trust, Virginia
Griffin Foundation, Rosa May
Griffin, Sr., Foundation, C. V.
Grigg-Lewis Trust
Griswold Foundation, John C.
Gronewaldt Foundation, Alice Busch
Gross Charitable Trust, Walter L. and Nell R.
GSC Enterprises
Gunderson Trust, Helen Paulson
Guse Endowment Trust, Frank J. and Adelaide
H.C.S. Foundation
Haas Foundation, Paul and Mary
Habig Foundation, Arnold F.
Hackett Foundation
Haffenreffer Family Fund
Haffner Foundation
Hagedorn Fund
Haggar Foundation
Haggerty Foundation
Hales Charitable Fund
Hallett Charitable Trust
Halloran Foundation, Mary P. Dolciani
Hallowell Foundation
Halmos Foundation
Halstead Foundation
Hamilton Bank
Hamilton Foundation, Florence P.
Hamman Foundation, George and Mary Josephine
Hand Industries
Hanes Foundation, John W. and Anna H.
Hankamer Foundation, Curtis and Doris K.
Hannon Foundation, William H.
Hansen Foundation, Dane G.
Hanson Testamentary Charitable Trust, Anna Emery
HarCo. Drug
Harden Foundation
Harding Educational and Charitable Foundation
Harding Foundation, Charles Stewart
Hargis Charitable Foundation, Estes H. and Florence Parker

Harland Co., John H.
Harmon Foundation, Pearl M. and Julia J.
Harper Brush Works
Harper Foundation, Philip S.
Harrington Trust, George
Harris Brothers Foundation
Harris Foundation
Harris Foundation, James J. and Angelia M.
Harris Foundation, John H. and Lucille
Harris Foundation, William H. and Mattie Wattis
Harrison Foundation, Fred G.
Hartz Foundation
Harvey Foundation, Felix
Hatch Charitable Trust, Margaret Milliken
Havens Foundation, O. W.
Hawkins Foundation, Robert Z.
Hawn Foundation
Hayden Foundation, William R. and Virginia
Hazen Foundation, Edward W.
Health 1st Foundation
Heath Foundation, Ed and Mary
Hechinger Co.
Hecht-Levi Foundation
Heckscher Foundation for Children
Hedrick Foundation, Frank E.
Heginbotham Trust, Will E.
Helis Foundation
Helms Foundation
Hemby Foundation, Alex
Hemingway Foundation, Robert G.
Henderson Foundation, George B.
Hendrickson Brothers
Herndon Foundation
Herndon Foundation, Alonzo F. Herndon and Norris B.
Herrick Foundation
Hersey Foundation
Hess Charitable Trust, Myrtle E. and William C.
Heydt Fund, Nan and Matilda
Hiawatha Education Foundation
Higgins Charitable Trust, Lorene Sails
High Foundation
Hill and Family Foundation, Walter Clay
Hill Crest Foundation
Hill Foundation
Hillman Foundation, Henry L.
Hills Fund, Edward E.
Hillsdale Fund
Hitchcock Foundation, Gilbert M. and Martha H.
Hobart Memorial Fund, Marion W.
Hobbs Foundation
Hobbs Foundation, Emmert
Hoffer Plastics Corp.
Hoffer Plastics Corp.
Hofheinz Foundation, Irene Cafcalas
Hofstetter Trust, Bessie
Holley Foundation
Hollis Foundation
Homasote Co.
Homeland Foundation
Hooper Foundation, Elizabeth S.
Hoover Fund-Trust, W. Henry
Hopewell Foundation
Hopkins Foundation, John Jay
Hopkins Foundation, Josephine Lawrence
Hopper Memorial Foundation, Bertrand
Hopwood Charitable Trust, John M.
Horne Trust, Mabel
Houchens Foundation, Ervin G.
Houston Endowment

Hovnanian Foundation, Hirair and Anna
Howe and Mitchell B. Howe Foundation, Lucite Horton
Howell Fund
Hoyt Foundation, Stewart W. and Willma C.
Hubbard Broadcasting
Hugoton Foundation
Huisking Foundation
Huizenga Family Foundation
Huizenga Foundation, Jennie
Hulme Charitable Foundation, Milton G.
Humphrey Foundation, Glenn & Gertrude
Hunt Alternatives Fund
Hunt Charitable Trust, C. Giles
Hunt Foundation
Hunt Foundation, Samuel P.
Hunt Trust for Episcopal Charitable Institutions, Virginia
Huntsman Foundation, Jon and Karen
Hurley Foundation, J. F.
Huston Foundation
Hutcheson Foundation, Hazel Montague
Huthsteiner Fine Arts Trust
Hutzell Foundation
Hyde and Watson Foundation
Hyde Foundation, J. R.
Hyde Manufacturing Co.
Iacocca Foundation
Illges Memorial Foundation, A. and M. L.
India Foundation
Indiana Gas and Chemical Corp.
Ingersoll Milling Machine Co.
Inman Mills
Interco
International Foundation
Iowa State Bank
Ireland Foundation
Irwin-Sweeney-Miller Foundation
Ix & Sons, Frank
J. D. B. Fund
Jacobson & Sons, Benjamin
Jaharis Family Foundation
Jameson Foundation, J. W. and Ida M.
Jasper Desk Co.
Jasper Table Co.
Jasper Wood Products Co.
Jenkins Foundation, George W.
Jennings Foundation, Alma
Jennings Foundation, Mary Hillman
Jensen Construction Co.
Jergens Foundation, Andrew
Jewett Foundation, George Frederick
Jinks Foundation, Ruth T.
Jockey Hollow Foundation
JOFCo., Inc.
Johnson Foundation, Burdine
Johnson Foundation, Howard
Johnson Fund, Edward C.
Johnston Trust for Charitable and Educational Purposes, James M.
Jones and Bessie D. Phelps Foundation, Cyrus W. and Amy F.
Jones Family Foundation, Eugenie and Joseph
Jones Foundation, Harvey and Bernice
Jones Foundation, Helen
Jones Fund, Blanche and George
Jones Intercable, Inc.
Jordan and Ettie A. Jordan Charitable Foundation, Mary Ranken
Joslin-Needham Family Foundation
Joslyn Foundation, Marcellus I.

Joukowsky Family Foundation
Journal Gazette Co.
Joy Family Foundation
Joyce Foundation, John M. and Mary A.
Kasal Charitable Trust, Father
Katzenberger Foundation
Kaufmann Foundation, Marion Esser
Kautz Family Foundation
Kavanagh Foundation, T. James
Kawabe Memorial Fund
Keating Family Foundation
Keck, Jr. Foundation, William M.
Kejr Foundation
Kellenberger Historical Foundation, May Gordon Latham
Kelley Foundation, Kate M.
Kellmer Co., Jack
Kelly Tractor Co.
Kemper Charitable Lead Trust, William T.
Kemper Charitable Trust, William T.
Kemper Foundation, Enid and Crosby
Kemper Foundation, William T.
Kemper Memorial Foundation, David Woods
Kenan, Jr. Charitable Trust, William R.
Kenedy Memorial Foundation, John G. and Marie Stella
Kennecott Corp.
Kennedy Family Foundation, Ethel and W. George
Kennedy Foundation, John R.
Kennedy Foundation, Quentin J.
Kent-Lucas Foundation
Kentland Foundation
Kerney Foundation, James
Kerr Foundation, A. H.
Kerr Foundation, Robert S. and Grayce B.
Kilcawley Fund, William H.
Killough Trust, Walter H. D.
Kilworth Charitable Foundation, Florence B.
Kimball International
Kimmelman Foundation, Helen & Milton
King Ranch
Kingsley Foundation, Lewis A.
Kinney-Lindstrom Foundation
Kirbo Charitable Trust, Thomas M. and Irene B.
Kirby Foundation, F. M.
Klau Foundation, David W. and Sadie
Klee Foundation, Conrad and Virginia
Kling Trust, Louise
Klingler Foundation, Helen and Charles
Klipstein Foundation, Ernest Christian
Knowles Charitable Memorial Trust, Gladys E.
Knox Family Foundation
Knox Foundation, Seymour H.
Knox, Sr., and Pearl Wallis Knox Charitable Foundation, Robert W.
Knudsen Charitable Foundation, Earl
Knudsen Foundation, Tom and Valley
Koch Foundation
Koch Sons, George
Koffler Family Foundation
Komes Foundation
Kopf Foundation
Kopf Foundation, Elizabeth Christy
Koulaieff Educational Fund, Trustees of Ivan Y.
Kowalski Sausage Co.

Churches (cont.)

Kress Foundation, George
Krimendahl II Foundation, H. Frederick
Kunkel Foundation, John Crain
Kuyper Foundation, Peter H. and E. Lucille Gaass
Kysor Industrial Corp.
L. L. W. W. Foundation
L and L Foundation
Laffey-McHugh Foundation
Lakeside Foundation
Lamb Foundation, Kirkland S. and Rena B.
Lane Foundation, Minnie and Bernard
Lane Memorial Foundation, Mills Bee
Lang Foundation, Eugene M.
Langendorf Foundation, Stanley S.
Lanier Brothers Foundation
Large Foundation
Lassus Brothers Oil
LaViers Foundation, Harry and Maxie
Lawrence Foundation, Lind
Leavey Foundation, Thomas and Dorothy
LeBrun Foundation
Lee Endowment Foundation
Lee Foundation, Ray M. and Mary Elizabeth
LEF Foundation
Lehrman Foundation, Jacob and Charlotte
Leighton-Oare Foundation
Lennon Foundation, Fred A.
Leonardt Foundation
Leonhardt Foundation, Dorothea L.
Leu Foundation
Leuthold Foundation
Levinson Foundation, Max and Anna
Lewis Foundation, Frank J.
Libby-Dufour Fund, Trustees of the
Liberty Hosiery Mills
Liberty National Bank
Lichtenstein Foundation, David B.
Lincoln Family Foundation
Lincolnshire
Lincy Foundation
Lindstrom Foundation, Kinney
Link, Jr. Foundation, George
Lizzadro Family Foundation, Joseph
Llagas Foundation
Lockwood Foundation, Byron W. and Alice L.
Loughran Foundation, Mary and Daniel
Louisiana Land & Exploration Co.
Loutit Foundation
Love Foundation, George H. and Margaret McClintic
Love Foundation, Lucyle S.
Lovett Foundation
Lowe Foundation, Joe and Emily
Loyola Foundation
Lozier Foundation
Luce Charitable Foundation, Stephen C.
Luchsinger Family Foundation
Luck Stone
Luckyday Foundation
Lurie Foundation, Louis R.
Lutheran Brotherhood Foundation
Luttrell Trust
Lytel Foundation, Bertha Russ
M. E. G. Foundation
M.E. Foundation

MacDonald Foundation, James A.
MacDonald Foundation, Marquis George
Maclellan Charitable Trust, R. J.
Maclellan Foundation
MacLeod Stewardship Foundation
Magee Christian Education Foundation
Magowan Family Foundation
Magruder Foundation, Chesley G.
Mailman Family Foundation, A. L.
Mandeville Foundation
Mann Foundation, John Jay
Manoogian Foundation, Alex and Marie
Mardigian Foundation
Markey Charitable Fund, John C.
Marpat Foundation
Marshall Foundation
Marshall Foundation, Mattie H.
Marshburn Foundation
Martin Family Fund
Martin Foundation
Martin Marietta Aggregates
Martini Foundation, Nicholas
Massey Charitable Trust
Massey Foundation
Massie Trust, David Meade
Mastronardi Charitable Foundation, Charles A.
Mautz Paint Co.
May Charitable Trust, Ben
Mayer Charitable Trust, Oscar G. & Elsa S.
Mazza Foundation
McAlister Charitable Foundation, Harold
McBean Charitable Trust, Alletta Morris
McCamish Foundation
McCann Foundation
McCarthy Charities
McCarthy Foundation, John and Margaret
McCarthy Foundation, Michael W.
McCasland Foundation
McCrea Foundation
McCullough Foundation, Ralph H. and Ruth J.
McDougall Charitable Trust, Ruth Camp
McEvoy Foundation, Mildred H.
McFeely-Rogers Foundation
McGraw Foundation, Curtis W.
McGraw Foundation, Donald C.
McIntosh Foundation
McIntosh Foundation
McIntyre Foundation, B. D. and Jane E.
McIntyre Foundation, C. S. and Marion F.
McKee Foundation, Robert E. and Evelyn
McLean Contributionship
McLendon Educational Fund, Violet H.
McMillan, Jr. Foundation, Bruce
McNutt Charitable Trust, Amy Shelton
McRae Foundation
McShain Charities, John
McVay Foundation
Mead Fund, Nelson
Meek Foundation
Meland Outreach
Mellen Foundation
Memton Fund
Mengle Foundation, Glenn and Ruth
Mercury Aircraft
Meredith Foundation
Mericos Foundation
Merillat Foundation, Orville D. and Ruth A.

Merrick Foundation, Robert G. and Anne M.
Merrill Foundation, R. D.
Merrion Foundation
Metal Industries
Meyer Family Foundation, Paul J.
Meyer Foundation
Meyer Foundation, Baron de Hirsch
Meyer Foundation, Bert and Mary
Meyer Foundation, George C.
Michigan Consolidated Gas Co.
Middendorf Foundation
Milbank Foundation, Dunlevy
Milken Family Medical Foundation
Milken Foundation, L. and S.
Milken Institute for Job and Capital Formation
Millbrook Tribute Garden
Miller Charitable Foundation, C. John and Reva
Miller Charitable Trust, Lewis N.
Miller-Mellor Association
Miller Memorial Trust, George Lee
Milliken & Co.
Milliken Foundation, Agnes G.
Mills Charitable Foundation, Henry L. and Kathryn
Mills Foundation, Ralph E.
Mills Fund, Frances Goll
Mitchell Foundation
Monadnock Paper Mills
Monadnock Paper Mills
Monaghan Charitable Trust, Rose
Moncrief Foundation, William A. and Elizabeth B.
Monfort Charitable Foundation
Monroe Foundation (1976), J. Edgar
Moore Foundation
Moore Foundation, C. F.
Moore Foundation, Edward S.
Moore Foundation, O. L.
Moore Memorial Foundation, James Starr
Moores Foundation, Harry C.
Moosehead Manufacturing Co.
Morania Foundation
Morgan Charitable Residual Trust, W. and E.
Morgan Foundation, Burton D.
Morgan Foundation, Louie R. and Gertrude
Morgan Trust for Charity, Religion, and Education
Morris Charitable Foundation, E. A.
Morris Foundation
Morrison Foundation, Harry W.
Morrison Trust, Louise L.
Moskowitz Foundation, Irving I.
Moss Foundation, Harry S.
Mostyn Foundation
Mulford Foundation, Vincent
Mulford Trust, Clarence E.
Mullan Foundation, Thomas F. and Clementine L.
Muller Foundation
Muller Foundation, C. John and Josephine
Munger Foundation, Alfred C.
Murdy Foundation
Murfee Endowment, Kathryn
Murphy Co., G.C.
Murphy Foundation
Murphy Foundation, Dan
Murphy Foundation, Katherine and John
Musson Charitable Foundation, R. C. and Katharine M.
Nanney Foundation, Charles and Irene
National Pro-Am Youth Fund
Nelson Foundation, Florence

New England Foundation
New York Mercantile Exchange
Noble Foundation, Vivian Bilby
Norcliffe Fund
Norgren Foundation, Carl A.
Norris Foundation, Dellora A. and Lester J.
North Carolina Foam Foundation
North Shore Foundation
Northern Star Foundation
Noyes, Jr. Memorial Foundation, Nicholas H.
O'Connor Foundation, A. Lindsay and Olive B.
O'Connor Foundation, Kathryn
O'Connor Foundation, Magee
OCRI Foundation
Oestreicher Foundation, Sylvan and Ann
O'Fallon Trust, Martin J. and Mary Anne
Offield Family Foundation
Ohrstrom Foundation
Oldham Little Church Foundation
Oliver Memorial Trust Foundation
Olsson Memorial Foundation, Elis
Onan Family Foundation
O'Neil Foundation, Cyril F. and Marie E.
O'Neil Foundation, M. G.
O'Neil Foundation, W.
O'Neill Charitable Corporation, F. J.
O'Neill Foundation, William J. and Dorothy K.
Orleton Trust Fund
Orscheln Co.
Osborn Charitable Trust, Edward B.
Osceola Foundation
O'Shaughnessy Foundation, I. A.
O'Sullivan Children Foundation
O'Toole Foundation, Theresa and Edward
Overbrook Foundation
Overlake Foundation
Overstreet Foundation
Owen Trust, B. B.
Owsley Foundation, Alvin and Lucy
Oxford Foundation
Pacific Western Foundation
Palin Foundation
Palisano Foundation, Vincent and Harriet
Palmer Fund, Francis Asbury
Palmer Fund, Frank Loomis
Pan-American Life Insurance Co.
Pappas Charitable Foundation, Thomas Anthony
Parker Drilling Co.
Parker, Jr. Foundation, William A.
Parsons - W.D. Charities, Vera Davis
Pasadena Area Residential Aid
Patterson-Barclay Memorial Foundation
Paul and C. Michael Paul Foundation, Josephine Bay
Paulucci Family Foundation
Payne Foundation, Frank E. and Seba B.
Peabody Foundation, Amelia
Pearson Foundation, E. M.
Peery Foundation
Pellegrino-Realmuto Charitable Foundation
Pendleton Memorial Fund, William L. and Ruth T.
Pennington Foundation, Irene W. and C. B.
Pennsylvania Dutch Co.
Penzance Foundation
Peppers Foundation, Ann
Perini Foundation, Joseph

Perkins Charitable Foundation
Perkins Foundation, Joe and Lois
Perkins Memorial Fund, James J. and Marie Richardson
Perkins-Prothro Foundation
Perley Fund, Victor E.
Perot Foundation
Perry-Griffin Foundation
Peters Foundation, Charles F.
Peters Foundation, Leon S.
Peters Foundation, R. D. and Linda
Petersen Foundation, Esper A.
Philibosian Foundation, Stephen
Phillipps Foundation
Phillips Charitable Trust, Dr. and Mrs. Arthur William
Phillips Foundation, A. P.
Phillips Foundation, Dr. P.
Phillips Foundation, Ellis L.
Phillips Foundation, Ellis L.
Phipps Foundation, Howard
Pierce Charitable Trust, Harold Whitworth
Pillsbury Foundation
Piper Foundation, Minnie Stevens
Piton Foundation
Pitts Foundation, William H. and Lula E.
Pitzman Fund
Plankenhorn Foundation, Harry
Plant Memorial Fund, Henry B.
Plaster Foundation, Robert W.
Plumsock Fund
Plym Foundation
Pope Foundation
Post Foundation of D.C., Marjorie Merriweather
Potomac Electric Power Co.
Pott Foundation, Herman T. and Phenie R.
Potts and Sibley Foundation
Powell Family Foundation
Prentice Foundation, Abra
Price Associates, T. Rowe
Price Foundation, Louis and Harold
Price Foundation, Lucien B. and Katherine E.
Priddy Foundation
Prince Corp.
Pritzker Foundation
Procter & Gamble Cosmetic & Fragrance Products
Proctor Trust, Mortimer R.
Prudential-Bache Securities
Puett Foundation, Nelson
Pukall Lumber
Pulitzer Publishing Co.
Quabaug Corp.
Quinlan Foundation, Elizabeth C.
Quivey-Bay State Foundation
Rachal Foundation, Ed
Ragan Charitable Foundation, Carolyn King
Ragen, Jr. Memorial Fund Trust No. 1, James M.
Raker Foundation, M. E.
Rales and Ruth Rales Foundation, Norman R.
Ransom Fidelity Company
Raskob Foundation for Catholic Activities
Rauch Foundation
Redman Foundation
Reed Foundation, Philip D.
Reeves Foundation
Reidler Foundation
Reily & Co., William B.
Reinberger Foundation
Reinhart Institutional Foods
Reinhold Foundation, Paul E. and Ida Klare
Replogle Foundation, Luther I.
Reynolds Foundation, Richard S.
Rhoades Fund, Otto L. and Hazel E.

Rhode Island Hospital Trust National Bank
Rhodebeck Charitable Trust
Rhoden Charitable Foundation, Elmer C.
Rice Charitable Foundation, Albert W.
Rice Family Foundation, Jacob and Sophie
Rice Foundation, Ethel and Raymond F.
Richardson Foundation, Frank E. and Nancy M.
Richardson Fund, Mary Lynn
Rienzi Foundation
Rinker Materials Corp.
Ritter Charitable Trust, George W. & Mary F.
Ritter Foundation, May Ellen and Gerald
River Branch Foundation
Roberts Foundation, Dora
Robinson Foundation
Robinson Fund, Maurice R.
Robison Foundation, Ellis H. and Doris B.
Robson Foundation, LaNelle
Rockwell Foundation
Rockwell Fund
Roddenberry Co., Inc., W.B.
Roddis Foundation, Hamilton
Roehl Foundation
Rogers Charitable Trust, Florence
Rogers Family Foundation
Rogers Foundation
Rogers Foundation, Mary Stuart
Rollins Luetkemeyer Charitable Foundation
Romill Foundation
RosaMary Foundation
Rosenstiel Foundation
Rosenthal Foundation, Benjamin J.
Rosenwald Family Fund, William
Ross Foundation
Ross Foundation, Arthur
Rotterman Trust, Helen L. and Marie F.
Ruddick Corp.
Rudy, Jr. Trust, George B.
Rukin Philanthropic Foundation, David and Eleanore
Russell Charitable Foundation, Tom
Ryan Foundation, David Claude
Ryan Foundation, Nina M.
Ryan Foundation, Patrick G. and Shirley W.
Sacharuna Foundation
Saemann Foundation, Franklin I.
Sage Foundation
Saint Gerard Foundation
St. Mary's Catholic Foundation
Salwil Foundation
Sams Foundation, Earl C.
Sandy Foundation, George H.
Sara Lee Hosiery
Sargent Foundation, Newell B.
Sasco Foundation
Sattler Beneficial Trust, Daniel A. and Edna J.
Saunders Charitable Foundation, Helen M.
Saunders Foundation
Sawyer Charitable Foundation
Scaler Foundation
Schey Foundation
Schieffelin Residuary Trust, Sarah I.
Schiff Foundation
Schilling Motors
Schimmel Foundation
Schiro Fund
Schmidlapp Trust No. 1, Jacob G.
Schmidt Charitable Foundation, William E.
Schneider Foundation Corp., Al J.

Scholl Foundation, Dr.
Schoonmaker J-Sewkly Valley Hospital Trust
Schowalter Foundation
Schramm Foundation
Schultz Foundation
Schust Foundation, Clarence L. and Edith B.
Schwartz Fund for Education and Health Research, Arnold and Marie
Scott Foundation, William E.
Scott, Jr. Charitable Foundation, Walter
Scurlock Foundation
Seaver Charitable Trust, Richard C.
Seaway Food Town
Seay Charitable Trust, Sarah M. and Charles E.
Semmes Foundation
Sewall Foundation, Elmina
Sewell Foundation, Warren P. and Ava F.
Sexton Foundation
Seymour and Troester Foundation
Shafer Foundation, Richard H. and Ann
Shaffer Family Charitable Trust
Share Foundation
Sharp Foundation, Charles S. and Ruth C.
Shea Co., John F.
Shea Foundation
Shea Foundation, Edmund and Mary
Shea Foundation, John and Dorothy
Shelton Cos.
Shenandoah Foundation
Sheppard Foundation, Lawrence B.
Shoney's Inc.
Shook Foundation, Barbara Ingalls
Siebert Lutheran Foundation
Simon Charitable Trust, Esther
Simon Foundation, William E. and Carol G.
Simone Foundation
Simpson Foundation
Simpson Investment Co.
Sioux Steel Co.
Slifka Foundation, Alan B.
Smith and W. Aubrey Smith Charitable Foundation, Clara Blackford
Smith Foundation, Gordon V. and Helen C.
Smith Foundation, Richard and Susan
Smock Foundation, Frank and Laura
Smucker Co., J.M.
Snite Foundation, Fred B.
Snow Foundation, John Ben
Snyder Foundation, Frost and Margaret
Snyder Foundation, Harold B. and Dorothy A.
Snyder Fund, Valentine Perry
Solheim Foundation
Solo Cup Co.
Souers Charitable Trust, Sidney W. and Sylvia N.
South Texas Charitable Foundation
Southern Furniture Co.
Special People In Need
Speer Foundation, Roy M.
Spiro Foundation, Donald W.
Sprague Educational and Charitable Foundation, Seth
Sprague, Jr. Foundation, Caryll M. and Norman F.
Springs Foundation
Stabler Foundation, Donald B. and Dorothy L.
Stackner Family Foundation

Stackpole-Hall Foundation
Stacy Foundation, Festus
Stamps Foundation, James L.
Starr Foundation
Stauffer Foundation, John and Beverly
Staunton Farm Foundation
Steinman Foundation, James Hale
Steinman Foundation, John Frederick
Stella D'Oro Biscuit Co.
Stemmons Foundation
Stephens Foundation Trust
Sterkel Trust, Justine
Stern Family Foundation, Alex
Stern Foundation, Leonard N.
Sterne-Elder Memorial Trust
Stevens Foundation, Abbot and Dorothy H.
Stevens Foundation, John T.
Stevens Foundation, Nathaniel and Elizabeth P.
Stewards Fund
Stewardship Foundation
Stewart Educational Foundation, Donnell B. and Elizabeth Dee Shaw
Stokely, Jr. Foundation, William B.
Stone Foundation, France
Stonecutter Mills Corp.
Stoneman Charitable Foundation, Anne and David
Stott Foundation, Robert L.
Stowe, Jr. Foundation, Robert Lee
Strake Foundation
Stratford Foundation
Straus Foundation, Martha Washington Straus and Harry H.
Strauss Foundation, Leon
Strong Foundation, Hattie M.
Stroud Foundation
Stry Foundation, Paul E.
Stuart Center Charitable Trust, Hugh
Stuart Foundation, Elbridge and Evelyn
Stubblefield, Estate of Joseph L.
Stupp Brothers Bridge & Iron Co.
Sudix Foundation
Sullivan Foundation, Ray H. and Pauline
Sulzer Family Foundation
Summerfield Foundation, Solon E.
Sunderland Foundation, Lester T.
Superior Tube Co.
Surrena Memorial Fund, Harry and Thelma
Sweatt Foundation, Harold W.
Swig Foundation
Synovus Financial Corp.
Tai and Co., J. T.
Tamko Asphalt Products
Taub Foundation, Joseph and Arlene
Taylor Foundation
Taylor Foundation, Fred and Harriett
Tell Foundation
Templeton Foundation, Herbert A.
Templeton Foundation, John
Terry Foundation, C. Herman
Thanksgiving Foundation
Thomas Foundation, Dorothy
Thornton Foundation
Thornton Foundation, Flora L.
Thrush-Thompson Foundation
Thurman Charitable Foundation for Children, Edgar A.
Thurston Charitable Foundation
Tibstra Charitable Foundation, Thomas and Gertrude

Timmis Foundation, Michael & Nancy
Tippit Charitable Trust, C. Carlisle and Margaret M.
Titmus Foundation
Tobin Foundation
Tomlinson Foundation, Kate and Elwyn
Tonkin Foundation, Tom and Helen
Tractor & Equipment Co.
Treakle Foundation, J. Edwin
Triford Foundation
True Trust, Henry A.
Truland Foundation
Trull Foundation
Truman Foundation, Mildred Faulkner
Trust Funds
Tucker Foundation, Marcia Brady
Turner Charitable Foundation 28:19
Tyndale House Foundation
Tyson Fund
Ukrop's Super Markets, Inc.
Union Camp Corp.
Union Foundation
Union Manufacturing Co.
United Service Foundation
U.S. Oil/Schmidt Family Foundation, Inc.
Uvas Foundation
Vale-Asche Foundation
Valentine Foundation, Lawson
Van Every Foundation, Philip L.
Van Huffel Foundation, I. J.
Van Nuys Foundation, I. N. and Susanna H.
Vanderbilt Trust, R. T.
Vanneck-Bailey Foundation
Vaughn Foundation
Vaughn, Jr. Foundation Fund, James M.
Veritas Foundation
Vermeer Investment Company Foundation
Vermeer Manufacturing Co.
Vetlesen Foundation, G. Unger
Vidda Foundation
Vidinha Charitable Trust, A. and E.
Vingo Trust II
Visciglia Foundation, Frank
Voelkerding Charitable Trust, Walter and Jean
Vollmer Foundation
Von der Ahe Foundation
Von der Ahe, Jr. Trust, Theodore Albert
Waggoner Charitable Trust, Crystelle
Wahlstrom Foundation
Walker Foundation, Archie D. and Bertha H.
Walker Foundation, L. C. and Margaret
Walker Foundation, Smith
Walker Foundation, W. E.
Walsh Foundation
Walthall Perpetual Charitable Trust, Marjorie T.
Ward Foundation, Louis L. and Adelaide C.
Wardlaw Fund, Gertrude and William C.
Ware Foundation
Warner Foundation, Lee and Rose
Warren and Beatrice W. Blanding Foundation, Riley J. and Lillian N.
Warren Charite
Warren Foundation, William K.
Warsh-Mott Legacy
Warwick Foundation
Washington Forrest Foundation
Washington Foundation
Wasily Family Foundation

Wasmer Foundation
Waters Foundation
Watkins Christian Foundation
Watumull Fund, J.
Wean Foundation, Raymond John
Weaver Foundation
Weaver Foundation, Gil and Dody
Webb Charitable Trust, Susan Mott
Webster Charitable Foundation
Webster Foundation, Edwin S.
Weckbaugh Foundation, Eleanore Mullen
Wedum Foundation
Weezie Foundation
Wehadkee Foundation
Weiler Foundation
Weinberg Foundation, John L.
Weinberg, Jr. Foundation, Sidney J.
Weininger Foundation, Richard and Gertrude
Weir Foundation Trust
Weisbrod Foundation Trust Dept., Robert and Mary
Weiss Foundation, William E.
Wendt Foundation, Margaret L.
Werner Foundation, Clara and Spencer
West Foundation
Westend Foundation
Westerman Foundation, Samuel L.
Western Shade Cloth Charitable Foundation
Western Southern Life Insurance Co.
Westport Fund
Westwood Endowment
Weyerhaeuser Memorial Foundation, Charles A.
Whalley Charitable Trust
Wharton Foundation
Wheeler Foundation, Wilmot
Wheless Foundation
Whirlpool Corp.
White Construction Co.
White Foundation, Erle and Emma
White Trust, G. R.
Whitehead Foundation
Whiteley Foundation, John and Elizabeth
Whitener Foundation
Whiting Foundation
Whiting Memorial Foundation, Henry and Harriet
Wickson-Link Memorial Foundation
Widgeon Foundation
Wilcox General Trust, George N.
Wilcox Trust, S. W.
Wildermuth Foundation, E. F.
Willard Foundation, Helen Parker
Willard Helping Fund, Cecilia Young
Williams Family Foundation of Georgia
Williams Foundation, C. K.
Williams Foundation, Edna Sproull
Willits Foundation
Willmott Foundation, Fred & Floy
Wilsey Bennet Co.
Wilson Foundation, Elaine P. and Richard U.
Wilson Foundation, Frances Wood
Wilson Foundation, Hugh and Mary
Wilson Foundation, John and Nevils
Winkler Foundation, Mark and Catherine
Wiseheart Foundation
Woltman Foundation, B. M.

Recipient Type Index

Churches (cont.)

Wood Charitable Trust, W. P.
Woodard Family Foundation
Woodland Foundation
Woods Foundation, James H.
Woods-Greer Foundation
Woodward Fund-Atlanta, David, Helen, Marian
Woolf Foundation, William C.
Word Investments
Wornall Charitable Trust and Foundation, Kearney
Wright Foundation, Lola
Wunsch Foundation
Wyne Foundation
Wyss Foundation
Yassenoff Foundation, Leo
Yeager Charitable Trust, Lester E.
Young Foundation, Irvin L.
Young Foundation, R. A.
Young Foundation, Robert R.
Zemurray Foundation
Ziegler Foundation
Zimmerman Foundation, Mary and George Herbert
Zink Foundation, John Steele
Zock Endowment Trust
Zuckerberg Foundation, Roy J.

General

Abrons Foundation, Louis and Anne
Hand Industries
Kennecott Corp.
Michael-Walters Industries
Minolta Corp.
Myers and Sons, D.
Padnos Iron & Metal Co., Louis

Missionary Activities

Aldeen Charity Trust, G. W.
Alma Piston Co.
Andersons Management Corp.
Andreas Foundation
Annenberg Foundation
Ansley Foundation, Dantzler Bond
Arbie Mineral Feed Co.
Artevel Foundation
Asgrow Seed Co.
Atkinson Foundation
Atkinson Foundation, Myrtle L.
Aurora Foundation
Bannan Foundation, Arline and Thomas J.
Bannerman Foundation, William C.
Bannon Foundation
Bauer Foundation, M. R.
Baughman Foundation
Beck Foundation, Elsie E. & Joseph W.
Beinecke Foundation
Bell Trust
Berry Foundation, Lowell
Boeckmann Charitable Foundation
Bolten Charitable Foundation, John
Bowers Foundation
Bozzone Family Foundation
Brach Foundation, Helen
Bridwell Foundation, J. S.
Brown Charitable Trust, Dora Maclellan
Bruno Foundation, Angelo
Bustard Charitable Permanent Trust Fund, Elizabeth and James
Butler Foundation, J. Homer
Caddock Foundation
Cameron Foundation, Harry S. and Isabel C.
Chartwell Foundation

Chatlos Foundation
Chilton Foundation Trust
Christian Training Foundation
Christian Workers Foundation
Clark Family Foundation, Emory T.
Clark Foundation
Collins Foundation, George and Jennie
Collins Foundation, James M.
Collins-McDonald Trust Fund
Colonial Oil Industries, Inc.
Community Enterprises
Connemara Fund
Cook Brothers Educational Fund
Cosmair, Inc.
Cottrell Foundation
Crandall Memorial Foundation, J. Ford
Crowell Trust, Henry P. and Susan C.
Dauch Foundation, William
Day Foundation, Cecil B.
DeMoss Foundation, Arthur S.
Deseranno Educational Foundation
DeVos Foundation, Richard and Helen
Diener Foundation, Frank C.
Disney Family Foundation, Roy
Douglas Charitable Foundation
Douglas Corp.
Dow Foundation, Herbert H. and Barbara C.
Drum Foundation
Edwards Foundation, Jes
Egenton Home
English Foundation, W. C.
Epaphroditus Foundation
Erickson Charitable Fund, Eben W.
Evinrude Foundation, Ralph
Fales Foundation Trust
Falk Medical Research Foundation, Dr. Ralph and Marian
Finley Charitable Trust, J. B.
First Fruit
Fish Foundation, Vain and Harry
Fleishhacker Foundation
Foster Foundation
Fox Foundation, John H.
Fruehauf Foundation
Gallagher Family Foundation, Lewis P.
Gavin Foundation, James and Zita
Generation Trust
Genesis Foundation
Gibson Foundation, E. L.
Ginter Foundation, Karl and Anna
Glaser Foundation
Glaze Foundation, Robert and Ruth
Glenmore Distilleries Co.
Glick Foundation, Eugene and Marilyn
Goldbach Foundation, Ray and Marie
Hamilton Bank
Hand Industries
Hankamer Foundation, Curtis and Doris K.
Hartz Foundation
Helis Foundation
Hersey Foundation
Hill-Snowdon Foundation
Hillsdale Fund
Homeland Foundation
Homeland Foundation
Houchens Foundation, Ervin G.
Huizenga Foundation, Jennie
Hunt Charitable Trust, C. Giles
Indiana Gas and Chemical Corp.
International Foundation
Jerome Foundation
Jones Intercable, Inc.

Kavanagh Foundation, T. James
Kejr Foundation
Kenedy Memorial Foundation, John G. and Marie Stella
Kerr Foundation, A. H.
Koch Foundation
Kutz Foundation, Milton and Hattie
Lamb Foundation, Kirkland S. and Rena B.
Lane Foundation, Minnie and Bernard
Lane Memorial Foundation, Mills Bee
Lewis Foundation, Frank J.
Libby-Dufour Fund, Trustees of the
Link, Jr. Foundation, George
Lockwood Foundation, Byron W. and Alice L.
Loridans Foundation, Charles
Loyola Foundation
Luce Charitable Trust, Theodore
Lutheran Brotherhood Foundation
M. E. G. Foundation
M.E. Foundation
Maclellan Charitable Trust, R. J.
Maclellan Foundation
Manoogian Foundation, Alex and Marie
Marriott Foundation, J. Willard
Marshburn Foundation
Martin Foundation
Mather Fund, Richard
Mazza Foundation
McCarthy Foundation, Michael W.
McDougall Charitable Trust, Ruth Camp
McGee Foundation
McGraw Foundation, Curtis W.
McMahon Charitable Trust Fund, Father John J.
McRae Foundation
Meland Outreach
Merillat Foundation, Orville D. and Ruth A.
Merrion Foundation
Millard Charitable Trust, Adah K.
Miller Charitable Foundation, C. John and Reva
Milliken Foundation, Agnes G.
Moore & Sons, B.C.
Moores Foundation, Harry C.
Morania Foundation
Morris Charitable Foundation, E. A.
Morris Foundation
Munger Foundation, Alfred C.
Nathan Foundation
Norgren Foundation, Carl A.
North Shore Foundation
Ogilvy & Mather Worldwide
O'Neil Foundation, W.
O'Neill Foundation, William J. and Dorothy K.
Overstreet Foundation
Owen Trust, B. B.
Owsley Foundation, Alvin and Lucy
Palmer Fund, Francis Asbury
Paulstan
Philibosian Foundation, Stephen
Phillips Foundation, Dr. P.
Pioneer Trust Bank, NA
Pritzker Foundation
Ragan Charitable Foundation, Carolyn King
Ragen, Jr. Memorial Fund Trust No. 1, James M.
Raskob Foundation for Catholic Activities
Richardson Fund, Mary Lynn
Roddis Foundation, Hamilton
Rolfs Foundation, Thomas J.
Rosenthal Foundation, Benjamin J.

Rotterman Trust, Helen L. and Marie F.
Ryan Family Charitable Foundation
Ryan Foundation, David Claude
S.G. Foundation
Schowalter Foundation
Sexton Foundation
SIT Investment Associates, Inc.
Snite Foundation, Fred B.
Solheim Foundation
Solo Cup Co.
Spring Arbor Distributors
Stacy Foundation, Festus
Stamps Foundation, James L.
Stephens Foundation Trust
Stewards Fund
Stewardship Foundation
Sullivan Foundation, Ray H. and Pauline
Tell Foundation
Tibstra Charitable Foundation, Thomas and Gertrude
Timmis Foundation, Michael & Nancy
Titmus Foundation
Trull Foundation
Tucker Foundation, Marcia Brady
28:19
Tyndale House Foundation
U.S. Oil/Schmidt Family Foundation, Inc.
Van Andel Foundation, Jay and Betty
Vermeer Investment Company Foundation
Visciglia Foundation, Frank
Ware Foundation
Washington Foundation
Watkins Christian Foundation
Weckbaugh Foundation, Eleanore Mullen
West Foundation
Westwood Endowment
Weyerhaeuser Foundation, Frederick and Margaret L.
Whitener Foundation
Willard Foundation, Helen Parker
Woltman Foundation, B. M.
Word Investments
Wouk Foundation, Abe
Yassenoff Foundation, Leo
Young Foundation, Irvin L.

Religious Organizations

Abelard Foundation
Abeles Foundation, Joseph and Sophia
Abney Foundation
Abraham Foundation
Abraham Foundation, Anthony R.
Abraham & Straus
Abrams Foundation
Abrams Foundation, Benjamin and Elizabeth
Abramson Family Foundation
Abroms Charitable Foundation
ACF Industries, Inc.
Action Industries, Inc.
Acushnet Co.
Aequus Institute
Aigner
Air France
Ala Vi Foundation of New York
Alco Standard Corp.
Aldeen Charity Trust, G. W.
Alexander Foundation, Joseph
Allen Brothers Foundation
Allen Foundation, Rita
Allendale Mutual Insurance Co.
Alma Piston Co.
Alperin/Hirsch Family Foundation
Altman Foundation
Altschul Foundation

Amado Foundation, Maurice
Amdur Braude Riley, Inc.
Ameribank
American Building Maintenance Industries
American Saw & Manufacturing Co.
American Society of Ephesus
Ames Department Stores
Amfac/JMB Hawaii
Amsterdam Foundation, Jack and Mimi Leviton
Andersen Corp.
Anderson Foundation
Anderson Foundation
Anderson Foundation, M. D.
Anderson Foundation, Robert C. and Sadie G.
Andersons Management Corp.
Andreas Foundation
Ansin Private Foundation, Ronald M.
AON Corp.
Applebaum Foundation
Appleby Foundation
Appleman Foundation
Arata Brothers Trust
Arbie Mineral Feed Co.
Arca Foundation
Arcadia Foundation
Archbold Charitable Trust, Adrian and Jessie
Archer-Daniels-Midland Co.
Argyros Foundation
Arkell Hall Foundation
Arkwright Foundation
Armstrong Foundation
Aron Charitable Foundation, J.
Arronson Foundation
Artevel Foundation
ASARCO
Asgrow Seed Co.
Asplundh Foundation
Associated Food Stores
Atalanta/Sosnoff Capital Corp.
Atherton Family Foundation
Atkinson Foundation
Atkinson Foundation, Myrtle L.
Atran Foundation
Attleboro Pawtucket Savings Bank
Auerbach Foundation, Beatrice Fox
Aurora Foundation
Austin Memorial Foundation
AVI CHAI - A Philanthropic Foundation
Azby Fund
Babson Foundation, Paul and Edith
Bacardi Imports
Bachmann Foundation
Baer Foundation, Alan and Marcia
Bag Bazaar, Ltd.
Bailey Foundation
Baird Charitable Trust, William Robert
Baird Foundation, Cameron
Baker & Baker
Baker Foundation, R. C.
Baker Foundation, Solomon R. and Rebecca D.
Baker Trust, Clayton
Baldwin, Jr. Foundation, Summerfield
Ball Brothers Foundation
Banc One Illinois Corp.
Banco Portugues do Atlantico, New York Branch
Banfi Vintners
Banfi Vintners
Bank Foundation, Helen and Merrill
Bank Hapoalim B.M.
Bank Leumi Trust Co. of New York
Bank of Louisville

Bannan Foundation, Arline and Thomas J.

Bannerman Foundation, William C.

Bantam Doubleday Dell Publishing Group, Inc.

Bargman Foundation, Theodore and Mina

Barnett Charitable Foundation, Lawrence and Isabel

Barra Foundation

Barry Corp., R. G.

Barstow Foundation

Bass and Edythe and Sol G. Atlas Fund, Sandra Atlas

Bastien Memorial Foundation, John E. and Nellie J.

Batts Foundation

Bauervic Foundation, Charles M.

Bauervic-Paisley Foundation

Baughman Foundation

Baum Family Fund, Alvin H.

Bay Branch Foundation

Beach Foundation Trust D for Baptist Village, Thomas N. and Mildred V.

Beaird Foundation, Charles T.

Beal Foundation

Beck Foundation, Elsie E. & Joseph W.

Beeghly Fund, Leon A.

Beerman Foundation

Behmann Brothers Foundation

Beir Foundation

Beitzell & Co.

Beitzell & Co.

Belding Heminway Co.

Belk Stores

Belk Stores

Bell Trust

Belmont Metals

Belmont Metals

Beloco Foundation

Belz Foundation

Benbough Foundation, Legler

Bender Foundation

Benenson Foundation, Frances and Benjamin

Benfamil Charitable Trust

Bennett Foundation, Carl and Dorothy

Benua Foundation

Bere Foundation

Beren Foundation, Robert M.

Berenson Charitable Foundation, Theodore W. and Evelyn

Beretta U.S.A. Corp.

Berger Foundation, Albert E.

Berger Foundation, H.N. and Frances C.

Bergstrom Manufacturing Co.

Berkman Charitable Trust, Allen H. and Selma W.

Berkman Foundation, Louis and Sandra

Berkowitz Family Foundation, Louis

Berlin Charitable Fund, Irving

Bernsen Foundation, Grace and Franklin

Bernstein & Co., Sanford C.

Bernstein Foundation, Diane and Norman

Berrie Foundation, Russell

Berry Foundation, Lowell

Bertha Foundation

Best Foundation, Walter J. and Edith E.

Bickerton Charitable Trust, Lydia H.

Biddle Foundation, Margaret T.

Bierhaus Foundation

Big V Supermarkets

Binswanger Co.

Birch Foundation, Stephen and Mary

Birmingham Foundation

Birnschein Foundation, Alvin and Marion

Bishop Foundation, Vernon and Doris

Bjorkman Foundation

Blackman Foundation, Aaron and Marie

Blade Communications

Blair Foundation, John

Blank Fund, Myron and Jacqueline

Blaustein Foundation, Jacob and Hilda

Blaustein Foundation, Louis and Henrietta

Bleibtreu Foundation, Jacob

Blinken Foundation

Bloch Foundation, Henry W. and Marion H.

Block Family Charitable Trust, Ephraim

Block Family Foundation, Emphraim

Block, H&R

Bloedel Foundation

Bloomfield Foundation, Sam and Rie

Blount

Blowitz-Ridgeway Foundation

Blue Bell, Inc.

Blue Cross & Blue Shield of Alabama

Blue Cross & Blue Shield of Kentucky Foundation

Blum Foundation, Edith C.

Blum Foundation, Harry and Maribel G.

Blum Foundation, Lois and Irving

Blum Foundation, Nathan and Emily S.

Blum-Kovler Foundation

BMW of North America, Inc.

Boatmen's First National Bank of Oklahoma

Bobst Foundation, Elmer and Mamdouha

Boeckmann Charitable Foundation

Boh Brothers Construction Co.

Bolten Charitable Foundation, John

Bolz Family Foundation, Eugenie Mayer

Booth-Bricker Fund

Borden

Borkee Hagley Foundation

Borman's

Borun Foundation, Anna Borun and Harry

Bossong Hosiery Mills

Botwinick-Wolfensohn Foundation

Boulevard Foundation

Bowers Foundation

Bowne Foundation, Robert

Bowyer Foundation, Ambrose and Gladys

Bozzone Family Foundation

Brach Foundation, Helen

Bradley-Turner Foundation

Brady Foundation, W. H.

Brand Cos.

Bravmann Foundation, Ludwig

Brencanda Foundation

Brenner Foundation

Briggs Family Foundation

Briggs Foundation, T. W.

Brinkley Foundation

British Airways

Broad Foundation, Shepard

Broadhurst Foundation

Brody Foundation, Frances

Bromley Residuary Trust, Guy I.

Bronstein Foundation, Sol and Arlene

Bronstein Foundation, Soloman and Sylvia

Brookdale Foundation

Brooklyn Benevolent Society

Brooks Brothers

Brooks Foundation, Gladys

Brotz Family Foundation, Frank G.

Brown Charitable Trust, Dora Maclellan

Brown Charitable Trust, Peter D. and Dorothy S.

Broyhill Family Foundation

Brunner Foundation, Fred J.

Brunner Foundation, Robert

Bruno Foundation, Angelo

Brush Foundation

Bryant Foundation

Bryce Memorial Fund, William and Catherine

Buchalter, Nemer, Fields, & Younger

Buhl Family Foundation

Bunbury Company

Burchfield Foundation, Charles E.

Burkitt Foundation

Burns Foundation

Burns Foundation, Fritz B.

Burns Foundation, Jacob

Burns International

Burress, J.W.

Business Incentives

Bustard Charitable Permanent Trust Fund, Elizabeth and James

Butler Family Foundation, George W. and Gladys S.

Butler Family Foundation, Patrick and Aimee

Butler Foundation, J. Homer

Bydale Foundation

C.I.O.S.

Cabell III and Maude Morgan Cabell Foundation, Robert G.

Caddock Foundation

Cahn Family Foundation

Callaway Foundation

Callister Foundation, Paul Q.

Cameron Foundation, Harry S. and Isabel C.

Cameron Memorial Fund, Alpin J. and Alpin W.

Camp Foundation

Campbell Foundation, J. Bulow

Candlesticks Inc.

Cannon Foundation

Canon U.S.A., Inc.

Cantor Foundation, Iris and B. Gerald

Capital Fund Foundation

Caplan Charity Foundation, Julius H.

Carlson Cos.

Carlyle & Co. Jewelers

Carpenter Foundation, E. Rhodes and Leona B.

Carstensen Memorial Foundation, Fred R. and Hazel W.

Carter Charitable Trust, Wilbur Lee

Carter Family Foundation

Carter Foundation, Amon G.

Cartinhour Foundation

Carylon Foundation

Casey Foundation, Eugene B.

Cassett Foundation, Louis N.

Castle Foundation, Samuel N. and Mary

Castle Trust, George P. and Ida Tenney

Cauthorn Charitable Trust, John and Mildred

Cayuga Foundation

Ceco Corp.

Cedars-Sinai Medical Center Section D Fund

Center for Educational Programs

Central Bank of the South

Central National-Gottesman

Central Soya Co.

CertainTeed Corp.

Chais Family Foundation

Chait Memorial Foundation, Sara

Chambers Development Co.

Chambers Memorial, James B.

Chapin Foundation, Frances

Chapin Foundation of Myrtle Beach, South Carolina

Charina Foundation

Charitable Foundation of the Burns Family

Chase Charity Foundation, Alfred E.

Chatham Valley Foundation

Chatlos Foundation

Chazen Foundation

Cheatham Foundation, Owen

Chernow Trust for the Benefit of Charity Dated 3/13/75, Michael

Childress Foundation, Francis and Miranda

Chiquita Brands Co.

Chisholm Foundation

Christian Training Foundation

Christian Workers Foundation

Cincinnati Foundation for the Aged

CIT Group Holdings

Citizens Bank

Citizens First National Bank

Clark Charitable Trust

Clark Charitable Trust, Frank E.

Clark Foundation

Clark-Winchcole Foundation

Clarke Trust, John

Clorox Co.

Clougherty Charitable Trust, Francis H.

Clowes Fund

Coats & Clark Inc.

Cockrell Foundation

Codrington Charitable Foundation, George W.

Coffey Foundation

Cohen Family Foundation, Saul Z. and Amy Scheuer

Cohen Foundation, George M.

Cohen Foundation, Manny and Ruthy

Cohen Foundation, Naomi and Nehemiah

Cohen Foundation, Wilfred P.

Cohn Family Foundation, Robert and Terri

Cohn Foundation, Peter A. and Elizabeth S.

Colburn Fund

Cole National Corp.

Cole Taylor Financial Group

Coleman Foundation

Collins Foundation

Collins Foundation, George and Jennie

Collins Foundation, James M.

Collins, Jr. Foundation, George Fulton

Columbia Foundation

Columbia Savings Charitable Foundation

Commerce Bancshares, Inc.

Commercial Metals Co.

Community Foundation

Community Hospital Foundation

Comprecare Foundation

Cone Mills Corp.

Connelly Foundation

Conston Corp.

Contempo Communications

Cook Brothers Educational Fund

Cook Charitable Foundation

Cook Foundation, Loring

Cook Foundation, Louella

Cooke Foundation

Copernicus Society of America

Corbin Foundation, Mary S. and David C.

Cornell Trust, Peter C.

Corpus Christi Exploration Co.

Cosmair, Inc.

Cottrell Foundation

Courts Foundation

Cove Charitable Trust

Cowden Foundation, Louetta M.

Cox Charitable Trust, A. G.

Crane Foundation, Raymond E. and Ellen F.

Cranston Print Works

Crels Foundation

CRL Inc.

Crowell Trust, Henry P. and Susan C.

Crown Charitable Fund, Edward A.

Crown Cork & Seal Co., Inc.

CTS Corp.

Cudahy Fund, Patrick and Anna M.

Cullen/Frost Bankers

Cuneo Foundation

Curran Foundation

Daily News

Dalton Foundation, Dorothy U.

Dammann Fund

Daniel Foundation, Gerard and Ruth

Danis Industries

Danner Foundation

Dart Group Corp.

Dater Foundation, Charles H.

Dauch Foundation, William

Davenport-Hatch Foundation

David-Weill Foundation, Michel

Davis Foundation, Joe C.

Davis Foundation, Ken W.

Davis Foundation, Simon and Annie

Day Foundation, Cecil B.

Daywood Foundation

DCB Corp.

de Hirsch Fund, Baron

de Kay Foundation

de Rothschild Foundation, Edmond

Decio Foundation, Arthur J.

Deer Creek Foundation

Delany Charitable Trust, Beatrice P.

Delavan Foundation, Nelson B.

DeMoss Foundation, Arthur S.

Demoulas Supermarkets

DeRoy Foundation, Helen L.

DeRoy Testamentary Foundation

Deseranno Educational Foundation

Deuble Foundation, George H.

Deutsch Co.

DeVos Foundation, Richard and Helen

Dexter Industries

Dial Corp.

Dickson Foundation

Diener Foundation, Frank C.

Dillon Foundation

Dimeo Construction Co.

Dimick Foundation

Dishman Charitable Foundation Trust, H. E. and Kate

Disney Family Foundation, Roy

Dodge Foundation, P. L.

Dodge Foundation, P. L.

Doheny Foundation, Carrie Estelle

Domino of California

Domino's Pizza

Donaldson Charitable Trust, Oliver S. and Jennie R.

Donaldson Co.

Donnelley Foundation, Elliott and Ann

Donnelley Foundation, Gaylord and Dorothy

Donnelly Foundation, Mary J.

Dorot Foundation

Religious Organizations (cont.)

Doss Foundation, M. S.
Doty Family Foundation
Dougherty, Jr. Foundation, James R.
Douglas Charitable Foundation
Douglas Corp.
Douglas & Lomason Company
Dover Foundation
Dow Foundation, Herbert H. and Barbara C.
Dower Foundation, Thomas W.
Downs Perpetual Charitable Trust, Ellason
Dreitzer Foundation
Dresser Industries
Driehaus Foundation, Richard H.
Drum Foundation
Dubow Family Foundation
Dula Educational and Charitable Foundation, Caleb C. and Julia W.
Duncan Foundation, Lillian H. and C. W.
Dunspaugh-Dalton Foundation
Dupar Foundation
duPont Foundation, Alfred I.
duPont Fund, Jessie Ball
Durst Foundation
Durst Foundation
Dweck Foundation, Samuel R.
E and M Charities
Early Foundation
East Foundation, Sarita Kenedy
Eaton Foundation, Edwin M. and Gertrude S.
Ebell of Los Angeles Rest Cottage Association
Ebert Charitable Foundation, Horatio B.
Eckman Charitable Foundation, Samuel and Rae
Eden Hall Foundation
Eder Foundation, Sidney and Arthur
Edison Foundation, Harry
Edison Foundation, Irving and Beatrice C.
Edouard Foundation
Edwards Foundation, Jes
Edwards Foundation, O. P. and W. E.
Egerton Home
Ehrman Foundation, Fred and Susan
Einstein Fund, Albert E. and Birdie W.
EIS Foundation
Eisenberg Foundation, Ben B. and Joyce E.
Eisenberg Foundation, George M.
El-An Foundation
Elco Charitable Foundation
Elkin Memorial Foundation, Neil Warren and William Simpson
Elkins, Jr. Foundation, Margaret and James A.
Ellis Foundation
Ellis Grant and Scholarship Fund, Charles E.
Ellsworth Trust, W. H.
EMI Records Group
Engelhard Foundation, Charles
English-Bonter-Mitchell Foundation
English Foundation, W. C.
English Memorial Fund, Florence C. and H. L.
Enright Foundation
Epaphroditus Foundation
Equitable Life Assurance Society of the U.S.
Erb Lumber Co.
Erickson Charitable Fund, Eben W.

Ernest & Julio Gallo Winery
Erving Paper Mills
Essel Foundation
Evinrude Foundation, Ralph
Ewald Foundation, H. T.
Eyman Trust, Jesse
FAB Industries
Fabick Tractor Co., John
Fabri-Kal Corp.
Fair Foundation, R. W.
Fair Oaks Foundation, Inc.
Fairchild Corp.
Fairfield Foundation, Freeman E.
Faith Charitable Trust
Fales Foundation Trust
Falk Foundation, Michael David
Falk Medical Research Foundation, Dr. Ralph and Marian
Fanwood Foundation
Farish Fund, William Stamps
Farnsworth Trust, Charles A.
Farwell Foundation, Drusilla
Fay Charitable Fund, Aubert J.
Federation Foundation of Greater Philadelphia
Feil Foundation, Louis and Gertrude
Feild Co-Operative Association
Fein Foundation
Feinstein Foundation, Myer and Rosaline
Feintech Foundation
Feldberg Family Foundation
Feldman Foundation
Fellner Memorial Foundation, Leopold and Clara M.
Fenton Foundation
Ferkauf Foundation, Eugene and Estelle
Fife Foundation, Elias and Bertha
Fifth Third Bancorp
Fig Tree Foundation
Filene Foundation, Lincoln and Therese
Fingerhut Family Foundation
Fink Foundation
Finley Charitable Trust, J. B.
Finnegan Foundation, John D.
Firan Foundation
Fireman Charitable Foundation, Paul and Phyllis
Firestone, Jr. Foundation, Harvey
First Fidelity Bancorporation
First Fruit
First Maryland Bancorp
First Mississippi Corp.
First Petroleum Corp.
Fischbach Foundation
Fischel Foundation, Harry and Jane
Fish Foundation, Ray C.
Fish Foundation, Vain and Harry
Fisher Foundation
Fisher Foundation, Max M. and Marjorie S.
Fishoff Family Foundation
Fitz-Gibbon Charitable Trust
Flagler Foundation
Flatley Foundation
Fleishhacker Foundation
Flemm Foundation, John J.
Flickinger Memorial Trust
Florence Foundation
Florida Steel Corp.
Fogel Foundation, Shalom and Rebecca
Fohs Foundation
Folger Fund
Forbes
Forbes Charitable Trust, Herman
Forchheimer Foundation
Ford Foundation
Ford Foundation, Joseph F. and Clara
Ford Fund, Benson and Edith
Ford Fund, Walter and Josephine

Ford III Memorial Foundation, Jefferson Lee
Forest Foundation
Forest Lawn Foundation
Formrite Tube Co.
Forster-Powers Charitable Trust
Fortin Foundation of Florida
Foster Charitable Foundation, M. Stratton
Foster Charitable Trust
Foster Foundation
Foster Foundation, Joseph C. and Esther
Foundation for Middle East Peace
Fox Charitable Foundation, Harry K. & Emma R.
Fox Foundation, Richard J.
Fox Steel Co.
Fraida Foundation
Frank Family Foundation, A. J.
Frank Foundation, Ernest and Elfriede
Frank Fund, Zollie and Elaine
Frankel Foundation, George and Elizabeth F.
Franklin Charitable Trust, Ershel
Frazier Foundation
Frear Eleemosynary Trust, Mary D. and Walter F.
Freed Foundation
Freeman Foundation, Carl M.
Frees Foundation
Fribourg Foundation
Friedland Family Foundation, Samuel
Friedman Brothers Foundation
Friedman Family Foundation
Friedman Foundation, Stephen and Barbara
Friendly Rosenthal Foundation
Friendship Fund
Frisch's Restaurants Inc.
Froderman Foundation
Fruchthandler Foundation, Alex and Ruth
Fruehauf Foundation
Fuchs Foundation, Gottfried & Mary
Fuchsberg Family Foundation
Fuchsberg Family Foundation, Abraham
Fuller Foundation
Fuller Foundation, C. G.
Fuller Foundation, George F. and Sybil H.
Funderburke & Associates
Furth Foundation
G.A.G. Charitable Corporation
Gage Foundation, Philip and Irene Toll
Gaisman Foundation, Catherine and Henry J.
Galkin Charitable Trust, Ira S. and Anna
Gallagher Family Foundation, Lewis P.
Gallo Foundation, Julio R.
Galter Foundation
Galvin Foundation, Robert W.
Garfinkle Family Foundation
Garner Charitable Trust, James G.
Garvey Texas Foundation
Gavin Foundation, James and Zita
Gavin Foundation, James and Zita
Geifman Family Foundation
Geist Foundation
Gellert Foundation, Celia Berta
Gelman Foundation, Melvin and Estelle
Generation Trust
Genesis Foundation
Geneva Foundation
Gerlach Foundation

German Protestant Orphan Asylum Association
Gershenson Foundation, Charles H.
Gershman Foundation, Joel
Gerson Family Foundation, Benjamin J.
Gerson Trust, B. Milfred
Getsch Family Foundation Trust
Giant Eagle
Giant Food
Giant Food Stores
Gibson Foundation, E. L.
Gifford Charitable Corporation, Rosamond
Giger Foundation, Paul and Oscar
Gilbane Foundation, Thomas and William
Giles Foundation, Edward C.
Gillette Co.
Gilman, Jr. Foundation, Sondra and Charles
Gilmore Foundation, Earl B.
Gindi Associates Foundation
Ginsberg Family Foundation, Moses
Ginter Foundation, Karl and Anna
Gitano Group
Glaze Foundation, Robert and Ruth
Glazer Foundation, Jerome S.
Glazer Foundation, Madelyn L.
Gleason Foundation, James
Glenmore Distilleries Co.
Glick Foundation, Eugene and Marilyn
Glickenhaus & Co.
Glosser Foundation, David A.
Goerlich Family Foundation
Goldbach Foundation, Ray and Marie
Goldberg Family Foundation
Goldberg Family Foundation, Israel and Matilda
Goldberg Family Foundation, Milton D. and Madeline L.
Goldberger Foundation, Edward and Marjorie
Goldie-Anna Charitable Trust
Goldman Charitable Trust, Sol
Goldman Foundation, Aaron and Cecile
Goldman Foundation, Herman
Goldman Foundation, William
Goldring Family Foundation
Goldsmith Family Foundation
Goldsmith Foundation
Goldstein Foundation, Alfred and Ann
Goldstein Foundation, Leslie and Roslyn
Golub Corp.
Goodman Family Foundation
Goodman Foundation, Edward and Marion
Goodman Memorial Foundation, Joseph C. and Clare F.
Goodstein Family Foundation, David
Goodstein Foundation
Goodyear Foundation, Josephine
Goody's Manufacturing Corp.
Gordon Charitable Trust, Peggy and Yale
Gordon Foundation, Meyer and Ida
Gore Family Memorial Foundation
Gorin Foundation, Nehemiah
Gottesman Fund
Grader Foundation, K. W.
Gradison & Co.
Grant Foundation, Charles M. and Mary D.
Grass Family Foundation
Grassmann Trust, E. J.
Graybar Electric Co.

Greater Construction Corp. Charitable Foundation, Inc.
Greeley Gas Co.
Green Foundation, Allen P. and Josephine B.
Green Fund
Greenberg Foundation, Alan C.
Greene Foundation, David J.
Greene Foundation, Jerome L.
Greene Foundation, Robert Z.
Greenspan Foundation
Greenville Foundation
Gregg-Graniteville Foundation
Gries Charity Fund, Lucile and Robert H.
Griffin Foundation, Rosa May
Griffin, Sr., Foundation, C. V.
Griffith Foundation, W. C.
Grigg-Lewis Trust
Groome Beatty Trust, Helen D.
Grossman Foundation, N. Bud
Group Health Plan Inc.
Gruber Research Foundation, Lila
Grumbacher Foundation, M. S.
Gruss Charitable and Educational Foundation, Oscar and Regina
Gruss Charitable Foundation, Emanuel and Riane
Gucci America Inc.
Gudelsky Family Foundation, Homer and Martha
Gudelsky Family Foundation, Isadore and Bertha
Guggenheim Foundation, Daniel and Florence
Gulton Foundation
Gurwin Foundation, J.
Guse Endowment Trust, Frank J. and Adelaide
Gussman Foundation, Herbert and Roseline
Guttag Foundation, Irwin and Marjorie
Guttman Foundation, Stella and Charles
H.C.S. Foundation
Haas Foundation, Paul and Mary
Habig Foundation, Arnold F.
Hackett Foundation
Hagedorn Fund
Haggar Foundation
Haggerty Foundation
Haigh-Scatena Foundation
Hale Foundation, Crescent Porter
Hallett Charitable Trust, Jessie F.
Halsell Foundation, O. L.
Hamilton Bank
Hamman Foundation, George and Mary Josephine
Hammer Foundation, Armand
Hand Industries
Handleman Co.
Hanes Foundation, John W. and Anna H.
Hankamer Foundation, Curtis and Doris K.
Hannon Foundation, William H.
Hanson Testamentary Charitable Trust, Anna Emery
HarCo. Drug
Harding Foundation, Charles Stewart
Hargis Charitable Foundation, Estes H. and Florence Parker
Harland Co., John H.
Harmon Foundation, Pearl M. and Julia J.
Harris Family Foundation, Hunt and Diane
Harris Foundation, J. Ira and Nicki
Hartman Foundation, Jesse and Dorothy
Hartmarx Corp.
Hartz Foundation
Hartzell Industries, Inc.

Harvey Foundation, Felix
Hassenfeld Foundation
Havens Foundation, O. W.
Hawkins Foundation, Robert Z.
Hawley Foundation
Hayden Foundation, William R. and Virginia
Hayswood Foundation
Hazen Charitable Trust, Lita Annenberg
Hazen Foundation, Edward W.
Heath Foundation, Ed and Mary
Hebrew Technical Institute
Hechinger Co.
Hecht-Levi Foundation
Hedrick Foundation, Frank E.
Heilicher Foundation, Menahem
Heinz Co., H.J.
Heinz Endowment, Vira I.
Helfaer Foundation, Evan and Marion
Helis Foundation
Helms Foundation
Helzberg Foundation, Shirley and Barnett
Hemingway Foundation, Robert G.
Hendrickson Brothers
Henry Foundation, Patrick
Heritage Foundation
Herman Foundation, John and Rose
Herrick Foundation
Herschend Family Foundation
Herzstein Charitable Foundation, Albert and Ethel
Hess Charitable Foundation, Ronne and Donald
Hess Foundation
Heymann Special Account, Mr. and Mrs. Jimmy
Hidary Foundation, Jacob
Higginson Trust, Corina
Hill Crest Foundation
Hill Foundation
Hill-Snowdon Foundation
Hillman Family Foundation, Alex
Hillman Foundation
Hillsdale Fund
Hirschhorn Foundation, David and Barbara B.
Hobbs Foundation
Hobby Foundation
Hodge Foundation
Hoffberger Foundation
Hoffman Foundation, H. Leslie Hoffman and Elaine S.
Hoffman Foundation, Marion O. and Maximilian
Hofheinz Foundation, Irene Cafcalas
Holtzmann Foundation, Jacob L. and Lillian
Holzer Memorial Foundation, Richard H.
Homeland Foundation
Homeland Foundation
Honigman Foundation
Hooker Charitable Trust, Janet A.
Hoover Foundation
Hoover Foundation, H. Earl
Hopeman Brothers
Hopkins Foundation, John Jay
Hopkins Foundation, Josephine Lawrence
Hopper Memorial Foundation, Bertrand
Horncrest Foundation
Horowitz Foundation, Gedale B. and Barbara S.
Hospital Corp. of America
House of Gross
Houston Endowment
Hovnanian Foundation, Hirair and Anna
Hubbell Inc.
Hudson Neckwear

Hughes Charitable Trust, Mabel Y.
Hugoton Foundation
Huisking Foundation
Huizenga Family Foundation
Huizenga Foundation, Jennie
Hulme Charitable Foundation, Milton G.
Hume Foundation, Jaquelin
Hunt Trust for Episcopal Charitable Institutions, Virginia
Hurford Foundation
Hurley Foundation, J. F.
Huston Charitable Trust, Stewart
Huston Foundation
Hutcheson Foundation, Hazel Montague
Hutchins Foundation, Mary J.
Hutzell Foundation
Hyde and Watson Foundation
Hyde Foundation, J. R.
I. and L. Association
I and G Charitable Foundation
Illges Memorial Foundation, A. and M. L.
Imerman Memorial Foundation, Stanley
In His Name
India Foundation
Indiana Desk Co.
Indiana Gas and Chemical Corp.
Ingersoll Milling Machine Co.
Inman Mills
Innovating Worthy Projects Foundation
Interco
Interstate Packaging Co.
Ix & Sons, Frank
J. D. B. Fund
Jackson Family Foundation, Ann
Jacobson Foundation, Bernard H. and Blanche E.
Jacobson & Sons, Benjamin
Jacoby Foundation, Lela Beren and Norman
Jaffe Foundation
Jaharis Family Foundation
Jameson Foundation, J. W. and Ida M.
Janssen Foundation, Henry
Jarson-Stanley and Mickey Kaplan Foundation, Isaac & Esther
Jasam Foundation
Jasper Desk Co.
Jasper Table Co.
Jasper Wood Products Co.
Jaydor Corp.
Jellison Benevolent Society
Jenkins Foundation, George W.
Jennings Foundation, Alma
Jennings Foundation, Mary Hillman
Jensen Construction Co.
Jerome Foundation
Jesselson Foundation
Jinks Foundation, Ruth T.
JMK-A M Micallef Charitable Foundation
JOFCo., Inc.
Johnson Fund, Edward C.
Johnston-Fix Foundation
Johnston-Hanson Foundation
Jones Charitable Trust, Harvey and Bernice
Jones Foundation, Harvey and Bernice
Jones Foundation, Montfort Jones and Allie Brown
Jones Fund, Blanche and George
Jones Intercable, Inc.
Joselow Foundation
Joslin-Needham Family Foundation
Joukowsky Family Foundation
Journal Gazette Co.
Joyce Foundation, John M. and Mary A.

JSJ Corp.
Jurodin Fund
Jurzykowski Foundation, Alfred
Kahn Memorial Trust
Kaiser Foundation, Betty E. and George B.
Kangesser Foundation, Robert E., Harry A., and M. Sylvia
Kapiloff Foundation, Leonard
Kaplan Foundation, Charles I. and Mary
Kaplan Foundation, Mayer and Morris
Kaplan Foundation, Rita J. and Stanley H.
Kaplen Foundation
Kaplun Foundation, Morris J. and Betty
Kasal Charitable Trust, Father
Kasle Steel Corp.
Katten, Muchin, & Zavis
Katzenberger Foundation
Kaufman Foundation, Henry & Elaine
Kaufman Memorial Trust, Chaim, Fanny, Louis, Benjamin, and Anne Florence
Kaufmann Foundation, Henry
Kavanagh Foundation, T. James
Kawabe Memorial Fund
Kayser Foundation
Keating Family Foundation
Keebler Co.
Keene Trust, Hazel R.
Keith Foundation Trust, Ben E.
Kejr Foundation
Keller Family Foundation
Kelley Foundation, Kate M.
Kellmer Co., Jack
Kellogg's
Kelly Tractor Co.
Kemper Foundation, Enid and Crosby
Kemper Memorial Foundation, David Woods
Kenedy Memorial Foundation, John G. and Marie Stella
Kennecott Corp.
Kennedy Foundation, John R.
Kennedy Foundation, Quentin J.
Kentland Foundation
Kepco, Inc.
Kern Foundation Trust
Kerr Foundation, A. H.
Kerr Foundation, Robert S. and Grayce B.
Kerr-McGee Corp.
Kest Family Foundation, Sol and Clara
Kevorkian Fund, Hagop
Key Food Stores Cooperative Inc.
Kiewit Foundation, Peter
Kilcawley Fund, William H.
Killough Trust, Walter H. D.
Kilroy Foundation, William S. and Lora Jean
Kilworth Charitable Foundation, Florence B.
Kimball Co., Miles
Kimball International
Kimmelman Foundation, Helen & Milton
King Ranch
Kirbo Charitable Trust, Thomas M. and Irene B.
Kirby Foundation, F. M.
Kirkland & Ellis
Klau Foundation, David W. and Sadie
Klee Foundation, Conrad and Virginia
Klein Fund, Nathan J.
Kline Foundation, Charles and Figa
Klipstein Foundation, Ernest Christian
Klosk Fund, Louis and Rose

Knott Foundation, Marion I. and Henry J.
Knox, Sr., and Pearl Wallis Knox Charitable Foundation, Robert W.
Knudsen Charitable Foundation, Earl
Knudsen Foundation, Tom and Valley
Kobacker Co.
Koch Foundation
Koch Sons, George
Koffler Family Foundation
Kohl Charitable Foundation, Allen D.
Kohl Charities, Herbert H.
Kohl Foundation, Sidney
Kohn-Joseloff Fund
Komes Foundation
Koopman Fund
Kopf Foundation, Elizabeth Christy
Koret Foundation
Korman Family Foundation, Hyman
Kowalski Sausage Co.
Kramer Foundation
Kramer Foundation, C. L. C.
Kravis Foundation, Henry R.
Kress Foundation, George
Kugelman Foundation
Kutz Foundation, Milton and Hattie
Kuyper Foundation, Peter H. and E. Lucille Gaass
Kysor Industrial Corp.
Lacy Foundation
Ladish Co.
Laffey-McHugh Foundation
Lakeside Foundation
Lamb Foundation, Kirkland S. and Rena B.
Lane Foundation, Minnie and Bernard
Langdale Co.
Langendorf Foundation, Stanley S.
Lapham-Hickey Steel Corp.
Larsh Foundation Charitable Trust
Lasdon Foundation
Lasky Co.
Lassus Brothers Oil
Lastfogel Foundation, Abe and Frances
Lautenberg Foundation
Lavanburg-Corner House
LaViers Foundation, Harry and Maxie
Law Foundation, Robert O.
Lawrence Foundation, Alice
Lazar Foundation
Leavey Foundation, Thomas and Dorothy
Lebovitz Fund
LeBrun Foundation
Lederer Foundation, Francis L.
Lee Foundation, James T.
Legg Mason Inc.
Lehmann Foundation, Otto W.
Lehrman Foundation, Jacob and Charlotte
Leibovitz Foundation, Morris P.
Leidy Foundation, John J.
Leighton-Oare Foundation
Lemberg Foundation
Lender Family Foundation
Lennon Foundation, Fred A.
Leonardt Foundation
Leu Foundation
Leu Foundation, Harry P.
Leucadia National Corp.
Leuthold Foundation
Levin Foundation, Philip and Janice
Levine Family Foundation, Hyman

Levinson Foundation, Max and Anna
Levinson Foundation, Morris L.
Levit Family Foundation, Joe
Leviton Manufacturing Co.
Levitt Foundation
Levitt Foundation, Richard S.
Levy Foundation, Betty and Norman F.
Levy Foundation, Charles and Ruth
Levy Foundation, Edward C.
Levy Foundation, Hyman Jebb
Levy Foundation, June Rockwell
Levy's Lumber & Building Centers
Lewis Foundation, Frank J.
Lewis Foundation, Lillian Kaiser
Libby-Dufour Fund, Trustees of the
Liberman Foundation, Bertha & Isaac
Liberty Diversified Industries Inc.
Liberty Hosiery Mills
Lichtenstein Foundation, David B.
Lieberman Enterprises
Lightner Sams Foundation
Lilly Endowment
Lincoln Family Foundation
Lincy Foundation
Lindner Foundation, Fay J.
Link, Jr. Foundation, George
Lipsky Foundation, Fred and Sarah
Lipton Foundation
List Foundation, Albert A.
Littauer Foundation, Lucius N.
Livingston Foundation, Milton S. and Corinne N.
Livingston Memorial Foundation
Lizzadro Family Foundation, Joseph
Loeb Foundation, Frances and John L.
Loewenberg Foundation
Loose Trust, Carrie J.
Lopata Foundation, Stanley and Lucy
Louis Foundation, Michael W.
Louisiana Land & Exploration Co.
Loutit Foundation
Lowe Foundation, Joe and Emily
Lowenstein Brothers Foundation
Lowenstein Foundation, William P. and Marie R.
Loyola Foundation
Lubo Fund
Luce Charitable Foundation, Stephen C.
Luce Foundation, Henry
Luckyday Foundation
Ludwick Institute
Lupin Foundation
Lurcy Charitable and Educational Trust, Georges
Lutheran Brotherhood Foundation
Lyons Foundation
M. E. G. Foundation
M.E. Foundation
M.T.D. Products
Maas Foundation, Benard L.
Mabee Foundation, J. E. and L. E.
MacDonald Foundation, James A.
MacDonald Foundation, Marquis George
Mack Foundation, J. S.
Maclellan Charitable Trust, R. J.
Maclellan Foundation
Maclellan Foundation, Robert L. and Kathrina H.
MacLeod Stewardship Foundation
Maddox Foundation, J. F.

Recipient Type Index

Religious Organizations (cont.)

Recipient Type Index

Religious Organizations (cont.)

Ware Foundation
Warner Fund, Albert and Bessie
Warren and Beatrice W. Blanding Foundation, Riley J. and Lillian N.
Warren Charite
Warren Foundation, William K.
Warsh-Mott Legacy
Washington Forrest Foundation
Washington Foundation
Wasmer Foundation
Wasserman Foundation
Wasserman Foundation, George
Watkins Christian Foundation
Watumull Fund, J.
Wausau Paper Mills Co.
Wauwatosa Savings & Loan Association
Wean Foundation, Raymond John
Weaver Foundation, Gil and Dody
Webb Educational and Charitable Trust, Torrey H. and Dorothy K.
Webb Foundation
Webster Charitable Foundation
Weckbaugh Foundation, Eleanore Mullen
Wedum Foundation
Weezie Foundation
Wegener Foundation, Herman and Mary
Weil, Gotshal & Manges Foundation
Weiler Foundation, Theodore & Renee
Weinberg Foundation, John L.
Weinberg, Jr. Foundation, Sidney J.
Weiner Foundation
Weininger Foundation, Richard and Gertrude
Weinstein Foundation, Alex J.
Weinstein Foundation, J.
Weintraub Family Foundation, Joseph
Weiss Foundation, Stephen and Suzanne
Weisz Foundation, David and Sylvia
Wellons Foundation
Wells Foundation, Franklin H. and Ruth L.
Wendt Foundation, Margaret L.
Werblow Charitable Trust, Nina W.
Werner Foundation, Clara and Spencer
Werthan Foundation
West Co.
West Texas Corp., J. M.
Western Shade Cloth Charitable Foundation
Western Southern Life Insurance Co.
Westwood Endowment
Wexner Foundation
Weyerhaeuser Foundation, Frederick and Margaret L.
Wharton Foundation
Wheeler Foundation
Wheeler Foundation, Wilmot
Whirlpool Corp.
Whitaker Charitable Foundation, Lyndon C.
White Coffee Pot Family Inns
White Foundation, Erle and Emma
White Trust, G. R.
Whiteley Foundation, John and Elizabeth
Whitener Foundation
Whiting Memorial Foundation, Henry and Harriet

Whitney Fund, David M.
Widgeon Foundation
Wien Foundation, Lawrence A.
Wildermuth Foundation, E. F.
Wilf Family Foundation
Wilkof Foundation, Edward and Ruth
Willard Helping Fund, Cecilia Young
Williams Charitable Trust, John C.
Williams Foundation, Edna Sproull
Wilsey Bennet Co.
Wilson Foundation, Hugh and Mary
Wilson Public Trust, Ralph
Winston Research Foundation, Harry
Wisdom Foundation, Mary F.
Wiseheart Foundation
Witco Corp.
Woldenberg Foundation
Wolens Foundation, Kalman and Ida
Wolf Foundation, Melvin and Elaine
Wolff Memorial Foundation, Pauline Sterne
Wolff Shoe Co.
Wolfson Family Foundation
Wollenberg Foundation
Woltman Foundation, B. M.
Wolverine World Wide, Inc.
Woman's Seamen's Friend Society of Connecticut
Wood Charitable Trust, W. P.
Woods Foundation, James H.
Woods-Greer Foundation
Woodward Fund-Atlanta, David, Helen, Marian
Woolf Foundation, William C.
Word Investments
Wornall Charitable Trust and Foundation, Kearney
Wouk Foundation, Abe
Wrape Family Charitable Trust
Wunsch Foundation
Wurts Memorial, Henrietta Tower
Wurzburg, Inc.
Wyne Foundation
Wyomissing Foundation
Wyss Foundation
XTEK Inc.
Xtra Corp.
Yassenoff Foundation, Leo
Young Foundation, Irvin L.
Young Foundation, R. A.
Young & Rubicam
Youth Foundation
Yulman Trust, Morton and Helen
Yulman Trust, Morton and Helen
Zaban Foundation
Zacharia Foundation, Isaac Herman
Zale Foundation
Zale Foundation, William and Sylvia
Zamoiski Co.
Zarkin Memorial Foundation, Charles
Zenkel Foundation
Ziegler Foundation for the Blind, E. Matilda
Ziegler Foundation, Ruth/Allen
Zilkha & Sons
Zimmerman Family Foundation, Raymond
Zuckerberg Foundation, Roy J.

Synagogues

Abrams Foundation
Abrams Foundation, Benjamin and Elizabeth
Abramson Family Foundation
Abroms Charitable Foundation
Ahmanson Foundation

Alexander Foundation, Joseph
Alperin/Hirsch Family Foundation
Amado Foundation, Maurice
Ames Department Stores
Amfac/JMB Hawaii
Annenberg Foundation
Ansin Private Foundation, Ronald M.
Applebaum Foundation
Appleman Foundation
Arakelian Foundation, Mary Alice
Aron Charitable Foundation, J.
Asgrow Seed Co.
AVI CHAI - A Philanthropic Foundation
Baer Foundation, Alan and Marcia
Baker Foundation, Solomon R. and Rebecca D.
Barry Corp., R. G.
Bass and Edythe and Sol G. Atlas Fund, Sandra Atlas
Baum Family Fund, Alvin H.
Beerman Foundation
Beir Foundation
Belding Heminway Co.
Belfer Foundation
Belz Foundation
Bennett Foundation, Carl and Dorothy
Berenson Charitable Foundation, Theodore W. and Evelyn
Berkman Charitable Trust, Allen H. and Selma W.
Berkman Foundation, Louis and Sandra
Berkowitz Family Foundation, Louis
Bernstein & Co., Sanford C.
Blackman Foundation, Aaron and Marie
Blank Family Foundation
Blaustein Foundation, Jacob and Hilda
Bloch Foundation, Henry W. and Marion H.
Bloomfield Foundation, Sam and Rie
Blowitz-Ridgeway Foundation
Blum Foundation, Harry and Maribel G.
Blum-Kovler Foundation
Borman's
Braun Foundation
Bravmann Foundation, Ludwig
Brenner Foundation
Broad Foundation, Shepard
Brody Foundation, Frances
Bronstein Foundation, Sol and Arlene
Bronstein Foundation, Soloman and Sylvia
Brown Charitable Trust, Peter D. and Dorothy S.
Buchalter, Nemer, Fields, & Younger
Burns Foundation, Fritz B.
Burns Foundation, Jacob
Cantor Foundation, Iris and B. Gerald
Capital Fund Foundation
Caplan Charity Foundation, Julius H.
Carnival Cruise Lines
Carylon Foundation
Cedars-Sinai Medical Center Section D Fund
Chapin Foundation of Myrtle Beach, South Carolina
Charina Foundation
Chatham Valley Foundation
Chazen Foundation
Cheatham Foundation, Owen
Chernow Trust for the Benefit of Charity Dated 3/13/75, Michael
Cohen Foundation, George M.

Cohen Foundation, Manny and Ruthy
Cohen Foundation, Wilfred P.
Cohn Family Foundation, Robert and Terri
Coleman Foundation
Columbia Foundation
Columbia Savings Charitable Foundation
Commercial Metals Co.
Conston Corp.
Cosmair, Inc.
Cummings Foundation, Nathan
Daniel Foundation, Gerard and Ruth
Davis Foundation, Simon and Annie
Deutsch Co.
Dewar Foundation
Dimeo Construction Co.
Douglas Charitable Foundation
Duncan Trust, John G.
Eckman Charitable Foundation, Samuel and Rae
Eder Foundation, Sidney and Arthur
Ehrman Foundation, Fred and Susan
Einstein Fund, Albert E. and Birdie W.
EIS Foundation
Eisenberg Foundation, Ben B. and Joyce E.
Eisenberg Foundation, George M.
El-An Foundation
FAB Industries
Factor Family Foundation, Max
Falk Foundation, Michael David
Federation Foundation of Greater Philadelphia
Feinberg Foundation, Joseph and Bessie
Feinstein Foundation, Myer and Rosaline
Feintech Foundation
Fellner Memorial Foundation, Leopold and Clara M.
Fig Tree Foundation
Fireman Charitable Foundation, Paul and Phyllis
First Petroleum Corp.
Fischel Foundation, Harry and Jane
Fishoff Family Foundation
Flemm Foundation, John J.
Florence Foundation
Fogel Foundation, Shalom and Rebecca
Forbes Charitable Trust, Herman
Foster Charitable Trust
Fox Steel Co.
Frank Fund, Zollie and Elaine
Frankel Foundation, George and Elizabeth F.
Fribourg Foundation
Friedland Family Foundation, Samuel
Friedman Brothers Foundation
Friedman Foundation, Stephen and Barbara
Friendly Rosenthal Foundation
Fruchthandler Foundation, Alex and Ruth
Fuchsberg Family Foundation, Abraham
Galkin Charitable Trust, Ira S. and Anna
Galter Foundation
Garfinkle Family Foundation
Geifman Family Foundation
Geist Foundation
Gelman Foundation, Melvin and Estelle
Gerlach Foundation
Gershenson Foundation, Charles H.
Gerson Family Foundation, Benjamin J.

Gerson Trust, B. Milfred
Giant Eagle
Gindi Associates Foundation
Ginsberg Family Foundation, Moses
Gitano Group
Glazer Foundation, Jerome S.
Glazer Foundation, Madelyn L.
Glick Foundation, Eugene and Marilyn
Glosser Foundation, David A.
Goldberg Family Foundation
Goldberg Family Foundation, Israel and Matilda
Goldberger Foundation, Edward and Marjorie
Goldie-Anna Charitable Trust
Goldman Foundation, Aaron and Cecile
Goldman Foundation, William
Goldring Family Foundation
Goldsmith Family Foundation
Goldsmith Foundation
Goldstein Foundation, Leslie and Roslyn
Golub Corp.
Goodman Family Foundation
Goodman Foundation, Edward and Marion
Goodstein Family Foundation, David
Gordon Charitable Trust, Peggy and Yale
Gorin Foundation, Nehemiah
Gottesman Fund
Grass Family Foundation
Green Fund
Greenberg Foundation, Alan C.
Greene Foundation, David J.
Greenspan Foundation
Gries Charity Fund, Lucile and Robert H.
Gruber Research Foundation, Lila
Grumbacher Foundation, M. S.
Gruss Charitable and Educational Foundation, Oscar and Regina
Gruss Charitable Foundation, Emanuel and Riane
Gudelsky Family Foundation, Homer and Martha
Gudelsky Family Foundation, Isadore and Bertha
Gumenick Foundation, Nathan and Sophie
Gurwin Foundation, J.
Gussman Foundation, Herbert and Roseline
Gutman Foundation, Edna and Monroe C.
Guttag Foundation, Irwin and Marjorie
Haas Fund, Miriam and Peter
Hafif Family Foundation
Hassenfeld Foundation
Hechinger Co.
Hecht-Levi Foundation
Heilicher Foundation, Menahem
Helzberg Foundation, Shirley and Barnett
Herman Foundation, John and Rose
Herzstein Charitable Foundation, Albert and Ethel
Hess Charitable Foundation, Ronne and Donald
Hess Foundation
Heymann Special Account, Mr. and Mrs. Jimmy
Hidary Foundation, Jacob
Higgins Foundation, Aldus C.
Hillman Family Foundation, Alex
Himmelfarb Foundation, Paul and Annetta
Hoffberger Foundation
Hofmann Co.
Holtzmann Foundation, Jacob L. and Lillian

Holzer Memorial Foundation, Richard H.
Horowitz Foundation, Gedale B. and Barbara S.
House of Gross
Hudson Neckwear
Imerman Memorial Foundation, Stanley
India Foundation
Irmas Charitable Foundation, Audrey and Sydney
Jacoby Foundation, Lela Beren and Norman
Jaffe Foundation
Jaydor Corp.
Jergens Foundation, Andrew
Jesselson Foundation
Joselow Foundation
Jurodin Fund
Jurzykowski Foundation, Alfred
Kaiser Foundation, Betty E. and George B.
Kapiloff Foundation, Leonard
Kaplan Foundation, Rita J. and Stanley H.
Kaufman Foundation, Henry & Elaine
Kawaler Foundation, Morris and Nellie L.
Kellenberger Historical Foundation, May Gordon Latham
Kepco, Inc.
Kest Family Foundation, Sol and Clara
Kimmelman Foundation, Helen & Milton
Klau Foundation, David W. and Sadie
Klein Charitable Foundation, Raymond
Klein Fund, Nathan J.
Kline Foundation, Charles and Figa
Koffler Family Foundation
Koopman Fund
Koret Foundation
Korman Family Foundation, Hyman
Kraft Foundation
Kramer Foundation
Kugelman Foundation
Lang Foundation, Eugene M.
Lasdon Foundation
Lautenberg Foundation
Lawrence Foundation, Alice
Lazar Foundation
Lederer Foundation, Francis L.
Lehrman Foundation, Jacob and Charlotte
Lemberg Foundation
Lender Family Foundation
Leo Burnett Co.
Levine Family Foundation, Hyman
Levinson Foundation, Max and Anna
Levinson Foundation, Morris L.
Levy Foundation, Betty and Norman F.
Levy Foundation, Charles and Ruth
Levy Foundation, Hyman Jebb
Lewis Foundation, Lillian Kaiser
Lipsky Foundation, Fred and Sarah
Livingston Foundation, Milton S. and Corinne N.
Loewenberg Foundation
Lopata Foundation, Stanley and Lucy
Lowe Foundation, Joe and Emily
Lowenstein Brothers Foundation
Lowenstein Foundation, William P. and Marie R.
Maas Foundation, Benard L.
MacAndrews & Forbes Holdings
Mailman Foundation

MalCo Products Inc.
Mamiye Brothers
Manat Foundation
Mandel Foundation, Jack N. and Lilyan
Mandel Foundation, Joseph and Florence
Manilow Foundation, Nathan
Mann Foundation, Ted
Marcus Brothers Textiles Inc.
Mattus Foundation, Reuben and Rose
May Department Stores Co.
Mayerson Foundation, Manuel D. and Rhoda
Mazer Foundation, Jacob and Ruth
McGonagle Foundation, Dextra Baldwin
McGregor Foundation, Thomas and Frances
Melohn Foundation
Mendel Foundation
Messing Family Charitable Foundation
Messing Foundation, Morris M. and Helen F.
Metropolitan Theatres Corp.
Meyer Fund, Milton and Sophie
Meyer Memorial Foundation, Aaron and Rachel
Meyerhoff Fund, Joseph
Milken Foundation, L. and S.
Millstein Charitable Foundation
Millstone Foundation
Milstein Family Foundation
Mnuchin Foundation
Morgenstern Foundation, Morris
Morris Charitable Trust, Charles M.
Morris Foundation, Norman M.
Morse, Jr. Foundation, Enid and Lester S.
Moskowitz Foundation, Irving I.
Nelco Sewing Machine Sales Corp.
Neu Foundation, Hugo and Doris
Neuberger Foundation, Roy R. and Marie S.
New York Mercantile Exchange
Newbrook Charitable Foundation
Newhouse Foundation, Samuel I.
Newman Charitable Trust, Calvin M. and Raquel H.
Novotny Charitable Trust, Yetta Deitch
Number Ten Foundation
N've Shalom Foundation
Obernauer Foundation
Odyssey Partners
Ottenstein Family Foundation
Padnos Iron & Metal Co., Louis
Parnes Foundation, E. H.
Parthenon Sportswear
Phillips Family Foundation, Jay and Rose
Phillips Family Foundation, L. E.
Polinger Foundation, Howard and Geraldine
Pope Foundation, Lois B.
Posnack Family Foundation of Hollywood
Pottstown Mercury
Premier Dental Products Co.
Prentis Family Foundation, Meyer and Anna
Price Foundation, Louis and Harold
Pritzker Foundation
Propp Sons Fund, Morris and Anna
Prudential-Bache Securities
Rabb Charitable Foundation, Sidney and Esther
Rabb Charitable Trust, Sidney R.
Radiator Specialty Co.
Radin Foundation

Rales and Ruth Rales Foundation, Norman R.
Raskin Foundation, Hirsch and Braine
Regis Corp.
Reicher Foundation, Anne & Harry J.
Resnick Foundation, Jack and Pearl
Rittenhouse Foundation
Ritter Foundation
Rochlin Foundation, Abraham and Sonia
Rosen Foundation, Joseph
Rosenberg Family Foundation, William
Rosenberg, Jr. Family Foundation, Louise and Claude
Rosenbloom Foundation, Ben and Esther
Rosenthal Foundation, Richard and Lois
Rosenthal Foundation, Samuel
Rosenthal-Statter Foundation
Ross Foundation, Lyn & George M.
Roth Foundation, Louis T.
Rubenstein Foundation, Philip
Rubin Foundation, Rob E. & Judith O.
Rudin Foundation
Sang Foundation, Elsie O. and Philip D.
Sapirstein-Stone-Weiss Foundation
Sawyer Charitable Foundation
Schaffer Foundation, H.
Schaffer Foundation, Michael & Helen
Schermer Charitable Trust, Frances
Scheuer Family Foundation, S. H. and Helen R.
Schiro Fund
Schloss & Co., Marcus
Schwartz and Robert Schwartz Foundation, Bernard
Schwartz Foundation, Bernard Lee
Schwartz Foundation, David
Schwartz Fund for Education and Health Research, Arnold and Marie
Schwob Foundation, Simon
Seaway Food Town
Shapell Foundation, Nathan and Lilly
Shapero Foundation, Nate S. and Ruth B.
Shapiro Foundation, Charles and M. R.
Shemanski Testamentary Trust, Tillie and Alfred
Sherman Family Charitable Trust, George and Beatrice
Shiffman Foundation
Shorenstein Foundation, Walter H. and Phyllis J.
Simon Foundation, Sidney, Milton and Leoma
Slant/Fin Corp.
Slifka Foundation, Alan B.
Slifka Foundation, Joseph and Sylvia
Smith Foundation, Richard and Susan
Soref Foundation, Samuel M. Soref and Helene K.
Speyer Foundation, Alexander C. and Tillie S.
Spiegel Family Foundation, Jerry and Emily
Spingold Foundation, Nate B. and Frances
Stein Foundation, Joseph F.
Stein Foundation, Louis
Steinberg Family Foundation, Meyer and Jean

Steinhardt Foundation, Judy and Michael
Steinsapir Family Foundation, Julius L. and Libhie B.
Stern Family Foundation, Harry
Stern Foundation, Gustav and Irene
Stern Foundation, Irvin
Stern Foundation, Leonard N.
Stern Foundation, Max
Stern Memorial Trust, Sidney
Stone Family Foundation, Norman H.
Strauss Foundation
Stuart Foundation
Sulzberger Foundation
Sutton Foundation
Swig Charity Foundation, Mae and Benjamin
Swig Foundation
Tamarkin Co.
Taub Foundation, Henry and Marilyn
Taub Foundation, Joseph and Arlene
Tauber Foundation
Taubman Foundation, Herman P. and Sophia
Taylor Family Foundation, Jack
Thalheimer Foundation, Alvin and Fanny Blaustein
Thalhimer, Jr. and Family Foundation, William B.
Tisch Foundation
Titan Industrial Co.
Union Camp Corp.
United Togs Inc.
Valley National Bancorp
Volen Charitable Trust, Benjamin
Waldbaum Family Foundation, I.
Wasserman Foundation
Wasserman Foundation, George
Weiner Foundation
Weinstein Foundation, Alex J.
Weinstein Foundation, J.
Weintraub Family Foundation, Joseph
Weisz Foundation, David and Sylvia
Werthan Foundation
Wexner Foundation
Wien Foundation, Lawrence A.
Wilkof Foundation, Edward and Ruth
Winston Foundation, Norman and Rosita
Winston Research Foundation, Harry
Woldenberg Foundation
Wolens Foundation, Kalman and Ida
Wolff Shoe Co.
Wouk Foundation, Abe
Wurzburg, Inc.
Yassenoff Foundation, Leo
Zaban Foundation
Zacharia Foundation, Isaac Herman
Zale Foundation
Zale Foundation, William and Sylvia
Ziegler Foundation, Ruth/Allen
Zimmerman Family Foundation, Raymond
Zuckerberg Foundation, Roy J.

Science

General

Arkla
Control Data Corp.
GenRad
Kennecott Corp.
Oki America Inc.
Roseburg Forest Products Co.

Observatories & Planetariums

Abbott Laboratories
Algonquin Energy, Inc.
Ameritech Services
Amsted Industries
Armco Inc.
Atlanta Gas Light Co.
Beech Aircraft Corp.
Berwind Corp.
Bishop Trust for the SPCA of Manatee County, Florida, Lillian H.
Blair and Co., William
Brooks Foundation, Gladys
Buchanan Family Foundation
Buhl Foundation
Bunbury Company
Burdines
Cahill Foundation, John R.
Chevron Corp.
Chicago Board of Trade
Commerce Clearing House
CT Corp. System
Deposit Guaranty National Bank
Donaldson Co.
Dumke Foundation, Dr. Ezekiel R. and Edna Wattis
Equifax
Ethyl Corp.
Fikes Foundation, Leland
Fireman's Fund Insurance Co.
First Interstate Bank of Arizona
First National Bank & Trust Co. of Rockford
First NH Banks, Inc.
First Union Corp.
Foulds Trust, Claiborne F
Freedom Forum
Genentech
GenRad
George Foundation
Grass Foundation
Haffner Foundation
Hales Charitable Fund
Illinois Tool Works
Jenkins Foundation, George W.
Johnson Co., E. F.
Keating Family Foundation
Keck Foundation, W. M.
Kellwood Co.
Kennecott Corp.
Kettering Family Foundation
Laclede Gas Co.
MacArthur Foundation, John D. and Catherine T.
Mallinckrodt Specialty Chemicals Co.
Mellam Family Foundation
Mine Safety Appliances Co.
Motorola
Navistar International Corp.
New England Business Service
The New Yorker Magazine, Inc.
Norris Foundation, Kenneth T. and Eileen L.
Northern Trust Co.
Norton Co.
O'Brien Foundation, Alice M.
Ogilvy & Mather Worldwide
Peoples Energy Corp.
Perkin Fund
Phillips Foundation, A. P.
Pittway Corp.
PPG Industries
Raymond Educational Foundation
Rubin Family Fund, Cele H. and William B.
San Diego Gas & Electric
Sara Lee Corp.
Searle & Co., G.D.
Sedgwick James Inc.
Shenandoah Life Insurance Co.
TCF Banking & Savings, FSB
Teleflex Inc.

Observatories & Planetariums (cont.)

Thermo Electron Corp.
Tomlinson Foundation, Kate and Elwyn
Trull Foundation
United Airlines
West Co.
Winona Corporation
Wolff Foundation, John M.
Wollenberg Foundation

Science Exhibits & Fairs

Air Products & Chemicals
Alabama Power Co.
Alumax
Aluminum Co. of America
American Electric Power
American Natural Resources Co.
Asea Brown Boveri
Atlanta Gas Light Co.
Battelle
Benwood Foundation
Bertha Foundation
BFGoodrich
Block, H&R
Boehringer Mannheim Corp.
Booz Allen & Hamilton
Boston Edison Co.
Briggs & Stratton Corp.
Burdines
Cabot Corp.
Campbell Foundation, J. Bulow
Carter Foundation, Amon G.
Carter Foundation, Beirne
Cascade Natural Gas Corp.
Central Hudson Gas & Electric Corp.
Central Maine Power Co.
Central Vermont Public Service Corp.
Chevron Corp.
Ciba-Geigy Corp. (Pharmaceuticals Division)
Clorox Co.
Cowles Media Co.
CTS Corp.
Dayton Power and Light Co.
Dibner Fund
Digital Equipment Corp.
Dodge Foundation, P. L.
Douglas & Lomason Company
Dow Corning Corp.
du Pont de Nemours & Co., E. I.
Duke Power Co.
Edgerton Foundation, Harold E.
Ethyl Corp.
Federal-Mogul Corp.
Fikes Foundation, Leland
Fireman's Fund Insurance Co.
First Fidelity Bancorporation
First Union Corp.
Fluor Corp.
Freeport-McMoRan
Genentech
General Motors Corp.
GenRad
Griffith Laboratories Foundation, Inc.
Gulfstream Aerospace Corp.
Haggar Foundation
Halmos Foundation
Hawley Foundation
Hecla Mining Co.
Hoblitzelle Foundation
Hospital Corp. of America
IBM Corp.
Illinois Power Co.
Illinois Tool Works
Indiana Bell Telephone Co.
Inland Steel Industries
Johnson Co., E. F.
Jones Construction Co., J.A.

Kennecott Corp.
Kiplinger Foundation
Lafarge Corp.
Liberty National Bank
Lincoln National Corp.
Little, Arthur D.
Litton/Itek Optical Systems
Long Island Lighting Co.
Louisiana Land & Exploration Co.
Louisiana-Pacific Corp.
Louisiana Power & Light Co./New Orleans Public Service
Lubrizol Corp.
Maritz Inc.
McCasland Foundation
McDonnell Douglas Corp.
McKenna Foundation, Katherine Mabis
Merck & Co.
Merck Human Health Division
Mettler Instrument Corp.
Michigan Bell Telephone Co.
Michigan Gas Utilities
Mitchell Energy & Development Corp.
Mobil Oil Corp.
Motorola
MTS Systems Corp.
National Computer Systems
NBD Bank
New York Telephone Co.
Norfolk Shipbuilding & Drydock Corp.
Northern Indiana Public Service Co.
Northern Telecom Inc.
Northwest Natural Gas Co.
Norton Co.
NYNEX Corp.
Oglebay Norton Co.
Ohio Bell Telephone Co.
Phillips Foundation, Dr. P.
Piper Foundation, Minnie Stevens
Portland Food Products Co.
Portland General Electric Co.
PPG Industries
Public Service Electric & Gas Co.
Questar Corp.
Rockwell Fund
Rockwell International Corp.
Rohm and Haas Company
Rohr Inc.
San Diego Gas & Electric
Schrafft and Bertha E. Schrafft Charitable Trust, William E.
Seaway Food Town
Shell Oil Co.
Shenandoah Life Insurance Co.
Shoney's Inc.
Signet Bank/Maryland
Simpson Investment Co.
Sonoco Products Co.
Southern California Edison Co.
Southern California Gas Co.
Springs Industries
Stanley Works
Syntex Corp.
Taubman Foundation, A. Alfred
Tenneco
Texas Commerce Bank Houston, N.A.
Texas Instruments
Textron
Thermo Electron Corp.
Thomas & Betts Corp.
3M Co.
Torchmark Corp.
Tracor, Inc.
Transco Energy Company
Union Camp Corp.
Unisys Corp.
United Technologies Corp.
Unocal Corp.

Varian Associates
Vulcan Materials Co.
Washington Water Power Co.
Washington Water Power Co.
West Co.
Wetterau
Whirlpool Corp.
Williams Cos.

Scientific Institutes

Abramson Family Foundation
Ada Foundation, Julius
AMAX
American Electric Power
American Natural Resources Co.
AMETEK
AON Corp.
Atherton Family Foundation
Atlantic Foundation
Banbury Fund
Barra Foundation
Bay Foundation
BCR Foundation
Beckman Foundation, Arnold and Mabel
Bernstein Foundation, Diane and Norman
Berwind Corp.
BFGoodrich
Blanchard Foundation
Bohen Foundation
Borman's
Bozzone Family Foundation
Burroughs Wellcome Co.
Castle Foundation, Harold K. L.
CBI Industries
Central Maine Power Co.
Chase Manhattan Bank, N.A.
Chevron Corp.
Christodora
Cleveland-Cliffs
Clowes Fund
Columbia Foundation
Commercial Metals Co.
Crown Central Petroleum Corp.
Crown Cork & Seal Co., Inc.
de Rothschild Foundation, Edmond
Detroit Edison Co.
Devonshire Associates
Dietrich Foundation, William B.
Doherty Charitable Foundation, Henry L. and Grace
Donaldson Charitable Trust, Oliver S. and Jennie R.
Dorr Foundation
Dow Foundation, Herbert H. and Barbara C.
Dow Foundation, Herbert H. and Grace A.
Dresser Industries
Driscoll Foundation
du Pont de Nemours & Co., E. I.
Duke Power Co.
Earl-Beth Foundation
Eastman Kodak Co.
Ellsworth Foundation, Ruth H. and Warren A.
Erb Lumber Co.
Ethyl Corp.
Exxon Corp.
Falcon Foundation
Federal-Mogul Corp.
Fellner Memorial Foundation, Leopold and Clara M.
First Fidelity Bancorporation
First Union Corp.
Fluor Corp.
Ford Foundation
Ford Fund, William and Martha
Ford III Memorial Foundation, Jefferson Lee
Forest Foundation
Foster-Davis Foundation
Foster-Davis Foundation
Foster Foundation

Fox Foundation, Richard J.
Frick Educational Commission, Henry C.
Frisch's Restaurants Inc.
Frohlich Charitable Trust, Ludwig W.
Galter Foundation
Garvey Memorial Foundation, Edward Chase
General Dynamics Corp.
General Electric Co.
General Motors Corp.
GenRad
Georgia Power Co.
Gerber Products Co.
German Protestant Orphan Asylum Association
Getz Foundation, Emma and Oscar
Glenn Foundation for Medical Research, Paul F.
Goddard Foundation, Charles B.
Goldberg Family Foundation
Goldman Foundation, Morris and Rose
Goldman Foundation, Morris and Rose
Goldsmith Family Foundation
Goldsmith Foundation, Horace W.
Goody's Manufacturing Corp.
Grainger Foundation
Grant Foundation, William T.
Grass Foundation
Graybar Electric Co.
Grede Foundries
Greenspan Foundation
Gruss Petroleum Corp.
H. B. B. Foundation
Handleman Co.
Hankamer Foundation, Curtis and Doris K.
Hansen Memorial Foundation, Irving
Harrington Foundation, Francis A. and Jacquelyn H.
Harris Family Foundation, Hunt and Diane
Harris Foundation, William H. and Mattie Wattis
Harvard Apparatus Foundation
Hechinger Co.
Heineman Foundation for Research, Educational, Charitable, and Scientific Purposes
Heinz Endowment, Howard
Hills Fund, Edward E.
Himmelfarb Foundation, Paul and Annetta
Hoechst Celanese Corp.
Hoffmann-La Roche
Holt Foundation, William Knox
Hooper Foundation, Elizabeth S.
Hume Foundation, Jaquelin
Hunt Foundation, Samuel P.
Imerman Memorial Foundation, Stanley
IMT Insurance Co.
Indiana Gas and Chemical Corp.
Inland Steel Industries
Iowa State Bank
Ishiyama Foundation
Jacobson Foundation, Bernard H. and Blanche E.
Johnson Co., E. F.
Johnson Controls
Johnson Foundation, Willard T. C.
Jones Foundation, W. Alton
Journal Gazette Co.
Keck Foundation, W. M.
Kentland Foundation
Kimmelman Foundation, Helen & Milton
Kleberg Foundation for Wildlife Conservation, Caesar

Klingenstein Fund, Esther A. and Joseph
Kohl Charitable Foundation, Allen D.
Komes Foundation
Kowalski Sausage Co.
Kresge Foundation
Lane Memorial Foundation, Mills Bee
Langendorf Foundation, Stanley S.
Levinson Foundation, Morris L.
Levitt Foundation
Levitt Foundation, Richard S.
Life Investors Insurance Company of America
Link Foundation
Little, Arthur D.
Littlefield Foundation, Edmund Wattis
Litton/Itek Optical Systems
Lockheed Sanders
Long Island Lighting Co.
Lopata Foundation, Stanley and Lucy
LTV Corp.
Ludwick Institute
MacArthur Foundation, John D. and Catherine T.
Mailman Family Foundation, A. L.
Mallinckrodt Specialty Chemicals Co.
Markey Charitable Trust, Lucille P.
Masco Corp.
Masserini Charitable Trust, Maurice J.
Maxfield Foundation
McDonnell Douglas Corp.
McDonnell Douglas Corp.-West
McEachern Charitable Trust, D. V. & Ida J.
McEvoy Foundation, Mildred H.
McGonagle Foundation, Dextra Baldwin
MCI Communications Corp.
McKenna Foundation, Philip M.
McKnight Foundation, Sumner T.
McLean Contributionship
Meadows Foundation
Mellam Family Foundation
Mellon Foundation, Andrew W.
Merck & Co.
Merck Human Health Division
Merrick Foundation
Meyer Foundation, Robert R.
Milliken Co.
Mine Safety Appliances Co.
Mobil Oil Corp.
Moorman Manufacturing Co.
National Computer Systems
National Fuel Gas Co.
NBD Bank
New England Biolabs Foundation
The New Yorker Magazine, Inc.
Newman Assistance Fund, Jerome A. and Estelle R.
Nichols Foundation
Noble Foundation, Samuel Roberts
Norfolk Southern Corp.
Norton Co.
Oakley Foundation, Hollie and Anna
Ogden Foundation, Ralph E.
Olin Corp.
Olsson Memorial Foundation, Elis
O'Neill Foundation, William J. and Dorothy K.
PACCAR
Peabody Foundation, Amelia
Pepsi-Cola Bottling Co. of Charlotte
Perkin-Elmer Corp.
PHH Corp.
Phillips Foundation, Dr. P.

Phillips Petroleum Co.
Piedmont Health Care Foundation
Pierce Charitable Trust, Harold Whitworth
Pitzman Fund
PPG Industries
PQ Corp.
Premier Dental Products Co.
Procter & Gamble Cosmetic & Fragrance Products
Public Service Electric & Gas Co.
R. P. Foundation
Ralston Purina Co.
Raskin Foundation, Hirsch and Braine
Recognition Equipment
Rice Charitable Foundation, Albert W.
Rockefeller Foundation
Rockwell International Corp.
Rodman Foundation
Rohm and Haas Company
Roseburg Forest Products Co.
Rosenstiel Foundation
Rouse Co.
Rowland Foundation
Sachs Fund
Schaffer Foundation, Michael & Helen
Science Applications International Corp.
Searle & Co., G.D.
Security Life of Denver
Seven Springs Foundation
Shawmut National Corp.
Shelton Cos.
Shorenstein Foundation, Walter H. and Phyllis J.
Snee-Reinhardt Charitable Foundation
Snider Foundation
Sonat
South Waite Foundation
Southern California Edison Co.
Sprague Educational and Charitable Foundation, Seth
Stroud Foundation
Stulsaft Foundation, Morris
Stupp Foundation, Norman J.
Texas Instruments
Textron
Thomas & Betts Corp.
Three Swallows Foundation
3M Co.
Thrush-Thompson Foundation
Tinker Foundation
Trust Co. Bank
Unocal Corp.
Uvas Foundation
Vetlesen Foundation, G. Unger
Waters Foundation
Webb Charitable Trust, Susan Mott
Webster Foundation, Edwin S.
Wehr Foundation, Todd
Weinstein Foundation, J.
West Co.
West Texas Corp., J. M.
Wharton Trust, William P.
Whirlpool Corp.
Whitehall Foundation
Winona Corporation
Zemurray Foundation

Scientific Organizations

Abell-Hanger Foundation
Aerospace Corp.
Air France
Alco Standard Corp.
Allegheny Foundation
Alumax
Aluminum Co. of America
AMAX

American Electric Power
American Natural Resources Co.
Annenberg Foundation
Arcadia Foundation
Aristech Chemical Corp.
Atlanta Gas Light Co.
Babcock & Wilcox Co.
Battelle
Becton Dickinson & Co.
Beneficia Foundation
Benetton
BFGoodrich
Bingham Foundation, William
Blair and Co., William
BMW of North America, Inc.
Booth-Bricker Fund
Borden
Borman's
Bridgestone/Firestone
Briggs & Stratton Corp.
Brown & Williamson Tobacco Corp.
Burroughs Wellcome Co.
Cabot Corp.
Carnegie Corporation of New York
Castle Foundation, Harold K. L.
Central Maine Power Co.
Charles River Laboratories
Chase Manhattan Bank, N.A.
Chevron Corp.
Church & Dwight Co.
Ciba-Geigy Corp. (Pharmaceuticals Division)
Cincinnati Bell
Clark Foundation, Edna McConnell
Clowes Fund
Constantin Foundation
Cullen/Frost Bankers
DeCamp Foundation, Ira W.
DeKalb Genetics Corp.
Detroit Edison Co.
Dibner Fund
Doelger Charitable Trust, Thelma
Dresser Industries
Dreyfus Foundation, Camille and Henry
du Pont de Nemours & Co., E. I.
Duke Power Co.
Eastman Kodak Co.
Edison Fund, Charles
Eka Nobel
Ellsworth Foundation, Ruth H. and Warren A.
Ethyl Corp.
Exxon Corp.
Field Foundation of Illinois
Fikes Foundation, Leland
First Maryland Bancorp
First Union Corp.
Foerderer Foundation, Percival E. and Ethel Brown
Ford Foundation
Ford Fund, Walter and Josephine
Foster-Davis Foundation
Fowler Memorial Foundation, John Edward
Fox Charitable Foundation, Harry K. & Emma R.
Fraser Paper Ltd.
Freed Foundation
Freeport-McMoRan
Freightliner Corp.
Friends' Foundation Trust, A.
Friendship Fund
General Electric Co.
General Motors Corp.
General Service Foundation
GenRad
George Foundation
Gifford Charitable Corporation, Rosamond
Golden Family Foundation
Gorin Foundation, Nehemiah
Gould Inc.
Grace & Co., W.R.

Grainger Foundation
Grant Foundation, William T.
Grass Foundation
Grassmann Trust, E. J.
Griggs and Mary Griggs Burke Foundation, Mary Livingston
Haas Fund, Walter and Elise
Hancock Foundation, Luke B.
Harkness Ballet Foundation
Harris Corp.
Hartzell Industries, Inc.
Hawley Foundation
Hebrew Technical Institute
Heinz Co., H.J.
Hewlett-Packard Co.
Hobby Foundation
Hofheinz Foundation, Irene Cafcalas
Hofheinz Fund
Hooper Foundation, Elizabeth S.
Houston Industries
Humana
IBM Corp.
ICI Americas
Illinois Power Co.
Indiana Bell Telephone Co.
Inland Steel Industries
Intel Corp.
ITT Corp.
Jackson Hole Preserve
Jennings Foundation, Mary Hillman
Johnson Fund, Edward C.
Jones Foundation, Daisy Marquis
Jones Foundation, Helen
Jones Foundation, Helen
Jones Foundation, W. Alton
Keck Foundation, W. M.
Kennecott Corp.
Kentland Foundation
Kettering Family Foundation
Knox Foundation, Seymour H.
Knudsen Foundation, Tom and Valley
Koh-I-Noor Rapidograph Inc.
Kyocera International Inc.
Law Foundation, Robert O.
Lehman Foundation, Edith and Herbert
Lipton, Thomas J.
List Foundation, Albert A.
Loeb Foundation, Frances and John L.
Long Island Lighting Co.
Lounsbery Foundation, Richard
Luce Foundation, Henry
Ludwick Institute
Magma Copper Co.
Marpat Foundation
Maxfield Foundation
McBean Family Foundation
McCormick & Co.
McDonnell Douglas Corp.
McDonnell Foundation, James S.
McLean Contributionship
Mead Foundation, Giles W. and Elise G.
Meadows Foundation
Merck & Co.
Merck Human Health Division
Mercury Aircraft
Meredith Corp.
Meyer Foundation, Alice Kleberg Reynolds
Michigan Consolidated Gas Co.
Mitchell Energy & Development Corp.
Mitsubishi International Corp.
Mobil Oil Corp.
Montgomery Street Foundation
Morris Foundation, Margaret T.
Mott Fund, Ruth
National Computer Systems
National Starch & Chemical Corp.
National Westminster Bank New Jersey

NBD Bank
New England Foundation
New York Life Insurance Co.
The New Yorker Magazine, Inc.
Noble Foundation, Edward John
Norton Co.
Oak Foundation U.S.A.
Onan Family Foundation
Orchard Corp. of America.
PACCAR
Packard Foundation, David and Lucile
Palmer Fund, Frank Loomis
Peabody Foundation, Amelia
Perkin-Elmer Corp.
Phillips Petroleum Co.
Pick, Jr. Fund, Albert
Pittway Corp.
Portland General Electric Co.
PPG Industries
Quaker Oats Co.
Reily & Co., William B.
Riordan Foundation
River Blindness Foundation
Rockefeller Brothers Fund
Rockefeller Foundation
Rockefeller Trust, Winthrop
Rockwell International Corp.
Rodman Foundation
Rohm and Haas Company
Rowland Foundation
Russell Charitable Foundation, Tom
San Diego Gas & Electric
Scholl Foundation, Dr.
Schroeder Foundation, Walter
Science Applications International Corp.
Scrivner, Inc.
Sedgwick James Inc.
Shell Oil Co.
Sloan Foundation, Alfred P.
Smith 1980 Charitable Trust, Kelvin
Southern California Edison Co.
Stare Fund
Sterling Winthrop
Strake Foundation
Stroud Foundation
Texaco
3M Co.
Tracor, Inc.
Tropicana Products, Inc.
TRW Corp.
TU Electric Co.
Unilever United States
Union Bank of Switzerland Los Angeles Branch
Union Bank of Switzerland New York Branch
Union Camp Corp.
Universal Foods Corp.
UST
USX Corp.
Valley Foundation
Varian Associates
Wallace Genetic Foundation
Wenner-Gren Foundation for Anthropological Research
Whirlpool Corp.
Whitaker Charitable Foundation, Lyndon C.
Whitney Fund, David M.
Williams Cos.
Wisconsin Energy Corp.
Witco Corp.
Wyman-Gordon Co.
Xerox Corp.
Younkers, Inc.

Social Services

Aged

Abel Construction Co.
Abell-Hanger Foundation
Abernethy Testamentary Charitable Trust, Maye Morrison
Abitibi-Price
Abrams Foundation, Benjamin and Elizabeth
Abramson Family Foundation
Abrons Foundation, Louis and Anne
Achelis Foundation
Ada Foundation, Julius
Ahmanson Foundation
Air Products & Chemicals
Alabama Power Co.
Albertson's
Alexander Foundation, Joseph
Allegheny Foundation
Allegheny Ludlum Corp.
AlliedSignal
Alltel/Western Region
ALPAC Corp.
Altman Foundation
Alumax
Aluminum Co. of America
Amado Foundation, Maurice
AMAX
AMCORE Bank, N.A. Rockford
Amdur Braude Riley, Inc.
American Electric Power
American Express Co.
American Financial Corp.
American Home Products Corp.
American Microsystems, Inc.
American United Life Insurance Co.
Americana Foundation
Ameritas Life Insurance Corp.
Ames Department Stores
AMETEK
Amfac/JMB Hawaii
Amoco Corp.
Anderson Foundation
Anderson Foundation, M. D.
Anschutz Family Foundation
AON Corp.
Apache Corp.
Apple Computer, Inc.
Appleman Foundation
Appleton Papers
Arcadia Foundation
Archer-Daniels-Midland Co.
Archibald Charitable Foundation, Norman
ARCO
ARCO Chemical
Arkansas Power & Light Co.
Arkell Hall Foundation
Armbrust Chain Co.
Armco Inc.
Arrillaga Foundation
Ashland Oil
Atherton Family Foundation
Atkinson Foundation
Atlanta Gas Light Co.
Atran Foundation
Attleboro Pawtucket Savings Bank
Auerbach Foundation, Beatrice Fox
Aurora Foundation
Avon Products
Backer Spielvogel Bates U.S.
Bacon Trust, Charles F.
Badgeley Residuary Charitable Trust, Rose M.
Baier Foundation, Marie
Baker Foundation, R. C.
Baker Foundation, Solomon R. and Rebecca D.
Baker Trust, Clayton
Baltimore Gas & Electric Co.

Aged (cont.)

Banbury Fund
Bancorp Hawaii
Banfi Vintners
Bank of Boston Corp.
Barnes Group
Barra Foundation
Barry Corp., R. G.
Bass and Edythe and Sol G. Atlas Fund, Sandra Atlas
Bassett Foundation, Norman
Bastien Memorial Foundation, John E. and Nellie J.
Battelle
Bauer Foundation, M. R.
Baumker Charitable Foundation, Elsie and Harry
Beaird Foundation, Charles T.
Beck Foundation
Beckman Foundation, Leland D.
Bedminster Fund
Bedsole Foundation, J. L.
Beech Aircraft Corp.
Beecher Foundation, Florence Simon
Beidler Charitable Trust, Francis
Bekins Foundation, Milo W.
Bel Air Mart
Belding Heminway Co.
Bell Industries
Bemis Company
Ben & Jerry's Homemade
Bender Foundation
Benedum Foundation, Claude Worthington
Bennett Memorial Corporation, James Gordon
Benwood Foundation
Benz Trust, Doris L.
Bernstein & Co., Sanford C.
Berwind Corp.
Best Products Co.
Bethlehem Steel Corp.
Beveridge Foundation, Frank Stanley
BFGoodrich
Bierhaus Foundation
Bigelow Foundation, F. R.
Birnschein Foundation, Alvin and Marion
Bissell Foundation, J. Walton
Blair and Co., William
Blaustein Foundation, Jacob and Hilda
Block, H&R
Blount
BMW of North America, Inc.
Boatmen's First National Bank of Oklahoma
Bodman Foundation
Boeing Co.
Boettcher Foundation
Boise Cascade Corp.
Bonfils-Stanton Foundation
Borman's
Borun Foundation, Anna Borun and Harry
Boston Edison Co.
Boston Fatherless and Widows Society
Bothin Foundation
Bovaird Foundation, Mervin
Boynton Fund, John W.
Bozzone Family Foundation
Brace Foundation, Donald C.
Brach Foundation, Helen
Bradford Foundation, George and Ruth
Brand Foundation, C. Harold and Constance
Bremer Foundation, Otto
Brochsteins Inc.
Bronstein Foundation, Soloman and Sylvia
Brookdale Foundation

Brown Foundation, James Graham
Brown Foundation, M. K.
Brown & Williamson Tobacco Corp.
Browning Masonic Memorial Fund, Otis Avery
Bruening Foundation, Eva L. and Joseph M.
Brunswick Corp.
Bryan Family Foundation, Kathleen Price and Joseph M.
Bryce Memorial Fund, William and Catherine
Buchalter, Nemer, Fields, & Younger
Buckley Trust, Thomas D.
Bucyrus-Erie
Bunbury Company
Burden Foundation, Florence V.
Burndy Corp.
Bush Charitable Foundation, Edyth
Bush Foundation
C.P. Rail Systems
Cabot Corp.
Cadbury Beverages Inc.
Cafritz Foundation, Morris and Gwendolyn
Cahn Family Foundation
Cameron Foundation, Harry S. and Isabel C.
Campbell and Adah E. Hall Charity Fund, Bushrod H.
Cannon Foundation
Capital Cities/ABC
Capital Fund Foundation
Capital Holding Corp.
Carolyn Foundation
Carpenter Foundation
Carrier Corp.
Carter Foundation, Amon G.
Carvel Foundation, Thomas and Agnes
Cascade Natural Gas Corp.
Catlin Charitable Trust, Kathleen K.
Cauthorn Charitable Trust, John and Mildred
Centel Corp.
Centerior Energy Corp.
Central Fidelity Banks, Inc.
Central Hudson Gas & Electric Corp.
Central Maine Power Co.
Chadwick Fund, Dorothy Jordan
Chandler Foundation
Chapman Charitable Trust, H. A. and Mary K.
Charina Foundation
Charlesbank Homes
Chartwell Foundation
Chase Manhattan Bank, N.A.
Chatham Valley Foundation
CHC Foundation
Cheney Foundation, Ben B.
Chesebrough-Pond's
Chevron Corp.
Chicago Sun-Times, Inc.
Chicago Title and Trust Co.
Chrysler Corp.
Churches Homes Foundation
Ciba-Geigy Corp. (Pharmaceuticals Division)
Cincinnati Foundation for the Aged
Citizens Bank
Civitas Fund
Clark Foundation
Clark-Winchcole Foundation
Cleveland-Cliffs
Clipper Ship Foundation
Clorox Co.
CM Alliance Cos.
CNG Transmission Corp.
Coast Federal Bank
Codrington Charitable Foundation, George W.

Coen Family Foundation, Charles S. and Mary
Cohen Foundation, George M.
Cohen Foundation, Naomi and Nehemiah
Colonial Life & Accident Insurance Co.
Colonial Penn Group, Inc.
Colorado Trust
Colt Foundation, James J.
Columbus Dispatch Printing Co.
Commonwealth Fund
Comprecare Foundation
Cone-Blanchard Machine Co.
Connecticut Natural Gas Corp.
Connelly Foundation
Consolidated Freightways
Consolidated Natural Gas Co.
Contraves USA
Cooke Foundation
Cooke Foundation Corporation, V. V.
Cooper Industries
Coors Brewing Co.
Copley Press
Copperweld Steel Co.
Cosmair, Inc.
County Bank
Covington and Burling
Cowan Foundation Corporation, Lillian L. and Harry A.
Cowles Charitable Trust
Cowles Foundation, Gardner and Florence Call
CPC International
Craig Foundation, J. Paul
Cremer Foundation
Crestlea Foundation
Crown Memorial, Arie and Ida
Crum and Forster
CTS Corp.
Cudahy Fund, Patrick and Anna M.
Cullen/Frost Bankers
Cummins Engine Co.
Cunningham Foundation, Laura Moore
Curtice-Burns Foods
Dain Bosworth/Inter-Regional Financial Group
Danner Foundation
Davey Tree Expert Co.
Davis Charitable Foundation, Champion McDowell
Davis Hospital Foundation
Day Family Foundation
DEC International, Inc.
Deere & Co.
Delacorte Fund, George
Deluxe Corp.
Deposit Guaranty National Bank
DeRoy Testamentary Foundation
Deutsch Co.
DeVos Foundation, Richard and Helen
Dietrich Foundation, William B.
Digital Equipment Corp.
Dillon Foundation
Dimeo Construction Co.
Dodge Foundation, Cleveland H.
Dodson Foundation, James Glenwell and Clara May
Doelger Charitable Trust, Thelma
Doheny Foundation, Carrie Estelle
Donnelley Foundation, Gaylord and Dorothy
Doss Foundation, M. S.
Doty Family Foundation
Douty Foundation
Dover Foundation
Doyle Charitable Foundation
Dresser Industries
Dreyfus Foundation, Jean and Louis
Dreyfus Foundation, Max and Victoria
du Pont de Nemours & Co., E. I.

Duke Foundation, Doris
Duke Power Co.
Duncan Trust, James R.
Dunspaugh-Dalton Foundation
duPont Foundation, Alfred I.
Durham Merchants Association Charitable Foundation
Dweck Foundation, Samuel R.
Dynamet, Inc.
East Ohio Gas Co.
Eaton Corp.
Ebell of Los Angeles Rest Cottage Association
Eccles Charitable Foundation, Willard L.
Eccles Foundation, George S. and Dolores Dore
Eccles Foundation, Marriner S.
Echlin Inc.
Eckman Charitable Foundation, Samuel and Rae
Eden Hall Foundation
Eder Foundation, Sidney and Arthur
Educational Foundation of America
Einstein Fund, Albert E. and Birdie W.
EIS Foundation
Eisenberg Foundation, Ben B. and Joyce E.
El Pomar Foundation
Elkin Memorial Foundation, Neil Warren and William Simpson
Emergency Aid of Pennsylvania Foundation
Emerson Electric Co.
Emerson Foundation, Fred L.
EMI Records Group
Engelhard Foundation, Charles
English Foundation, Walter and Marian
Enron Corp.
Equifax
Equitable Life Assurance Society of the U.S.
Ernsthausen Charitable Foundation, John F. and Doris E.
Eureka Co.
European American Bank
Evjue Foundation
Exxon Corp.
Eyman Trust, Jesse
Factor Family Foundation, Max
Fairfield Foundation, Freeman E.
Faith Home Foundation
Falk Foundation, David
Farnsworth Trust, Charles A.
Faulkner Trust, Marianne Gaillard
Fay's Incorporated
Federal Express Corp.
Federated Department Stores and Allied Stores Corp.
Fein Foundation
Fels Fund, Samuel S.
Fidelity Bank
Fifth Third Bancorp
Fikes Foundation, Leland
Finch Foundation, Thomas Austin
Finnegan Foundation, John D.
Fireman's Fund Insurance Co.
First Fidelity Bancorporation
First Hawaiian
First Interstate Bank of Arizona
First Interstate Bank of California
First Interstate Bank of Oregon
First Interstate Bank of Texas, N.A.
First Union Corp.
Firstar Bank Milwaukee NA
FirsTier Bank N.A. Omaha
Fisher Foundation
Flagler Foundation
Flinn Foundation
Florence Foundation

Florida Power & Light Co.
Florida Rock Industries
FMR Corp.
Fohs Foundation
Forbes
Forbes Charitable Trust, Herman
Forchheimer Memorial Foundation Trust, Louise and Josie
Ford III Memorial Foundation, Jefferson Lee
Ford Meter Box Co.
Fort Worth Star Telegram
Foster Co., L.B.
Foster Foundation
Foundation for Seacoast Health
Fox Inc.
Fox Steel Co.
Frank Fund, Zollie and Elaine
Frankel Foundation
Franklin Foundation, John and Mary
Freedom Forum
Freeport Brick Co.
Freeport-McMoRan
Friends' Foundation Trust, A.
Frohring Foundation, Paul & Maxine
Frost Foundation
Frueauff Foundation, Charles A.
Fry Foundation, Lloyd A.
Fuchs Foundation, Gottfried & Mary
Funderburke & Associates
Fusenot Charity Foundation, Georges and Germaine
Galkin Charitable Trust, Ira S. and Anna
Gallo Foundation, Julio R.
Gannett Co.
Gannett Publishing Co., Guy
Garner Charitable Trust, James G.
Gates Foundation
GATX Corp.
Gellert Foundation, Carl
Gelman Foundation, Melvin and Estelle
General American Life Insurance Co.
General Electric Co.
General Mills
General Railway Signal Corp.
GenRad
Georgia Power Co.
Gerondelis Foundation
Gershman Foundation, Joel
Gerson Trust, B. Milfred
Gerstacker Foundation, Rollin M.
Giant Eagle
Giant Food
Giant Food Stores
Gifford Charitable Corporation, Rosamond
Gilmore Foundation, Earl B.
Ginter Foundation, Karl and Anna
Glaxo
Gleason Foundation, Katherine
Glenn Foundation for Medical Research, Paul F.
Goldman Foundation, Aaron and Cecile
Goldman Foundation, Herman
Goldsmith Foundation, Horace W.
Goldstein Foundation, Leslie and Roslyn
Goldstein Foundation, Leslie and Roslyn
Goldwyn Foundation, Samuel
Goodman & Company
Goodman Foundation, Edward and Marion
Goody's Manufacturing Corp.
Gore Family Memorial Foundation
Gorin Foundation, Nehemiah

Grace & Co., W.R.
Grader Foundation, K. W.
Gradison & Co.
Graphic Controls Corp.
Grassmann Trust, E. J.
Graybar Electric Co.
Great Western Financial Corp.
Green Foundation, Allen P. and Josephine B.
Green Fund
Greene Foundation, Robert Z.
Gregg-Graniteville Foundation
Griffin Foundation, Rosa May
Grigg-Lewis Trust
Grotto Foundation
GTE Corp.
Guaranty Bank & Trust Co.
Gucci America Inc.
Gulf Power Co.
Guttman Foundation, Stella and Charles
Haas Fund, Walter and Elise
Haas, Jr. Fund, Evelyn and Walter
Habig Foundation, Arnold F.
Hadson Corp.
Hagedorn Fund
Hale Foundation, Crescent Porter
Hall Family Foundations
Hall Foundation
Hallmark Cards
Hancock Foundation, Luke B.
Hankamer Foundation, Curtis and Doris K.
Hansen Foundation, Dane G.
Harden Foundation
Harper Brush Works
Harper Foundation, Philip S.
Harris Brothers Foundation
Hartmarx Corp.
Hartz Foundation
Hartzell Industries, Inc.
Hatch Charitable Trust, Margaret Milliken
Hayden Foundation, William R. and Virginia
Haynes Foundation, John Randolph and Dora
Healy Family Foundation, M. A.
Hearst Foundation
Hearst Foundation, William Randolph
Hechinger Co.
Hecla Mining Co.
Hedco Foundation
Hedrick Foundation, Frank E.
Heileman Brewing Co., Inc., G.
Heinz Co., H.J.
Heinz Endowment, Vira I.
Herbst Foundation
Hermann Foundation, Grover
Herndon Foundation, Alonzo F. Herndon and Norris B.
Hess Foundation
Heymann Special Account, Mr. and Mrs. Jimmy
Hillcrest Foundation
Hillman Foundation
Himmelfarb Foundation, Paul and Annetta
Hirschl Trust for Charitable Purposes, Irma T.
Hobart Memorial Fund, Marion W.
Hoffman Foundation, H. Leslie Hoffman and Elaine S.
Hofstetter Trust, Bessie
Home for Aged Men
Honeywell
Honigman Foundation
Hopper Memorial Foundation, Bertrand
Hopper Memorial Foundation, Bertrand
Horowitz Foundation, Gedale B. and Barbara S.
Hospital Corp. of America
Household International

Houston Industries
Howell Foundation, Eric and Jessie
Hoyt Foundation, Stewart W. and Willma C.
Hugoton Foundation
Humana
Hunt Foundation, Samuel P.
Huntsman Foundation, Jon and Karen
Hurley Foundation, J. F.
Hyams Foundation
IBM Corp.
ICI Americas
Iddings Benevolent Trust
IES Industries
Illinois Power Co.
Illinois Tool Works
Indiana Bell Telephone Co.
Indiana Insurance Cos.
Inland Container Corp.
Inland Steel Industries
Innovating Worthy Projects Foundation
International Flavors & Fragrances
International Paper Co.
Ishiyama Foundation
ITT Corp.
ITT Hartford Insurance Group
ITT Rayonier
Ittleson Foundation
Ivakota Association
J.P. Morgan & Co.
Jackson Family Foundation, Ann
Jackson Foundation
Janirve Foundation
Jewish Healthcare Foundation of Pittsburgh
John Hancock Mutual Life Insurance Co.
Johnson Controls
Johnson Foundation, Helen K. and Arthur E.
Johnson Foundation, M. G. and Lillie A.
Johnson Foundation, Robert Wood
Johnson Foundation, Willard T. C.
Johnson & Higgins
Johnson & Johnson
Johnston Trust for Charitable and Educational Purposes, James M.
Jones Foundation, Daisy Marquis
Joslyn Foundation, Marcellus I.
Journal Gazette Co.
Julia R. and Estelle L. Foundation
Kanematsu-Gosho U.S.A. Inc.
Kantzler Foundation
Kaplen Foundation
Kaufmann Foundation, Henry
Kaufmann Foundation, Marion Esser
Kawabe Memorial Fund
Kellenberger Historical Foundation, May Gordon Latham
Keller-Crescent Co.
Kellogg Foundation, W. K.
Kemper Charitable Lead Trust, William T.
Kennecott Corp.
Kerney Foundation, James
Kevorkian Fund, Hagop
Kieckhefer Foundation, J. W.
Kiewit Foundation, Peter
Kimball International
Kimberly-Clark Corp.
King Ranch
Kingsbury Corp.
Kiplinger Foundation
Klau Foundation, David W. and Sadie
Klosk Fund, Louis and Rose

Knowles Charitable Memorial Trust, Gladys E.
Kobacker Co.
Koehler Foundation, Marcia and Otto
Koffler Family Foundation
Kohl Charitable Foundation, Allen D.
Kohl Foundation, Sidney
Koret Foundation
Kramer Foundation
Kramer Foundation, Louise
Kuhne Foundation Trust, Charles
Kysor Industrial Corp.
La-Z-Boy Chair Co.
Lacy Foundation
Ladish Co.
Laffey-McHugh Foundation
Lasdon Foundation
Lauder Foundation
Laurel Foundation
Leach Foundation, Tom & Frances
Leavey Foundation, Thomas and Dorothy
Lee Enterprises
Lee Foundation, Ray M. and Mary Elizabeth
Leibovitz Foundation, Morris P.
Lender Family Foundation
Leucadia National Corp.
Levin Foundation, Philip and Janice
Levy Foundation, Betty and Norman F.
Levy Foundation, Hyman Jebb
Lewis Foundation, Frank J.
Liberty National Bank
Life Insurance Co. of Georgia
Lightner Sams Foundation
Lincoln Fund
Lincoln National Corp.
Lincy Foundation
Lindsay Foundation
Lindsay Trust, Agnes M.
Link, Jr. Foundation, George
Lipsky Foundation, Fred and Sarah
Lipsky Foundation, Fred and Sarah
Liquid Air Corp.
Littauer Foundation, Lucius N.
Litwin Foundation
Livingston Foundation
Long Foundation, J.M.
Long Island Lighting Co.
Longwood Foundation
Louisiana Power & Light Co./New Orleans Public Service
Loutit Foundation
Lowe Foundation, Joe and Emily
Lowenstein Brothers Foundation
Lowenstein Foundation, William P. and Marie R.
LTV Corp.
Lukens
Lydall, Inc.
Lytel Foundation, Bertha Russ
Maas Foundation, Benard L.
Mabee Foundation, J. E. and L. E.
MacArthur Foundation, John D. and Catherine T.
MacDonald Foundation, Marquis George
Macy & Co., R.H.
Makita U.S.A., Inc.
Manville Corp.
Marathon Oil, Indiana Refining Division
Mardag Foundation
Marpat Foundation
Marriott Foundation, J. Willard
Mars Foundation
Marshall Trust in Memory of Sanders McDaniel, Harriet McDaniel

Masserini Charitable Trust, Maurice J.
Massey Charitable Trust
Massey Foundation, Jack C.
Mastronardi Charitable Foundation, Charles A.
May Charitable Trust, Ben
Mayerson Foundation, Manuel D. and Rhoda
Mayor Foundation, Oliver Dewey
Mazda Motors of America (Central), Inc.
Mazda North America
MBIA, Inc.
MCA
McBeath Foundation, Faye
McBride & Son Associates
McCann Foundation
McConnell Foundation
McCune Foundation
McDonald & Co. Securities
McDonald & Co. Securities
McDonald Foundation, J. M.
McDonnell Douglas Corp.-West
McGee Foundation
McGraw-Hill
McGregor Fund
McInerny Foundation
McIntosh Foundation
MCJ Foundation
McKee Foundation, Robert E. and Evelyn
McKnight Foundation
McLean Contributionship
McNutt Charitable Trust, Amy Shelton
MDU Resources Group, Inc.
Meadows Foundation
Measey Foundation, Benjamin and Mary Siddons
Medina Foundation
Medtronic
Memorial Foundation for Children
Menasha Corp.
Merrill Lynch & Co.
Metropolitan Health Foundation
Metropolitan Life Insurance Co.
Meyer Foundation, Baron de Hirsch
Meyer Foundation, Eugene and Agnes E.
Meyer Foundation, Robert R.
Meyer Fund, Milton and Sophie
Meyer Memorial Trust
MGIC Investment Corp.
Michigan Bell Telephone Co.
Michigan Gas Utilities
Mid-Iowa Health Foundation
Millbrook Tribute Garden
Miller Fund, Kathryn and Gilbert
Mills Foundation, Ralph E.
Mingenback Foundation, Julia J.
Minnegasco
Mitsubishi International Corp.
MNC Financial
Mobil Oil Corp.
Moncrief Foundation, William A. and Elizabeth B.
Montgomery Street Foundation
Moody Foundation
Moore Charitable Foundation, Marjorie
Moore Family Foundation
Moore Memorial Foundation, James Starr
Morris Charitable Foundation, E. A.
Morris Charitable Trust, Charles M.
Morris Foundation, Margaret T.
Morris Foundation, Norman M.
Morrison Trust, Louise L.
Moses Fund, Henry and Lucy
Motorola
Mutual of New York
Myra Foundation

National City Corp.
National Fuel Gas Co.
National Machinery Co.
National Medical Enterprises
National Steel
National Westminster Bank New Jersey
Nationwide Insurance Cos.
NBD Bank
Nelco Sewing Machine Sales Corp.
Nelson Foundation, Florence
Nelson Foundation, Florence
New England Mutual Life Insurance Co.
New England Telephone Co.
New-Land Foundation
New York Foundation
New York Life Insurance Co.
New York Mercantile Exchange
New York Telephone Co.
New York Times Co.
The New Yorker Magazine, Inc.
Newhouse Foundation, Samuel I.
Newmil Bancorp
News & Observer Publishing Co.
Nias Foundation, Henry
Nordson Corp.
North Shore Foundation
Northeast Utilities
Northern Indiana Public Service Co.
Northern States Power Co.
Northwest Natural Gas Co.
Northwestern National Life Insurance Co.
Norton Co.
NuTone Inc.
NYNEX Corp.
Occidental Oil & Gas Corp.
Odyssey Partners
Ogilvy & Mather Worldwide
Oglebay Norton Co.
Ohio Valley Foundation
Onan Family Foundation
O'Neil Foundation, W.
O'Neill Charitable Corporation, F. J.
Ontario Corp.
Oppenstein Brothers Foundation
Ortho Diagnostic Systems, Inc.
Ottenstein Family Foundation
Overbrook Foundation
Owen Trust, B. B.
Oxford Foundation
Oxford Industries, Inc.
Pacific Mutual Life Insurance Co.
Pacific Telesis Group
Packer Foundation, Horace B.
Panhandle Eastern Corp.
Paramount Communications Inc.
Parshelsky Foundation, Moses L.
Parsons Foundation, Ralph M.
Payne Foundation, Frank E. and Seba B.
Peery Foundation
Penn Foundation, William
Peoples Energy Corp.
Pepsi-Cola Bottling Co. of Charlotte
Perini Foundation, Joseph
Perkin-Elmer Corp.
Perkins Memorial Fund, James J. and Marie Richardson
Peters Foundation, R. D. and Linda
Petersen Foundation, Esper A.
Pew Charitable Trusts
Pfizer
Philip Morris Cos.
Phillips Family Foundation, Jay and Rose
Phillips Foundation, A. P.
Phillips Petroleum Co.
Piankova Foundation, Tatiana
Pickford Foundation, Mary
Pineywoods Foundation

Aged (cont.)

Pioneer Hi-Bred International
Pitts Foundation, William H. and Lula E.
Pittsburgh National Bank
Playboy Enterprises, Inc.
Polinger Foundation, Howard and Geraldine
Portland General Electric Co.
Post Foundation of D.C., Marjorie Merriweather
Potomac Electric Power Co.
Potts Memorial Foundation
Powers Foundation
PPG Industries
Pratt Memorial Fund
Prentiss Foundation, Elisabeth Severance
Price Foundation, Louis and Harold
Priddy Foundation
Prince Corp.
Principal Financial Group
Pritzker Foundation
Procter & Gamble Cosmetic & Fragrance Products
Providence Journal Company
Prudential-Bache Securities
Prudential Insurance Co. of America
Public Service Co. of Colorado
Public Service Electric & Gas Co.
Public Welfare Foundation
Puget Sound Power & Light Co.
Pulitzer Publishing Co.
Pyramid Foundation
Quaker Oats Co.
R. F. Foundation
R&B Tool Co.
Rabb Charitable Trust, Sidney R.
Rabb Foundation, Harry W.
Raker Foundation, M. E.
Ralston Purina Co.
Ramapo Trust
Randa
Raskob Foundation for Catholic Activities
Rauch Foundation
Recognition Equipment
Redfield Foundation, Nell J.
Reidler Foundation
Reilly Industries
Reliance Electric Co.
Republic New York Corp.
Retirement Research Foundation
Reynolds Charitable Trust, Kate B.
Reynolds Foundation, Richard S.
Rhone-Poulenc Inc.
Rice Foundation, Helen Steiner
Richardson Fund, Mary Lynn
Rider-Pool Foundation
Ridgefield Foundation
Rieke Corp.
Ritchie Memorial Foundation, Charles E. and Mabel M.
Ritter Foundation, May Ellen and Gerald
Rochester Telephone Corp.
Rochlin Foundation, Abraham and Sonia
Rockwell Fund
Rogers Charitable Trust, Florence
Rohm and Haas Company
Rohr Inc.
Roseburg Forest Products Co.
Rosenbaum Foundation, Paul and Gabriella
Rosenthal Foundation, Samuel
Ross Laboratories
Rothschild Foundation, Hulda B. and Maurice L.
Rouse Co.
Royal Group Inc.
Rudin Foundation

Russ Togs
Russell Charitable Foundation, Tom
SAFECO Corp.
Sailors' Snug Harbor of Boston
San Diego Gas & Electric
Sang Foundation, Elsie O. and Philip D.
Santa Fe Pacific Corp.
Sara Lee Corp.
Sara Lee Hosiery
Saul Foundation, Joseph E. & Norma G.
Schaffer Foundation, H.
Schamach Foundation, Milton
Scherman Foundation
Scheuer Family Foundation, S. H. and Helen R.
Schlink Foundation, Albert G. and Olive H.
Schmidlapp Trust No. 1, Jacob G.
Scholl Foundation, Dr.
Schottenstein Foundation, Jerome & Saul
Schroeder Foundation, Walter
Scott Foundation, William R., John G., and Emma
Scrivner, Inc.
Sealaska Corp.
Sealright Co., Inc.
Searle & Co., G.D.
Seaway Food Town
Seevak Family Foundation
Segal Charitable Trust, Barnet
Seid Foundation, Barre
Selby and Marie Selby Foundation, William G.
Self Foundation
Senior Citizens Foundation
Sentinel Communications Co.
Shawmut National Corp.
Shell Oil Co.
Siebert Lutheran Foundation
Signet Bank/Maryland
Silverman Foundation, Marty and Dorothy
Simpson Foundation
Simpson Investment Co.
Skandia America Reinsurance Corp.
Skinner Corp.
Slant/Fin Corp.
Smeal Foundation, Mary Jean & Frank P.
Smith Charitable Trust, W. W.
Smith Corp., A.O.
Smith Foundation, Lon V.
Smock Foundation, Frank and Laura
Smucker Co., J.M.
Snee-Reinhardt Charitable Foundation
SNET
Snider Foundation
Snyder Fund, Valentine Perry
Society for Savings
Solo Cup Co.
Sonat
Sooner Pipe & Supply Corp.
Sosland Foundation
Southern Bell
Southern California Edison Co.
Southwestern Bell Corp.
Speas Foundation, Victor E.
Special People In Need
Spiegel
Spingold Foundation, Nate B. and Frances
Spiro Foundation, Donald W.
Sprague Educational and Charitable Foundation, Seth
Springs Industries
Square D Co.
Star Bank, N.A.
Starr Foundation
Staunton Farm Foundation
Steelcase

Steele Foundation, Harry and Grace
Stein Foundation, Louis
Steinberg Family Foundation, Meyer and Jean
Steiner Charitable Fund, Albert
Steinhagen Benevolent Trust, B. A. and Elinor
Steinsapir Family Foundation, Julius L. and Libhie B.
Sterling Inc.
Sterling Winthrop
Stern Foundation, Irvin
Stern Memorial Trust, Sidney
Stevens Charitable Trust, Abbot and Dorothy H.
Stocker Foundation
Stone Foundation, David S.
Stranahan Foundation
Strong Foundation, Hattie M.
Summerfield Foundation, Solon E.
Sun Co.
Surdna Foundation
Swisher Foundation, Carl S.
Synovus Financial Corp.
Tamarkin Co.
Tandem Computers
Tandy Foundation, David L.
Taper Foundation, Mark
Taper Foundation, S. Mark
Taubman Foundation, A. Alfred
Taubman Foundation, Herman P. and Sophia
Taylor Family Foundation, Jack
Taylor Foundation, Ruth and Vernon
TCF Banking & Savings, FSB
Teleklew Productions
Temple Foundation, T. L. L.
Tenneco
Tesoro Petroleum Corp.
Tetley, Inc.
Texaco
Texas Commerce Bank Houston, N.A.
Texas Gas Transmission Corp.
Textron
Thermo Electron Corp.
Thomas Built Buses L.P.
Thompson Charitable Trust, Sylvia G.
Thompson Trust, Thomas
Thorpe Foundation, James R.
3M Co.
Time Warner Cable
Times Mirror Co.
Tisch Foundation
Titus Foundation, C. W.
Travelers Cos.
Trexler Trust, Harry C.
Trimble Family Foundation, Robert Mize and Isa White
TRINOVA Corp.
Tropicana Products, Inc.
Trull Foundation
Truman Foundation, Mildred Faulkner
Trust Co. Bank
Trust Funds
Tull Charitable Foundation
Twentieth Century-Fox Film Corp.
Tyson Fund
Union Camp Corp.
Union Electric Co.
Union Pacific Corp.
United Dominion Industries
United Parcel Service of America
United States Trust Co. of New York
United Technologies Corp.
United Togs Inc.
Unitrode Corp.
Universal Foods Corp.
UNUM Corp.
US Bancorp

UST
USX Corp.
Vale-Asche Foundation
Valero Energy Corp.
Valley Foundation
Van Buren Foundation
Van Nuys Charities, J. B. and Emily
Varian Associates
Veritas Foundation
Vernon Fund, Miles Hodsdon
Vevay-Switzerland County Foundation
Virginia Power Co.
Volen Charitable Trust, Benjamin
Vulcan Materials Co.
Waggoner Charitable Trust, Crystelle
Wahlert Foundation
Wal-Mart Stores
Waldbaum, Inc.
Walsh Charity Trust, Blanche M.
Ward Foundation, A. Montgomery
Ware Foundation
Warner-Lambert Co.
Washington Water Power Co.
Wasserman Foundation, George
Wean Foundation, Raymond John
Weaver Foundation
Weaver Foundation, Gil and Dody
Webster Foundation, Edwin S.
Wedum Foundation
Wege Foundation
Weiler Foundation, Theodore & Renee
Weinberg Foundation, Harry and Jeanette
Weinberg Foundation, John L.
Weinberg, Jr. Foundation, Sidney J.
Weintraub Family Foundation, Joseph
Weisz Foundation, David and Sylvia
Welfare Foundation
Wells Fargo & Co.
Werner Foundation, Clara and Spencer
West Co.
Western Resources
Western Southern Life Insurance Co.
Weyerhaeuser Co.
Wheless Foundation
Whirlpool Corp.
White Foundation, Erle and Emma
Whitehead Foundation, Joseph B.
Whitehead Foundation, Lettie Pate
Whiting Foundation
Wilf Family Foundation
Williams Charitable Trust, Mary Jo
Williams Family Foundation
Willmott Foundation, Fred & Floy
Wilson Foundation, Hugh and Mary
Wilson Foundation, Marie C. and Joseph C.
Winston Foundation, Norman and Rosita
Wisconsin Energy Corp.
Wisconsin Public Service Corp.
Witte, Jr. Foundation, John H.
Wolff Memorial Foundation, Pauline Sterne
Wolfson Family Foundation
Woods Charitable Fund
Woodward Governor Co.
Woolf Foundation, William C.
Wright Foundation, Lola
Wrigley Co., Wm. Jr.
Wurzburg, Inc.
Wyman-Gordon Co.

Xerox Corp.
Yassenoff Foundation, Leo
Young Foundation, Hugo H. and Mabel B.
Zacharia Foundation, Isaac Herman
Zarrow Foundation, Anne and Henry
Zemurray Foundation

Animal Protection

Abrons Foundation, Louis and Anne
Ahmanson Foundation
Alcon Laboratories, Inc.
Allendale Mutual Insurance Co.
ALPAC Corp.
American Foundation Corporation
American United Life Insurance Co.
Andersen Corp.
Andersen Foundation
Andersons Management Corp.
Animal Assistance Foundation
Annenberg Foundation
Arcadia Foundation
Avon Products
Bailey Wildlife Foundation
Baker Foundation, Elinor Patterson
Baker Foundation, George T.
Baker Foundation, Solomon R. and Rebecca D.
Baldwin Memorial Foundation, Fred
Banbury Fund
Banner Life Insurance Co.
Barbour Foundation, Bernice
Barra Foundation
Bartsch Memorial Trust, Ruth
Bartsch Memorial Trust, Ruth
Bass and Edythe and Sol G. Atlas Fund, Sandra Atlas
Bechtel, Jr. Foundation, S. D.
Beim Foundation
Benua Foundation
Berry Foundation, Loren M.
Besser Foundation
Bingham Foundation, William
Bishop Charitable Trust, A. G.
Bishop Trust for the SPCA of Manatee County, Florida, Lillian H.
Blank Family Foundation
Blum-Kovler Foundation
Bobst Foundation, Elmer and Mamdouha
Boehringer Mannheim Corp.
Booth-Bricker Fund
Borman's
Bostwick Foundation, Albert C.
Brach Foundation, Helen
Brenton Banks Inc.
Bright Charitable Trust, Alexander H.
Bristol-Myers Squibb Co.
Britton Fund
Brotz Family Foundation, Frank G.
Brown Foundation
Bryant Foundation
Buchanan Family Foundation
Burnand Medical and Educational Foundation, Alphonse A.
Burnham Donor Fund, Alfred G.
Burnham Foundation
Cabell III and Maude Morgan Cabell Foundation, Robert G.
Cahn Family Foundation
Caine Charitable Foundation, Marie Eccles
Callaway Foundation
Cameron Foundation, Harry S. and Isabel C.

Carvel Foundation, Thomas and
Agnes
Central Maine Power Co.
Champlin Foundations
Cheatham Foundation, Owen
Cherokee Foundation
Childs Charitable Foundation,
Roberta M.
Church & Dwight Co.
Ciba-Geigy Corp.
(Pharmaceuticals Division)
Clark-Winchcole Foundation
Colonial Life & Accident
Insurance Co.
Commerce Clearing House
Community Enterprises
Connelly Foundation
Cooper Industries
Corbin Foundation, Mary S. and
David C.
Cosmair, Inc.
Cowles Charitable Trust
Cox, Jr. Foundation, James M.
Crestlea Foundation
Curtice-Burns Foods
Davis Foundation, Edwin W. and
Catherine M.
Davis Foundation, Ken W.
DEC International, Inc.
Delaware North Cos.
Dell Foundation, Hazel
DeRoy Testamentary Foundation
Deutsch Co.
Dimeo Construction Co.
Dimick Foundation
Dodge Foundation, Geraldine R.
Doelger Charitable Trust, Thelma
Donaldson Charitable Trust,
Oliver S. and Jennie R.
Donnelley Foundation, Gaylord
and Dorothy
Dorminy Foundation, John Henry
Douglas & Lomason Company
Dresser Industries
Dreyfus Foundation, Max and
Victoria
du Bois Foundation, E. Blois
du Pont de Nemours & Co., E. I.
Duke Foundation, Doris
Duke Power Co.
Dula Educational and Charitable
Foundation, Caleb C. and Julia
W.
Dunn Foundation, Elizabeth
Ordway
Earl-Beth Foundation
Emerson Electric Co.
Engelhard Foundation, Charles
Enron Corp.
Everett Charitable Trust
Falcon Foundation
Falk Foundation, Elizabeth M.
Farish Fund, William Stamps
Federal-Mogul Corp.
Flemm Foundation, John J.
Ford Fund, Benson and Edith
Ford Fund, Walter and Josephine
Ford Meter Box Co.
Forest Oil Corp.
Formrite Tube Co.
Foster Co., L.B.
Franklin Mint Corp.
Fruehauf Foundation
Gage Foundation, Philip and
Irene Toll
GEICO Corp.
Gellert Foundation, Carl
GenRad
Gerard Foundation, Sumner
Glazer Foundation, Jerome S.
Goddard Foundation, Charles B.
Goldstein Foundation, Alfred
and Ann
Goodyear Foundation, Josephine
Grainger Foundation
Graphic Controls Corp.
Greater Lansing Foundation

Green Fund
Gronewaldt Foundation, Alice
Busch
Gulf Power Co.
Haghenbeck Foundation,
Antonio Y. De La Lama
Halstead Foundation
Harden Foundation
Harris Foundation, William H.
and Mattie Wattis
Hawkins Foundation, Robert Z.
Hayfields Foundation
Hechinger Co.
Hecla Mining Co.
Heinz Co., H.J.
Hermann Foundation, Grover
Hill Crest Foundation
Hobby Foundation
Hoblitzelle Foundation
Hoffman Foundation, Marion O.
and Maximilian
Hoffmann-La Roche
Hofmann Co.
Holden Fund, James and Lynelle
Hooker Charitable Trust, Janet A.
Hooper Foundation, Elizabeth S.
Hoover Foundation
Hopkins Foundation, Josephine
Lawrence
Hunt Foundation, Roy A.
Indiana Gas and Chemical Corp.
Innovating Worthy Projects
Foundation
Janirve Foundation
Jaqua Foundation
Jaqua Foundation
Jasper Desk Co.
Jellison Benevolent Society
Johnson & Son, S.C.
Julia R. and Estelle L.
Foundation
Keebler Co.
Kennecott Corp.
Kenworthy - Sarah H. Swift
Foundation, Marion E.
Killough Trust, Walter H. D.
Kimball Foundation, Horace A.
Kimball and S. Ella
King Foundation, Carl B. and
Florence E.
Kingsbury Corp.
Koch Charitable Trust, David H.
Koffler Family Foundation
Kysor Industrial Corp.
Laclede Gas Co.
Laffey-McHugh Foundation
Lane Charitable Trust, Melvin R.
Livingston Foundation
Loomis House
Louisiana Land & Exploration
Co.
Luster Family Foundation
Lyons Foundation
Maas Foundation, Benard L.
MacDonald Foundation, James A.
Marathon Oil, Indiana Refining
Division
Mardag Foundation
Mars Foundation
Marshall Foundation, Mattie H.
Marshall & Ilsley Bank
Martin Foundation
Martin Foundation, Bert William
Maxon Charitable Foundation
McAlister Charitable
Foundation, Harold
McCray Lumber Co.
McCrea Foundation
McInerny Foundation
McNutt Charitable Trust, Amy
Shelton
Mead Corp.
Meadows Foundation
Memton Fund
Menasha Corp.
Merkley Charitable Trust

Meyer Foundation, Baron de
Hirsch
Milken Foundation, L. and S.
Miller Charitable Trust, Lewis N.
Monell Foundation, Ambrose
Montgomery Street Foundation
MTS Systems Corp.
Murphy Foundation, Katherine
and John
Murphy Oil Corp.
Myra Foundation
Nathan Foundation
National Fuel Gas Co.
New England Foundation
Newhouse Foundation, Samuel I.
Northern Indiana Public Service
Co.
Northwest Natural Gas Co.
Oestreicher Foundation, Sylvan
and Ann
Ohrstrom Foundation
Oppenheimer Family Foundation
Overbrook Foundation
Owen Trust, B. B.
Penney Foundation, James C.
Philips Foundation, Jesse
Phipps Foundation, Howard
Porter Foundation, Mrs. Cheever
Potomac Electric Power Co.
Prairie Foundation
Price Foundation, Louis and
Harold
Prickett Fund, Lynn R. and Karl
E.
Pritzker Foundation
Quivey-Bay State Foundation
Randleigh Foundation Trust
Ransom Fidelity Company
Recognition Equipment
Redfield Foundation, Nell J.
Rice Foundation, Ethel and
Raymond F.
Rider-Pool Foundation
Rieke Corp.
Roberts Foundation
Roberts Foundation, Dora
Rockwell Fund
Rogers Foundation
Ross Foundation
Ross Laboratories
Russell Educational Foundation,
Benjamin and Roberta
Salwil Foundation
Sandy Foundation, George H.
Sara Lee Hosiery
Schieffelin Residuary Trust,
Sarah I.
Schroeder Foundation, Walter
Schwab & Co., Charles
Scott, Jr. Charitable Foundation,
Walter
Scurry Foundation, D. L.
Seebee Trust, Frances
Sefton Foundation, J. W.
Selby and Marie Selby
Foundation, William G.
Sewall Foundation, Elmina
Shapiro, Inc.
Shenandoah Foundation
Simon Foundation, William E.
and Carol G.
Slant/Fin Corp.
Smith Foundation
Snider Foundation
Sonat
South Branch Foundation
Southways Foundation
Sprague Educational and
Charitable Foundation, Seth
Steel, Sr. Foundation, Marshall
Stemmons Foundation
Stoddard Charitable Trust
Stranahan Foundation
Strauss Foundation, Judy and
Howard E.
Strawbridge Foundation of
Pennsylvania II, Margaret
Dorrance

Sudix Foundation
Summerlee Foundation
Taub Foundation
Tenneco
Thirty-Five Twenty, Inc.
Titus Foundation, C. W.
Triford Foundation
Trion
Turner Fund, Ruth
21 International Holdings
Universal Leaf Tobacco Co.
Upton Foundation, Frederick S.
Vermeer Charitable Foundation
Vulcan Materials Co.
W. W. W. Foundation
Wal-Mart Stores
Disney Co., Walt
Walter Family Trust, Byron L.
Walthall Perpetual Charitable
Trust, Marjorie T.
Waterfowl Research Foundation
Wean Foundation, Raymond John
Weatherwax Foundation
Weiler Foundation
Wellman Foundation, S. K.
Wendt Foundation, Margaret L.
Westerman Foundation, Samuel
L.
Western Shade Cloth Charitable
Foundation
Westvaco Corp.
Weyerhaeuser Family Foundation
Wharton Foundation
Wharton Trust, William P.
Whirlpool Corp.
Wilcox Trust, S. W.
Wisdom Foundation, Mary F.
Witter Foundation, Dean
Wouk Foundation, Abe
WWF Paper Corp.
Wyne Foundation
Zemurray Foundation

Child Welfare

Abbott Laboratories
Abelard Foundation
Abell Foundation, Charles S.
Abell Foundation, The
Abell-Hanger Foundation
Abercrombie Foundation
Abney Foundation
Abraham Foundation, Anthony R.
Abrons Foundation, Louis and
Anne
Ace Beverage Co.
Achelis Foundation
Acme United Corp.
Action Industries, Inc.
Acushnet Co.
Adams Foundation, Arthur F. and
Alice E.
Adams Trust, Charles E. and
Caroline J.
Advanced Micro Devices
AFLAC
Agape Foundation
Ahmanson Foundation
Air France
Air Products & Chemicals
Akzo Chemicals Inc.
Alabama Power Co.
Alberto-Culver Co.
Albertson's
Alcon Laboratories, Inc.
Aldeen Charity Trust, G. W.
Alexander & Baldwin, Inc.
Alexander Charitable Foundation
Alexander Foundation, Joseph
Alexander Foundation, Judd S.
Alice Manufacturing Co.
Allegheny Ludlum Corp.
Allen Foundation, Frances
Allendale Mutual Insurance Co.
Alliant Techsystems
AlliedSignal
Alltel/Western Region

Alma Piston Co.
ALPAC Corp.
Alro Steel Corp.
Altman Foundation
Aluminum Co. of America
AMAX
Amcast Industrial Corp.
AMCORE Bank, N.A. Rockford
American Brands
American Electric Power
American Express Co.
American Financial Corp.
American Foundation
American Home Products Corp.
American National Bank & Trust
Co. of Chicago
American Natural Resources Co.
American Saw & Manufacturing
Co.
American Schlafhorst
Foundation, Inc.
American Stock Exchange
American Telephone &
Telegraph Co.
American United Life Insurance
Co.
Ames Department Stores
Amfac/JMB Hawaii
Amoco Corp.
AMR Corp.
Andersen Corp.
Anderson Charitable Trust,
Josephine
Anderson Foundation
Anderson Foundation, M. D.
Anderson Foundation, Robert C.
and Sadie G.
Anderson Foundation, William P.
Andersons Management Corp.
Andres Charitable Trust, Frank
G.
Andrews Foundation
Anheuser-Busch Cos.
Annenberg Foundation
Anschutz Family Foundation
Ansley Foundation, Dantzler
Bond
AON Corp.
Apache Corp.
Apple Computer, Inc.
Applebaum Foundation
Appleton Papers
Arcadia Foundation
Arcana Foundation
Archbold Charitable Trust,
Adrian and Jessie
Archer-Daniels-Midland Co.
Archibald Charitable
Foundation, Norman
ARCO
Argyros Foundation
Arizona Public Service Co.
Arkansas Power & Light Co.
Arkla
Armco Inc.
Armstrong Foundation
Armstrong World Industries Inc.
Asea Brown Boveri
Ashland Oil
Astor Foundation, Vincent
Atherton Family Foundation
Atkinson Foundation
Atkinson Foundation, Myrtle L.
Atlanta Foundation
Atlanta Gas Light Co.
Atran Foundation
Attleboro Pawtucket Savings
Bank
Auerbach Foundation, Beatrice
Fox
Aurora Foundation
Autry Foundation
Autzen Foundation
Avon Products
Azadoutioun Foundation
Babcock Foundation, Mary
Reynolds

Child Welfare (cont.)

Bachmann Foundation
Backer Spielvogel Bates U.S.
Bacon Trust, Charles F.
Badgeley Residuary Charitable
  Trust, Rose M.
Baehr Foundation, Louis W. and
  Dolpha
Baer Foundation, Alan and
  Marcia
Baird & Co., Robert W.
Baird Foundation, Cameron
Baker Foundation, R. C.
Baker Foundation, Solomon R.
  and Rebecca D.
Baker, Jr. Memorial Fund,
  William G.
Baldwin Memorial Foundation,
  Fred
Baltimore Gas & Electric Co.
Bamberger and John Ernest
  Bamberger Memorial
  Foundation, Ruth Eleanor
Banbury Fund
Banc One Illinois Corp.
Bancroft, Jr. Foundation, Hugh
Banfi Vintners
Bank IV
Bank of A. Levy
Bank of America Arizona
Bank of Boston Corp.
Bank of New York
Bankers Trust Co.
Banyan Tree Foundation
BarclaysAmerican Corp.
Bargman Foundation, Theodore
  and Mina
Barker Foundation
Barker Welfare Foundation
Barnes Group
Barnett Charitable Foundation,
  Lawrence and Isabel
Barra Foundation
Barrows Foundation, Geraldine
  and R. A.
Barry Corp., R. G.
Baskin-Robbins USA CO.
Bass and Edythe and Sol G.
  Atlas Fund, Sandra Atlas
Bass Foundation, Harry
Bassett Foundation, Norman
Bastien Memorial Foundation,
  John E. and Nellie J.
Battelle
Bauer Foundation, M. R.
Bauervic Foundation, Peggy
Baumker Charitable Foundation,
  Elsie and Harry
Bay Foundation
BCR Foundation
Beaird Foundation, Charles T.
Beal Foundation
Bean Foundation, Norwin S. and
  Elizabeth N.
Beasley Foundation, Theodore
  and Beulah
Beazley Foundation
Beck Foundation
Beerman Foundation
Beidler Charitable Trust, Francis
Beim Foundation
Beir Foundation
Beitzell & Co.
Belz Foundation
Bemis Company
Benedum Foundation, Claude
  Worthington
Benenson Foundation, Frances
  and Benjamin
Benua Foundation
Benwood Foundation
Benz Trust, Doris L.
Bere Foundation
Berkowitz Family Foundation,
  Louis
Berry Foundation, Loren M.

Bersted Foundation
Berwind Corp.
Besser Foundation
Best Foundation, Walter J. and
  Edith E.
Best Western International
Bethlehem Steel Corp.
Bettingen Corporation, Burton G.
Betts Industries
Beveridge Foundation, Frank
  Stanley
Beynon Foundation, Kathryne
Bicknell Fund
Biddle Foundation, Margaret T.
Bigelow Foundation, F. R.
Bingham Foundation, William
Bingham Second Betterment
  Fund, William
Binney & Smith Inc.
Birch Foundation, Stephen and
  Mary
Bireley Foundation
Bishop Charitable Trust, A. G.
Bishop Foundation, E. K. and
  Lillian F.
Blair and Co., William
Blandin Foundation
Blank Family Foundation
Blaustein Foundation, Jacob and
  Hilda
Bleibtreu Foundation, Jacob
Block, H&R
Bloedorn Foundation, Walter A.
Blount
Blowitz-Ridgeway Foundation
Blue Bell, Inc.
Blue Cross & Blue Shield of
  Alabama
Blum Foundation, Edna F.
Blum Foundation, Harry and
  Maribel G.
Blum-Kovler Foundation
Board of Trustees of the Prichard
  School
Boatmen's Bancshares
Boatmen's First National Bank
  of Oklahoma
Bock Charitable Trust, George W.
Bodman Foundation
Boehm Foundation
Boeing Co.
Boettcher Foundation
Bolz Family Foundation,
  Eugenie Mayer
Booth-Bricker Fund
Booth Ferris Foundation
Booz Allen & Hamilton
Borden
Borden Memorial Foundation,
  Mary Owen
Borkee Hagley Foundation
Borman's
Borun Foundation, Anna Borun
  and Harry
Bossong Hosiery Mills
Boston Fatherless and Widows
  Society
Boswell Foundation, James G.
Botwinick-Wolfensohn
  Foundation
Bound to Stay Bound Books
  Foundation
Boutell Memorial Fund, Arnold
  and Gertrude
Bovaird Foundation, Mervin
Bowyer Foundation, Ambrose
  and Gladys
Boynton Fund, John W.
Bozzone Family Foundation
Brach Foundation, Edwin I.
Brach Foundation, Helen
Bradley-Turner Foundation
Brady Foundation
Brand Foundation, C. Harold and
  Constance
Bray Charitable Trust, Viola E.
Bremer Foundation, Otto
Brenner Foundation, Mervyn

Bridgestone/Firestone
Bridwell Foundation, J. S.
Briggs Foundation, T. W.
Bright Charitable Trust,
  Alexander H.
Britton Fund
Bromley Residuary Trust, Guy I.
Brooklyn Benevolent Society
Brooks Brothers
Brotman Foundation of
  California
Brotz Family Foundation, Frank
  G.
Brown Charitable Trust, Dora
  Maclellan
Brown Foundation
Brown Foundation, Joe W. and
  Dorothy Dorsett
Brown Foundation, M. K.
Brown & Williamson Tobacco
  Corp.
Bruening Foundation, Eva L. and
  Joseph M.
Brunner Foundation, Fred J.
Brunner Foundation, Robert
Brunswick Corp.
Bryan Family Foundation,
  Kathleen Price and Joseph M.
Bryant Foundation
Bryce Memorial Fund, William
  and Catherine
Buchalter, Nemer, Fields, &
  Younger
Buehler Foundation, Emil
Buell Foundation, Temple Hoyne
Buffett Foundation
Builder Marts of America
Bull Foundation, Henry W.
Bull HN Information Systems
  Inc.
Burchfield Foundation, Charles
  E.
Burden Foundation, Florence V.
Burlington Resources
Burnand Medical and
  Educational Foundation,
  Alphonse A.
Burndy Corp.
Burnham Foundation
Burns International
Bush Foundation
Butler Manufacturing Co.
C.P. Rail Systems
Cabell III and Maude Morgan
  Cabell Foundation, Robert G.
Cable & Wireless
  Communications
Cabot Corp.
Cain Foundation, Gordon and
  Mary
Calder Foundation, Louis
Caldwell Foundation, Hardwick
Callaway Foundation, Fuller E.
Cambridge Mustard Seed
  Foundation
Cameron Foundation, Harry S.
  and Isabel C.
Cameron Memorial Fund, Alpin
  J. and Alpin W.
Camp and Bennet Humiston
  Trust, Apollos
Camp Younts Foundation
Campbell Foundation, Ruth and
  Henry
Cannon Foundation
Capital Cities/ABC
Capital Fund Foundation
Capital Holding Corp.
Carnahan-Jackson Foundation
Carnegie Corporation of New
  York
Carolina Power & Light Co.
Carolyn Foundation
Carpenter Foundation
Carpenter Foundation, E. Rhodes
  and Leona B.
Carrier Corp.

Carter Charitable Trust, Wilbur
  Lee
Carter Foundation, Amon G.
Carvel Foundation, Thomas and
  Agnes
Casey Foundation, Annie E.
Castle Trust, George P. and Ida
  Tenney
Catlin Charitable Trust, Kathleen
  K.
Cauthorn Charitable Trust, John
  and Mildred
Cawsey Trust
Cayuga Foundation
CBI Industries
Centel Corp.
Centerior Energy Corp.
Central Bank of the South
Central Fidelity Banks, Inc.
Central Hudson Gas & Electric
  Corp.
Central Maine Power Co.
Central Soya Co.
Century Companies of America
Chadwick Fund, Dorothy Jordan
Challenge Foundation
Chamberlin Foundation, Gerald
  W.
Chambers Development Co.
Chanin Family Foundation, Paul
  R.
Chapin Foundation, Frances
Charina Foundation
Charitable Fund
Charities Foundation
Chartwell Foundation
Chase Charity Foundation,
  Alfred E.
Chase Manhattan Bank, N.A.
Chase Trust, Alice P.
Chastain Charitable Foundation,
  Robert Lee and Thomas M.
Chatham Valley Foundation
Chatlos Foundation
CHC Foundation
Chemical Bank
Cheney Foundation, Ben B.
Cherne Foundation, Albert W.
Chevron Corp.
Chicago Resource Center
Chicago Sun-Times, Inc.
Children's Foundation of Erie
  County
Childress Foundation, Francis
  and Miranda
Chiles Foundation
Chilton Foundation Trust
Chisholm Foundation
Chrysler Corp.
Churches Homes Foundation
Ciba-Geigy Corp.
  (Pharmaceuticals Division)
Cimarron Foundation
CIT Group Holdings
Citicorp
Citizens Bank
Citizens Commercial & Savings
  Bank
City of Hope 1989 Section E
  Foundation
Clapp Charitable and
  Educational Trust, George H.
CLARCOR
Clark Foundation
Clark Foundation
Clark Foundation, Edna
  McConnell
Clark Foundation, Robert
  Sterling
Clark-Winchcole Foundation
Clay Foundation
Clements Foundation
Clipper Ship Foundation
Clorox Co.
CM Alliance Cos.
CNA Insurance Cos.
Cobb Family Foundation
Cockrell Foundation

Codrington Charitable
  Foundation, George W.
Coen Family Foundation,
  Charles S. and Mary
Cogswell Benevolent Trust
Cohen Family Foundation, Saul
  Z. and Amy Scheuer
Cohen Foundation, George M.
Cohn Foundation, Peter A. and
  Elizabeth S.
Cole Foundation
Cole Foundation, Robert H. and
  Monica H.
Coleman Foundation
Coles Family Foundation
Collins Foundation
Collins Foundation, Carr P.
Collins Foundation, George and
  Jennie
Collins, Jr. Foundation, George
  Fulton
Collins Medical Trust
Colonial Life & Accident
  Insurance Co.
Colorado Trust
Coltec Industries
Columbus Dispatch Printing Co.
Comer Foundation
Comer Foundation
Commerce Bancshares, Inc.
Commerce Clearing House
Commonwealth Fund
Comstock Foundation
ConAgra
Cone Mills Corp.
Conn Memorial Foundation
Connelly Foundation
Connemara Fund
Contempo Communications
Continental Corp.
Contran Corp.
Cook Charitable Foundation
Cook Foundation
Cook Foundation, Loring
Cooke Foundation
Cooper Charitable Trust, Richard
  H.
Cooper Foundation
Cooper Industries
Coors Foundation, Adolph
Copley Press
Copperweld Steel Co.
Cord Foundation, E. L.
Cornell Trust, Peter C.
Cosmair, Inc.
Country Curtains, Inc.
Cowell Foundation, S. H.
Cowles Charitable Trust
Cowles Media Co.
Cox Foundation
CPC International
CPI Corp.
Craig Foundation, J. Paul
Crandall Memorial Foundation,
  J. Ford
Crane Co.
Crane Foundation, Raymond E.
  and Ellen F.
Crawford Estate, E. R.
Cremer Foundation
CRL Inc.
Crocker Trust, Mary A.
Crown Central Petroleum Corp.
Crown Memorial, Arie and Ida
Crum and Forster
Crummer Foundation, Roy E.
Crystal Trust
Cudahy Fund, Patrick and Anna
  M.
Cullen/Frost Bankers
Culpeper Memorial Foundation,
  Daphne Seybolt
Culver Foundation, Constans
Cummings Foundation, Nathan
Cummings Memorial Fund
  Trust, Frances L. and Edwin L.
Cummins Engine Co.

Cuneo Foundation
Curtice-Burns Foods
Daily News
Dain Bosworth/Inter-Regional Financial Group
Dalton Foundation, Dorothy U.
Daly Charitable Foundation Trust, Robert and Nancy
Dammann Fund
Dana Corp.
Daniel Foundation, Gerard and Ruth
Danner Foundation
Dart Group Corp.
Dater Foundation, Charles H.
Daugherty Foundation
Davenport-Hatch Foundation
Davidson Family Charitable Foundation
Davis Foundation, Edwin W. and Catherine M.
Davis Foundation, James A. and Juliet L.
Davis Foundation, Ken W.
Davis Foundation, Shelby Cullom
Davis Foundation, Simon and Annie
Day Foundation, Nancy Sayles
Day Foundation, Willametta K.
DCNY Corp.
de Hirsch Fund, Baron
Dean Witter Discover
DeCamp Foundation, Ira W.
Dee Foundation, Annie Taylor
Dee Foundation, Lawrence T. and Janet T.
Delano Foundation, Mignon Sherwood
Dell Foundation, Hazel
Deluxe Corp.
Demos Foundation, N.
Dennett Foundation, Marie G.
Deposit Guaranty National Bank
DeRoy Foundation, Helen L.
DeRoy Testamentary Foundation
Deuble Foundation, George H.
Deutsch Co.
DeVlieg Foundation, Charles
DeVore Foundation
DeVos Foundation, Richard and Helen
Dewing Foundation, Frances R.
Dexter Charitable Fund, Eugene A.
Dial Corp.
Digital Equipment Corp.
Dimeo Construction Co.
Dishman Charitable Foundation Trust, H. E. and Kate
Disney Family Foundation, Roy
Dixie Yarns, Inc.
Dodge Foundation, Cleveland H.
Dodge Foundation, Geraldine R.
Dodson Foundation, James Glenwell and Clara May
Doelger Charitable Trust, Thelma
Doheny Foundation, Carrie Estelle
Doherty Charitable Foundation, Henry L. and Grace
Domino's Pizza
Donaldson Charitable Trust, Oliver S. and Jennie R.
Donaldson Co.
Donnelley Foundation, Elliott and Ann
Donnelley Foundation, Gaylord and Dorothy
Donovan, Leisure, Newton & Irvine
Doss Foundation, M. S.
Dougherty, Jr. Foundation, James R.
Douglas Charitable Foundation
Douty Foundation
Dow Fund, Alden and Vada
Dow Jones & Co.

Downs Perpetual Charitable Trust, Ellason
Dreitzer Foundation
Dresser Industries
Dreyfus Foundation, Jean and Louis
Dreyfus Foundation, Max and Victoria
Driehaus Foundation, Richard H.
Driscoll Foundation
du Pont de Nemours & Co., E. I.
Duchossois Industries
Dues Charitable Foundation, Cesle C. and Mamie
Duke Endowment
Duke Foundation, Doris
Duke Power Co.
Dula Educational and Charitable Foundation, Caleb C. and Julia W.
Dumke Foundation, Dr. Ezekiel R. and Edna Wattis
Dun & Bradstreet Corp.
Dunagan Foundation
Duncan Foundation, Lillian H. and C. W.
Duncan Trust, James R.
Duncan Trust, John G.
Dunspaugh-Dalton Foundation
Dupar Foundation
duPont Foundation, Chichester
Durr-Fillauer Medical
Durst Foundation
Dyson Foundation
Earl-Beth Foundation
Early Foundation
Easley Trust, Andrew H. and Anne O.
Eaton Corp.
Eaton Foundation, Edwin M. and Gertrude S.
Eaton Memorial Fund, Georgiana Goddard
Ebell of Los Angeles Rest Cottage Association
Ebert Charitable Foundation, Horatio B.
Eccles Foundation, George S. and Dolores Dore
Eccles Foundation, Marriner S.
Echlin Foundation
Ecolab
Eddy Family Memorial Fund, C. K.
Eden Hall Foundation
Eder Foundation, Sidney and Arthur
Edison Foundation, Harry
Edouard Foundation
Educational Foundation of America
Edwards Foundation, Jes
Edwards Foundation, O. P. and W. E.
Edwards Industries
Egenton Home
Einstein Fund, Albert E. and Birdie W.
El Pomar Foundation
Elizabethtown Gas Co.
Elkin Memorial Foundation, Neil Warren and William Simpson
Ellis Foundation
Ellsworth Foundation, Ruth H. and Warren A.
Ellsworth Trust, W. H.
Ellwood Foundation
Emergency Aid of Pennsylvania Foundation
Emerson Electric Co.
Emerson Foundation, Fred L.
Emery Memorial, Thomas J.
Engelhard Foundation, Charles
English-Bonter-Mitchell Foundation
English Foundation, Walter and Marian

English Memorial Fund, Florence C. and H. L.
Enright Foundation
Enron Corp.
Ensign-Bickford Industries
Ensworth Charitable Foundation
Enterprise Rent-A-Car Co.
Equifax
Equitable Life Assurance Society of the U.S.
Erickson Charitable Fund, Eben W.
Erpf Fund, Armand G.
European American Bank
Everett Charitable Trust
Evinrude Foundation, Ralph
Evjue Foundation
Ewald Foundation, H. T.
Exxon Corp.
FAB Industries
Factor Family Foundation, Max
Failing Fund, Henry
Fairfield Foundation, Freeman E.
Faith Charitable Trust
Faith Home Foundation
Falcon Foundation
Falk Foundation, David
Falk Medical Research Foundation, Dr. Ralph and Marian
Farallon Foundation
Farish Fund, William Stamps
Farley Industries
Faulkner Trust, Marianne Gaillard
Favrot Fund
Fay's Incorporated
Federal Home Loan Mortgage Corp. (Freddie Mac)
Federal-Mogul Corp.
Federal National Mortgage Assn., Fannie Mae
Federal Screw Works
Federated Department Stores and Allied Stores Corp.
Federated Life Insurance Co.
Federation Foundation of Greater Philadelphia
Fein Foundation
Fels Fund, Samuel S.
Fidelity Bank
Field Foundation, Jamee and Marshall
Field Foundation, Jamee and Marshall
Field Foundation of Illinois
Fieldcrest Cannon
Fife Foundation, Elias and Bertha
Fifth Avenue Foundation
Fifth Avenue Foundation
Fikes Foundation, Leland
Finch Foundation, Doak
Finley Charitable Trust, J. B.
Finnegan Foundation, John D.
Fireman's Fund Insurance Co.
First Boston
First Fidelity Bancorporation
First Interstate Bank of Arizona
First Interstate Bank of California
First Interstate Bank of Oregon
First Maryland Bancorp
First National Bank & Trust Co. of Rockford
First Petroleum Corp.
First Union Corp.
Firstar Bank Milwaukee NA
FirsTier Bank N.A. Omaha
Fish Foundation, Ray C.
Fishback Foundation Trust, Harmes C.
Fisher-Price
Flagler Foundation
Flatley Foundation
Fleet Bank of New York
Fleet Financial Group
Fleishhacker Foundation
Fleming Foundation

Fletcher Foundation, A. J.
Flinn Foundation
Florida Rock Industries
Florida Steel Corp.
Foellinger Foundation
Fohs Foundation
Fondren Foundation
Foote, Cone & Belding Communications
Forbes
Forbes Charitable Trust, Herman
Ford Foundation
Ford Fund, Benson and Edith
Ford Fund, Walter and Josephine
Ford Fund, William and Martha
Ford II Fund, Henry
Ford Meter Box Co.
Forest City Enterprises
Forest Foundation
Fort Worth Star Telegram
Fortin Foundation of Florida
Fortis Benefits Insurance Company/Fortis Financial Group
Foster Charitable Foundation, M. Stratton
Foster Charitable Trust
Foster-Davis Foundation
Foster Foundation
Foulds Trust, Claiborne F
Foundation for Child Development
Fourth Financial Corp.
Fowler Memorial Foundation, John Edward
Fox Inc.
Fox Charitable Foundation, Harry K. & Emma R.
Frank Foundation, Ernest and Elfriede
Frankel Foundation
Frankel Foundation, George and Elizabeth F.
Franklin Foundation, John and Mary
Franklin Mint Corp.
Fraser Paper Ltd.
Frear Eleemosynary Trust, Mary D. and Walter F.
Freas Foundation
Frederick Foundation
Freed Foundation
Freedom Forum
Freeport-McMoRan
Frelinghuysen Foundation
French Foundation
Fribourg Foundation
Frick Educational Commission, Henry C.
Frohlich Charitable Trust, Ludwig W.
Frohman Foundation, Sidney
Frohring Foundation, William O. and Gertrude Lewis
Frost Foundation
Frueauff Foundation, Charles A.
Fry Foundation, Lloyd A.
Fuchs Foundation, Gottfried & Mary
Fuchsberg Family Foundation, Abraham
Fuller Foundation, C. G.
Fuller Foundation, George F. and Sybil H.
Fullerton Foundation
Funderburke & Associates
Fuqua Foundation, J. B.
Fusenot Charity Foundation, Georges and Germaine
Gaisman Foundation, Catherine and Henry J.
Gallagher Family Foundation, Lewis P.
Gallo Foundation, Julio R.
Galter Foundation
Galvin Foundation, Robert W.
Gannett Publishing Co., Guy
Gap, The

Garland Foundation, John Jewett and H. Chandler
Garner Charitable Trust, James G.
Garvey Memorial Foundation, Edward Chase
Garvey Texas Foundation
GATX Corp.
Gavin Foundation, James and Zita
Gaylord Foundation, Clifford Willard
Gebbie Foundation
GEICO Corp.
Geist Foundation
Gelb Foundation, Lawrence M.
Gellert Foundation, Carl
Gellert Foundation, Celia Berta
Gellert Foundation, Fred
General Dynamics Corp.
General Electric Co.
General Mills
General Motors Corp.
Geneseo Foundation
GenRad
George Foundation
Georgia Health Foundation
Georgia-Pacific Corp.
Georgia Power Co.
Gerber Products Co.
Gerbode Foundation, Wallace Alexander
German Protestant Orphan Asylum Association
Gerondelis Foundation
Gerson Family Foundation, Benjamin J.
Getsch Family Foundation Trust
Ghidotti Foundation, William and Marian
Giant Eagle
Giant Food
Giant Food Stores
Gifford Charitable Corporation, Rosamond
Gilder Foundation
Gill Foundation, Pauline Allen
Gilmore Foundation, Earl B.
Gilmore Foundation, Irving S.
Gindi Associates Foundation
Ginsberg Family Foundation, Moses
Ginter Foundation, Karl and Anna
Glancy Foundation, Lenora and Alfred
Glaser Foundation
Glaxo
Glazer Foundation, Jerome S.
Glenn Foundation, Carrie C. & Lena V.
Glickenhaus & Co.
Globe Newspaper Co.
Goddard Foundation, Charles B.
Goldberg Family Foundation, Israel and Matilda
Goldenberg Foundation, Max
Goldman Foundation, Aaron and Cecile
Goldman Foundation, Herman
Goldman Foundation, Morris and Rose
Goldring Family Foundation
Goldseker Foundation of Maryland, Morris
Goldstein Foundation, Leslie and Roslyn
Goldwyn Foundation, Samuel
Good Samaritan
Goodman Family Foundation
Goodstein Foundation
Goodwin Foundation, Leo
Goodyear Foundation, Josephine
Gordon Foundation, Meyer and Ida
Gorin Foundation, Nehemiah
Gould Inc.

Child Welfare (cont.)

Gould Foundation for Children, Edwin
Grace & Co., W.R.
Graco
Grader Foundation, K. W.
Gradison & Co.
Graham Charitable Trust, William L.
Graham Fund, Philip L.
Grainger Foundation
Grant Foundation, Charles M. and Mary D.
Grant Foundation, William T.
Graphic Controls Corp.
Grassmann Trust, E. J.
Gray Foundation, Garland
Graybar Electric Co.
Great Western Financial Corp.
Greater Lansing Foundation
Green Charitable Trust, Leslie H. and Edith C.
Green Foundation, Allen P. and Josephine B.
Green Fund
Greene Foundation, David J.
Greene Foundation, Robert Z.
Greenspan Foundation
Griffin, Sr., Foundation, C. V.
Grigg-Lewis Trust
Gross Charitable Trust, Stella B.
Gross Charitable Trust, Walter L. and Nell R.
Gruss Charitable Foundation, Emanuel and Riane
Gucci America Inc.
Gudelsky Family Foundation, Isadore and Bertha
Gulf Power Co.
Gulfstream Aerospace Corp.
Gund Foundation, George
Gurwin Foundation, J.
Guttman Foundation, Stella and Charles
Haas Foundation, Saul and Dayee G.
Haas Fund, Walter and Elise
Hachar Charitable Trust, D. D.
Hagedorn Fund
Haigh-Scatena Foundation
Hale Foundation, Crescent Porter
Halff Foundation, G. A. C.
Hall Charitable Trust, Evelyn A. J.
Hall Family Foundations
Hall Foundation
Hallett Charitable Trust
Hallett Charitable Trust, Jessie F.
Hallmark Cards
Halmos Foundation
Halsell Foundation, Ewing
Halsell Foundation, O. L.
Hamel Family Charitable Trust, D. A.
Hamilton Bank
Hamman Foundation, George and Mary Josephine
Hancock Foundation, Luke B.
Handleman Co.
Hansen Foundation, Dane G.
Harcourt Foundation, Ellen Knowles
Harcourt General
Hardin Foundation, Phil
Harding Educational and Charitable Foundation
Harding Educational and Charitable Foundation
Harding Foundation, Charles Stewart
Hargis Charitable Foundation, Estes H. and Florence Parker
Harper Brush Works
Harper Foundation, Philip S.
Harriman Foundation, Gladys and Roland

Harriman Foundation, Mary W.
Harrington Foundation, Don and Sybil
Harrington Trust, George
Harris Foundation, J. Ira and Nicki
Harris Foundation, John H. and Lucille
Hartmarx Corp.
Hartzell Industries, Inc.
Hasbro
Havens Foundation, O. W.
Hawley Foundation
Hay Foundation, John I.
Hayden Foundation, Charles
Hazen Charitable Trust, Lita Annenberg
Hazen Foundation, Edward W.
Hearst Foundation
Hearst Foundation, William Randolph
Hechinger Co.
Heckscher Foundation for Children
Hecla Mining Co.
Hedrick Foundation, Frank E.
Heginbotham Trust, Will E.
Heinz Co., H.J.
Heinz Foundation, Drue
Helfaer Foundation, Evan and Marion
Helis Foundation
Helmerich Foundation
Hendrickson Brothers
Herbst Foundation
Hermann Foundation, Grover
Herrick Foundation
Hersey Foundation
Hershey Foods Corp.
Hershey Foundation
Hervey Foundation
Hess Foundation
Heublein
Hewit Family Foundation
Hewlett Foundation, William and Flora
Heydt Fund, Nan and Matilda
Hill Crest Foundation
Hillcrest Foundation
Hillman Foundation
Hillsdale Fund
Hilton Foundation, Conrad N.
Himmelfarb Foundation, Paul and Annetta
Hirschhorn Foundation, David and Barbara B.
Hobbs Foundation
Hobby Foundation
Hoche-Scofield Foundation
Hodge Foundation
Hoffman Foundation, Marion O. and Maximilian
Hofmann Co.
Hogan Foundation, Royal Barney
Hollis Foundation
Home Depot
Homeland Foundation
Homeland Foundation
Honeywell
Hooper Foundation, Elizabeth S.
Hoover Foundation
Hopper Memorial Foundation, Bertrand
Horizons Foundation
Horne Foundation, Dick
Horowitz Foundation, Gedale B. and Barbara S.
Hospital Corp. of America
Household International
Houston Endowment
Houston Industries
Howell Foundation, Eric and Jessie
Howell Fund
Hubbard Broadcasting
Hubbell Inc.
Huffy Corp.

Hughes Memorial Foundation, Charles Evans
Hugoton Foundation
Huizenga Family Foundation
Hultquist Foundation
Humana
Humphrey Foundation, Glenn & Gertrude
Hunt Alternatives Fund
Hunt Alternatives Fund, Helen
Hunt Charitable Trust, C. Giles
Hunt Foundation
Hunt Manufacturing Co.
Hunter Trust, A. V.
Hunter Trust, Emily S. and Coleman A.
Hurst Foundation
Huston Foundation
Hutcheson Foundation, Hazel Montague
Hutchins Foundation, Mary J.
Hyams Foundation
Hyde and Watson Foundation
IBM Corp.
IBP, Inc.
Icahn Foundation, Carl C.
ICI Americas
IDS Financial Services
IES Industries
Illges Memorial Foundation, A. and M. L.
IMCERA Group Inc.
Imerman Memorial Foundation, Stanley
IMT Insurance Co.
Index Technology Corp.
Indiana Desk Co.
Ingalls Foundation, Louise H. and David S.
Inland Container Corp.
Inland Steel Industries
Innovating Worthy Projects Foundation
Insurance Management Associates
Interco
International Flavors & Fragrances
International Multifoods Corp.
International Paper Co.
Irvine Health Foundation
Isaly Klondike Co.
ITT Corp.
ITT Hartford Insurance Group
ITT Rayonier
Ittleson Foundation
Ivakota Association
J.P. Morgan & Co.
Jackson Charitable Trust, Marion Gardner
Jackson Foundation
Jacobson Foundation, Bernard H. and Blanche E.
Jacobson & Sons, Benjamin
Janeway Foundation, Elizabeth Bixby
Janirve Foundation
Jaqua Foundation
Jarson-Stanley and Mickey Kaplan Foundation, Isaac & Esther
Jasam Foundation
Jasper Desk Co.
Jefferson Smurfit Corp.
Jeffress Memorial Trust, Elizabeth G.
JELD-WEN, Inc.
Jenkins Foundation, George W.
Jennings Foundation, Alma
Jennings Foundation, Martha Holden
Jennings Foundation, Mary Hillman
Jergens Foundation, Andrew
Jewett Foundation, George Frederick
Jinks Foundation, Ruth T.

JMK-A M Micallef Charitable Foundation
Jockey Hollow Foundation
John Hancock Mutual Life Insurance Co.
Johnson Co., E. F.
Johnson Controls
Johnson Foundation, A. D.
Johnson Foundation, M. G. and Lillie A.
Johnson Foundation, Robert Wood
Johnson Foundation, Walter S.
Johnson & Higgins
Johnson & Son, S.C.
Jones Construction Co., J.A.
Jones Foundation, Daisy Marquis
Jones Foundation, Harvey and Bernice
Jones Foundation, Helen
Jones Intercable, Inc.
Jonsson Foundation
Joselow Foundation
Jost Foundation, Charles and Mabel P.
Journal Gazette Co.
Julia R. and Estelle L. Foundation
Jurzykowski Foundation, Alfred
Kamps Memorial Foundation, Gertrude
Kanematsu-Gosho U.S.A. Inc.
Kaplan Foundation, Mayer and Morris
Kaplan Fund, J. M.
Kaplun Foundation, Morris J. and Betty
Kapoor Charitable Foundation
Katten, Muchin, & Zavis
Katzenberger Foundation
Kaufmann Foundation, Henry
Kautz Family Foundation
Kayser Foundation
Keith Foundation Trust, Ben E.
Keller-Crescent Co.
Keller Family Foundation
Kelley and Elza Kelley Foundation, Edward Bangs
Kellogg Foundation, W. K.
Kelly, Jr. Memorial Foundation, Ensign C. Markland
Kemper Charitable Lead Trust, William T.
Kemper Educational and Charitable Fund
Kemper Foundation, Enid and Crosby
Kempner Fund, Harris and Eliza
Kenan Family Foundation
Kendall Foundation, George R.
Kenedy Memorial Foundation, John G. and Marie Stella
Kennecott Corp.
Kennedy Foundation, Ethel
Kennedy Foundation, Quentin J.
Kennedy, Jr. Foundation, Joseph P.
Kent-Lucas Foundation
Kentland Foundation
Kenworthy - Sarah H. Swift Foundation, Marion E.
Kepco, Inc.
Kern Foundation, Ilma
Kerney Foundation, James
Kerr Foundation, A. H.
Kerr Foundation, Robert S. and Grayce B.
Kettering Fund
Key Food Stores Cooperative Inc.
Kieckhefer Foundation, J. W.
Kiewit Foundation, Peter
Kilcawley Fund, William H.
Kilworth Charitable Foundation, Florence B.
Kimball Foundation, Horace A. Kimball and S. Ella
Kimball International
Kimberly-Clark Corp.

Kinder-Care Learning Centers
King Foundation, Carl B. and Florence E.
King Ranch
Kingston Foundation
Kiplinger Foundation
Kirby Foundation, F. M.
Kirchgessner Foundation, Karl
Klau Foundation, David W. and Sadie
Klein Fund, Nathan J.
Kline Foundation, Josiah W. and Bessie H.
Knight Foundation, John S. and James L.
Knistrom Foundation, Fanny and Svante
Knowles Charitable Memorial Trust, Gladys E.
Knox Family Foundation
Knox, Sr., and Pearl Wallis Knox Charitable Foundation, Robert W.
Knudsen Charitable Foundation, Earl
Koehler Foundation, Marcia and Otto
Kohl Charities, Herbert H.
Komes Foundation
Koopman Fund
Koret Foundation
Korman Family Foundation, Hyman
Kraft General Foods
Kramer Foundation, Louise
Kresge Foundation
Kress Foundation, George
Krieble Foundation, Vernon K.
Kuehn Foundation
Kugelman Foundation
Kysor Industrial Corp.
L. L. W. W. Foundation
L and L Foundation
Laclede Gas Co.
Lafarge Corp.
Laffey-McHugh Foundation
Lane Charitable Trust, Melvin R.
Lane Co., Inc.
Lang Foundation, Eugene M.
Langendorf Foundation, Stanley S.
Lanier Brothers Foundation
Lard Trust, Mary Potishman
Laros Foundation, R. K.
Larsen Fund
Lasky Co.
Lassen Foundation, Irving A.
Lauffer Trust, Charles A.
Laurel Foundation
Lavanburg-Corner House
Law Foundation, Robert O.
Lawrence Foundation, Lind
LBJ Family Foundation
LDI Charitable Foundation
Leach Foundation, Tom & Frances
Leavey Foundation, Thomas and Dorothy
Lee Endowment Foundation
Lee Foundation, James T.
Lee Foundation, Ray M. and Mary Elizabeth
Legg Mason Inc.
Lehman Foundation, Edith and Herbert
Lehmann Foundation, Otto W.
Lehrman Foundation, Jacob and Charlotte
Leidy Foundation, John J.
Lemberg Foundation
Leo Burnett Co.
Leonardt Foundation
Leuthold Foundation
Levine Family Foundation, Hyman
Levy Foundation, June Rockwell
Lewis Foundation, Frank J.
Lewis Foundation, Lillian Kaiser

Liberty Corp.
Liberty National Bank
Life Insurance Co. of Georgia
Lightner Sams Foundation
Lilly & Co., Eli
Lilly Foundation, Richard Coyle
Lincoln Electric Co.
Lincoln Fund
Lincoln National Corp.
Lindsay Trust, Agnes M.
Link, Jr. Foundation, George
Liquid Air Corp.
Little, Arthur D.
Litton Industries
Livingston Foundation, Milton S. and Corinne N.
Livingston Memorial Foundation
Liz Claiborne
Loats Foundation
Lockheed Sanders
Lockwood Foundation, Byron W. and Alice L.
Loews Corp.
Loewy Family Foundation
Logan Foundation, E. J.
Long Foundation, George A. and Grace
Longwood Foundation
Loose Trust, Carrie J.
Loose Trust, Harry Wilson
Loridans Foundation, Charles
Lost Tree Charitable Foundation
Louisiana Land & Exploration Co.
Louisiana-Pacific Corp.
Loutit Foundation
Love Foundation, George H. and Margaret McClintic
Love Foundation, Lucyle S.
Lowe Foundation
Lowe Foundation, Joe and Emily
Lowenstein Foundation, Leon
Lozier Foundation
LTV Corp.
Luce Charitable Trust, Theodore
Lukens
Lumpkin Foundation
Lurie Family Foundation
Lurie Foundation, Louis R.
Luse Foundation, W. P. and Bulah
Luttrell Trust
Lux Foundation, Miranda
Lydall, Inc.
Lyon Foundation
Lyons Foundation
Lytel Foundation, Bertha Russ
Maas Foundation, Benard L.
MacCurdy Salisbury Educational Foundation
MacDonald Foundation, James A.
Mack Foundation, J. S.
Maclellan Charitable Trust, R. J.
Maclellan Foundation, Robert L. and Kathrina H.
Macy & Co., R.H.
Maddox Foundation, J. F.
Magma Copper Co.
Magowan Family Foundation
Mailman Family Foundation, A. L.
Mailman Foundation
Makita U.S.A., Inc.
Mandel Foundation, Joseph and Florence
Mandel Foundation, Morton and Barbara
Mandeville Foundation
Maneely Fund
Mankato Citizens Telephone Co.
Mann Foundation, John Jay
Mann Foundation, Ted
Manoogian Foundation, Alex and Marie
Mapco Inc.
Marbrook Foundation
Marcus Brothers Textiles Inc.
Mardag Foundation

Maritz Inc.
Marley Co.
Marquette Electronics
Mars Foundation
Marsh & McLennan Cos.
Marshall Foundation
Marshall & Ilsley Bank
Martin & Deborah Flug Foundation
Martin Foundation
Martin Marietta Aggregates
Martin Marietta Corp.
Marx Foundation, Virginia & Leonard
Massengill-DeFriece Foundation
Massey Charitable Trust
Massey Foundation, Jack C.
Massie Trust, David Meade
Mastronardi Charitable Foundation, Charles A.
Mather Charitable Trust, S. Livingston
Mather Fund, Richard
Mathis-Pfohl Foundation
Mattel
Mattus Foundation, Reuben and Rose
May Department Stores Co.
May Mitchell Royal Foundation
Mayborn Foundation, Frank W.
Mayer Foundation, James and Eva
Maytag Family Foundation, Fred
Mazda Motors of America (Central), Inc.
Mazda North America
Mazza Foundation
MCA
McAlister Charitable Foundation, Harold
McAlonan Trust, John A.
McBean Charitable Trust, Alletta Morris
McBeath Foundation, Faye
McBride & Son Associates
McCarthy Charities
McCasland Foundation
McCray Lumber Co.
McCrea Foundation
McCune Charitable Trust, John R.
McCune Foundation
McDonald & Co. Securities
McDonald & Co. Securities
McDonald Foundation, J. M.
McDonald's Corp.
McDonnell Douglas Corp.-West
McDougall Charitable Trust, Ruth Camp
McEachern Charitable Trust, D. V. & Ida J.
McElroy Trust, R. J.
McEvoy Foundation, Mildred H.
McFawn Trust No. 2, Lois Sisler
McGee Foundation
McGonagle Foundation, Dextra Baldwin
McGraw Foundation
McGraw Foundation, Curtis W.
McGregor Fund
MCI Communications Corp.
MCJ Foundation
McKee Foundation, Robert E. and Evelyn
McKesson Corp.
McKnight Foundation
McKnight Foundation, Sumner T.
McMurray-Bennnett Foundation
McRae Foundation
McVay Foundation
Mead Corp.
Mead Fund, Nelson
Meadows Foundation
Mechanic Foundation, Morris A.
Mechanics Bank
Mellam Family Foundation
Mellon Foundation, Richard King

Melohn Foundation
Memorial Foundation for Children
Mengle Foundation, Glenn and Ruth
Menil Foundation
Mercantile Bancorp
Merck & Co.
Meredith Foundation
Mericos Foundation
Merit Oil Corp.
Merrill Lynch & Co.
Mertz Foundation, Martha
Mervyn's
Meserve Memorial Fund, Albert and Helen
Metropolitan Life Insurance Co.
Metropolitan Theatres Corp.
Meyer Family Foundation, Paul J.
Meyer Foundation, Alice Kleberg Reynolds
Meyer Foundation, Eugene and Agnes E.
Meyer Foundation, Robert R.
Meyer Memorial Foundation, Aaron and Rachel
Meyer Memorial Trust
Meyerhoff Fund, Joseph
Michael Foundation, Herbert I. and Elsa B.
Mid-Iowa Health Foundation
Middendorf Foundation
Milken Foundation, L. and S.
Millard Charitable Trust, Adah K.
Millbrook Tribute Garden
Miller Foundation, Steve J.
Miller Fund, Kathryn and Gilbert
Mills Charitable Foundation, Henry L. and Kathryn
Mine Safety Appliances Co.
Miniger Memorial Foundation, Clement O.
Mitchell Family Foundation, Edward D. and Anna
MNC Financial
Mobil Oil Corp.
Mohasco Corp.
Moncrief Foundation, William A. and Elizabeth B.
Monfort Charitable Foundation
Monsanto Co.
Montgomery Foundation
Montgomery Street Foundation
Moody Foundation
Moore Charitable Foundation, Marjorie
Moore Foundation
Moore Foundation, Edward S.
Moore Foundation, Martha G.
Moore Foundation, Roy C.
Moores Foundation, Harry C.
Morania Foundation
Morgan Foundation, Burton D.
Morgan Trust for Charity, Religion, and Education
Morgenstern Foundation, Morris
Morrill Charitable Foundation
Morris Foundation
Morris Foundation, Margaret T.
Morrison Foundation, Harry W.
Morrison-Knudsen Corp.
Moses Fund, Henry and Lucy
Mosher Foundation, Samuel B.
Moss Charitable Trust, Finis M.
Moss Foundation, Harry S.
Motorola
Mott Fund, Ruth
Mrs. Fields, Inc.
MTS Systems Corp.
Muller Foundation
Mulligan Charitable Trust, Mary S.
Multimedia, Inc.
Munger Foundation, Alfred C.
Murch Foundation
Murdock Charitable Trust, M. J.

Murphey Foundation, Lluella Morey
Murphy Foundation, Katherine and John
Murray Foundation
Musson Charitable Foundation, R. C. and Katharine M.
Mutual of New York
Myra Foundation
Nalco Chemical Co.
Nason Foundation
National City Corp.
National Computer Systems
National Machinery Co.
National Medical Enterprises
National Pro-Am Youth Fund
National Starch & Chemical Corp.
National Westminster Bank New Jersey
NationsBank Corp.
Nationwide Insurance Cos.
NBD Bank
Neilson Foundation, George W.
Nelson Foundation, Florence
Nesholm Family Foundation
New England Mutual Life Insurance Co.
New England Mutual Life Insurance Co.
New Horizon Foundation
New-Land Foundation
New Street Capital Corp.
New World Foundation
New York Foundation
New York Life Insurance Co.
New York Mercantile Exchange
New York Telephone Co.
The New Yorker Magazine, Inc.
Newhall Foundation, Henry Mayo
Newhouse Foundation, Samuel I.
Newman Charitable Trust, Calvin M. and Raquel H.
Newman's Own
Newmil Bancorp
News & Observer Publishing Co.
Nias Foundation, Henry
Nichols Foundation
Nike Inc.
Noble Foundation, Edward John
Noble Foundation, Samuel Roberts
Noble Foundation, Vivian Bilby
Norcross Wildlife Foundation
Nord Family Foundation
Nordson Corp.
Norfolk Shipbuilding & Drydock Corp.
Norgren Foundation, Carl A.
Norman Foundation, Andrew
Norman/Nethercutt Foundation, Merle
Norris Foundation, Dellora A. and Lester J.
Norris Foundation, Kenneth T. and Eileen L.
Northeast Utilities
Northern States Power Co.
Northern Trust Co.
Northwest Natural Gas Co.
Northwestern National Life Insurance Co.
Norton Co.
Norton Foundation Inc.
Norton Memorial Corporation, Geraldi
Norwest Bank Nebraska
NuTone Inc.
Occidental Oil & Gas Corp.
O'Connor Co.
Odell and Helen Pfeiffer Odell Fund, Robert Stewart
Oestreicher Foundation, Sylvan and Ann
Ogden Foundation, Ralph E.
Oglebay Norton Co.
Ohio Valley Foundation

Ohl, Jr. Trust, George A.
Ohrstrom Foundation
Onan Family Foundation
1525 Foundation
1957 Charity Trust
O'Neil Foundation, Casey Albert T.
O'Neil Foundation, M. G.
O'Neill Charitable Corporation, F. J.
Open Society Fund
Oppenheimer and Flora Oppenheimer Haas Trust, Leo
Oppenheimer Family Foundation
Oppenstein Brothers Foundation
Orange Orphan Society
Ordean Foundation
Orleans Trust, Carrie S.
Osborn Manufacturing Co.
O'Shaughnessy Foundation, I. A.
Oshkosh B'Gosh
O'Sullivan Children Foundation
Overbrook Foundation
Overlake Foundation
Overseas Shipholding Group
Owen Trust, B. B.
Oxford Foundation
Oxford Foundation
Oxford Industries, Inc.
PACCAR
Pacific Mutual Life Insurance Co.
Pacific Telesis Group
PacifiCorp
Packard Foundation, David and Lucile
Padnos Iron & Metal Co., Louis
Page Foundation, George B.
PaineWebber
Palin Foundation
Palisades Educational Foundation
Palmer-Fry Memorial Trust, Lily
Palmer Fund, Francis Asbury
Palmer Fund, Frank Loomis
Panhandle Eastern Corp.
Paramount Communications Inc.
Park Bank
Parker Foundation
Parker Foundation, Theodore Edson
Parsons Foundation, Ralph M.
Parsons - W.D. Charities, Vera Davis
Pasadena Area Residential Aid
Patterson Charitable Fund, W. I.
Paulucci Family Foundation
Pax Christi Foundation
PayLess Drug Stores
Payne Foundation, Frank E. and Seba B.
Peabody Foundation, Amelia
Pendergast-Weyer Foundation
Penn Foundation, William
Penney Foundation, James C.
Pennzoil Co.
Penzance Foundation
Peoples Energy Corp.
Peppers Foundation, Ann
Pepsi-Cola Bottling Co. of Charlotte
Perkin-Elmer Corp.
Perkin-Elmer Corp.
Perkins Charitable Foundation
Perkins Foundation, Edwin E.
Perkins Foundation, Joe and Lois
Perley Fund, Victor E.
Perpetual Benevolent Fund
Persis Corp.
Pesch Family Foundation
Pet
Petersen Foundation, Esper A.
Pew Charitable Trusts
Pfizer
Pforzheimer Foundation, Carl and Lily
Philadelphia Electric Co.
Philibosian Foundation, Stephen

Child Welfare (cont.)

Phillips Charitable Trust, Dr. and Mrs. Arthur William
Phillips Family Foundation, Jay and Rose
Phillips Foundation, Dr. P.
Phillips Foundation, Ellis L.
Phillips Petroleum Co.
Pick Charitable Trust, Melitta S.
Piedmont Health Care Foundation
Pillsbury Foundation
Pilot Trust
Pines Bridge Foundation
Pioneer Hi-Bred International
Pioneer Trust Bank, NA
Piper Jaffray Cos.
Pittsburgh Child Guidance Foundation
Pittsburgh National Bank
Pittway Corp.
Plankenhorn Foundation, Harry
Playboy Enterprises, Inc.
Plitt Southern Theatres
Plough Foundation
PMA Industries
Polinsky-Rivkin Family Foundation
Pollybill Foundation
Poorvu Foundation, William and Lia
Pope Foundation
Portland General Electric Co.
Post Foundation of D.C., Marjorie Merriweather
Potlatch Corp.
Potomac Electric Power Co.
Pott Foundation, Herman T. and Phenie R.
Powell Co., William
Powell Family Foundation
PPG Industries
Precision Rubber Products
Price Associates, T. Rowe
Price Foundation, Louis and Harold
Priddy Foundation
Prince Corp.
Prince Trust, Abbie Norman
Pritzker Foundation
Procter & Gamble Co.
Procter & Gamble Cosmetic & Fragrance Products
Providence Journal Company
Prudential Insurance Co. of America
Public Service Co. of Colorado
Public Service Electric & Gas Co.
Public Welfare Foundation
Pulitzer Publishing Co.
Puterbaugh Foundation
Quaker Chemical Corp.
Quaker Hill Foundation
Quaker Oats Co.
Questar Corp.
R. F. Foundation
Rabb Charitable Trust, Sidney R.
Radiator Specialty Co.
Ragen, Jr. Memorial Fund Trust No. 1, James M.
Ralston Purina Co.
Randa
Raskob Foundation for Catholic Activities
Ratshesky Foundation, A. C.
Rauch Foundation
Ray Foundation
Read Foundation, Charles L.
Redfield Foundation, Nell J.
Redman Foundation
Regenstein Foundation
Relations Foundation
Reliable Life Insurance Co.
Reliance Electric Co.
Rennebohm Foundation, Oscar

Replogle Foundation, Luther I.
Rexham Inc.
Reynolds Charitable Trust, Kate B.
Reynolds Foundation, Christopher
Reynolds Foundation, Donald W.
Reynolds Foundation, Edgar
Reynolds Foundation, J. B.
Reynolds Foundation, Richard S.
Reynolds Foundation, Z. Smith
Reynolds Metals Co.
Rice Foundation
Rich Co., F.D.
Richardson Foundation, Smith
Richardson Fund, Grace
Richardson Fund, Mary Lynn
Richmond Foundation, Frederick W.
Ricoh Corp.
Rieke Corp.
Rienzi Foundation
Riggs Benevolent Fund
Riley Foundation, Mabel Louise
Ringier-America
Rinker Materials Corp.
Ritchie Memorial Foundation, Charles E. and Mabel M.
Rite-Hite Corp.
Ritter Foundation, May Ellen and Gerald
Roberts Foundation
Robertshaw Controls Co.
Robinson Fund, Maurice R.
Roblee Foundation, Joseph H. and Florence A.
Roche Relief Foundation, Edward and Ellen
Rockford Products Corp.
Rockwell Foundation
Rockwell Fund
Rockwell International Corp.
Roddis Foundation, Hamilton
Rogers Foundation
Rogers Foundation, Mary Stuart
Rohm and Haas Company
Romill Foundation
RosaMary Foundation
Roseburg Forest Products Co.
Rosenbaum Foundation, Paul and Gabriella
Rosenberg Family Foundation, William
Rosenberg Foundation, Sunny and Abe
Rosenberg Foundation, William J. and Tina
Rosenberg, Jr. Family Foundation, Louise and Claude
Rosenthal Foundation, Benjamin J.
Rosenthal Foundation, Ida and William
Rosenthal Foundation, Richard and Hinda
Rosenwald Family Fund, William
Ross Foundation
Ross Foundation, Lyn & George M.
Ross Laboratories
Roth Family Foundation
Rouse Co.
Royal Group Inc.
Ruan Foundation Trust, John
Rubenstein Charitable Foundation, Lawrence J. and Anne
Rubinstein Foundation, Helena
Rudin Foundation
Rudy, Jr. Trust, George B.
Ruffin Foundation, Peter B. & Adeline W.
Russell Charitable Foundation, Tom
Russell Charitable Trust, Josephine S.
Russell Trust, Josephine G.
Ryan Foundation, Nina M.

Ryan Foundation, Patrick G. and Shirley W.
Saemann Foundation, Franklin I.
Sage Foundation
Sailors' Snug Harbor of Boston
Saint Croix Foundation
St. Faith's House Foundation
San Diego Gas & Electric
San Diego Trust & Savings Bank
Sandusky International Inc.
Sandy Foundation, George H.
Sandy Hill Foundation
Sanguinetti Foundation, Annunziata
Santa Fe Pacific Corp.
Sapirstein-Stone-Weiss Foundation
Sara Lee Corp.
Sara Lee Hosiery
Sarkeys Foundation
Sasco Foundation
Saturno Foundation
Sawyer Charitable Foundation
Scaife Family Foundation
Schadt Foundation
Schautz Foundation, Walter L.
Schenck Fund, L. P.
Scherer Foundation, Karla
Schermer Charitable Trust, Frances
Schieffelin Residuary Trust, Sarah I.
Schiff Foundation
Schiff Foundation, Dorothy
Schmidlapp Trust No. 1, Jacob G.
Schmitt Foundation, Arthur J.
Schneider Foundation Corp., Al J.
Scholl Foundation, Dr.
Scholler Foundation
Schroeder Foundation, Walter
Schultz Foundation
Schumann Fund for New Jersey
Schwartz Foundation, Arnold A.
Schwartz Foundation, David
Schwartz Fund for Education and Health Research, Arnold and Marie
Scott Foundation, William R., John G., and Emma
Scoular Co.
Scripps Foundation, Ellen Browning
Scrivner, Inc.
Scroggins Foundation, Arthur E. and Cornelia C.
Scurlock Foundation
Scurry Foundation, D. L.
Seafirst Corp.
Searle & Co., G.D.
Seaver Institute
Seaway Food Town
Seay Charitable Trust, Sarah M. and Charles E.
Seay Memorial Trust, George and Effie
Second Foundation
Security Life of Denver
See Foundation, Charles
Seid Foundation, Barre
Semple Foundation, Louise Taft
Sentinel Communications Co.
Sequoia Foundation
Setzer Foundation
Seybert Institution for Poor Boys and Girls, Adam and Maria Sarah
Seymour and Troester Foundation
Seymour Foundation, W. L. and Louise E.
Shapiro Foundation, Charles and M. R.
Share Foundation
Sharp Foundation, Evelyn
Shattuck Charitable Trust, S. F.
Shawmut National Corp.
Shaw's Supermarkets

Shea Foundation, John and Dorothy
Sheaffer Inc.
Sheldon Foundation, Ralph C.
Shell Oil Co.
Shemanski Testamentary Trust, Tillie and Alfred
Sheridan Foundation, Thomas B. and Elizabeth M.
Shirk Foundation, Russell and Betty
Shoenberg Foundation
Shoney's Inc.
Shoong Foundation, Milton
Shughart, Thomson & Kilroy, P.C.
Siebert Lutheran Foundation
Sierra Pacific Industries
Signet Bank/Maryland
Silverburgh Foundation, Grace, George & Judith
Simon Foundation, Robert Ellis
Simon Foundation, Sidney, Milton and Leoma
Simon Foundation, William E. and Carol G.
Simpson Foundation
Simpson Investment Co.
Sioux Steel Co.
Siragusa Foundation
SIT Investment Associates, Inc.
Sizzler International
Skillman Foundation
Skinner Corp.
Slant/Fin Corp.
Slaughter, Jr. Foundation, William E.
Slemp Foundation
Slifka Foundation, Alan B.
Slifka Foundation, Joseph and Sylvia
Smeal Foundation, Mary Jean & Frank P.
Smith and W. Aubrey Smith Charitable Foundation, Clara Blackford
Smith Charitable Foundation, Lou and Lutza
Smith Charitable Fund, Eleanor Armstrong
Smith Charitable Trust
Smith Charitable Trust, W. W.
Smith Corp., A.O.
Smith Foundation
Smith Foundation, Kelvin and Eleanor
Smith Foundation, Lon V.
Smith Foundation, Richard and Susan
Smith, Jr. Charitable Trust, Jack J.
Smith, Jr. Foundation, M. W.
Smith Memorial Fund, Ethel Sergeant Clark
Smithers Foundation, Christopher D.
Smucker Co., J.M.
SNET
Snider Foundation
Snow Foundation, John Ben
Somers Foundation, Byron H.
Sonat
Sooner Pipe & Supply Corp.
Sordoni Foundation
Soref Foundation, Samuel M. Soref and Helene K.
Sosland Foundation
Southern California Edison Co.
Southways Foundation
Southwestern Bell Corp.
Spang & Co.
Speas Foundation, Victor E.
Speas Memorial Trust, John W. and Effie E.
Special People In Need
Spiegel
Spiritus Gladius Foundation
Spiro Foundation, Donald W.

Sprague Educational and Charitable Foundation, Seth
Springs Industries
Spunk Fund
Square D Co.
Stabler Foundation, Donald B. and Dorothy L.
Stackner Family Foundation
Staley, Jr. Foundation, A. E.
Stanley Charitable Foundation, A. W.
Star Bank, N.A.
Starr Foundation
State Street Bank & Trust Co.
Statter Foundation, Amy Plant
Stauffer Foundation, John and Beverly
Staunton Farm Foundation
Stearns Charitable Foundation, Anna B.
Stearns Trust, Artemas W.
Steel, Sr. Foundation, Marshall
Steelcase
Stein Foundation, Jules and Doris
Steinhagen Benevolent Trust, B. A. and Elinor
Sterkel Trust, Justine
Sterling Inc.
Sterling Winthrop
Stern Foundation, Bernice and Milton
Stern Foundation, Irvin
Stern Foundation, Leonard N.
Stern Memorial Trust, Sidney
Sternberger Foundation, Sigmund
Sterne-Elder Memorial Trust
Stewardship Foundation
Stewart Trust under the will of Helen S. Devore, Alexander and Margaret
Stillwell Charitable Trust, Glen and Dorothy
Stock Foundation, Paul
Stocker Foundation
Stoddard Charitable Trust
Stokely, Jr. Foundation, William B.
Stone Charitable Foundation
Stone Container Corp.
Stone Family Foundation, Norman H.
Stone Foundation, David S.
Stone Foundation, France
Stonecutter Mills Corp.
Stonestreet Trust, Eusebia S.
Strake Foundation
Stranahan Foundation
Straus Foundation, Aaron and Lillie
Straus Foundation, Martha Washington Straus and Harry H.
Straus Foundation, Philip A. and Lynn
Strauss Foundation
Strawbridge Foundation of Pennsylvania II, Margaret Dorrance
Stride Rite Corp.
Strong Foundation, Hattie M.
Stuart Center Charitable Trust, Hugh
Stuart Foundations
Stulsaft Foundation, Morris
Stupp Brothers Bridge & Iron Co.
Stupp Foundation, Norman J.
Sturgis Charitable and Educational Trust, Roy and Christine
Subaru-Isuzu Automotive Inc.
Subaru of America Inc.
Summerfield Foundation, Solon E.
Sumners Foundation, Hatton W.
Sunderland Foundation, Lester T.
Surdna Foundation
Surrena Memorial Fund, Harry and Thelma

Swalm Foundation
Swift Memorial Health Care Foundation
Swig Charity Foundation, Mae and Benjamin
Swisher Foundation, Carl S.
Taconic Foundation
Tandem Computers
Tandy Corp.
Tandy Foundation, Anne Burnett and Charles
Tandy Foundation, David L.
Taper Foundation, Mark
Target Stores
Taub Foundation
Taylor Charitable Trust, Jack DeLoss
Taylor Foundation, Fred and Harriett
TCF Banking & Savings, FSB
Teichert
Teledyne
Teleklew Productions
Templeton Foundation, Herbert A.
Tennant Co.
Tension Envelope Corp.
Terner Foundation
Texaco
Texas Gas Transmission Corp.
Textron
Thagard Foundation
Thalhimer and Family Foundation, Charles G.
Thanksgiving Foundation
Thermo Electron Corp.
Thoman Foundation, W. B. and Candace
Thomas Foundation, Dorothy
Thomas Memorial Foundation, Theresa A.
Thompson Charitable Foundation, Marion G.
Thorne Foundation
Thorpe Foundation, James R.
3M Co.
Thurman Charitable Foundation for Children, Edgar A.
Thurston Charitable Foundation
Time Insurance Co.
Times Mirror Co.
Tisch Foundation
Titmus Foundation
TJX Cos.
Tomkins Industries, Inc.
Tonkin Foundation, Tom and Helen
Tosco Corp. Refining Division
Toyota Motor Sales, U.S.A.
Tracor, Inc.
Transamerica Corp.
Transco Energy Company
Trees Charitable Trust, Edith L.
Treuhaft Foundation
Trexler Trust, Harry C.
Trimble Family Foundation, Robert Mize and Isa White
Tropicana Products, Inc.
True Trust, Henry A.
Trull Foundation
Truman Foundation, Mildred Faulkner
Trust Co. Bank
TRW Corp.
Tuch Foundation, Michael
Tuohy Foundation, Alice Tweed
Tupancy-Harris Foundation of 1986
Turner Fund, Ruth
Turrell Fund
Twentieth Century-Fox Film Corp.
Union Bank of Switzerland Los Angeles Branch
Union Camp Corp.
Union Electric Co.
Union Pacific Corp.
United Conveyor Corp.

United Parcel Service of America
U.S. Bank of Washington
United States Sugar Corp.
United States Trust Co. of New York
United Technologies Corp.
Universal Foods Corp.
Universal Leaf Tobacco Co.
Universal Leaf Tobacco Co.
Upjohn Foundation, Harold and Grace
Upton Charitable Foundation, Lucy and Eleanor S.
Upton Foundation, Frederick S.
Uris Brothers Foundation
US WEST
USF&G Co.
Ushkow Foundation
UST
Utilicorp United
Vale-Asche Foundation
Vale Foundation, Ruby R.
Valley Foundation
Valley National Bank of Arizona
Valmont Industries
Van Camp Foundation
Van Every Foundation, Philip L.
Van Houten Charitable Trust
Van Nuys Charities, J. B. and Emily
Van Nuys Foundation, I. N. and Susanna H.
Van Wert County Foundation
Vance Charitable Foundation, Robert C.
Vanneck-Bailey Foundation
Varian Associates
Vaughn Foundation
Vernon Fund, Miles Hodsdon
Virginia Power Co.
Vollbrecht Foundation, Frederick A.
Von der Ahe Foundation
Vulcan Materials Co.
W. W. W. Foundation
Wachovia Bank & Trust Co., N.A.
Wade Endowment Fund, Elizabeth Firth
Waggoner Charitable Trust, Crystelle
Wagner Foundation, Ltd., R. H.
Wal-Mart Stores
Waldbaum, Inc.
Waldbaum Family Foundation, I.
Walgreen Co.
Walker Foundation, L. C. and Margaret
Walker Foundation, T. B.
Wallace Foundation, George R.
Wallach Foundation, Miriam G. and Ira D.
Wallin Foundation
Walsh Foundation
Walthall Perpetual Charitable Trust, Marjorie T.
Ward Foundation, A. Montgomery
Ward Foundation, Louis L. and Adelaide C.
Wardle Family Foundation
Ware Foundation
Wareheim Foundation, E. C.
Warfield Memorial Fund, Anna Emory
Warner Fund, Albert and Bessie
Warner-Lambert Co.
Warsh-Mott Legacy
Washington Forrest Foundation
Washington Foundation
Washington Mutual Savings Bank
Washington Post Co.
Washington Square Fund
Washington Water Power Co.
Wasserman Foundation
Watson Foundation, Walter E. and Caroline H.

Wean Foundation, Raymond John
Weaver Foundation
Weaver Foundation, Gil and Dody
Webb Charitable Trust, Susan Mott
Webb Educational and Charitable Trust, Torrey H. and Dorothy K.
Webb Foundation
Weber Charities Corp., Frederick E.
Webster Charitable Foundation
Webster Foundation, Edwin S.
Weckbaugh Foundation, Eleanore Mullen
Wedum Foundation
Weeden Foundation, Frank
Wege Foundation
Weinberg Foundation, John L.
Weinberg, Jr. Foundation, Sidney J.
Weingart Foundation
Weisbrod Foundation Trust Dept., Robert and Mary
Weiss Fund, Clara
Welch Testamentary Trust, George T.
Welfare Foundation
Wellman Foundation, S. K.
Wells Fargo & Co.
Wells Foundation, A. Z.
Wenger Foundation, Henry L. and Consuelo S.
West Co.
West Foundation, Neva and Wesley
Western New York Foundation
Western Southern Life Insurance Co.
Westinghouse Electric Corp.
Weyerhaeuser Co.
Wharton Foundation
Wheless Foundation
Whirlpool Corp.
Whitaker Charitable Foundation, Lyndon C.
White Consolidated Industries
White Construction Co.
White Foundation, Erle and Emma
White Trust, G. R.
Whitehead Foundation
Whitehead Foundation, Joseph B.
Whitener Foundation
Whiting Foundation
Whiting Memorial Foundation, Henry and Harriet
Whitney Fund, David M.
Whittenberger Foundation, Claude R. and Ethel B.
Wickes Foundation, Harvey Randall
Wickson-Link Memorial Foundation
Wiener Foundation, Malcolm Hewitt
Wilcox General Trust, George N.
Wildermuth Foundation, E. F.
Wilkof Foundation, Edward and Ruth
Willard Helping Fund, Cecilia Young
Williams Cos.
Willits Foundation
Wilson Foundation, Elaine P. and Richard U.
Wilson Foundation, Frances Wood
Wilson Foundation, Hugh and Mary
Wilson Foundation, Marie C. and Joseph C.
Wilson Public Trust, Ralph
Wimpey Inc., George
Winn-Dixie Stores
Winona Corporation
Wisconsin Energy Corp.

Wisconsin Power & Light Co.
Wolf Foundation, Melvin and Elaine
Wolff Memorial Foundation, Pauline Sterne
Wollenberg Foundation
Wood Charitable Trust, W. P.
Woodland Foundation
Woods Charitable Fund
Woods Foundation, James H.
Woodward Fund
Woodward Fund-Atlanta, David, Helen, Marian
Woodward Fund-Watertown, David, Helen, and Marian
Woodward Governor Co.
Woolley Foundation, Vasser
Wornall Charitable Trust and Foundation, Kearney
Wright Foundation, Lola
Wrigley Co., Wm. Jr.
Wurts Memorial, Henrietta Tower
Wyss Foundation
Xerox Corp.
Yassenoff Foundation, Leo
Yawkey Foundation II
Yeager Charitable Trust, Lester E.
Yost Trust, Elizabeth Burns
Youth Foundation
Zale Foundation
Zarkin Memorial Foundation, Charles
Zellerbach Family Fund
Ziegler Foundation
Zilkha & Sons
Zonas Trust, Steven K.
Zuckerberg Foundation, Roy J.

Community Centers

Abbott Laboratories
Abell Foundation, Charles S.
Abrams Foundation
Abrams Foundation, Benjamin and Elizabeth
Abrons Foundation, Louis and Anne
ACF Industries, Inc.
Ackerman Trust, Anna Keesling
Acme-McCrary Corp.
Action Industries, Inc.
Acushnet Co.
Adams Memorial Fund, Emma J.
Advanced Micro Devices
Aigner
Alabama Power Co.
Albertson's
Alcon Laboratories, Inc.
Alexander Charitable Foundation
Allegheny Ludlum Corp.
Allendale Mutual Insurance Co.
AlliedSignal
Alltel/Western Region
Alms Trust, Eleanora
ALPAC Corp.
Alperin/Hirsch Family Foundation
Alumax
Aluminum Co. of America
Amado Foundation, Maurice
AMCORE Bank, N.A. Rockford
American Brands
American Electric Power
American Express Co.
American Foundation
American National Bank & Trust Co. of Chicago
American Saw & Manufacturing Co.
American United Life Insurance Co.
Ames Department Stores
Amfac/JMB Hawaii
Andersen Foundation
Andersons Management Corp.
AON Corp.
Apache Corp.

Apple Computer, Inc.
ARCO Chemical
Arkansas Power & Light Co.
Armco Inc.
Astor Foundation, Vincent
Atherton Family Foundation
Atlanta Gas Light Co.
Attleboro Pawtucket Savings Bank
Auerbach Foundation, Beatrice Fox
Avon Products
Babcock & Wilcox Co.
Bacardi Imports
Backer Spielvogel Bates U.S.
Baird & Co., Robert W.
Baker Foundation, R. C.
Banc One Illinois Corp.
Banc One Wisconsin Corp.
Bank of America Arizona
Bank of Boston Corp.
Bank of Louisville
Bank South Corp.
Barden Corp.
Barker Welfare Foundation
Barry Corp., R. G.
Barstow Foundation
Barth Foundation, Theodore H.
Bassett Foundation, Norman
Bauervic Foundation, Peggy
Bauervic-Paisley Foundation
Bechtel Charitable Remainder Uni-Trust, Marie H.
Bedsole Foundation, J. L.
Beerman Foundation
Belding Heminway Co.
Beneficia Foundation
Benenson Foundation, Frances and Benjamin
Beretta U.S.A. Corp.
Berger Foundation, H.N. and Frances C.
Bernstein & Co., Sanford C.
Berwind Corp.
Bethlehem Steel Corp.
Beveridge Foundation, Frank Stanley
BFGoodrich
BHP Pacific Resources
Bing Fund
Binney & Smith Inc.
Blair and Co., William
Blandin Foundation
Block, H&R
Blowitz-Ridgeway Foundation
Blue Bell, Inc.
Blue Cross and Blue Shield United of Wisconsin Foundation
Blum-Kovler Foundation
Boatmen's First National Bank of Oklahoma
Bodman Foundation
Boeing Co.
Boettcher Foundation
Boise Cascade Corp.
Booth-Bricker Fund
Borg-Warner Corp.
Borman's
Bound to Stay Bound Books Foundation
Bowater Inc.
Bowne Foundation, Robert
BP America
Brach Foundation, Helen
Bradley Foundation, Lynde and Harry
Bradley-Turner Foundation
Bray Charitable Trust, Viola E.
Bremer Foundation, Otto
Brenton Banks Inc.
Bridgestone/Firestone
Brochsteins Inc.
Brody Foundation, Frances
Bromley Residuary Trust, Guy I.
Bronstein Foundation, Soloman and Sylvia

Community Centers (cont.)

Brookdale Foundation
Brown & Williamson Tobacco Corp.
Bruening Foundation, Eva L. and Joseph M.
Brunswick Corp.
Bryant Foundation
Buchalter, Nemer, Fields, & Younger
Buchanan Family Foundation
Buffett Foundation
Burchfield Foundation, Charles E.
Burlington Industries
Burlington Northern Inc.
Burns Foundation
Burns International
Burress, J.W.
Burroughs Wellcome Co.
Bush Foundation
Business Incentives
C.P. Rail Systems
Cable & Wireless Communications
Cabot Corp.
Cafritz Foundation, Morris and Gwendolyn
Cain Foundation, Effie and Wofford
Camp Younts Foundation
Campbell Soup Co.
Cantor Foundation, Iris and B. Gerald
Capital Holding Corp.
Carnahan-Jackson Foundation
Carrier Corp.
Carvel Foundation, Thomas and Agnes
Cary Charitable Trust, Mary Flagler
Carylon Foundation
Catlin Charitable Trust, Kathleen K.
CBI Industries
Ceco Corp.
Centel Corp.
Centerior Energy Corp.
Central Bank of the South
Central Hudson Gas & Electric Corp.
Central Life Assurance Co.
Central Maine Power Co.
Chamberlin Foundation, Gerald W.
Chambers Development Co.
Chanin Family Foundation, Paul R.
Charina Foundation
Charlton, Jr. Charitable Trust, Earle P.
Chartwell Foundation
Chase Charity Foundation, Alfred E.
Chase Manhattan Bank, N.A.
Chase Trust, Alice P.
Chazen Foundation
Cherne Foundation, Albert W.
Cherokee Foundation
Chevron Corp.
Chicago Sun-Times, Inc.
Children's Foundation of Erie County
Chilton Foundation Trust
Cincinnati Bell
Circuit City Stores
Citicorp
Citizens Bank
CLARCOR
Clark Foundation
Clarke Trust, John
Classic Leather
Clipper Ship Foundation
Clorox Co.
Coffey Foundation

Cohen Foundation, George M.
Cohen Foundation, Manny and Ruthy
Cohen Foundation, Manny and Ruthy
Cole Foundation, Olive B.
Coleman Co.
Collins Foundation
Colonial Life & Accident Insurance Co.
Colorado State Bank of Denver
Coltec Industries
Columbia Foundation
Columbus Dispatch Printing Co.
Commerce Clearing House
Comstock Foundation
Cone Mills Corp.
Connelly Foundation
Consolidated Natural Gas Co.
Consolidated Papers
Conston Corp.
Continental Corp.
Cooper Industries
Coors Foundation, Adolph
Copperweld Steel Co.
Corbin Foundation, Mary S. and David C.
Country Curtains, Inc.
Cowles Charitable Trust
Cowles Foundation, Gardner and Florence Call
Cowles Media Co.
CPC International
Craig Foundation, J. Paul
Crandall Memorial Foundation, J. Ford
Crestlea Foundation
Crocker Trust, Mary A.
Crum and Forster
Crystal Trust
Cudahy Fund, Patrick and Anna M.
Cullen/Frost Bankers
Cummings Foundation, Nathan
Cummings Memorial Fund Trust, Frances L. and Edwin L.
Cummins Engine Co.
Curtice-Burns Foods
Dalton Foundation, Dorothy U.
Dana Corp.
Darrah Charitable Trust, Jessie Smith
Dart Foundation
Davis Foundation, Joe C.
DEC International, Inc.
Deere & Co.
DeKalb Genetics Corp.
Delaware North Cos.
Demoulas Supermarkets
Deposit Guaranty National Bank
DeRoy Testamentary Foundation
Detroit Edison Co.
Deuble Foundation, George H.
Deutsch Co.
DeVos Foundation, Richard and Helen
Dexter Charitable Fund, Eugene A.
Diamond Foundation, Aaron
Diamond Shamrock
Dimeo Construction Co.
Doheny Foundation, Carrie Estelle
Domino's Pizza
Donaldson Charitable Trust, Oliver S. and Jennie R.
Donaldson Co.
Douglas & Lomason Company
Dow Corning Corp.
Dow Foundation, Herbert H. and Grace A.
Dow Fund, Alden and Vada
Dresser Industries
Dreyfus Foundation, Jean and Louis
du Pont de Nemours & Co., E. I.
Duke Power Co.

Dweck Foundation, Samuel R.
Dynamet, Inc.
Dyson Foundation
Earl-Beth Foundation
Eastern Fine Paper, Inc.
Eastover Corp.
Eaton Corp.
Eaton Foundation, Edwin M. and Gertrude S.
Ebell of Los Angeles Rest Cottage Association
Eccles Foundation, George S. and Dolores Dore
Eccles Foundation, Marriner S.
Eddy Family Memorial Fund, C. K.
Edison Foundation, Harry
Edwards Industries
Egenton Home
Einstein Fund, Albert E. and Birdie W.
Eisenberg Foundation, Ben B. and Joyce E.
Elco Charitable Foundation
Electronic Data Systems Corp.
Ellsworth Foundation, Ruth H. and Warren A.
Ellsworth Trust, W. H.
Emerson Electric Co.
Emery Memorial, Thomas J.
Engelhard Foundation, Charles
Ensign-Bickford Industries
Ensworth Charitable Foundation
Equifax
Ernsthausen Charitable Foundation, John F. and Doris E.
Evans Foundation, T. M.
Evjue Foundation
Eyman Trust, Jesse
FAB Industries
Fair Oaks Foundation, Inc.
Fairfield Foundation, Freeman E.
Falk Medical Fund, Maurice
Farr Trust, Frank M. and Alice M.
Faulkner Trust, Marianne Gaillard
Federal-Mogul Corp.
Federation Foundation of Greater Philadelphia
Fein Foundation
Feldberg Family Foundation
Fels Fund, Samuel S.
Ferkauf Foundation, Eugene and Estelle
Fidelity Bank
Fieldcrest Cannon
Fife Foundation, Elias and Bertha
Fingerhut Family Foundation
Finley Charitable Trust, J. B.
Finnegan Foundation, John D.
Fireman's Fund Insurance Co.
Firestone, Jr. Foundation, Harvey
First Fidelity Bancorporation
First Financial Bank FSB
First Interstate Bank of Arizona
First Interstate Bank of California
First Interstate Bank of Oregon
First Maryland Bancorp
First National Bank & Trust Co. of Rockford
First Union Corp.
Firstar Bank Milwaukee NA
FirsTier Bank N.A. Omaha
Fischbach Foundation
Fischel Foundation, Harry and Jane
Fisher Foundation
Fisher Foundation
Fleet Financial Group
Flemm Foundation, John J.
Fletcher Foundation
Florida Rock Industries
Flowers Charitable Trust, Albert W. and Edith V.
Forbes
Forbes Charitable Trust, Herman

Ford Fund, Benson and Edith
Forest Foundation
Forster-Powers Charitable Trust
Foster Charitable Trust
Foster Foundation
Foundation for Seacoast Health
Fox Steel Co.
Frank Fund, Zollie and Elaine
Fraser Paper Ltd.
Frear Eleemosynary Trust, Mary D. and Walter F.
Freas Foundation
Freedom Forum
Frees Foundation
French Oil Mill Machinery Co.
Frese Foundation, Arnold D.
Friedman Foundation, Stephen and Barbara
Friendly Rosenthal Foundation
Froderman Foundation
Frohman Foundation, Sidney
Frueauff Foundation, Charles A.
Fry Foundation, Lloyd A.
Fuchsberg Family Foundation, Abraham
Fuchsberg Family Foundation, Abraham
Funderburke & Associates
Fusenot Charity Foundation, Georges and Germaine
Gannett Publishing Co., Guy
Garvey Kansas Foundation
Gates Foundation
GATX Corp.
GEICO Corp.
Geifman Family Foundation
Gellert Foundation, Carl
Gellert Foundation, Fred
Gelman Foundation, Melvin and Estelle
General American Life Insurance Co.
General Electric Co.
General Machine Works
General Mills
General Motors Corp.
General Railway Signal Corp.
Georgia Health Foundation
Georgia Power Co.
Gerondelis Foundation
Gershenson Foundation, Charles H.
Gershman Foundation, Joel
Gerson Family Foundation, Benjamin J.
Gerson Trust, B. Milfred
Gerstacker Foundation, Rollin M.
Giant Eagle
Giant Food
Giant Food Stores
Gillette Co.
Gindi Associates Foundation
Gitano Group
Glaxo
Globe Corp.
Globe Newspaper Co.
Glosser Foundation, David A.
Goldberg Family Foundation, Israel and Matilda
Goldsmith Foundation
Goldstein Foundation, Alfred and Ann
Golub Corp.
Goodman Memorial Foundation, Joseph C. and Clare F.
Goodyear Foundation, Josephine
Gorin Foundation, Nehemiah
Grace & Co., W.R.
Graphic Controls Corp.
Gray Foundation, Garland
Graybar Electric Co.
Great Atlantic & Pacific Tea Co. Inc.
Greater Lansing Foundation
Grede Foundries
Green Fund
Greenheck Fan Corp.

Greentree Foundation
Gregg-Graniteville Foundation
Gries Charity Fund, Lucile and Robert H.
Grigg-Lewis Trust
Groves & Sons Co., S.J.
Grumbacher Foundation, M. S.
GTE Corp.
Guaranty Bank & Trust Co.
Gudelsky Family Foundation, Homer and Martha
Gudelsky Family Foundation, Isadore and Bertha
Gund Foundation, George
Guttman Foundation, Stella and Charles
Haas Fund, Walter and Elise
Haas, Jr. Fund, Evelyn and Walter
Hagedorn Fund
Halff Foundation, G. A. C.
Hall Foundation
Hallmark Cards
Halloran Foundation, Mary P. Dolciani
Halsell Foundation, O. L.
Hamel Family Charitable Trust, D. A.
Hansen Foundation, Dane G.
Hanson Foundation
Harding Foundation, Charles Stewart
Harkness Ballet Foundation
Harriman Foundation, Mary W.
Harrington Foundation, Don and Sybil
Harrington Foundation, Francis A. and Jacquelyn H.
Harris Brothers Foundation
Harris Foundation
Harris Foundation, James J. and Angelia M.
Harsco Corp.
Hartmarx Corp.
Hartz Foundation
Hartzell Industries, Inc.
Hatterscheidt Foundation
Hawley Foundation
Hawn Foundation
Hayden Foundation, Charles
Hechinger Co.
Hecla Mining Co.
HEI Inc.
Heilicher Foundation, Menahem
Heinz Co., H.J.
Helfaer Foundation, Evan and Marion
Helzberg Foundation, Shirley and Barnett
Henderson Foundation
Henderson Foundation, George B.
Herbst Foundation
Herman Foundation, John and Rose
Herndon Foundation, Alonzo F. Herndon and Norris B.
Hervey Foundation
Hidary Foundation, Jacob
Higgins Foundation, Aldus C.
Hillcrest Foundation
Hilliard Corp.
Hillman Foundation
Hoblitzelle Foundation
Hodge Foundation
Hoffer Plastics Corp.
Hofheinz Foundation, Irene Cafcalas
Hofstetter Trust, Bessie
Holley Foundation
Holzer Memorial Foundation, Richard H.
Home Depot
HON Industries
Honda of America Manufacturing, Inc.
Honeywell

Hopkins Foundation, Josephine Lawrence
Horne Foundation, Dick
Horne Trust, Mabel
Hospital Corp. of America
Houck Foundation, May K.
Household International
Houston Industries
Hoyt Foundation
Hoyt Foundation, Stewart W. and Willma C.
Hubbard Milling Co.
Hubbell Inc.
Hughes Charitable Trust, Mabel Y.
Huisking Foundation
Humana
Hunt Charitable Trust, C. Giles
Hunt Foundation
Hunter Trust, A. V.
Hurst Foundation
Hyams Foundation
Hyde and Watson Foundation
ICI Americas
IES Industries
IMT Insurance Co.
Indiana Bell Telephone Co.
Ingalls Foundation, Louise H. and David S.
Inland Container Corp.
Inland Steel Industries
Interco
Isaly Klondike Co.
ITT Rayonier
J. D. B. Fund
J.P. Morgan & Co.
Jackson Charitable Trust, Marion Gardner
Jackson Foundation
Jackson Mills
Janirve Foundation
Jarson-Stanley and Mickey Kaplan Foundation, Isaac & Esther
Jasper Seating Co.
JELD-WEN, Inc.
Jellison Benevolent Society
Jennings Foundation, Alma
Jergens Foundation, Andrew
Jerome Foundation
John Hancock Mutual Life Insurance Co.
Johnson Co., E. F.
Johnson Controls
Johnson Foundation, Helen K. and Arthur E.
Johnson Foundation, M. G. and Lillie A.
Jones Foundation, Daisy Marquis
Jones Foundation, Montfort Jones and Allie Brown
Jones Intercable, Inc.
Jonsson Foundation
Joslyn Foundation, Marcellus I.
Jostens
JSJ Corp.
Kaplan Foundation, Charles I. and Mary
Kaplan Foundation, Rita J. and Stanley H.
Kaplen Foundation
Kaufmann Foundation, Henry
Kawabe Memorial Fund
Keene Trust, Hazel R.
Keith Foundation Trust, Ben E.
Kemper Charitable Lead Trust, William T.
Kemper Foundation, Enid and Crosby
Kemper Memorial Foundation, David Woods
Kennecott Corp.
Kennedy Foundation, Ethel
Kerr Foundation
Kerr-McGee Corp.
Key Bank of Maine

Kilworth Charitable Trust, William
Kimberly-Clark Corp.
King Ranch
Kingsbury Corp.
Kiplinger Foundation
Kirbo Charitable Trust, Thomas M. and Irene B.
Kitzmiller/Bales Trust
Klee Foundation, Conrad and Virginia
Klein Charitable Foundation, Raymond
Kline Foundation, Charles and Figa
Kline Foundation, Josiah W. and Bessie H.
Knistrom Foundation, Fanny and Svante
Knott Foundation, Marion I. and Henry J.
Knox Family Foundation
Knudsen Charitable Foundation, Earl
Koehler Foundation, Marcia and Otto
Koret Foundation
Kramer Foundation, Louise
Kresge Foundation
Kuehn Foundation
Kuhns Investment Co.
Kysor Industrial Corp.
Ladd Charitable Corporation, Helen and George
Lamson & Sessions Co.
Lane Foundation, Minnie and Bernard
Laros Foundation, R. K.
Lassus Brothers Oil
Lavanburg-Corner House
Lee Enterprises
Lehrman Foundation, Jacob and Charlotte
Lennon Foundation, Fred A.
Lennox International, Inc.
Leo Burnett Co.
Leuthold Foundation
Levinson Foundation, Max and Anna
Levitt Foundation, Richard S.
Levy Foundation, Hyman Jebb
Liberty National Bank
Lightner Sams Foundation
Lilly Endowment
Lincoln Fund
Lincoln National Corp.
Lindsay Trust, Agnes M.
Lipton, Thomas J.
Littauer Foundation, Lucius N.
Little, Arthur D.
Litton Industries
Long Foundation, George A. and Grace
Long Island Lighting Co.
Longwood Foundation
Lowe Foundation, Joe and Emily
Lowenstein Brothers Foundation
Lowenstein Foundation, Leon
Lowenstein Foundation, William P. and Marie R.
Lubrizol Corp.
Lurie Foundation, Louis R.
Lux Foundation, Miranda
Lydall, Inc.
Lyon Foundation
Maas Foundation, Benard L.
Mabee Foundation, J. E. and L. E.
Mack Foundation, J. S.
Maclellan Charitable Trust, R. J.
MacLeod Stewardship Foundation
Macmillan, Inc.
Macy & Co., R.H.
Magma Copper Co.
Magruder Foundation, Chesley G.

MalCo Products Inc.
Mallinckrodt Specialty Chemicals Co.
Manat Foundation
Mandell Foundation, Samuel P.
Mankato Citizens Telephone Co.
Manville Corp.
Marcus Corp.
Mardag Foundation
Marinette Marine Corp.
Markey Charitable Fund, John C.
Marmot Foundation
Marquette Electronics
Mars Foundation
Marshall & Ilsley Bank
Martin Family Fund
Martin Foundation
Martin Marietta Corp.
Masserini Charitable Trust, Maurice J.
Massey Charitable Trust
Mattus Foundation, Reuben and Rose
Maxus Energy Corp.
May Department Stores Co.
Mayor Foundation, Oliver Dewey
Maytag Family Foundation, Fred
MBIA, Inc.
MCA
McAlister Charitable Foundation, Harold
McCann Foundation
McConnell Foundation
McCune Foundation
McDonald & Co. Securities
McDonald's Corp.
McDonnell Douglas Corp.-West
McDonough Foundation, Bernard
McEvoy Foundation, Mildred H.
McFawn Trust No. 2, Lois Sisler
McGraw-Hill
McKee Foundation, Robert E. and Evelyn
McKee Poor Fund, Virginia A.
McKesson Corp.
McKnight Foundation
McLean Contributionship
McMahon Foundation
McNeely Foundation
McNutt Charitable Trust, Amy Shelton
Meadows Foundation
Media General, Inc.
Medina Foundation
Medtronic
Mellon Bank Corp.
Memorial Foundation for Children
Mengle Foundation, Glenn and Ruth
Menil Foundation
Merchants Bancshares
Meridian Bancorp
Messing Foundation, Morris M. and Helen F.
Mettler Instrument Corp.
Meyer Foundation, Eugene and Agnes E.
Meyer Foundation, Robert R.
Meyer Fund, Milton and Sophie
Michigan Consolidated Gas Co.
Michigan Gas Utilities
Midmark Corp.
Mingenback Foundation, Julia J.
Miniger Memorial Foundation, Clement O.
Mitchell Family Foundation, Edward D. and Anna
Mitsubishi International Corp.
Mobil Oil Corp.
Monsanto Co.
Montgomery Street Foundation
Moore Charitable Foundation, Marjorie
Moore Foundation, Edward S.
Moore & Sons, B.C.

Moorman Manufacturing Co.
Morley Brothers Foundation
Morrison Foundation, Harry W.
Morrison-Knudsen Corp.
Moses Fund, Henry and Lucy
Moskowitz Foundation, Irving I.
Moss Foundation, Harry S.
Moss Heart Trust, Harry S.
Motter Printing Press Co.
Mullan Foundation, Thomas F. and Clementine L.
Munson Foundation, W. B.
Nalco Chemical Co.
National By-Products
National City Corp.
National Computer Systems
National Fuel Gas Co.
National Life of Vermont
National Machinery Co.
National Medical Enterprises
National Presto Industries
National Service Industries
National Starch & Chemical Corp.
National Westminster Bank New Jersey
NBD Bank
Nelco Sewing Machine Sales Corp.
Nestle U.S.A. Inc.
New England Business Service
New England Mutual Life Insurance Co.
New York Foundation
New York Life Insurance Co.
New York Telephone Co.
Newhouse Foundation, Samuel I.
Newman's Own
Newmil Bancorp
News & Observer Publishing Co.
Noble Foundation, Edward John
Nordson Corp.
Norfolk Southern Corp.
Nortek, Inc.
North Carolina Foam Foundation
Northeast Utilities
Northern Indiana Public Service Co.
Northern States Power Co.
Northwest Natural Gas Co.
Norton Co.
Norwest Bank Nebraska
Norwest Bank Nebraska
NuTone Inc.
O'Connor Foundation, A. Lindsay and Olive B.
Oglebay Norton Co.
Ohio National Life Insurance Co.
Ohio Valley Foundation
Ohrstrom Foundation
Olin Corp.
1525 Foundation
O'Neil Foundation, Cyril F. and Marie E.
Orchard Corp. of America.
Ordean Foundation
Orleans Trust, Carrie S.
O'Shaughnessy Foundation, I. A.
Ottenstein Family Foundation
Overbrook Foundation
Owen Trust, B. B.
Owens-Corning Fiberglas Corp.
Oxford Foundation
PacifiCorp
Parker-Hannifin Corp.
Parshelsky Foundation, Moses L.
Parsons Foundation, Ralph M.
Parsons - W.D. Charities, Vera Davis
Pasadena Area Residential Aid
Peabody Foundation, Amelia
Pella Corp.
Penn Foundation, William
Pennington Foundation, Irene W. and C. B.
Peoples Energy Corp.

Perkin-Elmer Corp.
Perkin-Elmer Corp.
Perkins Foundation, Edwin E.
Perley Fund, Victor E.
Pfizer
Phelps, Inc.
Philips Foundation, Jesse
Phillips Family Foundation, Jay and Rose
Pick Charitable Trust, Melitta S.
Pillsbury Foundation
Pinkerton Foundation
Pittsburgh National Bank
Playboy Enterprises, Inc.
Poinsettia Foundation, Paul and Magdalena Ecke
Polinger Foundation, Howard and Geraldine
Portland General Electric Co.
Posnack Family Foundation of Hollywood
Post Foundation of D.C., Marjorie Merriweather
Powell Family Foundation
PPG Industries
Preston Trust, Evelyn W.
Price Foundation, Louis and Harold
Primerica Corp.
Providence Journal Company
Provigo Corp. Inc.
Prudential Insurance Co. of America
Quivey-Bay State Foundation
Raleigh Linen Service/National Distributing Co.
Ramapo Trust
Recognition Equipment
Redman Foundation
Reinberger Foundation
Reinhart Institutional Foods
Reliance Electric Co.
Retirement Research Foundation
Rhodebeck Charitable Trust
Rice Foundation
Rice Foundation, Helen Steiner
Rich Foundation
Riley Foundation, Mabel Louise
Ritchie Memorial Foundation, Charles E. and Mabel M.
Robbins & Myers, Inc.
Roberts Foundation, Dora
Robinson Fund, Charles Nelson
Roche Relief Foundation, Edward and Ellen
Rockwell Fund
Rogers Family Foundation
Rohatyn Foundation, Felix and Elizabeth
Rohm and Haas Company
Rohr Inc.
Rose Foundation, Billy
Roseburg Forest Products Co.
Rosen Foundation, Joseph
Rosenberg, Jr. Family Foundation, Louise and Claude
Rosenthal Foundation, Ida and William
Rosenthal Foundation, Samuel
Ross Laboratories
Roth Foundation, Louis T.
Royal Group Inc.
Rubbermaid
Rubenstein Charitable Foundation, Lawrence J. and Anne
Rukin Philanthropic Foundation, David and Eleanore
Russ Togs
Russell Memorial Foundation, Robert
Sailors' Snug Harbor of Boston
San Diego Gas & Electric
Sandusky International Inc.

Community Centers (cont.)

Sanguinetti Foundation, Annunziata
Sapirstein-Stone-Weiss Foundation
Sara Lee Corp.
Scaife Family Foundation
Schaffer Foundation, H.
Schenck Fund, L. P.
Schmidlapp Trust No. 1, Jacob G.
Scholl Foundation, Dr.
Schroeder Foundation, Walter
Scrivner, Inc.
Sealright Co., Inc.
Seaway Food Town
Shatford Memorial Trust, J. D.
Shawmut National Corp.
Sheaffer Inc.
Shell Oil Co.
Shemanski Testamentary Trust, Tillie and Alfred
Shoney's Inc.
Simon Foundation, William E. and Carol G.
Simpson Investment Co.
SIT Investment Associates, Inc.
Skinner Corp.
Slant/Fin Corp.
Slaughter, Jr. Foundation, William E.
Slifka Foundation, Alan B.
Slifka Foundation, Joseph and Sylvia
Smith Charitable Fund, Eleanor Armstrong
Smith Charitable Trust, W. W.
Smith Corp., A.O.
Smith Family Foundation, Charles E.
Smith, Jr. Charitable Trust, Jack J.
Smith Memorial Fund, Ethel Sergeant Clark
Snyder Fund, Valentine Perry
Society Corp.
Solo Cup Co.
Sonat
Sonoco Products Co.
Sooner Pipe & Supply Corp.
Sosland Foundation
Southern California Edison Co.
Speas Foundation, Victor E.
Speas Memorial Trust, John W. and Effie E.
Spiegel
Sprague Educational and Charitable Foundation, Seth
Springs Industries
Square D Co.
Stackpole-Hall Foundation
Star Bank, N.A.
Starr Foundation
Starrett Co., L.S.
State Street Bank & Trust Co.
Steelcase
Steiger Memorial Fund, Albert
Stein Foundation, Joseph F.
Steinsapir Family Foundation, Julius L. and Libhie B.
Sterling Winthrop
Stern Foundation, Bernice and Milton
Stern Foundation, Irvin
Stern Foundation, Leonard N.
Stern Foundation, Max
Stern Memorial Trust, Sidney
Stewardship Foundation
Stone Container Corp.
Stone Foundation, David S.
Stone & Webster, Inc.
Strake Foundation
Strauss Foundation
Stride Rite Corp.
Strosacker Foundation, Charles J.

Stuart Center Charitable Trust, Hugh
Stulsaft Foundation, Morris
Summerfield Foundation, Solon E.
Sundstrand Corp.
Swig Charity Foundation, Mae and Benjamin
Synovus Financial Corp.
Taub Foundation, Henry and Marilyn
TCF Banking & Savings, FSB
Teleflex Inc.
Teleklew Productions
Tenneco
Tetley, Inc.
Texaco
Texas Instruments
Textron
Thomas & Betts Corp.
Thorpe Foundation, James R.
3M Co.
Times Mirror Co.
Tisch Foundation
Tisch Foundation
TJX Cos.
Tobin Foundation
Tonya Memorial Foundation
Tosco Corp. Refining Division
Totsy Manufacturing Co.
Tozer Foundation
Transamerica Corp.
Trexler Trust, Harry C.
Tropicana Products, Inc.
True North Foundation
Trull Foundation
Trust Co. Bank
Turrell Fund
Tyson Foods, Inc.
Unilever United States
Union Bank of Switzerland Los Angeles Branch
Union Camp Corp.
Union Electric Co.
Union Pacific Corp.
United Airlines
U.S. Leasing International
United States Sugar Corp.
United States Trust Co. of New York
Universal Leaf Tobacco Co.
Upton Foundation, Frederick S.
US Bancorp
UST
USX Corp.
Valley Foundation
Valley National Bank of Arizona
Vance Charitable Foundation, Robert C.
Vermeer Manufacturing Co.
Vicksburg Foundation
Virginia Power Co.
Von der Ahe, Jr. Trust, Theodore Albert
Vulcan Materials Co.
Wachovia Bank & Trust Co., N.A.
Wade Endowment Fund, Elizabeth Firth
Wal-Mart Stores
Waldbaum Family Foundation, I.
Wallach Foundation, Miriam G. and Ira D.
Disney Co., Walt
Washington Mutual Savings Bank
Wauwatosa Savings & Loan Association
Weaver Foundation, Gil and Dody
Webster Foundation, Edwin S.
Weckbaugh Foundation, Eleanore Mullen
Weiler Foundation, Theodore & Renee
Weiner Foundation
Weingart Foundation

Weiss Foundation, Stephen and Suzanne
Welfare Foundation
West Co.
West One Bancorp
Westerman Foundation, Samuel L.
Western New York Foundation
Weyerhaeuser Co.
Weyerhaeuser Foundation, Frederick and Margaret L.
Wharton Foundation
Wheat First Securites
Whirlpool Corp.
Whitaker Charitable Foundation, Lyndon C.
White Consolidated Industries
Whitehead Foundation, Joseph B.
Whitney Fund, David M.
WICOR, Inc.
Wilf Family Foundation
Wilmington Trust Co.
Wimpey Inc., George
Winnebago Industries, Inc.
Winter Construction Co.
Wisconsin Energy Corp.
Wisconsin Public Service Corp.
Wolff Memorial Foundation, Pauline Sterne
Woods Charitable Fund
Woodward Governor Co.
Wright Foundation, Lola
Wyomissing Foundation
Yassenoff Foundation, Leo
Yeager Charitable Trust, Lester E.
Zale Foundation
Zale Foundation, William and Sylvia

Community Service Organizations

Abbott Laboratories
Abell Foundation, Charles S.
Abell-Hanger Foundation
Abney Foundation
Abraham Foundation
Abrams Foundation
Abramson Family Foundation
Abreu Charitable Trust u/w/o May P. Abreu, Francis I.
Abroms Charitable Foundation
Abrons Foundation, Louis and Anne
Ace Beverage Co.
ACF Industries, Inc.
Achelis Foundation
Acme-Cleveland Corp.
Acme United Corp.
Action Industries, Inc.
Acushnet Co.
Adams Foundation, Arthur F. and Alice E.
Adams Memorial Fund, Emma J.
Adler Foundation Trust, Philip D. and Henrietta B.
Advanced Micro Devices
Aeroflex Foundation
Agway
AHS Foundation
Aid Association for the Blind
Aigner
Air Products & Chemicals
Akzo America
Akzo Chemicals Inc.
Alabama Power Co.
Albertson's
Alco Standard Corp.
Alcon Laboratories, Inc.
Aldeen Charity Trust, G. W.
Alexander Charitable Foundation
Alexander Foundation, Joseph
Alexander Foundation, Judd S.
Alexander Foundation, Walter
Alhambra Foundry Co., Ltd.
Alice Manufacturing Co.

Allegheny Ludlum Corp.
Allen Brothers Foundation
Allen Foundation, Frances
Allen Foundation, Rita
Allendale Mutual Insurance Co.
AlliedSignal
Allstate Insurance Co.
Alltel/Western Region
Allyn Foundation
Alma Piston Co.
ALPAC Corp.
Alperin/Hirsch Family Foundation
Alpert Foundation, Herb
Alro Steel Corp.
Alsdorf Foundation
Altman Foundation
Altschul Foundation
Alumax
Aluminum Co. of America
AMAX
Amcast Industrial Corp.
AMCORE Bank, N.A. Rockford
Amdur Braude Riley, Inc.
Ameribank
America West Airlines
American Aggregates Corp.
American Brands
American Building Maintenance Industries
American Electric Power
American Express Co.
American Foundation Corporation
American General Finance
American National Bank & Trust Co. of Chicago
American Natural Resources Co.
American President Cos.
American Saw & Manufacturing Co.
American Society of Ephesus
American Telephone & Telegraph Co.
American United Life Insurance Co.
Ameritech Publishing
Ames Charitable Trust, Harriett
Ames Department Stores
Amfac/JMB Hawaii
Amoco Corp.
AMP
AMR Corp.
Analog Devices
Andalusia Health Services
Andersen Corp.
Andersen Foundation
Andersen Foundation, Arthur
Anderson Charitable Trust, Josephine
Anderson Foundation
Anderson Foundation
Anderson Foundation, John W.
Anderson Foundation, M. D.
Anderson Foundation, Peyton
Anderson Foundation, Robert C. and Sadie G.
Anderson Foundation, William P.
Andres Charitable Trust, Frank G.
Anheuser-Busch Cos.
Anschutz Family Foundation
Ansley Foundation, Dantzler Bond
AON Corp.
Apple Computer, Inc.
Appleby Foundation
Appleby Trust, Scott B. and Annie P.
Appleton Papers
Arata Brothers Trust
Arbie Mineral Feed Co.
Archer-Daniels-Midland Co.
Archibald Charitable Foundation, Norman
Aristech Chemical Corp.
Arizona Public Service Co.

Arkansas Power & Light Co.
Arkelian Foundation, Ben H. and Gladys
Armco Inc.
Armstrong Foundation
Armstrong World Industries Inc.
Arnold Fund
Aron Charitable Foundation, J.
Arronson Foundation
Artevel Foundation
Asplundh Foundation
Atalanta/Sosnoff Capital Corp.
Atherton Family Foundation
Atkinson Foundation
Atlanta Foundation
Atlanta Gas Light Co.
Atran Foundation
Attleboro Pawtucket Savings Bank
Auerbach Foundation, Beatrice Fox
Augat, Inc.
Aurora Foundation
Austin Memorial Foundation
Autzen Foundation
AVI CHAI - A Philanthropic Foundation
Avis Inc.
Avon Products
Ayres Foundation, Inc.
Azby Fund
Babcock Foundation, Mary Reynolds
Babcock & Wilcox Co.
Bachmann Foundation
Backer Spielvogel Bates U.S.
Bacon Foundation, E. L. and Oma
Bacon Trust, Charles F.
Badgeley Residuary Charitable Trust, Rose M.
Badger Meter, Inc.
Baehr Foundation, Louis W. and Dolpha
Baer Foundation, Alan and Marcia
Bag Bazaar, Ltd.
Bailey Foundation
Baird Brothers Co.
Baird Charitable Trust, William Robert
Baker Foundation, George T.
Baker Foundation, R. C.
Baker Foundation, Solomon R. and Rebecca D.
Baker Trust, Clayton
Baldwin Foundation
Baldwin Foundation, David M. and Barbara
Ball Corp.
Banbury Fund
Banc One Illinois Corp.
Bancroft, Jr. Foundation, Hugh
Bank of A. Levy
Bank of America - Giannini Foundation
Bank of Boston Corp.
Bank of New York
Bank of Tokyo Trust Co.
Bank One, Texas-Houston Office
Bank One, Youngstown, NA
BankAmerica Corp.
Bankers Trust Co.
Bannan Foundation, Arline and Thomas J.
Bannerman Foundation, William C.
Banta Corp.
Barbour Foundation, Bernice
Barden Corp.
Bardes Corp.
Bargman Foundation, Theodore and Mina
Barker Welfare Foundation
Barnes Foundation
Barnes Group
Barra Foundation

Barry Corp., R. G.
Barstow Foundation
Barton-Malow Co.
Bartsch Memorial Trust, Ruth
Bass and Edythe and Sol G.
  Atlas Fund, Sandra Atlas
Bassett Foundation, Norman
Bauer Foundation, M. R.
Bauervic-Paisley Foundation
Baughman Foundation
Baum Family Fund, Alvin H.
Baumker Charitable Foundation,
  Elsie and Harry
Bausch & Lomb
Baxter International
Bay Branch Foundation
BayBanks
BCR Foundation
Beaird Foundation, Charles T.
Beal Foundation
Beasley Foundation, Theodore
  and Beulah
Beatty Trust, Cordelia Lunceford
Beazley Foundation
Bechtel Charitable Remainder
  Uni-Trust, Harold R.
Bechtel Charitable Remainder
  Uni-Trust, Marie H.
Beck Foundation
Bedford Fund
Bedsole Foundation, J. L.
Beech Aircraft Corp.
Beecher Foundation, Florence
  Simon
Beeghly Fund, Leon A.
Beerman Foundation
Behmann Brothers Foundation
Beidler Charitable Trust, Francis
Beim Foundation
Beinecke Foundation
Bekins Foundation, Milo W.
Belfer Foundation
Belk Stores
Bellamah Foundation, Dale J.
Bellini Foundation
Beloit Foundation
Belz Foundation
Bemis Company
Bend Millwork Systems
Bender Foundation
Benedum Foundation, Claude
  Worthington
Beneficia Foundation
Benenson Foundation, Frances
  and Benjamin
Benetton
Bennett Foundation, Carl and
  Dorothy
Bentley Foundation, Alvin M.
Benua Foundation
Benwood Foundation
Berenson Charitable Foundation,
  Theodore W. and Evelyn
Beretta U.S.A. Corp.
Berger Foundation, H.N. and
  Frances C.
Bergstrom Manufacturing Co.
Berkman Charitable Trust, Allen
  H. and Selma W.
Berkman Foundation, Louis and
  Sandra
Berkowitz Family Foundation,
  Louis
Bernsen Foundation, Grace and
  Franklin
Bernstein & Co., Sanford C.
Berry Foundation, Lowell
Bersted Foundation
Besser Foundation
Best Products Co.
Best Western International
Bethlehem Steel Corp.
Bettingen Corporation, Burton G.
Betts Industries
Beveridge Foundation, Frank
  Stanley
BFGoodrich
Bicknell Fund

Bierhaus Foundation
Big V Supermarkets
Bigelow Foundation, F. R.
Binswanger Co.
Birch Foundation, Stephen and
  Mary
Bird Inc.
Bireley Foundation
Birnschein Foundation, Alvin
  and Marion
Bishop Charitable Trust, A. G.
Bishop Foundation, E. K. and
  Lillian F.
Bishop Foundation, Vernon and
  Doris
Bjorkman Foundation
Blair and Co., William
Blake Foundation, S. P.
Blaustein Foundation, Jacob and
  Hilda
Blaustein Foundation, Louis and
  Henrietta
Bleibtreu Foundation, Jacob
Block Family Foundation,
  Emphraim
Block, H&R
Bloedorn Foundation, Walter A.
Bloomfield Foundation, Sam and
  Rie
Blount
Blount Educational and
  Charitable Foundation,
  Mildred Weedon
Blowitz-Ridgeway Foundation
Blue Bell, Inc.
Blue Cross & Blue Shield of
  Alabama
Bluhdorn Charitable Trust,
  Charles G. and Yvette
Blum Foundation, Edith C.
Blum Foundation, Harry and
  Maribel G.
Blum Foundation, Lois and
  Irving
Blum Foundation, Nathan and
  Emily S.
Blum-Kovler Foundation
BMC Industries
BMW of North America, Inc.
Boatmen's Bancshares
Boatmen's First National Bank
  of Oklahoma
Boatmen's First National Bank
  of Oklahoma
Bobst Foundation, Elmer and
  Mamdouha
Bodenhamer Foundation
Bodine Corp.
Boeckmann Charitable
  Foundation
Boehringer Mannheim Corp.
Boeing Co.
Boettcher Foundation
Boisi Family Foundation
Bonfils-Stanton Foundation
Booth-Bricker Fund
Booth Ferris Foundation
Boothroyd Foundation, Charles
  H. and Bertha L.
Booz Allen & Hamilton
Borchard Foundation, Albert and
  Elaine
Borden
Borkee Hagley Foundation
Borman's
Borun Foundation, Anna Borun
  and Harry
Bossong Hosiery Mills
Boston Edison Co.
Bothin Foundation
Botwinick-Wolfensohn
  Foundation
Boulevard Foundation
Bourns, Inc.
Bovaird Foundation, Mervin
Bowers Foundation
Bowne Foundation, Robert
Bowsher-Booher Foundation

Bowyer Foundation, Ambrose
  and Gladys
Boynton Fund, John W.
Bozzone Family Foundation
BP America
Brach Foundation, Edwin I.
Bradford Foundation, George
  and Ruth
Bradley-Turner Foundation
Brand Cos.
Brand Foundation, C. Harold and
  Constance
Branta Foundation
Bravmann Foundation, Ludwig
Bray Charitable Trust, Viola E.
Breidenthal Foundation, Willard
  J. and Mary G.
Bremer Foundation, Otto
Brencanda Foundation
Brenner Foundation
Brenner Foundation, Mervyn
Breyer Foundation
Bridgestone/Firestone
Briggs Family Foundation
Briggs Foundation, T. W.
Bright Family Foundation
Bristol-Myers Squibb Co.
Bristol Savings Bank
Britton Fund
Broadhurst Foundation
Broccoli Charitable Foundation,
  Dana and Albert R.
Brochsteins Inc.
Brody Foundation, Frances
Bromley Residuary Trust, Guy I.
Bronstein Foundation, Soloman
  and Sylvia
Brookdale Foundation
Brooklyn Benevolent Society
Brooks Brothers
Brother International Corp.
Brotz Family Foundation, Frank
  G.
Brown Charitable Trust, Peter D.
  and Dorothy S.
Brown Foundation, George
  Warren
Brown Foundation, James
  Graham
Brown Foundation, Joe W. and
  Dorothy Dorsett
Brown Foundation, M. K.
Brown Group
Brown, Jr. Charitable Trust,
  Frank D.
Brown & Williamson Tobacco
  Corp.
Browning-Ferris Industries
Broyhill Family Foundation
Bruening Foundation, Eva L. and
  Joseph M.
Brundage Charitable, Scientific,
  and Wildlife Conservation
  Foundation, Charles E. and
  Edna T.
Brunner Foundation, Robert
Bruno Charitable Foundation,
  Joseph S.
Bruno Foundation, Angelo
Brunswick Corp.
Bryce Memorial Fund, William
  and Catherine
Buchalter, Nemer, Fields, &
  Younger
Buchanan Family Foundation
Bucyrus-Erie
Budweiser of Columbia
Buehler Foundation, Emil
Builder Marts of America
Builder Marts of America
Bull Foundation, Henry W.
Burchfield Foundation, Charles
  E.
Burden Foundation, Florence V.
Burkitt Foundation
Burlington Industries

Burnand Medical and
  Educational Foundation,
  Alphonse A.
Burnham Foundation
Burns Family Foundation
Burns Foundation, Fritz B.
Burns Foundation, Jacob
Bush Foundation
Bushee Foundation, Florence
  Evans
Business Incentives
Bustard Charitable Permanent
  Trust Fund, Elizabeth and
  James
Butler Family Foundation,
  George W. and Gladys S.
Butler Foundation, J. Homer
Butler Manufacturing Co.
C.P. Rail Systems
Cabell III and Maude Morgan
Cabell Foundation, Robert G.
Cable & Wireless
  Communications
Cabot Corp.
Caestecker Foundation, Charles
  and Marie
Cafritz Foundation, Morris and
  Gwendolyn
Cahn Family Foundation
Cain Foundation, Gordon and
  Mary
Calder Foundation, Louis
California & Hawaiian Sugar Co.
Callaway Foundation
Callister Foundation, Paul Q.
Cameron Foundation, Harry S.
  and Isabel C.
Cameron Memorial Fund, Alpin
  J. and Alpin W.
Camp and Bennet Humiston
  Trust, Apollos
Camp Foundation
Camp Younts Foundation
Campbell Foundation
Campbell Foundation, J. Bulow
Campbell Foundation, Ruth and
  Henry
Campbell Soup Co.
Candlesticks Inc.
Cannon Foundation
Canon U.S.A., Inc.
Cantor Foundation, Iris and B.
  Gerald
Capital Cities/ABC
Capital Fund Corporation
Capital Holding Corp.
Caplan Charity Foundation,
  Julius H.
Cargill
Carlson Cos.
Carnahan-Jackson Foundation
Carnegie Corporation of New
  York
Carnival Cruise Lines
Carolina Power & Light Co.
Carolyn Foundation
Carpenter Foundation, E. Rhodes
  and Leona B.
Carpenter Technology Corp.
Carr Real Estate Services
Carteh Foundation
Carter Charitable Trust, Wilbur
  Lee
Carter Family Foundation
Carter Foundation, Amon G.
Cartier, Inc.
Carvel Foundation, Thomas and
  Agnes
Carylon Foundation
Cascade Natural Gas Corp.
Cassett Foundation, Louis N.
Castle & Co., A.M.
Castle Foundation, Samuel N.
  and Mary
Castle Trust, George P. and Ida
  Tenney
Caterpillar

Catlin Charitable Trust, Kathleen
  K.
Cawsey Trust
Cayuga Foundation
CBI Industries
Centel Corp.
Centerior Energy Corp.
Central Fidelity Banks, Inc.
Central Hudson Gas & Electric
  Corp.
Central Maine Power Co.
Central National-Gottesman
Central Soya Co.
Central Vermont Public Service
  Corp.
CertainTeed Corp.
Cessna Aircraft Co.
Chais Family Foundation
Chait Memorial Foundation, Sara
Chamberlin Foundation, Gerald
  W.
Chambers Memorial, James B.
Champion International Corp.
Chandler Foundation
Chapin Foundation of Myrtle
  Beach, South Carolina
Chapin-May Foundation of
  Illinois
Chapman Charitable Trust, H. A.
  and Mary K.
Charina Foundation
Charitable Fund
Charities Foundation
Charlesbank Homes
Charlton, Jr. Charitable Trust,
  Earle P.
Chartwell Foundation
Chase Charity Foundation,
  Alfred E.
Chase Manhattan Bank, N.A.
Chazen Foundation
Cheatham Foundation, Owen
Chemical Bank
Cheney Foundation, Ben B.
Cheney Foundation, Elizabeth F.
Cherne Foundation, Albert W.
Chernow Trust for the Benefit of
  Charity Dated 3/13/75, Michael
Cherokee Foundation
Chesapeake Corp.
Chesapeake & Potomac
  Telephone Co.
Chevron Corp.
Chicago Board of Trade
Chicago Resource Center
Chicago Sun-Times, Inc.
Chicago Title and Trust Co.
Children's Foundation of Erie
  County
Childs Charitable Foundation,
  Roberta M.
Chilton Foundation Trust
Chiquita Brands Co.
Christensen Charitable and
  Religious Foundation, L. C.
Christian Training Foundation
Christodora
Chrysler Corp.
Church & Dwight Co.
Churches Homes Foundation
Cincinnati Enquirer
Cincinnati Foundation for the
  Aged
CIT Group Holdings
Citicorp
Citizens Bank
Citizens First National Bank
Clabir Corp.
Claneil Foundation
Clapp Charitable and
  Educational Trust, George H.
CLARCOR
Clark Charitable Trust
Clark Foundation
Clark Foundation
Clark-Winchcole Foundation
Clarke Trust, John
Classic Leather

Community Service Organizations (cont.)

Cleary Foundation
Clements Foundation
Clorox Co.
Clowes Fund
CM Alliance Cos.
CNA Insurance Cos.
Cockrell Foundation
Codrington Charitable Foundation, George W.
Coen Family Foundation, Charles S. and Mary
Coffey Foundation
Cogswell Benevolent Trust
Cohen Family Foundation, Saul Z. and Amy Scheuer
Cohen Foundation, George M.
Cohen Foundation, Manny and Ruthy
Cohen Foundation, Wilfred P.
Cohn Family Foundation, Robert and Terri
Cohn Foundation, Peter A. and Elizabeth S.
Cole Foundation
Cole Foundation, Robert H. and Monica H.
Cole National Corp.
Cole Taylor Financial Group
Cole Trust, Quincy
Coleman Co.
Colket Foundation, Ethel D.
Collins Foundation
Collins Foundation, Carr P.
Collins Foundation, George and Jennie
Collins Foundation, James M.
Collins, Jr. Foundation, George Fulton
Colonial Life & Accident Insurance Co.
Colonial Oil Industries, Inc.
Colt Foundation, James J.
Coltec Industries
Columbia Foundation
Columbia Savings Charitable Foundation
Columbia Terminals Co.
Columbus Dispatch Printing Co.
Comer Foundation
Commerce Bancshares, Inc.
Commonwealth Edison Co.
Commonwealth Fund
Community Foundation
Community Health Association
Community Hospital Foundation
Comprecare Foundation
Compton Foundation
Concord Chemical Co.
Cone Mills Corp.
Conn Memorial Foundation
Connecticut Natural Gas Corp.
Connell Foundation, Michael J.
Consolidated Freightways
Consolidated Natural Gas Co.
Consolidated Papers
Conston Corp.
Conston Corp.
Consumer Farmer Foundation
Consumers Power Co.
Contempo Communications
Continental Corp.
Contraves USA
Cook Batson Foundation
Cook Charitable Foundation
Cook Foundation
Cook Foundation, Louella
Cooke Foundation
Cooper Charitable Trust, Richard H.
Cooper Industries
Coors Foundation, Adolph
Copernicus Society of America

Copley Press
Copolymer Rubber & Chemical Corp.
Copperweld Steel Co.
Cord Foundation, E. L.
Corestates Bank
Cornell Trust, Peter C.
Cottrell Foundation
Country Curtains, Inc.
Countrymark Cooperative
Cove Charitable Trust
Covington Foundation, Marion Stedman
Cowan Foundation Corporation, Lillian L. and Harry A.
Cowden Foundation, Louetta M.
Cowell Foundation, S. H.
Cowles Charitable Trust
Cowles Foundation, Harriet Cheney
Cowles Media Co.
Cox Charitable Trust, A. G.
Cox Charitable Trust, Jessie B.
Cox Enterprises
CPC International
CR Industries
Craig Foundation, J. Paul
Craigmyle Foundation
Crandall Memorial Foundation, J. Ford
Crane & Co.
Crane Co.
Crane Foundation, Raymond E. and Ellen F.
Cranston Print Works
Crapo Charitable Foundation, Henry H.
Crary Foundation, Bruce L.
Crawford & Co.
Credit Agricole
Crels Foundation
Cremer Foundation
Crescent Plastics
Crestlea Foundation
CRI Charitable Trust
CRL Inc.
Crocker Trust, Mary A.
Crown Books Foundation, Inc.
Crown Central Petroleum Corp.
Crown Central Petroleum Corp.
Crown Cork & Seal Co., Inc.
Crown Memorial, Arie and Ida
Crum and Forster
CTS Corp.
Cudahy Fund, Patrick and Anna M.
Cuesta Foundation
Cullen/Frost Bankers
Culpeper Memorial Foundation, Daphne Seybolt
Culver Foundation, Constans
Cummings Foundation, Nathan
Cummins Engine Co.
CUNA Mutual Insurance Group
Cuneo Foundation
Currey Foundation, Brownlee
Curtice-Burns Foods
Curtis Industries, Helene
Dai-Ichi Kangyo Bank of California
Daily News
Dalgety Inc.
Dalton Foundation, Harry L.
Daly Charitable Foundation Trust, Robert and Nancy
Dana Corp.
Danforth Foundation
Daniels Foundation, Fred Harris
Danis Industries
Darby Foundation
Darrah Charitable Trust, Jessie Smith
Dart Foundation
Dater Foundation, Charles H.
Dauch Foundation, William
Daugherty Foundation

Davidson Family Charitable Foundation
Davis Family - W.D. Charities, James E.
Davis Foundation, Edwin W. and Catherine M.
Davis Foundation, James A. and Juliet L.
Davis Foundation, Joe C.
Davis Foundation, Ken W.
Davis Foundation, Shelby Cullom
Day Family Foundation
Dayton Power and Light Co.
DCB Corp.
DCNY Corp.
de Dampierre Memorial Foundation, Marie C.
de Hirsch Fund, Baron
de Kay Foundation
De Lima Co., Paul
Dean Witter Discover
Decio Foundation, Arthur J.
Delacorte Fund, George
Delany Charitable Trust, Beatrice P.
Delavan Foundation, Nelson B.
Dell Foundation, Hazel
DelMar Foundation, Charles
Deluxe Corp.
Demco Charitable Foundation
Demos Foundation, N.
Demoulas Supermarkets
Dennison Manufacturing Co.
Dent Family Foundation, Harry
Dentsu, Inc., NY
DeRoy Foundation, Helen L.
DeRoy Testamentary Foundation
Deseranno Educational Foundation
DeSoto
Detroit Edison Co.
Deutsch Co.
Devereaux Foundation
DeVore Foundation
Dewar Foundation
Dewing Foundation, Frances R.
Dexter Charitable Fund, Eugene A.
Dexter Corp.
Dial Corp.
Diamond Foundation, Aaron
Dick Family Foundation
Diener Foundation, Frank C.
Dietrich Foundation, William B.
Digital Equipment Corp.
Dillard Paper Co.
Dillon Foundation
Dimeo Construction Co.
Dimick Foundation
Dishman Charitable Foundation Trust, H. E. and Kate
Dixie Yarns, Inc.
Dodge Foundation, Cleveland H.
Dodge Foundation, Geraldine R.
Dodge Jones Foundation
Dodson Foundation, James Glenwell and Clara May
Doelger Charitable Trust, Thelma
Doheny Foundation, Carrie Estelle
Doherty Charitable Foundation, Henry L. and Grace
Dole Food Company, Inc.
Domino of California
Donaldson Charitable Trust, Oliver S. and Jennie R.
Donaldson Co.
Donnelley Foundation, Elliott and Ann
Donnelly Foundation, Mary J.
Donovan, Leisure, Newton & Irvine
Dorot Foundation
Doss Foundation, M. S.
Doty Family Foundation
Dougherty, Jr. Foundation, James R.

Douglas Corp.
Douglas & Lomason Company
Douty Foundation
Dover Foundation
Dow Corning Corp.
Dow Fund, Alden and Vada
Downs Perpetual Charitable Trust, Ellason
Dreitzer Foundation
Dresser Industries
Dreyfus Foundation, Jean and Louis
Dreyfus Foundation, Max and Victoria
Driehaus Foundation, Richard H.
Drown Foundation, Joseph
Drum Foundation
du Pont de Nemours & Co., E. I.
Duchossois Industries
Dues Charitable Foundation, Cesle C. and Mamie
Duke Power Co.
Dumke Foundation, Dr. Ezekiel R. and Edna Wattis
Dun & Bradstreet Corp.
Duncan Trust, James R.
Duncan Trust, John G.
Dunning Foundation
Dunspaugh-Dalton Foundation
Dupar Foundation
duPont Foundation, Chichester
duPont Fund, Jessie Ball
Durfee Foundation
Durst Foundation
Dweck Foundation, Samuel R.
Dynamet, Inc.
Eagle-Picher Industries
Early Foundation
Easley Trust, Andrew H. and Anne O.
Eastern Bank Foundation
Eastern Fine Paper, Inc.
Eastman Foundation, Alexander
Eaton Corp.
Eaton Foundation, Edwin M. and Gertrude S.
Ebell of Los Angeles Rest Cottage Association
Ebert Charitable Foundation, Horatio B.
Eccles Foundation, George S. and Dolores Dore
Eccles Foundation, Marriner S.
Eccles Foundation, Ralph M. and Ella M.
Echlin Inc.
Eckman Charitable Foundation, Samuel and Rae
Ecolab
Eddy Family Memorial Fund, C. K.
Eden Hall Foundation
Eder Foundation, Sidney and Arthur
Edgewater Steel Corp.
Edison Foundation, Harry
Edison Foundation, Irving and Beatrice C.
Edmonds Foundation, Dean S.
Edouard Foundation
Edwards Foundation, O. P. and W. E.
Edwards Industries
EG&G Inc.
Ehrman Foundation, Fred and Susan
Einstein Fund, Albert E. and Birdie W.
EIS Foundation
Eisenberg Foundation, Ben B. and Joyce E.
Eisenberg Foundation, George M.
El-An Foundation
El Pomar Foundation
Electric Power Equipment Co.
Electronic Data Systems Corp.
Elf Atochem North America
Elgin Sweeper Co.

Elkin Memorial Foundation, Neil Warren and William Simpson
Elkins Foundation, J. A. and Isabel M.
Elkins, Jr. Foundation, Margaret and James A.
Ellis Foundation
Ellis Grant and Scholarship Fund, Charles E.
Ellsworth Trust, W. H.
Emergency Aid of Pennsylvania Foundation
Emerson Electric Co.
Emerson Foundation, Fred L.
Emery Memorial, Thomas J.
Engelhard Foundation, Charles
English-Bonter-Mitchell Foundation
English Foundation, W. C.
English Foundation, Walter and Marian
English Foundation, Walter and Marian
English Memorial Fund, Florence C. and H. L.
Enright Foundation
Enron Corp.
Ensworth Charitable Foundation
Epaphroditus Foundation
Equifax
Equitable Life Assurance Society of the U.S.
Erb Lumber Co.
Erickson Charitable Fund, Eben W.
Ernest & Julio Gallo Winery
Ernsthausen Charitable Foundation, John F. and Doris E.
Estes Foundation
Ethyl Corp.
Eureka Co.
Everett Charitable Trust
Evjue Foundation
Ewald Foundation, H. T.
Excel Industries (Elkhart, Indiana)
Exposition Foundation
Exxon Corp.
Eyman Trust, Jesse
FAB Industries
Fabick Tractor Co., John
Factor Family Foundation, Max
Failing Fund, Henry
Fair Oaks Foundation, Inc.
Fair Play Foundation
Fairchild Corp.
Fairfield Foundation, Freeman E.
Faith Charitable Trust
Faith Home Foundation
Fales Foundation Trust
Falk Foundation, David
Falk Foundation, Michael David
Falk Medical Research Foundation, Dr. Ralph and Marian
Fanuc U.S.A. Corp.
Farallon Foundation
Farish Fund, William Stamps
Farr Trust, Frank M. and Alice M.
Fay Charitable Fund, Aubert J.
Fay's Incorporated
Federal Express Corp.
Federal Home Loan Mortgage Corp. (Freddie Mac)
Federal-Mogul Corp.
Federal Screw Works
Federated Department Stores and Allied Stores Corp.
Federated Life Insurance Co.
Federation Foundation of Greater Philadelphia
Fein Foundation
Feinstein Foundation, Myer and Rosaline
Feintech Foundation

Fellner Memorial Foundation, Leopold and Clara M.
Fels Fund, Samuel S.
Femino Foundation
Fenton Foundation
Ferebee Endowment, Percy O.
Ferkauf Foundation, Eugene and Estelle
Fiat U.S.A., Inc.
Fibre Converters
Fidelity Bank
Field Foundation of Illinois
Fieldcrest Cannon
Fife Foundation, Elias and Bertha
Fifth Third Bancorp
Fig Tree Foundation
Fikes Foundation, Leland
FINA, Inc.
Finch Foundation, Doak
Finch Foundation, Thomas Austin
Fingerhut Family Foundation
Fink Foundation
Finley Charitable Trust, J. B.
Finley Foundation, A. E.
Finnegan Foundation, John D.
Firestone Foundation, Roger S.
First Boston
First Brands Corp.
First Fidelity Bancorporation
First Interstate Bancsystem of Montana
First Interstate Bank of Arizona
First Interstate Bank of California
First Interstate Bank of Oregon
First Maryland Bancorp
First Mississippi Corp.
First National Bank & Trust Co. of Rockford
First Tennessee Bank
First Union Corp.
First Union National Bank of Florida
Firstar Bank Milwaukee NA
Fischel Foundation, Harry and Jane
Fish Foundation, Ray C.
Fish Foundation, Vain and Harry
Fishback Foundation Trust, Harmes C.
Fisher Brothers
Fisher Foundation
Fisher Foundation
Fisher Foundation, Max M. and Marjorie S.
Fishoff Family Foundation
Flarsheim Charitable Foundation, Louis and Elizabeth
Flatley Foundation
Fleet Bank of New York
Flemm Foundation, John J.
Fletcher Foundation
Flickinger Memorial Trust
Flintridge Foundation
Florence Foundation
Florence Foundation
Florence Foundation
Florida Power Corp.
Florida Power & Light Co.
Florida Rock Industries
Florida Steel Corp.
Flowers Charitable Trust, Albert W. and Edith V.
Fluor Corp.
FMR Corp.
Foellinger Foundation
Folger Fund
Fondren Foundation
Foote Mineral Co.
Foothills Foundation
Forbes
Forbes Charitable Trust, Herman
Ford Foundation
Ford Foundation, Kenneth W.
Ford Fund, Walter and Josephine
Ford Fund, William and Martha

Ford II Fund, Henry
Ford III Memorial Foundation, Jefferson Lee
Ford Meter Box Co.
Ford Motor Co.
Forest City Enterprises
Forest Foundation
Forest Fund
Forest Lawn Foundation
Formrite Tube Co.
Forster-Powers Charitable Trust
Fort Worth Star Telegram
Fortin Foundation of Florida
Fortis Benefits Insurance Company/Fortis Financial Group
Foster and Gallagher
Foster Charitable Foundation, M. Stratton
Foster Charitable Trust
Foster Co., L.B.
Foster Foundation
Foster Foundation, Joseph C. and Esther
Foundation for Middle East Peace
Foundation for Seacoast Health
Foundation for the Needs of Others
Fox Charitable Foundation, Harry K. & Emma R.
Fox Foundation, John H.
Fox Steel Co.
Fraida Foundation
France Foundation, Jacob and Annita
Frank Family Foundation, A. J.
Frank Fund, Zollie and Elaine
Frankel Foundation
Frankel Foundation, George and Elizabeth F.
Franklin Charitable Trust, Ershel
Franklin Foundation, John and Mary
Fraser Paper Ltd.
Frazier Foundation
Frear Eleemosynary Trust, Mary D. and Walter F.
Frederick Foundation
Freedom Forum
Freeman Foundation, Ella West
Freeport Brick Co.
Freeport-McMoRan
Frees Foundation
Freightliner Corp.
Frelinghuysen Foundation
Frelinghuysen Foundation
French Oil Mill Machinery Co.
Freygang Foundation, Walter Henry
Fribourg Foundation
Frick Educational Commission, Henry C.
Friedman Brothers Foundation
Friedman Family Foundation
Friedman Foundation, Stephen and Barbara
Friendly Rosenthal Foundation
Friendship Fund
Frisch's Restaurants Inc.
Frohman Foundation, Sidney
Frohring Foundation, Paul & Maxine
Frohring Foundation, William O. and Gertrude Lewis
Fruchthandler Foundation, Alex and Ruth
Frueauff Foundation, Charles A.
Fry Foundation, Lloyd A.
Fuchs Foundation, Gottfried & Mary
Fuchsberg Family Foundation
Fuchsberg Family Foundation, Abraham
Fujitsu America, Inc.
Fujitsu Systems of America, Inc.
Fullerton Foundation
Funderburke & Associates

Furth Foundation
G.A.G. Charitable Corporation
Gabelli Foundation
Gaisman Foundation, Catherine and Henry J.
Galkin Charitable Trust, Ira S. and Anna
Gallagher Family Foundation, Lewis P.
Gallo Foundation, Julio R.
Galter Foundation
Gannett Co.
Gap, The
GAR Foundation
Garfinkle Family Foundation
Garland Foundation, John Jewett and H. Chandler
Garner Charitable Trust, James G.
Garvey Fund, Jean and Willard
Garvey Texas Foundation
Garvey Trust, Olive White
Gateway Apparel
GATX Corp.
Gault-Hussey Charitable Trust
Gavin Foundation, James and Zita
Gazette Co.
Geifman Family Foundation
Geist Foundation
Gellert Foundation, Carl
Gellert Foundation, Celia Berta
Gellert Foundation, Fred
Gelman Foundation, Melvin and Estelle
General American Life Insurance Co.
General Electric Co.
General Mills
General Motors Corp.
General Reinsurance Corp.
General Signal Corp.
General Tire Inc.
Geneseo Foundation
Geneva Foundation
GenRad
George Foundation
Georgia-Pacific Corp.
Georgia Power Co.
Gerber Products Co.
Gerbode Foundation, Wallace Alexander
Gerlach Foundation
Gershenson Foundation, Charles H.
Gershman Foundation, Joel
Gerson Family Foundation, Benjamin J.
Getsch Family Foundation Trust
Ghidotti Foundation, William and Marian
Giant Eagle
Giant Food
Giant Food Stores
Gibson Foundation, E. L.
Giddings & Lewis
Gifford Charitable Corporation, Rosamond
Gilbert, Jr. Charitable Trust, Price
Giles Foundation, Edward C.
Gill Foundation, Pauline Allen
Gilman Foundation, Howard
Gilman, Jr. Foundation, Sondra and Charles
Gilman Paper Co.
Gilmer-Smith Foundation
Gilmore Foundation, William G.
Gindi Associates Foundation
Ginsberg Family Foundation, Moses
Ginter Foundation, Karl and Anna
Glaser Foundation
Glaxo
Glaze Foundation, Robert and Ruth
Glazer Foundation, Jerome S.
Glazer Foundation, Madelyn L.

Gleason Foundation, James
Gleason Foundation, Katherine
Glenmore Distilleries Co.
Glick Foundation, Eugene and Marilyn
Glickenhaus & Co.
Globe Corp.
Globe Newspaper Co.
Glosser Foundation, David A.
Goddard Foundation, Charles B.
Goerlich Family Foundation
Goldbach Foundation, Ray and Marie
Goldberg Family Foundation
Goldie-Anna Charitable Trust
Goldman Foundation, Aaron and Cecile
Goldman Foundation, Herman
Goldman Foundation, William
Goldring Family Foundation
Goldsmith Family Foundation
Goldsmith Foundation
Goldsmith Foundation, Horace W.
Goldwyn Foundation, Samuel
Golub Corp.
Goodman Family Foundation
Goodman Foundation, Edward and Marion
Goodstein Family Foundation, David
Goodyear Foundation, Josephine
Goodyear Tire & Rubber Co.
Goody's Manufacturing Corp.
Gordon Charitable Trust, Peggy and Yale
Gordon Foundation, Meyer and Ida
Gorin Foundation, Nehemiah
Gottwald Foundation
Gould Inc.
Gould Foundation for Children, Edwin
Grace & Co., W.R.
Graco
Gradison & Co.
Graham Fund, Philip L.
Grant Foundation, Charles M. and Mary D.
Graphic Controls Corp.
Grass Family Foundation
Gray Foundation, Garland
Graybar Electric Co.
Great Atlantic & Pacific Tea Co. Inc.
Great-West Life Assurance Co.
Great Western Financial Corp.
Greater Construction Corp. Charitable Foundation, Inc.
Greater Lansing Foundation
Grede Foundries
Greeley Gas Co.
Green Foundation
Green Foundation, Allen P. and Josephine B.
Green Foundation, Burton E.
Greenberg Foundation, Alan C.
Greene Foundation, David J.
Greene Foundation, Robert Z.
Greenspan Foundation
Greentree Foundation
Greenville Foundation
Gregg-Graniteville Foundation
Gries Charity Fund, Lucile and Robert H.
Griffin Foundation, Rosa May
Griffin, Sr., Foundation, C. V.
Griffith Foundation, W. C.
Grigg-Lewis Trust
Gross Charitable Trust, Walter L. and Nell R.
Grossman Foundation, N. Bud
Groves & Sons Co., S.J.
Grumbacher Foundation, M. S.
Gruss Charitable and Educational Foundation, Oscar and Regina

Gruss Charitable Foundation, Emanuel and Riane
GTE Corp.
Guaranty Bank & Trust Co.
Guggenheim Foundation, Daniel and Florence
Gulf Power Co.
Gund Foundation
Gussman Foundation, Herbert and Roseline
Guttag Foundation, Irwin and Marjorie
Guttman Foundation, Stella and Charles
H.C.S. Foundation
Haas Foundation, Paul and Mary
Haas Fund, Walter and Elise
Haas, Jr. Fund, Evelyn and Walter
Habig Foundation, Arnold F.
Hackett Foundation
Haffner Foundation
Hafif Family Foundation
Haggar Foundation
Haggerty Foundation
Hagler Foundation, Jon L.
Haigh-Scatena Foundation
Hales Charitable Fund
Haley Foundation, W. B.
Halff Foundation, G. A. C.
Hall Charitable Trust, Evelyn A. J.
Hall Foundation
Hall Foundation
Hallmark Cards
Halmos Foundation
Halsell Foundation, Ewing
Halsell Foundation, O. L.
Hambay Foundation, James T.
Hamel Family Charitable Trust, D. A.
Hamilton Bank
Hamilton Foundation, Florence P.
Hamman Foundation, George and Mary Josephine
Hancock Foundation, Luke B.
Handleman Co.
Hankins Foundation
Hanna Co., M.A.
Hannon Foundation, William H.
Hanson Foundation
HarCo. Drug
Harden Foundation
Hardin Foundation, Phil
Harding Foundation, Charles Stewart
Hargis Charitable Foundation, Estes H. and Florence Parker
Harmon Foundation, Pearl M. and Julia J.
Harper Brush Works
Harper Foundation, Philip S.
HarperCollins Publishers
Harriman Foundation, Gladys and Roland
Harriman Foundation, Mary W.
Harrington Foundation, Don and Sybil
Harrington Foundation, Francis A. and Jacquelyn H.
Harris Brothers Foundation
Harris Brothers Foundation
Harris Family Foundation, Hunt and Diane
Harris Foundation
Harris Foundation, James J. and Angelia M.
Harris Foundation, John H. and Lucille
Harris Trust & Savings Bank
Harrison Foundation, Fred G.
Harsco Corp.
Hartmarx Corp.
Hartz Foundation
Hartzell Industries, Inc.
Harvest States Cooperative
Harvey Foundation, Felix
Hasbro

Community Service Organizations (cont.)

Haskell Fund
Hatterscheidt Foundation
Havens Foundation, O. W.
Hawley Foundation
Hay Foundation, John I.
Hayden Foundation, Charles
Hayden Foundation, William R. and Virginia
Hayfields Foundation
Hazen Foundation, Edward W.
Healy Family Foundation, M. A.
Hearst Foundation, William Randolph
Heath Foundation, Ed and Mary
Hebrew Technical Institute
Hechinger Co.
Hecht-Levi Foundation
Hecla Mining Co.
Hedco Foundation
Heginbotham Trust, Will E.
HEI Inc.
Heilicher Foundation, Menaham
Heinz Co., H.J.
Heinz Endowment, Vira I.
Helfaer Foundation, Evan and Marion
Helmerich Foundation
Helzberg Foundation, Shirley and Barnett
Hemingway Foundation, Robert G.
Henderson Foundation, George B.
Hendrickson Brothers
Heritage Pullman Bank & Trust
Herman Foundation, John and Rose
Hermann Foundation, Grover
Herndon Foundation
Herrick Foundation
Herschend Family Foundation
Hershey Foundation
Hervey Foundation
Hess Charitable Trust, Myrtle E. and William C.
Hess Foundation
Hettinger Foundation
Heublein
Hewit Family Foundation
Hewlett Foundation, William and Flora
Hewlett-Packard Co.
Hexcel Corp.
Heydt Fund, Nan and Matilda
Heymann Special Account, Mr. and Mrs. Jimmy
Heymann-Wolf Foundation
Hiawatha Education Foundation
Higgins Foundation, Aldus C.
Higginson Trust, Corina
High Foundation
Hill and Family Foundation, Walter Clay
Hill Foundation
Hill-Snowdon Foundation
Hillcrest Foundation
Hillman Family Foundation, Alex
Hillman Foundation
Hillsdale Fund
Hirschhorn Foundation, David and Barbara B.
Hoblitzelle Foundation
Hoche-Scofield Foundation
Hodge Foundation
Hoechst Celanese Corp.
Hoffberger Foundation
Hoffer Plastics Corp.
Hoffman Foundation, John Ernest
Hofheinz Foundation, Irene Cafcalas
Hofheinz Fund
Hofstetter Trust, Bessie
Hogan Foundation, Royal Barney

Holley Foundation
Hollis Foundation
Holmes Foundation
Holtzmann Foundation, Jacob L. and Lillian
Holzer Memorial Foundation, Richard H.
Home for Aged Men
HON Industries
Honda of America Manufacturing, Inc.
Honeywell
Honigman Foundation
Hook Drug
Hooker Charitable Trust, Janet A.
Hooper Foundation, Elizabeth S.
Hoover Foundation
Hoover Foundation, H. Earl
Hoover Fund-Trust, W. Henry
Hoover, Jr. Foundation, Margaret W. and Herbert
Hopedale Foundation
Hopeman Brothers
Hopkins Foundation, John Jay
Hopkins Foundation, Josephine Lawrence
Hopper Memorial Foundation, Bertrand
Hornblower Fund, Henry
Horncrest Foundation
Horowitz Foundation, Gedale B. and Barbara S.
Hospital Corp. of America
Houchens Foundation, Ervin G.
Houck Foundation, May K.
House Educational Trust, Susan Cook
House of Gross
Household International
Houston Endowment
Houston Industries
Howard and Bush Foundation
Howe and Mitchell B. Howe Foundation, Lucite Horton
Howell Foundation, Eric and Jessie
Howell Fund
Hubbard Foundation, R. Dee and Joan Dale
Hubbell Inc.
Hudson Neckwear
Huffy Corp.
Hughes Charitable Trust, Mabel Y.
Hugoton Foundation
Huisking Foundation
Huizenga Foundation, Jennie
Hulme Charitable Foundation, Milton G.
Hultquist Foundation
Humana
Hume Foundation, Jaquelin
Humphrey Foundation, Glenn & Gertrude
Humphrey Fund, George M. and Pamela S.
Hunt Alternatives Fund
Hunt Charitable Trust, C. Giles
Hunt Foundation
Hunt Foundation, Samuel P.
Hunt Trust for Episcopal Charitable Institutions, Virginia
Hunter Foundation, Edward and Irma
Hunter Trust, A. V.
Hunter Trust, Emily S. and Coleman A.
Huston Foundation
Hutcheson Foundation, Hazel Montague
Hutchins Foundation, Mary J.
Hyams Foundation
Hyde and Watson Foundation
Hyde Foundation, J. R.
I and G Charitable Foundation
IBM Corp.
Icahn Foundation, Carl C.
ICI Americas

Iddings Benevolent Trust
Ideal Industries
IES Industries
Illges Foundation, John P. and Dorothy S.
Illges Memorial Foundation, A. and M. L.
Illinois Bell
Illinois Power Co.
Imerman Memorial Foundation, Stanley
Imperial Electric
India Foundation
Indiana Bell Telephone Co.
Indiana Desk Co.
Indiana Gas and Chemical Corp.
Indiana Insurance Cos.
Ingalls Foundation, Louise H. and David S.
Ingersoll Milling Machine Co.
Inland Container Corp.
Inland Steel Industries
Inman Mills
Innovating Worthy Projects Foundation
Insurance Management Associates
Intel Corp.
Interco
International Paper Co.
Interstate Packaging Co.
Ireland Foundation
Irmas Charitable Foundation, Audrey and Sydney
Irwin Charity Foundation, William G.
Ishiyama Foundation
Island Foundation
ITT Corp.
ITT Hartford Insurance Group
Ittleson Foundation
Ivakota Association
Ix & Sons, Frank
J. D. B. Fund
J.P. Morgan & Co.
Jackson Charitable Trust, Marion Gardner
Jackson Foundation
Jackson Mills
Jacobson Foundation, Bernard H. and Blanche E.
Jacobson & Sons, Benjamin
Jaffe Foundation
Jameson Foundation, J. W. and Ida M.
Jameson Trust, Oleonda
Janesville Foundation
Janeway Foundation, Elizabeth Bixby
Janirve Foundation
Jaqua Foundation
Jarson-Stanley and Mickey Kaplan Foundation, Isaac & Esther
Jasam Foundation
Jasper Desk Co.
Jasper Seating Co.
Jasper Table Co.
Jasper Wood Products Co.
Jellison Benevolent Society
Jergens Foundation, Andrew
Jewett Foundation, George Frederick
JFM Foundation
Jinks Foundation, Ruth T.
JMK-A M Micallef Charitable Foundation
Jockey Hollow Foundation
JOFCo., Inc.
John Hancock Mutual Life Insurance Co.
Johnson Controls
Johnson Foundation, A. D.
Johnson Foundation, Helen K. and Arthur E.
Johnson Foundation, Robert Wood
Johnson Foundation, Walter S.

Johnson & Higgins
Johnson & Johnson
Johnson & Son, S.C.
Johnston-Hanson Foundation
Johnstone and H. Earle Kimball Foundation, Phyllis Kimball
Jones and Bessie D. Phelps Foundation, Cyrus W. and Amy F.
Jones Family Foundation, Eugenie and Joseph
Jones Foundation, Harvey and Bernice
Jones Foundation, Montfort Jones and Allie Brown
Jones Intercable, Inc.
Jonsson Foundation
Joselow Foundation
Joslin-Needham Family Foundation
Joslyn Corp.
Joslyn Foundation, Marcellus I.
Jostens
Journal Gazette Co.
Joyce Foundation, John M. and Mary A.
JSJ Corp.
Julia R. and Estelle L. Foundation
Jurodin Fund
Justus Trust, Edith C.
Kamps Memorial Foundation, Gertrude
Kangesser Foundation, Robert E., Harry A., and M. Sylvia
Kao Corp. of America (DE)
Kapiloff Foundation, Leonard
Kaplan Foundation, Charles I. and Mary
Kaplan Foundation, Rita J. and Stanley H.
Kaplen Foundation
Kaplun Foundation, Morris J. and Betty
Kasal Charitable Trust, Father
Katzenberger Foundation
Kaufman Endowment Fund, Louis G.
Kaufman Foundation, Henry & Elaine
Kaufman Memorial Trust, Chaim, Fanny, Louis, Benjamin, and Anne Florence
Kaufmann Foundation, Henry
Kaul Foundation Trust, Hugh
Kautz Family Foundation
Kavanagh Foundation, T. James
Kawabe Memorial Fund
Kayser Foundation
Keck Foundation, W. M.
Keeler Fund, Miner S. and Mary Ann
Keene Trust, Hazel R.
Keith Foundation Trust, Ben E.
Keller-Crescent Co.
Keller Family Foundation
Kelley and Elza Kelley Foundation, Edward Bangs
Kelley Foundation, Kate M.
Kellogg Foundation, J. C.
Kellogg Foundation, W. K.
Kellogg's
Kellwood Co.
Kelly Tractor Co.
Kemper Charitable Lead Trust, William T.
Kemper Memorial Foundation, David Woods
Kenan Family Foundation
Kendall Foundation, George R.
Kenedy Memorial Foundation, John G. and Marie Stella
Kennametal
Kennedy Foundation, Ethel
Kennedy Foundation, Quentin J.
Kennedy Memorial Fund, Mark H.
Kent-Lucas Foundation

Kentucky Foundation for Women
Kern Foundation Trust
Kerney Foundation, James
Kerr Foundation, Robert S. and Grayce B.
Kerr Fund, Grayce B.
Kerr-McGee Corp.
Kettering Family Foundation
Kevorkian Fund, Hagop
Key Bank of Maine
Kidder, Peabody & Co.
Kiewit Sons, Peter
Kilcawley Fund, William H.
Kilroy Foundation, William S. and Lora Jean
Kilworth Charitable Foundation, Florence B.
Kilworth Charitable Trust, William
Kimball Foundation, Horace A. Kimball and S. Ella
Kimball International
Kimberly-Clark Corp.
Kimmelman Foundation, Helen & Milton
King Foundation, Carl B. and Florence E.
Kingsbury Corp.
Kingston Foundation
Kiplinger Foundation
Kirby Foundation, F. M.
Kirkpatrick Foundation
Klau Foundation, David W. and Sadie
Klee Foundation, Conrad and Virginia
Klein Fund, Nathan J.
Kline Foundation, Charles and Figa
Kline Foundation, Josiah W. and Bessie H.
Kling Trust, Louise
Klipstein Foundation, Ernest Christian
Kloeckner-Pentaplast of America
Klosk Fund, Louis and Rose
Kmart Corp.
Knapp Foundation
Knight Foundation, John S. and James L.
Knistrom Foundation, Fanny and Svante
Knox Family Foundation
Knox, Sr., and Pearl Wallis Knox Charitable Foundation, Robert W.
Knudsen Charitable Foundation, Earl
Knudsen Foundation, Tom and Valley
Kobacker Co.
Koch Industries
Koch Sons, George
Koehler Foundation, Marcia and Otto
Koffler Family Foundation
Kohl Charitable Foundation, Allen D.
Kohl Charities, Herbert H.
Kohl Foundation, Sidney
Kohn-Joseloff Fund
Komes Foundation
Koopman Fund
Korman Family Foundation, Hyman
Kowalski Sausage Co.
Kraft Foundation
Kramer Foundation, C. L. C.
Kramer Foundation, Louise
Kresge Foundation
Kress Foundation, George
Kress Foundation, Samuel H.
Krieble Foundation, Vernon K.
Krimendahl II Foundation, H. Frederick
KSM Foundation
Kuehn Foundation
Kuhns Investment Co.

Kunkel Foundation, John Crain
Kutz Foundation, Milton and Hattie
Kuyper Foundation, Peter H. and E. Lucille Gaass
Kysor Industrial Corp.
La-Z-Boy Chair Co.
Laclede Gas Co.
Lacy Foundation
Ladd Charitable Corporation, Helen and George
Ladish Co.
Ladish Family Foundation, Herman W.
Lakeside Foundation
Lamson & Sessions Co.
Lancaster Colony
Lance, Inc.
Landegger Charitable Foundation
Landmark Communications
Lane Co., Inc.
Lane Foundation, Minnie and Bernard
Lang Foundation, Eugene M.
Lapham-Hickey Steel Corp.
Large Foundation
Laros Foundation, R. K.
Lasky Co.
Lassen Foundation, Irving A.
Lassus Brothers Oil
Lastfogel Foundation, Abe and Frances
Lauffer Trust, Charles A.
Laurel Foundation
Lautenberg Foundation
Lavanburg-Corner House
Law Foundation, Robert O.
Lawrence Foundation, Alice
Lazar Foundation
Lazarus Charitable Trust, Helen and Charles
LBJ Family Foundation
Lea Foundation, Helen Sperry
Leach Foundation, Tom & Frances
Lebovitz Fund
LeBrun Foundation
Lederer Foundation, Francis L.
Lee Endowment Foundation
Legg Mason Inc.
Lehigh Portland Cement Co.
Lehmann Foundation, Otto W.
Leibovitz Foundation, Morris P.
Leidy Foundation, John J.
Lender Family Foundation
Lennon Foundation, Fred A.
Lennox International, Inc.
Leonardt Foundation
Leonhardt Foundation, Dorothea L.
Leonhardt Foundation, Frederick H.
Leu Foundation
Leu Foundation, Harry P.
Leucadia National Corp.
Leuthold Foundation
Levee Charitable Trust, Polly Annenberg
Levine Family Foundation, Hyman
Levinson Foundation, Max and Anna
Levinson Foundation, Morris L.
Levit Family Foundation, Joe
Levitt Foundation, Richard S.
Levy Foundation, Betty and Norman F.
Levy Foundation, Edward C.
Levy Foundation, Hyman Jebb
Levy Foundation, Jerome
Levy's Lumber & Building Centers
Lewis Foundation, Lillian Kaiser
Libby-Dufour Fund, Trustees of the
Liberman Foundation, Bertha & Isaac
Liberty Corp.

Liberty Diversified Industries Inc.
Lichtenstein Foundation, David B.
Lied Foundation Trust
Life Insurance Co. of Georgia
Lightner Sams Foundation
Lilly Foundation, Richard Coyle
Lincoln Family Foundation
Lincoln Fund
Lincoln National Corp.
Lincy Foundation
Lindsay Foundation
Lipton Foundation
Lipton, Thomas J.
Liquid Air Corp.
Little, Arthur D.
Littlefield Memorial Trust, Ida Ballou
Litton Industries
Litton/Itek Optical Systems
Livingston Memorial Foundation
Lockhart Iron & Steel Co.
Loeb Partners Corp.
Loewenberg Foundation
Long Foundation, George A. and Grace
Longwood Foundation
Loose Trust, Carrie J.
Loose Trust, Harry Wilson
Lopata Foundation, Stanley and Lucy
Loughran Foundation, Mary and Daniel
Lounsbery Foundation, Richard
Loutit Foundation
Love Charitable Foundation, John Allan
Love Foundation, George H. and Margaret McClintic
Lovett Foundation
Lowe Foundation, Joe and Emily
Lowenstein Brothers Foundation
Lowenstein Foundation, William P. and Marie R.
Lozier Foundation
LTV Corp.
Lubo Fund
Luce Charitable Trust, Theodore
Luchsinger Family Foundation
Luckyday Foundation
Lumpkin Foundation
Lupin Foundation
Lutheran Brotherhood Foundation
Luttrell Trust
Lux Foundation, Miranda
Lyon Foundation
Lyons Foundation
Lytel Foundation, Bertha Russ
M. E. G. Foundation
M.T.D. Products
Maas Foundation, Benard L.
Mabee Foundation, J. E. and L. E.
MacAndrews & Forbes Holdings
MacArthur Foundation, John D. and Catherine T.
MacCurdy Salisbury Educational Foundation
MacDonald Foundation, James A.
MacDonald Foundation, Marquis George
Macht Foundation, Morton and Sophia
Mack Foundation, J. S.
Maclellan Charitable Trust, R. J.
Maclellan Foundation
MacLeod Stewardship Foundation
Macmillan, Inc.
Macy & Co., R.H.
Madison Gas & Electric Co.
Magee Christian Education Foundation
Magma Copper Co.
Magruder Foundation, Chesley G.

Mailman Family Foundation, A. L.
Mailman Foundation
Makita U.S.A., Inc.
MalCo Products Inc.
Mallinckrodt Specialty Chemicals Co.
Mamiye Brothers
Mandel Foundation, Jack N. and Lilyan
Mandel Foundation, Joseph and Florence
Mandel Foundation, Morton and Barbara
Mandell Foundation, Samuel P.
Mandeville Foundation
Maneely Fund
Manilow Foundation, Nathan
Mann Foundation, Ted
Mansfield Foundation, Albert and Anne
Manufacturers Life Insurance Co. of America
Marathon Oil, Indiana Refining Division
Marbrook Foundation
Marcus Corp.
Mardag Foundation
Mardigian Foundation
Margoes Foundation
Mark IV Industries
Marley Co.
Marmot Foundation
Marriott Corp.
Marsh & McLennan Cos.
Marshall Field's
Marshall Foundation, Mattie H.
Marshall Fund
Marshall & Ilsley Bank
Marshall Trust in Memory of Sanders McDaniel, Harriet McDaniel
Marshburn Foundation
Martin Foundation
Martin Foundation, Bert William
Martin Marietta Aggregates
Martin Marietta Corp.
Martini Foundation, Nicholas
Marubeni America Corp.
Masco Corp.
Massachusetts Mutual Life Insurance Co.
Massengill-DeFriece Foundation
Masserini Charitable Trust, Maurice J.
Massey Charitable Trust
Massey Foundation
Massey Foundation, Jack C.
Massie Trust, David Meade
Mather and William Gwinn Mather Fund, Elizabeth Ring
Mather Charitable Trust, S. Livingston
Mather Fund, Richard
Mathis-Pfohl Foundation
Matthews International Corp.
Mattus Foundation, Reuben and Rose
Matz Foundation — Edelman
Maxus Energy Corp.
May Charitable Trust, Ben
May Department Stores Co.
May Mitchell Royal Foundation
Mayborn Foundation, Frank W.
Mayer Charitable Trust, Oscar G. & Elsa S.
Mayer Foods Corp., Oscar
Mayor Foundation, Oliver Dewey
Maytag Family Foundation, Fred
Mazer Foundation, Jacob and Ruth
MBIA, Inc.
MCA
McBean Family Foundation
McCarthy Charities
McCarthy Foundation, Michael W.

McCarthy Memorial Trust Fund, Catherine
McConnell Foundation, Neil A.
McCormick & Co.
McCormick Tribune Foundation, Robert R.
McCullough Foundation, Ralph H. and Ruth J.
McCune Charitable Trust, John R.
McCune Foundation
McCutchen Foundation
McDermott
McDonald Industries, Inc., A. Y.
McDonnell Douglas Corp.
McDonnell Douglas Corp.-West
McDonough Foundation, Bernard
McEachern Charitable Trust, D. V. & Ida J.
McEvoy Foundation, Mildred H.
McFeely-Rogers Foundation
McGee Foundation
McGonagle Foundation, Dextra Baldwin
McGraw Foundation, Donald C.
McGraw-Hill
McGregor Foundation, Thomas and Frances
McGregor Fund
McInerny Foundation
McIntosh Foundation
McIntyre Foundation, B. D. and Jane E.
McIntyre Foundation, C. S. and Marion F.
MCJ Foundation
McKee Foundation, Robert E. and Evelyn
McKee Poor Fund, Virginia A.
McKesson Corp.
McKnight Foundation
McLean Contributionship
McMahon Charitable Trust Fund, Father John J.
McMillan Foundation, D. W.
McMillen Foundation
McMurray-Bennett Foundation
McNeely Foundation
McNutt Charitable Trust, Amy Shelton
McVay Foundation
MDU Resources Group, Inc.
Mead Corp.
Mead Fund, Nelson
Meadowood Foundation
Meadows Foundation
Mechanic Foundation, Morris A.
Mechanics Bank
Medina Foundation
Medtronic
Meek Foundation
Meland Outreach
Mellam Family Foundation
Mellam Family Foundation
Mellon Foundation, Richard King
Melohn Foundation
Memton Fund
Menasha Corp.
Mendel Foundation
Mengle Foundation, Glenn and Ruth
Menschel Foundation, Robert and Joyce
Mentor Graphics
Mercantile Bancorp
Merchants Bancshares
Merck & Co.
Merck Human Health Division
Meredith Corp.
Meredith Foundation
Merit Oil Corp.
Merrick Foundation
Merrion Foundation
Mertz Foundation, Martha
Mervyn's
Meserve Memorial Fund, Albert and Helen

Messing Family Charitable Foundation
Messing Foundation, Morris M. and Helen F.
Metal Industries
Metropolitan Health Foundation
Meyer Foundation, Alice Kleberg Reynolds
Meyer Foundation, Baron de Hirsch
Meyer Foundation, Eugene and Agnes E.
Meyer Foundation, George C.
Meyer Foundation, Robert R.
Meyer Fund, Milton and Sophie
Meyer Memorial Trust
Meyerhoff Fund, Joseph
MGIC Investment Corp.
Michael Foundation, Herbert I. and Elsa B.
Michigan Bell Telephone Co.
Michigan Gas Utilities
Microsoft Corp.
Mid-Iowa Health Foundation
Middendorf Foundation
Midwest Resources
Milbank Foundation, Dunlevy
Mill-Rose Co.
Millard Charitable Trust, Adah K.
Millbrook Tribute Garden
Miller Charitable Trust, Lewis N.
Miller Foundation
Miller Foundation, Steve J.
Miller Fund, Kathryn and Gilbert
Miller-Mellor Association
Miller Memorial Trust, George Lee
Milliken & Co.
Mills Foundation, Ralph E.
Mills Fund, Frances Goll
Millstone Foundation
Mine Safety Appliances Co.
Miniger Memorial Foundation, Clement O.
Minnegasco
Minnesota Foundation
Minnesota Power & Light Co.
Minster Machine Co.
Mitchell Energy & Development Corp.
Mitchell Family Foundation, Bernard and Marjorie
Mitchell Family Foundation, Bernard and Marjorie
Mitchell Family Foundation, Edward D. and Anna
Mitchell Foundation
Mitsubishi Heavy Industries America
Mitsubishi International Corp.
MNC Financial
Mnuchin Foundation
Mobil Oil Corp.
Model Foundation, Leo
Mohasco Corp.
Monaghan Charitable Trust, Rose
Monarch Machine Tool Co.
Monroe Auto Equipment Co.
Montgomery Elevator Co.
Montgomery Street Foundation
Montgomery Ward & Co.
Moore Business Forms, Inc.
Moore Charitable Foundation, Marjorie
Moore Foundation, C. F.
Moore Foundation, Edward S.
Moore Foundation, Martha G.
Moore Foundation, O. L.
Moore Foundation, Roy C.
Moores Foundation
Moorman Manufacturing Co.
Morania Foundation
Morgan and Samuel Tate
Morgan, Jr. Foundation, Marietta McNeil
Morgan Stanley & Co.
Morgenstern Foundation, Morris
Morley Brothers Foundation

Community Service Organizations (cont.)

Morrill Charitable Foundation
Morris Foundation
Morris Foundation, Margaret T.
Morris Foundation, Norman M.
Morrison-Knudsen Corp.
Morrison Trust, Louise L.
Morse Foundation, Richard P. and Claire W.
Mosbacher, Jr. Foundation, Emil
Moses Fund, Henry and Lucy
Mosinee Paper Corp.
Moskowitz Foundation, Irving I.
Moss Charitable Trust, Finis M.
Moss Foundation, Harry S.
Mostyn Foundation
Motorola
Mott Fund, Ruth
MTS Systems Corp.
Mulcahy Foundation
Mulford Foundation, Vincent
Mulford Trust, Clarence E.
Mullen Foundation, J. K.
Muller Foundation
Muller Foundation, C. John and Josephine
Mulligan Charitable Trust, Mary S.
Murphey Foundation, Lluella Morey
Murphy Co., G.C.
Murphy Foundation, Dan
Murphy Foundation, John P.
Murphy Oil Corp.
Murray Foundation
Musson Charitable Foundation, R. C. and Katharine M.
Muth Foundation, Peter and Mary
Myers and Sons, D.
Myra Foundation
Nalco Chemical Co.
Nanney Foundation, Charles and Irene
Nathan Foundation
National City Bank of Evansville
National City Corp.
National Gypsum Co.
National Machinery Co.
National Presto Industries
National Starch & Chemical Corp.
National Steel
National Westminster Bank New Jersey
Nationale-Nederlanden North America Corp.
NationsBank Corp.
NBD Bank
NCR Corp.
NEC Technologies, Inc.
NEC USA
Neenah Foundry Co.
Neese Family Foundation
Neilson Foundation, George W.
Nelson Foundation, Florence
Nelson Industries, Inc.
Neu Foundation, Hugo and Doris
Neuberger Foundation, Roy R. and Marie S.
New England Business Service
New England Foundation
New England Mutual Life Insurance Co.
New Hampshire Ball Bearings
New Horizon Foundation
New-Land Foundation
New Prospect Foundation
New Street Capital Corp.
New York Foundation
New York Life Insurance Co.
New York Stock Exchange
New York Telephone Co.
New York Times Co.
The New Yorker Magazine, Inc.

Newbrook Charitable Foundation
Newhall Foundation, Henry Mayo
Newhouse Foundation, Samuel I.
Newman Assistance Fund, Jerome A. and Estelle R.
Newman Charitable Trust, Calvin M. and Raquel H.
Newman's Own
News & Observer Publishing Co.
Nias Foundation, Henry
Nichols Co., J.C.
Nissan Motor Corporation in U.S.A.
Noble Foundation, Samuel Roberts
Noble Foundation, Vivian Bilby
Norcliffe Fund
Norcross Wildlife Foundation
Nordson Corp.
Nordstrom, Inc.
Norfolk Southern Corp.
Norman Foundation
Normandie Foundation
Norris Foundation, Kenneth T. and Eileen L.
North American Reinsurance Corp.
North Carolina Foam Foundation
North Shore Foundation
Northeast Utilities
Northern Indiana Public Service Co.
Northern States Power Co.
Northern Trust Co.
Northwestern National Insurance Group
Norton Co.
Norton Foundation Inc.
Norton Memorial Corporation, Geraldi
Noyes, Jr. Memorial Foundation, Nicholas H.
Number Ten Foundation
NuTone Inc.
N've Shalom Foundation
Oakley Foundation, Hollie and Anna
Oberkotter Family Foundation
Oberlaender Foundation, Gustav
Obernauer Foundation
Obernauer Foundation
O'Bleness Foundation, Charles G.
O'Brien Foundation, Cornelius and Anna Cook
Occidental Oil & Gas Corp.
O'Connor Co.
O'Connor Foundation, A. Lindsay and Olive B.
O'Connor Foundation, Kathryn
O'Connor Foundation, Magee
OCRI Foundation
Odell and Helen Pfeiffer Odell Fund, Robert Stewart
Oestreicher Foundation, Sylvan and Ann
O'Fallon Trust, Martin J. and Mary Anne
Ogden Foundation, Ralph E.
Ogilvy & Mather Worldwide
Ogle Foundation, Paul
Oglebay Norton Co.
Ohio Savings Bank
Ohio Valley Foundation
Ohrstrom Foundation
Oklahoma Gas & Electric Co.
Oklahoman Foundation
Old National Bank in Evansville
Oleson Foundation
Olin Charitable Trust, John M.
Olive Bridge Fund
Olmsted Foundation, George and Carol
Olsson Memorial Foundation, Elis
Onan Family Foundation
1525 Foundation

1957 Charity Trust
O'Neil Foundation, Cyril F. and Marie E.
O'Neil Foundation, M. G.
O'Neill Charitable Corporation, F. J.
O'Neill Foundation, William J. and Dorothy K.
Ontario Corp.
Oppenheimer and Flora Oppenheimer Haas Trust, Leo
Oppenheimer Family Foundation
Orange Orphan Society
Orleans Trust, Carrie S.
Orleton Trust Fund
Ormet Corp.
Osborn Manufacturing Co.
Oshkosh B'Gosh
Oshkosh Truck Corp.
O'Sullivan Children Foundation
O'Toole Foundation, Theresa and Edward
Ottenstein Family Foundation
Overbrook Foundation
Overlake Foundation
Owen Trust, B. B.
Oxford Foundation
Oxford Foundation
Oxford Industries, Inc.
Pacific Mutual Life Insurance Co.
Pacific Western Foundation
PacifiCorp
Packaging Corporation of America
Packard Foundation, David and Lucile
Packer Foundation, Horace B.
Padnos Iron & Metal Co., Louis
Page Belting Co.
Page Foundation, George B.
Palmer-Fry Memorial Trust, Lily
Palmer Fund, Francis Asbury
Palmer Fund, Frank Loomis
Pan-American Life Insurance Co.
Panhandle Eastern Corp.
Park National Bank
Parker Drilling Co.
Parker, Jr. Foundation, William A.
Parman Foundation, Robert A.
Parnes Foundation, E. H.
Parshelsky Foundation, Moses L.
Parvin Foundation, Albert
Pasadena Area Residential Aid
Patterson-Barclay Memorial Foundation
Patterson Charitable Fund, W. I.
Paulstan
Paulucci Family Foundation
Pax Christi Foundation
Payne Foundation, Frank E. and Seba B.
Peabody Foundation, Amelia
Pearce Foundation, Dr. M. Lee
Peck Foundation, Milton and Lillian
Peerless Insurance Co.
Peierls Foundation
Pella Corp.
Pellegrino-Realmuto Charitable Foundation
Pendleton Memorial Fund, William L. and Ruth T.
Penn Foundation, William
Penn Savings Bank, a division of Sovereign Bank Bank of Princeton, a division of Sovereign Bank
Penney Foundation, James C.
Pennington Foundation, Irene W. and C. B.
Pennzoil Co.
Peoples Energy Corp.
Pepsi-Cola Bottling Co. of Charlotte
PepsiCo
Perini Corp.
Perini Foundation, Joseph

Perkin-Elmer Corp.
Perkin-Elmer Corp.
Perkins Charitable Foundation
Perkins Foundation, Edwin E.
Perkins Foundation, Joe and Lois
Perot Foundation
Perpetual Benevolent Fund
Persis Corp.
Pet
Peterloon Foundation
Peters Foundation, Charles F.
Peters Foundation, Leon S.
Peterson Foundation, Fred J.
Petteys Memorial Foundation, Jack
Pettus Crowe Foundation
Pettus, Jr. Foundation, James T.
Pew Charitable Trusts
Pfister and Vogel Tanning Co.
Pfizer
Phelps, Inc.
Phelps Dodge Corp.
PHH Corp.
Philadelphia Industries
Philibosian Foundation, Stephen
Philip Morris Cos.
Phillips Family Foundation, Jay and Rose
Phillips Foundation, A. P.
Phillips Foundation, Dr. P.
Phillips Petroleum Co.
Phillips-Van Heusen Corp.
Phipps Foundation, William H.
Physicians Mutual Insurance
Pick Charitable Trust, Melitta S.
Pick, Jr. Fund, Albert
Piedmont Health Care Foundation
Pillsbury Foundation
Pilot Trust
Pincus Family Fund
Pine Tree Foundation
Pines Bridge Foundation
Pineywoods Foundation
Pinkerton Foundation
Pirelli Armstrong Tire Corp.
Pitney Bowes
Pitt-Des Moines Inc.
Pitts Foundation, William H. and Lula E.
Pittsburgh Child Guidance Foundation
Pittsburgh National Bank
Pittway Corp.
Pitzman Fund
Plankenhorn Foundation, Harry
Plant Memorial Fund, Henry B.
Playboy Enterprises, Inc.
Plough Foundation
Plym Foundation
Poindexter Foundation
Poinsettia Foundation, Paul and Magdalena Ecke
Polinger Foundation, Howard and Geraldine
Pollock Company Foundation, William B.
Poorvu Foundation, William and Lia
Porsche Cars North America, Inc.
Porter Foundation, Mrs. Cheever
Portland General Electric Co.
Potomac Electric Power Co.
Pott Foundation, Herman T. and Phenie R.
Pottstown Mercury
Powell Co., William
Powell Family Foundation
PPG Industries
Prairie Foundation
Prange Co., H. C.
Pratt Memorial Fund
Precision Rubber Products
Premier Bank
Premier Dental Products Co.
Premier Industrial Corp.

Prentis Family Foundation, Meyer and Anna
Preston Trust, Evelyn W.
Price Associates, T. Rowe
Price Foundation, Lucien B. and Katherine E.
Priddy Foundation
Prince Trust, Abbie Norman
Pritzker Foundation
Procter & Gamble Co.
Procter & Gamble Cosmetic & Fragrance Products
Proctor Trust, Mortimer R.
Propp Sons Fund, Morris and Anna
Providence Energy Corp.
Provident Life & Accident Insurance Co.
Prudential-Bache Securities
Prudential Insurance Co. of America
Public Service Co. of Colorado
Public Service Electric & Gas Co.
Public Welfare Foundation
Puett Foundation, Nelson
Pulitzer Publishing Co.
Puterbaugh Foundation
Putnam Foundation
Pyramid Foundation
Quaker Chemical Corp.
Quaker Oats Co.
Quanex Corp.
Questar Corp.
Quincy Newspapers
Quinlan Foundation, Elizabeth C.
Quivey-Bay State Foundation
R. F. Foundation
R. P. Foundation
R&B Tool Co.
Radin Foundation
Ragen, Jr. Memorial Fund Trust No. 1, James M.
Rahr Malting Co.
Raker Foundation, M. E.
Raleigh Linen Service/National Distributing Co.
Rales and Ruth Rales Foundation, Norman R.
Ralston Purina Co.
Ramapo Trust
Ramlose Foundation, George A.
Randa
Randolph Foundation
Rankin and Elizabeth Forbes Rankin Trust, William
Ranney Foundation, P. K.
Ransom Fidelity Company
Raskin Foundation, Hirsch and Braine
Raskob Foundation for Catholic Activities
Rasmussen Foundation
Ratshesky Foundation, A. C.
Ray Foundation
Raymond Corp.
Raymond Educational Foundation
Raytheon Co.
Read Foundation, Charles L.
Redfield Foundation, Nell J.
Redman Foundation
Reed Foundation
Reed Foundation, Philip D.
Reedman Car-Truck World Center
Regenstein Foundation
Regis Corp.
REI-Recreational Equipment, Inc.
Reicher Foundation, Anne & Harry J.
Reichhold Chemicals, Inc.
Reidler Foundation
Reilly Industries
Reily & Co., William B.
Reinhold Foundation, Paul E. and Ida Klare

Reliable Life Insurance Co.
Reliance Electric Co.
Rennebohm Foundation, Oscar
Replogle Foundation, Luther I.
Republic New York Corp.
Retirement Research Foundation
Revlon
Reynolds Foundation, Donald W.
Reynolds Foundation, Eleanor T.
Reynolds Foundation, J. B.
Reynolds Metals Co.
Rhoades Fund, Otto L. and
Hazel E.
Rhodebeck Charitable Trust
Rhoden Charitable Foundation,
Elmer C.
Rhone-Poulenc Inc.
Rhone-Poulenc Rorer
Rice Foundation, Helen Steiner
Rich Products Corp.
Richardson Benevolent
Foundation, C. E.
Richardson Foundation, Smith
Rider-Pool Foundation
Ridgefield Foundation
Rieke Corp.
Rienzi Foundation
Riggs Benevolent Fund
Riley Foundation, Mabel Louise
Ritchie Memorial Foundation,
Charles E. and Mabel M.
Rite-Hite Corp.
Rittenhouse Foundation
Ritter Charitable Trust, George
W. & Mary F.
Ritter Foundation
Ritter Foundation, May Ellen
and Gerald
RJR Nabisco Inc.
Robertson Brothers
Robin Family Foundation, Albert
A.
Robinson Foundation
Robinson Fund, Charles Nelson
Robinson Fund, Maurice R.
Robison Foundation, Ellis H. and
Doris B.
Roblee Foundation, Joseph H.
and Florence A.
Roche Relief Foundation,
Edward and Ellen
Rock Foundation, Milton and
Shirley
Rockford Products Corp.
Rockwell Foundation
Rockwell Fund
Rockwell International Corp.
Rodgers Foundation, Richard &
Dorothy
Roehl Foundation
Rogers Charitable Trust, Florence
Rogers Foundation
Rohatyn Foundation, Felix and
Elizabeth
Rohlik Foundation, Sigmund and
Sophie
Rohm and Haas Company
Rohr Inc.
Rolfs Foundation, Robert T.
RosaMary Foundation
Rosenberg Foundation
Rosenberg Foundation, Alexis
Rosenberg Foundation, Henry
and Ruth Blaustein
Rosenthal Foundation, Benjamin
J.
Rosenthal Foundation, Ida and
William
Rosenthal Foundation, Samuel
Rosenwald Family Fund, William
Ross Foundation
Ross Foundation, Lyn & George
M.
Ross Foundation, Walter G.
Ross Laboratories
Ross Memorial Foundation, Will
Roth Foundation, Louis T.

Rothschild Foundation, Hulda B.
and Maurice L.
Rotterman Trust, Helen L. and
Marie F.
Royal Group Inc.
Ruan Foundation Trust, John
Rubenstein Foundation, Philip
Ruddick Corp.
Rudin Foundation, Samuel and
May
Rudy, Jr. Trust, George B.
Ruffin Foundation, Peter B. &
Adeline W.
Rukin Philanthropic Foundation,
David and Eleanore
Rupp Foundation, Fran and
Warren
Russell Charitable Foundation,
Tom
Russell Charitable Trust,
Josephine S.
Russell Trust, Josephine G.
Ryan Family Charitable
Foundation
Ryan Foundation, David Claude
Ryan Foundation, Nina M.
Ryan Foundation, Patrick G. and
Shirley W.
Sachs Fund
SAFECO Corp.
Sagamore Foundation
Saint Croix Foundation
St. Faith's House Foundation
Saint Gerard Foundation
St. Mary's Catholic Foundation
Saint Paul Cos.
San Diego Gas & Electric
San Diego Trust & Savings Bank
Sanders Trust, Charles
Sandusky International Inc.
Sandy Hill Foundation
Sang Foundation, Elsie O. and
Philip D.
Santa Fe Pacific Corp.
Santa Maria Foundation
Sapirstein-Stone-Weiss
Foundation
Sara Lee Corp.
Sara Lee Hosiery
Sarkeys Foundation
Sasco Foundation
Saturno Foundation
Saul Foundation, Joseph E. &
Norma G.
Sawyer Charitable Foundation
Schaffer Foundation, H.
Schaffer Foundation, Michael &
Helen
Schautz Foundation, Walter L.
Schecter Private Foundation,
Aaron and Martha
Scheirich Co., H.J.
Schenck Fund, L. P.
Scheuer Family Foundation, S.
H. and Helen R.
Schey Foundation
Schieffelin Residuary Trust,
Sarah I.
Schiff Foundation
Schiff Foundation, Dorothy
Schilling Motors
Schiro Fund
Schlink Foundation, Albert G.
and Olive H.
Schmidlapp Trust No. 1, Jacob G.
Schmidlapp Trust No. 2, Jacob G.
Schmidt Charitable Foundation,
William E.
Schmitt Foundation, Arthur J.
Schneider Foundation Corp., Al
J.
Schoonmaker J-Sewkly Valley
Hospital Trust
Schottenstein Foundation,
Jerome & Saul
Schroeder Foundation, Walter
Schultz Foundation
Schultz Foundation

Schwab & Co., Charles
Schwartz and Robert Schwartz
Foundation, Bernard
Schwartz Foundation, Arnold A.
Schwartz Foundation, David
Schwartz Fund for Education
and Health Research, Arnold
and Marie
Schwob Foundation, Simon
Science Applications
International Corp.
Scott and Fetzer Co.
Scott Foundation, William E.
Scott Foundation, William R.,
John G., and Emma
Scrivner, Inc.
Scroggins Foundation, Arthur E.
and Cornelia C.
Scurlock Foundation
Seafirst Corp.
Sealright Co., Inc.
Sears Family Foundation
Seaver Charitable Trust, Richard
C.
Seaway Food Town
Seay Memorial Trust, George
and Effie
Sebastian Foundation
Security Life of Denver
Seevak Family Foundation
Segerstrom Foundation
Sehn Foundation
Seid Foundation, Barre
Seidman Family Foundation
Self Foundation
Semmes Foundation
Sentinel Communications Co.
Sentry Insurance Co.
Sewall Foundation, Elmina
Sexton Foundation
Seybert Institution for Poor Boys
and Girls, Adam and Maria
Sarah
Seymour and Troester Foundation
Shafer Foundation, Richard H.
and Ann
Shapell Foundation, Nathan and
Lilly
Shapero Foundation, Nate S. and
Ruth B.
Shapiro, Inc.
Shapiro Family Foundation,
Soretta and Henry
Share Foundation
Share Trust, Charles Morton
Sharon Steel Corp.
Sharp Electronics Corp.
Sharp Foundation
Sharp Foundation, Charles S.
and Ruth C.
Shaw Foundation, Arch W.
Shaw Foundation, Gardiner
Howland
Shawmut National Corp.
Shaw's Supermarkets
Sheaffer Inc.
Sheinberg Foundation, Eric P.
Shelden Fund, Elizabeth, Allan
and Warren
Sheldon Foundation, Ralph C.
Shell Oil Co.
Shelton Cos.
Shenandoah Life Insurance Co.
Shiffman Foundation
Shirk Foundation, Russell and
Betty
Shoemaker Fund, Thomas H.
and Mary Williams
Shoenberg Foundation
Shoney's Inc.
Shott, Jr. Foundation, Hugh I.
Sierra Pacific Resources
Sifco Industries Inc.
Signet Bank/Maryland
Simmons Family Foundation, R.
P.
Simon Foundation, Robert Ellis

Simon Foundation, William E.
and Carol G.
Simone Foundation
Simone Foundation
Simpson Foundation
Simpson Foundation, John M.
Simpson Industries
Simpson Investment Co.
Sioux Steel Co.
Siragusa Foundation
SIT Investment Associates, Inc.
Skandia America Reinsurance
Corp.
Skillman Foundation
Skinner Corp.
Slant/Fin Corp.
Slaughter, Jr. Foundation,
William E.
Slifka Foundation, Alan B.
Slifka Foundation, Joseph and
Sylvia
Smith Charitable Trust, W. W.
Smith Corp., A.O.
Smith Family Foundation,
Charles E.
Smith Family Foundation, Theda
Clark
Smith Foundation
Smith Foundation, Julia and
Albert
Smith Foundation, Lon V.
Smith, Jr. Charitable Trust, Jack
J.
Smith, Jr. Foundation, M. W.
Smith Memorial Fund, Ethel
Sergeant Clark
Smucker Co., J.M.
Smucker Co., J.M.
Snee-Reinhardt Charitable
Foundation
SNET
Snider Foundation
Snow Foundation, John Ben
Snyder Charitable Fund, W. P.
Snyder Foundation, Frost and
Margaret
Snyder Foundation, Harold B.
and Dorothy A.
Snyder Fund, Valentine Perry
Solheim Foundation
Solow Foundation
Somers Foundation, Byron H.
Sonat
Sony Corp. of America
Sooner Pipe & Supply Corp.
Sooner Pipe & Supply Corp.
Soref Foundation, Samuel M.
Soref and Helene K.
Sosland Foundation
South Branch Foundation
South Carolina Electric & Gas
Co.
South Waite Foundation
Southern California Edison Co.
Southern Furniture Co.
Southwest Gas Corp.
Southwestern Bell Corp.
Spang & Co.
Special People In Need
Spiegel
Spiegel Family Foundation, Jerry
and Emily
Spingold Foundation, Nate B.
and Frances
Spiritus Gladius Foundation
Sprague Educational and
Charitable Foundation, Seth
Springs Foundation
Sprint
SPS Technologies
Spunk Fund
SPX Corp.
Square D Co.
Stabler Foundation, Donald B.
and Dorothy L.
Stackner Family Foundation
Stacy Foundation, Festus
Stacy Foundation, Festus

Staley, Jr. Foundation, A. E.
Staley Manufacturing Co., A.E.
Standard Chartered Bank New
York
Standard Products Co.
Standard Register Co.
Standard Steel Speciality Co.
Stanley Charitable Foundation,
A. W.
Stanley Works
Starr Foundation
Starrett Co., L.S.
State Farm Mutual Automobile
Insurance Co.
State Street Bank & Trust Co.
Statler Foundation
Statter Foundation, Amy Plant
Stauffer Communications
Stauffer Foundation, John and
Beverly
Stearns Charitable Foundation,
Anna B.
Stearns Trust, Artemas W.
Steelcase
Steele Foundation
Steiger Memorial Fund, Albert
Stein Foundation, Joseph F.
Stein Foundation, Louis
Steinberg Family Foundation,
Meyer and Jean
Steiner Corp.
Steinhagen Benevolent Trust, B.
A. and Elinor
Steinhardt Foundation, Judy and
Michael
Steinman Foundation, James
Hale
Steinsapir Family Foundation,
Julius L. and Libhie B.
Stella D'Oro Biscuit Co.
Stemmons Foundation
Stephens Foundation Trust
Sterling Inc.
Sterling Winthrop
Stern Family Foundation, Alex
Stern Family Foundation, Harry
Stern Foundation, Bernice and
Milton
Stern Foundation, Gustav and
Irene
Stern Foundation, Irvin
Stern Foundation, Leonard N.
Stern Foundation, Max
Sternberger Foundation, Sigmund
Stevens Foundation, Abbot and
Dorothy H.
Stewards Fund
Stocker Foundation
Stoddard Charitable Trust
Stone Family Foundation,
Jerome H.
Stone Family Foundation,
Norman H.
Stone Foundation, W. Clement
and Jessie V.
Stone Trust, H. Chase
Stonecutter Mills Corp.
Stoneman Charitable
Foundation, Anne and David
Stonestreet Trust, Eusebia S.
Storage Technology Corp.
Storz Foundation, Robert Herman
Stott Foundation, Louis L.
Stowe, Jr. Foundation, Robert
Lee
Strake Foundation
Stranahan Foundation
Stratford Foundation
Straus Foundation, Aaron and
Lillie
Straus Foundation, Martha
Washington Straus and Harry
H.
Straus Foundation, Philip A. and
Lynn
Strauss Foundation
Stride Rite Corp.
Strong Foundation, Hattie M.

Community Service Organizations (cont.)

Strosacker Foundation, Charles J.
Stuart Center Charitable Trust, Hugh
Stuart Foundation
Stubblefield, Estate of Joseph L.
Stulsaft Foundation, Morris
Stupp Brothers Bridge & Iron Co.
Stupp Foundation, Norman J.
Subaru-Isuzu Automotive Inc.
Subaru of America Inc.
Sullivan Foundation, Ray H. and Pauline
Sumitomo Bank of California
Summerfield Foundation, Solon E.
Sumners Foundation, Hatton W.
Sun Co.
Sunderland Foundation, Lester T.
Sunmark Capital Corp.
Superior Tube Co.
Surrena Memorial Fund, Harry and Thelma
Sutton Foundation
Swalm Foundation
Swanson Foundation
Sweatt Foundation, Harold W.
Sweet Life Foods
Swift Memorial Health Care Foundation
Swig Charity Foundation, Mae and Benjamin
Swig Foundation
Swisher Foundation, Carl S.
Synovus Financial Corp.
Tait Foundation, Frank M.
Tamarkin Co.
Tamko Asphalt Products
Tandem Computers
Tandy Foundation, David L.
Tang Foundation
Taper Foundation, Mark
Taper Foundation, S. Mark
Tarmac America Inc.
Tasty Baking Co.
Taub Foundation
Taub Foundation, Joseph and Arlene
Taube Family Foundation
Taube Family Foundation
Taubman Foundation, A. Alfred
Taubman Foundation, Herman P. and Sophia
Taylor Foundation
Taylor Foundation, Fred and Harriett
Teagle Foundation
Teledyne
Teleklew Productions
Tell Foundation
Temple Foundation, T. L. L.
Templeton Foundation, Herbert A.
Tenneco
Tension Envelope Corp.
Terner Foundation
Terry Foundation, C. Herman
Tetley, Inc.
Texaco
Texas Commerce Bank Houston, N.A.
Texas Gas Transmission Corp.
Texas Instruments
Textron
Thagard Foundation
Thalheimer Foundation, Alvin and Fanny Blaustein
Thalhimer and Family Foundation, Charles G.
Thalhimer Brothers Inc.
Thalhimer, Jr. and Family Foundation, William B.
Thanksgiving Foundation
Thatcher Foundation

Thendara Foundation
Thirty-Five Twenty, Inc.
Thoman Foundation, W. B. and Candace
Thomas Foundation, Dorothy
Thomas Memorial Foundation, Theresa A.
Thomasville Furniture Industries
Thorne Foundation
Thorson Foundation
3M Co.
Thurman Charitable Foundation for Children, Edgar A.
Time Insurance Co.
Times Mirror Co.
Timken Co.
Timken Foundation of Canton
Tippens Foundation
Tiscornia Foundation
Titmus Foundation
Titus Foundation, C. W.
TJX Cos.
Tobin Foundation
Todd Co., A.M.
Tomlinson Foundation, Kate and Elwyn
Toms Foundation
Tonya Memorial Foundation
Torchmark Corp.
Tortuga Foundation
Tosco Corp. Refining Division
Towsley Foundation, Harry A. and Margaret D.
Transamerica Corp.
Transco Energy Company
Tranzonic Cos.
Travelers Cos.
Treakle Foundation, J. Edwin
Trees Charitable Trust, Edith L.
Trexler Trust, Harry C.
Triford Foundation
Trimble Family Foundation, Robert Mize and Isa White
TRINOVA Corp.
Tropicana Products, Inc.
True North Foundation
True Oil Co.
True Trust, Henry A.
Truland Foundation
Trull Foundation
Truman Foundation, Mildred Faulkner
Trust Co. Bank
Trust for Mutual Understanding
Trust Funds
Tuch Foundation, Michael
Tucker Foundation, Marcia Brady
Tull Charitable Foundation
Turner Fund, Ruth
Turrell Fund
Tyson Foods, Inc.
Unger Foundation, Aber D.
Unilever United States
Union Bank
Union Bank of Switzerland Los Angeles Branch
Union Camp Corp.
Union Central Life Insurance Co.
Union Electric Co.
Union Foundation
Union Manufacturing Co.
Union Pacific Corp.
United Co.
United Conveyor Corp.
United Dominion Industries
United Parcel Service of America
U.S. Oil/Schmidt Family Foundation, Inc.
U.S. Oil/Schmidt Family Foundation, Inc.
United States Sugar Corp.
United States Trust Co. of New York
United Technologies, Automotive
United Technologies Corp.
United Togs Inc.
Unitrode Corp.

Univar Corp.
Universal Foods Corp.
Universal Leaf Tobacco Co.
Unocal Corp.
Upjohn California Fund
Upjohn Foundation, Harold and Grace
Upton Foundation, Frederick S.
Uris Brothers Foundation
USG Corp.
Ushkow Foundation
Uslico Corp.
UST
Utica National Insurance Group
Vale-Asche Foundation
Valley National Bank of Arizona
Valspar Corp.
Van Andel Foundation, Jay and Betty
Van Every Foundation, Philip L.
Van Huffel Foundation, I. J.
van Loben Sels - Eleanor Slate van Lobel Sels Charitable Foundation, Ernst D.
Van Nuys Charities, J. B. and Emily
Van Wert County Foundation
Vance Charitable Foundation, Robert C.
Vanderbilt Trust, R. T.
Vanneck-Bailey Foundation
Varian Associates
Vaughan Foundation, Rachael and Ben
Vaughn Foundation
Veritas Foundation
Vermeer Investment Company Foundation
Vermeer Manufacturing Co.
Vernon Fund, Miles Hodsdon
Vicksburg Foundation
Victoria Foundation
Vidda Foundation
Vidinha Charitable Trust, A. and E.
Vilter Manufacturing Corp.
Virginia Power Co.
Visciglia Foundation, Frank
Vlasic Foundation
Vogt Machine Co., Henry
Vollbrecht Foundation, Frederick A.
Von der Ahe Foundation
Von der Ahe, Jr. Trust, Theodore Albert
Vulcan Materials Co.
Wachovia Bank of Georgia, N.A.
Wachovia Bank & Trust Co., N.A.
Wade Endowment Fund, Elizabeth Firth
Waffle House, Inc.
Waggoner Charitable Trust, Crystelle
Waggoner Foundation, E. Paul and Helen Buck
Wagner Manufacturing Co., E. R.
Wahlert Foundation
Wal-Mart Stores
Waldbaum, Inc.
Walker Foundation, Archie D. and Bertha H.
Walker Foundation, L. C. and Margaret
Walker Foundation, T. B.
Wallace Computer Services
Wallach Foundation, Miriam G. and Ira D.
Walter Family Trust, Byron L.
Walter Industries
Walthall Perpetual Charitable Trust, Marjorie T.
Ward Co., Joe L.
Ward Foundation, Louis L. and Adelaide C.
Wardle Family Foundation
Wareheim Foundation, E. C.

Warner Electric Brake & Clutch Co.
Warner Fund, Albert and Bessie
Warren and Beatrice W. Blanding Foundation, Riley J. and Lillian N.
Warren Foundation, William K.
Warwick Foundation
Washington Forrest Foundation
Washington Foundation
Washington Post Co.
Washington Square Fund
Washington Trust Bank
Washington Water Power Co.
Wasmer Foundation
Waters Foundation
Watson Foundation, Walter E. and Caroline H.
Wausau Paper Mills Co.
Wauwatosa Savings & Loan Association
Weaver Foundation
Weaver Foundation, Gil and Dody
Webb Charitable Trust, Susan Mott
Webb Foundation
Weber Charities Corp., Frederick E.
Webster Charitable Foundation
Weezie Foundation
Wege Foundation
Wegener Foundation, Herman and Mary
Wehadkee Foundation
Weil, Gotshal & Manges Foundation
Weiler Foundation, Theodore & Renee
Weinberg Foundation, John L.
Weiner Foundation
Weingart Foundation
Weininger Foundation, Richard and Gertrude
Weinstein Foundation, J.
Weir Foundation Trust
Weir Foundation Trust
Weisbrod Foundation Trust Dept., Robert and Mary
Weiss Foundation, Stephen and Suzanne
Weiss Fund, Clara
Welch Testamentary Trust, George T.
Wellman Foundation, S. K.
Wells Fargo & Co.
Wells Foundation, A. Z.
Wells Foundation, Franklin H. and Ruth L.
Wells Trust Fund, Fred W.
Wendt Foundation, Margaret L.
Werblow Charitable Trust, Nina W.
Werner Foundation, Clara and Spencer
Werthan Foundation
West Co.
West Foundation
West One Bancorp
Westend Foundation
Westerman Foundation, Samuel L.
Western New York Foundation
Western Resources
Westinghouse Electric Corp.
Westport Fund
Westvaco Corp.
Wexner Foundation
Weyerhaeuser Co.
Weyerhaeuser Foundation, Frederick and Margaret L.
Weyerhaeuser Memorial Foundation, Charles A.
Whalley Charitable Trust
Wharton Foundation
Wheat First Securites
Wheeler Foundation, Wilmot
Wheless Foundation

Whirlpool Corp.
Whitaker Charitable Foundation, Lyndon C.
Whitaker Foundation
White Coffee Pot Family Inns
White Foundation, Erle and Emma
White Foundation, W. P. and H. B.
Whitehead Foundation
Whiteley Foundation, John and Elizabeth
Whiteman Foundation, Edna Rider
Whiting Foundation
Whiting Memorial Foundation, Henry and Harriet
Whitney Benefits
Whitney Fund, David M.
Whittenberger Foundation, Claude R. and Ethel B.
Wickes Foundation, Harvey Randall
Wickson-Link Memorial Foundation
Widgeon Foundation
Wieboldt Foundation
Wiegand Foundation, E. L.
Wien Foundation, Lawrence A.
Wilbur Foundation, Marguerite Eyer
Wilcox General Trust, George N.
Wilcox Trust, S. W.
Wilder Foundation
Wildermuth Foundation, E. F.
Wiley & Sons, Inc., John
Wilkof Foundation, Edward and Ruth
Willard Foundation, Helen Parker
Willard Helping Fund, Cecilia Young
Williams Charitable Trust, John C.
Williams Charitable Trust, Mary Jo
Williams Cos.
Williams Family Foundation of Georgia
Williams Foundation, Arthur Ashley
Willits Foundation
Wilmington Trust Co.
Wilsey Bennet Co.
Wilson Fund, Matilda R.
Wilson Public Trust, Ralph
Wilson Trust, Lula C.
Wimpey Inc., George
Winchester Foundation
Winkler Foundation, Mark and Catherine
Winnebago Industries, Inc.
Winona Corporation
Wisconsin Energy Corp.
Wisconsin Power & Light Co.
Witco Corp.
Witter Foundation, Dean
Wolens Foundation, Kalman and Ida
Wolff Foundation, John M.
Wolff Memorial Foundation, Pauline Sterne
Wolff Shoe Co.
Wolfson Family Foundation
Wollenberg Foundation
Woltman Foundation, B. M.
Wolverine World Wide, Inc.
Wood Charitable Trust, W. P.
Wood-Claeyssens Foundation
Wood Foundation, Lester G.
Wood Foundation of Chambersburg, PA
Woodard Family Foundation
Woodland Foundation
Woods Charitable Fund
Woods Foundation, James H.
Woods-Greer Foundation
Woodward Fund

Woodward Fund-Atlanta, David, Helen, Marian
Woodward Fund-Watertown, David, Helen, and Marian
Word Investments
Wornall Charitable Trust and Foundation, Kearney
Wouk Foundation, Abe
Wright Foundation, Lola
Wrigley Co., Wm. Jr.
Wurts Memorial, Henrietta Tower
Wurzburg, Inc.
Wyman-Gordon Co.
Wyman Youth Trust
Wyomissing Foundation
Xerox Corp.
XTEK Inc.
Yassenoff Foundation, Leo
Yawkey Foundation II
York Barbell Co.
Yost Trust, Elizabeth Burns
Young Foundation, Hugo H. and Mabel B.
Young Foundation, R. A.
Yulman Trust, Morton and Helen
Zaban Foundation
Zacharia Foundation, Isaac Herman
Zale Foundation
Zale Foundation, William and Sylvia
Zamoiski Co.
Zarkin Memorial Foundation, Charles
Zarrow Foundation, Anne and Henry
Zenkel Foundation
Ziegler Foundation
Ziegler Foundation, Ruth/Allen
Ziemann Foundation
Zimmerman Family Foundation, Raymond
Zock Endowment Trust

Counseling

Abell-Hanger Foundation
Ahmanson Foundation
Air Products & Chemicals
Alexander Foundation, Walter
Allegheny Foundation
Allegheny Ludlum Corp.
Alliant Techsystems
Alliant Techsystems
AlliedSignal
Allstate Insurance Co.
Alltel/Western Region
ALPAC Corp.
Altman Foundation
Aluminum Co. of America
AMCORE Bank, N.A. Rockford
American Express Co.
American United Life Insurance Co.
Amfac/JMB Hawaii
Ansley Foundation, Dantzler Bond
AON Corp.
Apache Corp.
Apple Computer, Inc.
Appleton Papers
Archibald Charitable Foundation, Norman
Arkell Hall Foundation
Arkla
Asea Brown Boveri
Atherton Family Foundation
Atkinson Foundation
Attleboro Pawtucket Savings Bank
Badgeley Residuary Charitable Trust, Rose M.
Baird Charitable Trust, William Robert
Bank of America - Giannini Foundation
Bechtel Charitable Remainder Uni-Trust, Harold R.

Bedsole Foundation, J. L.
Beinecke Foundation
Belding Heminway Co.
Bemis Company
Bethlehem Steel Corp.
Bingham Second Betterment Fund, William
Bishop Foundation
Blair and Co., William
Blanchard Foundation
Block, H&R
Bodman Foundation
Boehringer Mannheim Corp.
Booz Allen & Hamilton
Borden Memorial Foundation, Mary Owen
Borun Foundation, Anna Borun and Harry
Boston Edison Co.
Bremer Foundation, Otto
Brencanda Foundation
Briggs Family Foundation
Briggs & Stratton Corp.
Brochsteins Inc.
Brown Foundation
Buchalter, Nemer, Fields, & Younger
Burlington Northern Inc.
Burndy Corp.
Burns Foundation, Fritz B.
Bush Charitable Foundation, Edyth
Bush Foundation
Butler Family Foundation, Patrick and Aimee
Cabot Corp.
Cafritz Foundation, Morris and Gwendolyn
Calder Foundation, Louis
Cameron Foundation, Harry S. and Isabel C.
Carolyn Foundation
Carter-Wallace
Central Life Assurance Co.
Central Maine Power Co.
Challenge Foundation
Charlesbank Homes
Chase Manhattan Bank, N.A.
Chastain Charitable Foundation, Robert Lee and Thomas M.
Cheney Foundation, Ben B.
Chicago Sun-Times, Inc.
Churches Homes Foundation
Clay Foundation
Clipper Ship Foundation
Clorox Co.
CNA Insurance Cos.
Collins Foundation
Collins Foundation, Carr P.
Collins, Jr. Foundation, George Fulton
Colonial Life & Accident Insurance Co.
Commerce Bancshares, Inc.
Comstock Foundation
Consolidated Natural Gas Co.
Constantin Foundation
Contran Corp.
Cook Family Trust
Copperweld Steel Co.
Corbin Foundation, Mary S. and David C.
Country Curtains, Inc.
Cowan Foundation Corporation, Lillian L. and Harry A.
Cowles Charitable Trust
Crystal Trust
Cullen/Frost Bankers
Cummings Foundation, Nathan
Cummings Memorial Fund Trust, Frances L. and Edwin L.
Cummins Engine Co.
DeCamp Foundation, Ira W.
Delavan Foundation, Nelson B.
Dell Foundation, Hazel
Deluxe Corp.
Deutsch Co.

Dewing Foundation, Frances R.
Diamond Walnut Growers
Dimeo Construction Co.
Dodge Foundation, P. L.
Donaldson Co.
Dreyfus Foundation, Max and Victoria
du Pont de Nemours & Co., E. I.
Duke Power Co.
Dunspaugh-Dalton Foundation
duPont Foundation, Chichester
Eaton Corp.
Ebell of Los Angeles Rest Cottage Association
Eccles Foundation, George S. and Dolores Dore
Eccles Foundation, Marriner S.
Ecolab
Eden Hall Foundation
Educational Foundation of America
Egenton Home
Electronic Data Systems Corp.
Emergency Aid of Pennsylvania Foundation
English-Bonter-Mitchell Foundation
Ensworth Charitable Foundation
Falk Foundation, David
Falk Medical Fund, Maurice
Fay Charitable Fund, Aubert J.
Federal Home Loan Mortgage Corp. (Freddie Mac)
Federated Life Insurance Co.
Fireman's Fund Insurance Co.
First Fidelity Bancorporation
First Interstate Bancsystem of Montana
First Interstate Bank of Arizona
First Union Corp.
Fish Foundation, Ray C.
Fisher Foundation
Forest Foundation
Foster Co., L.B.
Foundation for Middle East Peace
Franklin Charitable Trust, Ershel
Freas Foundation
Freed Foundation
Freedom Forum
Freeport-McMoRan
Frueauff Foundation, Charles A.
Frumkes Foundation, Alana and Lewis
Fry Foundation, Lloyd A.
Fuller Foundation, George F. and Sybil H.
Funderburke & Associates
Funderburke & Associates
Gallo Foundation, Julio R.
Gannett Co.
GATX Corp.
Gebbie Foundation
GEICO Corp.
General American Life Insurance Co.
General Mills
GenRad
George Foundation
German Protestant Orphan Asylum Association
Gheens Foundation
Giant Eagle
Gill Foundation, Pauline Allen
Glaser Foundation
Globe Newspaper Co.
Goldman Foundation, Herman
Goldman Foundation, William
Goldseker Foundation of Maryland, Morris
Goodwin Foundation, Leo
Grassmann Trust, E. J.
Graybar Electric Co.
Greentree Foundation
Griffith Foundation, W. C.
GTE Corp.

Guggenheim Foundation, Daniel and Florence
Haas Foundation, Paul and Mary
Haas Fund, Walter and Elise
Haigh-Scatena Foundation
Halff Foundation, G. A. C.
Hall Foundation
Hallmark Cards
Hamel Family Charitable Trust, D. A.
Hancock Foundation, Luke B.
Harrison Foundation, Fred G.
Hawn Foundation
Hearst Foundation
Hearst Foundation, William Randolph
Hechinger Co.
HEI Inc.
Heinz Co., H.J.
Helfaer Foundation, Evan and Marion
Hemingway Foundation, Robert G.
Henry Foundation, Patrick
Heritage Foundation
Herschend Family Foundation
Hervey Foundation
Heydt Fund, Nan and Matilda
Hill-Snowdon Foundation
Hillman Foundation
Hillsdale Fund
Hoblitzelle Foundation
Hoche-Scofield Foundation
Hoffer Plastics Corp.
Hoffman Foundation, Marion O. and Maximilian
Holley Foundation
Home Depot
Homeland Foundation
Honeywell
Hopkins Foundation, Josephine Lawrence
Houck Foundation, May K.
Household International
Humane Society of the Commonwealth of Massachusetts
Hunt Alternatives Fund
Hunt Charitable Trust, C. Giles
Hunt Manufacturing Co.
Huston Foundation
Hutchins Foundation, Mary J.
Hyams Foundation
I and G Charitable Foundation
Icahn Foundation, Carl C.
Illges Memorial Foundation, A. and M. L.
Inland Steel Industries
Innovating Worthy Projects Foundation
Insurance Management Associates
Island Foundation
ITT Rayonier
Ittleson Foundation
Ix & Sons, Frank
J.P. Morgan & Co.
Jackson Foundation
Jacobson Foundation, Bernard H. and Blanche E.
Jasper Seating Co.
Jennings Foundation, Mary Hillman
John Hancock Mutual Life Insurance Co.
Johnson Controls
Johnson Foundation, Walter S.
Jones Foundation, Harvey and Bernice
Jones Intercable, Inc.
JSJ Corp.
Julia R. and Estelle L. Foundation
Kaplan Foundation, Rita J. and Stanley H.
Kaufmann Foundation, Henry
Keating Family Foundation
Keene Trust, Hazel R.

Kejr Foundation
Keller-Crescent Co.
Kenan Family Foundation
Kenedy Memorial Foundation, John G. and Marie Stella
Kennecott Corp.
Kennedy, Jr. Foundation, Joseph P.
Kerr Fund, Grayce B.
Kieckhefer Foundation, J. W.
Kilworth Charitable Trust, William
Kimball International
Kimberly-Clark Corp.
King Foundation, Carl B. and Florence E.
King Ranch
Kirbo Charitable Trust, Thomas M. and Irene B.
L. L. W. W. Foundation
L and L Foundation
Laclede Gas Co.
Ladd Charitable Corporation, Helen and George
Laffey-McHugh Foundation
Lapham-Hickey Steel Corp.
Lassen Foundation, Irving A.
Laurel Foundation
Lavanburg-Corner House
Levinson Foundation, Max and Anna
Levy Foundation, Betty and Norman F.
Liberty National Bank
Lindstrom Foundation, Kinney
Little, Arthur D.
Livingston Foundation
Lizzadro Family Foundation, Joseph
Loats Foundation
Lockhart Iron & Steel Co.
Long Foundation, George A. and Grace
Louisiana Land & Exploration Co.
LTV Corp.
Luse Foundation, W. P. and Bulah
Lydall, Inc.
Maclellan Charitable Trust, R. J.
Macy & Co., R.H.
Maddox Foundation, J. F.
Magruder Foundation, Chesley G.
Mallinckrodt Specialty Chemicals Co.
Mandel Foundation, Joseph and Florence
Mardag Foundation
Margoes Foundation
Massengill-DeFriece Foundation
Mastronardi Charitable Foundation, Charles A.
Maxus Energy Corp.
May Department Stores Co.
Mayerson Foundation, Manuel D. and Rhoda
MBIA, Inc.
MCA
McAlister Charitable Foundation, Harold
McAlonan Trust, John A.
McBride & Son Associates
McCune Foundation
McDonald & Co. Securities
McDonald & Co. Securities
McDonnell Douglas Corp.-West
McEachern Charitable Trust, D. V. & Ida J.
McIntyre Foundation, B. D. and Jane E.
McKee Foundation, Robert E. and Evelyn
McKnight Foundation
Meadows Foundation
Medina Foundation
Merchants Bancshares
Mercy, Jr. Foundation, Sue and Eugene

Counseling (cont.)

Metropolitan Life Insurance Co.
Meyer Foundation, Alice
  Kleberg Reynolds
Meyer Foundation, Eugene and
  Agnes E.
Mid-Iowa Health Foundation
Midwest Resources
Milken Family Medical
  Foundation
Miller Foundation
Mnuchin Foundation
Mobil Oil Corp.
Montgomery Street Foundation
Moskowitz Foundation, Irving I.
Motorola
MTS Systems Corp.
Musson Charitable Foundation,
  R. C. and Katharine M.
Nalco Chemical Co.
National Pro-Am Youth Fund
Nationwide Insurance Cos.
New England Mutual Life
  Insurance Co.
New Horizon Foundation
New York Foundation
New York Life Insurance Co.
New York Mercantile Exchange
New York Telephone Co.
News & Observer Publishing Co.
Noble Foundation, Edward John
Nordson Corp.
Northeast Utilities
Northern Indiana Public Service
  Co.
Northern States Power Co.
Northwest Natural Gas Co.
Norton Co.
Norwest Bank Nebraska
Ohrstrom Foundation
Olympia Brewing Co.
Ontario Corp.
Oppenheimer and Flora
  Oppenheimer Haas Trust, Leo
Oppenstein Brothers Foundation
Orange Orphan Society
Ordean Foundation
Osher Foundation, Bernard
Overbrook Foundation
Overlake Foundation
Owen Trust, B. B.
Pacific Mutual Life Insurance Co.
Packard Foundation, David and
  Lucile
Page Foundation, George B.
Palmer-Fry Memorial Trust, Lily
Pendergast-Weyer Foundation
Penn Foundation, William
Penney Foundation, James C.
People's Bank
Perini Foundation, Joseph
Perkin-Elmer Corp.
Perkin-Elmer Corp.
Perkins-Prothro Foundation
Perley Fund, Victor E.
Pfizer
Phillips Family Foundation, Jay
  and Rose
Phillips Foundation, Dr. P.
Piankova Foundation, Tatiana
Pillsbury Foundation
Pitzman Fund
Plankenhorn Foundation, Harry
Price Foundation, Louis and
  Harold
Pritzker Foundation
Prudential Insurance Co. of
  America
Public Service Electric & Gas
  Co.
Quaker Hill Foundation
Quaker Oats Co.
Ramlose Foundation, George A.
Raskob Foundation for Catholic
  Activities
Ratshesky Foundation, A. C.

Reynolds Foundation, Donald W.
Rienzi Foundation
Riley Foundation, Mabel Louise
Roche Relief Foundation,
  Edward and Ellen
Rockwell Fund
Rockwell International Corp.
Rohr Inc.
Roseburg Forest Products Co.
Rosenberg Foundation, William
  J. and Tina
Rosenstiel Foundation
Royal Group Inc.
Rubinstein Foundation, Helena
San Diego Gas & Electric
Santa Fe Pacific Corp.
Sara Lee Corp.
Sara Lee Hosiery
Scaife Family Foundation
Scheuer Family Foundation, S.
  H. and Helen R.
Schmidlapp Trust No. 1, Jacob G.
Schoenleber Foundation
Sealright Co., Inc.
Seidman Family Foundation
Sequa Corp.
Seybert Institution for Poor Boys
  and Girls, Adam and Maria
  Sarah
Share Foundation
Sharp Foundation, Charles S.
  and Ruth C.
Shaw Foundation, Gardiner
  Howland
Shawmut National Corp.
Shenandoah Life Insurance Co.
Shoney's Inc.
Simon Foundation, Robert Ellis
SIT Investment Associates, Inc.
Skillman Foundation
Skinner Corp.
Smith Charities, John
Smith Foundation, Lon V.
Soling Family Foundation
Southern California Edison Co.
Sprague Educational and
  Charitable Foundation, Seth
Starr Foundation
State Street Bank & Trust Co.
Statter Foundation, Amy Plant
Staunton Farm Foundation
Stearns Charitable Foundation,
  Anna B.
Stearns Trust, Artemas W.
Steelcase
Stern Memorial Trust, Sidney
Stride Rite Corp.
Stubblefield, Estate of Joseph L.
Stulsaft Foundation, Morris
Sullivan Foundation, Ray H. and
  Pauline
Summerfield Foundation, Solon
  E.
Synovus Financial Corp.
Taconic Foundation
Taper Foundation, Mark
Teleklew Productions
Texas Gas Transmission Corp.
Texas Instruments
Textron
Thermo Electron Corp.
3M Co.
Thurston Charitable Foundation
Times Mirror Co.
TJX Cos.
Tozer Foundation
Trull Foundation
Trust Co. Bank
Turrell Fund
Union Bank of Switzerland Los
  Angeles Branch
Union Camp Corp.
Upton Foundation, Frederick S.
Uris Brothers Foundation
US Bancorp
van Ameringen Foundation

van Loben Sels - Eleanor Slate
  van Lobel Sels Charitable
  Foundation, Ernst D.
Varian Associates
Vidinha Charitable Trust, A. and
  E.
Vingo Trust II
Virginia Power Co.
Vulcan Materials Co.
Wal-Mart Stores
Walker Foundation, Archie D.
  and Bertha H.
Walthall Perpetual Charitable
  Trust, Marjorie T.
Wareheim Foundation, E. C.
Washington Foundation
Webb Educational and
  Charitable Trust, Torrey H.
  and Dorothy K.
Webster Foundation, Edwin S.
Weezie Foundation
Weinberg Foundation, John L.
Weingart Foundation
Welfare Foundation
Wendt Foundation, Margaret L.
West Co.
Westvaco Corp.
Weyerhaeuser Co.
Whirlpool Corp.
Wilson Public Trust, Ralph
Wolff Foundation, John M.
Woods Charitable Fund
Woodward Governor Co.
Wornall Charitable Trust and
  Foundation, Kearney
Wyman Youth Trust

Day Care

Ace Beverage Co.
Acushnet Co.
Allendale Mutual Insurance Co.
Alltel/Western Region
ALPAC Corp.
Alumax
AMCORE Bank, N.A. Rockford
American Brands
American Express Co.
American Schlafhorst
  Foundation, Inc.
American United Life Insurance
  Co.
Apache Corp.
Archbold Charitable Trust,
  Adrian and Jessie
Attleboro Pawtucket Savings
  Bank
Autzen Foundation
Azadoutioun Foundation
Babcock Foundation, Mary
  Reynolds
Bacardi Imports
Badger Meter, Inc.
Baird Foundation, Cameron
Baker Foundation, R. C.
Baker, Jr. Memorial Fund,
  William G.
Balfour Foundation, L. G.
Bancorp Hawaii
Bank One, Youngstown, NA
Barden Corp.
Barth Foundation, Theodore H.
Baughman Foundation
Beckman Foundation, Leland D.
Bethlehem Steel Corp.
Blair and Co., William
Block, H&R
Blue Cross & Blue Shield of
  Alabama
Borden Memorial Foundation,
  Mary Owen
Borman's
Bothin Foundation
Bovaird Foundation, Mervin
Bray Charitable Trust, Viola E.
Bucyrus-Erie
Burchfield Foundation, Charles
  E.

Burndy Corp.
Burns Foundation, Fritz B.
C.P. Rail Systems
Carter Foundation, Amon G.
Cassett Foundation, Louis N.
Catlin Charitable Trust, Kathleen
  K.
Central Life Assurance Co.
Central Maine Power Co.
Chase Manhattan Bank, N.A.
Chemical Bank
Chevron Corp.
Chicago Sun-Times, Inc.
Children's Foundation of Erie
  County
Ciba-Geigy Corp.
  (Pharmaceuticals Division)
Citicorp
Clipper Ship Foundation
CM Alliance Cos.
Cole Foundation, Olive B.
Colonial Life & Accident
  Insurance Co.
Coltec Industries
Comer Foundation
Conn Memorial Foundation
Constantin Foundation
Corpus Christi Exploration Co.
Cowell Foundation, S. H.
Cowles Media Co.
Cox Charitable Trust, A. G.
Crestlea Foundation
Crum and Forster
CUNA Mutual Insurance Group
Cyprus Minerals Co.
Daniel Foundation, Gerard and
  Ruth
Davis Foundation, James A. and
  Juliet L.
de Hirsch Fund, Baron
DeKalb Genetics Corp.
DeRoy Testamentary Foundation
Dewing Foundation, Frances R.
Dial Corp.
Diamond Foundation, Aaron
Dodge Jones Foundation
Donaldson Co.
Dreyfus Foundation, Max and
  Victoria
du Pont de Nemours & Co., E. I.
duPont Foundation, Chichester
Eastern Star Hall and Home
  Foundation
Eccles Foundation, Marriner S.
Eden Hall Foundation
Edwards Foundation, O. P. and
  W. E.
El Pomar Foundation
Emergency Aid of Pennsylvania
  Foundation
Equifax
Fairfield Foundation, Freeman E.
Fanwood Foundation
Fireman's Fund Insurance Co.
First Fidelity Bancorporation
First Hawaiian
First National Bank & Trust Co.
  of Rockford
First Union Corp.
Fishback Foundation Trust,
  Harmes C.
Florence Foundation
Florida Steel Corp.
Florida Steel Corp.
Foothills Foundation
Forbes Charitable Trust, Herman
Foundation for Child
  Development
Foundation for Seacoast Health
Frazier Foundation
Freedom Forum
French Foundation
Fuchs Foundation, Gottfried &
  Mary
Funderburke & Associates
Funderburke & Associates

Garner Charitable Trust, James
  G.
Gelman Foundation, Melvin and
  Estelle
General Railway Signal Corp.
Gershman Foundation, Joel
Giles Foundation, Edward C.
Glaxo
Glickenhaus & Co.
Gluck Foundation, Maxwell H.
Goddard Foundation, Charles B.
Goldwyn Foundation, Samuel
Good Samaritan
Goodwin Foundation, Leo
Grader Foundation, K. W.
Grassmann Trust, E. J.
Grinnell Mutual Reinsurance Co.
GTE Corp.
Harper Foundation, Philip S.
Harriman Foundation, Mary W.
Harrington Foundation, Don and
  Sybil
Hawley Foundation
Hechinger Co.
Herndon Foundation, Alonzo F.
  Herndon and Norris B.
Hershey Foundation
Hiawatha Education Foundation
Hillcrest Foundation
Hodge Foundation
Home Depot
Howell Foundation, Eric and
  Jessie
Huffy Corp.
Humphrey Foundation, Glenn &
  Gertrude
Hyams Foundation
IBP, Inc.
ICI Americas
IDS Financial Services
IMCERA Group Inc.
International Paper Co.
Irwin-Sweeney-Miller
  Foundation
ITT Rayonier
Jackson Foundation
JCPenney Co.
Jergens Foundation, Andrew
Jones Foundation, Daisy Marquis
Jones Foundation, Harvey and
  Bernice
Keller-Crescent Co.
Kemper Educational and
  Charitable Fund
Kendall Foundation, George R.
Kennedy, Jr. Foundation, Joseph
  P.
Kirbo Charitable Trust, Thomas
  M. and Irene B.
Knox Foundation, Seymour H.
Knudsen Charitable Foundation,
  Earl
Kugelman Foundation
Kuyper Foundation, Peter H. and
  E. Lucille Gaass
Laffey-McHugh Foundation
Lattner Foundation, Forrest C.
Lautenberg Foundation
Lavanburg-Corner House
Lehman Foundation, Edith and
  Herbert
Lewis Foundation, Lillian Kaiser
Lincoln National Corp.
Longwood Foundation
Lost Tree Charitable Foundation
Lukens
Lurie Family Foundation
M. E. G. Foundation
Maddox Foundation, J. F.
Magruder Foundation, Chesley
  G.
Mailman Family Foundation, A.
  L.
Mankato Citizens Telephone Co.
Mardag Foundation
Marmot Foundation
Marshall & Ilsley Bank

Mayer Foundation, James and
 Eva
MBIA, Inc.
McBeath Foundation, Faye
McCormick Tribune Foundation,
 Robert R.
McCune Foundation
McDonough Foundation, Bernard
McGraw Foundation, Curtis W.
McMillen Foundation
McMurray-Bennnett Foundation
Medina Foundation
Merck & Co.
Mericos Foundation
Merrick Foundation
Merrick Foundation, Robert G.
 and Anne M.
Mervyn's
Meyer Memorial Trust
Midwest Resources
Morrison-Knudsen Corp.
Moss Charitable Trust, Finis M.
Moss Foundation, Harry S.
Mutual of New York
National Computer Systems
National Life of Vermont
New England Mutual Life
 Insurance Co.
New York Life Insurance Co.
Norfolk Southern Corp.
Norris Foundation, Dellora A.
 and Lester J.
Northern States Power Co.
Northwest Natural Gas Co.
Noyes, Jr. Memorial Foundation,
 Nicholas H.
O'Connor Foundation, A.
 Lindsay and Olive B.
Odell and Helen Pfeiffer Odell
 Fund, Robert Stewart
Olive Bridge Fund
O'Neill Charitable Corporation,
 F. J.
Ontario Corp.
Ontario Corp.
Orange Orphan Society
Ore-Ida Foods, Inc.
Oxford Foundation
Pacific Telesis Group
Packard Foundation, David and
 Lucile
Parsons Foundation, Ralph M.
Penn Foundation, William
People's Bank
Pepsi-Cola Bottling Co. of
 Charlotte
Perkin-Elmer Corp.
Perkin-Elmer Corp.
Pick, Jr. Fund, Albert
Pitney Bowes
PPG Industries
Primerica Corp.
Principal Financial Group
Public Service Co. of New
 Mexico
Quaker Hill Foundation
Quaker Oats Co.
Questar Corp.
Raskob Foundation for Catholic
 Activities
Read Foundation, Charles L.
Recognition Equipment
Reily & Co., William B.
Reliable Life Insurance Co.
Reynolds Foundation, Z. Smith
Richardson Foundation, Sid W.
Riley Foundation, Mabel Louise
Robinson Fund, Charles Nelson
Rogers Family Foundation
Roseburg Forest Products Co.
SAFECO Corp.
St. Faith's House Foundation
San Diego Gas & Electric
Sara Lee Co.
Sara Lee Hosiery
Schmidlapp Trust No. 1, Jacob G.
Schmidlapp Trust No. 2, Jacob G.

Schmitt Foundation, Arthur J.
Scholler Foundation
Schramm Foundation
Schumann Fund for New Jersey
Scurlock Foundation
Sentinel Communications Co.
Seymour Foundation, W. L. and
 Louise E.
Shawmut National Corp.
Shoney's Inc.
Siebert Lutheran Foundation
Signet Bank/Maryland
Skinner Corp.
Snow Memorial Trust, John Ben
Soling Family Foundation
Stern Memorial Trust, Sidney
Stulsaft Foundation, Morris
Teleklew Productions
Temple Foundation, T. L. L.
Templeton Foundation, Herbert
 A.
Texas Gas Transmission Corp.
Thornton Foundation
3M Co.
Thurman Charitable Foundation
 for Children, Edgar A.
Tracor, Inc.
Treuhaft Foundation
Trull Foundation
Turrell Fund
Unilever United States
Union Camp Corp.
Universal Foods Corp.
Uris Brothers Foundation
Van Wert County Foundation
Victoria Foundation
Wachovia Bank & Trust Co.,
 N.A.
Ware Foundation
Welch Testamentary Trust,
 George T.
Welfare Foundation
Whittenberger Foundation,
 Claude R. and Ethel B.
Zale Foundation
Zarrow Foundation, Anne and
 Henry

Delinquency & Crime

Abbott Laboratories
Ahmanson Foundation
Air Products & Chemicals
Alabama Power Co.
AlliedSignal
Alltel/Western Region
Alumax
Aluminum Co. of America
AMCORE Bank, N.A. Rockford
American Express Co.
American United Life Insurance
 Co.
Amfac/JMB Hawaii
Anheuser-Busch Cos.
Anschutz Family Foundation
Apache Corp.
Atherton Family Foundation
Atlanta Gas Light Co.
Avon Products
Baird & Co., Robert W.
Baker Foundation, R. C.
Ball Corp.
Banc One Wisconsin Corp.
Berwind Corp.
Bethlehem Steel Corp.
Bionetics Corp.
Blair and Co., William
Block, H&R
Boatmen's Bancshares
Boehringer Mannheim Corp.
Boeing Co.
Borman's
Brown Foundation
Brunswick Corp.
Burden Foundation, Florence V.
Burlington Industries

Burndy Corp.
Bush Foundation
Cameron Foundation, Harry S.
 and Isabel C.
Carter Foundation, Amon G.
Casey Foundation, Annie E.
Centerior Energy Corp.
Central Maine Power Co.
Chase Manhattan Bank, N.A.
Chevron Corp.
Clark Foundation
Clark Foundation, Edna
 McConnell
Cleveland-Cliffs
Clorox Co.
CM Alliance Cos.
CNA Insurance Cos.
Cohen Foundation, Naomi and
 Nehemiah
Colonial Life & Accident
 Insurance Co.
Commerce Clearing House
Comstock Foundation
Conn Memorial Foundation
Continental Corp.
Copperweld Steel Co.
Corbin Foundation, Mary S. and
 David C.
Cowles Charitable Trust
Cowles Media Co.
Crown Central Petroleum Corp.
CT Corp. System
Cullen/Frost Bankers
Curtice-Burns Foods
Dana Corp.
Deposit Guaranty National Bank
Detroit Edison Co.
DeVos Foundation, Richard and
 Helen
Dexter Corp.
Diamond Walnut Growers
Donaldson Co.
Doss Foundation, M. S.
Dreyfus Foundation, Max and
 Victoria
du Pont de Nemours & Co., E. I.
Eaton Corp.
Enron Corp.
Equifax
Exxon Corp.
Federal Express Corp.
Federal-Mogul Corp.
Fidelity Bank
Fieldcrest Cannon
First Interstate Bank of Arizona
First Interstate Bank of California
First Union Corp.
Firstar Bank Milwaukee NA
Florida Power Corp.
Ford Foundation
Ford Motor Co.
Forest City Enterprises
Foundation for Child
 Development
Foxmeyer Corp.
Freedom Forum
Freeport-McMoRan
Fry Foundation, Lloyd A.
Funderburke & Associates
Funderburke & Associates
GATX Corp.
General Accident Insurance Co.
 of America
General Mills
GenRad
Georgia Power Co.
Goldman Fund, Richard and
 Rhoda
Grace & Co., W.R.
Grassmann Trust, E. J.
Graybar Electric Co.
Hallmark Cards
Harden Foundation
Harriman Foundation, Mary W.
Hechinger Co.
Heinz Co., H.J.
Hillcrest Foundation

Honeywell
Hospital Corp. of America
Household International
Houston Industries
Hoyt Foundation, Stewart W. and
 Willma C.
Hudson-Webber Foundation
Hulings Foundation, Mary
 Andersen
Hunt Alternatives Fund
Hunter Trust, A. V.
Hyams Foundation
IBM Corp.
IMCERA Group Inc.
Interco
Island Foundation
ITT Corp.
ITT Hartford Insurance Group
ITT Rayonier
Ittleson Foundation
James River Corp. of Virginia
Jennings Foundation, Mary
 Hillman
JMK-A M Micallef Charitable
 Foundation
John Hancock Mutual Life
 Insurance Co.
Johnson & Son, S.C.
Jones Foundation, Daisy Marquis
Kellogg Foundation, W. K.
Kennecott Corp.
Kerr Foundation, Robert S. and
 Grayce B.
Kimberly-Clark Corp.
King Ranch
Kysor Industrial Corp.
Lincoln National Corp.
Louisiana Land & Exploration
 Co.
LTV Corp.
Maclellan Foundation
Macy & Co., R.H.
Mardag Foundation
Maritz Inc.
Martin Marietta Corp.
May Foundation, Wilbur
MCA
McBeath Foundation, Faye
McBride & Son Associates
McCormick Tribune Foundation,
 Robert R.
McCune Foundation
McDonald & Co. Securities
McKesson Corp.
McKnight Foundation
McMillen Foundation
Meadows Foundation
Medina Foundation
Metropolitan Life Insurance Co.
Meyer Foundation, Eugene and
 Agnes E.
Meyer Memorial Trust
Midwest Resources
Mobil Oil Corp.
Nalco Chemical Co.
National City Corp.
National Computer Systems
National Fuel Gas Co.
National Westminster Bank New
 Jersey
New England Mutual Life
 Insurance Co.
New York Foundation
New York Times Co.
Newman's Own
News & Observer Publishing Co.
Nordson Corp.
Northeast Utilities
Northern Indiana Public Service
 Co.
Northern States Power Co.
Northwest Natural Gas Co.
Norton Co.
Occidental Oil & Gas Corp.
O'Connor Co.
Pacific Mutual Life Insurance Co.
Palmer Fund, Francis Asbury

Parsons Foundation, Ralph M.
Pennzoil Co.
Perkin-Elmer Corp.
Perkin-Elmer Corp.
Pfizer
Pillsbury Co.
Pittsburgh National Bank
Playboy Enterprises, Inc.
Portland General Electric Co.
Prudential Insurance Co. of
 America
Public Service Electric & Gas
 Co.
Public Welfare Foundation
Ralston Purina Co.
Reynolds Foundation, Z. Smith
Rockwell Fund
Rockwell International Corp.
Rohr Inc.
Rudin Foundation
Russell Educational Foundation,
 Benjamin and Roberta
Rutgers Community Health
 Foundation
SAFECO Corp.
Salomon
San Diego Gas & Electric
Shaw Foundation, Gardiner
 Howland
Shawmut National Corp.
Shell Oil Co.
Shoney's Inc.
SIT Investment Associates, Inc.
Skinner Corp.
SNET
Snow Memorial Trust, John Ben
Sprague Educational and
 Charitable Foundation, Seth
SPS Technologies
State Street Bank & Trust Co.
Staunton Farm Foundation
Steelcase
Stein Foundation, Jules and Doris
Stevens Foundation, Abbot and
 Dorothy H.
Stewardship Foundation
Stulsaft Foundation, Morris
Teleklew Productions
Tenneco
Texaco
Texas Commerce Bank Houston,
 N.A.
Texas Gas Transmission Corp.
3M Co.
Transco Energy Company
Trull Foundation
Trust Co. Bank
Union Bank of Switzerland Los
 Angeles Branch
Union Camp Corp.
Union Electric Co.
United States Trust Co. of New
 York
Unitrode Corp.
Universal Foods Corp.
US Bancorp
USF&G Co.
Varian Associates
Virginia Power Co.
Vulcan Materials Co.
W. W. W. Foundation
Wachovia Bank & Trust Co.,
 N.A.
Wareheim Foundation, E. C.
Washington Water Power Co.
Weingart Foundation
Weyerhaeuser Co.
Whirlpool Corp.
Woods Charitable Fund
Wrigley Co., Wm. Jr.

Disabled
Abbott Laboratories
Abell Foundation, Charles S.
Abell-Hanger Foundation
Abraham Foundation, Anthony R.
Abramson Family Foundation

Disabled (cont.)

Adams Foundation, Arthur F. and Alice E.
Adler Foundation
Advanced Micro Devices
Ahmanson Foundation
Aid Association for the Blind
Air Products & Chemicals
Akzo Chemicals Inc.
Alabama Power Co.
Alcon Laboratories, Inc.
Alden Trust, John W.
Alexander Charitable Foundation
Alexander Foundation, Joseph
Alexander Foundation, Judd S.
Allegheny Ludlum Corp.
Allen Foundation, Frances
Allen Foundation, Rita
Allendale Mutual Insurance Co.
Alliant Techsystems
AlliedSignal
Alltel/Western Region
Alltel/Western Region
Alltel/Western Region
Allyn Foundation
ALPAC Corp.
Altman Foundation
Alumax
Aluminum Co. of America
Amaturo Foundation
AMAX
AMCORE Bank, N.A. Rockford
American Brands
American Express Co.
American Foundation Corporation
American Home Products Corp.
American National Bank & Trust Co. of Chicago
American Natural Resources Co.
American Saw & Manufacturing Co.
American Telephone & Telegraph Co.
American United Life Insurance Co.
Amfac/JMB Hawaii
Amoco Corp.
AMP
Andersen Corp.
Andersen Foundation
Anderson Charitable Trust, Josephine
Anderson Foundation, John W.
Anderson Foundation, M. D.
Andrews Foundation
Angelica Corp.
Anheuser-Busch Cos.
Annenberg Foundation
Anschutz Family Foundation
AON Corp.
Apple Computer, Inc.
Applebaum Foundation
Appleby Trust, Scott B. and Annie P.
Appleman Foundation
Appleton Papers
Arcadia Foundation
Archbold Charitable Trust, Adrian and Jessie
Archibald Charitable Foundation, Norman
Aristech Chemical Corp.
Arkell Hall Foundation
Armco Inc.
Armstrong World Industries Inc.
Arrillaga Foundation
ASARCO
Ashland Oil
Asplundh Foundation
Atherton Family Foundation
Atkinson Foundation
Atkinson Foundation, Myrtle L.
Atlanta Gas Light Co.
Atran Foundation

Attleboro Pawtucket Savings Bank
Atwood Foundation
Auerbach Foundation, Beatrice Fox
Austin Memorial Foundation
Autotrol Corp.
Avon Products
Axe-Houghton Foundation
Ayres Foundation, Inc.
Bacardi Imports
Bacon Foundation, E. L. and Oma
Bacon Trust, Charles F.
Badgeley Residuary Charitable Trust, Rose M.
Badger Meter, Inc.
Baird & Co., Robert W.
Baird Foundation
Baker Foundation, R. C.
Baker Foundation, Solomon R. and Rebecca D.
Baldwin Foundation, David M. and Barbara
Ball Corp.
Bamberger and John Ernest Bamberger Memorial Foundation, Ruth Eleanor
Banc One Wisconsin Corp.
Bang & Olufsen of America, Inc.
Bank Foundation, Helen and Merrill
Bank IV
Bankers Trust Co.
Banner Life Insurance Co.
Barclays Bank of New York
Barker Foundation, Donald R.
Barker Welfare Foundation
Barnes Foundation
Barnes Group
Barra Foundation
Barry Corp., R. G.
Bartsch Memorial Trust, Ruth
Bass and Edythe and Sol G. Atlas Fund, Sandra Atlas
Bastien Memorial Foundation, John E. and Nellie J.
Battelle
Baughman Foundation
Bay Branch Foundation
BCR Foundation
Beal Foundation
Beazley Foundation
Beck Foundation
Beckman Foundation, Leland D.
Bedford Fund
Bedsole Foundation, J. L.
Beech Aircraft Corp.
Behmann Brothers Foundation
Beidler Charitable Trust, Francis
Bekins Foundation, Milo W.
Belding Heminway Co.
Belfer Foundation
Bell Atlantic Corp.
Bellini Foundation
Belz Foundation
Bemis Company
Benenson Foundation, Frances and Benjamin
Benetton
Benua Foundation
Berenson Charitable Foundation, Theodore W. and Evelyn
Berkowitz Family Foundation, Louis
Bernstein & Co., Sanford C.
Berry Foundation, Loren M.
Berry Foundation, Lowell
Best Foundation, Walter J. and Edith E.
Bethlehem Steel Corp.
Bettingen Corporation, Burton G.
Beveridge Foundation, Frank Stanley
BFGoodrich
Bicknell Fund
Biddle Foundation, Margaret T.
Biddle Foundation, Mary Duke

Birch Foundation, Stephen and Mary
Bireley Foundation
Bissell Foundation, J. Walton
Blair and Co., William
Blake Foundation, S. P.
Block, H&R
Bloedorn Foundation, Walter A.
Blowitz-Ridgeway Foundation
Blue Cross and Blue Shield of Minnesota Foundation Inc.
Blum Foundation, Nathan and Emily S.
Blum-Kovler Foundation
Boatmen's First National Bank of Oklahoma
Bodman Foundation
Boeing Co.
Boettcher Foundation
Boisi Family Foundation
Booth-Bricker Fund
Boots Pharmaceuticals, Inc.
Booz Allen & Hamilton
Borden
Borden Memorial Foundation, Mary Owen
Borman's
Bosque Foundation
Boston Fatherless and Widows Society
Bostwick Foundation, Albert C.
Boswell Foundation, James G.
Bothin Foundation
Botwinick-Wolfensohn Foundation
Bovaird Foundation, Mervin
Bowater Inc.
Boynton Fund, John W.
Bozzone Family Foundation
Brach Foundation, Helen
Bradley-Turner Foundation
Bremer Foundation, Otto
Bridgestone/Firestone
Bridwell Foundation, J. S.
Briggs Family Foundation
Briggs Foundation, T. W.
Bristol-Myers Squibb Co.
Brooks Brothers
Brooks Foundation, Gladys
Brotman Foundation of California
Brown Foundation, Joe W. and Dorothy Dorsett
Brown Foundation, W. L. Lyons
Broyhill Family Foundation
Bruening Foundation, Eva L. and Joseph M.
Brunetti Charitable Trust, Dionigi
Brunner Foundation, Fred J.
Brunswick Corp.
Bryan Family Foundation, Kathleen Price and Joseph M.
Bucyrus-Erie
Buhl Family Foundation
Bull Foundation, Henry W.
Bunbury Company
Burnand Medical and Educational Foundation, Alphonse A.
Burndy Corp.
Bush Charitable Foundation, Edyth
Bush Foundation
Bustard Charitable Permanent Trust Fund, Elizabeth and James
Butler Family Foundation, Patrick and Aimee
Butler Foundation, J. Homer
Butz Foundation
C.P. Rail Systems
Cabell III and Maude Morgan Cabell Foundation, Robert G.
Cabot Corp.
Cafritz Foundation, Morris and Gwendolyn
Cain Foundation, Effie and Wofford

Cameron Foundation, Harry S. and Isabel C.
Campbell and Adah E. Hall Charity Fund, Bushrod H.
Campbell Foundation, Charles Talbot
Campbell Foundation, J. Bulow
Campbell Foundation, Ruth and Henry
Canon U.S.A., Inc.
Capital Cities/ABC
Capital Fund Foundation
Capital Holding Corp.
Cargill
Carnahan-Jackson Foundation
Carpenter Foundation, E. Rhodes and Leona B.
Carrier Corp.
Carter Foundation, Amon G.
Carter-Wallace
Cassett Foundation, Louis N.
Castle Foundation, Harold K. L.
Castle Foundation, Samuel N. and Mary
CBI Industries
Centel Corp.
Centerior Energy Corp.
Central Bank of the South
Central Maine Power Co.
Central Newspapers, Inc.
Cessna Aircraft Co.
Chambers Memorial, James B.
Chandler Foundation
Chapman Charitable Trust, H. A. and Mary K.
Charina Foundation
Charities Foundation
Chartwell Foundation
Chase Charity Foundation, Alfred E.
Chase Manhattan Bank, N.A.
Chatham Valley Foundation
Chatlos Foundation
Cheney Foundation, Ben B.
Cherne Foundation, Albert W.
Chevron Corp.
Chicago Sun-Times, Inc.
Childs Charitable Foundation, Roberta M.
Christian Dior New York, Inc.
CIT Group Holdings
Citicorp
Clark Foundation
Clark Foundation
Clark-Winchcole Foundation
Clayton Fund
Cleveland-Cliffs
Clipper Ship Foundation
Clorox Co.
Close Foundation
Clowes Fund
CNA Insurance Cos.
Cobb Family Foundation
Codrington Charitable Foundation, George W.
Coen Family Foundation, Charles S. and Mary
Cogswell Benevolent Trust
Cohen Foundation, George M.
Cohen Foundation, Wilfred P.
Cole Foundation, Olive B.
Coleman Co.
Coleman Foundation
Collins & Aikman Holdings Corp.
Collins Foundation
Colonial Life & Accident Insurance Co.
Colorado State Bank of Denver
Colorado Trust
Commerzbank AG, New York
Community Health Association
Comstock Foundation
ConAgra
Conn Memorial Foundation
Connelly Foundation
Consolidated Freightways

Consolidated Natural Gas Co.
Consolidated Papers
Continental Corp.
Cook Charitable Foundation
Cook Foundation, Loring
Cooke Foundation
Cooke Foundation Corporation, V. V.
Cooper Industries
Coors Brewing Co.
Coors Foundation, Adolph
Copley Press
Copperweld Steel Co.
Cord Foundation, E. L.
Cornell Trust, Peter C.
Corvallis Clinic
Country Curtains, Inc.
Cowan Foundation Corporation, Lillian L. and Harry A.
Cowan Foundation Corporation, Lillian L. and Harry A.
Cowell Foundation, S. H.
Cowles Charitable Trust
Cowles Media Co.
Cox Charitable Trust, A. G.
CPC International
CR Industries
Craigmyle Foundation
Crane Foundation, Raymond E. and Ellen F.
Crane Fund for Widows and Children
Cremer Foundation
CRL Inc.
Crown Central Petroleum Corp.
Crown Memorial, Arie and Ida
Crum and Forster
Crystal Trust
Cudahy Fund, Patrick and Anna M.
Cullen/Frost Bankers
Cummings Memorial Fund Trust, Frances L. and Edwin L.
Cuneo Foundation
Cunningham Foundation, Laura Moore
Curtice-Burns Foods
Daily News
Dain Bosworth/Inter-Regional Financial Group
Daly Charitable Foundation Trust, Robert and Nancy
Dammann Fund
Dana Corp.
Davenport-Hatch Foundation
Davidson Family Charitable Foundation
Davis Foundation, Simon and Annie
DeCamp Foundation, Ira W.
Decio Foundation, Arthur J.
Deere & Co.
Delaware North Cos.
Deluxe Corp.
Demoulas Supermarkets
Dennett Foundation, Marie G.
Deposit Guaranty National Bank
Deuble Foundation, George H.
Deutsch Co.
DeVos Foundation, Richard and Helen
Dewing Foundation, Frances R.
Dexter Corp.
Dickenson Foundation, Harriet Ford
Digital Equipment Corp.
Dimick Foundation
Dodge Foundation, Geraldine R.
Dodge Jones Foundation
Doheny Foundation, Carrie Estelle
Doherty Charitable Foundation, Henry L. and Grace
Dolan Family Foundation
Donaldson Co.
Donnelley & Sons Co., R.R.
Dorot Foundation

Dougherty, Jr. Foundation, James R.
Douty Foundation
Downs Perpetual Charitable Trust, Ellason
Doyle Charitable Foundation
Dresser Industries
Dreyfus Foundation, Max and Victoria
Driehaus Foundation, Richard H.
du Pont de Nemours & Co., E. I.
Duchossois Industries
Dues Charitable Foundation, Cesle C. and Mamie
Duke Foundation, Doris
Duke Power Co.
Dumke Foundation, Dr. Ezekiel R. and Edna Wattis
Dun & Bradstreet Corp.
Duncan Foundation, Lillian H. and C. W.
Duncan Trust, James R.
Duncan Trust, John G.
Dunspaugh-Dalton Foundation
Dupar Foundation
duPont Fund, Jessie Ball
Durst Foundation
Dweck Foundation, Samuel R.
Dynamet, Inc.
Dyson Foundation
Earl-Beth Foundation
Eaton Corp.
Eaton Memorial Fund, Georgiana Goddard
Eccles Charitable Foundation, Willard L.
Eccles Foundation, George S. and Dolores Dore
Eccles Foundation, Marriner S.
Eckman Charitable Foundation, Samuel and Rae
Eckman Charitable Foundation, Samuel and Rae
Eden Hall Foundation
Eder Foundation, Sidney and Arthur
Edwards Memorial Trust
Egenton Home
Egenton Home
Eisenberg Foundation, George M.
El Pomar Foundation
Electronic Data Systems Corp.
Elf Aquitaine, Inc.
Elf Atochem North America
Elkins Foundation, J. A. and Isabel M.
Ellwood Foundation
Emergency Aid of Pennsylvania Foundation
Emery Memorial, Thomas J.
EMI Records Group
Engelhard Foundation, Charles
English-Bonter-Mitchell Foundation
Equifax
Erickson Charitable Fund, Eben W.
Ernest & Julio Gallo Winery
Essick Foundation
Exxon Corp.
Factor Family Foundation, Max
Faith Home Foundation
Fanwood Foundation
Farallon Foundation
Farish Fund, William Stamps
Farley Industries
Fay Charitable Fund, Aubert J.
Federal Express Corp.
Federal-Mogul Corp.
Federal National Mortgage Assn., Fannie Mae
Federated Department Stores and Allied Stores Corp.
Feil Foundation, Louis and Gertrude
Fein Foundation
Fels Fund, Samuel S.

Ferkauf Foundation, Eugene and Estelle
Fibre Converters
Field Foundation of Illinois
Fife Foundation, Elias and Bertha
Fifth Third Bancorp
Fikes Foundation, Leland
FINA, Inc.
Finnegan Foundation, John D.
Fireman's Fund Insurance Co.
Firestone, Jr. Foundation, Harvey
First Brands Corp.
First Fidelity Bancorporation
First Interstate Bank of Arizona
First Interstate Bank of California
First Interstate Bank of Oregon
First Interstate Bank of Texas, N.A.
First Petroleum Corp.
First Union Corp.
Firstar Bank Milwaukee NA
Fish Foundation, Ray C.
Fish Foundation, Vain and Harry
Fisher Foundation
Fisher Foundation, Max M. and Marjorie S.
Fleet Bank of New York
Florida Power Corp.
Florida Power & Light Co.
Forbes Charitable Trust, Herman
Ford Fund, Walter and Josephine
Forest Lawn Foundation
Forest Oil Corp.
Fortin Foundation of Florida
Fortis Benefits Insurance Company/Fortis Financial Group
Foster Charitable Trust
Foster-Davis Foundation
Foundation for Child Development
Fourth Financial Corp.
Frankel Foundation
Frankel Foundation, George and Elizabeth F.
Franklin Foundation, John and Mary
Franklin Mint Corp.
Frederick Foundation
Freedom Forum
Freeman Charitable Trust, Samuel
French Foundation
Frese Foundation, Arnold D.
Freygang Foundation, Walter Henry
Frick Educational Commission, Henry C.
Friedman Foundation, Stephen and Barbara
Froderman Foundation
Frohman Foundation, Sidney
Frohring Foundation, Paul & Maxine
Frohring Foundation, William O. and Gertrude Lewis
Frueauff Foundation, Charles A.
Fry Foundation, Lloyd A.
Fuchs Foundation, Gottfried & Mary
Fuller Foundation, George F. and Sybil H.
Funderburke & Associates
Funderburke & Associates
Fusenot Charity Foundation, Georges and Germaine
Gabelli Foundation
Gage Foundation, Philip and Irene Toll
Gallo Foundation, Julio R.
Gannett Co.
Garvey Kansas Foundation
Gates Foundation
Gateway Apparel
GATX Corp.
Gaylord Foundation, Clifford Willard
GEICO Corp.

Gellert Foundation, Carl
Gellert Foundation, Fred
Gelman Foundation, Melvin and Estelle
General Accident Insurance Co. of America
General American Life Insurance Co.
General Dynamics Corp.
General Electric Co.
General Mills
General Motors Corp.
General Reinsurance Corp.
GenRad
George Foundation
Georgia-Pacific Corp.
Georgia Power Co.
Gerber Products Co.
Gerson Trust, B. Milfred
Gheens Foundation
Giant Eagle
Giant Food
Giant Food Stores
Gilder Foundation
Giles Foundation, Edward C.
Gilmore Foundation, Irving S.
Glaser Foundation
Glaxo
Glickenhaus & Co.
Globe Corp.
Globe Newspaper Co.
Goerlich Family Foundation
Goldberg Family Foundation
Golden Family Foundation
Goldie-Anna Charitable Trust
Goldman Foundation, Herman
Goldring Family Foundation
Goldsmith Foundation
Goldsmith Foundation, Horace W.
Goldstein Foundation, Alfred and Ann
Goldstein Foundation, Leslie and Roslyn
Goldwyn Foundation, Samuel
Golub Corp.
Gore Family Memorial Foundation
Gorin Foundation, Nehemiah
Gould Foundation for Children, Edwin
Grace & Co., W.R.
Graco
Graham Fund, Philip L.
Graphic Controls Corp.
Grassmann Trust, E. J.
Gray Charitable Trust, Mary S.
Graybar Electric Co.
Great-West Life Assurance Co.
Green Foundation, Allen P. and Josephine B.
Green Foundation, Burton E.
Green Fund
Greene Foundation, Robert Z.
Gries Charity Fund, Lucile and Robert H.
Griffin Foundation, Rosa May
Griffin, Sr., Foundation, C. V.
Griffith Foundation, W. C.
Groome Beatty Trust, Helen D.
Gross Charitable Trust, Stella B.
GTE Corp.
Gudelsky Family Foundation, Homer and Martha
Gudelsky Family Foundation, Isadore and Bertha
Gulf Power Co.
Gund Foundation
Guttman Foundation, Stella and Charles
H.C.S. Foundation
Haas Foundation, Paul and Mary
Haas Foundation, Saul and Dayee G.
Haas Fund, Walter and Elise
Haffenreffer Family Fund
Hafif Family Foundation

Hagedorn Fund
Hales Charitable Fund
Halff Foundation, G. A. C.
Hall Charitable Trust, Evelyn A. J.
Hall Foundation
Hallett Charitable Trust
Hallett Charitable Trust, Jessie F.
Hallmark Cards
Halsell Foundation, Ewing
Hambay Foundation, James T.
Hammer Foundation, Armand
Hancock Foundation, Luke B.
Hansen Foundation, Dane G.
Harden Foundation
Hardin Foundation, Phil
Harmon Foundation, Pearl M. and Julia J.
Harper Foundation, Philip S.
Harriman Foundation, Gladys and Roland
Harriman Foundation, Mary W.
Harrington Foundation, Don and Sybil
Harrison and Conrad Memorial Trust
Hartford Courant Foundation
Hatterscheidt Foundation
Havens Foundation, O. W.
Hawn Foundation
Hayfields Foundation
Hazen Charitable Trust, Lita Annenberg
Hearst Foundation
Hearst Foundation, William Randolph
Hechinger Co.
Hecla Mining Co.
Hedrick Foundation, Frank E.
Heinz Co., H.J.
Helfaer Foundation, Evan and Marion
Helis Foundation
Helms Foundation
Hendrickson Brothers
Herbst Foundation
Hermann Foundation, Grover
Herrick Foundation
Hervey Foundation
Herzstein Charitable Foundation, Albert and Ethel
Hess Charitable Foundation, Ronne and Donald
Hess Foundation
Heublein
Hightower Foundation, Walter
Hill Crest Foundation
Hill Foundation
Hillcrest Foundation
Hillman Foundation
Hilton Foundation, Conrad N.
Himmelfarb Foundation, Paul and Annetta
Hoag Family Foundation, George
Hobbs Foundation, Emmert
Hodge Foundation
Hoechst Celanese Corp.
Hoffman Foundation, H. Leslie Hoffman and Elaine S.
Hoffman Foundation, Maximillian E. and Marion O.
Hogan Foundation, Royal Barney
Honeywell
Honigman Foundation
Hook Drug
Hooper Foundation, Elizabeth S.
Hornblower Fund, Henry
Horne Trust, Mabel
Hospital Corp. of America
Household International
Houston Industries
Howell Foundation, Eric and Jessie
Hubbard Broadcasting
Hubbell Inc.
Hughes Charitable Trust, Mabel Y.

Hulme Charitable Foundation, Milton G.
Humana
Humphrey Foundation, Glenn & Gertrude
Hunt Alternatives Fund
Hunt Charitable Trust, C. Giles
Hunt Foundation, Samuel P.
Hunter Trust, A. V.
Hyde and Watson Foundation
I. and L. Association
IBM Corp.
ICI Americas
IDS Financial Services
IES Industries
Illinois Bell
Illinois Tool Works
Imerman Memorial Foundation, Stanley
Indiana Bell Telephone Co.
Indiana Gas and Chemical Corp.
Indiana Insurance Cos.
Inland Container Corp.
Inland Steel Industries
Inman Mills
Innovating Worthy Projects Foundation
Interco
International Flavors & Fragrances
International Foundation
Iowa-Illinois Gas & Electric Co.
Irvine Health Foundation
Irwin Charity Foundation, William G.
ITT Corp.
ITT Hartford Insurance Group
Ittleson Foundation
Jackson Family Foundation, Ann
Jackson Foundation
Jackson Mills
Jacobson & Sons, Benjamin
Janirve Foundation
Jaqua Foundation
JCPenney Co.
Jefferson Endowment Fund, John Percival and Mary C.
JELD-WEN, Inc.
Jenkins Foundation, George W.
Jennings Foundation, Martha Holden
Jerome Foundation
Jewett Foundation, George Frederick
Jewish Healthcare Foundation of Pittsburgh
JM Foundation
John Hancock Mutual Life Insurance Co.
Johnson Controls
Johnson Foundation, Helen K. and Arthur E.
Johnson Foundation, Howard
Johnson Foundation, Robert Wood
Johnson & Higgins
Johnson & Johnson
Johnston Trust for Charitable and Educational Purposes, James M.
Jones Foundation, Daisy Marquis
Jones Foundation, Helen
Jones Intercable, Inc.
Jordan and Ettie A. Jordan Charitable Foundation, Mary Ranken
Jost Foundation, Charles and Mabel P.
Julia R. and Estelle L. Foundation
Kaman Corp.
Kamps Memorial Foundation, Gertrude
Kaplan Foundation, Mayer and Morris
Kaplan Foundation, Rita J. and Stanley H.

Disabled (cont.)

Kaplun Foundation, Morris J. and Betty
Katzenberger Foundation
Kaufmann Foundation, Henry
Kawabe Memorial Fund
Keating Family Foundation
Keebler Co.
Keller-Crescent Co.
Kellogg Foundation, W. K.
Kelly Tractor Co.
Kemper Educational and Charitable Fund
Kemper Foundation, Enid and Crosby
Kennecott Corp.
Kennedy Foundation, Ethel
Kennedy Foundation, Quentin J.
Kennedy, Jr. Foundation, Joseph P.
Kentland Foundation
Kenworthy - Sarah H. Swift Foundation, Marion E.
Kern Foundation Trust
Kerr-McGee Corp.
Kieckhefer Foundation, J. W.
Kiewit Foundation, Peter
Kiewit Sons, Peter
Kilcawley Fund, William H.
Kimberly-Clark Corp.
Kiplinger Foundation
Kirbo Charitable Trust, Thomas M. and Irene B.
Kirchgessner Foundation, Karl
Klau Foundation, David W. and Sadie
Klee Foundation, Conrad and Virginia
Kline Foundation, Josiah W. and Bessie H.
Klosk Fund, Louis and Rose
Knapp Foundation
Knistrom Foundation, Fanny and Svante
Knott Foundation, Marion I. and Henry J.
Knowles Foundation
Knox Family Foundation
Knox Foundation, Seymour H.
Kohn-Joseloff Fund
Koopman Fund
Kramer Foundation, C. L. C.
Krause Foundation, Charles A.
Kresge Foundation
KSM Foundation
Kuse Foundation, James R.
Kuyper Foundation, Peter H. and E. Lucille Gaass
Laclede Gas Co.
Ladish Co.
Lafarge Corp.
Laffey-McHugh Foundation
LamCo. Communications
Land O'Lakes
Lane Foundation, Minnie and Bernard
Lard Trust, Mary Potishman
Laros Foundation, R. K.
Lasdon Foundation
Lastfogel Foundation, Abe and Frances
Lattner Foundation, Forrest C.
Lauder Foundation
LBJ Family Foundation
Leavey Foundation, Thomas and Dorothy
Lederer Foundation, Francis L.
Lee Endowment Foundation
Lee Foundation, Ray M. and Mary Elizabeth
Legg Mason Inc.
Lehmann Foundation, Otto W.
Leidy Foundation, John J.
Lemberg Foundation
Leucadia National Corp.
Leuthold Foundation

Levy Foundation, Hyman Jebb
Levy Foundation, June Rockwell
Lewis Foundation, Frank J.
Liberty Diversified Industries Inc.
Lightner Sams Foundation
Lincoln Electric Co.
Lindsay Trust, Agnes M.
Link, Jr. Foundation, George
Linnell Foundation
Lipsky Foundation, Fred and Sarah
Lipton, Thomas J.
Liquid Air Corp.
Littlefield Foundation, Edmund Wattis
Littlefield Memorial Trust, Ida Ballou
Litton Industries
Litton/Itek Optical Systems
Lockwood Foundation, Byron W. and Alice L.
Loeb Partners Corp.
Logan Foundation, E. J.
Long Foundation, George A. and Grace
Long Island Lighting Co.
Longwood Foundation
Lost Tree Charitable Foundation
Louisiana-Pacific Corp.
Love Charitable Foundation, John Allan
Lowe Foundation
Lowenstein Foundation, Leon
LTV Corp.
Luce Charitable Trust, Theodore
Luse Foundation, W. P. and Bulah
Luttrell Trust
Lydall, Inc.
Lynn Foundation, E. M.
Lyon Foundation
Lyons Foundation
M.E. Foundation
Maas Foundation, Benard L.
MacDonald Foundation, James A.
Macy & Co., R.H.
Mailman Family Foundation, A. L.
Mallinckrodt Specialty Chemicals Co.
Manat Foundation
Mandel Foundation, Jack N. and Lilyan
Manville Corp.
Mardag Foundation
Maritz Inc.
Marmot Foundation
Marriott Corp.
Marriott Foundation, J. Willard
Mars Foundation
Marshall & Ilsley Bank
Martin Foundation
Martin Foundation, Bert William
Martin Marietta Corp.
Mary Kay Foundation
Massachusetts Charitable Mechanics Association
Massey Charitable Trust
Massey Foundation, Jack C.
Massie Trust, David Meade
Mastronardi Charitable Foundation, Charles A.
Mastronardi Charitable Foundation, Charles A.
Mather and William Gwinn Mather Fund, Elizabeth Ring
Matthews International Corp.
May Department Stores Co.
May Foundation, Wilbur
May Mitchell Royal Foundation
Mayerson Foundation, Manuel D. and Rhoda
Maytag Corp.
Maytag Family Foundation, Fred
Mazda Motors of America (Central), Inc.
Mazda North America
Mazza Foundation

MBIA, Inc.
MCA
McAlister Charitable Foundation, Harold
McAlonan Trust, John A.
McBeath Foundation, Faye
McBride & Son Associates
McCamish Foundation
McCasland Foundation
McCaw Cellular Communications
McCormick Tribune Foundation, Robert R.
McCune Charitable Trust, John R.
McCune Foundation
McDermott Foundation, Eugene
McDonald & Co. Securities
McDonald Foundation, J. M.
McDonald's Corp.
McDonnell Douglas Corp.-West
McEachern Charitable Trust, D. V. & Ida J.
McElroy Trust, R. J.
McGee Foundation
McGonagle Foundation, Dextra Baldwin
McGraw Foundation
McGraw-Hill
McInerny Foundation
McIntosh Foundation
MCJ Foundation
McKee Foundation, Robert E. and Evelyn
McKnight Foundation
McLean Contributionship
Mead Corp.
Meadows Foundation
Medina Foundation
Mellon Bank Corp.
Memorial Foundation for the Blind
Mengle Foundation, Glenn and Ruth
Merck Human Health Division
Mercy, Jr. Foundation, Sue and Eugene
Meredith Corp.
Merrick Foundation, Robert G. and Anne M.
Messing Foundation, Morris M. and Helen F.
Mettler Instrument Corp.
Meyer Foundation, Eugene and Agnes E.
Meyer Foundation, Robert R.
Michigan Consolidated Gas Co.
Michigan Gas Utilities
Mid-Iowa Health Foundation
Middendorf Foundation
Midwest Resources
Milken Family Medical Foundation
Milken Foundation, L. and S.
Milken Institute for Job and Capital Formation
Mill-Rose Co.
Miller Foundation, Steve J.
Miller Fund, Kathryn and Gilbert
Milliken & Co.
Mills Charitable Foundation, Henry L. and Kathryn
Mine Safety Appliances Co.
Mitrani Family Foundation
Mitsubishi Electric America
MNC Financial
Mobil Oil Corp.
Model Foundation, Leo
Mohasco Corp.
Moncrief Foundation, William A. and Elizabeth B.
Monell Foundation, Ambrose
Monroe Foundation (1976), J. Edgar
Montgomery Street Foundation
Moody Foundation
Moore Charitable Foundation, Marjorie

Moore Foundation, Edward S.
Moore Foundation, Martha G.
Moorman Manufacturing Co.
Morania Foundation
Morgan Foundation, Burton D.
Morris Foundation, Norman M.
Morton International
Moses Fund, Henry and Lucy
Moss Charitable Trust, Finis M.
Mostyn Foundation
Motch Corp.
Motorola
MTS Systems Corp.
Mueller Co.
Mullen Foundation, J. K.
Munger Foundation, Alfred C.
Murdock Charitable Trust, M. J.
Murphy Foundation, Dan
Murphy Foundation, John P.
Murphy Foundation, Katherine and John
Musson Charitable Foundation, R. C. and Katharine M.
Muth Foundation, Peter and Mary
Myers and Sons, D.
Nalco Chemical Co.
Nash Foundation
National City Corp.
National Computer Systems
National Fuel Gas Co.
National Gypsum Co.
National Medical Enterprises
National Steel
National Westminster Bank New Jersey
Nationwide Insurance Cos.
Navistar International Corp.
NBD Bank
NEC USA
Nelson Foundation, Florence
Neu Foundation, Hugo and Doris
Neuberger Foundation, Roy R. and Marie S.
New England Mutual Life Insurance Co.
New Horizon Foundation
New Prospect Foundation
New York Foundation
New York Life Insurance Co.
New York Mercantile Exchange
New York Telephone Co.
The New Yorker Magazine, Inc.
Newbrook Charitable Foundation
Newhouse Foundation, Samuel I.
Newman Assistance Fund, Jerome A. and Estelle R.
Newman's Own
News & Observer Publishing Co.
Nias Foundation, Henry
Nichols Co., J.C.
Nissan Motor Corporation in U.S.A.
Noble Charitable Trust, John L. and Ethel G.
Noble Foundation, Samuel Roberts
Nordson Corp.
Norgren Foundation, Carl A.
Norris Foundation, Kenneth T. and Eileen L.
North American Life & Casualty Co.
Northeast Utilities
Northern Indiana Public Service Co.
Northern States Power Co.
Northern Trust Co.
Northwest Natural Gas Co.
Norton Co.
Norwest Bank Nebraska
NuTone Inc.
Oak Foundation U.S.A.
Oberkotter Family Foundation
Occidental Oil & Gas Corp.
Oceanic Cablevision Foundation
O'Connor Co.

O'Connor Foundation, A. Lindsay and Olive B.
O'Connor Foundation, Magee
Odell and Helen Pfeiffer Odell Fund, Robert Stewart
Oestreicher Foundation, Sylvan and Ann
Offield Family Foundation
Ohl, Jr. Trust, George A.
Ohrstrom Foundation
Olive Bridge Fund
Olsson Memorial Foundation, Elis
1525 Foundation
1957 Charity Trust
O'Neill Charitable Corporation, F. J.
Oppenheimer and Flora Oppenheimer Haas Trust, Leo
Ordean Foundation
O'Shaughnessy Foundation, I. A.
Osher Foundation, Bernard
Oshkosh B'Gosh
Overbrook Foundation
Overseas Shipholding Group
Oxford Foundation
Pacific Mutual Life Insurance Co.
Pacific Telesis Group
Packard Foundation, David and Lucile
Page Foundation, George B.
Palmer-Fry Memorial Trust, Lily
Pappas Charitable Foundation, Bessie
Pappas Charitable Foundation, Thomas Anthony
Parke-Davis Group
Parker Foundation
Parshelsky Foundation, Moses L.
Parsons Foundation, Ralph M.
Patterson Charitable Fund, W. I.
Peabody Foundation
Peabody Foundation, Amelia
Peery Foundation
Peierls Foundation
Pennzoil Co.
Peppers Foundation, Ann
Perini Foundation, Joseph
Perkin-Elmer Corp.
Perkin-Elmer Corp.
Peterloon Foundation
Peters Foundation, Leon S.
Petersen Foundation, Esper A.
Pew Charitable Trusts
Pfizer
Philip Morris Cos.
Phillips Family Foundation, Jay and Rose
Phillips Foundation, Waite and Genevieve
Phillips Petroleum Co.
Phillips Trust, Edwin
Pickford Foundation, Mary
Pines Bridge Foundation
Pinkerton Foundation
Pioneer Electronics (USA) Inc.
Pioneer Fund
Pittsburgh National Bank
Pitzman Fund
Plankenhorn Foundation, Harry
Playboy Enterprises, Inc.
Porter Foundation, Mrs. Cheever
Porter Testamentary Trust, James Hyde
Portland General Electric Co.
Posey Trust, Addison
Posnack Family Foundation of Hollywood
Potomac Electric Power Co.
PPG Industries
Prairie Foundation
Prentiss Foundation, Elisabeth Severance
Price Associates, T. Rowe
Principal Financial Group
Pritzker Foundation

Procter & Gamble Cosmetic & Fragrance Products
Prudential-Bache Securities
Prudential Insurance Co. of America
Public Service Electric & Gas Co.
Puget Sound Power & Light Co.
Pyramid Foundation
Quabaug Corp.
Quaker Chemical Corp.
Quaker Oats Co.
Questar Corp.
Ragen, Jr. Memorial Fund Trust No. 1, James M.
Rahr Malting Co.
Ralston Purina Co.
Rankin and Elizabeth Forbes Rankin Trust, William
Rapp Foundation, Robert Glenn
Raskob Foundation for Catholic Activities
Raytheon Co.
Red Wing Shoe Co.
Redfield Foundation, Nell J.
Regenstein Foundation
Reily & Co., William B.
Reisman Charitable Trust, George C. and Evelyn R.
Reliable Life Insurance Co.
Reliance Electric Co.
Rennebohm Foundation, Oscar
Republic New York Corp.
Retirement Research Foundation
Reynolds Foundation, Christopher
Reynolds Foundation, Eleanor T.
Reynolds Foundation, Richard S.
Reynolds Metals Co.
Rhoades Fund, Otto L. and Hazel E.
Rhone-Poulenc Inc.
Rice Family Foundation, Jacob and Sophie
Rice Foundation, Ethel and Raymond F.
Rice Foundation, Helen Steiner
Rich Foundation
Richardson Foundation, Sid W.
Richardson Fund, Mary Lynn
Rieke Corp.
Rienzi Foundation
Riley Foundation, Mabel Louise
Ritter Foundation
Ritter Foundation, May Ellen and Gerald
Roberts Foundation
Roche Relief Foundation, Edward and Ellen
Rochester Telephone Corp.
Rockwell Fund
Rockwell International Corp.
Roddis Foundation, Hamilton
Rodgers Foundation, Richard & Dorothy
Rogers Charitable Trust, Florence
Rogers Family Foundation
Rogers Foundation
Rogers Foundation, Mary Stuart
Rohatyn Foundation, Felix and Elizabeth
Rohm and Haas Company
Rohr Inc.
Rosen Foundation, Joseph
Rosenthal Foundation, Richard and Hinda
Rowland Foundation
Royal Group Inc.
Rudin Foundation, Samuel and May
Russell Charitable Trust, Josephine S.
SAFECO Corp.
Sailors' Snug Harbor of Boston
St. Giles Foundation
Saltonstall Charitable Foundation, Richard
San Diego Gas & Electric

Sandy Foundation, George H.
Sandy Hill Foundation
Sang Foundation, Elsie O. and Philip D.
Sanguinetti Foundation, Annunziata
Santa Fe Pacific Corp.
Sara Lee Corp.
Sara Lee Hosiery
Sargent Foundation, Newell B.
Sarkeys Foundation
Sattler Beneficial Trust, Daniel A. and Edna J.
Sawyer Charitable Foundation
Scaife Family Foundation
Schenck Fund, L. P.
Scherer Foundation, Karla
Scheuer Family Foundation, S. H. and Helen R.
Schieffelin Residuary Trust, Sarah I.
Schiff Foundation
Schlink Foundation, Albert G. and Olive H.
Schlumberger Ltd.
Schmidlapp Trust No. 1, Jacob G.
Schmidt Charitable Foundation, William E.
Schmitt Foundation, Arthur J.
Schneider Foundation, Robert E.
Schoenbaum Family Foundation
Scholl Foundation, Dr.
Scholler Foundation
Schramm Foundation
Schroeder Foundation, Walter
Schust Foundation, Clarence L. and Edith B.
Schwab & Co., Charles
Schwartz Foundation, Arnold A.
Science Applications International Corp.
Scott Foundation, Walter
Scrivner, Inc.
Scurlock Foundation
Scurry Foundation, D. L.
Seafirst Corp.
Sealright Co., Inc.
Seaway Food Town
Selby and Marie Selby Foundation, William G.
Sewall Foundation, Elmina
Seymour Foundation, W. L. and Louise E.
Shafer Foundation, Richard H. and Ann
Shapiro Foundation, Charles and M. R.
Share Trust, Charles Morton
Sharp Foundation
Sharp Foundation, Evelyn
Shawmut National Corp.
Shea Foundation
Sheaffer Inc.
Shelden Fund, Elizabeth, Allan and Warren
Sheldon Foundation, Ralph C.
Shell Oil Co.
Shelter Mutual Insurance Co.
Shemanski Testamentary Trust, Tillie and Alfred
Sherman Family Charitable Trust, George and Beatrice
Sherwin-Williams Co.
Shoenberg Foundation
Shoong Foundation, Milton
Siebe North Inc.
Siebert Lutheran Foundation
Sierra Pacific Resources
Signet Bank/Maryland
Silver Spring Foundation
Simon Foundation, Sidney, Milton and Leoma
Simon Foundation, William E. and Carol G.
SIT Investment Associates, Inc.
Skinner Corp.
Slant/Fin Corp.
Slifka Foundation, Alan B.

Smeal Foundation, Mary Jean & Frank P.
Smith Charitable Fund, Eleanor Armstrong
Smith Charitable Trust
Smith Charitable Trust, W. W.
Smith Corp., A.O.
Smith Family Foundation, Charles E.
Smith Foundation
Smith Foundation, Kelvin and Eleanor
Smith Foundation, Lon V.
Smith, Jr. Charitable Trust, Jack J.
Smith, Jr. Foundation, M. W.
Smith Memorial Fund, Ethel Sergeant Clark
Smithers Foundation, Christopher D.
SmithKline Beecham
Smock Foundation, Frank and Laura
SNET
Snite Foundation, Fred B.
Snow Foundation, John Ben
Snyder Foundation, Harold B. and Dorothy A.
Snyder Fund, Valentine Perry
Society for Savings
Solo Cup Co.
Sonat
Sony Corp. of America
Souers Charitable Trust, Sidney W. and Sylvia N.
Southern California Edison Co.
Southwestern Bell Corp.
Spang & Co.
Speas Foundation, Victor E.
Spiegel
Spingold Foundation, Nate B. and Frances
Sprague Educational and Charitable Foundation, Seth
Spunk Fund
Square D Co.
Stanley Works
Star Bank, N.A.
Starr Foundation
Starrett Co., L.S.
Statter Foundation, Amy Plant
Stearns Trust, Artemas W.
Steelcase
Steele Foundation
Steele Foundation, Harry and Grace
Steinbach Fund, Ruth and Milton
Steinberg Family Foundation, Meyer and Jean
Steinhardt Foundation, Judy and Michael
Steinman Foundation, James Hale
Stemmons Foundation
Sterling Winthrop
Stern Family Foundation, Alex
Stevens Foundation, Abbot and Dorothy H.
Stewardship Foundation
Stewart Educational Foundation, Donnell B. and Elizabeth Dee Shaw
Stewart Trust under the will of Helen S. Devore, Alexander and Margaret
Stillwell Charitable Trust, Glen and Dorothy
Stocker Foundation
Stone Container Corp.
Storer Foundation, George B.
Strake Foundation
Stranahan Foundation
Straus Foundation, Aaron and Lillie
Straus Foundation, Martha Washington Straus and Harry H.

Straus Foundation, Philip A. and Lynn
Stride Rite Corp.
Strong Foundation, Hattie M.
Stuart Center Charitable Trust, Hugh
Stulsaft Foundation, Morris
Sumitomo Bank of California
Summerfield Foundation, Solon E.
Sun Co.
Super Valu Stores
Surrena Memorial Fund, Harry and Thelma
Swalm Foundation
Swanson Foundation
Tandem Computers
Tandy Foundation, Anne Burnett and Charles
Tarmac America Inc.
Tasty Baking Co.
Taube Family Foundation
Taubman Foundation, A. Alfred
Taylor Foundation, Ruth and Vernon
Tenneco
Tension Envelope Corp.
Terner Foundation
Teubert Charitable Trust, James H. and Alice
Texaco
Texas Commerce Bank Houston, N.A.
Texas Gas Transmission Corp.
Textron
Thagard Foundation
Thanksgiving Foundation
Thermo Electron Corp.
Thomas Foundation, Dorothy
Thompson Charitable Foundation, Marion G.
3M Co.
Time Insurance Co.
Times Mirror Co.
Tippit Charitable Trust, C. Carlisle and Margaret M.
Tisch Foundation
Titmus Foundation
Titus Foundation, C. W.
TJX Cos.
Tonkin Foundation, Tom and Helen
Torchmark Corp.
Toyota Motor Sales, U.S.A.
Tracor, Inc.
Transco Energy Company
Tranzonic Cos.
Treuhaft Foundation
Trexler Trust, Harry C.
Trimble Family Foundation, Robert Mize and Isa White
Trinity Foundation
TRINOVA Corp.
Tropicana Products, Inc.
Truland Foundation
Trust Co. Bank
Tuch Foundation, Michael
Tull Charitable Foundation
Turner Charitable Foundation
Turner Fund, Ruth
21 International Holdings
Unger Foundation, Aber D.
Unilever United States
Union Bank
Union Bank of Switzerland Los Angeles Branch
Union Camp Corp.
Union Carbide Corp.
Union Electric Co.
Union Foundation
Union Pacific Corp.
United Dominion Industries
U.S. Leasing International
United States Sugar Corp.
United States Trust Co. of New York
United Technologies Corp.

Universal Foods Corp.
Universal Leaf Tobacco Co.
Upjohn Foundation, Harold and Grace
Upton Foundation, Frederick S.
US Bancorp
USF&G Co.
USG Corp.
Ushkow Foundation
USX Corp.
Utica National Insurance Group
Valley Foundation
Valspar Corp.
van Ameringen Foundation
van Loben Sels - Eleanor Slate van Lobel Sels Charitable Foundation, Ernst D.
Van Nuys Charities, J. B. and Emily
Van Nuys Foundation, I. N. and Susanna H.
Van Wert County Foundation
Vance Charitable Foundation, Robert C.
Varian Associates
Vidda Foundation
Vidinha Charitable Trust, A. and E.
Virginia Power Co.
Vlasic Foundation
Vulcan Materials Co.
Waggoner Charitable Trust, Crystelle
Wal-Mart Stores
Waldbaum, Inc.
Walgreen Co.
Wallach Foundation, Miriam G. and Ira D.
Disney Co., Walt
Ward Foundation, Louis L. and Adelaide C.
Wareheim Foundation, E. C.
Warner-Lambert Co.
Warwick Foundation
Wasily Family Foundation
Wauwatosa Savings & Loan Association
Wean Foundation, Raymond John
Weaver Foundation, Gil and Dody
Webb Foundation
Webb Foundation, Del E.
Weckbaugh Foundation, Eleanore Mullen
Weiler Foundation
Weiler Foundation, Theodore & Renee
Weinberg, Jr. Foundation, Sidney J.
Weingart Foundation
Weinstein Foundation, J.
Weintraub Family Foundation, Joseph
Weisbrod Foundation Trust Dept., Robert and Mary
Weiss Fund, Clara
Welfare Foundation
Wells Fargo & Co.
Wells Foundation, Franklin H. and Ruth L.
Wendt Foundation, Margaret L.
Werblow Charitable Trust, Nina W.
West One Bancorp
Westerman Foundation, Samuel L.
Western New York Foundation
Westinghouse Electric Corp.
Westvaco Corp.
Weyerhaeuser Co.
Wheat First Securites
Whirlpool Corp.
Whitaker Charitable Foundation, Lyndon C.
White Foundation, Erle and Emma
White Trust, G. R.
Whitehead Foundation

Disabled (cont.)

Whitehead Foundation, Joseph B.
Whiting Foundation
Wickes Foundation, Harvey Randall
Wien Foundation, Lawrence A.
Wilcox General Trust, George N.
Willard Foundation, Helen Parker
Williams Cos.
Williams Family Foundation
Williams Family Foundation of Georgia
Willmott Foundation, Fred & Floy
Wilson Foundation, H. W.
Wilson Foundation, Marie C. and Joseph C.
Wilson Sanitarium for Children of Baltimore City, Thomas
Wilson Trust, Lula C.
Winn-Dixie Stores
Winston Research Foundation, Harry
Wisconsin Energy Corp.
Wisconsin Power & Light Co.
Wollenberg Foundation
Wolverine World Wide, Inc.
Woodland Foundation
Woods Charitable Fund
Woodward Fund-Atlanta, David, Helen, Marian
Woodward Governor Co.
Wornall Charitable Trust and Foundation, Kearney
Wright Foundation, Lola
Wrigley Co., Wm. Jr.
Xerox Corp.
Yassenoff Foundation, Leo
Yawkey Foundation II
Yeager Charitable Trust, Lester E.
Young Foundation, Hugo H. and Mabel B.
Young & Rubicam
Zacharia Foundation, Isaac Herman
Ziegler Foundation
Ziegler Foundation for the Blind, E. Matilda
Ziegler Foundation, Ruth/Allen
Ziemann Foundation
Zilkha & Sons
Zlinkoff Fund for Medical Research and Education, Sergei S.
Zuckerberg Foundation, Roy J.

Domestic Violence

Abell-Hanger Foundation
Abercrombie Foundation
Achelis Foundation
Ahmanson Foundation
Air Products & Chemicals
Alberto-Culver Co.
AlliedSignal
Alltel/Western Region
Alltel/Western Region
ALPAC Corp.
Altman Foundation
Aluminum Co. of America
AMAX
AMCORE Bank, N.A. Rockford
American Express Co.
American National Bank & Trust Co. of Chicago
American United Life Insurance Co.
Amfac/JMB Hawaii
Amoco Corp.
Andersen Foundation, Hugh J.
Anderson Charitable Trust, Josephine
Andrews Foundation
Apache Corp.
Appleton Papers
Arkansas Power & Light Co.

Arkell Hall Foundation
Arkla
Atherton Family Foundation
Attleboro Pawtucket Savings Bank
Bank of America Arizona
Bard, C. R.
Barker Foundation
Barrows Foundation, Geraldine and R. A.
Baughman Foundation
Beal Foundation
Beazley Foundation
Beecher Foundation, Florence Simon
Ben & Jerry's Homemade
Benbough Foundation, Legler
Benefit Trust Life Insurance Co.
Benetton
Bernsen Foundation, Grace and Franklin
Bethlehem Steel Corp.
Bishop Charitable Trust, A. G.
Block, H&R
Bodman Foundation
Boeing Co.
Boettcher Foundation
Borman's
Bowater Inc.
Bremer Foundation, Otto
Briggs Family Foundation
Britton Fund
Brown & Sons, Alex
Bucyrus-Erie
Burden Foundation, Florence V.
Burlington Northern Inc.
Burnand Medical and Educational Foundation, Alphonse A.
Burndy Corp.
Burroughs Wellcome Co.
Bush Foundation
C.P. Rail Systems
Cafritz Foundation, Morris and Gwendolyn
Campbell Foundation
Cannon Foundation
Carolyn Foundation
Central Hudson Gas & Electric Corp.
Central Maine Power Co.
Chapman Charitable Trust, H. A. and Mary K.
Charlesbank Homes
Chase Manhattan Bank, N.A.
Chevron Corp.
Chicago Resource Center
Chicago Sun-Times, Inc.
Clorox Co.
Codrington Charitable Foundation, George W.
Colonial Life & Accident Insurance Co.
Colorado Trust
Commerce Bancshares, Inc.
Commerce Clearing House
Consolidated Natural Gas Co.
Coors Brewing Co.
Coors Foundation, Adolph
Copperweld Steel Co.
Cord Foundation, E. L.
Cowell Foundation, S. H.
Cowles Media Co.
CPC International
CPI Corp.
CRL Inc.
Crown Memorial, Arie and Ida
Crum and Forster
Cullen/Frost Bankers
Cummins Engine Co.
Curtice-Burns Foods
Dater Foundation, Charles H.
Dee Foundation, Annie Taylor
Delano Foundation, Mignon Sherwood
Deluxe Corp.
Dexter Corp.

Diamond Walnut Growers
Digital Equipment Corp.
Dodge Foundation, Geraldine R.
Donaldson Co.
Donnelley & Sons Co., R.R.
Dougherty, Jr. Foundation, James R.
du Pont de Nemours & Co., E. I.
Dumke Foundation, Dr. Ezekiel R. and Edna Wattis
Edison Foundation, Harry
Egenton Home
El Pomar Foundation
Emergency Aid of Pennsylvania Foundation
EMI Records Group
Evjue Foundation
FAB Industries
Fales Foundation Trust
Federated Life Insurance Co.
Fel-Pro Incorporated
Fidelity Bank
Fikes Foundation, Leland
Firan Foundation
Fireman's Fund Insurance Co.
First Fidelity Bancorporation
First Interstate Bancsystem of Montana
First Interstate Bank of Arizona
First Union Corp.
Forest Foundation
Foundation for Child Development
Fourth Financial Corp.
Frederick Foundation
Freedom Forum
Freeport-McMoRan
Frost Foundation
Fry Foundation, Lloyd A.
Fund for New Jersey
Funderburke & Associates
Funderburke & Associates
Gates Foundation
GATX Corp.
Gebbie Foundation
General American Life Insurance Co.
General Mills
GenRad
Georgia Health Foundation
Giant Eagle
Giant Food Stores
Glaser Foundation
Globe Newspaper Co.
Goldseker Foundation of Maryland, Morris
Graco
Great-West Life Assurance Co.
Groome Beatty Trust, Helen D.
GTE Corp.
Gulfstream Aerospace Corp.
Haas Foundation, Saul and Dayee G.
Haas, Jr. Fund, Evelyn and Walter
Hadson Corp.
Hagedorn Fund
Haigh-Scatena Foundation
Hall Family Foundations
Hall Foundation
Hampden Papers
Harrington Foundation, Don and Sybil
Hawkins Foundation, Robert Z.
Hechinger Co.
Heinz Endowment, Vira I.
Henry Foundation, Patrick
Hermann Foundation, Grover
Hillcrest Foundation
Hilton Foundation, Conrad N.
Hoche-Scofield Foundation
Honeywell
Hospital Corp. of America
Houck Foundation, May K.
Howell Foundation, Eric and Jessie
Hunt Alternatives Fund

Hunt Alternatives Fund, Helen
Hunt Charitable Trust, C. Giles
Hunter Trust, A. V.
Hyams Foundation
Hyundai Motor America
I and G Charitable Foundation
Icahn Foundation, Carl C.
IDS Financial Services
IMCERA Group Inc.
Inland Steel Industries
Irvine Foundation, James
ITT Hartford Insurance Group
ITT Rayonier
J.P. Morgan & Co.
Jackson Foundation
Janirve Foundation
Jasper Seating Co.
Johnson Foundation, Burdine
Jones Foundation, Daisy Marquis
Kautz Family Foundation
Keating Family Foundation
Keene Trust, Hazel R.
Kennecott Corp.
Kentland Foundation
Kerr Foundation
Kimberly-Clark Corp.
Knistrom Foundation, Fanny and Svante
Ladd Charitable Corporation, Helen and George
Lattner Foundation, Forrest C.
Leach Foundation, Tom & Frances
Lederer Foundation, Francis L.
Life Insurance Co. of Georgia
Lincoln National Corp.
Liquid Air Corp.
Livingston Foundation
Livingston Memorial Foundation
Liz Claiborne
LTV Corp.
Lukens
Madison Gas & Electric Co.
Maneely Fund
Mardag Foundation
Maritz Inc.
Mary Kay Foundation
Maxus Energy Corp.
Mayerson Foundation, Manuel D. and Rhoda
MBIA, Inc.
McBeath Foundation, Faye
McBride & Son Associates
McCormick Tribune Foundation, Robert R.
McDonald & Co. Securities
McDonald & Co. Securities
McKee Foundation, Robert E. and Evelyn
MDU Resources Group, Inc.
Mead Corp.
Meadows Foundation
Medina Foundation
Mellon Bank Corp.
Menasha Corp.
Merit Oil Corp.
Meyer Foundation, Eugene and Agnes E.
Meyer Foundation, Robert R.
Meyer Memorial Trust
MGIC Investment Corp.
Midwest Resources
MNC Financial
Mobil Oil Corp.
Monsanto Co.
Montana Power Co.
Morgan Foundation, Burton D.
Myers and Sons, D.
Nalco Chemical Co.
National Computer Systems
National Life of Vermont
National Westminster Bank New Jersey
New England Mutual Life Insurance Co.
New York Foundation
New York Life Insurance Co.

The New Yorker Magazine, Inc.
Newman's Own
News & Observer Publishing Co.
Norman Foundation, Andrew
Northeast Utilities
Northern States Power Co.
Northern Trust Co.
Norton Co.
O'Brien Foundation, Alice M.
Occidental Oil & Gas Corp.
O'Neil Foundation, Casey Albert T.
Ordean Foundation
O'Shaughnessy Foundation, I. A.
Oshkosh B'Gosh
Overlake Foundation
Parke-Davis Group
Parsons Foundation, Ralph M.
Pearlstone Foundation, Peggy Meyerhoff
Pearlstone Foundation, Peggy Meyerhoff
Penn Savings Bank, a division of Sovereign Bank Bank of Princeton, a division of Sovereign Bank
Perkin-Elmer Corp.
Perkin-Elmer Corp.
Pesch Family Foundation
Pew Charitable Trusts
Phillips Petroleum Co.
Phipps Foundation, William H.
Piedmont Health Care Foundation
Pinkerton Foundation
Pittsburgh National Bank
Playboy Enterprises, Inc.
Portec, Inc.
Pott Foundation, Herman T. and Phenie R.
Pritzker Foundation
Procter & Gamble Cosmetic & Fragrance Products
Public Welfare Foundation
Quaker Oats Co.
Rahr Malting Co.
Raskob Foundation for Catholic Activities
Recognition Equipment
Redfield Foundation, Nell J.
Reliance Electric Co.
Reynolds Charitable Trust, Kate B.
Reynolds Foundation, Z. Smith
Reynolds Metals Co.
Richardson Charitable Trust, Anne S.
Richardson Foundation, Smith
Roche Relief Foundation, Edward and Ellen
Rockwell International Corp.
Rohr Inc.
Roseburg Forest Products Co.
Rosenberg Family Foundation, William
Rouse Co.
Rupp Foundation, Fran and Warren
Sandy Hill Foundation
Santa Fe Pacific Corp.
Sara Lee Corp.
Sara Lee Hosiery
Scherman Foundation
Schoenbaum Family Foundation
Scrivner, Inc.
Sealright Co., Inc.
Seaway Food Town
Second Foundation
Security Life of Denver
Segal Charitable Trust, Barnet
Shawmut National Corp.
Shoney's Inc.
Simpson Investment Co.
Skinner Corp.
Smith Memorial Fund, Ethel Sergeant Clark
Smithers Foundation, Christopher D.

Sonoco Products Co.
South Texas Charitable Foundation
Spiegel
Sprague Educational and Charitable Foundation, Seth
Steelcase
Sterling Inc.
Stewardship Foundation
Stulsaft Foundation, Morris
Sturgis Charitable and Educational Trust, Roy and Christine
Subaru of America Inc.
Sunnen Foundation
Swift Memorial Health Care Foundation
Swig Charity Foundation, Mae and Benjamin
Target Stores
Target Stores
Tarmac America Inc.
Teleklew Productions
Temple Foundation, T. L. L.
Tennant Co.
Tetley, Inc.
Texas Gas Transmission Corp.
3M Co.
Time Insurance Co.
TJX Cos.
Tosco Corp. Refining Division
Tracor, Inc.
Transco Energy Company
Tropicana Products, Inc.
Trull Foundation
Trust Co. Bank
Union Bank
Union Bank of Switzerland Los Angeles Branch
Union Camp Corp.
Union Pacific Corp.
United Dominion Industries
U.S. Leasing International
Uris Brothers Foundation
US Bancorp
UST
van Ameringen Foundation
Van Camp Foundation
Veritas Foundation
Waffle House, Inc.
Waggoner Charitable Trust, Crystelle
Wal-Mart Stores
Waldbaum, Inc.
Walker Foundation, Archie D. and Bertha H.
Wareheim Foundation, E. C.
Wells Foundation, Franklin H. and Ruth L.
West Foundation
West One Bancorp
Weyerhaeuser Co.
Wharton Foundation
Whirlpool Corp.
WICOR, Inc.
Williams Cos.
Wilson Foundation, Marie C. and Joseph C.
Wilson Trust, Lula C.
Wolf Foundation, Melvin and Elaine
Woods Charitable Fund
Wright Foundation, Lola
Wrigley Co., Wm. Jr.
Wurts Memorial, Henrietta Tower
Xerox Corp.

Drugs & Alcohol

Abbott Laboratories
Abell Foundation, The
Abell-Hanger Foundation
Acushnet Co.
AFLAC
Ahmanson Foundation
Air Products & Chemicals
Alabama Power Co.
Albertson's

AlliedSignal
Allstate Insurance Co.
Alltel/Western Region
ALPAC Corp.
Alumax
Aluminum Co. of America
AMCORE Bank, N.A. Rockford
American Brands
American Electric Power
American Express Co.
American Financial Corp.
American Home Products Corp.
American United Life Insurance Co.
American Welding & Manufacturing Co.
Amfac/JMB Hawaii
Andersen Corp.
Andersen Foundation
Anderson Charitable Trust, Josephine
Anderson Foundation, William P.
Anheuser-Busch Cos.
Anschutz Family Foundation
Apache Corp.
Apple Computer, Inc.
Appleton Papers
Archbold Charitable Trust, Adrian and Jessie
Archer-Daniels-Midland Co.
Archibald Charitable Foundation, Norman
ARCO Chemical
Arkansas Power & Light Co.
Arkla
Asea Brown Boveri
Atherton Family Foundation
Atkinson Foundation
Atlanta Gas Light Co.
Attleboro Pawtucket Savings Bank
Augat, Inc.
Avon Products
Badgeley Residuary Charitable Trust, Rose M.
Bailey Foundation
Baird Foundation
Baker Foundation, R. C.
Baldwin Foundation, David M. and Barbara
Ball Corp.
Bank of America - Giannini Foundation
Bank of New York
Bank One, Texas-Houston Office
Bankers Trust Co.
Barker Welfare Foundation
Baskin-Robbins USA CO.
Bassett Foundation, Norman
Battelle
Bauervic-Paisley Foundation
Bechtel Group
Beeghly Fund, Leon A.
Behmann Brothers Foundation
Belding Heminway Co.
Belk Stores
Bemis Company
Benetton
Benwood Foundation
Bertha Foundation
Bethlehem Steel Corp.
Beynon Foundation, Kathryne
BFGoodrich
BHP Pacific Resources
Blair and Co., William
Blandin Foundation
Block, H&R
Blum-Kovler Foundation
Boatmen's Bancshares
Boatmen's First National Bank of Oklahoma
Boeing Co.
Boise Cascade Corp.
Borg-Warner Corp.
Borman's
Bothin Foundation
Bovaird Foundation, Mervin

Bowater Inc.
Bremer Foundation, Otto
Bridgestone/Firestone
Bridwell Foundation, J. S.
Briggs & Stratton Corp.
Brillion Iron Works
Bristol-Myers Squibb Co.
Brooks Brothers
Brown & Williamson Tobacco Corp.
Broyhill Family Foundation
Bruening Foundation, Eva L. and Joseph M.
Brunswick Corp.
Burden Foundation, Florence V.
Burlington Northern Inc.
Burndy Corp.
Burns Family Foundation
Bush Foundation
C.P. Rail Systems
Cabot Corp.
Cadbury Beverages Inc.
Cafritz Foundation, Morris and Gwendolyn
Cain Foundation, Gordon and Mary
Callaway Foundation
Cameron Foundation, Harry S. and Isabel C.
Camp and Bennet Humiston Trust, Apollos
Cannon Foundation
Capital Cities/ABC
Capital Fund Foundation
Carolyn Foundation
Carter Foundation, Amon G.
Carter-Wallace
Cartier, Inc.
Cascade Natural Gas Corp.
Caterpillar
Catlin Charitable Trust, Kathleen K.
Central Life Assurance Co.
Central Maine Power Co.
Champion International Corp.
Chapman Charitable Trust, H. A. and Mary K.
Chase Manhattan Bank, N.A.
Cheatham Foundation, Owen
Chesebrough-Pond's
Chevron Corp.
Chicago Resource Center
Chicago Sun-Times, Inc.
Chilton Foundation Trust
Chrysler Corp.
City National Bank
Clark Foundation
Clark-Winchcole Foundation
Clorox Co.
Close Foundation
Clowes Fund
CNG Transmission Corp.
Codrington Charitable Foundation, George W.
Collins & Aikman Holdings Corp.
Colonial Life & Accident Insurance Co.
Colorado Trust
Comer Foundation
Commerce Bancshares, Inc.
Commerce Clearing House
Commonwealth Edison Co.
Comprecare Foundation
ConAgra
Conn Memorial Foundation
Connelly Foundation
Consumers Power Co.
Continental Corp.
Contraves USA
Cook Charitable Foundation
Cooke Foundation
Coors Brewing Co.
Copperweld Steel Co.
Cornell Trust, Peter C.
Cosmair, Inc.
Cowell Foundation, S. H.

Cowles Media Co.
Cox Charitable Trust, Jessie B.
CPC International
CR Industries
Crandall Memorial Foundation, J. Ford
CT Corp. System
Cudahy Fund, Patrick and Anna M.
Cullen/Frost Bankers
Cummins Engine Co.
Curtice-Burns Foods
Daly Charitable Foundation Trust, Robert and Nancy
Dammann Fund
Dana Corp.
Daniel Foundation of Alabama
Danner Foundation
Davidson Family Charitable Foundation
Dean Witter Discover
Decio Foundation, Arthur J.
Deere & Co.
DeKalb Genetics Corp.
Delaware North Cos.
Deluxe Corp.
Dennett Foundation, Marie G.
Deposit Guaranty National Bank
Detroit Edison Co.
Deutsch Co.
Dexter Corp.
Diamond Walnut Growers
Digital Equipment Corp.
Dimeo Construction Co.
Donaldson Co.
Donnelley & Sons Co., R.R.
Dougherty, Jr. Foundation, James R.
Dreyfus Foundation, Max and Victoria
Driscoll Foundation
Drown Foundation, Joseph
du Pont de Nemours & Co., E. I.
Duke Power Co.
Dupar Foundation
Dynamet, Inc.
Eccles Foundation, Marriner S.
Ecolab
Eden Hall Foundation
Educational Foundation of America
El Pomar Foundation
Electronic Data Systems Corp.
Emerson Electric Co.
EMI Records Group
English-Bonter-Mitchell Foundation
Equifax
Ernest & Julio Gallo Winery
Eureka Co.
European American Bank
Exxon Corp.
Factor Family Foundation, Max
Fairfield Foundation, Freeman E.
Farish Fund, William Stamps
Fay's Incorporated
Federal-Mogul Corp.
Federal National Mortgage Assn., Fannie Mae
Federated Department Stores and Allied Stores Corp.
Federated Life Insurance Co.
Feild Co-Operative Association
Fidelity Bank
Field Foundation of Illinois
Fig Tree Foundation
Fikes Foundation, Leland
Fireman's Fund Insurance Co.
First Hawaiian
First Interstate Bank of Arizona
First Interstate Bank of California
First Interstate Bank of Oregon
First Union Corp.
Firstar Bank Milwaukee NA
Fisher Foundation
Fisher Foundation, Max M. and Marjorie S.

Flatley Foundation
Fleming Foundation
Florida Power & Light Co.
Foellinger Foundation
Fondren Foundation
Forbes
Ford Fund, Benson and Edith
Ford Fund, William and Martha
Ford Meter Box Co.
Ford Motor Co.
Forest Oil Corp.
Fort Worth Star Telegram
Foster Co., L.B.
Foundation for Seacoast Health
Fourth Financial Corp.
Franklin Charitable Trust, Ershel
Frederick Foundation
Freedom Forum
Freeport-McMoRan
Friends' Foundation Trust, A.
Frueauff Foundation, Charles A.
Fry Foundation, Lloyd A.
Fuller Co., H.B.
Funderburke & Associates
Funderburke & Associates
Gates Foundation
GATX Corp.
Gazette Co.
GEICO Corp.
General Accident Insurance Co. of America
General American Life Insurance Co.
General Electric Co.
General Mills
General Motors Corp.
General Railway Signal Corp.
General Reinsurance Corp.
GenRad
Georgia-Pacific Corp.
Georgia Power Co.
Gerstacker Foundation, Rollin M.
Gheens Foundation
Giant Food Stores
Gifford Charitable Corporation, Rosamond
Glaxo
Glen Eagles Foundation
Glenmore Distilleries Co.
Globe Newspaper Co.
Goodall Rubber Co.
Grace & Co., W.R.
Grainger Foundation
Graphic Controls Corp.
Graybar Electric Co.
Great-West Life Assurance Co.
Greater Lansing Foundation
Greene Manufacturing Co.
Griffith Foundation, W. C.
GTE Corp.
Guardian Life Insurance Co. of America
Gucci America Inc.
Gulf Power Co.
Haas Foundation, Paul and Mary
Haas Fund, Walter and Elise
Hadson Corp.
Hafif Family Foundation
Hale Foundation, Crescent Porter
Halff Foundation, G. A. C.
Hall Family Foundations
Hall Foundation
Hallmark Cards
Halsell Foundation, Ewing
Hamel Family Charitable Trust, D. A.
Hamilton Oil Corp.
Hanley Family Foundation
Harriman Foundation, Mary W.
Hayden Foundation, Charles
Haynes Foundation, John Randolph and Dora
Hearst Foundation
Hearst Foundation, William Randolph
Hechinger Co.
HEI Inc.

Drugs & Alcohol (cont.)

Heileman Brewing Co., Inc., G.
Heinz Co., H.J.
Heinz Endowment, Vira I.
Herrick Foundation
Hershey Foods Corp.
Herzstein Charitable Foundation, Albert and Ethel
Hill-Snowdon Foundation
Hillcrest Foundation
Hilton Foundation, Conrad N.
Hoblitzelle Foundation
Hoechst Celanese Corp.
Honeywell
Hook Drug
Hoover Foundation
Hospital Corp. of America
Household International
Houston Industries
Hoyt Foundation, Stewart W. and Willma C.
Hubbard Broadcasting
Huffy Corp.
Humane Society of the Commonwealth of Massachusetts
Humphrey Fund, George M. and Pamela S.
Hunt Charitable Trust, C. Giles
Hunter Trust, A. V.
Hyams Foundation
Hyundai Motor America
IBM Corp.
ICI Americas
Illinois Bell
Illinois Tool Works
Indiana Bell Telephone Co.
Indiana Insurance Cos.
Inland Container Corp.
International Flavors & Fragrances
International Paper Co.
Irvine Health Foundation
Island Foundation
Israel Foundation, A. Cremieux
ITT Corp.
ITT Rayonier
Jackson Foundation
James River Corp. of Virginia
JCPenney Co.
Jenkins Foundation, George W.
Jennings Foundation, Martha Holden
Jennings Foundation, Mary Hillman
Jewish Healthcare Foundation of Pittsburgh
JM Foundation
John Hancock Mutual Life Insurance Co.
Johnson Co., E. F.
Johnson Controls
Johnson Foundation, Helen K. and Arthur E.
Johnson Foundation, Robert Wood
Johnson Foundation, Walter S.
Johnson & Higgins
Johnson & Johnson
Jones Family Foundation, Eugenie and Joseph
Julia R. and Estelle L. Foundation
Kanematsu-Gosho U.S.A. Inc.
Kaplen Foundation
Keck, Jr. Foundation, William M.
Keller-Crescent Co.
Kellogg's
Kellwood Co.
Kemper Foundation, Enid and Crosby
Kenedy Memorial Foundation, John G. and Marie Stella
Kennecott Corp.
Kenridge Fund

Kenworthy - Sarah H. Swift Foundation, Marion E.
Kerney Foundation, James
Kerr Foundation
Kimberly-Clark Corp.
King Ranch
Kingsbury Corp.
Kirkland & Ellis
Koehler Foundation, Marcia and Otto
Kresge Foundation
Kulas Foundation
Kysor Industrial Corp.
Lafarge Corp.
Laffey-McHugh Foundation
Large Foundation
Laros Foundation, R. K.
Lechmere
Leonhardt Foundation, Dorothea L.
Lewis Foundation, Frank J.
Liberty Diversified Industries Inc.
Life Insurance Co. of Georgia
Lincoln National Corp.
Lindsay Trust, Agnes M.
Lindstrom Foundation, Kinney
Lipton, Thomas J.
Liquid Air Corp.
Littlefield Foundation, Edmund Wattis
Litton/Itek Optical Systems
Lockheed Sanders
Longwood Foundation
Lost Tree Charitable Foundation
Louisiana Land & Exploration Co.
Louisiana-Pacific Corp.
Love Foundation, Lucyle S.
Lowenstein Foundation, Leon
LTV Corp.
Lurie Foundation, Louis R.
Lydall, Inc.
Mabee Foundation, J. E. and L. E.
Maclellan Foundation
Macy & Co., R.H.
Makita U.S.A., Inc.
Mallinckrodt Specialty Chemicals Co.
Manville Corp.
Mardag Foundation
Maritz Inc.
Mark IV Industries
Mars Foundation
Marsh & McLennan Cos.
Martin Marietta Corp.
Maxus Energy Corp.
May Mitchell Royal Foundation
Maytag Family Foundation, Fred
Mazda Motors of America (Central), Inc.
Mazda North America
Mazza Foundation
MBIA, Inc.
McBeath Foundation, Faye
McBride & Son Associates
McCasland Foundation
McCormick Tribune Foundation, Robert R.
McCune Charitable Trust, John R.
McCune Foundation
McDermott Foundation, Eugene
McDonald & Co. Securities
McDonald & Co. Securities
McDonald's Corp.
McDonnell Douglas Corp.
McDonnell Douglas Corp.-West
McElroy Trust, R. J.
McGovern Fund for the Behavioral Sciences
McGraw Foundation, Donald C.
McGraw-Hill
MCJ Foundation
McKesson Corp.
McMillen Foundation

McWane Inc.
Meadows Foundation
Mebane Packaging Corp.
Medina Foundation
Menasha Corp.
Metropolitan Life Insurance Co.
Meyer Foundation, Alice Kleberg Reynolds
Meyer Foundation, Eugene and Agnes E.
Meyer Foundation, Robert R.
Meyer Memorial Trust
MGIC Investment Corp.
Midwest Resources
Milken Family Medical Foundation
Miller Brewing Co.
Minnesota Mutual Life Insurance Co.
Mobil Oil Corp.
Monell Foundation, Ambrose
Monroe Auto Equipment Co.
Monsanto Co.
Montgomery Street Foundation
Moody Foundation
Moore Business Forms, Inc.
Morris Foundation
Motorola
MTS Systems Corp.
Murch Foundation
Murdy Foundation
Murphy Foundation
Murphy Foundation, John P.
Nalco Chemical Co.
National City Corp.
National Computer Systems
National Fuel Gas Co.
National Gypsum Co.
National Life of Vermont
National Machinery Co.
National Steel
National Westminster Bank New Jersey
Nationwide Insurance Cos.
New England Mutual Life Insurance Co.
New England Telephone Co.
New York Mercantile Exchange
New York Telephone Co.
The New Yorker Magazine, Inc.
News & Observer Publishing Co.
Noble Foundation, Samuel Roberts
Noble Foundation, Vivian Bilby
Nordson Corp.
Norfolk Southern Corp.
Norris Foundation, Kenneth T. and Eileen L.
Northeast Utilities
Northern States Power Co.
Northern Trust Co.
Northwest Natural Gas Co.
Northwestern National Life Insurance Co.
Norton Co.
Noyes, Jr. Memorial Foundation, Nicholas H.
Occidental Oil & Gas Corp.
Oglebay Norton Co.
Ohrstrom Foundation
Old National Bank in Evansville
Olin Corp.
Olympia Brewing Co.
O'Neill Charitable Corporation, F. J.
Ontario Corp.
Open Society Fund
Ormet Corp.
Osher Foundation, Bernard
O'Sullivan Children Foundation
Overbrook Foundation
Overlake Foundation
Overseas Shipholding Group
Owens-Corning Fiberglas Corp.
Oxford Foundation
Pacific Mutual Life Insurance Co.
Pacific Telesis Group

Palmer Fund, Frank Loomis
Panhandle Eastern Corp.
Parker-Hannifin Corp.
Pasadena Area Residential Aid
Pennzoil Co.
Pepsi-Cola Bottling Co. of Charlotte
Perini Corp.
Perkin-Elmer Corp.
Perkin-Elmer Corp.
Persis Corp.
Pew Charitable Trusts
Pfizer
PHH Corp.
Phillips Petroleum Co.
Pineywoods Foundation
Pittsburgh Child Guidance Foundation
Pittway Corp.
Pitzman Fund
Portland General Electric Co.
Potomac Electric Power Co.
Preferred Risk Mutual Insurance Co.
Premier Bank
Prentiss Foundation, Elisabeth Severance
Prickett Fund, Lynn R. and Karl E.
Principal Financial Group
Pritzker Foundation
Procter & Gamble Cosmetic & Fragrance Products
Providence Energy Corp.
Providence Journal Company
Provident Life & Accident Insurance Co.
Provigo Corp. Inc.
Prudential Insurance Co. of America
Public Service Electric & Gas Co.
Puterbaugh Foundation
Quaker Oats Co.
Quantum Chemical Corp.
Questar Corp.
Rachal Foundation, Ed
Ralston Purina Co.
Raskob Foundation for Catholic Activities
Ray Foundation
Recognition Equipment
Reliable Life Insurance Co.
Reliance Electric Co.
Republic New York Corp.
Reynolds Foundation, Z. Smith
Reynolds Metals Co.
Rhone-Poulenc Inc.
Rice Foundation, Ethel and Raymond F.
Riley Foundation, Mabel Louise
Rockwell Fund
Rockwell International Corp.
Rohm and Haas Company
Rohr Inc.
Roseburg Forest Products Co.
Royal Group Inc.
Rubbermaid
Rubinstein Foundation, Helena
Rudin Foundation, Samuel and May
Ryder System
S.G. Foundation
Sachs Fund
SAFECO Corp.
Salomon
Sams Foundation, Earl C.
San Diego Gas & Electric
Sandy Foundation, George H.
Santa Fe Pacific Corp.
Sara Lee Corp.
Sara Lee Hosiery
Sattler Beneficial Trust, Daniel A. and Edna J.
Scaife Family Foundation
Schering-Plough Corp.
Schieffelin & Somerset Co.

Schmidlapp Trust No. 1, Jacob G. Scrivner, Inc.
Seagram & Sons, Joseph E.
Sealright Co., Inc.
Seaver Institute
Seaway Food Town
Security Life of Denver
Sequa Corp.
Shawmut National Corp.
Sheaffer Inc.
Shell Oil Co.
Shoney's Inc.
Simon Foundation, William E. and Carol G.
Simpson Investment Co.
SIT Investment Associates, Inc.
Skandia America Reinsurance Corp.
Skillman Foundation
Skinner Corp.
Smeal Foundation, Mary Jean & Frank P.
Smith Corp., A.O.
Smith Foundation, Kelvin and Eleanor
Smithers Foundation, Christopher D.
SNET
Solo Cup Co.
Sonat
Sonoco Products Co.
Sooner Pipe & Supply Corp.
South Plains Foundation
South Waite Foundation
Southern California Edison Co.
Southwestern Bell Corp.
Speas Foundation, Victor E.
Spiegel
Sprague Educational and Charitable Foundation, Seth
Springs Foundation
Springs Industries
Sprint
Spunk Fund
Stackpole-Hall Foundation
Starr Foundation
Stauffer Foundation, John and Beverly
Steelcase
Sterling Inc.
Sterling Winthrop
Stern Memorial Trust, Sidney
Stewardship Foundation
Stewart Trust under the will of Helen S. Devore, Alexander and Margaret
Stocker Foundation
Stone Foundation
Storage Technology Corp.
Stott Foundation, Louis L.
Strake Foundation
Stratford Foundation
Stride Rite Corp.
Stulsaft Foundation, Morris
Sun Co.
Super Valu Stores
Swalm Foundation
Swift Co. Inc., John S.
Swift Memorial Health Care Foundation
Tandem Computers
Tandy Foundation, Anne Burnett and Charles
Tarmac America Inc.
Taub Foundation
Taubman Foundation, A. Alfred
Taylor Foundation, Ruth and Vernon
TCF Banking & Savings, FSB
Teledyne
Teleflex Inc.
Temple Foundation, T. L. L.
Temple-Inland
Templeton Foundation, Herbert A.
Tenneco
Tetley, Inc.

Texaco
Texas Commerce Bank Houston, N.A.
Texas Gas Transmission Corp.
Texas Instruments
Textron
Thomas Built Buses L.P.
Thorson Foundation
3M Co.
Time Insurance Co.
Tosco Corp. Refining Division
Towsley Foundation, Harry A. and Margaret D.
Toyota Motor Sales, U.S.A.
Tracor, Inc.
Transco Energy Company
Treuhaft Foundation
TRINOVA Corp.
Tropicana Products, Inc.
Trull Foundation
Trust Co. Bank
Turner Charitable Trust, Courtney S.
Unilever United States
Union Camp Corp.
Union Pacific Corp.
United Dominion Industries
United States Trust Co. of New York
United Technologies Corp.
Unitrode Corp.
Universal Foods Corp.
Unocal Corp.
Upjohn Foundation, Harold and Grace
US Bancorp
USF&G Co.
Uslico Corp.
UST
USX Corp.
Valley National Bank of Arizona
Victoria Foundation
Virginia Power Co.
Vogt Machine Co., Henry
Von der Ahe Foundation
Vulcan Materials Co.
Wachovia Bank & Trust Co., N.A.
Wal-Mart Stores
Walgreen Co.
Walker Foundation, Archie D. and Bertha H.
Ware Foundation
Warren Charite
Warren Foundation, William K.
Washington Water Power Co.
Wauwatosa Savings & Loan Association
Wean Foundation, Raymond John
Webb Charitable Trust, Susan Mott
Webster Foundation, Edwin S.
Weingart Foundation
West Co.
West Foundation
Western New York Foundation
Westvaco Corp.
Weyerhaeuser Co.
Weyerhaeuser Family Foundation
Wheless Foundation
Whirlpool Corp.
WICOR, Inc.
Williams Cos.
Wimpey Inc., George
Winnebago Industries, Inc.
Winslow Foundation
Wisconsin Bell, Inc.
Wisconsin Public Service Corp.
Wood Charitable Trust, W. P.
Woods Charitable Fund
Woodward Fund-Atlanta, David, Helen, Marian
Woolf Foundation, William C.
Wrigley Co., Wm. Jr.
Xerox Corp.
Young Foundation, Robert R.
Young & Rubicam

Zigler Foundation, Fred B. and Ruth B.

Emergency Relief

Abbott Laboratories
Adams Foundation, Arthur F. and Alice E.
Ahmanson Foundation
Albertson's
Alltel/Western Region
ALPAC Corp.
Alumax
Aluminum Co. of America
Alyeska Pipeline Service Co.
AMCORE Bank, N.A. Rockford
America West Airlines
American Natural Resources Co.
American United Life Insurance Co.
Ames Department Stores
Amfac/JMB Hawaii
Andersen Corp.
Andersen Foundation, Hugh J.
Anderson Foundation, Peyton
Appleton Papers
Archer-Daniels-Midland Co.
ARCO Chemical
Atherton Family Foundation
Atkinson Foundation, Myrtle L.
Attleboro Pawtucket Savings Bank
Bacardi Imports
Ball Corp.
Bank IV
Bank of America Arizona
Beazley Foundation
Bechtel Group
Bethlehem Steel Corp.
Beveridge Foundation, Frank Stanley
BFGoodrich
BHP Pacific Resources
Block, H&R
Booz Allen & Hamilton
Borman's
Braun Foundation
Brewer and Co., Ltd., C.
Bridgestone/Firestone
Buchalter, Nemer, Fields, & Younger
Burndy Corp.
Burns Foundation, Fritz B.
Cafritz Foundation, Morris and Gwendolyn
Cameron Foundation, Harry S. and Isabel C.
Campbell Foundation, J. Bulow
Carr Real Estate Services
Central Maine Power Co.
Challenge Foundation
Chase Manhattan Bank, N.A.
Chesebrough-Pond's
Chevron Corp.
Chicago Sun-Times, Inc.
Chrysler Corp.
Church & Dwight Co.
Citicorp
Cleveland-Cliffs
Clipper Ship Foundation
CNG Transmission Corp.
Collins & Aikman Holdings Corp.
Colonial Life & Accident Insurance Co.
Cone Mills Corp.
Connecticut Natural Gas Corp.
Cooper Industries
Coors Brewing Co.
Copperweld Steel Co.
Cosmair, Inc.
Cowles Charitable Trust
Cowles Media Co.
Crown Memorial, Arie and Ida
Cudahy Fund, Patrick and Anna M.
Cullen/Frost Bankers
Cummins Engine Co.

Curtice-Burns Foods
Dana Corp.
Davidson Family Charitable Foundation
Davis Foundation, Edwin W. and Catherine M.
Delaware North Cos.
Deluxe Corp.
Digital Equipment Corp.
Dodge Foundation, Cleveland H.
Dodson Foundation, James Glenwell and Clara May
Doheny Foundation, Carrie Estelle
Donaldson Co.
Driscoll Foundation
du Pont de Nemours & Co., E. I.
Duke Power Co.
duPont Foundation, Alfred I.
Durham Merchants Association Charitable Foundation
Eaton Corp.
El Pomar Foundation
English-Bonter-Mitchell Foundation
Enron Corp.
Equifax
Equitable Life Assurance Society of the U.S.
Federal National Mortgage Assn., Fannie Mae
Fidelity Bank
Fireman's Fund Insurance Co.
First Union Corp.
Fish Foundation, Ray C.
Forest Lawn Foundation
Fortis Benefits Insurance Company/Fortis Financial Group
Fowler Memorial Foundation, John Edward
Frederick Foundation
Freedom Forum
Freeport-McMoRan
Funderburke & Associates
Funderburke & Associates
GATX Corp.
GEICO Corp.
General Mills
Glenn Foundation, Carrie C. & Lena V.
Gordon/Rousmaniere/Roberts Fund
Graco
Graybar Electric Co.
GTE Corp.
Haas Fund, Walter and Elise
Hall Foundation
Hallmark Cards
Hancock Foundation, Luke B.
Hansen Foundation, Dane G.
Harmon Foundation, Pearl M. and Julia J.
Harsco Corp.
Hawn Foundation
HEI Inc.
Heinz Endowment, Vira I.
Hermann Foundation, Grover
Hess Charitable Foundation, Ronne and Donald
Hesston Corp.
Heublein
Hillcrest Foundation
Hobby Foundation
Hoffman Foundation, H. Leslie Hoffman and Elaine S.
Hofmann Co.
Honeywell
Hunter Trust, A. V.
IBM Corp.
Inland Container Corp.
ITT Corp.
ITT Hartford Insurance Group
Johnson Foundation, Helen K. and Arthur E.
Johnson & Son, S.C.
Kayser Foundation
Kentland Foundation

Kerr-McGee Corp.
Key Food Stores Cooperative Inc.
Kingsbury Corp.
Laffey-McHugh Foundation
Lawrence Foundation, Lind
Lincoln National Corp.
Lipton, Thomas J.
Little, Arthur D.
Lockheed Sanders
Louisiana Land & Exploration Co.
Louisiana-Pacific Corp.
Lowenstein Foundation, Leon
Lydall, Inc.
Lynn Foundation, E. M.
Macy & Co., R.H.
Manoogian Foundation, Alex and Marie
Mardag Foundation
Maritz Inc.
Mars Foundation
May Foundation, Wilbur
Mayer Foods Corp., Oscar
MCA
McBride & Son Associates
McCann Foundation
McCasland Foundation
McCormick Tribune Foundation, Robert R.
McCormick Trust, Anne
McDonald & Co. Securities
McDonnell Douglas Corp.-West
MCI Communications Corp.
Meadows Foundation
Medina Foundation
Mellon Bank Corp.
Michigan Gas Utilities
Midwest Resources
Mine Safety Appliances Co.
Minnesota Mutual Life Insurance Co.
Mobil Oil Corp.
Moores Foundation, Harry C.
Morton International
National Computer Systems
National Machinery Co.
National Starch & Chemical Corp.
Nationwide Insurance Cos.
New England Mutual Life Insurance Co.
New York Mercantile Exchange
News & Observer Publishing Co.
Normandie Foundation
Northeast Utilities
Northeast Utilities
Northern Indiana Public Service Co.
Northern States Power Co.
Norton Co.
Occidental Oil & Gas Corp.
Oglebay Norton Co.
Oklahoma Gas & Electric Co.
Ormet Corp.
Oxford Industries, Inc.
Pacific Mutual Life Insurance Co.
Packaging Corporation of America
Palmer Fund, Frank Loomis
Pappas Charitable Foundation, Thomas Anthony
Parke-Davis Group
Parsons Foundation, Ralph M.
Pearson Foundation, E. M.
Penn Savings Bank, a division of Sovereign Bank Bank of Princeton, a division of Sovereign Bank
Pennzoil Co.
Perkin-Elmer Corp.
Perkin-Elmer Corp.
Peters Foundation, Leon S.
Pfizer
PHH Corp.
Philip Morris Cos.
Phillips Petroleum Co.
Piper Jaffray Cos.

Pitt-Des Moines Inc.
Plankenhorn Foundation, Harry
Portland General Electric Co.
Premier Industrial Corp.
Price Foundation, Louis and Harold
Pritzker Foundation
Prudential Insurance Co. of America
Pulitzer Publishing Co.
Quaker Oats Co.
Rachal Foundation, Ed
Ritter Foundation, May Ellen and Gerald
Rockwell Fund
Rockwell International Corp.
Rohm and Haas Company
Rohr Inc.
Ross Foundation
Russell Educational Foundation, Benjamin and Roberta
SAFECO Corp.
Salomon
Sams Foundation, Earl C.
San Diego Gas & Electric
Santa Fe Pacific Corp.
Sara Lee Hosiery
Schmidlapp Trust No. 1, Jacob G.
Schwab & Co., Charles
Schwartz Foundation, Bernard Lee
Scott Foundation, Walter
Seabury Foundation
Sealright Co., Inc.
Second Foundation
Security Life of Denver
Shaffer Family Charitable Trust
Shapiro Foundation, Charles and M. R.
Shell Oil Co.
Shenandoah Life Insurance Co.
Shoney's Inc.
Simpson Investment Co.
Skinner Corp.
Smith Charitable Trust, W. W.
Smoot Charitable Foundation
Sonoco Products Co.
Sosland Foundation
South Texas Charitable Foundation
Southern California Edison Co.
Sprague Memorial Institute, Otho S. A.
Springs Industries
Square D Co.
Starr Foundation
Sterling Winthrop
Sun Co.
Tandy Foundation, Anne Burnett and Charles
Taylor Foundation, Ruth and Vernon
Teledyne
Tenneco
Texas Instruments
Textron
Thermo Electron Corp.
3M Co.
Torchmark Corp.
Tosco Corp. Refining Division
Tracor, Inc.
Trull Foundation
Trust Co. Bank
21 International Holdings
Union Bank of Switzerland Los Angeles Branch
Union Camp Corp.
Union Carbide Corp.
Union Electric Co.
Universal Foods Corp.
USG Corp.
Vogt Machine Co., Henry
Vulcan Materials Co.
Wal-Mart Stores
Ware Foundation
Washington Water Power Co.
Weingart Foundation

Recipient Type Index

3295

Emergency Relief (cont.)

West Co.
Wetterau
Williams Cos.
Woodward Governor Co.

Employment/Job Training

Abell-Hanger Foundation
Abraham & Straus
Achelis Foundation
Advanced Micro Devices
Ahmanson Foundation
AlliedSignal
Alltel/Western Region
ALPAC Corp.
Altman Foundation
Alumax
Aluminum Co. of America
AMAX
American Brands
American Electric Power
American Express Co.
American Financial Corp.
American Natural Resources Co.
American Stock Exchange
American Telephone & Telegraph Co.
American United Life Insurance Co.
Ameritech Corp.
Ames Department Stores
Amoco Corp.
Andersen Foundation, Hugh J.
Anheuser-Busch Cos.
AON Corp.
Apache Corp.
Apple Computer, Inc.
Arcana Foundation
ARCO
ARCO Chemical
Atkinson Foundation
Atlanta Gas Light Co.
Attleboro Pawtucket Savings Bank
Austin Memorial Foundation
Avon Products
Babcock Foundation, Mary Reynolds
Badger Meter, Inc.
Badgeley Residuary Charitable Trust, Rose M.
Badger Meter, Inc.
Bank of America Arizona
Bank of Boston Connecticut
Bank of Boston Corp.
Bank of Tokyo Trust Co.
Bankers Trust Co.
Battelle
Batts Foundation
Bauer Foundation, M. R.
Bausch & Lomb
Bechtel Charitable Remainder Uni-Trust, Marie H.
Bemis Company
Ben & Jerry's Homemade
Benedum Foundation, Claude Worthington
Bethlehem Steel Corp.
Bigelow Foundation, F. R.
Block, H&R
Boatmen's Bancshares
Boatmen's First National Bank of Oklahoma
Booth Ferris Foundation
Boston Edison Co.
Brach Foundation, Helen
Bradley Foundation, Lynde and Harry
Bridgestone/Firestone
Bristol-Myers Squibb Co.
Brown & Williamson Tobacco Corp.

Bruening Foundation, Eva L. and Joseph M.
Buchanan Family Foundation
Buhl Foundation
Burden Foundation, Florence V.
Burndy Corp.
Bush Foundation
C.P. Rail Systems
Cabot Corp.
Cafritz Foundation, Morris and Gwendolyn
Calder Foundation, Louis
Campbell Soup Co.
Capital Cities/ABC
Cargill
Carr Real Estate Services
Centerior Energy Corp.
Central Maine Power Co.
Chambers Development Co.
Chase Charity Foundation, Alfred E.
Chase Manhattan Bank, N.A.
Chemical Bank
Chevron Corp.
Chicago Sun-Times, Inc.
Chicago Title and Trust Co.
Chicago Tribune Co.
CIGNA Corp.
Citicorp
Clark Foundation
Clipper Ship Foundation
Clorox Co.
CM Alliance Cos.
CM Alliance Cos.
CNA Insurance Cos.
Coleman Co.
Colonial Life & Accident Insurance Co.
Columbia Foundation
Commerce Clearing House
Commonwealth Fund
Conn Memorial Foundation
Cooke Foundation
Coors Foundation, Adolph
Cowell Foundation, S. H.
Cowles Charitable Trust
Cowles Media Co.
CPC International
Crown Memorial, Arie and Ida
Cullen/Frost Bankers
Cummings Foundation, Nathan
Cummings Memorial Fund Trust, Frances L. and Edwin L.
Cummins Engine Co.
Curtice-Burns Foods
Danner Foundation
Davis Foundation, James A. and Juliet L.
Dayton Hudson Corp.
Devonshire Associates
Digital Equipment Corp.
Donaldson Co.
Donaldson Co.
Donnelley & Sons Co., R.R.
Donner Foundation, William H.
Dower Foundation, Thomas W.
Dresser Industries
Dreyfus Foundation, Max and Victoria
du Pont de Nemours & Co., E. I.
Duncan Trust, John G.
Eaton Corp.
Eccles Foundation, Marriner S.
Echlin Inc.
Electronic Data Systems Corp.
Elf Atochem North America
Ellis Grant and Scholarship Fund, Charles E.
Equifax
Equitable Life Assurance Society of the U.S.
Ernest & Julio Gallo Winery
Exxon Corp.
Federated Department Stores and Allied Stores Corp.
Fel-Pro Incorporated
Fidelity Bank

Fieldcrest Cannon
Fireman's Fund Insurance Co.
First Bank System
First Brands Corp.
First Interstate Bank of Arizona
First Interstate Bank of California
First Interstate Bank of Oregon
First Union Corp.
Fisher Foundation
Flagler Foundation
Flintridge Foundation
Florida Power Corp.
Florida Power & Light Co.
FMC Corp.
Ford Foundation
Ford Motor Co.
Forest Lawn Foundation
Fox Charitable Foundation, Harry K. & Emma R.
Frankel Foundation
Freedom Forum
Freeport-McMoRan
Friedman Family Foundation
Frueauff Foundation, Charles A.
Fry Foundation, Lloyd A.
Fuchs Foundation, Gottfried & Mary
Funderburke & Associates
Funderburke & Associates
Gallo Foundation, Julio R.
Gates Foundation
GATX Corp.
General Electric Co.
General Mills
General Motors Corp.
General Reinsurance Corp.
Georgia Power Co.
Giant Food
Gillette Co.
Glaxo
Glenn Foundation, Carrie C. & Lena V.
Glickenhaus & Co.
Globe Newspaper Co.
Goldman Foundation, Herman
Goldseker Foundation of Maryland, Morris
Grace & Co., W.R.
Graco
Gradison & Co.
Grainger Foundation
Graphic Controls Corp.
Great Western Financial Corp.
Greenfield Foundation, Albert M.
Greentree Foundation
Greenville Foundation
Griggs and Mary Griggs Burke Foundation, Mary Livingston
GTE Corp.
Haas, Jr. Fund, Evelyn and Walter
Haigh-Scatena Foundation
Hall Foundation
Hallmark Cards
Hancock Foundation, Luke B.
Harris Trust & Savings Bank
Harsco Corp.
Hartz Foundation
Hatterscheidt Foundation
Hayden Foundation, Charles
Hazen Foundation, Edward W.
Hearst Foundation
Hearst Foundation, William Randolph
Hechinger Co.
HEI Inc.
Heinz Co., H.J.
Hershey Foods Corp.
Hervey Foundation
Hewlett Foundation, William and Flora
Hill Foundation
Hillcrest Foundation
Hillman Foundation
Hoblitzelle Foundation
Holtzmann Foundation, Jacob L. and Lillian

Home Depot
Honeywell
Hospital Corp. of America
Household International
Hunt Alternatives Fund
Hunt Manufacturing Co.
Hunter Trust, A. V.
Hyams Foundation
Hyde and Watson Foundation
I. and L. Association
IBM Corp.
IBM South Africa Projects Fund
ICI Americas
IDS Financial Services
Illinois Tool Works
Indiana Bell Telephone Co.
Indiana Insurance Cos.
Inland Steel Industries
Interco
International Flavors & Fragrances
International Foundation
Irvine Foundation, James
ITT Corp.
ITT Hartford Insurance Group
Ivakota Association
J.P. Morgan & Co.
James River Corp. of Virginia
JCPenney Co.
Jennings Foundation, Mary Hillman
John Hancock Mutual Life Insurance Co.
Johnson Foundation, Helen K. and Arthur E.
Johnson & Johnson
Johnson & Son, S.C.
Jones Foundation, Harvey and Bernice
Kaiser Cement Corp.
Keebler Co.
Kellogg Foundation, W. K.
Kennecott Corp.
Kettering Fund
Kiewit Foundation, Peter
Kiplinger Foundation
Knott Foundation, Marion I. and Henry J.
Koret Foundation
Laffey-McHugh Foundation
Land O'Lakes
Lane Foundation, Minnie and Bernard
Lattner Foundation, Forrest C.
Legg Mason Inc.
Levi Strauss & Co.
Liberty National Bank
Life Insurance Co. of Georgia
Lincoln Fund
Lincoln National Corp.
Little, Arthur D.
Long Island Lighting Co.
Longwood Foundation
Lotus Development Corp.
Louisiana Power & Light Co./New Orleans Public Service
Lowenstein Foundation, Leon
LTV Corp.
Luce Charitable Trust, Theodore
Lurie Foundation, Louis R.
Lux Foundation, Miranda
Lytel Foundation, Bertha Russ
M. E. G. Foundation
Macy & Co., R.H.
Manville Corp.
Mardag Foundation
Maritz Inc.
Marriott Corp.
Marshall Field's
Maxon Charitable Foundation
May Department Stores Co.
MBIA, Inc.
MCA
McCormick Tribune Foundation, Robert R.
McCune Foundation

McDonald's Corp.
McGovern Fund for the Behavioral Sciences
McGraw-Hill
MCI Communications Corp.
MCJ Foundation
McKnight Foundation
Meadows Foundation
Meridian Bancorp
Metropolitan Life Insurance Co.
Meyer Foundation, Eugene and Agnes E.
MGIC Investment Corp.
Michigan Consolidated Gas Co.
Midwest Resources
Milken Institute for Job and Capital Formation
Minnesota Mutual Life Insurance Co.
Mitsubishi International Corp.
MNC Financial
Mobil Oil Corp.
Morgan Stanley & Co.
Motorola
Mott Foundation, Charles Stewart
MTS Systems Corp.
Murch Foundation
Murphy Foundation, John P.
Nalco Chemical Co.
National Computer Systems
National Fuel Gas Co.
National Steel
National Westminster Bank New Jersey
Nationwide Insurance Cos.
NEC USA
Nestle U.S.A. Inc.
New England Mutual Life Insurance Co.
New York Foundation
New York Life Insurance Co.
New York Telephone Co.
News & Observer Publishing Co.
Nissan Motor Corporation in U.S.A.
Nordson Corp.
Norfolk Southern Corp.
Northern Indiana Public Service Co.
Northern States Power Co.
Northern Trust Co.
Northwest Area Foundation
Northwestern National Life Insurance Co.
Noyes, Jr. Memorial Foundation, Nicholas H.
NuTone Inc.
NYNEX Corp.
Ohl, Jr. Trust, George A.
Olsson Memorial Foundation, Elis
1525 Foundation
O'Neill Charitable Corporation, F. J.
Ordean Foundation
Overbrook Foundation
PACCAR
Pacific Gas & Electric Co.
Pacific Mutual Life Insurance Co.
Packard Foundation, David and Lucile
Panhandle Eastern Corp.
Parsons Foundation, Ralph M.
Penn Foundation, William
People's Bank
Peoples Energy Corp.
Perkin-Elmer Corp.
Perkin-Elmer Corp.
Pew Charitable Trusts
Pfizer
Philip Morris Cos.
Philips Foundation, Jesse
Phillips Foundation, Dr. P.
Phillips Petroleum Co.
Phoenix Home Life Mutual Insurance Co.
Pick, Jr. Fund, Albert

Pillsbury Co.
Pines Bridge Foundation
Pioneer Hi-Bred International
Pitney Bowes
Pittsburgh National Bank
Playboy Enterprises, Inc.
Potomac Electric Power Co.
PPG Industries
Primerica Corp.
Principal Financial Group
Pritzker Foundation
Prudential Insurance Co. of America
Public Service Electric & Gas Co.
Public Welfare Foundation
Pulitzer Publishing Co.
Quaker Oats Co.
Ralston Purina Co.
Raskob Foundation for Catholic Activities
Relations Foundation
Republic New York Corp.
Retirement Research Foundation
Reynolds Foundation, Christopher
Reynolds Foundation, Richard S.
Reynolds Foundation, Z. Smith
Riley Foundation, Mabel Louise
Roche Relief Foundation, Edward and Ellen
Rockwell Fund
Rockwell International Corp.
Rohm and Haas Company
Rouse Co.
Rowland Foundation
Rubin Foundation, Samuel
Rubinstein Foundation, Helena
Russell Memorial Foundation, Robert
SAFECO Corp.
Salomon
San Diego Gas & Electric
Santa Fe Pacific Corp.
Sara Lee Corp.
Sarkeys Foundation
Scherman Foundation
Schrafft and Bertha E. Schrafft Charitable Trust, William E.
Schwab & Co., Charles
Science Applications International Corp.
Scrivner, Inc.
Seafirst Corp.
Sears Family Foundation
Sears, Roebuck and Co.
Seymour Foundation, W. L. and Louise E.
Shaw Foundation, Gardiner Howland
Shawmut National Corp.
Shawmut Worcester County Bank, N.A.
Sheaffer Inc.
Shenandoah Life Insurance Co.
Shoney's Inc.
Signet Bank/Maryland
Silverburgh Foundation, Grace, George & Judith
Silverman Foundation, Marty and Dorothy
Simpson Investment Co.
Skinner Corp.
Smoot Charitable Foundation
Sonat
Sosland Foundation
Spiegel
Sprague Educational and Charitable Foundation, Seth
Springs Industries
Stackpole-Hall Foundation
Starr Foundation
State Street Bank & Trust Co.
Stearns Charitable Foundation, Anna B.
Stein Foundation, Jules and Doris
Sterling Winthrop

Stern Memorial Trust, Sidney
Stewardship Foundation
Straus Foundation, Aaron and Lillie
Strong Foundation, Hattie M.
Stulsaft Foundation, Morris
Sumitomo Bank of California
Sun Co.
Sun Microsystems
Super Valu Stores
Taconic Foundation
Tandy Foundation, Anne Burnett and Charles
Taub Foundation, Henry and Marilyn
TDK Corp. of America
Teleklew Productions
Temple Foundation, T. L. L.
Tenneco
Texaco
Texas Commerce Bank Houston, N.A.
Textron
Thermo Electron Corp.
3M Co.
Time Insurance Co.
Times Mirror Co.
TJX Cos.
Town Creek Foundation
Tracor, Inc.
Transco Energy Company
Trees Charitable Trust, Edith L.
Tropicana Products, Inc.
Trull Foundation
Trust Co. Bank
Unilever United States
Union Camp Corp.
United Airlines
U.S. Leasing International
Unitrode Corp.
Universal Leaf Tobacco Co.
Uris Brothers Foundation
US Bancorp
US WEST
USX Corp.
Valley National Bank of Arizona
Victoria Foundation
Virginia Power Co.
Vogt Machine Co., Henry
Walker Foundation, Archie D. and Bertha H.
Wallace-Reader's Digest Fund, DeWitt
Wean Foundation, Raymond John
Webster Foundation, Edwin S.
Weinberg Foundation, John L.
Wells Fargo & Co.
Wendt Foundation, Margaret L.
Western Resources
Westvaco Corp.
Weyerhaeuser Co.
Whirlpool Corp.
Whitaker Foundation
Whitehead Foundation
Wickes Foundation, Harvey Randall
WICOR, Inc.
Winston Foundation, Norman and Rosita
Wisconsin Bell, Inc.
Woodward Fund-Atlanta, David, Helen, Marian
Wrigley Co., Wm. Jr.
Xerox Corp.
Young & Rubicam

Family Planning

Abell-Hanger Foundation
Abrons Foundation, Louis and Anne
Adler Foundation
Ahmanson Foundation
AKC Fund
Alexander Foundation, Joseph
Alltel/Western Region
Allyn Foundation

Allyn Foundation
Alms Trust, Eleanora
ALPAC Corp.
Altman Foundation
Aluminum Co. of America
Andersen Corp.
Andersen Foundation, Hugh J.
Anderson Foundation, John W.
Anderson Foundation, William P.
Andersons Management Corp.
Annenberg Foundation
Appleman Foundation
Archer-Daniels-Midland Co.
Armstrong World Industries Inc.
Atkinson Foundation
Ayres Foundation, Inc.
Babson Foundation, Paul and Edith
Baird Foundation, Cameron
Baker Trust, Clayton
Baldwin Foundation
Banbury Fund
Bank of A. Levy
Barker Welfare Foundation
Barra Foundation
Battelle
Batts Foundation
Bauer Foundation, M. R.
Bausch & Lomb
Beaver Foundation
Beecher Foundation, Florence Simon
Beerman Foundation
Beidler Charitable Trust, Francis
Beim Foundation
Belk Stores
Belmont Metals
Beloit Foundation
Bemis Company
Bender Foundation
Bergstrom Foundation, Erik E. and Edith H.
Bernstein Foundation, Diane and Norman
Berry Foundation, Loren M.
Berry Foundation, Lowell
Bersted Foundation
Berwind Corp.
Bettingen Corporation, Burton G.
Bicknell Fund
Bingham Second Betterment Fund, William
Bishop Foundation, E. K. and Lillian F.
Bissell Foundation, J. Walton
Blair Foundation, John
Blank Fund, Myron and Jacqueline
Bleibtreu Foundation, Jacob
Blinken Foundation
Block, H&R
Blum Foundation, Edna F.
Blum Foundation, Lois and Irving
Bodine Corp.
Borden Memorial Foundation, Mary Owen
Bovaird Foundation, Mervin
Brach Foundation, Edwin I.
Breidenthal Foundation, Willard J. and Mary G.
Brenner Foundation, Mervyn
Breyer Foundation
Britton Fund
Broccoli Charitable Foundation, Dana and Albert R.
Bronstein Foundation, Sol and Arlene
Brown Foundation
Brown Foundation, W. L. Lyons
Browning Charitable Foundation, Val A.
Brunswick Corp.
Brush Foundation
Buchanan Family Foundation
Buffett Foundation
Bull Foundation, Henry W.

Bunbury Company
Burndy Corp.
Burns Foundation, Fritz B.
Butler Family Foundation, Patrick and Aimee
Bydale Foundation
Cabot Family Charitable Trust
Cain Foundation, Gordon and Mary
Campbell and Adah E. Hall Charity Fund, Bushrod H.
Cannon Foundation
Capital Fund Foundation
Carnegie Corporation of New York
Carpenter Technology Corp.
Carter Foundation, Beirne
Carter-Wallace
Casey Foundation, Eugene B.
Cassett Foundation, Louis N.
Cayuga Foundation
Central Maine Power Co.
Chadwick Foundation
Chait Memorial Foundation, Sara
Champlin Foundations
Charter Manufacturing Co.
Chartwell Foundation
Chase Manhattan Bank, N.A.
Chatham Valley Foundation
CHC Foundation
Chicago Sun-Times, Inc.
Children's Foundation of Erie County
Clabir Corp.
Claneil Foundation
Clark Foundation
Clark Foundation, Robert Sterling
Clipper Ship Foundation
Clorox Co.
Clowes Fund
Cohen Family Foundation, Saul Z. and Amy Scheuer
Cohen Foundation, Naomi and Nehemiah
Cohen Foundation, Wilfred P.
Cohn Foundation, Herman and Terese
Collins Foundation
Collins Foundation, Carr P.
Colonial Life & Accident Insurance Co.
Columbus Dispatch Printing Co.
Comer Foundation
Commerce Bancshares, Inc.
Compton Foundation
Confidence Foundation
Consolidated Papers
Cooke Foundation
Copperweld Steel Co.
Cornell Trust, Peter C.
Country Curtains, Inc.
Cowell Foundation, S. H.
Cowles Charitable Trust
Cowles Foundation, Gardner and Florence Call
Cowles Media Co.
Crary Foundation, Bruce L.
Crestlea Foundation
CRI Charitable Trust
Crummer Foundation, Roy E.
Crystal Trust
Cudahy Fund, Patrick and Anna M.
Cuesta Foundation
Cummings Foundation, Nathan
Cummings Memorial Fund Trust, Frances L. and Edwin L.
Cummins Engine Co.
Curtice-Burns Foods
Dain Bosworth/Inter-Regional Financial Group
Dana Co.
Daniels Foundation, Fred Harris
Davenport-Hatch Foundation
Davis Foundation, James A. and Juliet L.

Day Foundation, Cecil B.
Day Foundation, Nancy Sayles
Dee Foundation, Lawrence T. and Janet T.
Delavan Foundation, Nelson B.
DeMoss Foundation, Arthur S.
Deuble Foundation, George H.
Deutsch Co.
Dewar Foundation
Diamond Foundation, Aaron
Dillon Foundation
Dimeo Construction Co.
Dimick Foundation
Dodge Foundation, Cleveland H.
Dodge Foundation, Geraldine R.
Donaldson Co.
Dougherty, Jr. Foundation, James R.
Douty Foundation
Dover Foundation
Dresser Industries
Dreyfus Foundation, Jean and Louis
Drown Foundation, Joseph
Duke Power Co.
Dumke Foundation, Dr. Ezekiel R. and Edna Wattis
Dunagan Foundation
Dunspaugh-Dalton Foundation
duPont Foundation, Chichester
Durst Foundation
Dyson Foundation
Earl-Beth Foundation
Eaton Foundation, Cyrus
Eccles Charitable Foundation, Willard L.
Eccles Foundation, Marriner S.
Educational Foundation of America
Edwards Foundation, O. P. and W. E.
Edwards Industries
Eisenberg Foundation, Ben B. and Joyce E.
Emery Memorial, Thomas J.
Engelhard Foundation, Charles
Ettinger Foundation
Falk Medical Fund, Maurice
Fanwood Foundation
Farish Fund, William Stamps
Favrot Fund
Federated Department Stores and Allied Stores Corp.
Federated Life Insurance Co.
Fels Fund, Samuel S.
Fidelity Bank
Fife Foundation, Elias and Bertha
Fikes Foundation, Leland
First Union Corp.
Fish Foundation, Ray C.
Fishback Foundation Trust, Harmes C.
Fisher Foundation
Forbes
Ford Foundation
Ford Fund, Benson and Edith
Ford Fund, Walter and Josephine
Forest Foundation
Forest Fund
Fort Worth Star Telegram
Foster Co., L.B.
Foundation for Child Development
Foundation for Seacoast Health
Foundation for the Needs of Others
Franklin Foundation, John and Mary
Freed Foundation
Freeman Charitable Trust, Samuel
Freeman Foundation, Ella West
Frees Foundation
French Foundation
French Oil Mill Machinery Co.
Frohring Foundation, Paul & Maxine

Family Planning (cont.)

Replogle Foundation, Luther I.
Reynolds Foundation, Z. Smith
Richardson Fund, Mary Lynn
Rigler-Deutsch Foundation
Riley Foundation, Mabel Louise
Ritter Foundation
River Branch Foundation
Robinson Fund, Charles Nelson
Robinson Mountain Fund, E. O.
Roblee Foundation, Joseph H. and Florence A.
Rockefeller Foundation
Rockwell Fund
Rohr Inc.
Rose Foundation, Billy
Rosenbaum Foundation, Paul and Gabriella
Rosenthal Foundation, Samuel
Roth Family Foundation
Rowland Foundation
Ruan Foundation Trust, John
Rubinstein Foundation, Helena
Rutgers Community Health Foundation
Sailors' Snug Harbor of Boston
St. Faith's House Foundation
Sara Lee Corp.
Sasco Foundation
Schadt Foundation
Schenck Fund, L. P.
Scherman Foundation
Schiff Foundation
Schiff Foundation, Dorothy
Schiro Fund
Schmidlapp Trust No. 1, Jacob G.
Schneiderman Foundation, Roberta and Irwin
Schoenleber Foundation
Schramm Foundation
Schultz Foundation
Schwartz Foundation, David
Sears Family Foundation
Seay Memorial Trust, George and Effie
Seevak Family Foundation
Segal Charitable Trust, Barnet
Sequoia Foundation
Sewall Foundation, Elmina
Seybert Institution for Poor Boys and Girls, Adam and Maria Sarah
Share Foundation
Sharp Foundation, Evelyn
Shawmut National Corp.
Shoenberg Foundation
Shwayder Foundation, Fay
Sierra Pacific Resources
Silver Spring Foundation
Simone Foundation
Simpson Foundation, John M.
Skinner Corp.
Smith Charitable Fund, Eleanor Armstrong
Smith Fund, George D.
Smithers Foundation, Christopher D.
Sprague Educational and Charitable Foundation, Seth
Stanley Charitable Foundation, A. W.
Starr Foundation
Stearns Charitable Foundation, Anna B.
Steel, Sr. Foundation, Marshall
Steelcase
Steele Foundation, Harry and Grace
Steele-Reese Foundation
Stein Foundation, Jules and Doris
Steinberg Family Foundation, Meyer and Jean
Steinman Foundation, James Hale
Steinman Foundation, John Frederick
Sterkel Trust, Justine
Stern Family Foundation, Alex
Stern Memorial Trust, Sidney

Sterne-Elder Memorial Trust
Stewardship Foundation
Stocker Foundation
Stone Charitable Foundation
Stone Container Corp.
Stott Foundation, Louis L.
Stowe, Jr. Foundation, Robert Lee
Straus Foundation, Aaron and Lillie
Straus Foundation, Philip A. and Lynn
Strawbridge Foundation of Pennsylvania II, Margaret Dorrance
Stulsaft Foundation, Morris
Sunnen Foundation
Swensrud Charitable Trust, Sidney A.
Taconic Foundation
Tandy Foundation, Anne Burnett and Charles
Taubman Foundation, A. Alfred
Taylor Foundation, Ruth and Vernon
Teleklew Productions
Tennant Co.
Textron
Thanksgiving Foundation
Thomas Memorial Foundation, Theresa A.
Three Swallows Foundation
Thurman Charitable Foundation for Children, Edgar A.
Time Insurance Co.
Times Mirror Co.
Tippit Charitable Trust, C. Carlisle and Margaret M.
Tiscornia Foundation
Tortuga Foundation
Tracor, Inc.
Treadwell Foundation, Nora Eccles
True North Foundation
Trull Foundation
Trust Funds
Tucker Charitable Trust, Rose E.
Tucker Foundation, Marcia Brady
Tuohy Foundation, Alice Tweed
Union Camp Corp.
Universal Foods Corp.
Uris Brothers Foundation
USF&G Co.
van Loben Sels - Eleanor Slate van Lobel Sels Charitable Foundation, Ernst D.
Vance Charitable Foundation, Robert C.
Vanderbilt Trust, R. T.
Vaughan Foundation, Rachael and Ben
Vaughn Foundation
Victoria Foundation
Wachovia Bank & Trust Co., N.A.
Walker Foundation, Smith
Walker Foundation, T. B.
Wallach Foundation, Miriam G. and Ira D.
Wallin Foundation
Walter Family Trust, Byron L.
Wardlaw Fund, Gertrude and William C.
Wardle Family Foundation
Washington Square Fund
Waters Foundation
Watumull Fund, J.
Wean Foundation, Raymond John
Webb Foundation
Weber Charities Corp., Frederick E.
Webster Foundation, Edwin S.
Weeden Foundation, Frank
Weil, Gotshal & Manges Foundation
Weiler Foundation
Weiss Fund, Clara

Welch Testamentary Trust, George T.
Wells Foundation, Franklin H. and Ruth L.
Wessinger Foundation
Westport Fund
Whirlpool Corp.
Wien Foundation, Lawrence A.
Wiener Foundation, Malcolm Hewitt
Willard Foundation, Helen Parker
Williams Cos.
Wimpey Inc., George
Winona Corporation
Witte, Jr. Foundation, John H.
Wolff Memorial Foundation, Pauline Sterne
Wollenberg Foundation
Women's Project Foundation
Wood Charitable Trust, W. P.
Wood-Claeyssens Foundation
Woodland Foundation
Woods Charitable Fund
Wright Foundation, Lola
Wurts Memorial, Henrietta Tower
Wyomissing Foundation
Wyss Foundation
Zarrow Foundation, Anne and Henry
Zemurray Foundation
Zlinkoff Fund for Medical Research and Education, Sergei S.

Family Services
Abell-Hanger Foundation
Abraham Foundation
Abrams Foundation
Achelis Foundation
Acushnet Co.
Adams Trust, Charles E. and Caroline J.
Ahmanson Foundation
Air Products & Chemicals
Alabama Power Co.
Alberto-Culver Co.
Alcon Laboratories, Inc.
Alexander Charitable Foundation
Allegheny Ludlum Corp.
Allendale Mutual Insurance Co.
AlliedSignal
Alltel/Western Region
Allyn Foundation
Allyn Foundation
Alms Trust, Eleanora
ALPAC Corp.
Altman Foundation
Aluminum Co. of America
AMAX
AMCORE Bank, N.A. Rockford
American Express Co.
American Home Products Corp.
American National Bank & Trust Co. of Chicago
American Saw & Manufacturing Co.
American Telephone & Telegraph Co.
American United Life Insurance Co.
Amfac/JMB Hawaii
Amoco Corp.
AMP
AMR Corp.
Andersen Corp.
Andersen Foundation
Andersen Foundation, Hugh J.
Anderson Foundation, John W.
Andersons Management Corp.
Ansin Private Foundation, Ronald M.
Ansley Foundation, Dantzler Bond
Apache Corp.
Apple Computer, Inc.
Appleman Foundation
Arcana Foundation

Arkell Hall Foundation
Arrillaga Foundation
Asea Brown Boveri
Atkinson Foundation
Atlanta Gas Light Co.
Attleboro Pawtucket Savings Bank
Auerbach Foundation, Beatrice Fox
Austin Memorial Foundation
Autzen Foundation
Avis Inc.
Avon Products
Ayres Foundation, Inc.
Babson Foundation, Paul and Edith
Bacardi Imports
Bacon Trust, Charles F.
Baker Foundation, R. C.
Baker, Jr. Memorial Fund, William G.
Baker Trust, Clayton
Ball Brothers Foundation
Banbury Fund
Banfi Vintners
Bank of America Arizona
Bank of Boston Corp.
Bank of New York
BankAmerica Corp.
Bannan Foundation, Arline and Thomas J.
Bard, C. R.
Barker Foundation, J. M. R.
Barker Welfare Foundation
Barry Corp., R. G.
Bassett Foundation, Norman
Bastien Memorial Foundation, John E. and Nellie J.
Battelle
Bauer Foundation, M. R.
Becton Dickinson & Co.
Bedsole Foundation, J. L.
Behmann Brothers Foundation
Beinecke Foundation
Beir Foundation
Beloit Foundation
Bemis Company
Bender Foundation
Benwood Foundation
Berry Foundation, Lowell
Besser Foundation
Bethlehem Steel Corp.
Betts Industries
Beveridge Foundation, Frank Stanley
Bierhaus Foundation
Binney & Smith Inc.
Bishop Foundation
Bishop Foundation, E. K. and Lillian F.
Bishop Trust for the SPCA of Manatee County, Florida, Lillian H.
Blair and Co., William
Blandin Foundation
Blank Fund, Myron and Jacqueline
Blaustein Foundation, Jacob and Hilda
Block, H&R
Blount
Blowitz-Ridgeway Foundation
Boettcher Foundation
Boisi Family Foundation
Bolz Family Foundation, Eugenie Mayer
Booth Ferris Foundation
Borden
Borden Memorial Foundation, Mary Owen
Borg-Warner Corp.
Borman's
Boston Edison Co.
Bostwick Foundation, Albert C.
Brach Foundation, Edwin I.
Brach Foundation, Helen

Bradley Foundation, Lynde and Harry
Brand Cos.
Breidenthal Foundation, Willard J. and Mary G.
Brenner Foundation, Mervyn
Bridgestone/Firestone
Broccoli Charitable Foundation, Dana and Albert R.
Brochsteins Inc.
Brooks Brothers
Brown Foundation
Brown Foundation, James Graham
Brown & Williamson Tobacco Corp.
Bruening Foundation, Eva L. and Joseph M.
Brunswick Corp.
Bryce Memorial Fund, William and Catherine
Bucyrus-Erie
Bull Foundation, Henry W.
Bunbury Company
Burden Foundation, Florence V.
Burlington Industries
Burndy Corp.
Bush Foundation
Bydale Foundation
C.P. Rail Systems
Caddock Foundation
Cahn Family Foundation
Calder Foundation, Louis
Calhoun Charitable Trust, Kenneth
Capital Cities/ABC
Capital Holding Corp.
Carnegie Corporation of New York
Carolyn Foundation
Carpenter Foundation
Carpenter Foundation, E. Rhodes and Leona B.
Carpenter Technology Corp.
Carter Foundation, Amon G.
Cascade Natural Gas Corp.
Casey Foundation, Annie E.
Castle Trust, George P. and Ida Tenney
Cayuga Foundation
Central Bank of the South
Central Fidelity Banks, Inc.
Central Life Assurance Co.
Central Maine Power Co.
Chartwell Foundation
Chase Manhattan Bank, N.A.
Chatham Valley Foundation
CHC Foundation
Chevron Corp.
Chicago Sun-Times, Inc.
Children's Foundation of Erie County
Childress Foundation, Francis and Miranda
Citicorp
Claneil Foundation
Clark Foundation, Edna McConnell
Clark-Winchcole Foundation
Clay Foundation
Clipper Ship Foundation
Clorox Co.
Clowes Fund
CNA Insurance Cos.
Cockrell Foundation
Codrington Charitable Foundation, George W.
Cogswell Benevolent Trust
Cohen Family Foundation, Saul Z. and Amy Scheuer
Cole National Corp.
Collins Foundation, Carr P.
Collins Medical Trust
Colonial Life & Accident Insurance Co.
Colonial Oil Industries, Inc.
Coltec Industries
Comer Foundation

Family Services
(cont.)

Comer Foundation
Commerce Clearing House
Community Hospital Foundation
Comstock Foundation
ConAgra
Conn Memorial Foundation
Connelly Foundation
Continental Corp.
Cooke Foundation
Coors Foundation, Adolph
Copperweld Steel Co.
Country Curtains, Inc.
Cowell Foundation, S. H.
Cowles Media Co.
Cox Enterprises
CPC International
Craigmyle Foundation
Crandall Memorial Foundation, J. Ford
Crapo Charitable Foundation, Henry H.
Cremer Foundation
Crown Memorial, Arie and Ida
Crystal Trust
CT Corp. System
CTS Corp.
Cudahy Fund, Patrick and Anna M.
Cuesta Foundation
Cullen/Frost Bankers
Culpeper Memorial Foundation, Daphne Seybolt
Cummings Memorial Fund Trust, Frances L. and Edwin L.
Cummins Engine Co.
CUNA Mutual Insurance Group
Curtice-Burns Foods
Dain Bosworth/Inter-Regional Financial Group
Dalton Foundation, Dorothy U.
Daly Charitable Foundation Trust, Robert and Nancy
Dana Corp.
Daniel Foundation, Gerard and Ruth
Davee Foundation
Davenport-Hatch Foundation
Davis Foundation, Edwin W. and Catherine M.
Day Foundation, Cecil B.
Deere & Co.
DeKalb Genetics Corp.
Delano Foundation, Mignon Sherwood
Delavan Foundation, Nelson B.
Deluxe Corp.
DeRoy Foundation, Helen L.
DeRoy Testamentary Foundation
Detroit Edison Co.
Dial Corp.
Diamond Walnut Growers
Dimick Foundation
Dishman Charitable Foundation Trust, H. E. and Kate
Dodge Foundation, Cleveland H.
Dodge Foundation, Geraldine R.
Doheny Foundation, Carrie Estelle
Dolan Family Foundation
Donaldson Charitable Trust, Oliver S. and Jennie R.
Donaldson Co.
Donnelley & Sons Co., R.R.
Douglas & Lomason Company
Dow Fund, Alden and Vada
Dresser Industries
Dreyfus Foundation, Max and Victoria
du Pont de Nemours & Co., E. I.
Duchossois Industries
Duke Power Co.
Dula Educational and Charitable Foundation, Caleb C. and Julia W.

Dunagan Foundation
duPont Fund, Jessie Ball
Durham Merchants Association Charitable Foundation
E and M Charities
Earl-Beth Foundation
Easley Trust, Andrew H. and Anne O.
Eastern Fine Paper, Inc.
Eaton Corp.
Ebell of Los Angeles Rest Cottage Association
Ecolab
Edwards & Sons, A.G.
Egenton Home
El Pomar Foundation
Electronic Data Systems Corp.
Emerson Electric Co.
Emery Memorial, Thomas J.
Equifax
Equitable Life Assurance Society of the U.S.
Erb Lumber Co.
Erteszek Foundation
Evjue Foundation
Exxon Corp.
Fairfield Foundation, Freeman E.
Falk Medical Fund, Maurice
Farallon Foundation
Federal Home Loan Mortgage Corp. (Freddie Mac)
Federated Life Insurance Co.
Feild Co-Operative Association
Fibre Converters
Fidelity Bank
Field Foundation, Jamee and Marshall
Fifth Third Bancorp
Fikes Foundation, Leland
Fink Foundation
Fireman's Fund Insurance Co.
Firestone, Jr. Foundation, Harvey
First Brands Corp.
First Fidelity Bancorporation
First Interstate Bank of Arizona
First Interstate Bank of Oregon
First Interstate Bank of Texas, N.A.
First Union Corp.
Firstar Bank Milwaukee NA
Fishback Foundation Trust, Harmes C.
Fisher Foundation
Flarsheim Charitable Foundation, Louis and Elizabeth
Fleet Bank of New York
Fleming Foundation
Florence Foundation
Florida Power & Light Co.
FMR Corp.
Fondren Foundation
Forbes
Ford Foundation
Forest Foundation
Fortis Benefits Insurance Company/Fortis Financial Group
Foster Charitable Foundation, M. Stratton
Foster Co., L.B.
Foster Co., L.B.
Foster Foundation
Foundation for Child Development
Foundation for the Needs of Others
Foxmeyer Corp.
Frankel Foundation, George and Elizabeth F.
Franklin Charitable Trust, Ershel
Frederick Foundation
Freed Foundation
Freedom Forum
Freeport-McMoRan
Frees Foundation
French Foundation
Frese Foundation, Arnold D.

Friendly Rosenthal Foundation
Frost Foundation
Fuchsberg Family Foundation, Abraham
Fullerton Foundation
Fund for New Jersey
Funderburke & Associates
Funderburke & Associates
Gage Foundation, Philip and Irene Toll
Gardner Charitable Foundation, Edith D.
Garfinkle Family Foundation
GATX Corp.
Geffen Foundation, David
GEICO Corp.
Gelb Foundation, Lawrence M.
Gellert Foundation, Carl
General Dynamics Corp.
General Mills
General Motors Corp.
GenRad
George Foundation
Georgia-Pacific Corp.
Georgia Power Co.
Gerber Products Co.
Gerbode Foundation, Wallace Alexander
German Protestant Orphan Asylum Association
Gerson Family Foundation, Benjamin J.
Gheens Foundation
Giant Eagle
Giant Food
Giant Food Stores
Gill Foundation, Pauline Allen
Glanville Family Foundation
Glaser Foundation
Glaxo
Glickenhaus & Co.
Globe Corp.
Globe Newspaper Co.
Goddard Foundation, Charles B.
Goldman Foundation, Herman
Goldseker Foundation of Maryland, Morris
Goldsmith Family Foundation
Goldsmith Foundation, Horace W.
Goldwyn Foundation, Samuel
Golub Corp.
Goodyear Foundation, Josephine
Graco
Grader Foundation, K. W.
Graham Fund, Philip L.
Graphic Controls Corp.
Grassmann Trust, E. J.
Graybar Electric Co.
Great-West Life Assurance Co.
Greeley Gas Co.
Green Fund
Greene Foundation, Jerome L.
Greenville Foundation
Grigg-Lewis Trust
Grousbeck Family Foundation
GTE Corp.
H.C.S. Foundation
Haas Foundation, Saul and Dayee G.
Haas Fund, Walter and Elise
Haas, Jr. Fund, Evelyn and Walter
Hagedorn Fund
Haigh-Scatena Foundation
Hale Foundation, Crescent Porter
Hall Foundation
Hallmark Cards
Hamilton Bank
Hancock Foundation, Luke B.
Handleman Co.
Harden Foundation
Harland Charitable Foundation, John and Wilhelmina D.
Harper Foundation, Philip S.
Harris Brothers Foundation
Hartford Courant Foundation

Hawley Foundation
Hearst Foundation
Hearst Foundation, William Randolph
Hechinger Co.
Heinz Co., H.J.
Heinz Endowment, Vira I.
Helms Foundation
Henry Foundation, Patrick
Hermann Foundation, Grover
Herschend Family Foundation
Hess Foundation
Heublein
Hill and Family Foundation, Walter Clay
Hill Crest Foundation
Hillcrest Foundation
Hoblitzelle Foundation
Hoffer Plastics Corp.
Hofmann Co.
Holley Foundation
Homeland Foundation
Honeywell
Horne Trust, Mabel
Hospital Corp. of America
Household International
Houston Industries
Hubbard Broadcasting
Hubbell Inc.
Huffy Corp.
Hulings Foundation, Mary Andersen
Hulme Charitable Foundation, Milton G.
Humphrey Fund, George M. and Pamela S.
Hunt Alternatives Fund
Hunt Foundation
Hunt Foundation, Samuel P.
Hunter Trust, A. V.
Hurst Foundation
Huston Foundation
Hutcheson Foundation, Hazel Montague
Hutchins Foundation, Mary J.
Hyams Foundation
Hyde and Watson Foundation
Hyundai Motor America
IBM Corp.
Ideal Industries
Illges Memorial Foundation, A. and M. L.
Illinois Tool Works
IMCERA Group Inc.
IMT Insurance Co.
Inland Steel Industries
Innovating Worthy Projects Foundation
International Paper Co.
Iowa-Illinois Gas & Electric Co.
Irmas Charitable Foundation, Audrey and Sydney
Irvine Foundation, James
Island Foundation
Ivakota Association
J.P. Morgan & Co.
Jackson Charitable Trust, Marion Gardner
Jackson Foundation
Jacobson & Sons, Benjamin
Jameson Trust, Oleonda
Janirve Foundation
Jennings Foundation, Mary Hillman
Jewett Foundation, George Frederick
John Hancock Mutual Life Insurance Co.
Johnson Controls
Johnson Foundation, Burdine
Johnson Foundation, Walter S.
Johnson & Son, S.C.
Jones Construction Co., J.A.
Jones Foundation, Daisy Marquis
Jones Foundation, Harvey and Bernice
Jostens

JSJ Corp.
Julia R. and Estelle L. Foundation
Jurzykowski Foundation, Alfred
Justus Trust, Edith C.
Kaplan Foundation, Mayer and Morris
Kaplun Foundation, Morris J. and Betty
Kaufman Endowment Fund, Louis G.
Kaufmann Foundation, Henry
Kaul Foundation Trust, Hugh
Keebler Co.
Kellogg Foundation, W. K.
Kennecott Corp.
Kennedy Foundation, Ethel
Kennedy Foundation, Ethel
Kerr Foundation
Kerr Foundation, A. H.
Kerr Foundation, Robert S. and Grayce B.
Kieckhefer Foundation, J. W.
Kiewit Foundation, Peter
Kilroy Foundation, William S. and Lora Jean
Kilworth Charitable Trust, William
Kimball International
Kimberly-Clark Corp.
King Ranch
Kiplinger Foundation
Kirchgessner Foundation, Karl
Klein Fund, Nathan J.
Kmart Corp.
Knight Foundation, John S. and James L.
Knistrom Foundation, Fanny and Svante
Koehler Foundation, Marcia and Otto
Koopman Fund
Koret Foundation
Kraft General Foods
Kresge Foundation
Kunstadter Family Foundation, Albert
Laffey-McHugh Foundation
Lane Memorial Foundation, Mills Bee
Lard Trust, Mary Potishman
Lassen Foundation, Irving A.
Lattner Foundation, Forrest C.
Lauder Foundation
Laurel Foundation
Lavanburg-Corner House
Leach Foundation, Tom & Frances
Leavey Foundation, Thomas and Dorothy
Lebovitz Fund
Lee Foundation, James T.
Leonhardt Foundation, Frederick H.
Leuthold Foundation
Levine Family Foundation, Hyman
Lewis Foundation, Frank J.
Life Insurance Co. of Georgia
Lightner Sams Foundation
Lincoln National Corp.
Lindner Foundation, Fay J.
Lindsay Foundation
Lintilhac Foundation
Linus Foundation
Lipsky Foundation, Fred and Sarah
Liquid Air Corp.
Littauer Foundation, Lucius N.
Little, Arthur D.
Liz Claiborne
Lockhart Iron & Steel Co.
Long Foundation, George A. and Grace
Long Island Lighting Co.
Lost Tree Charitable Foundation
Lowe Foundation
LTV Corp.

Lukens
Lurie Foundation, Louis R.
Luse Foundation, W. P. and Bulah
Luse Foundation, W. P. and Bulah
Lydall, Inc.
Lyons Foundation
Lyons Foundation
Lytel Foundation, Bertha Russ
MacArthur Foundation, John D. and Catherine T.
Maclellan Charitable Trust, R. J.
Maclellan Foundation
Madison Gas & Electric Co.
Magowan Family Foundation
Mailman Family Foundation, A. L.
Mailman Foundation
MalCo Products Inc.
Maneely Fund
Manilow Foundation, Nathan
Manville Corp.
Mardag Foundation
Marshall & Ilsley Bank
Martini Foundation, Nicholas
Marx Foundation, Virginia & Leonard
Massey Charitable Trust
Massey Foundation
Maxus Energy Corp.
May Mitchell Royal Foundation
Mayer Foods Corp., Oscar
Mayerson Foundation, Manuel D. and Rhoda
Maytag Corp.
Maytag Family Foundation, Fred
MBIA, Inc.
McBean Charitable Trust, Alletta Morris
McBeath Foundation, Faye
McBride & Son Associates
McConnell Foundation
McCormick & Co.
McCormick Tribune Foundation, Robert R.
McCune Charitable Trust, John R.
McCune Foundation
McCutchen Foundation
McDonald & Co. Securities
McDonald Foundation, J. M.
McDonald's Corp.
McDonnell Douglas Corp.-West
McEachern Charitable Trust, D. V. & Ida J.
McElroy Trust, R. J.
McFeely-Rogers Foundation
McGonagle Foundation, Dextra Baldwin
McGraw Foundation
McGraw Foundation, Curtis W.
McIntyre Foundation, B. D. and Jane E.
MCJ Foundation
McKenna Foundation, Philip M.
McKnight Foundation
McMahon Foundation
McWane Inc.
MDU Resources Group, Inc.
Mead Corp.
Meadows Foundation
Medina Foundation
Medtronic
Meland Outreach
Mellon Bank Corp.
Memorial Foundation for Children
Mercantile Bancorp
Mercy, Jr. Foundation, Sue and Eugene
Meredith Corp.
Merillat Foundation, Orville D. and Ruth A.
Merit Oil Corp.
Mertz Foundation, Martha
Mervyn's
Meserve Memorial Fund, Albert and Helen

Metal Industries
Metropolitan Life Insurance Co.
Metropolitan Theatres Corp.
Meyer Foundation, Eugene and Agnes E.
Meyer Memorial Trust
MGIC Investment Corp.
Michigan Bell Telephone Co.
Middendorf Foundation
Midwest Resources
Milken Family Medical Foundation
Milken Foundation, L. and S.
Mills Charitable Foundation, Henry L. and Kathryn
Mine Safety Appliances Co.
Mitchell Family Foundation, Edward D. and Anna
MNC Financial
Mobil Oil Corp.
Monroe-Brown Foundation
Monsanto Co.
Montgomery Street Foundation
Moore Foundation, Edward S.
Morgan Foundation, Burton D.
Morgan Stanley & Co.
Morris Foundation, Margaret T.
Morrison Trust, Louise L.
Morse Foundation, Richard P. and Claire W.
Moss Charitable Trust, Finis M.
Mott Charitable Trust/Spectemur Agendo, Stewart R.
Murphey Foundation, Lluella Morey
Murray Foundation
Musson Charitable Foundation, R. C. and Katharine M.
Mutual of New York
Nalco Chemical Co.
National By-Products
National City Corp.
National Forge Co.
National Machinery Co.
National Steel
National Westminster Bank New Jersey
Nationwide Insurance Cos.
NBD Bank, N.A.
Nesholm Family Foundation
New England Mutual Life Insurance Co.
New Horizon Foundation
New Prospect Foundation
New York Foundation
New York Life Insurance Co.
New York Mercantile Exchange
New York Telephone Co.
The New Yorker Magazine, Inc.
Newman Charitable Trust, Calvin M. and Raquel H.
Newman's Own
News & Observer Publishing Co.
Noble Foundation, Edward John
Nord Family Foundation
Nordson Corp.
Norris Foundation, Dellora A. and Lester J.
Northeast Utilities
Northern States Power Co.
Northern Trust Co.
Northwestern National Life Insurance Co.
Norton Co.
Norton Foundation Inc.
NuTone Inc.
OCRI Foundation
Ohl, Jr. Trust, George A.
Olin Corp.
Olin Foundation, Spencer T. and Ann W.
Olsson Memorial Foundation, Elis
O'Neill Charitable Corporation, F. J.
Oppenheimer and Flora Oppenheimer Haas Trust, Leo
Orange Orphan Society

Ordean Foundation
Ore-Ida Foods, Inc.
Orleans Trust, Carrie S.
Oxford Industries, Inc.
Pacific Mutual Life Insurance Co.
Packard Foundation, David and Lucile
Padnos Iron & Metal Co., Louis
Page Foundation, George B.
Palmer Fund, Frank Loomis
Pangburn Foundation
Parker Foundation
Parman Foundation, Robert A.
Peabody Charitable Fund, Amelia
Peabody Foundation, Amelia
Pearlstone Foundation, Peggy Meyerhoff
Peery Foundation
Pella Corp.
Penn Foundation, William
Peoples Energy Corp.
Peppers Foundation, Ann
Perini Foundation, Joseph
Perkin-Elmer Corp.
Perkin-Elmer Corp.
Perkins Charitable Foundation
Persis Corp.
Pew Charitable Trusts
Pfizer
Phillips Foundation, Dr. P.
Pick, Jr. Fund, Albert
Piedmont Health Care Foundation
Pillsbury Foundation
Pinkerton Foundation
Pioneer Electronics (USA) Inc.
Piper Jaffray Cos.
Pittsburgh Child Guidance Foundation
Pittway Corp.
Pitzman Fund
Plankenhorn Foundation, Harry
Plant Memorial Fund, Henry B.
Plym Foundation
Pollybill Foundation
Potomac Electric Power Co.
Pott Foundation, Herman T. and Phenie R.
Potter Foundation, Justin and Valere
Powell Family Foundation
Price Associates, T. Rowe
Prince Corp.
Prince Manufacturing, Inc.
Principal Financial Group
Pritzker Foundation
Prouty Foundation, Olive Higgins
Prudential Insurance Co. of America
Public Service Co. of Colorado
Pulitzer Publishing Co.
Puterbaugh Foundation
Quaker Oats Co.
Radin Foundation
Ramapo Trust
Raskob Foundation for Catholic Activities
Rauch Foundation
Redman Foundation
Reed Foundation, Philip D.
Reily & Co., William B.
Rennebohm Foundation, Oscar
Reynolds Foundation, Donald W.
Reynolds Foundation, Z. Smith
Rice Foundation
Richardson Foundation, Smith
Richardson Fund, Mary Lynn
Riggs Benevolent Fund
Robinson Fund, Maurice R.
Roblee Foundation, Joseph H. and Florence A.
Rockford Acromatics Products Co./Aircraft Gear Corp.
Rockwell Fund
Rockwell International Corp.
Rohm and Haas Company
Rohr Inc.

Rosenbaum Foundation, Paul and Gabriella
Rosenbaum Foundation, Paul and Gabriella
Rosenberg Foundation, William J. and Tina
Rosenberg, Jr. Family Foundation, Louise and Claude
Ross Foundation, Walter G.
Royal Group Inc.
Rubinstein Foundation, Helena
Ryan Family Charitable Foundation
Sage Foundation
Sailors' Snug Harbor of Boston
St. Faith's House Foundation
Salwil Foundation
Salwil Foundation
San Diego Gas & Electric
Sanders Trust, Charles
Sara Lee Corp.
Sara Lee Hosiery
Sarkeys Foundation
Sasco Foundation
Schenck Fund, L. P.
Scherman Foundation
Scheuer Family Foundation, S. H. and Helen R.
Schiff Foundation, Dorothy
Schiro Fund
Schmidt Charitable Foundation, William E.
Schoenleber Foundation
Scholl Foundation, Dr.
Schrafft and Bertha E. Schrafft Charitable Trust, William E.
Schroeder Foundation, Walter
Schumann Fund for New Jersey
Schwab & Co., Charles
Schwartz Foundation, Arnold A.
Schwartz Foundation, David
Scrivner, Inc.
Seafirst Corp.
Seaver Charitable Trust, Richard C.
Security Benefit Life Insurance Co.
Security Life of Denver
Segal Charitable Trust, Barnet
Selby and Marie Selby Foundation, William G.
Semmes Foundation
Semple Foundation, Louise Taft
Sentinel Communications Co.
Seybert Institution for Poor Boys and Girls, Adam and Maria Sarah
Sharp Foundation, Evelyn
Shawmut National Corp.
Sheaffer Inc.
Sheinberg Foundation, Eric P.
Shell Oil Co.
Shelton Cos.
Shemanski Testamentary Trust, Tillie and Alfred
Shoemaker Fund, Thomas H. and Mary Williams
Shoney's Inc.
Shwayder Foundation, Fay
Signet Bank/Maryland
Silverweed Foundation
Simon Foundation, Robert Ellis
Simon Foundation, William E. and Carol G.
SIT Investment Associates, Inc.
Skinner Corp.
Skirball Foundation
Smith Corp., A.O.
Smith Foundation, Lon V.
Snyder Charitable Fund, W. P.
Sooner Pipe & Supply Corp.
Sosland Foundation
Southern California Edison Co.
Southwestern Bell Corp.
Speas Foundation, Victor E.
Spiegel
Springs Industries
Spunk Fund

SPX Corp.
Stanley Charitable Foundation, A. W.
Stanley Works
Starr Foundation
State Street Bank & Trust Co.
Staunton Farm Foundation
Stearns Charitable Foundation, Anna B.
Steelcase
Stein Foundation, Jules and Doris
Steinhauer Charitable Foundation
Stemmons Foundation
Sterkel Trust, Justine
Sterling Inc.
Sterling Winthrop
Stern Family Foundation, Alex
Stern Memorial Trust, Sidney
Stewart Trust under the will of Helen S. Devore, Alexander and Margaret
Stillwell Charitable Trust, Glen and Dorothy
Stocker Foundation
Stone Charitable Foundation
Strake Foundation
Straus Foundation, Aaron and Lillie
Stride Rite Corp.
Strong Foundation, Hattie M.
Stry Foundation, Paul E.
Stuart Foundations
Stulsaft Foundation, Morris
Sturgis Charitable and Educational Trust, Roy and Christine
Subaru of America Inc.
Sumitomo Bank of California
Summerfield Foundation, Solon E.
Sunnen Foundation
Swalm Foundation
Swig Charity Foundation, Mae and Benjamin
Swig Foundation
Synovus Financial Corp.
Tandem Computers
Tang Foundation
Target Stores
Taube Family Foundation
Taubman Foundation, A. Alfred
Teledyne
Teleklew Productions
Tell Foundation
Templeton Foundation, Herbert A.
Templeton Foundation, John
Thanksgiving Foundation
Thatcher Foundation
Thomas Built Buses L.P.
Thomas Foundation, Joan and Lee
Thorne Foundation
3M Co.
Thurman Charitable Foundation for Children, Edgar A.
Times Mirror Co.
Tisch Foundation
Titus Foundation, C. W.
TJX Cos.
Tosco Corp. Refining Division
Towsley Foundation, Harry A. and Margaret D.
Tozer Foundation
Tracor, Inc.
Transamerica Corp.
TRINOVA Corp.
Tropicana Products, Inc.
True North Foundation
Trull Foundation
Trust Co. Bank
Trust Funds
Tull Charitable Foundation
Tuohy Foundation, Alice Tweed
Turrell Fund
Union Bank
Union Camp Corp.

Family Services (cont.)

Union Pacific Corp.
United Conveyor Corp.
United Parcel Service of America
United States Sugar Corp.
United Technologies Corp.
Universal Foods Corp.
Universal Leaf Tobacco Co.
Upjohn California Fund
Upton Foundation, Frederick S.
US WEST
UST
Utica National Insurance Group
van Ameringen Foundation
Van Camp Foundation
van Loben Sels - Eleanor Slate van Lobel Sels Charitable Foundation, Ernst D.
Van Nuys Charities, J. B. and Emily
Varian Associates
Vesuvius Charitable Foundation
Victoria Foundation
Vollbrecht Foundation, Frederick A.
Wade Endowment Fund, Elizabeth Firth
Waldbaum, Inc.
Walker Foundation, T. B.
Walter Family Trust, Byron L.
Wardle Family Foundation
Wareheim Foundation, E. C.
Warfield Memorial Fund, Anna Emory
Washington Square Fund
Waters Charitable Trust, Robert S.
Watson Foundation, Walter E. and Caroline H.
Watumull Fund, J.
Webb Charitable Trust, Susan Mott
Webb Foundation
Weber Charities Corp., Frederick E.
Webster Foundation, Edwin S.
Weingart Foundation
Wells Fargo & Co.
Wendt Foundation, Margaret L.
Werthan Foundation
West Co.
Weyerhaeuser Co.
Wharton Foundation
Whirlpool Corp.
Whiting Foundation
Whittenberger Foundation, Claude R. and Ethel B.
Wickes Foundation, Harvey Randall
Wiener Foundation, Malcolm Hewitt
Wilf Family Foundation
Wilkof Foundation, Edward and Ruth
Williams Cos.
Williams Foundation, Edna Sproull
Wisconsin Energy Corp.
Wisconsin Power & Light Co.
Witte, Jr. Foundation, John H.
Wolff Memorial Foundation, Pauline Sterne
Wood Charitable Trust, W. P.
Wood-Claeyssens Foundation
Woods Charitable Fund
Woodward Governor Co.
Wurts Memorial, Henrietta Tower
Wyomissing Foundation
Younkers, Inc.
Zale Foundation
Zarrow Foundation, Anne and Henry
Zellerbach Family Fund

Food/Clothing Distribution

Abell Foundation, Charles S.
Abell Foundation, The
Abney Foundation
Abraham Foundation
Ackerman Trust, Anna Keesling
Acme-Cleveland Corp.
Advanced Micro Devices
AEC Trust
Ahmanson Foundation
Air Products & Chemicals
Alabama Power Co.
Albertson's
Alcon Laboratories, Inc.
Alexander Foundation, Judd S.
Alexander Foundation, Robert D. and Catherine R.
Allegheny Ludlum Corp.
Allen Foundation, Frances
Allendale Mutual Insurance Co.
Alliant Techsystems
AlliedSignal
Alltel/Western Region
ALPAC Corp.
Alro Steel Corp.
Altman Foundation
Alumax
Aluminum Co. of America
AMAX
Amcast Industrial Corp.
AMCORE Bank, N.A. Rockford
American Brands
American Electric Power
American Express Co.
American Financial Corp.
American Natural Resources Co.
American United Life Insurance Co.
Ames Department Stores
Amfac/JMB Hawaii
Andersen Corp.
Andersons Management Corp.
Anschutz Family Foundation
AON Corp.
Apache Corp.
Apple Computer, Inc.
Appleton Papers
Arata Brothers Trust
Archer-Daniels-Midland Co.
ARCO
Argyros Foundation
Aristech Chemical Corp.
Arkansas Power & Light Co.
Armbrust Chain Co.
Armstrong World Industries Inc.
Arrillaga Foundation
Associated Foundations
Atkinson Foundation
Atkinson Foundation, Myrtle L.
Atlanta Gas Light Co.
Attleboro Pawtucket Savings Bank
Auerbach Foundation, Beatrice Fox
Avon Products
Awrey Bakeries
Ayres Foundation, Inc.
Babcock & Wilcox Co.
Bacardi Imports
Badgeley Residuary Charitable Trust, Rose M.
Badger Meter, Inc.
Baer Foundation, Alan and Marcia
Baird Charitable Trust, William Robert
Baird Foundation
Baird Foundation, Cameron
Baker Foundation, R. C.
Baker, Jr. Memorial Fund, William G.
Banc One Illinois Corp.
Banc One Wisconsin Corp.
Bancorp Hawaii
Banfi Vintners

Bank of America Arizona
Bank of Boston Connecticut
Bannerman Foundation, William C.
Banta Corp.
Banyan Tree Foundation
Barker Foundation
Barra Foundation
Bass and Edythe and Sol G. Atlas Fund, Sandra Atlas
Beazley Foundation
Bechtel Group
Beech Aircraft Corp.
Bemis Company
Bender Foundation
Benedum Foundation, Claude Worthington
Berger Foundation, H.N. and Frances C.
Bernsen Foundation, Grace and Franklin
Bernstein Foundation, Diane and Norman
Berry Foundation, Archie W. and Grace
Berry Foundation, Lowell
Berwind Corp.
Best Western International
Bethlehem Steel Corp.
Bicknell Fund
Biddle Foundation, Margaret T.
Bierhaus Foundation
Birnschein Foundation, Alvin and Marion
Bjorkman Foundation
Blade Communications
Bleibtreu Foundation, Jacob
Block, H&R
Bloedorn Foundation, Walter A.
Blount
Blue Bell, Inc.
Blum Foundation, Edith C.
Blum Foundation, Harry and Maribel G.
Blum-Kovler Foundation
Bobst Foundation, Elmer and Mamdouha
Boehringer Mannheim Corp.
Boeing Co.
Booz Allen & Hamilton
Borden
Borden Memorial Foundation, Mary Owen
Boston Edison Co.
Bovaird Foundation, Mervin Bowater Inc.
Bozzone Family Foundation
Brach Foundation, Edwin I.
Bradford Foundation, George and Ruth
Brand Cos.
Bremer Foundation, Otto
Brenner Foundation
Brewer and Co., Ltd., C.
Bridwell Foundation, J. S.
Brooklyn Benevolent Society
Brown and C. A. Lupton Foundation, T. J.
Brown Foundation, M. K.
Brown & Sons, Alex
Bucyrus-Erie
Burdines
Burlington Resources
Burndy Corp.
Burnham Foundation
Burns Foundation, Fritz B.
Burns International
Bush Foundation
Butler Family Foundation, George W. and Gladys S.
Bydale Foundation
C. E. and S. Foundation
C.P. Rail Systems
Cabell III and Maude Morgan Cabell Foundation, Robert G.
Cabot Corp.
Calhoun Charitable Trust, Kenneth

Cameron Foundation, Harry S. and Isabel C.
Campbell and Adah E. Hall Charity Fund, Bushrod H.
Campbell Soup Co.
Capital Cities/ABC
Capital Fund Foundation
Capital Holding Corp.
Cargill
Carter Foundation, Amon G.
Casey Foundation, Eugene B.
Castle Foundation, Harold K. L.
Castle Foundation, Samuel N. and Mary
Catlin Charitable Trust, Kathleen K.
Cawsey Trust
Central Hudson Gas & Electric Corp.
Central Life Assurance Co.
Central Maine Power Co.
Chambers Development Co.
Chapman Charitable Corporation, Howard and Bess
Chapman Charitable Trust, H. A. and Mary K.
Charlesbank Homes
Chartwell Foundation
Chase Charity Foundation, Alfred E.
Chase Manhattan Bank, N.A.
Chatham Valley Foundation
Chatlos Foundation
Chemical Bank
Cheney Foundation, Ben B.
Chevron Corp.
Chicago Board of Trade
Chicago Sun-Times, Inc.
Chicago Title and Trust Co.
Chilton Foundation Trust
Chrysler Corp.
Church & Dwight Co.
Cimarron Foundation
CIT Group Holdings
Citicorp
Citizens Bank
Citizens First National Bank
Clark Foundation
Clark-Winchcole Foundation
Cleveland-Cliffs
Clipper Ship Foundation
Clorox Co.
Clowes Fund
CM Alliance Cos.
CNA Insurance Cos.
Codrington Charitable Foundation, George W.
Coffey Foundation
Cohen Foundation, Naomi and Nehemiah
Cohn Family Foundation, Robert and Terri
Cole Foundation, Olive B.
Coleman Co.
Collins Foundation
Collins, Jr. Foundation, George Fulton
Colonial Life & Accident Insurance Co.
Colorado Trust
Coltec Industries
Columbia Foundation
Columbus Dispatch Printing Co.
Columbus Southern Power Co.
Commerce Bancshares, Inc.
Compaq Computer Corp.
Comstock Foundation
Cone Mills Corp.
Conn Memorial Foundation
Connecticut Natural Gas Corp.
Connelly Foundation
Consolidated Natural Gas Co.
Cook Foundation, Louella
Cooke Foundation
Cooper Industries
Corpus Christi Exploration Co.
Cowell Foundation, S. H.

Cowles Charitable Trust
Cowles Media Co.
CPI Corp.
Craigmyle Foundation
Crawford Estate, E. R.
Cremer Foundation
Crown Memorial, Arie and Ida
Crystal Trust
Cudahy Fund, Patrick and Anna M.
Cuesta Foundation
Cullen/Frost Bankers
Cummings Foundation, James H.
Cummins Engine Co.
Cuneo Foundation
Curtice-Burns Foods
Dain Bosworth/Inter-Regional Financial Group
Dana Corp.
Darby Foundation
Dater Foundation, Charles H.
Davidson Family Charitable Foundation
Davis Foundation, James A. and Juliet L.
Davis Foundation, Simon and Annie
De Lima Co., Paul
Deluxe Corp.
Demoulas Supermarkets
Detroit Edison Co.
Dettman Foundation, Leroy E.
Deuble Foundation, George H.
Deutsch Co.
Dexter Corp.
Digital Equipment Corp.
Dixie Yarns, Inc.
Dodge Jones Foundation
Doelger Charitable Trust, Thelma
Donaldson Co.
Doss Foundation, M. S.
Dougherty, Jr. Foundation, James R.
Downs Perpetual Charitable Trust, Ellason
Dreitzer Foundation
Dreyfus Foundation, Jean and Louis
Dreyfus Foundation, Max and Victoria
Drum Foundation
du Pont de Nemours & Co., E. I.
Duke Power Co.
Dupar Foundation
duPont Foundation, Alfred I.
Dynamet, Inc.
Eastern Bank Foundation
Eastern Enterprises
Eastman Foundation, Alexander
Eaton Corp.
Eccles Foundation, Marriner S.
Eddy Family Memorial Fund, C. K.
Eder Foundation, Sidney and Arthur
Edmondson Foundation, Joseph Henry
Edwards Foundation, Jes
Edwards Foundation, O. P. and W. E.
EG&G Inc.
Eisenberg Foundation, George M.
El Pomar Foundation
Elco Charitable Foundation
Ellsworth Trust, W. H.
Ellsworth Trust, W. H.
Ellwood Foundation
English Memorial Fund, Florence C. and H. L.
Enright Foundation
Enron Corp.
Ensworth Charitable Foundation
Enterprise Rent-A-Car Co.
Epaphroditus Foundation
Equifax
Erb Lumber Co.
Ettinger Foundation

Fabick Tractor Co., John
Fair Foundation, R. W.
Fairfield Foundation, Freeman E.
Faith Charitable Trust
Falk Medical Research Foundation, Dr. Ralph and Marian
Farallon Foundation
Federal-Mogul Corp.
Federal National Mortgage Assn., Fannie Mae
Federated Department Stores and Allied Stores Corp.
Federated Life Insurance Co.
Fein Foundation
Feinberg Foundation, Joseph and Bessie
Felburn Foundation
Fibre Converters
Fidelity Bank
Field Foundation of Illinois
Fikes Foundation, Leland
Finch Foundation, Thomas Austin
Finley Foundation, A. E.
Finnegan Foundation, John D.
Fireman's Fund Insurance Co.
First Brands Corp.
First Fidelity Bancorporation
First Fruit
First Interstate Bank of Arizona
First Interstate Bank of California
First Interstate Bank of Oregon
First Union Corp.
Flatley Foundation
Fleming Companies, Inc.
Florence Corp.
Florence Foundation
Ford Foundation, Kenneth W.
Forest Foundation
Forest Lawn Foundation
Formrite Tube Co.
Foster and Gallagher
Foster Co., L.B.
Foster Foundation
Fourth Financial Corp.
Fox Foundation, John H.
Frank Family Foundation, A. J.
Franklin Mint Corp.
Frear Eleemosynary Trust, Mary D. and Walter F.
Frederick Foundation
Freed Foundation
Freeport Brick Co.
Freeport-McMoRan
Frees Foundation
French Oil Mill Machinery Co.
Freygang Foundation, Walter Henry
Frueauff Foundation, Charles A.
Fry Foundation, Lloyd A.
Fuchs Foundation, Gottfried & Mary
Funderburke & Associates
Funderburke & Associates
Fusenot Charity Foundation, Georges and Germaine
G.A.G. Charitable Corporation
Gallagher Family Foundation, Lewis P.
Gallo Foundation, Julio R.
Gap, The
GAR Foundation
Garvey Texas Foundation
Garvey Trust, Olive White
GATX Corp.
Gavin Foundation, James and Zita
GEICO Corp.
Gellert Foundation, Carl
Gellert Foundation, Celia Berta
General American Life Insurance Co.
General Electric Co.
General Mills
General Reinsurance Corp.
General Signal Corp.

Georgia-Pacific Corp.
Georgia Power Co.
Gerber Products Co.
Gheens Foundation
Giant Eagle
Giant Food
Gibson Foundation, E. L.
Gifford Charitable Corporation, Rosamond
Gilbane Foundation, Thomas and William
Giles Foundation, Edward C.
Gillette Co.
Gilman Foundation, Howard
Gilmore Foundation, Earl B.
Gilmore Foundation, Irving S.
Ginter Foundation, Karl and Anna
Gleason Foundation, James
Gleason Foundation, James
Gleason Foundation, Katherine
Glen Eagles Foundation
Globe Newspaper Co.
Goldbach Foundation, Ray and Marie
Goldman Fund, Richard and Rhoda
Goldome F.S.B
Goldsmith Foundation
Golub Corp.
Goodyear Foundation, Josephine
Goodyear Foundation, Josephine
Gore Family Memorial Foundation
Gould Foundation for Children, Edwin
Graco
Grader Foundation, K. W.
Gradison & Co.
Graham Fund, Philip L.
Graphic Controls Corp.
Grassmann Trust, E. J.
Graybar Electric Co.
Greater Lansing Foundation
Green Fund
Greenville Foundation
Gregg-Graniteville Foundation
Griffith Foundation, W. C.
Gross Charitable Trust, Stella B.
Guardian Life Insurance Co. of America
Gudelsky Family Foundation, Homer and Martha
Gulf Power Co.
Haas Fund, Walter and Elise
Haas, Jr. Fund, Evelyn and Walter
Hachar Charitable Trust, D. D.
Halff Foundation, G. A. C.
Hall Foundation
Hallmark Cards
Halsell Foundation, O. L.
Hamman Foundation, George and Mary Josephine
Hancock Foundation, Luke B.
Hankamer Foundation, Curtis and Doris K.
Hanson Foundation
Harden Foundation
Harmon Foundation, Pearl M. and Julia J.
Harper Foundation, Philip S.
Harrington Foundation, Don and Sybil
Harris Brothers Foundation
Harris Foundation
Harsco Corp.
Hartzell Industries, Inc.
Harvey Foundation, Felix
Haskell Fund
Hatterscheidt Foundation
Hawley Foundation
Hayfields Foundation
Hechinger Co.
Hecla Mining Co.
Heinz Endowment, Vira I.
Helis Foundation

Herbst Foundation
Herrick Foundation
Hershey Foods Corp.
Hervey Foundation
Hiawatha Education Foundation
Hillcrest Foundation
Hilliard Corp.
Hillman Foundation
Hillsdale Fund
Himmelfarb Foundation, Paul and Annetta
Hirschhorn Foundation, David and Barbara B.
Hobbs Foundation
Hobby Foundation
Hoblitzelle Foundation
Hoche-Scofield Foundation
Hodge Foundation
Hoffman Foundation, H. Leslie Hoffman and Elaine S.
Hoffman Foundation, John Ernest
Hofheinz Foundation, Irene Cafcalas
Hofmann Co.
Homeland Foundation
Homeland Foundation
Hopedale Foundation
Hospital Corp. of America
House Educational Trust, Susan Cook
Household International
Hubbard Broadcasting
Hubbell Inc.
Hugoton Foundation
Hulme Charitable Foundation, Milton G.
Humana
Hunt Charitable Trust, C. Giles
Hunter Foundation, Edward and Irma
Hunter Trust, A. V.
Hutchins Foundation, Mary J.
Hyde and Watson Foundation
I and G Charitable Foundation
IBP, Inc.
Iddings Benevolent Trust
Ideal Industries
IES Industries
Illinois Power Co.
IMCERA Group Inc.
Inland Container Corp.
Inland Steel Industries
Inman Mills
Interco
International Foundation
International Paper Co.
Irwin Charity Foundation, William G.
ITT Corp.
ITT Hartford Insurance Group
ITT Rayonier
Ivakota Association
J. D. B. Fund
J.P. Morgan & Co.
Jackson Foundation
Janirve Foundation
Jasper Desk Co.
JCPenney Co.
Jenkins Foundation, George W.
Jennings Foundation, Alma
JFM Foundation
John Hancock Mutual Life Insurance Co.
Johnson Charitable Trust, Keith Wold
Johnson Controls
Johnson Foundation, Helen K. and Arthur E.
Johnstone and H. Earle Kimball Foundation, Phyllis Kimball
Jones and Bessie D. Phelps Foundation, Cyrus W. and Amy F.
Jones Foundation, Daisy Marquis
Jones Foundation, Fletcher
Jordan and Ettie A. Jordan Charitable Foundation, Mary Ranken

Joukowsky Family Foundation
Journal Gazette Co.
Joy Family Foundation
Joyce Foundation, John M. and Mary A.
Jurzykowski Foundation, Alfred
Kaplan Fund, J. M.
Kasal Charitable Trust, Father
Kaufman Memorial Trust, Chaim, Fanny, Louis, Benjamin, and Anne Florence
Kawabe Memorial Fund
Kayser Foundation
Keck, Jr. Foundation, William M.
Keeler Fund, Miner S. and Mary Ann
Keller Family Foundation
Kelley Foundation, Kate M.
Kellogg's
Kellwood Co.
Kendall Foundation, George R.
Kennedy Foundation, Ethel
Kennedy Foundation, Quentin J.
Kent-Lucas Foundation
Kentland Foundation
Kern Foundation, Ilma
Kerr Foundation, Robert S. and Grayce B.
Kieckhefer Foundation, J. W.
Kiewit Foundation, Peter
Kilcawley Fund, William H.
Kilworth Charitable Trust, William
Kimball Foundation, Horace A. Kimball and S. Ella
Kimball International
Kimberly-Clark Corp.
Kiplinger Foundation
Kirbo Charitable Trust, Thomas M. and Irene B.
Klau Foundation, David W. and Sadie
Kline Foundation, Josiah W. and Bessie H.
Kmart Corp.
Knistrom Foundation, Fanny and Svante
Knott Foundation, Marion I. and Henry J.
Knox, Sr., and Pearl Wallis Knox Charitable Foundation, Robert W.
Knudsen Charitable Foundation, Earl
Koch Industries
Koch Sons, George
Koopman Fund
Koret Foundation
Kramer Foundation, Louise
Kugelman Foundation
Kunstadter Family Foundation, Albert
Kysor Industrial Corp.
L. L. W. W. Foundation
Ladish Co.
Laffey-McHugh Foundation
Land O'Lakes
Lane Foundation, Minnie and Bernard
Langendorf Foundation, Stanley S.
Lapham-Hickey Steel Corp.
Lard Trust, Mary Potishman
Laros Foundation, R. K.
Lassen Foundation, Irving A.
Lassus Brothers Oil
Lattner Foundation, Forrest C.
LBJ Family Foundation
Leavey Foundation, Thomas and Dorothy
LeBrun Foundation
Leidy Foundation, John J.
Lender Family Foundation
Leo Burnett Co.
Leu Foundation
Leuthold Foundation
Levy Foundation, Edward C.
Levy Foundation, June Rockwell

Libby-Dufour Fund, Trustees of the
Lincoln Electric Co.
Lipton, Thomas J.
Liquid Air Corp.
Lockwood Foundation, Byron W. and Alice L.
Long Island Lighting Co.
Loughran Foundation, Mary and Daniel
Louisiana-Pacific Corp.
Love Foundation, Martha and Spencer
Lowenstein Foundation, William P. and Marie R.
Loyola Foundation
LTV Corp.
Luchsinger Family Foundation
Luckyday Foundation
Lurie Foundation, Louis R.
Luttrell Trust
Lydall, Inc.
Lynn Foundation, E. M.
M. E. G. Foundation
M.T.D. Products
Mabee Foundation, J. E. and L. E.
Maclellan Charitable Trust, R. J.
Maddox Foundation, J. F.
Magruder Foundation, Chesley G.
Mankato Citizens Telephone Co.
Manville Corp.
Marathon Oil, Indiana Refining Division
Mardag Foundation
Marion Merrell Dow
Maritz Inc.
Marmot Foundation
Mars Foundation
Marshall Foundation
Marshall & Ilsley Bank
Marshburn Foundation
Martin Marietta Corp.
Massey Charitable Trust
Massie Trust, David Meade
Matthews International Corp.
May Foundation, Wilbur
Mayer Foods Corp., Oscar
Mayerson Foundation, Manuel D. and Rhoda
Mazza Foundation
MBIA, Inc.
McAlister Charitable Foundation, Harold
McAlonan Trust, John A.
McBride & Son Associates
McCarthy Charities
McCormick & Co.
McCormick Tribune Foundation, Robert R.
McCullough Foundation, Ralph H. and Ruth J.
McCune Foundation
McCutchen Foundation
McDermott Foundation, Eugene
McDonnell Douglas Corp.-West
McDonough Foundation, Bernard
McEachern Charitable Trust, D. V. & Ida J.
McElroy Trust, R. J.
McGregor Fund
McIntyre Foundation, C. S. and Marion F.
MCJ Foundation
McKee Foundation, Robert E. and Evelyn
McKee Poor Fund, Virginia A.
McKenna Foundation, Philip M.
McKesson Corp.
McKnight Foundation
McMillan, Jr. Foundation, Bruce
Mead Corp.
Meadows Foundation
Medina Foundation
Melitta North America Inc.
Mellam Family Foundation

Food/Clothing Distribution (cont.)

Mellon Foundation, Richard King
Menasha Corp.
Merrick Foundation, Robert G. and Anne M.
Merrion Foundation
Metropolitan Life Insurance Co.
Mettler Instrument Corp.
Meyer Foundation, Alice Kleberg Reynolds
Meyer Foundation, Eugene and Agnes E.
Meyer Memorial Foundation, Aaron and Rachel
Meyer Memorial Trust
MGIC Investment Corp.
Michael Foundation, Herbert I. and Elsa B.
Michigan Bell Telephone Co.
Michigan Gas Utilities
Midwest Resources
Milken Foundation, L. and S.
Miller-Mellor Association
Milliken & Co.
Mills Charitable Foundation, Henry L. and Kathryn
Minnesota Mutual Life Insurance Co.
Mitchell Family Foundation, Bernard and Marjorie
Mitchell Family Foundation, Edward D. and Anna
MNC Financial
Mnuchin Foundation
Mobil Oil Corp.
Monaghan Charitable Trust, Rose
Monell Foundation, Ambrose
Monfort Charitable Foundation
Monroe Foundation (1976), J. Edgar
Monsanto Co.
Moody Foundation
Moore Foundation, Martha G.
Moore Foundation, Roy C.
Moores Foundation, Harry C.
Morgan and Samuel Tate Morgan, Jr. Foundation, Marietta McNeil
Morgan Stanley & Co.
Morris Foundation, Margaret T.
Moses Fund, Henry and Lucy
Motorola
MTS Systems Corp.
Mulcahy Foundation
Mullen Foundation, J. K.
Mulligan Charitable Trust, Mary S.
Murphy Co., G.C.
Nalco Chemical Co.
Nashua Trust Co.
National City Bank of Evansville
National City Corp.
National Presto Industries
Nationwide Insurance Cos.
NBD Bank
NBD Bank, N.A.
Nestle U.S.A. Inc.
New England Mutual Life Insurance Co.
New Prospect Foundation
New World Foundation
New York Foundation
New York Life Insurance Co.
New York Mercantile Exchange
New York Stock Exchange
The New Yorker Magazine, Inc.
Newhouse Foundation, Samuel I.
Newman Charitable Trust, Calvin M. and Raquel H.
Newman's Own
News & Observer Publishing Co.
Nike Inc.
Norgren Foundation, Carl A.
Normandie Foundation

Norris Foundation, Kenneth T. and Eileen L.
Northeast Utilities
Northern Indiana Public Service Co.
Northern States Power Co.
Northern Trust Co.
Northwest Natural Gas Co.
Norton Foundation Inc.
Norwest Bank Nebraska
Noyes, Jr. Memorial Foundation, Nicholas H.
NutraSweet Co.
NYNEX Corp.
Occidental Oil & Gas Corp.
O'Connor Co.
OCRI Foundation
O'Fallon Trust, Martin J. and Mary Anne
Old Dominion Box Co.
Olin Corp.
Olsson Memorial Foundation, Elis
1957 Charity Trust
O'Neill Foundation, William J. and Dorothy K.
Ordean Foundation
Ore-Ida Foods, Inc.
Orleans Trust, Carrie S.
Orleton Trust Fund
Osborn Charitable Trust, Edward B.
Osborn Manufacturing Co.
Osher Foundation, Bernard
Overbrook Foundation
Overstreet Foundation
Owen Trust, B. B.
Pacific Mutual Life Insurance Co.
Packaging Corporation of America
Packard Foundation, David and Lucile
Page Foundation, George B.
PaineWebber
Palmer Fund, Frank Loomis
Parshelsky Foundation, Moses L.
Parsons Foundation, Ralph M.
Parsons - W.D. Charities, Vera Davis
Patterson Charitable Fund, W. I.
Pax Christi Foundation
Payne Foundation, Frank E. and Seba B.
Peabody Charitable Fund, Amelia
Peabody Foundation, Amelia
Pearlstone Foundation, Peggy Meyerhoff
Penn Savings Bank, a division of Sovereign Bank Bank of Princeton, a division of Sovereign Bank
Penney Foundation, James C.
Pennington Foundation, Irene W. and C. B.
People's Bank
Pepsi-Cola Bottling Co. of Charlotte
Perkin-Elmer Corp.
Perkin-Elmer Corp.
Perot Foundation
Peterloon Foundation
Peters Foundation, Leon S.
PHH Corp.
Philip Morris Cos.
Phillips Foundation, A. P.
Phillips Foundation, Dr. P.
Phillips Petroleum Co.
Pieper Electric
Pillsbury Foundation
Pine Tree Foundation
Piper Jaffray Cos.
Pittsburgh National Bank
Pittway Corp.
Plough Foundation
Pope Foundation
Portec, Inc.
Portland General Electric Co.

Post Foundation of D.C., Marjorie Merriweather
Potomac Electric Power Co.
Pott Foundation, Herman T. and Phenie R.
Powell Family Foundation
PPG Industries
Premier Industrial Corp.
Price Associates, T. Rowe
Price Foundation, Louis and Harold
Priddy Foundation
Principal Financial Group
Procter & Gamble Cosmetic & Fragrance Products
Providence Energy Corp.
Provident Life & Accident Insurance Co.
Prudential Insurance Co. of America
Public Service Electric & Gas Co.
Pulitzer Publishing Co.
Quaker Oats Co.
Questar Corp.
Ralston Purina Co.
Randa
Raskob Foundation for Catholic Activities
Recognition Equipment
Redfield Foundation, Nell J.
Redman Foundation
Regenstein Foundation
Reilly Industries
Reily & Co., William B.
Relations Foundation
Reliable Life Insurance Co.
Rennebohm Foundation, Oscar
Republic New York Corp.
Retirement Research Foundation
Reynolds Metals Co.
Rhoades Fund, Otto L. and Hazel E.
Rhodebeck Charitable Trust
Rich Products Corp.
Richardson Foundation, Sid W.
Richardson Fund, Mary Lynn
Rienzi Foundation
Ritchie Memorial Foundation, Charies E. and Mabel M.
Ritter Foundation, May Ellen and Gerald
Roberts Foundation, Dora
Rochlin Foundation, Abraham and Sonia
Rockwell Fund
Rohm and Haas Company
Rohr Inc.
Rolfs Foundation, Robert T.
Rollins Luetkemeyer Charitable Foundation
Rosenthal Foundation, Samuel
Ross Foundation, Arthur
Rouse Co.
Russell Educational Foundation, Benjamin and Roberta
Ryan Family Charitable Foundation
Ryan Foundation, David Claude
Salomon
San Diego Gas & Electric
Sandy Foundation, George H.
Sandy Hill Foundation
Santa Fe Pacific Corp.
Sara Lee Corp.
Sara Lee Hosiery
Sarkeys Foundation
Scaife Family Foundation
Schadt Foundation
Scherman Foundation
Schlink Foundation, Albert G. and Olive H.
Schlumberger Ltd.
Schmitt Foundation, Arthur J.
Scholl Foundation, Dr.
Schumann Fund for New Jersey
Schwab & Co., Charles

Scroggins Foundation, Arthur E. and Cornelia C.
Seabury Foundation
Seaway Food Town
Security Life of Denver
Segal Charitable Trust, Barnet
Selby and Marie Selby Foundation, William G.
Senior Services of Stamford
Sentinel Communications Co.
Sexton Foundation
Seybert Institution for Poor Boys and Girls, Adam and Maria Sarah
Seymour and Troester Foundation
Shapiro, Inc.
Share Foundation
Shaw Foundation, Arch W.
Shawmut National Corp.
Shell Oil Co.
Shelton Cos.
Shenandoah Life Insurance Co.
Shoney's Inc.
Simon Foundation, William E. and Carol G.
Simpson Foundation
Simpson Foundation, John M.
Simpson Investment Co.
SIT Investment Associates, Inc.
Skinner Corp.
Skirball Foundation
Slant/Fin Corp.
Smith Benevolent Association, Buckingham
Smith Charitable Trust, W. W.
Smith Charities, John
Smith Foundation, Kelvin and Eleanor
Smith Foundation, Lon V.
Smith Foundation, Richard and Susan
Smucker Co., J.M.
Sonat
Sooner Pipe & Supply Corp.
South Texas Charitable Foundation
Square D Co.
Stamps Foundation, James L.
Standard Products Co.
Star Bank, N.A.
Starr Foundation
Statler Foundation
Statter Foundation, Amy Plant
Stauffer Foundation, John and Beverly
Stearns Trust, Artemas W.
Steelcase
Steele Foundation, Harry and Grace
Steele-Reese Foundation
Sterling Winthrop
Stern Foundation, Irvin
Stewards Fund
Stone Container Corp.
Stone Family Foundation, Norman H.
Stone Foundation, W. Clement and Jessie V.
Storage Technology Corp.
Stuart Center Charitable Trust, Hugh
Sullivan Foundation, Ray H. and Pauline
Summerfield Foundation, Solon E.
Sundstrand Corp.
Sunnen Foundation
Swalm Foundation
Sweet Life Foods
Swisher Foundation, Carl S.
Symmes Foundation, F. W.
Tamko Asphalt Products
Tandem Computers
Tandy Foundation, Anne Burnett and Charles
Tandy Foundation, David L.
Taylor Foundation, Fred and Harriett

TCF Banking & Savings, FSB
Teledyne
Tenneco
Texas Commerce Bank Houston, N.A.
Texas Gas Transmission Corp.
Texas Instruments
Textron
Thermo Electron Corp.
Thomas Built Buses L.P.
Thomas Foundation, Dorothy
3M Co.
Thurman Charitable Foundation for Children, Edgar A.
Time Insurance Co.
Times Mirror Co.
Timken Co.
Timmis Foundation, Michael & Nancy
Titus Foundation, C. W.
Tozer Foundation
Tracor, Inc.
Transamerica Corp.
Transco Energy Company
Tropicana Products, Inc.
True Trust, Henry A.
Trust Co. Bank
Trust for Mutual Understanding
TRW Corp.
Tucker Charitable Trust, Rose E.
Tull Charitable Foundation
Turner Charitable Foundation
Turrell Fund
21 International Holdings
Unger Foundation, Aber D.
Unilever United States
Union Bank of Switzerland Los Angeles Branch
Union Electric Co.
Union Pacific Corp.
United Parcel Service of America
U.S. Oil/Schmidt Family Foundation, Inc.
United States Trust Co. of New York
United Technologies Corp.
Universal Foods Corp.
Universal Leaf Tobacco Co.
Uris Brothers Foundation
USG Corp.
Utica National Insurance Group
Vale-Asche Foundation
Valero Energy Corp.
Valley Foundation
Valley National Bank of Arizona
Van Huffel Foundation, I. J.
Vaughn Foundation
Virginia Power Co.
Visciglia Foundation, Frank
Vollbrecht Foundation, Frederick A.
Vulcan Materials Co.
Wachovia Bank & Trust Co., N.A.
Waffle House, Inc.
Waggoner Charitable Trust, Crystelle
Wagner Foundation, Ltd., R. H.
Wal-Mart Stores
Walsh Charity Trust, Blanche M. Disney Co., Walt
Walter Family Trust, Byron L.
Wardle Family Foundation
Washington Forrest Foundation
Washington Trust Bank
Wasmer Foundation
Watkins Christian Foundation
Wauwatosa Savings & Loan Association
Wean Foundation, Raymond John
Weaver Foundation, Gil and Dody
Webb Charitable Trust, Susan Mott
Webster Charitable Foundation
Weckbaugh Foundation, Eleanore Mullen

Wegener Foundation, Herman and Mary
Weinberg Foundation, Harry and Jeanette
Weingart Foundation
Weir Foundation Trust
Weiss Foundation, William E.
Welch Testamentary Trust, George T.
Wells Fargo & Co.
Westend Foundation
Westinghouse Electric Corp.
Weyerhaeuser Co.
Wheeler Foundation
Whirlpool Corp.
White Consolidated Industries
Whitney Fund, David M.
Wickes Foundation, Harvey Randall
Wiener Foundation, Malcolm Hewitt
Wilkof Foundation, Edward and Ruth
Willard Foundation, Helen Parker
Wilsey Bennet Co.
Wilson Foundation, Frances Wood
Wilson Foundation, Marie C. and Joseph C.
Winn-Dixie Stores
Wisconsin Power & Light Co.
Wisconsin Public Service Corp.
Wolff Foundation, John M.
Wollenberg Foundation
Woodland Foundation
Woodward Fund-Atlanta, David, Helen, Marian
Woodward Governor Co.
Wright Foundation, Lola
Wrigley Co., Wm. Jr.
Wurzburg, Inc.
Young Foundation, Irvin L.
Young Foundation, Robert R.
Zale Foundation
Zarrow Foundation, Anne and Henry
Zenkel Foundation

General

ABB Process Automation
Addison-Wesley Publishing Co.
Aeroglide Corp.
AFG Industries, Inc.
AGA Gas, Inc.
Airborne Express Co.
Alabama Gas Corp. (An Energen Co.)
Aladdin Industries, Incorporated
Allegheny Power System, Inc.
Alyeska Pipeline Service Co.
AMCORE Bank, N.A. Rockford
Amdahl Corp.
American Filtrona Corp.
American General Corp.
American International Group, Inc.
American Mutual Insurance Cos.
American National Bank
American National Can Co.
American Re-Insurance Co.
American Stock Exchange
American Stores Co.
American Telephone & Telegraph Co./New York City Region
Ameritech Publishing
Amoskeag Co.
Ampacet Corp.
ARA Services
Arcata Corp.
Arkansas Best Corp.
Arkla
Asahi Glass America, Inc.
Associated Food Stores
Atlanta Journal & Constitution
Attleboro Pawtucket Savings Bank

Autodesk, Inc.
Autotrol Corp.
Avery Dennison Corp.
Awrey Bakeries
AXIA Incorporated
Baird & Co., Robert W.
Baker, Watts & Co.
Ball Corp.
Bally's - Las Vegas
Baltimore Life Insurance Co.
Bank of Boston Connecticut
Bank of Louisville
Bank of Oklahoma, N.A.
Bank One, Texas-Houston Office
Bank One, Texas, NA
Barry Corp., R. G.
Bartlett & Co.
Barton-Gillet Co.
Bayview Federal Bank
BDM International
Bean, L.L.
Beitzell & Co.
Belden Brick Co., Inc.
Bell Helicopter Textron
Benefit Trust Life Insurance Co.
Bergen Record Corp.
Berwind Corp.
Betz Laboratories
Bill Communications
Binney & Smith Inc.
Birmingham News Co.
Black & Decker Corp.
Blair and Co., William
Bloomingdale's
Boston Gas Co.
Boston Mutual Life Insurance Co.
Boulevard Bank, N.A.
Bourns, Inc.
Brakeley, John Price Jones Inc.
Branch Banking & Trust Co.
Brewer and Co., Ltd., C.
Briggs & Stratton Corp.
Brooklyn Union Gas Co.
Bryn Mawr Trust Co.
Burns International
Business Men's Assurance Co. of America
Caesar's World, Inc.
Caldwell Manufacturing Co.
Capital Holding Corp.
Carolina Telephone & Telegraph Co.
Carr Real Estate Services
Cascade Natural Gas Corp.
Casco Northern Bank
Castle & Cooke
CCB Financial Corp.
Centex Corp.
Central Life Assurance Co.
Central Maine Power Co.
Central Trust Co.
Charter Medical Corp.
Chase Lincoln First Bank, N.A.
Chemtech Industries
Chicago Sun-Times, Inc.
Chubb Life Insurance Co. of America
CIBA-GEIGY Corp.
Cincinnati Enquirer
Citizens Gas & Coke Utility
Clark Equipment Co.
CNA Insurance Cos.
Coachmen Industries
Coastal Corp.
Coleman Co.
Colgate-Palmolive Co.
Colonial Parking
Colorado Interstate Gas Co.
Colorado National Bankshares
Colorado State Bank of Denver
Commercial Federal Corp.
Commercial Intertech Corp.
Commonwealth Life Insurance Co.
Community Mutual Insurance Co.

Computer Associates International
Computer Sciences Corp.
Consolidated Rail Corp. (Conrail)
Continental Airlines
Control Data Corp.
Conwood Co. L.P.
Cooper Oil Tool
Cooper Tire & Rubber Co.
Corpus Christi Exploration Co.
Corvallis Clinic
Countrymark Cooperative
County Bank
Credit Agricole
Creditanstalt-Bankverein, New York
CSX Corp.
CT Corp. System
Cubic Corp.
Culbro Corp.
Curtis Industries, Helene
Cyprus Minerals Co.
Danforth Co., John W.
Dean Witter Discover
DEC International, Inc.
Delmarva Power & Light Co.
Diamond Shamrock
Diamond State Telephone Co.
Dibrell Brothers, Inc.
Didier Taylor Refractories Corp.
Diebold, Inc.
Digicon
Dime Savings Bank of New York
Dover Corp.
Dreyer's & Edy's Grand Ice Cream
Duquesne Light Co.
Duriron Co., Inc.
Eastland Bank
Ebsco Industries
Echlin Inc.
Educators Mutual Life Insurance Co.
Edwards & Sons, A.G.
Electronic Data Systems Corp.
Employers Insurance of Wausau, A Mutual Co.
Employers Mutual Casualty Co.
Encyclopaedia Britannica, Inc.
Enserch Corp.
Entex
Equimark Corp.
Equitable Resources
Evening Post Publishing Co.
Exchange Bank
Fabri-Kal Corp.
Fairfield Communities, Inc.
Farmers Group, Inc.
Federal Paper Board Co.
Federated Life Insurance Co.
Ferranti Tech
Ferro Corp.
Filene's Sons Co., William
First Alabama Bancshares
First Brands Corp.
First Commercial Bank N.A.
First Interstate Bank of Denver
First Interstate Bank & Trust Co.
First National Bank in Wichita
First NH Banks, Inc.
First of America Bank Corp.
First Security Bank of Idaho N.A.
First Security Bank of Utah N.A.
First Union National Bank of Florida
Fisher-Price
Fleet Bank
Fleet Bank N.A.
Florida Power & Light Co.
Foxmeyer Corp.
Frito-Lay
Fullerton Metals Co.
Galileo Electro-Optics Corp.
Gast Manufacturing Corp.
Gates Corp.
General Color Co.
General Housewares Corp.

General Railway Signal Corp.
General Signal Corp.
General Tire Inc.
Genesco
GenRad
Glatfelter Co., P.H.
Glendale Federal Bank
Grainger, W.W.
Grand Rapids Label Co.
Grand Trunk Corp.
Graphic Controls Corp.
Great Lakes Bancorp, FSB
Great Lakes Carbon Corp.
Greene Manufacturing Co.
Grinnell Mutual Reinsurance Co.
Grumman Corp.
Hammond Machinery
Hand Industries
Handy & Harman
Hanna Co., M.A.
Harbert Corp.
Harcourt General
Harleysville Mutual Insurance Co.
Harnischfeger Foundation
Harris Stores, Paul
Harris Trust & Savings Bank
Hartford Steam Boiler Inspection & Insurance Co.
Hawaii National Bank
Haworth, Inc.
Hecla Mining Co.
Heil Co.
Hercules Inc.
Hills Department Stores, Inc.
Hiram Walker & Sons Inc.
Hobart Corp.
Holly Sugar Corp.
Holyoke Mutual Insurance Co. in Salem
Homasote Co.
Home Savings of America, FA
Howmet Corp.
Huber, Hunt & Nichols
Huck International Inc.
Hudson Jewellers, J.B.
Huffy Corp.
Hughes Aircraft Co.
Hunt Oil Co.
Huntington Bancshares Inc.
ICH Corp.
Illinois Power Co.
Industrial Risk Insurers
Ingram Industries
Integra Bank/South
Intermark, Inc.
Interpublic Group of Cos.
Isaly Klondike Co.
IU International
Jaydor Corp.
Jefferson-Pilot
Jefferson-Pilot Communications
Jones Construction Co., J.A.
Journal Communications
Kaiser Aluminum & Chemical Corp.
Kaman Corp.
Kaneb Services, Inc.
Karmazin Products Corp.
Kaufman & Broad Home Corp.
Kaye, Scholer, Fierman, Hays & Handler
Keefe, Bruyette & Woods
Kellogg Co., M.W.
Kellwood Co.
Kendall Health Care Products
Kennecott Corp.
Kenwood U.S.A. Corp.
Ketchum & Co.
Kilmartin Industries
Kimball International
King Kullen Grocery Co., Inc.
KN Energy, Inc.
Kulicke & Soffa Industries
L.A. Gear
Lafarge Corp.
Lambda Electronics Inc.

LaSalle Bank Lake View
Law Companies Group
Law Company, Inc.
Leaseway Transportation Corp.
Libbey-Owens Ford Co.
Liberty Mutual Insurance Group/Boston
LIN Broadcasting Corp.
Lincoln Telecommunications Co.
Loctite Corp.
Lomas Financial Corp.
Longs Drug Stores
Lord Corp.
Louisville Gas & Electric Co.
Lowe's Cos.
Lykes Brothers Steamship Co.
MacLean-Fogg Co.
Maguire Oil Co.
Manitowoc Co.
Manufacturers Life Insurance Co. of America
Marine Midland Banks
Marion Fabrics
Maritz Inc.
Mascoma Savings Bank
Mass Merchandisers, Inc.
Massachusetts Mutual Life Insurance Co.
MBIA, Inc.
McDonald & Co. Securities
Measurex Corp.
Meenan Oil Co., Inc.
Mellon PSFS
Memphis Light Gas & Water Division
Mennen Co.
Mercantile Bankshares Corp.
Meridian Insurance Group Inc.
Merit Oil Corp.
Mesa Inc.
Metroquip
Mettler Instrument Corp.
Meyer, Inc., Fred
Michigan Mutual Insurance Corp.
Michigan National Corp.
Michigan Wheel Corp.
MidAmerica Radio Co.
MidCon Corp.
Midland Co.
Midmark Corp.
Milton Bradley Co.
Minnesota Power & Light Co.
Minolta Corp.
Mississippi Chemical Corp.
Mississippi Power & Light Co.
Missouri Public Service
Mitre Corp.
Monfort of Colorado, Inc.
Moore, Costello & Hart
Morse Shoe, Inc.
Motter Printing Press Co.
Mount Vernon Mills
MTS Systems Corp.
Mutual of America Life
Myers and Sons, D.
Nash-Finch Co.
National Car Rental System, Inc.
National City Bank, Columbus
National City Bank of Indiana
National Computer Systems
National Convenience Stores, Inc.
National Data Corp.
National Forge Co.
National Fuel Gas Co.
National Standard Co.
NationsBank Texas
New Jersey National Bank
New Jersey Resources Corp.
New York Mercantile Exchange
New York State Electric & Gas Corp.
The New Yorker Magazine, Inc.
Niagara Mohawk Power Corp.
NIBCO Inc.
Norfolk Shipbuilding & Drydock Corp.

General (cont.)

Nortek, Inc.
North American Coal Corp.
Northern Virginia Natural Gas
NorthPark National Bank
Northrop Corp.
Northwest Natural Gas Co.
Norton & Co., W.W.
NRC, Inc.
Oak Industries
Oakite Products
Ogilvy & Mather Worldwide
Ohio Casualty Corp.
Ohio Citizens Bank
Ohio Edison Corp.
Oki America Inc.
Old Kent Bank & Trust Co.
Old Republic International Corp.
One Valley Bank, N.A.
Ontario Corp.
Orange & Rockland Utilities, Inc.
Orion Capital Corp.
Ormet Corp.
Oster/Sunbeam Appliance Co.
Owens-Illinois
Packaging Corporation of
  America
Padnos Iron & Metal Co., Louis
Pamida, Inc.
Pan-American Life Insurance Co.
Park-Ohio Industries Inc.
Patrick Industries Inc.
Paxton Co., Frank
PayLess Drug Stores
Pennsylvania Power & Light
Pentair
People's Bank
Persis Corp.
PHH Corp.
Phoenix Resource Cos.
Pioneer Trust Bank, NA
Piper Jaffray Cos.
Plante & Moran, CPAs
PMI Food Equipment Group Inc.
PNC Bank
Ponderosa, Inc.
Preferred Risk Mutual Insurance
  Co.
Primark Corp.
PriMerit F.S.B.
Producers Livestock Marketing
  Association
Providence Energy Corp.
Provident Mutual Life Insurance
  Co. of Philadelphia
PSI Energy
Public Service Co. of Oklahoma
Quaker State Corp.
Questar Corp.
Raley's
Ranco, Inc.
Ransburg Corp.
Raytheon Engineers &
  Constructors
RB&W Corp.
Reading & Bates Corp.
Reasoner, Davis & Fox
Redlands Federal Bank
Reliable Life Insurance Co.
Reliance Group Holdings, Inc.
Reliance Insurance Cos.
Republic Automotive Parts, Inc.
Research-Cottrell Inc.
Riggs National Bank
Risdon Corp.
Riviana Foods
Rochester Community Savings
  Bank
Rochester Gas & Electric Corp.
Rochester Telephone Corp.
Rollins Inc.
Roseburg Forest Products Co.
Ross Laboratories
Royal Group Inc.
Ryland Group

Santa Fe International Corp.
Sara Lee Hosiery
Sargent Electric Co.
SCANA Corp.
Scientific-Atlanta
Scientific Brake & Equipment
  Co.
Scott, Foresman & Co.
Scotty's, Inc.
Sea-Land Service
Sealed Air Corp.
Sealright Co., Inc.
Security Life of Denver
Sedgwick James Inc.
Seneca Foods Corp.
ServiceMaster Co. L.P.
Seton Co.
Shaw Industries
Shawmut Bank of Franklin
  County
Sheldahl Inc.
Simkins Industries, Inc.
SNC Manufacturing Co.
Society for Savings
Somers Corp.
  (Mersman/Waldron)
Sonoco Products Co.
Southern Co. Services
Southern Indiana Gas & Electric
  Co.
Southland Corp.
Southtrust Corp.
Southwestern Public Service Co.
Sprint United Telephone
Standard Brands Paint Co.
State Mutual Life Assurance Co.
Steel Heddle Manufacturing Co.
Stein Roe & Farnham
  Investment Council
Steuart Petroleum Co.
Stewart & Stevenson Services
Stirtz, Bernards & Co.
Storage Technology Corp.
Storer Communications Inc.
Strawbridge & Clothier
Stroh Brewery Co.
Student Loan Marketing
  Association
Susquehanna-Pfaltzgraff Co.
T.T.X. Co.
Tampa Electric
TCF Banking & Savings, FSB
Thomson Information Publishing
  Group
Time Warner
Torrington Co.
Towle Manufacturing Co.
Trans-Apex
Transtar Inc.
Travelers Express Co.
Tremco Inc.
Tripifoods
Triskelion Ltd.
Trustmark National Bank
Tucson Electric Power Co.
Turner Corp.
Twentieth Century Insurance Co.
Tyler Corp.
UJB Financial Corp.
Unigard Security Insurance Co.
Union Equity Division of
  Farmland Industries
United Gas Pipe Line Co.
United Illuminating Co.
United Stationers Inc.
United Telephone Co. of Florida
United Telephone System
  (Eastern Group)
Universal Foods Corp.
US Bancorp
Vons Cos., Inc.
Washington National Insurance
  Co.
Washington Natural Gas Co.
Wausau Insurance Cos.
Webber Oil Co.
Welch Foods

West One Bancorp
Whittaker Corp.
WICOR, Inc.
Wilbur-Ellis Co.
Wimpey Inc., George
Wiremold Co.
Wisconsin Bell, Inc.
Wyman-Gordon Co.
Wynn's International, Inc.
Y.K.K. (U.S.A.) Inc.
Zapata Corp.
Zurn Industries

Homes

Abell-Hanger Foundation
Abernethy Testamentary
  Charitable Trust, Maye
  Morrison
Abney Foundation
Adams Memorial Fund, Emma J.
AFLAC
Ahmanson Foundation
Air Products & Chemicals
Alcon Laboratories, Inc.
Alden Trust, John W.
Alexander Foundation, Joseph
Allegheny Ludlum Corp.
Allendale Mutual Insurance Co.
Alliant Techsystems
AlliedSignal
Alltel/Western Region
ALPAC Corp.
Altman Foundation
Aluminum Co. of America
AMCORE Bank, N.A. Rockford
Amdur Braude Riley, Inc.
American Financial Corp.
American National Bank & Trust
  Co. of Chicago
American Schlafhorst
  Foundation, Inc.
AMETEK
Amfac/JMB Hawaii
AMP
Andersen Corp.
Andersen Foundation
Anderson Foundation, Robert C.
  and Sadie G.
Anschutz Family Foundation
Ansley Foundation, Dantzler
  Bond
AON Corp.
Apache Corp.
Applebaum Foundation
Arata Brothers Trust
Archbold Charitable Trust,
  Adrian and Jessie
Arkansas Power & Light Co.
Arkwright Foundation
Armbrust Chain Co.
Aron Charitable Foundation, J.
Asea Brown Boveri
Astor Foundation, Vincent
Atherton Family Foundation
Atkinson Foundation
Atkinson Foundation, Myrtle L.
Atlanta Gas Light Co.
Atran Foundation
Attleboro Pawtucket Savings
  Bank
Badgeley Residuary Charitable
  Trust, Rose M.
Badger Meter, Inc.
Baer Foundation, Alan and
  Marcia
Baier Foundation, Marie
Baird Charitable Trust, William
  Robert
Baker Charitable Foundation,
  Jessie Foos
Baker Trust, Clayton
Banbury Fund
Banc One Illinois Corp.
Bank IV
Bank of America Arizona
Bank of Boston Corp.
Bank One, Youngstown, NA

BarclaysAmerican Corp.
Barnes Group
Barra Foundation
Barstow Foundation
Bauer Foundation, M. R.
Bauervic Foundation, Peggy
Baumker Charitable Foundation,
  Elsie and Harry
Bausch & Lomb
Beazley Foundation
Beech Aircraft Corp.
Beecher Foundation, Florence
  Simon
Beitzell & Co.
Belk Stores
Bemis Company
Beneficial Corp.
Bernstein & Co., Sanford C.
Berwind Corp.
Best Foundation, Walter J. and
  Edith E.
Bigelow Foundation, F. R.
Bingham Second Betterment
  Fund, William
Birnschein Foundation, Alvin
  and Marion
Bishop Foundation
Blaustein Foundation, Jacob and
  Hilda
Bleibtreu Foundation, Jacob
Block, H&R
Blount
Blowitz-Ridgeway Foundation
Blue Bell, Inc.
Blum-Kovler Foundation
Boatmen's First National Bank
  of Oklahoma
Bodman Foundation
Boeing Co.
Boise Cascade Corp.
Booth-Bricker Fund
Borden
Borkee Hagley Foundation
Bossong Hosiery Mills
Bowyer Foundation, Ambrose
  and Gladys
Brach Foundation, Edwin I.
Bradley-Turner Foundation
Bremer Foundation, Otto
Brooks Foundation, Gladys
Brown Foundation, Joe W. and
  Dorothy Dorsett
Brunner Foundation, Robert
Bryce Memorial Fund, William
  and Catherine
Buckley Trust, Thomas D.
Bucyrus-Erie
Buehler Foundation, Emil
Bunbury Company
Burlington Resources
Burndy Corp.
Burns Foundation, Fritz B.
Bush Foundation
Business Incentives
C. E. and S. Foundation
Cabot Corp.
Cain Foundation, Gordon and
  Mary
Caldwell Foundation, Hardwick
Callaway Foundation, Fuller E.
Cameron Foundation, Harry S.
  and Isabel C.
Camp Younts Foundation
Campbell Foundation, J. Bulow
Capital Fund Foundation
Capital Holding Corp.
Caplan Charity Foundation,
  Julius H.
Carr Real Estate Services
Carter Charitable Trust, Wilbur
  Lee
Carter Foundation, Amon G.
Carter Foundation, Beirne
Caterpillar
Cauthorn Charitable Trust, John
  and Mildred
Centel Corp.

Central Bank of the South
Central Hudson Gas & Electric
  Corp.
Central Life Assurance Co.
Central Maine Power Co.
CertainTeed Corp.
Chambers Development Co.
Chapman Charitable Trust, H. A.
  and Mary K.
Chase Manhattan Bank, N.A.
Chesapeake Corp.
Chevron Corp.
Chicago Board of Trade
Chicago Sun-Times, Inc.
Childs Charitable Foundation,
  Roberta M.
Chiles Foundation
Cincinnati Bell
Cincinnati Foundation for the
  Aged
CIT Group Holdings
Citicorp
Citizens Bank
Civitas Fund
CLARCOR
Clark Foundation
Clark-Winchcole Foundation
Clay Foundation
Clipper Ship Foundation
Clowes Fund
CM Alliance Cos.
Coen Family Foundation,
  Charles S. and Mary
Coffey Foundation
Cohen Foundation, Naomi and
  Nehemiah
Cole Trust, Quincy
Collins Foundation
Colonial Life & Accident
  Insurance Co.
Columbia Foundation
Comstock Foundation
Cone Mills Corp.
Conn Memorial Foundation
Consolidated Natural Gas Co.
Constantin Foundation
Consumer Farmer Foundation
Continental Corp.
Cook Charitable Foundation
Cook Foundation, Louella
Cooper Charitable Trust, Richard
  H.
Copperweld Steel Co.
County Bank
Craig Foundation, J. Paul
Crane Co.
Crane Fund for Widows and
  Children
Cranston Print Works
Crels Foundation
CRL Inc.
Cudahy Fund, Patrick and Anna
  M.
Cummings Foundation, Nathan
Cummings Memorial Fund
  Trust, Frances L. and Edwin L.
Cuneo Foundation
Curtice-Burns Foods
Dana Corp.
Dater Foundation, Charles H.
Daugherty Foundation
Davenport-Hatch Foundation
Davidson Family Charitable
  Foundation
Day Foundation, Cecil B.
DCNY Corp.
DeCamp Foundation, Ira W.
Delany Charitable Trust,
  Beatrice P.
Deluxe Corp.
Demoulas Supermarkets
Deposit Guaranty National Bank
DeRoy Testamentary Foundation
DeVlieg Foundation, Charles
DeVos Foundation, Richard and
  Helen
Dewar Foundation

Dewing Foundation, Frances R.
Dial Corp.
Dickenson Foundation, Harriet Ford
Dickson Foundation
Dishman Charitable Foundation Trust, H. E. and Kate
Dodson Foundation, James Glenwell and Clara May
Doheny Foundation, Carrie Estelle
Donaldson Charitable Trust, Oliver S. and Jennie R.
Donaldson Co.
Donaldson Co.
Doss Foundation, M. S.
Dougherty, Jr. Foundation, James R.
Dover Foundation
Dow Foundation, Herbert H. and Grace A.
Dow Fund, Alden and Vada
Dower Foundation, Thomas W.
Dreiling and Albina Dreiling Charitable Trust, Leo J.
du Pont de Nemours & Co., E. I.
Duchossois Industries
Duke Endowment
Duncan Trust, James R.
Duncan Trust, John G.
Dunspaugh-Dalton Foundation
duPont Foundation, Alfred I.
duPont Foundation, Chichester
Durst Foundation
Dweck Foundation, Samuel R.
Earl-Beth Foundation
Easley Trust, Andrew H. and Anne O.
Eaton Corp.
Eaton Foundation, Edwin M. and Gertrude S.
Ebell of Los Angeles Rest Cottage Association
Ebell of Los Angeles Scholarship Endowment Fund
Ebert Charitable Foundation, Horatio B.
Eccles Foundation, Marriner S.
Eden Hall Foundation
Eder Foundation, Sidney and Arthur
Edwards Foundation, Jes
EIS Foundation
Eisenberg Foundation, George M.
El Pomar Foundation
Electronic Data Systems Corp.
Elkin Memorial Foundation, Neil Warren and William Simpson
Ellis Foundation
Emerson Electric Co.
Emerson Foundation, Fred L.
Emery Memorial, Thomas J.
English-Bonter-Mitchell Foundation
Enright Foundation
Enron Corp.
Erb Lumber Co.
Ernest & Julio Gallo Winery
Ernsthausen Charitable Foundation, John F. and Doris E.
Eyman Trust, Jesse
Factor Family Foundation, Max
Faith Charitable Trust
Faith Home Foundation
Fales Foundation Trust
Falk Foundation, David
Farnsworth Trust, Charles A.
Faulkner Trust, Marianne Gaillard
Federal National Mortgage Assn., Fannie Mae
Fein Foundation
Fels Fund, Samuel S.
Ferebee Endowment, Percy O.
Fidelity Bank
Fikes Foundation, Leland
Finch Foundation, Doak

Finley Charitable Trust, J. B.
Finley Foundation, A. E.
Finnegan Foundation, John D.
First Fidelity Bancorporation
First Interstate Bank of Arizona
First Interstate Bank of Texas, N.A.
First Petroleum Corp.
First Union Corp.
Fish Foundation, Ray C.
Fisher Foundation
Fleet Bank of New York
Fletcher Foundation
Fletcher Foundation, A. J.
Flickinger Memorial Trust
Flintridge Foundation
Florence Foundation
Florida Rock Industries
Forbes
Forbes Charitable Trust, Herman
Ford Fund, Benson and Edith
Ford Fund, William and Martha
Ford Meter Box Co.
Formrite Tube Co.
Foster Foundation
Foulds Trust, Claiborne F
Foundation for Seacoast Health
Fox Charitable Foundation, Harry K. & Emma R.
Fox Foundation, John H.
Fox Steel Co.
Frank Family Foundation, A. J.
Frank Foundation, Ernest and Elfriede
Frankel Foundation
Franklin Charitable Trust, Ershel
Freas Foundation
Frederick Foundation
Freedom Forum
Freeman Foundation, Carl M.
Frees Foundation
Frelinghuysen Foundation
Friedland Family Foundation, Samuel
Friendly Rosenthal Foundation
Frohlich Charitable Trust, Ludwig W.
Frueauff Foundation, Charles A.
Fuller Foundation, C. G.
Fullerton Foundation
Funderburke & Associates
Funderburke & Associates
Gage Foundation, Philip and Irene Toll
Galkin Charitable Trust, Ira S. and Anna
Gannett Publishing Co., Guy
Gannett Publishing Co., Guy
Gebbie Foundation
GEICO Corp.
Gellert Foundation, Carl
Gellert Foundation, Celia Berta
General American Life Insurance Co.
General Mills
General Motors Corp.
Georgia Power Co.
German Protestant Orphan Asylum Association
Gerson Family Foundation, Benjamin J.
Gerson Trust, B. Milfred
Gerstacker Foundation, Rollin M.
Gheens Foundation
Gifford Charitable Corporation, Rosamond
Giles Foundation, Edward C.
Gindi Associates Foundation
Ginter Foundation, Karl and Anna
Glaser Foundation
Glazer Foundation, Madelyn L.
Globe Newspaper Co.
Goddard Foundation, Charles B.
Goldbach Foundation, Ray and Marie
Goldman Foundation, Herman

Goldstein Foundation, Leslie and Roslyn
Goldstein Foundation, Leslie and Roslyn
Goldwyn Foundation, Samuel
Goodman Foundation, Edward and Marion
Goodyear Foundation, Josephine
Goody's Manufacturing Corp.
Gore Family Memorial Foundation
Gorin Foundation, Nehemiah
Gottesman Fund
Gottwald Foundation
Grace & Co., W.R.
Gradison & Co.
Graham Fund, Philip L.
Grant Foundation, Charles M. and Mary D.
Graybar Electric Co.
Green Charitable Trust, Leslie H. and Edith C.
Green Fund
Gries Charity Fund, Lucile and Robert H.
Griffin Foundation, Rosa May
Grigg-Lewis Trust
Gross Charitable Trust, Walter L. and Nell R.
Grotto Foundation
Group Health Plan Inc.
Grundy Foundation
Gulf Power Co.
Gulton Foundation
Guttman Foundation, Stella and Charles
Haas Foundation, Paul and Mary
Haas Fund, Walter and Elise
Haas, Jr. Fund, Evelyn and Walter
Habig Foundation, Arnold F.
Hagedorn Fund
Hall Family Foundations
Hall Foundation
Hall Foundation
Hallett Charitable Trust
Hallett Charitable Trust, Jessie F.
Hallmark Cards
Halmos Foundation
Hamilton Bank
Hamman Foundation, George and Mary Josephine
Hancock Foundation, Luke B.
Hanes Foundation, John W. and Anna H.
Harland Charitable Foundation, John and Wilhelmina D.
Harper Foundation, Philip S.
Harris Foundation, John H. and Lucille
Harsco Corp.
Hartford Courant Foundation
Hayden Foundation, William R. and Virginia
Hayfields Foundation
Hayswood Foundation
Hazen Foundation, Edward W.
Hechinger Co.
Hedrick Foundation, Frank E.
Heginbotham Trust, Will E.
Heilicher Foundation, Menahem
Heinz Co., H.J.
Heinz Endowment, Vira I.
Helis Foundation
Herbst Foundation
Herndon Foundation, Alonzo F. Herndon and Norris B.
Herrick Foundation
Hiawatha Education Foundation
Hill Crest Foundation
Hillcrest Foundation
Hillman Foundation
Hillsdale Fund
Himmelfarb Foundation, Paul and Annetta
Hirschl Trust for Charitable Purposes, Irma T.

Hobart Memorial Fund, Marion W.
Hoblitzelle Foundation
Hodge Foundation
Holden Fund, James and Lynelle
Holzer Memorial Foundation, Richard H.
Home Depot
Home for Aged Men
Hoover Foundation
Horowitz Foundation, Gedale B. and Barbara S.
Hospital Corp. of America
Houck Foundation, May K.
Household International
Houston Endowment
Howell Foundation, Eric and Jessie
Hubbard Broadcasting
Hugoton Foundation
Hulme Charitable Foundation, Milton G.
Hultquist Foundation
Humana
Humphrey Foundation, Glenn & Gertrude
Hunt Alternatives Fund
Hunt Foundation
Hunter Trust, Emily S. and Coleman A.
Hurst Foundation
Hutchins Foundation, Mary J.
Hutzell Foundation
Hyams Foundation
Hyde and Watson Foundation
Illinois Tool Works
Indiana Desk Co.
Inland Container Corp.
Inland Steel Industries
Interco
International Foundation
Interstate Packaging Co.
Irmas Charitable Foundation, Audrey and Sydney
Isaly Klondike Co.
ITT Hartford Insurance Group
Ivakota Association
J.P. Morgan & Co.
Jackson Charitable Trust, Marion Gardner
Jackson Foundation
Janeway Foundation, Elizabeth Bixby
Janirve Foundation
Janssen Foundation, Henry
Jaqua Foundation
Jasper Desk Co.
Jenkins Foundation, George W.
Jennings Foundation, Alma
Jergens Foundation, Andrew
John Hancock Mutual Life Insurance Co.
Johnson Foundation, Helen K. and Arthur E.
Johnstone and H. Earle Kimball Foundation, Phyllis Kimball
Jones Foundation, Daisy Marquis
Jones Foundation, Harvey and Bernice
Jones Foundation, Helen
Jost Foundation, Charles and Mabel P.
Kaiser Foundation, Betty E. and George B.
Kamps Memorial Foundation, Gertrude
Kangesser Foundation, Robert E., Harry A., and M. Sylvia
Kapiloff Foundation, Leonard
Kaplen Foundation
Kaplun Foundation, Morris J. and Betty
Kaufmann Foundation, Henry
Kautz Family Foundation
Kawabe Memorial Fund
Kawabe Memorial Fund
Kayser Foundation
Keebler Co.

Kennedy Foundation, Ethel
Kentland Foundation
Kerney Foundation, James
Kerr Foundation, Robert S. and Grayce B.
Kiewit Sons, Peter
Kilworth Charitable Trust, William
Kimball International
Kingston Foundation
Kiplinger Foundation
Klee Foundation, Conrad and Virginia
Klipstein Foundation, Ernest Christian
Klosk Fund, Louis and Rose
Knowles Charitable Memorial Trust, Gladys E.
Knox Family Foundation
Koehler Foundation, Marcia and Otto
Koffler Family Foundation
Kohl Charitable Foundation, Allen D.
Kohl Charities, Herbert H.
Koret Foundation
Kowalski Sausage Co.
Kramer Foundation
Kramer Foundation, Louise
Lacy Foundation
Ladish Co.
Lafarge Corp.
Lancaster Colony
Lapham-Hickey Steel Corp.
Laros Foundation, R. K.
Lasdon Foundation
Lattner Foundation, Forrest C.
Lauffer Trust, Charles A.
Laughlin Trust, George A.
Lavanburg-Corner House
Law Foundation, Robert O.
Lawrence Foundation, Lind
LBJ Family Foundation
LDI Charitable Foundation
Lee Enterprises
Lehrman Foundation, Jacob and Charlotte
Lender Family Foundation
Leonardt Foundation
Levin Foundation, Philip and Janice
Liberty Diversified Industries Inc.
Lieberman Enterprises
Lightner Sams Foundation
Lilly & Co., Eli
Lincoln Fund
Lincy Foundation
Lindsay Foundation
Link, Jr. Foundation, George
Lipsky Foundation, Fred and Sarah
Little, Arthur D.
Littlefield Memorial Trust, Ida Ballou
Loeb Partners Corp.
Logan Foundation, E. J.
Long Foundation, George A. and Grace
Lost Tree Charitable Foundation
Loughran Foundation, Mary and Daniel
Louis Foundation, Michael W.
Luck Stone
Lukens
M. E. G. Foundation
M.E. Foundation
Maas Foundation, Benard L.
Mack Foundation, J. S.
Maclellan Charitable Trust, R. J.
Maclellan Foundation
Maclellan Foundation, Robert L. and Kathrina H.
Macy & Co., R.H.
Mandel Foundation, Joseph and Florence
Maneely Fund
Manville Corp.

Homes (cont.)

Marcus Brothers Textiles Inc.
Mardag Foundation
Marion Merrell Dow
Markey Charitable Fund, John C.
Marshall Foundation
Marshburn Foundation
Martin Marietta Corp.
Martini Foundation, Nicholas
Masserini Charitable Trust,
Maurice J.
Massey Charitable Trust
Massey Foundation
Mather Charitable Trust, S.
Livingston
Mathis-Pfohl Foundation
Matthews International Corp.
Mautz Paint Co.
May Foundation, Wilbur
Mazza Foundation
MBIA, Inc.
McAlister Charitable
Foundation, Harold
McAlonan Trust, John A.
McCarthy Charities
McCormick Foundation,
Chauncey and Marion Deering
McCormick Tribune Foundation,
Robert R.
McCune Charitable Trust, John
R.
McCune Foundation
McDonald's Corp.
McDonnell Douglas Corp.
McDonnell Douglas Corp.-West
McDougall Charitable Trust,
Ruth Camp
McEachern Charitable Trust, D.
V. & Ida J.
McGraw Foundation
McGregor Fund
MCI Communications Corp.
McIntyre Foundation, C. S. and
Marion F.
MCJ Foundation
McLean Contributionship
McMahon Charitable Trust
Fund, Father John J.
McNutt Charitable Trust, Amy
Shelton
Mead Corp.
Meadows Foundation
Medina Foundation
Mellon Foundation, Richard King
Mengle Foundation, Glenn and
Ruth
Meredith Corp.
Meredith Foundation
Mertz Foundation, Martha
Metropolitan Health Foundation
Metropolitan Life Insurance Co.
Meyer Foundation, Alice
Kleberg Reynolds
Meyer Foundation, Baron de
Hirsch
Meyer Foundation, Eugene and
Agnes E.
Meyer Foundation, Robert R.
Michigan Gas Utilities
Midwest Resources
Millbrook Tribute Garden
Milliken & Co.
Mingenback Foundation, Julia J.
Miniger Memorial Foundation,
Clement O.
Mitchell Family Foundation,
Edward D. and Anna
Mobil Oil Corp.
Monaghan Charitable Trust, Rose
Monfort Charitable Foundation
Monsanto Co.
Moores Foundation
Moores Foundation, Harry C.
Morania Foundation
Morgan Stanley & Co.
Morrill Charitable Foundation

Morrison Trust, Louise L.
Muller Foundation
Murphy Co., G.C.
Murphy Foundation, Dan
National Machinery Co.
National Presto Industries
Nationwide Insurance Cos.
Nelson Foundation, Florence
Nestle U.S.A. Inc.
New England Mutual Life
Insurance Co.
New-Land Foundation
New York Foundation
New York Times Co.
Newman's Own
News & Observer Publishing Co.
Nichols Foundation
Noble Charitable Trust, John L.
and Ethel G.
Noble Foundation, Samuel
Roberts
Nordson Corp.
Nortek, Inc.
Northeast Utilities
Northern States Power Co.
Northwest Area Foundation
Northwest Natural Gas Co.
Norton Co.
Norton Foundation Inc.
Norwest Bank Nebraska
Noyes, Jr. Memorial Foundation,
Nicholas H.
O'Connor Co.
Odell and Helen Pfeiffer Odell
Fund, Robert Stewart
O'Fallon Trust, Martin J. and
Mary Anne
Oglebay Norton Co.
O'Neil Foundation, Casey Albert
T.
O'Neil Foundation, M. G.
Ontario Corp.
Oppenstein Brothers Foundation
Orange Orphan Society
Orbit Valve Co.
Ottenstein Family Foundation
Overbrook Foundation
Overstreet Foundation
Owen Trust, B. B.
Oxford Foundation
Pacific Mutual Life Insurance Co.
Pacific Telesis Group
Packard Foundation, David and
Lucile
Palisades Educational Foundation
Parker Foundation, Theodore
Edson
Parsons - W.D. Charities, Vera
Davis
Pasadena Area Residential Aid
Patterson Charitable Fund, W. I.
Pax Christi Foundation
Payne Foundation, Frank E. and
Seba B.
Peabody Foundation, Amelia
Pellegrino-Realmuto Charitable
Foundation
Pendleton Memorial Fund,
William L. and Ruth T.
Penn Foundation, William
Penney Foundation, James C.
Pennington Foundation, Irene W.
and C. B.
People's Bank
Peoples Energy Corp.
Perini Foundation, Joseph
Perkin-Elmer Corp.
Perkin-Elmer Corp.
Perkins Foundation, Joe and Lois
Perley Fund, Victor E.
Pet
Peters Foundation, R. D. and
Linda
Phillips Family Foundation, Jay
and Rose
Phillips Foundation, Dr. P.
Pick, Jr. Fund, Albert
Pickford Foundation, Mary

Pillsbury Foundation
Pitts Foundation, William H. and
Lula E.
Pott Foundation, Herman T. and
Phenie R.
Potts Memorial Foundation
Powers Foundation
PPG Industries
Prairie Foundation
Premier Bank
Premier Industrial Corp.
Prentiss Foundation, Elisabeth
Severance
Prince Corp.
Prudential Insurance Co. of
America
Public Welfare Foundation
Puett Foundation, Nelson
Pulitzer Publishing Co.
Puterbaugh Foundation
Quaker Chemical Corp.
Quaker Oats Co.
R&B Tool Co.
Rabb Foundation, Harry W.
Ralston Purina Co.
Randa
Raskob Foundation for Catholic
Activities
Rauch Foundation
Recognition Equipment
Regenstein Foundation
Reliable Life Insurance Co.
Resnick Foundation, Jack and
Pearl
Retirement Research Foundation
Reynolds Charitable Trust, Kate
B.
Rhodebeck Charitable Trust
Rice Family Foundation, Jacob
and Sophie
Richardson Foundation, Sid W.
Rienzi Foundation
Roberts Foundation, Dora
Robertson Brothers
Roblee Foundation, Joseph H.
and Florence A.
Rockwell Fund
Roehl Foundation
Rohm and Haas Company
Rollins Luetkemeyer Charitable
Foundation
RosaMary Foundation
Roseburg Forest Products Co.
Rosenberg Foundation, Sunny
and Abe
Rosenthal Foundation, Benjamin
J.
Rosenthal Foundation, Samuel
Ross Foundation, Walter G.
Ross Laboratories
Ross Memorial Foundation, Will
Roth Foundation, Louis T.
Rouse Co.
Royal Group Inc.
Ruan Foundation Trust, John
Rubbermaid
Rubin Foundation, Samuel
Sage Foundation
Sandy Foundation, George H.
Sandy Hill Foundation
Sanguinetti Foundation,
Annunziata
Santa Fe Pacific Corp.
Sapirstein-Stone-Weiss
Foundation
Sara Lee Corp.
Sargent Foundation, Newell B.
Sarkeys Foundation
Sattler Beneficial Trust, Daniel
A. and Edna J.
Saturno Foundation
Saul Foundation, Joseph E. &
Norma G.
Saunders Foundation
Schmidlapp Trust No. 1, Jacob G.
Schmitt Foundation, Arthur J.
Schneider Foundation Corp., Al
J.

Schottenstein Foundation,
Jerome & Saul
Schrafft and Bertha E. Schrafft
Charitable Trust, William E.
Schramm Foundation
Schroeder Foundation, Walter
Schultz Foundation
Scott Foundation, William R.,
John G., and Emma
Seabury Foundation
Sebastian Foundation
Segal Charitable Trust, Barnet
Seid Foundation, Barre
Sentinel Communications Co.
Seybert Institution for Poor Boys
and Girls, Adam and Maria
Sarah
Share Foundation
Shawmut National Corp.
Shelton Cos.
Shoney's Inc.
Signet Bank/Maryland
Simon Foundation, William E.
and Carol G.
SIT Investment Associates, Inc.
Sjostrom & Sons
Slant/Fin Corp.
Smith Charitable Trust, W. W.
Smith Charities, John
Smith Corp., A.O.
Smith Foundation, Kenneth L.
and Eva S.
Smith Foundation, Lon V.
Smith, Jr. Charitable Trust, Jack
J.
Smock Foundation, Frank and
Laura
Snyder Foundation, Harold B.
and Dorothy A.
Society for the Increase of the
Ministry
Sonat
Soref Foundation, Samuel M.
Soref and Helene K.
Speas Foundation, Victor E.
Special People In Need
Square D Co.
Stanley Works
State Street Bank & Trust Co.
Steelcase
Steele-Reese Foundation
Steiger Memorial Fund, Albert
Steiner Charitable Fund, Albert
Steinsapir Family Foundation,
Julius L. and Libhie B.
Stella D'Oro Biscuit Co.
Sterling Winthrop
Stern Memorial Trust, Sidney
Stevens Foundation, Abbot and
Dorothy H.
Stoddard Charitable Trust
Stone Foundation, David S.
Stone Foundation, France
Stonecutter Mills Corp.
Stonestreet Trust, Eusebia S.
Storer Foundation, George B.
Strake Foundation
Stranahan Foundation
Stratford Foundation
Straus Foundation, Aaron and
Lillie
Stride Rite Corp.
Stry Foundation, Paul E.
Stubblefield, Estate of Joseph L.
Stulsaft Foundation, Morris
Stupp Brothers Bridge & Iron Co.
Sunderland Foundation, Lester T.
Sundstrand Corp.
Swift Memorial Health Care
Foundation
Swig Foundation
Symmes Foundation, F. W.
Synovus Financial Corp.
Taper Foundation, Mark
Taylor Foundation
Taylor Foundation, Ruth and
Vernon
Teledyne

Texas Commerce Bank Houston,
N.A.
Thomas Foundation, Dorothy
Thomas Memorial Foundation,
Theresa A.
Thompson Trust, Thomas
Thorne Foundation
3M Co.
Thurman Charitable Foundation
for Children, Edgar A.
Times Mirror Co.
Titmus Foundation
Tonkin Foundation, Tom and
Helen
Tonya Memorial Foundation
Tozer Foundation
Tracor, Inc.
Tranzonic Cos.
Treuhaft Foundation
Trimble Family Foundation,
Robert Mize and Isa White
Trull Foundation
Trust Co. Bank
Turner Charitable Foundation
Tyson Foods, Inc.
Union Camp Corp.
Union Electric Co.
Union Manufacturing Co.
Union Pacific Corp.
United Service Foundation
United States Trust Co. of New
York
United Togs Inc.
Universal Leaf Tobacco Co.
Unocal Corp.
USF&G Co.
Valley Foundation
Van Every Foundation, Philip L.
Van Houten Charitable Trust
Van Nuys Foundation, I. N. and
Susanna H.
Vesuvius Charitable Foundation
Virginia Power Co.
Vlasic Foundation
Vogt Machine Co., Henry
Waggoner Foundation, E. Paul
and Helen Buck
Wagner Manufacturing Co., E. R.
Wal-Mart Stores
Wallin Foundation
Walthall Perpetual Charitable
Trust, Marjorie T.
Ward Foundation, A.
Montgomery
Ward Heritage Foundation,
Mamie McFaddin
Wardle Family Foundation
Washington Square Fund
Waters Charitable Trust, Robert
S.
Wauwatosa Savings & Loan
Association
Wean Foundation, Raymond John
Weaver Foundation
Webb Foundation
Webster Foundation, Edwin S.
Wedum Foundation
Weezie Foundation
Wege Foundation
Weiss Fund, Clara
Welch Testamentary Trust,
George T.
Wellons Foundation
Wendt Foundation, Margaret L.
West One Bancorp
Westend Foundation
Weyerhaeuser Foundation,
Frederick and Margaret L.
Whalley Charitable Trust
Whirlpool Corp.
Whitaker Charitable Foundation,
Lyndon C.
Whitehead Foundation
Whitehead Foundation, Joseph B.
Whitehead Foundation, Lettie
Pate
Whiteley Foundation, John and
Elizabeth

Whitener Foundation
Whiting Foundation
Whitney Fund, David M.
Willard Helping Fund, Cecilia Young
Williams Cos.
Wilson Fund, Matilda R.
Wilson Public Trust, Ralph
Wilson Trust, Lula C.
Winston Research Foundation, Harry
Wisconsin Energy Corp.
Wolff Foundation, John M.
Wolff Memorial Foundation, Pauline Sterne
Wolfson Family Foundation
Woodward Fund-Atlanta, David, Helen, Marian
Wright Foundation, Lola
Yassenoff Foundation, Leo
Yeager Charitable Trust, Lester E.
Zemurray Foundation

Legal Aid

Acushnet Co.
Ahmanson Foundation
Allendale Mutual Insurance Co.
Alltel/Western Region
Altman Foundation
Aluminum Co. of America
AMAX
American Brands
American Financial Corp.
American Home Products Corp.
American United Life Insurance Co.
Andersen Corp.
Anderson Foundation, John W.
Anderson Foundation, M. D.
Annenberg Foundation
Apple Computer, Inc.
Atherton Family Foundation
Attleboro Pawtucket Savings Bank
Avon Products
Babcock Foundation, Mary Reynolds
Banbury Fund
Banc One Illinois Corp.
Bank of Tokyo Trust Co.
Bauer Foundation, M. R.
Bechtel Group
Bechtel, Jr. Foundation, S. D.
Belding Heminway Co.
Ben & Jerry's Homemade
Bettingen Corporation, Burton G.
Bigelow Foundation, F. R.
Block, H&R
Blum-Kovler Foundation
Booz Allen & Hamilton
Bremer Foundation, Otto
Brunswick Corp.
Buchalter, Nemer, Fields, & Younger
Bull Foundation, Henry W.
Capital Holding Corp.
Carnegie Corporation of New York
Chase Manhattan Bank, N.A.
Chevron Corp.
Clark Foundation
Clark Foundation, Edna McConnell
Clipper Ship Foundation
Clorox Co.
CM Alliance Cos.
Colonial Life & Accident Insurance Co.
Columbia Foundation
Commerce Clearing House
Comstock Foundation
Confidence Foundation
Connemara Fund
Copperweld Steel Co.
Cowles Charitable Trust
Crum and Forster

Cummings Foundation, Nathan
Cummins Engine Co.
Deutsch Co.
Diamond Foundation, Aaron
DiRosa Foundation, Rene and Veronica
Donaldson Co.
Donovan, Leisure, Newton & Irvine
du Pont de Nemours & Co., E. I.
Duke Power Co.
Duncan Trust, John G.
Dunspaugh-Dalton Foundation
Dyson Foundation
Eaton Corp.
Eccles Foundation, George S. and Dolores Dore
Eccles Foundation, Marriner S.
EG&G Inc.
Equifax
Farnsworth Trust, Charles A.
Fein Foundation
Feinberg Foundation, Joseph and Bessie
Fidelity Bank
First Fidelity Bancorporation
First Union Corp.
Fletcher Foundation
Florida Steel Corp.
Forbes
Freedom Forum
French Oil Mill Machinery Co.
Frueauff Foundation, Charles A.
Fry Foundation, Lloyd A.
Fuchsberg Family Foundation, Abraham
Funderburke & Associates
Funderburke & Associates
Gerbode Foundation, Wallace Alexander
Giant Eagle
Gleason Foundation, Katherine
Glen Eagles Foundation
Goldman Foundation, Herman
Goldman Foundation, William
Goldseker Foundation of Maryland, Morris
Gottesman Fund
Grant Foundation, Charles M. and Mary D.
Grassmann Trust, E. J.
Green Fund
Greenfield Foundation, Albert M.
Guggenheim Foundation, Daniel and Florence
Haas, Jr. Fund, Evelyn and Walter
Haigh-Scatena Foundation
Hartmarx Corp.
Hastings Trust
Hastings Trust
Hazen Foundation, Edward W.
Hechinger Co.
Heinz Co., H.J.
Hemingway Foundation, Robert G.
Hermann Foundation, Grover
Hill Foundation
Hogan Foundation, Royal Barney
Hopeman Brothers
Hughes Memorial Foundation, Charles Evans
Humana
Hunt Alternatives Fund
Hyams Foundation
IBM South Africa Projects Fund
Illinois Tool Works
Indiana Desk Co.
International Foundation
Irmas Charitable Foundation, Audrey and Sydney
J.P. Morgan & Co.
Jackson Foundation
Jameson Foundation, J. W. and Ida M.
Janirve Foundation
Jones Foundation, Daisy Marquis

Kaplen Foundation
Kaye, Scholer, Fierman, Hays & Handler
Kennecott Corp.
Kerr-McGee Corp.
Kiplinger Foundation
Koret Foundation
Lennon Foundation, Fred A.
Lipton, Thomas J.
Little, Arthur D.
Livingston Foundation
MacArthur Foundation, John D. and Catherine T.
Macy & Co., R.H.
Mardag Foundation
Marshall Foundation
Mason Charitable Foundation
McCormick Tribune Foundation, Robert R.
McIntosh Foundation
McKenna Foundation, Philip M.
Meadows Foundation
Metropolitan Life Insurance Co.
Meyer Foundation, Eugene and Agnes E.
Mobil Oil Corp.
Monell Foundation, Ambrose
Montgomery Ward & Co.
Moses Fund, Henry and Lucy
Motorola
Nalco Chemical Co.
National Machinery Co.
New-Land Foundation
New World Foundation
New York Foundation
The New Yorker Magazine, Inc.
Nordson Corp.
Northeast Utilities
Northern States Power Co.
Ogilvy & Mather Worldwide
Overbrook Foundation
Pacific Mutual Life Insurance Co.
Perkin-Elmer Corp.
Perkin-Elmer Corp.
Peterloon Foundation
Pfizer
Philip Morris Cos.
Phillips Petroleum Co.
Pittsburgh National Bank
Playboy Enterprises, Inc.
Prudential Insurance Co. of America
Public Welfare Foundation
Quaker Oats Co.
Questar Corp.
Raskob Foundation for Catholic Activities
Reed Foundation
Revson Foundation, Charles H.
Reynolds Foundation, Z. Smith
Rockwell International Corp.
Rosenberg Foundation
Salomon
San Diego Gas & Electric
Santa Fe Pacific Corp.
Sara Lee Corp.
Scherman Foundation
Schiff, Hardin & Waite
Schlumberger Ltd.
Seagram & Sons, Joseph E.
Searle & Co., G.D.
Skirball Foundation
Stein Foundation, Jules and Doris
Stern Memorial Trust, Sidney
Stocker Foundation
Stone Container Corp.
Sunmark Capital Corp.
Tamko Asphalt Products
Tandy Foundation, Anne Burnett and Charles
Texaco
Textron
3M Co.
Tracor, Inc.
Transamerica Corp.
Trull Foundation
Trust Co. Bank

Tucker Charitable Trust, Rose E.
Turner Charitable Trust, Courtney S.
Union Camp Corp.
U.S. Leasing International
United States Sugar Corp.
United States Trust Co. of New York
Unocal Corp.
van Ameringen Foundation
Woodward Governor Co.
Wyomissing Foundation

Recreation & Athletics

Abel Construction Co.
Abell-Hanger Foundation
Ace Beverage Co.
Ahmanson Foundation
Air Products & Chemicals
Alcon Laboratories, Inc.
Alexander Foundation, Judd S.
Allegheny Ludlum Corp.
Allen Brothers Foundation
Allen Foundation, Frances
Alliant Techsystems
Alltel/Western Region
ALPAC Corp.
Alro Steel Corp.
Aluminum Co. of America
AMAX
America West Airlines
American Brands
American Fidelity Corp.
American Financial Corp.
American Foundation Corporation
American National Bank & Trust Co. of Chicago
American Natural Resources Co.
American Saw & Manufacturing Co.
American United Life Insurance Co.
American Welding & Manufacturing Co.
Amfac/JMB Hawaii
Amoco Corp.
AMP
Andersen Corp.
Anderson Foundation, Peyton
Andersons Management Corp.
Anheuser-Busch Cos.
Annenberg Foundation
AON Corp.
Appleton Papers
Archbold Charitable Trust, Adrian and Jessie
Archer-Daniels-Midland Co.
Aristech Chemical Corp.
Arkansas Power & Light Co.
Armco Inc.
Armstrong World Industries Inc.
Aron Charitable Foundation, J.
Arrillaga Foundation
Atherton Family Foundation
Avon Products
Badger Meter, Inc.
Baird Foundation
Baker Foundation, R. C.
Baldwin Foundation
Ball Corp.
Banc One Wisconsin Corp.
Bancroft, Jr. Foundation, Hugh
Banfi Vintners
Bank IV
Bankers Trust Co.
Barker Foundation, Donald R.
Barrows Foundation, Geraldine and R. A.
Bassett Foundation, Norman
Batchelor Foundation
Battelle
Bauer Foundation, M. R.
Baughman Foundation
Beatty Trust, Cordelia Lunceford

Bechtel Group
Belding Heminway Co.
Bellamah Foundation, Dale J.
Bemis Company
Bender Foundation
Berkman Foundation, Louis and Sandra
Bernstein & Co., Sanford C.
Bethlehem Steel Corp.
BFGoodrich
Bierlein Family Foundation
Bird Inc.
Bishop Foundation
Blank Family Foundation
Block, H&R
Blount
Blue Bell, Inc.
Blum-Kovler Foundation
Boatmen's Bancshares
Boatmen's First National Bank of Oklahoma
Boise Cascade Corp.
Booz Allen & Hamilton
Borden
Borden Memorial Foundation, Mary Owen
Borman's
Boswell Foundation, James G.
Bothin Foundation
Botwinick-Wolfensohn Foundation
Bradley-Turner Foundation
Brady Foundation
Bremer Foundation, Otto
Brennan Foundation, Robert E.
Bridgestone/Firestone
Bridwell Foundation, J. S.
Brother International Corp.
Brunswick Corp.
Bryant Foundation
Bucyrus-Erie
Bull Foundation, Henry W.
Burlington Industries
Burlington Resources
Burnham Donor Fund, Alfred G.
Burnham Foundation
Burns International
Cabot Corp.
Cafritz Foundation, Morris and Gwendolyn
Cain Foundation, Gordon and Mary
California & Hawaiian Sugar Co.
Cameron Foundation, Harry S. and Isabel C.
Camp and Bennet Humiston Trust, Apollos
Cannon Foundation
Capital Fund Foundation
Carpenter Foundation
Carter Foundation, Amon G.
Carter-Wallace
Carver Charitable Trust, Roy J.
Carylon Foundation
Cascade Natural Gas Corp.
Catlin Charitable Trust, Kathleen K.
Centel Corp.
Central Maine Power Co.
Central Soya Co.
Century Companies of America
Chambers Development Co.
Champlin Foundations
Charitable Foundation of the Burns Family
Chase Manhattan Bank, N.A.
Cheatham Foundation, Owen
Cheney Foundation, Ben B.
Cherokee Foundation
Children's Foundation of Erie County
Childress Foundation, Francis and Miranda
Chiles Foundation
Chilton Foundation Trust
Christensen Charitable and Religious Foundation, L. C.

Recreation & Athletics (cont.)

Chrysler Corp.
Cincinnati Bell
CIT Group Holdings
Clark Family Foundation, Emory T.
Clark-Winchcole Foundation
Cleveland-Cliffs
Clipper Ship Foundation
Clorox Co.
Clowes Fund
CNG Transmission Corp.
Cobb Family Foundation
Cockrell Foundation
Collins Foundation
Collins Foundation, George and Jennie
Collins, Jr. Foundation, George Fulton
Colonial Life & Accident Insurance Co.
Colorado State Bank of Denver
Comer Foundation
Commerce Clearing House
Comstock Foundation
Conn Memorial Foundation
Connelly Foundation
Consolidated Natural Gas Co.
Continental Corp.
Cook Foundation, Loring
Cooke Foundation
Coors Brewing Co.
Coors Foundation, Adolph
Copernicus Society of America
Copley Press
Copperweld Steel Co.
Cord Foundation, E. L.
Country Curtains, Inc.
Courts Foundation
Craigmyle Foundation
Crail-Johnson Foundation
Creel Foundation
CRL Inc.
Crown Central Petroleum Corp.
Cudahy Fund, Patrick and Anna M.
Cullen/Frost Bankers
Cuneo Foundation
Curtice-Burns Foods
Dain Bosworth/Inter-Regional Financial Group
Dalton Foundation, Harry L.
Dana Corp.
Daniel Foundation of Alabama
Danner Foundation
Dater Foundation, Charles H.
Daugherty Foundation
Davidson Family Charitable Foundation
Day Family Foundation
DCB Corp.
DCNY Corp.
Dell Foundation, Hazel
DelMar Foundation, Charles
Demoulas Supermarkets
Deposit Guaranty National Bank
DeRoy Testamentary Foundation
Detroit Edison Co.
Deutsch Co.
DeVos Foundation, Richard and Helen
Dewing Foundation, Frances R.
Dial Corp.
Dickenson Foundation, Harriet Ford
Dickson Foundation
Dillon Foundation
Dimick Foundation
Dixie Yarns, Inc.
Dobson Foundation
Dodson Foundation, James Glenwell and Clara May
Doheny Foundation, Carrie Estelle
Douglas & Lomason Company

Dreyfus Foundation, Max and Victoria
du Pont de Nemours & Co., E. I.
Duchossois Industries
Duke Power Co.
Dun & Bradstreet Corp.
Dupar Foundation
duPont Foundation, Chichester
Dyson Foundation
Eagle-Picher Industries
Eaton Corp.
Eccles Charitable Foundation, Willard L.
Eccles Foundation, George S. and Dolores Dore
Eccles Foundation, Marriner S.
Eddy Family Memorial Fund, C. K.
Edison Foundation, Harry
Edison Fund, Charles
Eisenberg Foundation, Ben B. and Joyce E.
El Pomar Foundation
Electronic Data Systems Corp.
Emergency Aid of Pennsylvania Foundation
Emerson Electric Co.
Emerson Foundation, Fred L.
Emery Memorial, Thomas J.
English-Bonter-Mitchell Foundation
English Memorial Fund, Florence C. and H. L.
Enright Foundation
Ensign-Bickford Industries
Ensworth Charitable Foundation
Enterprise Rent-A-Car Co.
Essick Foundation
Ettinger Foundation
Evans Foundation, Thomas J.
Ewald Foundation, H. T.
Eyman Trust, Jesse
Fairfield-Meeker Charitable Trust, Freeman E.
Falcon Foundation
Farish Fund, William Stamps
Faulkner Trust, Marianne Gaillard
Federal Home Loan Mortgage Corp. (Freddie Mac)
Federal-Mogul Corp.
Federated Life Insurance Co.
Ferguson Family Foundation, Kittie and Rugeley
Fidelity Bank
Fieldcrest Cannon
First Fidelity Bancorporation
First Interstate Bancsystem of Montana
First Maryland Bancorp
First Union Corp.
Firstar Bank Milwaukee NA
FirsTier Bank N.A. Omaha
Fish Foundation, Vain and Harry
Fleet Bank of New York
Flintridge Foundation
Florida Power Corp.
Florida Rock Industries
Florida Steel Corp.
Flowers Charitable Trust, Albert W. and Edith V.
Foellinger Foundation
Fohs Foundation
Foothills Foundation
Forbes
Ford Fund, Walter and Josephine
Ford Meter Box Co.
Forest Lawn Foundation
Formrite Tube Co.
Formrite Tube Co.
Fort Worth Star Telegram
Foster-Davis Foundation
Fourth Financial Corp.
Frankel Foundation, George and Elizabeth F.
Franklin Foundation, John and Mary
Freedom Forum

Frese Foundation, Arnold D.
Friedman Foundation, Stephen and Barbara
Friends' Foundation Trust, A.
Froderman Foundation
Frohlich Charitable Trust, Ludwig W.
Frueauff Foundation, Charles A.
Fullerton Foundation
Funderburke & Associates
Funderburke & Associates
Gabelli Foundation
Gallagher Family Foundation, Lewis P.
Gannett Co.
Garvey Kansas Foundation
Garvey Kansas Foundation
Gates Foundation
GEICO Corp.
Gellert Foundation, Carl
General American Life Insurance Co.
General Reinsurance Corp.
Geneseo Foundation
Geneseo Foundation
Georgia-Pacific Corp.
Georgia Power Co.
Gerber Products Co.
Gerson Trust, B. Milfred
Giant Eagle
Giant Food
Gillette Co.
Glick Foundation, Eugene and Marilyn
Globe Newspaper Co.
Goldbach Foundation, Ray and Marie
Goldberg Family Foundation, Israel and Matilda
Goldman Charitable Trust, Sol
Goldman Foundation, Herman
Goldman Foundation, William
Goldman Fund, Richard and Rhoda
Golub Corp.
Good Samaritan
Goodall Rubber Co.
Goody's Manufacturing Corp.
Gordon/Rousmaniere/Roberts Fund
Gould Foundation for Children, Edwin
Grainger Foundation
Grassmann Trust, E. J.
Gray Foundation, Garland
Graybar Electric Co.
Great Lakes Casting Corp.
Green Fund
Gregg-Graniteville Foundation
Griffith Foundation, W. C.
Grinnell Mutual Reinsurance Co.
Gulf Power Co.
Guttman Foundation, Stella and Charles
Haas Foundation, Paul and Mary
Hachar Charitable Trust, D. D.
Hagedorn Fund
Hagler Foundation, Jon L.
Hale Foundation, Crescent Porter
Hall Foundation
Hall Foundation
Halloran Foundation, Mary P. Dolciani
Halsell Foundation, O. L.
Hancock Foundation, Luke B.
Hansen Foundation, Dane G.
HarCo. Drug
Harcourt Foundation, Ellen Knowles
Harden Foundation
Harding Foundation, Charles Stewart
Harriman Foundation, Mary W.
Harris Brothers Foundation
Harrison Foundation, Fred G.
Harsco Corp.
Hartmarx Corp.

Hartz Foundation
Haskell Fund
Hatterscheidt Foundation
Hawkins Foundation, Robert Z.
Hawley Foundation
Hayden Foundation, Charles
Heath Foundation, Ed and Mary
Hechinger Co.
Heckscher Foundation for Children
Hecla Mining Co.
Heginbotham Trust, Will E.
Heinz Co., H.J.
Helfaer Foundation, Evan and Marion
Hemby Foundation, Alex
Henderson Foundation, George B.
Herrick Foundation
Herschend Family Foundation
Hershey Foods Corp.
Higgins Charitable Trust, Lorene Sails
Hilliard Corp.
Hillman Foundation
Hoag Family Foundation, George
Hodge Foundation
Hoffer Plastics Corp.
Hook Drug
Hopkins Foundation, Josephine Lawrence
Hopwood Charitable Trust, John M.
Hospital Corp. of America
Houston Endowment
Hoyt Foundation
Hoyt Foundation, Stewart W. and Willma C.
Hubbard Broadcasting
Huffy Corp.
Hughes Charitable Trust, Mabel Y.
Humphrey Fund, George M. and Pamela S.
Hunt Charitable Trust, C. Giles
Hunt Charitable Trust, C. Giles
Hunter Trust, A. V.
Hurst Foundation
Hyams Foundation
IES Industries
Indiana Desk Co.
Ingalls Foundation, Louise H. and David S.
Ingersoll Milling Machine Co.
Inland Container Corp.
Inland Steel Industries
Interco
Iowa Savings Bank
Irmas Charitable Foundation, Audrey and Sydney
Irwin-Sweeney-Miller Foundation
ITT Hartford Insurance Group
ITT Rayonier
Jackson Charitable Trust, Marion Gardner
Jackson Foundation
Jacobs Engineering Group
Jasper Desk Co.
Jasper Table Co.
Jefferson Endowment Fund, John Percival and Mary C.
JELD-WEN, Inc.
Jewell Memorial Foundation, Daniel Ashley and Irene Houston
Jinks Foundation, Ruth T.
JMK-A M Micallef Charitable Foundation
John Hancock Mutual Life Insurance Co.
Johnson Controls
Johnson Foundation, Helen K. and Arthur E.
Johnson & Son, S.C.
Johnstone and H. Earle Kimball Foundation, Phyllis Kimball
Jones Foundation, Daisy Marquis

Joslyn Foundation, Marcellus I.
Journal Gazette Co.
Journal Gazette Co.
Jurodin Fund
Kamps Memorial Foundation, Gertrude
Kaplen Foundation
Kaufman Endowment Fund, Louis G.
Keller-Crescent Co.
Kellogg Foundation, J. C.
Kellogg Foundation, Peter and Cynthia K.
Kelly, Jr. Memorial Foundation, Ensign C. Markland
Kemper Charitable Trust, William T.
Kemper Foundation, Enid and Crosby
Kemper Memorial Foundation, David Woods
Kennecott Corp.
Kennedy, Jr. Foundation, Joseph P.
Kent-Lucas Foundation
Kentland Foundation
Kerr Foundation, Robert S. and Grayce B.
Kerr-McGee Corp.
Key Bank of Maine
Kiewit Foundation, Peter
Kiewit Sons, Peter
King Foundation, Carl B. and Florence E.
Kingsley Foundation, Lewis A.
Kirkpatrick Foundation
Kitzmiller/Bales Trust
Klee Foundation, Conrad and Virginia
Knox Foundation, Seymour H.
Koret Foundation
Korman Family Foundation, Hyman
Kraft Foundation
Krimendahl II Foundation, H. Frederick
Kuyper Foundation, Peter H. and E. Lucille Gaass
Kysor Industrial Corp.
L and L Foundation
Ladish Co.
Laffey-McHugh Foundation
Lancaster Colony
Langdale Co.
Laros Foundation, R. K.
Lasky Co.
Lautenberg Foundation
Lazarus Charitable Trust, Helen and Charles
Leavey Foundation, Thomas and Dorothy
Lehigh Portland Cement Co.
Lehman Foundation, Edith and Herbert
Lehman Foundation, Edith and Herbert
Lennox International, Inc.
Leo Burnett Co.
Levee Charitable Trust, Polly Annenberg
Levi Strauss & Co.
Levy Foundation, Hyman Jebb
Lewis Foundation, Lillian Kaiser
Liberty Diversified Industries Inc.
Liberty National Bank
Lieberman Enterprises
Lied Foundation Trust
Lightner Sams Foundation
Lilly & Co., Eli
Lincoln National Corp.
Lindstrom Foundation, Kinney
Lintilhac Foundation
Lipton, Thomas J.
Litton/Itek Optical Systems
Logan Foundation, E. J.
Long Foundation, George A. and Grace

Louis Foundation, Michael W.
Louisiana Land & Exploration Co.
Louisiana Power & Light Co./New Orleans Public Service
Lowe Foundation
Lowe Foundation, Joe and Emily
Lubrizol Corp.
Lukens
Lyon Foundation
M.T.D. Products
Maas Foundation, Benard L.
Maclellan Charitable Trust, R. J.
MacLeod Stewardship Foundation
Macy & Co., R.H.
Magma Copper Co.
Manville Corp.
Maritz Inc.
Marmot Foundation
Marquette Electronics
Mars Foundation
Marsh & McLennan Cos.
Marshall & Ilsley Bank
Marshall Trust in Memory of Sanders McDaniel, Harriet McDaniel
Martin Foundation
Martin Marietta Corp.
Martini Foundation, Nicholas
Masco Corp.
Masserini Charitable Trust, Maurice J.
Massey Foundation
Massie Trust, David Meade
May Foundation, Wilbur
Mayerson Foundation, Manuel D. and Rhoda
Maytag Corp.
Maytag Family Foundation, Fred
MBIA, Inc.
MCA
McCann Foundation
McCarthy Foundation, Michael W.
McConnell Foundation
McCormick Tribune Foundation, Robert R.
McCray Lumber Co.
McCrea Foundation
McDermott Foundation, Eugene
McDonnell Douglas Corp.-West
McElroy Trust, R. J.
McGraw Foundation, Curtis W.
McGraw Foundation, Donald C.
McGregor Fund
MCI Communications Corp.
McIntosh Foundation
McIntyre Foundation, C. S. and Marion F.
McMillen Foundation
McWane Inc.
Mead Corp.
Meadows Foundation
Medina Foundation
Melitta North America Inc.
Mellon Foundation, Richard King
Messick Charitable Trust, Harry F.
Meyer Foundation, Eugene and Agnes E.
Michigan Bell Telephone Co.
Michigan Consolidated Gas Co.
Mid-Iowa Health Foundation
Middendorf Foundation
Midwest Resources
Mielke Family Foundation
Milken Family Medical Foundation
Milken Foundation, L. and S.
Millbrook Tribute Garden
Milliken & Co.
Mine Safety Appliances Co.
Minster Machine Co.
Mobil Oil Corp.
Mohasco Corp.

Monroe-Brown Foundation
Montgomery Foundation
Montgomery Street Foundation
Moody Foundation
Moorman Manufacturing Co.
Morgan and Samuel Tate Morgan, Jr. Foundation, Marietta McNeil
Morley Brothers Foundation
Morrill Charitable Foundation
Morris Foundation, Margaret T.
Morrison Charitable Trust, Pauline A. and George R.
Morrison-Knudsen Corp.
Moss Charitable Trust, Finis M.
Motorola
MTS Systems Corp.
Muller Foundation
Myers and Sons, D.
National Computer Systems
National Forge Co.
National Life of Vermont
National Presto Industries
National Starch & Chemical Corp.
NBD Bank
NBD Bank, N.A.
Nelson Foundation, Florence
Nelson Industries, Inc.
New England Mutual Life Insurance Co.
New York Foundation
New York Life Insurance Co.
Newhouse Foundation, Samuel I.
Newman Assistance Fund, Jerome A. and Estelle R.
Newmil Bancorp
Nichols Foundation
Nike Inc.
Norfolk Southern Corp.
Norgren Foundation, Carl A.
Norris Foundation, Kenneth T. and Eileen L.
Northern Indiana Public Service Co.
Norton Co.
Norton Memorial Corporation, Geraldi
Norwest Bank Nebraska
O'Connor Co.
O'Connor Foundation, Magee
Ohio National Life Insurance Co.
Ohl, Jr. Trust, George A.
Ohrstrom Foundation
Old Dominion Box Co.
O'Neill Charitable Corporation, F. J.
O'Neill Foundation, William J. and Dorothy K.
Ontario Corp.
Ontario Corp.
Open Society Fund
Oppenheimer Family Foundation
Oppenstein Brothers Foundation
Orange Orphan Society
Osborn Manufacturing Co.
O'Shaughnessy Foundation, I. A.
Osher Foundation, Bernard
Oshkosh B'Gosh
O'Sullivan Children Foundation
Outboard Marine Corp.
Overbrook Foundation
Overseas Shipholding Group
Owen Industries, Inc.
Oxford Foundation
PacifiCorp
Packaging Corporation of America
Packer Foundation, Horace B.
Page Belting Co.
Page Foundation, George B.
Palin Foundation
Palisades Educational Foundation
Palmer-Fry Memorial Trust, Lily
Palmer Fund, Francis Asbury
Palmer Fund, Frank Loomis
Pamida, Inc.

Panhandle Eastern Corp.
Pappas Charitable Foundation, Thomas Anthony
Paramount Communications Inc.
Parshelsky Foundation, Moses L.
Parsons Foundation, Ralph M.
Parsons - W.D. Charities, Vera Davis
Pella Corp.
Penn Foundation, William
Perkin-Elmer Corp.
Perkin-Elmer Corp.
Perkins Memorial Fund, James J. and Marie Richardson
Perot Foundation
Peterson Foundation, Fred J.
Pfaffinger Foundation
Pfizer
Phelps Dodge Corp.
Philips Foundation, Jesse
Phillips Family Foundation, Jay and Rose
Phillips Family Foundation, L. E.
Phillips Foundation, Dr. P.
Phillips Petroleum Co.
Phipps Foundation, William H.
Pittsburgh Child Guidance Foundation
Pittsburgh National Bank
Pope Foundation
Post Foundation of D.C., Marjorie Merriweather
Potomac Electric Power Co.
Powell Family Foundation
Premier Industrial Corp.
Price Associates, T. Rowe
Pritzker Foundation
Procter & Gamble Cosmetic & Fragrance Products
Prudential Insurance Co. of America
Public Service Electric & Gas Co.
Quaker Chemical Corp.
Quaker Oats Co.
Quincy Newspapers
Quivey-Bay State Foundation
Ralston Purina Co.
Raskob Foundation for Catholic Activities
Ratner Foundation, Milton M.
Raymond Corp.
Red Devil
Red Wing Shoe Co.
Redfield Foundation, Nell J.
REI-Recreational Equipment, Inc.
Reynolds Foundation, Donald W.
Reynolds Foundation, Edgar
Reynolds Foundation, Richard S.
Reynolds Metals Co.
Rhodebeck Charitable Trust
Rice Foundation
Rice Foundation, Ethel and Raymond F.
Rich Products Corp.
Richardson Benevolent Foundation, C. E.
Robinson Foundation
Rockwell International Corp.
Rogers Charitable Trust, Florence
Rohm and Haas Company
Roseburg Forest Products Co.
Ruan Foundation Trust, John
Rubin Foundation, Rob E. & Judith O.
Rubinstein Foundation, Helena
Rudin Foundation
Rudin Foundation, Samuel and May
Ryan Family Charitable Foundation
Sage Foundation
Salomon
San Diego Gas & Electric
Sandy Foundation, George H.
Sandy Hill Foundation

Sanguinetti Foundation, Annunziata
Scheuer Family Foundation, S. H. and Helen R.
Schmidlapp Trust No. 1, Jacob G.
Schneider Foundation, Robert E.
Scholl Foundation, Dr.
Scholler Foundation
Schumann Fund for New Jersey
Schwab & Co., Charles
Schwartz Fund for Education and Health Research, Arnold and Marie
Scott Foundation, Walter
Scoular Co.
Scroggins Foundation, Arthur E. and Cornelia C.
Seaver Institute
Seaway Food Town
Security Life of Denver
Sentry Insurance Co.
Sequoia Foundation
Setzer Foundation
Shafer Foundation, Richard H. and Ann
Share Foundation
Sharon Steel Corp.
Shawmut National Corp.
Sheinberg Foundation, Eric P.
Shelton Cos.
Shenandoah Life Insurance Co.
Sierra Pacific Industries
Simon Foundation, Sidney, Milton and Leoma
Simon Foundation, William E. and Carol G.
Simpson Industries
Sioux Steel Co.
Slant/Fin Corp.
Slemp Foundation
Slifka Foundation, Alan B.
Smith and W. Aubrey Smith Charitable Foundation, Clara Blackford
Smith Charitable Trust
Smith Corp., A.O.
Smoot Charitable Foundation
Snider Foundation
Snyder Fund, Valentine Perry
Sonat
Sonoco Products Co.
Sosland Foundation
Southern California Edison Co.
Southern Furniture Co.
Southwestern Bell Corp.
Sperry Fund
Sprague Educational and Charitable Foundation, Seth
Springs Foundation
Stackpole-Hall Foundation
Star Bank, N.A.
Starr Foundation
State Street Bank & Trust Co.
Staunton Farm Foundation
Steadley Memorial Trust, Kent D. and Mary L.
Stearns Charitable Foundation, Anna B.
Stearns Trust, Artemas W.
Steele Foundation, Harry and Grace
Steiner Corp.
Stella D'Oro Biscuit Co.
Stern Family Foundation, Alex
Stock Foundation, Paul
Stock Foundation, Paul
Stokely, Jr. Foundation, William B.
Stone Family Foundation, Norman H.
Storer Foundation, George B.
Stott Foundation, Robert L.
Strake Foundation
Stratford Foundation
Strauss Foundation
Stry Foundation, Paul E.
Stuart Foundation
Stulsaft Foundation, Morris

Stupp Brothers Bridge & Iron Co.
Sulzberger Foundation
Sulzer Family Foundation
Summerfield Foundation, Solon E.
Swig Charity Foundation, Mae and Benjamin
Swig Foundation
Synovus Financial Corp.
Taylor Foundation, Ruth and Vernon
Technical Foundation of America
Teledyne
Teubert Charitable Trust, James H. and Alice
Texas Commerce Bank Houston, N.A.
Texas Gas Transmission Corp.
Textron
Thompson Trust, Thomas
3M Co.
Thrush-Thompson Foundation
Times Mirror Co.
Timken Foundation of Canton
Tisch Foundation
Tiscornia Foundation
Titmus Foundation
Tonkin Foundation, Tom and Helen
Tosco Corp. Refining Division
Town Creek Foundation
Transco Energy Company
Treuhaft Foundation
Trexler Trust, Harry C.
Trinity Foundation
Trust Co. Bank
Turner Charitable Foundation
Turrell Fund
Tyler Corp.
Tyson Foods, Inc.
Ukrop's Super Markets, Inc.
Union Bank of Switzerland Los Angeles Branch
Union Camp Corp.
United Service Foundation
United States Sugar Corp.
Unitrode Corp.
Universal Leaf Tobacco Co.
Unocal Corp.
Upjohn Foundation, Harold and Grace
Valmont Industries
Van Buren Foundation
Van Every Foundation, Philip L.
Van Wert County Foundation
Vanneck-Bailey Foundation
Varian Associates
Vaughn Foundation
Vlasic Foundation
Vulcan Materials Co.
Wachovia Bank & Trust Co., N.A.
Wal-Mart Stores
Disney Co., Walt
Washington Forrest Foundation
Washington Trust Bank
Wausau Paper Mills Co.
Wean Foundation, Raymond John
Weber Charities Corp., Frederick E.
Weinberg Foundation, John L.
Weinberg, Jr. Foundation, Sidney J.
Weingart Foundation
Weir Foundation Trust
Weiss Foundation, Stephen and Suzanne
Welch Testamentary Trust, George T.
West Texas Corp., J. M.
Westinghouse Electric Corp.
Westvaco Corp.
Wetterau
Weyerhaeuser Co.
Whirlpool Corp.
Whitehead Foundation
Whitney Fund, David M.

Recipient Type Index

Recreation & Athletics (cont.)

Wickes Foundation, Harvey Randall
Wickson-Link Memorial Foundation
WICOR, Inc.
Williams Cos.
Wilson Trust, Lula C.
Wimpey Inc., George
Winston Foundation, Norman and Rosita
Wollenberg Foundation
Wolverine World Wide, Inc.
Woods Foundation, James H.
Woodward Fund-Atlanta, David, Helen, Marian
Woodward Governor Co.
Xerox Corp.
Yawkey Foundation II
Yeager Charitable Trust, Lester E.
Yost Trust, Elizabeth Burns
Young Charity Trust Northern Trust Company
Young Foundation, H and B
Young & Rubicam

Refugee Assistance

ALPAC Corp.
Altman Foundation
American President Cos.
Andersen Corp.
Andersons Management Corp.
AON Corp.
Arca Foundation
Bard, C. R.
Benetton
Bernstein & Co., Sanford C.
Block, H&R
Blum-Kovler Foundation
Booz Allen & Hamilton
Bremer Foundation, Otto
British Airways
Buffett Foundation
Bush Foundation
Cafritz Foundation, Morris and Gwendolyn
Chevron Corp.
Clark Charitable Trust
Clark Foundation, Edna McConnell
Clipper Ship Foundation
Colonial Life & Accident Insurance Co.
Columbia Foundation
Cowles Media Co.
CPC International
Crown Memorial, Arie and Ida
Davis Foundation, Edwin W. and Catherine M.
Dayton Hudson Corp.
Dewing Foundation, Frances R.
EMI Records Group
Field Foundation, Jamee and Marshall
Florida Power & Light Co.
Fohs Foundation
Ford Foundation
Frankel Foundation
Fry Foundation, Lloyd A.
Funderburke & Associates
Funderburke & Associates
General Mills
Gilbane Foundation, Thomas and William
Grotto Foundation
Honeywell
Houston Industries
Hyams Foundation
I and G Charitable Foundation
International Foundation
Johnson Foundation, Walter S.

Kaufman Memorial Trust, Chaim, Fanny, Louis, Benjamin, and Anne Florence
LeBrun Foundation
Lotus Development Corp.
Lowe Foundation, Joe and Emily
Mardag Foundation
McCormick Tribune Foundation, Robert R.
Meadows Foundation
Medina Foundation
Meyer Foundation, Eugene and Agnes E.
Meyer Memorial Trust
Mobil Oil Corp.
National Westminster Bank New Jersey
New World Foundation
New York Foundation
The New Yorker Magazine, Inc.
Norman Foundation
Northern States Power Co.
Noyes, Jr. Memorial Foundation, Nicholas H.
Parsons Foundation, Ralph M.
Pew Charitable Trusts
Playboy Enterprises, Inc.
Public Welfare Foundation
Quaker Oats Co.
Raskob Foundation for Catholic Activities
Reynolds Foundation, Christopher
Riley Foundation, Mabel Louise
Royal Group Inc.
Sara Lee Corp.
Sara Lee Hosiery
Scrivner, Inc.
Shapiro Foundation, Charles and M. R.
Shawmut National Corp.
Starr Foundation
State Street Bank & Trust Co.
Stulsaft Foundation, Morris
TCF Banking & Savings, FSB
Teledyne
Tennant Co.
Textron
Times Mirror Co.
Trull Foundation
21 International Holdings
Vaughan Foundation, Rachael and Ben

Religious Welfare

Achelis Foundation
Ada Foundation, Julius
Ahmanson Foundation
Akzo Chemicals Inc.
Alco Standard Corp.
Alcon Laboratories, Inc.
Allendale Mutual Insurance Co.
Altman Foundation
Aluminum Co. of America
American Natural Resources Co.
Ames Department Stores
Amfac/JMB Hawaii
Amoco Corp.
Anderson Foundation, Peyton
Andersons Management Corp.
Annenberg Foundation
Archer-Daniels-Midland Co.
Arkansas Power & Light Co.
Aron Charitable Foundation, J.
Atherton Family Foundation
Atkinson Foundation
Atkinson Foundation, Myrtle L.
Aurora Foundation
Badgeley Residuary Charitable Trust, Rose M.
Baker & Baker
Baker Foundation, R. C.
Bank Hapoalim B.M.
Bank South Corp.
Barra Foundation
Batts Foundation
Bauer Foundation, M. R.

Beazley Foundation
Beitzell & Co.
Belmont Metals
Beren Foundation, Robert M.
Beretta U.S.A. Corp.
Bergstrom Manufacturing Co.
Bernstein & Co., Sanford C.
Bettingen Corporation, Burton G.
Bierlein Family Foundation
Blank Family Foundation
Blaustein Foundation, Jacob and Hilda
Blount
Blue Cross & Blue Shield of Alabama
Boatmen's First National Bank of Oklahoma
Borden
Borman's
Bozzone Family Foundation
Brach Foundation, Helen
Bradley-Turner Foundation
Brooks Brothers
Brown Family Foundation, John Mathew Gay
Bruening Foundation, Eva L. and Joseph M.
Buchanan Family Foundation
Burndy Corp.
Burns Foundation, Fritz B.
Business Incentives
Bustard Charitable Permanent Trust Fund, Elizabeth and James
Cameron Foundation, Harry S. and Isabel C.
Campbell Foundation, J. Bulow
Capital Cities/ABC
Capital Fund Foundation
Carnival Cruise Lines
Carolyn Foundation
Carpenter Foundation, E. Rhodes and Leona B.
Casey Charitable Trust, Eugene B.
Caterpillar
Central Bank of the South
Chanin Family Foundation, Paul R.
Chapman Charitable Trust, H. A. and Mary K.
Chatlos Foundation
Cheney Foundation, Ben B.
CIT Group Holdings
Citizens Bank
Clark Foundation
Clipper Ship Foundation
Clorox Co.
Cockrell Foundation
Collins Foundation
Collins Foundation, Carr P.
Colorado Trust
Columbia Foundation
Columbus Dispatch Printing Co.
Commercial Metals Co.
Cone Mills Corp.
Conn Memorial Foundation
Connelly Foundation
Cook Charitable Foundation
Cooke Foundation
Coors Foundation, Adolph
Country Curtains, Inc.
Crowell Trust, Henry P. and Susan C.
Crown Books Foundation, Inc.
Cudahy Fund, Patrick and Anna M.
Cummings Foundation, Nathan
Davidson Family Charitable Foundation
Day Foundation, Cecil B.
DeMoss Foundation, Arthur S.
Deutsch Co.
DeVos Foundation, Richard and Helen
Dexter Industries
Dillon Foundation
Dishman Charitable Foundation Trust, H. E. and Kate

Dodge Foundation, P. L.
Dodson Foundation, James Glenwell and Clara May
Doheny Foundation, Carrie Estelle
Domino's Pizza
Doss Foundation, M. S.
Dougherty, Jr. Foundation, James R.
Dover Foundation
Dreyfus Foundation, Max and Victoria
Dubow Family Foundation
Duke Power Co.
Dupar Foundation
duPont Fund, Jessie Ball
Eaton Corp.
Ebell of Los Angeles Rest Cottage Association
Eden Hall Foundation
Ehrman Foundation, Fred and Susan
Elgin Sweeper Co.
Engelhard Foundation, Charles
English-Bonter-Mitchell Foundation
Epp Fund B Charitable Trust, Otto C.
Ernest & Julio Gallo Winery
Factor Family Foundation, Max
Fairchild Foundation, Sherman
Falk Foundation, Michael David
Farish Fund, William Stamps
Farnsworth Trust, Charles A.
Feil Foundation, Louis and Gertrude
Feintech Foundation
Feldman Foundation
Fibre Converters
Field Foundation of Illinois
Fifth Third Bancorp
FINA, Inc.
Fingerhut Family Foundation
Finley Charitable Trust, J. B.
Finnegan Foundation, John D.
First Maryland Bancorp
First Petroleum Corp.
Firstar Bank Milwaukee NA
Fish Foundation, Ray C.
Fondren Foundation
Forbes
Ford Fund, Walter and Josephine
Foster Charitable Trust
Foundation for Child Development
Fox Steel Co.
Frank Fund, Zollie and Elaine
Frear Eleemosynary Trust, Mary D. and Walter F.
Frederick Foundation
Friedman Brothers Foundation
Frueauff Foundation, Charles A.
Fry Foundation, Lloyd A.
Fuchsberg Family Foundation, Abraham
Fuller Foundation, George F. and Sybil H.
Funderburke & Associates
Funderburke & Associates
GAR Foundation
Geifman Family Foundation
Gelman Foundation, Melvin and Estelle
General American Life Insurance Co.
General Mills
General Motors Corp.
Georgia-Pacific Corp.
Gershenson Foundation, Charles H.
Gheens Foundation
Giant Eagle
Gilmore Foundation, Irving S.
Globe Corp.
Goldman Foundation, Herman
Golub Corp.
Grainger Foundation
Grassmann Trust, E. J.

Green Fund
Greene Manufacturing Co.
Gregg-Graniteville Foundation
Gudelsky Family Foundation, Homer and Martha
Guttman Foundation, Stella and Charles
Hafif Family Foundation
Hagedorn Fund
Haggar Foundation
Hale Foundation, Crescent Porter
Hall Charitable Trust, Evelyn A. J.
Halsell Foundation, Ewing
Hamilton Bank
Hancock Foundation, Luke B.
Handleman Co.
Hanson Testamentary Charitable Trust, Anna Emery
Hargis Charitable Foundation, Estes H. and Florence Parker
Harsco Corp.
Hazen Charitable Trust, Lita Annenberg
Hechinger Co.
Heckscher Foundation for Children
Heinz Co., H.J.
Herrick Foundation
Hess Charitable Foundation, Ronne and Donald
Hess Foundation
Hill Crest Foundation
Hilton Foundation, Conrad N.
Hofmann Co.
Homeland Foundation
HON Industries
Hospital Corp. of America
Houston Endowment
Howard and Bush Foundation
Hubbard Broadcasting
Hubbell Inc.
Huizenga Family Foundation
Huizenga Family Foundation
Huizenga Foundation, Jennie
Hulme Charitable Foundation, Milton G.
Hultquist Foundation
Humana
Hutzell Foundation
Hyde and Watson Foundation
Indiana Insurance Cos.
Interco
Irwin Charity Foundation, William G.
ITT Hartford Insurance Group
J C S Foundation
Jackson Foundation
Jacoby Foundation, Lela Beren and Norman
Jellison Benevolent Society
Jenkins Foundation, George W.
Jennings Foundation, Mary Hillman
Johnson Controls
Jones Foundation, Daisy Marquis
Journal Gazette Co.
Joyce Foundation, John M. and Mary A.
Julia R. and Estelle L. Foundation
Jurodin Fund
Jurzykowski Foundation, Alfred
Kahn Memorial Trust
Kaiser Foundation, Betty E. and George B.
Kaplan Foundation, Charles I. and Mary
Keebler Co.
Kemper Charitable Trust, William T.
Kemper Foundation, Enid and Crosby
Kempner Fund, Harris and Eliza
Kenedy Memorial Foundation, John G. and Marie Stella
Kerr-McGee Corp.
Kettering Fund

Key Food Stores Cooperative Inc.
Kieckhefer Foundation, J. W.
Kiewit Foundation, Peter
Kilroy Foundation, William S. and Lora Jean
Kimberly-Clark Corp.
King Ranch
Kirbo Charitable Trust, Thomas M. and Irene B.
Kirby Foundation, F. M.
Knapp Foundation
Koch Foundation
Koret Foundation
KSM Foundation
Kuyper Foundation, Peter H. and E. Lucille Gaass
Laffey-McHugh Foundation
Lauder Foundation
Leavey Foundation, Thomas and Dorothy
Leviton Manufacturing Co.
Lewis Foundation, Frank J.
Liberty Diversified Industries Inc.
Lieberman Enterprises
Life Insurance Co. of Georgia
Link. Jr. Foundation, George
Lipton Foundation
Littauer Foundation, Lucius N.
Loughran Foundation, Mary and Daniel
Louis Foundation, Michael W.
Louisiana Land & Exploration Co.
Lowe Foundation, Joe and Emily
Lowenstein Foundation, Leon
Lowenstein Foundation, William P. and Marie R.
Lurie Foundation, Louis R.
Lutheran Brotherhood Foundation
Mack Foundation, J. S.
Maclellan Foundation
Makita U.S.A., Inc.
Manat Foundation
Mann Foundation, Ted
Manville Corp.
Marcus Corp.
Marriott Foundation, J. Willard
Marshall & Ilsley Bank
Martini Foundation, Nicholas
Marx Foundation, Virginia & Leonard
Maytag Family Foundation, Fred
Mazza Foundation
McCarthy Foundation, John and Margaret
McCasland Foundation
McCormick Tribune Foundation, Robert R.
McCune Charitable Trust, John R.
McDonnell Douglas Corp.-West
McElroy Trust, R. J.
McGregor Fund
MCI Communications Corp.
McIntyre Foundation, C. S. and Marion F.
McMahon Foundation
McShain Charities, John
Meadows Foundation
Medina Foundation
Merrion Foundation
Metropolitan Theatres Corp.
Meyerhoff Foundation, Lyn P.
Michigan Bell Telephone Co.
Miller-Mellor Association
Milliken & Co.
Mine Safety Appliances Co.
Mirapaul Foundation
Mitchell Family Foundation, Edward D. and Anna
Mobil Oil Corp.
Monaghan Charitable Trust, Rose
Moore Foundation, Edward S.
Morris Charitable Foundation, E. A.

Morris Charitable Trust, Charles M.
Morris Foundation, William T.
Moskowitz Foundation, Irving I.
Motorola
Murphy Foundation
Murphy Foundation, Dan
Murphy Foundation, John P.
Myers and Sons, D.
Nashua Trust Co.
National Presto Industries
National Steel
National Westminster Bank New Jersey
Nationale-Nederlanden North America Corp.
NBD Bank
Nelco Sewing Machine Sales Corp.
Nelson Foundation, Florence
New World Foundation
Newhouse Foundation, Samuel I.
Newman's Own
Noble Charitable Trust, John L. and Ethel G.
Nordson Corp.
Norwest Bank Nebraska
Number Ten Foundation
O'Neil Foundation, Casey Albert T.
O'Neil Foundation, W.
O'Neill Charitable Corporation, F. J.
Orchard Foundation
Orleans Trust, Carrie S.
O'Shaughnessy Foundation, I. A.
Osher Foundation, Bernard
Overbrook Foundation
Overseas Shipholding Group
Owen Trust, B. B.
Pacific Western Foundation
Packard Foundation, David and Lucile
Parsons - W.D. Charities, Vera Davis
Peerless Insurance Co.
Pendleton Memorial Fund, William L. and Ruth T.
Perkins-Prothro Foundation
Phelps Dodge Corp.
Philips Foundation, Jesse
Phillips Family Foundation, Jay and Rose
Phillips Foundation, Dr. P.
Physicians Mutual Insurance
Pillsbury Foundation
Pinkerton Foundation
Pioneer Fund
Pitts Foundation, William H. and Lula E.
Pittway Corp.
Plough Foundation
Posey Trust, Addison
Post Foundation of D.C., Marjorie Merriweather
Potter Foundation, Justin and Valere
Powell Family Foundation
Price Foundation, Louis and Harold
Procter & Gamble Cosmetic & Fragrance Products
Pulitzer Publishing Co.
Ralston Purina Co.
Raskob Foundation for Catholic Activities
Regenstein Foundation
Reily & Co., William B.
Reinhold Foundation, Paul E. and Ida Klare
Relations Foundation
Resnick Foundation, Jack and Pearl
Rice Foundation
Ritchie Memorial Foundation, Charles E. and Mabel M.
Ritter Foundation, May Ellen and Gerald

Roberts Foundation
Roche Relief Foundation, Edward and Ellen
Rogers Foundation, Mary Stuart
RosaMary Foundation
Rose Foundation, Billy
Rowland Foundation
Rutgers Community Health Foundation
Sage Foundation
Sandy Hill Foundation
Sanguinetti Foundation, Annunziata
Sawyer Charitable Foundation
Scaife Family Foundation
Schapiro Fund, M. A.
Scheuer Family Foundation, S. H. and Helen R.
Schiff, Hardin & Waite
Schlink Foundation, Albert G. and Olive H.
Schmidlapp Trust No. 1, Jacob G.
Schneider Foundation Corp., Al J.
Schoenbaum Family Foundation
Scholl Foundation, Dr.
Schroeder Foundation, Walter
Scrivner, Inc.
Sealright Co., Inc.
Sebastian Foundation
Sequoia Foundation
Sexton Foundation
Shaffer Family Charitable Trust
Shapero Foundation, Nate S. and Ruth B.
Shapiro, Inc.
Shapiro Fund, Albert
Share Foundation
Shelton Cos.
Silverburgh Foundation, Grace, George & Judith
Skirball Foundation
Slant/Fin Corp.
Slusher Charitable Foundation, Roy W.
Smith, Jr. Charitable Trust, Jack J.
Snite Foundation, Fred B.
Snyder Foundation, Harold B. and Dorothy A.
Solo Cup Co.
Sosland Foundation
Speer Foundation, Roy M.
Spiegel
Sprague Educational and Charitable Foundation, Seth
Stanley Charitable Foundation, A. W.
Star Bank, N.A.
Starr Foundation
State Street Bank & Trust Co.
Stauffer Communications
Stein Foundation, Jules and Doris
Steinhagen Benevolent Trust, B. A. and Elinor
Steiniger Charitable Foundation, Edward & Joan
Stewardship Foundation
Stone Container Corp.
Storer Foundation, George B.
Strake Foundation
Stratford Foundation
Straus Foundation, Aaron and Lillie
Straus Foundation, Martha Washington Straus and Harry H.
Sturgis Charitable and Educational Trust, Roy and Christine
Summerfield Foundation, Solon E.
Swift Memorial Health Care Foundation
Tamarkin Co.
Tandy Foundation, Anne Burnett and Charles

Taubman Foundation, Herman P. and Sophia
Taylor Foundation, Ruth and Vernon
Teledyne
Textron
Thalheimer Foundation, Alvin and Fanny Blaustein
Thanksgiving Foundation
Thomas Foundation, Joan and Lee
Times Mirror Co.
Titan Industrial Co.
TJX Cos.
Towsley Foundation, Harry A. and Margaret D.
Transamerica Corp.
Trull Foundation
Trust for Mutual Understanding
Union Camp Corp.
United Merchants & Manufacturers
Unocal Corp.
Upton Foundation, Frederick S.
Valley Foundation, Wayne and Gladys
Van Every Foundation, Philip L.
Vance Charitable Foundation, Robert C.
Vlasic Foundation
Von der Ahe Foundation
Von der Ahe, Jr. Trust, Theodore Albert
Wachtell, Lipton, Rosen & Katz
Wahlert Foundation
Wal-Mart Stores
Wardle Family Foundation
Ware Foundation
Wasily Family Foundation
Wasserman Foundation
Wausau Paper Mills Co.
Wean Foundation, Raymond John
Weckbaugh Foundation, Eleanore Mullen
Weingart Foundation
Weir Foundation Trust
Weisz Foundation, David and Sylvia
Wendt Foundation, Margaret L.
Western Southern Life Insurance Co.
Westwood Endowment
Whirlpool Corp.
Whitaker Foundation
White Coffee Pot Family Inns
Wilsey Bennet Co.
Wilson Public Trust, Ralph
Wisdom Foundation, Mary F.
Witco Corp.
Woodward Fund-Atlanta, David, Helen, Marian
Woolf Foundation, William C.
Wurts Memorial, Henrietta Tower
Ziegler Foundation, Ruth/Allen
Zilkha & Sons

Shelters/ Homelessness

Abbott Laboratories
Abell Foundation, Charles S.
Abell Foundation, The
Abell-Hanger Foundation
Abraham Foundation
Abrons Foundation, Louis and Anne
Adams Memorial Fund, Emma J.
Advanced Micro Devices
AFLAC
Ahmanson Foundation
Air Products & Chemicals
Alabama Power Co.
Albertson's
Alcon Laboratories, Inc.
Alexander Foundation, Judd S.
Allendale Mutual Insurance Co.
AlliedSignal
Alltel/Western Region

ALPAC Corp.
Alro Steel Corp.
Altman Foundation
Aluminum Co. of America
Amaturo Foundation
Amcast Industrial Corp.
AMCORE Bank, N.A. Rockford
American Brands
American Electric Power
American Express Co.
American General Finance
American National Bank & Trust Co. of Chicago
American United Life Insurance Co.
AMETEK
Amfac/JMB Hawaii
AMP
Anderson Foundation, M. D.
Anderson Foundation, Peyton
Anheuser-Busch Cos.
Anschutz Family Foundation
Apple Computer, Inc.
Appleton Papers
Arkansas Power & Light Co.
Armstrong World Industries Inc.
Aron Charitable Foundation, J.
Atalanta/Sosnoff Capital Corp.
Atherton Family Foundation
Atkinson Foundation
Atlanta Gas Light Co.
Attleboro Pawtucket Savings Bank
Auerbach Foundation, Beatrice Fox
Avon Products
Ayres Foundation, Inc.
Bacardi Imports
Bacon Trust, Charles F.
Badgeley Residuary Charitable Trust, Rose M.
Badger Meter, Inc.
Baer Foundation, Alan and Marcia
Baird Charitable Trust, William Robert
Baker Foundation, Clark and Ruby
Baker Foundation, R. C.
Baker, Jr. Memorial Fund, William G.
Bamberger and John Ernest Bamberger Memorial Foundation, Ruth Eleanor
Banc One Illinois Corp.
Bank of America Arizona
Bank of Boston Connecticut
Bank of Boston Corp.
Bank of New York
Bannerman Foundation, William C.
Bannon Foundation
Barker Welfare Foundation
Barra Foundation
Baumker Charitable Foundation, Elsie and Harry
Beasley Foundation, Theodore and Beulah
Beeson Charitable Trust, Dwight M.
Bemis Company
Bernstein Foundation, Diane and Norman
Berry Foundation, Lowell
Besser Foundation
Best Foundation, Walter J. and Edith E.
Bethlehem Steel Corp.
BHP Pacific Resources
Bicknell Fund
Biddle Foundation, Margaret T.
Binney & Smith Inc.
Birnschein Foundation, Alvin and Marion
Bjorkman Foundation
Blanchard Foundation
Bleibtreu Foundation, Jacob

Shelters/ Homelessness (cont.)

Block Family Foundation, Emphraim
Block, H&R
Blowitz-Ridgeway Foundation
Blum Foundation, Edna F.
Blum Foundation, Lois and Irving
Blum-Kovler Foundation
Boatmen's First National Bank of Oklahoma
Boeing Co.
Booth-Bricker Fund
Booz Allen & Hamilton
Borden
Borman's
Boutell Memorial Fund, Arnold and Gertrude
Bowater Inc.
Bowsher-Booher Foundation
Bozzone Family Foundation
Bradford Foundation, George and Ruth
Bradley Foundation, Lynde and Harry
Bradley-Turner Foundation
Bremer Foundation, Otto
Britton Fund
Brooklyn Benevolent Society
Brown Foundation
Brown Foundation, James Graham
Brown & Sons, Alex
Browning-Ferris Industries
Bruening Foundation, Eva L. and Joseph M.
Brunswick Corp.
Bryan Family Foundation, Kathleen Price and Joseph M.
Bucyrus-Erie
Buhl Family Foundation
Bunbury Company
Burndy Corp.
Bush Foundation
Butler Family Foundation, George W. and Gladys S.
Butler Family Foundation, Patrick and Aimee
C.I.O.S.
Cabell III and Maude Morgan Cabell Foundation, Robert G.
Cafritz Foundation, Morris and Gwendolyn
Calhoun Charitable Trust, Kenneth
Cameron Foundation, Harry S. and Isabel C.
Camp Younts Foundation
Candlesticks Inc.
Capital Fund Foundation
Capital Holding Corp.
Carbon Fuel Co.
Carpenter Foundation, E. Rhodes and Leona B.
Carpenter Technology Corp.
Carr Real Estate Services
Carter Foundation, Amon G.
Carter Foundation, Beirne
Cascade Natural Gas Corp.
Casey Foundation, Eugene B.
Central Hudson Gas & Electric Corp.
Central Life Assurance Co.
Central Maine Power Co.
CertainTeed Corp.
Chapin Foundation, Frances
Chapman Charitable Trust, H. A. and Mary K.
Charlesbank Homes
Chartwell Foundation
Chase Charity Foundation, Alfred E.
Chase Manhattan Bank, N.A.
Chase Trust, Alice P.

Chatlos Foundation
Chemical Bank
Cheney Foundation, Ben B.
Chevron Corp.
Chicago Board of Trade
Chicago Resource Center
Chicago Sun-Times, Inc.
Childs Charitable Foundation, Roberta M.
Chilton Foundation Trust
Ciba-Geigy Corp. (Pharmaceuticals Division)
CIT Group Holdings
Citibank, F.S.B.
Citicorp
Citizens First National Bank
Clark Foundation
Clark Foundation
Clark Foundation, Edna McConnell
Clark-Winchcole Foundation
Clay Foundation
Clayton Fund
Clipper Ship Foundation
Clorox Co.
CM Alliance Cos.
CNA Insurance Cos.
Cockrell Foundation
Coffey Foundation
Cogswell Benevolent Trust
Cohen Foundation, Naomi and Nehemiah
Cole Trust, Quincy
Coleman Co.
Collins & Aikman Holdings Corp.
Collins Foundation, George and Jennie
Collins Foundation, James M.
Colorado Trust
Columbia Foundation
Columbus Southern Power Co.
Commerce Bancshares, Inc.
Commerce Clearing House
Community Health Association
Comstock Foundation
ConAgra
Connecticut Natural Gas Corp.
Connelly Foundation
Constantin Foundation
Continental Corp.
Contran Corp.
Cook Foundation, Louella
Coors Brewing Co.
Copperweld Steel Co.
Cord Foundation, E. L.
Cosmair, Inc.
Cottrell Foundation
Country Curtains, Inc.
Courts Foundation
Cowles Charitable Trust
Cowles Media Co.
Cox Enterprises
CPI Corp.
Craigmyle Foundation
Crandall Memorial Foundation, J. Ford
Crane Fund for Widows and Children
Cranston Print Works
Crestar Financial Corp.
Crum and Forster
CT Corp. System
Cudahy Fund, Patrick and Anna M.
Cummins Engine Co.
CUNA Mutual Insurance Group
Cuneo Foundation
Curtice-Burns Foods
Dain Bosworth/Inter-Regional Financial Group
Dalton Foundation, Dorothy U.
Daly Charitable Foundation Trust, Robert and Nancy
Dammann Fund
Dana Corp.
Davee Foundation

Davidson Family Charitable Foundation
Davis Foundation, Joe C.
Davis Foundation, Simon and Annie
Delaware North Cos.
Deluxe Corp.
Deposit Guaranty National Bank
Dexter Corp.
Dial Corp.
Dibner Fund
Dickson Foundation
Digital Equipment Corp.
Disney Family Foundation, Roy
Dodge Foundation, Cleveland H.
Doheny Foundation, Carrie Estelle
Donaldson Co.
Donnelley & Sons Co., R.R.
Dougherty, Jr. Foundation, James R.
Douglas Charitable Foundation
Dow Fund, Alden and Vada
Dreitzer Foundation
Dresser Industries
Dreyfus Foundation, Jean and Louis
Dreyfus Foundation, Max and Victoria
Driehaus Foundation, Richard H.
du Pont de Nemours & Co., E. I.
Dubow Family Foundation
Dula Educational and Charitable Foundation, Caleb C. and Julia W.
Dupar Foundation
duPont Foundation, Alfred I.
duPont Fund, Jessie Ball
Earl-Beth Foundation
Eastern Bank Foundation
Eastern Enterprises
Eaton Corp.
Eaton Foundation, Edwin M. and Gertrude S.
Eccles Foundation, George S. and Dolores Dore
Eccles Foundation, Marriner S.
Eden Hall Foundation
Einstein Fund, Albert E. and Birdie W.
Eisenberg Foundation, George M.
El Pomar Foundation
Electronic Data Systems Corp.
Engelhard Foundation, Charles
English-Bonter-Mitchell Foundation
Enright Foundation
Enron Corp.
Equifax
Ethyl Corp.
Ettinger Foundation
Exxon Corp.
Faith Charitable Trust
Fales Foundation Trust
Falk Medical Research Foundation, Dr. Ralph and Marian
Farnsworth Trust, Charles A.
Favrot Fund
Federal National Mortgage Assn., Fannie Mae
Federated Department Stores and Allied Stores Corp.
Fels Fund, Samuel S.
Fidelity Bank
Field Foundation of Illinois
Fifth Avenue Foundation
Fikes Foundation, Leland
Finnegan Foundation, John D.
Fireman's Fund Insurance Co.
First Boston
First Fidelity Bancorporation
First Hawaiian
First Interstate Bank NW Region
First Interstate Bank of Arizona
First Interstate Bank of California
First Interstate Bank of Oregon

First Interstate Bank of Texas, N.A.
First Union Corp.
Firstar Bank Milwaukee NA
Fleet Bank of New York
Fleet Financial Group
Fleming Foundation
Fletcher Foundation
Florence Foundation
Florence Foundation
Florida Power & Light Co.
Foellinger Foundation
Foerderer Foundation, Percival E. and Ethel Brown
Ford Foundation, Kenneth W.
Forest Lawn Foundation
Forest Oil Corp.
Foster Foundation
Foundation for Child Development
Fowler Memorial Foundation, John Edward
Fox Foundation, John H.
Frankel Foundation
Freed Foundation
Freedom Forum
Freeman Charitable Trust, Samuel
Frees Foundation
Frost Foundation
Frueauff Foundation, Charles A.
Fry Foundation, Lloyd A.
Fuchs Foundation, Gottfried & Mary
Fuller Co., H.B.
Fuller Foundation, C. G.
Funderburke & Associates
G.A.G. Charitable Corporation
Gallo Foundation, Ernest
Gallo Foundation, Julio R.
Gannett Co.
Gap, The
GAR Foundation
Garner Charitable Trust, James G.
Gates Foundation
GATX Corp.
Gellert Foundation, Celia Berta
General Dynamics Corp.
General Electric Co.
General Mills
General Motors Corp.
General Signal Corp.
General Tire Inc.
GenRad
Georgia Power Co.
Gheens Foundation
Giant Food
Gibson Foundation, E. L.
Gifford Charitable Corporation, Rosamond
Giles Foundation, Edward C.
Gill Foundation, Pauline Allen
Gillette Co.
Gilman Foundation, Howard
Ginter Foundation, Karl and Anna
Glaser Foundation
Gleason Foundation, James
Gleason Foundation, Katherine
Glenmore Distilleries Co.
Glenn Foundation, Carrie C. & Lena V.
Globe Newspaper Co.
Goldbach Foundation, Ray and Marie
Goldman Foundation, Aaron and Cecile
Goldman Foundation, Herman
Goldman Fund, Richard and Rhoda
Goldseker Foundation of Maryland, Morris
Goldsmith Foundation, Horace W.
Goodyear Foundation, Josephine
Gottesman Fund

Grace & Co., W.R.
Grader Foundation, K. W.
Graphic Controls Corp.
Grassmann Trust, E. J.
Graybar Electric Co.
Great Western Financial Corp.
Greater Construction Corp. Charitable Foundation, Inc.
Grundy Foundation
GTE Corp.
Gudelsky Family Foundation, Homer and Martha
Gulfstream Aerospace Corp.
Haas Fund, Walter and Elise
Haas, Jr. Fund, Evelyn and Walter
Hadson Corp.
Hagedorn Fund
Haigh-Scatena Foundation
Hall Family Foundations
Hall Foundation
Hallmark Cards
Halsell Foundation, O. L.
Hamel Family Charitable Trust, D. A.
Hamman Foundation, George and Mary Josephine
Hampden Papers
Hancock Foundation, Luke B.
Harris Foundation
Harrison Foundation, Fred G.
Harsco Corp.
Hartford Courant Foundation
Hasbro
Hawley Foundation
Hazen Foundation, Edward W.
Hearst Foundation
Hearst Foundation, William Randolph
Hechinger Co.
Heinz Endowment, Vira I.
Heinz Foundation, Drue
Hemingway Foundation, Robert G.
Hettinger Foundation
Heublein
Hiawatha Education Foundation
Hill Crest Foundation
Hill Foundation
Hillcrest Foundation
Hillman Foundation, Henry L.
Hobby Foundation
Hoblitzelle Foundation
Hodge Foundation
Home Depot
Homeland Foundation
Horizons Foundation
Hospital Corp. of America
Houck Foundation, May K.
Household International
Hunt Alternatives Fund
Hunt Charitable Trust, C. Giles
Hunter Foundation, Edward and Irma
Huston Foundation
Hutchins Foundation, Mary J.
Hyams Foundation
Hyundai Motor America
I and G Charitable Foundation
ICI Americas
Iddings Benevolent Trust
IDS Financial Services
IES Industries
IMCERA Group Inc.
Inland Container Corp.
Inland Steel Industries
International Paper Co.
Irmas Charitable Foundation, Audrey and Sydney
Irvine Foundation, James
Irwin Charity Foundation, William G.
Israel Foundation, A. Cremieux
ITT Corp.
ITT Hartford Insurance Group
ITT Rayonier
Ivakota Association

Ix & Sons, Frank
J.P. Morgan & Co.
Jackson Foundation
James River Corp. of Virginia
Jarson-Stanley and Mickey
  Kaplan Foundation, Isaac &
  Esther
Jeffress Memorial Trust,
  Elizabeth G.
Jenkins Foundation, George W.
Jockey Hollow Foundation
John Hancock Mutual Life
  Insurance Co.
Johnson Foundation, Helen K.
  and Arthur E.
Johnson Foundation, Walter S.
Jones Family Foundation,
  Eugenie and Joseph
Jones Foundation, Daisy Marquis
Jones Foundation, Helen
Joyce Foundation, John M. and
  Mary A.
Julia R. and Estelle L.
  Foundation
Jurodin Fund
Kapiloff Foundation, Leonard
Kaplan Fund, J. M.
Kasal Charitable Trust, Father
Katzenberger Foundation
Kavanagh Foundation, T. James
Kayser Foundation
Keating Family Foundation
Keith Foundation Trust, Ben E.
Kenedy Memorial Foundation,
  John G. and Marie Stella
Kennecott Corp.
Kennedy Foundation, Ethel
Kennedy Foundation, Quentin J.
Kern Foundation, Ilma
Kerr Foundation, Robert S. and
  Grayce B.
Kieckhefer Foundation, J. W.
Kiewit Foundation, Peter
Kimball Foundation, Horace A.
  Kimball and S. Ella
Kimberly-Clark Corp.
Kingsley Foundation, Lewis A.
Kiplinger Foundation
Kirbo Charitable Trust, Thomas
  M. and Irene B.
Klee Foundation, Conrad and
  Virginia
Knight Foundation, John S. and
  James L.
Knistrom Foundation, Fanny and
  Svante
Knott Foundation, Marion I. and
  Henry J.
Knox, Sr., and Pearl Wallis Knox
  Charitable Foundation, Robert
  W.
Koch Foundation
Koret Foundation
Kraft General Foods
Kramer Foundation, Louise
Kuhne Foundation Trust, Charles
Kysor Industrial Corp.
Ladish Co.
Lafarge Corp.
Laffey-McHugh Foundation
Land O'Lakes
Lapham-Hickey Steel Corp.
Lasdon Foundation
Lassen Foundation, Irving A.
Lassus Brothers Oil
Lavanburg-Corner House
LBJ Family Foundation
Legg Mason Inc.
Levinson Foundation, Max and
  Anna
Lewis Foundation, Frank J.
Lied Foundation Trust
Lightner Sams Foundation
Lincoln National Corp.
Link, Jr. Foundation, George
Little, Arthur D.
Long Foundation, George A. and
  Grace

Long Island Lighting Co.
Longwood Foundation
Louisiana Power & Light
  Co./New Orleans Public
  Service
Love Foundation, George H. and
  Margaret McClintic
Love Foundation, Martha and
  Spencer
Lowe Foundation, Joe and Emily
Lowenstein Foundation, Leon
LTV Corp.
Luce Charitable Trust, Theodore
Lydall, Inc.
M. E. G. Foundation
M.T.D. Products
Mabee Foundation, J. E. and L.
  E.
Maclellan Charitable Trust, R. J.
Maddox Foundation, J. F.
Mailman Family Foundation, A.
  L.
Makita U.S.A., Inc.
Mallinckrodt Specialty
  Chemicals Co.
Mansfield Foundation, Albert
  and Anne
Mardag Foundation
Maritz Inc.
Marmot Foundation
Mars Foundation
Marshall Foundation
Martin Foundation
Martin Marietta Corp.
Mary Kay Foundation
Massey Charitable Trust
Maxus Energy Corp.
Mayer Charitable Trust, Oscar
  G. & Elsa S.
Mayer Foods Corp., Oscar
Mayerson Foundation, Manuel
  D. and Rhoda
Maytag Family Foundation, Fred
Mazza Foundation
MBIA, Inc.
McAlonan Trust, John A.
McBean Family Foundation
McBride & Son Associates
McCarthy Charities
McCasland Foundation
McCormick Tribune Foundation,
  Robert R.
McCullough Foundation, Ralph
  H. and Ruth J.
McCune Foundation
McDonald & Co. Securities
McDonald & Co. Securities
McDonnell Douglas Corp.
McDonnell Douglas Corp.-West
McGraw-Hill
McGregor Foundation, Thomas
  and Frances
McGregor Fund
McIntosh Foundation
McKee Foundation, Robert E.
  and Evelyn
McKee Poor Fund, Virginia A.
McKesson Corp.
McKnight Foundation
McMillen Foundation
McRae Foundation
Mead Corp.
Meadows Foundation
Medina Foundation
Melitta North America Inc.
Mellon Bank Corp.
Mellon Foundation, Richard King
Menasha Corp.
Merck Human Health Division
Meridian Bancorp
Merrion Foundation
Metropolitan Health Foundation
Metropolitan Life Insurance Co.
Meyer Foundation, Eugene and
  Agnes E.
Meyer Memorial Foundation,
  Aaron and Rachel
MGIC Investment Corp.

Michigan Gas Utilities
Mid-Iowa Health Foundation
Middendorf Foundation
Midwest Resources
Miller-Mellor Association
Mills Charitable Foundation,
  Henry L. and Kathryn
Minnesota Mutual Life
  Insurance Co.
Mitchell Family Foundation,
  Bernard and Marjorie
MNC Financial
Mobil Oil Corp.
Monaghan Charitable Trust, Rose
Monell Foundation, Ambrose
Monroe Foundation (1976), J.
  Edgar
Monsanto Co.
Moore Foundation, Edward S.
Moores Foundation
Moores Foundation, Harry C.
Morgan Stanley & Co.
Moses Fund, Henry and Lucy
Moskowitz Foundation, Irving I.
Motorola
Mulligan Charitable Trust, Mary
  S.
Munson Foundation, W. B.
Murphy Foundation, Dan
Myra Foundation
Nanney Foundation, Charles and
  Irene
Nashua Trust Co.
National City Bank of Evansville
National Computer Systems
National Life of Vermont
National Presto Industries
Nationwide Insurance Cos.
NBD Bank
Neu Foundation, Hugo and Doris
New England Mutual Life
  Insurance Co.
New England Telephone Co.
New Prospect Foundation
New York Foundation
New York Life Insurance Co.
New York Mercantile Exchange
New York Stock Exchange
New York Telephone Co.
The New Yorker Magazine, Inc.
Newman's Own
Newmil Bancorp
News & Observer Publishing Co.
Nias Foundation, Henry
Nike Inc.
Noble Foundation, Samuel
  Roberts
Norgren Foundation, Carl A.
Norris Foundation, Kenneth T.
  and Eileen L.
Northeast Utilities
Northern Indiana Public Service
  Co.
Northern States Power Co.
Northern Trust Co.
Northwest Natural Gas Co.
Norton Co.
Norton Foundation Inc.
Noyes, Jr. Memorial Foundation,
  Nicholas H.
Occidental Oil & Gas Corp.
O'Connor Co.
OCRI Foundation
Ogilvy & Mather Worldwide
Ohio National Life Insurance Co.
Old National Bank in Evansville
Olin Corp.
Olsson Memorial Foundation,
  Elis
O'Neill Foundation, William J.
  and Dorothy K.
Oppenstein Brothers Foundation
Ordean Foundation
Ore-Ida Foods, Inc.
Orleans Trust, Carrie S.
Orleton Trust Fund
Osher Foundation, Bernard

Overbrook Foundation
Overstreet Foundation
Owen Trust, B. B.
Oxford Industries, Inc.
Pacific Gas & Electric Co.
Pacific Mutual Life Insurance Co.
Pacific Telesis Group
Packaging Corporation of
  America
Palmer-Fry Memorial Trust, Lily
Pan-American Life Insurance Co.
Panhandle Eastern Corp.
Parke-Davis Group
Parker Drilling Co.
Parker Foundation, Theodore
  Edson
Parman Foundation, Robert A.
Parsons Foundation, Ralph M.
Parsons - W.D. Charities, Vera
  Davis
Patterson Charitable Fund, W. I.
Pax Christi Foundation
Payne Foundation, Frank E. and
  Seba B.
Peabody Charitable Fund, Amelia
Peabody Foundation, Amelia
Penn Savings Bank, a division of
  Sovereign Bank Bank of
  Princeton, a division of
  Sovereign Bank
Penney Foundation, James C.
Pennington Foundation, Irene W.
  and C. B.
Pennzoil Co.
Penzance Foundation
People's Bank
Peoples Energy Corp.
Peppers Foundation, Ann
Pepsi-Cola Bottling Co. of
  Charlotte
Perkin-Elmer Corp.
Perkin-Elmer Corp.
Perley Fund, Victor E.
Pet
Peters Foundation, Leon S.
Pew Charitable Trusts
Pfister and Vogel Tanning Co.
Pfizer
PHH Corp.
Philip Morris Cos.
Philips Foundation, Jesse
Phillips Family Foundation, Jay
  and Rose
Phillips Foundation, Dr. P.
Phillips Foundation, Waite and
  Genevieve
Pickford Foundation, Mary
Pillsbury Foundation
Pine Tree Foundation
Pines Bridge Foundation
Pitney Bowes
Pittsburgh National Bank
Playboy Enterprises, Inc.
Plough Foundation
Portec, Inc.
Porter Testamentary Trust, James
  Hyde
Portland General Electric Co.
Potomac Electric Power Co.
Pott Foundation, Herman T. and
  Phenie R.
Pratt Memorial Fund
Price Associates, T. Rowe
Priddy Foundation
Primerica Corp.
Principal Financial Group
Procter & Gamble Cosmetic &
  Fragrance Products
Providence Energy Corp.
Provident Life & Accident
  Insurance Co.
Prudential-Bache Securities
Prudential Insurance Co. of
  America
Public Welfare Foundation
Quaker Oats Co.
Quanex Corp.
Questar Corp.

R. F. Foundation
Ralston Purina Co.
Raskob Foundation for Catholic
  Activities
Read Foundation, Charles L.
Recognition Equipment
Redfield Foundation, Nell J.
Reeves Foundation
Reilly Industries
Reliable Life Insurance Co.
Rennebohm Foundation, Oscar
Republic New York Corp.
Retirement Research Foundation
Revlon
Rhoades Fund, Otto L. and
  Hazel E.
Rhodebeck Charitable Trust
Rice Foundation
Rich Foundation
Richardson Fund, Mary Lynn
Ritter Foundation
Rockwell Fund
Rockwell International Corp.
Rogers Foundation, Mary Stuart
Rohm and Haas Company
Roseburg Forest Products Co.
Rosenstiel Foundation
Ross Foundation, Arthur
Ross Laboratories
Ross Memorial Foundation, Will
  Rouse Co.
Royal Group Inc.
Rubin Foundation, Samuel
Rubinstein Foundation, Helena
Ruffin Foundation, Peter B. &
  Adeline W.
Rupp Foundation, Fran and
  Warren
Russell Charitable Foundation,
  Tom
SAFECO Corp.
Salgo Charitable Trust, Nicholas
  M.
Sams Foundation, Earl C.
San Diego Gas & Electric
Sandy Foundation, George H.
Sandy Hill Foundation
Santa Fe Pacific Corp.
Sara Lee Corp.
Sara Lee Hosiery
Scaife Family Foundation
Scherman Foundation
Schlink Foundation, Albert G.
  and Olive H.
Schlumberger Ltd.
Schmidlapp Trust No. 1, Jacob G.
Schmitt Foundation, Arthur J.
Schneider Foundation Corp., Al
  J.
Scholl Foundation, Dr.
Schumann Fund for New Jersey
Schwab & Co., Charles
Schwartz Foundation, David
Scott Foundation, William R.,
  John G., and Emma
Scroggins Foundation, Arthur E.
  and Cornelia C.
Sealright Co., Inc.
Seaway Food Town
Security Life of Denver
Sentinel Communications Co.
Share Foundation
Shawmut National Corp.
Shawmut Worcester County
  Bank, N.A.
Shea Co., John F.
Shea Foundation, John and
  Dorothy
Shell Oil Co.
Shenandoah Life Insurance Co.
Shoong Foundation, Milton
Simon Foundation, William E.
  and Carol G.
Simpson PSB Foundation
SIT Investment Associates, Inc.
Skinner Corp.
Slant/Fin Corp.

Beal Foundation
Bean Foundation, Norwin S. and
    Elizabeth N.
Bean, L.L.
Beasley Foundation, Theodore
    and Beulah
Beatty Trust, Cordelia Lunceford
Beazley Foundation
Bechtel Charitable Remainder
    Uni-Trust, Harold R.
Bechtel Group
Bechtel, Jr. Foundation, S. D.
Beck Foundation
Becton Dickinson & Co.
Bedford Fund
Bedsole Foundation, J. L.
Beech Aircraft Corp.
Beecher Foundation, Florence
    Simon
Beeghly Fund, Leon A.
Beerman Foundation
Behmann Brothers Foundation
Beitzell & Co.
Bekins Foundation, Milo W.
Belden Brick Co., Inc.
Belk Stores
Belk Stores
Bell Communications Research
Bell Helicopter Textron
Beloit Foundation
Belz Foundation
Bemis Company
Bend Millwork Systems
Bender Foundation
Benedum Foundation, Claude
    Worthington
Beneficia Foundation
Benefit Trust Life Insurance Co.
Benetton
Bentley Foundation, Alvin M.
Benz Trust, Doris L.
Berenson Charitable Foundation,
    Theodore W. and Evelyn
Beretta U.S.A. Corp.
Bergner Co., P.A.
Berkey Foundation, Peter
Berkman Charitable Trust, Allen
    H. and Selma W.
Bernsen Foundation, Grace and
    Franklin
Bernstein & Co., Sanford C.
Bernstein Foundation, Diane and
    Norman
Berry Foundation, Loren M.
Bersted Foundation
Berwind Corp.
Best Foundation, Walter J. and
    Edith E.
Best Products Co.
Bethlehem Steel Corp.
Betts Industries
BFGoodrich
BHP Pacific Resources
Bicknell Fund
Bierhaus Foundation
Bierlein Family Foundation
Bigelow Foundation, F. R.
Bingham Second Betterment
    Fund, William
Binney & Smith Inc.
Binney & Smith Inc.
Binswanger Co.
Bionetics Corp.
Bishop Charitable Trust, A. G.
Bishop Foundation, E. K. and
    Lillian F.
Bishop Foundation, Vernon and
    Doris
Bjorkman Foundation
Blade Communications
Blank Fund, Myron and
    Jacqueline
Bloch Foundation, Henry W. and
    Marion H.
Block, H&R
Bloedorn Foundation, Walter A.
Blount

Blount Educational and
    Charitable Foundation,
    Mildred Weedon
Blue Bell, Inc.
Blue Cross and Blue Shield of
    Minnesota Foundation Inc.
Blue Cross and Blue Shield
    United of Wisconsin
    Foundation
Blue Cross & Blue Shield of
    Alabama
Blue Cross & Blue Shield of
    Kentucky Foundation
Blum Foundation, Edith C.
Blum Foundation, Harry and
    Maribel G.
Blum Foundation, Lois and
    Irving
Blum Foundation, Nathan and
    Emily S.
BMC Industries
BMW of North America, Inc.
Boatmen's Bancshares
Boatmen's First National Bank
    of Oklahoma
Bodenhamer Foundation
Bodine Corp.
Boehringer Mannheim Corp.
Boeing Co.
Boettcher Foundation
Boh Brothers Construction Co.
Boise Cascade Corp.
Boisi Family Foundation
Bolz Family Foundation,
    Eugenie Mayer
Boots Pharmaceuticals, Inc.
Borchard Foundation, Albert and
    Elaine
Bordeaux Foundation
Borden
Borden Memorial Foundation,
    Mary Owen
Borg-Warner Corp.
Borman's
Borun Foundation, Anna Borun
    and Harry
Bosch Corp., Robert
Bosque Foundation
Bossong Hosiery Mills
Boston Edison Co.
Boston Fatherless and Widows
    Society
Boston Gas Co.
Boulevard Foundation
Bourns, Inc.
Boutell Memorial Fund, Arnold
    and Gertrude
Bovaird Foundation, Mervin
Bowater Inc.
Bowers Foundation
Bowsher-Booher Foundation
Boynton Fund, John W.
Bozzone Family Foundation
BP America
Brach Foundation, Edwin I.
Bradford & Co., J.C.
Bradford & Co., J.C.
Bradley-Turner Foundation
Brady Foundation
Brand Cos.
Braun Foundation
Bray Charitable Trust, Viola E.
Breidenthal Foundation, Willard
    J. and Mary G.
Bremer Foundation, Otto
Brenner Foundation, Mervyn
Brewer and Co., Ltd., C.
Breyer Foundation
Bridgestone/Firestone
Bridwell Foundation, J. S.
Briggs Family Foundation
Briggs & Stratton Corp.
Bright Charitable Trust,
    Alexander H.
Bright Family Foundation
Bristol-Myers Squibb Co.
Bristol Savings Bank
Britton Fund

Broadhurst Foundation
Broccoli Charitable Foundation,
    Dana and Albert R.
Brody Foundation, Frances
Bromley Residuary Trust, Guy I.
Bronstein Foundation, Soloman
    and Sylvia
Brooks Brothers
Brown Charitable Trust, Dora
    Maclellan
Brown Foundation
Brown Foundation, George
    Warren
Brown Foundation, James
    Graham
Brown Foundation, M. K.
Brown Foundation, W. L. Lyons
Brown Group
Brown, Jr. Charitable Trust,
    Frank D.
Brown & Sharpe Manufacturing
    Co.
Brown & Sons, Alex
Brown & Williamson Tobacco
    Corp.
Browning-Ferris Industries
Broyhill Family Foundation
Bruening Foundation, Eva L. and
    Joseph M.
Brundage Charitable, Scientific,
    and Wildlife Conservation
    Foundation, Charles E. and
    Edna T.
Brunner Foundation, Fred J.
Brunswick Corp.
Buchalter, Nemer, Fields, &
    Younger
Buchanan Family Foundation
Bucyrus-Erie
Budweiser of Columbia
Buffett Foundation
Builder Marts of America
Burchfield Foundation, Charles
    E.
Burdines
Burkitt Foundation
Burlington Industries
Burlington Northern Inc.
Burlington Resources
Burnand Medical and
    Educational Foundation,
    Alphonse A.
Burndy Corp.
Burnham Donor Fund, Alfred G.
Burnham Foundation
Burns Family Foundation
Burns Foundation, Fritz B.
Burroughs Wellcome Co.
Burton Foundation, William T.
    and Ethel Lewis
Bush Foundation
Business Incentives
Bustard Charitable Permanent
    Trust Fund, Elizabeth and
    James
Butler Family Foundation,
    George W. and Gladys S.
Butler Family Foundation,
    Patrick and Aimee
Butler Foundation, J. Homer
Butler Manufacturing Co.
Bydale Foundation
C. E. and S. Foundation
C.P. Rail Systems
Cable & Wireless
    Communications
Cabot Corp.
Cabot-Saltonstall Charitable
    Trust
Cadbury Beverages Inc.
Cafritz Foundation, Morris and
    Gwendolyn
Cahn Family Foundation
Cain Foundation, Gordon and
    Mary
Caldwell Foundation, Hardwick
Calhoun Charitable Trust,
    Kenneth

California & Hawaiian Sugar Co.
Callaway Foundation
Callaway Foundation, Fuller E.
Cambridge Mustard Seed
    Foundation
Cameron Foundation, Harry S.
    and Isabel C.
Camp Younts Foundation
Campbell Foundation
Campbell Foundation, J. Bulow
Campbell Soup Co.
Canon U.S.A., Inc.
Capital Fund Foundation
Capital Holding Corp.
Caplan Charity Foundation,
    Julius H.
Cargill
Carlson Cos.
Carlyle & Co. Jewelers
Carnahan-Jackson Foundation
Carolina Power & Light Co.
Carpenter Foundation
Carpenter Technology Corp.
Carrier Corp.
Carteh Foundation
Carter Family Foundation
Carter Foundation, Amon G.
Carter-Wallace
Carvel Foundation, Thomas and
    Agnes
Carylon Foundation
Cassett Foundation, Louis N.
Castle Foundation, Harold K. L.
Castle Foundation, Samuel N.
    and Mary
Castle Trust, George P. and Ida
    Tenney
Caterpillar
Cawsey Trust
Cayuga Foundation
CBS Inc.
Ceco Corp.
Center for Educational Programs
Centex Corp.
Central Fidelity Banks, Inc.
Central Hudson Gas & Electric
    Corp.
Central Life Assurance Co.
Central Maine Power Co.
Central Soya Co.
Century Companies of America
CertainTeed Corp.
Cessna Aircraft Co.
Chamberlin Foundation, Gerald
    W.
Chambers Development Co.
Chambers Memorial, James B.
Chandler Foundation
Chapin-May Foundation of
    Illinois
Chapman Charitable
    Corporation, Howard and Bess
Chapman Charitable Trust, H. A.
    and Mary K.
Charitable Fund
Charities Foundation
Charlesbank Homes
Charlton, Jr. Charitable Trust,
    Earle P.
Charter Manufacturing Co.
Chase Charity Foundation,
    Alfred E.
Chase Manhattan Bank, N.A.
Chatham Valley Foundation
Cheatham Foundation, Owen
Chemical Bank
Cheney Foundation, Elizabeth F.
Cherokee Foundation
Chesapeake Corp.
Chesebrough-Pond's
Chevron Corp.
Chicago Board of Trade
Chicago Sun-Times, Inc.
Chicago Title and Trust Co.
Chicago Tribune Co.
Children's Foundation of Erie
    County

Childress Foundation, Francis
    and Miranda
Childs Charitable Foundation,
    Roberta M.
Chilton Foundation Trust
Chiquita Brands Co.
Chrysler Corp.
Church & Dwight Co.
Ciba-Geigy Corp.
    (Pharmaceuticals Division)
CIGNA Corp.
Cincinnati Bell
Cincinnati Enquirer
Cincinnati Milacron
Circuit City Stores
CIT Group Holdings
Citibank, F.S.B.
Citicorp
Citizens Bank
Citizens First National Bank
City National Bank
Clabir Corp.
Clapp Charitable and
    Educational Trust, George H.
CLARCOR
Clark Foundation
Clark-Winchcole Foundation
Cleary Foundation
Clements Foundation
Cleveland-Cliffs
Clipper Ship Foundation
Clorox Co.
Close Foundation
Clowes Fund
CM Alliance Cos.
CNA Insurance Cos.
CNG Transmission Corp.
Cobb Family Foundation
Cockrell Foundation
Codrington Charitable
    Foundation, George W.
Coen Family Foundation,
    Charles S. and Mary
Coffey Foundation
Cogswell Benevolent Trust
Cohen Foundation, George M.
Cohen Foundation, Naomi and
    Nehemiah
Cohen Foundation, Wilfred P.
Cohn Family Foundation, Robert
    and Terri
Cohn Foundation, Peter A. and
    Elizabeth S.
Cole Foundation
Cole Foundation, Olive B.
Cole Foundation, Robert H. and
    Monica H.
Cole National Corp.
Cole Taylor Financial Group
Cole Trust, Quincy
Coleman Co.
Coles Family Foundation
Colket Foundation, Ethel D.
Collins Foundation
Collins Foundation, Carr P.
Collins Foundation, George and
    Jennie
Collins Foundation, James M.
Collins-McDonald Trust Fund
Colonial Life & Accident
    Insurance Co.
Colonial Oil Industries, Inc.
Colorado State Bank of Denver
Colt Foundation, James J.
Coltec Industries
Columbia Savings Charitable
    Foundation
Columbus Dispatch Printing Co.
Columbus Southern Power Co.
Comer Foundation
Comerica
Cominco American Inc.
Commerce Bancshares, Inc.
Commerce Clearing House
Commerzbank AG, New York
Commonwealth Edison Co.
Community Enterprises

United Funds (cont.)

Community Foundation
Community Health Association
ConAgra
Cone Mills Corp.
Connecticut Natural Gas Corp.
Connemara Fund
Conoco Inc.
Consolidated Freightways
Consolidated Natural Gas Co.
Consolidated Papers
Consolidated Rail Corp. (Conrail)
Constantin Foundation
Conston Corp.
Consumers Power Co.
Continental Corp.
Contran Corp.
Contraves USA
Cook Batson Foundation
Cook Foundation
Cook Foundation, Loring
Cooper Charitable Trust, Richard
  H.
Cooper Foundation
Cooper Industries
Coors Foundation, Adolph
Copernicus Society of America
Copley Press
Copperweld Steel Co.
Corbett Foundation
Cord Foundation, E. L.
Cornell Trust, Peter C.
Corning Incorporated
Corpus Christi Exploration Co.
Corvallis Clinic
Cosmair, Inc.
Country Curtains, Inc.
Countrymark Cooperative
County Bank
Courts Foundation
Covington Foundation, Marion
  Stedman
Cowden Foundation, Louetta M.
Cowles Charitable Trust
Cowles Media Co.
Cox Charitable Trust, A. G.
CPC International
CR Industries
Craig Foundation, J. Paul
Craigmyle Foundation
Crandall Memorial Foundation,
  J. Ford
Crane & Co.
Crane Co.
Crane Foundation, Raymond E.
  and Ellen F.
Crane Fund for Widows and
  Children
Cranston Print Works
Crapo Charitable Foundation,
  Henry H.
Crawford Estate, E. R.
Credit Suisse
Crels Foundation
Cremer Foundation
Crescent Plastics
Crestar Financial Corp.
Crestlea Foundation
CRL Inc.
Crown Central Petroleum Corp.
Crum and Forster
Crummer Foundation, Roy E.
CT Corp. System
CTS Corp.
Cuesta Foundation
Cullen Foundation
Culpeper Memorial Foundation,
  Daphne Seybolt
Culver Foundation, Constans
Cummings Foundation, James H.
Cummins Engine Co.
CUNA Mutual Insurance Group
Currey Foundation, Brownlee
Curtice-Burns Foods
Cyprus Minerals Co.

Dai-Ichi Kangyo Bank of
  California
Daily News
Dain Bosworth/Inter-Regional
  Financial Group
Dalgety Inc.
Dalton Foundation, Dorothy U.
Dalton Foundation, Harry L.
Daly Charitable Foundation
  Trust, Robert and Nancy
Dan River, Inc.
Dana Corp.
Daniels Foundation, Fred Harris
Darby Foundation
Darrah Charitable Trust, Jessie
  Smith
Dart Foundation
Dart Group Corp.
Dater Foundation, Charles H.
Daugherty Foundation
Dauphin Deposit Corp.
Davenport-Hatch Foundation
Davey Tree Expert Co.
Davidson Family Charitable
  Foundation
Davis Family - W.D. Charities,
  Tine W.
Davis Foundation, Edwin W. and
  Catherine M.
Davis Foundation, James A. and
  Juliet L.
Davis Foundation, Joe C.
Davis Foundation, Ken W.
Davis Foundation, Shelby
  Cullom
Davis Foundation, Simon and
  Annie
Davis Foundations, Arthur Vining
Day Family Foundation
Day Foundation, Willametta K.
Dayton Hudson Corp.
Dayton Power and Light Co.
Daywood Foundation
DCB Corp.
DCNY Corp.
De Lima Co., Paul
Dean Witter Discover
DEC International, Inc.
DeCamp Foundation, Ira W.
Dee Foundation, Lawrence T.
  and Janet T.
Deere & Co.
Dekalb Energy Co.
Dekalb Energy Co.
DeKalb Genetics Corp.
Delano Foundation, Mignon
  Sherwood
Delany Charitable Trust,
  Beatrice P.
Dell Foundation, Hazel
DelMar Foundation, Charles
Deluxe Corp.
Dennett Foundation, Marie G.
Dennison Manufacturing Co.
Dent Family Foundation, Harry
Deposit Guaranty National Bank
DeSoto
DeSoto
Detroit Edison Co.
Deutsch Co.
Devonwood Foundation
DeVos Foundation, Richard and
  Helen
Dexter Corp.
Dexter Industries
Dibner Fund
Dick Family Foundation
Dickson Foundation
Dillard Paper Co.
Dillon Foundation
Dimick Foundation
Dishman Charitable Foundation
  Trust, H. E. and Kate
Dixie Yarns, Inc.
Dodge Jones Foundation
Doherty Charitable Foundation,
  Henry L. and Grace
Domino of California

Donaldson Charitable Trust,
  Oliver S. and Jennie R.
Donaldson Co.
Donnelley Foundation, Elliott
  and Ann
Donnelley & Sons Co., R.R.
Doty Family Foundation
Dougherty, Jr. Foundation, James
  R.
Douglas Corp.
Douglas & Lomason Company
Douty Foundation
Dover Corp.
Dover Foundation
Dow Corning Corp.
Dow Foundation, Herbert H. and
  Barbara C.
Dow Fund, Alden and Vada
Dow Jones & Co.
Downs Perpetual Charitable
  Trust, Ellason
Dreitzer Foundation
Dresser Industries
Driscoll Foundation
du Pont de Nemours & Co., E. I.
Dubow Family Foundation
Duchossois Industries
Duke Power Co.
Dula Educational and Charitable
  Foundation, Caleb C. and Julia
  W.
Dun & Bradstreet Corp.
Dunagan Foundation
Duncan Foundation, Lillian H.
  and C. W.
Duncan Trust, James R.
Dunn Research Foundation, John
  S.
Dunspaugh-Dalton Foundation
Dupar Foundation
duPont Foundation, Alfred I.
duPont Foundation, Chichester
Duquesne Light Co.
Durham Corp.
Durr-Fillauer Medical
Dweck Foundation, Samuel R.
Dynamet, Inc.
Eagle-Picher Industries
Earl-Beth Foundation
Early Foundation
Easley Trust, Andrew H. and
  Anne O.
Eastern Bank Foundation
Eastern Fine Paper, Inc.
Eastern Foundry Co.
Eastman Kodak Co.
Eaton Corp.
Ebert Charitable Foundation,
  Horatio B.
Echlin Foundation
Eckerd Corp., Jack
Ecolab
Eddy Family Memorial Fund, C.
  K.
Eden Hall Foundation
Edgewater Steel Corp.
Edison Brothers Stores
Edison Foundation, Harry
Edison Foundation, Irving and
  Beatrice C.
Edwards Industries
EG&G Inc.
Egenton Home
Ehrman Foundation, Fred and
  Susan
Einstein Fund, Albert E. and
  Birdie W.
EIS Foundation
Eisenberg Foundation, George M.
El Pomar Foundation
Elco Charitable Foundation
Electric Power Equipment Co.
Elf Aquitaine, Inc.
Elf Atochem North America
Elgin Sweeper Co.
Elkin Memorial Foundation, Neil
  Warren and William Simpson

Elkins Foundation, J. A. and
  Isabel M.
Ellsworth Foundation, Ruth H.
  and Warren A.
Ellsworth Trust, W. H.
Emerson Electric Co.
Emerson Foundation, Fred L.
Emery Memorial, Thomas J.
EMI Records Group
Employers Insurance of Wausau,
  A Mutual Co.
Encyclopaedia Britannica, Inc.
Engelhard Foundation, Charles
English-Bonter-Mitchell
  Foundation
English Foundation, Walter and
  Marian
English Memorial Fund,
  Florence C. and H. L.
Enright Foundation
Enron Corp.
Ensign-Bickford Industries
Ensworth Charitable Foundation
Enterprise Rent-A-Car Co.
Epaphroditus Foundation
Equifax
Equitable Life Assurance Society
  of the U.S.
Erb Lumber Co.
Ernsthausen Charitable
  Foundation, John F. and Doris
  E.
Essel Foundation
Essick Foundation
Estes Foundation
Ethyl Corp.
Eureka Co.
European American Bank
Everett Charitable Trust
Evinrude Foundation, Ralph
Evjue Foundation
Ewald Foundation, H. T.
Ewald Foundation, H. T.
Exposition Foundation
Exxon Corp.
Eyman Trust, Jesse
Fabick Tractor Co., John
Fabri-Kal Corp.
Factor Family Foundation, Max
Fair Foundation, R. W.
Fair Oaks Foundation, Inc.
Fairchild Corp.
Fairfield Foundation, Freeman E.
Faith Home Foundation
Falk Foundation, David
Falk Foundation, Michael David
Falk Medical Research
  Foundation, Dr. Ralph and
  Marian
Farallon Foundation
Farley Industries
Farwell Foundation, Drusilla
Faulkner Trust, Marianne
  Gaillard
Favrot Fund
Fay's Incorporated
Federal Express Corp.
Federal-Mogul Corp.
Federal National Mortgage
  Assn., Fannie Mae
Federal Screw Works
Federated Department Stores and
  Allied Stores Corp.
Federated Life Insurance Co.
Federated Life Insurance Co.
Federated Life Insurance Co.
Fein Foundation
Feinstein Foundation, Myer and
  Rosaline
Femino Foundation
Fenton Foundation
Fibre Converters
Fidelity Bank
Field Foundation, Jamee and
  Marshall
Field Foundation of Illinois
Fieldcrest Cannon
Fifth Avenue Foundation

Fifth Third Bancorp
Fikes Foundation, Leland
FINA, Inc.
Finch Foundation, Doak
Fingerhut Family Foundation
Finley Foundation, A. E.
Finnegan Foundation, John D.
Fireman Charitable Foundation,
  Paul and Phyllis
Fireman's Fund Insurance Co.
Firestone Foundation, Roger S.
Firestone, Jr. Foundation, Harvey
First Bank System
First Boston
First Fidelity Bancorporation
First Financial Bank FSB
First Financial Bank FSB
First Hawaiian
First Interstate Bancsystem of
  Montana
First Interstate Bank NW Region
First Interstate Bank of Arizona
First Interstate Bank of California
First Interstate Bank of Denver
First Interstate Bank of Oregon
First Interstate Bank of Texas,
  N.A.
First Maryland Bancorp
First Mississippi Corp.
First National Bank in Wichita
First National Bank & Trust Co.
  of Rockford
First NH Banks, Inc.
First Petroleum Corp.
First Tennessee Bank
First Union Corp.
Firstar Bank Milwaukee NA
FirsTier Bank N.A. Omaha
Fishback Foundation Trust,
  Harmes C.
Fisher Foundation
Fisher Foundation
FKI Holdings Inc.
Flagler Foundation
Flatley Foundation
Fleet Bank
Fleet Bank of New York
Fleet Financial Group
Fleming Companies, Inc.
Flemm Foundation, John J.
Fletcher Foundation
Flickinger Memorial Trust
Florida Power Corp.
Florida Power & Light Co.
Florida Rock Industries
Fluor Corp.
FMC Corp.
Foellinger Foundation
Foote, Cone & Belding
  Communications
Foothills Foundation
Forbes
Forchheimer Foundation
Forchheimer Memorial
  Foundation Trust, Louise and
  Josie
Ford Foundation
Ford Foundation, Kenneth W.
Ford Fund, Walter and Josephine
Ford Fund, William and Martha
Ford II Fund, Henry
Ford Meter Box Co.
Ford Motor Co.
Forest City Enterprises
Forest Fund
Forest Oil Corp.
Formrite Tube Co.
Fort Worth Star Telegram
Fortin Foundation of Florida
Fortis Inc.
Fortis Benefits Insurance
  Company/Fortis Financial
  Group
Foster and Gallagher
Foster Charitable Foundation, M.
  Stratton
Foster Charitable Trust

Foster Charitable Trust
Foster Co., L.B.
Foster Foundation
Foundation for Middle East Peace
Foundation for the Needs of Others
Fourth Financial Corp.
Fox Charitable Foundation, Harry K. & Emma R.
Fox Foundation, John H.
Fox Foundation, Richard J.
Foxmeyer Corp.
France Foundation, Jacob and Annita
Frank Foundation, Ernest and Elfriede
Frank Fund, Zollie and Elaine
Frankel Foundation
Frankino Charitable Foundation, Samuel J. and Connie
Franklin Foundation, John and Mary
Franklin Mint Corp.
Frear Eleemosynary Trust, Mary D. and Walter F.
Frederick Foundation
Freedom Forum
Freeman Foundation, Ella West
Freeport Brick Co.
Freeport-McMoRan
Frees Foundation
Freightliner Corp.
Frelinghuysen Foundation
French Oil Mill Machinery Co.
Frese Foundation, Arnold D.
Friedman Family Foundation
Friends' Foundation Trust, A.
Frisch's Restaurants Inc.
Frohman Foundation, Sidney
Frost Foundation
Fry Foundation, Lloyd A.
Fuchsberg Family Foundation
Fujitsu America, Inc.
Fujitsu Systems of America, Inc.
Fuller Co., H.B.
Fuller Foundation, George F. and Sybil H.
Fullerton Foundation
Fullerton Metals Co.
Funderburke & Associates
Furth Foundation
Fusenot Charity Foundation, Georges and Germaine
Gage Foundation, Philip and Irene Toll
Galkin Charitable Trust, Ira S. and Anna
Gallagher Family Foundation, Lewis P.
Gallo Foundation, Ernest
Galter Foundation
Gannett Publishing Co., Guy
Gap, The
GAR Foundation
Gardner Charitable Foundation, Edith D.
Garland Foundation, John Jewett and H. Chandler
Garner Charitable Trust, James G.
Garvey Kansas Foundation
Garvey Texas Foundation
Garvey Trust, Olive White
Gates Foundation
Gateway Apparel
GATX Corp.
Gault-Hussey Charitable Trust
Gaylord Foundation, Clifford Willard
Gazette Co.
Gear Motion
Gear Motion
Gebbie Foundation
Geffen Foundation, David
GEICO Corp.
Gelman Foundation, Melvin and Estelle

GenCorp
General Accident Insurance Co. of America
General American Life Insurance Co.
General Development Corp.
General Electric Co.
General Machine Works
General Mills
General Motors Corp.
General Railway Signal Corp.
General Reinsurance Corp.
General Signal Corp.
General Tire Inc.
Geneseo Foundation
Geneva Foundation
Genius Foundation, Elizabeth Morse
Georgia-Pacific Corp.
Georgia Power Co.
Gerber Products Co.
Gerlach Foundation
Gershman Foundation, Joel
Gerson Family Foundation, Benjamin J.
Gerson Trust, B. Milfred
Gerstacker Foundation, Rollin M.
Getsch Family Foundation Trust
Gheens Foundation
Ghidotti Foundation, William and Marian
Gholston Trust, J. K.
Giant Eagle
Giant Food
Giant Food Stores
Giddings & Lewis
Gifford Charitable Corporation, Rosamond
Gilbane Foundation, Thomas and William
Gilbert, Jr. Charitable Trust, Price
Giles Foundation, Edward C.
Gill Foundation, Pauline Allen
Gillette Co.
Gilman Paper Co.
Gilmer-Smith Foundation
Gilmore Foundation, Irving S.
Gilmore Foundation, William G.
Gindi Associates Foundation
Ginter Foundation, Karl and Anna
Gitano Group
Glancy Foundation, Lenora and Alfred
Glaser Foundation
Glaxo
Glaze Foundation, Robert and Ruth
Glazer Foundation, Madelyn L.
Gleason Foundation, Katherine
Gleason Memorial Fund
Glenmore Distilleries Co.
Glenn Foundation, Carrie C. & Lena V.
Glick Foundation, Eugene and Marilyn
Glickenhaus & Co.
Glidden Co.
Globe Corp.
Globe Newspaper Co.
Glosser Foundation, David A.
Goddard Foundation, Charles B.
Godfrey Co.
Goerlich Family Foundation
Goldbach Foundation, Ray and Marie
Goldberg Family Foundation
Goldman Foundation, William
Goldman Fund, Richard and Rhoda
Goldome F.S.B
Goldring Family Foundation
Goldsmith Foundation
Goldstein Foundation, Alfred and Ann
Goldstein Foundation, Leslie and Roslyn
Golub Corp.

Goodall Rubber Co.
Goodman Family Foundation
Goodstein Family Foundation, David
Goodstein Foundation
Goodyear Foundation, Josephine
Goodyear Tire & Rubber Co.
Goody's Manufacturing Corp.
Gottwald Foundation
Grace & Co., W.R.
Graco
Grader Foundation, K. W.
Gradison & Co.
Graphic Controls Corp.
Graybar Electric Co.
Great Atlantic & Pacific Tea Co. Inc.
Great Lakes Casting Corp.
Great-West Life Assurance Co.
Great Western Financial Corp.
Greater Lansing Foundation
Grede Foundries
Green Foundation
Green Foundation, Burton E.
Green Fund
Greene Foundation, David J.
Greene Foundation, Robert Z.
Greene Manufacturing Co.
Greenebaum, Doll & McDonald
Greenfield Foundation, Albert M.
Greenspan Foundation
Greentree Foundation
Gries Charity Fund, Lucile and Robert H.
Griffis Foundation
Griffith Foundation, W. C.
Grigg-Lewis Trust
Griggs and Mary Griggs Burke Foundation, Mary Livingston
Grinnell Mutual Reinsurance Co.
Gross Charitable Trust, Walter L. and Nell R.
Grossman Foundation, N. Bud
Groves & Sons Co., S.J.
Grumbacher Foundation, M. S.
Grundy Foundation
Gruss Charitable Foundation, Emanuel and Riane
GTE Corp.
Guaranty Bank & Trust Co.
Guardian Life Insurance Co. of America
Gucci America Inc.
Gudelsky Family Foundation, Isadore and Bertha
Gulf Power Co.
Gulfstream Aerospace Corp.
Gussman Foundation, Herbert and Roseline
Guttman Foundation, Stella and Charles
Haas Foundation, Paul and Mary
Haas Fund, Miriam and Peter
Haas, Jr. Fund, Evelyn and Walter
Habig Foundation, Arnold F.
Hachar Charitable Trust, D. D.
Haffenreffer Family Fund
Haffner Foundation
Hagedorn Fund
Haggar Foundation
Haggerty Foundation
Hale Foundation, Crescent Porter
Hales Charitable Fund
Haley Foundation, W. B.
Halff Foundation, G. A. C.
Hall Foundation
Hall Foundation
Hallmark Cards
Halmos Foundation
Halstead Foundation
Hambay Foundation, James T.
Hamel Family Charitable Trust, D. A.
Hamilton Bank
Hamilton Foundation, Florence P.
Hamilton Oil Corp.

Hammond Machinery
Hampden Papers
Handleman Co.
Handy & Harman
Hanes Foundation, John W. and Anna H.
Hankins Foundation
Hannon Foundation, William H.
Hanson Foundation
Harcourt Foundation, Ellen Knowles
Harden Foundation
Hargis Charitable Foundation, Estes H. and Florence Parker
Harland Co., John H.
Harper Foundation, Philip S.
Harriman Foundation, Mary W.
Harrington Foundation, Don and Sybil
Harrington Foundation, Francis A. and Jacquelyn H.
Harris Corp.
Harris Family Foundation, Hunt and Diane
Harris Foundation
Harris Foundation, J. Ira and Nicki
Harris Foundation, James J. and Angelia M.
Harris Foundation, John H. and Lucille
Harris Trust & Savings Bank
Harrison Foundation, Fred G.
Harsco Corp.
Hartford Steam Boiler Inspection & Insurance Co.
Hartman Foundation, Jesse and Dorothy
Hartmarx Corp.
Hartzell Industries, Inc.
Harvest States Cooperative
Haskell Fund
Hatch Charitable Trust, Margaret Milliken
Hatterscheidt Foundation
Hawkins Foundation, Robert Z.
Hawley Foundation
Hawn Foundation
Hayfields Foundation
Hazen Foundation, Edward W.
Heath Foundation, Ed and Mary
Hechinger Co.
Hecht-Levi Foundation
Hecla Mining Co.
Hedrick Foundation, Frank E.
HEI Inc.
Heileman Brewing Co., Inc., G.
Heilicher Foundation, Menahem
Heinz Co., H.J.
Heinz Endowment, Howard
Heinz Endowment, Vira I.
Heinz Foundation, Drue
Helfaer Foundation, Evan and Marion
Helis Foundation
Heller Financial
Heller Foundation, Walter E.
Helmerich Foundation
Hemby Foundation, Alex
Henderson Foundation
Henkel Corp.
Henry Foundation, Patrick
Herman Foundation, John and Rose
Herndon Foundation
Herndon Foundation, Alonzo F. Herndon and Norris B.
Herrick Foundation
Herschend Family Foundation
Hershey Foods Corp.
Hershey Foundation
Hervey Foundation
Herzstein Charitable Foundation, Albert and Ethel
Hess Charitable Foundation, Ronne and Donald
Hettinger Foundation
Heublein

Hewit Family Foundation
Hexcel Corp.
Heymann Special Account, Mr. and Mrs. Jimmy
Heymann-Wolf Foundation
Hiawatha Education Foundation
Hidary Foundation, Jacob
Higgins Foundation, Aldus C.
Higginson Trust, Corina
High Foundation
Hilliard Corp.
Hillsdale Fund
Himmelfarb Foundation, Paul and Annetta
Hirschl Trust for Charitable Purposes, Irma T.
Hobbs Foundation
Hoche-Scofield Foundation
Hodge Foundation
Hoechst Celanese Corp.
Hoffberger Foundation
Hoffer Plastics Corp.
Hoffman Foundation, John Ernest
Hoffman Foundation, Maximillian E. and Marion O.
Hofmann Co.
Hofstetter Trust, Bessie
Hogan Foundation, Royal Barney
Holden Fund, James and Lynelle
Holley Foundation
Hollis Foundation
Home for Aged Men
Home Savings of America, FA
HON Industries
Honeywell
Honigman Foundation
Hook Drug
Hooker Charitable Trust, Janet A.
Hoover Foundation
Hoover Foundation, H. Earl
Hoover Fund-Trust, W. Henry
Hopper Memorial Foundation, Bertrand
Hopwood Charitable Trust, John M.
Hornblower Fund, Henry
Hospital Corp. of America
Houchens Foundation, Ervin G.
Houck Foundation, May K.
Houghton Mifflin Co.
House Educational Trust, Susan Cook
Household International
Houston Industries
Howe and Mitchell B. Howe Foundation, Lucite Horton
Howell Fund
Hoyt Foundation
Hubbard Broadcasting
Hubbard Milling Co.
Hubbell Inc.
Hudson-Webber Foundation
Huffy Corp.
Hughes Charitable Trust, Mabel Y.
Hugoton Foundation
Huisking Foundation
Hulings Foundation, Mary Andersen
Hulme Charitable Foundation, Milton G.
Hultquist Foundation
Humana
Hume Foundation, Jaquelin
Humphrey Foundation, Glenn & Gertrude
Humphrey Fund, George M. and Pamela S.
Hunt Alternatives Fund
Hunt Foundation
Hunt Foundation, Roy A.
Hunter Foundation, Edward and Irma
Hunter Trust, Emily S. and Coleman A.
Hurst Foundation
Huston Foundation

United Funds (cont.)

Hutchins Foundation, Mary J.
I and G Charitable Foundation
IBM Corp.
Icahn Foundation, Carl C.
ICI Americas
Iddings Benevolent Trust
Ideal Industries
IES Industries
Illges Foundation, John P. and Dorothy S.
Illges Memorial Foundation, A. and M. L.
Illinois Bell
Illinois Power Co.
Illinois Tool Works
IMCERA Group Inc.
Imperial Bancorp
Imperial Electric
IMT Insurance Co.
Inco Alloys International
Indiana Bell Telephone Co.
Indiana Gas and Chemical Corp.
Indiana Insurance Cos.
Ingalls Foundation, Louise H. and David S.
Ingersoll Milling Machine Co.
Inland Container Corp.
Inland Steel Industries
Inman Mills
Insurance Management Associates
Intel Corp.
Interco
Intercontinental Hotels Corp.
International Flavors & Fragrances
International Multifoods Corp.
Interstate National Corp.
Interstate National Corp.
Interstate Packaging Co.
Iowa-Illinois Gas & Electric Co.
Iowa State Bank
Ireland Foundation
Iroquois Avenue Foundation
Irwin Charity Foundation, William G.
Irwin-Sweeney-Miller Foundation
ITT Hartford Insurance Group
ITT Rayonier
Ivakota Association
Ix & Sons, Frank
J C S Foundation
J.P. Morgan & Co.
Jackson Family Foundation, Ann
Jackson Foundation
Jacobs Engineering Group
Jacobson Foundation, Bernard H. and Blanche E.
Jacobson & Sons, Benjamin
Jacoby Foundation, Lela Beren and Norman
Jaffe Foundation
Jaharis Family Foundation
James River Corp. of Virginia
Jameson Trust, Oleonda
Janesville Foundation
Janeway Foundation, Elizabeth Bixby
Janssen Foundation, Henry
Jaqua Foundation
Jarson-Stanley and Mickey Kaplan Foundation, Isaac & Esther
JCPenney Co.
JELD-WEN, Inc.
Jellison Benevolent Society
Jenkins Foundation, George W.
Jennings Foundation, Mary Hillman
Jergens Foundation, Andrew
Jersey Central Power & Light Co.
Jewell Memorial Foundation, Daniel Ashley and Irene Houston

Jewett Foundation, George Frederick
JFM Foundation
Jockey Hollow Foundation
John Hancock Mutual Life Insurance Co.
Johnson Controls
Johnson Foundation, A. D.
Johnson Foundation, Helen K. and Arthur E.
Johnson & Higgins
Johnson & Johnson
Johnson & Son, S.C.
Johnston-Hanson Foundation
Johnstone and H. Earle Kimball Foundation, Phyllis Kimball
Jones Family Foundation, Eugenie and Joseph
Jones Foundation, Harvey and Bernice
Jones Foundation, Montfort Jones and Allie Brown
Jones Intercable, Inc.
Jordan and Ettie A. Jordan Charitable Foundation, Mary Ranken
Jordan Foundation, Arthur
Joslyn Corp.
Jost Foundation, Charles and Mabel P.
Jostens
Joukowsky Family Foundation
Journal Gazette Co.
JSJ Corp.
Julia R. and Estelle L. Foundation
Jurzykowski Foundation, Alfred
Justus Trust, Edith C.
Kaiser Foundation, Betty E. and George B.
Kamps Memorial Foundation, Gertrude
Kanematsu-Gosho U.S.A. Inc.
Kangesser Foundation, Robert E., Harry A., and M. Sylvia
Kantzler Foundation
Kaplan Foundation, Mayer and Morris
Kaplan Foundation, Rita J. and Stanley H.
Kaplun Foundation, Morris J. and Betty
Kasle Steel Corp.
Katten, Muchin, & Zavis
Katzenberger Foundation
Kaufman Endowment Fund, Louis G.
Kautz Family Foundation
Kawabe Memorial Fund
Kawaler Foundation, Morris and Nellie L.
Kawasaki Motors Corp., U.S.A.
Kaye, Scholer, Fierman, Hays & Handler
Kayser Foundation
Kearney Inc., A.T.
Keating Family Foundation
Keck, Jr. Foundation, William M.
Keebler Co.
Keeler Fund, Miner S. and Mary Ann
Keene Trust, Hazel R.
Keith Foundation Trust, Ben E.
Keller-Crescent Co.
Keller Family Foundation
Kelley and Elza Kelley Foundation, Edward Bangs
Kellogg Foundation, J. C.
Kelly, Jr. Memorial Foundation, Ensign C. Markland
Kemper Memorial Foundation, David Woods
Kenan Family Foundation
Kendall Foundation, George R.
Kennametal
Kennecott Corp.
Kennedy Foundation, Ethel
Kent-Lucas Foundation

Kenworthy - Sarah H. Swift Foundation, Marion E.
Kepco, Inc.
Kerr Fund, Grayce B.
Kerr-McGee Corp.
Key Bank of Maine
Key Food Stores Cooperative Inc.
Kiewit Foundation, Peter
Kiewit Sons, Peter
Kilcawley Fund, William H.
Kilroy Foundation, William S. and Lora Jean
Kilworth Charitable Foundation, Florence B.
Kilworth Charitable Trust, William
Kimball Co., Miles
Kimball International
Kimberly-Clark Corp.
King Foundation, Carl B. and Florence E.
Kingsbury Corp.
Kingsley Foundation
Kinney-Lindstrom Foundation
Kiplinger Foundation
Kirkland & Ellis
Kirkpatrick Foundation
Klau Foundation, David W. and Sadie
Klee Foundation, Conrad and Virginia
Klein Fund, Nathan J.
Kline Foundation, Charles and Figa
Kline Foundation, Josiah W. and Bessie H.
Klingler Foundation, Helen and Charles
Kloeckner-Pentaplast of America
Kmart Corp.
Knapp Foundation
Knight-Ridder, Inc.
Knistrom Foundation, Fanny and Svante
Knowles Charitable Memorial Trust, Gladys E.
Knox Family Foundation
Knox Foundation, Seymour H.
Knox, Sr., and Pearl Wallis Knox Charitable Foundation, Robert W.
Koch Industries
Koch Sons, George
Koffler Family Foundation
Koh-I-Noor Rapidograph Inc.
Kohl Charitable Foundation, Allen D.
Kohl Foundation, Sidney
Kohn-Joseloff Fund
Komes Foundation
Koopman Fund
Koret Foundation
Korman Family Foundation, Hyman
Kraft General Foods
Kramer Foundation, Louise
Kress Foundation, George
Krieble Foundation, Vernon K.
Kuehn Foundation
Kuhne Foundation Trust, Charles
Kuhns Investment Co.
Kulas Foundation
Kunkel Foundation, John Crain
Kuyper Foundation, Peter H. and E. Lucille Gaass
Kyocera International Inc.
Kysor Industrial Corp.
L and L Foundation
La-Z-Boy Chair Co.
Laclede Gas Co.
Ladd Charitable Corporation, Helen and George
Ladish Co.
Ladish Family Foundation, Herman W.
Laffey-McHugh Foundation
Lakeside Foundation
Lamson & Sessions Co.

Lancaster Colony
Lance, Inc.
Land O'Lakes
Landmark Communications
Lane Co., Inc.
Lane Foundation, Minnie and Bernard
Lanier Brothers Foundation
Lard Trust, Mary Potishman
Laros Foundation, R. K.
Lasky Co.
Lassen Foundation, Irving A.
Lassus Brothers Oil
Lauffer Trust, Charles A.
Laurel Foundation
Lavanburg-Corner House
Lawrence Foundation, Lind
Lawyers Title Foundation
Lazar Foundation
LBJ Family Foundation
LDI Charitable Foundation
Leach Foundation, Tom & Frances
Lebanon Mutual Insurance Co.
Lebovitz Fund
Lee Endowment Foundation
Lee Enterprises
Lee Foundation, James T.
Lee Foundation, Ray M. and Mary Elizabeth
Legg Mason Inc.
Lehigh Portland Cement Co.
Lehman Foundation, Edith and Herbert
Lehmann Foundation, Otto W.
Leidy Foundation, John J.
Leighton-Oare Foundation
Lemberg Foundation
Lender Family Foundation
Lennox International, Inc.
Leo Burnett Co.
Leu Foundation, Harry P.
Leucadia National Corp.
Levi Strauss & Co.
Levin Foundation, Philip and Janice
Levinson Foundation, Morris L.
Leviton Manufacturing Co.
Levitt Foundation
Levitt Foundation, Richard S.
Levy Foundation, Charles and Ruth
Levy Foundation, June Rockwell
Levy's Lumber & Building Centers
Lewis Foundation, Frank J.
Libby-Dufour Fund, Trustees of the
Liberty Corp.
Liberty Diversified Industries Inc.
Liberty National Bank
Lieberman Enterprises
Lied Foundation Trust
Life Insurance Co. of Georgia
Life Investors Insurance Company of America
Lightner Sams Foundation
Lilly & Co., Eli
Lilly Endowment
Lilly Foundation, Richard Coyle
Lincoln Electric Co.
Lincoln Family Foundation
Lincoln Fund
Lincoln National Corp.
Lincy Foundation
Lindsay Foundation
Lindstrom Foundation, Kinney
Link Foundation
Linnell Foundation
Lippitt Foundation, Katherine Kenyon
Lipsky Foundation, Fred and Sarah
Lipton, Thomas J.
Liquid Air Corp.
Little, Arthur D.

Litton Industries
Litwin Foundation
Livingston Foundation
Lockhart Iron & Steel Co.
Lockheed Sanders
Lockwood Foundation, Byron W. and Alice L.
Loeb Partners Corp.
Loews Corp.
Long Foundation, George A. and Grace
Long Island Lighting Co.
Longwood Foundation
Loose Trust, Carrie J.
Loose Trust, Harry Wilson
Lopata Foundation, Stanley and Lucy
Louisiana Land & Exploration Co.
Louisiana-Pacific Corp.
Louisiana Power & Light Co./New Orleans Public Service
Loutit Foundation
Love Charitable Foundation, John Allan
Love Foundation, George H. and Margaret McClintic
Lovett Foundation
Lowe Foundation
Lowenstein Brothers Foundation
Lozier Foundation
LTV Corp.
Lubo Fund
Lubrizol Corp.
Luce Charitable Trust, Theodore
Luchsinger Family Foundation
Lucky Stores
Luckyday Foundation
Lukens
Lurie Family Foundation
Lurie Foundation, Louis R.
Luttrell Trust
Lydall, Inc.
M. E. G. Foundation
M/A-COM, Inc.
M.T.D. Products
Maas Foundation, Benard L.
MacArthur Foundation, John D. and Catherine T.
MacDonald Foundation, James A.
MacDonald Foundation, Marquis George
Macht Foundation, Morton and Sophia
Mack Foundation, J. S.
Maclellan Charitable Trust, R. J.
Maclellan Foundation
Maclellan Foundation, Robert L. and Kathrina H.
MacLeod Stewardship Foundation
Macy & Co., R.H.
Madison Gas & Electric Co.
Magma Copper Co.
Magowan Family Foundation
Maier Foundation, Sarah Pauline
Mailman Foundation
Makita U.S.A., Inc.
Mallinckrodt Specialty Chemicals Co.
Mamiye Brothers
Mandel Foundation, Joseph and Florence
Mandell Foundation, Samuel P.
Maneely Fund
Manilow Foundation, Nathan
Manitou Foundation
Mankato Citizens Telephone Co.
Mann Foundation, Ted
Manville Corp.
Mapco Inc.
Marathon Oil, Indiana Refining Division
Marbrook Foundation
Marcus Corp.
Mardag Foundation
Mardigian Foundation

Marine Midland Banks
Marinette Marine Corp.
Maritz Inc.
Mark IV Industries
Marley Co.
Marmot Foundation
Marquette Electronics
Marsh & McLennan Cos.
Marshall Foundation
Marshall Fund
Marshall & Ilsley Bank
Martin Marietta Aggregates
Martin Marietta Corp.
Marx Foundation, Virginia & Leonard
Massengill-DeFriece Foundation
Massey Charitable Trust
Massey Foundation
Massey Foundation, Jack C.
Massie Trust, David Meade
Material Service Corp.
Mather and William Gwinn Mather Fund, Elizabeth Ring
Mather Charitable Trust, S. Livingston
Mather Fund, Richard
Matthews International Corp.
Matz Foundation — Edelman Division
Mautz Paint Co.
May Department Stores Co.
May Foundation, Wilbur
Mayer Foods Corp., Oscar
Mayer Foundation, James and Eva
Mayor Foundation, Oliver Dewey
Maytag Corp.
Maytag Family Foundation, Fred
Mazer Foundation, Jacob and Ruth
Mazza Foundation
MCA
McAlonan Trust, John A.
McBean Family Foundation
McCann Foundation
McCarthy Charities
McCarthy Foundation, John and Margaret
McCasland Foundation
McCaw Foundation
McCormick & Co.
McCormick Tribune Foundation, Robert R.
McCune Foundation
McCutchen Foundation
McDermott
McDermott Foundation, Eugene
McDonald & Co. Securities
McDonald & Co. Securities
McDonald Industries, Inc., A. Y.
McDonnell Douglas Corp.
McDonnell Douglas Corp.-West
McDonough Foundation, Bernard
McDougall Charitable Trust, Ruth Camp
McEachern Charitable Trust, D. V. & Ida J.
McEvoy Foundation, Mildred H.
McFawn Trust No. 2, Lois Sisler
McFeely-Rogers Foundation
McGee Foundation
McGovern Fund for the Behavioral Sciences
McGraw Foundation
McGraw-Hill
McGregor Foundation, Thomas and Frances
McGregor Fund
MCI Communications Corp.
McInerny Foundation
McIntyre Foundation, B. D. and Jane E.
McKee Foundation, Robert E. and Evelyn
McKee Poor Fund, Virginia A.
McKenna Foundation, Katherine Mabis

McKenna Foundation, Philip M.
McKnight Foundation
McLean Contributionship
McMahon Foundation
McMaster Foundation, Harold and Helen
McMurray-Bennnett Foundation
McNutt Charitable Trust, Amy Shelton
McRae Foundation
MDU Resources Group, Inc.
Mead Corp.
Mead Fund, Nelson
Mechanics Bank
Media General, Inc.
Medtronic
Meek Foundation
Mellon Bank Corp.
Mellon Foundation, Richard King
Memton Fund
Menasha Corp.
Menschel Foundation, Robert and Joyce
Mentor Graphics
Merchants Bancshares
Merck & Co.
Mercury Aircraft
Meredith Corp.
Meredith Foundation
Mericos Foundation
Meridian Bancorp
Merillat Foundation, Orville D. and Ruth A.
Merit Oil Corp.
Merrick Foundation
Mervyn's
Meserve Memorial Fund, Albert and Helen
Messick Charitable Trust, Harry F.
Messing Family Charitable Foundation
Metal Industries
Metropolitan Health Foundation
Metropolitan Life Insurance Co.
Metropolitan Theatres Corp.
Mettler Instrument Corp.
Meyer Foundation, Alice Kleberg Reynolds
Meyer Foundation, George C.
Meyer Foundation, Robert R.
Meyer Memorial Foundation, Aaron and Rachel
Meyerhoff Fund, Joseph
MGIC Investment Corp.
Michigan Bell Telephone Co.
Michigan Consolidated Gas Co.
Michigan Gas Utilities
Mid-Iowa Health Foundation
Midwest Resources
Miles Inc.
Milken Foundation, L. and S.
Mill-Rose Co.
Miller Charitable Trust, Lewis N.
Miller Foundation
Miller Foundation, Steve J.
Miller Fund, Kathryn and Gilbert
Miller-Mellor Association
Miller Memorial Trust, George Lee
Milliken & Co.
Mills Foundation, Ralph E.
Mine Safety Appliances Co.
Miniger Memorial Foundation, Clement O.
Minnegasco
Minnesota Mutual Life Insurance Co.
Minnesota Power & Light Co.
Minster Machine Co.
Misco Industries
Misco Industries
Mitchell Energy & Development Corp.
Mitchell Family Foundation, Edward D. and Anna
Mitrani Family Foundation

MNC Financial
Mobil Oil Corp.
Model Foundation, Leo
Mohasco Corp.
Monarch Machine Tool Co.
Monfort Charitable Foundation
Monroe Auto Equipment Co.
Monsanto Co.
Montana Power Co.
Montgomery Foundation
Montgomery Ward & Co.
Moody Foundation
Moog Automotive, Inc.
Moore Business Forms, Inc.
Moore Charitable Foundation, Marjorie
Moore Foundation, C. F.
Moore Foundation, Roy C.
Moores Foundation
Moores Foundation, Harry C.
Moorman Manufacturing Co.
Morania Foundation
Morgan and Samuel Tate Morgan, Jr. Foundation, Marietta McNeil
Morgan Construction Co.
Morgan Foundation, Burton D.
Morgan Trust for Charity, Religion, and Education
Morgenstern Foundation, Morris
Morrill Charitable Foundation
Morris Charitable Trust, Charles M.
Morris Foundation
Morris Foundation, Norman M.
Morris Foundation, William T.
Morrison Foundation, Harry W.
Morrison Trust, Louise L.
Morse Foundation, Richard P. and Claire W.
Morton International
Mosbacher, Jr. Foundation, Emil
Moses Fund, Henry and Lucy
Mosinee Paper Corp.
Moss Charitable Trust, Finis M.
Moss Foundation, Harry S.
Motch Corp.
Motorola
Motter Printing Press Co.
Mount Vernon Mills
MTS Systems Corp.
Mueller Co.
Mulcahy Foundation
Mulford Foundation, Vincent
Mulford Trust, Clarence E.
Multimedia, Inc.
Munson Foundation, W. B.
Murata Erie North America
Murch Foundation
Murphey Foundation, Lluella Morey
Murphy Co., G.C.
Murphy Foundation
Murphy Foundation, John P.
Murphy Foundation, Katherine and John
Myers and Sons, D.
Myers and Sons, D.
Nanney Foundation, Charles and Irene
Nashua Trust Co.
Nason Foundation
National By-Products
National City Bank of Evansville
National City Corp.
National Computer Systems
National Forge Co.
National Fuel Gas Co.
National Gypsum Co.
National Life of Vermont
National Machinery Co.
National Presto Industries
National Pro-Am Youth Fund
National Service Industries
National Starch & Chemical Corp.
National Steel

National Westminster Bank New Jersey
Nationale-Nederlanden North America Corp.
NationsBank Corp.
Nationwide Insurance Cos.
Navistar International Corp.
NBD Bank
NBD Bank, N.A.
NCR Corp.
Neenah Foundry Co.
Nelco Sewing Machine Sales Corp.
Nelson Foundation, Florence
Nelson Industries, Inc.
Nesholm Family Foundation
Nestle U.S.A. Inc.
Neuberger Foundation, Roy R. and Marie S.
New Cycle Foundation
New England Mutual Life Insurance Co.
New England Telephone Co.
New Hampshire Ball Bearings
New Jersey Bell Telephone Company
New York Life Insurance Co.
New York Telephone Co.
New York Times Co.
The New Yorker Magazine, Inc.
Newhall Foundation, Henry Mayo
Newhouse Foundation, Samuel I.
Newman Assistance Fund, Jerome A. and Estelle R.
Newmil Bancorp
Newmont Mining Corp.
News America Publishing Inc.
News & Observer Publishing Co.
Nias Foundation, Henry
Nichols Co., J.C.
Nichols Foundation
Nike Inc.
Nippon Life Insurance Co.
Noble Foundation, Vivian Bilby
Norcliffe Fund
Nordson Corp.
Nordstrom, Inc.
Norfolk Shipbuilding & Drydock Corp.
Norfolk Southern Corp.
Norgren Foundation, Carl A.
Normandie Foundation
Nortek, Inc.
North American Life & Casualty Co.
North American Philips Corp.
North American Reinsurance Corp.
North Carolina Foam Foundation
Northeast Utilities
Northern Indiana Public Service Co.
Northern States Power Co.
Northern Telecom Inc.
Northwest Natural Gas Co.
Northwestern National Insurance Group
Northwestern National Life Insurance Co.
Norton Co.
Norton Foundation Inc.
Norton Memorial Corporation, Geraldi
Norwest Bank Nebraska
Norwest Corp.
Noyes, Jr. Memorial Foundation, Nicholas H.
NuTone Inc.
NYNEX Corp.
Oakley Foundation, Hollie and Anna
Oberlaender Foundation, Gustav
Obernauer Foundation
O'Bleness Foundation, Charles G.
Occidental Oil & Gas Corp.
Occidental Petroleum Corp.

O'Connor Co.
O'Connor Foundation, A. Lindsay and Olive B.
O'Connor Foundation, Magee
Odell and Helen Pfeiffer Odell Fund, Robert Stewart
Oestreicher Foundation, Sylvan and Ann
O'Fallon Trust, Martin J. and Mary Anne
Offield Family Foundation
Ogilvy & Mather Worldwide
Ogle Foundation, Paul
Oglebay Norton Co.
Ohio Bell Telephone Co.
Ohio National Life Insurance Co.
Ohio Valley Foundation
Oklahoman Foundation
Old Dominion Box Co.
Old National Bank in Evansville
Oleson Foundation
Olin Charitable Trust, John M.
Olin Corp.
Olin Foundation, Spencer T. and Ann W.
Olive Bridge Fund
Oliver Memorial Trust Foundation
Onan Family Foundation
1957 Charity Trust
O'Neil Foundation, Cyril F. and Marie E.
O'Neil Foundation, M. G.
O'Neill Charitable Corporation, F. J.
Ontario Corp.
Ontario Corp.
Oppenheimer Family Foundation
Oppenstein Brothers Foundation
Orbit Valve Co.
Orleans Trust, Carrie S.
Orleton Trust Fund
Ormet Corp.
Orscheln Co.
Osborn Manufacturing Co.
OsCo. Industries
O'Shaughnessy Foundation, I. A.
Oshkosh B'Gosh
Oshkosh Truck Corp.
O'Sullivan Children Foundation
Outboard Marine Corp.
Overbrook Foundation
Overnite Transportation Co.
Overseas Shipholding Group
Overstreet Foundation
Owen Industries, Inc.
Owen Trust, B. B.
Owens-Corning Fiberglas Corp.
Oxford Industries, Inc.
PACCAR
Pacific Gas & Electric Co.
Pacific Mutual Life Insurance Co.
Pacific Telesis Group
PacifiCorp
Packaging Corporation of America
Packer Foundation, Horace B.
Page Belting Co.
Page Foundation, George B.
Palin Foundation
Palmer-Fry Memorial Trust, Lily
Panhandle Eastern Corp.
Paramount Communications Inc.
Park Bank
Park National Bank
Park-Ohio Industries Inc.
Parker Drilling Co.
Parker Foundation, Theodore Edson
Parker-Hannifin Corp.
Parman Foundation, Robert A.
Parsons - W.D. Charities, Vera Davis
Pasadena Area Residential Aid
Patterson-Barclay Memorial Foundation
Patterson Charitable Fund, W. I.

United Funds (cont.)

Paulucci Family Foundation
Peabody Foundation, Amelia
Pearce Foundation, Dr. M. Lee
Peerless Insurance Co.
Pella Corp.
PemCo. Corp.
Pendleton Construction Corp.
Pendleton Memorial Fund,
William L. and Ruth T.
Penn Foundation, William
Penn Savings Bank, a division of
Sovereign Bank Bank of
Princeton, a division of
Sovereign Bank
Pennington Foundation, Irene W.
and C. B.
Pennsylvania General Insurance
Co.
Pennzoil Co.
People's Bank
Peoples Energy Corp.
Pepsi-Cola Bottling Co. of
Charlotte
Perini Corp.
Perini Foundation, Joseph
Perkin-Elmer Corp.
Perkin-Elmer Corp.
Perkins Charitable Foundation
Perkins Foundation, Joe and Lois
Perkins Memorial Foundation,
George W.
Perot Foundation
Perpetual Benevolent Fund
Perry Drug Stores
Persis Corp.
Pet
Peterloon Foundation
Peters Foundation, Charles F.
Peterson Foundation, Fred J.
Pettus, Jr. Foundation, James T.
Pfaffinger Foundation
Pfizer
Phelps, Inc.
Phelps Dodge Corp.
PHH Corp.
Philadelphia Electric Co.
Philadelphia Industries
Phillips Family Foundation, Jay
and Rose
Phillips Family Foundation, L. E.
Phillips Foundation, A. P.
Phillips Foundation, Waite and
Genevieve
Phillips Petroleum Co.
Phillips-Van Heusen Corp.
Phoenix Home Life Mutual
Insurance Co.
Physicians Mutual Insurance
Pick Charitable Trust, Melitta S.
Pick, Jr. Fund, Albert
Picker International
Pieper Electric
Pineywoods Foundation
Pioneer Fund
Pioneer Hi-Bred International
Pioneer Trust Bank, NA
Piper Foundation
Piper Jaffray Cos.
Pirelli Armstrong Tire Corp.
Pitney Bowes
Piton Foundation
Pitt-Des Moines Inc.
Pittsburgh Child Guidance
Foundation
Pittsburgh National Bank
Pittway Corp.
Pitzman Fund
Plankenhorn Foundation, Harry
Plough Foundation
Plumsock Fund
Plym Foundation
Poinsettia Foundation, Paul and
Magdalena Ecke
Pollock Company Foundation,
William B.

Pollybill Foundation
Polychrome Corp.
Poole & Kent Co.
Porter Testamentary Trust, James
Hyde
Portland General Electric Co.
Potlatch Corp.
Potomac Electric Power Co.
Pott Foundation, Herman T. and
Phenie R.
Pottstown Mercury
Powell Co., William
PPG Industries
Prairie Foundation
Prange Co., H. C.
Pratt Memorial Fund
Preferred Risk Mutual Insurance
Co.
Premier Bank
Premier Industrial Corp.
Preston Trust, Evelyn W.
Price Associates, T. Rowe
Price Foundation, Louis and
Harold
Prickett Fund, Lynn R. and Karl
E.
Priddy Foundation
Prince Corp.
Prince Trust, Abbie Norman
Pritzker Foundation
Procter & Gamble Co.
Procter & Gamble Cosmetic &
Fragrance Products
Progressive Corp.
Promus Cos.
Propp Sons Fund, Morris and
Anna
Providence Energy Corp.
Providence Journal Company
Provident Life & Accident
Insurance Co.
Provigo Corp. Inc.
Prudential-Bache Securities
Prudential Insurance Co. of
America
PSI Energy
Public Service Co. of Colorado
Public Service Electric & Gas
Co.
Puget Sound Power & Light Co.
Pulitzer Publishing Co.
Puterbaugh Foundation
Putnam Foundation
Pyramid Foundation
Quabaug Corp.
Quaker Chemical Corp.
Quaker Oats Co.
Quality Metal Finishing
Foundation
Quanex Corp.
Questar Corp.
Quincy Newspapers
Quinlan Foundation, Elizabeth C.
Quivey-Bay State Foundation
R. F. Foundation
R&B Tool Co.
Rabb Charitable Trust, Sidney R.
Rabb Foundation, Harry W.
Ragen, Jr. Memorial Fund Trust
No. 1, James M.
Rahr Malting Co.
Ralston Purina Co.
Randa
Ransom Fidelity Company
Rapp Foundation, Robert Glenn
Ratner Foundation, Milton M.
Ratshesky Foundation, A. C.
Raymond Corp.
Raytheon Co.
Read Foundation, Charles L.
Rebsamen Companies, Inc.
Recognition Equipment
Red Wing Shoe Co.
Redfield Foundation, Nell J.
Reed Foundation, Philip D.
Reeves Foundation
Regenstein Foundation

Regis Corp.
Reichhold Chemicals, Inc.
Reidler Foundation
Reilly Industries
Reinhart Institutional Foods
Reisman Charitable Trust,
George C. and Evelyn R.
Relations Foundation
Reliance Electric Co.
Rennebohm Foundation, Oscar
Resnick Foundation, Jack and
Pearl
Revlon
Rexham Inc.
Reynolds Foundation, Donald W.
Reynolds Foundation, Edgar
Reynolds Foundation, J. B.
Reynolds Metals Co.
Rhone-Poulenc Rorer
Rice Charitable Foundation,
Albert W.
Rich Co., F.D.
Rich Foundation
Rich Products Corp.
Richardson Benevolent
Foundation, C. E.
Richardson Charitable Trust,
Anne S.
Richardson Foundation, Sid W.
Richardson Foundation, Smith
Rieke Corp.
Rienzi Foundation
Riggs Benevolent Fund
Ringier-America
Rinker Materials Corp.
Riordan Foundation
Ritchie Memorial Foundation,
Charies E. and Mabel M.
Rite-Hite Corp.
Rittenhouse Foundation
River Branch Foundation
RJR Nabisco Inc.
Roberts Foundation
Robertshaw Controls Co.
Robertson Brothers
Robin Family Foundation, Albert
A.
Robinson Foundation
Robinson Fund, Charles Nelson
Robison Foundation, Ellis H. and
Doris B.
Robson Foundation, LaNelle
Rochester Community Savings
Bank
Rochester Gas & Electric Corp.
Rochester Midland Corp.
Rock Foundation, Milton and
Shirley
Rockford Products Corp.
Rockwell Foundation
Rockwell Fund
Rockwell International Corp.
Roddis Foundation, Hamilton
Rodman Foundation
Rogers Charitable Trust, Florence
Rogers Family Foundation
Rogers Foundation
Rogers Foundation, Mary Stuart
Rohm and Haas Company
Rohr Inc.
Rolfs Foundation, Robert T.
Rollins Luetkemeyer Charitable
Foundation
Romill Foundation
RosaMary Foundation
Roseburg Forest Products Co.
Rosenberg Foundation, Alexis
Rosenberg Foundation, William
J. and Tina
Rosenberg, Jr. Family
Foundation, Louise and Claude
Rosenbloom Foundation, Ben
and Esther
Rosenthal Foundation, Benjamin
J.
Ross Foundation
Ross Foundation, Lyn & George
M.

Ross Laboratories
Ross Memorial Foundation, Will
Roth Foundation, Louis T.
Rothschild Foundation, Hulda B.
and Maurice L.
Rouse Co.
Rowland Foundation
Royal Group Inc.
Ruan Foundation Trust, John
Rubbermaid
Rubenstein Foundation, Philip
Rubinstein Foundation, Helena
Ruddick Corp.
Rudin Foundation
Ruffin Foundation, Peter B. &
Adeline W.
Rupp Foundation, Fran and
Warren
Russell Charitable Trust,
Josephine S.
Russell Memorial Foundation,
Robert
Russell Trust, Josephine G.
Ryan Foundation, David Claude
Ryan Foundation, Nina M.
Ryder System
Sachs Fund
Saemann Foundation, Franklin I.
SAFECO Corp.
Sagamore Foundation
Saint Croix Foundation
Saint Paul Cos.
Salomon Foundation, Richard &
Edna
Saltonstall Charitable
Foundation, Richard
San Diego Gas & Electric
Sanders Trust, Charles
Sandusky International Inc.
Sandy Hill Foundation
Sanguinetti Foundation,
Annunziata
Sapirstein-Stone-Weiss
Foundation
Sara Lee Corp.
Sara Lee Hosiery
Sasco Foundation
Saunders Foundation
Savin Corp.
Sawyer Charitable Foundation
Schadt Foundation
Schaffer Foundation, H.
Schautz Foundation, Walter L.
Scheirich Co., H.J.
Schering-Plough Corp.
Schermer Charitable Trust,
Frances
Scheuer Family Foundation, S.
H. and Helen R.
Schey Foundation
Schiff, Hardin & Waite
Schiff, Hardin & Waite
Schilling Motors
Schiro Fund
Schloss & Co., Marcus
Schloss & Co., Marcus
Schmidlapp Trust No. 1, Jacob G.
Schmidlapp Trust No. 2, Jacob G.
Schoonmaker J-Sewkly Valley
Hospital Trust
Schrafft and Bertha E. Schrafft
Charitable Trust, William E.
Schramm Foundation
Schroeder Foundation, Walter
Schultz Foundation
Schultz Foundation
Schust Foundation, Clarence L.
and Edith B.
Schwab & Co., Charles
Schwartz and Robert Schwartz
Foundation, Bernard
Science Applications
International Corp.
Scott and Fetzer Co.
Scott Foundation, William E.
Scott, Jr. Charitable Foundation,
Walter
Scrivner, Inc.

Scroggins Foundation, Arthur E.
and Cornelia C.
SCT Yarns
Scurlock Foundation
Scurlock Foundation
Seabury Foundation
Seafirst Corp.
Searle & Co., G.D.
Sears Family Foundation
Sears, Roebuck and Co.
Seay Charitable Trust, Sarah M.
and Charles E.
Seay Memorial Trust, George
and Effie
Sebastian Foundation
Security Benefit Life Insurance
Co.
Security Life of Denver
See Foundation, Charles
Seid Foundation, Barre
Seidman Family Foundation
Semmes Foundation
Semple Foundation, Louise Taft
Sentinel Communications Co.
Sentry Insurance Co.
Servco Pacific
Sewall Foundation, Elmina
Seymour Foundation, W. L. and
Louise E.
Shafer Foundation, Richard H.
and Ann
Shaffer Family Charitable Trust
Shaklee Corp.
Shapero Foundation, Nate S. and
Ruth B.
Shapiro, Inc.
Shapiro Charity Fund, Abraham
Shapiro Family Foundation,
Soretta and Henry
Shapiro Fund, Albert
Share Foundation
Sharon Steel Corp.
Sharp Electronics Corp.
Sharp Foundation, Charles S.
and Ruth C.
Shaw Foundation, Arch W.
Shawmut National Corp.
Shawmut Worcester County
Bank, N.A.
Shaw's Supermarkets
Shea Co., John F.
Sheaffer Inc.
Shelden Fund, Elizabeth, Allan
and Warren
Sheldon Foundation, Ralph C.
Shell Oil Co.
Shelton Cos.
Shemanski Testamentary Trust,
Tillie and Alfred
Shenandoah Life Insurance Co.
Sheppard Foundation, Lawrence
B.
Sherwin-Williams Co.
Shiffman Foundation
Shirk Foundation, Russell and
Betty
Shoemaker Fund, Thomas H.
and Mary Williams
Shoney's Inc.
Shook Foundation, Barbara
Ingalls
Shorenstein Foundation, Walter
H. and Phyllis J.
Shuwa Investments Corp.
Siebe North Inc.
Sierra Pacific Industries
Sierra Pacific Resources
Sifco Industries Inc.
Signet Bank/Maryland
Simmons Family Foundation, R.
P.
Simon Foundation, Robert Ellis
Simon Foundation, William E.
and Carol G.
Simpson Industries
Simpson Investment Co.
Sioux Steel Co.
SIT Investment Associates, Inc.

Sizzler International
Sjostrom & Sons
Skinner Corp.
Slant/Fin Corp.
Slaughter, Jr. Foundation, William E.
Slifka Foundation, Alan B.
Smith and W. Aubrey Smith Charitable Foundation, Clara Blackford
Smith Charitable Foundation, Lou and Lutza
Smith Charitable Fund, Eleanor Armstrong
Smith Charitable Trust
Smith Corp., A.O.
Smith Family Foundation, Charles E.
Smith Family Foundation, Theda Clark
Smith Foundation, Lon V.
Smith, Jr. Charitable Trust, Jack J.
Smith, Jr. Foundation, M. W.
Smith Memorial Fund, Ethel Sergeant Clark
Smith 1963 Charitable Trust, Don McQueen
Smithers Foundation, Christopher D.
Smoot Charitable Foundation
Smucker Co., J.M.
Snee-Reinhardt Charitable Foundation
SNET
Snite Foundation, Fred B.
Snyder Charitable Fund, W. P.
Society Corp.
Society for Savings
Solheim Foundation
Solow Foundation
Solow Foundation, Sheldon H.
Somers Foundation, Byron H.
Sonat Exploration
Sony Corp. of America
Soref Foundation, Samuel M. Soref and Helene K.
Sosland Foundation
Souers Charitable Trust, Sidney W. and Sylvia N.
South Bend Tribune
South Carolina Electric & Gas Co.
South Waite Foundation
Southern California Edison Co.
Southern Furniture Co.
Southwest Gas Corp.
Southwestern Bell Corp.
Spahn & Rose Lumber Co.
Spang & Co.
Spectra-Physics Analytical
Speyer Foundation, Alexander C. and Tillie S.
Spiegel
Springs Foundation
Springs Industries
Sprint
SPS Technologies
SPX Corp.
Square D Co.
Stabler Foundation, Donald B. and Dorothy L.
Stackpole-Hall Foundation
Staley, Jr. Foundation, A. E.
Standard Products Co.
Standard Register Co.
Standard Steel Speciality Co.
Stanley Charitable Foundation, A. W.
Stanley Consultants
Stanley Works
Stans Foundation
Star Bank, N.A.
Starrett Co., L.S.
State Farm Mutual Automobile Insurance Co.
State Street Bank & Trust Co.
Statter Foundation, Amy Plant

Stauffer Communications
Stearns Charitable Foundation, Anna B.
Stearns Trust, Artemas W.
Steelcase
Steiger Memorial Fund, Albert
Stein Foundation, Joseph F.
Steinbach Fund, Ruth and Milton
Steinberg Family Foundation, Meyer and Jean
Steiner Corp.
Steinman Foundation, James Hale
Steinman Foundation, John Frederick
Steinsapir Family Foundation, Julius L. and Libhie B.
Stella D'Oro Biscuit Co.
Sterkel Trust, Justine
Sterling Inc.
Sterling Winthrop
Stern Family Foundation, Alex
Stern Foundation, Leonard N.
Sternberger Foundation, Sigmund
Sterne-Elder Memorial Trust
Stevens Foundation, Abbot and Dorothy H.
Stevens Foundation, John T.
Stewards Fund
Stocker Foundation
Stockham Valves & Fittings
Stoddard Charitable Trust
Stone Container Corp.
Stone Family Foundation, Jerome H.
Stone Family Foundation, Norman H.
Stone Foundation, France
Stone Trust, H. Chase
Stonecutter Mills Corp.
Storer Foundation, George B.
Storz Foundation, Robert Herman
Stowe, Jr. Foundation, Robert Lee
Strake Foundation
Stranahan Foundation
Straus Foundation, Aaron and Lillie
Straus Foundation, Martha Washington Straus and Harry H.
Straus Foundation, Philip A. and Lynn
Strauss Foundation
Stride Rite Corp.
Strong Foundation, Hattie M.
Strosacker Foundation, Charles J.
Stuart Center Charitable Trust, Hugh
Stuart Foundation
Stubblefield, Estate of Joseph L.
Stupp Brothers Bridge & Iron Co.
Stupp Foundation, Norman J.
Subaru of America Inc.
Sulzberger Foundation
Sulzer Family Foundation
Sumitomo Bank of California
Sun Co.
Sunderland Foundation, Lester T.
Sundstrand Corp.
Sunshine Biscuits
Superior Tube Co.
Surrena Memorial Fund, Harry and Thelma
Susquehanna Investment Group
Swalm Foundation
Swanson Foundation
Sweatt Foundation, Harold W.
Swift Co. Inc., John S.
Swig Charity Foundation, Mae and Benjamin
Swig Foundation
Swisher Foundation, Carl S.
Swiss Bank Corp.
Synovus Financial Corp.
Tandy Foundation, Anne Burnett and Charles
Tanner Cos.

Tasty Baking Co.
Taub Foundation
Taub Foundation, Henry and Marilyn
Taub Foundation, Joseph and Arlene
Taube Family Foundation
Taubman Foundation, A. Alfred
Taubman Foundation, Herman P. and Sophia
Taylor Foundation
TBG, Inc.
TCF Banking & Savings, FSB
TDK Corp. of America
Teagle Foundation
Tektronix
Teledyne
Temple Foundation, T. L. L.
Temple-Inland
Templeton Foundation, Herbert A.
Tennant Co.
Tenneco
Tension Envelope Corp.
Terner Foundation
Tetley, Inc.
Texaco
Texas Commerce Bank Houston, N.A.
Texas Gas Transmission Corp.
Texas Instruments
Textron
Thagard Foundation
Thalheimer Foundation, Alvin and Fanny Blaustein
Thalhimer and Family Foundation, Charles G.
Thalhimer Brothers Inc.
Thanksgiving Foundation
Thatcher Foundation
Thendara Foundation
Thermo Electron Corp.
Thomas & Betts Corp.
Thomas Built Buses L.P.
Thomas Foundation, Dorothy
Thomas Industries
Thomas Memorial Foundation, Theresa A.
Thomasville Furniture Industries
Thorne Foundation
Thornton Foundation, Flora L.
Thornton Foundation, John M. and Sally B.
3M Co.
Thrush-Thompson Foundation
Thurman Charitable Foundation for Children, Edgar A.
Thurston Charitable Foundation
Thyssen Specialty Steels
Time Insurance Co.
Times Mirror Co.
Timken Co.
Tippens Foundation
Tippit Charitable Trust, C. Carlisle and Margaret M.
Tisch Foundation
Titan Industrial Co.
Titus Foundation, C. W.
TJX Cos.
Tobin Foundation
Todd Co., A.M.
Tokheim Corp.
Tomkins Industries, Inc.
Tomlinson Foundation, Kate and Elwyn
Toms Foundation
Tonya Memorial Foundation
Torchmark Corp.
Tosco Corp. Refining Division
Tozer Foundation
Tracor, Inc.
Tractor & Equipment Co.
Transco Energy Company
Tranzonic Cos.
Travelers Cos.
Travelli Fund, Charles Irwin
Treuhaft Foundation

Triford Foundation
TRINOVA Corp.
Trion
Tropicana Products, Inc.
True North Foundation
True Oil Co.
True Trust, Henry A.
Trull Foundation
Truman Foundation, Mildred Faulkner
Trust Co. Bank
TRW Corp.
TU Electric Co.
Tuch Foundation, Michael
Tucker Charitable Trust, Rose E.
Tucker Foundation, Marcia Brady
Tuohy Foundation, Alice Tweed
Turner Fund, Ruth
21 International Holdings
Tyler Corp.
Tyson Foods, Inc.
Ukrop's Super Markets, Inc.
Unilever United States
Union Bank
Union Bank of Switzerland Los Angeles Branch
Union Camp Corp.
Union Carbide Corp.
Union Electric Co.
Union Pacific Corp.
Unisys Corp.
United Airlines
United Conveyor Corp.
United Dominion Industries
United Merchants & Manufacturers
United States Borax & Chemical Corp.
U.S. Leasing International
United States Sugar Corp.
United Technologies, Automotive
United Togs Inc.
Univar Corp.
Universal Foods Corp.
Universal Leaf Tobacco Co.
Unocal Corp.
UNUM Corp.
Upjohn California Fund
Upjohn Co.
Upjohn Foundation, Harold and Grace
Upton Foundation, Frederick S.
US Bancorp
US WEST
USF&G Co.
USG Corp.
Uslico Corp.
USX Corp.
Utica National Insurance Group
Valdese Manufacturing Co., Inc.
Valley National Bancorp
Valley National Bank of Arizona
Valmont Industries
Valspar Corp.
Van Andel Foundation, Jay and Betty
Van Camp Foundation
Van Every Foundation, Philip L.
Van Nuys Charities, J. B. and Emily
Van Wert County Foundation
Vanderbilt Trust, R. T.
Vanneck-Bailey Foundation
Varian Associates
Vaughan Foundation, Rachael and Ben
Vaughn Foundation
Veritas Foundation
Vernon Fund, Miles Hodsdon
Vesper Corp.
Vesuvius Charitable Foundation
Vilter Manufacturing Corp.
Vlasic Foundation
Vogt Machine Co., Henry
Volkswagen of America, Inc.
Vollbrecht Foundation, Frederick A.

Von der Ahe Foundation
Vulcan Materials Co.
Wachovia Bank of Georgia, N.A.
Wachovia Bank & Trust Co., N.A.
Wachtell, Lipton, Rosen & Katz
Waggoner Charitable Trust, Crystelle
Waggoner Foundation, E. Paul and Helen Buck
Wagner Manufacturing Co., E. R.
Wahlert Foundation
Wal-Mart Stores
Waldbaum, Inc.
Waldbaum Family Foundation, I.
Walgreen Co.
Walker Foundation, L. C. and Margaret
Walker Foundation, T. B.
Walker Foundation, W. E.
Wallace Computer Services
Wallach Foundation, Miriam G. and Ira D.
Wallin Foundation
Walsh Foundation
Disney Co., Walt
Walter Family Trust, Byron L.
Walter Industries
Ward Co., Joe L.
Wardlaw Fund, Gertrude and William C.
Wardle Family Foundation
Wareheim Foundation, E. C.
Warner Electric Brake & Clutch Co.
Warren and Beatrice W. Blanding Foundation, Riley J. and Lillian N.
Warren Charite
Warwick Foundation
Washington Forrest Foundation
Washington Mutual Savings Bank
Washington Post Co.
Washington Trust Bank
Washington Water Power Co.
Watkins Christian Foundation
Watson Foundation, Walter E. and Caroline H.
Wausau Paper Mills Co.
Wean Foundation, Raymond John
Weaver Foundation
Weaver Foundation, Gil and Dody
Webb Charitable Trust, Susan Mott
Webb Foundation
Weber Charities Corp., Frederick E.
Webster Charitable Foundation
Webster Foundation, Edwin S.
Wegener Foundation, Herman and Mary
Wehadkee Foundation
Weil, Gotshal & Manges Foundation
Weinberg Foundation, John L.
Weinberg, Jr. Foundation, Sidney J.
Weiner Foundation
Weintraub Family Foundation, Joseph
Weir Foundation Trust
Weiss Foundation, William E.
Weiss Fund, Clara
Weisz Foundation, David and Sylvia
Welfare Foundation
Wells Fargo & Co.
Wells Foundation, A. Z.
Wells Foundation, Franklin H. and Ruth L.
Wendt Foundation, Margaret L.
Werthan Foundation
West Co.
West Foundation
West One Bancorp
Westchester Health Fund

United Funds (cont.)

Westend Foundation
Westerman Foundation, Samuel L.
Western New York Foundation
Western Resources
Western Shade Cloth Charitable Foundation
Western Southern Life Insurance Co.
Westinghouse Electric Corp.
WestLB New York Branch
Weston Associates/R.C.M. Corp.
Westport Fund
Westvaco Corp.
Wetterau
Weyerhaeuser Co.
Weyerhaeuser Foundation, Frederick and Margaret L.
Weyerhaeuser Memorial Foundation, Charles A.
Whalley Charitable Trust
Wharton Foundation
Wheat First Securites
Wheeler Foundation
Wheeler Foundation, Wilmot
Wheless Foundation
Whirlpool Corp.
Whitaker Charitable Foundation, Lyndon C.
Whitaker Foundation
White Consolidated Industries
White Construction Co.
White Foundation, Erle and Emma
White Trust, G. R.
Whitehead Foundation
Whiteley Foundation, John and Elizabeth
Whiteman Foundation, Edna Rider
Whiting Foundation
Whiting Memorial Foundation, Henry and Harriet
Whitney Fund, David M.
Whittenberger Foundation, Claude R. and Ethel B.
Wickes Foundation, Harvey Randall
Wickson-Link Memorial Foundation
WICOR, Inc.
Widgeon Foundation
Wiener Foundation, Malcolm Hewitt
Wigwam Mills
Wilbur-Ellis Co.
Wilcox General Trust, George N.
Wilcox Trust, S. W.
Wildermuth Foundation, E. F.
Wilkof Foundation, Edward and Ruth
Willard Foundation, Helen Parker
Williams Charitable Trust, Mary Jo
Williams Cos.
Williams Family Foundation
Williams Family Foundation of Georgia
Williams Foundation, Edna Sproull
Williamson Co.
Willits Foundation
Wilmington Trust Co.
Wilson Foundation, Elaine P. and Richard U.
Wilson Foundation, Hugh and Mary
Wilson Foundation, Marie C. and Joseph C.
Wilson Trust, Lula C.
Winn-Dixie Stores
Winnebago Industries, Inc.
Winona Corporation
Winston Research Foundation, Harry

Wisconsin Bell, Inc.
Wisconsin Centrifugal
Wisconsin Energy Corp.
Wisconsin Power & Light Co.
Wisconsin Public Service Corp.
Witco Corp.
Witte, Jr. Foundation, John H.
Wodecroft Foundation
Woldenberg Foundation
Wolf Foundation, Melvin and Elaine
Wolff Foundation, John M.
Wolfson Family Foundation
Wollenberg Foundation
Wolverine World Wide, Inc.
Wood Charitable Trust, W. P.
Wood-Claeyssens Foundation
Wood Foundation, Lester G.
Woodard Family Foundation
Woodland Foundation
Woods Charitable Fund
Woods Foundation, James H.
Woodward Fund-Atlanta, David, Helen, Marian
Woodward Fund-Watertown, David, Helen, and Marian
Woodward Governor Co.
Woolf Foundation, William C.
Woolley Foundation, Vasser
Wornall Charitable Trust and Foundation, Kearney
Wouk Foundation, Abe
Wrigley Co., Wm. Jr.
Wurts Memorial, Henrietta Tower
Wyman-Gordon Co.
Wyman Youth Trust
Wyomissing Foundation
Xerox Corp.
XTEK Inc.
Xtra Corp.
Yawkey Foundation II
Yeager Charitable Trust, Lester E.
Yellow Corp.
Yost Trust, Elizabeth Burns
Young Foundation, R. A.
Young Foundation, Robert R.
Young & Rubicam
Younkers, Inc.
Zachry Co., H. B.
Zarrow Foundation, Anne and Henry
Ziegler Foundation
Ziegler Foundation, Ruth/Allen
Zilkha & Sons
Zimmerman Family Foundation, Raymond
Zink Foundation, John Steele
Zollner Foundation
Zuckerberg Foundation, Roy J.

Volunteer Services

Abbott Laboratories
Abell Foundation, Charles S.
Abrons Foundation, Louis and Anne
Aerospace Corp.
Aid Association for the Blind
Air Products & Chemicals
Allendale Mutual Insurance Co.
Alliant Techsystems
AlliedSignal
Allstate Insurance Co.
Alltel/Western Region
ALPAC Corp.
Altman Foundation
Aluminum Co. of America
AMAX
AMCORE Bank, N.A. Rockford
America West Airlines
American Brands
American Express Co.
American Natural Resources Co.
American United Life Insurance Co.
Amfac/JMB Hawaii

Amoco Corp.
AMR Corp.
Andersen Corp.
Anheuser-Busch Cos.
AON Corp.
Apple Computer, Inc.
ARCO
Arizona Public Service Co.
Arkansas Power & Light Co.
Arkla
Armco Inc.
Asea Brown Boveri
Atherton Family Foundation
Atlanta Gas Light Co.
Atlantic Foundation of New York
Attleboro Pawtucket Savings Bank
Avon Products
Baker Foundation, R. C.
Baker Foundation, Solomon R. and Rebecca D.
Banc One Illinois Corp.
Bank of America Arizona
Bank of Boston Connecticut
Bank of Boston Corp.
Bank of New York
Bank One, Youngstown, NA
Barker Foundation, J. M. R.
Barker Welfare Foundation
Beaird Foundation, Charles T.
Bechtel, Jr. Foundation, S. D.
Becton Dickinson & Co.
Beech Aircraft Corp.
Benefit Trust Life Insurance Co.
Benfamil Charitable Trust
Bergstrom Foundation, Erik E. and Edith H.
Bethlehem Steel Corp.
Biddle Foundation, Margaret T.
Bing Fund
Binney & Smith Inc.
Block, H&R
Boeing Co.
Boettcher Foundation
Booz Allen & Hamilton
Borden
Boston Edison Co.
Bothin Foundation
Bovaird Foundation, Mervin
Brach Foundation, Helen
Bridgestone/Firestone
Brooks Foundation, Gladys
Broyhill Family Foundation
Bull Foundation, Henry W.
Burlington Resources
Burndy Corp.
Burns International
Bush Charitable Foundation, Edyth
Bush Foundation
Cafritz Foundation, Morris and Gwendolyn
Cahill Foundation, John R.
Capital Holding Corp.
Carrier Corp.
Carter Foundation, Amon G.
Carter Foundation, Beirne
Cawsey Trust
CBI Industries
Centel Corp.
Centerior Energy Corp.
Central Hudson Gas & Electric Corp.
Central Life Assurance Co.
Central Maine Power Co.
Chapman Charitable Trust, H. A. and Mary K.
Chase Manhattan Bank, N.A.
Cheney Foundation, Ben B.
Chevron Corp.
Chicago Sun-Times, Inc.
Chrysler Corp.
Ciba-Geigy Corp. (Pharmaceuticals Division)
CIT Group Holdings
Citicorp
Clay Foundation

Clipper Ship Foundation
Clorox Co.
CM Alliance Cos.
CNG Transmission Corp.
Coleman Co.
Collins Foundation
Colonial Life & Accident Insurance Co.
Colorado State Bank of Denver
Columbia Foundation
Columbus Southern Power Co.
Commerce Clearing House
Compaq Computer Corp.
ConAgra
Contran Corp.
Cooke Foundation
Coors Brewing Co.
Copperweld Steel Co.
Cosmair, Inc.
Cowles Charitable Trust
Cowles Media Co.
Crapo Charitable Foundation, Henry H.
Crown Central Petroleum Corp.
Cudahy Fund, Patrick and Anna M.
Cullen/Frost Bankers
Cummings Foundation, Nathan
Cummins Engine Co.
Curtice-Burns Foods
Dana Corp.
DEC International, Inc.
Deluxe Corp.
Deposit Guaranty National Bank
Deutsch Co.
Dishman Charitable Foundation Trust, H. E. and Kate
Douglas Corp.
Douglas & Lomason Company
Dow Jones & Co.
Dreyfus Foundation, Max and Victoria
du Pont de Nemours & Co., E. I.
Duncan Foundation, Lillian H. and C. W.
Eaton Corp.
Electronic Data Systems Corp.
Elgin Sweeper Co.
Enron Corp.
Equitable Life Assurance Society of the U.S.
Exxon Corp.
Farish Fund, William Stamps
Federal-Mogul Corp.
Federated Department Stores and Allied Stores Corp.
Federated Life Insurance Co.
Fidelity Bank
Fieldcrest Cannon
Fikes Foundation, Leland
Fireman's Fund Insurance Co.
First Boston
First Fidelity Bancorporation
First Tennessee Bank
First Union Corp.
Firstar Bank Milwaukee NA
Fluor Corp.
Fondren Foundation
Forbes
Ford Motor Co.
Freedom Forum
Freeport-McMoRan
Frisch's Restaurants Inc.
Frohman Foundation, Sidney
Fry Foundation, Lloyd A.
Funderburke & Associates
Gap, The
GenCorp
General American Life Insurance Co.
General Electric Co.
General Mills
General Motors Corp.
GenRad
Gerber Products Co.
German Protestant Orphan Asylum Association

Gillette Co.
Golden Family Foundation
Goldsmith Foundation, Horace W.
Graphic Controls Corp.
Graybar Electric Co.
Green Foundation, Burton E.
Green Fund
Greentree Foundation
Greenville Foundation
Grinnell Mutual Reinsurance Co.
Gudelsky Family Foundation, Homer and Martha
Haas Fund, Walter and Elise
Haas, Jr. Fund, Evelyn and Walter
Hafif Family Foundation
Hagedorn Fund
Hale Foundation, Crescent Porter
Hall Foundation
Hallmark Cards
Hancock Foundation, Luke B.
Hardin Foundation, Phil
Harmon Foundation, Pearl M. and Julia J.
Harriman Foundation, Gladys and Roland
Harsco Corp.
Hartford Steam Boiler Inspection & Insurance Co.
Hechinger Co.
Heckscher Foundation for Children
Hecla Mining Co.
Heineman Foundation for Research, Educational, Charitable, and Scientific Purposes
Heinz Co., H.J.
Hershey Foods Corp.
Hewlett Foundation, William and Flora
Hitachi
Honeywell
Hoover, Jr. Foundation, Margaret W. and Herbert
Hospital Corp. of America
Household International
Houston Industries
Hubbard Broadcasting
Hunt Alternatives Fund
Hunter Trust, A. V.
IBM Corp.
IBP, Inc.
Illinois Power Co.
Illinois Tool Works
International Paper Co.
Irvine Foundation, James
ITT Rayonier
Ittleson Foundation
J.P. Morgan & Co.
Jackson Foundation
Jacobs Engineering Group
James River Corp. of Virginia
JCPenney Co.
JELD-WEN, Inc.
Jewish Healthcare Foundation of Pittsburgh
John Hancock Mutual Life Insurance Co.
Johnson Foundation, Helen K. and Arthur E.
Johnson & Higgins
Jordan and Ettie A. Jordan Charitable Foundation, Mary Ranken
JSJ Corp.
Keebler Co.
Keller-Crescent Co.
Kepco, Inc.
Kimball International
Kimberly-Clark Corp.
King Ranch
Kingsbury Corp.
Kiplinger Foundation
Kline Foundation, Josiah W. and Bessie H.
Knight-Ridder, Inc.

Kraft General Foods
Kysor Industrial Corp.
Lafarge Corp.
Lawrence Foundation, Lind
LeBrun Foundation
Liberty National Bank
Lincy Foundation
Link, Jr. Foundation, George
Lipton, Thomas J.
Little, Arthur D.
Long Island Lighting Co.
Lowe Foundation, Joe and Emily
Lowenstein Foundation, Leon
Lund Foundation
Lytel Foundation, Bertha Russ
MacArthur Foundation, John D. and Catherine T.
Macmillan, Inc.
Macy & Co., R.H.
Mallinckrodt Specialty Chemicals Co.
Manville Corp.
Mardag Foundation
Marion Merrell Dow
Marmot Foundation
Mars Foundation
Marshall & Ilsley Bank
Mason Charitable Foundation
Massie Trust, David Meade
Maytag Family Foundation, Fred
MBIA, Inc.
MCA
McBride & Son Associates
McCasland Foundation
McCormick & Co.
McCormick Tribune Foundation, Robert R.
McCune Charitable Trust, John R.
McDonnell Douglas Corp.-West
McElroy Trust, R. J.
McGovern Fund for the Behavioral Sciences
McGraw-Hill
McInerny Foundation
MCJ Foundation
Meadows Foundation
Medina Foundation
Medtronic
Melitta North America Inc.
Merrick Foundation, Robert G. and Anne M.
Merrion Foundation
Mervyn's
Metropolitan Life Insurance Co.
Meyer Foundation, Alice Kleberg Reynolds
Meyer Foundation, Eugene and Agnes E.
Meyer Foundation, Robert R.
MGIC Investment Corp.
Midwest Resources
Mobil Oil Corp.
Monell Foundation, Ambrose
Morgan Stanley & Co.
Moskowitz Foundation, Irving I.
Motorola
Mott Foundation, Charles Stewart
National Computer Systems
National Westminster Bank New Jersey
Negaunee Foundation
New England Mutual Life Insurance Co.
New-Land Foundation
New Street Capital Corp.
New York Foundation
New York Life Insurance Co.
New York Telephone Co.
New York Times Co.
The New Yorker Magazine, Inc.
News & Observer Publishing Co.
Noble Foundation, Edward John
Norfolk Southern Corp.
Northeast Utilities
Northern Indiana Public Service Co.

Northern States Power Co.
Northern Telecom Inc.
Northern Trust Co.
Northwest Natural Gas Co.
Northwestern National Life Insurance Co.
Norton Co.
Ogilvy & Mather Worldwide
Oglebay Norton Co.
Olin Corp.
O'Neill Charitable Corporation, F. J.
Ore-Ida Foods, Inc.
Ormet Corp.
Overbrook Foundation
Pacific Mutual Life Insurance Co.
Pacific Telesis Group
Pan-American Life Insurance Co.
Panhandle Eastern Corp.
Parke-Davis Group
Pella Corp.
Penn Foundation, William
Penn Savings Bank, a division of Sovereign Bank Bank of Princeton, a division of Sovereign Bank
People's Bank
Peoples Energy Corp.
Perkin-Elmer Corp.
Perkin-Elmer Corp.
Perot Foundation
Persis Corp.
Pew Charitable Trusts
Pfizer
Phelps, Inc.
Phillips Family Foundation, Jay and Rose
Pinkerton Foundation
Portland General Electric Co.
Powers Foundation
PPG Industries
Premier Industrial Corp.
Priddy Foundation
Principal Financial Group
Pritzker Foundation
Prudential Insurance Co. of America
Public Service Co. of Colorado
Puget Sound Power & Light Co.
Questar Corp.
Ralston Purina Co.
Raskob Foundation for Catholic Activities
Ratner Foundation, Milton M.
Raymond Corp.
Recognition Equipment
Reliance Electric Co.
Rennebohm Foundation, Oscar
Retirement Research Foundation
Reynolds Foundation, Christopher
Robinson Foundation
Rochester Telephone Corp.
Rockwell Fund
Rockwell International Corp.
Rohm and Haas Company
Roseburg Forest Products Co.
Rouse Co.
Royal Group Inc.
Ryder System
SAFECO Corp.
San Diego Gas & Electric
Sandy Foundation, George H.
Santa Fe Pacific Corp.
Sara Lee Corp.
Sara Lee Hosiery
Scherman Foundation
Schmidlapp Trust No. 1, Jacob G.
Scholl Foundation, Dr.
Schroeder Foundation, Walter
Schultz Foundation
Schwab & Co., Charles
Scurlock Foundation
Security Life of Denver
Sentinel Communications Co.
Shapero Foundation, Nate S. and Ruth B.

Share Foundation
Shawmut National Corp.
Shell Oil Co.
Shoney's Inc.
Signet Bank/Maryland
Simpson Industries
SmithKline Beecham
SNET
Sonoco Products Co.
Sooner Pipe & Supply Corp.
South Texas Charitable Foundation
Southern California Edison Co.
Southwestern Bell Corp.
Speas Foundation, Victor E.
Sprague Educational and Charitable Foundation, Seth
Springs Industries
Sterling Winthrop
Stone Container Corp.
Strake Foundation
Stride Rite Corp.
Strong Foundation, Hattie M.
Stulsaft Foundation, Morris
Tandem Computers
Temple Foundation, T. L. L.
Tenneco
Terra Industries
Texaco
Texas Commerce Bank Houston, N.A.
Texas Gas Transmission Corp.
Textron
3M Co.
Times Mirror Co.
Tisch Foundation
TJX Cos.
Towsley Foundation, Harry A. and Margaret D.
Tozer Foundation
Tracor, Inc.
Turrell Fund
Union Bank of Switzerland Los Angeles Branch
Union Camp Corp.
Union Carbide Corp.
Union Electric Co.
United States Trust Co. of New York
United Technologies Corp.
Universal Foods Corp.
Valley Foundation
Virginia Power Co.
Wal-Mart Stores
Walker Foundation, T. B.
Disney Co., Walt
Wareheim Foundation, E. C.
Washington Mutual Savings Bank
Weingart Foundation
Wells Fargo & Co.
Westinghouse Broadcasting Co.
Weyerhaeuser Co.
Whirlpool Corp.
Whitaker Foundation
Whitehead Foundation, Joseph B.
Wilkof Foundation, Edward and Ruth
Winter Construction Co.
Woodward Governor Co.

Youth Organizations

Abbott Laboratories
Abel Construction Co.
Abell Foundation, Charles S.
Abell Foundation, The
Abell-Hanger Foundation
Abitibi-Price
Abney Foundation
Abraham Foundation
Abrams Foundation, Benjamin and Elizabeth
Abrams Foundation, Talbert and Leota
Abroms Charitable Foundation
Ace Beverage Co.

ACF Industries, Inc.
Achelis Foundation
Acme-Cleveland Corp.
Acme-McCrary Corp.
Acme United Corp.
Action Industries, Inc.
Acushnet Co.
Adams Trust, Charles E. and Caroline J.
Adler Foundation Trust, Philip D. and Henrietta B.
Advanced Micro Devices
Aeroflex Foundation
AGFA Division of Miles Inc.
Agway
Ahmanson Foundation
AHS Foundation
Air Products & Chemicals
Akzo Chemicals Inc.
Alabama Power Co.
Alberto-Culver Co.
Albertson's
Alco Standard Corp.
Alcon Laboratories, Inc.
Aldeen Charity Trust, G. W.
Alden Trust, George I.
Alden Trust, John W.
Alexander & Baldwin, Inc.
Alexander Charitable Foundation
Alexander Foundation, Joseph
Alexander Foundation, Judd S.
Alexander Foundation, Robert D. and Catherine R.
Alexander Foundation, Walter
Alice Manufacturing Co.
Allegheny Foundation
Allegheny Ludlum Corp.
Allen Foundation, Frances
Allendale Mutual Insurance Co.
AlliedSignal
Allstate Insurance Co.
Alltel/Western Region
Allyn Foundation
Allyn Foundation
Alma Piston Co.
ALPAC Corp.
Alperin/Hirsch Family Foundation
Alro Steel Corp.
Altman Foundation
Altschul Foundation
Alumax
Aluminum Co. of America
Alyeska Pipeline Service Co.
Amado Foundation, Maurice
Amaturo Foundation
AMAX
AMAX Coal Industries
Amcast Industrial Corp.
AMCORE Bank, N.A. Rockford
Amdahl Corp.
Ameribank
America West Airlines
American Aggregates Corp.
American Brands
American Electric Power
American Express Co.
American Financial Corp.
American Foundation
American Foundation Corporation
American General Finance
American Home Products Corp.
American International Group, Inc.
American National Bank & Trust Co. of Chicago
American Natural Resources Co.
American Optical Corp.
American President Cos.
American Saw & Manufacturing Co.
American Stock Exchange
American Telephone & Telegraph Co.
American United Life Insurance Co.

American Welding & Manufacturing Co.
Ameritas Life Insurance Corp.
Ames Department Stores
AMETEK
Amfac/JMB Hawaii
Amoco Corp.
AMP
AMR Corp.
Amsted Industries
Andersen Corp.
Andersen Foundation
Andersen Foundation, Arthur
Andersen Foundation, Hugh J.
Anderson Charitable Trust, Josephine
Anderson Foundation
Anderson Foundation
Anderson Foundation, John W.
Anderson Foundation, M. D.
Anderson Foundation, Peyton
Anderson Foundation, William P.
Andersons Management Corp.
Andreas Foundation
Andres Charitable Trust, Frank G.
Andrews Foundation
Anheuser-Busch Cos.
Annenberg Foundation
Anschutz Family Foundation
Ansin Private Foundation, Ronald M.
Ansley Foundation, Dantzler Bond
AON Corp.
Apple Computer, Inc.
Applebaum Foundation
Appleby Foundation
Appleby Trust, Scott B. and Annie P.
Appleton Papers
Arata Brothers Trust
Arbie Mineral Feed Co.
Arcadia Foundation
Arcana Foundation
Archbold Charitable Trust, Adrian and Jessie
Archer-Daniels-Midland Co.
Archibald Charitable Foundation, Norman
ARCO
ARCO Chemical
Argyros Foundation
Aristech Chemical Corp.
Arizona Public Service Co.
Arkansas Power & Light Co.
Arkelian Foundation, Ben H. and Gladys
Arkell Hall Foundation
Arkla
Arkwright-Boston Manufacturers Mutual
Arkwright Foundation
Armbrust Chain Co.
Armco Inc.
Armco Steel Co.
Armstrong Foundation
Armstrong World Industries Inc.
Arnold Fund
Aron Charitable Foundation, J.
Arrillaga Foundation
Arvin Industries
ASARCO
Asea Brown Boveri
Ashland Oil
Asplundh Foundation
Associated Foundations
Astor Foundation, Vincent
Atalanta/Sosnoff Capital Corp.
Atherton Family Foundation
Atkinson Foundation
Atkinson Foundation, Myrtle L.
Atlanta Foundation
Atlanta Gas Light Co.
Atran Foundation
Attleboro Pawtucket Savings Bank

Youth Organizations (cont.)

Atwood Foundation
Auerbach Foundation, Beatrice Fox
Aurora Foundation
Austin Memorial Foundation
Autzen Foundation
Avon Products
Awrey Bakeries
Axe-Houghton Foundation
Azadoutioun Foundation
Babcock Foundation, Mary Reynolds
Babson Foundation, Paul and Edith
Bachmann Foundation
Badgeley Residuary Charitable Trust, Rose M.
Badger Meter, Inc.
Baehr Foundation, Louis W. and Dolpha
Baer Foundation, Alan and Marcia
Baier Foundation, Marie
Bailey Foundation
Baird Charitable Trust, William Robert
Baird & Co., Robert W.
Baird Foundation, Cameron
Baker Foundation, George T.
Baker Foundation, R. C.
Baker Trust, Clayton
Baker Trust, George F.
Baldwin Foundation
Baldwin Foundation, David M. and Barbara
Baldwin Memorial Foundation, Fred
Ball Brothers Foundation
Ball Corp.
Ball Foundation, George and Frances
Baltimore Gas & Electric Co.
Bamberger and John Ernest Bamberger Memorial Foundation, Ruth Eleanor
Banc One Illinois Corp.
Banc One Wisconsin Corp.
Bancorp Hawaii
Banfi Vintners
Bang & Olufsen of America, Inc.
Bank Hapoalim B.M.
Bank IV
Bank of A. Levy
Bank of America Arizona
Bank of Boston Corp.
Bank of New York
Bank One, Texas-Houston Office
BankAmerica Corp.
Bankers Trust Co.
Banner Life Insurance Co.
Bannerman Foundation, William C.
Banta Corp.
Bantam Doubleday Dell Publishing Group, Inc.
Banyan Tree Foundation
BarclaysAmerican Corp.
Bardes Corp.
Barker Foundation
Barker Foundation, Donald R.
Barker Foundation, J. M. R.
Barker Welfare Foundation
Barlow Family Foundation, Milton A. and Gloria G.
Barnes Foundation
Barnes Group
Barnett Charitable Foundation, Lawrence and Isabel
Barra Foundation
Barrows Foundation, Geraldine and R. A.
Barstow Foundation
Barth Foundation, Theodore H.
Barton-Malow Co.

Bass and Edythe and Sol G. Atlas Fund, Sandra Atlas
Bass Foundation
Bass Foundation, Harry
Bassett Foundation, Norman
Battelle
Bauer Foundation, M. R.
Bauervic-Paisley Foundation
Baughman Foundation
Baumker Charitable Foundation, Elsie and Harry
Bausch & Lomb
Bay Branch Foundation
Bay Foundation
BCR Foundation
Beaird Foundation, Charles T.
Beal Foundation
Bean Foundation, Norwin S. and Elizabeth N.
Beasley Foundation, Theodore and Beulah
Beatty Trust, Cordelia Lunceford
Beaver Foundation
Beazley Foundation
Bechtel Charitable Remainder Uni-Trust, Harold R.
Bechtel Group
Bechtel, Jr. Foundation, S. D.
Beck Foundation
Becton Dickinson & Co.
Bedford Fund
Bedminster Fund
Bedsole Foundation, J. L.
Beech Aircraft Corp.
Beecher Foundation, Florence Simon
Beeghly Fund, Leon A.
Beerman Foundation
Beeson Charitable Trust, Dwight M.
Behmann Brothers Foundation
Beidler Charitable Trust, Francis
Beim Foundation
Beinecke Foundation
Beir Foundation
Beitzell & Co.
Bekins Foundation, Milo W.
Belding Heminway Co.
Belding Heminway Co.
Belfer Foundation
Belk Stores
Belk Stores
Bellamah Foundation, Dale J.
Bellini Foundation
Beloit Foundation
Belz Foundation
Bemis Company
Ben & Jerry's Homemade
Bend Millwork Systems
Bender Foundation
Benedum Foundation, Claude Worthington
Beneficia Foundation
Beneficial Corp.
Benenson Foundation, Frances and Benjamin
Benetton
Benua Foundation
Benz Trust, Doris L.
Bere Foundation
Beretta U.S.A. Corp.
Bergen Foundation, Frank and Lydia
Berger Foundation, H.N. and Frances C.
Bergner Co., P.A.
Bergstrom Manufacturing Co.
Berkey Foundation, Peter
Berkowitz Family Foundation, Louis
Bernsen Foundation, Grace and Franklin
Berry Foundation, Loren M.
Berry Foundation, Lowell
Bersted Foundation
Besser Foundation

Best Foundation, Walter J. and Edith E.
Best Products Co.
Bethlehem Steel Corp.
Bettingen Corporation, Burton G.
Betts Industries
Beveridge Foundation, Frank Stanley
Beynon Foundation, Kathryne
BFGoodrich
BHP Pacific Resources
Bicknell Fund
Bierhaus Foundation
Bierlein Family Foundation
Bing Fund
Bing Fund
Bingham Foundation, William
Bingham Second Betterment Fund, William
Binney & Smith Inc.
Binswanger Co.
Birch Foundation, Stephen and Mary
Bird Inc.
Bireley Foundation
Birnschein Foundation, Alvin and Marion
Bishop Charitable Trust, A. G.
Bishop Foundation
Bishop Foundation, E. K. and Lillian F.
Bishop Foundation, Vernon and Doris
Bishop Trust for the SPCA of Manatee County, Florida, Lillian H.
Bjorkman Foundation
Blair and Co., William
Blanchard Foundation
Blandin Foundation
Blank Fund, Myron and Jacqueline
Blaustein Foundation, Jacob and Hilda
Blaustein Foundation, Louis and Henrietta
Bleibtreu Foundation, Jacob
Block, H&R
Bloedorn Foundation, Walter A.
Blount
Blount Educational and Charitable Foundation, Mildred Weedon
Blowitz-Ridgeway Foundation
Blue Bell, Inc.
Blue Cross and Blue Shield United of Wisconsin Foundation
Blum Foundation, Edith C.
Blum Foundation, Edna F.
Blum Foundation, Lois and Irving
Blum-Kovler Foundation
BMC Industries
BMW of North America, Inc.
Board of Trustees of the Prichard School
Boatmen's Bancshares
Boatmen's First National Bank of Oklahoma
Bob Evans Farms
Bobst Foundation, Elmer and Mamdouha
Bodenhamer Foundation
Bodine Corp.
Boeckmann Charitable Foundation
Boehm Foundation
Boeing Co.
Boettcher Foundation
Boh Brothers Construction Co.
Boise Cascade Corp.
Boisi Family Foundation
Bolz Family Foundation, Eugenie Mayer
Bonfils-Stanton Foundation
Booth-Bricker Fund
Booth Ferris Foundation

Boots Pharmaceuticals, Inc.
Booz Allen & Hamilton
Borchard Foundation, Albert and Elaine
Bordeaux Foundation
Borden
Borden Memorial Foundation, Mary Owen
Borg-Warner Corp.
Borkee Hagley Foundation
Borman's
Borun Foundation, Anna Borun and Harry
Bosch Corp., Robert
Bosque Foundation
Bossong Hosiery Mills
Boston Edison Co.
Boston Fatherless and Widows Society
Bothin Foundation
Botwinick-Wolfensohn Foundation
Boulevard Bank, N.A.
Boulevard Foundation
Bound to Stay Bound Books Foundation
Boutell Memorial Fund, Arnold and Gertrude
Bovaird Foundation, Mervin
Bowater Inc.
Bowers Foundation
Bowsher-Booher Foundation
Bowyer Foundation, Ambrose and Gladys
Boynton Fund, John W.
Bozzone Family Foundation
BP America
Brach Foundation, Edwin I.
Brach Foundation, Helen
Brackenridge Foundation, George W.
Bradford & Co., J.C.
Bradley Foundation, Lynde and Harry
Bradley-Turner Foundation
Brady Foundation
Brand Cos.
Brand Foundation, C. Harold and Constance
Bray Charitable Trust, Viola E.
Breidenthal Foundation, Willard J. and Mary G.
Bremer Foundation, Otto
Bren Foundation, Donald L.
Brenner Foundation, Mervyn
Brewer and Co., Ltd., C.
Breyer Foundation
Bridgestone/Firestone
Bridwell Foundation, J. S.
Briggs Foundation, T. W.
Briggs & Stratton Corp.
Bright Charitable Trust, Alexander H.
Bright Family Foundation
Bristol-Myers Squibb Co.
Bristol Savings Bank
Britton Fund
Broadhurst Foundation
Broccoli Charitable Foundation, Dana and Albert R.
Brody Foundation, Frances
Bromley Residuary Trust, Guy I.
Brooklyn Union Gas Co.
Brooks Brothers
Brotman Foundation of California
Brotz Family Foundation, Frank G.
Brown and C. A. Lupton Foundation, T. J.
Brown Charitable Trust, Dora Maclellan
Brown Foundation
Brown Foundation, George Warren
Brown Foundation, James Graham

Brown Foundation, Joe W. and Dorothy Dorsett
Brown Foundation, M. K.
Brown Group
Brown, Jr. Charitable Trust, Frank D.
Brown & Sons, Alex
Browning-Ferris Industries
Broyhill Family Foundation
Bruening Foundation, Eva L. and Joseph M.
Brunner Foundation, Fred J.
Bruno Foundation, Angelo
Brunswick Corp.
Bryant Foundation
Bryce Memorial Fund, William and Catherine
Buchalter, Nemer, Fields, & Younger
Buchanan Family Foundation
Bucyrus-Erie
Buell Foundation, Temple Hoyne
Buell Foundation, Temple Hoyne
Buffett Foundation
Buhl Foundation
Builder Marts of America
Builder Marts of America
Bull Foundation, Henry W.
Bunbury Company
Burchfield Foundation, Charles E.
Burden Foundation, Florence V.
Burkitt Foundation
Burlington Industries
Burlington Northern Inc.
Burlington Resources
Burnand Medical and Educational Foundation, Alphonse A.
Burndy Corp.
Burnham Foundation
Burns Family Foundation
Burns Foundation, Fritz B.
Burns International
Burress, J.W.
Burton Foundation, William T. and Ethel Lewis
Bush Charitable Foundation, Edyth
Bush Foundation
Butler Family Foundation, George W. and Gladys S.
Butler Family Foundation, Patrick and Aimee
Butler Foundation, J. Homer
Butler Manufacturing Co.
C. E. and S. Foundation
C.I.O.S.
C.P. Rail Systems
Cabell III and Maude Morgan Cabell Foundation, Robert G.
Cable & Wireless Communications
Cabot Corp.
Cabot-Saltonstall Charitable Trust
Cadbury Beverages Inc.
Cadence Design Systems
Cafritz Foundation, Morris and Gwendolyn
Cahill Foundation, John R.
Cahn Family Foundation
Cain Foundation, Effie and Wofford
Cain Foundation, Gordon and Mary
Calder Foundation, Louis
Caldwell Foundation, Hardwick
Calhoun Charitable Trust, Kenneth
Callaway Foundation
Cambridge Mustard Seed Foundation
Cameron Foundation, Harry S. and Isabel C.
Cameron Memorial Fund, Alpin J. and Alpin W.

Camp and Bennet Humiston Trust, Apollos
Camp Foundation
Camp Younts Foundation
Campbell Foundation
Campbell Foundation
Campbell Foundation, J. Bulow
Campbell Foundation, Ruth and Henry
Campbell Foundation, Ruth and Henry
Campbell Soup Co.
Cannon Foundation
Canon U.S.A., Inc.
Capital Cities/ABC
Capital Fund Foundation
Capital Holding Corp.
Caplan Charity Foundation, Julius H.
Cargill
Carlson Cos.
Carnahan-Jackson Foundation
Carnegie Corporation of New York
Carolina Telephone & Telegraph Co.
Carolyn Foundation
Carpenter Foundation
Carpenter Foundation, E. Rhodes and Leona B.
Carpenter Technology Corp.
Carrier Corp.
Carteh Foundation
Carter Family Foundation
Carter Foundation, Amon G.
Carter Foundation, Beirne
Carter-Wallace
Cartinhour Foundation
Carvel Foundation, Thomas and Agnes
Carver Charitable Trust, Roy J.
Casey Foundation, Annie E.
Castle & Co., A.M.
Castle Foundation, Harold K. L.
Castle Foundation, Samuel N. and Mary
Castle Industries
Castle Trust, George P. and Ida Tenney
Caterpillar
Catlin Charitable Trust, Kathleen K.
Cauthorn Charitable Trust, John and Mildred
Cawsey Trust
Cayuga Foundation
CBI Industries
CBS Inc.
Ceco Corp.
CENEX
Centel Corp.
Centerior Energy Corp.
Centex Corp.
Central Fidelity Banks, Inc.
Central Hudson Gas & Electric Corp.
Central Maine Power Co.
Central National-Gottesman
Central & South West Services
Central Soya Co.
Central Trust Co.
Cessna Aircraft Co.
Challenge Foundation
Chamberlin Foundation, Gerald W.
Chambers Development Co.
Chambers Memorial, James B.
Champlin Foundations
Chapin Foundation, Frances
Chapin Foundation of Myrtle Beach, South Carolina
Chapin-May Foundation of Illinois
Chapman Charitable Corporation, Howard and Bess
Chapman Charitable Trust, H. A. and Mary K.
Charina Foundation

Charitable Fund
Charities Foundation
Charlesbank Homes
Charlton, Jr. Charitable Trust, Earle P.
Charter Manufacturing Co.
Chartwell Foundation
Chase Charity Foundation, Alfred E.
Chase Manhattan Bank, N.A.
Chase Trust, Alice P.
Chastain Charitable Foundation, Robert Lee and Thomas M.
Chatham Valley Foundation
Chemical Bank
Cheney Foundation, Ben B.
Cheney Foundation, Elizabeth F.
Cherne Foundation, Albert W.
Cherokee Foundation
Chesapeake Corp.
Chesapeake & Potomac Telephone Co.
Chesebrough-Pond's
Chevron Corp.
Chicago Board of Trade
Chicago Sun-Times, Inc.
Chicago Title and Trust Co.
Children's Foundation of Erie County
Childress Foundation, Francis and Miranda
Childs Charitable Foundation, Roberta M.
Chiles Foundation
Chilton Foundation Trust
Chisholm Foundation
Christian Dior New York, Inc.
Christian Training Foundation
Christian Workers Foundation
Chrysler Corp.
Church & Dwight Co.
Churches Homes Foundation
Ciba-Geigy Corp. (Pharmaceuticals Division)
Cincinnati Bell
Cincinnati Enquirer
Cincinnati Gas & Electric Co.
Circuit City Stores
CIT Group Holdings
Citibank, F.S.B.
Citicorp
Citizens Bank
Claneil Foundation
Clapp Charitable and Educational Trust, George H.
CLARCOR
Clark Foundation
Clark Foundation
Clark-Winchcole Foundation
Classic Leather
Clay Foundation
Cleary Foundation
Clements Foundation
Cleveland-Cliffs
Cline Co.
Clipper Ship Foundation
Clorox Co.
Close Foundation
Clowes Fund
CM Alliance Cos.
CNA Insurance Cos.
CNG Transmission Corp.
Coats & Clark Inc.
Cockrell Foundation
Codrington Charitable Foundation, George W.
Coen Family Foundation, Charles S. and Mary
Coffey Foundation
Cogswell Benevolent Trust
Cohen Family Foundation, Saul Z. and Amy Scheuer
Cohen Foundation, George M.
Cohen Foundation, Naomi and Nehemiah
Cohn Family Foundation, Robert and Terri

Cohn Foundation, Herman and Terese
Cohn Foundation, Peter A. and Elizabeth S.
Cole Foundation
Cole Foundation, Olive B.
Cole Foundation, Robert H. and Monica H.
Cole National Corp.
Cole Taylor Financial Group
Cole Trust, Quincy
Coleman Co.
Colket Foundation, Ethel D.
Collins & Aikman Holdings Corp.
Collins Foundation
Collins Foundation, Carr P.
Collins Foundation, James M.
Collins-McDonald Trust Fund
Colonial Life & Accident Insurance Co.
Colonial Oil Industries, Inc.
Colorado Trust
Colt Foundation, James J.
Coltec Industries
Columbia Foundation
Columbia Savings Charitable Foundation
Columbus Dispatch Printing Co.
Columbus Southern Power Co.
Comer Foundation
Comerica
Commerce Bancshares, Inc.
Commerce Clearing House
Commerzbank AG, New York
Commonwealth Edison Co.
Commonwealth Fund
Community Enterprises
Community Foundation
Community Health Association
Compaq Computer Corp.
Compton Foundation
Comstock Foundation
ConAgra
Cone-Blanchard Machine Co.
Cone Mills Corp.
Confidence Foundation
Conn Memorial Foundation
Connecticut Natural Gas Corp.
Connelly Foundation
Connemara Fund
Consolidated Freightways
Consolidated Natural Gas Co.
Consolidated Papers
Constantin Foundation
Conston Corp.
Consumers Power Co.
Contempo Communications
Continental Corp.
Contran Corp.
Contraves USA
Cook Batson Foundation
Cook Charitable Foundation
Cook Foundation
Cook Foundation, Loring
Cooke Foundation
Cooke Foundation Corporation, V. V.
Cooper Charitable Trust, Richard H.
Cooper Foundation
Cooper Industries
Coors Foundation, Adolph
Copley Press
Copperweld Corp.
Copperweld Steel Co.
Corbin Foundation, Mary S. and David C.
Cord Foundation, E. L.
Cornell Trust, Peter C.
Corning Incorporated
Cosmair, Inc.
Coughlin-Saunders Foundation
Country Curtains, Inc.
County Bank
Courtaulds Fibers Inc.
Courts Foundation

Cove Charitable Trust
Cowan Foundation Corporation, Lillian L. and Harry A.
Cowden Foundation, Louetta M.
Cowell Foundation, S. H.
Cowles Charitable Trust
Cowles Foundation, Gardner and Florence Call
Cowles Foundation, Harriet Cheney
Cowles Media Co.
Cox Charitable Trust, A. G.
Cox Enterprises
CPC International
CPI Corp.
Craig Foundation, J. Paul
Craigmyle Foundation
Crail-Johnson Foundation
Crandall Memorial Foundation, J. Ford
Cranshaw Corporation
Cranston Print Works
Crapo Charitable Foundation, Henry H.
Crawford & Co.
Crawford Estate, E. R.
Cremer Foundation
Crescent Plastics
Crestar Financial Corp.
Crestlea Foundation
CRL Inc.
Crocker Trust, Mary A.
Crown Central Petroleum Corp.
Crown Memorial, Arie and Ida
Crum and Forster
Crummer Foundation, Roy E.
Crystal Trust
CT Corp. System
CTS Corp.
Cudahy Fund, Patrick and Anna M.
Cuesta Foundation
Cullen Foundation
Cullen/Frost Bankers
Culpeper Memorial Foundation, Daphne Seybolt
Culver Foundation, Constans
Cummings Foundation, James H.
Cummings Foundation, Nathan
Cummings Memorial Fund Trust, Frances L. and Edwin L.
Cummins Engine Co.
CUNA Mutual Insurance Group
Cuneo Foundation
Currey Foundation, Brownlee
Curtice-Burns Foods
Dai-Ichi Kangyo Bank of California
Daily News
Dain Bosworth/Inter-Regional Financial Group
Dalgety Inc.
Dalton Foundation, Dorothy U.
Dalton Foundation, Harry L.
Dammann Fund
Dan River, Inc.
Dana Corp.
Danforth Foundation
Daniel Foundation of Alabama
Daniels Foundation, Fred Harris
Danis Industries
Danner Foundation
Darby Foundation
Darrah Charitable Trust, Jessie Smith
Dart Foundation
Dater Foundation, Charles H.
Daugherty Foundation
Davenport-Hatch Foundation
Davidson Family Charitable Foundation
Davis Family - W.D. Charities, James E.
Davis Family - W.D. Charities, Tine W.
Davis Foundation, Edwin W. and Catherine M.

Davis Foundation, James A. and Juliet L.
Davis Foundation, Ken W.
Day Family Foundation
Day Foundation, Cecil B.
Day Foundation, Nancy Sayles
Day Foundation, Willametta K.
Dayton Power and Light Co.
Daywood Foundation
DCB Corp.
DCNY Corp.
Dean Witter Discover
DEC International, Inc.
Dee Foundation, Annie Taylor
Dee Foundation, Lawrence T. and Janet T.
Deere & Co.
Delano Foundation, Mignon Sherwood
Dell Foundation, Hazel
DelMar Foundation, Charles
Deluxe Corp.
Demos Foundation, N.
DeMoss Foundation, Arthur S.
Demoulas Supermarkets
Dennett Foundation, Marie G.
Dennison Manufacturing Co.
Deposit Guaranty National Bank
DeRoy Foundation, Helen L.
DeRoy Testamentary Foundation
Detroit Edison Co.
Deuble Foundation, George H.
Deutsch Co.
Devereaux Foundation
DeVlieg Foundation, Charles
Devonshire Associates
DeVore Foundation
Dewar Foundation
Dexter Charitable Fund, Eugene A.
Dexter Corp.
Dial Corp.
Diamond Foundation, Aaron
Diamond Walnut Growers
Dibner Fund
Dick Family Foundation
Dickson Foundation
Digital Equipment Corp.
Dillard Paper Co.
Dillon Foundation
Dimick Foundation
Disney Family Foundation, Roy
Dively Foundation, George S.
Dixie Yarns, Inc.
Dodge Foundation, Cleveland H.
Dodge Foundation, Geraldine R.
Dodge Foundation, P. L.
Dodge Jones Foundation
Dodson Foundation, James Glenwell and Clara May
Doelger Charitable Trust, Thelma
Doheny Foundation, Carrie Estelle
Doherty Charitable Foundation, Henry L. and Grace
Domino of California
Donaldson Charitable Trust, Oliver S. and Jennie R.
Donaldson Co.
Donnelley Foundation, Elliott and Ann
Donnelley Foundation, Gaylord and Dorothy
Donnelley & Sons Co., R.R.
Donovan, Leisure, Newton & Irvine
Dorminy Foundation, John Henry
Doss Foundation, M. S.
Doty Family Foundation
Dougherty, Jr. Foundation, James R.
Douglas Corp.
Douglas & Lomason Company
Douty Foundation
Dover Foundation
Dow Corning Corp.

Youth Organizations (cont.)

Dow Foundation, Herbert H. and Barbara C.
Dow Fund, Alden and Vada
Dower Foundation, Thomas W.
Dreitzer Foundation
Dresser Industries
Dreyfus Foundation, Jean and Louis
Dreyfus Foundation, Max and Victoria
Driehaus Foundation, Richard H.
Driscoll Foundation
Drown Foundation, Joseph
du Pont de Nemours & Co., E. I.
Duchossois Industries
Duke Foundation, Doris
Duke Power Co.
Dun & Bradstreet Corp.
Dunagan Foundation
Duncan Foundation, Lillian H. and C. W.
Duncan Trust, James R.
Duncan Trust, John G.
Dunn Research Foundation, John S.
Dunspaugh-Dalton Foundation
Dupar Foundation
Dupar Foundation
duPont Foundation, Alfred I.
duPont Foundation, Chichester
duPont Fund, Jessie Ball
Duquesne Light Co.
Durfee Foundation
Durham Merchants Association Charitable Foundation
Durr-Fillauer Medical
Durst Foundation
Dweck Foundation, Samuel R.
Dyson Foundation
E and M Charities
Eagle-Picher Industries
Earl-Beth Foundation
Early Foundation
Easley Trust, Andrew H. and Anne O.
Eastern Bank Foundation
Eastern Enterprises
Eastern Fine Paper, Inc.
Eastman Foundation, Alexander
Eastman Kodak Co.
Eaton Corp.
Eaton Foundation, Edwin M. and Gertrude S.
Eaton Memorial Fund, Georgiana Goddard
Eberly Foundation
Ebert Charitable Foundation, Horatio S.
Eccles Foundation, George S. and Dolores Dore
Eccles Foundation, Marriner S.
Eccles Foundation, Ralph M. and Ella M.
Echlin Inc.
Echlin Foundation
Ecolab
Eddy Family Memorial Fund, C. K.
Eden Hall Foundation
Edgewater Steel Corp.
Edison Foundation, Harry
Edison Fund, Charles
Edouard Foundation
Edwards Foundation, O. P. and W. E.
Edwards Industries
EG&G Inc.
Egenton Home
Einstein Fund, Albert E. and Birdie W.
EIS Foundation
Eisenberg Foundation, Ben B. and Joyce E.
Eisenberg Foundation, George M.
El Pomar Foundation

Electric Power Equipment Co.
Electronic Data Systems Corp.
Elf Aquitaine, Inc.
Elf Atochem North America
Elkin Memorial Foundation, Neil Warren and William Simpson
Elkins Foundation, J. A. and Isabel M.
Ellison Foundation
Ellsworth Foundation, Ruth H. and Warren A.
Ellsworth Trust, W. H.
Emergency Aid of Pennsylvania Foundation
Emerson Electric Co.
Emerson Foundation, Fred L.
Emery Memorial, Thomas J.
EMI Records Group
Encyclopaedia Britannica, Inc.
Endries Fastener & Supply Co.
Endries Fastener & Supply Co.
Engelhard Foundation, Charles
English-Bonter-Mitchell Foundation
English Foundation, Walter and Marian
English Memorial Fund, Florence C. and H. L.
Enright Foundation
Enron Corp.
Ensign-Bickford Industries
Ensworth Charitable Foundation
Epaphroditus Foundation
Epp Fund B Charitable Trust, Otto C.
Equifax
Equitable Life Assurance Society of the U.S.
Erb Lumber Co.
Erickson Charitable Fund, Eben W.
Ernest & Julio Gallo Winery
Erpf Fund, Armand G.
Erteszek Foundation
Essick Foundation
Estes Foundation
Ethyl Corp.
Ettinger Foundation
European American Bank
Evans Foundation, Thomas J.
Everett Charitable Trust
Evinrude Foundation, Ralph
Evjue Foundation
Ewald Foundation, H. T.
Exchange Bank
Exposition Foundation
Exxon Corp.
FAB Industries
Fabick Tractor Co., John
Factor Family Foundation, Max
Failing Fund, Henry
Fair Foundation, R. W.
Fair Oaks Foundation, Inc.
Fairchild Corp.
Fairchild Foundation, Sherman
Fairfield Foundation, Freeman E.
Faith Charitable Trust
Faith Home Foundation
Fales Foundation Trust
Falk Foundation, David
Falk Medical Research Foundation, Dr. Ralph and Marian
Farallon Foundation
Farish Fund, William Stamps
Farley Industries
Farm & Home Savings Association
Farmland Industries, Inc.
Farnsworth Trust, Charles A.
Farr Trust, Frank M. and Alice M.
Farwell Foundation, Drusilla
Farwell Foundation, Drusilla
Faulkner Trust, Marianne Gaillard
Favrot Fund

Fay Charitable Fund, Aubert J.
Fay's Incorporated
Federal Express Corp.
Federal Home Loan Mortgage Corp. (Freddie Mac)
Federal-Mogul Corp.
Federal National Mortgage Assn., Fannie Mae
Federal Screw Works
Federated Department Stores and Allied Stores Corp.
Federated Life Insurance Co.
Federation Foundation of Greater Philadelphia
Feild Co-Operative Association
Fein Foundation
Fels Fund, Samuel S.
Femino Foundation
Ferguson Family Foundation, Kittie and Rugeley
Ferrell Cos.
Fibre Converters
Fidelity Bank
Field Foundation of Illinois
Fieldcrest Cannon
Fifth Avenue Foundation
Fifth Third Bancorp
Fig Tree Foundation
Fikes Foundation, Leland
FINA, Inc.
Finch Foundation, Doak
Finch Foundation, Thomas Austin
Finley Foundation, A. E.
Finnegan Foundation, John D.
Fireman's Fund Insurance Co.
Firestone Foundation, Roger S.
First Boston
First Fidelity Bancorporation
First Hawaiian
First Interstate Bancsystem of Montana
First Interstate Bank NW Region
First Interstate Bank of Arizona
First Interstate Bank of California
First Interstate Bank of Denver
First Interstate Bank of Oregon
First Interstate Bank of Texas, N.A.
First Maryland Bancorp
First Mississippi Corp.
First National Bank in Wichita
First National Bank & Trust Co. of Rockford
First NH Banks, Inc.
First Tennessee Bank
First Union Corp.
First Union National Bank of Florida
Firstar Bank Milwaukee NA
FirsTier Bank N.A. Omaha
Fish Foundation, Bert
Fish Foundation, Ray C.
Fish Foundation, Vain and Harry
Fishback Foundation Trust, Harmes C.
Fisher Foundation
Fisher Foundation
Fisher-Price
FKI Holdings Inc.
Flagler Foundation
Flarsheim Charitable Foundation, Louis and Elizabeth
Flatley Foundation
Fleet Bank
Fleet Bank of New York
Fleet Financial Group
Fleishhacker Foundation
Fleming Foundation
Flemm Foundation, John J.
Fletcher Foundation
Flickinger Memorial Trust
Florence Foundation
Florida Power Corp.
Florida Power & Light Co.
Florida Rock Industries

Flowers Charitable Trust, Albert W. and Edith V.
Fluor Corp.
FMR Corp.
Foellinger Foundation
Fohs Foundation
Foley, Hoag & Eliot
Folger Fund
Fondren Foundation
Foote, Cone & Belding Communications
Foothills Foundation
Forbes
Forbes Charitable Trust, Herman
Ford Foundation
Ford Foundation, Kenneth W.
Ford Fund, Benson and Edith
Ford Fund, Walter and Josephine
Ford Fund, William and Martha
Ford II Fund, Henry
Ford Meter Box Co.
Ford Motor Co.
Forest City Enterprises
Forest Foundation
Forest Fund
Forest Lawn Foundation
Forster Charitable Trust, James W. and Ella B.
Forster-Powers Charitable Trust
Fort Worth Star Telegram
Fortin Foundation of Florida
Fortis Benefits Insurance Company/Fortis Financial Group
Foster Charitable Foundation, M. Stratton
Foster Charitable Trust
Foster Co., L.B.
Foster-Davis Foundation
Foster Foundation
Foundation for Child Development
Foundation for Middle East Peace
Foundation for Seacoast Health
Foundation for the Needs of Others
Fourth Financial Corp.
Fowler Memorial Foundation, John Edward
Fox Inc.
Fox Charitable Foundation, Harry K. & Emma R.
Fox Foundation, John H.
Fox Foundation, Richard J.
Fraida Foundation
Frank Foundation, Ernest and Elfriede
Frank Fund, Zollie and Elaine
Frankel Foundation
Frankel Foundation, George and Elizabeth F.
Franklin Foundation, John and Mary
Fraser Paper Ltd.
Frear Eleemosynary Trust, Mary D. and Walter F.
Frederick Foundation
Freed Foundation
Freedom Forum
Freeman Charitable Trust, Samuel
Freeport Brick Co.
Freeport-McMoRan
Frees Foundation
Freightliner Corp.
French Oil Mill Machinery Co.
Frese Foundation, Arnold D.
Fribourg Foundation
Friedman Family Foundation
Friendly Rosenthal Foundation
Friends' Foundation Trust, A.
Frisch's Restaurants Inc.
Froderman Foundation
Frohlich Charitable Trust, Ludwig W.
Frohman Foundation, Sidney

Frohring Foundation, Paul & Maxine
Frohring Foundation, William O. and Gertrude Lewis
Frueauff Foundation, Charles A.
Frumkes Foundation, Alana and Lewis
Fry Foundation, Lloyd A.
Fuchs Foundation, Gottfried & Mary
Fuller Foundation, George F. and Sybil H.
Fullerton Foundation
Funderburke & Associates
Fuqua Foundation, J. B.
Furth Foundation
Fusenot Charity Foundation, Georges and Germaine
G.A.G. Charitable Corporation
Gage Foundation, Philip and Irene Toll
Gaisman Foundation, Catherine and Henry J.
Galkin Charitable Trust, Ira S. and Anna
Gallagher Family Foundation, Lewis P.
Gallo Foundation, Julio R.
Galter Foundation
Galvin Foundation, Robert W.
Gannett Co.
Gannett Publishing Co., Guy Gap, The
GAR Foundation
Garland Foundation, John Jewett and H. Chandler
Garner Charitable Trust, James G.
Garvey Kansas Foundation
Garvey Texas Foundation
Garvey Trust, Olive White
Gates Foundation
GATX Corp.
Gaylord Foundation, Clifford Willard
Gazette Co.
Gear Motion
Gebbie Foundation
Gelb Foundation, Lawrence M.
Gellert Foundation, Carl
Gellert Foundation, Celia Berta
Gellert Foundation, Fred
GenCorp
General Accident Insurance Co. of America
General American Life Insurance Co.
General Atlantic Partners L.P.
General Development Corp.
General Dynamics Corp.
General Electric Co.
General Mills
General Motors Corp.
General Signal Corp.
General Tire Inc.
Geneseo Foundation
GenRad
George Foundation
Georgia-Pacific Corp.
Georgia Power Co.
Gerber Products Co.
Gerbode Foundation, Wallace Alexander
Gerlach Foundation
German Protestant Orphan Asylum Association
Gerondelis Foundation
Gerson Family Foundation, Benjamin J.
Gerstacker Foundation, Rollin M.
Getsch Family Foundation Trust
Gheens Foundation
Ghidotti Foundation, William and Marian
Gholston Trust, J. K.
Giant Eagle
Giant Food
Giant Food Stores

Giddings & Lewis
Gifford Charitable Corporation, Rosamond
Giger Foundation, Paul and Oscar
Gilbane Foundation, Thomas and William
Gilbert, Jr. Charitable Trust, Price
Gilder Foundation
Giles Foundation, Edward C.
Gill Foundation, Pauline Allen
Gillette Co.
Gilman Paper Co.
Gilmer-Smith Foundation
Gilmore Foundation, Earl B.
Gilmore Foundation, Irving S.
Gilmore Foundation, William G.
Gindi Associates Foundation
Ginsberg Family Foundation, Moses
Ginter Foundation, Karl and Anna
Gitano Group
Givenchy, Inc.
Glaser Foundation
Glaxo
Glaze Foundation, Robert and Ruth
Glazer Foundation, Jerome S.
Glazer Foundation, Madelyn L.
Gleason Foundation, James
Gleason Foundation, Katherine
Gleason Memorial Fund
Gleason Works
Glen Eagles Foundation
Glenmore Distilleries Co.
Glick Foundation, Eugene and Marilyn
Globe Corp.
Globe Newspaper Co.
Goddard Foundation, Charles B.
Goerlich Family Foundation
Goldberger Foundation, Edward and Marjorie
Golden Family Foundation
Goldenberg Foundation, Max
Goldman Foundation, Herman
Goldman Foundation, Morris and Rose
Goldman Foundation, William
Goldman Fund, Richard and Rhoda
Goldome F.S.B
Goldring Family Foundation
Goldsmith Family Foundation
Goldstein Foundation, Leslie and Roslyn
Goldwyn Foundation, Samuel
Golub Corp.
Goodman Family Foundation
Goodman Memorial Foundation, Joseph C. and Clare F.
Goodstein Foundation
Goodwin Foundation, Leo
Goodyear Foundation, Josephine
Goodyear Tire & Rubber Co.
Goody's Manufacturing Corp.
Gordon Foundation, Meyer and Ida
Gordon/Rousmaniere/Roberts Fund
Gore Family Memorial Foundation
Gottwald Foundation
Gould Foundation for Children, Edwin
Grace & Co., W.R.
Graco
Grader Foundation, K. W.
Gradison & Co.
Graham Charitable Trust, William L.
Graham Fund, Philip L.
Grainger Foundation
Grant Foundation, Charles M. and Mary D.
Grant Foundation, William T.
Graphic Controls Corp.
Grassmann Trust, E. J.

Gray Foundation, Garland
Graybar Electric Co.
Great Atlantic & Pacific Tea Co. Inc.
Great-West Life Assurance Co.
Great Western Financial Corp.
Greater Lansing Foundation
Grede Foundries
Greeley Gas Co.
Green Charitable Trust, Leslie H. and Edith C.
Green Foundation, Allen P. and Josephine B.
Green Foundation, Burton E.
Green Fund
Greene Foundation, David J.
Greentree Foundation
Gregg-Graniteville Foundation
Griffin, Sr., Foundation, C. V.
Griffis Foundation
Griffith Foundation, W. C.
Grigg-Lewis Trust
Grimes Foundation
Grinnell Mutual Reinsurance Co.
Griswold Foundation, John C.
Gross Charitable Trust, Stella B.
Gross Charitable Trust, Walter L. and Nell R.
Groves & Sons Co., S.J.
Gruber Research Foundation, Lila
Grumbacher Foundation, M. S.
Grundy Foundation
GTE Corp.
Guardian Life Insurance Co. of America
Gucci America Inc.
Gudelsky Family Foundation, Isadore and Bertha
Guggenheim Foundation, Daniel and Florence
Gulf Power Co.
Gund Foundation, George
Gurwin Foundation, J.
Guttag Foundation, Irwin and Marjorie
Guttman Foundation, Stella and Charles
H.C.S. Foundation
Haas Foundation, Paul and Mary
Haas Foundation, Saul and Dayee G.
Haas Fund, Miriam and Peter
Haas Fund, Walter and Elise
Haas, Jr. Fund, Evelyn and Walter
Habig Foundation, Arnold F.
Hachar Charitable Trust, D. D.
Haffenreffer Family Fund
Haffner Foundation
Hafif Family Foundation
Hagedorn Fund
Haggar Foundation
Haggerty Foundation
Hagler Foundation, Jon L.
Haigh-Scatena Foundation
Hale Foundation, Crescent Porter
Haley Foundation, W. B.
Halff Foundation, G. A. C.
Hall Charitable Trust, Evelyn A. J.
Hall Family Foundations
Hall Foundation
Hall Foundation
Hallett Charitable Trust
Halliburton Co.
Hallmark Cards
Halmos Foundation
Halsell Foundation, O. L.
Halstead Foundation
Hambay Foundation, James T.
Hamilton Bank
Hamilton Oil Corp.
Hamman Foundation, George and Mary Josephine
Hammer Foundation, Armand
Hammond Machinery

Hancock Foundation, Luke B.
Hand Industries
Handleman Co.
Hanes Foundation, John W. and Anna H.
Hankins Foundation
Hannon Foundation, William H.
Hansen Foundation, Dane G.
Hanson Foundation
HarCo. Drug
Harcourt Foundation, Ellen Knowles
Harcourt General
Harden Foundation
Hardin Foundation, Phil
Harding Educational and Charitable Foundation
Harding Foundation, Charles Stewart
Hargis Charitable Foundation, Estes H. and Florence Parker
Harkness Ballet Foundation
Harland Charitable Foundation, John and Wilhelmina D.
Harland Co., John H.
Harper Brush Works
Harper Foundation, Philip S.
Harriman Foundation, Gladys and Roland
Harriman Foundation, Mary W.
Harrington Foundation, Don and Sybil
Harrington Foundation, Francis A. and Jacquelyn H.
Harris Corp.
Harris Family Foundation, Hunt and Diane
Harris Foundation
Harris Foundation, J. Ira and Nicki
Harris Foundation, James J. and Angelia M.
Harris Foundation, John H. and Lucille
Harris Foundation, William H. and Mattie Wattis
Harrison Foundation, Fred G.
Harsco Corp.
Hartford Courant Foundation
Hartmarx Corp.
Hartzell Industries, Inc.
Harvest States Cooperative
Hasbro
Haskell Fund
Hastings Trust
Hatch Charitable Trust, Margaret Milliken
Hatterscheidt Foundation
Havens Foundation, O. W.
Hawkins Foundation, Robert Z.
Hawley Foundation
Hawn Foundation
Hay Foundation, John I.
Hayden Foundation, Charles
Hayden Foundation, William R. and Virginia
Hazen Foundation, Edward W.
Hearst Foundation
Hearst Foundation, William Randolph
Hebrew Technical Institute
Hechinger Co.
Heckscher Foundation for Children
Hecla Mining Co.
Hedrick Foundation, Frank E.
HEI Inc.
Heileman Brewing Co., Inc., G.
Heilicher Foundation, Menahem
Heineman Foundation for Research, Educational, Charitable, and Scientific Purposes
Heinz Co., H.J.
Heinz Endowment, Vira I.
Helfaer Foundation, Evan and Marion
Helis Foundation

Heller Financial
Helmerich Foundation
Helms Foundation
Helzberg Foundation, Shirley and Barnett
Hemby Foundation, Alex
Henderson Foundation
Herbst Foundation
Herman Foundation, John and Rose
Hermann Foundation, Grover
Herndon Foundation
Herndon Foundation, Alonzo F. Herndon and Norris B.
Herrick Foundation
Herschend Family Foundation
Hersey Foundation
Hershey Foods Corp.
Hershey Foundation
Hervey Foundation
Hess Charitable Trust, Myrtle E. and William C.
Hess Foundation
Heublein
Hewit Family Foundation
Hewlett Foundation, William and Flora
Heydt Fund, Nan and Matilda
Hiawatha Education Foundation
Higgins Charitable Trust, Lorene Sails
Higgins Foundation, Aldus C.
Higginson Trust, Corina
High Foundation
Hill and Family Foundation, Walter Clay
Hill Crest Foundation
Hill-Snowdon Foundation
Hillcrest Foundation
Hilliard Corp.
Hillman Foundation
Hillsdale Fund
Hilton Foundation, Conrad N.
Himmelfarb Foundation, Paul and Annetta
Hitachi
Hitchcock Foundation, Gilbert M. and Martha H.
Hoag Family Foundation, George
Hobbs Foundation
Hobby Foundation
Hoblitzelle Foundation
Hoche-Scofield Foundation
Hodge Foundation
Hoechst Celanese Corp.
Hoffberger Foundation
Hoffer Plastics Corp.
Hoffman Foundation, H. Leslie Hoffman and Elaine S.
Hoffman Foundation, John Ernest
Hofmann Co.
Hofstetter Trust, Bessie
Hogan Foundation, Royal Barney
Holden Fund, James and Lynelle
Holding Foundation, Robert P.
Holley Foundation
Hollis Foundation
Holmes Foundation
Home Depot
Home for Aged Men
Home Savings of America, FA
Homeland Foundation
Homeland Foundation
HON Industries
Honda of America Manufacturing, Inc.
Honeywell
Hook Drug
Hooker Charitable Trust, Janet A.
Hooper Foundation, Elizabeth S.
Hooper Handling
Hoover Foundation
Hoover Foundation, H. Earl
Hoover Fund-Trust, W. Henry
Hopeman Brothers
Hopkins Foundation, Josephine Lawrence

Hopper Memorial Foundation, Bertrand
Hopwood Charitable Trust, John M.
Hornblower Fund, Henry
Horne Foundation, Dick
Horne Trust, Mabel
Horowitz Foundation, Gedale B. and Barbara S.
Hospital Corp. of America
Houchens Foundation, Ervin G.
Houck Foundation, May K.
House Educational Trust, Susan Cook
Household International
Houston Endowment
Houston Industries
Howard and Bush Foundation
Howe and Mitchell B. Howe Foundation, Lucite Horton
Howell Foundation, Eric and Jessie
Howell Fund
Hoyt Foundation
Hoyt Foundation, Stewart W. and Willma C.
Hubbard Broadcasting
Hubbard Foundation, R. Dee and Joan Dale
Hubbard Milling Co.
Hubbell Inc.
Huffy Corp.
Hughes Charitable Trust, Mabel Y.
Hugoton Foundation
Huisking Foundation
Huizenga Family Foundation
Hulme Charitable Foundation, Milton G.
Hultquist Foundation
Humana
Hume Foundation, Jaquelin
Humphrey Foundation, Glenn & Gertrude
Humphreys Foundation
Hunt Alternatives Fund
Hunt Charitable Trust, C. Giles
Hunt Foundation
Hunt Foundation, Roy A.
Hunt Foundation, Samuel P.
Hunter Foundation, Edward and Irma
Hunter Trust, A. V.
Hunter Trust, Emily S. and Coleman A.
Huntsman Foundation, Jon and Karen
Hurst Foundation
Huston Foundation
Hutchins Foundation, Mary J.
Huthsteiner Fine Arts Trust
Hyams Foundation
Hyde and Watson Foundation
Hyde Foundation, J. R.
Hyde Manufacturing Co.
I and G Charitable Foundation
IBM Corp.
IBP, Inc.
Icahn Foundation, Carl C.
Iddings Benevolent Trust
Ideal Industries
IDS Financial Services
IES Industries
Illges Foundation, John P. and Dorothy S.
Illges Memorial Foundation, A. and M. L.
Illinois Bell
Illinois Tool Works
Imerman Memorial Foundation, Stanley
IMT Insurance Co.
Index Technology Corp.
Indiana Bell Telephone Co.
Indiana Desk Co.
Indiana Gas and Chemical Corp.
Ingalls Foundation, Louise H. and David S.

Recipient Type Index

Youth Organizations (cont.)

Ingersoll Milling Machine Co.
Inland Container Corp.
Inland Steel Industries
Inman Mills
Insurance Management Associates
Intel Corp.
Interco
International Flavors & Fragrances
International Multifoods Corp.
International Paper Co.
Interstate National Corp.
Ireland Foundation
Irmas Charitable Foundation, Audrey and Sydney
Iroquois Avenue Foundation
Irvine Foundation, James
Irvine Health Foundation
Irwin Charity Foundation, William G.
Isaly Klondike Co.
Island Foundation
ITT Corp.
ITT Hartford Insurance Group
ITT Rayonier
Ivakota Association
J. D. B. Fund
J.P. Morgan & Co.
Jackson Charitable Trust, Marion Gardner
Jackson Foundation
Jacobs Engineering Group
Jacobson Foundation, Bernard H. and Blanche E.
Jacobson & Sons, Benjamin
Jaffe Foundation
James River Corp. of Virginia
Jameson Foundation, J. W. and Ida M.
Jameson Trust, Oleonda
Janesville Foundation
Janeway Foundation, Elizabeth Bixby
Janssen Foundation, Henry
Jaqua Foundation
Jarson-Stanley and Mickey Kaplan Foundation, Isaac & Esther
Jasam Foundation
Jasper Desk Co.
Jasper Table Co.
Jasper Wood Products Co.
JCPenney Co.
Jeffress Memorial Trust, Elizabeth G.
Jellison Benevolent Society
Jenkins Foundation, George W.
Jennings Foundation, Martha Holden
Jennings Foundation, Mary Hillman
Jergens Foundation, Andrew
Jerome Foundation
Jerusalem Fund for Education and Community Development
Jesselson Foundation
Jewett Foundation, George Frederick
JFM Foundation
Jinks Foundation, Ruth T.
JM Foundation
Jockey Hollow Foundation
John Hancock Mutual Life Insurance Co.
Johnson Controls
Johnson Foundation, A. D.
Johnson Foundation, Helen K. and Arthur E.
Johnson Foundation, Howard
Johnson Foundation, M. G. and Lillie A.
Johnson Foundation, Walter S.

Johnson Foundation, Willard T. C.
Johnson & Higgins
Johnson & Johnson
Johnson & Son, S.C.
Johnston-Fix Foundation
Johnston-Hanson Foundation
Johnstone and H. Earle Kimball Foundation, Phyllis Kimball
Jones Construction Co., J.A.
Jones Family Foundation, Eugenie and Joseph
Jones Foundation, Daisy Marquis
Jones Foundation, Harvey and Bernice
Jones Foundation, Helen
Jones Foundation, Montfort Jones and Allie Brown
Jones Intercable, Inc.
Jonsson Foundation
Jordan and Ettie A. Jordan Charitable Foundation, Mary Ranken
Jordan Foundation, Arthur
Joslyn Foundation, Marcellus I.
Jost Foundation, Charles and Mabel P.
Jostens
Journal Gazette Co.
Joy Family Foundation
Joyce Foundation
JSJ Corp.
Julia R. and Estelle L. Foundation
Justus Trust, Edith C.
Kamps Memorial Foundation, Gertrude
Kanematsu-Gosho U.S.A. Inc.
Kantzler Foundation
Kaplan Foundation, Mayer and Morris
Kaplen Foundation
Kaplun Foundation, Morris J. and Betty
Katten, Muchin, & Zavis
Katzenberger Foundation
Kaufman Endowment Fund, Louis G.
Kaufmann Foundation, Henry
Kautz Family Foundation
Kavanagh Foundation, T. James
Kawabe Memorial Fund
Kayser Foundation
Kearney Inc., A.T.
Keating Family Foundation
Keeler Fund, Miner S. and Mary Ann
Keene Trust, Hazel R.
Keith Foundation Trust, Ben E.
Keller-Crescent Co.
Keller Family Foundation
Kelley and Elza Kelley Foundation, Edward Bangs
Kelley Foundation, Kate M.
Kellogg Foundation, J. C.
Kellogg Foundation, W. K.
Kellogg's
Kellwood Co.
Kelly, Jr. Memorial Foundation, Ensign C. Markland
Kelly Tractor Co.
Kemper Charitable Lead Trust, William T.
Kemper Charitable Trust, William T.
Kemper Educational and Charitable Fund
Kemper Foundation, Enid and Crosby
Kemper Memorial Foundation, David Woods
Kempner Fund, Harris and Eliza
Kenan Family Foundation
Kendall Foundation, George R.
Kenedy Memorial Foundation, John G. and Marie Stella
Kennametal
Kennecott Corp.

Kennedy Family Foundation, Ethel and W. George
Kennedy Foundation, Ethel
Kennedy Memorial Fund, Mark H.
Kent-Lucas Foundation
Kentland Foundation
Kenworthy - Sarah H. Swift Foundation, Marion E.
Kepco, Inc.
Kerney Foundation, James
Kerr Foundation
Kerr Foundation, A. H.
Kerr Foundation, Robert S. and Grayce B.
Kerr Fund, Grayce B.
Kerr-McGee Corp.
Kettering Family Foundation
Kettering Fund
Key Bank of Maine
Key Food Stores Cooperative Inc.
Kieckhefer Foundation, J. W.
Kiewit Foundation, Peter
Kiewit Sons, Peter
Kilcawley Fund, William H.
Kilroy Foundation, William S. and Lora Jean
Kilworth Charitable Foundation, Florence B.
Kilworth Charitable Trust, William
Kimball Foundation, Horace A. Kimball and S. Ella
Kimball International
Kimberly-Clark Corp.
King Foundation, Carl B. and Florence E.
King Ranch
Kingsbury Corp.
Kingsley Foundation
Kingston Foundation
Kiplinger Foundation
Kirbo Charitable Trust, Thomas M. and Irene B.
Kirby Foundation, F. M.
Kirchgessner Foundation, Karl
Kirkhill Rubber Co.
Kirkpatrick Foundation
Klau Foundation, David W. and Sadie
Klee Foundation, Conrad and Virginia
Kline Foundation, Charles and Figa
Kline Foundation, Josiah W. and Bessie H.
Kling Trust, Louise
Kmart Corp.
Knapp Foundation
Knight Foundation, John S. and James L.
Knistrom Foundation, Fanny and Svante
Knott Foundation, Marion I. and Henry J.
Knowles Charitable Memorial Trust, Gladys E.
Knox Family Foundation
Knox, Sr., and Pearl Wallis Knox Charitable Foundation, Robert W.
Knudsen Charitable Foundation, Earl
Koch Industries
Koch Sons, George
Koehler Foundation, Marcia and Otto
Koffler Family Foundation
Kohl Foundation, Sidney
Kohn-Joseloff Fund
Komes Foundation
Koopman Fund
Korman Family Foundation, Hyman
Kowalski Sausage Co.
Kraft Foundation
Kraft General Foods
Kramer Foundation, Louise

Kresge Foundation
Kress Foundation, George
Krieble Foundation, Vernon K.
Krimendahl II Foundation, H. Frederick
KSM Foundation
Kuehn Foundation
Kugelman Foundation
Kuhne Foundation Trust, Charles
Kuhns Investment Co.
Kulas Foundation
Kunkel Foundation, John Crain
Kutz Foundation, Milton and Hattie
Kuyper Foundation, Peter H. and E. Lucille Gaass
Kysor Industrial Corp.
L. L. W. W. Foundation
L and L Foundation
La-Z-Boy Chair Co.
Laclede Gas Co.
Lacy Foundation
Ladd Charitable Corporation, Helen and George
Ladish Co.
Ladish Family Foundation, Herman W.
Ladish Malting Co.
Laffey-McHugh Foundation
Lakeside Foundation
LamCo. Communications
Lamson & Sessions Co.
Lancaster Colony
Lance, Inc.
Land O'Lakes
Landmark Communications
Lane Charitable Trust, Melvin R.
Lane Co., Inc.
Lane Foundation, Minnie and Bernard
Lane Memorial Foundation, Mills Bee
Lang Foundation, Eugene M.
Langdale Co.
Langendorf Foundation, Stanley S.
Lanier Brothers Foundation
Lard Trust, Mary Potishman
Large Foundation
Laros Foundation, R. K.
Larsen Fund
LaSalle National Bank
Lasdon Foundation
Lasky Co.
Lassen Foundation, Irving A.
Lassus Brothers Oil
Lauder Foundation
Lauffer Trust, Charles A.
Laurel Foundation
Lautenberg Foundation
Lavanburg-Corner House
Law Foundation, Robert O.
Lawrence Foundation, Lind
Lazar Foundation
LBJ Family Foundation
Leach Foundation, Tom & Frances
Lederer Foundation, Francis L.
Lee Endowment Foundation
Lee Enterprises
Lee Foundation, James T.
Lee Foundation, Ray M. and Mary Elizabeth
Legg Mason Inc.
Lehigh Portland Cement Co.
Lehmann Foundation, Otto W.
Leidy Foundation, John J.
Leighton-Oare Foundation
Lender Family Foundation
Lennon Foundation, Fred A.
Leo Burnett Co.
Leonhardt Foundation, Frederick H.
Leu Foundation
Leu Foundation, Harry P.
Leucadia National Corp.
Leuthold Foundation

Levee Charitable Trust, Polly Annenberg
Levi Strauss & Co.
Leviton Manufacturing Co.
Levy Foundation, Jerome
Levy Foundation, June Rockwell
Levy's Lumber & Building Centers
Lewis Foundation, Frank J.
Lewis Foundation, Lillian Kaiser
Libby-Dufour Fund, Trustees of the
Liberman Foundation, Bertha & Isaac
Liberty Corp.
Liberty Diversified Industries Inc.
Liberty Hosiery Mills
Lieberman Enterprises
Lied Foundation Trust
Life Insurance Co. of Georgia
Lightner Sams Foundation
Lilly & Co., Eli
Lilly Endowment
Lilly Foundation, Richard Coyle
Lincoln Electric Co.
Lincoln Family Foundation
Lincoln Fund
Lincoln National Corp.
Lincy Foundation
Lindsay Foundation
Lindsay Trust, Agnes M.
Lindstrom Foundation, Kinney
Link, Jr. Foundation, George
Linn-Henley Charitable Trust
Lintilhac Foundation
Lipton, Thomas J.
Liquid Air Corp.
Little, Arthur D.
Little Family Foundation
Littlefield Foundation, Edmund Wattis
Livingston Foundation
Livingston Memorial Foundation
Liz Claiborne
Loats Foundation
Lockhart Iron & Steel Co.
Lockheed Sanders
Lockwood Foundation, Byron W. and Alice L.
Logan Foundation, E. J.
Long Foundation, George A. and Grace
Long Island Lighting Co.
Longwood Foundation
Loose Trust, Carrie J.
Loose Trust, Harry Wilson
Lopata Foundation, Stanley and Lucy
Lotus Development Corp.
Loughran Foundation, Mary and Daniel
Louisiana Land & Exploration Co.
Louisiana-Pacific Corp.
Louisiana Power & Light Co./New Orleans Public Service
Lounsbery Foundation, Richard
Loutit Foundation
Love Charitable Foundation, John Allan
Love Foundation, George H. and Margaret McClintic
Love Foundation, Lucyle S.
Love Foundation, Martha and Spencer
Lovett Foundation
Lowe Foundation, Joe and Emily
Lowenstein Foundation, Leon
Lowenstein Foundation, William P. and Marie R.
Lozier Foundation
LTV Corp.
Lubo Fund
Lubrizol Corp.
Luce Charitable Trust, Theodore
Luck Stone

Luckyday Foundation
Lukens
Lumpkin Foundation
Lurie Family Foundation
Lurie Foundation, Louis R.
Luse Foundation, W. P. and Bulah
Lutheran Brotherhood
  Foundation
Luttrell Trust
Lux Foundation, Miranda
Lydall, Inc.
Lynn Foundation, E. M.
Lyon Foundation
Lyons Foundation
Lytel Foundation, Bertha Russ
M. E. G. Foundation
M/A-COM, Inc.
M.T.D. Products
Maas Foundation, Benard L.
Mabee Foundation, J. E. and L. E.
MacCurdy Salisbury Educational
  Foundation
MacDonald Foundation, James A.
Macht Foundation, Morton and
  Sophia
Mack Foundation, J. S.
Maclellan Foundation
Maclellan Foundation, Robert L.
  and Kathrina H.
MacLeod Stewardship
  Foundation
Macmillan, Inc.
Macy & Co., R.H.
Maddox Foundation, J. F.
Madison Gas & Electric Co.
Magma Copper Co.
Magowan Family Foundation
Magruder Foundation, Chesley
  G.
Maier Foundation, Sarah Pauline
Mailman Family Foundation, A.
  L.
Mailman Foundation
Makita U.S.A., Inc.
MalCo Products Inc.
Mallinckrodt Specialty
  Chemicals Co.
Mandel Foundation, Jack N. and
  Lilyan
Mandell Foundation, Samuel P.
Mandeville Foundation
Mankato Citizens Telephone Co.
Mann Foundation, Ted
Manoogian Foundation, Alex
  and Marie
Manville Corp.
Mapco Inc.
Marbrook Foundation
Marcus Corp.
Mardag Foundation
Marine Midland Banks
Marion Merrell Dow
Maritz Inc.
Markey Charitable Fund, John C.
Marley Co.
Marmot Foundation
Marriott Corp.
Marriott Foundation, J. Willard
Mars Foundation
Marshall Field's
Marshall Foundation
Marshall Fund
Marshall & Ilsley Bank
Martin Family Fund
Martin Foundation
Martin Marietta Aggregates
Martin Marietta Corp.
Martini Foundation, Nicholas
Marubeni America Corp.
Marx Foundation, Virginia &
  Leonard
Masco Corp.
Massachusetts Charitable
  Mechanics Association
Massengill-DeFriece Foundation

Masserini Charitable Trust,
  Maurice J.
Massey Charitable Trust
Massey Foundation
Massey Foundation, Jack C.
Massie Trust, David Meade
Mastronardi Charitable
  Foundation, Charles A.
Material Service Corp.
Mather Charitable Trust, S.
  Livingston
Mather Fund, Richard
Mathis-Pfohl Foundation
Matthews International Corp.
Mattus Foundation, Reuben and
  Rose
Matz Foundation — Edelman
  Division
Max Charitable Foundation
May Department Stores Co.
May Foundation, Wilbur
May Mitchell Royal Foundation
Mayborn Foundation, Frank W.
Mayer Charitable Trust, Oscar
  G. & Elsa S.
Mayer Foods Corp., Oscar
Mayer Foundation, James and
  Eva
Mayor Foundation, Oliver Dewey
Maytag Family Foundation, Fred
Mazda Motors of America
  (Central), Inc.
Mazda North America
Mazer Foundation, Jacob and
  Ruth
MBIA, Inc.
MCA
McAlister Charitable
  Foundation, Harold
McAlonan Trust, John A.
McBeath Foundation, Faye
McBride & Son Associates
McCarthy Charities
McCasland Foundation
McCaw Foundation
McConnell Foundation, Neil A.
McCormick & Co.
McCormick Tribune Foundation,
  Robert R.
McCormick Trust, Anne
McCray Lumber Co.
McCrea Foundation
McCune Charitable Trust, John
  R.
McCune Foundation
McCutchen Foundation
McDermott
McDermott Foundation, Eugene
McDonald & Co. Securities
McDonald & Co. Securities
McDonald Industries, Inc., A. Y.
McDonald's Corp.
McDonnell Douglas Corp.
McDonnell Douglas Corp.-West
McDonough Foundation, Bernard
McDougall Charitable Trust,
  Ruth Camp
McEachern Charitable Trust, D.
  V. & Ida J.
McElroy Trust, R. J.
McEvoy Foundation, Mildred H.
McFawn Trust No. 2, Lois Sisler
McFeely-Rogers Foundation
McGee Foundation
McGraw Foundation
McGraw-Hill
McGregor Foundation, Thomas
  and Frances
McGregor Fund
MCI Communications Corp.
McInerny Foundation
McIntosh Foundation
McIntyre Foundation, B. D. and
  Jane E.
McIntyre Foundation, C. S. and
  Marion F.
MCJ Foundation

McKee Foundation, Robert E.
  and Evelyn
McKee Poor Fund, Virginia A.
McKenna Foundation, Katherine
  Mabis
McKenna Foundation, Philip M.
McKnight Foundation
McKnight Foundation, Sumner T.
McLean Contributionship
McMahon Charitable Trust
  Fund, Father John J.
McMahon Foundation
McMaster Foundation, Harold
  and Helen
McMillan, Jr. Foundation, Bruce
McMurray-Bennett Foundation
McNutt Charitable Trust, Amy
  Shelton
McRae Foundation
McVay Foundation
McWane Inc.
MDU Resources Group, Inc.
Mead Corp.
Meadowood Foundation
Meadows Foundation
Mebane Packaging Corp.
Mechanic Foundation, Morris A.
Mechanics Bank
Medina Foundation
Meek Foundation
Mellon Bank Corp.
Mellon Foundation, Richard King
Memorial Foundation for
  Children
Memton Fund
Mendel Foundation
Mengle Foundation, Glenn and
  Ruth
Menschel Foundation, Robert
  and Joyce
Mentor Graphics
Mercantile Bancorp
Merchants Bancshares
Merck & Co.
Merck Human Health Division
Meredith Corp.
Meredith Foundation
Mericos Foundation
Merit Oil Corp.
Merrick Foundation
Merrill Lynch & Co.
Mertz Foundation, Martha
Mervyn's
Meserve Memorial Fund, Albert
  and Helen
Messick Charitable Trust, Harry
  F.
Messing Family Charitable
  Foundation
Metal Industries
Metropolitan Health Foundation
Metropolitan Life Insurance Co.
Metropolitan Theatres Corp.
Mettler Instrument Corp.
Meyer Family Foundation, Paul
  J.
Meyer Foundation, Alice
  Kleberg Reynolds
Meyer Foundation, Eugene and
  Agnes E.
Meyer Foundation, Robert R.
Meyer Memorial Foundation,
  Aaron and Rachel
MGIC Investment Corp.
Michael Foundation, Herbert I.
  and Elsa B.
Michael Foundation, Herbert I.
  and Elsa B.
Michigan Bell Telephone Co.
Michigan Consolidated Gas Co.
Michigan Gas Utilities
Mid-Iowa Health Foundation
Middendorf Foundation
Midwest Resources
Mill-Rose Co.
Millard Charitable Trust, Adah K.
Millbrook Tribute Garden

Miller Charitable Foundation,
  Howard E. and Nell E.
Miller Charitable Trust, Lewis N.
Miller Foundation
Miller Foundation, Steve J.
Miller Fund, Kathryn and Gilbert
Miller-Mellor Association
Miller Memorial Trust, George
  Lee
Milliken & Co.
Millipore Corp.
Mills Charitable Foundation,
  Henry L. and Kathryn
Mills Fund, Frances Goll
Mine Safety Appliances Co.
Miniger Memorial Foundation,
  Clement O.
Minnegasco
Minnesota Mutual Life
  Insurance Co.
Minolta Co.
Minster Machine Co.
Missouri Farmers Association
Mitchell Energy & Development
  Corp.
Mitchell Family Foundation,
  Edward D. and Anna
Mitrani Family Foundation
Mitsubishi Electric America
Mitsubishi International Corp.
MNC Financial
Mobil Oil Corp.
Mohasco Corp.
Monarch Machine Tool Co.
Monell Foundation, Ambrose
Monfort Charitable Foundation
Monroe Auto Equipment Co.
Monroe-Brown Foundation
Montana Power Co.
Montgomery Elevator Co.
Montgomery Foundation
Montgomery Street Foundation
Montgomery Ward & Co.
Moody Foundation
Moog Automotive, Inc.
Moore Business Forms, Inc.
Moore Charitable Foundation,
  Marjorie
Moore Charitable Foundation,
  Marjorie
Moore Family Foundation
Moore Foundation
Moore Foundation, C. F.
Moore Foundation, Edward S.
Moore Foundation, Martha G.
Moore Foundation, Roy C.
Moores Foundation
Moores Foundation, Harry C.
Moorman Manufacturing Co.
Morania Foundation
Morgan and Samuel Tate
  Morgan, Jr. Foundation,
  Marietta McNeil
Morgan Foundation, Burton D.
Morgan Stanley & Co.
Morgan Trust for Charity,
  Religion, and Education
Morgenstern Foundation, Morris
Morley Brothers Foundation
Morrill Charitable Foundation
Morris Charitable Foundation, E.
  A.
Morris Charitable Trust, Charles
  M.
Morris Foundation
Morris Foundation, Margaret T.
Morris Foundation, Norman M.
Morris Foundation, William T.
Morrison Foundation, Harry W.
Morrison-Knudsen Corp.
Morse Foundation, Richard P.
  and Claire W.
Morse, Jr. Foundation, Enid and
  Lester S.
Morton International
Mosbacher, Jr. Foundation, Emil
Mosher Foundation, Samuel B.
Mosinee Paper Corp.

Moskowitz Foundation, Irving I.
Moss Foundation, Harry S.
Motch Corp.
Motorola
Mott Foundation, Charles Stewart
Mott Fund, Ruth
MTS Systems Corp.
Mulcahy Foundation
Mulford Foundation, Vincent
Mulford Trust, Clarence E.
Mullen Foundation, J. K.
Muller Foundation
Mulligan Charitable Trust, Mary
  S.
Multimedia, Inc.
Munger Foundation, Alfred C.
Munson Foundation, W. B.
Murch Foundation
Murdock Charitable Trust, M. J.
Murdy Foundation
Murphey Foundation, Lluella
  Morey
Murphy Co., G.C.
Murphy Foundation
Murphy Foundation, Dan
Murphy Foundation, John P.
Murphy Foundation, Katherine
  and John
Murray Foundation
Musson Charitable Foundation,
  R. C. and Katharine M.
Myra Foundation
Nalco Chemical Co.
Nanney Foundation, Charles and
  Irene
Nashua Trust Co.
Nason Foundation
Nathan Foundation
National By-Products
National City Bank of Evansville
National City Corp.
National Computer Systems
National Fuel Gas Co.
National Gypsum Co.
National Life of Vermont
National Machinery Co.
National Presto Industries
National Pro-Am Youth Fund
National Service Industries
National Starch & Chemical
  Corp.
National Steel
National Westminster Bank New
  Jersey
Nationale-Nederlanden North
  America Corp.
Nationwide Insurance Cos.
Navajo Refining Co.
NBD Bank
NBD Bank, N.A.
NCR Corp.
Neenah Foundry Co.
Negaunee Foundation
Neilson Foundation, George W.
Nelco Sewing Machine Sales
  Corp.
Nelson Foundation, Florence
Nelson Industries, Inc.
Nesholm Family Foundation
Nestle U.S.A. Inc.
Neuberger Foundation, Roy R.
  and Marie S.
New Cycle Foundation
New England Biolabs Foundation
New England Foundation
New England Mutual Life
  Insurance Co.
New England Telephone Co.
New Horizon Foundation
New-Land Foundation
New Street Capital Corp.
New York Foundation
New York Life Insurance Co.
New York Mercantile Exchange
New York Stock Exchange
New York Telephone Co.
New York Times Co.

Youth Organizations (cont.)

The New Yorker Magazine, Inc.
Newhall Foundation, Henry Mayo
Newhouse Foundation, Samuel I.
Newman Assistance Fund, Jerome A. and Estelle R.
Newman Charitable Trust, Calvin M. and Raquel H.
Newman's Own
Newmil Bancorp
News & Observer Publishing Co.
Nias Foundation, Henry
Nichols Foundation
Nike Inc.
Nissan Motor Corporation in U.S.A.
Noble Foundation, Edward John
Noble Foundation, Samuel Roberts
Noble Foundation, Vivian Bilby
Nord Family Foundation
Nordson Corp.
Norfolk Southern Corp.
Norgren Foundation, Carl A.
Norman/Nethercutt Foundation, Merle
Norris Foundation, Dellora A. and Lester J.
Norris Foundation, Kenneth T. and Eileen L.
North American Life & Casualty Co.
North American Philips Corp.
North Carolina Foam Foundation
North Shore Foundation
Northeast Utilities
Northern Indiana Public Service Co.
Northern Star Foundation
Northern States Power Co.
Northern Trust Co.
Northwest Natural Gas Co.
Northwestern National Insurance Group
Northwestern National Life Insurance Co.
Norton Co.
Norton Foundation Inc.
Norton Memorial Corporation, Geraldi
Norwest Bank Nebraska
Norwest Bank Nebraska
Noyes, Jr. Memorial Foundation, Nicholas H.
Number Ten Foundation
NuTone Inc.
NutraSweet Co.
Oaklawn Foundation
Oakley Foundation, Hollie and Anna
Oberlaender Foundation, Gustav
Obernauer Foundation
O'Bleness Foundation, Charles G.
O'Brien Foundation, Cornelius and Anna Cook
Occidental Petroleum Corp.
O'Connor Co.
O'Connor Foundation, A. Lindsay and Olive B.
O'Connor Foundation, Magee
OCRI Foundation
Odell and Helen Pfeiffer Odell Fund, Robert Stewart
Oestreicher Foundation, Sylvan and Ann
O'Fallon Trust, Martin J. and Mary Anne
Offield Family Foundation
Ogden Foundation, Ralph E.
Ogilvy & Mather Worldwide
Oglebay Norton Co.
Ohio Valley Foundation
Ohl, Jr. Trust, George A.
Ohrstrom Foundation

Oklahoma Gas & Electric Co.
Oklahoman Foundation
Old Dominion Box Co.
Old National Bank in Evansville
Oleson Foundation
Olin Charitable Trust, John M.
Olin Corp.
Olive Bridge Fund
Oliver Memorial Trust Foundation
Olmsted Foundation, George and Carol
Olsson Memorial Foundation, Elis
Olympia Brewing Co.
Onan Family Foundation
1525 Foundation
1957 Charity Trust
1939 Foundation
O'Neil Foundation, Casey Albert T.
O'Neil Foundation, Cyril F. and Marie E.
O'Neil Foundation, M. G.
O'Neill Charitable Corporation, F. J.
Ontario Corp.
Ontario Corp.
Oppenheimer and Flora Oppenheimer Haas Trust, Leo
Oppenstein Brothers Foundation
Orange Orphan Society
Ordean Foundation
Ore-Ida Foods, Inc.
Orleans Trust, Carrie S.
Orleton Trust Fund
Ormet Corp.
Osborn Charitable Trust, Edward B.
Osborn Manufacturing Co.
OsCo. Industries
O'Shaughnessy Foundation, I. A.
Oshkosh B'Gosh
Oshkosh Truck Corp.
O'Sullivan Children Foundation
Overbrook Foundation
Overlake Foundation
Overseas Shipholding Group
Overstreet Foundation
Owen Industries, Inc.
Owen Trust, B. B.
Owens-Corning Fiberglas Corp.
Owsley Foundation, Alvin and Lucy
Oxford Foundation
Oxford Foundation
PACCAR
Pacific Gas & Electric Co.
Pacific Mutual Life Insurance Co.
Pacific Telesis Group
Pacific Western Foundation
PacifiCorp
Packaging Corporation of America
Packard Foundation, David and Lucile
Packer Foundation, Horace B.
Padnos Iron & Metal Co., Louis
Page Foundation, George B.
Paley Foundation, William S.
Palin Foundation
Palisades Educational Foundation
Palmer-Fry Memorial Trust, Lily
Palmer Fund, Frank Loomis
Pan-American Life Insurance Co.
Pangburn Foundation
Pappas Charitable Foundation, Thomas Anthony
Parke-Davis Group
Parker Drilling Co.
Parker Foundation
Parker Foundation, Theodore Edson
Parker-Hannifin Corp.
Parman Foundation, Robert A.
Parshelsky Foundation, Moses L.

Parsons Foundation, Ralph M.
Parsons - W.D. Charities, Vera Davis
Pasadena Area Residential Aid
Patterson-Barclay Memorial Foundation
Patterson Charitable Fund, W. I.
Paulucci Family Foundation
PayLess Drug Stores
Payne Foundation, Frank E. and Seba B.
Peabody Charitable Fund, Amelia
Peabody Foundation, Amelia
Pearlstone Foundation, Peggy Meyerhoff
Pearson Foundation, E. M.
Peerless Insurance Co.
Peery Foundation
Peierls Foundation
Pella Corp.
Pellegrino-Realmuto Charitable Foundation
PemCo. Corp.
Pendleton Construction Corp.
Pendleton Memorial Fund, William L. and Ruth T.
Penn Foundation, William
Penn Savings Bank, a division of Sovereign Bank Bank of Princeton, a division of Sovereign Bank
Penney Foundation, James C.
Pennington Foundation, Irene W. and C. B.
Pennsylvania Dutch Co.
Pennzoil Co.
Penzance Foundation
People's Bank
Peoples Energy Corp.
Peppers Foundation, Ann
Pepsi-Cola Bottling Co. of Charlotte
Perini Corp.
Perini Foundation, Joseph
Perkin-Elmer Corp.
Perkin Fund
Perkins Charitable Foundation
Perkins Foundation, Joe and Lois
Perkins Memorial Foundation, George W.
Perley Fund, Victor E.
Perot Foundation
Perpetual Benevolent Fund
Persis Corp.
Pesch Family Foundation
Pet
Peterloon Foundation
Peters Foundation, Charles F.
Peters Foundation, Leon S.
Petersen Foundation, Esper A.
Peterson Foundation, Fred J.
Pettus, Jr. Foundation, James T.
Pew Charitable Trusts
Pfizer
Pfriem Foundation, Norma F.
Phelps, Inc.
Phelps Dodge Corp.
PHH Corp.
Philadelphia Industries
Philibosian Foundation, Stephen
Philips Foundation, Jesse
Phillips Charitable Trust, Dr. and Mrs. Arthur William
Phillips Family Foundation, Jay and Rose
Phillips Family Foundation, L. E.
Phillips Foundation, A. P.
Phillips Foundation, Dr. P.
Phillips Foundation, Waite and Genevieve
Phillips Petroleum Co.
Phipps Foundation, Howard
Phipps Foundation, William H.
Physicians Mutual Insurance
Piankova Foundation, Tatiana
Pick Charitable Trust, Melitta S.
Pick, Jr. Fund, Albert

Picker International
Pickford Foundation, Mary
Piedmont Health Care Foundation
Pierce Charitable Trust, Harold Whitworth
Pillsbury Foundation
Pilot Trust
Pineywoods Foundation
Pinkerton Foundation
Pioneer Electronics (USA) Inc.
Pioneer Fund
Pioneer Trust Bank, NA
Piper Foundation, Minnie Stevens
Piper Jaffray Cos.
Piton Foundation
Pitt-Des Moines Inc.
Pittsburgh Child Guidance Foundation
Pittsburgh National Bank
Pittulloch Foundation
Pittway Corp.
Pitzman Fund
Plankenhorn Foundation, Harry
Plantronics, Inc.
Playboy Enterprises, Inc.
Plitt Southern Theatres
Plough Foundation
Plumsock Fund
Plym Foundation
Poinsettia Foundation, Paul and Magdalena Ecke
Polinsky-Rivkin Family Foundation
Pollock Company Foundation, William B.
Pollybill Foundation
Porsche Cars North America, Inc.
Portland General Electric Co.
Post Foundation of D.C., Marjorie Merriweather
Potlatch Corp.
Potomac Electric Power Co.
Pott Foundation, Herman T. and Phenie R.
Potter Foundation, Justin and Valere
Pottstown Mercury
Powell Co., William
Powell Family Foundation
Powers Foundation
PPG Industries
Prairie Foundation
Prange Co., H. C.
Pratt Memorial Fund
Precision Rubber Products
Premier Bank
Premier Industrial Corp.
Preston Trust, Evelyn W.
Price Associates, T. Rowe
Price Foundation, Louis and Harold
Prickett Fund, Lynn R. and Karl E.
Priddy Foundation
Primerica Corp.
Prince Corp.
Prince Trust, Abbie Norman
Principal Financial Group
Pritzker Foundation
Procter & Gamble Co.
Procter & Gamble Cosmetic & Fragrance Products
Proctor Trust, Mortimer R.
Prouty Foundation, Olive Higgins
Providence Energy Corp.
Providence Journal Company
Provident Life & Accident Insurance Co.
Provigo Corp. Inc.
Prudential-Bache Securities
Prudential Insurance Co. of America
PSI Energy
Public Service Co. of Colorado
Public Service Co. of New Mexico

Public Service Electric & Gas Co.
Pulitzer Publishing Co.
Puterbaugh Foundation
Pyramid Foundation
Quabaug Corp.
Quaker Chemical Corp.
Quaker Oats Co.
Quality Metal Finishing Foundation
Quanex Corp.
Questar Corp.
Quincy Newspapers
Quinlan Foundation, Elizabeth C.
R. P. Foundation
R&B Tool Co.
Rabb Charitable Trust, Sidney R.
Rabb Foundation, Harry W.
Radiator Specialty Co.
Ragen, Jr. Memorial Fund Trust No. 1, James M.
Raker Foundation, M. E.
Ralston Purina Co.
Ramapo Trust
Ramlose Foundation, George A.
Randa
Rankin and Elizabeth Forbes Rankin Trust, William
Ransom Fidelity Company
Raskin Foundation, Hirsch and Braine
Raskob Foundation for Catholic Activities
Rasmussen Foundation
Ratshesky Foundation, A. C.
Rauch Foundation
Ray Foundation
Raymond Corp.
Raytheon Co.
Read Foundation, Charles L.
Rebsamen Companies, Inc.
Recognition Equipment
Red Devil
Red Wing Shoe Co.
Redfield Foundation, Nell J.
Reed Foundation, Philip D.
Regenstein Foundation
Regis Corp.
Reichhold Chemicals, Inc.
Reidler Foundation
Reilly Industries
Reily & Co., William B.
Reinberger Foundation
Reinhart Institutional Foods
Reinhold Foundation, Paul E. and Ida Klare
Relations Foundation
Reliable Life Insurance Co.
Reliance Electric Co.
Rennebohm Foundation, Oscar
Replogle Foundation, Luther I.
Republic New York Corp.
Revson Foundation, Charles H.
Rexham Inc.
Reynolds Foundation, Donald W.
Reynolds Foundation, Edgar
Reynolds Foundation, Eleanor T.
Reynolds Foundation, J. B.
Reynolds Metals Co.
Rhodebeck Charitable Trust
Rhoden Charitable Foundation, Elmer C.
Rhone-Poulenc Inc.
Rice Charitable Foundation, Albert W.
Rice Foundation
Rice Foundation, Helen Steiner
Rich Co., F.D.
Rich Foundation
Rich Products Corp.
Richardson Benevolent Foundation, C. E.
Richardson Charitable Trust, Anne S.
Richardson Foundation, Sid W.
Richardson Fund, Mary Lynn

Richmond Foundation, Frederick W.
Ridgefield Foundation
Rieke Corp.
Rienzi Foundation
Riggs Benevolent Fund
Riley Foundation, Mabel Louise
Ringier-America
Rinker Materials Corp.
Ritchie Memorial Foundation, Charies E. and Mabel M.
Rite-Hite Corp.
Rittenhouse Foundation
Ritter Charitable Trust, George W. & Mary F.
Ritter Foundation, May Ellen and Gerald
River Branch Foundation
RJR Nabisco Inc.
Roberts Foundation
Roberts Foundation, Dora
Robertshaw Controls Co.
Robin Family Foundation, Albert A.
Robinson Foundation
Robinson Fund, Charles Nelson
Robison Foundation, Ellis H. and Doris B.
Roblee Foundation, Joseph H. and Florence A.
Robson Foundation, LaNelle
Roche Relief Foundation, Edward and Ellen
Rockford Acromatics Products Co./Aircraft Gear Corp.
Rockford Products Corp.
Rockwell Foundation
Rockwell Fund
Rockwell International Corp.
Roddis Foundation, Hamilton
Rodgers Foundation, Richard & Dorothy
Rodman Foundation
Rogers Charitable Trust, Florence
Rogers Family Foundation
Rogers Foundation
Rogers Foundation
Rogers Foundation, Mary Stuart
Rohm and Haas Company
Rohr Inc.
Rolfs Foundation, Robert T.
Romill Foundation
Rose Foundation, Billy
Roseburg Forest Products Co.
Rosenberg Foundation, Alexis
Rosenberg Foundation, William J. and Tina
Rosenthal Foundation, Benjamin J.
Rosenthal Foundation, Ida and William
Rosenthal Foundation, Richard and Hinda
Rosenthal Foundation, Richard and Lois
Rosenwald Family Fund, William
Ross Foundation
Ross Foundation
Ross Foundation, Lyn & George M.
Ross Foundation, Walter G.
Ross Laboratories
Ross Memorial Foundation, Will
Roth Family Foundation
Roth Foundation, Louis T.
Rouse Co.
Royal Group Inc.
RTM
Ruan Foundation Trust, John
Rubbermaid
Rubenstein Foundation, Philip
Rubin Family Fund, Cele H. and William B.
Rubin Foundation, Rob E. & Judith O.
Rubinstein Foundation, Helena
Ruddick Corp.
Rudin Foundation

Rudy, Jr. Trust, George B.
Ruffin Foundation, Peter B. & Adeline W.
Rukin Philanthropic Foundation, David and Eleanore
Rupp Foundation, Fran and Warren
Russ Togs
Russell Charitable Foundation, Tom
Russell Charitable Trust, Josephine S.
Russell Educational Foundation, Benjamin and Roberta
Russell Trust, Josephine G.
Ryan Family Charitable Foundation
Ryan Foundation, David Claude
Ryan Foundation, Nina M.
Ryan Foundation, Patrick G. and Shirley W.
Ryder System
Sachs Fund
Saemann Foundation, Franklin I.
SAFECO Corp.
Safeguard Scientifics Foundation
Sage Foundation
Saint Croix Foundation
St. Faith's House Foundation
Saint Paul Cos.
Salomon
Saltonstall Charitable Foundation, Richard
Salwil Foundation
Sams Foundation, Earl C.
San Diego Gas & Electric
San Diego Trust & Savings Bank
Sanders Trust, Charles
Sandusky International Inc.
Sandy Foundation, George H.
Sandy Hill Foundation
Sanguinetti Foundation, Annunziata
Santa Fe Pacific Corp.
Sara Lee Corp.
Sara Lee Hosiery
Sarkeys Foundation
Sasco Foundation
Saturno Foundation
Saunders Foundation
Sequa Corp.
Scaife Family Foundation
Schadt Foundation
Schaffer Foundation, Michael & Helen
Schautz Foundation, Walter L.
Schenck Fund, L. P.
Scherer Foundation, Karla
Schering-Plough Corp.
Scherman Foundation
Schermer Charitable Trust, Frances
Scheuer Family Foundation, S. H. and Helen R.
Schey Foundation
Schiff Foundation
Schiff Foundation, Dorothy
Schiff, Hardin & Waite
Schilling Motors
Schiro Fund
Schmidlapp Trust No. 1, Jacob G.
Schmidlapp Trust No. 2, Jacob G.
Schmitt Foundation, Arthur J.
Schneider Foundation Corp., Al J.
Schoenbaum Family Foundation
Scholl Foundation, Dr.
Schoonmaker J-Sewkly Valley Hospital Trust
Schrafft and Bertha E. Schrafft Charitable Trust, William E.
Schramm Foundation
Schroeder Foundation, Walter
Schultz Foundation
Schultz Foundation
Schust Foundation, Clarence L. and Edith B.
Schwab & Co., Charles
Schwartz Foundation, Arnold A.

Schwartz Foundation, David
Schwartz Fund for Education and Health Research, Arnold and Marie
Scott and Fetzer Co.
Scott Foundation, William E.
Scott Foundation, William R., John G., and Emma
Scott, Jr. Charitable Foundation, Walter
Scoular Co.
Scripps Foundation, Ellen Browning
Scrivner, Inc.
Scrivner of North Carolina Inc.
Scroggins Foundation, Arthur E. and Cornelia C.
SCT Yarns
Scurlock Foundation
Scurry Foundation, D. L.
Seabury Foundation
Seafirst Corp.
Seagram & Sons, Joseph E.
Sealright Co., Inc.
Searle & Co., G.D.
Seaver Institute
Seaway Food Town
Seay Charitable Trust, Sarah M. and Charles E.
Seay Memorial Trust, George and Effie
Sebastian Foundation
Second Foundation
Security Benefit Life Insurance Co.
Security Life of Denver
Security State Bank
Segal Charitable Trust, Barnet
Segerstrom Foundation
Seid Foundation, Barre
Seidman Family Foundation
Selby and Marie Selby Foundation, William G.
Self Foundation
Semmes Foundation
Semple Foundation, Louise Taft
Seneca Foods Corp.
Sentinel Communications Co.
Sentry Insurance Co.
Sequa Corp.
Sequoia Foundation
Setzer Foundation
Seven Springs Foundation
Sewall Foundation, Elmina
Sexton Foundation
Seybert Institution for Poor Boys and Girls, Adam and Maria Sarah
Seymour Foundation, W. L. and Louise E.
Shafer Foundation, Richard H. and Ann
Shaklee Corp.
Shapero Foundation, Nate S. and Ruth B.
Shapiro Family Foundation, Soretta and Henry
Shapiro Foundation, Charles and M. R.
Share Foundation
Share Trust, Charles Morton
Sharon Steel Corp.
Sharp Electronics Corp.
Sharp Foundation, Charles S. and Ruth C.
Sharp Foundation, Evelyn
Shattuck Charitable Trust, S. F.
Shaw Foundation, Arch W.
Shawmut National Corp.
Shaw's Supermarkets
Shea, er Inc.
Sheinberg Foundation, Eric P.
Shelden Fund, Elizabeth, Allan and Warren
Sheldon Foundation, Ralph C.
Shell Oil Co.
Shelter Mutual Insurance Co.
Shelton Cos.

Shemanski Testamentary Trust, Tillie and Alfred
Shenandoah Life Insurance Co.
Sheppard Foundation, Lawrence B.
Sheridan Foundation, Thomas B. and Elizabeth M.
Sherwin-Williams Co.
Shiffman Foundation
Shirk Foundation, Russell and Betty
Shoemaker Fund, Thomas H. and Mary Williams
Shoenberg Foundation
Shoney's Inc.
Shoong Foundation, Milton
Shorenstein Foundation, Walter H. and Phyllis J.
Shughart, Thomson & Kilroy, P.C.
Siebert Lutheran Foundation
Sierra Pacific Industries
Sierra Pacific Resources
Sifco Industries Inc.
Signet Bank/Maryland
Simmons Family Foundation, R. P.
Simon Foundation, Robert Ellis
Simon Foundation, Sidney, Milton and Leoma
Simon Foundation, William E. and Carol G.
Simpson Foundation
Simpson Foundation, John M.
Simpson Investment Co.
Sioux Steel Co.
Siragusa Foundation
SIT Investment Associates, Inc.
Sizzler International
Sjostrom & Sons
Skillman Foundation
Skinner Corp.
Skirball Foundation
Slant/Fin Corp.
Slaughter, Jr. Foundation, William E.
Slemp Foundation
Slifka Foundation, Alan B.
Slifka Foundation, Joseph and Sylvia
Slusher Charitable Foundation, Roy W.
Smeal Foundation, Mary Jean & Frank P.
Smith and W. Aubrey Smith Charitable Foundation, Clara Blackford
Smith Barney, Harris Upham & Co.
Smith Charitable Foundation, Lou and Lutza
Smith Charitable Trust
Smith Charitable Trust, W. W.
Smith Corp., A.O.
Smith Family Foundation, Theda Clark
Smith Foundation
Smith Foundation, Bob and Vivian
Smith Foundation, Gordon V. and Helen C.
Smith Foundation, Kelvin and Eleanor
Smith Foundation, Lon V.
Smith, Jr. Charitable Trust, Jack J.
Smith, Jr. Foundation, M. W.
Smith Memorial Fund, Ethel Sergeant Clark
Smith 1963 Charitable Trust, Don McQueen
Smithers Foundation, Christopher D.
SmithKline Beecham
Smoot Charitable Foundation
Smucker Co., J.M.
Snee-Reinhardt Charitable Foundation
SNET

Snite Foundation, Fred B.
Snow Foundation, John Ben
Snow Memorial Trust, John Ben
Snyder Charitable Fund, W. P.
Snyder Fund, Valentine Perry
Solheim Foundation
Solo Cup Co.
Solow Foundation
Solow Foundation, Sheldon H.
Somers Foundation, Byron H.
Sonat
Sonoco Products Co.
Sony Corp. of America
Sooner Pipe & Supply Corp.
Sordoni Foundation
Soref Foundation, Samuel M. Soref and Helene K.
Sosland Foundation
Sotheby's
Souers Charitable Trust, Sidney W. and Sylvia N.
South Bend Tribune
South Carolina Electric & Gas Co.
South Waite Foundation
Southern California Edison Co.
Southern Furniture Co.
Southways Foundation
Southwest Gas Corp.
Southwestern Bell Corp.
Spahn & Rose Lumber Co.
Spang & Co.
Special People In Need
Spectra-Physics Analytical
Sperry Fund
Spiegel
Spingold Foundation, Nate B. and Frances
Spiritus Gladius Foundation
Sprague Educational and Charitable Foundation, Seth
Springs Foundation
Springs Industries
Sprint
SPS Technologies
Spunk Fund
SPX Corp.
Square D Co.
Stabler Foundation, Donald B. and Dorothy L.
Stackner Family Foundation
Stackpole-Hall Foundation
Staley, Jr. Foundation, A. E.
Staley Manufacturing Co., A.E.
Stamps Foundation, James L.
Standard Products Co.
Standard Register Co.
Standard Steel Speciality Co.
Stanley Charitable Foundation, A. W.
Stanley Works
Star Bank, N.A.
Starr Foundation
Starrett Co., L.S.
State Street Bank & Trust Co.
Statter Foundation, Amy Plant
Stauffer Communications
Stauffer Foundation, John and Beverly
Stearns Charitable Foundation, Anna B.
Stearns Trust, Artemas W.
Steel, Sr. Foundation, Marshall
Steelcase
Steele Foundation
Steele Foundation, Harry and Grace
Steele-Reese Foundation
Steiger Memorial Fund, Albert
Stein Foundation, Joseph F.
Stein Foundation, Jules and Doris
Steinberg Family Foundation, Meyer and Jean
Steiner Corp.
Steinhagen Benevolent Trust, B. A. and Elinor

Youth Organizations (cont.)

Steinhardt Foundation, Judy and Michael
Steinman Foundation, James Hale
Steinman Foundation, John Frederick
Steinsapir Family Foundation, Julius L. and Libhie B.
Stella D'Oro Biscuit Co.
Stemmons Foundation
Sterkel Trust, Justine
Sterling Inc.
Sterling Winthrop
Stern Family Foundation, Alex
Stern Family Foundation, Harry
Stern Family Fund
Stern Foundation, Irvin
Stern Foundation, Leonard N.
Stern Memorial Trust, Sidney
Sternberger Foundation, Sigmund
Sterne-Elder Memorial Trust
Stevens Foundation, Abbot and Dorothy H.
Stevens Foundation, John T.
Stevens Foundation, Nathaniel and Elizabeth P.
Stewards Fund
Stewardship Foundation
Stewart Educational Foundation, Donnell B. and Elizabeth Dee Shaw
Stewart Trust under the will of Helen S. Devore, Alexander and Margaret
Stillwell Charitable Trust, Glen and Dorothy
Stock Foundation, Paul
Stocker Foundation
Stoddard Charitable Trust
Stokely. Jr. Foundation, William B.
Stone Charitable Foundation
Stone Container Corp.
Stone Family Foundation, Norman H.
Stone Foundation, David S.
Stone Foundation, France
Stone Trust, H. Chase
Stonecutter Mills Corp.
Stoneman Charitable Foundation, Anne and David
Stonestreet Trust, Eusebia S.
Storage Technology Corp.
Storer Foundation, George B.
Stott Foundation, Louis L.
Stowe, Jr. Foundation, Robert Lee
Strake Foundation
Stranahan Foundation
Straus Foundation, Aaron and Lillie
Straus Foundation, Martha Washington Straus and Harry H.
Straus Foundation, Philip A. and Lynn
Strauss Foundation
Strauss Foundation, Leon
Strong Foundation, Hattie M.
Stuart Center Charitable Trust, Hugh
Stuart Foundation
Stubblefield, Estate of Joseph L.
Stulsaft Foundation, Morris
Stupp Foundation, Norman J.
Sturgis Charitable and Educational Trust, Roy and Christine
Subaru of America Inc.
Sulzer Family Foundation
Sumitomo Bank of California
Sumitomo Corp. of America
Summerfield Foundation, Solon E.

Sumners Foundation, Hatton W.
Sun Co.
Sunderland Foundation, Lester T.
Sundstrand Corp.
Sunnen Foundation
Super Valu Stores
Superior Tube Co.
Surdna Foundation
Surrena Memorial Fund, Harry and Thelma
Susquehanna Investment Group
Susquehanna-Pfaltzgraff Co.
Swalm Foundation
Swanson Family Foundation, Dr. W.C.
Swanson Foundation
Sweatt Foundation, Harold W.
Sweet Life Foods
Swift Co. Inc., John S.
Swig Charity Foundation, Mae and Benjamin
Swig Foundation
Swisher Foundation, Carl S.
Swiss American Securities, Inc.
Swiss Bank Corp.
Synovus Financial Corp.
Tait Foundation, Frank M.
Talley Industries, Inc.
Tamko Asphalt Products
Tandem Computers
Tandy Foundation, Anne Burnett and Charles
Tandy Foundation, David L.
Tang Foundation
Tanner Cos.
Taub Foundation
Taub Foundation, Henry and Marilyn
Taubman Foundation, A. Alfred
Taubman Foundation, Herman P. and Sophia
Taylor Foundation
Taylor Foundation, Fred and Harriett
Taylor Foundation, Ruth and Vernon
TCF Banking & Savings, FSB
TDK Corp. of America
Teagle Foundation
Teichert
Teledyne
Teleflex Inc.
Teleklew Productions
Temple Foundation, T. L. L.
Temple-Inland
Templeton Foundation, Herbert A.
Tennant Co.
Tenneco
Tension Envelope Corp.
Terner Foundation
Terry Foundation, C. Herman
Tetley, Inc.
Teubert Charitable Trust, James H. and Alice
Texaco
Texas Commerce Bank Houston, N.A.
Texas Gas Transmission Corp.
Texas Instruments
Textron
Thagard Foundation
Thalheimer Foundation, Alvin and Fanny Blaustein
Thalhimer and Family Foundation, Charles G.
Thalhimer, Jr. and Family Foundation, William B.
Thanksgiving Foundation
Thomas & Betts Corp.
Thomas Built Buses L.P.
Thomas Foundation, Dorothy
Thomas Foundation, Joan and Lee
Thomas Industries
Thomas Memorial Foundation, Theresa A.
Thomasville Furniture Industries

Thorne Foundation
Thornton Foundation
Thorpe Foundation, James R.
Thorson Foundation
Three Swallows Foundation
3M Co.
Thrush-Thompson Foundation
Thurman Charitable Foundation for Children, Edgar A.
Thurston Charitable Foundation
Thyssen Specialty Steels
Time Insurance Co.
Times Mirror Co.
Timken Foundation of Canton
Timmis Foundation, Michael & Nancy
Tisch Foundation
Tiscornia Foundation
Titmus Foundation
Titus Foundation, C. W.
Tobin Foundation
Todd Co., A.M.
Tokheim Corp.
Tomkins Industries, Inc.
Tomlinson Foundation, Kate and Elwyn
Toms Foundation
Tonkin Foundation, Tom and Helen
Tonya Memorial Foundation
Torchmark Corp.
Tosco Corp. Refining Division
Towsley Foundation, Harry A. and Margaret D.
Tozer Foundation
Tracor, Inc.
Tractor & Equipment Co.
Transco Energy Company
Travelers Cos.
Treakle Foundation, J. Edwin
Treuhaft Foundation
Trexler Trust, Harry C.
Trimble Family Foundation, Robert Mize and Isa White
TRINOVA Corp.
Tropicana Products, Inc.
True Oil Co.
True Trust, Henry A.
Trull Foundation
Truman Foundation, Mildred Faulkner
Trusler Foundation
Trust Co. Bank
Trust Funds
TRW Corp.
Tuch Foundation, Michael
Tucker Charitable Trust, Rose E.
Tucker Foundation, Marcia Brady
Tucson Electric Power Co.
Tull Charitable Foundation
Tuohy Foundation, Alice Tweed
Tupancy-Harris Foundation of 1986
Turner Charitable Trust, Courtney S.
Turner Fund, Ruth
Turrell Fund
Twentieth Century-Fox Film Corp.
21 International Holdings
Tyndale House Foundation
Tyson Foods, Inc.
Ukrop's Super Markets, Inc.
Unilever United States
Union Bank
Union Bank of Switzerland Los Angeles Branch
Union Camp Corp.
Union Carbide Corp.
Union Electric Co.
Union Foundation
Union Manufacturing Co.
Union Pacific Corp.
United Airlines
United Co.
United Conveyor Corp.

United Dominion Industries
United Merchants & Manufacturers
U.S. Leasing International
U.S. Oil/Schmidt Family Foundation, Inc.
U.S. Silica Co.
United States Sugar Corp.
United States Trust Co. of New York
United Technologies Corp.
United Togs Inc.
Unitrode Corp.
Universal Foods Corp.
Universal Leaf Tobacco Co.
Unocal Corp.
Upjohn California Fund
Upjohn Foundation, Harold and Grace
Upton Charitable Foundation, Lucy and Eleanor S.
Upton Foundation, Frederick S.
Uris Brothers Foundation
US Bancorp
US WEST
USF&G Co.
USG Corp.
Uslico Corp.
USX Corp.
Utilicorp United
Valdese Manufacturing Co., Inc.
Valley Foundation
Valley Foundation, Wayne and Gladys
Valley National Bancorp
Valley National Bank of Arizona
Valmont Industries
Valspar Corp.
van Ameringen Foundation
Van Andel Foundation, Jay and Betty
Van Camp Foundation
Van Every Foundation, Philip L.
Van Houten Charitable Trust
van Loben Sels - Eleanor Slate van Lobel Sels Charitable Foundation, Ernst D.
Van Nuys Charities, J. B. and Emily
Van Nuys Foundation, I. N. and Susanna H.
Van Wert County Foundation
Vance Charitable Foundation, Robert C.
Vanderbilt Trust, R. T.
Vanneck-Bailey Foundation
Varian Associates
Vaughan Foundation, Rachael and Ben
Vaughn Foundation
Veritas Foundation
Vermeer Investment Company Foundation
Vernon Fund, Miles Hodsdon
Vesper Corp.
Vicksburg Foundation
Victoria Foundation
Vidda Foundation
Vilter Manufacturing Corp.
Virginia Power Co.
Vlasic Foundation
Voelkerding Charitable Trust, Walter and Jean
Vogt Machine Co., Henry
Vollbrecht Foundation, Frederick A.
Von der Ahe Foundation
Vulcan Materials Co.
W. W. W. Foundation
Wachovia Bank of Georgia, N.A.
Wachovia Bank & Trust Co., N.A.
Wade Endowment Fund, Elizabeth Firth
Waffle House, Inc.
Waggoner Charitable Trust, Crystelle

Waggoner Foundation, E. Paul and Helen Buck
Wagner Manufacturing Co., E. R.
Wahlert Foundation
Wal-Mart Stores
Waldbaum, Inc.
Waldbaum Family Foundation, I.
Walgreen Co.
Walker Foundation, L. C. and Margaret
Walker Foundation, Smith
Walker Foundation, T. B.
Walker Foundation, W. E.
Wallace Computer Services
Wallace Foundation, George R.
Wallace-Reader's Digest Fund, DeWitt
Wallach Foundation, Miriam G. and Ira D.
Walsh Foundation
Disney Co., Walt
Walter Family Trust, Byron L.
Walter Industries
Ward Co., Joe L.
Ward Foundation, A. Montgomery
Ward Foundation, Louis L. and Adelaide C.
Wardlaw Fund, Gertrude and William C.
Wardle Family Foundation
Ware Foundation
Wareheim Foundation, E. C.
Warner Electric Brake & Clutch Co.
Warner Fund, Albert and Bessie
Warren Foundation, William K.
Warsh-Mott Legacy
Washington Forrest Foundation
Washington Foundation
Washington Mutual Savings Bank
Washington Post Co.
Washington Square Fund
Washington Trust Bank
Washington Water Power Co.
Wasily Family Foundation
Wasmer Foundation
Wasserman Foundation, George
Watkins Christian Foundation
Watson Foundation, Walter E. and Caroline H.
Wausau Paper Mills Co.
Wauwatosa Savings & Loan Association
Wean Foundation, Raymond John
Weatherwax Foundation
Weaver Foundation
Weaver Foundation, Gil and Dody
Webb Charitable Trust, Susan Mott
Webb Educational and Charitable Trust, Torrey H. and Dorothy K.
Webb Foundation
Webber Oil Co.
Weber Charities Corp., Frederick E.
Webster Charitable Foundation
Webster Foundation, Edwin S.
Weckbaugh Foundation, Eleanore Mullen
Weezie Foundation
Wege Foundation
Wegener Foundation, Herman and Mary
Wehadkee Foundation
Weinberg Foundation, John L.
Weinberg, Jr. Foundation, Sidney J.
Weiner Foundation
Weingart Foundation
Weininger Foundation, Richard and Gertrude
Weir Foundation Trust
Weisbrod Foundation Trust Dept., Robert and Mary

Weiss Foundation, Stephen and
   Suzanne
Weiss Foundation, William E.
Weiss Fund, Clara
Weisz Foundation, David and
   Sylvia
Welfare Foundation
Wells Fargo & Co.
Wells Foundation, A. Z.
Wells Foundation, Franklin H.
   and Ruth L.
Wendt Foundation, Margaret L.
Wenger Foundation, Henry L.
   and Consuelo S.
Werthan Foundation
Wessinger Foundation
West Co.
West Foundation
West One Bancorp
Westend Foundation
Westerman Foundation, Samuel
   L.
Western New York Foundation
Western Resources
Western Shade Cloth Charitable
   Foundation
Westinghouse Electric Corp.
Westport Fund
Westvaco Corp.
Westwood Endowment
Wetterau
Weyerhaeuser Co.
Weyerhaeuser Foundation,
   Frederick and Margaret L.
Whalley Charitable Trust
Wharton Foundation
Wheat First Securites

Wheeler Foundation
Wheeler Foundation, Wilmot
Wheless Foundation
Whirlpool Corp.
Whitaker Charitable Foundation,
   Lyndon C.
Whitaker Foundation
White Construction Co.
White Foundation, Erle and
   Emma
White Trust, G. R.
Whitehead Foundation
Whitehead Foundation, Joseph B.
Whiteley Foundation, John and
   Elizabeth
Whiteman Foundation, Edna
   Rider
Whiteman Foundation, Edna
   Rider
Whitener Foundation
Whiting Foundation
Whiting Memorial Foundation,
   Henry and Harriet
Whitney Benefits
Whitney Fund, David M.
Whittenberger Foundation,
   Claude R. and Ethel B.
Whittier Foundation, L. K.
Wickes Foundation, Harvey
   Randall
Wickson-Link Memorial
   Foundation
WICOR, Inc.
Widgeon Foundation
Wiegand Foundation, E. L.
Wiggins Memorial Trust, J. J.
Wigwam Mills

Wilbur Foundation, Marguerite
   Eyer
Wilcox General Trust, George N.
Wilcox Trust, S. W.
Wildermuth Foundation, E. F.
Wilf Family Foundation
Wilkof Foundation, Edward and
   Ruth
Willard Foundation, Helen Parker
Willard Helping Fund, Cecilia
   Young
Williams Charitable Trust, John
   C.
Williams Cos.
Williams Family Foundation of
   Georgia
Williams Foundation, Arthur
   Ashley
Williams Foundation, C. K.
Williams Foundation, Edna
   Sproull
Willits Foundation
Willmott Foundation, Fred &
   Floy
Willmott Foundation, Peter S.
Wilmington Trust Co.
Wilson Foundation, Elaine P. and
   Richard U.
Wilson Foundation, Hugh and
   Mary
Wilson Foundation, Marie C.
   and Joseph C.
Wilson Fund, Matilda R.
Wilson Public Trust, Ralph
Wilson Trust, Lula C.
Wimpey Inc., George
Winn-Dixie Stores
Winnebago Industries, Inc.

Winona Corporation
Winston Foundation, Norman
   and Rosita
Winston Research Foundation,
   Harry
Wisconsin Centrifugal
Wisconsin Energy Corp.
Wisconsin Power & Light Co.
Wisconsin Public Service Corp.
Wise Foundation and Charitable
   Trust, Watson W.
Witco Corp.
Witte, Jr. Foundation, John H.
Wodecroft Foundation
Wolf Foundation, Melvin and
   Elaine
Wolff Foundation, John M.
Wollenberg Foundation
Wolverine World Wide, Inc.
Wood Charitable Trust, W. P.
Wood-Claeyssens Foundation
Wood Foundation, Lester G.
Woodard Family Foundation
Woodland Foundation
Woodruff Foundation, Robert W.
Woods Charitable Fund
Woods Foundation, James H.
Woodward Fund
Woodward Fund-Watertown,
   David, Helen, and Marian
Woodward Governor Co.
Woolf Foundation, William C.
Woolley Foundation, Vasser
Word Investments
Wornall Charitable Trust and
   Foundation, Kearney
Wortham Foundation

Wright Foundation, Lola
Wrigley Co., Wm. Jr.
Wurts Memorial, Henrietta Tower
Wurzburg, Inc.
Wyman-Gordon Co.
Wyman Youth Trust
Wyomissing Foundation
Xerox Corp.
XTEK Inc.
Yassenoff Foundation, Leo
Yawkey Foundation II
Yeager Charitable Trust, Lester
   E.
York Barbell Co.
Young Foundation, Hugo H. and
   Mabel B.
Young Foundation, Irvin L.
Young Foundation, R. A.
Young Foundation, Robert R.
Young & Rubicam
Youth Foundation
Yulman Trust, Morton and Helen
Zale Foundation
Zarkin Memorial Foundation,
   Charles
Zarrow Foundation, Anne and
   Henry
Zellerbach Family Fund
Ziegler Foundation
Zigler Foundation, Fred B. and
   Ruth B.
Zink Foundation, John Steele
Zollner Foundation
Zuckerberg Foundation, Roy J.

Recipient Type Index

Index to Corporations by Major Products/Industry

Agricultural Production—Crops (SIC 01)
Alexander & Baldwin, Inc.
American Tobacco Co.
Amfac/JMB Hawaii
Amstar Corp.
Andersons Management Corp.
Asgrow Seed Co.
Brewer and Co., Ltd., C.
Chiquita Brands Co.
Culbro Corp.
DeKalb Genetics Corp.
Diamond Walnut Growers
Dole Food Company, Inc.
Dole Fresh Vegetables
Ernest & Julio Gallo Winery
Godfrey Co.
Lubrizol Corp.
Newhall Land & Farming Co.
Ocean Spray Cranberries
Syntex Corp.
United States Sugar Corp.
Upjohn Co.
Watkins Associated Industries

Agricultural Production— Livestock (SIC 02)
Arbor Acres Farm, Inc.
Cactus Feeders Inc.
Charles River Laboratories
ConAgra
Continental Grain Co.
DeKalb Genetics Corp.
Foster Farms
Friona Industries L.P.
Globe Corp.
Godfrey Co.
Gold Kist, Inc.
Hubbard Farms
King Ranch
Merck & Co.
Monfort of Colorado, Inc.
Newhall Land & Farming Co.
North Star Universal Inc.
Pilgrim's Pride Corp.
Simplot Co., J.R.
Tyson Foods, Inc.

Agricultural Services (SIC 07)
Davey Tree Expert Co.
Diamond Walnut Growers
Dole Fresh Vegetables
Rollins Inc.
Seaboard Corp.
Sun-Diamond Growers of California

Amusement & Recreation Services (SIC 79)
American Amusement Arcades
Anheuser-Busch Cos.
Bally's - Las Vegas
Caesar's World, Inc.
Circus Circus Enterprises
Hershey Entertainment & Resort Co.
Hilton Hotels Corp.
Landmark Land Co., Inc.
Mirage Casino-Hotel
New York Racing Association
Promus Cos.

Six Flags Theme Parks Inc.
Turner Broadcasting System
Disney Co., Walt

Apparel & Accessory Stores (SIC 56)
Abraham & Straus
Alden's Inc.
Angelica Corp.
Bally Inc.
Brooks Brothers
Brooks Fashion Stores Inc.
Brown Group
Christian Dior New York, Inc.
Conston Corp.
Crystal Brands
Dollar General Corp.
Edison Brothers Stores
Fashion Bar
Federated Department Stores and Allied Stores Corp.
Florsheim Shoe Co.
Gap, The
Genesco
Gucci America Inc.
Harris Stores, Paul
Interco
Jacobson Stores, Inc.
Kobacker Co.
Laura Ashley Inc.
The Limited, Inc.
Marshalls Inc.
Melville Corp.
Merry-Go-Round Enterprises, Inc.
Morse Shoe, Inc.
National Dollar Stores, Ltd.
Neiman Marcus
Nordstrom, Inc.
Oak Hall, Inc.
Oshman's Sporting Goods, Inc.
Parisian Inc.
Phillips-Van Heusen Corp.
Prange Co., H. C.
Quaker Oats Co.
Rose's Stores, Inc.
Saks Fifth Ave.
Spiegel
Stride Rite Corp.
Toys "R" Us, Inc.
Tultex Corp.
US Shoe Corp.
Weiner's Stores

Apparel & Other Textile Products (SIC 23)
Acustar Inc.
Addison-Wesley Publishing Co.
Amoskeag Co.
Angelica Corp.
Aratex Services
Associated Products
Athlone Industries, Inc.
Becton Dickinson & Co.
Benetton
Bibb Co.
Bidermann Industries
Blue Bell, Inc.
Burlington Industries
Candlesticks Inc.
Carter Co., William
Champion Products, Inc.
Chase Packaging Corp.
Coachmen Industries
Coleman Co.

Concord Fabrics, Inc.
Crystal Brands
FAB Industries
Farley Industries
Fieldcrest Cannon
Friedman Bag Co.
Fruit of the Loom, Inc.
Fuqua Industries, Inc.
Genesco
Gerber Products Co.
Gitano Group
Goldman & Brothers, Inc., William P.
Haggar Apparel Corp.
Hampton Industries
Hudson Neckwear
Instrument Systems Corp.
Jantzen, Inc.
Jostens
K-Products
Kellwood Co.
Kendall Health Care Products
Kingspoint Industries
L.A. Gear
Lee Apparel Co.
Leslie Fay Cos., Inc.
Levi Strauss & Co.
Liz Claiborne
Mamiye Brothers
Marcade Group, Inc.
MCA
Munsingwear, Inc.
New Balance Athletic Shoe
Nike Inc.
North Face, The
Oshkosh B'Gosh
Oxford Industries, Inc.
Page Belting Co.
Palm Beach Co.
Phillips-Van Heusen Corp.
Prince Corp.
Russ Togs
Russell Corp.
Sara Lee Corp.
Schlegel Corp.
Seneca Foods Corp.
Springs Industries
Standard Textile Co., Inc.
Swank, Inc.
Thomaston Mills, Inc.
United Merchants & Manufacturers
United Togs Inc.
VF Corp.
W. L. T.

Automobile Repair, Services & Parking (SIC 75)
Arkansas Best Corp.
Avis Inc.
Cole National Corp.
Colonial Parking
Cummins Engine Co.
Enterprise Rent-A-Car Co.
Four Wheels, Inc.
National Car Rental System, Inc.
Penske Corp.
Pep Boys
PHH Corp.
Reedman Car-Truck World Center
Ryder System
U.S. Leasing International
Xtra Corp.

Automotive Dealers & Service Stations (SIC 55)
Brad Ragan, Inc.
Chevron Corp.
Colonial Oil Industries, Inc.
Crown Central Petroleum Corp.
Cumberland Farms
Dart Group Corp.
Diamond Shamrock
Fay's Incorporated
Grand Auto, Inc.
HarCo. Drug
Kaibab Industries
Lassus Brothers Oil
National Convenience Stores, Inc.
PACCAR
Penske Corp.
Pep Boys
Petroleum Marketers
Racetrac Petroleum
Reedman Car-Truck World Center
Republic Automotive Parts, Inc.
Rite Aid Corp.
Saab Cars USA, Inc.
Schilling Motors
Smith Oil Corp.
Star Enterprise
Steuart Petroleum Co.
Sun Electric Corp.
Thrifty Oil Co.
TSC STores, Inc.
Tyler Corp.
United Refining Co
UNO-VEN Co.
Valvoline Inc.
Victory Markets, Inc.

Building Materials & Garden Supplies (SIC 52)
Ace Hardware Corp.
Apogee Enterprises Inc.
Blue Circle Inc.
Erb Lumber Co.
Foodarama Supermarkets, Inc.
Franks Nursery and Crafts
Grow Group
Hechinger Co.
Home Depot
Levy's Lumber & Building Centers
Lowe's Cos.
Nuveen & Co., Inc., John
Payless Cashways Inc.
Pier 1 Imports, Inc.
PK Lumber Co.
Redman Industries
Scotty's, Inc.
Sherwin-Williams Co.
Standard Brands Paint Co.
Temple-Inland
TSC STores, Inc.
Washington Natural Gas Co.
Weatherford International, Inc.

Business Services (SIC 73)
Advertising Checking Bureau
Advo System Inc.
Affiliated Publications, Inc.
Alberto-Culver Co.
Aldus Corp.
American Building Maintenance Industries

Ameritech Corp.
Ameritech Information Systems
Ameritech Services
Anacomp, Inc.
Angeles Corp.
Apollo Computer Inc.
Arkansas Best Corp.
Atari Corp.
Autodesk, Inc.
Automatic Data Processing, Inc.
Ayco Corp.
Ayer Inc., N.W.
Backer Spielvogel Bates U.S.
Baker Hughes Inc.
Banc One - Colorado Corp.
Banta Corp.
BarclaysAmerican Corp.
BBDO Worldwide
BDM International
Bel Air Mart
Bell Communications Research
Berry & Co., L.M.
Best Western International
Bonner & Moore Associates
Borg-Warner Corp.
Bozell, Inc.
Brakeley, John Price Jones Inc.
Bristol Steel & Iron Works
Bull HN Information Systems Inc.
Business Records Corp.
Cadence Design Systems
Carrols Corp.
Chambers Development Co.
Christie, Manson & Woods International, Inc.
Cincinnati Financial Corp.
Cincom Systems, Inc.
Comcast Corp.
Commerce Clearing House
Computer Associates International
Computer Sciences Corp.
Contel Federal Systems
Continental Airlines
Control Data Corp.
Courier Corp.
CPI Corp.
D'Arcy Masius Benton & Bowles Inc.
DDB Needham Worldwide
Dean Witter Discover
Decision Data Computer Corp.
Dentsu, Inc., NY
Devon Group
Diebold, Inc.
Digicon
Digital Communications Associates, Inc.
Digital Equipment Corp.
Digital Sciences Corp.
Dimeo Construction Co.
Dow Jones & Co.
Dun & Bradstreet Corp.
Ebsco Industries
Eckerd Corp., Jack
EDS Corp.
Electronic Data Systems Corp.
Ellerbe Becket
Enterra Corp.
Equifax
Ernst & Young
Esselte Pendaflex Corp.
Fanuc U.S.A. Corp.
FMR Corp.
Foote, Cone & Belding Communications
Fuqua Industries, Inc.
Gannett Co.
GATX Corp.

Business Services (cont.)

GenRad
Gensler Jr. & Associates, M. Arthur
Gilbert Associates, Inc.
Grolier, Inc.
Grumman Corp.
Guardian Industries Corp.
Hall & Co. Inc., Frank B.
Handleman Co.
Harte-Hanks Communications, Inc.
Hartford Steam Boiler Inspection & Insurance Co.
Honeywell
Hopeman Brothers
Huffy Corp.
IBM Corp.
Insurance Systems, Inc.
Intelligent Controls
Intergraph Corp.
Interpublic Group of Cos.
ISS International Service System
Jacobs Engineering Group
Johnson & Son, S.C.
Josephson International Inc.
Kansas City Southern Industries
Keller-Crescent Co.
Kelly Services
Ketchum Communications
Kiplinger Washington Editors
Knight-Ridder, Inc.
Korn/Ferry International
Krelitz Industries
Lamar Corp.
LDB Corp.
Leaseway Transportation Corp.
Leo Burnett Co.
Lieberman Enterprises
Lincoln National Corp.
Little, Arthur D.
Lockheed Corp.
Lotus Development Corp.
Manpower, Inc.
Martin Marietta Corp.
McDonnell Douglas Corp.
McDonnell Douglas Corp.-West
McGraw-Hill
Mentor Graphics
Metromail Corp.
Metroquip
MicroSim Corp.
Microsoft Corp.
Midlantic Banks, Inc.
Moore Business Forms, Inc.
National Computer Systems
National Data Corp.
NCR Corp.
Nelson Industries, Inc.
New Valley
New York Times Co.
Novell Inc.
Ogilvy & Mather Worldwide
Olsten Corp.
Oracle Corp.
Paramount Communications Inc.
Pioneer Hi-Bred International
Pittston Co.
Planning Research Corp.
Polk & Co., R.L.
Primark Corp.
Prime Computer, Inc.
Primerica Corp.
Pyramid Technology Corp.
Recognition Equipment
Reed Publishing USA
Regis Corp.
Reynolds & Reynolds Co.
Risdon Corp.
Rollins Inc.
Scholastic Inc.
Seiler Corp.
ServiceMaster Co. L.P.
Shared Medical Systems Corp.

Shaw's Supermarkets
Silvestri Corp.
Simon & Schuster Inc.
Society Corp.
Software Toolworks
Somers Corp. (Mersman/Waldron)
Sotheby's
Sprint
Steelcase
Steiner Corp.
Sterling Software Inc.
Sun Microsystems
Synovus Financial Corp.
Tandem Computers
Tigon Corp.
Unilever United States
Union Planters Corp.
Unisys Corp.
U.S. Leasing International
United Technologies Corp.
Victaulic Co. of America
Wallace Computer Services
Wang Laboratories, Inc.
Wilsey Bennet Co.
Xerox Corp.
Young & Rubicam

Chemicals & Allied Products (SIC 28)

Abbott Laboratories
Acushnet Co.
AGA Gas, Inc.
Air Products & Chemicals
Akzo America
Akzo Chemicals Inc.
Alberto-Culver Co.
Alcan Aluminum Corp.
Alcon Laboratories, Inc.
Alfa-Laval, Inc.
Alice Manufacturing Co.
Allergan, Inc.
AlliedSignal
Aluminum Co. of America
American Cyanamid Co.
American Home Products Corp.
American Trading & Production Corp.
Ameron, Inc.
Amgen, Inc.
Amoco Corp.
Ampacet Corp.
Amway Corp.
APL Corp.
ARCO Chemical
Arden Group, Inc.
Aristech Chemical Corp.
Armor All Products Corp.
ASARCO
Astra Pharmaceutical Products, Inc.
Ausimont, U.S.A.
Avery Dennison Corp.
Avon Products
Ball Corp.
Banner Industries, Inc.
Baroid Corp.
BASF Corp.
Baxter International
Beckman Instruments
Bemis Company
Berlex Laboratories
Betz Laboratories
BFGoodrich
Big Three Industries
Binney & Smith Inc.
Black & Decker Corp.
Block Drug Co.
BOC Group
Boehringer Mannheim Corp.
Boots Pharmaceuticals, Inc.
Borden
Bridgestone/Firestone
Bristol-Myers Squibb Co.
Buffalo Color Corp.
Burroughs Wellcome Co.

Cabot Corp.
Cabot Stains
Calgon Corp.
Carey Industries
Carter-Wallace
Carus Corp.
Chattem, Inc.
Chemed Corp.
Chemtech Industries
Chesebrough-Pond's
Chiron Corp.
Chomerics, Inc.
Church & Dwight Co.
CIBA-GEIGY Corp.
Ciba-Geigy Corp. (Pharmaceuticals Division)
Clark Oil & Refining Corp.
Clorox Co.
Coastal Corp.
Colgate-Palmolive Co.
Cominco American Inc.
Concord Chemical Co.
Cookson America
Cooper Tire & Rubber Co.
Copolymer Rubber & Chemical Corp.
Corning Incorporated
Cosmair, Inc.
Countrymark Cooperative
Courtaulds Fibers Inc.
CPC International
Cranston Print Works
Crompton & Knowles Corp.
Curtis Industries, Helene
DeSoto
Dexter Corp.
Dial Corp.
Diasonics, Inc.
Difco Laboratories
Dow Chemical Co.
Dow Corning Corp.
du Pont de Nemours & Co., E. I.
Duriron Co., Inc.
Eagle-Picher Industries
Eastman Chemical Co.
Eastman Gelatine Corp.
Eastman Kodak Co.
Eka Nobel
Elf Aquitaine, Inc.
Elf Atochem North America
Elixir Industries
Enron Corp.
Ensign-Bickford Industries
Enterprises Inc.
Enterra Corp.
Ethyl Corp.
Everest & Jennings International
Farmland Industries, Inc.
FDL Foods/Dubuque Packing Co.
Fel-Pro Incorporated
Ferro Corp.
First Brands Corp.
First Mississippi Corp.
Fisons Corp.
Fleet Co., Inc., C.B.
FMC Corp.
Formosa Plastics Corp. U.S.A.
Freeport-McMoRan
Fuller Co., H.B.
GAF Corp.
GenCorp
Genentech
General Color Co.
Georgia Gulf Corp.
Georgia-Pacific Corp.
Gillette Co.
Glaxo
Glidden Co.
GNB Inc.
Gold Kist, Inc.
Goody's Manufacturing Corp.
Grace & Co., W.R.
Great Lakes Chemical Corp.
Grow Group
Gulf USA Corp.
Halliburton Co.

Handy & Harman
Hanna Co., M.A.
Hanson Office Products
Helena Chemical Co.
Helmerich & Payne Inc.
Henkel Corp.
Hercules Inc.
Hexcel Corp.
Himont Inc.
Hitachi
Hoechst Celanese Corp.
Hoffmann-La Roche
Houghton & Co., E.F.
Howell Corp.
Hunt Manufacturing Co.
ICC Industries
ICI Americas
Illinois Tool Works
IMCERA Group Inc.
Interface Inc.
International Flavors & Fragrances
Iroquois Brands, Ltd.
ITT Rayonier
Jafra Cosmetics, Inc. (U.S.)
Johnson & Johnson
Johnson & Son, S.C.
Kaisertech Ltd.
Kal Kan Foods, Inc.
Kao Corp. of America (DE)
Kerr-McGee Corp.
Koch Sons, George
Kolene Corp.
Krelitz Industries
L & F Products
La-Co. Industries, Inc.
Lafarge Corp.
Laporte Inc.
LeaRonal, Inc.
Lilly & Co., Eli
Liquid Air Corp.
Loctite Corp.
Lord Corp.
Lubrizol Corp.
Lydall, Inc.
MalCo Products Inc.
Mallinckrodt Specialty Chemicals Co.
Mapco Inc.
Marion Merrell Dow
Markem Corp.
Mary Kay Cosmetics
McDermott
McKesson Corp.
McNeil Consumer Products
Mead Corp.
Melville Corp.
Mennen Co.
Merck & Co.
Merck Human Health Division
Miles Inc.
Miles Inc., Diagnostic Division
Miles Inc., Pharmaceutical Division
Mississippi Chemical Corp.
Missouri Farmers Association
Mitsubishi Kasei America
Monsanto Co.
Mooney Chemicals
Morton International
Nalco Chemical Co.
National Service Industries
National Starch & Chemical Corp.
NCH Corp.
Nepera Inc.
Neutrogena Corp.
Neville Chemical Co.
NutraSweet Co.
Oakite Products
Occidental Petroleum Corp.
Olin Corp.
Ortho Diagnostic Systems, Inc.
Ortho-McNeil Pharmaceutical
Owens-Corning Fiberglas Corp.
Oxy Petrochemicals Inc.

Page Belting Co.
Pantasote Polymers
Park-Ohio Industries Inc.
Parke-Davis Group
Peabody Holding Company Inc.
Peridot Chemicals (NJ)
Petrolite Corp.
Pfizer
Phelps Dodge Corp.
Pirelli Armstrong Tire Corp.
Plastics Engineering Co.
PMC Inc.
Portland Food Products Co.
PPG Industries
PQ Corp.
Pratt & Lambert, Inc.
Premark International
Premier Industrial Corp.
Pro-line Corp.
Procter & Gamble Co.
Procter & Gamble Cosmetic & Fragrance Products
Publicker Industries, Inc.
Quaker Chemical Corp.
Quantum Chemical Corp.
Radiator Specialty Co.
Reckitt & Colman
Reichhold Chemicals, Inc.
Reilly Industries
Revlon
Rexene Products Co.
Rhone-Poulenc Inc.
Rhone-Poulenc Rorer
Rochester Midland Corp.
Rogers Corp.
Rohm and Haas Company
Ross Laboratories
RPM, Inc.
Rust-Oleum Corp.
Safety-Kleen Corp.
Sandoz Corp.
Schering Laboratories
Schering-Plough Corp.
Schulman Inc., A.
SCM Chemicals Inc.
Sealed Air Corp.
Searle & Co., G.D.
Sequa Corp.
ServiceMaster Co. L.P.
Seton Co.
Shell Oil Co.
Sherwin-Williams Co.
Sigma-Aldrich Corp.
Simplot Co., J.R.
SmithKline Beecham
Soft Sheen Products Co.
Sonoco Products Co.
Standard Brands Paint Co.
Stanhome Inc.
Starrett Co., L.S.
Stepan Co.
Sterling Chemicals Inc.
Sterling Winthrop
Sudbury Inc.
Sulzer Brothers Inc.
Sun Chemical Corp.
Syntex Corp.
Tennant Co.
Tenneco
Terra Industries
Texas Olefins Co.
3M Co.
Todd Co., A.M.
Tom's of Maine
Tracor, Inc.
Tremco Inc.
Tropicana Products, Inc.
Ulrich Chemical, Inc.
Union Camp Corp.
Union Carbide Corp.
Uniroyal Chemical Co. Inc.
United States Borax & Chemical Corp.
Universal Foods Corp.
Unocal Corp.
Upjohn Co.

Valspar Corp.
Valvoline Inc.
Vista Chemical Company
Voplex Corp.
Vulcan Materials Co.
Warner-Lambert Co.
Wellman Inc.
Westvaco Corp.
Weyerhaeuser Co.
Witco Corp.

Coal Mining (SIC 12)

Adams Resources & Energy, Inc.
Allegheny Power System, Inc.
AMAX
AMAX Coal Industries
American Natural Resources Co.
Arch Mineral Corp.
ARCO
Ashland Oil
B.H.P. Minerals
Berwind Corp.
Bethlehem Steel Corp.
BHP Utah International
Burlington Northern Inc.
Burlington Resources
Cleveland-Cliffs
Coastal Corp.
Consol Energy Inc.
Costain Holdings Inc.
Cyprus Minerals Co.
Drummond Co.
du Pont de Nemours & Co., E. I.
Enterprise Coal Co.
First Mississippi Corp.
General Dynamics Corp.
Grace & Co., W.R.
Gulf USA Corp.
Hanson Office Products
Houston Industries
James River Coal Co.
Kerr-McGee Corp.
KN Energy, Inc.
Mapco Inc.
Montana Power Co.
NACCO Industries
Nerco, Inc.
North American Coal Corp.
Oglebay Norton Co.
PacifiCorp
Panhandle Eastern Corp.
Peabody Holding Company Inc.
Pittsburgh & Midway Coal
    Mining Co.
Pittston Co.
Quaker State Corp.
Rochester & Pittsburgh Coal Co.
Sharon Steel Corp.
Sun Co.
Terra Industries
Transco Energy Company
United Co.
USX Corp.
Walter Industries
Washington Water Power Co.
Westmoreland Coal Co.

Communications (SIC 48)

AFLAC
ALLTEL Corp.
Alltel/Western Region
American Telephone &
    Telegraph Co.
Ameritech Corp.
Ameritech Mobile
    Communications
Ameritech Services
Bell Atlantic Corp.
Bell Communications Research
BellSouth Corp.
Bellsouth Telecommunications,
    Inc.
Belo Corp., A.H.
Blade Communications

Cable & Wireless
    Communications
Cablevision Systems Corp.
Capital Cities/ABC
Carolina Telephone & Telegraph
    Co.
CBS Inc.
Centel Corp.
Chesapeake & Potomac
    Telephone Co.
Chesapeake & Potomac
    Telephone Co. of West Virginia
Cincinnati Bell
Citizens Utilities Co.
Comcast Corp.
Communications Satellite Corp.
    (COMSAT)
Contel Federal Systems
Cook Inlet Region
Corporate Printing Co.
Cox Enterprises
Diamond State Telephone Co.
Discovery Channel/Cable
    Education Network
Durham Corp.
Fairchild Corp.
Freedom Newspapers Inc.
Gannett Co.
Harte-Hanks Communications,
    Inc.
Hearst Corp.
Home Box Office
Hubbard Broadcasting
Illinois Bell
Illinois Consolidated Telephone
    Co.
Indiana Bell Telephone Co.
ITT Corp.
Jefferson-Pilot Communications
Jones Intercable, Inc.
Journal Communications
Landmark Communications
Lee Enterprises
Liberty Corp.
LIN Broadcasting Corp.
Lincoln Telecommunications Co.
Mankato Citizens Telephone Co.
McCaw Cellular
    Communications
McDonnell Douglas Corp.
McGraw-Hill
MCI Communications Corp.
Media General, Inc.
Meredith Corp.
Michigan Bell Telephone Co.
Multimedia, Inc.
National Broadcasting Co., Inc.
New England Telephone Co.
New Jersey Bell Telephone
    Company
New Valley
New York Telephone Co.
New York Times Co.
News America Publishing Inc.
Northern States Power Co.
NYNEX Corp.
Ohio Bell Telephone Co.
Pacific Telesis Group
PacifiCorp
Paramount Communications Inc.
Park Communications Inc.
Playboy Enterprises, Inc.
Providence Journal Company
Pulitzer Publishing Co.
Quincy Newspapers
Rich Products Corp.
Rochester Telephone Corp.
Rock Hill Telephone Co.
St. Joe Paper Co.
Sammons Enterprises
SNET
Southern Bell
Southwestern Bell Corp.
Sprint
Sprint United Telephone
Stauffer Communications
Storer Communications Inc.

Tele-Communications, Inc.
Time Warner
Time Warner Cable
Times Mirror Co.
Turner Broadcasting System
United Telephone Co. of Florida
United Telephone System
    (Eastern Group)
US WEST
Viacom International Inc.
Washington Post Co.
WCVB-TV
Westinghouse Broadcasting Co.
Wisconsin Bell, Inc.
WJLA Inc.

Depository Institutions (SIC 60)

Advest Group, Inc.
Ahmanson & Co., H.F.
Altus Services Inc.
AMCORE Bank, N.A. Rockford
American Capital Corp.
American Express Co.
American National Bank
American National Bank & Trust
    Co. of Chicago
American Savings & Loan
    Association of Florida
AmSouth Bancorporation
Apple Bank for Savings
Attleboro Pawtucket Savings
    Bank
Bailey & Son, Bankers, M.S.
Baltimore Bancorp.
Banc One - Colorado Corp.
Banc One Illinois Corp.
Banc One Wisconsin Corp.
Banca Commerciale Italiana,
    New York Branch
Bancal Tri-State Corp.
Banco Portugues do Atlantico,
    New York Branch
Bancorp Hawaii
Bangor Savings Bank
Bank Hapoalim B.M.
Bank IV
Bank Leumi Trust Co. of New
    York
Bank of A. Levy
Bank of Alma
Bank of America
Bank of America Arizona
Bank of Boston Connecticut
Bank of Boston Corp.
Bank of New York
Bank of Oklahoma, N.A.
Bank of the Orient
Bank of Tokyo Trust Co.
Bank One, Cambridge, NA
Bank One, Cleveland, NA
Bank One, Columbus, NA
Bank One, Coshocton, NA
Bank One, Dayton, NA
Bank One, Dover, NA
Bank One, Portsmouth, NA
Bank One, Sidney, NA
Bank One, Texas-Houston Office
Bank One, Texas, NA
Bank One, Youngstown, NA
Bank South Corp.
BankAmerica Corp.
Bankers Trust Co.
Banque Francaise du Commerce
    Exterieur
Barclays Bank of New York
Barnett Banks
Bayview Federal Bank
BB&T Financial Corp.
Bell Federal Savings & Loan
    Association
Beverly Bank
Boatmen's Bancshares
Boatmen's First National Bank
    of Oklahoma

Branch Banking & Trust Co.
Brenton Banks Inc.
Bristol Savings Bank
Broad, Inc.
Brown Brothers Harriman & Co.
Bryn Mawr Trust Co.
CalFed Inc.
Canadian Imperial Bank of
    Commerce
Capital Group
Casco Northern Bank
CCB Financial Corp.
Central Bank of the South
Central Fidelity Banks, Inc.
Central Trust Co.
Chase Bank of Arizona
Chase Lincoln First Bank, N.A.
Chase Manhattan Bank, N.A.
Chemical Bank
Chevy Chase Savings Bank FSB
Chicago City Bank & Trust Co.
Citibank, F.S.B.
Citicorp
Citizens Bank
Citizens Commercial & Savings
    Bank
Citizens First National Bank
Citizens & Southern National
    Bank of Florida
Citizens Union Bank
City National Bank
Climatic Corp.
Coast Federal Bank
Cole Taylor Financial Group
Colorado National Bankshares
Columbia Savings & Loan
    Association
Comerica
Commerce Bancshares, Inc.
Commercial Bank
Commercial Federal Corp.
Commerzbank AG, New York
Community National Bank &
    Trust Co. of New York
Connecticut Savings Bank
Continental Bancorp, Inc.
Continental Bank N.A.
Corestates Bank
Credit Agricole
Credit Suisse
Creditanstalt-Bankverein, New
    York
Crestar Financial Corp.
Crossland Savings FSB
Cullen/Frost Bankers
CUNA Mutual Insurance Group
Dai-Ichi Kangyo Bank of
    California
Dauphin Deposit Corp.
DCB Corp.
Deposit Guaranty National Bank
Deutsche Bank AG
Dime Savings Bank of New York
Dollar Dry Dock Bank
Downey Savings & Loan
    Association
Eastland Bank
Eastover Bank for Savings
Equimark Corp.
European American Bank
Far West Financial Corp.
Farm & Home Savings
    Association
Farmers & Mechanics Bank
Federal National Mortgage
    Assn., Fannie Mae
Fidelity Bank
Fiduciary Trust Co.
Fifth Third Bancorp
Financial Corp. of Santa Barbara
First Alabama Bancshares
First American Corp. (Nashville,
    Tennessee)
First Bank System
First Chicago
First Citizens Bank and Trust Co.

First Colorado Bank & Trust,
    N.A.
First Commerce Corp.
First Commercial Bank N.A.
First Empire State Corp.
First Federal of Michigan
First Fidelity Bancorp, Inc.
First Fidelity Bancorporation
First Hawaiian
First Interstate Bancsystem of
    Montana
First Interstate Bank
First Interstate Bank NW Region
First Interstate Bank of Arizona
First Interstate Bank of California
First Interstate Bank of Denver
First Interstate Bank of Oregon
First Interstate Bank of Texas,
    N.A.
First Interstate Bank & Trust Co.
First Maryland Bancorp
First National Bank in Wichita
First National Bank of Atlanta
First National Bank & Trust Co.
    of Rockford
First NH Banks, Inc.
First of America Bank Corp.
First Pennsylvania Bank NA
First Security Bank of Idaho N.A
First Security Bank of Utah N.A.
First Security Corp. (Salt Lake
    City, Utah)
First Source Corp.
First Tennessee Bank
First Union National Bank of
    Florida
First Valley Bank
First Virginia Banks
Firstar Bank Milwaukee NA
Firstar Corp.
FirsTier Bank N.A. Omaha
Fleet Bank
Fleet Bank N.A.
Fleet Bank of Maine
Fleet Financial Group
Fortune Bank
Fourth Financial Corp.
Frost National Bank
Gardiner Savings Institution FSB
Glendale Federal Bank
Golden West Financial Corp.
Goldome F.S.B
Great Lakes Bancorp, FSB
Great Western Financial Corp.
Greater New York Savings Bank
Guaranty Bank & Trust Co.
Hamilton Bank
Hang Seng Bank
Harris Trust & Savings Bank
Hawkeye Bancorporation
HEI Inc.
Heritage Pullman Bank & Trust
Hibernia Corp.
Home Savings of America, FA
Howard Savings Bank
Huntington Bancshares Inc.
Independent Bankshares
Industrial Bank of Japan Trust
    Co.
Integra Bank
Integra Bank/South
Israel Discount Bank of New
    York
J.P. Morgan & Co.
Key Bank of Maine
Key Bank of Oregon
Lakeside National Bank
Landmark Land Co., Inc.
LaSalle Bank Lake View
LaSalle National Bank
Lasalle National Corp.
Leucadia National Corp.
Liberty National Bank
Manufacturers National Bank of
    Detroit
Marine Midland Banks
Marshall & Ilsley Bank

Depository Institutions (cont.)

Mascoma Savings Bank
Mechanics Bank
Mellon Bank Corp.
Mellon PSFS
Mercantile Bancorp
Mercantile Bankshares Corp.
Merchants Bancshares
Meridian Bancorp
Metropolitan Bank & Trust Co.
Michigan National Corp.
Midlantic Banks, Inc.
Nashua Trust Co.
National City Bank
National City Bank, Columbus
National City Bank of Evansville
National City Bank of Indiana
National City Corp.
National Westminster Bank New Jersey
NationsBank Corp.
NationsBank Texas
NBD Bank
NBD Bank, N.A.
NBD Genesee Bank
New Jersey National Bank
Northeast Savings, FA
Northern Trust Co.
NorthPark National Bank
Norwest Bank Nebraska
Norwest Corp.
Ohio Citizens Bank
Ohio Savings Bank
Old Kent Bank & Trust Co.
Old National Bank in Evansville
One Valley Bank, N.A.
Park National Bank
Penn Savings Bank, a division of Sovereign Bank Bank of Princeton, a division of Sovereign Bank
People's Bank
Peoples Heritage Savings Bank
PHM Corp.
Pioneer Group
Pioneer Trust Bank, NA
Pittsburgh National Bank
PNC Bank
PNC Bank
Premier Bank
Premier Bank Lafayette
Premier Bank of South Louisiana
PriMerit F.S.B.
Puget Sound National Bank
Redlands Federal Bank
Rhode Island Hospital Trust National Bank
Riggs National Bank
Rochester Community Savings Bank
St. Paul Federal Bank for Savings
San Diego Trust & Savings Bank
San Francisco Federal Savings & Loan Association
Sanwa Bank Ltd. New York
Seafirst Corp.
Security State Bank
Shawmut Bank of Franklin County
Shawmut Worcester County Bank, N.A.
Signet Bank/Maryland
Society Corp.
Society for Savings
Southtrust Corp.
Southwest Gas Corp.
Standard Chartered Bank New York
Standard Federal Bank
Standard Pacific Corp.
Star Bank, N.A.
State Street Bank & Trust Co.
Statesman Group, Inc.
Sumitomo Bank of California

Sumitomo Trust & Banking Co., Ltd.
Summit Bancorporation
Sun Banks Inc.
Sunwest Bank of Albuquerque, N.A.
Swiss Bank Corp.
Synovus Financial Corp.
TCF Banking & Savings, FSB
Team Banchares Inc.
Team Bank Houston
Texas Commerce Bank Houston, N.A.
Third National Corp.
Tokai Bank, Ltd.
TransOhio Savings Bank
Travelers Express Co.
Trust Co. Bank
Trustmark National Bank
UJB Financial Corp.
Union Bank
Union Bank of Switzerland New York Branch
Union Planters Corp.
Union Trust
United Missouri Bancshares, Inc.
United Savings Association of Texas
U.S. Bank of Washington
United States Trust Co. of New York
US Bancorp
Valley Bancorp
Valley National Bancorp
Valley National Bank of Arizona
Wachovia Bank of Georgia, N.A.
Wachovia Bank & Trust Co., N.A.
Washington Mutual Savings Bank
Washington Trust Bank
Wauwatosa Savings & Loan Association
Wells Fargo & Co.
West One Bancorp
West One Bank Idaho
WestLB New York Branch
WestStar Bank N.A.
Whitney National Bank
Wilber National Bank
Wilmington Trust Co.
World Savings & Loan Association
Zions Bancorp.

Eating & Drinking Places (SIC 58)

Albrecht Grocery Co., Fred W.
American Amusement Arcades
Atwood Industries
Baskin-Robbins USA CO.
Ben & Jerry's Homemade
Bob Evans Farms
Burger King Corp.
Carlson Cos.
Carrols Corp.
Chick-Fil-A, Inc.
Church's Fried Chicken, Inc.
ConAgra
Delaware North Cos.
Domino's Pizza
Dunkin' Donuts
Edison Brothers Stores
Friendly Ice Cream Corp.
Frisch's Restaurants Inc.
General Mills
Hershey Foods Corp.
Hilton Hotels Corp.
International Dairy Queen, Inc.
Kentucky Fried Chicken Corp.
LDB Corp.
Luby's Cafeterias
Marcus Corp.
Marriott Corp.
McDonald's Corp.
Meyer, Inc., Fred

Mirage Casino-Hotel
Morrison, Inc.
Ogden Corp.
OSF International, Inc.
PepsiCo
Pizza Hut
Ponderosa, Inc.
Restaurant Associates, Inc.
Rose's Stores, Inc.
Royal Crown Cos., Inc.
Seiler Corp.
Shoney's Inc.
Sky Chefs, Inc.
Specialty Restaurants Corp.
Waffle House, Inc.
Wendy's International, Inc.
White Castle System
White Coffee Pot Family Inns

Educational Services (SIC 82)

Development Dimensions International
Kinder-Care Learning Centers
Reynolds & Reynolds Co.

Electric, Gas & Sanitary Services (SIC 49)

Access Energy Corp.
Air Products & Chemicals
Air & Water Technologies Corp.
Alabama Gas Corp. (An Energen Co.)
Alabama Power Co.
Algonquin Energy, Inc.
Allegheny Power System, Inc.
Alyeska Pipeline Service Co.
American Electric Power
American Natural Resources Co.
American Water Works Co., Inc.
Anadarko Petroleum Corp.
Applied Energy Services
Arizona Public Service Co.
Arkansas Power & Light Co.
Arkla
Atlanta Gas Light Co.
Baltimore Gas & Electric Co.
BHP Pacific Resources
Boston Gas Co.
Brooklyn Union Gas Co.
Browning-Ferris Industries
Burlington Resources
Cabot Corp.
Carolina Power & Light Co.
Cascade Natural Gas Corp.
Centerior Energy Corp.
Central Hudson Gas & Electric Corp.
Central Illinois Public Service Co.
Central Maine Power Co.
Central Power & Light Co.
Central & South West Services
Central Vermont Public Service Corp.
Chambers Development Co.
Cincinnati Gas & Electric Co.
Citizens Gas & Coke Utility
Citizens Utilities Co.
CNG Transmission Corp.
Colorado Interstate Gas Co.
Columbia Gas Distribution Cos.
Columbus Southern Power Co.
Commonwealth Edison Co.
Commonwealth Energy System
Connecticut Natural Gas Corp.
Consolidated Edison Co. of New York Inc.
Consolidated Natural Gas Co.
Consumers Power Co.
Danis Industries
Dayton Power and Light Co.
Delhi Gas Pipeline Co.
Delmarva Power & Light Co.

Detroit Edison Co.
Diamond Shamrock
Duke Power Co.
Duquesne Light Co.
DWG Corp.
East Ohio Gas Co.
Eastern Enterprises
Elizabethtown Gas Co.
Elizabethtown Water Co.
Empire District Electric Co.
Enron Corp.
Enserch Corp.
Entergy Corp.
Entex
EnviroSource
Equitable Resources
Florida Power Corp.
Florida Power & Light Co.
General Public Utilities Corp.
Georgia Power Co.
Greeley Gas Co.
Hanna Co., M.A.
HEI Inc.
Houston Industries
IES Industries
Illinois Power Co.
Indiana Gas and Chemical Corp.
Indiana Gas Co.
Indianapolis Water Co.
Intermountain Gas Industries
Interstate Power Co.
Iowa-Illinois Gas & Electric Co.
IPALCO Enterprises
IU International
Jersey Central Power & Light Co.
Kaiser Steel Resources
Kansas City Power & Light Co.
Kansas Power & Light/Western Resources
Kentucky Utilities Co.
KN Energy, Inc.
Laclede Gas Co.
Lone Star Gas Co.
Long Island Lighting Co.
Louisiana Gas Services
Louisiana Power & Light Co./New Orleans Public Service
Louisville Gas & Electric Co.
Madison Gas & Electric Co.
Memphis Light Gas & Water Division
Michigan Consolidated Gas Co.
Michigan Gas Utilities
MidCon Corp.
Midwest Gas Co.
Midwest Resources
Minnegasco
Minnesota Power & Light Co.
Mississippi Power Co.
Mississippi Power & Light Co.
Missouri Public Service
Montana Power Co.
National Fuel Gas Co.
Nevada Power Co.
New England Electric System
New Jersey Resources Corp.
New York State Electric & Gas Corp.
Niagara Mohawk Power Corp.
Nicor, Inc.
Northeast Utilities
Northern Illinois Gas Co.
Northern Indiana Fuel & Light Co.
Northern Indiana Public Service Co.
Northern States Power Co.
Northwest Natural Gas Co.
Northwest Pipeline Corp.
NUI Corp.
Ogden Corp.
Ohio Edison Corp.
Oklahoma Gas & Electric Co.
ONEOK Inc.
Orange & Rockland Utilities, Inc.
Pacific Enterprises

Pacific Gas & Electric Co.
PacifiCorp
Panhandle Eastern Corp.
Parsons Corp.
Pennsylvania Power & Light
Peoples Energy Corp.
Philadelphia Electric Co.
Piedmont Natural Gas Co., Inc.
Portland General Electric Co.
Potomac Edison Co.
Potomac Electric Power Co.
Providence Energy Corp.
PSI Energy
Public Service Co. of Colorado
Public Service Co. of New Mexico
Public Service Co. of Oklahoma
Public Service Electric & Gas Co.
Puget Sound Power & Light Co.
Questar Corp.
Reading & Bates Corp.
Rochester Gas & Electric Corp.
Rollins Environmental Services, Inc.
Ross Corp.
San Diego Gas & Electric
Savannah Electric & Power Co.
SCANA Corp.
Sierra Pacific Resources
Sonat
South Carolina Electric & Gas Co.
South Jersey Industries
Southdown, Inc.
Southern California Edison Co.
Southern California Gas Co.
Southern Co. Services
Southern Connecticut Gas Co.
Southern Indiana Gas & Electric Co.
Southwest Gas Corp.
Southwestern Electric Power Co.
Southwestern Public Service Co.
Tampa Electric
Texas Gas Transmission Corp.
Texas-New Mexico Power Co.
Toledo Edison Co.
Transco Energy Company
TU Electric Co.
Tucson Electric Power Co.
UGI Corp.
Union Electric Co.
Union Texas Petroleum
United Gas Pipe Line Co.
United Illuminating Co.
Valero Energy Corp.
Valley Line Co.
Virginia Power Co.
Washington Natural Gas Co.
Washington Water Power Co.
Waste Management
West Texas Utilities Co.
Western Resources
WICOR, Inc.
Williams Cos.
Wisconsin Energy Corp.
Wisconsin Power & Light Co.
Wisconsin Public Service Corp.

Electronic & Other Electrical Equipment (SIC 36)

Acme-Cleveland Corp.
Acustar Inc.
ADC Telecommunications
Advanced Micro Devices
Aladdin Industries, Incorporated
Alcatel NA Cable Systems, Inc.
ALLTEL Corp.
Alpha Industries
Altec Lansing Corp.
American Electronics
American Microsystems, Inc.

Ameritech Development
Ameritech Information Systems
AMETEK
AMP
Amsco International
Amstar Corp.
Analog Devices
Analogic Corp.
Andrew Corp.
Applied Power, Inc.
Arden Group, Inc.
Arkla
Asea Brown Boveri
Augat, Inc.
Avnet, Inc.
Aydin Corp.
Babcock & Wilcox Co.
Bairnco Corp.
Ball Chain Manufacturing Co.
Ball Corp.
Bang & Olufsen of America, Inc.
Barber-Colman Co.
Bardes Corp.
BASF Corp.
Beckman Instruments
Bell Industries
Betts Industries
Black & Decker Corp.
BMC Industries
BOC Group
Boeing Co.
Bosch Corp., Robert
Bourns, Inc.
Brunswick Corp.
Brush Wellman Inc.
Burndy Corp.
Calex Manufacturing Co.
Carlisle Cos.
Carol Cable Co.
Champion Spark Plug Co.
Chomerics, Inc.
Christie Electric Corp.
Cincinnati Milacron
Commodore International Ltd.
Contraves USA
Cooper Industries
Cosco, Inc.
Crown International, Inc.
CTS Corp.
Cubic Corp.
Dana Corp.
Dataproducts Corp.
Delco Electronics Corp.
Deutsch Co.
Diebold, Inc.
Digital Equipment Corp.
Dover Corp.
Dresser Industries
DSC Communications Co.
Duchossois Industries
Ducommun Inc.
Duracell International
Dynatech Corp.
Dyneer Corp.
E-Systems
Echlin Inc.
Ecolab
EG&G Inc.
Elastimold Corp.
Eldec Corp.
Electric Power Equipment Co.
Emerson Electric Co.
Emerson Radio Corp.
EMI Records Group
Esterline Technologies Corp.
ETCO Inc.
Eureka Co.
Federal-Mogul Corp.
Ferranti Tech
Fischer & Porter Co.
Franklin Electric Company Inc.

(Bluffton, Indiana)
Gates Corp.
GenCorp
General Electric Co.
General Motors Corp.

General Railway Signal Corp.
General Signal Corp.
Gerber Products Co.
Gilbert Associates, Inc.
Gillette Co.
GNB Inc.
Gould Inc.
Great Lakes Carbon Corp.
GTE Corp.
Guth Lighting Co.
Hanson Office Products
Harris Corp.
Hazeltine Corp.
Hitachi
Honeywell
Hubbell Inc.
IBM Corp.
Ideal Industries
Instrument Systems Corp.
Intel Corp.
International Rectifier Corp.
International Standard Electric
Corp.
ITT Corp.
Johnson Co., E. F.
Johnson Controls
Joslyn Corp.
KDI Corp.
Kennametal
Kenwood U.S.A. Corp.
Kepco, Inc.
Kimball International
KitchenAid Inc.
Kuhlman Corp.
Kulicke & Soffa Industries
Kyocera International Inc.
Lambda Electronics Inc.
Lamson & Sessions Co.
Landis & Gyr, Inc.
Leviton Manufacturing Co.
Lincoln Electric Co.
Lionel Corp.
Litton Industries
Lockheed Sanders
LoJack Corp.
Loral Corp.
LPL Technologies Inc.
LSI Logic Corp.
M/A-COM, Inc.
MacLean-Fogg Co.
Macom-Venitz
Magic Chef
Magnatek
Mark IV Industries
Masco Corp.
Matsushita Electric Corp. of
America
Maytag Corp.
MCA
McGill Manufacturing Co.
Measurex Corp.
Melitta North America Inc.
Milton Bradley Co.
Mitsubishi Kasei America
Molex, Inc.
Moog, Inc.
Mor-Flo Industries, Inc.
Motorola
MTS Systems Corp.
Murata Erie North America
NACCO Industries
National Semiconductor Corp.
National Service Industries
NEC Electronics, Inc.
NEC USA
NMB (USA) Inc.
Nortek, Inc.
North American Philips Corp.
Northern Telecom Inc.
NuTone Inc.
Oak Industries
Oki America Inc.
Olivetti Office USA, Inc.
Onan Corp.
Onan Family Foundation
Oneida Ltd.

Osram Corp.
Oster/Sunbeam Appliance Co.
PemCo. Corp.
Pentair
Picker International
Pioneer Electronics (USA) Inc.
Pittway Corp.
Plantronics, Inc.
Portec, Inc.
PPG Industries
Preformed Line Products Co.
Premark International
Publicker Industries, Inc.
Racal-Milgo
Ralston Purina Co.
Ransburg Corp.
Rayovac Corp.
Reliance Electric Co.
Robbins & Myers, Inc.
Robertshaw Controls Co.
Rockwell International Corp.
Rogers Corp.
Rolm Systems
S.T.J. Group, Inc.
Sanyo Audio Manufacturing
(U.S.A.) Corp.
Sanyo Fisher U.S.A. Corp.
Sanyo Manufacturing Corp.
SCI Systems, Inc.
Scientific-Atlanta
Scott and Fetzer Co.
SGS-Thomson Microelectronics
Inc.
Sharp Electronics Corp.
Sheldahl Inc.
Silicon Systems Inc.
Silvestri Corp.
Simplex Time Recorder Co.
Singer Company
Slant/Fin Corp.
SNC Manufacturing Co.
Sony Corp. of America
Soundesign Corp.
Spang & Co.
Sparton Corp.
Spartus Corp.
Spectra-Physics Analytical
Square D Co.
Stabler Cos., Inc.
Standard Motor Products, Inc.
Stewart & Stevenson Services
Sunbeam-Oster
Tauber Oil Co.
TBG, Inc.
TDK Corp. of America
Teleflex Inc.
Teradyne, Inc.
Texas Instruments
Thomas & Betts Corp.
Time Warner
Timex Corp.
Tokheim Corp.
TRW Corp.
Unisys Corp.
United Industrial Corp.
United Technologies, Automotive
Unitrode Corp.
Varian Associates
Vernitron Corp.
Victaulic Co. of America
Wagner Manufacturing Co., E. R.
Wang Laboratories, Inc.
Watkins-Johnson Co.
Westinghouse Electric Corp.
Whirlpool Corp.
White Consolidated Industries
Wiremold Co.
Woodward Governor Co.
Wrap-On Co.
Yale Security Inc.
Zebco/Motorguide Corp.

Engineering & Management Services (SIC 87)

Advertising Checking Bureau
Aerospace Corp.
Alexander & Alexander
Services, Inc.
Altus Services Inc.
Ameritech Information Systems
Ameritech Services
APAC Inc.
ARA Services
Arvin Industries
Asea Brown Boveri
Automatic Data Processing, Inc.
Badger Co., Inc.
Barton-Gillet Co.
Barton-Malow Co.
Battelle
BDM International
BE&K Inc.
Bechtel Group
Bell Communications Research
Bernstein & Co., Sanford C.
Best Western International
Bill Communications
Black & Veatch
Bonner & Moore Associates
Booz Allen & Hamilton
Brakeley, John Price Jones Inc.
Brown Inc., John
Brown & Root, Inc.
Business Incentives
Caleb Brett U.S.A. Inc.
Chiron Corp.
Commonwealth Energy System
Communications Satellite Corp.
(COMSAT)
Contel Federal Systems
Continental Corp.
Control Data Corp.
Cook & Co., Frederic W.
Coopers & Lybrand
CRS Sirrine Engineers
CT Corp. System
DeKalb Genetics Corp.
Deloitte & Touche
Dentsu, Inc., NY
Development Dimensions
International
Dimeo Construction Co.
Dow Elanco Inc.
Duchossois Industries
DynCorp
EG&G Inc.
Ellerbe Becket
Eni-Chem America, Inc.
Enterprises Inc.
Ernst & Young
Ethyl Corp.
Factory Mutual Engineering
Corp.
Farley Industries
Fluor Corp.
FMR Corp.
Foster Wheeler Corp.
Freeport-McMoRan
Fru-Con Construction Corp.
Genentech
General Dynamics Corp.
Genetics Institute
Gensler Jr. & Associates, M.
Arthur
Gilbert Associates, Inc.
Grant Thornton
Great Lakes Chemical Corp.
GTE Corp.
Hall & Co. Inc., Frank B.
Halliburton Co.
Harcourt Brace Jovanovich
Hartford Steam Boiler Inspection
& Insurance Co.
Hazeltine Corp.
Holmes & Narver Services Inc.
Holzman USA, Philipp
Homestead Financial Corp.

Huber, Hunt & Nichols
Humana
Hyman Construction Co., George
IMS America Ltd.
Interpublic Group of Cos.
Jacobs Engineering Group
Kearney Inc., A.T.
Kellogg Co., M.W.
Ketchum Communications
KPMG Peat Marwick
Laclede Steel Co.
Law Companies Group
Lazard Freres & Co.
Lincoln Property Co.
Little, Arthur D.
Litton Industries
Lockheed Corp.
Lukens
Lummus Crest, Inc.
M/A/R/C Inc.
Management Compensation
Group/Dulworth Inc.
Maritz Inc.
Marsh & McLennan Cos.
McKinsey & Co.
Mitre Corp.
Morse-Diesel International
National Broadcasting Co., Inc.
National Gypsum Co.
Nationale-Nederlanden North
America Corp.
Nielsen Co., A.C.
Nortek, Inc.
North Star Universal Inc.
Obayashi America Corp.
Ogden Corp.
Ogilvy & Mather Worldwide
Parexel International Corp.
Parsons Corp.
PemCo. Corp.
Penn Central Corp.
Plante & Moran, CPAs
Price Waterhouse-U.S.
Raytheon Engineers &
Constructors
Reliance Group Holdings, Inc.
Research-Cottrell Inc.
Research Institute of America
Ross, Johnston & Kersting
Rust International Corp.
Sachs Electric Corp.
Sandia National Laboratories
Sandoz Corp.
Science Applications
International Corp.
Seiler Corp.
ServiceMaster Co. L.P.
Servico, Inc.
Skidmore, Owings & Merrill
SmithKline Beecham
Southern Co. Services
Stanley Consultants
Stone & Webster, Inc.
Sulzer Brothers Inc.
Tate & Lyle Inc.
Torchmark Corp.
Towers Perrin
Tracor, Inc.
Turner Construction Co.
Turner Corp.
United Conveyor Corp.
United Telephone Co. of Florida
Univar Corp.
Walbridge Aldinger Co.
Wyle Laboratories
Zurn Industries

Fabricated Metal Products (SIC 34)

Aarque Cos.
Acme-Cleveland Corp.
Acme United Corp.
Air Products & Chemicals
Aladdin Industries, Incorporated
Alcan Aluminum Corp.
Alfa-Laval, Inc.

Fabricated Metal Products (cont.)

Alhambra Foundry Co., Ltd.
Alliant Techsystems
Aluminum Co. of America
Amcast Industrial Corp.
American Electronics
American National Can Co.
American Saw & Manufacturing Co.
American Standard
American Welding & Manufacturing Co.
Amsco International
Amsted Industries
Anchor Fasteners
Andal Corp.
Anderson Industries
Apogee Enterprises Inc.
Applied Power, Inc.
Armbrust Chain Co.
Armco Inc.
Arvin Industries
Asea Brown Boveri
Augat, Inc.
Avondale Industries, Inc.
AXIA Incorporated
Babcock & Wilcox Co.
Badger Meter, Inc.
Bairnco Corp.
Ball Chain Manufacturing Co.
Ball Corp.
Banner Industries, Inc.
Barden Corp.
Barnes Group
Beech Aircraft Corp.
Beretta U.S.A. Corp.
Bethlehem Steel Corp.
Betts Industries
BFGoodrich
Billy Penn Corp
Binks Manufacturing Co.
BMW of North America, Inc.
Bridgestone/Firestone
Briggs & Stratton Corp.
Brillion Iron Works
Browning
Brunswick Corp.
Budd Co.
Buffalo Forge Co.
Butler Manufacturing Co.
Caldwell Manufacturing Co.
Cardinal Industries
Carlisle Cos.
Carol Cable Co.
Carolina Steel Corp.
Castle Industries
Cawsl Corp.
CBI Industries
Ceco Corp.
Celotex Corp.
Chamberlain Manufacturing Corp.
Charter Manufacturing Co.
CLARCOR
Cold Heading Co.
Coleman Co.
Commercial Intertech Corp.
Commercial Metals Co.
Continental Can Co.
Cooper Oil Tool
Crane Co.
Croft Metals
Crown Cork & Seal Co., Inc.
CTS Corp.
Curtiss-Wright Corp.
Daniel & Co., Gerard
Dayton-Walther Corp.
Deutsch Co.
Diebold, Inc.
Douglas & Lomason Company
Dover Corp.
Dresser Industries

Duriron Co., Inc.
Dynamet, Inc.
Eastern Foundry Co.
Eastern Stainless Corp.
Eaton Corp.
Ebsco Industries
Edgewater Steel Corp.
Edwards Industries
Elixir Industries
Emerson Electric Co.
Esterline Technologies Corp.
Federal-Mogul Corp.
Federal Screw Works
Fiat U.S.A., Inc.
FKI Holdings Inc.
Florida Steel Corp.
Ford Meter Box Co.
Formrite Tube Co.
Foster Co., L.B.
Foster Wheeler Corp.
Fox Steel Co.
GenCorp
General Housewares Corp.
General Signal Corp.
General Steel Fabricators
Gillette Co.
Gleason Works
Globe Valve Corp.
Gould Inc.
Greif Brothers Corp.
Grinnell Corp.
Hadson Corp.
Hampden Papers
Hand Industries
Harley-Davidson, Inc.
Harsco Corp.
Hartz Mountain Corp.
Harvard Industries
Hayes Albion Industries
Heil Co.
Hein-Werner Corp.
Hexcel Corp.
Hillenbrand Industries
HON Industries
Hopeman Brothers
Huck International Inc.
ICI Americas
Illinois Tool Works
Ingersoll-Rand Co.
Instrument Systems Corp.
International Aluminum Corp.
James River Corp. of Virginia
Jorgensen Co., Earle M.
JSJ Corp.
Kelco Industries, Inc.
Kerr Glass Manufacturing Corp.
Keystone International
Klein Tools
Koch Sons, George
Kohler Co.
Kolene Corp.
Kuhlman Corp.
Laclede Steel Co.
Ladish Co.
Lamson & Sessions Co.
Lapham-Hickey Steel Corp.
Louisiana-Pacific Corp.
M.T.D. Products
MacLean-Fogg Co.
Mark Controls Corp.
Marmon Group, Inc.
Masco Corp.
McDermott
McDonald Industries, Inc., A. Y.
McWane Inc.
Metal Industries
Michigan Bell Telephone Co.
Microdot, Inc.
Mor-Flo Industries, Inc.
Mueller Co.
National Forge Co.
National Machinery Co.
National Manufacturing Co.
National Standard Co.
NCH Corp.
New Hampshire Ball Bearings

NIBCO Inc.
North Star Steel Co.
Northern Engraving Corp.
Nucor Corp.
NuTone Inc.
Olin Corp.
Owen Industries, Inc.
Owens-Illinois
Packaging Corporation of America
Patrick Industries Inc.
Penn Central Corp.
Pentair
Phelps Dodge Corp.
Philadelphia Industries
Pitt-Des Moines Inc.
Pittway Corp.
Portec, Inc.
Powell Co., William
Premier Industrial Corp.
Radiator Specialty Co.
Ranco, Inc.
Ransburg Corp.
RB&W Corp.
Redman Industries
Rexham Inc.
Rieke Corp.
Riley Stoker Co.
Rinker Materials Corp.
Risdon Corp.
Rockford Products Corp.
Rockwell International Corp.
Scott and Fetzer Co.
SECO
Sharon Steel Corp.
Sifco Industries Inc.
Sigma-Aldrich Corp.
Skyline Corp.
Slant/Fin Corp.
Smith Corp., A.O.
Snap-on Tools Corp.
Sparton Corp.
SPS Technologies
SPX Corp.
Square D Co.
Standard Steel Speciality Co.
Standex International Corp.
Stanley Works
Starrett Co., L.S.
Steiner Corp.
Sterling Inc.
Stockham Valves & Fittings
Stupp Brothers Bridge & Iron Co.
Sudbury Inc.
Sundstrand Corp.
Teleflex Inc.
Tomkins Industries, Inc.
Toro Co.
Tracor, Inc.
Tredegar Industries
Trinity Industries, Inc.
TRINOVA Corp.
Tyco Laboratories, Inc.
UNC, Inc.
Uniform Tubes, Inc.
United Conveyor Corp.
United Dominion Industries
United Industrial Corp.
Valmont Industries
Varlen Corp.
Victaulic Co. of America
Vogt Machine Co., Henry
Vollrath Co.
Wagner Manufacturing Co., E. R.
Weirton Steel Corp.
West Co.
White Castle System
Williamson Co.
Wyman-Gordon Co.
Yale Security Inc.
Zurn Industries

Food & Kindred Products (SIC 20)

AG Processing Inc.

Agway
Alberto-Culver Co.
Alexander & Baldwin, Inc.
ALPAC Corp.
Alpert & Co., Inc., Herman
Amalgamated Sugar Co.
American Brands
American Home Products Corp.
American Maize Products
Anheuser-Busch Cos.
Arbie Mineral Feed Co.
Archer-Daniels-Midland Co.
Aura Cacia
Azteca Foods, Inc.
Baker Commodities
Ball Corp.
Banfi Vintners
Barbara's Bakery
Baskin-Robbins USA CO.
Beef America Inc.
Ben & Jerry's Homemade
Berkshire Hathaway
Blue Diamond Growers
Bob Evans Farms
Borman's
Brewer and Co., Ltd., C.
Brown-Forman Corp.
Bryan Foods
Bumble Bee Seafoods Inc.
Burlington Industries
Cadbury Beverages Inc.
California & Hawaiian Sugar Co.
Campbell Soup Co.
Campbell Taggart, Inc.
Carter-Wallace
Central Soya Co.
Cherry Hill Cooperative Cannery
Chesebrough-Pond's
Chiquita Brands Co.
Climatic Corp.
Clorox Co.
Coca-Cola Co.
Colgate-Palmolive Co.
Community Coffee Co.
ConAgra
Continental Grain Co.
Contran Corp.
Coors Brewing Co.
Cornnuts, Inc.
Countrymark Cooperative
CPC International
Crestar Food Products, Inc.
Crompton & Knowles Corp.
Cullum Cos.
Curtice-Burns Foods
Dairylea Cooperative Inc.
Dairymen, Inc.
Dean Foods Co.
DEC International, Inc.
Deer Valley Farm
Del Monte Foods
Dellwood Foods, Inc.
Dial Corp.
Dillons Super Markets
Dixie-Portland Flour Mills
Dole Food Company, Inc.
Dreyer's & Edy's Grand Ice Cream
DWG Corp.
Eden Foods
Elf Aquitaine, Inc.
Entenmann's Inc.
Ernest & Julio Gallo Winery
Excel Corp.
Famous Amos Chocolate Chip Cookie Co.
Fantastic Foods
Faribault Foods
Farmland Industries, Inc.
Farmstead Foods
Fast Food Merchandisers
FDL Foods/Dubuque Packing Co.
Fearn International, Inc.
Flowers Industries, Inc.
Foster Farms
Friendly Ice Cream Corp.

Friona Industries L.P.
Frito-Lay
Frozfruit Corp.
General Mills
Gerber Products Co.
Glenmore Distilleries Co.
Godfrey Co.
Gold Kist, Inc.
Golden Grain Macaroni Co.
Golden State Foods Corp.
Goya Foods
Grace & Co., W.R.
Great Atlantic & Pacific Tea Co. Inc.
Hanson Office Products
Hartz Mountain Corp.
Harvest States Cooperative
Heileman Brewing Co., Inc., G.
Heinz Co., H.J.
Herr Foods
Hershey Foods Corp.
Heublein
Hiram Walker & Sons Inc.
Hoechst Celanese Corp.
Holly Sugar Corp.
Hood Inc., H.P.
Hormel & Co., George A.
Hubbard Milling Co.
Hudson Foods
IBP, Inc.
Illinois Cereal Mills
Imagine Foods
IMCERA Group Inc.
Imperial Holly Corp.
International Flavors & Fragrances
International Multifoods Corp.
Interstate Brands Corp.
Isaly Klondike Co.
Jim Beam Brands Co.
Kal Kan Foods, Inc.
Kane-Miller Corp.
Kayem Foods, Inc.
Kellogg's
Kikkoman Foods, Inc.
Kikkoman International, Inc.
Kowalski Sausage Co.
Kraft General Foods
La Croix Water Co.
Ladish Malting Co.
Lamb-Weston Inc.
Lancaster Colony
Lance, Inc.
Land O'Lakes
Lender's Bagel Bakery
Lipton, Thomas J.
Marathon Cheese Corp.
Mariani Nut Co.
Mars, Inc.
Mayacamas Corp.
Mayer Foods Corp., Oscar
McCormick & Co.
McIlhenny and Sons Corp
Melitta North America Inc.
Merck & Co.
Mid-America Dairymen
Miller Brewing Co.
Missouri Farmers Association
Modern Maid Food Products, Inc.
Monfort of Colorado, Inc.
Moorman Manufacturing Co.
MorningStar Foods
Mrs. Fields, Inc.
Nabisco Foods Group
National By-Products
National Starch & Chemical Corp.
Nestle U.S.A. Inc.
New England Grocer Supply
North Star Universal Inc.
Norton Simon Inc.
Ocean Spray Cranberries
Ore-Ida Foods, Inc.
Pacific Coca-Cola Bottling Co.
Pepperidge Farm, Inc.

Pepsi-Cola Bottling Co. of
Charlotte
PepsiCo
Perdue Farms
Pet
Pfizer
Philip Morris Cos.
Pilgrim's Pride Corp.
Pillsbury Co.
Portland Food Products Co.
Procter & Gamble Co.
Quaker Oats Co.
Rahr Malting Co.
Ralston Purina Co.
Reckitt & Colman
Reily & Co., William B.
Reviva Labs
Rhone-Poulenc Inc.
Riceland Foods, Inc.
Rich Products Corp.
Riviana Foods
RJR Nabisco Inc.
Roddenbery Co., Inc., W.B.
Ross Laboratories
Royal Crown Cos., Inc.
Rykoff & Co., S.E.
St. Joe Paper Co.
Sara Lee Corp.
Schreiber Foods, Inc.
Schwan's Sales Enterprises
Seaboard Corp.
Seagram & Sons, Joseph E.
Sealaska Corp.
Seneca Foods Corp.
Simplot Co., J.R.
Smucker Co., J.M.
Smucker Co., J.M.
Southland Corp.
Staley Manufacturing Co., A.E.
Steiner Corp.
Stella D'Oro Biscuit Co.
Stroehmann Bakeries
Stroh Brewery Co.
Sun-Diamond Growers of
California
Sunkist Growers
Sunmark Capital Corp.
Sunshine Biscuits
Super Valu Stores
Swift-Eckrich Inc.
Tasty Baking Co.
Tetley, Inc.
Thorn Apple Valley, Inc.
Todd Co., A.M.
Tombstone Pizza Corp.
Tootsie Roll Industries, Inc.
Topps Company
Tropicana Products, Inc.
21st Century Foods
Tyson Foods, Inc.
Union Equity Division of
Farmland Industries
United States Sugar Corp.
Universal Foods Corp.
UST
Victory Markets, Inc.
Vons Cos., Inc.
Warner-Lambert Co.
Welch Foods
White Coffee Pot Family Inns
Wrigley Co., Wm. Jr.

Food Stores (SIC 54)

Acme Markets
Albertson's
Albrecht Grocery Co., Fred W.
Almac's, Inc.
Alpha Beta Stores, Inc.
American Stores Co.
Arden Group, Inc.
Arizona Supermarkets/Q-Fresh
Markets
Bel Air Mart
Big V Supermarkets
Borman's
Bruno's Inc.

Colonial Stores
Community Coffee Co.
Cullum Cos.
Cumberland Farms
Dairylea Cooperative Inc.
Delhi Gas Pipeline Co.
Demoulas Supermarkets
Dillons Super Markets
Entenmann's Inc.
Farm Fresh Inc. (Norfolk,
Virginia)
Fleming Companies, Inc.
Food Barn Stores, Inc.
Food Emporium
Food Lion Inc.
Foodarama Supermarkets, Inc.
Furr's Supermarkets
Giant Eagle
Giant Food
Giant Food Stores
Godfrey Co.
Golub Corp.
Great Atlantic & Pacific Tea Co.
Inc.
Harris-Teeter Super Markets
Hy-Vee Food Stores
King Kullen Grocery Co., Inc.
Kowalski Sausage Co.
Land O'Lakes
Lassus Brothers Oil
Lucky Stores
Marsh Supermarkets, Inc.
Mayfair Super Markets
Meijer Inc.
Meyer, Inc., Fred
Mrs. Fields, Inc.
Nash-Finch Co.
National Convenience Stores,
Inc.
Pay 'N Save Inc.
Penn Traffic Co.
Piggly Wiggly Southern
Publix Supermarkets
Quaker Oats Co.
Raley's
Red Food Stores, Inc.
Riser Foods
Roundy's Inc.
Ruddick Corp.
Safeway, Inc.
Schnuck Markets
Scrivner, Inc.
Seaway Food Town
Shaw's Supermarkets
Skaggs Alpha Beta Co.
Smith Oil Corp.
Smitty's Super Valu, Inc.
Southland Corp.
Star Markets Co.
Super Valu Stores
Tamarkin Co.
Tops Markets, Inc.
Ukrop's Super Markets, Inc.
United Refining Co
Victory Markets, Inc.
Vons Cos., Inc.
Wal-Mart Stores, Inc.
Waldbaum, Inc.
Winchell's Donut Houses
Operating Company
Winn-Dixie Stores

Forestry (SIC 08)

Continental Can Co.
Longview Fibre Co.
Murphy Oil Corp.
New York Times Co.
Scott Paper Co.

Furniture & Fixtures (SIC 25)

American Trading & Production
Corp.
Amsco International
Armstrong World Industries Inc.

Bassett Furniture Industries, Inc.
Brodart Co.
Butler Manufacturing Co.
Clopay Corp.
Cooper Industries
Cosco, Inc.
CTS Corp.
Dennison Manufacturing Co.
Douglas & Lomason Company
Ebsco Industries
Everest & Jennings International
Fisher-Price
Foldcraft Co.
Harvard Interiors Manufacturing

Co.
Hauserman, Inc.
Haworth, Inc.
Henkel-Harris Co., Inc.
Henredon Furniture Industries
Hillenbrand Industries
HMK Enterprises
HON Industries
Hunt Manufacturing Co.
Indiana Desk Co.
Interco
Jasper Desk Co.
Jasper Seating Co.
JOFCo., Inc.
Johnson Controls
Kenney Manufacturing Co.
Kimball International
Kohler Co.
La-Z-Boy Chair Co.
Lane Co., Inc.
Leggett & Platt, Inc.
Lehigh Portland Cement Co.
Masco Corp.
Miller Inc., Herman
Mohasco Corp.
Newell Co.
Pickering Industries
Reflector Hardware Corp.
Sealy, Inc.
Singer Company
Somers Corp.

(Mersman/Waldron)
Southern Furniture Co.
Standard Pacific Corp.
Steelcase
Thomasville Furniture Industries
Tranzonic Cos.

Furniture & Homefurnishings Stores (SIC 57)

Action Industries, Inc.
Baltimore Gas & Electric Co.
Circuit City Stores
Dollar General Corp.
EMI Records Group
Greeley Gas Co.
Haverty Furniture Cos., Inc.
Hechinger Co.
Heilig-Meyers Co.
Jacobson Stores, Inc.
Lappin Electric Co.
Laura Ashley Inc.
Lechmere
Lieberman Enterprises
Meyer, Inc., Fred
National Dollar Stores, Ltd.
Neiman Marcus
Parisian Inc.
Piedmont Natural Gas Co., Inc.
Pier 1 Imports, Inc.
Schottenstein Stores Corp.
Spiegel
Standard Brands Paint Co.
Tandy Corp.
Town & Country Corp.
Valmont Industries
Value City Furniture
Washington Natural Gas Co.

General Building Contractors (SIC 15)

Abel Construction Co.
Atkinson Co., Guy F.
Austin Industries
Badger Co., Inc.
Bardes Corp.
Barton-Malow Co.
BE&K Inc.
Bechtel Group
Blount
Brice Building Co., Inc.
Brown & Root, Inc.
Butler Manufacturing Co.
Centex Corp.
Cummings Properties
Management, Inc.
Danis Industries
Dick Corp.
Dimeo Construction Co.
Driscoll Co., L.F.
Edwards Industries
Ellerbe Becket
Enserch Corp.
Fairfield Communities, Inc.
FIP Corp.
Flagler Co.
Fluor Corp.
Fru-Con Construction Corp.
Gilbane Building Co.
Good Value Home, Inc.
Gulfstream Housing Corp.
Harbert Corp.
HCB Contractors
Holzman USA, Philipp
Homewood Corp.
Honeywell
Hovnanian Enterprises Inc., K.
Huber, Hunt & Nichols
Hyman Construction Co., George
Jones Construction Co., J.A.
Kajima International, Inc.
Kaufman & Broad Home Corp.
Korte Construction Co.
Law Company, Inc.
Lennar Corp.
Lewis Homes of California
Lincoln Property Co.
Lyon Co., William
M.D.C. Holdings
McDevitt Street Bovis Inc.
Mellon Stuart Construction Inc.
Morrison-Knudsen Corp.
Morse-Diesel International
Mortenson Co., M.A.
Murdock Development Co.
National Gypsum Co.
Newhall Land & Farming Co.
Obayashi America Corp.
OMNI Construction
Oxford Development Group
Pardee Construction Co.
Peck/Jones Construction Corp.
Pepper Cos.
Perina Corp
Perini Corp.
Phelps, Inc.
PHM Corp.
Pitt-Des Moines Inc.
Presley Cos.
Raytheon Engineers &
Constructors
Rouse Co.
Rust International Corp.
Ryland Group
Shapell Industries, Inc.
Shoemaker Co., R.M.
Sordoni Enterprises
Standard Pacific Corp.
Starrett Housing Corp.
Stone & Webster, Inc.
Swinerton & Walberg Co.
Turner Construction Co.
Turner Corp.

UDC-Universal Development LP
Walbridge Aldinger Co.
Walter Industries
Weitz Corp.
Wimpey Inc., George
Winter Construction Co.

General Merchandise Stores (SIC 53)

Abraham & Straus
Ames Department Stores
Ann & Hope
Anthony Co., C.R.
Belk Stores
Bergner Co., P.A.
Best Products Co.
Bloomingdale's
Borman's
Burdines
Cohn Co., M.M.
Cumberland Farms
Dayton Hudson Corp.
Dayton's
Dillard Department Stores, Inc.
Duckwall-Alco Stores
Fay's Incorporated
Fedco, Inc.
Federated Department Stores and
Allied Stores Corp.
Filene's Sons Co., William
Harcourt General
Hecht's
Hills Department Stores, Inc.
Jamesway Corp.
JCPenney Co.
Kmart Corp.
Kraus Co., Ltd.
Lord & Taylor
Luria's
Macy & Co., R.H.
Marshall Field's
May Department Stores Co.
McCrory Corp.
Mercantile Stores Co.
Mervyn's
Montgomery Ward & Co.
Moore & Sons, B.C.
Murphy Co., G.C.
National Dollar Stores, Ltd.
Neiman Marcus
Nordstrom, Inc.
Pamida, Inc.
PayLess Drug Stores
Pic 'N' Save Corp.
Prange Co., H. C.
Rose's Stores, Inc.
Saks Fifth Ave.
Schottenstein Stores Corp.
Sears, Roebuck and Co.
Smitty's Super Valu, Inc.
Strawbridge & Clothier
Target Stores
Thalhimer Brothers Inc.
Victory Markets, Inc.
Wal-Mart Stores
Wal-Mart Stores, Inc.
Weiner's Stores
Woolworth Co., F.W.
Younkers, Inc.

Health Services (SIC 80)

Basic American Medical, Inc.
Care Enterprises
Charter Medical Corp.
CIGNA Corp.
Community Psychiatric Centers
Comprehensive Care Corp.
Corning Incorporated
Damon Corp.
Enterprises Inc.
Forum Group, Inc.
Hoffmann-La Roche

Health Services
(cont.)

Hospital Corp. of America
Humana
Irvine Medical Center
Manor Care
National Medical Enterprises
Olsten Corp.
Ortho Diagnostic Systems, Inc.
Revlon
U.S. Healthcare, Inc.
Universal Health Services, Inc.

Heavy Construction Except Building Construction (SIC 16)

APAC Inc.
Ashland Oil
Atkinson Co., Guy F.
Austin Industries
Bechtel Group
Blount
Boh Brothers Construction Co.
Brice Building Co., Inc.
Brown & Root, Inc.
Burnett Construction Co.
CalMat Co.
CBI Industries
Danis Industries
DynCorp
Enserch Corp.
Fluor Corp.
Foster Wheeler Corp.
Fru-Con Construction Corp.
Goodyear Tire & Rubber Co.
Groves & Sons Co., S.J.
Hadson Corp.
Harbert Corp.
Hendrickson Brothers
Holmes & Narver Services Inc.
Holzman USA, Philipp
Huber, Hunt & Nichols
Hydraulic Co.
Irby Construction Co.
Jensen Construction Co.
Jones Construction Co., J.A.
Kaneb Services, Inc.
Kasler Corp.
Kellogg Co., M.W.
McDermott
Morrison-Knudsen Corp.
Obayashi America Corp.
Ohio Road Paving Co.
Parsons Corp.
Peck/Jones Construction Corp.
PemCo. Corp.
Perina Corp
Perini Corp.
Phelps, Inc.
Raytheon Co.
Rich Co., F.D.
Riley Stoker Co.
Santa Fe International Corp.
Shea Co., John F.
Stabler Cos., Inc.
Starrett Housing Corp.
Stone & Webster, Inc.
Turner Construction Co.
United Dominion Industries
Zachry Co., H.B.
Zurn Industries

Holding & Other Investment Offices (SIC 67)

Aarque Cos.
ACF Industries, Inc.
Advest Group, Inc.
AEGON USA, Inc.
AFLAC
Ahmanson & Co., H.F.

Air & Water Technologies Corp.
Alexander & Alexander Services, Inc.
Algonquin Energy, Inc.
Allegheny Power System, Inc.
ALLTEL Corp.
Alumax
AMAX Coal Industries
American Bankers Insurance Group
American Brands
American Capital Corp.
American Electric Power
American Express Co.
American General Corp.
American International Group, Inc.
American President Cos.
American Stores Co.
American Water Works Co., Inc.
Amoco Corp.
Amoskeag Co.
AMR Corp.
AmSouth Bancorporation
Amstar Corp.
Anderson Industries
Angeles Corp.
Anheuser-Busch Cos.
ARA Services
Arcata Corp.
Arden Group, Inc.
Argonaut Group
Arkansas Best Corp.
Asahi Glass America, Inc.
AXIA Incorporated
Baker Hughes Inc.
Baltimore Bancorp.
Banc One - Colorado Corp.
Banc One Illinois Corp.
Banc One Wisconsin Corp.
Bancal Tri-State Corp.
Bancorp Hawaii
Bandag, Inc.
Bank of Boston Connecticut
Bank of Boston Corp.
Bank of Oklahoma, N.A.
Bank South Corp.
BankAmerica Corp.
BarclaysAmerican Corp.
Bardes Corp.
Barnes Group
Barnett Banks
Baskin-Robbins USA CO.
BayBanks
BB&T Financial Corp.
Bekins Co.
Bell Atlantic Corp.
Ben & Jerry's Homemade
Bergner Co., P.A.
Berkshire Hathaway
Berwind Corp.
Best Products Co.
Bitco Corp.
Blade Communications
Boatmen's Bancshares
Boston Co., Inc.
BP America
Brenton Banks Inc.
Brewer and Co., Ltd., C.
Burger King Corp.
Burlington Northern Inc.
Business Men's Assurance Co. of America
C.P. Rail Systems
Caesar's World, Inc.
CalFed Inc.
Caltex Petroleum Corp.
Capital Group
Capital Holding Corp.
Care Enterprises
Carlson Cos.
Cawsl Corp.
CBI Industries
CCB Financial Corp.
Centerior Energy Corp.
Central Fidelity Banks, Inc.

Central & South West Services
Chase Manhattan Bank, N.A.
Chemical Bank
Chicago Milwaukee Corp.
Chick-Fil-A, Inc.
Christian Dior New York, Inc.
Chrysler Corp.
Chubb Corp.
CIGNA Corp.
Cincinnati Bell
Cincinnati Financial Corp.
Circus Circus Enterprises
CIT Group Holdings
Citicorp
Citizens Bank
Citizens & Southern National Bank of Florida
City National Bank
Clarity Holdings Corp.
Coastal Corp.
Coats & Clark Inc.
Cole Taylor Financial Group
Colonial Penn Group, Inc.
Colorado National Bankshares
Coltec Industries
Comerica
Commerce Bancshares, Inc.
Commercial Credit Co.
Commercial Federal Corp.
Commonwealth Energy System
Commonwealth Industries Corp.
Computer Associates International
Connecticut General Corp.
Consolidated Natural Gas Co.
Constar International Inc.
Continental Airlines
Continental Bancorp, Inc.
Continental Corp.
Contran Corp.
Cookson America
Corestates Bank
Costain Holdings Inc.
Crestar Financial Corp.
CRL Inc.
Crum and Forster
Crystal Brands
CSC Industries
CSX Corp.
Cullen/Frost Bankers
Dalgety Inc.
Dauphin Deposit Corp.
DCB Corp.
DCNY Corp.
Dean Witter Discover
DEC International, Inc.
Decision Data Computer Corp.
Delaware North Cos.
Domino's Pizza
Dreyfus Corp.
Dunkin' Donuts
Durham Corp.
DWG Corp.
Dyson-Kissner-Moran Corp.
Eastern Enterprises
Edwards & Sons, A.G.
Employers Mutual Casualty Co.
Equimark Corp.
European American Bank
Far West Financial Corp.
Farley Industries
Farmers Group, Inc.
Ferrell Cos.
Fifth Third Bancorp
Figgie International
FINA, Inc.
Financial Corp. of Santa Barbara
First Alabama Bancshares
First American Corp. (Nashville, Tennessee)
First American Financial Corp.
First Chicago
First Commerce Corp.
First Empire State Corp.
First Fidelity Bancorp, Inc.
First Hawaiian

First Interstate Bancsystem of Montana
First Maryland Bancorp
First Mississippi Corp.
First National Bank of Atlanta
First National Bank & Trust Co. of Rockford
First NH Banks, Inc.
First of America Bank Corp.
First Security Corp. (Salt Lake City, Utah)
First Source Corp.
First Tennessee Bank
First Union Corp.
First Virginia Banks
Firstar Corp.
Fleet Bank
Fleet Financial Group
Florida East Coast Industries
Fortis Inc.
Fortune Bank
Foster Wheeler Corp.
Fourth Financial Corp.
Fox Inc.
Foxmeyer Corp.
Franks Nursery and Crafts
Frisch's Restaurants Inc.
Gates Corp.
General Atlantic Partners L.P.
General Public Utilities Corp.
Gilbert Associates, Inc.
Glenmede Trust Corp.
Globe Corp.
Golden West Financial Corp.
Golub Corp.
Grand Trunk Corp.
Great Western Financial Corp.
Grumman Corp.
GSC Enterprises
GTE Corp.
Hadson Corp.
Hall Financial Group
Harcourt Brace Jovanovich
Hartmarx Corp.
Hawkeye Bancorporation
HEI Inc.
Hibernia Corp.
Hillman Co.
Hilton Hotels Corp.
Himont Inc.
HMK Enterprises
Home Beneficial Corp.
Homestead Financial Corp.
Houston Industries
Howell Corp.
Huntington Bancshares Inc.
ICH Corp.
IES Industries
Illinois Bell
Imperial Corp. of America
Independent Bankshares
Inland Steel Industries
Integrated Resources
Intermark, Inc.
International Dairy Queen, Inc.
International Data Group
International Multifoods Corp.
International Standard Electric Corp.
Interpublic Group of Cos.
IPALCO Enterprises
Iroquois Brands, Ltd.
J.P. Morgan & Co.
Jefferson-Pilot
Josephson International Inc.
Joslyn Corp.
Kansas City Southern Industries
Kemper National Insurance Cos.
Kentucky Fried Chicken Corp.
Ketchum & Co.
Kiewit Sons, Peter
Knight-Ridder, Inc.
Korte Construction Co.
Kraft General Foods
Lasalle National Corp.
LDB Corp.

Leucadia National Corp.
Lewis Homes of California
Liberty Corp.
Life Investors Insurance Company of America
Lincoln National Corp.
Lincoln Telecommunications Co.
Lionel Corp.
Liquid Air Corp.
Loews Corp.
Longs Drug Stores
Louisiana Land & Exploration Co.
Lukens
M/A/R/C Inc.
MacAndrews & Forbes Holdings
Manor Care
Manville Corp.
Marine Midland Banks
Marley Co.
Marmon Group, Inc.
Marsh & McLennan Cos.
Marshall & Ilsley Bank
Mayacamas Corp.
Mayflower Group
Mazda North America
MBIA, Inc.
McDonald's Corp.
Melitta North America Inc.
Mellon Bank Corp.
Mercantile Bancorp
Mercantile Bankshares Corp.
Merchants Bancshares
Meredith Corp.
Meridian Bancorp
Meridian Insurance Group Inc.
Meritor Financial Group
Merrill Lynch & Co.
Metallgesellschaft Corp.
Metallurg, Inc.
MGIC Investment Corp.
Miami Corp.
Michigan Mutual Insurance Corp.
Michigan National Corp.
MidCon Corp.
Midland Co.
Midlantic Banks, Inc.
Midwest Resources
Mitchell Energy & Development Corp.
Morrison-Knudsen Corp.
NACCO Industries
National City Bank of Indiana
National City Corp.
National Fuel Gas Co.
NationsBank Texas
Navistar International Corp.
NBD Bank
NEC USA
New England Electric System
New Jersey Resources Corp.
New Valley
Nichimen America, Inc.
Nicor, Inc.
Norfolk Southern Corp.
Northeast Utilities
Norton Simon Inc.
NUI Corp.
Nutri/System Inc.
Nuveen & Co., Inc., John
Occidental Oil & Gas Corp.
Odyssey Partners
Ohio Casualty Corp.
Old Republic International Corp.
Olsten Corp.
ONEOK Inc.
Orion Capital Corp.
Oshman's Sporting Goods, Inc.
Overstreet Investment Co.
Owen Industries, Inc.
Pacific Enterprises
Pacific Telesis Group
PaineWebber
Panhandle Eastern Corp.
Peabody Holding Company Inc.
Pechiney Corp.

Pennzoil Co.
Peoples Energy Corp.
PHM Corp.
Pioneer Group
Pizza Hut
Playboy Enterprises, Inc.
Ponderosa, Inc.
Porsche Cars North America, Inc.
Premier Bank
Premier Bank Lafayette
Premier Bank of South Louisiana
Primark Corp.
Progressive Corp.
Property Capital Trust
Providence Energy Corp.
Provigo Corp. Inc.
Raymark Corp.
Reckitt & Colman
Reed Publishing USA
Reliance Group Holdings, Inc.
Republic Financial Services, Inc.
Republic New York Corp.
Rexene Products Co.
Rexham Inc.
Rhone-Poulenc Rorer
Richley, Inc.
Rio Grande Railroad
Rite Aid Corp.
RJR Nabisco Inc.
Roadway Services, Inc.
Rouse Co.
Royal Group Inc.
Ruddick Corp.
SAFECO Corp.
Saint Johnsbury Trucking Co.
Sammons Enterprises
Sandoz Corp.
Santa Fe Pacific Corp.
Sanwa Bank Ltd. New York
Scholastic Inc.
Seafirst Corp.
Sealy, Inc.
Security Benefit Life Insurance
    Co.
Security Capital Corp.
Servico, Inc.
Shawmut National Corp.
Shaw's Supermarkets
Shearson, Lehman & Hutton
Shoney's Inc.
Sierra Pacific Resources
Simpson Investment Co.
Six Flags Theme Parks Inc.
Skandia America Reinsurance
    Corp.
SmithKline Beecham
Society Corp.
Society for Savings
Sogem Holding Ltd.
Sonat
Sordoni Enterprises
Sotheby's
South Jersey Industries
Southdown, Inc.
Southland Corp.
Southmark Corp.
Southtrust Corp.
Sprint
State Street Bank & Trust Co.
Statesman Group, Inc.
Sumitomo Corp. of America
Summit Bancorporation
Sweet Life Foods
Synovus Financial Corp.
Tate & Lyle Inc.
Taylor Corp.
Team Banchares Inc.
Telecom Corp.
Teledyne
Temple-Inland
Tenneco
Terra Industries
Third National Corp.
Thor Industries, Inc.
Toshiba America, Inc.
Transamerica Corp.

Transamerica Occidental Life
    Insurance Co.
Transco Energy Company
Transtar Inc.
Trump Group
Turner Corp.
Twentieth Century Insurance Co.
Tyler Corp.
UJB Financial Corp.
UniGroup, Inc.
Union Pacific Corp.
Union Planters Corp.
United Asset Management Corp.
United Industrial Corp.
United Missouri Bancshares, Inc.
United Parcel Service of America
United States Trust Co. of New
    York
UNUM Corp.
US Bancorp
US Shoe Corp.
US WEST
USF&G Co.
USG Corp.
Uslico Corp.
USLIFE Corp.
UST
Valley Bancorp
Valley National Bancorp
Valley National Bank of Arizona
Vanguard Group of Investment
    Cos.
Viacom International Inc.
Wachovia Bank of Georgia, N.A.
Waffle House, Inc.
WEA Enterprises Co.
Weitz Corp.
Wells Fargo & Co.
Wendy's International, Inc.
West One Bancorp
Wheeling-Pittsburgh Corp.
Whitman Corp.
WICOR, Inc.
Wisconsin Energy Corp.
Yellow Corp.
Zions Bancorp.

Hotels & Other Lodging Places (SIC 70)

Amfac/JMB Hawaii
Amfac/JMB Hawaii
Atwood Industries
Bally's - Las Vegas
Caesar's World, Inc.
Carlson Cos.
Circus Circus Enterprises
CSX Corp.
Frisch's Restaurants Inc.
Harrah's Hotels & Casinos
Hershey Entertainment & Resort
    Co.
Hilton Hotels Corp.
Intercontinental Hotels Corp.
La Quinta Motor Inns
Landmark Land Co., Inc.
Loews Corp.
Manor Care
Marcus Corp.
Marriott Corp.
Meridien Hotels
Mirage Casino-Hotel
Promus Cos.
Quality Inn International
Sammons Enterprises
Servico, Inc.
Sonesta International Hotels
    Corp.
Twentieth Century-Fox Film
    Corp.
United Inns, Inc.

Industrial Machinery & Equipment (SIC 35)

ABB Process Automation
Acme-Cleveland Corp.
Advanced Micro Devices
Aeroglide Corp.
AGA Gas, Inc.
AGFA Division of Miles Inc.
Air & Water Technologies Corp.
Albany International Corp.
Alfa-Laval, Inc.
AlliedSignal
Alma Piston Co.
Amdahl Corp.
American Filtrona Corp.
American Saw & Manufacturing
    Co.
American Standard
American Welding &
    Manufacturing Co.
AMETEK
Amstar Corp.
Amsted Industries
Anacomp, Inc.
Analogic Corp.
Anderson Industries
Apollo Computer Inc.
Apple Computer, Inc.
Applied Power, Inc.
APV Crepaco Inc.
Armco Inc.
AST Research, Inc.
Atari Corp.
Auto Specialties Manufacturing
    Co.
Avery Dennison Corp.
Avondale Industries, Inc.
AXIA Incorporated
Aydin Corp.
Babcock & Wilcox Co.
Baker Hughes Inc.
Bandag, Inc.
Banner Industries, Inc.
Barber-Colman Co.
Barber-Greene Co.
Barden Corp.
Bardes Corp.
Baroid Corp.
Bell Industries
Berwind Corp.
Besser Co.
Big Three Industries
Binks Manufacturing Co.
Bird Inc.
Black & Decker Corp.
Blount
Blount
Bodine Corp.
Borg-Warner Corp.
Bosch Corp., Robert
Bowater Inc.
Briggs & Stratton Corp.
Brillion Iron Works
Brown Inc., John
Brown & Sharpe Manufacturing
    Co.
Brunswick Corp.
Bucyrus-Erie
Buffalo Forge Co.
Bull HN Information Systems
    Inc.
CalComp, Inc.
Canon U.S.A., Inc.
Cardinal Industries
Carlisle Cos.
Carrier Corp.
Case Co., J.I.
Caterpillar
Champion Spark Plug Co.
Chicago Pneumatic Tool Co.
Cincinnati Milacron
Clabir Corp.
Clark Equipment Co.

Coltec Industries
Commercial Intertech Corp.
Commodore International Ltd.
Compaq Computer Corp.
Conair, Inc.
Cone-Blanchard Machine Co.
Connell LP
Conner Peripherals
Control Data Corp.
Cooper Industries
Cooper Oil Tool
Copeland Corp.
CR Industries
Crane Co.
Cranston Print Works
Cray Research
CRC Evans Pipeline
    International, Inc.
CRL Inc.
Crompton & Knowles Corp.
Crown Cork & Seal Co., Inc.
CSC Industries
Cubic Corp.
Cummins Engine Co.
Curtiss-Wright Corp.
Dana Corp.
Danaher Corp.
Dataproducts Corp.
DEC International, Inc.
Decision Data Computer Corp.
Deere & Co.
Dexter Co.
Dickey-John Corp.
Diebold, Inc.
Digital Communications
    Associates, Inc.
Digital Equipment Corp.
Donaldson Co.
Douglas & Lomason Company
Dover Elevator Systems Inc.
Dresser Industries
Ducommun Inc.
Duriron Co., Inc.
Dynamet, Inc.
Dynatech Corp.
Dyson-Kissner-Moran Corp.
E-Systems
Eagle-Picher Industries
Eaton Corp.
Ebco Manufacturing Co.
Echlin Inc.
EG&G Inc.
Egan Machinery Co.
Emerson Electric Co.
Enterra Corp.
Esselte Pendaflex Corp.
Esterline Technologies Corp.
ETCO Inc.
Fairchild Corp.
Fedders Corp.
Federal-Mogul Corp.
Fiat U.S.A., Inc.
FKI Holdings Inc.
FMC Corp.
Ford Motor Co.
Freeport Brick Co.
French Oil Mill Machinery Co.
Fujitsu America, Inc.
Fujitsu Systems of America, Inc.
Fuqua Industries, Inc.
Gast Manufacturing Corp.
GCA Corp.
General Electric Co.
General Motors Corp.
General Signal Corp.
Giddings & Lewis
Gleason Works
Goulds Pumps
Graco
Grinnell Corp.
GTE Corp.
Hartzell Industries, Inc.
Heil Co.
Hein-Werner Corp.
Hesston Corp.
Hilliard Corp.

Hitachi
Hobart Corp.
Honda of America
    Manufacturing, Inc.
Howmet Corp.
Hubbell Inc.
Huck International Inc.
Huffy Corp.
Hunt Manufacturing Co.
Hyster-Yale
IBM Corp.
IDEX Corp.
IMO Industries Inc.
Ingersoll Milling Machine Co.
Ingersoll-Rand Co.
Ingram Industries
Intel Corp.
Intergraph Corp.
Johnson Inc., Axel
Jupiter Industries, Inc.
Katy Industries Inc.
Kennametal
Kice Industries, Inc.
Kingsbury Corp.
Klein Tools
Koch Sons, George
Kohler Co.
Kolene Corp.
Kollsman Instrument Co.
Kulicke & Soffa Industries
Kyocera International Inc.
Kysor Industrial Corp.
Landis & Gyr, Inc.
Lanier Business Products, Inc.
Leesona Corp.
Lennox International, Inc.
Lincoln Electric Co.
Litton Industries
Lockheed Sanders
Longyear Co.
Loral Corp.
LSI Logic Corp.
M.T.D. Products
Makita U.S.A., Inc.
Marley Co.
Masco Corp.
Matthews International Corp.
Maxtor Corp.
Maytag Corp.
McDonald Industries, Inc., A. Y.
McDonnell Douglas Corp.
McGill Manufacturing Co.
Medalist Industries, Inc.
Memorex Telex Corp.
Mettler Instrument Corp.
Michigan Wheel Corp.
Microsoft Corp.
Mid-Continent Supply Co.
Minster Machine Co.
Monarch Machine Tool Co.
Montgomery Elevator Co.
Moog, Inc.
Moore Business Forms, Inc.
Moorman Manufacturing Co.
Morgan Construction Co.
Motch Corp.
Motter Printing Press Co.
MPB Corp.
Mueller Co.
Murray Ohio Manufacturing Co.
NACCO Industries
National Computer Systems
National Forge Co.
National Machinery Co.
National Semiconductor Corp.
National Service Industries
National Standard Co.
Navistar International Corp.
NCR Corp.
NCR Corp.
NEC Technologies, Inc.
Neenah Foundry Co.
Nelson Industries, Inc.
New England Aircraft Products
    Co.
New Hampshire Ball Bearings

Industrial Machinery & Equipment (cont.)

Newell Co.
NMB (USA) Inc.
Nordson Corp.
Nortek, Inc.
North American Philips Corp.
Norton Co.
Novell Inc.
NuTone Inc.
Oak Industries
Onan Corp.
Onan Family Foundation
Otis Elevator Co.
Outboard Marine Corp.
PACCAR
Pall Corp.
Park-Ohio Industries Inc.
Parker Drilling Co.
Parker-Hannifin Corp.
Penn Central Corp.
Penske Corp.
Pentair
Perkin-Elmer Corp.
Petrolite Corp.
Pioneer Hi-Bred International
Pitney Bowes
Ply-Gem Industries, Inc.
PMI Food Equipment Group Inc.
Portec, Inc.
Premark International
Premier Industrial Corp.
Prime Computer, Inc.
Pyramid Technology Corp.
Quaker Chemical Corp.
R&B Tool Co.
Ranco, Inc.
Ransburg Corp.
Raymark Corp.
Raymond Corp.
RB&W Corp.
Recognition Equipment
Reell Precision Manufacturing
Reliance Electric Co.
Remmele Engineering, Inc.
Reynolds & Reynolds Co.
Ricoh Corp.
Ricoh Electronics Inc.
Rieke Corp.
Riley Stoker Co.
Rite-Hite Corp.
Robbins & Myers, Inc.
Robertshaw Controls Co.
Rockford Acromatics Products

Co./Aircraft Gear Corp.
Rockwell International Corp.
Rolls-Royce Inc.
Rolm Systems
Safety-Kleen Corp.
San Diego Gas & Electric
Sandusky International Inc.
Sanyo Manufacturing Corp.
Schindler Elevator Corp.
Schlumberger Ltd.
Schreiber Foods, Inc.
SCI Systems, Inc.
Seagate Technology
Sequa Corp.
Sharp Electronics Corp.
Simplex Time Recorder Co.
Sioux Steel Co.
SKF USA, Inc.
Slant/Fin Corp.
Smith Corona Corp.
Smith Corp., A.O.
Smith International
Snap-on Tools Corp.
Snyder General Corp.
Sony Corp. of America
Sordoni Enterprises
Sprint
SPS Technologies
SPX Corp.
Standard Motor Products, Inc.

Standard Register Co.
Standard Steel Speciality Co.
Standex International Corp.
Stanley Works
Starrett Co., L.S.
Steel Heddle Manufacturing Co.
Steelcase
Steiger Tractor
Sterling Inc.
Stewart & Stevenson Services
Stone Container Corp.
Storage Technology Corp.
Sulzer Brothers Inc.
Sun Electric Corp.
Sun Microsystems
Sundstrand Corp.
Support Systems International
Tandem Computers
Tandon Corp.
TBG, Inc.
Tecumseh Products Co.
Tektronix
Telecom Corp.
Teleflex Inc.
Tennant Co.
Tenneco
Texas Instruments
Thermo Electron Corp.
Tidewater, Inc.
Timken Co.
Tokheim Corp.
Tomkins Industries, Inc.
Toro Co.
Torrington Co.
TRINOVA Corp.
TRW Corp.
Tyco Laboratories, Inc.
Unisys Corp.
United Conveyor Corp.
United Technologies, Automotive
United Technologies Corp.
Unitrode Corp.
Valmont Industries
Valvoline Inc.
Vermeer Charitable Foundation
Vermeer Investment Company Foundation
Vermeer Manufacturing Co.
Vilter Manufacturing Corp.
Vogt Machine Co., Henry
Wang Laboratories, Inc.
Ward Machinery Co.
Watkins-Johnson Co.
WEA Enterprises Co.
Weatherford International, Inc.
West Co.
Westinghouse Electric Corp.
Whirlpool Corp.
WICOR, Inc.
Williamson Co.
Woodward Governor Co.
Wynn's International, Inc.
Xerox Corp.
XTEK Inc.
York International Corp.
Zebco/Motorguide Corp.

Instruments & Related Products (SIC 38)

ABB Process Automation
Abbott Laboratories
Acme United Corp.
ADC Telecommunications
Air & Water Technologies Corp.
Alcon Laboratories, Inc.
Alfa-Laval, Inc.
Allergan, Inc.
American Electronics
American Home Products Corp.
American Optical Corp.
AMETEK
Amsco International
Analog Devices
Analogic Corp.

Asea Brown Boveri
Aydin Corp.
Badger Meter, Inc.
Bairnco Corp.
Barber-Colman Co.
Bard, C. R.
Basic American Medical, Inc.
Bausch & Lomb
Baxter International
Beckman Instruments
Becton Dickinson & Co.
Becton Dickinson & Co.
Beech Aircraft Corp.
Berwind Corp.
Betz Laboratories
Bio-Medicus, Inc.
Biomet
Block Drug Co.
BMC Industries
BOC Group
Boehringer Mannheim Corp.
Bourns, Inc.
Brown & Sharpe Manufacturing

Co.
Burron Medical
Canon U.S.A., Inc.
Carter-Wallace
CBI Industries
Chesebrough-Pond's
Christie Electric Corp.
Chrysler Corp.
COBE Laboratories, Inc.
Contraves USA
CooperVision, Inc.
Corning Incorporated
Coulter Corp.
Crompton & Knowles Corp.
Cubic Corp.
Delco Electronics Corp.
Dentsply International, Inc.
Diasonics, Inc.
Dickey-John Corp.
Dow Corning Corp.
Dresser Industries
Durr-Fillauer Medical
Dynatech Corp.
E-Systems
Eastman Kodak Co.
EG&G Inc.
Eldec Corp.
Emerson Electric Co.
Esterline Technologies Corp.
Everest & Jennings International
Fischer & Porter Co.
FMC Corp.
Ford Meter Box Co.
Ford Motor Co.
Galileo Electro-Optics Corp.
GCA Corp.
General Motors Corp.
General Signal Corp.
GenRad
Gleason Works
Graphic Controls Corp.
Grass Instrument Co.
Gruen Marketing
Grumman Corp.
Hand Industries
Hewlett-Packard Co.
Honeywell
Hughes Aircraft Co.
Ideal Industries
IMCERA Group Inc.
IMO Industries Inc.
Instron Corp.
James River Corp. of Virginia
Johnson Inc., Axel
Johnson Controls
Johnson & Johnson
Kaman Corp.
Kendall Health Care Products
Koh-I-Noor Rapidograph Inc.
Kollsman Instrument Co.
Krelitz Industries
Landis & Gyr, Inc.
Lincoln Telecommunications Co.

Litton Industries
Litton/Itek Optical Systems
Lockheed Corp.
Lockheed Sanders
Mallinckrodt Specialty Chemicals Co.
Mark Controls Corp.
Marquette Electronics
McDonnell Douglas Corp.-West
Medtronic
MEI Diversified, Inc.
Metromedia Co.
Miles Inc., Diagnostic Division
Mill-Rose Co.
Millipore Corp.
Mine Safety Appliances Co.
MTS Systems Corp.
Oak Industries
Ontario Corp.
Pall Corp.
Park Communications Inc.
Pearle Vision
Perkin-Elmer Corp.
Picker International
Polaroid Corp.
Polychrome Corp.
Preformed Line Products Co.
Premier Dental Products Co.
Ranco, Inc.
Ransburg Corp.
Raytheon Co.
Research-Cottrell Inc.
Ricoh Corp.
Ricoh Electronics Inc.
Robertshaw Controls Co.
Rosemount, Inc.
Schlumberger Ltd.
SCI Systems, Inc.
Scientific-Atlanta
Sequa Corp.
Sharp Electronics Corp.
Sherwood Medical Co.
Siebe North Inc.
Siemens Medical Systems Inc.
Simplex Time Recorder Co.
Sony Corp. of America
Sparton Corp.
Spartus Corp.
Spectra-Physics Analytical
Square D Co.
Storz Instrument Co.
Sun Electric Corp.
Sundstrand Corp.
Talley Industries, Inc.
Tasty Baking Co.
Tektronix
Teradyne, Inc.
Texas Instruments
Textron
Thermo Electron Corp.
Timex Corp.
Tokheim Corp.
TRINOVA Corp.
United States Surgical Corp.
United Technologies Corp.
Varian Associates
Vernitron Corp.
W. L. T.
Watkins-Johnson Co.
Whittaker Corp.
Zimmer Inc.

Insurance Agents, Brokers & Service (SIC 64)

Aetna Life & Casualty Co.
AFLAC
Alexander & Alexander Services, Inc.
Automatic Data Processing, Inc.
Ayco Corp.
Bankers Life & Casualty Co.
Banner Life Insurance Co.
Broad, Inc.
CIGNA Corp.

CNA Insurance Cos.
Columbus Life Insurance Co.
Corroon & Black of Illinois
Corroon & Black of Oregon
Country Cos.
Crawford & Co.
CUNA Mutual Insurance Group
Durham Corp.
Edwards & Sons, A.G.
Equifax
First National Bank of Atlanta
First Source Corp.
Great West Casualty Co.
Hall & Co. Inc., Frank B.
Industrial Risk Insurers
Insurance Management Associates
James & Co., Fred S.
Johnson & Higgins
Kemper National Insurance Cos.
Lazard Freres & Co.
Life Investors Insurance Company of America
Madison Mutual Insurance Co.
Marsh & McLennan Cos.
NationsBank Texas
New England Mutual Life Insurance Co.
Penn Central Corp.
Rebsamen Companies, Inc.
Security Capital Corp.
Sedgwick James Inc.
Skandia America Reinsurance Corp.
Sun Banks Inc.
Union Planters Corp.
Utica National Insurance Group
Wachovia Bank of Georgia, N.A.

Insurance Carriers (SIC 63)

Acacia Mutual Life Insurance Co.
AEGON USA, Inc.
Aetna Life & Casualty Co.
AFLAC
Allendale Mutual Insurance Co.
Allstate Insurance Co.
American Bankers Insurance Group
American Financial Corp.
American General Corp.
American General Finance
American General Life & Accident Insurance Co.
American International Group, Inc.
American Mutual Insurance Cos.
American National Insurance
American Re-Insurance Co.
American Security Bank
American United Life Insurance Co.
Ameritas Life Insurance Corp.
AON Corp.
Argonaut Group
Arkwright-Boston Manufacturers Mutual
Armco Inc.
Atlantic Mutual Cos.
Baltimore Life Insurance Co.
Bang & Olufsen of America, Inc.
Bang & Olufsen of America, Inc.
Bang & Olufsen of America, Inc.
Bankers Life & Casualty Co.
Banner Life Insurance Co.
BarclaysAmerican Corp.
Beneficial Corp.
Benefit Trust Life Insurance Co.
Berkshire Hathaway
Bitco Corp.
Blue Cross & Blue Shield of Alabama
Blue Cross/Blue Shield of Michigan
Boston Mutual Life Insurance Co.

Broad, Inc.
Capital Holding Corp.
Central Life Assurance Co.
Century Companies of America
Chicago Title and Trust Co.
Chubb Corp.
Chubb Life Insurance Co. of America
Church Mutual Insurance
CIGNA Corp.
Cincinnati Financial Corp.
CM Alliance Cos.
CNA Insurance Cos.
Collins & Aikman Holdings Corp.
Colonial Life & Accident Insurance Co.
Colonial Penn Group, Inc.
Columbus Life Insurance Co.
Commercial Credit Co.
Commonwealth Industries Corp.
Commonwealth Life Insurance Co.
Community Mutual Insurance Co.
Continental Corp.
Country Cos.
Crum and Forster
CUNA Mutual Insurance Group
Durham Corp.
Educators Mutual Life Insurance Co.
Employers Insurance of Wausau, A Mutual Co.
Employers Mutual Casualty Co.
Equitable Life Assurance Society of the U.S.
Equitable Variable Life Insurance Co.
Ethyl Corp.
Farmers Group, Inc.
Federated American Insurance
Federated Life Insurance Co.
Fidelity Mutual Life Insurance Co.
Fireman's Fund Insurance Co.
First American Financial Corp.
First National Bank in Wichita
First Security Corp. (Salt Lake City, Utah)
Fortis Inc.
Fortis Benefits Insurance Company/Fortis Financial Group
Fourth Financial Corp.
Franklin Life Insurance Co.
GEICO Corp.
General Accident Insurance Co. of America
General American Life Insurance Co.
General Reinsurance Corp.
Gerber Products Co.
Great West Casualty Co.
Great-West Life Assurance Co.
Grinnell Mutual Reinsurance Co.
Group Health Plan Inc.
Guardian Life Insurance Co. of America
Hall & Co. Inc., Frank B.
Halliburton Co.
Hanover Insurance Co.
Harcourt Brace Jovanovich
Harleysville Mutual Insurance Co.
Hartford Steam Boiler Inspection & Insurance Co.
Hawkeye Bancorporation
Hillenbrand Industries
Holyoke Mutual Insurance Co. in Salem
Home Beneficial Corp.
Humana
ICH Corp.
ICI Americas
Indiana Insurance Cos.
Industrial Risk Insurers
Integrated Resources

Inter-State Assurance Co.
Interstate National Corp.
ITT Hartford Insurance Group
Jackson National Life Insurance Co.
Jefferson-Pilot
John Hancock Mutual Life Insurance Co.
Kemper Investors Life Insurance Co.
Kemper National Insurance Cos.
Kentucky Central Life Insurance
Keyport Life Insurance Co.
Leucadia National Corp.
Liberty Corp.
Liberty Mutual Insurance Group/Boston
Life Insurance Co. of Georgia
Life Investors Insurance Company of America
Lincoln National Corp.
Loews Corp.
Madison Mutual Insurance Co.
Manufacturers Life Insurance Co. of America
Maryland Casualty Co.
Massachusetts Mutual Life Insurance Co.
Maxicare Health Plans
MBIA, Inc.
Meridian Insurance Group Inc.
Metropolitan Life Insurance Co.
MGIC Investment Corp.
Michigan Mutual Insurance Corp.
Middlesex Mutual Assurance Co.
Midland Mutual Life Insurance Co.
Minnesota Mutual Life Insurance Co.
MSI Insurance
Mutual of America Life
Mutual of New York
Mutual of Omaha Insurance Co.
Mutual Savings Life Insurance Co.
Mutual Service Life Insurance Cos.
National Life of Vermont
National Travelers Life Co.
Nationale-Nederlanden North America Corp.
Nationwide Insurance Cos.
New England Mutual Life Insurance Co.
New Jersey Manufacturers Insurance Co.
New Jersey National Bank
New York Life Insurance Co.
New York Marine & General Insurance Co.
Nippon Life Insurance Co.
North American Life & Casualty Co.
North American Reinsurance Corp.
Northwestern National Insurance Group
Northwestern National Life Insurance Co.
Ohio Casualty Corp.
Ohio National Life Insurance Co.
Old American Insurance Co.
Old Republic International Corp.
Oregon Mutual Insurance Co.
Orion Capital Corp.
Pan-American Life Insurance Co.
Peerless Insurance Co.
Penn Mutual Life Insurance Co.
Pennsylvania General Insurance Co.
Phoenix Home Life Mutual Insurance Co.
Physicians Mutual Insurance
Preferred Risk Mutual Insurance Co.
Primerica Corp.
Principal Financial Group
Progressive Corp.

Provident Life & Accident Insurance Co.
Provident Mutual Life Insurance Co. of Philadelphia
Prudential Insurance Co. of America
Reliable Life Insurance Co.
Reliance Group Holdings, Inc.
Reliance Insurance Cos.
Republic Financial Services, Inc.
Royal Group Inc.
Royal Insurance Co. of America
Ryder System
SAFECO Corp.
Saint Paul Cos.
Sammons Enterprises
Sears, Roebuck and Co.
Security Benefit Life Insurance Co.
Security Life Insurance Co. of America
Security Life of Denver
Sentry Insurance Co.
Shelter Mutual Insurance Co.
Shenandoah Life Insurance Co.
Skandia America Reinsurance Corp.
Southwestern Life Insurance Co.
State Farm Mutual Automobile Insurance Co.
State Mutual Life Assurance Co.
Statesman Group, Inc.
Sun Life Assurance Co. of Canada (U.S.)
Teledyne
Textron
Time Insurance Co.
Torchmark Corp.
Transamerica Occidental Life Insurance Co.
Travelers Cos.
Twentieth Century Insurance Co.
Unigard Security Insurance Co.
Union Central Life Insurance Co.
Union Mutual Fire Insurance Co.
United Fire & Casualty Co.
United Services Automobile Association
U.S. Healthcare, Inc.
UNUM Corp.
USF&G Co.
Uslico Corp.
USLIFE Corp.
Utica National Insurance Group
Washington National Insurance Co.
Wausau Insurance Cos.

Leather & Leather Products (SIC 31)

Acushnet Co.
Akzo America
Amdur Braude Riley, Inc.
Athlone Industries, Inc.
Bally Inc.
Barry Corp., R. G.
Blue Bell, Inc.
Brown-Forman Corp.
Brown Group
Brown Shoe Co.
Dexter Shoe Co.
Florsheim Shoe Co.
Genesco
Gucci America Inc.
Hartz Mountain Corp.
Hillenbrand Industries
Interco
Jostens
Justin Industries, Inc.
Klein Tools
L.A. Gear
Melville Corp.
New Balance Athletic Shoe
Nike Inc.
Page Belting Co.
Pfister and Vogel Tanning Co.

Phillips-Van Heusen Corp.
Red Wing Shoe Co.
Seton Co.
Stride Rite Corp.
Swank, Inc.
US Shoe Corp.
Wolff Shoe Co.
Wolverine World Wide, Inc.

Legal Services (SIC 81)

Buchalter, Nemer, Fields, & Younger
Covington and Burling
Donovan, Leisure, Newton & Irvine
Foley, Hoag & Eliot
Katten, Muchin, & Zavis
Kaye, Scholer, Fierman, Hays & Handler
Kirkland & Ellis
Schiff, Hardin & Waite
Wachtell, Lipton, Rosen & Katz

Local & Interurban Passenger Transit (SIC 41)

Dial Corp.
Fleming Companies, Inc.
Mayflower Group
PHH Corp.
Ryder System
SCANA Corp.

Lumber & Wood Products (SIC 24)

Abitibi-Price
Acme United Corp.
American Cyanamid Co.
Amoskeag Co.
Andersen Corp.
APL Corp.
Bend Millwork Systems
Bohemia Inc.
Boise Cascade Corp.
Butler Manufacturing Co.
Ceco Corp.
Celotex Corp.
CertainTeed Corp.
Champion International Corp.
Chesapeake Corp.
Clopay Corp.
Coachmen Industries
Collins & Aikman Holdings Corp.
Contran Corp.
Cooper Wood Products
Crane Co.
Erb Lumber Co.
Fleetwood Enterprises, Inc.
Foldcraft Co.
Frank Lumber Co.
Georgia-Pacific Corp.
Greif Brothers Corp.
Hartzell Industries, Inc.
Intercraft Co., Inc.
International Paper Co.
ITT Corp.
ITT Rayonier
Jasper Wood Products Co.
JELD-WEN, Inc.
Kaibab Industries
Louisiana-Pacific Corp.
Marsh Furniture Co.
Masonite Corp.
Medford Corp.
Menasha Corp.
Murphy Oil Corp.
National Manufacturing Co.
Packaging Corporation of America
Patrick Industries Inc.
Pella Corp.
Pfizer

Pickering Industries
PK Lumber Co.
Ply-Gem Industries, Inc.
Pope & Talbot, Inc.
Potlatch Corp.
Quaker Chemical Corp.
Redman Industries
Roseburg Forest Products Co.
Scheirich Co., H.J.
Scott Paper Co.
Sealaska Corp.
Sierra Pacific Industries
Skyline Corp.
Snap-on Tools Corp.
Sonoco Products Co.
Stone Forest Industries
Temple-Inland
Union Camp Corp.
Weyerhaeuser Co.
Willamette Industries, Inc.

Metal Mining (SIC 10)

AMAX
American Cyanamid Co.
ASARCO
B.H.P. Minerals
BHP Utah International
Cleveland-Cliffs
Cominco American Inc.
Costain Holdings Inc.
Cyprus Minerals Corp.
First Mississippi Corp.
Freeport-McMoRan
Gold Fields Mining Co.
Hanna Co., M.A.
Hecla Mining Co.
Homestake Mining Co.
Kaisertech Ltd.
Kennecott Corp.
Magma Copper Co.
Nerco, Inc.
Newmont Mining Corp.
Oglebay Norton Co.
PacifiCorp
Pegasus Gold Corp.
Phelps Dodge Corp.
Reynolds Metals Co.
Terra Industries
Union Carbide Corp.
Union Pacific Corp.
USX Corp.

Miscellaneous Manufacturing Industries (SIC 39)

Acushnet Co.
Amcast Industrial Corp.
American Biltrite
American Filtrona Corp.
American Greetings Corp.
Anchor Fasteners
Apex Oil Co.
Armbrust Chain Co.
Armstrong World Industries Inc.
Atari Corp.
Avon Products
Baccarat Inc.
Ballou & Co., B.A.
Belding Heminway Co.
Binney & Smith Inc.
Bristol-Myers Squibb Co.
Browning
Browning Charitable Foundation, Val A.
Cabot Corp.
Coats & Clark Inc.
Cross Co., A.T.
Crystal Brands
Dennison Manufacturing Co.
Douglas Corp.
Easton Aluminum
Enterra Corp.
Fisher-Price

Miscellaneous Manufacturing Industries (cont.)

Franklin Mint Corp.
Fuqua Industries, Inc.
Galileo Electro-Optics Corp.
General Housewares Corp.
Gillette Co.
Goodman Jewelers, Inc.
Graphic Controls Corp.
Gruen Marketing
Hand Industries
Harper Brush Works
Hartz Mountain Corp.
Hasbro
Huffy Corp.
IBM Corp.
Johnson & Son, S.C.
Jostens
Kelco Industries, Inc.
Kilmartin Industries
Kimball International
Koh-I-Noor Rapidograph Inc.
La-Co. Industries, Inc.
Loren Industries Inc.
Matchbox Toys (USA) Ltd.
Mattel
Matthews International Corp.
Medalist Industries, Inc.
Milton Bradley Co.
Mizuno Corporation of America
Murray Ohio Manufacturing Co.
Napier Co.
Northwestern Golf Co.
Oneida Ltd.
Osborn Manufacturing Co.
Oster/Sunbeam Appliance Co.
Parker Brothers and Company Inc.
Parker Pen USA Ltd.
Peoples Energy Corp.
Polk & Co., R.L.
Prince Manufacturing, Inc.
Quaker Oats Co.
Ricoh Electronics Inc.
Rite-Hite Corp.
Rochester Midland Corp.
Sheaffer Inc.
Sherwin-Williams Co.
Standex International Corp.
Stanhome Inc.
Swank, Inc.
Talley Industries, Inc.
Towle Manufacturing Co.
Town & Country Corp.
United Merchants & Manufacturers
Vollrath Co.
Wallace Computer Services
Western Publishing Co., Inc.
Y.K.K. (U.S.A.) Inc.
York Barbell Co.
Zebco/Motorguide Corp.
Zippo Manufacturing Co.

Miscellaneous Repair Services (SIC 76)

Brown & Sharpe Manufacturing Co.
Chemed Corp.
Magnatek
Metroquip
Sanyo Fisher Service Corp.
Savin Corp.
Sega of America
Smith International
Sun Electric Corp.
UNC, Inc.

Miscellaneous Retail (SIC 59)

Affiliated Publications, Inc.

Alco Standard Corp.
American Amusement Arcades
American Business Products, Inc.
American Stores Co.
Atwood Industries
AXIA Incorporated
Bartell Drug Co.
Bean, L.L.
Best Products Co.
Blair Corp.
Brodart Co.
Brown Group
Bruno's Inc.
Carlyle & Co. Jewelers
Cartier, Inc.
Cole National Corp.
CPI Corp.
Cullum Cos.
Dart Group Corp.
Delta Woodside Industries
Duty Free International
Earth Care Paper, Inc.
Eckerd Corp., Jack
Erving Paper Mills
Fay's Incorporated
Ferrell Cos.
Fingerhut Corp.
Foodarama Supermarkets, Inc.
Franklin Mint Corp.
Franks Nursery and Crafts
Giant Food
Goodman Jewelers, Inc.
HarCo. Drug
Hook Drug
Intermark, Inc.
JCPenney Co.
Kobacker Co.
Lanier Business Products, Inc.
Lechmere
Levinson's, Inc.
Lionel Corp.
Longs Drug Stores
Luria's
Marsh Supermarkets, Inc.
Mast Drug Co.
Mayacamas Corp.
Meenan Oil Co., Inc.
Melville Corp.
Meyer, Inc., Fred
Moore Medical Corp.
Neiman Marcus
Oshman's Sporting Goods, Inc.
Pacific Enterprises
Patagonia
Pay 'N Save Inc.
PayLess Drug Stores
Pearle Vision
Peoples Drug Stores Inc.
Perry Drug Stores
Petroleum Marketers
Philadelphia Industries
Pier 1 Imports, Inc.
Prange Co., H. C.
Raley's
Rebsamen Companies, Inc.
REI-Recreational Equipment, Inc.
Reily & Co., William B.
Reiss Coal Co., C.
Rite Aid Corp.
Rose's Stores, Inc.
Sears, Roebuck and Co.
Seaway Food Town
Seventh Generation
Shaklee Corp.
Skaggs Alpha Beta Co.
Smith Oil Corp.
Spiegel
Stanhome Inc.
Sterling Inc.
Steuart Petroleum Corp.
Thrift Drug, Inc.
Thrifty Corp.
Town & Country Corp.
Toys "R" Us, Inc.
UGI Corp.

Walgreen Co.
Webber Oil Co.
World Book Inc.
Zale Corp.

Motion Pictures (SIC 78)

Banta Corp.
Bergen Brunswig Corp.
Dartnell Corp.
Fox Inc.
Handleman Co.
Harcourt General
Home Box Office
Ingram Industries
Kajima International, Inc.
MacAndrews & Forbes Holdings
Marcus Corp.
MCA
Metromedia Co.
Metropolitan Theatres Corp.
News America Publishing Inc.
Paramount Communications Inc.
Playboy Enterprises, Inc.
Simon & Schuster Inc.
Tele-Communications, Inc.
Time Warner
Turner Broadcasting System
Twentieth Century-Fox Film Corp.
United Artists Theatre Circuits
Viacom International Inc.
Disney Co., Walt

Nonclassifiable Establishments (SIC 99)

Peterson & Co. Consulting

Nondepository Institutions (SIC 61)

Ahmanson & Co., H.F.
Allen & Co.
American Express Co.
American General Corp.
American General Finance
Ameritech Corp.
Bank of America
BarclaysAmerican Corp.
Boston Co., Inc.
Brenton Banks Inc.
Brewer and Co., Ltd., C.
CIT Group Holdings
CNA Insurance Cos.
Colorado National Bankshares
Commercial Credit Co.
Continental Corp.
Continental Wingate Co., Inc.
Dean Witter Discover
Farm Credit Banks of Springfield
Federal Home Loan Mortgage Corp. (Freddie Mac)
First Interstate Bancsystem of Montana
First Union Corp.
Fleetwood Enterprises, Inc.
Fortis Inc.
Heller Financial
Homestead Financial Corp.
Household International
Imperial Corp. of America
Kaufman & Broad Home Corp.
Leucadia National Corp.
Lomas Financial Corp.
M.D.C. Holdings
McDonnell Douglas Corp.
McDonnell Douglas Corp.-West
Midlantic Banks, Inc.
Nellie Mae
Newmont Mining Corp.
Ohio Casualty Corp.
Philip Morris Cos.

Primark Corp.
Primerica Corp.
PriMerit F.S.B.
Principal Financial Group
Rochester Community Savings Bank
Ryland Group
St. Paul Federal Bank for Savings
Salomon
Security Benefit Life Insurance Co.
Service Corp. International
Shuwa Investments Corp.
Statesman Group, Inc.
Steiger Tractor
Student Loan Marketing Association
Sun Banks Inc.
Third National Corp.
Tucker Anthony, Inc.
Tultex Corp.
UDC-Universal Development LP
UJB Financial Corp.
United Fire & Casualty Co.
Volvo North America Corp.
Wachovia Bank of Georgia, N.A.
Washington Water Power Co.
Williams Cos.

Nonmetallic Minerals Except Fuels (SIC 14)

American Aggregates Corp.
American Cyanamid Co.
Ameron, Inc.
APAC Inc.
Burlington Resources
CalMat Co.
Cominco American Inc.
Costain Holdings Inc.
Cyprus Minerals Co.
Elf Atochem North America
Florida Rock Industries
Freeport-McMoRan
Green Industries, A. P.
Hecla Mining Co.
Huber Corp., J.M.
International Paper Co.
Kaiser Cement Corp.
Kerr-McGee Corp.
Longyear Co.
Martin Marietta Aggregates
Martin Marietta Corp.
Pennzoil Co.
Pfizer
Rinker Materials Corp.
Shoemaker Co., R.M.
South Jersey Industries
Stabler Cos., Inc.
Tarmac America Inc.
United States Borax & Chemical Corp.
U.S. Silica Co.
Vulcan Materials Co.

Oil & Gas Extraction (SIC 13)

Adams Resources & Energy, Inc.
AMAX
Amerada Hess Corp.
American Natural Resources
American Trading & Production Corp.
Amoco Corp.
Anadarko Petroleum Corp.
Angeles Corp.
Apache Corp.
ARCO
Arkla
Ashland Oil
Atkinson Co., Guy F.
Baker Hughes Inc.
Baroid Corp.

BP Exploration
Brooklyn Union Gas Co.
Brown Inc., Tom
Burlington Resources
Burnett Construction Co.
Cabot Corp.
Chevron Corp.
Clarity Holdings Corp.
CNG Transmission Corp.
Coastal Corp.
Colorado Interstate Gas Co.
Conoco Inc.
Consolidated Natural Gas Co.
Contran Corp.
Cook Inlet Region
Crown Central Petroleum Corp.
DeBlois Oil Co.
Digicon
du Pont de Nemours & Co., E. I.
Elf Aquitaine, Inc.
Enron Corp.
Ensearch Corp.
Equitable Resources
Exxon Corp.
FINA, Inc.
Forest Oil Corp.
Grace & Co., W.R.
Grace Petroleum Corp.
Grant-Norpac, Inc.
Gulf USA Corp.
Hadson Corp.
Halliburton Co.
Hamilton Oil Corp.
Hanna Co., M.A.
Harbert Corp.
Helmerich & Payne Inc.
Howell Corp.
Hunt Oil Co.
Iowa-Illinois Gas & Electric Co.
Kaneb Services, Inc.
Katy Industries Inc.
Kerr-McGee Corp.
King Ranch
KN Energy, Inc.
Koch Industries
Louisiana Land & Exploration Co.
Maguire Oil Co.
Mapco Inc.
Maxus Energy Corp.
McDermott
Mesa Inc.
Mid-Continent Supply Co.
Mitchell Energy & Development Corp.
Mobil Oil Corp.
Montana Power Co.
Murphy Oil Corp.
New Jersey Resources Corp.
Newmont Mining Corp.
Nicor, Inc.
Noble Affiliates, Inc.
North American Royalties
Northwest Pipeline Corp.
Norton Co.
Occidental Oil & Gas Corp.
Occidental Petroleum Corp.
ONEOK Inc.
Pacific Enterprises
Panhandle Eastern Corp.
Parker Drilling Co.
Pennzoil Co.
Phibro Energy
Phillips Petroleum Co.
Phoenix Resource Cos.
Placid Oil Co.
Pogo Producing Co.
Pool Energy Services Co.
Presley Cos.
Questar Corp.
Raytheon Co.
Reading & Bates Corp.
Rowan Cos., Inc.
Santa Fe International Corp.
Santa Fe Pacific Corp.
Schlumberger Ltd.

Shell Oil Co.
Smith International
Sonat
Sonat Exploration
Sonat Offshore Drilling
South Jersey Industries
Southern California Gas Co.
Sparton Corp.
Stone Container Corp.
Sun Co.
Tesoro Petroleum Corp.
Texaco
Thums Long Beach Co.
Tidewater, Inc.
Tosco Corp. Refining Division
Transco Energy Company
UGI Corp.
Union Pacific Corp.
Union Texas Petroleum
United States Borax & Chemical
Corp.
Unocal Corp.
Unocal-Union Oil of California
USX Corp.
Valero Energy Corp.
Vista Chemical Company
Weatherford International, Inc.
WICOR, Inc.
Zapata Corp.

Paper & Allied Products (SIC 26)

Acorn Corrugated Box Co.
American Biltrite
American Business Products, Inc.
American Filtrona Corp.
American Greetings Corp.
American National Can Co.
APL Corp.
Appleton Papers
Avery Dennison Corp.
Bemis Company
Boise Cascade Corp.
Bowater Inc.
Champion International Corp.
Chase Packaging Corp.
Chemtech Industries
Chesapeake Corp.
CLARCOR
Clorox Co.
Consolidated Papers
Continental Can Co.
Crane & Co.
Dennison Manufacturing Co.
Eastern Fine Paper, Inc.
Erving Paper Mills
Esselte Pendaflex Corp.
Federal Paper Board Co.
Fibre Converters
First Brands Corp.
Fraser Paper Ltd.
Friedman Bag Co.
Gaylord Container Corp.
Gilman Investment Co.
Gilman Paper Co.
Glatfelter Co., P.H.
Graphic Controls Corp.
Greif Brothers Corp.
Hampden Papers
HON Industries
Hunt Manufacturing Co.
Inland Container Corp.
Instrument Systems Corp.
International Paper Co.
Interstate Packaging Co.
ITT Rayonier
James River Corp. of Virginia
Jefferson Smurfit Corp.
Johnson & Johnson
Kimberly-Clark Corp.
Liberty Diversified Industries
Inc.
Longview Fibre Co.
Louisiana-Pacific Corp.
Lydall, Inc.

Manville Corp.
Mead Corp.
Mebane Packaging Corp.
Media General, Inc.
Melitta North America Inc.
Menasha Corp.
Monadnock Paper Mills
Moore Business Forms, Inc.
Mosinee Paper Corp.
National Gypsum Co.
NVF Co.
Old Dominion Box Co.
Orchard Corp. of America.
Packaging Corporation of
America
Pantasote Polymers
Parsons and Whittemore Inc.
Pentair
Philadelphia Industries
Pitney Bowes
Ply-Gem Industries, Inc.
Pope & Talbot, Inc.
Potlatch Corp.
Printpack, Inc.
Procter & Gamble Co.
Rand-Whitney
Packaging-Delmar Corp.
Rexham Inc.
Rochester Midland Corp.
St. Joe Paper Co.
Scott Paper Co.
Sealed Air Corp.
Sealright Co., Inc.
Sheaffer Inc.
Simkins Industries, Inc.
Simpson Paper Co.
Solo Cup Co.
Sonoco Products Co.
Standard Register Co.
Stone Container Corp.
Tambrands Inc.
Temple-Inland
Tension Envelope Corp.
3M Co.
Times Mirror Co.
Tranzonic Cos.
Tropicana Products, Inc.
Union Camp Corp.
USG Corp.
W. L. T.
Warren Co., S.D.
Wausau Paper Mills Co.
Werthan Packaging, Inc.
Westvaco Corp.
Weyerhaeuser Co.
Willamette Industries, Inc.
Wurzburg, Inc.

Personal Services (SIC 72)

American Building Maintenance
Industries
American Linen Supply Co.
Angelica Corp.
Aratex Services
Ayco Corp.
Bachrach, Inc.
Block, H&R
CPI Corp.
Lincoln Telecommunications Co.
MEI Diversified, Inc.
National Service Industries
Nutri/System Inc.
Regis Corp.
Service Corp. International
ServiceMaster Co. L.P.
Steiner Corp.
Weight Watchers International

Petroleum & Coal Products (SIC 29)

Abitibi-Price
Agway
Akzo America
Amerada Hess Corp.

APAC Inc.
ARCO
Ashland Oil
Ausimont, U.S.A.
BHP Pacific Resources
Callanan Industries
CalMat Co.
Caltex Petroleum Corp.
Celotex Corp.
Chevron Corp.
Clark Oil & Refining Corp.
Conoco Inc.
Crown Central Petroleum Corp.
Diamond Shamrock
Exxon Corp.
Farmland Industries, Inc.
Fel-Pro Incorporated
FINA, Inc.
First Brands Corp.
GAF Corp.
Great Lakes Carbon Corp.
Great Lakes Chemical Corp.
Harsco Corp.
Houghton & Co., E.F.
Hunt Oil Co.
Iroquois Brands, Ltd.
Klein Tools
La-Co. Industries, Inc.
Levy Co., Edward C.
Lyondell Petrochemical Co.
Marathon Oil, Indiana Refining
Division
Mobil Oil Corp.
Murphy Oil Corp.
Nalco Chemical Co.
Navajo Refining Co.
Ohio Road Paving Co.
Pennzoil Co.
Phibro Energy
Phillips Petroleum Co.
Placid Oil Co.
Premier Industrial Corp.
Quaker Chemical Corp.
Quaker State Corp.
Reilly Industries
Rexene Products Co.
Safety-Kleen Corp.
Shell Oil Co.
Star Enterprise
Tamko Asphalt Products
Tesoro Petroleum Corp.
Texaco
Texas Olefins Co.
Thrifty Oil Co.
Tosco Corp. Refining Division
Tremco Inc.
Union Pacific Corp.
Uniroyal Chemical Co. Inc.
United Gas Pipe Line Co.
United Refining Co
UNO-VEN Co.
Unocal Corp.
Valvoline Inc.
Vulcan Materials Co.
Witco Corp.
Wynn's International, Inc.

Pipelines Except Natural Gas (SIC 46)

Alyeska Pipeline Service Co.
Kaneb Services, Inc.
Koch Industries
Mapco Inc.
Permian Corp.
Sun Co.
Tenneco
Texaco
Williams Cos.

Primary Metal Industries (SIC 33)

Aarque Cos.
Alcan Aluminum Corp.

Alcatel NA Cable Systems, Inc.
Alhambra Foundry Co., Ltd.
Allegheny Ludlum Corp.
Alumax
Aluminum Co. of America
AMAX
Amcast Industrial Corp.
Amsted Industries
Anchor Fasteners
Andal Corp.
Andrew Corp.
Armco Inc.
Armco Steel Co.
ASARCO
Athlone Industries, Inc.
Babcock & Wilcox Co.
Barden Corp.
Bethlehem Steel Corp.
Betts Industries
Brillion Iron Works
Brush Wellman Inc.
Budd Co.
Carol Cable Co.
Carpenter Technology Corp.
Cawsl Corp.
Champion Spark Plug Co.
Charter Manufacturing Co.
Chicago White Metal Casting
Commercial Metals Co.
Connell LP
Cookson America
Copperweld Corp.
Copperweld Steel Co.
Croft Metals
CSC Industries
Curtiss-Wright Corp.
Dayton-Walther Corp.
Delaware North Cos.
Dexter Co.
Diversified Industries, Inc.
Douglas Corp.
Dow Chemical Co.
Dynamet, Inc.
Easco Corp.
Eastern Foundry Co.
Eastern Stainless Corp.
Easton Aluminum
Edgewater Steel Corp.
Elastimold Corp.
Elixir Industries
Everest & Jennings International
Federal Screw Works
FKI Holdings Inc.
Florida Steel Corp.
Ford Meter Box Co.
Foster Co., L.B.
Galileo Electro-Optics Corp.
General Housewares Corp.
GNB Inc.
Goulds Pumps
Great Lakes Casting Corp.
Grede Foundries
Handy & Harman
Harvard Industries
Hayes Albion Industries
Hexcel Corp.
Hitachi
Hobart Corp.
Howmet Corp., Wichita Falls
Casting Division
Howmet Corp., Wichita Falls
Refurbishment Center
Howmet Corp., Winstead
Machining
Inco Alloys International
Inland Steel Industries
International Aluminum Corp.
IU International
J&L Specialty Products Corp.
Jessop Steel Co.
Johnson Matthey Investments
Jorgensen Co., Earle M.
Kaiser Aluminum & Chemical
Corp.
Kaisertech Ltd.
Kennametal

Kice Industries, Inc.
Kolene Corp.
Laclede Steel Co.
Lapham-Hickey Steel Corp.
Loral Corp.
Loren Industries Inc.
LPL Technologies Inc.
LTV Corp.
Lukens
Marmon Group, Inc.
Maynard Steel Casting Co.
McLouth Steel-An Employee
Owned Co.
McWane Inc.
Miller & Co.
Monsanto Co.
Mueller Co.
National Forge Co.
National Standard Co.
National Steel
Neenah Foundry Co.
New Hampshire Ball Bearings
Nortek, Inc.
North American Philips Corp.
North American Royalties
North Star Steel Co.
Northwestern Steel & Wire Co.
NRC, Inc.
Nucor Corp.
NVF Co.
Okonite Co.
Olin Corp.
Oneida Ltd.
Ormet Corp.
OsCo. Industries
Outokumpu-American Brass Co.
Padnos Iron & Metal Co., Louis
Pechiney Corp.
Phelps Dodge Corp.
Precision Castparts Corp.
Quanex Corp.
Ravenswood Aluminum Corp.
Raychem Corp.
Redman Industries
Republic Engineered Steels
Reynolds Metals Co.
Rouge Steel Co.
RSR Corp.
Sharon Steel Corp.
Smitty's Super Valu, Inc.
Southwire Co.
SPS Technologies
SPX Corp.
Standard Steel Speciality Co.
Stanley Works
Steel Heddle Manufacturing Co.
Stockham Valves & Fittings
Stupp Brothers Bridge & Iron Co.
Sudbury Inc.
Sulzer Brothers Inc.
Superior Tube Co.
Support Systems International
Texas Industries, Inc.
Thyssen Specialty Steels
Timken Co.
Tredegar Industries
Tyco Laboratories, Inc.
Tyler Corp.
United Conveyor Corp.
United Iron & Metal Co.
USX Corp.
Valmont Industries
Varlen Corp.
Victaulic Co. of America
Vollrath Co.
Wagner Manufacturing Co., E. R.
Walter Industries
Wayne Steel Inc.
Weirton Steel Corp.
Wheeling-Pittsburgh Corp.
Worthington Industries, Inc.
Wyman-Gordon Co.
XTEK Inc.

Major Products/Industry Index

Printing & Publishing (SIC 27)

Addison-Wesley Publishing Co.
Advertising Checking Bureau
Affiliated Publications, Inc.
American Bankers Insurance Group
American Brands
American Business Products, Inc.
American Decal & Manufacturing Co.
American Greetings Corp.
American Trading & Production Corp.
Ameritech Corp.
Ameritech Publishing
Amway Corp.
Arcata Corp.
Arcata Graphics Co.
Atlanta Journal & Constitution
Avery Dennison Corp.
Bancroft-Whitney Co.
Banta Corp.
Bantam Doubleday Dell Publishing Group, Inc.
Belo Corp., A.H.
Bemis Company
Bergen Record Corp.
Berkshire Hathaway
Bill Communications
Birmingham News Co.
Blade Communications
Bowater Inc.
Carus Corp.
Central Newspapers, Inc.
Chicago Sun-Times, Inc.
Chicago Tribune Co.
Commerce Clearing House
Conde Nast Publications, Inc.
Copley Press
Corporate Printing Co.
Courier Corp.
Courier-Journal & Louisville Times
Cowles Media Co.
Cox Enterprises
CRL Inc.
Culbro Corp.
Daily News
Dartnell Corp.
Delaware North Cos.
Deluxe Corp.
Dennison Manufacturing Co.
Devon Group
Donnelley & Sons Co., R.R.
Dow Jones & Co.
Dun & Bradstreet Corp.
Duplex Products, Inc.
Ebsco Industries
Encyclopaedia Britannica, Inc.
Esselte Pendaflex Corp.
Evening Post Publishing Co.
Forbes
Fort Worth Star Telegram
Franklin Mint Corp.
Freedom Newspapers Inc.
Gannett Co.
Gannett Publishing Co., Guy
Gazette Co.
Globe Newspaper Co.
Grand Rapids Label Co.
Graphic Controls Corp.
Graphic Printing Co.
Grolier, Inc.
Hallmark Cards
Harcourt Brace Jovanovich
Harland Co., John H.
HarperCollins Publishers
Harte-Hanks Communications, Inc.
Hearst Corp.
Higher Education Publications
Hoechst Celanese Corp.
Houghton Mifflin Co.
Houston Post Co.

Indianapolis Newspapers, Inc.
International Data Group
Interstate Packaging Co.
Jeppesen Sanderson
Jostens
Journal Communications
Justin Industries, Inc.
Keller-Crescent Co.
King Ranch
Kiplinger Washington Editors
Knight-Ridder, Inc.
Koch Industries
Ladies' Home Journal Magazine
Lancaster Newspapers
Landmark Communications
Lasky Co.
Lawyers Co-operative Publishing Co.
Lee Enterprises
Lehigh Press, Inc.
LIN Broadcasting Corp.
Little Brown & Co., Inc.
Macmillan, Inc.
Matthews International Corp.
MCA
McGraw-Hill
Mead Corp.
Media General, Inc.
Menasha Corp.
Meredith Corp.
Merrill Corp.
Messenger Publishing Co.
Moore Business Forms, Inc.
Multimedia, Inc.
National Computer Systems
NCR Corp.
New England Business Service
New York Post Corp.
New York Times Co.
The New Yorker Magazine, Inc.
Newhouse Publication Corp.
News America Publishing Inc.
Newsweek, Inc.
Northwest Publishing Co. — Portland
Norton & Co., W.W.
Paramount Communications Inc.
Park Communications Inc.
Penguin USA Inc.
Persis Corp.
Philadelphia Industries
Pitney Bowes
Pittway Corp.
Playboy Enterprises, Inc.
Polk & Co., R.L.
Polychrome Corp.
Pottstown Mercury
Providence Journal Company
Pulitzer Publishing Co.
Quebecor Printing (USA) Inc.
Quincy Newspapers
Rand McNally and Co.
Random House Inc.
Raytheon Co.
Reader's Digest Association
Rebsamen Companies, Inc.
Reed Publishing USA
Research Institute of America
Reynolds & Reynolds Co.
Richmond Newspapers
Ringier-America
Rodale Press
Ruddick Corp.
Salem News Publishing Co.
Scholastic Inc.
Scott and Fetzer Co.
Scott, Foresman & Co.
Scripps Co., E.W.
Seattle Times Co.
Sentinel Communications Co.
Shreveport Publishing Corp.
Simon & Schuster Inc.
South Bend Tribune
South-Western Publishing Co.
Standard Register Co.
Standex International Corp.

Stauffer Communications
Swift Co. Inc., John S.
Taylor Corp.
Textron
Thomson Information Publishing Group
Thomson Newspapers Corp.
Time Warner
Times Mirror Co.
Topps Company
Treasure Chest Advertising Co.
Twentieth Century-Fox Film Corp.
Uarco Inc.
U.S. News & World Report
Wallace Computer Services
Washington Post Co.
Webcraft Technologies
Weight Watchers International
West Publishing Co.
Western Publishing Co., Inc.
Wiley & Sons, Inc., John
World Book Inc.
Wurzburg, Inc.
Ziff Communications Co.

Railroad Transportation (SIC 40)

Burlington Northern Inc.
C.P. Rail Systems
Cincinnati Gas & Electric Co.
Consolidated Rail Corp. (Conrail)
CSX Corp.
Florida East Coast Industries
Gilman Investment Co.
Gilman Paper Co.
Goodyear Tire & Rubber Co.
Grand Trunk Corp.
Illinois Central Railroad Co.
Kansas City Southern Industries
Rio Grande Railroad
St. Joe Paper Co.
Santa Fe Pacific Corp.
Southern Pacific Transportation Co.

Real Estate (SIC 65)

Aladdin Industries, Incorporated
Almac's, Inc.
American Capital Corp.
American Investment Co.
Amoskeag Co.
Atlantic Realty Co.
Atwood Industries
Balcor Co.
Banc One - Colorado Corp.
Binswanger Co.
Carr Real Estate Services
Castle & Cooke
Centex Corp.
Central Vermont Public Service Corp.
Chicago Milwaukee Corp.
Chicago Title and Trust Co.
Chubb Corp.
Cincinnati Gas & Electric Co.
Continental Wingate Co., Inc.
Cook Inlet Region
Cummings Properties Management, Inc.
DeBartolo Corp., Edward J.
Deltona Corp.
Dole Food Company, Inc.
Edwards Industries
Erb Lumber Co.
Fairfield Communities, Inc.
Far West Financial Corp.
FIP Corp.
First Security Corp. (Salt Lake City, Utah)
Florida East Coast Industries
Forbes
Forest City Enterprises
Fortune Bank

Forum Group, Inc.
Four Wheels, Inc.
Fru-Con Construction Corp.
Globe Corp.
Good Value Home, Inc.
Grady Management
Gruss Petroleum Corp.
Gulf USA Corp.
Gulfstream Housing Corp.
Hall Financial Group
Helmerich & Payne Inc.
Hillman Co.
Holzman USA, Philipp
Homestead Financial Corp.
Homewood Corp.
Hovnanian Enterprises Inc., K.
Hydraulic Co.
Intermark, Inc.
Kaiser Steel Resources
Kaufman & Broad Home Corp.
Koger Properties
Lamar Corp.
Landmark Land Co., Inc.
Lennar Corp.
Liberty Corp.
Lincoln Property Co.
Lomas Financial Corp.
M.D.C. Holdings
Maguire Thomas Partners
Mays , Inc., J.W.
Meredith Corp.
Milwaukee Golf Development Co.
Mitchell Energy & Development Corp.
Murdock Development Co.
NationsBank Texas
New Jersey Resources Corp.
Nichols Co., J.C.
Obayashi America Corp.
Oregon Cutting Systems
Oxford Development Group
Paxton Co., Frank
Perini Corp.
Persis Corp.
Philip Morris Cos.
Pioneer Hi-Bred International
Presley Cos.
Primerica Corp.
Providence Energy Corp.
Rich Co., F.D.
Rouse Co.
SAFECO Corp.
San Diego Gas & Electric
Santa Fe International Corp.
Schulman Management Corp.
Security Capital Corp.
Service Corp. International
Shapell Industries, Inc.
Shelton Co.
Sierra Pacific Resources
Sotheby's
Southmark Corp.
Southwest Gas Corp.
Starrett Housing Corp.
Strouse, Greenberg & Co.
Sumitomo Corp. of America
Summa Development Corp.
T.T.X. Co.
Tredegar Industries
Trump Group
Turner Broadcasting System
Turner Corp.
UDC-Universal Development LP
United Iron & Metal Co.
USLIFE Corp.
Disney Co., Walt
Walter Industries
Washington Water Power Co.
Watkins Associated Industries
Watt Industry
Weitz Corp.
Westvaco Corp.
Weyerhaeuser Co.
Wimpey Inc., George

Rubber & Miscellaneous Plastics Products (SIC 30)

Abitibi-Price
Action Industries, Inc.
Acushnet Co.
Akzo America
Aladdin Industries, Incorporated
AlliedSignal
American Biltrite
American Filtrona Corp.
American National Can Co.
American Optical Corp.
American Standard
Ameron, Inc.
AMETEK
AMP
APL Corp.
Aristech Chemical Corp.
Arvin Industries
Atkinson Co., Guy F.
Augat, Inc.
Bandag, Inc.
Banner Industries, Inc.
BASF Corp.
Becton Dickinson & Co.
Bemis Company
BFGoodrich
Borden
Bridgestone/Firestone
Budd Co.
Carlisle Cos.
CertainTeed Corp.
Chomerics, Inc.
Cincinnati Milacron
Cincom Systems, Inc.
Clabir Corp.
CLARCOR
Clopay Corp.
Clorox Co.
Coleman Co.
Constar International Inc.
Continental Can Co.
Cooper Tire & Rubber Co.
Crane Co.
Crescent Plastics
CRL Inc.
Croft Metals
Dana Corp.
Douglas Corp.
Dow Chemical Co.
Dunlop Tire Corp.
Eagle-Picher Industries
Eastman Chemical Co.
Eastman Kodak Co.
Eaton Corp.
Egan Machinery Co.
Elf Atochem North America
Fabri-Kal Corp.
Federal-Mogul Corp.
Fel-Pro Incorporated
Ferro Corp.
FINA, Inc.
Gates Corp.
General Tire Inc.
Goodall Rubber Co.
Goodyear Tire & Rubber Co.
Harvard Industries
Hercules Inc.
Himont Inc.
Hoffer Plastics Corp.
ICI Americas
Illinois Tool Works
Innovation Packaging
Intercraft Co., Inc.
Interstate Packaging Co.
ITT Rayonier
James River Corp. of Virginia
Jefferson Smurfit Corp.
Johnson Controls
JSJ Corp.
Kerr Glass Manufacturing Corp.
Kimball International
Kloeckner-Pentaplast of America

Kuhlman Corp.
Kysor Industrial Corp.
L.A. Gear
Lamson & Sessions Co.
Lancaster Colony
Liberty Diversified Industries

Inc.
LoJack Corp.
Lord Corp.
MacLean-Fogg Co.
Mark IV Industries
McCormick & Co.
McKesson Corp.
Menasha Corp.
Michelin North America
Millipore Corp.
Milton Bradley Co.
Monsanto Co.
National Presto Industries
Neville Chemical Co.
Newell Co.
NIBCO Inc.
Norton Co.
NVF Co.
Occidental Petroleum Corp.
O'Sullivan Corp.
Owens-Corning Fiberglas Corp.
Owens-Illinois
Packaging Corporation of

America
Pantasote Polymers
Park-Ohio Industries Inc.
Pirelli Armstrong Tire Corp.
Pitney Bowes
Plastics Engineering Co.
PMC Inc.
Polychrome Corp.
Preformed Line Products Co.
Premark International
Quabaug Corp.
Radiator Specialty Co.
Reichhold Chemicals, Inc.
Rexham Inc.
Reynolds Metals Co.
Rhone-Poulenc Inc.
Rieke Corp.
Risdon Corp.
Rockwell International Corp.
Rogers Corp.
Rohm and Haas Company
RPM, Inc.
Rubbermaid
Schlegel Corp.
Schulman Inc., A.
Sealed Air Corp.
Sealright Co., Inc.
Sheldahl Inc.
Siebe North Inc.
Smith Corp., A.O.
Solo Cup Co.
Sonoco Products Co.
Standard Products Co.
Stone Container Corp.
Sudbury Inc.
Susquehanna Corp.
Talley Industries, Inc.
Teledyne
Teleflex Inc.
3M Co.
Tomkins Industries, Inc.
Toro Co.
Towle Manufacturing Co.
Tredegar Industries
TRINOVA Corp.
Union Carbide Corp.
United Industrial Corp.
United Merchants &

Manufacturers
USG Corp.
Varlen Corp.
Vollrath Co.
Voplex Corp.
West Co.
Wheaton Industries
Worthington Industries, Inc.

Security & Commodity Brokers (SIC 62)

Advest Group, Inc.
Alexander & Alexander
Services, Inc.
Allen & Co.
Alliance Capital Management
Corp.
American General Corp.
American Stock Exchange
Ameritas Life Insurance Corp.
Angeles Corp.
Atalanta/Sosnoff Capital Corp.
Automatic Data Processing, Inc.
Ayco Corp.
Baird & Co., Robert W.
Banc One Illinois Corp.
Bank of America
Bernstein & Co., Sanford C.
Blackstone Group LP
Blair and Co., William
Boston Co., Inc.
Brenton Banks Inc.
Broad, Inc.
Brown & Associates, Clayton
Brown & Sons, Alex
Capital Group
Chicago Board of Trade
CM Alliance Cos.
Columbus Dispatch Printing Co.
Commercial Credit Co.
Continental Wingate Co., Inc.
Dain Bosworth/Inter-Regional
Financial Group
Daiwa Securities America Inc.
DCNY Corp.
Dean Witter Discover
Deutsche Bank AG
Diversified Industries, Inc.
Donaldson, Lufkin & Jenrette
Dreyfus Corp.
Edwards & Sons, A.G.
First Boston
Ford Motor Co.
Glenmede Trust Corp.
Glickenhaus & Co.
Goldman Sachs & Co.
Gradison & Co.
Heffernan & Co.
IDS Financial Services
Integrated Resources
Jacobson & Sons, Benjamin
Kansas City Southern Industries
Keefe, Bruyette & Woods
Kemper Securities Inc.
Kidder, Peabody & Co.
King Ranch
Lazard Freres & Co.
Legg Mason Inc.
Loeb Partners Corp.
Loomis-Sayles & Co.
McDonald & Co. Securities
McGraw-Hill
Meridian Insurance Group Inc.
Merrill Lynch & Co.
Metallgesellschaft Corp.
Miami Corp.
Midland Montagu
Morgan Stanley & Co.
Morrison-Knudsen Corp.
National Life of Vermont
New England Mutual Life
Insurance Co.
New York Mercantile Exchange
New York Stock Exchange
Nomura Securities International
Nuveen & Co., Inc., John
Oppenheimer & Co., Inc.
Oppenheimer Management Corp.
Orion Capital Corp.
PaineWebber
PHM Corp.
Pioneer Group
Piper Jaffray Cos.

Price Associates, T. Rowe
Primerica Financial Services
Prudential-Bache Securities
Reich & Tang L.P.
SAFECO Corp.
Salomon
Schloss & Co., Marcus
Schwab & Co., Charles
Security Benefit Life Insurance
Co.
Shearson, Lehman & Hutton
SIT Investment Associates, Inc.
Skinner Corp.
Smith Barney, Harris Upham &
Co.
Southwestern Life Insurance Co.
Susquehanna Investment Group
Swiss American Securities, Inc.
Synovus Financial Corp.
Thomson Information Publishing
Group
Torchmark Corp.
Tucker Anthony, Inc.
UJB Financial Corp.
United Asset Management Corp.
United States Trust Co. of New
York
Uslico Corp.
USLIFE Corp.
Vanguard Group of Investment
Cos.
Wheat First Securites
Yamaichi International
(America) Inc.

Services Not Elsewhere Classified (SIC 89)

Ampacet Corp.
Bechtel Group
Charter Medical Corp.
Hartford Steam Boiler Inspection
& Insurance Co.

Social Services (SIC 83)

Forum Group, Inc.
Kinder-Care Learning Centers

Special Trade Contractors (SIC 17)

American Building Maintenance
Industries
Apogee Enterprises Inc.
Barton-Malow Co.
Boh Brothers Construction Co.
Brand Cos.
Bristol Steel & Iron Works
Carolina Steel Corp.
Ceco Corp.
Dimeo Construction Co.
DynCorp
Electric Power Equipment Co.
Grinnell Corp.
Groves & Sons Co., S.J.
Jupiter Industries, Inc.
Kajima International, Inc.
Kasler Corp.
KDI Corp.
Marley Co.
OMNI Construction
Pitt-Des Moines Inc.
Riley Stoker Corp.
Sachs Electric Corp.
Sargent Electric Co.
SECO
Swinerton & Walberg Co.
Tremco Inc.
Truland Systems Corp.
Tyco Laboratories, Inc.
Washington Natural Gas Co.
Weatherford International, Inc.

Stone, Clay & Glass Products (SIC 32)

Abex Inc.
Acustar Inc.
AFG Industries, Inc.
Alhambra Foundry Co., Ltd.
Amcast Industrial Corp.
American Aggregates Corp.
American Greetings Corp.
American National Can Co.
American Optical Corp.
American Standard
Ameron, Inc.
Anchor Glass Container Corp.
Apogee Enterprises Inc.
Armstrong World Industries Inc.
Asahi Glass America, Inc.
ASARCO
Baccarat Inc.
Ball-InCon Glass Packaging
Corp.
Belden Brick Co., Inc.
Blue Circle Inc.
Bristol Steel & Iron Works
Brown-Forman Corp.
Burnett Construction Co.
Callanan Industries
CalMat Co.
Caterpillar
Celotex Corp.
Centex Corp.
CertainTeed Corp.
Champion Spark Plug Co.
Cincinnati Milacron
Clarity Holdings Corp.
Coors Brewing Co.
Corning Incorporated
Didier Taylor Refractories Corp.
Eagle-Picher Industries
Elf Atochem North America
Ensign-Bickford Industries
Ferro Corp.
Fischer & Porter Co.
Florida Rock Industries
Foster Co., L.B.
Franklin Mint Corp.
Freeport Brick Co.
GAF Corp.
Galileo Electro-Optics Corp.
General Dynamics Corp.
General Housewares Corp.
Great Lakes Carbon Corp.
Green Industries, A. P.
Guardian Industries Corp.
Harvard Industries
Holman
International Aluminum Corp.
Justin Industries, Inc.
Kaiser Cement Corp.
Kerr Glass Manufacturing Corp.
Kohler Co.
Kyocera International Inc.
Lafarge Corp.
Lancaster Colony
Lehigh Portland Cement Co.
Levy Co., Edward C.
Libbey-Owens Ford Co.
Liberty Glass Co.
Manville Corp.
Martin Marietta Aggregates
Martin Marietta Corp.
Material Service Corp.
Metallurg, Inc.
Moore McCormack Resources
Nalco Chemical Co.
National Gypsum Co.
Newell Co.
Norton Co.
Oneida Ltd.
Osborn Manufacturing Co.
Owens-Corning Fiberglas Corp.
Owens-Illinois
Park-Ohio Industries Inc.
Pella Corp.
Pioneer Concrete of America Inc.
PPG Industries

PQ Corp.
Rinker Materials Corp.
Sealaska Corp.
Silvestri Corp.
Southdown, Inc.
Spang & Co.
Stabler Cos., Inc.
Standard Pacific Corp.
Steuart Petroleum Co.
Tarmac America Inc.
Texas Industries, Inc.
Textron
Towle Manufacturing Co.
Tracor, Inc.
Tropicana Products, Inc.
Uniform Tubes, Inc.
USG Corp.
Vesuvius Charitable Foundation
Vulcan Materials Co.
West Co.
Wheaton Industries
Zurn Industries

Textile Mill Products (SIC 22)

Albany International Corp.
Alice Manufacturing Co.
American Biltrite
Amoco Corp.
Armstrong World Industries Inc.
Associated Products
Belding Heminway Co.
Bibb Co.
Blue Bell, Inc.
Bossong Hosiery Mills
Bridgestone/Firestone
Burlington Industries
Carter Co., William
Chomerics, Inc.
Chrysler Corp.
Clopay Corp.
Coats & Clark Inc.
Collins & Aikman Corp.
Concord Fabrics, Inc.
Cone Mills Corp.
Country Curtains, Inc.
Courtaulds Fibers Inc.
Cranston Print Works
Dan River, Inc.
Delta Woodside Industries
Dixie Yarns, Inc.
du Pont de Nemours & Co., E. I.
DWG Corp.
Ensign-Bickford Industries
FAB Industries
Farley Industries
Fieldcrest Cannon
Fruit of the Loom, Inc.
General Tire Inc.
Greenwood Mills
Guilford Mills
Hampton Industries
Hexcel Corp.
HMK Enterprises
Hoechst Celanese Corp.
Inman Mills
Interface Inc.
Ix & Sons, Frank
Jackson Mills
Jockey International
Kendall Health Care Products
Keystone Weaving Mills
LoJack Corp.
Lydall, Inc.
Magee Carpet Co.
Malden Mills Industries
Marion Fabrics
Masland & Sons, C.H.
Midland Co.
Milliken & Co.
Monsanto Co.
National Spinning Co.
Page Belting Co.
Publicker Industries, Inc.
R. L. Stowe Mills Inc.

Textile Mill Products (cont.)

Raymark Corp.
Ruddick Corp.
Russell Corp.
Sara Lee Corp.
Sara Lee Hosiery
Scott Paper Co.
Seton Co.
Shaw Industries
Springs Industries
Standard Textile Co., Inc.
Stonecutter Mills Corp.
Thomaston Mills, Inc.
3M Co.
Tranzonic Cos.
Tultex Corp.
Unifi, Inc.
United Merchants & Manufacturers
Valdese Manufacturing Co., Inc.
VF Corp.
Voplex Corp.
Walton Monroe Mills
Wellman Inc.
World Carpets
Y.K.K. (U.S.A.) Inc.

Tobacco Products (SIC 21)

American Brands
American Maize Products
American Tobacco Co.
Brooke Group Ltd.
Brown & Williamson Tobacco Corp.
Conwood Co. L.P.
Culbro Corp.
Dibrell Brothers, Inc.
Loews Corp.
Lorillard Tobacco Inc.
Philip Morris Cos.
Pinkerton Tobacco Co.
RJR Nabisco Inc.
Sara Lee Corp.

Transportation by Air (SIC 45)

Air Express International Corp.
Air France
Airborne Express Co.
Alaska Airlines, Inc.
America West Airlines
AMR Corp.
Aviall, Inc.
Braniff International Airlines
British Airways
Burlington Air Express Inc.
Consolidated Freightways
Continental Airlines
Delta Air Lines
DHL Airways Inc.
Dial Corp.
Dillons Super Markets
DynCorp
E-Systems
Eastern Air Lines
Emery Worldwide
Holmes & Narver Services Inc.
Midway Airlines
Northwest Airlines, Inc.
Offshore Logistics
Ogden Corp.
Pittston Co.
Primark Corp.
Qantas Airways Ltd.
Rowan Cos., Inc.
Seneca Foods Corp.
Southwest Airlines Co.
Trans World Airlines
UNC, Inc.
United Airlines

Transportation Equipment (SIC 37)

Abex Inc.
ACF Industries, Inc.
Acustar Inc.
Aerojet
AlliedSignal
Alma Piston Co.
American Suzuki Motor Corp.
American Welding & Manufacturing Co.
Anderson Industries
Arvin Industries
Auto Specialties Manufacturing Co.
Aviall, Inc.
Avondale Industries, Inc.
Bairnco Corp.
Barnes Group
Beech Aircraft Corp.
Bell Helicopter Textron
Berkman Co., Louis
Bethlehem Steel Corp.
Betts Industries
BFGoodrich
Bird Inc.
Blue Circle Inc.
BMW of North America, Inc.
Boeing Co.
Boeing Co.
Borg-Warner Corp.
Bosch Corp., Robert
British Aerospace Inc.
Browning
Brunswick Corp.
Budd Co.
Cessna Aircraft Co.
Chrysler Corp.
Clark Equipment Co.
Coachmen Industries
Coleman Co.
Collins & Aikman Holdings Corp.
Coltec Industries
Cooper Industries
CR Industries
Curtiss-Wright Corp.
Dana Corp.
Danaher Corp.
Dayton-Walther Corp.
Delco Electronics Corp.
Douglas & Lomason Company
Duchossois Industries
Ducommun Inc.
Dyneer Corp.
Eaton Corp.
Echlin Inc.
Elixir Industries
Excel Industries (Elkhart, Indiana)
Fairchild Corp.
Fiat U.S.A., Inc.
FKI Holdings Inc.
Fleetwood Enterprises, Inc.
FMC Corp.
Ford Motor Co.
Freightliner Corp.
GenCorp
General Dynamics Corp.
General Electric Co.
General Motors Corp.
Gleason Works
Gould Inc.
Grumman Corp.
Gulfstream Aerospace Corp.
Handy & Harman
Harley-Davidson, Inc.
Harsco Corp.
Hayes Albion Industries
Hazeltine Corp.
Heil Co.
Hercules Inc.
HMK Enterprises
Honda of America Manufacturing, Inc.

Hopeman Brothers
Huffy Corp.
Hughes Aircraft Co.
Illinois Tool Works
Ingalls Shipbuilding
ITT Corp.
Kaman Corp.
Karmazin Products Corp.
Kysor Industrial Corp.
Lamson & Sessions Co.
Lancaster Colony
Learjet Inc.
Lockheed Corp.
LTV Corp.
Lydall, Inc.
Manitowoc Co.
Manitowoc Co.
Mark IV Industries
Martin Marietta Corp.
McDonnell Douglas Corp.-West
Midas International Corp.
Mitsubishi Heavy Industries America
Monroe Auto Equipment Co.
Moog, Inc.
Moog Automotive, Inc.
Morton International
Murray Ohio Manufacturing Co.
Navistar International Corp.
Nelson Industries, Inc.
New England Aircraft Products Co.
Newport News Shipbuilding & Dry Dock Co.
Nissan Motor Corporation in U.S.A.
Norfolk Shipbuilding & Drydock Corp.
Northrop Corp.
Olivetti Office USA, Inc.
Ontario Corp.
Oshkosh Truck Corp.
Outboard Marine Corp.
PACCAR
Pall Corp.
Peterson Builders
Polaris Industries, LP
Portec, Inc.
Precision Castparts Corp.
Ranco, Inc.
Raymark Corp.
Reebok International Ltd.
Robertshaw Controls Co.
Rockford Acromatics Products Co./Aircraft Gear Corp.
Rockford Products Corp.
Rohr Inc.
Rolls-Royce Inc.
Ryder System
Sequa Corp.
Simpson Industries
SKF USA, Inc.
Skyline Corp.
Smith Corp., A.O.
SPX Corp.
Standard Motor Products, Inc.
Standard Products Co.
Sterling Inc.
Stewart & Stevenson Services
Subaru-Isuzu Automotive Inc.
Sundstrand Corp.
Talley Industries, Inc.
TBG, Inc.
Tecumseh Products Co.
Teledyne
Thomas Built Buses L.P.
Thor Industries, Inc.
Tokheim Corp.
Tomkins Industries, Inc.
Torrington Co.
Trans-Apex
Trinity Industries, Inc.
Trustcorp, Inc.
TRW Corp.
UIS, Inc.
UNC, Inc.
Union City Body Co.

United Dominion Industries
United Technologies, Automotive
United Technologies Corp.
Varlen Corp.
Volvo North America Corp.
Voplex Corp.
Williamson Co.
Winnebago Industries, Inc.
Woodward Governor Co.
Wynn's International, Inc.

Transportation Services (SIC 47)

ACF Industries, Inc.
Airborne Express Co.
American Express Co.
American President Cos.
Bekins Co.
Caleb Brett U.S.A. Inc.
Caltex Petroleum Corp.
Carlson Cos.
Consolidated Freightways
Duchossois Industries
Federal Express Corp.
First Source Corp.
Fritz Cos.
GATX Corp.
Harper Group
Heritage Travel Inc./Thomas Cook Travel
Leaseway Transportation Corp.
Omega World Travel
PHH Corp.
Pittston Co.
Rosenbluth Travel Agency
T.T.X. Co.
UniGroup Inc.

Trucking & Warehousing (SIC 42)

Adams Resources & Energy, Inc.
Alexander & Baldwin, Inc.
American Natural Resources Co.
American Red Ball World Wide Movers
Ameritech Services
Apex Oil Co.
Archer-Daniels-Midland Co.
Arkansas Best Corp.
Bekins Co.
Choice Courier Systems Inc.
Consolidated Freightways
Dixie-Portland Flour Mills
Friona Industries L.P.
Global Van Lines
Houff Transfer, Inc.
Hunt Transport Services, J.B.
IU International
Jupiter Industries, Inc.
Kaplan Trucking Co.
Knight-Ridder, Inc.
Leaseway Transportation Corp.
Mayflower Group
Mayne Nickless
New Penn Motor Express
Overnite Transportation Co.
PHH Corp.
Polk & Co., R.L.
Preston Trucking Co., Inc.
Rio Grande Railroad
Roadway Services, Inc.
Saint Johnsbury Trucking Co.
Sea-Land Service
Seaboard Corp.
Southern Pacific Transportation Co.
Stone & Webster, Inc.
T & T United Truck Lines
UniGroup Inc.
United Parcel Service of America
United Van Lines, Inc.
Watkins Associated Industries
Yellow Corp.

U.S. Postal Service (SIC 43)

Burlington Air Express Inc.

Water Transportation (SIC 44)

Air Express International Corp.
Alco Standard Corp.
Alexander & Baldwin, Inc.
American President Cos.
Apex Oil Co.
Cincinnati Gas & Electric Co.
Consol Energy Inc.
Cook Inlet Region
CSX Corp.
Eastern Enterprises
GATX Corp.
HEI Inc.
Ingram Industries
Kloster Cruise Ltd.
Lykes Brothers Steamship Co.
Matson Navigation Co.
Midland Co.
Nicor, Inc.
Offshore Logistics
Oglebay Norton Co.
Overseas Shipholding Group
Pickering Industries
Sea-Land Service
Tidewater, Inc.
Tosco Corp. Refining Division
Valley Line Co.
Zapata Corp.

Wholesale Trade—Durable Goods (SIC 50)

Abex Inc.
Ace Hardware Corp.
Action Industries, Inc.
Action Products International
AGA Gas, Inc.
Airbus Industrie of America
Alberto-Culver Co.
Alcan Aluminum Corp.
Alco Standard Corp.
ALLTEL Corp.
Alro Steel Corp.
American Aggregates Corp.
American Building Maintenance Industries
American Honda Motor Co.
American Optical Corp.
American Suzuki Motor Corp.
Ameritech Information Systems
Amfac/JMB Hawaii
AMP
Andal Corp.
Apple Computer, Inc.
Applied Power, Inc.
Arrow Electronics, Inc.
Asahi Glass America, Inc.
Athlone Industries, Inc.
Aviall, Inc.
Avnet, Inc.
Bard, C. R.
Barnes Group
Baxter International
Bearings, Inc.
Bell Industries
Bergen Brunswig Corp.
Berkman Co., Louis
Big Three Industries
Binks Manufacturing Co.
Bird Inc.
BMW of North America, Inc.
Bohemia Inc.
Boise Cascade Corp.
Brad Ragan, Inc.
Briggs & Stratton Corp.
British Aerospace Inc.
Brother International Corp.

Brown-Forman Corp.
Browning
Browning Charitable
   Foundation, Val A.
Builder Marts of America
Burnett Construction Co.
Canon U.S.A., Inc.
Carlyle & Co. Jewelers
Carpenter Technology Corp.
Cartier, Inc.
Castle & Co., A.M.
Cawsl Corp.
CertainTeed Corp.
Chevron Corp.
Chicago Milwaukee Corp.
Cleveland-Cliffs
Climatic Corp.
COBE Laboratories, Inc.
Collins & Aikman Holdings
   Corp.
Collins Co.
Commercial Metals Co.
Compaq Computer Corp.
Consol Energy Inc.
Consolidated Electrical
   Distributors
Cotter & Co.
Cox Enterprises
Cray Research
Cubic Corp.
Dalgety Inc.
Daniel & Co., Gerard
Decision Data Computer Corp.
Delta Woodside Industries
Diasonics, Inc.
Dickey-John Corp.
Dollar General Corp.
DSC Communications Co.
Durr-Fillauer Medical
Edwards Industries
Emerson Radio Corp.
EMI Records Group
Erb Lumber Co.
Fabick Tractor Co., John
Fairchild Corp.
Fanuc U.S.A. Corp.
Fiat U.S.A., Inc.
Forest City Enterprises
Foster Co., L.B.
Fujitsu Systems of America, Inc.
GAF Corp.
General Railway Signal Corp.
Genuine Parts Co.
Georgia-Pacific Corp.
Georgia-Pacific Corp.
Grainger, W.W.
Graybar Electric Co.
Gulfstream Aerospace Corp.
Handleman Co.
Harris Corp.
Hazeltine Corp.
Hendrickson Brothers
Hesston Corp.
Hillman Co.
Hobart Corp.
Hughes Supply, Inc.
Hyundai Motor America
Ingram Industries
Inland Steel Industries
Intermark, Inc.
International Paper Co.
IPCO Corp.
Isuzu Motors America Inc.
Itoh (C.) International
   (America), Inc.
IU International
Jorgensen Co., Earle M.
Kaman Corp.
Kanematsu-Gosho U.S.A. Inc.
Kawasaki Motors Corp., U.S.A.
Kelly Tractor Co.
Kenwood U.S.A. Corp.
KitchenAid Inc.
Koch Sons, George
Kyocera International Inc.
Lafarge Corp.

Lanier Business Products, Inc.
Lapham-Hickey Steel Corp.
Lappin Electric Co.
Lawson Products, Inc.
Levy Circulating Co., Charles
Levy's Lumber & Building
   Centers
Lieberman Enterprises
Lowe's Cos.
Lyons Physician's Supply Co.
Makita U.S.A., Inc.
Martin-Brower Co., The
Marubeni America Corp.
Material Service Corp.
Matsushita Electric Corp. of
   America
Mazda Motors of America
   (Central), Inc.
McKesson Corp.
Mercedes-Benz of North
   America, Inc.
Metroquip
Mid-America Dairymen
Mid-Continent Supply Co.
Minolta Corp.
Mitsubishi Electric America
Mitsubishi International Corp.
Mitsubishi Motor Sales of
   America, Inc.
Mitsui & Co. (U.S.A.)
Moore Medical Corp.
National Metal & Steel
National Presto Industries
NEC Technologies, Inc.
NEC USA
Nelco Sewing Machine Sales
   Corp.
Nichimen America, Inc.
Nissan Motor Corporation in
   U.S.A.
Noland Co.
North Face, The
North Star Steel Co.
North Star Universal Inc.
Northern Telecom Inc.
NRC, Inc.
O'Connor Co.
Odessa Trading Co.
Oglebay Norton Co.
Ohio Road Paving Co.
Olivetti Office USA, Inc.
Olympus Corp.
Oshman's Sporting Goods, Inc.
Owens & Minor, Inc.
PACCAR
Padnos Iron & Metal Co., Louis
Patrick Industries Inc.
Paxton Co., Frank
Pay 'N Save Inc.
Peabody Holding Company Inc.
Pechiney Corp.
PemCo. Corp.
PGL Building Products
Pickering Industries
Pioneer Electronics (USA) Inc.
Pitt-Des Moines Inc.
Pittway Corp.
Ply-Gem Industries, Inc.
Polaris Industries, LP
Pool Energy Services Co.
Poole Equipment Co., Gregory
Porsche Cars North America, Inc.
Premier Dental Products Co.
Price Company
Publicker Industries, Inc.
Quaker State Corp.
RB&W Corp.
Rebsamen Companies, Inc.
Regis Corp.
REI-Recreational Equipment,
   Inc.
Reinhart Institutional Foods
Reiss Coal Co., C.
Republic Automotive Parts, Inc.
Reynolds Metals Co.
Rite-Hite Corp.
Roseburg Forest Products Co.

Roundy's Inc.
Saab Cars USA, Inc.
Samsung America Inc.
Sanyo Fisher Service Corp.
Sanyo Fisher U.S.A. Corp.
Savin Corp.
Schlegel Corp.
Science Applications
   International Corp.
Scientific Brake & Equipment
   Co.
Scott and Fetzer Co.
Sedco Inc.
Servistar Corp.
Sharon Steel Corp.
Snap-on Tools Corp.
Sogem Holding Ltd.
Sony Corp. of America
Sooner Pipe & Supply Corp.
Soundesign Corp.
Spring Arbor Distributors
Stanhome Inc.
Stanley Works
Steiger Tractor
Stewart & Stevenson Services
Subaru of America Inc.
Sumitomo Corp. of America
Tandem Computers
Tandon Corp.
Tandy Corp.
Tarmac America Inc.
Tate & Lyle Inc.
Teac America, Inc.
Telecom Corp.
Thyssen Specialty Steels
Titan Industrial Co.
Tomen America, Inc.
Towle Manufacturing Co.
Toyota Motor Sales, U.S.A.
Tractor & Equipment Co.
Union Camp Corp.
United Co.
United Dominion Industries
United Iron & Metal Co.
United Stationers Inc.
Valero Energy Corp.
Value City Furniture
Vesuvius Charitable Foundation
Volkswagen of America, Inc.
Volvo North America Corp.
Wayne Steel Inc.
Wellman Inc.
Wurzburg, Inc.
Wyle Laboratories
Xerox Corp.
Zamoiski Co.

Wholesale Trade — Nondurable Goods (SIC 51)

Abitibi-Price
Action Industries, Inc.
Action Products International
Adams Resources & Energy, Inc.
Agway
Albrecht Grocery Co., Fred W.
Alco Standard Corp.
ALPAC Corp.
Amalgamated Sugar Co.
Amerada Hess Corp.
Amway Corp.
Andersons Management Corp.
Apex Oil Co.
Archer-Daniels-Midland Co.
Armor All Products Corp.
Asahi Glass America, Inc.
Associated Milk Producers, Inc.
Avon Products
Bacardi Imports
Baccarat Inc.
Bag Bazaar, Ltd.
Baker Commodities
Banfi Vintners
Barry Corp., R. G.
Basic American Medical, Inc.

Baxter International
Bel Air Mart
Belding Heminway Co.
Ben & Jerry's Homemade
Bergen Brunswig Corp.
Betz Laboratories
Bindley Western Industries
Blue Diamond Growers
Boise Cascade Corp.
Borman's
Budweiser of Columbia
Cactus Feeders Inc.
Caltex Petroleum Corp.
Candlesticks Inc.
Care Enterprises
Cargill
CENEX
Central National-Gottesman
Central Soya Co.
Chemtech Industries
Chiquita Brands Co.
Christian Dior New York, Inc.
Colonial Oil Industries, Inc.
Community Coffee Co.
ConAgra
Connell Rice & Sugar Co.
Continental Grain Co.
Cookson America
Countrymark Cooperative
Crestar Food Products, Inc.
Cross Co., A.T.
Crown Central Petroleum Corp.
Culbro Corp.
Cumberland Farms
Dairylea Cooperative Inc.
Dalgety Inc.
Diamond Shamrock
Dibrell Brothers, Inc.
Dillard Paper Co.
DNP (America), Inc.
Dollar General Corp.
Dreyfus Corp., Louis
Duplex Products, Inc.
Durr-Fillauer Medical
Earth Care Paper, Inc.
Eastman Chemical Co.
Elf Aquitaine, Inc.
Eni-Chem America, Inc.
Enron Corp.
Ernest & Julio Gallo Winery
Famous Amos Chocolate Chip
   Cookie Co.
Fanuc U.S.A. Corp.
Farmland Industries, Inc.
Fast Food Merchandisers
First Petroleum Corp.
Fleming Companies, Inc.
Friedman Bag Co.
Frisch's Restaurants Inc.
GATX Corp.
Genesco
Genuine Parts Co.
Giant Eagle
Givenchy, Inc.
Glaxo
Glidden Co.
Golden State Foods Corp.
Grocers Supply Co.
Grow Group
Growmark, Inc.
GSC Enterprises
Hallmark Cards
Hampton Industries
Handleman Co.
Harper Brush Works
Harvest States Cooperative
Heublein
Hillman Co.
Hiram Walker & Sons Inc.
Holly Sugar Corp.
Hood Inc., H.P.
Hormel & Co., George A.
Howell Corp.
ICC Industries
IMCERA Group Inc.
Ingram Book Co.

Interco
International Multifoods Corp.
Iroquois Brands, Ltd.
Itoh (C.) International
   (America), Inc.
Kanematsu-Gosho U.S.A. Inc.
Keith Co., Ben E.
Ketchum & Co.
Key Food Stores Cooperative Inc.
Kikkoman International, Inc.
Koch Industries
Kowalski Sausage Co.
Kraft General Foods
Krelitz Industries
Land O'Lakes
Lawson Products, Inc.
LeaRonal, Inc.
Levy Circulating Co., Charles
Liz Claiborne
Marcus Brothers Textiles Inc.
Martin-Brower Co., The
Marubeni America Corp.
Mass Merchandisers, Inc.
McCormick & Co.
McKesson Corp.
Mead Corp.
Meenan Oil Co., Inc.
MEI Diversified, Inc.
Meijer Inc.
Mitsubishi International Corp.
Mitsui & Co. (U.S.A.)
Mobil Oil Corp.
Monfort of Colorado, Inc.
Moore Medical Corp.
Morse Shoe, Inc.
Nabisco Foods Group
Nash-Finch Co.
National Distributing Co., Inc.
Neville Chemical Co.
Nichimen America, Inc.
Nike Inc.
North Face, The
Odessa Trading Co.
Olivetti Office USA, Inc.
Owens & Minor, Inc.
Paddington Corp.
Paxton Co., Frank
PepsiCo
Permian Corp.
Petroleum Marketers
Phibro Energy
Phillips-Van Heusen Corp.
Pier 1 Imports, Inc.
Pillsbury Co.
Pioneer Hi-Bred International
Price Company
Pro-line Corp.
Producers Livestock Marketing
   Association
Provigo Corp. Inc.
Quaker State Corp.
Quantum Chemical Corp.
Racetrac Petroleum
Raleigh Linen Service/National
   Distributing Co.
Reebok International Ltd.
Reichhold Chemicals, Inc.
Reily & Co., William B.
Reinhart Institutional Foods
Riser Foods
Roundy's Inc.
RPM, Inc.
Rykoff & Co., S.E.
Samsung America Inc.
Sandoz Corp.
Santa Fe Pacific Corp.
Schieffelin & Somerset Co.
Scrivner, Inc.
Scrivner of North Carolina Inc.
Seaboard Corp.
Seventh Generation
Silvestri Corp.
Smith Oil Corp.
Sogem Holding Ltd.
Sordoni Enterprises
Southland Corp.

Wholesale Trade - Nondurable Goods (cont.)

Spring Arbor Distributors
Standard Brands Paint Co.
Standard Textile Co., Inc.
Star Enterprise
Stella D'Oro Biscuit Co.
Steuart Petroleum Co.
Stonecutter Mills Corp.
Sumitomo Corp. of America

Sun Co.
Sun-Diamond Growers of California
Sunkist Growers
Super Food Services
Super Valu Stores
Sweet Life Foods
Swift-Eckrich Inc.
Sysco Corp.
Tamarkin Co.
Tasty Baking Co.
Tate & Lyle Inc.

Tauber Oil Co.
Tesoro Petroleum Corp.
Texaco
Texas Olefins Co.
Tomen America, Inc.
Tyson Foods, Inc.
UGI Corp.
Ulrich Chemical, Inc.
Union Equity Division of Farmland Industries
United Grocers, Inc.
United Stationers Inc.

Univar Corp.
Universal Foods Corp.
Universal Leaf Tobacco Co.
Unocal Corp.
US Shoe Corp.
UST
Vons Cos., Inc.
Wallace Computer Services
Watkins Associated Industries
Webber Oil Co.
Webster Co., H. K.
Weight Watchers International

Wetterau
Wilbur-Ellis Co.
Witco Corp.
Wolff Shoe Co.
Wurzburg, Inc.
WWF Paper Corp.
Wyatt Energy, Inc.
Zamoiski Co.

Index to Officers and Directors

A

Aaron, Daniel, vchmn, dir: Comcast Corp.

Aaron, Roy Henry, pres, ceo, dir: Plitt Southern Theatres; trust: Plitt Southern Theatres, Inc., Employees Fund

Abbey, Donald C., Jr., trust: Goddard Homestead

Abbey, G. Marshall, pres, dir: Baxter Foundation

Abbott, Janet, vp: Drum Foundation

Abbott, Laura M., secy: AT&T Foundation

Abbrederis, Dale, cfo: Unigard Security Insurance Co.

Abdalla, Gerald M., exec vp, cfo: Croft Metals; trust: Croft Metal Products Educational Trust Fund

Abdoo, Richard A., chmn, ceo, pres: Wisconsin Energy Corp.; pres, dir: Wisconsin Energy Corp. Foundation

Abe, Christie, commun rels supervisor: Toyota Motor Sales, U.S.A.

Abe, Kobo, trust: Ise Cultural Foundation

Abegg, Edward, trust: Woodward Governor Co. Charitable Trust

Abel, Alice, dir: Abel Foundation

Abel, Elizabeth, dir: Abel Foundation

Abel, George P., pres: Abel Foundation

Abeles, Charles C., trust: Higginson Trust, Corina

Abeles, Joseph C., pres, vp: Abeles Foundation, Joseph and Sophia

Abeles, Sophia, treas: Abeles Foundation, Joseph and Sophia

Abell, Anthony F., trust: Abell Foundation, Charles S.

Abell, Christopher S., trust: Abell Foundation, Charles S.

Abell, D. Barry, treas, dir: Three Swallows Foundation

Abell, Gregory T., trust: Abell Foundation, Charles S.

Abell, Kevin O'Callaghan, trust: Abell Foundation, Charles S.

Abell, Pamela T., dir: Three Swallows Foundation

Abell, Patricia O'Callaghan, vp, trust: Abell Foundation, Charles S.

Abell, William Shepherdson, Jr., secy-treas, trust: Abell Foundation, Charles S.; trust: Abell Foundation, The

Abell, William Shepherdson, Sr., don, pres, trust: Abell Foundation, Charles S.

Abely, Joseph F., sr vp, cfo: LoJack Corp.

Abercrombie, Josephine E., don, pres, trust: Abercrombie Foundation

Abercrombie, Ralph L., trust: Chapman Charitable Trust, H. A. and Mary K.

Abernathy, Bruce, dir: Fort Pierce Memorial Hospital Scholarship Foundation

Abernethy, Claude S., Jr., trust: Abernethy Testamentary Charitable Trust, Maye Morrison

Abernethy, J.W., Jr., Abernethy Testamentary Charitable Trust, Maye Morrison

Abess, Alan T., Jr., dir: Jennings Foundation, Alma

Abia-Smith, Lisa, fdn asst: Gap Foundation

Ablon, R. Richard, pres, ceo: Ogden Corp.

Ablon, Ralph E., chmn: Ogden Corp.

Abraham, Alexander, pres: Abraham Foundation; pres: Bleibtreu Foundation, Jacob

Abraham, Anthony R., pres, dir: Abraham Foundation, Anthony R.

Abraham, Helene, secy: Abraham Foundation

Abraham, James, treas: Abraham Foundation

Abraham, Morris, secy: Parthenon Sportwear Foundation

Abraham, Nancy, vp: Abraham Foundation

Abraham, Thomas C., secy, dir: Abraham Foundation, Anthony R.

Abrahams, J.H., chmn, dir: Security Benefit Life Insurance Co.

Abrahams, Richard I., treas: Wolf Foundation, Benjamin and Fredora K.

Abrahamsen, Grace, secy: Larrabee Fund Association

Abramovic, A. Mark, vp, cfo: Connecticut Natural Gas Corp.

Abramovitz, Albert J., trust: Huntington Fund for Education, John

Abrams, Arthur, adv: Bronstein Foundation, Sol and Arlene

Abrams, Howard, dir: Strouse, Greenberg & Co. Charitable Fund

Abrams, James, vp (corporate communications): May Stores Foundation

Abrams, Robert H., dir: Uris Brothers Foundation

Abramson, Albert, off: Abramson Family Foundation

Abramson, Clarence Allen, secy: Merck Co. Foundation

Abramson, Gary M., secy: Abramson Family Foundation

Abramson, Leonard, pres, dir: U.S. Healthcare, Inc.

Abramson, Ronald D., treas: Abramson Family Foundation

Abrego, Judith A., secy: Carpenter Foundation

Abreu, Peter M., chmn: Abreu Charitable Trust u/w/o May P. Abreu, Francis I.

Abrew, Frederick H., exec vp, coo, dir: Equitable Resources

Abromovic, Mark, trust: Connecticut Energy Foundation, Inc.

Abromowitz, Charles, trust: Dayton Foundation Depository

Abroms, Harold L., pres, treas: Abroms Charitable Foundation

Abroms, James M., vp: Abroms Charitable Foundation

Abroms, Judith E., secy: Abroms Charitable Foundation

Abrons, Alix, dir: Abrons Foundation, Louis and Anne

Abrons, Anne, dir: Abrons Foundation, Louis and Anne

Abrons, Henry, dir: Abrons Foundation, Louis and Anne

Abrons, Herbert, vp, dir: Abrons Foundation, Louis and Anne

Abrons, John, dir: Abrons Foundation, Louis and Anne

Abrons, Leslie, dir: Abrons Foundation, Louis and Anne

Abrons, Peter, dir: Abrons Foundation, Louis and Anne

Abrons, Richard, pres, dir: Abrons Foundation, Louis and Anne

Abt, Walter L., pres, ceo: Mor-Flo Industries, Inc.

Aceves, Ann N., vp, dir: Neuberger Foundation, Roy R. and Marie S.

Acheson, Allen Morrow, trust: Black & Veatch Foundation

Acheson, George H., MD, dir: Grass Foundation

Achor, Robert L., vp, dir: Pearce Foundation, Dr. M. Lee

Ackeley, Ethel G., trust: Carteh Foundation

Acker, Albert E., trust: Charitable Fund

Acker, Janet, secy: Giger Foundation, Paul and Oscar

Ackerly, Mrs. John P., III, Memorial Foundation for Children

Ackerman, Asche, trust: Vale-Asche Foundation

Ackerman, Barbara B., trust: Berkman Charitable Trust, Allen H. and Selma W.

Ackerman, Don E., chmn: Decision Data Computer Corp.

Ackerman, F. Duane, exec vp: BellSouth Corp.; trust: BellSouth Foundation; exec vp: Bellsouth Tele-communications, Inc.

Ackerman, Jack Rossin, dir: Jewish Foundation for Education of Women

Ackerman, James H., vp, secy, dir: Bauer Foundation, M. R.

Ackerman, John Tryon, chmn, pres, ceo: Public Service Co. of New Mexico; dir: PNM Foundation

Ackerman, Lee James, dir: Bauer Foundation, M. R.

Ackerman, Lisa M., chief adm off: Kress Foundation, Samuel H.

Ackerman, Loraine E., vp, dir: Bauer Foundation, M. R.

Ackerman, Peter, secy, treas: Banyan Tree Foundation

Ackerman, Philip C., coo: National Fuel Gas Co.

Ackerman, Roger G., trust: Corning Incorporated Foundation

Ackerman, Vale Asche, pres, trust: Vale-Asche Foundation

Ackerson, Robert L., secy, treas: Schneider Foundation Corp., Al J.

Ackley, Kenneth E., pres, dir: Innovation Packaging

Acklin, Robert G., secy, treas: Bicknell Fund

Acord, H. K., dir: Mobil Foundation

Acton, Evelyn Meadows, trust, dir: Meadows Foundation

Acuff, Mary M., Cottrell Foundation

Adair, Charles E., pres, coo, dir: Durr-Fillauer Medical

Adair, Charles W., bd mem: Caring Foundation

Adam, J. Marc, dir: 3M Co.

Adam, Judith, cfo: TransOhio Savings Bank

Adam, Milton F., secy: CHC Foundation

Adam, P. J., chmn: Black & Veatch; trust: Black & Veatch Foundation

Adams, Allan B., vp, dir: Hunter Trust, A. V.

Adams, B.T., treas: CBI Foundation

Adams, Charles Francis, Jr., trust: Humane Society of the Commonwealth of Massachusetts

Adams, Chris G., pres, coo: Rykoff & Co., S.E.

Adams, D. Nelson, trust: Bugher Foundation; mem adv comm: Weezie Foundation

Adams, Daniel N., Jr., trust: Bugher Foundation

Adams, Edward, trust: Besser Foundation

Adams, Elizabeth Helms, vp, secy, treas, trust: Helms Foundation

Adams, Eugene E., treas, dir: Georgia Health Foundation

Adams, Glen, ceo, pres: Southmark Corp.

Adams, Harold C., dir: Mielke Family Foundation

Adams, James R., dir: Southwestern Bell Foundation

Adams, Janet Noyes, off: Noyes, Jr. Memorial Foundation, Nicholas H.

Adams, John, vp: Coughlin-Saunders Foundation

Adams, John C., pres, coo: Russell Corp.

Adams, John E., trust: Avery-Fuller Children's Center

Adams, John W., chmn, ceo: Care Enterprises

Adams, Kenneth Stanley, Jr., chmn, pres, ceo, dir: Adams Resources & Energy, Inc.

Adams, Kipling, Jr., contact: Alexander & Baldwin Foundation

Adams, Louise B., treas, trust: Barnes Foundation

Adams, Marsha H., dir: Hancock Companies, Luke B.

Adams, Minnie, vp: Mitchell Energy & Development Corp.

Adams, Nellie, dir: Coughlin-Saunders Foundation

Adams, Paul D., sr vp, cfo: Old Republic International Corp.

Adams, Paul W., trust: Stone Foundation

Adams, Peter Webster, pres, trust: Huntington Fund for Education, John

Adams, Richard, dir: Tennant Co. Foundation

Adams, Robert E., vp: Conway Scholarship Foundation, Carle C.

Adams, Robert M., trust: Newcombe Foundation, Charlotte W.

Adams, Roy M., dir: Prentice Foundation, Abra; dir: Siragusa Foundation

Adams, S. Kent, pres, dir: Moorman Co. Fund

Adams, Stephen, dir: Weight Watchers Foundation

Adams, Stewart E., dir: Zellerbach Family Fund

Adams, Warren Sanford, II, trust, gen coun: Whitehall Foundation

Adams, William H., trust: Michael Foundation, Herbert I. and Elsa B.

Adams, William W., chmn, pres, ceo: Armstrong World Industries Inc.; pres, dir: Armstrong Foundation

Adamson, Lynn, off mgr: Obayashi America Corp.

Adamson, Roland, exec dir, gen mgr: George Foundation

Adare, J.Robert, chmn: Buffalo Forge Co.

Adderley, Terence E., pres, ceo, dir: Kelly Services

Addington, Leonard M., vp, dir: Thorpe Foundation, James R.

Addington, Whitney Wood, trust: Sprague Memorial Institute, Otho S. A.

Addison, Edward L., chmn, dir: Southern Co. Services

Addison, Francis G., III, trust: Stewart Trust under the will of Helen S. Devore, Alexander and Margaret; trust: Stewart Trust under the will of Mary E. Stewart, Alexander and Margaret

Addison, Michael, dir: Flintridge Foundation

Addison, Susan A., secy: Flintridge Foundation

Addison, Tessa, dir: Flintridge Foundation

Addy, Frederick Seale, exec vp, cfo: Amoco Corp.; pres, dir: Amoco Foundation

Adel, Catherine, trust: Raymond Educational Foundation

Adelson, Andrew S., trust: Bernstein & Co. Foundation, Sanford C.

Adelsperger, J. W., dir: Union City Body Co. Foundation

Adelsperger, Steven L., pres: Union City Body Co.; pres, dir: Union City Body Co. Foundation

Adess, Melvin S., dir: Kirkland & Ellis Foundation

Adkins, Ruth F., trust: Yeager Charitable Trust, Lester E.

Adler, Henrietta B., trust: Adler Foundation Trust, Philip D. and Henrietta B.

Adler, Homer, dir: Coughlin-Saunders Foundation

Adler, Ira R., sr vp, cfo: Tucson Electric Power Co.

Adler, Irving, dir, vp: Stone Foundation, David S.

Adler, J., asst contr: Campbell Soup Foundation

Adler, John, pres, trust: Adler Foundation

Admire, Jack G., trust: Rosenberg Foundation, William J. and Tina

Adrean, Lee, sr vp, cfo: Capital Holding Corp.

Aeder, Arthur, dir: Bravmann Foundation, Ludwig

Aery, Valeen T., trust: Raymond Educational Foundation

Afkhami, Mahnaz, vp, exec dir: Foundation for Iranian Studies

Africk, Jack, exec vp, dir: UST

Aftoors, Patricia J., secy: B & O Railroad Museum

Agati, Giacomo, trust: Eastman Foundation, Alexander

Agee, Eloise R., vp, secy: Rogers Foundation

Agee, Mary Cunningham, chmn: Morrison Knudsen Corp. Foundation Inc.

Agee, Richard, pres, treas: Rogers Foundation

Agee, William F., treas: Board of Trustees of the Prichard School

Agee, William J., chmn, ceo, dir: Morrison-Knudsen Corp.

Ager, John Curtis, trust, exec dir: McClure Educational and Development Fund, James G. K.

Ager, Mrs. John C., Jr., trust: McClure Educational and Development Fund, James G. K.

Agger, David, dir: Osher Foundation, Bernard

Agnew, Dan F., pres: Grinnell Mutual Reinsurance Co.

Agnew, Patrick J., pres, coo: St. Paul Federal Bank for Savings

Agnich, Richard John, dir: Texas Instruments

Agocs, Elizabeth, secy, treas: Soros Foundation-Hungary

Agosti, Frank Emanuel, dir: Detroit Edison Foundation

Agresti, J.J., pres, coo, dir: Atkinson Co., Guy F.

Agricola, Hugh W., trust: Hill Crest Foundation

Aguina, Steve, dir: Chicago Tribune Foundation

Ahlstrom, A., Andres Charitable Trust, Frank G.

Ahmad, Parry Mead, dir: Mead Foundation, Giles W. and Elise G.

Ahmadi, Hoshand, vp, dir: Ala Vi Foundation of New York

Ahmanson, Howard Fieldstad, Jr., trust, don: Ahmanson Foundation

Ahmanson, Robert H., pres, trust: Ahmanson Foundation

Ahmanson, William H., vp, trust: Ahmanson Foundation

Ahnert, Edward F., mgr (Contributions): Exxon Corp.; exec dir: Exxon Education Foundation

Aigner, Rev. Frederick, dir: Aigner Foundation, G.J.

Aiken, Scott, trust: Cincinnati Bell Foundation

Aikenhead, David S., dir: Hayden Foundation, William R. and Virginia

Aikenhead, Kathleen, dir, secy, treas: Hannon Foundation, William H.

Ainslie, Michael Lewis, dir: Markle Foundation, John and Mary R.

Ainsworth, Laine, dir: Hedco Foundation

Airington, Harold A., chmn: Georgia-Pacific Foundation

Akerman, Walter, Jr., chmn, trust: Williams, Jr. Family Foundation, A. L.

Akers, Carl D., vp, dir: Cooper Wood Products Foundation

Akers, John Fellows, chmn, ceo, dir: IBM Corp.; dir: New York Times Co. Foundation

Akeson, Alan C., trust: Smyth Trust, Marion C.

Akin, Carol A., James River Corp. of Virginia

Akin, Gwynn, mem contributions comm: Syntex Corp.

Akos, Andrew, vp: Shapiro Foundation, Charles and M. R.

Akre, Charles Thomas, vp, dir: Marpat Foundation

Alafita, Carlos G., trust: Sandusky International Foundation

Aland, Dave, mng comm: Alliant Community Investment Foundation

Alandt, Lynn F., pres, trust: Ford Fund, Benson and Edith

Alban, Nina C., trust: Mill-Rose Foundation

Albe, Alvin R., Jr., cfo, treas: Day Foundation, Willametta K.

Alber, LaRose, chmn fin: Ebell of Los Angeles Rest Cottage Association; dir, chmn fin: Ebell of Los Angeles Scholarship Endowment Fund

Alber, Mrs. LaRose, finance chmn: Ebell of Los Angeles Scholarship Endowment Fund

Alberding, Ellen S., program off (culture): Joyce Foundation

Albers, C. Hugh, vp, dir: Coleman Foundation

Albers, F. B., secy, gen couns: C.P. Rail Systems

Albers, Genevieve, trust: Geneva Foundation

Alberthal, Les, ceo, pres: Electronic Data Systems Corp.

Alberthal, Lester M., Jr., chmn, pres, ceo, dir: EDS Corp.

Albertine, John M., dir: Farley Foundation, William F.

Albrecht, Frederick Ivan, chmn, dir: Albrecht Grocery Co., Fred W.

Albrecht, Paul Abraham, chmn comm research & grants, trust: Haynes Foundation, John Randolph and Dora

Albrecht, Randal A., chmn: DEC International, Inc.; dir: DEC International- Albrecht Foundation

Albrecht, Richard Raymond, exec vp: Boeing Co.

Albrecht, Steven, pres, dir: Albrecht Grocery Co., Fred W.

Albright, David, trust: Corbin Foundation, Mary S. and David C.

Albright, Harry, trust: Bodman Foundation

Albright, Harry W., Jr., trust: Achelis Foundation

Albright, Thomas E., exec vp, cro: Howard Savings Bank

Albritton, Oliver, dir: Navarro County Educational Foundation

Alcock, Nancy M., secy, dir: Herzog Foundation, Carl J.

Alcott, James Arthur, vp, dir: Cowles Media Foundation

Alda, Alan, trust: Rockefeller Foundation

Aldeen, Norris A., trust: Aldeen Charity Trust, G. W.

Alden, John, treas, asst secy, trust: Casey Foundation, Annie E.

Alderson, Anne W., contr: Burroughs Wellcome Fund

Alderson, David P., mem (contributions comm): Pennzoil Co.

Aldredge, Alison, trust: Coles Family Foundation

Aldrich, Charles R., pres: Louisiana Gas Services

Aldrich, Hope, trust: Rockefeller Family Fund

Aldridge, Edward C., Jr., chmn, dir: Aerospace Corp.

Aldridge, Elizabeth A., sec: Noble Foundation, Samuel Roberts

Aldridge, Susan B., cfo, sr vp (fin): Macmillan, Inc.; dir: Macmillan Foundation

Alegi, August P., dir: GEICO Philanthropic Foundation

Aleppo, Georgia, trust: Bayport Foundation; trust: Aurora Foundation

Aleppo, Joseph, exec dir, trust: Aurora Foundation

Alesi-Miller, Linda, trust: Mobility Foundation

Alessandrini, Charles A., treas: Graphic Arts Education & Research Foundation

Alessi, Keith E., exec vp, cfo: Farm Fresh Inc. (Norfolk, Virginia)

Alexander, Arthur W., exec secy: Schlumberger Foundation

Alexander, Beatrice, trust: Shiffman Foundation

Alexander, Brigitte, exec dir: Pittsburgh Child Guidance Foundation

Alexander, Camille, mgr (corp contributions): JCPenney Co.

Alexander, Caroline R., dir: Kleberg, Jr. and Helen C. Kleberg Foundation, Robert J.

Alexander, Catherine R., trust: Alexander Foundation, Robert D. and Catherine R.

Alexander, Cindy, secy, treas: Bass Foundation

Alexander, David, trust: Armco Steel Co. Foundation; dir: Seaver Institute

Alexander, Dorothy D., dir: Kleberg, Jr. and Helen C. Kleberg Foundation, Robert J.

Alexander, Edward H., trust: Goerlich Family Foundation

Alexander, Emory G., treas, dir: Kleberg, Jr. and Helen C. Kleberg Foundation, Robert J.

Alexander, George W., asst secy-treas, dir: Scholl Foundation, Dr.

Alexander, Helen C., vp, dir: Kleberg, Jr. and Helen C. Kleberg Foundation, Robert J.

Alexander, Henrietta K., dir: Kleberg, Jr. and Helen C. Kleberg Foundation, Robert J.

Alexander, Jack H., secy: Peppers Foundation, Ann

Alexander, John D., Jr., secy, dir: Kleberg, Jr. and Helen C. Kleberg Foundation, Robert J.

Alexander, John R., secy, dir: Hilliard Foundation

Alexander, Judith Dow, vp, trust: Towsley Foundation, Harry A. and Margaret D.

Alexander, Larry J., pres: Southwestern Bell Foundation

Alexander, Michael C., vp, exec dir: Aetna Foundation

Alexander, Norman E., chmn, ceo: Ampacet Corp.; chmn, ceo: Sequa Corp.; pres, trust: Sequa Foundation of Delaware

Alexander, Paule R., dir: Lincoln Fund

Alexander, Quentin, pres, mgr: Prentiss Foundation, Elisabeth Severance

Alexander, Richard G., trust: Douty Foundation

Alexander, Robert C., mem (contributions comm): SAFECO Corp.

Alexander, Ronald B., vp, cfo: Commodore International Ltd.

Alexander, S. Kenneth, III, pres, ceo, dir: Bank IV

Alexander, Sandrea Sue Goerlich, trust: Goerlich Family Foundation

Alexander, Stuart, dir: Deluxe Corp. Foundation

Alexander, W. R., trust: Hughes Charitable Trust, Mabel Y.

Alexander, W. Robert, trust: Colorado Trust; pres, dir: Hunter Trust, A. V.

Alexander, Willie S., trust: Strake Foundation

Alexnder, R. Denny, trust: Alexander Foundation, Robert D. and Catherine R.

Alexy, R. James, vp, trust: Presto Foundation

Aley, Paul Nathaniel, pres: National Machinery Co.; pres: National Machinery Foundation

Alfert, Arthur S., pres, dir: Alexander Foundation, Joseph

Alfiero, Sal H., chmn, dir: Mark IV Industries

Alfond, Dorothy, trust: Alfond Trust, Harold

Alfond, Harold, chmn, dir: Dexter Shoe Co.; trust: Alfond Trust, Harold

Alfond, Theodore, trust: Alfond Trust, Harold

Alford, A. L., Jr., trust: Potlatch Foundation for Higher Education/Potlatch Foundation II

Alford, Bryant K., secy, mem trust comm: Bergen Foundation, Frank and Lydia

Alford, John W., chmn, trust: Evans Foundation, Thomas J.; chmn exec comm: Park National Bank

Alford, Kenneth M., MD, vp, dir: Cummings Foundation, James H.

Alford, L. E., pres: Hale Foundation, Crescent Porter

Alford, Wende, trust: Cornell Trust, Peter C.

Alfred, Theodore Mark, dir: Acme-Cleveland Foundation

Algozin, Kenneth A., asst treas, secy, dir: Special People In Need

Ali, Mehdi Raza, pres, dir: Commodore International Ltd.

Aliber, James A., trust: Skillman Foundation

Alibrandi, Joseph Francis, chmn, ceo, dir: Whittaker Corp.

Alimard, Amin, trust: Foundation for Iranian Studies

Alistrom, R. W., trust: Andres Charitable Trust, Frank G.

Aljian, James D., pres: Lincy Foundation

Alkire, Durwood, adv: Archibald Charitable Foundation, Norman

Allaire, Paul Arthur, trust: Institute for Research on Learning; chmn, dir, ceo: Xerox Corp.

Allan, Karen C., secy, trust: Carpenter Foundation

Allard, Robert A., vp, trust: Foundation for Seacoast Health

Allardice, Edward, trust: Shiffman Foundation

Allardyce, Fred A., dir: American Standard Foundation

Allbee, Colleen, secy grants program: Murdock Charitable Trust, M. J.

Allbritton, Joe Lewis, owner, chmn, ceo: Riggs National Bank

Allday, Doris Fondren, trust: Fondren Foundation

Allen, Barbara K., secy: CP&L Foundation

Allen, Barry K., pres, ceo: Wisconsin Bell, Inc.

Allen, Brandt R., trust: Gould Foundation for Children, Edwin

Allen, C. Robert, III, trust: Allen Foundation, Frances

Allen, Charles C., Jr., secy, dir: Mallinckrodt, Jr. Foundation, Edward

Allen, Charles E., trust: Bates Memorial Foundation, George A.

Allen, Charles Robert, Jr., trust: Allen Foundation, Frances

Allen, Christine, dir: Bedminster Fund

Allen, Christine F., trust: Shore Fund

Allen, Darryl F., chmn, pres, ceo: TRINOVA Corp.; trust: TRINOVA Foundation

Allen, David F., mgr pub aff: Central Maine Power Co.

Allen, Douglas E., dir: Bedminster Fund

Allen, Douglas F., trust: Eastern Bank Foundation

Allen, E. Rudge, Jr., trust: Sarofim Foundation

Allen, Ethan A., Jr., trust: General Educational Fund

Allen, Eugene M., secy, treas: Dodge Jones Foundation

Allen, Gail E., pres, trust: Gerstacker Foundation, Rollin M.; pres: Pardee Foundation, Elsa U.

Allen, Gerald M., trust: Mary Kay Foundation

Allen, Glenn L., Jr., trust: Monticello College Foundation

Allen, Henry L, program dir: Hyams Foundation

Allen, Herbert Anthony, Jr., pres, mng dir: Allen & Co.; trust: Allen Foundation, Frances

Allen, Herbert Anthony, Sr., pres: Allen Brothers Foundation; trust: Allen Foundation, Frances

Allen, Ivan, Jr., trust: Woodruff Foundation, Robert W.

Allen, Jack W., trust: Patterson-Barclay Memorial Foundation

Allen, Joan G., trust: English Foundation, W. C.

Allen, John O., exec vp, gen mgr, dir: Inco Alloys International

Allen, Joseph H., trust: Enron Foundation

Allen, Lew, Jr., dir, mem dirs grant program comm: Keck Foundation, W. M.

Allen, Lloyd, trust: CENEX Foundation

Allen, M. George, dir: 3M Co.

Allen, Marjorie B., vp: Bolz Family Foundation, Eugenie Mayer

Allen, Marjorie Powell, pres, trust, don daughter: Powell Family Foundation

Allen, Martin, dir: Grand Rapids Label Foundation

Allen, Mayreta V., trust: Allen Charitable Trust, Phil N.

Allen, Patterson, trust: Patterson-Barclay Memorial Foundation

Allen, Paul G., pres, dir: Allen Foundation for Medical Research, Paul G.

Allen, Philip D., vp, dir: Bedminster Fund

Allen, Randy, dir: Deloitte & Touche Foundation

Allen, Richard, dir: Sordoni Foundation

Allen, Robert Eugene, chmn, ceo, dir: American Telephone & Telegraph Co.

Allen, Ronald W., chmn, ceo, dir: Delta Air Lines; pres, trust: Delta Air Lines Foundation

Allen, Shirley, vp, treas: Berger Foundation, H.N. and Frances C.

Allen, Susan J., secy, dir: Grand Rapids Label Foundation

Allen, Thomas F., secy: Bingham Foundation, William; trust, treas, secy: Dively Foundation, George S.; treas: Weatherhead Foundation

Allen, W. James, asst treas, asst secy: Pardee Foundation, Elsa U.

Allen, W. W., pres, coo, dir: Phillips Petroleum Co.

Allen, William Frederick, Jr., chmn, ceo, dir, pres: Stone & Webster, Inc.

Allen, William R., Jr., pres, ceo: Union Equity Division of Farmland Industries

Alles, Norbert C., chmn: DCB Corp.; dir: DCB Foundation

Allex, Kenneth R., vp, treas: Brencanda Foundation

Alley, William J., chmn, ceo: American Brands

Allin, William B., treas: Self Foundation

Allingham, Dennis, sr vp, cfo: Krelitz Industries

Allison, Ethelyn, trust: Snyder Foundation, Harold B. and Dorothy A.

Allison, Jim, pres, exec dir: Harrington Foundation, Don and Sybil

Allison, John, chmn, ceo: Branch Banking & Trust Co.

Allison, John Andrew, IV, chmn, ceo, dir: BB&T Financial Corp.

Allison, L. L., trust: McEachern Charitable Trust, D. V. & Ida J.

Allison, Robert J., Jr., chmn, ceo, dir: Anadarko Petroleum Corp.

Allison, Walter V., ceo, chmn: WestStar Bank N.A.

Allison, Walter W., vp, asst treas: Lyon Foundation

Allman, Edward L., trust: Edison Fund, Charles

Allmon, Barbara, pres: Block Foundation, H&R

Allocco, Nancy A., grants adm, asst secy: Hyde and Watson Foundation

Allsbrook, Bethany, program off: Hall Foundation

Allton, John D., treas, trust: Schlink Foundation, Albert G. and Olive H.

Allyn, Dawn, dir: Allyn Foundation

Allyn, Janet J., dir: Allyn Foundation

Allyn, John W., Jr., dir, vp: Allyn Foundation

Allyn, Lew F., vp, dir: Allyn Foundation

Allyn, Margaret B., dir, pres: Allyn Foundation

Allyn, Sonya, dir: Allyn Foundation

Allyn, William Finch, vp, dir: Allyn Foundation; dir: Emerson Foundation, Fred L.

Allyn, William G., pres, dir: Allyn Foundation

Alm, John, dir: Coca-Cola Foundation

Alm, Melanie, secy: Kemper Foundation, Enid and Crosby

Almquist, Donald J., chmn, ceo, pres: Delco Electronics Corp.

Almquist, L. Arden, dir: Young Foundation, Irvin L.

Alonso, Jose, asst treas: Gould Foundation for Children, Edwin

Alpaugh, Lewis F., pres: Hoechst Celanese Foundation

Alper, Hortense, vp: Herman Foundation, John and Rose

Alperin, Barry J., trust: Alperin/Hirsch Family Foundation

Alperin, Max, trust: Alperin/Hirsch Family Foundation

Alperin, Melvin G., trust: Alperin/Hirsch Family Foundation; trust: Haffenreffer Family Fund

Alperin, Ruth, trust: Alperin/Hirsch Family Foundation

Alpert, Arthur Malcolm, trust: Kempner Fund, Harris and Eliza

Alpert, Benjamin, trust, secy, treas: Geist Foundation

Alpert, Charles, ceo, pres, dir: Alpert & Co., Inc., Herman

Alpert, Gerald, vp (sales & mktg): Alpert & Co., Inc., Herman

Alpert, Herb, chmn, pres: Alpert Foundation, Herb

Alpert, Lani Hall, vchmn, vp: Alpert Foundation, Herb

Alpert, Saul, vp: Ann & Hope; dir: Chase Memorial Scholarship Foundation, Martin M.

Alpert, William T., sr program off: Donner Foundation, William H.

Alsdorf, Marilynn B., dir, vp, secy: Alsdorf Foundation; dir: Rice Foundation

Alsip, John, III, pres, coo: Rahr Malting Co.

Alstadt, Donald M., chmn, ceo: Lord Corp.

Alster, Iris B., secy: Zlinkoff Fund for Medical Research and Education, Sergei S.

Altamore, Ellen, advisor: Delano Foundation, Mignon Sherwood

Altenbaumer, Larry F., vp, cfo: Illinois Power Co.

Alter, Charles M, trust, treas: Pilgrim Foundation

Altermatt, Paul Barry, pres, dir: Harcourt Foundation, Ellen Knowles; mem distr comm: Meserve Memorial Fund, Albert and Helen

Altman, D. David, exec secy: Seasongood Good Government Foundation, Murray and Agnes

Altman, Drew, pres, trust: Kaiser Family Foundation, Henry J.

Altman, F.C., chmn, ceo: Spahn & Rose Lumber Co.

Altman, Lawrence K., MD, dir: Macy, Jr. Foundation, Josiah

Altobello, Daniel Joseph, trust: Loyola Foundation

Altomare, Arlene, vp: MBIA, Inc.

Alton, David C., vp, gen tax couns: Warner-Lambert Co.; first vp: Warner-Lambert Charitable Foundation

Altschul, Arthur Goodhart, vp, dir: Lehman Foundation, Edith and Herbert; pres, treas, dir: Overbrook Foundation; trust: Weinberg Foundation, John L.; trust: Whitehead Foundation

Altschul, Diana L., secy, dir: Overbrook Foundation

Altschul, Stephen F., dir: Overbrook Foundation

Altshuler, Sharman B., trust: Merck Family Fund

Alvarez, Ed, dir: Levi Strauss Foundation

Alvarez, Paul H., pres, ceo: Ketchum Communications

Alveres, Ken, pres: Sun Microsystems Foundation

Alvey, David W., trust: Faith Home Foundation

Alvin, Rose M., Pittsburgh Child Guidance Foundation

Alvord, Joel Barnes, chmn, ceo, dir: Shawmut National Corp.

Alyea, Mark, pres, dir: Alro Steel Corp.; trust: Alro Steel Corp. Charitable Trust

Amacher, Howard R., trust: Washington Foundation

Amado, Bernice, vp, secy, dir: Amado Foundation, Maurice

Amado, Ralph A., dir: Amado Foundation, Maurice

Amado, Ralph D., dir: Amado Foundation, Maurice

Amani, Sarada, mgr community rels: CNA Insurance Cos.

Amaral, Walter D., cfo: Maxtor Corp.

Amari, Yoko, adm asst Tokyo off: United States-Japan Foundation

Amato, A. J., pres, dir: Wisconsin Power & Light Foundation

Amato, Paul H., pres, ceo: Columbus Life Insurance Co.

Amato, Thomas G., secy: Amcast Industrial Foundation

Amaturo, Douglas Q., dir: Amaturo Foundation

Amaturo, Joseph C., don, dir: Amaturo Foundation

Amaturo, Lawrence V., dir: Amaturo Foundation

Amaturo, Lorna J., dir: Amaturo Foundation

Amaturo, Winifred, dir: Amaturo Foundation

Amaturo, Winifred L., dir: Amaturo Foundation

Ambasz, Emilio, dir: Skidmore, Owings & Merrill Foundation

Ambros, Dr. Dieter H., chmn, dir: Henkel Corp.

Ambrose, Mary Lou, dir: Alcoa Foundation

Ambrose, Patricia A., trust: Perry Drug Stores Charitable Foundation

Ambrozy, Sandra McAlister, program off: Kresge Foundation

Amelio, Gilbert F., pres, ceo: National Semiconductor Corp.

Amemiya, Koichi, pres, coo: American Honda Motor Co.

Amend, Lois, mgr (corp contributions & comm rels): CIBA-GEIGY Corp.

Amerman, John W., chmn, ceo, dir: Mattel

Ames, Aubin Z., trust: Schumann Fund for New Jersey

Ames, B. Charles, ceo: Acme-Cleveland Corp.

Ames, Edward A., trust: Cary Charitable Trust, Mary Flagler

Ames, George Joseph, secy, treas, dir: Meyer Foundation

Ames, James B., trust: Shaw Fund for Mariner's Children

Ames, Morgan P., treas: Price Foundation, Lucien B. and Katherine E.

Amino, Toshi, exec vp: Honda of America Foundation

Amiry, Reda, treas: Connelly Foundation

Amman, Robert J., ceo: New Valley

Ammann, William, trust: TRINOVA Foundation

Amodio, John J., pres: Community National Bank & Trust Co. of New York

Amore, Joseph, chmn exec comm, pres, ceo: Beef America Inc.

Amory, Walter, trust: Shaw Fund for Mariner's Children

Amos, Daniel P., ceo, pres, dir: AFLAC

Amos, Harold, PhD, hon dir: Macy, Jr. Foundation, Josiah

Amos, Paul S., chmn, dir: AFLAC

Amos, W.J., Jr., ceo, chmn: Lykes Brothers Steamship Co.

Amper, Robert, pres: Ladish Co.

Amsterdam, Gustave G., trust: Greenfield Foundation, Albert M.

Amsterdam, Jack, pres: Amsterdam Foundation, Jack and Mimi Leviton; ceo: Leviton Manufacturing Co.; secy-treas: Leviton Foundation New York

Amundson, Duane M., chmn, dir: Indiana Gas Co.

Amundson, W. R., trust: Stern Family Foundation, Alex

Anastasio, Carol, secy, trust: Hazen Foundation, Edward W.

Andeisan, Timothy B., dir: Baxter Foundation

Andelman, David, trust: Reisman Charitable Trust, George C. and Evelyn R.

Anders, Steven M., trust: Jefferson Endowment Fund, John Percival and Mary C.; vp: Wade Endowment Fund, Elizabeth Firth

Anders, William Alison, chmn: General Dynamics Corp.

Andersen, Anthony Lee, chmn, ceo, dir: Fuller Co., H.B.; dir: Fuller Co. Foundation, H.B.

Andersen, Arthur E., III, pres: Andersen Foundation, Arthur

Andersen, Arthur H., secy: Eden Hall Foundation

Andersen, Christine E., vp: Andersen Foundation, Hugh J.

Andersen, Frank N., trust: Wickes Foundation, Harvey Randall

Andersen, Joan N., vp, treas: Andersen Foundation, Arthur

Andersen, Katherine B., trust: Bayport Foundation; don: Andersen Foundation

Andersen, Sarah J., pres: Andersen Foundation, Hugh J.

Anderson, Alden M., chmn, pres, ceo, dir: Rhode Island Hospital Trust National Bank

Anderson, Andrew E., secy, treas, trust: Stone Foundation, France

Anderson, Andrew T., trust: Anderson Foundation

Anderson, Angela, vp, dir: Lizzadro Family Foundation, Joseph

Anderson, Ann Stewart, dir: Kentucky Foundation for Women

Anderson, Arthur, trust: Connecticut Energy Foundation, Inc.

Anderson, Bruce, acting pres: Danforth Foundation

Anderson, Bruce G., chmn: Mutual Service Life Insurance Cos.

Anderson, Catherine M., vp, trust: Markey Charitable Fund, John C.

Anderson, Charles M., pres: Anderson Foundation

Anderson, Charles Ralph Seibold, chmn, dir: IES Industries

Anderson, Chester M., secy: Berkman Foundation, Louis and Sandra

Anderson, David Boyd, chmn, pres, dir: Inland Steel-Ryerson Foundation

Anderson, David G., vp (fin), treas: Humana Foundation

Anderson, David H., vchmn, trust: Lennox Foundation

Anderson, Dorothy, dir: Noyes Foundation, Jessie Smith

Anderson, Dorothy I., secy, treas: Anderson Foundation

Anderson, Eugene Karl, treas: Simmons Foundation, Harold

Anderson, Evelyn M., trust: Anderson Foundation, Peyton

Anderson, Ford A., II, exec dir: Murdock Charitable Trust, M. J.

Anderson, Fred C., secy, dir: Norcross Wildlife Foundation

Anderson, G.F., pres, coo: Tampa Electric

Anderson, George W., dir: ASARCO Foundation

Anderson, Gordon Benjamin, dir: Phipps Foundation, William H.

Anderson, Gordon M., pres: Santa Fe International Corp.

Anderson, Gregory S., assoc: CHC Foundation

Anderson, Grenville, trust: Anderson Foundation, William P.

Anderson, Ivan V., Jr., pres, dir: Evening Post Publishing Co.; vp: Post & Courier Foundation

Anderson, J. D., dir: Werner Foundation, Clara and Spencer

Anderson, J. Robert, vchmn, cfo: Grumman Corp.

Anderson, James C., treas, contr: Teagle Foundation

Anderson, James G., trust: Kerr Foundation, Robert S. and Grayce B.

Anderson, James M., trust: Thendara Foundation

Anderson, Jeffrey W., trust: Anderson Foundation

Anderson, Jennifer A., dir fdns: Deluxe Corp. Foundation

Anderson, John, secy: Toshiba America Foundation

Anderson, John Edward, pres, dir, treas: Ace Beverage Co.; chmn, dir: Anderson Foundation, Marion & John E.

Anderson, John Firth, trust, chmn: Pineywoods Foundation

Anderson, John R., chmn, dir: Anderson Industries; pres: Anderson Industries Charitable Foundation; chmn, dir: Atwood Industries

Anderson, John T., chmn, dir: Joyce Foundation

Anderson, Joseph M., trust: Self Foundation

Anderson, Judy M., exec dir, sec, treas: Georgia Power Foundation

Anderson, Julaine F., secy, dir: Tombstone Pizza Foundation

Anderson, June C., trust: Aldeen Charity Trust, G. W.

Anderson, Kathleen, vp, secy, trust: Seymour and Troester Foundation

Anderson, Kenneth G., trust: Swisher Foundation, Carl S.

Anderson, Lee S., dir: Maclellan Foundation, Robert L. and Kathrina H.

Anderson, Lowell C., chmn, pres, coo: North American Life & Casualty Co.

Anderson, Marcia F., trust: Fink Foundation

Anderson, Margaret A., vp, cfo: Aerospace Corp.

Anderson, Marion, pres, dir: Anderson Foundation, Marion & John E.

Anderson, Michael Scott, dir: Overlake Foundation

Anderson, Mrs. Richardson, mem grants comm: Memorial Foundation for Children

Anderson, Nancy C., trust: Rockefeller Family Fund

Anderson, Patricia, secy, dir: Reed Foundation, Philip D.

Anderson, Paul J., chief personnel officer: Booz Allen & Hamilton

Anderson, R. Edward, sr vp, cfo: Rose's Stores, Inc.

Anderson, R. Quintus, chmn, pres: Aarque Cos.

Anderson, R. Wayne, vp (human resources): Amoco Corp.; chmn, dir: Amoco Foundation

Anderson, R.E. Olds, pres: Ransom Fidelity Company

Anderson, Ralph F., chmn, secy, dir: Anderson Industries; chmn: Anderson Industries Charitable Foundation

Anderson, Ray C., chmn, pres, ceo: Interface Inc.

Anderson, Richard L., trust: Brown Foundation, George Warren

Anderson, Richard P., pres, ceo: Andersons Management Corp.; trust: First Mississippi Corp. Foundation

Anderson, Robert, secy: Pioneer Fund

Anderson, Robert E., pres, ceo, coo: GenRad

Anderson, Robert P., Ph.D., exec dir, secy, treas: South Plains Foundation

Anderson, Roger E., vchmn, dir: Fry Foundation, Lloyd A.

Anderson, Roy A., dir: Weingart Foundation

Anderson, Sherwood L., secy, treas, dir: Bristol Savings Bank Foundation

Anderson, Stefan Stolen, dir: Ball Foundation, George and Frances

Anderson, Steve Craig, dir: Overlake Foundation

Anderson, Steven A., Confidence Foundation; vp: Mericos Foundation

Anderson, Suzanne, asst secy: Hertz Foundation, Fannie and John

Anderson, Ted M., dir: Behmann Brothers Foundation

Anderson, Thomas, trust: Anderson Foundation

Anderson, Thomas Harold, chmn: Andersons Management Corp.; chmn, trust: Anderson Foundation

Anderson, Timothy A., trust: Anderson Foundation

Anderson, Vernon R., vchmn: Johnson Inc., Axel

Anderson, William G., pres, treas, trust: Anderson Foundation, William P.

Anderson, William J., adm, asst sec: Pella Rolscreen Foundation

Anderson, William P., V, trust: Anderson Foundation, William P.

Andersson, Craig R., pres, coo, dir: Aristech Chemical Corp.; trust: Aristech Foundation

Ando, Kuri, pres: Sony Corp. of America

Andrasick, James Stephen, pres: Brewer Charitable Foundation, C.

Andreani, Alessandro, chmn: Eni-Chem America, Inc.

Andreas, Dorothy Inez, trust: Andreas Foundation

Andreas, Dwayne Orville, pres: Andreas Foundation; chmn, ceo: Archer-Daniels-Midland Co.

Andreas, John L., secy, treas, dir: McMillen Foundation

Andreas, Lowell Willard, exec vp, treas, dir: Andreas Foundation; pres: Archer-Daniels-Midland Foundation

Andreas, Michael Dwayne, vp, secy, trust: Andreas Foundation

Andreassen, Paul, chmn: ISS International Service System

Andreen, Brian, vp: Research Corporation

Andreoli, James M., pres, ceo, dir: Baker Commodities; pres: Jerome Foundation

Andres, F. William, trust: Charlesbank Homes

Andresen, Rolf S., sr vp, cfo: Eastern Air Lines

Andress, Charlotte F., vp, dir: Mertz Foundation, Martha

Andreuzzi, Denis, chmn exec comm, vchmn, pres, coo, dir: Witco Corp.

Andrew, Edward J., Andrew Corp.

Andrew, Phoebe Haffner, trust: Haffner Foundation

Andrews, Christie F., vp: Hewit Family Foundation

Andrews, Edward C., Jr.,MD, dir, mem budget comm: Dana Foundation, Charles A.; trust: Johnson Foundation, Robert Wood

Andrews, Gene, mem contributions comm: Puget Sound Power & Light Co.

Andrews, H. D., trust: Vicksburg Hospital Medical Foundation

Andrews, Joseph, Jr., secy: Luck Stone Foundation

Andrews, Mary Linda, mem contributions comm: Burroughs Wellcome Co.

Andrews, Oakley, secy, trust: Huntington Fund for Education, John

Andrews, Oliver R., Jr., exec dir: Ayling Scholarship Foundation, Alice S.; exec dir: Travelli Fund, Charles Irwin

Andrews, Paul R. P., adjunct dir: Educational Foundation of America

Andrews, Richard J., dir: Hewit Family Foundation

Andrews, Sheri L., trust: Lozier Foundation

Andrews, Sumner R., trust: Ayling Scholarship Foundation, Alice S.; pres: Travelli Fund, Charles Irwin

Andringa, Dale, dir: Vermeer Charitable Foundation

Andringa, Mary, dir: Vermeer Charitable Foundation

Andrus, John E., III, trust, dir: Marbrook Foundation; chmn emeritus, dir: Surdna Foundation

Angel, Albert D., pres: Merck Co. Foundation

Angel, J. T., pres, coo: Reading & Bates Corp.

Angelastro, Linda M., secy: Ensign-Bickford Foundation

Angelicchio, David J., coo: Gulf USA Corp.

Angelo, Bill, corp contr: Coachmen Industries

Angeloni, Arnold A., dir: Deluxe Corp. Foundation

Anglebeck, Eleanor, secy, asst treas: Hall Family Foundations; asst secy: Hallmark Cards

Anglin, Jesse B., Jr., dir: Durham Merchants Association Charitable Foundation

Angood, Arthur W., exec vp, coo, trust: Miller Foundation

Angulo, Valerie, mgr, comm rels: America West Airlines

Anlyan, William G., trust: Duke Endowment

Annable, Grant, pres: Gold Fields Mining Co.

Annenberg, Leonore A., vchmn, vp: Annenberg Foundation

Annenberg, Wallis, vp: Annenberg Foundation

Annenberg, Walter Hubert, trust: Ames Charitable Trust, Harriett; don, chmn, pres: Annenberg Foundation; trust: Hall Charitable Trust, Evelyn A. J.; trust: Hazen Charitable Trust, Lita Annenberg; trust: Hooker Charitable Trust, Janet A.; trust: Levee Charitable Trust, Polly Annenberg; trust: Simon Charitable Trust, Esther

Annette, Kathleen, trust: Blandin Foundation

Annon, David M., cfo: Ward Machinery Co.

Anschuetz, Robert R., trust: Monticello College Foundation

Anschuetz, Robert R., MD, trust: Monticello College Foundation

Anschutz, Fred B., don, trust: Anschutz Family Foundation

Anschutz, Nancy P., trust: Anschutz Family Foundation

Anschutz, Philip F., don, vp: Anschutz Family Foundation

Anschutz, Sarah, trust: Anschutz Family Foundation

Anselmo, Joseph F., secy: Steele Foundation

Ansin, Ronald M., trust: Ansin Private Foundation, Ronald M.

Anstine, Mary K., treas, dir: Hunter Trust, A. V.

Anter, George, trust: Citizens Charitable Foundation

Anthony, Barbara Cox, chmn: Cox Foundation of Georgia, James M.; trust, vp: Cox, Jr. Foundation, James M.

Anthony, Bob, chmn, dir: Anthony Co., C.R.

Anthony, Eiland E., dir, secy, treas: Andalusia Health Services

Anthony, Frederick W., secy: Palisades Educational Foundation

Anthony, J. Danford, Jr., trust: Bissell Foundation, J. Walton

Anthony, Nancy S., trust: Swensrud Charitable Trust, Sidney A.

Anthony, Otis, trust: Jones Intercable Tampa Trust

Anthony, Ralph F., pres, dir: Palisades Educational Foundation

Anti, Janet McCune Edwards, mem dispensing comm: McCune Charitable Trust, John R.

Antle, William S., III, pres, ceo: Oak Industries

Anton, Frederick W., chmn: PMA Industries

Anton, Frederick W., III, trust: PMA Foundation

Antonelli, Edward A., pres, dir: Morris Foundation, William T.

Antonini, Joseph E., chmn, pres, ceo, dir: Kmart Corp.

Antony, Frank S., secy, dir: Bird Cos. Charitable Foundation

Antoun, M. Lawreace, SJ, exec dir: McMannis and A. Haskell McMannis Educational Fund, William J.

Antrim, Joseph L., III, dir: Cabell III and Maude Morgan Cabell Foundation, Robert G.

Anuzis, Andris, asst treas: Dun & Bradstreet Corp. Foundation

Aoki, Harriet, dir: First Hawaiian Foundation

Apoliona, Haunani, alternate mem distribution comm: McInerny Foundation

App, Robert G., trust: Wickes Foundation, Harvey Randall

Appel, Gloria W., trust: Price Foundation, Louis and Harold

Appel, John, trust: Forster Charitable Trust, James W. and Ella B.

Appel, Robert J., dir: Levitt Foundation

Appel, Wendy, dir, trust: Schaffer Foundation, Michael & Helen

Appell, George N., vp: Susquehanna-Pfaltzgraff Foundation

Appell, Louis J., pres: Susquehanna-Pfaltzgraff Co.

Appell, Louis J., Jr., pres, treas: Susquehanna-Pfaltzgraff Foundation

Apple, Suzanne H., dir (commun aff): Home Depot

Applebaugh, Richard T., vp: Dewar Foundation

Applebaum, Leila, mgr: Applebaum Foundation

Appleby, Thomas, dir: Lee Foundation, James T.

Applegate, Timothy, gen couns: Forest Lawn Foundation

Appleman, Don, cfo: Enterprise Coal Co.

Appleman, Nathan, pres: Appleman Foundation

Apregan, Craig, dir: Peters Foundation, Leon S.

Apregan, George, dir: Peters Foundation, Leon S.

Aprigliano, Vincent, treas: Banfi Vintners Foundation

Aqarons, Morris, trust: Allied Educational Foundation Fund

Aqua, Ronald, vp: United States-Japan Foundation

Aquilon, Nora, secy: Brennan Foundation, Robert E.

Arahata, Y., vp: Dai-Ichi Kangyo Bank of California

Arai, Koichi, pres: Dentsu, Inc., NY

Araki, Keisuke, pres, ceo: Oki America Inc.

Aranow, Edward, treas, secy: Abrons Foundation, Louis and Anne

Aranow, Judith, dir: Abrons Foundation, Louis and Anne

Aranow, Rita, vp, dir: Abrons Foundation, Louis and Anne

Araskog, Rand Vincent, chmn, pres, ceo: International Standard Electric Corp.

Aratani, George T., chmn: Kenwood U.S.A. Corp.

Arbaugh, Eugene, pres, dir: PHH Foundation

Arbuckle, James E., pres, coo, dir: Besser Co.

Arbury, Dorothy D., vp, trust, don daughter: Dow Foundation, Herbert H. and Grace A.

Arbury, Julie Carol, trust, don great granddaughter: Dow Foundation, Herbert H. and Grace A.

Arcadipane, Mildred, vp, secy, dir: Carvel Foundation, Thomas and Agnes

Archabal, Nina, dir: Northwest Area Foundation

Archambault, Margaret M., trust: Kemper Educational and Charitable Fund

Archer, John H., Plankenhorn Foundation, Harry

Archer, Richard Allen, dir: Seaver Institute

Archibald, Nolan D., chmn, pres, ceo, dir: Black & Decker Corp.

Archibald, Read William, vp: Occidental Oil & Gas Charitable Foundation

Arconti, Gino, mem distr comm: Meserve Memorial Fund, Albert and Helen

Ardia, Stephen V., pres, ceo: Goulds Pumps

Area, Mary Lou, dir: Imperial Bank Foundation

Areddy, Joseph Michael, vp, dir: Inland Container Corp. Foundation

Arena, John J., vchmn: BayBanks

Arent, Albert E., dir, vp: Freeman Foundation, Carl M.

Argyris, George T., dir, secy: Foothills Foundation

Argyris, Marcia M., pres: McKesson Foundation

Argyros, George Leon, secy, dir: Argyros Foundation; dir: Beckman Foundation, Arnold and Mabel

Argyros, Julie A., pres, dir: Argyros Foundation

Ariail, Leslie, vp: Washington Forrest Foundation

Arias, Robert, dir: Gaisman Foundation, Catherine and Henry J.

Arison, Marilyn, trust: Arison Foundation

Arison, Micky, chmn, ceo: Carnival Cruise Lines

Arison, Shari, pres: Arison Foundation

Arison, Ted, owner, chmn, dir: Carnival Cruise Lines

Arkin, Norman A., dir: Taylor Family Foundation, Jack

Arkwright, Richard T., pres: St. Giles Foundation

Arledge, David A., treas: ANR Foundation; exec vp, cfo: Coastal Corp.

Arlen, Myron, dir: JJJ Foundation

Armacost, Samuel H., dir: Irvine Foundation, James

Armbrust, Adelaide P., trust: Armbrust Foundation

Armbrust, Howard W., chmn, dir: Armbrust Chain Co.; trust: Armbrust Foundation

Armbruster, Timothy, pres: Goldseker Foundation of Maryland, Morris

Armentrout, Eugene E., pres: Gradison & Co.

Armington, Catherine, adv: Armington Fund, Evenor

Armington, David E., adv: Armington Fund, Evenor

Armington, Paul S., adv: Armington Fund, Evenor

Armington, Peter, adv: Armington Fund, Evenor

Armington, Rosemary, adv: Armington Fund, Evenor

Armour, Vernon, pres, trust: Sprague Memorial Institute, Otho S. A.

Armstrong, Arthur O., secy, dir: Norman/Nethercutt Foundation, Merle

Armstrong, C. M., chmn, ceo: Hughes Aircraft Co.

Armstrong, James Sinclair, secy, asst treas: Reed Foundation

Armstrong, Norma, assoc: CHC Foundation

Armstrong, Paul, vp, dir: Knox Family Foundation

Armstrong, Rose Ann, vp, dir: Knox Family Foundation

Armstrong, T. G., pres, ceo: Standard Steel Speciality Co.

Armstrong, Theodore M., cfo: Angelica Corp.

Armstrong, Thomas K., pres: Armstrong Foundation

Armstrong, Thomas K., Jr., vp: Armstrong Foundation

Armstrong, Wallace F., trust: Community Coffee Co., Inc. Foundation

Arnault, Ronald J., dir: ARCO Foundation

Arndt, Ardean A., secy: Lincoln Family Foundation

Arndt, Celestine Favrot, trust: Favrot Fund

Arne, Marshall C., trust: CLARCOR Foundation

Arnett, James E., chmn: Senior Citizens Foundation

Arnhart, James R., exec dir: Christy-Houston Foundation

Arnn, Larry P., exec dir: Aequus Institute

Arnn, Nancy Miller, trust: Edison Fund, Charles

Arnof, Ian, pres, ceo, dir: First Commerce Corp.

Arnold, A. K., dir: Oaklawn Foundation

Arnold, Brian A., pres: New Milford Savings Bank Foundation

Arnold, David J., trust: Strosacker Foundation, Charles J.

Arnold, Edward H., chmn, pres, ceo: New Penn Motor

Express; off: Arnold Industries Scholarship Foundation

Arnold, F.W., pres: Newmil Bancorp

Arnold, Florence A., dir: Wilson Foundation, H. W.

Arnold, Frances A., dir: Amaturo Foundation

Arnold, Fred E., mem adv comm: Jordan and Ettie A. Jordan Charitable Foundation, Mary Ranken

Arnold, Isaac, Jr., trust, secy-treas: Cullen Foundation

Arnold, Jerry L., secy: Mayborn Foundation, Frank W.

Arnold, Kay, chmn (contributions comm): Arkansas Power & Light Co.

Arnold, Louise Wilson, pres, exec secy, dir: Jones Foundation, Helen

Arnold, Martha G., pres, trust: Strosacker Foundation, Charles J.

Arnold, Patricia, dir: Beim Foundation

Arnold, Phyllis H., pres, ceo: One Valley Bank, N.A.; trust: One Valley Bank Foundation

Arnold, Robert Neff, vp, secy, dir: Jones Foundation, Helen

Arnold, Roland R., vp, treas, trust: Halff Foundation, G. A. C.

Arnold, Ross, trust: Patterson-Barclay Memorial Foundation

Arnold, W. A., IV, dir: Oaklawn Foundation

Arnsperger, Elmer, mem trust fund comm: Ingram Trust, Joe

Arnstein, Leo H., trust: Kellstadt Foundation; secy, dir: Lederer Foundation, Francis L.

Aron, Jack R., don, pres, dir: Aron Charitable Foundation, J.

Aron, Peter A., don, exec dir: Aron Charitable Foundation, J.

Aron, Robert, don, vp, dir: Aron Charitable Foundation, J.

Aron, Sharron A., pres: Imperial Bank Foundation

Aronin, Jeff, vp, secy, dir: Rubenstein Foundation, Philip

Aronson, Hillel S., vp: Columbia Savings Charitable Foundation

Aronson, Mark B., Pittsburgh Child Guidance Foundation

Aronson, Nancy P., dir: Pforzheimer Foundation, Carl and Lily

Arrillaga, Frances C., vp: Arrillaga Foundation

Arrillaga, John, don, pres: Arrillaga Foundation; dir: Peery Foundation

Arrillaga, John, Jr., treas: Arrillaga Foundation

Arrison, Clement R., pres, dir: Mark IV Industries; pres: Mark IV Industries Foundation

Arth, Lawrence J., pres, coo, dir: Ameritas Life Insurance Corp.; vp, dir: Ameritas Charitable Foundation

Arthur, John M., vchmn: Buhl Foundation

Arthurs, Alberta Bean, dir (arts & humanities): Rockefeller Foundation

Arthurs, Heidi D., dir: Dent Family Foundation, Harry

Artis, Curtis R., trust: AT&T Foundation

Artzt, Edwin L., chmn, dir: Procter & Gamble Co.

Arundel, Edward M., secy: Neilson Foundation, George W.

as-Sayid, Farouk, dir: Bobst Foundation, Elmer and Mamdouha

Asano, K., chmn: Mazda North America

Asbury, Paul, comm mem: Sherman Educational Fund

Asch, George, trust: Price Foundation, Louis and Harold

Ash, Mary Kay, chmn emeritus, dir: Mary Kay Cosmetics; trust: Mary Kay Foundation

Ashby, Douglas H., pres, ceo: AMAX Coal Industries

Ashcraft, Kenneth J., trust: Whittell Trust for Disabled Veterans of Foreign Wars, Elia

Ashen, Nancy, fiscal off: New York Foundation

Asher, Thomas, vp, secy: Rich Foundation

Ashford, Clinton Rutledge, secy, dir: Watumull Fund, J.

Ashford, James K., trust: Monroe Auto Equipment Foundation Trust; ceo, pres: Steiger Tractor

Ashford, Theodore H., trust: Beinecke Foundation

Ashkenazi, Ely E., chmn: Soundesign Corp.

Ashley, Daniel J., dir, vp: Trimble Family Foundation, Robert Mize and Isa White

Ashley, James W., dir: Globe Foundation

Ashley, Perry, secy, dir: Osceola Foundation

Ashley, W. Seaborn, Jr., dir: Citizens Union Bank Foundation

Ashmun, Candace McKee, trust: Fund for New Jersey

Ashton, Barbara, secy: Widow's Society

Ashton, Clifford L., mem: Bamberger and John Ernest Bamberger Memorial Foundation, Ruth Eleanor

Ashton, Harris J., chmn, pres, ceo, dir: Franks Nursery and Crafts

Ashton, James, mem: Florence Foundation

Ashton, Peter Jack, exec vp (bearings), dir: Timken Co.

Ashton, Robert W., exec dir, secy: Bay Foundation

Ashworth, Brenda K., adm: Price Associates Foundation, T. Rowe

Askew, Elsie Joe, trust: Kyle Educational Trust, S. H. and D. W.

Askins, Wallace B., exec vp, cfo, dir: Armco Inc.; trust: Armco Foundation

Askow, Irwin J., trust: Graham Foundation for Advanced Studies in the Fine Arts

Aslin, Malcolm M., trust: Kemper Foundation, Enid and Crosby; pres, coo, dir: United Missouri Bancshares, Inc.

Asmeth, James E., trust: Chesapeake Corporate Foundation

Aspinwall, Valerie, trust: Altschul Foundation

Asplundh, Barr E., dir: Asplundh Foundation

Asplundh, Edward K., pres, dir: Asplundh Foundation

Asplundh, Robert H., dir: Asplundh Foundation

Aston, James William, chmn, ceo, dir: Hoblitzelle Foundation

Astor, Roberta Brooke Russell, pres, trust: Astor Foundation, Vincent

Astrom, Torgny, mgr: Goodall Rubber Co.

Astrove, Katherine A., trust: Adler Foundation

Atcheson, Elizabeth, trust: Crocker Trust, Mary A.

Atchison, Leon H., vp: MichCon Foundation

Athanassiades, Ted, pres, coo: Metropolitan Life Insurance Co.

Atherton, Alexander Simpson, pres, dir: Atherton Family Foundation

Atherton, Alfred Leroy, Jr., mem adv bd: Hariri Foundation

Atherton, Peter, treas: Connecticut Natural Gas Corp.

Atherton, Stevenson, dir: Holt Foundation, William Knox

Atieh, Michael Gerard, treas: Merck Co. Foundation

Atkins, George W. P., Jr., treas, dir: Wachovia Foundation of Geaorgia

Atkins, Rosie, secy: Cobb Educational Fund, Ty

Atkinson, Duane E., pres, dir: Atkinson Foundation

Atkinson, Harold S., secy: Camp Foundation; trust: Camp Younts Foundation

Atkinson, James W., vp, treas: Stein Roe & Farnham Foundation

Atkinson, Lavina M., dir: Atkinson Foundation

Atkinson, Rachel C., vp, dir: Atkinson Foundation, Myrtle L.

Atkinson, Ray N., vp, dir: Atkinson Foundation

Atkinson, W. K., secy, treas: Trinity Foundation

Atkiss, A. W., vp: Exxon Education Foundation

Atkisson, Curtis T., Jr., pres, coo: SPX Corp.

Atlas, Martin, pres, ceo, treas: Cafritz Foundation, Morris and Gwendolyn

Atnip, Michael Grant, dir: American General Finance Foundation

Atran, Max, pres, dir: Atran Foundation

Atterbury, Robert R., III, vp, secy, gen couns: Caterpillar; secy: Caterpillar Foundation

Attfield, Gillian, mem adv comm: Ford Foundation, Edward E.

Attias, Daniel R., asst secy, dir: Mitchell Family Foundation, Edward D. and Anna

Attwell, J. Evans, secy, dir: Welch Foundation, Robert A.

Attwood, Steven C., pres: Fisons Corp.

Attwood, William E., pres: Stanley Charitable Foundation, A. W.

Atwater, Charles B., dir: Bunbury Company

Atwater, Edward, dir: Gleason Memorial Fund

Atwater, Horace Brewster, Jr., chmn, ceo, dir: General Mills; chmn, trust: General Mills Foundation; trust: Merck Co. Foundation

Atwater, Verne Stafford, dir: Lee Foundation, James T.

Atwood, Bruce T., trust: Atwood Foundation

Atwood, Diane P., trust: Atwood Foundation

Atwood, Henry K., trust: Nash Foundation

Atwood, Robert, dir: First Union Foundation

Atwood, Robert B., dir, pres: Atwood Foundation

Atwood, Sara Elaine, vp, secy: Atwood Foundation

Atwood, Seth G., trust: Atwood Foundation

Atwood, Seth L., trust: Atwood Foundation

Aubrecht, Richard A., chmn, dir: Moog, Inc.

Aubry, Julia A. Moon, dir: Surdna Foundation

Auchincloss, Lily van Ameringen, vp: van Ameringen Foundation

Auchincloss, Louis S., dir, mem exec comm: Macy, Jr. Foundation, Josiah

Audet, Paul L., cfo: PNC Bank

Audibert, Jean-Marc, vchmn: Ketchum & Co.

Auellina, Thomas, secy: Kane Paper Scholarship Fund

Auen, Joan, secy, dir: Berger Foundation, H.N. and Frances C.

Auen, Ronald M., pres, dir: Berger Foundation, H.N. and Frances C.

Auer, Albert J., dir: Hoag Family Foundation, George

Auerbach, Mollie, vp, dir: Berkowitz Family Foundation, Louis

Augusciak, Maureen O., contact person: Sprague Educational and Charitable Foundation, Seth

August, B. A., secy, dir: Morris Foundation, William T.

Auguste, M., treas: ITT Rayonier Foundation

Augustine, Norman Ralph, chmn, ceo, dir: Martin Marietta Corp.

Aull, William E., vp, trust: Castle Foundation, Samuel N. and Mary

Aultman, Everett T., exec dir: German Protestant Orphan Asylum Association

Aumack, Arthur C., dir: Robinson Mountain Fund, E. O.

Aumann, Walter D., cfo: Ladish Co.; trust: Ladish Co. Foundation

Aument, W. Alan, pres, treas, dir: Uslico Foundation

Aurand, Calvin W., Jr., chmn, pres, ceo, dir: Banta Corp.

Aurand, Eloise C., dir (publ rels): Hamilton Bank; alternative contact person: Hamilton Bank Foundation

Austen, W. Gerald, vchmn, trust: Knight Foundation, John S. and James L.

Austermiller, Judy, exec dir, trust: Boehm Foundation

Austin, C. Merrill, secy, trust: Folsom Foundation, Maud Glover

Austin, Donald G., vp, trust: Austin Memorial Foundation

Austin, Donald G., Jr., pres, trust: Austin Memorial Foundation

Austin, Faith T., trust: Coffey Foundation

Austin, Glenn T., Jr., sr vp (southeastern regional office): Federal National Mortgage Assn. Foundation

Austin, James W., trust: Austin Memorial Foundation

Austin, Maurice, trust: Kaplan Fund, J. M.

Austin, Patrick J., asst secy: Daily News Foundation

Baker, Donald E., trust: Bay Branch Foundation; treas, trust: Sunburst Foundation

Baker, Donald W., trust: Baker Foundation, Elinor Patterson

Baker, Edward L., co-fdr, chmn, ceo, dir: Florida Rock Industries; vp: Florida Rock Industries Foundation

Baker, George F., III, trust: Baker Trust, George F.

Baker, Irma, trust, chmn: Baker Foundation, George T.

Baker, James E., treas: Gannett Foundation, Guy P.

Baker, James Gilbert, trust: Perkin Fund

Baker, James Kendrick, chmn, ceo, dir: Arvin Industries; chmn, dir: Arvin Foundation

Baker, John A., trust: Equifax Foundation

Baker, Julia Clayton, trust: Baker Trust, Clayton

Baker, Kane K., trust: Baker Trust, George F.

Baker, Katherine M., trust: Valencia Charitable Trust

Baker, Kent G., vp, cfo: United Fire & Casualty Co.

Baker, Larry, secy, treas, trust: National Machinery Foundation

Baker, Larry A., vp, adm, dir: Wausau Paper Mills Foundation

Baker, Laurel T., secy: Whitehall Foundation

Baker, Laurin M., dir: OMC Foundation

Baker, Lee, vp, secy, dir: Baker & Baker Foundation

Baker, Leslie Mayo, Jr., pres: Wachovia Bank & Trust Co., N.A.

Baker, Louis A., secy: Forest Fund

Baker, Norman D., Jr., trust: Kimball Foundation, Horace A. Kimball and S. Ella

Baker, Pam, dir (Lincoln Off): Woods Charitable Fund

Baker, Paula W., dir (corp support plans & controls): IBM Corp.

Baker, Rebecca D., vp, secy, treas: Baker Foundation, Solomon R. and Rebecca D.

Baker, Reginald, asst treas, asst secy, trust: Gerber Cos. Foundation

Baker, Richard C., secy: Fuller Co. Foundation, H.B.

Baker, Richard M., secy: Imperial Bank Foundation

Baker, Richard W., trust: Speer Foundation, Roy M.

Baker, Robbie L., trust: Kantzler Foundation

Baker, Robert E., exec adm, secy-treas: Moody Foundation

Baker, Robert W., exec vp oper: AMR Corp.

Baker, Roger W. W., secy comm contributions: American Brands

Baker, Roland C., chmn: Old American Insurance Co.

Baker, Russell S., Jr., vp: Nathan Foundation

Baker, Solomon R., pres: Baker Foundation, Solomon R. and Rebecca D.

Baker, Thompson S., pres: Florida Rock Industries Foundation

Baker, W. K., trust: Walter Foundation

Baker, William C., trust: Baker Trust, Clayton; trust: Clayton Fund

Baker, William Oliver, trust: Fund for New Jersey; dir: Guggenheim Foundation, Harry Frank

Bakke, Dennis W., pres: Applied Energy Services

Bakken, Douglas Adair, exec dir: Ball Brothers Foundation

Bakken, Earl Elmer, fdr, dir: Medtronic

Bakkensen, Ralph V. G., asst secy: M/A-COM Charitable Foundation

Balasses, Mike, regional chmn: Team Bank Houston

Balderston, Frederick E., dir: Osher Foundation, Bernard

Baldwin, Barbara, trust, vp, secy: Baldwin Foundation, David M. and Barbara

Baldwin, Bennet M., trust: Baldwin Memorial Foundation, Fred

Baldwin, David M., trust, pres: Baldwin Foundation, David M. and Barbara

Baldwin, Ernest R., vp, dir, secy: Bireley Foundation

Baldwin, Everett N., pres, ceo: Welch Foods

Baldwin, H. Furlong, chmn, ceo, dir: Mercantile Bankshares Corp.

Baldwin, James J., trust: Campbell Soup Foundation

Baldwin, John C., dir: Castle Foundation, Harold K. L.

Baldwin, Joyce, dir: Aigner Foundation, G.J.

Baldwin, Karren, secy: R. P. Foundation

Baldwin, Mark E., vp, cfo: Keystone International

Baldwin, Melvin Dana, II, trust: Baldwin Foundation

Baldwin, Mrs. Ralph B., trust: Baldwin Foundation

Baldwin, Peter, dir: Bancorp Hawaii Charitable Foundation

Baldwin, Ralph B., dir, vp: Baldwin Foundation

Baldwin, Robert H., dir: Weber Charities Corp., Frederick E.

Baldwin, Robert Hayes Burns, chmn, trust: Dodge Foundation, Geraldine R.

Baldwin, Ronald C., pres, coo: Banc One Wisconsin Corp.; vp, dir: Banc One Wisconsin Foundation

Baldwin, William P., trust: Yawkey Foundation II

Baldwin, William R., pres: River Blindness Foundation

Balemian, Robert, pres, ceo: Instrument Systems Corp.

Bales, Dan, mem: Boatmen's First National Bank of Oklahoma Foundation

Bales, Dane G., secy-treas, trust: Hansen Foundation, Dane G.

Balgooyen, Warren, dir: Norcross Wildlife Foundation

Balint, Michael J., exec dir: Piper Foundation, Minnie Stevens

Balk, Melvin W., dir: Charles River Foundation

Balkas, Denise M., dir: Hoyt Foundation, Stewart W. and Willma C.

Ball, Anne, dir: Hopper Foundation, May Templeton

Ball, Anne F., trust: Firestone, Jr. Foundation, Harvey

Ball, Braden, pres, dir: duPont Foundation, Alfred I.

Ball, Edmund Ferdinand, chmn, dir: Ball Brothers Foundation

Ball, Frank E., vp, dir: Ball Brothers Foundation

Ball, George L., couns, product devel: Prudential-Bache Securities

Ball, John K., ceo, pres: Shoemaker Co., R.M.

Ball, Kenneth L., pres, dir: Orchard Corp. of America.

Ballaine, Horace, trust: Zink Foundation, John Steele

Ballantine, Dewey, co-trust: Adams Foundation, Arthur F. and Alice E.

Ballantine, Elizabeth, trust: Cowles Foundation, Gardner and Florence Call

Ballantine, Morley Cowles, trust, don granddaughter: Cowles Foundation, Gardner and Florence Call

Ballantine, Richard O., secy, dir: Butler Manufacturing Co. Foundation

Ballantyne, Robert B., pres: Civitas Fund

Ballard, A. L., secy, treas: Hale Foundation, Crescent Porter

Ballard, Ernesta D., dir: Penn Foundation, William

Ballard, Larry C., chmn, pres, ceo: Sentry Insurance Co.

Ballard, William C., Jr., exec vp fin: Humana Foundation

Ballentine, Richard O., secy, trust: Butler Foundation, Alice

Ballmer, Steven Anthony, off pres, exec vp sales & systems: Microsoft Corp.

Ballou, F. Remington, pres, dir: Ballou & Co., B.A.

Balog, James, dir: Donner Foundation, William H.

Balousek, John B., pres, coo, dir: Foote, Cone & Belding Communications

Balter, William H., Peters Foundation, Charles F.

Baltimore, David, dir: Life Sciences Research Foundation

Balue, Mrs. Ronald M., public relations chmn: Ebell of Los Angeles Rest Cottage Association; public relations chmn: Ebell of Los Angeles Scholarship Endowment Fund

Balzer, Giorgio, chmn: Business Men's Assurance Co. of America

Bam, Foster, pres, dir: Foster-Davis Foundation

Bamber, Anthony P., vp, cfo: Decision Data Computer Corp.

Bamberger, Clarence, Jr., chmn: Bamberger and John Ernest Bamberger Memorial Foundation, Ruth Eleanor

Bamford, Thomas H., vp: Corestates Foundation; sr vp, dir corp commun: Hamilton Bank; chmn: Hamilton Bank Foundation

Bamonte, John D., vp: Switzer Foundation

Bampton, Rose, trust: Sullivan Musical Foundation, William Matheus

Bana, K. P., vp, dir: Joslyn Foundation

Bancker, Dorothy B., trust, don: Williams, Jr. Family Foundation, A. L.

Bancroft, Bettina, mem adv comm: Dow Jones Foundation

Bancroft, James Ramsey, vp: Witter Foundation, Dean

Bancroft, Joseph C., chmn, ceo: Croft Metals; trust: Croft Metal Products Educational Trust Fund

Bancroft, Thomas M., Jr., chmn: New York Racing Association

Bandarrae, Kathryn M., asst secy: Bechtel Foundation

Bandos, Kathleen, trust: Hunt Manufacturing Co. Foundation

Bandy, Miriam, trust: Flickinger Memorial Trust

Baney, Robert, pres: New England Aircraft Products Co.

Bank, Adrienne, mem (scholarship comm): Circuit City Foundation

Bank, Helen Shapiro, pres: Bank Foundation, Helen and Merrill

Bank, Melvin E., secy: American Foundation Corporation; trust: Oglebay Norton Foundation

Bank, Merrill Lee, vp, treas: Bank Foundation, Helen and Merrill

Bank, Michael D., treas: Arkwright Foundation

Banks, Henry H., trust: Wolfson Foundation, Louis E.

Banks, Paula A., pres, exec dir: Sears-Roebuck Foundation

Banks, Russell, pres, ceo: Grow Group

Banks, William L., Jr., mem allocations comm: Jeffress Memorial Trust, Thomas F. and Kate Miller

Bannan, Charles F., pres: Pacific Western Foundation

Bannan, Thomas J., pres: Bannan Foundation, Arline and Thomas J.

Banner, Stephen Edward, treas, trust: Bronfman Foundation, Samuel

Bannister, Daniel R., ceo, pres, dir: DynCorp

Bannister, Melvin A., dir: Valmont Foundation

Bannon, Mel B., trust: Beynon Foundation, Kathryne

Bannon, Robert D., trust: Beynon Foundation, Kathryne

Bantle, Louis Francis, chmn, ceo, pres, dir: UST

Banzhaf, Julie, dir, programs: Hitachi

Barach, Philip G., chmn, dir: US Shoe Corp.

Barad, Jill, pres: Mattel; dir: Mattel Foundation

Baranoff, W., gen couns: CIT Group Foundation

Barash, David, adv bd: Ben & Jerry's Foundation

Barassi, Louis W., trust: Van Schaick Scholarship Fund, Nellie

Baratta, Joan M., sr vp (trust): Harris Trust & Savings Bank

Barbato, Virginia N., treas: Nord Family Foundation

Barber, Joseph H., secy, treas, dir: Smith Foundation

Barber, Kathleen L., trust: Gund Foundation, George

Barber, Martin S., dir: MCJ Foundation

Barber, W. Craig, cfo, vp: Shoney's Inc.

Barberi, Kathleen, adm corp contributions: Melville Corp.

Barbey, Anne Murray, pres, dir: Murray Foundation

Barbour, Benny J., pres, coo: SECO

Barbour, Fleming A., trust: United States Sugar Corporate Charitable Trust

Barbre, Erwin S., pres, dir: Bancroft-Whitney Co.

Barclay, Kitty, trust, vp: Woman's Seamen's Friend Society of Connecticut

Barclay, Lee, trust: Patterson-Barclay Memorial Foundation

Barcroft, John H., vp: Spencer Foundation

Bardeen, Maxwell D., Vicksburg Foundation

Barder, Sarah D., dir: Bradley Foundation, Lynde and Harry; pres: SDB Foundation

Bardes, Judith L., exec dir, trust: Douty Foundation; adm: Foerderer Foundation, Percival E. and Ethel Brown

Bardige, Betty S., trust: Mailman Family Foundation, A. L.

Bardin, Christian, pres (intl div): Neutrogena Corp.

Bardoff, Ralph, vp, dir: Ishiyama Foundation

Bardusch, William E., Jr., trust, secy, treas: Jones Fund, Blanche and George; pres, trust: Sullivan Foundation, Algernon Sydney

Bardwell, Stanley, M.D., trust: Potts Memorial Foundation

Barell, Martin, trust: Bruner Foundation

Barents, Brian E., pres, ceo, dir: Learjet Inc.

Bares, William G., pres, coo, dir: Lubrizol Corp.; trust: Oglebay Norton Foundation

Barfield, W. L., secy, trust: Gordon Foundation, Meyer and Ida

Barger, A. Clifford, pres: Harvard Apparatus Foundation

Barger, J. P., co-fdr, chmn: Dynatech Corp.

Barham, Charles D., Jr., exec vp (fin & admin): Carolina Power & Light Co.; trust: CP&L Foundation

Bark, Dennis L., chmn, trust: Earhart Foundation

Bark, France de Sugny, pres, dir: de Dampierre Memorial Foundation, Marie C.

Barkeley, Norman A., chmn, pres, ceo, dir: Ducommun Inc.

Barker, Allan M., pres: Barker Foundation

Barker, Donald J., trust: Campbell and Adah E. Hall Charity Fund, Bushrod H.

Barker, Dorothy A., trust: Barker Foundation

Barker, Elizabeth S., vp, dir: Barker Foundation, J. M. R.

Barker, James R., vp, dir: Barker Foundation, J. M. R.

Barker, John, trust: Schultz Foundation

Barker, Judith, pres: Borden Foundation; pres: Unocal Foundation

Barker, Judy, pres: Borden Foundation

Barker, Margaret W., dir: Barker Foundation, J. M. R.

Barker, Norman, Jr., dir, mem audit comm, mem dirs grant comm: Keck Foundation, W. M.

Barker, P. T., mgr corporate contributions: Union Carbide Corp.

Barker, Richard, cfo: Sun Microsystems Foundation

Barker, Richard H., trust: Baker Foundation, Solomon R. and Rebecca D.

Barker, Robert C., vp: Heublein Foundation

Barker, Robert R., pres, dir: Barker Foundation, J. M. R.

Barker, William Benjamin, dir: Barker Foundation, J. M. R.

Barker, William P., trust: McFeely-Rogers Foundation

Barker, Willie G., Jr., pres, coo, dir: Dibrell Brothers, Inc.

Barkley, Barry R., cfo: Bank One, Texas-Houston Office

Barkley, Dennis, trust, treas: Leu Foundation

Barkow, Richard D., secy, dir: Siebert Lutheran Foundation

Barksdale, Chandlee M., dir: Tennant Co. Foundation

Barksdale, Robert M., trust: Besser Foundation

Barletta, Robert, treas: Prospect Hill Foundation

Barlow, Gloria G., vp: Barlow Family Foundation, Milton A. and Gloria G.

Barlow, Gregory P., exec dir: Medina Foundation

Barlow, James A., Jr., mem: Tonkin Foundation, Tom and Helen

Barlow, Kent M., vp, dir: Madison Gas & Electric Foundation

Barlow, Milton A., dir, pres: Barlow Family Foundation, Milton A. and Gloria G.

Barlow, Milton Allan, Jr., treas: Barlow Family Foundation, Milton A. and Gloria G.

Barlow, Robert C., vp: Crestlea Foundation; asst secy: Longwood Foundation; asst secy: Welfare Foundation

Barmore, Beryl, trust: Wilmington Trust Co. Foundation

Barna, Roger, dir: Mitsubishi Electric America Foundation

Barnard, Boyd T., trust: Presser Foundation

Barnard, Marla, mgr (community rels): Panhandle Eastern Corp.

Barnard, William J., chmn, trust: Monticello College Foundation

Barndardt, William M. M., trust: Anderson Foundation, Robert C. and Sadie G.

Barnebey, Kenneth Alan, trust: Terry Foundation, C. Herman

Barnedette, Curtis H., chmn, ceo, dir: Bethlehem Steel Corp.

Barnes, Andrew E., dir, pres: Poynter Fund

Barnes, B. Jack, pres, coo: Crane Co.

Barnes, Barbara H., scholarship coordinator: Flinn Foundation

Barnes, Carlyle Fuller, vp, dir: Barnes Group Foundation

Barnes, Charles, mem loan comm: Lindsay Student Aid Fund, Franklin

Barnes, Corbin, dir: Cook, Sr. Charitable Foundation, Kelly Gene

Barnes, Edwin L., dir, secy, treas: Hopewell Foundation

Barnes, Frances M., III, trust: Gaylord Foundation, Clifford Willard

Barnes, Frank S., Jr., dir, pres: Hopewell Foundation; pres: Rock Hill Telephone Co.

Barnes, Fuller F., II, treas, trust: Barnes Foundation

Barnes, Galen, pres, coo: Employers Insurance of Wausau, A Mutual Co.

Barnes, Harry G., Jr., trust: German Marshall Fund of the United States

Barnes, J.B., trust: Hubbard Farms Charitable Foundation

Barnes, Jack, trust: Americana Foundation

Barnes, James E., chmn, ceo, dir: Mapco Inc.

Barnes, John R., chmn, pres, ceo: Kaneb Services, Inc.

Barnes, John T., treas: Guggenheim Foundation, Daniel and Florence

Barnes, Ladson A., Jr., dir: Hopewell Foundation

Barnes, Robert E., ceo, pres: Bayview Federal Bank

Barnes, Ronald R., exec dir, trust: Norris Foundation, Kenneth T. and Eileen L.

Barnes, W. Michael, vp, cfo: Rockwell International Corp.; mem (trust comm): Rockwell International Corp. Trust

Barnes, Wallace, chmn, dir: Barnes Group; chmn, dir: Barnes Group Foundation

Barness, W.E., trust: McNeely Foundation

Barnett, Carol Jenkins, dir: Jenkins Foundation, George W.

Barnett, Charles D., secy, dir: Mills Foundation, Ralph E.

Barnett, Eugene, dir: Pittway Corp. Charitable Foundation

Barnett, Henry L., mem nominating comm, mem counc: Foundation for Child Development

Barnett, Isabel, vp, cfo, dir: Barnett Charitable Foundation, Lawrence and Isabel

Barnett, James Joseph, asst secy, dir: Barnett Charitable Foundation, Lawrence and Isabel

Barnett, Lawrence R., pres, don, dir: Barnett Charitable Foundation, Lawrence and Isabel

Barnett, Richard M., chmn, pres: Straus Foundation, Aaron and Lillie

Barnett, Robert Glenn, secy: Deposit Guaranty Foundation

Barnett, Robert L., pres: Ameritech Corp.

Barney, Austin D., II, dir: Ensign-Bickford Foundation

Barney, William H., mem allocations comm: Jeffress Memorial Trust, Thomas F. and Kate Miller

Barnhard, Sherwood A., chmn: Lasky Co.; pres: Lasky Co. Foundation

Barnhardt, C. C., Jr., secy: Fieldcrest Foundation

Barnhart, Lorraine, asst secy, exec dir: Huber Foundation

Barnhart, Victor J., ceo, pres: Brand Cos.

Barnwell, G.P., trust: Wehadkee Foundation

Baron, George C., McCrea Foundation

Baron, Jules M., dir: Goldman Foundation, Herman

Baron, Peter L., dir: Searle Charitable Trust

Baron, Raymond S., dir: Goldman Foundation, Herman

Baron, Richard K., exec dir, asst secy, asst treas: Goldman Foundation, Herman

Barone, Robert, dir: Lincolnshire

Barone, Robert J., vp: Chatam Inc.

Barone, Robert P., pres, coo, dir: Diebold, Inc.

Barr, Donald, trust: Lincoln Health Care Foundation

Barr, E. E., ceo, pres: Sun Chemical Corp.

Barr, George V., pres: Halsell Foundation, O. L.

Barr, Harry C., trust: Peabody Foundation

Barr, J. D., pres, coo: Valvoline Inc.

Barr, Kathryn, trust mortgaging mgr & pr specialist: Bank of Oklahoma, N.A.

Barr, Maxine, secy: Lincoln Health Care Foundation

Barr, Robert T., trust: Bingham Trust, The

Barrett, Charles J., trust: Colonial Stores Foundation

Barrett, Craig, coo, exec vp: Intel Corp.

Barrett, Jane Norton, vp, dir: Norton Foundation Inc.

Barrett, Joan R., program coordinator: Moore Foundation

Barrett, John F., trust: Western-Southern Life Foundation

Barrett, Richard W., chmn, trust: Wodecroft Foundation

Barrett, Ronald E., vp, dir: Stanley Consultants Charitable Foundation

Barrett, William L. D., trust: Schepp Foundation, Leopold

Barrette, Raymond, dir: Fireman's Fund Foundation

Barron, Blue, secy: Mechanic Foundation, Morris A.

Barron, Gary A., exec vp, coo: Southwest Airlines Co.

Barroner, Robert F., trust: Carbon Fuel Foundation

Barroso, Carmen, dir (population program): MacArthur Foundation, John D. and Catherine T.

Barrow, Craig, III, trust: Johnson, Lane, Space, Smith Foundation, Inc.

Barrows, Jordan E., treas: New Milford Savings Bank Foundation

Barrows, Sidney, trust: Alliss Educational Foundation, Charles and Ellora; vp, secy: Boulevard Foundation; dir: Pittway Corp. Charitable Foundation

Barry, Daniel P., cfo: Amsco International

Barry, David W., dir: Burroughs Wellcome Fund

Barry, Donald H., treas, contr: Chesebrough-Pond's; treas: Chesebrough Foundation

Barry, Elizabeth J., trust: Jewell Memorial Foundation, Daniel Ashley and Irene Houston

Barry, Elizabeth T., dir: Gazette Foundation

Barry, J. Raymond, trust: Mellen Foundation

Barry, Michael M., contributions manager: McIntyre Foundation, C. S. and Marion F.

Barry, Richard Francis, III, vchmn: Landmark Charitable Foundation

Barry, Robert, Jr., chmn: KPMG Peat Marwick Foundation

Barry, Thomas C., trust: Grant Foundation, William T.

Barry, William S., trust: Shinnick Educational Fund, William M.

Barsness, W. E. Bye, dir: Northwest Area Foundation

Barstow, Frederick E., pres, trust: Barstow Foundation

Barstow, Ormond E., trust: Barstow Foundation

Bartell, George, Jr., chmn, ceo, dir: Bartell Drug Co.

Bartell, George D., pres: Bartell Drug Co.

Bartell, Laurence A., trust: Laub Foundation

Bartelt, Sarah Caswell, dir: Beveridge Foundation, Frank Stanley

Bartenstein, Frederick, III, secy: Dayton Foundation Depository

Barth, C.M., treas: Bowers Foundation

Barth, Frederic C., dir: Dietrich Foundation, William B.

Barth, Richard, chmn, pres, ceo: CIBA-GEIGY Corp.

Bartha, Louis A., secy, treas: Prairie Foundation

Barthe, Michael, pres, ceo, dir: Koh-I-Noor Rapidograph Inc.

Bartholomay, William C., vchmn: Turner Broadcasting System

Bartl, James F., secy, dir: Phillips Family Foundation, L. E.

Bartleson, Leslie Sheridan, dir: Stauffer Foundation, John and Beverly

Bartlett, James F., trust: Baumberger Endowment

Bartlett, Pamela, dir: Ensign-Bickford Foundation

Bartlett, Paul D., chmn: Bartlett & Co.; trust: Bartlett & Co. Grain Charitable Foundation

Bartlett, Richard, pres, coo: Mary Kay Cosmetics

Bartlett, Richard M., pres: Lebanon Mutual Insurance Co.; dir: Lebanon Mutual Foundation

Bartlett, Thomas A., trust: United States-Japan Foundation

Bartlett, Walter E., chmn, ceo, pres: Multimedia, Inc.

Bartley, Anne, dir: New World Foundation; trust, vp: Rockefeller Family Fund

Bartley, Charles R., Sr., dir: Exchange Bank Foundation

Bartol, Mary Farr, trust: Bartol Foundation, Stockton Rush

Bartolo, A.M., coo, exec vp, dir: Imperial Holly Corp.

Barton, Dorothy R., trust: Eastern Star Hall and Home Foundation

Barton, Gerald G., chmn, pres, ceo: Landmark Land Co., Inc.

Barton, Gerard, vp: WestLB New York Branch

Barton, James F., chmn: Raymond Foundation

Barton, James T., pres: Prudential-Bache Securities

Barton, Lucille, dir: Schmidt Charitable Foundation, William E.

Barton, R. K., chmn: Rinker Materials Corp.

Barton, R. Keith, chmn, dir: American Aggregates Corp.

Barton, Robert M., dir: Berger Foundation, H.N. and Frances C.

Barton, Stephen, vp (corp commun): North American Reinsurance Corp.; asst treas: Travelers Cos. Foundation

Barton, Willis H., Jr., vp: New Milford Savings Bank Foundation

Bartos, Adam, dir: Pinewood Foundation

Bartos, Armand P., vp, dir: Pinewood Foundation

Bartos, Celeste G., don, pres, dir: Pinewood Foundation

Bartow, Edwin B., vchmn: Truman Foundation, Mildred Faulkner

Bartow, Jerome, mem contributions comm: ITT Hartford Insurance Group

Bartram, John C., trust: True Trust, Henry A.

Bartram, John Kline, trust: True Trust, Henry A.

Bartsch, Glenn Bartsch, trust: Gray Charitable Trust, Mary S.

Bartwink, Theodore S., secy, treas, dir: Harkness Ballet Foundation

Bartz, Carol, chmn, ceo, pres, dir: Autodesk, Inc.

Barun, Ken, exec vp, managing dir: McDonald's Corp.

Basey, James L., vchmn, chief admin off: Colorado National Bankshares

Bashara, George N., chmn contributions comm: Federal-Mogul Corp. Charitable Trust Fund

Bashinsky, Sloan Y., Sr., chmn, pres: Bashinsky Foundation

Baskin, Philip, chmn, trust: Falk Medical Fund, Maurice

Basler, Donald N., pres, dir: United Conveyor Corp.; trust: United Conveyor Foundation

Bass, Doris L., trust: Bass Foundation, Harry

Bass, Edward Perry, vp: Bass Foundation

Bass, Harry Wesley, Jr., don, trust: Bass Foundation, Harry

Bass, J. T., vp, treas, trust: Crowell Trust, Henry P. and Susan C.

Bass, Lee M., Jr., secy, treas: Bass Corporation, Perry and Nancy Lee

Bass, Lee Marshall, vp: Bass Foundation; vp, dir: Richardson Foundation, Sid W.

Bass, Morton M., trust: Bass and Edythe and Sol G. Atlas Fund, Sandra Atlas

Bass, Nancy Lee, vp, bd vchmn: Bass Corporation, Perry and Nancy Lee; vp, dir: Bass Foundation; vp, dir: Richardson Foundation, Sid W.

Bass, Perry R., don, pres, bd chmn: Bass Corporation, Perry and Nancy Lee; pres, dir, don: Bass Foundation; pres, dir: Richardson Foundation, Sid W.; vp, trust: Tandy Foundation, Anne Burnett and Charles

Bass, Robert P., Jr., dir: Bird Cos. Charitable Foundation

Bass, Sandra Atlas, pres, trust: Bass and Edythe and Sol G. Atlas Fund, Sandra Atlas

Bass, Sid Richardson, vp, dir: Richardson Foundation, Sid W.

Bassani, Giuseppe, pres: NCR Foundation

Bassermann, Michael, pres: Mercedes-Benz of North America, Inc.

Bassett, Balfour, trust: Urann Foundation

Bassett, Edward C., dir: Skidmore, Owings & Merrill Foundation

Bassuk, Richard, pres, coo: Starrett Housing Corp.

Bastian, Ann, sr program off: New World Foundation

Bastian, Frank W., secy, dir: Schoenleber Foundation

Bastian, R. Richard, III, chmn, ceo: First National Bank & Trust Co. of Rockford; chmn, dir: First National Bank & Trust Co. of Rockford Charitable Trust

Batchelor, Anne O., secy: Batchelor Foundation

Batchelor, George E., pres: Batchelor Foundation

Bate, David S., vp, trust: International Foundation; secy, treas, trust: Schumann Foundation, Florence and John

Bateman, Robert J., ceo: Rosemount, Inc.

Bateman, Walter R., II, pres, coo: Harleysville Mutual Insurance Co.

Bates, George E., trust: BHP Petroleum Americas (HI) Foundation

Bates, Janice W., dir commun aff: Questar Corp.

Bates, Jeanne M., vp, secy: Hallmark Cards

Bates, Malcom, chmn: Picker International

Bates, William F., pres, secy, treas: Goerlich Family Foundation

Bath, John S., trust: Eyman Trust, Jesse

Bato, Andrew G., dir, vp: Zimmerman Foundation, Mary and George Herbert

Bato, Doris S., dir, secy: Zimmerman Foundation, Mary and George Herbert

Batson, R. Neal, trust: Woolley Foundation, Vasser

Batt, Cindy, mem: Boatmen's First National Bank of Oklahoma Foundation

Batt, James J., vp: Goldome Foundation

Batt, John, exec vp, cfo: Bumble Bee Seafoods Inc.

Battaglia, Thomas, dir: American Standard Foundation

Batte, G. A., Jr., dir, mem: Cannon Foundation

Batten, Frank, pres, treas, secy, dir, don: Batten Foundation

Batten, Frank, Sr., chmn: Landmark Communications; chmn, dir: Landmark Charitable Foundation

Batten, James K., trust: Knight Foundation, John S. and James L.; chmn, ceo, dir: Knight-Ridder, Inc.

Battey, Charles W., chmn, ceo, dir: KN Energy, Inc.

Battinelli, Salvatore, fin mgr: Kendall Foundation, Henry P.

Battjes, Kenneth J., vp, dir: Guardian Industries Educational Foundation

Battram, Richard L., vchmn, dir: May Department Stores Co.

Batts, Eloise, treas: Batts Foundation

Batts, Warren, pres: Batts Foundation

Batts, Warren L., chmn, ceo, dir: Premark International

Battye, Kenneth, trust: Gordon Charitable Trust, Peggy and Yale

Battye, Kenneth S., pres, dir: Legg & Co. Foundation

Bau-Madsen, Emily, dir: Glencairn Foundation

Bauchiero, Frank E., trust: Warner Electric Foundation

Bauder, Lillian, trust: Skillman Foundation

Bauer, Chris M., pres: Firstar Milwaukee Foundation

Bauer, Douglas F., Bowne Foundation, Robert

Bauer, Gordon P., treas: Osborn Manufacturing Co. Educational & Charitable Fund

Bauer, Michael, custodian: Handleman Charitable Foundation

Bauernfeind, George G., vp (taxes): Humana Foundation

Bauervic-Wright, Rose, trust: Bauervic Foundation, Peggy; trust: Bauervic-Paisley Foundation

Baugh, John F., sr chmn: Sysco Corp.

Baughin, William, secy: Seasongood Good Government Foundation, Murray and Agnes

Baughman, James F., trust: GE Foundations

Baughman, Leroy, treas, dir: Kuyper Foundation, Peter H. and E. Lucille Gaass

Bauhs, David J., ceo: Schindler Elevator Corp.

Bauknight, Clarence B., trust: Builderway Foundation

Baum, Ann F., pres, treas: Baum Family Fund, Alvin H.

Baum, Erica B., PhD, asst to pres: Kaiser Family Foundation, Henry J.

Bauman, Charles J., secy: Castle & Cooke International Charitable Foundation

Bauman, James, vp, treas: Ucross Foundation

Bauman, James R., vp-bus devel: Apache Corp.

Bauman, Monica, secy: Walker Foundation, L. C. and Margaret

Bauman, Paul, trust: Winship Memorial Scholarship Foundation

Bauman, Robert, ceo: SmithKline Beecham

Baumer, Moe, dir, vp, secy: Rohlik Foundation, Sigmund and Sophie

Baumgardner, Anita A., secy, trust: Copley Foundation, James S.

Baumgardner, Roberta A., trust: Russell Educational Foundation, Benjamin and Roberta

Baumgarner, John C., Jr., dir: Williams Cos. Foundation

Baumgarten, Herbert Joseph, sr vp, gen coun, secy: National Starch & Chemical Corp.; secy, dir: National Starch & Chemical Foundation

Baumgartner, Howard E., trust: Schowalter Foundation

Baur, Philip J., Jr., trust, chmn: Tasty Baking Corporation

Baur, Walter, dir, treas: Gilman, Jr. Foundation, Sondra and Charles

Baute, Joseph, chmn, ceo: Markem Corp.

Bautz, Sheila M., asst treas: Taconic Foundation

Bavendick, Frank J., dir: Leach Foundation, Tom & Frances

Bavicchi, Ferris G., trust: Foundation for Seacoast Health

Baxter, Arthur C., treas: Gilbert, Jr. Charitable Trust, Price

Baxter, Barbara J., vp, trust: Andrews Foundation

Baxter, H. Vaughan, III, Polk Foundation

Baxter, James G., vp, treas, dir: Farber Foundation

Baxter, Joe E., secy, treas, dir: Meyer Family Foundation, Paul J.

Baxter, Karen, exec dir: Redman Foundation

Baxter, Laura S., trust: Andrews Foundation

Bay, Frederick, chmn, dir: Bay Foundation; pres, exec dir: Paul and C. Michael Paul Foundation, Josephine Bay

Bay-Hansen, Christopher, dir: Bay Foundation

Bayard, Jane, vp, dir: Uris Brothers Foundation

Bayless, Charles E., chmn, pres, ceo, dir: Tucson Electric Power Co.

Bayless, Mary C., dir: Connell Foundation, Michael J.

Bayley, Christopher T., vp: Burlington Resources Foundation

Bayliss, Harry G., treas, trust: Alden Trust, George I.

Bayne, J. E., treas: Exxon Education Foundation

Baynes, Lacy G., trust: ABC Foundation

Bazany, LeRoy, trust: Bemis Company Foundation

Beach, C. E., dir: Broyhill Family Foundation

Beach, E. D., secy, treas, dir: Broyhill Family Foundation

Beach, Richard F., vp: NCR Foundation; pres, trust: Tait Foundation, Frank M.

Beach, Ross, trust: Hansen Foundation, Dane G.

Beachamp, Pat, pub aff off: PNC Bank

Beachum, John, dir promotion & pubity: Bergner Co., P.A.

Beadle, Ann, trust: UNUM Charitable Foundation

Beadle, Bob, mem contributions comm: Diamond Shamrock

Beaird, Carolyn, vp: Beaird Foundation, Charles T.

Beaird, Charles T., pres: Beaird Foundation, Charles T.; pres, publ, treas: Shreveport Publishing Corp.

Beaird, John B., trust: Beaird Foundation, Charles T.

Beal, Barry A., trust: Beal Foundation

Beal, Carlton, don, chmn, trust: Beal Foundation

Beal, Carlton, Jr., trust: Beal Foundation

Beal, David, trust: Gilmer-Smith Foundation

Beal, Dick, treas: Gallo Foundation, Ernest

Beal, James E., dir, secy: Falk Foundation, Elizabeth M.

Beal, Keleen, vchmn: Beal Foundation

Beal, Spencer, trust: Beal Foundation

Beale, Deborah Kinsella, dir: Osceola Foundation

Beale, Michelle, dir: Coca-Cola Foundation

Beale, Susan M., dir: Detroit Edison Foundation

Beall, Donald Ray, chmn, ceo, dir: Rockwell International Corp.; mem (trust comm): Rockwell International Corp. Trust

Beall, Kenneth S., Jr., trust: Whitehall Foundation

Beals, Vaughn L., chmn: Harley-Davidson, Inc.

Beals, Vaughn Leroy, Jr., dir: Firstar Milwaukee Foundation

Beamer, William E., secy, treas, dir: Parker Foundation

Bean, Atherton, trust: Athwin Foundation

Bean, Barbara, trust: Carpenter Foundation

Bean, Bruce William, trust: Athwin Foundation

Bean, Donald, dir: Levinson Foundation, Max and Anna

Bean, Mary F., trust: Athwin Foundation

Bean, Michael A., treas: Central Bank Foundation

Bean, Ralph, trust: Consolidated Natural Gas Co. Foundation

Bean, Ralph J., Jr., trust: Benedum Foundation, Claude Worthington

Bean, Winifred W., trust: Athwin Foundation

Beane, Sydney, trust: Woods Charitable Fund

Beard, Anson McCook, trust: Morgan Stanley Foundation

Beard, D. Paul, treas: Pittsburgh National Bank Foundation

Beard, Marjorie J., secy, treas: Beaver Foundation

Beard, Wendell R., dir: Ryder System Charitable Foundation

Beardsley, George B., trust: Gates Foundation

Beargie, William T., trust: Lubrizol Foundation

Bearn, Alexander G., MD, trust: Hughes Medical Institute, Howard; dir: Macy, Jr. Foundation, Josiah; trust, mem: Whitney Foundation, Helen Hay

Beasley, Mary E., pres: Beasley Foundation, Theodore and Beulah

Beatle, Vivian, dir commun aff: Hoffmann-La Roche; admin dir: Hoffmann-La Roche Foundation

Beatrice, Dennis F., vp: Kaiser Family Foundation, Henry J.

Beatt, Bruce H., secy: Dexter Corp. Foundation

Beattie, Art P., vp, secy, treas: Alabama Power Co.; treas: Alabama Power Foundation

Beattie, Catherine Hamrick, dir: Fullerton Foundation

Beattie, Richard I., trust, mem fin & admin comm: Carnegie Corporation of New York; dir: Kravis Foundation, Henry R.

Beattie, William F., secy, trust: Colorado Trust

Beatty, Linda E., Campbell Foundation, Ruth and Henry

Beatus, E. Jack, secy, treas, dir: Tisch Foundation

Beaty, Harry N., MD, trust: Sprague Memorial Institute, Otho S. A.

Beaty, John T., trust: Hornblower Fund, Henry

Beaty, Julian B., Jr., secy, dir: Langeloth Foundation, Jacob and Valeria

Beauchamp, John Herndon, chmn, dir: Keith Foundation Trust, Ben E.

Beaudoin, Lyle F., vp bus devel: Pegasus Gold Corp.

Beaudoin, Roseann K., vp, dir: Knox Family Foundation

Beaumont, Dorothy, vp, cfo: Sierra Health Foundation

Beaver, Thomas A., trust: Wyomissing Foundation

Beaver, William S., trust: Westvaco Foundation Trust

Beavers, Darrell, trust: Alhambra Foundry Co., Ltd. Scholarship Foundation

Becherer, Hans Walter, chmn, ceo, dir: Deere & Co.; dir: Deere Foundation, John

Becht, Loretta J., asst secy: Hyde and Watson Foundation

Bechtel, Carolyn M., dir, vp: Foothills Foundation

Bechtel, Elizabeth H., dir, vp: Shenandoah Foundation

Bechtel, Elizabeth Hogan, vp, dir: Bechtel, Jr. Foundation, S. D.

Bechtel, Gary Hogan, dir, pres: Foothills Foundation

Bechtel, Laura P., vp, dir: Lakeside Foundation

Bechtel, Riley P., pres, dir, coo: Bechtel Group; chmn, dir: Bechtel Foundation; pres, dir: Hogan Foundation, Royal Barney

Bechtel, Robert W., dir: Potts and Sibley Foundation

Bechtel, Stephen Davison, Jr., chmn emeritus: Bechtel Group; pres, dir: Bechtel, Jr. Foundation, S. D.; investment mgr: Foothills Foundation; vp, dir: Hogan Foundation, Royal Barney; investment mgr: Shenandoah Foundation

Bechtel, Susan Peters, vp, dir: Hogan Foundation, Royal Barney

Bechtold, Ellen A., contact person: Frankel Foundation

Bechtold, Ned W., dir: Firstar Milwaukee Foundation

Beck, Audrey Jones, dir: Houston Endowment

Beck, Carol, program off health & human svcs: Abell Foundation, The

Beck, Eckardt C., chmn, pres, ceo, dir: Air & Water Technologies Corp.

Beck, Henry Constable, Jr., trust: Constantin Foundation

Beck, John C., trust: Beck Foundation

Beck, Margaret V., Titmus Foundation

Beck, Matthew B., trust: Kettering Family Foundation

Beck, Mrs. Frela Owl, awards adv comm: Ferebee Endowment, Percy O.

Beck, Raymond, trust: Star Bank, N.A., Cincinnati Foundation

Beck, Richard A., trust: Ward Foundation, A. Montgomery

Beck, Robert N., trust: BankAmerica Foundation

Beck, Susan K., vp, trust: Kettering Family Foundation; mem distribution comm: Kettering Fund

Beck, T. Edmund, trust, pres: Beck Foundation

Beck, T.E., Jr., trust: Beck Foundation

Becker, Allen, trust: Schowalter Foundation

Becker, Gerald, dir: Lytel Foundation, Bertha Russ

Becker, Harold M., chmn: Guaranty Bank & Trust Co.; dir: Guaranty Bank & Trust Co. Charitable Trust

Becker, Howard C., secy, trust: Ohio National Foundation

Becker, James William, dir: Burlington Resources Foundation

Becker, John A., pres, dir: Firstar Bank Milwaukee NA; vchmn: Firstar Milwaukee

Foundation; pres, dir: Firstar Corp.

Becker, Kathy, environment program dir: Bullitt Foundation

Becker, Katrina H., vp, secy, dir: Barker Welfare Foundation

Becker, Lovice, asst secy: Johnson Foundation

Becker, Max, Jr., dir: Dent Family Foundation, Harry

Becker, Patrick E., secy: Clark Foundation

Becker, Paul A., trust: First Mississippi Corp. Foundation

Becker, Richard Charles, dir: Schmitt Foundation, Arthur J.

Becker, Steve, personnel mgr: Kloeckner- Pentaplast of America

Becket, MacDonald, trust: Unocal Foundation

Beckett, John Douglas, mem adv comm: Generation Trust

Beckett, Steven J., trust: American Optical Foundation

Beckett, Wendy, Generation Trust

Beckham, Claud, trust: Orange Orphan Society

Beckham, J. Gordon, Jr., asst secy: McCamish Foundation

Beckman, Arnold Orville, PhD, fdr, chmn, pres, dir: Beckman Foundation, Arnold and Mabel

Beckwith, G. Nicholas, III, trust: Benedum Foundation, Claude Worthington

Beckwith, Peter, deputy chmn: Heileman Brewing Co., Inc., G.

Bedell, Catherine, dir: Noyes Foundation, Jessie Smith

Bedell, Rev. George Chester, vchmn: duPont Fund, Jessie Ball

Bedford, Ruth R., pres, trust: Bedford Fund

Bednarz, Edward J., chmn, trust: Pinkerton Foundation

Bedsole, J. G., Jr., mem distribution comm: Bedsole Foundation, J. L.

Bedsole, Palmer, mem distribution comm: Bedsole Foundation, J. L.

Bedsole, T. Massey, chmn distribution comm, trust: Bedsole Foundation, J. L.

Beeby, Thomas H., trust: Graham Foundation for Advanced Studies in the Fine Arts; dir: Skidmore, Owings & Merrill Foundation

Beech, Thomas F., exec vp: Tandy Foundation, Anne Burnett and Charles

Beecher, Thomas R., Jr., trust: LeBrun Foundation

Beecherl, Julia T., trust: Bosque Foundation

Beecherl, Louis A., Jr., trust: Bosque Foundation

Beeghly, James L., exec secy appointing comm: Beeghly Fund, Leon A.

Beeghly, John D., mem appointing comm: Beeghly Fund, Leon A.

Beeghly, R. Thornton, mem appointing comm: Beeghly Fund, Leon A.

Beeman, Richard E., secy: Prentiss Foundation, Elisabeth Severance

Beemer, K. Larry, trust: Gerber Cos. Foundation

Beer, R. A., trust: Berbecker Scholarship Fund, Walter J. and Lille

Beers, Charlotte, chmn, ceo: Ogilvy & Mather Worldwide

Beers, Julius H., treas: Oleson Foundation

Beers, William O., trust: Beinecke Foundation

Beeston, John J., MD, mgr: Brush Foundation

Beewwkes, Ranier, III, trust: Harvard Apparatus Foundation

Beggs, Robert W., sr vp corp commun: Society for Savings

Beghini, Victor Gene, pres, dir: Marathon Oil, Indiana Refining Division; trust: USX Foundation

Begin, William J., treas, dir: Hulings Foundation, Mary Andersen

Begreen, Bernard, pres: Gilman Investment Co.

Behnke, Alvin G., trust: Chicago Title and Trust Co. Foundation

Behnke, Carl, pres, ceo: ALPAC Corp.

Behnke, John S., trust: Skinner Foundation

Behnke, Richard F., trust: Holy Land Charitable Trust

Behnke, Sally S., mem: Washington Mutual Savings Bank Foundation

Behnke, Sally Skinner, trust: Skinner Foundation

Behnke, Shari Dunkelman, trust: Skinner Foundation

Behr, Linda C., secy: Bohen Foundation

Behrenhausen, Richard A., vp, coo: McCormick Tribune Foundation, Robert R.

Behrman, Nancy, vp: Terner Foundation

Behrmann, John A., trust: Dentsply International Foundation

Beidler, Francis, III, trust: Beidler Charitable Trust, Francis

Beighle, Douglas, corp sr vp: Boeing Co.

Beilstein, Frederick B., III, sr vp, cfo: Fuqua Industries, Inc.

Beim, David O., dir: Markle Foundation, John and Mary R.

Beim, Raymond N., vp, dir: Beim Foundation

Beim, William H., pres, dir: Beim Foundation

Beim, William H., Jr., secy, treas: Beim Foundation

Beimfohr, Edward George, treas, trust: Engelhard Foundation, Charles

Beinecke, Elizabeth G., vp, dir: Prospect Hill Foundation

Beinecke, Frederick W., dir: Prospect Hill Foundation; pres, dir: Sperry Fund

Beinecke, John B., vp, dir: Prospect Hill Foundation

Beinecke, Walter, III, dir: Osceola Foundation

Beinecke, Walter, Jr., pres, treas, dir: Osceola Foundation

Beinecke, William S., don, pres, dir: Prospect Hill Foundation; vp, dir: Sperry Fund

Beir, Joan S., vp, secy, dir: Beir Foundation

Beir, Robert L., pres, dir: Beir Foundation

Beisenherz, Robert L., pres, coo: ICH Corp.

Beito, Gene, pres: Hartz Foundation

Bekavac, Nancy Y., trust: Wenner-Gren Foundation for Anthropological Research

Beker, Harvey, vp, dir: Wiener Foundation, Malcolm Hewitt

Bekins, Jacqueline, trust: Bekins Foundation, Milo W.

Bekins, Michael, trust: Bekins Foundation, Milo W.

Bekins, Milo W., Jr., trust: Bekins Foundation, Milo W.

Belanger, Warren, MD, trust: Valley Foundation

Belcher, Benjamin M., Jr., pres: Moore & Sons Foundation, B.C.

Belcher, Edward L., vchmn: Caldwell Manufacturing Co.

Belden, William H., Jr., pres, dir: Belden Brick Co., Inc.; trust: Belden Brick Co. Charitable Trust

Belden, William H., Sr., chmn, dir: Belden Brick Co., Inc.; trust: Belden Brick Co. Charitable Trust

Belfer, Arthur Beier, don, pres: Belfer Foundation

Belfer, Robert Alexander, don, secy: Belfer Foundation

Belfiore, Anna Marie, asst secy: Newman Assistance Fund, Jerome A. and Estelle R.

Belic, Ellen Stone, dir: Stone Family Foundation, Jerome H.

Belin, Daniel N., trust: Ahmanson Foundation; trust: Kress Foundation, Samuel H.

Belin, Jacob Chapman, vp, treas, dir: duPont Foundation, Alfred I.

Belin, Oscar F., trust: Hansen Foundation, Dane G.

Beling, Betty, assoc dir: Borchard Foundation, Albert and Elaine

Beling, Willard A., dir: Borchard Foundation, Albert and Elaine

Belk, Claudia, mem bd advs: Belk Foundation Trust

Belk, Irwin, mem bd advs: Belk Foundation Trust

Belk, John Montgomery, chmn, ceo: Belk Stores; mem bd advs: Belk Foundation Trust; chmn, ceo: Belk Stores

Belk, Judy, dir, secy: Levi Strauss Foundation

Belk, Katherine McKay, dir: Anderson Foundation, Robert C. and Sadie G.; mem bd advs: Belk Foundation Trust

Belk, Lowell Warner, secy: Bibb Foundation, Inc.

Belk, Thomas Milburn, pres: Belk Stores; chmn bd advs: Belk Foundation Trust

Belkin, Richard B., vp, dir: Lee Foundation

Belknap, Robert Lamont, trust: Whiting Foundation, Mrs. Giles

Bell, Bradley, treas: Whirlpool Foundation

Bell, Charles M., vp: Ordean Foundation

Bell, Diane Fisher, vp, dir: Fisher Foundation

Bell, Donald R., chmn, ceo, dir: Hall & Co. Inc., Frank B.

Bell, Ed, chmn: Lane Foundation

Bell, Gary, sr human resources rep: Airbus Industrie of America

Bell, Howard, trust: Smith Charitable Trust

Bell, Howard E., pres, coo: Entex

Bell, Howard J., dir: First National Bank & Trust Co. of Rockford Charitable Trust

Bell, James W., pres, dir: Landis & Gyr, Inc.

Bell, Karl Z., Copley Press

Bell, Lola, mgr shareholder rels: Cyprus Minerals Co.

Bell, Malcolm, trust: Hodge Foundation

Bell, Peter B., trust: Allegheny Foundation

Bell, Peter D., pres, trust: Clark Foundation, Edna McConnell

Bell, R. E., mem (bd control): Ralston Purina Trust Fund

Bell, R. Terry, vp, trust: Rockwell Fund

Bell, R.F., Ryan Foundation, Nina M.

Bell, Richard, trust: Sarkeys Foundation

Bell, Richard E., pres, ceo: Riceland Foods, Inc.

Bell, Robert M., vp, bd mem, dir: Gregg-Graniteville Foundation

Bell, Sally, secy, dir: Perot Foundation

Bell, Stephen Helms, trust: Helms Foundation

Bell, Thomas, asst vp (group insurance): Sun Life Assurance Co. of Canada (U.S.)

Bell, W. J., vchmn: Cablevision Systems Corp.

Bell, Wayne L., secy, dir: United Coal Co. Charitable Foundation

Bellairs, Carrie Jane, trust: Bishop Charitable Trust, A. G.

Bellamy, Kathie, mgr, consumer aff: Baskin-Robbins USA Co.

Bellando, John W., vp: Macmillan Foundation

Bellavance, Joseph A., trust: Nashua Trust Co. Foundation

Belles, David S., trust: First Interstate Bank of Oregon Charitable Foundation

Belles, Lawrence, pres: Cheney Foundation, Elizabeth F.

Bellet, Marilyn, trust: Stein Foundation, Louis

Bellinger, Susan, trust: New York Foundation

Bellini, Michael J., vp: Bellini Foundation

Bellini, Patrick W., pres: Bellini Foundation

Bellis, G. Gordon, secy: Hills Fund, Edward E.

Bellisario, Earl J., sr vp, cfo: Acme-Cleveland Corp.

Belloff, Mary Gretchen, dir: Bush Charitable Foundation, Edyth

Bellor, Mary, pres, secy: Graham Fund, Philip L.

Bellwood, Wesley E., chmn, dir: Wynn's International, Inc.

Belmonte, Norman, vp, dir: Mitrani Family Foundation

Belsky, Nancy Kaplan, dir: Kaplan Foundation, Rita J. and Stanley H.

Belsom, Walter J., Jr., treas, dir: Zemurray Foundation

Belt, John L., dir: Kirkpatrick Foundation

Belton, Steven L., dir: Northwest Area Foundation

Belvin, Christy H., trust: Bean Foundation, Norwin S. and Elizabeth N.

Belz, Jack A., don, mgr: Belz Foundation

Belz, Martin S., mgr: Belz Foundation

Belz, Philip, don, mgr: Belz Foundation

Belzberg, William, chmn, ceo, pres, dir: Far West Financial Corp.

Belzer, Alan, pres, coo, dir: AlliedSignal

Belzer, Folkert, M.D., trust: Surgical Science Foundation for Research and Development

BeMiller, Linda P., dir: Forest Foundation; program off: New Horizon Foundation; program dir: Sequoia Foundation

Bemis, Michael B., pres, coo: Louisiana Power & Light Co./New Orleans Public Service

Benach, Henry, chmn, ceo: Starrett Housing Corp.

Benbough, Legler, pres: Benbough Foundation, Legler

Bencin, Georgiana, secy, dir: Osborn Manufacturing Co. Educational & Charitable Fund

Benckenstein, Eunice R., vchmn, trust: Stark Foundation, Nelda C. and H. J. Lutcher

Bender, Barbara, dir: Bender Foundation

Bender, David, mem comm: American National Bank & Trust Co. of Chicago Foundation

Bender, Dorothy G., dir: Bender Foundation

Bender, George A., trust: Van Nuys Foundation, I. N. and Susanna H.

Bender, Howard Marvin, vp: Bender Foundation

Bender, John C., dir: Macmillan Foundation

Bender, Richard, secy, treas: Eisenberg Foundation, Ben B. and Joyce E.

Bender, Robert E., vchmn: Nordstrom, Inc.

Bender, Sondra D., pres: Bender Foundation

Bender, Stanley Seymour, vp, secy: Bender Foundation

Bender, Stuart, trust: Schimmel Foundation

Bender, Thomas, pres: CooperVision, Inc.

Bendheim, John M., vp: Lowenstein Foundation, Leon

Bendheim, Robert Austin, pres: Lowenstein Foundation, Leon

Bendix, William Emanuel, ceo, pres, dir: Mark Controls Corp.

Bendush, William E., sr vp, cfo: Silicon Systems Inc.

Benedeck, Alan F., exec dir, secy, dir: Allstate Foundation

Benedict, Andrew Bell, Jr., trust: Washington Foundation

Benedict, Kennette, dir (peace & intl coop): MacArthur Foundation, John D. and Catherine T.

Benedict, Peter B., chmn, dir: Surdna Foundation

Benedict, R. M., Jr., asst treas: Hanna Co. Foundation, M.A.

Benedum, Paul G., Jr., chmn, trust: Benedum Foundation, Claude Worthington

Benefiet, Thane, III, secy, dir: Sperry Fund

Benell, L. Raymond, trust: Orange Orphan Society

Benenson, Charles Benjamin, pres: Benenson Foundation, Frances and Benjamin

Benenson, James, chmn, pres: Vesper Corp.

Benenson, James, Jr., trust: Vesper Foundation

Benenson, Lawrence A., trust: Hebrew Technical Institute

Benenson, Sharen, trust: Vesper Foundation

Benetton, Gilberto, chmn, vp fin: Benetton

Benetton, Luciano, pres: Benetton

Benfell, Stan, pres: Security Life of Denver

Benford, William L., exec vp, cfo: L.A. Gear

Bengel, Ella, dir: Kellenberger Historical Foundation, May Gordon Latham

Benisek, John Paul, secy: Ideal Industries Foundation

Benjamin, Adelaide W., trust: RosaMary Foundation; secy: Wisdom Foundation, Mary F.

Bennack, Frank A., pres, ceo: Hearst Corp.

Bennack, Frank Anthony, Jr., vp, dir: Hearst Foundation; dir: Hearst Foundation, William Randolph

Bennet, David W., bd mem: First Fruit

Bennet, James, secy: Maytag Corp. Foundation

Bennett, Bruce, dir: Bennett Foundation, Carl and Dorothy

Bennett, Carl, pres, dir: Bennett Foundation, Carl and Dorothy

Bennett, Charles, dir: German Protestant Orphan Asylum Association; vp: Glazer Foundation, Jerome S.

Bennett, Donald E., exec vp, cfo: Cascade Natural Gas Corp.

Bennett, Dorothy, treas, dir: Bennett Foundation, Carl and Dorothy

Bennett, Edward F., vp: Mastronardi Charitable Foundation, Charles A.

Bennett, Floyd, dir: First Interstate Bank NW Region; trust: First Interstate Bank of Oregon Charitable Foundation

Bennett, Franklin, trust: Pollock Company Foundation, William B.

Bennett, George F., trust: Benfamil Charitable Trust

Bennett, Helen F., trust: Benfamil Charitable Trust

Bennett, James Stark, trust: Jones Foundation, W. Alton

Bennett, Jay, dir, pres, treas: Wallestad Foundation

Bennett, JoAnn P., dir of admin: duPont Fund, Jessie Ball

Bennett, John J., Jr., secy: St. Giles Foundation

Bennett, Marc, vp, dir: Bennett Foundation, Carl and Dorothy

Bennett, Marcus C., sr vp, cfo: Martin Marietta Corp.

Bennett, Nina B., trust: Raskob Foundation, Bill

Bennett, Otes, Jr., chmn: North American Coal Corp.

Bennett, Peter C., trust: Benfamil Charitable Trust

Bennett, Robert E., exec vp, trust: Pickett and Hatcher Educational Fund

Bennett, Robert W., dir: Pullman Educational Foundation, George M.

Bennett, Sally, dir, vp, secy: Wallestad Foundation

Bennett, T.A., trust: Taylor Foundation

Bennett, Thompson, trust: Dalton Foundation, Dorothy U.

Bennett, William Gordon, co-fdr, chmn bd, ceo: Circus Circus Enterprises

Benninger, Edward C., exec vp, cfo: Valero Energy Corp.

Bennington, Ronald Kent, trust: Hoover Foundation

Bennyhoff, George R., trust: West Foundation, Herman O.

Benoliel, Peter A., chmn, ceo: Quaker Chemical Corp.

Bensinger, Steven J., exec vp, cfo: Skandia America Reinsurance Corp.

Bensley, Bruce N., trust, mem: Rippel Foundation, Fannie E.

Benson, Bill R., vp, dir: Physicians Mutual Insurance Co. Foundation

Benson, Clifton L., III, treas: Palin Foundation

Benson, Clifton L., Jr., pres: Palin Foundation

Benson, Donald E., pres, dir: MEI Diversified, Inc.

Benson, Jeanne, contributions program admin: Pentair

Benson, Keith W., III, pres: National Manufacturing Co.

Benson, Keith W., Jr., chmn: National Manufacturing Co.

Benson, Lucy Wilson, trust: Sloan Foundation, Alfred P.

Benson, Margaret P., secy: Palin Foundation

Benson, Paul E., trust: Attleboro Pawtucket Savings Bank Charitable Foundation

Benson, Suzanne R., secy: Smith Foundation, Bob and Vivian

Bentas, Lily Haseotes, chmn, pres, dir: Cumberland Farms

Benter, George, pres: City National Bank

Bentle, Jim, exec vp (mktg): Bankers Life & Casualty Co.

Bentley, Alvin M., trust, Bentley Foundation, Alvin M.

Bentley, Antoinette Cozell, trust: Crum and Forster Foundation

Bentley, Barbara F., trust: Factor Family Foundation, Max

Bentley, Clark H., trust: Bentley Foundation, Alvin M.

Bentley, Helen, trust: Bentley Foundation, Alvin M.

Bentley, Kenneth J., dir: First Hawaiian Foundation

Bentley, Michael D., trust: Bentley Foundation, Alvin M.

Bentley, Peter, pres, dir: Herzog Foundation, Carl J.; ptnr: Parker Pen USA Ltd.

Bentley, Ralph, trust: Davis Hospital Foundation

Benton, Charles, pres: Benton Foundation

Benton, Craig, dir: Benton Foundation

Benton, Sharon Sayles, secy, dir: Bush Foundation

Bentzen, Michael P., secy, trust: Fowler Memorial Foundation, John Edward

Benua, T.R., Jr., pres, treas: Ebco Manufacturing Co.

Benvenuto, Cheryl, chmn contributions comm: Orion Capital Corp.

Benziger, Adelrick, Jr., mem adv comm: Weezie Foundation

Berardi, Carol, secy: International Paper Co. Foundation

Berberian, Martin Ray, trust, pres: Buehler Foundation, Emil; coo: Pfister and Vogel Tanning Co.

Berberich, Karen, HarperCollins Publishers

Berde, Carol, vp: McKnight Foundation

Berdrow, Stanton K., dir, secy, treas: Sierra Pacific Resources Charitable Foundation

Bere, Barbara Van Dellen, secy, treas, dir: Bere Foundation

Bere, David I., vp, dir: Bere Foundation

Bere, James Frederick, pres, dir: Bere Foundation

Bere, Robert P., vp, dir: Bere Foundation

Berelson, Irving P., pres, treas, dir: Barth Foundation, Theodore H.

Berelson, Thelma D., secy, dir: Barth Foundation, Theodore H.

Beren, Robert M., pres, treas: Beren Foundation, Robert M.

Beren, S.O., chmn, ceo: Misco Industries; trust: Misco Charitable Trust

Berenato, Joseph J., vp, cfo: Ducommun Inc.

Berens, Martha L., fdn mgr, secy: Lubrizol Foundation

Berens, Sheldon L., dir, vp: Fribourg Foundation

Berenson, Evelyn G., trust: Berenson Charitable Foundation, Theodore W. and Evelyn

Beres, Mary Ellen, vp: Goldome Foundation

Berez, Steven H., trust: Action Industries Charitable Foundation

Berg, Harvey, dir: Associated Food Stores Charitable Foundation

Berg, John P., pres: Greif Brothers Corp.

Berg, Paul, dir: Life Sciences Research Foundation

Berg, Robert, pres, secy-treas: Bartlett & Co.

Berg, W.R., trust: Bartlett & Co. Grain Charitable Foundation

Bergbauer, Urban C., Jr., trust: Whitaker Charitable Foundation, Lyndon C.

Bergeman, Richard P., chmn (contributions comm): CPC International

Berger, Bruce, trust: Whirlpool Foundation

Berger, Charles, chmn, dir: Weight Watchers International; chmn: Weight Watchers Foundation

Berger, George V., trust: Thoresen Foundation

Berger, Irving, ptnr: Hudson Neckwear; pres, dir: Hudson Charitable Foundation

Berger, James, treas, asst secy: Great Lakes Casting Corp. Foundation

Berger, John N., vp, dir: Berger Foundation, H.N. and Frances C.

Berger, Miles Lee, pres: Berger Foundation, Albert E.; secy, treas, trust: Graham Foundation for Advanced Studies in the Fine Arts

Berger, Paul, trust: Gudelsky Family Foundation, Isadore and Bertha

Berger, Robert, secy, treas: Berger Foundation, Albert E.

Berger, Ronald, dir: Berger Foundation, Albert E.

Berger, William, ptnr: Hudson Neckwear; treas, dir: Hudson Charitable Foundation

Bergerac, Michel Christian, dir: CBS Foundation

Bergeron, S. W., treas, trust: Chrysler Corp. Fund

Bergerson, Ruth K., dir: Palmer Foundation, George M.

Bergethon, K. Roald, trust: Newcombe Foundation, Charlotte W.

Bergholz, David, trust: Frick Educational Commission, Henry C.; exec dir: Gund Foundation, George

Bergman, Charles Cabe, consultant: Falk Medical Fund, Maurice; exec vp: Pollock-Krasner Foundation

Bergman, Esther, secy, treas: Mann Foundation, Ted

Bergman, Klaus, chmn, ceo: Allegheny Power System, Inc.; chmn, ceo: Potomac Edison Co.

Bergmann, Horst, pres, ceo: Jeppesen Sanderson

Bergreen, Bernard D., dir: Gilman Foundation, Howard

Bergreen, Morris H., pres, trust: Skirball Foundation

Bergstrom, Edith H., vp: Bergstrom Foundation, Erik E. and Edith H.

Bergstrom, Erik E., pres, dir, mgr: Bergstrom Foundation, Erik E. and Edith H.

Bergstrom, Henry A., trust: Benedum Foundation, Claude Worthington; trust: Trees Charitable Trust, Edith L.

Berick, James H., pres: Tranzonic Foundation

Berini, Joseph R., scholarship comm: Mitchell, Jr. Trust, Oscar

Berish, Barry M., pres, ceo: Jim Beam Brands Co.

Berk, R, vp, dir: Turner Construction Co. Foundation

Berk, Tony B., trust: Parshelsky Foundation, Moses L.

Berke, Ivan H., cfo: Carus Corp.

Berkenstadt, James A., dir, adm: Cremer Foundation

Berkey, Andrew D., II, dir, pres: Berkey Foundation, Peter

Berkley, E. Bertram, treas: Tension Envelope Foundation

Berkley, Eliot S., secy: Tension Envelope Foundation

Berkley, Richard L., pres: Tension Envelope Foundation

Berkley, William S., pres, ceo, dir: Tension Envelope Corp.

Berklund, Elwood, trust: Clemens Foundation

Berkman, Allen H., trust: Berkman Charitable Trust, Allen H. and Selma W.

Berkman, Louis, pres, treas, dir: Berkman Co., Louis; pres, treas: Berkman Foundation, Louis and Sandra; trust, chmn: Fair Oaks Foundation, Inc.

Berkman, Marshall L., vp: Berkman Foundation, Louis and Sandra; trust, pres: Fair Oaks Foundation, Inc.

Berkman, Marshall Lee, vp, trust: Berkman Foundation, Louis and Sandra

Berkman, Richard L., trust: Berkman Charitable Trust, Allen H. and Selma W.

Berkman, Selma W., trust: Berkman Charitable Trust, Allen H. and Selma W.

Berkoff, Herbert, M.D., trust: Surgical Science Foundation for Research and Development

Berkopec, Robert N., asst sec: Bradley Foundation, Lynde and Harry

Berkowitz, Bernard S., trust: Orange Orphan Society

Berlin, Charles, dir: Littauer Foundation, Lucius N.

Berlin, Ronald, pres, ceo: Hall Financial Group

Berlinski, Edward C., treas, dir: Gleason Works Foundation

Berman, Alfred, dir: Axe-Houghton Foundation

Berman, Colleen B., vp: Kimberly-Clark Foundation

Berman, Herbert, trust: Segal Charitable Trust, Barnet

Berman, Jay, cfo: Carter Co., William

Berman, K.E., trust: Simpson Industries Fund

Berman, Kathy, trust: Fein Foundation

Berman, Michael P., off, trust: Manat Foundation

Berman, Philip I., trust: Trexler Trust, Harry C.

Bermas, Stephen, pres: Conway Scholarship Foundation, Carle C.

Bermingham, Richard P., Sizzler International; cfo: Sizzler International Foundation

Bernard, B. E., dir: Shell Oil Co. Foundation

Bernard, Carolyn, trust: Hawkins Foundation, Robert Z.

Bernard, Eugene L., trust: Ross Foundation, Walter G.

Bernard, James W., pres, ceo: Univar Corp.; pres, trust: Univar Foundation

Bernard, Lowell C., trust: Thompson Charitable Foundation, Marion G.

Bernard, Robert, mem grantmaking comm: Liz Claiborne Foundation

Bernbach, John L., pres: DDB Needham Worldwide

Bernberg, Bruce, cfo: Western Publishing Co., Inc.

Berndsen, Leo J. M., chmn: AEGON USA, Inc.

Berner, Edgar R., chmn: Republic Automotive Parts, Inc.

Berner, Richard O., Ryan Foundation, Nina M.

Berner, Thomas Roland, vp, treas: Ryan Foundation, Nina M.

Berner, Wilbur J., pres: Aarque Cos.

Berney, Joseph Henry, vchmn, dir: National Presto Industries

Bernhard, Robert A., treas, dir: Lehman Foundation, Robert

Bernhardt, Fred J., Jr., trust: Lawrence Foundation, Lind

Bernheim, Leonard H., trust: Lavanburg-Corner House

Bernick, Howard Barry, pres, coo, dir: Alberto-Culver Co.

Berning, Larry D., dir: Donnelley Foundation, Gaylord and Dorothy

Berns, Ted, dir: PacifiCorp Foundation

Bernstein, Alan S., trust: Lurcy Charitable and Educational Trust, Georges

Bernstein, Caryl Salomon, secy: Federal National Mortgage Assn. Foundation

Bernstein, Celia Ellen, trust: Bernstein Foundation, Diane and Norman

Bernstein, Cynthia, dir: Abrams Foundation, Benjamin and Elizabeth

Bernstein, Daniel Lewis, trust: Lurcy Charitable and Educational Trust, Georges

Bernstein, David H., chmn, dir: Duty Free International

Bernstein, Diane, trust: Bernstein Foundation, Diane and Norman

Bernstein, Erik, trust: Phillips Family Foundation, Jay and Rose

Bernstein, George Lurcy, trust: Lurcy Charitable and Educational Trust, Georges

Bernstein, Jay S., trust: Lawrence Foundation

Bernstein, Leonard S., pres, ceo: Candlesticks Inc.; trust: Lawrence Foundation

Bernstein, Loraine, trust: Gordon Charitable Trust, Peggy and Yale

Bernstein, Morton J., chmn, dir: Samuels Foundation, Fan Fox and Leslie R.

Bernstein, Norman, dir, trust: Bernstein Foundation, Diane and Norman

Bernstein, Paula P., trust: Phillips Family Foundation, Jay and Rose

Bernstein, Richard A., chmn: Western Publishing Co., Inc.

Bernstein, Rita, trust: Lawrence Foundation

Bernstein, Robert L., vp, dir: Diamond Foundation, Aaron

Bernstein, Tom, dir: Ross Foundation, Arthur

Bernstein, William, trust: Friedman Brothers Foundation; trust: Phillips Family Foundation, Jay and Rose

Bernstein, Zalman Chaim, chmn, treas: AVI CHAI - A Philanthropic Foundation; trust: Bernstein & Co. Foundation, Sanford C.

Bernstock, Robert F., trust: Campbell Soup Foundation

Bernthal, Frederick W., vchmn: BASF Corp.

Bernthal, Harold George, mem: Butler Foundation, Alice

Bero, Donald B., asst secy-treas: National Machinery Foundation

Bero, Robert D., pres: Menasha Corp.

Berolzheimer, Karl, sr vp, secy, gen coun: Centel Corp.

Berowsky, Kurt T., vp, dir: MCJ Foundation

Berra, John M., pres: Rosemount, Inc.

Berrard, Steven R., secy, dir: Huizenga Family Foundation

Berresford, Susan Vail, vp: Ford Foundation

Berrett, Edward J., secy, treas: Kasiska Family Foundation

Berrett, James, ceo: NEC Technologies, Inc.

Berrie, Russell, pres, trust: Berrie Foundation, Russell

Berrie, Scott, trust: Berrie Foundation, Russell

Berritt, Raymond, vp: Buhl Family Foundation

Berrodin, Anastasia M., vp, dir: Pope Foundation, Lois B.

Berrodin, Frank, treas, dir: Pope Foundation, Lois B.

Berry, A. W., Sr., trust, don: Berry Foundation, Archie W. and Grace

Berry, Alan M., secy, treas, dir: Keating Family Foundation

Berry, Andrew, mgr: Horne Foundation, Dick

Berry, Charles D., trust: Berry Foundation, Loren M.

Berry, Daniel E., assoc dir: Gund Foundation, George

Berry, David L., trust: Berry Foundation, Loren M.

Berry, Donald C., Jr., trust: McDonald Foundation, J. M.

Berry, Donald E., ceo, pres: Chesapeake & Potomac Telephone Co. of West Virginia

Berry, G. Dennis, pres: Atlanta Journal & Constitution

Berry, George W., trust: Berry Foundation, Loren M.

Berry, Heidi, vp: Lehrman Foundation, Jacob and Charlotte

Berry, Ilona M., secy: First National Bank of Chicago Foundation

Berry, James D., dir: Hoblitzelle Foundation

Berry, Joane, dir: Babcock Memorial Endowment, William

Berry, John William, Jr., pres, dir: Berry & Co., L.M.; vp, trust: Berry Foundation, Loren M.

Berry, John William, Sr., pres, trust: Berry Foundation, Loren M.

Berry, Joseph, vchmn: Keefe, Bruyette & Woods

Berry, Katherine C., trust: Laub Foundation

Berry, Robert B., Sr., trust: Berry Foundation, Archie W. and Grace

Berry, Robert V., trust: Thomas & Betts Charitable Trust

Berry, Robin, mem: Boatmen's First National Bank of Oklahoma Foundation

Berry, Roger D., pres: Intelligent Controls

Berry, Thomas E., asst secy: Turner Charitable Foundation

Berry, William S., dir: ITT Rayonier Foundation

Berry, William Wells, trust: Washington Foundation

Bershad, Stephen, chmn, ceo, dir: Vernitron Corp.

Berson, Joel J., secy, trust: Adler Foundation

Berstein, James D., dir: Rockefeller Foundation, Winthrop

Bersticker, Albert C., pres, ceo, dir: Ferro Corp.; pres, trust: Ferro Foundation

Bertea, Richard, chmn exec comm, dir: Parker-Hannifin Corp.

Berthold, James K., vp, dir, asst treas: Sunnen Foundation

Bertman, J. G., vp, treas, trust: Humphreys Foundation

Bertran, David R., dir: Nalco Foundation

Bertrand, Frederic H., chmn, ceo, dir: National Life of Vermont

Bertsch, James L., treas: Armco Foundation

Berube, D. T., dir: MPCo/Entech Foundation

Berwind, C. Graham, Jr., chmn, pres, ceo, dir: Berwind Corp.

Berylson, Amy S., trust: Smith Foundation, Richard and Susan

Berzins, Mirdza, acting dir (MacArthur Fellows): MacArthur Foundation, John D. and Catherine T.

Besaw, Kathleen, trust: Bay Branch Foundation

Bescherer, Edwin A., Jr., trust: Dun & Bradstreet Corp. Foundation

Beshar, Christine, trust: Branta Foundation

Besser, John E., secy, dir: Barnes Group Foundation

Bessey, Edward Cushing, dir, vchmn: Pfizer

Bessire, Henry E., vchmn, dir: Brakeley, John Price Jones Inc.

Besson, Michel Louis, vchmn, pres, ceo, coo: CertainTeed Corp.; pres, dir: CertainTeed Corp. Foundation; vchmn, pres, ceo, coo: Norton Co.; pres, ceo, dir: Norton Co. Foundation

Best, John S., dir: Peters Foundation, R. D. and Linda

Best, Marilyn, secy, treas: Perkins Charitable Foundation

Best, R., group vp, secy, dir: Toyota U.S.A. Foundation

Best, Robert M., dir: Utica National Group Foundation

Best, Robert W., pres, ceo: Texas Gas Transmission Corp.

Betson, Donald E., asst treas: KIHI/21 International Holding Foundation

Bettis, Harry Little, pres, dir: Cunningham Foundation, Laura Moore

Betts, R. E., trust: Betts Foundation

Betts, Richard T., pres, dir: Betts Industries; trust: Betts Foundation

Betty, Charles G., ceo, pres: Digital Communications Associates, Inc.

Betty, John W., trust: Jergens Foundation, Andrew

Betz, Bill B., dir: Jameson Foundation, J. W. and Ida M.

Betz, Claire S., trust: J. D. B. Fund

Betz, John Drew, trust: J. D. B. Fund

Beukema, Henry S., exec dir: McCune Foundation

Bevan, Mrs. Thomas, co-chmn distribution comm: Emergency Aid of Pennsylvania Foundation

Bevan, William, trust emeritus: Grant Foundation, William T.

Bever, Ellis D., consultant: Rice Foundation, Ethel and Raymond F.

Bever, Keith, chmn, dir: Bank of Alma Charitable Trust

Beverly, Joe E., vchmn, dir: Synovus Financial Corp.

Beverly, Joseph E., dir: Williams Family Foundation of Georgia

Beversdorf, William R., vp: Sentry Life Group Foundation

Bevilacqua, Dominic A., dir: American Welding & Manufacturing Co. Foundation

Beville, R. Harwood, trust: Rouse Co. Foundation

Bevins, Peter, vp: Goldome Foundation

Bevis, James Wayne, pres, ceo, dir: Pella Corp.; trust: Pella Rolscreen Foundation

Bevona, Devra A., treas: Seneca Foods Foundation

Beyer, David L., vp, cfo: Liberty Glass Co.

Beyer, Herbert Albert, pres, exec dir, trust: DeVlieg Foundation, Charles

Beyer, Jeffrey C., vp: Farmers Group Safety Foundation

Beyer, Joanne B., pres, trust: Allegheny Foundation; vp, treas: Scaife Family Foundation

Beyer, Michele, trust: Mandel Foundation, Joseph and Florence

Beyl, Earnest, publ rels off: Qantas Airways Ltd.

Beyster, J. Robert, chmn, ceo: Science Applications International Corp.

Bhasin, K. K., cfo: Picker International

Biale, Patricia, mem (contributions comm): CPC International

Bialla, Rowley, secy: Guggenheim Foundation, Daniel and Florence

Bianchini, Thomas J., secy, treas: Kirby Foundation, F. M.

Bianco, D., trust: Arkelian Foundation, Ben H. and Gladys

Bibby, Douglas Martin, vp: Federal National Mortgage Assn. Foundation

Bible, Geoffrey C., pres, chief auditor off: Philip Morris Cos.

Bichel, Willou R., trust: Simpson Foundation

Bicknell, Guthrie, Bicknell Fund

Bicknell, Warren, III, vp, trust: Bicknell Fund; pres: Cherokee Foundation

Bicknell, Wendy, trust: Cherokee Foundation

Bicknell, Wendy H., trust: Bicknell Fund

Bickner, Bruce P., chmn, ceo: Dekalb Energy Co.; trust: Dekalb Energy Foundation; chmn, ceo, dir: DeKalb Genetics Corp.

Biddy, Ralph L., MD, dir: Group Health Foundation

Bieber, Marcia McGee, pres, dir: McGee Foundation

Bieber, Richard R., secy, treas: Schaffer Foundation, H.

Biederman, Sylvia, dir: Jewish Foundation for Education of Women

Biegler, David W., chmn, ceo: Enserch Corp.; chmn, ceo: Lone Star Gas Co.

Biehl, Glenn E., treas: Loats Foundation

Bieker, Dennis L., trust: Dreiling and Albina Dreiling Charitable Trust, Leo J.

Bielli, Georgio, coo: Savin Corp.

Bierhaus, Robert V., Jr., mgr: Bierhaus Foundation

Bierman, Jacquin D., trust: Joselow Foundation; Mills Charitable Foundation, Henry L. and Kathryn

Biermann, Stephen L., trust: Monticello College Foundation

Bigelow, T. William, trust: Smyth Trust, Marion C.

Biggers, Covella H., treas, dir: Houchens Foundation, Ervin G.

Biggers, Gil E., dir: Houchens Foundation, Ervin G.

Biggers, Gil M., dir: Houchens Foundation, Ervin G.

Biggie, Carmelita, comm mem: Whitaker Fund, Helen F.

Biggins, J. Veronica, dir corp community rels: NationsBank Corp.

Biggs, Electra Waggoner, pres: Waggoner Foundation, E. Paul and Helen Buck

Biggs, Huntley, exec dir: Mississippi Power Foundation

Biggs, John H., trust: Danforth Foundation

Bigham, James J., cfo: Continental Grain Co.

Bilbao, Thomas, dir: Goldome Foundation

Bilbo, Robert, sr program dir: Commonwealth Fund

Bildman, Lars, mng dir: Astra Pharmaceutical Products, Inc.

Bildner, Allen I., pres: KSM Foundation

Bildner, James L., secy: KSM Foundation

Bildner, Jean L., vp: KSM Foundation

Bildner, Robert L., treas, asst secy: KSM Foundation

Bilich, John M., exec vp, exec dir: Armco Foundation

Bill, G. Dana, trust: Peabody Foundation, Amelia

Bill, James K., pres, coo: Travelers Express Co.

Billings, Chester, dir: Greenwall Foundation

Billingsley, Helen Lee, trust: Doherty Charitable Foundation, Henry L. and Grace

Billingsley, James Ray, vp, treas, trust: Doherty Charitable Foundation, Henry L. and Grace

Bills, Eldon, dir, evp: Raymond Educational Foundation

Bills, Elmer E., Jr., mem trust fund comm: Ingram Trust, Joe

Bilotti, Margaret Schultz, trust: Schultz Foundation

Bilotti, Richard, trust: Kerney Foundation, James

Bilski, Berthold, dir: Littauer Foundation, Lucius N.

Bilson, Ira E., secy, mem bd advs: Stern Memorial Trust, Sidney

Bilton, Stuart Douglas, trust: Chicago Title and Trust Co. Foundation

Binder, Gordon M., chmn, ceo, dir: Amgen, Inc.

Binder, James, pres, ceo: Wrap-On Co.

Bindley, William E., chmn, pres, ceo, dir: Bindley Western Industries

Binford, Thomas W., mem (community concerns comm): NBD Bank, N.A.

Bing, Anna H., trust: Bing Fund

Bing, Peter S., trust: Bing Fund

Bing, Ward, secy, treas: MacCurdy Salisbury Educational Foundation

Bingenheimer, J. Jeffrey, Sr., vp: Index Technology Foundation

Binger, Al, sr program off (global environment): Rockefeller Foundation

Binger, James H., dir: McKnight Foundation

Binger, James M., treas, dir: McKnight Foundation

Binger, Patricia S., asst secy, asst treas, dir: McKnight Foundation

Binger, Virginia McKnight, hon chmn, dir: McKnight Foundation

Bingham, Charles W., chmn, trust: Weyerhaeuser Co. Foundation

Binning, John H., vchmn, dir: Bitco Corp.

Binns, James W., pres: Timex Corp.

Binstock, Shelton M., dir, pres: Stone Foundation, David S.

Binswanger, Frank G., Jr., chmn, dir: Binswanger Co.; vchmn, dir: Binswanger Foundation

Binswanger, Frank G., Sr., chmn, dir: Binswanger Foundation

Binswanger, John K., pres: Binswanger Co.; treas, dir: Binswanger Foundation

Blattman, H. Eugene, pres, coo, dir: McCormick & Co.

Blau, Harvey R., chmn, ceo: Instrument Systems Corp.

Blau, Lawrence, dir, pres: Horncrest Foundation

Blau, Olivia, dir, vp, secy: Horncrest Foundation

Blaufuss, William, Jr., trust: KPMG Peat Marwick Foundation

Blaustein, Jeanne P., trust: Blaustein Foundation, Jacob and Hilda; vp, trust: Blaustein Foundation, Morton K. and Jane

Blaustein, Mary Jane, vp, trust: Blaustein Foundation, Jacob and Hilda; vp, trust: Blaustein Foundation, Morton K. and Jane

Blaustein, Susan M., trust: Blaustein Foundation, Jacob and Hilda; trust, vp: Blaustein Foundation, Morton K. and Jane

Blaxter, H. Vaughan, III, dir: Hillman Foundation; dir: Hillman Foundation, Henry L.

Blazek, Doris D., trust: Healy Family Foundation, M. A.

Blazek, Frank A., pres: Giger Foundation, Paul and Oscar

Bleakley, W. Greg, trust: White Consolidated Industries Foundation

Bleck, Eugene E., MD, dir: Hale Foundation, Crescent Porter

Bleck, Max Emil, pres, dir: Beech Aircraft Corp.; dir: Beech Aircraft Foundation; pres, dir: Raytheon Co.

Bleckner, Edward, Jr., chmn, ceo: Racal-Milgo

Bleeker, Alfred E., trust: First Evergreen Foundation

Bleibtreu, John N., secy, treas: Bleibtreu Foundation, Jacob

Bleier, Robert S., MD, dir: Washington Square Health Foundation

Blend, Dominick, vchmn, dir: Karmazin Products Corp.

Blewett, James, treas, dir: Premier Foundation

Bley, Russell, secy: Monsanto Fund

Blind, William C., trust: Craigmyle Foundation

Blinken, Alan J., vp: Blinken Foundation

Blinken, Donald M., pres, treas: Blinken Foundation

Blinken, Robert J., vp, secy: Blinken Foundation

Blinkenberg, Linda J., secy: Confidence Foundation; secy: I Have A Dream Foundation - Los Angeles; secy: L. L. W. W. Foundation; secy: W. W. W. Foundation; cfo, secy, contact person: Whittier Foundation, L. K.

Bliumis, Sarah W., trust: Bydale Foundation

Bloch, Daniel R., trust: Johnson's Wax Fund

Bloch, Ernest, II, exec dir: PacifiCorp Foundation

Bloch, Henry Wollman, ceo, pres, dir: Bloch Foundation, Henry W. and Marion H.; chmn, ceo: Block, H&R; chmn, treas, dir: Block Foundation, H&R

Bloch, Hiroko, exec secy, grant adm: United States-Japan Foundation

Bloch, Konrad Emil, dir: Life Sciences Research Foundation

Bloch, Marion H., vp, secy, dir: Bloch Foundation, Henry W. and Marion H.

Bloch, Mary, mem disbursement comm: Oppenstein Brothers Foundation

Bloch, Peter, exec dir: Mayerson Foundation, Manuel D. and Rhoda

Bloch, Robert L., vp, treas, dir: Bloch Foundation, Henry W. and Marion H.

Bloch, Thomas Morton, dir: Bloch Foundation, Henry W. and Marion H.

Block, Alan James, vchmn, dir: Blade Communications; vp, trust: Blade Foundation

Block, Ellen, secy: Hassenfeld Foundation

Block, Eugene, co-chmn: Rosenbluth Travel Agency

Block, F. H., dir: Jewish Foundation for Education of Women

Block, James A., chmn: Block Drug Co.; trust: de Hirsch Fund, Baron

Block, John R., vp, trust: Blade Foundation

Block, Lawrence, dir: Schiff, Hardin & Waite Foundation

Block, Leonard N., sr chmn, ceo: Block Drug Co.

Block, Leonard Nathan, dir: Kaufmann Foundation, Henry

Block, Philip D., III, dir: Barker Welfare Foundation

Block, Rabbi Irving, trust: Perley Fund, Victor E.

Block, Robert L., secy, program off: Block Foundation, H&R

Block, Thomas M., ceo, pres: Block, H&R

Block, Thomas R., pres, treas: Block Drug Co.

Block, William, Sr., chmn, dir: Blade Communications

Block, William Karl, Jr., pres, vp, trust: Blade Foundation

Bloebaum, William Douglas, Jr., treas: Mead Corp. Foundation

Bloedel, Prentice, trust, don: Bloedel Foundation

Bloedel, Virginia Merrill, trust: Bloedel Foundation; chmn: Merrill Foundation, R. D.

Bloedorn, John H., Jr., dir: Bloedorn Foundation, Walter A.

Bloem, James H., vp, cfo: Miller Inc., Herman

Blohm, Donald E., adm: La-Z-Boy Foundation

Blokker, Joanne W., pres: Mericos Foundation

Blom, Margaret, dir: Hopper Foundation, May Templeton

Bloom, Aimee Simon, dir: Simon Foundation, William E. and Carol G.

Bloom, Alan K., secy, trust: Schimmel Foundation

Bloom, Cliffton E., trust: Mulcahy Foundation

Bloom, David R., chmn, ceo: Peoples Drug Stores Inc.

Bloom, Geoffrey B., pres, coo: Wolverine World Wide, Inc.

Bloom, Kenneth A., pres: Matchbox Toys (USA) Ltd.

Bloom, Susan, mem: American Express Co.

Bloomfield, Coleman, chmn, ceo: Minnesota Mutual Life Insurance Co.; pres, dir: Minnesota Mutual Foundation

Bloomfield, Richard, Hornblower Fund, Henry

Bloomfield, Rie, pres, trust: Bloomfield Foundation, Sam and Rie

Bloomstein, Charles, treas, dir: Mertz-Gilmore Foundation, Joyce

Bloor, James, dir: Lee Foundation, James T.

Blossom, C. Bingham, trust, chmn (investment comm), treas: Bingham Foundation, William

Blossom, Dudley S., trust: Bingham Foundation, William

Blossom, Laurel, trust, chmn (investment ethics comm), Company Inc.: Bingham Foundation, William

Blotstein, David, dir: Life Sciences Research Foundation

Blount, Dan S., pres: Montgomery Elevator Co.; trust: Montgomery Elevator Co. Charitable Trust

Blount, Winton Malcolm, Jr., chmn, ceo, dir: Blount; dir: Blount Foundation

Blout, Mrs. George C., trust: Oxford Foundation

Bloxsom, Mrs. Daniel, Jr., chmn of scholarships: Ebell of Los Angeles Rest Cottage Association; chmn of scholarships: Ebell of Los Angeles Scholarship Endowment Fund

Blubaugh, Harry C., vp, secy: Goldseker Foundation of Maryland, Morris

Bludworth, Gladys, trust: Ross Foundation, Walter G.

Bluemle, Lewis W., Jr., vp fin, trust: Connelly Foundation

Bluestone, Stan, pres, coo: Bergner Co., P.A.

Bluhdorn, Dominique, trust: Bluhdorn Charitable Trust, Charles G. and Yvette

Bluhdorn, Paul, trust: Bluhdorn Charitable Trust, Charles G. and Yvette

Bluhdorn, Yvette, trust: Bluhdorn Charitable Trust, Charles G. and Yvette

Blum, Barbara B., pres, mem exec comm, mem counc, dir: Foundation for Child Development

Blum, David, dir: Chicago Board of Trade Educational Research Foundation

Blum, John R. H., vp, dir: Dreyfus Foundation, Camille and Henry

Blum, Lawrence A., secy, treas: Blum Foundation, Lois and Irving

Blum, Michael S., chmn, pres, ceo: Heller Financial

Blum, Richard C., dir: Koret Foundation

Blume, Wolfram, pres: MicroSim Corp.

Blumenthal, Alan, pres: Radiator Specialty Co.; trust: Blumenthal Foundation

Blumenthal, Anita, trust: Blumenthal Foundation

Blumenthal, Barbara J., secy: Nelco Foundation

Blumenthal, Herman, chmn, ceo: Radiator Specialty Co.; chmn, trust: Blumenthal Foundation

Blumenthal, Martin, vp: de Hirsch Fund, Baron; dir: Jewish Foundation for Education of Women

Blumenthal, Philip, trust: Blumenthal Foundation

Blumenthal, Samuel, PhD, trust: Blumenthal Foundation

Blundell, John, pres: Koch Charitable Foundation, Charles G.; pres: Lambe Charitable Foundation, Claude R.

Bluntzer, John L., vp, dir: Behmann Brothers Foundation

Boag, William W., Jr., exec dir, asst sec: Ohio Bell Foundation

Boardman, Cynthia R., trust: Rosenthal Foundation, Samuel

Boardman, Harold F., trust: Hoffmann-La Roche Foundation

Boardman, Kathryn, trust: General Educational Fund

Boatman, Dennis, dir: Hall Foundation

Bobins, Norman, pres: LaSalle National Bank

Bobo, William N., secy, treas: Abney Foundation

Bobrow, Edythe, exec dir: Schepp Foundation, Leopold

Bobrow, Irving S., vp, asst treas: Rosen Foundation, Joseph

Bobrow, Robert, treas, dir: Rosenhaus Peace Foundation, Sarah and Matthew

Bobst, Mamdouha S., pres, treas, dir: Bobst Foundation, Elmer and Mamdouha

Bocko, Miranda Fuller, trust: Fuller Foundation

Bodden, Mark L., mgr (corp contributions): Philip Morris Cos.

Bode, Barbara, dir: Richmond Foundation, Frederick W.

Bodeen, Kay, adm: Marriott Foundation, J. Willard

Bodenhamer, Lee, trust: Bodenhamer Foundation

Bodie, Carroll A., vp: Procter & Gamble/Noxell Foundation

Bodie, William C., MD, trust: Florence Foundation

Bodine, Edward F., chmn: Bodine Corp.; pres, dir: Bodine Foundation

Bodine, Jean, trust: McLean Contributionship

Bodine, Norman R., pres: United Technologies, Automotive

Bodine, Richard P., pres: Bodine Corp.; treas, dir: Bodine Foundation

Bodkin, Lawrence G., Jr., dir: Ziegler Foundation for the Blind, E. Matilda

Bodman, Samuel W., ceo: Cabot Corp.; pres, dir: Cabot Corp. Foundation

Bodner, Herbert, pres, ceo, dir: Fru-Con Construction Corp.

Boeckman, Duncan E., dir: O'Donnell Foundation

Boeckmann, Alan, trust: Fluor Foundation

Boeckmann, Herbert F., II, ceo: Boeckmann Charitable Foundation

Boeckmann, Jane, secy: Boeckmann Charitable Foundation

Boehl, Ronald C., pres: Corroon & Black of Oregon

Boehm, Robert L., pres, trust: Boehm Foundation

Boekenheide, Russell W., trust: Union Camp Charitable Trust

Boekhoff, Dennis D., dir: Quad City Osteopathic Foundation

Boerman, Lori J., staff acct: Gerber Cos. Foundation

Boero, Edward, DDS, 2nd vp, dir: Babcock Memorial Endowment, William

Boesen, James M., treas, dir: Dillon Foundation

Boettcher, Mrs. Charles, II, trust: Boettcher Foundation

Boettiger, John R., dir: Reynolds Foundation, Christopher

Bogart, Dawn, sr coordinator in-kind donations: America West Airlines

Boger, D. J., secy: Ormet Foundation

Bogert, Jeremiah M., dir: JM Foundation; vp, trust: Woodland Foundation

Bogert, Margot C., pres, trust: Woodland Foundation

Bogert, Milicient D., trust: Woodland Foundation

Bogert, Mrs. H. Lawrence, vp, dir: JM Foundation

Boghetich, Jilene, trust: Rapp Foundation, Robert Glenn

Bogle, Donald, pres, dir: ABB Process Automation

Bogner, Stephen B., mem distribution comm: Ford and Ada Ford Fund, S. N.

Bogomolny, Robert Lee, dir: Searle Charitable Trust

Bogus, Donald W., mem screening comm: PPG Industries Foundation

Boh, Robert Henry, co-fdr, chmn, pres: Boh Brothers Construction Co.; chmn, trust: Boh Foundation

Boh, Robert S., trust: Boh Foundation

Boham, Gloria, pres: Omega World Travel

Bohart, Barbara, adjunct dir: Educational Foundation of America

Bohart, James, Jr., adjunct dir: Educational Foundation of America

Bohay, Philbrick, vp: Beaver Foundation

Bohland, Jerome A., trust: Charities Foundation

Bohlig, Paul M., treas, dir: National By-Products Foundation

Bohm, Pete, bd mem: Salvatori Foundation, Henry

Bohn, Karen M., chmn corp contributions: Piper Jaffray Cos.

Bohne, P. W., vp, dir: German Protestant Orphan Asylum Association

Boice, John E., Jr., secy, treas, dir: Bloedorn Foundation, Walter A.

Boillot, Lynn H., dir: Langeloth Foundation, Jacob and Valeria

Boisi, Geoffrey T., trust: Boisi Family Foundation

Boisi, Norine I., trust: Boisi Family Foundation

Boisselle, Mary S., trust: Conn Memorial Foundation

Boissonnas, Eric, pres, dir: Scaler Foundation

Boissonnas, Sylvie, vp, dir: Scaler Foundation

Boitano, Caroline, asst secy: Bank of America - Giannini Foundation; pres, exec dir: BankAmerica Foundation

Bok, Joan T., chmn, dir: New England Electric System

Boklund, Thomas B., trust: Gilmore Foundation, William G.

Bolada, trust: Giddings & Lewis Foundation

Boland, Herbert, dir (personnel): Siebe North Inc.

Bowen, Arthur H., Jr., trust: Cowden Foundation, Louetta M.

Bowen, Freda, trust: Abercrombie Foundation

Bowen, Henry, dir: Bowen Foundation, Ethel N.

Bowen, James B., chmn, dir: Steel Heddle Manufacturing Co.

Bowen, Jean G., treas: Goodyear Foundation, Josephine

Bowen, Jimelle, exec dir: Teubert Charitable Trust, James H. and Alice

Bowen, Otis R., MD, dir: Lilly Endowment

Bowen, R.L., treas: Fuller Foundation

Bowen, Sheryl, treas: Edwards Foundation, Jes

Bowen, Suzanne, trust: Montgomery Foundation

Bowen, Virginia M., Bowen Foundation, Ethel N.

Bowen, William G., PhD, pres, trust: Mellon Foundation, Andrew W.; trust: Merck Co. Foundation; dir: Wallace-Reader's Digest Fund, DeWitt; dir: Wallace Reader's Digest Fund, Lila

Bower, Ellen E., asst secy: Kulas Foundation

Bower, Joseph L., trust: Brown Foundation, George Warren; dir: Sonesta Charitable Foundation

Bower, Roger N., trust: Russell Trust, Josephine G.

Bower, Sam R., secy-treas: Owen Foundation

Bowers, Anthony J., American Society of Ephesus

Bowers, Dave, cfo: Crown International, Inc.

Bowers, Hugh R., pres: Bowers Foundation

Bowers, Ryn R., vp: Bowers Foundation

Bowes, Donald, trust, secy: Howard and Bush Foundation

Bowles, Crandall C., vp: Springs Industries

Bowles, Howard, vp: Davey Co. Foundation

Bowles, Lillian Crandall Close, vp, treas, dir: Close Foundation; vp, treas, dir: Springs Foundation

Bowles, Margaret C., dir: Clowes Fund

Bowlin, John D., pres: Mayer Foods Corp., Oscar

Bowlin, Michael Ray, sr vp: ARCO; dir: ARCO Foundation

Bowling, James W., chmn, pres, dir: Formrite Tube Co.

Bowman, Bob, trust, secy: Pineywoods Foundation

Bowman, Faith, Acct Mgr: Morris Charitable Foundation, E. A.

Bowman, George A., Jr., vp: State Street Foundation

Bowman, Gloria G., secy: Barlow Family Foundation, Milton A. and Gloria D.

Bowman, Jon, 1st vp, dir: Haas Foundation, Saul and Dayee G.

Bowman, Robert W., trust: Fruehauf Foundation

Bowmer, Jim D., dir: Mayborn Foundation, Frank W.

Bowser, Shirley Dunlap, trust: Kellogg Foundation, W. K.

Bowser, Wayne, pres: Schlegel Corp.

Bowsher, John M., trust: Benua Foundation

Boxx, Linda McKenna, secy, dir: McKenna Foundation, Katherine Mabis

Boxx, T. William, treas: McKenna Foundation, Katherine Mabis; secy, treas, off: McKenna Foundation, Philip M.

Boy, John Buckner, vchmn: United States Sugar Corp.; trust: United States Sugar Corporate Charitable Trust

Boyan, William L., pres, coo, dir: John Hancock Mutual Life Insurance Co.

Boyarski, Margaret, secy: Alexander Charitable Foundation

Boyazis, James, vp, secy: Goodyear Tire & Rubber Company Fund

Boyce, Donald N., chmn, pres, ceo, dir: IDEX Corp.

Boyce, Doreen E., pres: Buhl Foundation; trust: Frick Educational Commission, Henry C.

Boyce, Ernest F., trust: Ramlose Foundation, George A.

Boyce, Phillip R., chmn: Valley Foundation

Boyce-Abel, Olivia, trust: Tilghman, Sr., Charitable Trust, Bell and Horace

Boycks, Barbara E., treas: Oshkosh Truck Foundation

Boyd, Alan S., chmn, ceo: Airbus Industrie of America

Boyd, Barbara, vp, dir: Glenn Foundation for Medical Research, Paul F.

Boyd, Dennis W., asst secy: MDU Resources Foundation

Boyd, Hallam, Jr., trust: Plough Foundation

Boyd, John W., dir: Hertz Foundation, Fannie and John

Boyd, Llewellyn, vp, dir: Brown Charitable Trust, Dora Maclellan

Boyd, Michael, dir, vp: Donaldson, Lufkin & Jenrette Foundation

Boyd, Richard A., exec dir: Jennings Foundation, Martha Holden

Boyd, Willard, trust: Carver Charitable Trust, Roy J.

Boyer, David S., pres: Teleflex Inc.

Boyer, James G., chmn, pres, dir: Premier Bank

Boyer, Joyce, secy, treas: Einstein Fund, Albert E. and Birdie W.

Boyer, Ray, dir (communs): MacArthur Foundation, John D. and Catherine T.

Boyer, Robert L., dir: Georgia Power Foundation

Boyette, John G., treas: Cox Foundation of Georgia, James M.

Boyle, Alexander R. M., pres: Chevy Chase Savings Bank FSB

Boyle, B. Snowden, Jr., adv: Van Vleet Foundation

Boyle, Dennis, trust: Vicksburg Foundation

Boyle, Dorothy R., trust: Booth-Bricker Fund

Boyle, Edwin T., trust: Buehler Foundation, Emil

Boyle, R. Emmett, chmn, pres, ceo: Ormet Corp.; pres, dir: Ormet Foundation; chmn, pres, ceo: Ravenswood Aluminum Corp.

Boyle, Richard James, vchmn, dir: Chase Manhattan Bank, N.A.

Boylston, A. D., Jr., trust: Glenn Memorial Foundation, Wilbur Fisk; chmn: Murphy Foundation, Katherine and John

Boynton, Cynthia Binger, pres, dir: McKnight Foundation

Boynton, Noa, dir: McKnight Foundation

Boyter, R.S., vp: Bibb Foundation, Inc.

Bozic, Michael, ceo, pres: Hills Department Stores, Inc.

Bozorth, Squire, dir: Hess Foundation

Bozzone, Robert P., pres, ceo, dir: Allegheny Ludlum Corp.; trust: Allegheny Ludlum Foundation; don, trust: Bozzone Family Foundation

Bracken, Frank A., pres, dir: Ball Foundation, George and Frances

Bracken, Rosemary B., dir: Ball Foundation, George and Frances

Bracken, S. Terry, trust: Hankamer Foundation, Curtis and Doris K.

Bracken, William M., dir: Ball Brothers Foundation

Bradbeer, Ann, dir: Abel Foundation

Braden, Katherine F., vp, treas: Castle Foundation, Harold K. L.

Bradford, Dalene D., vp: Loose Trust, Carrie J.; vp: Loose Trust, Harry Wilson

Bradford, Gary W., trust: Coffey Foundation

Bradford, James C., ptnr: Bradford & Co., J.C.

Bradford, James C., Jr., pres: Bradford & Co. Foundation, J.C.; chmn, dir: New York Stock Exchange Foundation

Bradford, Robert, trust: Bradford Foundation, George and Ruth

Bradford, Robert E., sr vp (pub aff): Safeway, Inc.

Bradford, William E., sr vp: Dresser Industries

Bradish, Mary E., secy: MichCon Foundation

Bradlee, Dudley H., II, vp, trust: Charlesbank Homes; trust: Hornblower Fund, Henry

Bradley, C. Richard, dir: Hayden Foundation, William R. and Virginia

Bradley, Darby, trust: Friendship Fund

Bradley, Elizabeth, trust, secy: Friendship Fund

Bradley, James, dir: Close Foundation; dir: Springs Foundation

Bradley, Jane C., trust: Cabot Family Charitable Trust

Bradley, John, vp (mktg): Cincinnati Financial Corp.

Bradley, John F., trust: Stillwell Charitable Trust, Glen and Dorothy

Bradley, Ronald, dir: Kenedy Memorial Foundation, John G. and Marie Stella

Bradley, S.L., asst treas: Halliburton Foundation

Bradley, William O., trust: Cord Foundation, E. L.

Bradshaw, Donald, trust: Chapman Foundation, William H.

Bradshaw, Lillian Moore, dir: Hoblitzelle Foundation

Bradshaw, Thomas I., trust: McNeil, Jr. Charitable Trust, Robert L.

Brady, Douglas, cfo: Plante & Moran, CPAs

Brady, James C., Jr., pres, treas, trust: Brady Foundation

Brady, Katherine D., trust: Darby Foundation

Brady, Martha, adm (contributions): Kerr-McGee Corp.

Brady, Nicholas F., trust: Darby Foundation

Brady, Nicholas Frederick, trust: Brady Foundation

Brady, Robert T., pres, ceo: Moog, Inc.

Brady, William H., III, dir: Brady Foundation, W. H.

Braga, Mary A., trust: Bodman Foundation

Braga, Mary B., trust: Achelis Foundation

Bragdon, Paul E., trust: Tektronix Foundation

Bragg, C. Bartley, adjunct dir: Educational Foundation of America

Bragg, Carole P., adjunct dir: Educational Foundation of America

Bragin, D. H., treas, asst secy, dir: Winn-Dixie Stores Foundation

Braitmayer, John W., trust: Braitmayer Foundation

Braitmayer, Karen L., trust: Braitmayer Foundation

Brakeley, George A., III, pres, dir: Brakeley, John Price Jones Inc.

Braksick, Norman A., pres: Asgrow Seed Co.

Braly, Hugh C., secy: Anschutz Family Foundation

Braly, Jack E., pres, dir: Beech Aircraft Corp.; dir: Beech Aircraft Foundation

Braman, Mary O'Connor, treas: O'Connor Foundation, Kathryn

Bramble, Forrest F., Jr., trust: Middendorf Foundation

Brame, Scott O., dir: Coughlin-Saunders Foundation

Bramley, Christopher W., pres, ceo: Shawmut Worcester County Bank, N.A.; pres, dir: Shawmut Charitable Foundation

Bramwell, Jerry, pres: Medford Corp.

Branagh, John Charles, pres, dir: Berry Foundation, Lowell

Branch, J. Read, pres, dir: Cabell III and Maude Morgan Cabell Foundation, Robert G.

Branch, J. Read, Jr., dir: Cabell III and Maude Morgan Cabell Foundation, Robert G.

Branch, Marti, admin (corp contributions): Compaq Computer Foundation

Branch, Patteson, Jr., dir: Cabell III and Maude Morgan Cabell Foundation, Robert G.

Branch, William J., Jr., pres, ceo, dir: Masland & Sons, C.H.

Branchini, Melinda L., secy, treas: McDonnell Douglas Foundation

Brand, Constance M., pres, treas: Brand Foundation, C. Harold and Constance

Brand, Elizabeth D., secy: Dalton Foundation, Harry L.

Brand, Louis, dir: Graphic Arts Education & Research Foundation

Brand, Mark J., pres: Amgen Foundation

Brandenburg, R. N., treas, dir: Glaser Foundation

Brandenburg, Shirley C., secy, treas: Ray Foundation

Brandes, Bernard E., dir: Harkness Ballet Foundation; exec dir: Harkness Foundation, William Hale

Brandes, JoAnne, trust: Johnson's Wax Fund

Brandman, Saul, dir: Domino Foundation

Brandon, Christopher, treas, dir: Glancy Foundation, Lenora and Alfred

Brandon, Edward B., chmn, ceo, dir: National City Corp.; trust: Standard Products Co. Foundation

Brandt, Dora, commun aff: Southern Co. Services

Brandt, E. N., vp, secy, trust: Gerstacker Foundation, Rollin M.

Brandt, Yale M., dir: Reynolds Metals Co. Foundation

Branham, William T., dir: Scholl Foundation, Dr.

Brann, Alton J., pres, ceo, dir: Litton Industries

Brannon, Ben W., pres: Livingston Foundation

Brannon, Marguerite, pres: Chicago Tribune Foundation

Brannon, Milton, dir: Livingston Foundation

Branson, James E., secy, treas, dir: Thalhimer Brothers Foundation

Brant, Keith, dir corp commun: Provident Mutual Life Insurance Co. of Philadelphia

Brant, Terri, asst exec secy: Raymond Foundation

Branton, Mary Shaw, sec-treas: Francis Families Foundation

Branum, Frances Daniel, dir: Daniel Foundation of Alabama

Bratton, Teresa, vp, dir: Snite Foundation, Fred B.

Bratwink, Theodore S., exec dir: Harkness Foundation, William Hale

Brauman, Ludwig, vp: Odyssey Partners Foundation

Braun, C. Allan, dir: Braun Foundation

Braun, Henry A., pres, dir: Braun Foundation; trust: Faith Home Foundation

Braun, Hugo E., Jr., vp, secy, trust: Wickes Foundation, Harvey Randall

Braun, John G., dir: Braun Foundation

Braun, Reto, pres, coo, dir: Unisys Corp.

Braun, Richard W., trust: Tilles Nonsectarian Charity Fund, Rosalie

Braun, Victor F., trust: Ladish Co. Foundation; vp, dir: Ladish Family Foundation, Herman W.; vp, dir: Ladish Malting Co. Foundation

Brauner, David A., vp: Goldman Foundation, Herman

Braunlich, Chris V., vp, cfo, treas: Atkinson Co., Guy F.

Brauntuch, Jack, special counsellor: JM Foundation

Brautigam, Virginia, dir: Kent Foundation, Ada Howe

Bravmann, Lotte, dir, secy, treas: Bravmann Foundation, Ludwig

Bravmann, Ludwig, dir, pres: Bravmann Foundation, Ludwig

Brawer, Catherine Coleman, pres, dir: Rosenthal Foundation, Ida and William

Brawer, Robert A., vp, dir: Rosenthal Foundation, Ida and William

Bray, Charles W., pres: Johnson Foundation

Bray, Thomas Joseph, trust: Earhart Foundation

Brayman, Beverly, dir: Pendergast-Weyer Foundation

Brazier, Robert G., pres, coo, dir: Airborne Express Co.

Bready, Richard L., chmn, pres, ceo: Nortek, Inc.; vchmn, dir: Papitto Foundation

Breall, Dr. William, dir: Blackman Foundation, Aaron and Marie

Brecher, Harvey, secy: Scheuer Family Foundation, S. H. and Helen R.

Breece, Margaret B., dir: Board of Trustees of the Prichard School

Breeden, James P., vchmn, dir: New World Foundation

Breeland, William, pres: Smith Oil Corp.

Breen, John Gerald, chmn, ceo, dir: Sherwin-Williams Co.; chmn, trust: Sherwin-Williams Foundation

Breen, Lyon, dir: Sjostrom & Sons Foundation

Breen, Marion I., vp, dir: Starr Foundation

Breene, William E., trust: Phillips Charitable Trust, Dr. and Mrs. Arthur William

Breese, Donald, cfo: Philipps Foundation

Breese, Lauren W., secy: Phillipps Foundation

Breeze, Tom, trust: Strauss Foundation, Leon

Breezley, Roger L., chmn, ceo, dir: US Bancorp

Bregande, Donald R., vp, dir: Fay's Foundation, Inc.

Bregar, H. H., secy, dir: Blum Foundation, Harry and Maribel G.; secy: Blum-Kovler Foundation

Breidenback, Fred A., pres, coo: Gulfstream Aerospace Corp.

Breidenthal, Gary, trust: Breidenthal Foundation, Willard J. and Mary G.

Breidenthal, Mary Ruth, trust: Breidenthal Foundation, Willard J. and Mary G.

Breitmeyer, Julie F., trust: Keller Family Foundation

Bremekamp, Theodore H., III, trust: Raskob Foundation, Bill

Bremer, Patsy R., trust: Raskob Foundation, Bill

Bremer, Richard H., adv: Central & South West Foundation; ceo, pres: Southwestern Electric Power Co.

Bremer, William S., trust: Raskob Foundation, Bill

Bren, Donald Leroy, pres, dir: Bren Foundation, Donald L.

Brenan, Michail R., pres, coo: Bank One, Youngstown, NA

Brendsel, Leland C., chmn, ceo: Federal Home Loan Mortgage Corp. (Freddie Mac); dir: Freddie Mac Foundation

Brengel, Douglas, dir: Nakamichi Foundation, E.

Brengel, Frederick L., chmn, dir: Johnson Controls; chmn adv bd, dir: Johnson Controls Foundation

Brennan, Bernard Francis, chmn, pres, ceo, dir: Montgomery Ward & Co.

Brennan, Edward A., chmn, pres, ceo, dir: Sears, Roebuck and Co.

Brennan, Edward J., Jr., co-trust: Brennan Foundation Trust

Brennan, Herbert J., secy: Sandoz Foundation Am

Brennan, James C., mem bd mgrs: Measey Foundation, Benjamin and Mary Siddons

Brennan, John J., pres: Vanguard Group of Investment Cos.

Brennan, John M., treas, dir: Fletcher Foundation, A. J.

Brennan, Judith S., Jr., co-trust: Brennan Foundation Trust

Brennan, Leo J., Jr., exec dir: Ford Motor Co. Fund

Brennan, Michael J., cfo: Binswanger Co.

Brennan, Patricia A., vp, trust: Brennan Foundation, Robert E.

Brennan, Patrick F., pres, coo, dir: Consolidated Papers; dir: Consolidated Papers Foundation

Brennan, Robert E., pres, trust: Brennan Foundation, Robert E.

Brennan, Sybil Ann, vp: Frank Foundation, Ernest and Elfriede

Brennan, Thomas Paul, mem (corp contributions comm): International Multifoods Corp.

Brennan, Virginia S., trust: Self Foundation

Brenneman, Howard L., dir: Hesston Foundation

Brenner, Abe, pres: Brenner Foundation

Brenner, Charles S., dir: Guttman Foundation, Stella and Charles

Brenner, D. H., pres, dir: Fearn International, Inc.

Brenner, Edgar H., vp, dir: Guttman Foundation, Stella and Charles

Brenner, Gertrude, secy, treas: Brenner Foundation

Brenner, Herb, vp: Brenner Foundation

Brenner, Paul R., trust: Calder Foundation, Louis

Brenninkmeyer, Anthony, pres, dir: Brencanda Foundation

Brenninkmeyer, Roland M., dir: Brencanda Foundation

Brent, Andrew J., secy, dir: Media General Foundation

Brenton, C. Robert, chmn: Brenton Banks Inc.; trust: Brenton Foundation

Brenton, J. C., pres: Brenton Banks Inc.; trust: Brenton Foundation

Brenton, William H., vchmn: Brenton Banks Inc.; trust: Brenton Foundation

Breon, Helen, trust: Montgomery Foundation

Bresky, H. H., pres: Seaboard Corp.

Breslauer, Gerald, pres, dir: Max Charitable Foundation

Breslaver, Benjamin F., trust: Soref Foundation, Samuel M. Soref and Helene K.

Breslin, Nancy K., dir: Noble Foundation, Edward John

Breslow, Warren, dir, secy: Goldrich Family Foundation

Bresnahan, William M., mktg & sales mgr: Boston Mutual Life Insurance Co.

Bresnahan, William W., vchmn, dir: Finnegan Foundation, John D.

Bressler, Alfred W., vp, treas, dir: Moses Fund, Henry and Lucy

Bressler, Richard M., chmn, dir: Burlington Resources; dir: Burlington Resources Foundation

Brettbard, Robert, trust: Burnham Foundation

Brevig, Yasue, allocation comm: Kawabe Memorial Fund

Brewer, Ann Fraser, trust: Vidda Foundation

Brewer, Candice, mem (contributions comm): PacifiCorp Foundation

Brewer, Cornelia B., asst secy: Georgia-Pacific Foundation

Brewer, Janet, trust: Reynolds & Reynolds Company Foundation

Brewer, Oliver Gordon, Jr., treas, dir: Alco Standard Foundation

Brewer, Sebert, Jr., pres, trust: Benwood Foundation

Brewerton, Iris G., dir: Redfield Foundation, Nell J.

Brewster, Andre W., trust: Isaacs Foundation, Harry Z.

Brewster, Pamela H., trust: Bullitt Foundation

Brewster, Walter W., secy: Brown & Sons Charitable Foundation, Alex

Brewton, Kenneth L., Jr., vp: Sandoz Foundation Am

Breyer, Henry W., III, dir, pres: Breyer Foundation

Breyer, Joanne, trust: Breyer Foundation

Breyer, Margaret McKee, dir, secy: Breyer Foundation

Brice, Deborah L., trust: Loeb Foundation, Frances and John L.

Brice, Houston A., Jr., chmn: Brice Building Co., Inc.

Bricker, John F., chmn, pres, trust: Booth-Bricker Fund; dir: Schlieder Educational Foundation, Edward G.

Brickner, Bulfour, vp: Reicher Foundation, Anne & Harry J.

Brickner, Ronald J., sr vp, cfo: Chemed Corp.

Brickson, Richard A., asst secy: May Stores Foundation

Bridge, Almon H., Jr., vp: Massachusetts Charitable Mechanics Association

Bridgeland, James R., Jr., secy, trust: Semple Foundation, Louise Taft; trust: Star Bank, N.A., Cincinnati Foundation

Bridgeman, Jeannette C., treas, asst secy: Beazley Foundation; treas, asst secy: Frederick Foundation

Bridges, Kathryn T., chmn: Tomlinson Foundation, Kate and Elwyn

Bridges, Kenneth, trust: McMahon Foundation

Bridges, Wilbur Y., pres, secy: Smith Charities, John

Bridgewater, B. A., Jr., chmn, trust: Brown Foundation, George Warren; chmn, ceo, pres, dir: Brown Group; mem bd control: Brown Group Incorporated Charitable Trust

Bridgforth, W.R., trust: Johnson Day Trust, Carl and Virginia

Bridwell, Ralph S., dir: Bridwell Foundation, J. S.

Brier, Harvey, chmn, ceo: Dellwood Foods, Inc.

Briesch, John, deputy pres (sales & mktg): Sony Corp. of America

Brigel, Barbara, secy: Crown Memorial, Arie and Ida

Briggs, Eleanore, dir: Griggs and Mary Griggs Burke Foundation, Mary Livingston

Briggs, Graham D., dir: General Motors Foundation

Briggs, John N., pres: Briggs Family Foundation

Briggs, Paul W., chmn exec & fin comm: Rochester Gas & Electric Corp.

Brigham, Dana P., mgr: Larsh Foundation Charitable Trust

Brigham, David, trust: Wenner-Gren Foundation for Anthropological Research

Brigham, Margaret Hoover, vp, secy, trust: Hoover, Jr. Foundation, Margaret W. and Herbert

Brigham, Sallie, pres, dir: Kentucky Foundation for Women

Bright, Calvin, pres: Bright Family Foundation

Bright, James R., trust: Tippit Charitable Trust, C. Carlisle and Margaret M.

Bright, Lyn, secy, treas: Bright Family Foundation

Bright, Marjorie, vp: Bright Family Foundation

Bright, S. J., chmn, pres, ceo: Iowa-Illinois Gas & Electric Co.

Bright, Sam Raymond, vp, dir: Fair Foundation, R. W.

Brightbill, Frederick M., vp (mktg): Carol Cable Co.

Brighton, Cynthia Zeigler, dir: Ziegler Foundation for the Blind, E. Matilda

Brill, Arthur W., treas, dir: Whitehead Charitable Foundation

Briloff, Abraham J., dir, vp: Eckman Charitable Foundation, Samuel and Rae

Brinberg, Simeon, dir: Wishnick Foundation, Robert I.

Brinckman, Donald W., chmn, pres, ceo, coo, dir: Safety-Kleen Corp.

Brine, Kevin R., trust: Bernstein & Co. Foundation, Sanford C.

Brinegar, Claude Stout, vchmn, exec vp, dir: Unocal Corp.; trust: Unocal Foundation

Briner, Daniel G., secy, dir: Mosinee Paper Corp. Foundation

Bring, Robert L., trust: Towsley Foundation, Harry A. and Margaret D.

Brink, W. P., treas, dir: Square D Foundation

Brinker, Norman, trust: Brinker Girls' Tennis Foundation, Maureen Connolly

Brinkerhoff, Philip R., chmn, pres, ceo, dir: Financial Corp. of Santa Barbara

Brinkley, N. B., vchmn, dir: Bank of America

Brinkman, Earl W., dir: Davenport-Hatch Foundation

Brinkman, Lloyd D., chmn, ceo: LDB Corp.

Brinkman, Robert J., dir: Davenport-Hatch Foundation

Brinn, Lawrence E., L and L Foundation

Brinn, Mildred C., dir, vp, treas: Piankova Foundation, Tatiana

Brinn, Mildred Cunningham, pres, treas, dir: L and L Foundation

Brinsfield, Shirley D., chmn, pres, ceo, coo: Curtiss-Wright Corp.

Brinton, S. Jervis, Jr., trust, mem: Rippel Foundation, Fannie E.

Brinzo, J. S., trust: Cleveland-Cliffs Foundation

Briscoe, Virginia Wolf, trust: Wolf Foundation, Benjamin and Fredora K.

Briselli, Iso, pres, dir: Fels Fund, Samuel S.

Briskin, Bernard, ceo, pres, dir: Arden Group, Inc.

Briskman, Louis J., trust: Westinghouse Foundation

Bristol, Barbara F., vp: Fruehauf Foundation

Bristow, Aurelia B., vp, trust: Barnes Foundation

Bristow, Elliot B., trust: Barnes Foundation

Brittain, Warner L., vp: Loats Foundation

Brittenham, Raymond Lee, secy, dir, mem exec, audit & fin comms: Tinker Foundation

Britton, Charles S., II, pres, trust: Britton Fund

Britton, Gertrude, vp, trust: Britton Fund

Britton, Lynda R., trust: Britton Fund

Broad, Eli L., co-fdr, chmn, pres, ceo: Broad, Inc.; co-fdr, chmn, pres, ceo: Kaufman & Broad Home Corp.

Broad, Morris N., vp, treas, dir: Broad Foundation, Shepard

Broad, Shepard, pres, dir: Broad Foundation, Shepard

Broad, William L., trust: Mather Fund, Richard

Broadbent, Robert R., vp, trust: Murphy Foundation, John P.

Broadfoot, John W., dir: Meadows Foundation

Broadfoot, Vela, trust, dir: Meadows Foundation

Broadhead, G., dir: Mobil Foundation

Broadhead, James L., ceo, dir: FPL Group Foundation

Broadus, Thomas R., Jr., managing dir: Price Associates, T. Rowe; vp: Price Associates Foundation, T. Rowe

Broccoli, Albert R., pres: Broccoli Charitable Foundation, Dana and Albert R.

Broccoli, Dana, Broccoli Charitable Foundation, Dana and Albert R.

Brochstein, Bertha, trust: Brochsteins Foundation

Brochstein, I. S., trust: Brochsteins Foundation

Brochstein, Joel, trust: Brochsteins Foundation

Brochstein, Mildred, trust: Brochsteins Foundation

Brochstein, Raymond D., ceo: Brochsteins Inc.

Brochstein, S. J., trust: Brochsteins Foundation

Brock, Frank A., trust: Maclellan Foundation

Brock, Harry, III, pres: Central Bank Foundation

Brock, Harry B., Jr., chmn, fdr: Central Bank of the South; trust: Central Bank Foundation; pres: Daniel Foundation of Alabama

Burns, Ingrid Lilly, trust: Frohlich Charitable Trust, Ludwig W.

Burns, J. W., chmn: Great-West Life Assurance Co.

Burns, Jacob, pres, treas: Burns Foundation, Jacob

Burns, Joan, admin: Honda of America Foundation

Burns, John, treas: National Pro-Am Youth Fund

Burns, John D., chmn, pres, ceo: Vista Chemical Company

Burns, Katherine S., trust: Associated Foundations; trust: Fusenot Charity Foundation, Georges and Germaine

Burns, Lucy Keating, dir, pres: Burns Family Foundation

Burns, M. Anthony, chmn, pres, ceo, dir: Ryder System; pres, dir: Ryder System Charitable Foundation

Burns, Rex, dir: Mid-Iowa Health Foundation

Burns, Ronald J., trust: Enron Foundation

Burns, Ruthelen Griffith, adv: Griffith Foundation, W. C.

Burns, Sheila O'Connor, dir: Burns Foundation

Burns, Thomas R., trust: Frohlich Charitable Trust, Ludwig W.

Burns, W. Haywood, trust: Boehm Foundation

Burns, William J., vp: Charitable Foundation of the Burns Family

Burns, William L., Jr., pres, ceo: CCB Financial Corp.

Burns, William R., pres: Burns International; pres, dir: Burns International Foundation

Burr, Francis Hardon, trust: Humane Society of the Commonwealth of Massachusetts; trust: River Road Charitable Corporation; trust: Vingo Trust II

Burr, Malcolm S., trust: Massachusetts Charitable Mechanics Association

Burrell, Craig D., vp: Sandoz Foundation Am

Burrell, Jack, trust: Luse Foundation, W. P. and Bulah

Burrell, Jack L., Jr., trust: Luse Foundation, W. P. and Bulah

Burrell, Richard L., treas: Barry Foundation

Burress, John W., III, pres, treas: Burress Foundation, J.W.

Burress, John W., pres: Burress, J.W.

Burress, Pam, vp, treas: Burress Foundation, J.W.

Burrill, W. Gregory, trust: Hopedale Foundation

Burroughs, Hugh C., vp: Kaiser Family Foundation, Henry J.

Burrow, Harold, vchmn, dir: American Natural Resources Co.; vchmn, dir: Colorado Interstate Gas Co.

Burrows, Sunny Harvey, asst secy: Harvey Foundation, Felix

Burrus, Clark D., vp, dir: First National Bank of Chicago Foundation

Burrus, Robert L., Jr., trust: Circuit City Foundation

Burrus, Robert Lewis, Jr., secy, dir: Best Products Foundation

Burstein, Jack D., pres, ceo, dir: American Capital Corp.

Burt, Barbara, dir: Foellinger Foundation

Burt, Eva M., program asst: Samuels Foundation, Fan Fox and Leslie R.

Burt, James Melvin, sr vp: California & Hawaiian Sugar Co.

Burt, Robert, comm mem: Pendleton Memorial Fund, William L. and Ruth T.

Burt, Robert N., chmn, pres, ceo: FMC Corp.; dir: FMC Foundation

Burton, Arthur H., Jr., vchmn: Prudential-Bache Securities

Burton, Courtney, chmn emeritus: Oglebay Norton Co.; pres, trust: Oglebay Norton Foundation

Burton, Donald E., trust: Lowe Foundation

Burton, Marion, trust: Rockefeller Trust, Winthrop

Burton, R.C., Jr., ceo, pres: T.T.X. Co.

Burton, Sally F., mgr: Brush Foundation

Burts, Stephen L., Jr., pres, treas, cfo: Synovus Financial Corp.

Bury, Anita, asst secy: Regenstein Foundation

Busboom, Larry, pres: Sun-Diamond Growers of California

Busby, Gail, secy: Daily News Foundation

Busch, August Adolphus, III, chmn, pres, dir: Anheuser-Busch Cos.

Busch, Howard, dir: Smith Foundation

Busche, Eugene Marvin, vchmn, trust: Jordan Foundation, Arthur

Buschmann, Siegfried, chmn, ceo: Budd Co.

Bush, Bob G., dir: Reynolds Foundation, Donald W.

Bush, Donald P., Jr., vp: Chubb Foundation

Bush, G. Kenner, pres, cfo, publ, treas: Messenger Publishing Co.

Bush, John, vp, dir: Animal Assistance Foundation

Bush, Nancy, dir: Bank of San Francisco Foundation

Bush, Robert, chmn: Schreiber Foods, Inc.; pres, dir: Bush-D.D. Nusbaum Foundation, M.G.

Bush, Travis, dir: Mills Foundation, Ralph E.

Bush, Werner F., exec vp, coo: Ferro Corp.

Bushardt, Jeff, mgr (empl rels): Chicago Pneumatic Tool Co.

Bushyeager, Peter, program off health & human svcs: Prudential Foundation

Buske, Wayne R., secy-treas: Wisconsin Centrifugal Charitable Foundation

Buss, Dennis, vp (technology): Analog Devices

Bussel, Ann B., vp, secy, dir: Broad Foundation, Shepard

Bussett, Fred W., dir: Davis Family - W.D. Charities, Tine W.

Bussmann, Charles Haines, vp, dir: Atlantic Foundation

Butcher, Robert, sr exec vp, cfo: Marine Midland Banks

Butkiewicz, Ronald M., pres: Inter-State Assurance Co.

Butler, Andrew J., trust: Dow Chemical Co.

Butler, Carol H., pres, trust: Humphrey Fund, George M. and Pamela S.

Butler, Clarence C., trust: Bradley-Turner Foundation

Butler, Eugene W., treas: Norris Foundation, Dellora A. and Lester J.

Butler, Fred M., pres, ceo: Manitowoc Co.

Butler, George, trust: Kyle Educational Trust, S. H. and D. W.

Butler, George A., ceo, chmn: First Pennsylvania Bank NA

Butler, George L., dir: Olmsted Foundation, George and Carol

Butler, Gladys A., trust: Butler Family Foundation, George W. and Gladys S.

Butler, Henry King, dir: Christy-Houston Foundation

Butler, Herbert Johnson, trust: Johnston-Hanson Foundation

Butler, J. Murfree, vcmn, dir: Grace & Co., W.R.; chmn, dir: Grace Foundation, Inc.

Butler, James G., dir: Lannan Foundation

Butler, Joann, coordinator commun svcs: SCANA Corp.

Butler, John G., vp, trust: Humphrey Fund, George M. and Pamela S.

Butler, John J., trust: Scott Paper Co. Foundation

Butler, John K., treas, trust: Butler Family Foundation, Patrick and Aimee

Butler, John P., hon trust: Abell-Hanger Foundation

Butler, John R., pres, treas, dir: JJJ Foundation

Butler, John W., vp: Chamberlin Foundation, Gerald W.

Butler, Katharine, trust: Brace Foundation, Donald C.

Butler, Lewis H., dir: Joyce Foundation

Butler, Lynne G., trust: Butler Family Foundation, George W. and Gladys S.

Butler, Mary D., secy, treas: Switzer Foundation

Butler, Patricia, trust: Butler Family Foundation, Patrick and Aimee

Butler, Patrick, Jr., vp, trust: Butler Family Foundation, Patrick and Aimee

Butler, Peter M., pres, trust: Butler Family Foundation, Patrick and Aimee

Butler, Rhett W., trust: Butler Family Foundation, George W. and Gladys S.

Butler, Sandra K., trust: Butler Family Foundation, Patrick and Aimee

Butler, Sarah T., trust: Bradley-Turner Foundation

Butler, Stephen T., chmn, trust: Bradley-Turner Foundation

Butler, Susan L., exec dir: Best Products Foundation

Butler, Susan Storz, trust: Storz Foundation, Robert Herman

Butler, William E., pres, coo, dir: Eaton Corp.

Butler, William G., trust: Shelden Fund, Elizabeth, Allan and Warren

Butler, William J., secy, dir: Richmond Foundation, Frederick W.; trust: Stark Foundation, Nelda C. and H. J. Lutcher

Butner, James S., dir: ABC Foundation

Butson, Lowell Anne, secy, exec dir: Murray Foundation

Butterbaugh, Bonnie S., exec secy: Wagnalls Memorial

Butterfield, Bruce B., trust: Merchants Bank Foundation

Butterfield, Donald G., MD, trust: Colorado Trust

Butterfield, Hazel L., trust, pres: Shinnick Educational Fund, William M.

Butterfield, Reeder, vp: Osher Foundation, Bernard

Butterfield, Sharon, trust: Eastman Foundation, Alexander

Butters, Gerald, pres: Northern Telecom Inc.

Butterwieser, Lawrence C., secy: Rodgers Foundation, Richard & Dorothy

Butterworth, Edward L., pres, ceo: Fedco, Inc.

Butterworth, George W., III, treas: Boston Fatherless and Widows Society; secy, dir: Harvard Musical Association

Butterworth, Kenneth W., chmn, dir: Loctite Corp.

Butz, Barbara, dir, vp, secy: Butz Foundation

Butz, Elvira M., trust: Butz Foundation

Butz, Herbert K., trust: Butz Foundation

Butz, Roger, M.D., mem (contributions comm): SAFECO Corp.

Butz, Theodore H., dir, treas: Butz Foundation

Butz, Thompson H., trust: Butz Foundation

Butzow, George N., chmn, dir: MTS Systems Corp.

Buxton, Charles I., II, chmn, ceo: Federated Life Insurance Co.; pres: Federated Life Insurance Foundation

Buxton, Winslow H., pres, coo: Pentair

Buya, Wallace Joseph, vp, secy, exec dir: AON Foundation

Buye, Susan, treas, dir: Cowles Media Foundation

Buyer, James G., asst to pres: Northern Indiana Public Service Co.

Buyers, John W. A., chmn, dir: Brewer and Co., Ltd., C.

Buzzard, Glen W., chmn, dir: Siebert Lutheran Foundation

Byard, Spencer, trust: Sullivan Musical Foundation, William Matheus

Bye, James E., bd mem: Piton Foundation

Byer, P. Roger, cfo: KDI Corp.

Byerly, Stacy S., dir: Stokely, Jr. Foundation, William B.

Byers, Allan, coo: FDL Foods/Dubuque Packing Co.

Byers, Deborah, contact person: Howard and Bush Foundation

Byers, Karen D., fin off: Markle Foundation, John and Mary R.

Byers, R. A., trust: Pittsburgh-Des Moines Inc. Charitable Trust

Byham, W. C., ceo, pres: Development Dimensions International

Byland, Peter, chmn: Holman Foundation

Byrd, Ann, dir: Kirkpatrick Foundation

Byrd, D. Harold, Jr., trust: Hillcrest Foundation

Byrd, Edward R., cfo: Pacific Mutual Charitable Foundation

Byrd, Richard E., trust: Sailors' Snug Harbor of Boston

Byrd, Richard H., treas: Borden Foundation

Byrne, Brendan, dir: Carvel Foundation, Thomas and Agnes

Byrne, Leonard, dir, chmn: Piedmont Health Care Foundation

Byrne, Margaret Lea, vp, treas, dir: McKenzie Family Foundation, Richard

Byrne, Patricia, coordinator: Primerica Foundation

Byrne, William J., Jr., pres: Pittston Co.

Byrns, Priscilla U., trust: Upton Foundation, Frederick S.

Byrom, Fletcher L., dir: New Street Foundation

Byron, Kimberly, community rels and fdn mgr: Toyota Motor Sales, U.S.A.

Bystrom, Marcia J., first vchmn, dir: Northwest Area Foundation

C

Caamano, Rafael F., trust: Homeland Foundation

Cabell, Charles, dir: Cabell III and Maude Morgan Cabell Foundation, Robert G.

Cabell, Robert G., vp: Cabell III and Maude Morgan Cabell Foundation, Robert G.

Cabell, Royal E., Jr., secy, dir: Cabell III and Maude Morgan Cabell Foundation, Robert G.; secy, trust: Scott Foundation, William R., John G., and Emma

Cable, Austin, trust: Rubenstein Charitable Foundation, Lawrence J. and Anne

Cable, Wade, pres: Presley Cos.

Cabot, Anne P., secy: Perkins Memorial Foundation, George W.

Cabot, John Godfrey Lowell, trust: Cabot Family Charitable Trust

Cabot, Louis Wellington, dir: Cabot Corp. Foundation; trust: Cabot Family Charitable Trust

Cabot, Maryellen, dir: Cabot Corp. Foundation

Cabot, Paul C., Jr., trust: Cabot-Saltonstall Charitable Trust

Cabot, Paul Codman, trust: Cabot-Saltonstall Charitable Trust

Cabot, Powell M., dir: Guggenheim Foundation, Daniel and Florence

Cabot, Samuel, III, pres: Cabot Stains

Cabot, Thomas Dudley, dir: Cabot Corp. Foundation

Cabot, Virginia C., trust: Cabot-Saltonstall Charitable Trust

Cabral, Mary L., asst contr: Weyerhaeuser Co. Foundation

Caccavaro, George, ceo: Cone-Blanchard Machine Co.

Caceres, Ann R., trust: Russell Educational Foundation, Benjamin and Roberta

Cacioppo, Joseph, Jr., pres: Cacioppo Foundation, Joseph & Mary

Cacioppo, Mary, vp: Cacioppo Foundation, Joseph & Mary

Cadbury, Dominic, ceo: Cadbury Beverages Inc.

Caddock, Anne M., vp: Caddock Foundation

Caddock, Richard E., pres: Caddock Foundation

Caddock, Richard E., Jr., treas: Caddock Foundation

Cadger, Laura, secy, treas, dir: Martin & Deborah Flug Foundation

Cadieux, Robert D., exec vp, dir: Amoco Corp.

Candlish, Malcolm, chmn, pres, ceo, dir: Sealy, Inc.

Cane, Myles A., pres: Slaughter Foundation, Charles

Canellos, Peter C., asst vp: Wachtell, Lipton, Rosen & Katz Foundation

Canepa, Patricia, pres, dir: Treadwell Foundation, Nora Eccles

Canham, Colin A., consultant: Shaw Fund for Mariner's Children

Cann, Samuel A., trust: Huston Charitable Trust, Stewart

Cannell, Timothy A., vp, gen mgr: Guth Lighting Co.

Cannestra, K. W., dir: Lockheed Leadership Fund

Canning, J.B., secy: ITT Rayonier Foundation

Cannon, Charles G., trust: Gates Foundation

Cannon, George, trust: Buell Foundation, Temple Hoyne

Cannon, James, vchmn, cfo, dir: BBDO Worldwide

Cannon, James W., mem (contributions comm): SAFECO Corp.

Cannon, Ted, secy, treas: Quivey-Bay State Foundation

Cannon, W. C., Jr., dir, mem: Cannon Foundation

Cannon, William Ragsdale, chmn: Pitts Foundation, William H. and Lula E.

Cano, Margarita, dir: Cintas Foundation

Canoles, LeRoy T., Jr., trust: Beazley Foundation; trust: Frederick Foundation

Canon, Joseph E., exec vp, dir: Dodge Jones Foundation

Cant, Donald R., trust: Brody Foundation, Carolyn and Kenneth D.

Cantacuzne, Melissa, dir: Post Foundation of D.C., Marjorie Merriweather

Canter, Roger, bd mem: Roberts Foundation, Dora

Canterbury, Ralph B., vchmn: CUNA Mutual Insurance Group; pres: CUNA Mutual Charitable Foundation

Cantor, Arthur, chmn, dir: Rose Foundation, Billy

Cantor, Bernard Gerald, don, vp, trust, mem: Cantor Foundation, Iris and B. Gerald

Cantor, Iris, pres, trust: Cantor Foundation, Iris and B. Gerald

Cantrell, Barbara B., secy, treas, dir: Strong Foundation, Hattie M.

Cantrell, J. C., dir: Collins Foundation, Carr P.

Cantrell, John K., chmn, ceo: Commonwealth Industries Corp.

Cantrell, Wesley E., Jr., pres, ceo: Lanier Business Products, Inc.

Capanna, Robert, trust: Presser Foundation

Capell, Odette, secy: Baker Foundation, Clark and Ruby

Capita, Robert, vp: Capita Charitable Trust, Emil

Capitano, Nick, trust: Jones Intercable Tampa Trust

Caplan, Eli, dir: Caplan Charity Foundation, Julius H.; pres, treas: Keystone Weaving Mills

Caplan, Helen, dir: Caplan Charity Foundation, Julius H.

Caplan, Perry, dir: Caplan Charity Foundation, Julius H.

Capo, T. P., asst treas: Chrysler Corp. Fund

Caporali, Renso L., chmn, pres, ceo: Grumman Corp.

Cappadonna, Mitchell A., trust: Beal Foundation

Capps, Edward, vp (human rels): Jones Construction Co., J.A.

Capps, Joanna, info systems: Newmont Mining Corp.

Capps, Robert P., chmn, cfo: Hadson Foundation

Caprancia, Ruth M., trust, secy: Knapp Educational Fund

Capranica, Ruth, secy: Knapp Foundation

Capron, Jeffery P., treas, trust: Fowler Memorial Foundation, John Edward

Capua, James V., pres: Donner Foundation, William H.

Carballada, R. Carlos, pres, ceo, dir: Central Trust Co.

Cardello, Ann L., adm: Boston Edison Foundation

Carden, Isabell, dir, special programs: Hanson Office Products

Carden, Willie, Jr., dir: New Orphan Asylum Scholarship Foundation

Cardoza, K. H., Crane Fund for Widows and Children

Cardwell, Charles P., III, pres: Metropolitan Health Foundation

Cardy, Robert W., chmn, pres, coo: Carpenter Technology Corp.; chmn: Carpenter Technology Corp. Foundation

Caren, Robert Poston, PhD, dir: Lockheed Leadership Fund

Carew, Martin J., Hornblower Fund, Henry

Carey, C. William, chmn, ceo: Town & Country Corp.

Carey, Chase, exec vp, coo: Twentieth Century-Fox Film Corp.

Carey, John J., chmn, ceo: Allendale Mutual Insurance Co.; dir: Allendale Insurance Foundation

Carey, Kathryn, exec dir: American Honda Foundation

Carey, Margaret H., trust, secy: O'Fallon Trust, Martin J. and Mary Anne

Carey, Raymond J., pres: Carey Industries

Carey, Robert R., pres, ceo: Central Power & Light Co.; adv: Central & South West Foundation

Cargill, James R., vp, dir: Cargill Foundation

Cargo, Robert C., secy: Mars Foundation

Carhart, Mary F., secy: Nalco Foundation

Carina, Arthur, cfo: Bank One, Youngstown, NA

Carl, John, vp: MPCo/Entech Foundation

Carley, Joan Davidson, secy, treas, dir: Cunningham Foundation, Laura Moore

Carley, John B., pres, coo, dir: Albertson's

Carlin, F. Taylor, adv: AMCORE Foundation, Inc.

Carlone, Marie, treas, mem trust comm: Bergen Foundation, Frank and Lydia

Carlos, Michael C., pres, ceo: National Distributing Co., Inc.; pres, ceo: Raleigh Linen Service/National Distributing Co.

Carlson, Arthur G., Jr., exec dir: Linnell Foundation

Carlson, C. Dean, pres, ceo: National By-Products; pres, dir: National By-Products Foundation

Carlson, Carl, Jr., vp, dir: Lytel Foundation, Bertha Russ

Carlson, Curtis Leroy, chmn, ceo, dir: Carlson Cos.

Carlson, Harry, vchmn, dir: Lincoln Electric Co.

Carlson, Herbert E., Jr., pres: Vance Charitable Foundation, Robert C.

Carlson, J. Charles, trust: Peabody Foundation

Carlson, James E., vchmn, dir: Spring Arbor Distributors

Carlson, John F., chmn, ceo, dir: Cray Research

Carlson, Kathleen, contact: Equitable Foundation

Carlson, Kathy, mgr community resources: Portland General Electric Co.

Carlson, Maxwell, trust: Bloedel Foundation

Carlson, Richard, scholarship comm: Mitchell, Jr. Trust, Oscar

Carlson, Richard H., exec dir: Alworth Memorial Fund, Marshall H. and Nellie

Carlson, Robert J., chmn, ceo: Case Co., J.I.

Carlson, Roderick, exec dir: Hewlett-Packard Co.

Carlstrom, R. W., exec dir: Glaser Foundation

Carlton, Jerry W., chmn, pres, trust: Day Foundation, Willametta K.

Carlucci, Frank, dir: Quaker Oats Foundation

Carmack, John M., asst secy: Bireley Foundation

Carmack, Marion D., Jr., trust: Loats Foundation

Carman, Peter, trust: Bernstein & Co. Foundation, Sanford C.

Carmany, James P., chmn, pres, ceo: Comprehensive Care Corp.

Carmichael, W.P., sr vp, cfo: Norton Simon Inc.

Carmody, Thomas Roswell, pres, ceo, dir: American Business Products, Inc.

Carnahan, Michael L., pres, trust: C & H Charitable Trust

Carnell, James E., Jr., dir: Life Sciences Research Foundation

Carner, Donald C., trust: Miller Foundation, Earl B. and Loraine H.

Carney, David, cfo: Corestates Bank

Carney, John, trust: Hunt Manufacturing Co. Foundation

Carney, Joseph D., vp, dir: Giddings & Lewis Foundation

Carney, Victoria, trust: Johnston-Hanson Foundation

Carney, W. Peter, secy, trust: Harris Foundation

Caro, Herman, dir: Neu Foundation, Hugo and Doris

Carothers, Lucille K., dir: Klau Foundation, David W. and Sadie

Carothers, Suzanne, Bowne Foundation, Robert

Carparelli, Peter, trust: First Interstate Banks of Billings Centennial Youth Foundation

Carpenter, Adelaide de Menil, dir: Menil Foundation

Carpenter, David R., exec vp, dir: Transamerica Fdn.; chmn, pres, ceo: Transamerica Occidental Life Insurance Co.

Carpenter, Donald P., treas, dir: Cuesta Foundation

Carpenter, Dunbar, treas, trust: Carpenter Foundation

Carpenter, Edmund M., chmn, ceo, dir: General Signal Corp.

Carpenter, Edmund N., II, secy, treas, dir: Good Samaritan

Carpenter, Gordon R., exec dir, trust: Sumners Foundation, Hatton W.

Carpenter, H. Daniel, trust: Perley Fund, Victor E.

Carpenter, Jane H., pres, trust: Carpenter Foundation

Carpenter, Karen H., trust: Parker Foundation, Theodore Edson

Carpenter, Lon P., sr vp: Cullen/Frost Bankers

Carpenter, Marshall L., cfo, vp: MTS Systems Corp.

Carpenter, Michael Alan, chmn, pres, ceo: Kidder, Peabody & Co.

Carpenter, Richard A., pres, ceo, treas: Index Technology Corp.; pres: Index Technology Foundation

Carpenter, Richard M., pres, ceo: Johnson & Son, S.C.

Carpenter, Robert Ruliph Morgan, Jr., trust, vp: Carpenter Foundation

Carpenter, Thomas W., secy, dir: Kuyper Foundation, Peter H. and E. Lucille Gaass

Carper, Patricia Ikeda, dir (commun rels): Federated Department Stores and Allied Stores Corp.

Carr, Barbara, Johnson Inc., Axel

Carr, F. William, Jr., trust: Dougherty, Jr. Foundation, James R.

Carr, Harold, vp (pub rels) Boeing Co: Boeing Co.

Carr, Howard E., dir: Sternberger Foundation, Sigmund

Carr, Hugh E., pres, ceo: Trion; trust: Trion Charitable Foundation

Carr, Justice M., dir: East Foundation, Sarita Kenedy

Carr, Kathleen D. H., trust: Loyola Foundation

Carr, Patricia, asst secy: China Medical Board of New York

Carr, Richard G., pres, trust: Tomkins Corporation Foundation

Carr, Robert, dir: Capezio-Ballet Makers Dance Foundation; pres, ceo: Carr Real Estate Services

Carr, Shirley Hall, trust: Hall Foundation

Carr, Thomas P., secy, dir: Thomas Memorial Foundation, Theresa A.

Carranza, Reuban, Marshall Foundation

Carras, Barbara D., trust: Dow Fund, Alden and Vada

Carraway, Gertrude S., vchmn, dir: Kellenberger Historical Foundation, May Gordon Latham

Carrell, Stewart, chmn, ceo: Diasonics, Inc.

Carrico, James T., treas: Wiegand Foundation, E. L.

Carrico, John D., secy, treas, trust: International Foundation

Carrico, John D., Jr., asst secy, asst treas: International Foundation

Carrigan, Geraldine, trust: Eaton Foundation, Edwin M. and Gertrude S.

Carrigan, Mike, vp, gm: Warner Electric Brake & Clutch Co.

Carrigg, James, chmn, pres, ceo, dir: New York State Electric & Gas Corp.

Carrington, Janet A., off: Noyes, Jr. Memorial Foundation, Nicholas H.

Carrol, Donald R., trust: Perkins Foundation, B. F. & Rose H.

Carroll, Barry J., trust: Carroll Foundation

Carroll, Daniel B., trust: Massey Charitable Trust

Carroll, David, mem adv comm: LTV Foundation

Carroll, Deborah, secy: Young & Rubicam Foundation

Carroll, Denis H., trust: Carroll Foundation

Carroll, Gordon G., bd mem: Precision Rubber Products Foundation

Carroll, J., ceo: Precision Rubber Products

Carroll, James, pres, ceo, dir: Wynn's International, Inc.

Carroll, Jane, dir, treas: Bauervic Foundation, Peggy; trust: HKH Foundation

Carroll, Jeffrey, trust: Bauervic Foundation, Peggy

Carroll, Joe J., vp, treas, contr: CIT Group Foundation

Carroll, John D., pres, ceo: Williamson Co.

Carroll, Joseph J., exec vp, cfo: CIT Group Holdings

Carroll, Leffert G., exec vp, cfo: IMO Industries Inc.

Carroll, Lynne M., dir, vp: Bauervic Foundation, Peggy

Carroll, Margaret, secy: GAR Foundation

Carroll, Milton, dir: Houston Endowment

Carroll, Philip Joseph, mem exec comm, dir: Shell Oil Co. Foundation

Carroll, Robert C., pres: Goldome Foundation

Carroll, Thomas F., asst secy: Rand McNally Foundation

Carroll, Thomas W., adv: Weezie Foundation

Carroll, Wallace E., Jr., trust: Carroll Foundation

Carroll, Wallace Edward, trust: Carroll Foundation

Carroll, Walter J., exec dir, trust: Massey Charitable Trust

Carruth, Allen H., chmn, pres: Wortham Foundation

Carruth, Brady F., vp, asst treas: Wortham Foundation

Carry, Jean K., pres, treas: Aid Association for the Blind

Carsky, Katherine, trust: Robinson Fund, Maurice R.

Carson, Carl, trust: Packer Foundation, Horace B.

Carson, David E.A., ceo, pres: People's Bank

Carson, Kenneth A., asst secy: Macmillan Foundation

Carstarphen, J.M., vchmn, ceo, treas: R. L. Stowe Mills Inc.

Carsten, Robert, pres: Deer Valley Farm

Carswell, Bruce, trust: GTE Foundation

Carswell, Gale Fisher, mem comm beneficiaries: Wilcox General Trust, George N.; trust: Wilcox Trust, S. W.

Carte, Ira F., chmn: Hubbard Farms Charitable Foundation

Carter, Anne Pitts, trust: Sage Foundation, Russell

Carter, Ashton Baldwin, trust: German Marshall Fund of the United States

Carter, Connie, mgr: PSI Foundation

Carter, David R., exec vp, cfo: Trustmark National Bank

Carter, E.L., secy: Solo Cup Foundation

Carter, Edward F., Ritchie Memorial Foundation, Charles E. and Mabel M.

Carter, Edwin L., mem distribution comm: Frear Eleemosynary Trust, Mary D. and Walter F.; chmn distribution comm: McInerny Foundation; chmn comm beneficiaries: Wilcox General Trust, George N.

Carter, Emma Leigh, Zachry Co., H. B.

Carter, Francis C., chmn distribution comm, mem investigating comm: Champlin Foundations

Carter, Frederic D., Jr., pres: Palmer Fund, Francis Asbury

Carter, George, dir: Carter Star Telegram Employees Fund, Amon G.

Carter, Gordon E., pres: Library Association of Warehoue Point

Carter, H. William, Jr., admin: Bailey Foundation

Carter, Hugh C., dir: Powell Foundation, Charles Lee

Carter, Imadell, secy, trust: Anderson Charitable Trust, Josephine

Carter, J. D., sr vp, secy: Bechtel Foundation

Carter, John Boyd, Jr., dir: Kleberg, Jr. and Helen C. Kleberg Foundation, Robert J.

Carter, Lee A., treas, trust: Emery Memorial, Thomas J.

Carter, Lisle C., trust: Prudential Foundation

Carter, Margaret J., asst secy: Holt Foundation, William Knox

Carter, Marie E. C., trust: Carter Charitable Trust, Wilbur Lee

Carter, Nicholas S. F., treas, dir: Clipper Ship Foundation

Carter, Ogden B., vp: Orange Orphan Society

Carter, Paul R., mem: Wal-Mart Foundation

Carter, Richard J., Jr., trust: Ferriday Fund Charitable Trust

Carter, Robert T., dir: Donnelley Foundation, Gaylord and Dorothy

Carter, Ruth Ann, trust: Eberly Foundation

Carter, Virginia P., manager: Brush Foundation

Carter, Wilbur L., Jr., trust: Carter Charitable Trust, Wilbur Lee

Cartinhour, Kathleen G., trust, pres: Cartinhour Foundation

Cartledge, Raymond Eugene, chmn, ceo, dir: Union Camp Corp.; trust: Union Camp Charitable Trust

Cartmell, Carvel H., trust: Schepp Foundation, Leopold

Carton, Robert W., MD, dir: Donnelley Foundation, Gaylord and Dorothy

Cartwright, Cheri D., asst secy-treas, dir of grants: Sarkeys Foundation

Cartwright, Herb, secy, treas, trust: Beal Foundation

Cartwright, J.D., pres: Champion Spark Plug Co.

Cartwright, Thomas H., vp fin, treas, secy: Banc One Illinois Corp.

Carty, Donald J., exec vp fin & planning: AMR Corp.; treas, vp: AMR/American Airlines Foundation

Carus, M. Blouke, chmn, pres, ceo, coo, dir: Carus Corp.

Caruth, Mabel P., trust, don dtr-in-law: Hillcrest Foundation

Carvel, Agnes, chmn, dir: Carvel Foundation, Thomas and Agnes

Carver, Eugene Pendleton, trust: Hoffman Foundation, H. Leslie Hoffman and Elaine S.

Carver, John P., dir bd trust: Gap Foundation

Carver, Lillian Ahrens, trust: Werblow Charitable Trust, Nina W.

Carver, Lucille Avis, trust: Carver Charitable Trust, Roy J.

Carver, Martin G., chmn, pres, ceo, dir: Bandag, Inc.

Carver, Roy J., Jr., chmn: Carver Charitable Trust, Roy J.

Carver, Spencer, trust: Owen Trust, B. B.

Carwile, Charles W., vp, dir: Burton Foundation, William T. and Ethel Lewis

Cary, Donna, mgr pub affs: Merck Human Health Division

Cary, Sturges F., trust: Robinson Fund, Maurice R.

Casabona, George, coo, exec vp: IPCO Corp.

Casady, Simon, dir: Mid-Iowa Health Foundation

Case, Charles W., Jr., trust: Carolyn Foundation

Case, Dean W., pres, coo, dir: Reliance Insurance Cos.

Case, Don L., trust: Hillcrest Foundation

Case, Jim, comm mem: Sherman Educational Fund

Case, Weldon Wood, trust: Morgan Foundation, Burton D.

Casey, A. Michael, secy, dir: Bothin Foundation

Casey, Betty Brown, chmn, pres, trust: Casey Foundation, Eugene B.

Casey, Charles F., chmn, pres, ceo, coo: Constar International Inc.

Casey, Coleman H., trust: Saunders Charitable Foundation, Helen M.

Casey, Jeremiah E., chmn: First Maryland Bancorp; chmn, trust: First Maryland Foundation

Casey, John, vp sales & mktg: Acorn Corrugated Box Co.

Casey, John K., vchmn, cfo: Wendy's International, Inc.

Casey, John P., fin off: Altman Foundation

Casey, Joseph T., vchmn, cfo, dir: Litton Industries

Casey, Lyman, pres, dir: Schwab Foundation, Charles and Helen

Casey, Lyman H., exec dir, treas: Bothin Foundation

Casey, Michael D., pres: Ortho-McNeil Pharmaceutical

Casey, Michael J., vp: Confidence Foundation

Casey, R. R., trust: Pennington Foundation, Irene W. and C. B.

Casey, Samuel Alexander, treas, dir: Alexander Charitable Foundation

Cash, Don, chmn, pres, ceo, dir: Questar Corp.

Cash, Hugh I., pres: Steel Heddle Manufacturing Co.

Cashman, Elizabeth E., trust: Goddard Foundation, Charles B.

Cashman, Kathryn Batchelber, trust: Schepp Foundation, Leopold

Cashman, Maurice J., treas: National Forge Foundation

Casner, Andrew James, trust: Rabb Charitable Trust, Sidney R.

Caspall, Ken, dir: MFA Foundation

Caspersen, Barbara M., dir, treas: Caspersen Foundation for Aid to Health and Education, O. W.

Caspersen, Erik Michael Westby, dir, vp: Caspersen Foundation for Aid to Health and Education, O. W.

Caspersen, Finn Michael Westby, chmn, ceo, dir: Beneficial Corp.; dir: Beneficial Foundation; vp, dir: Caspersen Foundation for Aid to Health and Education, O. W.

Caspersen, Finn Michael Westby, Jr., dir, vp: Caspersen Foundation for Aid to Health and Education, O. W.

Caspersen, Freda R., Caspersen Foundation for Aid to Health and Education, O. W.

Caspersen, Samuel Michael Westby, dir, vp: Caspersen Foundation for Aid to Health and Education, O. W.

Cass, William R., dir: Beveridge Foundation, Frank Stanley

Cassel, Christine K., MD, dir: Greenwall Foundation

Cassel, Milton E., pres, treas, dir: Allen Foundation, Rita

Cassell, J. T., trust: National Machinery Foundation

Cassens, Vern H., sr vp, treas: Woodward Governor Co.

Cassidy, Anna M., pres: Enright Foundation

Cassidy, John, Jr., trust: Broadhurst Foundation

Cassidy, Kathleen, dir, treas: Enright Foundation

Cassidy, L. J., treas: Enright Foundation

Cassidy, M. Sharon, asst secy: USX Foundation

Cassidy, Samuel M., pres, ceo, dir: Star Bank, N.A.; pres, trust: Star Bank, N.A., Cincinnati Foundation

Cassin, B. J., dir: Lucas Cancer Foundation, Richard M.

Cassity, Dean R., secy: Jellison Benevolent Society

Cassity, Dorothy J., vp: Jellison Benevolent Society

Cassullo, Joanne L., pres, dir: Leonhardt Foundation, Dorothea L.

Castaing, F. J., trust: Chrysler Corp. Fund

Casteel, Lauren, exec dir: Hunt Alternatives Fund

Castellani, Armand J., chmn emeritus: Tops Markets, Inc.

Castellani, Lawrence P., pres, coo: Tops Markets, Inc.

Castellano, Joseph, secy: CBS Foundation

Castellini, D. J., treas: Scripps Howard Foundation

Castelman, Peter, trust: Foundation for Middle East Peace

Castenskiold, Christian, dir: Knudsen Foundation, Tom and Valley

Castiglia, Joseph J., pres, ceo: Pratt & Lambert, Inc.

Castle, Alfred L., secy, trust: Castle Foundation, Samuel N. and Mary

Castle, James C., pres, dir: Castle Foundation, Harold K. L.; vp, trust: Castle Foundation, Samuel N. and Mary

Castle, James C., Jr., vp: Castle Foundation, Harold K. L.

Castle, William Donald, pres, trust: Castle Foundation, Samuel N. and Mary

Castleman, Riva, dir: Cintas Foundation

Castles, James B., trust: Murdock Charitable Trust, M. J.

Castonguay, Roger, pres: Fleet Bank of Maine

Castro, John W., ceo, pres, dir: Merrill Corp.

Castro, Nash, trust: Jackson Hole Preserve

Castruccio, Louis M., trust: Leavey Foundation, Thomas and Dorothy

Caswell, John Beveridge, dir: Beveridge Foundation, Frank Stanley

Caswell, Philip, pres, dir: Beveridge Foundation, Frank Stanley

Catacosinos, William J., chmn, ceo, dir: Long Island Lighting Co.

Cataiano, Joseph A., dir: Norcross Wildlife Foundation

Catalina, Ronald, asst treas: Stern Foundation, Leonard N.; asst treas: Stern Foundation, Max

Catanzaro, Michael J., vp, treas, dir: Link, Jr. Foundation, George

Cate, Patricia A., exec dir: Phillips Foundation, Ellis L.

Catell, Robert B., pres, ceo: Brooklyn Union Gas Co.

Cater, Charles O., trust: Brundage Charitable, Scientific, and Wildlife Conservation Foundation, Charles E. and Edna T.

Cater, June O., trust: Brundage Charitable, Scientific, and Wildlife Conservation Foundation, Charles E. and Edna T.

Cater, William B., trust, vp, treas: Brundage Charitable, Scientific, and Wildlife Conservation Foundation, Charles E. and Edna T.; trust: Upton Charitable Foundation, Lucy and Eleanor S.

Cater, William B., Jr., trust: Brundage Charitable, Scientific, and Wildlife Conservation Foundation, Charles E. and Edna T.

Cates, Bena, advisor: Briggs Foundation, T. W.

Cates, MacFarlane Lafferty, Sr., chmn, trust: Arkwright Foundation

Cathcart, Emelda M., pres: Time Warner; pres: Time Warner Foundation

Catherwood, Charles E., treas: McLean Contributionship

Catherwood, Susan, dir: Pew Charitable Trusts

Cathey, Molly McCune, mem dispensing comm: McCune Charitable Trust, John R.

Catlett, Stanley B., trust: Rapp Foundation, Robert Glenn

Catlin, Loring, trust: China Medical Board of New York; dir: Huston Foundation

Catlin, Richard A., chmn, dir: AMCORE Foundation, Inc.

Catlin, Sara H., pres, trust: Howard and Bush Foundation

Catola, Stanley G., dir: Detroit Edison Foundation

Caton, Ralph W., chmn: Roberts Foundation, Dora

Catron, Courtney, dir: Hancock Foundation, Luke B.

Catron, Linda, dir: Hancock Foundation, Luke B.

Catsimatidis, John Andreas, chmn, ceo: United Refining Co

Catsman, David P, trust: Ford III Memorial Foundation, Jefferson Lee

Cattarulla, Elliot Reynold, chmn, pres, trust: Exxon Education Foundation

Catterall, Elaine, secy: Engelhard Foundation, Charles

Cattivera, Joseph, pres, coo, dir: Angeles Corp.

Catto, Jessica Hobby, trust: Hobby Foundation

Cattoi, Robert Louis, mem (trust comm): Rockwell International Corp. Trust

Causey, J. P., vp, secy, gen coun: Chesapeake Corp.

Cavalier, E.M., dir: Lilly & Co. Foundation, Eli

Cavalire, Anthony, treas: Mobil Foundation

Cavanaugh, William, III, pres, coo: Carolina Power & Light Co.

Cave, Edwin F., trust: Peabody Foundation

Cavell, Walter E., exec dir: Fullerton Foundation

Cavenaugh, Gayle, exec secy: Scrivner of North Carolina Inc.

Cavins, Robert E., vp: Johnson Co. Foundation, E. F.

Cawley, Michael A., trust: Merrick Foundation; pres, trust: Noble Foundation, Samuel Roberts

Cawley, Thomas J., pres: Elizabethtown Water Co.

Cawthorn, Robert Elston, chmn, pres, ceo, dir: Rhone-Poulenc Rorer

Cay, John E., III, trust: Hodge Foundation

Cecala, Ted T., Jr., cfo: Wilmington Trust Co.

Cecil, A., trust: National Gypsum Foundation

Cecil, Arthur B., vp: Ebell of Los Angeles Rest Cottage Association; pres, dir: Ebell of Los Angeles Scholarship Endowment Fund

Cecil, Robert, pres, ceo: Plantronics, Inc.

Ceddia, Anthony Francis, dir: SICO Foundation

Celski, Vicki, mgr community affairs: International Multifoods Corp.

Cerino, Harry E., vp programs: Penn Foundation, William

Cerny, Howard F., treas, secy, trust: Hayden Foundation, Charles

Cerrato, Anthony, dir: Carvel Foundation, Thomas and Agnes

Cerrone, Luciano F., secy, treas: Evans Foundation, T. M.

Cerrutti, E. Val, pres: Stella D'Oro Biscuit Co.

Cerulli, Robert F., asst treas, dir: May Stores Foundation

Cervieri, John A., Jr., mgr trustee, ceo: Property Capital Trust

Cetera, Joan A., dir: Educational Foundation of America

Chadwick, Laura, trust: Chadwick Foundation; trust: Farish Fund, William Stamps

Chaffin, Lawrence, vp, trust: Van Nuys Charities, J. B. and Emily

Chaho, Bahij, treas: Hoffman Foundation, Maximillian E. and Marion O.

Chaho, Doris C., pres: Hoffman Foundation, Maximillian E. and Marion O.

Chaimov, Alan, M.D., trust: Corvallis Clinic Foundation

Chain, Mark, dir: Deloitte & Touche Foundation

Chais, Emily, vp, dir: Chais Family Foundation

Chais, Mark, vp, dir: Chais Family Foundation

Chais, Pamela, cfo, secy, dir: Chais Family Foundation

Chais, Stanley, chmn, pres, dir: Chais Family Foundation

Chais, William, vp, dir: Chais Family Foundation

Chait, Gerald, trust: Giant Eagle Foundation

Chait, Marilyn, secy, treas: Chait Memorial Foundation, Sara

Chalfant, William Y., secy: Davis Foundation, James A. and Juliet L.

Challita, Hanna, corp banking: Commerzbank AG, New York

Chalphin, Bernice S., secy, dir: Feinstein Foundation, Myer and Rosaline

Chalsty, John S., pres, ceo, dir: Donaldson, Lufkin & Jenrette

Chamberlain, David M., chmn, pres, ceo: Shaklee Corp.

Chamberlain, J. Boatner, pres, dir: Stulsaft Foundation, Morris

Chamberlain, Jim, treas: Pfaffinger Foundation

Chamberlin, Donald F., pres: Chamberlin Foundation, Gerald W.

Chamberlin, Patience, vp, trust: Merck Family Fund

Chambers, Anne Cox, chmn, trust: Cox Foundation of Georgia, James M.

Chambers, Christine, vp, dir: MCJ Foundation

Chambers, Jack H., vchmn, pres, ceo: Koger Properties

Chambers, Jennifer, dir: MCJ Foundation

Chambers, Michael, dir: MCJ Foundation

Chambers, Patricia A., dir: MCJ Foundation

Chambers, Raymond George, pres, dir: MCJ Foundation

Chambers, T.A., trust: Goody's Manufacturing Corp. Foundation

Chambers, T.H., Jr., trust: Goody's Manufacturing Corp. Foundation

Chambers, Thomas H., pres: Goody's Manufacturing Corp.

Chambers, William R., chmn, dir: Fleet Co., Inc., C.B.

Chamovitz, Irvin, M.D., trust: Pittsburgh Child Guidance Foundation

Champagne, Robert E., pres, ceo: Porter Paint Co.; dir: Porter Paint Foundation

Chan, Miriam, trust: Kevorkian Fund, Hagop

Chan, Stephen, chmn, exec vp, trust: Kevorkian Fund, Hagop

Chancellor, Glenn, dir: Temple-Inland Foundation

Chandler, Charles Q., chmn, ceo: First National Bank in Wichita

Chandler, Clarissa Haffner, vp, secy: Haffner Foundation

Chandler, Douglas A., trust: Wells Trust Fund, Fred W.

Chandler, J. Howard, vp: Grand Metropolitan Food Sector Foundation

Chandler, Kent, Jr., dir: Buchanan Family Foundation; trust: Special People In Need

Chandler, Richard B., treas: Holmes Foundation

Chandler, Richard D., Jr., trust: Woltman Foundation, B. M.

Chandler, Stephen M., dir: Valley Foundation, Wayne and Gladys

Chandler, Wallace Lee, vp, dir: Universal Leaf Foundation

Chaney, William R., dir: Tinker Foundation

Chanin, Jeffrey R., vp: Chanin Family Foundation, Paul R.

Chanin, Paul R., pres, treas: Chanin Family Foundation, Paul R.

Chanin, Steven H., vp: Chanin Family Foundation, Paul R.

Chanoki, Futoshi, pres: Murata Erie North America

Chao, Jessica, vp: Wallace-Reader's Digest Fund, DeWitt; vp: Wallace Reader's Digest Fund, Lila

Chapin, Charles, III, trust: Victoria Foundation

Chapin, Charles S., trust: Prickett Fund, Lynn R. and Karl E.

Chapin, Chester F., trust: Prickett Fund, Lynn R. and Karl E.

Chapin, E. Y., III, vp, trust: Benwood Foundation

Chapin, Mary Ann, asst treas: Magowan Family Foundation

Chapin, Monroe, trust: Greene Foundation, Robert Z.

Chapin, Richard, trust: Higgins Foundation, Aldus C.

Chapin, Samuel C., trust: Prickett Fund, Lynn R. and Karl E.

Chapman, Alger B., chmn, ceo: Chicago Board of Trade

Chapman, Alvah Herman, Jr., trust: Knight Foundation, John S. and James L.

Chapman, Austin, vp: Hersey Foundation

Chapman, Constance G., mgr: Dodson Foundation, James Glenwell and Clara May

Chapman, D.R., vp, trust: Crawford & Co. Foundation

Chapman, Duane, trust: Retirement Research Foundation

Chapman, George B., Jr., pres, trust: Jennings Foundation, Martha Holden

Chapman, Hugh M., vchmn, trust: Duke Endowment

Chapman, J. S., dir: Grainger Foundation

Chapman, James C., pres, ceo: Outboard Marine Corp.; pres, dir: OMC Foundation

Chapman, James Edward, secy, trust: Mellen Foundation; secy, trust: Standard Products Co. Foundation

Chapman, John S., Jr., Sullivan Foundation, Algernon Sydney

Chapman, Kenneth, dir: Plumsock Fund

Chapman, Lise P., dir: Pfeiffer Research Foundation, Gustavus and Louise

Chapman, Max C., Jr., co-chmn, ceo: Nomura Securities International

Chapman, Page, pres, dir: BT Foundation

Chapman, Richard H., mgr, contact person, vp (Southeast Bank): Adams Foundation, Arthur F. and Alice E.

Chapman, Robert H., III, pres, treas: Inman Mills; trust: Inman-Riverdale Foundation

Chapman, Robert H., Jr., vchmn, trust: Inman-Riverdale Foundation

Chapman, Tom, vp corp commun: Mitsubishi Electric America

Chapman, W. Marshall, chmn, ceo: Inman Mills; chmn, trust: Inman-Riverdale Foundation

Chapman, Warren K., program off (education): Joyce Foundation

Chappelear, Marilyn, acct mgr: Texas Commerce Bank Houston Foundation

Chappell, John S., dir: DCB Foundation

Chappell, M. E., treas: Richardson Foundation, Sid W.

Chappell, Sally Kitt, trust: Graham Foundation for Advanced Studies in the Fine Arts

Chappell, Thomas M., pres, ceo: Tom's of Maine

Charach, Manuel, don, mgr: Manat Foundation

Charach, Natalie, don, mgr: Manat Foundation

Charles, Clifford S., comm mem: Wells Foundation, Franklin H. and Ruth L.

Charles, Ellen MacNeille, pres: Post Foundation of D.C., Marjorie Merriweather

Charles, Gladys R., mem: Wells Foundation, Franklin H. and Ruth L.

Charles, Willis, vp, dir: Ogle Foundation, Paul

Charlestein, Gary M., ceo: Premier Dental Products Co.; secy, treas, dir: Julius & Ray Charlestein Foundation

Charlestein, Morton, chmn: Premier Dental Products Co.; pres, dir: Julius & Ray Charlestein Foundation

Charlton, Earle P., II, trust: Charlton, Jr. Charitable Trust, Earle P.

Charmichael, Jay, trust: Andres Charitable Trust, Frank G.

Charsky, Albert W., trust: Wells Trust Fund, Fred W.

Charter, Christine L., asst treas: ITT Hartford Insurance Group Foundation

Chase, Beverly, trust: Wenner-Gren Foundation for Anthropological Research

Chase, Dorothy, clerk: Loomis House

Chase, Irwin, pres: Ann & Hope; dir: Chase Memorial Scholarship Foundation, Martin M.

Chase, John P., trust: Whitney Benefits

Chase, Lavinia B., trust: Schrafft and Bertha E. Schrafft Charitable Trust, William E.

Chase, Rodney F., chmn, ceo: BP America; chmn, ceo: BP Exploration

Chase, Samuel N., secy, treas, gen couns: Ann & Hope; dir: Chase Memorial Scholarship Foundation, Martin M.

Chase-Lansdale, Lindsay, dir, mem counc: Foundation for Child Development

Chasin, Dana, trust: Rockefeller Family Fund

Chasin, Gail B., secy: de Hirsch Fund, Baron

Chasin, Laura Spelman Rockefeller, trust: Rockefeller Family Fund

Chasin, Richard M., trust: Rockefeller Family Fund

Chastain, Thomas M., trust: Chastain Charitable Foundation, Robert Lee and Thomas M.

Chatfield, Henry H., Peterloon Foundation

Chatham, Lucy Hanes, trust: Morehead Foundation, John Motley

Chatkis, Jacob, trust: Foster Foundation, Joseph C. and Esther

Chatlos, Alice E., chmn, sr vp, trust: Chatlos Foundation

Chatlos, William J., pres, treas, trust: Chatlos Foundation

Chauvel, Bernard, exec vp, gen mgr: Credit Agricole

Chavez, Julie, vp, treas; exec dir: Continental Bank Foundation

Chavis, Donna, dir: Noyes Foundation, Jessie Smith

Chazen, Jerome A., trust: Chazen Foundation; co-fdr, chmn, dir: Liz Claiborne

Chazen, Lawrence J., cfo, dir: G.P.G. Foundation; cfo: Getty Foundation, Ann and Gordon

Chazen, Simona A., trust: Chazen Foundation

Checchi, Alfred A., ptnr: Northwest Airlines, Inc.

Cheek, C. W., trust: Prickett Fund, Lynn R. and Karl E.

Cheek, H. Yvonne, dir: Jerome Foundation

Chelberg, Bruce Stanley, chmn, ceo, dir: Whitman Corp.

Chelini, Marjorie, trust: Mosher Foundation, Samuel B.

Chellgren, Paul Wilbur, pres, coo, dir: Ashland Oil; mem: Ashland Oil Foundation

Chen, Ida K., dir: Penn Foundation, William

Chenery, Robin, chmn, ceo, dir: Wheeling-Pittsburgh Corp.

Cheney, Bradbury, trust: Cheney Foundation, Ben B.

Cheney, Bradbury B., secy, dir: Cheney Foundation, Ben B.

Cheney, Ed, mgr: Unilever United States Foundation

Cheney, Eleanor M., secy: McCarthy Foundation, John and Margaret

Cheney, Eudine Meadows, trust, dir: Meadows Foundation

Cheney, Jeffrey P., treas: Kohler Foundation

Cheney, William H., pres: McCarthy Foundation, John and Margaret

Chenoweth, Arthur I., trust: Illges Memorial Foundation, A. and M. L.

Chenoweth, B.M., Jr., trust: Illges Memorial Foundation, A. and M. L.

Chenoweth, Richard A., trust: Morgan Foundation, Burton D.

Cheong, Thian C., cfo: PMC Inc.

Cherdiak, Steven M., vp, treas: Solow Foundation, Sheldon H.

Chereek, Robert A., dir: First Interstate Bank of Texas Foundation

Cherne, A. William, Jr., vp: Cherne Foundation, Albert W.

Cherne, Elizabeth B., vp, secy: Cherne Foundation, Albert W.

Cherniak, Steven, treas: Solow Foundation

Chernoff, David S., asst secy, assoc gen coun: MacArthur Foundation, John D. and Catherine T.

Cherrie, G. E., Jr., dir: Bank of America - Giannini Foundation

Cherry, Earl R., pres: Quivey-Bay State Foundation

Cherry, James R., vp, dir: Rose Foundation, Billy

Cherry, Wendell, vchmn, dir: Humana Foundation

Chesbro, Joan, dir: CHC Foundation

Chesebro, Marvin, trust: Fusenot Charity Foundation, Georges and Germaine

Chesebro, R.E., chmn: Wigwam Mills

Chesebro, R.E., Jr., pres: Wigwam Mills Fund

Chesnut, Mark E., dir: Cummins Engine Foundation

Chester, Anetra, dir: Rosenhaus Peace Foundation, Sarah and Matthew

Cheston, Brooke, vp: Ellis Grant and Scholarship Fund, Charles E.

Chew, Frank S., treas: Delta Air Lines Foundation

Chia, Pei-Yuan, sr exec vp: Citicorp

Chiara, Judith L., trust: Loeb Foundation, Frances and John L.

Chiaravalloti, Frank A., dir: Boston Edison Foundation

Chiarucci, Vincent A., pres: Figgie International

Chicoine, Jerry, sr vp, cfo: Pioneer Hi-Bred International

Chiesa, Robert L., managing trust: Lindsay Trust, Agnes M.

Chilcote, Hazel S., vp, secy: Fairchild Industries Foundation

Child, John L., vp: Foundation of the Litton Industries

Childers, James H., secy, treas: Garvey Kansas Foundation

Childress, Fielding, mem bd: Columbia Terminals Co. Charitable Trust

Childress, Miranda Y., trust, pres: Childress Foundation, Francis and Miranda

Childress, Owen F., vp: Webb Foundation, Del E.

Childress, Ruth, mem bd: Columbia Terminals Co. Charitable Trust

Childs, Daniel H., treas, dir: St. Faith's House Foundation

Childs, David M., mng ptnr, ceo: Skidmore, Owings & Merrill; dir: Skidmore, Owings & Merrill Foundation

Childs, Edward C., vp: AKC Fund

Childs, Frederick C., dir: Burden Foundation, Florence V.

Childs, Hope S., trust: AKC Fund

Childs, John W., treas: AKC Fund; chmn bd mgrs: Childs Memorial Fund for Medical Research, Jane Coffin

Childs, Margaret Burden, co-chair, dir: Burden Foundation, Florence V.

Childs, Richard S., Jr., secy, mem bd mgrs: Childs Memorial Fund for Medical Research, Jane Coffin

Chiles, Earle M., pres, trust: Chiles Foundation

Chiles, Virginia H., vp, trust: Chiles Foundation

Chill, C. Daniel, trust: Lawrence Foundation, Alice

Chin, Gloria, contributions adm: Marsh & McLennan Cos.

Ching, Gerry, mem distribution comm: McInerny Foundation

Ching, Meredith J., vp, dir: Alexander & Baldwin Foundation

Ching, Patrick D., treas: Servco Foundation

Ching, Philip H., vp, dir: First Hawaiian Foundation

Chinn, Louis, secy: Washington Square Fund

Chinski, Arthur, trust: Buchalter, Nemer, Fields, Chrystie & Younger Charitable Foundation

Chirco, Anne Marie, trust: Dalsimer Fund, Craig

Chisholm, Margaret A., Chisholm Foundation

Chisholm, William Hardenbergh, trust, treas: Grant Foundation, William T.

Chism, Billy, pers mgr: Coats & Clark Inc.

Chisolm, Donald H., trust: Loose Trust, Harry Wilson

Chisolm, William A., trust: Palmer Fund, Francis Asbury

Chisum, Clayton D., trust: Glendorn Foundation

Chisum, Gloria Twine, dir: Penn Foundation, William

Chitty, Charles Benjamin, treas: Lyndhurst Foundation

Chiu, Bob, gen mgr: Mizuno Corporation of America

Choate, Arthur B., pres: Mostyn Foundation

Choate, Jerry D., vp, trust: Allstate Foundation

Choi, John, sr vp (fin): Bantam Doubleday Dell Publishing Group, Inc.

Chomeau, Bernal T., chmn, ceo: Reliable Life Insurance Co.

Chomeau, Douglas D., pres: Reliable Life Insurance Co.

Chong, Arthur, trust: McKesson Foundation

Chookaszian, Dennis Haig, chmn, pres, ceo: CNA Insurance Cos.

Chopin, L. Frank, secy, treas, dir: Fortin Foundation of Florida

Choppin, Purnell W., MD, pres: Hughes Medical Institute, Howard

Choquette, Paul J., Jr., pres: Gilbane Building Co.

Choquette, Paul Joseph, Jr., trust: Haffenreffer Family Fund

Chormann, Richard F., pres, coo, dir: First of America Bank Corp.

Choromanski, Jerome J., vp, treas, dir: Wasie Foundation

Chou, Harry H.S., vchmn, dir: Wang Laboratories, Inc.

Chow, Kim, off: Hang Seng Bank

Christ, Chris T., trust: Kellogg Foundation, W. K.

Christ, Donald, trust: McBean Charitable Trust, Alletta Morris

Christakis, George, dir: Weight Watchers Foundation

Christensen, David Allen, vp: Hickory Tech Corp. Foundation

Christensen, Duane, sr vp corp commun: Maritz Inc.

Christensen, Harold K., Jr., pres: Christensen Charitable and Religious Foundation, L. C.

Christensen, Leslie N., trust: Kemper Educational and Charitable Fund

Christensen, Lydell L., treas, dir: Pacific Telesis Foundation

Christensen, Neil H., secy-treas: Valley Bank Charitable Foundation

Christian, Charles Leigh, MD, trust, mem: Whitney Foundation, Helen Hay

Christian, Frances R., chmn: Rupp Foundation, Fran and Warren

Christian, Malcolm M., mem allocations comm: Jeffress Memorial Trust, Thomas F. and Kate Miller

Christian, Nathalia E., secy: Roehl Foundation

Christian, Winslow, National Center for Automated Information Retrieval

Christians, F. Wilhelm, chmn: Deutsche Bank AG

Christiansen, Elva E., secy: 3M Co.

Christiansen, Paul J., pres, trust: Edison Fund, Charles; trust: Turrell Fund

Christiansen, R.E., chmn, pres: Midwest Gas Co.

Christiansen, Russell E., trust: Harvest States Foundation; vchmn, pres, coo, dir: Midwest Resources

Christianson, Carol, bd mem: Dain Bosworth/IFG Foundation

Christie, Tom E., chmn, ceo: Christie Electric Corp.

Christman, Anne K., appointing comm: Kilcawley Fund, William H.

Christman, Thomas H., secy to trust: Trexler Trust, Harry C.

Christoffersen, Ralph, vp (res): SmithKline Beecham

Christopherson, Weston R., dir: Quaker Oats Foundation

Christovich, Mary Lou M., vp, dir: Williams Foundation, Kemper and Leila

Christy, John Gilray, chmn, ceo: IU International

Christy, Joseph T., Pittsburgh Child Guidance Foundation

Chu, John C. K., trust: Chubb Foundation

Chubb, Corinne A., trust: Victoria Foundation

Chubb, Hendon, trust: Chubb Foundation

Chubb, Percy, III, vchmn: Chubb Corp.; pres of bd, trust: Victoria Foundation

Chubb, Sally, trust: Victoria Foundation

Chuck, Stutenroth, trust off: Epp Fund B Charitable Trust, Otto C.

Chucker, Harold, dir, treas: North Star Research Foundation

Chumney, William T., mgr: Morrison Trust, Louise L.

Chung, B. U., pres: Samsung America Inc.

Chung, David O., pres, ceo: Hyundai Motor America

Chupita, Kenneth J., dir: Deluxe Corp. Foundation

Church, Andrew, secy: Harden Foundation

Church, James E., Jr., bd mem: Gardiner Scholarship Foundation

Churchill, Clinton R., dir: Bancorp Hawaii Charitable Foundation

Churchill, Emma L. D., trust: Goodyear Foundation, Josephine

Churchill, Glen D., adv: Central & South West Foundation

Churchill, Winston J., dir: Cameron Memorial Fund, Alpin J. and Alpin W.

Churn, Margaret, vp, secy: Bing Fund

Chustz, J. Steven, asst gen couns: First Mississippi Corp. Foundation

Chuu, Ching-Chih, dir: China Times Cultural Foundation

Cialella, Toni, cfo: Access Energy Corp.

Ciani, Judith, dir: Osher Foundation, Bernard

Ciavaglia, James, vp: McMurray-Bennnett Foundation

Ciechanover, Joseph, vchmn: Israel Discount Bank of New York

Cifatte, Carol, trust: Valencia Charitable Trust

Cifu, Palma, treas: Ohrstrom Foundation

Cisco, Thomas, treas: Benbough Foundation, Legler

Ciskie, Roger D., pres, coo: Mercantile Stores Co.

Cisler, Walker L., trust: Holley Foundation

Cismoski, Jerome J., trust: First Evergreen Foundation

Cisneros, Henry G., trust: Rockefeller Foundation

Ciszewski, Robert, dir, pres: International Fund for Health and Family Planning

Cizik, Robert, chmn, pres, dir: Cooper Industries; chmn, trust: Cooper Industries Foundation

Clabes, Judy G., trust: Scripps Howard Foundation

Claeyssens, Ailene B., pres, dir: Wood-Claeyssens Foundation

Claeyssens, Pierre P., 1st vp, dir: Wood-Claeyssens Foundation

Claiborne, Herbert A., III, alternate trust: Whitehead Foundation, Lettie Pate

Claiborne, Herbert A., Jr., vchmn: Whitehead Foundation, Lettie Pate

Clair, Raymond C., trust: Grigg-Lewis Trust

Clancey, John P., pres, ceo: Sea-Land Service

Clancy, John G., secy, trust: Erpf Fund, Armand G.

Clapham, Clarence, secy: Lancaster Lens Foundation

Clapp, Jacqueline, sr vp: Medina Foundation

Clapp, James N., II, asst treas: Medina Foundation

Clapp, John S., Jr., pres, trust: Boston Fatherless and Widows Society

Clapp, Joseph M., chmn, pres, dir: Roadway Services, Inc.

Clapp, Joseph Mark, mem distribution comm: GAR Foundation

Clapp, K. Elizabeth, trust: Medina Foundation

Clapp, Kristina H., vp, trust: Medina Foundation

Clapp, Matthew N., Jr., asst secy, trust: Medina Foundation

Clapp, Melvin C., chmn, ceo, dir: Cascade Natural Gas Corp.

Clapp, Norton, pres, trust: Medina Foundation

Clardy, Harold D., chmn, dir: Chapin Foundation of Myrtle Beach, South Carolina

Clare, David R., trust: Johnson Foundation, Robert Wood

Clareman, Jack, secy, treas, dir: Reynolds Foundation, Christopher

Clark, Aaron, vp: May Foundation, Wilbur

Clark, Alfred Corning, dir: Clark Foundation

Clark, Alfred James, pres: Clark Charitable Foundation

Clark, Amy Plant Statter, trust: Statter Foundation, Amy Plant

Clark, Andrew L., trust: Clark Family Charitable Trust, Andrew L.

Clark, Barbara M., trust: Massey Foundation, Jack C.

Clark, Catherine H., program assoc: Markle Foundation, John and Mary R.

Clark, Dale H., treas: Hollis Foundation

Clark, Dennis, pres: CR Industries

Clark, Dick, dir: Arca Foundation

Clark, Donald C., chmn, ceo, dir: Household International

Clark, Duncan W., MD, trust: International Foundation

Clark, Edwin L., ceo, pres: Great Lakes Casting Corp.

Clark, Eugene V., vp, secy, trust: Homeland Foundation

Clark, Frank W., Jr., vp: Gilmore Foundation, Earl B.

Clark, G. Reynolds, pres: Westinghouse Foundation

Clark, Gary D., mem selection comm: Westlake Scholarship Fund, James L. and Nellie M.

Clark, Gary M., pres, ceo: Westinghouse Electric Corp.

Clark, Geoffrey A., chmn: Dillard Paper Co.; chmn, trust: Dillard Fund

Clark, H. Ray, vp, trust: Smucker Foundation, Willard E.

Clark, Hays, chmn, trust, don son: Clark Foundation, Edna McConnell; trust: Penzance Foundation

Clark, Henry B., Jr., vchmn distribution comm: McInerny Foundation

Clark, Howard L., chmn, ceo: Shearson, Lehman & Hutton

Clark, Irving, vp, dir: Grotto Foundation; treas, dir, mem corp: Jerome Foundation; trust: Northwest Area Foundation

Clark, Jack D., dir: Animal Assistance Foundation

Clark, James, Jr., trust, don grandson: Clark Foundation, Edna McConnell

Clark, James McConnell, vp, trust, treas: Penzance Foundation

Clark, Jane F., II, pres, don daughter, dir: Clark Foundation

Clark, John W., pres: Consumers Power Foundation

Clark, Kim N., corporator: Island Foundation

Clark, Malcolm D., pres, coo: Keystone International

Clark, Marcella S., exec vp, trust: Smucker Foundation, Willard E.

Clark, Mariana L., trust: Bedford Fund

Clark, Mary H., vp: Hollis Foundation; corporator: Island Foundation

Clark, Maurie D., pres, treas: Clark Foundation

Clark, Nolan P., trust: Rogers Charitable Trust, Florence

Clark, Noreen M., dir: Diamond Foundation, Aaron

Clark, Peggy, trust: Ross Foundation

Clark, R. Hix, secy, trust: Washington Foundation

Clark, Raymond R., trust: Cincinnati Bell Foundation

Clark, Richard McCourt, vp, trust: Kellogg Co. Twenty-Five Year Employees' Fund

Clark, Roger Arthur, secy: Cafritz Foundation, Morris and Gwendolyn

Clark, Roy Thomas, trust: Knudsen Charitable Foundation, Earl

Clark, Russell E., secy, dir: Eagles Memorial Foundation

Clark, Stephen, trust: New England Foundation

Clark, Stephen C., Jr., trust: Jockey Club Foundation

Clark, Stephen H., dir: Island Foundation

Clark, Sylvia, exec dir: NEC Foundation of America

Clark, Ted, trust: Heginbotham Trust, Will E.

Clark, Tim, dir: Atkinson Foundation

Clark, William J., chmn, dir: Massachusetts Mutual Life Insurance Co.

Clark, William P., dir, treas: Churches Homes Foundation

Clark, Witt, secy, treas: Daniels Charitable Foundation, Josephus

Clark, Worley H., Jr., chmn, ceo, dir: Nalco Chemical Co.

Clarke, Charles F., Jr., treas, trust: Sprague Memorial Institute, Otho S. A.

Clarke, David, dept chmn, ceo: Hanson Office Products

Clarke, Donna L., trust: Clabir Corp. Foundation

Clarke, Glenn S., pres, dir: Avon Products Foundation

Clarke, Henry D., Jr., chmn, pres, ceo: Clabir Corp.; trust: Clabir Corp. Foundation

Clarke, Howard P., dir: Ordean Foundation

Clarke, James L., secy: Haywood Foundation

Clarke, James McClure, trust, secy: McClure Educational and Development Fund, James G. K.

Clarke, Kathleen M., dir: McIntosh Foundation

Clarke, Kay Knight, trust: Aeroflex Foundation

Clarke, Lois A., treas, dir: United Coal Co. Charitable Foundation

Clarke, Mark C., cfo: Holmes & Narver Services Inc.

Clarke, Mary V., Haywood Foundation

Clarke, Meredith, trust: Vicksburg Foundation

Clarke, Peter, dir: Monsanto Fund

Clarke, Richard A., chmn, ceo, dir: Pacific Gas & Electric Co.

Clarke, Richard M., chmn: Akzo America

Clarke, Robert F., pres, dir: HEI Charitable Foundation

Clarke, Robert H., trust: Clabir Corp. Foundation

Clarke, T. Dexter, secy, treas, trust: Kimball Foundation, Horace A. Kimball and S. Ella

Clarke, William V. H., exec secy: Wortham Foundation

Clauson, Bronwyn Baird, trust: Baird Foundation, Cameron

Clauss, Valerie, treas: Corbin Foundation, Mary S. and David C.

Clay, Beth Anne, mgr (corp contributions): Transco Energy Company

Clay, Buckner W., vp: Clay Foundation

Clay, Hamilton G., treas: Clay Foundation

Clay, John W., Jr., chmn, pres, dir: Third National Corp.

Clay, Lyell Buffington, chmn: Clay Foundation

Clay, Orson C., pres, ceo, dir: American National Insurance

Clay, Richard, dir: Norton Foundation Inc.

Claybourn, Colleen, secy, treas, trust, mem contributions comm, exec dir: Trull Foundation

Claypool, James, pres: Alworth Memorial Fund, Marshall H. and Nellie

Claypool, William M., III, chmn: Cotter & Co.

Clayton, Constance E., dir: Connecticut Mutual Life Foundation

Clayton, Fred, pres, trust: Hedrick Foundation, Frank E.

Clayton, J. Kerry, pres, ceo: Fortis Benefits Insurance Company/Fortis Financial Group

Clayton, John, vp (headquarter svcs): Great-West Life Assurance Co.

Clayton, Myrna, secy, treas: Hedrick Foundation, Frank E.

Clayton, Richard R., pres, coo: Eastern Enterprises; trust: Eastern Enterprises Foundation

Cleary, Catherine B., vp, secy: Johnson Foundation

Cleary, Gail K., vp, secy, dir: Cleary Foundation

Cleary, James F., treas: Morrison Knudsen Corp. Foundation Inc.

Cleary, Kristine H., trust: Cleary Foundation

Cleary, Russell G., pres, treas, dir: Cleary Foundation

Cleary, Sandra G., trust: Cleary Foundation

Cleave, Jim, pres, ceo: Marine Midland Banks

Clem, George M., treas: Rice Foundation, Ethel and Raymond F.

Clemans, Jerald G., pres: Farmers Group Safety Foundation

Clemence, Richard R., trust: Hyde Foundation

Clemence, Robert U., chmn, ceo: Hyde Foundation

Clemens, Ethel M., pres, treas, trust: Clemens Foundation

Clemens, Peter J., III, vp, trust: Vulcan Materials Co. Foundation

Clement, James B., pres, ceo: Offshore Logistics

Clement, Josephine D., trust: Reynolds Foundation, Z. Smith

Clement, Leslie C., trust: King Ranch Family Trust

Clement, Ronald W., exec dir: Haigh-Scatena Foundation

Clements, B. Gill, vp: Clements Foundation; trust: Gill Foundation, Pauline Allen

Clements, Jamie, trust: Wilson Public Trust, Ralph

Clements, Keith R., treas, dir: Andersen Foundation

Clements, Rita C., vp: O'Donnell Foundation

Clements, Robert, pres: Marsh & McLennan Cos.

Clements, William Perry, Jr., pres: Clements Foundation

Clemo, William H., trust: Reinghardt Foundation, Albert

Clendenin, John L., dir: New York Stock Exchange Foundation

Clendenin, Michael C., chmn, dir: Bennett Memorial Corporation, James Gordon; mng dir: New York Telephone Co.

Cleveland, Barbara, exec dir: Tull Charitable Foundation

Cleveland, Harlan, dir: Mertz-Gilmore Foundation, Joyce

Cleveland, Leatrice F., dir: Piper Foundation, Minnie Stevens

Clevenger, Raymond C., III, dir: Markle Foundation, John and Mary R.

Clevenger, Thomas R., chmn, dir: Bank IV; chmn, ceo: Bank IV Charitable Trust

Click, Dennis W., asst vp, asst secy: Nationwide Insurance Foundation

Cliff, Walter Conway, asst treas, asst secy, dir: Gould Foundation, Florence J.

Clifford, Charles H., cfo, trust: Langendorf Foundation, Stanley S.

Clifford, Joseph P., vchmn, dir: TCF Banking & Savings, FSB

Clifford, Robert, vp: Weller Foundation

Clifford, William M., pres, ceo, dir: Saint Johnsbury Trucking Co.

Cline, Benjamin L., adv bd: Lipsky Foundation, Fred and Sarah

Cline, David M., secy: Cline Foundation

Cline, Martha A., vp: Cline Foundation

Cline, N.Q., chmn, pres, treas: Cline Co.

Cline, N.Q., Sr., pres: Cline Foundation

Cline, Platt C., trust: Raymond Educational Foundation

Cline, Richard Gordon, chmn, pres, ceo, dir: Nicor, Inc.; chmn, pres, ceo, dir: Northern Illinois Gas Co.

Cline, Robert S., chmn, ceo, dir: Airborne Express Co.

Cline, Robert T., trust: Raymond Foundation

Clinton, C. Kenneth, dir: Youth Foundation

Clites, Victoria, administrator: Giant Eagle Foundation

Clodfelter, Daniel G., trust: Reynolds Foundation, Z. Smith

Cloiseau, Jean-Pierre, sr vp, cfo: Lafarge Corp.

Cloninger, Kriss, III, exec vp, cfo, treas: AFLAC

Close, Anne Springs, chmn, dir: Close Foundation; don, chmn, dir: Springs Foundation

Close, David P., secy, dir: Post Foundation of D.C., Marjorie Merriweather

Close, Derick Springsteen, dir: Close Foundation; dir: Springs Foundation

Close, Elliot Springs, dir: Close Foundation; dir: Springs Foundation

Close, Hugh William, Jr., dir: Close Foundation; dir: Springs Foundation

Close, Katherine Anne, dir: Close Foundation; dir: Springs Foundation

Close, Leroy Springs, dir: Close Foundation; dir: Springs Foundation

Close, Pat, dir: Springs Foundation

Close, Sandy, dir: Levinson Foundation, Max and Anna

Cloud, Bruce B., pres: Zachry Co., H.B.

Cloud, Joe C., pres: Smoot Charitable Foundation

Cloudt, H. P., dir: Brencanda Foundation

Clough, Charles M., chmn, ceo, dir: Wyle Laboratories

Clough, Lisa, vp (admin): Indiana Insurance Cos.

Clougherty, Bernard J., trust: Clougherty Charitable Trust, Francis H.

Clougherty, Coleman F., vp, dir: Link, Jr. Foundation, George

Clougherty, Joseph D., trust: Clougherty Charitable Trust, Francis H.

Clouston, Brendan R., coo: Tele- Communications, Inc.

Cloutier, Francis H., vp, treas, trust: Hotchkiss Foundation, W. R.

Clowes, Alexander W., dir: Clowes Fund

Clowes, Allen W., pres, treas: Clowes Fund

Clowes, Margaret J., vp: Clowes Fund

Clowes, Thomas J., dir: Clowes Fund

Cluett, Robert, trust: Morehead Foundation, John Motley

Cluff, Leighton Eggertsen, MD, trust emeritus: Johnson Foundation, Robert Wood

Clumock, Gloria Goodman, dir: Goodman Foundation, Edward and Marion

Clyde, Aileen H., exec comm: Swanson Family Foundation, Dr. W.C.

Clyde, Calvin, trust: Wise Foundation and Charitable Trust, Watson W.

Clymer, John A., pres, coo: Minnesota Mutual Life Insurance Co.

Clymer, John H., chmn: Hyams Foundation; clerk: Sofia American Schools

Clymer, John Raymond, Jr., dir: Priddy Foundation

Coates, John M., dir: Woodson Foundation, Aytchmonde

Cobb, Calvin Hayes, Jr., vp, trust: Foundation for Middle East Peace

Cobb, Catherine R., trust: Herrick Foundation

Cobb, Charles E., Jr., trust: Cobb Family Foundation

Cobb, Charles K., Jr., trust: Sailors' Snug Harbor of Boston

Cobb, Christian M., trust: Cobb Family Foundation

Cobb, G., dir: Community Hospital Foundation

Cobb, Henry N., dir: Skidmore, Owings & Merrill Foundation

Cobb, Rhoda W., trust: Ware Foundation

Cobb, Sue M., trust: Cobb Family Foundation

Cobb, Tobin T., trust: Cobb Family Foundation

Cobban, Sharon, mgr corp affs svcs: Manufacturers Life Insurance Co. of America

Cobbe, Mary L., dir, secy: Lacy Foundation

Cobben, Sharon, corp aff svcs: Manufacturers Life Insurance Co. of America

Cobbin, W. Frank, Jr., trust: AT&T Foundation

Coble, Hugh K., trust: Fluor Foundation

Coble, R. Larry, treas: Richardson Foundation, Smith

Coblentz, William K., dir, secy: Friedman Family Foundation; dir: Koret Foundation

Coburn, Jean Crummer, pres: Crummer Foundation, Roy E.

Coburn, Milton, vp: Crummer Foundation, Roy E.

Cochener, Bruce G., trust: Fink Foundation

Cochran, Larry, pres, ceo: Six Flags Theme Parks Inc.

Cochran, Peyton S., Jr., dir: Guggenheim Foundation, Harry Frank

Cochran, Travis L., secy: Blue Cross & Blue Shield of Kentucky Foundation

Cochrane, Edward G., II, trust: Mount Vernon Mills Foundation

Cochrane, Luther, pres: McDevitt Street Bovis Inc.

Cocke, Frances F., trust, pres: Exposition Foundation

Cockrell, Ernest H., pres, dir: Cockrell Foundation

Cockrell, Janet S., dir: Cockrell Foundation

Cockrell, Mel, cfo: Keith Co., Ben E.

Cockroft, Don, pres: United Inns, Inc.

Cocroft, Duncan H., vp, treas: International Multifoods Charitable Foundation

Codell, J. C., Jr., dir: Robinson Mountain Fund, E. O.

Codington, John, trust: Davis Charitable Foundation, Champion McDowell

Cody, D. Thane, MD, pres: American Otological Society

Cody, Thomas G., exec vp (legal & human resources): Federated Department Stores and Allied Stores Corp.

Coe, Charles R., Jr., trust: Merrick Foundation

Coe, Donald M., pres: Hiram Walker & Sons Inc.

Coe, Elizabeth Merrick, pres, trust: Merrick Foundation

Coe, Henry E., III, chmn, dir: Waterfowl Research Foundation

Coe, Ward I., trust: Merrick Foundation

Coen, Earl, trust: Coen Family Foundation, Charles S. and Mary

Coffey, John, vp: State Farm Cos. Foundation

Coffey, Shelby, III, dir: Times Mirror Foundation

Coffey, William E., asst treas: Chatam Inc.

Coffin, David L., chmn, dir: Dexter Corp.; chmn, dir: Dexter Corp. Foundation

Coffin, Dwight C., secy, dir: Continental Grain Foundation; secy: Fribourg Foundation

Coffin, Harold W., trust: Comstock Foundation

Coffin, Steve, trust: CPI Corp.

Cofrin, David A., chmn adv comm: AEC Trust

Cofrin, David H., mem adv comm: AEC Trust

Cofrin, Edith D., mem adv comm: AEC Trust

Cofrin, Mary Ann H., mem adv comm: AEC Trust

Cogan, James Richard, treas, dir: Bunbury Company

Cogan, John F., Jr., pres: Pioneer Group

Cogan, Marshall S., chmn, ceo, dir: 21 International Holdings; pres: KIHI/21 International Holding Foundation

Cogen, Harry C., dir: Drown Foundation, Joseph

Coggeshall, Mary, trust: Victoria Foundation

Cogswell, Lourdes, dir (corp commun): NEC USA

Cohan, Eugene L., treas, trust: Ogden Foundation, Ralph E.

Cohen, Alan Norman, pres, dir: Andal Corp.

Cohen, Albert A., chmn, trust: Penn Knitted Outerwear Foundation

Cohen, Allie, trust: Wolfson Foundation, Louis E.

Cohen, Amy Scheuer, secy, treas: Cohen Family Foundation, Saul Z. and Amy Scheuer; vp: Scheuer Family Foundation, S. H. and Helen R.

Cohen, Bennett R., fdr, chp, ceo, dir: Ben & Jerry's Homemade

Cohen, Bluma D., vp, exec dir, mgr, trust: Jurzykowski Foundation, Alfred

Cohen, Cammie R., secy: Milken Family Medical Foundation

Cohen, Carolyn, trust: Cohen Foundation, George M.

Cohen, Charlotte McKee, trust: McKee Foundation, Robert E. and Evelyn

Cohen, Donald B., vp: Pyramid Foundation

Cohen, Edward B., vp: National Center for Automated Information Retrieval

Cohen, Edwin C., pres: General Atlantic Partners L.P.; chmn: Echoing Green Foundation

Cohen, Eileen Phillips, trust: Presto Foundation; dir: Phillips Family Foundation, L. E.

Cohen, George M., pres, mgr, trust: Cohen Foundation, George M.

Cohen, H. Robert, dir: Litwin Foundation

Cohen, H. William, trust, vp: Macht Foundation, Morton and Sophia

Cohen, Harold, treas: Scheuer Family Foundation, S. H. and Helen R.

Cohen, Herbert, contr: Arcata Graphics Co.; vp, dir:

Collins, Roy, mem adv comm: Pott Foundation, Herman T. and Phenie R.

Collins, Stephen W., vp, dir: Collins Foundation

Collins, T. Clyde, dir: Fletcher Foundation, A. J.

Collins, Truman W., Jr., trust: Collins Medical Trust

Collins, Velma J., trust: Jones Foundation, Montfort Jones and Allie Brown

Collins, Whitfield J., dir: Brown and C. A. Lupton Foundation, T. J.; pres: Fifth Avenue Foundation

Collins, William E., trust: Clapp Charitable and Educational Trust, George H.; trust: Green Foundation; trust: Redman Foundation

Collinson, John T., v chmn, trust: B & O Railroad Museum

Collision, Arthur, trust: Blowitz-Ridgeway Foundation

Collomb, Bertrand, chmn, dir: Lafarge Corp.

Collopy, Francis W., trust: Hill Foundation

Collored-Mansfeld, Ferdinand, trust: Humane Society of the Commonwealth of Massachusetts

Colman, John Charles, dir: Premier Industrial Corp.; trust: Premier Industrial Foundation

Colmar, Craig P., dir: Aigner Foundation, G.J.

Colopy, Hugh, trust, mem distribution comm: GAR Foundation

Colquhoun, Ross K., pres, ceo, dir: Raymond Corp.

Colson, Charles Wendell, vp, dir: M.E. Foundation

Colson, Wendell H., pres: Sun Banks Inc.

Colston, John W., chmn, pres, ceo: Beitzell & Co.; pres: Beitzell & Co. Charitable Foundation

Colston, John W., III, vp: Beitzell & Co. Charitable Foundation

Colt, James D., trust: Shaw Foundation, Gardiner Howland

Colton, Barnum L., Jr., trust: Johnston Trust for Charitable and Educational Purposes, James M.

Colton, E. T., Jr., trust: Libby-Dufour Fund, Trustees of the

Colton, Sterling, mgr: Marriott Foundation, J. Willard

Colussy, Dan A., chmn, pres, ceo, dir: UNC, Inc.

Colvard, Karen, program off: Guggenheim Foundation, Harry Frank

Colver, Dave, trust: Heginbotham Trust, Will E.

Colvin, Gerald O., Jr., chmn, trust: Hargis Charitable Foundation, Estes H. and Florence Parker

Colwell, W. Paul, pres, dir: Peppers Foundation, Ann

Comai, Barbara L., trust: Miller Foundation

Comb, Donald G., trust: New England Biolabs Foundation

Combs, B.V., trust: Combs Foundation, Earle M. and Virginia M.

Combs, Esther, Cook Inlet Region

Combs, Virginia M., secy: Combs Foundation, Earle M. and Virginia M.

Combs, W.G., vp, treas, trust: Long Foundation, J.M.

Comer, Adrian, trust: Thatcher Foundation

Comer, Clarence C., pres, ceo: Moore McCormack Resources; pres, ceo: Southdown, Inc.

Comer, Frances, vp, secy: Comer Foundation

Comer, Gary Campbell, pres, treas, dir: Comer Foundation

Comer, James P., trust, mem nominating comm: Carnegie Corporation of New York

Comer, John D., mem adv bd: Burke Foundation, Thomas C.

Comer, John D., Jr., trust: Anderson Foundation, Peyton

Comer, Richard J., chmn, trust: Comer Foundation

Comerchero, Leonard, vp, dir: Mitrani Family Foundation

Comerica Bank, trust: Monroe Auto Equipment Foundation Trust

Comine, Lawrence, Jr., coo, sr exec vp, dir: FirsTier Bank N.A. Omaha

Comisky, Marvin, trust: Bronstein Foundation, Soloman and Sylvia

Comly, Joseph P., III, pres: Kerney Foundation, James

Commes, Thomas Allen, pres, coo, dir: Sherwin-Williams Co.; asst secy, trust: Sherwin-Williams Foundation

Compton, James Randolph, pres, dir: Compton Foundation; vchmn, trust: Danforth Foundation

Compton, Ronald E., chmn, pres, dir: Aetna Life & Casualty Co.; pres, dir: Aetna Foundation; dir: Compton Foundation

Compton, W. Danforth, trust: Compton Foundation

Comstock, Robert L., Jr., trust, mem exec comm: Blandin Foundation

Conant, Colleen Christner, trust: Scripps Howard Foundation

Conant, John A., secy: Harland Charitable Foundation, John and Wilhelmina D.

Conant, Miriam Harland, pres: Harland Charitable Foundation, John and Wilhelmina D.

Conant, Roger R., chmn, dir: Northwest Area Foundation

Conard, Helen, trust: Jones Foundation, Walter S. and Evan C.

Conarroe, Joel Osborne, pres: Guggenheim Memorial Foundation, John Simon

Conaton, Michael J., pres, coo, dir: Midland Co.

Condon, James, treas: Hartmarx Charitable Foundation

Condon, Larry E., pres, dir: Mertz-Gilmore Foundation, Joyce

Cone, D. L., asst secy: Phillips Petroleum Foundation

Cone, Rev. Kady, trust: Colorado Trust

Conely, James, awards adv comm: Ferebee Endowment, Percy O.

Conerly, Richard Pugh, mem adv comm: Pott Foundation, Herman T. and Phenie R.

Confer, Ogden W., pres, dir: Palmer Foundation, George M.

Confer, Richard P., pres, ceo: Hubbard Milling Co.; secy,

dir: Palmer Foundation, George M.

Congdon, Elizabeth C., trust: Memorial Foundation for the Blind

Conger, Clement Ellis, trust, treas: Hopkins Foundation, John Jay

Conger, Harry M., chmn, ceo, dir: Homestake Mining Co.

Conger, Jay A., trust: Hopkins Foundation, John Jay

Conger, Kenneth W., vp (human resources), dir: Kohler Co.

Conger, Lianne H., trust, pres: Hopkins Foundation, John Jay

Congreve, Richard N., trust: Potlatch Foundation for Higher Education/Potlatch Foundation II

Coniglio, Peter J., trust: National Pro-Am Youth Fund

Conklin, Charles, secy adv comm: Blue Bell Foundation

Conklin, Donald R., pres (pharmaceutical opers): Schering-Plough Corp.; trust: Schering-Plough Foundation

Conklin, Thomas J., sr vp, secy: Mutual of New York; dir: Mutual of New York Foundation

Conley, Kathleen R., secy, dir: Hulings Foundation, Mary Andersen

Conley, R. Michael, dir: Northwestern National Life Insurance Co.

Conley, R.E., cfo: Standard Steel Speciality Co.

Conlin, William P., pres: CalComp, Inc.

Conn, Eric, sr adv mgr: American Honda Motor Co.

Conn, M. K., vp, secy: National Standard Foundation

Connable, Genevieve, trust: Wildermuth Foundation, E. F.

Connally, Norris L., treas, trust: Herndon Foundation, Alonzo F. Herndon and Norris B.

Connally, Ruth, trust: Winchester Foundation

Connell, James R., trust: Bernstein Foundation, Diane and Norman

Connell, Lawrence, pres, ceo: Society for Savings

Connell, Michael J., pres, dir: Connell Foundation, Michael J.

Connell, William F., chmn, ceo: Connell LP

Connelly, Brendan R., pres, ceo: North American Reinsurance Corp.

Connelly, Christine C., trust, don daughter: Connelly Foundation

Connelly, Daniele, trust: Connelly Foundation

Connelly, J. J., vp, dir: Joslyn Foundation

Connelly, John Edward, Jr., pres, dir: Kent Foundation, Ada Howe

Connelly, Joseph F., trust, pres: Kramer Foundation, Louise

Connelly, M. H., mem loan comm: Lindsay Student Aid Fund, Franklin

Connelly, Martha L., chmn, trust: Lattner Foundation, Forrest C.

Connelly, Thomas S., trust, don son: Connelly Foundation

Conner, Charles, vp: Clark Home for Aged People, Ella

Conner, Finis F., chmn, ceo: Conner Peripherals

Conner, Frank, press, coo: Mass Merchandisers, Inc.

Conner, James W., pres: Lyon Foundation

Conner, Maude, cfo: DiRosa Foundation, Rene and Veronica

Connolly, Arthur G., pres, dir: Laffey-McHugh Foundation

Connolly, Arthur G., Jr., treas, dir: Laffey-McHugh Foundation

Connolly, Charles H., pres: Whitman Corp. Foundation

Connolly, Cynthia S., trust: Sprague, Jr. Foundation, Caryll M. and Norman F.

Connolly, David, vp, treas: Albertson's

Connolly, Eugene B., Jr., chmn, ceo: USG Corp.

Connolly, Gerald E., trust: Reinhart Family Foundation, D.B.

Connolly, James F., mgr: Richardson Fund, Mary Lynn

Connolly, Joseph A., admin: Collins Medical Trust

Connolly, Ruth E., trust: Thirty-Five Twenty, Inc.

Connor, David J., pres: Carrols Corp.

Connor, Gordon R., vp, dir: Roddis Foundation, Hamilton

Connor, James Richard, exec dir: Kemper Foundation, James S.

Connor, Michael, McFawn Trust No. 2, Lois Sisler

Connor, Mrs. John T., vp: Lost Tree Charitable Foundation

Connor, Richard, pres, publ: Fort Worth Star Telegram

Connor, Robert P., treas, dir: Barker Foundation, J. M. R.

Connors, Kathryn, mem grantmaking comm: Liz Claiborne Foundation

Conomikes, John G., vp, dir, gen mgr (broadcasting): Hearst Foundation; vp, dir: Hearst Foundation, William Randolph

Cononelos, Louis J., mgr comm rels: Kennecott Corp.

Conover, Joseph I., dir: Oakley-Lindsay Foundation of Quincy Newspapers & Quincy Broadcasting Co.

Conrad, C. A., pres, coo: Quaker State Corp.

Conrad, Carol, secy: Castle Foundation, Harold K. L.

Conrad, Gene R., Upjohn Foundation, Harold and Grace

Conrad, Howard P., Jr., pres, treas: Northern Indiana Fuel & Light Co.

Conrad, Mrs. Howard P., chmn: Northern Indiana Fuel & Light Co.

Conrad, William C., exec secy: Stackpole-Hall Foundation

Conron, John J., Enright Foundation

Conroy, Janet, trust: Eastman Foundation, Alexander

Conroy, Roberta A., dir, secy: Capital Group Foundation

Considine, Frank W., chmn (exec comm), dir: American National Can Co.

Considine, Raymond, secy, exec dir: Hood Foundation, Charles H.

Constance, Marcia W., vp: W. W. W. Foundation

Constantine, Jim, treas, dir: Sears-Roebuck Foundation

Conston, Charles, mgr: Conston Foundation

Conte, James W., chmn, ceo: Community Psychiatric Centers

Conte, Richard L., pres, cfo: Community Psychiatric Centers

Contino, Francis A., treas, trust: B & O Railroad Museum

Contreras, Mitch, corp contributions: Mesa Inc.

Convisser, Theodora, trust: Boston Edison Foundation

Conway, E. Virgil, dir, chmn audit comm, mem exec & fin comms: Macy, Jr. Foundation, Josiah

Conway, Edward, trust: Nathan Foundation

Conway, Glenn, trust: Fairfield Foundation, Freeman E.

Conway, James F., III, pres, coo: Courier Corp.

Conway, James F., Jr., chmn, ceo: Courier Corp.

Conway, Jill Kathryn Ker, trust: Knight Foundation, John S. and James L.; dir: Kresge Foundation

Conway, John Harold, Jr., vchmn, secy, treas, trust: Mabee Foundation, J. E. and L. E.

Conway, John P., vp, secy, dir: Dillon Foundation

Conway, Michael J., pres, ceo, dir: America West Airlines

Conway, Peter P., pres, dir: CNA Foundation

Conway, W. Joseph, vchmn, dir: Southdown, Inc.

Conway, William Gaylord, dir: Griffis Foundation

Conwill, Kinshasha Holman, dir: Warhol Foundation for the Visual Arts, Andy

Cook, Cecile, chmn, mem: Florence Foundation

Cook, Charles Beckwith, Jr., dir: Ziegler Foundation for the Blind, E. Matilda

Cook, Charles W., secy, trust: Sullivan Foundation, Algernon Sydney

Cook, Daniel W., III, trust: Cook Foundation

Cook, David E., trust: Schey Foundation

Cook, Dee, mgr: Central Soya Foundation

Cook, Donald C., Britton Fund; Haskell Fund

Cook, Donald G., dir: American Welding & Manufacturing Co. Foundation

Cook, Edward D., Jr., trust: Shaw Fund for Mariner's Children

Cook, Emajean, don, treas, dir: Cook Charitable Foundation

Cook, Frank C., grants adm, trust: Cook Brothers Educational Fund

Cook, Franklin C., pres: Cook Family Trust; admin: Natural Heritage Foundation; vp: South Coast Foundation

Cook, Frederic W., pres: Cook & Co., Frederic W.

Cook, Gail B., trust: Cook Foundation

Cook, Gayland, pres, ceo: Integra Bank

Cook, George, chmn, ceo: Colonial Parking

Cook, Gerald S., trust: Teitel Charitable Trust, Ben N.

Cook, J. C., Jr., vp (product oper & corp engg): Lilly & Co., Eli; dir: Lilly & Co. Foundation, Eli

Cook, Jane Bancroft, chmn adv comm: Dow Jones Foundation

Cook, Jay Michael, chmn, ceo: Deloitte & Touche; chmn bd: Deloitte & Touche Foundation

Cook, Joe, dir: Eagles Memorial Foundation

Cook, John R., cfo, dir: Harcourt General

Cook, K. James, comm: Fairfield-Meeker Charitable Trust, Freeman E.

Cook, Kathleen M., secy, trust: Cook Brothers Educational Fund; secy: Cook Family Trust; pres: South Coast Foundation

Cook, L. D., trust: National Machinery Foundation

Cook, Lodwrick Monroe, chmn, ceo: ARCO; chmn, dir: ARCO Foundation; chmn, ceo: ARCO Chemical

Cook, Mary McDermott, pres, trust: Biological Humanics Foundation; secy, treas, trust: McDermott Foundation, Eugene

Cook, Mrs. Vannie E., Jr., secy, treas: Cook Foundation, Loring

Cook, Paul M., chmn: Raychem Corp.

Cook, Peggy J., pres: Cook, Sr. Charitable Foundation, Kelly Gene

Cook, Peter C., don, pres, secy, dir: Cook Charitable Foundation

Cook, Phyllis, pres, dir: Rosenberg Foundation

Cook, R., mem student loan adv comm: Jeffers Memorial Fund, Michael

Cook, Robert E., mem: Butler Foundation, Alice

Cook, Robert S., mem adv comm: Generation Trust

Cook, Stanton R., chmn: McCormick Tribune Foundation, Robert R.

Cook, Susan V., pres, trust: Cook Brothers Educational Fund; treas: Cook Family Trust; treas: South Coast Foundation

Cook, Thomas P., secy, trust: Phillips Family Foundation, Jay and Rose

Cook, Vannie E., Jr., dir, pres: Cook Foundation, Loring

Cook, Wallace Lawrence, mem bd dirs, chmn investment comm: Dana Foundation, Charles A.

Cook, William E., pres, trust: Whitney Benefits

Cook, William H., trust: Cook Brothers Educational Fund; vp: Cook Family Trust; pres: Natural Heritage Foundation; secy: South Coast Foundation

Cook, William R., pres, coo, dir: Betz Laboratories

Cooke, Alyson, program off ed: Abell Foundation, The

Cooke, Carole, sr vp (fin): Sky Chefs, Inc.

Cooke, Elva, treas, dir: Cooke Foundation Corporation, V. V.

Cooke, Geoffrey B., exec dir, mem contributions comm: NYNEX Corp.

Cooke, John D., trust: Willmott Foundation, Fred & Floy

Cooke, John Warren, pres, treas: Treakle Foundation, J. Edwin

Cooke, Joseph P., Jr., trust: Baldwin Memorial Foundation, Fred

Cooke, Maury W., pres: Portsmouth General Hospital Foundation

Cooke, Raymond J., secy: Amax Foundation

Cooke, Richard A., Jr., vp, trust: Cooke Foundation

Cooke, Ruth H., vp, secy: Westerman Foundation, Samuel L.

Cooke, Samuel A., pres, trust: Cooke Foundation

Cooke, V. V., Jr., pres, dir: Cooke Foundation Corporation, V. V.

Cookson, John S., trust: Kingsbury Fund

Cool, Judd R., vp (human resources): Inland Steel Industries; dir: Inland Steel-Ryerson Foundation

Cooley, Edward H., chmn, ceo: Precision Castparts Corp.

Cooley, Richard P., dir: PACCAR Foundation

Cooley, Richard Pierce, trust: Kaiser Family Foundation, Henry J.

Coolidge, E. David, III, vp: Blair and Co. Foundation, William

Coolidge, Lawrence, trust: Mifflin Memorial Fund, George H. and Jane A.; dir: Weber Charities Corp., Frederick E.

Coolidge, Thomas R., trust: Astor Foundation, Vincent

Coolidge, William A., pres, trust: River Road Charitable Corporation; trust: Vingo Trust II

Coolley, Paul, dir: Werner Foundation, Clara and Spencer

Coombe, Eva Jane, trust: Anderson Foundation, William P.

Coombe, Michael A., trust: Anderson Foundation, William P.

Coombe, Vachael Anderson, vp, trust: Anderson Foundation, William P.; chmn, dir: Powell Co., William; trust: Powell Co. Foundation, William

Coombs, John W., trust: Davenport Trust Fund

Coon, Jerome J., treas, pres: Physicians Mutual Insurance Co. Foundation

Cooper, Barry, trust: Klosk Fund, Louis and Rose

Cooper, Bob E., pres, ceo: Kennecott Corp.

Cooper, Cameron, dir: Seaver Institute

Cooper, David, treas: Castle & Cooke International Charitable Foundation

Cooper, Dennis E., chmn, exec dir: RTM Foundation

Cooper, Diane, office admin supervisor: Loctite Corp.

Cooper, Donald M., Jr., chmn, pres, ceo: Hamilton Bank

Cooper, Douglas C., bd mem: Gardiner Scholarship Foundation

Cooper, Douglas O., secy: Codrington Charitable Foundation, George W.

Cooper, Elaine, vp, secy: Terner Foundation

Cooper, Frank G., secy, dir: Dietrich Foundation, William B.

Cooper, Frederick Eansor, dir: Williams Family Foundation of Georgia

Cooper, Janet, treas: Quaker Oats Foundation

Cooper, Janis, vp (pub aff): Maytag Corp.; vp, trust: Maytag Corp. Foundation

Cooper, Jerry, dir: Amax Foundation

Cooper, Lana S., dir, secy: Cooper Charitable Trust, Richard H.

Cooper, Lance, cfo, vp fin: Iowa-Illinois Gas & Electric Co.

Cooper, Marsh A., dir, mem exec comm, mem grant program comm: Keck Foundation, W. M.

Cooper, Nathan, trust: Klosk Fund, Louis and Rose

Cooper, Peter T., secy, treas, trust: Cartinhour Foundation; treas, trust: Jewell Memorial Foundation, Daniel Ashley and Irene Houston; secy, treas: Woods-Greer Foundation

Cooper, R. John, III, pres, dir: Young & Rubicam Foundation

Cooper, Richard H., dir, pres, treas: Cooper Charitable Trust, Richard H.

Cooper, Richard W., trust: Guggenheim Memorial Foundation, John Simon

Cooper, Robert, trust: Bird Cos. Charitable Foundation

Cooper, Rose Mary, secy, treas: Fohs Foundation

Cooper, Russell, trust: Heath Foundation, Ed and Mary

Cooper, Suzanne S., chmn: Cooper Wood Products; pres, dir: Cooper Wood Products Foundation

Cooper, Theodore, MD, chmn, ceo, dir: Upjohn Co.

Cooper, W. L., III, pres: Cooper Wood Products

Cooper, W. Paul, vchmn, mem supervisory bd: Codrington Charitable Foundation, George W.

Cooper, Warren F., dir: Sears-Roebuck Foundation

Cooper, William A., chmn, ceo, dir: TCF Banking & Savings, FSB

Cooper, William L., trust: Mida Foundation

Coopersmith, Fran M., vp fin, treas: Penn Foundation, William

Coor, Lattie Finch, trust: Deer Creek Foundation

Coors, Jeffrey H., treas: Coors Foundation, Adolph

Coors, Peter Hanson, chmn, ceo: Coors Brewing Co.; vp: Coors Foundation, Adolph

Coors, William K., chmn, ceo, dir: Coors Brewing Co.; pres: Coors Foundation, Adolph; trust: Hunter Trust, A. V.

Coovert, Sander, pres, dir: CPI Corp.

Copaken, Richard, secy: Winston Research Foundation, Harry

Cope, E. Ray, exec dir, dir (poor & needy div): Reynolds Charitable Trust, Kate B.

Copeland, Alvin C., chmn, ceo: Church's Fried Chicken, Inc.

Copeland, Frederick, Jr., pres: Fleet Bank

Copeland, Gerret van Sweringen, trust: Longwood Foundation

Copeland, William John, trust: Frick Educational Commission, Henry C.

Copelin, Herman H., secy: Rogow Birken Foundation

Copenhaver, Don, dir: MFA Foundation

Copenhaver, John T., mem: Maier Foundation, Sarah Pauline

Copes, Paul, trust: Hartford Courant Foundation

Copes, Ronald, second vp: Massachusetts Mutual Life Insurance Co.

Coplan, Alfred I., secy, treas, trust: Straus Foundation, Aaron and Lillie

Copley, David C., pres, dir: Copley Press; pres, trust: Copley Foundation, James S.

Copley, Helen K., chmn, ceo, dir: Copley Press; chmn, trust: Copley Foundation, James S.; trust: Hughes Medical Institute, Howard

Copp, Eugenie T., trust: Carolyn Foundation

Copp, Mary Wagley, dir: Penney Foundation, James C.

Coppersmith, Jack, sr vp, cfo: NVF Co.

Coppersmith, S. James, vp, gen mgr: WCVB-TV

Coppola, Alfred, pres: Okonite Co.

Coquillette, James E., dir: Hall Foundation

Corbally, John E., dir: MacArthur Foundation, John D. and Catherine T.

Corbally, Richard V., secy, dir: McCann Foundation

Corbert, Patricia A., trust: Baker Foundation, George T.

Corbett, Cornelia, trust: Farish Fund, William Stamps

Corbett, Patricia A., trust: Corbett Foundation

Corbett, Richard E., treas, trust: Montgomery Foundation

Corbett, Steve, dir (mktg): Calex Manufacturing Co.

Corbett, Thomas R., pres, trust: Corbett Foundation

Corbin, Hunter W., vp, dir: Hyde and Watson Foundation

Corbin, Lee Harrison, dir, asst secy, asst treas: Hopkins Foundation, Josephine Lawrence

Corboy, James John, pres, dir: Dresser Industries

Corcoran, Walter G., vp bd dirs, mem investment comm: Dana Foundation, Charles A.

Corcoran, William G., trust: Clarke Trust, John

Corcoran, William J., treas: Harriman Foundation, Gladys and Roland; treas: Harriman Foundation, Mary W.

Cordaro, Nancy Anne, dir, pres: Alexander Foundation, Walter

Cordes, Donald L., secy: Koch Foundation, Fred C.

Cordes, James F., pres, dir: American Natural Resources Co.; pres, dir: ANR Foundation

Cordon, Frank Joseph, secy: Kingsley Foundation, Lewis A.

Core, Ruth T., dir: Chapin Foundation of Myrtle Beach, South Carolina

Corey, William G., MD, trust: MacKenzie Foundation; trust: Norris Foundation, Kenneth T. and Eileen L.

Cori, C. Tom, chmn, pres, ceo, dir: Sigma-Aldrich Corp.

Cori, Tom, vp, dir: Mallinckrodt, Jr. Foundation, Edward

Corkern, Wilton C., Jr., trust: Higginson Trust, Corina

Corlett, Robert, pres, dir: Lockheed Leadership Fund

Corley, Anne, dir corp commun: Twentieth Century-Fox Film Corp.

Corley, Margaret, mgr: Dewing Foundation, Frances R.

Corley, Mary Jo Ratner, pres, trust: Ratner Foundation, Milton M.

Corman, Stephen D., treas, dir: Burroughs Wellcome Fund

Cormany, Ralph L., dir: Livingston Memorial Foundation

Cormier, Margaret, secy, treas, trust: Zigler Foundation, Fred B. and Ruth B.

Corn, Elizabeth T., don, secy: Beloco Foundation; trust: Bradley-Turner Foundation

Corn, Jack W., chmn, ceo: Quaker State Corp.

Corn, Lovick P., pres, trust: Beloco Foundation; vchmn, trust: Bradley-Turner Foundation

Corneille, Barbara Berry, secy, dir: Berry Foundation, Lowell

Cornelius, Iris H., trust: Bigelow Foundation, F. R.

Cornelius, James M., dir: Lilly & Co. Foundation, Eli; treas: Noyes, Jr. Memorial Foundation, Nicholas H.

Cornelius, Julie, mem grants comm: First Bank System Foundation

Cornelius, Nelson O., trust: Frankel Foundation

Cornelius, William E., chmn, ceo, dir: Union Electric Co.; trust: Union Electric Co. Charitable Trust

Cornell, Harry M., Jr., chmn, ceo, dir: Leggett & Platt, Inc.

Cornell, N. Thomas, trust: Hauss-Helms Foundation

Cornell, R. Gary, admin: Johnson Co. Foundation, E. F.

Cornell, S. Douglas, trust: Cornell Trust, Peter C.

Cornelson, George Henry, mem adv comm: Bailey Foundation

Corning, Henry H., trust: American Foundation Corporation

Corning, Nathan E., trust: American Foundation Corporation

Corning, Ursula, trust: Vidda Foundation

Cornish, John M., trust: Harrington Trust, George; trust: Wharton Trust, William P.

Cornish, William G., trust: Harrington Trust, George

Cornog, Robert A., chmn, ceo, pres: Snap-on Tools Corp.

Cornu, Thomas W., trust: Charlesbank Homes

Cornwall, John W., trust: Fund for New Jersey

Cornwall, Joseph C., chmn, treas, trust: Fund for New Jersey

Cornwell, Diane, adm dir: Haynes Foundation, John Randolph and Dora

Coronella, Charles J., pres, ceo: Chase Bank of Arizona

Corpus, Janet, trust: Azadoutioun Foundation

Corpus-Perez, Chary, admin corp contributions: Bacardi Imports

Corr, J. M., vp, dir: CertainTeed Corp. Foundation

Corr, Paul J., mgr: J. D. B. Fund

Corrado, Fred, vchmn, exec vp (fin & admin): Great Atlantic & Pacific Tea Co. Inc.

Correll, Alston Dayton, pres, ceo: Georgia-Pacific Corp.

Correnti, John D., pres, coo: Nucor Corp.

Correra, Francis X., sr vp, cfo: Town & Country Corp.

Corrigan, Ann G., trust: Goddard Foundation, Charles B.

Corrigan, James H., Jr., pres, ceo, dir: Mebane Packaging Corp.

Corrigan, Wilfred J., chmn, ceo: LSI Logic Corp.

Corrigan, William E., Jr., sr vp (pers): Attleboro Pawtucket Savings Bank; exec trust: Attleboro Pawtucket Savings Bank Charitable Foundation

Corry, Charles A., chmn, ceo, dir: USX Corp.; chmn, trust: USX Foundation

Corsini, Andrew C., sr vp, cfo: Swank, Inc.

Corso, Joseph D., dir: Inland Steel-Ryerson Foundation

Corson, F. P., vp: Dow Chemical Co. Foundation

Corson, Keith, pres: Coachmen Industries

Corson, Madeline G., dir: Gannett Foundation, Guy P.

Corson, Maurice S., pres: Wexner Foundation

Corson, Thomas H., chmn: Coachmen Industries

Cort, Doris, asst secy: Gould Foundation for Children, Edwin

Cort, Kenneth J., coo: Ames Department Stores

Cortese, Arline Snyder, trust: Snyder Foundation, Harold B. and Dorothy A.

Cortines, Ramon C., treas: Institute for Research on Learning

Cortner, Nancy, trust: Sullivan Foundation, Algernon Sydney

Cortright, Earle D., Jr., pres: Deltona Corp.

Corvin, Mrs. Robert, dir: Stulsaft Foundation, Morris

Corvin, William, vp, dir: Stulsaft Foundation, Morris

Corwin, Bruce, pres: Metropolitan Theatres Corp.

Corwin, Bruce C., ceo, pres, cfo: Metropolitan Theatres Foundation

Corwin, Laura J., secy: New York Times Co. Foundation

Cory, William F., trust: Carver Charitable Trust, Roy J.

Corzo, Mignel Angel, dir (Getty Conservation Inst): Getty Trust, J. Paul

Cosgrove, Howard E., pres, ceo, coo: Delmarva Power & Light Co.

Cosgrove, Michael J., treas: GE Foundations

Cossman, Jerome, dir: Rosenhaus Peace Foundation, Sarah and Matthew

Costello, Albert Joseph, pres, dir: American Cyanamid Co.

Costello, John J., trust: Homeland Foundation

Costello, Joseph Ball, pres, ceo: Cadence Design Systems

Costello, Shirley J., adm: Herbst Foundation

Costello, Thomas Patrick, pres, dir: Westinghouse Electric Corp.; trust: Westinghouse Foundation

Coster, Nancy L., trust: Boehm Foundation

Costley, Gary Edward, trust: Miller Foundation

Costley, Lew, trust: Swanson Family Foundation, Dr. W.C.

Cota-Robles, Eugene H., trust, mem nominating comm: Carnegie Corporation of New York

Cote, Samuel A., vp, dir: Thorpe Foundation, James R.

Cotham, W. Robert, Jr., vp, asst secy: Bass Corporation, Perry and Nancy Lee

Cotrone, Marion, vp (corp commun): Barclays Bank of New York

Cotsen, Lloyd Edward, trust: Ahmanson Foundation; chmn, ceo: Neutrogena Corp.

Cotten, F. David, mgr pub rel: CNG Transmission Corp.

Cotter, Daniel, pres, ceo: Cotter & Co.

Cotter, Harvey S., vp (fin), treas: Freedom Forum

Cotter, Patrick William, dir: Bucyrus-Erie Foundation; vp, treas, dir: Evinrude Foundation, Ralph; secy, exec dir: Stackner Family Foundation

Cotter, Timothy P., secy: Coleman Charitable Trust

Cotting, James C., chmn, ceo, dir: Navistar International Corp.; dir: Navistar Foundation

Cottle, Robert DuQuemin, dir: Keating Family Foundation

Cottrell, Comer J., chmn, pres, ceo: Pro-line Corp.

Cottrell, G. Walton, vp, cfo: Carpenter Technology Corp.

Cottrell, Joseph, M.D., trust: Cottrell Foundation

Cottrell, Joseph J., Sr., trust: Cottrell Foundation

Cottrell, Mary M., trust: Cottrell Foundation

Couch, John Charles, pres, ceo, dir, coo: Alexander & Baldwin, Inc.; pres, dir: Alexander & Baldwin Foundation

Coudrai, Marcelle, dir: Larsen Fund

Coughenour, Katherine N., trust: Quaker Chemical Foundation

Coughenour, Wilda, Mingenback Foundation, Julia J.

Coughlan, Gary Patrick, cfo, sr vp fin: Abbott Laboratories; pres: Abbott Laboratories Fund

Coughlin, Barring, trust: Eaton Foundation, Cyrus

Coughlin, James P., pres: DCNY Corp.; dir: Discount Corp. of New York Charitable Foundation

Coughlin, Sister Magdalen, dir: Doheny Foundation, Carrie Estelle; trust: Getty Trust, J. Paul

Coughlin, Thomas Martin, mem: Wal-Mart Foundation

Coughlon, Timothy, pres: Norwest Bank Nebraska

Couilling, L. R., Jr., chmn, dir: Bowen Foundation, Ethel N.

Coulombe, Joseph H., co-chmn, dir: Thrifty Corp.

Coulson, Norman M., vchmn, pres: Glendale Federal Bank

Coulter, George S., pres, trust: Swisher Foundation, Carl S.

Coulter, Joan, secy, treas: Reily Foundation

Coulter, Joseph R., Jr., pres: Coulter Corp.

Coumelis, Linda, mgr corp community rels: Texas Instruments

Countryman, Gary L., chmn, ceo: Liberty Mutual Insurance Group/Boston

Counts, T., asst secy: Crawford & Co. Foundation

Couper, Richard Watrous, trust: Link Foundation; dir: Pforzheimer Foundation, Carl and Lily

Couri, John A., pres, ceo, dir: Duty Free International

Courter, James Andrew, secy: Ford Motor Co. Fund

Courts, Richard W., trust: Courts Foundation; trust: Gilbert, Jr. Charitable Trust, Price

Courts, Richard W., II, pres, trust: Courts Foundation; chmn, secy: Gilbert, Jr. Charitable Trust, Price

Courts, Richard Winn, II, chmn, pres, dir: Atlantic Realty Co.; vchmn, trust: Campbell Foundation, J. Bulow

Cousineau, Eileen P., secy: Curran Foundation

Couzens, Melinda A., trust: Anschutz Family Foundation

Cover, Fred W., trust: Southwest Gas Corp. Foundation

Coverdell, E. P., dir: Georgia Health Foundation

Covert, Calvin C., chmn, ceo, pres: Woodward Governor Co.

Covey, Kathleen D., trust: Strake Foundation

Covington, James W., trust: Barnett Charities

Covington, Joe S., MD, dir: Hardin Foundation, Phil

Covington, Marion S., trust: Covington Foundation, Marion Stedman

Covington, Olive W., dir: Strong Foundation, Hattie M.

Covitt, Regina, asst treas: Bettingen Corporation, Burton G.

Cowan, Ivy, Sr., sr chmn: Stonecutter Mills Corp.

Cowan, James R., chmn, ceo: Stonecutter Mills Corp.; vp, dir: Stonecutter Foundation

Cowan, Jill, secy: Metropolitan Theatres Foundation

Cowan, John C., Jr., trust: Burlington Industries Foundation

Cowan, John L., pres, coo: Kasler Corp.

Cowan, Marjorie, trust, vp, secy: Friedland Family Foundation, Samuel

Cowan, R. D., ceo, pres: Davey Tree Expert Co.; pres: Davey Co. Foundation

Cowan, Robert, mng dir: Lamb-Weston Foundation

Cowan, Rory J., exec vp, info tech: Donnelley & Sons Co., R.R.

Cowan, W. Maxwell, MD,PhD, vp, chief scientific off: Hughes Medical Institute, Howard

Cowart, D. Randy, pres: Powell Co.; William

Cowden, Jean, pub aff mgr: Mayer Foods Corp., Oscar

Cowdrey, Ruth F., trust: Walsh Charity Trust, Blanche M.

Cowell, John F., III, trust: First Boston Foundation Trust

Cowell, Marion Aubrey, Jr., dir: First Union Foundation

Cowen, Robert J., trust: Beal Foundation

Cowin, Peter G., trust: Hill Crest Foundation

Cowles, Charles, trust: Cowles Charitable Trust

Cowles, Donald T., vp, gen couns, secy, dir: Reynolds Metals Co. Foundation

Cowles, Gardner, III, don, pres, trust: Cowles Charitable Trust

Cowles, James Paine, vp, trust: Cowles Foundation, Harriet Cheney; vp, trust: Cowles Foundation, William H.

Cowles, Jan Streate, trust: Cowles Charitable Trust

Cowles, William Hutchinson, III, pres, trust: Cowles Foundation, Harriet Cheney; pres, trust: Cowles Foundation, William H.

Cowles Schroth, Virginia, trust: Cowles Charitable Trust

Cowley, Allen W., MD, comm mem: Whitaker Foundation

Cowman, Fairman C., trust: Mechanics Bank Foundation

Cox, Archibald, Jr., pres, ceo: First Boston

Cox, C.D., trust: SCT Foundation

Cox, Charles D., III, vp, cfo: Shenandoah Life Insurance Co.

Cox, Clint V., trust: Broadhurst Foundation

Cox, David Carson, pres, ceo, dir: Cowles Media Co.; vp, dir: Cowles Media Foundation

Cox, Donald M., chmn, dir: Teagle Foundation

Cox, Douglas L., sr vp (fin), cfo: Elf Atochem North America; trust: Elf Atochem North America Foundation

Cox, Frances S., asst dir: Watson Foundation, Thomas J.

Cox, Frederick K., pres, treas, trust: Gund Foundation, George

Cox, Howard F., dir: Preuss Foundation

Cox, John Francis, sr vp (commun): Avon Products

Cox, John W., vchmn, trust: Mabee Foundation, J. E. and L. E.

Cox, Kyle W., trust: Kettering Family Foundation

Cox, Lawrence W., treas, dir: Powell Foundation, Charles Lee

Cox, Mark A., trust: Kettering Family Foundation

Cox, Martha W., treas: Cox Foundation

Cox, Michael L., asst secy: Ontario Corporation Foundation

Cox, Robert G., pres, dir: Summit Bancorporation

Cox, Robert T., dir: Shelter Insurance Foundation

Cox, Russell N., trust: Linnell Foundation

Cox, Sid, vchmn, trust: Meredith Foundation

Cox, William, trust: Fish Foundation, Bert

Cox, William Coburn, Jr., trust: Cox Charitable Trust, Jessie B.; pres, don, dir: Cox Foundation

Cox Chambers, Anne, chmn, dir: Atlanta Journal & Constitution

Coxe, Eckley, IV, comm mem: Whitaker Foundation

Coxe, T. C., III, trust: Sonoco Products Foundation

Coxe, Tench C., secy: Turner Foundation

Coxhead, Peter C., pres, dir: Nichols Foundation

Coy, Lorreta, asst secy: Moriah Fund

Coye, Molly Joel, trust: China Medical Board of New York

Coyer, Patricia, trust: Graham Charitable Trust, William L.

Coyle, D. P., secy: FPL Group Foundation

Coyle, Patrick E., dir: Rennebohm Foundation, Oscar

Coyne, Francis J., pres, coo: General Accident Insurance Co. of America; trust: General Accident Charitable Trust

Coyne, James E., vp: Wyman-Gordon Foundation

Coyne, Mary V., mem scholarship comm: Zimmerman Foundation, Hans and Clara Davis

Coyne, Richard L., trust: Kiewit Foundation, Peter

Cozens, Elsian, asst secy: Menil Foundation

Cozzolino, Salvatore J., vp, treas, dir: Coltec Industries Charitable Foundation

Crabbe, Grace, asst treas: Clark Home for Aged People, Ella

Crabtree, David, trust: Innovating Worthy Projects Foundation

Cracchiolo, Andrea, III, dir: Steele Foundation

Cracchiolo, Daniel, pres: Steele Foundation

Craft, H. Spalding, exec dir: Lanier Brothers Foundation

Craft, Ira Q., trust: Day Foundation, Cecil B.

Craft, Lynn, dir: Collins Foundation, Carr P.

Craft, Sylvia W., dir: Wellons Foundation

Crafton, Robert, pres: Rand-Whitney Packaging-Delmar Corp.

Craig, Albert B., III, dir: Staunton Farm Foundation

Craig, Andrew Billings, III, chmn, ceo, pres: Boatmen's Bancshares

Craig, Eleanor L., trust: Benua Foundation

Craig, Floyd w., secy: SCT Foundation

Craig, George, pres, ceo, dir: HarperCollins Publishers

Craig, H. Curtis, trust: Brown Foundation, James Graham

Craig, John, pres: Lender's Bagel Bakery

Craig, John E., Jr., exec vp, treas: Commonwealth Fund

Craig, Mary Ellen, mem: American Express Co.

Craig, Nedenia R., trust: Spiritus Gladius Foundation

Craig, Nina Rumbough, dir: Post Foundation of D.C., Marjorie Merriweather

Craig, Randell C., vp (mktg): Chubb Life Insurance Co. of America

Craigmyle, Louise, trust: Craigmyle Foundation

Craigmyle, Ronald M., Jr., trust: Craigmyle Foundation

Crain, James F., secy, treas, dir: Bennett Memorial Corporation, James Gordon

Crain, James T., Jr., exec dir: Cralle Foundation

Crain, Richard, trust: Feinberg Foundation, Joseph and Bessie

Craine, Beatrice, trust: Feinberg Foundation, Joseph and Bessie

Cram, Douglas, secy: PepsiCo

Cram, John O., Jr., pres: Concord Chemical Co.

Cram, Katharine Neilson, pres: Neilson Foundation, George W.

Cram, Oliver S., pres, dir: Concord Foundation

Cramer, Douglas S., pres, dir, treas: Cramer Foundation

Cramer, Ellen R., comm mem: Wells Foundation, Franklin H. and Ruth L.

Cramer, Lee H., asst secy, mem (trust comm): Rockwell International Corp. Trust

Cramer, Richard A., trust: Hartford Foundation, John A.

Crampton, Stuart B., dir: Research Corporation

Crance, Gordon, pres: Apple and Eve

Crandall, Robert Lloyd, chmn, pres, ceo, dir: AMR Corp.; pres, dir: AMR/American Airlines Foundation

Crane, Alpo F., trust: Crane Foundation, Raymond E. and Ellen F.

Crane, Charles R., trust: Friendship Fund

Crane, Clarence, Jr., dir: Lytel Foundation, Bertha Russ

Crane, David J., Jr., trust: Crane Foundation, Raymond E. and Ellen F.

Crane, Edward M., Jr., trust: Curran Foundation

Crane, Les, pres, chmn: Software Toolworks

Crane, Lucia L., vp: Quinlan Foundation, Elizabeth C.

Crane, Robert, vp: Mertz-Gilmore Foundation, Joyce

Crane, Robert F., Jr., trust: Crane Foundation, Raymond E. and Ellen F.

Crane, S. R., trust: Crane Foundation, Raymond E. and Ellen F.

Crane, Sylvia E., trust, vp: Friendship Fund

Crane, Thomas, trust: Friendship Fund

Craner, Ernest C., dir: CHC Foundation

Cranor, John M., III, pres, ceo: Kentucky Fried Chicken Corp.

Crapple, George, vp, dir: Wiener Foundation, Malcolm Hewitt

Crary, Evans, Jr., secy: Haven Charitable Foundation, Nina

Crary, Judy, Jr., Haven Charitable Foundation, Nina

Crary, Miner D., Jr., secy, dir: Clark Foundation, Robert Sterling

Crary, Oliver, treas: Homeland Foundation

Crassweller, Donald B., treas, dir: Alworth Memorial Fund, Marshall H. and Nellie

Craugh, Joseph P., Jr., sr vp, govt aff couns: Harleysville Mutual Insurance Co.

Craven, David Laird, trust: Longwood Foundation

Crawford, Anne W., trust: Whitehead Foundation

Crawford, Donald D., secy, treas: Drum Foundation

Crawford, Donald D., Jr., treas, mem bd dirs: Skaggs Foundation, L. J. and Mary C.

Crawford, Earle W., trust: Wilson Foundation, John and Nevils

Crawford, Edward F., chmn, pres, ceo: Park-Ohio Industries Inc.

Crawford, G. Wayne, pres: Industrial Risk Insurers

Crawford, George, trust: Hargis Charitable Foundation, Estes H. and Florence Parker

Crawford, Helen, dir: Huisking Foundation

Crawford, James B., pres: James River Coal Co.

Crawford, James C., Jr., chmn, pres: Moore & Sons, B.C.

Crawford, Mac, pres: Charter Medical Corp.

Crawford, Mike, admin: Sumitomo Bank of California

Crawford, Milton W., Jr., vp, secy: Poole and Kent Foundation

Crawford, Richard, pres, ceo: Voplex Corp.

Crawford, Steve, trust: Scripps Howard Foundation

Crawford, Vernon, dir, educator: Georgia Scientific and Technical Research Foundation

Crawford, W.S., pres: Memphis Light Gas & Water Division

Crawford, William D., asst treas: Brenner Foundation, Mervyn; cfo, dir: Herbst Foundation

Crayton, Sam, mem comm: American National Bank & Trust Co. of Chicago Foundation

Creach, Dale, dir: MFA Foundation

Creach, Ormal C., pres, dir: MFA Foundation

Creagan, David J., contact person: Hammer Foundation, Armand

Crean, Donna C., secy: Crean Foundation

Crean, Eilean, asst secy: Dorot Foundation

Crean, John C., don, pres, treas: Crean Foundation; chmn, ceo, dir: Fleetwood Enterprises, Inc.

Crean, Johnnie R., vp: Crean Foundation

Cree, Nancy, trust: Dimick Foundation

Creed, Thomas G., pres, coo: Florida Steel Corp.; vp, dir: Florida Steel Foundation

Creedon, John, pres: Home for Aged Men

Creek, W. W., secy: General Motors Foundation

Creighton, John W., Jr., pres, dir, ceo: Weyerhaeuser Co.

Creighton, Neil, pres, ceo: McCormick Tribune Foundation, Robert R.

Cremer, H.L., dir, secy: Cremer Foundation

Crenshaw, Gordon L., chmn: Universal Leaf Tobacco Co.; mem: Universal Leaf Foundation

Crenshaw, H. W., dir: Stonecutter Foundation

Cresci, Andrew A., treas: Gellert Foundation, Celia Berta

Crespo, J. R., chmn, pres, ceo, dir: Southern Connecticut Gas Co.

Cress, Robert G., trust: Riggs Benevolent Fund

Cressman, Paul R., pres, trust: Lockwood Foundation, Byron W. and Alice L.

Cressman, Paul R., Jr., trust: Lockwood Foundation, Byron W. and Alice L.

Creticos, Angelo P., MD, vchmn, dir: Washington Square Health Foundation

Crew, Herbert A., Jr., trust: Greenville Foundation

Crikelair, D. C., treas: Texaco Foundation

Crim, Alonzo A., trust, mem long-range planning comm: Mott Foundation, Charles Stewart

Crim, Jack C., pres, coo: Talley Industries, Inc.

Crimmins, Robert J., chmn, dir: Metropolitan Life Foundation

Criniti, Steve, cfo: Ormet Corp.; treas, dir: Ormet Foundation

Cripe, Bruce A., chmn, dir: Forum Group, Inc.

Criscuoli, Phyllis M., admin dir, treas: Dodge Foundation, Cleveland H.

Crisp, Maggie Alice Sandlin, awards adv comm: Ferebee Endowment, Percy O.

Cristman, Bess, mem: Templeton Foundation, Herbert A.

Critchell, Simon, pres: Cartier, Inc.

Critchlow, Paul W., vp, trust: Merrill Lynch & Co. Foundation

Critser, Gary P., secy: Habig Foundation

Criuckshank, Joseph H., secy: Clark Foundation

Crockard, Jane S., trust: Comer Foundation

Crocker, Charles, trust: Crocker Trust, Mary A.

Crocker, William H., trust: Crocker Trust, Mary A.

Crockett, Bruce L., pres, ceo: Communications Satellite Corp. (COMSAT)

Crockett, Kathleen, trust: Covington Foundation, Marion Stedman

Crockett, Rex J., pres: Dexter Co.

Croft, Mary, treas: Cowles Charitable Trust

Cromling, Maureen M., chmn, pres: Ross Corp.; pres, dir: Ross Foundation

Cromling, William E., trust: Ross Foundation

Cromling, William E., II, trust: Ross Foundation

Cromwell, Robert L., trust: Jones Intercable Tampa Trust

Cronin, Jeremiah P., vp, cfo: Crane Co.; vp, treas: Crane Fund

Cronin, Jerry P., trust: Crane Fund for Widows and Children

Cronin, Mary Gittings, exec dir: Piton Foundation

Cronin, Robert, pres, ceo: Wallace Computer Services; pres, dir: Wallace Computer Services Foundation

Cronk, William F., III, pres, dir: Dreyer's & Edy's Grand Ice Cream

Cronkhite, Leonard Wolsey, Jr., trust: Day Foundation, Nancy Sayles

Cronkite, Walter, trust: CBS Foundation

Cronson, Mary, vp, trust: Sharp Foundation, Evelyn

Cronson, Paul, vp, trust: Sharp Foundation, Evelyn

Crook, Donald M., secy: Kimberly-Clark Foundation

Crook, James W., trust: First Mississippi Corp. Foundation

Crooke, Edward A., pres, coo: Baltimore Gas & Electric Co.; pres, dir: Baltimore Gas & Electric Foundation

Crooks, William B., Jr., dir: Hardin Foundation, Phil

Crosby, Edwin L., treas, trust: Carolyn Foundation

Crosby, Elizabeth J., vp, dir: Grand Rapids Label Foundation

Crosby, Ella P., trust: Southways Foundation

Crosby, Franklin M., III, trust: Carolyn Foundation

Crosby, G. Christian, trust: Carolyn Foundation

Crosby, Gordon E., Jr., chmn, ceo, dir: USLIFE Corp.

Crosby, Robert C., dir: HCA Foundation

Crosby, Sumner McKnight, Jr., trust: Carolyn Foundation

Crosby, Thomas M., Jr., trust: Carolyn Foundation

Crose, Jack, dir: Eagles Memorial Foundation

Crosland, Katherine, trust: Lyndhurst Foundation

Crosley, Britton E., Cook Inlet Region

Cross, Dewain Kingsley, treas, trust: Cooper Industries Foundation

Cross, Jane C., dir: Cooke Foundation Corporation, V. V.

Cross, Joe D., vp, dir: Cooke Foundation Corporation, V. V.

Cross, John W., III, pres, dir: Moore Foundation, Edward S.

Cross, Michael R., treas, corp secy: Bush Charitable Foundation, Edyth

Cross, Robert J., chmn: Nashua Trust Co.

Cross, Theodore L., trust: Guggenheim Memorial Foundation, John Simon

Cross, Travis, trust: Meyer Memorial Trust

Cross, Wallace, exec vp, cfo: Central Hudson Gas & Electric Corp.

Cross, William Redmond, Jr., pres, dir: Langeloth Foundation, Jacob and Valeria

Crossland, Christine H., community resources specialist: Portland General Electric Co.

Crossman, Elizabeth, vp: Weyerhaeuser Co. Foundation

Crossman, Patrick F., pres, dir: Bristol-Myers Squibb Foundation; dir: Childs Memorial Fund for Medical Research, Jane Coffin

Crosswhite, Randal, cfo: Independent Bankshares

Crosthwait, Rene, secy, treas: Millhollon Educational Trust Estate, Nettie

Crosthwaite, Kevin C., pres: Spartus Corp.

Crouch, Gary L., off, dir: Valmont Foundation

Crouse, William W., pres: Ortho Diagnostic Systems, Inc.

Crow, Bob J., exec dir: Carter Foundation, Amon G.

Crow, Chris, treas: Veritas Foundation

Crow, Danny, cfo: Scotty's, Inc.

Crow, I.A., vp: Veritas Foundation

Crowder, Juanita, trust: Jewell Memorial Foundation, Daniel Ashley and Irene Houston

Crowder, Sheffield L., adm: Conn Memorial Foundation

Crowe, Mary Jane, dir: McMillen Foundation

Crowe, Timothy J., vp, cfo: Knight Foundation, John S. and James L.

Crowell, Shirley M., secy: Noble Foundation, Edward John

Crowley, Daniel F., trust: Hawley Foundation

Crowley, James, cfo: Aladdin Industries, Incorporated

Crown, Arie Steven, trust: Crown Charitable Fund, Edward A.; vp, dir: Crown Memorial, Arie and Ida

Crown, James Schine, trust: Crown Charitable Fund, Edward A.; vp, dir: Crown Memorial, Arie and Ida

Crown, Lester, trust: Crown Charitable Fund, Edward A.; don, vp, treas, dir: Crown Memorial, Arie and Ida; mgr: Material Service Foundation

Crown, Susan, trust: Crown Charitable Fund, Edward A.; pres: Crown Memorial, Arie and Ida

Croxton, William M., vp, treas, dir: Jameson Foundation, J. W. and Ida M.

Crozer, Robert P., vchmn: Flowers Industries, Inc.

Crozier, Nancy R., trust, vp: McFeely-Rogers Foundation

Crozier, William Marshall, Jr., chmn, pres, ceo: BayBanks

Cruden, M. Patricia, secy: Pacific Western Foundation

Cruikshank, Robert J., vp, asst secy, trust: Fish Foundation, Ray C.

Cruikshank, Thomas Henry, trust: Goodyear Tire & Rubber Company Fund; chmn, ceo: Halliburton Co.; pres, trust: Halliburton Foundation

Crull, Timm F., chmn, ceo: Nestle U.S.A. Inc.; pres: Nestle USA Foundation

Crum, Lawrence Lee, mem loan comm: Lindsay Student Aid Fund, Franklin

Crumling, Robert, vp human resources: Glidden Co.

Crummer, M. Thomas, trust: Criss Memorial Foundation, Dr. C.C. and Mabel L.

Crump, Ed, secy, treas: Coughlin-Saunders Foundation

Crump, Robert W., fin off: Crystal Trust

Cruser, George E., trust: Westvaco Foundation Trust

Crutchfield, Edward Elliott, Jr., chmn, ceo: First Union Corp.; dir: First Union Foundation

Crutchfield, William, Jr., dir: Reflection Riding

Crutsinger, Robert Keane, chmn, chief exec off: Wetterau

Cruz, Amado G., trust: Fox Foundation Trust, Jacob L. and Lewis

Cryer, Arthur W., trust: Baird Foundation

Cryer, Margot, secy, treas, dir: Sharp Foundation, Charles S. and Ruth C.

Crystal, John, chmn: Iowa Savings Bank; pres: Iowa Savings Bank Charitable Trust

Crystal, Tom, dir: Iowa Savings Bank Charitable Trust

Cuatrecasas, Pedro, dir: Life Sciences Research Foundation

Cudahy, Daniel, dir, don grandson: Cudahy Fund, Patrick and Anna M.

Cudahy, Janet S., MD, pres, dir, don daughter-in-law: Cudahy Fund, Patrick and Anna M.

Cudahy, M. J., pres: Marquette Electronics; trust: Marquette Electronics Foundation

Cudahy, Richard D., chmn, dir, don son: Cudahy Fund, Patrick and Anna M.

Cudd, Barbara Lee, dir: Mertz Foundation, Martha

Cudd, Nancy H., dir: Mertz Foundation, Martha

Cudd, Robert A. N., treas, dir: Mertz Foundation, Martha

Cuff, S. P., pres: Calex Manufacturing Co.

Cuff, William, pres: Diamond Walnut Growers

Cuklerman, Roger, asst secy: de Rothschild Foundation, Edmond

Culbertson, Judy B., vp: Meadows Foundation

Cullen, Albert F., Jr., trust: Wolfson Foundation, Louis E.

Cullen, Claire, secy: Bronfman Foundation, Samuel

Cullen, Frederick Landis, chmn, ceo: Banc One Wisconsin Corp.; pres, dir: Banc One Wisconsin Foundation

Cullen, James G., pres: Bell Atlantic Corp.; pres, ceo, dir: New Jersey Bell Telephone Company

Cullen, John B., chmn, ceo: King Kullen Grocery Co., Inc.

Cullen, Roy Henry, vp, trust: Cullen Foundation

Cullenbine, Clair Stephens, trust: Gaylord Foundation, Clifford Willard; dir: Montgomery Street Foundation

Culley, Natalie C., secy, dir: Dick Family Foundation

Culliton, Edward F., vp: Castle & Co., A.M.; vp, dir: Castle Foundation

Cullman, Edgar M, Jr., pres, coo, dir: Culbro Corp.

Cullman, Edgar M., chmn, ceo, dir: Culbro Corp.

Cullum, Charles, vp, trust: McDermott Foundation, Eugene

Cullum, Charles G., chmn emeritus: Cullum Cos.

Cullum, Dorothy R., dir: Hoblitzelle Foundation

Cullum, K. H., pres, ceo: Bristol Steel & Iron Works

Cully, Mrs. John O., Dick Family Foundation

Culman, Anne LaFarge, vp: Abell Foundation, The

Culver, Catherine, trust: Thoresen Foundation

Culver, Ellsworth, dir: Arca Foundation

Culver, Margaret S., secy: Vogt Foundation, Henry

Culvertson, Richard, treas: Innovating Worthy Projects Foundation

Culwell, Elizabeth, mem: Maier Foundation, Sarah Pauline

Cuman, J. J., pres: Mizuno Corporation of America

Cumings, Charles B., trust emeritus: Mott Foundation, Charles Stewart

Cumming, Ian M., trust: American Investment Co. Foundation; chmn, ceo: Leucadia National Corp.; trust: Leucadia Foundation

Cummings, Bruce, dir human resources: Abitibi Co.

Cummings, D. Merril, mgr, vp, treas, secy, trust: Abercrombie Foundation

Cummings, Diane, mem bd, secy: Cummings Foundation, Nathan

Cummings, Douglas R., dir: Kirkpatrick Foundation

Cummings, Helen K., dir: HCA Foundation

Cummings, James K., vchmn, mem bd: Cummings Foundation, Nathan

Cummings, Jean B., trust: Wells Trust Fund, Fred W.

Cummings, Melbourne W., Founder: Addison-Wesley Publishing Co.

Cummings, Michael, mem bd: Cummings Foundation, Nathan

Cummings, Naurice G., dir, mem dirs grant program comm: Keck Foundation, W. M.

Cummings, Robert E., Jr., secy: Scott Fund, Olin

Cummings, Susan Hurd, trust: Payne Foundation, Frank E. and Seba B.

Cummings, William S., pres: Cummings Properties Management, Inc.

Cummins, Edgar J., sr vp, cfo: Allergan, Inc.

Cummins, Mark R., sr vp, treas, chief investment officer: Harleysville Mutual Insurance Co.

Cummins, T.J., Marshburn Foundation

Cundey, S.I., Jr., treas: North American Philips Foundation

Cundiff, Richard M., treas, trust: Ford Fund, Benson and Edith; treas: Ford Fund, Eleanor and Edsel; treas: Ford Fund, Walter and Josephine; treas, trust: Ford Fund, William and Martha; treas, trust: Ford II Fund, Henry

Cuneo, Herta, dir: Cuneo Foundation

Cuneo, John, Jr., genl ptnr: Milwaukee Golf Development Co.

Cuneo, John F., Jr., pres, dir: Cuneo Foundation

Cunin, John R., chmn distribution comm: Bruening Foundation, Eva L. and Joseph M.

Cunniffe, Maurice J., chmn, dir, secy: American Optical Corp.

Cunnigle, Edward J., trust: Pritchard Charitable Trust, William E. and Maude S.

Cunningham, Dan, trust off, sr vp (First Natl Bank): Bock Charitable Trust, George W.

Cunningham, Helen, exec dir: Fels Fund, Samuel S.

Cunningham, Ingersoll, trust: Shaw Fund for Mariner's Children

Cunningham, J. Oliver, chmn distribution comm: Oliver Memorial Trust Foundation

Cunningham, James, dir: MFA Foundation

Cunningham, John P., pres: International Aluminum Corp.

Cunningham, John W., vp, bd mem, dir: Gregg-Graniteville Foundation

Cunningham, M. E., indus rels dir: Inco Alloys International

Cunningham, Margaret S., trust: Snyder Foundation, Frost and Margaret

Cunningham, Nancy M., trust: Hannon Foundation, William H.

Cunningham, Richard, trust: Bass and Edythe and Sol G. Atlas Fund, Sandra Atlas

Cunningham, Jr., William J., chmn: Statler Foundation

Cunnningham, Kim, pub aff dept: Ricoh Electronics Inc.

Cuomo, Ralph, treas: Hearst Foundation; treas: Hearst Foundation, William Randolph

Cupps, Thomas Edward, vchmn, dir: Virginia Power Co.

Curbo, Gary W., dir, secy/treas: Schilling Foundation

Curby, Norma J., dir: Monsanto Fund

Curci, Frank, sr vp, cfo: Mayfair Super Markets

Curci, John L., Jr., dir: Hoag Family Foundation, George

Curci, John V., trust: Vesper Foundation

Curley, Ann L., asst secy, asst treas: Firstar Milwaukee Foundation

Curley, Charles, trust: Strauss Foundation, Leon

Curley, Jack R., treas, secy: Koret Foundation

Curley, John F., Jr., vchmn: Legg Mason Inc.

Curley, John J., chmn, pres, ceo: Gannett Co.

Curlin, Carol, trust: Baldwin Foundation

Curlin, Lemuel, trust: Baldwin Foundation

Curnes, Thomas J., trust: Buell Foundation, Temple Hoyne

Curran, Barbara Sanson, trust: Chubb Foundation; corp sec: ICI Americas

Curran, Carol Cockrell, dir: Cockrell Foundation

Curran, Charles, dir: Francis Families Foundation

Curran, Charles E., dir: Block Foundation, H&R

Curran, James J., chmn, pres, ceo: First Interstate Bank NW Region; chmn, pres, ceo, dir: First Interstate Bank of Oregon

Curran, Richard B., dir: Cockrell Foundation

Curran, S. H., sr vp, treas, cfo: Primark Corp.

Currey, Brownlee O., Jr., vp: Currey Foundation, Brownlee

Currey, R. J., pres, coo: Illinois Consolidated Telephone Co.

Currie, Gilbert A., asst treas, trust: Gerstacker Foundation, Rollin M.

Currie, Jack Thornton, trust: Kempner Fund, Harris and Eliza

Currie, Paula, dir: Chicago Tribune Foundation

Currie, Peter L. S., sr vp, cfo: McCaw Cellular Communications

Currier, Kevin, cfo: Dimeo Construction Co.

Currier, Lavinia, trust: Sacharuna Foundation

Currigan, Tom, dir external aff: Public Service Co. of Colorado

Curry, Bernard F., treas, trust, mem fin comm: Jones Foundation, W. Alton

Curry, Charles E., asst secy: Quaker Oats Foundation

Curry, David R., staff vp (pub affairs): Unisys Corp.

Curry, Irving G., III, secy: Endries Foundation, Ltd.

Curry, Natalie H., trust: Hulme Charitable Foundation, Milton G.

Curry, Roger, pres, ceo: Emery Worldwide

Curtin, John D., Jr., vp, treas: Cabot Corp. Foundation

Curtin, Thomas A., vp, cfo: Simplex Time Recorder Co.

Curtin, Timothy A., SJ, dir: Butler Foundation, J. Homer

Curtis, C. William, mem admin comm: Selby and Marie Selby Foundation, William G.

Curtis, Diane, dir: Barker Welfare Foundation

Curtis, Donna Streibich, recording secy: Harris Bank Foundation

Curtis, Elizabeth H., dir, adm: Atkinson Foundation

Curtis, Gerald L., trust: Ise Cultural Foundation

Curtis, Gregory Dyer, pres, secy: Laurel Foundation

Curtis, James E., Jr., vp, cfo: Luby's Cafeterias

Curtis, Kevin L., vp (mktg): Besser Co.

Curtis, Mabel E., pres: Havens Foundation, O. W.

Curtis, Therese D., secy: Anderson Foundation, Marion & John E.

Curtis, W. R., vp, secy, treas, trust: Plitt Southern Theatres, Inc., Employees Fund

Curtis, Wilson W., trust: Donaldson Charitable Trust, Oliver S. and Jennie R.

Curvin, Robert, Ph.D., trust: Victoria Foundation

Curzan, Myron P., dir: Connecticut Mutual Life Foundation

Cushman, Elizabeth, treas, dir: Dearborn Cable Communications Fund

Cushman, John C., dir: Howe and Mitchell B. Howe Foundation, Lucite Horton

Cushnie, Douglas J., trust: Kettering Family Foundation

Cushnie, Karen W., trust: Kettering Family Foundation

Cusmano, Christine, secy contributions comm: Federal-Mogul Corp. Charitable Trust Fund

Custer, Monford D., III, treas: Gallagher Family Foundation, Lewis P.

Cusumano, Gary M., pres, coo: Newhall Land & Farming Co.

Cutchins, Clifford Armstrong, III, dir: Camp Foundation

Cutchins, William W., dir: Camp Foundation

Cutler, Alexander M., mem contributions comm: Eaton Charitable Fund

Cutler, Richard M., trust, treas: Humane Society of the Commonwealth of Massachusetts

Cutlip, Randall Brower, trust: McNutt Charitable Trust, Amy Shelton

Cutter, Nancy L., secy: Foundation for Seacoast Health

Cutting, Richard W., trust: Children's Foundation of Erie County

Cuttitta, S.J., trust: Brunetti Charitable Trust, Dionigi

Cvengros, William D., vchmn, chief invest off: Pacific Mutual Life Insurance Co.; dir: Pacific Mutual Charitable Foundation

Cyphen, Irving, trust: Gerson Trust, B. Milfred

Cyphers, Judith, asst secy, dir: Strong Foundation, Hattie M.

Czepiel, Thomas P., trust: Scott Paper Co. Foundation

D

d'Alessio, Jon, trust: McKesson Foundation

D'Alonzo, Thomas W., secy, dir: Glaxo Foundation

D'Amato, Anthony S., chmn, ceo, coo, dir: Borden

D'Ambrosio, A. Daniel, chmn, mem trust comm: Bergen Foundation, Frank and Lydia

D'Ambrosio, Daniel, vp, trust: Bonner Foundation, Corella and Bertram

D'Andrade, Hugh Alfred, trust: Schering-Plough Foundation

D'Andrea, James A., trust: Copperweld Steel Co.'s Warren Employees' Trust

D'Arata, Joy E., vp, trust: Chatlos Foundation

d'Arbeloff, Alexander V., co-fdr, chmn, pres: Teradyne, Inc.

D'Arcy, June B., trust: Berkey Foundation, Peter

D'Orazio, Hal, pres: Ameritech Services

D'Souza, Dinesh, dir: Brady Foundation, W. H.

Dabah, Ezra, vchmn: Gitano Group; trust: Gitano Foundation

Dabah, Haim, pres, coo, dir: Gitano Group; trust: Gitano Foundation

Dabah, Isaac, vchmn: Gitano Group; trust: Gitano Foundation

Dabah, Morris, fdr, chmn, ceo, dir: Gitano Group; trust: Gitano Foundation

Dabney, Donna C., asst secy: Reynolds Metals Co. Foundation

Dabney, Thomas N., trust: Eaton Memorial Fund, Georgiana Goddard

Dachowski, Peter R., sr vp: CertainTeed Corp.

Dachs, Lauren B., dir: Hogan Foundation, Royal Barney

DaCunha, Milly, secy, contributions committee: New Jersey Bell Telephone Company

Daddario, Richard, cfo: Mutual of New York Foundation

Daddino, Anthony F., cfo: Donaldson, Lufkin & Jenrette; secy, treas: Donaldson, Lufkin & Jenrette Foundation

Dade, Malcom G., Jr., dir: Detroit Edison Foundation

Daering, Duane H., chmn, trust: CTS Foundation

Daggett, Christopher J., trust: Schumann Fund for New Jersey

Daghlian, Nazar, trust: Philibosian Foundation, Stephen

Daher, Thomas, vp, contr: Motch Corp.; pres, trust: Motch Corp. Foundation

Dahl, Arthur Ernest, trust: Carver Charitable Trust, Roy J.

Dahl, C. R., dir: Montgomery Street Foundation

Dahl, H. D., pres, dir: Drummond Co.

Dahl, Richard J., cfo: Bancorp Hawaii; vp, treas: Bancorp Hawaii Charitable Foundation

Dahlberg, Alfred William, III, pres, ceo, dir: Georgia Power Co.

Davis, Andrew P. Esq., secy: Goldsmith Foundation, Nathan and Louise

Davis, Anita T., trust: Louisiana-Pacific Foundation

Davis, Archie K., trust, chmn comm investments: Biddle Foundation, Mary Duke; trust: Duke Endowment

Davis, Bernard C., secy, trust: Clemens Foundation

Davis, Betty G., dir: Grede Foundation

Davis, Brian W., secy, asst treas: Potlatch Foundation for Higher Education/Potlatch Foundation II

Davis, C. E., trust: Griffin, Sr., Foundation, C. V.

Davis, C. S., III, pres: Dickey-John Corp.

Davis, Carle E., secy: Estes Foundation; secy, treas, trust: McCrea Foundation; secy, trust: Olsson Memorial Foundation, Elis

Davis, Carolyn P., vp: Community Foundation

Davis, Carolyne K., trust: Prudential Foundation

Davis, Carolyne Kahle, PhD, trust: Merck Co. Foundation

Davis, D. D., dir: 3M Co.

Davis, D. H., pres, ceo: Merchants Bancshares

Davis, Delmont A., pres, ceo, dir: Ball Corp.

Davis, Donald Walter, trust: Stanley Charitable Foundation, A. W.

Davis, Dudley H., pres, dir: Merchants Bank Foundation

Davis, Edward, pres: Advertising Checking Bureau; secy, dir: Katzenberger Foundation

Davis, Edwin, dir, treas: Murphy Co. Foundation, G.C.

Davis, Ellen P., trust: Preyer Fund, Mary Norris

Davis, Ellen Scripps, trust: Scripps Foundation, Ellen Browning

Davis, Errol Brown, Jr., pres, ceo: Wisconsin Power & Light Co.

Davis, Ethel F., trust: Foerderer Foundation, Percival E. and Ethel Brown

Davis, F. Elwood, pres, dir: Bloedorn Foundation, Walter A.

Davis, Florence N., dir: Davis Family - W.D. Charities, James E.

Davis, Frances, dir, secy: Churches Homes Foundation

Davis, Frederick W., II, secy, dir: Davis Foundation, Edwin W. and Catherine M.

Davis, G. Gordon, vp, secy, gov: Crary Foundation, Bruce L.

Davis, Gale E., trust: Criss Memorial Foundation, Dr. C.C. and Mabel L.

Davis, George W., Jr, sr vp: Boston Edison Co.; trust: Boston Edison Foundation

Davis, Gilbert S., dir, vp: Memorial Foundation for the Blind

Davis, Hal, treas: Amax Foundation

Davis, Harold O., secy, trust: Blade Foundation

Davis, Holbrook R., trust: Davis Foundations, Arthur Vining

Davis, J. Bradley, McGraw Foundation

Davis, J. Cody, trust: Lubrizol Foundation

Davis, J. H. Dow, trust: Davis Foundations, Arthur Vining

Davis, J. M., pres, coo: National Distributing Co., Inc.

Davis, Jack, chmn, pres, ceo, dir: Dataproducts Corp.

Davis, James, pres: New Balance Athletic Shoe

Davis, James Elsworth, pres, dir: Davis Family - W.D. Charities, James E.

Davis, James K., dir: Georgia Power Foundation

Davis, James N., treas, exec dir: Gheens Foundation

Davis, Jay M., vp: Davis Foundation, Inc.

Davis, Jayne C., vp, mem bd dirs: Skaggs Foundation, L. J. and Mary C.

Davis, Jeanette A., pres: Jasam Foundation

Davis, Jennifer, adm matching & in-kind programs: First Interstate Bank NW Region; bd mem: Seascape Senior Housing, Inc.

Davis, Joel P., trust: Davis Foundations, Arthur Vining

Davis, John, mem (contributions comm): Pennzoil Co.

Davis, John A., sr vp, gen coun, secy: United Dominion Industries

Davis, John B., asst treas, dir: Jerome Foundation

Davis, John B., Jr., trust: Alliss Educational Foundation, Charles and Ellora

Davis, John H., pres, dir: American Saw & Manufacturing Co.

Davis, John M. K., trust: Foerderer Foundation, Percival E. and Ethel Brown

Davis, John Phillips, Jr., Waters Charitable Trust, Robert S.

Davis, John S., pres, coo: United Gas Pipe Line Co.

Davis, Julianna B., trust: Bosque Foundation

Davis, Karyll A., secy, trust: Heinz Co. Foundation, H.J.

Davis, Kay, vp, secy, treas: Davis Foundation, Ken W.

Davis, Ken, mgr: Cherry Hill Cooperative Cannery

Davis, Ken W., Jr., pres: Davis Foundation, Ken W.

Davis, Laura A., vp (corporate affairs): Kellogg Foundation, W. K.

Davis, Laurianne T., secy, trust: Tiscornia Foundation

Davis, Lee, exec dir: Pacific Telesis Foundation

Davis, Lewin B., secy: Moorman Co. Fund

Davis, Linda Steigerwaldt, trust: Steigerwaldt Foundation, Donna Wolf

Davis, Lynn, vp: Mapplethorpe Foundation, Robert

Davis, Martin S., chmn, ceo, dir: Paramount Communications Inc.

Davis, Mary, American Saw & Manufacturing Co.

Davis, Mary E., vp, dir, mem, don daughter-in-law: Davis Foundation, Edwin W. and Catherine M.

Davis, Maxwell S., Jr., vp, dir: Centel Foundation

Davis, Maynard K., trust: Davis Foundations, Arthur Vining

Davis, Mignon Foerderer, trust: Foerderer Foundation, Percival E. and Ethel Brown

Davis, Mrs. J. Clarence, Jr., trust: Heckscher Foundation for Children

Davis, Nathanael V., chmn: Davis Foundations, Arthur Vining

Davis, Nelda, scholarship adm: Moody Foundation

Davis, O. C., chmn, dir: MidCon Corp.

Davis, Peggy C., trust: Sage Foundation, Russell

Davis, Perry, dir: New Orphan Asylum Scholarship Foundation

Davis, R. L., pres: Zimmer Inc.

Davis, Rita Langsam, asst secy: Mars Foundation

Davis, Robert, pres, dir: Carvel Foundation, Thomas and Agnes

Davis, Robert D., vp, asst secy: Davis Family - W.D. Charities, James E.; vp, dir: Parsons - W.D. Charities, Vera Davis

Davis, Robert E., dir: Bloedorn Foundation, Walter A.; pres, coo, dir: Sequa Corp.

Davis, Robert G., pres, coo: Bank One, Columbus, NA

Davis, Robert M., trust: Barden Foundation, Inc.

Davis, Robert S., treas, trust: Minnesota Foundation; pres, dir: Saint Croix Foundation; vp, dir: Tozer Foundation

Davis, Roger, secy, treas: Lastfogel Foundation, Abe and Frances; ceo, pres: Paxton Co., Frank

Davis, Sam H., vchmn, dir: Kohler Co.; dir: Kohler Foundation

Davis, Samuel Bernhard, trust: Jasam Foundation

Davis, Sharon, vp: Memorial Foundation for the Blind

Davis, Shelby Cullom, chmn: Davis Foundation, Shelby Cullom

Davis, Shelley S., admin: Morton International

Davis, Shelton, trust: Mott Fund, Ruth

Davis, Sidney P., Jr., mem: Maier Foundation, Sarah Pauline

Davis, Stephen A., vp, dir: American Saw & Manufacturing Co.

Davis, T.C., vp: Davis Foundation, Ken W.

Davis, Tine Wayne, Jr., pres, secy, treas: Davis Family - W.D. Charities, Tine W.

Davis, Trevor L., dir: Harris Bank Foundation

Davis, Troy, chmn: Best Western International

Davis, Ulla, consultant, dir: Hale Foundation, Crescent Porter

Davis, Virginia, trust: Snee-Reinhardt Charitable Foundation

Davis, W. Derek, trust: Dixie Yarns Foundation

Davis, Walter S., chmn: Thomas Industries

Davis, Warren, dir: Gateway Apparel Charitable Foundation

Davis, William H., pres, coo: Gilman Paper Co.

Davis, William W., trust: Cole Foundation, Robert H. and Monica H.

Davison, Daniel Pomeroy, vp, treas, dir: Gould Foundation, Florence J.

Davison, John S., pres, secy, treas: Stevens Foundation, John T.

Davison, William M., IV, treas: Ludwick Institute; trust: Presser Foundation

Davisson, Ralph M., trust: Potlatch Foundation for Higher Education/Potlatch Foundation II

Davy, Louise W., trust: Walker Foundation, Archie D. and Bertha H.

Dawdy, R. L., dir: Alexander & Baldwin Foundation

Dawes, Michael V., trust: Whitehall Foundation

Dawson, Edwin H., dir: Arvin Foundation

Dawson, Eugene E., trust: Buell Foundation, Temple Hoyne

Dawson, J.W., pres: Zebco/Motorguide Corp.

Dawson, Judith, vp, dir: Atherton Family Foundation

Dawson, Leighton B., pres: Caston Foundation, M. C. and Mattie; pres: Navarro County Educational Foundation

Dawson, Sue Ann, trust: Schepp Foundation, Leopold

Dawson-White, Gail, mgr: Sovereign Bank Foundation

Day, Ann, pres: Carpenter Foundation, E. Rhodes and Leona B.

Day, Carolyn C., asst secy, asst treas: Jenkins Foundation, George W.

Day, Clinton M., trust: Day Foundation, Cecil B.

Day, Dorothy J., trust: Day Family Foundation

Day, Frank, chmn, ceo: Trustmark National Bank

Day, Frank R., mgr: Luckyday Foundation

Day, Graham, chmn: Cadbury Beverages Inc.

Day, H. Corbin, trust: Day Family Foundation; trust: Friedman Foundation, Stephen and Barbara; treas, dir: Hyde and Watson Foundation

Day, Helen, secy: Research Corporation

Day, Howard M., trust: Day Foundation, Willametta K.; dir: Keck Foundation, W. M.

Day, Janice, pres, dir: Jafra Educational Development Grant Endowment

Day, Kathleen, trust: Day Foundation, Cecil B.

Day, Lon L., Jr., trust: Day Foundation, Cecil B.

Day, Lynn Weyerhaeuser, trust, don: Weyerhaeuser Family Foundation

Day, Michelle, off svc mgr: Bowater Inc.

Day, Paul, Jr., vp, secy, treas: Carpenter Foundation, E. Rhodes and Leona B.

Day, R. Pat, vchmn: Tartt Scholarship Fund, Hope Pierce

Day, Richard, vp, trust: Miniger Memorial Foundation, Clement O.

Day, Robert A., trust: Day Foundation, Willametta K.; vp, dir, mem exec & other comms: Keck Foundation, W. M.

Day, Susan C., MD, trust: Seybert Institution for Poor Boys and Girls, Adam and Maria Sarah

Day, Tammis M., trust: Day Foundation, Willametta K.; dir: Keck Foundation, W. M.

Day, Theodore J., trust: Day Foundation, Willametta K.; dir, mem dirs grant program

comm: Keck Foundation, W. M.

Dayan, Soloman, vp: Parthenon Sportwear Foundation

Days, Drew S., III, trust: Clark Foundation, Edna McConnell

Dayton, Bruce C., dir: Meadowood Foundation

Dayton, David Draper, dir: Meadowood Foundation

Dayton, Douglas J., pres, treas, dir: Meadowood Foundation

Dayton, Duncan N., dir: Oakleaf Foundation

Dayton, Edward Nelson, vp, dir: Chadwick Foundation

Dayton, John W., vp, dir: Chadwick Foundation

Dayton, Judson McDonald, dir: Oakleaf Foundation

Dayton, Julia, vp, secy, dir: Oakleaf Foundation

Dayton, K. N., pres, treas, dir: Oakleaf Foundation

Dayton, Kenneth Nelson, trust: Getty Trust, J. Paul

Dayton, Lucy Jackson, pres, treas, dir: Chadwick Foundation

Dayton, Robert Jackson, vp, secy, dir: Chadwick Foundation

Dayton, Shirley D., vp, dir: Meadowood Foundation

De Ambra, Robert, mem: American Express Co.

De Bakcsy, Alex, vp, trust: Copley Foundation, James S.

de Bekessy, Antal Post, dir: Post Foundation of D.C., Marjorie Merriweather

de Boer, Ton, vchmn, dir: European American Bank

de Bruin, Andre, pres: Boehringer Mannheim Corp.

de Brye, Barbara, trust: Smith Horticultural Trust, Stanley

de Chambrunn, Countess, chmn, dir: Baccarat Inc.

de Eseverri, Carolina V., secy: Vollmer Foundation

de Estrada, Ana Mercedes, dir: Vollmer Foundation

De Felippo, Olga, secy: Mastronardi Charitable Foundation, Charles A.

De Graaf, Clare, pres, treas: Word Investments

De Graaf, Susan, secy: Word Investments

De Gregory, Alfred D., treas, vp (fin): Blue Diamond Growers

De Gutierrez, Maria Josefina Katze, vp, treas, dir: Haghenbeck Foundation, Antonio Y. De La Lama

De Habsburgo, Inmaculada, trust: Kress Foundation, Samuel H.

De Jager, Harold G., off: K-Products Foundation

De Jong, Hubert, trust: Bronstein Foundation, Sol and Arlene

De Kruif, Robert M., trust: Ahmanson Foundation

de la Flor, Teresa, mgr pub rels: Ciba-Geigy Corp. (Pharmaceuticals Division)

De La Garza, Luis A., vp corp rels: Valero Energy Corp.

de la Renta, Anne Engelhard, trust: Engelhard Foundation, Charles

De La Vega, Frederick, trust: Stern Foundation, Charles H. and Anna S.

De Lima, Paul, chmn, ceo: De Lima Co., Paul

De Lima, Paul, Jr., trust: De Lima Foundation, Paul

De Luca, Victor, program off: Noyes Foundation, Jessie Smith

De Marzio, Alfredo, pres, ceo: Eni-Chem America, Inc.

de Menil, Dominique, don, pres, dir: Menil Foundation

de Menil, Francois, dir: Menil Foundation

de Menil, Marie Christophe, dir: Menil Foundation

De Michele, O. Mark, pres, ceo: Arizona Public Service Co.; pres, dir: APS Foundation

De Montmorin, Hugues, pres: Baccarat Inc.

de Rham, Casimir, dir, treas: Bushee Foundation, Florence Evans

de Rham, Casimir, Jr., treas, trust: Bushee Foundation, Florence Evans; trust: Campbell and Adah E. Hall Charity Fund, Bushrod H.

de Rothschild, Benjamin, asst secy, dir: de Rothschild Foundation, Edmond

de Rothschild, Edmond, chmn, dir: de Rothschild Foundation, Edmond

de Roulet, Sandra, trust, treas, mem: Whitney Foundation, Helen Hay

De Schutter, Richard U., dir: Searle Charitable Trust

de Souza, A. A., sr vp, dir: Joslyn Foundation

de Vegh, Diana, dir: Bayne Fund, Howard

de Vegh, Pierre J., dir: Bayne Fund, Howard

de Vink, Lodewijk, pres US oper: Warner-Lambert Co.

De Vitry, Arnaud, dir: Beaucourt Foundation

Deacy, Jean, trust: Halsell Foundation, Ewing

Deadwyler, John B., pres: Marion Merrell Dow Foundation

Deakins, Warren W., pres, ceo, dir: Fidelity Mutual Life Insurance Co.

Deakyne, Walter, selection comm: Gordy Family Educational Trust Fund, George E.

Deal, Kenneth A., dir: Alabama Power Foundation

Dealey, Joseph McDonald, trust: Dallas Morning News—WFAA Foundation, The

Dean, Brett, dir: Boatmen's First National Bank of Oklahoma Foundation

Dean, Howard M., Jr., chmn, ceo, dir: Dean Foods Co.

Dean, J. Simpson, Jr., vp, trust: Welfare Foundation

Dean, Paul Regis, vp, trust: Loyola Foundation

Dean, Sarah M., exec dir: McBeath Foundation, Faye

Dean, Tony, treas, trust: Blowitz-Ridgeway Foundation

Dean, Victoria Seaver, dir: Seaver Institute

Dean, Yvonne S., secy, treas: Civitas Fund

Deane, Barbara, vp: Ushkow Foundation

Deane, Maurice A., secy, treas: Ushkow Foundation

Dear, James, chmn, trust: Meredith Foundation

Deasey, Anthony P., vp, cfo: Church & Dwight Co.

Deats, Paul, Jr., trust: Carteh Foundation

Deavenport, Earnest W., pres: Eastman Chemical Co.

Deay, Stephen K., asst treas: Alco Standard Foundation

DeBartolo, Ed J., Jr., pres, chief admin off: DeBartolo Corp., Edward J.

Debartolo, Edward J., Jr., trust: Debartolo Foundation, Marie P.

DeBartolo, Edward J., Sr., chmn, ceo: DeBartolo Corp., Edward J.

Debartolo, M. Denise, Jr., trust: Debartolo Foundation, Marie P.

Deberroth, P., dir: Capital Fund Foundation

Debevoise, Dickinson Richards, trust: Fund for New Jersey

DeBlois, Arthur J., chmn: DeBlois Oil Co.

DeBlois, Robert E., pres, coo: DeBlois Oil Co.

DeBoer, Anne, exec dir: Dow Corning Corp.

DeBoer, Richard G., vp, trust: Kysor Industrial Corp. Foundation

DeBolt, Bruce R., sr vp, cfo: Northwest Natural Gas Co.

Debs, Barbara Knowles, trust: Dodge Foundation, Geraldine R.

Debuc, K. E., pres: Johnson Matthey Investments

deButts, Robert Edward Lee, vp: Norfolk Southern Foundation

DeCaro, Angelo, treas, dir: Goldman Sachs Fund

DeCastro, Donald, exec vp, cfo: Amfac/JMB Hawaii

Decherd, Robert, chmn, ceo: Belo Corp., A.H.; chmn, pres, trust: Dallas Morning News—WFAA Foundation, The

Decio, Arthur Julius, trust: Decio Foundation, Arthur J.; chmn, ceo: Skyline Corp.

Decio, Patricia C., trust: Decio Foundation, Arthur J.

Decker, A. Dean, trust: Geneseo Foundation

Decker, Don M., adm: Dana Corp. Foundation

Decker, Janet, gov: Crary Foundation, Bruce L.

Decker, Mary, trust: Woods Charitable Fund

Decker, Robert W., dir, pres: Scott Foundation, William E.

Decker, Thomas A., vp: CertainTeed Corp. Foundation

Decosimo, Joseph F., secy, dir: Maclellan Foundation, Robert L. and Kathrina H.

DeCosta, Alyce H., pres, dir: Heller Foundation, Walter E.

DeCosta, Edwin J., dir: Heller Foundation, Walter E.

DeCoudreaux, Alecia A., asst secy: Lilly & Co. Foundation, Eli

DeCrane, Alfred Charles, Jr., chmn: Texaco

Decyk, Roxanne J., dir: Navistar Foundation

DeDeyn, S. Anthony, chmn, mem admin comm: Selby and Marie Selby Foundation, William G.

Dedmon, Judith, dir: Federal National Mortgage Assn. Foundation

DeDomenico, Vincent, chmn, secy, treas: Golden Grain Macaroni Co.

Dee, David I., distribution comm, vchmn: Dee Foundation, Annie Taylor

Dee, David L., vp, dir: Dee Foundation, Lawrence T. and Janet T.

Dee, Thomas D., II, chmn, distribution comm: Dee Foundation, Annie Taylor; chmn, mgr: Dee Foundation, Lawrence T. and Janet T.

Dee, Thomas D., III, distribution comm, vchmn: Dee Foundation, Annie Taylor; vp, mgr: Dee Foundation, Lawrence T. and Janet T.

Deeb, Ziad, dir: Jerusalem Fund for Education and Community Development

Deegan, John E., Sr., trust: O'Brien Foundation, James W.

Deems, Richard E., vp, dir: Hearst Foundation; vp, dir: Hearst Foundation, William Randolph

Deen, R. B., Jr., secy, dir: Hardin Foundation, Phil

Deeney, Gerald D., secy: Hubbard Foundation

Deering, Joseph, pres: PMI Food Equipment Group Inc.

Deering, L. Patrick, vp, trust: Sheridan Foundation, Thomas B. and Elizabeth M.

DeFrange, Gary J., chmn, pres, ceo, dir: First Interstate Bank of Denver

DeFriece, Frank W., Jr., vp: Massengill-DeFriece Foundation

DeFriece, Mark W., dir: Massengill-DeFriece Foundation

DeFriece, Paul E., dir: Massengill-DeFriece Foundation

DeGaetano, Peter F., dir: Butler Foundation, J. Homer; secy, dir: L and L Foundation; dir, secy: Piankova Foundation, Tatiana

Degen, Joe I., trust: Wolfson Family Foundation

Degen, Sylvia W., trust: Wolfson Family Foundation

Degenhardt, Robert A., exec vp, coo: Ellerbe Becket

DeGeorge, Lawrence J., chmn, pres: LPL Technologies Inc.

Degheri, Chris, trust: O'Toole Foundation, Theresa and Edward

DeGive, Josephine, trust, pres: Friendship Fund

Degolia, Richard C., MD, trust: Miller Foundation, Earl B. and Loraine H.

DeGraff, Richard A., exec dir: Koch Foundation

DeGrandpre, Charles A., trust: Smith Charitable Foundation, Lou and Lutza

DeGreve, Stanley C., mem screening comm: PPG Industries Foundation

DeGroot, Shirley A., trust: Artevel Foundation

Dehaas, Tony, mgr commun rels: Browning-Ferris Industries

DeHart, Donald M., treas: Devonshire Associates

Dehaven, Michael A., mem adv comm: Jordan and Ettie A. Jordan Charitable Foundation, Mary Ranken

Dehavenon, Anna Lou, dir: Olive Bridge Fund

Deieso, Donald, pres, ceo: Research-Cottrell Inc.

Deihl, Richard H., chmn, ceo: Ahmanson & Co., H.F.; chmn, ceo: Home Savings of America, FA

Deikel, Beverly, dir: Fingerhut Family Foundation

Deikel, Theodore, chmn, pres, ceo, dir: Fingerhut Corp.

Deily, Linnet F., ceo: First Interstate Bank of Texas, N.A.; pres, ceo, dir: First Interstate Bank of Texas Foundation

Deitch, Sande, exec dir: Miles Inc. Foundation

Dekko, Chester E., Jr., pres: Dekko Foundation

Dekko, Erica, vp: Dekko Foundation

Dekko, Lorene, vp: Dekko Foundation

DeKnatel, Elizabeth, trust: Stoneman Charitable Foundation, Anne and David

DeKruif, Robert M., vchmn, dir: Ahmanson & Co., H.F.

Del Rosso, Sheila H., secy-treas: Burns International Foundation

Del Santo, Lawrence A., chmn, ceo: Lucky Stores

Del Spina, Anthony, pres: Capita Charitable Trust, Emil

del Toro, Duncan J., pres, dir: Bairnco Corp.

Delacorte, Albert P., secy: Delacorte Fund, George

Delacorte, George T., Jr., pres: Delacorte Fund, George

Delacorte, Valerie, vp, treas: Delacorte Fund, George

Delamar, Ned, dir: Perry-Griffin Foundation

Delamar, Ned, II, dir: Perry-Griffin Foundation

DeLancey, William J., mgr: Prentiss Foundation, Elisabeth Severance

Delaney, Wayne E., dir: Smith and W. Aubrey Smith Charitable Foundation, Clara Blackford

Delano, Winifred G., exec dir: Monticello College Foundation

Delape, Mary, asst secy: Mann Foundation, Ted

Delarios, Louise, trust: Luse Foundation, W. P. and Bulah

Delattre, Edwin J., trust: Quaker Chemical Foundation

DeLauro, Debra, secy: Greenfield Foundation, Albert M.

Delbridge, Ed, dir: Christy-Houston Foundation

Delehanty, Jeanne M., dir: Ensign-Bickford Foundation

Delfiner, Judith, trust: Mandell Foundation, Samuel P.

Delgado, Jane, mem nominating comm, mem counc, dir: Foundation for Child Development

Delia, Frank S., vp, dir: Mentor Graphics Foundation

Delibert, Steven, dir, vp, secy: International Fund for Health and Family Planning

DeLima, Richard Ford, trust: Polaroid Foundation

Delisi, Samuel P., trust: Miller Charitable Foundation, Howard E. and Nell E.

Delisle, Raymond C., chmn, dir: Comprecare Foundation

Dellamo, Frank A., vchmn: Crossland Savings FSB

Dellaporta, Angelo, dir: Lucas Cancer Foundation, Richard M.

Delman, Neil M., secy: O'Sullivan Children Foundation

delMar, Elizabeth Adams, trust, pres: DelMar Foundation, Charles

Delmontagne, Regis J., pres: Graphic Arts Education & Research Foundation

Delo, Robert P., treas: Chicago Tribune Foundation

DeLoache, Bond Davis, trust: Davis Foundation, Joe C.

DeLoache, William, trust: Davis Foundation, Joe C.

DeLoache, William R., Jr., trust: Davis Foundation, Joe C.

DeLong, Mary W., dir: McDonnell Douglas Corp.-West

Delonis, Robert J., pres, coo: Great Lakes Bancorp, FSB

DeLorenzo, David A., pres: Dole Food Company, Inc.

Delorme, Jean H., chmn: Liquid Air Corp.

Delouvrier, Judith C., trust, don daughter: Connelly Foundation

Delouvrier, Philippe, trust: Connelly Foundation

Delp, George C., chmn, trust: Crels Foundation

DeLuca, Anthony Peter, trust: Elf Atochem North America Foundation

DeLuca, Ronald, vchmn: Bozell, Inc.

Demaeyer, Bruce R., pres: Ameritech Mobile Communications

Demakes, Louis, mem: Gerondelis Foundation

Demakes, Thomas L., dir: Gerondelis Foundation

Demakis, Charles, pres, dir: Gerondelis Foundation

Demakis, Gregory C., mem: Gerondelis Foundation

Demakis, Paul C., dir: Gerondelis Foundation

Demakis, Thomas C., mem: Gerondelis Foundation

Demarest, Daniel A., dir: Bay Foundation; secy, dir: Paul and C. Michael Paul Foundation, Josephine Bay

DeMaria, Peter James, exec vp (admin), chief accounting off: American Electric Power

DeMars, Richard B., treas, trust: Jordan Foundation, Arthur

Demas, William G., secy, treas, dir: Prentice Foundation, Abra

DeMera, Marie C., trust: Diener Foundation, Frank C.

Demere, Robert H., ceo, dir: Colonial Oil Industries, Inc.; pres: Colonial Foundation

Demere, Robert H., Jr., pres, dir: Colonial Oil Industries, Inc.

Demetter, R.A., asst secy: Sifco Foundation

DeMeuse, Donald Howard, Cornerstone Foundation of Northeastern Wisconsin

Demkhael, Sue, mgr: LDI Charitable Foundation

DeMichele, Robert M., trust: Richardson Foundation, Smith

Deming, Bertie Murphy, Murphy Foundation

Deming, Claiborne P., exec vp, coo, dir: Murphy Oil Corp.

Deming, Grove W., trust: Plankenhorn Foundation, Harry

Deming, John Winton, dir: Murphy Foundation

Demme, James, pres: Shaw's Supermarkets

Demmer, Lawrence, trust: Demmer Foundation, Edward U.

Demming, Winifred, vp: Benbough Foundation, Legler

Demo, Bernell, vchmn, dir: Moore Foundation, Alfred

Demoratsky, Bernard, dir: Seibel Foundation, Abe and Annie

Demorest, Byron, MD, dir: Sierra Health Foundation

Demos, John, vchmn: Super Food Services

DeMoss, Charlotte A., dir: DeMoss Foundation, Arthur S.

DeMoss, Deborah L., dir: DeMoss Foundation, Arthur S.

DeMoss, Mark, dir: DeMoss Foundation, Arthur S.

DeMoss, Nancy L., dir: DeMoss Foundation, Arthur S.

DeMoss, Nancy S., chmn, ceo: DeMoss Foundation, Arthur S.

DeMoss, Robert G., pres: DeMoss Foundation, Arthur S.

DeMoss, Theodore G., secy/treas: DeMoss Foundation, Arthur S.

Demoulas, Arthur T., trust: Demoulas Foundation

Demoulas, Telemachus A., pres, ceo, dir: Demoulas Supermarkets; trust: Demoulas Foundation

Dempsey, James Howard, Jr., secy: Andrews Foundation; secy: Ingalls Foundation, Louise H. and David S.

Dempsey, John C., chmn, ceo: Greif Brothers Corp.

Dempsey, T. M., vp, dir: Oshkosh Truck Foundation

Dempsey, Timothy M., dir: SNC Foundation

Dempsey, Wallace Guy, secy, dir: IFF Foundation

Dempster, Jan, dir corp commun: Carolina Telephone & Telegraph Corp.

DeMuth, David Peter, treas: National Starch & Chemical Corp.

Denbrow, Victor, dir: Taylor Family Foundation, Jack

DeNecochea, Gloria, program off ed, arts & humanities programs: ARCO Foundation

deNeergaard, William F., trust, secy: Faith Home Foundation

Denegre, George, trust: Jones Family Foundation, Eugenie and Joseph

DeNero, Henry, vchmn: Dayton Hudson Corp.; trust: Dayton Hudson Foundation

Denham, Robert Edwin, chmn, ceo, dir: Salomon

Denius, Franklin W., exec vp, active dir: Cain Foundation, Effie and Wofford

Denkers, Stephen E., comm mem: Eccles Charitable Foundation, Willard L.

Denkers, Stephen G., comm mem: Eccles Charitable Foundation, Willard L.

Denkers, Susan E., comm mem: Eccles Charitable Foundation, Willard L.

Denkler, Margaret C. Woods, trust: Woods-Greer Foundation

Denkler, Margaret W., trust: Cartinhour Foundation

Denlea, Leo E., Jr., chmn, pres, ceo, dir: Farmers Group, Inc.; vp: Farmers Group Safety Foundation

Denman, Gilbert M., Jr., trust: Brackenridge Foundation, George W.; trust: Halsell Foundation, Ewing

Denman, Leroy G., Jr., trust: Brackenridge Foundation,

George W.; trust: Halsell Foundation, Ewing; trust: Kleberg Foundation for Wildlife Conservation, Caesar

Denney, Sharon, vchmn: Senior Citizens Foundation

Denney, Steve, mem (contributions comm): GATX Corp.

Denning, Bernadine N., trust: Skillman Foundation

Denning, Steven A., dir: Echoing Green Foundation

Dennis, Everette E., vp: Freedom Forum

Dennis, O. D., trust: Chesapeake Corporate Foundation

Dennis, Richard James, fdr, pres, dir: Chicago Resource Center

Dennis, Samuel Sibley, III, trust: Bolten Charitable Foundation, John

Dennis, Thomas A., vp: Chicago Resource Center

Denny, Charles Morton, Jr., chmn, dir: ADC Telecommunications

Denny, Charley W., coo: Square D Co.

Denny, Dwight D., dir: Ryder System Charitable Foundation

Denomme, Thomas Gerald, pres, trust: Chrysler Corp. Fund

Denova, James V., PhD, sr program off: Jewish Healthcare Foundation of Pittsburgh

Dent, F. B., chmn, trust: Armco Foundation

Dent, Gloria G., pres, dir: Dent Family Foundation, Harry

Dent, Harry M., III, treas, dir: Dent Family Foundation, Harry

Dent, John, dir: SmithKline Beecham Foundation

Dent, Lucy, chmn, dir: Dent Family Foundation, Harry

Denton, James M., III, trust: Washington Foundation

Denton, Jerry B., trust: Blount Educational and Charitable Foundation, Mildred Weedon

Denton, Lynne, trust: Whiteman Foundation, Edna Rider

Denworth, Raymond K., Jr., dir: Fels Fund, Samuel S.

DePaul, J. D., chmn, pres, ceo: Lehigh Press, Inc.

Depew, Robert H., contact person, bank rep: Jackson Foundation

DePree, Max O., chmn, dir: Miller Inc., Herman

DePriest, Rex, pres: Jasper Wood Products Co.

Deramus, W.N., III, chmn, dir: Kansas City Southern Industries

deRedon, Margaret, trust: Eastman Foundation, Alexander

DeRiemer, Charles O., vp, exec dir: Southwestern Bell Foundation

DeRienzo, Harold, vp, ceo: Consumer Farmer Foundation

Dern, James R., trust: Arkell Hall Foundation

DeRoo, Curt, treas, trust: DeVlieg Foundation, Charles

Derr, Kenneth Tindall, chmn, ceo: Chevron Corp.

Derr, Melvin H., dir, secy: Loats Foundation

Derr, Roger K., exec vp, coo: AMETEK

Derrer, Suzanne, dir: Reynolds Foundation, Christopher

Derrickson, Lloyd J., secy, trust: Freed Foundation

Derry, R. Michael, vp: HON Industries Charitable Foundation

Derry, William, dir: Rockford Products Corp. Foundation

Derry, William S., trust: Van Wert County Foundation

Derusha, James R., pres: Marinette Marine Foundation

Derusha, Roger H., chmn, pres: Marinette Marine Corp.; vp, secy: Marinette Marine Foundation

DeRusha, William C., chmn, ceo, dir: Heilig-Meyers Co.

des Granges, Pauline, trust: Burnham Foundation

Des Jardins, Jerry L., trust: Bentley Foundation, Alvin M.

Des Jardins, John R., trust: Bentley Foundation, Alvin M.

DesBarres, J.P., chmn, ceo, dir: Transco Energy Company

DeSerrano, Aline, dir, pres: Deseranno Educational Foundation

DeSerrano, Don, dir, vp: Deseranno Educational Foundation

Deshotel, Adrian, dir: American Standard Foundation

DeSimone, Livio Diego, chmn, ceo, dir: 3M Co.

DeSipio, George, secy, dir: Kaufman Foundation, Henry & Elaine; secy, treas, dir: Lehman Foundation, Edith and Herbert

Desmond, Thomas P., dir: Fairview Foundation

DeSole, Domenico, pres, ceo: Gucci America Inc.

DeSoto, Peter, pres, ceo: Metal Industries

Destino, Ralph, chmn: Cartier, Inc.

DeSutter, Robert J., asst secy, asst treas: Millstone Foundation

Detar, Robert, pres: Indiana Gas Co.

Deters, Laura Lee Brown, pres: Sutherland Foundation

Deters, Laura Lee Lyons, secy: Sutherland Foundation

Detmer, Don, trust: China Medical Board of New York

deTornvay, Rheba D., ED.D., trust: Johnson Foundation, Robert Wood

Detrick, Judson W., trust: Bancroft, Jr. Foundation, Hugh

Dettman, Douglas R., dir, pres: Dettman Foundation, Leroy E.

Dettman, Gregory L., dir, secy: Dettman Foundation, Leroy E.

Dettman, S. Barbara, trust: Dettman Foundation, Leroy E.

Detweiler, Frank H., mem adv comm: Ford Foundation, Edward E.

Deubel, George, dir: Sierra Health Foundation

Deuble, Andrew H., trust: Deuble Foundation, George H.

Deuble, Stephen G., trust: Deuble Foundation, George H.

Deuble, Walter C., pres, trust: Deuble Foundation, George H.

Deur, Grace J., adm, secy: Gerber Cos. Foundation

Deutsch, Alex, pres, dir: Deutsch Co.; pres: Deutsch Foundation

Deutsch, Carl, vp: Deutsch Foundation

Deutsch, Lester, secy: Deutsch Foundation

Devan, Charlotte S., vp: Sheppard Foundation, Lawrence B.

Devan, Lawrence S., trust: Sheppard Foundation, Lawrence B.

Devan, W. Todd, trust: Sheppard Foundation, Lawrence B.

Devanie, Anne, secy: Robinson Fund, Maurice R.

Devecchi, Betsy, mem adv comm: de Kay Foundation

DeVeer, Robert K., Jr., trust: First Boston Foundation Trust

Devel, Thomas R., dir: Mallinckrodt, Jr. Foundation, Edward

Devening, R. Randolph, exec vp, cfo, dir: Fleming Companies, Inc.

Devenny, Thomas A., mem: Piedmont Health Care Foundation

Devens, Charles, trust: Humane Society of the Commonwealth of Massachusetts

Dever, Dortha, secy: American Fidelity Corporation Founders Fund

Devereaux, Ann Thompson, trust: Devereaux Foundation

Devereaux, William Anderson, trust: Devereaux Foundation

Devereux, Kate D., trust: Farallon Foundation

Deverick, Percy F., trust: Coffey Foundation

Devilbiss, Thomas, exec secy, treas, trust: Miniger Memorial Foundation, Clement O.

Devine, Thomas F., Allen Brothers Foundation

DeVita, M. Christine, pres, dir: Wallace-Reader's Digest Fund, DeWitt; pres, dir: Wallace Reader's Digest Fund, Lila

DeVito, Mathias, chmn, pres, ceo, dir: Rouse Co.

Devito, Mathias J., pres, trust: Rouse Co. Foundation

Devlieg, Kathryn S., trust: DeVlieg Foundation, Charles

Devlin, James Richard, dir: Sprint Foundation

Devonshire, D. W., vp fin: Honeywell

DeVore, Richard A., pres, secy: DeVore Foundation

DeVore, William O., vp, treas: DeVore Foundation

DeVos, Helen J., don, vp: DeVos Foundation, Richard and Helen

DeVos, Richard Marvin, co-fdr, pres: Amway Corp.; don, pres: DeVos Foundation, Richard and Helen

Devries, Robert K., mem (admin comm): Nabisco Foundation Trust

DeWees, James H., pres, ceo: Godfrey Co.; pres, dir: Godfrey Foundation

Dewey, Francis H., III, chmn, trust: Alden Trust, George I.; trust: Mechanics Bank Foundation

Dewey, Robert F., pres, asst secy, trust: Gifford Charitable Corporation, Rosamond

DeWind, Adrian W., dir: Diamond Foundation, Aaron; dir: New World Foundation; dir: Revson Foundation, Charles H.

Dewing, Merlin E., dir: Bush Foundation

DeWolfe, L. Donald, vp: Farmers Group Safety Foundation

DeWoody, Beth Rudin, vp, dir: Rudin Foundation, Samuel and May

---

Di Giacomo, T. A., chmn, pres, ceo: Manufacturers Life Insurance Co. of America

di Rosa, Rene, pres: DiRosa Foundation, Rene and Veronica

di Rosa, Veronica, vp: DiRosa Foundation, Rene and Veronica

Di San Faustino, Genevieve Bothin Lyman, pres, dir: Bothin Foundation

Di Silvestri, Angelica, asst to pres: Fiat U.S.A., Inc.

Dial, Benton W., dir: Rosenberg Foundation

Dial, Ellen C., dir: Haas Foundation, Saul and Dayee G.

Dial, William Henry, trust: Griffin, Sr., Foundation, C. V.

Diamond, Henry L., trust: Jackson Hole Preserve

Diamond, Irene, pres, dir: Diamond Foundation, Aaron

Diamond, Richard E., asst secy, asst treas: Newhouse Foundation, Samuel I.

Diamond, Stephen C., vchmn: American National Bank & Trust Co. of Chicago

Dibbell, David, M.D., trust: Surgical Science Foundation for Research and Development

Dibner, David, pres, trust: Dibner Fund

Dibner, Frances K., vp, trust: Dibner Fund

DiBuono, Anthony J., vp, secy, dir: Coltec Industries Charitable Foundation

Dice, James R., secy, treas: Baldwin Foundation

Dicino, Daphne, sr dir corp commun: America West Airlines

Dick, Albert B., III, Dick Family Foundation

Dick, Dorsey W., chmn: Dick Corp.

Dick, Edison, dir, pres: Dick Family Foundation

Dick, John H., dir, secy: Dick Family Foundation

Dickason, John H., vp (fin admin): Markey Charitable Trust, Lucille P.

Dicke, Richard M., trust: Ferkauf Foundation, Eugene and Estelle

Dicken, Michael A., secy, dir: Levy's Lumber & Building Centers Foundation

Dickens, John, pres, dir: Bailey & Son, Bankers, M.S.

Dickerson, Kenneth R., dir: ARCO Foundation

Dickerson, Mark S., secy, dir: Talley Foundation

Dickes, Don D., secy, treas, trust: Timken Foundation of Canton

Dickes, Glenn P., asst secy: MacAndrews & Forbes Foundation

Dickey, Boh A., mem (contributions comm): SAFECO Corp.

Dickhoner, William H., chmn, dir: Cincinnati Gas & Electric Co.

Dickie, Elizabeth R., pres, treas: Replogle Foundation, Luther I.

Dickinson, Dallas P., dir: Frost Foundation

Dickinson, H. Tyndall, pres: Trinity Foundation

Dickinson, Haskell L., vp: Trinity Foundation

Dickinson, Karen, mgr bd rel: Guardian Life Insurance Co. of America

Dickler, Gerald, chmn, dir: Pollock-Krasner Foundation

Dickson, Alan Thomas, pres, dir: Dickson Foundation; chmn, trust: Morehead Foundation, John Motley; chmn: Ruddick Corp.; pres: Dickson Foundation

Dickson, Anthony G., pres: New Jersey Manufacturers Insurance Co.

Dickson, Colleen S., secy, treas: Dickson Foundation

Dickson, Donald, trust: Presto Foundation

Dickson, John, ceo, pres: Roundy's Inc.

Dickson, Margaret C., vp, treas: Harland Charitable Foundation, John and Wilhelmina D.

Dickson, R. Stuart, chmn: Harris-Teeter Super Markets; chmn: Ruddick Corp.; chmn: Dickson Foundation

Dickson, Robert J., cfo, vp fin: Dynamet, Inc.

Dickson, Rush S., II, vp: Dickson Foundation

Dickson, Rush S., III, vp, dir: Dickson Foundation

Dickson, Rush Stuart, chmn, dir: Dickson Foundation; trust (arts & sciences counc): Heineman Foundation for Research, Educational, Charitable, and Scientific Purposes

Dickson, Stanley, trust: Brown Foundation, James Graham

Dickson, Thomas W., vp, dir: Dickson Foundation

Dickson, W. W., dir: Glenn Foundation, Carrie C. & Lena V.

DiCorcia, Edward T., chmn, ceo: UNO-VEN Co.

Diebel, William C., dir, secy: Demos Foundation, N.

Diederich, John Leroy, dir: Alcoa Foundation

Diehl, Betty, dir: Lytel Foundation, Bertha Russ

Diehl, Harrison Lueders, Jr., dir: SICO Foundation

Diehl, John E., dir: Grotto Foundation

Diekman, Susan, exec dir: Pacific Telesis Foundation

Diener, Edward F., trust: Diener Foundation, Frank C.

Diener, Martha Stott, trust, chmn: Stott Foundation, Louis L.

Diener, Mary A., trust: Diener Foundation, Frank C.

Dienstbier, Daniel L., pres: Arkla

Dietel, William M., trust: Jackson Hole Preserve

Dieter, Barbara E., asst secy: BT Foundation

Dietrich, G. Phillip, trust: Delano Foundation, Mignon Sherwood

Dietrich, Loreine C., chmn, trust: Collins Foundation, George and Jennie; treas: Collins, Jr. Foundation, George Fulton

Dietrich, William B., pres, treas, dir: Dietrich Foundation, William B.

Dietz, Carolyn Emmerson, treas: Sierra Pacific Foundation

Dietz, Milton S., trust: Polaroid Foundation

Dietz, Philip E. L., Jr., secy, treas, trust: Town Creek Foundation

DiGesu, Jon, mgr (commun): Osram Corp.

Diggs, Walter Edward, Jr., pres: McDonnell Douglas Foundation

DiGiacomo, Karin, exec dir: Manitou Foundation

DiGirolamo, Vincent, pres, ceo: National City Bank of Indiana

Dik, Carolyn, trust: Memorial Foundation for the Blind

DiLeo, Victor, trust: Schwartz Foundation, Arnold A.

Dillard, John H., Sr., vp, trust: Dillard Fund

Dillard, John M., trust: Bannon Foundation

Dillard, Mary B., trust: Bosque Foundation

Dillard, William, II, pres, coo, dir: Dillard Department Stores, Inc.

Dillard, William T., chmn, ceo, dir: Dillard Department Stores, Inc.

Dillehay, L. B., pres, dir: Washington Square Health Foundation

Diller, A. C., Van Wert County Foundation

Diller, Whitney Clay, secy: Clay Foundation

Dillingham, Charles, chmn: Wills Foundation

Dillion, David B., pres, ceo: Dillons Super Markets

Dillion, Richard W., chmn: Dillons Super Markets

Dillivan, Marilyn J., treas: Bohen Foundation

Dillon, Carol L., asst secy: Reynolds Metals Co. Foundation

Dillon, Francis B., trust: Arata Brothers Trust

Dillon, George C., trust: Butler Manufacturing Co. Foundation

Dillon, George Chaffee, mem: Butler Foundation, Alice; trust: Manville Fund

Dillon, John Robert, III, sr vp (fin), cfo, dir: Cox Enterprises

Dillon, Margo, dir: Dillon Foundation

Dillon, Mary L., vp, dir: Snite Foundation, Fred B.

Dillon, Monika, trust: PaineWebber Foundation

Dillon, Peter W., pres, dir: Dillon Foundation

Dillon, Terrance J., pres, dir: Snite Foundation, Fred B.

Dills, Joan Nelson, adm: Stulsaft Foundation, Morris

Dilworth, J. Richardson, trust: Rockefeller Trust, Winthrop

DiMarco, James F., sr vp (consumer products, r&d, engg): Johnson & Son, S.C.

DiMartino, Joseph S., pres, coo, dir: Dreyfus Corp.

Dimeo, Thomas P., chmn, dir: Dimeo Construction Co.

Dimick, Neil F., cfo: Bergen Brunswig Corp.

Dimitriou, Theodore, chmn, dir: Wallace Computer Services

Dimon, James, pres, cfo, dir: Primerica Corp.; trust: Primerica Foundation

Dimson, Barry H., ceo: Woodner Family Collection, Ian

Dineen, Robert J., pres, ceo, dir: Marley Co.

Dinerman, Marshall, secy: Zaban Foundation

Dingell, Deborah I., pres: General Motors Foundation

Dingethal, Lorelei K., secy, admin gift matching program: Eaton Charitable Fund

Dingham, Michael D., dir: Lincolnshire

Dingle, Doris B., pres, mgr: Brush Foundation

Dingledy, Thomas, secy, dir: Hook Drug Foundation

Dingler, Ruth C., secy: General Service Foundation

Dingman, Elizabeth T., vp: Dingman Foundation, Michael D.

Dingman, Michael D., pres, cfo: Dingman Foundation, Michael D.

Dingman, Michael David, dir: Chatam Inc.; trust: Hartford Foundation, John A.

Dinner, Richard S., trust: Swig Charity Foundation, Mae and Benjamin; trust: Swig Foundation

Dinome, Anthony J., secy, treas: Benenson Foundation, Frances and Benjamin

Dinse, Ann G., trust: Turrell Fund

Dinsmoor, Dorothy, pres, dir: Dreyfus Foundation, Camille and Henry

Dinzole, John W., pres, ceo: Devon Group

Dion, Earnest E., trust: Lindsay Trust, Agnes M.

Dionne, Joseph L., chmn, ceo: McGraw-Hill

Diotte, Alfred Peter, vp, dir: Janesville Foundation

DiPaola, Robert, trust: Calvin Klein Foundation

Dircher, Dick, trust: National Gypsum Foundation

Dircks, Robert J., pres: Warner-Lambert Charitable Foundation

Dirickson, A.G. Mason, trust: Richfood Educational Trust

Disbrow, Richard Edwin, chmn, ceo: Columbus Southern Power Co.

Disher, J. W., mem bd adms: Van Every Foundation, Philip L.

Disher, J. William, chmn, pres, ceo: Lance, Inc.; dir: Lance Foundation

Dishman, Melanie, Jr., secy: Texas Energy Museum

Disney, Abigail E., vp, dir: Disney Family Foundation, Roy

Disney, Linda J., vp, dir: Disney Family Foundation, Roy

Disney, Martha H., dir: Disney Family Foundation, Roy

Disney, Patricia Ann, pres, dir: Disney Family Foundation, Roy

Disney, Roy Edward, vp, dir: Disney Family Foundation, Roy; vchmn, dir: Disney Co., Walt; trust: Disney Co. Foundation, Walt

Disney, Roy P., vp, dir: Disney Family Foundation, Roy

Disney, Susan M., secy, dir: Disney Family Foundation, Roy

Disney, Timothy J., vp, dir: Disney Family Foundation, Roy

Distanovich, Sophie, treas: Ritter Foundation, May Ellen and Gerald

Ditamassi, George R., pres: Milton Bradley Co.

Dittmann, Mrs. H. Carton, Jr., Wurts Memorial, Henrietta Tower

Dittmar-Cricler, Meghan, contributions/corp commun: Lafarge Corp.

Dittrich, Norbert, asst treas, asst secy, exec mgr: Welch Foundation, Robert A.

Dittus, Jay E., treas: Inland Steel-Ryerson Foundation

Ditze, Karl, chmn, dir: Koh-I-Noor Rapidograph Inc.

Ditzler, Hugh W., Jr., trust, chmn: Farallon Foundation

Ditzler, Nancy M., trust: Farallon Foundation

Dively, Juliette G., trust, vp: Dively Foundation, George S.

Dively, Michael A., trust, pres: Dively Foundation, George S.

Dix, Ronald H., dir: Badger Meter Foundation

Dix, W. L., chmn: Qantas Airways Ltd.

Dixon, C. Bailey, mem adv comm: Bailey Foundation

Dixon, Charles, secy: Classic Foundation

Dixon, Frank James, mem scientific adv comm: Whitney Foundation, Helen Hay

Dixon, Joseph S., pres: Carol Cable Co.

Dixon, Markus K., trust: Dentsply International Foundation

Dixon, Michele, pub aff rep: Sumitomo Bank of California

Dixon, Ruth B., trust: Barstow Foundation

Dixon, Steward Strawn, secy, trust: Sprague Memorial Institute, Otho S. A.

Dixon, Suzanne Searle, vp, secy, treas: Sudix Foundation

Dixon, Wesley Moon, Jr., pres: Sudix Foundation

Dixson, Thomas F., dir: Harriman Foundation, Gladys and Roland

Doan, Herbert Dow, secy: Dow Foundation, Herbert H. and Grace A.

Doan, Jeffrey W., assoc: Dow Foundation, Herbert H. and Grace A.

Doane, Lawrence S., vchmn: Skidmore, Owings & Merrill Foundation

Doar, Gael, dir (contributions & community support program): Champion International Corp.

Dobbin, Charles E., trust: Coffey Foundation

Dobbins, Z. E., pres, dir: Stonecutter Foundation

Dobbs, Harold S., trust: Meyer Fund, Milton and Sophie

Dobelman, Katherine B., exec dir, treas: Brown Foundation

Doberstein, Stephen C., dir: Crystal Trust

Dobkin, John Howard, dir: Ross Foundation, Arthur

Dobkin, Kendel Kennedy, dir: Kennedy Family Foundation, Ethel and W. George

Dobras, Mary Ann, trust: Stocker Foundation

Dobres, Barbara, adm: Lauder Foundation

Dobrowolski, John, treas, secy: Fabri-Kal Foundation

Dobson, Douglas R., trust: Stackpole-Hall Foundation

Dobson, Peter, pres, gen mgr North Am: Standard Chartered Bank New York

Dobson, Robert, trust: Cooper Foundation

Dockson, Robert Ray, first vp, trust: Haynes Foundation, John Randolph and Dora

Docter, Alan K., dir: Ridgefield Foundation

Dodd, Albert, pres: Ferranti Tech

Dodd, Ruth E., secy: Connell Foundation, Michael J.

Dodds, R. Harcourt, trust: New York Foundation

Dodge, Cleveland Earl, Jr., pres, chmn exec comm, mem fin comm, dir: Dodge Foundation, Cleveland H.; dir: Phelps Dodge Foundation

Dodge, David S., mem exec comm, dir: Dodge Foundation, Cleveland H.

Dodge, Douglas W., vchmn, dir: Mercantile Bankshares Corp.

Dodge, Douglas Walker, gov: Baker, Jr. Memorial Fund, William G.

Dodge, E. V., ceo, pres: C.P. Rail Systems

Dodge, James H., ceo, pres: Providence Energy Corp.

Dodge, Phillip R., dir: Mallinckrodt, Jr. Foundation, Edward

Dodge, Stuart P., vp, dir: Sachs Foundation

Dods, Walter Arthur, Jr., chmn, ceo: First Hawaiian; pres, dir: First Hawaiian Foundation

Dodson, Becky, dir: Harrington Foundation, Don and Sybil

Dodson, David, dir: Babcock Foundation, Mary Reynolds; trust: Bryan Family Foundation, Kathleen Price and Joseph M.

Dodson, Sheila, treas: Goldseker Foundation of Maryland, Morris

Doehring, Clarence, trust: Smysor Memorial Fund, Harry L. and John L.

Doehrman, Druscilla S., trust: Somers Foundation, Byron H.

Doelger, Susan, trust: Doelger Charitable Trust, Thelma

Doerfler, Ronald J., sr vp, cfo: Capital Cities/ABC; vp, dir: Capital Cities Foundation

Doermann, Humphrey, pres: Bush Foundation

Doerr, Henry, trust: Blandin Foundation

Doerr, Ronald H., pres, coo: National Steel

Doggett, James D., vp, trust: Green Foundation, Burton E.

Doggett, W. B., dir communs & commun rels: BP America

Doherty, Bernard J., secy: Mueller Co. Foundation

Doherty, Francis J., Jr., secy: CertainTeed Corp. Foundation; exec dir: Norton Co. Foundation

Doherty, J. B., vp (external aff): National Starch & Chemical Corp.; chmn, dir: National Starch & Chemical Foundation

Doherty, J. N., sr vp, mem exec comm, dir: Shell Oil Co. Foundation

Doherty, John H., pres: Corporate Printing Co.

Doherty, Leonard Edward, mem adv comm, adm off: Dow Jones Foundation

Dohrman, Pam, trust: Wilcox Trust, S. W.

Dohrmann, Fred G., pres, coo, dir: Winnebago Industries, Inc.

Doing, Robert B., vchmn: Community Health Association

Doiron, Don F., pres: Goldome F.S.B

Doke, Timothy J., secy, mgr: AMR/American Airlines Foundation

Dolan, Charles Francis, chmn, ceo: Cablevision Systems

Corp.; don, dir: Dolan Family Foundation

Dolan, Dennis M., cfo: Air Express International Corp.

Dolan, Helen A., don, dir: Dolan Family Foundation

Dolan, James F., trust: Heinz Foundation, Drue

Dolan, James Francis, secy, dir: Coral Reef Foundation; mem adv comm: Weezie Foundation

Dolan, Marianne, pres: Dolan Family Foundation

Dolan, Myles, trust, vp: Rabb Foundation, Harry W.

Dolan, Thomas Ironside, dir: Smith Corp., A.O.; vp, dir: Smith Foundation, A.O.

Dolanski, A. P., trust: KPMG Peat Marwick Foundation

Dolden, Roger, sr vp (fin): Cosmair, Inc.

Dole, Nancy, trust: Wells Trust Fund, Fred W.

Dole, S. R., exec vp, coo: Southland Corp.

Dolinsky, Alan, dir, treas: International Fund for Health and Family Planning

Doll, A. Robert, pres: Greenebaum, Doll & McDonald Foundation

Doll, Robert, pres: C. E. and S. Foundation

Dollar, Joann F., secy: Day Foundation, Cecil B.

Dollens, R. W., dir: Lilly & Co. Foundation, Eli

Dolohanty, Shane, cfo: Parker Pen USA Ltd.

Dominick, Robert I., trust: Harris Foundation, H. H.

Dompier, Sandra Smith, trust: Smith Foundation, Bob and Vivian

Donaghy, James E., pres, ceo, dir: Sheldahl Inc.

Donahue, Donald J., dir: Greenwall Foundation

Donahue, Donald Jordan, chmn: Magma Copper Co.

Donahue, Frank R., Jr., secy, dir: Barra Foundation

Donahue, Richard K., dir: Joyce Foundation; pres, coo: Nike Inc.

Donald, James, chmn, pres, ceo, dir: DSC Communications Co.

Donald, Judy, secy, treas, exec dir: Beldon Fund

Donaldson, Don, vp, asst secy: Lyon Foundation

Donaldson, F. A. Sandy, trust: Donaldson Foundation

Donaldson, Kenneth T., trust: Slaughter Foundation, Charles

Donaldson, Matthew S., Jr., secy: Measey Foundation, Benjamin and Mary Siddons

Donaldson, Patricia F., Green Charitable Trust, Leslie H. and Edith C.

Donaldson, Richard Miesse, treas, mgr: Brush Foundation

Donaldson, William, chmn, ceo: New York Stock Exchange

Donaldson, William H., chmn, dir: Aetna Foundation

Dondorf, Joseph L., pres, ceo: Hein-Werner Corp.

Donehue, Gerald F., trust: Fay Charitable Fund, Aubert J.

Donelan, Edward P., asst treas: Waterfowl Research Foundation

Donelson, Harold L., asst secy, asst treas: McMillen Foundation

Donian, Margaret L., trust: Lincoln Family Foundation

Donithen, Joe D., trust: True Trust, Henry A.

Donley, Edward, chmn, dir: American Standard

Donlon, Thomas B., asst treas: Aetna Foundation

Donlon, William J., chmn, ceo: Niagara Mohawk Power Corp.

Donnell, Bruce, trust: Sullivan Musical Foundation, William Matheus

Donnelley, David E., dir: Donnelley Foundation, Elliott and Ann

Donnelley, Dorothy Ranney, vp, dir, don: Donnelley Foundation, Gaylord and Dorothy

Donnelley, Elliott, vp, dir: Donnelley Foundation, Gaylord and Dorothy

Donnelley, Gaylord, chmn, dir: Donnelley Foundation, Gaylord and Dorothy

Donnelley, James R., dir: Barker Welfare Foundation; dir: Donnelley Foundation, Elliott and Ann; vchmn, dir: Donnelley & Sons Co., R.R.; trust, vp, treas: Griswold Foundation, John C.

Donnelley, Laura, vp, dir: Donnelley Foundation, Gaylord and Dorothy

Donnelley, Robert G., dir: Donnelley Foundation, Elliott and Ann

Donnelley, Strachan, vp, dir: Donnelley Foundation, Gaylord and Dorothy

Donnelley, Thomas E., II, dir: Donnelley Foundation, Elliott and Ann

Donnelly, Gerald, chmn, ceo: Prange Co., H. C.

Donnelly, James C., vp, dir: WICOR Foundation

Donnelly, Jane, exec dir, mem trust comm: Bergen Foundation, Frank and Lydia

Donnelly, Joan C., secy, dir: Brunner Foundation, Robert

Donnelly, John J., mgr: Sheadle Trust, Jasper H.; dir: Truman Foundation, Mildred Faulkner

Donnelly, John L., treas, dir: Gazette Foundation

Donnelly, Rosemary, secy: Plym Foundation

Donnelly, Thomas J., trust: Donnelly Foundation, Mary J.; dir, pres: Evinrude Foundation, Ralph

Donnely, Edward L., trust: Rider-Pool Foundation

Donner, Alexander, dir: Donner Foundation, William H.

Donner, Frederick H., vp, dir: Independence Foundation

Donner, Robert, Jr., vp, asst treas: Donner Foundation, William H.

Donohue, Daniel J., pres, trust: Murphy Foundation, Dan

Donohue, Elise R., dir: Weyerhaeuser Memorial Foundation, Charles A.

Donohue, Rosemary E., trust: Murphy Foundation, Dan

Donohue, Tom, mgr (commun aff): U.S. Leasing International

Donovan, Ann Fuller, trust: Fuller Foundation

Donovan, John M., secy, dir: Alworth Memorial Fund, Marshall H. and Nellie

Donovan, Thomas, trust: Mellon Bank Foundation

Donovan, Thomas F., chmn, pres, ceo: Mellon PSFS

Donovan, William, secy, dir: Horowitz Foundation, Gedale B. and Barbara S.

Donway, Walter, program off (education): Dana Foundation, Charles A.

Doochin, Jerald, chmn, pres: Interstate Packaging Co.; trust: Interstate Packaging Foundation Charitable Trust

Doochin, Michael, trust: Interstate Packaging Foundation Charitable Trust

Doody, John Robert, exec vp fin & admin: Sonat

Doolan, Victor H., exec vp (sales & mktg): BMW of North America, Inc.

Dooley, Michael F., program off: Exxon Education Foundation

Doolin, Thomas, pres: Pennbank

Doolittle, James, pres, dir: Time Warner Cable

Doolittle, Renee, gen admin coordinator: Fanuc U.S.A. Corp.

Doordan, Helen R., trust-at-large, mem communicating & coordinating & other comms: Raskob Foundation for Catholic Activities

Dopp, Melissa, dir: American Honda Foundation

Dopson, Arnold B., dir, chmn: Blount Educational and Charitable Foundation, Mildred Weedon

Doquette, Ernest A., trust: American Optical Foundation

Dor, Barbara, trust: Ferkauf Foundation, Eugene and Estelle

Dor, Benny, trust: Ferkauf Foundation, Eugene and Estelle

Dora, James E., dir: AUL Foundation

Dorann, Eileen, contr: Grant Foundation, William T.

Dorenbusch, John F., dir: Irwin-Sweeney- Miller Foundation

Dorety, J.C., trust: Finch Foundation, Doak

Dorf, Alfred R., trust: Large Foundation

Dorf, Jerome, vp: Hartmarx Charitable Foundation

Dorfman, Henry S., chmn, ceo, dir: Thorn Apple Valley, Inc.

Dorfman, Hiram A., pres: Maas Foundation, Benard L.

Dorfman, Joel, ceo, dir: Thorn Apple Valley, Inc.

Dorfman, Lucille F., trust: Maas Foundation, Benard L.

Dorkhom, George, pres, ceo: Contraves USA

Dorman, Gerald D., M.D., trust: Potts Memorial Foundation

Dormann, Juergen, chmn: Hoechst Celanese Corp.

Dorminy, John Henry, III, dir, vchmn: Dorminy Foundation, John Henry

Dorminy, William J., dir, chmn, pres: Dorminy Foundation, John Henry

Dormitzer, Henry, II, vp, dir: Wyman-Gordon Foundation

Dorn, Carl S., trust: Sofia American Schools

Dorn, David F., trust: Glendorn Foundation

Dorn, John C., trust: Glendorn Foundation

Dorn, Richard B., trust: Glendorn Foundation

Dorn, William L., chmn, pres, ceo, dir: Forest Oil Corp.

Dornbos, William, vp (human resources): Contraves USA

Dornsife, David H., vp, dir: Hedco Foundation

Dornsife, Ester M., pres, dir: Hedco Foundation

Dornsife, Harold W., cfo, dir: Hedco Foundation

Doroshow, Carol A., vp, dir: Levinson Foundation, Max and Anna

Doroshow, Helen L., dir: Levinson Foundation, Max and Anna

Doroshow, James E., dir: Levinson Foundation, Max and Anna

Doroshow, William, dir: Levinson Foundation, Max and Anna

Dorrance, G. Morris, Jr., trust rep CoreStates NA: Smith Charitable Trust, W. W.

Dorrenbacher, C. James, dir: McDonnell Douglas Foundation; chmn: McDonnell Douglas Employee's Community Fund-West

Dorris, Thomas B., trust: Beidler Charitable Trust, Francis

Dorsett, C. Powers, vp (gen coun): Springs Industries

Dorsey, Bob Rawls, dir, mem exec comm, chmn dirs grant comm: Keck Foundation, W. M.

Dorsey, Earl A., trust: Brown Foundation, W. L. Lyons

Dorsey, Gilbert L., pres, dir: Eureka Co.

Dorsey, Hugh M., trust: Beck Foundation, Lewis H.

Dorsey, Patrick, dir: Kellenberger Historical Foundation, May Gordon Latham

Dorskind, Albert A., vp, cfo, dir: Parsons Foundation, Ralph M.

Dorwart, Frederic, trust: Kaiser Foundation, Betty E. and George B.

Doss, Lawrence P., dir: ANR Foundation; trust: Hudson-Webber Foundation

Doss, Marion K., dir: Fieldcrest Foundation

Doty, Carl K., pres: Donnelley & Sons Co., R.R.

Doty, George E., secy, trust: Doty Family Foundation

Doty, George E., Jr., trust: Doty Family Foundation

Doty, Marie J., trust: Doty Family Foundation

Doty, William W., trust: Doty Family Foundation

Doucette, James W., vp (investment mgmt): Humana Foundation

Dougherty, Ada M., asst secy: Hyde and Watson Foundation

Dougherty, Gordon M., trust: Reinghardt Foundation, Albert

Dougherty, Mary Ellen, trust: Eaton Foundation, Edwin M. and Gertrude S.

Dougherty, Mary Patricia, secy, trust: Dougherty, Jr. Foundation, James R.

Dougherty, R. E., vchmn, dir: Aerospace Corp.

Dougherty, Stephen T., trust: Dougherty, Jr. Foundation, James R.

Doughty, H. C., Jr., secy: Borden Foundation

Douglas, Anne, mgr: Douglas Charitable Foundation

Douglas, Arthur, dir: Norcross Wildlife Foundation

Douglas, Colette, mgr (corp contributions): Comerica

Douglas, Francis W., mem adv comm: Michael Foundation, Herbert I. and Elsa B.

Douglas, Jean W., dir: Wallace Genetic Foundation

Douglas, Kenneth J., vchmn: Dean Foods Co.

Douglas, Kirk, mgr: Douglas Charitable Foundation

Douglas, Mary St. John, vp, trust: Whiting Foundation, Mrs. Giles

Douglas, Paul W., chmn, ceo, dir: Pittston Co.

Douglas, Robert D., Jr., chmn, dir: Kellenberger Historical Foundation, May Gordon Latham

Douglas, Walter E., trust: Skillman Foundation

Douglas, William A., pres, exec dir: Boettcher Foundation

Douglass, Arthur R., trust: Harding Educational and Charitable Foundation

Douglass, Katheryn Cowles, trust: Mason Charitable Foundation

Douglass, Kingman Scott, trust: Mason Charitable Foundation

Douglass, Louise J., trust: Mason Charitable Foundation

Douglass, Robert Dun, trust: Mason Charitable Foundation

Douglass, Robert Royal, trust: Chase Manhattan Bank, N.A.

Douglass, Timothy P., trust: Mason Charitable Foundation

Douglass, W. Birch, III, secy, trust: Gray Foundation, Garland

Douzinas, Nancy R., vp, dir: Rauch Foundation

Dow, Barbara C., secy, treas, trust: Dow Foundation, Herbert H. and Barbara C.

Dow, G. Lincoln, Jr., trust: Sailors' Snug Harbor of Boston

Dow, Herbert Henry, II, pres, trust: Dow Foundation, Herbert H. and Barbara C.; pres: Dow Foundation, Herbert H. and Grace A.

Dow, Michael I., treas: Dow Fund, Alden and Vada

Dow, Michael L., treas, trust, don grandson: Dow Foundation, Herbert H. and Grace A.

Dow, Pamela G., assoc: Dow Foundation, Herbert H. and Grace A.

Dow, Vada B., pres: Dow Fund, Alden and Vada

Dow, Willard H., II, trust: Dow Foundation, Herbert H. and Barbara C.

Dowd, Hector G., secy: Frese Foundation, Arnold D.

Dowd, James, cfo: Management Compensation Group/Dulworth Inc.

Dowd, James F., pres, ceo: Skandia America Reinsurance Corp.

Dowden, Albert R., pres, ceo: Volvo North America Corp.

Dowdle, James C., dir: McCormick Tribune Foundation, Robert R.

Dowling, Anne T., dir (corp contributions): Philip Morris Cos.

Downer, Edwin E., dir: Hardin Foundation, Phil

Downer, W. C., cfo: American Business Products, Inc.

Downes, Edward O., trust: Sullivan Musical Foundation, William Matheus

Downes, Laurence M., sr vp, cfo: New Jersey Resources Corp.

Downey, J. L., trust: Dow Chemical Co.

Downey, Thelma, asst secy, asst treas: Olsson Memorial Foundation, Elis

Downham, Max, chmn (contributions comm): NutraSweet Co. Charitable Trust

Downie, John F., secy: Cole National Foundation

Downing, John C., pres: Downing Foundation, J. C.

Downing, L. Marie, trust: Foundation for Seacoast Health

Downs, Harry S., chmn scholarship bd: Cobb Educational Fund, Ty

Downs, Sue, dir corp & commun aff: Shoney's Inc.

Downs, Tom, dir: Tanner Foundation

Doxsey, Judy, accounting dept: Stauffer Charitable Trust, John

Doyle, Alice P., trust: Valentine Foundation, Lawson

Doyle, Allen, trust: Valentine Foundation, Lawson

Doyle, Christopher M., pub rels coordinator: REI-Recreational Equipment, Inc.

Doyle, Donald W., trust: Gheens Foundation

Doyle, Francis A., Massachusetts Charitable Mechanics Association

Doyle, Francis C., Williams Foundation, Kemper and Leila

Doyle, Frank P., trust: GE Foundations

Doyle, John H., secy, trust: DelMar Foundation, Charles

Doyle, Michael P., dir: Research Corporation

Doyle, Patricia, grants admin: Morgan Stanley Foundation

Doyle, Robert A., dir: AMCORE Foundation, Inc.

Doyle, T. Lawrence, treas, dir: Wieboldt Foundation

Doyle, Terence N., secy: Butler Family Foundation, Patrick and Aimee

Doyle, Terrence N., mem: AHS Foundation

Doyle, Thomas M., secy, dir: East Foundation, Sarita Kenedy; vp, dir: Grace Foundation, Inc.

Doyle, Valentine, trust: Valentine Foundation, Lawson

Dozier, Ollin Kemp, treas: Universal Leaf Foundation

Drabik, Ronald C., vp, cfo: RB&W Corp.

Drachler, Sol, trust: Maas Foundation, Benard L.

Drack, Paul Edward, pres, coo, dir, chmn: Alumax; pres, coo, dir, chmn: AMAX

Drackett, Jeanne H., secy, trust: Wodecroft Foundation

Draeger, John K., trust: Giddings & Lewis Foundation

Dragone, Allan Rudolph, trust: Akzo America Foundation

Drain, Randall G., trust: Joukowsky Family Foundation

Drake, Carl Bigelow, Jr., chmn, trust: Bigelow Foundation, F. R.

Drake, Duane W., exec vp, cfo: San Diego Trust & Savings Bank

Drake, John Walter, secy: Pilgrim Foundation

Drake, Judy, trust: Shwayder Foundation, Fay

Drake, Philip M., vp, secy, treas, dir: Culpeper Foundation, Charles E.

Drake, William Frank, Jr., vchmn, dir: Alco Standard Corp.; vp, dir: Alco Standard Foundation

Draper, Anne, dir: Tucker Foundation, Marcia Brady

Draper, Cecil Vanoy, vp, treas: Manville Fund

Draper, Dana, dir: Guggenheim Foundation, Daniel and Florence

Draper, E. Linn, Jr., pres, coo: American Electric Power; pres, coo: Columbus Southern Power Co.

Draper, James, dir: Copernicus Society of America

Draper, James Avery, III, trust, vp: Carpenter Foundation

Draper, Renee Carpenter, trust: Carpenter Foundation

Draper, Ron, cfo: Sheaffer Inc.

Drapkin, D.G., vchmn, dir: MacAndrews & Forbes Holdings

Drasner, Fred, ceo: U.S. News & World Report

Draughon, Rob, vp: Fuqua Foundation, J. B.

Dray, Joseph F., dir: Van Huffel Foundation, I. J.

Drayton, Cynthia W., pres: Bartol Foundation, Stockton Rush

Drebin, Allan, treas: Cheney Foundation, Elizabeth F.

Dreby, Edwin C., III, trust: Scholler Foundation

Dreckshage, Ruth, secy, treas, trust: Laclede Gas Charitable Trust

Drees, Donna, secy, treas: Mid-Iowa Health Foundation

Dreiling, John G., trust: Dreiling and Albina Dreiling Charitable Trust, Leo J.

Dreiling, Norbert R., trust: Dreiling and Albina Dreiling Charitable Trust, Leo J.

Dreitzer, Shirley, trust: Dreitzer Foundation

Drell, Stuart, exec vp, gen mgr: Matchbox Toys (USA) Ltd.

Drell, William, vp: California Foundation for Biochemical Research

Drennan, Altie Don, treas: Frazier Foundation

Drennan, Dorothea F., vp: Freygang Foundation, Walter Henry

Drennan, Joseph A., trust: Freygang Foundation, Walter Henry

Drennan, Rudith A., vp: Frazier Foundation

Dressel, Daniel, sr vp (human resources): Kraft General Foods

Dressel, Henry R., Jr., trust: National Service Foundation

Dresser, Joyce G., trust: Arkell Hall Foundation

Dresser, Paul A., coo: Chesapeake Corp.

Drestruel, Jean E., dir: Exchange Bank Foundation

Drew, Elton F., trust: Ellison Foundation

Drew, Ernest Harold, pres, ceo, dir: Hoechst Celanese Corp.

Drew, Helen Hall, trust: Stackpole-Hall Foundation

Drew, Richard L., trust, secy: Pilgrim Foundation

Drew, Roy M., dir: Parker Foundation

Drexel, Noreen, trust: McBean Charitable Trust, Alletta Morris

Drexler, Millard S., pres, dir: Gap, The; trust: Gap Foundation

Driehaus, Margaret F., trust: Driehaus Foundation, Richard H.

Dries, William, vp, dir: AMCA Foundation

Driggers, Nathan B., pres, trust: Harder Foundation

Drinko, Diane Lynn, trust: Mellen Foundation

Drinko, Elizabeth G., vp, trust: Mellen Foundation

Drinko, John Deaver, pres, trust: Mellen Foundation

Driscoll, Edward C., chmn, ceo: Driscoll Co., L.F.

Driscoll, Elizabeth S., dir: Driscoll Foundation; secy, trust: Weyerhaeuser Family Foundation

Driscoll, Frank E., chmn, dir: Mebane Packaging Corp.

Driscoll, George E., dir: Siragusa Foundation

Driscoll, Mrs. C. Francis, trust: Chapman Foundation, William H.

Driscoll, Richard D., trust: Charlesbank Homes

Driscoll, Rudolph W., Jr., trust: Weyerhaeuser Family Foundation

Driscoll, Rudolph Weyerhaeuser, vp, dir, don: Driscoll Foundation

Driscoll, W. Daniel, Wildermuth Foundation, E. F.

Driscoll, W. John, pres, don, dir: Driscoll Foundation; trust, dir: Northwest Area Foundation

Droguett, Mrs. Rudy O., theater rentals chmn: Ebell of Los Angeles Rest Cottage Association

Drost, Charles M., dir: Burton Foundation, William T. and Ethel Lewis

Drost, Jill, trust: Eberly Foundation

Drought, David W., treas: First Financial Foundation

Drought, Richard M., trust, treas: Egenton Home

Drowota, Frank F., III, trust: Ansley Foundation, Dantzler Bond; dir: HCA Foundation

Druckenmiller, Rev. Bruce, trust: Plankenhorn Foundation, Harry

Drueding, Bernard J., vp: Drueding Foundation

Drueding, Frank J., pres: Drueding Foundation

Druley, Robert F., dir: Dana Corp. Foundation

Druliner, Kathryn, treas, trust: Cooper Foundation

Drummond, G. N., chmn, ceo, dir: Drummond Co.

Drummond, Gerard K., exec vp, dir: Nerco, Inc.; chmn: PacifiCorp Foundation

Drumwright, Elenita M., vp, dir: Memton Fund

Drury, David, pres, ceo: Principal Financial Group

Drury, Francis T., chmn: Rutgers Community Health Foundation

Drury, Robert E., vp, dir: AMCA Foundation

Drury, W. Roger, sr vp: Humana Foundation

Drushel, William H., Jr., trust: Cullen Foundation

Drye, Kathy, employee rels mgr: Yale Security Inc.

Drymalski, Raymond H., treas: Offield Family Foundation

Du Bain, Myron, chmn, dir: Irvine Foundation, James

du Bois, Alan, pres, dir: du Bois Foundation, E. Blois

du Pont, Alexis Felix, Jr., treas: duPont Foundation, Chichester

du Pont, Caroline J., trust: duPont Foundation, Chichester

du Pont, Christopher T., vp, trust: duPont Foundation, Chichester

du Pont, Edward Bradford, vp, trust: Longwood Foundation; treas, trust: Welfare Foundation

du Pont, Helena Allaire Crozer, trust: duPont Foundation, Chichester

du Pont, Irenee, Jr., adv trust, don son: Crystal Trust

du Pont, Lammot Joseph, trust: Marmot Foundation

du Pont, Miren de Amezola, trust: Marmot Foundation

du Pont, Pierre Samuel, IV, trust: Longwood Foundation

du Pont, Willis Harrington, trust: Marmot Foundation

Duane, Morris, trust: Presser Foundation

Dubes, Michael, dir: Northwestern National Life Insurance Co.

Dubiel, Robert, trust: Acushnet Foundation

Dubin, Melvin, pres, dir: Slant/Fin Corp.; pres, dir: Slant/Fin Foundation

Dubin, Stephen V., vp, secy, dir: Farber Foundation

Dubler, Robert, trust: Young Foundation, Hugo H. and Mabel B.

Duboc, Charles A., treas, dir: Loose Trust, Carrie J.; treas: Loose Trust, Harry Wilson

DuBois, Jennifer Land, trust, don daughter: Rowland Foundation

DuBois, Joan F., program vp: Keck Foundation, W. M.

DuBois, Philip, pres, trust: Rowland Foundation

DuBose, Vivian Noble, trust: Noble Foundation, Samuel Roberts

DuBow, Helen A., vp, ex admin: Dubow Family Foundation

Dubow, Isabella B., dir: Marpat Foundation

DuBow, Lawrence, pres, trust: Dubow Family Foundation

Dubow, Lawrence J., secy, trust: Cohen Foundation, George F.

DuBow, Linda, treas, trust: Dubow Family Foundation

DuBow, Michael, vp, trust: Dubow Family Foundation

DuBow, Susan, vp, trust: Dubow Family Foundation

DuBridge, Lee A., adv to bd: Weingart Foundation

Dubrow, Eli B., trust: Early Medical Research Trust, Margaret E.

Dubrow, Lowell H., trust: Goldman Foundation, William

Dubrul, Stephen M., Jr., dir: Acme-Cleveland Foundation

Dubuque, Loretta, dir: Jafra Educational Development Grant Endowment

Duch, Edward K., Jr., dir: Goldome Foundation

Duche, Jean-Pierre, chmn, ceo: Ketchum & Co.

Duchossois, Craig J., pres: Duchossois Industries; vp, treas: Duchossois Foundation

Duchossois, Dayle Paige, dir: Duchossois Foundation

Duchossois, R. Bruce, dir: Duchossois Foundation

Duchossois, Richard L., chmn, dir: Chamberlain Manufacturing Corp.

Duchossois, Richard Louis, chmn, ceo, dir: Duchossois Industries; secy: Duchossois Foundation

Duckworth, William, secy: Stauffer Communications Foundation

Ducournau, Jackson P., trust: Libby-Dufour Fund, Trustees of the

DuCray, Dean T., vp, cfo: York International Corp.

Dudas, Michael L., sr vp, cfo: ISS International Service System

Dudek, Susan, cfo: Miller & Co.

Dudley, Alfred E., chmn, ceo, dir: First Brands Corp.

Dudley, R.W., dir: CBI Foundation

Dudley, Richard D., treas, dir: Alexander Foundation, Judd S.

Dudte, James, pres, trust: Young Foundation, Hugo H. and Mabel B.

Duello, J. Donald, treas, dir: Shelter Insurance Foundation

Duemke, Emmett, dir, pres: Tandy Foundation, David L.

Duerksen, Erwin, chmn, dir: Union Equity Division of Farmland Industries

Duesenberg, Richard William, vp, dir: Monsanto Fund

Duff, Charles B., dir: Edmondson Foundation, Joseph Henry

Duff, Charles F., vp, trust: Gray Foundation, Garland

Duff, Christopher Bruce, dir: Edmondson Foundation, Joseph Henry

Duff, James George, chmn, ceo, dir: U.S. Leasing International

Duff, Patrick D., Jr., trust: Tiger Foundation

Duff, Sallie E., dir: Edmondson Foundation, Joseph Henry

Duff, Thomas M., pres, ceo: Wellman Inc.

Duffell, Carol, secy, treas: Semmes Foundation

Duffield, Michael, vp, dir: Wallace Computer Services Foundation

Duffy, Bernard J., Jr., mem: McGee Foundation

Duffy, Brian, pres, dir: Fleet Co., Inc., C.B.

Duffy, Edward W., dir: Utica National Group Foundation

Duffy, G. Chapman, comm: Thurman Charitable Foundation for Children, Edgar A.

Duffy, John J., Esq., co-trust: Badgeley Residuary Charitable Trust, Rose M.; secy, dir: Lee Foundation, James T.

Duffy, Michael G., 2nd vp: Raskob Foundation for Catholic Activities

Duffy, Paul, dir: Lee Foundation, James T.

Duffy, Robert A., dir: Hertz Foundation, Fannie and John

Duffy, Vivien Stiles, dir: Rohatyn Foundation, Felix and Elizabeth

Duffy, William, trust: Lynch Scholarship Foundation, John B.

DuFort, Beverly, mgr corp contributions volunteerism: Puget Sound Power & Light Co.

Dufournier, Beatrix R., trust: Hillsdale Fund

Dugan, Dennis O., dir: Ray Foundation

Dugan, Jay J., trust: Iacocca Foundation

Dugan, Michael K., pres: Henredon Furniture Industries

Dugdale, J. W., dir: Davee Foundation

Duggan, Patricia M., dir: Polk Foundation

Duhme, Carol M., pres, trust: Roblee Foundation, Joseph H. and Florence A.

Duhme, Warren, bd mem: Roblee Foundation, Joseph H. and Florence A.

Duke, Anthony, trust: Achelis Foundation; trust: Bodman Foundation

Duke, Barbara Foshay, vp, dir: Milbank Foundation, Dunlevy

Duke, Brian O. L., med dir: River Blindness Foundation

Duke, David A., vchmn (tech), dir: Corning Incorporated; trust: Corning Incorporated Foundation

Duke, Doris, trust, don daughter: Duke Endowment; don, pres, dir: Duke Foundation, Doris

Duke, Jennifer U. Johnson, dir: South Branch Foundation

Duke, Lani Lattin, dir (Getty Ctr Ed Arts): Getty Trust, J. Paul

Duke, Robin Chandler, trust: Packard Foundation, David and Lucile; trust: United States-Japan Foundation

Dulaney, Robert W., pres, dir: Norton Foundation Inc.

Dulany, Margaret Rockefeller, trust: Rockefeller Foundation

Dulin, Susan W., trust: Boswell Foundation, James G.

Dulin, William R., secy, treas, trust: Morgan Trust for Charity, Religion, and Education

Dullea, Charles, SJ, dir: Hale Foundation, Crescent Porter

Dulude, Donald, chmn, ceo: Kuhlman Corp.

Dulude, Richard, trust: Corning Incorporated Foundation

Duman, Louis J., dir: Bonfils-Stanton Foundation

Dumble, John S., pres: Glidden Co.

Dumke, Carol, dir: Browning Charitable Foundation, Val A.

Dumke, Edmund E., treas, dir: Dumke Foundation, Dr. Ezekiel R. and Edna Wattis

Dumke, Ezekiel R., Jr., pres, dir: Dumke Foundation, Dr. Ezekiel R. and Edna Wattis

Dumke, Valerie, asst secy, dir: Dumke Foundation, Dr. Ezekiel R. and Edna Wattis

Dummire, Robert W., vp, trust: Montgomery Foundation

Dumont, Mrs. Rene, ways and means chmn: Ebell of Los Angeles Scholarship Endowment Fund

Dumont, Rene, chmn of ways and means: Ebell of Los

Angeles Rest Cottage Association

DuMont, Vera, asst to dir: Dodge Foundation, Geraldine R.

Dunagan, J. Conrad, pres: Dunagan Foundation

Dunagan, John C., secy, treas: Dunagan Foundation

Dunagan, Kathlyn C., vp: Dunagan Foundation

Dunbar, C. Wendell, treas, trust: Towsley Foundation, Harry A. and Margaret D.

Dunbar, Leslie Wallace, vchmn, trust: Mott Fund, Ruth

Dunbar, Lynn S., asst dir: Gibson Foundation, Addison H.

Duncan, Anne S., dir: Duncan Foundation, Lillian H. and C. W.

Duncan, Baker, trust: Walker Foundation, W. E.

Duncan, Beverly R., secy, dir: Madison Gas & Electric Foundation

Duncan, Brenda, dir: Duncan Foundation, Lillian H. and C. W.

Duncan, Buell G., Jr., chmn: Sun Banks Inc.

Duncan, C. W., III, dir: Duncan Foundation, Lillian H. and C. W.

Duncan, Carolyn, asst secy: Duke Power Co. Foundation

Duncan, Charles William, Jr., chmn: Duncan Foundation, Lillian H. and C. W.; trust: Welch Foundation, Robert A.

Duncan, Diene P., dir: Beneficia Foundation

Duncan, George T., trust: Franklin Foundation, John and Mary

Duncan, Ian, trust: Tomkins Corporation Foundation

Duncan, Jeaneane, dir: Duncan Foundation, Lillian H. and C. W.

Duncan, John H., Jr., dir: Duncan Foundation, Lillian H. and C. W.

Duncan, John House, pres, dir: Duncan Foundation, Lillian H. and C. W.

Duncan, John L., pres, ceo: Murray Ohio Manufacturing Co.

Duncan, John W., treas: SDB Foundation

Duncan, Mary Anne, dir: Duncan Foundation, Lillian H. and C. W.

Duncan, Melvin D., Jr., ceo: American Red Ball World Wide Movers

Duncan, Nancy Young, treas: Post Foundation of D.C., Marjorie Merriweather

Duncan, Paul R., cfo, exec vp, dir: Reebok International Ltd.; cfo, trust: Reebok Foundation

Duncan, Richard J., sr vp, cfo: Brown & Sharpe Manufacturing Co.

Duncan, Susan M., vp, trust: Schlessman Foundation

Duncan, Thomas, pres: Lea County Electric Co-op

Duncan, Thurman, pres: Lea Country Electric Education Foundation

Duncan, W. P., Jr., cfo, treas: Thomas Built Buses L.P.

Duncan, William H., vp, dir: SICO Foundation

Dunckel, Jeanette M., secy, dir: Haigh-Scatena Foundation; dir: Zellerbach Family Fund

Duncombe, Harmon, pres, treas, dir: Monell Foundation, Ambrose; secy: van Ameringen Foundation; vp, treas: Vetlesen Foundation, G. Unger

Dunford, Betty P., vp, trust: Cooke Foundation

Dunford, Edsel D., pres, coo, dir: TRW Corp.

Dungan, Thomas N., chmn: Sunkist Growers

Dunham, R. S., trust: Powell Co. Foundation, William

Dunkerly, Allan S., pres: Quabaug Corp.

Dunkerton, Donald, trust: Rixson Foundation, Oscar C.

Dunkerton, Nathan E., vp, secy, dir: Rixson Foundation, Oscar C.

Dunlap, Charles Lee, pres, coo: Crown Central Petroleum Corp.

Dunlap, F. Thomas, Jr., secy, dir: Intel Foundation

Dunlap, J. A., trust: Monarch Machine Tool Co. Foundation

Dunlap, Paul D., chmn: Hawkeye Bancorporation

Dunlap, R. Thornwell, pres: County Bank

Dunlap, Stan, vp (human resources): Spectra-Physics Analytical

Dunleavy, Francis J., trust: Bird Cos. Charitable Foundation

Dunlop, John T., trust: Bird Cos. Charitable Foundation

Dunlop, Joy S., dir, secy: Dell Foundation, Hazel

Dunlop, R.T., trust: County Bank Foundation

Dunlop, Robert G., dir: Pew Charitable Trusts

Dunn, David, pres, dir: ETCO Inc.

Dunn, Edward K., Jr., treas, trust: Warfield Memorial Fund, Anna Emory; trust: Wilson Sanitarium for Children of Baltimore City, Thomas

Dunn, Edward S., Jr., pres: Harris-Teeter Super Markets

Dunn, Harry E., vp, dir: Treakle Foundation, J. Edwin

Dunn, James J., vchmn, dir: Forbes

Dunn, John S., Jr., vp, treas, trust: Dunn Research Foundation, John S.

Dunn, Joseph C., secy, treas: Richley, Inc.

Dunn, Joseph M., pres, dir: PACCAR

Dunn, Leslie W., pres: Corpus Christi Exploration Co.; secy-treas: Corpus Christi Exploration Co. Foundation

Dunn, Lisa, corp rels mgr: Mitsubishi Motor Sales of America, Inc.

Dunn, Marie, publ aff off: NationsBank Texas

Dunn, Milby Dow, pres, trust: Dunn Research Foundation, John S.

Dunn, Milo, trust: Harvest States Foundation

Dunn, Peter M., Jr., secy, gen coun: Chapman Charitable Corporation, Howard and Bess

Dunn, R. H., Jr., trust: Burroughs Educational Fund, N. R.

Dunn, Richard, dir: Burns Foundation, Fritz B.

Dunn, Richard C., pres: Richley, Inc.

Dunn, Richard S., treas, trust: Community Coffee Co., Inc. Foundation

Dunn, Robert H., exec vp: Levi Strauss Foundation

Dunn, William J., cfo, vp (fin): Pirelli Armstrong Tire Corp.

Dunnigan, Joseph J., trust: Upjohn Foundation, Harold and Grace

Dunnigan, T. Kevin, chmn, pres, ceo: Thomas & Betts Corp.

Dunning, Bill, dir: Dearborn Cable Communications Fund

Dunning, George A. V., dir: Dunning Foundation

Dunning, Richard E., vp, treas, trust: Gerber Cos. Foundation

Dunnington, Walter G., Jr., trust: Sprague Educational and Charitable Foundation, Seth; trust: Sullivan Foundation, Algernon Sydney

Dunphy, T.J. Dermot, pres, ceo, dir: Sealed Air Corp.

Dunwell, Kathleen, sec: Clipper Ship Foundation

Dunwiddie, Alan W., Jr., pres, exec dir: Janesville Foundation

Dunwody, Atwood, gen coun, dir: United States Sugar Corp.; trust: United States Sugar Corporate Charitable Trust

Dunwoody, Atwood, trust: Davis Foundations, Arthur Vining

Dunworth, Gerald J., Jr., treas: Palisades Educational Foundation

Dupar, Frank A., Jr., trust, pres: Dupar Foundation

Dupar, James W., trust: Dupar Foundation

Dupar, James W., Jr., trust, vp: Dupar Foundation

Dupar, Robert W., trust: Dupar Foundation

Dupar, Thomas E., trust: Dupar Foundation

DuPont, Elizabeth Lee, vp: Good Samaritan

Dupont, Mary L., trust: KPMG Peat Marwick Foundation

Dupper, Ross, asst treas: Porsche Foundation

DuPree, Donald E., 3rd vp, chmn: Ebell of Los Angeles Rest Cottage Association

Dupree, Mrs. Donald E., Ebell of Los Angeles Scholarship Endowment Fund

Durand, H. Whitney, secy, trust: Tonya Memorial Foundation

Durban, Barbara, trust: Stern Foundation, Charles H. and Anna S.

Durbin, Vaughn, secy, treas: Colt Foundation, James J.

Durden, J. C., vp, dir: Tractor & Equipment Company Foundation

Durein, Ted, pres: National Pro-Am Youth Fund

Durgin, Diane, secy: Georgia-Pacific Foundation

Durgin, Eugene J., secy: Johnson Foundation, Howard

Durham, G. Robert, pres, ceo: Walter Industries

Durham, Richard P., vp, treas, trust: Huntsman Foundation, Jon and Karen

Durkee, King, scholarship adv: Copley Foundation, James S.

Durney, Michael, dir: Lotus Development Corp.

Durocher, Francis W., chmn, pres, treas: Perina Corp

Durovsik, Thomas, pres: Franklin Mint Corp.

Durr, John W., trust: Durr-Fillauer Medical Foundation

Durrett, William E., chmn: American Fidelity Corp.; pres: American Fidelity Corporation Founders Fund

Durst, David M., don, vp, dir: Durst Foundation

Durst, Douglas, vp: Durst Foundation

Durst, Eli, treas: DEC International- Albrecht Foundation

Durst, Peter, vp: Durst Foundation

Durst, Robert, vp: Durst Foundation

Durst, Royal H., don, vp, dir: Durst Foundation

Durst, Seymour B., don, pres, dir: Durst Foundation

Dury, Joseph D., Jr., dir: Staunton Farm Foundation

Dusenberry, Philip B., vchmn, dir: BBDO Worldwide

Dussin, Guss, pres, treas: OSF International, Inc.

Dussling, Eric H., treas: Westinghouse Foundation

Duthie, David T., ceo: Courtaulds Fibers Inc.

Dutt, Mallika, program dir: Norman Foundation

Dutton, Anthony, secy: Tripifoods Foundation

Dutton, Uriel E., trust: Anderson Foundation, M. D.

Dutton, Warren C., dir: Exchange Bank Foundation

Duval, Daniel W., pres, ceo: Robbins & Myers, Inc.; pres, mgr: Robbins & Myers Foundation

Duvall, Bill, pres: Lincoln Property Co.

Duvall, Robert L., secy, treas: Tartt Scholarship Fund, Hope Pierce

Dweck, Ralph, dir: Dweck Foundation, Samuel R.

Dweck, Rena, dir: Dweck Foundation, Samuel R.

Dwek, Cyril S., vchmn, dir: Republic New York Corp.

Dwight, George H. P., pres, trust: Tortuga Foundation

Dwight, Thomas J., trust: O'Neil Foundation, Casey Albert T.

Dwyer, John J., mem supervisory bd: Codrington Charitable Foundation, George W.; vp, trust: Mellen Foundation; trust: Oglebay Norton Foundation

Dwyer, Maureen Ellen, dir: Meyer Foundation, Eugene and Agnes E.

Dyar, Mary Anna, trust: Nash Foundation

Dyck, Harold P., vp, dir: Hesston Foundation

Dye, E. R., secy, trust: O'Neil Foundation, M. G.

Dye, Robert, vp corp commun: Journal Communications

Dye, Sherman, mem: South Waite Foundation

Dyer, W. A., Jr., pres: Indianapolis Newspapers, Inc.

Dyke, Walter P., trust: Murdock Charitable Trust, M. J.

Dykes, E.W., trust: Curran Foundation

Dykes, Martha M., trust: Marshall Foundation, Mattie H.

Dykhuizen, Ronald H., asst secy, asst treas: Simon Foundation, Jennifer Jones

Dykstra, Charles, pres: Michigan Wheel Corp.

Dykstra, Herbert, trust: IMT Co. Charitable Trust

Dykstra, Rev. Dr. Craig, vp (religion): Lilly Endowment

Dyson, Anne E., MD, pres, dir: Dyson Foundation

Dyson, Charles Henry, fdr, don, vp, dir: Dyson Foundation; chmn emeritus, dir: Dyson-Kissner- Moran Corp.

Dyson, Margaret M., dir: Dyson Foundation

Dyson, Melvin A., pres, treas: Scott Fund, Olin

Dyson, Robert R., treas, dir: Dyson Foundation; pres, coo, dir: Dyson-Kissner- Moran Corp.

E

Eades, Pauline S., trust: Pitzman Fund

Eagle, Richard A., trust: Lauffer Trust, Charles A.

Eagleson, Arthur J., trust, vp: Hatterscheidt Foundation

Eamer, Richard Keith, chmn: National Medical Enterprises

Eames, G. Clifton, chmn, dir: Bangor Savings Bank

Eames, John, secy, treas, trust: Technical Foundation of America

Eardley, Vernon, pres, ceo: Korte Construction Co.

Earhart, Anne Catherine Getty, secy: Homeland Foundation

Earhart, John E., pres: Homeland Foundation

Earley, Anthony F., Jr., pres, coo, dir: Long Island Lighting Co.

Earley, Michael M., sr vp, cfo: Intermark, Inc.

Early, Jeannette B., pres: Early Foundation

Early, William Bernard, trust: JELD-WEN Foundation

Earnhardt, Stan, trust: Jones Foundation, Montfort Jones and Allie Brown

Easley, William K., mem (pub affairs comm): Springs Industries

Eason, Elizabeth, trust: Kyle Educational Trust, S. H. and D. W.

Eason, J. Rod, chmn, dir: Sierra Health Foundation

Eastham, Thomas, vp, western dir: Hearst Foundation; vp, western dir: Hearst Foundation, William Randolph

Eastman, Joseph, secy-treas: Johnson Co. Foundation, E. F.

Eastom, Timothy R., trust: Tokheim Foundation

Easton, James L., pres, ceo: Easton Aluminum

Easton, Kenneth, trust: McMahon Foundation

Easton, Richard, dir: Katzenberger Foundation

Eaton, Evelyn T., pres, trust: Eaton Foundation, Edwin M. and Gertrude S.

Eaton, Joseph E., trust: Sailors' Snug Harbor of Boston

Eaton, Larry E., dir: 3M Co.

Eaton, Mary Stephens, trust, vp: Eaton Foundation, Cyrus

Eaton, Robert James, vchmn, dir, coo: Chrysler Corp.

Ebeling, Henry, secy: Piper Foundation

Ebenshade, Richard D., secy, trust: Booth Foundation, Otis; vp, secy, trust: Munger Foundation, Alfred C.

Eber, Andrew, vp, dir: Haigh-Scatena Foundation

Eberhart, Guy, dir: Sears-Roebuck Foundation

Eberius, Klaus, pres, ceo: Motch Corp.

Eberle, William Denman, chmn bd trusts: United States-Japan Foundation

Eberly, Robert E., Jr., trust: Eberly Foundation

Eberly, Robert Edward, pres, treas: Eberly Foundation; chmn: Integra Bank/South

Ebert, Adrienne, trust: Ebert Charitable Foundation, Horatio B.

Ebert, Carroll Erich, dir: Bergner Foundation, P.A.

Ebert, Robert O., trust: Ebert Charitable Foundation, Horatio B.

Ebert, Viola R., trust: Ebert Charitable Foundation, Horatio B.

Ebrom, Charles E., exec vp, dir: Zachry Co., H. B.

Eccles, Dolores Dore, founding trst, don wife: Eccles Foundation, George S. and Dolores Dore

Eccles, John D., comm mem: Eccles Foundation, Marriner S.

Eccles, Lisa, exec asst to chmn: Eccles Foundation, George S. and Dolores Dore

Eccles, Ruth P., chmn: Eccles Charitable Foundation, Willard L.

Eccles, Sara M., chmn: Eccles Foundation, Marriner S.

Eccles, Spencer Fox, pres, dir: Eccles Foundation, George S. and Dolores Dore; comm mem: Eccles Foundation, Marriner S.; chmn, ceo, dir: First Security Bank of Idaho N.A.; dir: Treadwell Foundation, Nora Eccles

Echement, John R., Weisbrod Foundation Trust Dept., Robert and Mary

Echlin, Beryl G., trust: Echlin Foundation

Echlin, John E., dir, trust: Echlin Foundation

Echlin, John E., Jr., trust: Echlin Foundation

Eck, Dennis K., vchmn, coo, dir: Vons Cos., Inc.

Ecke, Paul, III, trust: Poinsettia Foundation, Paul and Magdalena Ecke

Ecke, Paul, Jr., dir, vp: Poinsettia Foundation, Paul and Magdalena Ecke

Eckel, Lee N., secy: Columbia Savings Charitable Foundation

Eckenrode, Robert J., vchmn, dir: NYNEX Corp.

Eckerle, David E., pres, ceo: DCB Corp.; pres, dir: DCB Foundation

Eckert, Carter H., pres, ceo, dir: Boots Pharmaceuticals, Inc.

Eckert, Constance L., trust: Hubbard Foundation

Eckert, J. P., pres, coo, dir: Babcock & Wilcox Co.

Eckert, Ralph J., chmn: Benefit Trust Life Insurance Co.

Eckert, V. E., dir: Jasper Wood Products Co. Foundation

Eckhardt, Kleberg, vp, trust: Vaughan Foundation, Rachael and Ben

Eckley, Robert Spence, dir: State Farm Cos. Foundation

Eckstein, Paul, trust: Marshall Fund

Eckstrom, Amy Lou, treas, dir: Murray Foundation

Economy, Stephen, exec asst to pres (corp contributions): Michigan Bell Telephone Co.

Eda, Minoru, gen mgr: Sanwa Bank Ltd. New York

Eddie, Gloria Jeneal, trust: Johnson Foundation, Walter S.

Eddy, Charles Russell, Jr., trust: Sailors' Snug Harbor of Boston

Eddy, Edith P., adm dir: Compton Foundation

Eddy, Erika G., exec dir: Pesch Family Foundation

Eddy, Jane Lee, secy, exec dir, trust: Taconic Foundation

Eddy, Maria, trust: Ivakota Association

Edelman, Manfred, vp (human resources): Sharp Electronics Corp.

Edelman, Marian Wright, dir: Aetna Foundation; dir: Diamond Foundation, Aaron

Edelman, Murray R., pres: Toledo Edison Co.

Edelman, Richard J., asst secy: Nias Foundation, Henry

Edelman, Richard M., trust: Matz Foundation — Edelman Division

Edelman, Stanley, MD, chmn: Nias Foundation, Henry

Edelson, Robert I., vp: Arell Foundation

Edelstein, Chaim, chmn, ceo: Abraham & Straus

Edelstein, Lester, pres, secy: Glosser Foundation, David A.

Edelstein, Morris, trust: Rales and Ruth Rales Foundation, Norman R.

Eden, Rose Mary, vp, dir: Dougherty Foundation

Edens, Jim Ben, pres: PGL Building Products

Eder, Andrew J., trust: Eder Foundation, Sidney and Arthur

Eder, Arthur, chmn, trust: Eder Foundation, Sidney and Arthur

Eder, Jo Ann, vp, dir: Edwards Foundation, O. P. and W. E.

Edey, Helen, MD, dir: Scherman Foundation

Edgar, Ann, dir: Butler Foundation, J. Homer

Edgar, Carol, secy: Lilly & Co. Foundation, Eli

Edge, Norris Lagrand, sr vp (customer & operating serv): Carolina Power & Light Co.

Edge, Robert G., chmn, trust: Loridans Foundation, Charles

Edgerly, Edward, Ph.D., off: Group Health Foundation

Edgerly, William Skelton, chmn: State Street Bank & Trust Co.

Edgerton, Bradford W., MD, vp, trust: Jones Foundation, W. Alton

Edgerton, Brenda Evans, treas, trust: Campbell Soup Foundation

Edgerton, Malcolm J., Jr., trust: Gould Foundation for Children, Edwin

Edgerton, Patricia Jones, pres, trust, mem fin comm, don daughter: Jones Foundation, W. Alton

Edgerton, William A., trust: Jones Foundation, W. Alton

Edison, Bernard Alan, dir: Edison Brothers Stores Foundation; vp, secy, dir: Edison Foundation, Harry; don, pres, dir: Edison Foundation, Irving and Beatrice C.

Edison, Marilyn, vp: Edison Foundation, Irving and Beatrice C.

Edison, Peter A., secy, dir: Edison Foundation, Irving and Beatrice C.

Edmond, Lisette S., vp, trust: McGraw Foundation, Curtis W.

Edmonds, Campbell S., trust: Slemp Foundation

Edmonds, Clarence, treas, trust: Massey Foundation, Jack C.

Edmonds, Dean S., III, trust: Edmonds Foundation, Dean S.

Edmonds, George P., trust: Fair Play Foundation

Edmonds, Mary Virginia, trust: Slemp Foundation

Edmondson, Arthur, dir: Kellenberger Historical Foundation, May Gordon Latham

Edmondson, John, pres, ceo, dir: Barclays Bank of New York

Edmunds, John W., chmn corp contributions: Rochester Gas & Electric Corp.

Edmunds, R. Larry, secy, treas: Comer Foundation

Edner, Leon E., trust: National Pro-Am Youth Fund

Edson, Catherine H., secy, trust: Halff Foundation, G. A. C.

Edson, Thomas H., trust: Halff Foundation, G. A. C.

Edwards, Albert G., vp: Stewards Fund

Edwards, B.F., III, chmn, pres, ceo, dir: Edwards & Sons, A.G.

Edwards, Barry L., treas, dir: Liberty Corp. Foundation

Edwards, Beverly A., pres: Burlington Northern Foundation

Edwards, Bruce C., sr vp, cfo: AST Research, Inc.

Edwards, Charles C., Jr., trust: Cowles Foundation, Gardner and Florence Call

Edwards, Charles W., trust: Arise Charitable Trust

Edwards, D.A., trust: Edwards Foundation

Edwards, David L., mem dispensing comm: McCune Charitable Trust, John R.

Edwards, Don Raby, trust: Scott Foundation, William R., John G., and Emma

Edwards, Earnest Jonathan, dir: Alcoa Foundation

Edwards, Edith W., trust: Wolfson Family Foundation

Edwards, Frank G., trust: Puterbaugh Foundation

Edwards, J.T., Jr., trust: Edwards Foundation

Edwards, James Burrows, dir: Guggenheim Foundation, Harry Frank

Edwards, James K., trust: Levy Foundation, June Rockwell

Edwards, James M., mem dispensing comm: McCune Charitable Trust, John R.; mem distribution comm, don nephew: McCune Foundation

Edwards, John H., mem dispensing comm: McCune Charitable Trust, John R.

Edwards, Kathleen Bryan, trust: Bryan Family Foundation, Kathleen Price and Joseph M.

Edwards, Mahlon D., asst secy: Norfolk Southern Foundation

Edwards, Marvin S., cfo: Alcatel NA Cable Systems, Inc.

Edwards, Michael M., mem dispensing comm: McCune Charitable Trust, John R.

Edwards, Morris D., trust: Wolfson Family Foundation

Edwards, Paul B., trust: Wagner Foundation, Ltd., R. H.

Edwards, Richard D., mem distribution comm: McCune Foundation

Edwards, Robert A., trust: O'Brien Foundation, Cornelius and Anna Cook

Edwards, Robert M., secy: Goldome Foundation

Edwards, Rodney J., trust: Eddy Foundation

Edwards, Ron, trust: Clemens Foundation

Edwards, Tracy, cfo: Bell Industries

Edwards, William H., vchmn, trust: Camp and Bennet Humiston Trust, Apollos; dir: Hilton Foundation, Conrad N.

Edwards, William J., trust: Bentley Foundation, Alvin M.

Edwardson, John A., exec vp, cfo: Ameritech Publishing

Eefting, Ilene B., treas: Taylor Family Foundation, Jack

Efird, Claire, dir: Belk-Simpson Foundation

Efrid, C. L., Jr., dir: Simpson Foundation

Efron, Miles E., pres, ceo: North Star Universal Inc.

Efroymson, Daniel C., mem (community concerns comm): NBD Bank, N.A.

Efroymson, Daniel R., treas, secy, vp, dir: Moriah Fund

Efroymson, Loralei M., asst vp: Moriah Fund

Efroymson-Kahn, Shirley G., dir: Moriah Fund

Egan, Estelle, contact person: Huston Charitable Trust, Stewart

Egan, Evelyn Wilson, trust, pres: Wilson Foundation, John and Nevils

Egan, Gerald F., vp (fin), cfo: Duty Free International

Egan, Gordon T., pres: Connell Rice & Sugar Co.

Egan, Thomas J., vp, chief adm off: Freeport-McMoRan

Egan, Thomas P., dir, off: Valmont Foundation

Ege, Hans A., treas, dir: Bay Foundation; dir, treas: Paul and C. Michael Paul Foundation, Josephine Bay

Egelston, Robert B., pres, dir: Capital Group Foundation

Eggum, John, secy, treas, dir: Regenstein Foundation

Egler, Gary L., dir (mktg): Indiana Desk Co.; secy, dir: Indiana Desk Foundation

Egler, Ruth D., trust: Donnelly Foundation, Mary J.

Eglinton, W. M., exec vp, coo, dir: Public Service Co. of New Mexico

Eglinton, William, dir: PNM Foundation

Egner, Andrew J., Jr., trust: Orange Orphan Society

Eguchi, Motoko, asst to pres: Nichimen America, Inc.

Ehlers, Charles H., pres: Chomerics, Inc.

Ehlers, Walter George, treas, trust: China Medical Board of New York

Ehrenfeld, David, dir: Educational Foundation of America

Ehrenkranz, Joel S., trust: Werblow Charitable Trust, Nina W.

Ehrensberger, Evangeline, chief adm: Rienzi Foundation

Ehrhardt, Orville W., trust: Giddings & Lewis Foundation

Ehrhardt, Thomas H., mem trust fund comm: Ingram Trust, Joe

Ehrlich, Delia F., dir: Fleishhacker Foundation

Ehrlich, Jodi, dir: Fleishhacker Foundation

Ehrlich, John Stephen, Jr., dir: Fleishhacker Foundation

Ehrlich, M. Gordon, trust: Orchard Foundation

Ehrlich, Philip S., Jr., secy, dir: Zellerbach Family Fund

Ehrling, Robert F., pres: Gear Motions Foundation

Ehrman, Fred, pres, treas, dir: Ehrman Foundation, Fred and Susan

Ehrman, Susan, vp, dir: Ehrman Foundation, Fred and Susan

Eibling, Stephen H., trust: Ohio Bell Foundation

Eichenberg, Joyce N., vp: Goodman Memorial Foundation, Joseph C. and Clare F.

Eichler, Franklin Roosevelt, treas, dir: SICO Foundation

Eichman, Thelma L., dir: Strong Foundation, Hattie M.

Eichmann, James, exec dir: Cincinnati Bell Foundation

Eidelman, Steven M., exec dir: Kennedy, Jr. Foundation, Joseph P.

Eidenberg, Eugene, dir: MCI Foundation

Eielson, Rodney S., pres: Culpeper Foundation, Daphne Seybolt

Eigner, Michael, pres, dir: Daily News Foundation

Eigsti, Roger Harry, pres, ceo, dir: SAFECO Corp.

Einhorn, David M., asst vp: Wachtell, Lipton, Rosen & Katz Foundation

Einiger, Carol B., vp, cfo: Clark Foundation, Edna McConnell

Eischens, Curt, trust: CENEX Foundation

Eisele, A. E., secy, dir: DeSoto Foundation

Eiseman, Constance, exec dir, secy: Prospect Hill Foundation

Eisen, Julius, dir: Rukin Philanthropic Foundation, David and Eleanore

Eisen, Susan, dir: Rukin Philanthropic Foundation, David and Eleanore

Eisenberg, David H., pres, coo: Peoples Drug Stores Inc.

Eisenberg, George M., trust: Eisenberg Foundation, George M.

Eisenberg, Marshall E., dir: Linde Foundation, Ronald and Maxine

Eisenberg, Richard, vp: Read Foundation, Charles L.

Eisenberg, Saul, treas: Read Foundation, Charles L.

Eisenberg, Sharon R., trust: Plough Foundation

Eisenberg-Keefer, Joyce E., pres: Eisenberg Foundation, Ben B. and Joyce E.

Eisenhardt, Dianne L., asst treas, asst secy: Gebbie Foundation

Eisenhardt, Elizabeth Haas, trust, don daughter: Haas, Jr. Fund, Evelyn and Walter

Eisenpreis, Alfred, secy, treas: J C S Foundation

Eisenstein, Elizabeth A., dir: Amaturo Foundation

Eisenstein, Joshua, asst treas: Dorot Foundation

Eisenstein, Marci, dir: Schiff, Hardin & Waite Foundation

Eisner, Dean, treas: Cox Enterprises

Eisner, Eric, trust: Geffen Foundation, David

Eisner, Margaret D., vp, dir: Dammann Fund

Eisner, Michael Dammann, chmn, ceo, dir: Disney Co., Walt; pres, trust: Disney Co. Foundation, Walt

Eitel, Karl E., chmn exec comm, trust: El Pomar Foundation

Eitelgeorge, John, mgr publ rels corp contributions: Sprint United Telephone

Eiting, James A., pres: Midmark Corp.; vp, secy: Midmark Foundation

Eitingon, Daniel, mem: First Interstate Bank of California Foundation

Ekern, George P., secy: Handy & Harman Foundation

Eklund, Dariel Ann, vp: Norton Memorial Corporation, Geraldi

Eklund, Dariel P., vp: Norton Memorial Corporation, Geraldi

Eklund, Roger P., pres, treas: Norton Memorial Corporation, Geraldi

Eklund, Sally S., secy: Norton Memorial Corporation, Geraldi

Ekman, Richard, secy: Mellon Foundation, Andrew W.

El-Gohary, Joanne, vp: BankAmerica Foundation; adm: California Educational Initiatives Fund

Elam, Ed, dir: Christy-Houston Foundation

Elam, Lloyd Charles, trust: Merck Co. Foundation; trust: Sloan Foundation, Alfred P.

Elbel, Christine, exec dir: Fleishhacker Foundation

Elbert, P. O., chmn: Pitt-Des Moines Inc.

Elbright, Mitchell, secy, treas: Jerome Foundation

Eldred, Janice R., dir (CA grants program): Kaiser Family Foundation, Henry J.

Eldred, Robert C., trust: Raymond Foundation

Eldridge, Dorothy, vp, dir: Gardiner Scholarship Foundation

Eldridge, Huntington, dir: Buchanan Family Foundation

Eldridge, Huntington, Jr., dir: Buchanan Family Foundation

Eldridge, James W., mem contributios comm: Puget Sound Power & Light Co.

Elfers, William, dir: Fairchild Foundation, Sherman

Elgin, Jack, cfo: Thrifty Oil Co.

Elia, Mary C., secy: Stans Foundation

Elias, Albert J., trust: Cassett Foundation, Louis N.

Elias, Clifford E., trust: Russell Trust, Josephine G.; trust: Stearns Trust, Artemas W.

Elias, Marsha K., Stearns Trust, Artemas W.

Elias, Norma, trust: Douty Foundation

Elion, Gertrude Belle, dir: Burroughs Wellcome Fund

Eliot, Allen E., treas: Snite Foundation, Fred B.

Elish, Herbert, chmn, pres, ceo: Weirton Steel Corp.

Elisha, Walter Y., chmn, ceo, dir: Springs Industries

Elkerton, Bonnie, asst secy, asst treas: Butler Family Foundation, Patrick and Aimee

Elkin, Irvin J., pres, dir: Associated Milk Producers, Inc.

Elkins, James Anderson, III, trust: Elkins Foundation, J. A. and Isabel M.; treas: Elkins, Jr. Foundation, Margaret and James A.

Elkins, James Anderson, Jr., trust: Elkins Foundation, J. A. and Isabel M.; pres: Elkins, Jr. Foundation, Margaret and James A.

Ellcessor, Steven J., secy: Smucker Foundation, Willard E.

Ellen, Martin M., exec vp, cfo: Sun Electric Corp.

Ellerbrake, Richard P., dir: Group Health Foundation

Elliman, Christopher J., trust: Dodge Foundation, Geraldine R.

Elliman, Edward H., trust: Christodora

Elliman, Edward S., pres: Christodora

Elliot, Charles W., exec vp, cfo: Kellogg's; trust: Kellogg Co. Twenty-Five Year Employees' Fund

Elliot, J. A., dir: Beech Aircraft Foundation

Elliot, Lloyd H., dir: Bloedorn Foundation, Walter A.; chmn, trust: Ross Foundation, Walter G.

Elliot, Robert H., secy, dir: Zarrow Foundation, Anne and Henry

Elliot, Steven, treas: Mellon Bank Foundation

Elliot, Thomas J., pres, dir: Rixson Foundation, Oscar C.

Elliot, Thomas J., Jr., mem: Rixson Foundation, Oscar C.

Elliott, Anson Wright, trust: Chase Manhattan Bank, N.A.

Elliott, Carol K., secy, treas: Montgomery Street Foundation

Elliott, Charles W., trust: Winship Memorial Scholarship Foundation

Elliott, Daniel Robert, Jr., chmn: White Consolidated Industries Foundation

Elliott, David H., pres, ceo, dir: MBIA, Inc.

Elliott, Eleanor Thomas, trust: Clark Foundation, Edna McConnell; mem nominating comm, mem counc, dir: Foundation for Child Development

Elliott, Irma B., secy, treas: Oklahoma Gas & Electric Co. Foundation

Elliott, J. W., trust: Cauthorn Charitable Trust, John and Mildred

Elliott, Michael, pres: Jasper Seating Co.; pres, dir: Jasper Seating Foundation

Elliott, William H., chmn, ceo, dir: Angeles Corp.

Elliott, William T., pres: Schmidt & Sons, C.

Elliott Jr., John, vp, dir: Ogilvy Foundation

Ellis, Alpheus Lee, dir: Ellis Foundation

Ellis, Belle I., trust: Thagard Foundation

Ellis, Charles D., trust: Ellis Fund

Ellis, Charles R., pres, ceo: Wiley & Sons, Inc., John

Ellis, Darlene S., asst secy: Deere Foundation, John

Ellis, David B., asst treas: Sara Lee Foundation

Ellis, David W., vchmn: Gradison & Co.; trust: Gradison & Co. Foundation

Ellis, J. K., pres, ceo, dir: B.H.P. Minerals

Ellis, James D., dir: Southwestern Bell Foundation

Ellis, John B., chmn investment comm, trust: Campbell Foundation, J. Bulow; trust: Courts Foundation; trust: Franklin Foundation, John and Mary

Ellis, John W., chmn: Puget Sound Power & Light Co.

Ellis, Letitia, trust: Dick Family Foundation

Ellis, Libby, grants dir: Patagonia

Ellis, Peter S., trust: Hopedale Foundation

Ellis, W. Douglas, Jr., trust: Beck Foundation, Lewis H.

Ellis, Wiley, trust: Hodge Foundation

Ellis, William Ben, pres, dir: Connecticut Mutual Life Foundation; chmn, ceo, dir: Northeast Utilities

Ellis, William D., Jr., comm mem: Woodward Fund-Atlanta, David, Helen, Marian

Ellis, William Edward, Jr., secy, trust: Barry Foundation

Ellis, William H., pres, coo, dir: Piper Jaffray Cos.

Ellison, Edward, chmn: Harvest States Cooperative; trust: Harvest States Foundation

Ellison, Jody, trust: Morgan Charitable Residual Trust, W. and E.

Ellison, Lawrence J., co-fdr, chmn, pres, ceo: Oracle Corp.

Ellison, Sara, secy corporate dues & contributions comm: Northeast Utilities

Ellspermann, Stanley, mem contributions comm: James River Corp. of Virginia

Ellsworth, Barry, dir: Kentucky Foundation for Women

Ellsworth, David H., trust: Ellsworth Foundation, Ruth H. and Warren A.

Ellsworth, John E., chmn emeritus, dir: Ensign-Bickford Industries; dir: Ensign-Bickford Foundation

Ellsworth, Peter K., secy: Benbough Foundation, Legler

Ellsworth, Phoebe C., trust: Sage Foundation, Russell

Ellwood, Scott, pres, dir: Morton Memorial Fund, Mark

Ellyson, Mrs. William G., secy: Memorial Foundation for Children

Elmer, Richard A., MD, dir: Georgia Health Foundation

Elmore, Dave, trust: Zigler Foundation, Fred B. and Ruth B.

Elmore, John Michael, trust: Zigler Foundation, Fred B. and Ruth B.

Elrod, Scott M., McGraw Foundation

Elsberry, Paul S., trust: Conn Memorial Foundation

Elser, Arlon, trust: Winship Memorial Scholarship Foundation

Elston, Frances Beinecke, dir: Prospect Hill Foundation

Eltinge, George M., chmn: Imperial Bancorp; dir: Imperial Bank Foundation

Elverman, Timothy J., vp, dir: Banc One Wisconsin Foundation

Elwick, Keith, trust: Winnebago Industries Foundation

Elworth, James F., Lehmann Foundation, Otto W.

Ely, Hiram B., Jr., trust: Sullivan Foundation, Algernon Sydney

Ely, Rae H., trust: Tilghman, Sr., Charitable Trust, Bell and Horace

Ely, Richard, trust: Edwards Scholarship Fund

Ely, William L., dir: Davenport-Hatch Foundation

Eman, Alain, exec vp, coo: Meridien Hotels

Emblidge, Warren E., Jr., trust: Children's Foundation of Erie County

Embry, Robert C., Jr., pres, trust: Abell Foundation, The

Emden, Craig A., trust: Kapiloff Foundation, Leonard

Emerson, C. Lee, vp, trust, treas: Gilmore Foundation, William G.

Emerson, David L., treas, dir: Emerson Foundation, Fred L.

Emerson, Edward L., trust: Parker Foundation, Theodore Edson

Emerson, Frederick George, vp, secy: Dial Corporation Fund

Emerson, H. Truxton, Jr., secy, trust: Wodecroft Foundation

Emerson, Kristen D., dir: Emerson Foundation, Fred L.

Emerson, Lori C., dir: Emerson Foundation, Fred L.

Emerson, Peter J., vp, dir: Emerson Foundation, Fred L.

Emerson, W. Gary, dir: Emerson Foundation, Fred L.

Emery, Ethan, trust: Peterloon Foundation

Emery, John C., Jr., vp, trust: Emery Air Freight Educational Foundation

Emery, John M., trust: Clark Foundation, Edna McConnell; vp, trust, secy: Penzance Foundation

Emery, S. W., vp, group exec: Honeywell

Emke, Robert W., Jr., Shelden Fund, Elizabeth, Allan and Warren

Emmanuel, Michael G., secy, dir: Saunders Foundation

Emmerich, Karol Denise, vp, treas: Dayton Hudson Corp.

Emmerling, Paul E., dir: American Welding & Manufacturing Co. Foundation

Emmerson, A.A., pres, dir: Sierra Pacific Industries

Emmerson, Ida, pres: Sierra Pacific Foundation

Evans, Daniel J., chmn, trust: Kaiser Family Foundation, Henry J.

Evans, David, dir, secy: Piedmont Health Care Foundation

Evans, David W., Jr., secy: Jones Foundation, Walter S. and Evan C.

Evans, Donald L., chmn, pres, ceo, dir: Brown Inc., Tom

Evans, Dwight H., dir: Georgia Power Foundation

Evans, Edward P., don, trust: Evans Foundation, Edward P.

Evans, Edward Parker, trust: Evans Foundation, T. M.

Evans, Eli N., pres: Revson Foundation, Charles H.

Evans, H. L., trust: Wurlitzer Foundation, Farny R.

Evans, Harold, vp: Phelps Foundation, Hensel

Evans, Jack B., dir: Hall Foundation

Evans, Jack W., chmn, pres, ceo: Cullum Cos.

Evans, John C., vp, dir: Luce Foundation, Henry

Evans, John H., trust: Willits Foundation

Evans, John Robert, chmn bd trusts: Rockefeller Foundation

Evans, Kenneth M., pres, ceo, dir: Armor All Products Corp.

Evans, Linda, vp, trust, dir: Meadows Foundation

Evans, Maureen B., Michaels Scholarship Fund, Frank J.

Evans, Mike, mgr: JMK-A M Micallef Charitable Foundation

Evans, Morgan J., pres, dir: First Security Corp. (Salt Lake City, Utah)

Evans, Paul, pres: CRC Evans Pipeline International, Inc.

Evans, Richard E., dir: Amoco Foundation

Evans, Richard H., vp corp comm: Delmarva Power & Light Co.

Evans, Richard W., Jr., pres: Frost National Bank

Evans, Robert, trust: Collins-McDonald Trust Fund

Evans, Robert E., trust: McDonough Foundation, Bernard; pres, coo, dir: TCF Banking & Savings, FSB

Evans, Robert S., chmn, pres, ceo, dir: Crane Co.; chmn, pres: Crane Fund; trust: Evans Foundation, Edward P.

Evans, Ronald A., pres, ceo: Best Western International

Evans, Thomas Mellon, pres, don, trust: Evans Foundation, T. M.

Evans, Thomas Mellon, Jr., trust: Evans Foundation, T. M.

Evans, V. Bond, pres, ceo: Alumax

Evard, Timothy F., vp (mktg): Time Warner Cable

Evarts, William M., Jr., dir: Clark Foundation

Evelt, Sibylle, dir: Heineman Foundation for Research, Educational, Charitable, and Scientific Purposes

Evenhouse, Janet, pres: Huizenga Foundation, Jennie

Everbach, Otto George, pres, dir: Kimberly-Clark Foundation

Everett, C. Taylor, trust: Gray Foundation, Garland

Everett, Graham, pres: Caleb Brett U.S.A. Inc.

Everett, Michael T., vp, chief legal off, sec: Raychem Corp.

Everett, Morris, treas, trust: Huntington Fund for Education, John

Everingham, Lyle J., trust: Cincinnati Milacron Foundation

Everitt, Robert H., trust: O'Brien Foundation, Cornelius and Anna Cook

Everitt, William, vp (corp commun): Kyocera International Inc.

Eversman, George, dir: Ayer Foundation, N.W.

Every, Russell B., pres: Sudbury Inc.

Evoy, Martin, dir: Smith Foundation

Ewald, Carolyn T., secy, treas: Ewald Foundation, H. T.

Ewald, Henry T., Jr., pres: Ewald Foundation, H. T.

Ewald, Robert H., exec vp, dir: Cray Research

Ewalt, H. Ward, pres: Wildermuth Foundation, E. F.

Ewan, George E., trust: Whitney Benefits

Ewen, Daniel C., trust: Heisey Foundation

Ewen, Elaine S., trust: Hannon Foundation, William H.

Eweson, Dorothy Anne Dillon, pres, dir: Bedminster Fund

Ewing, Brenda, Dewing Foundation, Frances R.

Ewing, Nancy Best, secy, assoc gen coun: MacArthur Foundation, John D. and Catherine T.

Ewing, Robert P., dir: MacArthur Foundation, John D. and Catherine T.; trust, secy: Retirement Research Foundation

Ewing, Rumsey, pres: Love Charitable Foundation, John Allan

Ewing, Ruth D., trust: Dewing Foundation, Frances R.

Ewing, Stephen E., pres, coo, dir: Michigan Consolidated Gas Co.

Ewing, Virginia Wilson, vp, trust: Wilson Foundation, John and Nevils

Ex, Merri, program consultant: Sara Lee Foundation

Exley, Charles Errol, Jr., trust: Mellon Foundation, Andrew W.; trust: Merck Co. Foundation

Eyre, Stephen A., exec dir, treas: Hartford Foundation, John A.

F

Faber, Elizabeth, trust: Meek Foundation

Faber, Herbert H., trust: DeCamp Foundation, Ira W.

Fabick, Harry, pres, coo, dir: Fabick Tractor Co., John; pres, dir: Fabick Charitable Trust

Fabick, John, chmn, dir: Fabick Tractor Co., John

Fabick, III, John, vp, dir: Fabick Charitable Trust

Factor, Gerald, trust: Factor Family Foundation, Max

Factor, Max, III, trust: Factor Family Foundation, Max

Factor, Max III, dir: Luster Family Foundation

Fad, Otto C., secy: Crestlea Foundation

Fahey, Joseph F., Jr., dir: Culpeper Foundation, Charles E.; pres: Rich Foundation, Inc.

Fahrenkopf, Frank J., Jr., trust: Wiegand Foundation, E. L.

Fahrni, Fritz, pres, ceo, dir: Sulzer Brothers Inc.

Failing, Barbara M., trust: Potlatch Foundation for Higher Education/Potlatch Foundation II

Fain, Mary, secy, dir: Premier Foundation

Fair, James W., sr vp, dir, don son: Fair Foundation, R. W.

Fair, Kenneth R., secy: Oglebay Norton Foundation

Fair, Vicki, mng comm: Alliant Community Investment Foundation

Fair, Wilton H., pres, dir, don son: Fair Foundation, R. W.

Fairbank, Catherine, dir: Van Camp Foundation

Fairbanks, J. Nelson, pres, dir: United States Sugar Corp.

Faircloth, Anne B., vp: Stewards Fund

Faircloth, Nancy B., pres: Stewards Fund

Fairfax, Matthew L., pres: New Orphan Asylum Scholarship Foundation

Fairman, Endsley P., secy, trust: Marmot Foundation

Fairweather, Ross, trust: Wilson Public Trust, Ralph

Faisant, J. A., trust: Cooper Tire & Rubber Foundation

Faith, Marshall E., pres, ceo: Scoular Co.; pres: Scoular Foundation

Faith, Mona, trust: Faith Charitable Trust

Faivre, Jean-Francois, exec vp, cfo: Pechiney Corp.

Falbaum, Berl, trust: Perry Drug Stores Charitable Foundation

Falcon, Angelo, trust: New York Foundation

Falcone, Sam, trust: Messing Foundation, Morris M. and Helen F.

Falcone, Tasha, dir: Allyn Foundation

Falconio, Patrick, cfo: AEGON USA, Inc.

Faldet, Marion M., vp, secy: Spencer Foundation

Falencki, Karin, trust: Jurzykowski Foundation, Alfred

Fales, Haliburton, II, trust: Victoria Foundation

Fales, John R., Jr., trust: Johnstone and H. Earle Kimball Foundation, Phyllis Kimball

Fales, Judith S., trust: Seeley Foundation

Falk, EuGene L., dir: Pfaffinger Foundation

Falk, Harvey L., pres, vchmn, dir: Liz Claiborne; mem grantmaking comm: Liz Claiborne Foundation

Falk, Isidore, mgr: Falk Foundation, Michael David

Falk, Marian C., pres, treas: Falk Medical Research Foundation, Dr. Ralph and Marian

Falk, Mary Irene McKay, chmn: Falk Foundation, David

Falk, Maurice, mgr: Falk Foundation, Michael David

Falk, Myron S., Jr., trust: Hebrew Technical Institute

Falk, Sigo, ceo: Falk Medical Fund, Maurice

Falk, Stephen, dir, pres: Falk Foundation, Elizabeth M.

Falla, Enrique Crabb, trust: Dow Chemical Co.

Fallenstein, Al, cfo: Taylor Corp.

Fallon, Gail A., trust: Dell Foundation, Hazel

Fallon, James P., trust: Frueauff Foundation, Charles A.

Falsgraf, William W., secy: Frohring Foundation, Paul & Maxine

Falsgraf, William Wendell, trust: Frohring Foundation, William O. and Gertrude Lewis

Famularo, Joseph J., trust: Perley Fund, Victor E.

Fancher, Edwin, pres: Plumsock Fund

Fanning, Karl P., trust: Frueauff Foundation, Charles A.

Fanning, Katherine, trust: Mott Foundation, Charles Stewart

Fannon, J. J., pres, dir: Simpson Paper Co.

Fanton, Jonathan F., trust: Rockefeller Brothers Fund

Faraci, John V., pres, ceo: Masonite Corp.

Farber, Jack, pres: Philadelphia Industries; pres, dir: Farber Foundation

Farber, John J., chmn: ICC Industries

Farber, William A., trust: Levin Foundation, Philip and Janice

Fares, Sally, trust: Raper Foundation, Tom

Fargo, Wilson D., secy: Compaq Computer Foundation

Farkas, Bonnie, human resource asst: Gould Inc.

Farkas, Carol, treas, trust: Mayer Foundation, Louis B.

Farland, Melanie Taylor, trust elect: Bryan Family Foundation, Kathleen Price and Joseph M.

Farley, Barbara, dir: Farley Foundation, William F.

Farley, James Bernard, chmn, dir, ceo, trust: Mutual of New York

Farley, James D., trust: Dennett Foundation, Marie G.; chmn, trust: Hartford Foundation, John A.

Farley, John F., dir: Farley Foundation, William F.

Farley, Terrence M., ptnr: Brown Brothers Harriman & Co.

Farley, Terrence Michael, dir: Harriman Foundation, Gladys and Roland

Farley, William Francis, vchmn: First Bank System; vchmn: Fruit of the Loom, Inc.

Farling, Robert J., chmn, ceo, dir, pres: Centerior Energy Corp.; chmn: Centerior Energy Foundation; chmn, ceo, dir, pres: Toledo Edison Co.

Farman, Richard Donald, chmn, ceo, dir: Southern California Gas Co.

Farman, Walter E., chmn, ceo, dir: Pennsylvania General Insurance Co.

Farmer, Bill J., trust: Hervey Foundation

Farmer, F. J., trust: Chrysler Corp. Fund

Farmer, Forest J., pres: Acustar Inc.

Farmer, Kenneth Wayne, vp, chmn (contributions comm): Abbott Laboratories Fund

Farnam, Walter E., chmn, ceo: General Accident Insurance Co. of America

Farnet, Stewart, dir: Azby Fund

Farnham, Nicholas H., sec: Johnson Endeavor Foundation, Christian A.

Farnsworth, Philip R., secy: Capital Cities/ABC; secy: Capital Cities Foundation

Farnsworth, Thomas C., adv: Van Vleet Foundation

Farr, C. Sims, chmn: Commonwealth Fund; vp, dir: Iroquois Avenue Foundation

Farr, F. W. Elliott, vp, trust: Kynett Memorial Foundation, Edna G.

Farr, F.W. Elliott, vp: Ludwick Institute

Farr, Olivia H., mem: Merck Family Fund

Farrar, Marjorie M., dir: Memton Fund

Farrell, Ann M., trust: Loyola Foundation

Farrell, David C., chmn, ceo, dir: May Department Stores Co.; vp, dir: May Stores Foundation

Farrell, James, dir: Illinois Tool Works Foundation

Farrell, Neal Francis, vp, treas: Borg-Warner Foundation

Farrell, Thomas J., trust: Connelly Foundation

Farrington, Ann, secy: Little Foundation, Arthur D.

Farris, G. Steven, sr vp domestic expl & prod: Apache Corp.

Farsoun, Samih, dir: Jerusalem Fund for Education and Community Development

Farstow, Roland J., chmn, dir: Bell Federal Savings & Loan Association

Farver, Mary Joan Kuyper, pres, dir: Kuyper Foundation, Peter H. and E. Lucille Gaass; chmn, dir: Pella Corp.; trust: Pella Rolscreen Foundation

Farver, Suzanne, vp, dir: Kuyper Foundation, Peter H. and E. Lucille Gaass

Fasken, Andrew, trust: Fasken Foundation

Fasken, Barbara T., dir, pres: Prairie Foundation

Fasken, Murray, pres, trust: Fasken Foundation

Fasken, Steven P., secy, treas, trust: Fasken Foundation

Fass, Peter J., co-chmn: Peridot Chemicals (NJ)

Fasseas, Peter A., chmn, pres, ceo: Metropolitan Bank & Trust Co.

Fassett, John H., trust: Hilliard Foundation

Fate, Martin E., Jr., adv: Central & South West Foundation

Fatzinger, Walter Robert, Jr., pres, dir: Loughran Foundation, Mary and Daniel

Fauerbach, George, Jr., dir: Cummins Engine Foundation

Faulders, C. Thomas, III, vp, cfo: Communications Satellite Corp. (COMSAT)

Faulkner, Edwin Jerome, trust: Cooper Foundation

Faulkner, H. George, pres: Huck International Inc.

Faulkner, Karen, exec dir: Schrafft and Bertha E. Schrafft Charitable Trust, William E.

Faulstrich, George L., Jr., sr vp, cfo: Ceco Corp.

Faulwell, Gerald E., treas: Farmers Group Safety Foundation

Fauntleroy, Gaylord, trust: Gaylord Foundation, Clifford Willard

Faust, Michael L., contributions comm: Kiewit Cos Foundation

Faust, Mike, contributions comm: Kiewit Cos Foundation

Faust, Robert J., secy, treas: Duncan Foundation, Lillian H. and C. W.

Faversham, Harry, pres: National Metal & Steel; vp: National Metal & Steel Foundation

Favrot, Johanna A., pres, trust: Favrot Fund

Favrot, Laurence de Kanter, trust: Favrot Fund

Favrot, Leo Mortimer, trust: Favrot Fund

Favrot, Romelia, trust: Favrot Fund

Favrot-Anderson, Marcia, trust: Favrot Fund

Fawcett, Daniel W., trust: Thompson Trust, Thomas

Fawcett, George T., Jr., trust: Gilmer-Smith Foundation

Fay, Barbara L., fdn admin: Butler Manufacturing Co. Foundation

Fay, Patricia R., dir: Lurie Foundation, Louis R.

Fay, Paul B., Jr., trust: Odell and Helen Pfeiffer Odell Fund, Robert Stewart

Fazzano, Mary Louise, dir: Hasbro Charitable Trust

Feaga, Garland P., trust: Loats Foundation

Feagin, Louise Milby, dir: Hamman Foundation, George and Mary Josephine

Fearnley, John, treas, trust: Bedford Fund

Fearon, Greer J., exec secy: Boswell Foundation, James G.

Fearon, Janet A., trust, exec dir: Newcombe Foundation, Charlotte W.

Fearon, Robert H., Jr., vp: Chapman Charitable Corporation, Howard and Bess

Featherman, Sandra, PhD, vp, dir: Fels Fund, Samuel S.

Fechtel, Patricia, adm off: Davis Foundations, Arthur Vining

Fechter, John P., mem adv comm: Pott Foundation, Herman T. and Phenie R.

Fedak, Marilyn Goldstein, trust, treas: Wenner-Gren Foundation for Anthropological Research

Federal, Most Rev. Joseph L., trust: Price Foundation, Lucien B. and Katherine E.

Federman, Daniel D., trust: Wolfson Foundation, Louis E.

Fedoruk, Tanya, secy: Ryan Foundation, Nina M.

Feduniak, Robert, trust: Morgan Stanley Foundation

Fee, Frank H., III, dir: Fort Pierce Memorial Hospital Scholarship Foundation

Feeney, Helen M., vp, dir: Amax Foundation

Feeney, James E., trust: Charitable Fund

Feeney, John R., exec vp, cfo: Summit Bancorporation

Feeney, Thomas E., trust: Sandy Foundation, George H.

Feest, Ronald L., vp, dir: Formrite Foundation

Fegan, Ann B., vp: Reidler Foundation

Fegan, Howard D., dir: Reidler Foundation

Fehl, Mark, trust: Zigler Foundation, Fred B. and Ruth B.

Fehlman, Bruce, trust: Geneseo Foundation

Fehr, David S., sr vp: Dun & Bradstreet Corp.; vp: Dun & Bradstreet Corp. Foundation

Fehr, Robert O., dir: Heineman Foundation for Research, Educational, Charitable, and Scientific Purposes

Feibel, J. B., secy: Electric Power Equipment Co. Foundation

Feierstein, Cathy E., vp, secy, dir: Time Insurance Foundation

Feil, Gertrude, pres, dir: Feil Foundation, Louis and Gertrude

Feil, Jeffrey, vp, dir: Feil Foundation, Louis and Gertrude

Feil, Louis, secy, treas, dir: Feil Foundation, Louis and Gertrude

Feild, Reginald H., chmn, dir: McMillan, Jr. Foundation, Bruce

Fein, Bernard, trust: Fein Foundation; chmn, pres: United Industrial Corp.

Fein, David, trust: Fein Foundation

Feinberg, Barbara L., adv bd: Lipsky Foundation, Fred and Sarah

Feinberg, Frances, secy: Feinberg Foundation, Joseph and Bessie

Feinberg, Herbert D., trust, dir: Weinstein Foundation, Alex J.

Feinberg, Janie, trust: Feinberg Foundation, Joseph and Bessie

Feinberg, Paul, asst secy: Kangesser Foundation, Robert E., Harry A., and M. Sylvia

Feinberg, Ruben, pres: Feinberg Foundation, Joseph and Bessie

Feinblatt, Eugene M., pres, treas: Unger Foundation, Aber D.

Feinblatt, John, trust: Unger Foundation, Aber D.

Feinblatt, Lois Blum, pres: Blum Foundation, Lois and Irving

Feinblatt, Marjorie W., trust: Unger Foundation, Aber D.

Feiner, Gordon A., trust: Johnstone and H. Earle Kimball Foundation, Phyllis Kimball

Feinman, Alfred, vp: Glickenhaus Foundation

Feinstein, Karen Wolk, PhD, pres: Jewish Healthcare Foundation of Pittsburgh

Feinstein, Samuel, vp, dir: Feinstein Foundation, Myer and Rosaline

Feintech, Irving, vp: Feintech Foundation

Feintech, Norman, pres: Feintech Foundation

Feitler, Joan, mem: Smart Family Foundation

Feitler, Robert, chmn: Smart Family Foundation

Fejes, Frank S., treas: Hugoton Foundation

Felburn, J. Phil, pres, treas: Felburn Foundation

Feldberg, Charles, mem (contributions comm): CPC International

Feldberg, Stanley H., trust: Feldberg Family Foundation

Feldberg, Sumner Lee, trust: Feldberg Family Foundation;

chmn: TJX Cos.; dir: TJX Foundation

Feldhouse, Lynn A., mgr, secy: Chrysler Corp. Fund

Feldman, B. Inez, trust: Saemann Foundation, Franklin I.

Feldman, D. E., trust: Feldman Foundation

Feldman, Irwin Miles, trust: Treuhaft Foundation

Feldman, Moses, trust: Feldman Foundation

Feldman, Oscar H., secy, dir: Guardian Industries Educational Foundation

Feldman, R. L., trust: Feldman Foundation

Feldman, Ronald Arthur, trust: Grant Foundation, William T.

Feldman, Sandra, trust: German Marshall Fund of the United States

Feldman, Steven M., pres: Totsy Manufacturing Co.; trust: Totsy Foundation

Feldstein, Lewis, treas, trust: Hazen Foundation, Edward W.

Feldstein, Richard, chmn: Silvestri Corp.

Felheim, Lasalle, dir: Jewish Foundation for Education of Women

Felicetti, Armondo, pres, dir: Fidelity Federal Savings & Loan

Felix, Patricia Berry, dir: Berry Foundation, Lowell

Felker, Arthur G., trust: Bryan Foundation, Dodd and Dorothy L.

Felker, G. Stephen, pres, ceo, treas: Walton Monroe Mills

Felker, George W., III, chmn: Walton Monroe Mills

Feller, J. L., chmn, ceo: Kasler Corp.

Feller, Nancy P., assoc gen coun & dir legal services: Ford Foundation

Fellner, Jamie, program off: Noyes Foundation, Jessie Smith

Felmeth, William H., trust: Willits Foundation

Felsenthal, Steven A., secy: Chanin Family Foundation, Paul R.

Felton, John Walter, vp (corp commun): McCormick & Co.

Femino, James J., pres: Femino Foundation

Femino, Sue, vp: Femino Foundation

Feng, Tscheng S., dir: Lannan Foundation

Fenlon, Thomas Bolger, trust: Schieffelin Residuary Trust, Sarah I.

Fenner, David L., trust: Moores Foundation, Harry C.

Fenno, Harold W., vp: Gear Motions Foundation

Fenoglio, William R., pres, coo: Barnes Group; vp, dir: Barnes Group Foundation

Fenton, Arlene, mem adv & distribution comm: Jennings Foundation, Martha Holden

Fenton, Elinor P., dir, secy: Fenton Foundation

Fenton, Frank M., dir, treas: Fenton Foundation

Fenton, Gary, trust: Heath Foundation, Ed and Mary

Fenton, John L., dir: Youth Foundation

Fenton, Silvia, dir: Hoyt Foundation, Stewart W. and Willma C.

Fenton, Thomas K., dir, vp: Fenton Foundation

Fenton, Wilmer C., dir, pres: Fenton Foundation

Ferger, Jane, secy: Jasam Foundation

Ferguson, A. Barlow, vp, secy, dir: Bechtel, Jr. Foundation, S. D.; dir: Lakeside Foundation; dir, secy: Shenandoah Foundation

Ferguson, C. David, pres, ceo: Gould Inc.; pres, dir: Gould Foundation

Ferguson, Charlotte B., trust: Wills Foundation

Ferguson, Daniel C., chmn: Newell Co.

Ferguson, Daryl A., pres, coo: Citizens Utilities Co.

Ferguson, David, dir: Hyde and Watson Foundation

Ferguson, Donald C., pres: Rust-Oleum Corp.

Ferguson, Donald L., trust: Manville Fund

Ferguson, H. Rugeley, fdr: Ferguson Family Foundation, Kittie and Rugeley

Ferguson, Isaac C., exec comm: Swanson Family Foundation, Dr. W.C.

Ferguson, Joseph E., dir: Amaturo Foundation

Ferguson, Kittie N., fdr: Ferguson Family Foundation, Kittie and Rugeley

Ferguson, Mary Jo, dir: Cooper Wood Products Foundation

Ferguson, Robert H.M., secy, dir: Hertz Foundation, Fannie and John

Ferguson, Robert Harry Munro, secy: China Medical Board of New York; secy, treas: Whiting Foundation, Mrs. Giles

Ferguson, Ronald Eugene, chmn, dir, pres, ceo: General Reinsurance Corp.

Ferguson, Sanford B., pres: Scaife Family Foundation

Ferguson, Thomas A., pres, coo: Newell Co.

Ferguson, William Charles, chmn, ceo: NYNEX Corp.

Fergusson, Frances D., trust: Ford Foundation

Ferkauf, Estelle, trust: Ferkauf Foundation, Eugene and Estelle

Ferkauf, Eugene, trust: Ferkauf Foundation, Eugene and Estelle

Ferland, E. James, chmn, pres, ceo: Public Service Electric & Gas Co.

Fernandes, Alvin C., Jr., vp, secy, dir: Ayres Foundation, Inc.

Fernandez, Antonio, cfo: Oppenheimer & Co., Inc.

Fernandez, Olimpio, exec vp: Banco Portugues do Atlantico, New York Branch

Fernandez, Rolando E., asst treas: Magowan Family Foundation

Ferra, Dennis J., cfo: ALLTEL Corp.

Ferrante, Anthony F., pres: Kaplan Trucking Co.

Ferranti, Anthony L., comptr: Pforzheimer Foundation, Carl and Lily

Ferrara, Arthur V., pres, ceo: Guardian Life Insurance Co. of America

Ferrara, Charles J., dir(admin): Kresevich Foundation

Ferraresi, Daniel J., treas: Batchelor Foundation

Ferrari, Clarence J., Jr., secy: Maxfield Foundation

Ferrell, James E., ceo, pres: Ferrell Cos.

Ferrero, Louis Peter, chmn, ceo, dir: Anacomp, Inc.

Ferrill, Sharon A., first vp: Lannan Foundation

Ferris, Dick, mem distribution comm: Greater Lansing Foundation

Ferris, Sally, dir admin: Rockefeller Foundation

Ferry, George F., dir: Hopper Memorial Foundation, Bertrand

Ferry, Richard M., pres: Korn/Ferry International

Ferry, Robert E., mem adv & distribution comm: Jennings Foundation, Martha Holden

Fery, John Bruce, chmn, ceo, dir, coo: Boise Cascade Corp.

Fessler, Kathryn M., contributions adm: Virginia Power Co.

Fetridge, Clarke W., chmn, pres, ceo: Dartnell Corp.

Fetro, Alice, secy, dir: Rosenhaus Peace Foundation, Sarah and Matthew

Fetterer, Peter, mgr (media & civic services): Kohler Co.

Fetzer, Carol J., exec dir, secy, trust: Carolyn Foundation

Feuerstein, Aaron, pres: Malden Mills Industries

Feulner, Edwin J., Jr., mgr: Aequus Institute; vchmn, trust: Roe Foundation; trust: Scaife Foundation, Sarah

Fey, Eugene E., treas, trust: Pinkerton Foundation

ffolliott, Sheila, trust: Northwest Area Foundation

Fibiger, John A., exec vp, cfo: Transamerica Occidental Life Insurance Co.

Fichthorn, Luke, III, chmn, dir: Bairnco Corp.

Ficke, Carl H., dir: Baier Foundation, Marie

Fidler, J. T., dir (corp affs): General Public Utilities Corp.

Fiduciary Trust Company, trust: Tupancy-Harris Foundation of 1986

Fiedler, Gary W., chmn, ceo, dir: Equimark Corp.

Fiedler, J. F., chmn: Brad Ragan, Inc.

Field, Arthur Norman, trust: Ramapo Trust

Field, Benjamin R., trust: Bemis Company Foundation

Field, Frances K., trust: Gould Foundation for Children, Edwin

Field, Jamee J., vp, dir: Field Foundation, Jamee and Marshall

Field, Lyman, trust: Kress Foundation, Samuel H.; trust: Murphy Charitable Fund, George E. and Annette Cross

Field, Marshall, V, pres, dir: Field Foundation, Jamee and Marshall; dir: Field Foundation of Illinois

Fielder, Charles Robert, vp, treas: Halliburton Foundation

Fieldhouse, Katharine Schultz, trust: Schultz Foundation

Fielding, Craig, dir: Glenn Foundation, Carrie C. & Lena V.

Fielding, William G., pres: Excel Corp.

Fields, Bill, mem: Wal-Mart Foundation

Fields, Debra Jane, fdr, ceo, pres: Mrs. Fields, Inc.

Fields, Joyce M., Hartford
Courant Foundation
Fields, Kenneth H., asst treas:
Steinbach Fund, Ruth and
Milton
Fields, Laura Kemper, vp,
treas, dir: Kemper Memorial
Foundation, David Woods;
mem disbursement comm:
Oppenstein Brothers
Foundation
Fields, Leo, dir: Zale Foundation
Fields, Murray M., trust:
Buchalter, Nemer, Fields,
Chrystie & Younger Charitable
Foundation
Fields, Randall K., chmn: Mrs.
Fields, Inc.
Fields, Randolph, vp: Farwell
Foundation, Drusilla
Fields, Rosemary, trust:
Wegener Foundation, Herman
and Mary
Fierce, Hughlyn F., trust: Chase
Manhattan Bank, N.A.
Fies, Larry R., treas, corp secy:
Irvine Foundation, James
Fiesler, Nancy, commun
specialist: Volvo North
America Corp.
Fiez, Terry, asst secy-treas:
CUNA Mutual Charitable
Foundation
Fife, Arlene, dir: Fife
Foundation, Elias and Bertha
Fife, Bernard, pres, dir: Fife
Foundation, Elias and Bertha;
co-chmn, co-ceo, dir: Standard
Motor Products, Inc.
Fife, William J., Jr., chmn, ceo:
Giddings & Lewis; vp, dir:
Giddings & Lewis Foundation
Figgie, Harry E., Jr., chmn,
ceo, dir: Figgie International
Fike, Marilyn, dir admin: Bullitt
Foundation
Fikes, Amy L., trust: Fikes
Foundation, Leland
Fikes, Catherine W., chmn,
trust: Fikes Foundation, Leland
Fikes, Lee, pres, treas, trust:
Fikes Foundation, Leland
Files, Glen, adv: Central &
South West Foundation
Files, Glenn, pres, ceo: West
Texas Utilities Co.
Fillius, Milton F., chmn, dir:
Drown Foundation, Joseph
Fillo, Stephen W., dir: Markle
Foundation, John and Mary R.
Finberg, Barbara Denning,
exec vp, program chmn
(special projects): Carnegie
Corporation of New York
Finch, Arnold, trust: Edouard
Foundation
Finch, David, chmn fdn comm:
Finch Foundation, Thomas
Austin
Finch, Edward Ridley, Jr.,
Adams Memorial Fund, Emma
J.; gen coun: St. Giles
Foundation; trust: Whittell
Trust for Disabled Veterans of
Foreign Wars, Elia
Finch, Harold B., Jr., chmn,
ceo, dir: Nash-Finch Co.
Finch, Helen, trust: Finch
Foundation, Doak
Finch, James A., III, trust:
Pettus, Jr. Foundation, James T.
Finch, James C., trust: New
Hampshire Ball Bearings
Foundation
Finch, John, mem fdn comm:
Finch Foundation, Thomas
Austin
Finch, Lyliane D., dir, pres:
Edouard Foundation

Finch, M. L., Jr., vp: Daniels
Charitable Foundation,
Josephus
Finch, Pauline Swayze, trust:
Adams Memorial Fund, Emma
J.
Finch, Richard J., trust: Finch
Foundation, Doak
Finch, Sumner, mem fdn comm:
Finch Foundation, Thomas
Austin
Findlay, Robert W., trust:
Morrison Charitable Trust,
Pauline A. and George R.
Findley, T. J., Jr., treas:
ASARCO Foundation
Findorff, Robert L., sr vp:
Donaldson Co.; trust:
Donaldson Foundation
Fine, Jeffrey M., dir: Jennings
Foundation, Alma
Fine, Margie, pres, dir:
Common Giving Fund
Fine, Peter A., trust: Wharton
Trust, William P.
Fine, Roger S., pres: Johnson &
Johnson Family of Cos.
Contribution Fund
Fine, Stuart, trust: MacKall and
Evanina Evans Bell MacKall
Trust, Paul
Finegan, William F., vp, trust:
Monroe Foundation (1976), J.
Edgar
Finerman, R., asst secy, treas,
dir: Center for Educational
Programs
Finerman, Ralph, dir: Capital
Fund Foundation; dir: Milken
Family Medical Foundation
Finger, Gregory, trust: Carteh
Foundation
Finger, Harold M., trust:
Hooper Foundation
Fingerhut, Manny, dir:
Fingerhut Family Foundation
Fingerhut, Ronald, pres, dir:
Fingerhut Family Foundation
Fingerhut, Rose, vp, dir:
Fingerhut Family Foundation
Fingleton, Thomas D., chmn:
Hecht's
Fink, Donald W., MD, trust:
Colorado Trust
Fink, H. Bernerd, vp, trust:
Fink Foundation
Fink, John E., dir:
Leighton-Oare Foundation
Fink, Norman S., trust:
Killough Trust, Walter H. D.
Fink, Richard M., dir: Koch
Charitable Foundation,
Charles G.; vp, dir: Koch
Foundation, Fred C.; dir:
Lambe Charitable Foundation,
Claude R.
Fink, Ruth Garvey, pres, trust,
don: Fink Foundation
Finkbeiner, James V., pres,
trust: Wickes Foundation,
Harvey Randall
Finkelstein, Bernard, trust:
Altman Foundation; vp:
Gutman Foundation, Edna and
Monroe C.
Finkelstein, Michael, asst secy,
asst treas: Fisher Foundation
Finkelstein, Robert J., exec dir:
Christodora
Finlay, John David, Jr., trust:
McMillan Foundation, D. W.
Finlay, Louis E., pres, treas,
trust: Oldham Little Church
Foundation
Finlay, Louis M., Jr., mem:
Smith, Jr. Foundation, M. W.
Finlay, Robert Derek, trust:
Heinz Co. Foundation, H.J.
Finley, A. Earle, II, secy, dir:
Finley Foundation, A. E.

Finley, David A., dir: IBM
South Africa Projects Fund
Finley, John H., trust: Humane
Society of the Commonwealth
of Massachusetts
Finley, Warren, trust: Argyros
Foundation
Finn, Richard Galletly Francis,
pres, ceo, dir:
Chesebrough-Pond's
Finn, Richard H., pres, ceo, dir:
Transamerica Corp.; dir:
Transamerica Fdn.
Finn, Richard L., secy:
Reynolds Foundation, J. B.
Finnegan, Lawrence J., chmn.
pres, dir: Boston Mutual Life
Insurance Co.
Finnegan, W. N., III, trust:
Smith Foundation, Bob and
Vivian
Finnegan, William J., mem
contributions comm: Puget
Sound Power & Light Co.
Finnell, Lisa J., asst secy:
Prudential Securities
Foundation
Finneran, Gerard B., trust:
Trimble Family Foundation,
Robert Mize and Isa White
Finneran, Gerard I., dir, pres:
Trimble Family Foundation,
Robert Mize and Isa White
Finneran, Laurey, trust: LEF
Foundation
Finney, Graham S., dir: Penn
Foundation, William; trust:
Seybert Institution for Poor
Boys and Girls, Adam and
Maria Sarah
Finney, Redmond C. S., dir:
France Foundation, Jacob and
Annita
Fino, Raymond M., vp (human
resources): Warner-Lambert
Co.; second vp:
Warner-Lambert Charitable
Foundation
Finucane, Richard Daniel, MD,
dir, pres: Westchester Health
Fund
Fiola, Janet S., vchmn, chmn
(ed comm): Medtronic
Foundation
Fiorani, R. P., vp, dir: Square D
Foundation
Fioratti, Helen, dir: Richmond
Foundation, Frederick W.
Fireman, Paul, ceo, trust:
Fireman Charitable
Foundation, Paul and Phyllis;
chmn, pres, ceo, coo: Reebok
International Ltd.
Fireman, Phyllis, trust: Fireman
Charitable Foundation, Paul
and Phyllis
Firestien, Larry, mem
scholarship selection comm:
Ritter Charitable Trust, George
W. & Mary F.
Firestone, D. Morgan, trust:
Firan Foundation
Firestone, John D., trust:
Firestone Foundation, Roger S.
Firestone, Lisa, trust: Firestone
Foundation, Roger S.
Firman, Pamela, trust:
Cherokee Foundation
First Wisconsin Trust
Company, trust: Pfister and
Vogel Tanning Co. Foundation
Firth, Nicholas L. D., vp:
Dreyfus Foundation, Jean and
Louis
Firth, Valli V. Dreyfus, pres:
Dreyfus Foundation, Jean and
Louis
Fischbach, Jerome, pres:
Fischbach Foundation
Fischer, Aaron, trust: Deer
Creek Foundation

Fischer, Adam B., trust:
Thompson Charitable Trust,
Sylvia G.
Fischer, Christopher, trust:
Christodora
Fischer, Diane, corp secy, dir:
Atran Foundation
Fischer, Don R., trust: UPS
Foundation
Fischer, Duane A., dir: Scoular
Foundation
Fischer, Henry F., vp: TCF
Foundation
Fischer, Jack L., secy: Kettering
Family Foundation; contact
person: Kettering Fund
Fischer, Lynn T., trust: Saul
Foundation, Joseph E. &
Norma G.
Fischer, M. Peter, trust: Deer
Creek Foundation
Fischer, Marie, trust: Woods
Charitable Fund
Fischer, Miles P., vp, secy:
Brencanda Foundation
Fischer, Richard Lawrence, dir:
Alcoa Foundation
Fischer, Teresa m., trust: Deer
Creek Foundation
Fischer, William D., pres, coo,
dir: Dean Foods Co.
Fischer, William J., Jr., trust:
Hagedorn Fund
Fischman, Arnie, pres:
Seascape Senior Housing, Inc.
Fischman, Bernard D., trust:
Boehm Foundation
Fish, Eugene C., chmn, secy,
dir: Eastern Foundry Co.;
trust: EAFCO Foundation; dir:
Reidler Foundation
Fish, L.M., trust: Greenville
Foundation
Fishbein, Peter M., trust: Kaye
Foundation
Fisher, A.J., trust: Holley
Foundation
Fisher, Adrienne A., grants mgr:
Commonwealth Fund
Fisher, Allan Herbert, Jr., secy,
trust: Leidy Foundation, John J.
Fisher, Arnold, dir: Fisher
Brothers Foundation
Fisher, Arthur E., vp: Smith
Benevolent Association,
Buckingham
Fisher, Benjamin, Jr., trust:
Shore Fund
Fisher, Bernard, dir: Uris
Brothers Foundation
Fisher, Charles Thomas, III,
chmn, pres, ceo, dir: NBD
Bank
Fisher, David, cfo: Rosenbluth
Travel Agency
Fisher, David S., dir: Young
Foundation, Irvin L.
Fisher, Donald George, fdr,
chmn, ceo: Gap, The; chmn,
ceo: Gap Foundation
Fisher, Doris F., treas: Gap
Foundation
Fisher, E. Gayle, exec dir: Frese
Foundation, Arnold D.
Fisher, Ellen Kingman,
program off: Gates Foundation
Fisher, Everett, secy, treas,
trust: Dennett Foundation,
Marie G.
Fisher, Francis M., Jr., trust:
Gulf Power Foundation
Fisher, Frederick W., dir:
Woodson Foundation,
Aytchmonde
Fisher, George Myles Cordell,
chmn, ceo, dir: Motorola; pres,
dir: Motorola Foundation
Fisher, Herbert, chmn, pres,
ceo: Jamesway Corp.
Fisher, Hinda N., pres, treas,
dir: Fisher Foundation

Fisher, James P., dir, vp:
Ramlose Foundation, George
A.
Fisher, James W., secy, treas,
dir: Martin Foundation, Bert
William
Fisher, John, trust: Fisher
Foundation
Fisher, John E., gen chmn, dir:
Wausau Insurance Cos.
Fisher, John Edwin, dir:
Nationwide Insurance Cos.;
chmn, trust: Nationwide
Insurance Foundation
Fisher, John Wesley, pres, dir:
Ball Brothers Foundation
Fisher, Judith, trust: Fisher
Foundation
Fisher, Kenneth, secy, treas, dir:
Scurlock Foundation
Fisher, Lawrence, dir: Fisher
Brothers Foundation
Fisher, Lawrence N., secy:
Fluor Foundation
Fisher, Lillian, trust: Shore Fund
Fisher, M. Anthony, dir: Fisher
Brothers Foundation
Fisher, Max Martin, pres, trust:
Taubman Foundation, A.
Alfred
Fisher, Mrs. Bruce C., trust:
Friendship Fund
Fisher, Orville Earl, Jr., treas,
mem contributions comm:
Jostens Foundation
Fisher, R. S., dir: Legg & Co.
Foundation
Fisher, Richard, dir: Fisher
Brothers Foundation
Fisher, Richard B., chmn:
Morgan Stanley & Co.
Fisher, Richard W., sr vp
(human resources): Reichhold
Chemicals, Inc.
Fisher, Robert J., trust: Gap
Foundation
Fisher, Suzanne, treas, trust:
Cantor Foundation, Iris and B.
Gerald
Fisher, Thomas L., pres, ceo,
dir: Northern Illinois Gas Co.
Fisher, W. S., dir, mem: Cannon
Foundation
Fisher, Zachary, dir: Fisher
Brothers Foundation
Fishkin, Stuart, treas: Tarmac
America Inc.
Fishman, Fred N., trust: Kaye
Foundation
Fishman, Jerald G., pres, coo,
dir: Analog Devices
Fishman, Joseph L., vp, dir:
Moses Fund, Henry and Lucy
Fishoff, Benjamin, trust: Fishoff
Family Foundation
Fisk, Charles B., trust: Seabury
Foundation
Fisk, Mary A., dir: Harriman
Foundation, Mary W.
Fiske, Guy W., trust: Bird Cos.
Charitable Foundation
Fist, David, trust: Taubman
Foundation, Herman P. and
Sophia
Fister, Richard E., secy, trust:
Webb Foundation
Fister, Virginia M., mem adv
comm, trust: Webb Foundation
Fitch, Stona James, vp, trust:
Procter & Gamble Fund
Fitchhorn, Davie, dir: MFA
Foundation
Fite, Clyde, dir:
Christy-Houston Foundation
Fiterman, Ben, secy, dir:
Fiterman Foundation, Jack and
Bessie
Fiterman, Michael, pres:
Liberty Diversified Industries
Inc.; pres, dir: Fiterman
Foundation, Jack and Bessie

Fites, Donald Vester, chmn, ceo: Caterpillar; dir: Caterpillar Foundation

Fitterman, Miles Q., trust: Fiterman Charitable Foundation, Miles and Shirley

Fitterman, Shirley, trust: Fiterman Charitable Foundation, Miles and Shirley

Fitterman, Steven C., trust: Fiterman Charitable Foundation, Miles and Shirley

Fitts, Harriet W., treas, trust: Walker Foundation, Archie D. and Bertha H.

Fitzgerald, Brian, chmn, dir: Security Capital Corp.

Fitzgerald, Dennis M., vp, secy, dir: Vernon Fund, Miles Hodsdon

Fitzgerald, Dennis W., McGraw Foundation

FitzGerald, Frances, trust: Rockefeller Foundation

Fitzgerald, John A., pres, trust: Merrill Lynch & Co. Foundation

Fitzgerald, Leslie Law, trust: Law Foundation, Robert O.

Fitzgerald, Margaret Boles, dir, mem: Luce Foundation, Henry

Fitzgerald, Paul M., pres: Factory Mutual Engineering Corp.

Fitzgerald, William A., pres, ceo, dir: Commercial Federal Corp.

FitzGibbon, D. J., dir: Bardes Corp.

Fitzgibbons, James M., dir: Fieldcrest Cannon

Fitzmorris, Ann, dir: Azby Fund

Fitzpatrick, Henry B., trust: McShain Charities, John

Fitzpatrick, Jane P., chmn, ceo, treas: Country Curtains, Inc.; chmn: High Meadow Foundation

Fitzpatrick, Jean R., trust: Stoneman Charitable Foundation, Anne and David

Fitzpatrick, John H., vchmn, chmn (plan and fin comm): Country Curtains, Inc.; pres: High Meadow Foundation

Fitzpatrick, Nancy J., dir: High Meadow Foundation

Fitzpatrick, Jr., Robert R., vp, secy: Procter & Gamble Fund

Fitzsimmons, Hugh A., Jr., trust: Halsell Foundation, Ewing

Fitzsimonds, Roger L., ceo, dir: Firstar Bank Milwaukee NA; chmn: Firstar Milwaukee Foundation; ceo, dir: Firstar Corp.

Fitzsimons, John H., secy: Dyson Foundation

Fix, Duard, trust: Kitzmiller/Bales Trust

Fix, William C., pres: Johnston-Fix Foundation

Fizdale, Richard B., chmn, ceo: Leo Burnett Co.

Fizer, Don, secy, dir: Mathers Charitable Foundation, G. Harold and Leila Y.

Fjellman, Carl Gustaf, trust: Turrell Fund

Fjelstul, Dean M., cfo: Alliant Techsystems; dir: Alliant Community Investment Foundation

Flad, Eleanor Beecher, dir: Beecher Foundation, Florence Simon

Flad, Erle L., dir: Beecher Foundation, Florence Simon

Flad, Ward Beecher, dir: Beecher Foundation, Florence Simon

Flagler, Tom, chmn: Flagler Co.

Flagler, III, Thorne, pres: Flagler Co.

Flaherty, G. S., group pres: Caterpillar; trust: Caterpillar Foundation

Flaherty, John, pres: Singer Company

Flaherty, Patrick F., dir: Wasie Foundation

Flaherty, W. J., trust: Eastern Enterprises Foundation

Flaherty, Walter J., sr vp, cfo, chief adm off: Eastern Enterprises

Flaherty, William E., chmn: Great Lakes Carbon Corp.

Flammang, Donna M., secy, treas, dir: Acme-Cleveland Foundation

Flamouropoulour, Elise M., first vp: Michael-Walters Industries Foundation

Flanagan, David T., sr vp, coo, dir: Central Maine Power Co.

Flanagan, Edward P., secy: Price Foundation, Lucien B. and Katherine E.

Flanagan, Jack, trust: Christodora

Flanagan, Martha L., secy: Cincinnati Enquirer Foundation

Flanagan, Tom A., Jr., chmn: Lakeside National Bank

Flanagin, Neil, dir: Scholl Foundation, Dr.

Flanders, Grame L., trust: Acushnet Foundation

Flanigan, Peter M., trust: Olin Foundation, John M.

Flannery, P., pres: Bank of San Francisco Co.

Flannery, W.W., trust: Morrison Trust, Louise L.

Flans, A., vp, dir: Milken Family Medical Foundation

Flasher, H. T., trust: Kuhns Brothers Co. Foundation

Flaten, Alfred N., Jr., pres, coo: Nash-Finch Co.

Flather, Newell, pres, trust: Parker Foundation, Theodore Edson; adm: Riley Foundation, Mabel Louise

Flatley, Thomas John, trust: Flatley Foundation

Flaville, Victoria K., vp, secy: Connelly Foundation

Fleck, Ernest R., pres, dir: Leach Foundation, Tom & Frances

Fleckenstein, Janie Holley, trust: Earl-Beth Foundation

Fleet, Mary Anne, mgr (corp contributions): Coors Brewing Co.

Fleetwood, Shirley, exec asst: Kao Corp. of America (DE)

Fleischauer, Emil, Jr., secy, dir: Sentry Life Group Foundation

Fleischer, Charles H., dir: Strong Foundation, Hattie M.

Fleischman, Charles D., vp, treas: Nias Foundation, Henry

Fleischman, Henry L., pres emeritus: Nias Foundation, Henry

Fleischmann, Donald, cfo: Ampacet Corp.

Fleischmann, Ruth H., exec dir: Wilson Foundation, Marie C. and Joseph C.

Fleisher, David L., cfo, sr exec vp: Maritz Inc.

Fleishhacker, David, pres, dir: Fleishhacker Foundation

Fleishhacker, Mortimer, III, treas, dir: Fleishhacker Foundation

Fleishman, Joel L., mem: Bryan Family Foundation, Kathleen Price and Joseph M.; chmn, dir: Markle Foundation, John and Mary R.

Fleming, Barbara Jane, vp: Dettman Foundation, Leroy E.

Fleming, David D., pres, trust: Mellinger Educational Foundation, Edward Arthur

Fleming, Dean, secy, treas: Weller Foundation

Fleming, Richard Harrison, vp, treas: USG Corp.; treas, trust: USG Foundation

Fleming, Robert J., trust: Hawley Foundation

Fleming, Walter L., Jr., trust: Constantin Foundation

Fleming-McGrath, Lucy, trust: Homeland Foundation

Flescher, Sharon, dir (programs & grants): Equitable Foundation

Fletcher, Allen W., trust: Fletcher Foundation; trust: Stoddard Charitable Trust

Fletcher, Atheda W., dir: Hadson Foundation

Fletcher, Betty B., dir: Haas Foundation, Saul and Dayee G.

Fletcher, Bob, contributions mgr: Nike Inc.

Fletcher, Frank U., grant coordinator: Fletcher Foundation, A. J.

Fletcher, Marion S., trust, vchmn: Fletcher Foundation; trust, asst treas, don daughter: Stoddard Charitable Trust

Fletcher, Mary S., trust: Fletcher Foundation

Fletcher, Maureen T., asst secy: Hayden Foundation, Charles

Fletcher, Nina M., trust: Fletcher Foundation

Fletcher, Pamela W., secy, dir: Dana Corp. Foundation

Fletcher, Paris, trust, chmn: Fletcher Foundation

Fletcher, Patricia A., trust: Fletcher Foundation

Fletcher, Philip B., ceo, pres: ConAgra

Fletcher, Richard, Jr., mem: Phillips Foundation, Dr. P.

Fletcher, Terry B., vp, dir: Bristol Savings Bank Foundation

Fletcher, Warner S., secy, trust: Alden Trust, George I.; trust: Fletcher Foundation; chmn, trust: Stoddard Charitable Trust

Flettrich, Albert J., dir: German Protestant Orphan Asylum Association

Flewellen, Marvin E., mem: Northern Trust Co. Charitable Trust

Flicker, Irving, pres: Homasote Co.; pres: Homasote Foundation

Flicker, Shanely E., vp: Homasote Foundation

Flickinger, Bonnie G., trust: Children's Foundation of Erie County

Flickinger, F. Miles, M.D., trust, chmn: Flickinger Memorial Trust

Flickinger, Irma L., trust: Flickinger Memorial Trust

Flickinger, Marhl P., trust, treas: Flickinger Memorial Trust

Fliegelman, Amy, secy: IBM South Africa Projects Fund

Flieth, Holger, pres, coo: Thyssen Specialty Steels

Flink, Richard A., vp, gen coun, secy: Bard, C. R.; secy: Bard Foundation, C. R.

Flinn, David B., trust: Avery-Fuller Children's Center

Flinn, Eleanor, trust: India Foundation

Flinn, Patrick L., chmn, pres, ceo, dir: Bank South Corp.

Flint, Dennis, chmn, ceo, dir: FKI Holdings Inc.

Flippin, Doreen, communications off: Davis Foundations, Arthur Vining

Flom, Doug, cfo: Burdines

Flom, Edward L., vice chmn, ceo: Florida Steel Corp.; pres, dir: Florida Steel Foundation

Flood, Al, chmn, ceo: Canadian Imperial Bank of Commerce

Flood, H., McFawn Trust No. 2, Lois Sisler

Flood, Joan M., asst treas: KIHI/21 International Holding Foundation

Flora, Louis A., dir: Stewardship Foundation

Florence, David, mem: Florence Foundation

Florio, Emil, publ rels mgr: Ricoh Corp.

Florio, Steven T., pres, ceo: The New Yorker Magazine, Inc.

Flory, L. J., vp, secy: Grainger, W.W.

Flory, Lee J., vp, secy, asst treas, dir: Grainger Foundation

Flournoy, Houston I., vp, trust: Jones Foundation, Fletcher; dir: Lockheed Leadership Fund

Flower, Walter C., III, dir: German Protestant Orphan Asylum Association

Flowers, Langdon S., trust: Campbell Foundation, J. Bulow

Flowers, Rockne G., pres: Nelson Industries, Inc.

Flowers, Thomas J., pres, dir: Hultquist Foundation

Flowers, Wilford, dir: Wright Foundation, Lola

Flowers, Worthington C., trust: Hambay Foundation, James T.

Floyd, Franklin B., trust: Wellman Foundation, S. K.

Floyd, Mary Bell, vp, secy, treas, don: Floyd Family Foundation

Floyd, Robert K., vp, cfo: Tracor, Inc.

Floyd, William S., pres, don: Floyd Family Foundation

Flug, Jeremy, vp, dir: Martin & Deborah Flug Foundation

Flug, Laura Gurwin, dir: Gurwin Foundation, J.

Flug, Martin, dir, pres: Martin & Deborah Flug Foundation

Fluke, John Maurice, Jr., dir: PACCAR Foundation

Flummerfelt, J.K., pres: Lechmere

Fluno, Jere D., vchmn, dir: Grainger, W.W.

Fluor, John Robert, II, pres, trust: Fluor Foundation

Flynn, Edward J., trust: Martin Foundation, Della

Flynn, James A., pres: Church's Fried Chicken, Inc.

Flynn, James L., vp, trust: Corning Incorporated Foundation

Flynn, Robert E., chmn, ceo: NutraSweet Co.

Flynn, Thomas G., sr vp: Bechtel Foundation; vp: Bechtel, Jr. Foundation, S. D.

Flynn, Thomas Joseph, exec vp, gen coun, dir: Humana Foundation

Flynn, William J., chmn, pres, ceo, dir: Mutual of America Life

Focht, James L., dir: Powell Foundation, Charles Lee

Foege, William, dir: MacArthur Foundation, John D. and Catherine T.

Foell, Ronald R., pres: Standard Pacific Corp.

Foerstner, George C., vp, dir: Hall Foundation

Fogarty, W. Philip, dir, pres: Loats Foundation

Fogel, Alexandra Wolf, secy: Wolf Foundation, Benjamin and Fredora K.

Fogel, Rebecca, vp, secy: Fogel Foundation, Shalom and Rebecca

Fogel, Shalom, pres: Fogel Foundation, Shalom and Rebecca

Fogelson, David, vp, secy, trust: Lowe Foundation, Joe and Emily

Fogelson, Gayle D., trust: Los Trigos Foundation

Fogelsong, Roger, trust: Forster-Powers Charitable Trust

Fogerty, Arthur Joseph, chmn, trust: Agway Foundation

Foissac, Louis, chmn bd: Miles Inc., Diagnostic Division

Folender, Joseph, dir: Weight Watchers Foundation

Foley, Eileen D., trust: Foundation for Seacoast Health

Foley, Joy, contributions mgr: Humana Foundation

Foley, Patricia Ann, secy, treas, dir: Inland Container Corp. Foundation

Foley, Patrick, chmn, ceo: DHL Airways Inc.

Foley, Thomas C., chmn, pres, coo, dir: Bibb Co.

Folger, Elizabeth, asst secy: Hayden Foundation, William R. and Virginia

Folger, John Dulin, trust: Folger Fund

Folger, Kathrine Dulin, pres, treas: Folger Fund

Folger, Lee Merritt, vp, secy: Folger Fund

Folger, P., dir: McBean Family Foundation

Folk, Mark A., vp, treas: Nationwide Insurance Foundation

Folkert, R. A., dir: Koulaieff Educational Fund, Trustees of Ivan Y.

Follis, R. Gwen, dir: McBean Family Foundation

Fonda, Jane, dir: Turner Foundation

Fondren, Robert E., trust: Fondren Foundation

Fondren, Walter W., III, secy/treas: Fondren Foundation

Fonseca, Bruno, trust: Kaplan Fund, J. M.

Fonseca, Caio, trust: Kaplan Fund, J. M.

Fonseca, Elizabeth K., vp, trust: Kaplan Fund, J. M.

Fonseca, Isabel, trust: Kaplan Fund, J. M.

Fonseca, Quina, trust: Kaplan Fund, J. M.

Fontaine, George, trust: Lyndhurst Foundation

Fontaine, Jack, trust: Lyndhurst Foundation

Fried, Robert, dir: Abraham Foundation, Anthony R.

Fried, Wendy R., asst vp, asst secy: Discount Corp. of New York Charitable Foundation

Friede, Barbara, secy, dir: Fireman's Fund Foundation

Friedholm, R., pres: Stroh Brewery Co.

Friedlaender, Helmut N., dir: AMETEK Foundation

Friedland, Harold, trust, vp: Friedland Family Foundation, Samuel

Friedland, Jack, trust, vp, treas: Friedland Family Foundation, Samuel; trust: Gilman, Jr. Foundation, Sondra and Charles

Friedlander, Lillian, trust: Chatham Valley Foundation

Friedli, Floyd E., secy, trust: Montgomery Foundation

Friedman, Alan D., trust: Lard Trust, Mary Potishman

Friedman, Albert, trust: Friedman Brothers Foundation

Friedman, Arthur N. K., trust: Tamarkin Foundation

Friedman, Barbara, trust: Friedman Foundation, Stephen and Barbara

Friedman, Bayard H., dir: Brown and C. A. Lupton Foundation, T. J.; trust: Lard Trust, Mary Potishman

Friedman, Cyrus, Jr., vchmn: Booz Allen & Hamilton

Friedman, D. Sylvan, dir: Hobbs Foundation, Emmett

Friedman, Darlene, mem contributions comm: Syntex Corp.

Friedman, Darrell, trust: Straus Foundation, Aaron and Lillie

Friedman, David, sr vp: Heller Financial

Friedman, Ephraim, trust: Friedman Brothers Foundation

Friedman, Frances M., trust: Blum Foundation, Edith C.

Friedman, Harold Edward, secy: Fox Charitable Foundation, Harry K. & Emma R.

Friedman, Harris C., chmn, ceo: American Savings & Loan Association of Florida

Friedman, Harvey, ceo: Friedman Bag Co.; trust: Friedman Brothers Foundation

Friedman, Howard A., dir, vp: Friedman Family Foundation

Friedman, Joel M., trust: Baum Family Fund, Alvin H.

Friedman, Louis, treas: Gallo Foundation; asst secy, asst treas: Gallo Foundation, Julio R.

Friedman, Louis Frank, dir: Hobbs Foundation, Emmett

Friedman, Milton, dir: Glosser Foundation, David A.

Friedman, Phyllis C., dir: Hobbs Foundation, Emmett

Friedman, Phyllis K., pres, treas: Friedman Family Foundation

Friedman, Robert, dir: Levi Strauss Foundation

Friedman, Robert F., dir: Rosenberg Foundation

Friedman, Robert S., secy, treas: Rubinstein Foundation, Helena

Friedman, Saul, trust: Schermer Charitable Trust, Frances

Friedman, Sidney O., trust: Lurcy Charitable and Educational Trust, Georges

Friedman, Stephen, trust: Cook Foundation; trust: Day Family Foundation; trust: Friedman Foundation, Stephen and Barbara; vchmn, mem mgmt comm, vchmn: Goldman Sachs & Co.

Friedman, Walker C., trust: Lard Trust, Mary Potishman

Friedman, Wilbur Harvey, trust: Blum Foundation, Edith C.; secy, dir: Gelb Foundation, Lawrence M.

Friedman, William, Jr., trust: Hawley Foundation

Friedman, William B., dir: Washington Square Health Foundation

Friedman, William E., dir, pres, treas: Eckman Charitable Foundation, Samuel and Rae; secy, treas: Slaughter Foundation, Charles

Friedman, William K., trust: Bronfman Foundation, Samuel

Friedwald, W., dir: Metropolitan Life Foundation

Frieland, Leonard, trust, pres: Friedland Family Foundation, Samuel

Frieling, Gerald H., Jr., treas: Hunter Foundation, Edward and Irma; chmn: Tokheim Corp.

Friend, Eugene L., pres, dir: Koret Foundation

Friend, Robert, dir: Osher Foundation, Bernard

Friend, W. L., exec vp, dir: Bechtel Foundation

Friendly, Melvyn C., trust: Friendly Rosenthal Foundation

Frierson, Daniel K., chmn, ceo, dir: Dixie Yarns, Inc.; pres, trust: Dixie Yarns Foundation

Frierson, J. Burton, Jr., vp, trust: Westend Foundation

Friesen, William L., dir: Hesston Foundation

Friley, Charles B., vp, dir: Phillips Petroleum Foundation

Frink, George R., chmn: IMT Insurance Co.; trust: IMT Co. Charitable Trust

Frisbee, Don Calvin, chmn: PacifiCorp; dir: Wessinger Foundation

Frisch, Maureen, pres, dir: Matlock Foundation

Frist, Thomas F., trust: Ansley Foundation, Dantzler Bond

Frist, Thomas Fearn, Jr., chmn, ceo, pres: Hospital Corp. of America; chmn, pres: HCA Foundation

Fristedt, Hans, pres: American Trading & Production Corp.

Fritsch, Robert Bruce, vp, gen mgr (off products div): Hunt Manufacturing Co.

Fritsche, William S., trust: Consolidated Natural Gas Co. Foundation

Fritz, Bertha G., trust: Gorin Foundation, Nehemiah

Fritz, Lynn C., ceo, pres: Fritz Cos.

Fritz, Sandra, advisor: Cayuga Foundation

Fritz, William J., treas: Moore & Sons Foundation, B.C.

Fritz, William W., vp (fin): Kellogg Foundation, W. K.

Frizen, Edwin L., Jr., pres, trust: Crowell Trust, Henry P. and Susan C.; pres, mgr: Tyndale House Foundation

Froderman, Carl M., pres: Froderman Foundation

Froehlich, Meghan, dir: Freddie Mac Foundation

Froelich, Eugene, exec vp, cfo: Maxicare Health Plans

Froelich, Georgia A., trust: Hershey Foundation

Froelicher, F. Charles, trust: Gates Foundation

Frohlich, William O., vp: Dun & Bradstreet Corp. Foundation

Frohman, Daniel C., trust: Frohman Foundation, Sidney

Frohring, Glenn H., chmn, trust: Frohring Foundation, William O. and Gertrude Lewis

Frohring, Lloyd W., treas, trust: Frohring Foundation, William O. and Gertrude Lewis

Frohring, Maxine A., vp, treas: Frohring Foundation, Paul & Maxine

Frohring, Paul R., pres: Frohring Foundation, Paul & Maxine

Froio, Anthony, treas: Home for Aged Men

Fromel, Robert A., vp, dir: Hutchins Foundation, Mary J.

Frommelt, Andrew E.R., Jr., trust: Schamach Foundation, Milton

Fromstein, Mitchell S., chmn, ceo: Manpower, Inc.

Fronterhouse, Gerald W., dir: Hoblitzelle Foundation

Fronterhouse, Jerry, dir: Texas Instruments

Fross, Roger R., dir: Joyce Foundation

Frost, Camilla Chandler, dir: Irvine Foundation, James

Frost, Charles H., vchmn: Tektronix Foundation

Frost, Gordon T., secy, trust: Sefton Foundation, J. W.

Frost, H. G., Jr., dir, mgr: Jones Charitable Trust, Harvey and Bernice

Frost, Herbert G., Jr., dir: Jones Foundation, Harvey and Bernice

Frost, Louis B., trust: Hansen Memorial Foundation, Irving

Frost, T. C., Jr., chmn, ceo, dir: Cullen/Frost Bankers; trust: Morrison Trust, Louise L.

Frost, T.C., chmn: Frost National Bank

Frost, Virginia, sr vp (pub aff): Comerica

Frost, William Lee, pres, treas, dir: Littauer Foundation, Lucius N.

Frost National Bank, trust: Ferguson Family Foundation, Kittie and Rugeley

Fruchtenbaum, Edward, pres, coo, dir: American Greetings Corp.

Fruchthandler, Abraham, pres: Fruchthandler Foundation, Alex and Ruth

Frueauff, David, exec dir, secy: Frueauff Foundation, Charles A.

Frueauff, Sue M., trust: Frueauff Foundation, Charles A.

Fruehauf, Harvey C., Jr., pres, dir: Fruehauf Foundation; trust: Wiegand Foundation, E. L.

Frumkes, Alana, vp: Frumkes Foundation, Alana and Lewis

Frumkes, Beatrice, trust: Frumkes Foundation, Alana and Lewis

Frumkes, Lewis, pres: Frumkes Foundation, Alana and Lewis

Frumkes, Timothy, trust: Frumkes Foundation, Alana and Lewis

Fry, Caroline M., trust: Palmer-Fry Memorial Trust, Lily

Fry, Charles L., chmn, secy: Searle Charitable Trust

Fry, James, vp (admin): Big Three Industries

Fry, John D., pres, coo: Sharon Steel Corp.

Fry, Lloyd A., Jr., pres, dir: Fry Foundation, Lloyd A.

Fry, Marjorie Walthall, trust: Walthall Perpetual Charitable Trust, Marjorie T.

Fry, Michael D., dir: Olmsted Foundation, George and Carol

Fry, Sandra, dir: Skinner Foundation

Fryberger, Carol, dir: Alworth Memorial Fund, Marshall H. and Nellie

Frye, Clayton W., Jr., trust: Jackson Hole Preserve

Frye, Doyle, trust: Conn Memorial Foundation

Frye, W. Vance, dir (health care div): Reynolds Charitable Trust, Kate B.

Fryer, J. Robert, trust: Leesona Charitable Foundation

Fryer, Marna C., trust: Callister Foundation, Paul Q.

Fryling, Victory J., Jr., dir: Consumers Power Foundation

Fthenakis, Emanuel J., pres, coo: Banner Industries, Inc.

Fu, Norman C. C., vp: China Times Cultural Foundation

Fuchs, David, chmn, ceo: Hampton Industries

Fuchs, Michael J., chmn, ceo: Home Box Office

Fuchsberg, Abraham, pres: Fuchsberg Family Foundation, Abraham

Fuchsberg, Frances, dir: Fuchsberg Family Foundation

Fuchsberg, Jacob David, chmn: Fuchsberg Family Foundation

Fuchsberg, Meyer, pres, treas: Fuchsberg Family Foundation; treas: Fuchsberg Family Foundation, Abraham

Fuchsberg, Seymour, vp, dir: Fuchsberg Family Foundation; secy: Fuchsberg Family Foundation, Abraham

Fucito, F., contact: Marubeni America Corp.

Fuegner, Jane Ellen, asst secy: Brand Foundation, C. Harold and Constance

Fuegner, Robert C., vp: Brand Foundation, C. Harold and Constance

Fuellgraf, Charles Louis, Jr., trust: Nationwide Insurance Foundation

Fuellkemper, Horst T., joint chmn N Am: WestLB New York Branch

Fuges, Frederick L., secy, trust: Scholler Foundation

Fuhriman, Addie, exec comm: Swanson Family Foundation, Dr. W.C.

Fuhrman, Gary R., secy: Baltimore Gas & Electric Foundation

Fuhs, Wendy L., pres, dir: Brunswick Foundation

Fujie, Kensuke, exec vp: Dentsu, Inc., NY

Fujii, Hiro, exec vp, treas: Minolta Corp.

Fujii, Kenji, pres, ceo: Olympus Corp.

Fujii, Sharon, dir: Zellerbach Family Fund

Fujishama, Mary, trust: Alsdorf Foundation

Fujita, P. K., pres, ceo, dir: Dunlop Tire Corp.

Fujiwara, Kenj, asst secy: Mitsubishi Kasei America

Fukanaga, George J., chmn, ceo: Servco Pacific

Fukanaga, Thomas I., pres, coo: Servco Pacific

Fukukawa, Shinji, trust: United States-Japan Foundation

Fukunaga, Mark H., alternate mem distribution comm: McInerny Foundation

Fukutani, H., pres: Mitsubishi Kasei America

Fuldner, Henry E., asst secy, dir: Jeffris Family Foundation

Fulford, John H., sr vp (western regional office): Federal National Mortgage Assn. Foundation

Fuller, Afrea, trust: Charlton, Jr. Charitable Trust, Earle P.

Fuller, Alfred W., trust: Ellison Foundation

Fuller, Andrew P., pres: Fuller Foundation

Fuller, Carl W., trust: Blount Educational and Charitable Foundation, Mildred Weedon

Fuller, Charles A., Jr., foundation mgr: Slusher Charitable Foundation, Roy W.

Fuller, Cynthia, trust: Union Foundation

Fuller, Don E., dir: Oakley-Lindsay Foundation of Quincy Newspapers & Quincy Broadcasting Co.

Fuller, Ernest M., trust: Fuller Foundation, George F. and Sybil H.

Fuller, H. Laurence, dir: Skidmore, Owings & Merrill Foundation

Fuller, Harry Laurance, chmn, pres, ceo, dir: Amoco Corp.

Fuller, Jack W., dir: McCormick Tribune Foundation, Robert R.

Fuller, James E., treas: Herman Foundation, John and Rose

Fuller, Joyce I., asst treas: Fuller Foundation, George F. and Sybil H.

Fuller, Julia G., trust: Russell Educational Foundation, Benjamin and Roberta

Fuller, Lincoln E., trust: Fuller Foundation, George F. and Sybil H.

Fuller, Mark, trust: Fuller Foundation, George F. and Sybil H.

Fuller, Mary Jane, dir (community rels): Promus Cos.

Fuller, Orville, chmn, dir: Bank One, Coshocton, NA

Fuller, Peter, pres, trust: Fuller Foundation

Fuller, Peter D., Jr., trust: Fuller Foundation

Fuller, Russell E., chmn, trust, treas: Fuller Foundation, George F. and Sybil H.

Fuller, Steven, chmn: World Book Inc.

Fuller, Thomas R., pres, ceo: Thomas Industries

Fuller, William M., vp: Fuller Foundation

Fullerton, Marna W., dir: Wagner Manufacturing Co. Foundation, E. R.

Fulleylove, Brian, pres: Courtaulds Fibers Inc.

Fullinwider, Carol C., vp: Falk Medical Research Foundation, Dr. Ralph and Marian

Fullinwider, Jerome M., trust: Abell-Hanger Foundation

Gignilliat, Arthur M., Jr., pres, ceo: Savannah Electric & Power Co.

Gigray, Margaret, vchmn: Whittenberger Foundation, Claude R. and Ethel B.

Gilbane, Jean A., trust: Gilbane Foundation, Thomas and William

Gilbane, William J., chmn: Gilbane Building Co.; trust: Gilbane Foundation, Thomas and William

Gilbert, G. Jean, exec secy, clerk: Hayden Recreation Center, Josiah Willard

Gilbert, James M., mem: Rixson Foundation, Oscar C.

Gilbert, John Neely, Jr., trust: Davis Hospital Foundation

Gilbert, Lee, trust: Moss Charitable Trust, Finis M.

Gilbert, Louisa, dir: Moore Foundation, Edward S.

Gilbert, Marion Moore, vp, dir: Moore Foundation, Edward S.

Gilbert, Paul W., exec vp, cfo: Jacobson Stores, Inc.

Gilbert, Rodney C., chmn, ceo: Rust International Corp.

Gilbert, Roy W., Jr., pres, dir: Southtrust Corp.

Gilbert, S. Parker, dir: Macy, Jr. Foundation, Josiah; trust, mem: Sloan Foundation, Alfred P.

Gilbertson, Gene R., cfo, dir: Banner Life Insurance Co.

Gilder, Richard, Jr., pres: Gilder Foundation

Gildred, Stuart C., pres, dir: M. E. G. Foundation; pres: S.G. Foundation

Giles, Clark P., secy: Eccles Charitable Foundation, Willard L.

Giles, Gordon L., trust: Nicol Scholarship Foundation, Helen Kavanagh

Giles, Lucille P., pres, treas: Giles Foundation, Edward C.

Gilgore, Sheldon Gerald, MD, chmn, ceo, dir: Searle & Co., G.D.; vchmn: Searle Charitable Trust

Gill, Barbara, admin asst: Security Life of Denver

Gill, Brendan, chmn, dir: Warhol Foundation for the Visual Arts, Andy

Gill, Daniel E., chmn, ceo, dir: Bausch & Lomb

Gill, Donald, vp: Packer Foundation, Horace B.

Gill, George, pres: Courier-Journal & Louisville Times

Gill, George A., Jr., asst secy: Hopewell Foundation

Gill, Juliann, adm: Dun & Bradstreet Corp. Foundation

Gill, Lawrence, vp, dir: Dodge Jones Foundation

Gill, Lisa, vp, dir: Wasserman Foundation, George

Gill, Sherry B., trust: Gordon Charitable Trust, Peggy and Yale

Gillan, George M., asst treas: Brencanda Foundation

Gillen, Blake, vp: Caston Foundation, M. C. and Mattie; vp: Navarro County Educational Foundation

Gillen, James Robert, trust: Prudential Foundation

Gillen, Lori, program off econ devel: Abell Foundation, The

Gillespie, Anneliese, trust, secy, treas: Buehler Foundation, Emil

Gillespie, George Joseph, III, mem adv comm: Ford Foundation, Edward E.; trust: Joyce Foundation, John M. and Mary A.; treas, secy, trust, mem exec comm: Olin Foundation, John M.; dir: Paley Foundation, William S.; pres, trust: Pinkerton Foundation; secy, dir: Ross Foundation, Arthur

Gillespie, J. Samuel, Jr., adv: Carter Foundation, Beirne; adv: Jeffress Memorial Trust, Thomas F. and Kate Miller

Gillespie, Larry, dir: Jasper Desk Foundation

Gillespie, Lee Day, trust: Day Foundation, Nancy Sayles

Gillespie, Phil G., treas: Kramer Foundation, Louise

Gillespie, Ramon E., secy: Ford Meter Box Foundation

Gillespie, Robert W., chmn, ceo, dir: Society Corp.

Gillespie, Thomas G., Jr., vp: Arell Foundation

Gillespie, Thomas J., III, pres: Lockhart Iron & Steel Co.

Gillespie, Tyrone W., grant comm: May Mitchell Royal Foundation

Gillett, Elesabeth I., chmn, pres, dir: Gillett Foundation, Elesabeth Ingalls

Gillett, F. Warrington, Jr., secy, treas, dir: Gillett Foundation, Elesabeth Ingalls

Gillette, Edmond S., Jr., trust: Lux Foundation, Miranda; trust: Witter Foundation, Dean

Gillette, Howard G., bd mem: Precision Rubber Products Foundation

Gillette, James R., cfo: Swinerton & Walberg Co.

Gilley, R. Stevens, trust: Delta Tau Delta Educational Fund

Gillfillan, Michael, vchmn: Wells Fargo & Co.; dir: Wells Fargo Foundation

Gilliam, James H., Jr., treas: Beneficial Foundation; trust: Hughes Medical Institute, Howard

Gillies, Archibald L., pres, dir: Warhol Foundation for the Visual Arts, Andy

Gillies, Linda, dir, trust: Astor Foundation, Vincent

Gillig, Edward C., pres: Myra Foundation

Gilligan, Matthew, trust: UNUM Charitable Foundation

Gillilan, William J., pres, coo, dir: Centex Corp.

Gillin, Alelia, exec dir: Babcock Memorial Endowment, William

Gillingham, Frank, trust: Fish Foundation, Bert

Gillstrom, Mary, asst secy: Andersen Foundation

Gilman, Charles, III, trust: Gilman, Jr. Foundation, Sondra and Charles

Gilman, Douglas E., vp: Whiteley Foundation, John and Elizabeth

Gilman, E. Atwill, trust: Boettcher Foundation

Gilman, Howard, pres, dir: Gilman Foundation, Howard; chmn, ceo: Gilman Paper Co.; pres, dir: Gilman Paper Co. Foundation

Gilman, Howard L., chmn, ceo: Gilman Investment Co.

Gilman, Ralph W., dir, treas: Webster Charitable Foundation

Gilman, Sondra, dir, chmn: Gilman, Jr. Foundation, Sondra and Charles

Gilman, Sylvia P., dir: Gilman Foundation, Howard

Gilmar, Leonard, trust: Merit Gasoline Foundation

Gilmartin, John A., chmn, pres, ceo,coo: Millipore Corp.; trust: Millipore Foundation

Gilmartin, Raymond V., pres, ceo, dir: Becton Dickinson & Co.

Gilmore, Elizabeth Burke, secy, dir: Mertz-Gilmore Foundation, Joyce

Gilmore, Hugh R., Jr., trust: Phillips Charitable Trust, Dr. and Mrs. Arthur William

Gilmore, Patrick T., pres: Brother International Corp.

Gilmore, Voit, trust: Anderson Foundation, Robert C. and Sadie G.

Gilmour, Allan Dana, trust: Ford Motor Co. Fund

Gilrain, Ronald F., vp (pub affairs): Stanley Works Foundation

Giltinan, David M., Jr., trust: Carbon Fuel Foundation

Gimon, Eleanor H., dir: Hewlett Foundation, William and Flora

Gin, Yuen T., trust: Nelson Foundation, Florence

Gindes, Joan L., vp: Kaplan Foundation, Charles I. and Mary

Gindi, Abraham, trust: Gindi Associates Foundation

Gindi, Ralph I., trust: Gindi Associates Foundation

Gindi, Sam, trust: Gindi Associates Foundation

Ginger, Lyman V., pres, dir: Robinson Mountain Fund, E. O.

Gingher, Deborah J., vp, secy: Prudential Foundation

Ginn, Regis C., secy, dir: Wilbur Foundation, Marguerite Eyer

Ginn, Robert Martin, trust: Huntington Fund for Education, John; trust: Jennings Foundation, Martha Holden

Ginn, Sam L., chmn, ceo, dir, pres: Pacific Telesis Group

Ginn, William Denton, secy: Nord Family Foundation

Ginnis, Sandra, dir: Ensign-Bickford Foundation

Ginsberg, Calmon J., pres: Ginsberg Family Foundation, Moses

Ginsberg, Daniel R., Ginsberg Family Foundation, Moses

Ginsberg, Donald C., vp: Ginsberg Family Foundation, Moses

Ginsberg, Ernest, vchmn, gen coun, dir: Republic New York Corp.

Ginsberg, Morris, Ginsberg Family Foundation, Moses

Ginsberg, Stanley, sr vp mktg comm: Daiwa Securities America Inc.

Ginsburg, Marianne L., secy, program off: German Marshall Fund of the United States

Gintel, Robert, vchmn, dir: Xtra Corp.

Ginther, Louis A., trust: Massie Trust, David Meade

Giocolo, Anthony, secy: Capezio-Ballet Makers Dance Foundation

Gioia, Lucy, adm asst: Dreyfus Foundation, Max and Victoria

Giordano, Joseph, mem: Rixson Foundation, Oscar C.

Giordano, Salvatore, chmn: Fedders Corp.

Giordano, Salvatore, Jr., vchmn, pres, ceo, coo: Fedders Corp.

Giovanisci, Stephen J., dir: ARCO Foundation

Gipe, Dagmar Dunn Pickens, vp, trust: Dunn Research Foundation, John S.

Giramita, Phillip S., chmn: Martin Marietta Corp. Foundation

Gire, Leroy M., treas: Bireley Foundation

Girouard, Marvin, pres, coo, dir: Pier 1 Imports, Inc.

Gische, Samuel R., fin dir, contr: Hartford Foundation, John A.

Gisel, William George, pres, dir: Cummings Foundation, James H.

Gitlin, Paul, trust: Brace Foundation, Donald C.

Gittell, Marilyn, trust: New York Foundation

Gitter, Allan E., trust: Amdur Leather Association Foundation

Gitter, Richard L., pres: Amdur Braude Riley, Inc.; trust: Amdur Leather Association Foundation

Gittis, Howard, vchmn, dir: MacAndrews & Forbes Holdings; vchmn, dir: Revlon

Giuggio, John Peter, vchmn, dir: Globe Newspaper Co.; dir: Boston Globe Foundation

Giuliani, Albert H., secy-treas: Cadillac Products Foundation

Giurgiu, Alexandra, mng dir: Olivetti Office USA, Inc.

Givan, Boyd, corp sr vp, cfo: Boeing Co.

Given, Hugh, contr; mem contributions comm: National Steel

Given, Rev. Davis, trust: Davis Foundations, Arthur Vining

Givens, David W., mem (community concerns comm): NBD Bank, N.A.

Givens, William P., chmn: Marsh Supermarkets, Inc.

Glade, Fred M., Jr., chmn, dir: Reynolds Foundation, Edgar

Gladfelter, Millard E., trust emeritus: Newcombe Foundation, Charlotte W.

Gladstein, Gary, vp, secy: Open Society Fund

Gladstone, Henry A., trust: Strauss Foundation

Glancy, Alfred R., III, vchmn, dir: Glancy Foundation, Lenora and Alfred; trust: Hudson-Webber Foundation; chmn, ceo, dir: Michigan Consolidated Gas Co.

Glanville, James W., pres: Glanville Family Foundation

Glanville, Nancy H., vp: Glanville Family Foundation

Glanzer, Aaron, trust: CENEX Foundation

Glaser, Daniel E., vp, treas: Blue Cross & Blue Shield of Kentucky Foundation

Glaser, Gary A., ceo, pres, dir: National City Bank, Columbus

Glaser, Miles, exec vp, treas, dir: Menil Foundation

Glaser, Robert J., MD, dir med science, trust: Markey Charitable Trust, Lucille P.; trust: Packard Foundation, David and Lucile

Glaser, William P., trust: Trion Charitable Foundation

Glasgow, William Jacob, dir: PacifiCorp Foundation

Glasple, Ray, trust: Millhollon Educational Trust Estate, Nettie

Glass, David D., pres, ceo, dir: Wal-Mart Stores; trust: Wal-Mart Foundation; pres, ceo, dir: Wal-Mart Stores, Inc.

Glass, Gwendolyn, pres: Loomis House

Glass, Margaret, trust: Markey Charitable Trust, Lucille P.

Glass, Sandra A., program vp: Keck Foundation, W. M.

Glasscock, Jim, secy: McRae Foundation

Glasser, Gene, trust: Schecter Private Foundation, Aaron and Martha

Glasser, James J., chmn, ceo, pres: GATX Corp.

Glassmoyer, Thomas P., trust: Newcombe Foundation, Charlotte W.

Glauberman, J. D., exec vp, treas: MalCo Products Inc.

Glauberman, Stuart C., pres: MalCo Products Inc.

Glaudel, Robert H., trust: M/A-COM Charitable Foundation

Glave, Mrs. James M., chmn grants comm: Memorial Foundation for Children

Glaze, dir, vp, secy: Glaze Foundation, Robert and Ruth

Glaze, Robert E., dir, pres, treas: Glaze Foundation, Robert and Ruth

Glazer, Bradford A., secy-treas: Glazer Foundation, Jerome S.

Glazer, Donald, trust: Cowan Foundation Corporation, Lillian L. and Harry A.

Glazer, Edward, vp: Glazer Foundation, Madelyn L.

Glazer, Ellen, vp: Cowan Foundation Corporation, Lillian L. and Harry A.

Glazer, Jerome S., pres: Glazer Foundation, Jerome S.

Glazer, Madelyn L., pres: Glazer Foundation, Madelyn L.

Gleason, Alfred M., pres, ceo, dir: PacifiCorp

Gleason, James S., pres, dir: Gleason Memorial Fund; chmn, pres, ceo, dir: Gleason Works

Gleason, Janis F., dir: Gleason Memorial Fund

Gleason, Patricia, dir, vp: Gleason Foundation, James; vp, dir: Gleason Foundation, Katherine

Gleason, Thomas D., chmn, ceo: Wolverine World Wide, Inc.

Gleason, Walter M., dir, pres, treas, mgr: Gleason Foundation, James; pres, treas, dir: Gleason Foundation, Katherine

Gleason, William F., Jr., vp: Continental Corp. Foundation

Gleixner, E. H., pres, trust: St. Mary's Catholic Foundation

Glen, Thomas, II, trust: Abreu Charitable Trust u/w/o May P. Abreu, Francis I.; trust: Beck Foundation, Lewis H.

Glendening, Brad, trust: Mary Kay Foundation

Glenn, Diane, dir: Wieboldt Foundation

Glenn, Don T., secy, treas: 28:19

Goldstein, Alfred R., pres, secy: Goldstein Foundation, Alfred and Ann

Goldstein, Ann L., treas, dir: Goldstein Foundation, Alfred and Ann

Goldstein, Bruce, dir: Haigh-Scatena Foundation

Goldstein, Cynthia, dir: Goldstein Foundation, Alfred and Ann

Goldstein, Diane R., trust: Plough Foundation

Goldstein, Elliott, secy, treas, trust: Chatham Valley Foundation

Goldstein, Emanuel, dir: Goldman Foundation, Herman

Goldstein, Frederic S., treas, dir: Fischel Foundation, Harry and Jane

Goldstein, Gabriel F., pres, dir: Fischel Foundation, Harry and Jane

Goldstein, George J., chmn, dir: Acorn Corrugated Box Co.; pres: Acorn Corrugated Box Co. Foundation

Goldstein, Harriet, vchmn, trust: Chatham Valley Foundation

Goldstein, Jack, chmn, pres: Loren Industries Inc.

Goldstein, Jan, mgr (grants): Equitable Foundation

Goldstein, Leonard J., pres, ceo: Miller Brewing Co.

Goldstein, Leslie, trust: Goldstein Foundation, Leslie and Roslyn

Goldstein, Lester, trust: Glosser Foundation, David A.

Goldstein, Marvin, chmn, ceo: Dayton's

Goldstein, Michael, vchmn, cfo: Toys "R" Us, Inc.

Goldstein, Phillip M., pres, dir: Acorn Corrugated Box Co.; treas: Acorn Corrugated Box Co. Foundation

Goldstein, Richard A., chmn, ceo: Unilever United States

Goldstein, Richard E., dir: Goldstein Foundation, Alfred and Ann

Goldstein, Robert, MD, dir: Zlinkoff Fund for Medical Research and Education, Sergei S.

Goldstein, Roslyn, trust: Goldstein Foundation, Leslie and Roslyn

Goldstein, Samuel R., chmn, dir: Apex Oil Co.

Goldstein, Seth M., dir: Fischel Foundation, Harry and Jane

Goldstein, Simeon H. F., dir: Fischel Foundation, Harry and Jane

Goldstein, Stanley P., chmn, pres: Melville Corp.

Goldstein, Steven R., dir: Goldstein Foundation, Alfred and Ann

Goldstein, Susan, secy, trust: Rosenberg Foundation, Sunny and Abe

Goldsten, Janice W., pres, treas, dir: Wasserman Foundation, George

Goldston, Mark R., pres, coo: L.A. Gear

Goldwyn, Anthony, trust: Goldwyn Foundation, Samuel

Goldwyn, Francis, trust: Goldwyn Foundation, Samuel

Goldwyn, John, trust: Goldwyn Foundation, Samuel

Goldwyn, Peggy E., trust: Goldwyn Foundation, Samuel

Goldwyn, Samuel, Jr., ceo: Goldwyn Foundation, Samuel

Golieb, Abner J., pres, dir: Katzenberger Foundation

Gollihue, Alan E., exec dir: Portsmouth General Hospital Foundation

Golliver, Robert R., pres, coo: Washington Natural Gas Co.

Golteus, Hans, pres: Kloster Cruise Ltd.

Golub, Alan, pres, coo: Leslie Fay Cos., Inc.

Golub, Harvey, ceo: American Express Co.

Gomi, Yasumasa, chmn, pres, ceo, dir: Bancal Tri-State Corp.

Gomory, Ralph E., pres, trust, mem exec & investment comms: Sloan Foundation, Alfred P.

Gonnason, Jeff, Cook Inlet Region

Gonnerman, Mary Frances, secy, treas: MFA Foundation

Gonring, Mathew P., trust: USG Foundation

Gonzales, Robert, vp, secy: Macht Foundation, Morton and Sophia

Gonzalez, C. D., asst secy: ASARCO Foundation

Gonzalez, Celso M., dir, pres: Gilman, Jr. Foundation, Sondra and Charles

Gonzalez, Fausto, dir: Butler Foundation, J. Homer

Gonzalez, Patricia W., contributions coordinator: Niagara Mohawk Power Corp.

Gonzalez, Roy Diaz, dir: Haghenbeck Foundation, Antonio Y. De La Lama

Gonzalez-Falla, Celson M., vp: Gilman and Gonzalez-Falla Theatre Foundation

Gonzalez-Falla, Sondra Gilman, pres: Gilman and Gonzalez-Falla Theatre Foundation

Gooch, Walter L., trust: Ashland Oil Foundation

Good, Kenneth M., chmn: Gulfstream Housing Corp.

Good, Lewis R., dir: Smith Foundation

Good, Robert Alan, MD, trust: Dana Charitable Trust, Eleanor Naylor

Goodale, Irene E., trust: Peterloon Foundation

Goodall, John C., III, dir, secy: Thorson Foundation

Goodall, John C., Jr., treas: Hay Foundation, John I.

Goodall, Virginia T., dir, vp, treas: Thorson Foundation

Goodalls, Kimberly, secy economics: Akzo Chemicals Inc.

Goodban, Nicholas, vp (philanthropy): McCormick Tribune Foundation, Robert R.

Goode, David R., vp: Norfolk Southern Foundation

Goodell, Joseph, pres, ceo: Outokumpu- American Brass Co.

Goodell, Richard, pres: U.S. Silica Co.

Gooden, Andrea, program mgr (ed grants): Apple Computer

Goodes, Melvin Russell, chmn, ceo, dir: Warner-Lambert Co.

Goodhardt, Alan, trust, vp: Macht Foundation, Morton and Sophia

Gooding, Lucy B., trust: Gooding Charitable Foundation, Luca

Goodley-Thomas, Mary, vp, fin and admin: Grant Foundation, William T.

Goodman, Alvin S., trust: Schamach Foundation, Milton

Goodman, Barbara F., trust: Goodman Family Foundation

Goodman, Charles B., trust: Crown Charitable Fund, Edward A.; vp, dir: Crown Memorial, Arie and Ida; dir: Goodman Foundation, Edward and Marion

Goodman, David L., vp: Clorox Company Foundation

Goodman, Harold S., trust: Messing Family Charitable Foundation

Goodman, Jack, secy, treas: Schamach Foundation, Milton

Goodman, Marian, trust: Goldenberg Foundation, Max

Goodman, Maurice, trust: Harvard Apparatus Foundation

Goodman, Morris, pres: Goodman Jewelers, Inc.

Goodman, Roy M., trust: Goodman Family Foundation

Goodmon, James F., pres, dir: Fletcher Foundation, A. J.

Goodmon, Raymond H., III, dir: Fletcher Foundation, A. J.

Goodpaster, Andrew J., trust: German Marshall Fund of the United States

Goodrich, Dennett W., trust: Dennett Foundation, Marie G.

Goodrich, Dorothy, treas: Truman Foundation, Mildred Faulkner

Goodrich, Enid, vchmn: Thirty-Five Twenty, Inc.; vchmn: Winchester Foundation

Goodrich, Harry Lee, secy: Dan River Foundation

Goodrich, John A., trust: Dennett Foundation, Marie G.

Goodrich, M. K., chmn, pres, ceo: Moore Business Forms, Inc.

Goodrich, T. Michael, pres, dir: BE&K Inc.

Goodsell, Jill, adm, dir: Foster Foundation

Goodson, R. Eugene, chmn, ceo: Oshkosh Truck Corp.

Goodstein, Carol, dir: Goodstein Family Foundation, David

Goodstein, Robert, vp: Goodstein Family Foundation, David

Goodwin, David A., asst secy, asst treas, dir: Finley Foundation, A. E.

Goodwin, David P., trust: Cogswell Benevolent Trust

Goodwin, Francis B., pres: Goodwin Foundation, Leo

Goodwin, Neva R., trust: Rockefeller Brothers Fund

Goodwin, P. J., pres, ceo: Miller & Co.

Goodwin, Peter, vp (fin monitoring): Johnson Foundation, Robert Wood

Goodwin, Robert L., trust: Booth-Bricker Fund

Goodwin, Todd, chmn: Ladish Co.

Goodwin, William M., treas, secy: Lilly Endowment

Goodwyn, William H., Jr., trust: Lawyers Title Foundation

Goody, John J., vp, cfo: Rust International Corp.

Goodyear, Frank H., trust: Goodyear Foundation, Josephine; pres: Independence Foundation

Goodyear, Patricia O., secy: Price Associates Foundation, T. Rowe

Goodyear, Robert M., vp: Goodyear Foundation, Josephine

Goolsby, Durward M., trust: Fasken Foundation

Goolsby, John L., ceo, pres: Summa Development Corp.

Gorant, Anthony, vp: Ohio Edison Corp.

Gordan, Patricia, trust: Gould Foundation for Children, Edwin

Gordan, Roger L., ceo, pres: San Francisco Federal Savings & Loan Association

Gordon, Alvin A., pres, exec dir: Lowenstein Foundation, William P. and Marie R.

Gordon, Aron Samuel, vp, treas, trust: Gordon Foundation, Meyer and Ida

Gordon, Bernard Marshall, vchmn, dir: Analogic Corp.; trust: Gordon Foundation

Gordon, Bernice W., secy: Gordon Family Foundation, Joel C. and Bernice W.

Gordon, Elaine K., trust: Lowenstein Foundation, William P. and Marie R.

Gordon, Ellen R., pres: Rubin Family Fund, Cele H. and William B.; pres, coo, dir: Tootsie Roll Industries, Inc.

Gordon, George M., trust: Norris Foundation, Kenneth T. and Eileen L.

Gordon, H. Roy, trust: Foster Charitable Trust

Gordon, Harry B., pres, trust: Gordon Foundation, Meyer and Ida

Gordon, J. M., pres: Mid-Continent Supply Co.

Gordon, James C., vp, trust: Gordon Foundation, Meyer and Ida

Gordon, Jeffrey W., vp (corp commun rels): Meridian Bancorp

Gordon, Joel C., pres: Gordon Family Foundation, Joel C. and Bernice W.

Gordon, John E., pres, trust: Bloedel Foundation

Gordon, Jonathan R., trust: Mailman Family Foundation, A. L.

Gordon, Joseph G., treas, trust: Reynolds Foundation, Z. Smith

Gordon, Joseph K., trust: McLean Contributionship

Gordon, Lois, vp, dir: Fleishhacker Foundation

Gordon, Marshall D., trust: Lowenstein Foundation, William P. and Marie R.

Gordon, Melvin J., chmn, ceo: Tootsie Roll Industries, Inc.

Gordon, Melvin Jay, vp, dir: Rubin Family Fund, Cele H. and William B.

Gordon, Raymond J., trust: Gordon Charitable Trust, Peggy and Yale

Gordon, Richard, pres: Columbia Gas Distribution Cos.

Gordon, Robert, trust: Lowenstein Foundation, William P. and Marie R.

Gordon, Sophia, trust: Gordon Foundation

Gordon, Steven C., pres, ceo: Domino of California; dir: Domino Foundation

Gordon, Thomas Christian, Jr., trust: Gray Foundation, Garland

Gordon, Thomas J., vp: Colorado State Bank Foundation

Gordon, William W., pres: Stern Foundation, Charles H. and Anna S.

Gore, Carol, Cook Inlet Region

Gore, George H., trust: Gore Family Memorial Foundation

Gore, Robert H., Jr., trust: Gore Family Memorial Foundation

Gore, Theodore H., trust: Gore Family Memorial Foundation

Gore, Thomas P., II, vp (communications): Johnson Foundation, Robert Wood

Gorham, David L., sr vp, treas: New York Times Co. Foundation

Gorham, John, mem distribution comm, mem investigating comm: Champlin Foundations

Gorin, William, trust: Gorin Foundation, Nehemiah

Goriup, Mary A., mgr: Hedco Foundation

Gorman, Edmund J., sr vp, cfo: Morrison-Knudsen Corp.

Gorman, Joseph M., secy: General American Charitable Foundation

Gorman, Joseph Tolle, chmn, ceo: TRW Corp.

Gorman, Kenneth J., pres, dir: Atlantic Mutual Cos.

Gorman, Leon A., pres, dir: Bean, L.L.

Gorman, Marguerite, treas: Kellogg Foundation, Peter and Cynthia K.

Gorman, Maureen V., vp: GTE Foundation

Gorman, Michael R., exec dir: Irwin Charity Foundation, William G.

Gormley, Dennis James, chmn, ceo, dir: Federal-Mogul Corp.; mem contributions comm: Federal-Mogul Corp. Charitable Trust Fund

Gormley, Patrick A., vp: Bacon Foundation, E. L. and Oma

Gormley, T. P., dir (mktg): Buffalo Color Corp.

Gorr, Ivan W., chmn, ceo: Cooper Tire & Rubber Co.

Gorran, Gary M., asst treas: Johnson & Johnson Family of Cos. Contribution Fund; treas: Rutgers Community Health Foundation

Gorski, Walter Joseph, vp, dir: Connecticut Mutual Life Foundation

Gorsuch, Charles A., treas: McIntire Educational Fund, John

Gorzynski, Gregory, trust: Johnson Foundation, Barbara P.

Goschi, Nicholas P., trust: Comer Foundation

Gosline, Walter W., bd mem: Gardiner Scholarship Foundation

Gosnell, M. Ann, asst secy: Corning Incorporated Foundation

Goss, Janet Reed, trust: Thendara Foundation

Gossage, Thomas L., chmn, ceo: Hercules Inc.

Gossen, Jim, dir: Norwest Foundation

Gossett, William T., vp, dir: Hughes Memorial Foundation, Charles Evans

Gostomski, Michael, dir: Hiawatha Education Foundation

Gother, Ronald E., asst secy: Lund Foundation

Gotlieb, Jacquelin, MD, dir: Georgia Health Foundation

Gotschall, G.D., secy: Sifco Foundation

Gotschall, Jeffrey P., ceo, pres: Sifco Industries Inc.; trust: Sifco Foundation

Gottesman, David Sanford, pres, dir: Gottesman Fund

Gottesman, Esther, vp, dir: Gottesman Fund

Gottesman, Jerome W., trust: de Hirsch Fund, Baron

Gottesman, Milton M., secy: Gottesman Fund

Gottesman, Robert W., treas: Gottesman Fund

Gottesman, Ruth L., vp, dir: Gottesman Fund

Gottleib, Robert, secy: Mayer Foundation, Louis B.

Gottlieb, Art, dir: Gumbiner Foundation, Josephine

Gottlieb, Harold, trust: Shinnick Educational Fund, William M.

Gottlieb, Jerome H., first vp: Israel Discount Bank of New York

Gottlieb, Meyer, treas, dir: Goldwyn Foundation, Samuel

Gottlieb, Richard D., pres, ceo, dir: Lee Enterprises

Gottlieb, Richard Douglas, vp, dir: Lee Foundation

Gottscalk, Alfred, MD, adv: Bronstein Foundation, Sol and Arlene

Gottschalk, Ernest J., pres: Weller Foundation

Gottstein, Robert, Cook Inlet Region

Gottwald, Anne Cobb, vp: Gottwald Foundation

Gottwald, Bruce Cobb, ceo, pres, coo, dir: Ethyl Corp.; secy, treas: Gottwald Foundation

Gottwald, Elisabeth S., trust: Herndon Foundation

Gottwald, Floyd Dewey, Jr., chmn, chmn exec comm, dir: Ethyl Corp.; pres: Gottwald Foundation; trust: Herndon Foundation

Gottwald, John D., chmn, pres, ceo: Tredegar Industries

Gotwalt, Norma, dir: Shoemaker Trust for Shoemaker Scholarship Fund, Ray S.

Goudy, Garry A., mem screening comm: PPG Industries Foundation

Goudy, Grace Collins, fdr, vp, dir: Collins Foundation

Gould, David, vp (corp commun): Fujitsu America, Inc.

Gould, Edward P., chmn distribution comm: English Memorial Fund, Florence C. and H. L.; chmn distribution comm: Marshall Trust in Memory of Sanders McDaniel, Harriet McDaniel; chmn: Trust Co. Bank

Gould, Hermia, secy, treas: Reicher Foundation, Anne & Harry J.

Gould, Irving, chmn, ceo, dir: Commodore International Ltd.

Gould, Lawrence K., Jr., trust: Martin Foundation, Della

Gould, Michael, chmn, ceo: Bloomingdale's

Gould, Paul A., vp: Allen Brothers Foundation

Gould, Robert L., pres: Eastern Air Lines

Gould, W. Thomas, chmn, dir: Younkers, Inc.

Gould, William Thomas, pres: Younkers Foundation

Goulet, Victor N., chmn, dir: Imperial Corp. of America

Gow, Anne Paxton Wagley, dir: Penney Foundation, James C.

Gowan, Alastair C., pres, ceo, dir: Brown Inc., John

Gowen, George W., trust: Christodora

Gowen, May A., trust: Attleboro Pawtucket Savings Bank Charitable Foundation

Gower, Bob G., pres, ceo, dir: Lyondell Petrochemical Co.

Gowland, Brian, coo: San Diego Trust & Savings Bank

Grabel, Jeffrey N., dir, secy: Loewenberg Foundation

Graber, Robert, dir: Lee Foundation, James T.

Graber, Samuel W., mem bd govs: Mayor Foundation, Oliver Dewey

Grabiak, Nancy L., secy, treas: Vicksburg Foundation

Grable, Minnie K., Grable Foundation

Grabowski, Gary G., exec dir, treas, dir: Beloit Foundation; treas, evec dir: Neese Family Foundation

Grace, Caroline, dir: Alice Manufacturing Co. Foundation

Grace, Helen K., vp (programming): Kellogg Foundation, W. K.

Grace, J. Peter, chmn, dir: Grace & Co., W.R.; pres, dir: Santa Maria Foundation

Grace, Karl, dir, treas: Hornblower Fund, Henry

Grace, Margaret F., pres, dir: East Foundation, Sarita Kenedy; trust: Santa Maria Foundation

Grace, Mary A., advisory com: Powers Higher Educational Fund, Edward W. and Alice R.

Grace, Patrick P., dir, secy: Santa Maria Foundation

Grace, Philip M., treas: MacArthur Foundation, John D. and Catherine T.

Grace, Timothy, Stanley Charitable Foundation, A. W.

Gracia-Kennedy, Norma, trust: McKesson Foundation

Gracida, Rev. Rene Henry, pres, dir: Kenedy Memorial Foundation, John G. and Marie Stella

Grade, Donald L., secy-treas: Greenheck Foundation

Grader, Evelyn L., vp: Grader Foundation, K. W.

Gradison, Willis David, Jr., trust: Rice Foundation, Helen Steiner

Grado, John, Jr., trust: Wallace Foundation, George R.

Gradowski, Stanley Joseph, Jr., secy, dir: Chicago Tribune Foundation

Grady, G. J., gen mgr: Harper Brush Works

Grady, Henry W., Jr., dir: Zimmermann Fund, Marie and John

Grady, John, chmn: Grady Management

Grady, Stafford Robert, dir: Mead Foundation, Giles W. and Elise G.

Graf, Alan B., Jr., sr vp, cfo: Federal Express Corp.

Graf, Bayard M., secy, treas: Arronson Foundation

Graf, Joseph C., exec secy: Cullen Foundation

Graf, Kenneth F., trust: Smith Charitable Foundation, Lou and Lutza

Graf, Paul E., pres, ceo: Johnson Inc., Axel

Graf, Thomas J., vp: Principal Financial Group; chmn: Principal Financial Group Foundation

Grafer, W. D., treas: National Standard Foundation

Grafton, Stephen J., chmn, ceo: Glendale Federal Bank

Gragstein, Bernice, dir: Grass Foundation

Graham, Arnold Harold, trust: Jones Foundation, Walter S. and Evan E.

Graham, Betty Harrison, trust: Graham Charitable Trust, William L.

Graham, Bruce J., chmn: Skidmore, Owings & Merrill Foundation

Graham, Carolyn C., trust: Carolyn Foundation

Graham, Donald, dir: Rice Foundation

Graham, Donald E., pres, ceo, dir: Washington Post Co.

Graham, Donald Edward, trust: Graham Fund, Philip L.

Graham, Edith A., vp, dir: Overbrook Foundation

Graham, Irene T., secy-treas: Homasote Foundation

Graham, J. Leonard, vp: Bryan Foundation, Dodd and Dorothy L.

Graham, J.H., secy, trust: Crawford & Co. Foundation

Graham, John K., vp, secy, dir: Knox Family Foundation

Graham, Katharine Meyer, trust, don wife: Graham Fund, Philip L.; chmn, dir: Washington Post Co.

Graham, M.F., dir, vp: Bordeaux Foundation

Graham, Martha, mgr (precollegiate pub ed): Chemical Bank

Graham, Patricia Albjerg, PhD, trust: Hitachi Foundation; mem exec comm: Macy, Jr. Foundation, Josiah; pres, dir: Spencer Foundation

Graham, Randy A., sr vp: Bank One, Texas-Houston Office

Graham, Robert C., Jr., dir: Overbrook Foundation

Graham, Robert M., treas: Eccles Foundation, George S. and Dolores Dore

Graham, Stan, cfo: Consolidated Electrical Distributors

Graham, Stanley E., trust: Hill Crest Foundation

Graham, W. E., Jr., vchmn, dir: Carolina Power & Light Co.; vp, secy: CP&L Foundation

Graham, William B., sr chmn, dir: Baxter International; dir: Baxter Foundation

Grainger, David W., pres, treas, dir, don: Grainger Foundation; chmn, pres: Grainger, W.W.

Grainger, J. P., vp, asst secy, dir: Grainger Foundation

Graitcer, Leslie, assoc dir: BellSouth Foundation

Gralen, Donald John, dir: Bergner Foundation, P.A.

Gram, W. Dunbar, trust: Johnston Trust for Charitable and Educational Purposes, James M.

Gramelspacher, Eugene J., secy, treas, dir: Jasper Wood Products Co. Foundation

Gramelspacher, G. H., vp, dir: Jasper Wood Products Co. Foundation

Gramelspacher, G. W., dir: Jasper Wood Products Co. Foundation

Gramelspacher, Glenn H., DCB Foundation; dir: Jasper Seating Foundation

Gramelspacher, John W., pres: Jasper Desk Co.; dir: Jasper Desk Foundation; pres, dir: Jasper Wood Products Co. Foundation

Grammer, Carrie, asst dir: Wal-Mart Foundation

Grandinetti, James, secy, treas: Havens Foundation, O. W.

Grandis, Harry, secy: Gumenick Foundation, Nathan and Sophie

Grandon, Carleen, dir: Hall Foundation

Granger, Jack, dir: Morrison Knudsen Corp. Foundation Inc.

Granieri, Vincent J., vp, cfo: Midland Mutual Life Insurance Co.

Graniero, Mary, secy: Reader's Digest Foundation

Granitow, W. W., secy, dir: Koulaieff Educational Fund, Trustees of Ivan Y.

Granoff, Clement N., trust: Hilliard Foundation

Granoff, Leonard, trust: Koffler Family Foundation

Granoien, Linda J., mem exec contributions comm: Northern States Power Co.

Granson, Peter A., trust: Reynolds & Reynolds Company Foundation

Grant, Debra Ann, trust: Dauch Foundation, William

Grant, Fred Russell, trust: Irwin Charity Foundation, William G.; dir: McIntire Educational Fund, John

Grant, H. L., pres: Grant-Norpac, Inc.

Grant, Harold A., sr vp (mktg & sales): Brooke Group Ltd.

Grant, Irene, trust: Swasey Fund for Relief of Public School Teachers of Newburyport

Grant, Joseph M., vp, cfo: Electronic Data Systems Corp.

Grant, Munro J., trust, pres: Pittsburgh Child Guidance Foundation

Grant, R. Gene, pres, dir: Cheney Foundation, Ben B.

Grant, Raymond, treas: Hopedale Foundation

Grant, Richard A., Jr., vp, trust: Murphy Foundation, Dan

Grant, Stephen, Sofia American Schools

Grant, William A., co-chmn oper: Ernst & Young

Grant, William R., trust: Cary Charitable Trust, Mary Flagler

Grant, William W., III, trust: Gates Foundation

Grantham, J., vp: Manville Fund

Granucci, Judy D., fin off: BankAmerica Foundation

Grasmere, Robert H., pres, trust: Turrell Fund

Grass, A. M., pres: Grass Instrument Co.

Grass, Albert M., vp, dir: Grass Foundation

Grass, Alexander, chmn, dir: Grass Family Foundation; chmn: Rite Aid Corp.

Grass, E. R., treas: Grass Instrument Co.

Grass, Ellen R., pres, dir: Grass Foundation

Grass, Henry J., MD, dir: Grass Foundation

Grass, Martin Lehrman, dir: Grass Family Foundation; vchmn: Rite Aid Corp.

Grass, Mary G., secy, dir: Grass Foundation

Grasso, Richard A., exec vchmn, pres: New York Stock Exchange

Gratton, James, trust: Eastman Foundation, Alexander

Grau, Juan, pres, ceo: Bacardi Imports

Graubard, Seymour, vchmn bd, vchmn exec comm: Gulf USA Corp.

Gravelle, Frederick, contributions mgr: Wilson Trust, Lula C.

Gravelle, Peter W., vp, cfo, treas: Kysor Industrial Corp.

Graver, Irene C., exec dir: Truman Foundation, Mildred Faulkner

Graves, A. P., mem: Cannon Foundation

Graves, Beverly Garner, trust: Garner Charitable Trust, James G.

Graves, Frances B., vp, secy: Graves Foundation

Graves, Michael, dir: Skidmore, Owings & Merrill Foundation

Graves, Milton T., vp, assoc dir: Cockrell Foundation

Graves, William M., pres, treas, don: Graves Foundation

Gray, Barry W., vp, dir: Israel Foundation, A. Cremieux

Gray, Bruce B., trust: Gray Foundation, Garland

Gray, Charles, trust: Demos Foundation, N.

Gray, Charles C., treas: Wood-Claeyssens Foundation

Gray, Charles D., III, trust: Nanney Foundation, Charles and Irene

Gray, D. L., exec dir, mem, dir: Cannon Foundation

Gray, Elizabeth B., trust: Berry Foundation, Loren M.

Gray, Elmon T., pres, treas, trust: Gray Foundation, Garland

Gray, Garland, II, trust: Gray Foundation, Garland

Gray, Hanna H., PhD, dir: Ameritech Foundation; dir: Cummins Engine Foundation; dir: Field Foundation of Illinois; trust: Hughes Medical Institute, Howard; trust: Mellon Foundation, Andrew W.

Gray, James, pres: Burdines

Gray, James W., Jr., chmn: Conn Memorial Foundation

Gray, John B., exec dir, exec secy, dir: Cooke Foundation Corporation, V. V.; pres, coo, dir: Dennison Manufacturing Co.; trust: Dennison Foundation

Gray, Lawrence, pres: Heil Co.

Gray, Lyons, trust: Whitehead Foundation, Lettie Pate

Gray, Malinda E., asst secy: Jones Intercable Tampa Trust

Gray, Margaret Owen, trust: Owen Foundation

Gray, Mrs. J. Ronald, trust: Wolf Foundation, Benjamin and Fredora K.

Gray, R.S., trust: Sifco Foundation

Gray, Walter Franklin, vchmn: Mercantile Bank Co. Charitable Trust

Gray, Winnifred P., trust: Perkin Fund

Graybill, Charles S., MD, chmn, trust: McMahon Foundation

Graziadio, George L., vice-chmn, pres: Imperial Bancorp; dir: Imperial Bank Foundation

Greaney, L. J., contr: Campbell Soup Foundation

Greathead, R. Scott, dir: Sperry Fund

Grecky, Joseph M., dir: Reader's Digest Foundation

Greco, Jerome D., sr vp, dir commun aff: First Fidelity Bancorporation

Greco, Mary, mem adv comm: Pott Foundation, Herman T. and Phenie R.

Greehey, William E., chmn, ceo, dir: Valero Energy Corp.

Greelee, Bertha A., trust, pres, treas: Anderson Foundation

Greeley, Gwen, commun mgr: Peerless Insurance Co.

Greeley, Joseph B., trust: Bernstein & Co. Foundation, Sanford C.

Green, Amelia, program assoc: HCA Foundation

Green, B. J., secy: Alexander & Baldwin Foundation

Green, Carl, trust: Hitachi Foundation

Green, Cecil Howard, trust: Green Foundation

Green, Cyril, pres, coo: Meyer, Inc., Fred

Green, Don C., dir: Mid-Iowa Health Foundation

Green, Dorothy, Green Foundation, Burton E.

Green, Ellen Z., MD, dir: Bush Foundation

Green, Friday A., trust: Taylor Foundation, Ruth and Vernon

Green, Jean McGreevy, vp, secy: Westport Fund

Green, Joe M., Jr., pres, fdn mgr: Rockwell Fund

Green, Joshua, III, vchmn, ceo: U.S. Bank of Washington

Green, Kenneth R., dir (contributions): United Technologies Corp.

Green, Michael, vp, dir: Loewy Family Foundation

Green, Nancy H., pres: Equitable Foundation

Green, Patricia, dir: Green Fund

Green, Pauline, dir: Feinstein Foundation, Myer and Rosaline

Green, R. Thomas, secy: McVay Foundation; chmn, pres, ceo: Oglebay Norton Co.

Green, Raymond S., trust: Presser Foundation

Green, Richard, pres: Barton-Gillet Co.

Green, Richard C., Jr., vp: Utilicorp United Charitable Foundation

Green, S. William, secy, treas, don son: Green Fund

Green, Sharon, mktg asst: Ryland Group

Greenawalt, Diane, secy contributions comm: Delmarva Power & Light Co.

Greenawalt, Eileen, secy, trust: Bonfils-Stanton Foundation

Greenbaum, Maurice C., secy, dir: Mandeville Foundation; secy: Rosenstiel Foundation

Greenberg, Alan C., pres, treas: Greenberg Foundation, Alan C.

Greenberg, Barbara R., exec dir: Burden Foundation, Florence V.

Greenberg, David H., trust: Berenson Charitable Foundation, Theodore W. and Evelyn

Greenberg, Frank Standard, chmn, ceo: Burlington Industries

Greenberg, Jack, secy: Cohen Foundation, Wilfred P.

Greenberg, Martin S., DDS, dir: Group Health Foundation

Greenberg, Maurice Raymond, chmn: American International Group, Inc.; chmn bd, dir: Starr Foundation

Greenberg, Maynard, vp, secy, dir: Greenberg Foundation, Alan C.

Greenberg, Michael, treas: Newman Assistance Fund, Jerome A. and Estelle R.

Greenberg, Steven, dir: Three Swallows Foundation

Greenberg, Susan, dir: Buffett Foundation

Greenblatt, Maurice, chmn, ceo: United Van Lines, Inc.

Greene, A. Crawford, Jr., dir: Babcock Memorial Endowment, William

Greene, Alan I., pres, dir: Greene Foundation, David J.

Greene, Andrew R., exec vp (fin), treas, trust: Johnson Foundation, Robert Wood

Greene, Anne Johnston, trust: Orleton Trust Fund

Greene, Anne S., vp, trust: Dayton Foundation Depository

Greene, Dana, secy, treas: Murphy Foundation

Greene, Danita, vp: McVay Foundation

Greene, David E., cfo, exec vp: Young & Rubicam; treas, dir: Young & Rubicam Foundation

Greene, Dawn, dir: Greene Foundation, Jerome L.

Greene, Donald Ray, pres, dir: Coca-Cola Foundation

Greene, Emory, mgr: Porter Testamentary Trust, James Hyde

Greene, Hal, trust: Seafirst Foundation

Greene, James R., treas, dir: Greene Foundation, David J.

Greene, Jeanne M., dir: Lincoln Fund

Greene, Jerome L., pres, dir: Greene Foundation, Jerome L.

Greene, John Frederick, dir: Louisiana Land & Exploration Co. Foundation

Greene, John K., trust: Kaul Foundation Trust, Hugh

Greene, Marion E., pres: LEF Foundation

Greene, Michael, dir: Greene Foundation, David J.

Greene, O. G., pres, ceo: National Data Corp.

Greene, Oscar, trust: Eastman Foundation, Alexander

Greene, Richard L., dir: Koret Foundation

Greenebaum, L. M., dir: Legg & Co. Foundation

Greenewalt, David, adv trust, don grandson: Crystal Trust

Greenfield, Bruce Harold, trust: Greenfield Foundation, Albert M.

Greenfield, Jerry, co-fdr, vchp, dir: Ben & Jerry's Homemade; fdr, pres: Ben & Jerry's Foundation

Greenfield, Julius, trust: Goldie-Anna Charitable Trust

Greenfield, Majorie H., trust: Hanson Testamentary Charitable Trust, Anna Emery

Greenfield, Robert Kauffman, trust, pres: Rosenberg Foundation, Alexis

Greenheck, Bernard A., pres, treas: Greenheck Fan Corp.; pres: Greenheck Foundation

Greenheck, Robert C., vp: Greenheck Foundation

Greenhill, Hy, chmn: Fraida Foundation

Greenhill, Mark A., vp: Fraida Foundation

Greenhill, Michael L., vp: Fraida Foundation

Greenland, Thomas, asst secy, asst treas: Kentland Foundation

Greenleaf, Arline Ripley, trust: Sprague Educational and Charitable Foundation, Seth

Greenleaf, Gracemary B., secy, dir: Animal Assistance Foundation

Greenlee, P.E., trust: Nelson Foundation, Florence

Greenman, Norman L., prees, ceo: Rogers Corp.

Greenough, Benjamin, dir: Bank of the Orient Foundation

Greenough, Julia M., dir: Morania Foundation

Greenspan, Ethel, vp: Greenspan Foundation

Greenspan, Saul, pres: Greenspan Foundation

Greenstein, Rachel, community affairs mgr: Unilever United States Foundation

Greenwalt, Clifford L., pres, ceo, dir: Central Illinois Public Service Co.

Greenway, Diane V., trust: Verney Foundation, Gilbert

Greenwood, Fred M., secy: Ashland Oil Foundation

Greenwood, John L., trust: Geneseo Foundation

Greer, C. Scott, pres, dir: Echlin Inc.

Greer, Colin, pres: New World Foundation

Greer, David S., trust: Jaffe Foundation

Greer, George C., dir: Eden Hall Foundation

Greer, Jackie, admin comm mem: McDonald Foundation, Tillie and Tom

Greer, Margaret Weyerhaeuser Jewett, trust: Jewett Foundation, George Frederick

Greer, William Hershey, Jr., trust: Jewett Foundation, George Frederick

Greevy, Charles F., III, dir, vp: Plankenhorn Foundation, Harry

Grefenstette, C. G., vp, dir: Hillman Foundation

Grefenstette, C.G., dir: Polk Foundation

Grefenstette, Carl G., pres, ceo, dir: Hillman Co.

Gregg, Davis Weinert, trust: Kynett Memorial Foundation, Edna G.

Gregoire, Jerome D., vp, dir: ITT Rayonier Foundation

Gregorian, Vartan, dir: Diamond Foundation, Aaron; trust: Getty Trust, J. Paul

Gregory, C. E., III, dir: Livingston Foundation

Gregory, Jean E., vp, treas: Skillman Foundation

Gregory, Paul S., bd mem: Salvatori Foundation, Henry

Gregory, R. Neal, exec secy: Bradley-Turner Foundation

Gregory, Victor A., secy distribution comm: English Memorial Fund, Florence C. and H. L.; secy distribution comm: Marshall Trust in Memory of Sanders McDaniel, Harriet McDaniel; secy: Trust Co. of Georgia Foundation; trust: Wardlaw Fund, Gertrude and William C.

Gregson, Darryl R., pres, ceo, dir: Victory Markets, Inc.

Greif, Arnon C., admin, trust: Agway Foundation

Greil, Gail Danner, dir: Danner Foundation

Greilsheimer, Louise, trust: Lavanburg-Corner House

Grein, David E., sr vp, treas: Lipton Foundation, Thomas J.

Greiveldinger, Harold, treas: Johnson Foundation

Gremban, Joe L., dir, pres: Sierra Pacific Resources Charitable Foundation

Grenier, Helen P., trust: Philippe Foundation

Grenz, M. Kay, dir: 3M Co.

Grenzebach, Martin, chmn: Grenzebach & Associates, John

Gresham, J. T., pres, gen mgr, treas: Callaway Foundation; pres, gen mgr, treas: Callaway Foundation, Fuller E.

Gressette, Lawrence, ceo, chmn: South Carolina Electric & Gas Co.

Gressette, Lawrence M., Jr., chmn, pres, ceo: SCANA Corp.; trust: Summer Foundation

Grewcock, William L., vchmn: Kiewit Sons, Peter

Grey, Carol M., asst secy: CertainTeed Corp. Foundation

Grieb, Warren, dir: Katzenberger Foundation

Grieb, Warren E., chmn: Advertising Checking Bureau

Grier, Joseph W., Jr., dir: Ginter Foundation, Karl and Anna

Grier, Joseph Williamson, Jr., vp: Giles Foundation, Edward C.

Grier, Patricia, mgr, trust: Langendorf Foundation, Stanley S.

Gries, Robert D., comm: Gries Charity Fund, Lucile and Robert H.; pres, trust: Gries Family Foundation

Gries, Sally P., secy, treas, trust: Gries Family Foundation

Grieve, Pierson MacDonald, chmn, pres, ceo: Ecolab

Griffin, Dale G., trust: Miller Foundation

Griffin, Donald R., dir: Guggenheim Foundation, Harry Frank

Griffin, Donald W., trust: Olin Corp. Charitable Trust

Griffin, Elsie R., chmn, trust: Griffin, Sr., Foundation, C. V.

Griffin, Glenn J., exec vp, cfo: Bruno's Inc.

Griffin, James B., dir: Ryder System Charitable Foundation

Griffin, James T., vp, asst secy, gen coun: MacArthur Foundation, John D. and Catherine T.

Griffin, John A., Jr., trust: Tiger Foundation

Griffin, John H., Jr., chmn, trust: Smyth Trust, Marion C.

Griffin, Leslie, dir: Boston Globe Foundation

Griffin, Louis Austin, secy: Blount Foundation

Griffin, Michelle D., mem: Northern Trust Co. Charitable Trust

Griffin, Patrick, vp: Makita U.S.A., Inc.

Griffin, Terry, sr vp: TU Electric Co.

Griffin, W.L. Hadley, trust: Brown Foundation, George Warren

Griffin, William Lester Hadley, mem bd control: Brown Group Incorporated Charitable Trust

Griffin, William M., vp: Hillman Family Foundation, Alex

Griffis, Hughes, secy, treas, dir: Griffis Foundation

Griffis, Nixon, pres, dir: Griffis Foundation

Griffith, Alan Richard, pres, coo: Bank of New York

Griffith, Charles P., Jr., adv: Griffith Foundation, W. C.

Griffith, David H., pres, trust: Walker Foundation, Archie D. and Bertha H.

Griffith, Elwanda, mem loan comm: Lindsay Student Aid Fund, Franklin

Griffith, J. Larry, trust: Carver Charitable Trust, Roy J.

Griffith, James M., dir: Amoco Foundation

Griffith, Jim, vp (pub aff): BFGoodrich

Griffith, Katherine S., vp (corp commun): Canadian Imperial Bank of Commerce

Griffith, Katherine W., trust: Walker Foundation, Archie D. and Bertha H.

Griffith, Lawrence S. C., vp, dir: Surdna Foundation

Griffith, Mary Lavinia, vp: Summerlee Foundation

Griffith, Patricia K., secy: Warren Charite; asst secy: Warren Foundation, William K.

Griffith, Vincent A., Jr., contact person: Pfriem Foundation, Norma F.

Griffith, W. C., Jr., adv: Griffith Foundation, W. C.

Griffith, Walter S., adv: Griffith Foundation, W. C.

Griffith, William C., III, adv: Griffith Foundation, W. C.

Griffiths, Andrea Q., vp, dir: Staunton Farm Foundation

Griffiths, Clark, trust: Mascoma Savings Bank Foundation

Griffiths, Richard, dir: Beech Aircraft Foundation

Grigal, Dennis, trust: Donaldson Foundation

Grigg, William Humphrey, pres: Duke Power Co. Foundation

Griggs, C. E. Bayliss, dir: Griggs and Mary Griggs Burke Foundation, Mary Livingston

Griggs, Karen, dir: Quad City Osteopathic Foundation

Griggs, T. H., asst secy: Hillsdale Fund

Grigsby, Lonnie O., dir: IBP Foundation, Inc., The

Grimes, Charles B., Jr., trust: Homeland Foundation

Grimes, J. William, pres, coo: Multimedia, Inc.

Grimes, L. E., treas, trust: Fair Play Foundation

Grimes, Susan H., corp secy, program off: Weingart Foundation

Grimm, Debra Mills, trust: Mills Charitable Foundation, Henry L. and Kathryn

Grimm, Jeffrey, cfo: Portland Food Products Co.

Grimm, Ronald L., secy, treas, trust: Toms Foundation

Grindstaff, E. Douglas, pres, ceo: Genesco

Grinstein, Gerald, chmn, ceo: Burlington Northern Inc.

Grinstien, Gerald, vchmn, dir: Burlington Resources

Grisanti, Eugene Philip, chmn, pres, ceo, dir: International Flavors & Fragrances; pres, dir: IFF Foundation; dir: Monell Foundation, Ambrose; dir: Vetlesen Foundation, G. Unger

Grisi, Jeanmarie C., treas: Carnegie Corporation of New York

Grissom, S. L., secy, treas, dir: Lumpkin Foundation

Griswold, Benjamin Howell, IV, chmn, managing dir: Brown & Sons, Alex; chmn: Brown & Sons Charitable Foundation, Alex

Gritton, Mark T., dir: Deluxe Corp. Foundation

Grodin, Jay, secy, dir: Weisz Foundation, David and Sylvia

Groh, Donna, vp, coo: Irvine Medical Center

Groman, Arthur, pres: Occidental Petroleum Charitable Foundation

Groner, E. B., MD, secy, dir: Kenedy Memorial Foundation, John G. and Marie Stella

Gronewaldt, Alice Busch, pres, dir: Gronewaldt Foundation, Alice Busch

Grooms, Jack D., pres, treas: Valdese Manufacturing Co., Inc.; pres, treas, dir: Valdese Manufacturing Co. Foundation

Groos, Alexander M., secy, treas, trust: Buell Foundation, Temple Hoyne

Grosberg, Julius, asst treas, trust: Gerstacker Foundation, Rollin M.

Grosc, Harriet, dir: Rosenhaus Peace Foundation, Sarah and Matthew

Grose, William E., trust: Warfield Memorial Fund, Anna Emory

Gross, Bert, asst secy: Regis Foundation

Gross, Carl R., trust: Cox Foundation of Georgia, James M.; trust, treas: Cox, Jr. Foundation, James M.

Gross, Charles T., trust: Durr-Fillauer Medical Foundation

Gross, Eugene, vp (human resources): TBG, Inc.

Gross, Hillel A., dir: House of Gross Foundation

Gross, Jack M., pres: House of Gross; dir: House of Gross Foundation

Gross, Jenard M., trust: Wolff Memorial Foundation, Pauline Sterne

Gross, Jerome, MD, trust, mem, mem scientific adv comm: Whitney Foundation, Helen Hay

Gross, Ronald Martin, chmn, ceo, pres: ITT Rayonier; chmn, pres, dir: ITT Rayonier Foundation

Gross, Ronald N., dir: Chadwick Foundation; secy, dir: Meadowood Foundation

Gross, Ted, vp, asst secy: Weinberg Foundation, Harry and Jeanette

Gross, Thomas R., mem adv bd: Gross Charitable Trust, Walter L. and Nell R.

Gross, Valerie, exec asst to pres: Getty Trust, J. Paul

Gross, Walter L., Jr., mem adv bd: Gross Charitable Trust, Walter L. and Nell R.

Grosse, Rose B., pres, dir: Buehler Foundation, A. C.

Grosser, Sharon, mgr (commun support programs): Grumman Corp.

Grossett, Duane R., pres, ceo, dir: Easco Corp.

Grossman, N. Bud, pres: Boulevard Foundation

Grossman, N.M., secy, treas: Bannan Foundation, Arline and Thomas J.

Grossman, Nathan M., vp, secy: Baum Family Fund, Alvin H.

Grote, Deborah A., secy: Veritas Foundation

Groth, Frederick H., treas, dir: Siebert Lutheran Foundation

Groth, Paul H., dir: Mielke Family Foundation

Grousbeck, Anne, cfo: Grousbeck Family Foundation

Grousbeck, H. Irving, pres: Grousbeck Family Foundation

Grousbeck, Susanne B., vp: Grousbeck Family Foundation

Grousbeck, Wycliffe K., secy, treas: Grousbeck Family Foundation

Groussman, Dean, chmn, pres, ceo: Zale Corp.

Grove, Alan, vp (law), secy: North American Life & Casualty Co.

Grove, Andrew S., pres, ceo, dir: Intel Corp.

Grove, Hugh, Jr., treas, asst secy: Dougherty, Jr. Foundation, James R.

Grover, Martha E., dir: Estes Foundation

Groves, C. T., vp, trust: Groves Foundation

Groves, David D., chmn: SCT Foundation

Groves, Franklin Nelson, chmn, pres: Groves & Sons Co., S.J.; pres, trust: Groves Foundation

Groves, Helen Kleberg, pres: Kleberg, Jr. and Helen C. Kleberg Foundation, Robert J.

Groves, I. M., Jr., trust: Burroughs Educational Fund, N. R.

Groves, Ray John, chmn: Ernst & Young

Groves, Robert A., dir: Hilton Foundation, Conrad N.

Grubb, David H., pres: Swinerton & Walberg Co.

Grubb, Edger H., sr vp: Transamerica Corp.; dir: Transamerica Fdn.

Grube, Lewis Blaine, pres, trust: Mack Foundation, J. S.

Gruber, Alan R., chmn, ceo, dir: Orion Capital Corp.

Gruber, Carl E., mgr: Baird Foundation

Gruber, Marilyn L., vp: Bristol-Myers Squibb Foundation

Gruber, Murray P., trust: Gruber Research Foundation, Lila

Gruber, Roy, dir: Humphrey Foundation, Glenn & Gertrude

Gruber, W. W., dir: La-Z-Boy Foundation

Grubman, Stanley D., secy: Warner-Lambert Charitable Foundation

Gruen, Carol A., adm off: Boatmen's Bancshares Charitable Trust

Gruener, Garret, cfo, secy: Downing Foundation, J. C.

Gruetner, Donald W., trust, secy, treas: South Waite Foundation

Gruhl, Robert H., sr vp, cfo, treas: Liberty Mutual Insurance Group/Boston

Gruhn, Fred, vchmn, dir: Missouri Farmers Association

Grum, Clifford J., chmn, ceo: Temple-Inland; dir: Temple-Inland Foundation

Grumbacher, Jack Egon, trust: McNutt Charitable Trust, Amy Shelton

Grumbacher, R., trust: Grumbacher Foundation, M. S.

Grumhaus, Margaret A., vp, trust: Austin Memorial Foundation

Grumman, Carol B., dir, vp: Carteh Foundation

Grumman, David L., dir: Phillips Foundation, Ellis L.

Grumman, Elizabeth S., dir, secy: Carteh Foundation

Grumman, Helen Burr, dir, pres: Carteh Foundation

Grumman, Paul Martin, dir, treas: Carteh Foundation

Grumman, Sandra Martin, trust: Carteh Foundation

Grun, Ann Kissel, treas, dir: Manning and Emma Austin Manning Foundation, James Hilton

Grundhofer, J. A., vchmn, dir: Bank of America

Grundhofer, John Francis, chmn, pres, ceo: First Bank System; chmn: First Bank System Foundation

Grundman, Eileen L., trust: Quinlan Foundation, Elizabeth C.

Grune, George V., chmn, pres, ceo, coo: Reader's Digest Association; chmn, dir: Reader's Digest Foundation; chmn, dir: Wallace-Reader's Digest Fund, DeWitt; chmn, dir: Wallace Reader's Digest Fund, Lila

Gruner, Nancy E., dir: Staunton Farm Foundation

Grunewald, Dale, dir: Mid-Iowa Health Foundation

Grunfeld, Ernst, chmn: Metallurg, Inc.

Grupka, R.A., dir: Danforth Co. Foundation, John W.

Grushack, Cynthia, secy: Belding Foundation, Hausman

Gruss, Brenda, dir: Gruss Charitable Foundation, Emanuel and Riane

Gruss, Emanuel, secy: Gruss Charitable and Educational Foundation, Oscar and Regina; vp, secy, dir: Gruss Charitable Foundation, Emanuel and Riane

Gruss, Leslie, dir: Gruss Charitable Foundation, Emanuel and Riane

Gruss, Martin, pres: Gruss Petroleum Corp.

Gruss, Regina, pres: Gruss Charitable and Educational Foundation, Oscar and Regina

Gruss, Riane, treas: Gruss Charitable and Educational Foundation, Oscar and Regina; pres, treas, dir: Gruss Charitable Foundation, Emanuel and Riane

Gryttenholm, Jerry A., vp, dir: NMC Projects

Grzelecki, Frank E., vchmn, dir: Handy & Harman

Guarneschelli, Philip George, dir: AMP Foundation

Gudelsky, John, vp, treas: Gudelsky Family Foundation, Homer and Martha

Gudelsky, Martha, pres: Gudelsky Family Foundation, Homer and Martha

Gudelsky, Medda, dir: Gudelsky Family Foundation, Homer and Martha

Gudger, Robert H., vp: Xerox Foundation

Guenther, Jack Egon, trust: McNutt Charitable Trust, Amy Shelton

Guenther, Paul, trust: PaineWebber Foundation

Guerra, John C., Jr., trust: AT&T Foundation

Guerrera, S., vp, treas, dir: Valspar Foundation

Guerrero, Anthony R., Jr., dir: First Hawaiian Foundation

Guerrero, Linda H., dir: Wright Foundation, Lola

Guerri, William Grant, mem adv comm: Pott Foundation, Herman T. and Phenie R.

Guerry, Alexander, III, coo: Chattem, Inc.

Guerry, Zan, Jr., chmn, pres, ceo: Chattem, Inc.

Guess, Francis, exec dir: Danner Foundation

Gueterman, John, cfo: Murray Ohio Manufacturing Co.

Guethie, K.R., dir: Group Health Foundation

Guffee, Ruth M., trust: KH Foundation

Guffey, John W., Jr., pres, coo: Coltec Industries

Guggenheim, Charles, trust: Danforth Foundation

Guggenheim, Daniel, Guggenheim Foundation, Daniel and Florence

Guggenheim, Robert, Jr., dir: Guggenheim Foundation, Daniel and Florence

Guggenhime, Richard J., pres, trust: Langendorf Foundation, Stanley S.

Guggimio, Kathleen, dir: Bellamah Foundation, Dale J.

Guido, James V., dir: Truman Foundation, Mildred Faulkner

Guidone, Rosemary, exec vp, asst treas, asst secy, trust: Price Foundation, Louis and Harold

Guild, Henry Rice, Jr., trust: Henderson Foundation, George B.

Guilden, Paul B., dir: Bulova Fund

Guilford, Frank W., Jr., dir: Jennings Foundation, Alma

Guinan, Tom, pres: Pinkerton Tobacco Co.

Guinn, Kenny C., chmn, ceo: PriMerit F.S.B.; chmn, ceo: Southwest Gas Corp.; trust: Southwest Gas Corp. Foundation

Guinn, Paul T., secy: Riordan Foundation

Guinnessey, Kathleen, treas: Macmillan Foundation

Gulda, Edward J., pres: Dayton-Walther Corp.

Gulick, Alice J., trust, vp, treas: Eaton Foundation, Cyrus

Gulick, Henry W., trust, pres: Eaton Foundation, Cyrus

Gullen, David J., MD, trust: Flinn Foundation

Gullett, J. E., secy: Noland Co. Foundation

Gulton, Edith, pres: Gulton Foundation

Gumbiner, Alis, cfo, dir: Gumbiner Foundation, Josephine

Gumbiner, Josephine S., pres, dir: Gumbiner Foundation, Josephine

Gumbiner, Lee, dir: Gumbiner Foundation, Josephine

Gumenick, Nathan S., pres, treas: Gumenick Foundation, Nathan and Sophie

Gumenick, Sophie, vp: Gumenick Foundation, Nathan and Sophie

Gummere, John, chmn, ceo: Phoenix Home Life Mutual Insurance Co.

Gund, Agnes, dir: Warhol Foundation for the Visual Arts, Andy

Gund, Ann L., secy, trust: Gund Foundation, George

Gund, Geoffrey, trust: Gund Foundation, Geoffrey

Gund, Geoffrey de Conde, vp, trust: Gund Foundation, George

Gund, George, III, trust: Gund Foundation, George

Gund, Llura A., trust: Gund Foundation, George

Gund, Louise L., trust: Women's Project Foundation

Gundersen, K.E., pres: Epaphroditus Foundation

Gundersen, M.C., vp, treas: Epaphroditus Foundation

Gunderson, Charles H., Jr., secy, treas, dir: Foote, Cone & Belding Foundation

Gundlach, Susan Jones, vp, trust: Jones Family Foundation, Eugenie and Joseph

Gunji, Hiromi, chmn, ceo: Brother International Corp.

Gunn, Barbara, trust: Glick Foundation, Eugene and Marilyn

Gunn, Colin, trust: Palisades Educational Foundation

Gunning, David H., secy, trust: Kulas Foundation

Gunnon, Judy, Joslin-Needham Family Foundation

Gunterman, Antnony, trust: Page Foundation, George B.

Gunther, D. J., exec vp, dir: Bechtel Foundation

Gunther, Herbert Chao, dir: New World Foundation

Gunther, Peter, mgr: Tyndale House Foundation

Gunzenhauser, Lynn C., trust: Prickett Fund, Lynn R. and Karl E.

Gupta, Ramesh C., exec vp, cfo: Crossland Savings FSB

Gurash, John T., chmn, dir: CertainTeed Corp.; dir, mem audit comm: Weingart Foundation

Guren, Debra S., trust, secy: Hershey Foundation

Gurin, Richard, pres, ceo: Binney & Smith Inc.

Gurnitz, Robert N., ceo, pres: Northwestern Steel & Wire Co.

Halbreich, Kathy, dir: Warhol Foundation for the Visual Arts, Andy

Hale, Edwin F., Sr., chmn, dir: Baltimore Bancorp.

Hale, Elfreda, dir: Hale Foundation, Crescent Porter

Hale, Michael V., trust: Cauthorn Charitable Trust, John and Mildred

Hale, Roger L., pres, ceo, dir: Tennant Co.

Hale, Roger Loucks, dir: Tennant Co. Foundation

Hale, Roger W., chmn, pres, ceo, dir: Louisville Gas & Electric Co.

Haleen, Tobi, vp, secy: Rosen Foundation, Michael Alan

Halepeska, Robert, exec vp: Johnson Foundation, M. G. and Lillie A.

Hales, Burton W., Jr., secy, treas, dir: Hales Charitable Fund

Hales, Marion J., dir: Hales Charitable Fund

Hales, Mary C., dir: Hales Charitable Fund

Hales, William M., pres, dir: Hales Charitable Fund

Haley, Alex Palmer, dir: Parsons Foundation, Ralph M.

Haley, Eloise, pres: Haley Foundation, W. B.

Haley, Frederick Thomas, dir: Haas Foundation, Saul and Dayee G.

Haley, Mrs. Daniel J., Jr., dir, secy: Emergency Aid of Pennsylvania Foundation

Halff, Hugh, Jr., pres, trust: Halff Foundation, G. A. C.

Halff, Marie M., trust: Halff Foundation, G. A. C.

Hall, Andrew J., chmn, ceo: Salomon

Hall, Brent, trust: Davis Foundations, Arthur Vining

Hall, Charles T., dir: Gebbie Foundation

Hall, Charles W., trust: Anderson Foundation, M. D.

Hall, Craig, chmn: Hall Financial Group

Hall, Daniel S., treas, dir: Lattner Foundation, Forrest C.

Hall, David E., pres, trust: Technical Foundation of America

Hall, David N., vp, treas, dir: Eagle-Picher Foundation

Hall, Dennis J., exec vp, cfo: Carlisle Cos.

Hall, Donald, pres: Red Devil

Hall, Donald Joyce, chmn, dir: Hall Family Foundations; chmn: Hallmark Cards

Hall, Euphemia V., gov: Crary Foundation, Bruce L.

Hall, George A., vchmn: Little Brown & Co., Inc.

Hall, Gerald N., pres, trust: Hall Foundation

Hall, Giles S., Peppers Foundation, Ann

Hall, Gordon R., mem adv comm: Michael Foundation, Herbert I. and Elsa B.

Hall, Harry A., vp, dir: Giddings & Lewis Foundation

Hall, J. Edward, pres, dir: Reader's Digest Foundation; dir: Wallace-Reader's Digest Fund, DeWitt; dir: Wallace Reader's Digest Fund, Lila

Hall, Jesse C., trust: Elkin Memorial Foundation, Neil Warren and William Simpson

Hall, Jesse Seaborn, mem distribution comm: English

Memorial Fund, Florence C. and H. L.; mem distribution comm: Marshall Trust in Memory of Sanders McDaniel, Harriet McDaniel; mem: Trust Co. of Georgia Foundation

Hall, John, trust: Bishop Foundation

Hall, John F., secy, trust: Bloedel Foundation; vp, treas: Seaver Institute

Hall, John M., trust: Ellison Foundation

Hall, John Richard, chmn, ceo: Ashland Oil

Hall, Joseph S., dir: France Foundation, Jacob and Annita; dir: Merrick Foundation, Robert G. and Anne M.

Hall, Larry D., pres, coo, dir: KN Energy, Inc.

Hall, Leo J., trust: Hosler Memorial Educational Fund, Dr. R. S.

Hall, Lowell K., secy, treas, trust: Kinney-Lindstrom Foundation

Hall, Lyle G., trust: Stackpole-Hall Foundation

Hall, Marion T., dir: Joyce Foundation

Hall, Mortimer W., treas: Schiff Foundation, Dorothy

Hall, R. A., dir: Vilter Foundation

Hall, Richard A., trust: Phillips Trust, Edwin

Hall, Robert, trust: Clemens Foundation

Hall, Robert E., secy, treas, trust: Hall Foundation

Hall, Stephen G., pres, coo: Colonial Life & Accident Insurance Co.

Hall, Terry L., treas: United Airlines Foundation

Hall, Thomas H. III, secy, treas: Georgia Scientific and Technical Research Foundation

Hall, William A., pres: Hall Family Foundations; pres: Hallmark Cards

Hall, William K., pres, dir: Elastimold Corp.

Halla, Lee, off: Grenfell Association of America

Hallagan, Kevin, secy: Continental Bank Foundation

Hallam, Howard, dir: Keith Foundation Trust, Ben E.

Hallam, Howard P., pres: Keith Co., Ben E.

Hallam, Robert Gaston, dir: Keith Foundation Trust, Ben E.

Hallaran, Iris, dir: Hopper Foundation, May Templeton

Hallen, Philip Burgh, pres: Falk Medical Fund, Maurice

Hallene, Alan Montgomery, mem: Butler Foundation, Alice; dir: MacArthur Foundation, John D. and Catherine T.

Haller, Calvin J., pres: Children's Foundation of Erie County

Haller, J. Gary, secy, dir: German Protestant Orphan Asylum Association

Haller, Richard, cfo: Walbridge Aldinger Co.

Hallett, Anne C., exec dir, secy: Wieboldt Foundation

Hallgren, Carl R., dir: SICO Foundation

Hallinan, Cornelia I., trust: Mather and William Gwinn Mather Fund, Elizabeth Ring

Halling, William R., trust: Lutheran Brotherhood Foundation

Hallock, David P., secy: Fuller Foundation, George F. and Sybil H.

Hallock, Richard W., vp, dir: Knox Family Foundation

Halloran, Concepcion G., vp: Halloran Foundation, Mary P. Dolciani

Halloran, James J., pres: Halloran Foundation, Mary P. Dolciani

Halloran, Michael J., vp, dir: Wallace Computer Services Foundation

Hallowell, Barclay, secy, trust: Kynett Memorial Foundation, Edna G.

Hallowell, Dorothy W., trust: Hallowell Foundation

Hallowell, Howard T., III, trust: Hallowell Foundation

Hallowell, Merritt W., trust: Hallowell Foundation

Halmos, Peter, trust: Halmos Foundation

Halmos, Steven, trust: Halmos Foundation

Halperin, James R., Spingold Foundation, Nate B. and Frances

Halperin, Richard E., pres, dir: MacAndrews & Forbes Foundation; pres, dir: Revlon Foundation

Halpern, C., secy, treas: Woldenberg Foundation

Halpern, Charles R., pres, mem bd: Cummings Foundation, Nathan

Halpern, Susan, pres, dir: Uris Brothers Foundation

Halpin, Kenneth J., vp, treas: Discount Corp. of New York Charitable Foundation

Halpin, Stephen R., cfo: Chevy Chase Savings Bank FSB

Halton, Dale, chmn, pres, ceo: Pepsi-Cola Bottling Co. of Charlotte; pres, dir: Pepsi-Cola of Charlotte Foundation

Halton, Phil, vp, treas, dir: Pepsi-Cola of Charlotte Foundation

Halvorsen, Andrew Christian, cfo, mem off pres: Beneficial Corp.; trust: Schumann Fund for New Jersey

Halvorsen, Bradley W., communications off: Flinn Foundation

Halvorson, Newman T., Jr., secy, dir: Covington and Burling Foundation; asst secy/treas chmn emeritus: Meyer Foundation, Eugene and Agnes E.

Hamacher, Charles, Jr., trust: Young Charity Trust Northern Trust Company

Hamamoto, Howard, mem distribution comm: Frear Eleemosynary Trust, Mary D. and Walter F.

Hamamoto, T., trust: Armco Steel Co. Foundation

Hamann, Leonard, comm mem: Fromm Scholarship Trust, Walter and Mabel

Hamblett, David C., trust: Nashua Trust Co. Foundation

Hamblett, Stephen, chmn, ceo: Providence Journal Company; trust: Providence Journal Charitable Foundation

Hamblin, Lynn T., trust: Towsley Foundation, Harry A. and Margaret D.

Hamboyan, Denis, trust: Technical Training Foundation

Hamburg, Beatrix Ann, MD, dir: Bush Foundation; pres, trust: Grant Foundation,

William T.; dir: Greenwall Foundation; dir: Revson Foundation, Charles H.

Hamburg, David A., pres, trust, mem fin & admin comm: Carnegie Corporation of New York

Hamby, Rob, dir, treas: Piedmont Health Care Foundation

Hamby, Robert E., Jr., cfo, treas: Multimedia, Inc.; trust: Multimedia Foundation

Hamel, Dana A., trust: Hamel Family Charitable Trust, D. A.

Hamel, Jane M., mgr (corp contributions program): Digital Equipment Corp.

Hamel, Kathryn P., trust: Hamel Family Charitable Trust, D. A.

Hamett, Gordan D., ceo, pres, chmn: Brush Wellman Inc.

Hamill, John P., vchmn: Shawmut National Corp.

Hamilton, Ann Oppenheimer, trust: Kempner Fund, Harris and Eliza

Hamilton, Bruce B., pres, dir: Eastern Fine Paper, Inc.

Hamilton, Don, comm: Fairfield-Meeker Charitable Trust, Freeman E.

Hamilton, Donald L., pres: North American Philips Foundation

Hamilton, Dorothy C., treas: Huston Foundation

Hamilton, Edward K., dir: Aetna Foundation

Hamilton, Frank T., secy, trust: Emery Memorial, Thomas J.; trust: Peterloon Foundation

Hamilton, Frederic C., chmn, ceo, pres, dir: Hamilton Oil Corp.

Hamilton, George E., III, trust: Stewart Trust under the will of Helen S. Devore, Alexander and Margaret; trust: Stewart Trust under the will of Mary E. Stewart, Alexander and Margaret

Hamilton, Gordon C., mem (contributions comm): SAFECO Corp.

Hamilton, J. Richard, trust: Mellen Foundation

Hamilton, Jack H., secy: Fink Foundation; trust: Teledyne Charitable Trust Foundation

Hamilton, James L., III, gen mgr: USX Foundation

Hamilton, James M., chmn: Greene Manufacturing Co.

Hamilton, James M., Jr., trust: Greene Manufacturing Co. Foundation

Hamilton, James M., Sr., trust: Greene Manufacturing Co. Foundation

Hamilton, John D., pres, dir: Gebbie Foundation

Hamilton, L.E., pres: Dover Elevator Systems Inc.

Hamilton, Louise, trust: Greene Manufacturing Co. Foundation

Hamilton, Lyman C., pres, ceo: Imperial Corp. of America

Hamilton, Mrs. James C., treas: Memorial Foundation for Children

Hamilton, Peter Bannerman, dir: Cummins Engine Foundation

Hamilton, Robert, trust: Hamilton Foundation, Florence P.

Hamilton, Thomas, mem (contributions comm): Pennzoil Co.

Hamister, Donald B., chmn, ceo: Joslyn Corp.; chmn, dir: Joslyn Foundation

Hamm, Candace S., vp: Northern Star Foundation

Hamm, Edward H., pres, treas: Hersey Foundation; vp, treas, dir: Northern Star Foundation

Hamm, William H., pres, dir: Northern Star Foundation

Hammack, John A., trust, dir: Meadows Foundation

Hamman, Ann L., dir: Hamman Foundation, George and Mary Josephine

Hamman, Henry R., secy, dir: Hamman Foundation, George and Mary Josephine

Hamman, Marilyn P., vp, treas, dir: Tell Foundation

Hammel, J. Carter, cfo, trust: International Foundation

Hammele, Joseph F., vchmn, dir: Rochester Community Savings Bank

Hammer, C.W., trust: SCT Foundation

Hammer, Carolyn S., dir: Staunton Farm Foundation

Hammer, Dru, dir: Hammer Foundation, Armand

Hammer, L.R., Jr., comm: Craig Foundation, J. Paul

Hammer, Michael, trust: Hammer United World College Trust, Armand

Hammer, Michael A., dir: Hammer Foundation, Armand

Hammer, Roy A., trust: Cox Charitable Trust, Jessie B.

Hammer, Thomas J., dir: Teichert Foundation

Hammerly, Harry Allan, dir: 3M Co.

Hammerman, Harry, dir, treas: Millstone Foundation

Hammes, Michael N., vchmn, dir: Black & Decker Corp.

Hammes, Robert M., secy, corp coun: Barber-Colman Co.

Hammill, Donald D., pres, treas: Hammill Foundation, Donald D.

Hammill, Ruth, secy: Hammill Foundation, Donald D.

Hammond, Christine A., trust: Hammond Foundation

Hammond, Donna, admin asst: American Honda Foundation

Hammond, Dr. J. David, dir: Emerson Foundation, Fred L.

Hammond, Frank Joseph, trust: Alliss Educational Foundation, Charles and Ellora; gen coun: Bush Foundation; chmn, trust: Minnesota Foundation

Hammond, Franklin T., Jr., dir: Weber Charities Corp., Frederick E.

Hammond, Hazel, trust: Hammond Foundation

Hammond, R. M., trust: Crandall Memorial Foundation, J. Ford

Hammond, Robert E., trust: Hammond Foundation

Hammonds, Donald R., chmn, dir: Addison-Wesley Publishing Co.

Hammons, Royce, trust: Kerr Foundation

Hamolsky, Milton, MD, pres: Zlinkoff Fund for Medical Research and Education, Sergei S.

Hamolsky, Sandra, dir: Zlinkoff Fund for Medical Research and Education, Sergei S.

Hamp, Sheila F., trust: Ford Motor Co. Fund

Hampton, Archie, dir: Strouse, Greenberg & Co. Charitable Fund

Hampton, John C., dir: Wessinger Foundation

Hampton, Louis R., mem distribution comm: Champlin Foundations

Hampton, Robert K., exec dir, secy, asst treas: Bryan Family Foundation, Kathleen Price and Joseph M.

Hamrick, Charles F., dir: Fullerton Foundation

Hamrick, Harvey B., secy: Dover Foundation

Hamrick, John M., chmn, dir: Fullerton Foundation

Hamrick, William J., trust: Williams Foundation, Edna Sproull

Hamrick, Wylie L., vchmn, treas, dir: Fullerton Foundation

Hanasen, Marty Voelkel, dir: Knott Foundation, Marion I. and Henry J.

Hanavan, Claire F., dir: Huisking Foundation

Hanavan, Taylor W., trust: Huisking Foundation

Hanawalt, Frank S., exec dir: Haas Foundation, Saul and Dayee G.

Hance, William Adams, dir: Axe-Houghton Foundation

Hancock, Carol E., dir: Hancock Foundation, Luke B.

Hancock, Denise, dir: Hancock Foundation, Luke B.

Hancock, Gary T., ceo, pres: Helena Chemical Co.

Hancock, Jane, vp, dir: Hancock Foundation, Luke B.

Hancock, John S., trust: Mather Fund, Richard

Hancock, Kimberly, secy, dir: Hancock Foundation, Luke B.

Hancock, Lorraine, chmn, dir: Hancock Foundation, Luke B.

Hancock, Margo, dir: Quad City Osteopathic Foundation

Hancock, Noble, pres, dir: Hancock Foundation, Luke B.

Hancock, Wesley, dir: Hancock Foundation, Luke B.

Hand, Avery, vp, trust: Young Foundation, Hugo H. and Mabel B.

Hand, Donna, trust: Pickett and Hatcher Educational Fund

Hand, Elbert O., pres, coo, dir: Hartmarx Corp.

Hand, John G., mgr: Hand Industries Foundation

Hand, Marion, trust: Medina Foundation

Hand, Ronald D., vp, dir: Hand Industries Foundation

Hand, Terry E., pres: Hand Industries; secy, treas, dir: Hand Industries Foundation

Hand, William Brevard, dir: Mitchell Foundation

Hand, William F., chmn: Hand Industries; pres, dir: Hand Industries Foundation

Handelman, Blanche B., MacDonald Foundation, James A.

Handelman, Donald, pres, dir: Mathers Charitable Foundation, G. Harold and Leila Y.

Handelman, Donald E., vp, secy, treas: Spiritus Gladius Foundation

Handelman, James H., exec dir: Mathers Charitable Foundation, G. Harold and Leila Y.

Handelman, Jay, dir (pub rels): Freeport-McMoRan

Handelman, Joseph W., treas, asst secy, dir: Mathers Charitable Foundation, G. Harold and Leila Y.; trust: Spiritus Gladius Foundation

Handelman, Walter J., secy, dir: MacDonald Foundation, James A.

Handelman, William, asst secy, treas: Spiritus Gladius Foundation

Handelman, William R., vp, dir: Mathers Charitable Foundation, G. Harold and Leila Y.

Handlan, Raymond, secy, treas, dir: Atlantic Foundation of New York

Handler, Cherie, trust: Geifman Family Foundation

Handler, Geoffrey, secy: Gerschel Foundation, Patrick A.

Handler, Leslie, secy: Lehrman Foundation, Jacob and Charlotte

Handler, Mark S., coo: Macy & Co., R.H.

Hanes, Frank, trust: Morehead Foundation, John Motley

Hanes, Frank Borden, Jr., trust: Hanes Foundation, John W. and Anna H.

Hanes, Frank Borden, Sr., trust: Hanes Foundation, John W. and Anna H.

Hanes, Gordon, trust: Hanes Foundation, John W. and Anna H.

Hanes, Ralph Philip, Jr., trust: Hanes Foundation, John W. and Anna H.

Haney, Curtis B., trust: First Interstate Banks of Billings Centennial Youth Foundation

Haney, William J., pres: Kirkhill Rubber Co.; vp: Kirkhill Foundation

Hangs, George L., Jr., secy, treas, trust: Harmon Foundation, Pearl M. and Julia J.

Hangs, George L., Sr., chmn, trust: Harmon Foundation, Pearl M. and Julia J.

Hank, Bernard J., Jr., chmn: Montgomery Elevator Co.; trust: Montgomery Elevator Co. Charitable Trust

Hank, Ron, dir (mktg): Cincom Systems, Inc.

Hankamer, Doris K., trust: Hankamer Foundation, Curtis and Doris K.

Hankamer, Raymond E., vp: Oldham Little Church Foundation

Hanke, G. F. Robert, exec vp, dir: Flagler Foundation

Hankin, Michael D., trust: Isaacs Foundation, Harry Z.

Hankins, James M., trust, pres: Sunburst Foundation

Hankins, Ruth Leale, trust: Hankins Foundation

Hanks, Stephan G., secy: Morrison Knudsen Corp. Foundation Inc.

Hanley, John, dir: Hanley Family Foundation

Hanley, John W., dir: Hanley Family Foundation

Hanley, Mary Jane, dir: Hanley Family Foundation

Hanley, Susan Jane, dir: Hanley Family Foundation

Hanley, William Lee, Jr., treas, dir: JM Foundation

Hanley, William T., pres, ceo: Galileo Electro-Optics Corp.

Hanlin, Russell L., pres, ceo, coo: Sunkist Growers

Hanlon, Tim, vp: Wells Fargo Foundation

Hanman, Gary, pres, ceo: Mid-America Dairymen

Hanna, Richard, second vchmn, dir: Land O'Lakes

Hanna, Robert C., trust: George Foundation; pres, ceo, dir: Holly Sugar Corp.; pres, ceo, dir: Imperial Holly Corp.

Hanna, William W., pres, coo: Koch Industries

Hannah, John, trust, vp: Thoman Foundation, W. B. and Candace

Hannah, John R., dir: Semmes Foundation

Hannah, Thomas E., ceo, pres: Collins & Aikman Corp.

Hannan, Robert W., pres: Thrift Drug, Inc.

Hannaway, Peter, pres: Sargent Electric Co.

Hannefield, Jim, cfo: Hyundai Motor America

Hanning, Stephen E., exec dir: Chambers Memorial, James B.

Hannon, Patrick H., trust: Hannon Foundation, William H.

Hannon, William Herbert, chmn, asst secy, dir: Burns Foundation, Fritz B.; chmn, pres, dir: Hannon Foundation, William H.

Hanrahan, Charles J., trust: Kingsbury Fund

Hanrahan, Clement E., exec dir: UPS Foundation

Hansen, A.G., secy: Burnand Medical and Educational Foundation, Alphonse A.

Hansen, C.W., secy-treas: Abel Foundation

Hansen, Julia S., dir: Barker Welfare Foundation

Hansen, Julie A., secy: Sears-Roebuck Foundation

Hansen, Kenneth, trust: Presto Foundation

Hansen, Kenneth N., vchmn: ServiceMaster Co. L.P.

Hansen, Lois E., secy, asst treas: Caspersen Foundation for Aid to Health and Education, O. W.

Hansen, Richard L., dir: Huston Foundation

Hansen, Robert, trust: Petteys Memorial Foundation, Jack

Hansen, Robert F., secy, treas: Myra Foundation

Hansen, Robert U., trust: Kitzmiller/Bales Trust

Hansen, Robert V., trust: Joslin-Needham Family Foundation

Hansen, Rodney S., trust: Olympia Brewing Co. Employees Beneficial Trust

Hansler, John F., treas, dir: Cheney Foundation, Ben B.

Hansmann, Ralph E., asst secy: Olive Bridge Fund

Hansmann, Ralph Emil, treas, dir: Golden Family Foundation; vp, treas: Zlinkoff Fund for Medical Research and Education, Sergei S.

Hansmeyer, Herbert, chmn, ceo: Fireman's Fund Insurance Co.

Hanson, Allen D., ceo, pres: Harvest States Cooperative; 2nd vchmn: Harvest States Foundation; asst secy, asst treas: Phillips Family Foundation, L. E.

Hanson, Elizabeth, pres, secy, treas: Johnston-Hanson Foundation

Hanson, Eric, trust: Johnston-Hanson Foundation

Hanson, Erling A., Jr., pres: Massachusetts Charitable Mechanics Association

Hanson, Frances A., exec dir: Winship Memorial Scholarship Foundation

Hanson, Fred, trust: Johnston-Hanson Foundation

Hanson, Herman H., trust, treas: Charitable Fund

Hanson, James R., dir: Forest Foundation; mem: Sequoia Foundation; secy, dir: Stewardship Foundation

Hanson, Joann, secy: Conway Scholarship Foundation, Carle C.

Hanson, John K., trust: Hanson Foundation; chmn, ceo, dir: Winnebago Industries, Inc.

Hanson, Jon E., trust: Prudential Foundation

Hanson, Lillian P., vp, exec dir, dir: Sentry Life Group Foundation

Hanson, Luise V., trust: Hanson Foundation; trust: Winnebago Industries Foundation

Hanson, Marv, trust: Harvest States Foundation

Hanson, Mrs. Fred, Johnston-Hanson Foundation

Hanson, Paul D., trust: Winnebago Industries Foundation

Hanson, Peggy, contributions coordinator: Minnesota Power & Light Co.

Hanson, Richard E., vp, dir: 3M Co.

Hanson, T. E., trust: KPMG Peat Marwick Foundation

Hanson, Victor H., II, pres, ceo, dir: Birmingham News Co.

Hanzalek, Astrid T., pres: Connecticut Natural Gas Corp.; trust: Connecticut Energy Foundation, Inc.

Hapgood, Elaine P., dir: Educational Foundation of America; vp, trust: Ettinger Foundation

Happ, Joyce O., trust: Steiner Charitable Fund, Albert

Haqq, Constance T., exec dir: Nordson Corporation Foundation

Hara, Kuwa, mgr human resources & gen aff: Itoh (C.) International (America), Inc.

Hara, Makota, treas: Armco Steel Co. Foundation

Harada, Curtis Y., treas, dir: HEI Charitable Foundation

Harada, Takeshi, pres: Sanyo Audio Manufacturing (U.S.A.) Corp.

Harbeck, Eugene O., Jr., trust: Loutit Foundation

Harbert, Bill Lebold, pres, coo: Harbert Corp.

Harbert, David L., cfo: Applied Power, Inc.

Harbert, John Murdoch, III, chmn, ceo: Harbert Corp.

Harbison, Elizabeth, treas: Female Association of Philadelphia

Harbottle, Gerald K., vp: Servco Foundation

Hard, Michael, bd mem: Valley Bank Charitable Foundation

Hardee, Ernest F., vp: Portsmouth General Hospital Foundation

Hardegree, William B., trust: Pickett and Hatcher Educational Fund

Hardeman, Greg, trust: Stephens Foundation Trust

Harden, O.C., Jr., trust: Blount Educational and Charitable Foundation, Mildred Weedon

Hardenbergh, Gabrielle, dir, secy: Saint Croix Foundation

Harder, Henry U., secy: Christodora

Harder, Henry Upham, trust: Dodge Foundation, Geraldine R.

Harder, William Ewald, secy: Dayton Hudson Foundation

Harder, William H., trust: Children's Foundation of Erie County

Harder, Willis, trust: Schowalter Foundation

Hardie, Donald, Jr., dir: Imlay Foundation

Hardie, Eben, pres, trust: Libby-Dufour Fund, Trustees of the

Hardie, James C., trust: Dively Foundation, George S.

Hardin, Joe, mem: Wal-Mart Foundation

Hardin, P. Russell, secy, treas: Evans Foundation, Lettie Pate; secy, treas: Whitehead Foundation, Joseph B.; secy, treas: Whitehead Foundation, Lettie Pate; secy, treas: Woodruff Foundation, Robert W.

Hardine, Robert C., chmn: Freedom Newspapers Inc.

Harding, David, trust: Camp and Bennet Humiston Trust, Apollos

Harding, Frank I., III, mgr: Sheadle Trust, Jasper H.

Harding, John H., pres, coo, dir: National Life of Vermont

Harding, Louis, vp: Schwartz Foundation, Arnold A.

Harding, Robert L., Jr., trust: Harding Educational and Charitable Foundation

Hardis, Stephen R., vchmn, cfo, adm off, dir: Eaton Corp.

Hardison, Roy L., asst treas, asst secy: American General Finance Foundation

Hardle, Betty, ceo: Good Value Home, Inc.

Hardle, Donald L., pres: Good Value Home, Inc.

Hardon, Allen, secy, trust: Dorr Foundation

Hardon, Roger, trust: Dorr Foundation

Hardten, R. D., mng ptnr: Black & Veatch; trust: Black & Veatch Foundation

Hardwick, Ambrose H., trust: Orange Orphan Society

Hardwick, Ann M., mgr (corp support programs): Pfizer

Hardwig, Brenda K., asst secy: Pacific Mutual Charitable Foundation

Hardy, Ann Steinwedell Donnelley, dir, pres, treas: Donnelley Foundation, Elliott and Ann

Hardy, Gene M., dir: La-Z-Boy Foundation

Hardy, Joan, trust: McBeath Foundation, Faye

Hardy, Maurice G., pres, ceo, dir: Pall Corp.

Hardy, R. Hubbard, secy: Collins Foundation, Carr P.; treas: Collins Foundation, James M.

Hartmann, David B., M.D., trust: Pittsburgh Child Guidance Foundation

Hartmann, Virginia L., Jockey Hollow Foundation

Hartong, Hendrick Johan, Jr., chmn, dir: Air Express International Corp.

Hartshorn, Gary S., dir: General Service Foundation

Hartshorne, Harold, Jr., dir: Chapin Foundation of Myrtle Beach, South Carolina

Hartung, Paul W., Jr., trust: Belden Brick Co. Charitable Trust

Hartung, Suzanne R., trust: Rupp Foundation, Fran and Warren

Hartz, Onealee, secy, treas: Hartz Foundation

Hartz, Shelly Ames, trust: Foerderer Foundation, Percival E. and Ethel Brown

Harvey, Constance, vp, dir: New-Land Foundation

Harvey, F. Barton, Jr., trust: Brown & Sons Charitable Foundation, Alex

Harvey, Felix, pres: Harvey Foundation, Felix

Harvey, Frank H., Jr., secy, treas: Wilkof Foundation, Edward and Ruth

Harvey, George Burton, chmn, pres, ceo: Pitney Bowes

Harvey, Hal, trust: Mertz-Gilmore Foundation, Joyce; vp, dir: New-Land Foundation

Harvey, James D., mem scholarship selection comm: Ritter Charitable Trust, George W. & Mary F.

Harvey, James R., pres, coo, dir: Washington Water Power Co.

Harvey, James Ross, chmn, dir: Transamerica Corp.; chmn, dir: Transamerica Fdn.

Harvey, Joan, dir: New-Land Foundation

Harvey, Joseph, dir: New-Land Foundation

Harvey, Margaret B., treas: Harvey Foundation, Felix

Harvey, Nellie G., vchmn: Builder Marts of America

Harvey, Paul, dir: MacArthur Foundation, John D. and Catherine T.

Harvey, Philip D., dir, vp: International Fund for Health and Family Planning

Harvey, Thomas B., trust: Douty Foundation

Harvley, G. Bonner, chmn: County Bank; trust: County Bank Foundation

Harvy, Ashton, treas: Stony Wold Herbert Fund

Harwood, John K., pres, secy, treas, dir: Genesis Foundation

Harwood, William B., exec dir: Martin Marietta Philanthropic Trust

Hasbargen, Vernae, secy, trust: Blandin Foundation

Hasch, J. Bruce, pres, coo: Peoples Energy Corp.

Haseotes, Demetrious B., dir: Cumberland Farms

Hash, Jack, dir: Bravmann Foundation, Ludwig

Hashim, Carlisle V., dir: Knott Foundation, Marion I. and Henry J.

Hashimoto, Sidney I., dir: Bancorp Hawaii Charitable Foundation

Hashorva, Tanya, vp: Arcadia Foundation

Haskell, Antoinette M., dir: Public Welfare Foundation

Haskell, Coburn, trust, pres: Haskell Fund

Haskell, Francis W., trust: Adams Memorial Fund, Emma J.

Haskell, John G., pres: Chapman Charitable Corporation, Howard and Bess

Haskell, Mary D. F., dir: Adams Memorial Fund, Emma J.

Haskell, Melville H., Jr., trust: Haskell Fund

Haskell, Robert G., pres, dir: Pacific Mutual Charitable Foundation

Haskell, Robert H., dir: Public Welfare Foundation

Haskell, Schuyler A., trust, vp: Haskell Fund

Haskey, A.F., chmn, mem: Tonkin Foundation, Tom and Helen

Haskins, Caryl Parker, hon trust, mem fin & admin comm: Carnegie Corporation of New York

Haskins, Ralph, trust: Wells Trust Fund, Fred W.

Haslam, Anne S., secy: Teichert Foundation

Hasler, Joseph W., ceo, pres: Illinois Cereal Mills

Hassenfeld, Alan Geoffrey, chmn, pres, ceo, dir: Hasbro; pres: Hasbro Charitable Trust; vp, treas: Hassenfeld Foundation

Hassenfeld, Sylvia, pres: Hassenfeld Foundation

Hastings, Alfred B., Jr., trust: Murphey Foundation, Lluella Morey

Hastings, Carl D., vp, secy: Keck, Jr. Foundation, William M.

Hastings, David R., II, trust: Mulford Trust, Clarence E.

Hastings, Donald F., chmn, ceo: Lincoln Electric Co.

Hastings, John A., trust: Hastings Trust

Hastings, John T., Jr., trust, asst secy: Helms Foundation

Hastings, Joseph V., secy, treas: Mailman Foundation

Hastings, Patricia Close, dir: Close Foundation

Hastings, Peter G., trust: Mulford Trust, Clarence E.

Hastings, Robert C., trust: Hastings Trust

Hatch, Ann M., trust: Walker Foundation, T. B.

Hatch, Francis W., chmn, trust: Merck Fund, John

Hatch, Francis W., III, secy, trust: Merck Family Fund

Hatch, George W. M., mem: Merck Family Fund

Hatch, Rakia I., trust: Hatch Charitable Trust, Margaret Milliken

Hatch, Richard L., trust: Hatch Charitable Trust, Margaret Milliken

Hatch, Robert A., trust: Eccles Charitable Foundation, Willard L.

Hatch, Robert W., chmn, pres, ceo: Mohasco Corp.

Hatch, Serena M., trust: Merck Family Fund; trust: Merck Fund, John

Hatcher, Jack, chmn, ceo, dir: SECO

Hatcher, James A., secy: Cox, Jr. Foundation, James M.

Hatcher, Joe B., dir: Jones Charitable Trust, Harvey and Bernice; dir: Rockefeller Foundation, Winthrop

Hatcher, Robert V., Jr., chmn, ceo, dir: Johnson & Higgins

Hatcher, William K., pres, trust: Pickett and Hatcher Educational Fund

Hatfield, Elizabeth, secy: Hutchins Foundation, Mary J.

Hatfield, Paul Harold, pres (protein technologies intl): Ralston Purina Co.

Hathaway, Donald, treas: Cincinnati Foundation for the Aged

Hathaway, E. Phillips, pres, trust: Middendorf Foundation

Hathaway, Harold Grant, pres, dir: MNC Financial; pres, dir: MNC Financial Foundation

Hathaway, John M., trust: Wiggins Memorial Trust, J. J.

Hathaway, Philips, trust: Middendorf Foundation

Hatsopoulos, G.N., chmn, pres: Thermo Electron Corp.

Hatsopoulos, John N., exec vp, cfo: Thermo Electron Corp.

Hattem, Gary S., treas: BT Foundation

Hattemer, Val P., treas: Beerman Foundation

Hattendorf, W. C., trust: Cooper Tire & Rubber Foundation

Hattersley, Gordon B., pres, secy: Uniform Tubes, Inc.

Hattier, Robert L., treas, dir: German Protestant Orphan Asylum Association

Hattler, Andrea M., trust: Loyola Foundation

Hattler, Denise M., pres, treas, trust: Loyola Foundation

Hattler, Hilary A., trust: Loyola Foundation

Hatton, Barbara K., trust: Hazen Foundation, Edward W.

Hattori, Noriyasu, pres: Makita U.S.A., Inc.

Hattox, Brock A., sr vp, cfo: Babcock & Wilcox Co.

Hattox, Brock Alan, cfo, sr vp: McDermott

Hatzfeldt, Hermann, trust: HKH Foundation

Haubein, Robert H., dir: Georgia Power Foundation

Hauben, Helen G., vp, trust: Lowe Foundation, Joe and Emily

Hauber, William M., chmn, pres, ceo: Matthews International Corp.; trust: Matthews and Co. Educational and Charitable Trust, James H.

Haufler, George J., chmn, ceo, pres, dir: Bird Inc.; pres, dir: Bird Cos. Charitable Foundation

Haugen, Gerald Alan, sr vp, cfo: Jostens; dir: Jostens Foundation

Hauger, Joshua, pres: Lambda Electronics Inc.

Haugeu, Richard M, coo: Allergan, Inc.

Hauk, Donald B., exec vp, cfo: Republic Automotive Parts, Inc.

Haupert, Ruth C., treas, asst secy: Jackson Hole Preserve

Haupt, E.W., vp: Davey Co. Foundation

Hauser, David, treas: Duke Power Co. Foundation

Hauser, Gustave, vp: Hauser Foundation

Hauser, Pierre N., III, dir: Disney Family Foundation, Roy

Hauser, Rita, pres: Hauser Foundation

Hauser, Russell L., trust: Loyola Foundation

Hauserman, Jackie, pres: Centerior Energy Foundation

Hauserman, William F., chmn, ceo: Hauserman, Inc.

Hauserman, William Foley, vp, trust: Jennings Foundation, Martha Holden

Hauslein, R. E., vp, dir, mem (contributions comm): Dresser Industries

Hausman, Jack, vchmn, dir: Belding Heminway Co.; admin: Belding Foundation, Hausman

Hausman, Leo, vchmn, dir, chmn exec comm: Belding Heminway Co.

Hausman, Richard D., chmn, ceo, dir: Belding Heminway Co.

Hausmann, W.D., secy: Schlegel Foundation, Oscar C. and Augusta

Hausner, Barbara, pub rels: Melitta North America Inc.

Havemeyer, Harry W., vp, trust: Whiting Foundation, Mrs. Giles

Havens, Louise A., grant adm: Smith Charitable Trust, W. W.

Havens, Philip V., exec dir: Ford Foundation, Edward E.

Haversat, Robert A., pres: Amstar Corp.

Haverty, Harold V., chmn, pres, ceo, dir: Deluxe Corp.; dir: Deluxe Corp. Foundation

Haverty, John Rhodes, MD, chmn, dir: Georgia Health Foundation

Haverty, Rawson, chmn: Haverty Furniture Cos., Inc.

Haviland, David, trust: Howard and Bush Foundation

Hawes, Alexander Boyd, Jr., treas: Boston Globe Foundation

Hawken, E. Robert, Jr., secy: McDonald & Co. Securities Foundation

Hawkes, Daphne, trust: Borden Memorial Foundation, Mary Owen

Hawkins, Annice Hawkins, trust: Kenan Family Foundation

Hawkins, Chaille W., trust: Turner Charitable Foundation

Hawkins, Harman, mem bd govs: Brooks Foundation, Gladys

Hawkins, Jack Wade, vp, trust: Mobility Foundation

Hawkins, Mo, pres: Hubbard Farms

Hawkins, Prince A., trust: Hawkins Foundation, Robert Z.

Hawkins, Thomas G., vchmn: The Limited, Inc.

Hawkins, W. Witley, pres, coo, dir: Delta Air Lines; trust: Delta Air Lines Foundation

Hawkins, Wendy, program adm: Intel Foundation

Hawkinson, Gary M., treas: Centerior Energy Foundation

Hawley, Jean Gannett, pres: Gannett Foundation, Guy P.

Hawley, Jess, dir: Morrison Knudsen Corp. Foundation Inc.

Hawley, Marion E., asst treas: Noble Foundation, Edward John

Hawley, Philip Metschan, trust: Haynes Foundation, John Randolph and Dora

Hawley, Wendell Charles, mgr: Tyndale House Foundation

Hawn, Bruce Sams, dir: Sams Foundation, Earl C.

Hawn, Gates H., dir: Clark Foundation

Hawn, Joe V., Jr., secy, treas, dir: Hawn Foundation

Hawn, W. A., Jr., dir: Hawn Foundation

Hawn, William Russell, pres, dir: Hawn Foundation

Hawn, William Russell, Jr., dir: Hawn Foundation

Haworth, Gerrard Wendell, fdr, chmn: Haworth, Inc.

Haworth, Richard G., pres, ceo, dir: Haworth, Inc.

Hawthoren, David E., ceo: Servico, Inc.

Hay, Bonita, dir: Lizzadro Family Foundation, Joseph

Hay, Gary W., sr vp mktg: Cessna Aircraft Co.; dir: Cessna Foundation

Hay, Jess, chmn, pres, ceo, dir: Lomas Financial Corp.

Hay, John, vp, dir: Mathers Charitable Foundation, G. Harold and Leila Y.

Hay, Roger, vp, cfo: International Rectifier Corp.

Hayashi, H., asst mgr (gen aff): Tokai Bank, Ltd.

Hayashi, Joji, vchmn: American President Cos.; sr vp: American President Companies Foundation

Haycraft, Howard, chmn, dir: Wilson Foundation, H. W.

Haydan, J. P., Jr., chmn, ceo, dir: Midland Co.

Hayden, Joseph Page, Jr., trust: Star Bank, N.A., Cincinnati Foundation

Hayden, Marcia A., dir: Hayden Foundation, William R. and Virginia

Hayden, Rod, exec vp, coo: Hyundai Motor America

Hayden, Stanley D., pres, dir: Hayden Foundation, William R. and Virginia

Haydock, Francis B., trust: Peabody Foundation

Hayes, Arthur H., Jr., dir: Macy, Jr. Foundation, Josiah

Hayes, Betty Frost, chmn, trust: Johnston Trust for Charitable and Educational Purposes, James M.

Hayes, Carl, coo: Church's Fried Chicken, Inc.

Hayes, Charles A., chmn, pres, ceo, dir: Guilford Mills

Hayes, Denis A., pres: Bullitt Foundation

Hayes, John E., Jr., chmn, pres, ceo, dir: Kansas Power & Light/Western Resources; chmn, pres, ceo, dir: Western Resources; chmn, pres, ceo: Western Resources Foundation

Hayes, John R., dir: Federal National Mortgage Assn. Foundation

Hayes, Mariam C., pres, dir, mem: Cannon Foundation

Hayes, Merrick C., dir: Shirk Foundation, Russell and Betty

Hayes, Patricia Ann, trust: RGK Foundation

Hayes, R. C., dir, mem: Cannon Foundation

Hayes, Russell, pres: Wimpey Inc., George

Hayes, Samuel Banks, III, vchmn, dir: Boatmen's Bancshares

Hayes, Synnova B., dir, chmn: Paul and C. Michael Paul Foundation, Josephine Bay

Hayes, Synnova Bay, pres, dir: Bay Foundation

Hayling, Charles, dir: Fort Pierce Memorial Hospital Scholarship Foundation

Haymon, Monte, ceo, pres: Packaging Corporation of America

Hayner, H. H., trust: Stubblefield, Estate of Joseph L.

Hayner, James K., trust: Stubblefield, Estate of Joseph L.

Haynes, Alethia P., trust: Reynolds Foundation, Eleanor T.

Haynes, David Bruce, trust: Reynolds Foundation, Eleanor T.

Haynes, David S., trust: Reynolds Foundation, Eleanor T.

Haynes, Harold J., dir: PACCAR Foundation

Haynes, I.M., trust, pres: Haynes Foundation

Haynes, Larry N., dir: Christy-Houston Foundation

Haynes, Noris R., Jr., exec dir, trust: Plough Foundation

Hays, Frances McKee, vp, trust: McKee Foundation, Robert E. and Evelyn

Hays, Lydia L., exec dir: CIRI Foundation

Hays, Mary Ann, vp, trust: Jergens Foundation, Andrew

Hays, Patricia A., secy: Navistar Foundation

Hays, Thomas A., pres, dir: May Department Stores Co.; vp, dir: May Stores Foundation

Hays, Thomas C., pres, coo, dir: American Brands

Hays, William H., III, mem adv comm: Weezie Foundation

Hayssen, Charles N., cfo: Piper Jaffray Cos.

Hayward, Charles E., pres: Little Brown & Co., Inc.

Hayward, John T., dir: Hertz Foundation, Fannie and John

Hayward, Thomas B., dir: Bancorp Hawaii Charitable Foundation

Haywood, Alice V., secy: Pickett and Hatcher Educational Fund

Haywood, Mary H., Haskell Fund

Haywood, T. C., secy, treas, dir, mem: Cannon Foundation

Hazard, Robert C., Jr., pres, ceo: Quality Inn International

Hazel, Lewis F., treas: Children's Foundation of Erie County

Hazel, R.D., trust: Summer Foundation

Hazeltine, Herbert Samuel, Jr., trust: Hoffman Foundation, H. Leslie Hoffman and Elaine S.

Hazelton, Robert, secy, trust: McKee Foundation, Robert E. and Evelyn

Hazelton, Warren, dir corp rels: Packaging Corporation of America

Hazen, Donald, dir: New World Foundation

Hazen, Paul Mandeville, pres, coo, dir: Wells Fargo & Co.

Hazleton, Richard A., pres: Dow Corning Corp.

Head, Beverly P. III, trust: Kaul Foundation Trust, Hugh

Head, Carol, asst treas: Fund for New Jersey

Head, Head, vp: Continental Divide Electric Education Foundation

Head, R. J., dir: Parsons - W.D. Charities, Vera Davis

Heafey, Edwin Austin, Jr., dir: Valley Foundation, Wayne and Gladys

Heagney, Lawrence, trust: Kingsley Foundation; mem adv comm, contact: Milliken Foundation; treas: Milliken Foundation, Agnes G.; treas: Romill Foundation

Heagney, W. Dennis, pres: Sonat Offshore Drilling

Healey, James E., mem (contributions comm): CPC International

Healey, Judith K., pres: Minnesota Foundation

Healey, Kevin, ed mgr: UNUM Charitable Foundation

Healey, Melissa, trust: Hunt Manufacturing Co. Foundation

Healy, Edmund, dir, vp: Healy Family Foundation, M. A.

Healy, James T., cfo, vp, dir: Trust Funds

Healy, Jill, sr admin: Polaroid Foundation

Healy, Martha Ann Dumke, vp, dir: Dumke Foundation, Dr. Ezekiel R. and Edna Wattis; dir, pres: Healy Family Foundation, M. A.

Healy, Patricia K., pres, dir: Winona Corporation

Healy, Shevy, dir: Luster Family Foundation

Heaney, Cornelius A., Sr., secy: Brooklyn Benevolent Society

Heaney, Joe, ceo, pres: Cornnuts, Inc.

Heard, Anita C., Colt Foundation, James J.

Heard, Drew R., off: McMillan, Jr. Foundation, Bruce

Heard, Thomas H, vp: Colt Foundation, James J.

Hearin, William Jefferson, trust: Chandler Foundation

Hearn, Ruby Puryear, PhD, vp: Johnson Foundation, Robert Wood

Hearn, Thomas A., vp, dir: Russell Charitable Foundation, Tom

Hearon, J. Erick, treas: Cook, Sr. Charitable Foundation, Kelly Gene

Hearst, George Randolph, Jr., pres, dir: Hearst Foundation; vp, dir: Hearst Foundation, William Randolph

Hearst, John Randolph, Jr., vp, dir: Hearst Foundation; vp, dir: Hearst Foundation, William Randolph

Hearst, Randolph Apperson, chmn: Hearst Corp.; vp, dir: Hearst Foundation; pres, dir: Hearst Foundation, William Randolph

Hearst, William Randolph, III, dir: Skidmore, Owings & Merrill Foundation

Heasley, Karen I., trust: Snee-Reinhardt Charitable Foundation

Heasley, Paul A., dir, chmn: Snee-Reinhardt Charitable Foundation

Heasley, Timothy, trust: Snee-Reinhardt Charitable Foundation

Heath, Charles K., pres: Allen-Heath Memorial Foundation

Heath, Mary Lou, trust: Schenck Fund, L. P.

Heath, Ruth, secy: Harvey Foundation, Felix

Heath, Vernon H., chmn, ceo: Rosemount, Inc.

Heaton, James W., trust: Kennametal Foundation

Heaton, Mary Alice J., trust: Whiting Foundation

Heaton, Robert E., sr vp: Lukens

Heatwole, David, Cook Inlet Region

Heaviside, Robert C., dir: Allyn Foundation

Heazel, Francis James, Jr., secy, treas, trust: Courts Foundation

Hebe, James L., pres, ceo, dir: Freightliner Corp.

Hebert, William L., asst sec, asst treas: Louisiana-Pacific Foundation

Hechinger, John Walter, Sr., trust: Hechinger Foundation

Hechinger, June Ross, trust: Hechinger Foundation

Hecht, Ira, vp, dir: Mitrani Family Foundation

Hecht, Margaret W., vp, dir: Winkler Foundation, Mark and Catherine

Hecht, William F., chmn, pres, ceo: Pennsylvania Power & Light

Heck, Joan, secy: Armco Steel Co. Foundation

Heckel, Ben, trust: Swift Co. Inc. Charitable Trust, John S.

Heckel, Jack L., pres, coo, dir: GenCorp

Hecken, Kenneth A., vchmn: Johnson & Higgins

Heckman, Al A., secy, exec dir: Grotto Foundation; chmn, treas, dir: Jerome Foundation

Hecktman, Melvin L., vchmn, dir: United Stationers Inc.

Hector, Louis Julius, chmn, trust: Markey Charitable Trust, Lucille P.

Hed, Gordon E., dir, treas: Weyerhaeuser Foundation, Frederick and Margaret L.; dir: Weyerhaeuser Memorial Foundation, Charles A.

Hedberg, Victor, trust: Lewis Foundation, Frank J.

Hedges, Gary, vp: Sundstrand Corp. Foundation

Hedges, James R., III, vp, asst secy, trust: Tonya Memorial Foundation

Hedges, M. D., trust: Betts Foundation

Hedien, Wayne Evans, chmn, ceo, dir: Allstate Insurance Co.; pres, trust: Allstate Foundation

Hedley, John C., vp: Morton International

Hedling, Susan, trust: Shwayder Foundation, Fay

Hedlund, Donna, trust: Donaldson Foundation

Hedrick, Charles L., vchmn, dir: Zurn Industries

Hedrick, Harriet E., chmn, trust: Hedrick Foundation, Frank E.

Heegaard, Peter A., trust, mem exec comm: Blandin Foundation

Heenan, David A., dir: Bancorp Hawaii Charitable Foundation

Heenan, Earl I., trust: Earhart Foundation

Heerlyn, Vickie G., exec dir, secy: Upjohn Co. Foundation

Heeschen, Paul, vp: Environment Now

Heffern, Gordon Emory, trust: Knight Foundation, John S. and James L.

Heffernan, Daniel E., pres: Heffernan & Co.

Heffernan, Elizabeth Blossom, pres, trust: Bingham Foundation, William

Heffner, Jane E., vp corp contributions: Salomon

Heffner, Ralph H., chmn, dir: Agway

Heffner, Richard H., dir: Maclellan Foundation, Robert L. and Kathrina H.

Hefler, Richard, mgr: Sarkeys Foundation

Heflin, James, vchmn: Tartt Scholarship Fund, Hope Pierce

Hefner, Christie A., chmn, ceo: Playboy Enterprises, Inc.; dir: Playboy Foundation

Hefner, Hugh M., chmn emeritus: Playboy Enterprises, Inc.

Hefni, Ibrahim, trust: Technical Training Foundation

Hefni, Wensley, trust: Technical Training Foundation

Heftler, Pierre V., secy, trust: Ford Fund, Benson and Edith; secy, trust, mem: Ford Fund, Eleanor and Edsel; secy, trust, mem: Ford Fund, Walter and Josephine; secy, trust: Ford Fund, William and Martha; secy, trust: Ford II Fund, Henry; vp, trust: Wilson Fund, Matilda R.

Hefty, Noel M., trust: Messing Family Charitable Foundation

Hegarty, William Edward, vp, secy, dir: Gould Foundation, Florence J.

Hegel, Garret, cfo: Central Bank of the South

Hegener, Joseph L., dir: Dunning Foundation

Hegman, Trygue, chmn: Kloster Cruise Ltd.

Heher, Garret M., trust, dir: Atlantic Foundation

Hehl, David K., dir: La-Z-Boy Foundation

Heiberg, Kenneth S., trust: Faith Home Foundation

Heid, Karen, program off Focus on Children: Prudential Foundation

Heidakka, Edwin F., trust: Presser Foundation

Heide, Stan, coo: Michigan Wheel Corp.

Heidelmark, Edward J., trust: Community Health Association

Heider, Jon Vinton, vp: BFGoodrich Foundation

Heidman, Julia W., trust: Weyerhaeuser Family Foundation

Heidt, John M., trust: Van Nuys Charities, J. B. and Emily

Heil, Joseph F., Jr., chmn: Heil Co.

Heil, Russell H., exec vp (tech oper): Delta Air Lines; trust: Delta Air Lines Foundation

Heilala, John A., trust: Vulcan Materials Co. Foundation

Heilenman, Norman E., trust: Robertson Brothers Co. Charitable Foundation

Heilicher, Amos, American Amusement Arcades; pres: Heilicher Foundation, Menaham

Heilicher, Daniel, vp, treas: Heilicher Foundation, Menaham

Heiligbrodt, L. William, pres, coo, dir: Service Corp. International

Heiling, Blanche, vp, dir: Berkowitz Family Foundation, Louis

Heilmeier, George, pres, ceo: Bell Communications Research

Heim, Mark, secy, cfo: Segerstrom Foundation

Heiman, Gary, pres: Standard Textile Co., Inc.

Heiman, Paul, chmn, ceo: Standard Textile Co., Inc.

Heimann, John G., dir: Markle Foundation, John and Mary R.

Heimann, Sandra W., secy: American Financial Corp. Foundation; vp, secy, dir: United Brands Foundation

Heimerman, Quentin O., dir, vp: Saint Croix Foundation

Heimlich, Lydia, vp, dir: Rudin Foundation, Louis and Rachel

Heine, Spencer H., pres: Montgomery Ward Foundation

Heineman, Benjamin Walter, Jr., trust: GE Foundations

Heineman, Harry, vp, dir: Alexander Foundation, Judd S.

Heineman, James H., dir: Heineman Foundation for Research, Educational, Charitable, and Scientific Purposes

Heineman, Melvin L., secy, treas: Rohatyn Foundation, Felix and Elizabeth

Heineman, William M., trust: de Hirsch Fund, Baron

Heiner, Lawrence, dir: PacifiCorp Foundation

Heiner, Lawrence E., pres: Nerco, Inc.

Heinlein, Charles H., Faith Home Foundation

Heinrich, John E., vp: Universal Foods Foundation

Heins, Richard M., deputy ceo: Century Companies of America; pres, ceo: CUNA Mutual Insurance Group; ceo, treas, secy: CUNA Mutual Charitable Foundation

Heintz, W., chmn, ceo: Dole Fresh Vegetables

Heinz, Drue, trust: Heinz Foundation, Drue

Heinz, H. John, IV, trust: Heinz Endowment, Howard

Heinz, Martha H., trust: Illges Memorial Foundation, A. and M. L.

Heinz, Teresa F., trust: Carnegie Corporation of New York; chmn: Heinz Endowment, Howard; trust: Heinz Family Foundation

Heinz, Theresa, trust: Winslow Foundation

Heiseke, F.H., secy: Federated Life Insurance Foundation

Heisey, W. Lawrence, dir: Kimball Foundation, Miles

Heiskell, Marian Sulzberger, dir: New York Times Co. Foundation; pres, dir: Sulzberger Foundation

Heisler, William H., III, trust: Haffenreffer Family Fund

Heist, Lewis Clark, pres, coo, dir: Champion International Corp.

Heist, Mrs. Lee H., Jr., co-chmn, distribution comm: Emergency Aid of Pennsylvania Foundation

Hildebrandt, Milton H., treas: Minnesota Mutual Foundation

Hildestad, Terry D., dir: MDU Resources Foundation

Hildreth, G. R., asst secy: Armco Foundation

Hilen, Andrew G., Sr., trust: Gilmore Foundation, Earl B.

Hilger, W. D., MD, secy, dir: Treadwell Foundation, Nora Eccles

Hilgers, William, vp, dir: Wright Foundation, Lola

Hilinski, Chester C., vp, trust, gen counc: Connelly Foundation

Hill, Allen M., pres, ceo, coo: Dayton Power and Light Co.

Hill, Anita, dir corp contributions: CSX Corp.

Hill, B. Harvey, Jr., trust: Loridans Foundation, Charles

Hill, Caroline N., trust: Steinman Foundation, James Hale

Hill, Charlotte Bishop, vchmn, mem adv comm: O'Connor Foundation, A. Lindsay and Olive B.

Hill, David N., vp, dir: Newhall Foundation, Henry Mayo

Hill, E. Eldred, dir: Lincoln Fund

Hill, Edward F., pres, ceo, dir: BarclaysAmerican Corp.; chmn, pres: Barclays Foundation Inc.

Hill, F. Trent, Jr., trust: Sonoco Products Foundation

Hill, Frederick W., chmn, trust: Westinghouse Foundation

Hill, G. Paul, trust: Monroe Auto Equipment Foundation Trust

Hill, George, trust: Burchfield Foundation, Charles E.

Hill, George R., trust: Lubrizol Foundation

Hill, Harriet, trust: Artevel Foundation

Hill, J. M., secy, treas: Ferro Foundation

Hill, Jackie, vp pub rels: San Diego Trust & Savings Bank

Hill, Jesse, Jr., pres, trust: Herndon Foundation, Alonzo F. Herndon and Norris B.

Hill, Julian W., trust: Lalor Foundation

Hill, Leonard F., trust: Johnson Foundation, Robert Wood

Hill, Linda Bourns, vp, trust: Bourns Foundation

Hill, Linda K., pres, dir: Tyler Foundation

Hill, Louis F., dir: Grotto Foundation

Hill, Louis W., Jr., pres, dir: Grotto Foundation; trust: Northwest Area Foundation

Hill, Luther Lyons, Jr., secy, trust: Cowles Foundation, Gardner and Florence Call

Hill, Marvin F., secy, treas, dir: Florida Steel Foundation

Hill, Norman A., dir: Scott Foundation, Walter

Hill, R.H., mem (contributions comm): Virginia Power Co.

Hill, Richard S., trust: Tektronix Foundation

Hill, Robert E., mem bd govs: Brooks Foundation, Gladys

Hill, Roger W., pres, ceo, dir: Holly Sugar Corp.

Hill, Sally B., trust, vp: Burchfield Foundation, Charles E.

Hill, Steven Richard, trust: Weyerhaeuser Co. Foundation

Hill, Sylvia I., dir: New World Foundation

Hill, Thomas K., pres: Kirkhill Foundation

Hill, W.W., pres, treas: Thirty-Five Twenty, Inc.

Hill, Walter Clay, trust: Hill and Family Foundation, Walter Clay

Hill, William R., MD, trust: Davis Hospital Foundation

Hillard, R. G., ceo: Security Life of Denver

Hillburger, Robert E., pres: Tripifoods

Hillen, Frances Gilmore, dir, vp: Gilmore Foundation, Earl B.

Hillenbrand, Daniel A., chmn, dir: Hillenbrand Industries

Hillenbrand, W. August, ceo, pres, coo, dir: Hillenbrand Industries

Hillenmeyer, E.B., Jr., Hayswood Foundation

Hilliard, Thomas J., Jr., trust: Frick Foundation, Helen Clay

Hilliard, III, Landon, trust: Brown Brothers Harriman & Co. Undergraduate Fund

Hillin, Betty S., exec dir: Constantin Foundation

Hillman, Elsie H., dir: Hillman Foundation

Hillman, Henry Lea, chmn: Hillman Co.; chmn, dir, don son: Hillman Foundation; don, pres, dir: Hillman Foundation, Henry L.; pres, dir: Polk Foundation

Hillman, Rita K., pres: Hillman Family Foundation, Alex

Hillman, Tommy, vchmn: Riceland Foods, Inc.

Hills, Lee, chmn, trust: Knight Foundation, John S. and James L.

Hills, Reuben W., III, pres: Hills Fund, Edward E.

Hillyard, Gerald R., Jr., secy, trust: Johnson Foundation, Helen K. and Arthur E.

Hilsabeck, Frank H., pres, ceo: Lincoln Telecommunications Co.

Hilsberg, Marshall, chmn, ceo: Lord & Taylor

Hilsman, Joseph, comm mem: Woodward Fund-Atlanta, David, Helen, Marian

Hilton, Andrew C., vp, dir: Coltec Industries Charitable Foundation

Hilton, Barron, dir, don son: Hilton Foundation, Conrad N.; chmn, pres, ceo, dir: Hilton Hotels Corp.

Hilton, Eric M., dir, don son: Hilton Foundation, Conrad N.

Hilton, Robert W., Jr., trust: Seasongood Good Government Foundation, Murray and Agnes

Hilton, Steve M., vp programs, dir, don grandson: Hilton Foundation, Conrad N.

Hilton, William B., Jr., dir, don grandson: Hilton Foundation, Conrad N.

Hilty, Henry L., Jr., dir, vp, secy: Gilmore Foundation, Earl B.

Hiltz, Francie S., trust: H.C.S. Foundation

Hiltz, L. Thomas, trust: H.C.S. Foundation

Himmelman, Bonnie, dir: Fairchild Foundation, Sherman

Hinchliff, James D., vp: Replogle Foundation, Luther I.

Hindley, George, mgr: Lytel Foundation, Bertha Russ

Hindy, James, dir: Health 1st Foundation

Hiner, Glen A., chmn, pres, ceo, dir: Owens-Corning Fiberglas Corp.

Hines, B. E., trust: Duriron Co. Foundation

Hines, Catherine G., trust: Scheirich Co. Foundation, H.J.

Hines, Lurley, dir: Perry-Griffin Foundation

Hinn, Dallas H., exec vp (mktg): Chicago City Bank & Trust Co.

Hinshaw, Juanita, treas: Monsanto Fund

Hinson, David R., chmn, ceo: Midway Airlines

Hinson, J. A., pres, chmn, dir: Phillips Foundation, Dr. P.

Hinton, J.R., pres, trust: Kellogg Co. Twenty-Five Year Employees' Fund

Hipp, Francis Moffett, chmn bd, chmn exec comm, dir: Liberty Corp.; chmn, dir: Liberty Corp. Foundation

Hipp, William Hayne, pres, ceo, dir: Liberty Corp.; pres, dir: Liberty Corp. Foundation

Hipps, J. Robert, mgr, trust: National Service Foundation

Hipwell, Arthur P., vp, assoc gen couns: Humana Foundation

Hird, Janice, dir corp pub involvement: UNUM Charitable Foundation

Hirooka, Sueyuki, chmn, pres: Sharp Electronics Corp.

Hirsch, Andrea S., asst secy: Macmillan Foundation

Hirsch, Anita T., vp, dir: Taube Family Foundation

Hirsch, Arthur L., vp: Gordon Foundation, Charles and Gertrude

Hirsch, David M., trust: Alperin/Hirsch Family Foundation

Hirsch, Gary D., chmn: Penn Traffic Co.

Hirsch, Gerald B., pres: Gordon Foundation, Charles and Gertrude

Hirsch, Jacob, trust: Julia Foundation, Laura

Hirsch, Laurence E., chmn, ceo, dir: Centex Corp.

Hirsch, Leon Charles, chmn, pres, ceo: United States Surgical Corp.

Hirsch, Philip J., vp, treas, dir: Miller Fund, Kathryn and Gilbert

Hirsch, Robert, dir: Taube Family Foundation

Hirsch, Sanford, exec dir, secy, treas: Gottlieb Foundation, Adolph and Esther

Hirsch, Vigal, vp, dir: Moskowitz Foundation, Irving I.

Hirschberg, William S., hon dir: Dana Foundation, Charles A.

Hirschfeld, A. Barry, trust: Boettcher Foundation

Hirschfield, Ira S., pres, trust: Haas, Jr. Fund, Evelyn and Walter

Hirschfield, Sylvia Weisz, pres, dir: Weisz Foundation, David and Sylvia

Hirschhorn, Barbara A., trust, chmn: Hirschhorn Foundation, David and Barbara B.

Hirschhorn, Barbara B., don, vp, trust: Blaustein Foundation, Jacob and Hilda

Hirschhorn, Daniel B., trust, vp: Hirschhorn Foundation, David and Barbara B.

Hirschhorn, David, don, pres, trust: Blaustein Foundation, Jacob and Hilda; vp, trust: Blaustein Foundation, Louis and Henrietta; trust, pres: Hirschhorn Foundation, David and Barbara B.

Hirschhorn, Michael J., trust: Blaustein Foundation, Jacob and Hilda; trust, vp: Hirschhorn Foundation, David and Barbara B.

Hirschman, Frank Frederick, pres, dir: Inland Container Corp. Foundation

Hirshberg, Elizabeth P., secy, dir: Tell Foundation

Hirshorn, Lynn B., dir: Kline Foundation, Charles and Figa

Hirsig, Alan R., pres, dir: ARCO Chemical

Hiscano, Ralph A., trust: Orange Orphan Society

Hiser, Harold Russell, Jr., trust: Schering-Plough Foundation

Hishmeh, George, dir: Jerusalem Fund for Education and Community Development

Histen, Deborah, adm asst: UNUM Charitable Foundation

Hitchcock, Meacham, vp, mgr: Brush Foundation

Hitchcox, Laura C., dir: Bingham Foundation, William

Hitching, Harry James, chmn, trust: Tonya Memorial Foundation

Hitchings, George Herbert, dir: Burroughs Wellcome Fund

Hitchner, Ruth, asst secy: Sordoni Foundation

Hite, B. J., vp: Manville Fund

Hite, James W., vp, trust: Harris Foundation, William H. and Mattie Wattis

Hite, Lawrence, pres: Hite Foundation

Hite, Marilyn Harris, secy, trust: Harris Foundation, William H. and Mattie Wattis

Hite, Sybil, vp: Hite Foundation

Hitt, David, Jr., treas: Texas Energy Museum

Hitt, Wendy M., trust: Glendorn Foundation

Hixon, Alexander P. Jr., adv bd: Hixon Fund for Religion and Education, Alexander & Adelaide

Hixon, Sheila K., adv bd: Hixon Fund for Religion and Education, Alexander & Adelaide

Hixson, Christina M., trust: Lied Foundation Trust

Hladky, J.F., III, pres, dir: Gazette Foundation

Hladky, J.F., Jr., dir: Gazette Foundation

Hladky, Joe, pres: Gazette Co.

Hlavac, Bernard C., dir: Sentry Life Group Foundation

Hlavenka, J. A., mgr community affairs: Union Carbide Corp.

Ho, Stuart T. K., dir: Bancorp Hawaii Charitable Foundation

Hoag, Carl, dir: Bank of the Orient Foundation

Hoag, David H., chmn, pres, ceo, dir: LTV Corp.; trust: LTV Foundation

Hoag, George Grant, II, pres, dir: Hoag Family Foundation, George

Hoag, John A., vp, dir: First Hawaiian Foundation

Hoag, Merritt E., mem scholarship bd: Cobb Educational Fund, Ty

Hoag, Patricia H., vp, dir: Hoag Family Foundation, George

Hoagland, Karl King, Jr., treas, trust: Monticello College Foundation

Hoaglund, Robert W., vp (control & information sys): Premark International

Hoar, Fred W., trust: Fusenot Charity Foundation, Georges and Germaine

Hobart, Sharon L., asst secy: Wheat Foundation

Hobbes, Julius, dir commun rels: Tampa Electric

Hobbs, F. Worth, pres, dir: Alcoa Foundation

Hobbs, John H., dir: Foundation for Child Development; trust: Hobbs Charitable Trust, John H.

Hobbs, Joyce C., dir: Hobbs Foundation

Hobbs, Truman M., pres, treas, dir: Hobbs Foundation

Hobbs, Truman M., Jr., vp, secy, dir: Hobbs Foundation

Hobby, Diana P., trust: Hobby Foundation

Hobby, Oveta Culp, pres, trust: Hobby Foundation

Hobby, William Pettus, Jr., vp, trust: Hobby Foundation

Hoben, John H., trust: Bean Foundation, Norwin S. and Elizabeth N.

Hober, Margo, cfo: Software Toolworks

Hoberg, Arthur P., vp: Rolfs Foundation, Robert T.; vp: Rolfs Foundation, Thomas J.

Hoblitzell, Alan P., Jr., exec vp, cfo: Ryland Group

Hobson, Henry W., Jr., pres, trust: Emery Memorial, Thomas J.; trust, secy: Griswold Foundation, John C.

Hoch, Orion Lindel, chmn, dir: Litton Industries

Hochman, Kenneth G., vp: Kenridge Fund

Hochreiter, Edward Joseph, pres, coo: Fischer & Porter Co.

Hochschild, Adam, trust: HKH Foundation; dir: Langeloth Foundation, Jacob and Valeria

Hock, Bernice, mem adv comm, trust: Webb Foundation

Hock, Delwin D., chmn, pres, ceo, dir: Public Service Co. of Colorado

Hock, W. Fletcher, Jr., secy: Jaqua Foundation

Hockaday, Irvine O., Jr., trust: Continental Corp. Foundation; dir: Hall Family Foundations; pres, ceo: Hallmark Cards

Hockberger, John J., dir: Morrison Foundation, Harry W.

Hockenbrocht, David W., pres, coo: Sparton Corp.

Hockenjos, G. Frederick, trust, mem: Rippel Foundation, Fannie E.

Hockert, Lorance, vp, treas: Spingold Foundation, Nate B. and Frances

Hodapp, Siegfried, pres, coo: Metallgesellschaft Corp.

Hodder, William A., chmn, pres, ceo: Donaldson Co.

Hoddy, George W., trust: Bentley Foundation, Alvin M.

Hodes, Richard S., trust: Jones Intercable Tampa Trust

Hodge, Lynn W., trust: Self Foundation

Holloway, James Lemuel, III, dir: Olmsted Foundation, George and Carol

Hollowell, Heather, dir (community rels): Sterling Winthrop

Holm, Herbert W., vp (fin), dir: Bush Charitable Foundation, Edyth; treas: Genius Foundation, Elizabeth Morse

Holm, Richard T., asst treas: Davis Foundation, Edwin W. and Catherine M.

Holman, David, mem: First Interstate Bank of California Foundation

Holman, John W., Jr., dir: Barker Foundation, J. M. R.; chmn, dir: Hyde and Watson Foundation

Holman, Morton, dir, vp, secy, treas: Philippe Foundation

Holman, Virginia, trust: Haley Foundation, W. B.

Holmberg, Cathy A., asst treas: Lutheran Brotherhood Foundation

Holmberg, Ronald Keith, sr exec vp, chief adm off, dir: AON Corp.; dir: AON Foundation

Holmberg, Ruth Sulzberger, dir: New York Times Co. Foundation; vp, dir: Sulzberger Foundation

Holmes, Carlette F., trust: Abney Foundation

Holmes, Christian R., trust: Holmes Foundation

Holmes, David R., chmn, pres, ceo: Reynolds & Reynolds Co.

Holmes, Edward A., grants chmn, trust: International Foundation

Holmes, G. Burtt, OD, comm mem: Whitaker Foundation

Holmes, Harry B., Jr., secy: Snite Foundation, Fred B.

Holmes, Jacqueline M., dir, vp: Holmes Foundation

Holmes, John Peter, dir, pres: Holmes Foundation

Holmes, John S., Jr., dir: Christy-Houston Foundation

Holmes, Kay, trust: Morgan Charitable Residual Trust, W. and E.

Holmes, Lee, trust, vp: Wegener Foundation, Herman and Mary

Holmes, Reva A., vp, secy, trust: Johnson's Wax Fund

Holmes, Robert W., Jr., trust: Riley Foundation, Mabel Louise

Holmes, Roger, secy (contributions comm): Westvaco Foundation Trust

Holmes, Ruth W., PhD, chmn: Whitaker Foundation; comm mem: Whitaker Fund, Helen F.

Holmquist, Marilyn L., asst secy: Schlegel Foundation, Oscar C. and Augusta

Holoman, John, sr vp: Home Savings of America, FA

Holsey, Neven C., pres, ceo: Jorgensen Co., Earle M.

Holst, Eugene R., pres, ceo: Quad City Osteopathic Foundation

Holt, David E., secy, trust: Brown Foundation, M. K.

Holt, John C., chmn, ceo: Nielsen Co., A. C.

Holt, Leon C., Jr., trust: Rider-Pool Foundation

Holt, Melvin W., vp, dir: Dodge Jones Foundation

Holt, Robert A., pres: Ontario Corporation Foundation

Holt, Sharon, secy: Hunter Trust, A. V.

Holtman, W. J., chmn, pres: Rio Grande Railroad

Holton, A. Linwood, Jr., dir: Loughran Foundation, Mary and Daniel

Holton, Earl D., pres, dir: Meijer Inc.

Holtz, Doris, dir: Knudsen Foundation, Tom and Valley

Holtz, Harry Lawrence, trust: Alliss Educational Foundation, Charles and Ellora

Holtz, Jean, dir: Cudahy Fund, Patrick and Anna M.

Holtzhauser, J. R., cfo: Mooney Chemicals

Holtzman, Robert, vp: Winston Research Foundation, Harry

Holtzmann, Howard Marshall, trust: Holtzmann Foundation, Jacob L. and Lillian

Holzer, Alan, contr: New York Stock Exchange Foundation

Holzer, Erich, secy, treas: Holzer Memorial Foundation, Richard H.

Holzer, Eva, pres: Holzer Memorial Foundation, Richard H.

Holzman, Steven D., secy: Day Foundation, Willametta K.

Hom, Gloria, dir: Haigh-Scatena Foundation

Homburger, Eric, secy: Julia Foundation, Laura

Homer, Arthur F., trust: Dalton Foundation, Dorothy U.

Honea, T. Milton, Jr., chmn, ceo: Arkla

Honigman, Daniel M., pres: Honigman Foundation

Honigman, David M., trust: Honigman Foundation

Honigman, Edith, vp: Honigman Foundation

Honsho, H., vp: JTB Cultural Exchange Corp.

Hood, Charles H., II, pres, treas, mem: Hood Foundation, Charles H.

Hood, Leroy Edward, dir: Seaver Institute

Hood, M. Gerald, dir: Health 1st Foundation

Hook, Clifford, cfo: Kaye, Scholer, Fierman, Hays & Handler

Hook, Harold Swanson, chmn, ceo, pres, dir: American General Corp.; dir: American General Finance Foundation

Hook, Henry B., vp: Lee Endowment Foundation

Hook, June C., dir: Cooke Foundation Corporation, V. V.

Hook, Robert L., secy, dir: Cooke Foundation Corporation, V. V.

Hooker, Jane, trust, secy: Woman's Seamen's Friend Society of Connecticut

Hooker, Raymond C., Jr., dir: Metropolitan Health Foundation

Hoolihan, James, trust: Blandin Foundation

Hooper, Adrian S., pres, dir: Hooper Foundation, Elizabeth S.

Hooper, Bruce H., secy, dir: Hooper Foundation, Elizabeth S.

Hooper, Jack H., trust: McCullough Foundation, Ralph H. and Ruth J.

Hooper, Lois A., trust: Hooper Foundation

Hooper, Ralph W., treas, dir: Hooper Foundation, Elizabeth S.

Hooper, Ruth R., vp: Allen-Heath Memorial Foundation

Hooper, Thomas, vp, dir: Hooper Foundation, Elizabeth S.

Hooper, W. Stanley, trust: Hooper Foundation

Hootkin, Pamela N., secy: Phillips-Van Heusen Foundation

Hootnick, Laurence R., pres, ceo: Maxtor Corp.

Hooton, Paula, secy: Fish Foundation, Ray C.

Hoover, Herbert, III, pres, trust: Hoover, Jr. Foundation, Margaret W. and Herbert

Hoover, Lawrence Richard, chmn, trust: Hoover Foundation

Hoover, Lyle, trust: Clorox Company Foundation

Hoover, Lynn C., trust: Plaster Foundation, Robert W.

Hoover, Miriam W., trust: Hoover Foundation, H. Earl

Hoover, Rose, secy: Fair Oaks Foundation, Inc.

Hoover, Thomas H., trust: Hoover Foundation

Hoover, William R., chmn, pres, coo, ceo, dir: Computer Sciences Corp.

Hopeman, A. A., pres, trust: Hopeman Memorial Fund

Hopeman, H. W., secy, treas, trust: Hopeman Memorial Fund

Hopeman, Harriet M., vp, trust: Hopeman Memorial Fund

Hopiak, George A., secy: Cowell Foundation, S. H.

Hopkins, David, Jr., vp, secy, dir: Reflection Riding

Hopkins, Edward D., chmn, pres, ceo, dir: Medalist Industries, Inc.

Hopkins, Henry H., managing dir: Price Associates, T. Rowe

Hopkins, Henry Tyler, exec vp, trust: Weisman Art Foundation, Frederick R.

Hopkins, K.H., trust: Lubrizol Foundation

Hopkins, L. Nelson, Jr., dir: Dent Family Foundation, Harry

Hopkins, L.N., Jr., dir: Danforth Co. Foundation, John W.

Hopkins, Maureen A., secy, adm: Barker Foundation, J. M. R.

Hopkins, R. E., Jr., trust: Montgomery Foundation

Hopkins, Virginia, treas: Holding Foundation, Robert P.

Hopkinson, Rachel R., treas: Female Association of Philadelphia

Hopmayer, Marlene, trust: Mansfield Foundation, Albert and Anne

Hopp, Daniel F., secy: KitchenAid Inc.

Hoppel, Thomas H., treas: IFF Foundation

Hopper, Bertrand C., dir, pres: Hopper Memorial Foundation, Bertrand

Hopper, Carol, mem: Boatmen's First National Bank of Oklahoma Foundation

Hopper, Frederick C., trust: Hopper Memorial Foundation, Bertrand

Hopper, Max Dean, sr vp information sys: AMR Corp.

Hopper, William B., trust: Hopper Memorial Foundation, Bertrand

Hopper, William David, trust: Rockefeller Foundation

Hopwood, Barry, trust: Pottstown Mercury Foundation

Hopwood, William T., trust: Hopwood Charitable Trust, John M.

Horack, Thomas Borland, vp, dir: Lance Foundation

Horan, John J., trust: Johnson Foundation, Robert Wood; trust: Merck Co. Foundation

Hori, Takeaki, vp, dir: United States-Japan Foundation

Hori, Tokeaki, dir: United States-Japan Foundation

Horike, Tsuyoshi, allocation comm: Kawabe Memorial Fund

Horn, Audrey, secy: Hobby Foundation

Horn, Carl, Jr., trust: Anderson Foundation, Robert C. and Sadie G.

Horn, Charles G., pres,coo: Fieldcrest Cannon; pres, dir: Fieldcrest Foundation

Horn, Craig W., trust: Wickes Foundation, Harvey Randall

Horn, David, gen mgr: Sun Life Assurance Co. of Canada (U.S.)

Horn, James C., pres: Star Markets Co.

Horn, Karen Nicholson, chmn, ceo, dir: Bank One, Cleveland, NA; trust: Huntington Fund for Education, John; trust: Rockefeller Foundation

Horn, Robert J., dir: Olmsted Foundation, George and Carol

Horn, William B., vp, dir: Olin Foundation, F. W.

Hornbeck, Daniel L., asst secy: Yellow Corporate Foundation

Horne, Gail B., secy, treas, dir: du Bois Foundation, E. Blois

Horne, John R., pres, coo: Navistar International Corp.

Horne, L. Donald, chmn, pres, ceo, dir: Mennen Co.

Horne, Michael S., dir: Covington and Burling Foundation

Horne, Robert C., vp, dir: du Bois Foundation, E. Blois

Horner, Donald G., vp, dir: First Hawaiian Foundation

Horner, Matina, chmn: Revson Foundation, Charles H.

Horner, Rich, asst vp, dir publ rels: Norwest Bank Nebraska

Horning, J. A., asst secy: Kenridge Fund

Horning, Jackie A., secy, treas: Humphrey Fund, George M. and Pamela S.

Hornor, Townsend, trust: Kelley and Elza Kelley Foundation, Edward Bangs

Horovitz, Samuel, trust: Steinsapir Family Foundation, Julius L. and Libhie B.

Horowitz, Barbara S., treas, dir: Horowitz Foundation, Gedale B. and Barbara S.

Horowitz, Barry M., ceo, pres: Mitre Corp.

Horowitz, David, admin: Horowitz Foundation, Gedale B. and Barbara S.

Horowitz, Gedale Bob, pres, dir: Horowitz Foundation, Gedale B. and Barbara S.

Horowitz, Ruth, dir: Horowitz Foundation, Gedale B. and Barbara S.

Horowitz, Seth, dir: Horowitz Foundation, Gedale B. and Barbara S.

Horrow, Harry R., secy: Littlefield Foundation, Edmund Wattis

Horsch, Lawrence L., chmn, dir: Munsingwear, Inc.

Horsky, Charles A., chmn emeritus: Meyer Foundation, Eugene and Agnes E.

Horsley, Richard D., vchmn, dir: First Alabama Bancshares

Horton, Alice Kirby, dir: Kirby Foundation, F. M.

Horton, Jack King, second vp, trust: Haynes Foundation, John Randolph and Dora

Horton, Jacob F., trust: Gulf Power Foundation

Horton, Raymond D., dir: Clark Foundation, Robert Sterling

Horvitz, Harry R., trust: H. R. H. Family Foundation

Horvitz, Jane R., trust: Rosenthal Foundation, Samuel

Horvitz, Michael J., trust: H. R. H. Family Foundation

Horvitz, Peter A., trust: H. R. H. Family Foundation

Horwich, Allan, secy, dir: Schiff, Hardin & Waite Foundation

Horwitz, Laurence, trust: Corbett Foundation

Hoshino, Hiroaki, treas: Kajima Foundation

Hosie, William C., chmn: Diamond Walnut Growers

Hosiosky, Issai, dir: Littauer Foundation, Lucius N.

Hoskins, Lowell, pres, dir: Arbor Acres Farm, Inc.

Hoskins, T., chmn: Bridgestone/ Firestone Trust Fund

Hoskinson, Beverly A., secy, treas: California Educational Initiatives Fund; secy, treas, exec dir: McDonnell Douglas Corp.-West

Hosler, Jerry, cfo: Acme Markets

Hostetter, G. Richard, trust: Maclellan Foundation

Hotchkis, John, dir, treas: Janeway Foundation, Elizabeth Bixby

Hotchkis, Preston B., dir, vp: Janeway Foundation, Elizabeth Bixby

Hotchner, Aaron E., co-chmn: Newman's Own; vp: Newman's Own Foundation

Houchens, Ervin G., pres, dir: Houchens Foundation, Ervin G.

Houchens, George Suel, dir: Houchens Foundation, Ervin G.

Houff, Douglas E., vp: Houff Transfer, Inc.

Hough, John, mgr: Harris Foundation, H. H.

Hough, Lawrence Alan, pres, ceo: Student Loan Marketing Association

Hough, Richard Ralston, trust: Turrell Fund

Houghton, James L., trust: Mabee Foundation, J. E. and L. E.

Houghton, James Richardson, chmn, ceo, dir: Corning Incorporated; trust: Corning Incorporated Foundation

Houghton, Leroy B., vp: Parsons Foundation, Ralph M.

Hourihan, Thomas J., dir: Norton Co. Foundation

Housen, Charles B., pres, treas, dir: Erving Paper Mills; pres, dir: Housen Foundation

Housen, Morris, secy, dir: Housen Foundation

Houser, Christopher I. M., pres: Union Bank Foundation

Houser, Dwane R., chmn, pres, ceo, dir: Community Mutual Insurance Co.

Houser, F. C., secy: Bridgestone/ Firestone Trust Fund

Houser, Henry C., secy, dir: Autzen Foundation

Houson, R. E., chmn, ceo: Babcock & Wilcox Co.

Houston, Ben, dir: Phillips Foundation, Dr. P.

Houston, F.E., trust: Millhollon Educational Trust Estate, Nettie

Houston, John D., II, trust, vp: Pittsburgh Child Guidance Foundation

Houtsma, Margaret E., trust: Artevel Foundation

Hoven, M. Patricia, vp: Honeywell Foundation

Hovnanian, Anna, pres: Hovnanian Foundation, Hirair and Anna

Hovnanian, Ara K., pres: Hovnanian Enterprises Inc., K.

Hovnanian, Armen, vp: Hovnanian Foundation, Hirair and Anna

Hovnanian, Edele, treas: Hovnanian Foundation, Hirair and Anna

Hovnanian, Hirair, chmn: Hovnanian Foundation, Hirair and Anna

Hovnanian, Kevork S., fdr, chmn, ceo: Hovnanian Enterprises Inc., K.

Hovnanian, Leela, vp: Hovnanian Foundation, Hirair and Anna

Hovnanian, Siran, vp: Hovnanian Foundation, Hirair and Anna

Hovnanian, Tanya, secy: Hovnanian Foundation, Hirair and Anna

Hovrihan, Thomas J., vp: CertainTeed Corp. Foundation

Howard, A. E., dir: Finley Foundation, A. E.

Howard, Alton E., secy, treas: Stewards Fund

Howard, Carole Margaret, dir: Reader's Digest Foundation

Howard, Ernestine Broadhurst, trust: Broadhurst Foundation

Howard, Frances L., trust: Arkell Hall Foundation

Howard, J. L., treas, dir: FPL Group Foundation

Howard, J. Myrick, trust: Covington Foundation, Marion Stedman

Howard, Jay M., secy: Israel Foundation, A. Cremieux

Howard, Jerome L., vp, trust: Dunn Research Foundation, John S.

Howard, John A., pres, dir: Ingersoll Foundation

Howard, John D., secy, treas, dir: Gellert Foundation, Fred

Howard, Melvin, vchmn, dir: Xerox Corp.

Howard, R. Robert, vp, dir: Badger Meter Foundation

Howard, Robert D., treas: Abrams Foundation, Talbert and Leota

Howard, Robert G., treas: Staley Foundation, Thomas F.

Howard, Robert Staples, dir: Reynolds Foundation, Donald W.

Howard, Scott, comm: Hope Memorial Fund, Blanche and Thomas; secy: Ward Foundation, Louis L. and Adelaide C.

Howard, T. J., asst secy: Shell Oil Co. Foundation

Howard, Wayne L., trust: Clemens Foundation

Howard, III, James J., chmn, ceo, dir, pres: Northern States Power Co.

Howat, Jr, Bruce Bradshaw, asst secy: Ameritech Foundation

Howatt, Robert A., trust: Massachusetts Charitable Mechanics Association

Howe, J. Franklin, trust: Davenport Trust Fund

Howe, James E., trust, chmn investment comm: Edison Fund, Charles

Howe, Linda, asst secy: Alexander & Baldwin Foundation; arts adm, gen adm: Zellerbach Family Fund

Howe, Mitchell B., Jr., pres, treas: Howe and Mitchell B. Howe Foundation, Lucite Horton

Howe, Robert M., pres, coo, dir: Mapco Inc.

Howe, Stanley M., chmn: HON Industries; pres: HON Industries Charitable Foundation

Howe, Wesley J., chmn, dir: Becton Dickinson & Co.

Howell, Alfred H., trust: Sofia American Schools

Howell, Alfred Hunt, vp, mem exec & fin comms, dir: Dodge Foundation, Cleveland H.

Howell, Arthur, exec dir: Arnold Fund

Howell, Clark, III, trust: Howell Fund

Howell, George L., trust: Hilliard Foundation

Howell, J. Smith, awards adv comm: Ferebee Endowment, Percy O.

Howell, John R., vchmn, dir: UJB Financial Corp.

Howell, Paul N., chmn, ceo, dir: Howell Corp.

Howell, W. Barrett, trust: Howell Fund

Howell, William Robert, chmn, ceo, dir: JCPenney Co.

Hower, Frank B. Jr., vchmn: Blue Cross & Blue Shield of Kentucky Foundation

Hower, Frank Beard, Jr., trust: Brown Foundation, James Graham

Howes, Davis C., treas: Crapo Charitable Foundation, Henry H.

Howes, Esther, Kelley and Elza Kelley Foundation, Edward Bangs

Howes, William B., pres, coo: Inland Container Corp.; vp, dir: Inland Container Corp. Foundation

Howie, John S., vchmn, dir: Mississippi Chemical Corp.

Howison, George Everett, treas: Burlington Resources Foundation

Howland, Mary G., vp: Children's Foundation of Erie County

Howland, Weston, III, treas, trust: Devonshire Associates

Howland, Weston, Jr., pres: Devonshire Associates

Howley, John J., secy, treas: Falk Foundation, David

Howling, G. E., sr vp (America): Qantas Airways Ltd.

Howson, Robert Edward, ceo, pres, dir: McDermott

Howze, Patricia, dir: Wells Fargo Foundation

Hoyem, David S., trust: United Conveyor Foundation

Hoyert, Robert S., trust: Stewart Memorial Trust, J. C.

Hoying, John C., pres, dir: Bank One, Sidney, NA

Hoyt, Charles Orcutt, chmn exec comm, dir: Carter-Wallace; secy: Carter-Wallace Foundation

Hoyt, Henry Hamilton, Jr., chmn, ceo, dir: Carter-Wallace; pres: Carter-Wallace Foundation

Hoyt, John W., secy, treas: Harris Foundation, John H. and Lucille

Hoyt, L. Douglas, trust: Morrison Charitable Trust, Pauline A. and George R.

Hrdlicka, Richard F., vchmn, sr vp, secy, gen coun, dir: Hesston Corp.

Hsu, F. Richard, secy: Tai and Co. Foundation, J. T.

Hsu, Ta Chun, pres, dir: Starr Foundation

Huang, Chao Sung, secy: China Times Cultural Foundation

Huang, Shuang R., vp: Merck Co. Foundation

Hubacker, Fredrick L., treas, vp: Acustar Inc.

Hubbard, Albert C., Jr., chmn, pres: Price Associates Foundation, T. Rowe

Hubbard, Charles W., asst secy, asst treas: Cockrell Foundation

Hubbard, Frank M., Friends' Foundation Trust, A.; mem: Phillips Foundation, Dr. P.

Hubbard, G. Morrison, Jr., dir: Hyde and Watson Foundation

Hubbard, Joan D., vp, dir: Hubbard Foundation, R. Dee and Joan Dale

Hubbard, John Barry, mem loan comm: Lindsay Student Aid Fund, Franklin

Hubbard, Karen H., vp, trust: Hubbard Foundation

Hubbard, L. Evans, bd mem: Friends' Foundation Trust, A.

Hubbard, R. Carl, vp, secy, dir: Close Foundation

Hubbard, R. D., chmn, pres, ceo, dir: AFG Industries, Inc.

Hubbard, Randall Dee, chmn, pres, ceo, dir: Clarity Holdings Corp.

Hubbard, Robert C., vp: Sofia American Schools

Hubbard, Stanley Eugene, pres: Hubbard Foundation

Hubbard, Stanley Stub, chmn, pres, ceo: Hubbard Broadcasting; vp, treas: Hubbard Foundation

Hubbard, T. Sewell, secy: Nathan Foundation

Hubbard, Thomas J., secy, asst treas: Dreyfus Foundation, Jean and Louis

Hubbard Rominski, Kathryn, dir: Hubbard Foundation

Hubbell, James W., Jr., trust, treas: Hawley Foundation

Hubbs, Donald H., pres, dir: Hilton Foundation; Conrad N.

Huber, D. M., chmn: PemCo. Corp.

Huber, David G., vp, trust: Huber Foundation

Huber, Dianne, asst secy: Enterprise Leasing Foundation

Huber, Gary L., pres, coo: United Fire & Casualty Co.

Huber, Hans A., pres, trust: Huber Foundation

Huber, Michael S., cfo: Andal Corp.

Huber, Michael W., chmn, dir: Huber Corp., J.M.; secy: Huber Foundation

Huber, Richard Leslie, vchmn, dir: Continental Bank N.A.

Hubler, John O., trust: Rotterman Trust, Helen L. and Marie F.

Huck, John Lloyd, trust: Dodge Foundation, Geraldine R.

Huckaba, John, dir: Reflection Riding

Huddleston, Anita, pres, dir: Precision Rubber Products Foundation

Huddleston, William H., Christy-Houston Foundation

Hudiburg, John J., chmn, ceo, dir: Florida Power & Light Co.

Hudner, Philip, pres: Drum Foundation

Hudnut, Stewart S., secy, dir: Illinois Tool Works Foundation

Hudson, Bannus B., pres, ceo, dir: US Shoe Corp.

Hudson, Charles D., vp, trust: Callaway Foundation; vp, trust: Callaway Foundation, Fuller E.

Hudson, Edward R., Jr., vp, trust, secy: Tandy Foundation, Anne Burnett and Charles

Hudson, Gilbert, pres, trust, ceo: Hudson-Webber Foundation

Hudson, Harry H., secy, treas, trust: Vale-Asche Foundation

Hudson, Ida Callaway, trust: Callaway Foundation; trust: Callaway Foundation, Fuller E.

Hudson, James T., chmn, ceo: Hudson Foods

Hudson, Joseph L., IV, trust: Hudson-Webber Foundation

Hudson, Joseph Lowthian, Jr., chmn, trust: Hudson-Webber Foundation

Hudson, Michael T., pres, coo: Hudson Foods

Hudson, Remy L., chmn, trust: Joslyn Foundation, Marcellus I.

Hudson, Thomas, secy: Kravis Foundation, Henry R.

Hudson, Vincent G., vp: Hauss-Helms Foundation

Hudson, William J., Jr., ceo, pres: AMP

Huesmans, Spike, chmn: Courtaulds Fibers Inc.

Huey, John W., trust: Butler Foundation, Alice; trust: Butler Manufacturing Co. Foundation

Huey, Ward L., Jr., vchmn, dir: Belo Corp., A.H.; trust: Dallas Morning News—WFAA Foundation, The

Huff, D. R., vp, asst treas: Federated Life Insurance Foundation

Huff, Glynn D., secy, treas: Perkins Foundation, Joe and Lois; secy: Perkins-Prothro Foundation

Huff, Margaret, secy, trust: Cooper Foundation

Huff, W. C., MD, vp, dir: Livingston Memorial Foundation

Huff, William B., cfo: Affiliated Publications, Inc.

Huffaker, Robert F., vp, dir: Brown Charitable Trust, Dora Maclellan

Huffer, Duane G., trust: Saemann Foundation, Franklin I.

Huffington, Michael, trust: Huffington Foundation

Huffington, Phyliss G., trust: Huffington Foundation

Huffington, Roy M., trust: Huffington Foundation

Huffington, Terry L., trust: Huffington Foundation

Huffman, Robert R., pres: Pasadena Area Residential Aid

Hufford, Jack R., secy, treas, trust: Whitney Benefits

Hufstedler, Shirley Mount, dir: MacArthur Foundation, John D. and Catherine T.

Hugenberg, Stanley, Jr., trust: Brown Foundation, James Graham

Huger, Eugenie Jones, pres: Jones Family Foundation, Eugenie and Joseph

Huger, Killian L., Jr., secy, treas, trust: Jones Family Foundation, Eugenie and Joseph

Hughes, Al E., secy, trust: Wahlert Foundation

Hughes, Bill M., trust: Buckley Trust, Thomas D.

Hughes, Bob, vp (mktg): Bryan Foods

Hughes, Bruce, trust, treas: DelMar Foundation, Charles

Hughes, David H., dir: Hall Family Foundations; vchmn, dir: Hughes Supply, Inc.

Hughes, Donald R., vchmn, dir: Burlington Industries; trust: Burlington Industries Foundation

Hughes, Frederick W., chmn emeritus, dir: Warhol Foundation for the Visual Arts, Andy

Hughes, H. Stuart, dir: Hughes Memorial Foundation, Charles Evans

Hughes, Harriette, dir: Stauffer Foundation, John and Beverly

Hughes, John E., pres, treas, dir: Coleman Foundation

Hughes, Kathy, mem contributions comm: Diamond Shamrock

Hughes, Lois J., vp, secy, dir: Wahlstrom Foundation

Hughes, Louis R., exec vp: General Motors Corp.

Hughes, Lulu, secy, dir: Weiss Foundation, William E.

Hughes, Mareen D., trust, vp: DelMar Foundation, Charles

Hughes, Marianne H., asst secy: Plumsock Fund

Hughes, Mark F., pres, trust: Collins Foundation, Joseph

Hughes, Mary Ellen, treas, trust: Norcliffe Fund

Hughes, O. P., dir: Koulaieff Educational Fund, Trustees of Ivan Y.

Hughes, Robert, pres: Armbrust Chain Co.

Hughes, Roger A., exec adm: Carver Charitable Trust, Roy J.

Hughey, Richard M., pres, trust: Gilmore Foundation, Irving S.

Hugonnet, Barbara M., adm dir: Whitney Foundation, Helen Hay

Huhn, David R., mem: Scripps Howard Foundation

Huhn, Les M., pres, dir: Jameson Foundation, J. W. and Ida M.

Huhndorf, Roy M., Cook Inlet Region

Huidekoper, Peter G., program off: Gates Foundation

Huiner, June, secy, treas: Huizenga Foundation, Jennie

Huisking, Frank R., treas: Huisking Foundation

Huisking, Richard V., Jr., secy: Huisking Foundation

Huisking, Richard V., Sr., trust: Huisking Foundation

Huisking, William, Jr., vp: Huisking Foundation

Huitt, J. Fred, vchmn bd trusts, mem investment comm: Trull Foundation

Huizenga, G. Harry, treas, dir: Huizenga Family Foundation

Huizenga, H. Wayne, don, pres, dir: Huizenga Family Foundation

Huizenga, Marti, vp, dir: Huizenga Family Foundation

Hulbert, Henry L., mgr, trust: Warren and Beatrice W. Blanding Foundation, Riley J. and Lillian N.

Hulings, Albert Dewayne, chmn exec comm, dir: Andersen Corp.; vp: Bayport Foundation; vp, dir: Hulings Foundation, Mary Andersen

Hulings, Mary A., vp: Bayport Foundation

Hulings, Mary Andersen, pres, dir: Hulings Foundation, Mary Andersen

Hull, Addis E., dir: Heller Foundation, Walter E.

Hull, Cordell William, vchmn, dir: Bechtel Foundation

Hull, Floyd V., Jr., trust: Nicol Scholarship Foundation, Helen Kavanagh

Hull, Gerry, chmn, dir: Glancy Foundation, Lenora and Alfred

Hull, Nancy M., secy, treas, dir: Atlantic Foundation of New York

Hulman, Mary F., comm mem: Indiana Chemical Trust

Hulme, Aura P., trust: Hulme Charitable Foundation, Milton G.

Hulme, Helen C., trust: Hulme Charitable Foundation, Milton G.

Hulsebosch, C. J., treas, dir: Oshkosh Truck Foundation

Hulseman, J. F., vp: Solo Cup Foundation

Hulseman, Robert L., pres, dir, ceo: Solo Cup Co.; pres: Solo Cup Foundation

Hultgren, Dennis N., dir (environmental & pub aff): Appleton Papers

Hultin, Donna d., dir: Animal Assistance Foundation

Humann, L. Phillip, mem: Trust Co. of Georgia Foundation

Humann, Phillip L., trust: Camp Younts Foundation

Hume, Caroline H., dir, srvp: Hume Foundation, Jaquelin

Hume, George H., vp, secy: Hume Foundation, Jaquelin

Hume, William J., dir, vp, treas: Hume Foundation, Jaquelin

Humke, Ramon L., chmn: IPALCO Enterprises

Huml, Donald, vp, cfo: CertainTeed Corp.; vp, dir: CertainTeed Corp. Foundation

Humleker, Margaret Banta, vp, dir: Banta Co. Foundation

Hummer, Paul F., pres, coo: Green Industries, A. P.

Hummer, Philip, dir: Field Foundation of Illinois

Humphrey, Benjamin C., trust: Wagnalls Memorial

Humphrey, Gertrude, chmn, dir: Humphrey Foundation, Glenn & Gertrude

Humphrey, H. Dean, dir (publ rels): Cessna Aircraft Co.; secy, treas: Cessna Foundation

Humphrey, Howard C., chmn, ceo: Franklin Life Insurance Co.

Humphrey, Hubert, trust: Reynolds Foundation, Z. Smith

Humphrey, James, III, vp, dir: Wilson Foundation, H. W.

Humphrey, Louise Ireland, pres, treas, trust: Ireland Foundation

Humphrey, William A., pres, coo: Homestake Mining Co.

Humphrey, William R., Jr., dir: Marbrook Foundation

Humphreys, B. J., vp, secy: Wickson-Link Memorial Foundation

Humphreys, Cecil C., trust: Plough Foundation

Humphreys, Ethel Mae Craig, trust: Craig Foundation, E. L.

Humphreys, Ethelmae Craig, chmn, secy, dir: Modern Maid Food Products, Inc.

Humphreys, Henry C., pres: National Spinning Co.

Humphreys, Jay P., pres: Tamko Asphalt Products

Humphreys, John Patrick, pres: Tamko Asphalt Products; pres, dir: Craig Foundation, E. L.

Humphreys, Robert, Jr., dir: Royal Insurance Foundation

Hundt, Paul Robert, vp, secy: Crane Fund; trust: Crane Fund for Widows and Children

Hungerpiller, James, trust: Hodge Foundation

Hunia, Edward M., vp, treas: Kresge Foundation

Hunsaker, Scott, trust: Hankamer Foundation, Curtis and Doris K.

Hunsberger, Ruby, chmn: Crown International, Inc.

Hunsucker, Glenn, pres, coo, dir: Bassett Furniture Industries, Inc.

Hunt, Alan Reeve, mgr: Shoemaker Fund, Thomas H. and Mary Williams

Hunt, Andrew McQ., trust: Hunt Foundation; trust: Hunt Foundation, Roy A.

Hunt, Christopher M., trust: Hunt Foundation

Hunt, Christopher M., MD, trust: Hunt Foundation, Roy A.

Hunt, Daniel Kilner, trust: Hunt Foundation; trust: Hunt Foundation, Roy A.

Hunt, David P., trust: Consolidated Natural Gas Co. Foundation

Hunt, Donald Samuel, exec vp & dir: Harris Trust & Savings Bank; dir: Harris Bank Foundation

Hunt, Erica, sr program off: New World Foundation

Hunt, Gary H., secy, dir: Irvine Health Foundation

Hunt, Gayle G., vp, trust: Cimarron Foundation

Hunt, Helen, dir, don: Hunt Alternatives Fund; dir: Hunt Alternatives Fund, Helen

Hunt, Helen M., trust: Hunt Foundation; trust: Hunt Foundation, Roy A.

Hunt, Jack L., trust: Cimarron Foundation

Hunt, Joan Lepley, trust: Campbell Foundation

Hunt, John B., trust: Hunt Foundation; trust: Hunt Foundation, Roy A.

Hunt, John D., chmn: Shawmut Worcester County Bank, N.A.; vp, dir: Shawmut Charitable Foundation

Hunt, Johnnie Bryan, fdr, chmn: Hunt Transport Services, J.B.

Hunt, Judith McBean, dir: McBean Family Foundation

Hunt, Katherine W., secy: Detroit Edison Foundation

Hunt, Michael S., vp, treas: Lilly & Co. Foundation, Eli

Hunt, Penny, dir: Medtronic Foundation

Hunt, Ray Lee, chmn, dir, ceo: Hunt Oil Co.

Hunt, Richard M., trust: Hunt Foundation; trust, don son: Hunt Foundation, Roy A.

Hunt, Robert G., trust: Campbell Foundation; pres: Huber, Hunt & Nichols

Hunt, Robert J., exec vp, cfo: Price Company

Hunt, Roy Arthur, III, trust: Hunt Foundation; trust: Hunt Foundation, Roy A.

Hunt, Swanee, dir: Hunt Alternatives Fund; dir: Hunt Alternatives Fund, Helen

Hunt, Theresa, secy: Clorox Company Foundation

Hunt, Torrence M., trust: Hunt Foundation; trust, don son: Hunt Foundation, Roy A.

Hunt, Torrence M., Jr., trust: Hunt Foundation; pres, trust: Hunt Foundation, Roy A.

Hunt, V. William, dir: Arvin Foundation

Hunt, William E., trust: Hunt Foundation; trust: Hunt Foundation, Roy A.

Hunt, Woody L., pres, trust: Cimarron Foundation

Hunt-Badiner, Marion M., trust: Hunt Foundation; trust: Hunt Foundation, Roy A.

Hunter, Allan B., dir: Hertz Foundation, Fannie and John

Hunter, Andrew A., Shaw Fund for Mariner's Children

Hunter, Charles David, vp, dir: Walgreen Benefit Fund

Hunter, Christine F., chmn: Fisher Foundation, Gramma

Hunter, E. K., secy, treas: Brown Foundation, Joe W. and Dorothy Dorsett

Hunter, Hugh V., dir: Howe and Mitchell B. Howe Foundation, Lucite Horton

Hunter, Kathryn M., Ritchie Memorial Foundation, Charies E. and Mabel M.

Hunter, Matthew, pres, ceo, dir: Central Maine Power Co.

Hunter, Raymond P., dir: Post Foundation of D.C., Marjorie Merriweather

Hunter, Richard N., dir: First Financial Foundation

Hunter, Robert D., trust: Chase Manhattan Bank, N.A.

Hunter, Shirley H., trust: Staley Foundation, Thomas F.

Hunter, Thelma E., asst secy: Jerome Foundation

Hunter, William T., treas: Fisher Foundation, Gramma

Hunting, David Dyer, Jr., trust: Steelcase Foundation

Hunting, John R., pres: Beldon Fund; pres, dir: Beldon II Fund

Huntington, Lawrence S., dir: Commonwealth Fund; dir, mem fin comm, mem audit comm: Macy, Jr. Foundation, Josiah

Huntington Trust Company, trust: Baker Charitable Foundation, Jessie Foos

Huntley, Linda, trust: Ross Foundation

Huntley-James, Ladonna, corporate pub involvement off: Lincoln National Corp.

Huntsman, Jon M., pres, trust: Huntsman Foundation, Jon and Karen

Huntsman, Karen H., vp, trust: Huntsman Foundation, Jon and Karen

Huntsman, Peter R., vp, trust: Huntsman Foundation, Jon and Karen

Huot, Paul, dir: Fuller Co. Foundation, H.B.

Hupp, John W., secy: Knowles Foundation

Hurack, Thomas Borland, mem bd adms: Van Every Foundation, Philip L.

Hurd, G. David, chmn, ceo, dir: Principal Financial Group

Hurd, George A., trust: Payne Foundation, Frank E. and Seba B.

Hurd, Priscilla Payne, trust: Payne Foundation, Frank E. and Seba B.

Hurford, Gary, pres: Hunt Oil Co.

Hurford, John B., dir, pres: Hurford Foundation

Hurlbut, Sally D., trust: Peabody Foundation

Hurlbut, Wendell P., chmn, pres, ceo, dir: Esterline Technologies Corp.

Hurley, Beatrice M., trust: Bickerton Charitable Trust, Lydia H.

Hurley, Doris Mattus, vp: Mattus Foundation, Reuben and Rose

Hurley, Gordon P., pres, dir: Hurley Foundation, J. F.

Hurley, Haden, vp, dir: Hurley Foundation, J. F.

Hurley, J. F., III, chmn, secy, dir: Hurley Foundation, J. F.

Hurley, James G., trust: Palisano Foundation, Vincent and Harriet

Hurley, James H., Jr., secy: Wood-Claeyssens Foundation

Hurley, John, trust: Bickerton Charitable Trust, Lydia H.

Hurley, Joseph G., pres, dir: Parsons Foundation, Ralph M.

Hurley, Willard L., trust: Hill Crest Foundation

Hurley, William D., chmn, ceo: Harvard Industries; chmn, ceo: Hayes Albion Industries

Hurley, William P., dir, asst secy, asst treas: Hopkins Foundation, Josephine Lawrence

Hurley, William S., vp, dir: Wyman-Gordon Foundation

Hursh, David M., pres: Kimball Co., Miles

Hursh, Robert D., chmn: Lawyers Co-operative Publishing Co.

Hurst, Anthony P., trust: Hurst Foundation

Hurst, Dean W., comm: Shaw Charitable Trust, Mary

Elizabeth Dee; mem: Stewart Educational Foundation, Donnell B. and Elizabeth Dee Shaw

Hurst, Elizabeth S., trust: Hurst Foundation

Hurst, Peggy, dir pub affs: Burdines

Hurst, Ronald F., trust: Hurst Foundation

Hurtig, Mary Wolf, secy: Wolf Foundation, Benjamin and Fredora K.

Hurtig, Peggy Helms, pres: Helms Foundation

Hurwit, Roger, mem disbursement comm: Oppenstein Brothers Foundation

Hurwitz, Charles Edwin, trust: RGK Foundation

Hurwitz, Stephen A., dir: Preuss Foundation

Husarik, Ernest A., mem adv & distribution comm: Jennings Foundation, Martha Holden

Husbands, Thomas F., trust: Borkee Hagley Foundation

Hushen, John Wallace, chmn contributions comm: Eaton Charitable Fund

Husking, Mildred, trust: Davis Hospital Foundation

Hussain, J. Mansoor, Sagamore Foundation

Hussey, Derrick, trust: Aeroflex Foundation

Hussing, Howard, pres, dir: Olmsted Foundation, George and Carol

Hussman, William H., trust: Kapiloff Foundation, Leonard

Husted, Ralph W., trust: Thirty-Five Twenty, Inc.

Husted, Thalia Barbara, trust: Orange Orphan Society

Huston, Charles L. III, trust: Huston Charitable Trust, Stewart

Huston, Charles Lukens, III, dir: Huston Foundation

Huston, Edwin Allen, sr exec vp, cfo: Ryder System; vp, dir: Ryder System Charitable Foundation

Huston, John A., dir: Culpeper Foundation, Charles E.

Huston, Robert L., dir: St. Faith's House Foundation

Hutchcraft, A. Stephen, pres, coo: Kaisertech Ltd.

Hutchcraft, A. Stephens, Jr., pres, coo, dir: Kaiser Aluminum & Chemical Corp.

Hutchens, Rita D., dir: Ordean Foundation

Hutcherson, Edward C., Jr., pres, coo, dir: Baroid Corp.

Hutcheson, Betty R., trust: Hutcheson Foundation, Hazel Montague

Hutcheson, Mary Ross Carter, pres: Carter Foundation, Beirne

Hutcheson, Suzanne Lilly, dir: Lilly Foundation, Richard Coyle

Hutcheson, Theodore M., trust: Hutcheson Foundation, Hazel Montague

Hutcheson, W. Frank, trust: Hutcheson Foundation, Hazel Montague

Hutchings, Gregory, trust: Tomkins Corporation Foundation

Hutchings, John A., trust: Ward Foundation, A. Montgomery

Hutchings, Peter L., exec vp, cfo: Guardian Life Insurance Co. of America

Johnson, Madeleine Rudin, dir: Rudin Foundation, Samuel and May

Johnson, Marjory Hughes, dir: Hughes Memorial Foundation, Charles Evans

Johnson, Mark L., dir: Carter Foundation, Amon G.; dir: Carter Star Telegram Employees Fund, Amon G.

Johnson, Martin, trust: JSJ Foundation

Johnson, Marvin Donald, vp (corp pub affairs): Coors Brewing Co.

Johnson, Mary W., dir: Pasadena Area Residential Aid

Johnson, Mayo, pres, treas: Wedum Foundation

Johnson, Michael P., vp, dir: Banc One Wisconsin Foundation

Johnson, Mrs. J. Dorsey, trust: Nathan Foundation

Johnson, Mrs. James D., trust: Washington Square Fund

Johnson, N. E., trust: Weyerhaeuser Co. Foundation

Johnson, Norman E., trust: CLARCOR Foundation

Johnson, P. Greer, trust: Anderson Foundation, Robert C. and Sadie G.

Johnson, P.J., vp (advertising & pub rels): Nomura Securities International

Johnson, Patricia Bates, trust: Johnson Foundation, Howard

Johnson, Paul A., trust: JSJ Foundation; trust, pres: Loutit Foundation

Johnson, Paul H., pres, ceo, dir: Connecticut Savings Bank

Johnson, Peter J., dir: Alworth Memorial Fund, Marshall H. and Nellie

Johnson, Peter Lawson, dir: Donner Foundation, William H.

Johnson, Phillip Royce, secy: Halsell Foundation, O. L.

Johnson, R. C., pres, ceo: Barber-Greene Co.

Johnson, Raymond, trust: Geneseo Foundation

Johnson, Richard E., treas: Grader Foundation, K. W.

Johnson, Richard J. V., pres, dir: Welch Foundation, Robert A.

Johnson, Richard R., program off: Exxon Education Foundation

Johnson, Robert A., trust: Whittenberger Foundation, Claude R. and Ethel B.

Johnson, Robert Gibson, pres, trust: Van Nuys Charities, J. B. and Emily

Johnson, Robert H., pres, dir: Webb Foundation, Del E.

Johnson, Robert O., treas: Wolfson Family Foundation

Johnson, Robert W. IV, trust: Johnson Charitable Trust, Keith Wold

Johnson, Robert Wood, IV, chmn: Johnson Foundation, Willard T. C.

Johnson, Roland H., secy, sr program off: Penn Foundation, William

Johnson, Ruth, trust: McNutt Charitable Trust, Amy Shelton

Johnson, Samuel Curtis, chmn, dir: Johnson & Son, S.C.; chmn, pres, trust: Johnson's Wax Fund

Johnson, Sanfra, asst to pres: River Blindness Foundation

Johnson, Stuart C., pres: Contel Federal Systems

Johnson, Sylvia R., asst dir: Hyams Foundation

Johnson, Thomas, trust: Knight Foundation, John S. and James L.; dir: Rockford Products Corp. Foundation

Johnson, Thomas Nelson Page, Jr., trust, chmn: Fitz-Gibbon Charitable Trust

Johnson, Thomas Page, III, trust: Fitz-Gibbon Charitable Trust

Johnson, Tom, secy, treas, trust: Mellinger Educational Foundation, Edward Arthur; trust: Rockefeller Foundation

Johnson, V. S., III, dir: Aladdin Industries Foundation

Johnson, W. Martin, vp, dir: Old Dominion Box Co. Foundation

Johnson, W.C., sales mgr: Hammond Machinery

Johnson, Walt, cfo: Besser Co.

Johnson, Wayne J., pres, treas: Johnson Foundation, A. D.

Johnson, Willa Ann, trust: Earhart Foundation

Johnson, William C., ceo: Grolier, Inc.

Johnson, William E., chmn, ceo, dir: Scientific-Atlanta

Johnson, William J., pres, coo: Apache Corp.

Johnson, William T., trust: Johnson Foundation, Burdine

Johnson-Bly, Ann, mem ed grant comm: Northeast Utilities

Johnston, Fred, dir: Fort Pierce Memorial Hospital Scholarship Foundation

Johnston, Frederick Thomas, pres, trust: Besser Foundation

Johnston, George A., pres, ceo, dir: American Water Works Co., Inc.

Johnston, George Sim, dir: Allen Foundation, Rita

Johnston, Gerald Andrew, pres, dir: McDonnell Douglas Corp.

Johnston, Harry A., II, trust: Chastain Charitable Foundation, Robert Lee and Thomas M.

Johnston, James, dir: La-Z-Boy Foundation

Johnston, John, pres: Easton Aluminum

Johnston, John R., trust: Boston Fatherless and Widows Society

Johnston, John S., vp, secy, dir: Marsh Foundation

Johnston, Lynn H., chmn, ceo, dir: Life Insurance Co. of Georgia

Johnston, Martha L., secy: Lamb Foundation, Kirkland S. and Rena B.

Johnston, Murray Lloyd, Jr., vp, secy, gen coun, dir: Zachry Co., H. B.

Johnston, Nelle C., secy: Jonsson Foundation

Johnston, R. A., exec vp (sales & mktg): APV Crepaco Inc.

Johnston, Ray V., trust: Whitney Benefits

Johnston, Robert L., trust: Gerber Cos. Foundation

Johnston, Verna Lee, treas: First Security Foundation

Johnston, W., pres: Thomson Newspapers Corp.

Johnston, Wendell G., pres: Lamb Foundation, Kirkland S. and Rena B.

Johnston, William, dir: Lannan Foundation

Johnstone, Clarence, dir, vp: Cook Foundation, Loring

Johnstone, F. T., vp, treas: Llagas Foundation

Johnstone, Frederick T., vp, treas, asst secy: Lakeside Foundation

Johnstone, John William, Jr., chmn, pres, ceo, dir: Olin Corp.; trust: Olin Corp. Charitable Trust; dir: Research Corporation

Johnstone, Michael, pres, ceo: Sheaffer Inc.

Johnstone, Nancy, trust: Woman's Seamen's Friend Society of Connecticut

Johnstone, R. C., sr vp, treas, dir: Bechtel Foundation

Johnstone, Shana B., dir: Hogan Foundation, Royal Barney; dir, pres: Shenandoah Foundation

Joiner, Webb F., pres: Bell Helicopter Textron

Jolson, Leon, pres: Nelco Foundation

Jonas, Charles F., secy: Lurie Foundation, Louis R.

Jones, Alan C., pres, ceo, secy, gen mgr: United Grocers, Inc.

Jones, Arleigh T., trust: Lassen Foundation, Irving A.

Jones, B. L., exec dir, trust: Fasken Foundation

Jones, Belle, asst secy, asst treas: McGonagle Foundation, Dextra Baldwin

Jones, Ben, vice-chmn: Kasle Steel Corp.; vp, secy: Kasle Foundation

Jones, Bernard B., II, chmn, dir: Feild Co-Operative Association

Jones, Bernard Bryan, III, 1st vp, dir: Feild Co-Operative Association

Jones, Bernice, dir: Jones Charitable Trust, Harvey and Bernice; co-chmn: Jones Foundation, Harvey and Bernice

Jones, Betty Alyce, dir: Redfield Foundation, Nell J.

Jones, Bucky, pres: Dairymen, Inc.

Jones, C. M., bd mem: Caring Foundation

Jones, Carol, commun coordinator: BOC Group

Jones, Carroll Payne, bd mem: Pitts Foundation, William H. and Lula E.

Jones, Charles H., mem, trust: Harris Foundation, H. H.

Jones, Clifford L., pres, dir: Anchor Glass Container Corp.

Jones, D. C., dir: Lockheed Leadership Fund

Jones, D. L. E., treas: National Starch & Chemical Foundation

Jones, D. Michael, asst secy: Reynolds Metals Co. Foundation; pres: West One Bancorp

Jones, D. Paul, chmn, ceo: Central Bank of the South; trust: Central Bank Foundation

Jones, D. Whitman, trust: Whittenberger Foundation, Claude R. and Ethel B.

Jones, Dale P., pres: Halliburton Co.; trust: Halliburton Foundation

Jones, David Allen, co-fdr, chmn, ceo, dir: Humana; chmn, ceo, dir: Humana Foundation

Jones, David R., pres, ceo, dir: Atlanta Gas Light Co.

Jones, Donald Richard, vp, dir: Motorola Foundation

Jones, Douglas C., trust: SIT Investment Associates Foundation

Jones, E. Lee, treas: Chambers Memorial, James B.

Jones, Edward L., dir: Arcadia Foundation

Jones, Elizabeth, mem (contributions comm): SAFECO Corp.

Jones, Emily J., asst vp: Meadows Foundation

Jones, Farrell, dir: Levitt Foundation

Jones, Frank H., asst secy: USX Foundation

Jones, G. Wayne, secy: Great Lakes Casting Corp. Foundation

Jones, George F., Jr., pres, ceo: NorthPark National Bank

Jones, George L., pres, ceo: Rose's Stores, Inc.

Jones, George M., III, pres, trust: Miniger Memorial Foundation, Clement O.

Jones, Glenn R., chmn, ceo: Jones Intercable, Inc.

Jones, H. L., vp: Caring Foundation

Jones, Heidi Hall, trust: Meyer-Ceco Foundation

Jones, Helen Devitt, dir: Jones Foundation, Helen

Jones, Helen Jeane, dir: Redfield Foundation, Nell J.

Jones, Hubert E., trust: Foley, Hoag & Eliot Foundation

Jones, Ingrid Saunders, chmn, dir: Coca-Cola Foundation

Jones, J. Bruce, vp: Alabama Power Co.; dir: Alabama Power Foundation

Jones, J. Stephen, trust: Jones Foundation, Walter S. and Evan C.

Jones, Jack, sr vp human resources: Jostens

Jones, James H., asst treas: Coleman Foundation

Jones, James R., chmn, ceo, dir: American Stock Exchange

Jones, Jerry D., McGraw Foundation

Jones, Jerve, pres, ceo: Peck/Jones Construction Corp.

Jones, Joan, secy to the pres: DNP (America), Inc.

Jones, John E., chmn, ceo, pres: CBI Industries; dir: CBI Foundation

Jones, John M., adv: O'Bleness Foundation, Charles G.

Jones, Joseph A., trust: Eastern Bank Foundation

Jones, Joseph Merrick, Jr., vp, trust: Jones Family Foundation, Eugenie and Joseph

Jones, Joseph W., chmn, trust: Evans Foundation, Lettie Pate; chmn, trust: Whitehead Foundation, Joseph B.

Jones, Joseph West, secy, dir: Coca-Cola Foundation; chmn, trust: Woodruff Foundation, Robert W.

Jones, Judith B., dir: Browning Charitable Foundation, Val A.

Jones, Judith H., asst secy: Aetna Foundation

Jones, Keith O., pres, ceo: Blue Circle Inc.

Jones, Lawrence M., dir: Coleman Co.; chmn: Coleman Charitable Trust

Jones, Leonade, asst treas: Graham Fund, Philip L.

Jones, Leslie A., trust: Dentsply International Foundation

Jones, M. William, secy: Armstrong Foundation

Jones, Malcolm E., pres, dir: Bangor Savings Bank

Jones, Marilyn Penny, mgr govt & pub aff: Matsushita Electric Corp. of America

Jones, Mary Duke Trent, 2cd vchmn, asst secy, asst treas, trust: Biddle Foundation, Mary Duke; trust: Duke Endowment

Jones, Mickey, dir: Wells Fargo Foundation

Jones, Norman T., ceo: Growmark, Inc.

Jones, Patrick, dir: Badger Meter Foundation

Jones, Patrick S., vp, cfo: LSI Logic Corp.

Jones, Paul, trust: Monticello College Foundation

Jones, Raymond E., secy, dir: Shelter Insurance Foundation

Jones, Rebecca S., dir charitable contributions: Southern California Edison Co.

Jones, Rev. Luther, pres: Dodge Foundation, P. L.

Jones, Robert D., dir: Bergner Foundation, P.A.

Jones, Robert G., Winchester Foundation

Jones, Robert M, trust: Sattler Beneficial Trust, Daniel A. and Edna J.

Jones, Robert T., trust: Anderson Foundation

Jones, Ross, treas: Reader's Digest Foundation

Jones, Russell, vp: Kaman Corp.

Jones, Stephany, mgr (intl programs & product giving): Johnson & Johnson Family of Cos. Contribution Fund

Jones, Stephen N., trust: Casey Foundation, Eugene B.

Jones, Thomas K., trust: Smith Foundation, Kenneth L. and Eva S.

Jones, Thomas S., III, secy, dir: Pasadena Area Residential Aid

Jones, Trevor M., dir: Burroughs Wellcome Fund

Jones, Wayne C., pres, dir: Eastman Gelatine Corp.

Jones, William B., trust: Sofia American Schools

Jones, William C., trust: Moores Foundation, Harry C.

Jones, William M., dir: Deposit Guaranty Foundation

Jones, Willliam, trust: Hugg Trust, Leoia W. and Charles H.

Jones-Saxey, Ruth, vp: California Educational Initiatives Fund; secy, treas: First Interstate Bank of California Foundation

Jongebloed, J. T., pres: Pool Energy Services Co.

Jonklaas, Anthony, trust: Kenridge Fund

Jonklaas, Claire H., trust: Kenridge Fund

Jonklaas, Claire H. B., pres: Kenridge Fund

Jonsen, Albert R., dir: Sierra Health Foundation

Jonsson, J. E., trust: Jonsson Foundation

Jonsson, Kenneth A., pres, treas, trust: Jonsson Foundation

Jonsson, Philip R., vp, treas, trust: Jonsson Foundation

Joralemon, Jane G., trust: Anderson Foundation

Jordan, Ann K., trust: Kaufman Endowment Fund, Louis G.

Jordan, Barbara C., dir: Freddie Mac Foundation

Jordan, Barbara M., vp, dir: Claneil Foundation

Jordan, Don D., pres, ceo, dir: Houston Industries

Jordan, E. B., trust: Rinker Cos. Foundation

Jordan, Eugene F., secy bd control: Brown Group Incorporated Charitable Trust

Jordan, Henry A., exec dir: Claneil Foundation

Jordan, J. Luther, Jr., dir: Frost Foundation

Jordan, J.W., secy: Phillips Foundation, A. P.

Jordan, James E., Jr., trust: American Investment Co. Foundation; trust: Leucadia Foundation

Jordan, Jerry, dir: Ayer Foundation, N.W.

Jordan, John W., II, trust: American Investment Co. Foundation; trust: Leucadia Foundation

Jordan, Juanita T., trust: Anderson Foundation, Peyton

Jordan, Leria L., vp: Sonat Foundation

Jordan, Neal A., vchmn: Kasiska Family Foundation

Jordan, Richard D., trust: Barnett Charities

Jordan, Richard E., vp, dir: Kline Foundation, Josiah W. and Bessie H.; trust: Stabler Foundation, Donald B. and Dorothy L.

Jordan, Robert E., M.D., trust: Swift Memorial Health Care Foundation

Jordan, Vernon E., Jr., trust: Ford Foundation

Jordan, Warren, comm: Craig Foundation, J. Paul

Jordan, William B., III, dir: Scholl Foundation, Dr.

Jordan, William M., pres, coo, dir: Duriron Co., Inc.

Jordan-Fellner, Lydia, dir: Quad City Osteopathic Foundation

Jordin, John N., vp, dir: Armstrong Foundation

Jorgensen, Ann Bentley, trust: Bentley Foundation, Alvin M.

Jorgensen, Earle M., chmn, dir: Jorgensen Co., Earle M.

Jorndt, L. Daniel, pres, coo, dir: Walgreen Co.

Jorstad, Josephine, secy, treas: Briggs Family Foundation

Joseph, Burton, chmn, dir: Playboy Foundation

Joseph, Geri M., trust: German Marshall Fund of the United States

Joseph, Marcel P., chmn, pres, ceo, dir: Augat, Inc.

Joseph, Meril, trust: Fortis Foundation

Josephs, Arthur C., pres: Ordean Foundation

Josephson, Marvin, chmn, pres, ceo: Josephson International Inc.

Josey, Jack S., pres emeritus, dir: Welch Foundation, Robert A.

Josey, Lenoir M., vp, mgr, trust: Favrot Fund

Joslin, Roger, asst treas: State Farm Cos. Foundation

Joslyn, Robert B., trust: Fruehauf Foundation

Joson, Yvonne, dir: Bank of the Orient Foundation

Joss, Robert L., vchmn: Wells Fargo & Co.

Josse, Constance B., trust: Olin Charitable Trust, John M.

Jouan, Sylvie, dir (publ rels): Baccarat Inc.

Joukowsky, Artemis A. W., dir: Joukowsky Family Foundation

Joukowsky, Martha Content, dir: Joukowsky Family Foundation

Jovanovich, Peter, pres, ceo: Harcourt Brace Jovanovich

Joy, Daniel W., trust: Gould Foundation for Children, Edwin

Joy, H. Joan, trust: Joy Family Foundation

Joy, J.W., chmn: Davey Co. Foundation

Joy, Paul W., trust, don: Joy Family Foundation

Joy, Stephen T., trust: Joy Family Foundation

Joy Reinhold, Paula, trust: Joy Family Foundation

Joy Sullivan, Marsha, trust: Joy Family Foundation

Joyce, Bernard F., vp, secy, dir: Link, Jr. Foundation, George

Joyce, Burton M., pres, ceo, dir: Terra Industries

Joyce, Catherine P., pres, treas, trust: Joyce Foundation, John M. and Mary A.

Joyce, E. P., secy, treas: O'Neill Charitable Corporation, F. J.

Joyce, Eileen, human resources mgr: General Signal Corp.

Joyce, Elizabeth W., vp: Wiseheart Foundation

Joyce, Hugh D., asst secy, asst treas: Hillman Foundation; asst treas: Hillman Foundation, Henry L.; asst secy: Polk Foundation

Joyce, Michael Stewart, pres, dir: Bradley Foundation, Lynde and Harry; vp, dir: Brady Foundation, W. H.; trust: Pinkerton Foundation

Joyce, Micheal J., dir: Deloitte & Touche Foundation

Joyce, Severn, trust: Miniger Memorial Foundation, Clement O.

Joyroe, Jane, vp, trust: Sarkeys Foundation

Juarez, Robert, trust: Swift Memorial Health Care Foundation

Juday, David W., pres: Ideal Industries Foundation

Judd, Barbara E., treas: White Coffee Pot Restaurants Foundation

Judd, Wendell W., trust: Owen Trust, B. B.

Judson, Ray W., pres: Parsons Corp.

Judy, Leonard P., chmn, ceo: Rust-Oleum Corp.

Jukowsky, Susan, trust: Brundage Charitable, Scientific, and Wildlife Conservation Foundation, Charles E. and Edna T.

Julian, Leon, mem scholarship comm: Zimmerman Foundation, Hans and Clara Davis

Julian, Michael E., chmn, pres, dir: Farm Fresh Inc. (Norfolk, Virginia)

Juliber, Lois, dir: Brookdale Foundation

Jung, Raymond C., vp, secy-treas: Poole & Kent Co.; pres: Poole and Kent Foundation

Junge, Brandon, dir: Glencairn Foundation

Junge, Dirk, secy, dir: Glencairn Foundation

Junkins, Jerry Ray, chmn, pres, ceo, dir: Texas Instruments

Jurck, James T., mgr: Equimark Charitable Foundation

Jurdem, Ann, trust: Goldberger Foundation, Edward and Marjorie

Jurjens, J., vp: Nationale-Nederlanden North America Corp.

Jurzykowski, M. Christine, secy, treas, trust: Jurzykowski Foundation, Alfred

Jurzykowski, Yolande L., exec vp, trust: Jurzykowski Foundation, Alfred

Just, Myron, trust: Harvest States Foundation

Justice, Brady R., Jr., pres, ceo, dir: Basic American Medical, Inc.

Justice, Franklin Pierce, Jr., vp, trust: Ashland Oil Foundation

Justin, John S., Jr., chmn, pres, ceo, coo: Justin Industries, Inc.

Justus, Ralph, dir: Covington and Burling

Jutila, William L., trust: Massachusetts Charitable Mechanics Association

K

Kabacinski, M. M., treas: Marquette Electronics Foundation

Kabay, John, trust: Calvin Klein Foundation

Kabbani, Raja, dir: Bobst Foundation, Elmer and Mamdouha

Kabler, Elizabeth R., vp: Rosenstiel Foundation

Kabureck, George R., pres, cfo: Union Trust

Kachel, Theodore, pres, ceo: Esselte Pendaflex Corp.

Kaddaras, James C., treas, dir: Gerondelis Foundation

Kade, Fritz, Jr., dir: Kade Foundation, Max

Kade, Fritz, Sr., dir: Kade Foundation, Max

Kagan, Donald, mem bd govs: Richardson Foundation, Smith

Kahana, Aron, chmn, pres: Israel Discount Bank of New York

Kahler, Cynthia W., dir: Wagner Manufacturing Co. Foundation, E. R.

Kahlor, Robert A., chmn: Journal Communications

Kahn, Alan R., treas, dir: Jewish Foundation for Education of Women

Kahn, Albert B., Jr., secy: Kerney Foundation, James

Kahn, Harold, pres: Montgomery Ward & Co.

Kahn, Hugo, pres: Kraus Co., Ltd.

Kahn, Joan F., trust: Freed Foundation

Kahn, Louise W., trust: Kahn Dallas Symphony Foundation, Louise W. and Edmund J.

Kahn, Marilyn, fin off: Davis Foundations, Arthur Vining

Kahn, Michael, pres, dir: Reynolds Foundation, Christopher

Kahn, Richard Dreyfus, dir: Barker Foundation, J. M. R.

Kahn, Richard L., trust: Perkins Foundation, Edwin E.

Kai, Gary K., dir: First Hawaiian Foundation

Kaichen, Lisa, trust: Shiffman Foundation

Kain, Herbert, MD, trust: Valley Foundation

Kaiser, David W., trust: Rockefeller Family Fund

Kaiser, Ferdinand C., secy, trust: Arkell Hall Foundation

Kaiser, Gladys, secy: Buffett Foundation

Kaiser, Jackie, vp: Dearborn Cable Communications Fund

Kaiser, Kim J., trust: Kaiser Family Foundation, Henry J.

Kaiser, Lloyd Eugene, trust: Frick Educational Commission, Henry C.

Kaiser, Philip Mayer, vp, dir: Soros Foundation-Hungary

Kaising, Elmer, cfo: South-Western Publishing Co.

Kaito, Ben F., dir: HEI Charitable Foundation

Kajima, Dr. Shoichi, pres: Kajima Foundation

Kakita, Hon. Edward Y., dir: Nakamichi Foundation, E.

Kaku, Ryuzaburo, chmn: Canon U.S.A., Inc.

Kalaher, Richard Alan, vp, dir: Amax Foundation

Kalaidjian, Edward C., trust: Orange Orphan Society

Kalail, Edward, dir of corp commun: General Tire Inc.

Kalajian, Harry, exec vp, chief fin off: Michigan Bell Telephone Co.

Kalangis, Ike, ceo: Sunwest Bank of Albuquerque, N.A.

Kalb, Bettie A., secy: Wildermuth Foundation, E. F.

Kalb, Marianne Bernstein, trust: Bernstein Foundation, Diane and Norman

Kalfus, Blache, dir: New Orphan Asylum Scholarship Foundation

Kaliakin, N. A., dir: Koulaieff Educational Fund, Trustees of Ivan Y.

Kalikow, P., ceo: New York Post Corp.

Kalish, Bernard, chmn, ceo: Lawson Products, Inc.

Kalish, Kathy, mgr: Porter Testamentary Trust, James Hyde

Kalisman, Gayle T., trust: Taubman Foundation, A. Alfred

Kalivrentos, George, dir: Ryan Family Charitable Foundation

Kalka, Howard, dir: Litwin Foundation

Kalleward, Howard, vp, trust: Dalton Foundation, Dorothy U.

Kallman, Ellen B., pres, dir: Jewish Foundation for Education of Women

Kalnow, C. F., trust: National Machinery Foundation

Kalsi, Sarla, vp, treas, dir: Irwin-Sweeney-Miller Foundation

Kaltenbach, Hubert Leonard, vchmn, dir, mem exec com: Copley Press; vp, trust: Copley Foundation, James S.

Kaltenbacher, Philip D., chmn, ceo, dir: Seton Co.

Kaluza, Diane Basinet, grants adm: Hunt Alternatives Fund

Kaman, Charles H., chmn, ceo, dir: Kaman Corp.

Kamen, Harry, chmn, ceo: Metropolitan Life Insurance Co.

Kamerschen, Robert, chmn, pres, ceo, coo, dir: Advo System Inc.

Kamezaki, Takeomi, asst treas: Mazda Foundation (USA), Inc.

Kamimura, Tetsuo, pres, ceo: Mitsubishi International Corp.

Kaminaka, Muriel M., trust: BHP Petroleum Americas (HI) Foundation

Kaminer, Benjamin, trust: Harvard Apparatus Foundation

Kaminow, Ed, pres, ceo: Palm Beach Co.

Kaminski, Kenneth W., pres: KitchenAid Inc.

Kamiya, K., pres: Asahi Glass America, Inc.

Kamiya, Kanichi, chmn: Makita U.S.A., Inc.

Kamm, Solomon M., dir: Capital Group Foundation

Kampen, Emerson, chmn, pres, ceo, dir: Great Lakes Chemical Corp.

Kampfer, Merlin W., MD, trust, vp admin: Flinn Foundation

Kampouris, Emmanuel Andrew, pres, ceo, dir: American Standard

Kamprath, Stan, vp, exec dir: Johnson Foundation, Helen K. and Arthur E.

Kanai, Hisao, chmn: NEC Technologies, Inc.

Kanarek, Robin Bennett, dir: Bennett Foundation, Carl and Dorothy

Kandel, Richard, secy, treas: Weiler Foundation, Theodore & Renee

Kane, Charles J., dir: HCA Foundation

Kane, Daniel, chmn: Kane-Miller Corp.

Kane, Douglas C., vp, dir: MDU Resources Foundation

Kane, Elissa, secy: Heilicher Foundation, Menahem

Kane, James G., treas: Kane Paper Scholarship Fund

Kane, John C., pres: Ross Laboratories

Kane, John F., treas, asst secy: Lyon Foundation

Kane, Richard, pres, coo, dir: Bank Leumi Trust Co. of New York

Kane, Thomas, dir, treas: Clover Foundation

Kaneko, Hisashi, pres, ceo: NEC USA; pres: NEC Foundation of America

Kaner, Richard I., trust: Rubenstein Charitable Foundation, Lawrence J. and Anne

Kangas, Edward A., ceo: Deloitte & Touche

Kangesser, David G., pres, trust: Kangesser Foundation, Robert E., Harry A., and M. Sylvia

Kangesser, Hedy, treas, trust: Kangesser Foundation, Robert E., Harry A., and M. Sylvia

Kangesser, Helen, vp, trust: Kangesser Foundation, Robert E., Harry A., and M. Sylvia

Kangisser, Dianne, vp, exec dir, trust: Bowne Foundation, Robert

Kanitz, Betsy, asst secy: Domino's Foundation

Kann, Peter Robert, chmn, ceo, dir: Dow Jones & Co.; mem adv comm: Dow Jones Foundation

Kanne, Frank J., Jr., trust: Helms Foundation

trust: Randleigh Foundation Trust

Kenary, James, trust: Stone Fund, Albert H. and Reuben S.

Kendall, Donald M., chmn exec comm, dir, pres, ceo: PepsiCo; chmn: PepsiCo Foundation

Kendall, G. Preston, trust: Kendall Foundation, George R.

Kendall, George P., Jr., trust: Kendall Foundation, George R.

Kendall, Henry W., trust: Kendall Foundation, Henry P.

Kendall, J. William, chmn gifts comm, dir: Arvin Foundation

Kendall, James A., secy: Pardee Foundation, Elsa U.

Kendall, Jane C., trust: Bryan Family Foundation, Kathleen Price and Joseph M.

Kendall, John P., pres, trust: Kendall Foundation, Henry P.

Kendall, Thomas C., trust: Kendall Foundation, George R.

Kendrick, Benjamin, dir: Wieboldt Foundation

Kendrick, Edmund H., trust: Higgins Foundation, Aldus C.

Kendrick, Schaefer B., mgr: Piedmont Health Care Foundation

Kenealy, J. Robert, treas, trust: Sheridan Foundation, Thomas B. and Elizabeth M.

Kenerson, John B., trust: Charlesbank Homes

Keneven, Richard G., trust: Rice Family Foundation, Jacob and Sophie

Keniry, Joseph P., vp, treas: Rexham Corp. Foundation

Kenna, E. Douglas, chmn, dir: Carlisle Cos.

Kennamer, Rexford, M.D., pres: Western Cardiac Foundation

Kennan, Christopher J., Jr., dir: Rockefeller Fund, David

Kennan, Joan, exec dir: Arcana Foundation

Kennard, Janice M., vp: Bionetics Corp. Charitable Trust

Kennare, Arlene J., grants off adm, contact person: Fuld Health Trust, Helene

Kennedy, Bernard D., pres, coo: King Kullen Grocery Co., Inc.

Kennedy, Bernard J., chmn, pres, ceo, dir: National Fuel Gas Co.

Kennedy, Craig, dir: Joyce Foundation

Kennedy, David B., pres, trust: Earhart Foundation

Kennedy, Donald P., pres: First American Financial Corp.

Kennedy, Duff, dir: Haas Foundation, Saul and Dayee G.

Kennedy, Edward Moore, pres, trust: Kennedy, Jr. Foundation, Joseph P.

Kennedy, Elizabeth, dir: Kennedy Foundation, John R.

Kennedy, George D., chmn, ceo, dir: IMCERA Group Inc.; trust: Kemper Foundation, James S.

Kennedy, Harold E., vchmn, dir: Foster Wheeler Corp.

Kennedy, Holly, secy: Arcana Foundation

Kennedy, Jack E., dir: Hewit Family Foundation

Kennedy, James A., pres, ceo, dir: National Starch & Chemical Corp.; dir: National Starch & Chemical Foundation

Kennedy, James Cox, chmn, ceo, dir: Cox Enterprises;

trust: Cox Foundation of Georgia, James M.; pres, trust: Cox, Jr. Foundation, James M.

Kennedy, James Waite, vp, secy: Kennedy Foundation, John R.

Kennedy, John R., pres, ceo, dir: Federal Paper Board Co.

Kennedy, John R., III, vp: Kennedy Foundation, John R.

Kennedy, John Raymond, Jr., pres: Kennedy Foundation, John R.

Kennedy, Kathleen P., secy, dir: Kennedy Family Foundation, Ethel and W. George

Kennedy, Keith F., pres, secy, dir: Rexham Corp. Foundation

Kennedy, Mary Ann, trust: Merrion Foundation

Kennedy, Mary Elizabeth, vp: Kennedy Foundation, Quentin J.

Kennedy, Murry D., vp, secy, trust: Dunn Research Foundation, John S.

Kennedy, Parker S., trust: Jones Foundation, Fletcher

Kennedy, Patricia A., secy: AMCORE Foundation, Inc.

Kennedy, Paula, dir: Kennedy Foundation, John R.

Kennedy, Quentin J., pres, treas: Kennedy Foundation, Quentin J.

Kennedy, Quentin J., Jr., secy: Kennedy Foundation, Quentin J.

Kennedy, Robert D., chmn, pres, ceo, dir: Union Carbide Corp.

Kennedy, Robert Meyer, vp: Halliburton Foundation

Kennedy, Roger W., trust, mgr: Colonial Stores Foundation

Kennedy, Susan K., asst treas: Ogden Foundation, Ralph E.

Kennedy, Theodore C., chmn, ceo, dir: BE&K Inc.

Kennedy, Thomas B., sr vp: BayBanks

Kennedy, Thomas J., secy, treas: Smoot Charitable Foundation

Kennedy, Thomas N., trust: Matthews and Co. Educational and Charitable Trust, James H.

Kennedy, W. Keith, Jr., pres, ceo: Watkins-Johnson Co.

Kennedy, Wayne G., pres, dir: Kennedy Family Foundation, Ethel and W. George

Kennedy, Wayne J., trust: Millipore Foundation

Kennedy, William Jesse, III, dir: Quaker Oats Foundation

Kennedy, William M., dir: Kennedy Family Foundation, Ethel and W. George

Kenney, Edward F., trust: Yawkey Foundation II

Kenney, G. Dickson, chmn, pres, ceo: Kenney Manufacturing Co.

Kenney, Richard J., dir: Consolidated Papers Foundation

Kenney, Robert P., pres, ceo, dir: Elizabethtown Gas Co.

Kenny, John, secy, treas, trust: Loews Foundation

Kenny, Margaret Rosita, trust: Valencia Charitable Trust

Kenny, Maugha, asst secy: Wenner-Gren Foundation for Anthropological Research

Kenny, Pat, cfo: Hyman Construction Co., George

Kenny, Wey D., vp, dir: Beech Aircraft Foundation

Kenny, William F., III, chmn, pres, ceo: Meenan Oil Co., Inc.

Kent, Conrad S., pres: Akzo Chemicals Inc.

Kent, Helene D., pres: Kentland Foundation

Kent, Jack, pres, trust: Buell Foundation, Temple Hoyne

Kent, Plympton C., Jr., bd mem: Gardiner Scholarship Foundation

Kent, Robert Warren, vp, secy: Armco Foundation

Kent, Wendel, mem admin comm: Selby and Marie Selby Foundation, William G.

Keny-Guyer, Alissa C., dir: Penney Foundation, James C.

Kenyon, Bruce D., pres, coo: South Carolina Electric & Gas Co.; vp: Summer Foundation

Kenyon, Mark J., vp, cfo: Blackstone Group LP

Kenyon, Mrs. Robert, trust: Chapman Foundation, William H.

Kenyon, Robert O., trust: Stubblefield, Estate of Joseph L.

Kenyon, Robert W., mem distribution comm: Champlin Foundations

Kenzie, Ross Bruce, dir: Goldome Foundation

Keough, William H., sr vp, cfo: Pioneer Group

Kepler, Charles G., pres: Stock Foundation, Paul

Kerbel, Robert N., exec secy: Kutz Foundation, Milton and Hattie

Kerby, J. W., secy-treas: Sooner Pipe & Supply Corp. Foundation

Kerley, James J., chmn: Rohr Inc.

Kerley, Marsha L., secy, treas, dir: Peterson Foundation, Fred J.

Kerlin, Gilbert, secy, mem exec & fin comms, dir: Dodge Foundation, Cleveland H.

Kern, John C., trust: Kern Foundation Trust

Kerney, J. Regan, treas: Kerney Foundation, James

Kerney, T. Lincoln, II, trust: Kerney Foundation, James

Kerr, Alexander H., Jr., pres, dir: Kerr Foundation, A. H.

Kerr, Breen M., treas, trust: Kerr Fund, Grayce B.

Kerr, David G., trust: Falk Foundation, David

Kerr, Deborah, treas: Hilton Foundation, Conrad N.

Kerr, Donald M., trust: EG&G Foundation

Kerr, Donald Maclean, Jr., trust: EG&G Foundation

Kerr, Jo Arthur G., chmn: Kerr Foundation, Robert S. and Grayce B.

Kerr, Joffa, trust: Kerr Foundation, Robert S. and Grayce B.

Kerr, John, pres, ceo: Volkswagen of America, Inc.

Kerr, Lou C., vp, secy: Kerr Foundation

Kerr, Merle D., cfo, treas: BMC Industries; treas, dir: BMC Foundation

Kerr, Robert Samuel, Jr., pres: Kerr Foundation

Kerr, Sharon, trust: Kerr Foundation

Kerr, Sheryl V., pres: Kerr Fund, Grayce B.

Kerr, Steven, trust: Kerr Foundation

Kerr, William A., vp, treas, dir: Kerr Foundation, A. H.

Kerr, William G., pres, treas, trust: Kerr Foundation, Robert S. and Grayce B.

Kerschen, R., ceo, pres: Law Company, Inc.

Kerslake, John A., chmn, dir: BarclaysAmerican Corp.

Kerst, A. F., pres: Calgon Corp.

Kerst, Richard N., trust: Heckscher Foundation for Children

Kerstein, David A., vp, trust: Helis Foundation

Kerstein, Ruth, secy, dir: Schwartz Fund for Education and Health Research, Arnold and Marie

Kersteiner, James A., asst treas: Armco Steel Co. Foundation

Kersting, Donald L., trust: Johnson Endeavor Foundation, Christian A.

Kerwin, Thomas Hugh, treas: Norfolk Southern Foundation

Kese, Barbara, program off: Weingart Foundation

Kesel, George F., chmn: Integra Bank

Kesler, Charles, dir: Salvatori Foundation, Henry

Kessel, William W., trust: Wickes Foundation, Harvey Randall

Kessinger, Tom George, trust: China Medical Board of New York

Kessler, Barbara, secy, dir: Relations Foundation

Kessler, Dennis L., pres, dir: Fel-Pro/ Mecklenburger Foundation; vp, dir: Relations Foundation

Kest, Clara, secy, dir: Kest Family Foundation, Sol and Clara

Kest, Michael, treas, dir: Kest Family Foundation, Sol and Clara

Kest, Newell, vp, trust: Blade Foundation

Kest, Sol, pres, dir: Kest Family Foundation, Sol and Clara

Kestenboum, Joseph, branch mgr: Bank Hapoalim B.M.

Kester, Kathleen Carpenter, trust: Shapiro Charitable Trust, J. B. & Maurice C.

Kestner, R. Steven, asst secy, asst treas: Mellen Foundation

Ketcherside, James Lee, dir: Mingenback Foundation, Julia J.

Ketchum, Ezekiel Sargent, pres, ceo, dir: Meridian Bancorp

Ketchum, William K., trust: AT&T Foundation

Kettering, Charles F., III, pres, trust: Kettering Family Foundation

Kettering, Lisa S., trust: Kettering Family Foundation

Kettering, Virginia W., trust: Kettering Family Foundation; mem distribution comm: Kettering Fund

Ketterman, Alda, trust: Hoffman Foundation, Bob

Keune, Donald J., adv: Cayuga Foundation

Keusch, Suzanne H., vp, dir: Jewish Foundation for Education of Women

Keuthen, Catherine J., legal adv: Boston Edison Foundation

Kevorkian, Marjorie, pres, curator, trust: Kevorkian Fund, Hagop

Key, James W., trust: Pickett and Hatcher Educational Fund

Key Trust Company, trust: Kingston Foundation

Keydel, Frederick R., secy: Fruehauf Foundation

Keyes, James Henry, pres, ceo, dir: Johnson Controls; adv: Johnson Controls Foundation

Keyser, Alan J., trust: Quaker Chemical Foundation

Keyser, F. Ray, Jr., chmn, dir: Central Vermont Public Service Corp.

Keyston, David, mgr: Aequus Institute

Kiburis, Doris, secy: Oakley Foundation, Hollie and Anna

Kice, James V., chmn: Kice Industries, Inc.

Kice, Thomas F., pres: Kice Industries, Inc.

Kick, Frank J., treas: Bydale Foundation

Kickliter, Ben F., trust: Gulf Power Foundation

Kidd, Mrs. Wilmot H., pres, trust: Johnson Endeavor Foundation, Christian A.

Kidd, Vallee, trust: Grimes Foundation, Otha H.

Kidde, John L., trust, mem: Rippel Foundation, Fannie E.

Kidder, C. Robert, chmn, pres, ceo: Duracell International

Kidder, Rushworth M., trust: Mott Foundation, Charles Stewart

Kiebach, Olivia M., pres: Bardes Foundation

Kieckhafer, Allan C., vchmn: Schlegel Foundation, Oscar C. and Augusta

Kieckhefer, John I., trust: Kieckhefer Foundation, J. W.

Kieckhefer, Robert H., trust: Kieckhefer Foundation, J. W.

Kiefer, Raymond H., vp, trust: Allstate Foundation

Kiehne, E. C., vp, treas, dir: Legg & Co. Foundation

Kieley, Leo, pres: Coors Brewing Co.

Kien, Gerald A., chmn, pres, ceo: Sun Electric Corp.

Kierlin, Robert A., pres: Hiawatha Education Foundation

Kiersznowski, Demi Lloyd, dir: Share Foundation

Kies, William S., III, dir: Oaklawn Foundation

Kieschnick, Gerald B., trust: Woltman Foundation, B. M.

Kiewit, Marjorie H., trust: Kiewit Foundation, Peter

Kiewit, Peter, Jr., trust: Kiewit Foundation, Peter

Kiggen, James D., chmn, pres, ceo: XTEK Inc.; pres, dir: XTEK Foundation

Kihneman, David M., pres: Delhi Gas Pipeline Co.

Kilborn, Jane, asst vp publ aff: Washington Natural Gas Co.

Kilduff, Tim, dir (pub aff): Bull HN Information Systems Inc.

Kile, James, trust: CENEX Foundation

Kilgore, Ronald N., secy, treas, trust: Dalton Foundation, Dorothy U.

Kilhenny, Valerie, secy: Mutual of New York Foundation

Kilius, Paul, treas: Brunswick Foundation

Killinger, Kerry K., pres, chmn, ceo: Washington Mutual Savings Bank

Killinger, Kerry Kent, mem: Washington Mutual Savings Bank Foundation

Killion, Linda T., Jr., dir: Stowers Foundation

Killip, Wilfred, trust: Raymond Educational Foundation

Killpack, J. Robert, mgr: Prentiss Foundation, Elisabeth Severance

Kilman, George F., cfo, dir: Beckman Instruments

Kilmartin, David F., pres: Kilmartin Industries Charitable Foundation

Kilmartin, David F., Jr., pres, treas: Kilmartin Industries; vp: Kilmartin Industries Charitable Foundation

Kilpatrick, Joseph E., asst dir: Reynolds Foundation, Z. Smith

Kilpatrick, Kay M., contributions adm: Harcourt General

Kilroy, W. Terrence, trust: Shughart, Thomson & Kilroy Charitable Foundation Trust

Kilroy, William S., trust: Kilroy Foundation, William S. and Lora Jean

Kim, Young, gen mgr (gen affs div): Samsung America Inc.

Kimball, Alberta S., pres: Kimball Foundation, Miles

Kimball, Richard W., ceo, pres, dir: Teagle Foundation

Kimball, Sheila, assoc trust: Carpenter Foundation

Kimball, Shirley, trust: Carpenter Foundation

Kimbell, David A., trust: Wilson Foundation, John and Nevils

Kimberly, Susan L., dir: Dent Family Foundation, Harry

Kime, Jack E., cfo, assoc dir, chief adm off: Heinz Endowment, Howard; assoc dir, cfo, chief adm off: Heinz Endowment, Vira I.

Kimmel, Ceasar P., dir: Colt Foundation, James J.

Kimmel, O. M., Jr., secy, treas, trust: Leuthold Foundation

Kimmelman, Helen, trust: Kimmelman Foundation, Helen & Milton

Kimmelman, Peter, treas, dir: Diamond Foundation, Aaron

Kimmett, Gary, dir: Gleason Memorial Fund

Kimoto, Shari, secy: Environment Now

Kimport, Ken, dir: Mautz Paint Foundation

Kimsey, C. Windon, MD, adm: Hurlbut Memorial Fund, Orion L. and Emma S.

Kimzey, Lane Anne, trust: Alexander Foundation, Robert D. and Catherine R.

Kincaid, Warren, comm: Craig Foundation, J. Paul

Kind, Patricia, dir: van Ameringen Foundation

Kinder, Richard Dan, trust: Enron Foundation

Kinderman, Larry, exec vp, coo: Stockham Valves & Fittings; trust: Stockham Foundation, William H. & Kate F.

Kindle, Jo Ann, exec vp: Enterprise Leasing Foundation

King, Alan, pres: Silicon Systems Inc.

King, Arthur, selection comm: Gordy Family Educational Trust Fund, George E.

King, Basil, dir: Fort Pierce Memorial Hospital Scholarship Foundation

King, Betty S., secy: Richardson Benevolent Foundation, C. E.

King, Carolyn, dir: Reflection Riding

King, D. Christine, Jr., trust: Tiger Foundation

King, D. E., trust: National Machinery Foundation

King, David A., exec dir, mem distribution & investigating comms: Champlin Foundations

King, Delutha H., Jr., chmn, dir: Health 1st Foundation

King, Dennis B., dir: Herbst Foundation

King, Doris, vp: Ford III Memorial Foundation, Jefferson Lee

King, Dorothy, trust: Whitney Benefits

King, Dorothy E., pres, dir: King Foundation, Carl B. and Florence E.

King, Dorothy Warren, secy, dir: Warren Foundation, William K.

King, Edward H., pres, dir: Walgreen Benefit Fund

King, Edward M., trust: Doelger Charitable Trust, Thelma

King, Gary, dir: Sylvester Foundation, Harcourt M. and Virginia W.

King, Harry R., chmn, dir: Student Loan Marketing Association

King, Henry J., treas: SmithKline Beecham Foundation

King, Hugh, dir, vp: Andalusia Health Services

King, James D., secy, dir: Quad City Osteopathic Foundation

King, Jodie, asst secy: Hearst Foundation; asst secy: Hearst Foundation, William Randolph

King, John J., Jr., dir: Warren Foundation, William K.

King, John T., III, gov: Baker, Jr. Memorial Fund, William G.

King, Judith S., trust, treas: Stoddard Charitable Trust

King, Lord, chmn: British Airways

King, Louise Straus, pres, trust: Straus Foundation, Martha Washington Straus and Harry H.

King, Margaret, trust: Weyerhaeuser Family Foundation

King, Mary E., secy, dir: Arca Foundation

King, May Dougherty, chmn, trust: Dougherty, Jr. Foundation, James R.

King, Octavo P., clerk, dir: Clipper Ship Foundation

King, Olin B., chmn: SCI Systems, Inc.

King, Patricia, dir: General Service Foundation

King, Reatha Clark, dir: Fuller Co. Foundation, H.B.; pres, exec dir: General Mills Foundation

King, Richard Hood, treas: Hartford Courant Foundation

King, Robert L., pres, ceo: Foxmeyer Corp.

King, Robert R., pres, coo: Northwestern National Insurance Group

King, Roger J., secy, treas, trust: Straus Foundation, Martha Washington Straus and Harry H.

King, Roger Leo, treas, dir: Graco Foundation

King, Russell C., Jr., pres, coo, dir: Sonoco Products Co.; trust: Sonoco Products Foundation

King, T.L., pres, ceo: Standex International Corp.

King, Thomas E., secy: Enright Foundation

King, Timothy L., treas: Banc One Wisconsin Foundation

King, Victor R., trust: Fanwood Foundation

King, William Joseph, chmn, ceo: Dauphin Deposit Corp.; treas, dir: Kline Foundation, Josiah W. and Bessie H.; chmn, trust: Stabler Foundation, Donald B. and Dorothy L.

Kingman, Edward R., cfo: Chesapeake & Potomac Telephone Co.

Kingsbury, Frederick Hutchinson, III, vp: Johnson & Higgins

Kingsbury-Smith, Joseph, vp, dir: Hearst Foundation; vp, dir: Hearst Foundation, William Randolph

Kingsland, Richard M., vp: Valley Foundation, Wayne and Gladys

Kingsley, Alfred D., vchmn: ACF Industries, Inc.; vp, dir: ACF Foundation

Kingsley, Charles, vp, secy, dir: JJJ Foundation

Kingsley, Ora Rimes, trust: Kingsley Foundation

Kingston, Maureen P., secy: Price Waterhouse Foundation

Kinkel, Walter J., mem distribution comm: Ford and Ada Ford Fund, S. N.

Kinnamon, David L., secy, dir: Ross Memorial Foundation, Will

Kinnear, James Wesley, III, pres, ceo, dir: Texaco

Kinney, Annabelle, secy: Shinnick Educational Fund, William M.

Kinney, Douglas, dir: Farley Foundation, William F.

Kinney, Harry A., vp: Oldham Little Church Foundation

Kinning, Robert K., mem distribution comm: Greater Lansing Foundation

Kinosh, Diana, mgmt information supvr: Aetna Life & Casualty Co.

Kinsolving, Augustus Blagden, dir: ASARCO Foundation

Kintz, Margie, exec dir: Intel Foundation

Kiplinger, Austin H., chmn, pres: Kiplinger Washington Editors

Kiplinger, Austin Huntington, pres, trust: Kiplinger Foundation

Kiplinger, Knight A., trust: Kiplinger Foundation

Kiplinger, Todd L., trust: Kiplinger Foundation

Kipp, Robert Almy, dir: Hall Family Foundations

Kippen, Christina McKnight, dir: McKnight Foundation, Sumner T.

Kipper, Barbara Levy, chwm, treas: Levy Foundation, Charles and Ruth

Kipper, David, dir: Levy Foundation, Charles and Ruth

Kirbo, Bruce W., trust: Kirbo Charitable Trust, Thomas M. and Irene B.

Kirbo, Charles Hughes, chmn, trust: Kirbo Charitable Trust, Thomas M. and Irene B.

Kirby, Ann Pfohl, Mathis-Pfohl Foundation

Kirby, Fred M., III, dir: Kirby Foundation, F. M.

Kirby, Jefferson W., dir: Kirby Foundation, F. M.

Kirby, Keith, dir (Harkness Fellowships): Commonwealth Fund

Kirby, Philip L., vp, trust: Chambers Memorial, James B.

Kirby, Robert Stephen, dir: Washington Square Health Foundation

Kirby, S. Dillard, dir: Kirby Foundation, F. M.

Kirby, Walker D., vp, dir: Kirby Foundation, F. M.

Kirby, William Joseph, vp, dir: FMC Foundation

Kircaldie, James, trust: Jones Fund, Paul L.

Kirchhof, Anton Conrad, secy, gen couns: Louisiana-Pacific Corp.; secy: Louisiana-Pacific Foundation

Kircos, Louis, treas: Handleman Charitable Foundation

Kirk, Chuck, Hayswood Foundation

Kirk, Edward, trust: Edwards Scholarship Fund

Kirk, Garrett, Jr., trust: Randleigh Foundation Trust

Kirk, Grayson Louis, vp, dir, chmn exec comm, mem audit comm: Tinker Foundation

Kirk, J. W., contr: Chesapeake Corp.

Kirk, James R., trust: Campbell Soup Foundation

Kirk, Jill Powers, trust: Tektronix Foundation

Kirk, Katharine, secy, dir: Babcock Memorial Endowment, William

Kirk, Richard J., asst to exec dir: Hayden Recreation Center, Josiah Willard

Kirk, Russell, trust, pres: Wilbur Foundation, Marguerite Eyer

Kirker, John A., PhD, mem adv & distribution comm: Jennings Foundation, Martha Holden

Kirkham, George D., Bicknell Fund

Kirkham, Kate B., pres, trust: Bicknell Fund

Kirkland, Benjamin B., trust: Large Foundation

Kirkland, James H., secy, treas: Summer Foundation

Kirkland, John Cyril, asst secy, asst treas: Arkwright Foundation

Kirkland, Robin H., pres: Jafra Cosmetics, Inc. (U.S.)

Kirkman, Bruce, dir: Coca-Cola Foundation

Kirkman, Larry, exec dir: Benton Foundation

Kirkpatrick, Eleanor B., treas, dir: Kirkpatrick Foundation

Kirkpatrick, Jean, pres: Swasey Fund for Relief of Public School Teachers of Newburyport

Kirkpatrick, Joan E., pres, dir: Kirkpatrick Foundation

Kirkpatrick, John, trust: Young Foundation, Hugo H. and Mabel B.

Kirkpatrick, John Elson, chmn, dir: Kirkpatrick Foundation

Kirkpatrick, Susan T., trust: Taylor Foundation

Kirkpatrick, William A., Upjohn Foundation, Harold and Grace

Kirkwood, John H., pres, dir: Edgewater Steel Corp.

Kirsch, R. Craig, chmn, pres, ceo, dir: Action Industries, Inc.

Kirschner, Sidney, pres, ceo, dir: National Service Industries; trust: National Service Foundation

Kirtley, Donald, vp pub aff: Hercules Inc.

Kiser, Anthony C. M., pres, dir: Greve Foundation, William and Mary

Kiser, John W., III, chmn: Greve Foundation, William and Mary

Kish, Stephen A., dir: Allyn Foundation

Kish, Susan, Jr., secy: Tsai Foundation, Gerald

Kishimoto, Muneo, pres, trust: Mazda Foundation (USA), Inc.

Kishner, Judith Z., dir: Zarrow Foundation, Anne and Henry

Kissinger, Henry Alfred, dir: CBS Foundation; chmn, dir: Paley Foundation, William S.

Kissling, Walter, pres, coo, exec vp, dir: Fuller Co., H.B.

Kissner, Naida, adm & program asst: Fuller Co. Foundation, H.B.

Kisting, A. J., trust: Wahlert Foundation

Kistler, William H., trust: Johnson Foundation, Helen K. and Arthur E.

Kitabjian, Mary, asst secy: Pforzheimer Foundation, Carl and Lily

Kitamura, Toshi, chmn: Hitachi

Kitchell, William, cfo: Zamoiski Co.

Kitchen, Thomas M., vp, cfo, dir: Avondale Industries, Inc.

Kitchens, John L., admin: FPL Group Foundation

Kitka, Jack, Vevay-Switzerland County Foundation

Kitko, Paulette, secy, treas: Kenridge Fund

Kittredge, Robert P., chmn: Fabri-Kal Corp.; pres: Fabri-Kal Foundation

Kiuchi, Takashi, dir: Mitsubishi Electric America Foundation

KixMiller, Richard W., asst treas, dir: Hyde and Watson Foundation

Kizer, John, asst secy, treas, dir: Daywood Foundation; vp, dir: Robertshaw Controls Co. Charitable & Ed Foundation

Kiziah, Clyde, vp: Hurley Foundation, J. F.

Klasinski, Debbie, admin asst: Sentry Life Group Foundation

Klateu, Robert E., cfo: Arrow Electronics, Inc.

Klatsky, Bruce J., pres, coo, dir: Phillips-Van Heusen Corp.; pres: Phillips-Van Heusen Foundation

Klau, James D., dir: Klau Foundation, David W. and Sadie

Klau, Richard J., pres: Eastern Enterprises

Klau, Sadie K., pres, dir: Klau Foundation, David W. and Sadie

Klauber, Philip M., trust: Burnham Foundation

Klaus, Joan, dir: American National Bank & Trust Co. of Chicago Foundation

Klayman, Ron, trust: Scripps Howard Foundation

Klebba, Kenneth J., trust, pres, treas: Vollbrecht Foundation, Frederick A.

Kleberg, Richard Mifflin, III, trust: King Ranch Family Trust

Kleberg, Stephen J., trust: Kleberg Foundation for Wildlife Conservation, Caesar

Kledzik, Gary S., vp: Glenn Foundation for Medical Research, Paul F.

Kleier, George O., asst treas: Reynolds Foundation, Donald W.

Klein, Amelia, trust: Klein Fund, Nathan J.

Klein, Anne L., trust: Quinlan Foundation, Elizabeth C.

Klein, Arthur Luce, pres, treas: Rittenhouse Foundation

Klein, Bertram W., chmn, dir: Bank of Louisville Charities

Klein, Beth Paxton, dir: Bank of Louisville Charities

Klein, Charles T., vp, trust: Frueauff Foundation, Charles A.

Klein, David, dir: Bank of Louisville Charities

Klein, David M., mem contributions comm: ITT Hartford Insurance Group

Klein, Edith Miller, dir: Morrison Foundation, Harry W.

Klein, Edward J., trust: Klein Fund, Nathan J.

Klein, Ernest, trust: Klein Fund, Nathan J.

Klein, Esther, dir, exec. vp: Rittenhouse Foundation

Klein, Jeffrey, pres: Liberman Foundation, Bertha & Isaac

Klein, Marilyn, exec dir: Goldman Foundation, William

Klein, Michael S., chmn, pres, ceo: Klein Tools

Klein, Raymond, pres: Klein Charitable Foundation, Raymond

Klein, Richard A., pres, treas: Quinlan Foundation, Elizabeth C.

Klein, Richard D., vchmn, dir: First of America Bank Corp.

Klein, Richard L., trust: Durr-Fillauer Medical Foundation

Klein, Richard T., Jr., pres: Klein Tools

Klein, Russell R., MD, dir: Babcock Memorial Endowment, William

Klein, Saul, secy: Arell Foundation

Klein, Stanley M., pres: Goldman Foundation, Herman

Klein, Starr T., secy, treas: Dixie Yarns Foundation

Klein, Steven G., treas: Dun & Bradstreet Corp. Foundation

Klein, Vicki, dir: Abrons Foundation, Louis and Anne

Kleinfeldt, Richard C., vp, cfo: Giddings & Lewis; pres, dir: Giddings & Lewis Foundation

Kleinpell, Susan, trust: Mott Fund, Ruth

Kleinz, Louise, trust: Whiteman Foundation, Edna Rider

Klemens, J. F., trust: Lubrizol Foundation

Klementik, David, trust: Whalley Charitable Trust

Klender, Paul P., treas: Nathan Foundation

Klepfer, Robert O., Jr., exec dir: Sternberger Foundation, Sigmund

Kleppel, Lee D., dir: Grader Foundation, K. W.

Klett, Frank, Cook Inlet Region

Klich, William R., trust: Jones Intercable Tampa Trust

Kliem, Peter Otto, trust: Polaroid Foundation

Kligler, Seymour H., dir: Goldman Foundation, Herman

Kline, C. Bob, chmn, pres, ceo: Kansas City Power & Light Co.

Kline, Cheryl, asst treas, dir: Dana Corp. Foundation

Kline, Daniel, vp, trust: Blowitz-Ridgeway Foundation

Kline, Gary, dir: Field Foundation of Illinois

Kline, Gary H., dir, secy: Special People In Need

Kline, James Edward, trust: TRINOVA Foundation

Kline, John R., trust, vp: Haynes Foundation

Kline, Karen, contributions coordinator: Fisher-Price Foundation

Kline, Logan, dir: Three Swallows Foundation

Kline, Lowell L., exec dir, secy: Crowell Trust, Henry P. and Susan C.

Kline, Robin T., dir: Three Swallows Foundation

Kline, Sidney D., Jr., trust: Wyomissing Foundation

Klinedinst, Thomas J., trust: Star Bank, N.A., Cincinnati Foundation

Klinefelter, Stanard T., trust: Isaacs Foundation, Harry Z.

Klinfelter, Marjorie, secy: Webb Foundation, Del E.

Kling, Breckenridge, mem bd mgrs: Wilson Foundation, Marie C. and Joseph C.

Klingenberger, Mary A., dir: Harris Bank Foundation

Klingenstein, Frederick A., vp, secy, asst treas, don son: Klingenstein Fund, Esther A. and Joseph; vp, secy, dir: Steinbach Fund, Ruth and Milton

Klingenstein, John, pres, treas, don son: Klingenstein Fund, Esther A. and Joseph; pres, treas, dir: Steinbach Fund, Ruth and Milton

Klingenstein, Patricia D., dir: Steinbach Fund, Ruth and Milton

Klingenstein, Sharon L., dir: Steinbach Fund, Ruth and Milton

Klinger, Andrew W., trust: Mex-Am Cultural Foundation

Klinger, Ernest T., cfo: Arden Group, Inc.

Klinger, Harry, vp, dir: Wilson Foundation, Hugh and Mary

Klinger, Helen W., trust: Klingler Foundation, Helen and Charles

Klinger, Linda L., exec dir: McElroy Trust, R. J.

Klingner, Linda, treas: Morrison Foundation, Harry W.

Klingsberg, David, trust: Kaye Foundation

Klipstein, David H., vp, treas: Klipstein Foundation, Ernest Christian

Klipstein, Kenneth H., pres: Klipstein Foundation, Ernest Christian

Kloska, Ronald F., trust: Decio Foundation, Arthur J.; pres: Skyline Corp.

Kloss, Lester K., mgr, dir: Kearney & Co. Foundation, A.T.

Klotzbach, H.B., dir: Cremer Foundation

Klug, Jerry L., treas: Werner Foundation, Clara and Spencer

Kluge, John Werner, chmn, pres, dir: Metromedia Co.; vp: Shubert Foundation

Klugman, Craig, editor: Journal Gazette Co.

Klusener, Shirley B., dir: Smithers Foundation, Christopher D.

Klutch, Alan J., comptr: Dun & Bradstreet Corp. Foundation

Klyce, Dorothy, dir commun: Louisiana Power & Light Co./New Orleans Public Service

Kmentt, Cornel A., secy, treas: CSC Industries Foundation

Knab, James, vchmn: Brooks Fashion Stores Inc.

Knabusch, Charles T., chmn, pres, dir: La-Z-Boy Chair Co.; chmn: La-Z-Boy Foundation

Knafel, Susan R., asst treas: Jewish Foundation for Education of Women

Knapp, Dorothy W., secy: Carnegie Corporation of New York

Knapp, Harry K., dir, treas: Bafflin Foundation

Knapp, Hugh J., trust: Houck Foundation, May K.

Knapp, J. Linsalm, trust: Shinnick Educational Fund, William M.

Knapp, M. P., pres: Mettler Instrument Corp.

Knapp, Maurice, pres: Mettler Instrument Corp.

Knapp, Susan Garwood, trust: Henry Foundation, Patrick

Knapp, W. A., vp, dir: McDonald Manufacturing Co. Charitable Foundation, A. Y.

Knappenberger, Dianne, dir: Van Huffel Foundation, I. J.

Knaup, Marianne, dir: Enterprise Leasing Foundation

Knauss, Dalton L., trust: Kemper Foundation, James S.

Knecht, Raymond L., trust: C & H Charitable Trust

Knecht, Sandra Stone, trust: Stone Foundation, W. Clement and Jessie V.

Knell, Theresa N., secy, trust: Middendorf Foundation

Knese, William, chmn, trust: CLARCOR Foundation

Knez, Brian J., vp: Harcourt General

Knez, Debra S., trust: Smith Foundation, Richard and Susan

Knicely, Howard V., pres: TRW Foundation

Knickerbocker, Marilyn, vp: Mette Foundation

Knickman, James R., PhD, vp: Johnson Foundation, Robert Wood

Knie, Laura R., trust: Wyne Foundation

Kniefel, Christopher, dir: Pesch Family Foundation

Kniefel, Linda, dir: Pesch Family Foundation

Kniffen, Jan Rogers, vp, secy, treas, dir: May Stores Foundation

Knight, Charles Field, chmn, ceo: Emerson Electric Co.; trust: Olin Foundation, John M.

Knight, David, program dir, asst secy: Skaggs Foundation, L. J. and Mary C.

Knight, George W., trust: Woodland Foundation

Knight, Herbert Borwell, vp, dir: Borwell Charitable Foundation

Knight, Howard A., pres: Prudential Securities Foundation

Knight, Kathleen C., dir: Staunton Farm Foundation

Knight, Lester B., dir: Baxter Foundation

Knight, Merrill D., dir: GEICO Philanthropic Foundation

Knight, Newell S., Jr., vchmn selection comm: Westlake Scholarship Fund, James L. and Nellie M.

Knight, Philip, chmn, ceo: Nike Inc.

Knight, Roger D., Jr., trust: Johnson Foundation, Helen K. and Arthur E.

Knight, Townsend J., vp, asst treas: Banbury Fund

Knight, Will, trust: Wise Foundation and Charitable Trust, Watson W.

Knight, Will A., dir: Fair Foundation, R. W.

Knighton, Elizabeth, mgr: Tyndale House Foundation

Knirko, Leonard J., treas: Scholl Foundation, Dr.

Knizel, Anthony C., vp, contr, asst treas: Pet; vp, treas: Pet Inc. Community Support Foundation

Knobbe, Urban, chmn, dir: AG Processing Inc.

Knoblauch, L. W., vp intl bus devel: Honeywell

Knoedler, Gunther H., coo, dir: Bell Federal Savings & Loan Association

Knoefel, Renate, pers mgr: Thyssen Specialty Steels

Knott, Carol D., dir: Knott Foundation, Marion I. and Henry J.

Knott, Francis X., dir: Knott Foundation, Marion I. and Henry J.

Knott, Henry J., Jr., treas, dir: Knott Foundation, Marion I. and Henry J.

Knott, Henry Joseph, dir: Knott Foundation, Marion I. and Henry J.

Knott, James E., dir: Knott Foundation, Marion I. and Henry J.

Knott, Marion I., dir: Knott Foundation, Marion I. and Henry J.

Knott, Martin G., dir: Knott Foundation, Marion I. and Henry J.

Knott, Teresa H., dir: Knott Foundation, Marion I. and Henry J.

Knotts, Dale, comm mem: Sherman Educational Fund

Knowles, Chester, trust: Knowles Trust A, Leonora H.

Knowles, Merry, trust: Rapp Foundation, Robert Glenn

Knowles, Mrs. Peter I. C., II, corresponding secy: Memorial Foundation for Children

Knowles, Nancy W., vp: Knowles Foundation

Knowles, Rachel M. Hunt, trust: Hunt Foundation; trust: Hunt Foundation, Roy A.

Knowles-Sorokin, Cheryl, secy: Bank of America - Giannini Foundation

Knowlton, Richard L., chmn, pres, ceo, dir: Hormel & Co., George A.

Knox, I. C., Jr., vp: Vicksburg Hospital Medical Foundation

Knox, Northrop Rand, pres, treas: Knox Foundation, Seymour H.

Knox, Northrup Rand, Jr., dir: Knox Foundation, Seymour H.

Knox, Seymour H., III, chmn: Knox Foundation, Seymour H.

Knox, Seymour Horace, IV, dir: Knox Foundation, Seymour H.

Knox, W. Graham, MD, vp, trust: Collins Foundation, Joseph

Knudsen, Richard, Cooper Foundation

Knudson, Darrell G., chmn, ceo: Fourth Financial Corp.

Knudson, Geoffry, pres: Pepper Cos.

Knudtsen, Darwin, trust: Geneseo Foundation

Knue, Paul Frederick, trust: Scripps Howard Foundation

Knuth, Robert H., secy: Wisconsin Public Service Foundation

Kobacker, Arthur J., chmn: Kobacker Co.

Kobayashi, Takaji, pres: Shuwa Investments Corp.

Kobel, R. J., pres, coo, dir: Atalanta/Sosnoff Capital Corp.

Kober, A. R., ceo, dir: Indiana Insurance Cos.

Kober, Albert, ceo: Peerless Insurance Co.

Kober, Roger W., chmn, pres, ceo: Rochester Gas & Electric Corp.

Kobrin, Lawrence Alan, dir: Ehrman Foundation, Fred and Susan

Koch, Charles de Ganahl, dir: Koch Charitable Foundation, Charles G.; chmn: Koch Industries; trust: Lambe Charitable Foundation, Claude R.

Koch, Curtis J., trust: Schlink Foundation, Albert G. and Olive H.

Koch, D. G., trust: Frohman Foundation, Sidney

Koch, David Andrew, chmn, pres, ceo, dir: Graco; pres: Graco Foundation

Koch, David Hamilton, pres: Koch Charitable Trust, David H.; dir: Koch Foundation, Fred C.

Koch, Elizabeth B., vp, dir: Koch Charitable Foundation, Charles G.; vp, dir: Koch Foundation, Fred C.; vp, dir: Lambe Charitable Foundation, Claude R.

Koch, Kenneth, trust: Van Wert County Foundation

Koch, Paula, don, pres emeritus, dir: Koch Foundation

Koch, Robert L., vp human resources: Bally Inc.

Koch, Robert L., II, pres, treas, dir: Koch Sons, George; pres, treas, dir: Koch Sons Foundation, George

Koch, W., cfo: Development Dimensions International

Koch, William Ingraham, pres, dir: Falcon Foundation

Koch-Weser, Reimer, secy, dir: Kade Foundation, Max

Kocher, E. J., vp, dir: Vilter Foundation

Kochis, Frank, trust: Clemens Foundation

Kociba, Richard J., PhD, trust, chmn med comm: Pardee Foundation, Elsa U.

Kock, E. James, Jr., secy, trust: Libby-Dufour Fund, Trustees of the

Kocmand, Howard, vp, contr: Minolta Corp.

Kodweis, J. B., pres, dir: Gleason Works Foundation

Kodweis, John, vp (admin), dir: Gleason Memorial Fund

Koedel, John G., Jr., secy, treas, dir: National Forge Foundation

Koehler, Kenneth T., pres, ceo: Dollar Dry Dock Bank

Koehler, Mary C., vp, dir: Palmer Foundation, George M.

Koehn, Thomas, pres, treas: Waldinger Corp. Foundation

Koelbel, Gene N., secy, dir: Norgren Foundation, Carl A.

Koelling, Herbert L., ceo: Uarco Inc.

Koenemann, Carl F., vp, dir: Motorola Foundation

Koenig, Fred, dir: MFA Foundation

Koenig, Harry C., dir: Cuneo Foundation

Koenigsberger, Joseph A., treas: Guggenheim Foundation, Harry Frank

Koenitzer, John E., vchmn, dir: Siebert Lutheran Foundation

Koepke, James E., trust: Farr Trust, Frank M. and Alice M.

Koerner, Edgar R., treas, mem bd mgrs: Childs Memorial Fund for Medical Research, Jane Coffin

Koerner, James D., consultant: Klingenstein Fund, Esther A. and Joseph

Koerselman, James E., pres, dir: Demco Charitable Foundation

Koestler, Alfred, vp (corp human resources): Bosch Corp., Robert

Kofalt, James A., pres, coo: Cablevision Systems Corp.

Koffler, Lillian, trust: Koffler Family Foundation

Koffler, Sol, trust: Koffler Family Foundation

Kogan, Richard Jay, pres, coo, dir: Schering-Plough Corp.; trust, mem: Schering-Plough Foundation

Koger, Ira M., chmn, ceo: Koger Properties

Kogod, Arlene R., dir: Smith Family Foundation, Charles E.

Kogod, Robert P., vp, dir: Smith Family Foundation, Charles E.

Kogovsek, C. J., trust: St. Mary's Catholic Foundation

Kohl, Allen D., pres, dir: Kohl Charitable Foundation, Allen D.; vp, dir: Kohl Charities, Herbert H.

Kohl, Bonnie A., vp, dir: Kohl Charitable Foundation, Allen D.

Kohl, Dorothy, trust: Kohl Foundation, Sidney

Kohl, Herbert H., pres, dir: Kohl Charities, Herbert H.

Kohl, Mary, dir: Kohl Charitable Foundation, Allen D.; dir, vp: Kohl Foundation, Sidney

Kohl, Nicole, secy: Falk Medical Research Foundation, Dr. Ralph and Marian

Kohl, Sidney, dir, pres: Kohl Foundation, Sidney

Kohl, Sidney A., secy, dir: Kohl Charities, Herbert H.

Kohlberg, Jerome Spiegel, Jr., dir: Kravis Foundation, Henry R.

Kohler, Charlotte M., vp, dir: Windway Foundation, Inc.

Kohler, Herbert Vollrath, Jr., chmn, pres, dir: Kohler Co.; chmn, ceo, dir: Kohler Foundation

Kohler, Laura, exec dir: Kohler Foundation

Kohler, Mary S., vp, dir: Windway Foundation, Inc.

Kohler, R. H., trust: Rinker Cos. Foundation

Kohler, R. Hagan, Jr., treas: Rinker, Sr. Foundation, M. E.

Kohler, Ruth DeYoung, II, pres, coo, dir: Kohler Foundation

Kohler, Terry J., pres, dir: Windway Foundation, Inc.

Kohn, Bernhard L., Jr., vp, dir: Kohn-Joseloff Fund

Kohn, Bernhard L., Sr., pres, dir: Kohn-Joseloff Fund

Kohn, Edith, vp: Arronson Foundation

Kohn, Harold E., pres: Arronson Foundation

Kohn, Henry, dir: Edison Foundation, Harry; trust: Lavanburg-Corner House

Kohn, Janet S., trust, secy: Shiffman Foundation

Kohn, Joan J., vp, secy, dir, treas: Kohn-Joseloff Fund

Kohn, Joseph C., vp: Arronson Foundation

Kohn, Max, pres: Wolf Foundation, Benjamin and Fredora K.

Kohn, Robert I., Jr., trust, vp: Shiffman Foundation

Kohnhorst, Earl, coo: Brown & Williamson Tobacco Corp.

Kohnstamm, P.L., pres, chmn, treas: General Color Co.

Kohout, Thomas J., pres: K-Products; pres, dir: K-Products Foundation

Kohut, Andrew J., vp (fin), cfo: Chesapeake Corp.

Kohut, Robert J., MD, secy, treas: American Otological Society

Koide, Megumi, cfo: Calgon Corp.

Koike, Isamu, dir: IBJ Foundation

Kokjer, Ralph L., pres, treas, dir: Harden Foundation

Kolakowski, Al H., trust: Delta Air Lines Foundation

Kolb, John E., dir, mem exec comm, chmn legal comm,: Keck Foundation, W. M.

Kolbe, Robert G., vp, cfo: Ameritech Foundation

Kolde, Bert, secy: Allen Foundation for Medical Research, Paul G.

Kolin, Elizabeth, asst secy: Mack Foundation, J. S.

Kolin, Oscar, pres emeritus: Rubinstein Foundation, Helena

Kolk, Fritz, vp, cfo: Meijer Inc.

Kolvig, Ann B., dir: Barker Foundation, J. M. R.

Komaroff, Stanley, dir: de Rothschild Foundation, Edmond

Komes, Flora, Komes Foundation

Komes, Jerome W., pres, vp: Komes Foundation

Kometer, Clyde W., corp contr: Kohler Co.

Komiya, Toyosaburo, secy: IBJ Foundation

Koncelik, Dabid G., sr vp, cfo: California & Hawaiian Sugar Co.

Kondo, Keijiro, secy, treas: Mazda Foundation (USA), Inc.

Konishi, Hiro, trust: Armco Steel Co. Foundation

Konrad, Beth, chmn (contributions & mem comm): NBD Charitable Trust

Konrad, Peter A., vp admin: Colorado Trust

Kontny, Vincent L., pres, coo, dir: Fluor Corp.; trust: Fluor Foundation

Koo, Timothy T., dir: Fireman's Fund Foundation

Koodray, George R., commun & pub rels mgr: Jersey Central Power & Light Co.

Koontz, James L., pres, ceo: Kingsbury Corp.; trust: Kingsbury Fund

Koontz, Richard Harvey, trust: Bowne Foundation, Robert

Koop, Dick, trust: Johnson Foundation, M. G. and Lillie A.

Koopman, Beatrice, trust: Koopman Fund

Koopman, Georgette A., pres, trust: Auerbach Foundation, Beatrice Fox; pres, trust: Koopman Fund; trust: Schiro Fund

Koopman, Rena, trust: Auerbach Foundation, Beatrice Fox; trust: Koopman Fund

Koopman, Richard, Jr., trust: Koopman Fund

Kopelman, Frank, trust: Rubenstein Charitable Foundation, Lawrence J. and Anne

Kopf, Eugene, pres: Litton/Itek Optical Systems

Kopidlansky, Victor Raymond, secy: Motorola Foundation

Kopp, Barbara, dir: Caring and Sharing Foundation

Kopp, LeRoy, dir: Caring and Sharing Foundation

Kopp, Russel T., trust: Clark Charitable Trust

Koppele, Gary S., sr vp (admin), cfo, dir: Big V Supermarkets

Koppelman, Charles, pres: EMI Records Group

Koppleman, Charles, Schlink Foundation, Albert G. and Olive H.

Koprowski, John J., treas, dir fin services: Ford Foundation

Koprowski, W. M., secy, dir: Joslyn Foundation

Korb, Donald B., dir: Crescent Plastics Foundation

Korba, Robert, pres: Sammons Enterprises

Korduf, Lynn, mgr pub rels: Wausau Insurance Cos.

Kordus, Lynn, sr pub rels coordinator: Employers Insurance of Wausau, A Mutual Co.

Koren, M. Robert, trust: Statler Foundation

Koret, Susan, chmn: Koret Foundation

Korinek, Gerge J., ceo, pres: NRC, Inc.

Korman, Berton E., trust: Korman Family Foundation, Hyman

Korman, Leonard I., trust: Korman Family Foundation, Hyman

Korman, Samuel J., trust: Korman Family Foundation, Hyman

Korman, Steven H., trust: Korman Family Foundation, Hyman

Korn, Lester B., chmn: Korn/Ferry International

Korn, Robert, dir, secy: Hebrew Technical Institute

Kornberg, Arthur, dir: Life Sciences Research Foundation

Kornegay, S. Dock, vp, exec dir: Duke Power Co. Foundation

Kornfeld, Allan A., exec vp, cfo: AMETEK

Korpics, David, sr vp, cfo: Volvo North America Corp.

Korshin, C. G., secy, program mgr: Exxon Education Foundation

Kortbein, Donald, trust: Andres Charitable Trust, Frank G.

Korte, Ralph, chmn: Korte Construction Co.

Kortendick, Russel I., Sr., vp: Christensen Charitable and Religious Foundation, L. C.

Kortepeter, Wendy G., adv: Griffith Foundation, W. C.

Kortjohn, Martin D., dir, treas: Gloeckner Foundation, Fred

Kory, Geraldine A., dir, secy: Abrams Foundation, Benjamin and Elizabeth

Kosarek, Charles L., pres, dir: Behmann Brothers Foundation

Kosarek, Willie J., treas, dir: Behmann Brothers Foundation

Koscielack, Frank A., trust: McNeely Foundation

Koski, Jean, secy, treas: Bentley Foundation, Alvin M.

Koskinen, Donald Steward, vp, dir: Banta Co. Foundation

Koskiner, Jean A., vp, dir: Alexander Foundation, Walter

Kosky, Patricia A., vp: Pacific Mutual Charitable Foundation

Koslan, Spencer L., secy: Ogden Foundation, Ralph E.

Kosnik, Edward F., pres, ceo: S.T.J. Group, Inc.

Kosofsky, Evelyn E., adv bd: Lipsky Foundation, Fred and Sarah

Koss, James M., dir: Health 1st Foundation

Kostanecki, Sheila, trust: Ruffin Foundation, Peter B. & Adeline W.

Kostecky, James F., dir corp support programs: Bethlehem Steel Corp.

Kostelnick, Rose, asst secy: Forest Lawn Foundation

Koster, Eugene S., sr vp (mktg), dir: Acacia Mutual Life Insurance Co.

Koster, Sherry, exec dir: Dain Bosworth/IFG Foundation

Kostishack, John, exec dir: Bremer Foundation, Otto

Kostmayer, Rosmary, dir communications: AEGON USA, Inc.

Kotik, Charlotta, trust: Gottlieb Foundation, Adolph and Esther

Kott, H. Stephen, vp, trust: Boston Fatherless and Widows Society

Koulaieff, B. J., dir: Koulaieff Educational Fund, Trustees of Ivan Y.

Kountze, Charles, trust: Hitchcock Foundation, Gilbert M. and Martha H.

Kountze, Denman, pres, trust: Hitchcock Foundation, Gilbert M. and Martha H.

Kountze, Neely, vp, trust: Hitchcock Foundation, Gilbert M. and Martha H.

Koutnik, Thomas A., asst secy: O'Neil Foundation, M. G.

Kovacevic, Lilly, corp commun specialist: Security Life of Denver

Kovacevich, Richard M., vchmn, pres, coo: Norwest Corp.; dir: Norwest Foundation

Kovach, Gerald J., dir: MCI Foundation

Kovacs, G. M., asst secy: Exxon Education Foundation

Kovats, George S., exec dir: Stewardship Foundation

Koven, Joan F., secy, treas, dir: Marpat Foundation

Kovler, Everett, pres: Blum-Kovler Foundation

Kovler, H. Jonathan, pres, dir: Blum Foundation, Harry and Maribel G.; treas: Blum-Kovler Foundation

Kovler, Peter, dir: Blum Foundation, Harry and Maribel G.; asst secy: Blum-Kovler Foundation

Kowalski, Agnes, trust: Kowalski Sausage Co. Charitable Trust

Kowalski, Audrey J., pres: Kowalski Sausage Co.

Kowalski, Donald, pres, dir: Kowalski Sausage Co. Charitable Trust

Kowalski, Kenneth, trust: Kowalski Sausage Co. Charitable Trust

Kowalski, Stephen, chmn, dir: Kowalski Sausage Co. Charitable Trust

Kowert, Marie F., asst secy: Steele Foundation, Harry and Grace

Kozan, Lillian M., secy: Renner Foundation

Koziar, Stephen F., pres, trust: Dayton Power and Light Co. Foundation

Kozlowski, J. A., asst secy: Chrysler Corp. Fund

Kozlowski, L. Dennis, pres: Grinnell Corp.; pres: Mueller Co.; pres, dir: Mueller Co. Foundation; pres: Tyco Laboratories, Inc.

Kozmetsky, Cynthia, trust: RGK Foundation

Kozmetsky, George, trust: RGK Foundation

Kozmetsky, Gregory, don, pres, treas, trust: RGK Foundation

Kozmetsky, Ronya, chmn, secy, trust: RGK Foundation

Kozusko, Donald, trust: Gund Foundation, Geoffrey

Kraemer, Richard C., pres, treas, coo: UDC-Universal Development LP

Kraft, John C., Leo Burnett Co.

Kraft, John F., Jr., vp, trust: Laurel Foundation

Kraft, Richard, pres, coo: Matsushita Electric Corp. of America; pres, dir: Panasonic Foundation

Krain, Leon J., treas: General Motors Foundation

Krakoff, Robert, chmn, ceo: Reed Publishing USA

Krakower, Victor, mgr: McGregor Foundation, Thomas and Frances

Krakowiecki, Marion J., treas: Sentry Life Group Foundation

Kral, Richard F., chmn, ceo: Crystal Brands

Krall, Leo P., MD, chmn, pres: Diabetes Research and Education Foundation

Kramarsky, Sarah-Ann, secy: Schiff Foundation, Dorothy

Kramer, Charlotte R., trust: Rosenthal Foundation, Samuel

Kramer, Earl, pres: Concord Fabrics, Inc.

Kramer, Elizabeth Abrams, pres, treas, dir: Abrams Foundation, Benjamin and Elizabeth

Kramer, Irwin H., vp: Allen Brothers Foundation

Kramer, Janet, dir: Jewish Foundation for Education of Women

Kramer, Jeffrey L., pres, ceo: Frontier Oil & Refining Co.

Kramer, Karl, Jr., cfo: Kirchgessner Foundation, Karl

Kramer, Mark R., trust: Rosenthal Foundation, Samuel

Kramer, Saul, mgr: Kramer Foundation

Kramer, William Joseph, contact person: DeCamp Foundation, Ira W.

Krane, Howard, legal counsel: Skidmore, Owings & Merrill Foundation

Krannich, Beverly Turner, pres: Sonat Foundation

Kransoff, Abraham, chmn, dir: Pall Corp.

Kranson, Bernice G., vp, trust: Norman Foundation, Andrew

Krantzler, Robert, treas: Glosser Foundation, David A.

Krapek, Karl J., chmn, pres, ceo: Carrier Corp.

Krasnansky, Marvin L., trust, mem (policy bd): McKesson Foundation

Krasne, Hale S., trust: Steinman Foundation, James Hale

Kratovil, Edward D., mem (corp contributions comm): UST

Kratt, Myra H., trust: Kraft Foundation

Kratz, Anne S., Berkey Foundation, Peter

Kraus, John P., trust: Anderson Foundation

Krause, Charles A., secy, treas, dir: Krause Foundation, Charles A.; trust: McBeath Foundation, Faye

Krause, James W., vchmn, trust: Lutheran Brotherhood Foundation

Krause, Jim L., asst treas: Mott Foundation, Charles Stewart

Krause, Lester W., asst secy: Mayborn Foundation, Frank W.

Krause, Raymond R., dir: Grand Metropolitan Food Sector Foundation

Krause, Sandra S., trust: Strauss Foundation

Krauskopf, Jack A., trust: Lavanburg-Corner House

Krauss, George, vp, treas: Baer Foundation, Alan and Marcia

Krave, Helmuth, secy: Farwell Foundation, Drusilla

Krave, Hugo, pres: Farwell Foundation, Drusilla

Kravis, Allen B., sr vp, cfo: United Stationers Inc.

Kravitz, Anne Goldman, trust: Goldman Foundation, William

Kraynak, Michael, dir: Brunner Foundation, Robert

Kreamer, Janice C., pres: Loose Trust, Carrie J.; pres: Loose Trust, Harry Wilson

Kreamer, Marion E., secy, dir: Loose Trust, Carrie J.; secy: Loose Trust, Harry Wilson

Krebs, Robert Duncan, chmn, pres, ceo, coo: Santa Fe Pacific Corp.

Krehbiel, Frederick A., vchmn: Molex, Inc.

Krehbiel, John H., Jr., pres: Molex, Inc.

Krehbiel, John H., Sr., chmn: Molex, Inc.

Kreick, John R., pres: Lockheed Sanders

Kreid, Leland F., trust: Monticello College Foundation

Kreider, Esther S., dir, fdr daughter: Sunnen Foundation

Kreiger, Janet F., trust: Pittsburgh Child Guidance Foundation

Krein, William A., cfo: Alpha Industries

Kreindler, Peter M., dir: AlliedSignal Foundation

Kreisberg, Barrett G., pres, dir: Harkness Ballet Foundation

Krelitz, Barry M., pres, ceo, treas: Krelitz Industries

Kremer, George, Jr., adv bd: Kremer Foundation Trust, George

Kremer, Juergen, cfo, exec vp: Metallgesellschaft Corp.

Kremer, Mary, Jr., adv bd: Kremer Foundation Trust, George

Kremer, Richard E., sr vp (mktg): Coast Federal Bank

Krempp, Andrew B., dir: DCB Foundation

Krempp, K. L., treas, dir: Indiana Desk Foundation

Krems, Nathan, secy: Wood Foundation of Chambersburg, PA

Krenitsky, Thomas Anthony, dir: Burroughs Wellcome Fund

Kreps, Juanita M., trust: Duke Endowment

Kresa, Kent, chmn, pres, ceo: Northrop Corp.

Kresevich, Angela, chmn: Stella D'Oro Biscuit Co.

Kresge, Bruce Anderson, MD, vp: Kresge Foundation

Kresky, Edward M., dir: Greenwall Foundation

Kress, George F., dir. pres: Kress Foundation, George

Kress, James F., dir, vp: Kress Foundation, George

Kresse, Robert J., secy, trust: Wendt Foundation, Margaret L.

Kressly, Caroline W., corporator: Island Foundation

Kretschmar, Lanie, coordinator: Dexter Corp. Foundation

Kretzer, William T., pres, ceo: Unifi, Inc.

Kretzmann, John, dir: Wieboldt Foundation

Kreuch, Paul C., Jr., mem (contributions comm): National Westminster Bank New Jersey

Kreulen, Grace, trust: Artevel Foundation

Kreutz, Charles B., dir: Priddy Foundation

Kreuzberger, Donald, trust: Knistrom Foundation, Fanny and Svante

Kreuzberger, Douglas, trust: Knistrom Foundation, Fanny and Svante

Kreuzberger, Virginia, pres, trust: Knistrom Foundation, Fanny and Svante

Kriak, John M., vp, cfo: Penn Traffic Co.

Kridel, William J., pres: Turner Fund, Ruth

Krider, Harold H., treas: Marinette Marine Foundation

Krieble, Frederick B., vp: Krieble Foundation, Vernon K.

Krieble, Nancy B., secy: Krieble Foundation, Vernon K.

Krieg, Iris J., exec dir: Field Foundation, Jamee and Marshall

Krieger, John J., dir: GEICO Philanthropic Foundation

Krieger, Sharron, program adm: Whirlpool Foundation

Kriesberg, Barnett G., pres, dir: Harkness Foundation, William Hale

Krietemery, George, secy, trust: Crescent Plastics Foundation

Krimendahl, Constance M., trust: Krimendahl II Foundation, H. Frederick

Krimendahl, Frederick, II, trust: Krimendahl II Foundation, H. Frederick

Krimendahl, H. Frederick, II, trust: Brody Foundation, Carolyn and Kenneth D.

Krimm, Bernard, secy: Quaker Oats Foundation

Kring, Gary S., secy: Schramm Foundation

Kring, Lesley E., pres: Schramm Foundation

Krinsky, Josephine B., trust: Parshelsky Foundation, Moses L.

Krinsky, Robert Daniel, trust: Parshelsky Foundation, Moses L.

Kripal, D. Francis, trust: Buckley Trust, Thomas D.

Kripowcz, Mary Jo, asst secy, asst treas: Consumers Power Foundation

Krise, Dorothy, dir: Gumbiner Foundation, Josephine

Krissoff, Robert, secy: Ada Foundation, Julius; secy: Grateful Foundation; secy: Linus Foundation

Kritzler, J. H., vp: Community Hospital Foundation

Krivsky, William A., exec vp, cfo: Bird Inc.; treas, dir: Bird Cos. Charitable Foundation

Krizanic, Tina M., asst secy: Shelden Fund, Elizabeth, Allan and Warren

Krodel, William J., vp, dir: Jasper Table Co. Foundation

Kroeber, C. Kent, chmn contributions comm: Interpublic Group of Cos.

Kroeger, Thomas, asst secy, trust: Sherwin-Williams Foundation

Kroenlein, David F., asst secy: Penzance Foundation

Kroger, Joan A., assoc secy: Humana Foundation

Kroger, Joseph, pres: Decision Data Computer Corp.

Krogh, H. M., pres, coo: Oshkosh B'Gosh

Krohn, Robert F., chmn, dir: Commercial Federal Corp.

Kroll, Alexander S., chmn, ceo: Young & Rubicam

Krome, Margery Loomis, dir: Lincoln-Lane Foundation

Kromholz, Steven S., pres: Menasha Corporate Foundation

Krone, Bruce A., secy, trust: Dater Foundation, Charles H.

Krone, Paul W., pres, trust: Dater Foundation, Charles H.

Krongard, Alvin B., chmn, ceo, mng dir: Brown & Sons, Alex; pres: Brown & Sons Charitable Foundation, Alex

Kronk, Claude F., pres, ceo: J&L Specialty Products Corp.

Kronstadt, Annette, dir: Himmelfarb Foundation, Paul and Annetta

Kronstadt, Lillian, treas, exec dir, dir: Himmelfarb Foundation, Paul and Annetta

Kropf, Robert L., treas, dir: Animal Assistance Foundation

Krows, Wayne W., Griswold Foundation, John C.

Krueger, Harvey M., trust: Barry Foundation

Krug, Eleanor C., vp, trust: Toms Foundation

Kruidenier, David, pres, trust: Cowles Foundation, Gardner and Florence Call; chmn, dir: Cowles Media Co.; chmn, dir: Cowles Media Foundation

Kruidenier, Elizabeth Stuart, trust: Cowles Foundation, Gardner and Florence Call

Krukowski, Rev. Francis, trust: Price Foundation, Lucien B. and Katherine E.

Krul, Joseph, sr vp, cfo: Standard Federal Bank

Krulewitch, Peter E., dir: Innisfree Foundation

Krull, Margaret, chmn contributions comm: Cable & Wireless Communications

Krumholz, Stephen B., sr vp 7-Eleven Stores: Southland Corp.

Kryshak, Thomas E., exec vp (fin): Nationwide Insurance Foundation

Krzemienski, Alexander J., contr: NYNEX Corp.

Kubale, Bernard S., vp, secy, dir: Wagner Manufacturing Co. Foundation, E. R.

Kubelick, Cheryl L., secy: Westinghouse Foundation

Kubo, Hisashi, chmn: Ricoh Corp.

Kucharski, John M., chmn, ceo, dir: EG&G Inc.; trust: EG&G Foundation

Kucharski, Robert Joseph, treas: IES Industries Charitable Foundation

Kuchler, Ray, asst vp (commun): Sumitomo Trust & Banking Co., Ltd.

Kuczinski, Anthony J., coo: New York Marine & General Insurance Co.

Kuczmanski, Lee, vp, cfo: Ameritech Services

Kudish, Selwyn A., trust: Xtra Corp. Charitable Foundation

Kuechle, Urban T., hon dir: Bradley Foundation, Lynde and Harry

Kuechler, Henry N., III, trust: Booth-Bricker Fund

Kuehl, Hal Charles, dir: Firstar Milwaukee Foundation

Kuehn, Phillip Gregg, Jr., trust: Holley Foundation

Kuehn, Ronald L., Jr., chmn, pres, ceo, dir: Sonat

Kuehne, Norman, secy: Douglas Foundation

Kuester, D.J., pres, dir: Marshall & Ilsley Bank

Kufeldt, James, pres, dir: Winn-Dixie Stores; vp, dir: Winn-Dixie Stores Foundation

Kugelman, D. Jack, chmn: Kugelman Foundation

Kugle, J. Alan, vp: Brewer Charitable Foundation, C.

Kugler, Frank J., Jr., chmn, ceo: Union Trust

Kuhlin, Michael E., secy, staff dir: Ameritech Foundation

Kuhlman, J. T., pres: Intercontinental Hotels Corp.

Kuhlman, Ron, pres: Kuhlman Corp.

Kuhn, Jim, dir: Berger Foundation, H.N. and Frances C.

Kuhn, Mary L., secy, treas, exec dir: Bartol Foundation, Stockton Rush

Kuhn, Robert J., trust: Best Foundation, Walter J. and Edith E.

Kuhn, Thomas E., dir: Millstone Foundation

Kuhne, Lucy S., dir: Belk-Simpson Foundation

Kuhns, R. W., trust: Kuhns Brothers Co. Foundation

Kuhns, Ronald L., secy: Shell Oil Co. Foundation

Kuhrt, Friedrich, chmn, dir: Siemens Medical Systems Inc.

Kuhrts, G.J., III, treas: Burnand Medical and Educational Foundation, Alphonse A.

Kuhrtz, Steve, mem (contributions comm): GATX Corp.

Kulicke, C. Scott, chmn, ceo: Kulicke & Soffa Industries

Kullgren, Elwood M., chmn: Colorado State Bank of Denver

Kully, Robert I., secy, trust: Livingston Foundation, Milton S. and Corinne N.

Kummer, Glenn F., pres, coo, dir: Fleetwood Enterprises, Inc.

Kump, Edwina, dir, secy, treas: Nelson Foundation, Florence

Kunce, Marquita L., asst treas: Olin Foundation, Spencer T. and Ann W.

Kundert, David Jon, vp, dir: Banc One Wisconsin Foundation

Kunin, Myron, chmn, pres, ceo: Regis Corp.; pres: Regis Foundation

Kunisch, Robert Dietrich, chmn, pres, ceo, dir: PHH Corp.; chmn, dir: PHH Foundation

Kunkel, W. Minster, trust: Kunkel Foundation, John Crain

Kunstadter, Christopher, dir, vp: Kunstadter Family Foundation, Albert

Kunstadter, Elizabeth, trust: Kunstadter Family Foundation, Albert

Kunstadter, Geraldine S., dir, chmn: Kunstadter Family Foundation, Albert

Kunstadter, John W., dir, pres, treas: Kunstadter Family Foundation, Albert

Kunstadter, Lisa, dir, secy: Kunstadter Family Foundation, Albert

Kunstadter, Peter, dir, vp: Kunstadter Family Foundation, Albert

Kunstadter, Sally Lennington, trust: Kunstadter Family Foundation, Albert

Kuntz, Jean M., trust: Harmon Foundation, Pearl M. and Julia J.

Kuntzman, Ronald G., trust: Hoffmann-La Roche Foundation

Kunz, Daniel, dir: Morrison Knudsen Corp. Foundation Inc.

Kunz, Larry P., pres, coo, dir: Payless Cashways Inc.

Kunzel, Herbert, chmn, dir: Powell Foundation, Charles Lee

Kunzman, Edwin D., pres: Schwartz Foundation, Arnold A.

Kunzman, Kenneth, secy: Bonner Foundation, Corella and Bertram

Kunzman, Steven, secy, treas: Schwartz Foundation, Arnold A.

Kupferberg, Jack, pres: Kupferberg Foundation

Kupferberg, Jesse, vp: Kupferberg Foundation

Kupferberg, Kenneth, vp: Kupferberg Foundation

Kupferberg, Marty, cfo: Kepco, Inc.

Kupferberg, Max, pres: Kepco, Inc.; secy-tres: Kupferberg Foundation

Kupis, Alexandra M., asst treas: Raskob Foundation, Bill

Kuprionis, Denise, secy: Scripps Howard Foundation

Kurack, Sandra, vp, trust: PemCo. Foundation

Kurczewski, W. W., pres, dir: Square D Foundation

Kurland, Philip B., trust: Deer Creek Foundation

Kurman, Elizabeth K., mem: Northern Trust Co. Charitable Trust

Kuroda, Kunihiro, treas: Mitsubishi Electric America Foundation

Kurras, Herbert L., trust: Ford III Memorial Foundation, Jefferson Lee

Kurtz, Bernard D., Sr., trust, vp: Hawley Foundation

Kurtz, Daniel L., pres, ceo: Spingold Foundation, Nate B. and Frances

Kurtz, F. Anthony, pres, coo: Downey Savings & Loan Association

Kurtz, Melvin H., secy, dir: Chesebrough Foundation

Kurtz, Samuel B., dir: Lebanon Mutual Foundation

Kurtz, Samuel G., chmn: Lebanon Mutual Insurance Co.; dir: Lebanon Mutual Foundation

Kurtz, Steven G., trust: Ellis Fund

Kurtze, A. Allan, sr vp: Centel Corp.; vp, dir: Centel Foundation

Kurtzman, Allan H., pres, coo: Neutrogena Corp.

Kury, Mark C., trust: McDonough Foundation, Bernard

Kurzman, H. Michael, vp, dir: Lurie Foundation, Louis R.

Kurzman, Jayne M., coun: Fuld Health Trust, Helene; dir, vp: Hurford Foundation

Kusche, William R., Jr., trust: Rixson Foundation, Oscar C.

Kuse, James R., chmn, dir: Georgia Gulf Corp.; trust: Kuse Foundation, James R.

Kuse, Shirley R., trust: Kuse Foundation, James R.

Kushen, Allan Stanford, pres: Schering-Plough Foundation

Kushner, Marilyn, dir: Goodstein Family Foundation, David

Kuslan, Paula Frohring, trust: Frohring Foundation, Paul & Maxine

Kuster, Gerald, trust: Harvest States Foundation

Kusumoto, Sadahei, chmn, ceo: Minolta Corp.

Kuth, Dean, vp: LEF Foundation

Kuth, Lyda Ebert, secy, cfo: LEF Foundation

Kylynych, Petro, pres, chmn: Lowe's Charitable & Educational Foundation

L

La Boon, Bruce, vp: Kayser Foundation

la Fond, Laura Jane Van Evera, adv: Van Evera Foundation, Dewitt Caroline

La Rosa, Gloria, asst secy: Pforzheimer Foundation, Carl and Lily

LaBahn, Mary Ann, treas, dir: Ross Memorial Foundation, Will

LaBalme, George, Jr., vp, asst treas, dir: Langeloth Foundation, Jacob and Valeria

Labanowski, Elizabeth J., trust: Enron Foundation

Labaree, Frances L., dir: Overbrook Foundation

Labin, Emanuel, vp: Benenson Foundation, Frances and Benjamin

Laborde, John P., chmn, pres, ceo, dir: Tidewater, Inc.

Labrecque, Thomas Goulet, chmn: Chase Manhattan Bank, N.A.

Lacey, Frank M., Jr., pres: Pannill Scholarship Foundation, William Letcher

Lacey, Graham F., chmn, pres, ceo: Gulf USA Corp.

Lacey, W. H., pres (grocery products group), vp: Ralston Purina Co.

Lacey, William F., trust: Massachusetts Charitable Mechanics Association

Lachman, Marguerite Leanne, trust: Chicago Title and Trust Co. Foundation

Lackland, David, trust: Schwartz Foundation, Arnold A.

Laconi, Reggie, chmn: Sherman Educational Fund

LaCounte, Maage, trust: Johnston-Hanson Foundation

LaCroix, Anthony A., chmn, dir: Advest Group, Inc.

Lacy, Alan Jasper, mem contributions comm: Kraft General Foods

Lacy, Benjamin H., pres, dir: Clipper Ship Foundation

Lacy, Chuck, pres, dir: Ben & Jerry's Homemade

Lacy, Frank M., Jr., dir, pres: Lacy Foundation

Lacy, Lois D., secy, treas: Rhoden Charitable Foundation, Elmer C.

Lacy, William H., pres, ceo, dir: MGIC Investment Corp.

Ladd, Edward, trust: Forster Charitable Trust, James W. and Ella B.

Ladd, G. Michael, dir: Filene Foundation, Lincoln and Therese

Ladd, George E., III, vp, dir: Filene Foundation, Lincoln and Therese

Ladd, Joseph C., chmn, dir: Fidelity Mutual Life Insurance Co.

Ladd, Lincoln F., dir: Filene Foundation, Lincoln and Therese

Ladd, Robert M., dir: Filene Foundation, Lincoln and Therese

Ladd, Virginia S., trust: Stockham Foundation, William H. & Kate F.

Ladds, Herbert P., Jr., dir: Utica National Group Foundation

Ladehoff, Leo W., chmn, ceo, pres, dir: Amcast Industrial Corp.

Ladehoff, Leo William, pres, trust: Amcast Industrial Foundation

Ladish, John H., trust: Armco Foundation; trust: Ladish Co. Foundation; pres, dir: Ladish Family Foundation, Herman W.; chmn: Ladish Malting Co.; pres, treas, dir: Ladish Malting Co. Foundation

Ladish, William J., pres: Ladish Malting Co.

LaDuc, John, cfo, vp: Kaisertech Ltd.

Lafer, Fred S., dir, secy: Taub Foundation, Joseph and Arlene

Lafer, Fred Seymour, secy: Lautenberg Foundation; secy: Taub Foundation, Henry and Marilyn

Lafferty, Frederick W., exec dir: France Foundation, Jacob and Annita; exec dir: Merrick Foundation, Robert G. and Anne M.

Laffont, Frederic J., pres, coo, secy: Grolier, Inc.

LaFleur, David J., dir: IBP Foundation, Inc., The

LaForce, Dr. J. Clayburn, dir: Bradley Foundation, Lynde and Harry

LaFreniere, Norma B., secy distribution comm: Champlin Foundations

Lagerlof, Stanley C., trust, chmn: Stillwell Charitable Trust, Glen and Dorothy

Lagges, James, trust: Kearney & Co. Foundation, A.T.

LaGrone, Troy, dir: Keith Foundation Trust, Ben E.

Lahiff, Mary Elizabeth, secy: Quinlan Foundation, Elizabeth C.

Lahn, John L., vp: Smith Foundation, Lon V.

Lahrer, Howard, pres: Thalhimer Brothers Inc.

Laird, Edwin Cody, Jr., chmn exec comm: Life Insurance Co. of Georgia

Laird, Helen, trust: Presser Foundation

Laird, John R., chmn bd, chmn exec comm, ceo: Boston Co., Inc.

Laird, Melvin R., dir: Wallace-Reader's Digest Fund, DeWitt; dir: Wallace Reader's Digest Fund, Lila

Laird, Walter J., Jr., dir: Glencoe Foundation

Lake, F. Edward, vp: Dial Corporation Fund

Lake, Thomas H., dir: Group Health Foundation; hon chmn: Lilly Endowment

Lakey, Ronald L., secy: Shea Co. Foundation, J. F.; cfo: Shea Foundation

Lakin, Charles, trust: Lytel Foundation, Bertha Russ

Lakovos, Bishop, Demos Foundation, N.

Lally, John P., asst secy, asst treas, dir: Hooper Foundation, Elizabeth S.

LaLonde, Joseph, vp, dir: Fay's Foundation, Inc.

LaMacchia, John Thomas, pres, dir, coo: Cincinnati Bell; trust: Cincinnati Bell Foundation

Lamade, Howard, dir: LamCo. Foundation

Lamade, J. Robert, dir: LamCo. Foundation

Lamade, James S., dir: LamCo. Foundation

LaMantia, Charles R., pres, ceo, dir: Little, Arthur D.

Lamar, Charles C., secy, treas: Harper Foundation, Philip S.

Lamb, Brigid Shanley, trust: Chubb Foundation

Lamb, Dorothy, vchmn, dir: OCRI Foundation

Lamb, Edna, OCRI Foundation

Lamb, F. Gilbert, secy, dir: OCRI Foundation

Lamb, Frank G., dir: OCRI Foundation

Lamb, George, dir: Manitou Foundation

Lamb, George C., Jr., hon trust: Casey Foundation, Annie E.

Lamb, George Richard, pres, trust: Jackson Hole Preserve

Lamb, Helen, secy, dir: OCRI Foundation

Lamb, Isabelle, dir: Bishop Foundation, E. K. and Lillian F.

Lamb, John R., trust: Barker Foundation, Donald R.

Lamb, Joseph P., secy: Mohasco Memorial Fund

Lamb, Maryann, dir: OCRI Foundation

Lamb, Paula L., dir: OCRI Foundation

Lamb, Peter, dir: OCRI Foundation

Lamb, Robert L., pres, dir: Empire District Electric Co.

Lamb, Teri M., secy, trust: Walker Foundation, Archie D. and Bertha H.

Lambe, James F., dir: Nalco Foundation

Lamberg, Harold, pres: Reicher Foundation, Anne & Harry J.

Lambert, Charles A., chmn: Gulf Power Foundation

Lambert, Clement T., trust, treas: Williams Foundation, Arthur Ashley

Lambert, Harry W., trust: Eckerd Corp. Foundation, Jack

Lambert, Samuel W., III, pres, ceo, dir: Bunbury Company; secy, trust: McGraw Foundation, Curtis W.

Lambert, Samuel W. III, trust: Winslow Foundation

Lambeth, Thomas W., exec dir, secy, asst treas: Reynolds Foundation, Z. Smith

Lamear, Robert, dir: Schmidt Charitable Foundation, William E.

LaMendola, Walter, dir rsch & info sys: Colorado Trust

Lamkin, J.C., mgr: Johnson Day Trust, Carl and Virginia

Lamkin, Martha D., exec dir (corp & govt affaris): Cummins Engine Co.

Lamm, Donald S., chmn, pres, dir: Norton & Co., W.W.

Lamm, Henry, trust: Thompson Charitable Trust, Sylvia G.

Lamm, Robert B., secy: Grace Foundation, Inc.

Lamond, Alice, trust: Pilgrim Foundation

LaMothe, William E., trust: Kellogg Foundation, W. K.

LaMotta, Steven, ceo, pres: Oppenheimer & Co., Inc.

Lamphere, Gilbert H., chmn: Recognition Equipment

Lampman, Charles, gen mgr: Georgia Scientific and Technical Research Foundation

Lancashire, Ben John, chmn, pres, ceo, dir: Inland Container Corp.; vp, dir: Inland Container Corp. Foundation

Lancaster, R. C., sr vp fin, cfo: Bowater Inc.

Lancaster, Rose C., trust, mem contributions comm: Trull Foundation

Lancaster, Ruth, treas: Mingenback Foundation, Julia J.

Lancaster, Sally R., exec vp, trust, dir: Meadows Foundation

Lancaster, Spencer, trust: Chapman Foundation, William H.

Lance, Walter, secy, treas, dir: Ayer Foundation, N.W.

Land, Edwin Herbert, don, pres, trust: Rowland Foundation

Land, Helen Maislen, vp, treas, trust: Rowland Foundation

Land, John, exec vp, ceo: Cohn Co., M.M.

Land, Lillie S., secy, dir: duPont Foundation, Alfred I.

Landaker, James, trust: Durell Foundation, George Edward

Landau, James, mem: Bank of America - Giannini Foundation

Landau, Richard, office mgr: Mitsubishi Heavy Industries America

Lande, Nelson P., trust: Prentis Family Foundation, Meyer and Anna

Landefeld, Charles W., chmn adv & distribution comm: Jennings Foundation, Martha Holden

Landegger, Carl Clement, treas, dir: Landegger Charitable Foundation; chmn, dir: Parsons and Whittemore Inc.

Landegger, George Francis, pres, dir: Landegger Charitable Foundation; ceo: Parsons and Whittemore Inc.

Landegger, Lena, pres, dir: Landegger Charitable Foundation

Landel, Michel, pres: Seiler Corp.

Lander, Raymond A., Jr., chmn: Voplex Corp.

Landers, M.B., III, trust: Lincoln Health Care Foundation

Landers, M.B., M.D., pres, treas: Lincoln Health Care Foundation

Landers, Sara Jane Turner, trust: Turner Charitable Foundation, Harry and Violet

Landers, Stephen, vp: Lincoln Health Care Foundation

Landers, Virginia V., trust: Lincoln Health Care Foundation

Landes, Robert Nathan, vp, dir: McGraw-Hill Foundation

Landes, Stephanie, trust: Philibosian Foundation, Stephen

Landesman, Heidi P., dir: Educational Foundation of America

Landesman, Rocco, treas: Ettinger Foundation

Landgon, Roy, mgr (personnel): Astra Pharmaceutical Products, Inc.

Landgrebe, George, pres: Thomson Information Publishing Group

Landgrebe, Karl L., trust: North American Royalties Welfare Fund

Landin, Thomas Milton, vp (govt & pub aff): SmithKline Beecham

Landman, Bernard, Jr., vp: Glick Foundation, Eugene and Marilyn

Landon, David, pres: Pardee Construction Co.

Landon, R. Kirk, chmn, ceo, dir: American Bankers Insurance Group

Landon, S. Whitney, trust: Turrell Fund

Landry, Edward A., trust: Hume Foundation, Jaquelin; trust: Murphy Foundation, Dan; trust: Thornton Foundation, Flora L.

Landry, Lawrence L., vp, cfo: MacArthur Foundation, John D. and Catherine T.

Landsberg, Gloria, dir: Zale Foundation

Landy, Jean, sr human resources rep: Indiana Insurance Cos.

Lane, George, pres, dir: Ogle Foundation, Paul

Lane, J. S., III, secy: Groves Foundation

Lane, Jeffrey B., vchmn, dir: Smith Barney, Harris Upham & Co.

Lane, Joan F., trust: Brown Foundation, George Warren; dir: Irvine Foundation, James

Lane, Nancy Wolfe, vp: Wolfe Associates, Inc.

Lane, R. W., mem distribution comm: Mead Corp. Foundation

Lane, Richard, pres: Merck Human Health Division

Lane, Robert, ceo, pres: West One Bank Idaho

Lane, Robert B., pres, dir: NationsBank Texas

Lane, Stuart, trust: Stuart Foundation, Edward C.

Lane, Tom, chmn, trust: Lane Memorial Foundation, Mills Bee

Lane, William A., Jr., pres, trust: Dunspaugh-Dalton Foundation

Laney, Emsley A., trust: Davis Charitable Foundation, Champion McDowell

Laney, James Thomas, dir: Luce Foundation, Henry

Laney, John, vp, program off: Hall Family Foundations

Lanfeld, Alvin, pres, treas, dir: Friedman Bag Co.

Lang, Charles J., comptr: Rockefeller Foundation

Lang, David, trust: Lang Foundation, Eugene M.

Lang, Eugene Michael, trust: Lang Foundation, Eugene M.

Lang, Howard B., dir: Shelter Insurance Foundation

Lang, Jane, trust: Lang Foundation, Eugene M.

Lang, Margaret A., vp, dir: Overbrook Foundation

Lang, Robert Todd, trust: Hirschl Trust for Charitable Purposes, Irma T.; chmn, dir: Weil, Gotshal & Manges Foundation

Lang, Stanley, pres: Waldbaum, Inc.

Lang, Stephen, trust: Lang Foundation, Eugene M.

Lang, Theresa, trust: Lang Foundation, Eugene M.

Lang, treas, Simpson Foundation, John M.

Langbauer, Del, vp, trust: Harder Foundation

Langbauer, Eldon N., trust: Harder Foundation

Langbauer, Lucille E., vp, treas, trust: Harder Foundation

Langbauer, Robert L., trust: Harder Foundation

Langbauer, William H., trust: Harder Foundation

Langbo, Arnold G., chmn, ceo: Kellogg's

Langdale, Harley, chmn: Langdale Co.

Langdale, Harley, Jr., vp: Langdale Foundation

Langdale, John W., pres: Langdale Foundation

Langdon, George Dorland, Jr., dir: Kresge Foundation; trust: Wenner-Gren Foundation for Anthropological Research

Langdon, John J., pres, coo: Topps Company

Lange, Beverly J., contact: Anderson Foundation

Langenberg, Donald Newton, trust: Sloan Foundation, Alfred P.

Langenberg, E. L., vp, dir: Shoenberg Foundation

Langenberg, Frederick Charles, dir: Carpenter Technology Corp. Foundation

Langenberg, Oliver M., pres, treas, dir: Mallinckrodt, Jr. Foundation, Edward

Langfitt, Thomas W., MD, pres, dir: Pew Charitable Trusts

Langford, J. Beverly, treas, trust: Ratner Foundation, Milton M.

Langford, Thomas A., trust: Duke Endowment

Langhorst, Fred, vp, dir: Mentor Graphics Foundation

Langlais, Ann, trust: Citizens Charitable Foundation

Langley, W. B., treas, dir: Electric Power Equipment Co. Foundation

Langner, Jay B., trust: Mailman Family Foundation, A. L.

Langsdorf, John, mgr commun rels: Church & Dwight Co.

Langstaff, Carol, dir: Guggenheim Foundation, Harry Frank

Langston, Charles, vp: Hoechst Celanese Foundation

Langton, Raymond B., pres, dir: SKF USA, Inc.

Lanier, Bruce N., Jr., vp: Wehadkee Foundation

Lanier, Bruce N., Sr., pres: Wehadkee Foundation

Lanier, George M., trust, secy: Charitable Fund

Lanier, Helen S., trust: Lanier Brothers Foundation

Lanier, I. Hicks, vchmn, secy: Oxford Foundation

Lanier, J. Hicks, chmn, pres, ceo: Oxford Industries, Inc.; chmn, pres, trust: Oxford Industries Foundation

Lanier, John Reese, trust: Lanier Brothers Foundation

Lanier, Joseph, chmn, ceo: Dan River, Inc.

Lanier, Joseph L., Jr., pres, dir: Dan River Foundation

Lanier, Lawrence L., treas, dir: Lincoln Fund

Lanier, Melissa Emery, vp: Peterloon Foundation

Lanier, Mike, vp preconstruction svcs: Winter Construction Co.

Lanier, Richard, trust: Trust for Mutual Understanding

Lanier, Sartain, trust: Lanier Brothers Foundation; chmn, treas: Oxford Foundation

Lanigan, Bernard, Jr., treas, dir: Williams Family Foundation of Georgia

Lanigan, Joanne, trust: Blowitz-Ridgeway Foundation

Lanigar, Mary, trust: Johnson Foundation, Walter S.

Lanka, Alan S., vp (fin), cfo: Harper Group

Lannan, Anne, dir: Lannan Foundation

Lannan, J. Patrick, Jr., pres: Lannan Foundation

Lannan, John J., asst secy, asst treas: Lannan Foundation

Lannan, John R., vp: Lannan Foundation

Lannan, Lawrence, Jr., dir: Lannan Foundation

Lannert, Robert C., treas: Navistar Foundation

Lanni, J. Terrence, pres, coo, dir: Caesar's World, Inc.

Lannon, John J., sr vp, cfo: Nicor, Inc.

Lansaw, Judy W., secy, trust: Dayton Power and Light Co. Foundation

Lansdale, Daryl L., chmn, ceo: Scotty's, Inc.

Lansing, John Cook, trust: Cook Foundation, Louella

Lanthorne, Rodney, pres: Kyocera International Inc.

Lantz, Joanne B., dir: Foellinger Foundation

Lanum, Robert, secy, dir: Ogle Foundation, Paul

Lanz, John R., sr vp, cfo: Utica National Insurance Group

Lanza, Frank C., pres, coo: Loral Corp.

LaPierre, Donald J., trust: Wells Trust Fund, Fred W.

Lapins, Douglas, pres, ceo, dir: Staley Manufacturing Co., A.E.

LaPlaca, Frank, admin: Rinker Cos. Foundation

LaPorte, Cloyd, Jr., secy, legal couns: Dover Corp.

Lappen, Craig S., asst treas: Aetna Foundation

Lappin, Gerald D., chmn: Lappin Electric Co.

Lappin, R. Todd, pres: Lappin Electric Co.

Lappin, Richard, pres, coo: Farley Industries

Lappin, Richard C., vchmn, dir: Fruit of the Loom, Inc.

Lappin, W. R., pres, trust: Hansen Foundation, Dane G.

Lapyowker, Andrew, esquire: Crown Central Petroleum Foundation

Laraia, William J., chmn, ceo, dir: Apple Bank for Savings

Larance, Charles L., pres: General American Charitable Foundation

Lardner, Peter, chmn, pres, ceo, dir: Bitco Corp.

Largay, George H., pres, dir: Anchor Fasteners

Largay, Vincent B., chmn, dir: Anchor Fasteners

Large, Edwin K., Jr., pres, trust: Large Foundation

Lark, J. Andrew, co-trust: Cummings Memorial Fund Trust, Frances L. and Edwin L.

Larkin, Frank Y., treas, dir: Noble Foundation, Edward John

Larkin, Jean M., trust: Morehead Foundation, John Motley

Larkin, June Noble, chmn, pres, dir: Noble Foundation, Edward John

Laros, R.K., Jr., pres: Laros Foundation, R. K.

LaRosa, William R., MD, trust: Hayward Foundation Charitable Trust, John T. and Winifred

Larrieu, Marie-Josette, trust: Philippe Foundation

Larry, Richard M., treas: Carthage Foundation; dir: McKenna Foundation, Philip M.; pres, trust: Scaife Foundation, Sarah

Larsen, Christopher, vp, dir: Larsen Fund

Larsen, Clifford, trust: Timme Revocable Trust, Abigail S.

Larsen, Jonathan Zerbe, secy, dir: Larsen Fund

Larsen, Marianne, mgr contribution programs: International Paper Co. Foundation

Larsen, Ralph S., ceo, dir, mem exec comm: Johnson & Johnson; chmn: McNeil Consumer Products

Larsen, Robert R., pres, treas, dir: Larsen Fund

Larsen, Stephen C., trust: Hammill Foundation, Donald D.

Larson, Allan, trust: Faith Home Foundation

Larson, Carl E., dir: Julia R. and Estelle L. Foundation

Larson, Carol, dir: Wieboldt Foundation

Larson, Clint O., dir: Honeywell Foundation

Larson, Daniel N., pres: Kaiser Steel Resources

Larson, Davis J., secy, coun: Lutheran Brotherhood Foundation

Larson, Elwin S., trust: Faith Home Foundation

Larson, Gaylen Nevoy, group vp, chief acctg off: Household International

Larson, George, Hornblower Fund, Henry

Larson, Kenneth, pres: Polaris Industries, LP

Larson, Lyle, trust: Taylor Charitable Trust, Jack DeLoss

Larson, Marie, secy, dir: Offield Family Foundation

Larson, Peggy, dir corp contributions: Wisconsin Bell, Inc.

Larson, Richard, pres: Brillion Iron Works; vp, dir: Brillion Foundation

Larson, Steve, dir: Murray Foundation

Larson, Terrence, chmn, ceo: Corestates Bank

LaRue, Mary, chmn contributions comm: Berwind Corp.

LaRussa, Benny M., Jr., vp, treas: Bruno Charitable Foundation, Joseph S.

Lary, Jacqueline, trust: Mascoma Savings Bank Foundation

LaSalle, Nancy L., vp, secy: Normandie Foundation

Lasdon, Gene S., dir, vp: Lasdon Foundation

Lasdon, Jeffrey S., vp, dir: Lasdon Foundation

Lasdon, Mildred D., dir, vp: Lasdon Foundation

Lasdon, Stanley S., dir, pres, treas: Lasdon Foundation

Lasell, Raymond E., secy, dir: HON Industries Charitable Foundation

Lash, Wendy, vp, dir: Lehman Foundation, Edith and Herbert

Lashley, Eleanor H., dir: Huston Foundation

Laske, A. C., Jr., treas, dir: Morris Foundation, William T.

Laske, Arthur C., Sr., dir: Morris Foundation, William T.

Lasker, Joan, vp (corp pub aff): Cosmair, Inc.

Lasker, Joel Marc, adv: Bronstein Foundation, Sol and Arlene

Laskowski, Richard E., chmn, dir: Ace Hardware Corp.

Lasley, Robert, trust: Moss Charitable Trust, Finis M.

Lasota, John A., Jr., pres, dir: Dougherty Foundation

Lassalle, Honor, dir: Norman Foundation

Lassalle, Nancy Norman, vp, dir: Norman Foundation

Lassalle, Philip E., dir: Norman Foundation

Lasser, Miles L., treas, dir: Sheldon Foundation, Ralph C.

Lassiter, John W., trust: Belk Foundation Trust

Lassiter, Ronald C., chmn, ceo, dir: Zapata Corp.

Lassus, John F., ceo, pres: Lassus Brothers Oil; trust: Lassus Brothers Oil Foundation

Last, Barbara B., trust, pres: Sullivan Musical Foundation, William Matheus

Lastavica, Catherine C., trust: River Road Charitable Corporation

Lastavica, John, trust: Vingo Trust II

Lastinger, Allen L., Jr., pres, coo, dir: Barnett Banks; pres: Barnett Charities

Lasty, David, trust: Ford Foundation, Joseph F. and Clara

Latednesse, Gary, cfo: Rouge Steel Co.

Latham, John Brace, trust: Brace Foundation, Donald C.

Latimer, Ray, trust: Andalusia Health Services

Lattner, F. P. G., dir: Morton Memorial Fund, Mark

Laube, H. R., asst secy, asst treas: Freeport Brick Co. Charitable Trust

Laube, III, F. H., trust: Freeport Brick Co. Charitable Trust

Laubenstein, John R., asst secy: Amoco Foundation

Lauck, Joseph, dir: Lebanon Mutual Foundation

Lauder, Estee, pres: Lauder Foundation

Lauder, Leonard Alan, secy-treas: Lauder Foundation

Lauder, Ronald Stephen, vp: Lauder Foundation

Lauderbach, C. Ward, dir: Wickson-Link Memorial Foundation

Lauer, John N., pres, coo: BFGoodrich

Lauer, Robert Lee, pres, dir: Sara Lee Foundation

Laufer, Harry, dir: Associated Food Stores Charitable Foundation

Laughery, Jack A., ceo: Fast Food Merchandisers

Laughlin, Alexander M., treas: Waterfowl Research Foundation

Laughlin, Alexander Mellon, trust: Hartford Foundation, John A.

Laurance, Dale R., exec vp, sr oper off: Occidental Petroleum Corp.; dir: Occidental Petroleum Charitable Foundation

Lauren, Charles B., trust: Hagedorn Fund

Laurie, Marilyn, chmn, trust: AT&T Foundation

Laurie, William D., Jr., vchmn, trust: Earhart Foundation

Lauritzen, Dean G., trust: McDonald & Co. Securities Foundation

Lausche, Frank J., trust: Grimes Foundation

Lautenberg, Frank Raleigh, pres: Lautenberg Foundation

Lautenberg, Lois, vp: Lautenberg Foundation

Lavelle, James C., vp, dir: Banc One Wisconsin Foundation

Lavender, Patricia, secy/treas: Rebsamen Fund

Laventhol, David Abram, trust: Hartford Courant Foundation; pres: Times Mirror Co.; dir: Times Mirror Foundation

LaVeque, Edgar G., MD, trust: Valley Foundation

Laver, J. Michael, exec vp, cfo: MGIC Investment Corp.

Laverage, Hendrick J., treas: Fribourg Foundation

Lavey, Gilbert L., asst treas: MichCon Foundation

Lavezzo, Nellie, trust: Arata Brothers Trust

Lavezzorio, Joan F., vp: Mazza Foundation

Lavezzorio, Tina, vp, secy: Mazza Foundation

Laviers, Barbara P., secy, treas, trust: LaViers Foundation, Harry and Maxie

Laviers, Harry, Jr., pres, trust: LaViers Foundation, Harry and Maxie

Lavin, Leonard H., chmn, ceo, dir: Alberto-Culver Co.

Lavin, William K., exec vp, cfo: Woolworth Co., F.W.

Lavinia, Robert, pres: Phibro Energy

Lavis, Stella A., pres, dir: Amado Foundation, Maurice

Lavis, Victor R., dir: Amado Foundation, Maurice

Lavoie, Rosemary, trust: UNUM Charitable Foundation

Law, Caroline, dir: Menil Foundation

Law, H. Grant, Jr., pres, dir: Reflection Riding

Law, Jack R., trust: Nashua Trust Co. Foundation

Law, Mansel, dir: Hopper Foundation, May Templeton

Law, Mary Jane, trust: Law Foundation, Robert O.

Law, Robert O., III, pres: Law Foundation, Robert O.

Lawford, Patricia Kennedy, trust: Kennedy, Jr. Foundation, Joseph P.

Lawler, Dell R., dir: 1939 Foundation

Lawler, F. Rodney, pres, dir: 1939 Foundation

Lawler, Frank, dir: Lannan Foundation

Lawler, Jon R., dir: 1939 Foundation

Lawler, Oscar Thom, vp, trust: Murphy Foundation, Dan

Lawler, Patricia, sec: Lannan Foundation

Lawless, R. F., pres, ceo: Grand Trunk Corp.

Lawrence, Alice Kaplan, don, pres: Lawrence Foundation, Alice

Lawrence, Anne, dir: Gap Foundation

Lawrence, Anne I., trust: Ingalls Foundation, Louise H. and David S.

Lawrence, Barbara Childs, pres: AKC Fund

Lawrence, Barbara I., vp: Anderson Foundation

Lawrence, Charles M., pres, dir: Lytel Foundation, Bertha Russ

Lawrence, Dr. Elizabeth Atwood, trust: Donaldson Charitable Trust, Oliver S. and Jennie R.

Lawrence, Emily D., secy, treas: Willits Foundation

Lawrence, George D., Jr., pres, ceo: Phoenix Resource Cos.

Lawrence, George E., trust: Faith Home Foundation

Lawrence, J. Vinton, trust: AKC Fund

Lawrence, John E., secy: Colorado State Bank Foundation; trust, pres: Humane Society of the Commonwealth of Massachusetts

Lawrence, John T., Jr., trust: Emery Memorial, Thomas J.; trust: Semple Foundation, Louise Taft

Lawrence, Kent, pres, dir: Bauer Foundation, M. R.

Lawrence, Larry E., secy, treas: Beech Aircraft Foundation

Lawrence, Louis J., vp, dir: Giddings & Lewis Foundation

Lawrence, Pauline W., trust: Meyer Memorial Trust

Lawrence, Pelham, V, pres: Perdue Farms

Lawrence, Richard Wesley, Jr., pres, gov: Crary Foundation, Bruce L.

Lawrence, Robert Ashton, trust: Saltonstall Charitable Foundation, Richard

Lawrence, Robert J., treas, asst secy, dir: Bauer Foundation, M. R.

Lawrence, Robert S., dir (health sciences): Rockefeller Foundation

Lawrence, Starling R., vchmn bd mgrs: Childs Memorial Fund for Medical Research, Jane Coffin

Lawrence, Sull, secy, dir: Pickford Foundation, Mary

Lawrence, Warren, trust: Vicksburg Foundation

Lawrenz, Ruthmarie, dir: Schroeder Foundation, Walter

Laws, D. P., mem adv comm: Blue Bell Foundation

Lawson, Charles E., chmn, ceo, treas, dir: Brakeley, John Price Jones Inc.

Lawson, Jay Bird, trust: Glendorn Foundation

Lawson, Philip O., secy: 1939 Foundation

Lawson, William H., chmn, pres, ceo: Franklin Electric Company Inc. (Bluffton, Indiana)

Lawson-Johnston, Peter, II, dir: Guggenheim Foundation, Harry Frank

Lawson-Johnston, Peter O., chmn, dir: Guggenheim Foundation, Harry Frank

Lawton, Barbara P., trust: Gaylord Foundation, Clifford Willard

Lawton, Jack E., pres, dir: Burton Foundation, William T. and Ethel Lewis

Lawton, William Burton, chmn, dir: Burton Foundation, William T. and Ethel Lewis

Lay, Kenneth Lee, chmn, pres, ceo, coo: Enron Corp.; trust: Enron Foundation

Laybourne, Everett B., vp, dir: Parsons Foundation, Ralph M.

Layden, Donald W., asst secy, asst treas, trust: Casey Foundation, Annie E.; trust: UPS Foundation

Layton, Thomas C., dir: Cow Hollow Foundation; asst secy, exec dir: Gerbode Foundation, Wallace Alexander

Lazar, Helen B., pres, trust: Lazar Foundation

Lazar, William, vp, trust: Lazar Foundation

Lazarof, Janice A., vp, treas, dir: Taper Foundation, S. Mark

Lazarof, Janice Taper, vp, treas, dir: Taper Foundation, Mark

Lazarus, Charles, pres: Lazarus Charitable Trust, Helen and Charles; fdr, chmn, ceo: Toys "R" Us, Inc.

Lazarus, John T., Jr., trust: Emery Memorial, Thomas J.; trust: Semple Foundation

Lazarus, Cynthia A. Cecil, exec dir: Yassenoff Foundation, Leo

Lazarus, Ellen, asst treas: Cummings Foundation, Nathan

Lazarus, Leonard, secy: Solow Foundation

Le Buhn, Robert, pres, trust: Dodge Foundation, Geraldine R.

Le Clair, Laurie A., Azadoutioun Foundation

Le Comte, Maryanne, asst secy: Dingman Foundation, Michael D.

Le Grand, Clay, trust: Carver Charitable Trust, Roy J.

Le Maistre, Charles A., trust: Biological Humanics Foundation

Lea, Anna, dir, vp: Lea Foundation, Helen Sperry

Lea, Charles I., treas, trust: Community Coffee Co., Inc. Foundation

Lea, Helena, dir, vp: Lea Foundation, Helen Sperry

Lea, L. Bates, dir, vp: Wood Foundation, Lester G.

Lea, Marcia W., trust: Wood Foundation, Lester G.

Lea, R. Brooke, II, dir, vp: Lea Foundation, Helen Sperry

Lea, Sperry, dir, pres, treas: Lea Foundation, Helen Sperry

Leabo, Karen, trust: Cherokee Foundation

Leach, Diana Crow, pres, exec dir: Veritas Foundation

Leach, Duane M., trust: Kleberg Foundation for Wildlife Conservation, Caesar

Leach, Phillip M., exec dir, gen couns, trust: Temple Foundation, T. L. L.

Leach, Willis R., trust: Stamps Foundation, James L.

Leachtell, Michael, dir (mktg): Buchalter, Nemer, Fields, & Younger

Leahy, B. W., trust: Hemby Foundation, Alex

Leahy, Michael S., MD, trust, mem med comm: Pardee Foundation, Elsa U.

Leahy, Richard, trust: Peabody Charitable Fund, Amelia

Leaman, Richard, pres: Warren Co., S.D.

Leamon, Joyce, trust: Raymond Educational Foundation

Leander, Henry A., pres: Ford Meter Box Co.

Lear, William S., vp, dir: First National Bank of Chicago Foundation

Leary, Edward J., dir: Stanley Works Foundation

Leary, Ellen P., asst secy, treas: Pearlstone Foundation, Peggy Meyerhoff

Leary, Hugh K., mem allocations comm: Jeffress Memorial Trust, Thomas F. and Kate Miller

Leary, Pat, contact: Tetley, Inc.

Leask, Janie, Cook Inlet Region

Leath, Berneice R., secy, treas, exec dir: Priddy Foundation

Leather, Richard Brenk, trust: Frohlich Charitable Trust, Ludwig W.

Leatherdale, Douglas West, chmn, pres, ceo: Saint Paul Cos.

Leatherman, Laramie L., vp, trust: Gheens Foundation; chmn: Greenebaum, Doll & McDonald; dir: Greenebaum, Doll & McDonald Foundation

Leatherwood, Richard L., pres, trust: B & O Railroad Museum

Leavensworth, David S., pres, ceo: Campbell Taggart, Inc.

Leaver, Walter C., III, trust: Stephens Foundation Trust

Leavey, Dorothy, don, trust: Leavey Foundation, Thomas and Dorothy

Leavey, Joseph James, trust: Leavey Foundation, Thomas and Dorothy

Leavitt, Jeffrey S., asst treas: Kulas Foundation

Leavitt, Julian, mgr, trust: Sweet Life Foundation

Leavitt, Julian J., pres: Sweet Life Foods

LeBeau, Ben, dir: Imperial Bank Foundation

Lebedoff, Randy, secy, dir: Cowles Media Foundation

Lebensfeld, Harry, ceo: Trustcorp, Inc.; pres, ceo: UIS, Inc.

LeBlanc, Ray A., chmn, ceo: Keystone International

Leblois, Axel, pres, ceo: Bull HN Information Systems Inc.

LeBoeuf, Raymond W., vp, dir: PPG Industries Foundation

Lebovitz, Clara H., pres: Lebovitz Fund

Lebovitz, Herbert C., treas: Lebovitz Fund

Lebovitz, James, dir: Lebovitz Fund

LeBow, Bennett, chmn: New Valley

LeBrescu, Betty, mgr gen services: Murphy Oil Corp.

Lebsack, Chester W., trust: Doelger Charitable Trust, Thelma

Leckart, Ida G., trust: Gorin Foundation, Nehemiah

Ledbetter, J. Lee, pres: Oregon Cutting Systems

Ledbetter, Patricia L., secy: CTS Foundation

Ledell, Paul T., cfo: Hubbard Farms; treas: Hubbard Farms Charitable Foundation

Lederberg, Joshua, dir: Dreyfus Foundation, Camille and Henry; dir: Revson Foundation, Charles H.

Lederer, Adrienne, vp, dir: Lederer Foundation, Francis L.

Lederer, Francis L., II, pres, treas, dir: Lederer Foundation, Francis L.

Lederman, Carol, vp: Terner Foundation

Ledsinger, Charles Albert, Jr., sr vp, cfo: Promus Cos.

Lee, Charles R., chmn, pres, ceo, coo: GTE Corp.

Lee, Dwight E., vp, dir: Barker Foundation, J. M. R.

Lee, Earl V., secy: Gulf Power Foundation

Lee, Elliot D., program off: Victoria Foundation

Lee, Essie, dir: Jewish Foundation for Education of Women

Lee, Francis Childress, trust, vp: Childress Foundation, Francis and Miranda

Lee, George L., chmn: Red Devil

Lee, George L., Jr., trust: Red Devil Foundation

Lee, H. Clifford, vchmn, dir: Bush Charitable Foundation, Edyth

Lee, Homer W., trust: Shafer Foundation, Richard H. and Ann; treas: Wildermuth Foundation, E. F.

Lee, Irene, program off: Meyer Foundation, Eugene and Agnes E.

Lee, J. Philip, pres: Plant Memorial Fund, Henry B.

Lee, Jane T., mgr: Red Devil Foundation

Lee, Joanne Brown, treas: Prudential Foundation

Lee, Joe R., vchmn, cfo: General Mills; trust: General Mills Foundation

Lee, John, trust: Deseranno Educational Foundation

Lee, John J., pres, coo, dir: Tosco Corp. Refining Division; chmn exec comm, dir: Xtra Corp.

Lee, John L., trust: Red Devil Foundation

Lee, Kimary, mgr pub affairs: Walgreen Benefit Fund

Lee, Lewis S., trust, treas: Childress Foundation, Francis and Miranda

Lee, Lydia, chairperson contributions comm: Valley Bank Charitable Foundation

Lee, Madeline, exec dir: New York Foundation

Lee, Philip R., MD, trust: Kaiser Family Foundation, Henry J.

Lee, R. William, Jr., secy, trust: Oxford Industries Foundation

Lee, Richard H., pres, trust: Fowler Memorial Foundation, John Edward

Lee, Robert W., trust: Wildermuth Foundation, E. F.

Lee, Theodore K., vp, dir: Shoong Foundation, Milton

Lee, Thomas H., pres: Hills Department Stores, Inc.

Lee, Thomas L., chmn, ceo, dir: Newhall Land & Farming Co.

Lee, Valeria L., program off: Reynolds Foundation, Z. Smith

Lee, Victoria C., trust: Mitchell Family Foundation, Bernard and Marjorie

Lee, William States, chmn, pres, ceo: Duke Power Co.; chmn: Duke Power Co. Foundation; chmn, mgr: Harris Foundation, James J. and Angelia M.

Leedom-Ackerman, Joanne, pres: Banyan Tree Foundation

Leedy, Harriet V., trust: V and V Foundation

Leegant, Bernard, treas: Fish Foundation, Vain and Harry

Leemhuis, Andrew J., MD, med dir, dir: Wasie Foundation

Leeming, E. Janice, trust: Little Family Foundation

Leemon, Daniel J., trust: Vulcan Materials Co. Foundation

Leer, Steven, pres, ceo, dir: Arch Mineral Corp.

Leet, Mildred Robbins, trust: Joselow Foundation

Leff, Carl, chmn emeritus: National Spinning Co.

Leff, Deborah, pres, dir: Joyce Foundation

Leff, Joseph, chmn: National Spinning Co.

Lefferts, Peter A., pres: Citibank, F.S.B.

Lefkowitz, Elise G., vp: Gelman Foundation, Melvin and Estelle

Lefkowitz, Sidney M., trust: Wolfson Family Foundation

Leftwich, S. E., dir: Centel Foundation

Legg, Joan, Greater Lansing Foundation

Legg, Louis, Jr., trust: Thoman Foundation, W. B. and Candace

Leggat, John E., trust: Walsh Charity Trust, Blanche M.

Leggat, Thomas E., trust: Parker Foundation, Theodore Edson

Legge, Albert V., sr vp, cfo: Key Bank of Oregon

Lehman, Brenda L., dir: Jewish Foundation for Education of Women

Lehman, Edward, trust: Boettcher Foundation

Lehman, Elliot, dir: New Prospect Foundation

Lehman, Frances, treas, dir: Fel-Pro/Mecklenburger Foundation; pres, dir: New Prospect Foundation

Lehman, John R., pres, dir: Lehman Foundation, Edith and Herbert

Lehman, Kenneth, co-chmn: Fel-Pro Incorporated; asst secy: Fel-Pro/Mecklenburger Foundation; dir: New Prospect Foundation

Lehman, Lucy, dir: New Prospect Foundation

Lehman, Paul, pres, dir: Fel-Pro/Mecklenburger Foundation; dir: New Prospect Foundation

Lehman, Ronna Stamm, dir: New Prospect Foundation

Lehmann, Anne, American Society of Ephesus

Lehmann, Richard J., chmn, ceo, dir: Valley National Bank of Arizona

Lehn, Alan J., trust, treas: Corbett Foundation

Lehnhart, Rev. M. H., secy, trust: Johnson Foundation, M. G. and Lillie A.

Lehr, Gustav J., chmn, ceo, dir: Shelter Mutual Insurance Co.; pres, dir: Shelter Insurance Foundation

Lehr, Ronald L., trust: Johnson Foundation, Helen K. and Arthur E.

Lehr, William N., Jr., sr vp, secy, assoc gen coun: Hershey Foods Corp.

Lehrer, Sander, secy: United States-Japan Foundation

Lehrman, Fredrica, vp: Lehrman Foundation, Jacob and Charlotte

Lehrman, Robert, pres: Lehrman Foundation, Jacob and Charlotte

Lehrman, Samuel, vp, dir: Giant Food Foundation; vp: Lehrman Foundation, Jacob and Charlotte

Lehrolf, Patti, trust: Brody Foundation, Frances

Leib, Joseph, chmn, dir: Fidelity Federal Savings & Loan

Leiberman, Patricia S., trust: Mailman Family Foundation, A. L.

Leiblein, Frank, trust: Swift Memorial Health Care Foundation

Leibovitz, Morris P., trust: Leibovitz Foundation, Morris P.

Leibrick, Ann P., Pittsburgh Child Guidance Foundation

Leibrock, Robert M., vp, trust: Abell-Hanger Foundation

Leick, Frederick W., ceo, pres: Seneca Foods Corp.; pres, ceo, dir: Seneca Foods Foundation

Leifert, Leonard, exec vp, coo, dir: APL Corp.

Leighner, William H., trust: Moores Foundation, Harry C.

Leighton, Judd C., secy, treas, dir: Leighton-Oare Foundation

Leighton, Mary Morris, pres, dir: Leighton-Oare Foundation

Leighton, Paul J., secy, asst treas: Midwest Resources

Leiman, Joan, vchmn: New York Foundation

Leinbach, Harold O., trust, pres: Oberlaender Foundation, Gustav

Leinbach, Paula, Oberlaender Foundation, Gustav

Leinbach, Richard O., trust, vp: Oberlaender Foundation, Gustav

Leininger, Jeffrey, trust: Mellon Bank Foundation

Leipziger, Marcelo, dir: Ridgefield Foundation

Leir, Henry J., pres, dir: Ridgefield Foundation

Leis, Barbara E., mgr: Ix Foundation

Leisure, George S., Jr., dir: Donovan, Leisure, Newton & Irvine Foundation

Leland, Katherine A., M.D., Kelley and Elza Kelley Foundation, Edward Bangs

Leland, Leslie S., secy: Burlington Resources Foundation

Leland, Marc E., trust: German Marshall Fund of the United States

Leland, Marc Ernest, vp, dir: G.P.G. Foundation

LeLaura, Dr. James, trust: Connecticut Energy Foundation, Inc.

Leman, Eugene D., dir: IBP Foundation, Inc., The

Lemann, Thomas Berthelot, secy, treas, dir: Azby Fund; secy, dir: Zemurray Foundation

Lemberg, Thomas Michael, clerk, dir: Lotus Development Corp.

Lemeris, James R., secy, treas: Stanley Charitable Foundation, A. W.

Lemieux, Joseph H., chmn, ceo: Owens-Illinois

Lemk, Louis G., secy, treas, trust: Stern Foundation, Percival

Lemke, Carl R., secy: Consolidated Papers Foundation

Lemole, Daniel A., asst secy: Continental Corp. Foundation

Lemon, L. Gene, vp: Dial Corporation Fund

Lemons, Wishard, trust: Broadhurst Foundation

Lempka, Arnold W., MD, chmn: Physicians Mutual Insurance

Lemunyon, Ralph H., pres distribution comm: Ford and Ada Ford Fund, S. N.

Lenaburg, David S., chmn, pres, ceo, dir: Banner Life Insurance Co.

Lenahan, Helen Dent, dir: Dent Family Foundation, Harry

Lenahan, Marilyn S., trust: Swim Foundation, Arthur L.

Lenczuk, Kimberly Duchossois, pres: Duchossois Foundation

Lender, Marvin K., treas: Lender Family Foundation

Lender, Murray, pres: Lender Family Foundation

Lenehan, James T., pres: McNeil Consumer Products

Lenhart, Carole S., treas: Beveridge Foundation, Frank Stanley

Lenig, Larry E., Jr., pres, coo, asst secy, dir: Digicon

Lenker, Max V., pres: Racetrac Petroleum

Lenkowsky, Leslie, PhD, trust: Achelis Foundation; trust: Bodman Foundation

Lennings, Joseph L., pres, coo: Mount Vernon Mills

Lennings, Joseph L., Jr., trust: Mount Vernon Mills Foundation

Lennon, A. P., vp: Lennon Foundation, Fred A.

Lennon, Fred A., pres: Lennon Foundation, Fred A.

Lennon-Rzeszut, Mary, contributions adm: Colgate-Palmolive Co.

Lenoir, James S., dir: Deposit Guaranty Foundation

Lenox, John W., vchmn, exec vp, dir: Shelter Mutual Insurance Co.; dir: Shelter Insurance Foundation

Lents, Max R., dir, mem exec comm, chmn dirs grant comm: Keck Foundation, W. M.

Lentz, Hover T., vchmn, trust: Boettcher Foundation

Leny, Jean-Claude, chmn: Burndy Corp.

Lenzie, Charles A., chmn, ceo: Nevada Power Co.

Leo, M. S., sr vp, chief admin off, gen couns, dir: Rhone-Poulenc Inc.

Leon, Cecilia Vega, asst treas: Haghenbeck Foundation, Antonio Y. De La Lama

Leonard, George E., trust: Shughart, Thomson & Kilroy Charitable Foundation Trust

Leonard, J. Wayne, vp, cfo: PSI Energy

Leonard, James P., Bauervic Foundation, Charles M.

Leonard, John, secy-treas: Beitzell & Co. Charitable Foundation

Leonard, Judith S., dir: Bedminster Fund

Leonard, Kathryn, treas: Bauervic Foundation, Charles M.

Leonard, Patricia A., pres, secy: Bauervic Foundation, Charles M.

Leonard, Theodore J., treas: Bauervic Foundation, Charles M.

Leonard, Timothy J., dir: Bauervic Foundation, Charles M.

Leonard, William, pres: Aratex Services

Leonard, William J., secy, treas: Law Foundation, Robert O.

Leongomez, Carol W., secy, trust: Chatlos Foundation

Leonhardt, Anne S., pres, secy, dir: Leonhardt Foundation, Frederick H.

Leonhardt, Barbara A., vp, dir: Leonhardt Foundation, Frederick H.

Leonhardt, Frederick H., vp, treas, dir: Leonhardt Foundation, Frederick H.

Leonhardt, Melissa A., vp, dir: Leonhardt Foundation, Frederick H.

Leonhauser, Maria E., mgr pubic rels: Volkswagen of America, Inc.

Leonian, Edith, exec vp: Rosenbaum Foundation, Paul and Gabriella

Leopold, Michael, trust: Warner Electric Foundation

Lepak, Robert R., American Saw & Manufacturing Co.

Leppen, Michael A., trust: Hoover Foundation, H. Earl

Leppert, Tom, dir pub aff: Castle & Cooke

Lerch, Michael, treas: Salem Lutheran Foundation

Lerchen, Edward H., dir: Kresge Foundation

Lerman, Philip, dir: Cudahy Fund, Patrick and Anna M.

Lerner, Irwin, pres, ceo, dir: Hoffmann-La Roche; trust: Hoffmann-La Roche Foundation

Lerner, Sandra K., chmn, pres: Bosack and Bette M. Kruger Foundation, Leonard X.

LeRoux, Tamara Brown, trust: Dauch Foundation, William

Leroyer, Maxime F., trust: Ellison Foundation

Leschley, Jan, coo: SmithKline Beecham

Leser, Lawrence Arthur, pres, ceo, dir: Scripps Co., E.W.; mem: Scripps Howard Foundation

Leshion, Arthur, cfo: Gucci America Inc.

Lesko, Klementik G., trust: Whalley Charitable Trust

Lesley, J. K., trust: Burlington Industries Foundation

Leslie, Charles M., trust: Comstock Foundation

Leslie, Gaylord E., trust: Van Wert County Foundation

Leslie, M., dir: Oaklawn Foundation

Leslie, Marc, legal counsel: Fleet Financial Group

Leslie, Mary, exec dir: Pacific Telesis Foundation

Lesner, J., pres, dir: Center for Educational Programs; treas, secy, dir: Milken Institute for Job and Capital Formation

Lesner, Julius, exec vp, cfo, exec dir: Capital Fund Foundation; asst secy, dir: Milken Family Medical Foundation; cfo, secy, dir: Milken Foundation, L. and S.

Lesser, Bernard, pres: Conde Nast Publications, Inc.

Lesser, F. A. S., chmn: United States Borax & Chemical Corp.

Lesser, Richard, sr vp: TJX Cos.; vp, dir: TJX Foundation

Lessler, Edith, mem bd advs: Stern Memorial Trust, Sidney

Lester, Charles R., vp, dir: Alexander Charitable Foundation

Lester, Margaret, trust: English Foundation, W. C.

LeSuer, William Monroe, trust: Lubrizol Foundation

Lethbridge, Caryl A., asst secy: Hyde and Watson Foundation

Lettenberger, Peter J., dir: Brady Foundation, W. H.

Leu, Cynthia, trust: Leu Foundation

Leu, Frank, trust, pres, mgr: Leu Foundation

Leube, H., trust: Lehigh Portland Cement Charitable Trust

Leum, Mark E., pres, coo: Woodward Governor Co.

Leuthold, Betty B., vp, trust: Leuthold Foundation

Leuthold, Caroline E., trust: Leuthold Foundation

Leuthold, John H., pres, trust: Leuthold Foundation

Leuthye, Mrs. George G., dir, recording secy: Ebell of Los Angeles Scholarship Endowment Fund

Leva, James R., pres, coo: Jersey Central Power & Light Co.

Levan, B. W., vp, dir: Shell Oil Co. Foundation

Levan, John A., dir: Frost Foundation

Levas, Dimitri, vp: Mapplethorpe Foundation, Robert

Levavy, Zvi, pres: Kaplun Foundation, Morris J. and Betty

Level, Leon J., vp, cfo: Computer Sciences Corp.

Levenson, Harvey S., pres, coo, dir: Kaman Corp.

Lever, Ben R., Jr., trust: Love Foundation, Lucyle S.

Levering, Walter B., pres, dir: Oaklawn Foundation

Levett, Edith, secy: Greenwall Foundation

Levey, N. James, trust, pres: Shiffman Foundation

Levey, Richard, trust, vp: Shiffman Foundation

Levi, Alexander H., dir: Hecht-Levi Foundation

Levi, Arlo Dane, pres: 3M Co.

Levi, Constance M., dir: Mardag Foundation

Levi, Richard H., dir: Hecht-Levi Foundation

Levi, Robert Henry, pres, dir: Hecht-Levi Foundation

Levi, Ryda H., vp, dir: Hecht-Levi Foundation

Levin, Benjamin B., dir: Federation Foundation of Greater Philadelphia

Levin, Charles, trust: Rohlik Foundation, Sigmund and Sophie

Levin, Gail, trust: Seasongood Good Government Foundation, Murray and Agnes

Levin, Gerald Manuel, chmn, pres, ceo, dir: Time Warner; dir: Time Warner Foundation

Levin, Harold L., treas, trust: Wexner Foundation

Levin, Jack I., trust: Phillips Family Foundation, Jay and Rose

Levin, Janice H., pres, treas, trust: Levin Foundation, Philip and Janice

Levin, Jerry W., chmn: Burger King Corp.

Levin, John, trust: Phillips Family Foundation, Jay and Rose

Levin, John P., Jr., dir: Rosenberg, Jr. Family Foundation, Louise and Claude

Levin, Joseph, trust: Rohlik Foundation, Sigmund and Sophie

Levin, Michael S., pres: Titan Industrial Co.

Levin, Simon, secy, treas: Hite Foundation

Levin, Suzan, trust: Phillips Family Foundation, Jay and Rose

Levine, A. L., vp, trust: Meyer Memorial Foundation, Aaron and Rachel

Levine, Joseph, dir: Forchheimer Foundation

Levine, K. N., asst secy, asst treas: Ohrstrom Foundation

Levine, Larry, secy: Panasonic Foundation

Levine, Malden, treas: Levine Family Foundation, Hyman

Levine, Rachmiel, MD, dir: Diabetes Research and Education Foundation

Levine, Richard A., pres: Kutz Foundation, Milton and Hattie

LeVine, Robert A., dir: Spencer Foundation

Levine, Ronald Jay, vp: Levine Family Foundation, Hyman

Levine, Seymour, trust: Greene Foundation, Robert Z.

Levine, Sid B., pres: Levine Family Foundation, Hyman

Levings, Margaret Carr, trust: Howell Fund

Levings, Willard S., trust: Boston Fatherless and Widows Society

Levinson, Anna B., dir: Levinson Foundation, Max and Anna

Levinson, Barbara S., vp, dir: Levinson Foundation, Morris L.

Levinson, Beatrice, secy: Fischbach Foundation

Levinson, Carl A., pres, treas, dir: Levinson Foundation, Max and Anna; trust: Merit Gasoline Foundation

Levinson, Charlotte J., dir: Levinson Foundation, Max and Anna

Levinson, Donald M., dir: CIGNA Foundation

Levinson, Gordon, dir: Levinson Foundation, Max and Anna

Levinson, Harry, pres: Levinson's, Inc.

Levinson, Jo List, treas: List Foundation, Albert A.

Levinson, Julian, dir: Levinson Foundation, Max and Anna

Levinson, Julius, asst treas: Coltec Industries Charitable Foundation

Levinson, Lynda B., dir: Levinson Foundation, Max and Anna

Levinson, Mary, trust: Levy Foundation, Achille

Levinson, Morris L., pres, dir: Levinson Foundation, Morris L.

Levinson, S. Jarvin, dir: Georgia Health Foundation

Levit, Max, dir: Levit Family Foundation, Joe

Levit, Milton, chmn, pres, dir: Grocers Supply Co.; dir: Levit Family Foundation, Joe

Levitan, David M., vp: Fink Foundation

Levitan, Melvyn C., Spingold Foundation, Nate B. and Frances

Leviton, Harold, pres: Leviton Manufacturing Co.; pres: Leviton Foundation New York

Leviton, Louis, treas, asst secy: Weisz Foundation, David and Sylvia

Leviton, Shirley, treas: Leviton Foundation New York

Levitt, Alvin T., dir, secy, treas: Seven Springs Foundation

Levitt, Arthur, Jr., dir: Revson Foundation, Charles H.; trust: Rockefeller Foundation; dir: Winston Foundation, Norman and Rosita

Levitt, Charles H., Neuberger Foundation, Roy R. and Marie S.

Levitt, Gerald S., vp, cfo: South Jersey Industries

Levitt, Jeanne, secy: Levitt Foundation, Richard S.

Levitt, Lawrence, secy-treas: Odyssey Partners Foundation

Levitt, Mark, vp: Levitt Foundation, Richard S.

Levitt, Randall, vp: Levitt Foundation, Richard S.

Levitt, Richard, pres, treas: Levitt Foundation, Richard S.

Levitt, Richard S., dir: Northwest Area Foundation

Levitt, William J., Jr., pres, dir: Levitt Foundation

Levy, Andrew H., dir: Newman Assistance Fund, Jerome A. and Estelle R.

Levy, Bill, pres: Oak Hall, Inc.

Levy, Candy, vp (admin): Global Van Lines

Levy, David, trust: National Service Foundation

Levy, David B., treas, dir: Rudin Foundation

Levy, Donna, secy: Levy Foundation, Hyman Jebb

Levy, Edward C., Jr., pres, treas: Levy Co., Edward C.

Levy, Edward Charles, Jr., trust: Levy Foundation, Edward C.

Levy, Francis N., vp, dir: Levy Foundation, Betty and Norman F.

Levy, G., pres, ceo: Liquid Air Corp.

Levy, Gaston Raymond, vp, group mgr (Latin Am): Gillette Co.

Levy, Gerard, chmn: Big Three Industries

Levy, Hyman, pres, treas: Levy Foundation, Hyman Jebb

Levy, Irwin L., pres: NCH Corp.

Levy, J. Leonard, trust: Jones Intercable Tampa Trust

Levy, John, pres, dir: Fashion Bar

Levy, Julie R., treas: Honigman Foundation

Levy, Leon, trust: Guggenheim Memorial Foundation, John Simon; trust: Levy Foundation, Jerome

Levy, Lester A., chmn: NCH Corp.

Levy, Louis, vp: Material Service Foundation

Levy, Louis, II, MD, dir: Lupin Foundation

Levy, Madeline, trust: Messing Foundation, Morris M. and Helen F.

Levy, Martin, dir: Seibel Foundation, Abe and Annie

Levy, Norman F., pres, dir: Levy Foundation, Betty and Norman F.

Levy, Philip J., chmn, ceo: Levy's Lumber & Building Centers

Levy, Reynold, pres, trust: AT&T Foundation; mem bd: Cummings Foundation, Nathan

Levy, Roberta Morse, trust: Ratshesky Foundation, A. C.

Levy, S. Jay, trust: Levy Foundation, Jerome

Levy, Susan M., secy contributions comm: Donnelley & Sons Co., R.R.

Levy, Sylvia, trust: Hartford Courant Foundation

Levy Kipper, Barbara, chmn: Levy Circulating Co., Charles

Lewin, Natalie, treas, dir: Rudin Foundation, Louis and Rachel

Lewis, Andrew Lindsay, Jr., chmn, pres, ceo, dir: Union Pacific Corp.; chmn, trust: Union Pacific Foundation

Lewis, Arlyce K., mgr corp commun: Storage Technology Corp.

Lewis, C. Stephen, trust: Weyerhaeuser Co. Foundation

Lewis, Craig, vp, trust: Middendorf Foundation

Lewis, Delancey B., secy, treas, dir: Quest for Truth Foundation

Lewis, Delano E., pres: Chesapeake & Potomac Telephone Co.; chmn: Meyer Foundation, Eugene and Agnes E.

Lewis, Diana, mem corp contributions comm: Ecolab; trust: Lewis Foundation, Frank J.

Lewis, Edward D., pres, trust: Lewis Foundation, Frank J.

Lewis, Frances Aaronson, trust: Circuit City Foundation

Lewis, G. Wade, vp, cfo: Duracell International

Lewis, George, trust: Sanders Trust, Charles

Lewis, Harriet G., chmn: Globe Valve Corp.

Lewis, Harry T., Jr., trust: Boettcher Foundation

Lewis, Henrietta G., trust: Grigg-Lewis Trust

Lewis, Henry R., vchmn, cso, dir: Dennison Manufacturing Co.; trust: Dennison Foundation

Lewis, James R., trust: Callaway Foundation; trust: Callaway Foundation, Fuller E.

Lewis, Jan H., dir: Compton Foundation

Lewis, Janet P., dir: Flagler Foundation

Lewis, Jeffrey R., mgr: Heinz Family Foundation

Lewis, John, chmn, dir: Amdahl Corp.; exec vp: Comerica

Lewis, John D., trust: Packer Foundation, Horace B.

Lewis, John Furman, dir: Williams Cos. Foundation

Lewis, John M., trust: Hirschl Trust for Charitable Purposes, Irma T.

Lewis, Julius, dir, secy: Rhoades Fund, Otto L. and Hazel E.

Lewis, Karen Yoak, off mgr, secy: Reynolds Charitable Trust, Kate B.

Lewis, Kenneth W., vp, dir: BMC Foundation

Lewis, Laurie M., mem dispensing comm: McCune Charitable Trust, John R.

Lewis, Lawrence, vp, dir: Lastfogel Foundation, Abe and Frances

Lewis, Lawrence, Jr., pres, treas, dir: Flagler Foundation

Lewis, Lloyd E., Jr., trust: Dayton Foundation Depository

Lewis, Lydia, dir: Tell Foundation

Lewis, Marilyn W., chmn, dir: American Water Works Co., Inc.

Lewis, Marilyn Ware, vp, secy: Oxford Foundation

Lewis, Maryon Davies, trust: Davies Charitable Trust

Lewis, Max B., secy, mgr, dir: Dumke Foundation, Dr. Ezekiel R. and Edna Wattis; pres, mgr, trust: Harris Foundation, William H. and Mattie Wattis

Lewis, Megan, trust: Lewis Foundation, Frank J.

Lewis, Merwin, vp, dir: Oestreicher Foundation, Sylvan and Ann; secy: Salomon Foundation, Richard & Edna

Lewis, Mrs. Thomas J., pres, dir: Murphy Co. Foundation, G.C.

Lewis, Peter Benjamin, chmn, pres, ceo, dir: Progressive Corp.

Lewis, Philip D., trust: Lewis Foundation, Frank J.

Lewis, Ralph M., fdr, chmn: Lewis Homes of California

Lewis, Richard A., pres, reg mgr: Lewis Homes of California

Lewis, Robert J., sr vp: First NH Banks, Inc.; pres: First Capital Bank Foundation

Lewis, Roger, dir mktg: Commercial Federal Corp.

Lewis, Ronald L., admin, dir: Tell Foundation

Lewis, Sharon, vp, trust: Harris Foundation, William H. and Mattie Wattis

Lewis, Sydney, pres: Best Products Foundation

Lewis, T. Michael, trust: Butler Manufacturing Co. Foundation

Lewis, Thomas E., dir co commun: Texas Gas Transmission Corp.

Lewis, W. Ashton, trust: Beazley Foundation; secy, trust: Frederick Foundation

Lewis, W. Henry, cfo: Bonner & Moore Associates

Lewis, Warren, dir: Lebanon Mutual Foundation

Lewis, William, cfo: Nutri/System Inc.

Lewiton, Jacob, trust: Sherman Family Charitable Trust, George and Beatrice

Lewy, Ralph I., treas, dir: Pick, Jr. Fund, Albert

Lexiner, Timothy C., chmn: National Center for Automated Information Retrieval

Ley, Watson, trust: Van Wert County Foundation

Leyasmeyer, Archibald, vchmn: Jerome Foundation

Leydorf, Frederick Leroy, dir: Jameson Foundation, J. W. and Ida M.

Leyhe, Edward F., secy: Kimball Foundation, Miles

Lhota, William J., exec vp: American Electric Power

Li, Philip, asst vp: Marine Midland Banks

Li, Victor H., dir: HEI Charitable Foundation

Libassi, Frank Peter, chmn: Travelers Cos. Foundation

Liberate, Anthony W., Jr., trust: Debartolo Foundation, Marie P.

Liberman, Jack, chmn, dir: Victory Markets, Inc.

Liberman, Lee Marvin, chmn: Laclede Gas Co.

Libicki, Henry J., trust: Nord Family Foundation

Licata, Steven V., exec dir: Watson Foundation, Thomas J.

Lichtenstein, Daniel B., mgr, trust: Lichtenstein Foundation, David B.

Lichtenstein, David B., Jr., trust: Lichtenstein Foundation, David B.

Lichtenstein, Mary, trust: Lichtenstein Foundation, David B.

Lichter, Robert L., exec dir: Dreyfus Foundation, Camille and Henry

Lichtman, Judith, dir: Moriah Fund

Lichtman, Moshe, vp, trust: Community Cooperative Development Foundation

Liddell, Donald M., Jr., dir: Youth Foundation

Liddy, Richard A., pres, ceo, coo: General American Life Insurance Co.

Lidow, Eric, chmn, ceo, pres: International Rectifier Corp.

Lidvall, John Gabrielson, vp, exec dir: Hall Foundation

Liebaert, Michael, managing dir: Azby Fund

Lieber, Constance, pres: Essel Foundation

Lieber, Leo, Hudson Neckwear

Lieber, Samuel, vp: Essel Foundation

Lieber, Stephen, secy, treas: Essel Foundation

Lieberman, Adele, pres, dir: Lieberman-Okinow Foundation

Lieberman, Cynthia, dir (corp communs): Fox Inc.

Lieberman, David, vp, dir: Lieberman-Okinow Foundation

Lieberman, Leonard, trust: Fund for New Jersey

Lieberman, Stephen, secy, dir: Lieberman-Okinow Foundation

Lieberman, William K., vchmn: Jewish Healthcare Foundation of Pittsburgh

Liebhardt, Nadine, dir: Jewish Foundation for Education of Women

Liebling, Norman R., secy: Rosenbaum Foundation, Paul and Gabriella

Liebovitz, Mitchell, ceo, pres: Pep Boys

Liedtke, John Hugh, chmn, ceo: Pennzoil Co.

Liedtke, William C., Jr., chmn, pres, ceo, dir: Pogo Producing Co.

Lieser, W. E., treas, trust: Reeves Foundation

Lietz, Robert C., secy, treas: Hauss-Helms Foundation

Liffers, William Albert, vchmn: American Cyanamid Co.

Liftin, John Matthew, secy: Kidder Peabody Foundation

Lifton, Robert, co-chmn: Marcade Group, Inc.

Lifvendahl, Harold R., pres, publ, dir: Sentinel Communications Co.

Liggett, William Newton, trust: Star Bank, N.A., Cincinnati Foundation

Light, Dorothy K., chmn: Prudential Foundation

Light, Nathan, chmn, pres, ceo: Sterling Inc.

Light, Virginia, secy: Cincinnati Foundation for the Aged

Lightfoot, Sara Lawrence, dir: MacArthur Foundation, John D. and Catherine T.

Lightner, Earl Sams, trust: Lightner Sams Foundation

Lightner, Larry, trust: Lightner Sams Foundation

Lightner, Robin, trust: Lightner Sams Foundation

Lightner, Sue B., trust: Lightner Sams Foundation

Ligon, Bill A., trust: Hawkins Foundation, Robert Z.

Ligon, Ed D., Jr., dir: Orbit Valve Foundation

Ligon, Ed. D., chmn: Orbit Valve Co.

Liguori, Frank W., chmn, ceo: Olsten Corp.

Liles, Arthur D., secy, treas, exec dir: Lincoln-Lane Foundation

Lilienthal, Sally L., pres: Cow Hollow Foundation

Liljebeck, Roy C., cfo: Airborne Express Co.

Lillard, Peter T., vchmn, mem trust comm: Bergen Foundation, Frank and Lydia

Lilley, Jack, dir: Smith and W. Aubrey Smith Charitable Foundation, Clara Blackford

Lillian, Jeffrey S., asst secy: First National Bank of Chicago Foundation

Lillie, John Mitchell, pres, ceo, dir, coo: American President Cos.

Lillie, Richard H., MD, vp, dir: Bradley Foundation, Lynde and Harry

Lillo, Frances, trust: Hunt Manufacturing Co. Foundation

Lilly, Bruce A., dir: Lilly Foundation, Richard Coyle

Lilly, David M., pres, dir: Lilly Foundation, Richard Coyle

Lilly, David M., Jr., secy, dir: Lilly Foundation, Richard Coyle

Lilly, Diane P., pres: Norwest Foundation

Lilly, Eli, II, dir: Lilly Endowment

Lilly, Elizabeth M., vp, dir: Lilly Foundation, Richard Coyle

Lilly, Katherine V., dir: Mardag Foundation

Lilly, Leslie, dir: Rockefeller Foundation, Winthrop

Lilly, Marcella, trust: Seymour and Troester Foundation

Lilly, Maria, dir corp contributions: First Boston Foundation Trust

Liman, Arthur L., dir: Paley Foundation, William S.

Limes, Edward J., pres, treas, trust: Weckbaugh Foundation, Eleanore Mullen

Lincoln, George A., trust, pres: Lincoln Family Foundation

Lincoln, Olivia G., trust, vp: Lincoln Family Foundation

Lincoln, William T., treas, trust: Berry Foundation, Loren M.; trust: Kramer Foundation, Louise

Lindberg, Jerome, vp, trust: Buell Foundation, Temple Hoyne

Lindblom, Lance E., pres: MacArthur Foundation, J. Roderick

Linde, Maxine H., pres, dir: Linde Foundation, Ronald and Maxine

Linde, Ronald K., chmn, secy, treas: Linde Foundation, Ronald and Maxine

Lindeman, Donald L., ceo, pres: Citizens Gas & Coke Utility

Lindemer, Lawrence, trust: Bentley Foundation, Alvin M.

Lindenbaum, Armand, vp: Stern Foundation, Leonard N.; secy, dir: Stern Foundation, Max

Lindenberg, David R., pres: Hickory Tech Corp. Foundation

Lindenberg, George, trust: Winship Memorial Scholarship Foundation

Linder, Eric, pres: Colonial Parking

Linder, May L., secy: Olive Bridge Fund

Linder, Richard A., trust: Westinghouse Foundation

Linder, Susan E., vp, dir: Olive Bridge Fund

Linder-Scholer, William C., exec dir, secy, dir: Cray Research

Lindfeth, Michael, exec vp, cfo, dir: Cray Research

Lindholm, Darralu, assoc: Medtronic Foundation

Lindholm, John T., trust: Whiting Foundation

Lindholm, Richard, pres, dir: Fabyan Foundation

Lindig, Bill M., pres, coo: Sysco Corp.

Lindley, F. Haynes, Jr., pres, trust: Haynes Foundation, John Randolph and Dora

Lindley, Lucia Woods, pres, trust: Woods Charitable Fund

Lindley, Robert, pres: Jantzen, Inc.

Lindner, Carl, pres, dir: United Brands Foundation

Lindner, Carl H., III, pres, coo: Penn Central Corp.

Lindner, Carl Henry, III, pres, coo: American Financial Corp.; pres, dir: American Financial Corp. Foundation; pres, coo: Chiquita Brands Co.

Lindner, Jim, pres: Memorex Telex Corp.

Lindner, Keith E., pres, coo: Chiquita Brands Co.; vp, dir: United Brands Foundation

Lindner, Robert David, vchmn, sr vp, dir: American Financial Corp.; vp, dir: American Financial Corp. Foundation

Lindquist, Jack B., vp, trust: Disney Co. Foundation, Walt

Lindquist, John, dir: Russell Charitable Foundation, Tom

Lindsay, Arthur O., dir: Oakley-Lindsay Foundation of Quincy Newspapers & Quincy Broadcasting Co.

Lindsay, Donald, dir: Oakley-Lindsay Foundation of Quincy Newspapers & Quincy Broadcasting Co.

Lindsay, F. M., Jr., vp, dir: Oakley-Lindsay Foundation of Quincy Newspapers & Quincy Broadcasting Co.

Lindsay, James, ceo: AG Processing Inc.

Lindsay, Nancy D., trust: Dodge Foundation, Geraldine R.

Lindsay, Robert Van Cleef, chmn, trust: Guggenheim Memorial Foundation, John Simon

Lindsey, Connie L., treas: Ameritech Foundation

Lindsey, Douglas G., trust: Ivakota Association

Lindsey, Handy, Jr., exec dir, treas: Field Foundation of Illinois

Lindsey, Jean C., pres: Chisholm Foundation

Lindsley, Donald B., dir: Grass Foundation

Linehan, John Charles, sr vp, cfo: Kerr-McGee Corp.

Lineker, Rev. George, secy: Packer Foundation, Horace B.

Liner, R.A., trust: County Bank Foundation

Linge, H. Kennedy, mem screening comm: PPG Industries Foundation

Linge, Hope S., dir: Staunton Farm Foundation

Lingenfelter, Paul E., dir program evaluation & program-related investments: MacArthur Foundation, John D. and Catherine T.

Lingle, Walter L., vp, trust: Emery Memorial, Thomas J.; trust: Semple Foundation, Louise Taft

Lingnau, Lutz, chmn, dir: Berlex Laboratories

Link, Arthur, trust: Bonner Foundation, Corella and Bertram

Link, Eleanor Irene Higgins, chmn bd dirs: Link, Jr. Foundation, George

Link, Marilyn C., secy, treas, trust: Link Foundation

Link, Robert Emmett, vchmn, dir: Link, Jr. Foundation, George

Link, William M., mem tech assistance bd: Link Foundation

Link, William M., Jr., 2nd vp, dir: Feild Co-Operative Association

Linn, Milman H., pres: McIntire Educational Fund, John

Linn, Milman H., III, dir: McIntire Educational Fund, John

Linnan, Cynthia, dir, vp, treas: Ziemann Foundation

Linnell, John W., mem distribution comm: Champlin Foundations

Linnemann, Patricia G., Gross Charitable Trust, Walter L. and Nell R.

Linnert, Terrence Gregory, vp: Centerior Energy Foundation

Linsey, Joseph M., trust: Ford Foundation, Joseph F. and Clara

Lintilhac, Crea S., vp, secy, dir: Lintilhac Foundation

Lintilhac, Philip M., pres, dir: Lintilhac Foundation

Linus, James J., dir: Sylvester Foundation, Harcourt M. and Virginia W.

Linville, C. Edwin, trust: Schepp Foundation, Leopold

Linz, Andrew, pres, dir: Loewy Family Foundation

Linzer, Don A., trust: Pittsburgh Child Guidance Foundation

Lioi, Margaret, exec dir: Dana Charitable Trust, Eleanor Naylor

Liotta, Kathy, exec dir: Chambers Development Charitable Foundation

Lipani, John F., trust: Boh Foundation

Lipchitz, Yulla, pres: Lipchitz Foundation, Jacques and Yulla

Lipford, Ralph, dir: Dana Corp. Foundation

Lipford, Rocque Edward, dir: La-Z-Boy Foundation; trust:

McIntyre Foundation, B. D. and Jane E.; trust: McIntyre Foundation, C. S. and Marion F.

Lipkin, Gerald H., chmn, ceo, dir: Valley National Bancorp

Lipkin, John O., vp: Zlinkoff Fund for Medical Research and Education, Sergei S.

Lipkin, Mack, Jr., trust: New York Foundation; vp: Zlinkoff Fund for Medical Research and Education, Sergei S.

Lipkowitz, Irving, trust: Hebrew Technical Institute

Lipman, A.M., Jr., pres, coo, dir: Amalgamated Sugar Co.

Lipman, Bernard L., M.D., trust: Steiner Charitable Fund, Albert

Lipman, David, dir: Pulitzer Publishing Co. Foundation

Lipman, Stanley, dir: Weight Watchers Foundation

Lipner, Carol, dir: Bravmann Foundation, Ludwig

Lipoff, Norman H., trust: Russell Memorial Foundation, Robert

Lipp, Robert I., vchmn, dir: Primerica Corp.; vp, treas, trust: Primerica Foundation

Lippe, Gary, trust: Sapirstein-Stone-Weiss Foundation

Lipper, Evelyn, trust: Lipper Foundation, Kenneth & Evelyn

Lipper, Kenneth, trust: Lipper Foundation, Kenneth & Evelyn; trust: Rockefeller Brothers Fund

Lippert, John D., pres, ceo: National City Bank of Evansville

Lippes, Gerald S., secy: Mark IV Industries Foundation

Lippincott, H. Mather, Jr., mgr: Shoemaker Fund, Thomas H. and Mary Williams

Lippincott, Philip Edward, chmn, ceo, dir: Scott Paper Co.; trust: Scott Paper Co. Foundation

Lipschultz, William H., trust: Bremer Foundation, Otto

Lipshy, Bruce, dir: Zale Foundation

Lipsky, Burton, secy, treas: Mapplethorpe Foundation, Robert

Lipsman, William, asst secy: Sara Lee Foundation

Lipstein, Sanford, secy, treas: Snider Foundation

Lipton, Alan, trust: Lipton Foundation

Lipton, Harvey L., vp, dir, secy: Hearst Foundation; vp, dir: Hearst Foundation, William Randolph

Lipton, Janice, trust: Lipton Foundation

Lipton, Louis J., vp, dir: Ridgefield Foundation

Lipton, Martin, ptnr: Wachtell, Lipton, Rosen & Katz; pres: Wachtell, Lipton, Rosen & Katz Foundation; pres, treas, trust: Zarkin Memorial Foundation, Charles

Lipton, Susan, trust: Zarkin Memorial Foundation, Charles

Liquori, Michele M., secy: BT Foundation

Lis, Walter S., trust: Eastern Star Hall and Home Foundation

Lishman, Ruth C., grant comm: May Mitchell Royal Foundation

Lisimachia, Jean Louis, chmn: Grolier, Inc.

Lisle, L. W., trust: Markey Charitable Fund, John C.

Lison, S.A., vp, trust: SPX Foundation

Lissau, W. R., dir, vp: Warren Charite; pres, dir: Warren Foundation, William K.

List, Claire, vp: Klingenstein Fund, Esther A. and Joseph

List, D. H., mem student loan comm: Jeffers Memorial Fund, Michael

List, John D., sr vp, cfo: Lykes Brothers Steamship Co.

List, Viki, secy: List Foundation, Albert A.

Litt, Mark D., trust: Lavanburg-Corner House

Littenberg, Celia, dir: Feintech Foundation

Littick, Norma, trust: Shinnick Educational Fund, William M.

Little, Arthur Dehon, trust: Little Family Foundation

Little, Cameron R., trust: Little Family Foundation

Little, Dennis Gage, exec vp, cfo: Textron

Little, Jack Edward, mem exec comm, dir: Shell Oil Co. Foundation

Little, Jacqueline, trust: Barbour Foundation, Bernice

Little, James S., dir: Hedco Foundation

Little, John M., Jr., vp: Moss Foundation, Harry S.

Little, Louisa, trust: Goldman Charitable Trust, Sol

Little, Michael, cfo: GNB Inc.

Little, Stephen, trust: Edwards Scholarship Fund; pres, trust: Sailors' Snug Harbor of Boston

Little, William G., pres, ceo: West Co.

Little, William S., trust: Barbour Foundation, Bernice

Littlefield, Edmund Wattis, pres, treas: Littlefield Foundation, Edmund Wattis

Littlefield, Jeannik M., vp: Littlefield Foundation, Edmund Wattis

Littlefield, Priscilla, secy to the chmn: Elf Aquitaine, Inc.

Littlejohn, Carl W., Jr, dir, bd mem: Gregg-Graniteville Foundation

Littrel, Harold U., trust: Ackerman Trust, Anna Keesling

Litwin, Gordon, trust: Borden Memorial Foundation, Mary Owen

Litwin, Leonard, pres, dir: Litwin Foundation

Litwin, Ruth, secy, dir: Litwin Foundation

Litzerman, Mark R., clerk: Nashua Trust Co. Foundation

Liu, Lee, ceo, pres, dir: IES Industries; pres: IES Industries Charitable Foundation

Liuigni, Russell, trust: GenCorp Foundation

Lively, Keith, pres, ceo: Famous Amos Chocolate Chip Cookie Co.

Livengood, Lesly, mgr (corp contributions): Indiana Bell Telephone Co.

Livingston, Gladys Ritter, pres, trust: Ritter Foundation

Livingston, John H., vp: St. Giles Foundation

Livingston, Johnston R., dir: Bonfils-Stanton Foundation

Livingston, Mary, dir: Hopper Foundation, May Templeton

Livingston, Patricia P., vp, trust: Tortuga Foundation

Livingston, Robert C., trust: Tortuga Foundation

Livingstone, Mari W., advisor: English Foundation, Walter and Marian

Livy, Barbara, trust: Americana Foundation

Lizzadro, Frank C., dir: Lizzadro Family Foundation, Joseph

Lizzadro, John S., secy, treas, dir: Lizzadro Family Foundation, Joseph

Lizzadro, Joseph, Jr., pres, dir: Lizzadro Family Foundation, Joseph

Lizzadro, Mary, dir: Lizzadro Family Foundation, Joseph

Llewellyn, Frederick Eaton, pres, chmn, trust: Forest Lawn Foundation

Llewellyn, John, vp, secy, treas, dir: Forest Lawn Foundation

Llewellyn, John S., Jr., pres, ceo: Ocean Spray Cranberries

Lloyd, Constance L., secy, dir: Georgia Health Foundation

Lloyd, David, trust, exec dir: Sullivan Musical Foundation, William Matheus

Lloyd, Edward B., vp, trust: Bedford Fund

Lloyd, Frank V.D., trust: Barbour Foundation, Bernice

Lloyd, Harry J., pres, treas: Share Foundation

Lloyd, Heidi, dir: General Service Foundation

Lloyd, Margene West, trust: West Texas Corp., J. M.

Lloyd, Marion M., pres, dir: Forest Fund; hon dir: General Service Foundation

Lloyd, P. B., chmn, ceo: Reading & Bates Corp.

Lloyd, Patricia A., asst treas: Share Foundation

Lloyd, William B., trust: Bedford Fund

Lloyd, William R., Jr., trust, pres: West Texas Corp., J. M.

Lobbia, John E., chmn, pres, ceo, coo: Detroit Edison Co.

Lobeck, Elfriede M., exec dir, asst secy: Groves Foundation

Lober, Richard D., chmn, pres, dir: Alhambra Foundry Co., Ltd.

Lobman, Theodore E., pres: Stuart Foundations

Lochmann, Lee, pres: Swift-Eckrich Inc.

Lochtenberg, Bernard Hendrik, chmn: ICI Americas

Locke, Charles Stanley, chmn, ceo, dir: Morton International

Locke, Fred, trust: Community Health Association

Locker, John, treas: Barnes Group Foundation

Lockett, Robert P., Jr., treas, trust: Libby-Dufour Fund, Trustees of the

Lockhart, George D., trust: Frick Educational Commission, Henry C.

Lockhart, James Blakeley, vp (pub affairs): Transamerica Corp.; pres, dir: Transamerica Fdn.

Lockhart, Paul A., Jr., trust: Constantin Foundation

Lockhart, Robert, trust: Christian Workers Foundation

Lockwood, Edward J., trust: Hankins Foundation

Lockwood, Rhodes Greene, trust: Wharton Trust, William P.

Lockwood, Robert J., sr vp: Harleysville Mutual Insurance Co.

Lockwood, Theodore Davidge, dir: Guggenheim Foundation, Harry Frank

Lodder, Ron M., dir: Group Health Foundation

Loden, Elliot H., trust: Holy Land Charitable Trust

Lodge, Carolyn W., treas, dir: Borwell Charitable Foundation

Lodge, Thomas S., secy: Laffey-McHugh Foundation

Loeb, Anna Frank, dir: New-Land Foundation

Loeb, Arthur L., trust: Loeb Foundation, Frances and John L.

Loeb, Charles W., trust: Jacobson Foundation, Bernard H. and Blanche E.

Loeb, Frances Lehman, pres, trust: Loeb Foundation, Frances and John L.

Loeb, Henry A., trust: Lavanburg-Corner House

Loeb, Henry Alfred, dir, treas: Langeloth Foundation, Jacob and Valeria; vchmn, dir: Loeb Partners Corp.

Loeb, Jerome Thomas, vchmn, cfo, dir: May Department Stores Co.; pres, dir: May Stores Foundation

Loeb, John H., Lavanburg-Corner House

Loeb, John Langeloth, chmn, dir: Langeloth Foundation, Jacob and Valeria; vp, dir: Loeb Foundation, Frances and John L.; vchmn, dir: Loeb Partners Corp.

Loeb, John Langeloth, Jr., dir, asst treas: Langeloth Foundation, Jacob and Valeria; dir: Loeb Foundation, Frances and John L.

Loeb, Peter Kenneth, dir: Langeloth Foundation, Jacob and Valeria

Loeb, Steven M., Lehman Foundation, Edith and Herbert

Loeffler, Ann R., trust: Austin Memorial Foundation

Loeffler, David H., trust, chmn: Jones Foundation, Montfort Jones and Allie Brown

Loeffler, Richard, pres, coo, dir: Standard Brands Paint Co.

Loesser, Roland, group vp (fin), cfo: Sandoz Corp.

Loew, Ralph William, trust: Wendt Foundation, Margaret L.

Loewe, Leslie F., chmn emeritus, dir: Angelica Corp.

Loewenbaum, G. Walter, III, chmn, dir: Southdown, Inc.

Loewenberg, Ralph E., dir, pres: Loewenberg Foundation

Loewy, Arthur F., chmn (fin comm): TJX Cos.; dir: TJX Foundation

Loffelbein, Roger, ceo, pres: Bryan Foods

Loftin, Nancy Carol, secy, dir: APS Foundation

Lofton, Thomas M., secy: Clowes Fund; chmn: Lilly Endowment

Loftus, John W., dir: Frost Foundation

Logan, Elinor F., secy: Green Foundation, Burton E.

Logan, Henry W., trust: Page Foundation, George B.

Logan, John A., dir, vp: Ramlose Foundation, George A.

Logan, Rhonda, asst secy: See Foundation, Charles

Logan, Robert F. B., pres, coo: Valley National Bank of Arizona

LoGatto, James, mem contributions comm: Republic New York Corp.

Logwood, Donna, asst treas: McCaw Foundation

Lohan, Diane Legge, secy-treas: Skidmore, Owings & Merrill Foundation

Lohman, Eugene, trust: Geneseo Foundation

Lohman, Gordon R., pres, ceo, dir: Amsted Industries; trust: Amsted Industries Foundation

Lohman, James J., chmn, pres, ceo, dir: Excel Industries (Elkhart, Indiana); pres: Excel Industries Charitable Foundation

Lohrman, John J., chmn, ceo, dir: RB&W Corp.

Lohse, Ashby I., secy, treas: Mulcahy Foundation

Lomason, Harry A., II, pres, ceo, dir: Douglas & Lomason Company

Lomax, Howard, cfo: Risdon Corp.

Lombard, Jane K., secy, treas, trust: Kettering Family Foundation; mem distribution comm: Kettering Fund

Lombard, Richard J., trust: Kettering Family Foundation

Lombardi, Florian, trust: Havens Foundation, O. W.

Lombardi, Thomas J., treas: Magowan Family Foundation; treas: Merrill Lynch & Co. Foundation

Lonan, V. H., treas: Stonecutter Foundation

Lonati, John, vp (human resources): SKF USA, Inc.

Loncto, Denis, trust: Coleman, Jr. Foundation, George E.

London, Irving, trust: Philippe Foundation

Long, Alvin William, trust: Chicago Title and Trust Co. Foundation

Long, Beverly, program mgr (nonpr grants): Apple Computer

Long, Cathy, asst treas, asst secy: Cherne Foundation, Albert W.

Long, Charles E., chmn, dir: SKF USA, Inc.

Long, David Bourne, trust: Sumners Foundation, Hatton W.

Long, David S., vp, trust: Carbon Fuel Foundation

Long, Francis A., exec vp, coo: Pennsylvania Power & Light

Long, Gordon G., trust: Hankins Foundation

Long, J. H., trust: Pittsburgh-Des Moines Inc. Charitable Trust

Long, John F., Jr., adv comm: Martin Marietta Philanthropic Trust

Long, Josephus, trust: Harvard Apparatus Foundation

Long, Margro R., vp: Avon Products

Long, R.M., chmn, ceo, dir: Longs Drug Stores

Long, Robert A., mem: McGee Foundation

Long, Robert F., dir, vp: Harris Foundation

Long, Robert Merril, pres, trust: Long Foundation, J.M.

Long, Ron, dir: Harper Brush Works Foundation

Long, T. Dixon, trust: American Foundation Corporation

Long, Tom, comptr: Pacific Gas & Electric Co.

Longaker, Robert G., trust: Snyder Foundation, Harold B. and Dorothy A.

Longbrake, Mary, vp, dir: Young Foundation, Irvin L.

Longbrake, William Arthur, sr exec vp, cfo: Washington Mutual Savings Bank; mem: Washington Mutual Savings Bank Foundation

Longenecker, E. A., vp, dir: Krause Foundation, Charles A.

Longenecker, Kent, trust: Davis Foundation, James A. and Juliet L.

Longfield, William Herman, pres, coo, dir: Bard, C. R.

Longley, Elizabeth, vp corp affairs: Prudential Securities Foundation

Longley, Robert F., mem adv comm: de Kay Foundation

Longstreth, Bevis, mem bd: Cummings Foundation, Nathan; chmn fin comm: Rockefeller Family Fund

Longstreth, William, trust, vp: Wilbur Foundation, Marguerite Eyer

Longtin, Joel, cfo: LDB Corp.

Longto, Frank J., vp, treas: Phelps Dodge Foundation

Looker, Charles, trust, vp: Hartman Foundation, Jesse and Dorothy; dir: Kaufmann Foundation, Henry; secy: Kramer Foundation, C. L. C.; pres, dir: Miller Fund, Kathryn and Gilbert

Lookstein, Haskel, pres: Goldsmith Foundation, Nathan and Louise

Loomans, Leslie Louis, treas, dir: Detroit Edison Foundation

Loomis, Amelia B., program off: Stuart Foundations

Loomis, Carol, dir: Buffett Foundation

Loomis, George P., mgr: Delta Tau Delta Educational Fund

Loomis, Lois C., contact person: McInerny Foundation

Loomis, Worth, trust: Hartford Courant Foundation

Looney, H. Ray, pres, ceo: Ball-InCon Glass Packaging Corp.

Looney, Wilton, trust: Woodruff Foundation, Robert W.

Loos, Henry J., secy: Charter Manufacturing Co. Foundation

Lopata, Lucy, trust: Lopata Foundation, Stanley and Lucy

Lopata, Monte L., trust: Lopata Foundation, Stanley and Lucy

Lopata, Stanley L., mgr: Lopata Foundation, Stanley and Lucy

Loper, Graham B., vp, trust: Brown Foundation, James Graham

Loper, Larry, vp, dir: Mentor Graphics Foundation

Loper, Ray, trust: Brown Foundation, James Graham

Lopez, Ramon, dir: Shell Oil Co. Foundation

LoPrete, James H., pres: Westerman Foundation, Samuel L.

Lorah, Clay, vp: United States Borax & Chemical Corp.

Lorch, Ernest H., chmn, ceo, dir: Dyson-Kissner- Moran Corp.; chmn: Varlen Corp.

Lorch, Frank, trust: Golub Foundation

Lord, Albert L., exec vp, coo: Student Loan Marketing Association

Lord, Bette Bao, trust: Freedom Forum

Lord, Diana H., pres: Hopper Foundation, May Templeton

Lord, Joseph, treas: Borden Memorial Foundation, Mary Owen

Lord, Raymond Morrieson, vp, trust: Vulcan Materials Co. Foundation

Lord, Winston, trust: United States-Japan Foundation

Lorden, Lesley, pres asst: CalFed Inc.

Loren, William, vp: Kentland Foundation

Lorenson, Edward P., chmn; pres: Bristol Savings Bank; dir: Bristol Savings Bank Foundation

Lorenzen, Dale, dir: Chicago Board of Trade Educational Research Foundation

Lorenzo, Francisco A., chmn, dir: Eastern Air Lines

Lorezini, Paul, mem (contributions comm): PacifiCorp Foundation

Lorimer, Rodric Alan, trust: Clorox Company Foundation

Loring, Caleb, Jr., trust: Fidelity Foundation; trust: Johnson Fund, Edward C.

Loring, Jonathan B., treas, trust: Levy Foundation, June Rockwell

Loring, Melinda, trust: UNUM Charitable Foundation

Loring, Peter B., trust: Mifflin Memorial Fund, George H. and Jane A.

Loring, Robert W., trust: Sailors' Snug Harbor of Boston

Loring, Valerie S., trust, secy: Stoddard Charitable Trust

Lorman, Judith Ann Turner, trust: Turner Charitable Foundation, Harry and Violet

Lorton, Donald M., pres: Magic Chef

Losinger, Sara McCune, mem dispensing comm: McCune Charitable Trust, John R.

Loss, R.R., treas: Bryan Foundation, Dodd and Dorothy L.

Lostus, William, pres: PMA Industries

Lothrop, Francis B., Jr., treas, trust: Sailors' Snug Harbor of Boston

Lott, Charles H., chmn, ceo, dir: Keefe, Bruyette & Woods

Lott, William C., dir, bd mem: Gregg-Graniteville Foundation

Lottman, Martha K., trust: Klein Fund, Nathan J.

Loucks, Vernon Reece, Jr., chmn, ceo, dir: Baxter International

Louden, G. Malcolm, treas, secy, gen mgr: Fleming Foundation; secy, dir: Walsh Foundation

Loufek, Joseph R., treas, dir: Hall Foundation

Loughlin, Caroline K., trust: Keller Family Foundation

Loughman, Martin W., dir: Disney Family Foundation, Roy

Loughman, Thomas F., treas: Barden Foundation, Inc.

Loughrey, F. Joseph, dir: Cummins Engine Foundation

Loughridge, Dennis, pres, gen mgr: BHP Pacific Resources

Louis, Michael W., chmn: Louis Foundation, Michael W.

Louise, Sister Stella, trust: Retirement Research Foundation

Loux, Lloyd Fox, Jr., trust: Mellen Foundation

Love, Ben F., vp, dir: Scurlock Foundation

Love, Charles E., dir: Love Foundation, Martha and Spencer

Love, Cornelia S., dir: Love Foundation, Martha and Spencer

Love, Dennis M., pres: Love Foundation, Gay and Erskine; pres: Printpack, Inc.

Love, G. Donald, chmn: Oxford Development Group

Love, Gay M., vp: Love Foundation, Gay and Erskine

Love, George H., dir distribution: Love Foundation, George H. and Margaret McClintic

Love, Howard M., trust: Heinz Endowment, Howard; dir: Love Foundation, George H. and Margaret McClintic

Love, Hugh M., Sr., trust: Johnson Day Trust, Carl and Virginia

Love, Jon E., pres: Oxford Development Group

Love, Julian, dir: Love Foundation, Martha and Spencer

Love, Lela Porter, dir: Love Foundation, Martha and Spencer

Love, Martin E., dir: Love Foundation, Martha and Spencer

Love, S. L., asst treas: Duke Power Co. Foundation

Lovejoy, Joseph E., chmn, dir: Ensign-Bickford Industries

Lovelace, Charles E., Jr., exec dir: Morehead Foundation, John Motley

Lovelace, Jon B., dir: Capital Group Foundation

Lovelace, Jon B., Jr., chmn bd trusts: Getty Trust, J. Paul

Lovell, James C., vchmn, dir: Mercantile Stores Co.

Lovell, Richard H., trust: King Trust, Charles A.

Lovell, Sue, corp fdn adm: USF&G Foundation

Lovely, Edward, pres: Ausimont, U.S.A.

Lovett, Fred, trust: Davis Hospital Foundation

Lovett, Joel L., vchmn, dir: American Stock Exchange

Lovitz, David D., pres, coo: Hartz Mountain Corp.

Low, David A., pres: Sherwood Medical Co.

Lowden, F. V., III, secy: Universal Leaf Foundation

Lowe, Irving, vp, secy: Peck Foundation, Milton and Lillian

Lowe, King F., pres, coo, dir: American Security Bank

Lowe, Mary Ralph, pres, trust: Lowe Foundation

Lowe, Miriam, trust: Peck Foundation, Milton and Lillian

Lowe, William C., chmn, ceo: Gulfstream Aerospace Corp.

Lowell, John, mgr, trust: Lowell Institute, Trustees of the; trust: Shaw Foundation, Gardiner Howland

Lowengard, A. G., trust: Grumbacher Foundation, M. S.

Lowengard, Benjamin, dir: Shoemaker Trust for

Shoemaker Scholarship Fund, Ray S.

Lowengart, Sanford P., Jr., secy, treas: Cow Hollow Foundation

Lowenstein, Laurinda V., trust: Hillsdale Fund

Lowenstein, Sharon, trust: Lowenstein Brothers Foundation

Lowenstein, William B., trust: Lowenstein Brothers Foundation

Lowenthal, Henry, sr vp (fin): American Greetings Corp.; vp, off: American Greetings Corp. Foundation

Lower, James P., dir, mem legal comm, mem grants program comm: Keck Foundation, W. M.

Lower, Louis Gordon, II, vp, trust: Allstate Foundation

Lowry, Brinck, trust: Hixon Fund for Religion and Education, Alexander & Adelaide

Lowry, Kathleen, dir consumer aff: Big V Supermarkets

Lowet, Henry A., vp, secy, dir: Littauer Foundation, Lucius N.

Lowrie, John, contact person, trust, secy, treas: Anderson Foundation, M. D.

Lowry, A. Leon, trust: Jones Intercable Tampa Trust

Lowry, Noreen, dir commun rels: Brooklyn Union Gas Co.

Lowther, David, trust: Clemens Foundation

Lowther, Fred, trust: Clemens Foundation

Lowther, Steven, trust: Clemens Foundation

Lowy, Philip B., pres, trust: Meyer Memorial Foundation, Aaron and Rachel

Lowy, Rudy, trust: Friedman Brothers Foundation

Loy, Frank E., pres, trust: German Marshall Fund of the United States

Lozier, Allan George, trust: Lozier Foundation

Lubar, Sheldon B., dir: Firstar Milwaukee Foundation

Lubarsky, Jared, exec secy: Ise Cultural Foundation

Lubcher, Frederick, trust: Ogden Foundation, Ralph E.

Lubcher, Frederik, trust: Dollard Charitable Trust

Lubeker, Frederick, trust: Loewenberg Foundation

Luber, F. G., trust: Marquette Electronics Foundation

Lubetkin, Alvin N., vchmn, pres, ceo, dir: Oshman's Sporting Goods, Inc.

Lubin, Arline J., trust: Morris Foundation, Norman M.

Lubin, Donald G., dir: Levy Foundation, Charles and Ruth

Lubin, Kenneth A., trust: Morris Foundation, Norman M.

Lubin, Marvin, vp, trust: Morris Foundation, Norman M.

Lubin, Ronda H., secy: Stuart Foundation

Lubsen, Sigismundus W., pres, coo: Quaker Chemical Corp.

Luca, Raymond J., dir: Graphic Arts Education & Research Foundation

Lucarell, Louis, pres, ceo: Research Institute of America

Lucas, Donald Leo, chmn: Cadence Design Systems; dir: Lucas Cancer Foundation, Richard M.

Lucas, Herbert L., Jr., trust: Getty Trust, J. Paul

Lucas, John W., dir: Lucas Cancer Foundation, Richard M.

Lucas, Mary G., dir: Lucas Cancer Foundation, Richard M.

Lucas, Wilfred J., dir: Baxter Foundation

Lucckese, Deborah, member: Washington Forrest Foundation

Luce, Dwain G., trust: Florence Foundation

Luce, Henry, III, chmn, ceo, dir: Luce Foundation, Henry

Luce, Priscella, vp: Greenfield Foundation, Albert M.

Luchsinger, Amelia D., pres, trust: Luchsinger Family Foundation

Luchsinger, John W., secy, treas, trust: Luchsinger Family Foundation

Luchsinger, Mary M., vp, trust: Luchsinger Family Foundation

Luchsinger, Patricia E., vp, trust: Luchsinger Family Foundation

Lucia, Elsie, corp admin: Alfa-Laval, Inc.

Luciana, Eugene D., cfo, treas, vp: Chase Packaging Corp.

Luciano, Robert Peter, chmn, ceo, dir: Schering-Plough Corp.; trust: Schering-Plough Foundation

Lucido, Chester C., Jr., pres, ceo: South-Western Publishing Co.

Lucien, Kent T., treas: Brewer Charitable Foundation, C.

Luck, C.S., pres: Luck Stone

Luck, C.S., III, pres: Luck Stone Foundation

Luck, Mary Jo, vp pub aff: National City Bank, Columbus

Luckey, James C., trust: Moore Foundation, O. L.

Lucks, Sandra, admin, govt & comm rels: Honda of America Manufacturing, Inc.

Lucy, Paul E., vp, dir: Foote, Cone & Belding Foundation

Ludes, John T., trust: Acushnet Foundation

Ludington, John Samuel, asst treas, trust: Strosacker Foundation, Charles J.

Ludington, William F., pres, ceo: Chase Packaging Corp.

Ludlow, Jean W., chmn: duPont Fund, Jessie Ball

Ludwig, George E., Jr., vp: Metropolitan Health Council of Indianapolis

Luers, William Henry, trust: Rockefeller Brothers Fund

Luerssen, Frank Wonson, chmn, ceo, dir, chmn exec comm: Inland Steel Industries; dir: Inland Steel-Ryerson Foundation

Luethye, George G., 2nd vp: Ebell of Los Angeles Rest Cottage Association

Luetkemeyer, Anne A., secy, dir: Rollins Luetkemeyer Charitable Foundation

Luetkemeyer, John A., Jr., dir: Rollins Luetkemeyer Charitable Foundation

Luetkemeyer, John A., Sr., pres, dir: Rollins Luetkemeyer Charitable Foundation

Luffy, Robert H., ceo: Mellon Stuart Construction Inc.

Luggi, Richard D., vp (human resources): Lukens; trust: Lukens Foundation

Luhn, Catherine H., trust: Halff Foundation, G. A. C.

Luhn, George M., trust: Halff Foundation, G. A. C.

Luiso, Anthony, chmn, pres, ceo: International Multifoods Corp.

Luke, David Lincoln, III, dir, mem exec comm: Macy, Jr. Foundation, Josiah; chmn, pres, ceo: Westvaco Corp.

Luke, John Anderson, pres, dir, ceo: Westvaco Corp.

Luke, Kan Jung, chmn: Hawaii National Bank; chmn: Hawaii National Foundation

Luke, Warren Kwan Lee, vice-chmn: Hawaii National Bank; pres: Hawaii National Foundation

Luker, Howard E., dir: Westwood Endowment

Lukins, Scott, trust: Johnston-Hanson Foundation

Lukosius, Frank, trust: Eastman Foundation, Alexander

Lukowski, Stanley J., trust: Eastern Bank Foundation

Lumar-Johnson, Eileen, mgr pub rels: Pan-American Life Insurance Co.

Lummis, William R., Esq., trust: Hughes Medical Institute, Howard

Lummus, Lynn F., vp, dir, secy: Dunn Foundation, Elizabeth Ordway

Lumpkin, Mary G., vp, dir: Lumpkin Foundation

Lumpkin, Richard A., chmn, ceo: Illinois Consolidated Telephone Co.

Lumpkin, Richard Anthony, pres, dir: Lumpkin Foundation

Lunasco, Gladys, asst secy: Weinberg Foundation, Harry and Jeanette

Lunceford, Michael, trust: Mary Kay Foundation

Lund, Arthur K., trust: Stuart Center Charitable Trust, Hugh

Lund, Margaret McKee, vp, trust: McKee Foundation, Robert E. and Evelyn

Lund, Victor L., vchmn, ceo, dir: American Stores Co.

Lundback, Lee C., dir: Staunton Farm Foundation

Lunder, Peter H., pres, dir, asst treas: Dexter Shoe Co.

Lundgren, Terry, pres, ceo: Neiman Marcus

Lundin, Janet R., secy: CLARCOR Foundation

Lundin, Leif, coo: Bang & Olufsen of America, Inc.

Lundstrom, Charles, secy: Wege Foundation

Lundy, Marjorie W., secy (contributions comm): Northern Trust Co. Charitable Trust

Lung, David D., pres, coo: Patrick Industries Inc.

Lung, Mervin D., chmn, ceo: Patrick Industries Inc.

Lunger, Francis J., treas: Haigh-Scatena Foundation

Luning, Thomas P., Schiff, Hardin & Waite; pres: Schiff, Hardin & Waite Foundation

Lunt, Katherine Selma Bartol, trust: Bartol Foundation, Stockton Rush

Lunt, Thomas D., trust: Wendt Foundation, Margaret L.

Luongo, Angelo C., treas: River Road Charitable Corporation

Lupin, Arnold Mitchel, don, pres: Lupin Foundation

Lupin, Ellis Ralph, don, dir: Lupin Foundation

Lupin, Jay S., MD, dir: Lupin Foundation

Lupin, Louis, dir: Lupin Foundation

Lupin, Samuel, MD, vp, dir: Lupin Foundation

Lupper, Edgar B., advisor: Baker Charitable Foundation, Jessie Foos

Lupton, Edward D., mgr: Perry-Griffin Foundation

Luria, Leonard, chmn, ceo, treas: Luria's

Luria, Peter P., pres, coo: Luria's

Lurie, B. Ann, vp: Lurie Family Foundation

Lurie, Elizabeth B., pres, treas, dir: Brady Foundation, W. H.

Lurie, Robert Alfred, pres, treas: Lurie Family Foundation; pres, don, dir: Lurie Foundation, Louis R.

Lurton, H. William, chmn, ceo, dir: Jostens; dir: Jostens Foundation

Luse, Richard, secy, treas: Younkers Foundation

Lusk, William C., sr vp, treas: Shaw Industries

Lussier, James D., dir: Evjue Foundation

Lussier, John H., pres, dir: Evjue Foundation

Lussier, Richard H., chmn, pres, ceo: Pyramid Technology Corp.

Lustenberger, Louis C., Jr., dir: Donovan, Leisure, Newton & Irvine Foundation

Luster, Amy, secy: Luster Family Foundation

Luster, Andrew, vp, cfo: Luster Family Foundation

Luster, Elizabeth, pres, dir: Luster Family Foundation

Lustgarten, Ira H., vp, trust: Lavanburg-Corner House

Lustig, Gerald I., vp, dir: Rauch Foundation

Lustine, Doris, exec secy: Stewart Trust under the will of Mary E. Stewart, Alexander and Margaret

Lustman, Bruce S., exec vp (fin), coo: United States Surgical Corp.

Lutenski, Richard P., cfo: Michigan Mutual Insurance Corp.

Luther, Anne, sr vp (pub rels), chmn: Schieffelin & Somerset Co.

Luther, Janet E., treas: Rippel Foundation, Fannie E.

Luthey, Graydon Dean, Jr., secy: Occidental Oil & Gas Charitable Foundation

Luttgens, Leslie L., treas, dir: Rosenberg Foundation

Luttrell, James, trust: Luttrell Trust

Luttrell, Robert Grant, pres, dir: Temple-Inland Foundation

Lutz, Christopher H., dir: Plumsock Fund

Lutz, James, chmn, dir: Washington Square Health Foundation

Lutz, Robert Anthony, vchmn, dir: Chrysler Corp.

Lutz, Sarah L., dir: Plumsock Fund

Lutz, Theodore C., vchmn, investment comm: Meyer Foundation, Eugene and Agnes E.

Lux, Clifton L., vp, treas, asst secy, dir: Globe Foundation

Lux, Raymond H., consultant: Goldman Foundation, Herman

Lyall, Katharine C., trust: Kemper Foundation, James S.

Lybarger, Stanley A., chmn, ceo: Bank of Oklahoma, N.A.

Lyddon, John Knight, trust: Seven Springs Foundation

Lyddon, pres, Seven Springs Foundation

Lydon, John M., secy-treas: Shawmut Charitable Foundation

Lydon, Patricia A., vp: Fairchild Foundation, Sherman

Lyle, Paul, trust: Mayer Foundation, James and Eva

Lyman, J. Garrett, dir: O'Shaughnessy Foundation, I. A.

Lyman, Richard P., pres: Whiteley Foundation, John and Elizabeth

Lyman, Robert W., dir: St. Faith's House Foundation

Lynagh, John J., secy, dir: Surdna Foundation

Lynam, M.W., Jr., dir: Durham Merchants Association Charitable Foundation

Lynch, Albert F., Jr., cfo: Donovan, Leisure, Newton & Irvine

Lynch, David A., asst secy: USX Foundation

Lynch, Dorothy D., trust, secy, treas: Dupar Foundation

Lynch, Harry H., dir: Maddox Foundation, J. F.

Lynch, James E., trust: Collins-McDonald Trust Fund

Lynch, Jim, ceo: Macom-Venitz

Lynch, Joe, vchmn, dir: Farm & Home Savings Association

Lynch, John H., secy, dir: Gifford Charitable Corporation, Rosamond

Lynch, John T., chmn, pres, ceo: Towers Perrin

Lynch, John W., pres: Siebe North Inc.

Lynch, Kevin P., pres: Amoco Corp.; dir: Amoco Foundation

Lynch, Luba H., exec secy: Mailman Family Foundation, A. L.

Lynch, Nancy A., secy, treas: Dewar Foundation

Lynch, Patrick J., dir: Texaco Foundation

Lynch, Pauline, mem student loan comm: Jeffers Memorial Fund, Michael

Lynch, Rita E., asst secy: Burns Family Foundation

Lynch, Robert, vp: CUNA Mutual Charitable Foundation

Lynch, Robert Lee Kempner, secy, treas: Kempner Fund, Harris and Eliza

Lynch, Ronald P., dir: Culpeper Foundation, Charles E.

Lynch, Stephen A., III, trust: duPont Fund, Jessie Ball

Lynch, Thomas C., trust: Chase Manhattan Bank, N.A.

Lynch, Thomas G., pres, coo: First National Bank & Trust Co. of Rockford

Lynch, Thomas M., exec vp, cfo: Sudbury Inc.

Lynch, Thomas P., vp, trust: Stamps Foundation, James L.

Lynch, William T., pres, gen couns: Leo Burnett Co.

Lynde, Marguerite, dir: First Interstate Bank NW Region

Lynden, Margo, trust: Washington Square Fund

Lynham, John M., Jr., trust: Dimick Foundation

Lynn, E. M., trust: Lynn Foundation, E. M.

Lynn, John P., chmn, dir: American Welding & Manufacturing Co.

Lynne, Lois, secy, dir: Houchens Foundation, Ervin G.

Lynne, Seybourn Harris, mem adv comm: Meyer Foundation, Robert R.

Lyon, Frank, Sr., chmn: Climatic Corp.

Lyon, Sally A., secy: Lakeside Foundation

Lyon, Wayne Barton, pres, dir, coo: Masco Corp.

Lyon, William, chmn, ceo: Lyon Co., William

Lyons, Bernard E., dir: Colburn Fund; secy, dir: Negaunee Foundation

Lyons, Fred W., Jr., pres, dir: Marion Merrell Dow

Lyons, G. Sage, trust: Florence Foundation

Lyons, James F., pres, ceo: Bio-Medicus, Inc.

Lyons, James F., M.D., trust, vp: Baker Foundation, George T.

Lyons, Leo M., chmn, trust: Jones Foundation, Daisy Marquis

Lyons, Louis, trust: Camp and Bennet Humiston Trust, Apollos

Lyons, Melanie, dir, mem grantmaking comm: Liz Claiborne Foundation

Lyons, Michael H., II, pres, trust: Baldwin Memorial Foundation, Fred

Lyons, Tony J., mem bd govs: Mayor Foundation, Oliver Dewey

Lyons, William W., chmn (contributions comm): PacifiCorp Foundation

Lysinger, Rex Jackson, chmn, ceo, dir: Alabama Gas Corp. (An Energen Co.)

Lytle, Richard H., secy: Van Buren Foundation

Lytton, Don, pres: La-Co. Industries, Inc.

M

M.S. Bailey & Sons, Bankers, trust: Bailey Foundation

Maas, Suzanne W., exec dir: Boston Globe Foundation

Maatman, Gerald Leonard, chmn, pres, ceo, dir: Kemper National Insurance Cos.; chmn, pres, trust: Kemper Foundation, James S.

Mabee, Guy R., chmn, trust: Mabee Foundation, J. E. and L. E.

Mabee, Joe, vchmn, trust: Mabee Foundation, J. E. and L. E.

MacAffer, Kenneth S., trust: Kelley and Elza Kelley Foundation, Edward Bangs

Macaleer, R. J., chmn, ceo: Shared Medical Systems Corp.

MacAllaster, Archie F., dir: Clark Foundation

MacArthur, C. J., mgr, trust: CRI Charitable Trust

MacArthur, Gregoire, vchmn: MacArthur Foundation, J. Roderick

MacArthur, John R., chmn: MacArthur Foundation, J. Roderick

MacArthur, Solange D., secy, treas: MacArthur Foundation, J. Roderick

Macaskill, Brigette, pres: Oppenheimer Management Corp.

MacBeth, Anita L., trust: Bourns Foundation

MacColl, Stephanie, dir: Bothin Foundation

MacColl, William B., Jr., treas: Hills Fund, Edward E.

MacConnell, Jocelyn H., trust: Hulme Charitable Foundation, Milton G.

MacCrellish, William H., Jr., pres: Devonshire Associates

MacDonald, A. Ewan, pres, ceo: Del Monte Foods

MacDonald, Catherine, vp, dir: MacDonald Foundation, Marquis George

MacDonald, Florence C., dir: Burden Foundation, Florence V.

MacDonald, Gerald, pres, dir: MacDonald Foundation, Marquis George

MacDonald, Gerald V., chmn, ceo: Manufacturers National Bank of Detroit

MacDonald, Harold C., contr: Moody Foundation

MacDonald, James Henry, dir: McDonnell Douglas Foundation

MacDonald, John A., vp, treas: Hall Family Foundations; treas: Hallmark Cards

MacDonald, Joseph, dir: MacDonald Foundation, Marquis George

MacDonald, Kenneth, trust: Cowles Foundation, Gardner and Florence Call

MacDonald, Michael, exec vp (fin): Bergner Co., P.A.

MacDonald, Nicole de Sugny, vp: de Dampierre Memorial Foundation, Marie C.

Macdonald, Peter M., pres: Davis Foundation, James A. and Juliet L.

MacDonald, Reid V., pres: Faribault Foods

MacDonald, Robert, pres: Cranshaw Corporation

MacDonald, Roger L., vp, treas, dir: Gifford Charitable Corporation, Rosamond

MacDonald, William, Jr., chmn, ceo, coo: Houghton & Co., E.F.

MacDougal, Gary E., trust: Casey Foundation, Annie E.; trust: Grant Foundation, William T.

MacElree, Jane Cox, trust: Cox Charitable Trust, Jessie B.

MacEwen, Edward Carter, pres, trust: GTE Foundation

MacFarlane, Robert S., Jr., managing dir, trust: Durfee Foundation

MacFarlane, Roger I., ceo: Burlington Air Express Inc.

MacGrath, Andrew A., dir: Greenwall Foundation

MacGrath, C. Richard, treas, dir: Greenwall Foundation

MacGrath, Francis F., dir: Greenwall Foundation

MacGrath, Susan A., dir: Greenwall Foundation

MacGregor, David Lee, treas, dir: Stackner Family Foundation

Mach, John, trust: Capita Charitable Trust, Emil

Machado, Markele, dir: McDonnell Douglas Employee's Community Fund-West

Machiz, Leon, chmn, ceo, dir: Avnet, Inc.

Macht, Amy, trust, pres: Macht Foundation, Morton and Sophia

Macht, Philip, trust, vp: Macht Foundation, Morton and Sophia

MacInnes, Mildred Blair Bartol, chmn: Bartol Foundation, Stockton Rush

MacInnes, Viola, treas, dir: Independence Foundation

MacIntosh, John, trust: Joslyn Foundation, Marcellus I.

MacIntyre, John A., trust: Giddings & Lewis Foundation

Macisonald, Jean, treas: Swasey Fund for Relief of Public School Teachers of Newburyport

Mack, Donna, dir: Welk Foundation, Lawrence

Mack, Henry C., pres: Arkelian Foundation, Ben H. and Gladys

Mack, Henry C., Jr., vp: Arkelian Foundation, Ben H. and Gladys

Mack, John Duncan, trust: South Branch Foundation

Mack, John E., III, chmn, ceo, dir: Central Hudson Gas & Electric Corp.

Mack, Joseph N., secy, treas, trust: Mack Foundation, J. S.

Mack, Olga List, pres: List Foundation, Albert A.

Mack, Raymond P., dir: Arvin Foundation

Mackall, John R., dir: Tuohy Foundation, Alice Tweed

Mackay, Calder M., secy, treas, dir: Mead Foundation, Giles W. and Elise G.

MacKay, Malcolm, trust: Hayden Foundation, Charles

Mackay, Richard N., pres, dir: Baxter Foundation, Donald E. and Delia B.; dir: Mead Foundation, Giles W. and Elise G.

Mackay, Robert B., trust: St. Giles Foundation

Macke, Kenneth A., chmn, ceo, dir, chmn exec comm: Dayton Hudson Corp.; trust: Dayton Hudson Foundation

MacKechnie, John G., dir: Hyde and Watson Foundation

Mackenbach, Frederick W., pres: Lincoln Electric Co.

MacKenzie, Brian, pres: Builder Marts of America

MacKenzie, H. C., chmn (contributions comm): Northeast Utilities

MacKenzie, Tod, vp pub aff: Frito-Lay

Mackenzie, William B., vp, trust: Arkell Hall Foundation

Mackey, Diane, trust: Seafirst Foundation

Mackey, Susan, vp, community affairs: First Interstate Bank NW Region

Mackey, William R., vp, trust: Gilmore Foundation, William G.

Mackin, J. Stanley, chmn, pres, ceo, dir: First Alabama Bancshares

Mackin, Peter C., trust: Wells Trust Fund, Fred W.

MacKinnon, Robert, pres, ceo: Siemens Medical Systems Inc.

Mackirgan, Mary E., trust: Manger and Audrey Cordero Plitt Trust, Clarence

Mackler, Alfred, vp, dir: Alexander Foundation, Joseph

Mackler, Harvey A., dir: Alexander Foundation, Joseph

Mackler, Helen, treas, dir: Alexander Foundation, Joseph

MacLead, Gordon A., trust: Fisher Foundation

MacLean, Barry L., pres, ceo, dir: MacLean-Fogg Co.

MacLean, Joan, dir: Butler Foundation, J. Homer

MacLean, Mary Anna H., trust: Hanson Testamentary Charitable Trust, Anna Emery

Maclellan, Hugh O., Jr., trust, pres, treas: Maclellan Charitable Trust, R. J.; pres, treas, trust: Maclellan Foundation

Maclellan, Hugh O., Sr., chmn: Maclellan Charitable Trust, R. J.; chmn, trust: Maclellan Foundation

Maclellan, Kathrina H., vp, trust: Maclellan Foundation; pres, treas, dir: Maclellan Foundation, Robert L. and Kathrina H.

Maclellan, Robert H., dir: Maclellan Foundation, Robert L. and Kathrina H.

MacLeod, Cynthia, trust: MacLeod Stewardship Foundation

Macleod, Donald, sr vp, cfo: National Semiconductor Corp.

MacLeod, Gary, treas, trust: Medina Foundation

MacLeod, John Amend, dir, pres, secy: MacLeod Stewardship Foundation

MacLeod, Monica S., trust: MacLeod Stewardship Foundation

MacLeod, Muriel D., trust: MacLeod Stewardship Foundation

MacLeod, Roderick A., trust: MacLeod Stewardship Foundation

MacMillan, Cargill, Jr., vp, dir: Cargill Foundation

MacMillan, Pat, trust: Maclellan Foundation

MacMillan, Whitney, chmn, ceo, dir: Cargill

MacMillen, William C., Jr., trust: Jockey Club Foundation

MacMorran, Henry G., ceo, pres: LaSalle Bank Lake View

MacNeary, John D., trust: Heckscher Foundation for Children

MacPhee, Chester R., Jr., trust: Sandy Foundation, George H.

Macrae, Edwin W., vp: Upjohn California Fund

Macrae, Howard T., Jr., secy: Wheat Foundation

Macy, Bill C., treas: Lincoln Family Foundation

Madar, William P., pres, ceo, dir: Nordson Corp.; chmn, trust: Nordson Corporation Foundation

Madden, Frank, pres, trust: International Foundation

Madden, Jean J., dir: Shelter Insurance Foundation

Madden, Peter E., pres, dir: State Street Bank & Trust Co.

Madden, Richard Blaine, chmn, pres, ceo, dir: Potlatch Corp.

Madden, Wales Hendrix, Jr., dir: Harrington Foundation, Don and Sybil

Madding, Bruce W., vp: Kaiser Family Foundation, Henry J.

Maddock, Charles S., trust: Curran Foundation

Maddox, Don, pres, dir: Maddox Foundation, J. F.

Maddox, F.L., dir, trust: Fortis Foundation

Maddox, James M., vp, treas, dir: Maddox Foundation, J. F.

Maddrey, E. E., II, pres, ceo: Delta Woodside Industries

Maddux, Thomas H., trust: Warfield Memorial Fund, Anna Emory

Madera, Cornelius J. J., Jr., sr vp, secy, gen coun, real estate exec: Big V Supermarkets

Madigan, John William, ceo, prin: Chicago Tribune Co.; chmn, dir: Chicago Tribune Foundation; dir: McCormick Tribune Foundation, Robert R.

Madonick, Marjorie, dir: Jewish Foundation for Education of Women

Madonna, Jon C., chmn, ceo: KPMG Peat Marwick

Madsen, Ellen P., trust: Maytag Family Foundation, Fred

Maestre, Charles Hey, dir: New World Foundation

Maffei, Gary R., trust: Louisiana-Pacific Foundation

Maffeo, Mary J., secy, treas, dir: Dougherty Foundation

Maffie, Michael Otis, pres, coo, dir: Southwest Gas Corp.; trust: Southwest Gas Corp. Foundation

Magallawes, Gene, mng comm: Alliant Community Investment Foundation

Magaram, Philip S., secy, treas, dir: Drown Foundation, Joseph

Magee, James A., pres: Magee Carpet Co.

Magee, John, pres: Earth Care Paper, Inc.

Magee, John F., chmn, dir: Little, Arthur D.

Magee, Wayne E., fin grants analyst: Moody Foundation

Mager, Ezra Pascal, trust: de Hirsch Fund, Baron

Mager, Reva, dir: Jewish Foundation for Education of Women

Maggio, Elizabeth, mgr corp contributions: Consolidated Rail Corp. (Conrail)

Maginn, James, cfo: Watt Industry

Magliochetti, Joseph, pres, dir: Dana Corp. Foundation

Maglione, Louis, trust: Corbin Foundation, Mary S. and David C.

Magness, Bob John, chmn, dir: Tele- Communications, Inc.

Magowan, Charles M., asst vp: Magowan Family Foundation

Magowan, Doris M., vp: Magowan Family Foundation

Magowan, James, asst vp: Magowan Family Foundation

Magowan, Kimberly, asst vp: Magowan Family Foundation

Magowan, Mark E., vp: Magowan Family Foundation

Magowan, Merrill L., vp: Magowan Family Foundation

Magowan, Peter Alden, pres: Magowan Family Foundation; chmn, ceo, dir: Safeway, Inc.

Magowan, Robert A., Jr., asst vp: Magowan Family Foundation

Magowan, Stephen C., vp: Magowan Family Foundation

Magowan, Thomas A., asst vp: Magowan Family Foundation

Maguire, Cary, pres: Maguire Oil Co.

Maguire, Lynne M., dir: Irwin-Sweeney- Miller Foundation

Maguire, Robert F., III, mng ptnr: Maguire Thomas Partners

Mahaffee, Pamela Scholl, dir: Scholl Foundation, Dr.

Mahan, Paul D., treas, trust: Bloomfield Foundation, Sam and Rie

Mahan, Randolph R., trust: Summer Foundation

Mahaney, L., pres: Webber Oil Co.

Maher, Howard M., trust: Bernsen Foundation, Grace and Franklin

Maher, John F., pres, coo, dir: Great Western Financial Corp.

Mahon, Arthur Joseph, trust: Archbold Charitable Trust, Adrian and Jessie; secy: Bobst Foundation, Elmer and Mamdouha

Mahon, David, trust: Alro Steel Corp. Charitable Trust

Mahoney, David J., chmn: Dana Charitable Trust, Eleanor Naylor; chmn bd dirs, mem investment & other comms: Dana Foundation, Charles A.

Mahoney, Donald K., exec dir: Hayden Recreation Center, Josiah Willard

Mahoney, Edward P., pres, coo: American Savings & Loan Association of Florida

Mahoney, Elaine, dir: Drown Foundation, Joseph

Mahoney, J. Edward, chmn, dir: Beverly Bank

Mahoney, Margaret E., pres, dir: Commonwealth Fund; dir: MacArthur Foundation, John D. and Catherine T.

Mahoney, P. Michael, dir: Park Banks Foundation

Mahoney, R. D. Patrick, trust: Durell Foundation, George Edward

Mahoney, Richard, dir: Benton Foundation

Mahoney, Richard John, chmn, ceo: Monsanto Co.

Mahoney, Robert W., chmn, ceo, dir: Diebold, Inc.

Mahoney, William M., sr vp, cfo: Mechanics Bank

Mahoney, William P., Jr., vp, dir: Dougherty Foundation

Mahr, Helen, dir: Kirkhill Foundation

Mahuna, Dee Anne, secy: Moore Foundation, O. L.

Maibach, Ben C., Jr., chmn, dir: Barton-Malow Co.

Maibach, III, Ben C., pres: Barton-Malow Co.; trust: Barton-Malow Foundation

Maichel, Joseph R., dir: MDU Resources Foundation

Maier, Craig F., pres, ceo, dir: Frisch's Restaurants Inc.

Maier, Edward Handy, pres: Maier Foundation, Sarah Pauline

Maier, Jack C., chmn, dir: Frisch's Restaurants Inc.

Maier, John, vp, comptr: Lukens

Maier, Pauline, chmn: Maier Foundation, Sarah Pauline

Maier, Russell, pres, ceo: Republic Engineered Steels

Maier, William J., III, vp: Maier Foundation, Sarah Pauline

Mailman, Joshua L., vp, trust: Mailman Foundation

Mailman, Phyllis, pres, trust: Mailman Foundation

Main, Ross, mgr: Three Swallows Foundation

Main, Ruby E., asst secy: Hallmark Cards

Maine, Jerry I., trust: Morrison Charitable Trust, Pauline A. and George R.

Maino, Patricia McGee, vp, dir: McGee Foundation

Mainwaring, A. Bruce, chmn, treas: Uniform Tubes, Inc.

Maio, Nathalie P., vp, secy: Prudential Securities Foundation

Maiorini, Denis N., trust: M/A-COM Charitable Foundation

Mairs, Helen M., trust: Lassen Foundation, Irving A.

Mairs, Thomas G., trust, prin off: Mardag Foundation

Maitland, Peggy L., dir, pres, secy: Bauervic Foundation, Peggy

Maitland, Stuart, trust: Bauervic Foundation, Peggy

Makela, June, secy, treas, dir: Common Giving Fund

Maki, Dennis G., dir: Rennebohm Foundation, Oscar

Makihara, Minoru, chmn: Mitsubishi International Corp.

Makin, Robert E., dir (indust rels): NuTone Inc.

Makoski, Milton, vp human resources: Echlin Inc.

Makous, Norman B., MD, trust: Kynett Memorial Foundation, Edna G.

Malamud, Neil, trust: MalCo Charitable Foundation

Malato, Stephen A., dir: Petersen Foundation, Esper A.

Malcolm, Allen R., exec vp, secy, dir: Snow Foundation, John Ben; trust: Snow Memorial Trust, John Ben

Malcolm, Barbara H., trust: Schumann Fund for New Jersey

Malcolm, Bruce, dir: Snow Foundation, John Ben

Malcolm, Daniel, secy: Gulton Foundation

Malcolm, John D., trust: Massachusetts Charitable Mechanics Association

Malcolm, Marian G., vp, treas: Gulton Foundation

Malcom, Shirley M., trust: Carnegie Corporation of New York

Maldonado, Adelfa B., secy: Rachal Foundation, Ed

Malecek, Joseph E., treas: Wells Foundation, Lillian S.

Malek, Frederic Vincent, vchmn: Northwest Airlines, Inc.

Malenick, Donald H., pres, coo, dir: Worthington Industries, Inc.

Maler, Maurice, mgr: Fish Foundation, Bert

Maletta, Tom, cfo: Gulfstream Aerospace Corp.

Mali, Jane L., trust: AKC Fund

Malik, R. R., dir: Joslyn Foundation

Malin, Edward G., trust: Wheelwright Scientific School

Malino, Jerome R., mem distr comm: Meserve Memorial Fund, Albert and Helen

Malinski, Mark A., mem (contributions comm): Pennzoil Co.

Malinsky, Randie, dir: Waldbaum Family Foundation, I.

Malkerson, Elizabeth Ann, mem grants comm: First Bank System Foundation

Malkin, Isabel W., dir: Wien Foundation, Lawrence A.

Malkin, Peter Laurence, secy, dir: Wien Foundation, Lawrence A.

Mallardi, Joseph L., pres, ceo: Howmet Corp.

Mallardi, Michael P., sr vp, pres (broadcasting group): Capital Cities/ABC; vp, dir: Capital Cities Foundation

Mallender, William H., chmn, ceo: Talley Industries, Inc.; pres, dir: Talley Foundation

Mallott, Byron, ceo, pres: Sealaska Corp.

Malloy, James B., pres, ceo, dir: Jefferson Smurfit Corp.

Malm, Harry, chmn: Bio-Medicus, Inc.

Malmberg, David C., vchmn: National Computer Systems

Malo, John F., secy, dir: Mullen Foundation, J. K.

Malon, Anita Engel, secy: Lambert Memorial Foundation, Gerard B.

Malone, Frank M., Jr., trust: Franklin Foundation, John and Mary

Malone, John Charles Custer, pres, ceo, dir: Tele- Communications, Inc.

Malone, Thomas J., pres, dir: Milliken & Co.

Malone, Wallace D., Jr., chmn, ceo, dir: Southtrust Corp.

Maloney, Estelle Cameron, co-trust: Cameron Foundation, Harry S. and Isabel C.

Maloney, George Thomas, chmn, ceo, pres, dir: Bard, C. R.; pres: Bard Foundation, C. R.

Maloney, Gerald P., exec vp, cfo, dir: American Electric Power

Maloney, Lillian R., asst secy, asst treas: Emery Air Freight Educational Foundation

Maloney, William A., vp, treas: Schmitt Foundation, Arthur J.

Maloni, William R., dir: Federal National Mortgage Assn. Foundation

Maloof, Maurice N., exec dir: Graves Foundation

Malott, C. Taxon, secy-treas: Bradford & Co. Foundation, J.C.

Malott, Robert Harvey, dir: FMC Foundation

Malouf, Donald J., vp, secy, dir: Overlake Foundation

Maloy, William, trust: Mascoma Savings Bank Foundation

Malry, Cassandra, treas: Times Mirror Foundation

Malstrom, Robert A., dir, pres: Kelly Foundation, T. Lloyd

Malti, George M., dir: Holt Foundation, William Knox

Maltz, Albert L., secy, dir: Levy Foundation, Betty and Norman F.

Maltzman, Dorothy, pub rels specialist: Brother International Corp.

Mamary, Albert, dir: Hoyt Foundation, Stewart W. and Willma C.

Mamiye, Charles, vp: Mamiye Foundation

Mamiye, David, secy: Mamiye Foundation

Mamiye, Jack C., chmn, pres: Mamiye Brothers; pres: Mamiye Foundation

Mamiye, Michael, vp: Mamiye Foundation

Manaut, Frank J., dir: Bancorp Hawaii Charitable Foundation

Manbeck, Clarence, dir: Lebanon Mutual Foundation

Mancasola, John A., dir: McConnell Foundation

Mancheski, Frederick J., chmn, ceo, dir: Echlin Inc.

Manchester, Gilbert M., secy, trust: Commercial Intertech Foundation

Manczak, John E., pres: Michigan Gas Utilities

Mand, Martin G., trust: Kutz Foundation, Milton and Hattie

Mandekic, Alex, cfo, secy: Lincy Foundation

Mandel, Barbara A., vp, trust: Mandel Foundation, Morton and Barbara

Mandel, Florence, vp, trust: Mandel Foundation, Joseph and Florence

Mandel, Jack N., pres, trust: Mandel Foundation, Jack N. and Lilyan; chmn fin comm, dir: Premier Industrial Corp.

Mandel, Joseph C., pres, trust: Mandel Foundation, Joseph and Florence; chmn exec comm, dir: Premier Industrial Corp.; trust: Premier Industrial Foundation

Mandel, Lawrence, dir: Key Food Stores Foundation

Mandel, Lilyan, vp: Mandel Foundation, Jack N. and Lilyan

Mandel, Morton Leon, secy, treas, trust: Mandel Foundation, Jack N. and Lilyan; pres, trust: Mandel Foundation, Morton and Barbara; chmn, ceo, dir: Premier Industrial Corp.; trust: Premier Industrial Foundation

Mandell, Gerald, MD, trust: Mandell Foundation, Samuel P.

Mandell, Lester, pres, dir: Greater Construction Corp. Charitable Foundation, Inc.

Mandell, Morton, MD, trust: Mandell Foundation, Samuel P.

Mandell, Ronald, trust: Mandell Foundation, Samuel P.

Mandell, Seymour, trust: Mandell Foundation, Samuel P.

Mandelstam, Charles L., secy: Rubin Foundation, Samuel

Mandeville, Deborah S., Mandeville Foundation

Mandeville, Hubert T., pres, dir: Mandeville Foundation

Mandeville, Josephine C., ceo, pres, trust, don daughter: Connelly Foundation

Mandeville, Matthew T., dir: Mandeville Foundation

Mandeville, Owen A., trust: Connelly Foundation

Mandeville, P. Kempton, vp, dir: Mandeville Foundation

Mandeville, Robert, trust: Cranston Foundation

Manes, Mathew, dir: Bennett Foundation, Carl and Dorothy

Manfredi, John F., mem (admin comm): Nabisco Foundation Trust

Mangan, Rt. Rev. Msgr. B.P., trust, treas: Kasal Charitable Trust, Father

Manger, Robert E., vp, dir: Cornerstone Foundation of Northeastern Wisconsin

Mangino, Terri C., exec dir, asst secy: Rose Foundation, Billy

Mangione, Ellen J., dir: Comprecare Foundation

Mangold, Robert, trust: Gottlieb Foundation, Adolph and Esther

Manice, Pamela, trust: Christodora

Manigault, Peter, chmn, dir: Evening Post Publishing Co.; pres: Post & Courier Foundation

Manilow, Barbara Goodman, vp, dir: Crown Memorial, Arie and Ida

Manilow, Barbara N., trust: Crown Charitable Fund, Edward A.

Manilow, Lewis, pres, treas: Manilow Foundation, Nathan

Manilow, Susan, secy: Manilow Foundation, Nathan

Manley, James I., asst secy: American General Finance Foundation

Manley, Terrell Stans, dir: Stans Foundation

Manley, William, vp, dir: Stans Foundation

Manlin, Geraldine, Nestle USA Foundation

Mann, Carol B., dir, vp, secy: Mann Foundation, John Jay

Mann, John Jay, dir, pres, treas: Mann Foundation, John Jay

Mann, John Jay, Jr., trust: Mann Foundation, John Jay

Mann, Lydia B., pres, dir, don: Iroquois Avenue Foundation

Mann, Marvin, vp: Mann Foundation, Ted

Mann, Milton, trust, secy: Hartman Foundation, Jesse and Dorothy

Mann, Ralph S., vchmn: Josephson International Inc.

Mann, Sally B., vp, secy: Aid Association for the Blind

Mann, Sheva Stern, dir: Stern Family Foundation, Harry

Mann, Theodore, don, pres: Mann Foundation, Ted

Mann-Benson, Roberta, dir: Mann Foundation, Ted

Mannes, Karen, secy: Rittenhouse Foundation

Manning, Bayless A., trust: China Medical Board of New York

Manning, Dana, vp: Grateful Foundation; pres: Linus Foundation

Manning, Henry P., Jr., Community Health Association

Manning, Janine, mgr: UNUM Charitable Foundation

Manning, John A., chmn: Van Buren Foundation

Manning, Kenneth Paul, chmn, coo, dir: Universal Foods Corp.; vp, dir: Universal Foods Foundation

Manning, Michael, trust: Montgomery Foundation

Manny, Carter H., Jr., dir: Graham Foundation for Advanced Studies in the Fine Arts

Manoogian, Alex, pres, dir: Manoogian Foundation, Alex and Marie

Manoogian, Richard Alexander, chmn, ceo, dir: Masco Corp.

Mansell, Edmona Lyman, vp, dir: Bothin Foundation

Mansell, Thomas V., pres, secy, dir: Hoyt Foundation

Mansfield, Anne, trust: Mansfield Foundation, Albert and Anne

Mansfield, Benetta, trust: Mansfield Foundation, Albert and Anne

Mansfield, Cindy, admin asst: Syntex Corp.

Mansfield, Elinor, gen curator: Ebell of Los Angeles Rest Cottage Association; gen curator: Ebell of Los Angeles Scholarship Endowment Fund

Mansfield, Harry K., trust: Stare Fund

Mansfield, Seymour, trust: Mansfield Foundation, Albert and Anne

Manson, T.J., trust: SCT Foundation

Mantegani, Peter, vp, dir: Shoong Foundation, Milton

Manton, Edwin Alfred Grenville, dir: Starr Foundation

Manuel, William D., mgr: Helms Foundation

Manz, Myna, secy: Bank of America - Giannini Foundation

Manz, Terry, cfo: Cactus Feeders Inc.

Manzi, James Paul, chmn, ceo, pres, dir: Lotus Development Corp.

Mapel, Frank, secy: Scroggins Foundation, Arthur E. and Cornelia C.

Mapelli, Roland L., chmn, sr vp: Monfort of Colorado, Inc.

Maples, Larry, cfo: Peterson Builders

Maples, Mike, off pres, exec vp prod: Microsoft Corp.

Maples, Roger C., dir: Christy-Houston Foundation

Mar, Donna, program mgr (Bay area): Apple Computer

Mara, Thomas E., trust: Leucadia Foundation

Marafino, Vincent Norman, vchmn, cfo, chief admin off, dir: Lockheed Corp.

Marangi, Leonard M., trust: Murphey Foundation, Lluella Morey

Marbut, Robert G., pres, ceo, dir: Harte-Hanks Communications, Inc.

Marcella, Paul A., secy: Dow Corning Corp.

March, Don, cfo: Cosco, Inc.

March, James E., chmn, trust: Sage Foundation, Russell

March, Nancy, editor: Pottstown Mercury

Marcuccilli, Joseph, cfo, treas: Commonwealth Life Insurance Co.

Marcum, Joseph L., chmn, ceo: Ohio Casualty Corp.

Marcum, Kenneth W., treas, trust: Commercial Intertech Foundation

Marcus, Arthur, secy, treas, dir: Marcus Foundation

Marcus, Ben, fdr, dir, chmn fin comm: Marcus Corp.; pres, dir: Marcus Corp. Foundation

Marcus, Bernard, chmn, ceo, dir: Home Depot

Marcus, James S., trust: Krimendahl II Foundation, H. Frederick

Marcus, Leonard, pres, coo: Abraham & Straus

Marcus, Lorraine, secy: Boothroyd Foundation, Charles H. and Bertha L.

Marcus, Martin, pres: Marcus Brothers Textiles Inc.; pres: Marcus Foundation

Marcus, Richard C., chmn: Neiman Marcus

Marcus, Richard G., pres, coo: American Biltrite

Marcus, Roger S., chmn, ceo, dir: American Biltrite

Marcus, Samuel, pres: Marcus Brothers Textiles Inc.; pres, dir: Marcus Foundation

Marcus, Stephen, pres, coo, ceo: Marcus Corp.

Marcus, Stephen Howard, secy, dir: Marcus Corp. Foundation

Marcuse, Edgar K., MD, dir: Nesholm Family Foundation

Marden, Robert A., Sr., chmn: Peoples Heritage Savings Bank

Marder, Ruth R., trust: Rosenberg Foundation, Henry and Ruth Blaustein

Mardigian, Edward S., Sr., pres, dir: Mardigian Foundation

Mardigian, Helen, dir: Mardigian Foundation

Marek, Michael, dir admin & treas: Bang & Olufsen of America, Inc.

Mares, Fidencio M., trust: BHP Petroleum Americas (HI) Foundation

Marett, James J., dir: Ziegler Foundation for the Blind, E. Matilda

Margenthaler, Donald R., pres, dir: Deere Foundation, John

Margerison, Rick W., vp, dir: Tyler Foundation

Marget, Michael, dir admin: Katten, Muchin, & Zavis

Margolin, Abraham E., dir: Tension Envelope Foundation

Margolis, Arthur I., secy, dir: Washington Square Health Foundation

Margolis, David I., chmn, ceo, dir: Coltec Industries; pres, dir: Coltec Industries Charitable Foundation

Margolis, Jay, vchmn, dir: Liz Claiborne; mem grantmaking comm: Liz Claiborne Foundation

Margolius, Edwin A., secy: Edouard Foundation

Margolius, Philip N., secy, treas: Gudelsky Family Foundation, Isadore and Bertha

Margolius, Richard, trust: Gerson Family Foundation, Benjamin J.

Mariani, Dennis, vp: Mariani Nut Co. Foundation

Mariani, Harry F., pres, coo: Banfi Vintners; dir: Banfi Vintners Foundation

Mariani, J. Dennis, dir: Mariani Nut Co. Foundation

Mariani, Jack M., pres: Mariani Nut Co.; pres: Mariani Nut Co. Foundation

Mariani, John J., Jr., chmn: Banfi Vintners; dir: Banfi Vintners Foundation

Mariani, Martin, dir: Mariani Nut Co. Foundation

Maricich, Marian S., vp, trust: McGraw Foundation, Curtis W.

Marin, Lawrence, vp: Kaplun Foundation, Morris J. and Betty

Marinella, Sabino, chmn: Keyport Life Insurance Co.

Mariner, Joseph V., Jr., dir: Dyson Foundation

Marino, P. A., pres, coo, dir: Fairchild Corp.

Marino, Patricia J., pres: Clorox Company Foundation

Marinos, G. T., cfo: Modern Maid Food Products, Inc.

Mario, Ernest, chmn: Glaxo; dir: Glaxo Foundation

Marion, Anne W., pres, trust: Tandy Foundation, Anne Burnett and Charles

Marion, John L., chmn, dir: Sotheby's; trust: Tandy Foundation, Anne Burnett and Charles

Maris, Edward G., cfo: Northwestern Steel & Wire Co.

Maritz, William Edward, chmn, ceo, dir: Maritz Inc.

Mark, Caroline Schumann, vp, trust: Schumann Foundation, Florence and John

Mark, Hans, dir: Hertz Foundation, Fannie and John

Mark, Melvyn I., secy, dir: Herbst Foundation

Mark, Reuben, chmn, pres, ceo, dir: Colgate-Palmolive Co.

Mark-Ross, Florine, dir: Weight Watchers Foundation

Markel, Erich H., treas, dir: Baier Foundation, Marie; pres, dir: Kade Foundation, Max

Markel, Iris, trust: Gudelsky Family Foundation, Isadore and Bertha

Markel, Larry G., asst secy: Lyon Foundation

Markel, Virginia, trust: Fusenot Charity Foundation, Georges and Germaine

Marker, Lela E., secy, treas: Glazer Foundation, Madelyn L.

Markey, Andrew Joseph, treas: Johnson & Johnson Family of Cos. Contribution Fund

Markey, Carol S., mgr (community involvement): Eaton Charitable Fund

Markey, John R., pres, treas, trust: Markey Charitable Fund, John C.

Markey, Shirley K., trust: Klein Fund, Nathan J.

Markland, Frank P., pres: Hay Foundation, John I.

Markle, Joyce B., secy: Seid Foundation, Barre

Markley, William C., III, secy, dir: Jacobs Engineering Foundation

Markopoulos, George J., dir: Gerondelis Foundation

Markos, Arthur C., pres: Gardiner Savings Institution FSB; pres, dir: Gardiner Scholarship Foundation

Markow, Irwin, asst treas: Pinewood Foundation

Marks, David, treas: Kramer Foundation, C. L. C.

Marks, Davis, treas: Kawaler Foundation, Morris and Nellie L.

Marks, Edwin M., vp, trust: Goldsmith Foundation

Marks, Leon, secy: US WEST Foundation

Marks, Lowell, secy, dir: Brotman Foundation of California

Marks, Martha S., dir: Green Foundation, Allen P. and Josephine B.

Marks, Michael J., vp, asst secy: Alexander & Baldwin Foundation

Marks, Paul Camp, dir: Camp Foundation; trust: Camp Younts Foundation; dir: Campbell Foundation, Ruth and Henry; dir: McDougall Charitable Trust, Ruth Camp

Marks, Randolph A., dir: Knox Foundation, Seymour H.

Marks, Raymond, secy, treas, dir: Stulsaft Foundation, Morris

Marks, S.E., secy: CBI Foundation

Marks, William L., chmn, ceo: Whitney National Bank

Marland, Sidney P., Jr., pres, trust: Robinson Fund, Maurice R.

Marlar, Donald F., trust: Bernsen Foundation, Grace and Franklin

Marley, James Earl, chmn: AMP; dir: Kline Foundation, Josiah W. and Bessie H.

Marlo, Philip, trust: Leader Foundation

Marlowe, C. P., treas, trust: Occidental Oil & Gas Charitable Foundation

Marlowe, Ed, trust: Lowenstein Foundation, William P. and Marie R.

Maroney, Eleanor S., secy: Borkee Hagley Foundation; adv trust, don granddaughter: Crystal Trust

Marquard, William A., chmn, dir: Arkansas Best Corp.

Marquardt, Clifford, coo: MorningStar Foods

Marquardt, Tim, cfo: Sunwest Bank of Albuquerque, N.A.

Marquart, Rex, vp: Rogers Foundation

Marquart, William, trust: Voelkerding Charitable Trust, Walter and Jean

Marquitz, D. J., pres: Valley Line Co.

Marran, Elizabeth, vp: Kennedy Foundation, Ethel

Marran, Ethel K., pres, treas: Kennedy Foundation, Ethel

Marran, Laura, secy: Kennedy Foundation, Ethel

Marriott, Alice, don, off: Marriott Foundation, J. Willard

Marriott, John Willard, Jr., chmn, ceo, pres, dir: Marriott Corp.; don, off: Marriott Foundation, J. Willard

Marriott, Richard Edwin, vchmn, exec vp, dir: Marriott Corp.; off: Marriott Foundation, J. Willard

Marron, Donald Baird, mem bd dirs, mem investment comm: Dana Foundation, Charles A.; chmn, ceo: PaineWebber

Marrow, Deborah, dir (Getty Grant Program): Getty Trust, J. Paul

Mars, Bernard S., trust: Foster Charitable Trust

Mars, Forrest Edward, Jr., chmn, ceo, co-pres: Mars, Inc.; vp: Mars Foundation

Mars, John Franklyn, co-pres: Mars, Inc.; vp: Mars Foundation

Marsden, Charles J., vp, cfo: Crompton & Knowles Corp.

Marsella, Al, asst secy, trust: Baker Foundation, Solomon R. and Rebecca D.

Marsh, Alberta A., exec vp, treas: Corbett Foundation

Marsh, Claudia Haines, dir emeritus: Public Welfare Foundation

Marsh, Colleen, secy, trust: Walker Foundation, T. B.

Marsh, David E., vp, cfo: Central Maine Power Co.

Marsh, Don E., pres, ceo: Marsh Supermarkets, Inc.

Marsh, G Alex, III, vp, dir: Marsh Foundation

Marsh, George M., chmn: Marsh Furniture Co.

Marsh, Gilbert Reid, III, pres, ceo: Marsh Furniture Co.

Marsh, Harold, treas: Fireman's Fund Foundation

Marsh, Kevin B., trust: Summer Foundation

Marsh, Lex, pres, treas, dir: Marsh Foundation

Marsh, Miles L., chmn, ceo, pres: Pet; trust: Pet Inc. Community Support Foundation

Marsh, Myron L., trust: Tokheim Foundation

Marsh, Richard S. T., trust: Foundation for Middle East Peace; treas, dir: Strong Foundation, Hattie M.

Marshall, Anthony D., vp, trust: Astor Foundation, Vincent

Marshall, Colin, ceo: British Airways

Marshall, David B., pres, dir: Contempo Communications Foundation for the Arts, Inc.

Marshall, David L., pres: Burlington Air Express Inc.; secy, treas, dir: Contempo Communications Foundation for the Arts, Inc.; vchmn, cfo: Pittston Co.

Marshall, Gerald Robert, treas: Kerr Foundation

Marshall, Joan F., vp, dir: Contempo Communications Foundation for the Arts, Inc.

Marshall, John Elbert, III, pres, secy: Kresge Foundation

Marshall, Jonathan, dir, pres: Marshall Fund

Marshall, Leonard B., Jr., dir: Habig Foundation

Marshall, Maxine B., dir, vp: Marshall Fund

Marshall, Robert C., sr vp, coo, dir: Tandem Computers

Marshall, Ron, asst secy: Crown Books Foundation, Inc.; contact: Dart Group Foundation

Marshall, Rose M., dir: Arakelian Foundation, Mary Alice

Marshall, Thomas, cfo, dir: Aristech Chemical Corp.; trust: Aristech Foundation

Marshall, Thomas C., vp, dir: Drown Foundation, Joseph

Marshall, Thomas O., chmn, secy: Marshall Foundation, Mattie H.

Marshall, Thomas O., Jr., bd mem: Pitts Foundation, William H. and Lula E.

Marshall, William H., dir: Clowes Fund

Marshall-Sapon, Laura, trust: Marshall Fund

Marshburn, D.C., trust: Marshburn Foundation

Marshburn, F.K., trust: Marshburn Foundation

Marshburn, L. C., trust: Marshburn Foundation

Marshburn, R. A., trust: Marshburn Foundation

Marsico, Lou, treas: McCormick Tribune Foundation, Robert R.

Marsten, Richard, contact: Fraser Paper Ltd.

Marston, Randolph B., trust: Mobility Foundation

Marston, Ted Leroy, consultant: Cummins Engine Co.; dir: Cummins Engine Foundation

Mart, William E., trust: Brown Foundation, George Warren

Martaus, Cecilia M., secy, trust: Ohio Bell Foundation

Martello, M. E., asst treas: Bechtel Foundation

Martens, Ernesto R., vchmn, dir: Anchor Glass Container Corp.

Martin, Alvin, trust: Mineral Trust

Martin, Bobby, mem: Wal-Mart Foundation

Martin, C. Cecil, dir: Houchens Foundation, Ervin G.

Martin, C. Virgil, dir: Mertz-Gilmore Foundation, Joyce

Martin, Carmel C., Jr., secy: National Pro-Am Youth Fund

Martin, Carol E., pres, dir: Ellis Foundation

Martin, Casper, dir: Martin Foundation

Martin, Dan M., dir world environment & resources program, population program: MacArthur Foundation, John D. and Catherine T.

Martin, David, chmn, ceo, dir: Occidental Oil & Gas Corp.

Martin, Dorothy G., Zachry Co., H. B.

Martin, Edgar, pres: Commercial Bank

Martin, Elio L., treas: Johnson Foundation, Walter S.

Martin, Elizabeth, secy, dir: Martin Foundation

Martin, G. Eugene, vp, trust: Technical Foundation of America

Martin, Geraldine F., pres, dir: Martin Foundation

Martin, Gertrude A., secy: Martin Family Fund

Martin, Glenn R., vp, dir: Reynolds Foundation, Richard S.

Martin, Grace, mgr corp pub rels: Hartford Steam Boiler Inspection & Insurance Co.

Martin, Herve, vp (mktg): Cartier, Inc.

Martin, Ian Alexander, ceo, mng dir, coo: Pillsbury Co.

Martin, J. Landis, chmn, ceo, dir: Baroid Corp.

Martin, Jennifer, treas, dir: Martin Foundation

Martin, John, mem: Smith, Jr. Foundation, M. W.

Martin, John C., pres, dir: American Schlafhorst Foundation, Inc.

Martin, John R., trust: Reynolds & Reynolds Company Foundation

Martin, John W., asst treas: Ontario Corporation Foundation

Martin, John W., Jr., trust: Ford Motor Co. Fund

Martin, Judith W., mem bd mgrs: Wilson Foundation, Marie C. and Joseph C.

Martin, Justin M., vp: Merrill Foundation, R. D.

Martin, Karen C., program supvr: Corning Incorporated Foundation

Martin, Lee, dir: Martin Foundation; chmn: NIBCO Inc.

Martin, Lee P., Jr., trust: Lawrence Foundation, Lind

Martin, M. D., pres: Lakeside National Bank

Martin, Mahlon A., pres: Rockefeller Foundation, Winthrop

Martin, Malcolm Elliot, secy, dir: Bennett Foundation, Carl and Dorothy

Martin, Margaret, dir community programs: Carrier Corp.

Martin, Maurice H., pres, treas, trust: Tonya Memorial Foundation

Martin, Mrs. John M., dir: Reflection Riding

Martin, Ralph H., trust: Reinhold Foundation, Paul E. and Ida Klare

Martin, Ray, ceo, chmn: Coast Federal Bank

Martin, Rex, pres: NIBCO Inc.

Martin, Robert Allan, pres: Martin Family Fund

Martin, Roger L., trust: Steelcase Foundation

Martin, Ron, vp, cfo: Mayflower Group

Martin, Ruth, vp, dir: Berkowitz Family Foundation, Louis

Martin, S. Walter, mem scholarship bd: Cobb Educational Fund, Ty

Martin, Stephen E., trust: Beckman Foundation, Leland D.

Martin, Susan J., exec dir: Maytag Corp. Foundation

Martin, Thomas C., vp, dir: Banc One Wisconsin Foundation

Martin, Wanda, sr pub rels specialist grants & community service: Federal Express Corp.

Martin, Webb, trust: Mott Foundation, Charles Stewart

Martin, William T., trust: Arkell Hall Foundation

Martinenza, Stephen A., treas: Crestlea Foundation; asst treas: Longwood Foundation; asst treas: Welfare Foundation

Martinez, Andre, pres, ceo: Meridien Hotels

Martinez, Arthur, vchmn, dir: Saks Fifth Ave.

Martinez, Ignacio J., trust: Clorox Company Foundation

Martinez, Vicente, program off: New York Foundation

Martinez, Vilma S., vchmn, trust: Hazen Foundation, Edward W.

Marting, Isabel, trust: Treuhaft Foundation

Martini, A. P., mem charitable comm: Foster Charitable Trust, L.B.

Martini, Robert E., chmn, ceo, dir: Bergen Brunswig Corp.

Martini, William J., trust: Martini Foundation, Nicholas

Martinson, David, dir corp rels: East Ohio Gas Co.

Martix, Lucy C., Pannill Scholarship Foundation, William Letcher

Martonchik, Richard, dir (human resources): Schieffelin & Somerset Co.

Martone, Joan Dalis, Goodman & Company

Martorella, Joseph, treas: Kidder Peabody Foundation

Martus, Rose, treas: Mattus Foundation, Reuben and Rose

Marty, Mary, vice treas: Boston Globe Foundation

Martyn, Jack T., Jr., pres: Ivakota Association

Maruhashi, M., sr vp: Toyota Motor Sales, U.S.A.

Marusin, Mary Lou, exec dir: Scripps Howard Foundation

Maruta, Yasao, pub resources coordinator: Mazda North America

Maruta, Yoshio, chmn: Kao Corp. of America (DE)

Marvin, Charles H., III, dir, bd mem: Gregg-Graniteville Foundation

Marvin, Dennis H., secy: Consumers Power Foundation

Marwell, Edward M., trust: Sofia American Schools

Marx, Leonard, Jr., trust: Marx Foundation, Virginia & Leonard

Marx, Leonard, Sr., dir: Gluck Foundation, Maxwell H.

Marx, Virginia, trust: Marx Foundation, Virginia & Leonard

Mary, Charles C., Jr., secy, dir: Lupin Foundation

Mary, Pauline, trust: McShain Charities, John

Maryles, Mathew, dir: Bravmann Foundation, Ludwig

Marzelli, Alan, treas: Jockey Club Foundation

Marzocchi, Robert A., treas: Chubb Foundation

Mascari, Patricia, dir: Strong Foundation, Hattie M.

Mascotte, John Pierre, chmn, ceo, dir: Continental Corp.; chmn, pres, trust: Continental Corp. Foundation; dir: Hall Family Foundations

Masi, Joseph L., treas, dir: Hancock Foundation, Luke B.

Masi, Susan H., chmn (finance comm), dir: Hancock Foundation, Luke B.

Masi, Wendy S., trust: Mailman Family Foundation, A. L.

Masilla, Thomas A., Jr., chmn: Hibernia Corp.

Masket, David C., vp, treas, dir: Rosenthal Foundation, Ida and William

Masket, Steven N., secy: Rosenthal Foundation, Ida and William

Maslick, Joseph R., trust: Griffith Laboratories Foundation, Inc.

Maslowski, Clem, cfo: Rite-Hite Corp.

Mason, Elaine, vp, dir: Keating Family Foundation

Mason, Frederick T., asst secy, asst treas: Sulzberger Foundation

Mason, James K., MD, dir: Livingston Memorial Foundation

Mason, James N., dir (civic affairs): CIGNA Foundation

Mason, Jeffrey N., secy, dir: Uslico Foundation

Mason, John L., pres: Monsanto Fund

Mason, Paul W., secy, treas, dir: Carter Foundation, Amon G.

Mason, Rausey W., vchmn, dir: Fortune Bank

Mason, Raymond A., chmn, ceo: Legg Mason Inc.

Mason, Robert H., dir, pres: Layne Foundation

Mason, Steve J., pres: Ingram Book Co.

Mason, Steven Charles, vchmn bd: Mead Corp.

Mason, W. Bruce, chmn, ceo, dir: Foote, Cone & Belding Communications

Mason, Wesley M., dir, secy, treas: Layne Foundation

Massa, John A., trust: Heileman Old Style Foundation

Massam, Ronald A., sr vp (fin), cfo: Hamilton Bank

Massey, E. Morgan, treas: Massey Foundation

Massey, Frank, vp, treas: Keebler Co.

Massey, Ike, publ: Houston Post Co.

Massey, Jack C., trust: Massey Foundation, Jack C.

Massey, James P., trust: Osborn Manufacturing Co. Educational & Charitable Fund

Massey, Joe B., trust: Massey Charitable Trust

Massey, William Blair, pres: Massey Foundation

Massey, William E., Jr., pres: Massey Foundation

Massi, Frank, vp, dir: Hearst Foundation; vp, dir: Hearst Foundation, William Randolph

Massie, Dale, dir (mktg): Cominco American Inc.

Massie, Edward L., pres, ceo, dir: Commerce Clearing House

Massimino, Gary L., exec vp, cfo: Care Enterprises

Mast, John, dir: McIntire Educational Fund, John

Mast, William H., chmn, pres: Mast Drug Co.

Masters, Jane J., asst secy, asst treas: Mather and William Gwinn Mather Fund, Elizabeth Ring

Masterson, Carroll S., trust: Rienzi Foundation

Masterson, Harris, trust: Rienzi Foundation

Mastriana, J. Ronald, Jr., trust: Debartolo Foundation, Marie P.

Mastro, Anthony F., trust: Aristech Foundation

Mastronardi, Carrie, pres: Mastronardi Charitable Foundation, Charles A.

Mastronardi, Joseph, treas: Mastronardi Charitable Foundation, Charles A.

Mastronardi, Nicholas D., vp: Mastronardi Charitable Foundation, Charles A.

Mastrota, Joan T., treas: Heublein Foundation

Masure, Morton, cfo: Rigler-Deutsch Foundation

Matchett, Terri E., trust: Winchester Foundation

Mateo, Laura Davies, dir: Lakeside Foundation; vp, dir: Llagas Foundation; dir, vp: Uvas Foundation

Mateo, Segundo, vp, dir: Llagas Foundation; dir, vp: Uvas Foundation

Mather, Karen W., grants mgr: Gates Foundation

Mather, Russell R., secy, treas, dir: Leach Foundation, Tom & Frances

Matherne, Louis K., Jr., treas: Chesapeake Corp.

Mathers, William L., exec dir, mgr: Wareheim Foundation, E. C.

Mathes, Stephen, secy, dir: Levitt Foundation

Matheson, Alline, dir: Barker Welfare Foundation

Matheson, Gordon H., trust: Harvest States Foundation

Mathews, Jessica Tuchman, trust: Rockefeller Brothers Fund

Mathews, L.David, VP: Sonat Foundation

Mathews, Paul, mgr: Tyndale House Foundation

Mathias, Charles McC., Jr., dir: Tinker Foundation

Mathias, Edward Joseph, managing dir: Price Associates, T. Rowe

Mathias, James H., treas, dir: Beir Foundation

Mathiasen, Karl, dir: Moriah Fund

Mathieson, Andrew Wray, trust: Mellon Foundation, Richard King

McBride, Kevin, treas, trust: Biological Humanics Foundation

McBride, Mary, vp mktg: Pioneer Hi-Bred International

McBride, Richard C., chmn: McBride Charitable Foundation, Joseph & Elsie

McBride, Robert D., pres, ceo: McLouth Steel-An Employee Owned Co.

McBride, Thomas J., dir: McBride Charitable Foundation, Joseph & Elsie

McBroom, Russell D., pres: Trans-Apex

McCabe, Daniel Marie, trust: Valencia Charitable Trust

McCabe, Eleanora W., pres, treas, dir: Wahlstrom Foundation

McCabe, Nancy, development off: Guggenheim Memorial Foundation, John Simon

McCafferty, Michael Gilbert, treas: Mattel Foundation

McCaffrey, Thomas R., pres, coo: Columbus Southern Power Co.

McCahill, Eugene P., trust: Quinlan Foundation, Elizabeth C.

McCaig, Nancy C., MD, trust: Monticello College Foundation

McCain, James A., asst secy, asst treas: Burkitt Foundation

McCain, John B., Merrill Corp: Merrill Corp.

McCall, Dorothy R., vp, trust: Doherty Charitable Foundation, Henry L. and Grace

McCall, James W., pres, dir: Chesebrough Foundation

McCall, Jeffrey G., asst to pres: Provident Life & Accident Insurance Co.

McCallie, Allen, secy: Lyndhurst Foundation

McCallie, Thomas H., dir: Maclellan Foundation, Robert L. and Kathrina H.

McCallie, Thomas H., III, secy: Maclellan Foundation

McCallister, Alice, dir: Harcourt Foundation, Ellen Knowles

McCallum, W. T., ceo: Great-West Life Assurance Co.

McCallum, W.W., hon chmn: Lost Tree Charitable Foundation

McCamish, Henry F., Jr., vp: McCamish Foundation

McCamish, Margaret P., pres: McCamish Foundation

McCammon, David Noel, treas, trust: Ford Motor Co. Fund

McCandliss, Len, pres, dir: Sierra Health Foundation

McCanley, Richard G., secy-treas, trust: Rouse Co. Foundation

McCann, James P., vchmn, pres, coo: Bridgestone/Firestone

McCann, Joseph F., pres: PepsiCo

McCann, Nancy W., asst vp: Murphy Foundation, John P.

McCann, Thomas, dir: Hertz Foundation, Fannie and John

McCanne, Robert H., mgr: Woltman Foundation, B. M.

McCannell, Dana D., trust: Walker Foundation, Archie D. and Bertha H.

McCannell, Laurie H., trust: Walker Foundation, Archie D. and Bertha H.

McCannell, Louise Walker, vp, trust: Walker Foundation, Archie D. and Bertha H.

McCants, Debbie, fdn asst: Travelers Cos. Foundation

McCardle, M. A., secy: Beneficial Foundation

McCardle, Thomas F., pres, coo: Kolene Corp.

McCarrick, Theodore Edgar, trust: Loyola Foundation

McCarter, Michael G., sr vp, cfo, actuary: Harleysville Mutual Insurance Co.

McCarter, Thomas N., III, chmn, trust: Christodora

McCarthy, Albert, vp (admin & human resources): NEC Technologies, Inc.

McCarthy, Albert Gregory, III, secy, trust: Loyola Foundation

McCarthy, Albert Gregory, IV, trust: Loyola Foundation

McCarthy, Barry, trust: Perley Fund, Victor E.

McCarthy, Charles V., trust: Campbell Soup Foundation; pres: Pepperidge Farm, Inc.

McCarthy, Edward, Jr., trust: Williams Foundation, Edna Sproull

McCarthy, Edward Q., vp (mktg): Chicago Title and Trust Co.

McCarthy, Gerald P., dir: Daily News Foundation

McCarthy, J. Thomas, chmn, trust: Leavey Foundation, Thomas and Dorothy

McCarthy, James A., vp: McCarthy Charities

McCarthy, John E., mem: Burkitt Foundation

McCarthy, Kathleen Leavey, trust: Leavey Foundation, Thomas and Dorothy

McCarthy, Lucy R., pres, dir: Weyerhaeuser Memorial Foundation, Charles A.

McCarthy, Lynn L., chmn, pres, dir: Nichols Co., J.C.; trust: Nichols Co. Charitable Trust

McCarthy, Madeline B., secy, dir: Flagler Foundation

McCarthy, Marion P., secy: McCarthy Charities

McCarthy, Mary, dir corp contributions: Time Warner

McCarthy, Michael A., dir: Skidmore, Owings & Merrill Foundation

McCarthy, Michael D., dir: Goldman Sachs Fund

McCarthy, Michael W., trust: McCarthy Foundation, Michael W.

McCarthy, Patricia A., adm off: Schumann Foundation, Florence and John

McCarthy, Peter F., pres, treas: McCarthy Charities

McCarthy, Roblee, Jr., bd mem: Roblee Foundation, Joseph H. and Florence A.

McCarthy, Thomas M., asst secy: BT Foundation

McCarthy, William, vp, dir: Montgomery Ward Foundation

McCartin, William Robert, treas: Procter & Gamble Cosmetic & Fragrance Products

McCarty, John B., treas: McCarthy Foundation, John and Margaret

McCarty, Maclyn, MD, vp, trust, mem, chmn scientific adv comm: Whitney Foundation, Helen Hay

McCarty, Marilu H., trust: Franklin Foundation, John and Mary

McCary, Paul, trust: Connecticut Energy Foundation, Inc.

McCashin, Helen B., trust: Bedford Fund

McCaskey, Donald L., Weisbrod Foundation Trust Dept., Robert and Mary

McCaskey, Mary M., secy corporate contributions comm: Pitney Bowes

McCaskill, Beverly, vp, treas: Texas Commerce Bank Houston Foundation

McCasland, Thomas H., Jr., trust: McCasland Foundation

McCathron, Peggy, sr admin secy: Cadbury Beverages Inc.

McCaughan, John F., chmn, ceo, dir: Betz Laboratories

McCauley, James, treas, comptr: Warhol Foundation for the Visual Arts, Andy

McCaw, Bruce R., secy, treas: McCaw Foundation

McCaw, Craig O., chmn, ceo: LIN Broadcasting Corp.; chmn, ceo: McCaw Cellular Communications; vp: McCaw Foundation

McCaw, John E., vp: McCaw Foundation

McCaw, Keith W., vp: McCaw Foundation

McClane, Robert S., pres, dir: Cullen/Frost Bankers

McClarren, Libby, treas: Dresser Industries

McClaughry, Paul D., secy: Miller Foundation, Earl B. and Loraine H.

McClean, Roy W., Lund Foundation

McCleary, S., dir: Legg & Co. Foundation

McClellan, J., pres: Awrey Bakeries

McClellan, Rowland J., dir: Janesville Foundation

McClelland, Rex Arnold, sr vp (admin svcs): Delta Air Lines; trust: Delta Air Lines Foundation

McClelland, W. Craig, pres, coo, dir: Union Camp Corp.

McClintock, Emily, trust: Nord Family Foundation

McClintock, George D., dir: Palmer Foundation, George M.

McClintock, John R.D., trust: Childs Charitable Foundation, Roberta M.

McCloskey, John J., secy, dir: R. P. Foundation

McCloy, Ellen Z., pres: Mobil Foundation

McClung, James Allen, vp, dir: FMC Foundation

McClure, Ann Cunningham, mem distribution comm: Oliver Memorial Trust Foundation

McClure, John V. N., mem: Northern Trust Co. Charitable Trust

McCluskey, Joseph L., secy: Meyer Foundation, George C.

McColl, Hugh Leon, Jr., chmn: NationsBank Corp.; chmn: NationsBank Texas

McCollow, Thomas J., vchmn: McBeath Foundation, Faye

McCollum, H. W., chmn fin comm, dir: Amerada Hess Corp.

McComas, Harold J., trust: Demmer Foundation, Edward U.

McComas, Harrold J., trust: Pick Charitable Trust, Melitta S.; vp, dir: Ziegler Foundation

McComas, Murray Knabb, chmn, pres: Blair Corp.

McCombs, A. Parks, dir: Zimmermann Fund, Marie and John

McConn, Christiana R., trust: Turner Charitable Foundation

McConnell, B. Scott, vp, trust: McConnell Foundation, Neil A.

McConnell, David M., vp: Stowe, Jr. Foundation, Robert Lee

McConnell, James M., ceo, pres: Instron Corp.

McConnell, John Henderson, fdr, chmn, ceo, dir: Worthington Industries, Inc.

McConnell, John P., vchmn: Worthington Industries, Inc.

McConnell, John W., pres, ceo: Fairfield Communities, Inc.

McConnell, Leah F., fdr, don, dir: McConnell Foundation

McConnell, Neil A., pres, trust: McConnell Foundation, Neil A.

McConnell, Robert B., chmn: Indianapolis Water Co.

McConnell, William T., chmn: Park National Bank; pres, dir: Park National Corporation Foundation

McConnon, Van, dir: Hiawatha Education Foundation

McCord, Patrick J., pres: Yale Security Inc.

McCord, William C., sr chmn: Enserch Corp.; sr chmn: Lone Star Gas Co.

McCorkindale, Douglas Hamilton, vchmn, cfo, chief admin off: Gannett Co.

McCormack, Elizabeth J., chmn, dir: MacArthur Foundation, John D. and Catherine T.; trust: Trust for Mutual Understanding

McCormack, John A., pres, ceo, dir: Bank of Alma

McCormack, Robert C., dir: Pullman Educational Foundation, George M.

McCormack, William J., pres, treas, dir: Morania Foundation

McCormick, Charles Deering, pres, dir, don son: McCormick Foundation, Chauncey and Marion Deering; trust: Silver Spring Foundation

McCormick, E.F., pres: Lykes Brothers Steamship Co.

McCormick, Elena, asst treas, assoc fin & admin: New World Foundation

McCormick, J. L., trust: Stern Family Foundation, Alex

McCormick, Richard David, chmn, pres, ceo, dir: US WEST; pres: US WEST Foundation

McCormick, Thomas J., dir: Alexander Charitable Foundation

McCormick, William C., pres, ceo: Precision Castparts Corp.

McCormick, William Thomas, Jr., chmn, dir: Consumers Power Co.; chmn: Consumers Power Foundation; trust: McGregor Fund

McCortney, John H., vp, treas, dir: White Foundation, W. P. and H. B.

McCourt, K. W., ceo, pres: Buffalo Color Corp.

McCown, James R., gen mgr: Kenedy Memorial Foundation, John G. and Marie Stella

McCoy, Carolyn, fdn off: Fifth Third Foundation

McCoy, Carolyn F., fdn off (Fifth Third Bank): Schmidlapp Trust No. 1, Jacob G.

McCoy, Donald Richard, dir, secy: Wellons Foundation

McCoy, Louise Boney, trust: Hillsdale Fund

McCoy, Michael, cfo: FDL Foods/Dubuque Packing Co.

McCoy, Nelson, secy: McIntire Educational Fund, John

McCoy, William O., vchmn: BellSouth Corp.

McCracken, Paul W., trust: Earhart Foundation; trust: German Marshall Fund of the United States

McCrackin, William K., vchmn, cfo, dir: Michigan Consolidated Gas Co.

McCraig, Joseph J., chmn, ceo: Colonial Stores; trust: Colonial Stores Foundation

McCrary, Charles D., sr vp: Alabama Power Co.; pres: Alabama Power Foundation

McCrary, Charles W., Jr., chmn, pres: Acme-McCrary Corp.; vp: Acme-McCrary and Sapona Foundation

McCrary, Giles C., trust: Franklin Charitable Trust, Ershel

McCraw, J.R., contr: Texas Industries Foundation

McCraw, Leslie G., ceo, dir, chmn: Fluor Corp.; trust, chmn: Fluor Foundation

McCray, Ann W., trust: McCray Charitable Foundation

McCray, Harry Claxton, Jr., chmn, pres: McCray Lumber Co.

McCray, Steward, trust: McCray Charitable Foundation

McCreight, Paul W., secy: Board of Trustees of the Prichard School

McCue, Howard, III, secy: Cheney Foundation, Elizabeth F.

McCue, Howard M., III, secy, dir: Fry Foundation, Lloyd A.; asst secy, asst treas: Lannan Foundation

McCue, Howard McDowell, III, dir: Washington Square Health Foundation

McCulloch, Albert Donald, Jr., chmn, ceo, pres, dir: Nutri/System Inc.

McCulloch, Mervyn J., cfo: Armor All Products Corp.

McCullough, F.E., distribution comm: Flowers Charitable Trust, Albert W. and Edith V.

McCullough, George R., vchmn: Carthage Foundation

McCullough, Hubert, dir: Christy-Houston Foundation

McCullough, J. W., pres, mgr, trust: McCullough Foundation, Ralph H. and Ruth J.

McCullough, J. W., Jr., trust, mgr, pres: McCullough Foundation, Ralph H. and Ruth J.

McCullough, James T., trust: McCullough Foundation, Ralph H. and Ruth J.

McCullough, Ouida, dir: Gallo Foundation

McCullough, R. Michael, sr chmn: Booz Allen & Hamilton

McCullough, Samuel Alexander, chmn, ceo, dir: Meridian Bancorp

McHenry, Merl, trust: Irwin Charity Foundation, William G.

McHugh, Ann, vp, treas, dir: Carvel Foundation, Thomas and Agnes

McHugh, John A., dir: Bush Foundation; mem adv comm: Minnesota Foundation

McHugh, Katherine S., adm: Cox Charitable Trust, Jessie B.

McHugh, Marie L., vp, dir: Laffey-McHugh Foundation

McIlraith, Kenneth J., vchmn, dir: Moog, Inc.

McInerney, Henry F., ceo, pres: Tetley, Inc.

McIninch, Bonnie, trust: Wilson Public Trust, Ralph

McInnes, Duncan Joseph, pres, dir: Blount Foundation

McInnis, James I., trust: O'Brien Foundation, James W.

McInnis, Patricia C., corp secy: Powell Foundation, Charles Lee

McIntosh, DeCourcy E., exec dir, secy: Frick Foundation, Helen Clay

McIntosh, Diane H., vp, secy, dir: McIntosh Foundation

McIntosh, James C., dir: Castle Foundation, Harold K. L.

McIntosh, Joan H., vp, asst treas, dir: McIntosh Foundation

McIntosh, Marilyn D., trust: Dupar Foundation

McIntosh, Michael A., pres, dir: McIntosh Foundation

McIntosh, Peter H., vp, treas, dir: McIntosh Foundation

McIntosh, Thomas B., dir: McIntosh Foundation

McIntosh, William A., pres, treas, dir: McIntosh Foundation

McIntosh, Winsome D., vp, asst treas, dir: McIntosh Foundation

McIntyre, Charles S., III, trust: McIntyre Foundation, B. D. and Jane E.

McIntyre, David I., trust: McIntyre Foundation, C. S. and Marion F.

McIntyre, Diane, pres, dir: Dreyer's & Edy's Grand Ice Cream Charitable Fdn.

McIntyre, John, dir: Katzenberger Foundation; trust: Tull Charitable Foundation

McIntyre, Scott, Jr., chmn, dir: United Fire & Casualty Co.

McJicker, Linda K., asst secy, asst treas: Santa Fe Pacific Foundation

McJunkin, Donald R., trust: McDonald Foundation, J. M.

McJunkin, Eleanor F., pres, trust: McDonald Foundation, J. M.

McJunkin, Reed L., secy, trust: McDonald Foundation, J. M.

McKay, Herbert G., pres: Falk Foundation, David; pres, dir: Saunders Foundation

McKay, Robert B., Zarkin Memorial Foundation, Charles

McKay, Shaun L., vp, trust: Baldwin Memorial Foundation, Fred

McKay, T. Todd, vp: McVay Foundation

McKay, Vernon, secy, trust: Bloomfield Foundation, Sam and Rie

McKean, Hugh F., pres: Genius Foundation, Elizabeth Morse

McKean, Lawrence, corp vp: Boeing Co.

McKean, Linda B., trust: Schepp Foundation, Leopold

McKean, Q. A. Shaw, Jr., pres, trust: Borden Memorial Foundation, Mary Owen

McKee, C. David, vp, trust: McKee Foundation, Robert E. and Evelyn

McKee, C. Steven, trust: McKee Foundation, Robert E. and Evelyn

McKee, Clyde V., Jr., secy-treas, trust: Stark Foundation, Nelda C. and H. J. Lutcher

McKee, John S., vp, trust: McKee Foundation, Robert E. and Evelyn

McKee, Louis B., pres, treas, trust: McKee Foundation, Robert E. and Evelyn

McKee, Louis B., Jr., trust: McKee Foundation, Robert E. and Evelyn

McKee, Philip Russell, trust: McKee Foundation, Robert E. and Evelyn

McKee, Philip S., vp, trust: McKee Foundation, Robert E. and Evelyn

McKee, Robert E., III, trust: McKee Foundation, Robert E. and Evelyn

McKee, W. W., pres, ceo: Pitt-Des Moines Inc.

McKeel, Sam, pres, ceo: Chicago Sun-Times, Inc.

McKellar, C. H., vp, dir: Winn-Dixie Stores Foundation

McKelvey, Barbara, trust: Christodora

McKelvey, Patricia E., secy: Strosacker Foundation, Charles J.

McKenna, Alex George, chmn, dir: McKenna Foundation, Katherine Mabis; chmn, off: McKenna Foundation, Philip M.

McKenna, Andrew, trust: Decio Foundation, Arthur J.

McKenna, Andrew James, dir: AON Foundation

McKenna, Anne, trust: Simon Foundation, Jennifer Jones

McKenna, Bill, cfo: Bourns, Inc.

McKenna, Florence, dir: Bristol-Myers Squibb Foundation

McKenna, Joseph, sr vp (pub rels): Paddington Corp.

McKenna, Mark, mgr (commun aff): Kaiser Cement Corp.

McKenna, Matthew M., trust: Merrill Lynch & Co. Foundation

McKenna, Quentin C., chmn, ceo: Kennametal; trust: Kennametal Foundation

McKenna, T. M., dir: Moorman Co. Fund

McKenna, William J., chmn, pres, ceo, dir: Kellwood Co.; pres: Kellwood Foundation

McKenna, Wilma F., chmn, dir: McKenna Foundation, Katherine Mabis

McKennon, Keith Robert, Dow Corning Corp.

McKenny, Jere Wesley, pres, coo, dir: Kerr-McGee Corp.

McKenzie, Clyde E., vp, treas: Apache Corp.

McKenzie, Eileen Grace, secy, dir: McKenzie Family Foundation, Richard

McKenzie, John, dir: Haas Foundation, Saul and Dayee G.

McKenzie, Kenneth, chmn: GSC Enterprises

McKenzie, Michael K., pres, ceo: GSC Enterprises

McKenzie, Richard C. Jr., pres, dir: McKenzie Family Foundation, Richard

McKeon, Gerard J., pres: New York Racing Association

McKeown, Edward C., dir: Moore Foundation

McKeown, James A., trust: Cummings Properties Foundation

McKeown, Thomas, exec vp, chief adm off: Saint Paul Cos.

McKernan, Leo J., ceo, chmn, pres: Clark Equipment Co.

McKewen, George E., chmn, pres: CRL Inc.

McKim, Judith, dir: Beim Foundation

McKim, Karen P., secy, exec dir: Corbett Foundation

Mckinley, Kimsey, treas: Senior Citizens Foundation

McKinley, Terry L., asst secy: Ashland Oil Foundation

McKinnell, Henry A., cfo, exec vp: Pfizer

McKinney, Bill, mgr banking & admin svcs: Cominco American Inc.

McKinney, Clifford P., Jr., trust: Fulbright and Monroe L. Swyers Foundation, James H.

McKinney, David E., exec secy, mem adv bd: Watson Foundation, Thomas J.

McKinney, Dean B., dir: Bergner Foundation, P.A.

McKinney, J. Bruce, pres, ceo: Hershey Entertainment & Resort Co.

McKinney, John, trust: Love Charitable Foundation, John Allan

McKinney, John B., pres, ceo: Laclede Steel Co.

McKinney, Joseph F., chmn, ceo, pres, dir: Tyler Corp.; chmn: Tyler Foundation

McKinney, Luther C., vp, dir: Quaker Oats Foundation

McKinney, Mike, mgr: TU Electric Co.

McKinney, Roy L., III, gov: Munson Foundation, W. B.

McKinney, Walker, treas, trust: Walker Foundation, L. C. and Margaret

McKinnon, Oriana McArthur, trust: Beazley Foundation; trust: Frederick Foundation

McKinzie, Philip, mem bd govs: Mayor Foundation, Oliver Dewey

McKissick, Elizabeth P., dir: Alice Manufacturing Co. Foundation

McKissick, Ellison S., III, dir: Alice Manufacturing Co. Foundation

McKissick, Ellison S., Jr., ceo: Alice Manufacturing Co.; pres, treas, dir: Alice Manufacturing Co. Foundation

McKissick, Noel P., secy, dir: Alice Manufacturing Co. Foundation

McKissock, David L., vp, secy: Psychists

McKitrick, James, pres: Murphy Co., G.C.

McKittrick, David J., vchmn, coo: Collins & Aikman Holdings Corp.; vp: Collins & Aikman Holdings Foundation

McKleroy, John P., Jr., secy: Bashinsky Foundation

McKnight, Gregory W., treas: Ashland Oil Foundation

McKnight, H. Turney, pres: McKnight Foundation, Sumner T.

McKnight, Sumner T., II, vp, dir: McKnight Foundation, Sumner T.

McKone, Francis L., pres, dir: Albany International Corp.

McLafferty, Bernard J., dir: Copernicus Society of America

McLain, Christopher M., vp, secy, dir: Transamerica Fdn.

McLamore, A. Thomas, trust: Pittsburgh Child Guidance Foundation

McLanahan, Duer, vp, dir: Lincoln Fund

McLane, John Roy, Jr., trust: Bean Foundation, Norwin S. and Elizabeth N.

McLane, Malcolm, trust: Jameson Trust, Oleonda

McLaughlin, A. T., pres: Dick Corp.

McLaughlin, Andrew J., Jr., trust: Loeb Rhoades Employee Welfare Fund

McLaughlin, Lester S., trust: Massachusetts Charitable Mechanics Association

McLaughlin, Michael T., gen coun: Pacific Mutual Charitable Foundation

McLaughlin, Patric J., pres, coo: American Maize Products

McLaughlin, Sandra J., vp, trust: Frick Educational Commission, Henry C.; chmn, pres: Mellon Bank Foundation

McLaughlin, Walter, sr pub rels specialist (grants & community service): Federal Express Corp.

McLean, Carol Ann, trust: Bass Foundation, Harry

McLean, J. Lacy, mem: Piedmont Health Care Foundation

McLean, Justina W., trust: Walker Foundation, W. E.; trust: Walker Wildlife Conservation Foundation

McLean, William L., III, chmn, trust: McLean Contributionship

McLellan, William J., dir: 3M Co.

McLendon, Barbara, trust: Schepp Foundation, Leopold

McLendon, Charles A., trust: Burlington Industries Foundation

McLennan, R.G., trust: Epaphroditus Foundation

McLeod, E. Douglas, dir devel: Moody Foundation

McLeod, Katherine T., dir: Irwin-Sweeney- Miller Foundation

McLeod, Kaye, trust: Gerber Cos. Foundation

McLeod, Margaret, secy: Monroe-Brown Foundation

Mcleod, Marilyn P., vp, secy, trust, don daughter: Powell Family Foundation

McLoone, Michael E., asst treas: General Accident Charitable Trust

McLoraine, Helen M., pres, treas: Pioneer Fund

McLoughlin, John P., vp: Roberts Foundation

McMahon, J.J., Jr., pres, secy, treas, dir: McWane Inc.

McMahon, John, trust: McWane Foundation

McMahon, Robert, trust: McMahon Charitable Trust Fund, Father John F.

McManus, Joseph, secy, treas: Olmsted Foundation, George and Carol

McManus, M. John, vp: Schlegel Corp.

McManus, Patrick J., treas: Raymond Foundation

McMaster, Andrew G., dir: Deloitte & Touche Foundation

McMaster, D. G., pres, coo: Bowater Inc.

McMaster, Harold A., pres, treas: McMaster Foundation, Harold and Helen

McMaster, Helen E., vp, secy: McMaster Foundation, Harold and Helen

McMaster, Ronald A., trust: McMaster Foundation, Harold and Helen

McMeekin, Ronald S., dir: Bank of the Orient Foundation

McMenamin, Louise A., secy, treas: Cudahy Fund, Patrick and Anna M.

McMenamin, Mrs. Edward B., dir: Clark Foundation

McMenemy, Mark, exec vp, cfo: Brooks Brothers

McMennamin, Michael J., chmn, ceo, dir: Bank One, Columbus, NA

McMichael, R. Daniel, secy: Carthage Foundation; secy: Scaife Foundation, Sarah

McMillan, Ed Leigh, II, managing trust: McMillan Foundation, D. W.

McMillan, Elizabeth M., Mather Charitable Trust, S. Livingston

McMillan, George M., trust, vchmn: Jewell Memorial Foundation, Daniel Ashley and Irene Houston

McMillan, Howard L., Jr., pres, coo, dir: Deposit Guaranty National Bank; vp, dir: Deposit Guaranty Foundation

McMillan, Hugh, chmn, treas, trust: Dorr Foundation

McMillan, James, cfo: Blue Circle Inc.

McMillan, John A., co-chmn: Nordstrom, Inc.

McMillan, Mary Bigelow, trust: Bigelow Foundation, F. R.

McMillan, Robert Allan, vp: BFGoodrich; treas: BFGoodrich Foundation

McMillan, Samuel Sterling, III, Mather Charitable Trust, S. Livingston

McMillan, Toney D., trust: Ross Foundation

McMillen, Dale W., III, dir: McMillen Foundation

McMillen, John F., pres, dir: McMillen Foundation

McMillian, Jackie, secy-treas: Lea Country Electric Education Foundation

McMillian, Sterling, III, trust: Mather Fund, Richard

McMillin, John P., pres: Grace Petroleum Corp.

McMorrow, Richard Mark, asst vp (community affairs): American Electric Power

McMorrow, William J., off: Gillette Charitable and Educational Foundation

McMullan, James M., vp: Blair and Co. Foundation, William

McMullen, Jack, Jr., trust: Pineywoods Foundation

McMullen, Thomas, trust: Americana Foundation

McMullian, Amos R., chmn, ceo, dir: Flowers Industries, Inc.

McMullin, Anne, program mgr (regional & intl programs): Apple Computer

Moore, Jacqueline G., trust, pres: Griswold Foundation, John C.

Moore, James F., chmn (contributions comm): American General Corp.

Moore, James S., trust: Westinghouse Foundation

Moore, Jane Petit, dir: Beloit Foundation

Moore, Janet B., secy: Female Association of Philadelphia

Moore, Jim S., Ph.D., dir: South Plains Foundation

Moore, Joe F., pres, ceo: Bonner & Moore Associates

Moore, John, vp: Armco Steel Co. Foundation; pres, coo: Penguin USA Inc.

Moore, John Eddy, sr vp (pers): Cessna Aircraft Co.; vp, dir: Cessna Foundation; pres, trust: Dayton Foundation Depository

Moore, John R., pres, ceo: Midas International Corp.

Moore, John S., vp, dir: Lance, Inc.

Moore, Jonathan, trust: Moore Foundation, C. F.

Moore, Joseph A., trust: Barker Foundation, Donald R.

Moore, Joseph D., dir: SICO Foundation

Moore, Kenneth G., trust: Moore Family Foundation

Moore, Lewis O., chmn, pres: Grimes Foundation

Moore, M. Eugene, Jr., chmn: Caring Foundation

Moore, M. Thomas, chmn, ceo, pres: Cleveland-Cliffs; chmn, pres, trust: Cleveland-Cliffs Foundation

Moore, Mark B., dir: Moore Foundation

Moore, Martin J., pres: Moore Foundation

Moore, Martin L., Jr., trust: Patterson Charitable Fund, W. I.

Moore, Maurice T., vp, dir: Luce Foundation, Henry

Moore, Michael H., pres: Longyear Co.

Moore, Michael J., corporator: Island Foundation

Moore, Michael Q., dir: Moore Foundation

Moore, O. H., secy, treas: Caston Foundation, M. C. and Mattie

Moore, O.H., secy, treas: Navarro County Educational Foundation

Moore, Peter C., trust: Staley Foundation, Thomas F.

Moore, Peter M., grants off: Moody Foundation

Moore, R. A., asst comptr: Armco Foundation

Moore, R. D., trust: Barden Foundation, Inc.

Moore, R. Stuart, chmn: Lane Co., Inc.

Moore, R.C., secy: Texas Industries Foundation

Moore, Randolph, exec vp: Castle Foundation, Harold K. L.

Moore, Richard A., vp, dir: Griggs and Mary Griggs Burke Foundation, Mary Livingston; trust: Minnesota Foundation

Moore, Robert, cfo: Sara Lee Hosiery

Moore, Ronald L., chmn, pres, ceo, dir: Banc One - Colorado Corp.

Moore, Royanna, secy: Cacioppo Foundation, Joseph & Mary

Moore, Sara Giles, chmn, trust: Moore Memorial Foundation, James Starr

Moore, Scott D., sr vp, cfo: Skandia America Reinsurance Corp.

Moore, Starr, trust: Moore Memorial Foundation, James Starr

Moore, Stephen A, trust: Hoffman Foundation, John Ernest

Moore, Stephen O., dir: Hardin Foundation, Phil

Moore, Steven E., trust: Moore Family Foundation

Moore, T. Justin, Jr., vp, trust: Scott Foundation, William R., John G., and Emma

Moore, Taylor F., dir: Frost Foundation

Moore, Thomas N., trust: Criss Memorial Foundation, Dr. C.C. and Mabel L.

Moore, Thomas R., secy, dir: Wiener Foundation, Malcolm Hewitt

Moore, Tom, pres: Remmele Engineering, Inc.

Moore, Virlyn B., Jr., chmn: Baker Foundation, Clark and Ruby; secy, trust, mem exec comm: Franklin Foundation, John and Mary

Moore, Wenda Weekes, trust: Kellogg Foundation, W. K.

Moore, William B., secy: Whitman Corp. Foundation

Moore, William C., trust: Enron Foundation

Moore, William E., dir, vp: Moore Foundation, O. L.

Moore, Winston C., dir: Martin Foundation, Bert William

Moores, Jennifer A., trust, secy: Moores Foundation

Moores, John, bd chmn, don: River Blindness Foundation

Moores, John J., Jr., trust, vp: Moores Foundation

Moores, John Jay, pres, trust: Moores Foundation

Moores, Rebecca A., trust, treas: Moores Foundation

Moorhead, Thomas Leib, Esq., trust: Nordson Corporation Foundation

Moorman, Albert J., treas, dir, mem, don son-in-law: Davis Foundation, Edwin W. and Catherine M.

Moorman, Bette D., pres, dir, mem, don daughter: Davis Foundation, Edwin W. and Catherine M.

Moorman, Elizabeth Davis, trust: Weyerhaeuser Family Foundation

Moot, John R., secy, trust: Western New York Foundation

Moot, Richard, treas, trust: Western New York Foundation

Moot, Welles V., Jr., pres, trust: Western New York Foundation

Mooty, John W., chmn: International Dairy Queen, Inc.

Morak, Del, cfo: Jessop Steel Co.

Moran, Bob, mem (contributions comm): GATX Corp.

Moran, Charles, dir: Sears-Roebuck Foundation

Moran, Edward P., Jr., trust: Barker Foundation

Moran, Elizabeth R., comm mem: 1957 Charity Trust

Moran, James M., Jr., comm mem: 1957 Charity Trust

Moran, John L., vp domestic expl & prod svc: Apache Corp.

Moran, John R., Jr., pres: Colorado Trust; trust: Hill Foundation

Moran, Robert L., dir: Louis Foundation, Michael W.

Moran, Susan B., vp: Barker Foundation

Morath, Carl, dir, secy: Deseranno Educational Foundation

Morath, Paul, pres: Cold Heading Co.; dir, treas: Deseranno Educational Foundation

Moravitz, Stanley, trust: Giant Eagle Foundation

Morawetz, Cathleen Synge, trust, mem audit comm: Sloan Foundation, Alfred P.

Morby, Carolyn, vp, trust: Gerber Cos. Foundation

Morchio, G., pres: Pirelli Armstrong Tire Corp.

Morcott, Southwood J., chmn, pres, ceo, coo, dir: Dana Corp.

Moreau, Gary L., pres, coo: Oneida Ltd.

Moreau, Ronald A., trust: CLARCOR Foundation

Morehead, John H., pres: Richardson County Bank and Trust Co.

Morehouse, L. Clark, III, dir: Daily News Foundation

Morel, Bernard, vp, gen mgr: Air France

Morency, Jeanne L., secy, trust: Lazar Foundation

Moret, Pamela J., vp (commun): IDS Financial Services

Moreton, Charles P., trust: First Mississippi Corp. Foundation

Moreton, Robert D., MD, vp, med adv: Dunn Research Foundation, John S.

Morey, Joseph H., Jr., trust: Cornell Trust, Peter C.

Morf, Claudia, vp: PepsiCo

Morf, Darrel A., secy, atty, dir: Hall Foundation

Morford, Donald K., pres: Sedgwick James Inc.

Morgan, Anne Hodges, dir: Kirkpatrick Foundation

Morgan, Barbara J., dir: Reader's Digest Foundation

Morgan, Charles A., trust: Deuble Foundation, George H.

Morgan, Charles O., trust: Chatlos Foundation

Morgan, D. D., trust: Hanna Co. Foundation, M.A.

Morgan, Daniel M., dir: Morgan-Worcester, Inc.

Morgan, Edward L., vp, dir: ITT Hartford Insurance Group Foundation

Morgan, Elizabeth E., trust: Morgan Trust for Charity, Religion, and Education

Morgan, Evalyn, trust: Morgan Charitable Residual Trust, W. and E.

Morgan, Gayle, program dir (music): Cary Charitable Trust, Mary Flagler

Morgan, Geraldine K., mgr (corp contributions): UST

Morgan, Glenn R., comm mem: Hartmarx Charitable Foundation

Morgan, Helen Fairley, secy: Forest City Enterprises Charitable Foundation

Morgan, James A., secy, trust: Rubbermaid Foundation

Morgan, James F., Jr., vp, dir: Atherton Family Foundation

Morgan, James L., chmn, trust: Morgan Trust for Charity, Religion, and Education

Morgan, John, chmn disbursement comm: Oppenstein Brothers Foundation

Morgan, John L., ceo, pres, dir: American Filtrona Corp.

Morgan, L. J., vp fin, cfo: ADC Telecommunications

Morgan, M. Morrison, trust: Morgan Trust for Charity, Religion, and Education

Morgan, Patricia M., exec dir, secy: Baxter Foundation; dir: Priddy Foundation

Morgan, Paul B., Jr., dir: Morgan-Worcester, Inc.

Morgan, Paul R., ceo, pres: Morgan Construction Co.

Morgan, Paul S., dir: Morgan-Worcester, Inc.

Morgan, Peter S., pres, treas, dir: Morgan-Worcester, Inc.

Morgan, Philip R., dir: Morgan-Worcester, Inc.

Morgan, Robert B., ceo, pres, dir: Cincinnati Financial Corp.

Morgan, Roy Edward, dir: Sordoni Foundation

Morgan, Steve, vp: Cohen Foundation, Manny and Ruthy

Morgan, Walter L., trust, pres: Lovett Foundation

Morgan, Warren, trust: Morgan Charitable Residual Trust, W. and E.

Morgensen, Jerry L., pres: Phelps, Inc.

Morgenstein, Alvin, pres: Cohen Foundation, Manny and Ruthy

Morgenstein, Getrude, treas: Cohen Foundation, Manny and Ruthy

Morgenstein, Melvin, secy: Cohen Foundation, Manny and Ruthy

Morgenstein, Norman, Cohen Foundation, Manny and Ruthy

Morgenstern, Frank N., trust: Morgenstern Foundation, Morris

Morgenstern, Jerry, pres: Phelps Foundation, Hensel

Morgenthaler, George J., sr vp, gen counc, corp secy: Apache Corp.

Morgenthau, Jennie, trust: de Hirsch Fund, Baron

Mori, Faith Harding, trust: Harding Educational and Charitable Foundation

Morian, Robert, pres: Conair, Inc.

Morie, G. Glen, secy: PACCAR Foundation

Morimoto, Jumpei, pres: Obayashi America Corp.

Morin, Eliane, vchmn, ceo: Burndy Corp.

Morita, Masaaki, chmn, ceo, dir: Sony Corp. of America; chmn, dir: Sony USA Foundation

Moritz, Charles Worthington, chmn, ceo, dir: Dun & Bradstreet Corp.; pres, trust: Dun & Bradstreet Corp. Foundation

Moritz, Donald I., pres, ceo, dir: Equitable Resources

Moriyoshi, Hiroshi, trust: Mazda Foundation (USA), Inc.

Mork, Philip W., pres, dir: Bucyrus-Erie

Mork, Richard G., pres, ceo: Castle & Co., A.M.

Morley, Burrows, trust: Morley Brothers Foundation

Morley, Burrows, Jr., trust: Morley Brothers Foundation

Morley, Catherine W., trust: Weyerhaeuser Family Foundation

Morley, Edward B., Jr., pres, trust: Morley Brothers Foundation

Morley, John C., pres, ceo, dir: Reliance Electric Co.

Morley, John D., trust: Morley Brothers Foundation

Morley, Peter B., treas, trust: Morley Brothers Foundation

Morley, Robert S., trust: Morley Brothers Foundation

Morning, John, dir: Culpeper Foundation, Charles E.

Morningstar, John M., dir, vchmn: Special People In Need

Morningstar, Leslie H., dir, vp: Special People In Need

Moroney, James McQueen, Jr., trust: Dallas Morning News—WFAA Foundation, The

Morrell, Hugh W., trust: Akzo America Foundation

Morrell, James Lloyd, bd mem: Dain Bosworth/IFG Foundation

Morressey, Karen M., dir: Cabot Corp. Foundation

Morrill, Amy B., trust: Morrill Charitable Foundation

Morrill, James A., trust: Scott Paper Co. Foundation

Morrill, Vaughan, secy, trust: Monticello College Foundation

Morrione, Paolo, pres, ceo: Himont Inc.

Morris, Ann, contact: Wachovia Foundation of Geaorgia

Morris, Ann A., vp: Flintridge Foundation

Morris, Barbara Young, treas, dir: Baxter Foundation

Morris, Benjamin H., trust: Brown Foundation, W. L. Lyons

Morris, Clea, dir: Flintridge Foundation

Morris, David H., pres, ceo: Toro Co.

Morris, Donna T., asst secy, trust: Strosacker Foundation, Charles J.

Morris, E. A., don, pres: Morris Charitable Foundation, E. A.

Morris, Edward A., vp: Farmers Group Safety Foundation

Morris, Ernest, trust: Americana Foundation

Morris, Florence, Kilworth Charitable Foundation, Florence B.

Morris, George N., trust: General Accident Charitable Trust

Morris, Irving, trust: Kutz Foundation, Milton and Hattie

Morris, Jack B., trust: Morris Foundation

Morris, James T., dir: AUL Foundation; chmn, pres, ceo: Indianapolis Water Co.

Morris, John H., Jr., mem (bd control): Ralston Purina Trust Fund

Morris, Joseph, secy, treas, trust: Sarkeys Foundation

Morris, Joseph E., treas: Morris Charitable Foundation, E. A.

Morris, Leland M., trust: Morris Foundation, Norman M.

Morris, Lester, trust: Shiffman Foundation

Morris, Linda C., trust: Morris Foundation

Morris, Louis Fisk, trust: Seabury Foundation

Morris, Marcia C., clerk, dir: Stride Rite Charitable Foundation

Morris, Mary Lou, secy: Morris Charitable Foundation, E. A.

Morris, Max King, exec dir: Davis Foundations, Arthur Vining

Morris, Michael H., secy, dir: Sun Microsystems Foundation

Morris, Mike G., exec vp, coo: Consumers Power Co.; dir: Consumers Power Foundation

Morris, Norman M., pres, trust: Morris Foundation, Norman M.

Morris, Robert, dir: Fel-Pro/Mecklenburger Foundation

Morris, Robert E., secy, treas, trust: Morris Foundation, Norman M.

Morris, Sally, trust: Kelly Foundation, T. Lloyd

Morris, Samuel W., trust: Waldorf Educational Foundation

Morris, Sarah, asst secy, asst treas: Mitsubishi Electric America Foundation

Morris, Stewart, secy: Oldham Little Church Foundation

Morris, William Carloss, Jr., vp: Oldham Little Church Foundation; secy, treas, trust: Woltman Foundation, B. M.

Morris, William T., vp, dir: Briggs Foundation, T. W.

Morrisett, Lloyd N., pres, dir: Markle Foundation, John and Mary R.

Morrison, David F., vp, treas: Emery Air Freight Educational Foundation

Morrison, Donald K., vp, treas: Southways Foundation

Morrison, Douglas W., trust: Sargent Foundation, Newell B.

Morrison, Howard Jackson, Jr., treas, trust: Lane Memorial Foundation, Mills Bee

Morrison, J. Holmes, chmn: One Valley Bank, N.A.; trust: One Valley Bank Foundation

Morrison, J. M., chmn, pres: Morrison, Inc.

Morrison, Jack R., vp, trust: Johnson Foundation, M. G. and Lillie A.

Morrison, Jacqueline, dir: Aron Charitable Foundation, J.

Morrison, James K., secy, dir: Lytel Foundation, Bertha Russ

Morrison, James S., dir: ARCO Foundation

Morrison, Lucian L., Jr., dir: Semmes Foundation

Morrison, Mills Lane, secy, trust: Lane Memorial Foundation, Mills Bee

Morrison, Myles C., IV, trust: Sullivan Foundation, Algernon Sydney

Morrison, Velma Vivian, pres, don: Morrison Foundation, Harry W.

Morrisroe, David W., treas: Beckman Foundation, Arnold and Mabel

Morrisroe, Susan H., secy: Paramount Communications Foundation

Morrissey, Thomas I., trust, vp, secy: Brundage Charitable, Scientific, and Wildlife Conservation Foundation, Charles E. and Edna T.

Morrissey, Thomas L., trust: Upton Charitable Foundation, Lucy and Eleanor S.

Morrow, G. E., mgr, trust: Garland Foundation, John Jewett and H. Chandler

Morrow, Peter C., mgr corp contributions, exec secy, comm contributions: du Pont de Nemours & Co., E. I.

Morrow, Richard Towson, dir: Disney Family Foundation, Roy

Morrow, W.E., trust: Millhollon Educational Trust Estate, Nettie

Morse, Alan R., Jr., trust, treas: Ratshesky Foundation, A. C.

Morse, Claire W., trust: Morse Foundation, Richard P. and Claire W.

Morse, Enid, vp: Morse, Jr. Foundation, Enid and Lester S.

Morse, Enid W., dir: Wien Foundation, Lawrence A.

Morse, Eric Robert, trust, secy: Ratshesky Foundation, A. C.

Morse, Everett, Jr., trust: Sailors' Snug Harbor of Boston

Morse, John, Jr., trust, vp: Ratshesky Foundation, A. C.

Morse, John A., trust: Miniger Memorial Foundation, Clement O.

Morse, John H., vchmn: National Forge Co.; vp, dir: National Forge Foundation

Morse, Lester S., Jr., Morse Foundation, Richard P. and Claire W.; pres: Morse, Jr. Foundation, Enid and Lester S.; dir: Wien Foundation, Lawrence A.

Morse, Peter C., dir: JM Foundation

Morse, Richard, treas: Morse, Jr. Foundation, Enid and Lester S.

Morse, Richard P., trust: Morse Foundation, Richard P. and Claire W.

Morse, Robert A., contr: Aetna Foundation

Morse, Sarah D., dir: Daniels Foundation, Fred Harris

Morse, Stephan A., dir: Bunbury Company

Morse, Theresa, trust, pres: Ratshesky Foundation, A. C.

Morse, Theresa J., trust: Hyams Foundation

Morse, Timothy, trust: Ratshesky Foundation, A. C.

Mort, Hanno D., vp: Lipchitz Foundation, Jacques and Yulla

Mortenson, M. A., pres, ceo: Mortenson Co., M.A.

Mortenson, Robert S., secy, trust: Meyer Memorial Foundation, Aaron and Rachel

Mortenson, Vernon, trust: Epaphroditus Foundation

Mortimer, Edward Albert, Jr., Brush Foundation

Mortimer, Kathleen H., chmn counc: Foundation for Child Development; pres, dir: Harriman Foundation, Mary W.

Mortimer, Robert J., vp, secy, treas, dir: Johnson Foundation, Willard T. C.

Mortin, Linda, CHC Foundation

Morton, Dean O., trust: Packard Foundation, David and Lucile

Morton, Margaret H., program off: Fidelity Foundation

Morton, Marshall N., sr vp, cfo: Media General, Inc.; treas: Media General Foundation

Morton, Mary, pres: Larrabee Fund Association

Morton, Terry L., trust: Foundation for Seacoast Health

Morton, Vincent P., Jr., trust: Stearns Trust, Artemas W.

Morton, Warren A., mem: Tonkin Foundation, Tom and Helen

Mosbacher, Emil, III, trust: Mosbacher, Jr. Foundation, Emil

Mosbacher, Emil, Jr., trust: Frese Foundation, Arnold D.; pres, dir: Mosbacher, Jr. Foundation, Emil

Mosbacher, John D., vp: Mosbacher, Jr. Foundation, Emil

Mosbacher, Patricia, vp, secy: Mosbacher, Jr. Foundation, Emil

Mosbacher, R. Bruce, trust: Mosbacher, Jr. Foundation, Emil

Moschello, Joan, vp: Swiss Bank Corp.

Mosco, Robert, pres, dir: Younkers, Inc.

Moscoso, Jose T., trust, secy: Sullivan Musical Foundation, William Matheus

Moscow, David, pres: Levy Circulating Co., Charles

Moseley, Alexander, pres: Flintridge Foundation

Moseley, Carlos Dupre, trust: Dana Charitable Trust, Eleanor Naylor; vp, dir: Samuels Foundation, Fan Fox and Leslie R.

Moseley, Cassandra, dir: Flintridge Foundation

Moseley, Elaine R., vp, treas: Rosenthal Foundation, Benjamin J.

Moseley, Frederick Strong, III, trust: Humane Society of the Commonwealth of Massachusetts

Moseley, Furman Colin, pres, dir: Simpson Investment Co.; dir: Matlock Foundation

Moseley, Jacki, dir: Flintridge Foundation

Moseley, James B., managing trust: Jockey Club Foundation

Moseley, Jaylene L., mgr, dir: Flintridge Foundation

Moseley, Lloyd W., dir, pres: Ramlose Foundation, George A.

Moseley, Peter, treas: Flintridge Foundation

Moseley, Sarah, dir: Flintridge Foundation

Mosely, Furman C., chmn, dir: Simpson Paper Co.

Moser, Eyvonne, asst secy, asst treas: Turner Charitable Foundation

Moser, John, dir, secy: Gilman, Jr. Foundation, Sondra and Charles

Moser, M. Peter, secy: Number Ten Foundation

Moser, Robert W., mem (pub affairs comm): Springs Industries

Moses, Alexandra, trust: Agape Foundation

Moses, Billy, dir: Burton Foundation, William T. and Ethel Lewis

Moses, Bruce H., pres, coo: Uarco Inc.

Moses, Stephen E., pres, treas: Waldinger Corp.

Mosher, Greg, trust: Gilman and Gonzalez-Falla Theatre Foundation

Mosher, Margaret C., pres, trust: Mosher Foundation, Samuel B.

Mosier, Ronald, vp (mktg): Browning

Moskin, Morton, trust, pres: Blackmer Foundation, Henry M.

Moskowitz, Cherna, dir, secy, treas: Moskowitz Foundation, Irving I.

Moskowitz, Irving I., M.D., pres, dir: Moskowitz Foundation, Irving I.

Mosley, Daniel L., sec: Paley Foundation, William S.; trust: Pinkerton Foundation; mem adv bd: Watson Foundation, Thomas J.

Mosley, I. Sigmund, Jr., vp, secy: Imlay Foundation

Mosley, W. Kelly, chmn, trust, mem exec comm: Franklin Foundation, John and Mary

Mosner, John H., Jr., pres, dir: Mercantile Bankshares Corp.

Moss, Ann H., vp: Moss Foundation

Moss, Diane, pres, ceo: Rubinstein Foundation, Helena

Moss, Harold Gene, program off: Kresge Foundation

Moss, I. Barney, trust: Korman Family Foundation, Hyman

Moss, Jerome S., pres: Moss Foundation

Moss, Morrie, trust: Hammer United World College Trust, Armand

Moss, Morrie Alfred, vp: Occidental Petroleum Charitable Foundation

Moss, Robert, dir: Rubinstein Foundation, Helena

Moss, Roger, secy: Ludwick Institute

Mostue, Emily C., vp, trust: Carpenter Foundation

Mota, Kathy, dir pub aff: EMI Records Group

Motley, John, dir: Travelers Cos. Foundation

Motono, Moriyuki, trust: United States-Japan Foundation

Motsinger, Jean K., trust: Casey Foundation, Eugene B.

Mott, Charles H., mem fin comm: Rockefeller Family Fund

Mott, Charles Stewart Harding, II, pres, treas, ceo, trust: Harding Foundation, Charles Stewart; trust: Mott Foundation, Charles Stewart

Mott, Isabel S., trust: Harding Foundation, Charles Stewart

Mott, Kerry K., dir: Keck Foundation, W. M.

Mott, Maryanne T., trust: Mott Foundation, Charles Stewart; pres, trust: Mott Fund, Ruth; pres, don: Warsh-Mott Legacy

Mott, Paul B., Jr., exec dir: Kirby Foundation, F. M.

Mott, Paula Kee, trust: Harding Foundation, Charles Stewart

Mott, Ruth Rawlings, trust emeritus: Mott Foundation, Charles Stewart

Mott, Stewart Rawlings, fdr, don, trust: Mott Charitable Trust/Spectemur Agendo, Stewart R.

Mottaz, Rolla, trust: Olin Foundation, Spencer T. and Ann W.

Motte, Camilz, dir: Kentucky Foundation for Women

Motter, Edward, secy: Motter Printing Press Co.; trust: Motter Foundation

Motter, Frank, chmn, pres: Motter Printing Press Co.; chmn, dir: Motter Foundation

Motter, John C., Jr., dir: Motter Foundation

Moulding, Mary B., secy: Wells Foundation, Lillian S.

Moulton, Carl R., pres: Jessop Steel Co.

Moulton, Franklin F., secy, treas, trust: Van Nuys Charities, J. B. and Emily

Moulton, Hugh G., secy: Alco Standard Foundation

Mountcastle, Katharine Babcock, dir: Babcock Foundation, Mary Reynolds; trust: Reynolds Foundation, Z. Smith

Mountcastle, Katharine Reynolds, dir: Babcock Foundation, Mary Reynolds

Mountcastle, Kenneth F., III, dir: Babcock Foundation, Mary Reynolds

Mountcastle, Kenneth F., Jr., secy, dir: Babcock Foundation, Mary Reynolds; dir: Sears-Roebuck Foundation

Mountcastle, Laura, dir: Babcock Foundation, Mary Reynolds

Mountcastle, Mary, dir: Babcock Foundation, Mary Reynolds; pres, trust: Reynolds Foundation, Z. Smith

Moursund, Travis M., secy, trust: Baumberger Endowment

Mowrer, Gordon B., off: Laros Foundation, R. K.

Moxley, Lucina B., dir: Ball Brothers Foundation

Moye, Michael, pres: Security State Bank

Moyer, R. W., pres, ceo: Wilber National Bank

Moyers, Bill, pres: Schumann Foundation, Florence and John

Moyers, Donald P., vchmn, trust: Mabee Foundation, J. E. and L. E.

Moyers, E. L., chmn, pres, ceo: Illinois Central Railroad Co.

Moyler, J. Edward, Jr., dir: Camp Foundation

Moyles, Denise L., trust: Bourns Foundation

Moynahan, John Daniel, Jr., dir: Metropolitan Life Foundation

Moyse, Hollis Weaver, treas: Wrigley Co. Foundation, Wm. Jr.

Muchin, Allan B., dir: Katten, Muchin, & Zavis Foundation

Mudd, John Philip, vp, dir: Pearce Foundation, Dr. M. Lee

Mudd, Stephen B., vp, dir: Handy & Harman Foundation

Muehlbauer, James Herman, vp, secy, dir: Koch Sons Foundation, George

Mueller, Gerd Dieter, exec vp, cfo, dir: Miles Inc.; pres: Miles Inc. Foundation

Mueller, Jim, sr vp, cfo: Dairymen, Inc.

Mueller, Joseph P., dir: Kenedy Memorial Foundation, John G. and Marie Stella

Mueller, Marvin A., dir: Group Health Foundation

Mueller, Nancy Sue, vp: Kopf Foundation; vp: Kopf Foundation, Elizabeth Christy

Mueller, P. Henry, chmn: Saab Cars USA, Inc.

Mueller, Ronald J., pres: Florsheim Shoe Co.; pres, dir: Florsheim Shoe Foundation

Mueller, Stanley R., dir: Phillips Petroleum Foundation

Mugar, Carolyn G., trust: Azadoutioun Foundation

Mugavero, Fedele, trust: Chapman Foundation, William H.

Muhlenberg, Nicholas, trust: Wyomissing Foundation

Muir, Edward D., trust: McNutt Charitable Trust, Amy Shelton

Muir, James W., coo, exec vp: Circus Circus Enterprises

Muir, Kathleen, dir: Grand Rapids Label Foundation

Muir, Keith H., treas: Westerman Foundation, Samuel L.

Muir, William W., Jr., pres: Grand Rapids Label Co.; pres, dir: Grand Rapids Label Foundation

Muire, Annie S., trust: Richardson Benevolent Foundation, C. E.

Mulcahy, Betty Jane, trust: H.C.S. Foundation

Mulcahy, Kimberly Kennedy, dir: Kennedy Family Foundation, Ethel and W. George

Mulcock, James B., pres, dir: PNM Foundation

Muldowney, John J., treas: Titmus Foundation

Mulford, Donald L., trust: Mulford Foundation, Vincent

Mulford, Vincent, Jr., trust: Mulford Foundation, Vincent

Mulhall, Dennis, cfo: Tomkins Industries, Inc.; vp: Tomkins Corporation Foundation

Mulhearn, Patrick F. X., vp: New York Telephone Co.

Mulholland, Charles Bradley, exec vp, dir: Alexander & Baldwin Foundation

Mulholland, Richard G., dir: Hutchins Foundation, Mary J.

Mulholland, Robert A., treas, dir: Zarrow Foundation, Anne and Henry

Mulkey, Larry S., dir: Ryder System Charitable Foundation

Mullally, Mary, contributions mgr: Michigan Bell Telephone Co.

Mullan, C. Louise, secy: Mullan Foundation, Thomas F. and Clementine L.

Mullan, Charles A., vp: Mullan Foundation, Thomas F. and Clementine L.

Mullan, Joseph, treas: Mullan Foundation, Thomas F. and Clementine L.

Mullan, Thomas F., Jr., pres: Mullan Foundation, Thomas F. and Clementine L.

Mullane, Denis Francis, pres, ceo, dir: CM Alliance Cos.; dir: Connecticut Mutual Life Foundation

Mullane, Donald A., dir: Bank of America - Giannini Foundation; exec vp: BankAmerica Corp.; pres: California Educational Initiatives Fund

Mullane, Robert E., chmn: Bally's - Las Vegas

Mullarkey, Thomas F. X., secy, treas: David-Weill Foundation, Michel

Mullen, Carol, trust: Swasey Fund for Relief of Public School Teachers of Newburyport

Mullen, Charles H., chmn, pres, ceo: American Tobacco Co.

Mullen, Daniel P., vp, treas, dir: Talley Foundation

Mullen, David P., chmn, ceo, dir: Filene's Sons Co., William

Mullen, Donald, treas: Annenberg Foundation

Mullen, F., ceo, pres, dir: American National Bank & Trust Co. of Chicago

Mullen, Gina, asst dir: Sara Lee Foundation

Mullen, Hugh M., dir, treas: Green Foundation, Burton E.

Mullen, Lynda, secy: Rockefeller Foundation

Mullen, Theresa A., exec dir: Jewett Foundation, George Frederick

Mullen, William J., dir: Finnegan Foundation, John D.

Muller, C. John, dir: Muller Foundation, C. John and Josephine

Muller, George T., exec vp, dir: Subaru of America Inc.

Muller, Henry James, trust: Carnegie Corporation of New York

Muller, James, dir: Muller Foundation

Muller, Jean, vp: Index Technology Foundation

Muller, John, treas, dir: Muller Foundation

Muller, John H., Jr., chmn: General Housewares Corp.

Muller, Karen P., exec dir: Fuller Co. Foundation, H.B.

Muller, Sheila, vp: Muller Foundation

Muller, Tim, dir: Muller Foundation

Mullholland, C. Bradley, pres, coo: Matson Navigation Co.

Mulligan, Terrence, dir: Baxter Foundation

Mullin, C. H., trust: Upjohn Foundation, Harold and Grace

Mullin, J. Shan, advisor: Archibald Charitable Foundation, Norman

Mullin, Leo F., exec vp: American National Bank & Trust Co. of Chicago; trust: American National Bank & Trust Co. of Chicago Foundation

Mullin, Peter, ceo, pres: Management Compensation Group/Dulworth Inc.

Mullins, Shelley Dru, trust: Noble Foundation, Samuel Roberts

Mullis, Harold H., dir: Robinson Mountain Fund, E. O.

Mullitz, Shelley G., vp: Gudelsky Family Foundation, Isadore and Bertha

Mulloney, Peter Black, pres, trust: USX Foundation

Mulnix, Frances, trust: Baldwin Foundation

Mulnix, L.V., Jr., trust: Baldwin Foundation

Mulreany, Robert H., secy, trust: Hartford Foundation, John A.; trust: Richardson Foundation, Smith

Mulroney, John Patrick, pres, coo, dir: Rohm and Haas Company

Mulshine, Robert, dir: Price Waterhouse Foundation

Muma, Dorothy E., vchmn, dir: Noyes Foundation, Jessie Smith

Muma, Edith N., dir: Noyes Foundation, Jessie Smith

Mund, Richard Gordon, secy, exec dir: Mobil Foundation

Munder, Barbara A., pres, dir: McGraw-Hill Foundation

Mundt, Ray B., chmn, ceo, dir: Alco Standard Corp.; pres, dir: Alco Standard Foundation

Mundy, Donna, vp, trust: UNUM Charitable Foundation

Munford, Dillard, adv trust: Freedom Forum

Munford, John Durburrow, dir: Camp Foundation

Munger, Charles T., vchmn, dir: Berkshire Hathaway; vp, treas, trust: Booth Foundation, Otis

Munger, Charles Thomas, pres, trust: Munger Foundation, Alfred C.; trust: Sprague, Jr. Foundation, Caryll M. and Norman F.

Munger, D., dir: Union City Body Co. Foundation

Munger, Nancy B., treas, trust: Munger Foundation, Alfred C.

Munger, Sharon M., pres, coo, dir: M/A/R/C Inc.

Munn, Stephen P., pres, ceo: Carlisle Cos.

Munroe, George Barber, dir: New York Times Co. Foundation; dir: Phelps Dodge Foundation

Munroe, Jack F., Jr., mem contributions comm: Burroughs Wellcome Co.

Munroe, Tom, trust: Walker Foundation, L. C. and Margaret

Muns, James N., trust: Bell Trust

Munshower, Stephen A., mem contributions comm: Burroughs Wellcome Co.

Munson, Edwin Palmer, trust: Scott Foundation, William R., John G., and Emma

Munson, W. B., III, gov: Munson Foundation, W. B.

Munts, Polly T., sr program off: Dayton Hudson Foundation

Munyan, Winthrop R., pres: Clark Foundation, Robert Sterling

Munzer, Rudolph James, trust: Jones Foundation, Fletcher

Mura, David, dir: Jerome Foundation

Murakami, Edward S., vp: Jerome Foundation

Murakawi, T., contr: Mitsui & Co. (U.S.A.)

Murata, Ernest, treas: Hawaii National Foundation

Murch, Creighton B., vp, secy, trust: Murch Foundation

Murch, Maynard H., IV, pres, treas, trust: Murch Foundation; chmn: Robbins & Myers, Inc.; chmn: Robbins & Myers Foundation

Murch, Robert B., vp, trust: Murch Foundation

Murchie, Edward, pres, coo, dir: Vernitron Corp.

Murchison, John, II, trust: Davis Charitable Foundation, Champion McDowell

Murdoch, Keith Rupert, chmn: Fox Inc.; chmn: HarperCollins Publishers; chmn: News America Publishing Inc.

Murdock, Daniel R., dir: Donovan, Leisure, Newton & Irvine Foundation

Murdough, Thomas G., trust: Morgan Foundation, Burton D.

Murdy, James L., sr vp (fin), cfo, dir: Allegheny Ludlum Corp.; trust: Allegheny Ludlum Foundation

Murdy, Wayne W., cfo: Apache Corp.

Murfree, Matt B., III, dir: Christy-Houston Foundation

Murfrey, Spencer L., Jr., trust: American Foundation Corporation

Murfrey, William W., trust: American Foundation Corporation

Murphy, Alex, advisory com: Powers Higher Educational Fund, Edward W. and Alice R.

Murphy, Amy B., mem selection comm: Westlake Scholarship Fund, James L. and Nellie M.

Murphy, Barth T., pres, dir: Bankers Life & Casualty Co.

Murphy, Charles E., Jr., vchmn, trust: Hartford Foundation, John A.

Murphy, Charles F., dir: Graco Foundation

Murphy, Charles Haywood, Jr., dir: Murphy Foundation; chmn, dir: Murphy Oil Corp.

Murphy, Christopher J., III, pres, dir: First Source Corp.; vp: First Source Corp. Foundation

Murphy, David R., vp, treas, trust: Johnson Foundation, Helen K. and Arthur E.

Murphy, Diana E., dir: Bush Foundation

Murphy, Donald B., treas: Sofia American Schools

Murphy, Edward, coo: Brooks Brothers

Murphy, Franklin D., trust: Murphy Charitable Fund, George E. and Annette Cross

Murphy, Franklin David, MD, trust: Ahmanson Foundation; chmn, trust: Kress Foundation, Samuel H.

Murphy, Greg, pres, ceo: Entenmann's Inc.

Murphy, Henry L., Jr., admin mgr: Kelley and Elza Kelley Foundation, Edward Bangs

Murphy, James, mem adv comm: Pott Foundation, Herman T. and Phenie R.

Murphy, James F., chmn: Hiram Walker & Sons Inc.

Murphy, James W., vp (corp fin): American United Life Insurance Co.; treas: AUL Foundation

Murphy, Jeffrey John, asst secy: Ryder System Charitable Foundation

Murphy, Jo, dir: Houston Endowment

Murphy, Joellyn, vp, dir: PNM Foundation

Murphy, Johanna, mem adv comm: Ensworth Charitable Foundation

Murphy, John Davis, chmn, dir: Wiremold Co.

Murphy, John Joseph, chmn, ceo, pres: Dresser Industries

Murphy, John Reginald, dir: Truman Foundation, Mildred Faulkner

Murphy, John W., exec dir, asst secy: Flinn Foundation

Murphy, Johnie W., pres, dir: Murphy Foundation

Murphy, Marguerite M., secy, treas: Smith Foundation, Lon V.

Murphy, Mark M., secy, exec dir: Fund for New Jersey

Murphy, Mary Lou, mem: Ragen, Jr. Memorial Fund Trust No. 1, James M.

Murphy, Michael, pres: Kal Kan Foods, Inc.

Murphy, Michael E., dir: Sara Lee Foundation

Murphy, Patrick F., pres, dir: AGA Gas, Inc.

Murphy, R. Madison, exec vp, cfo, dir: Murphy Oil Corp.

Murphy, Raymond R., Jr., secy, dir: Brown Charitable Trust, Dora Maclellan

Murphy, Richard F., trust: EG&G Foundation

Murphy, Robert B., secy, dir: NMC Projects

Murphy, Robert Earl, pres, treas: McMurray-Bennnett Foundation

Murphy, Robert F., Jr., trust: Walsh Charity Trust, Blanche M.

Murphy, Robert G., trust: Chase Manhattan Bank, N.A.

Murphy, Robert H., vchmn, dir: Wiremold Co.

Murphy, Robert L., pres: Holmes & Narver Services Inc.

Murphy, Sue, pub aff rep: Fleet Bank

Murphy, Thomas, chmn: National Car Rental System, Inc.

Murphy, Thomas B., chmn, dir: Spring Arbor Distributors

Murphy, Thomas E., dir: Olmsted Foundation, George and Carol

Murphy, Thomas Sawyer, pres, dir: Buffett Foundation; chmn, dir: Capital Cities/ABC

Murphy, Walter Young, mem scholarship bd: Cobb Educational Fund, Ty; bd mem: Pitts Foundation, William H. and Lula E.

Murphy, William H., pres, coo: Katy Industries Inc.

Murphy, William J., mem adv comm: O'Connor Foundation, A. Lindsay and Olive B.

Murrah, Alfred P., Jr., trust: Sumners Foundation, Hatton W.

Murrah, Jack, pres, trust: Lyndhurst Foundation

Murray, Al, trust: Winship Memorial Scholarship Foundation

Murray, Allen Edward, chmn, pres, ceo: Mobil Oil Corp.

Murray, Arthur G., pres, coo: Sunshine Biscuits

Murray, Arthur W., II, vp, trust: Mellinger Educational Foundation, Edward Arthur

Murray, Bettyann Asche, vp, trust: Vale-Asche Foundation

Murray, Dennis, bd mem: Dain Bosworth/IFG Foundation

Murray, Dennis J., dir: McCann Foundation

Murray, Diana T., dir: Markle Foundation, John and Mary R.

Murray, Douglas P., pres: Lingnan Foundation

Murray, H. R., trust: Amsted Industries Foundation

Murray, Haydn H., trust: Grassmann Trust, E. J.

Murray, Haydn Herbert, trust: Union Foundation

Murray, J. Terrance, dir: Martin Foundation, Bert William

Murray, J. Terrence, chmn, pres, ceo: Fleet Financial Group

Murray, L. T., Jr., vp, dir: Murray Foundation

Murray, Lawrence D., Jr., trust: Mercury Aircraft Foundation

Murray, Michael J., M.D., trust: Wills Foundation

Neibacher, Rev. Albert, trust: Perley Fund, Victor E.

Neier, Aryeh, dir: Open Society Fund

Neikirk, Joseph Randolph, vp, exec dir: Norfolk Southern Foundation

Neill, Mary G., trust: Gardner Foundation

Neilly, Andrew H., Jr., trust: Institute for Research on Learning

Neib, Jeffrey J., treas: Ensign-Bickford Foundation

Nelson, C. William, trust: Griffin, Sr., Foundation, C. V.

Nelson, C.A., chmn: Schlegel Foundation, Oscar C. and Augusta

Nelson, Catherine B., McGraw Foundation

Nelson, Charles, trust: Griffin, Sr., Foundation, C. V.

Nelson, Charles E., dir: Kirkpatrick Foundation

Nelson, Clarence J., secy, trust: Crels Foundation

Nelson, Clark, secy, treas: McBean Family Foundation

Nelson, Clarke A., trust: Stuart Foundation, Elbridge and Evelyn

Nelson, Daniel R., chmn, ceo, dir: West One Bancorp

Nelson, David, vp, grant dir: Houston Endowment

Nelson, David A., chmn, pres, ceo, dir: Amsco International

Nelson, Earl W., chmn, pres: Independent Financial Corp.; trust: Independent Financial Corp. Charitable Trust

Nelson, Edna, trust: Leu Foundation

Nelson, Eric G., vp, trust: Procter & Gamble Fund

Nelson, Frederick, pres: Kaiser Cement Corp.

Nelson, Frederick T., chmn: Associated Foundations

Nelson, Fredric C., dir: Cowell Foundation, S. H.

Nelson, Glen David, M.D., vchmn, dir: Medtronic

Nelson, Grant, cfo: West Publishing Co.

Nelson, H. Alan, trust: Mabee Foundation, J. E. and L. E.

Nelson, H. Joe, III, pres, dir: Houston Endowment

Nelson, Harry, trust: Smith Fund, Horace

Nelson, Helen R., trust: Nelson Foundation, Florence

Nelson, Hugh T., trust: Terry Foundation, C. Herman

Nelson, John M., chmn, ceo: Wyman-Gordon Co.; pres: Wyman-Gordon Foundation

Nelson, Joyce, treas: International Paper Co. Foundation

Nelson, Katherine E., program dir: Danforth Foundation

Nelson, Kent C., chmn, trust: Casey Foundation, Annie E.

Nelson, Kent Charles, chmn, ceo, dir: United Parcel Service of America; chmn: UPS Foundation

Nelson, L. Scott, chmn, pres, ceo, dir: First Security Bank of Utah N.A.

Nelson, Leonard B., dir: McConnell Foundation

Nelson, Lyle Morgan, dir: Hewlett Foundation, William and Flora

Nelson, Marilyn C., vchmn: Carlson Cos.

Nelson, Maurice, trust: Woodward Governor Co. Charitable Trust

Nelson, Merlin, chmn: IBJ Foundation

Nelson, Nancy A., treas: Foster-Davis Foundation

Nelson, Nancy J., asst secy: Meadows Foundation

Nelson, Nels A., Jr., trust: Whitney Benefits

Nelson, P. Erik, exec dir: Copernicus Society of America

Nelson, Robert B., trust, secy: Laub Foundation

Nelson, Robert N., treas: KIHI/21 International Holding Foundation

Nelson, Ronald D., cfo: Scoular Co.; secy-treas: Scoular Foundation

Nelson, Ronald G., vp, treas: Dial Corporation Fund

Nelson, Roy, secy: Waffle House Foundation

Nelson, Stuart K., trust: Bernstein & Co. Foundation, Sanford C.

Nelson, Thomas G., dir: Guaranty Bank & Trust Co. Charitable Trust

Nelson, Thomas P., trust: General Mills Foundation

Nelson, W.O., Jr., dir: Luck Stone Foundation

Nelson, Wilbur, Jr., trust: Clarke Trust, John

Nelson, William, dir: AMCORE Foundation, Inc.

Nelson, William A., vp, trust: Presto Foundation

Nelson, William E., vp: Kikkoman Foods, Inc.

Nelson, William F., Jr., trust: Wickes Foundation, Harvey Randall

Nelson-Heathrow, Larry W., dir, treas: Paulucci Family Foundation

Nemchik, Rita, dir: Diabetes Research and Education Foundation

Nemer, Stanley, vp, secy, treas, dir: Fingerhut Family Foundation

Nemetz, Marion, dir: Mielke Family Foundation

Nemirow, Arnold M., pres, ceo: Wausau Paper Mills Co.

Neppl, Walter Joseph, trust: Dodge Foundation, Geraldine R.

Nerren, Evonne, vp: Temple-Inland Foundation

Nesbeda, Lucy, trust, don granddaughter: Clark Foundation, Edna McConnell

Nesbeda, Lucy H., pres: Island Foundation

Nesbeda, Peter J., corporator: Island Foundation

Nesholm, John F., pres, dir: Nesholm Family Foundation

Nesholm, Laurel, exec dir: Nesholm Family Foundation

Ness, Howard L., trust: Baumker Charitable Foundation, Elsie and Harry

Nessier, Stephen, trust: Witter Foundation, Dean

Nestor, Alexander R., trust, vp: Jones and Bessie D. Phelps Foundation, Cyrus W. and Amy F.; chmn, pres, trust: Jost Foundation, Charles and Mabel P.

Netek, Rudolph, asst secy, treas: Coral Reef Foundation

Nethercutt, Dorothy S., vp, dir: Norman/Nethercutt Foundation, Merle

Nethercutt, Jack B., pres, dir: Norman/Nethercutt Foundation, Merle

Nett, Roy, treas, dir: Ogle Foundation, Paul

Netzer, Dick, pres: Gottlieb Foundation, Adolph and Esther

Netzer, Leon, vchmn: Jewish Healthcare Foundation of Pittsburgh

Neu, Doris, pres, treas, dir: Neu Foundation, Hugo and Doris

Neu, John L., vp, secy, dir: Neu Foundation, Hugo and Doris

Neu, Richard W., exec vp, cfo: First Federal of Michigan; vp, dir: Neu Foundation, Hugo and Doris

Neubauer, Joseph, chmn, pres, ceo, dir: ARA Services

Neuberger, James A., vp, dir: Neuberger Foundation, Roy R. and Marie S.

Neuberger, Marie S., vp, dir: Neuberger Foundation, Roy R. and Marie S.

Neuberger, Roy R., pres, treas, dir: Neuberger Foundation, Roy R. and Marie S.

Neuberger, Roy S., vp, dir: Neuberger Foundation, Roy R. and Marie S.

Neuenfeldt, Bonnie, community rels dir: Land O'Lakes

Neuerman, Marc, dir: Brand Cos. Charitable Foundation

Neufeld, D.H., pres: Copolymer Foundation

Neuharth, Allen Harold, chmn: Freedom Forum

Neuhauser, Raymond, trust: Harvest States Foundation

Neuhoff, Edward D., trust: Cord Foundation, E. L.

Neuman, Gerald David, mgr: Newbrook Charitable Foundation

Neumann, Roland M., trust: Brotz Family Foundation, Frank G.

Neumann, Roland M., Jr., treas, dir: Windway Foundation, Inc.

Neumer, Steven M., dir: Katten, Muchin, & Zavis Foundation

Neun, Carl W., sr vp, cfo: Conner Peripherals

Neustadt, Richard M., gen coun, treas, dir: Benton Foundation

Neuwirth, Gloria S., secy: Turner Fund, Ruth

Neville, James Morton, mem (bd control): Ralston Purina Trust Fund

Neville, Whit N., Jr., asst secy, asst treas: Fletcher Foundation, A. J.

Neville, William, mgr: Luckyday Foundation

Nevins, Elizabeth P., trust: Burnham Donor Fund, Alfred G.

Nevins, John A., secy, treas: Model Foundation, Leo

Nevius, Blake Reynolds, dir: Scott Foundation, Virginia Steele

Nevius, John A., dir: Strong Foundation, Hattie M.

Newbegin, Kenneth R., pres, co-publ: Salem News Publishing Co.

Newbegin, William B., Salem News Publishing Co.

Newberger, May W., dir: Levitt Foundation

Newbery, Charles C., vp: Mostyn Foundation

Newburg, Elsie V., trust: Gould Foundation for Children, Edwin

Newburger, Frank Lieberman, Jr., vp, dir: Federation Foundation of Greater Philadelphia

Newbury, Nathan, III, trust: Killam Trust, Constance; trust: Rodgers Trust, Elizabeth Killam

Newbury, Sarah, dir: Clipper Ship Foundation

Newcom, Jennings J., dir: Hubbard Foundation, R. Dee and Joan Dale

Newcomb, David R., dir: Utica National Group Foundation

Newcomb, Margaret P., trust: Knapp Foundation

Newcomer, Arthur S., secy, trust: Markey Charitable Fund, John C.

Newell, David, vp pub aff: Fidelity Bank

Newell, Frank William, MD, chmn, dir: Heed Ophthalmic Foundation

Newhall, George, pres, dir: Newhall Foundation, Henry Mayo

Newhall, Henry K., dir: McBean Family Foundation

Newhall, Jane, dir: Newhall Foundation, Henry Mayo

Newhall, John B., vp, dir: Clipper Ship Foundation; trust: Killam Trust, Constance; treas: Ladd Charitable Corporation, Helen and George

Newhall, John Breed, trust: Rodgers Trust, Elizabeth Killam

Newhall, Jon, vp, dir: Newhall Foundation, Henry Mayo

Newhall, Roger, dir: Newhall Foundation, Henry Mayo

Newhall, Scott, dir: Newhall Foundation, Henry Mayo

Newhouse, Donald Edward, vp, secy: Newhouse Foundation, Samuel I.

Newhouse, Samuel I., Jr., chmn: Conde Nast Publications, Inc.; pres, treas: Newhouse Foundation, Samuel I.

Newkam, Scott J., cfo: Hershey Entertainment & Resort Co.

Newkirk, Judith A., vp, treas, trust: Durfee Foundation

Newkirk, Michael, trust: Durfee Foundation

Newland, Hope R., dir: Deluxe Corp. Foundation; trust: Hotchkiss Foundation, W. R.

Newlin, George W., dir: Irwin-Sweeney- Miller Foundation

Newman, Allen, ceo: Key Food Stores Cooperative Inc.; trust, dir: Key Food Stores Foundation

Newman, Andrew Edison, chmn, ceo, dir: Edison Brothers Stores; dir: Edison Brothers Stores Foundation

Newman, Elizabeth L., vp, dir: Newman Assistance Fund, Jerome A. and Estelle R.

Newman, Eric Pfeiffer, pres, dir: Edison Foundation, Harry

Newman, Frances Moody, chmn, trust: Moody Foundation

Newman, Frank H., dir: Moriah Fund

Newman, Frank N., vchmn, ceo, dir: Bank of America

Newman, Frank Neil, vchmn, cfo, treas, dir: BankAmerica Corp.

Newman, Gordon Harold, vp, secy: Sara Lee Foundation

Newman, H. S., pres, coo, dir: Indiana Insurance Cos.

Newman, Harold J., dir: Hertz Foundation, Fannie and John

Newman, Howard A., chmn, dir: Newman Assistance Fund, Jerome A. and Estelle R.

Newman, John M., chmn, dir: Finnegan Foundation, John D.

Newman, Jule M., pres, trust: Livingston Foundation, Milton S. and Corinne N.

Newman, Louise K., trust: Smith Charitable Foundation, Lou and Lutza

Newman, M. S., trust: Marquette Electronics Foundation

Newman, Martha S., pres, trust: Hartford Courant Foundation

Newman, Miriam A., trust: Arnold Fund

Newman, Murray H., trust: Livingston Foundation, Milton S. and Corinne N.

Newman, Paul L., co-chmn: Newman's Own; pres, dir, don: Newman's Own Foundation

Newman, Raquel H., trust: Newman Charitable Trust, Calvin M. and Raquel H.

Newman, Stephanie K., trust: New York Foundation

Newman, William C., pres, dir: Newman Assistance Fund, Jerome A. and Estelle R.

Newmarch, Michael G., chmn: Jackson National Life Insurance Co.

Newton, Alice Faye, secy: Humana Foundation

Newton, Charles, pres, dir: Scott Foundation, Virginia Steele

Newton, Jack E., dir: DCB Foundation; dir: Jasper Wood Products Co. Foundation

Newton, John T., chmn, pres, ceo, dir: Kentucky Utilities Co.

Newton, Sally A., asst treas, asst secy: Wisconsin Energy Corp. Foundation

Ney, Dr. Lillian V., dir: Gebbie Foundation

Ney, Edward, dir: Mattel Foundation

Ng, Henry, chief adm off, treas: Kaplan Fund, J. M.

Niarakis, Ursula C., pres: Hoffman Foundation, Marion O. and Maximilian

Niblock, W.R., pres: Porter Paint Foundation

Nicandros, Constantine S., pres, ceo, dir: Conoco Inc.

Nicastro, Francis E., trust: Colonial Stores Foundation

Nicholas, C. R., cfo: Andrew Corp.

Nicholas, Colombe, pres: Christian Dior New York, Inc.

Nicholas, Diane, dir: Lizzadro Family Foundation, Joseph

Nichols, C. Walter, III, treas, dir: Nichols Foundation

Nichols, Carlton E., Jr., trust: Stone Fund, Albert H. and Reuben A.

Nichols, Carlton E., Sr., trust: Stone Fund, Albert H. and Reuben A.

Nichols, David H., vp, dir: Nichols Foundation

Nichols, David L., chmn, ceo: Mercantile Stores Co.

Nichols, H. Gilman, pres, ceo, dir: Fiduciary Trust Co.

O'Sullivan, Benjamin C., trust: Holtzmann Foundation, Jacob L. and Lillian

O'Sullivan, Carole, vp, treas: O'Sullivan Children Foundation

O'Sullivan, Emmet P., pres, ceo: Modern Maid Food Products, Inc.

O'Sullivan, Kevin P., dir, pres: O'Sullivan Children Foundation

O'Toole, Austin Martin, secy: ANR Foundation

O'Toole, Lawrence W., pres: Nellie Mae

O'Toole, Robert J., dir: Firstar Milwaukee Foundation; pres, ceo, chmn: Smith Corp., A.O.; vp: Smith Foundation, A.O.

Oakes, John Bertram, dir: Axe-Houghton Foundation

Oakes, R. K., dir: Aladdin Industries Foundation

Oakley, Allen M., dir: Oakley-Lindsay Foundation of Quincy Newspapers & Quincy Broadcasting Co.

Oakley, David, dir: Oakley-Lindsay Foundation of Quincy Newspapers & Quincy Broadcasting Co.

Oakley, Peter A., secy, dir: Oakley-Lindsay Foundation of Quincy Newspapers & Quincy Broadcasting Co.

Oakley, Thomas A., pres: Quincy Newspapers; pres, dir: Oakley-Lindsay Foundation of Quincy Newspapers & Quincy Broadcasting Co.

Oana, Yuko, chmn: CIT Group Holdings

Oates, Dennis, sr vp: Lukens

Oatsman, Thomas A., dir, treas: Winship Memorial Scholarship Foundation

Obasanjo, Olusegun, trust: Ford Foundation

Obayashi, Becky, corp contributions admin: San Diego Gas & Electric

Obayashi, Yoshiro, chmn: Obayashi America Corp.

Ober, Gayle M., vp, dir: Mardag Foundation

Ober, Richard B., treas, dir: Mardag Foundation

Ober, Timothy M., dir: Mardag Foundation

Oberbeck, Christian L., trust: SharonSteel Foundation

Oberkotter, Paul, trust emeritus: Casey Foundation, Annie E.

Obernauer, Joan S., dir, vp: Obernauer Foundation

Obernauer, Marne, dir, pres: Obernauer Foundation

Obernauer, Marne, Jr., chmn, ceo, dir: Devon Group; vp, dir: Obernauer Foundation

Oberndorf, Joseph, Cassett Foundation, Louis N.

Oberwetter, Jim, vp govt aff: Hunt Oil Co.

Oberzut, Lorraine, mgr (corporate pub affairs): Unisys Corp.

Obolensky, Ivan, pres, treas, dir: Hopkins Foundation, Josephine Lawrence

Obrow, Norman C., trust: Civitas Fund; pres, dir: Drown Foundation, Joseph

Obser, Fred, trust: Heckscher Foundation for Children

Occhipinti, Raymond A., treas: Robinson Fund, Maurice R.

Ochiltree, Ned A., Jr., trust: Meyer-Ceco Foundation

Ochoa, Hilda, mem fin comm: Rockefeller Family Fund

Ochs, Gail J., vp, bd mem: First Fruit

Ochs, Peter M., pres, bd mem: First Fruit

Ockene, Alan L., pres, ceo: General Tire Inc.

Ockerbloom, Richard C., pres, coo: Globe Newspaper Co.

Ockers, Paul H., trust: Shaw Fund for Mariner's Children

Odahowski, David A., pres: Bush Charitable Foundation, Edyth; dir: Wasie Foundation

Oddo, Nancy E., vp, dir: Dreyfus Foundation, Max and Victoria

Odeen, Phillip A., dir: BDM International

Odelgard, Richard E., pres: Seafirst Foundation

Odem, Martha, trust: Ware Foundation

Odgers, Richard W., secy, dir: Pacific Telesis Foundation

Odom, F. A., dir: Seibel Foundation, Abe and Annie

Odom, William E., mem bd govs: Richardson Foundation, Smith

Oehme, Richard B., trust: UPS Foundation

Oehmig, Daniel W., trust: Westend Foundation

Oehmig, L.W., pres, trust: Westend Foundation

Oehmig, Margaret W., vp: Cain Foundation, Gordon and Mary

Oehmig, William C., secy, treas, cfo: Cain Foundation, Gordon and Mary

Oelbaum, Harold, pres: Kane-Miller Corp.

Oelman, Bradford Coolidge, chmn contributions comm: Owens-Corning Fiberglas Corp.

Oelman, Robert S., trust: Grimes Foundation

Oelsner, John W., dir: Phillips Foundation, Ellis L.

Oenslager, Mary P., trust: Schenck Fund, L. P.

Oeschger, E.H., vp: Wigwam Mills Fund

Oess, George, pres, ceo: Western Publishing Co., Inc.

Oesterreicher, James E., pres: JCPenney Co.

Oestreicher, Ann, pres, dir: Oestreicher Foundation, Sylvan and Ann

Offenberg, William, pres, gen mgr: Spectra-Physics Analytical

Office, Gerald S., Jr., chmn, pres: Ponderosa, Inc.

Offield, Edna Jean, vp, dir: Offield Family Foundation

Offield, James S., dir: Offield Family Foundation

Offield, Paxson H., dir: Offield Family Foundation

Offutt, James A., dir: Shelter Insurance Foundation

Offutt, Madeleine M., Mather Charitable Trust, S. Livingston

Ogan, Mark, pres: Oster/Sunbeam Appliance Co.

Ogburn, W. Gary, trust: Fuld Health Trust, Helene; vp: Killough Trust, Walter H. D.

Ogden, Alfred, dir: Guggenheim Foundation, Daniel and Florence

Ogden, K. S., pres: Global Van Lines

Ogden, R. L., dir: Liberty Corp. Foundation

Ogden, Scott, chmn: Global Van Lines

Ogle, Elizabeth C., vp, trust: Beloco Foundation; trust: Bradley-Turner Foundation

Ogilivie, Donna Brace, trust: Brace Foundation, Donald C.

Ogilvy, David, founder, dir: Ogilvy Foundation

Oglesby, Mary Norris Preyer, trust: Preyer Fund, Mary Norris

Ogrodnik, Richard W., treas, dir: Key Bank of Central Maine Foundation

Ohashi, Hitoshi, dir: Toshiba America Foundation

Ohlig, Charles J., ceo, chmn: Greater New York Savings Bank

Ohman, Richard W., chmn, pres, ceo: Colonial Penn Group, Inc.

Ohnmacht, Susan, secy: Sams Foundation, Earl C.

Ohrstrom, George Lewis, Jr., asst secy, trust: Ohrstrom Foundation

Ohrstrom, Ricard Riggs, Jr., vp, trust: Ohrstrom Foundation

Oishei, Julian R., mem: Julia R. and Estelle L. Foundation

Okada, Alan, vp (health programs): Citicorp

Oken, Loretta M., adm: Heinz Co. Foundation, H.J.

Okieffe, Patricia S., trust: Simpson Foundation, John M.

Okinow, Harold, treas, dir: Lieberman-Okinow Foundation

Okonak, James R., trust, secy: McFeely-Rogers Foundation

Okorow, Dale S., cfo: HMK Enterprises

Okumura, Masaya, dir: Toshiba America Foundation

Olander, Chris K., exec dir, asst treas: JM Foundation

Olander, Ray Gunmar, vchmn, chief legal & commercial off, dir: Bucyrus-Erie

Olberding, David L., trust: Dater Foundation, Charles H.

Oldfield, Joseph, trust: Polaroid Foundation

Oldham, Mary E., asst secy: Brown Foundation

Oldham, Theodore H., Earl-Beth Foundation

Oldland, Jerry, comm: Fairfield-Meeker Charitable Trust, Freeman E.

Olds, Astrida R., asst vp, exec dir: Connecticut Mutual Life Foundation

Olds, Jane Fagan, pres, trust: Irwin Charity Foundation, William G.

Olds, William Lee, Jr., vp, trust: Irwin Charity Foundation, William G.

Oleck, Estelle, Zarkin Memorial Foundation, Charles

Olesen, Douglas Eugene, pres, ceo: Battelle

Oleson, Frances M., trust: Oleson Foundation

Oleson, Gerald W., pres: Oleson Foundation

Olfe, D. C., vp, secy, dir: Valspar Foundation

Oliensis, Sheldon, trust: Kaye Foundation

Olincy, Dan, secy, treas, trust: Norman Foundation, Andrew

Olincy, Virginia G., pres, trust: Norman Foundation, Andrew

Oliphant, Charles W., chmn, dir: Cuesta Foundation

Oliphant, Eric B., pres, dir: Cuesta Foundation

Oliphant, Gertrude O., trust: Cuesta Foundation

Oliva, George, III, trust: Perkins Charitable Foundation

Olive, G. Scott, Jr., treas: Metropolitan Health Council of Indianapolis

Oliveira, George, trust: Citizens Charitable Foundation

Oliver, A. Gordon, pres, ceo: Citizens & Southern National Bank of Florida

Oliver, Ann, dir: Osceola Foundation

Oliver, Christine Bireley, vp: Bireley Foundation

Oliver, Garrett, dir: Bridwell Foundation, J. S.

Oliver, Harry Maynard, Jr., secy: Pullman Educational Foundation, George M.

Oliver, James, trust: Heath Foundation, Ed and Mary

Oliver, Joseph W., trust: Heinz Endowment, Howard

Oliver, Louise, trust: Coleman, Jr. Foundation, George E.; dir: Donner Foundation, William H.

Oliver, Roberta M., secy-treas: Hesston Foundation

Olivetti, Alfred, vp, dir: Olivetti Foundation

Olivetti, Philip, vp, dir: Olivetti Foundation

Olivetti, Rosamond, pres, dir: Olivetti Foundation

Olivia, Gertrude, Cherokee Foundation

Olliff, Charleen, secy: Community Health Association

Olmsted, Carol S., dir: Olmsted Foundation, George and Carol

Olmsted, George Hamden, dir: Olmsted Foundation, George and Carol

Olmsted, Robert M., dir: Bunbury Company

Olofson, Elizabeth, exec dir: Guttman Foundation, Stella and Charles

Olrogg, Elgin E., vp, dir: Cheney Foundation, Ben B.

Olschwang, Alan P., secy: Mitsubishi Electric America Foundation

Olsen, Charles, off: Grenfell Association of America

Olsen, David Alexander, chmn, ceo: Johnson & Higgins

Olsen, Eeva-Liisa Aulikki, trust: Stratford Foundation

Olsen, Harold B., Jr., dir: Mobil Foundation

Olsen, Harry G., cfo, vp: Delco Electronics Corp.

Olsen, John Robert, trust: Templeton Foundation, Herbert A.

Olsen, John V., pres: Abitibi Co.

Olsen, Kenneth H., don, trust: Stratford Foundation

Olsen, T. F., chmn: Timex Corp.

Olsen, Thomas, trust: Kelley and Elza Kelley Foundation, Edward Bangs

Olsen, William G., trust: Associated Foundations

Olson, A. Craig, cfo: Albertson's

Olson, Amy, trust: DAO Foundation

Olson, Beverly Knight, trust: Knight Foundation, John S. and James L.

Olson, Dean A., II, chmn: Rockford Acromatics Products Co./Aircraft Gear Corp.

Olson, Gaylord, trust: CENEX Foundation

Olson, Gene, sr vp, cfo: Golden State Foods Corp.

Olson, Gilbert N., dir: Leach Foundation, Tom & Frances

Olson, Gregory L., secy: DeKalb Genetics Foundation

Olson, Keith D., secy, treas: Bayport Foundation

Olson, Nancy N., trust: DAO Foundation

Olson, Nobel, trust: DAO Foundation

Olson, Pat, trust: DAO Foundation

Olson, Paul M., pres: Blandin Foundation

Olson, R. Thomas, secy, dir: Glaser Foundation

Olson, Russel E., mem contributions comm: Puget Sound Power & Light Co.

Olson, Steven C., Jr., trust: Tiger Foundation

Olsson, John, trust: Cooper Foundation

Olsson, Shirley C., vp, treas, trust: Olsson Memorial Foundation, Elis

Olsson, Sture Gordon, trust: Chesapeake Corporate Foundation; pres, trust: Olsson Memorial Foundation, Elis

Olsten, Stuart, pres, coo: Olsten Corp.

Olsten, William, chmn: Olsten Corp.

Olvey, Daniel R., vp, secy, treas, dir: Wausau Paper Mills Foundation

Olwell, Margaret D., mem: Bamberger and John Ernest Bamberger Memorial Foundation, Ruth Eleanor

Olwell, William H., secy, treas, mem: Bamberger and John Ernest Bamberger Memorial Foundation, Ruth Eleanor

Oman, Norma J., pres, ceo: Meridian Insurance Group Inc.

Oman, Richard Heer, secy: Reinberger Foundation

Omaru, Mikio, dir: Mitsubishi Electric America Foundation

Onan, David W., II, pres, treas, trust: Onan Family Foundation

Onan, David W., III, trust: Onan Family Foundation

Onan, Lois C., trust: Onan Family Foundation

Onderdonk, Andrew Michael, trust: Jordan Charitable Trust, Martha Annie

Ong, John Doyle, chmn, ceo, dir: BFGoodrich; chmn: BFGoodrich Foundation; McFawn Trust No. 2, Lois Sisler; Ritchie Memorial Foundation, Charies E. and Mabel M.

Onstott, Marilyn, secy, treas: White Foundation, Erle and Emma

Onstott, Steve, dir: White Foundation, Erle and Emma

Opham, David L., secy distribution comm: Ford and Ada Ford Fund, S. N.

Oppenheim, David J., pres, dir: Dreyfus Foundation, Max and Victoria

Oppenheim, Paula K., vp, secy, treas, dir: Klau Foundation, David W. and Sadie

Oppenheimer, Deanna, mem: Washington Mutual Savings Bank Foundation

Oppenheimer, Edward H., pres: Oppenheimer Family Foundation

Oppenheimer, Gerald H., pres, dir: Stein Foundation, Jules and Doris

Oppenheimer, Hamilton G., dir: Stein Foundation, Jules and Doris

Oppenheimer, Harry D., vp, treas: Oppenheimer Family Foundation

Oppenheimer, James K., vp: Oppenheimer Family Foundation

Oppenheimer, James R., trust: Blandin Foundation; dir: Tozer Foundation

Oppenheimer, Jessie Halff, asst secy: Meyer Foundation, Alice Kleberg Reynolds

Oppenheimer, John, dir, secy, treas: Burnham Donor Fund, Alfred G.

Oppenheimer, Mildred, dir: Weight Watchers Foundation

Opperman, Dwight D., pres, ceo: West Publishing Co.

Oram, John, pres: ICC Industries

Orchard, Jack, secy-treas: Orchard Foundation

Orchard, Lois, vp: Orchard Foundation

Orchard, Robert H., chmn, dir: Orchard Corp. of America.; pres: Orchard Foundation

Orcutt, Gilbert F., pres, treas, dir: Northen, Mary Moody

Orden, Ted, pres: Thrifty Oil Co.

Orders, William H., trust: Symmes Foundation, F. W.

Oreffice, Paul Fausto, chmn, dir: Dow Chemical Co.; trust: Gerstacker Foundation, Rollin M.

Orendorf, Jo Tilden, Ogden College Fund

Oresman, Donald, trust: Colt Foundation, James J.; trust: Paramount Communications Foundation

Orick, Millard, trust: Hervey Foundation

Oriel, Patrick J., trust: Pardee Foundation, Elsa U.

Orlando, Philip A., asst vp: M/A-COM Charitable Foundation

Orlando, Robert, asst treas: Chesebrough Foundation

Orlikoff, Richard, secy: Herald Newspapers Foundation

Orman, Traci, vp (commun rels): PNC Bank

Ormsby, David G., secy: Gear Motions Foundation

Ormsby, Priscilla, secy, dir: Key Bank of Central Maine Foundation

Ormseth, Milo, trust: Tucker Charitable Trust, Rose E.

Orr, David, dir: Noyes Foundation, Jessie Smith

Orr, Dudley W., trust: Jameson Trust, Oleonda

Orr, James F., III, pres: Colonial Life & Accident Insurance Co.; pres: UNUM Corp.; pres, trust: UNUM Charitable Foundation

Orr, Sam W., Jr., chmn, dir: Wausau Paper Mills Co.; dir: Wausau Paper Mills Foundation

Orr, San W., Jr., chmn: Mosinee Paper Corp.; vp, dir: Mosinee Paper Corp. Foundation

Orr, San Watterson, Jr., treas, dir: Woodson Foundation, Aytchmonde

Orr, Susan Packard, vp, trust: Packard Foundation, David and Lucile

Orr, Tilda R., secy: Schwartz Foundation, Bernard Lee

Orscheln, Donald W., chmn, dir: Orscheln Co.; secy: Orscheln Industries Foundation

Orscheln, Gerald A., pres: Orscheln Industries Foundation

Orscheln, Phillip A., vp: Orscheln Industries Foundation

Orscheln, W. L., treas: Orscheln Industries Foundation

Orser, James S., trust: UNUM Charitable Foundation

Orser, William S., exec vp (nuclear generation): Carolina Power & Light Co.

Orswell, Lois, dir, pres: Bafflin Foundation

Orta, Phyllis, mgr: Revlon Foundation

Ortenberg, Arthur, don, trust, dir: Claiborne Art Ortenberg Foundation, Liz

Ortenberg, Elisabeth Claiborne, don, dir, trust: Claiborne Art Ortenberg Foundation, Liz

Orthwein, P.B., vchmn, treas: Thor Industries, Inc.

Ortino, Hector R., exec vp, cfo: Ferro Corp.; vp, trust: Ferro Foundation

Ortiz, Ana, dir: Harris Bank Foundation

Osborn, Donald Robert, secy, treas, dir: Milbank Foundation, Dunlevy

Osborn, Guy A., pres, coo: Universal Foods Corp.; pres, dir: Universal Foods Foundation

Osborn, June Elaine, MD, trust: Kaiser Family Foundation, Henry J.

Osborne, C. M., dir: Hotchkiss Foundation, W. R.

Osborne, Charles M., dir: Deluxe Corp. Foundation

Osborne, Dee S., trust: McCullough Foundation, Ralph H. and Ruth J.

Osborne, James L., chmn: Oregon Mutual Insurance Co.

Osborne, John M., trust: Chipman-Union Foundation

Osborne, Ray C., trust: Bay Branch Foundation

Osborne, Richard de Jongh, chmn, pres, ceo, dir: ASARCO; dir: ASARCO Foundation

Osborne, Robert C., secy, treas: Puett Foundation, Nelson

Osborne, Robert E., dir: Knudsen Foundation, Tom and Valley

Osborne, Robert S., treas, secy: Kirkland & Ellis Foundation

Osgood, Edward H., chmn, pres, trust: Levy Foundation, June Rockwell

Osgood, Kay M., trust: Monroe Auto Equipment Foundation Trust

Osheowitz, Michael W., pres, treas, trust: Gould Foundation for Children, Edwin

Osher, Barbro, pres: Osher Foundation, Bernard

Osher, Bernard A., treas: Osher Foundation, Bernard

Osheron, Shepard D., off: Atalanta/Sosnoff Charitable Foundation

Oshman Efron, Jeanette, chmn, dir: Oshman's Sporting Goods, Inc.

Osiecki, Clarice, mem distr comm: Meserve Memorial Fund, Albert and Helen

Oskins, J. C., treas: Koch Sons Foundation, George

Osmond, Gordon C., dir: Donovan, Leisure, Newton & Irvine Foundation

Osnos, Gilbert, pres: Webcraft Technologies

Osteen, Carolyn M., clerk: River Road Charitable Corporation; mem: Shaw Fund for Mariner's Children

Ostergard, Paul Michael, vp, dir (corporate contributions): Citicorp

Osterhoff, James Marvin, treas: US WEST Foundation

Osterloh, Wellington F., dir pub rels: Coastal Corp.

Ostern, Rolf, pres: Ostern Foundation

Ostler, Clyde, vchmn: Wells Fargo & Co.

Ostling, Paul James, pres: Ernst & Young Foundation

Ostrow, Barnett D., chmn: LeaRonal, Inc.

Ostrow, Jack M., cfo: Alpert Foundation, Herb; treas: Moss Foundation

Ostrow, Ronald F., pres, ceo, coo: LeaRonal, Inc.

Oswald, Charles W., chmn, ceo: National Computer Systems

Oswald, Ellen, mem: Smart Family Foundation

Oswalt, William, trust: Vicksburg Foundation

Otake, Yoshiki, vchmn AFLAC Intl: AFLAC

Otani, Tim, program adm: Washington Mutual Savings Bank Foundation

Otero, Carlos, asst dir: Piper Foundation, Minnie Stevens

Otis, James, Jr., trust: Graham Foundation for Advanced Studies in the Fine Arts

Otis, Kimberly, exec dir: Hunt Alternatives Fund

Otjen, Carl N., trust: Demmer Foundation, Edward U.

Otsuka, Jeanette Y., allocation comm: Kawabe Memorial Fund

Ott, Alan W., trust: Gerstacker Foundation, Rollin M.; trust: Pardee Foundation, Elsa U.

Ottaway, James Haller, Jr., sr vp, dir: Dow Jones & Co.; mem adv comm: Dow Jones Foundation

Ottenstein, Adam S., trust: Ottenstein Family Foundation

Ottenstein, Paul F., trust: Ottenstein Family Foundation

Ottenstein, Victor H., trust: Ottenstein Family Foundation

Ottinber, Betty A., dir: Winslow Foundation

Otto, Diether B., chmn, ceo: Burron Medical

Otto, Norman A., trust, pres: Cox Foundation, James M.

Otto, Peter, vchmn: Lehigh Portland Cement Co.

Ouchi, Rev. Sadamori, allocation comm: Kawabe Memorial Fund

Ousley, Joann, mem trust fund comm: Ingram Trust, Joe

Oustalet, A. J. M., trust: Zigler Foundation, Fred B. and Ruth B.

Overbaugh, Joseph, dir: AMP Foundation

Overby, Charles L., pres, ceo, trust: Freedom Forum

Overholt, J. C., vchmn, dir: Freeport Brick Co. Charitable Trust

Overlock, Willard J., Jr., trust: Boisi Family Foundation

Overstreet, Mildred, trust: Overstreet Foundation

Overstrom, Gunnar S., Jr., pres, coo: Shawmut National Corp.

Overton, Carter, trust: Terry Foundation

Overton, Francine, sr staff adv (human res): Ringier-America

Ovitz, J.D., dir, secy: Wurlitzer Foundation, Farny R.

Ovrom, Arthur P., treas: Van Buren Foundation

Owada, Takeshi, pres: TDK Corp. of America

Owen, Brian T., vp, treas, dir: Sonesta Charitable Foundation

Owen, C. Leevon, vp: Burns International Foundation

Owen, Claude B., Jr., chmn, ceo, dir: Dibrell Brothers, Inc.

Owen, Dolores C., trust: Owen Foundation

Owen, E.F., chmn: Owen Industries, Inc.

Owen, Edward F., pres, trust: Owen Foundation

Owen, Elizabeth Laviers, vp, trust: LaViers Foundation, Harry and Maxie

Owen, Gene V., trust: Mayer Foundation, James and Eva

Owen, George A., mgr, trust: Crane Foundation, Raymond E. and Ellen F.

Owen, Harry, pres, treas, dir: Foellinger Foundation

Owen, Jack W., trust: Johnson Foundation, Robert Wood

Owen, James Churchill, trust: Bancroft, Jr. Foundation, Hugh

Owen, John J., trust: Love Charitable Foundation, John Allan

Owen, Richard F., trust: Owen Foundation

Owen, Robert E., vp, trust: Owen Foundation

Owen, Rosalyn, secy: Medina Foundation

Owen, Terry, pres, ceo: Champion Products, Inc.

Owen, William I, dir: Utilicorp United Charitable Foundation

Owens, August I., Childress Foundation, Francis and Miranda

Owens, Jack B., vp, gen couns: Ernest & Julio Gallo Winery; asst secy: Gallo Foundation

Owens, James, vp, cfo: MPB Corp.

Owens, James B., treas: Gallo Foundation, Julio R.

Owens, Kenneth R., vp: Pickett and Hatcher Educational Fund

Owens, Maureen A., vp: Goldome Foundation

Owens, Samuel H., treas: St. Giles Foundation

Owsley, Alvin, chmn, dir: Ball Corp.; gen mgr, trust: Owsley Foundation, Alvin and Lucy

Owsley, David Thomas, trust: Owsley Foundation, Alvin and Lucy

Oxler, Ann Bixby, trust: Reynolds Foundation, J. B.

Oxman, David, off: Grenfell Association of America

Oxman, David C., dir: Coral Reef Foundation; secy: Jurodin Fund

Oxman, Phyllis S., vp: Plant Memorial Fund, Henry B.

Oyler, Robert B., pres: Rice Foundation, Ethel and Raymond F.

Ozinga, Kenneth, pres, ceo: First National Bank of Evergreen Park

Ozinga, Martin, chmn: First National Bank of Evergreen Park

Ozinga, Martin, Jr., trust: First Evergreen Foundation

Ozley, Marvin W., chmn, pres, ceo: Sealright Co., Inc.

Ozorkiewicz, Ralph L., pres, coo: Wyle Laboratories

P

Pabor, Louis, trust: Woltman Foundation, B. M.

Pace, Glenn L., chmn, exec comm: Swanson Family Foundation, Dr. W.C.

Pace, James C., Jr., trust: Inman-Riverdale Foundation

Pace, Joann N., pres: Norris Foundation, Dellora A. and Lester J.

Pachacek, Ginger, asst secy, asst treas: Moss Foundation, Harry S.

Pacheco, Alberto, dir, vp: Clover Foundation

Packard, Charles, trust: Argyros Foundation

Packard, David, chmn bd: Hewlett-Packard Co.; pres, chmn: Packard Foundation, David and Lucile

Packard, David Woodley, vp, trust: Packard Foundation, David and Lucile

Packard, Jack W., trust: Elco Charitable Foundation

Packard, Julie, vp, exec dir: Monterey Bay Aquarium Foundation

Packard, Julie Elizabeth, trust: Packard Foundation, David and Lucile

Packard, Watten C., pres, dir: Wiremold Co.

Packard, Winifred A., vp: Terner Foundation

Packer, Augusta L., secy, treas, trust: Collins Foundation, Joseph

Packer, Edward E., trust: Innovating Worthy Projects Foundation

Packer, Estelle, trust: Innovating Worthy Projects Foundation

Packer, H. L., trust: Bell Trust

Packer, Irving M., chmn, trust: Innovating Worthy Projects Foundation

Pacle, Bernard, chmn: Bull HN Information Systems Inc.

Pacocha, Betty F., secy: New Milford Savings Bank Foundation

Paddock, David S., trust: Smith Charitable Trust

Paddock, James W., secy: Rice Foundation, Ethel and Raymond F.

Paden, Carter, Jr., chmn: Wisconsin Centrifugal Charitable Foundation

Paden, Jack G., chmn: Hill Crest Foundation

Paden, James R., trust: Brown Foundation

Padgett, Edward, trust: Seasongood Good Government Foundation, Murray and Agnes

Padley, Edward, pres: Howson-Algraphy, Inc.

Padnos, Jeffrey, pres: Padnos Iron & Metal Co., Louis

Padnos, Seymour K., chmn, ceo: Padnos Iron & Metal Co., Louis

Paetzold, Frank, dir: American Schlafhorst Foundation, Inc.

Pagano, Ralph J., treas: Panasonic Foundation

Pagano, Richard C., secy: Centel Foundation

Paganucci, Paul D., dir: Fairchild Foundation, Sherman; dir: Grace Foundation, Inc.

Page, Beatrice H., treas: Ziegler Foundation for the Blind, E. Matilda

Page, Cary L., Jr., chmn, dir: Moore Foundation, Alfred

Page, David A., dir: Kresge Foundation

Page, David Keith, dir: Kresge Foundation

Page, Forrest H., assoc dir: Morehead Foundation, John Motley

Page, George B., trust: Page Foundation, George B.

Page, Henry A., Jr., trust: Charities Foundation

Page, J. Robert, trust: Cole Foundation, Robert H. and Monica H.

Page, Michael F., secy, treas: Appleman Foundation

Page, Pilar M., mgr: PHH Foundation

Page, Rheta Haas, trust: Haas Foundation, Paul and Mary

Page, Richard M., chmn, pres, ceo: James & Co., Fred S.

Page, Robert A., trust: Salgo Charitable Trust, Nicholas M.

Page, Seaver T., trust: Thomas Medical Foundation, Roy E.

Page, Stephen F., cfo: Black & Decker Corp.

Page, Thomas A., chmn, ceo, dir: San Diego Gas & Electric

Pagen, Barbara Pauley, trust: Pauley Foundation, Edwin W.

Pagen, William Roland, trust: Pauley Foundation, Edwin W.

Pahlavi, Princess Ashraf, chmn: Foundation for Iranian Studies

Pahle, Marriane L., dir: Salwil Foundation

Paige, S. H., dir: Dick Family Foundation

Paight, A. S., treas, dir: Oaklawn Foundation

Paine, Andrew J., Jr., secy, trust: Jordan Foundation, Arthur; pres, coo, dir: NBD Bank, N.A.

Paine, Betty L., vp, secy: Marley Fund

Paine, Peter S., adv trust: Astor Foundation, Vincent

Paine, Stephen D., trust: Peabody Foundation

Paine, W. K., pres, treas: Community Foundation

Paine, Walter C., dir: Phillips Foundation, Ellis L.

Painter, Alan S., vp, exec dir: AlliedSignal Foundation

Painter, John W., pres: Eagle-Picher Industries

Painter, Rev. Bordern W., pres: Society for the Increase of the Ministry

Paioni, A. T., dir: Bank of America - Giannini Foundation

Paisley, Beverly, dir, pres, secy: Bauervic-Paisley Foundation

Paisley, Peter W., dir, treas: Bauervic-Paisley Foundation

Pajcic, James P., mem: Morton International

Pajor, Robert E., pres, coo, dir: Valspar Corp.

Pake, George E., trust: Danforth Foundation

Pakula, Randall H., dir: Utica National Group Foundation

Palay, Gilbert, exec vp, cfo: Manpower, Inc.

Palenchar, David J., vp (programs): El Pomar Foundation

Palermo, Alfonsine, trust: Ford III Memorial Foundation, Jefferson Lee

Palermo, Anthony, trust: Ford III Memorial Foundation, Jefferson Lee

Paley, Kate C., dir: Paley Foundation, William S.

Paley, William S., trust: Paley Foundation, Goldie

Palisano, Charles J., trust: Palisano Foundation, Vincent and Harriet

Palisano, Joseph S., trust: Palisano Foundation, Vincent and Harriet

Pallotti, Marianne, vp, corp secy: Hewlett Foundation, William and Flora

Palmer, Bruce A., chmn exec contributions comm: Northern States Power Co.

Palmer, C. Robert, chmn, pres, ceo, dir: Rowan Cos., Inc.

Palmer, Charles W., chmn, ceo: Autotrol Corp.

Palmer, Curtis H., chmn, dir: Arden Group, Inc.

Palmer, James D., trust: Herndon Foundation, Alonzo F. Herndon and Norris B.

Palmer, James R., secy, treas, trust: Lockwood Foundation, Byron W. and Alice L.

Palmer, Joseph Beveridge, dir: Beveridge Foundation, Frank Stanley

Palmer, L. Guy, II, mem bd dirs, mem investment comm: Dana Foundation, Charles A.

Palmer, Robert B., pres: Corestates Bank; pres: Corestates Foundation; pres, ceo: Digital Equipment Corp.; trust: Musson Charitable Foundation, R. C. and Katharine M.

Palmer, William, mem student loan adv comm: Jeffers Memorial Fund, Michael

Palmieri, Peter C., vchmn, dir: Fidelity Bank; vchmn, dir: First Fidelity Bancorporation

Palmore, B. B., dir: Fair Foundation, R. W.

Palms, Deborah Holley, trust: Earl-Beth Foundation

Palumbo, Lillian, trust: Snyder Foundation, Harold B. and Dorothy A.

Pam, Ann Petersen, dir: Petersen Foundation, Esper A.

Pamer, Lulu E., trust: Simpson Foundation

Pamplin, Robert B., chmn, ceo: Mount Vernon Mills; trust: Mount Vernon Mills Foundation

Pampusch, Anita M., dir, second vchmn: Bush Foundation

Panar, Manuel, vchmn, exec dir, comm on ed aid: du Pont de Nemours & Co., E. I.

Panaritis, Andrea, exec dir: Reynolds Foundation, Christopher

Panasci, David H., pres, coo: Fay's Incorporated; vp, dir: Fay's Foundation, Inc.

Panasci, Henry A., Jr., chmn, ceo: Fay's Incorporated

Pancetti, John A., vchmn, dir: Republic New York Corp.

Pancoast, Terrence Russell, secy, treas: Templeton Foundation, Herbert A.

Panes, Emanuel, mgr: Parnes Foundation, E. H.

Panettiere, John Michael, pres, coo: Blount; dir: Blount Foundation

Pang, Gerald M., dir: First Hawaiian Foundation

Pangle, W. F., treas: Bannerman Foundation, William C.

Panitch, Michael B., vchmn, dir: Smith Barney, Harris Upham & Co.

Pannell, William C., trust: Sumners Foundation, Hatton W.

Pannill, William L., treas: Pannill Scholarship Foundation, William Letcher

Pansini, Rev. F. David, dir: Doheny Foundation, Carrie Estelle

Pantages, Lloyd A., dir: Duke Foundation, Doris

Pantleon, Heinz, vp, dir: Loewy Family Foundation

Pantone, D. J., auditor: Brooklyn Benevolent Society

Pao, Norman, treas: NCR Foundation

Papo, Michael A., exec dir, ceo: Koret Foundation

Papone, Aldo, trust: American Express Co.

Papp, L. Roy, trust: Solomon Foundation, Sarah M.

Pappas, Betsy Z., clerk, dir devel: Pappas Charitable Foundation, Bessie; clerk, dir: Pappas Charitable Foundation, Thomas Anthony

Pappas, Charles A., pres, treas, dir: Pappas Charitable Foundation, Bessie; pres, dir: Pappas Charitable Foundation, Thomas Anthony

Pappas, Helen K., vp, dir: Pappas Charitable Foundation, Bessie; vp, dir: Pappas Charitable Foundation, Thomas Anthony

Pappas, Nicholas, pres, coo, dir: Rollins Environmental Services, Inc.

Pappas, Sophia, trust: Pappas Charitable Foundation, Bessie; asst clerk: Pappas Charitable Foundation, Thomas Anthony

Pappert, E. T., trust: Chrysler Corp. Fund

Papworth, Richard, cfo: Wimpey Inc., George

Paquet, Joseph F., trust: Collins Medical Fund

Paquette, Joseph F., Jr., chmn, ceo: Philadelphia Electric Co.

Paradis, Daisy, dir: Bayne Fund, Howard

Pardee, Scott E., chmn, dir: Yamaichi International (America) Inc.

Parducci, Lelio G., pres, ceo: Weight Watchers International; dir: Weight Watchers Foundation

Parent, Carmen, coord (corp contributions): Liquid Air Corp.

Parente, Emil J., trust: Fluor Foundation

Parenti, Renato R., trust: Arata Brothers Trust

Parfet, Donald R., pres: Upjohn Co. Foundation

Parfet, William Upjohn, pres, dir: Upjohn Co.; vp, treas: Upjohn Co. Foundation

Parish, Richard L., Jr., pres, treas: Psychists

Parish, Suzanne D., pres, trust: Dalton Foundation, Dorothy U.

Parisi, Franklin Joseph, vp, dir: Cray Research

Park, Bruce G., coo: Beverly Bank

Park, Charles B. III, dir: American Schlafhorst Foundation, Inc.

Park, Dale, Jr., secy, dir: Buehler Foundation, A. C.; pres, trust: Kemper Educational and Charitable Fund

Park, Jane M., vchmn, dir: Hoyt Foundation, Stewart W. and Willma C.

Park, Roy Hampton, chmn, ceo: Park Communications Inc.

Parkel, James G., dir (corp support programs): IBM Corp.; pres, dir: IBM South Africa Projects Fund

Parker, Alan M., pres, dir: Oak Foundation U.S.A.

Parker, Arthur, trust: Schrafft and Bertha E. Schrafft Charitable Trust, William E.

Parker, Bertram B., dir: Gebbie Foundation

Parker, Blanc A., exec consultant: Schlieder Educational Foundation, Edward G.

Parker, Briscoe K., Jr., pres, ceo: Parker Brothers and Company Inc.

Parker, Carol Himmelfarb, vp, dir: Himmelfarb Foundation, Paul and Annetta

Parker, Charles A., vp: Continental Corp. Foundation

Parker, Dale I., treas, vp: Centel Corp.; treas: Centel Foundation

Parker, Diane W., secy, dir: Williams Family Foundation of Georgia

Parker, Franklin Eddy, secy, trust: Jackson Hole Preserve

Parker, George, Jr., dir: Texaco Foundation

Parker, George E., III, vp, secy: Whitney Fund, David M.

Parker, George R., chmn, ceo: Newmont Mining Corp.

Parker, George S., chmn, dir: Janesville Foundation

Parker, Geraldine M., dir: Gebbie Foundation

Parker, Gordon R., chmn: Peabody Holding Company Inc.

Parker, Gray S., dir: Booth-Bricker Fund

Parker, J. L., trust: Matthews and Co. Educational and Charitable Trust, James H.

Parker, J.H., III, treas: Luck Stone Foundation

Parker, Jack W., exec vp, cfo: Union Planters Corp.

Parker, Jette, vp, secy, dir: Oak Foundation U.S.A.

Parker, John, vp: Ritter Foundation, May Ellen and Gerald

Parker, John O., mem: Hood Foundation, Charles H.

Parker, Karr, Jr., trust: Western New York Foundation

Parker, L. G., Frohman Foundation, Sidney

Parker, Liza, vp (policy & adm): AT&T Foundation

Parker, Maclyn T., secy, dir: Cole Foundation, Olive B.

Parker, Margaret H., vp of bd, trust: Victoria Foundation

Parker, Michelle, secy: Autry Foundation

Parker, Mrs. Robert M., vp: Ebell of Los Angeles Rest Cottage Association; vp: Ebell of Los Angeles Scholarship Endowment Fund

Parker, Patrick, mgr: Aequus Institute

Parker, Patrick Streeter, chmn: Parker-Hannifin Corp.; pres, trust: Parker-Hannifin Foundation

Parker, R. David, trust: Whitney Benefits

Parker, Robert L., Jr., pres, coo: Parker Drilling Co.

Parker, Robert L., Sr., chmn, ceo: Parker Drilling Co.

Parker, Ronald C., treas: Ford Family Foundation

Parker, Terry S., trust: GTE Foundation

Parker, W. J., dir: Camp Foundation

Parker, William A., trust, vchmn: Beck Foundation, Lewis H.

Parker, William Anderson, Jr., chmn, trust: Campbell Foundation, J. Bulow; trust: Courts Foundation

Parker, William I., secy, dir: Gebbie Foundation

Parker, Winifred B., pres: Ryan Foundation, Nina M.

Parkin, J. Stanley, trust: Jephson Educational Trust No. 1

Parkin, Joe L., pres, trust: Retirement Research Foundation

Parkinson, Roger P., pres, dir: Cowles Media Foundation

Parkos, Gregory T., pres, coo, dir: Whittaker Corp.

Parks, Carol S., exec dir, trust: Sawyer Charitable Foundation

Parks, Edward M., ptnr: Plante & Moran, CPAs

Parks, Floyd L., vp, treas, trust: Gilmore Foundation, Irving S.; secy, treas: Upjohn Foundation, Harold and Grace

Parks, James C., chmn, ceo, dir: Besser Co.

Parks, Lewis H., Devonshire Associates

Parks, R.J., Jr., trust: Johnson Day Trust, Carl and Virginia

Parmelee, David W., trust, treas: Fox Foundation Trust, Jacob L. and Lewis; trust, treas: Howard and Bush Foundation

Parmelee, Harold J., pres, ceo: Turner Construction Co.

Parmelee, Jean, exec dir: Johnson Foundation, Walter S.

Parnes, Herschel, mgr: Parnes Foundation, E. H.

Parode, Anne, Jr., trust: Girard Foundation

Parodneck, Meyer, trust: Consumer Farmer Foundation

Parravano, Teresa Haggerty, secy, treas: Haggerty Foundation

Parriott, Jackson C., trust: Love Charitable Foundation, John Allan

Parris, John, chmn, awards adv comm: Ferebee Endowment, Percy O.

Parrish, J. J., trust: Griffin, Sr., Foundation, C. V.

Parrish, Jere Paul, mem exec comm, dir: Shell Oil Co. Foundation

Parrish, Randee, exec secy: Lynn Foundation, E. M.

Parrott, J. R., asst secy: ITT Rayonier Foundation

Parrott, Marion A., dir: Pioneer Fund

Parrott, Roy E., pres, coo: Simpson Industries; trust: Simpson Industries Fund

Parry, Charles William, trust: Goodyear Tire & Rubber Company Fund

Parry, Frances, trust: Stranahan Foundation

Parry, Gwyn, dir: Hoag Family Foundation, George

Parry, Tom C., pres, ceo, dir: Mississippi Chemical Corp.

Parshall, Daryl, vp: Millbrook Tribute Garden

Parshooto, C., pres, dir: Koulaieff Educational Fund, Trustees of Ivan Y.

Parsley, Georganna S., vp, secy: Strake Foundation

Parsley, Robert Horace, trust, secy, treas: West Texas Corp., J. M.

Parsonnet, Victor, pres: Sagamore Foundation

Parsons, B., pres: Support Systems International

Parsons, Barbara, trust: Connecticut Energy Foundation, Inc.

Parsons, Bernie H., pres: Corvallis Clinic; adm: Corvallis Clinic Foundation

Parsons, Earl B., Jr., trust: Gulf Power Foundation

Parsons, J. A., exec vp, cfo: Willamette Industries, Inc.

Parsons, Myers B., dir: Christy-Houston Foundation

Parsons, Richard D., chmn, ceo: Dime Savings Bank of New York; trust: Rockefeller Brothers Fund

Parsons, Robert W., Jr., pres, prin off, dir: Hyde and Watson Foundation

Parsons, Roger B., pres: Elgin Sweeper Co.; pres: Elgin Sweeper Foundation; vp, secy, dir: Hyde and Watson Foundation

Parsons, Stuart N., secy, treas, dir: Park National Corporation Foundation

Parsons, Warren F., secy, treas, dir: Mielke Family Foundation

Parsons, Willis, Jr., trust: Long Foundation, George A. and Grace

Partee, Sue Garrett, bd mem: Roberts Foundation, Dora

Parvin, Albert B., vp, dir: Parvin Foundation, Albert

Parvin, Phyllis, secy, dir: Parvin Foundation, Albert

Parvin, Stanley, dir: Parvin Foundation, Albert

Parzen, Julia A., program off: Joyce Foundation

Pasant, David, pres, ceo: Jackson National Life Insurance Co.

Pascal, Edward, vp, secy, dir: Valdese Manufacturing Co. Foundation

Pascal, Nancy W., trust: Ware Foundation

Pascal, Roger, dir: Schiff, Hardin & Waite Foundation

Paschel, Marilyn, asst treas: Creditanstalt- Bankverein, New York

Pasewark, Richard, dir (advertising): Giant Food Stores

Pasman, Jim, chmn: Permian Corp.

Pasqual, Leandro, dir: Harcourt Foundation, Ellen Knowles

Pasquale, Vince, pres: Intercraft Co., Inc.

Passage, Ray, trust: Gerber Cos. Foundation

Passante, John, sr vp (human resources): Moog Automotive, Inc.

Passen, Richard B., trust: Shepherd Foundation

Passman, David, dir: Deloitte & Touche Foundation

Pasternak, Ed, asst treas: General Motors Foundation

Pastin, Max, pres, trust: Blowitz-Ridgeway Foundation

Pastore, Roger C., vchmn, cfo: American Savings & Loan Association of Florida

Pastrana, Glenn M., research asst, matching gifts coordinator: ARCO Foundation

Patrick, Courtney C., secy: Clark Charitable Foundation

Patane, Joe S., asst vp: Clayton Fund

Patch, Lauren N., pres: Ohio Casualty Corp.

Patch, Thomas N., dir: Irwin-Sweeney- Miller Foundation

Pate, Glenn, Feild Co-Operative Association

Pate, J. M., vp, trust: Wilson Foundation, Frances Wood

Pate, James Leonard, pres, ceo, dir: Pennzoil Co.

Patek, Christopher, vp, trust: Birch Foundation, Stephen and Mary

Patek, Patrick J., pres, trust: Birch Foundation, Stephen and Mary

Patek, Rose B., secy-treas, trust: Birch Foundation, Stephen and Mary

Patel, Tushar, dir: Mitsubishi Electric America Foundation

Paterson, Phillip D., Jr., asst secy: Plankenhorn Foundation, Harry

Paterson, V. P., mem loan comm: Lindsay Student Aid Fund, Franklin

Patey, Edmund M., trust: Massachusetts Charitable Mechanics Association

Patin, Robert, ceo: Washington National Insurance Co.

Patkin, Jordan E., adv bd: Lipsky Foundation, Fred and Sarah

Patmore, Thomas Eugene, trust: Alhambra Foundry Co., Ltd. Scholarship Foundation

Paton, Leland B., group pres capital mkts, mem exec comm: Prudential-Bache Securities

Patric, Lowell C., pres, coo, dir: Rochester Community Savings Bank

Patrick, Charles F., treas, trust: Copley Foundation, James S.

Patrick, Michael E., exec vp, cfo: Lomas Financial Corp.

Patrick, Patrick F., vp, dir: Glaser Foundation

Patrick, Thomas J., Jr., dir: Brown Charitable Trust, Dora Maclellan

Patten, Z. Cartter, III, dir: Reflection Riding

Patterson, David K., secy, dir: Klee Foundation, Conrad and Virginia

Patterson, David R., asst to pres, trust: Wildermuth Foundation, E. F.

Patterson, David T., trust: Wildermuth Foundation, E. F.

Patterson, Don, chmn: Harrington Foundation, Don and Sybil

Patterson, Donald H., trust: Abell Foundation, The

Patterson, E. H., treas, dir: Reynolds Foundation, Donald W.

Patterson, James T., pres, trust: Lalor Foundation

Patterson, Jane S., trust: Reynolds Foundation, Z. Smith

Patterson, M. K., Jr., vp, dir biomed div, head nutrition section: Noble Foundation, Samuel Roberts

Patterson, Marvin Breckinridge, pres, dir: Marpat Foundation

Patterson, Melissa, trust: Mott Fund, Ruth

Patterson, Pat J., dir, secy, treas: Harris Foundation

Patterson, Remington Perrigo, pres, dir: Axe-Houghton Foundation

Patterson, Robert P., Jr., chmn bd trusts: Grant Foundation, William T.

Patterson, Thomas J., Jr., vp: Corestates Foundation

Patterson, W. Calvin, III, exec dir, asst secy: McGregor Fund

Pattillo, Elizabeth M., dir: Pittulloch Foundation

Pattillo, H. G., chmn, dir: Pittulloch Foundation

Pattillo, Lynn L., pres, treas, dir: Pittulloch Foundation

Pattillo, Robert A., dir: Pittulloch Foundation

Pattison, Margot A., trust: Anderson Foundation, William P.

Patton, Henry, dir: Guggenheim Foundation, Daniel and Florence

Patton, James Lewis, mng ptnr: Black & Veatch; trust: Black & Veatch Foundation

Patton, Leland R., trust: Davenport Trust Fund

Patton, Macon G., trust: Builderway Foundation

Patton, Thomas J., trust: Reeves Foundation

Patty, F.M., Jr., trust: Johnson Day Trust, Carl and Virginia

Patty, Frank L., trust: Bull Foundation, Henry W.

Paty, John C., Jr., secy, treas: Massengill-DeFriece Foundation

Paul, Alice, exec dir, secy: Uris Brothers Foundation

Paul, Carlisle, dir: First Interstate Bank of Texas Foundation

Paul, Douglas L., trust: First Boston Foundation Trust

Paul, Gerald, chmn: Harris Stores, Paul

Paul, James Robert, chmn, dir: American Natural Resources Co.; chmn, dir: ANR Foundation; pres, ceo, dir: Coastal Corp.

Paul, Lee Gilmour, dir: Pasadena Area Residential Aid

Paul, Robert A., vp: Berkman Foundation, Louis and Sandra

Paul, Robert Arthur, vp: Berkman Foundation, Louis and Sandra; vp, trust: Fair Oaks Foundation, Inc.; treas: Jewish Healthcare Foundation of Pittsburgh

Pauley, Janet A., dir: Noyes, Jr. Memorial Foundation, Nicholas H.

Pauley, Robert I., dir, chmn: Gellert Foundation, Celia Berta

Pauli, W., natl contributions and communications mgr: Toyota Motor Sales, U.S.A.

Paulis, Raymond, trust: Andres Charitable Trust, Frank G.

Paulucci, Gina J., trust: Paulucci Family Foundation

Paulucci, Lois M., dir, vp: Paulucci Family Foundation

Paulucci, Luigino Francisco, dir, pres: Paulucci Family Foundation

Paulucci, Michael J., dir, vp: Paulucci Family Foundation

Paulus, David J., pres, dir: First National Bank of Chicago Foundation

Paulus, Henry P., trust: New England Biolabs Foundation

Pauly, Marilyn B., trust: Bank IV Charitable Trust

Pauly, Robert L., vp, dir: Gellert Foundation, Carl

Paumgarten, Nicholas B., mem: Scripps Howard Foundation

Pavlick, Kathleen, mgr (corp contributions): Chemical Bank

Paxson, Howard H., vp, trust: Tiscornia Foundation

Paxton, Frank, Jr., chmn: Paxton Co., Frank

Payne, Delbert S., mgr corp social investment: Rohm and Haas Company

Payne, Doris, admin asst: Gates Corp.

Payne, James O., trust: Berry Foundation, Loren M.

Payne, John H., trust, vp: Buehler Foundation, Emil

Payne, John L., trust: One Valley Bank Foundation

Payne, Johnny, trust: Wilson Public Trust, Ralph

Payne, Karen, dir commun rels: Gulfstream Aerospace Corp.

Payne, L. Kirk, pres: Washington Square Fund

Payne, Lauren I., program assoc: Fidelity Foundation

Payne, M. Lee, pres, dir: Lincoln-Lane Foundation

Payne, Thomas R., dir: Ginter Foundation, Karl and Anna

Payne, Thomas W., trust: Hess Charitable Trust, Myrtle E. and William C.

Payne, W. Anderson, vp: Love Charitable Foundation, John Allan

Payne, W. J., vp, trust, secy: Rinker Cos. Foundation

Payne, Walter F., pres: Blue Diamond Growers

Payson, Mary Stone, trust: Stone Foundation

Payton, Sylvia, secy: Boston Globe Foundation

Pazol, James L., trust: Schermer Charitable Trust, Frances

Pazony, Bill, ceo: Kobacker Co.

Pddy, Richard D., treas, dir: Tombstone Pizza Foundation

Peach, John M., treas, trust: Johnson Foundation, Barbara P.

Peacock, Carl, ceo: Bourns, Inc.

Peacock, John, asst secy: Haghenbeck Foundation, Antonio Y. De La Lama

Peacock, John E.D., pres, dir: Ayres Foundation, Inc.

Peak, Chandos H., trust: Price Educational Foundation, Herschel C.

Pear, Henry E., treas, trust: Leidy Foundation, John J.

Pearce, Harry J., exec vp: General Motors Corp.

Pearce, James T., vchmn: Budweiser of the Carolinas Foundation

Pearce, M. Lee, MD, pres, dir: Pearce Foundation, Dr. M. Lee

Pearce, Nora Lodge, vp, dir: Pearce Foundation, Dr. M. Lee

Pearce, R. Roy, secy: Budweiser of the Carolinas Foundation

Pearce, William R., vchmn: Cargill, Inc.; pres: Cargill Foundation

Peard, Richard T. C., dir: Lambert Memorial Foundation, Gerard B.

Pearl, Frank H., dir: MCJ Foundation

Pearl, Melvin E., treas, dir: Katten, Muchin, & Zavis Foundation

Pearlman, Samuel, secy, treas: Tranzonic Foundation

Pearlstone, Esther S., pres: Pearlstone Foundation, Peggy Meyerhoff

Pearlstone, Richard L., vp, secy, treas: Pearlstone Foundation, Peggy Meyerhoff

Pearsall, Amos C., Jr., trust, secy, exec dir: Hawley Foundation

Pearson, Alexander, trust: Faith Home Foundation

Pearson, George H., adm: Koch Charitable Trust, David H.; pres: Koch Foundation, Fred C.

Pearson, John Edgar, vp, dir: Cargill Foundation

Pearson, Leonard, adv: Bronstein Foundation, Sol and Arlene

Pearson, Maida, chmn: Smith, Jr. Foundation, M. W.

Pearson, R. Dugald, exec secy: Wellman Foundation, S. K.

Pearson, Ron, pres: Hy-Vee Food Stores

Pease, Noreen, trust: Egenton Home

Peasley, Regina Hallowell, mgr: Shoemaker Fund, Thomas H. and Mary Williams

Peau, Alphone, dir: Jasper Desk Foundation

Pech, Warner, vp sales: Huber, Hunt & Nichols

Peck, A. John, Jr., secy: Corning Incorporated Foundation

Peck, Bernard, dir, pres, treas: Peck Foundation, Milton and Lillian

Peck, Clair, chmn, coo: Peck/Jones Construction Corp.

Peck, Elaine Z., dir, exec vp: Zimmerman Foundation, Mary and George Herbert

Peck, Joanne, dir commun: Burndy Corp.

Peck, Martha G., exec dir, secy: Burroughs Wellcome Fund

Peck, Miriam, trust: Peck Foundation, Milton and Lillian

Peck, Richard, dir: General Railway Signal Foundation

Peck, Sidney, trust: Azadoutioun Foundation

Peckham, Eugene E., mem adv comm: O'Connor Foundation, A. Lindsay and Olive B.

Peckham, Judith, exec dir: Hoyt Foundation, Stewart W. and Willma C.

Pedersen, Gilbert John, dir: Dent Family Foundation, Harry

Pederson, Jerrold P., vp, cfo: Montana Power Co.

Pederson, O. N., pres, trust: Griffin Foundation, Rosa May

Peebler, Charles D., Jr., ceo: Bozell, Inc.

Peed, Nancy F., comm rels mgr: Sentinel Communications Co.

Peek, Duncan G., dir, pres: Churches Homes Foundation

Peeler, Stuart T., trust: Getty Trust, J. Paul

Peeples, C. E., dir: Fair Foundation, R. W.

Peerce, Stuart B., dir: Donovan, Leisure, Newton & Irvine Foundation

Peery, Dennis, treas: Peery Foundation

Peery, J. K., vp, dir: Quanex Foundation

Peery, Mildred D., vp: Peery Foundation

Peery, Richard Taylor, dir: Arrillaga Foundation; pres: Peery Foundation

Peery, Troy A., Jr., pres, coo, dir: Heilig-Meyers Co.

Peete, Lindsey, exec dir: Washington Forrest Foundation

Peete, Margaret S., pres: Washington Forrest Foundation

Peierls, Brian Eliot, vp, treas: Peierls Foundation

Peierls, E. J., pres: Peierls Foundation

Peierls, Ethel, secy: Peierls Foundation

Peiffer, Jack O., trust: GE Foundations

Peins, Rudolph M., Jr., treas, trust: Hunt Manufacturing Co. Foundation

Peipers, David H., vp, dir: Bedminster Fund

Peirce, Neal R., trust: German Marshall Fund of the United States

Pelino, Dennis, dir: Fritz Cos.

Pell, Nuala, trust: Hartford Foundation, John A.

Pella, Katherine G., activities admin: Lukens Foundation

Pellecrino, Allison G., secy: Chatam Inc.

Pellegrino, A. Robert, pres: Foster and Gallagher

Pellegrino, Joseph, dir, treas: Pellegrino-Realmuto Charitable Foundation

Pellegrino, Joseph P., dir, secy: Pellegrino-Realmuto Charitable Foundation

Pelletier, Edith, mem selection comm: Woodward Fund-Watertown, David, Helen, and Marian

Pellish, Walter, vp (admin): U.S. Silica Co.

Pellisier, Jack E., secy: Bryan Foundation, Dodd and Dorothy L.

Pellizzi, Francesco, dir: Menil Foundation

Peltz, Nelson, chmn, ceo: Triangle Industries; trust: Triangle Foundation

Pelzer, Gerald E., pres, chmn: Brown & Associates, Clayton; secy, treas, dir: Brown Foundation, Clayton

Pemerton, Chloe, dir (pers): Robertshaw Controls Co.

Pence, Margaret H., program off, dir: Hall Family Foundations

Penchoen, Ruth C., dir: Allyn Foundation

Pendergast, Beverly B., pres, dir: Pendergast-Weyer Foundation

Pendergast, Mary Elizabeth, staff dir corp philanthropy: New York Telephone Co.

Pendergast, Thomas J., Jr., chmn, secy, treas, dir: Pendergast-Weyer Foundation

Pendergraft, Ross, asst treas: Reynolds Foundation, Donald W.

Pendexter, Harold E., Jr., sr vp (admin), chief admin off: USG Corp.; pres, dir: USG Foundation

Pendleton, E., cfo: Pendleton Construction Corp.

Pendleton, Edmund, pres, treas: Pendleton Construction Corp.

Pendleton, Edmund, Jr., dir: Pendleton Construction Corp. Foundation

Pendleton, Laird, treas, dir: Glencairn Foundation

Pendleton, William N., dir: Pendleton Construction Corp. Foundation

Penfield, William N., exec dir: Society for the Increase of the Ministry

Penglase, Frank D., vp, treas: McGraw-Hill Foundation

Penhoet, Edward E., PhD, ceo: Chiron Corp.

Penick, Theodore, trust: Wells Trust Fund, Fred W.

Penn, Arthur S., treas: Christodora

Penn, John, trust: Wolfson Foundation, Louis E.

Penn, Milton L., dir, vp, treas: Kelley and Elza Kelley Foundation, Edward Bangs

Penner, Betty J., asst secy: Johnson Foundation, Helen K. and Arthur E.

Penney, Caroline A., dir: Penney Foundation, James C.

Pennington, Claude Bernard, trust: Pennington Foundation, Irene W. and C. B.

Pennington, George F., dir: Clipper Ship Foundation

Pennington, Irene W., trust: Pennington Foundation, Irene W. and C. B.

Pennink, Eshowe P., dir: Beneficia Foundation

Pennink, Mark J., treas, dir: Beneficia Foundation

Pennock, George Tennant, dir: Tennant Co. Foundation

Pennoyer, Robert M., trust: Merck Fund, John; pres, trust: Whiting Foundation, Mrs. Giles

Pennoyer, Russell P., second vp, trust: Achelis Foundation; second vp: Bodman Foundation

Penny, George L., trust: Knapp Foundation

Penny, Roger P., pres, coo, dir: Bethlehem Steel Corp.

Penny, Sylvia V., trust: Knapp Educational Fund; trust: Knapp Foundation

Pennypacker, N. Ramsay, secy, trust: Foerderer Foundation, Percival E. and Ethel Brown

Penske, Roger S., chmn, pres, ceo, coo, dir: Penske Corp.

Pentecost, Mark P., MD, trust: Campbell Foundation, J. Bulow

Pepin, E. Lyle, secy: Centerior Energy Foundation

Peppas, John, mgr corp contributions: Bell Communications Research

Pepper, Richard S., chmn, ceo: Pepper Cos.

Pepski, Kathleen, vp, cfo: Johnson Co., E. F.

Perabo, Fred H., secy (bd control): Ralston Purina Trust Fund

Perachio, Elaine, exec dir: Kempner Fund, Harris and Eliza

Peraino, Roy T., chmn, ceo: Continental Bancorp, Inc.

Percio, Janis T., asst secy: Centerior Energy Foundation

Percy, Charles H., chmn, pres, dir: Hariri Foundation

Percy, David F., trust: Renner Foundation

Percy, Frank E., trust: Renner Foundation

Percy, Ruth A., trust: Renner Foundation

Percy, Steven W., pres: BP America

Percy, William A., II, trust: First Mississippi Corp. Foundation

Perdue, Franklin Parsons, chmn, dir: Perdue Farms

Pereira, J. G., vchmn: First Empire State Corp.

Perelman, Ronald Owen, chmn, ceo, dir: MacAndrews & Forbes Holdings; dir: MacAndrews & Forbes Foundation; chmn, ceo, dir: Revlon

Perenchio, Andrew Jerrold, pres: Chartwell Foundation

Perenchio, John, vp: Chartwell Foundation

Perera, Guido R., Jr., trust: Shaw Foundation, Gardiner Howland

Perera, Lawrence Thatcher, trust: Humane Society of the Commonwealth of Massachusetts

Peressinni, William, mem (contributions comm): PacifiCorp Foundation

Peretz, Martin, dir: Clark Foundation

Perez, Joseph, trust: Connecticut Energy Foundation, Inc.

Perez, Paul B., sr vp mktg: Action Industries, Inc.

Perfido, Dee, exec secy to the pres: Waldbaum, Inc.

Perini, Bart W., treas: Perini Memorial Foundation; treas: Perini Foundation, Joseph

Perini, Charles B., vp: Perini Memorial Foundation; vp: Perini Foundation, Joseph

Perini, David B., chmn, pres, ceo, dir: Perini Corp.; pres: Perini Memorial Foundation; pres: Perini Foundation, Joseph

Perini, Joseph R., vchmn, sr vp, dir: Perini Corp.

Peritz, Richard M., exec vp, dir: Coleman Foundation

Perkin, John T., trust: Perkin Fund

Perkin, Richard S., chmn, trust: Perkin Fund

Perkin, Richard T., trust: Perkin Fund

Perkin, Robert S., trust: Perkin Fund

Perkins, Arnold, dir: Haigh-Scatena Foundation

Perkins, Donald S., chmn, dir: AON Foundation

Perkins, Dorothy, secy: Clark Home for Aged People, Ella

Perkins, George W., Jr., vp: Perkins Memorial Foundation, George W.

Perkins, Homer G., dir: Beveridge Foundation, Frank Stanley

Perkins, Jacob B., trust: Perkins Charitable Foundation

Perkins, John Allen, trust: Sailors' Snug Harbor of Boston

Perkins, Leigh H., trust: Huntington Fund for

Education, John; trust: Perkins Charitable Foundation

Perkins, Linn M., pres: Perkins Memorial Foundation, George W.

Perkins, Phil, dir: MFA Foundation

Perkins, Priscilla C., trust: Schepp Foundation, Leopold

Perkins, Richard S., adv trust: Astor Foundation, Vincent

Perkins, Robert, trust: North Carolina Foam Foundation

Perkins, Robert E., adm agent: Beattie Foundation Trust, Cordelia Lee; exec dir: Selby and Marie Selby Foundation, William G.

Perkins, Roswell B., dir: Commonwealth Fund

Perkins, Tanga, adm (corp contributions): Eaton Charitable Fund

Perkins, Thomas J., chmn: Tandy Corp.

Perle, Elizabeth, trust: de Hirsch Fund, Baron

Perlman, Ira, dir: Panasonic Foundation

Perlman, Julian S., dir: Winston Foundation, Norman and Rosita

Perlman, Lawrence, pres, ceo, dir: Control Data Corp.

Perlmuth, William Alan, trust: Aeroflex Foundation; dir: Harkness Ballet Foundation; vp, dir: Harkness Foundation, William Hale; vp, secy: Weininger Foundation, Richard and Gertrude

Perlow, Rita, secy: Jewish Healthcare Foundation of Pittsburgh

Perna, Frank, Jr., pres, coo, dir: Magnatek

Pero, Perry R., sr vp, chief fin off: Northern Trust Co.

Perona, Dale F., pres, dir: Foote, Cone & Belding Foundation

Perot, H. Ross, Jr., trust: Perot Foundation

Perot, Margaret B., vp, dir: Perot Foundation

Perpich, Joseph G., MD, JD, vp grants & special programs: Hughes Medical Institute, Howard

Perracciano, Anthony P., ceo, dir: Fidelity Bank

Perralla, James E., pres: Ingersoll-Rand Co.

Perrella, James S., pres: Torrington Co.

Perret, Robert, Jr., dir: Zimmermann Fund, Marie and John

Perrigo, David W., asst treas: Castle & Cooke International Charitable Foundation

Perrin, Geoffrey, treas: Lowe Foundation

Perrin, Melinda, trust: Lowe Foundation

Perrine, Irene H., chmn, dir: Hall Foundation

Perrotte, Alisa S., dir: Siragusa Foundation

Perry, Alice Ann, trust: Oakley Foundation, Hollie and Anna

Perry, C. W., trust: Marshburn Foundation

Perry, Carrolle, trust: Douty Foundation

Perry, Charles A., ceo: Wauwatosa Savings & Loan Association; trust: Wauwatosa Savings & Loan Foundation

Perry, Edwin H., secy: Greenebaum, Doll & McDonald Foundation

Perry, Eston Lee, trust: Oakley Foundation, Hollie and Anna

Perry, Francis F., trust: Eastern Bank Foundation

Perry, Geoffrey, vp, treas, dir: Jafra Educational Development Grant Endowment

Perry, James M., pres: Stonecutter Mills Corp.

Perry, James N., vchmn: ISS International Service System

Perry, Jeffrey J., trust: Oakley Foundation, Hollie and Anna

Perry, Julie, trust: Oakley Foundation, Hollie and Anna

Perry, Kelly, matching gifts coordinator: Sedgwick James Inc.

Perry, Kenneth Walter, vp: FINA Foundation

Perry, Larry D., chmn, dir: Missouri Farmers Association

Perry, Manuel, chmn, dir: First Commercial Bank N.A.

Perry, Marilyn, pres, trust: Kress Foundation, Samuel H.

Perry, Martha J., assoc exec dir: McCune Foundation

Perry, Mary Mayne, trust: Toms Foundation

Perry, Michael D., cfo: Belo Corp., A.H.

Perry, Raymond J., dir: Siebert Lutheran Foundation; trust: Wauwatosa Savings & Loan Foundation

Perry, Raymond J., Jr., pres: Wauwatosa Savings & Loan Association

Perry, Susan, adm asst: Hyams Foundation

Pershetz, Arthur D., secy: Royal Insurance Foundation

Persinger, Jesse, trust: Eyman Trust, Jesse

Person, Meredith Slane, mem fdn comm: Finch Foundation, Thomas Austin

Perteys, Robert A., trust: Petteys Memorial Foundation, Jack

Pertschuk, Michael, dir: Benton Foundation

Pertzik, Marvin J., secy, treas, dir: Griggs and Mary Griggs Burke Foundation, Mary Livingston

Pesce, Pasquale, dir (Bellagio Study & Conf Ctr): Rockefeller Foundation

Pesch, Alida, dir: Pesch Family Foundation

Pesch, Brian, secy, dir: Pesch Family Foundation

Pesch, Christopher, dir: Pesch Family Foundation

Pesch, Daniel, dir: Pesch Family Foundation

Pesch, Ellen, dir: Pesch Family Foundation

Pesch, Gerri, dir: Pesch Family Foundation

Pesch, Leroy Allen, pres, treas, dir: Pesch Family Foundation

Peschka, Thomas Alan, secy, dir: Commerce Foundation

Pesky, Wendy S., vp: Stern Foundation, Bernice and Milton

Pestillo, Peter J., trust: Ford Motor Co. Fund

Petas, John, vp, dir: American Honda Foundation

Peter, Harry W., III, mem (corp contributions comm): UST

Peterman, Bruce Edgar, sr vp (oper): Cessna Aircraft Co.; dir: Cessna Foundation

Peternell, Ben C., sr vp (human resources): Promus Cos.

Plym, Lawrence John, pres, dir: Plym Foundation

Pobasco, Scott L., Jr., trust: Cartinhour Foundation

Poddar, Mayurika, trust: India Foundation

Podell, Jeffrey, pres: Pantasote Polymers

Podlipny, Ann R., secy: Heineman Foundation for Research, Educational, Charitable, and Scientific Purposes

Poesch, Gustav H., pres: Gloeckner Foundation, Fred

Poff, W. Herbert, III, trust: Plankenhorn Foundation, Harry

Pogue, Alfred Mack, chmn, pres, ceo, dir: Lincoln Property Co.

Pogue, Richard W., vp, trust: Kulas Foundation

Pohl, Susan W., trust: Norcliffe Fund

Pohlad, Carl Ray, chmn, dir: MEI Diversified, Inc.

Pohls, Ronald C., trust: McKesson Foundation

Poindexter, Christian Herndon, chmn, ceo: Baltimore Gas & Electric Co.; chmn, dir: Baltimore Gas & Electric Foundation

Poindexter, R.D., pres: Poindexter Foundation

Poinsette, Cheryl, trust: McKesson Foundation

Point, Warren W., mem: Maier Foundation, Sarah Pauline

Pointer, Deborah Battle, trust: Chubb Foundation

Poist, William G., chmn, ceo: Commonwealth Energy System

Pokelwaldt, Robert N., pres, ceo: York International Corp.

Pokorny, Gene, dir: Benton Foundation

Polachek, Thomas A., dir, treas: Special People In Need

Polakovic, Michael, trust: Weckbaugh Foundation, Eleanore Mullen

Polakovic, Teresa, vp, trust: Weckbaugh Foundation, Eleanore Mullen

Polanowska, D. S., pres, coo: Ketchum & Co.

Polansky, Ellen Woods, trust: Cartinhour Foundation; trust: Woods-Greer Foundation

Polansky, Sol, trust: Sofia American Schools

Polevoy, Martin D., trust: Kevorkian Fund, Hagop

Poli, Darrel, trust: Smith Benevolent Association, Buckingham

Polin, Jane L., comptr, chair (arts & culture comm): GE Foundations

Poling, Harold A., chmn, ceo, dir: Ford Motor Co.

Polinger, Arnold, dir, vp: Polinger Foundation, Howard and Geraldine

Polinger, David, dir, treas: Polinger Foundation, Howard and Geraldine

Polinger, Geraldine, dir, secy: Polinger Foundation, Howard and Geraldine

Polinger, Howard, dir, pres: Polinger Foundation, Howard and Geraldine

Polinger, Lorre Beth, dir, vp: Polinger Foundation, Howard and Geraldine

Polinsky, Jessie W., pres: Polinsky-Rivkin Family Foundation

Polis, Nancy E., mgr: General Motors Foundation

Polite, L. John, Jr., chmn, ceo: Peridot Chemicals (NJ)

Polite, Sandra Lynn Getz, dir: Globe Foundation

Politeo, Janet L., pres, dir: Glaser Foundation

Polito, Edward, asst secy: Stuart Foundation

Polito, Michael, pres: Kingsley Foundation, Lewis A.

Polk, Eugene P., dir: Charina Foundation; adm off, trust: Kieckhefer Foundation, J. W.; trust: Morris Foundation, Margaret T.

Polk, Samuel S., dir: Memton Fund

Pollack, Anne F., treas: New York Life Foundation

Pollack, Gerald J., comptr: ITT Rayonier Foundation

Pollack, James L., trust: Eisenberg Foundation, George M.

Pollack, Lester, Zarkin Memorial Foundation, Charles

Pollack, Philip, pres, secy: Billy Penn Corp

Pollack, Robert Elliot, trust: New York Foundation

Pollard, A. J., contr: Liberty Corp. Foundation

Pollard, C. William, chmn, ceo, dir: ServiceMaster Co. L.P.

Pollard, Carl Faulkner, chmn, ceo: Humana; pres, coo, dir: Humana Foundation

Pollard, Richard F., vchmn, dir: BayBanks

Polley, David, pres: World Carpets

Pollicino, Joseph A., vchmn: CIT Group Holdings; exec vp: CIT Group Foundation

Pollock, C. William, chmn, ceo, dir: United Gas Pipe Line Co.

Pollock, Davis E., pres: Van Buren Foundation

Pollock, John Phleger, pres, trust: Jones Foundation, Fletcher

Polzin, Dave, asst vp (programs): State Farm Cos. Foundation

Pomerantz, John J., chmn, ceo: Leslie Fay Cos., Inc.

Pomerantz, Marvin A., chmn, ceo: Gaylord Container Corp.

Ponchick, E. T., pres: Bannerman Foundation, William C.

Pond, Byron O., pres, coo, dir: Arvin Industries

Pontz, Curis M., asst secy: CertainTeed Corp. Foundation

Pool, Wendell, trust: Heath Foundation, Ed and Mary

Poole, James F., Jr., vp, cfo: Fay's Incorporated; vp, dir: Fay's Foundation, Inc.

Poole, James G., Jr., ceo, chmn: Poole Equipment Co., Gregory

Poole, Richard G., dir: Langeloth Foundation, Jacob and Valeria

Poon, Clarence, dir: Bank of the Orient Foundation

Poore, Edgar E., trust: Richfood Educational Trust

Poorvu, Lia G., trust: Poorvu Foundation, William and Lia

Poorvu, William J., trust: Poorvu Foundation, William and Lia; dir: Sonesta Charitable Foundation

Pope, Anthony, vp, secy, dir, don son: Pope Foundation

Pope, Blanche, pres: Pope Family Foundation, Blanche & Edker

Pope, Catherine, pres, dir, don wife: Pope Foundation

Pope, Edker III, vp: Pope Family Foundation, Blanche & Edker

Pope, Fortune, vp, treas, dir, don son: Pope Foundation

Pope, G. Phillip, treas: Caring Foundation

Pope, James W., vp, cfo: E-Systems

Pope, John A., Jr., dir: Reader's Digest Foundation

Pope, John C., pres, dir, coo: United Airlines; dir: United Airlines Foundation

Pope, John L., vp: McMillan, Jr. Foundation, Bruce

Pope, Larry, cfo: Blue Cross & Blue Shield of Alabama

Pope, Lois B., pres, dir: Pope Foundation, Lois B.

Pope, Mary Ann, vp, secy, treas, dir: Bren Foundation, Donald L.

Pope, Norwood W., dir: First Hawaiian Foundation

Pope, Peter T., chmn, pres, ceo, dir: Pope & Talbot, Inc.

Pope, Robert G., vchmn, cfo, dir: Southwestern Bell Corp.

Pope, Viola B., trust: Ivakota Association

Popoff, Frank Peter, chmn pres, ceo, dir: Dow Chemical Co.

Popoff, Jean U., trust: Gerstacker Foundation, Rollin M.

Popovich, Jane H., trust: Hoffman Foundation, H. Leslie Hoffman and Elaine S.

Popowcer, Leonard H., vp: Fraida Foundation

Poppa, R. R., chmn, pres, ceo: Storage Technology Corp.

Popper, Robert L., pres, trust: Lavanburg-Corner House

Poppleton, Jay K., trust: Metal Industries Foundation

Poppleton, Terry L., vp: Goldome Foundation

Porges, Carol Leigh Simon, dir: Simon Foundation, William E. and Carol G.

Portaro, Sam A., Jr., dir: Pullman Educational Foundation, George M.

Portea, Vito S., vchmn: Republic New York Corp.

Portee, Barbara C., pres: Meyer Foundation, Bert and Mary

Portenoy, Norman S., vp, dir: Dreyfus Foundation, Max and Victoria

Portenoy, Winifred Riggs, secy, treas, dir: Dreyfus Foundation, Max and Victoria

Porter, Don E., dir: Bucyrus-Erie Foundation

Porter, Dudley, Jr., trust: Maclellan Charitable Trust, R. J.

Porter, Irwin, chmn: Giant Eagle; trust: Giant Eagle Foundation

Porter, John W., trust, chmn audit comm: Mott Foundation, Charles Stewart

Porter, M., chmn exec comm: Foster Co., L.B.; mem charitable comm: Foster Charitable Trust, L.B.

Porter, Marc, vp, cfo: Law Company, Inc.

Porter, Mark M., vp, dir: Hardin Foundation, Phil

Porter, Milton, trust: Foster Charitable Trust

Porter, Richard, pres: Lamb-Weston Inc.

Porter, Robert, Jr., 1st vp: Cincinnati Foundation for the Aged

Porter, Robert Chamberlain, pres: Lost Tree Charitable Foundation

Porter, Russell M., trust: Bismarck Charitable Trust, Mona

Porter, Sue, trust: Scripps Howard Foundation

Porter, Victor B., dir: Cole Foundation, Olive B.

Porter, W. Thomas, exec vp: Seafirst Corp.; trust: Seafirst Foundation

Portlock, Carver A., trust: Seybert Institution for Poor Boys and Girls, Adam and Maria Sarah

Portman, William, trust: Star Bank, N.A., Cincinnati Foundation

Portney, David, second vp pub rels: State Mutual Life Assurance Co.

Posey, Frances, dir: Georgia Health Foundation

Posey, W. M., Jr., treas: Armstrong Foundation

Posner, Ernest G., secy, dir: PQ Corp. Foundation

Posner, Roy Edward, sr vp, cfo: Loews Corp.; trust: Loews Foundation

Posner, Steve, vchmn: DWG Corp.

Posner, Steven, vchmn, chmn exec comm, dir: APL Corp.; vchmn, chmn exec comm, dir: NVF Co.; vchmn, chmn exec comm, dir: Royal Crown Cos., Inc.

Posner, Victor N., chmn, ceo, pres, dir: APL Corp.; chmn, ceo, pres, dir: DWG Corp.; chmn, ceo, pres, dir: NVF Co.; chmn, ceo, pres, dir: Royal Crown Cos., Inc.

Poss, Ellen M., trust: Kapor Family Foundation

Poss, Mike, treas, dir: Perot Foundation

Possnecker, Paul, dir: Weller Foundation

Post, Judith, trust, vp: Flemm Foundation, John J.

Post, Leona, trust: Flemm Foundation, John J.

Post, Robert, trust, secy: Flemm Foundation, John J.

Post, Scott, trust: Insurance Management Associates Foundation

Post, William J., vp, dir: APS Foundation

Poston, Met R., vchmn: Janirve Foundation

Poteat, Janis T., trust: Towsley Foundation, Harry A. and Margaret D.

Potenziani, A. F., mgr, dir: Bellamah Foundation, Dale J.

Potenziani, Frank A., dir: Bellamah Foundation, Dale J.

Potenziani, Martha M., dir: Bellamah Foundation, Dale J.

Potenziani, William, dir: Bellamah Foundation, Dale J.

Pott, Phenie, mem adv comm: Pott Foundation, Herman T. and Phenie R.

Potter, Bruce, scholarship comm: Mitchell, Jr. Trust, Oscar

Potter, Charles, dir: Kellenberger Historical Foundation, May Gordon Latham

Potter, Delcour Stephen, III, dir: Lee Foundation, James T.

Potter, Helen, treas: Adler Foundation

Potter, Janet, supvr: Kmart Corp.

Potter, John R., secy, dir: Papitto Foundation

Potter, Nancy, pres: Eden Foods

Potter, Robert, off: Grenfell Association of America

Pottruck, David S., pres, ceo, dir: Schwab & Co., Charles

Potts, Charles F., pres: APAC Inc.

Poulos, Michael J., chmn, dir: American General Finance

Poulos, Michael James, dir: American General Finance Foundation

Poulson, Howard D., vchmn: Growmark, Inc.

Poulson, Richard J. M., vp, dir: Loughran Foundation, Mary and Daniel

Pounder, Elizabeth, trust: Eastern Star Hall and Home Foundation

Pounds, William F., vp (human resources): Copperweld Steel Co.

Poundstone, William N., secy: Lost Tree Charitable Foundation

Poupore-Haats, Antoinette, secy/treas, exec dir: Ordean Foundation

Powell, Arlene B., trust: Baird Brothers Co. Foundation

Powell, David G., pres, dir: AlliedSignal Foundation

Powell, E. Bryson, trust: Scott Foundation, William R., John G., and Emma

Powell, George Everett, III, treas: Powell Family Foundation; pres, ceo, dir: Yellow Corp.; trust: Yellow Corporate Foundation

Powell, George Everett, Jr., dir: Powell Family Foundation; chmn, dir: Yellow Corp.; trust: Yellow Corporate Foundation

Powell, H. Robert, exec vp, chief investment off: AON Corp.

Powell, Jeanette, asst secy: Hunt Manufacturing Co. Foundation

Powell, Jerry W., secy: Central Bank Foundation

Powell, John B., Jr., trust: Baker Trust, Clayton

Powell, Joseph B., Jr., trust: Haley Foundation, W. B.

Powell, L.R., vp, secy, treas: Copolymer Foundation

Powell, Lavatus V., Jr., trust: Jergens Foundation, Andrew

Powell, Mary Catherine, trust, chmn: Kuehn Foundation

Powell, Myrtis H., dir: Public Welfare Foundation

Powell, Nancy G., vp, dir: Universal Leaf Foundation

Powell, Nicholas A., dir: Powell Family Foundation

Powell, Nicholas K., secy: Kuehn Foundation

Powell, Peter E., trust: Kuehn Foundation

Powell, Richardson K., trust: Kuehn Foundation

Powell, Robert E., dir: Inland Steel-Ryerson Foundation

Powell, Sandra T., treas, asst secy: Potlatch Foundation for Higher Education/Potlatch Foundation II

Powell, W. H., dir: National Starch & Chemical Foundation

Powell, William A., pres, dir: AmSouth Bancorporation

Powelson, Leo, trust: Woodward Governor Co. Charitable Trust

Power, Eugene B., vp: Domino's Foundation

Power, Richard D., cfo: Tyco Laboratories, Inc.

Powers, Betty J., exec asst: Progressive Corp.

Powers, Ed, trust: Acushnet Foundation

Powers, James Frances, trust: LTV Foundation

Powers, John A., chmn, dir: Heublein; dir: Grand Metropolitan Food Sector Foundation

Powers, John P., dir: Educational Foundation of America

Powers, June M, dir, pres: Dell Foundation, Hazel

Powers, P. J., trust: Acme-Cleveland Foundation

Powers, Paul J., chmn, pres, ceo: Commercial Intertech Corp.

Powers, Richard P., mem contributions comm: Syntex Corp.

Powers, Thomas E., treas: Brooklyn Benevolent Society

Poynter, Marion K., trust: Poynter Fund

Prager, Denis J., dir (health program): MacArthur Foundation, John D. and Catherine T.

Prager, William W., pres, trust: Summerfield Foundation, Solon E.

Prager, William W., Jr., dir, vp: Raskin Foundation, Hirsch and Braine

Prager, William W., Sr., dir, secy: Raskin Foundation, Hirsch and Braine

Pralle, Robert, vp: Muth Foundation, Peter and Mary

Pramberg, John H., Jr., pres, dir: Arakelian Foundation, Mary Alice; trust: Swasey Fund for Relief of Public School Teachers of Newburyport; trust: Wheelwright Scientific School

Pramberg, John W., trust: Wheelwright Scientific School

Prancan, Jane, exec dir: US WEST Foundation

Prater, Ed, mem contributions comm: Diamond Shamrock

Pratt, Alice Evans, pres, treas: Wills Foundation

Pratt, David W., trust: Wilcox Trust, S. W.

Pratt, Donald H., pres: Butler Manufacturing Co.; vp, trust: Butler Manufacturing Co. Foundation

Pratt, Donald Henry, vp, trust: Butler Foundation, Alice

Pratt, G. A., cfo: Atari Corp.

Pratt, G. Gerald, trust: Meyer Memorial Trust

Pratt, Harold I., trust: Pierce Charitable Trust, Harold Whitworth

Pratt, Lincoln, trust: Providence Journal Charitable Foundation

Pratt, Marsha, trust: Wells Trust Fund, Fred W.

Pratt, Michael G., pres, ceo: Coats & Clark Inc.

Pratt, Peter E., vp, secy: Wills Foundation

Pratt, Richard W., mgr: Bishop Trust for the SPCA of Manatee County, Florida, Lillian H.

Pratt, Richardson, Jr., treas: Clark Foundation, Robert Sterling

Pratt, William H., dir: Kirkland & Ellis Foundation

Praulins, Pam, trust: Ziemann Foundation

Pray, Donald E., trust: Bernsen Foundation, Grace and Franklin; secy: Reynolds Foundation, Donald W.

Precourt, Lyman A., trust: Klingler Foundation, Helen and Charles

Preece, William H. S., Jr., treas: Motorola Foundation

Preis, Gladys M., trust, mgr: Baumker Charitable Foundation, Elsie and Harry

Preis, Nancy, trust: Baumker Charitable Foundation, Elsie and Harry

Preiskel, Barbara Scott, trust: Ford Foundation

Prelack, Steven, cfo: Alden's Inc.

Prendergast, Joseph, pres, dir: Wachovia Bank of Georgia, N.A.

Prendergast, Larry, trust: Turrell Fund

Prendergast, R. F., secy, dir: Bowyer Foundation, Ambrose and Gladys

Prentiss, John, trust: Sunmark Foundation

Prepouses, Nicholas T., treas, dir: Treadwell Foundation, Nora Eccles

Prescott, Betty, trust, secy: Wilson Public Trust, Ralph

Presley, W. Dewey, dir: Collins Foundation, Carr P.

Press, Frank D., trust, mem exec comm: Sloan Foundation, Alfred P.

Pressley, Barbara, mem trust fund comm: Ingram Trust, Joe

Prest, Eleanor, secy, dir: Briggs Foundation, T. W.

Preston, Burton, vp distribution comm: Ford and Ada Ford Fund, S. N.

Preston, Carole, secy, dir: Himmelfarb Foundation, Paul and Annetta

Preston, Dana D., asst treas: Amoco Foundation

Preston, Ed, trust: Stern Family Foundation, Alex

Preston, James Edward, chmn, pres, ceo, dir: Avon Products; vp, dir: Avon Products Foundation

Preston, James Y., secy: Giles Foundation, Edward C.

Preston, Kasandra K., secy, treas, dir: Briggs & Stratton Corp. Foundation

Preston, Lewis Thompson, trust, chmn audit comm: Sloan Foundation, Alfred P.

Preston, Michael, dir: Dunning Foundation

Preston, Ralph L., vp, dir: Herbst Foundation; cfo, secy: Newhall Foundation, Henry Mayo

Preston, Seymour Stotler, III, pres, dir, ceo: Elf Atochem North America; trust: Elf Atochem North America Foundation

Prestrud, Stuart Holmes, adv: Archibald Charitable Foundation, Norman

Preucil, Frank M., fdn mgr: Ernst & Young Foundation

Preuss, Peggy L., secy: Preuss Foundation

Preuss, Peter G., pres: Preuss Foundation

Preuss, R. J., vp, secy, treas, dir: Bush-D.D. Nusbaum Foundation, M.G.

Previte, Richard, pres, coo, dir: Advanced Micro Devices

Prewitt, Kenneth, sr vp: Rockefeller Foundation

Preyer, Fred L., trust: Preyer Fund, Mary Norris

Preyer, Jill, trust: Preyer Fund, Mary Norris

Preyer, Kelly Anne, trust: Preyer Fund, Mary Norris

Preyer, Lunsford Richardson, treas, dir: Babcock Foundation, Mary Reynolds; trust: Preyer Fund, Mary Norris; mem bd govs: Richardson Foundation, Smith

Preyer, Norris W., trust: Preyer Fund, Mary Norris

Preyer, Norris W., Jr., trust: Preyer Fund, Mary Norris

Preyer, Robert Otto, trust: Preyer Fund, Mary Norris

Preyer, William Yost Jr., trust: Preyer Fund, Mary Norris; trust: Richardson Fund, Mary Lynn

Price, Alfred L, secy, gen counsel: First Mississippi Corp. Foundation

Price, Carol Swanson, trust: Hamilton Foundation, Florence P.

Price, Charles H., vp, dir: Hultquist Foundation

Price, Charles H., II, chmn, pres, ceo: Ameribank; trust: Hamilton Foundation, Florence P.

Price, Clarence L., dir: Foundation of the Litton Industries

Price, Don K., vp, trust: Weatherhead Foundation

Price, Donna S., coordinator (gifts and grants): Martin Marietta Corp. Foundation

Price, George G., asst secy: Cincinnati Milacron Foundation

Price, Gordon A., cfo: McDonald & Co. Securities; treas: McDonald & Co. Securities Foundation

Price, H. Lyons, pres: Citizens Union Bank

Price, Harold, chmn, treas, trust: Price Foundation, Louis and Harold

Price, Harvey L., vp (grants): Weingart Foundation

Price, Hugh B., vp: Rockefeller Foundation

Price, JoAnn, trust: Price Educational Foundation, Herschel C.

Price, L. L., chmn: Budweiser of the Carolinas Foundation

Price, Melia, asst secy: Moriah Fund

Price, Michael J., pres, dir: Alden's Inc.

Price, Pauline, vp, secy, trust: Price Foundation, Louis and Harold

Price, R. A., trust: Thomas Foundation

Price, Richard H., PhD, trust: Grant Foundation, William T.

Price, Robert E., chmn, pres, ceo, dir: Price Company

Price, Robert W., asst treas: Sioux Steel Co. Foundation

Price, Sol, dir: Weingart Foundation

Price, W. James, IV, trust: Casey Foundation, Eugene B.

Price, W. S., Jr., dir: Kellenberger Historical Foundation, May Gordon Latham

Prickett, F. Daniel, trust: Hyams Foundation

Priddy, Charles Horne, vp, dir: Priddy Foundation

Priddy, Hervey Amsler, dir: Priddy Foundation

Priddy, Robert T., pres, dir: Priddy Foundation

Priddy, Ruby N., dir: Priddy Foundation

Pridgen, Martha, asst secy, dir admin: Reynolds Foundation, Z. Smith

Priesmeyer, Bill, cfo: Onan Corp.

Priest, H. Sam, pres, trust: Gaylord Foundation, Clifford Willard

Priestly, Eric, pres, ceo: Rexham Inc.

Prime, Meredith, gov: Crary Foundation, Bruce L.

Prince, Alan Norton, trust: Chicago Title and Trust Co. Foundation

Prince, Charles O., III, sec, trust: Primerica Foundation

Prince, Edgar D., pres, trust: Prince Foundation

Prince, Edward R., Jr., chmn, ceo, dir: Digicon

Prince, Elsa D., vp, secy, trust: Prince Foundation

Prince, Frederick Henry, trust: Prince Trust, Abbie Norman

Prince, Larry I., trust: Tull Charitable Foundation

Prince, Larry L., chmn, ceo: Genuine Parts Co.

Prince, Mark S., pres, dir: Bank One, Portsmouth, NA

Prince, Mary Martha, vp, dir: Dougherty Foundation

Prince, William Norman Wood, Prince Trust, Abbie Norman

Princing, Tom, pres: Scientific Brake & Equipment Co.

Prindle, R. L., trust: Montgomery Foundation

Printz, Albert, distribution comm: Flowers Charitable Trust, Albert W. and Edith V.

Priory, Sheila McNeil, trust: Kerney Foundation, James

Pritchard, David, pres, ceo: Alyeska Pipeline Service Co.

Pritchard, Gil, pres, ceo: Barbara's Bakery

Pritchard, Lee E., asst secy, asst treas: Broyhill Family Foundation

Pritzker, Daniel F., vp, dir: Pritzker Foundation

Pritzker, James N., don, vp, dir: Pritzker Foundation

Pritzker, Jay Arthur, don, pres, dir: Pritzker Foundation

Pritzker, John A., vp, dir: Pritzker Foundation

Pritzker, Nicholas J., don, vp, secy, dir: Pritzker Foundation

Pritzker, Penny F., vp, asst secy, dir: Pritzker Foundation

Pritzker, Robert Alan, ceo, pres, dir: Marmon Group, Inc.; chmn, vp, dir: Pritzker Foundation

Pritzker, Thomas Jay, don, vp, treas, asst secy, dir: Pritzker Foundation

Pritzlaff, John C., trust: Olin Foundation, Spencer T. and Ann W.

Pritzlaff, Mary O., trust: Monticello College Foundation; vp, trust: Olin Foundation, Spencer T. and Ann W.

Privette, Ray, treas, dir: Nakamichi Foundation, E.

Probasco, Scott L., Jr., vchmn, dir: Third National Corp.

Probert, Edward W., vp, secy: Rippel Foundation, Fannie E.

Prochnow, Lisa B., trust: Prickett Fund, Lynn R. and Karl E.; trust: Richardson Fund, Mary Lynn

Procknow, Donald E., trust: Prudential Foundation

Procter, Mary E., trust: Clark Foundation, Edna McConnell

Proctor, George H., dir, pres: Andalusia Health Services

Proctor, Venable B., secy: O'Connor Foundation, Kathryn

Proctor, William Z., trust: Hawley Foundation

Profeta, Nicholas J., vp, corp secy, mem contributions comm: Polychrome Corp.

Propp, Ephraim, dir: Propp Sons Fund, Morris and Anna

Propp, M. J., dir: Propp Sons Fund, Morris and Anna

Propp, Seymour, dir: Propp Sons Fund, Morris and Anna

Prosser, John W., Jr., treas, dir: Jacobs Engineering Foundation

Prosser, Max W., vp, secy, treas: Santa Fe Pacific Foundation

Prosser, Walter, secy: Sofia American Schools

Prothro, Charles N., vp, dir: Perkins Foundation, Joe and Lois; pres, trust: Perkins-Prothro Foundation

Prothro, Charles V., dir: Perkins Foundation, Joe and Lois

Prothro, Elizabeth P., pres, dir: Perkins Foundation, Joe and Lois; vp, trust: Perkins-Prothro Foundation

Prothro, James E., dir: Perkins Foundation, Joe and Lois

Prothro, Joe N., dir: Perkins Foundation, Joe and Lois; vp, trust: Perkins-Prothro Foundation

Prothro, Mark H., vp, dir: Perkins Foundation, Joe and Lois; treas, trust: Perkins-Prothro Foundation

Prothroe-Stith, Deborah, trust: Hyams Foundation

Protz, Edward L., vp, secy, dir: Northen, Mary Moody

Proudfoot, Allin, trust: Blowitz-Ridgeway Foundation

Prout, Curtis, trust: Humane Society of the Commonwealth of Massachusetts

Prout, Curtis, MD, trust: Campbell and Adah E. Hall Charity Fund, Bushrod H.

Prout, Elissa R., secy, treas: Robison Foundation, Ellis H. and Doris B.

Prouty, Jack Warren, vp: Younkers Foundation

Prouty, Lewis I., treas: Prouty Foundation, Olive Higgins

Prouty, Richard, trust, pres: Prouty Foundation, Olive Higgins

Provencal, Donald L., cfo, dir: FIP Corp.

Provence, Herbert H., dir: Graphic Arts Education & Research Foundation

Prud'homme, Laurence, cfo: Tarmac America Inc.

Pruet, Ron B., Jr., cfo: Sonat Exploration

Pruis, John J., dir: Ball Brothers Foundation; exec vp, dir: Ball Foundation, George and Frances

Pruitt, Peter T., pres, coo, dir: Hall & Co. Inc., Frank B.

Prus, Francis Vincent, exec vp (research & devel), dir: Goodyear Tire & Rubber Co.

Pryor, Millard H., Jr., trust: Hartford Courant Foundation

Pschirrer, Martin E., trust: Applied Power Foundation

Psiol, A. D., treas, dir: Koulaieff Educational Fund, Trustees of Ivan Y.

Ptacin, Gregory J., dir: Oakley-Lindsay Foundation of Quincy Newspapers & Quincy Broadcasting Co.

Puccetti, Patricia I., program dir: Homeland Foundation

Puchta, Charles G., trust: Smith, Jr. Charitable Trust, Jack J.

Puck, Robert J., treas, secy: Blank Family Foundation

Puckett, Julie, vp, dir: Phillips Foundation, Waite and Genevieve

Puckett, Marlene, dir: Morrison Knudsen Corp. Foundation Inc.

Puckett, Sam L., dir: Burton Foundation, William T. and Ethel Lewis

Puelicher, John A., Marshall & Ilsley Bank; pres, dir: Marshall & Ilsley Foundation; pres, dir: Schroeder Foundation, Walter

Puerner, John, dir: Chicago Tribune Foundation

Puett, Nelson, pres: Puett Foundation, Nelson

Puett, Ruth B., vp: Puett Foundation, Nelson

Pugh, Lawrence R., chmn, pres, ceo, dir: VF Corp.

Pugh, Linda, asst secy: Winchester Foundation

Pugh, Robert D., chmn: Rockefeller Foundation, Winthrop

Pugh, W. D., dir: Price Waterhouse Foundation

Pugsley, Nancy, trust, vp: Woman's Seamen's Friend Society of Connecticut

Pukall, Mary, dir: Pukall Lumber Foundation

Pukall, Robert L., pres: Pukall Lumber

Pukall, Roger L., dir: Pukall Lumber Foundation

Pukall-Christiansen, Debra, dir: Pukall Lumber Foundation

Pulaski, John, vp: Swiss American Securities, Inc.

Pulitzer, Joseph, Jr., chmn, dir: Pulitzer Publishing Co.

Pulitzer, Michael Edgar, pres, ceo, dir: Pulitzer Publishing Co.; vchmn, pres, dir: Pulitzer Publishing Co. Foundation

Pulitzer IV, Joseph, dir: Pulitzer Publishing Co. Foundation

Pullen, D.E., vp: Manville Fund

Pullen, Raymond, CHC Foundation

Pulles, Gregory J., secy: TCF Foundation

Pulliam, Eugene Smith, vp, dir: Central Newspapers Foundation

Pulliam, Larry, vp, treas, cfo: Noble Foundation, Samuel Roberts

Pulling, Thomas L., dir: Luce Foundation, Henry

Pulling, Thomas Leffingwell, trust: Mulford Foundation, Vincent

Pulver, Joyce M., dir commun: Avery Dennison Corp.

Pundsack, Fred L., chmn, pres, ceo, dir: Susquehanna Corp.

Punzelt, Shirley M., trust: Dorr Foundation

Purcell, Patrick E., pres: News America Publishing Inc.; trust, treas: O'Fallon Trust, Martin J. and Mary Anne

Purcell, Philip J., chmn, ceo: Dean Witter Discover

Purdom, Douglas J., vp finance: Magma Copper Co.

Purdum, Robert L., chmn, ceo, pres: Armco Inc.; pres, trust: Armco Foundation

Purdy, Raymond J., exec dir: Massachusetts Charitable Mechanics Association

Purks, W. K., MD, pres: Vicksburg Hospital Medical Foundation

Purl, Doris G., charities coordinator: Brown Group Incorporated Charitable Trust

Purmort, Paul W., Jr., trust: Van Wert County Foundation

Purvis, G. Frank, Jr., chmn, dir: Pan-American Life Insurance Co.

Purvis, Sarah Banda, mgr, secy: Consolidated Natural Gas Co. Foundation

Puryear, Mary, program off (culture & arts): Prudential Foundation

Pusateri, Elizabeth A., secy, asst treas: Benedum Foundation, Claude Worthington

Putman, Paukl, vp: Goerlich Family Foundation

Putnam, David F., dir: Putnam Foundation

Putnam, George, III, trust: Putnam Prize Fund for the Promotion of Scholarship, William Lowell

Putnam, James A., dir: Putnam Foundation

Putnam, Rosamund P., dir: Putnam Foundation

Putnam, Thomas, pres, treas: Markem Corp.

Putney, Jessie M., trust: Babson-Webber-Mustard Fund

Putney, Mark W., chmn, ceo, dir: Midwest Resources

Pyka, William, MD, trust: Jurzykowski Foundation, Alfred

Pyke, John S., Jr., trust: Hanna Co. Foundation, M.A.

Pyle, Edwin T., dir: Mingenback Foundation, Julia J.

Pyle, Ida M., trust: Ward Heritage Foundation, Mamie McFaddin

Pyle, Juanita Abeil, trust: Abell Education Trust, Jennie G. and Pearl

Pyle, Judith D., vchmn: Rayovac Corp.

Pyle, Thomas F., chmn, pres, ceo: Rayovac Corp.

Pyne, Eben W., dir: Grace Foundation, Inc.

Pyra, Thomas, cfo: Intercraft Co., Inc.

Pyrcik, Paul, dir: Waste Management

Pytte, Agnar, dir: Fairchild Foundation, Sherman; trust: Goodyear Tire & Rubber Company Fund

Q

Quadros, Joseph J., Jr., vp, trust: Beazley Foundation; vp: Frederick Foundation

Quaintance, Dave, dir: McDonnell Douglas Corp.-West

Qualls, Robert C., trust: Haggar Foundation

Qualls, T. L., asst secy: Winn-Dixie Stores Foundation

Quammen, David, dir: Claiborne Art Ortenberg Foundation, Liz

Quarles, Pam, mgr (human resources): Murata Erie North America

Quatman, George W., Jr., pres: American Society of Ephesus

Quatman, John D., American Society of Ephesus

Quatman, Joseph B., vp, trust: American Society of Ephesus

Quatman, Joseph E., Jr., trust: American Society of Ephesus

Quattlebaum, Ann, mem: Piedmont Health Care Foundation

Queenan, Charles J., trust: Evans Foundation, Edward P.

Queller, Robert L., trust: Earhart Foundation

Querido, Arthur J., trust, secy: Fox Foundation Trust, Jacob L. and Lewis

Quern, Arthur Foster, dir: Field Foundation of Illinois

Quesnel, Greg, sr vp, cfo: Consolidated Freightways; vp: Emery Air Freight Educational Foundation

Questrom, Allen I., res 1992: Federated Department Stores and Allied Stores Corp.

Queyssac, Daniel, pres: SGS-Thomson Microelectronics Inc.

Quick, Elizabeth L., dir, mem: Cannon Foundation

Quick, Robert F., treas: Bedminster Fund

Quigg, William M., mgr: Central Broadcasting Corp. Charitable Trust

Quigley, Lynn P., Mathis-Pfohl Foundation

Quigley, Thomas J., trust: Hotchkiss Foundation, W. R.

Quillin, Debra J., treas: Garvey Texas Foundation

Quillman, Sandra, trust: Cherokee Foundation

Quilter, James F., vp, secy, treas, dir: McGraw Foundation

Quin, Joseph Marvin, trust: Ashland Oil Foundation

Quine, Douglas B., pres: Triskelion Inc.

Quinlan, Donald P., ceo, chmn: Graphic Controls Corp.

Quinlan, Kathleen, asst secy: Zilkha Foundation

Quinlan, Michael, chmn, dir, ceo: McDonald's Corp.

Quinlan, Robert, dir: Freddie Mac Foundation

Quinn, Ann, sr vp mktg div: Bank One, Texas, NA

Quinn, David W., dir, exec vp, cfo: Centex Corp.

Quinn, E. V., dir: Bowyer Foundation, Ambrose and Gladys

Quinn, James, secy, dir: Gardiner Scholarship Foundation

Quinn, James W., asst secy: Allen Brothers Foundation

Quinn, Jane, program dir: Wallace-Reader's Digest Fund, DeWitt

Quinn, Mrs. Thomas F., dir, chmn: Emergency Aid of Pennsylvania Foundation

Quinn, Rick, chmn contributions comm: Dollar General Corp.

Quinn, Tracy A., vp (communications): Freedom Forum

Quint, Ira, chmn, pres: Conston Corp.

Qureshey, Safi U., co-chmn, pres, ceo: AST Research, Inc.

R

Raab, G. Kirk, ceo, pres: Genentech

Raabin, Gertrude, dir: Goodstein Family Foundation, David

Rabb, Esther V., trust: Rabb Charitable Trust, Sidney R.

Rabb, Irving W., trust: Ford Foundation, Joseph F. and Clara

Rabb, Norman S., trust: Ford Foundation, Joseph F. and Clara

Rabert, Dean F., Plankenhorn Foundation, Harry

Rabin, Paul I., asst treas: AON Foundation

Rabin, Stanley A., pres, ceo, dir: Commercial Metals Co.

Rabinowitch, Victor, vp (programs): MacArthur Foundation, John D. and Catherine T.

Raborn, Donald D., pres: Croft Metals

Racer, Elizabeth E., trust: Durell Foundation, George Edward

Rachmiel, George J., trust: Crum and Forster Foundation

Rackmore, Martin, trust: Allied Educational Foundation Fund

Raclin, Ernestine M., chmn: First Source Corp.; pres: First Source Corp. Foundation

Radcliff, Sarah Jeffords, secy: Dobson Foundation

Radcliffe, R. Stephen, sr vp, chief actuary: American United Life Insurance Co.

Radecki, Martin, pres: Metropolitan Health Council of Indianapolis

Rader, I. Andrew, chmn, dir: Bradley Foundation, Lynde and Harry

Radin, H. Marcus, pres, dir: Radin Foundation

Rados, Alexander, vp: Smith Foundation, Lon V.

Radosh, Alice, trust: New York Foundation

Radov, Joseph, pres, dir: Relations Foundation

Radov, Sylvia, secy, dir: Fel-Pro/ Mecklenburger Foundation

Radov, Sylvia M., vp, dir: Relations Foundation

Radt, Richard L., pres, ceo: Mosinee Paper Corp.; pres, dir: Mosinee Paper Corp. Foundation

Radtke, H. Helmut, pres, ceo: Melitta North America Inc.

Raff, Douglass A., trust: Bullitt Foundation

Raff, K. Nerator, pres: First Tennessee Bank

Raffin, Margaret, dir: Ishiyama Foundation

Rafsky, Steven M., secy, treas: Leader Foundation

Raftery, Kate, trust: Homeland Foundation

Ragan, Anna Laura, asst secy: Cherokee Foundation

Ragatz, Thomas R., secy: Bassett Foundation, Norman

Ragen, Francis W., mem: Ragen, Jr. Memorial Fund Trust No. 1, James M.

Ragen, Robert E., mem: Ragen, Jr. Memorial Fund Trust No. 1, James M.

Ragen, Virginia E., mem: Ragen, Jr. Memorial Fund Trust No. 1, James M.

Rager, Robert L., chmn: Wagnalls Memorial

Ragland, John C., chmn, pres, ceo, dir: Liberty National Bank

Ragone, David Vincent, dir: Luce Foundation, Henry; Sifco Industries Inc.

Rahdert, George, trust: Poynter Fund

Rahill, Richard E., trust: Corning Incorporated Foundation

Rahjes, Doyle Dean, vp, trust: Hansen Foundation, Dane G.

Rahm, C. R., dir: Legg & Co. Foundation

Rahm, Susan B., trust: Berkman Charitable Trust, Allen H. and Selma W.

Rahr, Frederick W., vp, dir: Rahr Foundation

Rahr, Guido R., Jr., chmn, ceo: Rahr Malting Co.; pres, dir: Rahr Foundation

Raiffa, Howard, trust: Sage Foundation, Russell

Raiffe, Herbert, pres, trust: Gund Foundation

Rainbolt, Harold E., vp, secy: Southwestern Bell Foundation

Raines, Franklin D., vchmn: Federal National Mortgage Assn., Fannie Mae; dir: Federal National Mortgage Assn. Foundation; chmn, trust: German Marshall Fund of the United States; trust: Johnson Foundation, Robert Wood

Raines, Mary E., corp secy: Delta Air Lines; asst secy: Delta Air Lines Foundation

Raines, Osborne L., Jr., dir: Fieldcrest Foundation

Rainey, Evelyn, corp personnel supervisor: FKI Holdings Inc.

Rainey, William, secy, dir: Cabot Corp. Foundation

Rainger, Charles W., pres: Sandusky International Inc.; trust: Sandusky International Foundation

Rainsford, Bettis C., cfo, exec vp: Delta Woodside Industries

Rainwater, Betty Gregg, vchmn: BCR Foundation

Rainwater, Crawford, chmn: BCR Foundation

Rainwater, Crawford, Jr., treas: BCR Foundation

Rainwater, Freddie B., secy: BCR Foundation

Rainwater, Karen E., secy: Rainwater Charitable Foundation

Rainwater, Nancy Gregg, vp: BCR Foundation

Rainwater, Richard E., pres: Rainwater Charitable Foundation

Raiser, Herbert A., trust: Hebrew Technical Institute

Raithel, Michael L., trust: Crane Fund for Widows and Children

Rearwin, Kenneth R., pres, dir: Parker Foundation

Reath, Mrs. Henry T., Wurts Memorial, Henrietta Tower

Reaves, Patricia, trust: Leader Foundation

Reavis, Lincoln, trust: Switzer Foundation

Recanati, Michael A., vp, secy, treas, dir: OSG Foundation

Recanati, Raphael, chmn fin & devel comms, dir: Overseas Shipholding Group; pres, dir: OSG Foundation

Recchia, Richard D., coo, exec vp: Mitsubishi Motor Sales of America, Inc.

Recchuite, Martin C., treas: ARCO Foundation

Reckler, Henry, secy, treas, dir: Wolf Foundation, Melvin and Elaine

Reckling, Isla C., trust: Rienzi Foundation; asst secy: Turner Charitable Foundation

Reckling, James S., trust: Turner Charitable Foundation

Reckling, T. R., III, pres, trust: Turner Charitable Foundation

Reckling, Thomas R., IV, trust: Turner Charitable Foundation

Recknagel, Fred, III, secy: Florida Rock Industries Foundation

Rectanus, William R., trust: Ohio Bell Foundation

Reda, K., trust: Motch Corp. Foundation

Redden, Roger Duffy, treas: Life Sciences Research Foundation

Redding, T. H., pres: Acme-McCrary and Sapona Foundation

Reddy, Thomas, dir: Carvel Foundation, Thomas and Agnes

Redell, Helene E., prog dir Luce Scholars Prog: Luce Foundation, Henry

Reder, Carl P., trust: Olympia Brewing Co. Employees Beneficial Trust

Redgrave, Martyn, cfo: Kentucky Fried Chicken Corp.

Redies, Robert D., chmn: R&B Tool Co.; trust: Redies Foundation, Edward F.

Redle, W.D., pres: Bryan Foundation, Dodd and Dorothy L.

Redle, William D., trust: Perkins Foundation, B. F. & Rose H.

Redlin, Gerald G., trust: Harvest States Foundation

Redman, James, trust: Redman Foundation

Redman, Manville, vchmn: McMahon Foundation

Redmann, Usher, secy, treas: Browning Masonic Memorial Fund, Otis Avery

Redmond, Charles Robert, chmn, dir: Pfaffinger Foundation; pres, ceo, dir: Times Mirror Foundation

Redmond, Paul A., chmn, ceo, dir: Washington Water Power Co.

Redpath, Frederick L., treas, trust: Sullivan Foundation, Algernon Sydney

Redstone, Sumner Murray, chmn, dir: Viacom International Inc.

Reece, Disney, Memorex Telex Corp.

Reed, A. Lachlan, trust: Sweatt Foundation, Harold W.

Reed, C. Lawson, trust: Thendara Foundation

Reed, C.L., III, trust: Thendara Foundation

Reed, Carlton D., Jr., chmn, dir: Central Maine Power Co.

Reed, Charles L., pres, treas, dir: Thomas Memorial Foundation, Theresa A.

Reed, Cordell, mem (corp responsibility comm): Commonwealth Edison Co.

Reed, David W., trust: Reed Foundation

Reed, Donald B., exec vp, coo, dir: New England Telephone Co.

Reed, Dorothy W., trust: Anderson Foundation, William P.; trust: Thendara Foundation

Reed, Earl F., Jr., trust: Gibson Foundation, Addison H.

Reed, Elizabeth C., secy: Britton Fund; secy: Haskell Fund

Reed, Foster A., trust: Thendara Foundation

Reed, Harold S., trust: Sweatt Foundation, Harold W.

Reed, Ina N., dir: Wasie Foundation

Reed, J. Brad, trust: Massey Foundation, Jack C.

Reed, James J., secy: Davey Co. Foundation

Reed, James M., trust: Union Camp Charitable Trust

Reed, John, trust: Sunmark Foundation

Reed, John M., dir: PQ Corp. Foundation

Reed, John Shepard, chmn, ceo: Citicorp; trust: Sage Foundation, Russell; dir: Spencer Foundation

Reed, Martha S., trust: Sweatt Foundation, Harold W.

Reed, Maurice T., Jr., trust: First Mississippi Corp. Foundation

Reed, Nancy, dir: Dreyer's & Edy's Grand Ice Cream Charitable Fdn.

Reed, Paul H., dir: Hoyt Foundation

Reed, Peter S., trust: Thendara Foundation

Reed, Philip D., chmn, pres: Reed Foundation, Philip D.

Reed, Robert, trust: Matthews and Co. Educational and Charitable Trust, James H.

Reed, Robert A., ceo, pres: Physicians Mutual Insurance; pres, dir: Physicians Mutual Insurance Co. Foundation

Reed, Robert W., pres, dir: Intel Foundation

Reed, Scott Eldridge, sr exec vp, cfo: Branch Banking & Trust Co.

Reed, Vincent Emory, trust: Graham Fund, Philip L.; dir: Strong Foundation, Hattie M.

Reed, William Garrard, Jr., chmn: Simpson Investment Co.; dir: Matlock Foundation

Reed, William S., trust: Sweatt Foundation, Harold W.

Reeder, William, trust: Wilson Public Trust, Ralph

Reedman, Herbert, dir: Reedman FCS Foundation

Reedman, Ralph, off: Reedman FCS Foundation

Reedman, Ralph, Jr., pres: Reedman Car-Truck World Center

Reedman, Stanley, dir: Reedman FCS Foundation

Reedman, Thomas, dir: Reedman FCS Foundation

Reepmeyer, Lorraine, mem (contributions comm): Northern Trust Co. Charitable Trust

Rees, Charles W., Jr., dir: Powell Foundation, Charles Lee

Rees, Diane D., dir: Cornerstone Foundation of Northeastern Wisconsin

Reese, Evelyn M., dir: Van Huffel Foundation, I. J.

Reese, Harry C., treas, dir: Comprecare Foundation

Reese, J. Gilbert, pres, trust: Evans Foundation, Thomas J.

Reese, John, trust: Shafer Foundation, Richard H. and Ann

Reese, L.H., dir, secy, treas: Heath Foundation, Ed and Mary

Reese, Lowell, dir: Brillion Foundation

Reese, Roger A., cfo: AMCORE Bank, N.A. Rockford

Reese, Stanley, trust: Sullivan Musical Foundation, William Matheus

Reese, Terry W., asst treas: Vulcan Materials Co. Foundation

Reese, Thomas, acting dir: Getty Trust, J. Paul

Reeves, Charles B., Jr., pres, trust: Warfield Memorial Fund, Anna Emory

Reeves, J. Paul, vp, bd mem, dir: Gregg-Graniteville Foundation

Reeves, Margaret H., pres, trust: Reeves Foundation

Reeves, Woodie, vp: Vevay-Switzerland County Foundation

Regal, Melryo R., treas: Foster & Gallagher Foundation

Regan, Andrew W., secy, dir: Gronewaldt Foundation, Alice Busch

Regan, Douglas P., mem: Northern Trust Co. Charitable Trust

Regan, Grace O'Neil, vp: O'Neil Foundation, W.

Regan, Joseph J., vp, dir: Martin Foundation, Bert William

Regan, Lois M., adm, program off (urban environment): Cary Charitable Trust, Mary Flagler

Regan, Peter M., dir: Uslico Foundation

Regazzi, John, cfo: Avnet, Inc.

Regenstein, Joseph, Jr., pres, dir: Regenstein Foundation

Regnery, Anne, trust: Western Shade Cloth Charitable Foundation

Regnery, Patrick B., trust: Western Shade Cloth Charitable Foundation

Regnery, William H. II, trust: Western Shade Cloth Charitable Foundation

Rego, Anthony C., co-chmn, co-ceo: Riser Foods

Reherman, Ronald G., pres, ceo, dir: Southern Indiana Gas & Electric Co.

Rehm, Jack D., chmn, pres, ceo, dir: Meredith Corp.

Rehmke, Jane, mem: AHS Foundation

Rehn, E.L., trust: Wasmer Foundation

Rehr, Helen, trust: New York Foundation

Reice, Charles T., vp, treas, dir: Bergner Foundation, P.A.

Reich, E., dir, secy: Lawrence Foundation, Alice

Reich, Lawrence A., dir: Bauer Foundation, M. R.

Reichard, David E., vp, cfo: Buffalo Forge Co.

Reichard, William E., secy: Saint Gerard Foundation

Reichardt, Carl E., chmn, ceo, dir: Wells Fargo & Co.

Reichel, Aaron I., dir: Fischel Foundation, Harry and Jane

Reichel, Hillel, assoc dir: Fischel Foundation, Harry and Jane

Reichel, O. Asher, chmn, dir: Fischel Foundation, Harry and Jane

Reichert, Jack Frank, chmn, pres, ceo, dir: Brunswick Corp.; dir: Brunswick Foundation

Reichert, James A., vp: West Texas Corp., J. M.

Reichling, George, sr vp (sales): Schieffelin & Somerset Co.

Reichman, Vivian C., secy, treas, trust: Altschul Foundation

Reickert, Erick Arthur, chmn: Acustar Inc.

Reid, Ala H., adm: Parker Foundation, Theodore Edson; treas: Stoneman Charitable Foundation, Anne and David

Reid, Charles M., dir: Sternberger Foundation, Sigmund

Reid, Fergus, III, treas, trust: Astor Foundation, Vincent

Reid, Jack P., pres, coo: Navajo Refining Co.

Reid, James, exec vp: Lipton Foundation, Thomas J.

Reid, James Sims, Jr., chmn, ceo, dir: Standard Products Co.; pres, trust: Standard Products Co. Foundation

Reid, Jean, chmn: Bernstein & Co. Foundation, Sanford C.

Reid, John A., trust: Slemp Foundation

Reid, Martin J., pres, coo, dir: Alpha Industries

Reid, Richard, trust: Gillespie Memorial Fund, Boynton

Reidler, Carl J., dir: Reidler Foundation

Reidler, Paul G., pres: Reidler Foundation

Reidy, Ann, Bushee Foundation, Florence Evans

Reiff, Doug, sr vp (sales & mktg): Boots Pharmaceuticals, Inc.

Reiff, J., cfo: Cornnuts, Inc.

Reifsnyder, Frank, trust: Foundation for Middle East Peace

Reighley, H. Ward, chmn, mem adv comm: Ford Foundation, Edward E.

Reilly, Donald C., pres, ceo: Superior Tube Co.

Reilly, Edward, grants consultant: Rice Foundation

Reilly, Edward A., secy-treas, dir: Dreyfus Foundation, Camille and Henry

Reilly, Elizabeth C., trust: Reilly Foundation

Reilly, J. P., chmn, pres: Monroe Auto Equipment Co.

Reilly, John E., chmn: Isuzu Motors America Inc.

Reilly, John H., Jr., trust: Statter Foundation, Amy Plant

Reilly, John Richard, secy, treas: Schultz Foundation

Reilly, Jonathan, pres, dir: Mertz Foundation, Martha

Reilly, Kevin, Jr., pres: Lamar Corp.

Reilly, Kevin, Sr., chmn: Lamar Corp.

Reilly, Lawrence H., pres, dir: Union Mutual Fire Insurance Co.

Reilly, Marie Ford, trust: Pittsburgh Child Guidance Foundation

Reilly, Richard R., cultural & the arts adv: Copley Foundation, James S.

Reilly, Thomas E., Jr., chmn (community concerns): NBD Bank, N.A.; chmn, pres, dir: Reilly Industries; trust: Reilly Foundation

Reilly, Wayne R., trust: Danforth Co. Foundation, John W.

Reilly, William K., trust: German Marshall Fund of the United States

Reily, H. Eustis, pres, dir: Reily Foundation

Reily, Robert D., vp, dir: Reily Foundation

Reily, William Boatner, III, pres, dir: Reily & Co., William B.; dir: Reily Foundation

Reiman, Robert W., M.D., trust: Blair Foundation, John

Reiman, Thomas J., pres: Indiana Bell Telephone Co.

Rein, Catherine A., exec vp: Metropolitan Life Insurance Co.; dir: Metropolitan Life Foundation

Reinberger, Robert N., co-dir, trust: Reinberger Foundation

Reinberger, William C., co-dir, trust: Reinberger Foundation

Reinemund, Steve S., ceo, pres: Pizza Hut

Reiner, John P., secy, treas, dir: Loewy Family Foundation

Reiners, Jan, dir: American Schlafhorst Foundation, Inc.

Reinhard, Keith L., chmn, ceo, chmn exec comm: DDB Needham Worldwide

Reinhard, Martin, dir: Eagles Memorial Foundation

Reinhardt, Edith A., trust: Presser Foundation

Reinhardt, J. Alec, exec vp, cfo: Cooper Tire & Rubber Co.; trust: Cooper Tire & Rubber Foundation

Reinhart, DeWayne B., pres: Reinhart Institutional Foods; trust: Reinhart Family Foundation, D.B.

Reinhart, Harold, pres: Tombstone Pizza Corp.

Reinhart, James, trust: Eastman Foundation, Alexander

Reinhart, M. H., dir: Carpenter Foundation, E. Rhodes and Leona B.

Reinhart, Marjorie A., trust: Reinhart Family Foundation, D.B.

Reinhold, Peter E., dir: Weber Charities Corp., Frederick E.

Reinking, C. William, pres, ceo: Exchange Bank; dir: Exchange Bank Foundation

Reinowski, Dave, dir: Dearborn Cable Communications Fund

Reins, Ralph E., dir: AlliedSignal Foundation

Reinschreiber, Mitchell L., exec vp, cfo, trust: Weisman Art Foundation, Frederick R.

Reintjes, Robert J., dir: Francis Families Foundation

Reis, Jean S., trust: Corbett Foundation

Richardson, Elliot Lee, chmn, dir: Hitachi Foundation

Richardson, Eudora L., trust: Hillsdale Fund

Richardson, Frank E., trust: Richardson Foundation, Frank E. and Nancy M.

Richardson, Frank H., pres, ceo, dir: Shell Oil Co.

Richardson, H. A., vp: Avery-Fuller Children's Center

Richardson, Heather S., trust: Randolph Foundation; trust, mem bd govs: Richardson Foundation, Smith

Richardson, Henry Smith, Jr., trust: Randolph Foundation; chmn, trust, mem bd govs, don son: Richardson Foundation, Smith; trust: Richardson Fund, Grace

Richardson, Joan, trust: Bradford Foundation, George and Ruth; secy, dir: Gerbode Foundation, Wallace Alexander

Richardson, Joseph N., secy: Texas Instruments

Richardson, Lunsford, Jr., pres, trust: Hillsdale Fund; mem bd govs: Richardson Foundation, Smith

Richardson, Nancy, bd mem: Roblee Foundation, Joseph H. and Florence A.

Richardson, Nancy M., trust: Richardson Foundation, Frank E. and Nancy M.

Richardson, Peter L., trust: Randolph Foundation; pres: Richardson Foundation, Smith

Richardson, Robert Randolph, trust: Randolph Foundation; trust: Richardson Fund, Grace

Richardson, Ronald, cfo: Bank One, Cleveland, NA

Richardson, Sarah Beinecke, dir: Prospect Hill Foundation

Richardson, Stuart Smith, trust: Randolph Foundation; trust, mem bd govs: Richardson Foundation, Smith

Richardson, Susan H., trust: Holtzmann Foundation, Jacob L. and Lillian

Richardson, T.H., trust: Wasmer Foundation

Richardson, William Chase, PhD, trust: Kaiser Family Foundation, Henry J.; dir: Pew Charitable Trusts

Richey, H.S., trust: Sifco Foundation

Richey, Herbert S., trust: Oglebay Norton Foundation

Richey, Kevin, trust: Warner Foundation, Lee and Rose

Richey, Ronald Kay, chmn, ceo, dir: Torchmark Corp.

Richey, S. W., trust: Warner Foundation, Lee and Rose

Richie, L. C., trust: Chrysler Corp. Fund

Richman, Martin Franklin, secy: Pforzheimer Foundation, Carl and Lily

Richman, Sidney, trust: Forbes Charitable Fund, Herman

Richmond, Charles P., dir: Arakelian Foundation, Mary Alice

Richmond, Frederick W., dir: Richmond Foundation, Frederick W.

Richmond, John L., asst treas: USX Foundation

Richmond, Julia A., asst secy: MCJ Foundation

Richmond, Julius B., mem counc, dir: Foundation for Child Development

Richmond, Ruth B., pres, trust: Templeton Foundation, Herbert A.

Richmond, William C., adv: Van Vleet Foundation

Richstone, Ellen B., cfo: Augat, Inc.

Richter, Alice, trust: KPMG Peat Marwick Foundation

Richter, Charles H., treas: Gerschel Foundation, Patrick A.

Richter, David W., secy: Gordon Foundation, Charles and Gertrude

Richter, James, vp, dir: Hook Drug Foundation

Richter, Linda, asst treas: CBS Foundation

Richter, Maria Heilbron, secy, dir: Cintas Foundation

Richter, Michael, trust: Woltman Foundation, B. M.

Rick, David F., trust: Janssen Foundation, Henry

Ricker, Sally Richards, trust: Bray Charitable Trust, Viola E.

Ricketts, John L., exec secy: Mandell Foundation, Samuel P.

Ricketts, Thomas R., chmn, pres: Standard Federal Bank

Rickman, Ronald L., vp, dir: Lee Foundation

Ricks, Gary R., trust, ceo: Wilbur Foundation, Marguerite Eyer

Ricksen, John C., vp: Beaver Foundation

Ridder, Jane I., secy: Epaphroditus Foundation

Ridder, Kathleen C., trust: Bigelow Foundation, F. R.

Ridder, Paul Anthony, pres, dir: Knight-Ridder, Inc.

Riddle, Dennis Raymond, First National Bank of Atlanta

Rider, Christine, dir: Chicago Tribune Foundation

Rider, D. Brickford, pres: Reynolds Metals Co. Foundation

Ridgley, Robert L., pres, ceo, dir: Northwest Natural Gas Co.

Ridgway, Ronald H., secy, treas, dir: Pulitzer Publishing Co. Foundation

Ridings, Dorothy S., dir: Benton Foundation; trust: Ford Foundation

Ridler, Gregory L., dir: Beecher Foundation, Florence Simon; dir: Finnegan Foundation, John D.

Riecken, Henry W., vchmn bd dirs, vchmn exec comm, mem counc: Foundation for Child Development; trust: Grant Foundation, William T.

Riecker, John E., secy: Towsley Foundation, Harry A. and Margaret D.

Riecker, Margaret Ann, trust, don granddaughter: Dow Foundation, Herbert H. and Grace A.; pres, trust: Towsley Foundation, Harry A. and Margaret D.

Riedel, Alan Ellis, trust: Cooper Industries Foundation

Riedel, Walter G., III, trust: Stark Foundation, Nelda C. and H. J. Lutcher

Rieger, H. Victor, Jr., exec vp, trust: Signet Bank/Maryland Charitable Trust

Rieger, Kathryn K., vp, dir: Kohn-Joseloff Fund

Riehl, Susan O., dir: Knott Foundation, Marion I. and Henry J.

Rieke, Glenn T., trust: Rieke Corp. Foundation

Rieke, Mahloh E., trust: Rieke Corp. Foundation

Rieke, William O., MD, exec dir: Cheney Foundation, Ben B.

Riemersma, James, vp (fin rels): Hamilton Oil Corp.

Riemke, John W., dir: Cole Foundation, Olive B.

Rienhoff, William F., IV, trust: Brown & Sons Charitable Foundation, Alex

Riepe, James Sellers, mng dir: Price Associates, T. Rowe

Ries, E. Carey, pres: Myers and Sons, D.; pres: D. Myers & Sons Foundation

Riesbeck, James E., trust: Corning Incorporated Foundation

Riester, Jeffrey, pres, dir: Mielke Family Foundation

Rietfors, Gene, vp: Share Foundation

Riethman, R. B., treas, secy: Monarch Machine Tool Co. Foundation

Rife, L. Merle, secy, treas, trust: Mack Foundation, J. S.

Riffel, Frances R., secy, treas, dir: Jasper Desk Foundation

Rifkind, Richard, dir: Winston Foundation, Norman and Rosita

Rifkind, Richard A., trust: Guggenheim Memorial Foundation, John Simon

Rifkind, Simon H., chmn emeritus, dir: Winston Foundation, Norman and Rosita

Rigas, John, asst treas: Sofia American Schools

Rigg, Douglas C., trust: Schultz Foundation

Rigg, Elizabeth Schultz, vp, trust: Schultz Foundation

Rigg, Geoffrey B., trust: Schultz Foundation

Rigg, Gerald B., chmn, pres: Donaldson, Lufkin & Jenrette Foundation

Riggins, Larry D., treas: Fink Foundation

Riggs, Adelaide C., dir, pres emeritus: Post Foundation of D.C., Marjorie Merriweather

Riggs, John A., III, trust: Riggs Benevolent Fund

Riggs, Judson T., dir: Teichert Foundation

Riggs, Louis V., pres, ceo: Teichert

Rigler, Donald, secy: Rigler-Deutsch Foundation

Rigler, James, vp: Rigler-Deutsch Foundation

Rigler, Lloyd E., pres, don, dir: Rigler-Deutsch Foundation

Rigot, J. M., secy: Robbins & Myers Foundation

Rike, Linda, secy: Rosenkranz Foundation

Riker, Bernard, trust: Delano Foundation, Mignon Sherwood

Riklas, Meshulam, chmn, ceo: McCrory Corp.

Riley, Ann Marie, dir: Dana Corp. Foundation

Riley, C. Ronald, dir: Royal Insurance Foundation

Riley, Christine, admin (corp contributions): Pacific Gas & Electric Co.

Riley, David, secy: Fort Pierce Memorial Hospital Scholarship Foundation

Riley, Emily C., exec vp, trust, don daughter: Connelly Foundation

Riley, Francis, secy, dir: Bodine Foundation

Riley, J. J., dir: Fieldcrest Foundation

Riley, James B., cfo: Republic Engineered Steels

Riley, James S., vp: Oldham Little Church Foundation

Riley, John, trust: Raymond Foundation

Riley, Joseph Harry, vp, trust: Clark-Winchcole Foundation

Riley, Joseph R., trust: Dimick Foundation

Riley, Michael J., treas, dir: Lee Foundation

Riley, Patrick V., dir: Weber Charities Corp., Frederick E.

Riley, Rebecca, dir (community initiatives program), vp (Chicago aff): MacArthur Foundation, John D. and Catherine T.

Riley, Rhett E., bd mem: Caring Foundation

Riley, Richard W., trust: Duke Endowment

Rilott, James H., pres, dir: Atwood Industries

Rimel, Rebecca W., exec dir: Pew Charitable Trusts

Rincker, William, secy, treas, dir: Hoyt Foundation, Stewart W. and Willma C.

Rinebarger, Opal, trust: Thompson Charitable Trust, Sylvia G.

Rinehart, Charles R., pres, coo, dir: Ahmanson & Co., H.F.; pres, coo, dir: Home Savings of America, FA

Rinella, Bernard B., dir: McGraw Foundation

Rines, Fred W., bd mem: Gardiner Scholarship Foundation

Rinfret, Pierre A., dir: Brunswick Foundation

Ring, Gerald J., dir: CUNA Mutual Charitable Foundation

Ring, Robert, pres: Coleman Co.; dir: Coleman Charitable Trust

Ring, Robert L., pres, coo: Coleman Co.

Ringdahl, Robert E., vchmn: Northern Engraving Corp.

Ringe, Lillian M., Essick Foundation

Ringhofer, Jerry, corp admin: National Computer Systems

Ringoen, Richard Miller, dir: Ball Brothers Foundation

Ringter, James M., pres, coo: Premark International

Rinke, Francis, trust: Hatterscheidt Foundation

Rinker, David B., Sr., pres: Rinker, Sr. Foundation, M. E.

Rinker, John J., Sr., vp: Rinker, Sr. Foundation, M. E.

Rinker, Marshall E., Sr., ceo: Rinker, Sr. Foundation, M. E.

Rinker, Marshall Edison, Sr., trust: Rinker Cos. Foundation

Rinsch, Charles E., pres, dir: Argonaut Group

Riordan, Geraldo R., dir: Ryder System Charitable Foundation

Riordan, J. F., pres, ceo, dir: MidCon Corp.

Riordan, Jill, chmn: Riordan Foundation

Riordan, Richard J., dir: Capital Fund Foundation; ceo: Riordan Foundation

Ripley, Sidney Dillon, II, dir emeritus: Hitachi Foundation

Ripley, W. E., Jr., secy: Winn-Dixie Stores Foundation

Ripley, William, pres: Silvestri Corp.

Riposanu, Marguerite M., secy: Ridgefield Foundation

Rippel, Eric R., pres, trust, mem: Rippel Foundation, Fannie E.

Rippey, A. Gordon, treas, trust: Colorado Trust

Risch, William H., vp: Firstar Milwaukee Foundation

Riser, Mary M., secy: Smith, Jr. Foundation, M. W.

Rish, Stephen A., vp: Nationwide Insurance Foundation

Rishel, Jane, pres, treas, dir: Donnelley Foundation, Gaylord and Dorothy

Rishel, Richard C., pres: Continental Bancorp, Inc.

Riskind, Kenneth J., chmn: Fullerton Metals Co.; treas: Fullerton Metals Foundation

Riskind, Phillip A., trust: Fullerton Metals Foundation

Risley, Parker C., trust: Hunt Trust for Episcopal Charitable Institutions, Virginia

Rismiller, David A., chmn, pres, ceo, dir: FirsTier Bank N.A. Omaha

Risner, Ollie J., vp, trust: Stone Foundation, France

Ristav, Josephine, mgr: Great Western Financial Corp.

Ristine, Kenneth I., program off: Cheney Foundation, Ben B.

Ritchey, S. Donley, vp, dir: Rosenberg Foundation

Ritchie, Jane Olds, trust: Irwin Charity Foundation, William G.

Ritchie, Kathryn A., exec secy: Greentree Foundation

Ritchin, Hyman B., trust: Hebrew Technical Institute

Ritsch, Malcolm E., Jr., dir: Metropolitan Health Foundation

Ritter, Alan I., treas, trust: Ritter Foundation

Ritter, David, vp, trust: Ritter Foundation

Ritter, Jerry E., vp, group exec, cfo, chief admin off: Anheuser-Busch Cos.

Ritter, Toby G., vp, secy, trust: Ritter Foundation

Rittinghaus, Erherd, pres: AGFA Division of Miles Inc.

Ritzen, Evy Kay, dir: Meadows Foundation

Ritzmann, Maryalice, mgr (corp events): Mercedes-Benz of North America, Inc.

Rivel, Robert, Lee Foundation, James T.

Rivel, Wesley, dir: Lee Foundation, James T.

Rivera, Sonia, dir: Chicago Tribune Foundation

Rives, Claude G., III, vp, dir: Frost Foundation; trust: Woolf Foundation, William C.

Rives, Howard P., trust: Hayward Foundation Charitable Trust, John T. and Winifred

Rivitz, Jan, exec dir, trust: Straus Foundation, Aaron and Lillie

Rivkin, Arthur L., vp: Polinsky-Rivkin Family Foundation

Rivkin, Jeannie P., secy, treas: Polinsky-Rivkin Family Foundation

Rivlin, Alice Mitchell, dir: Meyer Foundation, Eugene and Agnes E.

Rizk, Frederick E., dir: Hariri Foundation

Rizley, Robert, pres, trust: Sarkeys Foundation

Rizner, Dean B., secy, treas: Citizens Union Bank Foundation

Rizzardi, Frances, secy: Scott Paper Co. Foundation

Rizzo, Paul J., vchmn: IBM Corp.

Roach, John L., trust: Kahn Dallas Symphony Foundation, Louise W. and Edmund J.

Roach, Michele C., asst secy, asst treas, trust: Chatlos Foundation

Roach, Randa R., trust: Rienzi Foundation

Roache, James P., dir pub policy: Curtis Industries, Helene

Roadman, Ross, exec dir: Ryder System Charitable Foundation

Roaf, Andree, dir: Rockefeller Foundation, Winthrop

Roballey, Tracey, contact: Chesebrough Charitable Trust

Robarts, Richard C., trust: Sofia American Schools

Robb, Felix Compton, trust: Presser Foundation

Robb, Lynda J., trust: LBJ Family Foundation

Robbie, Art, mgr, consumer & exec rels: Hiram Walker & Sons Inc.

Robbins, Charles E., Jr., pres, trust: Orange Orphan Society

Robbins, Deborah A., vp: Farnsworth Trust, Charles A.

Robbins, Dick, trust: Woodward Governor Co. Charitable Trust

Robbins, Donald M., asst secy: Hasbro Charitable Trust

Robbins, Edward H., proposal manager: Johnson Foundation, Robert Wood

Robbins, F. J., mem distribution comm: Mead Corp. Foundation

Robbins, Jacob M., trust: Oppenheimer and Flora Oppenheimer Haas Trust, Leo

Robbins, John, dir: Durell Foundation, George Edward

Robbins, Joy C., secy, treas: Chamberlin Foundation, Gerald W.

Robbins, N. Clay, vp (comm devel): Lilly Endowment

Robbins, Peggy, secy: Orange Orphan Society

Robbins, Walter S., trust: Ayling Scholarship Foundation, Alice S.

Robbins, William C., III, vp: Beaver Foundation

Robbins, William L., trust: Fuller Foundation, George F. and Sybil H.

Robert, Curtis D., pres: Rachal Foundation, Ed

Robert, Curtis D., Jr., vp, secy: Rachal Foundation, Ed

Roberti, William V., ceo: Brooks Brothers

Roberts, Ann M., secy, treas: Stemmons Foundation

Roberts, Anne Lee, pres: Summerlee Foundation

Roberts, B. J., vp, dir: Tractor & Equipment Company Foundation

Roberts, Bert C., Jr., chmn, ceo: MCI Communications Corp.

Roberts, Brooke, MD, mem bd mgrs: Measey Foundation, Benjamin and Mary Siddons

Roberts, Burnell Richard, trust: Dayton Foundation Depository

Roberts, Charles C., secy, treas, dir: R. F. Foundation

Roberts, Chris, pres: Credit Suisse

Roberts, Claude C., vp, secy, trust: Humphreys Foundation

Roberts, Darrell C., mem scholarship bd: Cobb Educational Fund, Ty

Roberts, David R., pres emeritus, dir: Bush Charitable Foundation, Edyth

Roberts, Donald M., vchmn, treas, dir: United States Trust Co. of New York

Roberts, Edith M., dir: Mullen Foundation, J. K.

Roberts, Edward P., trusts: Xtra Corp. Charitable Foundation

Roberts, Ellen F., trust: Seeley Foundation

Roberts, Eugene, dir, pres: California Foundation for Biochemical Research

Roberts, Frank, trust: Packard Foundation, David and Lucile; trust: Witter Foundation, Dean

Roberts, George Adam, chmn, ceo, dir: Teledyne; trust: Teledyne Charitable Trust Foundation

Roberts, George Rosenberg, don, vp, secy-treas: Roberts Foundation

Roberts, Harry, dir: Youth Foundation

Roberts, James C., vp, dir: Thomas Memorial Foundation, Theresa A.

Roberts, Jill A., vp: Appleman Foundation

Roberts, John D., trust: Martin Foundation, Della

Roberts, John Joseph, dir: Starr Foundation

Roberts, John K., Jr., pres, ceo, dir: Pan-American Life Insurance Co.

Roberts, Judith V., vp: Morrison Foundation, Harry W.

Roberts, Kenneth Lewis, pres: HCA Foundation

Roberts, Leanne B., pres, dir: Roberts Foundation

Roberts, Mary Eleanor, vp, dir: R. F. Foundation

Roberts, Mary G., trust: Gordon/Rousmaniere/Roberts Fund

Roberts, Ralph H., Jr., trust: Hilliard Foundation

Roberts, Robby, secy: Smith and W. Aubrey Smith Charitable Foundation, Clara Blackford

Roberts, Theodore H., chmn, ceo, dir: Lasalle National Corp.

Roberts, Thomas H., Jr., treas: R. F. Foundation

Roberts, Tim, pres: Boston Co., Inc.

Robertson, David A., Jr., dir: Filene Foundation, Lincoln and Therese

Robertson, David W., trust: Robertson Brothers Co. Charitable Foundation

Robertson, E. Lorrie, mem distribution comm: Bruening Foundation, Eva L. and Joseph M.

Robertson, Heather M., trust: Spiritus Gladius Foundation

Robertson, Hugh D., trust: Christodora

Robertson, Jim, vp, dir (mktg): First Union National Bank of Florida

Robertson, John J., pres, dir: Filene Foundation, Lincoln and Therese

Robertson, John L., vp: Banbury Fund

Robertson, Judith, dir, vp: Bushee Foundation, Florence Evans

Robertson, Julian H., Jr., don, trust: Tiger Foundation

Robertson, K. N., trust: Exxon Education Foundation

Robertson, Kent L., sr vp, cfo: Pyramid Technology Corp.

Robertson, Oran B., trust: Meyer Memorial Trust

Robertson, R.M., mem: Tonkin Foundation, Tom and Helen

Robertson, Stuart, treas, dir: Doss Foundation, M. S.

Robertson, Wilhelmina Cullen, pres, trust: Cullen Foundation

Robertson, William S., pres: Banbury Fund

Robertson, Wyndham, dir: Babcock Foundation, Mary Reynolds

Robin, Albert A., pres: Robin Family Foundation, Albert A.

Robin, Constance, dir: Robin Family Foundation, Albert A.

Robin, Richard J., secy, treas: Robin Family Foundation, Albert A.

Robin, Stephen H., vp: Robin Family Foundation, Albert A.

Robinett, P. Ward, Jr., trust: Beazley Foundation; trust: Frederick Foundation

Robins, Marjorie M., trust: Roblee Foundation, Joseph H. and Florence A.

Robins, Steven, cfo: Builder Marts of America

Robinson, Barbara, secy/treas: Staunton Farm Foundation

Robinson, Barbara Paul, chmn bd dir, chmn exec comm, mem counc, dir: Foundation for Child Development

Robinson, Charles A., trust: Lynch Scholarship Foundation, John B.

Robinson, D.T., vp (mktg): Stroehmann Bakeries

Robinson, Dana P., trust-at-large: Raskob Foundation for Catholic Activities

Robinson, Daniel E., trust: Robinson Foundation

Robinson, David, vp: Freddie Mac Foundation

Robinson, Dorothy K., trust: Wenner-Gren Foundation for Anthropological Research

Robinson, E. B., Jr., chmn, ceo, dir: Deposit Guaranty National Bank; pres, dir: Deposit Guaranty Foundation

Robinson, E. Wayne, trust: Sprague Memorial Institute, Otho S. A.

Robinson, Edgar Allen, trust: Exxon Education Foundation

Robinson, Edna L., secy, treas: Beaird Foundation, Charles T.

Robinson, Edward H., dir, pres: Raskob Foundation, Bill; first vp: Raskob Foundation for Catholic Activities

Robinson, Elizabeth H., dir, pres, treas: Widgeon Foundation

Robinson, Fred, dir: Reflection Riding

Robinson, G. D., pres: Cominco American Inc.

Robinson, George Anderson, pres, trust: Robinson Foundation

Robinson, Guy Norman, pres, dir: Youth Foundation

Robinson, Harry L., chmn, ceo: Baltimore Bancorp.

Robinson, Horace B. B., dir: Youth Foundation

Robinson, J. H., chmn, pres: Harper Group

Robinson, J. Mack, trust: Robinson Foundation, J. Mack

Robinson, J.W., chmn, dir: Harland Co., John H.

Robinson, Jack A., ceo, chmn: Perry Drug Stores; trust: Perry Drug Stores Charitable Foundation

Robinson, Jamie Abercrombie, vp, trust: Robinson Foundation

Robinson, Jean A., treas: Buhl Foundation

Robinson, John C., pres, coo, dir: Bearings, Inc.

Robinson, John F., trust: Crowell Trust, Henry P. and Susan C.

Robinson, John H., secy, treas: Carter Star Telegram Employees Fund, Amon G.

Robinson, John H., Jr., mng ptnr: Black & Veatch; trust: Black & Veatch Foundation

Robinson, John R., fdn mgr: Beinecke Foundation

Robinson, Joseph A., cfo: Excel Industries (Elkhart, Indiana); secy: Excel Industries Charitable Foundation; treas, trust: Standard Products Co. Foundation

Robinson, Joseph G.S., Jr., asst treas: Goddard Homestead

Robinson, Joseph R., treas, trust: Mott Fund, Ruth

Robinson, Josephine R., trust: Lynch Scholarship Foundation, John B.

Robinson, Kerry A., northeast area trust: Raskob Foundation for Catholic Activities

Robinson, Laura A., trust: Robinson Foundation

Robinson, Lee, mgr: Porter Testamentary Trust, James Hyde

Robinson, Leroy, mem bd advs: Belk Foundation Trust

Robinson, Michael, treas, dir: Illinois Tool Works Foundation

Robinson, Michael J., III, trust, vp: Lovett Foundation

Robinson, Norman L., vchmn: Lakeside National Bank

Robinson, Peter, exec vp, dir: Brencanda Foundation

Robinson, R.J., exec vp, coo: AXIA Incorporated

Robinson, Ralph C., trust: Surrena Memorial Fund, Harry and Thelma

Robinson, Ralph S., Jr., trust: Anderson Foundation, Robert C. and Sadie G.

Robinson, Richard, chmn, ceo: Scholastic Inc.; dir, vp: Widgeon Foundation

Robinson, Robert A., cfo: Ohio Citizens Bank; trust: Ohio Citizens Bank Minority Scholarship Trust Fund

Robinson, Robert Armstrong, trust: Bugher Foundation

Robinson, Russell M., II, trust: Duke Endowment

Robinson, Sam, pres, coo: Super Food Services

Robinson, Stanley D., trust: Kaye Foundation

Robinson, Steve, vp (mktg): Chick-Fil-A, Inc.

Robinson, Susan Beaird, trust: Beaird Foundation, Charles T.

Robinson, Sylvia B., trust: Beinecke Foundation

Robinson, W. T., trust: Chesapeake Corporate Foundation

Robinson, Warren R., asst treas: MDU Resources Foundation

Robinson, William, pres, dir: Harland Co. Foundation, John H.

Robirds, Donald M., secy, treas: Stock Foundation, Paul

Robison, Earl F., trust: Houck Foundation, May K.

Robison, James A., pres: Robison Foundation, Ellis H. and Doris B.

Robison, Richard G., vp: Robison Foundation, Ellis H. and Doris B.

Robson, Don, exec vp, cfo: Neiman Marcus

Robson, Edward J., pres, dir: Robson Foundation, LaNelle

Robson, Hannah Davis, mng dir: Williams Cos. Foundation

Robson, Kimberly A., vp: Robson Foundation, LaNelle

Robson, Leah K., McGraw Foundation

Robson, Mark E., vp: Robson Foundation, LaNelle

Robson, Robert D., vp: Robson Foundation, LaNelle

Robson, Steven S., vp, treas, dir: Robson Foundation, LaNelle

Robson-Weiser, Lynda, secy, dir: Robson Foundation, LaNelle

Roby, Carolyn, asst secy, asst treas, program mgr: Norwest Foundation

Roby, Katherine W., chmn bd mgrs: Wilson Foundation, Marie C. and Joseph C.

Roche, Burke B., pres, ceo, dir: Binks Manufacturing Co.

Roche, George A., mng dir, cfo, vp: Price Associates, T. Rowe

Roche, Peter T., dir: First National Bank & Trust Co. of Rockford Charitable Trust

Rochelle, Deborah, secy: Cook, Sr. Charitable Foundation, Kelly Gene

Rochlin, Larry, pres: Rochlin Foundation, Abraham and Sonia

Rock, Arthur, fdr, prin: Intel Corp.

Rock, Douglas L., chmn, ceo: Smith International

Rock, Milton L., dir, pres: Rock Foundation, Milton and Shirley

Rock, Robert H., dir, vp: Rock Foundation, Milton and Shirley

Rock, Terry Haake, asst secy: Baxter Foundation, Donald E. and Delia B.

Rockefeller, Abby, Jr., dir: Rockefeller Fund, David

Rockefeller, David, Jr., trust: Rockefeller Brothers Fund; don, pres, dir: Rockefeller Fund, David

Rockefeller, David, Sr., hon trust: Rockefeller Family Fund

Rockefeller, Diana Newell-Rowan, trust: Rockefeller Family Fund

Rockefeller, Frederic L., chmn: Cranston Print Works; trust: Cranston Foundation

Rockefeller, Laurance, trust: Jackson Hole Preserve

Rockefeller, Laurance Spelman, chmn, trust: Jackson Hole Preserve; hon trust: Rockefeller Family Fund; dir: Wallace-Reader's Digest Fund, DeWitt; dir: Wallace Reader's Digest Fund, Lila

Rockefeller, Mary French, dir: Bobst Foundation, Elmer and Mamdouha

Rockefeller, Richard Gilder, trust: Rockefeller Brothers Fund; pres, trust, mem fin comm: Rockefeller Family Fund

Rockefeller, Rodman Clark, chmn, dir: Arbor Acres Farm, Inc.; trust: Rockefeller Brothers Fund

Rockefeller, Steven Clark, vchmn, trust: Rockefeller Brothers Fund; trust: Rockefeller Family Fund

Rockefeller, Wendy Gordon, vp, trust: Rockefeller Family Fund

Rockefeller, Winthrop Paul, dir: Rockefeller Foundation, Winthrop; trust: Rockefeller Trust, Winthrop

Rockmore, John, vp: Kenworthy - Sarah H. Swift Foundation, Marion E.

Rockwell, D. M., secy, trust: Bissell Foundation, J. Walton

Rockwell, George Peter, secy, trust: Rockwell Foundation

Rockwell, Hays, mem adv comm: de Kay Foundation

Rockwell, Russell A., trust: Rockwell Foundation

Rockwell, Willard Frederick, Jr., trust: Rockwell Foundation

Rodale, Robert H., chmn, dir: Rodale Press

Roddenbery, Julian B., Jr., ceo, pres: Roddenbery Co., Inc., W.B.; secy, treas, dir: Roddenbery Foundation

Roddenbery, Julian B., Sr., chmn, dir: Roddenbery Foundation

Roddenbery, Ralph J., vchmn, dir: Roddenbery Foundation

Roddis, Augusta D., secy, treas, dir: Roddis Foundation, Hamilton

Roddis, Richard Stiles Law, chmn, pres, dir: Haas Foundation, Saul and Dayee G.

Roddis, William H., II, pres, dir: Roddis Foundation, Hamilton

Rodecker, Arthur, pres, trust: DeRoy Foundation, Helen L.; vp, trust: DeRoy Testamentary Foundation

Roden, Thomas E., sr vp: Harleysville Mutual Insurance Co.

Rodenbach, Edward F., vp, secy, dir: Foster-Davis Foundation

Rodenbaugh, Edwin M., trust: Knudsen Charitable Foundation, Earl

Rodenberg, Clinton, sr vp (mktg): Schieffelin & Somerset Co.

Rodenberg, Louis B., Jr., secy, treas: Ivakota Association

Rodes, Harold P., trust emeritus: Mott Foundation, Charles Stewart

Rodes, Joe M., chmn, trust: Brown Foundation, James Graham

Rodewig, John S., mem corp contributions comm: Eaton Charitable Fund

Rodgers, Bowmar, trust: Avery-Fuller Children's Center

Rodgers, David A., treas, trust: Austin Memorial Foundation

Rodgers, Dorothy F., pres, treas: Rodgers Foundation, Richard & Dorothy

Rodgers, James R., trust: Beatty Trust, Cordelia Lunceford

Rodgers, James T., pres, coo, dir: Anadarko Petroleum Corp.

Rodgers, John H., treas, asst secy, trust: Foundation for Seacoast Health

Rodgers, John Hunter, sr vp, chief admin off, gen couns, secy: Southland Corp.

Rodgers, Melissa A., trust: Anschutz Family Foundation

Rodgers, Sue Anschutz, don, pres, exec dir: Anschutz Family Foundation

Rodgers, Susan E., trust: Anschutz Family Foundation

Rodgers, William W., trust: Beatty Trust, Cordelia Lunceford

Rodman, L.C., mng ptnr: Black & Veatch; trust: Black & Veatch Foundation

Rodman, Michael, mem (community concerns comm): NBD Bank, N.A.

Rodriguez, Daisy, mgr (corporate contributions): SNET

Rodriguez, Jay, contact person: Hafif Family Foundation

Rodriguez, Mike, mem bd: Pacific Telesis Foundation

Rodriques, Joe E., exec vp, cfo: Seaboard Corp.

Roe, Benson, trust: Avery-Fuller Children's Center

Roe, Benson Bertheau, MD, pres: Lux Foundation, Miranda

Roe, David H., chmn, dir: Uslico Foundation

Roe, John H., pres, ceo, dir: Bemis Company

Roe, Robert, mem contributions comm: Syntex Corp.

Roe, Shirley W., secy, trust: Roe Foundation

Roe, Thomas Anderson, chmn, treas, trust: Roe Foundation

Roeck, Thomas J., Jr., sr vp (fin), cfo: Delta Air Lines; trust: Delta Air Lines Foundation

Roedel, Paul R., ceo, dir: Carpenter Technology Corp.

Roedel, Paul Robert, trust: Wyomissing Foundation

Roeder, Michael, chmn, dir: Quad City Osteopathic Foundation

Roedig, John B., dir: Ayer Foundation, N.W.

Roehl, Janet L., trust: Roehl Foundation

Roehl, Ora C., pres: Roehl Foundation

Roehl, Peter G., vp, treas: Roehl Foundation

Roenisch, Davis, dir: Morton Memorial Fund, Mark

Roesch, John R., dir: Hook Drug Foundation

Rogal, Alvin, chmn: Jewish Healthcare Foundation of Pittsburgh

Rogala, Judith A., mem: Butler Foundation, Alice

Roge, Paul E., secy: Abbott Laboratories Fund

Rogers, Bernard W., trust: Kemper Foundation, James S.

Rogers, C. B., Jr., chmn, ceo: Equifax; trust: Equifax Foundation

Rogers, Catherine, trust: Stanley Charitable Foundation, A. W.

Rogers, Charles B., treas, dir: Pickford Foundation, Mary

Rogers, Christopher W., trust: Stevens Foundation, Abbot and Dorothy H.

Rogers, David H., pres, coo: PriMerit F.S.B.

Rogers, Deborah, secy: Weinberg Foundation, John L.

Rogers, F. Patrick, dir: Butler Foundation, J. Homer

Rogers, Fred M., pres: McFeely-Rogers Foundation

Rogers, Irving E., Jr., trust: Rogers Family Foundation

Rogers, James, cfo: McKinsey & Co.

Rogers, James B., trust: McFeely-Rogers Foundation

Rogers, James E., Jr., chmn, pres, ceo: PSI Energy

Rogers, Joe W., Jr., pres: Waffle House, Inc.

Rogers, Joe W., Sr., chmn: Waffle House, Inc.

Rogers, John C., trust: Robertson Brothers Co. Charitable Foundation

Rogers, Joseph E., dir: St. Faith's House Foundation

Rogers, Julie L., pres: Meyer Foundation, Eugene and Agnes E.

Rogers, Justin Towner, Jr., McFawn Trust No. 2, Lois Sisler

Rogers, Louise H., dir: Rogers Foundation

Rogers, Margaret J., vp, trust: Jonsson Foundation

Rogers, Martha B., trust: Rogers Family Foundation

Rogers, Mary Stuart, pres, dir: Rogers Foundation, Mary Stuart

Rogers, N. Stewart, treas, dir: Univar Foundation

Rogers, Nancy, mem grantmaking comm: Liz Claiborne Foundation

Rogers, Philip O., secy, dir: Legg & Co. Foundation

Rogers, R.B., chmn: Texas Industries Foundation

Rogers, Rebecca J., dir: Rogers Foundation

Rogers, Richard J., asst secy: Duchossois Foundation

Rogers, Richard R., chmn, ceo: Mary Kay Cosmetics

Rogers, Richard Raymond, trust: Mary Kay Foundation

Rogers, Robert D., ceo, pres: Texas Industries, Inc.

Rogers, Robert McDonald, dir: Rogers Foundation

Rogers, Robert W., vchmn, coo, dir: National City Bank

Rogers, Rutherford David, dir: Wilson Foundation, H. W.

Rogers, Samuel S., trust: Stevens Foundation, Abbot and Dorothy H.; trust: Stevens Foundation, Nathaniel and Elizabeth P.

Rogers, Shelby, secy: Texas Commerce Bank Houston Foundation

Rogers, T. Gary, chmn, ceo, dir: Dreyer's & Edy's Grand Ice Cream

Rogers, Tom, trust: Brown Family Foundation, John Mathew Gay

Rogers, Walter R., Jr., dir: Fletcher Foundation, A. J.

Rogers, William, pres, dir: Babcock Foundation, Mary Reynolds

Rogers, William Pierce, dir: Cafritz Foundation, Morris and Gwendolyn; dir: Hariri Foundation

Rogerson, Charles E., II, secy, treas, trust: Sailors' Snug Harbor of Boston

Rogerson, Francis C., Jr., trust: Phillips Trust, Edwin

Rogerson, Thomas, trust: Sailors' Snug Harbor of Boston

Roggin, Gary, trust: Shapiro Charitable Trust, J. B. & Maurice C.

Rogin, Edward, trust: Rogow Birken Foundation

Rogoff, Alice, cfo: U.S. News & World Report

Rogow, Bruce, trust: Rogow Birken Foundation

Rogow, Louis B., pres, treas: Rogow Birken Foundation

Rohan, Helen, vp: Ritter Foundation, May Ellen and Gerald

Rohatyn, Elizabeth, vp: Rohatyn Foundation, Felix and Elizabeth

Rohatyn, Felix George, pres: Rohatyn Foundation, Felix and Elizabeth

Rohde, Leroy, mgr: Bagnall Foundation

Rohde, Ronda L., mgr: Bagnall Foundation

Rohlfing, Joan H., vp, dir: Atherton Family Foundation

Rohlik, Sophie, pres, treas: Rohlik Foundation, Sigmund and Sophie

Rohm, John M., dir: Moore Foundation

Rohm, Robert F., Jr., secy, treas, dir: Hultquist Foundation

Rohner, Paul E., sr vp, cfo: Alexander & Alexander Services, Inc.

Rohr, James Edward, chmn, ceo, dir: Pittsburgh National Bank

Rohr, Loren, pres: Community Hospital Foundation

Rohrbasser, Markus, ceo: Union Bank of Switzerland New York Branch

Rohrer, Charles, trust: First Interstate Banks of Billings Centennial Youth Foundation

Rohrkemper, Paul H., vp, treas: CIGNA Foundation

Rohrmann, Guenter, pres, ceo: Air Express International Corp.

Rohsenow, Warren M., hon chmn, dir: Dynatech Corp.

Roisman, Milton, vp, trust: Philips Foundation, Jesse

Rokus, Josef U., vp, cfo: Galileo Electro-Optics Corp.

Roland, B.R., dir, vp, treas: Tandy Foundation, David L.

Roland, Catherine D., trust: Andalusia Health Services

Roland, Kenneth S., trust: Grant Foundation, William T.

Rolfs, Robert T., pres: Rolfs Foundation, Robert T.

Rolfs, Thomas J., pres: Rolfs Foundation, Thomas J.

Rolfsen, Carl D., treas: Dekko Foundation; chmn bd: Foellinger Foundation

Roll, G. Frederick, dir: Upjohn California Fund

Roll, Richard R., vp, dir: Pacific Telesis Foundation

Rolland, Ian Mckenzie, chmn, ceo, dir: Lincoln National Corp.

Rollans, James, cfo: Fluor Corp.; trust: Fluor Foundation

Roller, Donald E., vp: USG Foundation

Roller, Marilee, cfo: Pacific Mutual Charitable Foundation

Rolling, Ken, assoc dir: Woods Charitable Fund

Rollins, Gary W., pres, coo, dir: Rollins Inc.

Rollins, John William, Sr., fdr, chmn, ceo, dir: Rollins Environmental Services, Inc.

Rollins, Mary E., dir: Rollins Luetkemeyer Charitable Foundation

Rollins, O. Randolph, asst secy: Best Products Foundation

Rollins, R. Randall, chmn, ceo, dir: Rollins Inc.

Rolting, William A., dir, pres: Wurlitzer Foundation, Farny R.

Romaine, Henry S., dir: American General Finance Foundation

Romaine, Michael F., pres, dir: Zale Foundation

Roman, Steve, bd mem: Valley Bank Charitable Foundation

Romaniello, Lee Larssen, secy, trust: Weisman Art Foundation, Frederick R.

Romano, Maryanne, trust: Glaze Foundation, Robert and Ruth

Romans, Connie G., treas: Collins Foundation, Carr P.

Romans, John, dir: Clark Foundation, Robert Sterling

Romanucci, L., dir: Oaklawn Foundation

Ronald, John C., pres, publ: Graphic Printing Co.

Ronchi, Giorgio, chmn, ceo: Memorex Telex Corp.

Rones, Louis, trust, pres: Geist Foundation

Rones, Steven, trust, vp: Geist Foundation

Roob, Richard, chmn, ceo: Moore & Sons, B.C.; trust: Moore & Sons Foundation, B.C.

Rood, Anthony M., Jr., comm mem: Pfister and Vogel Tanning Co. Foundation

Rooks, Charles Shelby, exec dir: Meyer Memorial Trust

Rooney, Patrick W., pres, coo: Cooper Tire & Rubber Co.

Rooney, Phillip B., pres, coo, dir, mem exec comm: Waste Management

Roos, Linda Pillsbury, vp: Pillsbury Foundation

Roosevelt, Laura D., vp (community rels & pub affairs): J.P. Morgan & Co.

Roosevelt, William D., treas, trust: Donner Foundation, William H.

Root, Glenn, vp: Library Association of Warehouse Point

Roper, John L., III, pres, ceo: Norfolk Shipbuilding & Drydock Corp.

Roper, Ray, secy: Graphic Arts Education & Research Foundation

Roper, Wayne J., secy, dir: Bradley Foundation, Lynde and Harry

Rorabaugh, Barre L., pres, ceo, dir: Everest & Jennings International

Rorison, Wilbur, trust: Copperweld Steel Co.'s Warren Employees' Trust

Rork, Valerie, Dumke Foundation, Dr. Ezekiel R. and Edna Wattis

Rosa, Bruce L., pres: Lancaster Lens Foundation

Rosa, Karen L., exec dir: Altman Foundation

Rosacker, Jo Helen, secy, assoc dir: Richardson Foundation, Sid W.

Rosasco, Nat, Jr., pres: Northwestern Golf Co.

Roscitt, Frank, asst secy: Stern Foundation, Leonard N.

Rose, David, pres: Heineman Foundation for Research, Educational, Charitable, and Scientific Purposes

Rose, Frederick Phineas, dir: Kaufmann Foundation, Henry

Rose, John C., dir: Culpeper Foundation, Charles E.

Rose, Marian, dir: Heineman Foundation for Research, Educational, Charitable, and Scientific Purposes

Rose, Michael David, chmn, ceo, dir: Promus Cos.

Rose, Michael E., cfo: Anadarko Petroleum Corp.

Rose, Michel, pres, ceo: Lafarge Corp.

Rose, Milton Curtiss, dir: Bobst Foundation, Elmer and Mamdouha; dir: Pfeiffer Research Foundation, Gustavus and Louise

Rose, Mrs. Frederick, trust: Hebrew Technical Institute

Rose, Sally A., trust: Abney Foundation

Rose, Simon M. D., treas: Heineman Foundation for Research, Educational, Charitable, and Scientific Purposes

Rose, W.M., dir, vp: Quanex Foundation

Rosen, Abraham A., pres, dir: Rosen Foundation, Joseph

Rosen, Arlene, pres, treas: Rosen Foundation, Michael Alan

Rosen, Benjamin M., chmn: Compaq Computer Corp.

Rosen, James M., pres: Fantastic Foods

Rosen, Jonathan P., vp, secy, dir: Rosen Foundation, Joseph

Rosen, Leonard M., ptnr: Wachtell, Lipton, Rosen & Katz; vp, trust: Zarkin Memorial Foundation, Charles

Rosen, Marcella, dir: Ayer Foundation, N.W.

Rosen, Miriam, treas, dir: Rosen Foundation, Joseph

Rosen, Robert L., chmn, ceo: Damon Corp.

Rosenbaum, Francis F., Jr., pres, trust: de Hirsch Fund, Baron

Rosenbaum, Gabriella, chmn, vp: Rosenbaum Foundation, Paul and Gabriella

Rosenbaum, S. A., pres, dir: Hardin Foundation, Phil

Rosenbaum, Steven K., trust: de Hirsch Fund, Baron

Rosenberg, Abraham, pres, dir: Guttman Foundation, Stella and Charles; pres, treas: Rosenberg Foundation, Sunny and Abe

Rosenberg, Albert J., pres: Nias Foundation, Henry

Rosenberg, Ann, dir, vp, secy: Rosenberg Family Foundation, William

Rosenberg, Carol Kuyper, vp, dir: Kuyper Foundation, Peter H. and E. Lucille Gaass

Rosenberg, Claude N., Jr., secy, dir: Rosenberg, Jr. Family Foundation, Louise and Claude

Rosenberg, David, dir: Jewish Foundation for Education of Women

Rosenberg, Edward L., pres, treas, dir: Crown Central Petroleum Foundation

Rosenberg, Gary Aron, chmn: UDC-Universal Development LP

Rosenberg, Henry A., Jr., vp, trust: Blaustein Foundation, Louis and Henrietta; chmn, chmn exec comm, ceo, dir: Crown Central Petroleum Corp.; dir: Crown Central Petroleum Foundation; pres, trust: Rosenberg Foundation, Henry and Ruth Blaustein; vp: Thalheimer Foundation, Alvin and Fanny Blaustein

Rosenberg, Louise J., pres, dir: Rosenberg, Jr. Family Foundation, Louise and Claude

Rosenberg, Manuel, chmn, ceo, dir: Morse Shoe, Inc.

Rosenberg, Michael, secy, trust: Rosenberg Foundation, Sunny and Abe

Rosenberg, Norman, MD, trust: Johnson Foundation, Robert Wood

Rosenberg, Richard M., chmn, ceo, dir: Bank of America; chmn, ceo, dir: BankAmerica Corp.

Rosenberg, Robert M., chmn, ceo: Dunkin' Donuts

Rosenberg, Ruth Blaustein, trust: Blaustein Foundation, Jacob and Hilda; chmn, trust: Blaustein Foundation, Louis and Henrietta; chmn, trust: Rosenberg Foundation, Henry and Ruth Blaustein; trust: Thalheimer Foundation, Alvin and Fanny Blaustein

Rosenberg, Sonia, secy, dir: Guttman Foundation, Stella and Charles; vp, secy: Rosenberg Foundation, Sunny and Abe

Rosenberg, Stanley, asst secy: Wallace Genetic Foundation

Rosenberg, Sydney Julian, vp: American Building Maintenance Foundation

Rosenberg, Theodore T., pres: American Building Maintenance Foundation

Rosenberg, William, pres, treas: Rosenberg Family Foundation, William

Rosenberg, William F., vp, secy: Nias Foundation, Henry

Rosenberger, Henry, trust: Roth Foundation

Rosenberger, J.D., Jr., treas: Hill Crest Foundation

Rosenberry, Charles W., II, dir: Weyerhaeuser Memorial Foundation, Charles A.

Rosenberry, Walter Samuel, III, treas, trust, don: Weyerhaeuser Family Foundation; Weyerhaeuser Memorial Foundation, Charles A.

Rosenblatt, Bruce, contact person: Green Fund; vp, dir: Radin Foundation

Rosenblatt, Joseph, trust: Boehm Foundation

Rosenblatt, Roslyn, exec dir: PPG Industries Foundation

Rosenbloom, Ben, chmn: Rosenbloom Foundation, Ben and Esther

Rosenbloom, Esther, vp: Rosenbloom Foundation, Ben and Esther

Rosenbloom, Howard, pres: Rosenbloom Foundation, Ben and Esther

Rosenbloom, Robert, mgr (urban affairs): Chemical Bank

Rosenblum, Phyllis, 1st vp: Republic New York Corp.

Rosenbluth, Hal F., pres, ceo: Rosenbluth Travel Agency

Rosenbluth, Harold S., co-chmn: Rosenbluth Travel Agency

Rosenburg, Sarah, trust: Block Family Charitable Trust, Ephraim; trust: Block Family Foundation, Emphraim

Rosenfeld, Camila M., Lehman Foundation, Edith and Herbert

Rosenfeld, George, vchmn, trust: Fox Charitable Foundation, Harry K. & Emma R.

Rosenfeld, Mark K., pres, ceo: Jacobson Stores, Inc.

Rosenfield, Patricia L., program chmn (human resources in developing countries): Carnegie Corporation of New York

Rosengarten, Susan, trust: Brody Foundation, Frances

Rosengren, William R., chmn corp contributions comm: Ecolab

Rosenhaus, Albert, dir: Rosenhaus Peace Foundation, Sarah and Matthew

Rosenhaus, Irving R., managing dir: Rosenhaus Peace Foundation, Sarah and Matthew

Rosenhaus, Lawrence, dir: Rosenhaus Peace Foundation, Sarah and Matthew

Rosenkilde, Herbert C., MD, exec dir: Diabetes Research and Education Foundation

Rosenkranz, Margaret, treas, dir: Rosenkranz Foundation

Rosenkranz, Robert, pres, dir: Rosenkranz Foundation

Rosenman, Herm, vchmn, cfo: Rexene Products Co.

Rosenow, Mary V., dir, secy: Wyne Foundation

Rosenow, Thomas L., dir, pres, treas: Wyne Foundation

Rosenshine, Allen, chmn, ceo, dir: BBDO Worldwide

Rosenstein, Anita May, pres: May Foundation, Wilbur

Rosenstiel, Blanka A., pres: Rosenstiel Foundation

Rosenthal, Alan, trust: Schumann Fund for New Jersey

Rosenthal, Arthur, trust: Swanson Foundation

Rosenthal, Betty M., secy, treas: Rosenthal Foundation

Rosenthal, Hinda Gould, pres, trust: Rosenthal Foundation, Richard and Hinda

Rosenthal, Leighton A., trust: Rosenthal Foundation, Samuel

Rosenthal, Lois, vp, dir: Rosenthal Foundation, Richard and Lois

Rosenthal, Richard L., Jr., vp, trust: Rosenthal Foundation, Richard and Hinda

Rosenthal, Richard Laurence, chmn, trust: Rosenthal Foundation, Richard and Hinda

Rosenthal, Robert, trust: Hebrew Technical Institute

Rosenthal, Stuart, pres: Furr's Supermarkets

Rosenthal, Warren W., pres, mgr: Rosenthal Foundation

Rosenwald, Nina K., vp, dir: Rosenwald Family Fund, William

Rosenwald, William, pres, treas, dir: Rosenwald Family Fund, William

Rosenzweig, Elias, secy, treas: Goldman Foundation, Herman

Rosett, Richard Nathaniel, trust: Kemper Foundation, James S.

Rosi, Frances, exec dir: Circuit City Foundation

Rosilier, Glenn D., sr vp, cfo: Central & South West Services

Rosin, Axel G., pres, dir: Scherman Foundation

Rosin, Katharine S., secy, dir: Scherman Foundation

Rosinski, Martin J., treas, asst secy, dir: Rand McNally Foundation

Roslonic, James, treas, trust: Van Andel Foundation, Jay and Betty

Rosner, Bernat, secy: Magowan Family Foundation

Rosner, Myron, trust: Berrie Foundation, Russell

Rosovsky, Henry, vp, trust: Weatherhead Foundation

Ross, Alexander B., dir: Barker Welfare Foundation

Ross, Arthur, pres, treas, dir: Ross Foundation, Arthur

Ross, Barbara, secy, treas: Levy Foundation, Achille

Ross, Charles F., trust: Van Wert County Foundation

Ross, Clifford A., exec vp, dir: Ross Foundation, Arthur

Ross, D. P., Jr., trust: Fair Play Foundation

Ross, Daniel G., secy, dir: Levinson Foundation, Morris L.

Ross, David H., treas, asst secy: Hillman Foundation; treas: Hillman Foundation, Henry L.; asst treas: Polk Foundation

Ross, David P., bank rep, contact person: Speas Foundation, Victor E.; bank rep, contact person: Speas Memorial Trust, John W. and Effie E.

Ross, Dickinson C., trust: Jones Foundation, Fletcher

Ross, Dominick F., Jr., pres, dir: Ayer Inc., N.W.

Ross, Donald E., vchmn: MPB Corp.; trust: Wheelabrator MPB Corporate Fund

Ross, Donald K., dir, secy: Rockefeller Family Fund

Ross, Dorothy May, asst treas: Allegheny Foundation

Ross, Edward W., pres: Betz Foundation; pres: Jupiter Industries, Inc.

Ross, Eleanor, asst secy, asst treas: Oxford Foundation

Ross, Emerson J., treas: Owens-Corning Fiberglas Corp.

Ross, Emrys J., trust: Bowles and Robert Bowles Memorial Fund, Ethel Wilson

Ross, Gary R., vp, dir: Ross Foundation

Ross, George Martin, trust: Ross Foundation, Lyn & George M.

Ross, Hal, vp: Ross Foundation

Ross, J. David, chmn, pres, ceo: Ross, Johnston & Kersting

Ross, J. G., dir: Hedco Foundation

Ross, Jane, trust mgr: Ross Foundation

Ross, Janet C., vp, dir: Ross Foundation, Arthur

Ross, John, dir: Davenport-Hatch Foundation

Ross, Joseph J., dir: Elgin Sweeper Foundation

Ross, Katherine, vp museum svcs: Sotheby's

Ross, Loren D., mem fin comm: Rockefeller Family Fund; treas: Sage Foundation, Russell

Ross, Lyn M., trust: Ross Foundation, Lyn & George M.

Ross, Malcom, pres: Segerstrom Foundation

Ross, Mary Caslin, secy, exec dir: Achelis Foundation; exec dir, secy: Bodman Foundation; dir: JM Foundation

Ross, Ralph, vchmn: Valley Foundation

Ross, Raymond E., secy: Cincinnati Milacron Foundation

Ross, Richard S., trust: Merck Co. Foundation

Ross, Robert T., vp, dir: Butler Foundation, J. Homer

Ross, Roger W., dir, vp: Nelson Foundation, Florence

Ross, Samuel D., Jr., trust: Kline Foundation, Josiah W. and Bessie H.

Ross, Sarane H., pres, dir: Barker Welfare Foundation

Ross, Sharryn, trust: Azadoutioun Foundation

Ross, T. L., dir, mem: Cannon Foundation

Ross, Thomas T., dir: Phillips Foundation, Dr. P.

Ross, William W., secy, treas, dir: Shoenberg Foundation

Rosser, Nancy Frees, secy, treas: Frees Foundation

Rossi, Anthony T., pres, dir: Bible Alliance

Rossi, Eugene, trust: CSC Industries Foundation

Rossi, Jerome, pres: Marshalls Inc.

Rossi, Patrick, treas: Crum and Forster Foundation

Rossi, Ralph L., vchmn, dir: UST

Rossi, Sanna B., trust: Aurora Foundation

Rossi, Steven, dir (pub rels): Saab Cars USA, Inc.

Rossin, Ada E., trust: Dynamet Foundation

Rossin, Peter C., chmn, trust: Dynamet Foundation

Rossin, Peter S., chmn, ceo: Dynamet, Inc.

Rossley, Paul Robert, trust: McEvoy Foundation, Mildred H.

Rosson, William M., chmn, dir: Conwood Co. L.P.

Rossway, Melvin, trust: Kaufman Endowment Fund, Louis G.

Rosta, Fannie, trust: Martini Foundation, Nicholas

Roswell, Arthur E., vp, trust: Blaustein Foundation, Jacob and Hilda

Roswell, Elizabeth B., vp, trust, don daughter: Blaustein Foundation, Jacob and Hilda

Rotan, Caroline P., secy: Farish Fund, William Stamps

Roth, Bruce J., treas: Roth Foundation, Louis T.

Roth, David G., dir (mktg): Builder Marts of America

Roth, David M., secy: Roth Foundation, Louis T.

Roth, Edythe M., trust: Roth Foundation

Roth, Gerald Bart, vp: Younkers Foundation

Roth, Greg, vp, secy: Waldinger Corp. Foundation

Roth, Joseph, chmn: Twentieth Century-Fox Film Corp.

Roth, Joseph S., secy: Schering-Plough Foundation

Roth, L.M., coo: Lummus Crest, Inc.

Roth, Linda, mgr (corp contributions): Philadelphia Electric Co.

Roth, Louis T., pres: Roth Foundation, Louis T.

Roth, Michael, ceo, coo: Mutual of New York; dir: Roth Family Foundation

Roth, Patricia, dir: Roth Family Foundation

Roth, Robert G., treas: Knowles Foundation

Roth, Robert W., dir: Montgomery Street Foundation

Roth, Roland, trust: Roth Foundation

Roth, Susan, dir: Roth Family Foundation

Roth, Walter, secy: Fullerton Metals Foundation; secy, treas: Shaw Foundation, Walden W. and Jean Young

Rothblatt, Ben, exec dir: Fry Foundation, Lloyd A.

Rothchild, Kennon V., dir: Bush Foundation

Rothenburg, Elaine, trust: Circuit City Foundation

Rothman, Herbert, vp: Kaplun Foundation, Morris J. and Betty

Rothmeier, S. G., chmn, dir: Alliant Techsystems

Rothschild, M.J., Randa

Rothschild, Steven James, trust: Kutz Foundation, Milton and Hattie

Rothschild, Walter N., Jr., trust: Clark Foundation, Edna McConnell; former dir Josiah Macy fdn: Macy, Jr. Foundation, Josiah

Rothstein, David, trust: Reisman Charitable Trust, George C. and Evelyn R.

Rothstein, Edward, trust: Havens Foundation, O. W.

Rothstein, Louis, vp, trust: Altschul Foundation

Rothstein, Phyllis, pres, trust: Altschul Foundation

Rothstein, Susan, trust: Altschul Foundation

Rothstein, William, trust: Altschul Foundation

Rottenberg, Alan, trust: Stoneman Charitable Foundation, Anne and David

Rottenberg, Alan W., trust: Sherman Family Charitable Trust, George and Beatrice

Rotter, Steven J., asst secy, dir: Resnick Foundation, Jack and Pearl

Roub, Bryan R., treas, trust: Harris Foundation

Roubos, Gary L., chmn, pres, ceo, dir: Dover Corp.

Roundtree, Stephen D., dir (oper & planning): Getty Trust, J. Paul

Rounsaville, Guy, Jr., dir: Wells Fargo Foundation

Rountree, Robert B., trust: Franklin Foundation, John and Mary

Rouse, Eloise M., vp, dir: Meadows Foundation

Rouss, Ruth, vp, secy: Edmondson Foundation, Joseph Henry

Rousso, Eli L., chmn, dir: Russ Togs; trust: Russ Togs Foundation

Routh, Robert F., secy, treas: Cuneo Foundation

Rover, Edward F., vp, secy, treas: Cranshaw Corporation

Rovira, Luis D., pres, trust: Lowe Foundation

Rowan, Eugene F., pres, dir: Brunner Foundation, Robert

Rowan, F. J., II, pres, ceo: Lee Apparel Co.

Rowan, Rita H., dir, secy: Trimble Family Foundation, Robert Mize and Isa White

Rowe, A. Prescott, mem contributions mgmt comm: Ethyl Corp.

Rowe, George, Jr., vp, secy, dir: Monell Foundation, Ambrose; pres: Vetlesen Foundation, G. Unger

Rowe, Irwin D., trust: Loeb Rhoades Employee Welfare Fund

Rowe, John W., pres, ceo, dir: New England Electric System

Rowe, Joseph E., vp, dir: PPG Industries Foundation

Rowe, Sara M., secy, treas: Maier Foundation, Sarah Pauline

Rowell, Harry B., trust: Hubbell Foundation, Harvey

Rowell, Lester J., Jr., chmn, pres, ceo: Provident Mutual Life Insurance Co. of Philadelphia

Rowen, Henry S., mem bd govs: Richardson Foundation, Smith

Rowland, L.H., pres, ceo, dir: Kansas City Southern Industries

Rowland, Sallie, mem (community concerns comm): NBD Bank, N.A.

Rowley, Edward D., pres, secy, trust: Charlesbank Homes

Rowney, Ray W., trust, vp: Charitable Fund

Roy, Deborah Donner, dir: Donner Foundation, William H.

Roy, Delwin A., pres, ceo: Hitachi Foundation

Royal, Darrell K., trust: Terry Foundation

Royall, Kenneth C., Jr., dir: Glaxo Foundation

Royce, Joseph W., secy: McCullough Foundation, Ralph H. and Ruth J.

Royer, Robert Lewis, trust: Brown Foundation, James Graham

Rozek, John F., secy, treas: Rolfs Foundation, Robert T.; secy, treas: Rolfs Foundation, Thomas J.

Rozell, Martha, 2nd vp: Tuch Foundation, Michael

Rozelle, Frank I., Jr., trust, secy, treas: Exposition Foundation

Ruan, Elizabeth J., trust: Ruan Foundation Trust, John

Ruan, John, III, trust: Ruan Foundation Trust, John

Ruane, Thomas G., cfo: NEC Technologies, Inc.

Ruane, William, dir: Amaturo Foundation

Ruben, Lawrence, vp: Belfer Foundation

Rubenstein, Ernest, dir: Guttman Foundation, Stella and Charles

Rubenstein, Herbert, vp, dir: Rubenstein Foundation, Philip

Rubenstein, Jay, trust: Schamach Foundation, Milton

Rubenstein, Leonard Mark, exec vp, treas: General American Life Insurance Co.; vp, dir: General American Charitable Foundation

Rubenstein, Terry M., pres, treas: Meyerhoff Foundation, Lyn P.

Rubenstein, William H., secy, treas: Andersen Foundation, Hugh J.

Rubin, Carolyn, treas: Dettman Foundation, Leroy E.

Rubin, Donald S., sr vp (corp aff): McGraw-Hill; vp, dir: McGraw-Hill Foundation

Rubin, Gerald Mayer, mem scientific adv comm: Whitney Foundation, Helen Hay

Rubin, Jack L., treas, dir: Youth Foundation

Rubin, Jane Gregory, treas: Reed Foundation

Rubin, Jeffrey S., sr vp (fin), cfo: NYNEX Corp.

Rubin, Judith O., trust: Rubin Foundation, Rob E. & Judith O.

Rubin, Lewis, pres, ceo, dir: Xtra Corp.

Rubin, Pearl W., pres, trust: Jones Foundation, Daisy Marquis

Rubin, Reed, pres: Reed Foundation

Rubin, Robert E., mem mgmt comm, ptnr, co chmn: Goldman Sachs & Co.; trust: Rubin Foundation, Rob E. & Judith O.

Rubin, Sydney R., gen coun: Jones Foundation, Daisy Marquis

Rubin, Warren, trust: Shuster Memorial Trust, Herman

Rubinelli, Joseph O., vp: Mazza Foundation

Rubinelli, Mary Jane, secy, treas: Mazza Foundation

Rubino, Bill, vp, secy, dir: Jasper Office Furniture Foundation

Rubino, John A., asst secy, asst treas, dir: Walgreen Benefit Fund

Rubino, Robert C., pres: Eastern Stainless Corp.

Rubino, William, treas, dir: Jasper Seating Foundation

Rubino, William A., pres: JOFCo., Inc.

Rubinovitz, Samuel, trust: EG&G Foundation

Ruch, Richard H., pres, ceo, dir: Miller Inc., Herman

Ruckelshaus, William D., chmn, ceo: Browning-Ferris Industries

Rucker, Adin Henry, Jr., vp, dir: Stonecutter Foundation

Rucker, Robert, cfo: Levy Co., Edward C.

Rudd, Jean, exec dir: Woods Charitable Fund

Rudder, Paul R., exec vp (oper): Norfolk Southern Corp.; vp: Norfolk Southern Foundation

Ruddy, E. Peter, Jr., dir: Goldome Foundation

Rude, N. Jean, trust: Hallett Charitable Trust

Ruder, Brian, dir: Weight Watchers Foundation

Ruder, Charles J., chmn, dir: Sears-Roebuck Foundation

Rudin, Danylle, vp: Brookdale Foundation; compliance off: Ramapo Trust

Rudin, Eric C., vp, dir: Rudin Foundation, Samuel and May

Rudin, Jack, pres, dir: Rudin Foundation; pres, dir: Rudin Foundation, Louis and Rachel; pres, dir: Rudin Foundation, Samuel and May

Rudin, Katherine L., dir: Rudin Foundation, Samuel and May

Rudin, Lewis, vp, dir: Rudin Foundation; secy, dir: Rudin Foundation, Louis and Rachel; exec vp, secy, treas, dir: Rudin Foundation, Samuel and May

Rudin, May, dir: Rudin Foundation; chmn, dir: Rudin Foundation, Samuel and May

Rudin, William, dir: Rudin Foundation, Samuel and May

Ruding, H. Onno, vchmn, dir: Citicorp

Rudner, Jocelyn P., trust: Plough Foundation

Rudnick, Alford P., treas, trust: Stone Charitable Foundation

Rudnick, Allen, vp, gen couns: CSX Corp.

Rudolf, Keith J., secy: Stein Roe & Farnham Foundation

Rudolph, Mary J., ceo: Erteszek Foundation

Rudolph, William D., asst secy: Coltec Industries Charitable Foundation

Rue, C. J., chmn contributions comm: Northwest Natural Gas Co.

Ruebhausen, Oscar, chmn emeritus: Greenwall Foundation

Rueckert, William Dodge, mem exec & fin comms, dir: Dodge Foundation, Cleveland H.

Ruehlmann, Eugene P., trust: Rice Foundation, Helen Steiner

Ruemenapp, Harold A., trust: Besser Foundation

Ruey, John S., treas: Amoco Foundation

Ruff, Charles F. C., dir: Covington and Burling Foundation

Ruffin, Thomas, Jr., vp, trust: Dillard Fund

Ruffle, John Frederick, vchmn, dir: J.P. Morgan & Co.

Ruffner, Jay S., vp, secy, trust: Flinn Foundation

Ruge, Lois Fisher, vp, dir: Fisher Foundation

Ruggiero, Lou, pres: Food Emporium

Ruggles, Rudy Lamont, Jr., dir: Guggenheim Foundation, Harry Frank

Rugo, Paul R., trust, secy: Sunburst Foundation

Ruh, Ronald R., trust: Hitchcock Foundation, Gilbert M. and Martha H.

Ruhlman, Jon R., pres, dir: Preformed Line Products Co.

Ruisch, R. G., mng ptnr: Black & Veatch; trust: Black & Veatch Foundation

Rukeyser, Robert J., chmn contributions comm: American Brands

Rukin, Barnett, dir: Rukin Philanthropic Foundation, David and Eleanore

Rukin, Eleanore, dir: Rukin Philanthropic Foundation, David and Eleanore

Rumbough, J. Wright, Jr., vp: Whitehall Foundation

Rumbough, Stanley H., dir: Post Foundation of D.C., Marjorie Merriweather; trust: Spiritus Gladius Foundation

Ruml, Alvin, trust: Holmes Foundation

Rummel, Mrs. Mason, grants dir: Brown Foundation, James Graham

Rumple, Norman C., asst treas: Pardee Foundation, Elsa U.

Runde, James, trust: Morgan Stanley Foundation

Runk, Fred, treas, dir: United Brands Foundation

Runk, Lee H., pres, coo: Harvard Industries

Runk, Leroy H., pres, coo: Hayes Albion Industries

Running, Harry T., secy: Oleson Foundation

Runser, C. Allan, trust: Van Wert County Foundation

Runzer, Carolyn, trust: Raper Foundation, Tom

Ruocco, Roberta A., vp (community rels & pub affairs dept): J.P. Morgan & Co.

Rupp, Fran, Rupp Foundation, Fran and Warren

Rupp, Gerald E., mgr, trust: Vidda Foundation

Rupp, John P., dir: Covington and Burling Foundation

Rupp, Linda E., trust: Stone Foundation, W. Clement and Jessie V.

Rupp, Sheron A., trust: Rupp Foundation, Fran and Warren

Ruppert, Barbara L., asst secy: Bunbury Company

Rupple, Brenton H., dir: Bucyrus-Erie Foundation

Rupprecht, Peter W., asst treas: Sofia American Schools

Ruscha, Edward, trust: Weisman Art Foundation, Frederick R.

Rush, Avery, Jr., dir: Harrington Foundation, Don and Sybil

Rush, Helen P., trust: Heinz Endowment, Vira I.

Rush, Raymond J., asst treas: Hayden Foundation, Charles

Rush, Rebecca, treas, dir: Badger Meter Foundation

Rusher, William, treas, dir: Wilbur Foundation, Marguerite Eyer

Rushton, William J., III, mem adv comm: Meyer Foundation, Robert R.

Ruskin, Uzi, pres, ceo, coo, dir: United Merchants & Manufacturers; vp: United Merchants Foundation

Ruslander, Julian, secy, trust: Falk Medical Fund, Maurice

Russ, Charles Paul, III, secy: NCR Foundation

Russ, Gina S., asst secy: Ryder System Charitable Foundation

Russ, Jack, dir: Lytel Foundation, Bertha Russ

Russell, Allan David, dir: Youth Foundation

Russell, Benjamin, dir, vp: Russell Educational Foundation, Benjamin and Roberta

Russell, C. Edward, Jr., secy: Portsmouth General Hospital Foundation

Russell, Charles P., vp: Columbia Foundation

Russell, Christine H., treas, don, dir: Columbia Foundation

Russell, Dan C., comm mem: Caine Charitable Foundation, Marie Eccles

Russell, Don G., chmn: Sonat Exploration

Russell, Donald B., chmn, dir: Farm & Home Savings Association; trust: Moss Charitable Trust, Finis M.

Russell, Edith L., trust: Russell Educational Foundation, Benjamin and Roberta

Russell, Evelyn Beveridge, dir: Beveridge Foundation, Frank Stanley

Russell, Frank E., ceo, pres: Central Newspapers, Inc.; asst secy-treas, dir: Central Newspapers Foundation

Russell, Frank Eli, trust: Jordan Foundation, Edward A.

Russell, Fred McFerrin, trust: Ansley Foundation, Dantzler Bond

Russell, George A., Jr., chmn, dir: State Street Foundation

Russell, Grover B., vp, treas, trust: Clark-Winchcole Foundation

Russell, Harry A., vchmn: Pantasote Polymers

Russell, Henry E., trust: Humane Society of the Commonwealth of Massachusetts

Russell, Jenny D., exec secy: Island Foundation

Russell, John C., trust: Sheafer Charitable Trust, Emma A.

Russell, John F., chmn, dir: Hoyt Foundation, Stewart W. and Willma C.

Russell, Julia W., trust: Russell Educational Foundation, Benjamin and Roberta

Russell, Madeline Haas, pres, don, dir: Columbia Foundation; dir: Levi Strauss Foundation

Russell, Manon C., comm mem: Caine Charitable Foundation, Marie Eccles

Russell, Marvin W., Ogden College Fund

Russell, Maurice V., chmn, pres: Kenworthy - Sarah H. Swift Foundation, Marion E.

Russell, Peter E., dir: Castle Foundation, Harold K. L.

Russell, Richard C., sr vp, cfo: Danis Foundation

Russell, Robert B., II, treas, trust: Middendorf Foundation

Russell, T. Alan, exec vp, secy, treas: Illinois Cereal Mills

Russell, Terence L., dir: Ryder System Charitable Foundation

Russell-Shapiro, Alice C., secy, dir: Columbia Foundation

Russo, Freda, secy: Chubb Foundation

Russo, Kathleen M., trust: EG&G Foundation

Russo, Louis T., chmn, pres, ceo, dir: Beckman Instruments

Russoli, Charles E., exec vp, cfo: Pennsylvania Power & Light

Russom, Mary S., secy, treas: Vulcan Materials Co. Foundation

Rust, Edward B., Jr., chmn, pres, ceo: State Farm Mutual Automobile Insurance Co.; pres, treas: State Farm Cos. Foundation

Rust, Judge Lloyd, trust: Johnson Foundation, M. G. and Lillie A.

Ruszin, T. E., Jr., asst secy, asst treas: Baltimore Gas & Electric Foundation

Ruth, Mary E., dir: Glenn Foundation for Medical Research, Paul F.

Rutherford, Alan W., sr vp, cfo: Crown Cork & Seal Co., Inc.

Rutherford, Clyde E., chmn, pres, dir: Dairylea Cooperative Inc.

Rutherford, J. Larry, pres: Gulfstream Housing Corp.

Rutherfurd, Guy G., pres, treas, trust: Achelis Foundation; pres, treas, trust: Bodman Foundation

Rutherfurd, Winthrop, Jr., trust: Woodland Foundation

Rutkowski, Cynthia K., secy: Park Banks Foundation

Rutland, George P., chmn, pres, ceo: Northeast Savings, FA

Rutledge, William, pres, ceo, dir: Teledyne

Rutman, Michael, secy, treas, dir: Max Charitable Foundation

Rutstein, David W., secy: Giant Food Foundation; secy, treas: Meyer Foundation, Eugene and Agnes E.

Rutter, Pamela B., trust: Humphrey Fund, George M. and Pamela S.

Ruvane, Joseph J., dir: Glaxo Foundation

Ruwe, Dean M., pres, coo: Copeland Corp.

Ruwitch, Robert S., dir: Bergner Foundation, P.A.

Ruyle, Bob, secy: Phelps Foundation, Hensel

Ryan, Arthur F., pres, coo: Chase Manhattan Bank, N.A.

Ryan, Barbara M., dir: Ryan Family Charitable Foundation

Ryan, Carl E., trust: Burkitt Foundation

Ryan, Cornelius O'Brien, pres, trust: Burkitt Foundation

Ryan, Daniel M., dir: Ryan Family Charitable Foundation

Ryan, Edwin L., Jr, secy: Tomkins Corporation Foundation

Ryan, Edwin L., Jr., secy, trust: Philips Foundation, Jesse

Ryan, Gerald F., mem: Burkitt Foundation

Ryan, Gladys B., vp, secy, treas: Ryan Foundation, David Claude

Ryan, Gregory R., vp, secy: Keck Foundation, W. M.

Ryan, H. Eugene, trust: Sterkel Trust, Justine

Ryan, J. T., III, chmn, pres, ceo, dir: Mine Safety Appliances Co.

Ryan, James P., Jr., dir: Ryan Family Charitable Foundation

Ryan, James Patrick, Jockey Club Foundation; vp: Ryan Family Charitable Foundation

Ryan, Jerome D., pres: Ryan Foundation, David Claude

Ryan, Jill, chmn (contributions comm): SAFECO Corp.

Ryan, John, dir (pub rels): Oppenheimer & Co., Inc.

Ryan, John T., Jr., trust: Heinz Endowment, Vira I.; chmn exec comm, dir: Mine Safety Appliances Co.

Ryan, Joseph W., vp, secy, treas, trust: Burkitt Foundation

Ryan, Kathleen C., dir: Ryan Family Charitable Foundation

Ryan, Linda M., pres: Ryan Family Charitable Foundation

Ryan, Louis, asst secy: Batten Foundation

Ryan, M. Catherine, bank rep, contact person: Payne Foundation, Frank E. and Seba B.

Ryan, M.C., dir, treas: Kelly Foundation, T. Lloyd

Ryan, Nancy L., asst secy: Rippel Foundation, Fannie E.

Ryan, Patrick G., chmn, ceo, pres: AON Corp.; pres, dir: AON Foundation; vp, dir: Ryan Foundation, Patrick G. and Shirley W.

Ryan, Patrick J., vp, dir: Oklahoma Gas & Electric Co. Foundation

Ryan, Peter D., dir: Ryan Family Charitable Foundation

Ryan, Richard O., pres, coo, dir: DeKalb Genetics Corp.; pres: DeKalb Genetics Foundation

Ryan, Sayville, exec dir: New Cycle Foundation

Ryan, Shirley W., pres, dir: Ryan Foundation, Patrick G. and Shirley W.

Ryan, Stephen M., vp: Ryan Foundation, David Claude

Ryan, Thomas F., treas: Dell Foundation, Hazel

Ryan, Thomas W., treas: Smith Foundation, A.O.

Ryan, W. James, vp, cfo: Huber Corp., J.M.

Ryan, William F., pres, ceo, coo: South Jersey Industries

Ryan, William J., pres, ceo: Peoples Heritage Savings Bank

Ryberg, Claire Dumke, pres: Dumke Foundation, Dr. Ezekiel R. and Edna Wattis

Rybnick, William, secy: G.A.G. Charitable Corporation

Ryburn, Frank M., Jr., vp: Moss Foundation, Harry S.; trust: Moss Heart Trust, Harry S.

Ryburn, Frank S., pres: Moss Foundation, Harry S.

Ryburn, Mary Jane, vp: Moss Foundation, Harry S.

Rydberg, Charles R., vp, dir: Jeffris Family Foundation

Rydell, David, trust: Bergstrom Foundation, Erik E. and Edith H.

Ryder, Douglas C., pres, ceo, dir: Holyoke Mutual Insurance Co. in Salem

Rydin, Wesley F., cfo: Malden Mills Industries

Ryland, Neil, cfo: Boston Co., Inc.

Rylander, Carole, dir: Wright Foundation, Lola

Rynne, David J., sr vp, cfo: Tandem Computers

Ryon, Mortimer, secy: Akzo America Foundation

Rysdon, Jimmie, asst secy: Sioux Steel Co. Foundation

Rysdon, Lorraine, dir: Sioux Steel Co. Foundation

Rysdon, P. M., pres, treas: Sioux Steel Co.

Rysdon, Phillip M., vp, secy, dir: Sioux Steel Co. Foundation

Ryskamp, Charles Andrew, trust: Guggenheim Memorial Foundation, John Simon; vp, dir: Lambert Memorial Foundation, Gerard B.; trust: Mellon Foundation, Andrew W.

S

Sa, Sophie, exec dir: Panasonic Foundation

Saad, Michael, secy: Salem Lutheran Foundation

Saah, Michael, secy, treas, dir: Jerusalem Fund for Education and Community Development

Saal, William Dunne, trust: H.C.S. Foundation

Saario, Terry, trust: Cowles Foundation, Gardner and Florence Call

Saario, Terry Tinson, pres, secy, asst treas: Northwest Area Foundation

Saba, Fred, vp: Browning Masonic Memorial Fund, Otis Avery

Sabater, J. M., vp: IBM South Africa Projects Fund

Sabath, Robert, trust: Kearney & Co. Foundation, A.T.

Sacco, Rita, asst secy: Schering-Plough Foundation

Sachs, Carolyn, dir: Benton Foundation

Sachs, Louis S., chmn: Sachs Electric Corp.; trust: Sachs Fund

Sachs, Mary L., trust: Sachs Fund

Sack, Daniel J., pres, trust: Armco Steel Co. Foundation

Sackley, Margaret, vp, dir: Snite Foundation, Fred B.

Sada, Federico G., chmn, ceo, dir: Anchor Glass Container Corp.

Saddlemire, Carl, chmn: Truman Foundation, Mildred Faulkner

Sadler, Gale, secy, treas: McMahon Foundation

Sadler, Shelley, dir (human resources): Penguin USA Inc.

Saemann, Irene L., trust: Saemann Foundation, Franklin I.

Saengswang, Dolly, program dir: Echoing Green Foundation

Saevre, Phyllis, secy, treas: Janesville Foundation

Safe, Kenneth S., Jr., trust: Eaton Memorial Fund, Georgiana Goddard; trust: Shaw Foundation, Gardiner Howland

Saffold, Gordon E., Jr., treas: Portsmouth General Hospital Foundation

Safir, Alan, pres: Weiler Foundation, Theodore & Renee

Sagalyn, Louis E., trust: Matz Foundation — Edelman Division

Sagan, Bruce, pres: Herald Newspapers Foundation

Sage, Andrew G. C., III, trust: Bostwick Foundation, Albert C.

Sage, Genevieve R., trust: Sage Foundation

Sager, Sheldon M., trust, secy: O'Neill Foundation, William J. and Dorothy K.

Sagerser-Brown, Margaret, pres: CIRI Foundation

Saggerse, Joseph J., cfo: Driscoll Co., L.F.

Sahm, Roland K., chmn, ceo, dir: Elixir Industries

Saigeon, Katherine L., asst vp (fin): Kellogg Foundation, W. K.

Saika, Peggy Kyoko, dir: New World Foundation

Saine, Carroll L., chmn, ceo: Central Fidelity Banks, Inc.;

dir: Central Fidelity Banks Foundation

Saint-Amand, Cynthia C., secy: Chisholm Foundation

Saint-Amand, Nathan E., dir: Chisholm Foundation

Saito, Kunishiro, pres, ceo: NEC Electronics, Inc.

Sakaguchi, Russell G., prog off community & environmental programs: ARCO Foundation

Sakahara, Toru, allocation comm: Kawabe Memorial Fund

Sakai, S., pres, dir: Toyota U.S.A. Foundation

Sakane, Hideo, sr vp, dir: Mitsubishi Semiconductor America, Inc. Funds

Saker, Joseph J., chmn, pres, dir: Foodarama Supermarkets, Inc.

Sakmann, Charles, pres (golf-tennis): Crystal Brands

Sakurai, George S., vp: Servco Foundation

Sakurai, Takeshi, pres: Mitsubishi Electric America; pres, dir: Mitsubishi Electric America Foundation

Salanitri, Marie, trust: Martini Foundation, Nicholas

Salant, Dorothy, pres, dir: G.A.G. Charitable Corporation

Salant, Peter, treas: G.A.G. Charitable Corporation

Salas, Sylvia, dir: Nellie Mae Fund for Education

Salas-Porras, Josefina A., trust: Freedom Forum

Salazar, Arsenio, secy-treas: Continental Divide Electric Education Foundation

Salb, J. P., dir: Jasper Seating Foundation

Saldich, Robert J., pres, ceo: Raychem Corp.

Salerno, Mary Beth, mem: American Express Co.

Sales, Michael, vchmn, dir: North American Reinsurance Corp.

Saliba, Jacob, chmn, ceo: Katy Industries Inc.

Salinger, Robert M., secy: First Financial Foundation

Salisbury, Charles H., Jr., managing dir: Price Associates, T. Rowe

Salk, Jonas Edward, MD, dir: MacArthur Foundation, John D. and Catherine T.

Salka, E., dir: Milken Foundation, L. and S.

Sallee, Margaret F., adm asst: Jordan Foundation, Arthur

Sallee, Roger K., secy-treas: Utilicorp United Charitable Foundation

Salmen, Stanley, Weatherhead Foundation

Salomon, Edna, dir: Salomon Foundation, Richard & Edna

Salomon, Richard B., pres, dir: Salomon Foundation, Richard & Edna

Salomon, Richard E., dir: Salomon Foundation, Richard & Edna

Salomon, Richard E., Jr., secy: Rockefeller Fund, David

Salter, Lee W., dir, exec dir: McConnell Foundation

Saltonstall, G. West, trust: Sailors' Snug Harbor of Boston

Saltonstall, William I., trust: Sanders Trust, Charles

Saltonstall, William Lawrence, trust: Sailors' Snug Harbor of Boston

Saltus, Lloyd, II, mem adv comm: de Kay Foundation

Saltz, Anita, pres: Saltz Foundation, Gary

Saltz, Jack, treas: Belfer Foundation

Saltz, Leonard, treas: Saltz Foundation, Gary

Saltz, Ronald, vp: Saltz Foundation, Gary

Saltz, Susan, secy: Saltz Foundation, Gary

Salvatori, Henry, pres: Salvatori Foundation, Henry

Salvi, Walter E., mgr: Boston Edison Foundation

Salzer, Richard L., vp, dir: Greenwall Foundation

Salzer, Richard L., Jr.,MD, dir: Greenwall Foundation

Samelson, Judy Y., vp (communications): Mott Foundation, Charles Stewart

Samide, Michael, pres: New Hampshire Ball Bearings

Samide, Michael R., trust: New Hampshire Ball Bearings Foundation

Samly, Abdol H., treas: Foundation for Iranian Studies

Sampedro, Hortensia, treas, dir: Cintas Foundation

Sample, Mary W., dir: Wieboldt Foundation

Sample, William, pres: Harvard Interiors Manufacturing Co.

Samples, R. E., chmn: Arch Mineral Corp.

Sampson, Bernard, trust: Brochsteins Foundation

Sampson, Norma, secy: Loomis House

Sampson, Ronald Gary, pres: Harvard Musical Association

Sams, David E., Jr., chmn, dir: Commonwealth Life Insurance Co.

Sams, Thomas, mem (community concerns comm): NBD Bank, N.A.

Samuel, Michael, secy: MCA Foundation

Samuelian, Karl, mgr: Douglas Charitable Foundation

Samuelian, Karl M., dir, vp: Gilmore Foundation, Earl B.

Samuels, Ruth, vp, trust: Meyer Memorial Foundation, Aaron and Rachel

Samuels, Victoria Woolner, dir: Newman Assistance Fund, Jerome A. and Estelle R.

Sanan, Denis R., pres: Jafra Cosmetics, Inc. (U.S.)

Sanber, Charles F., treas, dir: Young Foundation, H and B

Sanborn, Robert B., pres, coo, dir: Orion Capital Corp.

Sanchez, Jose Antonio, secy, dir: Haghenbeck Foundation, Antonio Y. De La Lama

Sanchez, Marjorie, secy, treas: Sachs Foundation

Sand, Ann, trust: Lavanburg-Corner House

Sand, Morton, trust: Merit Gasoline Foundation

Sandbach, George A., trust: Borkee Hagley Foundation

Sandbach, Henry A., mem (admin comm): Nabisco Foundation Trust

Sandberg, Paul W., dir: Gebbie Foundation

Sandbulte, Arend J., chmn, pres, ceo, dir: Minnesota Power & Light Co.

Sandefur, L. Keith, secy: National Center for Automated Information Retrieval

Sandefur, Thomas E., Jr., chmn, ceo: Brown & Williamson Tobacco Corp.

Sander, Malvin G., trust: SharonSteel Foundation

Sander, Richard G., secy: Rand McNally Foundation

Sanders, Arthur D., treas: Spiegel Family Foundation, Jerry and Emily

Sanders, Charles A., dir: Commonwealth Fund; treas: Day Foundation, Cecil B.; trust: Guggenheim Memorial Foundation, John Simon

Sanders, Charles Addison, ceo: Glaxo; chmn, pres: Glaxo Foundation

Sanders, D. Faye, chmn, trust: Citizens Charitable Foundation

Sanders, Dean, mem: Wal-Mart Foundation

Sanders, Frank K., Jr., dir: Ziegler Foundation for the Blind, E. Matilda

Sanders, Gail H., asst vp: Signet Bank/Maryland Charitable Trust

Sanders, Henry M., mem: Hood Foundation, Charles H.

Sanders, Irwin T., pres: Sofia American Schools

Sanders, Lewis A., pres, coo: Bernstein & Co., Sanford C.; trust: Bernstein & Co. Foundation, Sanford C.

Sanders, Morton, dir: Litwin Foundation

Sanders, Virginia, pub aff dept: Abraham & Straus

Sanders, Walter Jeremiah, III, chmn, ceo, dir: Advanced Micro Devices

Sanders, Wayne R., chmn, ceo, dir: Kimberly-Clark Corp.

Sandford, J. W., pres, coo: Rolls-Royce Inc.

Sandler, David P., secy: Arcadia Foundation

Sandler, E., dir: Capital Fund Foundation; secy, cfo, dir: Milken Family Medical Foundation

Sandler, Gilbert, dir communs: Abell Foundation, The

Sandler, Herbert M., chmn, ceo: Golden West Financial Corp.; chmn, ceo: World Savings & Loan Association

Sandler, Marion O., Golden West Financial Corp.

Sandler, Perry L., trust: Shapiro Charitable Trust, J. B. & Maurice C.

Sandler, R. V., dir: Milken Foundation, L. and S.

Sandman, Dan D., gen couns, secy: USX Foundation

Sandoni, Linda, admin asst: Interpublic Group of Cos.

Sandri, Michael A., asst secy: Crum and Forster Foundation

Sandrick, Kristine, dir: Sears-Roebuck Foundation

Sandridge, T.L., vp (intl div): Phillips Petroleum Co.

Sands, Bliss Lewis, trust: Garvey Memorial Foundation, Edward Chase

Sands, Don W., pres, ceo: Gold Kist, Inc.

Sandson, John I., trust: Wolfson Foundation, Louis E.

Sandweiss, Jerome W., trust: Sachs Fund

Sandy, Lewis, MD, vp: Johnson Foundation, Robert Wood

Sane, E. R., dir: Love Foundation, Martha and Spencer

Saneishi-Kim, Sherelee, secy: BHP Petroleum Americas (HI) Foundation

Sanem, Michael L., pres, ceo: Monfort of Colorado, Inc.

Sanford, Charles Steadman, Jr., chmn, dir, ceo: Bankers Trust Co.

Sanford, Mary Cameron, trust: Baldwin Memorial Foundation, Fred

Sang, Bernard, secy: Sang Foundation, Elsie O. and Philip D.

Sang, Elsie O., pres: Sang Foundation, Elsie O. and Philip D.

Sanger, Linda, vp, dir: Uris Brothers Foundation

Sanger, Michael, dir: JM Foundation

Sanger, Stephen W., trust: General Mills Foundation

Sant, John W., dir: Hoyt Foundation

Sant, Roger West, chmn: Applied Energy Services

Santangelo, Joseph, asst treas, trust: Arkell Hall Foundation; dir (pub affairs): ITT Corp.

Santo, James M., vp, gen couns, secy: Eckerd Corp., Jack; chmn: Eckerd Corp. Foundation, Jack

Santos, John F., trust: Retirement Research Foundation

Santry, Arthur, chmn, dir: North American Reinsurance Corp.

Sapiente, Rebecca Wallace, dir: Gibson Foundation, Addison H.

Saporta, Herman, trust: Russ Togs Foundation

Saporta, Sam, pres: United Togs Inc.; pres, dir: United Togs Foundation

Sapp, A. Eugene, Jr., pres: SCI Systems, Inc.

Sapp, Charles, vp: Kayser Foundation

Sapp, Hubert, chmn, trust: Meyer Foundation, Bert and Mary

Sardanac-Studney, Sylvie, commun off: Credit Agricole

Sardas, Jacques Raphael, exec vp, coo, dir: Goodyear Tire & Rubber Co.

Sardi, Maurice Charles, trust: Westinghouse Foundation

Sargent, Frederic B., ceo: Sargent Electric Co.

Sargent, Hugh A. A., pres: Ludwick Institute

Sargent, James C., pres, dir: Lincoln Fund

Sargent, John A., dir: Post Foundation of D.C., Marjorie Merriweather

Sargent, John C., trust: Stark Foundation, Nelda C. and H. J. Lutcher

Sargent, Newell B., trust: Sargent Foundation, Newell B.

Sarney, George W., chmn, dir: Raytheon Engineers & Constructors

Sarni, Vincent Anthony, chmn, ceo, dir: PPG Industries; chmn, dir: PPG Industries Foundation

Sarnie, Gerard J., cfo: Amoskeag Co.

Sarnoff, Merton, pres: Dreyfus Corp., Louis

Sarnoff, Robert W., trust: United States-Japan Foundation

Sarofim, Christopher B., trust: Brown Foundation

Sarofim, Fayez Shalaby, trust: Sarofim Foundation

Sarofim, Louisa Stude, pres, trust: Brown Foundation; trust: Sarofim Foundation

Saroni, Louis, II, vp, treas, dir: Zellerbach Family Fund

Sarow, Robert D., secy: Kantzler Foundation

Saroyan, Cosette, trust: Saroyan Foundation, William

Sarsten, Gunnar E., pres, coo: Morrison-Knudsen Corp.

Sarsten, Marie, dir: Morrison Knudsen Corp. Foundation Inc.

Sartor, C. Lane, trust: Woolf Foundation, William C.

Sartwelle, James D., trust: George Foundation

Sarver, James H., secy, treas: Hunnicutt Foundation, H. P. and Anne S.

Sasakawa, Yohei, trust: United States-Japan Foundation

Sasaki, Marlene H., secy: Brewer Charitable Foundation, C.

Sasaki, Robert K., dir: Alexander & Baldwin Foundation

Sass, Gerald M., sr vp: Freedom Forum

Sassano, Rosalie, vp, dir: Common Giving Fund

Sasser, Barbara Weston, trust: Kempner Fund, Harris and Eliza

Satchell, Harold, pres: Einstein Fund, Albert E. and Birdie W.

Satcher, David, PhD, dir: Macy, Jr. Foundation, Josiah

Satin, Robert A., asst treas: Rosen Foundation, Michael Alan

Satinsky, Alex, trust: Paley Foundation, Goldie

Sato, Takao, pres, ceo: Hawaii National Bank; vp: Hawaii National Foundation

Satre, Philip G., pres, coo: Harrah's Hotels & Casinos; pres, coo: Promus Cos.

Satrum, Jerry R., pres, ceo, dir: Georgia Gulf Corp.

Satterfield, B. K., dir: Bowen Foundation, Ethel N.

Satterlee, F. F., dir: Mid-Iowa Health Foundation

Sattinger, Mr. Loren R., chmn grants comm: Badgeley Residuary Charitable Trust, Rose M.

Sattler, Omega C., secy: Massey Foundation, Jack C.

Satut, Miguel A., vp: Kresge Foundation

Sauer, Bradford B, asst secy, asst treas: Flagler Foundation

Saufley, Zack, dir: Mills Foundation, Ralph E.

Saul, Andrew Marshall, dir: Saul Foundation, Joseph E. & Norma G.

Saul, Bernard, trust: CENEX Foundation

Saul, Bernard Francis, II, chmn: Chevy Chase Savings Bank FSB

Saul, Charles F., pres, ceo: Agway

Saul, Joseph E., pres, treas: Saul Foundation, Joseph E. & Norma G.

Saul, Norma G., secy, trust: Saul Foundation, Joseph E. & Norma G.

Saul, Ralph, pres, dir: New Street Foundation

Saul, William J., chmn: Remmele Engineering, Inc.

Saunders, Carol H., trust: Hastings Trust

Saunders, Carolyn, dir: Coughlin-Saunders Foundation

Saunders, Dan, trust: Millhollon Educational Trust Estate, Nettie

Saunders, Gary, exec vp, cfo: Bosch Corp., Robert

Saunders, R. R., pres: Coughlin-Saunders Foundation

Sauntry, Jean, trust: Valencia Charitable Trust

Saurage, H. Norman, III, chmn, trust: Community Coffee Co., Inc. Foundation

Saurage, L. Cary, II, trust: Community Coffee Co., Inc. Foundation

Savage, Arthur V., vp, treas, gov: Crary Foundation, Bruce L.

Savage, Terry, dir: American Express Co.

Savage, Toy D., Jr., dir: Camp Foundation; secy, treas, dir: North Shore Foundation

Savard, Claude A., pres, coo: Provigo Corp. Inc.

Savedge, Henry S., Jr., exec vp, cfo: Reynolds Metals Co.; dir: Reynolds Metals Co. Foundation

Savett, Stuart H., vp: Arronson Foundation

Savin, Robert, chmn: IPCO Corp.

Savitske, Michael B., pres, ceo: National Standard Co.

Savoie, JoAnne, dir (corp aff): Cookson America

Savory, Wallace E., vp, asst treas: Howard Benevolent Society

Sawagari, Osamu, vchmn: National Steel

Sawhill, Isabel Van Devanter, trust: German Marshall Fund of the United States

Sawhill, John D., pres, ceo: WJLA Inc.

Sawicz, Edward J., chmn, ceo: DCNY Corp.; CHMN: Discount Corp. of New York Charitable Foundation

Sawyer, D. Jack, Jr., secy, treas, trust: Williams, Jr. Family Foundation, A. L.

Sawyer, Frank, trust: Sawyer Charitable Foundation

Sawyer, Mildred F., trust: Sawyer Charitable Foundation

Sawyer, Raymond Terry, chmn: Codrington Charitable Foundation, George W.

Sawyer, Tom, mng comm: Alliant Community Investment Foundation

Sawyer, William Dale, MD, pres, trust: China Medical Board of New York

Sax, Ward L., trust: Fales Foundation Trust

Saxton, G. William, trust, chmn: Fox Foundation Trust, Jacob L. and Lewis

Saxton, John A., pres: Procter & Gamble/Noxell Foundation

Saxton, Paul A., pres, ceo, coo: General Housewares Corp.

Sayad, Homer Elisha, dir: Green Foundation, Allen P. and Josephine B.

Sayatovic, Wayne P., vp, cfo: IDEX Corp.

Sayler, J. William, Jr., pres, ceo: Business Men's Assurance Co. of America

Sayles, Thomas D., Jr., chmn, ceo, dir: Summit Bancorporation

Sayres, Edwin J., trust emeritus: Dodge Foundation, Geraldine R.

Scaife, Curtis S., trust: Laurel Foundation

Scaife, David N., co-chmn, trust: Scaife Family Foundation

Scaife, Jennie K., co-chmn, trust: Scaife Family Foundation

Scaife, Margaret R., trust: Allegheny Foundation

Scaife, Richard Mellon, don, chmn: Allegheny Foundation; chmn, don: Carthage Foundation; chmn, trust: Scaife Foundation, Sarah

Scala, C. George, chmn, pres, ceo: Lechmere

Scalia, Frank, cfo: Coopers & Lybrand

Scammell, Deborah L., trust: Large Foundation

Scammell, F. W., trust, adm: Washington Trust Bank Foundation

Scangas, Christopher, dir: Gerondelis Foundation

Scanlan, C. R., dir: Lockheed Leadership Fund

Scanlan, Carlin, mgr corp communications: Union Electric Co. Charitable Trust

Scanlan, Sallie A., trust: Kahn Dallas Symphony Foundation, Louise W. and Edmund J.

Scanlan, Thomas M., Jr., pres: Ward Machinery Co.

Scanlon, Mary Ann, dir: McDonnell Douglas Corp.-West

Scanlon, Thomas J., vp, dir: Public Welfare Foundation

Scarborough, Ann Hanson, dir: Johnston-Hanson Foundation

Scarborough, Collin Wesley, dir: Kerr Fund, Grayce B.

Scarborough, T. A., secy, treas: Acme-McCrary and Sapona Foundation

Scarbrough, Arlan E., chmn: Gulf Power Foundation

Scarff, Edward L., chmn, dir: Arcata Corp.; chmn, dir: Arcata Graphics Co.

Scarfoss, D. Gerald, secy, treas: Deloitte & Touche Foundation

Scarlett, Joseph, pres, coo: TSC Stores, Inc.

Scarperi, Peter, exec vp, cfo: Ogilvy & Mather Worldwide; treas, dir: Ogilvy Foundation

Schaad, H. Ronald, pres, ceo: Kemper Investors Life Insurance Co.

Schaar, William H., contr: Armco Foundation

Schaber, Gordon Duane, dir: Sierra Health Foundation

Schacht, Henry Brewer, chmn, ceo, dir: Cummins Engine Co.; chmn, dir: Cummins Engine Foundation; chmn bd: Ford Foundation

Schadt, Charles F., Jr., trust: Schadt Foundation

Schadt, Charles F., Sr., trust: Schadt Foundation

Schadt, Harry E., Jr., trust: Schadt Foundation

Schadt, Reid, trust: Schadt Foundation

Schadt, Stephen C., Sr., dir, pres: Schadt Foundation

Schaefer, Charles V., III, trust: Shepherd Foundation

Schaefer, Charles V., Jr., chmn: New Jersey Manufacturers Insurance Co.; trust: Shepherd Foundation

Schaefer, Cheryl I., trust: Plaster Foundation, Robert W.

Schaefer, Donald A., vp, dir: Palisades Educational Foundation

Schaefer, Elizabeth H., trust: Mather Fund, Richard

Schaefer, George A., Jr., pres, dir: Fifth Third Bancorp

Schaefer, George C., trust, treas: Faith Home Foundation

Schaefer, John Paul, pres, ceo, dir: Research Corporation

Schaefer, Patricia, vp: Morgan Stanley Foundation; mem: Ragen, Jr. Memorial Fund Trust No. 1, James M.

Schaefer, Robert Wayne, secy, treas, trust: First Maryland Foundation

Schaeffer, Glenn, pres, cfo: Circus Circus Enterprises

Schaeffer, Howard J., pres, dir: Burroughs Wellcome Fund

Schaeffer, Wayne G., sr vp, cfo: Citizens Commercial & Savings Bank

Schaenen, Lee, trust: Sullivan Musical Foundation, William Matheus

Schafer, Betsy, trust: Cherokee Foundation

Schafer, Carl Walter, pres, trust, dir: Atlantic Foundation

Schafer, Oscar S., Jr., dir: Guggenheim Foundation, Daniel and Florence

Schaff, Theresa R., vp: Washington Square Fund

Schaffer, Forest R., dir: SICO Foundation

Schaffer, Helen, mgr: Schaffer Foundation, Michael & Helen

Schaffer, Mark, trust: Miniger Memorial Foundation, Clement O.

Schaffer, Michael J., mgr: Schaffer Foundation, Michael & Helen

Schaffer, Peter, dir, trust: Schaffer Foundation, Michael & Helen

Schaller, Harry W., chmn: Citizens First National Bank; trust: Citizens First National Bank Foundation

Schamach, Gene, pres: Schamach Foundation, Milton

Schamach, Howard, trust: Schamach Foundation, Milton

Schamach, Rhoda, trust: Schamach Foundation, Milton

Schamach, Robert, trust: Schamach Foundation, Milton

Schampier, Robert, human resources: Kanematsu-Gosho U.S.A. Inc.

Schanfield, Leonard, dir: Seid Foundation, Barre

Schantz, Frederick W., vp: Tait Foundation, Frank M.

Schaper, David, trust: Stabler Foundation, Donald B. and Dorothy L.

Schapiro, Donald, dir: Neu Foundation, Hugo and Doris

Schapiro, Douglas, secy: National Metal & Steel Foundation

Schapiro, Joseph, pres: National Metal & Steel Foundation

Schapiro, Morris A., pres, dir: Schapiro Fund, M. A.

Schara, Charles Gerard, treas: GEICO Corp.; asst treas, dir: GEICO Philanthropic Foundation

Scharf, Willis A., vp: Endries Foundation, Ltd.

Scharp, Anders, chmn, dir: White Consolidated Industries

Schatz, Joan L., member: One Valley Bank Foundation

Schatz, Myrna, trust: Gilman, Jr. Foundation, Sondra and Charles

Schatz, Susan J., 1st vp, dir: Jewish Foundation for Education of Women

Schautz, Madalene I., pres: Schautz Foundation, Walter L.

Schautz, Walter I., Jr., treas: Schautz Foundation, Walter L.

Schechter, Arthur L., trust: Lewis Foundation, Lillian Kaiser

Schechter, Dana, secy: Levine Family Foundation, Hyman

Schechter, Loren, vp: Prudential Securities Foundation

Schechter, Robert, treas, dir: Lotus Development Corp.

Schechter, Sol, pres: Hampton Industries

Scheckter, I. Jerome, pres, treas, dir: Eastern Foundry Co.; trust: EAFCO Foundation

Schecter, Aaron, trust: Schecter Private Foundation, Aaron and Martha

Schecter, Martha, trust: Schecter Private Foundation, Aaron and Martha

Scheer, Julian Weisel, chmn: LTV Foundation

Scheer, Ruth C., exec dir: Cabot Family Charitable Trust

Scheffer, Thomas R., vp, trust: Reeves Foundation

Scheid, Gerald H., exec dir: CHC Foundation

Scheid, Karen, trust: Brace Foundation, Donald C.

Scheidig, Frederick, vp: Harris Brothers Foundation

Schein, Richard, trust: Cranston Foundation

Scheinbart, Leo, dir, pres: Foster Foundation, Joseph C. and Esther

Scheinbart, Marcia J., secy: Foster Foundation, Joseph C. and Esther

Scheiner, J. David, vchmn: Burdines

Scheirich, H. J., III, chmn: Scheirich Co., H.J.; chmn, trust: Scheirich Co. Foundation, H.J.

Schelinski, Linda K., vp (admin): Joyce Foundation

Schell, Braxton, dir, secy: Kenan Family Foundation

Scheller, Sanford G., pres, ceo: Treasure Chest Advertising Co.

Schelling, Dennis E., dir: Christensen Charitable and Religious Foundation, L. C.

Schelter, Walter, dir: Odessa Trading Co. Educational Trust

Schenk, George, pres, coo, dir: Huber Corp., J.M.

Schenk, Susan, investor rels: Pegasus Gold Corp.

Schenkel, Gregory A., mem (community concerns comm): NBD Bank, N.A.

Schenker, Martine, Banque Francaise du Commerce Exterieur

Scheper, Fran, trust: CPI Corp.

Scher, Norman A., exec vp, cfo: Tredegar Industries

Scherck, Louis E., trust: Ellwood Foundation; vp, treas: Nason Foundation

Scherer, Karla, chmn, don: Scherer Foundation, Karla

Scherer, Robert B., cfo: Chicago Title and Trust Co.

Schermer, Harry Angus, vp: Nationwide Insurance Foundation

Schermer, Lloyd G., chmn: Lee Enterprises; chmn: Lee Foundation

Schettelkotte, Albert J., pres, ceo, trust, mem: Scripps Howard Foundation

Scheu, Robert S., dir: Cummings Foundation, James H.; vp, trust: Western New York Foundation

Scheuer, Richard J., pres: Scheuer Family Foundation, S. H. and Helen R.

Scheumann, Theiline P., pres, trust: Norcliffe Fund

Schey, Lucille L., trust: Schey Foundation

Schey, Ralph E., pres, trust: Schey Foundation; chmn, ceo: Scott and Fetzer Co.; chmn: Scott and Fetzer Foundation

Schichtel, Gerald F., pres: Hilliard Corp.; trust: Hilliard Foundation

Schick, Thomas E., trust: American Express Co.; pres, coo: Midway Airlines

Schiefer, Fredrich, chmn, pres, coo: Bosch Corp., Robert

Schiek, Fred A., exec vp, coo: Employers Mutual Casualty Co.

Schiek, Lisa, dir pub rels: Gucci America Inc.

Schierbaum, Wayne D., trust: White Consolidated Industries Foundation

Schierbeek, Robert H., asst sec-treas: DeVos Foundation, Richard and Helen

Schierholz, William F., pres: Chemtech Industries

Schierl, Carol A., vp, dir: Cornerstone Foundation of Northeastern Wisconsin

Schierl, Michael J., vp, dir: Cornerstone Foundation of Northeastern Wisconsin

Schierl, Paul G., mem adv comm: AEC Trust

Schierl, Paul J., pres: Cornerstone Foundation of Northeastern Wisconsin

Schifano, Thomas J., pres: Blue Cross & Blue Shield of Kentucky Foundation

Schiff, Andrew N., treas: Schiff Foundation

Schiff, David Tevele, pres, dir: Schiff Foundation

Schiff, Debra, secy: Shorenstein Foundation, Walter H. and Phyllis J.

Schiff, Harold L., secy, treas: Hillman Family Foundation, Alex

Schiff, John Jefferson, chmn, don: Schiff Foundation, John J. and Mary R.

Schiff, Marcia, exec dir, secy, mem oper comm: Polaroid Foundation

Schiff, Peter G., vp, dir: Schiff Foundation

Schiff, Thomas R., trust: Schiff Foundation, John J. and Mary R.

Schildecker, William, exec vp: Fish Foundation, Bert

Schilke, Susanne A., asst treas: Banc One Wisconsin Foundation

Schiller, Jerry A., exec vp, cfo, dir: Maytag Corp.; treas, trust: Maytag Corp. Foundation

Schiller, Jonathan D., dir: Irwin-Sweeney- Miller Foundation

Schilling, Alfred R., secy, trust: Griffin, Sr., Foundation, C. V.

Schilling, Constance L., General Mills Foundation

Schilling, Leslie W., cfo, secy: Tang Foundation

Schilling, Richard M., dir: Sundstrand Corp. Foundation

Schilmoeller, Denis, trust: CENEX Foundation

Schiltz, Timothy D., trust: Hoover Foundation

Schimmelbusch, Heinz, chmn, ceo: Metallgesellschaft Corp.

Schimpf, Glenn P., pres, coo: Danis Industries

Schimpff, Barbara S., exec vp: Olmsted Foundation, George and Carol

Schindler, Ralph, Jr., trust: Young Charity Trust Northern Trust Company

Schine, Wendy Wachtell, vp, program dir: Drown Foundation, Joseph

Schink, James Harvey, pres: Kirkland & Ellis Foundation

Schipke, Roger W., chmn, pres, ceo: Ryland Group

Schiro, Bernard, chmn, trust: Auerbach Foundation, Beatrice Fox; pres, trust: Schiro Fund

Schiro, Dorothy A., vp, treas, trust: Auerbach Foundation, Beatrice Fox; trust: Koopman Fund; secy, treas, trust: Schiro Fund

Schiro, Elizabeth, secy: Auerbach Foundation, Beatrice Fox

Schlachenhaufen, Kari, vp programs: Skillman Foundation

Schlag, Darwin W., Jr., dir: Group Health Foundation

Schlageter, William J., trust: Ohio Bell Foundation

Schlauch, W. F., vp (adhesives & resins): National Starch & Chemical Corp.; dir: National Starch & Chemical Foundation

Schlegel, Leland D., Jr., vp, dir: Vogt Foundation, Henry

Schleicher, Raymond M., vp, treas, dir: Salomon Foundation, Richard & Edna

Schlein, Dov C., pres, coo, dir: Republic New York Corp.

Schlesinger, James R., chmn: Mitre Corp.

Schlessman, Dolores J., trust: Schlessman Foundation

Schlessman, Gary L., vp, trust: Schlessman Foundation

Schlessman, Lee E., pres, ceo: Greeley Gas Co.; pres, trust: Schlessman Foundation

Schlichting, H. Jurgen, joint chmn N Am: WestLB New York Branch

Schlichting, Raymond C., pres, chmn: Hesston Foundation

Schliesman, Paul D., dir: Leach Foundation, Tom & Frances

Schlindwein, Timothy A., pres: Stein Roe & Farnham Investment Council

Schlinger, James A., trust: Murphey Foundation, Lluella Morey

Schlinker, Margie, sr commun assoc: Mallinckrodt Specialty Chemicals Co.

Schlit, Timothy R., Jr., trust: Tiger Foundation

Schlosberg, Richard, III, trust: Hartford Courant Foundation

Schlosberg, Richard T., III, dir: Pfaffinger Foundation; dir: Times Mirror Foundation

Schloss, Douglas, dir: Rexford Fund

Schloss, Irwin, secy, dir: Rexford Fund

Schloss, Richard, dir: Rexford Fund

Schlossberg, Lillian, dir, secy: Cohn Foundation, Peter A. and Elizabeth S.

Schlossberg, Thomas, dir: Mutual of New York Foundation

Schlosser, Frank, pres, coo: Pamida, Inc.

Schlottman, Richard A., pres, ceo, dir: Old National Bank in Evansville

Schlozman, Kay, dir: New Prospect Foundation

Schlozman, Stanley, dir: New Prospect Foundation

Schlumberger, Pierre Marcel, secy: Menil Foundation; dir: Schlumberger Foundation

Schlussel, Mark E., trust: Bargman Foundation, Theodore and Mina; secy: Imerman Memorial Foundation, Stanley

Schmalzried, Erma L., vp: Ebell of Los Angeles Rest Cottage Association; dir, vp: Ebell of Los Angeles Scholarship Endowment Fund

Schmechel, Warren Paul, chmn, ceo dir: Montana Power Co.; dir: MPCo/Entech Foundation

Schmeling, Roger, dir: First National Bank & Trust Co. of Rockford Charitable Trust

Schmergel, G., pres, dir: Genetics Institute

Schmick, William F., Jr., trust: Warfield Memorial Fund, Anna Emory

Schmid, Daniel J., Jr., trust: Heileman Old Style Foundation

Schmider, Mary Ellen, trust: Lutheran Brotherhood Foundation

Schmidhammer, Joseph E., treas: Lancaster Lens Foundation

Schmidt, Alice Oakley, pres: Oakley Foundation, Hollie and Anna

Schmidt, Arthur J., dir, pres: U.S. Oil/Schmidt Family Foundation, Inc.

Schmidt, Clifford, secy: Edwards Foundation, Jes

Schmidt, David G., treas: Hexcel Foundation

Schmidt, E.J., trust: Sifco Foundation

Schmidt, George P., dir: Livingston Foundation

Schmidt, Jareen E., pres: Edwards Foundation, Jes

Schmidt, John, dir: Schmidt Charitable Foundation, William E.

Schmidt, John G., vp: Oakley Foundation, Hollie and Anna

Schmidt, Kathryn G., mgr: Fisher-Price Foundation

Schmidt, Michael K., trust: Olympia Brewing Co. Employees Beneficial Trust

Schmidt, Nicholas M., trust: Olympia Brewing Co. Employees Beneficial Trust

Schmidt, Peter, secy: Slifka Foundation, Alan B.

Schmidt, Peter G., trust: Olympia Brewing Co. Employees Beneficial Trust

Schmidt, Peter W., secy, treas: Buhl Family Foundation; pres, ceo: Holzman USA, Philipp

Schmidt, Raymond, dir, secy: U.S. Oil/Schmidt Family Foundation, Inc.

Schmidt, Robert A., trust: Olympia Brewing Co. Employees Beneficial Trust

Schmidt, Ronald, trust: Baumberger Endowment

Schmidt, Stanley H., chmn, trust: Baumberger Endowment

Schmidt, Theodore F., trust: Olympia Brewing Co. Employees Beneficial Trust

Schmidt, Thomas, trust: U.S. Oil/Schmidt Family Foundation, Inc.

Schmidt, W. C., cfo, vp: Dow Elanco Inc.

Schmidt, Walter F., trust: Monaghan Charitable Trust, Rose

Schmidt, William, dir, vp: U.S. Oil/Schmidt Family Foundation, Inc.

Schmidt, William J., treas, dir: Olin Foundation, F. W.

Schmidt, William L., trust: Benua Foundation

Schmidtchen, Bernd, vp, cfo: Rolm Systems

Schmied, William F., trust: Link Foundation

Schmimmel, Stephen B., trust: Schimmel Foundation

Schmitt, Carl, trust: Homeland Foundation

Schmitt, Henry A., vp corp rels: Consolidated Freightways; vp, trust: Emery Air Freight Educational Foundation

Schmitt, Wolfgang R., co-chmn: Rubbermaid; trust: Rubbermaid Foundation

Schmitz, Michael, secy: Brunswick Foundation

Schmude, D.H., pres, ceo: Star Enterprise

Schmults, Edward Charles, trust: Clark Foundation, Edna McConnell; trust: GTE Foundation

Schnachenberg, Shirley, trust: Goldman Foundation, Morris and Rose

Schneckenburger, Karen, treas: Fairchild Industries Foundation

Schneebacher, Alex T., Jr., pres, dir: Educators Mutual Life Insurance Co.

Schneeweiss, Dr. Steven, treas: Chapman Charitable Corporation, Howard and Bess

Schneider, Al J., pres, trust: Schneider Foundation Corp., Al J.

Schneider, Eulalie Bloedel, trust: Bloedel Foundation

Schneider, Frederic, trust: Schneider Foundation, Robert E.

Schneider, Gail, dir: Goldman Foundation, Herman

Schneider, Gene F., trust: Bastien Memorial Foundation, John E. and Nellie J.

Schneider, George, cfo: Group Health Plan Inc.

Schneider, Henry, pres, dir: Moses Fund, Henry and Lucy

Schneider, Hubert H., pres: 1525 Foundation; pres, dir: Second Foundation

Schneider, Melvin, dir, pres: Schneider Foundation, Robert E.

Schneider, Melvyn H., dir: Siragusa Foundation

Schneider, P. C., vp, dir: Indiana Desk Foundation

Schneider, Pam H., trust: H. R. H. Family Foundation

Schneider, Phyllis, secy, treas: Schneider Foundation, Robert E.

Schneider, Richard, trust: Schneider Foundation, Robert E.

Schneider, Stanley, treas, dir: Autry Foundation

Schneider, Steve, pres: Tomkins Industries, Inc.

Schneider, Thelma E., vp: Schneider Foundation Corp., Al J.

Schneider-Manoury, Michel, chmn, pres: Elf Aquitaine, Inc.

Schneiderman, Irwin, dir, pres, secy: Schneiderman Foundation, Roberta and Irwin

Schneiderman, Roberta, dir, vp, treas: Schneiderman Foundation, Roberta and Irwin

Schneier, Lance W., ceo: Access Energy Corp.

Schnell, Carlton B., trust: Renner Foundation

Schnick, Thomas H., pres, ceo, dir: Commonwealth Life Insurance Co.

Schnuck, Craig, chmn, ceo: Schnuck Markets

Schnurr, Andrew V., trust: Kaplen Foundation

Schoeder, Nanette D., trust, secy: Nash Foundation

Schoeller, Peters, Peters Foundation, Charles F.

Schoellkopf, Wolfgang, vchmn, dir: Fidelity Bank; vchmn, dir: First Fidelity Bancorporation

Schoen, Gena, secy: Montgomery Ward Foundation

Schoenbachler, Carl L., sr vp, cfo: Brown & Williamson Tobacco Corp.

Schoenberg, Robert H., pres, dir: Shoenberg Foundation

Schoenberg, Sydney M., Jr., chmn, dir: Shoenberg Foundation

Schoendorf, Anthony, dir: Norcross Wildlife Foundation

Schoenecker, L. Guy, pres: Business Incentives; pres: Business Incentives Foundation

Schoenfeld, Gerald, chmn: Shubert Foundation

Schoenholz, W. W., dir: Joslyn Foundation

Schoenwetter, L. J., dir: 3M Co.

Schofield, George H., chmn, ceo, dir: Zurn Industries

Scholl, Jack E., exec dir, dir: Scholl Foundation, Dr.

Scholl, Michael L., dir: Scholl Foundation, Dr.

Scholl, William H., pres, dir: Scholl Foundation, Dr.

Scholle, Donald W., trust: Adams Memorial Fund, Emma J.

Schollmaier, Edgar H., chmn, pres, ceo, dir: Alcon Laboratories, Inc.

Scholten, Harvey I., trust, vp: Loutit Foundation

Scholtens, Martin A., Acme Markets

Scholz, Garret Arthur, vp (fin), treas: McKesson Corp.

Schomaker, Richard W., trust: Brown Foundation, George Warren

Schooler, Seward D., trust: Montgomery Foundation

Schoon, Susan Wylie, trust: Chase Manhattan Bank, N.A.

Schornack, John J., trust: Graham Foundation for

Advanced Studies in the Fine Arts

Schorr, Lisbeth Bamberger, chmn nominating comm, mem counc, dir: Foundation for Child Development

Schorrak, Walter, dir: Schoenleber Foundation

Schoshinski, James J., vp, dir: Cornerstone Foundation of Northeastern Wisconsin

Schott, Francis H., mem fin comm, mem counc, dir: Foundation for Child Development

Schott, Milton B., Jr., trust: H.C.S. Foundation

Schott, Owen, ceo, dir: Schott Foundation

Schottenstein, Jay L., treas, dir: El-An Foundation; treas: Schottenstein Foundation, Jerome & Saul; vchmn, exec vp, dir: Schottenstein Stores Corp.; vchmn, exec vp, dir: Value City Furniture

Schottenstein, Jerome, chmn, dir: Schottenstein Stores Corp.; chmn, dir: Value City Furniture

Schottenstein, Jerome M., chmn, dir: El-An Foundation; vp: Schottenstein Foundation, Jerome & Saul

Schottenstein, Melvin L., chmn, trust: Yassenoff Foundation, Leo

Schottenstein, Saul, secy, dir: El-An Foundation; pres: Schottenstein Foundation, Jerome & Saul; pres, dir: Schottenstein Stores Corp.

Schowalter, Robert E., pres, ceo: Ohio Citizens Bank

Schrader, Thomas F., vp, dir: WICOR Foundation

Schramm, Carl, pres: Time Insurance Co.

Schrank, Douglas, cfo: Sealy, Inc.

Schregel, Paul N., trust: Scott Paper Co. Foundation

Schreiber, Elliot S., vp: Miles Inc. Foundation

Schreier, Andrew, trust: Ramapo Trust

Schreier, William, trust: Ramapo Trust

Schreiner, Joan, dir (taxes): UST

Schreyer, John Y., dir: Hess Foundation

Schreyer, William Allen, dir: Hariri Foundation; chmn: Merrill Lynch & Co.

Schrickel, Patrick D., mem bd: Wisconsin Public Service Foundation

Schriner, Miriam, trust: Community Health Association

Schroeder, Anders U., vchmn: DeSoto

Schroeder, Carol, trust: Bates Memorial Foundation, George A.

Schroeder, Charles E., secy, treas, dir: McCormick Foundation, Chauncey and Marion Deering; pres: Miami Corp.; trust: Silver Spring Foundation

Schroeder, Diane, trust: Dell Foundation, Hazel

Schroeder, Jane S., trust: Whitney Benefits

Schroeder, John C., dir: Crescent Plastics Foundation

Schroeder, John H., chmn, ceo, pres: Crescent Plastics; pres, dir: Crescent Plastics Foundation

Schroeder, John J., mem: Piedmont Health Care Foundation

Schroeder, John M., treas: Johnson's Wax Fund

Schroeder, Lorraine D., trust: Reilly Foundation

Schroeder, Mare, trust: Salem Lutheran Foundation

Schroeder, Richard A., dir: Crescent Plastics Foundation

Schroeder, Robert A., Jr., sec: Girard Foundation

Schroeder, Steven A., MD, pres, trust: Johnson Foundation, Robert Wood

Schroeder, Walter, cfo: Titan Industrial Co.

Schroll, Maud Hill, trust, don daughter: Northwest Area Foundation

Schroter, William, dir: Jenkins Foundation, George W.

Schubach, J.J., adv: Timken Co. Charitable Trust

Schubert, Christopher, mem: AHS Foundation

Schubert, David A., mem: AHS Foundation

Schubert, Gage A., dir, vp: AHS Foundation

Schubert, Helen D., mem: AHS Foundation

Schubert, James, MD, dir: Sierra Health Foundation

Schubert, John D., dir, vp: AHS Foundation

Schubert, Leland, mem: AHS Foundation

Schubert, Leland W., Jr., dir, pres: AHS Foundation

Schubert, Rolf, dir: Fuller Co. Foundation, H.B.

Schuberth, Kenneth, trust: Wilson Sanitarium for Children of Baltimore City, Thomas

Schuchardt, Daniel Norman, secy, treas: FMC Foundation

Schuchart, John A., chmn, ceo: MDU Resources Group, Inc.

Schueppert, George L., exec vp, cfo: CBI Industries; dir: CBI Foundation

Schuette, Sheri R., secy: Cornerstone Foundation of Northeastern Wisconsin

Schuette, William D., trust: Gerstacker Foundation, Rollin M.; trust: Pardee Foundation, Elsa U.

Schuffler, Loraine E., secy: Birnschein Foundation, Alvin and Marion; pres, dir: Humphrey Foundation, Glenn & Gertrude

Schuhmacher, Peter, chmn: Lehigh Portland Cement Co.

Schuler, C. Barr, vp: Thomas Foundation

Schuler, Michael, chmn, pres, dir: Zippo Manufacturing Co.

Schuler, Steven T., vp, cfo, treas: Brenton Banks Inc.

Schulhof, Michael Peter, vchmn, ceo, pres: Sony Corp. of America; dir: Sony USA Foundation

Schuller, Ida, Baier Foundation, Marie

Schullinger, John N., MD, trust: Edison Fund, Charles

Schulman, David R., dir: Katten, Muchin, & Zavis Foundation

Schulman, S.J., trust: Westchester Health Fund

Schulot, Erben J., asst treas: Santa Fe Pacific Foundation

Schulte, Anthony M., dir: Scherman Foundation

Seawright, G. William, pres, ceo: Paddington Corp.

Seay, Charles E., trust: Seay Charitable Trust, Sarah M. and Charles E.

Seay, Charles E., Jr., trust: Seay Charitable Trust, Sarah M. and Charles E.

Seay, Nancy Clements, vp, treas: Clements Foundation; trust: Gill Foundation, Pauline Allen

Seay, Sarah M., trust: Seay Charitable Trust, Sarah M. and Charles E.

Seay, Stephen M., trust: Seay Charitable Trust, Sarah M. and Charles E.

Seay, Thomas P., mem: Wal-Mart Foundation

Sebastian, Audrey M., trust: Sebastian Foundation

Sebastian, David S., trust: Sebastian Foundation

Sebastian, James R., trust: Sebastian Foundation

Sebastian, John O., trust: Sebastian Foundation

Sebastian, Paul E., pres: Jockey International

Sebastian, Thomas A., cfo: American National Bank

Sebion, Diane L., secy: Marshall & Ilsley Foundation

Sebod, D. David, vp, dir: Tombstone Pizza Foundation

Sebrell, Henry, exec dir emeritus: Weight Watchers Foundation

Sebrell, J. E., vchmn, exec vp, reg mgr: McDevitt Street Bovis Inc.

Secrest, Richard B., dir: Emerson Foundation, Fred L.

Sederberg, Jean, scholarship comm: Mitchell, Jr. Trust, Oscar

Sedford, Holly, program dir: Wallace Reader's Digest Fund, Lila

Sedor, Robert S., cfo: Angeles Corp.

See, Anne R., vp, secy, dir: See Foundation, Charles

See, Charles B., pres, dir: See Foundation, Charles

See, Harry A., dir: See Foundation, Charles

See, Richard W., dir: See Foundation, Charles

Seed, Harris Waller, pres, dir: Tuohy Foundation, Alice Tweed

Seelenfreund, Alan J., chmn: Mass Merchandisers, Inc.

Seeley, Dana M., trust: Seeley Foundation

Seeley, David C., mem: American General Finance Foundation

Seeley, Miles G., trust: Seeley Foundation

Seeley, Miles P., trust: Seeley Foundation

Seeling, Laurel, secy, treas: Alliant Community Investment Foundation

Seely, Christopher W., trust: Huber Foundation

Seevak, Elinor A., trust: Seevak Family Foundation

Seevak, Sheldon, trust: Doty Family Foundation; trust: Seevak Family Foundation

Sefton, Donna K., vp, trust: Sefton Foundation, J. W.

Sefton, Thomas W., pres, trust: Sefton Foundation, J. W.

Segal, Beth Ann, secy: Lebovitz Fund

Segal, D. Robert, pres: Freedom Newspapers Inc.

Segal, Marilyn M., chmn, trust: Mailman Family Foundation, A. L.

Segal, Martin Eli, dir: Rubinstein Foundation, Helena

Segal, Richard D., pres, trust: Mailman Family Foundation, A. L.

Segal, Zalman, chmn, ceo, dir: Bank Leumi Trust Co. of New York

Segall, Harold Abraham, vp, treas, dir: Reed Foundation, Philip D.

Segall, Margaret T., grants coordinator: Noyes Foundation, Jessie Smith

Segers, Ben, trust: Musson Charitable Foundation, R. C. and Katharine M.

Segerstrom, Harold, Jr., trust, dir: Segerstrom Foundation

Segerstrom, Henry T., trust, dir: Segerstrom Foundation

Segerstrom, Nellie Ruth, trust: Segerstrom Foundation

Segerstrom, Ted, trust: Segerstrom Foundation

Segner, Edmund P., III, trust: Enron Foundation

Sehgal, Raghbir K., ceo: Law Companies Group

Sehn, Francis J., pres: Sehn Foundation

Seid, Barre, pres, treas: Seid Foundation, Barre

Seidenberg, Ivan G., vchmn: NYNEX Corp.; trust: Westchester Health Fund

Seidensticker, Robert B., ceo: Pinkerton Tobacco Co.

Seidl, J. M., chmn, ceo: Kaisertech Ltd.

Seidl, John M., chmmn, ceo, dir: Kaiser Aluminum & Chemical Corp.

Seidler, Lee J., treas: Shubert Foundation

Seidler, Lynn L., exec dir: Shubert Foundation

Seidman, I. William, trust: Seidman Family Foundation

Seidman, O. Thomas, trust: Seidman Family Foundation

Seidman, Sarah B., trust: Seidman Family Foundation

Seifert, James A., pres, dir: Jasper Desk Foundation

Seifert, St. Clare Pratt, trust: Wills Foundation

Seigel, Daniel A., pres, dir: Thrifty Corp.

Seigle, John T., treas: Brenner Foundation, Mervyn; pres: Herbst Foundation

Seigler, Larry, mem contributions comm: Burroughs Wellcome Co.

Seitz, Collins Jacques, vp, dir: Laffey-McHugh Foundation

Seitz, David W., vchmn, dir: Quad City Osteopathic Foundation

Seitz, Frederick, dir: Lounsbery Foundation, Richard

Seitz, Maurie, scholarship comm: Mitchell, Jr. Trust, Oscar

Sejima, Ryuzo, trust: United States-Japan Foundation

Selby, Charles W., secy, dir: Lyon Foundation

Selby, John R., chmn, ceo: SPS Technologies; trust: SPS Foundation

Selden, Jean, secy, dir: Gumbiner Foundation, Josephine

Selden, Jo Hershey, Hershey Foundation

Selden, Marvin R., chmn: Iowa State Bank

Selden, Marvin R., Jr., trust: Iowa State Bank Foundation

Selesko, Barrie W., trust, dir: Weinstein Foundation, Alex J.

Self, Dr. Sally E., trust: Self Foundation

Self, Evelyn, dir commun aff: Parke-Davis Group; asst secy-treas: Warner-Lambert Charitable Foundation

Self, James C., trust: Duke Endowment; pres, trust: Self Foundation

Self, James C., Jr., chmn, dir: Greenwood Mills; vp, trust: Self Foundation

Self, W. M., pres, dir: Greenwood Mills; secy, trust: Self Foundation

Selfe, Jane B., trust: Comer Foundation

Selig, Stephen F., dir, secy: Eckman Charitable Foundation, Samuel and Rae

Seligson, Aaron, vp: Kaplun Foundation, Morris J. and Betty

Selinger, Maurice A., Jr., trust: Altman Foundation

Selis, Pamela A., vp, trust: Louisiana-Pacific Foundation

Sell, E. S., Jr., trust: Anderson Foundation, Peyton

Sell, Ed S. III, Jr., trust: Anderson Foundation, Peyton

Sell, James T., trust: Copperweld Steel Co.'s Warren Employees' Trust

Sell, Neil I., asst secy: Phillips Family Foundation, Jay and Rose

Sella, George John, Jr., chmn, ceo: American Cyanamid Co.

Sellars, Richard B., trust: Johnson Foundation, Robert Wood

Seller, Eric P., asst clerk: Harcourt General

Sellers, Bruce, trust: Winship Memorial Scholarship Foundation

Sellers, Edna E., trust: Fairfield Foundation, Freeman E.

Sellers, Henry B., Oberlaender Foundation, Gustav

Sellers, Laurisa, dir: Honeywell Foundation

Sellers, Merl F., trust: Davis Foundation, James A. and Juliet L.

Sellers, Robert D., treas: Confidence Foundation; cfo: L. L. W. W. Foundation

Sellitti, W.J., vp, contr: Lipton Foundation, Thomas J.

Sellke, Dennis, dir, chmn (health comm): Medtronic Foundation

Sells, Harold E., chmn, ceo: Woolworth Co., F.W.

Seltzer, John, mgr corp planning: Super Valu Stores

Seltzer, Louis N., trust: Huston Charitable Trust, Stewart

Seltzer, Maryanne, secy: Farmers Group Safety Foundation

Selvidge, Glenn E., vp: FINA Foundation

Selznick, L. Jeffrey, pres, trust: Mayer Foundation, Louis B.

Semans, James H., MD, chmn, trust, secy grants comm: Biddle Foundation, Mary Duke

Semans, Mary Duke Biddle Trent, vchmn, chmn grants comm, don daughter: Biddle Foundation, Mary Duke; chmn, trust: Duke Endowment

Semans, Truman Thomas, trust: Brown & Sons Charitable Foundation, Alex

Sembler, Debbie, secy, secy: Ira-Hiti Foundation for Deep Ecology

Semegen, Susan F., trust: Firestone Foundation, Roger S.

Semelsberger, Ken J., pres: Scott and Fetzer Foundation

Semelsberger, Kenneth J., pres, coo: Scott and Fetzer Co.

Semerad, Roger D., pres: RJR Nabisco Inc.

Semha, Renee, cfo: Christian Dior New York, Inc.

Seminara, Joseph E., pres: Goodman Memorial Foundation, Joseph C. and Clare F.

Semler, Jerry D., chmn, pres, ceo: American United Life Insurance Co.; chmn, dir: AUL Foundation

Semmer, Rebecca F., secy: Hillman Foundation

Semmes, D. R., Jr., dir: Semmes Foundation

Semmes, Julia Yates, dir: Semmes Foundation

Semmes, Thomas R., pres: Semmes Foundation

Semran, Thomas J., secy, treas, dir: Rite-Hite Corp. Foundation

Semrod, T. Joseph, chmn, pres, ceo, dir: UJB Financial Corp.

Senanis, Dolores, trust: Heinz Family Foundation

Sendaba, Sheleme, vp (fin), cfo: Nissan Motor Corp. in U.S.A.

Senecal, H. Jess, co-trust: Stauffer Charitable Trust, John; trust: Stillwell Charitable Trust, Glen and Dorothy

Seneker, Stanley A., trust: Ford Motor Co. Fund

Sener, Joseph W., Jr., dir: Legg & Co. Foundation

Seng, Carl F., vp, dir: Jasper Desk Foundation

Seng, Orris, trust: Smysor Memorial Fund, Harry L. and John L.

Senger, Alan F., vp: TRW Foundation

Senter, Allan Z., treas: Xerox Foundation

Sentman, David K., treas, trust: CTS Foundation

Senturia, Brenda Baird, trust: Baird Foundation, Cameron

Seramur, John C., pres, ceo: First Financial Bank FSB; dir: First Financial Foundation

Serchuck, Jerome, vp: Ushkow Foundation

Serchuck, Joan, pres: Ushkow Foundation

Seremet, Peter M., pres: Heublein Foundation

Sergi, Vincent A. F., dir: Katten, Muchin, & Zavis Foundation

Sergio, Alexandria M., secy: Hartford Courant Foundation

Serkland, Wayne C., sr vp, chief legal off: C.P. Rail Systems

Serra-Badue, Daniel Francisco, dir: Cintas Foundation

Serranti, Tesi, mgr (pub aff): Eni-Chem America, Inc.

Sertell, T., pres, coo, dir: Seton Co.

Seshina, Ryozo, trust: Ise Cultural Foundation

Sessums, T. Terrell, secy: Jones Intercable Tampa Trust

Setrakian, Robert, trust: Saroyan Foundation, William

Setterstrom, William N., chmn (contributions comm): Northern Trust Co. Charitable Trust

Setzer, G. Cal, trust: Setzer Foundation

Setzer, Gene Willis, vp, trust: Jackson Hole Preserve

Setzer, Hardie C., trust: Setzer Foundation

Setzer, Leonard, pres: Pic 'N' Save Corp.

Setzer, Mark, trust: Setzer Foundation

Seulean, David, trust: Carpenter Foundation

Seuthe, Brenda, cfo: Anderson Foundation, Marion & John E.

Sevier, Sheila, dir: Mullen Foundation, J. K.

Seward, B., trust: Johnson Day Trust, Carl and Virginia

Seward, George Chester, trust: Gould Foundation for Children, Edwin

Sewey, Stacey, vp: Edwards Foundation, Jes

Sexter, Alan S., pres: Rexford Fund

Sexton, Philip, vp (mktg): Campbell Taggart, Inc.

Seydel, John R., trust: Woolley Foundation, Vasser

Seydel, Paul V., trust: Woolley Foundation, Vasser

Seymour, B. A., Jr., pres, treas, trust: Seymour and Troester Foundation

Seymour, B. A., Sr., chmn, trust: Seymour and Troester Foundation

Sganga, John B., treas: Mohasco Memorial Fund

Shabel, Fred A., trust: Snider Foundation

Shaddix, James W., gen couns: Pennzoil Co.

Shade, Thomas L., chmn, ceo, dir: Moorman Manufacturing Co.; dir: Moorman Co. Fund

Shafer, Fannie L., trust, mgr: Shafer Foundation, Richard H. and Ann

Shafer, Fanny L., pres, treas: Ohio Road Paving Co.

Shafer, Richard A., pres: Deloitte & Touche Foundation

Shaffer, Cecile, don, trust: Shaffer Family Charitable Trust

Shaffer, David, chmn, pres, ceo: Macmillan, Inc.; pres, dir: Macmillan Foundation; don, trust: Shaffer Family Charitable Trust

Shaffer, Jack M., don, trust: Shaffer Family Charitable Trust

Shaffer, James, pres: Gannett Publishing Co., Guy

Shaffer, Rebecca, trust: Ramapo Trust

Shaffer, Richard W., trust: Baker Foundation, Dexter F. and Dorothy H.

Shaffer, Robert, vp commun: AMCA Foundation

Shaffer, Rose, don, trust: Shaffer Family Charitable Trust

Shaffer, Susan, don, trust: Shaffer Family Charitable Trust

Shaffer, Thomas Lindsay, vp, dir: Cornerstone Foundation of Northeastern Wisconsin

Shaffir, Melvyn L., dir: Sperry Fund

Shafran, Nathan, vchmn, dir: Forest City Enterprises; treas, asst secy: Forest City Enterprises Charitable Foundation

Shaft, V. Carol, trust: Davis Foundation, James A. and Juliet L.

Shafto, Robert A., chmn, pres, ceo: New England Mutual Life Insurance Co.

Shahan, Norman D., pres: Cooper Oil Tool

Shaikun, Michael G., dir: Greenebaum, Doll & McDonald Foundation

Shainberg, Raymond, mgr: Belz Foundation

Shakely, Jack, dir: Dunning Foundation

Shaker, Anthony, dir: Abraham Foundation, Anthony R.

Shaker, Joseph, treas, dir: Abraham Foundation, Anthony R.

Shakespeare, Frank, dir: Bradley Foundation, Lynde and Harry

Shalala, Donna Edna, dir: Spencer Foundation

Shaler, Steven M., treas, trust: Blandin Foundation

Shalom, Henry, vp, secy: N've Shalom Foundation

Shalom, Joseph, pres: N've Shalom Foundation

Shalom, Stephen, treas: N've Shalom Foundation

Shama, Isadore, pres: Parthenon Sportswear

Shamah, Alan, treas: Parthenon Sportwear Foundation

Shamah, Isadore, dir: Parthenon Sportwear Foundation

Shames, Ervin, pres, ceo, chmn: Stride Rite Corp.

Shamoon, Alan, cfo: Apple Bank for Savings

Shanahan, Edmond M., pres, ceo, dir: Bell Federal Savings & Loan Association

Shanahan, James A., Jr., trust: Bean Foundation, Norwin S. and Elizabeth N.

Shaner, Wayne F., trust: Martin Marietta Corp. Foundation

Shanes, E., chmn: Entenmann's Inc.

Shank, Glenn, pres, dir: Duckwall-Alco Stores

Shanks, Brice D., mgr: Bagnall Foundation

Shanks, Donald K., pres: Unigard Security Insurance Co.

Shanler, Nadine B., secy: Rutgers Community Health Foundation

Shanley, Kevin, treas, trust: Victoria Foundation

Shannahan, William P., vp, secy: Gildred Foundation; vp, secy: M. E. G. Foundation; vp, secy: S.G. Foundation

Shannon, James P., dir: General Service Foundation

Shannon, John Sanford, vp: Norfolk Southern Foundation

Shannon, Ralph L., pres (retail): Crystal Brands

Shansby, J. Gary, chmn: Famous Amos Chocolate Chip Cookie Co.

Shapell, Lilly, secy, treas: Shapell Foundation, Nathan and Lilly

Shapell, Nathan, pres: Shapell Foundation, Nathan and Lilly; chmn, pres: Shapell Industries, Inc.

Shapero, J.E., treas: Shapero Foundation, Nate S. and Ruth B.

Shapero, Ray A., chmn: Shapero Foundation, Nate S. and Ruth B.

Shapira, Albert C., trust: Steinsapir Family Foundation, Julius L. and Libhie B.

Shapira, Amy, trust: Ferkauf Foundation, Eugene and Estelle

Shapira, David, pres, ceo: Tamarkin Co.

Shapira, David S., trust: Action Industries Charitable Foundation; ceo, pres, dir: Giant Eagle; trust: Giant Eagle Foundation

Shapira, Israel, trust: Ferkauf Foundation, Eugene and Estelle

Shapiro, Albert, pres: Shapiro Fund, Albert

Shapiro, Alexander, vp: Sagamore Foundation

Shapiro, Carl, pres: Shapiro Foundation, Carl and Ruth

Shapiro, Eileen C., vp: Shapiro Fund, Albert

Shapiro, George, trust: Shapiro Charity Fund, Abraham

Shapiro, George M., pres, dir: de Rothschild Foundation, Edmond

Shapiro, Harold Tafler, trust, mem exec & investment comms: Sloan Foundation, Alfred P.

Shapiro, Henry, trust: Shapiro Family Foundation, Soretta and Henry

Shapiro, Irving S., chmn, trust: Hughes Medical Institute, Howard

Shapiro, Isaac, trust: Ise Cultural Foundation

Shapiro, Linda Grass, secy, dir: Grass Family Foundation

Shapiro, Lucille, mem scientific adv comm: Whitney Foundation, Helen Hay

Shapiro, Marc J., chmn, pres, ceo: Texas Commerce Bank Houston, N.A.; trust: Texas Commerce Bank Houston Foundation; trust: Wolff Memorial Foundation, Pauline Sterne

Shapiro, Robert, trust: Schwartz Foundation, Arnold A.

Shapiro, Robert B., pres, coo, dir: Monsanto Co.

Shapiro, Robert F., dir: New Street Foundation

Shapiro, Romie, pres: Fink Foundation

Shapiro, Ruth, secy: Shapiro Foundation, Carl and Ruth

Shapiro, Sarah H., trust, vp: Hirschhorn Foundation, David and Barbara B.

Shapiro, Sarah Hirschhorn, program off health & human services: Abell Foundation, The

Shapiro, Vivian B., trust: Turrell Fund

Shapleigh, Warren, trust: Brown Foundation, George Warren

Shapleigh, Warren M., pres, trust: Olin Foundation, Spencer T. and Ann W.

Sharabi, Hisham, chmn, dir: Jerusalem Fund for Education and Community Development

Sharbel, Leslie, asst vp, trust off (AmSouth Bank, NA): Beach Foundation Trust A for Brunswick Hospital, Thomas N. and Mildred V.; asst vp, trust off (AmSouth Bank,

NA): Beach Foundation Trust D for Baptist Village, Thomas N. and Mildred V.; asst vp, trust off (AmSouth Bank, NA): Beach Foundation Trust for First Baptist Church, Thomas N. and Mildred V.; mgr; trust off (AmSouth Bank, NA): Beach Foundation Trust for the University of Alabama-Birmingham Diabetes Hospital, Thomas N. and Mildred V.

Sharp, Charles S., Jr., dir: Sharp Foundation, Charles S. and Ruth C.

Sharp, Eugene E., Collins-McDonald Trust Fund

Sharp, Hugh Rodney, III, pres, trust: Longwood Foundation

Sharp, Paul, trust: Sarkeys Foundation

Sharp, Peter J., pres: Sharp Foundation; vp, trust: Sharp Foundation, Evelyn

Sharp, Richard L., pres, ceo, dir: Circuit City Stores; trust: Circuit City Foundation

Sharp, Robert G., pres, ceo: Keyport Life Insurance Co.

Sharp, Ruth Collins, pres, dir: Collins Foundation, Carr P.; pres, dir: Sharp Foundation, Charles S. and Ruth C.

Sharp, Thomas S., trust: Delta Tau Delta Educational Fund

Sharpe, Frank A., Jr., vp, secy, trust: Dillard Fund

Sharpe, Henry D., Jr., chmn: Brown & Sharpe Manufacturing Co.; trust: Brown & Sharpe Foundation

Sharpe, P.M., secy: Gilmer-Smith Foundation

Sharpe, Richard S., program dir: Hartford Foundation, John A.

Sharr, Sandra A., mem (contributions comm): ITT Hartford Insurance Group

Shattuck, Clinton H., trust: Boston Fatherless and Widows Society

Shattuck, Mayo A., III, pres, coo, dir: Brown & Sons, Alex; trust: Brown & Sons Charitable Foundation, Alex

Shattuck, Sarah D., mgr: Abell Education Trust, Jennie G. and Pearl

Shaughnessy, Dennis R., coun, secy: Charles River Foundation

Shaw, Albert T., pres: Hofmann Co.; secy: Hofmann Foundation

Shaw, Arch W., II, trust: Shaw Foundation, Arch W.

Shaw, Charles H., trust: Graham Foundation for Advanced Studies in the Fine Arts

Shaw, Francis G., pres: Shaw Fund for Mariner's Children

Shaw, George E., chmn, dir: Shaw Industries

Shaw, George T., trust: Cox Charitable Trust, Jessie B.

Shaw, Harry A., III, chmn, ceo: Huffy Corp.; pres, trust: Huffy Foundation, Inc.

Shaw, J. Stanley, chmn, ceo: Community National Bank & Trust Co. of New York

Shaw, Jay, pres (mens wear): Crystal Brands

Shaw, Jeanette, vp: Goldome Foundation

Shaw, Jerome, mem adv comm: de Kay Foundation

Shaw, John I., trust: Shaw Foundation, Arch W.

Shaw, Joseph A., treas, dir: Tennant Co. Foundation

Shaw, Klare S., asst dir: Boston Globe Foundation

Shaw, L. Edward, Jr., trust: Chase Manhattan Bank, N.A.

Shaw, Marguerite G., trust: Shaw Fund for Mariner's Children

Shaw, Morgan L., dir: Schlieder Educational Foundation, Edward G.

Shaw, Ned, cfo: Bristol Steel & Iron Works

Shaw, Robert, pres: Irvine Medical Center

Shaw, Robert E., pres, ceo: Shaw Industries

Shaw, Robert T., Bankers Life & Casualty Co.; chmn, ceo: ICH Corp.

Shaw, Roger D., trust: Shaw Foundation, Arch W.

Shaw, Ruth C., secy: Stewart Trust under the will of Helen S. Devore, Alexander and Margaret

Shaw, S. Parkman, trust: Shaw Fund for Mariner's Children

Shaw, Stephen, asst treas: MichCon Foundation

Shaw, William W., trust: Shaw Foundation, Arch W.

Shayne, Herbert M., treas, asst secy: Werthan Foundation

Shea, Barry F., treas, dir: Dan River Foundation

Shea, Edmund H., secy: Shea Co. Foundation, J. F.

Shea, Felice K., dir: Klau Foundation, David W. and Sadie

Shea, James, trust: Kynett Memorial Foundation, Edna G.

Shea, Jeremiah Patrick, trust: Kutz Foundation, Milton and Hattie

Shea, John F., pres: Shea Co., John F.; pres: Shea Co. Foundation, J. F.; pres, trust: Shea Foundation

Shea, John J., pres, ceo, dir: Spiegel

Shea, Joseph F., trust: Link Foundation

Shea, Julie V., trust: Altman Foundation

Shea, Peter O., treas: Shea Co. Foundation, J. F.

Shea, Richard A., pres: Pepperidge Farm, Inc.

Shealey, Janet B., asst secy: First Mississippi Corp. Foundation

Sheard, J. L., vp, asst treas: Federated Life Insurance Foundation

Sheble-Hall, Alexander, trust: Stackpole-Hall Foundation

Shecter, Barry, vp, dir: United Togs Foundation

Sheehan, Charles, chmn: Kidder Peabody Foundation

Sheehan, D.W., chmn, pres, ceo, dir: AXIA Incorporated

Sheehan, Frank X., vp: Bibb Foundation, Inc.

Sheehan, James P., pres, coo, dir: Belo Corp., A.H.; trust: Dallas Morning News—WFAA Foundation, The

Sheehan, Kevin E., vp (components group): Cummins Engine Co.

Sheeran, Patricia, dir-intl grant making: Alcoa Foundation

Sheeran, William James, vp (tech): General Electric Co.

Sheesley, Devere Lamar, Jr., trust: Mengle Foundation, Glenn and Ruth

Sheets, Susan Ross, secy, treas: Ross Foundation

Sheetz, Richard Smedley, mem adv & distribution comm: Jennings Foundation, Martha Holden; Park-Ohio Industries Inc.

Sheikman, Philip, secy, treas: Gershman Foundation, Joel

Sheinbaum, Moshe, vp: Kaplun Foundation, Morris J. and Betty

Sheinberg, Eric P., trust: Sheinberg Foundation, Eric P.

Sheinberg, Sidney Jay, pres, coo, dir: MCA; pres, dir: MCA Foundation

Shelby, Jerome, dir: Ridgefield Foundation

Shelden, Virginia D., vp, trust: Shelden Fund, Elizabeth, Allan and Warren

Shelden, W. Warren, vp, trust: McGregor Fund; pres, trust: Shelden Fund, Elizabeth, Allan and Warren

Shelden, William W., Jr., treas, trust: Shelden Fund, Elizabeth, Allan and Warren

Sheldon, Edith S., trust: Quaker Hill Foundation

Sheldon, J. Elizabeth, pres, dir: Sheldon Foundation, Ralph C.

Sheldon, Robin O., trust: Overstreet Foundation

Shelist, Michael R., trust: Steigerwaldt Foundation, Donna Wolf

Shell, George, dir, vp: Churches Homes Foundation

Shelley, Evelyn D., dir: Kelly Foundation

Shelley, Jim, Sonoco Products Co.

Shellington, Kathleen, dir: Arcadia Foundation

Shelton, Charles M., pres: Shelton Cos.; pres: Shelton Foundation

Shelton, James J., trust: Baker Foundation, R. C.

Shelton, R. Edwin, vp: Shelton Foundation

Shelton, Talbot, vp: Laros Foundation, R. K.

Shelton, Wayne, chmn, pres, ceo: Planning Research Corp.

Shenk, Janet, exec dir: Arca Foundation

Shenk, Jim, trust: Midmark Foundation

Shenk, Willis Weidman, chmn, dir: Lancaster Newspapers; treas, trust: Steinman Foundation, James Hale; treas: Steinman Foundation, John Frederick

Shenkman, Barry A., asst secy: Burns Foundation, Jacob

Shep, Clarence, trust: Stern Foundation, Percival

Shepard, Andrew J., chmn: Exchange Bank; chmn: Exchange Bank Foundation

Shepard, Donald, pres: Life Investors Insurance Company of America

Shepard, Donald C., chmn, ceo: Menasha Corp.; dir: Menasha Corporate Foundation

Shepard, Donald James, pres, ceo, dir: AEGON USA, Inc.

Shepard, Henry B., Jr., trust: Wallace Foundation, George R.

Shepard, Robert, exec vp: Kawasaki Motors Corp., U.S.A.

Shepard, Yvonne M., trust: AT&T Foundation

Shephard, Richard G., dir: Montgomery Street Foundation

Shephard, William C., pres, ceo: Allergan, Inc.

Shepherd, Donald R., chmn, ceo: Loomis-Sayles & Co.

Shepherd, E. M., vp, trust: Washington Foundation

Shepherd, Gordon, bd mem: Seascape Senior Housing, Inc.

Shepherd, Kathleen S. M., dir: Daily News Foundation

Shepherd, Mark, Jr., dir: Texas Instruments

Shepherd, Sandie D., secy: Tyler Foundation

Sheplow, Marvin B., trust: Maas Foundation, Benard L.

Sheppard, Thomas Richard, trust: Martin Foundation, Della

Sher, Marcia L., adm: General American Charitable Foundation

Sherbrooke, Ross E., trust: Fidelity Foundation

Sherer, Joseph F., pres, dir: AMCA Foundation

Sheridan, Betrice, vp, dir: Rice Foundation

Sheridan, J.M., pres, trust: SPX Foundation

Sheridan, John J., secy, treas: Brach Foundation, Helen

Sheridan, Katherine Stauffer, dir: Stauffer Foundation, John and Beverly

Sherin, Willis B., trust, pres: Wegener Foundation, Herman and Mary

Sherman, Alison A., dir: Pforzheimer Foundation, Carl and Lily

Sherman, Donald, vp, cfo: Champion Products, Inc.

Sherman, George M., pres, ceo: Danaher Corp.

Sherman, J. L., vp: Sherman-Standard Register Foundation

Sherman, Jeffrey, pres, coo: Bloomingdale's

Sherman, Kathy, commun rels coordinator: PayLess Drug Stores

Sherman, Kelly, trust: Nichols Co. Charitable Trust

Sherman, L. J., secy, dir: McDonald Manufacturing Co. Charitable Foundation, A. Y.

Sherman, L.G., Jr., trust: Steiner Charitable Fund, Albert

Sherman, Linda K., trust: Edgerton Foundation, Harold E.

Sherman, M. Eugene, MD, dir: Comprecare Foundation

Sherman, Michael B., pres, dir: Brotman Foundation of California

Sherman, Norton L., trust: Sherman Family Charitable Trust, George and Beatrice

Sherman, Richard, trust: Geffen Foundation, David

Sherman, Saul, vchmn, dir: 21 International Holdings

Sherman, William E., dir: Graphic Arts Education & Research Foundation

Sherman, William P., pres: Sherman-Standard Register Foundation

Sherr, Sidney S., trust: Gordon Charitable Trust, Peggy and Yale

Sherratt, J.D., pres, ceo: Kendall Health Care Products

Sherrets, Amelia, trust: Children's Foundation of Erie County

Sherriff, Fred, hon trust: Kellogg Foundation, W. K.

Sherrill, Henry W., pres, dir: Good Samaritan

Sherrill, Hugh Virgil, dir: Kleberg, Jr. and Helen C. Kleberg Foundation, Robert J.

Sherrill, Joe, Jr., vp: West Foundation

Sherrill, Joseph N., Jr., trust, vp: Wilson Foundation, John and Nevils

Sherrod, Lonnie R., vp programs: Grant Foundation, William T.

Sherwin, Brian, trust, pres: South Waite Foundation

Sherwin, Dennis, mem: South Waite Foundation

Sherwin, Douglas F., vp: Lee Endowment Foundation

Sherwin, James T., vchmn, cao: GAF Corp.

Sherwin, Margaret H., trust, vp: South Waite Foundation

Sherwin, Peter, mem: South Waite Foundation

Sherwood, Frances K., asst secy: Pasadena Area Residential Aid

Sherwood, John F., vp, secy, dir: New Horizon Foundation

Sherwood, John R., trust: Warfield Memorial Fund, Anna Emory

Sherwood, Lynne, trust: JSJ Foundation

Sherwood, R. M., asst treas: Chrysler Corp. Fund

Shevlin, Patricia, dir: Schmitt Foundation, Arthur J.

Shibata, Y., pres, ceo: Dai-Ichi Kangyo Bank of California

Shideler, Shirley A., dir: Central Newspapers Foundation

Shields, Elizabeth B., Bayne Fund, Howard

Shields, John J., pres, ceo: Prime Computer, Inc.

Shiels, Richard A., Jr., vp: Goddard Homestead

Shiely, John S., vp, dir: Briggs & Stratton Corp. Foundation

Shiffman, Joellen M., mgr, grants & contributions: RJR Nabisco Inc.

Shiffman, Victor, trust: Shiffman Foundation

Shifler, George R., vp, treas: Eden Hall Foundation

Shiflett, B. B., fdr: Trull Foundation

Shiflett, Laura Trull, fdr: Trull Foundation

Shifrin, Edwin G., vp: Leader Foundation

Shifrin, George D., chmn: Corporate Printing Co.

Shih, Daphne B., vp, dir: Bayne Fund, Howard

Shikes, Ralph, dir: Rubin Foundation, Samuel

Shiki, Moriya, dir: Mitsubishi Electric America Foundation

Shillingburg, J. Edward, vp: National Center for Automated Information Retrieval

Shimamura, Eiri, corp staff: Oki America Inc.

Shimer, Dale J., pres, dir: PQ Corp. Foundation

Shimizu, Kenji, chmn, pres: American Suzuki Motor Corp.; chmn, pres: Suzuki Automotive Foundation for Life

Shimizu, Taisuke, pres, ceo: Union Bank

Shine, Warren, trust: Dibner Fund

Shinehouse, Jim, pres, ceo: Ferranti Tech

Shineman, Edward W., Jr., pres, trust: Arkell Hall Foundation

Shiney, Richard D., sr vp: Bank IV Charitable Trust

Shinkel, Donald, mem: Wal-Mart Foundation

Shinn, George Latimer, trust: Markey Charitable Trust, Lucille P.; dir: New York Times Co. Foundation

Shinn, Richard Randolph, exec vchmn, dir: New York Stock Exchange

Shinners, William L., vp: McShain Charities, John

Shinoda, Shunji, dir: Nakamichi Foundation, E.

Shipley, Walter Vincent, mem, dir: Wallace-Reader's Digest Fund, DeWitt; mem, dir: Wallace Reader's Digest Fund, Lila

Shipley, Zachary, treas: Falcon Foundation

Shir, Philip, trust: Shapiro Charity Fund, Abraham

Shirai, Scott, dir: HEI Charitable Foundation

Shire, Donald T., chmn, bd trust: Air Products Foundation

Shirk, B. J., secy, treas: Shirk Foundation, Russell and Betty

Shirk, James A., vp, dir: Shirk Foundation, Russell and Betty

Shirk, Russell O., pres, dir: Shirk Foundation, Russell and Betty

Shirlee, Janet, admin, grants coordinator: Chicago Tribune Foundation

Shirley, Betsy B., trust: Jockey Hollow Foundation

Shirley, Carl, vp, trust: Jockey Hollow Foundation

Shirley, Paul, Jr., trust: Hitchcock Foundation, Gilbert M. and Martha H.

Shiva, Andrew, vp, dir: Stein Foundation, Jules and Doris

Shivery, Charles W., treas, secy: Baltimore Gas & Electric Foundation

Shivley, Albert, vchmn, dir: Farmland Industries, Inc.

Shoaff, Thomas M., dir: McMillen Foundation

Shoch, David Eugene, MD, exec secy, dir: Heed Ophthalmic Foundation

Shoemaker, Edwin J., vchmn: La-Z-Boy Foundation

Shoemaker, Robert H., chmn, ceo: Kolene Corp.

Shoemate, Charles Richard, chmn, pres, ceo, dir: CPC International

Shoffeitt, T. Farrell, pres, coo: DeSoto; pres, dir: DeSoto Foundation

Shogren, Daniel, dir human resources: Grant Thornton

Sholtens, Clarence, dir: Mosinee Paper Corp. Foundation

Shomaker, Richard W., pres: Brown Shoe Co.

Shomber, D. K., dir: Union City Body Co. Foundation

Shonsey, Edward T., sr vp intl oper: Pioneer Hi-Bred International

Shontere, James G., secy: Shea Foundation

Shook, Barbara Ingalls, chmn, treas, dir: Shook Foundation, Barbara Ingalls

Shook, Elesabeth Ridgely, trust: Shook Foundation, Barbara Ingalls

Shook, Ellen Gregg, trust: Shook Foundation, Barbara Ingalls

Shook, Mark L., trust: Tilles Nonsectarian Charity Fund, Rosalie

Shook, Robert P., pres, secy, dir: Shook Foundation, Barbara Ingalls

Shoong, Milton W., pres, dir: Shoong Foundation, Milton

Shoong, Milton W., Sr., chmn, pres: National Dollar Stores, Ltd.

Shooter, Eric M., ScD, special adv dir med science: Markey Charitable Trust, Lucille P.

Shope, D.J., vp: Davey Co. Foundation

Shopis, David T., chmn, pres, ceo, dir: FIP Corp.

Shore, William, vp, dir: St. Faith's House Foundation

Shorenstein, Douglas W., treas: Shorenstein Foundation, Walter H. and Phyllis J.

Shorenstein, Phyllis J., vp: Shorenstein Foundation, Walter H. and Phyllis J.

Shorenstein, Walter H., pres: Shorenstein Foundation, Walter H. and Phyllis J.

Shores, Thomas H., chmn: Classic Leather; pres: Classic Foundation

Shorin, Arthur T., chmn, ceo: Topps Company

Shorris, Earl, dir: Ayer Foundation, N.W.

Shorstein, Samuel R., treas, trust: Cohen Foundation, George M.

Short, Jack E., trust: Parker Foundation, Robert L.

Short, Robert Louis, trust: Lane Foundation, Minnie and Bernard

Shott, Robert B., trust: Gradison & Co. Foundation

Shott, Scott, vp: Shott, Jr. Foundation, Hugh I.

Shoup, Helen H., trust: Hulme Charitable Foundation, Milton G.

Shourd, Roy Ray, dir: Schlumberger Foundation

Shouse, Catherine F., dir: Filene Foundation, Lincoln and Therese

Showen, Margaret Woo, trust: Haynes Foundation

Shriner, Ed, trust: Brown Family Foundation, John Mathew Gay

Shriver, Eunice Kennedy, exec vp, trust: Kennedy, Jr. Foundation, Joseph P.

Shrontz, Frank Anderson, chmn, ceo, dir: Boeing Co.

Shropshire, Thomas B., dir: Rockefeller Foundation, Winthrop

Shubert, Roy A., vp: CertainTeed Corp. Foundation

Shuck, V. Dewitt, vp, dir: Parker Foundation

Shuey, John M., Amcast Industrial Corp.; vp: Poindexter Foundation

Shuford, Harry A., trust: Hillcrest Foundation

Shugart, Alan F., chmn, ceo: Seagate Technology

Shuler, John F., trust: Horne Foundation, Dick

Shulman, Joel, off, trust: Manat Foundation

Shulman, Lee S., dir: Spencer Foundation

Shulman, Lloyd J., pres: Mays, Inc., J.W.; vp, dir: Weinstein Foundation, J.

Shulman, Louis T., trust: Rotterman Trust, Helen L. and Marie F.

Shulman, Max L., chmn, ceo: Mays, Inc., J.W.; pres, dir: Weinstein Foundation, J.

Shulman, Sylvia W., vp, dir: Weinstein Foundation, J.

Shumadine, William F., dir: Central Fidelity Banks Foundation

Shumake, William, trust: Thompson Charitable Trust, Sylvia G.

Shumaker, John W., trust: Stanley Charitable Foundation, A. W.

Shumaker, Portia W., comm mem: Whitaker Foundation

Shuman, Stanley S., dir: Markle Foundation, John and Mary R.

Shumate, James Bernard, cfo: American Bankers Insurance Group

Shumway, Floyd, trust, treas: Woman's Seamen's Friend Society of Connecticut

Shumway, Forrest Nelson, dir: Irvine Foundation, James

Shunichi, Oyama, dir: JTB International, Inc.; pres: JTB Cultural Exchange Corp.

Shurtz, Bruce, trust: Winship Memorial Scholarship Foundation

Shust, Robert B., trust: Patterson Charitable Fund, W. I.

Shuster, George W., pres: Cranston Print Works; trust: Cranston Foundation

Shuster, Walter, trust: Shuster Memorial Trust, Herman

Shute, Benjamin R., Jr., secy, treas: Rockefeller Brothers Fund

Shute, David, dir: Sears-Roebuck Foundation

Shuyler, Richard H., vp, cfo: Continental Airlines

Shwayder, Fay, dir, pres: Shwayder Foundation, Fay

Siano, Jerry J., chmn, ceo, dir: Ayer Inc., N.W.; dir: Ayer Foundation, N.W.

Sibley, D. J., Jr., dir: Potts and Sibley Foundation

Sibley, Horace Holden, comm mem: Woodward Fund-Atlanta, David, Helen, Marian

Sibley, James Malcolm, trust: Evans Foundation, Lettie Pate; trust: Harland Charitable Foundation, John and Wilhelmina D.; vchmn, trust: Whitehead Foundation, Joseph B.; vchmn, trust: Woodruff Foundation, Robert W.

Siceloff, Millie L., trust: Tortuga Foundation

Sichel, Leonard J., vchmn, cfo, dir: Mennen Co.

Sichler, Edward H., III, treas: Earhart Foundation

Siciliano, Rocco Carmine, trust: Getty Trust, J. Paul

Sick, William N., vice-chmn: Triangle Industries

Sickles, Martin, cfo: Winter Construction Co.

Sidamon-Eristoff, Anne Phipps, trust: Phipps Foundation, Howard

Sidhu, Jay S., pres, ceo: Penn Savings Bank, a division of

Sovereign Bank Bank of Princeton, a division of Sovereign Bank; dir: Sovereign Bank Foundation

Sieben, Todd W., trust: Geneseo Foundation

Sieber, Fred B., trust: McMannis and A. Haskell McMannis Educational Fund, William J.

Sieckman, Walter, co-chmn, ceo: Sharon Steel Corp.

Sieg, Dennis A., sr vp: Missouri Public Service

Siegel, Arthur, dir: Price Waterhouse Foundation

Siegel, Bernard, pres, dir: Weinberg Foundation, Harry and Jeanette

Siegel, Bernard I., treas: Kutz Foundation, Milton and Hattie

Siegel, David, sr vp, cfo: Presley Cos.

Siegel, Harvey, off: Atalanta/Sosnoff Charitable Foundation

Siegel, L. Pendelton, trust: Potlatch Foundation for Higher Education/Potlatch Foundation II

Siegel, Marvin, trust: Allen Charitable Trust, Phil N.

Siegel, Samuel, cfo, treas: Nucor Corp.; dir: Nucor Foundation

Siegel, Sarah, Goldberger Foundation, Edward and Marjorie

Siegel, Steven G., vp, secy: McMurray-Bennnett Foundation

Siegel, Victor H., exec vp, secy, cfo: Peck/Jones Construction Corp.

Siegert, Marvin, vp, cfo: Rayovac Corp.

Siegfried, Peter C., secy: Dorot Foundation; secy: Pinewood Foundation; secy: Wallach Foundation, Miriam G. and Ira D.

Siegfried, Robert E., chmn, dir: Commonwealth Energy System

Siegle, Helen, adm: Lipton Foundation, Thomas J.

Siegler, Thomas, dir, vp: Donaldson, Lufkin & Jenrette Foundation

Siegmund, Frederick, secy, dir: Berkowitz Family Foundation, Louis

Sielaff, Max, dir: Kress Foundation, George

Siemens, John, Jr., dir: Hesston Foundation

Sieracke, John M., secy, treas, dir: Prange Co. Fund, H. C.

Sieve, Richard, MD, secy: Valley Foundation

Sievers, Bruce R., exec dir, secy, treas: Haas Fund, Walter and Elise

Sievert, James L., exec vp, cfo: Medalist Industries, Inc.

Siewert, Robert J., pres: Monarch Machine Tool Co.

Sigelman, Alice Rosenwald, vp, dir: Rosenwald Family Fund, William

Sigfusson, Becky B., vp, dir: Bere Foundation

Sigler, Andrew Clark, chmn, ceo, dir: Champion International Corp.

Signorile, A. J., treas: Dana Charitable Trust, Eleanor Naylor

Sikkema, Karen Ann, trust: Unocal Foundation

Silas, C. J. Pete, chmn, ceo, dir, mem exec comm: Phillips Petroleum Co.

Silberkleit, Alexa, consultant: New Street Foundation

Silberman, A. L., chmn, ceo, treas, dir: Billy Penn Corp

Silberman, Samuel J., trust: AVI CHAI - A Philanthropic Foundation; chmn: Paramount Communications Foundation

Silberman, Sidney, trust: Kaye Foundation

Silberman, Sidney J., trust: Saul Foundation, Joseph E. & Norma G.

Silberman, Walter, MD, trust: Valley Foundation

Silbersack, Donna C., asst secy/treas: France Foundation, Jacob and Annita; asst secy, treas: Merrick Foundation, Robert G. and Anne M.

Silbert, Bernard, dir: Parvin Foundation, Albert

Silbert, H., dir: Capital Fund Foundation

Silk, Susan Clark, exec dir: Columbia Foundation

Silk, Tom, asst secy, asst treas: Haas Fund, Walter and Elise

Silla, Barbara, contributions mgr: Riggs National Bank

Silliman, Henry Harper, trust: Borkee Hagley Foundation

Silliman, Henry Harper, Jr., pres: Borkee Hagley Foundation; treas, trust: Longwood Foundation

Silliman, Jael M., program off: Noyes Foundation, Jessie Smith

Silliman, John E., vp: Borkee Hagley Foundation

Silliman, Robert M., vp, treas: Borkee Hagley Foundation

Sills, Barbara A., dir (community rels): Battelle

Sills, David G., dir: Irvine Health Foundation

Sills, Lawrence I., pres, coo, dir: Standard Motor Products, Inc.

Sills, Nathaniel L., secy, treas, dir: Fife Foundation, Elias and Bertha; co-chmn, co-ceo, dir: Standard Motor Products, Inc.

Sills, Ruth, dir: Fife Foundation, Elias and Bertha

Silva, Jacques, trust: Orange Orphan Society

Silvati, John D., trust: Dater Foundation, Charles H.

Silver, Julius, pres, treas, trust: Jurodin Fund; secy: Rowland Foundation

Silver, Leanor H., trust, secy: Lovett Foundation

Silver, Michael, pres: Jaydor Corp.

Silver, Paul A., dir, secy: Bafflin Foundation

Silver, Ralph P., treas: Getz Foundation, Emma and Oscar

Silver, Robert C., trust: Linnell Foundation

Silver, Roslyn, vp: Jurodin Fund

Silverboard, Lewis, trust: Steinsapir Family Foundation, Julius L. and Libhie B.

Silverman, A. A., chmn, pres: Vilter Manufacturing Corp.

Silverman, Albert A., pres, dir: Vilter Foundation

Silverman, Arnold P., pres, coo: Winter Construction Co.

Silverman, Arthur Esq., vp: Goldsmith Foundation, Nathan and Louise

Silverman, Barry S., chmn: Jaydor Corp.

Silverman, Fred, mgr (community affairs): Apple Computer

Silverman, Gilbert B., don, pres: Silverman Fluxus Collection Foundation, Gilbert and Lila

Silverman, Jacob, trust: Forbes Charitable Trust, Herman

Silverman, Jeffrey S., chmn, pres, ceo, dir: Ply-Gem Industries, Inc.

Silverman, Lila, don, secy, treas: Silverman Fluxus Collection Foundation, Gilbert and Lila

Silverman, Lorin, secy, treas, don, dir: Silverman Foundation, Marty and Dorothy

Silverman, Marty, pres, don, dir: Silverman Foundation, Marty and Dorothy

Silverman, Robert L., chmn, ceo: Winter Construction Co.

Silverman, Sandra, dir, asst secy: Scherman Foundation

Silverman, Saul S., dir: Taylor Family Foundation, Jack

Silverman, Sydel, pres, secy, trust ex-officio: Wenner-Gren Foundation for Anthropological Research

Silvernale, Rex, dir: Babcock Memorial Endowment, William

Silverstein, Duane, exec dir, asst secy, asst treas: Goldman Fund, Richard and Rhoda

Silverstein, Jules, trust: Kellmer Co. Foundation, Jack

Silverstein, Stephen H., chmn, ceo: Balcor Co.

Sim, Richard G., chmn, ceo, pres, dir: Applied Power, Inc.; trust: Applied Power Foundation

Simek, R. L., ceo: Tombstone Pizza Corp.

Simensen, Kim, bd mem: Dain Bosworth/IFG Foundation

Simeone, Fiorindo Anthony, MD, dir: Grass Foundation

Simkins, Leon J., chmn, pres, dir: Simkins Industries, Inc.

Simmons, Adele Smith, pres, dir: MacArthur Foundation, John D. and Catherine T.

Simmons, Christopher J., pres: Eastern Enterprises

Simmons, Edward M., pres: McIlhenny and Sons Corp

Simmons, Frederick L., trust: Fellner Memorial Foundation, Leopold and Clara M.

Simmons, Gaylon H., pres: Permian Corp.

Simmons, Glenn Reuben, vchmn: Contran Corp.

Simmons, Harold Clark, chmn, ceo, dir: Amalgamated Sugar Co.; chmn, ceo, dir: Contran Corp.; chmn, dir: Simmons Foundation, Harold

Simmons, Harris H., pres, ceo, dir: Zions Bancorp.

Simmons, Hildy J., mng dir (commun rels & pub affs): J.P. Morgan & Co.

Simmons, Lisa K., pres: Simmons Foundation, Harold

Simmons, Marion, secy: Ruffin Foundation, Peter B. & Adeline W.

Simmons, Richard P., chmn, ceo, dir: Allegheny Ludlum Corp.; trust: Simmons Family Foundation, R. P.

Simmons, Roy W., chmn, dir: Zions Bancorp.

Simmons, Roy William, mem: Bamberger and John Ernest Bamberger Memorial Foundation, Ruth Eleanor

Simmons, S. Stoney, Wurts Memorial, Henrietta Tower

Simmons, Samuel J., dir: Federal National Mortgage Assn. Foundation

Simms, Victoria, dir: Mann Foundation, Ted

Simock, Debbie, commun rels coordinator: Washington Water Power Co.

Simon, Allison S., vp: Stemmons Foundation

Simon, Carol G., pres, dir: Simon Foundation, William E. and Carol G.

Simon, Donald, trust: Simon Foundation, Robert Ellis

Simon, Heinz K., vp: Stemmons Foundation

Simon, J. Peter, vp, secy, dir: Simon Foundation, William E. and Carol G.

Simon, Jennifer Jones, chmn, pres, trust: Simon Foundation, Jennifer Jones

Simon, Johanna K., dir: Simon Foundation, William E. and Carol G.

Simon, John Gerald, pres, treas, trust: Taconic Foundation

Simon, Julie A., dir: Simon Foundation, William E. and Carol G.

Simon, Leonard S., chmn, ceo, dir: Rochester Community Savings Bank

Simon, Louis, trust: Page Foundation, George B.

Simon, Marc S., pres: Fraida Foundation

Simon, Norton, trust: Simon Foundation, Jennifer Jones

Simon, Paul, trust: Strauss Foundation, Leon

Simon, Peter, pres: Weininger Foundation, Richard and Gertrude

Simon, R. A., exec vp, dir: Phillips Foundation, Dr. P.

Simon, R. Matthew, dir: Brach Foundation, Helen

Simon, Raymond F., pres: Brach Foundation, Helen

Simon, William E., Jr., treas, dir: Simon Foundation, William E. and Carol G.

Simon, William Edward, pres, trust, mem exec comm: Olin Foundation, John M.; chmn, dir: Simon Foundation, William E. and Carol G.

Simone, Christine, secy, dir: Manoogian Foundation, Alex and Marie; vp: Simone Foundation

Simone, David, secy, treas: Simone Foundation

Simone, Louise, dir: Manoogian Foundation, Alex and Marie; pres: Simone Foundation

Simone, Mark, dir: Simone Foundation

Simone, Peter J., pres, ceo: GCA Corp.

Simone, Virginia, secy: Dun & Bradstreet Corp. Foundation

Simonet, J. Thomas, dir: Tozer Foundation

Simonnard, Michel A., chmn, pres, ceo: Pechiney Corp.

Simons, Anne M., asst sec: Medina Foundation

Simons, Carl, chmn, ceo: Gateway Apparel

Simons, Dolph C., Jr., trust: Freedom Forum

Simons, John Farr, dir: Marpat Foundation

Simons, W. Lucas, vp: Bradford & Co. Foundation, J.C.

Simonson, Anne Larsen, vp, dir: Larsen Fund

Simore, Joseph A., dir, secy: Gloeckner Foundation, Fred

Simpkins, Jacqueline DeNeuflize, trust: Sprague Educational and Charitable Foundation, Seth

Simplot, John Richard, fdr, chmn: Simplot Co., J.R.

Simpson, Abby Rockefeller, trust: Rockefeller Family Fund

Simpson, Andrea Lynn, pres: BHP Petroleum Americas (HI) Foundation

Simpson, Barclay, pres: Simpson PSB Foundation

Simpson, Bruce, pres, ceo: Tigon Corp.

Simpson, Carolyn, coordinator: WICOR Foundation

Simpson, David, II, off: American Snuff Co. Charitable Trust

Simpson, Frank, III, trust: Martin Foundation, Della

Simpson, Gary, chmn contributions comm: Varian Associates

Simpson, George L., vchmn, dir: Pittulloch Foundation

Simpson, Howard B., trust: Simpson Foundation, John M.

Simpson, Irma E., program adm: Gannett Co.

Simpson, James A., trust: Stanley Charitable Foundation, A. W.

Simpson, Judith, sr program off: Gund Foundation, George

Simpson, Kate M., dir: Belk-Simpson Foundation

Simpson, Louis A., vchmn, dir: GEICO Corp.

Simpson, Marie, treas, dir: Gellert Foundation, Carl

Simpson, Michael, chmn: Castle & Co., A.M.; pres, dir: Castle Foundation

Simpson, Nancy, trust, mgr: Friedland Family Foundation, Samuel

Simpson, Nancy T., pres: Simpson Foundation, John M.

Simpson, Phyllis T., asst secy: Duke Power Co. Foundation

Simpson, Roderic H., pres: Scroggins Foundation, Arthur E. and Cornelia C.

Simpson, Stanley D., treas: Scroggins Foundation, Arthur E. and Cornelia C.

Simpson, William, trust: Simpson Foundation, John M.

Simpson, William A., pres, dir: USLIFE Corp.

Simpson, William H., secy: Susquehanna-Pfaltzgraff Foundation

Sims, Howard F., trust: Kellogg Foundation, W. K.

Sims, M. Owen, Sr., vp: Bashinsky Foundation

Sims, Nancy A., mgr grant proposals: Kellogg Foundation, W. K.

Sims, Philip Stuart, secy, treas: Mandel Foundation, Joseph and Florence; vchmn, treas: Premier Industrial Corp.

Sinclair, James L., pres, trust: Sheridan Foundation, Thomas B. and Elizabeth M.

Sinclair, John B., secy, trust: Sheridan Foundation, Thomas B. and Elizabeth M.

Sinclair, John P., dir: Glencoe Foundation

Sinclair, K. Richard C., trust: One Valley Bank Foundation

Sinclair, Mark, treas, trust: Mobility Foundation

Sinclair, Michael R., PhD, dir (health & devel South Africa): Kaiser Family Foundation, Henry J.

Sinclair, Norman, trust: Grigg-Lewis Trust

Sinclair, Robey T., Jr., trust: Davis Charitable Foundation, Champion McDowell

Sinding, Steven W., dir (population sciences): Rockefeller Foundation

Sindscheffel, Steve, bd mem: Salvatori Foundation, Henry

Sines, Virginia, dir: Fort Pierce Memorial Hospital Scholarship Foundation

Singer, Arthur Louis, Jr., vp: Sloan Foundation, Alfred P.

Singer, Edwin McMahon, trust: Rice Family Foundation, Jacob and Sophie

Single, Richard W., Sr., chmn (charitable contributions comm): McCormick & Co.

Singletary, L. H., Cherokee Foundation

Singleton, Dean, chmn: Houston Post Co.

Singleton, Richard L., vp, cfo, treas: Landmark Land Co., Inc.

Singleton, Robert F., cfo, sr vp fin: Knight-Ridder, Inc.

Sink, Ronald E., asst treas: Norfolk Southern Foundation

Sinnerte, Charles, comm: Hope Memorial Fund, Blanche and Thomas

Sinon, Frank A., secy, trust: Stabler Foundation, Donald B. and Dorothy L.

Sinrod, Allison R., trust: McMillan Foundation, D. W.

Sinton, Robert E., vp, dir: Zellerbach Family Fund

Sinykin, Gerald B., MD, dir: Irvine Health Foundation

Sinykin, Gordon, dir: Evjue Foundation

Sipp, Donald C., vp (investments), treas: Scaife Foundation, Sarah

Siragusa, John Robert, vp, dir: Siragusa Foundation

Siragusa, Martha P., dir: Siragusa Foundation

Siragusa, Richard Donald, dir: Siragusa Foundation

Siragusa, Ross David, Jr., dir: Siragusa Foundation

Siragusa, Ross David, Sr., don: Siragusa Foundation

Siragusa, Theodore M., dir: Siragusa Foundation

Sirkin, Sidney, dir: Baier Foundation, Marie

Sirota, Wilbert H., secy, dir: Hecht-Levi Foundation

Sisco, Jean Head, trust: Higginson Trust, Corina

Sisk, John F., trust: Donaldson Charitable Trust, Oliver S. and Jennie R.

Sisley, Christine, secy, exec dir: Parsons Foundation, Ralph M.

Sissel, Mary R., dir: Ball Foundation, George and Frances

Sission, June E., secy: Obernauer Foundation

Sit, Eugene C., pres, ceo, treas: SIT Investment Associates, Inc.; trust: SIT Investment Associates Foundation

Sitkoff, Samuel, treas, dir: Ridgefield Foundation

Sitomer, Kenneth, pres, ceo: Russ Togs Inc.; trust: Russ Togs Foundation

Sittenfeld, Paul G., trust: Gradison & Co. Foundation

Sittenfeld, Paul George, trust: Peterloon Foundation

Sitwick, Irving, vp, dir: Moses Fund, Henry and Lucy

Sivertsen, Robert J., vp, dir: Weyerhaeuser Memorial Foundation, Charles A.

Six, Julie G., treas: Greenfield Foundation, Albert M.

Sizemore, H. Mason, pres: Seattle Times Co.

Sjoquist, Gregg D., exec dir, secy, dir: Wasie Foundation

Sjostrom, Joel, pres: Sjostrom & Sons; dir: Sjostrom & Sons Foundation

Sjostrom, Kristopher, dir: Sjostrom & Sons Foundation

Skadden, Donald H., vp: National Center for Automated Information Retrieval

Skadon, Janet T., dir: Bishop Foundation, E. K. and Lillian F.

Skaggs, James B., pres: Tracor, Inc.

Skaggs, Leonard Sam, Jr., chmn, dir: American Stores Co.

Skaggs, Mary C., pres, mem bd dirs: Skaggs Foundation, L. J. and Mary C.

Skala, Marjorie, trust: Leu Foundation

Skanse, C. Theodore, chmn, dir: Douglas Corp.

Skanse, C.A., vp: Douglas Foundation

Skanse, Douglas R., pres, dir: Douglas Corp.; pres: Douglas Foundation

Skarbek, Cynthia, dir: Smith Foundation, Gordon V. and Helen C.

Skeddle, Ronald W., pres, ceo, dir: Libbey-Owens Ford Co.

Skeebo, Eugene B., secy, trust: Barstow Foundation

Skeen, William, sr vp (admin): Fujitsu Systems of America, Inc.

Skelly, Thomas Francis, off: Gillette Charitable and Educational Foundation

Skelton, Allyn R., II, vp, cfo: Howell Corp.

Skelton, H. J., pres, dir, asst treas: Parsons - W.D. Charities, Vera Davis

Skestos, George A., ceo: Homewood Corp.

Skiles, Robin, pub rels mgr: Mitsubishi Motor Sales of America, Inc.

Skilling, Raymond I., exec vp, chief coun: AON Corp.; dir: AON Foundation

Skinner, Catherine E., chmn, trust: Skinner Foundation

Skinner, David, trust: Skinner Foundation

Skinner, Frank, trust: Tull Charitable Foundation

Skinner, Kathryn L., trust: Skinner Foundation

Skinner, Paul, chmn, pres, ceo, dir: Skinner Corp.

Skinner, R. Franklin, pres, ceo: Southern Bell

Skinner, Samuel K., pres, dir: Commonwealth Edison Co.

Skinner, Stanley T., pres, coo, dir: Pacific Gas & Electric Co.

Skinner, W. K., exec vp, secy-treas, dir: Burns Foundation, Fritz B.

Skirball-Kenis, Audrey, don, vp: Skirball Foundation

Sklar, David A., cfo: Imperial Bank Foundation

Sklenar, Herbert A., chmn, pres, ceo, dir: Vulcan Materials Co.; chmn, trust: Vulcan Materials Co. Foundation

Skloot, Edward, exec dir: Surdna Foundation

Skoda, Daniel, pres: Marshall Field's

Skolersky, Paul, trust: Levin Foundation, Philip and Janice

Skolaski, Steven, pres, treas, dir: Rennebohm Foundation, Oscar

Skolnick, Irwin, asst treas: Luce Foundation, Henry

Skou, Harold, dir: Knudsen Foundation, Tom and Valley

Skouby, Alan D., vp fin, treas, cfo: DeKalb Genetics Corp.

Skoug, John L., trust: Goldbach Foundation, Ray and Marie

Skrzypczak, Casimir S., mem contributions comm: NYNEX Corp.

Skutt, J. B., dir: Hotchkiss Foundation, W. R.

Skutt, Thomas J., chmn, ceo: Mutual of Omaha Insurance Co.

Skyes, J. T., pres: Cremer Foundation

Slack, D. Stephen, sr vp, cfo: Pogo Producing Co.

Sladoje, George, vp, secy, dir: Chicago Board of Trade Educational Research Foundation

Slaggie, Stephen, treas: Hiawatha Education Foundation

Slaney, Barbara L., vp, asst secy: Scaife Foundation, Sarah

Slapnicker, Gary L., exec dir: Renner Foundation

Slate, Donald, vp: Levine Family Foundation, Hyman

Slaten, Paul E., tresa: Sunnen Foundation

Slater, Arthur, chmn: Iroquois Brands, Ltd.

Slater, Ross, pres: Leesona Corp.

Slattery, Edward F., dir: Burns Foundation, Fritz B.

Slaughter, GLoria, trust: Slaughter, Jr. Foundation, William E.

Slaughter, James C., ceo, dir: Goldsmith Foundation, Horace W.

Slaughter, Ken, cfo: Gazette Co.; dir, vp: Gazette Foundation

Slaughter, Kent C., trust: Slaughter, Jr. Foundation, William E.

Slaughter, Thomas R., dir: Goldsmith Foundation, Horace W.

Slaughter, William, trust off: Synovus Charitable Trust

Slaughter, William A., dir: Goldsmith Foundation, Horace W.

Slaughter, William E., IV, dir, vp: Slaughter, Jr. Foundation, William E.

Slaughter, William E., Jr., pres, treas, dir: Slaughter, Jr. Foundation, William E.; treas, dir: Wenger Foundation, Henry L. and Consuelo S.

Slavik, Frank, dir: Piper Foundation, Minnie Stevens

Slavin, Albert, dir, pres, treas: Cowan Foundation Corporation, Lillian L. and Harry A.

Slavin, Beatrice, dir, clerk: Cowan Foundation Corporation, Lillian L. and Harry A.

Slavin, Morton A., clerk, dir: Housen Foundation

Slaymaker, Eugene W., pres, trust: Baughman Foundation

Slesin, Louis E., dir: Rubinstein Foundation, Helena

Slesin, Suzanne, dir: Rubinstein Foundation, Helena

Slette, Gary, vp: Wedum Foundation

Slife, Harry G., dir: McElroy Trust, R. J.

Slifka, Alan B., pres: Slifka Foundation, Alan B.; treas: Slifka Foundation, Joseph and Sylvia

Slifka, Alfred, pres: First Petroleum Corp.; trust: First Petroleum Corp. Charitable Trust

Slifka, Barbara, trust: Slifka Foundation, Joseph and Sylvia

Slifka, Joseph, pres: Slifka Foundation, Joseph and Sylvia

Slifka, Richard, trust: First Petroleum Corp. Charitable Trust

Slifka, Sylvia, vp: Slifka Foundation, Joseph and Sylvia

Slifka, Virginia, vp: Slifka Foundation, Alan B.

Sligar, James S., coun: Rockefeller Family Fund

Slinde, Stephen R., pres, dir: NMC Projects

Slipsager, Henrik, pres, ceo, coo: ISS International Service System

Sliwinski, Robert A., asst treas: Centerior Energy Foundation

Sloan, Albert Frazier, chmn, dir: Lance, Inc.; dir: Lance Foundation; mem bd adms: Van Every Foundation, Philip L.

Sloan, Lane E., vp, dir: Shell Oil Co. Foundation

Sloan, Meribeth, dir (corp commun): Scrivner, Inc.

Sloane, Ann Brownell, adm: Mayer Foundation, Louis B.; mgr: National Center for Automated Information Retrieval

Sloane, Douglas, IV, treas: Wheelwright Scientific School

Sloane, Howard G., pres, trust: Heckscher Foundation for Children

Sloane, Howard Grant, trust: Heckscher Foundation for Children

Slobadin, Stephen, trust: Christodora

Slocombe, Walter, vp, dir: Stern Family Fund

Slosburg, Stanley J., treas, trust: Livingston Foundation, Milton S. and Corinne N.

Sloss, Deborah, dir: Fleishhacker Foundation

Sloss, Laurie, dir: Fleishhacker Foundation

Sloss, Leon, vp, dir: Fleishhacker Foundation

Sloss, Merle, pres, ceo: Bally Inc.

Slovin, Bruce, pres, dir: MacAndrews & Forbes Holdings; dir: MacAndrews & Forbes Foundation; pres, dir: Revlon

Sly, Helen S., pres, dir, fdr daughter: Sunnen Foundation

Smadbeck, Arthur J., trust: Heckscher Foundation for Children

Smadbeck, Louis, chmn bd trusts: Heckscher Foundation for Children

Smadbeck, Mina, trust: Heckscher Foundation for Children

Smadbeck, Paul, trust: Heckscher Foundation for Children

Smale, John G., chmn, dir: General Motors Corp.

Smalheiser, Harvey, vp: Ryder System Charitable Foundation

Small, George M., vp, cfo: Offshore Logistics

Small, Lawrence M., pres, ceo: Federal National Mortgage Assn., Fannie Mae; pres: Federal National Mortgage Assn. Foundation

Small, Malinda B., asst secy, asst treas: Baltimore Gas & Electric Foundation

Smallwood, Thomas L., adm, trust: Helfaer Foundation, Evan and Marion

Smart, Louis Edwin, trust: Continental Corp. Foundation

Smart, Mary, secy: Smart Family Foundation

Smart, Nancy, mem: Smart Family Foundation

Smart, Paul M., vchmn: Toledo Edison Co.

Smart, Raymond, pres: Smart Family Foundation

Smeal, Frank P., trust: Smeal Foundation, Mary Jean & Frank P.

Smeal, Mary Jean, trust: Smeal Foundation, Mary Jean & Frank P.

Smeby, Kyhl S., dir: Bank of America - Giannini Foundation

Smelser, Neil J., trust: Sage Foundation, Russell

Smerling, Julian M., vchmn, dir: Dreyfus Corp.

Smialek, Bob, pres: Ranco, Inc.

Smiaroski, Donald, trust: Wells Trust Fund, Fred W.

Smickley, Robert J., pres: Wisconsin Centrifugal; pres: Wisconsin Centrifugal Charitable Foundation

Smiley, Michael, secy: Travelers Cos. Foundation

Smilow, Michael A., vp: Federal National Mortgage Assn. Foundation

Smith, A. J. C., pres, dir: Marsh & McLennan Cos.

Smith, Adrian, contact person: Skidmore, Owings & Merrill Foundation

Smith, Albert J., Jr., secy, treas: Smith Foundation, Julia and Albert

Smith, Albert J. III, Jr., dir: Smith Foundation, Julia and Albert

Smith, Alexander F., chmn, pres, ceo: Gilbert Associates, Inc.

Smith, Alexander Wyly, Jr., trust: Franklin Foundation, John and Mary

Smith, Alice T., trust: Brown Foundation, M. K.

Smith, Andrew J., ceo, pres: Rexene Products Co.

Smith, Arthur M., Jr., dir, mem exec & other comms: Keck Foundation, W. M.

Smith, Arthur O., vp, dir: Smith Foundation, A.O.

Smith, B.G., trust: Falk Foundation, David

Smith, Barry W., treas, trust: Folsom Foundation, Maud Glover

Smith, Benjamin A., II, mem: Gerondelis Foundation

Smith, Benjamin M., Jr., secy, treas: Washington Forrest Foundation

Smith, Bill, trust: Cooper Foundation

Smith, Bonnie H., trust: Gooding Charitable Foundation, Luca

Smith, Boyd C., dir: Peery Foundation

Smith, Bradley C., pres: Raymark Corp.

Smith, Brian J., pres, dir: Grace Foundation, Inc.

Smith, Bruce G., dir: Smith Foundation, Gordon V. and Helen C.

Smith, Bruce R., secy, trust: Onan Family Foundation

Smith, Bryan, trust: Green Foundation

Smith, C. A., contr: Chrysler Corp. Fund

Smith, C. Gordon, trust: Smith Charitable Trust

Smith, C.R., chmn, dir: Bordeaux Foundation

Smith, Camilla M., asst secy, asst treas: Smith Fund, George D.

Smith, Carroll George, dir: Sentry Life Group Foundation

Smith, Carter, trust: Charities Foundation

Smith, Cecil I., trust: Sattler Beneficial Trust, Daniel A. and Edna J.

Smith, Charles A., trust: Chase Manhattan Bank, N.A.

Smith, Charles C., vchmn, trust: CTS Foundation

Smith, Charles E., pres, dir: Smith Family Foundation, Charles E.

Smith, Charles H., Jr., chmn: Sifco Industries Inc.; pres: Sifco Foundation

Smith, Charles W., trust: Sargent Foundation, Newell B.

Smith, Clarice R., dir: Smith Family Foundation, Charles E.

Smith, Clark R., pres: Smith Family Foundation, Theda Clark

Smith, Clifford Vaughn, Jr., pres: GE Foundations

Smith, Clyde, cfo: BE&K Inc.

Smith, Cooper R., Jr., Regent: Ogden College Fund

Smith, Daniel R., chmn, ceo, dir: First of America Bank Corp.

Smith, David, mem (contributions comm): Dresser Industries

Smith, David Byron, dir: Wausau Paper Mills Foundation

Smith, David L., exec dir: Abell-Hanger Foundation

Smith, David S., Jr., dir: Noble Foundation, Edward John

Smith, David Shiverick, chmn, dir: Olmsted Foundation, George and Carol

Smith, Diane M., vp, dir: First National Bank of Chicago Foundation

Smith, Dolores J., asst secy, dir: Wieboldt Foundation

Smith, Don McQueen, trust: Smith 1963 Charitable Trust, Don McQueen

Smith, Donald, pres, dir: Friendly Ice Cream Corp.; secy, treas: Rupp Foundation, Fran and Warren

Smith, Donald D., secy, trust: Lee Foundation, Ray M. and Mary Elizabeth

Smith, Donald K., sr vp, gen coun, dir: GEICO Corp.; pres, gen coun, dir: GEICO Philanthropic Foundation

Smith, Donald R., secy, treas: MCJ Foundation

Smith, Doris Anita, secy: Disney Co. Foundation, Walt

Smith, Doris B., treas, dir: Livingstone Charitable Foundation, Betty J. and J. Stanley

Smith, Dorothy D., dir: Davis Family - W.D. Charities, James E.

Smith, Douglas F., trust: Oberlaender Foundation, Gustav

Smith, Douglas I., dir: Smith Foundation, Gordon V. and Helen C.

Smith, E. Berry, secy, treas: Schurz Communications Foundation, Inc.

Smith, E. Lee, III, trust: Associated Foundations

Smith, E. N., Jr., chmn: Tartt Scholarship Fund, Hope Pierce

Smith, Edward A., dir: Bloch Foundation, Henry W. and Marion H.; vchmn, dir: Block Foundation, H&R; vchmn, dir: Loose Trust, Carrie J.; vchmn: Loose Trust, Harry Wilson

Smith, Edward D., chmn: Woodward Fund-Atlanta, David, Helen, Marian

Smith, Edward G., vp, treas: Poole and Kent Foundation

Smith, Eleanor A., trust: Smith Charitable Fund, Eleanor Armstrong

Smith, Elizabeth B., exec dir: Hyams Foundation

Smith, Elizabeth Morris, trust: McBean Charitable Trust, Alletta Morris

Smith, Elizabeth W., trust: Weinberg, Jr. Foundation, Sidney J.

Smith, Elton O., Jr., trust: Children's Foundation of Erie County

Smith, Emil L., trust: California Foundation for Biochemical Research

Smith, Ernie, vp (fin): Giant Food Stores

Smith, Estella, mgr commun rels: Duquesne Light Co.

Smith, Eugene, mem trust fund comm: Ingram Trust, Joe

Smith, Eva S., trust: Smith Foundation, Kenneth L. and Eva S.

Smith, Everett, trust: Meredith Foundation

Smith, Fannie, dir: Doss Foundation, M. S.

Smith, Frank G., Jr., trust: First Mississippi Corp. Foundation

Smith, Fred, trust: Jackson Hole Preserve

Smith, Fred G., vp, treas, trust: General Educational Fund; treas, dir: Merchants Bank Foundation

Smith, Fred M., secy, treas, dir: Williams Foundation, Kemper and Leila

Smith, Fred Wesley, pres, dir: Reynolds Foundation, Donald W.

Smith, Frederick Coe, chmn, trust: Huffy Foundation, Inc.

Smith, Frederick Wallace, fdr, chmn, pres, ceo, dir: Federal Express Corp.

Smith, Gary M., secy: American General Finance Foundation

Smith, George D., Jr., pres, secy, treas, trust: Smith Fund, George D.

Smith, George E., chmn, trust: Tull Charitable Foundation

Smith, Gerald C., dir: Redfield Foundation, Nell J.

Smith, Gerald J., program off: Moody Foundation

Smith, Gordon C., pres: Simplot Co., J.R.

Smith, Gordon H., dir, pres: Demos Foundation, N.

Smith, Gordon L., Jr., trust: North American Royalties Welfare Fund

Smith, Gordon V., dir: Smith Foundation, Gordon V. and Helen C.

Smith, Graham Wood, vp, dir: Dent Family Foundation, Harry

Smith, Gregory L., treas, trust: Duriron Co. Foundation

Smith, Greta, trust: Oberlaender Foundation, Gustav

Smith, H. K., chmn, pres: Riley Stoker Co.

Smith, H.D., trust: Sifco Foundation

Smith, Hamilton Othanel, dir: Life Sciences Research Foundation

Smith, Harlan W., chmn, dir: Dyneer Corp.

Smith, Harold Byron, Jr., chmn, pres, dir: Illinois Tool Works Foundation

Smith, Harold W., vp, trust: Swisher Foundation, Carl S.

Smith, Harry L., dir, pres: Schilling Foundation

Smith, Helen C., dir: Smith Foundation, Gordon V. and Helen C.

Smith, Herbert J., Ogden College Fund

Smith, Horace E., secy: Sheppard Foundation, Lawrence B.

Smith, Howard W., Jr., secy: Bryant Foundation

Smith, Hulett C., emeritus trust: Benedum Foundation, Claude Worthington

Smith, Irwin N., dir: Chicago Board of Trade Educational Research Foundation

Smith, J. Armistead, vchmn, dir: Union Planters Corp.

Smith, J. Burleson, dir: Piper Foundation, Minnie Stevens

Smith, J. Frank, vp, dir: Georgia Scientific and Technical Research Foundation

Smith, J. Phil, dir: Robinson Mountain Fund, E. O.

Smith, James C., Jr., vp: Pannill Scholarship Foundation, William Letcher

Smith, James F., chmn, ceo, dir: Orange & Rockland Utilities, Inc.

Smith, James F., Jr., chmn, dir: First American Corp. (Nashville, Tennessee)

Smith, James H., cfo, dir: Anchor Glass Container Corp.

Smith, James S., pres, treas: Frese Foundation, Arnold D.

Smith, Jane Prouty, trust, vp: Prouty Foundation, Olive Higgins

Smith, Jane R., ceo: Cooke Foundation

Smith, Jean K., dir, v chmn: Bordeaux Foundation

Smith, Jean Kennedy, trust: Kennedy, Jr. Foundation, Joseph P.

Smith, Jean M., vchmn (community concerns comm): NBD Bank, N.A.

Smith, Jefferson V., III, dir: Smith Charities, John

Smith, Joe W., secy, treas, trust: Arkwright Foundation

Smith, John, treas: Goddard Homestead

Smith, John F., Jr., ceo, pres, dir: General Motors Corp.

Smith, John Francis, Jr., trust: General Motors Foundation

Smith, John J., chmn, ceo: Sparton Corp.

Smith, John M., trust: Gheens Foundation

Smith, Joseph E., pres: Parke-Davis Group

Smith, Julia A., dir: McIntosh Foundation

Smith, Julia C., Jr., pres: Smith Foundation, Julia and Albert

Smith, Kathleen D., dir, treas: Raskob Foundation, Bill

Smith, Kathryn R., trust: Reed Foundation, Philip D.

Smith, Kaylon, cfo: Smith Oil Corp.

Smith, Kenneth, trust: India Foundation

Smith, L. Edwin, treas, dir: Jones Foundation, Helen

Smith, L. L., dir: Shell Oil Co. Foundation

Smith, LaDonna, contributions admin: Owens-Illinois

Smith, Langhorne B., treas, dir: Claneil Foundation

Smith, Larry T., trust: Layne Foundation

Smith, Leonard W., pres, secy, trust: Skillman Foundation

Smith, Lewis W., trust: Morgan Foundation, Louie R. and Gertrude

Smith, Ley S., vchmn, dir: Upjohn Co.; dir: Upjohn Co. Foundation

Smith, Lin, pub affairs asst: Matlock Foundation

Smith, Lloyd Bruce, pres, dir: Smith Foundation, A.O.

Smith, Lucien T., chmn, dir: Duplex Products, Inc.

Smith, M. Munson, trust, asst secy: Johnson Foundation, M. G. and Lillie A.

Smith, M. T., vchmn, pres: Hughes Aircraft Co.

Smith, Malcolm, pres, dir: Brand Cos. Charitable Foundation; treas: New York Foundation

Smith, Malcolm Bernard, trust: Guggenheim Memorial Foundation, John Simon

Smith, Malcolm D., bd mem: Caring Foundation

Smith, Margaret A., vp: Ontario Corporation Foundation

Smith, Margaret T., dir: Kresge Foundation

Smith, Mark D., MD, vp: Kaiser Family Foundation, Henry J.

Smith, Mary E., dir: Schilling Foundation

Smith, Mary L., trust: Smith Charitable Trust, W. W.

Smith, Mary Mills Abel, trust: duPont Foundation, Chichester

Smith, Mary Welles, vp, dir: Hilliard Foundation

Smith, May, trust: Smith Horticultural Trust, Stanley

Smith, Melinda Hoag, dir: Hoag Family Foundation, George

Smith, Melvin E., trust: Chiles Foundation

Smith, Menlo F., trust: Sunmark Foundation

Smith, Michael L., ceo: Mayflower Group

Smith, Molly R., trust: Hillsdale Fund

Smith, Mrs. Deen Day, vchmn: Day Foundation, Cecil B.

Smith, Myron, trust: Forest Lawn Foundation

Smith, Nancy E., trust: Slemp Foundation

Smith, Noble, exec dir: Noble Foundation, Edward John

Smith, Norvel, dir: Rosenberg Foundation

Smith, Oliver C., chmn: Menasha Corporate Foundation

Smith, Ora K., trust: Kingsley Foundation

Smith, Orville D., trust: McMahon Foundation

Smith, Pamela C., trust: Donaldson Charitable Trust, Oliver S. and Jennie R.

Smith, Patricia M., secy, treas: Harrington Foundation, Don and Sybil

Smith, Peter, vp (sales & mktg): Meridien Hotels

Smith, Peter G., pres, coo: Lawson Products, Inc.

Smith, Philip N., Jr., secy: KIHI/21 International Holding Foundation

Smith, Philip S., sr vp, cfo: Mitchell Energy & Development Corp.

Smith, Phillip R., adv: Johnson Controls Foundation

Smith, Phillips Guy, mem adv comm: Ford Foundation, Edward E.

Smith, Pomerly, trust: Beal Foundation

Smith, R. J., Jr., vp, active dir: Cain Foundation, Effie and Wofford

Smith, R.N., vp: North American Philips Foundation

Smith, Rachel B., trust: Gilmer-Smith Foundation

Smith, Randy, vp, gen couns: Heileman Brewing Co., Inc., G.

Smith, Randy P., vp, cfo: Rosemount, Inc.

Smith, Raymond W., chmn, ceo: Bell Atlantic Corp.

Smith, Richard Alan, treas, dir: Arvin Foundation; vp, secy, dir: Biddle Foundation, Margaret T.; chmn, dir: Harcourt General

Smith, Richard C., dir: Sprint Foundation; treas, dir: Stanley Consultants Charitable Foundation

Smith, Richard D., pres, dir: Chubb Corp.

Smith, Richard Ferree, Wurts Memorial, Henrietta Tower

Smith, Richard G., III, trust: Hillsdale Fund

Smith, Richard L., vp: Sierra Pacific Foundation

Smith, Richard M., pres, dir: Newsweek, Inc.

Smith, Richard P., exec vp, ceo: Dairylea Cooperative Inc.

Smith, Robert, trust: Stoneman Charitable Foundation, Anne and David

Smith, Robert A., dir: Harcourt General; trust: Smith Foundation, Richard and Susan

Smith, Robert A., III, pres, dir: Doheny Foundation, Carrie Estelle

Smith, Robert Howard, secy, treas: Smith Family Foundation, Charles E.

Smith, Roger B., trust: Sloan Foundation, Alfred P.

Smith, Rosemarie, trust: Beidler Charitable Trust, Francis

Smith, Roy C., trust: Coles Family Foundation

Smith, S. Garry, secy, treas, fdn mgr: Daniel Foundation of Alabama

Smith, S. H., Jr., pres: CP&L Foundation

Smith, S. Kinnie, Jr., vchmn, gen counc, dir: Consumers Power Co.; dir: Consumers Power Foundation

Smith, Sara C., program off (poor & needy div): Reynolds Charitable Trust, Kate B.

Smith, Sherry, mgr commun rels: Target Stores

Smith, Sherwood Hubbard, Jr., chmn, ceo, dir: Carolina Power & Light Co.; pres: CP&L Foundation; trust: Reynolds Foundation, Z. Smith

Smith, Sidney Oslin, Jr., trust: Loridans Foundation, Charles

Smith, Spencer N., pres, treas, dir: Time Insurance Foundation

Smith, Stephen, secy: Christensen Charitable and Religious Foundation, L. C.

Smith, Stephen Byron, dir: Illinois Tool Works Foundation

Smith, Stephen J., cfo: Community Coffee Co.

Smith, Steven James, exec vp: Continental Corp. Foundation

Smith, Susan F., trust: Smith Foundation, Richard and Susan

Smith, Susan J., exec dir: Onan Family Foundation

Smith, Susan Jensen, mgr corp contributions: Electronic Data Systems Corp.

Smith, Tablin C., vp: Smith Family Foundation, Theda Clark

Smith, Ted R., trust: McKee Foundation, Robert E. and Evelyn

Smith, Tefft W., dir: Kirkland & Ellis Foundation

Smith, Thelma G., vp: 1525 Foundation; vp, dir: Second Foundation

Smith, Thomas R., trust, pres, treas: Carpenter Foundation

Smith, Tim S., secy, treas: Rupp Foundation, Fran and Warren

Smith, Tom, chmn, pres, ceo, dir: Food Lion Inc.

Smith, Van P., chmn, pres: Ontario Corp.; chmn: Ontario Corporation Foundation

Smith, Vivian L., pres, trust: Smith Foundation, Bob and Vivian

Smith, W. Keith, trust: Mellon Bank Foundation

Smith, W. R., dir, chmn: Heath Foundation, Ed and Mary

Smith, W. Thomas, vp, treas: Smith Charities, John

Smith, Wally, pres, ceo: REI-Recreational Equipment, Inc.

Smith, Wayne, dir: Humana Foundation

Smith, William, trust: Bend Foundation

Smith, William A., vp: Sonat Foundation

Smith, William C., pres, dir: Ameritas Charitable Foundation

Smith, William J., commun rels mgr: Minnesota Mutual Life Insurance Co.

Smith, William K., pres: United Telephone System (Eastern Group)

Smith, William M., III, trust: Prouty Foundation, Olive Higgins

Smith, William T., vchmn, coo: Savin Corp.

Smith, Wm. C., Jr., dir: Smith Foundation, Julia and Albert

Smith, Zachary Taylor, II, dir: Babcock Foundation, Mary Reynolds; vp, trust: Reynolds Foundation, Z. Smith

Smith-Ganey, Anne L., contact person: Sprague Educational and Charitable Foundation, Seth; treas, dir: Zimmermann Fund, Marie and John

Smithburg, William D., chmn, ceo, dir: Quaker Oats Co.

Smithers, Adele C., pres, dir: Smithers Foundation, Christopher D.

Smithers, Charles F., Jr., treas, dir: Smithers Foundation, Christopher D.

Smithers, Christopher B., dir: Smithers Foundation, Christopher D.

Smithers, R. Brinkley, chmn, dir: Smithers Foundation, Christopher D.

Smithgall, Charles, III, dir: Georgia Health Foundation

Smithhart, Claude, trust: Pineywoods Foundation

Smoak, Joseph F., secy, treas: Post & Courier Foundation

Smock, Frederick, secy, dir: Kentucky Foundation for Women

Smolik, Ellis F., sr vp (fin), secy, treas, cfo, dir: Lincoln Electric Co.; secy: Lincoln Electric Foundation Trust

Smoot, J. Thomas, Jr., trust: Edison Fund, Charles

Smoot, Richard L., pres, ceo: PNC Bank

Smoot, William H., vp, trust: Community Cooperative Development Foundation

Smucker, Lillian, trust: Thoman Foundation, W. B. and Candace

Smucker, Lorraine E., vp, trust: Smucker Foundation, Willard E.

Smucker, Paul Highnam, chmn exec comm, ceo, dir: Smucker Co., J.M.; pres, treas: Smucker Foundation, Willard E.

Smucker, Richard Kim, trust: Smucker Foundation, Willard E.

Smucker, Timothy Paul, trust: Smucker Foundation, Willard E.

Smurfit, Michael W. J., chmn, dir: Jefferson Smurfit Corp.

Smyth, Donald, vchmn: Servistar Corp.

Smyth, Frances G., secy: Banc One Wisconsin Foundation

Smyth, Geralynn D., secy, dir: Knott Foundation, Marion I. and Henry J.

Smyth, John C., secy, dir: Knott Foundation, Marion I. and Henry J.

Smyth, Maureen H., vp (programs): Mott Foundation, Charles Stewart

Smyth, Patricia K., vp, dir: Knott Foundation, Marion I. and Henry J.

Smythe, John W., exec dir, treas: Jones Foundation, Fletcher

Smythe, Thomas, chmn, pres, dir: Keller-Crescent Co.

Sneden, Kathleen M., mem: Davenport Foundation, M. E.

Sneden, Marcia A., mem: Davenport Foundation, M. E.

Sneden, Margaret D., vp, secy, dir: Davenport Foundation, M. E.

Sneden, Margaret E., mem: Davenport Foundation, M. E.

Sneden, Robert W., pres, dir: Davenport Foundation, M. E.

Sneider, Martin K., pres, dir: Edison Brothers Stores

Snell, Richard, chmn: Arizona Public Service Co.

Snetzer, Michael A., chmn, ceo: Medford Corp.

Snetzer, Michael Alan, pres, dir: Contran Corp.

Snider, Arnold H., Jr., trust: Tiger Foundation

Snider, Edward Malcolm, pres: Snider Foundation

Snodgrass, John F., trust: Noble Foundation, Samuel Roberts

Snow, David H., dir: Snow Foundation, John Ben

Snow, James, dir, secy: Clover Foundation

Snow, John W., chmn, pres, ceo, dir: CSX Corp.; chmn, pres, ceo, dir: Sea-Land Service

Snow, Joseph Z., dir: Foster & Gallagher Foundation

Snow, Mike, sr vp: Union Bank of Switzerland New York Branch

Snow, Vernon F., pres, dir: Snow Foundation, John Ben; trust: Snow Memorial Trust, John Ben

Snow, Vivienne B., adm, dir: Autzen Foundation

Snowden, Edward W., Jr., trust: Hill-Snowdon Foundation

Snowdon, Edward W., Jr., trust: Hill-Snowdon Foundation

Snowdon, Lee Hill, trust: Hill-Snowdon Foundation

Snowdon, Marguerite H., trust: Hill-Snowdon Foundation

Snowdon, Richard W., trust: Hill-Snowdon Foundation

Snyder, Audrey, trust: Snyder Foundation, Harold B. and Dorothy A.

Snyder, Barbara J., grants adm, secy: Wortham Foundation

Snyder, C. Robert, chmn, ceo: Northwestern National Insurance Group; chmn, trust: Northwestern National Insurance Foundation

Snyder, Dennis, trust: Meland Outreach

Snyder, Donald P., accounting mgr: Flinn Foundation

Snyder, Frank Ronald, II, trust: Lehigh Portland Cement Charitable Trust

Snyder, G. Whitney, trust: Snyder Charitable Fund, W. P.

Snyder, Geraldine, secy: Meland Outreach

Snyder, Leonard N., trust: Grundy Foundation

Snyder, Mary Ann, secy, treas, dir: Chicago Resource Center; dir: High Meadow Foundation

Snyder, Patricia H., dir: Habig Foundation

Snyder, Phillip, vp: Wilson Public Trust, Ralph

Snyder, Phyllis Johnson, trust: Snyder Foundation, Harold B. and Dorothy A.

Snyder, Richard A., vp, cfo, treas: Tennant Co.

Snyder, Richard E., ceo, pres: Simon & Schuster Inc.

Snyder, Richard Wesley, fdr, pres, ceo: Snyder General Corp.

Snyder, Robert C., pres, ceo, coo: Quanex Corp.; pres, dir: Quanex Foundation

Snyder, Ronald R., sec, dir: Arvin Foundation

Snyder, William B., chmn, ceo, dir: GEICO Corp.; dir: GEICO Philanthropic Foundation

Snyder, William L., ceo, dir, pres: Rinker Materials Corp.; pres, trust: Rinker Cos. Foundation

Snyder, William Penn, III, trust: Snyder Charitable Fund, W. P.

Sobel, Seymour, pres: Chait Memorial Foundation, Sara

Society Bank & Trust, trust: Cayuga Foundation; trust: Generation Trust

Socol, Howard, chmn, ceo: Burdines

Socolofsky, Robert D., secy, dir: Maddox Foundation, J. F.

Soderberg, Elsa A., dir: Allyn Foundation

Soderberg, Peter, dir: Allyn Foundation

Soderberg, Robert C., dir: Allyn Foundation

Soderquist, Donald G., vchmn, coo, dir: Wal-Mart Stores; trust: Wal-Mart Foundation; vchmn, coo, dir: Wal-Mart Stores, Inc.

Soderstrom, C. S., dir: Morton Memorial Fund, Mark

Soffa, Albert, vchmn: Kulicke & Soffa Industries

Sofia, Zuheir, pres, coo, dir: Huntington Bancshares Inc.

Sohn, Donald R., pres: Heritage Travel Inc./Thomas Cook Travel

Sohn, Edward, trust: Fohs Foundation

Sohn, Frances F., chmn: Fohs Foundation

Sohn, Fred, vchmn: Fohs Foundation

Sohn, Howard, trust: Fohs Foundation

Sohn, Ruth, trust: Fohs Foundation

Solana, Nancy, secy: Fikes Foundation, Leland

Solano, Patrick, dir: Sordoni Foundation

Solari, Jerome P., treas: Wilsey Foundation

Soleberg, Larry, exec vp, cfo: National Car Rental System, Inc.

Solender, Sanford, trust: Lavanburg-Corner House

Soles, W. Roger, chmn, pres, dir: Jefferson-Pilot

Solheim, Allan O., trust: Solheim Foundation

Solheim, John A., trust: Solheim Foundation

Solheim, K. Louis, trust: Solheim Foundation

Solheim, Karsten, trust: Solheim Foundation

Solheim, Louise C., trust: Solheim Foundation

Sollins, Karen R., dir: Scherman Foundation

Solmon, L., dir: Capital Fund Foundation; pres, dir: Milken Institute for Job and Capital Formation

Solnit, Albert J., dir: New-Land Foundation

Solomon, Anthony, dir: Warhol Foundation for the Visual Arts, Andy

Solomon, Charles M., vchmn, dir: Austin Industries

Solomon, Dianne, contributions adm: Rhone-Poulenc Rorer

Solomon, L. R., secy, dir: Florsheim Shoe Foundation

Solomon, Milton D., vp, secy, trust: Bydale Foundation

Solomon, Peter J., dir: Littauer Foundation, Lucius N.

Solomon, William T., chmn, pres, ceo, dir: Austin Industries

Solovy, Delores Kohl, treas, dir: Kohl Charities, Herbert H.

Solow, Robert M., trust: Sloan Foundation, Alfred P.

Solow, Sheldon Henry, don, pres: Solow Foundation; pres, treas: Solow Foundation, Sheldon H.

Solso, Theodore Mathew, dir: Cummins Engine Foundation

Solt, Jerry A., trust: Wagnalls Memorial

Solt, Russell, exec vp, cfo: Belk Stores

Somers, Stephen, PhD, assoc vp: Johnson Foundation, Robert Wood

Somers, W., pres: Somers Corp. (Mersman/Waldron)

Somerset, Harold Richard, ceo, pres, dir: California & Hawaiian Sugar Co.; trust: C & H Charitable Trust

Sommer, C. S., mem (bd control): Ralston Purina Trust Fund

Sommerfield, Esthel, secy: Abell Foundation, The

Sommerfield, Michele S., trust: Strake Foundation

Sommers, Davidson, chmn emeritus: Meyer Foundation, Eugene and Agnes E.

Somnolet, Michel, coo, dir: Cosmair, Inc.

Somrock, John D., pres, ceo: Johnson Co., E. F.; pres: Johnson Co. Foundation, E. F.

Sonderegger, John L., secy, dir: Rennebohm Foundation, Oscar

Sonderegger, Leona A., asst secy, dir: Rennebohm Foundation, Oscar

Sonderman, James J., dir: DCB Foundation

Sondheim, Walter, Jr., trust: Abell Foundation, The; gov: Baker, Jr. Memorial Fund, William G.

Song, Carole, secy: Soling Family Foundation

Song, Chester, pres: Soling Family Foundation

Song, Unmi, program off (econ devel): Joyce Foundation

Sonn, David E., trust: Raymond Foundation

Sonnabend, Paul, pres, dir: Sonesta International Hotels Corp.; vp, dir: Sonesta Charitable Foundation

Sonnabend, Peter J., clerk, dir: Sonesta Charitable Foundation

Sonnabend, Roger P., chmn, ceo, dir: Sonesta International Hotels Corp.; pres, dir: Sonesta Charitable Foundation

Sonne, Christian R., trust: Mulford Foundation, Vincent

Stack, Edward W., vp, dir: Clark Foundation

Stack, Richard L., trust: Darling Foundation, Hugh and Hazel

Stackpole, Harrison Clinton, chmn, trust: Stackpole-Hall Foundation

Stackpole, R. Dauer, trust: Stackpole-Hall Foundation

Stacy, Deloris E., trust: USG Foundation

Stacy, Festus, trust: Stacy Foundation, Festus

Stacy, Helen, trust: Stacy Foundation, Festus

Stacy, Mary, adm asst, secy: Hoblitzelle Foundation

Stadler, Gerald P., vchmn: United Van Lines, Inc.

Stadler, Martin F., trust: Hoffmann-La Roche Foundation

Stafford, Jack, chmn: Sherwood Medical Co.

Stafford, John R., chmn, ceo, dir: American Home Products Corp.

Stafford, Kathleen A., treas: Amgen Foundation

Stafford, Richard H., vp, dir: Rutledge Charity, Edward

Stafford, William P., pres: Hunnicutt Foundation, H. P. and Anne S.

Staheli, Donald L., pres, ceo: Continental Grain Co.; vp, dir: Continental Grain Foundation

Stahl, Dale E., pres, coo: Gaylord Container Corp.

Stahl, Jack L., treas, dir: Coca-Cola Foundation

Staiger, Charles, secy: Whiting Memorial Foundation, Henry and Harriet

Staines, Joseph J., secy: Amgen Foundation

Stairs, Michael, trust: Presser Foundation

Stajduhar, Michael W., mem: One Valley Bank Foundation

Staley, Harry L., secy, exec dir: Westchester Health Fund

Staley, Robert, vchmn, chief admin off, dir: Emerson Electric Co.; chmn, dir: Emerson Charitable Trust

Staley, Thomas F., pres: Staley Foundation, Thomas F.

Staley, Walter G., secy, treas, dir: Green Foundation, Allen P. and Josephine B.

Staley, Walter G., Jr., dir: Green Foundation, Allen P. and Josephine B.

Stall, Herman, pres: Schaffer Foundation, H.

Stalla, Gloria, secy: Shapero Foundation, Nate S. and Ruth B.

Stallings, Vici, dir: First Interstate Bank of Texas Foundation

Stalter, J. Neil, trust: Campbell Soup Foundation

Stamas, Stephen, dir: Greenwall Foundation

Stancato, Kenneth J., contr: Weyerhaeuser Co. Foundation

Stancil, Joann Barnette, adm: Rogers Charitable Trust, Florence

Stancliff, Carol, trust: Woman's Seamen's Friend Society of Connecticut

Standen, Michael, pres: Metallurg, Inc.

Standish, J. S., chmn, dir: Albany International Corp.

Standish, Victor J., pres, treas: York Barbell Co.

Stanely, Thomas Bahnson, III, exec dir: Landmark Charitable Foundation

Stanfill, Dennis Carothers, dir: Weingart Foundation

Stanford, Henry King, trust: Knight Foundation, John S. and James L.

Stangarone, Robert, vp (pub affs): Rolls-Royce Inc.

Stangeland, Roger E., chmn, ceo, dir: Vons Cos., Inc.

Stanger, L. Winn, secy: Elgin Sweeper Foundation

Staniar, Burton B., ceo, chmn: Westinghouse Broadcasting Co.

Stanley, Brian C., off: Valmont Foundation

Stanley, David, chmn, ceo, dir: Payless Cashways Inc.

Stanley, David M., pres, treas, dir: E and M Charities

Stanley, Edmund Allport, Jr., pres, trust: Bowne Foundation, Robert; pres, exec dir, trust: Town Creek Foundation

Stanley, Jean Leu, vp, secy, dir: E and M Charities

Stanley, Jennifer, vp, trust: Bowne Foundation, Robert; vp: Town Creek Foundation

Stanley, Kelly N., secy: Ontario Corporation Foundation

Stanley, L. W., asst contr: Exxon Education Foundation

Stanley, Lisa A., trust: Town Creek Foundation

Stanley, Richard H., vchmn, dir: Stanley Consultants; pres, dir: Stanley Consultants Charitable Foundation

Stanley, Richard Holt, dir: E and M Charities

Stanley, Talcott, trust: Stanley Charitable Foundation, A. W.

Stanley, Thomas O., trust: Bowne Foundation, Robert

Stans, Diane, dir: Stans Foundation

Stans, Maurice Hubert, chmn, treas, dir: Stans Foundation

Stans, Steven H., pres, dir: Stans Foundation

Stans, Susan, dir: Stans Foundation

Stans, Theodore M., vp, dir: Stans Foundation

Stanth, Robert A., pres, coo, dir: Fleming Companies, Inc.

Stanton, Frank, trust: Stanton Fund, Ruth and Frank

Stanton, J. Michael, Jr., trust: Raskob Foundation, Bill

Stanton, J.A., trust: Kuhns Brothers Co. Foundation

Stanton, Peter F., pres, ceo: Washington Trust Bank; trust: Washington Trust Bank Foundation

Stanton, Philip H., trust: Washington Trust Bank Foundation

Stanton, Robert E., pres, treas, trust: Bonfils-Stanton Foundation

Stanwood, JoAnn, vp, dir: Island Foundation

Stanworth, R. Howard, pres, ceo: Pearle Vision

Staples, Emily Anne, vchmn, trust: Minnesota Foundation

Staples, Stanley F., Jr., pres: Alexander Foundation, Judd S.; secy, dir: Alexander Foundation, Walter; treas, dir: Mosinee Paper Corp. Foundation; dir: Wausau Paper Mills Foundation

Stapleton, Benjamin F., vp, trust: Bonfils-Stanton Foundation

Stapleton, Katharine H., trust: Fishback Foundation Trust, Harmes C.

Stapp, Raymond L., treas, contrl: Thums Long Beach Co.

Stare, David S., trust: Stare Fund

Stare, Fredrick John, trust: Stare Fund

Stare, Irene M., trust: Stare Fund

Stark, Carlyn Kaiser, trust: Kaiser Family Foundation, Henry J.

Stark, Donald B., treas: Ahmanson Foundation

Stark, H. Allan, trust: Rhoades Fund, Otto L. and Hazel E.

Stark, K. R., trust: Kunkel Foundation, John Crain

Stark, Nathan Julius, trust: Allegheny Foundation

Stark, Nelda Childers, chmn: Stark Foundation, Nelda C. and H. J. Lutcher

Stark, Richard Alvin, secy, treas, dir: Leonhardt Foundation, Dorothea L.

Stark, Richard I., vchmn: Hubbard Farms Charitable Foundation

Stark, William B., pres, treas, trust: Lee Foundation, Ray M. and Mary Elizabeth

Starkins, Clifford E., trust: Porter Foundation, Mrs. Cheever

Starling, James R., M.D., trust: Surgical Science Foundation for Research and Development

Starr, Frederick B., pres, ceo: Thomasville Furniture Industries; chmn, mem adm comm: Thomasville Furniture Industries Foundation

Starr, Joe F., trust: Tyson Foundation

Starr, Karen, sr program off: Bremer Foundation, Otto

Starr, Kenneth I., vp, dir: Lambert Memorial Foundation, Gerard B.

Starr, Nat, exec dir: Swig Foundation

Starr, Paul G., trust: Insurance Management Associates Foundation

Starr, Richard W., cfo: Pope Family Foundation, Blanche & Edker

Starr, Stephen Frederick, trust: Rockefeller Brothers Fund

Starrett, D. A., dir: Starrett Co. Charitable Foundation, L.S.

Starrett, Douglas R., pres: Starrett Co., L.S.; dir: Starrett Co. Charitable Foundation, L.S.

Startzel, D. C., asst treas: PHH Foundation

Stasior, William F., chmn, ceo: Booz Allen & Hamilton

Stata, Ray S., chmn, pres, dir: Analog Devices

Staton, Jimmy, trust: Norman Foundation, Summers A.

Stauber, Karl N., vp program, asst secy: Northwest Area Foundation

Stauder, Lloyd P., coo: Carter Co., William

Staudt, John E., pres, coo: Banc One Illinois Corp.

Staudt, Ronald W., vp: National Center for Automated Information Retrieval

Stauffer, John H., chmn, pres, ceo, dir: Stauffer Communications; mem:

Stauffer Communications Foundation

Stauffer, Stanley H., chmn: Stauffer Communications Foundation

Stauffer, William D., vp: Halsell Foundation, O. L.

Stavely, Richard W., trust: Misco Charitable Trust

Staven, Ralph R., pres, mgr: First Financial Foundation

Stavropoulos, W. S., trust: Dow Chemical Co. Foundation

Stead, Jerre Lee, NCR Corp.

Steadman, Richard C., trust: German Marshall Fund of the United States; chmn, dir: National Convenience Stores, Inc.

Stebman, Betty J., dir: Hughes Memorial Foundation, Charles Evans

Stec, Cynthia M., vp: Foundation of the Litton Industries

Stecher, Patsy Palmer, dir: Beveridge Foundation, Frank Stanley

Stedham, Austin W., chmn, pres, ceo: Sierra Pacific Resources; vp, dir: Sierra Pacific Resources Charitable Foundation

Stedman, Betty Ann West, trust: West Foundation, Neva and Wesley

Stedman, Sheila, asst vp: Kentland Foundation

Stedman, Stuart West, trust: West Foundation, Neva and Wesley

Steedman, Martin, dir, secy: Meyer Foundation, Baron de Hirsch

Steel, Eric, trust: Steel, Sr. Foundation, Marshall

Steel, Gordon, trust: Steel, Sr. Foundation, Marshall

Steel, Jane, trust: Steel, Sr. Foundation, Marshall

Steel, Lauri, trust: Steel, Sr. Foundation, Marshall

Steel, Marshall, Jr., trust: Steel, Sr. Foundation, Marshall

Steele, Arthur J., trust: Warner Fund, Albert and Bessie

Steele, Finley M., trust: Hilliard Foundation

Steele, Harold J., comm mem: Eccles Foundation, Marriner S.

Steele, John H., ScD, trust: Johnson Foundation, Robert Wood

Steele, Lela Emery, pres, treas: Peterloon Foundation

Steele, Lewis M., trust: Warner Fund, Albert and Bessie

Steele, Richard, treas: Steele Foundation, Harry and Grace

Steele, Ruth M., trust: Warner Fund, Albert and Bessie

Steele, William W., pres, coo: American Building Maintenance Industries

Steenberg, Lawrence, dir: National City Bank of Evansville Foundation

Steenburgh, E. L., pres, coo: Ricoh Corp.

Steere, William C., Jr., chmn, ceo, chmn exec comm, dir: Pfizer

Stefanski, Stephen A., trust: Winn Educational Trust, Fanny Edith

Steffens, Marian I., asst secy: Robinson Fund, Maurice R.

Steffensen, Dwight A., pres, coo, dir: Bergen Brunswig Corp.

Steffes, Don C., dir: Mingenback Foundation, Julia J.

Steffner, John E., dir: Brown Charitable Trust, Dora Maclellan

Stegall, James W., mem loan comm: Lindsay Student Aid Fund, Franklin

Stegall, Ruth, asst secy: Taper Foundation, Mark; asst secy: Taper Foundation, S. Mark

Stegemeier, Richard Joseph, chmn, ceo, dir: Unocal Corp.; trust: Unocal Foundation

Steiger, Albert E., III, dir: Steiger Memorial Fund, Albert

Steiger, Albert E., Jr., pres, dir: Steiger Memorial Fund, Albert

Steiger, Allen, treas: Steiger Memorial Fund, Albert

Steiger, Phillip C., Jr., trust: Steiger Memorial Fund, Albert

Steiger, Ralph A., Jr., vp: Steiger Memorial Fund, Albert

Steiger, Robert K., trust: Steiger Memorial Fund, Albert

Steigerwaldt, Donna Wolf, chmn, ceo, dir: Jockey International; pres, treas, dir: Steigerwaldt Foundation, Donna Wolf

Steigerwaldt, William, dir, vp: Steigerwaldt Foundation, Donna Wolf

Stein, Carey M., secy: Hartmarx Charitable Foundation

Stein, Dieter, chmn, pres: BASF Corp.

Stein, Donald L., vp, dir: Consolidated Papers Foundation

Stein, Eric, trust: Stoneman Charitable Foundation, Anne and David

Stein, Howard, chmn, ceo, dir: Dreyfus Corp.

Stein, Jane, trust: Stoneman Charitable Foundation, Anne and David

Stein, Jean, vp, dir: Stein Foundation, Jules and Doris

Stein, John S., Sr., vp: Bashinsky Foundation

Stein, Joyce, trust: Philibosian Foundation, Stephen

Stein, Kenneth, trust: Goldie-Anna Charitable Trust

Stein, Louis, trust: Stein Foundation, Louis

Stein, Mark S., trust: Stern Foundation, Percival

Stein, Mary Ann Efroymson, pres, dir: Moriah Fund

Stein, Melvin M., pres, dir: Stein Foundation, Joseph F.

Stein, Robert J., dir human resources: BASF Corp.; dir: Moriah Fund

Stein, Ronald, dir: Aron Charitable Foundation, J.

Stein, Stuart M., secy, dir: Stein Foundation, Joseph F.

Stein, Suzanne, secy: Wouk Foundation, Abe

Stein, William S., trust: Friedman Brothers Foundation

Steinberg, Jean, vp, secy: Steinberg Family Foundation, Meyer and Jean

Steinberg, Joseph S., trust: American Investment Co. Foundation; pres, dir: Leucadia National Corp.; trust: Leucadia Foundation

Steinberg, Meyer, pres, treas: Steinberg Family Foundation, Meyer and Jean

Steinberg, Milton, trust: Blowitz-Ridgeway Foundation

Steinberg, Robert A., trust: Gordon Charitable Trust, Peggy and Yale

Steinberg, Robert M., chmn, ceo: Reliance Group Holdings, Inc.; chmn, ceo: Reliance Insurance Cos.

Steinberg, Saul Philip, fdr, chmn, ceo: Reliance Group Holdings, Inc.; fdr, chmn, ceo: Reliance Insurance Cos.

Steinbock, Mark A., vp, cfo: Tremco Inc.; trust: Tremco Foundation

Steinbright, Edith C., don, dir emeritus: Arcadia Foundation

Steinbright, Marilyn L., don, pres: Arcadia Foundation

Steiner, Daniel L., pres, dir: Olive Bridge Fund

Steiner, Gilbert Y., mem counc, dir: Foundation for Child Development

Steiner, Jeffrey, chmn, ceo: Banner Industries, Inc.

Steiner, Jeffrey Josef, chmn: Fairchild Industries Foundation

Steiner, Kevin K., pres, dir: Steiner Foundation

Steiner, L., trust: Bissell Foundation, J. Walton

Steiner, Lawrence G., pres, dir: American Linen Supply Co.

Steiner, Lisa Amelia, MD, trust, mem: Whitney Foundation, Helen Hay

Steiner, Prudence L., vp, dir: Olive Bridge Fund

Steiner, Richard R., pres, ceo: Steiner Corp.

Steingraber, Fred G., ceo, treas: Kearney Inc., A.T.

Steinhardt, Judith, trust: Steinhardt Foundation, Judy and Michael

Steinhardt, Michael, trust: Sheinberg Foundation, Eric P.; trust: Steinhardt Foundation, Judy and Michael

Steinhart, Ronald G., chmn, ceo: Team Bancshares Inc.

Steinhauer, Bruce W., MD, trust: McGregor Fund

Steinhoff, Edward, pres: Dow Corning Corp.

Steinkraus, Eric M., dir: Ziegler Foundation for the Blind, E. Matilda

Steinkraus, Helen Z., secy, dir: Ziegler Foundation for the Blind, E. Matilda

Steinman, Beverly R., vchmn, trust: Steinman Foundation, James Hale

Steinman, Lewis, dir: Rudin Foundation; dir: Rudin Foundation, Louis and Rachel

Steinmann, David P., secy: Rosenwald Family Fund, William

Steinschneider, Jean M., trust: Huisking Foundation

Steinschneider, Richard, Jr., Huisking Foundation

Steinweg, Bernard, trust: Fribourg Foundation

Steiss, Albert J., pres, dir: Trust Funds

Steitz, Joan Argetsinger, dir: Childs Memorial Fund for Medical Research, Jane Coffin

Stekas, Lynn, pres: Mutual of New York Foundation

Stella, Ethel, exec vp, dir: Norcross Wildlife Foundation

Stelyn, Denise Alice, trust: Bates Memorial Foundation, George A.

Stelzel, Walter T., cfo: American National Can Co.

Stemen, Milton E., trust: Redies Foundation, Edward F.

Stemmler, Edward Joseph, trust: Kynett Memorial Foundation, Edna G.

Stemmons, John M., hon dir: Hoblitzelle Foundation

Stemmons, John M., Jr., secy, treas: Stemmons Foundation

Stemmons, John M., Sr., pres: Stemmons Foundation

Stemmons, Ruth T., vp: Stemmons Foundation

Stempel, Ernest Edward, vchmn, dir: American International Group, Inc.; dir: Starr Foundation

Stender, Bruce W., chmn, mem exec comm: Blandin Foundation

Stenftenagel, Ed J., dir: DCB Foundation

Stenson, Glen E., trust: Heginbotham Trust, Will E.

Stensrud, Richard L., dir: Group Health Foundation

Stepan, F. Quinn, chmn, pres, coo, ceo, dir: Stepan Co.

Stepanian, Ira, chmn, ceo, dir: Bank of Boston Corp.

Stepanian, Tania W., chmn, ceo, trust: Crocker Trust, Mary A.

Stepelman, Jay, dir: Fischel Foundation, Harry and Jane

Stepelton, Virlee Stacy, trust: Stacy Foundation, Festus

Stephan, Edmund Anton, chmn, dir: Fry Foundation, Lloyd A.; secy: Schmitt Foundation, Arthur J.

Stephan, John S., vp, trust: BankAmerica Foundation

Stephan, Richard C., vp, contr: Dial Corporation Fund

Stephanoff, Katherine, trust: Trexler Trust, Harry C.

Stephans, Joan R., trust: Dynamet Foundation

Stephans, Peter N., pres: Dynamet, Inc.; pres, trust: Dynamet Foundation

Stephans, William W. T., vp, treas: Scott and Fetzer Foundation

Stephen, J. W., mem charitable comm: Foster Charitable Trust, L.B.

Stephenitch, Mark, dir, treas: H. B. B. Foundation

Stephens, Ann C., vp, dir: Compton Foundation

Stephens, D.R., chmn, ceo: Bank of San Francisco Co.

Stephens, Dianne E., secy, trust: First Interstate Bank of Arizona Charitable Foundation

Stephens, E. Barrie, chmn, ceo: Ranco, Inc.; chmn, pres: Robertshaw Controls Co.

Stephens, Elton B., chmn, dir: Ebsco Industries

Stephens, George Edward, Jr., secy: G.P.G. Foundation

Stephens, J. T., chmn exec comm, pres, ceo, dir: Ebsco Industries

Stephens, Juanita, trust: Stephens Foundation Trust

Stephens, Kathryn Fong, dir: True North Foundation

Stephens, Louis C., Jr., vchmn, trust: Duke Endowment

Stephens, Martha Roby, secy, trust: Cowles Charitable Trust

Stephens, Norval B., Jr., trust: Delta Tau Delta Educational Fund

Stephens, Richard T., pres, coo: Delaware North Cos.

Stephens, W.E., Jr., trust, chmn: Stephens Foundation Trust

Stephens, William Thomas, chmn, pres, ceo, dir: Manville Corp.; trust: Manville Fund

Stephenson, Ann, secy: Feild Co-Operative Association

Stephenson, Bryan W., pres, ceo: Independent Bankshares

Stephenson, Donald G., mgr: Porter Testamentary Trust, James Hyde

Stephenson, H. Howard, chmn: Bancorp Hawaii; pres, dir: Bancorp Hawaii Charitable Foundation

Stephenson, John D., trust: Heisey Foundation

Stephenson, John W., exec dir: Campbell Foundation, J. Bulow

Stephenson, Joseph E., III, pres, ceo, dir: Shenandoah Life Insurance Co.

Stephenson, Louise S., secy: Fletcher Foundation, A. J.

Stephenson, Thomas E., cfo, asst secy: Forest Lawn Foundation

Stephenson, William V., pres, coo, dir: First Brands Corp.

Sterlacci, Michael V., trust: WSP&R Charitable Trust Fund

Sterling, Helen N., secy, treas, trust: Rockwell Fund

Sterling, Mary K., secy: Phelps Dodge Foundation

Sterling, Sonja J., secy: Deere Foundation, John

Stern, Alfred R., dir: Commonwealth Fund

Stern, Amram, dir: Stern Family Foundation, Harry

Stern, Beatrice, trust: Ogden Foundation, Ralph E.

Stern, Bernard, pres, treas, trust: Lowe Foundation, Joe and Emily

Stern, Bernice, pres: Stern Foundation, Bernice and Milton

Stern, Edwin H., III, trust: de Hirsch Fund, Baron

Stern, Elisabeth Ellen, trust: Ogden Foundation, Ralph E.

Stern, Erica, dir: Stern Foundation, Marjorie and Michael

Stern, Fritz R., trust: German Marshall Fund of the United States

Stern, Gerald M., trust: Hammer United World College Trust, Armand

Stern, Ghity, dir: Stern Foundation, Max

Stern, H. Peter, pres, trust: Ogden Foundation, Ralph E.

Stern, Harry, pres: Stern Family Foundation, Harry

Stern, I. Jerome, exec vp, dir: Feinstein Foundation, Myer and Rosaline; secy, dir: Stern Family Foundation, Harry

Stern, Irene, pres: Stern Foundation, Gustav and Irene

Stern, Jean L., trust: Blum Foundation, Edna F.; trust: Kern Foundation, Ilma

Stern, John Peter, trust: Ogden Foundation, Ralph E.

Stern, Joseph A., pres, treas: Bionetics Corp.; pres: Bionetics Corp. Charitable Trust

Stern, Judi H., vp: Stone Family Foundation, Norman H.

Stern, Lawrence, cfo: Goldrich Family Foundation

Stern, Leonard Norman, owner, chmn, ceo: Hartz Mountain Corp.; pres, dir:

Stern Foundation, Leonard N.; pres, dir: Stern Foundation, Max

Stern, Marjorie, secy: Stern Foundation, Marjorie and Michael

Stern, Mark, dir: Stern Foundation, Marjorie and Michael

Stern, Michael, pres, treas: Stern Foundation, Marjorie and Michael

Stern, Philip M., pres, treas, dir: Stern Family Fund

Stern, Richard J., trust: Stern Foundation for the Arts, Richard J.

Stern, Robert A., trust: Blum Foundation, Edna F.; trust: Kern Foundation, Ilma

Stern, Robert A.A., dir: Skidmore, Owings & Merrill Foundation

Stern, Roy, treas: Stern Foundation, Gustav and Irene

Stern, Sidney J., Jr., secy, dir: Sternberger Foundation, Sigmund

Stern, Steven, vp: Stern Foundation, Gustav and Irene

Stern, Zelda, dir: Stern Family Foundation, Harry

Sterne, Dorothy Elder, dir: Sterne-Elder Memorial Trust

Sterne, Edwin L., mgr: Dodson Foundation, James Glenwell and Clara May

Sterner, Frank M., vchmn, ceo: Wagner Manufacturing Co., E. R.

Stetson, E. William, III, mem bd govs: Richardson Foundation, Smith

Stetson, Grace R., trust: Richardson Fund, Grace

Stetson, John Charles, trust: Kemper Foundation, James S.

Stettinius, Wallace, vp, trust: Gray Foundation, Garland

Steurer, Joseph F., chmn, ceo: JOFCo., Inc.; pres, dir: Jasper Office Furniture Foundation

Stevens, Bill, mgr, marketing & media: Teac America, Inc.

Stevens, Clara R., secy: Brand Foundation, C. Harold and Constance

Stevens, E.W. Dann, secy: Goodyear Foundation, Josephine

Stevens, Edith, Quaker Hill Foundation

Stevens, Elizabeth, dir, vp: Deseranno Educational Foundation

Stevens, George L., trust: Kaul Foundation Trust, Hugh

Stevens, John P., III, trust: Quaker Hill Foundation

Stevens, L. G., dir: La-Z-Boy Foundation

Stevens, Lee, vp, dir: Lastfogel Foundation, Abe and Frances

Stevens, Mike, dir: Medtronic Foundation

Stevens, Paul L., chmn, dir: Mankato Citizens Telephone Co.

Stevens, Philip A., vp, trust: National Machinery Foundation

Stevens, Ray, selection comm: Gordy Family Educational Trust Fund, George E.

Stevens, Raymond D., Jr., chmn: Pratt & Lambert, Inc.

Stevens, Richard L., secy, treas, dir: Wyman-Gordon Foundation

Stevens, Robert, owner: Lyons Physician's Supply Co.

Stevens, Robert E., trust: Fox Foundation Trust, Jacob L. and Lewis

Stevens, Robert L., pres, dir: Bryn Mawr Trust Co.

Stevens, Robert T., Jr., trust: Fanwood Foundation

Stevens, Rowland, Jr., trust: Chapman Charitable Corporation, Howard and Bess

Stevens, Whitney, mgr, trust: Fanwood Foundation

Stevenson, A. Robert, chmn (contributions comm): Kmart Corp.

Stevenson, Brent M., secy, trust: Huntsman Foundation, Jon and Karen

Stevenson, J. A., chmn: Johnson Matthey Investments

Stevenson, John Reese, trust: Mellon Foundation, Andrew W.

Stevenson, Lloyd C., trust: Mellinger Educational Foundation, Edward Arthur

Stevenson, Ruth Carter, pres, dir: Carter Foundation, Amon G.

Stevenson, T.J., Jr., vp, treas: Weininger Foundation, Richard and Gertrude

Steward, Faye H., treas, dir: Bohemia Foundation

Steward, H. Leighton, chmn, coo, dir: Louisiana Land & Exploration Co.; pres, dir: Louisiana Land & Exploration Co. Foundation

Steward, L. L., pres, dir: Bohemia Foundation

Stewart, C. Jim, II, chmn, dir: Stewart & Stevenson Services

Stewart, Charles, sr vp: First Commercial Bank N.A.

Stewart, Charles J., dir: Durham Merchants Association Charitable Foundation

Stewart, Cheryl, trust: UNUM Charitable Foundation

Stewart, D. Riley, pres: Brice Building Co., Inc.

Stewart, Donald M., dir: New York Times Co. Foundation

Stewart, Donnell B., vchmn: Shaw Charitable Trust, Mary Elizabeth Dee; vchmn: Stewart Educational Foundation, Donnell B. and Elizabeth Dee Shaw

Stewart, Elizabeth D.S., chmn: Shaw Charitable Trust, Mary Elizabeth Dee; chmn: Stewart Educational Foundation, Donnell B. and Elizabeth Dee Shaw

Stewart, Elizabeth T., dir: Glenn Foundation, Carrie C. & Lena V.

Stewart, J., trust: Davis Hospital Foundation

Stewart, J. B., dir: St. Faith's House Foundation

Stewart, J. Benjamin, MD, mem adv bd: Burke Foundation, Thomas C.

Stewart, J. Benton, trust: Jones Intercable Tampa Trust

Stewart, James C., trust, vp, treas: Curran Foundation

Stewart, James G., dir: CIGNA Foundation

Stewart, John H., treas: IBM South Africa Projects Fund

Stewart, John R., trust: Simpson Foundation

Stewart, Joseph M., trust: Kellogg Co. Twenty-Five Year Employees' Fund

Stewart, Mark, sr vp, cfo: Brooke Group Ltd.

Stewart, Max, Jr., trust: Jones Foundation, Walter S. and Evan C.

Stewart, Peter, vp, trust: Mack Foundation, J. S.

Stewart, Ralph E., pres: Abex Inc.

Stewart, Robert H., III, dir: Collins Foundation, Carr P.

Stewart, S. Jay, pres, coo, dir: Morton International

Stewart, Vivien, program chmn (education & development of youth): Carnegie Corporation of New York

Stewart, William H., sr vp admin: California & Hawaiian Sugar Co.; trust: C & H Charitable Trust

Stewart, William R., legal counsel: Austin Memorial Foundation

Stickney, William P., trust: Massachusetts Charitable Mechanics Association

Stiefler, Jeffrey E., pres, ceo: IDS Financial Services

Stieren, Arthur T., trust: Stieren Foundation, Arthur T. and Jane J.

Stieren, Jane J., trust: Stieren Foundation, Arthur T. and Jane J.

Stierwalt, Max E., Frohman Foundation, Sidney

Stiles, Meredith N., Jr., vp, dir: Hopkins Foundation, Josephine Lawrence

Stiles, Thomas E., cfo: Penn Mutual Life Insurance Co.

Stilley, John, dir, treas: Raymond Educational Foundation

Stillman, Ellen, trust: Urann Foundation

Stillwell, Gerald A., treas: Gear Motions Foundation

Stimson, Bruce, cfo: Teichert Foundation

Stine, Charles E., pres, dir: Montgomery Street Foundation

Stine, Jon C., trust: Leu Foundation, Harry P.

Stine, Joseph P., trust: Leu Foundation, Harry P.

Stine, Lynn B., vp, dir: Bere Foundation

Stine, Thomas Henry, trust: Thanksgiving Foundation

Stinnette, Joe L., dir: Fireman's Fund Foundation

Stinson, George A., emeritus trust: Benedum Foundation, Claude Worthington

Stinson, Kenneth E., vp, dir: Kiewit Sons, Peter

Stiritz, William Paul, chmn, ceo, pres, dir: Ralston Purina Co.

Stirn, Cara S., vp, trust: Smith Foundation, Kelvin and Eleanor

Stirn, Howard F., trust: Smith 1980 Charitable Trust, Kelvin

Stiska, John C., pres, dir: Intermark, Inc.

Stith, David L., chmn, ceo: Bank One, Texas-Houston Office

Stitle, S. A., dir: Lilly & Co. Foundation, Eli

Stitzer, Phyllis J., trust, pres: Jones Fund, Blanche and George

Stivers, William Charles, treas, trust: Weyerhaeuser Co. Foundation

Stock, Anne, vp (pub rels): Bloomingdale's

Stock, John, dir: Valley Foundation, Wayne and Gladys

Stock, Otto F., secy: Sherman-Standard Register Foundation

Stock, Richard, contr: Mobil Foundation

Stocker, Beth K., pres, trust: Stocker Foundation

Stocker, Kurt, pres: Continental Bank Foundation

Stockham, Charles E., trust: Stockham Foundation, William H. & Kate F.

Stockham, Herbert C., chmn: Stockham Valves & Fittings; chmn, trust: Stockham Foundation, William H. & Kate F.

Stockham, Kate, trust: Stockham Foundation, William H. & Kate F.

Stockham, Richard J., Jr., trust: Stockham Foundation, William H. & Kate F.

Stockholm, Charles M., treas: Gerbode Foundation, Wallace Alexander

Stockholm, Maryanna G., chmn, pres: Gerbode Foundation, Wallace Alexander

Stockly, Doris Silliman, trust: Borkee Hagley Foundation

Stockton, Cleveland J., vp, dir: Rogers Foundation, Mary Stuart

Stockton, Robert G., dir: Brenner Foundation

Stoddard, Helen E., vchmn, trust: Stoddard Charitable Trust

Stoddard, James A., exec dir: Hubbard Foundation, R. Dee and Joan Dale

Stoddard, Richard E., chmn, ceo, dir: Kaiser Steel Resources

Stoddard, William S., dir: Berry Foundation, Lowell

Stoeckle, Marilyn, secy: Bardes Foundation

Stoel, Thomas B., secy: Collins Foundation; trust: Tucker Charitable Trust, Rose E.; secy, dir: Wessinger Foundation

Stofer, Wolfgang, exec vp (fin): BMW of North America, Inc.

Stokar, Suzanne, dir: Lupin Foundation

Stoke, Wesley W., trust: Chapman Foundation, William H.

Stokely, Kay H., exec vp, dir: Stokely, Jr. Foundation, William B.

Stokely, William B., III, pres, dir: Stokely, Jr. Foundation, William B.

Stokely, William B., IV, dir: Stokely, Jr. Foundation, William B.

Stokes, Burt, dir: General Railway Signal Foundation

Stokes, Gerald L., trust: Town Creek Foundation

Stokes, Jerome W. D., dir: Public Welfare Foundation

Stokes, Patricia, treas: Drueding Foundation

Stokes, Spencer, pres: Chatam Inc.

Stokes, Thomas C., exec dir, secy: Gates Foundation

Stoll, Reiner G., dir: Dreyfus Foundation, Camille and Henry

Stollenwerk, Robert T., secy, treas: Ladish Family Foundation, Herman W.; secy, dir: Ladish Malting Co. Foundation

Stollings, Juanita, secy, treas: Robinson Mountain Fund, E. O.

Stoltzman, Kent, vp gen aff: Kajima International, Inc.

Stolz, Otto, secy, trust: Van Andel Foundation, Jay and Betty

Stolz, Paul H., pres: LIN Broadcasting Corp.

Stone, Alan, pres, don: Stone Family Foundation, Norman H.

Stone, Anne, trust: KPMG Peat Marwick Foundation

Stone, Anne L., dir: Rollins Luetkemeyer Charitable Foundation

Stone, Barbara, dir, vp: Stone Foundation, W. Clement and Jessie V.

Stone, Barbara West, trust: Stone Foundation, W. Clement and Jessie V.

Stone, Charles Lynn, Jr., trust, pres: Stone Foundation

Stone, Donald, vchmn, dir: New York Stock Exchange; dir: New York Stock Exchange Foundation

Stone, Doris Zemurray, pres: Zemurray Foundation

Stone, Edward Eldredge, trust, vp: Stone Foundation

Stone, Elmer L., treas: Pacific Western Foundation

Stone, George E., chmn: Jackson Mills

Stone, Guy Arnold, trust: Fusenot Charity Foundation, Georges and Germaine

Stone, Harry, MD, adm: Hurlbut Memorial Fund, Orion L. and Emma S.

Stone, Holly, secy: Gudelsky Family Foundation, Homer and Martha

Stone, Ida F., dir, vp: Stone Family Foundation, Norman H.

Stone, Ira N., vp, secy: Stone Family Foundation, Norman H.

Stone, Irving I., fdr/chmn, chmn exec comm, dir: American Greetings Corp.; vp, off: American Greetings Corp. Foundation; pres: Sapirstein-Stone-Weiss Foundation

Stone, Jacques J., secy, treas: Tuch Foundation, Michael

Stone, James D., dir: Rollins Luetkemeyer Charitable Foundation

Stone, James Howard, vp: Stone Family Foundation, Jerome H.

Stone, Jerome H., pres: Stone Family Foundation, Jerome H.

Stone, Jerome N., vp, secy, treas: Stone Foundation

Stone, Jerry S., cfo: Perry Drug Stores; trust: Perry Drug Stores Charitable Foundation

Stone, Jessie V., dir, vp: Stone Foundation, W. Clement and Jessie V.

Stone, John, vp, finance: Orbit Valve Co.

Stone, John K. P., III, secy, treas, dir: Filene Foundation, Lincoln and Therese

Stone, Joshua J., trust: Levy Foundation, Edward C.

Stone, Marvin N., dir: Stone Foundation

Stone, Michael, trust: Stone Foundation, W. Clement and Jessie V.

Stone, Morris S., vchmn: American Greetings Corp.

Stone, Norah Sharp, trust: Stone Foundation, W. Clement and Jessie V.

Stone, Norman J., dir: Berlin Charitable Fund, Irving

Stone, Patricia H., trust: Fusenot Charity Foundation, Georges and Germaine

Stone, Robert G., dir: Exchange Bank Foundation

Stone, Robert S., vp: IBM South Africa Projects Fund

Stone, Roger D., dir: Cintas Foundation; trust: Erpf Fund, Armand G.

Stone, Roger Warren, chmn, ceo, dir: Stone Container Corp.; pres: Stone Foundation; chmn, ceo, dir: Stone Forest Industries

Stone, Ronald N., cfo: Pioneer Electronics (USA) Inc.

Stone, Samuel Z., vp, dir: Zemurray Foundation

Stone, Sara S., trust: Stone Foundation

Stone, Stephen A., pres, trust: Stone Charitable Foundation

Stone, Steven, dir, vp, secy, treas: Stone Foundation, W. Clement and Jessie V.

Stone, Sue Smart, mem: Smart Family Foundation

Stone, Thomas D., dir: Delta Air Lines Foundation

Stone, Viveca Ann, trust: Fusenot Charity Foundation, Georges and Germaine

Stone, W. O., Jr., vp, dir: Fieldcrest Foundation

Stone, Warren R., ceo: Addison-Wesley Publishing Co.

Stone, William Clement, dir, chmn: Stone Foundation, W. Clement and Jessie V.

Stone-Cipher, Harry C., chmn, pres, ceo, dir: Sundstrand Corp.

Stonecipher, David, pres: Life Insurance Co. of Georgia

Stoneman, Miriam H., pres: Stoneman Charitable Foundation, Anne and David

Stoner, Debra A., asst treas: O'Neill Foundation, William J. and Dorothy K.

Stoner, Richard Burkett, pres, dir: Irwin-Sweeney- Miller Foundation

Stoner, Robert F., sr vp, cfo: Kelly Services

Stonier, Daryle L., vchmn: Growmark, Inc.

Stoochton, V., dir: SmithKline Beecham Foundation

Stookey, John Hoyt, dir: Clark Foundation; chmn, ceo, pres, dir: Quantum Chemical Corp.

Stopak, Carolyn, vp, secy, dir: Wasserman Foundation, George

Stophal, Leslie, vp: Connecticut Natural Gas Corp.

Stopher, Joseph E., pres, trust: Gheens Foundation

Stoppelmoor, Wayne H., chmn, pres, ceo, dir: Interstate Power Co.

Storer, James, secy, dir: Storer Foundation, George B.

Storer, Peter, pres, treas, dir: Storer Foundation, George B.

Storey, Venna, comm: Shaw Charitable Trust, Mary Elizabeth Dee

Storms, John W., trust: Terry Foundation

Storr, Hans George, exec vp, cfo: Philip Morris Cos.

Storrs, Norman B., pres, ceo: Nashua Trust Co.; vchmn, dir: Nashua Trust Co. Foundation

Story, Herbert B., pres: Bridwell Foundation, J. S.; dir: Perkins Foundation, Joe and Lois

Story, Robert P., Jr., sr vp, cfo: Courier Corp.

Storz, Robert Herman, trust: Storz Foundation, Robert Herman

Stotsenberg, Edward G., pres, ceo, dir: Pickford Foundation, Mary

Stott, Benjamin W., trust: Stott Foundation, Louis L.

Stott, Donald B., dir, secy, treas: Stott Foundation, Robert L.

Stott, Edward Barrington, trust: Stott Foundation, Louis L.

Stott, Jonathan D., trust: Stott Foundation, Louis L.

Stott, Robert L., Jr., dir, pres: Stott Foundation, Robert L.

Stottlemyer, Charles E., mem admin comm: Selby and Marie Selby Foundation, William G.

Stout, Charles I., dir, pres: Wilson Sanitarium for Children of Baltimore City, Thomas

Stout, Frank D., trust: Kemper Educational and Charitable Fund

Stout, Joan K., pres, treas: Hugoton Foundation

Stout, Joan M., secy, dir: Hugoton Foundation

Stout, John B., pres: Dixie-Portland Flour Mills

Stout, Michael W., pres: Mapplethorpe Foundation, Robert

Stout, William J., dir: Ayres Foundation, Inc.

Stover, Harry M., chmn, ceo: Green Industries, A. P.

Stover, James Robert, chmn, ceo, dir: Eaton Corp.

Stover, Matthew J., chmn contributions comm: NYNEX Corp.

Stover, William R., chmn: Old Republic International Corp.

Stowe, Daniel Harding, pres: Stowe, Jr. Foundation, Robert Lee

Stowe, Daniel J., chmn, pres: R. L. Stowe Mills Inc.

Stowe, David H., pres, coo, dir: Deere & Co.; dir: Deere Foundation, John

Stowe, Nonni, vp (corp aff): Life Insurance Co. of Georgia

Stowe, Richmond H., vp: Stowe, Jr. Foundation, Robert Lee

Stowe, Robert Lee, III, vp: Stowe, Jr. Foundation, Robert Lee

Stowers, James E., Jr., dir, pres: Stowers Foundation

Stowers, James E. III, Jr., dir, secy: Stowers Foundation

Stowers, Virginia G., Jr., dir, treas: Stowers Foundation

Strader, Timothy L., treas, dir: Irvine Health Foundation

Strafford, William, cfo: Sealaska Corp.

Strahan, Kathleen Haggerty, trust: Haggerty Foundation

Strahm, E. R., secy: Whiteman Foundation, Edna Rider

Straight, George, trust: Kaiser Family Foundation, Henry J.

Strait, Rex, vp: Van Buren Foundation

Straltor, George A., asst treas: Ford Fund, Benson and Edith; asst treas: Ford Fund, Eleanor and Edsel; asst treas: Ford Fund, Walter and Josephine; asst treas: Ford Fund, William and Martha

Strake, George W., Jr., pres, treas: Strake Foundation

Stranahan, Abbot, chmn: Needmor Fund

Stranahan, Ann, dir: Needmor Fund

Stranahan, Dinny, trust: Stranahan Foundation

Stranahan, Duane, trust: Stranahan Foundation

Stranahan, Duane, Jr., trust: Stranahan Foundation

Stranahan, Mark, trust: Stranahan Foundation

Stranahan, Mary C., dir: Needmor Fund

Stranahan, Mescal, trust: Stranahan Foundation

Stranahan, Molly L., dir: Needmor Fund

Stranahan, Robert A., Jr., trust: Stranahan Foundation

Stranahan, Sarah, dir: Needmor Fund

Stranahan, Stephen, dir: Needmor Fund

Strandjord, M. Jeannie, dir: Sprint Foundation

Strasser, F. Lee, secy, trust: Chambers Memorial, James B.

Strassler, David H., pres: Barrington Foundation

Strassler, Robert B., secy, treas: Barrington Foundation

Strassler, Stephen, pres: Reviva Labs

Straton, Bob, sr vp: Colonial Life & Accident Insurance Co.

Stratton, Frederick Prescott, Jr., chmn, pres, ceo, dir: Briggs & Stratton Corp.; pres, dir: Briggs & Stratton Corp. Foundation

Stratton, James W., trust: Foerderer Foundation, Percival E. and Ethel Brown

Straub, Chester John, vp, trust: Collins Foundation, Joseph

Straub, Jennifer, dir: Wieboldt Foundation

Straub, John, trust: Lichtenstein Foundation, David B.

Straube, Joey Holter, dir: Pendergast-Weyer Foundation

Straughn, A. Pickney, secy, trust: Wardlaw Fund, Gertrude and William C.

Straughn, Edward L., pres: Freeport Brick Co.

Straus, Betty B., vp, trust: Straus Foundation, Martha Washington Straus and Harry H.

Straus, Harry H., III, trust: Straus Foundation, Martha Washington Straus and Harry H.

Straus, Lynn G., vp, treas, trust: Straus Foundation, Philip A. and Lynn

Straus, Oscar S., II, pres, dir: Guggenheim Foundation, Daniel and Florence

Straus, Oscar S., III, vp, dir: Guggenheim Foundation, Daniel and Florence

Straus, Philip A., pres, trust: Straus Foundation, Philip A. and Lynn

Straus, Roger W., Jr., dir: Guggenheim Foundation, Harry Frank; trust emeritus: Guggenheim Memorial Foundation, John Simon

Strauss, Barbara Bachmann, vp, dir: Bachmann Foundation

Strauss, Benjamin, trust: Strauss Foundation

Strauss, Diana, vp, trust: Lowe Foundation

Strauss, Donald A., vp, secy, dir: Beckman Foundation, Arnold and Mabel

Strauss, Joseph, Jr., chmn: Strouse, Greenberg & Co.; dir: Strouse, Greenberg & Co. Charitable Fund

Strauss, Peter, vp, asst treas, dir: Hertz Foundation, Fannie and John

Strauss, Robert Perry, trust: Strauss Foundation

Strauss, Robert Schwarz, dir: Hawn Foundation

Strauss, Thomas W., treas, dir: Bachmann Foundation

Strauss, William D., cfo: American Stock Exchange

Strausse, Donald, trust: Wahlert Foundation

Strawbridge, Francis R., III, chmn: Strawbridge & Clothier

Strawbridge, George, Jr., pres, sec: Strawbridge Foundation of Pennsylvania I, Margaret Dorrance

Strawbridge, Herbert Edward, pres, treas, trust: Kulas Foundation; pres, treas, secy, trust: Murphy Foundation, John P.

Strawbridge, Marie S., vp, trust: Murphy Foundation, John P.

Strawbridge, Nina S., vp, secy: Strawbridge Foundation of Pennsylvania I, Margaret Dorrance

Strawbridge, Peter S., pres: Strawbridge & Clothier

Strawbridge, Steven L., vp, treas, secy: Strawbridge & Clothier

Strawderman, Dennis L., mgr, secy, dir: Bucyrus-Erie Foundation

Strawn, Kathryn, adm off: Mead Corp. Foundation

Strayer, Robert L., vp, dir: Smith Foundation

Strecker, A. M., vp, dir: Oklahoma Gas & Electric Co. Foundation

Streep, Mary B. Simon, dir: Simon Foundation, William E. and Carol G.

Street, Alice Ann, pres, dir: Bertha Foundation

Street, E. Bruce, dir: Bertha Foundation

Street, Gordon P., Jr., chmn, pres: North American Royalties

Street, M. Boyd, dir: Bertha Foundation

Streetcar, Charles M., trust: Anderson Foundation

Strehle, Diane T., trust: Chubb Foundation

Streiff, David R., vp: Kingsley Foundation, Lewis A.

Stribling, Jera G., exec dir: Alabama Power Foundation

Strichartz, Gary, dir: Grass Foundation

Stricker, Jerome A., exec vp, cfo: Gradison & Co.

Strickland, Carol A., adm: United States Trust Co. of New York Foundation

Strickland, D. Gordon, sr vp (fin), cfo: Kerr Glass Manufacturing Corp.

Strickland, Frances, dir: Citizens Union Bank Foundation

Strickland, R. M., Jr., trust: Rinker, Sr. Foundation, M. E.

Strickland, Robert, mem distribution comm: English Memorial Fund, Florence C. and H. L.; mem distribution

comm: Marshall Trust in Memory of Sanders McDaniel, Harriet McDaniel; bd mem: Pitts Foundation, William H. and Lula E.

Strickland, Robert L., chmn: Lowe's Cos.; vp: Lowe's Charitable & Educational Foundation

Stricklin, Mary A., dir: Hadson Foundation

Strigl, Dennis F., vp (oper), coo, dir: New Jersey Bell Telephone Company

Stringer, N. Martin, secy, trust: Kerr Foundation, Robert S. and Grayce B.

Stroble, Francis Anthony, chmn, dir: Monsanto Fund

Stroemel, Amelia R., treas, secy, dir: GSC Enterprises Foundation

Stroh, Peter Wetherill, trust: McGregor Fund; chmn, ceo: Stroh Brewery Co.

Strohm, Thomas G., exec vp (planning & corp affs): Meridian Bancorp

Strohmeier, Barbara, vp: Bennett Scholarship Fund, Margaret A. and Lawrence J.

Stromberg, C.W., comm: Shaw Charitable Trust, Mary Elizabeth Dee

Strome, Stephen, pres, ceo, dir: Handleman Co.; pres: Handleman Charitable Foundation

Strome, William, secy: Pittsburgh National Bank Foundation

Strong, C. Peter, dir: Strong Foundation, Hattie M.

Strong, George V., Jr., dir, secy: Widgeon Foundation

Strong, Hanne E., pres: Manitou Foundation

Strong, Henry, dir: Post Foundation of D.C., Marjorie Merriweather; chmn, pres, dir: Strong Foundation, Hattie M.

Strong, Henry L., vp, dir: Strong Foundation, Hattie M.

Strong, John D., Jr., trust: Bernsen Foundation, Grace and Franklin

Strong, Mary S., trust: Fund for New Jersey

Strong, Maurice E., treas: Manitou Foundation

Stroock, Mark Edwin, II, vp, dir: Young & Rubicam Foundation

Strother, Jack W., trust: Commercial Bank Foundation

Strother, Jack W., Jr., trust: Commercial Bank Foundation

Stroud, Douglas A., vp, dir: Bertha Foundation

Stroud, Joan M., mgr: Stroud Foundation

Stroud, Morris W., mgr: Stroud Foundation

Stroud, R.R., dir: Cremer Foundation

Stroud, W. B. Dixon, mgr: Stroud Foundation

Stroup, Paul, mem bd adms: Van Every Foundation, Philip L.

Stroup, Paul A., dir: Lance Foundation

Stroup, Robert N., dir: Rosenthal Foundation, Ida and William

Stroup, Stanley Stephenson, sr vp, secy, gen coun: Norwest Corp.

Strouse, Jean, trust: Guggenheim Memorial Foundation, John Simon

Strubel, Ella, secy: Leo Burnett Co. Charitable Foundation

Strubel, Richard P., ceo, pres: Microdot, Inc.

Struble, Susan, secy, dir: Merchants Bank Foundation

Struble, Susan D., trust: General Educational Fund

Struchen, J Maurice, trust: Forest City Enterprises Charitable Foundation

Strudwick, Lewis C., trust: Warfield Memorial Fund, Anna Emory

Strumpf, Linda B., vp, chief investment off: Ford Foundation

Struthers, Harvey J., Jr., dir: St. Faith's House Foundation

Struttmann, Ken, grants coordinator: Archer-Daniels-Midland Foundation

Strutz, George A., Jr., pres, dir: Clopay Corp.

Strzelczyk, Frank A., secy, treas: Blaustein Foundation, Jacob and Hilda; secy, treas: Blaustein Foundation, Louis and Henrietta; secy, treas: Blaustein Foundation, Morton K. and Jane; secy, treas: Hirschhorn Foundation, David and Barbara B.; secy, treas: Rosenberg Foundation, Henry and Ruth Blaustein; secy, treas: Thalheimer Foundation, Alvin and Fanny Blaustein

Stuart, Alan L., dir, vp, secy: Stuart Foundation

Stuart, Carolyn A., dir: Stuart Foundation

Stuart, David K., pres, ceo, dir: Integra Bank/South

Stuart, James G., dir: Glenn Foundation, Carrie C. & Lena V.

Stuart, James M., Jr., dir: Stuart Foundation

Stuart, James M., Sr., pres, dir: Stuart Foundation

Stuart, John, mem loan comm: Lindsay Student Aid Fund, Franklin

Stuart, John T., mem: Florence Foundation

Stuart, Karen S., vp, secy: Halliburton Foundation

Stuart, Margrette M, pres: Stuart Foundation, Edward C.

Stuart, Nancy S., trust: Stuart Foundation, Edward C.

Stuart, Robert M., vchmn, trust: Community Coffee Co., Inc. Foundation

Stuart, Susan W., dir: Seneca Foods Foundation

Stuart, William H., trust: Stuart Foundation, Edward C.

Stuart, William H., Jr., vp: Stuart Foundation, Edward C.

Stubblefield, Nelson, trust: Cauthorn Charitable Trust, John and Mildred

Stuber, Fred M., ceo, pres: Brown & Sharpe Manufacturing Co.

Stubing, William C., pres, dir: Greenwall Foundation

Stuck, David T., chmn, treas: Fibre Converters; pres: Fibre Converters Foundation

Stuck, J.D., pres, gen mgr: Fibre Converters

Stuck, Vivian K., adm off: Dayton Hudson Foundation

Stuckemann, Herman Campbell, secy, trust: Rockwell Foundation

Stuckey, Julia A., Jr., dir: Smith Foundation, Julia and Albert

Stude, Anita, trust: Lowe Foundation

Stude, M. S., first vp, trust: Brown Foundation

Studebaker, Joel, trust: Sofia American Schools

Stuebe, D. C., pres, ceo: Auto Specialties Manufacturing Co.

Stuebe, David, pres: Diversified Industries, Inc.

Stuebe, Patricia D., asst secy: Bank of New York

Stuebgen, William J., treas: American President Companies Foundation

Stuecker, Phillip J., secy-treas: Thomas Foundation

Stuever, Fred Ray, asst secy: Ryder System Charitable Foundation

Stumpf, E. A., III, vp, asst treas: Wortham Foundation

Stupp, Erwin P., Jr., trust: Stupp Brothers Bridge & Iron Co. Foundation

Stupp, John P., Jr., trust: Stupp Brothers Bridge & Iron Co. Foundation

Stupp, Robert P., pres, ceo, dir: Stupp Brothers Bridge & Iron Co.; trust: Stupp Brothers Bridge & Iron Co. Foundation

Stupski, Lawrence J., vchmn, dir: Schwab & Co., Charles

Sturges, Robert, vp: Arison Foundation

Sturm, Glen M., vp, secy, dir: Jasper Table Co. Foundation

Sturm, Gregory W., vp, treas, dir: Jasper Table Co. Foundation; vp, treas, dir: Jasper Office Furniture Foundation

Sturm, Omer, pres, dir: Jasper Table Co. Foundation

Sturn, David, mem trust fund comm: Ingram Trust, Joe

Sturtevant, Robert, secy: Hay Foundation, John I.

Sturtley, Cynthia A., trust: Allyn Foundation

Suarez, Rocio, exec dir: Baker Trust, George F.

Subramaniam, Shivan Sivaswamy, pres: Allendale Mutual Insurance Co.; dir: Allendale Insurance Foundation

Sudderth, Nelson, trust: Lyndhurst Foundation

Sudderth, Robert J., Jr., secy, treas, trust: Benwood Foundation

Sudduth, Charlotte P., trust: Cove Charitable Trust

Sudmann, William, mem bd: GenCorp Foundation

Sudoff, Robert J., secy, treas, dir: Minster Machine Co. Foundation

Sue, Ed, vp: Shoong Foundation, Milton

Sugiura, Tatsuya, chmn: Mitsubishi Electric America; dir: Mitsubishi Electric America Foundation

Sugiyama, Genji, pres, ceo, dir: Yamaichi International (America) Inc.

Sullivan, Antony T., secy, program off, trust: Earhart Foundation

Sullivan, Barbara D., trust: Robinson Fund, Maurice R.

Sullivan, Barry F., cfo: Alfa-Laval, Inc.

Sullivan, Benjamin J., chmn, ceo, dir: Crane & Co.

Sullivan, Cathlin E., asst treas, asst secy: Stokely, Jr. Foundation, William B.

Sullivan, Charles A., chmn, pres, ceo: Interstate Brands Corp.

Sullivan, D. Harold, trust: Demoulas Foundation

Sullivan, D.J., treas: Dennison Foundation

Sullivan, Dennis W., exec vp, coo: Parker-Hannifin Corp.

Sullivan, Donald M., pres, ceo, dir: MTS Systems Corp.

Sullivan, Dorothy L., secy: Greater Lansing Foundation

Sullivan, Eleanor T., dir: Krause Foundation, Charles A.

Sullivan, Elizabeth C., program off: Kresge Foundation

Sullivan, G. Craig, chmn, ceo, dir: Clorox Co.

Sullivan, James N., vchmn, dir: Chevron Corp.

Sullivan, John M., pres, ceo: Prince Manufacturing, Inc.

Sullivan, Joseph T., sr vp: CIBA-GEIGY Corp.

Sullivan, Kerry H., trust off: Balfour Foundation, L. G.

Sullivan, Kevin I., vp: Children's Foundation of Erie County

Sullivan, Kevin J., exec vp, cfo: PriMerit F.S.B.

Sullivan, Laura, vp, secy, dir: State Farm Cos. Foundation

Sullivan, Margaret B., secy: Teagle Foundation

Sullivan, Mary P., mem: Davenport Foundation, M. E.

Sullivan, Michael D., pres, ceo, dir: Merry-Go-Round Enterprises, Inc.

Sullivan, Michael P., pres, ceo: International Dairy Queen, Inc.

Sullivan, Paul B., secy, exec dir: Sheldon Foundation, Ralph C.

Sullivan, Pauline Gill, pres: Gill Foundation, Pauline Allen

Sullivan, Richard J., pres, trust: Fund for New Jersey

Sullivan, Richard T., dir: McBride Charitable Foundation, Joseph & Elsie

Sullivan, Robert, exec vp, general mgr: Eastern Fine Paper, Inc.

Sullivan, Robert E., vp, trust: Harris Foundation

Sullivan, Sallie P., trust: Perkins Charitable Foundation

Sullivan, T. Dennis, fin vp: Mellon Foundation, Andrew W.

Sullivan, Thomas C., chmn, ceo: RPM, Inc.

Sullivan, Thomas J., vp, dir: McGraw-Hill Foundation

Sullivan, Timothy, contr: Mazda Foundation (USA), Inc.

Sullivan, W.T., asst vp, dir: Ogle Foundation, Paul

Sullivan, Walter F., pres, dir: Stone & Webster, Inc.

Sullivan, Walter Francis, trust: McMahon Charitable Trust Fund, Father John J.

Sullivan, Walter H., Jr., trust: Hume Foundation, Jaquelin

Sullivan, William J., trust: Connecticut Mutual Life Foundation; trust: Dell Foundation, Hazel

Sultana, Joan, asst secy, asst treas: DeRoy Testamentary Foundation

Sulzberger, Arthur Ochs, Jr., chmn, ceo, dir: New York Times Co.

Sulzberger, Arthur Ochs, Sr., chmn, ceo: New York Times Co.; chmn, dir: New York Times Co. Foundation; vp,

secy, treas, dir: Sulzberger Foundation

Sulzberger, Judith P., dir: New York Times Co. Foundation; vp, dir: Sulzberger Foundation

Sulzer, Joseph P., trust: Massie Trust, David Meade

Sumansky, John, pres: Toshiba America Foundation

Sumikawa, Kunio, dir: Toshiba America Foundation

Summerall, Robert, Jr., dir, vp, treas: Morgan Foundation, Louie R. and Gertrude

Summerford, R. Michael, vp, cfo: First Mississippi Corp. Foundation

Summers, Anita Arrow, dir: Penn Foundation, William

Summers, Catherine C., trust: Cooke Foundation

Summers, Everett H., vp, asst secy: Bass Corporation, Perry and Nancy Lee

Summers, Stuart G., asst secy, trust: Ohio National Foundation

Summers, William B., Jr., pres: McDonald & Co. Securities

Summey, Mark L., dir: Stonecutter Foundation

Sumner, Sally, coordinator: First Bank System Foundation

Sump, Carl H., dir, secy: Plankenhorn Foundation, Harry

Sun, Alice Yu, dir: China Times Cultural Foundation

Sunderland, James P., dir: Francis Families Foundation; chmn, dir: Loose Trust, Carrie J.; chmn, trust: Loose Trust, Harry Wilson; vp, secy, dir: Sunderland Foundation, Lester T.

Sunderland, Paul, pres, trust: Sunderland Foundation, Lester T.

Sunderland, Robert, vp, treas, dir: Sunderland Foundation, Lester T.

Sunderwirth, Alfred, trust: Staley Foundation, Thomas F.

Sundet, Leland N., pres: Sundet Foundation

Sundet, Louise C., vp: Sundet Foundation

Sundet, Scott A., secy, treas: Sundet Foundation

Sunyer, Xavier P., exec dir: Weight Watchers Foundation

Supplee, Henderson, III, pres, trust: Presser Foundation

Surdam, Robert M., treas, trust: McGregor Fund; trust: Shelden Fund, Elizabeth, Allan and Warren; treas, trust: Wilson Fund, Matilda R.

Surface, Majorie L., asst secy: Noyes, Jr. Memorial Foundation, Nicholas H.

Surfus, Donald, secy, dir: Formrite Foundation

Surrey, Mary P., vp, dir: Dreyfus Foundation, Max and Victoria

Suskind, Ralph, dir: Stern Foundation, Gustav and Irene

Susman, Barbara G., trust: Goldman Foundation, William

Sussman, Ralph M., dir: Ross Foundation, Arthur

Sutcliffe, James, coo: Jackson National Life Insurance Co.

Sutherland, Alfred E., Fay Charitable Fund, Aubert J.

Sutherland, Dean, secy, treas, dir: Cooper Wood Products Foundation

Sutherland, Edmund R., trust, treas: Holley Foundation

Sutherland, Robert G., chmn, dir: Everest & Jennings International

Sutter, Ken, trust: Reynolds & Reynolds Company Foundation

Sutter, William P., pres, trust: Markey Charitable Trust, Lucille P.

Suttle, Harold L., trust: Adams Memorial Fund, Emma J.

Suttles, William Maurrelle, trust: Franklin Foundation, John and Mary

Suttmiller, Tom, trust: Reynolds & Reynolds Company Foundation

Sutton, Altoon, treas: Sutton Foundation

Sutton, David, ceo: Bag Bazaar, Ltd.; trust: Sutton Family Foundation, Abraham, David and Solomon

Sutton, Donald C., trust: Van Wert County Foundation

Sutton, Elie S., pres: Sutton Foundation

Sutton, James A., chmn, pres, ceo, coo, dir: UGI Corp.

Sutton, Joseph S., vp: Sutton Foundation

Sutton, Kelso F., chmn: Little Brown & Co., Inc.

Sutton, Ralph S., secy: Sutton Foundation

Sutton, Solomon, trust: Sutton Family Foundation, Abraham, David and Solomon

Sutton, Thomas C., chmn, ceo, dir: Pacific Mutual Life Insurance Co.; chmn: Pacific Mutual Charitable Foundation

Suzuki, Chihoro, chmn: Oki America Inc.

Suzuki, Hiroshi, pres: Sanyo Fisher U.S.A. Corp.

Suzuki, Yuji, pres: Industrial Bank of Japan Trust Co.; pres, dir: IBJ Foundation

Svanholm, Bert Olof, pres: Asea Brown Boveri

Sveen, Donald E., pres, coo: Nuveen & Co., Inc., John

Svendsbye, LLoyd August, trust: Lutheran Brotherhood Foundation

Svendsen, Arthur, chmn, ceo: Standard Pacific Corp.

Svenson, Lennart, coo: Miami Corp.

Svigals, Philip, dir: Clark Foundation, Robert Sterling

Svitek, John, vp, dir: Slant/Fin Foundation

Svwyn, Mark A., dir: International Paper Co. Foundation

Swaim, Joseph Carter, Jr., secy, treas, trust: Frick Educational Commission, Henry C.

Swain, Kristin A., pres: Corning Incorporated Foundation

Swalm, Dave C., vp, trust: Swalm Foundation

Swalm, David C., chmn, pres, ceo: Texas Olefins Co.

Swalm, Jo Beth Camp, pres, trust: Swalm Foundation

Swaminathan, Monkombu S., trust: Ford Foundation

Swan, Frank, pres: Cadbury Beverages Inc.

Swan, Philip V., dir: Pasadena Area Residential Aid

Swan, William C., dir: Weber Charities Corp., Frederick E.

Swander, Ann P., trust: Switzer Foundation

Swaney, Robert E., Jr., vp, chief investment off: Mott Foundation, Charles Stewart

Swanson, Armour F., asst treas, dir: Siebert Lutheran Foundation

Swanson, David H., pres, ceo: Central Soya Co.

Swanson, David W., trust, secy, treas: Blackmer Foundation, Henry M.

Swanson, Donald F., chmn: C.P. Rail Systems

Swanson, E. William, dir: Hale Foundation, Crescent Porter

Swanson, Earl C., trust: Bayport Foundation; vp, secy, dir: Andersen Foundation; dir: Katzenberger Foundation; trust: Tozer Foundation

Swanson, Edward N., pres: Gilmer-Smith Foundation

Swanson, Gerock H., trust: Hamilton Foundation, Florence P.

Swanson, Glen E., don: Swanson Foundation

Swanson, Lynwood W., trust: Murdock Charitable Trust, M. J.

Swanson, Marilyn Kress, dir: Kress Foundation, George

Swanson, Neil H., Jr., secy, treas, trust: Baldwin Memorial Foundation, Fred

Swanson, Robert A., chmn: Genentech

Swanson, Robert M., Ph.D., dir: Group Health Foundation

Swanson, Rudolph, cfo: Cone-Blanchard Machine Co.

Swanson, Thomas A., dir: Fireman's Fund Foundation

Swanson, W. Charles, mgr: Swanson Family Foundation, Dr. W.C.

Swanson, W. Clark, Jr., trust: Hamilton Foundation, Florence P.

Swantak, Judy L., pres, trust, secy: Union Pacific Foundation

Swart, Richard D., pres: Ford Meter Box Foundation

Swartsel, Vernon, dir: Bush Charitable Foundation, Edyth

Swartwout, Shirley, secy, treas: Crestar Foundation

Swartz, Arnold, trust: Tobin Foundation

Swartz, Donald A., secy-treas: General Machine Works Foundation

Swartz, Glenn, treas: United States Borax & Chemical Corp.

Swartz, Robert, pres: Stry Foundation, Paul E.

Swasey, Hope Halsey, trust: Fuller Foundation

Sweasy, William G., chmn, pres: Red Wing Shoe Co.; pres: Red Wing Shoe Co. Foundation

Sweasy, William J., vp: Red Wing Shoe Co. Foundation

Sweat, Carol G., trust: Garvey Texas Foundation

Sweeney, Bonnie, asst treas: Swiss Bank Corp.

Sweeney, Robert H., mem trust fund comm: Ingram Trust, Joe

Sweeney, Thomas Joseph, Jr., trust: Pinkerton Foundation

Sweet, Adele Hall, pres: Schiff Foundation, Dorothy

Sweeterman, John W., trust: Graham Fund, Philip L.

Swenson, Eric P., vchmn: Norton & Co., W.W.

Swensrud, Steven B., trust: Swensrud Charitable Trust, Sidney A.

Swerc, D.C., secy, treas, dir: Federal Screw Works Foundation

Swetland, David Sears, trust: Sears Family Foundation

Swetland, David W., trust: Sears Family Foundation

Swetland, Polly M., Sears Family Foundation

Swift, David L., pres, ceo, dir: Acme-Cleveland Corp.

Swift, Hampden M., pres, treas, dir: Swift Co. Inc., John S.; trust: Swift Co. Inc. Charitable Trust, John S

Swift, Ray, trust: Swift Memorial Health Care Foundation

Swift, Sara Taylor, trust, don daughter: Taylor Foundation, Ruth and Vernon

Swift, William D., trust: Hugg Trust, Leoia W. and Charles H.

Swig, Melvin M., dir: Koret Foundation; trust: Swig Charity Foundation, Mae and Benjamin

Swig, Richard L., trust: Swig Charity Foundation, Mae and Benjamin; trust: Swig Foundation

Swigon, Catherine, exec dir: FMC Foundation

Swilley, Monroe F., Jr., vchmn, trust: Moore Memorial Foundation, James Starr

Swim, Gaylord K., trust: Swim Foundation, Arthur L.

Swim, Katherine M., trust: Swim Foundation, Arthur L.

Swim, Roger C., trust: Swim Foundation, Arthur L.

Swindells, William, Jr., chmn, ceo, dir: Willamette Industries, Inc.

Swindle, Patricia Warren, don, dir: Warren Foundation, William K.

Swinehart, Robert E., exec vp, coo: McGill Manufacturing Co.

Swinney, Jo Ann, dir (community affairs): Tenneco

Switzenbaum, Samuel, pres: Strouse, Greenberg & Co.

Switzer, Fred E., trust: Switzer Foundation

Switzer, Marge, trust: Switzer Foundation

Switzer, Patricia D., trust: Switzer Foundation

Switzer, Paul E., trust: Switzer Foundation

Switzer, Robert, trust: Switzer Foundation

Switzer, Toccoa W., mem adv comm: Bailey Foundation

Swojenski, Irene, dir: Goldberg Family Foundation, Milton D. and Madeline L.

Swope, John F., pres: Chubb Life Insurance Co. of America

Swope, Marie, natl mktg coordinator: Life Investors Insurance Company of America

Sword, William H., trust: Palmer Fund, Francis Asbury

Syal, Vermder, pres: Golden Grain Macaroni Co.

Sydnor, E. Starke, pres, trust: Vulcan Materials Co. Foundation

Sykes, James W., Jr., dir: Greve Foundation, William and Mary

Sykora, Don D., vp, dir: Houston Industries

Sylte, Richard M., vp, treas: Conway Scholarship Foundation, Carle C.

Sylvester, Harcourt M., II, pres, dir: Sylvester Foundation, Harcourt M. and Virginia W.

Symington, J. Fife, III, trust: Frick Foundation, Helen Clay

Symons, John W., exec vp (blades & razors, North Atlantic): Gillette Co.

Synder, Abram M., dir, treas: Plankenhorn Foundation, Harry

Synder, John J., secy, treas: Mette Foundation

Synder, Ruth B., trust: Breidenthal Foundation, Willard J. and Mary G.

Syrmis, Pamela, vp, dir: Ittleson Foundation

Syrmis, Victor, MD, dir: Ittleson Foundation

Szabad, George Michael, secy, treas: Dibner Fund

Szabo, Raymond, trust, vp, secy: Eaton Foundation, Cyrus

Szilagyi, Elaine A., trust: Frohring Foundation, William O. and Gertrude Lewis

T

Tabak, Mark, pres: Group Health Plan Inc.

Tabankin, Margery, dir: Arca Foundation

Tabata, Kimio, vchmn: Ise America

Tabb, Bonnie G., mgr: Microsoft Corp.

Taber, George H., vp, dir, trust: Mellon Foundation, Richard King

Taboni, Viola G., treas, asst secy, trust: Dynamet Foundation

Tabuchi, Mamoru, pres: Mitsui & Co. (U.S.A.)

Tacelli, Elizabeth, contributions mgr: Kendall Health Care Products

Taff, Phillip W., cfo: American Trading & Production Corp.

Taffet, Edward, secy, treas: United Merchants Foundation

Tafoya, Linda S., exec dir, secy: Coors Foundation, Adolph

Taft, Dudley S., pres, trust: Semple Foundation, Louise Taft

Taft, Katharine W., trust: Anderson Foundation, William P.

Taft, Robert A., II, trust: Semple Foundation, Louise Taft

Taft, Robert A., Jr., trust: Semple Foundation, Louise Taft

Taggart, William, trust: Washington Square Fund

Tagney, Alvin R., trust: O'Brien Foundation, James W.

Taguchi, Tadao, chmn, ceo: Toshiba America, Inc.; chmn: Toshiba America Foundation

Tai, Jun Tset, pres, mang dir: Tai and Co. Foundation, J. T.

Tai, Ping Y., off: Tai and Co. Foundation, J. T.

Tait, John E., chmn, pres, ceo, dir: Penn Mutual Life Insurance Co.

Takagi, Shinichi, pres: Sony Corp. of America

Takagi, Tadasu, exec vp: Sumitomo Corp. of America

Takahashi, Masahiro, dir, gen mgr: Industrial Bank of Japan Trust Co.

Takahashi, Stanley S., dir: Bancorp Hawaii Charitable Foundation

Takaki, Donald M., dir: Bancorp Hawaii Charitable Foundation

Takebayashi, Mamoru, trust: Mazda Foundation (USA), Inc.

Takeda, Kaneo, gen mgr: Tokai Bank, Ltd.

Takeda, Kent M., trust: AT&T Foundation

Takemura, Kunihiko, gen mgr: DNP (America), Inc.

Talbert, J. Michael, pres, coo: Lone Star Gas Co.

Talbot, Deborah L., trust: Chase Manhattan Bank, N.A.

Talbot, Phillips, trust: United States-Japan Foundation

Talbot, Samuel S., trust: Fuller Foundation

Taliaferro, W.C., pres, ceo: Richfood Holdings

Tallacksen, Harry, chmn contrib comm: Woodward Governor Co. Charitable Trust

Taller, Joe A., corp dir (community & ed rels): Boeing Co.

Talley, Chris I., trust: Thirty-Five Twenty, Inc.

Talley, Chris L., secy: Winchester Foundation

Talley, Mrs. Daniel D., III, vp: Memorial Foundation for Children

Talley, Tim, asst adm: Loughran Foundation, Mary and Daniel

Talley, Wilson K., pres, dir: Hertz Foundation, Fannie and John

Tallichet, David, chmn, ceo, pres: Specialty Restaurants Corp.

Tallman, Gene, vp: Abel Foundation

Tally, John C., trust: Rogers Charitable Trust, Florence

Talmage, John H., chmn: Hood Inc., H.P.

Talman, Mrs. E. Armistead, pres: Memorial Foundation for Children

Tamarkin, Bertram, pres, trust: Tamarkin Foundation

Tamarkin, Jack B., treas, trust: Tamarkin Foundation

Tamarkin, Jerry P., vp, trust: Tamarkin Foundation

Tamblyn, Ken C., exec vp, cfo: Tidewater, Inc.

Tamblyn, Wayne I., pres, treas: Georgia-Pacific Foundation

Tamura, Norio, chmn, pres: Teac America, Inc.

Tanaka, Hide, treas: Suzuki Automotive Foundation for Life

Tanaka, Hiroshi, chmn: Restaurant Associates, Inc.

Tanaka, Masuo, pres: Fujitsu America, Inc.

Tanaka, Ted, dir: Nakamichi Foundation, E.

Tandon, Sirjang Lal, chmn, pres, ceo: Tandon Corp.

Tandy, A.R., Jr., vp: Tandy Foundation, David L.

Tanenbaum, Charles J., secy: Jewish Foundation for Education of Women

Tanenbaum, Robert M., asst treas: Skirball Foundation

Tang, Jack C. C., pres, dir: Tang Foundation

Tang, Madeleine H., vp: Tang Foundation

Tang, Martin Y., vp: Tang Foundation

Tang, Oscar L., pres, ceo: Reich & Tang L.P.

Tangeman, Carolyn S., dir: Irwin-Sweeney- Miller Foundation

Tangeman, Clementine M., chmn, dir: Irwin-Sweeney-Miller Foundation

Tangeman, John, dir: Irwin-Sweeney- Miller Foundation

Tangney, Charles L., pres: Goodstein Foundation

Tank, E. A., cfo: Ball-InCon Glass Packaging Corp.

Tanler, Ronald F., pres: Lord & Taylor

Tannenbaum, A. J., pres, dir: Sternberger Foundation, Sigmund

Tannenbaum, Jeanne, dir: Sternberger Foundation, Sigmund

Tannenbaum, Sigmund I., MD, dir: Sternberger Foundation, Sigmund

Tanner, Estelle, trust: Lavanburg-Corner House

Tanner, Harold, trust: Sage Foundation, Russell

Tanner, James T., pres, ceo: Tanner Cos.; pres: Tanner Foundation

Tanner, K. S., Jr., dir: Stonecutter Foundation

Tanner, Michael S., secy: Tanner Foundation

Tanner, Simpson B., III, vp: Tanner Foundation

Tannet, Robin C., asst secy, asst treas: Strong Foundation, Hattie M.

Tanquist, Dwight, vp: Hartz Foundation

Tanselle, George Thomas, vp: Guggenheim Memorial Foundation, John Simon

Tansky, Burton, Saks Fifth Ave.

Taper, Barry H., vp, secy, dir: Taper Foundation, Mark; vp, secy, dir: Taper Foundation, S. Mark

Taper, S. Mark, pres, dir: Taper Foundation, S. Mark

Taper, Sydney Mark, pres, dir: Taper Foundation, Mark

Taplick, Robert W., treas: Bassett Foundation, Norman

Taracido, Lita, secy: New York Foundation

Taranda, Margaret, secy: Swasey Fund for Relief of Public School Teachers of Newburyport

Tarantino, Dominic, co-chmn, mng ptnr: Price Waterhouse-U.S.

Taratus, Kenneth, trust: Beck Foundation, Lewis H.

Tarbel, Swannie Zink, trust: Zink Foundation, John Steele

Tarica, Regina A., vp, cfo, dir: Amado Foundation, Maurice

Tarica, Samuel R., asst secy: Amado Foundation, Maurice

Tarnow, Robert L., chmn: Goulds Pumps; dir: Utica National Group Foundation

Tarplee, Marjorie C., secy: Central Newspapers Foundation

Tarpley, James M., pres, ceo: Texas-New Mexico Power Co.

Tarr, Robert J., Jr., Harcourt General

Tartiere, Gladys R., pres: Rosenthal Foundation, Benjamin J.

Tarwater, Janet L., trust: Hankins Foundation

Tasch, Edward, treas, dir: Noyes Foundation, Jessie Smith

Task, Arnold S., dir: Sternberger Foundation, Sigmund

Tate, Dorothy P., pres, dir: Sams Foundation, Earl C.

Tate, Jim, mem: Piedmont Health Care Foundation

Tate, Linda Crowe, vp, dir: McMillen Foundation

Tate, Lloyd P., Jr., trust: Reynolds Foundation, Z. Smith

Tate, Royce D., dir: Sams Foundation, Earl C.

Tate, Warren E., treas: Gulf Power Foundation

Tatel, David S., dir: Spencer Foundation

Tatsuta, Akira, pres: Kenwood U.S.A. Corp.

Tatum, Lofton L., trust: Higgins Charitable Trust, Lorene Sails

Tatum, Nenetta, pres: Carter Star Telegram Employees Fund, Amon G.

Tatzer, Richard, vp, dir, chief investment off: Transamerica Fdn.

Taub, Arlene, dir, treas: Taub Foundation, Joseph and Arlene

Taub, H. Ben, trust: Taub Foundation

Taub, Henry, pres, dir: Taub Foundation, Henry and Marilyn

Taub, Henry J. N., trust: Taub Foundation; trust: Wolff Memorial Foundation, Pauline Sterne

Taub, Henry J. N., II, trust: Taub Foundation; trust: Wolff Memorial Foundation, Pauline Sterne

Taub, Joseph, dir, pres: Taub Foundation, Joseph and Arlene

Taub, Marcy E., trust: Taub Foundation

Taub, Marilyn, treas, dir: Taub Foundation, Henry and Marilyn

Taube, Thaddeus N., dir: Koret Foundation; pres, dir: Taube Family Foundation

Tauber, Hans, MD, dir: Heineman Foundation for Research, Educational, Charitable, and Scientific Purposes

Tauber, Laszlo Nandor, don, pres: Tauber Foundation

Tauber, O. J., Jr., pres: Tauber Oil Co.

Tauberleim, Gordon R., chmn, ceo: EnviroSource

Taubman, A. Alfred, chmn, treas, trust: Taubman Foundation, A. Alfred

Taubman, Lois, trust: Taubman Foundation, Herman P. and Sophia

Taubman, Morris G., trust: Taubman Foundation, Herman P. and Sophia

Taubman, Robert S., trust: Taubman Foundation, A. Alfred

Taubman, William S., trust: Taubman Foundation, A. Alfred

Taubner, Valentine J., Jr., pres, chief engineer: Ball Chain Manufacturing Co.

Taura, Y., pres: Mazda North America; pres: Mazda Foundation (USA), Inc.

Tausig, Eva Maria, vp: Frank Foundation, Ernest and Elfriede

Tauvaga, Julie, pres: Marion Fabrics

Taylor, A. Leavitt, dir, treas: Ramlose Foundation, George A.

Taylor, Alexander S., trust: Bicknell Fund

Taylor, Alfred Hendricks, Jr., chmn, ceo, trust: Kresge Foundation

Taylor, Alice, dir, pres: Memorial Foundation for the Blind

Taylor, Allen M., vchmn, dir: Bradley Foundation, Lynde and Harry

Taylor, Andrew C., vp, treas: Enterprise Leasing Foundation

Taylor, Anita, trust: Alexander Foundation, Robert D. and Catherine R.

Taylor, Barbara O., trust: Olin Foundation, Spencer T. and Ann W.

Taylor, Benjamin B., dir: Boston Globe Foundation

Taylor, Bernard J., II, chmn, ceo, dir: Wilmington Trust Co.; trust: Wilmington Trust Co. Foundation

Taylor, Bruce W., vchmn: Cole Taylor Financial Group

Taylor, Carol B., trust: Bjorkman Foundation

Taylor, Catherine, trust: Taylor Charitable Trust, Jack DeLoss

Taylor, Chuck, vp: IBM South Africa Projects Fund

Taylor, David H., vp, dir: Davenport-Hatch Foundation

Taylor, David L., dir, secy: Ramlose Foundation, George A.

Taylor, Douglas F., dir: Davenport-Hatch Foundation

Taylor, Elly, vp, dir: Taylor Family Foundation, Jack

Taylor, Elmer L., Jr., vchmn, dir: M/A/R/C Inc.

Taylor, Emmett, mem (contributions comm): Dresser Industries

Taylor, Erik S., exec dir: Animal Assistance Foundation

Taylor, F. Morgan, trust: Olin Foundation, Spencer T. and Ann W.

Taylor, George, trust: Smith Horticultural Trust, Stanley

Taylor, Glenhall E., Jr., vchmn: BankAmerica Corp.

Taylor, Glenn, pres: Taylor Corp.

Taylor, Hart, dir: Davenport-Hatch Foundation

Taylor, Herbert J., trust: Christian Workers Foundation

Taylor, I. N., dir: Hawn Foundation

Taylor, J. P., bd mem: Roberts Foundation, Dora

Taylor, J. Seaton, dir: Board of Trustees of the Prichard School

Taylor, Jack, pres, dir: Taylor Family Foundation, Jack

Taylor, Jack C., pres: Enterprise Leasing Foundation

Taylor, James W. Z., Bull Foundation, Henry W.

Taylor, Janet C., mgr, corp contributions: Raytheon Co.

Taylor, Jeanne E., secy: Hopper Foundation, May Templeton

Taylor, Jeffrey W., vchmn: Cole Taylor Financial Group

Taylor, John Guest, trust: Bryan Family Foundation, Kathleen Price and Joseph M.

Taylor, John J., dir: Jasper Desk Foundation

Taylor, John R., trust: Institute for Research on Learning; sr vp: Merck Co. Foundation

Taylor, Jonathan F., vchmn, dir: Arbor Acres Farm, Inc.

Taylor, Joni S., trust: Driehaus Foundation, Richard H.

Taylor, Julian Howard, vp, treas, dir: Reynolds Metals Co. Foundation

Taylor, Kenneth, dir: Guggenheim Foundation, Daniel and Florence

Taylor, Kenneth Nathaniel, mgr: Tyndale House Foundation

Taylor, L. James, Jr., cfo, sr vp: Fast Food Merchandisers

Taylor, Larry A., chmn, dir: Berry & Co., L.M.

Taylor, Laurie, grant adm: UNUM Charitable Foundation

Taylor, Leslie M., vp: Taylor Foundation

Taylor, Lucille, dir: Harper Brush Works Foundation

Taylor, Margaret C., trust: Dula Educational and Charitable Foundation, Caleb C. and Julia W.

Taylor, Margaret W., secy, treas, mgr: Tyndale House Foundation

Taylor, Mark D., mgr: Tyndale House Foundation

Taylor, Marshall B., pres: Aviall, Inc.

Taylor, Martha, secy: Howe and Mitchell B. Howe Foundation, Lucite Horton

Taylor, Mitchell, secy, dir: Taylor Family Foundation, Jack

Taylor, Norman, pres: Didier Taylor Refractories Corp.

Taylor, Paul E., Jr., dir: Ross Foundation, Arthur

Taylor, Robert C., trust: Brinker Girls' Tennis Foundation, Maureen Connolly; trust: Washington Foundation

Taylor, Robert M., dir: Acme-Cleveland Foundation

Taylor, Robert T., pres: Taylor Foundation

Taylor, S. Martin, pres, dir: Detroit Edison Foundation

Taylor, Sarah Willard, dir, vp: Willard Foundation, Helen Parker

Taylor, Sidney J., chmn, pres, ceo: Cole Taylor Financial Group

Taylor, Teddy O., trust: Blount Educational and Charitable Foundation, Mildred Weedon

Taylor, Terrence J., treas: Nalco Foundation

Taylor, Timothy A., trust: Clark Charitable Trust

Taylor, Trude C., dir: Pasadena Area Residential Aid

Taylor, Vernon F., Jr., trust, don son: Taylor Foundation, Ruth and Vernon

Taylor, Wanda, adm asst: Sunnen Foundation

Taylor, William Osgood, chmn, dir: Affiliated Publications, Inc.; chmn, dir: Globe Newspaper Co.; pres, dir: Boston Globe Foundation

Taylor, Wilson H., chmn, ceo, dir: CIGNA Corp.

Tchekmeian, Vartank, pres: Servico, Inc.

te Velde, Harm, pres: Artevel Foundation

te Velde, John, trust: Artevel Foundation

te Velde, Marvin, trust: Artevel Foundation

te Velde, Ralph, trust: Artevel Foundation

te Velde, Zwaantina, vp: Artevel Foundation

Teaff, Bob, trust: Cauthorn Charitable Trust, John and Mildred

Teague, Carroll H., vp (quality systems & customer svcs):

Brown & Williamson Tobacco Corp.

Teague, Lawrence B., trust: Campbell Foundation, J. Bulow

Teal, Norwood, vchmn: Van Buren Foundation

Teerlink, Richard F., pres, ceo: Harley-Davidson, Inc.

Teeter, Harry, trust: Hopkins Foundation, John Jay

Teets, John W., chmn, pres, ceo, dir: Dial Corp.; pres, ceo: Dial Corporation Fund

Teft, John, sr vp (bus strategies): Shaklee Corp.

Teichert, Erma M., dir: Teichert Foundation

Teichert, Frederick, exec dir: Teichert Foundation

Teichert, Frederick A., exec dir,: Teichert Foundation

Teichner, Thomas, trust: General Steel Fabricators College Scholarship Foundation

Teig, Eva S., mem (contributions comm): Virginia Power Co.

Teitelbaum, David, secy: Abeles Foundation, Joseph and Sophia

Teiwes, William M, exec vp, cfo: United Missouri Bancshares, Inc.

Teleser, Arthur, treas: Sulzer Family Foundation

Tell, Mary J., pres, dir: Tell Foundation

Tellalian, Aram H., Jr., chmn, pres, trust: Carstensen Memorial Foundation, Fred R. and Hazel W.; trust, chmn, pres, treas: Jones and Bessie D. Phelps Foundation, Cyrus W. and Amy F.; secy, trust: Jost Foundation, Charles and Mabel P.

Tellalian, Robert S., trust, secy: Carstensen Memorial Foundation, Fred R. and Hazel W.; secy, trust: Jones and Bessie D. Phelps Foundation, Cyrus W. and Amy F.; vp, trust: Jost Foundation, Charles and Mabel P.

Tellep, Daniel M., chmn, ceo, dir: Lockheed Corp.

Teller, Edward, dir: Hertz Foundation, Fannie and John

Tellez, Cora, dir: Bancorp Hawaii Charitable Foundation

Temerlin, J. Liener, chmn: Bozell, Inc.

Temin, Michael Lehman, secy: Rittenhouse Foundation

Tempest, Harrison F., chmn: European American Bank

Temple, Alvis, exec secy: Ogden College Fund

Temple, Arthur, Jr., chmn, trust: Temple Foundation, T. L. L.; dir: Temple-Inland Foundation

Temple, Arthur (Buddy), III, trust: Temple Foundation, T. L. L.

Temple, Diane E., secy, dir: Three Swallows Foundation

Temple, Esther, 2nd vp, dir: Hopper Foundation, May Templeton

Temple, Joseph George, Jr., chmn, ceo, dir: Merrill Corp.

Temple, Nancy L., dir: Three Swallows Foundation

Temple, Paul N., Jr., pres, dir: Three Swallows Foundation

Temple, Thomas D., dir: Three Swallows Foundation

Temple-Greenberg, Lise, dir: Three Swallows Foundation

Templer, Charles E., vp, treas: Commerce Foundation

Temples, Dent L., secy, dir: Piggly Wiggly Southern Foundation

Templeton, Coulter, trust: Meredith Foundation

Templeton, Hall, trust: Templeton Foundation, Herbert A.

Templeton, Harvey Maxwell, III, secy: Templeton Foundation, John

Templeton, John Marks, Jr., pres: Templeton Foundation, John

Templeton, Robert, mem: Templeton Foundation, Herbert A.

Templin, Gary, dir: Haigh-Scatena Foundation

Ten Haken, Mary L., secy, dir: Windway Foundation, Inc.

Tengi, Frank R., treas: Starr Foundation

Tenney, Daniel Gleason, Jr., secy, dir: JM Foundation

Tenney, Delbert, trust: Hartman Foundation, Jesse and Dorothy

Tenney, Margot Hartman, trust: Hartman Foundation, Jesse and Dorothy

Tenney, Stuart, pres: Haven Charitable Foundation, Nina

Tenniman, Nicholas G., IV, dir: Pulitzer Publishing Co. Foundation

Tennison, Gloria Lupton, dir: Brown and C. A. Lupton Foundation, T. J.

Tenny, Barron M., vp, secy, gen coun: Ford Foundation

Tenpas, Paul, secy, dir: Kohler Foundation

Teplow, Theodore Herzl, secy, trust: Stone Charitable Foundation

Tepperman, F.L., exec vp, cfo, dir: MacAndrews & Forbes Holdings

Tepperman, Fred L., vp, treas, dir: MacAndrews & Forbes Foundation

Tepperman, Marvin T., vp: Brenner Foundation, Mervyn

Teramura, Soji, secy: Hitachi Foundation

Terasawa, Yoshio, trust: United States-Japan Foundation

Terlizzi, Alfred, pres: Ballet Makers; pres: Capezio-Ballet Makers Dance Foundation

Terlizzi, Donald, vp: Ballet Makers

Terlizzi, Nick, vp: Capezio-Ballet Makers Dance Foundation

Termondt, M. James, treas, dir: Buehler Foundation, A. C.; vp, treas: Fry Foundation, Lloyd A.; dir: Heller Foundation, Walter E.; secy, dir: Wehr Foundation, Todd

Termondt, M.J., vp: Falk Medical Research Foundation, Dr. Ralph and Marian

Terner, Emmanuel M, chmn: Terner Foundation

Terner, Mathilda, pres, treas: Terner Foundation

Ternes, Barbara, program off: New York Foundation

Terpaik, Sr., John B., chmn: York Barbell Co.

Terpenning, L. M., mem charitable comm: Foster Charitable Trust, L.B.

Terracciano, Anthony P., chmn, pres, ceo, dir: First Fidelity Bancorp, Inc.; chmn, pres, ceo, dir: First Fidelity Bancorporation

Terrel, Billy G., pres: Preston Trucking Co., Inc.

Terrien, Linda, asst treas: Weyerhaeuser Co. Foundation

Terrill, Mildred K., vp, trust: Kemper Educational and Charitable Fund

Terry, C. Herman, trust: Terry Foundation, C. Herman

Terry, Charles R., Sr., vchmn: Hill Crest Foundation

Terry, Frederick Arthur, Jr., pres, dir: Flagler Foundation; trust: HKH Foundation; secy, dir: McIntosh Foundation

Terry, Howard L., trust: Terry Foundation

Terry, J. Fletcher, vp: Bibb Foundation, Inc.

Terry, Mary Virginia, trust: Terry Foundation, C. Herman

Terry, Richard E., chmn, ceo: Peoples Energy Corp.

Terry, Sally A., trust: Bowles and Robert Bowles Memorial Fund, Ethel Wilson

Terry, William, dir: Autotrol Corp. Charitable Trust

Teschner, Richard R., vp, dir: Ross Memorial Foundation, Will

Tessler, C., secy: Long Foundation, J.M.

Testa, M. David, managing dir: Price Associates, T. Rowe

Testa, Richard J., treas: Beaucourt Foundation; trust: Stratford Foundation

Testerman, Philip, 1st vchmn: Harvest States Foundation

TeStrake, Harvey D., secy, mgr: Miller Foundation, Steve J.

Tetlow, Horace G., chmn, trust: Crandall Memorial Foundation, J. Ford

Teufel, Robert, pres, dir: Rodale Press

Tewart, Donna, dir: Levi Strauss Foundation

Thacher, Albert Cardinal, trust: Heyward Memorial Fund, DuBose and Dorothy

Thacher, Carter P., vp, dir: Wilbur Foundation, Brayton

Thacher, William A., Law Foundation, Robert O.

Thacker, Frank, trust: National Pro-Am Youth Fund

Thagard, George F., Jr., trust, pres: Thagard Foundation

Thagard, Raymond G., Sr., trust, vp: Thagard Foundation

Thaler, Manley, pres: Howell Foundation, Eric and Jessie

Thalheimer, Louis B., chmn, ceo, dir: American Trading & Production Corp.; vp, trust: Blaustein Foundation, Louis and Henrietta; pres, trust: Thalheimer Foundation, Alvin and Fanny Blaustein

Thalhimer, Barbara J., dir, secy, treas: Thalhimer, Jr. and Family Foundation, William B.

Thalhimer, Charles G., Jr., vp: Thalhimer and Family Foundation, Charles G.

Thalhimer, Charles G., Sr., pres, dir: Thalhimer and Family Foundation, Charles G.

Thalhimer, Harry R., vp: Thalhimer and Family Foundation, Charles G.

Thalhimer, Rhonda R., secy, treas: Thalhimer and Family Foundation, Charles G.

Thalhimer, Robert L., dir, vp: Thalhimer, Jr. and Family Foundation, William B.

Thalhimer, William B., III, dir: Thalhimer Brothers

Foundation; vp: Thalhimer, Jr. and Family Foundation, William B.

Thalhimer, William B., Jr., vp: Thalhimer and Family Foundation, Charles G.; Thalhimer Brothers Inc.; pres, dir, dn: Thalhimer Brothers Foundation; vp, dir, don: Thalhimer, Jr. and Family Foundation, William B.

Thames, Susan Hawn, dir: Sams Foundation, Earl C.

Tharin, Judson, program off: Davis Foundations, Arthur Vining

Thatcher, Elizabeth N., trust: Schenck Fund, L. P.

Thatcher, Joseph W., chmn: SCT Yarns

Thaw, Eugene Victor, pres, dir: Pollock-Krasner Foundation

Thawerbhoy, Nazim G., controller: Jacobs Engineering Foundation

Thayer, Francis W., trust: Mobility Foundation

Thayer, Thomas C., trust: Moore Foundation, O. L.

Thelen, Max, Jr., vp: Cowell Foundation, S. H.

Theobald, Jon A., trust: Bigelow Foundation, F. R.

Theobald, Thomas C., chmn, ceo: Continental Bank N.A.; vchmn counc: Foundation for Child Development

Theriot, Charles H., mem adv comm: Weezie Foundation

Thiele, Randy, trust: Donaldson Foundation

Thien, William G., vp, dir: Walgreen Benefit Fund

Thieriot, Charles H., Jr., dir: Oxnard Foundation

Thigpenn, Anthony, dir: New World Foundation

Thilmony, Priscilla, treas: Clorox Company Foundation

Thomas, Albert L., trust: Thomas Foundation

Thomas, Ann D., dir, corp contributions: First Union Foundation

Thomas, Ann Freda, dir: Jewish Foundation for Education of Women

Thomas, B. L., trust: Thomas Foundation

Thomas, Bailey A., chmn, ceo, dir: McCormick & Co.

Thomas, Brian G., ceo, pres: British Aerospace Inc.

Thomas, Bruce, dir: Piper Foundation, Minnie Stevens

Thomas, Carolyn, secy: Sundstrand Corp. Foundation

Thomas, Christopher R., secy: Sizzler International Foundation

Thomas, David, pres: Alltel/Western Region

Thomas, David A., Jr., pres, ceo: Citizens Commercial & Savings Bank

Thomas, Denise Halloran, vp: Halloran Foundation, Mary P. Dolciani

Thomas, Donald, vp: Younkers Foundation

Thomas, Franklin Augustine, dir: CBS Foundation; pres, trust: Ford Foundation

Thomas, George, trust: Pilgrim Foundation

Thomas, Gladys R., vp: Starr Foundation

Thomas, Glenn E., Jr., dir: Thomas Foundation, Joan and Lee

Thomas, Gregory N., secy: Blair and Co. Foundation, William

Thomas, H. Seely, Jr., trust: Large Foundation

Thomas, Hon. David A., dir, chmn dirs grant program comm: Keck Foundation, W. M.

Thomas, Jack E., pres: San Diego Gas & Electric

Thomas, James A., mng ptnr: Maguire Thomas Partners

Thomas, James E., secy, trust: Thomas Foundation

Thomas, Jane R., trust: Skillman Foundation

Thomas, Jeannette M., secy: Foundation of the Litton Industries

Thomas, Joan E., Jr., dir: Thomas Foundation, Joan and Lee

Thomas, John C., dir: Kellenberger Historical Foundation, May Gordon Latham

Thomas, John R., trust: Bannon Foundation

Thomas, John S., vp, exec dir: Morris Charitable Foundation, E. A.

Thomas, John W., treas, dir: Charles River Foundation

Thomas, John W., Jr., chmn, pres, ceo: Thomas Built Buses L.P.; treas, trust: Thomas Foundation

Thomas, Jonathan, trust: Americana Foundation

Thomas, Joyce, mng comm: Alliant Community Investment Foundation

Thomas, Judy B., pres, trust: Ashland Oil Foundation

Thomas, Kenneth B., pres: Jones Foundation, Walter S. and Evan C.

Thomas, L. Newton, Jr., trust: Carbon Fuel Foundation; pres, dir: Daywood Foundation; trust: Jacobson Foundation, Bernard H. and Blanche E.

Thomas, Lee B., Jr., don, dir: Thomas Foundation, Joan and Lee

Thomas, Lewis, MD, dir: Diamond Foundation, Aaron; dir: Life Sciences Research Foundation; dir: Lounsbery Foundation, Richard

Thomas, Lilliam, trust, vchmn: Fox Foundation Trust, Jacob L. and Lewis

Thomas, Loyd A., cfo: Alma Piston Co.

Thomas, Lyda Ann Quinn, chmn: Kempner Fund, Harris and Eliza

Thomas, Lynn Schadt, dir, secy: Schadt Foundation

Thomas, Margaret, exec dir, secy: Grotto Foundation

Thomas, Mary Hager, vp, dir: Gronewaldt Foundation, Alice Busch

Thomas, Michael, dir, chmn, treas: Thomas Foundation, Dorothy

Thomas, Michael M., dir: Lehman Foundation, Robert

Thomas, Mrs. William, dir, vchmn: Emergency Aid of Pennsylvania Foundation

Thomas, Nancy, natl contributions mgr: Hewlett-Packard Co.

Thomas, P. A., trust: Thomas Foundation

Thomas, Richard, dir: American Honda Foundation

Thomas, Richard Lee, chmn, pres, ceo, dir: First Chicago; vp, dir: First National Bank of Chicago Foundation

Thomas, Richard M., dir: Detroit Edison Foundation

Thomas, Robert, dir, vchmn: Thomas Foundation, Dorothy

Thomas, Robert M., pres, trust: Montgomery Foundation

Thomas, Roger M., trust: Hoffman Foundation, John Ernest

Thomas, Thomas L., pres, trust: Chambers Memorial, James B.

Thomas, Tom, treas: Trusler Foundation

Thomas, Walter J., treas/secy, trust: Tull Charitable Foundation

Thomas, Wright M., pres, coo, treas, dir: Park Communications Inc.

Thomas, II, James R., pres, trust: Carbon Fuel Foundation

Thomason, D. W., trust: Kellogg Co. Twenty-Five Year Employees' Fund

Thomason, Jerry M., trust: Parman Foundation, Robert A.

Thomasson, Dan, trust: Scripps Howard Foundation

Thome, Dennis W., secy, treas, bd mem: First Fruit

Thomopulos, Gregs G., pres: Stanley Consultants

Thompson, A. A., vp, dir: Graybar Foundation

Thompson, B. Ray, Jr., dir: Thompson Charitable Foundation

Thompson, Billie, secy, dir: Doss Foundation, M. S.

Thompson, Brian, mem tech assistance bd: Link Foundation

Thompson, C. A., trust: Delta Air Lines Foundation

Thompson, Carole, dir (civic affairs): CIGNA Foundation

Thompson, Charles M., dir: Parsons - W.D. Charities, Vera Davis

Thompson, Dean A., vp, dir: Thrush-Thompson Foundation

Thompson, E. Arthur, pres, trust: Cooper Foundation

Thompson, E. Edward, mem selection comm: Woodward Fund-Watertown, David, Helen, and Marian

Thompson, E. N., chmn: Cooper Foundation

Thompson, Edward F., cfo: Amdahl Corp.

Thompson, Edward R., Jr., trust: Kempner Fund, Harris and Eliza

Thompson, Eve Lloyd, trust: Barbour Foundation, Bernice

Thompson, G. Lee, chmn, ceo: Smith Corona Corp.

Thompson, Gene, trust: Jones Foundation, Harvey and Bernice

Thompson, George C., treas, dir: Phillips Foundation, Ellis L.

Thompson, George S., mem trust fund comm: Ingram Trust, Joe

Thompson, Harry A., II, mgr: Heinz Foundation, Drue

Thompson, J. Cleo, Jr., trust: Sumners Foundation, Hatton W.

Thompson, Jack, Cooper Foundation

Thompson, James, chmn, pres, ceo, dir: Glenmore Distilleries Co.; treas: Loomis House

Thompson, Janet W., vp, dir (community devel programs): Citicorp

Thompson, Jerry T., vp, dir: Thrush-Thompson Foundation

Thompson, Jesse J., dir: Thompson Charitable Foundation

Thompson, Joan, dir community rels: GenCorp Foundation

Thompson, Joe, Jr., trust: Foster Charitable Foundation, M. Stratton

Thompson, John, bd mem: Dain Bosworth/IFG Foundation

Thompson, John D., treas: Dexter Corp. Foundation

Thompson, John F., treas: Christensen Charitable and Religious Foundation, L. C.

Thompson, Josephine H., dir, pres: Special People In Need

Thompson, Keith M., pres, ceo: Republic Automotive Parts, Inc.

Thompson, Kirk, pres, ceo: Hunt Transport Services, J.B.

Thompson, Lawrence M., pres: Sovereign Bank Foundation

Thompson, Leonora Kempner, chmn emeritus: Kempner Fund, Harris and Eliza

Thompson, Lucille S., emeritus chmn: Thompson Family Fund, Lucille S.

Thompson, Marcia T., dir: Scherman Foundation

Thompson, Mark E., asst treas: Amoco Foundation

Thompson, Mary M., vp, dir: Muller Foundation

Thompson, Mona, trust: Coen Family Foundation, Charles S. and Mary

Thompson, Paul, pres: DEC International, Inc.

Thompson, Paul F., pres, treas, dir: Thrush-Thompson Foundation

Thompson, Peter, dir: Mitsubishi Electric America Foundation

Thompson, Raybourne, Jr., trust: Ellwood Foundation

Thompson, Renold D., vchmn: Oglebay Norton Co.; vp, trust: Oglebay Norton Foundation

Thompson, Richard L, exec vp, cfo: Key Bank of Maine

Thompson, Robert I., trust: Gordy Family Educational Trust Fund, George E.

Thompson, Robert L., vp (pub aff): Springs Industries; secy, dir: Thrush-Thompson Foundation

Thompson, Roger Kennedy, trust: Van Wert County Foundation

Thompson, Russell, sr vp: Branch Banking & Trust Co.

Thompson, Theresa, trust: Washington Square Fund

Thompson, Thomas C., Jr., vp, secy, trust: Clark-Winchcole Foundation

Thompson, Timothy, trust: Harding Educational and Charitable Foundation

Thompson, Verneice D., dir: Zellerbach Family Fund

Thompson, Virgil, mem contributions comm: Syntex Corp.

Thompson, W. F. B., chmn, pres, ceo, dir: Thor Industries, Inc.

Thompson, William Reid, chmn, dir: Potomac Electric Power Co.

Thompson, William W., pres: General Machine Works

Thompson, William W., Jr., pres: General Machine Works Foundation

Thompson, Winifred H., trust: Levy Foundation, June Rockwell

Thomsen, C. J., trust: McDermott Foundation, Eugene

Thomson, Eleanor C., dir: Vernon Fund, Miles Hodsdon

Thomson, Lucy M., vp, trust: Morley Brothers Foundation

Thomson, Robert C., Jr., pres, treas, dir: Vernon Fund, Miles Hodsdon

Thoreen, John F., dir: Tozer Foundation

Thoresen, Michael, trust: Thoresen Foundation

Thoresz, Jamie L., mgr (corp contributions): American Cyanamid Co.

Thorn, George W., MD, trust, chmn emeritus: Hughes Medical Institute, Howard

Thorn, Therese M., trust: Hess Charitable Trust, Myrtle E. and William C.; mng trust: NBD Charitable Trust

Thornburg, James F., vp, dir: Leighton-Oare Foundation

Thorndike, W. Nicholas, trust: Peabody Foundation

Thorne, David H., vp: Thorne Foundation

Thorne, Felicitas S., trust: Millbrook Tribute Garden

Thorne, Jane W., trust: Fund for New Jersey

Thorne, Jean D., exec dir, vp, dir: Coleman Foundation

Thorne, Jeanne, trust: Callister Foundation, Paul Q.

Thorne, John D., finance/grants off: Coleman Foundation

Thorne, Miriam A., pres: Thorne Foundation

Thorne, Oakleigh B., pres: Millbrook Tribute Garden

Thorne, Oakleigh Blakeman, chmn, dir: Commerce Clearing House; chmn, pres, treas, dir: Thorne Foundation, Oakleigh L.

Thorne, Samuel, Jr., treas, trust: Schepp Foundation, Leopold

Thorner, Peter, dir: Ames Department Stores; vp, treas: Ames Foundation, Inc.

Thornhill, Carrie L., dir: Meyer Foundation, Eugene and Agnes E.

Thornton, B. H., trust: Share Trust, Charles Morton

Thornton, Charles B., Jr., pres, trust: Thornton Foundation

Thornton, Flora L., trust: Thornton Foundation, Flora L.

Thornton, John McBride, secy, dir: Thornton Foundation, John M. and Sally B.

Thornton, John T., cfo, exec vp: Norwest Corp.; treas: Norwest Foundation

Thornton, Mark B., dir: Thornton Foundation, John M. and Sally B.

Thornton, Martha L., dir: Ameritech Foundation

Thornton, Maureen, dir: Farley Foundation, William F.

Thornton, MelloDee, mgr commun aff: West One Bancorp

Thornton, Sally B., pres, dir: Thornton Foundation, John M. and Sally B.

Thornton, Steven B., dir: Thornton Foundation, John M. and Sally B.

Thornton, William Laney, vp, trust: Thornton Foundation; trust: Thornton Foundation, Flora L.

Thornton, William T., group sr vp: European American Bank

Thornton, Winfred L., chmn, pres, dir: Florida East Coast Industries

Thorp, Peter C., vp (univ rels): Citicorp

Thorpe, Edith D., dir: Surdna Foundation; pres, dir: Thorpe Foundation, James R.

Thorpe, James A., chmn, ceo: Washington Natural Gas Co.

Thorpe, Merle, Jr., pres, treas, trust: Foundation for Middle East Peace

Thorpe, Neal O., sr program off: Murdock Charitable Trust, M. J.

Thorpe, Samuel S., III, pres, dir: Surdna Foundation; treas, dir: Thorpe Foundation, James R.

Thorsen, Jamie, dir: Harris Bank Foundation

Thorson, Dorothy W., dir, pres: Thorson Foundation

Thorstenson, T., vp: Caterpillar Foundation

Thrall, Gordon, trust: Norman Foundation, Summers A.

Thrasher, E. Gene, pres: Blue Cross & Blue Shield of Alabama; pres: Caring Foundation

Thrasher, E.W. Al, vchmn, exec comm: Swanson Family Foundation, Dr. W.C.

Thrasher, Kenneth L., sr vp, cfo: Meyer, Inc., Fred

Threatt, Robert, dir, vp: Churches Homes Foundation

Threet, LaMonica, dir: Chicago Tribune Foundation

Thrune, Charles J., asst vp, trust: Strosacker Foundation, Charles J.

Thun, David L., trust: Wyomissing Foundation

Thun, Ferdinand, trust: Wyomissing Foundation

Thun, Louis, trust: Wyomissing Foundation

Thun, Peter, vp, dir: Wyomissing Foundation

Thunell, Arthur E., secy, treas: Doheny Foundation, Carrie Estelle

Thurber, Peter P., pres: Whitney Fund, David M.

Thurber, Peter Palms, secy, trust: McGregor Fund

Thurman, David M., pres, ceo, dir: National City Bank

Thurman, John D., treas: Merillat Foundation, Orville D. and Ruth A.

Thurmond, Harriet R., treas, dir: Hermann Foundation, Grover

Thurston, Kenneth P., vp, cfo: CSC Industries

Thurston, Robert H., vp: Thurston Charitable Foundation

Thurston, Severt W., Jr., pres: Thurston Charitable Foundation

Thurston, Susan E., treas: Thurston Charitable Foundation

Thurston, William R., chmn, dir: GenRad

Thye, Pamela M., chmn, trust: Steinman Foundation, John Frederick

Thyen, James C., dir: Habig Foundation

Thyen, Ronald J., dir: Habig Foundation

Tiano, Joseph A., secy, treas, trust: Summerfield Foundation, Solon E.

Tibaldo, Lanny, comm mem: Fromm Scholarship Trust, Walter and Mabel

Tibstra, Gertrude, secy: Tibstra Charitable Foundation, Thomas and Gertrude

Tibstra, Larry, trust: Tibstra Charitable Foundation, Thomas and Gertrude

Tibstra, Thomas, pres: Tibstra Charitable Foundation, Thomas and Gertrude

Ticknor, David, pres: Delano Foundation, Mignon Sherwood

Ticknor, William S., trust: Winship Memorial Scholarship Foundation

Tideman, Selim N., Jr., vp: Lost Tree Charitable Foundation

Tieken, Elizabeth B., dir, pres: H. B. B. Foundation

Tieken, Mrs. Theodore D., trust: Demos Foundation, N.

Tieken, Theodore D., Jr., dir, vp, secy: H. B. B. Foundation

Tieken, Theodore D., Sr., trust: H. B. B. Foundation

Tienda, Marta, PhD, trust: Kaiser Family Foundation, Henry J.; trust: Sage Foundation, Russell

Tierney, Gerald M., Jr., dir: GSC Enterprises Foundation

Tierney, Joseph, dir: Humphrey Foundation, Glenn & Gertrude

Tierney, Patricia, dir: Intercontinental Hotels Corp.

Tierney, Philip, trust, secy: Hopkins Foundation, John Jay

Tietel, Martin, vp, exec dir: Warsh-Mott Legacy

Tietze, Arnold, vp: Schramm Foundation

Tifft, Bela C., trust, secy: Anderson Foundation

Tigerman, Stanley, dir: Skidmore, Owings & Merrill Foundation

Tikkanen, Paul, ceo, pres: Ix & Sons, Frank

Tilden, Charles R., trust: GenCorp Foundation

Tilghman, Richard Granville, chmn, ceo, dir, pres: Crestar Financial Corp.; chmn, ceo, dir, pres: Crestar Food Products, Inc.

Till, A. Grey, Jr., secy: Caring Foundation

Tillery, Homer W., chmn: Jones Intercable Tampa Trust

Tilley, R. McFarland, secy, dir: Harcourt Foundation, Ellen Knowles

Tilley, Ralph W., pres: Vevay-Switzerland County Foundation

Tilley, W. J., chmn: Bristol Steel & Iron Works

Tillinghast, Charles C., Jr., dir, mem: Luce Foundation, Henry

Tillman, Robert, trust: Lowe's Charitable & Educational Foundation

Tillotson, Cheri, secy, treas: C & H Charitable Trust

Tilton, David L., vchmn, dir: Financial Corp. of Santa Barbara

Tilton, Sumner B., treas: White Companies Charitable Trust

Tilton, Sumner B., Jr., trust: Ellsworth Foundation, Ruth H. and Warren A.; trust: Harrington Foundation, Francis A. and Jacquelyn H.; trust: McEvoy Foundation, Mildred H.

Timken, Ward J., off: Timken Co. Charitable Trust; pres, trust: Timken Foundation of Canton

Timken, William R., vp, trust: Timken Foundation of Canton

Timken, William Robert, Jr., chmn, chmn exec comm, chmn fin comm, dir: Timken Co.; vp, trust: Timken Foundation of Canton

Timmerman, Robert P., bd mem, dir: Gregg-Graniteville Foundation

Timmerman, W. B., cfo: SCANA Corp.

Timmis, Michael T., pres, treas: Timmis Foundation, Michael & Nancy

Timmis, Nancy E., vp: Timmis Foundation, Michael & Nancy

Timms, Leonard J., Jr., pres: CNG Transmission Corp.

Timms, Leonard Joseph, trust: Consolidated Natural Gas Co. Foundation

Timoshuk, Walter W., vp, treas, trust, secy: Simon Foundation, Jennifer Jones

Timperman, Charles, dir: Borden Foundation

Tingley, Janice C., trust: Phillips Trust, Edwin

Tinney, Linda, secy: Beasley Foundation, Theodore and Beulah

Tinney, Richard D., pres, ceo: Bohemia Inc.; vp, dir: Bohemia Foundation

Tinsley, Clifford G., secy, treas: Bridwell Foundation, J. S.

Tippett, Henry H., treas, trust: Tiscornia Foundation

Tippit, Carl J., trust: Tippit Charitable Trust, C. Carlisle and Margaret M.

Tipton, Gwendlyn I., scholarship adm, dir: Cole Foundation, Olive B.

Tipton, Ronald D., dir: MDU Resources Foundation

Tirman, John, consultant: Kendall Foundation, Henry P.

Tirrell, Stanley A., trust: Goodyear Foundation, Josephine

Tisch, Andrew H., pres, ceo: Lorillard Tobacco Inc.

Tisch, Joan M., dir, don wife: Tisch Foundation

Tisch, Laurence Alan, trust, mem fin & admin comm: Carnegie Corporation of New York; chmn, pres, ceo, dir: CBS Inc.; chmn, pres, ceo, dir: Loews Corp.; trust: Loews Foundation; sr vp, don: Tisch Foundation

Tisch, Preston Robert, chmn, dir: CBS Foundation; pres, co-ceo: Loews Corp.; trust: Loews Foundation; pres, don: Tisch Foundation

Tisch, Wilma S., dir, don wife: Tisch Foundation

Tiscornia, Bernice, trust: Tiscornia Foundation

Tiscornia, Edward, trust: Tiscornia Foundation

Tiscornia, Lester, chmn: Auto Specialties Manufacturing Co.

Tiscornia, Lester Clinton, pres, trust: Tiscornia Foundation

Tisdale, Stuart W., chmn, ceo: WICOR, Inc.; pres, dir: WICOR Foundation

Titas, F. G., secy: Hanna Co. Foundation, M.A.

Titchell, Haskell, vp, dir: Herbst Foundation

Titcomb, Bruce L., dir: Rodman Foundation

Titcomb, Daniel C., dir: Rodman Foundation

Titcomb, E. Rodman, Jr., vp, treas, dir: Dunn Foundation, Elizabeth Ordway; dir, pres: Rodman Foundation

Titcomb, Edward Rodman, dir: Rodman Foundation

Titcomb, Frederic W., dir: Rodman Foundation

Titcomb, Julie C., vp, dir: Rodman Foundation

Titcomb, Peter, trust: Weyerhaeuser Family Foundation

Titmus, Edward T., pres: Titmus Foundation

Tizzio, Thomas R., pres: American International Group, Inc.

Tkachyk, Vince, trust: Dekalb Energy Foundation

Toal, Lawrence J., pres, coo: Dime Savings Bank of New York

Tobias, Barry, treas: Sharp Foundation, Evelyn

Tobias, Harold S., secy: Herman Foundation, John and Rose

Tobias, Randall L., vchmn, dir: American Telephone & Telegraph Co.

Tobin, James Robert, pres, coo, dir: Baxter International

Tobin, Marie L., community rels specialist: IDS Financial Services

Tobin, R.L.B., pres: Tobin Foundation

Tobisman, Stuart P., vp, dir, coun: Bettingen Corporation, Burton G.

Tobler, D. Lee, vp: BFGoodrich Foundation

Tobolowsky, George, secy, treas: Zale Foundation

Toda, Keishi, pres: Hitachi

Toda, Terrance M., allocation comm: Kawabe Memorial Fund

Todaro, Michael P., treas, dir: Compton Foundation

Todd, A. J., III, pres: Todd Co., A.M.; trust: Todd Co. Foundation, A.M.

Todd, Jane B., treas, trust: Monroe-Brown Foundation

Todd, T. W., chmn, ceo, dir: United Telephone Co. of Florida

Todd, Vivian E., secy: Wright Foundation, Lola

Todd, Webb, chmn corp contributions comm: First Interstate Bank of Arizona Charitable Foundation

Toder, Charles, vp, dir: Amax Foundation

Todewils, Robert, ceo, pres: Sogem Holding Ltd.

Toelle, Michael, trust: CENEX Foundation

Toft, Richard P., chmn, ceo, pres: Chicago Title and Trust Co.; trust: Chicago Title and Trust Co. Foundation

Togo, Yukiyasu, pres, ceo: Toyota Motor Sales, U.S.A.

Togut, Deborah, supv (advertising): TDK Corp. of America

Toland, Henry, secy: Thomas Foundation, Dorothy

Tolbert-Glover, Sharon, community affairs program mgr: Saint Paul Cos.

Tolin, Stephen Wise, secy, treas: Kenworthy - Sarah H. Swift Foundation, Marion E.

Toll, Daniel R., trust: Brown Foundation, George Warren; trust: Kemper Foundation, James S.

Tollenaere, Lawrence R., chmn, ceo, pres, dir: Ameron, Inc.

Toller, William R., chmn, ceo, dir: Witco Corp.

Tolleson, Anne E., trust: Overstreet Foundation

Tollett, Leland E., pres, ceo: Tyson Foods, Inc.

Tolley, Joan D., dir: Filene Foundation, Lincoln and Therese

Tolliver, Sharon, fdn adm: Dayton Power and Light Co. Foundation

Tolonen, James R., sr vp, cfo: Novell Inc.

Tolson, Bridgit, exec dir: Kerr Fund, Grayce B.

Tolson, Jay H., chmn, ceo: Fischer & Porter Co.

Tomaszewski, James M., sr vp, cfo: Lechmere

Tomberlin, M. C., secy, dir: Wolfson Family Foundation

Tomer, Richard S., pres, treas, trust: Andrews Foundation

Tomich, Rosemary, dir: Occidental Petroleum Charitable Foundation

Tominaga, K., pres: Sanyo Fisher Service Corp.

Tomlinson, Barbara, pres: Tomlinson Family Foundation

Tomlinson, Kate, treas: Tomlinson Family Foundation

Tomlinson, Kenneth Y., dir: Reader's Digest Foundation

Tomlinson, Mark P., vchmn: Tomlinson Foundation, Kate and Elwyn

Tomlinson, Norman, secy: Tomlinson Family Foundation

Tommaney, John J., secy, dir: Greve Foundation, William and Mary

Tompkins, Douglas R., pres: Ira-Hiti Foundation for Deep Ecology

Tompkins, Mary K., secy-treas: McShain Charities, John

Tompkins, Quincey, dir: Ira-Hiti Foundation for Deep Ecology

Tompkins, Summer, dir: Ira-Hiti Foundation for Deep Ecology

Tompson, Edythe, secy, treas: Community Hospital Foundation

Toms, William, trust: Ghidotti Foundation, William and Marian

Tone, Amy, sr program off: American Honda Foundation

Tong, Virginia M., secy, dir: Bank of the Orient Foundation

Toohey, Edward Joseph, vp, dir: Bunbury Company

Tooker, Gary L., pres, coo, dir: Motorola

Tookmanian, Donna, treas: Mailman Family Foundation, A. L.

Toole, Allan H., asst secy, asst treas, trust: Leuthold Foundation; trust: Wasmer Foundation

Toole, I., Jr., dir: Santa Fe Pacific Foundation

Toomey, Barbara Knight, trust: Knight Foundation, John S. and James L.

Toomey, Michael J., dir: Shawmut Charitable Foundation

Toot, Joseph Frederick, Jr., pres, dir: Timken Co.

Topazi, Anthony J., dir: Alabama Power Foundation

Topel, Henry, trust: Kutz Foundation, Milton and Hattie

Topham, Neil, sr vp, cfo: HarperCollins Publishers

Topham, Verl, dir: PacifiCorp Foundation

Topkis, William M., trust: Kutz Foundation, Milton and Hattie

Topol, Dee, pres, trust: Primerica Foundation

Topor, Frederic S., trust: AT&T Foundation

Topping, Brian B., treas, dir: Arca Foundation

Topping, Karin, dir (publ rels): Shaklee Corp.

Topping, Melissa Stutsman, vp, secy: Luce Foundation, Henry

Torgerson, William, vp, gen couns: Potomac Electric Power Co.

Tormey, John L., mem distribution comm: GAR Foundation

Torregrossa, Bernice C., grants analyst: Moody Foundation

Torrenzano, Richard, sr vp (corp aff): SmithKline Beecham; pres: SmithKline Beecham Foundation

Torrey, S. K., secy: USG Foundation

Tosh, Dennis A., asst treas: Ford Motor Co. Fund

Tosh, E. C., asst secy: Media General Foundation

Tossell, Sherrie, secy: Thurston Charitable Foundation

Tostengard, Stanford, trust: Lutheran Brotherhood Foundation

Toth, Mary L., secy: Ellis Foundation

Totten, H. W., Jr., dir: Smith and W. Aubrey Smith Charitable Foundation, Clara Blackford

Totten, William, dir: Reader's Digest Foundation

Touchard, William A., pres: Poole & Kent Co.

Touchton, J. Thomas, dir: Beveridge Foundation, Frank Stanley

Toundas, Mary G., contact person: Catlin Charitable Trust, Kathleen K.

Toupin, Arthur Vernon, dir: Bank of America - Giannini Foundation

Touscany, Susan M., dir: Cornerstone Foundation of Northeastern Wisconsin

Tow, Leonard, chmn, ceo: Citizens Utilities Co.

Tower, Caroline, dir: Haigh-Scatena Foundation

Tower, H.L., chmn, dir: Stanhome Inc.

Tower, Marsha, mem: Boatmen's First National Bank of Oklahoma Foundation

Towers, T. R., pres, dir: Universal Leaf Foundation

Towle, Timothy, pres: Boulevard Bank, N.A.; trust: Boulevard Foundation

Towns, Edward R., secy: Reliance Electric Co. Charitable, Scientific & Educational Trust

Vermeer, Matilda, dir: Vermeer Charitable Foundation

Vermeer, Michael, vchmn: Vermeer Investment Company Foundation

Vermeer, Robert L., dir: Vermeer Charitable Foundation; ceo: Vermeer Manufacturing Co.; pres, dir: Vermeer Foundation Co.

Vermillion, Mark, exec dir: Sun Microsystems Foundation

Vernam, Claude, dir: Sundstrand Corp. Foundation

Verney, E. Geoffrey, trust: Verney Foundation, Gilbert

Verney, Richard G., chmn, ceo: Monadnock Paper Mills; pres, dir: Verney Foundation, Gilbert

Verrecchia, Alfred J., treas, trust: Hasbro Charitable Trust

Verret, Paul A., secy, treas: Bigelow Foundation, F. R.; secy: Mardag Foundation; secy: Minnesota Foundation

Verville, Norbert J., treas, dir: Bucyrus-Erie Foundation

Vesce, Joseph, pres, ceo: Mervyn's

Vesce, Joseph C., trust: Dayton Foundation Depository

Vest, George Graham, vp, trust: Doherty Charitable Foundation, Henry L. and Grace

Vestner, Eliot N., trust: Bank of Boston Corp. Charitable Foundation

Vetrovec, Pauline, secy, dir: Jameson Foundation, J. W. and Ida M.

Vett, Thomas W., secy, treas, dir: King Foundation, Carl B. and Florence E.

Vette, John L., III, ceo: SNC Manufacturing Co.; dir: SNC Foundation

Vetter, Charles R., trust: OsCo. Industries Foundation

Veysey, M. C., vp, dir: Gould Foundation

Vezeris, David J., asst secy: Brencanda Foundation

Vezino, Patrick, trust: Marshall Foundation

Viall, William A., trust: Littlefield Memorial Trust, Ida Ballou

Viccellio, Henry, dir: Olmsted Foundation, George and Carol

Vickery, James A., pres: IMT Insurance Co.

Victor, Edward G., dir: Capital Fund Foundation

Victor, Lois B., trust: Merit Gasoline Foundation

Vidal, David, asst vp: Continental Corp. Foundation

Viederman, Stephen, pres: Noyes Foundation, Jessie Smith

Viera, John Joseph, mem (corp responsibility comm): Commonwealth Edison Co.

Viermetz, Kurt F., vchmn: J.P. Morgan & Co.

Vignolo, Biag, Jr., cfo: Sun Chemical Corp.

Vignos, Edith Ingalls, vp, trust: Ingalls Foundation, Louise H. and David S.

Vila, Robert, trust: CSC Industries Foundation

Villanueva, Edward, trust: Circuit City Foundation

Vilmure, Richard A., pres, dir: Muller Foundation

Vinardi, John J., trust: Criss Memorial Foundation, Dr. C.C. and Mabel L.

Vincent, Adele J., exec dir: Cummins Engine Foundation

Vincent, Donna, asst secy: State Farm Cos. Foundation

Vincent, Francis T., Jr., trust: Continental Corp. Foundation

Vincent, Robert C., Jr., chmn, dir: Barclays Bank of New York

Vine, Herbert, contr: Dana Foundation, Charles A.

Viner, Kim, dir commun rels: Colorado National Bankshares

Vingo, J. Ray, cfo: Alaska Airlines, Inc.

Vinovich, William, trust: Anderson Foundation, John W.

Vinson, Frank B., Jr., vp, dir: Mitchell Foundation

Vinson, William T., secy: Lockheed Leadership Fund

Vinton, Mary H., secy: Nichols Foundation

Virtue, Tecla M., pres: Phillipps Foundation

Visceglia, Frank D., mgr: Visciglia Foundation, Frank

Vischer, Dinah B., mem: Merck Family Fund

Visser, Donald, trust: California Foundation for Biochemical Research

Vitale, Alberto, chmn, pres, ceo: Random House Inc.

Vitale, David J., vp, dir: First National Bank of Chicago Foundation

Vititoe, William Paul, trust: Hudson-Webber Foundation

Vittem, Dan, ptnr: Kirkland & Ellis

Vitti, Linda, trust: Price Foundation, Louis and Harold

Vitulli, William, vp (commun & govt rels): Great Atlantic & Pacific Tea Co. Inc.

Viviano, Joseph P., trust: Hershey Foods Corp.

Vjiie, Junichi, co-chmn, coo: Nomura Securities International

Vladeck, Bruce Charney, PhD, trust: Kaiser Family Foundation, Henry J.

Vlasic, James, trust, secy, treas: Vlasic Foundation

Vlasic, Michael A., trust: Vlasic Foundation

Vlasic, Richard R., trust, vp: Vlasic Foundation

Vlasic, Robert Joseph, chmn, chmn exec comm, dir: Campbell Soup Co.; pres, trust, don: Vlasic Foundation

Vlasic, William, trust, vp: Vlasic Foundation

Vleishel, Victor, treas: Fish Foundation, Bert

Vlock, Daniel R., vp, dir: Vlock Family Foundation

Vlock, Jay I., chmn, pres, ceo: Fox Steel Co.; pres, dir: Vlock Family Foundation

Vlock, Laurel F., secy, dir: Vlock Family Foundation

Vodonik, R., sec, trust: Donaldson Foundation

Voelkel, Alice K., pres, dir: Knott Foundation, Marion I. and Henry J.

Voelkerding, David J., trust: Voelkerding Charitable Trust, Walter and Jean

Vogel, Jacqueline Mars, pres: Mars Foundation

Vogel, Stephanie, dir (pub rels): Christian Dior New York, Inc.

Vogelsang, Peter J., dir: Hayden Foundation, William R. and Virginia

Vogelstein, Deborah H., trust, vp: Hirschhorn Foundation, David and Barbara B.

Vogt, Phyllis P., secy: Pet Inc. Community Support Foundation

Vogt, Theodore, adv: O'Bleness Foundation, Charles G.

Voilleque, Anne S., dir: CHC Foundation

Vojvoda, Antoinette, pres: Knapp Foundation

Vojvoda, Robert B., vp: Knapp Foundation

Volk, Harry J., chmn, ceo, dir: Weingart Foundation

Volk, Norman H., vchmn, trust: Hartford Foundation, John A.

Volk, Spencer, ceo: Brooke Group Ltd.

Volk, Spencer J., pres, coo: Church & Dwight Co.

Vollmer, Gustavo A., dir: Vollmer Foundation

Vollmer, Gustavo J., pres, dir: Vollmer Foundation

Vollum, Jean E., chmn, trust: Tektronix Foundation

von Arx, Carol R., bd mem: Roblee Foundation, Joseph H. and Florence A.

Von Boecklin, August, trust: Snyder Foundation, Frost and Margaret

Von der Ahe, Charles K., bd mem: Von der Ahe Foundation

Von der Ahe, Clyde W., MD, vp, dir: Von der Ahe Foundation

Von der Ahe, Frederick T., bd mem: Von der Ahe Foundation; trust: Von der Ahe, Jr. Trust, Theodore Albert

Von der Ahe, Thomas R., bd mem: Von der Ahe Foundation

Von der Ahe, Vincent M., secy, treas, dir: Von der Ahe Foundation

Von der Ahe, Wilfred L., pres, dir: Von der Ahe Foundation

von Echt, John Bachhofen, chmn, ceo: Diversified Industries, Inc.

Von Essen, H. C., dir: Bank of America - Giannini Foundation

von Gontard, Jutta, secy, dir: Levinson Foundation, Max and Anna

von Hoffmann, Beatrix, vp: Arcana Foundation

von Hoffmann, Ladislaus, pres, treas: Arcana Foundation

von Hollen, James, mem adv comm: Bailey Foundation

von Kalinowski, Julian O., vp, dir, mem exec & other comms: Keck Foundation, W. M.

Von Lehman, John I., vp, cfo, treas: Midland Co.

von Mehren, Robert Brandt, vp, dir: Axe-Houghton Foundation

von Rohr, Hans Christoph, chmn, ceo: Kloeckner-Pentaplast of America

Von Rusten, John, secy, treas, dir: PNM Foundation

von Schack, Wesley W., chmn, pres, ceo, dir: Duquesne Light Co.

Von Steen, Verna, secy: Morrison Foundation, Harry W.

von Ziegesar, Franz, vp, trust: Bowne Foundation, Robert

Vonckx, Paul N., Jr., chmn, pres, ceo, dir: Bank of Boston Connecticut

Vondrasek, Frank C., chmn, ceo: Madison Gas & Electric Co.

VonRickenbach, Josef H., pres, treas: Parexel International Corp.

Voorhees, Vernon, sr vp: Business Men's Assurance Co. of America

Voran, Reed D., secy, dir: Ball Brothers Foundation

Vorhees, Charles A., dir: Brach Foundation, Helen

Vorhees, Charles M., chmn, dir, don brother: Brach Foundation, Helen

Voss, Bill, coo: Pilgrim's Pride Corp.

Voss, George, vp: Scroggins Foundation, Arthur E. and Cornelia C.

Vossler, Robert P., trust: Strauss Foundation, Leon

Vout, Murray C., trust: National Pro-Am Youth Fund

Vowles, Joan Hoover, vp, treas, trust: Hoover, Jr. Foundation, Margaret W. and Herbert

Voyles, Bobby, chmn, dir: Citizens Union Bank Foundation

Voyvoda, Antoinette P., trust, vp, treas: Knapp Educational Fund

Vraney, Inge, vp, dir: Koch Foundation

Vraney, Lawrence, dir: Koch Foundation

VumbacCo., J. V., secy, dir: Turner Construction Co. Foundation

W

Wabiszewski, Edmund D., pres: Maynard Steel Casting Co.

Wachenfeld, William, pres, trust: Hayden Foundation, Charles

Wachenheim, Edgar, III, vp: Dorot Foundation; trust: New York Foundation; vp: Pinewood Foundation; dir: Ross Foundation, Arthur; vp, dir: Wallach Foundation, Miriam G. and Ira D.

Wachenheim, Sue W., dir: Wallach Foundation, Miriam G. and Ira D.

Wachs, Elizabeth T., trust: Thalheimer Foundation, Alvin and Fanny Blaustein

Wachtel, Michael A., secy, dir: Oshkosh B'Gosh Foundation

Wachtell, Herbert M., ptnr: Wachtell, Lipton, Rosen & Katz; vp, treas: Wachtell, Lipton, Rosen & Katz Foundation

Wachter, James P., vp, dir: Leach Foundation, Tom & Frances

Wacker, Jerry, ceo: Odessa Trading Co.; mgr, dir: Odessa Trading Co. Educational Trust

Wacker, Roger, sr vp: Union Bank of Switzerland Los Angeles Branch

Wackerman, Dorothy C., vp, dir: CertainTeed Corp. Foundation

Wad, Bernard, mgr: Kramer Foundation

Wada, Yori, dir: Stulsaft Foundation, Morris

Waddell, Douglas M., dir: Heublein Foundation

Waddell, John C., chmn, dir: Arrow Electronics, Inc.

Waddell, Oliver W., trust: Corbett Foundation

Waddell, Oliver Wendell, chmn, dir: Star Bank, N.A.;

vp, trust: Star Bank, N.A., Cincinnati Foundation

Waddell, Theodore H., dir: Hughes Memorial Foundation, Charles Evans

Waddle, Allen C., adm: National City Corporation Charitable Foundation Trust

Wade, Charles B., Jr., trust: Duke Endowment

Wade, Florence, trust: Hargis Charitable Foundation, Estes H. and Florence Parker

Wade, Ormand Joseph, vchmn: Ameritech Corp.

Wade, William, sr vp (adv): Alpha Beta Stores, Inc.

Wadleigh, Theodore, trust: Cogswell Benevolent Trust

Wadsworth, Ermine, pres, dir: Azby Fund

Wadsworth, Frank W., trust: Wenner-Gren Foundation for Anthropological Research

Wadsworth, John S., Jr., trust: United States-Japan Foundation

Waechter, A. J., Jr., trust: Jones Family Foundation, Eugenie and Joseph

Waechter, J. H., trust: Weyerhaeuser Co. Foundation

Wagar, James Lee, mgr: Carter-Wallace Foundation

Wagele, James, vp: BankAmerica Foundation

Waggershauer, William, vchmn: Diamond Walnut Growers

Waggoner, J. Virgil, ceo, pres: Sterling Chemicals Inc.

Wagley, James F., dir: Penney Foundation, James C.

Wagley, Mary Frances, vp, treas, dir: Penney Foundation, James C.

Wagner, Ann, secy, trust: Langendorf Foundation, Stanley S.

Wagner, C.L., Jr., dir: RTM Foundation

Wagner, Corydon, Jr., pres: Merrill Foundation, R. D.

Wagner, David J., pres, ceo: Old Kent Bank & Trust Co.

Wagner, Eulalie Merrill, trust: Merrill Foundation, R. D.

Wagner, Harold A., chmn, pres, ceo, dir: Air Products & Chemicals

Wagner, James, treas: Landmark Charitable Foundation

Wagner, Jeffry, trust: Reeves Foundation

Wagner, Jerome, Jr., pres: Bank One, Sidney, NA

Wagner, John, trust: Winship Memorial Scholarship Foundation

Wagner, Lawrence M., dir: Hillman Foundation; treas: Polk Foundation

Wagner, Lucinda A., trust: Plankenhorn Foundation, Harry

Wagner, Martin S., secy: Institute for Research on Learning

Wagner, Marty, secy: Xerox Foundation

Wagner, Norman P., chmn, dir: Southern Indiana Gas & Electric Co.

Wagner, Richard C., vp-indv ins svcs: Shenandoah Life Insurance Co.

Wagner, Richard H., trust: Wagner Foundation, Ltd., R. H.

Wagner, Robert S., chmn: Wagner Manufacturing Co., E. R.; pres, dir: Wagner

Manufacturing Co.
Foundation, E. R.
Wagner, Roberta, secy, treas:
Wagner Foundation, Ltd., R. H.
Wagner, Seymour, secy:
Garrigues Trust, Edwin B.
Wagner, Thomas Joseph,
chmn: CIGNA Foundation
Wagniere, Daniel C., pres:
Sandoz Foundation Am
Wagoner, G. Richard, cfo, exec
vp: General Motors Corp.
Wahl, Beth Ann, secy:
Axe-Houghton Foundation
Wahlberg, Allen H., pres, treas,
dir: Turner Construction Co.
Foundation; sr vp, cfo: Turner
Corp.
Wahlert, David, trust: Wahlert
Foundation
Wahlert, Donna, trust: Wahlert
Foundation
Wahlert, Jim, trust: Wahlert
Foundation
Wahlert, R. C., trust: Wahlert
Foundation
Wahlert, R. C., III, trust:
Wahlert Foundation
Wahlert, Robert H., ceo, pres:
FDL Foods/Dubuque Packing
Co.; pres, treas, trust: Wahlert
Foundation
Wahlig, Michael J., asst secy,
corp atty: Dayton Hudson
Foundation
Wahlstedt, Robert, pres: Reell
Precision Manufacturing
Wahlstrom, Mats, pres: COBE
Laboratories, Inc.
Wahlstrom, Robert, pres:
Valley Bank Charitable
Foundation
Waid, John M., trust:
Booth-Bricker Fund
Waidmann, Laura M., assoc
vp: Edwards & Sons, A.G.
Waidner, Robert A., treas: Lost
Tree Charitable Foundation
Wainer, Stanley A., chmn exec
comm: Wyle Laboratories
**Wainwright, Carroll
Livingston, Jr.,** dir: Noble
Foundation, Edward John; vp,
secy, dir: Waterfowl Research
Foundation
Wainwright, Cynthia C., dir
(corp social policy): Chemical
Bank
Wainwright, Robin W., dir:
Westwood Endowment
Wainwright, Stuyvesant, III,
treas, trust: Lingnan
Foundation
Waite, Clark G., sr vp, cfo:
Brush Wellman Inc.
Waite, David H., chmn: First
Financial Foundation
Waite, Donald L., sr vp, cfo:
Seagate Technology
Waitzman, James W., Jr., pres,
dir: Tractor & Equipment
Company Foundation
Wajnert, Thomas C., trust:
AT&T Foundation
Wakairo, Kazuo, chief admin
off: Nomura Securities
International
Wakefield, David, exec secy:
Longwood Foundation; exec
secy: Welfare Foundation
Wakefield, Thomas, secy, treas,
trust: Dunspaugh-Dalton
Foundation
Wakley, James T., pres, dir:
McDonough Foundation,
Bernard
Walch, W. Stanley, mem adv
comm: Jordan and Ettie A.
Jordan Charitable Foundation,
Mary Ranken

Walcott, Lee E., Jr., vp,
managing dir: Ahmanson
Foundation
Walda, Julia Inskeep, dir:
Journal Gazette Foundation
Waldbaum, Bernice, treas:
Waldbaum Family Foundation,
I.
Waldbaum, Ira, chmn, pres, dir:
Waldbaum, Inc.; pres:
Waldbaum Family Foundation,
I.
Waldbaum, Julia, dir:
Waldbaum Family Foundation,
I.
Waldman, Eric W., dir:
Gaisman Foundation,
Catherine and Henry J.
Waldman, Saul Joseph, dir:
Detroit Edison Foundation
Waldref, Grant T., pres, dir:
Tozer Foundation
Waldron, Joan, secy:
Bedminster Fund
Waldroup, John, awards adv
comm: Ferebee Endowment,
Percy O.
Wales, Jane, program chmn
(cooperative security):
Carnegie Corporation of New
York
Waletzky, Jeremy P., mem fin
comm: Rockefeller Family
Fund
**Walgreen, Charles Rudolph,
III,** chmn, ceo, dir: Walgreen
Co.; dir: Walgreen Benefit
Fund
Walker, Abigail M., trust:
Walker Foundation, Archie D.
and Bertha H.
Walker, Amy C., trust: Walker
Foundation, Archie D. and
Bertha H.
Walker, Archie D., III, trust:
Walker Foundation, Archie D.
and Bertha H.
Walker, Archie D., Jr., trust:
Walker Foundation, Archie D.
and Bertha H.
Walker, Barrett C., trust:
Walker Educational and
Charitable Foundation, Alex C.
Walker, Berta, vp, trust: Walker
Foundation, Archie D. and
Bertha H.
Walker, Bill, awards adv comm:
Ferebee Endowment, Percy O.
Walker, Billy J., dir: First Union
Foundation
Walker, Brooks, Jr., treas, trust:
Walker Foundation, T. B.
Walker, C. E., trust: Smith
Benevolent Association,
Buckingham
Walker, Charles B., mem
contributions mgmt comm:
Ethyl Corp.
Walker, Charles W., comm:
Thurman Charitable
Foundation for Children,
Edgar A.
Walker, Charlotte M.,
contributions off: Air Products
Foundation
Walker, Dale W., dir: Nalco
Foundation
Walker, Denis J., pres, ceo:
Oregon Mutual Insurance Co.
Walker, Elaine B., trust: Walker
Foundation, Archie D. and
Bertha H.
Walker, Ellen, program exec:
Zellerbach Family Fund
Walker, Fergus, exec vp, cfo:
Redman Industries
Walker, G. P., asst treas:
Armstrong Foundation
Walker, Gene, trust:
Avery-Fuller Children's Center

Walker, George M., III, vp, cfo:
Robbins & Myers, Inc.; treas:
Robbins & Myers Foundation
Walker, George R., trust:
Schepp Foundation, Leopold
Walker, Gloria M., trust:
Walker Foundation, W. E.;
trust: Walker Wildlife
Conservation Foundation
Walker, H. Webster, III, dir:
Campbell Foundation, Ruth
and Henry
Walker, Harry W., trust: Camp
Younts Foundation; dir:
McDougall Charitable Trust,
Ruth Camp
Walker, Harvey L., exec dir,
secy, treas: Cain Foundation,
Effie and Wofford
Walker, Helene, secy, treas:
Kentland Foundation
Walker, James T., Jr., pres,
trust: Metal Industries
Foundation
Walker, Joan Castleberry,
trust: Creel Foundation
Walker, John C., pres, trust:
Walker Foundation, T. B.
Walker, John E., dir: Williams
Foundation, Kemper and Leila
Walker, Joseph P., chmn, pres,
ceo, dir: CTS Corp.
Walker, K. Grahame, pres, ceo,
dir: Dexter Corp.; pres: Dexter
Corp. Foundation
Walker, Kenneth G., dir:
Redfield Foundation, Nell J.
Walker, Leigh Earle, mem:
Piedmont Health Care
Foundation
Walker, Leslie D., cfo: Jensen
Construction Co.
Walker, Mallory, dir: Federal
National Mortgage Assn.
Foundation; chmn emeritus,
mem investment comm:
Meyer Foundation, Eugene
and Agnes E.
Walker, Martin D., chmn, ceo:
Hanna Co., M.A.
Walker, Mary H., trust: Haskell
Fund
Walker, Nancy, trust: Corbett
Foundation
Walker, Norman, pres: Price
Waterhouse Foundation
Walker, Patricia, trust: Walker
Foundation, Archie D. and
Bertha H.
Walker, R. Lance, trust: Walker
Foundation, T. B.
Walker, Richard F., chmn,
trust: Colorado Trust
Walker, Robert, trust: Simon
Foundation, Jennifer Jones
Walker, Ronald F., pres, coo,
dir: American Financial Corp.
Walker, S. Adrian, trust: Walker
Foundation, T. B.
Walker, Shaw, pres, trust:
Walker Foundation, L. C. and
Margaret
Walker, T. P., secy: Stonecutter
Foundation
Walker, T. Urling, trust: Walker
Educational and Charitable
Foundation, Alex C.
Walker, Thomas, chmn:
Servico, Inc.
Walker, Thomas S., trust:
Sumners Foundation, Hatton
W.
Walker, W. E., Jr., trust: Walker
Foundation, W. E.
Walker, W. Evelyn, secy, adm:
Lukens Foundation
Walker, W.E., Jr., trust: Walker
Wildlife Conservation
Foundation

Walker, Walter W., vp, trust:
Walker Foundation, Archie D.
and Bertha H.
Walker, William, trust: Jones
Foundation, Harvey and
Bernice
Walker, William D., trust:
Tektronix Foundation
Walker, Winston W., ceo, pres:
Provident Life & Accident
Insurance Co.
Wall, Irving M., secy: Shubert
Foundation
Wallace, Arthur, pres:
International Paper Co.
Foundation
Wallace, Christine, trust:
Egenton Home
Wallace, David, trust: Egenton
Home; trust: Wickes
Foundation, Harvey Randall
Wallace, David William, pres,
trust: Young Foundation,
Robert R.
Wallace, George R., III, trust:
Wallace Foundation, George R.
Wallace, Henry B., dir: Wallace
Genetic Foundation
Wallace, Jean W., dir: Young
Foundation, Robert R.
Wallace, John A., comm mem:
Abreu Charitable Trust u/w/o
May P. Abreu, Francis I.
Wallace, John C., dir: Mariani
Nut Co. Foundation
Wallace, John D., chmn, pres,
ceo: New Jersey National Bank
Wallace, Keith, pres: BHP Utah
International
Wallace, Paul G., trust, secy:
Anderson Foundation, John W.
Wallace, Robert B., don, dir:
Wallace Genetic Foundation
Wallace, Robert F., pres, coo,
dir: National Westminster
Bank New Jersey
Wallace, Ronnie, dir: Keith
Foundation Trust, Ben E.
Wallace, Sally, Jr., dir, asst
secy: Bordeaux Foundation
Wallace, Sarah R., secy, trust:
Evans Foundation, Thomas J.
Wallace, W. Ray, pres, ceo:
Trinity Industries, Inc.
Wallace, Wayne D., treas:
Central Newspapers
Foundation
Wallace, William H., chmn:
Hawkins Foundation, Robert Z.
Wallach, Diane Gates, vp, trust:
Gates Foundation
Wallach, Ira D., pres, dir:
Wallach Foundation, Miriam
G. and Ira D.
Wallach, James G., pres, ceo:
Central National-Gottesman;
pres: Central National-
Gottesman Foundation; vp,
dir: Wallach Foundation,
Miriam G. and Ira D.
Wallach, Judith, trust: Dreitzer
Foundation
Wallach, Kate B., dir: Wallach
Foundation, Miriam G. and Ira
D.
Wallach, Kenneth L., vp:
Central National- Gottesman
Foundation; vp, dir: Wallach
Foundation, Miriam G. and Ira
D.
Wallach, Mary K., dir: Wallach
Foundation, Miriam G. and Ira
D.
Wallach, Miriam G., vp, dir:
Wallach Foundation, Miriam
G. and Ira D.
Wallach, Susan S., dir: Wallach
Foundation, Miriam G. and Ira
D.

Waller, Debra Steigerwaldt,
dir, vp: Steigerwaldt
Foundation, Donna Wolf
Waller, Kathryn, dir:
Rockefeller Foundation,
Winthrop
Wallestad, Victor C., dir:
Wallestad Foundation
Walley, John, mem adv comm:
Smock Foundation, Frank and
Laura
Wallfisch, Nathan, trust: Helis
Foundation
Wallin, Franklin Whittelsey,
dir: Mertz-Gilmore
Foundation, Joyce
Wallis, Gordon T., treas, chmn
fin comm, mem exec comm:
Tinker Foundation
Wallis, Jeff, trust: Washington
Square Fund
Wallis, Mark, cfo: Lincoln
Property Co.
Wallman, Susan A., vp, secy:
McGraw-Hill Foundation
Wallrabe, H. K., pres: Miles
Inc., Pharmaceutical Division
**Walnutwood, Margaret F.
McKean,** trust: Shore Fund
Walruff, Judy, coordinator,
adolescent pregnancy
program: Flinn Foundation
Walsh, Donald Francis, trust:
Equifax Foundation
Walsh, Edward F., Jr., secy:
Children's Foundation of Erie
County; trust: Goodyear
Foundation, Josephine
Walsh, Edward T., Jr., secy,
asst treas: Rose Foundation,
Billy
Walsh, F. Howard, Jr., trust:
Fleming Foundation
Walsh, F. Howard, Sr., vp,
trust: Fleming Foundation;
pres, don: Walsh Foundation
Walsh, Frank E., Jr., dir: MCJ
Foundation; don, pres, dir:
Sandy Hill Foundation
Walsh, G. M., vp, secy:
Buchanan Family Foundation
Walsh, James, pres, dir: Aydin
Corp.
Walsh, James P., vp, dir:
Dougherty Foundation
Walsh, Jeffrey R., Jr., mgr:
Sandy Hill Foundation
Walsh, John, dir corp rels: Rohr
Inc.
Walsh, John, Jr., dir (J Paul
Getty Museum): Getty Trust,
J. Paul
Walsh, John F., trust: Thomas &
Betts Charitable Trust
Walsh, John N., III, trust:
Western New York Foundation
Walsh, John N., Jr., dir:
Cummings Foundation, James
H.
Walsh, Joseph W., vp: Beck
Foundation, Elsie E. & Joseph
W.
Walsh, Linda D., trust: Strake
Foundation
Walsh, Mary D., pres, trust:
Fleming Foundation; vp:
Walsh Foundation
Walsh, Mary D., Jr., secy, dir:
Sandy Hill Foundation
Walsh, Mason, Jr., trust: Mellon
Foundation, Richard King
Walsh, Michael H., chmn, ceo:
Tenneco
Walsh, Michael J., treas:
CertainTeed Corp. Foundation
Walsh, Michael W., treas, trust:
Kynett Memorial Foundation,
Edna G.
Walsh, Semmes G., gov: Baker,
Jr. Memorial Fund, William G.

Walsh, William M., Jr., trust: Fitz-Gibbon Charitable Trust

Walshok, Mary, Jr., trust: Girard Foundation

Walter, Donald F., pres: Hunter Foundation, Edward and Irma

Walter, Gerald K., trust: Amsted Industries Foundation

Walter, Henry C., dir: Dreyfus Foundation, Camille and Henry

Walter, Henry G., Jr., dir: Monell Foundation, Ambrose; trust: United States-Japan Foundation; dir: van Ameringen Foundation; trust: Vetlesen Foundation, G. Unger

Walter, James W., chmn: Walter Industries; trust: Walter Foundation

Walter, John R., chmn, ceo, dir: Donnelley & Sons Co., R.R.

Walter, John T., Jr., trust: Perot Foundation

Walter, Joseph J., SJ, pres, dir: Butler Foundation, J. Homer

Walter, Robert A., trust: Walter Foundation

Waltermire, Thomas, vp: BFGoodrich Foundation

Walters, Carole H., trust, vp: Hershey Foundation

Walters, Geoffrey King, dir: Research Corporation

Walters, Harry N., pres, ceo: Great Lakes Carbon Corp.

Walters, J. A., co-chmn: Alcon Foundation

Walters, Kirk W., cfo: Northeast Savings, FA

Walters, Rick, comm mem: Sherman Educational Fund

Walters, Robert, secy: Kloster Cruise Ltd.

Walters, Sumner J., trust: Van Wert County Foundation

Walthall, Paul T., trust: Walthall Perpetual Charitable Trust, Marjorie T.

Walthall, Wilson J., III, trust: Walthall Perpetual Charitable Trust, Marjorie T.

Walther, Jules G., trust: Capita Charitable Trust, Emil

Walton, Alice L., trust: Walton Foundation; dir: Walton Family Foundation

Walton, Helen Robson, trust: Walton Foundation; don, dir: Walton Family Foundation

Walton, James C., trust: Walton Foundation; dir: Walton Family Foundation

Walton, James Mellon, chmn: Heinz Endowment, Vira I.; trust: Scaife Family Foundation; trust: Scaife Foundation, Sarah

Walton, John T., trust: Walton Foundation; dir: Walton Family Foundation

Walton, Jon D., trust: Allegheny Ludlum Foundation

Walton, Jonathan Taylor, trust: Kellogg Foundation, W. K.

Walton, Richard, trust: Bank of Alma Charitable Trust; comm: Hope Memorial Fund, Blanche and Thomas

Walton, Richard E., secy, dir: Heublein Foundation

Walton, S. Robson, chmn: Wal-Mart Stores; chmn: Wal-Mart Stores, Inc.; trust: Walton Foundation; dir: Walton Family Foundation

Walton, Samuel M., chmn, dir: Wal-Mart Stores, Inc.

Waltrip, Robert L., chmn, ceo, dir: Service Corp. International

Waltz, Walter, Sheaffer Inc.

Walzel, James V., trust: Murfee Endowment, Kathryn

Wander, Herbert, secy, dir: Katten, Muchin, & Zavis Foundation

Wang, Charles B., ceo, pres: Computer Associates International

Wang, Tso-Yun, dir: China Times Cultural Foundation

Wang, Yung-ching, chmn, dir: Formosa Plastics Corp. U.S.A.

Wangstad, Kristi Rollag, pres: Alliant Community Investment Foundation

Wanlass, George R., comm mem: Caine Charitable Foundation, Marie Eccles

Wanlass, Kathryn C., comm mem: Caine Charitable Foundation, Marie Eccles

Wanner, Erk, pres, trust: Sage Foundation, Russell

Warburg, James P., Jr., trust: Bydale Foundation

Warburg, Jenny, trust: Bydale Foundation

Warburg, Joan M., pres, trust: Bydale Foundation

Warburg, Philip N., trust: Bydale Foundation

Ward, Adelaide C., vp, treas: Ward Foundation, Louis L. and Adelaide C.

Ward, Carl, secy: Fish Foundation, Bert

Ward, Dick, cfo: Schreiber Foods, Inc.

Ward, Douglas, pres: Hooper Handling

Ward, Frank A., Jr., dir: Durham Merchants Association Charitable Foundation

Ward, George B. P., Jr., secy, treas: MNC Financial Foundation

Ward, Harold A., III, secy: Genius Foundation, Elizabeth Morse

Ward, J., dir: Community Hospital Foundation

Ward, James J., vp, secy, dir: Trust Funds

Ward, Joe L., chmn: Ward Co., Joe L.

Ward, Joe L., Jr., trust: Ward Co. Ltd. Charitable Trust, Joe L.

Ward, John P., asst secy: Ashland Oil Foundation

Ward, Lawrence W., Jr., cfo: Plantronics, Inc.

Ward, Lester L., Jr., secy, treas: Thatcher Foundation

Ward, Loraine, secy, treas: Whitener Foundation

Ward, Louis Larrick, pres: Ward Foundation, Louis L. and Adelaide C.

Ward, Mabel B., exec dir: Bedsole Foundation, J. L.

Ward, Martha, asst secy, dir: Aron Charitable Foundation, J.

Ward, Martha B., trust: Richfood Educational Trust

Ward, Milton H., chmn, ceo, dir: Cyprus Minerals Co.

Ward, Patrick J., chmn, pres, ceo: Caltex Petroleum Corp.

Ward, Ralph, pres, treas, dir: McMillan, Jr. Foundation, Bruce

Ward, Ralph, Jr., secy, dir: McMillan, Jr. Foundation, Bruce

Ward, Robert F., dir: Hardin Foundation, Phil

Ward, Rodman, Jr., trust: Lalor Foundation

Ward, Suzanne, dir pub aff: Syntex Corp.

Ward, Terry W., treas: Farish Fund, William Stamps

Ward, William R., Jr., asst secy, asst treas: Vaughan Foundation, Rachael and Ben

Wardeberg, George E., dir: WICOR Foundation

Warden, Bert M., vp, dir: Martin Foundation, Bert William

Warden, William G., III, dir: Superior-Pacific Fund

Warden, Winifred M., pres, dir: Martin Foundation, Bert William

Wardlaw, Ednabelle Raine, chmn, trust: Wardlaw Fund, Gertrude and William C.

Wardlaw, William C., III, trust: Wardlaw Fund, Gertrude and William C.

Wardle, Corinne G., trust: Wardle Family Foundation

Wardle, Robert V., trust: Wardle Family Foundation

Wardley, George P., III, secy: Utica National Group Foundation

Ware, John H., III, chmn emeritus: Oxford Foundation

Ware, John H., IV, vp: Oxford Foundation

Ware, K. E., trust: Acme-Cleveland Foundation

Ware, Marian S., chmn, pres: Oxford Foundation

Ware, Paul W., vp: Oxford Foundation

Ware, Rhoda C., chmn, trust: Ware Foundation

Ware, Richard A., pres emeritus, trust: Earhart Foundation

Wareham, James L., pres, coo, dir: Wheeling-Pittsburgh Corp.

Wareing, Elizabeth B., dir: Scurlock Foundation

Waren, Wilbert W., Jr., dir: Baird Brothers Co. Foundation

Wargo, Bruce W., trust: Anderson Foundation, John W.

Warhola, John, vp, dir: Warhol Foundation for the Visual Arts, Andy

Waring, Bayard D., trust: Peabody Foundation, Amelia

Waring, Lloyd B., trust: Peabody Foundation, Amelia

Waring, P., trust: Peabody Foundation, Amelia

Wark, Robert R., dir: Scott Foundation, Virginia Steele

Warnemunde, Bradley L., chmn, ceo: Ohio National Life Insurance Co.; pres, trust: Ohio National Foundation

Warner, C. Elizabeth, dir: Public Welfare Foundation

Warner, David, vp, cfo: Microdot, Inc.

Warner, Donald T., chmn, dir: Public Welfare Foundation

Warner, Douglas A., III, pres, dir: J.P. Morgan & Co.

Warner, Joseph C., trust: Simon Foundation, Sidney, Milton and Leoma

Warner, Meryl, trust: Simon Foundation, Sidney, Milton and Leoma

Warner, Norton E., trust: Cooper Foundation

Warner, Philip G., dir: Houston Endowment

Warner, Robert S., trust: Van Nuys Charities, J. B. and Emily

Warner, Theodore K., Jr., dir: Independence Foundation

Warner, Walter D., pres, dir: Gildred Foundation

Warner, William S., chmn, ceo, dir: Hydraulic Co.

Warnick, William V., mem screening comm: PPG Industries Foundation

Warnke, Karl J., vp: Davey Co. Foundation

Warr, Gene, pres: 28:19

Warrell, Jonas E., chmn: Pennsylvania Dutch Co.; chmn: Pennsylvania Dutch Co. Foundation

Warrell, Lincoln A., pres: Pennsylvania Dutch Co.; secy: Pennsylvania Dutch Co. Foundation

Warren, Arthur M., sr vp, cfo: MBIA, Inc.

Warren, Charles O., gov: Crary Foundation, Bruce L.

Warren, David, vp, mgr commun affs: Sumitomo Trust & Banking Co., Ltd.

Warren, H. David, pres, ceo: Tremco Inc.

Warren, Ingrid R., mem exec comm, dir: Dodge Foundation, Cleveland H.

Warren, John A., pres: Summer Foundation

Warren, Natalie O., don, vchmn, dir: Warren Foundation, William K.

Warren, Peter F., Jr., trust: Martin Marietta Corp. Foundation

Warren, Rupert, pres,dir: Julia R. and Estelle L. Foundation

Warren, W. K., Jr., vchmn, dir: Warren Foundation, William K.

Warren, William B., pres, dir: Cintas Foundation

Warren, William K., pres, dir: Warren Charite

Warren, William Michael, Jr., pres, coo, dir: Alabama Gas Corp. (An Energen Co.)

Warriner, Jane Cunningham, mem distribution comm: Oliver Memorial Trust Foundation

Warsh, Herman E., trust: Mott Fund, Ruth; secy, cfo: Warsh-Mott Legacy

Warshaver, Shirley, secy: Goldman Foundation, Morris and Rose

Warson, Toby Gene, pres, ceo, dir: Alliant Techsystems; dir: Alliant Community Investment Foundation

Warwick, William J., vchmn: New Jersey Manufacturers Insurance Co.

Wasch, Susan Beck, trust: Beck Foundation

Wash, James R., secy, treas: Temple-Inland Foundation

Washborn, Lynn S., vp, dir: Flagler Foundation

Washburn, Frank, vp: Pamida Foundation

Washburn, Wilcomb Edward, dir: Donner Foundation, William H.

Washington, Don, mgr (commun & investor rels): Babcock & Wilcox Co.; mem (contributions comm): McDermott

Washington, Leroy M., treas, trust: Community Cooperative Development Foundation

Washington, Valora, vp (programming): Kellogg Foundation, W. K.

Wasik, Vincent A., pres, ceo, dir: National Car Rental System, Inc.

Wasserman, Bronna, mem (contributions comm): GATX Corp.

Wasserman, Edith, vp, cfo, secy: Wasserman Foundation

Wasserman, Harry Hershal, dir: Dreyfus Foundation, Camille and Henry

Wasserman, Lew Robert, chmn, ceo, dir, mem exec comm: MCA; chmn: Stein Foundation, Jules and Doris; pres: Wasserman Foundation

Wasserman, Michael G., asst secy: Georgia Scientific and Technical Research Foundation

Watanabe, Jeffrey N., dir: HEI Charitable Foundation

Watanabe, Lorraine, asst secy: Institute for Research on Learning

Watari, A., pres: Nichimen America, Inc.

Waterbury, James B., dir: McElroy Trust, R. J.

Waterman, Herb, treas: Larrabee Fund Association

Waterman, Irwin G., chmn, dir: Levy's Lumber & Building Centers Foundation

Waterman, William M., secy, dir: Morania Foundation

Waters, Bill W., chmn, trust: Brown Foundation, M. K.

Waters, Faith P., trust: Waters Foundation

Waters, J. Gary, trust: Trion Charitable Foundation

Waters, James L., trust: Waters Foundation

Waters, Richard C., trust: Waters Foundation

Waters, Robert N., trust: Baker Foundation, R. C.

Waters, Sandra, trust: Brown Foundation, M. K.

Watkins, Bill, chmn: Watkins Associated Industries; pres, dir: Watkins Christian Foundation

Watkins, Dean A., chmn: Watkins-Johnson Co.

Watkins, Edward G., chmn, pres: Simplex Time Recorder Co.

Watkins, Edwin H., secy, treas, dir: Field Foundation, Jamee and Marshall

Watkins, George, pres: Watkins Associated Industries; vp, dir: Watkins Christian Foundation

Watkins, Hays T., chmn: B & O Railroad Museum; chmn emeritus: CSX Corp.

Watkins, James D., trust: Carnegie Corporation of New York

Watkins, John, trust: Wagnalls Memorial

Watkins, Joseph R., trust: Stearns Charitable Foundation, Anna B.

Watkins, Randall A., contr, asst treas: Regenstein Foundation

Watkins, Ruth Ann, trust: Retirement Research Foundation

Watkins, Wallace H., vp, dir: Utica National Group Foundation

Watkins, Wallace W., pres: Utica National Insurance Group

Watrous, Bruce H., treas: Rockfall Foundation

Watrous, Helen, Joslin-Needham Family Foundation

Watrous, Helen C., trust: Petteys Memorial Foundation, Jack

Watson, Alonzo Wallace, Jr., secy, dir: Eccles Foundation, George S. and Dolores Dore; comm mem: Eccles Foundation, Marriner S.; secy, dir: Treadwell Foundation, Nora Eccles

Watson, Bernard C., PhD, pres, ceo, dir: Penn Foundation, William

Watson, Charles H., dir: Arvin Foundation

Watson, Donna, asst mgr commun rels: Ameritech Publishing

Watson, Douglas G., pres: Ciba-Geigy Corp. (Pharmaceuticals Division)

Watson, Hugh, dir: Keith Foundation Trust, Ben E.

Watson, Jack M., consultant: Starling Foundation, Dorothy Richard

Watson, James, dir: Life Sciences Research Foundation

Watson, Jane W., asst secy, asst treas: Ingalls Foundation, Louise H. and David S.

Watson, John, pres: American Foundation; trust: Arise Charitable Trust

Watson, John C., pres, coo: Franklin Life Insurance Co.

Watson, K. H., treas, trust: Rinker Cos. Foundation

Watson, Larry, vchmn: Mississippi Power Foundation

Watson, Michael B., secy: Mellon Foundation, Richard King

Watson, Noel G., vp, dir: Jacobs Engineering Foundation

Watson, P. K., trust: Vicksburg Hospital Medical Foundation

Watson, Philip, Jr., secy, treas: Vicksburg Hospital Medical Foundation

Watson, Roslyn M., trust: Hyams Foundation

Watson, Solomon Brown, IV, vp: New York Times Co. Foundation

Watson, Stephen E., pres: Dayton Hudson Corp.; trust: Dayton Hudson Foundation

Watson, Steven L., vp, secy, dir: Simmons Foundation, Harold

Watson, Stuart, secy: Haley Foundation, W. B.

Watson, Thomas J., III, mem adv bd: Watson Foundation, Thomas J.

Watson, Wendy Everett, dir: Sierra Health Foundation

Watt, Charles H., vp: Cherokee Foundation

Watt, Charles H., III, treas: Cherokee Foundation

Watt, J. Scott, ceo, vchmn: Watt Industry

Watt, Raymond A., ceo: Watt Industry

Wattles, Elizabeth C., dir: Bayne Fund, Howard

Wattles, Gurdon B., pres, dir: Bayne Fund, Howard

Wattles, John C., trust: Monroe-Brown Foundation

Wattleton, Faye, trust: Kaiser Family Foundation, Henry J.

Wattman, K. E., pres: Kao Corp. of America (DE)

Watts, Carl S., pres, ceo: Tasty Baking Co.; trust: Tasty Baking Foundation

Watts, Chene, secy: Library Association of Warehouse Point

Watts, Dave Henry, vp: Norfolk Southern Foundation

Watts, Elise Phillips, secy, dir: Phillips Foundation, Ellis L.

Watts, John H., III, dir, mem exec comm: Burden Foundation, Florence V.

Watts, Vinson A., dir: Robinson Mountain Fund, E. O.

Watumull, Gulab, pres, dir: Watumull Fund, J.

Watumull, Khubchand, vp, dir: Watumull Fund, J.

Watumull, Sundri R., treas: Watumull Fund, J.

Waxenberg, Richard, trust: Giant Food Foundation

Waxlax, Lorne R., exec vp (diversified oper): Gillette Co.

Way, Janice H., trust: Thomas & Betts Charitable Trust

Wayburn, Laurie A., dir: Compton Foundation

Weale, Ross, dir, chmn: Westchester Health Fund

Wean, Gordon B., mem bd adms: Wean Foundation, Raymond John

Wean, Raymond J., III, vchmn bd adms: Wean Foundation, Raymond John

Wean, Raymond J., Jr., don, chmn bd adms: Wean Foundation, Raymond John

Wearing, Raymond, vchmn, dir: Joyce Foundation

Wearn, Wilson C., trust: Symmes Foundation, F. W.

Weary, Dale J., treas: Jellison Benevolent Society

Weary, Daniel C., trust: Turner Charitable Trust, Courtney S.

Weary, Robert K., pres: Jellison Benevolent Society

Weary, Thomas S., dir: Cameron Memorial Fund, Alpin J. and Alpin W.

Weatherby, H. Allen, trust: Starling Foundation, Dorothy Richard

Weatherford, T. L., mem adv comm: Blue Bell Foundation

Weatherhead, Albert J., III, pres, trust: Weatherhead Foundation

Weatherhead, Celia, vp, trust: Weatherhead Foundation

Weatherhead, Dwight S., vp, secy, trust: Weatherhead Foundation

Weatherhead, John P., vp, trust: Weatherhead Foundation

Weatherhead, Michael H., vp, trust: Weatherhead Foundation

Weatherstone, Dennis, ceo, dir: J.P. Morgan & Co.; trust: Merck Co. Foundation

Weatherwax, David E., trust: Consolidated Natural Gas Co. Foundation

Weatherwax, Peter A., trust: Weatherwax Foundation

Weaver, Ashley E., trust: Weaver Foundation

Weaver, Connie, contributions adm: Boise Cascade Corp.

Weaver, Dale M., mgr: United Service Foundation

Weaver, Edith H., trust: Weaver Foundation

Weaver, Eudora J., trust, Weaver Foundation, Gil and Dody

Weaver, George W., trust: Buehler Foundation, Emil

Weaver, H. M., pres, chmn, trust: Weaver Foundation

Weaver, Henry O., trust, pres: Kayser Foundation

Weaver, James D., pres, coo: Cain Foundation, Gordon and Mary

Weaver, James R., secy: Kent-Lucas Foundation

Weaver, Jean J., trust: Orleton Trust Fund

Weaver, John F., dir: La-Z-Boy Foundation

Weaver, Michele D., trust: Weaver Foundation

Weaver, Neal C., secy, treas, trust: Bourns Foundation

Weaver, R. H., bd mem: Roberts Foundation, Dora

Weaver, Sharyn A., vp: Cain Foundation, Gordon and Mary

Weaver, Sterling L., chmn, dir: Gleason Memorial Fund

Weaver, Terrance R., vp pub & govt affairs: Amoco Corp.

Weaver, Thomas A., dir: Hertz Foundation, Fannie and John

Weaver, Thomas C., trust: Acushnet Foundation

Weaver, Tom, vp human resources: Isuzu Motors America Inc.

Weaver, Warren W., pres, dir: Commerce Foundation

Weaver, William R., M.D., trust: Weaver Foundation, Gil and Dody

Webb, Anne B., Jr., trust: Braitmayer Foundation

Webb, Charles B., Jr., trust: Webb Charitable Trust, Susan Mott

Webb, Charles G., pres: Packer Foundation, Horace B.

Webb, Clinton, treas, asst to pres: Scott Foundation, William R., John G., and Emma

Webb, Jack, trust: Ackerman Trust, Anna Keesling

Webb, Jim, pres: Indiana Desk Co.

Webb, Lewis, Jr., dir: Berger Foundation, H.N. and Frances C.

Webb, O. Glenn, chmn: Growmark, Inc.

Webb, Thomas C., pres, ceo, dir: Central Vermont Public Service Corp.

Webb, William A., M.D., bd mem: Caring Foundation

Webber, Howard C., dir: Graphic Arts Education & Research Foundation

Webber, I. E., chmn: Mayne Nickless

Webber, W. Temple, vchmn: Temple Foundation, T. L. L.

Webber, William B., trust: Templeton Foundation, Herbert A.

Weber, Carol, dir cust satisfaction: Knight-Ridder, Inc.

Weber, Clement C., exec dir: Leach Foundation, Tom & Frances

Weber, Dr. Robert W., vp: Smoot Charitable Foundation

Weber, Edward, trust: Miniger Memorial Foundation, Clement O.

Weber, Joy, secy: Sharp Foundation

Weber, Judy, vp: Haven Charitable Foundation, Nina

Weber, Maynard, trust: Abrams Foundation

Weber, Nancy W., dir program admin: Markey Charitable Trust, Lucille P.

Weber, Roy E., chmn, ceo, dir: Great Lakes Bancorp, FSB

Weber, William, vp, dir: Texas Instruments

Webre, John F., trust: Burkitt Foundation

Webster, Arthur E., Jr., dir, secy: Rockfall Foundation

Webster, Cindy, vp: Cherokee Foundation

Webster, Curtis, secy: Columbia Savings Charitable Foundation

Webster, Curtis M., exec vp, trust: McGraw Foundation, Curtis W.

Webster, David W., pres, trust: General Educational Fund

Webster, Dean K., Webster Charitable Foundation; pres: Webster Co., H. K.

Webster, Eliza, secy, dir: Webster Charitable Foundation

Webster, Elizabeth McGraw, pres, trust: McGraw Foundation, Curtis W.

Webster, Elroy, pres, trust: CENEX Foundation

Webster, Marjorie K., vp, treas, dir: Winona Corporation

Webster, Martin H., pres, dir: Kirchgessner Foundation, Karl

Webster, R. Kingman, trust: Webster Charitable Foundation

Webster, Susan, admin: Reynolds & Reynolds Company Foundation

Webster, Wally, vp, mgr: Seafirst Corp.; trust: Seafirst Foundation

Webster, Walter N., Webster Charitable Foundation; chmn: Webster Co., H. K.

Wechsler, Alan, trust: Simon Foundation, Sidney, Milton and Leoma

Wechsler, Irving A., treas: Jennings Foundation, Mary Hillman

Weckbaugh, Anne H., dir: Mullen Foundation, J. K.

Weckbaugh, J. Kernan, pres, dir: Mullen Foundation, J. K.

Weckbaugh, John K., vp, dir: Mullen Foundation, J. K.

Weckbaugh, Walter S., treas, dir: Mullen Foundation, J. K.

Weckstein, Wendy H., dir: Goldstein Foundation, Alfred and Ann

Wedding, Matthew, secy, treas, dir: Wallace Computer Services Foundation

Wedum, John A., vp: Wedum Foundation

Wedum, Mary Beth, secy: Wedum Foundation

Weeden, Alan Norman, pres, dir: Weeden Foundation, Frank

Weeden, Curt, vp: Johnson & Johnson Family of Cos. Contribution Fund

Weeden, John D., secy, treas, dir: Weeden Foundation, Frank

Weeden, William F., vp, dir: Weeden Foundation, Frank

Weedman, Sidney, vp govt rels: National City Bank of Indiana

Weedon, D. Reed, Jr., trust: Little Foundation, Arthur D.

Weekley, Harold J., treas: Brown Charitable Trust, Dora Maclellan

Weekly, John W., pres, coo: Mutual of Omaha Insurance Co.

Weeks, Charles E., vchmn: Citizens Commercial & Savings Bank

Weeks, John F., Jr., chmn: Page Belting Co.

Weeks, Joshua J., trust: Johnson Foundation, Howard

Weeks, Lee G., dir: Edison Brothers Stores Foundation

Weeks, W. E., treas, dir: Warren Charite; dir: Warren Foundation, William K.

Weeks, William H., trust: Johnson Foundation, Howard

Weese, Benjamin Horace, trust: Graham Foundation for Advanced Studies in the Fine Arts

Weese, Elizabeth Grass, dir: Grass Family Foundation

Wege, Peter M., vchmn, dir: Steelcase; trust: Steelcase Foundation; pres: Wege Foundation

Wege, Peter M., II, vp: Wege Foundation

Wegener, C. D., secy, dir: Vilter Foundation

Wegener, Clenard, trust, treas: Wegener Foundation, Herman and Mary

Wegener, Kenneth, trust: Wegener Foundation, Herman and Mary

Wegener, Raymond Lee, trust: Wegener Foundation, Herman and Mary

Wegener, Willis B., trust: Wegener Foundation, Herman and Mary

Weger, James E., pres: Hauss-Helms Foundation

Weger, Ronald E., trust, treas: Thoman Foundation, W. B. and Candace

Wegmann, Karen, pres, dir: Wells Fargo Foundation

Wegner, Arthur E., dir: Dexter Corp. Foundation

Wegner, K., cfo: Vilter Manufacturing Corp.

Wehling, Robert Louis, pres, trust: Procter & Gamble Fund

Wehmeier, Helge H., pres, ceo: Miles Inc.

Wehr, Martha J., secy, treas: DCB Foundation

Wehrle, L. F., vchmn, dir: Electric Power Equipment Co. Foundation

Weide, William W., vchmn, dir: Fleetwood Enterprises, Inc.

Weidlein, Edward R., Jr., trust: Frick Foundation, Helen Clay

Weidlein, Mary Rea, dir: Dodge Foundation, Cleveland H.

Weidman, John N., dir: SICO Foundation

Weiesner, John J., pres, ceo: Anthony Co., C.R.

Weigel, Rainer R., trust: Hanson Testamentary Charitable Trust, Anna Emery

Weigell, Bonnie R., chmn: McBeath Foundation, Faye

Weigman, Julie, trust: Lassen Foundation, Irving A.

Weiksner, George B., Jr., dir: Markle Foundation, John and Mary R.

Weil, Adolf, Jr., trust: Randa

Weil, Amanda E., dir: Norman Foundation

Weil, Andrew L., secy: Jennings Foundation, Mary Hillman

Weil, David S., pres, dir: Ampacet Corp.

Weil, Erwin A., trust: Sussman Trust, Otto

Weil, Frank A., pres, dir: Norman Foundation

Weil, Jack, mgr: Belz Foundation

Weil, Paul P., trust: Tilles Nonsectarian Charity Fund, Rosalie

Weil, Rae, trust: Gerson Family Foundation, Benjamin J.

Weil, Robert S., trust: Randa

Weil, Sandison E., dir: Norman Foundation

Weil, William S., dir: Norman Foundation

Weiler, Alan G., don, trust: Pines Bridge Foundation

Weiler, Elaine, trust: Pines Bridge Foundation

Weiler, Rhoda, dir: Weiler Foundation, Theodore & Renee

Weiler, Timothy L., secy, dir: Steiner Foundation

Weill, Sanford I., chmn, ceo, dir: Primerica Corp.; chmn: Primerica Foundation

Weiller, Margaret S., trust: Rich Foundation

Wein, Lawrence A., trust: Morse, Jr. Foundation, Enid and Lester S.

Weinberg, Carol, vp, dir: Relations Foundation

Weinberg, Daniel C., vp, dir: Relations Foundation

Weinberg, David, co-chmn: Fel-Pro Incorporated; asst treas: Fel-Pro/ Mecklenburger Foundation; treas, dir: Relations Foundation; asst treas: Weinberg Foundation, Harry and Jeanette

Weinberg, Ed, secy, treas: Gardner Charitable Foundation, Edith D.

Weinberg, Harvey A., chmn, ceo, dir: Hartmarx Corp.

Weinberg, Jean H., trust: Weinberg Foundation, John L.

Weinberg, John H., trust: Weinberg Foundation, John L.

Weinberg, John Livingston, sr chmn: Goldman Sachs & Co.; chmn, pres, dir: Goldman Sachs Fund; trust: Weinberg Foundation, John L.; trust: Whitehead Foundation

Weinberg, Martin S., pres: Gardner Charitable Foundation, Edith D.; dir: Rosenthal Foundation

Weinberg, Nathan, vp, secy, dir: Weinberg Foundation, Harry and Jeanette

Weinberg, Paul, exec vp, cfo: San Francisco Federal Savings & Loan Association

Weinberg, Penni, trust: Mandel Foundation, Joseph and Florence

Weinberg, Peter A., trust: Weinberg, Jr. Foundation, Sidney J.

Weinberg, Sidney J., Jr., trust: Weinberg, Jr. Foundation, Sidney J.

Weinberg, Sue Ann, trust: Weinberg Foundation, John L.

Weinberg, Sydney H., trust: Weinberg, Jr. Foundation, Sidney J.

Weinberg, William, vp, dir: Weinberg Foundation, Harry and Jeanette

Weinberger, Judah, vp: Tauber Foundation

Weiner, Gila Rosenhaus, dir: Rosenhaus Peace Foundation, Sarah and Matthew

Weiner, Leon, secy, treas, dir: Weiner Foundation; chmn, ceo: Weiner's Stores

Weiner, Leonard H., vp, trust: DeRoy Foundation, Helen L.; pres, trust: DeRoy Testamentary Foundation

Weiner, Sol B., vp, dir: Weiner Foundation; pres: Weiner's Stores

Weiner, Walter, chmn, ceo, dir: Republic New York Corp.

Weingart, Florence B., secy, dir: Greene Foundation, David J.

Weinglass, Leonard Michael, chmn: Merry-Go-Round Enterprises, Inc.

Weingrow, Howard, co-chmn: Marcade Group, Inc.

Weinheimer, Terri, secy, treas: Kellwood Foundation

Weinman, Charles H., trust: Eisenberg Foundation, George M.

Weinroth, Stephen D., chmn, ceo: Integrated Resources

Weins, Leo M., pres, treas, dir: Wilson Foundation, H. W.

Weinstein, A. J., dir: Lilly & Co. Foundation, Eli

Weinstein, Alvin, chmn: Concord Fabrics, Inc.

Weinstein, Frank, vchmn: Concord Fabrics, Inc.

Weinstein, Judith R., trust: Blaustein Foundation, Jacob and Hilda

Weintraub, Allen, pres, ceo, dir: Advest Group, Inc.

Weintraub, Hortense, treas: Weintraub Family Foundation, Joseph

Weintraub, Leonard, treas: Silverburgh Foundation, Grace, George & Judith

Weintraub, Michael, pres: Weintraub Family Foundation, Joseph

Weintraub, Robert M., secy, dir: Alexander Foundation, Joseph

Weir, Charles D., trust: Weir Foundation Trust

Weir, Gavin, chmn, pres: Chicago City Bank & Trust Co.

Weir, William C., MD, Brush Foundation

Weis, James J., vp, cfo: Publicker Industries, Inc.

Weis, Konrad M., chmn, dir: AGFA Division of Miles Inc.

Weisberg, Harry M., vp: Batchelor Foundation

Weisberg, Michael C., vp, dir: Thalhimer Brothers Foundation

Weisbruch, Doug, vp commun aff: Enserch Corp.

Weisenbeck, Arnold, vp: CENEX Foundation

Weisenburger, Randall J., co-chmn, dir: Collins & Aikman Holdings Foundation

Weiser, Irving, pres, ceo, dir: Dain Bosworth/Inter- Regional Financial Group

Weiser, J. W., pres, dir: Bechtel Foundation

Weisglass, Celeste C., pres, dir: Cheatham Foundation, Owen

Weisglass, Stephen S., vp, treas, dir: Cheatham Foundation, Owen

Weishaus, Enid R., mem: American Express Co.

Weisheit, Bowen P., vp, dir: Kelly, Jr. Memorial Foundation, Ensign C. Markland

Weisheit, Bowen P., Jr., treas, dir: Kelly, Jr. Memorial Foundation, Ensign C. Markland

Weisl, Edwin L., Jr., vp, dir: Lehman Foundation, Robert

Weisman, Frances R., Ritter Foundation

Weisman, Frederick R., don: Weisman Art Foundation, Frederick R.

Weisman, Marcia S., trust: Weisman Art Foundation, Frederick R.

Weiss, Andrew H., trust: Stanton Fund, Ruth and Frank

Weiss, Arthur D., trust: Weiss Fund, Clara

Weiss, Betty J., publ aff coordinator: Rochester Telephone Corp.

Weiss, Catherine, trust: Huber Foundation

Weiss, Cora, pres: Rubin Foundation, Samuel

Weiss, Daniel, dir: Rubin Foundation, Samuel

Weiss, David C., trust, mgr: Weiss Fund, Clara

Weiss, David R., trust: AVI CHAI - A Philanthropic Foundation

Weiss, Donald L., chmn, pres: First Colorado Bank & Trust, N.A.

Weiss, Gary, vp, secy, trust: Sapirstein-Stone-Weiss Foundation

Weiss, Jeffrey, trust: Sapirstein-Stone-Weiss Foundation

Weiss, Judy, vp: Rubin Foundation, Samuel

Weiss, Konrad M., chmn: Miles Inc., Diagnostic Division

Weiss, Mary K., dir: Weiss Foundation, William E.

Weiss, Morry, chmn, ceo: American Greetings Corp.; off: American Greetings Corp. Foundation; vp, treas: Sapirstein-Stone-Weiss Foundation

Weiss, Peter, treas: Rubin Foundation, Samuel

Weiss, Richard M., trust: Eder Foundation, Sidney and Arthur

Weiss, Robert E., vp admin: Meadows Foundation

Weiss, Robert L., trust: Foss Memorial Employees Trust, Donald J.; trust: Weiss Fund, Clara

Weiss, Roger J., secy, treas: Weiss Foundation, Stephen and Suzanne

Weiss, Stephen, secy, trust: Innovating Worthy Projects Foundation; pres: Weiss Foundation, Stephen and Suzanne

Weiss, Suzanne, vp: Weiss Foundation, Stephen and Suzanne

Weiss, Tamara, dir: Rubin Foundation, Samuel

Weiss, William D., pres, dir: Weiss Foundation, William E.

Weiss, William Lee, chmn, ceo: Ameritech Corp.; dir: Ameritech Foundation; chmn, ceo: Ameritech Publishing; dir: Quaker Oats Foundation

Weissburg, Lawrence, chmn, ceo: Homestead Financial Corp.

Weissfeld, Joachim A., trust: Littlefield Memorial Trust, Ida Ballou

Weissinger, Walt, secy: New York Life Foundation

Weissman, Robert Evan, pres, coo, dir: Dun & Bradstreet Corp.; trust: Dun & Bradstreet Corp. Foundation

Weissman, Seymour J., vchmn: Lasky Co.; vp, secy: Lasky Co. Foundation

Weisz, William J., vchmn, dir: Motorola

Weitz, Fred W., chmn, pres, ceo: Weitz Corp.

Weizenbaum, Norman, trust: Giant Eagle Foundation

Welander, Bo, pres: Eka Nobel

Welch, Don E., chmn: Winchester Foundation

Welch, Jerry, pres: Compaq Computer Foundation

Welch, John Francis, Jr., chmn, ceo, dir: General Electric Co.

Welch, Josiah H., secy: Wheelwright Scientific School

Welch, L. Dean, pres, ceo: Ladish Co.

Welch, Michael J., pres, dir: Deluxe Corp. Foundation; pres, trust: Hotchkiss Foundation, W. R.

Welch, Robert F., secy, dir: Oestreicher Foundation, Sylvan and Ann

Welch, Russell, secy: RTM Foundation

Welch, Tom, trust: Beal Foundation

Welch, W. Perry, trust, mem: Whitney Foundation, Helen Hay

Welch, Whiting, pres: Avery-Fuller Children's Center

Weld, Edward, trust: Bright Charitable Trust, Alexander H.

Welder, Paul E., trust: Self Foundation

Weldon, Henry, trust: Adams Memorial Fund, Emma J.

Weldy, Erma Sue, trust: Mississippi Power Foundation

Welk, Lawrence L., dir: Welk Foundation, Lawrence

Welker, Norris J., trust: Puterbaugh Foundation

Well, Hugh, III, trust, secy: Kramer Foundation, Louise

Wellek, Richard L., pres, ceo: Varlen Corp.

Weller, Frances W., dir: Weller Foundation

Weller, Jane, secy: Morgan Foundation, Louie R. and Gertrude

Weller, Joe M., pres: Nestle U.S.A. Inc.

Weller, Robert C., treas: Chapman Foundation, William H.

Weller, Stevens, Jr., mgr: Viele Scholarship Trust, Frances S.

Wellignton, Herbert C., trust: Pritchard Charitable Trust, William E. and Maude S.

Wellin, Nancy Brown, vp, trust: Brown Foundation

Welling, Truman, mgr: Stroud Foundation

Wellington, Roger U., Jr., cfo, treas: Starrett Co., L.S.; dir: Starrett Co. Charitable Foundation, L.S.

Wellman, Barclay O., trust: Sheldon Foundation, Ralph C.

Wellman, W. Arvid, pres: Andersen Corp.

Wellons, John H., Jr., dir, vp: Wellons Foundation

Wellons, John H., Sr., dir, pres: Wellons Foundation

Wells, A. E., trust: Wiggins Memorial Trust, J. J.

Wells, Christine, vp (admin): Freedom Forum

Wells, Frank G., don, pres: Environment Now; trust: Getty Trust, J. Paul; pres, coo, dir: Disney Co., Walt; treas: Disney Co. Foundation, Walt

Wells, Herman B., dir: Lilly Endowment

Wells, Hoyt M., trust: Goodyear Tire & Rubber Company Fund

Wells, J. Ralston, trust: Cartinhour Foundation

Wells, James F., pres: Armco Inc.

Wells, James M., III, pres: Crestar Financial Corp.

Wells, John, Sr., trust: One Valley Bank Foundation

Wells, John M., Sr., trust: Carbon Fuel Foundation

Wells, Kappy Jo, trust: Mott Charitable Trust/Spectemur Agendo, Stewart R.

Wells, Karyn L., dir corp contributions: Masco Corp. Charitable Trust

Wells, L.A., trust: Phillips Foundation, A. P.

Wells, Luanne, don, vp: Environment Now

Wells, M.W., Jr., Phillips Foundation, A. P.

Wells, Preston A., Jr., vp: Wells Foundation, Lillian S.

Wells, Richard, vp (fin), dir: Kohler Co.

Welsh, David D., trust: McCrea Foundation

Welsh, Edward C., trust: McCrea Foundation

Welsh, John L., III, trust: McCrea Foundation

Welsh, John L., Jr., pres, trust: McCrea Foundation

Welsh, Margaret S., trust: Boston Fatherless and Widows Society

Welsh, Martin E., Federal-Mogul Corp. Charitable Trust Fund

Welsh, Matthew E., trust: Hartford Foundation, John A.

Welsh, William F., II, pres, ceo, dir: Valmont Industries; dir: Valmont Foundation

Wendel, James F., asst secy, asst treas: Knox Foundation, Seymour H.

Wendel, Larry L., vp: Van Wert County Foundation

Wendel, W. Hall, Jr., chmn, ceo: Polaris Industries, LP

Wendelken, Ben S., vp, dir: Sachs Foundation

Wendell, Stephen A., vp, cfo, treas: Bohemia Inc.

Wendlandt, Gary, cfo: Massachusetts Mutual Life Insurance Co.

Wendt, Henry, chmn: SmithKline Beecham

Wendt, Nancy, trust: JELD-WEN Foundation

Wendt, R.C., trust, secy: JELD-WEN Foundation

Wendt, Richard L., pres, treas: JELD-WEN, Inc.; trust: JELD-WEN Foundation

Wendt, Rod, sr vp, secy: JELD-WEN, Inc.

Wendte, David L., cfo: Tractor & Equipment Co.

Wenger, Henry Penn, pres, dir: Wenger Foundation, Henry L. and Consuelo S.

Wennesland, Kathleen W., pres, dir: Winkler Foundation, Mark and Catherine

Wenschlof, Donald E., vp (mktg): Castle & Co., A.M.

Wentling, Thomas L., Jr., dir: Staunton Farm Foundation

Wentworth, Elizabeth B., trust: Bishop Charitable Trust, A. G.

Wentworth, G.O., pres: Moosehead Manufacturing Co.

Wentworth, Jack R., dir: Habig Foundation

Wentz, Sidney F., chmn bd trusts: Johnson Foundation, Robert Wood

Wentzell, C. John, treas: Budweiser of the Carolinas Foundation

White, Edward L., Jr., pres: Day Foundation, Cecil B.

White, Elton, pres, dir: NCR Corp.

White, Emma, chmn: White Foundation, Erle and Emma

White, Eugene A., vp, secy: Collins & Aikman Holdings Foundation

White, Eugene R., vchmn: Amdahl Corp.

White, H. Blair, dir, secy: Kelly Foundation, T. Lloyd; pres, dir: R. F. Foundation

White, H. Hunter, Jr., trust: Booth-Bricker Fund

White, Helen T., trust, vp: Thatcher Foundation

White, J. M., gen couns: Universal Leaf Foundation

White, J. Spratt, mem (pub affairs comm): Springs Industries

White, James A., cfo: Bank of Oklahoma, N.A.

White, James M., Jr., trust: Levy Foundation, June Rockwell

White, Jane, vchmn: Greater Lansing Foundation

White, Jeff V., trust: Equifax Foundation

White, Jessica, trust: Swift Memorial Health Care Foundation

White, Jim, treas: Sundstrand Corp. Foundation

White, John, cfo: United Grocers, Inc.

White, John, Jr., pres, dir: Country Cos.

White, Jonathan R., secy: Whiteley Foundation, John and Elizabeth

White, L. A., managing trust: Anderson Charitable Trust, Josephine

White, Leonard H., chmn: White Construction Co.; pres: White Companies Charitable Trust

White, Lynn, contributions mgr: Spiegel

White, Mahlon T., III, trust: Thatcher Foundation

White, Margaret R., trust: Hillsdale Fund

White, Marion C., secy: Klipstein Foundation, Ernest Christian

White, Michael H., chmn: Rite-Hite Corp.; pres, dir: Rite-Hite Corp. Foundation

White, Molly, fdn asst: Gap Foundation

White, Morgan P., dir: Rite-Hite Corp. Foundation

White, Moss, Jr., secy: New Orphan Asylum Scholarship Foundation

White, Pamela, dir: Memton Fund

White, Phillis R., pres: Board of Trustees of the Prichard School

White, Raymond M., pres, coo: Christie Electric Corp.

White, Richard K., chmn: Trexler Trust, Harry C.

White, Robert C., vp, cfo: Hughes Medical Institute, Howard

White, Robert F., trust: Charlesbank Homes

White, Robert N., pres: Ore-Ida Foods, Inc.

White, Robert P., dir: White Foundation, W. P. and H. B.

White, Roger B., pres, dir: White Foundation, W. P. and H. B.

White, Sara Margaret, vp: Powers Foundation

White, Steven R., secy, dir: White Foundation, W. P. and H. B.

White, Thomas A., pres, coo, dir: Crane & Co.; trust: Crane & Co. Fund

White, Tom, M.D., dir: Navarro County Educational Foundation

White, Tony L., dir: Baxter Foundation

White, W. N., trust: Monroe Auto Equipment Foundation Trust

White, Walter L., secy, treas, trust: Kemper Foundation, James S.

White, William, treas, dir: Travelers Cos. Foundation

White, William Bew, Jr., trust: Comer Foundation; trust: Shook Foundation, Barbara Ingalls; trust: Webb Charitable Trust, Susan Mott

White, William P., Jr., dir: White Foundation, W. P. and H. B.

White, William S., trust: Harding Foundation, Charles Stewart

White, William Samuel, chmn, pres, ceo, trust, chmn several comms: Mott Foundation, Charles Stewart; chmn, dir: United States Sugar Corp.

White-Randall, Andrea A., vp, secy, treas: Stokely, Jr. Foundation, William B.

White-Thomson, I. L., pres: United States Borax & Chemical Corp.

Whited, Edwin F., pres emeritus, dir: Frost Foundation

Whited, Mary Amelia Douglas, pres, dir: Frost Foundation

Whited-Howell, Mary Amelia, exec vp, dir: Frost Foundation

Whitehair, T. E., sr vp (intl): Brown & Williamson Tobacco Corp.

Whitehead, A. Pennington, dir: Clark Foundation

Whitehead, David W., asst treas: Centerior Energy Foundation

Whitehead, Edward E., mem (community concerns comm): NBD Bank, N.A.

Whitehead, Jack D., dir: Pasadena Area Residential Aid

Whitehead, John Cunningham, chmn, trust: Mellon Foundation, Andrew W.; trust: Whitehead Foundation

Whitehead, John G., trust: Getty Trust, J. Paul

Whitehead, John Gregory, trust: Whitehead Foundation

Whitehead, John J., pres, dir: Whitehead Charitable Foundation

Whitehead, Nancy D., trust: Whitehead Foundation

Whitehead, Peter J., vp, dir: Whitehead Charitable Foundation

Whitehead, Rosalind C., dir: Educational Foundation of America; secy, dir: Whitehead Charitable Foundation

Whitehead, Susan, dir: Whitehead Charitable Foundation

Whitehill, Clifford Lane, secy, trust: General Mills Foundation

Whitehill, D. B., asst secy: Warren Charite

Whitehorn, Nathaniel, treas: Schapiro Fund, M. A.

Whitehouse, Janet, trust: UNUM Charitable Foundation

Whitehouse, Neil, pres: TCF Foundation

Whitelaw, Robert I., trust: Vincent Trust, Anna M.

Whiteman, Jack W., pres: Whiteman Foundation, Edna Rider

Whiteman, Jeffrey, trust: Whiteman Foundation, Edna Rider

Whiteman, Joseph David, secy, trust: Parker-Hannifin Foundation

Whiten, Bennie E., Jr., secy, trust: Community Cooperative Development Foundation

Whitener, Orin, pres: Whitener Foundation

Whiteside, Hoyle L., trust: Davis Hospital Foundation

Whiteside, Thomas, vp: Shaw Fund for Mariner's Children

Whitfield, Sue Trammell, trust: Fondren Foundation

Whitfield, William F., Sr., trust: Fondren Foundation

Whitia, Eleanore T., trust: Charitable Fund

Whiting, A. Milton, chmn, ceo, dir: Kaibab Industries

Whiting, Eleanor W., trust: Plankenhorn Foundation, Harry

Whiting, Elizabeth L., secy, treas: Golden West Foundation

Whiting, Frank S., pres: Golden West Foundation

Whiting, Helen Dow, treas, trust: Whiting Foundation, Macauley and Helen Dow

Whiting, Mary MacAuley, secy, trust: Whiting Foundation, Macauley and Helen Dow

Whiting, McCauley, pres, trust: Whiting Foundation, Macauley and Helen Dow

Whiting, R. Bruce, pres, coo, dir: Kaibab Industries

Whiting, R. M., mem student loan comm: Jeffers Memorial Fund, Michael

Whiting, Robert C., dir: Louis Foundation, Michael W.

Whiting, Sara, trust: Whiting Foundation, Macauley and Helen Dow

Whitley, Michael R., sr vp, cfo: Kentucky Utilities Co.

Whitman, Charles, Jr., vp: Stony Wold Herbert Fund

Whitman, Martin J., dir: Wiener Foundation, Malcolm Hewitt

Whitmer, Richard E., ceo, pres: Blue Cross/Blue Shield of Michigan

Whitmore, Kay Rex, chmn, pres, ceo, dir: Eastman Kodak Co.

Whitmore, Susan H., vp, dir: Hopkins Foundation, Josephine Lawrence

Whitney, Betsey Cushing Roosevelt, pres, don: Greentree Foundation

Whitney, Betsy, trust: Dayton Foundation Depository

Whitney, George H., trust: Van Nuys Foundation, I. N. and Susanna H.

Whitney, Helen G., vchmn, trust: Jones Foundation, Daisy Marquis

Whitney, John R., pres: Colorado Interstate Gas Co.

Whitney, Kate R., vp, secy: Greentree Foundation

Whitney, L. C., chmn, ceo: National Data Corp.

Whitney, Lewis, secy, dir: Kirchgessner Foundation, Karl

Whitney, Marjorie T., dir: Ordean Foundation

Whitney, Mrs. E.C., vp: Tandy Foundation, Anna M.

Whitney, Wallace F., Jr., secy, treas: Wyman-Gordon Foundation

Whitridge, Frederick, trust: Wilson Sanitarium for Children of Baltimore City, Thomas

Whitridge, Frederick W., trust: Crocker Trust, Mary A.

Whitridge, Serena H., mem: Merck Family Fund

Whitsett, Elizabeth A., pres, dir: Atkinson Foundation, Myrtle L.

Whitsett, John F., treas, dir: Atkinson Foundation, Myrtle L.

Whitsett, Kirsten H., dir: Atkinson Foundation, Myrtle L.

Whitt, David C., pres, dir: Elixir Industries

Whitt, John J., Jr., vp: Titmus Foundation

Whittaker, E. William, trust: Anderson Foundation

Whittaker, Ethel A., trust, vp: Anderson Foundation

Whittaker, Harry W., vp, trust: Anderson Foundation, William P.

Whittemore, Clark M., Jr., secy-treas bd dirs, chmn budget comm: Dana Foundation, Charles A.

Whittum, Charles H., Jr., ceo, dir: Baltimore Bancorp.

Whitty, Julia B., secy: Perry-Griffin Foundation

Whitwam, David Ray, chmn, pres, ceo, dir: Whirlpool Corp.

Whitworth, J. Bryan, vp, dir: Phillips Petroleum Foundation

Whyel, George S., trust emeritus: Mott Foundation, Charles Stewart

Whyte, Joseph L., dir: Loughran Foundation, Mary and Daniel

Wiborg, James H., dir: PACCAR Foundation

Wice, David H., dir: Fels Fund, Samuel S.

Wichman, Charles R., dir: Bancorp Hawaii Charitable Foundation

Wichser, Robert J., pres (women's wear): Crystal Brands

Wick, J. Everett, trust: Quaker Chemical Foundation

Wickersham, John, pres, ceo, dir: Bill Communications

Wickham, Woodward A., vp (pub affairs), dir (gen program): MacArthur Foundation, John D. and Catherine T.

Wideman, Frank J., Jr., exec vp: Self Foundation

Widerman, Clark L., dir: Oakley-Lindsay Foundation of Quincy Newspapers & Quincy Broadcasting Co.

Wieboldt, Anne L., dir: Wieboldt Foundation

Wieboldt, Nancy, dir: Wieboldt Foundation

Wiedemann, Dorothy E., vp, trust: Schlink Foundation, Albert G. and Olive H.

Wiedemann, Robert A., pres, secy, trust: Schlink Foundation, Albert G. and Olive H.

Wiedenman, Jeanne M., secy: Vanneck-Bailey Foundation

Wiederholt, J. Lee, vp: Hammill Foundation, Donald D.

Wiegal, David, treas: Mutual of New York Foundation

Wieland, Robert Richard, secy: Huffy Foundation, Inc.

Wien, Lawrence A., vp: Schaffer Foundation, H.

Wiener, A. B., vp, secy, treas, dir: Pearce Foundation, Dr. M. Lee

Wiener, Ann Findlay, dir: Noyes Foundation, Jessie Smith

Wiener, Carolyn S., dir: Wiener Foundation, Malcolm Hewitt

Wiener, Malcolm Hewitt, don, pres, treas: Wiener Foundation, Malcolm Hewitt

Wiener, Ronald M., trust: Goldman Foundation, William

Wierman, Jane, asst secy: Wickes Foundation, Harvey Randall

Wies, Catherine, dir: Knott Foundation, Marion I. and Henry J.

Wiesner, Carol A., treas, dir: Foundation of the Litton Industries

Wiesner, Jerome B., dir: MacArthur Foundation, John D. and Catherine T.

Wiess Jr., Harry J., pres: Overstreet Investment Co.

Wigdale, James B., vchmn, dir: Marshall & Ilsley Bank; vp, dir: Marshall & Ilsley Foundation

Wiggins, W. Frank, pres, dir: Werner Foundation, Clara and Spencer

Wightman, John C., Jr., trust: Attleboro Pawtucket Savings Bank Charitable Foundation

Wightman, Julia P., trust: Dula Educational and Charitable Foundation, Caleb C. and Julia W.

Wightman, Orrin S., III, trust: Dula Educational and Charitable Foundation, Caleb C. and Julia W.

Wiksten, Barry Frank, pres: CIGNA Foundation

Wilbanks, Danile P., vchmn: Blount Educational and Charitable Foundation, Mildred Weedon

Wilbur, Brayton, Jr., pres: Wilbur-Ellis Co.; pres, dir: Wilbur Foundation, Brayton

Wilbur, Colburn S., exec dir: Packard Foundation, David and Lucile

Wilcanskas, Eugene, pres: Akzo America

Wilcha, George, cfo: Associated Products

Wilcock, James W., chmn, dir: Foster Co., L.B.

Wilcott, Harry W., pres, ceo: Republic Financial Services, Inc.

Wilcox, Gail M., secy, treas: Morgan-Worcester, Inc.

Wilcox, Julia O'Brien, pres: O'Brien Foundation, Alice M.

Wilcox, R. W., vp: National Fuel Gas Co.

Wilcox, Thomas R., dir, mem exec comm, mem dirs grant comm: Keck Foundation, W. M.

Wilcoxson, Melvin, bd mem: Salvatori Foundation, Henry

Wilczura, Christiane S., mgr (community affairs): GATX Corp.

Wild, Carter W., 1st vp: Board of Trustees of the Prichard School

Wild, Heidi Karen, trust: BHP Petroleum Americas (HI) Foundation

Wild, Robert M., 2nd vp: Board of Trustees of the Prichard School

Wilde, Wilson, pres, ceo, dir: Hartford Steam Boiler Inspection & Insurance Co.

Wildenstein, Daniel Leopold, vp, dir: Gould Foundation, Florence J.

Wilder, Betty, treas, trust: Orange Orphan Society

Wilder, G. Warren, trust: Foundation for Seacoast Health

Wilder, Gary, vp: Wilder Foundation

Wilder, Michael S., vp, dir: ITT Hartford Insurance Group Foundation

Wilder, Michel S., mem (contributions comm): ITT Hartford Insurance Group

Wilder, Rita, pres: Wilder Foundation

Wilder, Robert O., chmn, pres, ceo: National Forge Co.; pres, dir: National Forge Foundation

Wilderson, Frank B., Jr., dir, first vchmn: Bush Foundation

Wiley, Barbara M., dir: Badger Meter Foundation

Wiley, Bill, sr vp (industrial rels): Y.K.K. (U.S.A.) Inc.

Wiley, Bill G., III, dir: Washington Square Health Foundation

Wiley, Mary L. F., vp, dir: Flagler Foundation

Wiley, Robert, treas, dir: Berry Foundation, Lowell

Wiley, S. Donald, vchmn, trust: Heinz Co. Foundation, H.J.; trust: Heinz Endowment, Vira I.

Wiley, W. Bradford, chmn: Wiley & Sons, Inc.; John

Wilf, Elizabeth, trust: Wilf Family Foundation

Wilf, Harry, pres: Wilf Family Foundation

Wilf, Joseph, secy: Wilf Family Foundation

Wilf, Judith, trust: Wilf Family Foundation

Wilfley, George M., treas, trust: Boettcher Foundation

Wilfley, Mike, trust: Gates Foundation

Wilford, Sara R., vp, treas: Greentree Foundation

Wilhelm, Clarke L., trust: Reilly Foundation

Wilhelm, Roger, sr vp mktg: Alpha Beta Stores, Inc.

Wilhide, Margaret, trust: Davis Hospital Foundation

Wilhoit, Ray B., comm mem: Abreu Charitable Trust u/w/o May P. Abreu, Francis I.; trust: Howell Fund

Wilk, Gerald M., treas: Safeguard Scientifics Foundation

Wilke, J.F., secy-treas: Wigwam Mills Fund

Wilke, Robert D., vchmn, cfo: Newhall Land & Farming Co.

Wilkenfeld, Delores, trust: Lewis Foundation, Lillian Kaiser

Wilkening, Laurel Lynn, dir: Research Corporation

Wilkening, Leonard H., trust: Minnesota Foundation

Wilkerson, Thomas D., trust: One Valley Bank Foundation

Wilkes, Andrea, secy, dir: Kiplinger Foundation

Wilkes, Elizabeth W., dir: Bayne Fund, Howard

Wilkes, Jack D., trust: Merrick Foundation

Wilkes, Lester, coo: Star Enterprise

Wilkes, Robert E., ceo, pres: First Valley Bank

Wilkie, Jack, vp (corp commun): Franklin Mint Corp.

Wilkie, Valleau, Jr., vp, asst secy: Bass Corporation, Perry and Nancy Lee; exec dir: Bass Foundation; exec vp, exec dir: Richardson Foundation, Sid W.

Wilkin, Abra Prentice, chmn, pres, dir: Prentice Foundation, Abra

Wilkins, Michael D., mem scholarship comm: Ritter Charitable Trust, George W. & Mary F.

Wilkins, Wilfred G., vchmn, trust: Anderson Foundation, John W.

Wilkinson, Bruce, chmn, ceo, pres: CRS Sirrine Engineers

Wilkinson, Carol C., dir: Kerr Fund, Grayce B.

Wilkinson, F. McKinnon, trust: Symmes Foundation, F. W.

Wilkinson, Harry J., pres, coo: SPS Technologies

Wilkinson, John F., Jr., dir: Brand Foundation, C. Harold and Constance

Wilkinson, John G., pres: Colorado State Bank of Denver; pres: Colorado State Bank Foundation

Wilkinson, Julia Matthews, dir: Dodge Jones Foundation

Wilkinson, Mary S., trust: Stare Fund

Wilkinson, Noreen A., dir, secy: Steigerwaldt Foundation, Donna Wolf

Wilkinson, Richard W., secy, treas: Bowen Foundation, Ethel N.; pres: Shott, Jr. Foundation, Hugh I.

Wilkinson, Russell C., vp: Christodora

Wilkof, Richard, Jr., trust: Wilkof Foundation, Edward and Ruth

Will, Fred, trust: Walter Family Trust, Byron L.

Willaims, W. Robert, trust: Gordy Family Educational Trust Fund, George E.

Willard, Eugenia B., trust: Schepp Foundation, Leopold

Willard, Henry A., II, dir, secy, treas: Willard Foundation, Helen Parker

Willard, Larry, mgr gen acct: Sara Lee Hosiery

Willard, William B., dir, pres: Willard Foundation, Helen Parker

Wille, Robert H., treas, trust: Arkell Hall Foundation

Willemetz, J. Lester, treas, trust: Olin Foundation, Spencer T. and Ann W.

Willens, Joan G., trust: Simon Foundation, Robert Ellis

Willens, Sherwin, dir: Sulzer Family Foundation

Willes, Mark Hinckley, vchmn: General Mills

Willey, Joshua W., Jr., dir: Kellenberger Historical

Foundation, May Gordon Latham

William, David P., III, hon dir: Ayres Foundation, Inc.

Williams, A. Morris, Jr., dir, pres: Pine Tree Foundation

Williams, Alexander J., trust: Tait Foundation, Frank M.

Williams, Allison F., trust: Harland Charitable Foundation, John and Wilhelmina D.

Williams, Alyce, trust: Kyle Educational Trust, S. H. and D. W.

Williams, Barbara Coull, vp (human resources): Pacific Gas & Electric Co.

Williams, Barbara Steele, asst secy: Steele Foundation, Harry and Grace

Williams, Benjamin, trust: Sailors' Snug Harbor of Boston

Williams, Bernadette, contributions adm: Capital Cities Foundation

Williams, Carolyn R., contributions adm: Southern California Gas Co.

Williams, Charles J., III, trust: Williams Foundation, Edna Sproull

Williams, Charles K., dir: Williams Foundation, C. K.

Williams, Curtis A., trust: Wenner-Gren Foundation for Anthropological Research

Williams, Dave H., chmn, dir: Alliance Capital Management Corp.

Williams, David P., pres, coo: Budd Co.

Williams, David R., trust: Finch Foundation, Doak

Williams, David S., trust: Williams Foundation, Arthur Ashley

Williams, Dawn M., vp, treas, dir: Housen Foundation

Williams, Douglas, treas: Stevens Foundation, John T.

Williams, E. Belvin, exec dir, secy, trust: Turrell Fund

Williams, Edward, coo: Casco Northern Bank

Williams, Edward F., trust: French Foundation

Williams, Edward Joseph, sr vp, dir: Harris Trust & Savings Bank; pres, dir: Harris Bank Foundation

Williams, Elynor A., dir: Sara Lee Foundation

Williams, Emory, trust: Kellstadt Foundation

Williams, Eugene Flewellyn, Jr., mem (charitable contributions comm): Emerson Charitable Trust; trust: Olin Foundation, John M.

Williams, F. B., trust: Sonoco Products Foundation

Williams, G. E., pres: Budweiser of the Carolinas Foundation

Williams, Gray, Jr., trust: Sullivan Foundation, Algernon Sydney

Williams, H. L., dir: Moorman Co. Fund

Williams, Harold M., pres, ceo: Getty Trust, J. Paul; trust: Simon Foundation, Robert Ellis

Williams, J. Harold, Long Foundation, George A. and Grace

Williams, J. Kelley, chmn, pres, ceo, dir: First Mississippi Corp.; pres, ceo: First Mississippi Corp. Foundation

Williams, J. T., secy, treas, dir: Grede Foundation

Williams, James Bryan, trust: Evans Foundation, Lettie Pate; mem: Trust Co. of Georgia Foundation; trust: Woodruff Foundation, Robert W.

Williams, James E., pres, ceo: Golden State Foods Corp.

Williams, Jane, trust: Quaker Chemical Foundation

Williams, Jim, treas: Seafirst Foundation

Williams, Jim L., cfo: Law Companies Group

Williams, Jimmie D., mgr: Belz Foundation

Williams, Joel T., Jr., trust: Constantin Foundation

Williams, John O., dir: Beneficial Foundation; secy, dir: Caspersen Foundation for Aid to Health and Education, O. W.

Williams, Joseph Hill, chmn, ceo, dir: Williams Cos.; chmn, dir: Williams Cos. Foundation

Williams, Josephine C., dir: Williams Foundation, C. K.

Williams, Karen Hastie, dir: Federal National Mortgage Assn. Foundation

Williams, Katherine B., vp, dir: Snite Foundation, Fred B.

Williams, L. Neil, Jr., dir: Love Foundation, Gay and Erskine; chmn, trust: Woolley Foundation, Vasser

Williams, L. Stanton, dir: Texaco Foundation

Williams, Lamar Harper, vp: Harper Foundation, Philip S.

Williams, Larry, pres, coo: NutraSweet Co.

Williams, Lee R., Jr., dir: Durham Merchants Association Charitable Foundation

Williams, Lillian L., vp: Lamb Foundation, Kirkland S. and Rena B.

Williams, Lindsey, pres: Mattel

Williams, Lou, pres: Mayacamas Corp.

Williams, Louise, trust: Eastern Star Hall and Home Foundation

Williams, Lowell, sr vp, chief admin off, gen couns: Elf Aquitaine, Inc.

Williams, Luke G., trust: Comstock Foundation

Williams, Marguerite N., pres, dir: Williams Family Foundation of Georgia

Williams, Marie, dir, vp: Meyer Foundation, Baron de Hirsch

Williams, Marvin S., secy: Meyerhoff Fund, Joseph

Williams, Mary C., vp: New Milford Savings Bank Foundation

Williams, Maude O'Connor, pres: South Texas Charitable Foundation

Williams, Michael P., vp: Cadillac Products Foundation

Williams, Murat Willis, dir: Public Welfare Foundation

Williams, Nancy, corp commun: BMW of North America, Inc.

Williams, P. Greggory, vp-investment, treas: Shenandoah Life Insurance Co.

Williams, Patrick M., trust: Williams Foundation, Edna Sproull

Williams, Phillip L., vchmn, dir: Times Mirror Co.; dir: Times Mirror Foundation

Williams, Ray, trust: Meredith Foundation

Williams, Richard A., treas: Lamb Foundation, Kirkland S. and Rena B.

Williams, Richard L., vp, dir: Dan River Foundation

Williams, Robert, secy: Truman Foundation, Mildred Faulkner

Williams, Robert A., pres, dir: Animal Assistance Foundation

Williams, Robert C., co-fdr, chmn, pres, ceo: James River Corp. of Virginia; mem corp comm: Meridian Bancorp

Williams, Robert J., chmn, pres: Cadillac Products; pres: Cadillac Products Foundation

Williams, Roger K., treas: Cadillac Products Foundation

Williams, Roger P., vp: South Texas Charitable Foundation

Williams, Ronald W., dir, bd mem: Piton Foundation

Williams, Ruth W., dir, secy, treas: Pine Tree Foundation

Williams, Samuel C., Jr., pres, trust: Brundage Charitable, Scientific, and Wildlife Conservation Foundation, Charles E. and Edna T.; trust: Upton Charitable Foundation, Lucy and Eleanor S.

Williams, Sarah P., trust: Appleby Foundation; trust: Appleby Trust, Scott B. and Annie P.

Williams, Stella R., asst secy: Kent-Lucas Foundation

Williams, Stephen J., dir: Raker Foundation, M. E.

Williams, Sterling L., pres, ceo, dir: Sterling Software Inc.

Williams, Steve L., vp: Stevens Foundation, John T.

Williams, T. A., pres: Foote Mineral Co.

Williams, T. E., dir: Holding Foundation, Robert P.

Williams, Theodore E., chmn, pres, dir: Bell Industries

Williams, Thomas B., Jr., trust: Sailors' Snug Harbor of Boston

Williams, Thomas L., trust: Western-Southern Life Foundation

Williams, Thomas L., III, dir: Williams Family Foundation of Georgia

Williams, Trish, trust: Avery-Fuller Children's Center

Williams, W. W., trust: Pennington Foundation, Irene W. and C. B.

Williams, William J., trust: Jennings Foundation, Martha Holden; chmn, ceo: Western Southern Life Insurance Co.

Williams, William J., Jr., trust: Sofia American Schools

Williamson, Debra L., vp, trust: Kettering Family Foundation

Williamson, Douglas E., trust: Kettering Family Foundation

Williamson, Douglas F., Jr., secy: McConnell Foundation, Neil A.

Williamson, H. D., vp, dir: HEI Charitable Foundation

Williamson, Harold E., exec dir, trust: Buell Foundation, Temple Hoyne

Williamson, Henry, coo: Branch Banking & Trust Co.

Williamson, Henry G., Jr., pres, coo, dir: BB&T Financial Corp.

Williamson, Hugh H., ceo: Carolina Steel Corp.

Williamson, Jack, trust: Williams Charitable Trust, Mary Jo

Williamson, Jeanette L., trust: Raymond Foundation

Williamson, Leslie G., trust: Kettering Family Foundation

Williamson, P. D., trust: Kettering Family Foundation

Williamson, Sheila, trust: Orange Orphan Society

Williamson, Susan K., trust: Kettering Family Foundation; mem distribution comm: Kettering Fund

Williamson, W. A., Jr., chmn, ceo, dir: Durr-Fillauer Medical

Willie, Louis J., mem adv comm: Meyer Foundation, Robert R.

Willingham, Gene W., dir: Waggoner Foundation, E. Paul and Helen Buck

Willingham, Helen Biggs, secy, treas: Waggoner Foundation, E. Paul and Helen Buck

Willis, Bertrum C., secy: Campbell Soup Foundation

Willis, Dudlee H., trust: Sanders Trust, Charles

Willis, Dudley H., trust: Saltonstall Charitable Foundation, Richard

Willis, Gordon A., asst treas, asst secy: Wisconsin Energy Corp. Foundation

Willis, Lois Cross, dir: Moore Foundation, Edward S.

Willis, Patricia, pres, exec dir: BellSouth Foundation

Willis, Ralph N., trust: Wilson Sanitarium for Children of Baltimore City, Thomas

Willison, Bruce, chmn, pres, ceo: First Interstate Bank of California; chmn: First Interstate Bank of California Foundation

Willison, Robert E., trust: Laurel Foundation

Willits, Harris L., pres: Willits Foundation

Willits, Itto A., trust: Willits Foundation

Willits, John F., trust: Willits Foundation

Willmott, Peter S., pres, dir: Bergner Foundation, P.A.; pres, treas, don: Willmott Foundation, Peter S.

Willoughby, Colleen S., dir: Haas Foundation, Saul and Dayee G.

Wills, Kenneth, dir: Feild Co-Operative Association

Wills, Rosemary C., asst secy, asst treas: duPont Foundation, Alfred I.

Willson, George C., III, dir: Green Foundation, Allen P. and Josephine B.

Willumstadt, Bob, pres: Commercial Credit Co.

Wilmer, John, trust: Gilman and Gonzalez-Falla Theatre Foundation

Wilmers, Robert G., pres, coo: First Empire State Corp.

Wilmington Trust Commpany is corporate trustee.orp, purpose of funds sought, benefi, Harrington Charitable Trust, Charles J.

Wilmouth, Robert K., chmn: LaSalle National Bank

Wilner, Alvin G., dir: Harris Bank Foundation

Wilsen, Rev. Oscar, trust, vp: Baker Foundation, George T.

Wilsey, A.S., pres: Wilsey Foundation

Wilsey, Alfred, dir: Osher Foundation, Bernard

Wilsey, Alfred S., Jr., secy: Wilsey Foundation

Wilsey, Diane B., vp: Wilsey Foundation

Wilsey, Michael W., chmn, pres, dir: Wilsey Bennet Co.; vp: Wilsey Foundation

Wilson, Blenda J., dir: Commonwealth Fund

Wilson, C.J., comm: Fairfield-Meeker Charitable Trust, Freeman E.

Wilson, Chuck W., exec vp (products), dir: Shell Oil Co.

Wilson, Cleo A., exec dir: Playboy Foundation

Wilson, Cornelius, treas: New Orphan Asylum Scholarship Foundation

Wilson, Diane Wenger, vp, dir: Wenger Foundation, Henry L. and Consuelo S.

Wilson, Donald Malcolm, trust: Schumann Fund for New Jersey

Wilson, Donna Danner, dir: Danner Foundation

Wilson, Doris E., contr, research assoc: Block Foundation, H&R

Wilson, Dorothy B., trust: Toms Foundation

Wilson, Dorothy Clarke, dir: Meadows Foundation

Wilson, Eugene R., pres, dir: ARCO Foundation

Wilson, Evelyn, Ph.D., dir: South Plains Foundation

Wilson, Faye, secy: Gilmore Foundation, William G.

Wilson, Frank S., dir: Ensign-Bickford Foundation

Wilson, Frederick C., pres: Ingersoll Milling Machine Co.

Wilson, G. Dale, trust: Van Wert County Foundation

Wilson, G. W., dir: Finley Foundation, A. E.

Wilson, Gary Lee, co-chmn: Northwest Airlines, Inc.

Wilson, Glen Wesley, adv: AMCORE Foundation, Inc.

Wilson, Harry, trust: Haley Foundation, W. B.

Wilson, Harry B., mem: Northern Trust Co. Charitable Trust

Wilson, Herbert J., treas, trust: Holden Fund, James and Lynelle

Wilson, Howard O., dir, treas: Falk Foundation, Elizabeth M.; treas, dir: Peppers Foundation, Ann; mem bd advs: Stern Memorial Trust, Sidney

Wilson, Isabel Brown, chmn, trust: Brown Foundation

Wilson, J. G., comptr: Phillips Petroleum Foundation

Wilson, J. Lawrence, chmn, ceo, dir: Rohm and Haas Company

Wilson, J. R., vp, trust: Besser Foundation

Wilson, J.S., Jr., pres, ceo: Conwood Co. L.P.

Wilson, Jackie, publ aff: Lyondell Petrochemical Co.

Wilson, James, trust: Wilson Public Trust, Ralph

Wilson, James B., dir: Siragusa Foundation

Wilson, James N., chmn, coo: Syntex Corp.

Wilson, James Quinn, mem bd govs: Richardson Foundation, Smith

Wilson, Janet, comm mem: Pendleton Memorial Fund, William L. and Ruth T.

Wilson, Janet C., pres bd mgrs: Wilson Foundation, Marie C. and Joseph C.

Wilson, Janice J., trust: First Interstate Bank of Oregon Charitable Foundation

Wilson, Jess C., Jr., vp, trust: Jones Foundation, Fletcher

Wilson, Jim, pres: Wilson Public Trust, Ralph

Wilson, John H., II, dir: Piper Foundation, Minnie Stevens

Wilson, John Hill Tucker, chmn, trust: Morgan Stanley Foundation

Wilson, John M., pres, ceo: Pegasus Gold Corp.

Wilson, John M., Jr., pres, trust: Wellman Foundation, S. K.

Wilson, Joseph R., mem bd mgrs: Wilson Foundation, Marie C. and Joseph C.

Wilson, Josephine D., vp: Massengill-DeFriece Foundation

Wilson, Justin P., chmn, trust: Potter Foundation, Justin and Valere

Wilson, Kenneth, dir, vp: Ramlose Foundation, George A.

Wilson, Kenneth Pat, pres: Rebsamen Fund

Wilson, Kirke P., exec dir, secy: Rosenberg Foundation

Wilson, Lawrence A., pres, ceo: HCB Contractors

Wilson, Lee Anne, trust: Sarkeys Foundation

Wilson, Lucy C., secy: Pannill Scholarship Foundation, William Letcher

Wilson, Lynton R., chmn: Tate & Lyle Inc.

Wilson, Malcolm, dir: Carvel Foundation, Thomas and Agnes; dir: Clark Foundation

Wilson, Michael G., cfo: Broccoli Charitable Foundation, Dana and Albert R.

Wilson, Patricia W., trust: Wellman Foundation, S. K.

Wilson, Penelope P., vp: Perkins Memorial Foundation, George W.

Wilson, Peter A., exec dir: Stratford Foundation

Wilson, Richard A., vp, dir: Connell Foundation, Michael J.

Wilson, Rita P., vp, trust: Allstate Foundation; dir: Sears-Roebuck Foundation

Wilson, Robert A., pres: Pfizer Foundation

Wilson, Robert B., trust: Weyerhaeuser Co. Foundation

Wilson, Robert F., vp, treas: Rollins Luetkemeyer Charitable Foundation

Wilson, Robert L., vp, secy, treas: Lund Foundation

Wilson, Roderick, pres, ceo: Amfac/JMB Hawaii

Wilson, Rosine M., trust: Ward Heritage Foundation, Mamie McFaddin

Wilson, Sandra C., vp: International Paper Co. Foundation

Wilson, Sandra H., trust: Jones Intercable Tampa Trust

Wilson, Spence, dir: Briggs Foundation, T. W.

Wilson, Sunny, hon chmn: Wilson Public Trust, Ralph

Wilson, Thornton Arnold, dir: PACCAR Foundation

Wilson, Walter C., dir: Hadson Foundation

Wilson, William C., chmn, pres, trust: Toms Foundation

Wilson, William Julius, dir: Pullman Educational Foundation, George M.; trust: Sage Foundation, Russell; dir: Spencer Foundation

Wilson, William L., trust: Yeager Charitable Trust, Lester E.

Wilson, William N., pres: Chubb Foundation

Wilton, Doug, cfo: UniGroup Inc.

Wilton, Douglas H., cfo: United Van Lines, Inc.

Wiltse, Leon L., MD, trust: Miller Foundation, Earl B. and Loraine H.

Wiltshire, Richard W., Jr., pres, dir: Home Beneficial Corp.

Wiltshire, Richard W., Sr., chmn, ceo, coo, dir: Home Beneficial Corp.

Wimbish, Schaeffer, Jr., vp (mktg): Colonial Oil Industries, Inc.

Wimer, William J., cfo: Armstrong World Industries Inc.

Wimpey, P. A., sr vp, cfo: ONEOK Inc.

Win, Raymond B., Jr., trust, secy, treas: Westend Foundation

Winakur, Harbert S., Jr., chmn, dir: DynCorp

Winant, Rivington R., trust: Grant Foundation, William T.

Winch, John, pres: Minster Machine Co.; vp: Minster Machine Co. Foundation

Winchester, David P., dir: Rice Foundation

Windahl, Ronald, exec dir: LTV Foundation

Winder, Patricia S., trust: Sheppard Foundation, Lawrence B.

Winding, Charles A., trust, vp: Anderson Foundation

Windle, Timothty J., asst secy: American President Companies Foundation

Windon, Bernard M., sr vp: Ameritech Corp.; dir: Ameritech Foundation

Windship, William B., trust: Bingham Second Betterment Fund, William

Wine, L. Mark, dir: Kirkland & Ellis Foundation

Winegarden, Joel, vp, asst secy: Weinberg Foundation, Harry and Jeanette

Wineston, Ted M., trust: Lowenstein Foundation, William P. and Marie R.

Winford, B.F., dir: Tractor & Equipment Company Foundation

Winford, Benny F., secy-treas: Tractor & Equipment Company Foundation

Winfree, Lynn, secy, dir: Precision Rubber Products Foundation

Winger, C. Nelson, treas: Beck Foundation, Elsie E. & Joseph W.

Winger, Dennis L., sr vp, cfo: Chiron Corp.

Winger, G. Leo, trust: Charitable Fund

Wingfield, W. T., pres, trust: Wilson Foundation, Frances Wood

Winkelmann, Herman, vp: Havens Foundation, O. W.

Winkelstern, Philip N., sr vp, cfo: Commercial Intertech Corp.; vp, cfo: Commercial Intertech Foundation

Winkler, Carolyn, secy, dir: Winkler Foundation, Mark and Catherine

Winkler, Charles P., MD, pres: Metropolitan Health Foundation

Winkler, Henry R., vp: Seasongood Good Government Foundation, Murray and Agnes

Winkler, Paul, dir: Menil Foundation

Winkler, Virginia, trust: Hallberg Foundation, E. L. and R. F.

Winkler, William R., treas, trust: Tomkins Corporation Foundation

Winmill, Mark C., trust: Thanksgiving Foundation

Winn, David, trust: Klingensmith Charitable Foundation, Agnes

Winn, Kay, trust: Klingensmith Charitable Foundation, Agnes

Winn, William R., trust: Iacocca Foundation

Winn, Willis J., mem bd mgrs: Measey Foundation, Benjamin and Mary Siddons

Winnowski, T. R., chmn, ceo: Key Bank of Oregon

Winslow, Alicia B., trust: Burnham Donor Fund, Alfred G.

Winslow, Enid, vp: Jurodin Fund

Winsor, Curtin, Jr., secy: Donner Foundation, William H.

Winsor, James D., III, trust: Presser Foundation

Winston, Bert F., trust: Rienzi Foundation

Winston, Bert F., Jr., vp, trust: Turner Charitable Foundation

Winston, Charles F., dir: Waggoner Foundation, E. Paul and Helen Buck

Winston, Elecra Biggs, 1st vp, dir: Waggoner Foundation, E. Paul and Helen Buck

Winston, Gail, corp commun dept: Cartier, Inc.

Winston, Hathily, secy, trust: Johnson Foundation, Walter S.

Winston, James H., trust: Terry Foundation, C. Herman

Winston, Lynn David, trust: Rienzi Foundation

Winston, Ronald, pres: Winston Research Foundation, Harry

Winston, Samuel, trust: Blowitz-Ridgeway Foundation

Winter, Arthur, trust: Stern Foundation, Irvin

Winter, Barbara Ecke, dir, secy: Poinsettia Foundation, Paul and Magdalena Ecke

Winter, Charles K., trust: Simpson Industries Fund

Winter, Dorothy G., trust: Stern Foundation, Irvin

Winter, Irwin W., vp, treas: Phillips-Van Heusen Foundation

Winter, J. Burgess, pres, ceo: Magma Copper Co.

Winter, Stanley, trust: Stern Foundation, Irvin

Winter, William Bergford, pres, dir: Bucyrus-Erie; pres, dir: Bucyrus-Erie Foundation

Winters, Deborah, adm asst: UNUM Charitable Foundation

Winters, Robert Cushing, chmn, ceo, dir: Prudential Insurance Co. of America

Winthrop, John, dir: Brookdale Foundation

Winthrop, Robert, Waterfowl Research Foundation

Winvick, Stanley, secy, dir: Advanced Micro Devices Charitable Foundation

Wire, William S., II, chmn: Genesco

Wirkkala, Brian, mem (contributions comm): PacifiCorp Foundation

Wirtanen, Donald G., dir: Ordean Foundation

Wirth, Conrad L., trust: Jackson Hole Preserve

Wirth, Earle, mgr: Autotrol Corp. Charitable Trust

Wirth, Leland, pres: Farmstead Foods

Wirth, Wren W., trust: Winslow Foundation

Wirtz, Arthur M., vp, dir: Washington Square Health Foundation

Wisdom, Betty, trust: RosaMary Foundation

Wisdom, Mary E., pres: Wisdom Foundation, Mary F.

Wise, Daniel P., dir: Weber Charities Corp., Frederick E.

Wise, Emma F., trust: Wise Foundation and Charitable Trust, Watson W.

Wise, John, vp, dir: Mentor Graphics Foundation

Wise, John James, dir: Mobil Foundation

Wise, Robert E., cfo, vp, treas: Meadows Foundation

Wise, Robert Edward, MD, trust: Dana Charitable Trust, Eleanor Naylor

Wise, Stephanie, vp, dir: Lehman Foundation, Edith and Herbert

Wise, Urban G., exec vp, cfo: Ameribank

Wiseheart, Malcolm B., Jr., pres: Wiseheart Foundation

Wiseman, Ellen E., mgr: English Foundation, Walter and Marian

Wishart, Alfred W., Jr., exec dir: Heinz Endowment, Howard; exec dir: Heinz Endowment, Vira I.

Wishart, Steven, dir: Northwestern National Life Insurance Co.

Wishnack, Marshall B., pres, dir: Wheat First Securites; dir: Wheat Foundation

Wishnia, Steven, trust: Plough Foundation

Wishnick, Lisa, dir: Wishnick Foundation, Robert I.

Wishnick, William, pres, dir: Wishnick Foundation, Robert I.

Wislocki, George S., dir: Innisfree Foundation

Wismer, Steven H., cfo: Crane & Co.; trust: Crane & Co. Fund

Wisner, Edwin, trust: Wagnalls Memorial

Wisnom, David, secy, treas: Avery-Fuller Children's Center

Wisnom, David, Jr., vp: Lux Foundation, Miranda

Wisnom, Ruth, trust: Avery-Fuller Children's Center

Wissinger, Randy S., vp, treas: Elgin Sweeper Foundation

Witcher, Robert Campbell, trust: Killough Trust, Walter H. D.

Witherspoon, David H., vp: Fletcher Foundation, A. J.

Witherspoon, Douglas C., dir: Scholl Foundation, Dr.

Witherspoon, Jere Wathen, exec dir: Duke Endowment

Withington, Nathan N., dir, pres: Hornblower Fund, Henry

Withrow, David, trust: Whitney Benefits

Witt, Raymond B., Jr., secy, treas: Westend Foundation

Witt, Robert L., chmn, pres, ceo: Hexcel Corp.; pres, dir: Hexcel Foundation

Witt, Sherman E., Jr., secy, treas, trust: Carbon Fuel Foundation

Witte, R. F., program off: Exxon Education Foundation

Wittenborn, John R., trust: Cape Branch Foundation

Wittenstein, Joseph, mem: Phillips Foundation, Dr. P.

Witter, Dean, III, pres, dir: Witter Foundation, Dean

Witter, William D., secy, treas: Witter Foundation, Dean

Witunski, Michael, dir: McDonnell Foundation, James S.

Witz, Carol A., secy, dir: Kelly, Jr. Memorial Foundation, Ensign C. Markland

Witz, Herbert E., pres, dir: Kelly, Jr. Memorial Foundation, Ensign C. Markland

Witzling, Morton, secy, dir: Rudin Foundation

Wo, Robert, Jr., dir: Bancorp Hawaii Charitable Foundation

Wobst, Frank, chmn, ceo, dir: Huntington Bancshares Inc.

Woeltae, Gary, mem grants comm: First Bank System Foundation

Woessner, William M., trust: German Marshall Fund of the United States

Wohlert, Roger W., vp, treas: Southwestern Bell Foundation

Wohlstetter, Charles, pres, dir: Rose Foundation, Billy

Wojtak, Barry, treas: Abbott Laboratories Fund

Wolak, Karen A., secy, treas: Castle Foundation

Wolcott, Arthur S., chmn, dir: Seneca Foods Foundation

Wold, Elaine Johnson, trust: Bay Branch Foundation

Wold, Keith C., Bay Branch Foundation

Woldenberg, Dorothy, pres: Woldenberg Foundation

Wolf, Brian J., advisory com: Powers Higher Educational Fund, Edward W. and Alice R.

Wolf, Daniel A., vp: Plumsock Fund

Wolf, Elaine, vp, dir: Wolf Foundation, Melvin and Elaine

Wolf, Elizabeth K., trust: Krimendahl II Foundation, H. Frederick

Wolf, Flora Barth, trust: Wolf Foundation, Benjamin and Fredora K.

Wolf, Harold, dir: Peters Foundation, R. D. and Linda

Wolf, Harold J., secy, treas, dir: Brillion Foundation

Wolf, Howard, chmn: Offshore Logistics

Wolf, J. W., vp, treas, dir: Graybar Foundation

Wolf, Jamie G. R., vp, trust: Rosenthal Foundation, Richard and Hinda

Wolf, John W., Sr., dir: Kaufmann Foundation, Henry

Wolf, Lee J., trust: Raymond Foundation

Wolf, Lester K., trust: Patterson Charitable Fund, W. I.

Wolf, Melvin, pres, dir: Wolf Foundation, Melvin and Elaine

Wolf, Peter, trust: Baldwin Foundation

Wolf, Richard L., vp, secy, treas, dir: Julia R. and Estelle L. Foundation

Wolf, Robert, pres: New-Land Foundation

Wolf, Stephanie R., exec dir: Cowell Foundation, S. H.

Wolf, Stephen M., chmn, ceo, pres: United Airlines; dir: United Airlines Foundation

Wolf, Thomas, pres, trust: American Foundation Corporation; dir: Dana Corp. Foundation

Wolf, William, dir pub rels: Hyundai Motor America

Wolfberg, Stephen, secy: Falcon Foundation

Wolfe, C. Holmes, trust: Donnelly Foundation, Mary J.; trust: Frick Foundation, Helen Clay

Wolfe, Jerry, pres, ceo, dir: Andersen Corp.

Wolfe, Joan M., vp, asst secy: Mailman Foundation

Wolfe, John F., vp: Wolfe Associates, Inc.

Wolfe, John Walton, pres, dir: Wolfe Associates, Inc.

Wolfe, Judson, vp, asst trust: Mailman Foundation

Wolfe, Kenneth L., pres, coo, dir: Hershey Foods Corp.

Wolfe, Laurence A., vp (admin): Weingart Foundation

Wolfe, Maryalice, Jr., vp: Tsai Foundation, Gerald

Wolfe, Merle, dir: Thompson Charitable Foundation

Wolfe, William C., Jr., vp: Wolfe Associates, Inc.

Wolfen, Werner, secy: Alpert Foundation, Herb

Wolfen, Werner F., secy: Moss Foundation

Wolfensohn, Elaine, secy: Botwinick-Wolfensohn Foundation

Wolfensohn, James D., chmn: Botwinick-Wolfensohn Foundation; trust: Hughes Medical Institute, Howard

Wolfensohn, Naomi, treas: Botwinick-Wolfensohn Foundation

Wolfensohn, Sara, asst treas: Botwinick-Wolfensohn Foundation

Wolfensperger, Diana Potter, trust: Lux Foundation, Miranda

Wolff, Byron, vp: Pamida Foundation

Wolff, Elaine, dir: Wolff Shoe Foundation

Wolff, Herbert E., secy, dir: First Hawaiian Foundation

Wolff, Jesse D., treas, dir: Weil, Gotshal & Manges Foundation

Wolff, John M., III, trust: Wolff Foundation, John M.

Wolff, Paula, dir: Joyce Foundation

Wolff, Rosalie S., vp: Solow Foundation

Wolff, William, pres: Wolff Shoe Co.; mgr, dir: Wolff Shoe Foundation

Wolford, Stephen T., trust: Ferre Revocable Trust, Joseph C.

Wolfson, Cecil, chmn, dir: Wolfson Family Foundation

Wolfson, Gary L., trust: Wolfson Family Foundation

Wolfson, Marv, dir, vp: Mentor Graphics Foundation

Wolfson, Nathan, trust: Wolfson Family Foundation

Wolfson, Stephen P., trust: Wolfson Family Foundation

Wolfson, Warren D., secy, treas, dir: Fay's Foundation, Inc.

Wolkenbrod, Simon C., treas: Ginsberg Family Foundation, Moses

Wollen, Carolyn S., trust: Bingham Second Betterment Fund, William

Wollen, Dori, vp: Silverburgh Foundation, Grace, George & Judith

Wollen, Roger C., pres: Silverburgh Foundation, Grace, George & Judith

Wollenberg, J. Roger, trust: Wollenberg Foundation

Wollenberg, R.P., chmn, pres, ceo, dir: Longview Fibre Co.

Wollenberg, Richard Peter, trust: Wollenberg Foundation

Woller, Gary Lee, comm mem: Fromm Scholarship Trust, Walter and Mabel

Wollman, Jack, asst treas: Koh-I-Noor Rapidograph Inc.

Wolman, J. Martin, vp: Lee Endowment Foundation

Wolman, Philip J., pres: Buchalter, Nemer, Fields, & Younger; trust: Buchalter, Nemer, Fields, Chrystie & Younger Charitable Foundation

Wolpe, Gerald I., trust: Bronstein Foundation, Soloman and Sylvia

Wolski, Lawrence G., sr vp, treas, dir: Joslyn Foundation

Wolszon, Mary Rush Bartol, trust: Bartol Foundation, Stockton Rush

Wolters, Kate Pew, exec dir: Steelcase Foundation

Woltman, W. J., pres, trust: Woltman Foundation, B. M.

Womack, C. Suzanne, corp secy: Lincoln National Corp.

Womack, Christopher C., dir: Alabama Power Foundation

Womack, James S., chmn, dir: Sheldahl Inc.

Womack, Robert P., pres, coo: IMO Industries Inc.

Woman, Paul C., III, trust: Unger Foundation, Aber D.

Womble, G.M., chmn, pres, dir: Durham Corp.

Wommack, William Walton, trust: Star Bank, N.A., Cincinnati Foundation

Wondergem, Casey, secy, treas: Amway Environmental Foundation

Wong, Evelyn S., asst secy-treas: Occidental Petroleum Charitable Foundation

Wong, G. Ron, pres, dir: Bel Air Mart

Wong, Louisa, treas: China Times Cultural Foundation

Woo, William Franklin, dir: Pulitzer Publishing Co. Foundation

Wood, Al, cfo: Balcor Co.

Wood, Anthony C., chief program off: Kaplan Fund, J. M.

Wood, Barbara M. J., dir: Rice Foundation

Wood, C.O., III, trust: Wood Foundation of Chambersburg, PA

Wood, Charles, vp (human resources): Picker International

Wood, Cynthia S., 2nd vp, dir: Wood-Claeyssens Foundation

Wood, D. Dale, chmn, pres, ceo, dir: Enterra Corp.

Wood, Davis S., trust: Wood Foundation of Chambersburg, PA

Wood, Dick, mem (contributions comm): GATX Corp.

Wood, Fran, consumer aff rep: Giant Food Stores

Wood, Francis C., MD, mem bd mgrs: Measey Foundation, Benjamin and Mary Siddons

Wood, Hayden R., trust: Williams Foundation, Arthur Ashley

Wood, James, chmn, pres, ceo: Great Atlantic & Pacific Tea Co. Inc.; dir: Jewish Foundation for Education of Women; Metropolitan Health Foundation

Wood, James F., dir: McMahon Foundation

Wood, John M., Jr., trust: Schrafft and Bertha E. Schrafft Charitable Trust, William E.

Wood, John R., pres, dir: Wilson Foundation, Hugh and Mary

Wood, Joshua Warren, III, vp, secy, gen coun: Johnson Foundation, Robert Wood

Wood, Kate B., dir: Hyde and Watson Foundation

Wood, Lawrence M., trust: Pilot Trust

Wood, Lloyd, treas: Tanner Foundation

Wood, Lowell L., dir: Hertz Foundation, Fannie and John

Wood, Miriam M., trust: Wood Foundation of Chambersburg, PA

Wood, Peter, dir: Menil Foundation

Wood, R. Ray, dir: First National Bank & Trust Co. of Rockford Charitable Trust; chmn, pres, ceo: Rockford Products Corp.; pres, dir: Rockford Products Corp. Foundation

Wood, Robert A., dir: Green Foundation, Allen P. and Josephine B.

Wood, Robert C., secy, dir: XTEK Foundation

Wood, Robert E., pres, dir: MDU Resources Foundation

Wood, Robert S., vchmn, dir: Bob Evans Farms

Wood, Roger E., chmn, trust: Moore Foundation, Martha G.

Wood, Sadie L., secy, dir: Wilson Foundation, Hugh and Mary

Wood, Susan, dir: Wilson Foundation, Hugh and Mary

Wood, Susannah C. L., trust: AKC Fund

Wood, Sylvia Upton, secy, trust: Upton Foundation, Frederick S.

Wood, William, dir: Shoemaker Trust for Shoemaker Scholarship Fund, Ray S.

Wood, William Philler, trust: Grundy Foundation; trust, secy: Stott Foundation, Louis L.

Woodard, Carlton, pres: Woodard Family Foundation

Woodard, Dutee, vp: Woodard Family Foundation

Woodard, Kim, secy, treas: Woodard Family Foundation

Woodard, Milton P., dir: Bush Charitable Foundation, Edyth

Woodard, Mitchell R., secy, treas: Frost Foundation

Woodd-Cahusac, Sydney A., vp, dir: Herzog Foundation, Carl J.

Wooden, Ruth A., trust: Clark Foundation, Edna McConnell

Woodhouse, John F., chmn, ceo: Sysco Corp.

Woodhull, Nancy, trust: Freedom Forum

Woodling, Anne, trust: Stocker Foundation

Woodling, Nancy Elizabeth, trust: Stocker Foundation

Woodman, Ralph, asst secy: Foundation for Seacoast Health

Woodman, Victor E., vp: Genius Foundation, Elizabeth Morse

Woodner, Andrea, pres, secy, treas: Woodner Family Collection, Ian

Woodner, Dian, pres, secy, treas: Woodner Family Collection, Ian

Woodruff, D. Straton, Jr., trust: Kynett Memorial Foundation, Edna G.

Woodruff, Fred M., Jr., trust: Miller Foundation

Woodruff, J. Barnett, vp: Illges Memorial Foundation, A. and M. L.

Woods, C. Carl, dir: Durham Merchants Association Charitable Foundation

Woods, Carol, trust: Shoemaker Trust for Shoemaker Scholarship Fund, Ray S.

Woods, Caroline T., trust: Cartinhour Foundation

Woods, Carolyn Taylor, trust: Woods-Greer Foundation

Woods, Chuck, trust: McKesson Foundation

Woods, Cindy, coordinator commun rels: Central & South West Foundation

Woods, David F., clerk, dir: Beveridge Foundation, Frank Stanley

Woods, Earl C., dir: Azby Fund

Woods, Edwin Newhall, dir: Newhall Foundation, Henry Mayo

Woods, J. Mark, coo: Anacomp, Inc.

Woods, Jacqueline F., pres, ceo, dir: Ohio Bell Telephone Co.

Woods, James D., chmn, pres, ceo, dir: Baker Hughes Inc.

Woods, John W., chmn, ceo, dir: AmSouth Bancorporation

Woods, John W., III, comm: Hope Memorial Fund, Blanche and Thomas

Woods, Laura-Lee Whittier, pres: L. L. W. W. Foundation; pres: Whittier Foundation, L. K.

Woods, Marie Carinhour, trust, vp: Cartinhour Foundation

Woods, Marie Cartinhour, vchmn: Woods-Greer Foundation

Woods, Prudence, dir: Newhall Foundation, Henry Mayo

Woods, Robert A., trust: Bates Memorial Foundation, George A.

Woods, Thomas C., III, chmn: Lincoln Telecommunications Co.; vp, trust: Woods Charitable Fund

Woods, Very Rev C. Cecil, Jr., chmn: Woods-Greer Foundation

Woodside, William S., chmn: Sky Chefs, Inc.

Woodson, Robert R., pres, ceo, dir: Harland Co., John H.; secy, dir: Harland Co. Foundation, John H.

Woodson, Robert Ray, trust: Campbell Foundation, J. Bulow

Woodson, Sam P., III, pres, managing dir: Brown and C. A. Lupton Foundation, T. J.

Woodward, Catherine M., trust: Williams Family Foundation

Woodward, Gina, asst to ceo: Overnite Transportation Co.

Woodward, Joanne, dir: Newman's Own Foundation

Woodward, M. Cabell, vchmn, cfo, dir: ITT Corp.

Woodward, M. Cabell, Jr., vchmn: International Standard Electric Corp.

Woodward, Paul E., trust: Williams Family Foundation

Woodward, Reid T., Woodward Fund

Woodward, Richmond B., treas, dir: Grass Foundation

Woodward, Robert J., sr vp: Nationwide Insurance Foundation

Woodward, S.L., dir: Union City Body Co. Foundation

Woodward, Stephen S., mgr: Woodward Fund

Woodward, William S., mgr: Woodward Fund

Woodwell, George Masters, chmn, trust: Mott Fund, Ruth

Woodworth, Mrs. John K., vp, treas, dir: Reflection Riding

Woofter, R.D., chmn: Texas-New Mexico Power Co.

Woolard, Edgar Smith, Jr., chmn, ceo, dir: du Pont de Nemours & Co., E. I.

Woolbert, Richard E., mem (contributions comm): McDermott

Wooldredge, William, pres, ceo: TransOhio Savings Bank

Woolf, Harry, trust: Rockefeller Foundation

Woolf, Kenneth, trust: BCR Foundation

Woolfe, Walter L., trust: River Branch Foundation

Woollam, Tina F., trust: Freeman Foundation, Ella West

Woollcott, James, dir: Janirve Foundation

Woollems, J. Michael, asst treas, asst secy: Advanced Micro Devices Charitable Foundation

Woolley, Michele, Jr., trust: Girard Foundation

Woolley, R. B., Jr., ceo: Girard Foundation

Wootton, Mack, vp, admin: Central Soya Foundation

Worcester, Frederick C., treas, trust: Charlesbank Homes

Worfel, C. Christopher, trust, secy, treas: Loutit Foundation

Workman, John L., vp (fin): Montgomery Ward & Co.; dir: Montgomery Ward Foundation

Workman, Leanne M., adm: Ames Charitable Trust, Harriett; adm: Hall Charitable Trust, Evelyn A. J.; adm: Hazen Charitable Trust, Lita Annenberg; adm: Hooker Charitable Trust, Janet A.; adm: Levee Charitable Trust, Polly Annenberg; adm: Simon Charitable Trust, Esther

Workman, Maurice C., pres: Moore & Sons, B.C.; trust: Moore & Sons Foundation, B.C.

Workum, David, pres: United Iron & Metal Co.

Worley, Jack, trust: Sewell Foundation, Warren P. and Ava F.

Worley, Kenneth, dir: Group Health Foundation

Worlledge, Donald W., pres, coo: Ravenswood Aluminum Corp.

Woronoff, Patricia, dir: Daniels Charitable Foundation, Josephus

Worrell, Charles T., exec vp, dir: Subaru of America Inc.

Worth, M. W., trust: Delta Air Lines Foundation

Worth, Robert, trust: HKH Foundation

Wortham, R. W., III, vp, asst treas: Wortham Foundation

Worthington, C. Wayne, secy, treas, dir: National City Bank of Evansville Foundation

Worthington, John R., sr vp, gen coun, dir: MCI Communications Corp.; dir: MCI Foundation

Worthington, Margaret C., trust: Campbell Foundation

Wortman, J. John, ceo, pres: Michigan Mutual Insurance Corp.

Wouk, Betty Saraha, treas: Wouk Foundation, Abe

Wouk, Herman, pres, trust: Wouk Foundation, Abe

Wouk, Joseph, vp, trust: Wouk Foundation, Abe

Wouk, Nathaniel, vp: Wouk Foundation, Abe

Woy, Frank V., dir: MPCo/Entech Foundation

Wragg, Richard G., pres: Clark Home for Aged People, Ella

Wrape, A. J., III, trust: Wrape Family Charitable Trust

Wrape, A. J., Jr., mgr, trust: Wrape Family Charitable Trust

Wrape, Tom, trust: Wrape Family Charitable Trust

Wrape, W. R., II, trust: Wrape Family Charitable Trust

Wray, Gay F., trust: Firestone Foundation, Roger S.

Wray, Gilda G., vp: Hayden Foundation, Charles

Wray, Mrs. Michael B., recording secy: Memorial Foundation for Children

Wren, William C., vp (corporate rels): Northwest Airlines, Inc.

Wrenn, Peter J., dir: Schmitt Foundation, Arthur J.

Wright, Arnold W., Jr., exec dir: CIGNA Foundation

Wright, Barbara, secy, trust: Packard Foundation, David and Lucile

Wright, Carolyn, dir, pres: Ziemann Foundation

Wright, Donald Franklin, dir: Pfaffinger Foundation; dir: Times Mirror Foundation

Wright, Dwight, vp, dir: Shoong Foundation, Milton

Wright, Elizabeth J., secy: Baker Foundation, George T.

Wright, Emmett, Jr., trust: Sullivan Foundation, Algernon Sydney

Wright, Felix E., pres, coo, dir: Leggett & Platt, Inc.

Wright, George, pres, dir: National City Bank of Evansville Foundation

Wright, Hasbrouck S., exec trust: Kunkel Foundation, John Crain

Wright, J., trust: Cranston Foundation

Wright, James, dir: Fairchild Foundation, Sherman; trust: GenRad Foundation

Wright, James O., chmn, dir: Badger Meter, Inc.; pres, dir: Badger Meter Foundation; dir: Marshall & Ilsley Foundation

Wright, James W., vp, treas: Park Banks Foundation

Wright, Jan, dir: Wallestad Foundation

Wright, John E., dir: Alexander Charitable Foundation

Wright, Joseph R., Jr., vchmn, dir: Grace & Co., W.R.

Wright, Lawrence A., dir: Atkinson Foundation

Wright, Linda, secy contributions comm: US Bancorp

Wright, Michael W., chmn, pres, ceo, dir: Super Valu Stores

Wright, Mrs. James O. B., dir: Reflection Riding

Wright, Nancy, 1st vp, dir: Hopper Foundation, May Templeton

Wright, Patricia D., exec dir, secy: Amoco Foundation

Wright, Richard E., III, secy, dir: Cuesta Foundation

Wright, Robert C., pres, ceo: National Broadcasting Co., Inc.

Wright, Robert F., pres, coo, dir: Amerada Hess Corp.

Wright, Robert G., vp, trust: Murphy Foundation, John P.; vp, dir: Sheldon Foundation, Ralph C.

Wright, Robert I., trust: Mobility Foundation

Wright, Roger Ellerton, trust: Consolidated Natural Gas Co. Foundation

Wright, Ronald H., pres: Kollsman Instrument Co.

Wright, Rose Bauervic, vp: Bauervic Foundation, Charles M.

Wright, Samuel H., secy: PHH Foundation

Wright, Spencer D., III, treas, trust: Foerderer Foundation, Percival E. and Ethel Brown

Wright, Stanley C., dir corp contributions: Eastman Kodak Co.

Wright, Virginia Bloedel, chmn, trust: Bloedel Foundation; vp, treas: Merrill Foundation, R. D.

Wright, W. F., Jr., secy, treas, assoc dir: Cockrell Foundation

Wright, W.J., secy: Merrill Foundation, R. D.

Wright, Wesley, mem: Wal-Mart Foundation

Wright, William B., dir: Bunbury Company

Wright, William L., vp, dir: Hultquist Foundation

Wright, William R., trust: Davis Foundations, Arthur Vining

Wrightsman, Jayne L., pres, dir: Coral Reef Foundation

Wrightson, J. Wallace, trust: Bastien Memorial Foundation, John E. and Nellie J.

Wrightson, Lois I., trust: Birmingham Foundation

Wrigley, Julie Ann, dir, secy: Burns Family Foundation

Wrigley, William, pres, ceo, dir: Wrigley Co., Wm. Jr.

Wrigley, William, Jr., vp, dir: Wrigley Co. Foundation, Wm. Jr.

Wriston, Kathryn D., trust: Hartford Foundation, John A.

Wrobley, Ralph G., secy: Helzberg Foundation, Shirley and Barnett

Wrona, Diane, secy, treas: Motch Corp. Foundation

Wu, M. H., treas: Kellogg Co. Twenty-Five Year Employees' Fund

Wuensch, Ronald W., dir: American General Finance Foundation

Wuest, Teresa, cfo: Chase Bank of Arizona

Wuester, William O., MD, trust: Union Foundation

Wuesthoff, Winfred W., dir: Wehr Foundation, Todd

Wugalter, Harry, trust: Hazen Foundation, Edward W.

Wulff, Dr. Harald P., pres, ceo: Henkel Corp.

Wunderlich, Hermann, chmn: Miles Inc.

Wunsch, Eric M., vp: WEA Enterprises Co.; pres: Wunsch Foundation

Wunsch, Ethel, secy: Wunsch Foundation

Wunsch, Peter, secy, treas: WEA Enterprises Co.

Wurtele, C. A., chmn, ceo: Valspar Corp.; pres, dir: Valspar Foundation

Wurtele, C. Angus, dir: Bush Foundation

Wurtzel, Alan Leon, chmn, dir: Circuit City Stores; chmn: Circuit City Foundation

Wurzburg, Reginald, ceo, vp: Wurzburg, Inc.

Wyatt, Grady, dir, vchmn: Piedmont Health Care Foundation

Wyatt, Oscar Sherman, Jr., chmn, dir: Coastal Corp.

Wyckoff, Ann P., trust: Norcliffe Fund

Wyckoff, Clinton R., Jr., pres: Goodyear Foundation, Josephine

Wyckoff, Dorothy G., trust: Goodyear Foundation, Josephine

Wyckoff, E. Lisk, Jr., pres, treas, trust: Homeland Foundation

Wyckoff, Raymond W., vp, dir: Florida East Coast Industries

Wycoff, Robert E., pres, coo, dir: ARCO

Wyeth, Phyllis Mills, trust: duPont Foundation, Chichester

Wyland, Susan T., trust: Towsley Foundation, Harry A. and Margaret D.

Wyler, Michael, trust: Julia Foundation, Laura

Wyler, Veit, chmn, trust: Julia Foundation, Laura

Wylie, Joan H., exec dir: Hancock Foundation, Luke B.

Wyly, Charles Joseph, Jr., co-fdr, vchmn, dir: Sterling Software Inc.

Wyly, Sam, chmn, dir: Sterling Software Inc.

Wyman, Ann McCall, Wyman Youth Trust

Wyman, David C., trust: Wyman Youth Trust

Wyman, David E., trust: Wyman Youth Trust

Wyman, Deehan M., Wyman Youth Trust

Wyman, Hal, Wyman Youth Trust

Wyman, Henry W., chmn: Pantasote Polymers

Wyman, Ralph M., vchmn: Pantasote Polymers

Wyman, Richard M., trust: Rogers Family Foundation

Wyman, Thomas H., trust: Ford Foundation

Wyman, Thomas R., pres, dir: Oshkosh B'Gosh Foundation

Wyman, Timothy E., pres, dir: Richmond Foundation, Frederick W.

Wynbrandt, Dennis, treas, secy: Kohl Charitable Foundation, Allen D.

Wyne, Jon R., treas: Miles Inc. Foundation

Wynia, Ann, dir: Bush Foundation; dir: Fuller Co. Foundation, H.B.

Wynn, Elaine, treas: Golden Nugget Scholarship Fund

Wynn, Kevin, trust: Golden Nugget Scholarship Fund

Wynn, Stephen A., chmn, pres, ceo, dir: Mirage Casino-Hotel; trust: Golden Nugget Scholarship Fund

Wynne, John Oliver, pres, dir: Landmark Charitable Foundation

Wynne, Marjorie West, secy, dir: West Foundation

Wynne, Richard B., dir: Janirve Foundation

Wynne, Robert C., vp, dir: West Foundation

Wyper, Janet, community rels specialist: Bean, L.L.

Wyse, Alden M., secy, treas, dir: Kelly Foundation

Wyszomierski, Jack L., treas: Schering-Plough Foundation

Wythes, Carol Krause, pres, dir: Krause Foundation, Charles A.

X

Xydiaris, Tina, off (accounts payable): Standard Chartered Bank New York

Y

Yablon, Leonard Harold, pres: Forbes Foundation

Yaconetti, Dianne M., vp (admin), corp secy: Brunswick Corp.; vp, dir: Brunswick Foundation

Yaeger, Thomas A., secy, treas, dir: General Railway Signal Foundation

Yagi, Nobuhito, secy: NEC Foundation of America

Yahagi, Hiroka, planning dept: Bank of Tokyo Trust Co.

Yakel, Daniel J., comm mem: Pfister and Vogel Tanning Co. Foundation

Yakira, M. W., vp: FPL Group Foundation

Yakushiji, Hiromasa, dir, gen mgr: Sumitomo Trust & Banking Co., Ltd.

Yale, Charles E., M.D., trust: Surgical Science Foundation for Research and Development

Yamada, Masayuki, treas: Hitachi Foundation

Yamada, Shoichi, pres, ceo: Pioneer Electronics (USA) Inc.

Yamamoto, Frances, asst secy: Bancorp Hawaii Charitable Foundation

Yamamoto, Tamon, pres: Subaru-Isuzu Automotive Inc.

Yamane, Y., gen mgr, gen aff: Sumitomo Corp. of America

Yamano, Toshiya, exec vp, cfo: Mitsubishi Motor Sales of America, Inc.

Yamasaki, Koichi, dir: Nakamichi Foundation, E.

Yamashita, Yoshio, vchmn: Shuwa Investments Corp.

Yamazaki, Yas, pres, dir: Nakamichi Foundation, E.

Yampol, Barry, trust: Mineral Trust

Yampol, David, trust: Mineral Trust

Yancey, Benjamin W., pres, dir: Williams Foundation, Kemper and Leila

Yancey, Helen Lund, trust: McKee Foundation, Robert E. and Evelyn

Yancey, James D., vchmn, dir: Synovus Financial Corp.

Yancy, Mary Garwood, trust, secy: Henry Foundation, Patrick

Yanitelli, Victor R., SJ, trust: Loyola Foundation

Yannarell, Robert W., secy, treas: AMETEK Foundation

Yarbrough, C. Richard, trust: BellSouth Foundation

Yarter, David, adm; trust off (Sovran Bank): Bustard Charitable Permanent Trust Fund, Elizabeth and James

Yashiki, Toyoji, pres: Honda of America Manufacturing, Inc.

Yasinsky, John B., trust: Westinghouse Foundation

Yasutake, Chiyoko, allocation comm: Kawabe Memorial Fund

Yasutake, W. T., allocation comm: Kawabe Memorial Fund

Yates, Kathryn A., vp, trust: UNUM Charitable Foundation

Yates, Mary-Alice, secy: Guggenheim Foundation, Harry Frank

Yatsko, Helen D., adm: MCA Foundation

Yawkey, Jean R., trust: Yawkey Foundation II

Yawman, J. Gregory, asst secy: Crown Central Petroleum Foundation

Yeager, Charles G., dir, trust: Stranahan Foundation

Yeager, Kathryn Prothro, dir: Perkins Foundation, Joe and Lois; vp, trust: Perkins-Prothro Foundation

Yeakel, Judith P., trust: Arise Charitable Trust

Yearely, Douglas Cain, chmn, pres, ceo, dir: Phelps Dodge Corp.; dir: Phelps Dodge Foundation

Yeates, Jean W., trust: Walker Foundation, T. B.

Yeates, Jeffrey L., trust: Walker Foundation, T. B.

Yeckel, Carl, vp, dir: King Foundation, Carl B. and Florence E.

Yee, K. Tim, dir: Bancorp Hawaii Charitable Foundation

Yehle, Eugene C., chmn, trust: Strosacker Foundation, Charles J.

Yeiser, Charles F., vp: Hayfields Foundation

Yeiser, Eric P., pres: Hayfields Foundation

Yeisley, R., cfo: Six Flags Theme Parks Inc.

Yellott, Kinloch N., III, dir, vp: Wilson Sanitarium for Children of Baltimore City, Thomas

Yemenidjian, Alex, vp: Lincy Foundation

Yeo, Lloyd J., treas, trust: Wickes Foundation, Harvey Randall; pres, treas: Wickson-Link Memorial Foundation

Yesko, Michael A., treas: Sperry Fund

Yeskoo, Richard, mem: Rixson Foundation, Oscar C.

Yielding, F. Brooks, III, secy: Hill Crest Foundation

Yingling, John, chief adm, fin off: Dodge Foundation, Geraldine R.

Yingling, William E., chmn, ceo, dir: Thrifty Corp.

Yochum, Doreen S., trust: AT&T Foundation

Yocum, Robert, secy: Harsco Corp. Fund

Yoder, Elvin D., trust: Schowalter Foundation

Yohe, Merrill A., chmn contributions comm: AMP Foundation

Yoho, Bill I., trust: Stewart Memorial Trust, J. C.

Yonekura, Isao, chmn: Itoh (C.) International (America), Inc.

Yoneyama, Koji, chmn, pres, cfo: Daiwa Securities America Inc.

Yonker, Michael T., pres, ceo: Portec, Inc.

Yontz, Merle R., vp, trust: Mellinger Educational Foundation, Edward Arthur

Yoo, Ronald J., vchmn: Shearson, Lehman & Hutton

York, J. B., exec vp, cfo: Chrysler Corp.

York, John C., treas, dir: Washington Square Health Foundation

York, R.B., secy-treas: Porter Paint Foundation

York, Theodore, pres, coo: Burndy Corp.

Yoshida, Katsumi, pres: Ricoh Electronics Inc.

Yoshida, Tadashi, treas: NEC Foundation of America

Yoshino, Teruomi, pres: DNP (America), Inc.

Yoshioka, Marche H., asst secy: Gellert Foundation, Fred

Yosomiya, Masao, pres, dir: Kanematsu-Gosho U.S.A. Inc.

Yost, Lyle E., vp, dir: Hesston Foundation

Young, A. Thomas, pres, coo, dir: Martin Marietta Corp.

Young, Andrew B., trust: Lovett Foundation

Young, Andrew Brodbeck, Michaels Scholarship Fund, Frank J.

Young, C., dir: Capital Fund Foundation

Young, Charles, II, treas: Cacioppo Foundation, Joseph & Mary

Young, Donald J., dir: Pappas Charitable Foundation, Bessie; dir: Pappas Charitable Foundation, Thomas Anthony

Young, Douglas, cfo, vp, secy: Copperweld Corp.; trust: Copperweld Foundation

Young, Edmond C., pres, dir: Ross Memorial Foundation, Will

Young, Emily, trust: Baldwin Memorial Foundation, Fred

Young, F. Chandler, vp: Bassett Foundation, Norman

Young, Fern D., pres, treas, dir: Young Foundation, Irvin L.

Young, Henry C., pres: Howard Benevolent Society

Young, J. Will, dir: Eastover Foundation

Young, James H., gen dir, asst secy: John Hancock Mutual Life Insurance Co.

Young, John R., pres: Gould Foundation, Florence J.; dir: Grace Foundation, Inc.; dir: Mathers Charitable Foundation, G. Harold and Leila Y.; dir: Schneiderman Foundation, Roberta and Irwin

Young, Lawrence J., chmn, pres, ceo, dir: Angelica Corp.

Young, Leslie D., trust: Glendorn Foundation

Young, Lindsay, dir: Thompson Charitable Foundation

Young, Madeleine R., trust: Raymond Foundation

Young, Maureen O'Shaughnessy, dir: O'Shaughnessy Foundation, I. A.

Young, Merrilynn, asst secy: Grable Foundation

Young, Paschall H., treas, trust: Washington Foundation

Young, Peter V., vchmn: Union Trust

Young, Philip W., trust: Presser Foundation

Young, R. A., vp, dir: MFA Foundation

Young, R. R., MD, dir: Grass Foundation

Young, Raymond A., pres, trust: Young Foundation, R. A.

Young, Richard B., trust: Acushnet Foundation

Young, Richard C., dir: McElroy Trust, R. J.

Young, Robert A., III, pres, ceo, dir: Arkansas Best Corp.

Young, Roderick A., pres, coo: Diasonics, Inc.

Young, Samuel A., pres: Buffalo Forge Co.

Young, Stuart A., Jr., trust: Borden Memorial Foundation, Mary Owen

Young, Verna N., secy, treas, trust: Young Foundation, R. A.

Young, Virginia S., pres: Foundation of the Litton Industries

Young, William H., dir: Rennebohm Foundation, Oscar

Youngblood, Melvin R., treas, dir: Levy's Lumber & Building Centers Foundation

Younger, John F., trust: Abell-Hanger Foundation

Younglove, Eileen M., secy: United Airlines Foundation

Youngs, Joseph, pres: Nationale-Nederlanden North America Corp.

Yoxall, James R., secy, treas, trust: Baughman Foundation

Yu, Alice Tsai, dir: China Times Cultural Foundation

Yu, Chi-Chung, pres: China Times Cultural Foundation

Yu, Franklin, dir: China Times Cultural Foundation

Yudofsky, Stuart C., trust: Dollard Charitable Trust

Yuen, Thomas C. K., co-chmn, coo, dir: AST Research, Inc.

Yuhjtman, Alexander, exec vp & regional mgr-w hemisphere: Bank Hapoalim B.M.

Yulman, Helen Morton, investment mgr: Yulman Trust, Morton and Helen

Yurko, A. J., pres, coo, dir: Barber-Colman Co.

Yuschak, Philip, asst treas: Smucker Foundation, Willard E.

Z

Zaar, Carl L., secy, treas, dir: Universal Foods Foundation

Zaban, Erwin, chmn, dir: National Service Industries; trust: National Service Foundation; pres, treas: Zaban Foundation

Zabel, R. L., treas, trust: Harvest States Foundation

Zabel, William D., trust: Valentine Foundation, Lawson

Zabel, William David, dir: Open Society Fund; vp, dir: Soros Foundation-Hungary

Zabelle, Robert, trust: Bass and Edythe and Sol G. Atlas Fund, Sandra Atlas; pres: Kawaler Foundation, Morris and Nellie L.; pres: Kramer Foundation, C. L. C.

Zable, Walter C., vchmn, dir: Cubic Corp.

Zabotin, Mischa A., asst secy, dir: Loewy Family Foundation

Zaccaria, A., exec vp, dir: Bechtel Foundation

Zacharia, Issac Herman, pres: Zacharia Foundation, Isaac Herman

Zacharoff, Peter T., trust: Frankino Charitable Foundation, Samuel J. and Connie

Zachem, Harry M., chmn, trust: Ashland Oil Foundation

Zachry, Henry Bartell, Jr., chmn, dir: Zachry Co., H. B.; chmn, dir: Zachry Co., H.B.

Zachry, Mollie S., Zachry Co., H. B.

Zacks, Gordon, chmn, pres, ceo, dir: Barry Corp., R. G.; pres, trust: Barry Foundation

Zafris, James A., Jr., trust: Wheelwright Scientific School

Zahid, Amira, treas, asst secy, trust: Dahesh Museum

Zahid, Amr, vp, trust: Dahesh Museum

Zahid, Hoda, secy, trust: Dahesh Museum

Zahid, Mahmoud, trust: Dahesh Museum

Zahid, Mervat, pres, trust: Dahesh Museum

Zahn, J. Hillman, dir: Bloedorn Foundation, Walter A.; trust: Ross Foundation, Walter G.

Zahnow, Melvin J., chmn, trust: Wickes Foundation, Harvey Randall

Zainer, A.L., trust: Kellogg Co. Twenty-Five Year Employees' Fund

Zak, Leonard, dir: Morton Memorial Fund, Mark

Zaks, Jerry, trust: Gilman and Gonzalez-Falla Theatre Foundation

Zale, Abe, dir: Zale Foundation

Zale, David, dir: Zale Foundation

Zale, Donald, chmn bd dirs: Zale Foundation

Zale, Eugene, trust: Zale Foundation, William and Sylvia

Zale, Lew D., trust: Zale Foundation, William and Sylvia

Zale, Theodore, trust: Zale Foundation, William and Sylvia

Zaleznik, Abraham, vchmn: Ogden Corp.

Zalkin, Larry, exec vp, cfo: Westmoreland Coal Co.

Zalkin, Leonard, vp: Reicher Foundation, Anne & Harry J.

Zalokar, Robert H., chmn, dir: First Virginia Banks

Zambetti, Felice M., ceo: Stella D'Oro Biscuit Co.; pres, dir: Kresevich Foundation

Zambie, Allan J., asst secy: Murphy Foundation, John P.

Zammit, Valentine J., cfo: Bozell, Inc.

Zamoiski, Calman J., chmn, pres, ceo: Zamoiski Co.

Zamoiski, Calman J., Jr., pres, dir: Zamoiski Foundation

Zamora, Gloria, trust: Whirlpool Foundation

Zander, Glenn R., sr vp, cfo: Trans World Airlines

ZanDeWoestyne, Judy, advertising supervisor: Iowa-Illinois Gas & Electric Co.

Zankel, Arthur, trust: New York Foundation

Zanotti, John P., pres: Cincinnati Enquirer

Zapanta, Edward, MD, dir: Irvine Foundation, James

Zapapas, J. Richard, dir: AUL Foundation

Zapisek, John R., treas, dir: Utica National Group Foundation

Zapton, Daniel T., trust: Boulevard Foundation

Zarak, William J., Jr., trust: Harvest States Foundation

Zarb, Frank Gustave, chmn, pres, ceo, dir: Primerica Corp.; vp. trust: Primerica Foundation; chmn, pres, ceo, dir: Smith Barney, Harris Upham & Co.

Zarell, Elwin J., dir: Ladish Family Foundation, Herman W.

Zarick, Thomas, pres, coo, dir: Arizona Supermarkets/Q-Fresh Markets

Zarin, Gerald, chmn, pres, ceo, dir: Emerson Radio Corp.

Zarlengo, Richard A., trust, secy, treas: Rabb Foundation, Harry W.

Zarrella, Ronald L., pres, coo, dir: Bausch & Lomb

Zarrow, Anne, vp, dir: Zarrow Foundation, Anne and Henry

Zarrow, Henry, pres, dir: Zarrow Foundation, Anne and Henry

Zarrow, Henry H., pres: Sooner Pipe & Supply Corp.; pres: Sooner Pipe & Supply Corp. Foundation

Zarrow, Jack, exec vp: Shelton Foundation

Zarrow, Stuart A., dir: Zarrow Foundation, Anne and Henry

Zavis, Michael W., pres, dir: Katten, Muchin, & Zavis Foundation

Zawadzki, Joseph, cfo: Brooks Fashion Stores Inc.

Zazulia, Irwin, pres, ceo: Hecht's

Zeagler, M. F., asst exec dir, contr: Temple Foundation, T. L. L.

Zealy, James M., vp, dir: Bryan Foundation, James E. and Mary Z.

Zecca, Christine Van Camp, vp, secy, dir: Van Camp Foundation

Zechel, William, trust: Nashua Trust Co. Foundation

Zeckhouser, Sally H., trust: Lalor Foundation

Zedaker, Michael R., trust: Van Wert County Foundation

Zeeh, Lenor, dir: Rennebohm Foundation, Oscar

Zehfuss, Lawrence T., pres, ceo: Servistar Corp.

Zehms, Roger, trust: Salem Lutheran Foundation

Zeidman, Elizabeth G., secy, trust: Greenfield Foundation, Albert M.

Zeien, Alfred M., chmn, ceo: Gillette Co.

Zeigler, Susan, chmn (contributions comm): Laura Ashley Inc.

Zeigon, James W., trust: Chase Manhattan Bank, N.A.

Zeimer, C.O., vp, dir: CBI Foundation

Zeiss, Michael G., trust: First Boston Foundation Trust

Zelinsky, David, mem grants comm: First Bank System Foundation

Zellars, John B., trust: Tull Charitable Foundation

Zellerbach, John W., vp, dir: Zellerbach Family Fund

Zellerbach, Thomas H., dir: Zellerbach Family Fund

Zellerbach, William Joseph, pres, dir: Zellerbach Family Fund

Zellerbach-Boschwitz, Nancy, dir: Zellerbach Family Fund

Zelnak, Stephen P., Jr., pres: Martin Marietta Aggregates

Zemanek, Robert L., adv: Central & South West Foundation; pres, ceo: Public Service Co. of Oklahoma

Zemke, Joseph, pres, coo: Amdahl Corp.

Zemmin, Richard W., pres: MichCon Foundation

Zengerl, Roderic, vp, comm mem: 1957 Charity Trust

Zenkel, Bruce L., treas, dir: Zenkel Foundation

Zenkel, Daniel R., secy, dir: Zenkel Foundation

Zenkel, Gary B., dir: Zenkel Foundation

Zenkel, Lisa R., dir: Zenkel Foundation

Zenkel, Lois S., pres, dir: Zenkel Foundation

Zenko, Jere Scott, dir: Prentice Foundation, Abra

Zenorini, Henry J., SJ, dir: Butler Foundation, J. Homer

Zepf, J. Stephen, cfo, treas: Hughes Supply, Inc.

Zerner, David M., secy: Berkey Foundation, Peter

Zervas, Nicholas T., MD, mem: Gerondelis Foundation

Zervigon, Mary K., trust: Keller Family Foundation

Zetterberg, Anne D., dir: Bedminster Fund

Zettlemoyer, Anthony, dir: AMP Foundation

Zezima, Stephen P., vp: M/A-COM Charitable Foundation

Ziaylek, Theodore, Jr., dir: Sovereign Bank Foundation

Ziegenbein, Lyn L. Wallin, exec dir, secy: Kiewit Foundation, Peter

Ziegler, Allen S., don, pres: Ziegler Foundation, Ruth/Allen

Ziegler, Arthur P., Jr., trust: Allegheny Foundation

Ziegler, Bernard C., pres, dir: Ziegler Foundation

Ziegler, Henry Steinway, secy, dir: Smithers Foundation, Christopher D.

Ziegler, J. B., dir: SmithKline Beecham Foundation

Ziegler, R. Douglas, adv: Johnson Controls Foundation; vp, secy, treas, dir: Ziegler Foundation

Ziegler, Ruth B., don, secy: Ziegler Foundation, Ruth/Allen

Ziegler, Victor E., trust: West Foundation, Herman O.

Ziegler, William, III, chmn, ceo, dir: American Maize Products; pres, dir: Ziegler Foundation for the Blind, E. Matilda

Ziegler, William Alexander, secy, dir: Wilson Foundation, H. W.

Ziegler, William P., vchmn: Kolene Corp.

Ziemba, Ronald S., vp (corp rels): Eastern Enterprises; contact: Eastern Enterprises Foundation

Ziemer, Jean L., trust: Oberlaender Foundation, Gustav

Zier, Ronald Edward, vp (pub affairs): Warner-Lambert Co.; third vp: Warner-Lambert Charitable Foundation

Zieselman, Jerold, secy, dir: Miller Fund, Kathryn and Gilbert

Ziff, William Bernard, Jr., chmn: Ziff Communications Co.

Zifkin, Walter, pres, dir: Lastfogel Foundation, Abe and Frances

Zike, David, pres: Cosco, Inc.

Zilkha, Cecile E., vp, secy: Zilkha Foundation

Zilkha, Ezra Khedouri, pres: Zilkha & Sons; pres, treas: Zilkha Foundation

Ziltz, Carl, vp: Younkers Foundation

Ziminsky, Victor D., Jr., trust: Altman Foundation

Zimmer, Jack A., sr vp, cfo: Bankers Life & Casualty Co.

Zimmer, Mark, dir: Shelter Insurance Foundation

Zimmer, Max, pres: Wood Foundation of Chambersburg, PA

Zimmer, Theodore F., dir, secy: Evinrude Foundation, Ralph

Zimmerman, Arlene G., pres: Gudelsky Family Foundation, Isadore and Bertha; trust: Zimmerman Family Foundation, Raymond

Zimmerman, Donald J., trust: Ohio National Foundation

Zimmerman, Fred E., trust: Zimmerman Family Foundation, Raymond

Zimmerman, G.H., treas: Zimmerman Foundation, Mary and George Herbert

Zimmerman, James M., pres, coo, dir: Federated

Department Stores and Allied Stores Corp.

Zimmerman, Jetta M., chmn scholarship comm: Zimmerman Foundation, Hans and Clara Davis

Zimmerman, Joan Goodman, managing dir: Goodman Foundation, Edward and Marion

Zimmerman, Joe, pres, dir: Bend Millwork Systems

Zimmerman, L. Wilbur, vp: Ludwick Institute

Zimmerman, Lannette, trust: Chicago Title and Trust Co. Foundation

Zimmerman, Leroy S., trust: Hall Foundation

Zimmerman, Louis G., dir, pres: Zimmerman Foundation, Mary and George Herbert

Zimmerman, Raymond, trust: Zimmerman Family Foundation, Raymond

Zimmerman, Richard, trust: Stabler Foundation, Donald B. and Dorothy L.

Zimmerman, Richard Anson, chmn, ceo, dir: Hershey Foods Corp.

Zimmerman, Robyn, trust: Zimmerman Family Foundation, Raymond

Zimmerman, W. E., exec vp: Reeves Foundation

Zimmerman, W. M., trust: Caterpillar Foundation

Zimmerman, William, chmn: Pay 'N Save Inc.

Zimmermann, John C., III, pres, dir: Zimmermann Fund, Marie and John

Zinbarg, Edward Donald, trust: Prudential Foundation

Zink, Jacqueline A., trust: Zink Foundation, John Steele

Zink, John Smith, trust: Zink Foundation, John Steele

Zinko, Donald T., vp (mktg): Colorado Interstate Gas Co.

Zinn, Douglas C., asst to chmn: Biddle Foundation, Mary Duke

Zinn, Harold, dir: Taylor Family Foundation, Jack

Zipf, A.R., dir, chmn: Margoes Foundation

Zipf, Alfred R., dir: Lurie Foundation, Louis R.

Zirbel, Irving, dir: Autotrol Corp. Charitable Trust

Zischke, Peter H., trust: Farallon Foundation

Zises, Seymour, trust: de Hirsch Fund, Baron

Zisson, Adelaide Rudin, dir: Rudin Foundation

Zitterbart, Gilbert A., treas, trust: Teledyne Charitable Trust Foundation

Zitting, R. T., dir: Santa Fe Pacific Foundation

Zitzloff, Wayne, dir: Wallestad Foundation

Zlomek, Joseph M., publ: Pottstown Mercury

Zobeidi, Habib, vp, treas: Ala Vi Foundation of New York

Zock, Robert A., trust: Zock Endowment Trust

Zock, Sara M., trust: Zock Endowment Trust

Zodrow, Charles Francis, mem distribution comm: GAR Foundation

Zoernig, Elizabeth, secy, treas, dir: McGee Foundation

Zoffmann, Beth C., trust: Georgia-Pacific Foundation

Zollman, William J., III, trust: Voelkerding Charitable Trust, Walter and Jean

Zolot, Stanley L., trust: Novotny Charitable Trust, Yetta Deitch

Zonus, Irwin S., pres, coo: Peridot Chemicals (NJ)

Zook, Thomas W., trust: Foss Memorial Employees Trust, Donald J.

Zook, Woodrow J., trust: Foss Memorial Employees Trust, Donald J.

Zorn, Edward L., trust: Williams Family Foundation

Zottoli, Steven J., dir: Grass Foundation

Zubay, Mary E., Jr., dir: Imlay Foundation

Zuber, Harold L., Jr., vp, cfo: Teleflex Inc.

Zucaro, A. C., pres, ceo: Old Republic International Corp.

Zuccaro, Edward R., dir: Bunbury Company

Zucker, Henry L., secy, treas, trust: Mandel Foundation, Morton and Barbara

Zuckerberg, Barbara, trust: Zuckerberg Foundation, Roy J.

Zuckerberg, Dina R., trust: Zuckerberg Foundation, Roy J.

Zuckerberg, Lloyd P., trust: Zuckerberg Foundation, Roy J.

Zuckerberg, Paul J., treas, dir: Rexford Fund

Zuckerberg, Roy J., dir: Brookdale Foundation; trust: Kautz Family Foundation; trust: Rubin Foundation, Rob E. & Judith O.; trust: Zuckerberg Foundation, Roy J.

Zuckerman, Harriet, vp: Mellon Foundation, Andrew W.

Zuendt, William F., vchmn, exec vp: Wells Fargo & Co.

Zumbrun, Ruth, secy, dir: Jafra Educational Development Grant Endowment

Zunamon, Simon, asst treas: Pritzker Foundation

Zunker, Richard, mem (contributions comm): SAFECO Corp.

Zurn, James A., sr vp: Zurn Industries

Zurschmiede, W. T., Jr., chmn, ceo: Federal Screw Works; trust: Federal Screw Works Foundation

Zurschmiede, III, W. T., trust: Federal Screw Works Foundation

Zutz, Denise M., secy adv bd, dir: Johnson Controls Foundation

Zuzelo, Andrew, dir (mktg): Cardinal Industries

Zuzelo, Edward A., pres: Cardinal Industries

Zwald, Robert, vchmn, dir: Georgia Health Foundation

Zweifel, Ronald F., secy, treas, dir: Giddings & Lewis Foundation

Zweigart, Robert, mem: Hayswood Foundation

Zylstra, Stan, chmn, dir: Land O'Lakes

Index to Grant Recipients by State

Alabama

Alabama A&M University see Boeing Co.

Alabama A&M University ($24,550) see Simpson Foundation

Alabama Association of Independent Colleges see Alabama Power Co.

Alabama Child Caring ($692,610) see Blue Cross & Blue Shield of Alabama

Alabama Child Caring Foundation — health services to children ($13,200) see Hill Crest Foundation

Alabama Children's Hospital ($25,000) see Kaul Foundation Trust, Hugh

Alabama Children's Hospital Foundation see Alabama Power Co.

Alabama Conservancy see Alabama Power Co.

Alabama Council on Economic Education see Alabama Power Co.

Alabama Educational Enrichment Resource Agency see Alabama Power Co.

Alabama High School of Mathematics and Science Foundation see Alabama Power Co.

Alabama Independent Colleges — fund scholarship ($10,000) see Hill Crest Foundation

Alabama Independent Colleges ($2,500) see Moore & Sons, B.C.

Alabama Independent Colleges ($4,500) see Wehadkee Foundation

Alabama Institute for Deaf and Blind ($50,000) see Chandler Foundation

Alabama Institute for Deaf and Blind ($20,000) see Comer Foundation

Alabama Institute for Deaf and Blind ($100,000) see Daniel Foundation of Alabama

Alabama Institute for Deaf and Blind ($55,000) see Meyer Foundation, Robert R.

Alabama Poison Control Systems ($239,500) see Blue Cross & Blue Shield of Alabama

Alabama Public Television ($10,000) see Linn-Henley Charitable Trust

Alabama Public Television ($25,000) see Russell Educational Foundation, Benjamin and Roberta

Alabama School of Fine Arts ($25,000) see Fig Tree Foundation

Alabama School of Fine Arts ($25,000) see Hess Charitable Foundation, Ronne and Donald

Alabama School of Fine Arts ($10,000) see Kaul Foundation Trust, Hugh

Alabama School of Fine Arts Foundation ($10,000) see Abroms Charitable Foundation

Alabama School of Mathematics and Science — building fund ($10,000) see Chandler Foundation

Alabama Shakespeare Festival ($100,000) see Blount

Alabama Shakespeare Festival ($25,000) see Union Camp Corp.

Alabama Sheriff's Boys and Girls Ranches — upkeep and maintenance of its physical facilities and purchase of equipment ($40,822) see Beeson Charitable Trust, Dwight M.

Alabama Sheriffs Boys Ranch ($20,000) see Hargis Charitable Foundation, Estes H. and Florence Parker

Alabama Sports Festival ($15,000) see Central Bank of the South

Alabama State Troopers Association ($21,500) see Hess Charitable Foundation, Ronne and Donald

Alabama State University ($9,500) see Simpson Foundation

Alabama Symphony ($1,000) see Bruno Foundation, Angelo

Alabama Symphony Association see Alabama Power Co.

Alabama Symphony Orchestra ($20,000) see Blue Cross & Blue Shield of Alabama

Alabama Symphony Orchestra ($50,000) see Daniel Foundation of Alabama

Alabama Symphony Orchestra ($20,000) see Fig Tree Foundation

Alcohol and Drug Abuse Council — capital improvements ($25,000) see Hill Crest Foundation

Alcoholism Council of Central Alabama ($25,000) see Russell Educational Foundation, Benjamin and Roberta

Alexander City Board of Education ($105,000) see Russell Educational Foundation, Benjamin and Roberta

Amateur Athletes Society ($10,000) see Winn-Dixie Stores

American Cancer Society ($18,000) see Forchheimer Memorial Foundation Trust, Louise and Josie

American Heart Association ($18,000) see Forchheimer Memorial Foundation Trust, Louise and Josie

American Lung Association ($30,000) see Florence Foundation

American Lung Association of North Central Alabama see Alabama Power Co.

American Sports Medicine ($11,000) see Dodson Foundation, James Glenwell and Clara May

Amistad Foundation ($7,500) see Three Swallows Foundation

Apple Hill Scholarship ($20,000) see Fig Tree Foundation

Aspen Foundation ($6,250) see Shook Foundation, Barbara Ingalls

Auburn University ($50,000) see Blue Bell, Inc.

Auburn University see Boeing Co.

Auburn University — scholarships ($45,601) see Comer Foundation

Auburn University ($7,000) see Hargis Charitable Foundation, Estes H. and Florence Parker

Auburn University ($5,000) see McWane Inc.

Auburn University ($40,585) see Simpson Foundation

Auburn University — academic tournament ($1,000) see Stuart Foundation, Edward C.

Auburn University ($25,000) see Vulcan Materials Co.

Auburn University — supplement for renovation of Comer Hall on campus ($100,000) see Comer Foundation

Auburn University Foundation ($10,000) see Crawford & Co.

Auburn University Foundation ($25,000) see Russell Educational Foundation, Benjamin and Roberta

Auburn University Foundation ($24,906) see Teledyne

Auburn University — research study of environmental conditions in Lake West Point ($43,000) see Callaway Foundation, Fuller E.

Auburn University at Montgomery ($4,245) see Durr-Fillauer Medical

Auburn University at Montgomery ($10,250) see Simpson Foundation

Auburn University — Mosley distinguished professor ($85,000) see Franklin Foundation, John and Mary

Auburn University — supplement for renovation of Ralph Brown Draughon Library ($30,000) see Comer Foundation

Ballet and Theatre Arts — community welfare ($2,000) see Smith, Jr. Foundation, M. W.

Baptist Health Services Foundation ($6,600) see Blue Cross & Blue Shield of Alabama

Baptist Hospital Foundation ($25,000) see Shook Foundation, Barbara Ingalls

Baptist Hospitals Foundation of Birmingham — aid to the poor and needy who are under treatment at the Birmingham Baptist Medical Center at Montclair ($40,822) see Beeson Charitable Trust, Dwight M.

Baptist Medical Center Foundation, Mission 2000 — capital campaign ($20,000) see Comer Foundation

Baptist Montclair and Princeton Hospitals ($10,000) see Linn-Henley Charitable Trust

Baylor School ($3,000) see McWane Inc.

Bayside Academy ($25,000) see Mitchell Foundation

B'ham Jewish Federation ($54,000) see Fig Tree Foundation

Big Oak Ranch ($7,500) see Tractor & Equipment Co.

Birmingham Area Chamber of Commerce ($5,000) see Linn-Henley Charitable Trust

Birmingham Botanical Society ($1,000) see HarCo. Drug

Birmingham Boys Club/Girls Club ($50,000) see Meyer Foundation, Robert R.

Birmingham Boys and Girls Clubs — support operations ($25,000) see Hill Crest Foundation

Birmingham Jewish Federation ($41,000) see Abroms Charitable Foundation

Birmingham Jewish Federation ($41,000) see Abroms Charitable Foundation

Birmingham Jewish Federation ($31,000) see Abroms Charitable Foundation

Birmingham Jewish Federation ($25,000) see Abroms Charitable Foundation

Birmingham Jewish Federation ($126,000) see Fig Tree Foundation

Birmingham Jewish Federation ($36,000) see Fig Tree Foundation

Birmingham Jewish Federation ($595,500) see Hess Charitable Foundation, Ronne and Donald

Birmingham Jewish Foundation ($15,000) see Abroms Charitable Foundation

Birmingham Jewish Foundation ($15,000) see Abroms Charitable Foundation

Birmingham Landmarks ($30,000) see Meyer Foundation, Robert R.

Birmingham Museum of Art ($150,000) see Daniel Foundation of Alabama

Birmingham Museum of Art ($100,000) see Day Family Foundation

Birmingham Museum of Art ($35,000) see Fig Tree Foundation

Birmingham Museum of Art ($35,000) see Hess Charitable Foundation, Ronne and Donald

Birmingham Museum of Art ($60,000) see Meyer Foundation, Robert R.

Birmingham Museum of Art ($60,000) see Meyer Foundation, Robert R.

Birmingham Museum of Art ($15,000) see Stockham Valves & Fittings

Birmingham Museum of Art ($51,120) see Weisman Art Foundation, Frederick R.

Birmingham Public Library ($15,000) see Kaul Foundation Trust, Hugh

Birmingham Southern College ($20,000) see Abroms Charitable Foundation

Birmingham Southern College ($25,000) see Bruno Charitable Foundation, Joseph S.

Birmingham-Southern College ($10,000) see Central Bank of the South

Birmingham-Southern College ($6,500) see Central Bank of the South

Birmingham Southern College ($100,000) see Daniel Foundation of Alabama

Birmingham Southern College ($5,000) see Durr-Fillauer Medical

Birmingham Southern College ($20,000) see Hess Charitable Foundation, Ronne and Donald

Birmingham-Southern College ($33,333) see Kaul Foundation Trust, Hugh

Birmingham Southern College — general support ($77,125) see Sonat

Birmingham Southern College ($50,000) see Stockham Valves & Fittings

Birmingham Southern College ($5,225) see Tractor & Equipment Co.

Birmingham Southern College ($78,333) see Vulcan Materials Co.

Birmingham Southern Theatre ($15,000) see Fig Tree Foundation

Birmingham State University ($1,000) see Tractor & Equipment Co.

BJDS Foundation ($35,000) see Fig Tree Foundation

Boy Scouts of America ($5,000) see Blount Educational and Charitable Foundation, Mildred Weedon

Boy Scouts of America ($3,000) see Blount Educational and Charitable Foundation, Mildred Weedon

Boy Scouts of America ($6,250) see Tamko Asphalt Products

Boys Club of Tuscaloosa ($1,000) see HarCo. Drug

Boys and Girls Club ($4,000) see Tractor & Equipment Co.

Boys and Girls Club ($25,000) see Webb Charitable Trust, Susan Mott

Boys and Girls Clubs of Birmingham ($50,000) see Daniel Foundation of Alabama

Brentwood Children's Home ($16,666) see Blount

Calhoun College Foundation ($6,000) see Gibson Foundation, E. L.

Camp ASCA ($12,500) see Hill Crest Foundation

Camp Rap-A-Hope ($1,000) see Florence Foundation

Capstone Foundation ($1,500) see HarCo. Drug

Cathedral Church of Advent ($16,666) see Webb Charitable Trust, Susan Mott

Center of Concern ($5,000) see Bruno Foundation, Angelo

Center of Concern ($200) see Bruno Foundation, Angelo

Champ ($5,000) see Blue Cross & Blue Shield of Alabama

Chattahoochee Valley Educational Foundation ($5,000) see Cook Batson Foundation

Chattahoochee Valley Educational Society ($25,000) see Illges Foundation, John P. and Dorothy S.

Chattahoochee Valley Educational Society ($25,000) see Wehadkee Foundation

Alabama (cont.)

Chattahoochee Valley Hospital Society ($25,000) see Cook Batson Foundation

Chattahoochee Valley Medical ($10,000) see Luchsinger Family Foundation

Child Day Care Association — building fund ($30,000) see Chandler Foundation

Child Day Care Association ($2,000) see Florence Foundation

Children's Hospital ($50,000) see Meyer Foundation, Robert R.

Children's Hospital — capital campaign ($25,125) see Sonat

Children's Hospital of Alabama ($168,750) see Blue Cross & Blue Shield of Alabama

Children's Hospital of Alabama ($25,000) see Stockham Valves & Fittings

Children's Hospital of Birmingham — support for the new Ambulatory Care Center ($50,000) see Comer Foundation

Children's Hospital Foundation ($10,100) see Shook Foundation, Barbara Ingalls

Children's Oncology Services of Alabama ($10,000) see Kaul Foundation Trust, Hugh

City of Tallassee ($11,000) see Blount Educational and Charitable Foundation, Mildred Weedon

Civic Club Foundation ($75,000) see Vulcan Materials Co.

Community Health Foundation ($49,000) see Blue Cross & Blue Shield of Alabama

Community Hospital ($20,000) see Blount Educational and Charitable Foundation, Mildred Weedon

Covington County Commission — to employ two homemakers for personal care and cleaning households ($30,000) see Andalusia Health Services

Covington County Health Department — emergency medical equipment ($2,962) see Andalusia Health Services

Covington County Health Department — to employ additional workers, two nurses, one home health aide, one physical therapist and secretary ($53,750) see Andalusia Health Services

Cumberland School of Law ($5,000) see Linn-Henley Charitable Trust

DCH Foundation ($1,000) see HarCo. Drug

Diabetic Clinic of Mobile ($18,000) see Forchheimer Memorial Foundation Trust, Louise and Josie

Discovery Place — Educational ($2,500) see Bruno Charitable Foundation, Joseph S.

Elmore County High School ($10,000) see Blount Educational and Charitable Foundation, Mildred Weedon

Episcopal Church of Advent ($5,000) see Shook Foundation, Barbara Ingalls

Episcopal Foundation of Jefferson County ($10,000) see Tractor & Equipment Co.

Eufaula Carnegie Library — supplement for renovation and addition to library ($20,000) see Comer Foundation

Explore Center ($45,000) see Mitchell Foundation

Eye Foundation Hospital ($6,000) see Shook Foundation, Barbara Ingalls

Eye Research Foundation ($26,000) see Randa

Family and Child Services — capital campaign ($30,000) see Comer Foundation

Family and Child Services ($50,000) see Webb Charitable Trust, Susan Mott

Father Flanagan's Boys Home ($200) see Bruno Foundation, Angelo

Faulkner University ($30,000) see Davis Family - W.D. Charities, Tine W.

First Baptist Church of Center Point ($10,000) see Tractor & Equipment Co.

First Bible Church ($6,000) see Gibson Foundation, E. L.

Forward Calhoun County ($7,700) see Central Bank of the South

Girls Preparatory School ($5,000) see McWane Inc.

Glenwood Mental Health ($25,000) see Webb Charitable Trust, Susan Mott

Glenwood Mental Health Service ($4,000) see Tractor & Equipment Co.

Greater Birmingham Foundation — health research and health care for the poor and relief of poverty ($40,827) see Beeson Charitable Trust, Dwight M.

Greater Birmingham Ministries ($15,000) see Grant Foundation, Charles M. and Mary D.

Greater Birmingham Ministries ($10,000) see Hargis Charitable Foundation, Estes H. and Florence Parker

Gulf Shores First Presbyterian Church ($1,000) see Meyer Foundation, George C.

Henley Research Library ($50,000) see Linn-Henley Charitable Trust

Henley Research Library ($50,000) see Linn-Henley Charitable Trust

Heritage Commission of Tuscaloosa County ($300,000) see Brown Foundation, James Graham

Hobson State Technical College, Thomasville, AL — pulp, paper, and chemical program ($14,000) see Boise Cascade Corp.

Hospice ($6,000) see Gibson Foundation, E. L.

Huntsville Hospital Foundation ($3,300) see Durr-Fillauer Medical

Huntsville/Madison County Public Library ($10,000) see Morton International

Indian Springs School ($10,000) see Abroms Charitable Foundation

Indian Springs School ($20,175) see Hess Charitable Foundation, Ronne and Donald

International Outreach Ministries ($22,000) see Generation Trust

Jasper-Curry Church of Christ — missions ($43,000) see Frazier Foundation

John Carol High School, Birmingham — building fund for new school ($10,000) see Bashinsky Foundation

John M. Will Scholarship Fund — scholarships ($10,000) see Chandler Foundation

Junior Achievement see Michigan Mutual Insurance Corp.

Junior Achievement ($10,000) see Stockham Valves & Fittings

Kings Ranch — capital improvements ($25,000) see Hill Crest Foundation

L.B.W. State Junior College — emergency medical courses for nurses and rescue squad members ($14,499) see Andalusia Health Services

Livingston University ($17,750) see Simpson Foundation

Lyman Ward Military Academy ($75,000) see Russell Educational Foundation, Benjamin and Roberta

Methodist Homes for the Aging ($30,000) see Meyer Foundation, Robert R.

Metropolitan Arts Council — general support ($83,706) see Sonat

Metropolitan Arts Council ($85,000) see Vulcan Materials Co.

Metropolitan Development Board — general support ($25,000) see Sonat

Mobile Area Boys Scouts — community welfare ($3,000) see Smith, Jr. Foundation, M. W.

Mobile Area Chamber of Commerce Foundation ($100,000) see Bedsole Foundation, J. L.

Mobile Area Chamber of Commerce Foundation ($100,000) see Bedsole Foundation, J. L.

Mobile Area United Way ($36,000) see Forchheimer Memorial Foundation Trust, Louise and Josie

Mobile Association for Retarded Citizens — community welfare ($10,000) see Smith, Jr. Foundation, M. W.

Mobile College — library building expansion ($375,000) see Bedsole Foundation, J. L.

Mobile College — scholarships ($26,400) see Bedsole Foundation, J. L.

Mobile College ($25,000) see Mitchell Foundation

Mobile College — education ($50,000) see Smith, Jr. Foundation, M. W.

Mobile College — Division of Business and Science ($100,000) see Bedsole Foundation, J. L.

Mobile College Forest Resource Learning Center ($25,000) see Landegger Charitable Foundation

Mobile Community Foundation ($137,280) see Chandler Foundation

Mobile Community Organization ($10,000) see Mitchell Foundation

Mobile County Public Schools — "Sixth Day Academic Program" see Scott Paper Co.

Mobile Infirmary ($25,000) see Florence Foundation

Mobile Infirmary Medical Center ($120,000) see Bedsole Foundation, J. L.

Mobile Public School System — help with homework hotline ($36,000) see Bedsole Foundation, J. L.

Mobile Rescue Mission ($1,000) see Florence Foundation

Montgomery Area Food Bank ($25,500) see Randa

Montgomery Area Zoological Society ($50,000) see Blount

Montgomery Area Zoological Society ($25,000) see Blount

Montgomery Bell Academy ($50,000) see Potter Foundation, Justin and Valere

Montgomery Symphony Orchestra ($26,000) see Randa

Montgomery YMCA ($16,320) see Smith 1963 Charitable Trust, Don McQueen

Montgomery Zoo ($34,500) see Randa

Morgan County — Meals on Wheels ($5,000) see Gibson Foundation, E. L.

Mountain Brook Athletic Complex ($3,000) see HarCo. Drug

North Alabama Sheriffs Boys Ranch ($6,000) see Gibson Foundation, E. L.

Oncology Services of Alabama ($25,000) see Webb Charitable Trust, Susan Mott

Parker Evangelical Association ($6,000) see Gibson Foundation, E. L.

Penelope House — building fund ($40,000) see Chandler Foundation

Pickens Academy ($4,100) see Hutcheson Foundation, Hazel Montague

Pioneer Ministries ($9,000) see Christian Workers Foundation

Planned Parenthood of Alabama ($33,000) see Sunnen Foundation

Prattville YMCA ($12,000) see Smith 1963 Charitable Trust, Don McQueen

Prescott House ($200) see Bruno Foundation, Angelo

Providence Hospital ($25,000) see Florence Foundation

Reeltown High School ($10,000) see Blount Educational and Charitable Foundation, Mildred Weedon

Resource Advisory ($15,000) see Webb Charitable Trust, Susan Mott

Reynolds Historical Library ($5,000) see Linn-Henley Charitable Trust

Robert W. Woodruff Arts Center — general support ($25,000) see Sonat

Russell Hospital ($124,700) see Russell Educational Foundation, Benjamin and Roberta

St. Bernard Homes ($500) see Bruno Foundation, Angelo

St. Francis Xavier Church ($5,000) see Tractor & Equipment Co.

St. Vincent de Paul Catholic Church ($15,000) see Blount Educational and Charitable Foundation, Mildred Weedon

St. Vincent's Hospital ($5,000) see Bruno Charitable Foundation, Joseph S.

St. Vincent's Hospital ($10,000) see Linn-Henley Charitable Trust

St. Vincent's Hospital Foundation ($26,600) see Shook Foundation, Barbara Ingalls

Salvation Army ($10,000) see Bruno Charitable Foundation, Joseph S.

Salvation Army ($1,000) see Bruno Foundation, Angelo

Salvation Army ($1,000) see Florence Foundation

Salvation Army Capital Campaign ($10,000) see Blue Cross & Blue Shield of Alabama

Samford University ($16,500) see Central Bank of the South

Samford University ($8,500) see Central Bank of the South

Samford University ($225,000) see Daniel Foundation of Alabama

Samford University ($2,000) see HarCo. Drug

Samford University ($10,000) see Hess Charitable Foundation, Ronne and Donald

Samford University ($5,000) see Linn-Henley Charitable Trust

Samford University ($10,000) see Stockham Valves & Fittings

Samford University ($30,000) see Vulcan Materials Co.

Samford University — capital campaign; matching gift ($30,325) see Sonat

School of Commerce and Business ($1,500) see HarCo. Drug

Seaside Mission ($8,000) see Gibson Foundation, E. L.

Senior Citizens Service — building fund ($25,000) see Chandler Foundation

Sentencing Institute — for development of a center for corrections and sentencing policy in Alabama ($315,000) see Clark Foundation, Edna McConnell

Shoulder ($5,000) see Florence Foundation

Siloam Baptist Church ($14,000) see Ragan Charitable Foundation, Carolyn King

Siloam Baptist Church ($13,000) see Ragan Charitable Foundation, Carolyn King

South Central Alabama Mental Health Board — to increase care of mental patients ($10,000) see Andalusia Health Services

Southeastern Bible College — support operations ($20,000) see Hill Crest Foundation

Southern Poverty Law Center ($25,000) see Davee Foundation

Southern Poverty Law Center ($1,000) see Goldman Foundation, William

Southern Poverty Law Center ($11,500) see Kaplen Foundation

Southern Poverty Law Center ($3,000) see Prentis Family Foundation, Meyer and Anna

Southern Research Institute ($10,000) see Central Bank of the South

Southern Research Institute — support operations ($100,000) see Hill Crest Foundation

Southern Research Institute ($80,000) see Meyer Foundation, Robert R.

Southern Research Institute ($30,000) see Randa

Southern Research Institute ($5,000) see Shook Foundation, Barbara Ingalls

Southern Research Institute ($25,000) see Webb Charitable Trust, Susan Mott

Spring Hill College ($10,000) see Chandler Foundation

Spring Hill College ($23,000) see Huisking Foundation

Spring Hill College ($5,000) see Loeb Partners Corp.

Springhill Avenue Temple ($54,000) see Forchheimer Memorial Foundation Trust, Louise and Josie

State of Alabama Ballet ($5,000) see Kaul Foundation Trust, Hugh

Stillman College ($1,000) see HarCo. Drug

Stillman College — support of programs ($5,000) see Trull Foundation

Stillman College — support of programs ($5,000) see Trull Foundation

Stockham Literacy Program ($12,875) see Stockham Valves & Fittings

STRATE (Tallassee) ($4,800) see Blount Educational and Charitable Foundation, Mildred Weedon

Streetscapes — city beautification ($20,000) see Chandler Foundation

Sylacauga Park and Recreation Board — supplement for operations and programs ($30,000) see Comer Foundation

Tallassee City Schools — O'Brien Stadium ($10,000) see Blount Educational and Charitable Foundation, Mildred Weedon

Tallassee Community Library ($7,500) see Blount Educational and Charitable Foundation, Mildred Weedon

Temple Emanu-El ($12,167) see Hess Charitable Foundation, Ronne and Donald

Tuscaloosa Symphony Orchestra ($1,000) see HarCo. Drug

Tuskegee Institute ($5,500) see New Orphan Asylum Scholarship Foundation

Tuskegee University ($2,605,000) see Kellogg Foundation, W. K.

Tuskegee University ($30,000) see Vulcan Materials Co.

Tuskegee University — to provide a $1,000,000 one-for-one endowment-challenge grant ($1,000,000) see Mott Foundation, Charles Stewart

21st Century Youth Leadership Training Project — support youth organizing project for public school reform in 11 Alabama counties ($30,000) see Hazen Foundation, Edward W.

United Cerebral Palsy of Greater Birmingham — improvement of its physical facilities and the purchase of additional equipment ($40,823) see Beeson Charitable Trust, Dwight M.

United Funds ($1,600) see Joslyn Corp.

U.S. Space Academy — "Space Orientation: A Hands-On Approach for Educators" see Rockwell International Corp.

United Way ($86,200) see Blue Cross & Blue Shield of Alabama

United Way ($3,432) see Blue Cross & Blue Shield of Alabama

United Way ($10,000) see Bruno Foundation, Angelo

United Way ($26,091) see CBI Industries

United Way ($6,423) see CBI Industries

United Way ($14,000) see Durr-Fillauer Medical

United Way ($20,000) see Hess Charitable Foundation, Ronne and Donald

United Way ($3,000) see Meyer Foundation, George C.

United Way ($5,000) see Mueller Co.

United Way ($1,500) see Pieper Electric

United Way ($34,000) see PPG Industries

United Way ($25,000) see Randa

United Way ($11,000) see Randa

United Way ($6,000) see Shook Foundation, Barbara Ingalls

United Way ($10,000) see Smith 1963 Charitable Trust, Don McQueen

United Way ($65,000) see Stockham Valves & Fittings

United Way ($7,840) see Tractor & Equipment Co.

United Way ($25,000) see Webb Charitable Trust, Susan Mott

United Way-Autauga County ($40,000) see Union Camp Corp.

United Way of Birmingham ($51,500) see Vulcan Materials Co.

United Way of Morgan County ($69,838) see Monsanto Co.

United Way of Shoals ($15,000) see Reynolds Metals Co.

University of Alabama ($2,968) see Bruno Foundation, Angelo

University of Alabama ($100,000) see Daniel Foundation of Alabama

University of Alabama ($13,500) see Davis Family - W.D. Charities, Tine W.

University of Alabama ($15,000) see Durr-Fillauer Medical

University of Alabama ($3,000) see Durr-Fillauer Medical

University of Alabama ($5,000) see Florence Foundation

University of Alabama ($10,000) see Gillett Foundation, Elesabeth Ingalls

University of Alabama ($4,000) see HarCo. Drug

University of Alabama ($2,000) see Harris Foundation, H. H.

University of Alabama ($9,500) see Hutcheson Foundation, Hazel Montague

University of Alabama ($5,000) see Multimedia, Inc.

University of Alabama ($37,700) see Simpson Foundation

University of Alabama ($20,300) see Simpson Foundation

University of Alabama ($11,000) see Simpson Foundation

University of Alabama ($66,666) see Vulcan Materials Co.

University of Alabama at Birmingham ($600,000) see BellSouth Corp.

University of Alabama at Birmingham — building project ($500,000) see Callaway Foundation

University of Alabama at Birmingham ($50,000) see Gibson Foundation, E. L.

University of Alabama at Birmingham ($100,000) see Meyer Foundation, Robert R.

University of Alabama at Birmingham ($10,000) see Randa

University of Alabama in Birmingham ($125,000) see Russell Educational Foundation, Benjamin and Roberta

University of Alabama at Birmingham ($6,000) see Swisher Foundation, Carl S.

University of Alabama at Birmingham ($50,000) see Webb Charitable Trust, Susan Mott

University of Alabama Birmingham — Camellia Pavilion ($40,000) see Shook Foundation, Barbara Ingalls

University of Alabama Birmingham Medical and Education Foundation ($60,000) see Shook Foundation, Barbara Ingalls

University of Alabama Diabetes Hospital ($244,966) see Beach Foundation Trust for the University of Alabama-Birmingham Diabetes Hospital, Thomas N. and Mildred V.

University of Alabama-Huntsville ($30,000) see GenCorp

University of Alabama John S. Stone Chair of Law ($100,000) see Daniel Foundation of Alabama

University of Alabama Medical and Education — general support ($202,500) see Sonat

University of Alabama School of Law — general support ($25,000) see Sonat

University of Montevallo ($5,250) see Simpson Foundation

University of South Alabama ($1,000) see May Charitable Trust, Ben

University of South Alabama College of Medicine ($50,000) see Florence Foundation

WBHM Public Radio Station ($5,000) see Linn-Henley Charitable Trust

Westminster Christian Academy ($33,400) see Teledyne

Wilmer Hall ($10,000) see Chandler Foundation

YMCA — capital fund ($50,000) see Blount

YMCA ($15,000) see Comer Foundation

YMCA ($30,000) see Meyer Foundation, Robert R.

YMCA ($10,000) see Stockham Valves & Fittings

YMCA ($4,000) see Tractor & Equipment Co.

YMCA ($25,000) see Webb Charitable Trust, Susan Mott

Zoo Foundation ($508,885) see Meyer Foundation, George C.

Alaska

Alaska Center for the Performing Arts ($54,500) see Atwood Foundation

Alaska Conservation Foundation ($35,000) see McIntosh Foundation

Alaska Conservation Foundation ($25,000) see New-Land Foundation

Alaska Pacific University ($164,350) see Atwood Foundation

Alaska Public Radio Network see American Express Co.

Alaska Public Radio Network ($15,000) see Town Creek Foundation

Anchorage Festival of Music ($1,000) see Atwood Foundation

Anchorage Museum Foundation ($200,000) see Kreielsheimer Foundation Trust

Arkansas Institute for Social Justice — to conduct research and public education campaigns on the role of private money in state and local politics ($50,000) see Arca Foundation

Gwichin Steering Committee — public education campaign ($50,000) see Ira-Hiti Foundation for Deep Ecology

Harding University ($100,000) see Kendall Foundation, George R.

Steering Committee ($25,000) see Mead Foundation, Giles W. and Elise G.

United Way of Anchorage — corporate pledge ($345,000) see BP America

United Way of Anchorage ($13,360) see Skinner Corp.

University of Alaska ($75,000) see Atwood Foundation

University of Central Arkansas ($4,216) see Phelps, Inc.

Winrock International Institute for Agriculture — goat breeding, nutrition, management ($39,000) see International Foundation

Arizona

Achievement Rewards for College Scientists — to provide scholarships ($10,000) see Fish Foundation, Vain and Harry

Actors Theatre of Phoenix see Dial Corp.

Aid to Adoption of Special Kids ($20,000) see Marshall Fund

Aid for AIDS ($10,000) see Kapoor Charitable Foundation

Alhambra School District see America West Airlines

All Saints Church ($2,860) see Robson Foundation, LaNelle

Alliance for the Mentally Ill ($10,000) see Stocker Foundation

Alzheimer's Disease and Related Disorders Association ($28,381) see Pendleton Memorial Fund, William L. and Ruth T.

Alzheimers Foundation see Best Western International

American Cancer Society ($50) see Fink Foundation

American Cancer Society — 13 locations see America West Airlines

American Diabetes Association ($40,000) see Pendleton Memorial Fund, William L. and Ruth T.

American Graduate School of International Management see American Express Co.

American Graduate School of International Management see Dial Corp.

American Heart Association see Dial Corp.

American Heart Association ($25,000) see Robson Foundation, LaNelle

American Heart Association ($7,000) see Talley Industries, Inc.

American School of International Management ($25,000) see Burns Family Foundation

American Voluntary Medical Team ($100) see Burns International

Angel Charity for Children ($5,000) see Chapin Foundation, Frances

Angel Charity for Children ($20,000) see Marshall Foundation

Angel Charity for Children see Valley National Bank of Arizona

Arizona AIDS ($10,000) see Marshall Fund

Arizona Alliance of Business see Valley National Bank of Arizona

Arizona Boys Ranch ($15,000) see Brach Foundation, Edwin I.

Arizona Boys Ranch ($5,000) see Woodward Fund

Arizona Boys Ranch — aid to troubled youth; general purposes ($15,000) see Kieckhefer Foundation, J. W.

Arizona Cactus Girl Scouts ($25,000) see Pendleton Memorial Fund, William L. and Ruth T.

Arizona Cancer Center ($59,600) see Bannerman Foundation, William C.

Arizona Children's Home Association — aid to youth ($20,000) see Kieckhefer Foundation, J. W.

Arizona Clean and Beautiful see Valley National Bank of Arizona

Arizona College of the Bible ($300,000) see Solheim Foundation

Arizona Community Foundation ($16,667) see Cherne Foundation, Albert W.

Arizona Community Foundation ($90,000) see Globe Corp.

Arizona Community Foundation, Children's Action Alliance ($60,000) see Steele Foundation

Arizona Department of Education ($83,336) see Shea Co., John F.

Arizona Department of Education ($83,336) see Shea Co., John F.

Arizona Department of Education ($83,336) see Shea Co., John F.

Arizona Department of Education ($83,336) see Shea Co., John F.

Arizona Department of Education ($83,336) see Shea Co., John F.

Arizona Department of Education ($83,320) see Shea Co., John F.

Arizona Educational Foundation — special projects ($46,320) see First Interstate Bank of Arizona

Arizona Educational Foundation see Valley National Bank of Arizona

Arizona Educational Foundation — Arizona Literacy Initiative for Children ($100,000) see Citicorp

Arizona Friends of Foster Children see Dial Corp.

Arizona Heart Institute ($1,200) see Burns International

Arizona Heart Institute — to support the comprehensive programs at this multi-faceted outpatient clinic ($5,000) see Fish Foundation, Vain and Harry

Arizona Hispanic Chamber of Commerce see Valley National Bank of Arizona

Arizona Hispanic Chamber of Commerce — first of a three-year $634,004 grant for REVIVE! Arizona, a rural

Arizona (cont.)

development partnership ($210,100) see US WEST

Arizona Historical Society Centennial Foundation ($5,000) see Whiteman Foundation, Edna Rider

Arizona Historical Society Foundation — education; in support of library and archives ($20,000) see Kieckhefer Foundation, J. W.

Arizona Museum of Science and Technology ($10,000) see Globe Corp.

Arizona Museum for Youth ($5,000) see Whiteman Foundation, Edna Rider

Arizona Nature Conservancy ($25,000) see Arizona Public Service Co.

Arizona Nature Conservancy ($5,000) see Simpson Foundation, John M.

Arizona Opera see Valley National Bank of Arizona

Arizona Opera Company see Dial Corp.

Arizona Opera Company ($6,000) see Miller Foundation, Steve J.

Arizona Opera Company ($6,654) see Mulcahy Foundation

Arizona Opera Company ($25,000) see Phelps Dodge Corp.

Arizona Opera Company — support mortgage reduction and production of Aida ($10,000); towards purchase of Phoenix building ($15,000) ($25,000) see Morris Foundation, Margaret T.

Arizona Opera Company — Arizona's principal visual and performing arts institutions to attract and retain new audiences ($200,000) see Flinn Foundation

Arizona Rainbow Girls Foundation ($37,500) see Pendleton Memorial Fund, William L. and Ruth T.

Arizona Rainbow Girls Foundation ($25,000) see Pendleton Memorial Fund, William L. and Ruth T.

Arizona Sonora Desert Museum — capital funds ($25,000) see First Interstate Bank of Arizona

Arizona-Sonora Desert Museum ($267,250) see Stratford Foundation

Arizona State University ($7,500) see Central Newspapers, Inc.

Arizona State University ($51,441) see du Bois Foundation, E. Blois

Arizona State University — to support interdisciplinary research on motor systems neurobiology ($499,985) see Flinn Foundation

Arizona State University ($4,340) see Mulcahy Foundation

Arizona State University ($200,000) see PepsiCo

Arizona State University ($38,000) see Phelps Dodge Corp.

Arizona State University ($25,000) see Southwest Gas Corp.

Arizona State University — aid museum research on tooth morphology and prehistory of Austramelanesian populations, Australia ($10,000) see

Wenner-Gren Foundation for Anthropological Research

Arizona State University College of Business ($2,000) see Seidman Family Foundation

Arizona State University — Engineering Excellence Program ($100,000) see AlliedSignal

Arizona State University — Engineering and School of Business programs ($144,000) see Honeywell

Arizona State University Foundation see American Express Co.

Arizona State University Foundation ($18,000) see Kapoor Charitable Foundation

Arizona State University Foundation ($125,000) see Michigan Bell Telephone Co.

Arizona State University Foundation ($125,000) see Motorola

Arizona State University Foundation ($125,000) see Motorola

Arizona State University — Undergraduate Biological Sciences Education Program ($1,500,000) see Hughes Medical Institute, Howard

Arizona Theatre Company see America West Airlines

Arizona Theatre Company ($25,000) see Phelps Dodge Corp.

Arizona Theatre Company ($50,000) see Steele Foundation

Arizona Zoological Society ($21,350) see Globe Corp.

Arthritis Foundation see Dial Corp.

Ashfork School District ($1,224) see Burns International

Assistance League of Tucson ($2,850) see Arkelian Foundation, Ben H. and Gladys

Association of Arizona Food Banks see America West Airlines

Ballet Arizona ($15,000) see Arizona Public Service Co.

Ballet Arizona see Dial Corp.

Ballet Arizona ($25,000) see Phelps Dodge Corp.

Ballet Arizona ($10,000) see Talley Industries, Inc.

Beatitude Center ($8,000) see Marshall Fund

Believers International ($46,000) see Dauch Foundation, William

Better Business Bureau of Central Arizona Foundation see Dial Corp.

Big Brothers/Big Sisters — nine locations see America West Airlines

Bisbee Poetry ($6,000) see Marshall Fund

Boy Scouts of America ($1,000) see Burns International

Boy Scouts of America see Dial Corp.

Boy Scouts of America ($22,000) see Prince Trust, Abbie Norman

Boys Club of America ($25,000) see Hankins Foundation

Boys and Girls Club ($3,750) see Whiteman Foundation, Edna Rider

Boys/Girls Club of Metro Phoenix ($1,250) see Burns International

Boys and Girls Clubs — 16 locations see America West Airlines

Boys Ranch ($2,500) see Robson Foundation, LaNelle

Brandeis University Womens Committee see America West Airlines

Brophy College Preparatory see America West Airlines

Camelback Charitable Trust ($15,000) see Hervey Foundation

Cancer Research Institute, Arizona State University — in support of building renovation ($75,000) see Kieckhefer Foundation, J. W.

Center — support operating expenses, furnishings and endowment funds ($25,000) see Morris Foundation, Margaret T.

Center for National Independence in Politics — to set up 900-number order processing mechanism ($2,500) see Benton Foundation

Chicanos Por La Causa ($100) see Burns International

Children with AIDS Project of America ($15,000) see Innovating Worthy Projects Foundation

Children's Action Alliance — support "Arizona's Homeless Children and Youth" project ($30,000) see Morris Foundation, Margaret T.

Children's Action Alliance — Early Childhood Development ($147,950) see Honeywell

Childrens Legal Foundation ($200,000) see American Financial Corp.

Childsplay ($3,000) see Whiteman Foundation, Edna Rider

Christian Athlete Ministries see Dial Corp.

Christian Care Center ($44,926) see Pendleton Memorial Fund, William L. and Ruth T.

Christian Care Management ($21,322) see Pendleton Memorial Fund, William L. and Ruth T.

Christian Family Care Agency ($7,400) see Tell Foundation

Christian Family Care Agency — aid to troubled families; in support of the volunteer program ($15,000) see Kieckhefer Foundation, J. W.

Coconino Center for the Arts ($2,500) see Whiteman Foundation, Edna Rider

Colorado River Union High School District — program to meet the needs of pregnant and parenting teenagers ($380,130) see Flinn Foundation

Community Design Resources Center ($10,000) see Keating Family Foundation

Community Food Bank ($2,000) see Mulcahy Foundation

Comstock Children's Foundation ($2,500) see Marshall Foundation

Crisis Nursery ($5,000) see Globe Corp.

Del E. Webb Memorial Hospital — building fund campaign ($500,000) see Webb Foundation, Del E.

Delta Community Development Corporation ($15,000) see Grant Foundation, Charles M. and Mary D.

Desert Foothills Library Association ($3,000) see Fish Foundation, Vain and Harry

Easter Seals see Best Western International

Fellowship Ministries — video study kit ($31,905) see Lutheran Brotherhood Foundation

First Christian Church Guiding Light School ($28,600) see Pendleton Memorial Fund, William L. and Ruth T.

Flagstaff Festival of Arts ($1,000) see Raymond Educational Foundation

Flagstaff Health Management Corporation ($10,000) see Arizona Public Service Co.

Flagstaff Symphony ($10,000) see Raymond Educational Foundation

Flagstaff Unified School ($1,500) see Raymond Educational Foundation

Food for the Hungry ($78,210) see First Fruit

Foothills Equestrian Nature Center ($7,000) see Haskell Fund

Fountain of Life Ministry ($12,300) see Hutcheson Foundation, Hazel Montague

Friend of Our Little Brother ($10,000) see Von der Ahe Foundation

Ganado Unified School District — program to meet the needs of pregnant and parenting teenagers ($258,178) see Flinn Foundation

Goldwater Institute ($2,500) see Robson Foundation, LaNelle

Gompers Center for the Handicapped — providing rehabilitation therapy and other services for the disadvantaged persons suffering from disabilities ($5,000) see Fish Foundation, Vain and Harry

Grand Canyon University ($5,000) see Central Newspapers, Inc.

Grand Canyon University ($500,000) see Solheim Foundation

Grand Canyon University ($5,400) see Tell Foundation

Green Valley Community Church Foundation ($8,000) see Atkinson Foundation, Myrtle L.

Greenfields School ($2,705) see Sehn Foundation

Harrington Arthritis Research Center ($441,597) see Harrington Foundation, Don and Sybil

Harrington Arthritis Research Center ($3,250) see Robson Foundation, LaNelle

Heard Museum ($15,000) see Arizona Public Service Co.

Heard Museum ($25,000) see Phelps Dodge Corp.

Heard Museum ($5,000) see Whiteman Foundation, Edna Rider

Heard Museum — Barry M. Goldwater Center Building Fund ($25,000) see Globe Corp.

Hendrix College — introducing scientific enquiry into the high school ($68,000) see Research Corporation

Herberger Theater Center ($25,000) see Arizona Public Service Co.

Herberger Theatre Center ($2,000) see Whiteman Foundation, Edna Rider

Homeward Bound ($30,450) see Lannan Foundation

Homeward Bound ($5,000) see Whiteman Foundation, Edna Rider

Hopi Foundation ($80,000) see Hitachi

Hopi Foundation — for restoration of clan houses, to revitalize Hopi building crafts, to promote self-sufficiency, and to preserve the Hopi culture and architecture ($10,000) see Anschutz Family Foundation

House of Refuge ($10,000) see Pendleton Memorial Fund, William L. and Ruth T.

Jewish Federation of Phoenix ($7,500) see Cohn Family Foundation, Robert and Terri

Kingman Regional Medical Center Foundation — partial funding to furnish additional operating room ($100,000) see Webb Foundation, Del E.

Life's Journey ($2,000) see Robson Foundation, LaNelle

Listen — hearing tests ($24,700) see Innovating Worthy Projects Foundation

Local Initiatives Support Corporation ($5,000) see Talley Industries, Inc.

Lowell Observatory ($3,500) see Raymond Educational Foundation

Lowell Observatory ($143,500) see Wolff Foundation, John M.

Make-A-Wish Foundation see Best Western International

Maricopa Colleges Foundation ($6,000) see Talley Industries, Inc.

Maricopa County Treasurer ($164,247) see Quaker Oats Co.

Marshall Fund ($20,332) see Marshall Fund

Marshall Home for Men ($16,583) see Marshall Foundation

Mayo Clinic-Scottsdale — endowment for molecular genetic research ($100,000) see Hearst Foundation, William Randolph

Mobile Meals ($6,000) see Brach Foundation, Edwin I.

Mohave County Library District — construction of library building ($40,000) see JELD-WEN, Inc.

Multiple Sclerosis Society ($200) see Burns International

Muscular Distrophy see Best Western International

Museum of Northern Arizona ($12,000) see Marshall Fund

National Family Foundation ($50,000) see Prince Corp.

National Historical Fire Foundation ($100,500) see Globe Corp.

National Merit Scholarship Corporation: Phelps Dodge Scholarships ($37,220) see Phelps Dodge Corp.

Nau/Ralph M. Bilby Fund for Excellence ($25,000) see Arizona Public Service Co.

Navajo Nation Health Foundation — purchase trauma X-ray system for the Emergency Medical Service ($90,000) see Webb Foundation, Del E.

Neues Leben International ($50,000) see Solheim Foundation

North Arizona University ($100,600) see Raymond Educational Foundation

Northern Arizona University ($6,000) see Central Newspapers, Inc.

Northern Arizona University — scholarship ($7,950) see du Bois Foundation, E. Blois

Northern Arizona University ($3,700) see Mulcahy Foundation

Northern Arizona University ($4,000) see Raymond Educational Foundation

Northern Arizona University — music camp ($2,400) see Raymond Educational Foundation

Northern Arizona University — National Undergraduate Research Observatory ($56,121) see Research Corporation

Northland Hospice ($4,000) see Raymond Educational Foundation

Old Pueblo Trolley ($2,500) see Marshall Foundation

Orme School ($2,000) see Atwood Foundation

Orme School ($10,000) see Hogan Foundation, Royal Barney

Orme School ($100,000) see Mosher Foundation, Samuel B.

Orme School ($25,000) see Shenandoah Foundation

Phoenix Art Museum ($4,000) see Talley Industries, Inc.

Phoenix Art Museum ($10,000) see Whiteman Foundation, Edna Rider

Phoenix Art Museum — to establish endowment for Best of Show Award for Cowboy Artists of America exhibitions ($33,750) see Kieckhefer Foundation, J. W.

Phoenix Christian High School ($41,000) see Tell Foundation

Phoenix Gospel Mission ($100,000) see Solheim Foundation

Phoenix Performing Arts Center ($15,000) see Robson Foundation, LaNelle

Phoenix Special Programs ($5,000) see Wolff Foundation, John M.

Phoenix Symphony ($15,000) see Ray Foundation

Phoenix Symphony ($6,000) see Southwest Gas Corp.

Phoenix Symphony ($201,200) see Steele Foundation

Phoenix Symphony ($5,000) see Talley Industries, Inc.

Phoenix Symphony ($6,000) see Whiteman Foundation, Edna Rider

Phoenix Symphony Association ($50,000) see Globe Corp.

Phoenix Symphony Guild ($19,700) see Pendleton Memorial Fund, William L. and Ruth T.

Phoenix Symphony Orchestra ($20,000) see Arizona Public Service Co.

Phoenix Zoo ($11,200) see Talley Industries, Inc.

Pima Community College ($10,500) see Marshall Foundation

Pima Community College ($2,876) see Mulcahy Foundation

Pima County Juvenile Court ($2,500) see Marshall Foundation

Pioneer Historical Society ($3,500) see Raymond Educational Foundation

Planned Parenthood ($10,000) see Marshall Fund

Planned Parenthood Federation of America ($15,000) see Brach Foundation, Edwin I.

Planned Parenthood Federation of America — national assistance family planning ($33,350) see Morris Foundation, Margaret T.

Rising STAR ($3,500) see Talley Industries, Inc.

Roosevelt School District 66 ($18,000) see Ray Foundation

Roots and Wings for Infants ($40,000) see Miller Foundation, Steve J.

St. Barnabas on the Desert ($15,000) see Woods Foundation, James H.

St. Barnabas on the Desert ($10,000) see Woods Foundation, James H.

St. Luke's Foundation — purchase of bone densitometry equipment ($69,000) see Webb Foundation, Del E.

St. Luke's Hospital ($100,000) see Olin Foundation, Spencer T. and Ann W.

St. Mary's Food Bank ($6,000) see Smucker Co., J.M.

St. Stevens Church ($12,500) see Robson Foundation, LaNelle

Salpoint High School ($5,000) see Mulcahy Foundation

Salpointe Catholic High School — toward capital campaign ($45,000) see Raskob Foundation for Catholic Activities

Salvation Army ($1,000) see Burns International

Salvation Army ($7,000) see Smucker Co., J.M.

Scotsdale Christian Academy ($5,150) see Tell Foundation

Scottsdale Girls Club ($20,000) see Marshall Fund

Scottsdale Memorial Health Foundation ($25,000) see Fish Foundation, Vain and Harry

Southwest Indian Foundation ($50,000) see Edouard Foundation

Southwestern College ($25,000) see Tell Foundation

Summer Camp "A Leg Up" Program — for handicapped children conducted by Therapeutic Riding Center for the Handicapped ($108,129) see Reynolds Foundation, Eleanor T.

Sun Angel Foundation ($50,000) see Steele Foundation

Sunkist Kids ($1,000) see Burns International

Sunshine Rescue Mission — aid to poor ($3,500) see Raymond Educational Foundation

Techo ($7,300) see Marshall Fund

Tempe Union High School District — program to meet the needs of pregnant and parenting teenagers ($375,000) see Flinn Foundation

Thunderbirds ($7,700) see Talley Industries, Inc.

Tuba City Unified School District No. 15 ($161,017) see Macy, Jr. Foundation, Josiah

Tucson Association for the Blind ($5,000) see Miller Foundation, Steve J.

Tucson Medical Center Foundation ($14,500) see Simpson Foundation, John M.

Tucson Museum of Art ($10,000) see Chapin Foundation, Frances

Tucson Shalom House ($12,500) see Stocker Foundation

Tucson Tabernacle ($6,000) see Dauch Foundation, William

Tucson Young Men's Association ($14,650) see Mulcahy Foundation

United Community Fund ($5,000) see Brach Foundation, Edwin I.

United Methodist Outreach ($1,000) see Burns International

United Way ($3,200) see Federated Life Insurance Co.

United Way ($9,000) see Mulcahy Foundation

United Way ($10,000) see Robson Foundation, LaNelle

United Way — Alexis de Tocqueville Society ($10,000) see Globe Corp.

United Way of Sun Valley — general purpose fund ($7,600) see Walgreen Co.

United Way Tucson — general support ($29,125) see First Interstate Bank of Arizona

United Way Tucson — general support ($29,125) see First Interstate Bank of Arizona

United Way Tucson — general support ($29,125) see First Interstate Bank of Arizona

United Way Tucson — general support ($29,125) see First Interstate Bank of Arizona

United Way Valley of the Sun ($153,000) see AlliedSignal

United Way-Valley of the Sun ($267,310) see Arizona Public Service Co.

United Way-Valley of the Sun — general support ($62,500) see First Interstate Bank of Arizona

United Way-Valley of the Sun — general support ($62,500) see First Interstate Bank of Arizona

United Way-Valley of the Sun — general support ($62,500) see First Interstate Bank of Arizona

United Way-Valley of the Sun — general support ($62,500) see First Interstate Bank of Arizona

United Way-Valley of the Sun — general support ($62,500) see First Interstate Bank of Arizona

University of Arizona ($12,000) see Associated Foundations

University of Arizona — endowment for scholarships ($1,380,000) see Berger Foundation, H.N. and Frances C.

University of Arizona ($7,500) see Central Newspapers, Inc.

University of Arizona ($12,000) see Chapin Foundation, Frances

University of Arizona ($15,800) see du Bois Foundation, E. Blois

University of Arizona — to support research which explores ways in which the brain supports basic human mental capacities ($500,000) see Flinn Foundation

University of Arizona — to support interdisciplinary research and training in genetics ($499,765) see Flinn Foundation

University of Arizona — scholarship awards ($291,200) see Flinn Foundation

University of Arizona ($418,000) see Intel Corp.

University of Arizona ($36,177) see Margoes Foundation

University of Arizona ($112,640) see Marshall Foundation

University of Arizona ($5,000) see Marshall Foundation

University of Arizona ($5,000) see Marshall Foundation

University of Arizona ($27,100) see Miller Foundation, Steve J.

University of Arizona ($25,500) see Moores Foundation

University of Arizona ($64,000) see Phelps Dodge Corp.

University of Arizona ($20,000) see Pulitzer Publishing Co.

University of Arizona ($67,935) see Ramapo Trust

University of Arizona ($2,000) see Robson Foundation, LaNelle

University of Arizona ($20,000) see Southwest Gas Corp.

University of Arizona-College of Business and Public Administration ($50,000) see Arizona Public Service Co.

University of Arizona College of Pharmacy ($35,685) see Pfeiffer Research Foundation, Gustavus and Louise

University of Arizona Committee of Biological Science Departments — support for core undergraduate and graduate programs common to all of the 21 biological science departments ($375,000) see Flinn Foundation

University of Arizona Foundation suppressed ($250,000) see Anheuser-Busch Cos.

University of Arizona and Foundation ($67,648) see Mulcahy Foundation

University of Arizona Health Sciences Center ($100,000) see Marshall Foundation

University of Arizona Health Sciences Center ($131,411) see Wallace Genetic Foundation

University of Arizona — aid Hopi Dictionary Project, Arizona ($12,000) see Wenner-Gren Foundation for Anthropological Research

University of Arizona Medical Hospital ($10,000) see Brach Foundation, Edwin I.

University of Arizona — to support the training of pre- and post-doctoral investigators in developmental neurosciences ($497,803) see Flinn Foundation

University of Arizona Scholarship Fund ($16,000) see Haskell Fund

University of Arizona, School of Pharmacy ($2,000) see Long Foundation, J.M.

Up with People ($200,000) see Heinz Co., H.J.

Up With People — to provide leadership for worldwide program ($333,000) see Boswell Foundation, James G.

Up With People ($50,000) see Cook Foundation

Up With People ($500,000) see Hilton Foundation, Conrad N.

Up With People ($152,360) see Mandeville Foundation

Up With People Endowed Scholarship Fund ($10,000) see McKnight Foundation, Sumner T.

Up With People — "Golden Circle Fund" ($100,000) see Boswell Foundation, James G.

Up With People — to help relocate the Up With People office in Colorado ($20,000) see Anschutz Family Foundation

Valley of the Sun United Way — general support ($35,775) see Medtronic

Valley of the Sun United Way ($250,000) see Michigan Bell Telephone Co.

Valley of the Sun United Way ($250,000) see Motorola

World Neighbors — Ecuador development project ($50,000) see M. E. G. Foundation

YMCA of Phoenix and Valley of the Sun ($15,000) see Arizona Public Service Co.

Arkansas

Aerospace Education Center ($5,000) see Riggs Benevolent Fund

Aerospace Education Center ($25,000) see Trinity Foundation

Agriculture Development ($100,000) see Tyson Foods, Inc.

Arkadelphia Public Schools — math/science project ($75,000) see Ross Foundation

Arkadelphia Public Schools — mini-grants ($10,000) see Ross Foundation

Arkansas Adult Literacy Foundation ($25,000) see Tyson Foods, Inc.

Arkansas Adult Literacy Fund ($3,000) see Orbit Valve Co.

Arkansas Advocates for Children and Families — enhance organizational strength and decrease dependency on foundation grants ($47,821) see Rockefeller Foundation, Winthrop

Arkansas Advocates for Children and Families ($60,000) see Sturgis Charitable and Educational Trust, Roy and Christine

Arkansas Art Center — MacArthur Park ($5,220) see Weisman Art Foundation, Frederick R.

Arkansas Arts Center see International Paper Co.

Arkansas Arts Center — support museum school program ($15,000) see Jonsson Foundation

Arkansas Arts Center ($6,000) see Rebsamen Companies, Inc.

Arkansas Arts Center ($22,000) see Trinity Foundation

Arkansas Association of Hearing Impaired Children ($10,000) see Trinity Foundation

Arkansas Aviation Historical Society ($54,000) see Rockefeller Trust, Winthrop

Arkansas Baptist Children's Home ($100,000) see Jones Foundation, Harvey and Bernice

Arkansas Baptist Convention/Siloam ($260,000) see Jones Charitable Trust, Harvey and Bernice

Arkansas Baptist Convention/Siloam ($260,000) see Jones Charitable Trust, Harvey and Bernice

Arkansas Baptist Convention/Siloam ($225,000) see Jones Charitable Trust, Harvey and Bernice

Arkansas Business Council Foundation — earmarked for grant to Southern Arkansas University Tech ($86,105) see Walton Family Foundation

Arkansas Business Council Foundation — earmarked for

Arkansas (cont.)

grant to Westark Community College ($110,000) see Walton Family Foundation

Arkansas Cancer Research Center ($2,000) see Cohn Co., M.M.

Arkansas Center for Eye Research ($5,000) see Rebsamen Companies, Inc.

Arkansas Childrens Hospital see Arkla

Arkansas Children's Hospital — training of health professionals ($35,000) see Hearst Foundation

Arkansas Children's Hospital ($500,000) see Jones Charitable Trust, Harvey and Bernice

Arkansas Children's Hospital ($500,000) see Jones Charitable Trust, Harvey and Bernice

Arkansas Children's Hospital ($5,000) see Riggs Benevolent Fund

Arkansas Children's Hospital — funding helicopter/emergency patient transport ($5,000) see Jonsson Foundation

Arkansas Department of Health ($10,000) see Johnson & Johnson

Arkansas Education Renewal Consortium — to help selected Arkansas schools address the needs of children in middle-grade schools ($70,000) see Rockefeller Foundation, Winthrop

Arkansas Game and Fish Foundation — big timber area ($21,550) see Ross Foundation

Arkansas Institute for Social Justice — a four-year grant to ACORN of Brooklyn, New York ($250,000) see Schumann Foundation, Florence and John

Arkansas Repertory Theater ($2,857) see Cohn Co., M.M.

Arkansas Repertory Theatre — to meet the $2.5 million of the first capital campaign in the ten-year "history" of Arkansas Repertory Theatre ($25,000) see Frost Foundation

Arkansas Repertory Theatre Company ($150,000) see Sturgis Charitable and Educational Trust, Roy and Christine

Arkansas Research Center ($2,000) see Orbit Valve Co.

Arkansas Research Center ($5,000) see Riggs Benevolent Fund

Arkansas Research Center — start-up funds ($10,000) see Ross Foundation

Arkansas Rice Depot ($60,000) see Sturgis Charitable and Educational Trust, Roy and Christine

Arkansas River Education Service ($10,000) see Trinity Foundation

Arkansas State University Foundation ($10,000) see Reynolds Foundation, Donald W.

Arkansas Symphony Orchestra ($4,000) see Rebsamen Companies, Inc.

Baptist Medical Foundation, Nursing School ($10,000) see Riggs Benevolent Fund

Baptist Medical System Support Center — Nursing School

($5,000) see Rebsamen Companies, Inc.

Barton Library — endowment fund ($17,063) see Murphy Foundation

Bentonville United Way ($50,404) see Wal-Mart Stores

Boy Scouts of America ($5,000) see Rebsamen Companies, Inc.

Boy Scouts of America ($5,000) see Rebsamen Companies, Inc.

Boys Club of America ($20,000) see Riggs Benevolent Fund

Carmelite Fathers ($836,217) see Wrape Family Charitable Trust

Carmelite Fathers ($305,000) see Wrape Family Charitable Trust

Carmelite Sisters ($135,691) see Wrape Family Charitable Trust

Carmelite Sisters ($43,127) see Wrape Family Charitable Trust

Center for Youth and Families ($6,000) see Riggs Benevolent Fund

Centers for Youth and Families ($100,000) see Sturgis Charitable and Educational Trust, Roy and Christine

Clark County ($20,000) see Ross Foundation

Clark County ($10,000) see Ross Foundation

College of Ozarks ($50,000) see Pfeiffer Research Foundation, Gustavus and Louise

Dawson Educational Co-op — mini-grants ($44,504) see Ross Foundation

Delta Community Development Corporation — to address causes and conditions of economic depression and under- and unemployment in eastern Arkansas ($48,500) see Rockefeller Foundation, Winthrop

Diocese of Little Rock ($118,500) see Wrape Family Charitable Trust

EOA of Washington County ($50,000) see Walton Family Foundation

Fayettville Public Education ($9,000) see Bodenhamer Foundation

First Presbyterian Endowment Fund for Missions ($50,000) see National Presto Industries

Florence Crittenton Home ($1,000) see Orbit Valve Co.

Friends of Cross County Library ($3,000) see Halstead Foundation

Good Shepherd Center ($2,500) see Halstead Foundation

Harding University ($400,000) see Jones Charitable Trust, Harvey and Bernice

Harding University ($1,500,000) see Mabee Foundation, J. E. and L. E.

Harding University ($850,000) see Walton Family Foundation

Harding University ($2,000) see Winchester Foundation

Heifer Project International ($4,000) see Cayuga Foundation

Heifer Project International ($1,000) see Orbit Valve Co.

Heifer Project International ($3,000) see Reidler Foundation

Heifer Project International ($10,000) see Woodward Fund

Henderson State University — field-based study ($12,500) see Ross Foundation

Hendrix College — scholarship endowment ($50,000) see

Frueauff Foundation, Charles A.

Hendrix College ($1,000,000) see Mabee Foundation, J. E. and L. E.

Hendrix College ($500,000) see Rockefeller Trust, Winthrop

Hendrix College ($100,000) see Sturgis Charitable and Educational Trust, Roy and Christine

HIPPY-McGehee School District — target ($27,000) see Potlatch Corp.

Huttig Ambulance Service ($20,000) see Manville Corp.

Independent College Fund ($170,000) see Trinity Foundation

Independent College Fund of Arkansas ($12,000) see Walton Family Foundation

Independent Colleges of Arkansas ($5,000) see Rebsamen Companies, Inc.

John Brown University ($5,000) see Broadhurst Foundation

John Brown University ($50,000) see Chapman Charitable Trust, H. A. and Mary K.

John Brown University ($675,000) see Walton Family Foundation

Joint Educational Consortium — 1990-91 budget ($35,000) see Ross Foundation

Joint Educational Consortium — 1991-92 budget ($20,000) see Ross Foundation

Joseph Pfeiffer Kiwanis Camp ($50,000) see American Honda Motor Co.

Kingsland Public Schools ($65,000) see Sturgis Charitable and Educational Trust, Roy and Christine

Linden Hill School ($5,000) see Riggs Benevolent Fund

Little Rock Boys Club ($2,000) see Orbit Valve Co.

Little Rock Public Education ($25,000) see Bodenhamer Foundation

Little Rock Public Education ($8,000) see Bodenhamer Foundation

Little Rock Public Education ($5,000) see Bodenhamer Foundation

Little Rock Public Museum ($2,500) see Bodenhamer Foundation

Little Rock School District ($3,000) see Bodenhamer Foundation

Little Rock School District ($16,716) see Trinity Foundation

McCurtan County Sports Center ($50,000) see Tyson Foods, Inc.

Miss Polly's Learning Center ($2,500) see Halstead Foundation

NAACP see Arkla

New Futures for Little Rock Youth — New Futures Youth Initiative ($1,649,343) see Casey Foundation, Annie E.

Nonprofit Resources — to increase knowledge in grassroots fund raising ($51,140) see Rockefeller Foundation, Winthrop

Northwest Arkansas Adult Day Care Center ($75,000) see Jones Foundation, Harvey and Bernice

Old Ft. Museum ($12,000) see Reynolds Foundation, Donald W.

Ouachita Baptist University ($750,000) see Jones Charitable Trust, Harvey and Bernice

Ouachita Baptist University ($500,000) see Jones Charitable Trust, Harvey and Bernice

Ouachita Baptist University ($459,000) see Jones Charitable Trust, Harvey and Bernice

Ouachita Baptist University ($250,000) see Jones Charitable Trust, Harvey and Bernice

Ouachita Baptist University ($4,800) see Phelps, Inc.

Ouchita Baptist University ($13,000) see Atkinson Foundation, Myrtle L.

Philander Smith College — year-round evening program to allow working students time to complete their college degree requirements ($72,334) see Rockefeller Foundation, Winthrop

Pine Bluff Parks and Recreation ($12,000) see Trinity Foundation

Pine Bluff Public Schools ($13,758) see Trinity Foundation

Rape Crisis Center see Arkla

S.E. Arkansas Community Action Corporation see Arkla

St. Vincent Development Foundation ($1,000) see Orbit Valve Co.

Salvation Army — endowment fund ($23,888) see Murphy Foundation

Salvation Army Building Fund — operating budget ($20,000) see Murphy Foundation

Searcy County Airport Commission — support a grassroots attempt to design a local economy by building on existing resources ($50,000) see Rockefeller Foundation, Winthrop

Shiloh Museum ($50,000) see Tyson Foods, Inc.

South Arkansas Art Center — operating budget ($15,287) see Murphy Foundation

South Arkansas Arts Center — endowment fund ($34,925) see Murphy Foundation

South Arkansas Symphony — endowment fund ($17,063) see Murphy Foundation

Southeast Arkansas Arts and Science Center ($5,700) see Coltec Industries

Southern Arkansas University ($25,000) see Tyson Foods, Inc.

UAMS Foundation Fund — foundation fund ($25,000) see Murphy Foundation

United Fund ($5,000) see Standard Register Co.

United Way ($47,500) see Ladish Co.

United Way ($1,159) see Old Dominion Box Co.

United Way ($7,600) see Orbit Valve Co.

United Way ($3,750) see Orbit Valve Co.

United Way ($28,000) see Rebsamen Companies, Inc.

United Way ($48,500) see Riggs Benevolent Fund

United Way-Ft. Smith ($25,454) see American Standard

United Way of Pulaski County ($65,000) see Union Pacific Corp.

United Way of Union County — endowment fund ($34,125) see Murphy Foundation

United Way of White County ($9,935) see TRINOVA Corp.

University of Arkansas ($20,000) see Tyson Foods, Inc.

University of Arkansas at Fayetteville ($700,000) see Sturgis Charitable and Educational Trust, Roy and Christine

University of Arkansas Foundation ($55,500) see Phillips Petroleum Co.

University of Arkansas Foundation — a leadership and organizational development training program ($100,000) see Rockefeller Foundation, Winthrop

University of Arkansas Foundation ($15,000) see Rockefeller Trust, Winthrop

University of Arkansas — KUAF radio station ($10,000) see Walton Family Foundation

University of Arkansas Little Rock ($15,000) see Jonsson Foundation

University of Arkansas Little Rock ($4,000) see Orbit Valve Co.

University of Arkansas Little Rock ($30,000) see Trinity Foundation

University of Arkansas at Little Rock/School of Law — fellowships for Black law scholars ($49,550) see Rockefeller Foundation, Winthrop

University of Arkansas Medical Science see Arkla

University of Arkansas-Monticello — Department of Forest Resources ($100,000) see Sturgis Charitable and Educational Trust, Roy and Christine

University of the Ozarks ($32,500) see Grimes Foundation, Otha H.

University of the Ozarks ($625,000) see Walton Family Foundation

VAMS Foundation ($10,000) see Riggs Benevolent Fund

Vera Lloyd Presbyterian Home ($50,000) see Riggs Benevolent Fund

Wildwood ($3,000) see Orbit Valve Co.

Winrock International Institute for Agricultural Development ($3,702,952) see Rockefeller Trust, Winthrop

Winrock International Institute for Agriculture — for goat breeding, nutrition, management, farming development ($5,000) see Rebsamen Companies, Inc.

Winthrop Rockefeller Foundation ($690,000) see Rockefeller Trust, Winthrop

California

A Friendly Place — general support for a daytime hospitality center for homeless women ($5,000) see Gannett Co.

A.R.C.S. — scholarship fund ($21,600) see Kingsley Foundation, Lewis A.

A.T. Medical Research Foundation ($2,500) see Rales

and Ruth Rales Foundation, Norman R.

Academy Foundation ($25,000) see Daly Charitable Foundation Trust, Robert and Nancy

Academy Foundation ($10,000) see Goldwyn Foundation, Samuel

Academy Foundation ($25,000) see Max Charitable Foundation

Academy Foundation ($50,000) see MCA

Academy Foundation ($50,000) see Paramount Communications Inc.

Academy Foundation ($50,000) see Disney Co., Walt

Academy Foundation ($50,000) see Wasserman Foundation

Academy of Motion Picture Arts ($20,000) see Pickford Foundation, Mary

Academy of St. Martin's in the Fields Building Foundation ($25,000) see Colburn Fund

ACLU Foundation ($27,500) see Geffen Foundation, David

Adat Ariel ($22,500) see Beren Foundation, Robert M.

Adelante Corporation ($25,000) see Mott Fund, Ruth

Advocates for Self Government ($3,000) see Hastings Trust

Advocates for Self-Government ($20,000) see Tamko Asphalt Products

AFF Rose Bowl Aquatics Center ($4,000) see Jacobs Engineering Group

African Enterprise ($100,000) see Stewardship Foundation

African Team Ministries ($5,000) see Mostyn Foundation

African Team Ministries ($5,000) see Plant Memorial Fund, Henry B.

Agricultural Education Foundation — capital campaign ($300,000) see Boswell Foundation, James G.

Agricultural Education Foundation — funding for agricultural leadership training seminars ($120,000) see Boswell Foundation, James G.

Agricultural Workers Health Center ($10,000) see van Loben Sels - Eleanor Slate van Lobel Sels Charitable Foundation, Ernst D.

Ahead With Horses — general budget ($5,000) see Smith Trust, May and Stanley

AIDS Legal Referral Panel ($10,000) see Friedman Family Foundation

AIDS Project L.A. ($25,000) see Brotman Foundation of California

AIDS Project L.A. ($10,000) see Lastfogel Foundation, Abe and Frances

AIDS Project Los Angeles ($20,000) see Geffen Foundation, David

AIDS Project Los Angeles see Great Western Financial Corp.

AIDS Project of Los Angeles ($10,000) see Levy Foundation, Edward C.

Aimansor Center ($5,000) see Robinson Foundation

Alameda County Court — to support a program for youthful offenders integrating services of three independent agencies ($96,500) see Donner Foundation, William H.

Alano Club of Redding — building improvements

($75,000) see McConnell Foundation

Albert Baker Fund ($15,000) see Aequus Institute

Alcoholism Information Center — support for 1989 ($10,000) see Bank of America - Giannini Foundation

Alexis de Toqueville Institute ($5,000) see Durell Foundation, George Edward

Ali Akbar College of Music ($20,000) see Bayne Fund, Howard

All Saints AIDS Center ($1,500) see Femino Foundation

Alliance for Children's Rights ($150,000) see Bettingen Corporation, Burton G.

Allied Fellowship Service ($25,000) see Haigh-Scatena Foundation

Alta Bates Herrick Foundation ($2,000) see Uvas Foundation

Alternative Living for the Aging see Great Western Financial Corp.

Alzheimers Association — four locations see America West Airlines

Alzheimer's Disease and Related Disorders Association ($8,000) see Bellini Foundation

Alzheimer's Disease and Related Disorders Association ($10,000) see Benbough Foundation, Legler

Alzheimer's Disease and Related Disorders Association ($10,000) see Stillwell Charitable Trust, Glen and Dorothy

Alzheimer's Disease and Related Disorders Association ($1,000) see Taper Foundation, Mark

Alzheimer's Disease and Related Disorders Association ($20,000) see Wood-Claeyssens Foundation

Alzheimer's Services of the East Bay — for the start-up of the In-Home Registry Respite Project and to assume operations of the San Leandro Alzheimer's Day Care Resource Center ($50,000) see Haas, Jr. Fund, Evelyn and Walter

American Academy of Achievement ($7,500) see Farley Industries

American Academy of Achievement ($7,500) see Fireman Charitable Foundation, Paul and Phyllis

American Academy of Achievement ($50,000) see Roberts Foundation

American Academy of Achievement ($11,000) see Tauber Foundation

American Armenian International College ($201,000) see Manoogian Foundation, Alex and Marie

American Cancer Society ($100) see Baker Foundation, Solomon R. and Rebecca D.

American Cancer Society ($81,636) see Brunetti Charitable Trust, Dionigi

American Cancer Society ($2,000) see Burnand Medical and Educational Foundation, Alphonse A.

American Cancer Society ($2,000) see Green Foundation, Burton E.

American Cancer Society ($4,500) see Imperial Bancorp

American Cancer Society ($15,000) see Rogers Foundation, Mary Stuart

American Center for Music Theater ($5,000) see Van Nuys Charities, J. B. and Emily

American Cinema Awards Foundation — library building fund ($12,000) see Shoong Foundation, Milton

American Cinemateque ($62,500) see MCA

American Civil Liberties Union Foundation ($10,000) see van Loben Sels - Eleanor Slate van Lobel Sels Charitable Foundation, Ernst D.

American Civil Liberties Union Foundation of Northern California ($70,000) see Prickett Fund, Lynn R. and Karl E.

American Committee for Weizmann Institute ($100,000) see Rochlin Foundation, Abraham and Sonia

American Communications Foundation — earthbreak radio series ($25,000) see Goldman Fund, Richard and Rhoda

American Congress of Jews — monument ($25,000) see Eisenberg Foundation, Ben B. and Joyce E.

American Conservatory Theater ($5,000) see Brenner Foundation, Mervyn

American Conservatory Theater ($25,000) see Fleishhacker Foundation

American Conservatory Theatre ($100,000) see Osher Foundation, Bernard

American Diabetes Association ($8,000) see Bellini Foundation

American Film Foundation ($25,000) see Colburn Fund

American Film Institute — production of program guide for national video festival ($2,000) see Benton Foundation

American Film Institute ($100,000) see Mayer Foundation, Louis B.

American Film Institute ($22,000) see Plitt Southern Theatres

American Film Institute ($17,000) see Weiler Foundation, Theodore & Renee

American Foundrymen's Society ($1,000) see Alhambra Foundry Co., Ltd.

American Friends of Assad Harrofeh Medical Center ($5,000) see Feintech Foundation

American Friends of the Hebrew University ($5,000) see Schoenbaum Family Foundation

American Friends of Hebrew University — for the Harry S. Truman Institute for the Advancement of Peace ($35,000) see Columbia Foundation

American Friends Service Committee ($15,000) see Greenville Foundation

American Friends of Tel Aviv University ($25,000) see Feintech Foundation

American Friends of Weizmann Institute ($25,000) see Fellner Memorial Foundation, Leopold and Clara M.

American Friends of Weizmann Institute ($11,000) see

Levinson Foundation, Morris L.

American Graduate School of International Management ($40,000) see Continental Grain Co.

American Graduate School of International Management ($50,000) see Stuart Foundation, Elbridge and Evelyn

American Heart Association ($81,636) see Brunetti Charitable Trust, Dionigi

American Heart Association ($6,100) see Buchalter, Nemer, Fields, & Younger

American Heart Association ($5,000) see City of Hope 1989 Section E Foundation

American Heart Association ($30,000) see Favrot Fund

American Heart Association ($2,000) see Green Foundation, Burton E.

American Heart Association ($15,000) see Rogers Foundation, Mary Stuart

American Heart Association see San Diego Trust & Savings Bank

American Heart Association ($5,000) see Van Nuys Charities, J. B. and Emily

American Himalayan Foundation ($3,500) see Davies Charitable Trust

American Lung Association ($15,000) see Fairfield Foundation, Freeman E.

American Lung Association ($2,000) see Green Foundation, Burton E.

American Lung Association ($25,000) see Smith Foundation, Lon V.

American Lung Association of Los Angeles County see International Paper Co.

American Medical Flight Team ($25,000) see Smith Foundation, Lon V.

American Ornithologist's Union ($10,000) see Sefton Foundation, J. W.

American Red Cross ($5,500) see Ace Beverage Co.

American Red Cross ($10,000) see Bellini Foundation

American Red Cross ($50,000) see Clorox Co.

American Red Cross ($7,500) see Forest Lawn Foundation

American Red Cross ($2,000) see Green Foundation, Burton E.

American Red Cross ($5,000) see Muth Foundation, Peter and Mary

American Red Cross ($5,000) see Nelson Foundation, Florence

American Red Cross ($27,521) see Saturno Foundation

American Red Cross ($13,761) see Saturno Foundation

American Red Cross ($100,000) see Taper Foundation, Mark

American Red Cross ($100,000) see Taper Foundation, S. Mark

American Red Cross ($2,000) see Upjohn California Fund

American Red Cross ($1,500) see Upjohn California Fund

American Red Cross — funding toward expansion of the new facility ($100,000) see Valley Foundation

American Red Cross ($5,000) see Van Nuys Charities, J. B. and Emily

American Red Cross ($5,000) see Van Nuys Charities, J. B. and Emily

American Red Cross, Los Angeles Chapter ($2,500) see Rasmussen Foundation

American Service to India Medical and Educational Foundation ($7,960) see India Foundation

American Technion Society ($25,700) see Deutsch Co.

American Youth Symphony ($28,123) see Ziegler Foundation, Ruth/Allen

Americare ($5,000) see Weiler Foundation

Amie Karen Cancer Fund for Children ($5,000) see Gallo Foundation, Julio R.

Amigos de Los Ninos ($2,500) see Autry Foundation

Amity International Education Foundation ($70,000) see Van Camp Foundation

Amity International Foundation ($65,640) see Van Camp Foundation

Angeles Girl Scout Council ($5,000) see Van Nuys Charities, J. B. and Emily

Animal Alliance ($10,000) see Seebee Trust, Frances

Animal Protection Institute ($18,000) see Summerlee Foundation

Ann and Gordon Getty Foundation ($9,562,328) see G.P.G. Foundation

Anti-Defamation League ($4,200) see Buchalter, Nemer, Fields, & Younger

Anti-Defamation League ($3,876) see Metropolitan Theatres Corp.

Applied Behavioral and Cognitive Sciences — support of the Consortium for Workforce Education and Lifelong Learning ($450,000) see Hewlett Foundation, William and Flora

Aquatic Habitat Institute see Tosco Corp. Refining Division

Ararat Home ($20,000) see Philibosian Foundation, Stephen

Ararat Home of Los Angeles ($1,000,000) see Lincy Foundation

Ararat Home of Los Angeles ($650,000) see Lincy Foundation

Arcadia Methodist Hospital ($5,000) see Markey Charitable Fund, John C.

Arcata Little League ($2,775) see Sierra Pacific Resources

Arcata Little League and Babe Ruth League ($2,500) see Nelson Foundation, Florence

Archdiocese Education Foundation — Grant a Dream program see United Airlines

Archdiocese of Los Angeles ($55,000) see Hayden Foundation, William R. and Virginia

Archdiocese of Los Angeles ($305,000) see Hilton Foundation, Conrad N.

Archdiocese of Los Angeles ($1,050,000) see Leavey Foundation, Thomas and Dorothy

Archdiocese of Los Angeles ($360,993) see Shea Foundation, John and Dorothy

Archdiocese of Los Angeles ($222,807) see Shea Foundation, John and Dorothy

California (cont.)

Archdiocese of Los Angeles ($193,714) see Shea Foundation, John and Dorothy

Archdiocese of Los Angeles — for a computer-based literacy program in Archdiocesan schools and to add a science component to the program see Keck Foundation, W. M.

Archdiocese of Los Angeles Department of Education ($63,500) see Garland Foundation, John Jewett and H. Chandler

Archdiocese of Los Angeles Education Foundation ($50,000) see Unocal Corp.

Archdiocese of San Francisco ($1,500) see Eaton Foundation, Edwin M. and Gertrude S.

ARCS Foundation — scientific scholarships ($20,000) see Genentech

ARISE ($25,000) see Russell Educational Foundation, Benjamin and Roberta

Armand Hammer United World College ($100,000) see Huntsman Foundation, Jon and Karen

Armand Hammer World College ($10,000) see Getz Foundation, Emma and Oscar

Armory Center for the Arts ($35,000) see Connell Foundation, Michael J.

Armory Center for the Arts ($5,000) see Scott Foundation, Virginia Steele

Army and Navy Academy (San Diego) — computer memory boards ($500) see Sefton Foundation, J. W.

Arrowhead United Way ($1,078) see Lawyers Title Foundation

Art Against AIDS ($10,000) see Heller Foundation, Walter E.

Art Center College of Design ($26,565) see Porsche Cars North America, Inc.

Art Center College of Design ($4,000) see Scott Foundation, Virginia Steele

Art Center College of Design — to name the Ralph M. Parsons Foundation Computer-Aided Industrial Design Center as part of a capital building expansion of the South Wing ($150,000) see Parsons Foundation, Ralph M.

Art Fund Campaign/Community Foundation — funds to go toward the development of a permanent endowment for stability of the arts in Santa Clara County ($100,000) see Valley Foundation

Art Institute of Southern California ($150,000) see Van Camp Foundation

Arthritis Foundation ($2,000) see Green Foundation, Burton E.

Arthritis Foundation ($32,791) see Seebee Trust, Frances

Arthritis Foundation of Northern California ($12,204) see Brunetti Charitable Trust, Dionigi

Asia Foundation ($10,000) see Wilbur-Ellis Co.

Asia Foundation — to support a project to strengthen the rule of law in east and southeast Asia ($200,000) see Luce Foundation, Henry

Asian American Journalist Association ($1,000) see Gleason Foundation, James

Asian Art Foundation of San Francisco — for the Endowment Fund ($34,000) see Columbia Foundation

Asian Art Museum Foundation ($7,566) see Wilbur-Ellis Co.

Asian Law Caucus ($15,000) see van Loben Sels - Eleanor Slate van Lobel Sels Charitable Foundation, Ernst D.

Asian Pacific Amreican Legal Center of Southern California — Language Rights project ($85,000) see Rosenberg Foundation

Assistance Guild of S. Clarita ($1,000) see Rasmussen Foundation

Assistance League of California ($5,000) see Bekins Foundation, Milo W.

Assistance League of East San Gabriel Valley — clothe needy school children through "Operation School Bell" ($3,000) see American Foundation

Assistance League of Long Beach ($5,000) see Miller Foundation, Earl B. and Loraine H.

Assistance League of Southern California ($11,000) see Beynon Foundation, Kathryne

Assistance League of Southern California ($100,000) see Bing Fund

Assistance League of Southern California — toward construction of new facility and specifically for senior services center see Keck Foundation, W. M.

Assistance League of Southern California ($50,000) see McAlister Charitable Foundation, Harold

Assistance League of Southern California — Children's Club Los Angeles ($11,000) see Beynon Foundation, Kathryne

Association of Children's Services ($15,000) see Hedco Foundation

Association for Retarded Citizens ($15,000) see Jackson Family Foundation, Ann

Association of University Professors of Ophthalmology — goodwill ($25,000) see Alcon Laboratories, Inc.

Assumption School ($32,000) see OCRI Foundation

AT&T Junior Golf Association ($7,259) see National Pro-Am Youth Fund

Aububon Canyon Ranch ($50,000) see Gilman Foundation, Howard

Aurora School ($2,000) see Uvas Foundation

Aurora School ($2,000) see Uvas Foundation

Autism Society of America — camp fund ($35,000) see Baker Foundation, Solomon R. and Rebecca D.

Autism Society of America — camp fund ($25,000) see Baker Foundation, Solomon R. and Rebecca D.

Autism Society of America — purchaser of facilitator ($5,000) see Baker Foundation, Solomon R. and Rebecca D.

Azusa Pacific University ($6,000) see Associated Foundations

Azusa Pacific University ($11,000) see Atkinson Foundation, Myrtle L.

Azusa Pacific University — scholarships ($24,000) see Stamps Foundation, James L.

B.E.C.A. Foundation ($40,000) see Joslyn Foundation, Marcellus I.

Bakersfield College Athletic Foundation ($2,500) see Arkelian Foundation, Ben H. and Gladys

Bakersfield Memorial Hospital ($9,540) see Arkelian Foundation, Ben H. and Gladys

Bakersfield Rescue Mission ($3,600) see Arkelian Foundation, Ben H. and Gladys

Bar Association of San Francisco ($1,000) see Friedman Family Foundation

Bar Association of San Francisco ($10,000) see Furth Foundation

Barbara Sinatra Children's Center at Eisenhower ($2,000) see Broccoli Charitable Foundation, Dana and Albert R.

Barbara Sinatra Children's Center at Eisenhower ($1,000) see Broccoli Charitable Foundation, Dana and Albert R.

Barlow Hospital ($1,000) see Borun Foundation, Anna Borun and Harry

Bay Area Boys and Girls Clubs Fine Arts Programs — after school and summer fine arts programs with local artists as teachers ($50,300) see Gap, The

Bay Area Council — funding for a model project which will provide interaction between four high schools and four community colleges ($25,000) see Hancock Foundation, Luke B.

Bay Area Council for Soviet Jews — funds for the Soviet Jewry Communications and Publications project ($25,000) see Levinson Foundation, Max and Anna

Bay Area Crisis Nursery see Tosco Corp. Refining Division

Bay Area Discovery Museum ($5,000) see Baum Family Fund, Alvin H.

Bay Area Discovery Museum ($3,500) see Baum Family Fund, Alvin H.

Bay Area Discovery Museum ($3,000) see Baum Family Fund, Alvin H.

Bay Area Discovery Museum ($20,000) see Schwab Foundation, Charles and Helen

Bay Area Discovery Museum — towards implementation of their 1991 plans for programming ($25,000) see Jurzykowski Foundation, Alfred

Bay Area Independent Elders Program — coalitions in the San Francisco Bay Area who join together to identify the most pressing needs of frail elders in their communities and find ways to address those needs ($1,200,000) see Kaiser Family Foundation, Henry J.

Bay Area Institute — Pacific News Service ($20,000) see van Loben Sels - Eleanor Slate van Lobel Sels Charitable Foundation, Ernst D.

Bay Area Institute — support of its Youth in the Media Project

($30,000) see Gerbode Foundation, Wallace Alexander

Bay Area Tumor Institute ($30,000) see Gilmore Foundation, William G.

Bay Area Tumor Institute — general support ($25,000) see Lakeside Foundation

Bay Area Women's Philharmonic ($21,000) see Fleishhacker Foundation

Bay Area Women's Philharmonic ($100,000) see Whitaker Fund, Helen F.

Baykeeper ($5,000) see Prairie Foundation

Beckman Laser Institute and Medical Clinic ($100,000) see Beckman Foundation, Arnold and Mabel

Beckman Laser Institute and Medical Clinic ($25,000) see Mead Foundation, Giles W. and Elise G.

Beckman Research Institute, City of Hope ($20,000) see Diabetes Research and Education Foundation

Bel Air Presbyterian Church ($138,500) see Kerr Foundation, A. H.

Bel Air Presbyterian Church ($4,714) see Kerr Foundation, A. H.

Bel Air Presbyterian Church ($4,650) see Kerr Foundation, A. H.

Bellarmine College Preparatory ($75,000) see de Dampierre Memorial Foundation, Marie C.

Bellarmine College Preparatory ($8,000) see Muller Foundation

Bellarmine College Prepartory School ($400,000) see Valley Foundation, Wayne and Gladys

Berkeley Crisis Pregnancy Center ($10,000) see Trust Funds

Berkeley Friends of Baroque Music ($18,000) see Weston Associates/R.C.M. Corp.

Berkeley Hillel Foundation ($10,000) see Meyer Fund, Milton and Sophie

Berkeley Repertory Theatre — bridge to the future campaign ($25,000) see True North Foundation

Berkeley Waterfront ($15,000) see LEF Foundation

Bet Tzedek ($10,000) see Metropolitan Theatres Corp.

Bet Tzedek Legal Services ($400) see Borun Foundation, Anna Borun and Harry

Bethane Theatre ($28,000) see Crean Foundation

Betty Ford Center at Eisenhower ($2,500) see Israel Foundation, A. Cremieux

Betty Ford Foundation ($6,000) see Rales and Ruth Rales Foundation, Norman R.

Beverly Hills Hadassah ($2,500) see National Metal & Steel

Beverly Hills Police Officers Association ($100,000) see Columbia Savings Charitable Foundation

Beverly Hills Presbyterian Church ($3,000) see Berkey Foundation, Peter

Beynon Children's Education Trust ($10,000) see Sizzler International

Beyond Shelter ($360,000) see Columbia Savings Charitable Foundation

Beyond Shelter ($100,000) see Seaver Institute

Biblical Archaeological Society ($4,500) see Fellner Memorial Foundation, Leopold and Clara M.

Bienvenidos Children's Center — care and treatment of abused or neglected children ($3,000) see American Foundation

Big Brothers and Big Sisters ($20,000) see Webb Educational and Charitable Trust, Torrey H. and Dorothy K.

Big Sisters of Los Angeles — general operating support ($26,500) see Mattel

Bighorn Institute ($8,000) see Autry Foundation

Bill Wilson Counseling Center — for purchase and construction of a twelve-bed youth shelter ($20,000) see Stulsaft Foundation, Morris

Biola University — scholarships ($24,000) see Stamps Foundation, James L.

Birthright of San Francisco ($700) see Eaton Foundation, Edwin M. and Gertrude S.

Bishop of Fresno Catholic Diocese ($5,000) see Diener Foundation, Frank C.

Bishop Garcia Diego High School ($10,000) see Wade Endowment Fund, Elizabeth Firth

Bishop O'Dowd High School ($325,000) see Valley Foundation, Wayne and Gladys

Bishop's Ranch — expansion and refurbishment of retreat center ($5,000) see Smith Trust, May and Stanley

Bishop's School ($11,600) see Copley Press

Bishop's School ($50,000) see Ford Foundation, Edward E.

Bishops School ($50,000) see Scripps Foundation, Ellen Browning

Black Business Association of Los Angeles see Great Western Financial Corp.

Blind Children's Center ($5,000) see Bull Foundation, Henry W.

Blind Children's Learning Center — to provide funding for preschool scholarships ($15,000) see Kirchgessner Foundation, Karl

B'nai B'rith ($3,500) see Webb Educational and Charitable Trust, Torrey H. and Dorothy K.

Bob Hope Cultural Center ($25,000) see Autry Foundation

Bob Hope Cultural Center ($50,000) see Columbia Savings Charitable Foundation

Bonnie Doon Elementary School ($10,000) see Osceola Foundation

Border Ecology Project ($9,000) see Abelard Foundation

Borrego Community Health Foundation ($10,000) see Burnand Medical and Educational Foundation, Alphonse A.

Borrego Springs Children's Center ($2,000) see Burnand Medical and Educational Foundation, Alphonse A.

Borrego Springs Educational Scholarship Committee ($6,000) see Burnand Medical and Educational Foundation, Alphonse A.

Borrego Springs Unified School District ($8,650) see Burnand

Medical and Educational Foundation, Alphonse A.

Boy and Girls Scout of Santa Clarita Valley ($10,000) see Rasmussen Foundation

Boy Scouts of America ($20,000) see Arata Brothers Trust

Boy Scouts of America ($115,787) see Argyros Foundation

Boy Scouts of America ($6,000) see Bekins Foundation, Milo W.

Boy Scouts of America ($5,000) see Bing Fund

Boy Scouts of America ($5,000) see Bing Fund

Boy Scouts of America ($23,857) see Bright Family Foundation

Boy Scouts of America ($5,000) see Burns Family Foundation

Boy Scouts of America ($16,000) see Fairfield Foundation, Freeman E.

Boy Scouts of America ($2,000) see Femino Foundation

Boy Scouts of America ($300,000) see Forest Lawn Foundation

Boy Scouts of America ($10,000) see Forest Lawn Foundation

Boy Scouts of America ($10,000) see Gross Charitable Trust, Stella B.

Boy Scouts of America ($17,000) see Halsell Foundation, O. L.

Boy Scouts of America ($20,000) see Montgomery Street Foundation

Boy Scouts of America ($10,000) see Moore Family Foundation

Boy Scouts of America ($4,000) see Nelson Foundation, Florence

Boy Scouts of America ($5,000) see Page Foundation, George B.

Boy Scouts of America ($2,000) see Peery Foundation

Boy Scouts of America ($5,000) see Pratt Memorial Fund

Boy Scouts of America ($15,000) see Rogers Foundation, Mary Stuart

Boy Scouts of America ($11,000) see Sizzler International

Boy Scouts of America ($7,600) see Sizzler International

Boy Scouts of America ($25,000) see Smith Foundation, Lon V.

Boy Scouts of America ($5,000) see Thagard Foundation

Boy Scouts of America — Mount Diablo ($200,000) see Hofmann Co.

Boy Scouts of America-Western Los Angeles ($25,000) see Occidental Petroleum Corp.

Boy Scouts of the Bay Area ($8,750) see U.S. Leasing International

Boys Choir School of Orange County ($20,000) see Hoag Family Foundation, George

Boys Club ($9,600) see Teleklew Productions

Boys Club of America ($55,000) see Beaver Foundation

Boys Club of America ($10,000) see Bellini Foundation

Boys Club of America ($2,250) see Fox Foundation, John H.

Boys Club of America ($10,000) see Friedman Family Foundation

Boys Club of America ($15,000) see Prairie Foundation

Boys Club of Palm Springs ($5,000) see Lindsay Foundation

Boys Club of Palm Springs ($18,000) see Walker Foundation, Smith

Boys Club of Palm Springs ($18,000) see Walker Foundation, Smith

Boys and Girls Club ($6,000) see Bank of A. Levy

Boys and Girls Club ($7,500) see Beaver Foundation

Boys and Girls Club ($16,000) see Beynon Foundation, Kathryne

Boys and Girls Club ($50,000) see Confidence Foundation

Boys and Girls Club ($2,100) see Farallon Foundation

Boys and Girls Club ($17,000) see Halsell Foundation, O. L.

Boys and Girls Club ($8,568) see Howe and Mitchell B. Howe Foundation, Lucite Horton

Boys and Girls Club ($5,000) see Polinsky-Rivkin Family Foundation

Boys and Girls Club ($20,000) see Sandy Foundation, George H.

Boys and Girls Club ($44,500) see Segal Charitable Trust, Barnet

Boys and Girls Club ($8,000) see Stauffer Foundation, John and Beverly

Boys and Girls Club ($1,500) see Upjohn California Fund

Boys and Girls Club ($46,200) see W. W. W. Foundation

Boys and Girls Club of America ($62,500) see Nestle U.S.A. Inc.

Boys and Girls Club of Harbor Area ($10,000) see Hoag Family Foundation, George

Boys and Girls Club — The Key Council ($34,320) see Sun Microsystems

Boys Republic ($10,000) see Hoag Family Foundation, George

Boys Republic ($5,100) see Stillwell Charitable Trust, Glen and Dorothy

Boys Town of Italy — homeless children ($5,250) see Shoong Foundation, Milton

Braille Institute ($250,000) see Forest Lawn Foundation

Braille Institute — building program ($10,000) see Fusenot Charity Foundation, Georges and Germaine

Braille Institute of America ($501) see Martin Foundation, Bert William

Braille Institute of America ($25,000) see Peppers Foundation, Ann

Braille Institute of America ($40,000) see Van Nuys Foundation, I. N. and Susanna H.

Braille Institute — to continue funding of its Pre-School Assistants program ($20,000) see Kirchgessner Foundation, Karl

Branson School ($10,000) see Goodman Foundation, Edward and Marion

Braun Programs ($3,000) see AHS Foundation

Brentwood School ($15,000) see Darling Foundation, Hugh and Hazel

Brentwood Union School District ($500,000) see Cowell Foundation, S. H.

Bridge Focus see Home Depot

Bridge Housing Corporation ($250,000) see Cowell Foundation, S. H.

Bridge Housing Corporation ($150,000) see Cowell Foundation, S. H.

Bridge Housing Corporation ($25,000) see Transamerica Corp.

Buckley School ($10,000) see Disney Family Foundation, Roy

Buckley School ($10,000) see Sasco Foundation

Bureau of Jewish Education ($5,000) see Fellner Memorial Foundation, Leopold and Clara M.

Bureau of Jewish Education ($1,200) see Newman Charitable Trust, Calvin M. and Raquel H.

Bureau of Jewish Education of Greater Los Angeles ($8,200) see Fellner Memorial Foundation, Leopold and Clara M.

Burlingame United Methodist Church — toward costs of repairs ($10,000) see Atkinson Foundation

Business Enterprise Trust ($90,000) see Common Giving Fund

Business Enterprise Trust ($60,000) see Common Giving Fund

Cal Farley's Boys Ranch ($7,500) see Page Foundation, George B.

Cal State Dominguez Hills/Challenger Learning Center — space shuttle replication and science curriculum ($100,000) see Sega of America

Cal Summer School for Arts ($6,000) see Philibosian Foundation, Stephen

Calaveras Library ($5,000) see Tiscornia Foundation

Caleb Project ($2,000) see Morris Charitable Foundation, E. A.

California Academy of Math and Science, California State University at Dominguez Hills — to fund four-year public high school emphasizing math and science ($50,000) see American Honda Motor Co.

California Academy of Mathematics and Science — to support a four-year high school program dedicated to educating women and under-represented minorities in mathematics and science ($50,000) see Toyota Motor Sales, U.S.A.

California Academy of Science ($500,000) see Herbst Foundation

California Academy of Science ($50,000) see Hume Foundation, Jaquelin

California Academy of Science ($76,300) see Osher Foundation, Bernard

California Academy of Sciences ($11,500) see Foster-Davis Foundation

California Academy of Sciences ($5,000) see Littlefield Foundation, Edmund Wattis

California Academy of Sciences ($2,500) see Llagas Foundation

California Academy of Sciences ($12,500) see Uvas Foundation

California Academy of Sciences Department of Entomology ($250,000) see Schlinger Foundation

California Agricultural Leadership Foundation ($2,500) see Clougherty Charitable Trust, Francis H.

California Arboretum Foundation ($250,000) see Garland Foundation, John Jewett and H. Chandler

California Armenian Home ($50,000) see Peters Foundation, Leon S.

California Baptist Church College ($1,500) see Bourns, Inc.

California Baptist College ($1,500) see Bourns, Inc.

California Channel ($8,000) see Lea Foundation, Helen Sperry

California Channel — toward the first-year capitalization and operating budget for CAL-SPAN, the governmental affairs cable television network for California ($300,000) see Irvine Foundation, James

California Christian Home ($10,000) see Ebell of Los Angeles Rest Cottage Association

California Christian Home ($30,000) see Ebell of Los Angeles Scholarship Endowment Fund

California College of Arts and Crafts ($25,000) see Clorox Co.

California College of Arts and Crafts ($30,000) see Simpson PSB Foundation

California Community Foundation — arts support ($100,000) see Banyan Tree Foundation

California Community Foundation ($150,000) see Bauer Foundation, M. R.

California Community Foundation ($64,132) see Dunning Foundation

California Community Foundation ($20,000) see Durfee Foundation

California Community Foundation ($250) see Hench Foundation, John C.

California Confederation of the Arts — support, over a three-year period, of its Media Outreach Program ($30,000) see Gerbode Foundation, Wallace Alexander

California Educational Initiatives Fund ($25,000) see Union Bank

California Educational Initiatives Fund — foundation-initiated grant for the 1992/1993 school year California grants program ($70,000) see First Interstate Bank of California

California Educational Initiatives Fund, San Francisco, CA ($25,000) see McDonnell Douglas Corp.-West

California Foundation for the Improvement of Employer-Employee Relations — to provide training, networking, and research services ($250,000) see Stuart Foundations

California Foundation for the Retarded ($4,000) see American President Cos.

California Foundation for the Retarded ($100) see Dreyer's & Edy's Grand Ice Cream

California Foundation for the Retarded — Day Training Activity Center ($15,000) see Odell and Helen Pfeiffer Odell Fund, Robert Stewart

California Handicapped Skiers ($5,000) see Hoffman Foundation, H. Leslie Hoffman and Elaine S.

California Home for the Aged ($750,000) see Lincy Foundation

California Home for the Deaf ($5,000) see Pfaffinger Foundation

California Hospital Medical Center ($1,000,000) see Leavey Foundation, Thomas and Dorothy

California Housing Partnership Corporation see Great Western Financial Corp.

California Institute of the Arts ($40,000) see Blum-Kovler Foundation

California Institute of Arts ($630,000) see Disney Family Foundation, Roy

California Institute of Arts ($500,540) see Lund Foundation

California Institute of Arts ($75,000) see Newhall Foundation, Henry Mayo

California Institute of the Arts — general operations ($500,000) see Disney Co., Walt

California Institute of the Arts — character animation program ($50,000) see Disney Co., Walt

California Institute of the Arts — character animation program equipment ($50,000) see Disney Co., Walt

California Institute of the Arts — to support collaborations between the Institute and community-based arts groups ($150,000) see Cummings Foundation, Nathan

California Institute of the Arts — scholarship support 1991-92 ($260,000) see Ahmanson Foundation

California Institute of the Arts — matched ticket sales benefit premier "Rescuers Down Under" ($150,000) see Disney Co., Walt

California Institute of Technology ($235,663) see American Telephone & Telegraph Co.

California Institute of Technology ($10,000) see Associated Foundations

California Institute of Technology ($100,000) see BankAmerica Corp.

California Institute of Technology — develop automated human chromosomal mapper ($300,000) see Baxter Foundation, Donald E. and Delia B.

California Institute of Technology ($3,460,000) see Beckman Foundation, Arnold and Mabel

California Institute of Technology ($100,000) see Booth Ferris Foundation

California Institute of Technology ($84,000) see

California (cont.)

Bowles and Robert Bowles Memorial Fund, Ethel Wilson

California Institute of Technology ($300,000) see Bren Foundation, Donald L.

California Institute of Technology ($19,000) see California Foundation for Biochemical Research

California Institute of Technology — cancer research ($50,000) see Early Medical Research Trust, Margaret E.

California Institute of Technology ($4,500) see Essick Foundation

California Institute of Technology — distinguished scholars program ($925,000) see Fairchild Foundation, Sherman

California Institute of Technology ($6,000) see Fusenot Charity Foundation, Georges and Germaine

California Institute of Technology ($350,000) see Gates Foundation

California Institute of Technology ($250,000) see Glanville Family Foundation

California Institute of Technology ($100,000) see Golden Family Foundation

California Institute of Technology ($4,000) see Kingsley Foundation, Lewis A.

California Institute of Technology ($45,000) see Knudsen Foundation, Tom and Valley

California Institute of Technology ($1,000) see Linde Foundation, Ronald and Maxine

California Institute of Technology ($10,500) see Monticello College Foundation

California Institute of Technology ($20,000) see Neu Foundation, Hugo and Doris

California Institute of Technology — to micromachine integrated microdevices ($500,000) see Packard Foundation, David and Lucile

California Institute of Technology ($63,375) see Pasadena Area Residential Aid

California Institute of Technology ($15,000) see Peppers Foundation, Ann

California Institute of Technology ($40,000) see Pfeiffer Research Foundation, Gustavus and Louise

California Institute of Technology ($608,750) see Powell Foundation, Charles Lee

California Institute of Technology ($5,000) see Robinson Foundation

California Institute of Technology ($150,000) see Schlinger Foundation

California Institute of Technology ($15,000) see Schlumberger Ltd.

California Institute of Technology ($400,000) see Seaver Institute

California Institute of Technology ($100,000) see Texaco

California Institute of Technology ($100,000) see Unocal Corp.

California Institute of Technology ($36,429) see Van Nuys Foundation, I. N. and Susanna H.

California Institute of Technology ($250,000) see Watson Foundation, Thomas J.

California Institute of Technology — postdoctoral fellows support in neurology ($75,000) see Webb Foundation, Del E.

California Institute of Technology — Biological Imaging Center ($250,000) see Jones Foundation, Fletcher

California Institute of Technology — Center for Computational Research in Biology ($262,000) see Fairchild Foundation, Sherman

California Institute of Technology, Division of Earth and Planetary Sciences ($45,000) see Schlumberger Ltd.

California Institute of Technology — matching grant to fund research on the expression of human visual genes in Drosphilia to be conducted by Dr. Seymour Benzer ($18,000) see Kirchgessner Foundation, Karl

California Institute of Technology — to establish the Earthquake Media and Exhibit Center ($150,000) see Times Mirror Co.

California Institute of Technology — support development of Gene Analyzer for DNA research ($200,000) see Whittier Foundation, L. K.

California Institute of Technology Industrial Relations Center ($20,000) see Peppers Foundation, Ann

California Institute of Technology — Office of the President ($75,000) see Norris Foundation, Kenneth T. and Eileen L.

California Institute of Technology — Science and Engineering Scholarships ($15,000) see Peppers Foundation, Ann

California Institute of Technology — for a biological research study, How the Gene Regulatory System Transforms an Egg into an Embryo ($333,000) see Parsons Foundation, Ralph M.

California Institute of Technology — "TERRAscope" earthquake-monitoring network for Southern California ($1,000,000) see ARCO

California Institute of Technology — Undergraduate Biological Sciences Education Program ($2,000,000) see Hughes Medical Institute, Howard

California Institute of Technology — support Whittier Advanced Geophysical Observatory ($495,410) see Whittier Foundation, L. K.

California International Sailing Association — general operating support ($66,667) see Avis Inc.

California International Sailing Association ($25,000) see Philips Foundation, Jesse

California International Sailing Association ($25,000) see Philips Foundation, Jesse

California International Studies Project ($39,713) see Industrial Bank of Japan Trust Co.

California Jesuit Missionaries ($2,000) see Diener Foundation, Frank C.

California Marine Mammal Center ($10,000) see Doelger Charitable Trust, Thelma

California Museum Associates ($5,000) see Pauley Foundation, Edwin W.

California Museum Foundation ($5,000) see Sizzler International

California Museum of Photography ($25,000) see Warhol Foundation for the Visual Arts, Andy

California Museum of Science and Industry ($6,000) see Bekins Foundation, Milo W.

California Nature Conservancy ($400) see Borun Foundation, Anna Borun and Harry

California Nature Conservancy ($2,000) see Luster Family Foundation

California Neighborhood Housing Services Foundation ($20,000) see Union Bank

California Pacific Medical Center — research in limb preservation ($75,000) see Drown Foundation, Joseph

California Pacific Medical Center ($809,099) see Hartford Foundation, John A.

California Pacific Medical Center Foundation ($15,000) see Wilbur-Ellis Co.

California Parkinsons Foundation ($200,000) see Ostern Foundation

California Parkinson's Foundation ($26,000) see Strauss Foundation, Leon

California Parkinson's Foundation ($26,000) see Strauss Foundation, Leon

California Polytechnic State University ($110,176) see Pacific Telesis Group

California Polytechnic State University see Tandem Computers

California Polytechnic University School of Business ($2,000) see Long Foundation, J.M.

California Province of Society of Jesus ($2,000) see Sattler Beneficial Trust, Daniel A. and Edna J.

California Rural Legal Assistance Foundation ($8,000) see Abelard Foundation

California School of Professional Psychology ($45,963) see Simon Foundation, Robert Ellis

California Society of Pioneers ($40,000) see Wells Fargo & Co.

California Special Olympics ($5,000) see Essick Foundation

California Spinal Cord Injury Network ($10,000) see Luster Family Foundation

California State Bakersfield Foundation ($13,000) see Arkelian Foundation, Ben H. and Gladys

California State Polytechnic University ($25,000) see Sizzler International

California State Polytechnic University, Pomona — Laboratory Revitalization Project ($40,000) see Fluor Corp.

California State Summer School Arts Foundation ($85,000) see Burlington Resources

California State University ($18,000) see Bright Family Foundation

California State University ($5,000) see Bright Family Foundation

California State University ($2,400) see California Foundation for Biochemical Research

California State University ($35,200) see Peters Foundation, Leon S.

California State University ($35,000) see Rogers Foundation, Mary Stuart

California State University ($21,500) see Stern Memorial Trust, Sidney

California State University ($8,000) see Technical Foundation of America

California State University — capital grant ($75,000) see Times Mirror Co.

California State University — payment on $1 million pledge to support the establishment and continuing operation of the California Academy of Math and Science ($100,000) see TRW Corp.

California State University, Chico ($2,000) see Long Foundation, J.M.

California State University, Chico Foundation ($150,000) see Pacific Telesis Group

California State University, Chico Foundation ($110,176) see Pacific Telesis Group

California State University Foundation ($50,000) see Miller Foundation, Earl B. and Loraine H.

California State University Fresno Foundation ($25,000) see Heublein

California State University Fresno Foundation ($45,000) see Radin Foundation

California State University Los Angeles ($25,000) see MCA

California State University, Northridge ($20,000) see Collins & Aikman Holdings Corp.

California State University, Northridge — to establish a laboratory in the School of Education for training science and mathematics teachers see Keck Foundation, W. M.

California State University-San Jose ($1,253,932) see Hewlett-Packard Co.

California State University Stanislaus ($101,000) see Ernest & Julio Gallo Winery

California Tomorrow ($25,000) see Connell Foundation, Michael J.

California, University of Berkeley — support for three years for the Consortium on Competitiveness and Cooperation at Berkeley, Columbia, Stanford,

Harvard/MIT ($1,486,125) see Sloan Foundation, Alfred P.

California Waterfowl Association ($20,000) see Witter Foundation, Dean

California Wildlife Protection ($10,000) see Wouk Foundation, Abe

CALM ($15,000) see Jackson Family Foundation, Ann

CalTech — payment on $750,000 pledge to support the R. F. Mettler Chair of Engineering and Applied Science ($150,000) see TRW Corp.

Camp Hess Kramer ($25,000) see Irmas Charitable Foundation, Audrey and Sydney

Campaign for Scripps ($25,000) see Ishiyama Foundation

Campbell Hall School ($10,000) see Von der Ahe Foundation

Campus Crusade for Christ ($100) see Arbie Mineral Feed Co.

Campus Crusade for Christ ($32,300) see Atkinson Foundation, Myrtle L.

Campus Crusade for Christ — staff support ($36,925) see Brown Charitable Trust, Dora Maclellan

Campus Crusade for Christ ($5,200) see Demco Charitable Foundation

Campus Crusade for Christ ($5,000) see Fruehauf Foundation

Campus Crusade for Christ ($3,000) see Getsch Family Foundation Trust

Campus Crusade for Christ ($20,000) see Lamb Foundation, Kirkland S. and Rena B.

Campus Crusade for Christ ($15,000) see Leu Foundation

Campus Crusade for Christ — working capital ($250,000) see Maclellan Foundation

Campus Crusade for Christ ($18,860) see Marshburn Foundation

Campus Crusade for Christ ($15,182) see Meland Outreach

Campus Crusade for Christ ($40,000) see Overstreet Foundation

Campus Crusade for Christ ($61,200) see Paulstan

Campus Crusade for Christ ($200,000) see Stranahan Foundation

Campus Crusade for Christ ($30,000) see 28:19

Campus Crusade for Christ ($10,000) see Ware Foundation

Campus Crusade for Christ ($20,050) see Word Investments

Campus Crusade for Christ ($1,000) see Youth Foundation

Campus Crusade for Christ International — Arrowhead Springs ($100,000) see Chatlos Foundation

Canary Islands Gospel Mission ($10,620) see Kerr Foundation, A. H.

Cancer Foundation of Santa Barbara ($5,000) see Page Foundation, George B.

Cancer Foundation of Santa Barbara ($23,600) see Sattler Beneficial Trust, Daniel A. and Edna J.

Cancer Foundation of Santa Barbara ($20,000) see Wood-Claeyssens Foundation

Cancer Foundation, Santa Barbara, CA see Kmart Corp.

Canine Companions for Independence ($5,000) see Beim Foundation

Canine Companions for Independence ($7,000) see Burnand Medical and Educational Foundation, Alphonse A.

Canine Companions for Independence ($7,000) see Copley Press

Canine Companions for Independence — handicapped assistance programs ($15,000) see Dreyfus Foundation, Max and Victoria

Canine Companions for Independence — support of a dog ($3,000) see Exchange Bank

Canine Companions for Independence ($12,500) see Hubbard Foundation, R. Dee and Joan Dale

Capp Street Project ($25,000) see Warhol Foundation for the Visual Arts, Andy

Cardiovascular Institute ($5,000) see Arell Foundation

CARE Education Endowment Fund ($250,000) see Banyan Tree Foundation

Carina ($13,761) see Saturno Foundation

Caring for Children ($12,500) see Davies Charitable Trust

Caring for Children ($1,000) see Newman Charitable Trust, Calvin M. and Raquel H.

Caring for Children — program for emotionally disturbed children ($5,000) see Smith Trust, May and Stanley

Carmel Music Society ($26,000) see Segal Charitable Trust, Barnet

Carriage Museum ($11,000) see Mosher Foundation, Samuel B.

Casa de Amparo ($15,000) see Teleklew Productions

Casa De LasAmigas ($10,000) see Beynon Foundation, Kathryne

Casa for Riverside County ($1,500) see Borun Foundation, Anna Borun and Harry

Casa Youth Center ($35,000) see Halsell Foundation, O. L.

Casa Youth Shelter ($5,000) see Vesper Corp.

Castilleja School ($50,200) see Arrillaga Foundation

Catalina Conservancy ($105,000) see Offield Family Foundation

CATE ($10,000) see Crummer Foundation, Roy E.

Cate School — capital campaign ($50,000) see Boswell Foundation, James G.

Cate School ($15,000) see Littlefield Foundation, Edmund Wattis

Cate School ($5,000) see Sprague, Jr. Foundation, Caryll M. and Norman F.

Cate School ($12,000) see Wilbur-Ellis Co.

Catholic Charities ($19,200) see Fairfield Foundation, Freeman E.

Catholic Charities ($5,000) see Gallo Foundation, Julio R.

Catholic Charities ($20,000) see Gross Charitable Trust, Stella B.

Catholic Charities ($25,000) see Hale Foundation, Crescent Porter

Catholic Charities ($17,500) see Hayden Foundation, William R. and Virginia

Catholic Charities — home care program ($15,000) see Odell and Helen Pfeiffer Odell Fund, Robert Stewart

Catholic Charities ($10,000) see Pacific Western Foundation

Catholic Charities — job placement for the mentally ill ($32,562) see Sun Microsystems

Catholic Charities ($10,000) see van Loben Sels - Eleanor Slate van Lobel Sels Charitable Foundation, Ernst D.

Catholic Charities of Los Angeles — Angel's Flight Program ($170,000) see Bettingen Corporation, Burton G.

Catholic Charities of Los Angeles — Good Shepherd Center ($200,000) see Bettingen Corporation, Burton G.

Catholic Health Association of the United States ($8,000) see Teleklew Productions

Catholic Relief Services ($50,000) see Snite Foundation, Fred B.

Catholic Relief Services ($10,000) see Von der Ahe Foundation

Catholic Relief Services ($10,000) see Von der Ahe, Jr. Trust, Theodore Albert

Catholic Social Services ($10,000) see Von der Ahe Foundation

Catholic Social Services ($10,000) see Von der Ahe, Jr. Trust, Theodore Albert

Cedars Development Foundation — capital support ($10,000) see Bank of America - Giannini Foundation

Cedars-Sinai Medical Center ($60,000) see Andreas Foundation

Cedars-Sinai Medical Center ($50,000) see Bannerman Foundation, William C.

Cedars-Sinai Medical Center ($10,000) see Broccoli Charitable Foundation, Dana and Albert R.

Cedars-Sinai Medical Center ($5,500) see Buchalter, Nemer, Fields, & Younger

Cedars-Sinai Medical Center ($7,024) see Cedars-Sinai Medical Center Section D Fund

Cedars-Sinai Medical Center ($6,000) see Coleman Foundation

Cedars-Sinai Medical Center ($9,000) see Domino of California

Cedars-Sinai Medical Center ($25,000) see Douglas Charitable Foundation

Cedars-Sinai Medical Center — cancer research ($50,000) see Early Medical Research Trust, Margaret E.

Cedars Sinai Medical Center ($102,000) see Factor Family Foundation, Max

Cedars-Sinai Medical Center ($61,820) see Feintech Foundation

Cedars-Sinai Medical Center ($82,600) see Irmas Charitable Foundation, Audrey and Sydney

Cedars-Sinai Medical Center ($1,000,000) see Max Charitable Foundation

Cedars-Sinai Medical Center ($9,000) see Petersen Foundation, Esper A.

Cedars-Sinai Medical Center ($5,500) see Petersen Foundation, Esper A.

Cedars-Sinai Medical Center ($4,500) see Shapell Foundation, Nathan and Lilly

Cedars-Sinai Medical Center ($25,000) see Strauss Foundation

Cedars-Sinai Medical Center ($25,000) see Strauss Foundation

Cedars-Sinai Medical Center ($25,000) see Strauss Foundation

Cedars-Sinai Medical Center ($2,000) see Weintraub Family Foundation, Joseph

Cedars-Sinai Medical Center ($202,650) see Weisz Foundation, David and Sylvia

Cedars-Sinai Medical Center ($101,000) see Western Cardiac Foundation

Cedars-Sinai Medical Center — State of Israel Bonds ($25,000) see Price Foundation, Louis and Harold

Celia and Harold Littenberg Foundation ($25,000) see Feintech Foundation

Centenila Hospital Foundation ($25,000) see Goldsmith Family Foundation

Center for Asian-Pacific Affairs ($10,000) see Wilbur-Ellis Co.

Center for Children ($5,000) see Benbough Foundation, Legler

Center for Children see San Diego Trust & Savings Bank

Center for Community Advocacy — Farm Worker Housing project ($69,000) see Rosenberg Foundation

Center for Economic Policy Research ($10,000) see Moore Family Foundation

Center for Economic Policy Research ($50,000) see Witter Foundation, Dean

Center for Elderly Suicide Prevention and Grief Related Services — to evaluate the effectiveness and efficiency of three intervention techniques in the prevention of suicide in older adults ($271,550) see Retirement Research Foundation

Center for the Family in Transition — underachievement among teens program ($94,943) see Johnson Foundation, Walter S.

Center for Family in Transition ($15,000) see van Loben Sels - Eleanor Slate van Lobel Sels Charitable Foundation, Ernst D.

Center for Independent Living ($5,000) see Margoes Foundation

Center for Individual Recovery Services ($40,000) see Prickett Fund, Lynn R. and Karl E.

Center for Investigative Reporting — to support investigation of the environmental backlash movement ($105,000) see Schumann Foundation, Florence and John

Center for Investigative Reporting ($4,000) see Seven Springs Foundation

Center for Living Skills ($4,500) see Farallon Foundation

Center for Motion Picture Study ($20,000) see Douglas Charitable Foundation

Center for Natural Lands Management ($5,000) see Teichert

Center for Neurologic Study — ALS Research ($58,333) see Drown Foundation, Joseph

Center for Neurological Study ($65,000) see Thagard Foundation

Center for a New Democracy — Tides Foundation - to study the decline of party competition in American political life and devise solutions at state and local levels ($75,000) see Arca Foundation

Center for the Partially Sighted ($7,500) see Bull Foundation, Henry W.

Center for Policy Development ($5,000) see Seven Springs Foundation

Center to Prevent Handgun Violence — to help Oakland students to prevent firearm violence ($15,000) see Stulsaft Foundation, Morris

Center for Senior Employment ($10,000) see Gallo Foundation, Julio R.

Center Theatre Group — special grant for performances ($250,000) see ARCO

Center for Third World Organizing — for People United for a Better Oakland/Youth of Oakland United ($20,000) see Hazen Foundation, Edward W.

Center for US/USSR Initiatives ($75,000) see Trust for Mutual Understanding

Centinela Hospital ($13,500) see Shea Foundation

Central Catholic High School ($10,875) see Gallo Foundation, Ernest

Central City Hospitality House — to support journalism interns ($5,496) see Lux Foundation, Miranda

Central City Hospitality House ($5,000) see Wilsey Bennet Co.

Central Coast Visiting Nurses Association ($1,500) see Upjohn California Fund

Central Valley Amputee Support Group ($5,000) see Gallo Foundation, Julio R.

Centro de Ninos see Great Western Financial Corp.

Century High School ($100) see Alhambra Foundry Co., Ltd.

Century High School see Ricoh Electronics Inc.

Chabad House ($5,000) see Goodman Foundation, Edward and Marion

Channel 6 (KVIE) ($25,000) see Arata Brothers Trust

Chanticlear ($21,000) see Fleishhacker Foundation

Chaplaincy Program/Stanford Hospital ($8,000) see Atkinson Foundation, Myrtle L.

Chapman College ($68,675) see Argyros Foundation

Chapman College ($175,000) see Muth Foundation, Peter and Mary

Chapman University — to renovate the science lecture/demonstration hall and purchase equipment for the Division of Natural and Applied Sciences ($500,000) see Irvine Foundation, James

Charles Armstrong School ($20,000) see Oxnard Foundation

Charles Armstrong School ($500) see Schwab Foundation, Charles and Helen

Chestnut Fund — support to remodel a residence for university students ($25,000) see Clover Foundation

Child Abuse Council of Sacramento ($25,036) see Haigh-Scatena Foundation

Child Care Employee Project ($10,000) see Abelard Foundation

Child Care Employee Project — to help pay the salary of a development director ($35,000) see Rockefeller Family Fund

Child Development Center Emergency Rescue Fund — subsidy of child care costs of Mt. Sac students who are low income, single, needy parents ($5,000) see American Foundation

Child Help USA ($2,500) see See Foundation, Charles

Child S.H.A.R.E. Program ($40,000) see Smith Foundation, Lon V.

Child Victims in Court Foundation ($400,000) see Taper Foundation, Mark

Childhelp U.S.A. ($2,000) see City of Hope 1989 Section E Foundation

Childhelp USA ($11,500) see Stauffer Foundation, John and Beverly

Children of the Night ($300,000) see Bettingen Corporation, Burton G.

Children Now — communications program ($75,000) see Drown Foundation, Joseph

Children Now ($40,000) see W. W. Foundation

Children Now — Building a Child Support System for the Twenty-first Century project ($75,000) see Rosenberg Foundation

Children's Action Network ($250,000) see Aetna Life & Casualty Co.

Children's Bureau of Los Angeles ($7,900) see Norman/Nethercutt Foundation, Merle

Children's Bureau of Los Angeles ($12,000) see Stillwell Charitable Trust, Glen and Dorothy

Children's Bureau of Los Angeles — for continued support of the Family Connection Program ($150,000) see Stuart Foundations

Children's Cancer Research Institute — travel fund ($20,000) see Davis Foundation, Edwin W. and Catherine M.

Children's Club Assistance League ($5,000) see Ragen, Jr. Memorial Fund Trust No. 1, James M.

Children's Council of San Francisco — for coordinator for Bayview/Hunters Point children's programs ($15,000) see Stulsaft Foundation, Morris

Children's Dental Clinic ($20,000) see Fairfield Foundation, Freeman E.

California (cont.)

Children's Diabetes Foundation at Denver ($25,000) see Chartwell Foundation

Children's Discovery Museums ($5,000) see GenRad

Children's Garden ($5,000) see See Foundation, Charles

Children's Health Council — child development and prevention services ($77,222) see Johnson Foundation, Walter S.

Children's Health Council Summer Symphony ($15,000) see Walker Foundation, T. B.

Children's Home Society of California ($10,000) see Bireley Foundation

Children's Home Society of California ($59,891) see Herbst Foundation

Children's Home Society of California — Foster Family Care Program ($15,000) see Odell and Helen Pfeiffer Odell Fund, Robert Stewart

Children's Hospital ($20,000) see Borchard Foundation, Albert and Elaine

Children's Hospital ($100,000) see Burns Foundation, Fritz B.

Children's Hospital ($15,000) see Halsell Foundation, O. L.

Children's Hospital ($11,000) see Howe and Mitchell B. Howe Foundation, Lucite Horton

Children's Hospital ($25,000) see McAlister Charitable Foundation, Harold

Children's Hospital ($14,662) see Mead Foundation, Giles W. and Elise G.

Children's Hospital ($232,800) see Murphy Foundation, Dan

Children's Hospital ($15,000) see Rogers Foundation, Mary Stuart

Childrens Hospital see San Diego Trust & Savings Bank

Children's Hospital ($7,500) see Sunshine Biscuits

Children's Hospital ($200,000) see Taper Foundation, Mark

Children's Hospital Foundation ($30,000) see Masserini Charitable Trust, Maurice J.

Children's Hospital Foundation of Los Angeles see Great Western Financial Corp.

Children's Hospital Foundation of Orange County — capital campaign ($25,000) see Fluor Corp.

Children's Hospital and Health Center — to create in interagency collaborative system ($240,636) see Stuart Foundations

Children's Hospital Los Angeles ($16,000) see Bekins Foundation, Milo W.

Children's Hospital of Los Angeles ($66,000) see Bowles and Robert Bowles Memorial Fund, Ethel Wilson

Children's Hospital of Los Angeles ($20,000) see Braun Foundation

Children's Hospital of Los Angeles ($100,000) see Connell Foundation, Michael J.

Children's Hospital of Los Angeles — cancer research ($50,000) see Early Medical Research Trust, Margaret E.

Children's Hospital of Los Angeles — cancer research

($50,000) see Early Medical Research Trust, Margaret E.

Children's Hospital of Los Angeles ($150,000) see Garland Foundation, John Jewett and H. Chandler

Children's Hospital of Los Angeles ($3,000) see Jerome Foundation

Children's Hospital of Los Angeles — toward construction costs of Imaging and Diagnosis Center ($1,000,000) see Weingart Foundation

Children's Hospital of Los Angeles — toward construction and outfitting of the new six-story Outpatient Tower ($500,000) see Ahmanson Foundation

Children's Hospital Medical Center ($50,000) see Bireley Foundation

Children's Hospital Medical Center ($30,000) see Bireley Foundation

Children's Hospital Medical Center ($30,000) see Bireley Foundation

Children's Hospital Medical Center ($24,491) see Brunetti Charitable Trust, Dionigi

Children's Hospital Medical Center ($15,000) see Rogers Foundation, Mary Stuart

Children's Hospital Medical Center ($20,000) see Stuart Foundation, Elbridge and Evelyn

Children's Hospital Medical Center ($25,000) see Van Nuys Charities, J. B. and Emily

Children's Hospital Medical Center ($43,724) see Van Nuys Foundation, I. N. and Susanna H.

Children's Hospital of Orange ($5,000) see Jerome Foundation

Children's Hospital — San Diego ($4,000) see City of Hope 1989 Section E Foundation

Children's Hospital of San Francisco Foundation ($30,000) see Herbst Foundation

Children's Hospital of Stanford ($66,000) see Bowles and Robert Bowles Memorial Fund, Ethel Wilson

Children's Hospital at Stanford ($25,000) see Gallo Foundation, Ernest

Children's Hospital at Stanford ($1,000) see Ishiyama Foundation

Children's Institute International ($6,500) see Sprague, Jr. Foundation, Caryll M. and Norman F.

Children's Self Help ($10,000) see Van Camp Foundation

Children's Self-Help Center ($20,000) see Van Camp Foundation

Children's Television and Research Education Center — general support ($40,000) see Warsh-Mott Legacy

Chinese for Affirmative Action ($10,000) see Tang Foundation

Choices for Change — publish teacher training manuals for educational programs in abuse education and intervention ($2,500) see Exchange Bank

Chriopic Institute ($1,000) see Agape Foundation

Christian Anti-Communism Crusade ($150,000) see Kirby Foundation, F. M.

Christian Brothers ($1,000) see Diener Foundation, Frank C.

Christian National Partner ($5,050) see Meland Outreach

Christian World Publishers ($19,500) see Meland Outreach

Christian World Publishers ($10,000) see Tyndale House Foundation

Church Divinity School of Pacific ($16,833) see Society for the Increase of the Ministry

Church Divinity School of Pacific ($13,972) see Society for the Increase of the Ministry

Church of Latter Day Saints ($13,560) see Peery Foundation

Church on the Way ($100,000) see Boeckmann Charitable Foundation

CIL Computer Training — capital support ($15,000) see Bank of America - Giannini Foundation

Cities in Schools ($50,000) see Chartwell Foundation

Citizens Scholarship Fund America ($29,560) see McKesson Corp.

Citrus College Child Development Center — subsidy of child care costs of Citrus College students who are low income, single, needy parents ($5,000) see American Foundation

City of Beverly Hills ($15,000) see Green Foundation, Burton E.

City Celebration ($21,000) see Fleishhacker Foundation

City Celebration ($40,000) see McKesson Corp.

City of Daly City — recreational facilities improvements ($10,000) see Gellert Foundation, Carl

City of Daly City ($32,100) see Gellert Foundation, Fred

City of Downey — purchase of organ ($65,000) see Stamps Foundation, James L.

City of Englewood Board of Education ($2,000) see Kajima International, Inc.

City of Fresno ($30,000) see Cobb Family Foundation

City of Hope ($10,000) see Altschul Foundation

City of Hope ($500) see American Building Maintenance Industries

City of Hope ($300,000) see Beckman Foundation, Arnold and Mabel

City of Hope ($66,000) see Bowles and Robert Bowles Memorial Fund, Ethel Wilson

City of Hope ($11,000) see Brotman Foundation of California

City of Hope ($30,000) see California Foundation for Biochemical Research

City of Hope ($20,000) see City of Hope 1989 Section E Foundation

City of Hope ($10,000) see Lastfogel Foundation, Abe and Frances

City of Hope — civic ($50,000) see Mann Foundation, Ted

City of Hope ($2,500) see Marcus Brothers Textiles Inc.

City of Hope ($200,000) see Parvin Foundation, Albert

City of Hope ($30,000) see Strauss Foundation, Leon

City of Hope ($30,000) see Strauss Foundation, Leon

City of Hope ($17,000) see Valspar Corp.

City of Hope — support of medical services for children without insurance coverage ($600,000) see Weingart Foundation

City of Hope ($10,000) see Weisz Foundation, David and Sylvia

City of Hope ($59,398) see Ziegler Foundation, Ruth/Allen

City of Monterey — sports center building fund ($100,000) see Segal Charitable Trust, Barnet

City of San Buenaventura ($5,000) see Bank of A. Levy

City of San Jose — funding for the City of San Jose Mayor's College Motivation Program ($30,000) see Hancock Foundation, Luke B.

City of Santa Barbara Rose Garden ($5,000) see Wade Endowment Fund, Elizabeth Firth

City Team Ministries — funds toward relocation and program expansion ($100,000) see Valley Foundation

City of Yreka — recreation center improvements ($128,500) see McConnell Foundation

Clair Burgener Foundation for Developmentally Disabled ($4,000) see Burnand Medical and Educational Foundation, Alphonse A.

Clairbourn School ($16,500) see Robinson Foundation

Clare Foundation — capital support ($10,000) see Bank of America - Giannini Foundation

Claremont College ($2,500) see American Building Maintenance Industries

Claremont Graduate School, Center for Politics and Policy ($70,360) see Haynes Foundation, John Randolph and Dora

Claremont Institute for the Study of Statesmanship and ($100,000) see Aequus Institute

Claremont Institute for Study of Statesmanship and Political Philosophy — seminar for teachers on the founding principles ($175,000) see Salvatori Foundation, Henry

Claremont McKenna College — salaries ($50,000) see Athwin Foundation

Claremont McKenna College — science pledge ($50,000) see Athwin Foundation

Claremont McKenna College ($250,000) see Burns Foundation, Fritz B.

Claremont McKenna College ($120,000) see Day Foundation, Willametta K.

Claremont McKenna College ($12,500) see Day Foundation, Willametta K.

Claremont McKenna College — computer equipment ($220,000) see Jones Foundation, Fletcher

Claremont McKenna College ($9,000) see Lebus Trust, Bertha

Claremont McKenna College — achievement awards pledge ($330,000) see McKenna Foundation, Philip M.

Claremont McKenna College — science center pledge ($200,000) see McKenna Foundation, Philip M.

Claremont McKenna College ($25,000) see Pickford Foundation, Mary

Claremont McKenna College ($50,000) see Tuohy Foundation, Alice Tweed

Claremont McKenna College ($2,000) see Warner Foundation, Lee and Rose

Claremont McKenna College Bauer Center — scholarship fund ($1,002,000) see Berger Foundation, H.N. and Frances C.

Claremont University Center ($25,000) see Moskowitz Foundation, Irving I.

Claremont University Center ($12,500) see Wilbur-Ellis Co.

Claremont University Center — toward an endowment fund for book acquisitions for the Honnold and Seeley G. Mudd libraries ($450,000) see Ahmanson Foundation

Claremount McKenna College — endowment of scholarship funds ($100,000) see Litton Industries

Cloistered Carmelite Monastery ($50,000) see Hayden Foundation, William R. and Virginia

Clovis Unified School District — literacy insurance for tomorrow program ($65,670) see Johnson Foundation, Walter S.

Coalition for Elders' Independence — toward the start-up of Coalition for Elders' Independence ($50,000) see Haas, Jr. Fund, Evelyn and Walter

Coalition on Environmental and Occupational Health Hazards ($10,000) see Beldon II Fund

Coalition for Immigrant and Refugee Rights ($8,000) see Ben & Jerry's Homemade

Coastside Youth Center Project — in general support for new organization ($15,000) see Atkinson Foundation

Coleman Chamber Music Association ($2,500) see Scott Foundation, Virginia Steele

Collectors Forum ($2,500) see DiRosa Foundation, Rene and Veronica

College of the Canyon Foundation ($1,800) see Rasmussen Foundation

College of Canyons ($25,253) see Newhall Foundation, Henry Mayo

College of Marin ($15,000) see Sandy Foundation, George H.

College of Notre Dame ($25,000) see Drum Foundation

College of Notre Dame ($10,000) see Gellert Foundation, Carl

College of Notre Dame ($150,000) see Gleason Foundation, Katherine

College of Notre Dame ($30,000) see Hale Foundation, Crescent Porter

College of Notre Dame ($30,000) see Ritter Foundation, May Ellen and Gerald

College of Notre Dame ($5,300) see Taube Family Foundation

College of Notre Dame ($10,093) see Trust Funds

College Preparatory School
($50,000) see Ford
Foundation, Edward E.

College Preparatory School —
construction of two classrooms
($100,000) see Irwin Charity
Foundation, William G.

Columbia Park Boys Club —
clothing samples sales to raise
funds for Boys Club in San
Francisco ($220,000) see Gap,
The

Coming Together Foundation
($3,500) see Poinsettia
Foundation, Paul and
Magdalena Ecke

Commonweal ($10,000) see
Central National-Gottesman

Commonweal ($50,000) see
Pinewood Foundation

Commonweal — support
audio-video component of
their Training Institute in
Patient-Centered Cancer Care
($35,000) see Jurzykowski
Foundation, Alfred

Commonwealth Club ($500) see
Prairie Foundation

Community Arts Music
Association ($10,000) see
Wood-Claeyssens Foundation

Community Church of Los
Angeles ($11,000) see
Vermeer Manufacturing Co.

Community Church of Palm
Springs ($11,000) see
Philibosian Foundation,
Stephen

Community Connection ($2,250)
see Arkelian Foundation, Ben
H. and Gladys

Community Counseling Service
— support for 1989 ($10,000)
see Bank of America -
Giannini Foundation

Community Early Childhood
Health & Drug Education —
develop drug education
curriculum for second graders
in Healdsburg Schools
($2,500) see Exchange Bank

Community Education Services
— to support English literacy
and life skills program
($12,000) see Lux Foundation,
Miranda

Community Educational
Services ($5,000) see Tang
Foundation

Community Educational
Services of San Francisco
($35,000) see Haigh-Scatena
Foundation

Community Environmental
Council ($10,000) see Bothin
Foundation

Community Foundation ($3,000)
see Fox Foundation, John H.

Community Foundation see San
Diego Trust & Savings Bank

Community Foundation of
Monterey Peninsula ($15,000)
see Warner Foundation, Lee
and Rose

Community Foundation of Santa
Clara County — leadership
gift for the Silicon Valley Arts
Fund campaign ($1,000,000)
see Packard Foundation,
David and Lucile

Community Foundation of Santa
Clara County — for support of
the Silicon Valley Arts Fund
and the Partners Regranting
Program ($575,000) see
Hewlett Foundation, William
and Flora

Community Hospice ($200,000)
see Gallo Foundation, Julio R.

Community Hospice Foundation
($8,000) see Sanguinetti
Foundation, Annunziata

Community Hospice Foundation
of the Bay Area ($35,000) see
Hearst Foundation

Community Hospital — general
support ($75,000) see
Dunspaugh-Dalton Foundation

Community Hospital of Chula
Vista ($10,000) see Copley
Press

Community Hospital Foundation
($5,000) see Upjohn
California Fund

Community Hospital of
Monterey County ($10,000)
see McGee Foundation

Community Hospital of the
Monterey Peninsula ($5,000)
see Lindsay Foundation

Community Housing ($10,000)
see Lennox International, Inc.

Community Housing Partnership
($250,000) see Cowell
Foundation, S. H.

Community Music Center
($11,845) see Bothin
Foundation

Community Rehabilitation
Industries ($27,000) see
Fairfield Foundation, Freeman
E.

Community School of Music and
Arts see Raytheon Co.

Community Services Agency
($5,000) see Moore Family
Foundation

Community Task Force on
Homes for Children — a Bay
Area regional project to recruit
and improve services for foster
and adoptive parents ($98,398)
see Zellerbach Family Fund

Community Television of
Southern California/KCET —
toward LIFE and TIMES, a
new program initiative
focusing on the individuals
and opinions that influence
Southern California issues
($750,000) see Irvine
Foundation, James

CompuMentor — national
expansion of its mentoring
model for computerization
assistance for nonprofits
($10,000) see Benton
Foundation

Concern II ($50,000) see Alpert
Foundation, Herb

Concerned Businessmen's
Association of America
($10,000) see Memton Fund

Congregation B'nai Sholom —
building fund ($5,000) see
Geifman Family Foundation

Congregation Emanu-El — for
the cost of renovation and for
community service programs
($50,000) see Columbia
Foundation

Congregation Emanu-El —
capital campaign for building
renovation ($1,500,000) see
Haas Fund, Walter and Elise

Congregation Emanu-El —
capital campaign for building
renovation ($600,000) see
Haas Fund, Walter and Elise

Congregation Emanu-El
($50,000) see Lurie
Foundation, Louis R.

Congregation Emanu-El
($25,000) see Rosenberg, Jr.
Family Foundation, Louise
and Claude

Congregation Emanu-El — for
Community Service Program
($100,000) see Haas, Jr. Fund,
Evelyn and Walter

Congregation Emanuel
($100,000) see Swig Charity
Foundation, Mae and Benjamin

Congregation Sherith Israel
($28,825) see Goodman
Foundation, Edward and
Marion

Congregation Sherith Israel
($525) see Newman Charitable
Trust, Calvin M. and Raquel H.

Congregational Church
($345,000) see Lytel
Foundation, Bertha Russ

Congregational Church
($45,000) see Lytel
Foundation, Bertha Russ

Congregational Church, Sierra
Madre ($20,000) see Jameson
Foundation, J. W. and Ida M.

Constitutional Rights Foundation
($50,000) see Hancock
Foundation, Luke B.

Consumer Credit Counselors of
Los Angeles ($15,000) see
Pfaffinger Foundation

Consumer Credit Counselors of
Orange County ($3,000) see
Pfaffinger Foundation

Contra Costa Child Care Council
see Tosco Corp. Refining
Division

Contra Costa County School
Volunteer Program see Tosco
Corp. Refining Division

Contra Costa Food Bank see
Tosco Corp. Refining Division

Cooperative Ministries in Higher
Education — support of
campus ministries in the Bay
Area ($10,000) see Atkinson
Foundation

Corcoran Community
Foundation — Corcoran
Community Park Project
($777,117) see Boswell
Foundation, James G.

Corcoran Scholarship Committee
— Colonel James G. Boswell
Scholarship Fund ($65,000)
see Boswell Foundation,
James G.

Costume Council of LACMA —
Doris Stein Research and
Design Center for Costumes
and Textiles ($57,550) see
Stein Foundation, Jules and
Doris

Council of Christmas Cheer
($15,000) see Jackson Family
Foundation, Ann

Court Appointed Advocate of
Humboldt ($2,000) see Sierra
Pacific Resources

Court Appointed Special
Advocates ($8,000) see Bank
of A. Levy

Coyote Point Museum ($50,000)
see Doelger Charitable Trust,
Thelma

Coyote Point Museum — for the
Mildred M. Atkinson Pavilion
and Entry Plaza of the new
Wildlife Center ($50,000) see
Atkinson Foundation

Craft and Folk Art Museum
($10,000) see Brotman
Foundation of California

Craft and Folk Arts Museum
($2,500) see Rasmussen
Foundation

Crane School — faculty
endowment fund ($25,000) see
Jackson Family Foundation,
Ann

Creighton University School of
Medicine ($49,932) see Stern
Foundation, Charles H. and
Anna S.

Crippled Children's Society —
general fund ($26,000) see
Stuart Center Charitable Trust,
Hugh

Crippled Children's Society of
Santa Clara Co. ($3,000) see
Nelson Foundation, Florence

Crocker Art Museum ($5,000)
see Setzer Foundation

Crockett Recreation Association
($1,000) see California &
Hawaiian Sugar Co.

Crossroads School for the Arts
and Sciences ($50,000) see
Alpert Foundation, Herb

Crossroads School — support
toward summer enrichment
program for at-risk youth
($23,000) see Mattel

Crutcher's Serenity House
($5,000) see Leonardt
Foundation

Crystal Cathedral ($1,000,000)
see Crean Foundation

Crystal Cathedral ($500,000) see
Fuqua Foundation, J. B.

Crystal Springs and Uplands
Schools ($15,000) see
Littlefield Foundation,
Edmund Wattis

Cultural Heritage Foundation
($25,000) see Knudsen
Foundation, Tom and Valley

Cultural Heritage Foundation of
Southern California ($50,000)
see Associated Foundations

Curtis School ($5,000) see
Seaver Charitable Trust,
Richard C.

CYO Youth Activities ($25,000)
see Hale Foundation, Crescent
Porter

Cystic Fibrosis ($33,000) see
City of Hope 1989 Section E
Foundation

Cystic Fibrosis Foundation
($1,000) see Barry Corp., R. G.

Cystic Fibrosis Foundation
($15,000) see Pauley
Foundation, Edwin W.

Cystic Fibrosis Foundation
($25,000) see Wasserman
Foundation

D.A.R.E. ($10,000) see
Benbough Foundation, Legler

D.A.R.E. California ($250,000)
see Milken Foundation, L. and
S.

Dale McIntosh Center for the
Disabled ($12,075) see
Stillwell Charitable Trust,
Glen and Dorothy

Daughters of St. Joseph
($300,000) see Murphy
Foundation, Dan

Davis Joint Unified School
District ($5,500) see Walker
Foundation, T. B.

Dayle McIntosh Center for the
Disabled — access Irvine
project ($37,500) see Irvine
Health Foundation

Dede Hersch Mental Health
Center ($22,986) see Simon
Foundation, Robert Ellis

Delancey Street Foundation
($5,000) see Wilsey Bennet Co.

Delancy Street Foundation
($25,000) see Lurie
Foundation, Louis R.

Delhaven Community Center —
to provide for the local poor
and needy ($2,000) see
American Foundation

DeMolay Foundation of
California ($16,000) see
Sandy Foundation, George H.

Denali Foundation ($25,000) see
Mason Charitable Foundation

Dental Health Foundation — to
support the dissemination to
the general public of
information regarding Dental
Health obtained by analysis,
study and research ($10,000)
see Quest for Truth Foundation

Desert Hospital Foundation
($3,000) see Autry Foundation

Developmental Studies Center
($73,895) see Rosenberg, Jr.
Family Foundation, Louise
and Claude

Developmental Studies Center
— to extend the Child
Development Project
($220,000) see Stuart
Foundations

Developmental Studies Center
— support of the Child
Development Study
($1,000,000) see Hewlett
Foundation, William and Flora

Devil Mountain Run 1990
($500) see Dreyer's & Edy's
Grand Ice Cream

Diabetes Research Institute —
Analysis of Data in a
Transplant Registry to Clarify
Major Histocompatibility
Association in Diabetes
($20,000) see Diabetes
Research and Education
Foundation

Diabetes Society ($5,600) see
Weiler Foundation

Diablo Valley College ($2,000)
see Long Foundation, J.M.

Diadmes of Children Care
League (Merman School)
($1,100) see Ace Beverage Co.

Digit Fund ($25,000) see Seebee
Trust, Frances

Diocese of Los Angeles,
Episcopal ($50,000) see
Munger Foundation, Alfred C.

Diocese of San Jose ($10,000)
see Hayden Foundation,
William R. and Virginia

Direct Relief International —
medical commodities/general
assistance ($100,000) see M.
E. G. Foundation

Disabled Children's Computer
Group — individual
consultation program ($5,000)
see Smith Trust, May and
Stanley

Disaster Relief Fund, Greater
Santa Cruz Community
Foundation ($20,000) see Life
Investors Insurance Company
of America

Discovery Fund for Eye
Research ($25,000) see Factor
Family Foundation, Max

Discovery Museum of Orange
County ($25,000) see Fluor
Corp.

Dodar County 4-H Society
($2,500) see Keene Trust,
Hazel R.

Doheny Eye Clinic ($50,000) see
Autry Foundation

Doheny Eye Foundation
($13,000) see Bekins
Foundation, Milo W.

Doheny Eye Institute ($26,000)
see Argyros Foundation

Doheny Eye Institute
($1,010,000) see Doheny
Foundation, Carrie Estelle

Doheny Eye Institute ($79,816)
see Hoover, Jr. Foundation,
Margaret W. and Herbert

Doheny Eye Institute ($25,000)
see Munger Foundation,
Alfred C.

Doheny Eye Institute ($150,000)
see Seaver Institute

Dominican College ($5,000) see
Bannan Foundation, Arline
and Thomas J.

Dominican College ($12,500)
see Drum Foundation

Dominican College ($11,758)
see Kaplen Foundation

Dominican College —
renovation of Guzman and
Bertrand Halls ($100,000) see

California (cont.)

Irwin Charity Foundation, William G.

Dominican College of San Rafael — for multicultural focus for student-teaching candidates ($25,000) see Stulsaft Foundation, Morris

Dominion College ($10,000) see Pacific Western Foundation

Don Bosco Technical Institute ($31,000) see Connell Foundation, Michael J.

Don Bosco Technical Institute ($275,000) see Murphy Foundation, Dan

Don Bosco Technical Institute — to purchase equipment for the chemistry and biology laboratories ($113,422) see Parsons Foundation, Ralph M.

Downtown Senior Center — general funding ($800,000) see Civitas Fund

Dream Street ($25,000) see Lipton Foundation

Drug Abuse Resistance Education — purchase student workbooks ($100,000) see Drown Foundation, Joseph

Drug Abuse Resistance Education California ($152,000) see Columbia Savings Charitable Foundation

Dunn School — new dormitory ($100,000) see Irwin Charity Foundation, William G.

Dunn School — girls dormitory ($25,000) see Jackson Family Foundation, Ann

Dunn School ($200,000) see Roberts Foundation

Dunn School ($200,000) see Roberts Foundation

Dunn School ($200,000) see Roberts Foundation

Dunn School ($150,000) see Roberts Foundation

Dystonia Medical Research Foundation ($1,000) see Rasmussen Foundation

Eagle Lake Camp ($4,800) see Setzer Foundation

Earth Day 1990 ($5,000) see Seven Springs Foundation

Earth Island Institute ($50,000) see Ira-Hiti Foundation for Deep Ecology

Earth Trust ($17,000) see Davies Charitable Trust

Earth Trust ($12,500) see Davies Charitable Trust

Earth Trust ($8,300) see Davies Charitable Trust

Earthwatch ($30,000) see Bing Fund

Earthwatch ($6,000) see Vesuvius Charitable Foundation

East Bay Activity Center — Personal Adjustments and Life Skills Program ($86,750) see Johnson Foundation, Walter S.

East Bay Community Foundation ($100,000) see Valley Foundation, Wayne and Gladys

East Bay Funders ($50,000) see Clorox Co.

East Bay Zoological Society ($25,000) see Clorox Co.

East County Performing Arts Center ($10,000) see Masserini Charitable Trust, Maurice J.

East Oakland Youth Development Foundation ($5,000) see American President Cos.

East Oakland Youth Development Foundation ($70,000) see Clorox Co.

East Palo Alto Youth Development Center — Hispanic Mentor Advocates ($50,000) see Sun Microsystems

East Side Union High School District (S.T.Y.L.E.) — funding for the S.T.Y.L.E. Volunteer Program ($39,420) see Hancock Foundation, Luke B.

Easter Seal Society ($25,268) see Lytel Foundation, Bertha Russ

Easter Seal Society ($13,000) see Sanguinetti Foundation, Annunziata

Eastfield-Ming Quong Foundation ($10,000) see Gross Charitable Trust, Stella B.

Ebell Kingsley Care Program ($10,000) see Ebell of Los Angeles Rest Cottage Association

Ebell Kingsley Care Program ($30,000) see Ebell of Los Angeles Scholarship Endowment Fund

Ecology Action — general support ($20,000) see Warsh-Mott Legacy

Eden Hospital Trauma Unit ($10,000) see Bellini Foundation

Eden Housing ($250,000) see Cowell Foundation, S. H.

Edna Hill Middle — Math Counts 4 Every 1 ($12,766) see California Educational Initiatives Fund

Education Foundation's Challenge Fund ($10,000) see Sizzler International

Education Fund of the Archdiocese of Los Angeles ($100,000) see Bettingen Corporation, Burton G.

Education Training and Research Associates — contemporary health series ($62,500) see Johnson Foundation, Walter S.

Educational Resource and Service Center ($25,000) see Milken Foundation, L. and S.

Educational Services Exchange with China ($50,000) see First Fruit

Eisenhower Medical Center ($10,000) see Israel Foundation, A. Cremieux

Eisenhower Medical Center ($131,159) see Joslyn Foundation, Marcellus I.

Eisenhower Medical Center ($50,000) see Kiewit Sons, Peter

Eisenhower Medical Center ($2,000) see Webb Educational and Charitable Trust, Torrey H. and Dorothy K.

Eisenhower Medical Center Auxiliary — Voices of Christmas ($4,000) see Bannan Foundation, Arline and Thomas J.

Eisenhower Medical Center — to benefit the Eisenhower Medical, Annenberg Center, Betty Ford Center, and Barbara Sinatra Children's Center ($9,800) see Barker Foundation, Donald R.

El Adobe Corporation ($460,000) see Jackson Family Foundation, Ann

El Camino High School/Escondido High School/Ramona High School/Santana High School — "GO FOR THE GOLD" Academic Excellence Program ($15,601) see California Educational Initiatives Fund

El Camino Hospital Foundation ($10,000) see Moore Family Foundation

El Camino Hospital Foundation ($25,000) see Syntex Corp.

El Concilio Del Condado De Ventura ($10,000) see Bank of A. Levy

El Dorado School ($4,000) see Teichert

El Nido Services ($17,830) see Simon Foundation, Robert Ellis

El Rescate ($10,000) see Von der Ahe Foundation

El Rescate ($10,000) see Von der Ahe, Jr. Trust, Theodore Albert

Elizabeth Gamble Garden Center ($5,000) see Arrillaga Foundation

Elmwood Institute ($50,000) see Ira-Hiti Foundation for Deep Ecology

Emanuel Lutheran ($12,000) see Keck, Jr. Foundation, William M.

Emek Hebrew Academy ($5,000) see Domino of California

Emergency Housing Consortium, San Jose, CA — to shelter and assist the homeless see Tandem Computers

Emergency Housing Consortium of Santa Clara County — general budget ($5,000) see Smith Trust, May and Stanley

Emergency Housing Consortium of Santa Clara County — support toward the Family Case Management Program ($100,000) see Valley Foundation

Encino Chapter of Hadassah ($1,300) see Lipton Foundation

English Language Institute ($5,000) see Fruehauf Foundation

English Language Institute of China ($30,000) see Huston Foundation

English Language Institute China ($10,000) see Morris Charitable Foundation, E. A.

English Language Institute of China — Mongolia ($234,433) see Maclellan Foundation

Environment Action Committee of West Marin ($9,700) see Witter Foundation, Dean

Environmental Traveling Companions — handicapped support ($10,000) see Bradford Foundation, George and Ruth

Episcopal Chaplaincy ($9,000) see Hume Foundation, Jaquelin

Episcopal Community Services of San Francisco ($10,000) see de Dampierre Memorial Foundation, Marie C.

Episcopal Community Services of San Francisco ($3,000) see Wilsey Bennet Co.

Episcopal Diocese of Los Angeles ($26,000) see Stuart Foundation, Elbridge and Evelyn

Episcopal Home ($15,000) see Ebell of Los Angeles Rest Cottage Association

Episcopal Sanctuary ($10,000) see Gleason Foundation, James

Episcopal Sanctuary ($25,000) see McBean Family Foundation

Equestrian Therapy for Handicapped Riders ($2,000) see Shoong Foundation, Milton

Esalen Institute ($5,000) see Hunt Foundation

Escondido Joslyn Senior Center ($30,923) see Joslyn Foundation, Marcellus I.

ETR Associates ($250,000) see Cowell Foundation, S. H.

ETR Associates ($250,000) see Syntex Corp.

ETR Associates — to establish and manage a training system ($157,370) see Stuart Foundations

Evangelical Lutheran Church in America ($50,000) see Edouard Foundation

Evangelical Lutheran Church in America — senior outreach ministry program ($5,000) see Smith Trust, May and Stanley

Evelyn M. and Norman Feintech Foundation ($35,000) see Feintech Foundation

EVO Schools Project — support towards Parents Union in Los Angeles County schools ($25,000) see Mattel

Exceptional Children's Foundation ($20,000) see Stern Memorial Trust, Sidney

Exchange Club Center — prevention of child abuse ($30,000) see Irvine Health Foundation

Exploratorium, San Francisco, CA — for activities at science museum see Tandem Computers

Eye Research ($11,000) see Weisz Foundation, David and Sylvia

F.A.I.R. ($20,000) see Munger Foundation, Alfred C.

Family Enrichment Network ($15,700) see van Loben Sels - Eleanor Slate van Lobel Sels Charitable Foundation, Ernst D.

Family Life Center ($15,000) see Bothin Foundation

Family Outreach Project, San Mateo County — to support public health-mental health-social services collaborative approach to providing outreach and in-home services to at-risk families ($51,100) see Zellerbach Family Fund

Family Research Council ($500,000) see Prince Manufacturing, Inc.

Family Resource Center — building fund ($37,500) see Segal Charitable Trust, Barnet

Family School ($10,000) see Friedman Family Foundation

Family School — general fund ($25,000) see True North Foundation

Family Service Agency ($15,000) see Hale Foundation, Crescent Porter

Family Service Agency ($10,000) see Jefferson Endowment Fund, John Percival and Mary C.

Family Service Agency ($5,000) see Page Foundation, George B.

Family Service Agency ($10,000) see Wood-Claeyssens Foundation

Family Service of Long Beach Homemaker Service ($21,854) see Fairfield Foundation, Freeman E.

Family Services ($15,000) see Van Camp Foundation

Family Services of Butte and Glenn Counties ($41,000) see Sierra Health Foundation

Family Stress Center — Proud Fathers program ($15,000) see Odell and Helen Pfeiffer Odell Fund, Robert Stewart

Far East Broadcasting ($15,000) see Marshburn Foundation

Farm School University of California ($10,000) see Appleby Trust, Scott B. and Annie P.

Fellowship Academy ($10,000) see Bothin Foundation

Fellowship Academy ($556,904) see Herbst Foundation

Fellowship Academy — for career week, math lab and head teacher support ($10,000) see Atkinson Foundation

Fern Cottage — cost of instituting an archives facility at Fern Cottage ($15,000) see Lytel Foundation, Bertha Russ

Ferndale Museum — operating expenses ($15,000) see Lytel Foundation, Bertha Russ

Ferndale Union High School — purchase van, travel expenses and remodel shop ($11,600) see Lytel Foundation, Bertha Russ

Fine Arts Museum of San Francisco ($11,000) see Davies Charitable Trust

Fine Arts Museum of San Francisco ($200,000) see Hills Fund, Edward E.

Fine Arts Museum of San Francisco ($62,000) see Magowan Family Foundation

Fine Arts Museum of San Francisco ($25,000) see McBean Family Foundation

Fine Arts Museum of San Francisco ($25,000) see McKesson Corp.

Fine Arts Museum of San Francisco ($150,000) see Roberts Foundation

Fine Arts Museum of San Francisco ($105,000) see Thornton Foundation

Fine Arts Museum of San Francisco ($30,000) see Transamerica Corp.

Fine Arts Museum of San Francisco — to conserve/restore painting ($13,000) see Post Foundation of D.C., Marjorie Merriweather

Fine Arts Museums of San Francisco ($13,000) see U.S. Leasing International

Firechiefs Association of Trinity County ($3,000) see Sierra Pacific Resources

First Baptist Church — choir tour ($38,000) see Stamps Foundation, James L.

First Baptist Church — intern program ($25,000) see Stamps Foundation, James L.

First Covenant Church ($20,000) see Berry Foundation, Lowell

First United Methodist Church ($5,000) see Bright Family Foundation

First United Methodist Church ($14,377) see Ryan Foundation, David Claude

Five Acres — caring for abused or abandoned children ($2,000) see American Foundation

Flo Riford Library of La Jolla ($5,000) see Polinsky-Rivkin Family Foundation

Florence Crittenton Services ($10,000) see Stillwell

California (cont.)

Guide Dogs for the Blind ($15,000) see Bireley Foundation

Guide Dogs for the Blind ($10,000) see Brotman Foundation of California

Guide Dogs for the Blind ($6,123) see Brunetti Charitable Trust, Dionigi

Guide Dogs for the Blind — training program ($10,000) see Gellert Foundation, Carl

Guide Dogs for the Blind ($12,000) see Kirchgessner Foundation, Karl

Guide Dogs for the Blind ($34,979) see Posey Trust, Addison

Guide Dogs for the Blind ($500) see Prairie Foundation

Guide Dogs for the Blind ($20,000) see Rogers Foundation, Mary Stuart

Guide Dogs for the Blind ($11,800) see Sattler Beneficial Trust, Daniel A. and Edna J.

Guild of Pasadena Children's Hospital ($4,200) see Shea Foundation, Edmund and Mary

H.C.S.F. Foundation ($8,000) see Brenner Foundation, Mervyn

Habitat for Humanity ($7,500) see Bull Foundation, Henry W.

Haggin Museum — maintenance of Holt Wing and staffing ($65,000) see Holt Foundation, William Knox

Haight-Asbury Food Program ($15,000) see Langendorf Foundation, Stanley S.

Hamblin School of San Francisco ($25,000) see Hamilton Foundation, Florence P.

Hamburger Home (Aviva) ($100,000) see Bettingen Corporation, Burton G.

Hamlin School ($100,000) see Hills Fund, Edward E.

Hamlin School — computer equipment ($25,000) see Holt Foundation, William Knox

Hanford Community Hospital Fund ($2,500) see Standard Register Co.

Happy Valley School ($19,000) see Kern Foundation Trust

Harbor House ($25,000) see Berry Foundation, Lowell

Harey Mudd College ($5,000) see Robinson Foundation

Hart High School District ($33,000) see Newhall Foundation, Henry Mayo

Hartnell College Foundation ($4,500) see National Pro-Am Youth Fund

Harvard School ($10,000) see Deutsch Co.

Harvard-Westlake School ($7,000) see Gilmore Foundation, Earl B.

Harvard-Westlake School ($20,000) see May Foundation, Wilbur

Harvard-Westlake School ($258,698) see Munger Foundation, Alfred C.

Harvard-Westlake School ($15,000) see Seaver Charitable Trust, Richard C.

Harvard-Westlake School ($25,000) see Thornton Foundation

Harvest Evangelism ($37,500) see First Fruit

Harvest Evangelism — church planting survey ($250,000) see Maclellan Foundation

Harvey Mudd College ($49,655) see Baker Foundation, R. C.

Harvey Mudd College ($800,000) see Beckman Foundation, Arnold and Mabel

Harvey Mudd College ($5,000) see Broccoli Charitable Foundation, Dana and Albert R.

Harvey Mudd College ($100,000) see Keck, Jr. Foundation, William M.

Harvey Mudd College ($45,000) see Knudsen Foundation, Tom and Valley

Harvey Mudd College ($15,000) see Linde Foundation, Ronald and Maxine

Harvey Mudd College ($1,027,000) see Olin Foundation, F. W.

Harvey Mudd College — produce audio tapes teaching children about founding fathers ($31,275) see Salvatori Foundation, Henry

Harvey Mudd College ($12,550) see Sprague, Jr. Foundation, Caryll M. and Norman F.

Harvey Mudd College ($31,000) see Watson Foundation, Thomas J.

Harvey Mudd College — Fletcher Jones Endowed Chair ($582,991) see Jones Foundation, Fletcher

Hathaway Children's Service ($20,000) see Van Nuys Foundation, I. N. and Susanna H.

Hathaway Children's Services ($7,000) see Van Nuys Charities, J. B. and Emily

Hathaway Children's Services — for continued support of the In-Home Services Project ($150,000) see Stuart Foundations

Haven Hills Family Center ($15,000) see Ebell of Los Angeles Rest Cottage Association

Haven House — capital support ($10,000) see Bank of America - Giannini Foundation

Haven House ($10,000) see Ebell of Los Angeles Rest Cottage Association

Hawaii Heart Association ($17,500) see Cuneo Foundation

Hawaiian Gardens Social Services Agency ($360,000) see Moskowitz Foundation, Irving I.

Hayfork Little League ($2,500) see Sierra Pacific Resources

Hayward Rotary Club ($495) see Dreyer's & Edy's Grand Ice Cream

Head-Royce School ($50,000) see Bechtel, Jr. Foundation, S. D.

Head-Royce School ($50,000) see Bechtel, Jr. Foundation, S. D.

Head-Royce School ($10,000) see Hogan Foundation, Royal Barney

Head-Royce School ($2,500) see Llagas Foundation

Head-Royce School ($6,500) see Shenandoah Foundation

Head-Royce School ($2,500) see Uvas Foundation

Head-Royce School — 2nd Century Fund ($25,000) see Shenandoah Foundation

Headlands Center for the Arts ($20,000) see LEF Foundation

Heal the Bay ($10,000) see Daly Charitable Foundation Trust, Robert and Nancy

Health Access ($10,000) see Friedman Family Foundation

Health Champions ($35,000) see Chartwell Foundation

Healthy Mothers, Healthy Babies ($12,500) see Sierra Health Foundation

Hearing Society of Bay Area ($2,000) see Ishiyama Foundation

Heart of America Bone Marrow Donor Registry — donor registration ($20,000) see Maxfield Foundation

Heart Institute ($5,000) see Munger Foundation, Alfred C.

Heart of Jesus Retreat Center — non-restricted ($400,000) see Birch Foundation, Stephen and Mary

Hebrew Academy for Long Beach ($32,000) see Morgenstern Foundation, Morris

Hebrew Academy Lubavitch ($23,000) see AVI CHAI - A Philanthropic Foundation

Hebrew Christian Witness ($9,000) see Caddock Foundation

Hebrew Union College ($100) see Taper Foundation, S. Mark

Hebrew Union College — toward the construction of the Skirball Cultural Center in Los Angeles ($400,000) see Koret Foundation

Hebrew University ($10,500) see Brody Foundation, Frances

Hebrew University ($4,000) see Shapell Foundation, Nathan and Lilly

Hebrew University ($20,200) see Weisz Foundation, David and Sylvia

Hebrew University of Jerusalem ($2,000) see Cedars-Sinai Medical Center Section D Fund

Helen Woodward Animal Care Center ($1,450,000) see W. W. W. Foundation

Hemopet ($15,000) see Seebee Trust, Frances

Henry E. Huntington Library and Art Gallery ($212,267) see Scott Foundation, Virginia Steele

Henry E. Huntington Library and Art Gallery ($14,571) see Van Nuys Foundation, I. N. and Susanna H.

Henry Mayo Newall Memorial Health Foundation ($56,211) see Joslyn Foundation, Marcellus I.

Henry Mayo Newhall Hospital ($57,179) see Newhall Foundation, Henry Mayo

Henry Mayo Newhall Memorial Health Foundation ($10,900) see Rasmussen Foundation

Hereditary Disease Foundation ($90,000) see Chartwell Foundation

Hereditary Disease Foundation ($33,000) see Simon Foundation, Jennifer Jones

Hermano Pablo Ministries ($6,000) see Marshburn Foundation

Hierveme School District ($5,700) see Bank of A. Levy

High Hopes Head Injury Program — speech therapy ($35,000) see Irvine Health Foundation

High Hopes Head Injury Program ($12,000) see Stillwell Charitable Trust, Glen and Dorothy

Hillel Hebrew Academy ($10,000) see Taubman Foundation, Herman P. and Sophia

Hillside Home for Children ($20,000) see Beynon Foundation, Kathryne

Hillside House ($11,800) see Sattler Beneficial Trust, Daniel A. and Edna J.

Hindsdale Hospital Foundation ($74,948) see Joslyn Foundation, Marcellus I.

Hispanic Chamber of Commerce Scholarship see Tosco Corp. Refining Division

Hoag Hospital Foundation ($2,000,000) see Hoag Family Foundation, George

Hoag Hospital Foundation — public relations fund ($10,000) see Hoag Family Foundation, George

Hoag Memorial Hospital ($100,000) see Shaw Foundation, Walden W. and Jean Young

Hoag Memorial Hospital ($5,000) see Walker Foundation, Smith

Holistic Medicine Foundation ($30,470) see New Cycle Foundation

Hollywood Bowl ($5,400) see Goldsmith Family Foundation

Hollywood Entertainment Museum ($5,000) see Gilmore Foundation, Earl B.

Hollywood Memorial Hospital ($5,000) see Friedland Family Foundation, Samuel

Holocaust Oral History ($2,500) see Goodman Foundation, Edward and Marion

Holy Family Church ($5,000) see Leonardt Foundation

Holy Family Services ($5,000) see Bannan Foundation, Arline and Thomas J.

Holy Name of Jesus Church ($5,000) see Gellert Foundation, Celia Berta

Holy Names College ($25,000) see Hale Foundation, Crescent Porter

Holy Names College — for the performing arts center ($500,000) see Irvine Foundation, James

Holy Names College ($25,000) see Ritter Foundation, May Ellen and Gerald

Holy Names College ($390,000) see Valley Foundation, Wayne and Gladys

Holy Trinity Orthodox Seminary ($11,500) see Koulaieff Educational Fund, Trustees of Ivan Y.

Home of the Good Shepherd ($1,000) see Warner Foundation, Lee and Rose

Home-Safe Child Care Center ($20,000) see Stern Memorial Trust, Sidney

Homeless Children Health Fund ($75,000) see Douglas Charitable Foundation

Homemaker Service of Pasadena ($4,000) see Howe and Mitchell B. Howe Foundation, Lucite Horton

Hoover Foundation ($8,000) see R. P. Foundation

Hoover Institute ($25,000) see Munger Foundation, Alfred C.

Hoover Institute on War, Revolution and Peace

($250,000) see Monell Foundation, Ambrose

Hoover Institution ($30,000) see FMC Corp.

Hoover Institution ($100,000) see Frese Foundation, Arnold D.

Hoover Institution — general support ($70,000) see Goldman Fund, Richard and Rhoda

Hoover Institution ($100,000) see Henry Foundation, Patrick

Hoover Institution ($20,000) see Krieble Foundation, Vernon K.

Hoover Institution ($27,500) see Llagas Foundation

Hoover Institution of War, Revolution and Peace — to support the John M. Olin Program in Soviet and East European Studies ($250,000) see Olin Foundation, John M.

Hoover Institutions — Russia/E. Europe, general fund fund ($25,000) see Lakeside Foundation

Horatio Alger Association ($20,000) see Reinhart Institutional Foods

Horseless Carriage Foundation ($30,000) see Scripps Foundation, Ellen Browning

Hospice ($2,500) see Fox Foundation, John H.

Hospice ($20,000) see Warner Foundation, Lee and Rose

Hospice of the Monterey Peninsula — challenge grant for capital campaign ($900,000) see Hermann Foundation, Grover

Hospice of Monterey Peninsula ($5,000) see Upjohn California Fund

Hospital De Familia ($500) see Prairie Foundation

Hospital of Good Samaritan ($10,000) see Ebell of Los Angeles Rest Cottage Association

Hospital of the Good Samaritan ($30,000) see Ebell of Los Angeles Scholarship Endowment Fund

Hospital of Good Samaritan ($30,000) see Essick Foundation

Hospital of Good Samaritan ($75,000) see Thomas Medical Foundation, Roy E.

Hospital of Good Samaritan ($25,000) see Thomas Medical Foundation, Roy E.

Hospital of Good Samaritan ($344,280) see Van Nuys Foundation, I. N. and Susanna H.

Hospitaller Foundation of California ($5,300) see Gilmore Foundation, Earl B.

Hospitaller Foundation of California ($5,350) see Leonardt Foundation

Hospitaller Foundation of California ($15,350) see Stauffer Foundation, John and Beverly

House Ear Institute ($65,000) see Confidence Foundation

House Ear Institute ($2,000) see Femino Foundation

House Ear Institute ($20,000) see Fuqua Foundation, J. B.

House Ear Institute ($50,000) see Grace & Co., W.R.

House Ear Institute ($25,000) see Hoffman Foundation, H. Leslie Hoffman and Elaine S.

House Ear Institute ($76,787) see Hoover, Jr. Foundation, Margaret W. and Herbert

House Ear Institute ($3,500) see Imperial Bancorp

House Ear Institute ($30,000) see Jameson Foundation, J. W. and Ida M.

House Ear Institute ($25,000) see Kemper Educational and Charitable Fund

House Ear Institute — construction ($1,000,000) see Lied Foundation Trust

House Ear Institute ($42,500) see McAlister Charitable Foundation, Harold

House Ear Institute ($20,000) see Mead Foundation, Giles W. and Elise G.

House Ear Institute — support for 1989 ($10,000) see Bank of America - Giannini Foundation

House Ear Institute — building fund for Otologic Research Wing ($250,000) see Webb Foundation, Del E.

Hugh O'Brien Youth Foundation ($5,000) see Hume Foundation, Jaquelin

Human Options ($50,000) see Mericos Foundation

Humboldt State University ($9,700) see Sierra Pacific Industries

Hunger Project ($10,000) see Berry Foundation, Archie W. and Grace

Hunters Point Boys Club ($8,000) see Walker Foundation, T. B.

Hunters Point Community Youth Center ($50,000) see Hafif Family Foundation

The Huntington — to provide for research on development of natural gardens in England during the 18th Century ($25,000) see Skaggs Foundation, L. J. and Mary C.

Huntington History Fellowships ($21,600) see Haynes Foundation, John Randolph and Dora

Huntington Hospital ($4,000) see Femino Foundation

Huntington Library ($25,000) see Munger Foundation, Alfred C.

Huntington Library ($5,000) see Munger Foundation, Alfred C.

Huntington Library and Art Gallery ($100,000) see Durfee Foundation

Huntington Library and Art Gallery ($23,000) see Essick Foundation

Huntington Library and Art Gallery ($25,000) see Garland Foundation, John Jewett and H. Chandler

Huntington Library and Art Gallery ($66,000) see Mead Foundation, Giles W. and Elise G.

Huntington Medical Research Institute ($100,000) see Braun Foundation

Huntington Medical Research Institute ($76,000) see Howe and Mitchell B. Howe Foundation, Lucite Horton

Huntington Medical Research Institute ($50,000) see Jameson Foundation, J. W. and Ida M.

Huntington Medical Research Institute ($115,600) see Lucas Cancer Foundation, Richard M.

Huntington Medical Research Institute ($125,000) see Whittier Foundation, L. K.

Huntington Memorial Hospital ($7,500) see Forest Lawn Foundation

Huntington Memorial Hospital ($3,500) see Stans Foundation

Huntington Memorial Library Foundation ($7,500) see Warren and Beatrice W. Blanding Foundation, Riley J. and Lillian N.

I Have A Dream Foundation ($50,000) see Mericos Foundation

I Have a Dream Foundation — education ($1,000,000) see Berger Foundation, H.N. and Frances C.

I Have a Dream Foundation ($92,500) see Confidence Foundation

Idyllwild Arts Foundation ($210,000) see SDB Foundation

Immaculate Conception Academy ($25,000) see de Dampierre Memorial Foundation, Marie C.

Immaculate Conception Academy ($15,000) see Drum Foundation

Immaculate Conception Academy ($10,000) see Gellert Foundation, Celia Berta

Immaculate Conception Academy ($5,000) see Weiler Foundation

Immaculate Conception Academy ($7,500) see Wilsey Bennet Co.

Immaculate Conception School ($100,000) see Burns Foundation, Fritz B.

Immigrant Legal Resource Center — Immigrant Children's project ($87,565) see Rosenberg Foundation

In Spirit — general budget ($5,000) see Smith Trust, May and Stanley

Independent Colleges of Southern California ($16,000) see Bekins Foundation, Milo W.

Independent Colleges of Southern California — support campaign ($10,000) see Imperial Bancorp

Independent Colleges of Southern California ($30,000) see Litton Industries

Independent Colleges of Southern California ($20,000) see Pacific Mutual Life Insurance Co.

Independent Colleges of Southern California ($36,000) see Pfaffinger Foundation

Independent Colleges of Southern California — annual support ($185,000) see Times Mirror Co.

Independent Colleges of Southern California ($15,000) see Union Bank

Independent Institute ($5,000) see Durell Foundation, George Edward

Independent Institute ($6,000) see Garvey Fund, Jean and Willard

Independent Institute ($27,500) see Garvey Kansas Foundation

Industry Initiatives for Science and Math Education see Raytheon Co.

Infant Parents Friends ($2,000) see Farallon Foundation

Institute for Civil Justice ($200,000) see Aetna Life & Casualty Co.

Institute for Civil Justice ($50,000) see Continental Corp.

Institute for Contemporary Studies ($1,000) see Burns Foundation

Institute for Contemporary Studies ($125,000) see Randolph Foundation

Institute for the Future — Health Reform Synthesis Program ($250,000) see Commonwealth Fund

Institute of Human Origins ($698,392) see Getty Foundation, Ann and Gordon

Institute of Human Origins ($200,000) see Koch Charitable Trust, David H.

Institute of Journalism Education ($7,500) see Daily News

Institute for Journalism Education ($25,000) see Dow Jones & Co.

Institute for Journalism Education — for the institute's core programs in management training and advancement for minorities in journalism ($75,000) see Graham Fund, Philip L.

Institute for Journalism Education-North Gate Hall/University of California — renewed support ($100,000) see Freedom Forum

Institute of Noetic Sciences ($10,000) see Seven Springs Foundation

Institute of Noetic Sciences ($116,896) see Three Swallows Foundation

Institute for the Study of Educational Differences ($100,000) see Pioneer Fund

Instituto Evangeleco ($13,200) see Marshburn Foundation

Inter-Community Medical Center Foundation — hospice endowment ($6,000) see American Foundation

Inter-Mountain Fair of Shasta County — renovation of Ingram Hall ($63,572) see McConnell Foundation

Intercommunity Medical Center Foundation ($74,948) see Joslyn Foundation, Marcellus I.

Interface Institute ($32,000) see Haigh-Scatena Foundation

Interfaith Network for Community Help — support to work with churches and homeless shelters in San Mateo County ($10,000) see Atkinson Foundation

International Aerospace Hall of Fame ($5,000) see Pratt Memorial Fund

International Center for Economic Growth ($15,000) see Walker Educational and Charitable Foundation, Alex C.

International Fund for Education and Career Development ($250,000) see Mitchell Family Foundation, Edward D. and Anna

International Fund for Education and Career Development ($30,000) see Ridgefield Foundation

International Lincoln Foundation ($8,000) see Phillipps Foundation

International Medical Corps. — medical training and supplies ($30,000) see International Foundation

International Psoriasis Research Foundation ($75,000) see

Hayden Foundation, William R. and Virginia

International School of Theology ($7,500) see Atkinson Foundation, Myrtle L.

International Services Assistance Fund — general fund ($30,000) see Laurel Foundation

Internews Network ($75,000) see Wallach Foundation, Miriam G. and Ira D.

Interns for Peace ($2,500) see Newman Charitable Trust, Calvin M. and Raquel H.

Interplast, Inc. — operating support ($5,000) see Davis Foundation, Edwin W. and Catherine M.

Interplast, Inc. — medical programs ($20,000) see Dreyfus Foundation, Max and Victoria

Interplast ($25,181) see Frees Foundation

Intervarsity Christian Fellowship ($7,500) see Boeckmann Charitable Foundation

Intervarsity Christian Fellowship ($5,000) see Hargis Charitable Foundation, Estes H. and Florence Parker

Irish Education Redevelopment, Archbishop Mahoney Fund for Irish Seminaries ($10,000) see Hayden Foundation, William R. and Virginia

Irving Feintech Family Foundation ($35,000) see Feintech Foundation

Irwin Memorial Blood Bank ($200,000) see Herbst Foundation

Irwin Memorial Blood Bank — building purchase ($250,000) see Irwin Charity Foundation, William G.

ISKCON of San Diego ($2,000) see India Foundation

Israel Defense Fund ($25,000) see Plitt Southern Theatres

Israel Emergency Fund ($140,000) see Price Foundation, Louis and Harold

Italian Red Cross ($82,563) see Saturno Foundation

Italian Welfare Agency ($55,042) see Saturno Foundation

ITP — healing research ($55,155) see Maxfield Foundation

J. David Gladstone Foundation — support research in genetic mutation and blood cholesterol ($127,739) see Whittier Foundation, L. K.

J. Paul Getty Trust ($50,000) see Stuart Foundation, Elbridge and Evelyn

Japanese American Museum ($3,000) see Autry Foundation

Japanese American Museum ($25,000) see Servco Pacific

Japanese Community Youth Council ($5,000) see Gleason Foundation, James

Japanese Community Youth Council ($5,205) see Tang Foundation

Jefferson Union High School District — toward a bilingual acculturation/counseling program ($10,000) see Atkinson Foundation

Jesuit High School ($25,000) see Arata Brothers Trust

Jesuit High School ($25,000) see Gilmore Foundation, William G.

Jesus Film Project ($14,200) see Meland Outreach

Jesus Film Project ($236,000) see Paulstan

Jewish Agency ($25,000) see Fellner Memorial Foundation, Leopold and Clara M.

Jewish Big Brothers ($400) see Borun Foundation, Anna Borun and Harry

Jewish Community Center ($5,000) see Burns Foundation

Jewish Community Center ($100,000) see Rosenberg, Jr. Family Foundation, Louise and Claude

Jewish Community Endowment Fund ($35,000) see Newman Charitable Trust, Calvin M. and Raquel H.

Jewish Community Endowment Fund ($5,000) see Taube Family Foundation

Jewish Community Endowment Fund — for Operation Exodus ($375,000) see Columbia Foundation

Jewish Community Federation ($36,000) see Goodman Foundation, Edward and Marion

Jewish Community Federation — general campaign support ($750,000) see Haas Fund, Walter and Elise

Jewish Community Federation ($200,000) see Haas, Jr. Fund, Evelyn and Walter

Jewish Community Federation ($90,000) see Langendorf Foundation, Stanley S.

Jewish Community Federation ($200,000) see Lurie Foundation, Louis R.

Jewish Community Federation ($25,000) see Lurie Foundation, Louis R.

Jewish Community Federation ($25,000) see Lurie Foundation, Louis R.

Jewish Community Federation ($83,000) see Rosenberg, Jr. Family Foundation, Louise and Claude

Jewish Community Federation ($100,000) see Taube Family Foundation

Jewish Community Federation — Operation Exodus ($225,000) see Haas Fund, Walter and Elise

Jewish Community Federation of San Francisco, the Peninsula, Marin and Sonoma Counties — for the 1991 Annual Campaign ($714,000) see Koret Foundation

Jewish Community Federation of San Francisco, the Peninsula, Marin and Sonoma Counties — for Operation Exodus; resettlement of Soviet Jewish emigres in Israel ($2,220,000) see Koret Foundation

Jewish Community Foundation ($50,000) see Baker Foundation, Solomon R. and Rebecca D.

Jewish Community Foundation ($75,000) see Eisenberg Foundation, Ben B. and Joyce E.

Jewish Community Foundation ($101,150) see Fellner Memorial Foundation, Leopold and Clara M.

Jewish Family and Children Services — for partnership to improve learning for troubled youth ($25,000) see Stulsaft Foundation, Morris

Jewish Family and Children's Services ($75,000) see

California (cont.)

Rosenberg, Jr. Family Foundation, Louise and Claude

Jewish Family Service of Santa Monica ($27,500) see Irmas Charitable Foundation, Audrey and Sydney

Jewish Family Services ($1,000) see Goldberg Family Foundation, Milton D. and Madeline L.

Jewish Federation ($25,000) see Douglas Charitable Foundation

Jewish Federation ($33,000) see Goldsmith Family Foundation

Jewish Federation ($2,500) see Schermer Charitable Trust, Frances

Jewish Federation ($109,000) see Stern Foundation, Irvin

Jewish Federation ($17,000) see Stern Foundation, Irvin

Jewish Federation Council ($49,042) see Ziegler Foundation, Ruth/Allen

Jewish Federation Council ($27,948) see Ziegler Foundation, Ruth/Allen

Jewish Federation Council of Greater Los Angeles ($489,000) see Capital Fund Foundation

Jewish Federation Council of Greater Los Angeles — civic ($62,500) see Mann Foundation, Ted

Jewish Federation Council of Greater Los Angeles ($100,000) see Milken Foundation, L. and S.

Jewish Federation Council of Greater Los Angeles — United Jewish Fund ($62,500) see Mann Foundation, Ted

Jewish Federation Council, United Jewish Fund ($18,000) see Deutsch Co.

Jewish Federation of the Greater East Bay — for Operation Exodus; resettlement of Soviet Jewish emigres in Israel ($450,000) see Koret Foundation

Jewish Federation of Greater San Jose — for Operation Exodus; resettlement of Soviet Jewish emigres in Israel ($330,000) see Koret Foundation

Jewish Federation of Palm Springs ($50,000) see Wouk Foundation, Abe

Jewish Federation of Palm Springs ($15,000) see Wouk Foundation, Abe

Jewish Home for the Aged ($28,500) see Goodman Foundation, Edward and Marion

Jewish Home for the Aged — for the construction of the Howard A. Friedman Pavilion ($62,500) see Haas, Jr. Fund, Evelyn and Walter

Jewish Home for the Aging ($2,003,100) see Eisenberg Foundation, Ben B. and Joyce E.

Jewish Home for the Aging ($35,000) see Pickford Foundation, Mary

Jewish Homes for the Aging of Greater Los Angeles ($106,560) see Amado Foundation, Maurice

Jewish National Fund ($31,500) see Amado Foundation, Maurice

Jewish National Fund ($101,000) see Chais Family Foundation

Jewish National Fund ($25,000) see Feinberg Foundation, Joseph and Bessie

Jewish National Fund ($500,000) see Soref Foundation, Samuel M. Soref and Helene K.

Jewish Television Network ($250,000) see Capital Fund Foundation

Jewish Welfare Federation ($10,000) see Taubman Foundation, Herman P. and Sophia

JFCS ($3,000) see Goodman Foundation, Edward and Marion

Joan Shorenstein Barone Foundation for Harvard ($172,000) see Shorenstein Foundation, Walter H. and Phyllis J.

John Muir Foundation — for a chemotherapy program for cancer patients in Contra Costa County, CA ($120,000) see Pardee Foundation, Elsa U.

John O'Connell High School — for purchase of computer equipment for acceleration center ($47,374) see Lux Foundation, Miranda

John Swett High School ($7,000) see California & Hawaiian Sugar Co.

John Tracy Clinic ($5,000) see Pauley Foundation, Edwin W.

John Wayne Cancer Clinic ($49,000) see Eisenberg Foundation, Ben B. and Joyce E.

John Wayne Cancer Clinic ($20,000) see Steele Foundation

Joslyn Cove Communities Senior Center ($30,923) see Joslyn Foundation, Marcellus I.

Judah Magnee Museum ($20,000) see Langendorf Foundation, Stanley S.

Jules and Doris Stein University of California Los Angeles Support Group ($113,125) see Wasserman Foundation

Jules Stein Eye Institute ($75,000) see May Foundation, Wilbur

Jules Stein Eye Institute ($1,000) see Parvin Foundation, Albert

Jules Stein Eye Institute — Susan Stein Shiva Memorial Fund ($743,110) see Stein Foundation, Jules and Doris

Junior Achievement ($10,000) see Bank of America - Giannini Foundation

Junior Achievement ($1,800) see California & Hawaiian Sugar Co.

Junior Achievement ($500) see Dreyer's & Edy's Grand Ice Cream

Junior Achievement ($4,000) see Pacific Western Foundation

Junior Achievement ($6,000) see Sizzler International

Junior Achievement of Southern California ($20,000) see McDonnell Douglas Corp.-West

Junior Achievement of Southern California — headquarters and training facilities (final payment) ($500,000) see ARCO

Junior Center for Art and Science ($2,257) see Farallon Foundation

Junior League ($5,350) see Gilmore Foundation, Earl B.

Junior League of Palo Alto ($10,000) see Hogan Foundation, Royal Barney

Junior League of Pasadena ($10,000) see Gilmore Foundation, Earl B.

Junior Statesman Foundation ($40,000) see Tuohy Foundation, Alice Tweed

Just Say No ($28,225) see Buchalter, Nemer, Fields, & Younger

Just Say No to Drugs — drug prevention and education ($50,000) see Sega of America

Justin-Siena High School ($5,000) see Wilsey Bennet Co.

Juvenile Diabetes Foundation ($3,000) see Imperial Bancorp

Juvenile Diabetes Foundation ($20,000) see Norman Foundation, Andrew

JVS Scholarship Foundation ($5,000) see Fellner Memorial Foundation, Leopold and Clara M.

JWB Associates ($6,250) see Goldsmith Family Foundation

K.A.R.A. ($5,000) see Weiler Foundation

K.A.R.E. League ($6,000) see Marshburn Foundation

Kainos — retarded adults ($7,000) see Bradford Foundation, George and Ruth

Kaiser Family Foundation, Health Promotion Program — to continue community-wide pregnancy and substance abuse prevention programs ($245,000) see Stuart Foundations

KARA ($2,000) see Nelson Foundation, Florence

Kare Youth League ($20,000) see Peppers Foundation, Ann

Kare Youth League — building of cabins at Wrightwood Camp ($30,000) see Stamps Foundation, James L.

KCET ($500) see Chais Family Foundation

KCET ($250,000) see Connell Foundation, Michael J.

KCET ($20,000) see Disney Family Foundation, Roy

KCET ($125,000) see Durfee Foundation

KCET ($19,000) see Durfee Foundation

KCET ($4,000) see Green Foundation, Burton E.

KCET ($2,500) see Negaunee Foundation

KCET ($125,000) see Norris Foundation, Kenneth T. and Eileen L.

KCET ($25,000) see Roth Family Foundation

KCET ($10,000) see Thornton Foundation

KCET ($50,000) see Thornton Foundation, Flora L.

KCET ($500,000) see Weingart Foundation

KCET Community Television ($20,000) see Stern Memorial Trust, Sidney

KCET Los Angeles — support "The Human Quest" program ($500,000) see Whittier Foundation, L. K.

KCET, Public Television ($2,500) see Rasmussen Foundation

KCET — community outreach activities (second of five payments) ($100,000) see ARCO

KCRW ($10,835) see Roth Family Foundation

KCSM — public broadcasting ($20,000) see Bradford Foundation, George and Ruth

KCSM TV ($8,000) see Weiler Foundation

Keisen Jogakuen ($10,000) see Ishiyama Foundation

Kelter Center ($7,000) see Stauffer Foundation, John and Beverly

Kern County Library Foundation ($35,000) see Arkelian Foundation, Ben H. and Gladys

Kern Kiwanis ($4,000) see Arkelian Foundation, Ben H. and Gladys

Kern Soccer Foundation ($5,000) see Arkelian Foundation, Ben H. and Gladys

Keystone Conference on Diabetes ($5,000) see Iacocca Foundation

Kids Inventing and Discovering Science, University of California at Irvine — to fund a national model program of elementary science, grades K-6 ($100,000) see American Honda Motor Co.

Kids Turn ($5,000) see Furth Foundation

Kidspace ($10,000) see Hoffman Foundation, H. Leslie Hoffman and Elaine S.

KIXE ($4,316) see Sierra Pacific Industries

KIXE ($8,600) see Sierra Pacific Resources

KMTF Channel 18 ($10,000) see Radin Foundation

Koncepts Cultural Gallery ($31,500) see Fleishhacker Foundation

KPBS ($5,000) see Polinsky-Rivkin Family Foundation

KPBS ($23,000) see R. P. Foundation

KQED ($10,400) see Fireman's Fund Insurance Co.

KQED ($3,000) see G.A.G. Charitable Corporation

KQED ($20,000) see Gellert Foundation, Fred

KQED ($15,000) see GenRad

KQED ($75,000) see Herbst Foundation

KQED — model video classrooms project ($62,509) see Johnson Foundation, Walter S.

KQED ($246,800) see Osher Foundation, Bernard

KRCB, Community Public TV for North Bay ($15,000) see Fireman's Fund Insurance Co.

Krotona Institute of Theosophy ($97,844) see Kern Foundation Trust

KUSC ($25,000) see Negaunee Foundation

KUSC-FM ($56,150) see Nakamichi Foundation, E.

KVIE Public Television — operating fund to purchase new equipment ($20,000) see Allen-Heath Memorial Foundation

KVIE Public Television ($10,000) see Setzer Foundation

KVPR Valley Public Radio ($18,000) see Peters Foundation, Leon S.

KXPR Public Radio ($20,000) see Allen-Heath Memorial Foundation

KXPR Public Radio — operating funds to purchase new equipment ($15,000) see Allen-Heath Memorial Foundation

L.A. County Sheriff's Youth Foundation ($26,400) see Irmas Charitable Foundation, Audrey and Sydney

L.A. Family Housing ($120,928) see Irmas Charitable Foundation, Audrey and Sydney

L.A. Philharmonic Young Musician Institute ($25,000) see Pickford Foundation, Mary

La Familia Counseling Center ($29,806) see Haigh-Scatena Foundation

La Habra Children's Museum ($1,000) see Jerome Foundation

La Jolla Cancer Research foundation ($100,000) see Burnham Foundation

La Jolla Cancer Research Foundation ($12,500) see Pratt Memorial Fund

La Jolla Country Day School ($2,000) see Klipstein Foundation, Ernest Christian

La Jolla Playhouse ($3,000) see Thornton Foundation, John M. and Sally B.

La Jolla Stage Company ($15,600) see Parker Foundation

La Jolla Youth ($8,500) see Stauffer Foundation, John and Beverly

La Pena Cultural Center ($21,000) see Fleishhacker Foundation

Labor/Community Strategy Center — to organize low-income and people of color communities in Los Angeles to address urban environmental issues ($60,000) see Noyes Foundation, Jessie Smith

Ladies Home Society of Oakland: Special Support — general fund ($100,000) see Lakeside Foundation

Laguna Playhouse — to underwrite one performance during their Youth's Theater's '91-92 season ($1,000) see Subaru of America Inc.

LaJolla Cancer Research Foundation — medical research ($339,344) see Mathers Charitable Foundation, G. Harold and Leila Y.

Lake Avenue Congregational Church ($7,000) see Howe and Mitchell B. Howe Foundation, Lucite Horton

Lake Forest Academy ($2,000) see Howe and Mitchell B. Howe Foundation, Lucite Horton

Lake Forest Academy ($5,000) see Plym Foundation

Lake Tahoe Summer Music Festival ($100) see Dreyer's & Edy's Grand Ice Cream

LAMP — mentally ill training program ($25,000) see M. E. G. Foundation

Las Positas Park Foundation ($25,000) see Tuohy Foundation, Alice Tweed

LaSalle High School ($10,000) see Clougherty Charitable Trust, Francis H.

Latin American Consortium on Agroecology and Development — to strengthen development of agroecology in Latin America ($80,000) see Noyes Foundation, Jessie Smith

Lawrence Hall of Science ($25,000) see Gilmore Foundation, William G.

Lawrence Hall of Science — education, laser science technology and lab equipment ($213,180) see Holt Foundation, William Knox

Lawrence University — education ($10,000) see Menasha Corp.

LEAD ($5,000) see Burnham Foundation

Leakey Foundation ($12,500) see Seebee Trust, Frances

Legal Aid Society ($20,000) see van Loben Sels - Eleanor Slate van Lobel Sels Charitable Foundation, Ernst D.

Legal Services of Northern California — child support project ($70,000) see Rosenberg Foundation

Legal Services for Seniors ($24,200) see Segal Charitable Trust, Barnet

Leland Stanford Junior University — Eastern European document collecting ($250,000) see Hoover, Jr. Foundation, Margaret W. and Herbert

Leland Stanford Junior University — Renovation ($300,000) see Hoover, Jr. Foundation, Margaret W. and Herbert

Lets Go Fishing ($4,600) see Meland Outreach

Leukemia Society of America, Los Angeles, CA ($24,500) see McDonnell Douglas Corp.-West

Liahona Club ($3,000) see Peery Foundation

Liaison Citizen Program ($25,000) see Connell Foundation, Michael J.

Liberty Hill Foundation ($3,000) see Rosenthal Foundation, Richard and Hinda

Library Foundation of San Francisco ($5,000) see Cow Hollow Foundation

Library Foundation of San Francisco — capital ($30,000) see Gap, The

Library Foundation of San Francisco ($25,000) see Gilmore Foundation, William G.

Library Foundation of San Francisco — capital campaign ($60,000) see U.S. Leasing International

Lick-Wilmerding/Extension ($17,143) see Langendorf Foundation, Stanley S.

Lick-Wilmerding High School ($20,000) see Gellert Foundation, Fred

Life and Mission Foundation and World Vision ($20,000) see Lamb Foundation, Kirkland S. and Rena B.

Life on the Water, People's Theatre Coalition ($4,500) see Walker Foundation, T. B.

Lighthouse for the Blind and Visually Impaired — to send children to Enchanted Hills Camp ($5,000) see Smith Trust, May and Stanley

Linda Vista Health Care Center ($5,000) see Pratt Memorial Fund

Linda Vista Library ($5,000) see Polinsky-Rivkin Family Foundation

Lindsay Museum see Tosco Corp. Refining Division

Linus Pauling Institute of Science and Medicine ($3,000) see Glenn Foundation for Medical Research, Paul F.

Linus Pauling Institute of Science and Medicine ($15,000) see McGonagle Foundation, Dextra Baldwin

Linus Pauling Institute of Science and Medicine ($25,000) see Schaffer Foundation, Michael & Helen

Linus Pauling Institute of Science and Medicine ($3,900) see Thrush-Thompson Foundation

Little Children's Aid Junior Auxiliary ($5,000) see Gellert Foundation, Celia Berta

Little Sisters of Poor ($100,000) see Gellert Foundation, Carl

Little Sisters of Poor ($10,000) see Gellert Foundation, Celia Berta

Little Sisters of Poor ($10,000) see Gleason Foundation, Katherine

Little Sisters of Poor ($3,000) see Gleason Foundation, Katherine

Live Again Ministries ($5,000) see Boeckmann Charitable Foundation

Live Oak Adult Day Services ($5,000) see Nelson Foundation, Florence

Livingston Memorial Visiting Nurse Association ($125,000) see Livingston Memorial Foundation

Lobero Theater Foundation ($30,000) see Tuohy Foundation, Alice Tweed

Logan Heights Family Health Center ($102,500) see Union Bank

Loma Linda University ($50,000) see Hedco Foundation

Loma Linda University ($45,000) see Knudsen Foundation, Tom and Valley

Loma Linda University Medical Center — purchase of equipment for cancer treatment ($100,000) see Webb Foundation, Del E.

Loma Linda University School of Medicine ($72,866) see Bugher Foundation

Loma Linda University School of Medicine ($44,000) see MacKenzie Foundation

Long Beach Civic Light Opera ($200) see Robertshaw Controls Co.

Long Beach Day Nursery ($125,000) see Fairfield Foundation, Freeman E.

Long Beach Medical Center ($100,000) see Miller Foundation, Earl B. and Loraine H.

Long Beach Memorial Hospital ($2,000) see Dettman Foundation, Leroy E.

Long Marine Laboratory Visitors Center ($25,000) see Witter Foundation, Dean

Loretta High School ($17,516) see Arata Brothers Trust

Los Angeles Center for Economic Survival — Affordable Housing Preservation project ($70,000) see Rosenberg Foundation

Los Angeles Chamber Orchestra ($75,000) see Nakamichi Foundation, E.

Los Angeles Child Guidance Clinic ($25,000) see Disney Family Foundation, Roy

Los Angeles Children's Museum ($35,000) see Brotman Foundation of California

Los Angeles Children's Museum ($10,200) see Metropolitan Theatres Corp.

Los Angeles Children's Theatre ($5,000) see Bannerman Foundation, William C.

Los Angeles County Museum ($5,000) see Taper Foundation, S. Mark

Los Angeles County Museum of Art ($100,000) see Bren Foundation, Donald L.

Los Angeles County Museum of Art ($15,000) see Day Foundation, Willametta K.

Los Angeles County Museum of Art ($400,000) see Ford Motor Co.

Los Angeles County Museum of Art — general ($6,000) see Fusenot Charity Foundation, Georges and Germaine

Los Angeles County Museum of Art ($13,875) see Geffen Foundation, David

Los Angeles County Museum of Art ($5,000) see Goldsmith Family Foundation

Los Angeles County Museum of Art ($3,000) see Jones Fund, Blanche and George

Los Angeles County Museum of Art ($1,500) see National Metal & Steel

Los Angeles County Museum of Art ($18,000) see Schimmel Foundation

Los Angeles County Museum of Art ($10,000) see Seaver Charitable Trust, Richard C.

Los Angeles County Museum of Art ($5,000) see Shapell Foundation, Nathan and Lilly

Los Angeles County Museum of Art ($5,000) see Sprague, Jr. Foundation, Caryll M. and Norman F.

Los Angeles County Museum of Art ($5,000) see Taper Foundation, Mark

Los Angeles County Museum of Art — annual support ($90,000) see Times Mirror Co.

Los Angeles County Museum of Art ($10,000) see Weiler Foundation

Los Angeles County Museum of Natural History Foundation ($7,287) see Van Nuys Foundation, I. N. and Susanna H.

Los Angeles Education Alliance for Restructuring Now (LEARN) — business/community initiative for school reform ($150,000) see ARCO

Los Angeles Educational Alliance for Restructuring Now ($25,000) see MCA

Los Angeles Educational Partnership ($5,000) see Jonsson Foundation

Los Angeles Educational Partnership ($5,000) see Roth Family Foundation

Los Angeles Educational Partnership — for Humanitas program ($150,000) see Stuart Foundations

Los Angeles Educational Partnership — Interactive Mathematics ($15,000) see Toshiba America, Inc.

Los Angeles Educational Partnership — to fund the 1992 Toyota Math and Science Grants for Teachers in the LAUSD ($168,300) see Toyota Motor Sales, U.S.A.

Los Angeles Educational Partnership — to fund the

1992 Toyota Math and Science Grants for Teachers in the LAUSD ($78,800) see Toyota Motor Sales, U.S.A.

Los Angeles Educational Partnership — to support and expand PLUS, a program geared toward the reform of mathematics instruction ($200,000) see Parsons Foundation, Ralph M.

Los Angeles Educational Partnership — helps to fund a program to assist schools in implementing School Based Management see New Street Capital Corp.

Los Angeles Educational Partnership — Students Explore Science with Technology ($25,940) see Toshiba America, Inc.

Los Angeles Family Housing — charitable loans ($1,468,900) see Berger Foundation, H.N. and Frances C.

Los Angeles Family Housing Corporation ($5,000) see Goldsmith Family Foundation

Los Angeles Free Clinic ($10,000) see Bireley Foundation

Los Angeles Free Clinic ($500,000) see Taper Foundation, Mark

Los Angeles Free Clinic ($20,000) see Weisz Foundation, David and Sylvia

Los Angeles Heart Institute ($240,000) see McAlister Charitable Foundation, Harold

Los Angeles Holocaust Monument ($25,000) see Eisenberg Foundation, Ben B. and Joyce E.

Los Angeles Library — Save the Books ($50,000) see Rigler-Deutsch Foundation

Los Angeles — Make A Wish Foundation ($2,500) see City of Hope 1989 Section E Foundation

Los Angeles Mission ($5,000) see Bannerman Foundation, William C.

Los Angeles Mission ($50,000) see Douglas Charitable Foundation

Los Angeles Mission ($10,000) see Douglas Charitable Foundation

Los Angeles Mission ($10,000) see Hafif Family Foundation

Los Angeles Municipal Art Gallery ($14,000) see Chartwell Foundation

Los Angeles Music and Art School ($10,000) see Bull Foundation, Henry W.

Los Angeles Music and Art School ($7,500) see Bull Foundation, Henry W.

Los Angeles Music Center ($5,450) see Kingsley Foundation, Lewis A.

Los Angeles Music Center ($25,000) see Seaver Charitable Trust, Richard C.

Los Angeles Music Center Foundation ($46,000) see Wells Fargo & Co.

Los Angeles Music Center Opera ($202,000) see Getty Foundation, Ann and Gordon

Los Angeles Music Center Opera ($50,000) see Nakamichi Foundation, E.

Los Angeles Music Center Opera ($44,200) see Petersen Foundation, Esper A.

Los Angeles Music Center Opera ($250,000) see Skirball Foundation

Los Angeles Music Center Opera Association ($203,200) see Colburn Fund

Los Angeles Music Center Opera Association ($200,000) see Thornton Foundation, Flora L.

Los Angeles Music Center Opera Association ($6,350) see Thornton Foundation, John M. and Sally B.

Los Angeles Music Center Unified Fund ($25,000) see Union Bank

Los Angeles Orphanage Guild ($10,000) see Mosher Foundation, Samuel B.

Los Angeles Philharmonic ($5,000) see Negaunee Foundation

Los Angeles Philharmonic Association ($90,500) see Colburn Fund

Los Angeles Philharmonic Association ($150,000) see Getty Foundation, Ann and Gordon

Los Angeles Philharmonic Association ($15,000) see Witco Corp.

Los Angeles Planned Parenthood — support medical equipment for South Bay clinic ($75,000) see Whittier Foundation, L. K.

Los Angeles Police Department ($750) see Dreyer's & Edy's Grand Ice Cream

Los Angeles Regional Foodbank ($5,000) see Bannerman Foundation, William C.

Los Angeles Times Summer Camp Fund ($80,000) see Pfaffinger Foundation

Los Angeles Unified School District ($47,000) see Alpert Foundation, Herb

Los Angeles Unified School District ($150,000) see Center for Educational Programs

Los Angeles Unified School District ($5,000) see Roth Family Foundation

Los Angeles Unified School District — "earthmobile" ($22,400) see Gluck Foundation, Maxwell H.

Los Angeles Unified School District — Gluck Children's Center ($306,766) see Gluck Foundation, Maxwell H.

Los Angeles Unified Schools ($15,000) see Deutsch Co.

Los Positas College ($200) see Dreyer's & Edy's Grand Ice Cream

Love Foundation for American Music, Entertainment and Art ($450,000) see Kraft General Foods

Love Foundation for American Music, Entertainment and Art ($366,429) see Kraft General Foods

Love Foundation for American Music, Entertainment and Art ($366,429) see Kraft General Foods

Love Foundation for American Music, Entertainment and Art ($366,429) see Kraft General Foods

Love Is Feeding Everyone (LIFE) ($80,000) see Milken Foundation, L. and S.

Lovers of Holy Cross-Vietnamese Sisters ($37,000) see Morania Foundation

California (cont.)

Loyola High School ($150,000) see Clougherty Charitable Trust, Francis H.

Loyola High School ($12,500) see Hayden Foundation, William R. and Virginia

Loyola Law School ($1,500,000) see Burns Foundation, Fritz B.

Loyola Marymount University see American Electronics

Loyola Marymount University see Argonaut Group

Loyola-Marymount University ($1,400,000) see Burns Foundation, Fritz B.

Loyola Marymount University ($39,000) see Clougherty Charitable Trust, Francis H.

Loyola Marymount University ($200,000) see Darling Foundation, Hugh and Hazel

Loyola Marymount University ($64,132) see Dunning Foundation

Loyola Marymount University ($2,500) see Jacobs Engineering Group

Loyola Marymount University — scholarship fund ($25,000) see Kingsley Foundation, Lewis A.

Loyola Marymount University ($45,000) see Knudsen Foundation, Tom and Valley

Loyola Marymount University ($1,000) see McCarthy Foundation, Michael W.

Loyola Marymount University ($10,000) see Pacific Western Foundation

Loyola Marymount University see Richley, Inc.

Loyola Marymount University ($441,000) see Weingart Foundation

Loyola Marymount University — Scholarship Grant ($1,000) see Darling Foundation, Hugh and Hazel

Loyola Marymount University — to renovate and equip the Werts Electronics Laboratory ($189,000) see Parsons Foundation, Ralph M.

Lucile Salter Packard Children's Hospital at Stanford — pediatric advice line ($100,000) see Sega of America

Luden Center ($100) see Shapell Foundation, Nathan and Lilly

Luminaries, Jr. ($2,500) see Bannan Foundation, Arline and Thomas J.

Lutheran Bible Institute — Hispanic Conferences ($60,000) see Lutheran Brotherhood Foundation

Lutheran Social Services of Northern California — AIDS ministries ($34,175) see Lutheran Brotherhood Foundation

Madison Elementary School see Ricoh Electronics Inc.

Make A Circus — to support Teen Apprenticeship Program ($7,500) see Lux Foundation, Miranda

Mandela Freedom Fund ($10,000) see Lastfogel Foundation, Abe and Frances

Manressa ($5,000) see Crean Foundation

Maple Center of Beverly Hills ($25,000) see Smith Foundation, Lon V.

Marantha High School ($2,500) see Howe and Mitchell B.

Howe Foundation, Lucite Horton

March of Dimes ($500) see Martin Foundation, Bert William

Mardan — special education facility ($100,000) see Irvine Health Foundation

Marianne Frostig Center ($55,100) see Lund Foundation

Marianne Frostig Center of Educational Therapy ($5,000) see Arrillaga Foundation

Marianne Frostig Center of Educational Therapy ($18,000) see Borchard Foundation, Albert and Elaine

Marin Abused Women Services ($30,000) see Van Camp Foundation

Marin General Hospital ($25,000) see Fireman's Fund Insurance Co.

Marin General Hospital ($100,000) see Prairie Foundation

Marin General Hospital — new Emergency Department ($100,000) see Irwin Charity Foundation, William G.

Marin Heart Association ($1,000) see Gleason Foundation, James

Marin Humane Society ($70,000) see Doelger Charitable Trust, Thelma

Marin Humane Society ($500) see Prairie Foundation

Marin Institute for Prevention of Alcohol and Other Drug Problems ($200,000) see Cowell Foundation, S. H.

Marin Jewish Community Center ($10,000) see Goodman Foundation, Edward and Marion

Marin Symphony ($10,000) see Fireman's Fund Insurance Co.

Marin Therapy and Training Institute ($20,000) see Van Camp Foundation

Mark Taper Forum ($150,000) see Shubert Foundation

Marlborough College ($10,000) see Braitmayer Foundation

Marlborough School ($11,000) see Munger Foundation, Alfred C.

Marlborough School ($7,500) see Van Nuys Charities, J. B. and Emily

Marycrest Manor ($5,000) see Bannan Foundation, Arline and Thomas J.

Marycrest Manor ($10,000) see Pacific Western Foundation

Maryknoll Fathers and Brothers — current fund ($10,000) see Dolan Family Foundation

Marymount High School ($300,000) see Leavey Foundation, Thomas and Dorothy

Marymount School of Santa Barbara ($11,800) see Sattler Beneficial Trust, Daniel A. and Edna J.

Masonic Homes of California ($56,724) see Hobart Memorial Fund, Marion W.

Mateo Lodge ($16,212) see Bothin Foundation

Mathematics, Engineering, Science Achievement (MESA) at the University of California at Berkeley — Saturday Academy math and science program ($75,000) see Sega of America

Mayfield Junior School ($50,000) see Clougherty Charitable Trust, Francis H.

Mayfield Senior School ($40,000) see Clougherty Charitable Trust, Francis H.

Mayflower Church ($20,000) see Braun Foundation

Mayflower Congregational Church ($3,000) see Schlinger Foundation

Mazon ($2,000) see Bronstein Foundation, Soloman and Sylvia

Mazon A Jewish Response to Hunger ($5,000) see Thalheimer Foundation, Alvin and Fanny Blaustein

McGeorge School of Law — new law library research center ($96,000) see Cord Foundation, E. L.

McKinley Home for Boys ($15,000) see Leonardt Foundation

Meals on Wheels ($6,000) see Fusenot Charity Foundation, Georges and Germaine

Medical Research Institute ($50,000) see Gilmore Foundation, William G.

Medical Research Institute ($2,100) see Shoong Foundation, Milton

Medical Research Institute — Post Graduate Fellowship ($27,500) see Margoes Foundation

Medical Research Institute of San Francisco ($20,000) see Oxnard Foundation

Mendocino Coast Humane Society ($15,000) see Doelger Charitable Trust, Thelma

Mendocino Community Library ($1,000) see R. P. Foundation

Mendocino Music Festival ($2,500) see R. P. Foundation

Menlo School ($39,000) see Arrillaga Foundation

Menlo School ($1,000) see Woodard Family Foundation

Menlo School and College — academic assistance ($97,500) see Chiles Foundation

Menlo School and College ($26,000) see McAlister Charitable Foundation, Harold

Mental Health Association ($15,000) see Bradford Foundation, George and Ruth

Mental Health Association ($48,700) see Simon Foundation, Robert Ellis

Mercy High School — to upgrade computer equipment ($6,800) see Lux Foundation, Miranda

Mercy High School ($25,000) see Ritter Foundation, May Ellen and Gerald

Mercy High School — Burlingame ($15,000) see Hale Foundation, Crescent Porter

Mercy High School — repair and restoration of Kohl Mansion ($100,000) see Irwin Charity Foundation, William G.

Mercy Hospital Foundation of San Diego ($5,000) see Pratt Memorial Fund

Mercy Medical Center Redding ($268,761) see Offield Family Foundation

Merola Opera Program ($250) see Newman Charitable Trust, Calvin M. and Raquel H.

Merritt Peralta Foundation ($40,000) see Gilmore Foundation, William G.

Merritt Peralta Medical Center: Samuel Merritt College — nursing master's degree

program ($50,000) see Lakeside Foundation

Methodist Hospital ($42,979) see Arata Brothers Trust

Methodist Hospital of Southern California San Gabriel Arcadia Methodist Hospital — nursing scholarships and equipment purchases ($1,000,000) see Berger Foundation, H.N. and Frances C.

Mexican American Legal Defense and Education Fund ($20,000) see Hogan Foundation, Royal Barney

Mexican American Legal Defense and Education Fund — toward the purchase of a building in Los Angeles as a permanent site ($400,000) see Irvine Foundation, James

Mexican-American Legal Defense and Educational Fund — support broader implementation of a model parent leadership development program ($50,000) see Hazen Foundation, Edward W.

Mexican American Legal Defense and Educational Fund — California Language Rights program ($75,000) see Rosenberg Foundation

Mid-Peninsula Community Housing Coalition ($150,000) see Cowell Foundation, S. H.

Mid-Peninsula YWCA — Women Entrepreneurs Program ($36,000) see Sun Microsystems

Mid-Valley Community Police Council — general ($10,000) see Fusenot Charity Foundation, Georges and Germaine

Midnight Mission ($50,000) see Keck, Jr. Foundation, William M.

Midnight Missions ($7,500) see Forest Lawn Foundation

Mills College — endowed scholarship fund ($250,000) see Jones Foundation, Fletcher

Mills College — scholarship fund ($500,000) see Steele Foundation, Harry and Grace

Mills College ($400,000) see Valley Foundation, Wayne and Gladys

Mills College-Carnegie Hall — educational programs ($15,000) see Genentech

Milton Shoong Chinese Cultural Center ($154,000) see Shoong Foundation, Milton

Mission Aviation ($2,000) see City of Hope 1989 Section E Foundation

Mission Aviation Fellowship ($5,040) see Marshburn Foundation

Mission Aviation Fellowship ($80,000) see Ryan Foundation, David Claude

Mission Aviation Fellowship — purchase of radios for safety training pilots ($25,000) see Stamps Foundation, James L.

Mission Aviation Fellowship — used plane for Mexico ($50,000) see Young Foundation, Irvin L.

Mission Aviation Fellowship — plane for New Guinea ($25,000) see Young Foundation, Irvin L.

Mission Dolores — restoration of historic California mission ($25,000) see Skaggs Foundation, L. J. and Mary C.

Mission Training and Resource Center ($15,000) see Westwood Endowment

Modesto Rotary Club ($5,000) see Bright Family Foundation

Monsignor Kennedy Education Foundation ($25,000) see Gallo Foundation, Ernest

Monterey Bay Aquarium Research Institute — operating expenses and capital projects ($8,500,000) see Packard Foundation, David and Lucile

Monterey College of Law ($20,000) see Segal Charitable Trust, Barnet

Monterey Institute — general support ($39,500) see Dunspaugh-Dalton Foundation

Monterey Institute of International Studies ($5,000) see Littlefield Foundation, Edmund Wattis

Monterey Institute of International Studies ($5,000) see National Pro-Am Youth Fund

Monterey Institute of International Studies ($5,000) see National Pro-Am Youth Fund

Monterey Institute of International Studies — building fund ($50,000) see Segal Charitable Trust, Barnet

Monterey Institute of International Studies ($1,000) see Warner Foundation, Lee and Rose

Monterey Peninsula College ($11,000) see National Pro-Am Youth Fund

Monterey Peninsula College ($11,000) see National Pro-Am Youth Fund

Monterey Peninsula Museum — general support ($50,000) see Dunspaugh-Dalton Foundation

Monterey Sports Center ($2,500) see Upjohn California Fund

Morning Star Outreach ($10,000) see de Dampierre Memorial Foundation, Marie C.

Morris Animal Foundation ($18,295) see Barbour Foundation, Bernice

Morris Animal Foundation ($10,000) see Seebee Trust, Frances

Motion Picture Country Home ($50,000) see Pickford Foundation, Mary

Motion Picture and Television Fund ($75,000) see Douglas Charitable Foundation

Motion Picture and Television Fund ($100,300) see Geffen Foundation, David

Motion Picture and Television Fund ($10,000) see Lastfogel Foundation, Abe and Frances

Motion Picture and Television Fund ($100,000) see Disney Co., Walt

Motion Picture and Television Fund ($48,500) see Wasserman Foundation

Motion Picture and Television Relief Fund ($100,000) see MCA

Motion Picture TV Fund ($482,067) see Goldwyn Foundation, Samuel

Mount Diablo Council Boy Scouts of America see Tosco Corp. Refining Division

Mount Diablo Hospital Foundation ($200,000) see Hofmann Co.

Mt. Diablo Hospital Foundation — cancer center building fund

California (cont.)

NRDC — energy efficiency work ($20,000) see True North Foundation

O.C. Center for Performing Arts ($246,082) see Argyros Foundation

Oak Creek Church ($27,652) see Meland Outreach

Oak Valley District Hospital ($10,000) see Ernest & Julio Gallo Winery

Oakland Ballet Company ($30,000) see Clorox Co.

Oakland Boys Clubs — delinquency prevention ($15,000) see Odell and Helen Pfeiffer Odell Fund, Robert Stewart

Oakland Museum Foundation ($5,000) see DiRosa Foundation, Rene and Veronica

Oakland Youth Works ($10,000) see Friedman Family Foundation

Obstetrics and Gynecology Research and Education Foundation ($25,000) see Gellert Foundation, Fred

Occidental College ($20,000) see Atkinson Foundation, Myrtle L.

Occidental College ($50,000) see Connell Foundation, Michael J.

Occidental College ($20,000) see Greenville Foundation

Occidental College ($45,000) see Knudsen Foundation, Tom and Valley

Occidental College ($11,500) see MacKenzie Foundation

Occidental College ($10,000) see Mann Foundation, John Jay

Occidental College ($75,000) see Norris Foundation, Kenneth T. and Eileen L.

Occidental College ($2,600) see Psychists

Occidental College — Fletcher Jones Chair in Chemistry ($500,000) see Jones Foundation, Fletcher

Occidental College/Oxford University ($30,000) see Sperry Fund

O'Conner Hospital — cardiac equipment ($74,000) see Wiegand Foundation, E. L.

O'Connor Hospital Foundation Society — general fund ($50,000) see Stuart Center Charitable Trust, Hugh

O'Connor Hospital Foundation Society — general fund ($11,500) see Stuart Center Charitable Trust, Hugh

ODC/San Francisco ($21,000) see Fleishhacker Foundation

Ojai Valley School ($15,000) see Littlefield Foundation, Edmund Wattis

Ojai Valley School ($1,500) see New England Foundation

Old Globe Theater ($10,000) see Fox Foundation, John H.

Old Globe Theatre ($5,000) see Burnham Foundation

Old Globe Theatre ($100,000) see Parker Foundation

Old Globe Theatre ($19,000) see Poinsettia Foundation, Paul and Magdalena Ecke

Old Globe Theatre ($100,000) see Polinsky-Rivkin Family Foundation

Old Globe Theatre ($4,195) see Thornton Foundation, John M. and Sally B.

Olive Crest Orange County ($10,000) see Halsell Foundation, O. L.

Olive Crest Treatment Center ($10,450) see Argyros Foundation

Olympia Institute ($35,000) see Van Camp Foundation

On Lok Senior Health Services — toward purchase and renovation of new facility for senior housing, adult day health care, and day care center for intergenerational activities and for technical assistance to Coalition for Elder's Independence replication of On Lok's Program ($68,400) see Haas, Jr. Fund, Evelyn and Walter

1990 Deaf Olympiad ($100) see Dreyer's & Edy's Grand Ice Cream

One Voice ($1,000) see Parvin Foundation, Albert

Opera Pacific ($100,000) see Crean Foundation

Opera Pacific ($19,206) see Murdy Foundation

Opera Pacific ($25,000) see Segerstrom Foundation

Operation Exodus ($25,000) see Amado Foundation, Maurice

Operation Exodus ($149,000) see Chais Family Foundation

Operation Exodus ($250,000) see Deutsch Co.

Operation Exodus ($16,500) see Goodman Foundation, Edward and Marion

Operation Exodus ($202,000) see Irmas Charitable Foundation, Audrey and Sydney

Operation Exodus — civic ($250,000) see Mann Foundation, Ted

Operation Exodus ($51,000) see Taubman Foundation, Herman P. and Sophia

Operation Exodus ($26,667) see Weisz Foundation, David and Sylvia

Opportunities Industrialization Center West, Menlo Park, CA — for employment training work with minorities see Tandem Computers

Opportunities Industrialization Center West — The Industry Specific Training Program ($49,973) see Sun Microsystems

Opportunities Industrialization Centers of America (OIC), Job Training Center ($1,325,000) see Chevron Corp.

Optimist Club of Buena Park ($1,000) see Jerome Foundation

Or Lok Senior Health Services ($291,667) see Herbst Foundation

Orange County Bar Association ($12,500) see Stillwell Charitable Trust, Glen and Dorothy

Orange County Burn Association, Orange, CA ($20,000) see McDonnell Douglas Corp.-West

Orange County Council ($3,000) see Vesper Corp.

Orange County Performing Arts ($25,000) see Nestle U.S.A. Inc.

Orange County Performing Arts Center ($100,000) see Segerstrom Foundation

Orange County Performing Arts Center — to support the Center's fifth Anniversary Benefit Galas ($28,000) see Fluor Corp.

Orange County Performing Arts Center — funding to underwrite Opera ($516,875) see Steele Foundation, Harry and Grace

Orange County Trauma Society ($10,000) see Halsell Foundation, O. L.

Orangewood-A New Home for Dependent Children ($32,500) see Argyros Foundation

Orangewood Children's Foundation — children's nursery ($50,000) see Irvine Health Foundation

Organization of Chinese Americans ($1,000) see Gleason Foundation, James

Organization for the Needs of Elderly ($250,000) see Taper Foundation, Mark

Orgone Biophysical Research Laboratory — Israel Water Project Research ($16,080) see Fox Foundation, Richard J.

Orthopaedic Hospital Los Angeles ($6,000) see Bekins Foundation, Milo W.

Orthopaedic Hospital of Los Angeles ($22,000) see Beynon Foundation, Kathryne

Osteoporosis Research Foundation ($15,000) see Llagas Foundation

Otis Parsons ($10,000) see Weisz Foundation, David and Sylvia

Otis Parsons Institute ($20,000) see Irmas Charitable Foundation, Audrey and Sydney

Our Lady of Fatima Church ($20,000) see Gallo Foundation, Ernest

Our Lady of Guadalupe ($25,000) see Furth Foundation

Our Lady of Guadalupe ($9,500) see Stauffer Foundation, John and Beverly

Our Lady of Malibu School ($16,809) see Chartwell Foundation

Our Lady of Mercy Church ($3,000) see Wilsey Bennet Co.

Our Lady of Sacred Heart School ($10,000) see R. P. Foundation

Outpatient Ophthalmic Surgery Society — goodwill ($15,000) see Alcon Laboratories, Inc.

Outward Bound — support for education program aimed at risk youth ($25,000) see Mattel

Outward Bound — support for educational program aimed at risk youth ($25,000) see Mattel

Overseas Crusades ($2,400) see Meland Outreach

P.G.A. Foundation ($5,000) see Hoffman Foundation, H. Leslie Hoffman and Elaine S.

P.I.C.H. — choices for a healthier lifestyle program ($150,000) see Irvine Health Foundation

P.I.C.H. — health promotion ($51,027) see Irvine Health Foundation

Pacific Asia Museum ($5,000) see Scott Foundation, Virginia Steele

Pacific Asia Museum ($12,000) see Weisman Art Foundation, Frederick R.

Pacific Basin Institute — in support of translation services ($10,200) see Matsushita Electric Corp. of America

Pacific Children's Center ($250) see Dreyer's & Edy's Grand Ice Cream

Pacific Crest Outward Bound — funds are being used to run four in-school programs of 100 at-risk students each and two summer programs ($45,000) see Hancock Foundation, Luke B.

Pacific Graduate School of Psychology ($1,500) see Taube Family Foundation

Pacific Hospital of Long Beach ($29,557) see McDonnell Douglas Corp.-West

Pacific Institute — to develop practical strategies to prevent conflict ($25,000) see Mertz-Gilmore Foundation, Joyce

Pacific Legal Foundation ($15,000) see Bull Foundation, Henry W.

Pacific Legal Foundation ($5,000) see Bull Foundation, Henry W.

Pacific Legal Foundation ($5,000) see Hastings Trust

Pacific Legal Foundation ($25,000) see Jameson Foundation, J. W. and Ida M.

Pacific Legal Foundation — litigation in the public interest ($25,000) see Montgomery Street Foundation

Pacific Legal Foundation ($5,000) see Weiler Foundation

Pacific Legal Foundation — College of Public Interest Law, Judicial Responsibility Project, Limited Government Project ($375,000) see Hermann Foundation, Grover

Pacific Lutheran Theological Seminaries — Center for Church Growth and Mission ($58,000) see Lutheran Brotherhood Foundation

Pacific Oaks College ($1,780) see Norman Foundation, Andrew

Pacific Presbyterian ($20,000) see Langendorf Foundation, Stanley S.

Pacific Presbyterian Family Therapy Clinic ($4,000) see Walker Foundation, T. B.

Pacific Presbyterian Medicine Foundation ($2,500) see Davies Charitable Trust

Pacific Public Radio ($200,000) see Burlington Resources

Pacific Research Institute ($20,000) see Koch Charitable Foundation, Charles G.

Pacific Research Institute for Public Policy ($5,000) see Durell Foundation, George Edward

Pacific Research Institute for Public Policy ($3,500) see Hume Foundation, Jaquelin

Pacific Research Institute for Public Policy ($2,500) see Komes Foundation

Pacific Research Institute for Public Policy ($5,000) see Thirty-Five Twenty, Inc.

Pacific Research Institute for Public Policy ($15,000) see Witter Foundation, Dean

Pacific School of Religion ($100,000) see Atkinson Foundation, Myrtle L.

Pacific Symphony ($50,000) see Segerstrom Foundation

Pacific University ($4,500) see ASARCO

Pacific Vision Foundation ($100,000) see Gellert Foundation, Fred

Pacific Vision Foundation ($5,000) see Wilsey Bennet Co.

Pacifica Foundation ($6,000) see Von der Ahe, Jr. Trust, Theodore Albert

Palace of Fine Arts ($10,000) see Swig Foundation

Palm Springs Desert Museum ($15,350) see Douglas Charitable Foundation

Palm Springs Desert Museum ($10,000) see Robin Family Foundation, Albert A.

Palm Springs Desert Museum ($400) see Robin Family Foundation, Albert A.

Palm Springs Desert Museum ($3,160) see Stone Family Foundation, Jerome H.

Palm Springs Friends of the Los Angeles Philharmonics ($1,000) see Storz Foundation, Robert Herman

Palm Springs Friends of Philharmonic ($6,270) see Philibosian Foundation, Stephen

Palm Springs Museum ($6,000) see Stauffer Foundation, John and Beverly

Palm Springs Senior Center ($252,500) see Frank Fund, Zollie and Elaine

Palo Alto Community Church ($5,000) see Arrillaga Foundation

Palo Alto Community Players ($15,000) see Driscoll Foundation

Palo Alto High School ($2,000) see Peery Foundation

Palo Alto Medical Foundation ($20,000) see Lennox International, Inc.

Palo Alto Medical Foundation ($5,000) see Littlefield Foundation, Edmund Wattis

Palo Alto Medical Foundation — President's Discretionary Fund ($333,000) see Boswell Foundation, James G.

Palo Alto Police Department ($92,165) see Guggenheim Foundation, Daniel and Florence

Palo Alto Unified School District ($20,000) see Crocker Trust, Mary A.

Palomar High — Exhibit A ($12,450) see California Educational Initiatives Fund

Para Los Ninos ($10,000) see Bannerman Foundation, William C.

Parent Empowerment Project — (Mission Reading Clinic); to fund a program of support groups, educational activities and leadership training for parents of elementary and middle school children ($66,502) see Zellerbach Family Fund

Parent Services Project ($11,250) see Haigh-Scatena Foundation

Parent Services Project — PSP brings mutual support, leadership development and other activities to low-income parents with children in child care centers in Alameda, Marin and San Francisco counties ($82,294) see Zellerbach Family Fund

Partner's International — Rajasthan Bible Institute and the New Life Community Development Society ($150,000) see Maclellan Charitable Trust, R. J.

Pasadena City College ($50,000) see Durfee Foundation

Pasadena City College Foundation ($5,000) see Howe and Mitchell B. Howe Foundation, Lucite Horton

Pasadena Council on Alcoholism and Drug Abuse ($36,000) see Beynon Foundation, Kathryne

Pasadena Historical Society ($5,000) see Howe and Mitchell B. Howe Foundation, Lucite Horton

Pasadena Historical Society ($10,000) see Murphey Foundation, Lluella Morey

Pasadena Historical Society — History Center Construction ($20,000) see Beynon Foundation, Kathryne

Pasadena Hospital Association ($20,000) see Braun Foundation

Pasadena Housing Alliance ($10,000) see Peppers Foundation, Ann

Pasadena Playhouse ($5,000) see Brotman Foundation of California

Pasadena Public Library ($5,000) see Shea Foundation, Edmund and Mary

Pasadena School District ($200,000) see Shea Foundation, John and Dorothy

Pasadena Symphony Association ($5,000) see Scott Foundation, Virginia Steele

Pasadena Symphony Orchestra ($3,000) see Howe and Mitchell B. Howe Foundation, Lucite Horton

Pasadena Unified School District ($25,000) see Knudsen Foundation, Tom and Valley

Pasadena Unified School District ($200,000) see Riordan Foundation

Pasadena Unified Schools ($300,000) see Shea Foundation, John and Dorothy

Pasadena United School District ($25,000) see Mead Foundation, Giles W. and Elise G.

Pathfinders of Palm Springs ($5,000) see Lindsay Foundation

Pathfinders of Palm Springs ($10,000) see Webb Educational and Charitable Trust, Torrey H. and Dorothy K.

Patient Assistance Fund ($500) see Levy Foundation, Edward C.

Paulist Productions ($20,000) see Hayden Foundation, William R. and Virginia

Paulist Productions — toward production costs on a film on Dorothy Day ($25,000) see Raskob Foundation for Catholic Activities

Peace and Justice Center of Southern California ($6,000) see Von der Ahe, Jr. Trust, Theodore Albert

Pediatric AIDS Foundation ($200,000) see Milken Family Medical Foundation

Pediatric AIDS Foundation see New York Mercantile Exchange

Pediatric AIDS Foundation ($5,000) see Rosenthal Foundation, Richard and Hinda

Pediatric AIDS Foundation — "Educating Our Children" video project ($300,000) see Sega of America

Pediatric Cancer Research Foundation of Orange County ($117,500) see Shaw

Foundation, Walden W. and Jean Young

Pen Center USA West ($40,000) see Banyan Tree Foundation

Peniel Mission ($15,000) see Berry Foundation, Lowell

Peninsula Center for the Blind ($7,200) see Arrillaga Foundation

Peninsula Center for the Blind ($25,000) see Stuart Center Charitable Trust, Hugh

Peninsula Center for the Blind ($15,000) see Stuart Center Charitable Trust, Hugh

Peninsula Center for the Blind ($1,500) see Taube Family Foundation

Peninsula Humane Society ($70,000) see Doelger Charitable Trust, Thelma

Peninsula Open Space Trust ($26,000) see Herbst Foundation

Peninsula Open Space Trust ($500,000) see Moore Family Foundation

Peninsula Open Space Trust — Phleger property acquisition ($75,000) see Compton Foundation

Peninsula Outreach Welcome House — food and shelter for the homeless ($80,000) see Segal Charitable Trust, Barnet

Peninsula Volunteers ($10,000) see Walker Foundation, T. B.

Peoples Self-Help Housing — low-income housing ($50,000) see M. E. G. Foundation

Pepperdine University ($25,000) see Confidence Foundation

Pepperdine University ($25,000) see Crummer Foundation, Roy E.

Pepperdine University ($60,000) see Darling Foundation, Hugh and Hazel

Pepperdine University ($200,000) see Joslyn Foundation, Marcellus I.

Pepperdine University ($15,200) see Kingsley Foundation, Lewis A.

Pepperdine University ($30,400) see Moores Foundation

Pepperdine University ($17,500) see Peppers Foundation, Ann

Pepperdine University ($3,063) see Staley Foundation, Thomas F.

Pepperdine University ($50,000) see Stephens Foundation Trust

Pepperdine University ($424,695) see Weingart Foundation

Pepperdine University — for expansion of Odell McConnell Law Center ($75,000) see Stauffer Charitable Trust, John

Performing Arts Center ($10,000) see Bull Foundation, Henry W.

Performing Arts Council of the Music Center ($30,000) see McDonnell Douglas Corp.-West

Performing Group for Youth ($15,100) see Peery Foundation

Permanent Charities Com ($64,000) see CBS Inc.

Permanent Charities Committee ($40,000) see MCA

Permanent Charities Committee of Entertainment Industries ($31,000) see Paramount Communications Inc.

Permanent Charities Committee of the Entertainment Industries ($50,000) see Disney Co., Walt

Pet Protection Society ($15,000) see Seebee Trust, Frances

Petaluma People Services Center — assist with expenses for meal service to home-bound senior citizens ($3,000) see Exchange Bank

Petaluma Valley Hospital Foundation — second third of $10,000 to build new emergency room facility ($3,334) see Exchange Bank

Philharmonia Foundation ($100,000) see Meyer Foundation

Phillips Brooks School ($10,000) see Hogan Foundation, Royal Barney

Phillips Brooks School ($2,000) see Smith Charitable Fund, Eleanor Armstrong

Phoenix House of California ($950,000) see Bettingen Corporation, Burton G.

Pickle Family Circus ($21,000) see Fleishhacker Foundation

Piedmont Community Church ($50,000) see Bechtel, Jr. Foundation, S. D.

Piedmont Community Church ($50,000) see Bechtel, Jr. Foundation, S. D.

Piedmont Community Church ($3,350) see Farallon Foundation

Piedmont Community Church ($200,000) see Lakeside Foundation

Piedmont Community Church ($10,000) see Lakeside Foundation

Piedmont Community Church ($11,604) see Llagas Foundation

Piedmont Community Church ($20,000) see Uvas Foundation

Pilgrim Pines United Church of Christ ($50,000) see Confidence Foundation

Pilgrimage County Center ($12,000) see Stillwell Charitable Trust, Glen and Dorothy

Pinewood High School ($10,000) see Peery Foundation

Piru Elementary School ($15,995) see Newhall Foundation, Henry Mayo

Planned Parenthood ($5,000) see Polinsky-Rivkin Family Foundation

Planned Parenthood Association of San Mateo County — toward support of Parent Education program ($10,000) see Atkinson Foundation

Planned Parenthood Federation of America ($100,000) see Beaver Foundation

Planned Parenthood Federation of America ($57,000) see Beaver Foundation

Planned Parenthood Federation of America ($45,000) see Beaver Foundation

Planned Parenthood Federation of America ($25,000) see Beaver Foundation

Planned Parenthood Federation of America ($10,000) see Bergstrom Foundation, Erik E. and Edith H.

Planned Parenthood Federation of America ($4,000) see Brenner Foundation, Mervyn

Planned Parenthood Federation of America ($73,900) see Confidence Foundation

Planned Parenthood Federation of America ($20,000) see Favrot Fund

Planned Parenthood Federation of America ($5,000) see Fusenot Charity Foundation, Georges and Germaine

Planned Parenthood Federation of America ($4,000) see Haskell Fund

Planned Parenthood Federation of America ($25,000) see Keck, Jr. Foundation, William M.

Planned Parenthood Federation of America ($20,000) see McGee Foundation

Planned Parenthood Federation of America ($20,000) see McGee Foundation

Planned Parenthood Federation of America — national assistance family planning ($100,000) see Mericos Foundation

Planned Parenthood Federation of America ($115,000) see Munger Foundation, Alfred C.

Planned Parenthood Federation of America ($35,000) see Parker Foundation

Planned Parenthood Federation of America ($8,250) see Roth Family Foundation

Planned Parenthood Federation of America ($3,822) see Sierra Pacific Resources

Planned Parenthood Federation of America ($30,000) see Stern Memorial Trust, Sidney

Planned Parenthood/Orange and San Bernardino Counties — general support ($250,000) see Steele Foundation, Harry and Grace

Planned Parenthood of San Diego and Riverside counties ($200,000) see Cowell Foundation, S. H.

Planned Parenthood of San Mateo County — donation to assist with renovation and expansion of facility ($30,000) see Atkinson Foundation

Planned Parenthood of Santa Barbara ($10,000) see Walker Foundation, Smith

Playwrights Project — theater operations ($15,000) see Favrot Fund

Plaza de la Raza ($8,092) see Durfee Foundation

Ploughshares Fund ($60,000) see Cow Hollow Foundation

Ploughshares Fund ($60,000) see Cow Hollow Foundation

Ploughshares Fund ($50,000) see Cow Hollow Foundation

Ploughshares Fund ($50,000) see Cow Hollow Foundation

Point Loma High School ($10,000) see Abel Construction Co.

Point Reyes Bird Observatory ($15,000) see Bothin Foundation

Point Reyes Bird Observatory ($10,000) see Oliver Memorial Trust Foundation

Polytechnic School ($125,000) see Mead Foundation, Giles W. and Elise G.

Polytechnic School ($10,000) see Peppers Foundation, Ann

Polytechnic Schools ($50,000) see Garland Foundation, John Jewett and H. Chandler

Pomona College ($1,200) see California Foundation for Biochemical Research

Pomona College ($5,000) see Harris Family Foundation, Hunt and Diane

Pomona College ($11,000) see MacKenzie Foundation

Pomona College — faculty leave program ($649,688) see Steele Foundation, Harry and Grace

Pomona College Torchbearers, Claremont ($5,500) see Hafif Family Foundation

Pomona Valley Hospital Foundation — direct incidental needs of poor or needy patients ($1,000) see American Foundation

Poverello House ($2,000) see Eaton Foundation, Edwin M. and Gertrude S.

Poverello House ($15,000) see Peters Foundation, Leon S.

Pre-School Coordinating Council see Tosco Corp. Refining Division

President Children's Bureau ($1,500) see Ace Beverage Co.

Presidio Little League — baseball field ($22,650) see Sefton Foundation, J. W.

Pro-Choice ($1,800) see Domino of California

Product Donations Program ($6,636) see California & Hawaiian Sugar Co.

Project Concern International ($34,907) see Lane Foundation, Minnie and Bernard

Project Concern International ($1,000) see R. P. Foundation

Project Nishma ($2,600) see Newman Charitable Trust, Calvin M. and Raquel H.

Project Open Hand ($15,000) see de Dampierre Memorial Foundation, Marie C.

Project Open Hand ($5,000) see Woodland Foundation

Project Open Hand — Earthquake relief ($10,000) see Bank of America - Giannini Foundation

Project SCC ($1,500) see Ishiyama Foundation

Project Second Chance ($1,000) see California & Hawaiian Sugar Co.

Providence Hospital ($200,000) see Valley Foundation, Wayne and Gladys

Providence Speech and Hearing ($5,000) see Muth Foundation, Peter and Mary

Proyecto Pastoral ($5,000) see Roth Family Foundation

Proyecto Pastoral ($10,000) see Teleklew Productions

Psoriasis Research Foundation ($6,000) see Bellini Foundation

Psoriasis Research Institute — research into the causes and cures of skin diseases ($20,000) see Montgomery Street Foundation

Psychiatric Clinic for Youth ($49,800) see Simon Foundation, Robert Ellis

Public Communicators ($20,000) see Magowan Family Foundation

Public Counsel ($100,000) see Bettingen Corporation, Burton G.

Public Counsel — capital campaign to purchase and refurbish a new site to house the agency ($200,000) see Parsons Foundation, Ralph M.

Public Media Center — Green Marketing Task Force ($15,000) see Beldon Fund

Quality Education Project ($300,000) see Capital Fund Foundation

Quality Education Project ($90,000) see Milken Foundation, L. and S.

California (cont.)

Quality of Life ($5,000) see Burns Family Foundation

Queen of Angels — Hollywood Presbyterian Foundation; pneumatic tube system ($72,500) see Stauffer Charitable Trust, John

Queen of Angels — Hollywood Presbyterian Foundation; Emergency Center capital fund ($83,000) see Stauffer Charitable Trust, John

R.C. Baker Memorial Museum ($77,750) see Baker Foundation, R. C.

R.D. Colburn School ($125,000) see Colburn Fund

R House ($30,000) see Haigh-Scatena Foundation

R.P. Foundation ($5,000) see Andersen Foundation, Arthur

Radio Bilingue — Noticiero Latino ($90,000) see Rosenberg Foundation

Rain Forest Action Network ($25,000) see HKH Foundation

Rancho Bernado Joslyn Senior Center ($35,341) see Joslyn Foundation, Marcellus I.

Rand Corporation — support for a drug policy research center ($2,050,000) see Ford Foundation

Rand Corporation ($225,000) see General Electric Co.

Rand Corporation ($303,200) see Hilton Foundation, Conrad N.

RAND Corporation — to support the Center's graduate training program ($300,000) see Bradley Foundation, Lynde and Harry

Rape Crises ($5,000) see National Pro-Am Youth Fund

Rape Foundation ($15,400) see Deutsch Co.

Raphael House ($10,000) see Friedman Family Foundation

Raphael House — for resource development staff and in general support as the agency makes a transition from a largely volunteer organization to one with paid staff ($50,000) see Haas, Jr. Fund, Evelyn and Walter

Ravenswood City School District — training in developmental education ($27,000) see Hancock Foundation, Luke B.

Reason Foundation ($100,000) see Chicago Resource Center

Reason Foundation ($42,175) see Confidence Foundation

Reason Foundation ($20,000) see Hastings Trust

Reason Foundation — Grover Hermann Research Fellows program ($54,840) see Hermann Foundation, Grover

Rebuild L.A. ($600,000) see Pioneer Electronics (USA) Inc.

Rebuild LA — program developed by Mayor's office to fund restoration, job training, mediation and other community rebuilding efforts ($50,000) see Gap, The

Recording for the Blind — to continue funding of Studio Director's salary ($34,020) see Kirchgessner Foundation, Karl

Recovery Partnership ($15,000) see Ware Foundation

Recreation Center for the Handicapped ($15,000) see Gellert Foundation, Carl

Recreation Center for the Handicapped ($200,000) see Herbst Foundation

Recreation Center for the Handicapped ($30,000) see Sandy Foundation, George H.

Red Bluff Union School District ($7,550) see Sierra Pacific Resources

Redwood City School District ($270,000) see Cowell Foundation, S. H.

Redwoods United ($53,000) see Lytel Foundation, Bertha Russ

Redwoods United — financial assistance for homemakers for the elderly ($53,000) see Lytel Foundation, Bertha Russ

Regents of University of California — needy patients ($66,000) see Bowles and Robert Bowles Memorial Fund, Ethel Wilson

Regents of University of California — support medical school ($66,000) see Bowles and Robert Bowles Memorial Fund, Ethel Wilson

Regents of the University of California ($225,000) see Columbia Savings Charitable Foundation

Regents of University of California ($10,000) see Ernest & Julio Gallo Winery

Regents of the University of California ($75,000) see Frasch Foundation for Chemical Research (under the will of Elizabeth B. Frasch), Herman

Regents of the University of California ($259,000) see Milken Family Medical Foundation

Regents of the University of California ($40,000) see Mosher Foundation, Samuel B.

Regents of the University of California ($9,200) see Simpson PSB Foundation

Regents of the University of California ($10,000) see Sprague, Jr. Foundation, Caryll M. and Norman F.

Regents of the University of California — support of the Gerbode Professional Development Program ($44,000) see Gerbode Foundation, Wallace Alexander

Regents of University of California Los Angeles Campus ($113,824) see Hoover, Jr. Foundation, Margaret W. and Herbert

Regional Center for the Arts ($2,000) see California & Hawaiian Sugar Co.

Regional Institute of Southern California and the Environmental Defense Fund — for "Research for Southern California to Develop an Equitable Transportation System" ($113,000) see Haynes Foundation, John Randolph and Dora

Rehabilitation Institute ($185,000) see Mericos Foundation

Rehabilitation Institute ($30,000) see Wood-Claeyssens Foundation

Reiss-Davis Child Guidance ($25,000) see Deutsch Co.

Reiss-Davis Child Study Center — for a new audio visual center see Keck Foundation, W. M.

Renaissance Technical Training Institute — to support student opportunity and resource program ($20,000) see Lux Foundation, Miranda

Research and Education Center ($500) see Foundation for Iranian Studies

Resource Renewal Institute ($11,000) see G.A.G. Charitable Corporation

Resource Renewal Institute ($10,000) see Seven Springs Foundation

Rhonda Fleming Foundation — civic ($50,000) see Mann Foundation, Ted

Richard J. Donovan Correctional Facility — refurbishing ($3,000) see Sefton Foundation, J. W.

Richard J. and Nancy M. Muth Foundation ($62,250) see Muth Foundation, Peter and Mary

Richard M. Lucas Prostatic Research Fund ($175,000) see Lucas Cancer Foundation, Richard M.

Richard Nixon Library and Birthplace Foundation ($1,500,000) see Annenberg Foundation

River Oak Center for Children ($10,000) see Setzer Foundation

River Oak Center for Children ($100,000) see Sierra Health Foundation

River Oak Center for Children ($5,000) see Teichert

River Oak Center Service ($17,000) see Arata Brothers Trust

River Switchboard/River Community Services ($25,000) see Haigh-Scatena Foundation

Riverside Art Museum ($2,500) see Bourns, Inc.

Robert Louis Stevenson School ($100,000) see Day Foundation, Willametta K.

Robert Louis Stevenson School ($5,000) see Merrion Foundation

Robert Schuller Ministries ($1,000) see Bishop Foundation, Vernon and Doris

Roman Catholic Archbishop of Los Angeles ($3,980,194) see Murphy Foundation, Dan

Romani Opera Foundation ($3,500) see Wyne Foundation

Ronald McDonald House ($20,000) see W. W. W. Foundation

Ronald McDonald House ($20,000) see W. W. W. Foundation

Ronald Reagan Presidential Foundation ($45,000) see Argyros Foundation

Ronald Reagan Presidential Foundation ($20,000) see Boeckmann Charitable Foundation

Ronald Reagan Presidential Foundation ($15,000) see Helms Foundation

Rose Dirve Friends Church ($17,200) see Marshburn Foundation

Roserer House ($5,000) see Burns Foundation

Ross School ($5,000) see Goodman Foundation, Edward and Marion

RSVP ($15,000) see Jackson Family Foundation, Ann

Rudolph Steiner College ($5,000) see Setzer Foundation

Rudolph Steiner College ($78,000) see Waldorf Educational Foundation

Rural Community Assistance Corporation — San Diego Farmworker Housing ($85,000) see Rosenberg Foundation

Russian Choral Society ($18,000) see Koulaieff Educational Fund, Trustees of Ivan Y.

RX for Reading — support for computer learning lab project ($206,256) see Mattel

Ryan Hill Research Foundation ($50,000) see Braun Foundation

Ryan Hill Research Foundation ($35,000) see Norcliffe Fund

Sacramento Blood Center ($10,000) see Setzer Foundation

Sacramento Citizens Crime Alert Reward Program — "California Crackdown ($5,000) see Teichert

Sacramento Life Center ($18,000) see Trust Funds

Sacramento Police Athletic League ($5,000) see Teichert

Sacramento Public Library ($10,000) see Teichert

Sacramento Regional Foundation ($20,000) see Setzer Foundation

Sacramento Symphony Association ($10,000) see Teichert

Sacred Heart Cathedral Preparatory ($20,000) see Hale Foundation, Crescent Porter

Sacred Heart Schools ($25,000) see de Dampierre Memorial Foundation, Marie C.

Sacred Heart Schools ($5,000) see Gellert Foundation, Celia Berta

Sacred Hearts School ($100,000) see Castle Foundation, Harold K.L.

St. Agnes Foundation ($5,000) see Diener Foundation, Frank C.

St. Agnes Medical Center ($59,000) see Radin Foundation

St. Agnes Medical Center Foundation ($5,000) see Gallo Foundation, Julio R.

St. Andrews School — building fund ($62,500) see Maxfield Foundation

St. Annes Home for the Aged ($33,250) see Ritter Foundation, May Ellen and Gerald

St. Anne's Maternity Home — toward construction of new facilities ($500,000) see Ahmanson Foundation

St. Annes Maternity Home ($10,000) see Ragen, Jr. Memorial Fund Trust No. 1, James M.

St. Annes Maternity Hospital ($300,000) see Burns Foundation, Fritz B.

St. Anthony's Catholic Church ($76,818) see Greiner Trust, Virginia

St. Anthony's Dining Room ($15,000) see Gellert Foundation, Carl

St. Anthony's Dining Room ($30,000) see Gleason Foundation, James

St. Anthony's High School Foundation — David R. Crumby, Jr. Memorial

Foundation ($10,000) see Imperial Bancorp

St. Barnabas Senior Center ($10,000) see Hoffman Foundation, H. Leslie Hoffman and Elaine S.

St. Brendans Church ($5,000) see Ragen, Jr. Memorial Fund Trust No. 1, James M.

St. Catherine Hospital ($25,000) see Doelger Charitable Trust, Thelma

St. Dominica Catholic Church ($25,000) see Burns Foundation

St. Elizabeth Parish ($5,000) see Gallo Foundation, Ernest

St. Emydius School ($10,000) see de Dampierre Memorial Foundation, Marie C.

St. Felicitas Church ($2,000) see Clougherty Charitable Trust, Francis H.

St. Francis of Assisi ($10,000) see Bannan Foundation, Arline and Thomas J.

St. Francis of Assisi ($5,000) see Bannan Foundation, Arline and Thomas J.

St. Francis of Assisi Church ($1,700) see Eaton Foundation, Edwin M. and Gertrude S.

St. Francis of Assisi Church ($5,200) see McCarthy Foundation, Michael W.

St. Francis Hospital — purchase of cardiac catheterization laboratory equipment ($375,000) see Mathers Charitable Foundation, G. Harold and Leila Y.

St. Francis Medical Center ($5,000) see Pacific Western Foundation

St. George Pathfinders ($20,000) see Koulaieff Educational Fund, Trustees of Ivan Y.

St. Herman Orthodox Seminary ($6,500) see Koulaieff Educational Fund, Trustees of Ivan Y.

St. Ignatious College Preparatory — general construction purposes ($300,000) see Irwin Charity Foundation, William G.

St. Ignatius College Preparatory ($5,000) see Bannan Foundation, Arline and Thomas J.

St. Ignatius College Preparatory ($10,000) see Gellert Foundation, Celia Berta

St. Ignatius College Preparatory ($10,000) see Leonardt Foundation

St. James School ($10,000) see Hannon Foundation, William H.

St. Jerome School ($10,000) see Hannon Foundation, William H.

St. John Chrysostom School ($10,000) see Hannon Foundation, William H.

St. John the Evangelist School ($10,000) see Hannon Foundation, William H.

St. John of God Hospital ($10,000) see Clougherty Charitable Trust, Francis H.

St. John's Educational Threshhold's Center ($5,000) see Wilsey Bennet Co.

St. John's Hospital ($5,000) see Pyramid Foundation

St. John's Hospital ($10,000) see Stuart Foundation, Elbridge and Evelyn

St. Johns Hospital ($15,000) see Teleklew Productions

St. John's Hospital and Health Care ($20,000) see Ace Beverage Co.

St. John's Hospital and Health Center ($225,000) see McAlister Charitable Foundation, Harold

St. Johns Volunteers ($300,000) see Koulaieff Educational Fund, Trustees of Ivan Y.

St. Joseph Center ($10,000) see Chartwell Foundation

St. Joseph Center ($10,000) see Teleklew Productions

St. Joseph Hospital Foundation — for a linear accelerator ($25,000) see Lytel Foundation, Bertha Russ

St. Joseph Hospital Foundation ($10,000) see Stillwell Charitable Trust, Glen and Dorothy

St. Joseph Medical Center ($250) see Hench Foundation, John C.

St. Joseph's ($12,600) see Argyros Foundation

St. Jude Hospital Foundation ($10,000) see Lastfogel Foundation, Abe and Frances

St. Jude's Hospital Foundation ($25,000) see Plitt Southern Theatres

St. Lukes Hospital ($11,300) see Bothin Foundation

St. Luke's Hospital Foundation ($10,000) see Sanguinetti Foundation, Annunziata

St. Margaret's Church ($13,500) see Philibosian Foundation, Stephen

St. Marks-In-The-Valley ($15,000) see Jackson Family Foundation, Ann

St. Marks in the Valley Episcopal Church ($100,000) see Braun Foundation

St. Martin of Tours ($10,000) see Hannon Foundation, William H.

St. Mary Medical Center/Bauer Hospital ($75,000) see Bauer Foundation, M. R.

St. Marys Academy ($10,000) see Hannon Foundation, William H.

St. Mary's Cathedral ($14,700) see Eaton Foundation, Edwin M. and Gertrude S.

St. Mary's College ($25,000) see Clougherty Charitable Trust, Francis H.

St. Mary's College ($10,000) see Gellert Foundation, Celia Berta

St. Mary's College — scholarship ($20,000) see Sandy Foundation, George H.

St. Mary's College ($250,000) see Valley Foundation, Wayne and Gladys

St. Mary's College of California ($60,000) see Disney Family Foundation, Roy

St. Mary's College of California — toward a comprehensive program to become a more effective multicultural academic community ($750,000) see Irvine Foundation, James

St. Mary's College of California ($50,000) see Transamerica Corp.

St. Mary's Foundation/Mcauley Neuropsychiatric Institute ($8,000) see Sanguinetti Foundation, Annunziata

St. Matthew's Church ($25,000) see Stuart Foundation, Elbridge and Evelyn

St. Patrick Home ($30,000) see Arata Brothers Trust

St. Patrick/St. Vincent High ($25,000) see Hale Foundation, Crescent Porter

St. Patrick's Seminary ($10,000) see Trust Funds

St. Paul the Apostle Church ($5,000) see Leonardt Foundation

St. Paul Philoptochos Greek Orthodox Community Church ($125,300) see Argyros Foundation

St. Paul's Church ($5,000) see Bull Foundation, Henry W.

St. Paul's Episcopal Homes ($5,000) see Fox Foundation, John H.

St. Paul's Episcopal School ($15,000) see Crocker Trust, Mary A.

St. Paul's Health Care Center ($2,500) see Fox Foundation, John H.

St. Pauls Manor ($100,000) see Masserini Charitable Trust, Maurice J.

St. Paul's Manor Health Care Center ($5,000) see Pratt Memorial Fund

St. Peter's School ($10,000) see Trust Funds

St. Philip the Apostle Parish ($48,000) see Hayden Foundation, William R. and Virginia

St. Stanislaus Church ($5,000) see Gallo Foundation, Ernest

St. Stanislaus School ($11,000) see Gallo Foundation, Ernest

St. Theresa ($2,140) see Llagas Foundation

St. Tichon Orthodox Theological Seminary ($6,500) see Koulaieff Educational Fund, Trustees of Ivan Y.

St. Vincent de Paul Dining Room ($10,000) see Gleason Foundation, James

St. Vincent de Paul Society ($5,000) see Gallo Foundation, Julio R.

St. Vincent de Paul Society ($20,000) see Rogers Foundation, Mary Stuart

St. Vincents ($23,600) see Sattler Beneficial Trust, Daniel A. and Edna J.

St. Vincents Day Home ($100) see Dreyer's & Edy's Grand Ice Cream

St. Vladimir Orthodox Theological Seminary ($6,500) see Koulaieff Educational Fund, Trustees of Ivan Y.

Salk Institute — building fund ($350,000) see Berger Foundation, H.N. and Frances C.

Salk Institute ($200,000) see Burns Foundation, Fritz B.

Salk Institute — general support ($165,000) see Hammer Foundation, Armand

Salk Institute ($66,666) see Klingenstein Fund, Esther A. and Joseph

Salk Institute — support for new construction ($666,667) see Mathers Charitable Foundation, G. Harold and Leila Y.

Salk Institute — medical research ($416,666) see Mathers Charitable Foundation, G. Harold and Leila Y.

Salk Institute — building fund to expand laboratory space ($200,000) see Webb Foundation, Del E.

Salk Institute ($50,000) see Whitaker Charitable Foundation, Lyndon C.

Salk Institute — for AIDS research ($25,000) see Alexander Foundation, Joseph

Salk Institute for Biological Studies ($35,000) see Adler Foundation

Salk Institute for Biological Studies ($30,000) see Anderson Foundation

Salk Institute for Biological Studies ($10,000) see Anderson Foundation

Salk Institute for Biological Studies ($25,000) see Ferkauf Foundation, Eugene and Estelle

Salk Institute for Biological Studies ($26,390) see Foulds Trust, Claiborne F

Salk Institute for Biological Studies ($75,000) see Frasch Foundation for Chemical Research (under the will of Elizabeth B. Frasch), Herman

Salk Institute for Biological Studies ($10,000) see Hansen Memorial Foundation, Irving

Salk Institute for Biological Studies ($5,000) see Jones and Bessie D. Phelps Foundation, Cyrus W. and Amy F.

Salk Institute for Biological Studies ($10,000) see Law Foundation, Robert O.

Salk Institute for Biological Studies ($5,000) see Law Foundation, Robert O.

Salk Institute for Biological Studies ($25,000) see Masserini Charitable Trust, Maurice J.

Salk Institute for Biological Studies ($26,500) see Moore Foundation, Martha G.

Salk Institute for Biological Studies — plant cell biology project ($535,663) see Noble Foundation, Samuel Roberts

Salk Institute for Biological Studies ($5,000) see Norton Memorial Corporation, Geraldi

Salk Institute for Biological Studies ($10,000) see Pacific Western Foundation

Salk Institute for Biological Studies ($5,000) see Pioneer Fund

Salk Institute for Biological Studies ($5,100) see Pratt Memorial Fund

Salk Institute for Biological Studies ($12,500) see Rapp Foundation, Robert Glenn

Salk Institute for Biological Studies ($10,000) see Rupp Foundation, Fran and Warren

Salk Institute for Biological Studies ($25,000) see Schlink Foundation, Albert G. and Olive H.

Salk Institute for Biological Studies ($60,000) see Stock Foundation, Paul

Salk Institute for Biological Studies ($100) see Volkswagen of America, Inc.

Salk Institute for Biological Studies ($5,000) see Williams Family Foundation

Salk Institute for Biological Studies — Noble/Salk Plant Cell Biology fellowships ($151,154) see Noble Foundation, Samuel Roberts

Salvation Army ($10,000) see Bellini Foundation

Salvation Army ($9,000) see Borun Foundation, Anna Borun and Harry

Salvation Army ($5,000) see Bourns, Inc.

Salvation Army ($5,000) see Edison Foundation, Irving and Beatrice C.

Salvation Army ($3,900) see Farallon Foundation

Salvation Army ($7,500) see Forest Lawn Foundation

Salvation Army ($201,000) see Gallo Foundation, Julio R.

Salvation Army ($15,000) see Gellert Foundation, Fred

Salvation Army ($25,000) see Gilmore Foundation, Earl B.

Salvation Army ($8,500) see Gilmore Foundation, Earl B.

Salvation Army ($42,000) see Halsell Foundation, O. L.

Salvation Army ($5,000) see Nelson Foundation, Florence

Salvation Army ($5,000) see Page Foundation, George B.

Salvation Army ($664,612) see Posey Trust, Addison

Salvation Army ($15,000) see Rogers Foundation, Mary Stuart

Salvation Army ($6,000) see Ryan Foundation, David Claude

Salvation Army see San Diego Trust & Savings Bank

Salvation Army ($10,000) see Thagard Foundation

Salvation Army ($2,500) see Upjohn California Fund

Salvation Army — the grant went to the East Bay Fire Relief fund ($7,500) see Crum and Forster

Salvation Army-Oakland ($30,000) see Clorox Co.

Salvation Army, San Francisco — for capital funding of a new central kitchen in San Francisco ($200,000) see Koret Foundation

Samuel Merritt College — reimbursement for nurses' theorist series ($66,571) see Fuld Health Trust, Helene

Samuel Merritt College of Nursing ($2,500) see Llagas Foundation

Samuel Merritt College of Nursing ($2,500) see Uvas Foundation

San Diego Aerospace Museum ($28,000) see Parker Foundation

San Diego Art Museum ($2,000) see Bloomfield Foundation, Sam and Rie

San Diego Automotive Muse ($10,000) see Gildred Foundation

San Diego Center for Children ($5,000) see Hollis Foundation

San Diego City Schools ($12,500) see Parker Foundation

San Diego City Schools — "Young At Heart" program ($288,507) see Gluck Foundation, Maxwell H.

San Diego Community Foundation ($25,000) see Hollis Foundation

San Diego Community Foundation ($30,000) see Masserini Charitable Trust, Maurice J.

San Diego Community Foundation — non-restricted ($100,000) see Birch Foundation, Stephen and Mary

San Diego Foundation for the Arts ($15,000) see Thornton Foundation, John M. and Sally B.

San Diego Historical Society ($40,000) see Parker Foundation

San Diego Historical Society ($25,000) see Scripps Foundation, Ellen Browning

San Diego Historical Society — to support the research and publication of "San Diego History" ($10,000) see Quest for Truth Foundation

San Diego Hospice ($15,000) see Masserini Charitable Trust, Maurice J.

San Diego Maritime Museum ($25,000) see Sefton Foundation, J. W.

San Diego Museum of Art ($75,000) see Benbough Foundation, Legler

San Diego Museum of Art ($10,167) see Goldberg Family Foundation, Milton D. and Madeline L.

San Diego Museum of Art ($45,000) see Masserini Charitable Trust, Maurice J.

San Diego Museum of Art ($100,000) see Parker Foundation

San Diego Museum of Art ($100,420) see Thornton Foundation, John M. and Sally B.

San Diego Museum of Art ($816,791) see Weisman Art Foundation, Frederick R.

San Diego Museum of Art — "Young At Heart" program ($183,527) see Gluck Foundation, Maxwell H.

San Diego Museum of Contemporary Art ($5,000) see American President Cos.

San Diego Museum of Man ($30,000) see Parker Foundation

San Diego National Sports Training Foundation ($33,000) see Burnham Foundation

San Diego National Sports Training Foundation — construction of United States Olympic Training Center ($1,000,000) see Boswell Foundation, James G.

San Diego Natural History Museum ($25,000) see Hollis Foundation

San Diego Natural History Museum ($10,000) see Masserini Charitable Trust, Maurice J.

San Diego Natural History Museum ($5,000) see Thornton Foundation, John M. and Sally B.

San Diego Opera ($3,000) see Fox Foundation, John H.

San Diego Opera ($10,000) see Lincolnshire

San Diego Opera ($5,000) see Pratt Memorial Fund

San Diego Opera ($11,966) see Thornton Foundation, John M. and Sally B.

San Diego Opera Association ($6,250) see Burnham Foundation

San Diego Opera — "Rosenkavalier" production ($135,752) see Gluck Foundation, Maxwell H.

San Diego Police Department — firearms training ($20,000) see Sefton Foundation, J. W.

San Diego Police Department — honor awards ($911) see Sefton Foundation, J. W.

San Diego Rescue League ($6,000) see Ryan Foundation, David Claude

California (cont.)

San Diego Rescue Mission ($3,000) see Fox Foundation, John H.

San Diego Rescue Mission ($10,000) see Lincolnshire

San Diego Sheriff Department — awards ($515) see Sefton Foundation, J. W.

San Diego State University see San Diego Trust & Savings Bank

San Diego State University Aztecs ($5,000) see Burnham Foundation

San Diego State University Foundation — non-restricted ($182,000) see Birch Foundation, Stephen and Mary

San Diego Symphony ($10,000) see Fusenot Charity Foundation, Georges and Germaine

San Diego Symphony ($12,727) see Goldberg Family Foundation, Milton D. and Madeline L.

San Diego Symphony Orchestra ($90,000) see Parker Foundation

San Diego Youth for Christ ($27,500) see Ryan Foundation, David Claude

San Diego Youth Symphony ($25,000) see R. P. Foundation

San Diego Zoological Society ($10,000) see Benbough Foundation, Legler

San Diego Zoological Society ($2,500) see Burnand Medical and Educational Foundation, Alphonse A.

San Diego Zoological Society ($900,000) see Dingman Foundation, Michael D.

San Diego Zoological Society ($55,000) see Scripps Foundation, Ellen Browning

San Diego Zoological Society — aviaries ($90,000) see Sefton Foundation, J. W.

San Diego Zoological Society — San Pasqual Wild Animal Park ($55,000) see Scripps Foundation, Ellen Browning

San Domenica School Foundation ($25,000) see McBean Family Foundation

San Domenico School ($20,000) see Hills Fund, Edward E.

San Domenico School foundation — to support student opportunity and resource program ($7,500) see Lux Foundation, Miranda

San Fernando Mission ($10,000) see Hannon Foundation, William H.

San Fernando Valley Child Guidance Clinic ($250,000) see Bettingen Corporation, Burton G.

San Francisco Art Institute ($2,000) see DiRosa Foundation, Rene and Veronica

San Francisco Art Institute ($25,000) see McBean Family Foundation

San Francisco Art Institute ($4,000) see Walker Foundation, T. B.

San Francisco Art Museum ($5,000) see Weiler Foundation

San Francisco Arts Commission ($7,500) see LEF Foundation

San Francisco Artspace ($35,000) see Manoogian Foundation, Alex and Marie

San Francisco Ballet — studio completion ($34,000) see Buck Foundation, Carol Franc

San Francisco Ballet ($15,000) see Fireman's Fund Insurance Co.

San Francisco Ballet ($25,000) see Hills Fund, Edward E.

San Francisco Ballet ($22,500) see Langendorf Foundation, Stanley S.

San Francisco Ballet ($14,500) see Rosenberg, Jr. Family Foundation, Louise and Claude

San Francisco Ballet ($3,000) see Swig Foundation

San Francisco Ballet ($8,000) see U.S. Leasing International

San Francisco Ballet ($1,000) see Weiss Foundation, Stephen and Suzanne

San Francisco Ballet Auxiliary ($16,523) see Bank of San Francisco Co.

San Francisco Ballet/Opera Service Corporation ($717,000) see Hewlett-Packard Co.

San Francisco Bay Columbus Quincentenary Jubilee Committee — in support of organization's program ($25,000) see Jewett Foundation, George Frederick

San Francisco Chamber of Commerce ($4,000) see Swig Foundation

San Francisco Clothing Bank — donation of samples and distressed clothing for community clothing bank ($182,565) see Gap, The

San Francisco Committee for Aid to Vets ($20,500) see Koulaieff Educational Fund, Trustees of Ivan Y.

San Francisco Conservation Corps — funding to provide youth with the opportunity to earn their GED's ($35,000) see Hancock Foundation, Luke B.

San Francisco Conservatory of Music ($7,500) see Komes Foundation

San Francisco Conservatory of Music ($20,000) see Swig Foundation

San Francisco Conservatory of Music ($10,000) see Swig Foundation

San Francisco Conservatory of Music ($10,000) see Swig Foundation

San Francisco Day School ($50,000) see Hills Fund, Edward E.

San Francisco Day School ($50,000) see Hume Foundation, Jaquelin

San Francisco Day School ($30,000) see Lurie Foundation, Louis R.

San Francisco Day School ($107,500) see Thornton Foundation, Flora L.

San Francisco Day School ($10,000) see Thornton Foundation, Flora L.

San Francisco Day School 1980 ($16,666) see Langendorf Foundation, Stanley S.

San Francisco Education Fund ($36,000) see McKesson Corp.

San Francisco Education Fund ($75,000) see Osher Foundation, Bernard

San Francisco Education Fund ($7,500) see U.S. Leasing International

San Francisco Education Fund — San Francisco Arts Project

($85,000) see Haas Fund, Walter and Elise

San Francisco Food Bank ($200) see Newman Charitable Trust, Calvin M. and Raquel H.

San Francisco Foundation ($25,000) see McBean Family Foundation

San Francisco Foundation ($10,000) see Sierra Health Foundation

San Francisco Foundation ($1,826,587) see Steel, Sr. Foundation, Marshall

San Francisco Foundation ($170,000) see Switzer Foundation

San Francisco Foundation — support of its Audience Development Initiative Program ($35,000) see Gerbode Foundation, Wallace Alexander

San Francisco Foundation School Linked Services Consortium ($500,000) see Hewlett Foundation, William and Flora

San Francisco Hearing and Speech Center ($10,696) see Bothin Foundation

San Francisco Institute on Aging — to expand facilities for servicing the elderly ($10,000) see Montgomery Street Foundation

San Francisco Japanese American Citizens League ($1,000) see Gleason Foundation, James

San Francisco Japanese American Citizens League ($1,500) see Gleason Foundation, Katherine

San Francisco Library ($100,000) see Langendorf Foundation, Stanley S.

San Francisco Library Foundation ($650,000) see Osher Foundation, Bernard

San Francisco Montessori School — scholarships ($15,000) see Odell and Helen Pfeiffer Odell Fund, Robert Stewart

San Francisco Museum of Modern Art ($10,000) see Cow Hollow Foundation

San Francisco Museum of Modern Art ($5,000) see Cow Hollow Foundation

San Francisco Museum of Modern Art ($12,000) see Davies Charitable Trust

San Francisco Museum of Modern Art — offering reduced admission and special programs ($50,000) see Gap, The

San Francisco Museum of Modern Art — new building ($40,000) see Gap, The

San Francisco Museum of Modern Art ($29,000) see Gilmore Foundation, William G.

San Francisco Museum of Modern Art — construction of new museum building ($2,450,000) see Haas Fund, Walter and Elise

San Francisco Museum of Modern Art ($1,040,000) see Haas, Jr. Fund, Evelyn and Walter

San Francisco Museum of Modern Art ($10,000) see Hume Foundation, Jaquelin

San Francisco Museum of Modern Art — exhibition ($50,000) see Lannan Foundation

San Francisco Museum of Modern Art ($2,500) see Simpson PSB Foundation

San Francisco Museum of Modern Art ($5,000) see Swig Foundation

San Francisco Museum of Modern Art ($11,000) see Thornton Foundation

San Francisco Museum of Modern Art ($125,000) see Transamerica Corp.

San Francisco Museum of Modern Art ($18,250) see U.S. Leasing International

San Francisco Museum of Modern Art — capital campaign ($15,000) see U.S. Leasing International

San Francisco Museum of Modern Art ($10,500) see Walker Foundation, T. B.

San Francisco Museum of Modern Art ($5,500) see Walker Foundation, T. B.

San Francisco Museum of Modern Art ($52,500) see Wilbur-Ellis Co.

San Francisco Museum of Modern Art — for the construction costs and endowment for the new museum to be constructed in the Yerba Buena Center ($200,000) see Columbia Foundation

San Francisco Opera ($16,523) see Bank of San Francisco Co.

San Francisco Opera ($10,000) see Ernest & Julio Gallo Winery

San Francisco Opera ($10,000) see Fireman's Fund Insurance Co.

San Francisco Opera — general support ($33,000) see Goldman Fund, Richard and Rhoda

San Francisco Opera ($87,500) see Hills Fund, Edward E.

San Francisco Opera ($10,000) see Hume Foundation, Jaquelin

San Francisco Opera — purchase a stage turntable ($105,000) see Irwin Charity Foundation, William G.

San Francisco Opera ($25,000) see Langendorf Foundation, Stanley S.

San Francisco Opera ($25,000) see McBean Family Foundation

San Francisco Opera ($150,000) see Osher Foundation, Bernard

San Francisco Opera ($25,000) see Thornton Foundation

San Francisco Opera ($11,500) see U.S. Leasing International

San Francisco Opera Association ($565,000) see Getty Foundation, Ann and Gordon

San Francisco Opera Association ($33,000) see Northern Star Foundation

San Francisco Opera — to underwrite production of Verdi's I Vesperi Siciliani for fall 1993 ($250,000) see Skaggs Foundation, L. J. and Mary C.

San Francisco Opera — to help underwrite a new production of "War and Peace" ($100,000) see Columbia Foundation

San Francisco Opera — Western opera theatre ($25,000) see True North Foundation

San Francisco Performing Arts Library and Museum ($5,000) see Brenner Foundation, Mervyn

San Francisco Phoenix Project — support for capital building project ($25,000) see Mattel

San Francisco S.P.C.A. ($70,000) see Doelger Charitable Trust, Thelma

San Francisco School ($5,000) see Thendara Foundation

San Francisco School Volunteers ($15,000) see Crocker Trust, Mary A.

San Francisco Senators ($81,862) see Herbst Foundation

San Francisco Senators ($25,000) see Stern Memorial Trust, Sidney

San Francisco SPCA ($20,000) see Barbour Foundation, Bernice

San Francisco SPCA ($75,000) see Roberts Foundation

San Francisco SPCA ($45,000) see Sandy Foundation, George H.

San Francisco State University — Bay Area Homelessness Program ($62,500) see Johnson Foundation, Walter S.

San Francisco Suicide Prevention ($28,000) see Transamerica Corp.

San Francisco Symphony ($8,050) see American President Cos.

San Francisco Symphony ($16,523) see Bank of San Francisco Co.

San Francisco Symphony ($1,000) see California & Hawaiian Sugar Co.

San Francisco Symphony ($20,000) see Fireman's Fund Insurance Co.

San Francisco Symphony ($1,335,848) see Getty Foundation, Ann and Gordon

San Francisco Symphony — for acoustical renovations ($100,000) see Goldman Fund, Richard and Rhoda

San Francisco Symphony ($95,000) see Haas, Jr. Fund, Evelyn and Walter

San Francisco Symphony ($8,550) see Hume Foundation, Jaquelin

San Francisco Symphony — acoustics project ($250,000) see Irwin Charity Foundation, William G.

San Francisco Symphony ($15,000) see Langendorf Foundation, Stanley S.

San Francisco Symphony ($25,000) see McBean Family Foundation

San Francisco Symphony ($75,000) see Osher Foundation, Bernard

San Francisco Symphony ($100,000) see Roberts Foundation

San Francisco Symphony ($10,000) see Schwab Foundation, Charles and Helen

San Francisco Symphony ($50,000) see Swig Charity Foundation, Mae and Benjamin

San Francisco Symphony ($15,500) see U.S. Leasing International

San Francisco Symphony Adventures ($10,000) see Rosenberg, Jr. Family Foundation, Louise and Claude

San Francisco Symphony — capital campaign; permanent endowment for Adventures in Music ($100,000) see Haas Fund, Walter and Elise

San Francisco Symphony Orchestra see Sumitomo Bank of California

San Francisco Symphony Volunteer ($2,500) see Schwab Foundation, Charles and Helen

San Francisco Symphony — general support for the Youth Education Program ($25,000) see Hancock Foundation, Luke B.

San Francisco Symphony/Youth Orchestra ($75,000) see Osher Foundation, Bernard

San Francisco Theological Seminary — Lloyd Center counselling services ($20,000) see Driscoll Foundation

San Francisco Unified School District — Algebra GATE ($20,000) see Toshiba America, Inc.

San Francisco Unified School District — in support of the Arts Leadership Project ($24,000) see Jewett Foundation, George Frederick

San Francisco Unified School District — scientific kits Biotech program ($25,000) see Genentech

San Francisco Unified School District — Biotechnology in the Classroom ($20,000) see Toshiba America, Inc.

San Francisco Unified School District — Center for the Advancement and Renewal of Educators ($250,000) see Haas Fund, Walter and Elise

San Francisco University High School ($52,500) see Thornton Foundation

San Francisco Zoological Society ($200,000) see Doelger Charitable Trust, Thelma

San Francisco Zoological Society ($2,000) see Llagas Foundation

San Francisco Zoological Society ($17,500) see Magowan Family Foundation

San Francisco Zoological Society ($2,500) see Shoong Foundation, Milton

San Francisco Zoological Society ($20,000) see Swig Foundation

San Gabriel Cemetary Association ($55,000) see Garland Foundation, John Jewett and H. Chandler

San Joaquin AIDS Foundation ($24,500) see Sierra Health Foundation

San Joaquin Memorial High School ($11,500) see Diener Foundation, Frank C.

San Joquain College ($10,300) see Radin Foundation

San Jose Conservation Corps — funding for the education component ($25,250) see Hancock Foundation, Luke B.

San Jose Museum of Art ($30,000) see FMC Corp.

San Jose Museum of Art ($40,000) see Swig Charity Foundation, Mae and Benjamin

San Jose Museum of Art ($35,000) see Syntex Corp.

San Jose State University ($90,000) see Teagle Foundation

San Jose Symphony ($10,000) see Gross Charitable Trust, Stella B.

San Jose Symphony ($10,000) see Mentor Graphics

San Marino Guico Huntington Memorial Hospital ($1,000)

see Martin Foundation, Bert William

San Marino Schools Foundation ($25,750) see Hoffman Foundation, H. Leslie Hoffman and Elaine S.

San Mateo Arboretum Society — landscaping and planting ($30,000) see Smith Horticultural Trust, Stanley

San Mateo Public Library ($4,000) see Brenner Foundation, Mervyn

Sangua Union School District ($11,000) see Newhall Foundation, Henry Mayo

Sansum Medical Research Foundation ($6,000) see Bull Foundation, Henry W.

Sansum Medical Research Foundation ($37,474) see Joslyn Foundation, Marcellus I.

Santa Ana High — University Mentors at Santa Ana Schools ($14,000) see California Educational Initiatives Fund

Santa Barbara Christian School ($15,000) see Snite Foundation, Fred B.

Santa Barbara Contemporary Arts ($20,000) see Wade Endowment Fund, Elizabeth Firth

Santa Barbara Council on Alcoholism ($11,800) see Sattler Beneficial Trust, Daniel A. and Edna J.

Santa Barbara County Vietnam Veterans ($10,000) see Wade Endowment Fund, Elizabeth Firth

Santa Barbara Foundation ($23,600) see Sattler Beneficial Trust, Daniel A. and Edna J.

Santa Barbara Historical Society ($50,000) see Mericos Foundation

Santa Barbara Historical Society ($33,226) see Walker Foundation, Smith

Santa Barbara International Film Festival ($5,000) see Metropolitan Theatres Corp.

Santa Barbara Meals on Wheels ($5,000) see Page Foundation, George B.

Santa Barbara Medical Foundation Clinic ($4,000) see Haskell Fund

Santa Barbara Museum of Natural History ($32,000) see Braun Foundation

Santa Barbara Museum of Natural History ($50,000) see Mericos Foundation

Santa Barbara New House ($25,000) see Tuohy Foundation, Alice Tweed

Santa Barbara Rescue Mission — new life rehabilitation program ($100,000) see M. E. G. Foundation

Santa Barbara Scholarship Foundation ($6,000) see Jefferson Endowment Fund, John Percival and Mary C.

Santa Barbara Scholarship Foundation ($22,894) see Tuohy Foundation, Alice Tweed

Santa Barbara Special Olympics ($2,000) see Jefferson Endowment Fund, John Percival and Mary C.

Santa Barbara Special Olympics ($5,000) see Page Foundation, George B.

Santa Barbara Visiting Nurses Association ($100,000) see Mericos Foundation

Santa Barbara Zoological Gardens ($10,000) see Mosher Foundation, Samuel B.

Santa Barbara Zoological Gardens ($3,700) see Page Foundation, George B.

Santa Catalina School — general support ($35,100) see Dunspaugh-Dalton Foundation

Santa Catalina School — annual fund ($10,000) see Foothills Foundation

Santa Catalina School ($10,000) see Hogan Foundation, Royal Barney

Santa Catalina School ($10,000) see Shenandoah Foundation

Santa Clara County — general support ($50,000) see Compton Foundation

Santa Clara County Chapter, National Multiple Sclerosis Community Services — multiple sclerosis community research ($1,000) see Allen Charitable Trust, Phil N.

Santa Clara County Office of Education — for Regional Office of Child Care to increase quality of care ($15,000) see Stulsaft Foundation, Morris

Santa Clara University ($500,000) see Bannan Foundation, Arline and Thomas J.

Santa Clara University — scholarship fund ($25,000) see Kingsley Foundation, Lewis A.

Santa Clara University ($75,000) see Komes Foundation

Santa Clara University ($1,000,000) see Leavey Foundation, Thomas and Dorothy

Santa Clara University ($3,000) see Moore Family Foundation

Santa Clara University ($87,000) see Pacific Western Foundation

Santa Clara University ($10,000) see Shea Foundation, Edmund and Mary

Santa Clara University — general fund ($10,000) see Stuart Center Charitable Trust, Hugh

Santa Clara University — to provide full-tuition scholarships for four pre-medical students ($52,489) see Valley Foundation

Santa Clara University Law School ($10,000) see Gross Charitable Trust, Stella B.

Santa Clarita Special Children's Center ($29,120) see Newhall Foundation, Henry Mayo

Santa Marguerita ($10,000) see Burns Family Foundation

Santa Maria Joint Union High School District ($16,000) see Newhall Foundation, Henry Mayo

Santa Marta Hospital Foundation ($10,000) see Ace Beverage Co.

Santa Marta Hospital Foundation ($25,000) see Smith Foundation, Lon V.

Santa Monica Civic Light Opera ($500) see Norman/Nethercutt Foundation, Merle

Santa Monica Hospital ($500,000) see Norman/Nethercutt Foundation, Merle

Santa Monica Hospital Medical Center, Rape Treatment Center — for start-up and operating expenses ($201,745) see Stuart Foundations

Santa Monica Senior Health and Peer Counseling Center ($250,000) see Taper Foundation, Mark

Santa Monica Senior Health and Peer Counseling Center ($250,000) see Taper Foundation, S. Mark

Santa Teresita Hospital — general ($10,000) see Fusenot Charity Foundation, Georges and Germaine

Santa Ynez Valley Hospital —equipment and study ($25,000) see Jackson Family Foundation, Ann

Saratoga Federated Church ($3,000) see Nelson Foundation, Florence

Save-A-Heart Foundation ($1,000) see Parvin Foundation, Albert

Save-A-Heart Foundation ($5,000) see Western Cardiac Foundation

Save the Books ($15,000) see Norman Foundation, Andrew

School of Theology at Claremont ($50,000) see Greenville Foundation

Science 2000 City School Service Fund — scientific educational kits ($39,500) see Genentech

Scripps Clinic — establish day-care center ($375,000) see Gluck Foundation, Maxwell H.

Scripps Clinic and Research foundation ($50,000) see Hawn Foundation

Scripps Clinic and Research Foundation ($25,000) see Baker Foundation, R. C.

Scripps Clinic and Research Foundation ($7,000) see Bellini Foundation

Scripps Clinic and Research Foundation ($25,000) see Florence Foundation

Scripps Clinic and Research Foundation ($250,000) see Hazen Charitable Trust, Lita Annenberg

Scripps Clinic and Research Foundation — research and training in the field of molecular cell biology ($32,850) see Kade Foundation, Max

Scripps Clinic and Research Foundation ($2,500) see Ottenstein Family Foundation

Scripps Clinic and Research Foundation ($5,000) see Schwartz Foundation, Bernard Lee

Scripps Clinic and Research Foundation ($60,000) see Scripps Foundation, Ellen Browning

Scripps Clinic and Research Foundation ($94,600) see Walker Foundation, W. E.

Scripps Clinic and Research Foundation — final installment of 3- year pledge for Scripps Health Resource Center's "Health Education Lecture Series" ($16,580) see Barker Foundation, Donald R.

Scripps College — faculty ($25,000) see Athwin Foundation

Scripps College ($18,000) see Borchard Foundation, Albert and Elaine

Scripps College ($150,000) see Garland Foundation, John Jewett and H. Chandler

Scripps College ($50,000) see Glanville Family Foundation

Scripps College ($55,190) see Pasadena Area Residential Aid

Scripps College ($50,000) see Scripps Foundation, Ellen Browning

Scripps College ($3,000) see Shattuck Charitable Trust, S. F.

Scripps College — capital improvements ($500,000) see Steele Foundation, Harry and Grace

Scripps College ($25,000) see Weinberg Foundation, John L.

Scripps College ($250,000) see Weinberg, Jr. Foundation, Sidney J.

Scripps College ($15,000) see Weinberg, Jr. Foundation, Sidney J.

Scripps College Scholarship Fund ($7,500) see Schlinger Foundation

Scripps College — Sidney Weinberg Chair in Natural Science ($20,000) see Glanville Family Foundation

Scripps Institute of Oceanography ($20,000) see Harris Foundation, William H. and Mattie Wattis

Scripps Institution of Oceanography — in support of endowment fund for Innovative Oceanographic Research ($25,000) see Kieckhefer Foundation, J. W.

Scripps Institution of Oceanography — support endowment fund for Innovative Oceanographic Research ($25,000) see Morris Foundation, Margaret T.

Scripps Memorial Hospital ($10,000) see Bloomfield Foundation, Sam and Rie

Scripps Memorial Hospital ($50,000) see Scripps Foundation, Ellen Browning

Scripps Memorial Hospital Foundation ($230,000) see Confidence Foundation

Scripps Memorial Hospital Foundation ($100,000) see Confidence Foundation

Scripps Memorial Hospital Foundation ($25,000) see Poinsettia Foundation, Paul and Magdalena Ecke

Scripps Memorial Hospital Foundation ($37,000) see Schwartz Foundation, Bernard Lee

Scripps Memorial Hospital Foundation ($200,000) see W. W. W. Foundation

Scripps Oceanographic Institute ($500,000) see Vetlesen Foundation, G. Unger

Seaside High School ($6,700) see National Pro-Am Youth Fund

Season of Sharing — general fund ($75,000) see True North Foundation

See Surgical Eye — eye diseases ($25,000) see International Foundation

Self Help for Hard of Hearing People ($4,000) see Green Foundation, Burton E.

Self-Realization Fellowship Church ($50,000) see Duke Foundation, Doris

Sempervirens Fund ($10,000) see Bradford Foundation, George and Ruth

Sempervirens Fund ($11,800) see Witter Foundation, Dean

Senior Adult Services ($7,500) see Pratt Memorial Fund

California (cont.)

Senior Coordination Council ($20,200) see Arrillaga Foundation

Senior Gleaners ($5,000) see Bannerman Foundation, William C.

Senior Health and Peer Counseling ($5,000) see Buchalter, Nemer, Fields, & Younger

Senior Health and Peer Counseling ($5,000) see Imperial Bancorp

Senior Health and Peer and Wise ($10,000) see Teleklew Productions

SeniorNet — to continue strengthening the SeniorNet organization ($1,205,000) see Markle Foundation, John and Mary R.

Sephardic Educational Center ($27,500) see Levy Foundation, Hyman Jebb

Sephardic Educational Center ($17,000) see Levy Foundation, Hyman Jebb

Sephardic Hebrew Academy ($10,000) see Levy Foundation, Hyman Jebb

Sephardic Temple Tifereth Israel ($10,000) see Levy Foundation, Hyman Jebb

Sephardic Temple Tifereth Israel ($10,000) see Levy Foundation, Hyman Jebb

Sephardic Temple Tifereth Israel ($5,000) see Levy Foundation, Hyman Jebb

Sephardic Temple Tifereth Israel — Maurice Amado Perpetual Building Fund ($82,296) see Amado Foundation, Maurice

Sephardic Temple Tifereth Israel — Mortgage Retirement Challenge Grant ($27,923) see Amado Foundation, Maurice

Services for Seniors ($9,200) see Bradford Foundation, George and Ruth

Seton Health Services Foundation ($2,500) see Gleason Foundation, Katherine

Seton Medical Center ($20,000) see de Dampierre Memorial Foundation, Marie C.

Seton Medical Center ($50,000) see Doelger Charitable Trust, Thelma

Seton Medical Center — emergency room renovations ($25,000) see Gellert Foundation, Carl

Seton Medical Center ($11,500) see Gellert Foundation, Celia Berta

Seton Medical Center ($50,000) see Gellert Foundation, Fred

Seton Medical Center — cardiac imaging system ($73,500) see Wiegand Foundation, E. L.

Seton Medical Center — Carl Gellert Emergency Center ($25,000) see Gellert Foundation, Carl

Seva — J. Watumull Memorial Scholarship ($50,000) see Watumull Fund, J.

Seventh On Sale — Gap, GapKids and Banana Republic samples contributed to be sold at San Francisco AIDS fundraiser ($160,384) see Gap, The

Shaare Zeddek ($30,000) see Plitt Southern Theatres

Shakespeare Festival of California ($3,000) see Farallon Foundation

Share ($10,000) see Plitt Southern Theatres

SHARE ($6,000) see Shoong Foundation, Milton

Sharing Place ($5,000) see Setzer Foundation

Sharp Health Care ($85,000) see Benbough Foundation, Legler

Sharp Hospital ($500,000) see Polinsky-Rivkin Family Foundation

Sharp Hospital Foundation ($20,000) see Burnham Foundation

Sharp Hospital Foundation ($5,000) see Fox Foundation, John H.

Sharp Hospital Foundation ($50,000) see Parker Foundation

Sharp Hospital Foundation ($30,000) see Pratt Memorial Fund

Sharp Hospitals Foundation — non-restricted ($1,000,000) see Birch Foundation, Stephen and Mary

Shasta College Physical Education/Athletic Division — track and field bleachers ($139,057) see McConnell Foundation

Shasta County Sheriff's Department — film processing lab ($81,000) see McConnell Foundation

Shasta Natural Science Association — Redding Arboretum, Phase One ($195,000) see McConnell Foundation

Shefa Fund ($6,000) see Newman Charitable Trust, Calvin M. and Raquel H.

Shriners Hospital ($6,000) see Bellini Foundation

Shriners Hospital ($10,000) see Setzer Foundation

Shriners Hospital for Crippled Children ($5,000) see Martin Foundation, Bert William

Shriner's Hospital for Crippled Children — general ($25,000) see Thompson Charitable Foundation, Marion G.

Sierra Club ($2,000) see Bright Charitable Trust, Alexander H.

Sierra Club Foundation ($2,250) see Agape Foundation

Sierra Club Foundation — conservation programs ($60,000) see Baird Foundation, Cameron

Sierra Club Foundation ($102,000) see Harder Foundation

Sierra Club Foundation ($22,500) see Radiator Specialty Co.

Sierra Club Legal Defense Fund ($20,000) see Borun Foundation, Anna Borun and Harry

Sierra Club Legal Defense Fund ($5,000) see DiRosa Foundation, Rene and Veronica

Sierra Club Legal Defense Fund ($50,000) see General Atlantic Partners L.P.

Sierra Club Legal Defense Fund ($25,000) see Glen Eagles Foundation

Sierra Club Legal Defense Fund ($90,500) see McIntosh Foundation

Sierra Club Legal Defense Fund ($20,000) see Town Creek Foundation

Sierra Foothills AIDS Foundation ($37,000) see Sierra Health Foundation

Sierra Legal Defense Fund — Northwest Forests/Salmon ($100,000) see Bullitt Foundation

Sierra Repertory Theater ($20,000) see Allen-Heath Memorial Foundation

Sierra Repertory Theatre — operating funds for the artist in residence program ($16,000) see Allen-Heath Memorial Foundation

Simi Covenant Church ($25,000) see Boeckmann Charitable Foundation

Simon Wiesenthal Center ($25) see Amdur Braude Riley, Inc.

Simon Wiesenthal Center ($2,000) see Candlesticks Inc.

Simon Wiesenthal Center ($2,000) see Chanin Family Foundation, Paul R.

Simon Wiesenthal Center ($25) see Falk Foundation, Michael David

Simon Wiesenthal Center ($1,500) see Goldman Foundation, William

Simon Wiesenthal Center ($200,000) see Kohl Charitable Foundation, Allen D.

Simon Wiesenthal Center ($12,500) see Mitchell Family Foundation, Edward D. and Anna

Simon Wiesenthal Center ($5,000) see Rasmussen Foundation

Simon Wiesenthal Center ($25,000) see Resnick Foundation, Jack and Pearl

Simon Wiesenthal Center ($250,000) see Rigler-Deutsch Foundation

Simon Wiesenthal Center ($300,000) see Snider Foundation

Simon Wiesenthal Center of Holocaust ($33,000) see Stern Memorial Trust, Sidney

Siskiyou County Office of Education ($5,250) see Sierra Pacific Resources

Sisters of Nazareth ($10,000) see Pacific Western Foundation

Sisters of Nazareth House ($10,000) see Diener Foundation, Frank C.

Sisters of Pious Disciples of Divine Master ($1,000) see Diener Foundation, Frank C.

Sisters of St. Dominic — intensive care nursery ($40,000) see Thompson Charitable Foundation, Marion G.

Skid Row Charity Fund ($1,000) see Ace Beverage Co.

Skin Disease Society ($10,000) see Hansen Memorial Foundation, Irving

Slide Ranch ($20,000) see Crocker Trust, Mary A.

Social Service Auxiliary ($64,132) see Dunning Foundation

Society of American Foresters ($3,000) see Setzer Foundation

Society for the Propagation of Faith ($2,100) see Eaton Foundation, Edwin M. and Gertrude S.

Solano AIDS Tasks Force ($23,500) see Sierra Health Foundation

Solid Foundation, Mandela House — to support family maintenance and reunification, healthy child development and community outreach programs for drug-addicted mothers and

their infants ($41,500) see Zellerbach Family Fund

Solvang Friendship House — Alzheimer's residential facility ($160,000) see M. E. G. Foundation

Song Writers Hall of Fame ($5,000) see Autry Foundation

Sonoma County Faith Based Community Organizing Project ($13,560) see Haigh-Scatena Foundation

Sonoma County Family YMCA — building campaign for new activities center ($5,000) see Exchange Bank

Sonoma County Foundation — underwrite foundation's newsbriefs ($3,000) see Exchange Bank

Sonoma State University — two scholarships and annual contribution to athletic association ($4,500) see Exchange Bank

South Bay Syndicate — non-restricted ($70,000) see Birch Foundation, Stephen and Mary

South Central Family Health Center — repairs of extensive damage caused by looters ($10,000) see Gannett Co.

South Coast Repertory Theater ($11,500) see Argyros Foundation

South Coast Repertory Theater ($50,000) see Segerstrom Foundation

Southern African Freedom Through Education Foundation ($25,000) see Weyerhaeuser Family Foundation

Southern California Building Fund ($15,000) see Forest Lawn Foundation

Southern California Building Funds ($55,000) see Unocal Corp.

Southern California Building Funds — contribution to be distributed as follows: Los Angeles County $48,110; Orange County $6,000; and San Bernardino County $890 ($55,000) see First Interstate Bank of California

Southern California Children's Cancer Services ($20,000) see Lee Foundation, James T.

Southern California Children's Cancer Services ($905,714) see Milken Family Medical Foundation

Southern California Children's Cancer Services — Ronald McDonald House expansion ($5,000) see Imperial Bancorp

Southern California College ($5,000) see RTM

Southern California Psychoanalytic Facility ($15,000) see See Foundation, Charles

Southern California School of Theology, Claremont ($40,000) see Jameson Foundation, J. W. and Ida M.

Southwest Museum ($29,050) see Sprague, Jr. Foundation, Caryll M. and Norman F.

Southwest Yearly Friends Meeting Church ($22,150) see Marshburn Foundation

Spastic Children's Endowment Foundation ($50,000) see 21 International Holdings

SPCA ($200) see Steel, Sr. Foundation, Marshall

Spencer Education Foundation ($2,500) see Crawford & Co.

Spreckles Organ Society ($6,000) see Ryan Foundation, David Claude

Stanford Graduate School of Business ($20,000) see Alexander Foundation, Robert D. and Catherine R.

Stanford Graduate School of Business ($8,900) see Peierls Foundation

Stanford Graduate School of Business ($125,000) see Wells Fargo & Co.

Stanford Graduate School of Business, Palo Alto ($150,000) see Rosenberg, Jr. Family Foundation, Louise and Claude

Stanford Home for Children ($35,265) see Arata Brothers Trust

Stanford Home for Children ($6,155) see Teichert

Stanford Medical Center ($30,000) see Allen Foundation, Rita

Stanford School of Medicine — nuclear magnetic resonance spectroscopy imaging center, scholarship support, research of lymphocyte proteins ($349,500) see Baxter Foundation, Donald E. and Delia B.

Stanford Theater Foundation — construction, painting, architectural, and legal costs of the Stanford Theater ($880,000) see Packard Foundation, David and Lucile

Stanford University ($120,000) see Ada Foundation, Julius

Stanford University — multiple sclerosis research ($445,000) see Allen Charitable Trust, Phil N.

Stanford University ($325,795) see American Telephone & Telegraph Co.

Stanford University ($250,000) see American Telephone & Telegraph Co.

Stanford University ($265,000) see Arell Foundation

Stanford University ($283,317) see Arrillaga Foundation

Stanford University ($2,000) see Barnett Charitable Foundation, Lawrence and Isabel

Stanford University ($400,000) see Beckman Foundation, Arnold and Mabel

Stanford University ($150,000) see Berry Foundation, Lowell

Stanford University ($50,000) see Berry Foundation, Lowell

Stanford University ($120,000) see Bing Fund

Stanford University ($200,000) see Bing Fund

Stanford University ($120,000) see Bing Fund

Stanford University ($20,000) see Bradford Foundation, George and Ruth

Stanford University ($250,000) see Burnham Foundation

Stanford University ($100,000) see Cantor Foundation, Iris and B. Gerald

Stanford University — research and training in international security and arms control ($1,141,000) see Carnegie Corporation of New York

Stanford University ($243,000) see Chevron Corp.

Stanford University ($147,500) see Chevron Corp.

Stanford University — fellowship program for reseach training of physicians

California (cont.)

Town School ($25,000) see Hills Fund, Edward E.

Trauma Foundation — Teens on Targets, a gun violence prevention project for Oakland youth ($30,000) see Goldman Fund, Richard and Rhoda

Tree of Life Fund ($250) see American Building Maintenance Industries

Tree People ($3,000) see Negaunee Foundation

Tri-Cities Children's Center — services for abused and neglected children ($5,000) see Smith Trust, May and Stanley

Trinity Broadcasting Network ($12,000) see Stacy Foundation, Festus

Trinity County Junior Livestock ($2,977) see Sierra Pacific Resources

Trinity United Methodist Church ($12,000) see Harper Foundation, Philip S.

Trojan League of Orange County ($10,000) see Webb Educational and Charitable Trust, Torrey H. and Dorothy K.

Troy High School ($11,800) see Robinson Foundation

Trust for Hidden Valley ($11,272) see Bradford Foundation, George and Ruth

Trust for Historic Preservation ($20,000) see Tuohy Foundation, Alice Tweed

Trust for Public Land ($20,000) see Crocker Trust, Mary A.

Trust for Public Land ($10,000) see Dorr Foundation

Trust for Public Land ($37,500) see Kellogg Foundation, J. C.

Trust for Public Land ($7,500) see Witter Foundation, Dean

Trustees of University of California, San Francisco — for the Pew Health Professions Commission ($4,608,500) see Pew Charitable Trusts

Tuolome County Preservation Society ($6,000) see Allen-Heath Memorial Foundation

Turlock High School Auditorium Restoration Fund ($5,000) see Bright Family Foundation

Turnpike Road Congregation — Campus Ministry Program ($9,000) see Bell Trust

Tustin Unified School District see Ricoh Electronics Inc.

Twin Creeks Foundation ($23,000) see Gross Charitable Trust, Stella B.

U.C.S.A. Foundation ($95,000) see Mericos Foundation

UCLA Foundation see Brakeley, John Price Jones Inc.

UCSD, School of Medicine — modernization/expansion of UCSD Medical Center-Hillcrest comp ($500,000) see Weingart Foundation

Uncle Claude Fund-UCLA Mobile Eye Clinic — to provide continued funding of activities of Mobile Eye Clinic ($123,000) see Kirchgessner Foundation, Karl

UNICEF ($1,000) see Parvin Foundation, Albert

Union Rescue Mission ($5,600) see Marshburn Foundation

Union Rescue Mission ($20,000) see Sizzler International

Union Station Foundation ($50,000) see Garland Foundation, John Jewett and H. Chandler

Unitarian Universalist Fellowship ($40,000) see Cook Brothers Educational Fund

United Animal Nations USA ($100,000) see Brach Foundation, Helen

United Animal Nations USA ($100,000) see Brach Foundation, Helen

United Armenian Fund ($143,184) see Lincy Foundation

United Armenian Fund ($132,596) see Lincy Foundation

United Armenian Fund ($130,406) see Lincy Foundation

United Armenian Fund ($117,340) see Lincy Foundation

United Armenian Fund ($116,667) see Lincy Foundation

United Boys Club ($25,000) see Mosher Foundation, Samuel B.

United Cerebral Palsy Association ($15,000) see Foote, Cone & Belding Communications

United Cerebral Palsy/Spastic Children's Foundation of Los Angeles County ($50,000) see 21 International Holdings

United Friends of the Children ($20,000) see Daly Charitable Foundation Trust, Robert and Nancy

United Friends of the Children ($10,000) see Daly Charitable Foundation Trust, Robert and Nancy

United Funds ($5,360) see Joslyn Corp.

United Funds ($440) see Joslyn Corp.

United Funds ($200) see Joslyn Corp.

United Jewish Appeal Federation of Jewish Philanthropies ($5,000) see Borun Foundation, Anna Borun and Harry

United Jewish Appeal Federation of Jewish Philanthropies ($16,055) see Buchalter, Nemer, Fields, & Younger

United Jewish Appeal Federation of Jewish Philanthropies ($50,000) see Chais Family Foundation

United Jewish Appeal Federation of Jewish Philanthropies ($51,000) see Douglas Charitable Foundation

United Jewish Appeal Federation of Jewish Philanthropies ($20,000) see Feintech Foundation

United Jewish Appeal Federation of Jewish Philanthropies ($50,000) see Goldberg Family Foundation, Milton D. and Madeline L.

United Jewish Appeal Federation of Jewish Philanthropies ($13,334) see Goldberg Family Foundation, Milton D. and Madeline L.

United Jewish Appeal Federation of Jewish Philanthropies ($55,000) see Goldsmith Family Foundation

United Jewish Appeal Federation of Jewish Philanthropies ($1,500) see Parvin Foundation, Albert

United Jewish Appeal Federation of Jewish Philanthropies ($5,500) see Shapell Foundation, Nathan and Lilly

United Jewish Appeal Federation of Jewish Philanthropies ($56,500) see Weisz Foundation, David and Sylvia

United Jewish Community Centers — to provide daycare/day camp at thirteen sites in Marin, San Mateo and San Francisco counties ($55,000) see Stulsaft Foundation, Morris

United Jewish Community Centers — Marin Jewish Community Center ($240,000) see Koret Foundation

United Jewish Fund ($50,000) see Bernstein & Co., Sanford C.

United Jewish Fund ($400,000) see Columbia Savings Charitable Foundation

United Jewish Fund ($25,250) see Eisenberg Foundation, Ben B. and Joyce E.

United Jewish Fund ($275,000) see Factor Family Foundation, Max

United Jewish Fund ($211,000) see Irmas Charitable Foundation, Audrey and Sydney

United Jewish Fund ($30,000) see Price Foundation, Louis and Harold

United Jewish Fund ($254,531) see Wasserman Foundation

United Jewish Welfare Fund ($50,000) see Lastfogel Foundation, Abe and Frances

United Jewish Welfare Fund ($25,000) see Levine Family Foundation, Hyman

United Jewish Welfare Fund ($10,000) see Taubman Foundation, Herman P. and Sophia

United Jewish Welfare Fund ($10,000) see Taubman Foundation, Herman P. and Sophia

United Jewish Welfare Fund ($10,000) see Taubman Foundation, Herman P. and Sophia

United Jewish Welfare Fund ($10,000) see Taubman Foundation, Herman P. and Sophia

United Methodist Church ($13,000) see Walker Foundation, Smith

United Methodist Church ($10,000) see Walker Foundation, Smith

United Negro College Fund ($85,000) see Wollenberg Foundation

United Services Organization — 50th Anniversary ($20,000) see Chambers Development Co.

United States Catholic Conference — Don Bosco Technical Institute; upgrade and renovate science building ($300,000) see Berger Foundation, H.N. and Frances C.

United Way ($5,500) see ACF Industries, Inc.

United Way ($40,000) see Bank of A. Levy

United Way ($8,000) see Bekins Foundation, Milo W.

United Way ($2,000) see Bourns, Inc.

United Way ($10,000) see Burnham Foundation

United Way ($46,946) see California & Hawaiian Sugar Co.

United Way ($5,000) see California & Hawaiian Sugar Co.

United Way ($185,000) see Chevron Corp.

United Way ($25,000) see Circuit City Stores

United Way ($16,000) see Coltec Industries

United Way ($60,000) see Deutsch Co.

United Way ($50,000) see Goldman Fund, Richard and Rhoda

United Way ($15,000) see Green Foundation, Burton E.

United Way ($460,000) see GTE Corp.

United Way ($1,500) see Halstead Foundation

United Way ($25,000) see Hogan Foundation, Royal Barney

United Way ($3,100) see Hume Foundation, Jaquelin

United Way ($70,000) see Imperial Bancorp

United Way ($8,085) see Inland Container Corp.

United Way ($2,500) see Jacobs Engineering Group

United Way ($40,000) see Lakeside Foundation

United Way ($2,247) see Lawyers Title Foundation

United Way ($1,727) see Lawyers Title Foundation

United Way ($1,052) see Lawyers Title Foundation

United Way ($315,000) see Litton Industries

United Way ($15,000) see McBean Family Foundation

United Way ($155,000) see McDonnell Douglas Corp.

United Way ($269,342) see McKesson Corp.

United Way ($8,000) see Metropolitan Theatres Corp.

United Way ($10,000) see Poinsettia Foundation, Paul and Magdalena Ecke

United Way ($30,000) see Rosenberg, Jr. Family Foundation, Louise and Claude

United Way ($261,000) see Shorenstein Foundation, Walter H. and Phyllis J.

United Way ($200,000) see Shorenstein Foundation, Walter H. and Phyllis J.

United Way ($105,000) see Shorenstein Foundation, Walter H. and Phyllis J.

United Way ($75,000) see Shorenstein Foundation, Walter H. and Phyllis J.

United Way ($75,000) see Shorenstein Foundation, Walter H. and Phyllis J.

United Way ($50,000) see Shorenstein Foundation, Walter H. and Phyllis J.

United Way ($35,000) see Shorenstein Foundation, Walter H. and Phyllis J.

United Way ($35,000) see Shorenstein Foundation, Walter H. and Phyllis J.

United Way ($42,054) see Sizzler International

United Way see Sumitomo Bank of California

United Way ($250,000) see Taube Family Foundation

United Way ($10,000) see Thornton Foundation, Flora L.

United Way ($350,000) see TRW Corp.

United Way ($4,500) see Vesper Corp.

United Way ($1,500) see Wallace Computer Services

United Way ($800) see Wallace Computer Services

United Way ($10,000) see Wilbur-Ellis Co.

United Way ($355,000) see Xerox Corp.

United Way ($26,883) see Ziegler Foundation, Ruth/Allen

United Way of the Bay Area ($274,000) see Bechtel Group

United Way-Bay Area — unrestricted ($1,200,000) see Chevron Corp.

United Way of the Bay Area ($100,000) see Clorox Co.

United Way of the Bay Area ($20,000) see Crum and Forster

United Way of the Bay Area ($7,500) see Kidder, Peabody & Co.

United Way of the Bay Area ($100,000) see Levi Strauss & Co.

United Way of the Bay Area ($60,000) see Levi Strauss & Co.

United Way of the Bay Area ($1,150,843) see Pacific Telesis Group

United Way of the Bay Area ($200,000) see Pacific Telesis Group

United Way of the Bay Area ($250,000) see Transamerica Corp.

United Way of the Bay Area ($55,000) see Transamerica Corp.

United Way, Bay Area ($45,000) see Union Bank

United Way Bay Area ($1,400,000) see Wells Fargo & Co.

United Way of the Bay Area ($82,000) see Xerox Corp.

United Way of the Bay Area — 1991-1992 campaign ($149,850) see First Interstate Bank of California

United Way Campaign ($34,000) see Teledyne

United Way Campaign ($34,000) see Teledyne

United Way Campaign ($34,000) see Teledyne

United Way Campaign ($34,000) see Teledyne

United Way of Greater Los Angeles ($40,000) see Smith Foundation, Lon V.

United Way of Humboldt County — operating ($26,450) see Simpson Investment Co.

United Way of Los Angeles ($600,000) see BankAmerica Corp.

United Way of Los Angeles ($300,000) see BankAmerica Corp.

United Way Los Angeles — annual giving ($71,204) see Enterprise Rent-A-Car Co.

United Way of Los Angeles ($873,030) see Pacific Telesis Group

United Way of Los Angeles — annual support ($600,000) see Times Mirror Co.

United Way, Los Angeles, CA ($260,424) see McDonnell Douglas Corp.-West

United Way of Los Angeles County ($36,000) see Pfaffinger Foundation

United Way, Los Angeles County ($280,000) see Union Bank

United Way of Los Angeles — 1991-1992 campaign

California (cont.)

Charitable Trust, Lita Annenberg

University of California Los Angeles ($31,330) see Stern Memorial Trust, Sidney

University of California Los Angeles ($9,000) see Teleklew Productions

University of California at Los Angeles — final payment on $400,000 pledge to support chair in electrical engineering, and graduate minority engineering program ($145,000) see TRW Corp.

University of California at Los Angeles, Anderson Graduate School of Management — to establish the John M. Olin Center for Policy ($350,000) see Olin Foundation, John M.

University of California Los Angeles Athletics Department ($25,000) see Autry Foundation

University of California Los Angeles California Institute ($20,000) see Jonsson Foundation

University of California at Los Angeles — emergency care; geriatrics ($18,750) see Factor Family Foundation, Max

University of California Los Angeles Children's Neurological Research ($15,000) see Rosenthal Foundation, Richard and Hinda

University of California, Los Angeles — the Compton Fellowship Program supports minority Ph.D. candidates preparing for careers in college and university teaching ($105,000) see Danforth Foundation

University of California Los Angeles Film and Television Archives ($10,000) see Pickford Foundation, Mary

University of California Los Angeles Foundation ($6,150) see Ace Beverage Co.

University of California Los Angeles Foundation ($50,000) see Goldsmith Family Foundation

University of California Los Angeles Foundation ($240,000) see Iacocca Foundation

University of California Los Angeles Foundation ($40,000) see Jameson Foundation, J. W. and Ida M.

University of California Los Angeles Foundation ($5,000) see Kajima International, Inc.

University of California Los Angeles Foundation ($10,025) see Sizzler International

University of California at Los Angeles Foundation — Chancellor's Discretionary Fund ($5,000) see American President Cos.

University of California at Los Angeles Foundation-General — toward a pilot study on water reclamation technology ($400,000) see Ahmanson Foundation

University of California at Los Angeles Foundation — Medical University of California at Los Angeles School of Medicine ($333,000) see Mann Foundation, Ted

University of California at Los Angeles Foundation — University of California at Los Angeles School of Medicine; frontiers of medical science program ($100,000) see Drown Foundation, Joseph

University of California at Los Angeles Foundation/William Andrews Clark Memorial Library — toward additonal endowment for book acquisition ($500,000) see Ahmanson Foundation

University of California at Los Angeles Graduate School of Business ($70,834) see Wells Fargo & Co.

University of California Los Angeles Hope of Hearing ($1,000) see Cedars-Sinai Medical Center Section D Fund

University of California at Los Angeles — support Human Values and Communications in Medicine program ($300,707) see Whittier Foundation, L. K.

University of California at Los Angeles, Institute for Social Science Research — study on urban inequality in Los Angeles ($89,943) see Haynes Foundation, John Randolph and Dora

University of California Los Angeles Kennamer Foundation ($60,000) see Parvin Foundation, Albert

University of California at Los Angeles, Latin American Center — for support of the program on U.S.-Mexico relations ($525,000) see Hewlett Foundation, William and Flora

University of California at Los Angeles Law School — for expansion of law library ($200,000) see Stauffer Charitable Trust, John

University of California at Los Angeles, Lewis Center for Regional Policy Studies ($124,745) see Haynes Foundation, John Randolph and Dora

University of California Los Angeles Medical Center ($145,000) see Lawrence Foundation, Lind

University of California Los Angeles Medical Center — arthritis research ($125,000) see Treadwell Foundation, Nora Eccles

University of California Los Angeles Medical Center — diabetes research ($125,000) see Treadwell Foundation, Nora Eccles

University of California Los Angeles Oral History Program ($10,000) see Scott Foundation, Virginia Steele

University of California Los Angeles — Parkinsons research ($20,000) see Murdy Foundation

University of California Los Angeles Pediatric Neuro Research ($50,000) see Columbia Savings Charitable Foundation

University of California at Los Angeles — Regents of the University of California ($262,000) see Hilton Foundation, Conrad N.

University of California Los Angeles Scholarship Fund ($5,000) see Buchalter, Nemer, Fields, & Younger

University of California Los Angeles School of Dentistry ($15,000) see Borchard Foundation, Albert and Elaine

University of California Los Angeles School of Medicine ($25,000) see Norman Foundation, Andrew

University of California Los Angeles School of Medicine ($200,000) see Oberkotter Family Foundation

University of California Los Angeles School of Medicine ($800,000) see Revlon

University of California Medical Center Department of Psychiatry ($22,500) see Schlinger Foundation

University of California — olfactory perception: empirical honeybee studies and neural network models ($45,000) see Whitehall Foundation

University of California Press ($2,500) see Cow Hollow Foundation

University of California Regent Leadership Award ($2,000) see Ace Beverage Co.

University of California — Regents ($225,000) see Anheuser-Busch Cos.

University of California — Regents ($200,000) see Anheuser-Busch Cos.

University of California Regents ($261,500) see Borun Foundation, Anna Borun and Harry

University of California Regents ($11,000) see Brenner Foundation, Mervyn

University of California Regents — educational programs ($75,000) see Genentech

University of California Regents ($4,000) see Gilmore Foundation, Earl B.

University of California Regents ($5,000) see Jacobs Engineering Group

University of California Regents ($6,050) see Metropolitan Theatres Corp.

University of California Regents ($27,500) see Preuss Foundation

University of California Regents ($10,000) see R. P. Foundation

University of California Regents ($50,000) see Simon Foundation, Jennifer Jones

University of California Regents ($45,000) see Simon Foundation, Jennifer Jones

University of California Regents ($26,000) see Simon Foundation, Jennifer Jones

University of California Regents ($12,500) see Simon Foundation, Jennifer Jones

University of California Regents ($10,000) see Simon Foundation, Jennifer Jones

University of California Regents ($10,000) see Simon Foundation, Jennifer Jones

University of California Regents ($10,000) see Simon Foundation, Jennifer Jones

University of California Regents ($3,000) see Simon Foundation, Jennifer Jones

University of California Regents ($75,000) see Smithers Foundation, Christopher D.

University of California Regents ($47,000) see Wills Foundation

University of California Regents ($30,804) see Wills Foundation

University of California Regents ($30,000) see Wills Foundation

University of California Regents ($30,000) see Wills Foundation

University of California Regents ($25,000) see Wills Foundation

University of California Regents ($25,000) see Wills Foundation

University of California Regents University Art Museum ($4,500) see Walker Foundation, T. B.

University of California Riverside ($1,000) see Warner Foundation, Lee and Rose

University of California, Riverside, California Museum of Photography ($105,665) see Haynes Foundation, John Randolph and Dora

University of California Riverside Foundation ($1,500) see Bourns, Inc.

University of California Riverside Foundation ($1,500) see Bourns, Inc.

University of California Riverside Foundation ($5,000) see Essick Foundation

University of California San Diego — externships ($24,000) see Flintridge Foundation

University of California at San Diego ($1,160,778) see Powell Foundation, Charles Lee

University of California San Diego ($27,500) see Preuss Foundation

University of California San Diego ($500,000) see Thornton Foundation, John M. and Sally B.

University of California San Diego Foundation ($83,333) see Moore Family Foundation

University of California San Diego Lung Center ($7,700) see Ottenstein Family Foundation

University of California, San Diego — non-restricted ($1,500,000) see Birch Foundation, Stephen and Mary

University of California San Diego — School of Medicine ($39,800) see Stern Foundation, Charles H. and Anna S.

University of California San Diego Scripps Institute of Oceanography ($35,000) see Masserini Charitable Trust, Maurice J.

University of California, San Francisco — medical science scholar ($108,000) see Culpeper Foundation, Charles E.

University of California at San Francisco — degenerative diseases research ($450,000) see Fairchild Foundation, Sherman

University of California at San Francisco ($30,000) see Lurie Foundation, Louis R.

University of California San Francisco ($290,000) see Syntex Corp.

University of California, San Francisco ($250,000) see Valley Foundation, Wayne and Gladys

University of California, San Francisco ($25,262) see Whitney Foundation, Helen Hay

University of California, San Francisco — for the program in Biological Sciences ($1,213,520) see Markey Charitable Trust, Lucille P.

University of California at San Francisco — psychobiologic reactivity and health in primary school children: a longitudinal study ($200,000) see Grant Foundation, William T.

University of California, San Francisco — for the Clearinghouse for Drug Exposed Infants and Children ($25,000) see Stulsaft Foundation, Morris

University of California San Francisco Foundation ($9,500) see Brenner Foundation, Mervyn

University of California San Francisco Foundation ($5,000) see Hamilton Foundation, Florence P.

University of California San Francisco Foundation ($40,000) see Hills Fund, Edward E.

University of California San Francisco Foundation ($145,287) see Leonhardt Foundation, Frederick H.

University of California San Francisco Foundation ($2,000) see Nelson Foundation, Florence

University of California San Francisco Foundation ($1,844) see Schwartz Foundation, Bernard Lee

University of California San Francisco Foundation ($5,000) see Wilsey Bennet Co.

University of California, San Francisco — to support program on Health of the Public ($1,239,601) see Rockefeller Foundation

University of California at San Francisco — Institute for Health and Aging; for a study of residential care facilities and their residents ($300,000) see Kaiser Family Foundation, Henry J.

University of California, San Francisco — Neurology Fellowship ($56,332) see Osher Foundation, Bernard

University of California, San Francisco — 1988 Medical Science Scholar ($108,000) see Culpeper Foundation, Charles E.

University of California, San Francisco, School of Medicine — program to stimulate academic health centers to become more responsive to the health needs of populations and communities ($3,899,833) see Johnson Foundation, Robert Wood

University of California, San Francisco, School of Pharmacy ($5,400) see Long Foundation, J.M.

University of California, San Francisco, School of Pharmacy — prize for excellence ($4,600) see Long Foundation, J.M.

University of California San Francisco Science and Health — scientific educational kits ($47,260) see Genentech

University of California at Santa Barbara — to design computer system prototype to track future extinction of plants and animals ($1,190,000) see IBM Corp.

University of California, Santa Barbara, Department of Sociology — Santa Barbara, CA to enable a study of the Los Angeles garment industry ($81,186) see Haynes

Foundation, John Randolph and Dora

University of California Santa Barbara Foundation ($15,000) see Comer Foundation

University of California at Santa Barbara Foundation ($2,500) see Shea Foundation, Edmund and Mary

University of California Santa Cruz Foundation — general fund ($15,000) see Stuart Center Charitable Trust, Hugh

University of California School of Engineering ($5,000) see Gleason Foundation, Katherine

University of California School of Medicine ($5,000) see Broadhurst Foundation

University of California School of Medicine — arthritis research ($125,000) see Treadwell Foundation, Nora Eccles

University of California University of Medicine ($75,000) see Western Cardiac Foundation

University Children's Medical Group — fellowship in pediatric plastic surgery ($100,000) see Vidda Foundation

University of Judaism ($17,000) see Beren Foundation, Robert M.

University of Judaism ($7,200) see Beren Foundation, Robert M.

University of Judaism ($39,800) see Levine Family Foundation, Hyman

University of Judaism ($295,313) see Ziegler Foundation, Ruth/Allen

University of Judaism ($193,898) see Ziegler Foundation, Ruth/Allen

University of Judaism ($99,241) see Ziegler Foundation, Ruth/Allen

University of Judaism ($98,435) see Ziegler Foundation, Ruth/Allen

University of Judaism Foundation ($520,000) see Eisenberg Foundation, Ben B. and Joyce E.

University of La Verne ($10,000) see Peppers Foundation, Ann

University of La Verne — toward expanding and renovating Wilson Library ($450,000) see Irvine Foundation, James

University-Oakland Metropolitan Forum ($10,000) see American President Cos.

University of Pacific — student fitness center ($25,000) see Foothills Foundation

University of the Pacific ($25,000) see Gellert Foundation, Fred

University of Redlands ($4,250) see Associated Foundations

University of Redlands ($10,000) see Bekins Foundation, Milo W.

University of Redlands ($45,000) see Knudsen Foundation, Tom and Valley

University of Redlands ($1,510) see Natural Heritage Foundation

University of Redlands ($18,500) see Stuart Foundation, Elbridge and Evelyn

University of Redlands — equipment fund for Chemistry

Department ($125,000) see Stauffer Charitable Trust, John

University of Redlands — Fletcher Jones Chair ($500,000) see Jones Foundation, Fletcher

University of Redlands, Office of the President ($60,000) see Norris Foundation, Kenneth T. and Eileen L.

University of San Diego — toward implementing a cultural diversity program ($1,000,000) see Irvine Foundation, James

University of San Diego see San Diego Trust & Savings Bank

University of San Diego ($529,975) see Weingart Foundation

University of San Francisco ($15,000) see Gellert Foundation, Carl

University of San Francisco ($20,000) see Sandy Foundation, George H.

University of San Francisco ($35,000) see Swig Charity Foundation, Mae and Benjamin

University of San Francisco — Electronic Scientific Community ($200,000) see Jones Foundation, Fletcher

University of San Francisco — for construction costs of the Koret Health and Recreation Center ($600,000) see Koret Foundation

University of San Francisco Pacific Rim ($30,000) see Hale Foundation, Crescent Porter

University of Santa Barbara ($10,000) see Petersen Foundation, Esper A.

University of Santa Clara ($8,500) see Associated Foundations

University of Santa Clara ($100,000) see Clougherty Charitable Trust, Francis H.

University of Santa Clara ($10,000) see Foundation for the Needs of Others

University of Santa Clara ($60,000) see Hayden Foundation, William R. and Virginia

University of Santa Clara — excellence ($100,000) see Lockheed Corp.

University of Southern California ($1,901,000) see Annenberg Foundation

University of Southern California ($6,500) see Atkinson Foundation, Myrtle L.

University of Southern California ($200,000) see BankAmerica Corp.

University of Southern California ($52,000) see Bannerman Foundation, William C.

University of Southern California ($170,000) see Bauer Foundation, M. R.

University of Southern California — research fellowship laboratory for molecular biology and genetics ($182,200) see Baxter Foundation, Donald E. and Delia B.

University of Southern California ($18,000) see Borchard Foundation, Albert and Elaine

University of Southern California — support medical school ($66,000) see Bowles

and Robert Bowles Memorial Fund, Ethel Wilson

University of Southern California ($158,388) see Brookdale Foundation

University of Southern California ($30,000) see California Foundation for Biochemical Research

University of Southern California ($100,000) see Connell Foundation, Michael J.

University of Southern California ($25,000) see Connell Foundation, Michael J.

University of Southern California — construction of new teaching library ($250,000) see Cord Foundation, E. L.

University of Southern California ($120,000) see Darling Foundation, Hugh and Hazel

University of Southern California ($5,000) see Domino of California

University of Southern California — loan repayment assistance program ($100,000) see Drown Foundation, Joseph

University of Southern California ($64,132) see Dunning Foundation

University of Southern California — cancer research ($50,000) see Early Medical Research Trust, Margaret E.

University of Southern California ($48,794) see Ernst & Young

University of Southern California — capital campaign for unrestricted endowment ($50,000) see First Interstate Bank of California

University of Southern California ($8,000) see Hafif Family Foundation

University of Southern California ($1,261,621) see Hewlett-Packard Co.

University of Southern California ($1,256,577) see Hewlett-Packard Co.

University of Southern California ($53,000) see Hoffman Foundation, H. Leslie Hoffman and Elaine S.

University of Southern California ($50,000) see Hoffman Foundation, H. Leslie Hoffman and Elaine S.

University of Southern California ($3,750) see Jackson Mills

University of Southern California — scholarship fund ($26,500) see Kingsley Foundation, Lewis A.

University of Southern California ($45,000) see Knudsen Foundation, Tom and Valley

University of Southern California ($133,233) see KPMG Peat Marwick

University of Southern California — library ($1,000,000) see Leavey Foundation, Thomas and Dorothy

University of Southern California ($2,500) see Levine Family Foundation, Hyman

University of Southern California — excellence awards ($100,000) see Lockheed Corp.

University of Southern California ($90,000) see

McAlister Charitable Foundation, Harold

University of Southern California ($858,750) see Powell Foundation, Charles Lee

University of Southern California ($10,000) see Weiler Foundation

University of Southern California ($100,000) see Wells Fargo & Co.

University of Southern California — payment on $1 million pledge to support construction of new Electrical Engineering center ($100,000) see TRW Corp.

University of Southern California — Arthur C. Bartner Endowment Fund ($12,500) see Keck, Jr. Foundation, William M.

University of Southern California Associated ($50,000) see Femino Foundation

University of Southern California, Cancer Hospital and Research Institute ($52,000) see Litton Industries

University of Southern California Cancer Research Associates ($6,000) see Jones Fund, Blanche and George

University of Southern California Cancer Research Center ($32,791) see Seebee Trust, Frances

University of Southern California Cinema Circulus ($5,000) see Broccoli Charitable Foundation, Dana and Albert R.

University of Southern California Comprehensive Cancer Center ($200,000) see Thornton Foundation, Flora L.

University of Southern California Davis School of Gerontology ($55,000) see Pickford Foundation, Mary

University of Southern California Dentistry ($10,000) see Femino Foundation

University of Southern California, Department of Geological Sciences ($20,000) see Schlumberger Ltd.

University of Southern California — Division of Neurology ($64,000) see Norris Foundation, Kenneth T. and Eileen L.

University of Southern California Drama Center ($10,000) see Cramer Foundation

University of Southern California Ethel Percy Andrus Gerontology Center — establish a university chair in gerontology ($333,000) see Prudential Insurance Co. of America

University of Southern California/General University Support — toward construction of and endowment for the new Teaching Library ($2,000,000) see Ahmanson Foundation

University of Southern California — Las Floristas ($100,000) see Norris Foundation, Kenneth T. and Eileen L.

University of Southern California Law Center ($53,350) see Irmas Charitable Foundation, Audrey and Sydney

University of Southern California Leonard Davis School ($50,000) see Martin Foundation, Bert William

University of Southern California Library ($5,500) see Femino Foundation

University of Southern California — Loker Hydrocarbon Institute; for transformer and spectrometer ($100,000) see Stauffer Charitable Trust, John

University of Southern California — support Petroleum Engineering Fellowship program ($250,000) see Whittier Foundation, L. K.

University of Southern California — for the construction of the Ralph M. Parsons Auditorium ($1,000,000) see Parsons Foundation, Ralph M.

University of Southern California Scholarship Fund ($80,000) see Thagard Foundation

University of Southern California School of Business ($10,000) see Deutsch Co.

University of Southern California, School of Cinema and Television ($25,000) see Mayer Foundation, Louis B.

University of Southern California School of Cinema/TV ($3,000) see Jones Fund, Blanche and George

University of Southern California — School of Education and School of Public Administration ($106,862) see Haynes Foundation, John Randolph and Dora

University of Southern California School of Medicine ($50,000) see Borchard Foundation, Albert and Elaine

University of Southern California School of Medicine ($69,258) see Hoover, Jr. Foundation, Margaret W. and Herbert

University of Southern California School of Medicine ($46,000) see MacKenzie Foundation

University of Southern California School of Medicine ($135,518) see Martin Foundation, Della

University of Southern California School of Medicine ($12,075) see Potts Memorial Foundation

University of Southern California School of Medicine/C.J. Berne Professorship ($7,500) see Sprague, Jr. Foundation, Caryll M. and Norman F.

University of Southern California School of Medicine — for construction of a major laboratory suite in the new University of Southern California Center for Molecular Medicine ($200,000) see Webb Foundation, Del E.

University of Southern California, School of Pharmacy ($5,000) see Long Foundation, J.M.

University of Southern California — School of Public Administration, Sacramento Campus ($333,333) see Jones Foundation, Fletcher

California (cont.)

University of Southern California, School of Social Work — for an evaluation of in-home family support programs ($218,363) see Stuart Foundations

University of Southern California, School of Urban and Regional Planning ($64,346) see Haynes Foundation, John Randolph and Dora

UNS Project Handclasps ($4,000) see Miller-Mellor Association

Urban School of San Francisco ($15,000) see Crocker Trust, Mary A.

US Academic Decathlon ($50,000) see Lennox International, Inc.

US Conference of Mayors ($1,000) see Benbough Foundation, Legler

US-El Salvador Institute for Democratic Development ($29,000) see Prickett Fund, Lynn R. and Karl E.

US International University ($17,835) see Kerr Foundation, A. H.

US Ski Team Education Association ($3,000) see Blum Foundation, Harry and Maribel G.

US State Department ($12,000) see Boeckmann Charitable Foundation

USC-Library — toward library component of 21st Century Campaign ($500,000) see Weingart Foundation

USD-Regulatory Commission — support of Children's Advocacy Institute ($498,917) see Weingart Foundation

USS San Diego CL53 ($1,200) see Benbough Foundation, Legler

Vallejo Symphony ($1,000) see California & Hawaiian Sugar Co.

Valley Baptist Fellowship ($25,225) see Stamps Foundation, James L.

Valley Community Clinic — to provide visual examinations and prescription glasses to low income individuals, uninsured and homeless children and adults ($20,000) see Kirchgessner Foundation, Karl

Valley Medical Center Foundation ($30,000) see Syntex Corp.

Valley Medical Center Foundation — funding to provide expanded and renovated space for the main pharmacy ($100,000) see Valley Foundation

Valley Medical Center Foundation, Santa Clara Valley see Tandem Computers

Valley Rescue Mission ($1,000) see Clark Charitable Foundation

Vally Children's Hospital ($35,611) see Radin Foundation

Variety Children's Charities ($8,600) see Metropolitan Theatres Corp.

Variety Club International ($25,000) see Plitt Southern Theatres

Venice Family Clinic ($19,250) see Goldwyn Foundation, Samuel

Venice Family Clinic ($41,250) see Milken Foundation, L. and S.

Venice Family Clinic ($26,883) see Ziegler Foundation, Ruth/Allen

Venice Family Clinic — to help pay for a part-time optometrist's service only ($32,500) see Kirchgessner Foundation, Karl

Ventura Community College — refuge for homeless animals ($80,336) see Falk Foundation, Elizabeth M.

Ventura County Community Foundation ($32,500) see Bank of A. Levy

Ventura County Symphony Association ($12,500) see Bank of A. Levy

Verbum Dei High School ($25,000) see Nestle U.S.A. Inc.

Viking Charities ($30,500) see McAlister Charitable Foundation, Harold

Villa Esperanza ($20,000) see Braun Foundation

Vintage High School Peer Support Program ($5,000) see DiRosa Foundation, Rene and Veronica

Vista Del Mar ($50,000) see Alpert Foundation, Herb

Vista Del Mar ($50,000) see Factor Family Foundation, Max

Vista Del Mar ($3,000) see National Metal & Steel

Vista Del Mar ($5,000) see Shapell Foundation, Nathan and Lilly

Vistas for Blind Children Center ($87,500) see Milken Family Medical Foundation

Volunteer Auxiliary of Youth Guidance ($20,000) see Sandy Foundation, George H.

Volunteers of America ($100) see Baker Foundation, Solomon R. and Rebecca D.

Volunteers of America ($2,000) see Green Foundation, Burton E.

Volunteers of America ($5,000) see Robinson Foundation

Voyager Company — Program-Related Investment to produce and publish interactive multimedia products ($212,780) see Markle Foundation, John and Mary R.

Walden School ($10,000) see Peppers Foundation, Ann

Walden School of California ($12,000) see Beynon Foundation, Kathryne

Waldorf Institute of Southern California ($11,500) see Waldorf Educational Foundation

Walnut Creek Christian School ($3,870) see Meland Outreach

Walter Haas School of Business ($60,000) see Witter Foundation, Dean

Walter Hays PTA ($1,000) see Ishiyama Foundation

Webb Schools ($25,000) see Garland Foundation, John Jewett and H. Chandler

Welb School of California ($25,000) see Van Nuys Foundation, I. N. and Susanna H.

Welk Heritage ($30,000) see Teleklew Productions

Wellness Community — assistance for cancer patients

($50,000) see Irvine Health Foundation

Wellness Community ($25,000) see Markey Charitable Fund, John C.

Wellness Community ($20,000) see Stauffer Foundation, John and Beverly

Wellness Community, Santa Monica, CA ($25,000) see McDonnell Douglas Corp.-West

Wellsley ($2,000) see Femino Foundation

Westchester Academic Boys Club ($10,000) see Hannon Foundation, William H.

Western Cardiac Foundation ($50,000) see May Foundation, Wilbur

Western Diocese Religious Camp ($32,000) see Peters Foundation, Leon S.

Westminister Woods ($5,000) see Ryan Foundation, David Claude

Westmont College ($89,221) see Kerr Foundation, A. H.

Westmont College ($38,000) see Tuohy Foundation, Alice Tweed

Westpark Elementary School see Ricoh Electronics Inc.

Westside Neighborhood Clinic, Prenatal Care ($30,000) see Fairfield Foundation, Freeman E.

Whittier College ($4,250) see Associated Foundations

Whittier College ($17,500) see Murdy Foundation

Whittier College — toward implementing a comprehensive strategic plan to increase enrollment, improve the academic program, and strengthen development operations in preparation for a major development campaign ($500,000) see Irvine Foundation, James

Whittier Institute ($5,000) see Benbough Foundation, Legler

Whittier Institute ($50,000) see Stern Foundation, Charles H. and Anna S.

Whittier Institute ($5,000) see Thornton Foundation, John M. and Sally B.

Willow Creek Fire Department ($3,000) see Sierra Pacific Resources

Wilshire Boulevard Temple ($25,000) see Factor Family Foundation, Max

Winrock International ($10,000) see Stuart Foundation, Elbridge and Evelyn

WISE ($10,000) see Seven Springs Foundation

WomenCare Clinic ($15,000) see Deer Creek Foundation

Women's/Child Crisis Center ($15,000) see Ebell of Los Angeles Rest Cottage Association

Women's Foundation ($60,000) see Women's Project Foundation

Womens Haven ($3,000) see Burnand Medical and Educational Foundation, Alphonse A.

Woodland High — Biotechnology Study Center ($13,350) see California Educational Initiatives Fund

Woodlawn Avenue Elementary — Student and Parent Education in Computer Instruction and Literacy

(SPECIAL) ($12,463) see California Educational Initiatives Fund

Woodside School ($25,000) see Sudix Foundation

WORKNET — urban disadvantaged career development ($35,000) see M. E. G. Foundation

World College West ($20,000) see Crocker Trust, Mary A.

World Emergency Relief — Romania target development ($195,316) see M. E. G. Foundation

World Impact ($105,000) see First Fruit

World Impact ($7,500) see S.G. Foundation

World Opportunities ($10,000) see Atkinson Foundation, Myrtle L.

World Research ($25,000) see Smith Foundation, Lon V.

World Research Foundation ($10,000) see Boeckmann Charitable Foundation

World Vision ($2,000) see Carter Family Foundation

World Vision ($2,000) see Douglas Corp.

World Vision ($300) see Gilbane Foundation, Thomas and William

World Vision ($42,800) see Hedco Foundation

World Vision ($42,266) see Hedco Foundation

World Vision ($1,200,000) see Hilton Foundation, Conrad N.

World Vision ($1,000) see Kobacker Co.

World Vision ($54,000) see M. E. G. Foundation

World Vision ($13,500) see Overstreet Foundation

World Vision ($11,000) see Western Shade Cloth Charitable Foundation

World Vision ($40,000) see Westwood Endowment

World Vision International — Mali ($201,400) see Maclellan Foundation

World Vision Organization see Best Western International

World Vision — funding for Parent Empowerment Program ($35,000) see Hancock Foundation, Luke B.

Writing to Read Project/Rx for Reading in Wisconsin — computer programs/studies ($25,000) see Firstar Bank Milwaukee NA

Wycliffe Bible Translators ($26,000) see Artevel Foundation

Wycliffe Bible Translators ($5,000) see Corestates Bank

Wycliffe Bible Translators ($9,500) see Kejr Foundation

Wycliffe Bible Translators ($3,000) see Leu Foundation

Wycliffe Bible Translators ($20,000) see M.E. Foundation

Yellow Springs Institute for Contemporary Studies ($315,000) see Bohen Foundation

YMCA ($12,621) see Ace Beverage Co.

YMCA ($4,000) see American Foundation

YMCA ($28,058) see Arata Brothers Trust

YMCA ($21,000) see Arrillaga Foundation

YMCA ($36,666) see Burnham Foundation

YMCA ($15,000) see Crummer Foundation, Roy E.

YMCA ($5,500) see Davey Tree Expert Co.

YMCA ($12,500) see Day Foundation, Willametta K.

YMCA ($13,000) see Fairfield Foundation, Freeman E.

YMCA ($75,000) see Forest Lawn Foundation

YMCA ($15,000) see Fusenot Charity Foundation, Georges and Germaine

YMCA ($25,000) see Gellert Foundation, Fred

YMCA ($59,000) see Hoffman Foundation, H. Leslie Hoffman and Elaine S.

YMCA ($1,000) see Jerome Foundation

YMCA ($30,000) see Lux Foundation, Miranda

YMCA ($19,000) see Masserini Charitable Trust, Maurice J.

YMCA ($10,000) see Peery Foundation

YMCA ($12,000) see Poinsettia Foundation, Paul and Magdalena Ecke

YMCA ($19,000) see Sandy Foundation, George H.

YMCA ($80,000) see Van Camp Foundation

YMCA Metropolitan Los Angeles ($31,250) see Baker Foundation, R. C.

YMCA-Metropolitan Los Angeles — expand early childhood programs ($2,474,500) see Weingart Foundation

YMCA of Orange County ($50,500) see Baker Foundation, R. C.

YMCA-San Diego County ($106,000) see Copley Press

Yorba Linda Friends Church ($12,000) see Marshburn Foundation

Yosemite Association ($2,000) see Schlinger Foundation

Yosemite Institute — outdoor environmental education ($15,000) see Odell and Helen Pfeiffer Odell Fund, Robert Stewart

Yosemite Institute — capital needs ($50,000) see Sequoia Foundation

Young Life ($12,600) see Berry Foundation, Lowell

Young Life San Francisco ($43,814) see McKesson Corp.

Yours for Life Ministries ($19,000) see Norgren Foundation, Carl A.

Youth Advocates — teen HIV education ($30,000) see Goldman Fund, Richard and Rhoda

Youth for Christ ($5,800) see Kerr Foundation, A. H.

Youth for Christ/San Gabriel and Inland Valleys ($25,000) see Stamps Foundation, James L.

Youth Communications ($14,000) see Bannerman Foundation, William C.

Youth and Community Service see San Diego Trust & Savings Bank

Youth Development ($6,500) see Stauffer Foundation, John and Beverly

Youth and Family Services ($10,000) see Greenville Foundation

Youth Guidance Center — to purchase computer equipment for Computer Literacy

Program ($8,200) see Lux Foundation, Miranda

Youth Law Center — project to ensure preventive health screening for foster children ($30,000) see Goldman Fund, Richard and Rhoda

Youth Law Center ($15,956) see Haigh-Scatena Foundation

Youth for Service ($141,700) see Cahill Foundation, John R.

YWCA ($7,800) see Eaton Foundation, Edwin M. and Gertrude S.

YWCA ($17,000) see Halsell Foundation, O. L.

YWCA ($10,000) see Segerstrom Foundation

YWCA of Oakland ($40,000) see Clorox Co.

Zen Center ($150,000) see Johnson Fund, Edward C.

Zonta Children's Center — Project Reach program ($65,579) see Johnson Foundation, Walter S.

Zoological Society ($20,000) see Favrot Fund

Zoological Society ($3,000) see Fox Foundation, John H.

Zoological Society ($20,000) see Jameson Foundation, J. W. and Ida M.

Zoological Society ($6,100) see Thornton Foundation, John M. and Sally B.

Zoological Society of San Diego ($150,000) see Lincolnshire

Zoological Society of San Diego ($3,000) see Ryan Foundation, David Claude

Zoological Society of San Diego — Heart of the Zoo project ($500,000) see Steele Foundation, Harry and Grace

Zwemer Institute for Muslim Studies ($47,500) see First Fruit

Zwemer Institute of Muslim Studies ($7,225) see Kerr Foundation, A. H.

Colorado

Academy Research and Development Institute ($10,000) see Aristech Chemical Corp.

Adams Community Mental Health Center see Coors Brewing Co.

Adams County Historical Society see Public Service Co. of Colorado

Adult Learning Source ($25,000) see Hill Foundation

Adventure/Unlimited ($25,000) see Harding Foundation, Charles Stewart

Aesthetic Institute of Colorado ($2,500) see Burgess Trust, Ralph L. and Florence R.

Aims Community College ($6,229) see Phelps, Inc.

Air Force Academy Academic Development Fund — endowed chair program ($20,000) see Buell Foundation, Temple Hoyne

Allied Housing ($5,000) see Wolf Foundation, Melvin and Elaine

Allied Jewish Federation ($100,000) see Goodstein Foundation

Allied Jewish Federation ($25,000) see Martin & Deborah Flug Foundation

Allied Jewish Federation ($24,000) see Rabb Foundation, Harry W.

Alpine Institute see Coors Brewing Co.

Alzheimer's Association — Metro Denver Chapter ($10,000) see Anschutz Family Foundation

Alzheimer's Disease and Related Disorders Association ($5,063) see Wolf Foundation, Melvin and Elaine

AMC Cancer Research ($20,000) see Schramm Foundation

AMC Cancer Research Center ($5,000) see Duncan Trust, John G.

AMC Cancer Research Center ($18,000) see Forchheimer Memorial Foundation Trust, Louise and Josie

American Diabetes Association — camperships see Johnson Foundation, Helen K. and Arthur E.

American Humane Association ($100,000) see Animal Assistance Foundation

American Indian Science and Engineering Society — chemical engineering scholarship see Nalco Chemical Co.

American Indian Science and Engineering Society ($35,825) see Santa Fe Pacific Corp.

American Legion Post #68 ($15,000) see Joslin-Needham Family Foundation

American Numismatic Society ($145,100) see Bass Foundation, Harry

American Numismatic Society ($3,000) see Bass Foundation, Harry

American Numismatic Society ($1,000) see Salgo Charitable Trust, Nicholas M.

American Red Cross — operations ($20,000) see Hunter Trust, A. V.

American Red Cross, Pikes Peak Chapter — for purchasing property as a shelter for the homeless ($400,000) see El Pomar Foundation

American Wildlands ($25,000) see Jackson Hole Preserve

American Wildlands Alliance ($30,000) see New-Land Foundation

Anchor Center for Blind Children — therapy programs see Johnson Foundation, Helen K. and Arthur E.

Anderson Ranch Arts Center ($20,000) see Kuyper Foundation, Peter H. and E. Lucille Gaass

Anti-Defamation League ($10,000) see Wolf Foundation, Melvin and Elaine

Anti-Defamation League of B'nai B'rith ($11,000) see Goodstein Foundation

Arapahoe Community College see Coors Brewing Co.

Arapahoe House — advocacy case management see Johnson Foundation, Helen K. and Arthur E.

Archdiocese of Denver ($10,000) see Disney Family Foundation, Roy

Arvada Center for Arts/Humanities ($2,500) see Dekalb Energy Co.

Arvada Hockey see Public Service Co. of Colorado

Asher Student Foundation ($10,000) see Harding Foundation, Charles Stewart

Aspen Community School ($1,000) see Domino of California

Aspen Country Day School ($5,000) see Thendara Foundation

Aspen Foundation ($2,000) see Chanin Family Foundation, Paul R.

Aspen Foundation ($6,000) see Domino of California

Aspen Foundation ($6,000) see Parker, Jr. Foundation, William A.

Aspen Foundation ($11,000) see Strawbridge Foundation of Pennsylvania I, Margaret Dorrance

Aspen Institute ($25,000) see Lauder Foundation

Aspen Jewish Center ($10,000) see Chanin Family Foundation, Paul R.

Aspen Music Festival ($90,000) see Nakamichi Foundation, E.

Aspen Music Festival — for general funding, advancement of listening pleasure of violin ($30,000) see Starling Foundation, Dorothy Richard

Aspen School for the Deaf ($10,000) see Chanin Family Foundation, Paul R.

Aspen Valley Medical Center ($2,500) see Chanin Family Foundation, Paul R.

Aspen Valley Medical Foundation ($1,000) see Domino of California

Aspen Valley Medical Foundation ($1,000) see Domino of California

Aspen Winter Club ($1,000) see Gershman Foundation, Joel

Aspens Celebration of Indigenous Cultures — to fund start-up costs for the "Celebrating the Earth: A Festival of Indigenous Peoples" Event ($10,000) see Amway Corp.

Assistance League of Colorado Springs — to provide clothing for needy school children ($5,000) see Stone Trust, H. Chase

Association of Graduates Endowment Fund ($300,000) see Ackerman Trust, Anna Keesling

Association for the Retarded Citizens of Mesa County see Lowe Foundation

Association for Volunteer Administration see Coors Brewing Co.

Auraria Foundation see Public Service Co. of Colorado

BACA Center for High Altitude Sustainable Agriculture ($18,746) see Manitou Foundation

Bayaud Industries ($10,000) see Mullen Foundation, J. K.

Benedictine Sisters ($5,000) see Frank Family Foundation, A. J.

Berthoud Senior Center — purchase van see Johnson Foundation, Helen K. and Arthur E.

Beth Israel at Shalom Park — for construction costs ($15,000) see Bonfils-Stanton Foundation

Beth Israel at Shalom Park — building fund ($125,000) see Phillips Family Foundation, Jay and Rose

Beth Jacob High School ($7,500) see Jacoby Foundation, Lela Beren and Norman

Big Sisters of Colorado ($3,300) see Dekalb Energy Co.

Boulder County Humane Society ($64,000) see Animal Assistance Foundation

Boulder County Safe House ($5,000) see Duncan Trust, John G.

Boulder School for Student Urantia ($2,000) see Shea Foundation

Boy Scouts of America ($15,000) see First Interstate Bank of Denver

Boy Scouts of America ($10,000) see Hewit Family Foundation

Boy Scouts of America ($1,000) see Pioneer Fund

Boy Scouts of America see United Airlines

Boy Scouts of America-Denver Area Council ($10,000) see Martin Marietta Corp.

Boy Scouts of America — Troop 457 see Public Service Co. of Colorado

Boy Scouts-Denver Area Council — handicapped program see Johnson Foundation, Helen K. and Arthur E.

Boys Club of America ($5,000) see Hewit Family Foundation

Boys Clubs of Metro Denver ($10,000) see Slaughter, Jr. Foundation, William E.

Boys and Girls Club ($35,000) see Hunter Trust, A. V.

Boys and Girls Club ($20,750) see Monfort Charitable Foundation

Boys and Girls Club ($500) see Pioneer Fund

Boys and Girls Club of Pueblo — purchase equipment see Johnson Foundation, Helen K. and Arthur E.

Bravo Colorado Music Festival ($10,000) see Fair Play Foundation

Breckenridge Development Fund ($5,000) see Scott Foundation, Walter

Breckenridge Music Institute see Public Service Co. of Colorado

Breckenridge Outdoor Education Center see Public Service Co. of Colorado

Bridge Trust ($5,000) see Sterne-Elder Memorial Trust

Broomfield Economic Development Corp see Public Service Co. of Colorado

Brothers Redevelopment ($50,000) see Piton Foundation

Brush High School ($2,000) see Joslin-Needham Family Foundation

Cal-Wood ($174,620) see Pilot Trust

Callae McIntosh Duke Memorial Scholarship Fund ($5,000) see Sterne-Elder Memorial Trust

Camp Hope see Lowe Foundation

Capuchin Province of Mid-America ($5,000) see Butler Foundation, J. Homer

Cat Care Society ($14,510) see Animal Assistance Foundation

Cenikor Foundation — Lawncare and Landscape Equipment ($13,000) see O'Fallon Trust, Martin J. and Mary Anne

Centennial Task Force/Drug Free Youth — program support see Johnson Foundation, Helen K. and Arthur E.

Center for Hearing, Speech, and Language see Lowe Foundation

Center for Nonprofit Excellence — to help develop excellence in the Third Sector in Colorado ($10,000) see Anschutz Family Foundation

Center for Science Technology and Political Thought ($1,100) see True Oil Co.

Central City Opera Association ($30,000) see Sterne-Elder Memorial Trust

Central City Opera House Association — season budget see Johnson Foundation, Helen K. and Arthur E.

Central City Opera House — opening night sponsorship of "Italian Girl in Algiers" opera ($30,000) see Bonfils-Stanton Foundation

Channel Six — Public Television see Security Life of Denver

Cheetah Preservation Fund — for project in Namibia home to largest populatons of cheetahs ($10,000) see Bay Foundation

Cheyenne Mountain Zoo — underwrite cost for constructing Outdoor Siberian Tiger exhibit ($200,000) see Coors Foundation, Adolph

Cheyenne Mountain Museum and Zoological Society — toward "A Zoo For All Reasons" capital campaign, total grant $500,000 ($100,000) see Boettcher Foundation

Cheyenne Mountain Zoo — general support ($250,000) see El Pomar Foundation

Cheyenne Mountain Zoo — for "Zoo for All Reasons" capital campaign ($1,000,000) see El Pomar Foundation

Cheyenne Mountain Zoological Park ($175,000) see Gates Foundation

Cheyenne Village ($5,000) see Ackerman Trust, Anna Keesling

Children's Diabetes Foundation ($25,000) see Geffen Foundation, David

Children's Diabetes Foundation ($15,000) see Lastfogel Foundation, Abe and Frances

Children's Hospital ($10,000) see Hewit Family Foundation

Children's Hospital ($20,000) see Mullen Foundation, J. K.

Children's Hospital ($64,000) see Richardson Fund, Grace

Children's Hospital ($2,250) see Williams Family Foundation

Children's Hospital ($10,000) see Wolf Foundation, Melvin and Elaine

Children's Hospital Foundation ($4,025) see Dekalb Energy Co.

Children's Hospital Foundation — blood bank see Johnson Foundation, Helen K. and Arthur E.

Children's Hospital Foundation — child health clinic ($30,000) see Kaufmann Foundation, Marion Esser

Children's Hospital Foundation ($5,000) see Sterne-Elder Memorial Trust

Children's Hospital Foundation — portable EMG machine ($30,000) see Kaufmann Foundation, Marion Esser

Children's Museum ($5,000) see First Interstate Bank of Denver

Children's Museum ($150,000) see Gates Foundation

Church of Holy Ghost ($25,000) see Hill Foundation

Colorado (cont.)

Church of the Holy Redeemer Youth Leadership Tutorial Program — tutorial program for inner city youth ($10,000) see Anschutz Family Foundation

Church of Risen Christ ($10,000) see Weckbaugh Foundation, Eleanore Mullen

Citizens Goals — for three-year support of the Pikes Peak Tomorrow Program ($180,000) see El Pomar Foundation

City of Brush ($29,000) see Joslin-Needham Family Foundation

City of Brush ($10,000) see Petteys Memorial Foundation, Jack

City of Greeley — civic center improvements ($100,000) see Monfort Charitable Foundation

City of Pueblo ($20,000) see Thatcher Foundation

City of Wray ($5,016) see Kitzmiller/Bales Trust

City of Wray ($3,000) see Kitzmiller/Bales Trust

City of Wray ($1,325) see Kitzmiller/Bales Trust

CMA Headquarters ($154,500) see Paulstan

Collage Children's Museum ($10,600) see Thendara Foundation

Colorado Action for Healthy People — for operation and evaluation of statewide program ($210,734) see Colorado Trust

Colorado Action for Healthy People ($39,000) see Comprecare Foundation

Colorado AIDS Project — educational programs see Johnson Foundation, Helen K. and Arthur E.

Colorado AIDS Project see Security Life of Denver

Colorado Alliance of Business ($5,000) see Manville Corp.

Colorado Amateur Sports Corporation — for purchase of building for NGB's ($875,000) see El Pomar Foundation

Colorado Amateur Sports Corporation — refund from U.S. Olympic Hall of Fame construction project ($200,000) see Boettcher Foundation

Colorado Ballet see Public Service Co. of Colorado

Colorado Chautauqua see Public Service Co. of Colorado

Colorado Children's Chorale ($2,500) see Burgess Trust, Ralph L. and Florence R.

Colorado Coalition for the Homeless see Apache Corp.

Colorado Coalition for the Homeless ($50,250) see Hill Foundation

Colorado College ($580,569) see Boettcher Foundation

Colorado College — toward construction of new science facility ($200,000) see Boettcher Foundation

Colorado College ($12,500) see Colket Foundation, Ethel D.

Colorado College — scholarship fund ($10,000) see Creel Foundation

Colorado College ($5,000) see Darby Foundation

Colorado College — scholarship support ($260,000) see El Pomar Foundation

Colorado College ($5,000) see Gross Charitable Trust, Walter L. and Nell R.

Colorado College — annual fund ($10,000) see Kenan Family Foundation

Colorado College — lecture fund ($15,000) see Norman Foundation, Andrew

Colorado College ($15,000) see Stone Trust, H. Chase

Colorado College — presidential fund ($25,000) see Winkler Foundation, Mark and Catherine

Colorado Council on Economic Education ($27,000) see McKenna Foundation, Philip M.

Colorado Department of Education — second portion of a three-year $200,000 commitment ($100,000) see Gates Foundation

Colorado Domestic Violence Coalition — support for domestic violence program ($20,000) see Hunter Trust, A. V.

Colorado Easter Seal Society see Lowe Foundation

Colorado Episcopal Foundation ($431,360) see Colorado Trust

Colorado 4-H Youth Fund ($4,000) see Norgren Foundation, Carl A.

Colorado Historical Foundation — for the joint project of Denver Art Museum, Colorado Historical Society and the Denver Art Museum to prepare a master plan for the Civic Center Cultural Complex ($125,000) see Bonfils-Stanton Foundation

Colorado Historical Society ($5,000) see Fishback Foundation Trust, Harmes C.

Colorado Housing Assistance Corporation — payment on general operations ($30,000) see Piton Foundation

Colorado Masons Benevolent Fund — scholarships ($25,000) see Slusher Charitable Foundation, Roy W.

Colorado Northwestern Community College/Meeker Campus — courses at Fairfield Center ($2,535) see Fairfield-Meeker Charitable Trust, Freeman E.

Colorado Opera Festival — for the 1991 summer production expenses ($5,000) see Stone Trust, H. Chase

Colorado Outdoor Education Center ($6,500) see Norgren Foundation, Carl A.

Colorado Outward Bound School ($4,000) see Obernauer Foundation

Colorado Outward Bound School — Denver urban program for indigent youth ($35,000) see Hunter Trust, A. V.

Colorado Rocky Mountain School ($100,000) see Gates Foundation

Colorado Rocky Mountain School — scholarship program ($35,000) see Holt Foundation, William Knox

Colorado School of Mines ($30,000) see Phelps Dodge Corp.

Colorado School of Mines ($56,500) see Phillips Petroleum Co.

Colorado School of Mines Foundation ($10,000) see AMAX

Colorado School of Mines Foundation ($100,000) see ASARCO

Colorado School of Mines Foundation ($178,000) see Mobil Oil Corp.

Colorado School of Mines Foundation ($21,300) see Sussman Fund, Edna Bailey

Colorado School of Mines Foundation — Herman F. Coors Professorial Chair in Ceramics ($115,000) see Coors Foundation, Adolph

Colorado Springs Company ($10,000) see Bodenhamer Foundation

Colorado State University ($15,000) see NCR Corp.

Colorado State University ($21,000) see Petteys Memorial Foundation, Jack

Colorado State University ($22,500) see Stone Foundation, France

Colorado State University — College of Veterinary Medicine ($127,955) see Animal Assistance Foundation

Colorado State University Foundation — student programs ($103,000) see Monfort Charitable Foundation

Colorado State University Foundation ($7,500) see Norgren Foundation, Carl A.

Colorado State University Foundation ($10,000) see Phelps, Inc.

Colorado Symphony ($10,000) see Shwayder Foundation, Fay

Colorado Symphony Association — challenge grant ($50,000) see Bonfils-Stanton Foundation

Colorado Symphony Association ($5,000) see Fishback Foundation Trust, Harmes C.

Colorado Symphony Association ($100,000) see Sterne-Elder Memorial Trust

Colorado Symphony Association — in support of 1990-91 symphony season ($100,000) see Boettcher Foundation

Colorado Symphony Association — in support of 1991-92 symphony season ($100,000) see Boettcher Foundation

Colorado Symphony Orchestra ($17,000) see Burgess Trust, Ralph L. and Florence R.

Colorado Symphony Orchestra ($10,000) see First Interstate Bank of Denver

Colorado Trust — direct charitable contributions ($159,892) see Colorado Trust

Colorado Women's Employment and Education ($5,000) see Duncan Trust, John G.

Community Action Program — for general support; University of Denver ($25,000) see Hunt Alternatives Fund

Community Courthouse Addition ($102,500) see Heginbotham Trust, Will E.

Community Hospital Foundation ($15,000) see Bacon Foundation, E. L. and Oma

Community Technical Skills Center ($12,000) see Duncan Trust, John G.

Council for Public Television ($1,210) see Dekalb Energy Co.

Council for Public Television Channel 6 ($20,000) see Anschutz Family Foundation

Council for Public Television KRMA-TV Channel 6 — first portion of a six-year $500,000 commitment ($250,000) see Gates Foundation

Craig Rehabilitation Center ($5,000) see Blackmer Foundation, Henry M.

Crested Butte Center for Arts ($19,770) see C.I.O.S.

Crow Canyon Archaeological Center ($5,000) see Maxfield Foundation

Crow Canyon Archaeological Center ($25,000) see Morrison Charitable Trust, Pauline A. and George R.

Crow Canyon Center for Southwestern Archeology — to help establish an endowment ($10,000) see Anschutz Family Foundation

CSM Foundation ($10,000) see Shwayder Foundation, Fay

Cystic Fibrosis Foundation ($500) see Ackerman Trust, Anna Keesling

Dance Aspen ($2,000) see Chanin Family Foundation, Paul R.

Denver Area Council, Boy Scouts of America — in support of Family Enrichment Camp ($500,000) see Boettcher Foundation

Denver Art Museum ($17,000) see Burgess Trust, Ralph L. and Florence R.

Denver Art Museum ($35,500) see First Interstate Bank of Denver

Denver Art Museum ($5,000) see Fishback Foundation Trust, Harmes C.

Denver Art Museum ($15,000) see Frohlich Charitable Trust, Ludwig W.

Denver Art Museum ($400,000) see JFM Foundation

Denver Art Museum ($50,000) see JFM Foundation

Denver Art Museum ($17,000) see JFM Foundation

Denver Art Museum ($11,000) see Kuyper Foundation, Peter H. and E. Lucille Gaass

Denver Art Museum ($5,000) see Martin Marietta Corp.

Denver Art Museum — exhibition: "Gio Ponti (1891-1979)" ($10,000) see Graham Foundation for Advanced Studies in the Fine Arts

Denver Art Museum — participation in Second Century Fund for endowment of exhibition fund ($125,000) see Coors Foundation, Adolph

Denver Arts Center Foundation — capital campaign pledge ($25,000) see Bonfils-Stanton Foundation

Denver Arts Museum see Security Life of Denver

Denver Association of Life Underwriters see Security Life of Denver

Denver Botanic Gardens see Security Life of Denver

Denver Botanic Gardens ($10,000) see Shwayder Foundation, Fay

Denver Botanic Gardens — for continuation of Bonfils-Stanton Foundation lecture series ($20,000) see Bonfils-Stanton Foundation

Denver Boys — maintain counseling/activities program for boys ($1,000) see Buell Foundation, Temple Hoyne

Denver Center for the Performing Arts see Amoco Corp.

Denver Center for the Performing Arts ($1,000) see CRL Inc.

Denver Civic Ventures — support the work of other office ($27,000) see Piton Foundation

Denver Dumb Friends League ($180,000) see Animal Assistance Foundation

Denver Dumb Friends League ($17,000) see Barbour Foundation, Bernice

Denver Ear Institute see Lowe Foundation

Denver Foundation ($10,000) see Hughes Charitable Trust, Mabel Y.

Denver Mobility ($22,653) see Comprecare Foundation

Denver Museum of Natural History ($250,000) see Colorado Trust

Denver Museum of Natural History ($5,000) see Forest Oil Corp.

Denver Museum of Natural History — study of program ($18,000) see Harris Foundation, William H. and Mattie Wattis

Denver Museum of Natural History ($10,000) see Hewit Family Foundation

Denver Museum of Natural History ($4,000) see Norgren Foundation, Carl A.

Denver National Historical Society see Security Life of Denver

Denver Parks and Recreation Foundation ($150,000) see Morrison Charitable Trust, Pauline A. and George R.

Denver Public Library ($20,090) see Mullen Foundation, J. K.

Denver Public Library ($20,000) see Mullen Foundation, J. K.

Denver Public Library see Security Life of Denver

Denver Public Library ($6,000) see Shwayder Foundation, Fay

Denver Rescue Mission ($10,000) see Anschutz Family Foundation

Denver Victims Service Project ($10,000) see Comprecare Foundation

Denver Young Artists Orchestra ($5,000) see Burgess Trust, Ralph L. and Florence R.

Denver Zoological Foundation ($10,000) see Blackmer Foundation, Henry M.

Denver Zoological Foundation ($500,000) see Gates Foundation

Denver Zoological Foundation ($10,000) see Hewit Family Foundation

Denver Zoological Foundation ($250,000) see Morrison Charitable Trust, Pauline A. and George R.

Denver Zoological Foundation ($6,500) see Mullen Foundation, J. K.

Denver Zoological Foundation ($5,500) see Norgren Foundation, Carl A.

Denver Zoological Foundation ($13,000) see O'Fallon Trust, Martin J. and Mary Anne

Digit Fund ($2,000) see Northern Star Foundation

Dream Team — student scholarships ($315,000) see Monfort Charitable Foundation

Colorado (cont.)

Medicine ($10,000) see Helis Foundation

National Jewish Center for Immunology and Respiratory Medicine ($10,000) see Hughes Charitable Trust, Mabel Y.

National Jewish Center for Immunology and Respiratory Medicine ($60,000) see Kramer Foundation, C. L. C.

National Jewish Center for Immunology and Respiratory Medicine ($5,000) see Lewis Foundation, Lillian Kaiser

National Jewish Center of Immunology and Respiratory Medicine ($100,000) see Milken Family Medical Foundation

National Jewish Center for Immunology and Respiratory Medicine ($300) see Nortek, Inc.

National Jewish Center for Immunology and Respiratory Medicine ($4,000) see Russ Togs

National Jewish Center for Immunology and Respiratory Medicine ($10,000) see Shwayder Foundation, Fay

National Jewish Center for Immunology and Respiratory Medicine ($10,000) see Simon Foundation, Sidney, Milton and Leoma

National Jewish Center for Immunology and Respiratory Medicine ($10,000) see Stern Foundation, Leonard N.

National Jewish Center for Immunology and Respiratory Medicine ($10,000) see Strauss Foundation, Leon

National Jewish Center for Immunology and Respiratory Medicine ($5,000) see Trimble Family Foundation, Robert Mize and Isa White

National Jewish Center for Immunology and Respiratory Medicine ($5,000) see Williams Family Foundation

National Jewish Center for Immunology and Respiratory Medicine ($10,000) see Wolf Foundation, Melvin and Elaine

National Jewish Center for Immunology and Respiratory Medicine — capital equipment and educational materials to upgrade National Jewish Center's telephone health information service, the "Lung Line" ($100,000) see Boettcher Foundation

National Junior Achievement — general operating support to the National Junior Achievement office ($3,500) see Owens-Corning Fiberglas Corp.

National Sports Center for the Disabled — to assist with establishing an outdoor center ($37,500) see Bonfils-Stanton Foundation

National Sports Center for the Disabled — sponsor an athlete ($250) see Colorado State Bank of Denver

National Sports Center for the Disabled ($10,000) see Hughes Charitable Trust, Mabel Y.

National Sports Center for the Disabled ($6,500) see Norgren Foundation, Carl A.

National Western Stock Show ($3,500) see Norgren Foundation, Carl A.

Native American Rights Fund — for general support for legal services program ($15,000) see Bay Foundation

Native American Rights Fund ($30,000) see General Service Foundation

Nature Conservancy ($10,000) see Disney Family Foundation, Roy

Navigators ($46,000) see Solheim Foundation

NEWSED ($15,000) see Piton Foundation

North Colorado Medical Center Foundation ($20,000) see Phelps, Inc.

Northeast Denver Housing Center ($30,000) see Piton Foundation

Northeastern Junior College ($10,380) see Petteys Memorial Foundation, Jack

Northeastern Junior College — scholarship ($9,056) see Petteys Memorial Foundation, Jack

Open Colorado ($7,500) see First Interstate Bank of Denver

Opera Colorado ($5,000) see Burgess Trust, Ralph L. and Florence R.

Opera Colorado ($2,500) see Fishback Foundation Trust, Harmes C.

Opera Colorado ($2,650) see Rabb Foundation, Harry W.

Opera Colorado — to assist with the Opera Production of La Boheme ($30,000) see Bonfils-Stanton Foundation

Osage Initiatives — for program development ($490,000) see US WEST

P/SL Community Foundation — Block Grant ($829,067) see Colorado Trust

Paramount Theatre ($2,500) see Dekalb Energy Co.

Parkinsons Association of Rockies ($10,000) see Schramm Foundation

Pearl St. Temple Emanuel Foundation ($5,000) see Rabb Foundation, Harry W.

Penrose-St. Francis Healthcare Foundation — for Penrose Cancer Center ($10,000) see Stone Trust, H. Chase

Penrose-St. Francis Healthcare System — for support of cancer center and Webb Memorial Library ($121,750) see El Pomar Foundation

Performing Arts Center Foundation ($10,000) see Fishback Foundation Trust, Harmes C.

Pikes Peak Chapter American Red Cross — for operating expenses ($10,000) see Stone Trust, H. Chase

Pikes Peak United Way — general support in 1991 ($100,000) see El Pomar Foundation

Pikes Peak Y/USO — for the city-wide Gulf War Program ($5,000) see Stone Trust, H. Chase

Pikes Peak Y/USO — for the Youth Leadership Institute ($5,000) see Stone Trust, H. Chase

Pioneers Hospital — mammography system ($5,000) see Fairfield-Meeker Charitable Trust, Freeman E.

Planned Parenthood Federation of America ($83,837) see Hunter Trust, A. V.

Planned Parenthood Federation of America ($6,000) see O'Fallon Trust, Martin J. and Mary Anne

Porter Memorial Hospital Foundation — to provide funding support for the establishment of a third Center of Excellence, the Oncology Center ($30,000) see Frost Foundation

Presbyterian St. Luke's Community Foundation ($10,000) see Hughes Charitable Trust, Mabel Y.

Presbyterian/St. Luke's Institute of Limb Preservation ($2,500) see Fishback Foundation Trust, Harmes C.

Presbytery of Denver — 1985 agreement ($425,000) see Colorado Trust

Pueblo Symphony Association ($6,901) see Chamberlin Foundation, Gerald W.

Pueblo Symphony Association ($10,000) see Thatcher Foundation

Pueblo Zoological Society ($30,100) see Thatcher Foundation

Rankin Presbyterian Church ($3,000) see Joslin-Needham Family Foundation

RE-1J School ($22,500) see Heginbotham Trust, Will E.

RE-1J School ($13,850) see Heginbotham Trust, Will E.

RE-2J School ($50,000) see Heginbotham Trust, Will E.

Regis College ($59,134) see Birmingham Foundation

Regis College ($7,300) see Gerondelis Foundation

Regis College ($30,000) see Hill Foundation

Regis College ($10,000) see Hughes Charitable Trust, Mabel Y.

Regis College ($20,000) see Weckbaugh Foundation, Eleanore Mullen

Regis College — conversion of the existing football stadium and adjacent land to a multi-purpose athletic and intramural playing field ($200,000) see Coors Foundation, Adolph

Regis College for Women — replacement of Loyola Hall heating/cooling equipment ($104,000) see O'Shaughnessy Foundation, I. A.

Regis High School ($37,134) see Frank Family Foundation, A. J.

Regis High School ($25,000) see Mullen Foundation, J. K.

Regis High School ($23,980) see Weckbaugh Foundation, Eleanore Mullen

Regis/Loretto Heights College ($25,000) see Mullen Foundation, J. K.

Right to Read of Weld County — general operations ($48,752) see Monfort Charitable Foundation

Rio Bianco Board of Cooperative — computers and software for Meeker Elementary ($7,000) see Fairfield-Meeker Charitable Trust, Freeman E.

Rio Bianco County Golf Association — free golf lesson, video instructional equipment, two golf carts ($5,000) see Fairfield-Meeker Charitable Trust, Freeman E.

Riverview Christian School ($2,500) see Joslin-Needham Family Foundation

Rocky Mountain Center for Health Promotion and Education ($320,000) see Comprecare Foundation

Rocky Mountain Institute ($4,000) see G.A.G. Charitable Corporation

Rocky Mountain Institute ($25,770) see Harder Foundation

Rocky Mountain Institute ($67,000) see Merck Family Fund

Rocky Mountain Institute — to improve the accessibility, attractiveness, and dissemination of RMI's Competitek, a six-volume encyclopedia of information on electricity-saving technologies ($1,500,000) see MacArthur Foundation, John D. and Catherine T.

Rocky Mountain Multiple Sclerosis Center ($20,000) see Hunter Trust, A. V.

Rocky Mountain National Park Association ($1,500) see Dekalb Energy Co.

Rocky Mountain National Park — Moraine park restoration ($20,000) see Monfort Charitable Foundation

Rocky Mountain Poison and Drug ($15,708) see Animal Assistance Foundation

Rocky Mountain Program for Senior Executives — for leadership training for Denver Public Schools principals; University of Colorado at Denver Graduate School of Public Affairs ($35,000) see Hunt Alternatives Fund

Rose Foundation ($2,200) see Rabb Foundation, Harry W.

Rose Foundation — Rose Medical Center ($230,000) see Goodstein Foundation

Rose Medical Center ($75,000) see Wolf Foundation, Melvin and Elaine

Rural Healthcare Initiative — administrative and technical support ($188,676) see Colorado Trust

S.E.T. Ministry of Denver ($15,000) see Comprecare Foundation

Sacred Heart House ($5,000) see O'Fallon Trust, Martin J. and Mary Anne

Sacred Heart House ($2,250) see Rabb Foundation, Harry W.

Sacred Heart House ($30,000) see Weckbaugh Foundation, Eleanore Mullen

Safe House ($1,000) see CRL Inc.

Safehouse for Batted Women — completion of challenge grant ($25,000) see Bonfils-Stanton Foundation

St. Anthony Hospital ($7,500) see Schramm Foundation

St. Francis Center ($2,000) see Fishback Foundation Trust, Harmes C.

St. John Cathedral of Denver ($10,000) see Sterne-Elder Memorial Trust

St. Joseph Hospital Foundation ($50,000) see Sterne-Elder Memorial Trust

St. Joseph's Hospital Foundation ($25,000) see Hill Foundation

St. Mary's Academy ($3,500) see Fishback Foundation Trust, Harmes C.

St. Mary's Academy ($22,700) see Weckbaugh Foundation, Eleanore Mullen

St. Thomas Seminary ($9,500) see Burgess Trust, Ralph L. and Florence R.

St. Thomas Seminary ($12,500) see Mullen Foundation, J. K.

St. Thomas Seminary ($12,500) see Mullen Foundation, J. K.

Salvation Army ($10,000) see Ackerman Trust, Anna Keesling

Salvation Army ($1,000) see JFM Foundation

San Luis Valley Tibetan Project ($9,050) see Manitou Foundation

Sangre de Christo Arts and Conference Center ($42,250) see Thatcher Foundation

Sangre de Cristo Arts Center — remodeling of facility ($20,000) see Chamberlin Foundation, Gerald W.

Sangre de Cristo Arts Center — special projects ($6,000) see Chamberlin Foundation, Gerald W.

School District #50 — scholarship ($16,500) see Williams Family Foundation

School District #3 — scholarship ($88,750) see Williams Family Foundation

School District #20 — scholarship ($3,000) see Williams Family Foundation

School District #2 — scholarship ($64,500) see Williams Family Foundation

Senior Diabetic Outreach Program ($10,000) see Comprecare Foundation

Seniors, Inc. see Apache Corp.

Seniors Day Care Training Program ($6,000) see O'Fallon Trust, Martin J. and Mary Anne

Servicio De La Raza ($7,500) see Duncan Trust, John G.

Sewall Child Development Center ($8,815) see Schramm Foundation

Sewall Rehabilitation Center Foundation ($5,000) see Norgren Foundation, Carl A.

Shalom Park ($100,000) see Goodstein Foundation

Shining Mountain Waldorf School — operating fund ($125,000) see Grainger Foundation

South Suburban Park ($2,500) see Sterne-Elder Memorial Trust

Special Olympics see Lowe Foundation

Sri Aurgbindo Learning Center ($5,854) see Manitou Foundation

Stanley British Primary School ($10,000) see Duncan Trust, John G.

Stanley British Primary School ($250,000) see Gates Foundation

Step 13 ($5,000) see Manville Corp.

Sterling Regional Medical Center Foundation ($5,000) see Petteys Memorial Foundation, Jack

Suicide Project ($10,000) see Comprecare Foundation

Summit Foundation ($3,000) see CRL Inc.

Summit Ministries ($156,000) see Prince Corp.

Swedish Medical Center Foundation ($350) see Colorado State Bank of Denver

Temple Center ($10,000) see Duncan Trust, John G.

Thatcher Learning Center at Parkview ($10,000) see Thatcher Foundation

Total Longterm Care — health care services to elderly people ($308,272) see Colorado Trust

Total Longterm Care — project to replicate the On Lok Senior Health Services model for frail elderly ($371,084) see Colorado Trust

Town of Haxtun ($15,000) see Heginbotham Trust, Will E.

Town of Meeker — Christmas decorations ($3,000) see Fairfield-Meeker Charitable Trust, Freeman E.

United Methodist Foundation ($2,500) see Bacon Foundation, E. L. and Oma

United Mountain Trial Park Cultural Research ($14,000) see Morrison Charitable Trust, Pauline A. and George R.

United Sates Space Foundation — for teacher education program ($5,000) see Stone Trust, H. Chase

United States Air Force Academy ($11,969) see Delta Air Lines

United States Air Force Academy ($5,500) see Olmsted Foundation, George and Carol

United States Figure Skating Association — Memorial Fund ($10,000) see Frankino Charitable Foundation, Samuel J. and Connie

U.S. Figure Skating Association Memorial Fund ($61,056) see McGraw Foundation, Curtis W.

U.S. Olympic Committee ($9,000) see Luce Charitable Trust, Theodore

United Way ($10,000) see Bacon Foundation, E. L. and Oma

United Way ($75,456) see First Interstate Bank of Denver

United Way ($50,018) see First Interstate Bank of Denver

United Way ($10,000) see Glaze Foundation, Robert and Ruth

United Way — general operations ($60,000) see Monfort Charitable Foundation

United Way ($1,100) see National By-Products

United Way ($10,000) see Pioneer Fund

United Way see Security Life of Denver

United Way ($25,000) see Sterne-Elder Memorial Trust

United Way ($40,000) see Thatcher Foundation

United Way-Ft. Collins Area ($70,000) see Woodward Governor Co.

United Way-Mile High — operating ($28,000) see Sundstrand Corp.

United Way-Mile High — for annual support ($530,616) see US WEST

United Way of Mile High — general purpose fund ($7,281) see Walgreen Co.

University of Colorado ($120,000) see Banbury Fund

University of Colorado ($100,000) see Bechtel, Jr. Foundation, S. D.

University of Colorado ($15,884) see Bradish Trust, Norman C.

University of Colorado ($75,000) see Crail-Johnson Foundation

University of Colorado ($137,000) see Hedco Foundation

University of Colorado ($10,986) see Petteys Memorial Foundation, Jack

University of Colorado ($10,428) see Phelps, Inc.

University of Colorado ($6,523) see Stone Trust, H. Chase

University of Colorado ($20,000) see Thatcher Foundation

University of Colorado ($56,537) see Wolf Foundation, Melvin and Elaine

University of Colorado at Boulder ($371,632) see Boettcher Foundation

University of Colorado — renovation of Dal Ward Center on Boulder campus ($500,000) see Coors Foundation, Adolph

University of Colorado Foundation ($35,000) see MCI Communications Corp.

University of Colorado Foundation ($4,000) see Norgren Foundation, Carl A.

University of Colorado Foundation ($25,000) see Phelps, Inc.

University of Colorado Foundation ($7,500) see Schramm Foundation

University of Colorado Foundation ($3,000) see Shwayder Foundation, Fay

University of Colorado Foundation ($16,225) see Sussman Fund, Edna Bailey

University of Colorado Foundation — for Colorado Institute for Technology Transfer Implementation ($3,150,000) see El Pomar Foundation

University of Colorado Foundation — improvements in program for the School of Architecture and Planning ($100,000) see Buell Foundation, Temple Hoyne

University of Colorado Health Sciences Center ($10,000) see Hewit Family Foundation

University of Colorado Health Sciences Center ($35,000) see Hill Foundation

University of Colorado Health Sciences Center ($15,000) see Weight Watchers International

University Corporation for Atmospheric Research — toward the projected total cost of $200,000 needed to construct the Frost Biotic Research Facility ($45,000) see Frost Foundation

University of Denver ($12,000) see AMAX

University of Denver ($186,012) see Boettcher Foundation

University of Denver ($2,000) see Buell Foundation, Temple Hoyne

University of Denver ($5,000) see Dekalb Energy Co.

University of Denver ($5,000) see Fishback Foundation Trust, Harmes C.

University of Denver ($8,400) see Mansfield Foundation, Albert and Anne

University of Denver ($5,050) see Shwayder Foundation, Fay

University of Denver — establish the Center for Management Communication

($300,000) see Coors Foundation, Adolph

University of Denver-Lamont School of Music ($15,000) see Burgess Trust, Ralph L. and Florence R.

University of Denver — to support the development and implementation of an office for strategic long-range planning ($30,000) see Frost Foundation

University of Denver-Theater Program ($17,000) see Burgess Trust, Ralph L. and Florence R.

University North Colorado Foundation Grant ($37,626) see Watson Foundation, Thomas J.

University of Northern Colorado — student programs ($111,000) see Monfort Charitable Foundation

University of Northern Colorado ($9,600) see Phelps, Inc.

University of Southern Colorado ($10,350) see Potts Memorial Foundation

Uptown Partnership ($35,000) see Piton Foundation

Urban League of Pikes Peak ($5,000) see Ackerman Trust, Anna Keesling

US Olympic Committee — purchase of equipment ($100,000) see Bellamah Foundation, Dale J.

US Olympic Committee ($2,010) see Northern Star Foundation

USFSA Memorial Fund ($12,500) see Kemper Foundation, Enid and Crosby

Vail Valley Foundation ($15,000) see Fair Play Foundation

Vail Valley Foundation ($16,000) see Mercy, Jr. Foundation, Sue and Eugene

Vail Valley Foundation ($24,340) see Wertheim Foundation, Dr. Herbert A.

Vail Valley Foundation ($24,340) see Wertheim Foundation, Dr. Herbert A.

Vail Valley Medical Center ($20,000) see McGraw Foundation, Curtis W.

Vail Valley Medical Center ($450) see Wertheim Foundation, Dr. Herbert A.

Vail Valley Medical Center ($450) see Wertheim Foundation, Dr. Herbert A.

Volunteers for Outdoor Colorado ($120) see Colorado State Bank of Denver

Volunteers for Outdoor Colorado see Security Life of Denver

Webb-Waring Lung Institute ($10,000) see Stone Trust, H. Chase

Webb-Waring Lung Institute ($2,000) see Williams Family Foundation

We'll Have Equitable Relocation ($25,000) see Piton Foundation

Wellness Community ($10,000) see Hughes Charitable Trust, Mabel Y.

Western Colorado Healthcare Alliance — develop consortium representing 14 rural hospitals to improve quality of services ($167,588) see Colorado Trust

Wilderness on Wheels Foundation ($500) see Colorado State Bank of Denver

Women's Foundation of Colorado ($6,000) see Beaird Foundation, Charles T.

Women's Foundation of Colorado — for the endowment ($50,000) see Hunt Alternatives Fund

Women's Foundation of Colorado ($5,625) see Salwil Foundation

Woptura Ti O'Spave ($30,125) see Manitou Foundation

World Senior Golf Federation ($10,000) see Creel Foundation

World Youth Cultural Exchange — sponsors travel program for boy's club ($5,000) see Buell Foundation, Temple Hoyne

Wray Community District Hospital ($2,000) see Kitzmiller/Bales Trust

Wray Public Library ($1,000) see Kitzmiller/Bales Trust

Wray Rehabilitation and Activities Center ($318,000) see Kitzmiller/Bales Trust

YMCA ($10,000) see Ackerman Trust, Anna Keesling

YMCA ($2,500) see Colorado State Bank of Denver

YMCA ($10,000) see Hughes Charitable Trust, Mabel Y.

Young Life ($5,000) see Aigner

Young Life ($500) see Beitzell & Co.

Young Life ($65,000) see McCarthy Foundation, John and Margaret

Young Life ($20,900) see Norman/Nethercutt Foundation, Merle

Young Life Campaign — mission advance fund ($90,000) see Stewardship Foundation

Youth for Christ International — Jericho Wall Project ($233,500) see Maclellan Foundation

Youth For Christ/USA ($255,000) see Merillat Foundation, Orville D. and Ruth A.

YWCA ($10,000) see Hughes Charitable Trust, Mabel Y.

Connecticut

Achievement Unlimited ($3,000) see Robinson Fund, Charles Nelson

AIDS Project Greater New Britain ($10,000) see Stanley Works

Alzheimer's Disease and Related Disorders Association ($100) see Sweet Life Foods

American Cancer Society ($15,000) see Bedford Fund

American Cancer Society ($10,000) see Carstensen Memorial Foundation, Fred R. and Hazel W.

American Cancer Society ($13,000) see Jones and Bessie D. Phelps Foundation, Cyrus W. and Amy F.

American Center for Polish Culture ($20,000) see Rosenstiel Foundation

American Diabetes Association ($20) see Bodine Corp.

American Foundation ($15,000) see Pellegrino-Realmuto Charitable Foundation

American Heart Association ($3,000) see Safeguard Scientifics Foundation

American Heart Association ($100) see Sweet Life Foods

American Red Cross ($15,000) see Bedford Fund

American Red Cross ($8,000) see Meserve Memorial Fund, Albert and Helen

American Red Cross ($5,100) see Schiro Fund

American Red Cross ($50,000) see Woodward Fund-Watertown, David, Helen, and Marian

American School for the Deaf ($15,000) see Bissell Foundation, J. Walton

American School for the Deaf ($10,000) see Long Foundation, George A. and Grace

Americares ($210,000) see Chevron Corp.

AmeriCares — to airlift medical supplies to Catholic hospitals in Croatia ($50,000) see Koch Foundation

AmeriCares Foundation ($10,000) see Barker Foundation, J. M. R.

AmeriCares Foundation ($2,000) see G.A.G. Charitable Corporation

Americares Foundation — supplies for refugees ($25,000) see International Foundation

AmeriCares Foundation ($20,000) see Ruffin Foundation, Peter B. & Adeline W.

Androscoggin Home Health Services ($42,500) see Bingham Second Betterment Fund, William

Antiquarian and Landmark Society of Connecticut ($30,000) see Ferriday Fund Charitable Trust

Armenian Church of Holy Ascension ($5,000) see Jones and Bessie D. Phelps Foundation, Cyrus W. and Amy F.

Artist Collective ($5,000) see Preston Trust, Evelyn W.

Asylum Hill Foundation — neighborhood improvement program ($25,000) see CM Alliance Cos.

Avon Old Farms School ($50,000) see Jennings Foundation, Mary Hillman

Barnum Festival see People's Bank

Barnum Museum ($5,000) see Carstensen Memorial Foundation, Fred R. and Hazel W.

Barnum Museum ($10,000) see Hubbell Inc.

Barnum Museum ($5,000) see Jones and Bessie D. Phelps Foundation, Cyrus W. and Amy F.

The Barnum Museum see People's Bank

Bi-Cultural Day School ($3,000) see Read Foundation, Charles L.

Bishop's Annual Appeal ($6,000) see Mann Foundation, John Jay

B'nai B'rith ($150) see Fox Steel Co.

Bob Hope School of Comedy ($12,000) see Belding Heminway Co.

Bowers Elementary School ($5,000) see Barnes Foundation

Boys Club of New Britain ($75,000) see Stanley Works

Boys and Girls Club ($5,000) see Johnson Foundation, Howard

Boys and Girls Club ($25,000) see Vance Charitable Foundation, Robert C.

Boy's and Girl's Club of Bridgeport — purchase van

Connecticut (cont.)

($20,000) see Pfriem Foundation, Norma F.

Boys Village Youth and Family Services — to help complete and equip the Student Center ($10,000) see Culpeper Memorial Foundation, Daphne Seybolt

Branford Counseling ($10,000) see Freas Foundation

Bridgeport Area Foundation — to establish the Magnus Wahlstorm Leadership award fund ($64,100) see Wahlstrom Foundation

Bridgeport Economic Development Corporation see People's Bank

Bridgeport Hospital ($2,500) see Acme United Corp.

Bridgeport Hospital ($7,500) see Jones and Bessie D. Phelps Foundation, Cyrus W. and Amy F.

Bridgeport Hospital ($6,000) see Switzer Foundation

Bridgeport Hospital Foundation ($8,500) see Campbell Foundation, Ruth and Henry

Bridgeport Hospital Foundation ($75,000) see Morris Foundation, William T.

Bridgeport Hospital Foundation ($28,900) see Noble Charitable Trust, John L. and Ethel G.

Bridgeport Hospital Foundation ($25,000) see Perkin Fund

Bridgeport Hospital Foundation ($30,500) see Pfriem Foundation, Norma F.

Bridgeport Hospital Foundation — operational support for pastoral care ($1,000) see Wahlstrom Foundation

Bridgeport Public Education Fund ($4,000) see Carstensen Memorial Foundation, Fred R. and Hazel W.

Bridgeport Public Education Fund see People's Bank

Bridgeport Public Library ($15,000) see Boutell Memorial Fund, Arnold and Gertrude

Bridgeport Rehabilitation Center ($25,000) see Jost Foundation, Charles and Mabel P.

Bristol Regional Environmental Center ($10,000) see Barnes Foundation

Broad Park Development Corporation ($13,275) see Connecticut Natural Gas Corp.

Bruce Museum ($5,000) see Dennett Foundation, Marie G.

Bruce Museum see Merrill Lynch & Co.

Bruce Museum Association ($15,000) see Chesebrough-Pond's

Brunswick School ($50,000) see Ford Foundation, Edward E.

Bushnell Arts in Education Program ($10,000) see Long Foundation, George A. and Grace

Bushnell Memorial Hall ($10,000) see Barnes Group

Bushnell Memorial Hall ($12,500) see Dexter Corp.

Bushnell Memorial Hall ($52,500) see Kohn-Joseloff Fund

Bushnell Memorial Hall ($30,000) see Krieble Foundation, Vernon K.

Bushnell Memorial Hall see People's Bank

Bushnell Park Foundation ($5,000) see Robinson Fund, Charles Nelson

Camp Courant ($30,000) see Hartford Courant Foundation

Camp Courant ($5,000) see Robinson Fund, Charles Nelson

Camp Hemlocks ($4,000) see Jost Foundation, Charles and Mabel P.

Catholic Family Services ($30,000) see Stanley Charitable Foundation, A. W.

Catholic Family Services ($17,500) see Vance Charitable Foundation, Robert C.

Catholic Home Bureau ($50,000) see Noble Charitable Trust, John L. and Ethel G.

CCSU Foundation ($18,694) see Vance Charitable Foundation, Robert C.

Center A Drop In Community ($28,613) see Palmer Fund, Frank Loomis

Center City Churches ($5,000) see Connecticut Natural Gas Corp.

Center for Connecticut's Future ($10,000) see Ensworth Charitable Foundation

Center for Hope ($15,000) see Ruffin Foundation, Peter B. & Adeline W.

Center for Youth Ministry Development ($84,500) see Brencanda Foundation

Central Connecticut Association of Retarded Citizens ($12,000) see Moore Charitable Foundation, Marjorie

Chapin School ($5,000) see Dennett Foundation, Marie G.

Charles Ives Center ($70,000) see Weeden Foundation, Frank

Charter Oak Terrace Health Center ($12,000) see Hartford Courant Foundation

Cheshire Academy ($75,000) see Manger and Audrey Cordero Plitt Trust, Clarence

Children in Placement/Connecticut ($3,000) see Carstensen Memorial Foundation, Fred R. and Hazel W.

Children's Center ($10,000) see Freas Foundation

Children's Center ($7,000) see Harcourt Foundation, Ellen Knowles

Children's Center of New Milford ($750) see Newmil Bancorp

Children's Community School ($5,000) see Barnes Foundation

Children's Fund ($200,000) see Aetna Life & Casualty Co.

Choate Rosemary Hall ($2,000) see Bishop Foundation, Vernon and Doris

Choate Rosemary Hall ($27,980) see Cheatham Foundation, Owen

Choate Rosemary Hall ($150,000) see Gelb Foundation, Lawrence M.

Choate Rosemary Hall ($25,000) see Hoffman Foundation, John Ernest

Choate-Rosemary Hall ($12,000) see Hunt Foundation, Roy A.

Choate Rosemary Hall ($15,000) see Kelly Foundation, T. Lloyd

Choate Rosemary Hall ($20,000) see MacDonald Foundation, James A.

Choate Rosemary Hall ($10,000) see New Prospect Foundation

Choate Rosemary Hall ($40,000) see Nichols Foundation

Choate Rosemary Hall ($50,500) see Overbrook Foundation

Choate Rosemary Hall ($4,500) see Rosenthal Foundation, Richard and Hinda

Choate School ($5,000) see Dennett Foundation, Marie G.

Choate School ($10,000) see Krause Foundation, Charles A.

Choate School ($10,000) see Messing Foundation, Morris M. and Helen F.

Christ Church ($7,500) see Plant Memorial Fund, Henry B.

Christ Church — religious ($25,000) see Young Foundation, Robert R.

Christ Episcopal Church ($3,500) see Carstensen Memorial Foundation, Fred R. and Hazel W.

Christian Heritage School ($25,000) see Aldeen Charity Trust, G. W.

Christian Heritage School ($1,500) see Heritage Foundation

Chrysalis Center ($12,000) see Hartford Courant Foundation

Chrysalis Center ($3,000) see Robinson Fund, Charles Nelson

Church Street Foundation ($10,000) see Bissell Foundation, J. Walton

Citizens for Justice ($25,000) see Moskowitz Foundation, Irving I.

City of New London ($10,000) see Griffis Foundation

Colby-Sawyer College ($9,100) see Greenspan Foundation

Collegiate Schools ($5,000) see Dennett Foundation, Marie G.

Community Child Guidance Clinic ($10,000) see Long Foundation, George A. and Grace

Community Renewal Team ($25,000) see Travelers Cos.

Community of the Way Sunset Hill ($5,000) see Hettinger Foundation

Congregation Agudath Shalom ($4,000) see Bennett Foundation, Carl and Dorothy

Connecticut AIDS Consortium ($20,000) see Schiro Fund

Connecticut Association for Human Services — for "Growing Strong" ($60,000) see Cox Charitable Trust, Jessie B.

Connecticut Association of Independent Schools ($5,000) see Barnes Foundation

Connecticut Audubon Society ($30,000) see Dorr Foundation

Connecticut Audubon Society ($5,000) see Johnson Foundation, Howard

Connecticut Audubon Society ($5,000) see Sasco Foundation

Connecticut Braille Association ($15,000) see Bedford Fund

Connecticut Braille Association ($5,000) see Biddle Foundation, Margaret T.

Connecticut Burn Care Foundation ($15,000) see Jost Foundation, Charles and Mabel P.

Connecticut Business for Education Coalition see People's Bank

Connecticut Chamber Symphony ($3,000) see Preston Trust, Evelyn W.

Connecticut College ($6,000) see Barnes Foundation

Connecticut College ($7,500) see Dexter Shoe Co.

Connecticut College ($5,000) see Griffis Foundation

Connecticut College ($60,000) see Mercy, Jr. Foundation, Sue and Eugene

Connecticut College — high school students advancement program ($12,500) see Nellie Mae

Connecticut College ($5,000) see V and V Foundation

Connecticut College ($5,000) see Zenkel Foundation

Connecticut College International Center ($2,000) see Sifco Industries Inc.

Connecticut College — Wiesel Chair ($250,000) see Fig Tree Foundation

Connecticut Community Care ($25,000) see Noble Charitable Trust, John L. and Ethel G.

Connecticut Community Care ($5,000) see Schiro Fund

Connecticut Early Music Society ($6,500) see Griffis Foundation

Connecticut Fund for the Environment ($10,000) see Connemara Fund

Connecticut Grand Opera ($7,000) see Jones and Bessie D. Phelps Foundation, Cyrus W. and Amy F.

Connecticut Grand Opera ($2,000) see Wheeler Foundation, Wilmot

Connecticut Historical Society ($25,000) see Krieble Foundation, Vernon K.

Connecticut Housing Coalition ($10,000) see Ensworth Charitable Foundation

Connecticut Humane Society ($10,000) see Baker Foundation, Elinor Patterson

Connecticut Humane Society ($7,500) see Barbour Foundation, Bernice

Connecticut Province of the Sisters of St. Joseph of Chambery ($210,000) see Valencia Charitable Trust

Connecticut Public Broadcasting ($10,500) see Hartford Courant Foundation

Connecticut Public Broadcasting ($12,500) see Stanley Charitable Foundation, A. W.

Connecticut Public Television ($5,000) see Harcourt Foundation, Ellen Knowles

Connecticut Public Television ($50,000) see Hoffman Foundation, Maximillian E. and Marion O.

Connecticut Public Television see People's Bank

Connecticut Small Business Development Center ($30,000) see Travelers Cos.

Connecticut Valley Railroad Museum ($7,000) see Edmonds Foundation, Dean S.

Constructive Workshop ($20,000) see Hartford Courant Foundation

Constructive Workshop ($30,000) see Stanley Charitable Foundation, A. W.

Constructive Workshop ($15,000) see Vance Charitable Foundation, Robert C.

Convent of Sacred Heart, Sprout Creek Farm ($105,000) see Beinecke Foundation

Council of Churches of Greater Bridgeport ($2,000) see Carstensen Memorial Foundation, Fred R. and Hazel W.

Creative Recreation ($5,980) see Meserve Memorial Fund, Albert and Helen

Curbstone Press ($36,500) see Plumsock Fund

Danbury Hospital ($9,000) see Meserve Memorial Fund, Albert and Helen

Danbury Hospital Development ($1,150) see Newmil Bancorp

Danbury Music Centre ($6,467) see Meserve Memorial Fund, Albert and Helen

Danbury Scott-Fenton Museum ($8,934) see Meserve Memorial Fund, Albert and Helen

Day Kimball Hospital ($10,000) see Jones Fund, Paul L.

Diocese of Bridgeport ($10,000) see Kennedy Foundation, John R.

Downtown Bridgeport Cabaret Theatre ($100) see Bodine Corp.

Downtown Evening Soup Kitchen ($46,000) see Carolyn Foundation

Drugs Don't Work! — substance abuse prevention ($75,000) see CM Alliance Cos.

Eagle Hill School ($12,000) see Bayne Fund, Howard

Easter Seal Rehabilitation ($27,850) see Bennett Foundation, Carl and Dorothy

Easter Seal Rehabilitation Center of Greater Waterbury ($45,000) see Woodward Fund-Watertown, David, Helen, and Marian

El Hogar del Futuro ($10,000) see Ensworth Charitable Foundation

El Hogar del Futuro ($12,500) see Fisher Foundation

Eliot Pratt Education Center ($9,190) see Meserve Memorial Fund, Albert and Helen

Elliot Pratt Education ($4,000) see Harcourt Foundation, Ellen Knowles

Elms 65th Anniversary Fund ($25,000) see Firestone, Jr. Foundation, Harvey

Endowment Foundation ($50,000) see Fisher Foundation

Episcopal Church at Yale ($7,500) see Mostyn Foundation

Ethel Walker School ($8,750) see Bay Branch Foundation

Ethel Walker School ($4,000) see Haffner Foundation

Ethel Walker School ($250,000) see Prentice Foundation, Abra

Ethel Walker School ($10,000) see Statter Foundation, Amy Plant

Eugene O'Neill Theater Center ($35,000) see Spiritus Gladius Foundation

Explorer Post 53-Emergency Medical Service ($25,000) see Ziegler Foundation for the Blind, E. Matilda

Fairfield Country Day School ($15,000) see Wodecroft Foundation

Fairfield Fire Department ($2,200) see Dell Foundation, Hazel

Fairfield Police Department ($2,200) see Dell Foundation, Hazel

Fairfield University ($1,000) see Acme United Corp.

Fairfield University ($35,000) see Bennett Foundation, Carl and Dorothy

Fairfield University ($200) see Bristol Savings Bank

Fairfield University ($100) see Burndy Corp.

Fairfield University — purchase new computer network system ($61,000) see Cord Foundation, E. L.

Fairfield University — for financial aid and purchase of scientific equipment ($300,000) see DeCamp Foundation, Ira W.

Fairfield University — building fund ($118,034) see Dolan Family Foundation

Fairfield University ($20,000) see Jones Fund, Paul L.

Fairfield University ($25,000) see Jost Foundation, Charles and Mabel P.

Fairfield University ($20,000) see McIntosh Foundation

Fairfield University ($50,000) see Morris Foundation, William T.

Fairfield University ($50,000) see Pope Foundation

Fairfield University ($1,500) see Union Manufacturing Co.

Fairfield University School of Nursing ($10,000) see Pfriem Foundation, Norma F.

Faith Seventh Day Adventist Church ($11,200) see Valentine Foundation, Lawson

Families in Crisis ($15,000) see Fisher Foundation

Family Center ($10,000) see Firestone, Jr. Foundation, Harvey

Family and Childrens Aid of Greater Norwalk ($15,000) see Avon Products

Family Planning Clinic of Lock Haven — operating expenses ($4,000) see Piper Foundation

Family Services ($30,000) see Stanley Charitable Foundation, A. W.

Family Services ($7,500) see Vance Charitable Foundation, Robert C.

Farmington River Association ($15,000) see Ensign-Bickford Industries

Farmington Valley Jewish Congregation ($15,500) see Schiro Fund

Fidelco Guide Dog Foundation ($10,000) see Kohn-Joseloff Fund

First Church of Round Hill ($25,000) see Weinberg, Jr. Foundation, Sidney J.

FISH — transportation to medical appointments ($1,000) see Senior Services of Stamford

Five Town Foundation ($10,000) see Glanville Family Foundation

Florence Griswold Museum ($4,257) see MacCurdy Salisbury Educational Foundation

Foresight ($35,000) see Ziegler Foundation for the Blind, E. Matilda

Fort Nathan Hale Restoration Project ($21,800) see Woman's Seamen's Friend Society of Connecticut

Foundation for Higher Education ($1,427,500) see Sears, Roebuck and Co.

Foundation for IHE ($45,000) see CBS Inc.

Foundation for Independent Higher Education ($5,000) see Graybar Electric Co.

Foundation for Shamanic Studies — healing research ($20,000) see Maxfield Foundation

Francais Ouimet Caddie Scholarship ($10,000) see Dennett Foundation, Marie G.

Francais Ouimet Caddie Scholarship ($25,000) see Ellison Foundation

Friends of Animals — stop elephant poaching ($24,000) see Harris Foundation, William H. and Mattie Wattis

Friendship Center ($55,000) see Stanley Charitable Foundation, A. W.

Friendship Center ($28,000) see Vance Charitable Foundation, Robert C.

Friendship Service Center ($15,000) see Hartford Courant Foundation

Garde Arts Center — arts education project ($70,000) see Palmer Fund, Frank Loomis

Garde Arts Center — outreach program ($55,000) see Palmer Fund, Frank Loomis

Garden Area Neighborhood Council ($6,334) see Preston Trust, Evelyn W.

Garden Area Neighborhood Council ($6,333) see Preston Trust, Evelyn W.

Garden Area Neighborhood Council ($6,333) see Preston Trust, Evelyn W.

Garrison and Arterton — to continue supporting the coordination of grantees' activities in states participating in state-centered reform efforts ($261,100) see Clark Foundation, Edna McConnell

Glastonbury ABC ($12,500) see Hartford Courant Foundation

Goodwill Industries ($7,500) see Jones and Bessie D. Phelps Foundation, Cyrus W. and Amy F.

Goodwill Industries of Western Connecticut — purchase of van ($19,516) see Pfriem Foundation, Norma F.

Governor's Partnership to Protect Connecticut's Workforce — Drugs Don't Work program ($25,000) see Heublein

Grace Lutheran Church ($20,000) see Barth Foundation, Theodore H.

Granby Pentecostal Tabernacle — new building ($50,000) see Baker Trust, George F.

Greater Bridgeport Campus Ministry ($7,500) see Carstensen Memorial Foundation, Fred R. and Hazel W.

Greater Bridgeport Symphony ($22,000) see Carstensen Memorial Foundation, Fred R. and Hazel W.

Greater Bridgeport Youth Symphony ($3,000) see Carstensen Memorial Foundation, Fred R. and Hazel W.

Greater Hartford Academy of Performing Arts ($10,000) see Ensworth Charitable Foundation

Greater Hartford Arts Council ($192,500) see Aetna Life & Casualty Co.

Greater Hartford Arts Council ($8,000) see Barnes Group

Greater Hartford Arts Council — federated arts drive ($70,000) see CM Alliance Cos.

Greater Hartford Arts Council ($12,000) see Dexter Corp.

Greater Hartford Arts Council ($68,250) see Heublein

Greater Hartford Arts Council ($105,000) see ITT Hartford Insurance Group

Greater Hartford Arts Council — annual operating gift ($3,500) see Saunders Charitable Foundation, Helen M.

Greater Hartford Arts Council ($20,000) see Stanley Works

Greater Hartford Arts Council ($17,000) see Wiremold Co.

Greater Hartford Arts Council (GHAC) ($100,000) see Travelers Cos.

Greater Hartford Association ($15,000) see Fisher Foundation

Greater Hartford Association for Retarded Citizens ($15,000) see Hartford Courant Foundation

Greater Hartford Chamber of Commerce ($346,500) see Aetna Life & Casualty Co.

Greater Hartford Council ($6,500) see Ensign-Bickford Industries

Greater Hartford Jewish Community Center ($100,000) see Rosen Foundation, Joseph

Greater Hartford Jewish Federation ($100,000) see Fisher Foundation

Greater Hartford Jewish Federation — endowment fund ($32,000) see Koopman Fund

Greater Hartford Jewish Federation — annual appeal ($25,000) see Koopman Fund

Greater Hartford Operation ($15,000) see Fisher Foundation

Green Farms Academy ($10,000) see Dunagan Foundation

Greenwich Academy Annual Fund ($10,000) see Messing Foundation, Morris M. and Helen F.

Greenwich Adult Day Care ($10,000) see Lehman Foundation, Edith and Herbert

Greenwich Adult Day Care Center ($10,000) see Dennett Foundation, Marie G.

Greenwich Health Association ($13,000) see Dammann Fund

Greenwich Health Association ($8,000) see Firestone, Jr. Foundation, Harvey

Greenwich Hospital ($100,000) see Klau Foundation, David W. and Sadie

Greenwich Hospital ($100,000) see Zenkel Foundation

Greenwich Hospital Association ($50,000) see Jurodin Fund

Greenwich Hospital Association ($200,000) see Lowenstein Foundation, Leon

Greenwich Hospital Association ($30,000) see Moore Foundation, Edward S.

Greenwich Hospital Association ($2,000) see Psychists

Greenwich Hospital Association — cancer center building campaign ($62,500) see Schultz Foundation

Greenwich Hospital Hospice Fund ($10,000) see Dennett Foundation, Marie G.

Greenwich House ($25,000) see Nichols Foundation

Greenwich House ($25,000) see Nichols Foundation

Greenwich Jewish Federation ($30,500) see Bennett Foundation, Carl and Dorothy

Greenwich Jewish Federation ($18,000) see Brody Foundation, Frances

Greenwich Jewish Federation ($41,333) see Mazer Foundation, Jacob and Ruth

Greenwich Jewish Federation ($5,000) see Messing Foundation, Morris M. and Helen F.

Greenwich Jewish Federation ($70,000) see Morris Foundation, Norman M.

Greenwich Land Trust ($11,000) see Jurodin Fund

Greenwich Library ($150,000) see Lowenstein Foundation, Leon

Greenwich Teen Center ($100,000) see Pollybill Foundation

Gunnery ($5,156) see Ellsworth Trust, W. H.

Gunnery School — repair of hockey rink ($10,000) see Barnes Foundation

Habitat for Humanity ($9,000) see Connecticut Natural Gas Corp.

Habitat for Humanity ($500) see Newmil Bancorp

Hall-Brooke Hospital ($3,100) see Dell Foundation, Hazel

Hall Neighborhood House ($500) see Bodine Corp.

Hanahoe Children's Clinic ($10,000) see Meserve Memorial Fund, Albert and Helen

Hartford Action Plan on Infant Health — infant mortality and teen pregnancy prevention ($85,000) see CM Alliance Cos.

Hartford Area Child Care ($5,000) see Robinson Fund, Charles Nelson

Hartford Area Training Center ($4,500) see Wiremold Co.

Hartford Art School Scholarship Fund ($32,500) see Krieble Foundation, Vernon K.

Hartford Art School Visiting Artists ($25,000) see Krieble Foundation, Vernon K.

Hartford Business School ($2,750) see SIT Investment Associates, Inc.

Hartford College for Women — scholarship fund ($50,000) see Auerbach Foundation, Beatrice Fox

Hartford College for Women ($15,000) see Bissell Foundation, J. Walton

Hartford College for Women — scholarship ($25,500) see Koopman Fund

Hartford College for Women — University of Hartford Affiliation ($2,500) see Saunders Charitable Foundation, Helen M.

Hartford Community Mental Health Center ($13,200) see Connecticut Natural Gas Corp.

Hartford Easter Seal Rehabilitation Center — general support ($5,125) see Koopman Fund

Hartford Foundation for Public Giving — advise fund ($78,000) see Auerbach Foundation, Beatrice Fox

Hartford Foundation for Public Giving — general support ($50,140) see Koopman Fund

Hartford Foundation for Public Giving ($77,600) see Schiro Fund

Hartford Foundation for Public Giving — Bushnell ($100,000) see Auerbach Foundation, Beatrice Fox

Hartford Health Department ($225,000) see Aetna Life & Casualty Co.

Hartford Hebrew Home for the Aged ($2,000) see EIS Foundation

Hartford Hospital — cardiology fund ($100,000) see Auerbach Foundation, Beatrice Fox

Hartford Hospital — expansion and renovation ($50,000) see CM Alliance Cos.

Hartford Hospital ($20,000) see Fisher Foundation

Hartford Hospital ($20,000) see Hartford Courant Foundation

Hartford Hospital ($100,000) see ITT Hartford Insurance Group

Hartford Hospital ($67,000) see Kohn-Joseloff Fund

Hartford Hospital — capital campaign ($5,000) see Koopman Fund

Hartford Hospital — for the Campaign for Hartford Hospital ($5,000) see Saunders Charitable Foundation, Helen M.

Hartford Hospital Capital Campaign ($40,000) see Heublein

Hartford Jewish Federation — annual appeal ($150,000) see Auerbach Foundation, Beatrice Fox

Hartford Jewish Federation ($111,100) see Kohn-Joseloff Fund

Hartford Monthly Meeting of Friends ($4,000) see Valentine Foundation, Lawson

Hartford Neighborhood Centers ($3,500) see Robinson Fund, Charles Nelson

Hartford Public Schools — computer literacy ($60,000) see Travelers Cos.

Hartford Public Schools — "Building Blocks" Montessori School ($25,000) see Heublein

Hartford Public Schools — School Development Program (Comer Model) ($81,742) see Travelers Cos.

Hartford Seminary ($13,000) see Palmer Fund, Francis Asbury

Hartford Stage ($25,000) see Aeroflex Foundation

Hartford Stage Company ($12,500) see Bissell Foundation, J. Walton

Hartford Stage Company ($10,000) see Kohn-Joseloff Fund

Hartford Stage Company — capital campaign ($5,000) see Koopman Fund

Hartford Stage Company ($12,500) see Larsen Fund

Hartford Symphony ($5,000) see Ensign-Bickford Industries

Hartford Symphony ($5,334) see Preston Trust, Evelyn W.

Hartford Symphony Orchestra — Capriccio newsletter for 91-92 ($6,000) see Saunders Charitable Foundation, Helen M.

HAS-Soros Foundation Secretariat ($554,022) see Soros Foundation-Hungary

Connecticut (cont.)

Hathaway Brown School ($11,000) see Kohn-Joseloff Fund

Heal the Children ($6,000) see Harcourt Foundation, Ellen Knowles

Health Foundation of Greater Stamford ($25,000) see Barker Foundation, J. M. R.

Hebrew Home and Satellite ($30,000) see Fisher Foundation

High Hopes Therapeutic Riding ($50,000) see Ingalls Foundation, Louise H. and David S.

Hillside Elderly Housing ($500) see Newmil Bancorp

Hillstead Museum ($7,500) see Ensign-Bickford Industries

Historical Society of Town of Greenwich ($86,000) see Vanderbilt Trust, R. T.

Historical Society of Town of Greenwich ($10,000) see Vanderbilt Trust, R. T.

Hole in the Wall Gang Camp — funding to establish and equip a health care dispensary at this recretaional facility ($100,000) see Dyson Foundation

Hole in the Wall Gang Fund ($5,500) see Bozzone Family Foundation

Hole in the Wall Gang Fund ($50,000) see Wardle Family Foundation

Horace Bushnell Memorial Hall ($180,000) see Aetna Life & Casualty Co.

Horace Bushnell Memorial Hall — annual fund ($2,500) see Saunders Charitable Foundation, Helen M.

Hotchkiss School ($15,000) see Clapp Charitable and Educational Trust, George H.

Hotchkiss School ($18,834) see Ford Fund, William and Martha

Hotchkiss School ($200,000) see Garland Foundation, John Jewett and H. Chandler

Hotchkiss School — capital campaign ($100,000) see Mars Foundation

Hotchkiss School — unrestricted ($27,280) see Stackpole-Hall Foundation

Hotchkiss School ($25,000) see Weinberg Foundation, John L.

Hotchkiss School ($57,500) see Whiting Foundation, Macauley and Helen Dow

Housatonic Mental Health Institute ($30,000) see Weiss Foundation, William E.

Human Resources Agency of New Britain ($7,018) see Connecticut Natural Gas Corp.

Hungarian Reformed Church — for building fund ($10,000) see Culpeper Memorial Foundation, Daphne Seybolt

Industrial Museum ($5,000) see Freas Foundation

Institute for Community Research ($63,500) see Hitachi

Institute of World Affairs ($5,000) see Kunstadter Family Foundation, Albert

Institute of World Affairs ($5,000) see Kunstadter Family Foundation, Albert

Interfaith Caregivers — senior visitor program ($5,000) see Senior Services of Stamford

Interlude ($50,000) see Bingham Trust, The

Interlude ($8,000) see Meserve Memorial Fund, Albert and Helen

Jane Coffin Childs Memorial Fund for Medical Research ($22,500) see AKC Fund

Jewish Center Adult Program — scholarships for summer "camp" ($400) see Senior Services of Stamford

Jewish Family Services — transportation for companions to elderly ($924) see Senior Services of Stamford

Jewish Federation ($35,300) see Schiro Fund

Jewish Home for the Aged ($16,000) see Eder Foundation, Sidney and Arthur

Jewish Home for the Aged ($1,500) see Fox Steel Co.

Jewish Welfare Federation ($8,000) see Ratner Foundation, Milton M.

John Pettigone Memorial Scholarship Fund ($6,000) see Harcourt Foundation, Ellen Knowles

Julie Gould Fund for Medical Research ($2,000) see Iroquois Avenue Foundation

Junior Achievement ($2,000) see Acme United Corp.

Junior Achievement ($630) see Bristol Savings Bank

Junior Achievement ($6,200) see Hubbell Inc.

Junior Achievement ($4,800) see Wiremold Co.

Junior Achievement of North Central Connecticut (J.A.) ($28,000) see Travelers Cos.

Junior Achievement, Stamford, CT see Rhone-Poulenc Rorer

Juvenile Diabetes Foundation ($10,000) see Bernstein & Co., Sanford C.

Keep America Beautiful ($14,000) see Reynolds Metals Co.

Kent School ($100,000) see Brooks Foundation, Gladys

Kent School ($50,000) see Mather and William Gwinn Mather Fund, Elizabeth Ring

Kingswood-Oxford School ($2,200) see Bristol Savings Bank

Klingberg Family Centers ($12,000) see Hartford Courant Foundation

Laurel House ($410,000) see Bingham Trust, The

Lawrence and Memorial Hospital ($37,500) see Palmer Fund, Frank Loomis

Lawrence and Memorial Hospital ($37,500) see Palmer Fund, Frank Loomis

Lawrence and Memorial Hospital ($37,500) see Palmer Fund, Frank Loomis

Liberation Programs ($30,000) see Olin Corp.

Liberation Programs ($25,000) see Olin Corp.

Literacy Volunteers of America — to support the implementation of a strategic plan to improve the quality of literacy instruction while increasing the number of learners served see United Parcel Service of America

Little Sisters of the Poor ($50,000) see Noble Charitable Trust, John L. and Ethel G.

Long Wharf Theatre ($100,000) see Shubert Foundation

Loomis-Chaffee School ($82,000) see Kohn-Joseloff Fund

Loomis-Chaffee School ($15,000) see Mercy, Jr. Foundation, Sue and Eugene

Loomis Chaffee School ($100,000) see Olin Foundation, Spencer T. and Ann W.

Lyme Academy ($5,000) see MacCurdy Salisbury Educational Foundation

Lyme/Old Lyme School ($2,500) see MacCurdy Salisbury Educational Foundation

Manchester Area Conference of Churches ($5,000) see Connecticut Natural Gas Corp.

Manchester Community College ($16,000) see Jones Fund, Paul L.

Manchester Memorial Hospital ($5,000) see Price Foundation, Lucien B. and Katherine E.

Maritime Center at Norwalk ($25,000) see Ziegler Foundation for the Blind, E. Matilda

Marvelwood School ($6,000) see Barnes Foundation

Matilda Ziegler Publishing Company for the Blind ($230,000) see Ziegler Foundation for the Blind, E. Matilda

McLean Association — hospice program ($50,000) see Auerbach Foundation, Beatrice Fox

Meadowbrook School Capital ($10,000) see Dennett Foundation, Marie G.

Meals on Wheels ($23,725) see Senior Services of Stamford

Mental Health Association of Union County ($2,000) see Psychists

Mid-Fairfield Hospice ($20,000) see Bedford Fund

Middlebury College — scholarships ($54,000) see Ayling Scholarship Foundation, Alice S.

Middlebury College ($45,000) see Trust for Mutual Understanding

Middlebury College Parents Fund ($2,000) see Darby Foundation

Miss Porter's School ($20,000) see Bissell Foundation, J. Walton

Miss Porter's School ($26,500) see Firestone, Jr. Foundation, Harvey

Miss Porter's School ($120,000) see Olin Foundation, Spencer T. and Ann W.

Miss Porter's School — capital and endowment campaign ($500,000) see Tandy Foundation, Anne Burnett and Charles

Miss Porter's School — student center ($250,000) see Wean Foundation, Raymond John

Miss Porter's School ($120,000) see Weezie Foundation

Mitchell College ($30,000) see Palmer Fund, Frank Loomis

Montville Broncos ($3,000) see Lehman Foundation, Edith and Herbert

Mooreland Hill School ($30,000) see Vance Charitable Foundation, Robert C.

Moses Stern Memorial ($20,000) see Schiro Fund

Mount Olive Towers ($2,331) see Community Cooperative Development Foundation

Museum of Art, Science and Industry ($1,000) see Acme United Corp.

Music Foundation for the Handicapped of Connecticut ($5,000) see Ziegler Foundation for the Blind, E. Matilda

My Sister's Place II ($10,000) see Long Foundation, George A. and Grace

Mystic Museum ($10,000) see Plant Memorial Fund, Henry B.

Mystic Seaport Museum ($25,000) see Falcon Foundation

Mystic Seaport Museum ($30,000) see Moore Foundation, Edward S.

National Association of Electrical Distributors Educational Foundation ($5,000) see Wiremold Co.

National Executive Service Corps see General Signal Corp.

National Schools Committee for Economic Education ($15,000) see Curran Foundation

Natural Hygiene ($10,000) see Connemara Fund

Nature Conservancy-Connecticut Chapter ($30,000) see Carolyn Foundation

Nature Conservatory ($12,000) see Seeley Foundation

Nature Conservatory ($2,000) see Seeley Foundation

Neighborhood Housing Services ($8,300) see Connecticut Natural Gas Corp.

New Britain Institute ($11,000) see Vance Charitable Foundation, Robert C.

New Britain Museum of American Art ($69,500) see Stanley Charitable Foundation, A. W.

New Britain Museum of American Art ($25,000) see Stanley Works

New Britain Symphony ($15,000) see Stanley Charitable Foundation, A. W.

New Canaan Country School ($2,750) see Coleman Foundation

New Canaan County School System ($100,000) see Nason Foundation

New England Carousel Museum ($500) see Bristol Savings Bank

New Fairfield Community Playground ($500) see Newmil Bancorp

New Haven Colony Historical Society ($12,200) see Woman's Seamen's Friend Society of Connecticut

New Haven Crypt Association — to restore and preserve gravestone in crypt ($25,000) see Culpeper Memorial Foundation, Daphne Seybolt

New Haven Hebrew Day School ($25,100) see Lender Family Foundation

New Haven Jewish Community Center ($100) see Fox Steel Co.

New Haven Jewish Federation ($175,400) see Eder Foundation, Sidney and Arthur

New Haven Jewish Federation ($11,250) see Fox Steel Co.

New Haven Jewish Federation ($7,000) see Fox Steel Co.

New Haven Symphony see People's Bank

New Haven Symphony Orchestra ($30,000) see Carolyn Foundation

New Haven Symphony Orchestra ($2,000) see Eder Foundation, Sidney and Arthur

New Milford Creative Playground ($2,000) see Harcourt Foundation, Ellen Knowles

New Milford Hospital ($10,000) see Harcourt Foundation, Ellen Knowles

New Milford Hospital ($63,000) see Hettinger Foundation

New Milford Hospital Foundation ($5,200) see Harcourt Foundation, Ellen Knowles

New Milford Hospital Foundation ($5,750) see Meserve Memorial Fund, Albert and Helen

New Milford Hospital Foundation ($27,600) see Newmil Bancorp

New Milford Interfaith Housing ($5,000) see Meserve Memorial Fund, Albert and Helen

Noroton Presbyterian Church ($76,000) see Glanville Family Foundation

North American Maritime Ministry Association ($20,000) see Woman's Seamen's Friend Society of Connecticut

Norwalk Community College ($4,000) see Jones Fund, Paul L.

Norwalk Hospital ($100,000) see Bedford Fund

Norwalk Hospital — ambulatory surgical suite ($150,000) see Culpeper Foundation, Charles E.

Norwalk Hospital ($2,200) see Dell Foundation, Hazel

Norwalk Hospital ($2,200) see Dell Foundation, Hazel

Norwalk Hospital ($25,000) see Hagedorn Fund

Norwalk Hospital ($5,000) see Kennedy Foundation, John R.

Norwalk Hospital ($10,000) see Weinstein Foundation, Alex J.

Norwalk Hospital Association ($80,000) see Levee Charitable Trust, Polly Annenberg

Norwalk Hospital — to purchase PCA pumps ($15,000) see Culpeper Memorial Foundation, Daphne Seybolt

Norwalk Maritime Center ($16,357) see Stone Foundation

Norwich Public Schools ($15,000) see Barnes Foundation

Olivet Congregational Church ($7,000) see Jones and Bessie D. Phelps Foundation, Cyrus W. and Amy F.

Ona M. Wilcox School of Nursing ($6,000) see Jones Fund, Paul L.

Open Hearth ($5,000) see Connecticut Natural Gas Corp.

Our Lady of Sorrows Church ($4,000) see Vanderbilt Trust, R. T.

Outward Bound ($12,500) see Ogilvy & Mather Worldwide

Outward Bound ($200,000) see Whitehead Foundation

Park City Hospital ($4,000) see Jost Foundation, Charles and Mabel P.

Person to Person ($5,000) see Horncrest Foundation

PIMMS see General Signal Corp.

Planned Parenthood of Connecticut ($200,000) see Auerbach Foundation, Beatrice Fox

Planned Parenthood of Connecticut ($100,000) see Educational Foundation of America

Planned Parenthood of Connecticut ($25,000) see Penzance Foundation

Planned Parenthood Federation of America ($500) see Bodine Corp.

Planned Parenthood Federation of America ($10,000) see Hartman Foundation, Jesse and Dorothy

Planned Parenthood Federation of America ($10,750) see Schiro Fund

Pomfret School ($5,000) see Cranshaw Corporation

Pomfret School ($6,167) see Schwartz Foundation, Bernard Lee

Pomfret School ($10,000) see Statter Foundation, Amy Plant

Pomfret School Parents Fund ($3,000) see Bedminster Fund

Project Oceanology ($10,153) see Woman's Seamen's Friend Society of Connecticut

Prudence Crandall Center ($10,750) see Stanley Charitable Foundation, A. W.

Quinnipiac College ($3,500) see Blake Foundation, S. P.

Quinnipiac College ($20,000) see Jones Fund, Paul L.

Quinnipiac College ($25,000) see Lender Family Foundation

Rawhide Boys Ranch ($10,000) see Alexander Charitable Foundation

Real Art Ways ($5,333) see Preston Trust, Evelyn W.

Regional Y Building Fund ($2,000) see Newmill Bancorp

Regional 'Y' of Western Connecticut ($16,000) see Huiskíng Foundation

Rehabilitation Center ($100) see Bodine Corp.

Rehabilitation Center of Eastern Fairfield County ($15,000) see Bedford Fund

Rehabilitation Center for Fairfield ($155,000) see Noble Charitable Trust, John L. and Ethel G.

Renbrook School ($22,000) see Kohn-Joseloff Fund

Riverfront Recapture (RRI) ($80,000) see Travelers Cos.

Roaring Brook Nature ($7,000) see Ensign-Bickford Industries

Round Hill Community Church ($33,000) see Evans Foundation, T. M.

Sacred Heart University ($1,500) see Acme United Corp.

Sacred Heart University ($100) see Burndy Corp.

Sacred Heart University ($4,000) see Jost Foundation, Charles and Mabel P.

St. Agnes Family Center ($10,000) see Long Foundation, George A. and Grace

St. Clement's Parish Development Fund ($250) see Sweet Life Foods

St. Francis Hospital Medical Center ($20,000) see Ensign-Bickford Industries

St. Francis Hospital and Medical Center — cardiac catherization laboratory ($650,000) see

Hoffman Foundation, Maximillian E. and Marion O.

St. Francis Hospital School of Nursing ($6,000) see Jones Fund, Paul L.

St. Francis School ($5,000) see United States Surgical Corp.

St. James Retirement Fund ($5,000) see Price Foundation, Lucien B. and Katherine E.

St. James School — library fund ($8,000) see Price Foundation, Lucien B. and Katherine E.

St. James School ($18,000) see Price Foundation, Lucien B. and Katherine E.

St. Joseph College ($20,000) see Jones Fund, Paul L.

St. Joseph Hospital Foundation ($21,500) see Mann Foundation, John Jay

St. Luke's Foundation ($15,000) see Connemara Fund

St. Margarets-McTernan School ($60,000) see Woodward Fund-Watertown, David, Helen, and Marian

St. Marks Episcopal Church ($5,000) see Doherty Charitable Foundation, Henry L. and Grace

St. Marys Church ($2,000) see Doherty Charitable Foundation, Henry L. and Grace

St. Mary's Church Building Fund ($10,000) see Dennett Foundation, Marie G.

St. Mary's School of Nursing ($5,000) see Jones Fund, Paul L.

St. Matthew Church — to purchase carillons ($10,000) see Culpeper Memorial Foundation, Daphne Seybolt

St. Pauls Flax Hill Cooperative ($2,331) see Community Cooperative Development Foundation

St. Thomas Aquinas High School — scholarships ($37,000) see Hoffman Foundation, Maximillian E. and Marion O.

St. Timothy School ($5,000) see Freas Foundation

St. Vincents Hospital ($50,000) see Psychists

St. Vincent's Medical Center ($2,500) see Acme United Corp.

St. Vincent's Medical Center ($5,000) see Jones Fund, Paul L.

St. Vincent's Medical Center Foundation ($7,500) see Jones and Bessie D. Phelps Foundation, Cyrus W. and Amy F.

St. Vincent's Medical Center Foundation ($75,000) see Morris Foundation, William T.

St. Vincents Medical Center Foundation ($25,000) see Noble Charitable Trust, John L. and Ethel G.

St. Vincent's Medical Center Foundation ($32,000) see Pfriem Foundation, Norma F.

Salisbury School ($10,000) see AKC Fund

Salisbury School — environmental program ($10,000) see Day Family Foundation

Salisbury School ($50,000) see Ingalls Foundation, Louise H. and David S.

Save the Children ($204,000) see Banyan Tree Foundation

Save the Children ($50,000) see Edouard Foundation

Save the Children ($500) see Hirschhorn Foundation, David and Barbara B.

Save the Children ($49,536) see TJX Cos.

Save the Children Federation ($10,000) see Joselow Foundation

Schooner ($53,000) see Woman's Seamen's Friend Society of Connecticut

Science Museum of Connecticut for Family Science Program ($30,000) see Heublein

Seaman's Church Institute ($6,000) see Woman's Seamen's Friend Society of Connecticut

Second Stone Ridge Cooperative Corporation ($2,331) see Community Cooperative Development Foundation

Senior Friends ($20,000) see Russell Charitable Foundation, Tom

Senior Neighborhood Support — meal program, recreation and outreach ($34,500) see Senior Services of Stamford

Seniors Job Bank ($11,000) see Fisher Foundation

Sharon Creative Arts Foundation ($13,342) see Kramer Foundation, C. L. C.

Sisters of St. Dominic Our Lady of Elms ($25,000) see Firestone, Jr. Foundation, Harvey

Sisters of St. Joseph ($3,000) see Price Foundation, Lucien B. and Katherine E.

Society for the Arts ($1,000) see Seeley Foundation

Sound School ($13,910) see Woman's Seamen's Friend Society of Connecticut

South End Community Center ($100) see Bodine Corp.

South Kent School ($32,000) see Bicknell Fund

South Kent School ($20,000) see Hanson Testamentary Charitable Trust, Anna Emery

South Kent School ($10,000) see Vale Foundation, Ruby R.

South Kent School — Bartlett Fund ($40,000) see Ingalls Foundation, Louise H. and David S.

South Park Inn ($8,000) see Connecticut Natural Gas Corp.

South Park Inn ($12,000) see Long Foundation, George A. and Grace

South Park Inn ($4,000) see Robinson Fund, Charles Nelson

Southeastern Connecticut AIDS Project ($3,000) see Williams Foundation, Arthur Ashley

Sphere Watkins School ($9,999) see Long Foundation, George A. and Grace

Stamford Center for the Arts ($2,500) see Brace Foundation, Donald C.

Stamford Center for the Arts ($1,000) see Goldstein Foundation, Leslie and Roslyn

Stamford Family Housing Corporation — fund inner-city senior center ($23,000) see Senior Services of Stamford

Stamford Hospital ($52,305) see Overbrook Foundation

Stamford Hospital Development Fund ($50,000) see Leonhardt Foundation, Frederick H.

Stamford Hospital Foundation ($300,000) see Brace Foundation, Donald C.

Stamford Symphony ($1,500) see Goldstein Foundation, Leslie and Roslyn

Stamford Theatre Works ($3,000) see Hartman Foundation, Jesse and Dorothy

Stamford University ($25,000) see Whitney Foundation, Helen Hay

Stamford Women's Mentoring Project — project pairs women entering the work force for the first time after being on public assistance with professional women from the community who will act as mentors see New Street Capital Corp.

Stanford Law School ($2,500) see Mosbacher, Jr. Foundation, Emil

STAR Center (Society to Advance the Retarded) ($25,000) see Bedford Fund

State of Connecticut Department of Human Resources ($8,000) see Ziegler Foundation for the Blind, E. Matilda

Suffield High School Safe Parties ($100) see Sweet Life Foods

Symphony Society of Greater Hartford ($25,000) see Bissell Foundation, J. Walton

Taft School ($15,000) see Blinken Foundation

Taft School ($18,000) see Landegger Charitable Foundation

Taft School ($75,000) see Semple Foundation, Louise Taft

Taft School ($5,000) see Triford Foundation

Taft School ($100,000) see Woodward Fund-Watertown, David, Helen, and Marian

Taft School — in support of the 100th Anniversary campaign ($100,000) see Hillman Foundation, Henry L.

Taino Housing and Development ($12,170) see Connecticut Natural Gas Corp.

Technoserve ($5,000) see West Foundation

Temple Shalom ($26,000) see Bennett Foundation, Carl and Dorothy

Temple Sinai ($3,450) see Coleman Foundation

Thames Science Center — project robotacts ($55,000) see Palmer Fund, Frank Loomis

Thames Science Center — implement project magnet ($50,000) see Palmer Fund, Frank Loomis

Tip of the Mitt Watershed Council ($5,000) see Triford Foundation

Town of Avon ($8,210) see Ensign-Bickford Industries

Town of Simsbury ($12,900) see Ensign-Bickford Industries

Trinity College — new academic building ($60,000) see Baker Trust, George F.

Trinity College ($10,000) see Bissell Foundation, J. Walton

Trinity College — scholarship aid ($30,000) see Johnston Trust for Charitable and Educational Purposes, James M.

Trinity College ($100,000) see Strawbridge Foundation of Pennsylvania I, Margaret Dorrance

Trinity College Capital Campaign ($30,000) see Heublein

Ukranian Catholic Diocese of Stamford ($150,000) see Morania Foundation

United Cerebral Palsy Association ($9,000) see Long Foundation, George A. and Grace

United Community Services ($60,000) see Vance Charitable Foundation, Robert C.

United Congregational Church ($14,000) see Carstensen Memorial Foundation, Fred R. and Hazel W.

United Congregational Church ($19,200) see McDougall Charitable Trust, Ruth Camp

United Jewish Appeal - Federation of Jewish Philanthropies ($78,275) see Liz Claiborne

United Negro College Fund ($500) see Bodine Corp.

U.S. Coast Guard Academy Foundation — visiting lecture program ($2,000) see Olmsted Foundation, George and Carol

United Way ($16,000) see Acme United Corp.

United Way ($700) see Attleboro Pawtucket Savings Bank

United Way ($50,000) see Bedford Fund

United Way ($20,000) see Bedford Fund

United Way ($2,800) see Bristol Savings Bank

United Way ($100) see Burndy Corp.

United Way — federated drive for social and health services ($59,431) see CM Alliance Cos.

United Way — federated drive for social and health services ($59,431) see CM Alliance Cos.

United Way — federated drive for social and health services ($59,431) see CM Alliance Cos.

United Way — federated drive for social and health services ($59,431) see CM Alliance Cos.

United Way ($10,000) see Culpeper Memorial Foundation, Daphne Seybolt

United Way ($27,304) see Ensign-Bickford Industries

United Way ($18,782) see Ensign-Bickford Industries

United Way ($5,000) see Firestone, Jr. Foundation, Harvey

United Way ($2,500) see Goldstein Foundation, Leslie and Roslyn

United Way ($24,000) see Handy & Harman

United Way ($3,000) see Harcourt Foundation, Ellen Knowles

United Way ($3,000) see Hartman Foundation, Jesse and Dorothy

United Way ($2,500) see Hartman Foundation, Jesse and Dorothy

United Way ($11,000) see Hubbell Inc.

United Way ($7,500) see Hubbell Inc.

United Way ($17,607) see ITT Rayonier

United Way ($10,000) see Koopman Fund

United Way ($20,000) see Mead Fund, Nelson

Connecticut (cont.)

United Way ($3,000) see Mosbacher, Jr. Foundation, Emil

United Way ($500) see Newmil Bancorp

United Way ($500) see Newmil Bancorp

United Way see People's Bank

United Way ($5,000) see Robinson Fund, Charles Nelson

United Way ($11,750) see Schiro Fund

United Way ($10,000) see Schwartz Fund for Education and Health Research, Arnold and Marie

United Way ($125,000) see Stanley Charitable Foundation, A. W.

United Way ($58,300) see Wiremold Co.

United Way of Capital Area/Combined Health Appeal ($1,350,000) see Aetna Life & Casualty Co.

United Way of the Capital Area and Combined Health Appeal — to support a wide range of health and human service agencies ($540,000) see CIGNA Corp.

United Way of the Capital Area and Combined Health Appeal ($925,000) see Travelers Cos.

United Way Capital-Hartford Area ($127,313) see ITT Hartford Insurance Group

United Way/Capital-Hartford Area ($84,875) see ITT Hartford Insurance Group

United Way/Capital-Hartford Area ($84,875) see ITT Hartford Insurance Group

United Way/Capital-Hartford Area ($42,438) see ITT Hartford Insurance Group

United Way Central Naugatuck Valley ($15,000) see Illinois Tool Works

United Way/Chapter-Hartford Area ($84,875) see ITT Hartford Insurance Group

United Way of Eastern Fairfield County ($15,000) see Chesebrough-Pond's

United Way of Eastern Fairfield County ($16,000) see Hubbell Inc.

United Way of Eastern Fairfield County ($16,000) see Hubbell Inc.

United Way of Eastern Fairfield County ($89,000) see Textron

United Way - Eastern Fairfield County ($15,000) see Thomas & Betts Corp.

United Way of Greater New Haven ($18,500) see Miles Inc.

United Way of Greenwich ($30,000) see Chesebrough-Pond's

United Way of Greenwich — general charities ($15,000) see Young Foundation, Robert R.

United Way of Meriden-Wallingford ($28,000) see Allegheny Ludlum Corp.

University of Bridgeport ($2,000) see Acme United Corp.

University of Bridgeport ($100) see Burndy Corp.

University of Bridgeport ($25,000) see Dibner Fund

University of Bridgeport ($40,000) see Hubbell Inc.

University of Bridgeport ($90,000) see Palisades Educational Foundation

University of Bridgeport Law School ($11,000) see Jones and Bessie D. Phelps Foundation, Cyrus W. and Amy F.

University of Bridgeport Law School — support of Law Library and the Law Annual Fund ($15,000) see Culpeper Memorial Foundation, Daphne Seybolt

University of Connecticut ($500) see Bristol Savings Bank

University of Connecticut ($60,000) see Brookdale Foundation

University of Connecticut ($3,500) see Leonhardt Foundation, Frederick H.

University of Connecticut ($10,000) see Sweatt Foundation, Harold W.

University of Connecticut Extension Center Haddam ($1,000) see Rockfall Foundation

University of Connecticut Foundation/Travelers Center on Aging ($250,000) see Travelers Cos.

University of Connecticut Health Center ($150,000) see Patterson and Clara Guthrie Patterson Trust, Robert Leet

University of Hartford ($4,125) see Saunders Charitable Foundation, Helen M.

University of Hartford ($10,000) see Wiremold Co.

University of Hartford — ASK House ($160,000) see Auerbach Foundation, Beatrice Fox

University of Hartford — Educational Main Street Transitions Program ($12,500) see Nellie Mae

University of Hartford — support services for half-tuition students ($25,000) see Heublein

University of New Haven ($100) see Burndy Corp.

University of New Haven ($60,000) see Echlin Foundation

Vassar College see Brakeley, John Price Jones Inc.

Visiting Nurse Services ($1,500) see Bodine Corp.

Wadsworth Atheneum — challenge grant ($100,000) see Auerbach Foundation, Beatrice Fox

Wadsworth Atheneum ($10,000) see Barnes Group

Wadsworth Atheneum ($15,000) see Fisher Foundation

Wadsworth Atheneum ($52,060) see Kohn-Joseloff Fund

Wadsworth Atheneum — capital funding ($96,000) see Koopman Fund

Wadsworth Atheneum ($12,500) see Larsen Fund

Wadsworth Atheneum — endowment pledge ($17,000) see Saunders Charitable Foundation, Helen M.

Walks Foundation ($20,000) see Barnes Foundation

Walks Foundation ($10,000) see Bissell Foundation, J. Walton

Walks Foundation ($3,000) see Wiremold Co.

Warehouse Point Library Building Fund ($24,378) see Library Association of Warehouse Point

Washington Community Housing Trust ($500) see Newmil Bancorp

Watkinson School ($50,000) see Beveridge Foundation, Frank Stanley

Watkinson School ($15,000) see Ensworth Charitable Foundation

Watkinson School ($10,000) see Long Foundation, George A. and Grace

Wesleyan University ($15,000) see Beck Foundation

Wesleyan University ($100,000) see Berbecker Scholarship Fund, Walter J. and Lille

Wesleyan University ($7,500) see Binswanger Co.

Wesleyan University ($10,000) see Braitmayer Foundation

Wesleyan University — scholarship aid ($125,000) see Johnston Trust for Charitable and Educational Purposes, James M.

Wesleyan University ($9,500) see Kaplan Foundation, Mayer and Morris

Wesleyan University ($10,000) see Zilkha & Sons

Wesleyan University — Brodhead Scholarship ($250,000) see Barra Foundation

West Haven Community House ($15,000) see Miles Inc.

Westminster School ($37,500) see Heinz Family Foundation

Westminster School ($10,000) see Hollis Foundation

Westminster School ($201,000) see Kohn-Joseloff Fund

Westover School ($5,000) see Love Foundation, George H. and Margaret McClintic

Westover School ($48,169) see Mandeville Foundation

Westover School ($15,000) see Winona Corporation

Westport '89 Committee ($10,000) see Reynolds Foundation, J. B.

Westport Police Department ($2,500) see Dell Foundation, Hazel

WHC-TV W. Hartford Community TV 26 Access ($3,500) see Wiremold Co.

Wheeler Clinic Golf Classic ($1,000) see Bristol Savings Bank

Wilbur Cross High School Parent Teachers Student Association ($30,000) see Carolyn Foundation

Williams School — scholarships ($29,600) see Palmer Fund, Frank Loomis

Winsted Memorial Hospital ($5,000) see AKC Fund

Woman's League — day care center ($100,000) see Auerbach Foundation, Beatrice Fox

Wooster School — transition to Full K-2 Program ($75,000) see Wean Foundation, Raymond John

World Wildlife Fund ($25,000) see Taylor Foundation, Ruth and Vernon

Yale Alumni Fund ($10,000) see Hersey Foundation

Yale-China Association ($10,000) see Kunstadter Family Foundation, Albert

Yale Comprehensive Cancer Center ($12,500) see Pines Bridge Foundation

Yale Institute — couturier project ($42,915) see Menil Foundation

Yale Law School ($16,000) see CIT Group Holdings

Yale Law School ($300,000) see Goldsmith Foundation, Horace W.

Yale Law School ($35,000) see Littauer Foundation, Lucius N.

Yale Law School — Samuel S. Flug scholarship fund ($35,000) see Martin & Deborah Flug Foundation

Yale-New Haven Hospital ($100,000) see Carolyn Foundation

Yale-New Haven Hospital ($5,000) see Fox Steel Co.

Yale-New Haven Hospital ($85,783) see Patterson and Clara Guthrie Patterson Trust, Robert Leet

Yale/New Haven Teachers Institute — for teacher training and curriculum enhancement ($15,000) see Bay Foundation

Yale School of Nursing — to support the development of a Home-Health-Care-Nursing curriculum ($290,000) see Baxter International

Yale University ($5,000) see AKC Fund

Yale University see Brakeley, John Price Jones Inc.

Yale University ($92,000) see Bugher Foundation

Yale University ($160,000) see C. E. and S. Foundation

Yale University ($25,000) see Colt Foundation, James J.

Yale University ($10,000) see Connemara Fund

Yale University ($5,000) see Cowles Foundation, William H.

Yale University ($200,000) see Crown Memorial, Arie and Ida

Yale University ($4,200) see DiRosa Foundation, Rene and Veronica

Yale University ($1,665,000) see Ellis Fund

Yale University ($5,000) see Fink Foundation

Yale University — equipment for child study center ($10,000) see Fisher Foundation

Yale University ($125,000) see Ford II Fund, Henry

Yale University ($57,250) see Foster-Davis Foundation

Yale University ($50,000) see Foster-Davis Foundation

Yale University ($25,000) see Foster-Davis Foundation

Yale University ($200) see Fox Steel Co.

Yale University ($50,000) see Gelb Foundation, Lawrence M.

Yale University ($10,000) see Gelb Foundation, Lawrence M.

Yale University ($15,000) see Goldman Sachs & Co.

Yale University ($10,490) see Goldman Sachs & Co.

Yale University ($25,000) see Greentree Foundation

Yale University ($11,000) see Gries Charity Fund, Lucile and Robert H.

Yale University ($50,000) see Gund Foundation, Geoffrey

Yale University ($150,000) see Harriman Foundation, Gladys and Roland

Yale University ($7,000) see Holtzmann Foundation, Jacob L. and Lillian

Yale University ($5,000) see Holtzmann Foundation, Jacob L. and Lillian

Yale University ($4,000) see Holtzmann Foundation, Jacob L. and Lillian

Yale University ($20,000) see Humphrey Fund, George M. and Pamela S.

Yale University ($5,000) see Israel Foundation, A. Cremieux

Yale University ($50,000) see JFM Foundation

Yale University ($6,000) see JFM Foundation

Yale University ($75,000) see Jockey Hollow Foundation

Yale University ($30,000) see Julia Foundation, Laura

Yale University ($25,000) see Kilroy Foundation, William S. and Lora Jean

Yale University ($27,300) see Knox Foundation, Seymour H.

Yale University — for construction of center for molecular medicine ($1,000,000) see Kresge Foundation

Yale University ($80,000) see Lehman Foundation, Robert

Yale University — child study center ($100,000) see Lowenstein Foundation, Leon

Yale University ($15,000) see Lumpkin Foundation

Yale University ($500,000) see Macmillan, Inc.

Yale University ($19,000) see Mandeville Foundation

Yale University ($11,500) see Mandeville Foundation

Yale University — medical research ($517,131) see Mathers Charitable Foundation, G. Harold and Leila Y.

Yale University ($33,333) see Mazer Foundation, Jacob and Ruth

Yale University ($3,000) see Mazer Foundation, Jacob and Ruth

Yale University ($92,000) see McNeil, Jr. Charitable Trust, Robert L.

Yale University ($6,000) see Meek Foundation

Yale University — religion and arts ($12,000) see Menil Foundation

Yale University — scared music ($10,000) see Menil Foundation

Yale University ($25,000) see New England Foundation

Yale University ($5,500) see Northern Star Foundation

Yale University ($10,000) see Oaklawn Foundation

Yale University ($16,000) see Obernauer Foundation

Yale University ($35,000) see Olin Corp.

Yale University ($13,000) see Palmer Fund, Francis Asbury

Yale University ($70,650) see Patterson and Clara Guthrie Patterson Trust, Robert Leet

Yale University ($8,900) see Peierls Foundation

Yale University ($50,000) see Poorvu Foundation, William and Lia

Yale University — provide seminars in modern journalism ($20,000) see Poynter Fund

Yale University ($6,000) see Rosen Foundation, Joseph

Yale University ($27,984) see Salomon

Yale University ($8,000) see Scott Foundation, Walter

Yale University — unrestricted ($27,280) see Stackpole-Hall Foundation

Yale University ($8,000) see Sussman Fund, Edna Bailey

Yale University ($10,000) see Webb Educational and Charitable Trust, Torrey H. and Dorothy K.

Yale University ($40,000) see Wien Foundation, Lawrence A.

Yale University ($40,000) see Yawkey Foundation II

Yale University — education ($15,000) see Young Foundation, Robert R.

Yale University ($65,000) see Ziegler Foundation for the Blind, E. Matilda

Yale University Alumni Fund ($15,000) see Mars Foundation

Yale University Art Gallery ($20,000) see Barker Welfare Foundation

Yale University — Branford College Entryway ($150,000) see Wean Foundation, Raymond John

Yale University-Bush Center ($330,000) see Richardson Foundation, Smith

Yale University — for construction of the Center for Molecular Medicine and support of the Medical Informatics Program ($100,000) see DeCamp Foundation, Ira W.

Yale University, Department of History — to support John M. Olin Doctoral and Post-doctoral Scholars in Military and Strategic History ($210,000) see Olin Foundation, John M.

Yale University Forestry School ($40,000) see Camp Younts Foundation

Yale University — to support the Henry R. Luce International Center at Yale University ($2,500,000) see Luce Foundation, Henry

Yale University — Hillhouse High School Program ($47,055) see Herzog Foundation, Carl J.

Yale University Medical School — multiple sclerosis research ($30,000) see Allen Charitable Trust, Phil N.

Yale University — support of program in Molecular Oncology ($2,741,200) see Markey Charitable Trust, Lucille P.

Yale University Press ($25,000) see Joukowsky Family Foundation

Yale University — for basic heart research; over five year period ($6,000,000) see American Cyanamid Co.

Yale University School of Drama ($10,000) see Matz Foundation — Edelman Division

Yale University, School of Medicine ($50,000) see Berbecker Scholarship Fund, Walter J. and Lille

Yale University School of Medicine ($92,500) see Burroughs Wellcome Co.

Yale University School of Medicine ($50,000) see Hood Foundation, Charles H.

Yale University School of Medicine ($10,000) see Hubbell Inc.

Yale University School of Medicine — medical research ($44,000) see Spunk Fund

Yale University School of Medicine — abuse/neglect prevention ($40,000) see Spunk Fund

Yale University — School of Nursing; teaching endowment ($250,000) see Independence Foundation

Yale University — in support of renovation and redesign of the Sterling Library Reference Center ($1,000,000) see Starr Foundation

Yale University — Yale Campaign ($150,000) see Moore Foundation, Edward S.

Yale Weizmann Institute ($1,000) see Guttag Foundation, Irwin and Marjorie

YMCA ($7,000) see Appleby Foundation

YMCA ($100,000) see Bedford Fund

YMCA ($4,000) see Knox Family Foundation

YMCA ($10,000) see Long Foundation, George A. and Grace

YMCA ($25,000) see Vance Charitable Foundation, Robert C.

YMCA ($7,000) see Wiremold Co.

Youth Challenge of Greater Hartford ($7,000) see Robinson Fund, Charles Nelson

Youth Under Severe Stress ($5,000) see Robinson Fund, Charles Nelson

YWCA ($50,000) see Stanley Charitable Foundation, A. W.

YWCA ($25,000) see Woodward Fund-Watertown, David, Helen, and Marian

Delaware

A.C.E.S. see ICI Americas

Arthritis Foundation ($25,000) see Fair Play Foundation

Boys Club of America ($30,000) see Crestlea Foundation

Boys Club of Delaware — capital needs ($200,000) see Crystal Trust

Boys Club of Delaware see ICI Americas

Boys Club of Delaware — capital campaign ($500,000) see Longwood Foundation

Boys Clubs of Delaware — capital campaign ($100,000) see Laffey-McHugh Foundation

Boys Clubs of Delaware — capital campaign ($125,000) see Welfare Foundation

Catholic Diocese of Wilmington — Diocese of Wilmington Educational Trust ($75,000) see Laffey-McHugh Foundation

Chesapeake Bay Girl Scout Council — capital campaign ($35,000) see duPont Foundation, Chichester

Chesapeake Bay Girl Scout Council ($25,000) see Marmot Foundation

Children's Beach House — operating budget, endowment fund ($290,000) see duPont Foundation, Chichester

Children's Bureau ($5,000) see Kutz Foundation, Milton and Hattie

Children's Bureau of Delaware ($25,000) see Vale Foundation, Ruby R.

Christina Cultural Arts — building acquisition ($575,000) see Longwood Foundation

Church Home Foundation ($9,000) see Borkee Hagley Foundation

Claymont Community Center — building renovations ($1,000,000) see Longwood Foundation

Community Legal Aid Society — capital campaign ($100,000) see Welfare Foundation

Cranston Heights Fire Company ($2,722) see Downs Perpetual Charitable Trust, Ellason

Delaware Academy of Medicine — capital fund drive ($25,000) see Crestlea Foundation

Delaware Council on Economic Education ($2,000) see Curran Foundation

Delaware Council on Economic Education see ICI Americas

Delaware Foundation for Retarded Children ($2,722) see Downs Perpetual Charitable Trust, Ellason

Delaware Hospice see ICI Americas

Delaware Nature Education ($10,000) see Vale Foundation, Ruby R.

Delaware Nature Education Society ($7,000) see Borkee Hagley Foundation

Delaware Nature Society ($15,000) see Fair Play Foundation

Delaware Nature Society see ICI Americas

Delaware State College — a computer center ($125,000) see Crystal Trust

Delaware State College see ICI Americas

Delaware State College — capital campaign ($500,000) see Longwood Foundation

Delaware State College ($3,245) see Lynch Scholarship Foundation, John B.

Delaware State College ($33,000) see SICO Foundation

Delaware State College — capital campaign ($100,000) see Welfare Foundation

Delaware State College ($10,000) see Wilmington Trust Co.

Delaware Symphony Association ($13,500) see Wilmington Trust Co.

Delaware Technical and Community College — capital campaign ($750,000) see Longwood Foundation

Delaware Theater Company ($1,000) see Stroud Foundation

Delaware Theatre Company — endowment campaign ($50,000) see Laffey-McHugh Foundation

Delaware Theatre Company — endowment campaign ($75,000) see Welfare Foundation

Delaware Theatre Company ($8,500) see Wilmington Trust Co.

Delaware Volunteer Legal Services — tuition for law students ($4,200) see Kutz Foundation, Milton and Hattie

Diocese of Wilmington Educational Trust ($100,000) see Good Samaritan

Diocese of Wilmington — consultant fees/salaries/operating costs of a development/endowment campaign for Diocesan elementary and secondary schools ($50,000) see Raskob Foundation for Catholic Activities

Diocese of Wilmington School Fund ($10,000) see Huisking Foundation

Easter Seal Society ($5,000) see Vale Foundation, Ruby R.

Easter Seal Society Del-Mar see ICI Americas

Episcopal Diocese of Delaware ($12,722) see Downs Perpetual Charitable Trust, Ellason

Goldey-Beacon College ($9,000) see Wilmington Trust Co.

Hagley Museum ($25,000) see Fair Play Foundation

Hagley Museum and Library — memorial fund ($50,000) see Crestlea Foundation

Hagley Museum and Library ($40,500) see Lukens

Hagley Museum and Library ($100,000) see McShain Charities, John

Harry Francis DuPont Museum ($30,000) see Moore Memorial Foundation, James Starr

Henry DuPont Winterthur Museum ($115,000) see Fair Play Foundation

Henry Francis duPont Winterthur Museum — new exhibition building ($100,000) see duPont Foundation, Chichester

Henry Francis duPont Winterthur Museum — new exhibition building ($50,000) see Johnson Fund, Edward C.

Henry Francis du Pont Winterthur Museum ($50,000) see Wood Foundation of Chambersburg, PA

Historical Society of Delaware — building acquisition ($500,000) see Longwood Foundation

Hockessin Public Library — capital campaign ($75,000) see Welfare Foundation

Independence School — expansion campaign ($500,000) see Longwood Foundation

Jewels of Charity — non-restricted ($770,000) see Birch Foundation, Stephen and Mary

Jewish Federation ($28,000) see Federation Foundation of Greater Philadelphia

Jewish Federation of Delaware — community/family services ($14,000) see Kutz Foundation, Milton and Hattie

Jewish Federation of Delaware — Jewish resettlement costs ($18,500) see Kutz Foundation, Milton and Hattie

Jewish Federation of Delaware — Jewish family campus ($13,500) see Kutz Foundation, Milton and Hattie

Kalmar Nyckel Foundation — boat construction ($40,000) see duPont Foundation, Chichester

Kent-Sussex Industries — capital campaign ($75,000) see Welfare Foundation

Latin American Community Center ($25,000) see Marmot Foundation

Literacy Volunteers of America see ICI Americas

Little Sisters of the Poor — general support ($50,000) see Solo Cup Co.

Long Term Research Project ($10,000) see Gerard Foundation, Sumner

Middlesex School ($6,000) see Gerard Foundation, Sumner

Middletown-Odessa-Townsend Senior Center — capital campaign ($100,000) see Welfare Foundation

Milford Public Library ($8,334) see Dentsply International, Inc.

Milford Public Library Building Fund ($8,500) see Wilmington Trust Co.

Milton and Hattie Kutz Home — architectural plans ($5,500) see Kutz Foundation, Milton and Hattie

Ministry of Caring — distribution center ($135,000) see Crystal Trust

Ministry of Caring ($50,000) see Good Samaritan

Museum Trustee Association 1991 Fall Conference ($8,500) see Wilmington Trust Co.

Neighborhood House of South Wilmington ($25,000) see Marmot Foundation

Newark Day Nursery ($8,500) see Wilmington Trust Co.

Operation Help ($15,000) see O'Neil Foundation, W.

Opportunity Center — capital campaign ($25,000) see Crestlea Foundation

Opportunity Center — new building ($260,000) see Crystal Trust

Opportunity Center — capital expansion ($50,000) see Laffey-McHugh Foundation

Opportunity Center — capital campaign ($800,000) see Longwood Foundation

Opportunity Center — capital campaign ($100,000) see Welfare Foundation

Peninsula United Methodist Homes and Hospitals ($9,000) see Borkee Hagley Foundation

Pilot School — operating deficits ($137,500) see Crystal Trust

Pilot School — endowment fund ($50,000) see duPont Foundation, Chichester

Planned Parenthood Federation of America ($25,000) see Crestlea Foundation

Polish Assistance ($2,000) see Gerard Foundation, Sumner

Read-Aloud Delaware see ICI Americas

Rehoboth Kiwanis Club ($15,000) see McGregor Foundation, Thomas and Frances

St. Andre's School — construction of swimming pool ($150,000) see duPont Foundation, Chichester

St. Andrew's School ($25,000) see Crestlea Foundation

St. Francis Hospital — mobile health van ($75,000) see Crystal Trust

St. Michaels Day Nursery ($15,000) see Good Samaritan

Salvation Army ($2,722) see Downs Perpetual Charitable Trust, Ellason

Delaware (cont.)

Salvation Army ($40,000) see Laffey-McHugh Foundation

SPCA ($25,000) see Crestlea Foundation

Technoserve ($3,250) see Gerard Foundation, Sumner

United Negro College Fund — annual campaign ($38,000) see Laffey-McHugh Foundation

United Thank Offering ($2,722) see Downs Perpetual Charitable Trust, Ellason

United Way ($6,000) see Dentsply International, Inc.

United Way ($2,722) see Downs Perpetual Charitable Trust, Ellason

United Way of Delaware — capital campaign ($21,000) see Crestlea Foundation

United Way of Delaware — annual campaign ($165,000) see Laffey-McHugh Foundation

United Way of Delaware ($24,750) see Westvaco Corp.

University of Delaware — baseball program ($5,000) see Carpenter Foundation

University of Delaware — gallery exhibition ($30,000) see Crestlea Foundation

University of Delaware — chemistry building ($700,000) see Crystal Trust

University of Delaware — for internships ($250,000) see Getty Trust, J. Paul

University of Delaware — program expansion ($1,080,000) see Longwood Foundation

University of Delaware ($58,375) see Lynch Scholarship Foundation, John B.

University of Delaware ($25,000) see Marmot Foundation

University of Delaware ($100,000) see Pioneer Fund

University of Delaware ($69,000) see SICO Foundation

University of Delaware ($10,500) see Wilmington Trust Co.

University of Delaware — expand Colburn lab ($25,000) see Air Products & Chemicals

University of Delaware Convocation Center ($100,000) see Carpenter Foundation

University Delaware Library Association ($2,722) see Downs Perpetual Charitable Trust, Ellason

University of Delaware — Olympic Arena ($50,000) see Carpenter Foundation

Ursuline Academy — capital expansion ($100,000) see Laffey-McHugh Foundation

We Care in Delaware ($5,000) see Carpenter Foundation

Wesley College ($8,000) see Wilmington Trust Co.

Williams College Alumni Fund ($10,000) see Brown, Jr. Charitable Trust, Frank D.

Wilmington College — automation of the library ($320,000) see Crystal Trust

Wilmington Firefighters Benevolence Fund ($2,722) see Downs Perpetual Charitable Trust, Ellason

Wilmington Friends School ($10,000) see Borkee Hagley Foundation

Wilmington Garden Center — capital campaign ($75,000) see Welfare Foundation

Wilmington Garden Center ($5,000) see Williams Foundation, C. K.

Wilmington Institute ($10,000) see Curran Foundation

Wilmington Montessori School — new addition ($100,000) see Crystal Trust

Wilmington Senior Center — to support the Tenant Survival Project ($190,000) see duPont Fund, Jessie Ball

Winterthur — naming of second floor central hall in new exhibition ($200,000) see Kirby Foundation, F. M.

Winterthur Museum and Gardens ($10,000) see Brown, Jr. Charitable Trust, Frank D.

Winterthur Museum and Gardens ($5,000) see Hopkins Foundation, John Jay

Winterthur Museum and Gardens ($15,000) see Kingsley Foundation

Winterthur Museum and Gardens — for construction of exhibition building ($1,000,000) see Kresge Foundation

Winterthur Museum and Gardens — capital expansion ($50,000) see Laffey-McHugh Foundation

Winterthur Museum and Gardens ($25,000) see Marmot Foundation

Winterthur Museum and Gardens ($10,000) see Osborn Charitable Trust, Edward B.

Winterthur Museum and Gardens ($17,000) see Wilmington Trust Co.

YMCA ($15,000) see Davis Charitable Foundation, Champion McDowell

Youth Missions to Israel ($2,000) see Kutz Foundation, Milton and Hattie

YWCA of New Castle County see ICI Americas

District of Columbia

A.G.C. Education and Research Foundation ($25,000) see Boh Brothers Construction Co.

Academy of Natural Sciences — Chesapeake Bay Project ($10,000) see Freed Foundation

Accuracy in Media ($25,000) see Aequus Institute

Accuracy in Media ($120,000) see Carthage Foundation

Accuracy in Media ($10,000) see Davis Foundation, Shelby Cullom

ACP-Project Vote ($1,000) see Herald News

Adas Israel Congregation ($43,071) see Gelman Foundation, Melvin and Estelle

Adas Israel Congregation ($10,000) see Goldman Foundation, Aaron and Cecile

Adas Israel Mens Club ($1,000) see Wasserman Foundation, George

Adhesive and Sealant Council Education Foundation ($35,000) see National Starch & Chemical Corp.

Adhesive and Sealant Council Education Foundation — advancement grants ($35,000)

see National Starch & Chemical Corp.

Aesculapius International Medicine ($15,000) see Greenville Foundation

African Continuum Theatre Coalition ($1,000) see Best Products Co.

African Wildlife Foundation ($36,000) see Chadwick Fund, Dorothy Jordan

African Wildlife Foundation ($22,000) see Fair Play Foundation

African Wildlife Foundation ($60,000) see Moores Foundation

African Wildlife Foundation ($5,000) see Salwil Foundation

African Wildlife Foundation — in support of "Neighbors as Partners" project ($10,000) see Bedminster Fund

Africare — career development internship program ($500,201) see IBM South Africa Projects Fund

Africare ($10,000) see LeBrun Foundation

Agricultural Cooperative Development International ($4,800) see CENEX

Alexander Graham Bell Foundation for the Deaf ($5,000) see LBJ Family Foundation

Alexander Graham Bell Foundation for the Deaf ($300,000) see Oberkotter Family Foundation

Allen Chapel Outreach Center — food program and social worker salary ($28,000) see Abell Foundation, Charles S.

Allen Community Outreach Center ($45,000) see Penzance Foundation

Alliance to Save Energy ($2,500) see Thermo Electron Corp.

American Architectural Foundation ($15,000) see Brady Foundation, W. H.

American Architectural Foundation — restoration of Octagon historical building ($250,000) see Buell Foundation, Temple Hoyne

American Association for the Advancement of Science ($250,000) see Bell Atlantic Corp.

American Association for the Advancement of Science see du Pont de Nemours & Co., E. I.

American Association for the Advancement of Science — to explore barriers in engineering education for disabled students and to identify technolgy that gives them easier access to education ($40,000) see NEC USA

American Association of Colleges of Nursing — for annual John P. McGovern Award ($22,000) see McGovern Fund for the Behavioral Sciences

American Cancer Society ($25,606) see Gelman Foundation, Melvin and Estelle

American Cancer Society — cancer aid plan ($110,000) see Stewart Trust under the will of Mary E. Stewart, Alexander and Margaret

American Chemical Society ($40,000) see Dow Corning Corp.

American Chemical Society ($50,000) see Hoechst Celanese Corp.

American Chemical Society ($25,000) see National Starch & Chemical Corp.

American Chemical Society "Campaign for Chemistry" ($20,000) see Hoffmann-La Roche

American Civil Liberties Union Foundation — for the prison and jail litigation activities of the National Prison Project ($505,000) see Clark Foundation, Edna McConnell

American College of Nurse-Midwives — to assist midwives in training for medical assistance in Ghana ($60,798) see Williams, Jr. Family Foundation, A. L.

American Council for Capital Formation — support for ACCF's Center for Policy Research see Ameritech Corp.

American Council on Germany ($100) see Volkswagen of America, Inc.

American Council of Life Insurance — medical research fund ($2,500) see Ohio National Life Insurance Co.

American Defense Institute ($10,000) see Woods Foundation, James H.

American Diabetes Association see Crestar Financial Corp.

American Diabetes Association ($30,000) see Hagedorn Fund

American Diabetes Foundation ($22,000) see Smith Foundation, Lon V.

American Education Trust, Library Endowment ($7,500) see Lea Foundation, Helen Sperry

American Enterprise Institute ($20,000) see Blount

American Enterprise Institute ($1,000,000) see Brady Foundation, W. H.

American Enterprise Institute see du Pont de Nemours & Co., E. I.

American Enterprise Institute ($45,000) see FMC Corp.

American Enterprise Institute ($10,900) see Fuqua Foundation, J. B.

American Enterprise Institute ($5,000) see Johnson Foundation, Willard T. C.

American Enterprise Institute — policy research ($250,000) see Monell Foundation, Ambrose

American Enterprise Institute ($500,000) see Potlatch Corp.

American Enterprise Institute — general ($65,000) see Potlatch Corp.

American Enterprise Institute ($78,000) see Randolph Foundation

American Enterprise Institute ($500) see Simpson Industries

American Enterprise Institute — to support a study of the international economic, social, and political effects of American popular culture ($100,000) see Donner Foundation, William H.

American Enterprise Institute for Public Policy Research — to support general program activities ($350,000) see Bradley Foundation, Lynde and Harry

American Enterprise Institute for Public Policy Research

($100,000) see Chase Manhattan Bank, N.A.

American Enterprise Institute for Public Policy Research ($25,000) see JM Foundation

American Enterprise Institute for Public Policy Research ($40,000) see NBD Bank

American Enterprise Institute for Public Policy Research ($50,000) see Rose Foundation, Billy

American Enterprise Institute for Public Policy Research ($100,000) see SmithKline Beecham

American Enterprise Institute for Public Policy Research see United Airlines

American Enterprise Institute for Public Policy Research — for preparation of a book on the Bill of Rights ($50,000) see Earhart Foundation

American Enterprise Institute for Public Policy Research, Washington, D.C. see Kmart Corp.

American Environment ($25,000) see Beldon Fund

American Farmland Trust ($25,000) see Clayton Fund

American Farmland Trust — to continue programs to protect farmlands through the expansion of conservation agreements and easements ($750,000) see Mellon Foundation, Richard King

American Farmland Trust ($50,000) see Wallace Genetic Foundation

American Farmland Trust — continued support for the membership development component of the organization's five-year capital campaign ($1,000,000) see Rockefeller Brothers Fund

American Federation of Teachers Educational Foundation ($20,000) see Banyan Tree Foundation

American Film Institute ($40,000) see Bohen Foundation

American Film Institute ($40,000) see CBS Inc.

American Film Institute ($7,500) see Rosenthal Foundation, Richard and Hinda

American Forestry Association see Alpert & Co., Inc., Herman

American Forestry Association ($100,000) see Texaco

American Forestry Association — Reforestation Program see Discovery Channel/Cable Education Network

American Heart Association ($10,000) see Steele Foundation

American Inns of Court Foundation — general fund ($20,000) see Stuart Center Charitable Trust, Hugh

American Institute for Contemporary German Studies ($100) see Volkswagen of America, Inc.

American Institute for Contemporary German Studies — disbursed over three years (from Daimler-Benz G.m.b.H., Stuttgart) ($120,000) see Mercedes-Benz of North America, Inc.

American Institute of Public Service ($25,000) see Heinz Family Foundation

American-Israel Friendship League ($20,000) see

Gudelsky Family Foundation, Isadore and Bertha

American-Israel Friendship League ($7,500) see Meyer Fund, Milton and Sophie

American Legislative Exchange Council — renewed operating support ($100,000) see Allegheny Foundation

American Legislative Exchange Council — support for research and analysis programs for state legislators see Ameritech Corp.

American Legislative Exchange Council ($25,000) see JM Foundation

American Legislative Exchange Council ($10,000) see Vollrath Co.

American Legislative Exchange Council ($10,000) see Vollrath Co.

American Mental Health Fund see Crestar Financial Corp.

American Museum of Natural History see Bank of New York

American Museum of Natural History see Freeport-McMoRan

American Museum of Natural History ($100,000) see Klingenstein Fund, Esther A. and Joseph

American National Red Cross see American Express Co.

American National Red Cross Disaster Relief Fund ($150,000) see Aetna Life & Casualty Co.

American National Red Cross — Gulf Crisis Fund ($25,000) see Fluor Corp.

American Political Science Association — sponsor participation in APSA''s Congressional Fellowship Program ($40,000) see Poynter Fund

American Red Cross ($500,000) see Andreas Foundation

American Red Cross see Capital Holding Corp.

American Red Cross see Coors Brewing Co.

American Red Cross ($40,000) see Davenport-Hatch Foundation

American Red Cross ($5,000) see Lindsay Foundation

American Red Cross ($100,000) see Norfolk Southern Corp.

American Red Cross ($1,000) see Salgo Charitable Trust, Nicholas M.

American Red Cross ($1,498) see Smith Foundation, Gordon V. and Helen C.

American Red Cross ($5,000) see Van Nuys Charities, J. B. and Emily

American Red Cross — support for the American Red Cross Disaster Relief Fund see Ameritech Corp.

American Red Cross Disaster Relief Fund ($250,000) see Metropolitan Life Insurance Co.

American Red Cross, District of Columbia Chapter — general support ($30,000) see Clark-Winchcole Foundation

American Red Cross-Gulf Crisis ($250,000) see American Financial Corp.

American Red Cross Gulf Crisis Fund ($100,000) see Borden

American Red Cross (National Headquarters) ($300,000) see Mobil Oil Corp.

American Rivers ($30,000) see Dunn Foundation, Elizabeth Ordway

American Rivers ($15,000) see Goldman Charitable Trust, Sol

American Rivers ($10,000) see Harder Foundation

American Rivers ($25,000) see Town Creek Foundation

American Society of Newspaper Editors Foundation — renewed support ($50,000) see Freedom Forum

American Symphony Orchestra League ($200,000) see Whitaker Fund, Helen F.

American University ($25,000) see Abramson Family Foundation

American University ($100,000) see Bender Foundation

American University — education ($30,000) see Clark-Winchcole Foundation

American University ($50,000) see Daly Charitable Foundation Trust, Robert and Nancy

American University ($11,000) see Dart Group Corp.

American University ($2,000) see Fortis Inc.

American University ($2,000) see Fortis Inc.

American University ($1,000) see Fortis Inc.

American University ($30,000) see Loughran Foundation, Mary and Daniel

American University ($10,000) see Summerfield Foundation, Solon E.

American University ($10,000) see Tauber Foundation

Americans for Peace Now ($20,000) see HKH Foundation

America's Clean Water Foundation ($40,000) see Union Camp Corp.

Amnesty International ($4,000) see Flemm Foundation, John J.

Amnesty International ($500) see Foster Foundation, Joseph C. and Esther

Amnesty International ($20,000) see North Shore Foundation

Amnesty International ($2,000) see See Foundation, Charles

Amnesty International ($10,000) see Von der Ahe, Jr. Trust, Theodore Albert

Anacostia/Congress Heights Partnership — expansion of outreach and case management services to families at risk of homelessness in the Sheridan Terrace, Barry Farms and Congress Park developments in Ward 8 ($60,000) see Meyer Foundation, Eugene and Agnes E.

Anacostia Coordinating Council — neighborhood planning enrichment course for 8th and 9th graders at Kramer Junior High School ($6,000) see Strong Foundation, Hattie M.

ANERA ($1,000) see Foundation for Middle East Peace

Animal Welfare Institute ($15,000) see Wouk Foundation, Abe

Anthony Bowen Landmark Building Trust — to restore and redevelop the historic Anthony Bowen Landmark Building ($50,000) see Meyer Foundation, Eugene and Agnes E.

Anti-Defamation League ($5,000) see Lehrman

Foundation, Jacob and Charlotte

Anti-Defamation League of B'nai B'rith ($7,000) see Polinger Foundation, Howard and Geraldine

Archdiocese of Washington ($30,000) see Loughran Foundation, Mary and Daniel

Archdiocese of Washington ($10,000) see Tauber Foundation

Archdiocese of Washington — Bowie Farm ($30,000) see Loughran Foundation, Mary and Daniel

Arena Stage ($5,000) see Bernstein Foundation, Diane and Norman

Arena Stage ($350,000) see Cafritz Foundation, Morris and Gwendolyn

Arena Stage ($2,000) see Kaplan Foundation, Charles I. and Mary

Arena Stage ($6,000) see McGregor Foundation, Thomas and Frances

Arena Stage Guild ($20,000) see Hill-Snowdon Foundation

Armenian Assembly ($45,500) see Philibosian Foundation, Stephen

Armenian Assembly of America ($156,300) see Hovnanian Foundation, Hirair and Anna

Arms Control Association ($30,000) see Greve Foundation, William and Mary

Arms Control Association ($50,000) see Kendall Foundation, Henry P.

Arms Control Association — inform the media, Congress and specialist community of current arms control and disarmament initiatives through ACA's press program and the publication Arms Control Today ($220,000) see Jones Foundation, W. Alton

Art Services International ($10,000) see Dimick Foundation

Ashoka ($40,000) see Zlinkoff Fund for Medical Research and Education, Sergei S.

Aspen Institute ($100,000) see Gordon/Rousmaniere/Roberts Fund

Aspen Institute ($62,500) see Reynolds Foundation, Christopher

ASPIRA Association ($50,000) see Borden

ASPIRA Association — internships for Public Policy Leadership Program ($160,000) see Toyota Motor Sales, U.S.A.

Association of American Medical Colleges (AAMC) — to create the first national database on minority physicians ($490,000) see Kaiser Family Foundation, Henry J.

Association for Community Based Education — to support comprehensive literacy instructor training programs for community based organizations in eight communities see United Parcel Service of America

Association for Community Based Education — partial support of a mini-grant program in functional literacy ($100,000) see Donner Foundation, William H.

Association of Performing Arts Presenters ($1,000,000) see Wallace Reader's Digest Fund, Lila

Association of Performing Arts Presenters ($1,000,000) see Wallace Reader's Digest Fund, Lila

Association of Science-Technology Centers see du Pont de Nemours & Co., E. I.

Atlantic Council of the United States ($25,000) see Harriman Foundation, Mary W.

B. Bush Foundation for Literacy ($100,000) see O'Donnell Foundation

Barbara Bush Foundation for Family Literacy ($25,000) see Cook Foundation

Barbara Bush Foundation for Family Literacy ($25,000) see Cook Foundation, Louella

Barbara Bush Foundation for Family Literacy see Merrill Lynch & Co.

Barbara Bush Foundation for Family Literacy ($200,000) see Newhouse Foundation, Samuel I.

Barbara Bush Foundation for Family Literacy — general support ($500,000) see RJR Nabisco Inc.

Bell Multicultural High School (ADVANCE) — evening prevention dropout program ($12,500) see Strong Foundation, Hattie M.

Benedictine School for Handicapped Children ($20,000) see Loughran Foundation, Mary and Daniel

Bens Education Fund ($10,000) see Beidler Charitable Trust, Francis

Bens Education Fund ($17,500) see Salomon Foundation, Richard & Edna

Best Buddies of America — matching people with mental retardation with college students as buddies ($51,978) see Kennedy, Jr. Foundation, Joseph P.

Better World Society ($10,000) see Manitou Foundation

Bicycle Federation of America — energy and transportation ($125,000) see Bullitt Foundation

Black Student Fund see Crestar Financial Corp.

Blind Awareness Project ($10,000) see Aid Association for the Blind

B'nai B'rith ($1,000) see Wasserman Foundation, George

B'nai B'rith Hillel Foundations ($60,000) see Meyerhoff Fund, Joseph

B'nai Israel — Cemetery ($10,000) see Kaplan Foundation, Charles I. and Mary

Boy Scouts of America ($12,000) see Memton Fund

Boy Scouts of America ($25,000) see Ross Foundation, Walter G.

Boy Scouts of America ($2,500) see Smith Foundation, Gordon V. and Helen C.

Boys Clubs of Washington, D.C. ($10,000) see Appleby Foundation

Boys and Girls Club ($70,000) see Fowler Memorial Foundation, John Edward

Boys and Girls Club ($3,708) see Smith Foundation, Gordon V. and Helen C.

Boys and Girls Club ($8,500) see Strong Foundation, Hattie M.

Boys and Girls Club ($5,000) see Willard Foundation, Helen Parker

Bread for the City — distribution of food and clothing to poor of the city ($10,000) see Abell Foundation, Charles S.

Bread for the World Institute ($15,000) see Greenville Foundation

British-American Arts Association — general support of donee ($35,000) see Hammer Foundation, Armand

Brookings Institute ($25,000) see Cabot Family Charitable Trust

Brookings Institute ($10,000) see CertainTeed Corp.

Brookings Institute ($35,000) see Friedman Foundation, Stephen and Barbara

Brookings Institute ($5,000) see Gottesman Fund

Brookings Institute ($59,500) see Lurcy Charitable and Educational Trust, Georges

Brookings Institute ($25,800) see Milstein Family Foundation

Brookings Institute ($10,000) see Walker Educational and Charitable Foundation, Alex C.

Brookings Institution ($40,000) see Cabot Corp.

Brookings Institution ($25,000) see Harriman Foundation, Mary W.

Brookings Institution see International Paper Co.

Brookings Institution see Merrill Lynch & Co.

Brookings Institution — support for Brookings 75th Anniversary Campaign see Ameritech Corp.

Business Executives for National Security ($25,000) see Smeal Foundation, Mary Jean & Frank P.

Business Higher Education Forum ($17,500) see Cabot Corp.

Business and Professional Women's Foundation — special project ($62,500) see New York Life Insurance Co.

C.I.S.P.E.S. Education Fund ($29,000) see Prickett Fund, Lynn R. and Karl E.

C-Media ($1,000) see Neese Family Foundation

Camp Himmelfarb ($15,000) see Himmelfarb Foundation, Paul and Annetta

Campaign for New Priorities — Partnership for Democracy - to mobilize public and institutional support for transferring funds from military budget to domestic needs ($50,000) see Arca Foundation

Cancer Research Institute ($25,000) see Blum Foundation, Edith C.

Capital Area Health Foundation ($25,000) see Kline Foundation, Josiah W. and Bessie H.

Capital Research Center — research library ($25,000) see McKenna Foundation, Philip M.

Capital Research Center ($10,000) see Roe Foundation

District of Columbia (cont.)

Capital Research Center ($8,000) see Sunmark Capital Corp.

Cardinal's Appeal for Charity ($4,000) see Straus Foundation, Martha Washington Straus and Harry H.

Carnegie Endowment for International Peace — projects on nonproliferation and regional security ($800,000) see Carnegie Corporation of New York

Carnegie Institute of Washington ($90,000) see Flintridge Foundation

Carnegie Institute of Washington ($35,000) see Massey Charitable Trust

Carnegie Institute of Washington ($650,000) see Monell Foundation, Ambrose

Carnegie Institute of Washington ($250,000) see Weinberg, Jr. Foundation, Sidney J.

Carnegie Institute of Washington ($25,000) see Weinberg, Jr. Foundation, Sidney J.

Carnegie Institution of Washington ($30,000) see Allen Foundation, Rita

Catholic University — education ($30,000) see Clark-Winchcole Foundation

Catholic University ($5,000) see McMahon Charitable Trust Fund, Father John J.

Catholic University ($100,000) see McShain Charities, John

Catholic University ($35,000) see Mullen Foundation, J. K.

Catholic University ($25,000) see Paulucci Family Foundation

Catholic University of America ($2,000) see Copernicus Society of America

Catholic University of America — capital expansion ($50,000) see Laffey-McHugh Foundation

Catholic University of America ($11,000) see Ontario Corp.

Catholic University of America ($10,000) see O'Sullivan Children Foundation

Catholic University of America ($10,000) see Ritter Foundation, May Ellen and Gerald

Catholic University of America ($14,500) see Rotterman Trust, Helen L. and Marie F.

Catholics for a Free Choice — expand utilization of actions speak ($20,000) see Brush Foundation

Catholics for a Free Choice ($100,000) see Sunnen Foundation

Cato Institute ($50,000) see Cain Foundation, Gordon and Mary

CATO Institute ($15,000) see Connemara Fund

Cato Institute ($200,000) see Koch Charitable Foundation, Charles G.

CATO Institute ($1,500,000) see Koch Charitable Trust, David H.

CATO Institute ($250,000) see Koch Charitable Trust, David H.

Cato Institute — general ($400,000) see Lambe Charitable Foundation, Claude R.

Cato Institute ($250,000) see Lambe Charitable Foundation, Claude R.

Cato Institute ($150,000) see Lambe Charitable Foundation, Claude R.

CATO Institute ($25,000) see Seid Foundation, Barre

CATO Institute ($50,000) see Tamko Asphalt Products

CATO Institute ($10,000) see Walker Educational and Charitable Foundation, Alex C.

CATO Institute ($35,000) see Waters Foundation

Center for the Book ($100) see HarperCollins Publishers

Center on Budget and Policy Priorities ($10,000) see Friedman Family Foundation

Center on Budget and Policy Priorities — improve coordination among federal programs for children ($175,000) see Prudential Insurance Co. of America

Center on Budget and Policy Priorities ($150,000) see Public Welfare Foundation

Center on Budget and Policy Priorities — to develop public policy initiatives on a wide range of issues affecting low-income people ($30,000) see Rockefeller Family Fund

Center for Community Change ($25,000) see Prince Trust, Abbie Norman

Center for Community Change — general support for this national technical assistance/policy/advocacy organization ($125,000) see Surdna Foundation

Center for Community Change — assistance and training for community-based organizations ($100,000) see Federal National Mortgage Assn., Fannie Mae

Center for Community Change — support to provide technical assistance for local community development organizations in the Great Lakes region see Ameritech Corp.

Center for Community Change — in support of the Housing Trust Fund ($20,000) see Taconic Foundation

Center for Community Change/National CRA Coalition — establishment of a national coalition ($163,000) see Surdna Foundation

Center for Defense Information ($50,000) see Glickenhaus & Co.

Center for Defense Information ($2,500) see Schecter Private Foundation, Aaron and Martha

Center for Democracy ($5,000) see Fruehauf Foundation

Center for Democracy ($25,000) see Furth Foundation

Center for Democracy ($25,000) see Furth Foundation

Center for Democracy ($25,000) see Furth Foundation

Center for Democracy ($25,000) see Furth Foundation

Center for Democracy ($25,000) see Furth Foundation

Center for Development and Population Activities ($25,000) see Bergstrom Foundation, Erik E. and Edith H.

Center for Development and Population Activities — support options for a better life program ($20,000) see Brush Foundation

Center for Immigration Studies — support for International Immigration Seminary ($30,000) see Laurel Foundation

Center for International Policy ($50,000) see General Service Foundation

Center for International Policy ($3,000) see Mott Charitable Trust/Spectemur Agendo, Stewart R.

Center for International Policy ($10,000) see Rubin Foundation, Samuel

Center of International Policy ($5,000) see Schecter Private Foundation, Aaron and Martha

Center for Law and Social Policy — activities to increase FSA benefits for at-risk children and their families ($75,000) see Foundation for Child Development

Center for Marine Conservation ($25,000) see Beneficia Foundation

Center for Marine Conservation ($50,000) see Homeland Foundation

Center for Marine Conservation ($50,000) see Homeland Foundation

Center for Marine Conservation ($20,000) see Kettering Family Foundation

Center for Marine Conservation ($20,000) see Seebee Trust, Frances

Center for Marine Conservation — to conserve marine biological diversity and improve fisheries conservation and management ($125,000) see Surdna Foundation

Center for Marine Conservation ($25,000) see Town Creek Foundation

Center for Marine Conservation see Waste Management

Center for Marine Conservation ($10,000) see Weiss Foundation, William E.

Center for Marine Conservation — California marine debris action plan ($25,000) see True North Foundation

Center for Marine Conservation — N.J. Marine Debris Project ($10,000) see Freed Foundation

Center for Media and Public Affairs ($10,000) see Davis Foundation, Shelby Cullom

Center of National Labor Policy ($25,000) see Sunmark Capital Corp.

Center for National Policy ($5,000) see Blinken Foundation

Center for National Policy ($67,275) see Claiborne Art Ortenberg Foundation, Liz

Center for National Policy ($5,000) see Gruss Petroleum Corp.

Center for National Policy ($20,000) see Rubin Foundation, Rob E. & Judith O.

Center for Policy Alternatives — for the center's sustainable development program ($225,000) see Rockefeller Brothers Fund

Center for Policy Alternatives — to support the Collaborative Project on Reproductive Health ($100,000) see Cummings Foundation, Nathan

Center for Population Options ($20,000) see Bergstrom Foundation, Erik E. and Edith H.

Center for Population Options ($30,000) see Tortuga Foundation

Center for Population Options — AIDS Prevention Project ($15,000) see Freed Foundation

Center to Prevent Handgun Violence ($15,000) see Dreyfus Foundation, Jean and Louis

Center to Prevent Handgun Violence ($5,000) see Norman Foundation, Andrew

Center for Public Integrity ($15,000) see Deer Creek Foundation

Center for Public Integrity ($25,000) see Stern Family Fund

Center for Responsive Politics — support ($200,000) see Schumann Foundation, Florence and John

Center for Responsive Politics — for the Center's Federal Election Commission Watch ($50,000) see Arca Foundation

Center for Responsive Politics — for the "Money in Politics Connection" project ($30,000) see Rockefeller Family Fund

Center for Security Policy ($25,000) see Aequus Institute

Center for Sight ($75,000) see Aid Association for the Blind

Center for Strategic and International Studies ($50,000) see Archer-Daniels-Midland Co.

Center for Strategic and International Studies ($50,000) see BDM International

Center for Strategic and International Studies ($55,000) see de Rothschild Foundation, Edmond

Center for Strategic and International Studies ($50,000) see FMC Corp.

Center for Strategic International Studies ($5,000) see Salgo Charitable Trust, Nicholas M.

Center for Strategic and International Studies ($353,000) see Scaife Foundation, Sarah

Center for Strategic and International Studies — renewed support ($500,000) see Starr Foundation

Center for Strategic and International Studies — funding to support Quadrangular Forum ($200,000) see Scholl Foundation, Dr.

Center for the Study of Responsive Law — education ($200,000) see Hoffman Foundation, Maximillian E. and Marion O.

Center for the Study of Social Policy — to support technical assistance for states implementing family preservation services ($495,000) see Clark Foundation, Edna McConnell

Center for the Study of Social Policy — child welfare reform, New Futures evaluation ($2,798,240) see Casey Foundation, Annie E.

Center for Teaching Peace ($14,500) see Lea Foundation, Helen Sperry

Center for Youth Services ($20,000) see Fowler Memorial Foundation, John Edward

Central Union Mission ($10,000) see Willard Foundation, Helen Parker

Centre for Development and Population Activities — family planning project in Peru ($10,000) see Campbell and Adah E. Hall Charity Fund, Bushrod H.

Cetner for the Study of Commercialism — public awareness ($25,000) see Hoffman Foundation, Maximillian E. and Marion O.

Chesapeake Bay Foundation ($20,000) see Marpat Foundation

Children's Defense Fund ($10,000) see Baker Trust, Clayton

Children's Defense Fund ($45,000) see Bleibtreu Foundation, Jacob

Children's Defense Fund see Bloomingdale's

Children's Defense Fund ($30,000) see Grant Foundation, Charles M. and Mary D.

Children's Defense Fund ($25,000) see Hughes Memorial Foundation, Charles Evans

Children's Defense Fund ($5,000) see Kautz Family Foundation

Children's Defense Fund ($30,000) see Merck Family Fund

Children's Defense Fund ($40,000) see Primerica Corp.

Children's Defense Fund — to support the Crusade for Children/Challenge to the Community ($1,000,000) see Schumann Foundation, Florence and John

Children's Defense Fund — health-related portion of the Black Community Crusade for Children ($371,767) see Kaiser Family Foundation, Henry J.

Children's Defense Fund — provides technical assistance to states and helps ensure that low-income children receive the full benefit of new federal child care and Head Start funds ($30,000) see Rockefeller Family Fund

Children's Defense Fund — helping states take advantage of federal child care and Medicaid legislation ($75,000) see Foundation for Child Development

Children's Hospital see Banner Life Insurance Co.

Children's Hospital see Booz Allen & Hamilton

Children's Hospital ($10,950) see Crown Books Foundation, Inc.

Children's Hospital National medical Center — AIDS diagnostic and care center ($200,000) see Stewart Trust under the will of Helen S. Devore, Alexander and Margaret

Children's Hospital National Medical Center ($15,000) see Brownley Trust, Walter

Children's Hospital National Medical Center — cancer care program ($292,000) see Stewart Trust under the will of

Helen S. Devore, Alexander and Margaret

Children's Hospital Research Foundation ($100,000) see Nationwide Insurance Cos.

Children's National Medical Center ($5,000) see Bernstein Foundation, Diane and Norman

Children's National Medical Center see Johnson & Johnson

Children's Oncology Center ($25,000) see Shapiro, Inc.

Choral Arts Society of Washington — support the arts ($30,000) see Clark-Winchcole Foundation

Choral Arts Society of Washington ($1,750) see Crown Books Foundation, Inc.

Choral Arts Society of Washington ($9,500) see Dart Group Corp.

Christian Anti-Communism Crusade ($10,000) see Sunmark Capital Corp.

Christian College Coalition ($10,000) see Westwood Endowment

Christmas in April ($3,000) see Garvey Trust, Olive White

Christmas in April — for projects across the United States see Home Depot

Christmas Pageant of Peace — support world peace ($30,000) see Clark-Winchcole Foundation

Christmas Pageant of Peace ($20,000) see Dimick Foundation

Christopher Columbus Quincentennary ($20,000) see Decio Foundation, Arthur J.

Church of the Epiphany ($5,000) see Baird Brothers Co.

Churches Center for Theology and Public Policy ($5,000) see Woods-Greer Foundation

Cities in Schools ($160,000) see Alpert Foundation, Herb

Cities in Schools ($65,000) see Capital Cities/ABC

Cities in Schools — toward the training center for CIS and for programs in New Jersey ($200,000) see Dodge Foundation, Geraldine R.

Citizens for Congressional Reform Foundation ($125,000) see Koch Charitable Trust, David H.

Citizens for Congressional Reform Foundation — general ($175,000) see Lambe Charitable Foundation, Claude R.

Citizens for Constitutional Concerns ($100,000) see Common Giving Fund

Citizens for Constitutional Concerns ($95,000) see Common Giving Fund

Citizens Fund — to study the influence of special interest money in politics and conduct a public education campaign on the need for reform ($100,000) see Arca Foundation

Citizens for a Sound Economy Foundation ($1,000) see Eberly Foundation

Citizens for a Sound Economy Foundation ($250,000) see Koch Charitable Trust, David H.

Citizens for a Sound Economy Foundation ($250,000) see Koch Charitable Trust, David H.

Citizens for a Sound Economy Foundation — general

($300,000) see Lambe Charitable Foundation, Claude R.

City Lights — renovation costs for the school program which serves emotionally disturbed adolescents ($50,000) see Meyer Foundation, Eugene and Agnes E.

City Lights School ($10,000) see Fowler Memorial Foundation, John Edward

City Lights School — high school for emotionally disturbed children; support fundraiser position ($50,000) see Arcana Foundation

Clean Water Fund — to protect groundwater by strengthening and expanding grassroots organizing in the southern tier of the United States ($55,000) see Noyes Foundation, Jessie Smith

Climate Institute — for general support ($50,000) see Bingham Foundation, William

College of Preachers ($20,000) see Chisholm Foundation

Columbia Hospital for Women ($15,000) see Brownley Trust, Walter

Columbia Hospital for Women Foundation ($10,000) see IMCERA Group Inc.

Columbia Hospital for Women (Teen Health Center) — health education outreach program providing classes and workshops to DC schools and the community, targeting young women ages 13-19 ($7,500) see Strong Foundation, Hattie M.

Columbia Road Health Services ($20,000) see Fowler Memorial Foundation, John Edward

Commission on Peace ($2,000) see Foundation for Middle East Peace

Commission on Presidential Debates — educational programs and preparation for 1992 debates ($125,000) see Prudential Insurance Co. of America

Committee on the Constitution System ($10,000) see Oakleaf Foundation

Committee of Peace ($4,000) see Sexton Foundation

Committee for the Restoration of Treasury Building ($125,000) see Darby Foundation

Committee for the Study of the American Electorate — research on constitutional alternatives to present system of unregulated political advertising on television ($2,500) see Benton Foundation

Communications Consortium — for series of four regional media training and strategy workshops ($20,000) see Benton Foundation

Communications Consortium ($40,000) see Huber Foundation

Communications Consortium ($50,000) see Sunnen Foundation

Community of Caring — educational programs of adolescent pregnancy ($333,910) see Kennedy, Jr. Foundation, Joseph P.

Community Consortium ($5,000) see Hunt Alternatives Fund, Helen

Community for Creative Non-Violence ($25,000) see Shapiro, Inc.

Community for Creative Non-Violence ($10,000) see Von der Ahe Foundation

Community for Creative Non-Violence ($10,000) see Von der Ahe, Jr. Trust, Theodore Albert

Community Foundation for Greater Washington ($30,000) see Atlantic Foundation of New York

Community of Hope — care/treatment of sick or handicapped children ($65,000) see Stewart Trust under the will of Helen S. Devore, Alexander and Margaret

Competitive Enterprise Institute ($25,000) see Koch Charitable Foundation, Charles G.

Competitive Enterprise Institute ($7,500) see Thirty-Five Twenty, Inc.

Competitive Enterprise Institute ($15,000) see Walker Educational and Charitable Foundation, Alex C.

Concerned Women for America ($25,000) see Strake Foundation

Congregation Bar Shalom ($9,075) see McGregor Foundation, Thomas and Frances

Congress of National Black Churches ($32,000) see Hoffmann-La Roche

Congressional Cemetery ($3,100) see Bloedorn Foundation, Walter A.

Congressional Charity Golf Tournament ($2,500) see Talley Industries, Inc.

Congressional Human Rights Foundation ($20,000) see New Cycle Foundation

Connie Goldman Productions ($10,000) see Dammann Fund

Conservation International ($35,000) see Beneficia Foundation

Conservation International ($10,000) see Durfee Foundation

Conservation International ($225,000) see Engelhard Foundation, Charles

Conservation International ($50,000) see General Atlantic Partners L.P.

Conservation International ($250,000) see Moore Family Foundation

Conservation International ($63,000) see Overbrook Foundation

Conservation International ($5,000) see Rahr Malting Co.

Conservation International ($52,700) see Weeden Foundation, Frank

Conservation International Foundation ($25,000) see Rosenberg, Jr. Family Foundation, Louise and Claude

Conservation International Foundation — program support ($203,750) see Sequoia Foundation

Conservation International Foundation — issues of environmental and natural resource degradation in Central America ($50,000) see Tinker Foundation

Conservation International — Sea of Cortez ($40,000) see Flintridge Foundation

Consortium for Advancement of Private Higher Education — to improve funding capabilities of small private colleges through a national grant competition and special grant programs ($50,000) see NYNEX Corp.

Consumer Cooperative Development Corporation-National Cooperative Bank — initiative promoting the development of integrated systems of care for the frail elderly ($6,531,516) see Johnson Foundation, Robert Wood

Cooperative Assistance Fund — support development of small and minority-owned businesses serving low-income and minority communities ($83,000) see Guttman Foundation, Stella and Charles

Corcoran Gallery ($100,000) see Gould Foundation, Florence J.

Corcoran Gallery of Art ($28,250) see Abramson Family Foundation

Corcoran Gallery of Art ($10,000) see Dart Group Corp.

Corcoran Gallery of Art ($15,000) see Firestone Foundation, Roger S.

Corcoran Gallery of Art — publishing fund ($34,695) see Folger Fund

Corcoran Gallery of Art ($6,000) see Lehrman Foundation, Jacob and Charlotte

Corcoran Gallery of Art ($30,000) see Prince Trust, Abbie Norman

Corcoran Gallery of Art ($5,000) see Seidman Family Foundation

Corcoran Gallery of Art ($25,000) see Warhol Foundation for the Visual Arts, Andy

Corcoran Gallery of Art, Trustees of ($15,000) see Kiplinger Foundation

Corcoran Hall ($3,250) see Dart Group Corp.

Cornerstone for Tomorrow, Archdiocese of Washington ($100,000) see Casey Foundation, Eugene B.

Cosmetic, Toiletry and Fragrance Association ($45,000) see Procter & Gamble Cosmetic & Fragrance Products

Council of Ambassadors ($1,000) see Salgo Charitable Trust, Nicholas M.

Council for Basic Education ($15,000) see Chadwick Fund, Dorothy Jordan

Council on Foundations — general operating support ($2,600) see Morgan Foundation, Burton D.

Council on Foundations ($500) see Taper Foundation, Mark

Council on Foundations ($1,800) see Whiting Foundation, Mrs. Giles

Council on Foundations — in support of 1991 film and video festival ($10,000) see Benton Foundation

Council of Independent Colleges — information technologies for independent colleges - to launch project to assist small colleges take advantage of latest technological advances in access and delivery info ($62,000) see Buhl Foundation

Council for a Sound Economy Foundation ($50,000) see Tamko Asphalt Products

Crafted With Pride In USA Council ($7,613) see Stowe, Jr. Foundation, Robert Lee

Crossway Community ($5,000) see Higginson Trust, Corina

Cuban-American Committee RESearch and Education Fund — to educate the public on the humanitarian effects of U.S. economic embargo of Cuba and increase contact between Cuban-Americans and Cubans ($70,000) see Arca Foundation

D.C. Center for Citizen Education in the Law — capital campaign ($50,000) see Meyer Foundation, Eugene and Agnes E.

D.C. Housing Equity Foundation ($5,000) see Truland Foundation

D.C. Institute for Mental Health — to support a capital campaign for expansion and remodeling of facilities for mental health services ($75,000) see Graham Fund, Philip L.

D.C. Jewish Community Center ($27,360) see Gelman Foundation, Melvin and Estelle

D.C. Society for Crippled Children ($5,000) see Appleby Trust, Scott B. and Annie P.

D.C. Treas/2nd Street Shelter Project ($20,000) see Three Swallows Foundation

Dance USA ($13,000) see Ballet Makers

DC Prisoners Legal Services — HIV Education and Advocacy Program ($25,000) see Glen Eagles Foundation

Defenders of Wildlife ($150) see Linnell Foundation

Desert Storm Homecoming Foundation ($60,000) see Marriott Foundation, J. Willard

Development Corporation of Columbia Heights — pre-development costs ($50,000) see Meyer Foundation, Eugene and Agnes E.

Diplomatic Rooms Endowment Fund — special fund ($175,000) see Grainger Foundation

Direct Selling Educational Foundation ($15,000) see Scott and Fetzer Co.

Direct Selling Educational Foundation ($15,000) see Scott and Fetzer Co.

District of Columbia Bar Foundation ($5,000) see Covington and Burling

District of Columbia Hotline ($5,000) see Hill-Snowdon Foundation

District of Columbia Institute for Mental Health — care/treatment of sick or handicapped children ($100,000) see Stewart Trust under the will of Helen S. Devore, Alexander and Margaret

District of Columbia Institute of Mental Health — mental health/low-income families; Center for Family Health/92-93 budget ($75,000) see Arcana Foundation

District of Columbia Public Schools — education award ($3,600) see Washington Post Co.

District of Columbia (cont.)

District of Columbia Public Schools Foundation — renewed support ($80,000) see Freedom Forum

Dole Foundation see Oki America Inc.

Dole Foundation for the Handicapped — first payment-four year $80,000 pledge ($20,000) see Cessna Aircraft Co.

Dominican Fathers ($10,000) see Morania Foundation

Drug Policy Foundation ($150,000) see Chicago Resource Center

Drug Policy Foundation ($83,334) see Chicago Resource Center

Drug Policy Foundation ($83,334) see Chicago Resource Center

Drug Policy Foundation ($83,334) see Chicago Resource Center

Drug Policy Foundation ($40,000) see Chicago Resource Center

Drug Policy Foundation ($40,000) see Chicago Resource Center

Earth Conservation Corps ($25,000) see Union Camp Corp.

Earthwatch ($60,000) see Klingenstein Fund, Esther A. and Joseph

Easter Seal Society of DC — care/treatment of sick or handicapped children ($40,000) see Stewart Trust under the will of Helen S. Devore, Alexander and Margaret

Edmund Burke School ($9,000) see Lehrman Foundation, Jacob and Charlotte

Education for Parish Service Foundation ($15,000) see Kentland Foundation

Edward C. Mazique Parent Child Center — to establish day care centers at Hart Junior High, Dunbar and Cardozo High Schools ($160,000) see Cafritz Foundation, Morris and Gwendolyn

El Salvador Democracy Project U.S. Forum — to support Salvadoran nonprofit organizations for non-partisan voter registration and education, constitutional reform and public opinion analysis needs ($70,000) see Arca Foundation

Electronic Industries Partnership with Industry Scholarships see General Signal Corp.

Entertainment Industries Foundation CIS ($35,000) see Alpert Foundation, Herb

Environmental Defense Fund ($2,000) see Litwin Foundation

Environmental Defense Fund ($47,825) see Prickett Fund, Lynn R. and Karl E.

Environmental Defense Fund — Columbia River Basin/Salmon ($125,000) see Bullitt Foundation

Environmental and Energy Study Institute ($80,000) see Educational Foundation of America

Environmental and Energy Study Institute — to promote action to prevent global warming ($20,000) see Mertz-Gilmore Foundation, Joyce

Environmental Law Institute — partial support of project to strengthen environmental protection institutions in Latin America and the Caribbean through education and training ($60,000) see Tinker Foundation

Environmental Policy Institute ($25,000) see Beldon II Fund

Environmental Research Foundation — for technical assistance to grassroots environmental groups ($30,000) see Rockefeller Family Fund

Environmental Support Center ($15,000) see Beldon Fund

Environmental Support Center — to strengthen state environmental groups by providing coordinated fundraising and technical assistance ($40,000) see Rockefeller Family Fund

Environmental Support Center ($35,000) see Tortuga Foundation

Essential Information — environmental information ($33,000) see Hoffman Foundation, Maximillian E. and Marion O.

Ethics and Public Policy Center ($200,000) see Richardson Foundation, Smith

Ethics Resource ($30,000) see First Boston

FADICA ($15,000) see Loyola Foundation

FAIR ($20,000) see Americana Foundation

Families USA Foundation ($200,000) see Public Welfare Foundation

Family and Child Services ($8,000) see Ivakota Association

Family Place — general support for institutional development ($60,000) see Meyer Foundation, Eugene and Agnes E.

Family Research Council of America — sponsorship of the Marian Pfister Anschutz award to honor American families ($75,000) see Anschutz Family Foundation

Federal City Council — DC Committee on Public Education's implementation of recommendations made by the Committee to improve the local public schools ($10,000) see Strong Foundation, Hattie M.

Federal City Council — to support an initiative in early childhood development, family and community education at the Frederick Douglass and Stanton Dwellings in Anacostia ($150,000) see Graham Fund, Philip L.

Federal City Council — Smarter Schools Program ($375,912) see Citicorp

Federation for American Immigration Reform ($100,000) see Buffett Foundation

Federation for American Immigration Reform ($11,100) see Davis Foundation, Shelby Cullom

Federation for American Immigration Reform ($50,000) see Pioneer Fund

Federation of Parents and Friends of Lesbians and Gays — The Family AIDS Support Program serves those with HIV/AIDS through a national network of volunteer organizers and educators ($50,000) see van Ameringen Foundation

Fellowship Foundation ($78,000) see Timmis Foundation, Michael & Nancy

Fine Arts Committee ($25,000) see Masco Corp.

Folger Shakespeare Library — matching grant toward acquisition ($100,000) see Arcana Foundation

Folger Shakespeare Library ($25,000) see Marpat Foundation

Folger Shakespeare Library — education/operations ($85,300) see Folger Fund

Food Industry Crusade Against Hunger ($7,000) see Tripifoods

Food Research and Action Center ($150,000) see Public Welfare Foundation

Food Research and Action Center — program support ($62,500) see Sequoia Foundation

For Love of Children ($150,000) see Public Welfare Foundation

For Love of Children — funds will renovate a property in the District of Columbia into two apartments managed by FLOC's Hope and a Home program ($50,000) see Federal Home Loan Mortgage Corp. (Freddie Mac)

For Love of Children (FLOC) — education advocacy component for at-risk, school-age children living in Hope and A Home Housing units ($10,000) see Strong Foundation, Hattie M.

Ford's Theater ($10,000) see Getz Foundation, Emma and Oscar

Ford's Theater ($25,000) see Occidental Petroleum Corp.

Ford's Theater Society — endowment fund ($100,000) see Freed Foundation

Ford's Theater Society ($50,000) see Unocal Corp.

Ford's Theatre ($5,000) see Martin Marietta Corp.

Ford's Theatre Society ($7,000) see Dart Group Corp.

Foundation for American Economics Competitiveness — partial funding for the support of research on the time horizon on U.S. industrial investment for the Council of Competitiveness and the Harvard Business School ($624,183) see Sloan Foundation, Alfred P.

Foundation on Economic Trends ($100,000) see Ira-Hiti Foundation for Deep Ecology

Foundation on Economic Trends — genetic engineering ($100,000) see Ira-Hiti Foundation for Deep Ecology

Foundation on Economic Trends ($50,000) see Ira-Hiti Foundation for Deep Ecology

Foundation for Health Services Research — The Baxter Health Policy Review ($173,337) see Baxter International

Foundations and Donors Interested in Catholic Activities ($100,000) see Brencanda Foundation

Franciscan of Holy Land ($5,000) see Diener Foundation, Frank C.

Free Congress Foundation — special projects support ($100,000) see Allegheny Foundation

Free Congress Foundation ($100,000) see DeVos Foundation, Richard and Helen

Free Congress Foundation ($5,000) see Henry Foundation, Patrick

Free Congress Foundation ($55,000) see Roe Foundation

Free Congress Research and Education Foundation ($565,000) see Carthage Foundation

Free Congress Research and Education Foundation ($30,000) see JM Foundation

Free Congress Research and Education Foundation ($100,000) see Krieble Foundation, Vernon K.

Free Congress Research and Education Foundation ($50,000) see Milliken & Co.

Free Congress Research and Education Foundation ($325,000) see Scaife Foundation, Sarah

Free Congress Research and Education Foundation — support of the Center for State Policy Program to help shape policy reform ($150,000) see Coors Foundation, Adolph

Friends of the Children's Inn at National Institute of Health ($10,000) see Searle & Co., G.D.

Friends of the Children's Inn at National Institute of Health ($10,000) see United States Sugar Corp.

Friends of the Earth — environmental tax project ($15,000) see Beldon Fund

Friends of the Earth ($250,000) see Public Welfare Foundation

Friends of the Earth — project support ($10,000) see Warsh-Mott Legacy

Friends of Earth Foundation ($1,500) see Bright Charitable Trust, Alexander H.

Friends of the Earth International — project support ($15,000) see Warsh-Mott Legacy

Fund for Investigative Journalism — project support ($15,000) see Warsh-Mott Legacy

Funding and Donors Interested in Catholic Activities — 1991 membership dues and program expenses ($25,000) see Raskob Foundation for Catholic Activities

Funding Partnership for People with Disabilities ($5,000) see Roche Relief Foundation, Edward and Ellen

Funds for the Community's Future — to support this newly established organization which revitalizes communities by inspiring residents in low income neighborhoods to unite in support of educating their youth ($29,450) see Federal Home Loan Mortgage Corp. (Freddie Mac)

Gallaudet University ($7,000) see Appleby Trust, Scott B. and Annie P.

Gallaudet University ($10,000) see Himmelfarb Foundation, Paul and Annetta

Gallaudet University ($44,000) see Newcombe Foundation, Charlotte W.

Gallaudet University ($20,000) see Oaklawn Foundation

Gallaudet University ($15,000) see Ross Foundation, Walter G.

General Commission for Better Government ($25,000) see Chambers Development Co.

General Conference of Seventh Day Adventists — general support ($30,000) see Johnston Trust for Charitable and Educational Purposes, James M.

George C. Marshall Institute ($130,000) see Carthage Foundation

George Washington University see Applied Energy Services

George Washington University see Berlex Laboratories

George Washington University — for professorship of administrative medicine ($225,000) see Bloedorn Foundation, Walter A.

George Washington University ($67,417) see Burns Foundation, Jacob

George Washington University see Chiron Corp.

George Washington University ($20,000) see Cohen Foundation, Naomi and Nehemiah

George Washington University ($30,000) see Gelman Foundation, Melvin and Estelle

George Washington University ($5,000) see Lea Foundation, Helen Sperry

George Washington University ($30,000) see Loughran Foundation, Mary and Daniel

George Washington University ($100,000) see Marriott Foundation, J. Willard

George Washington University see Olympus Corp.

George Washington University see Parexel International Corp.

George Washington University ($100,000) see Ross Foundation, Walter G.

George Washington University ($25,000) see Ross Foundation, Walter G.

George Washington University see Ross Laboratories

George Washington University ($3,000,000) see Shapiro, Inc.

George Washington University ($100,000) see Souers Charitable Trust, Sidney W. and Sylvia N.

George Washington University — cancer home care program ($170,000) see Stewart Trust under the will of Mary E. Stewart, Alexander and Margaret

George Washington University see Vanguard Group of Investment Cos.

George Washington University see Weitz Corp.

George Washington University — Eugene B. Casey Revolving Loan Fund ($200,000) see Casey Foundation, Eugene B.

George Washington University Hospital ($25,000) see Upjohn Co.

George Washington University — toward a campaign for capital improvements, including renovations to Lisner Auditorium ($100,000) see Graham Fund, Philip L.

George Washington University National Law Center ($5,650) see Covington and Burling

Georgetown Annual Fund ($500) see Tripifoods

Georgetown Day School ($5,000) see Hecht-Levi Foundation

Georgetown Memorial Hospital ($15,000) see Manning and Emma Austin Manning Foundation, James Hilton

Georgetown Preparatory School ($3,000) see DelMar Foundation, Charles

Georgetown University ($50,000) see Banfi Vintners

Georgetown University ($15,000) see Banfi Vintners

Georgetown University — restricted ($10,000) see Beck Foundation, Elsie E. & Joseph W.

Georgetown University ($10,000) see Bostwick Foundation, Albert C.

Georgetown University ($5,000) see Cameron Memorial Fund, Alpin J. and Alpin W.

Georgetown University ($1,001,875) see Connelly Foundation

Georgetown University ($100,000) see Continental Corp.

Georgetown University ($5,000) see Cottrell Foundation

Georgetown University ($10,000) see Dexter Shoe Co.

Georgetown University ($7,500) see Dower Foundation, Thomas W.

Georgetown University ($50,000) see Gudelsky Family Foundation, Homer and Martha

Georgetown University — general support ($50,000) see Jewett Foundation, George Frederick

Georgetown University ($10,000) see Kennedy Foundation, Quentin J.

Georgetown University ($100,000) see Landegger Charitable Foundation

Georgetown University ($100,000) see Landegger Charitable Foundation

Georgetown University ($75,000) see Landegger Charitable Foundation

Georgetown University ($50,000) see Landegger Charitable Foundation

Georgetown University ($50,000) see Landegger Charitable Foundation

Georgetown University ($50,000) see Landegger Charitable Foundation

Georgetown University ($25,000) see Landegger Charitable Foundation

Georgetown University ($30,000) see Loughran Foundation, Mary and Daniel

Georgetown University ($125,000) see McDonough Foundation, Bernard

Georgetown University ($5,000) see Parvin Foundation, Albert

Georgetown University ($5,000) see Pittulloch Foundation

Georgetown University ($9,005) see Plym Foundation

Georgetown University ($15,000) see Rosenthal Foundation, Samuel

Georgetown University ($16,500) see Seymour and Troester Foundation

Georgetown University ($20,000) see Shea Foundation, John and Dorothy

Georgetown University ($15,000) see Shenandoah Foundation

Georgetown University ($6,600) see Shenandoah Foundation

Georgetown University ($30,000) see Sperry Fund

Georgetown University — cancer home care program ($316,906) see Stewart Trust under the will of Mary E. Stewart, Alexander and Margaret

Georgetown University ($57,000) see Tauber Foundation

Georgetown University ($5,000) see Weininger Foundation, Richard and Gertrude

Georgetown University — refugee medicine program ($75,000) see Winkler Foundation, Mark and Catherine

Georgetown University Hospital ($15,000) see Brownley Trust, Walter

Georgetown University Hospital ($7,000) see Straus Foundation, Martha Washington Straus and Harry H.

Georgetown University Law Center ($20,000) see Loyola Foundation

Georgetown University Medical Center — endow academic professorship and support pediatric project ($150,000) see Scholl Foundation, Dr.

Georgetown University Medical Center, Stephen M. Jones Revolving Loan Fund ($100,000) see Casey Foundation, Eugene B.

Georgetown University School of Nursing — nursing training programs ($30,000) see Johnston Trust for Charitable and Educational Purposes, James M.

Georgetown University — Vincent T. Lombardi Cancer Research Center ($150,000) see Citicorp

Georgetown University Vincent T. Lombardi Cancer Research Center — to establish the cancer prevention and control program ($150,000) see Hearst Foundation, William Randolph

Germantown Academy ($5,000) see Binswanger Co.

Girl Scout Council of the Nation's Capital — support for troops in homeless shelters and public housing projects ($10,000) see Gannett Co.

Global Tomorrow Coalition ($10,000) see Beldon II Fund

Good Shepherd Ministries — educational, mentoring, and vocational programs provided to at-risk, low-income youth ages 13 through 18 at Teen Center ($7,500) see Strong Foundation, Hattie M.

Government Accountability Project — for the Development Fund and for the Worker Health and Safety Project ($40,000) see Babcock Foundation, Mary Reynolds

Grand Canyon Trust ($25,000) see Pincus Family Fund

Grand Canyon Trust ($2,500) see Seven Springs Foundation

Greater Southeast Community Hospital ($15,000) see Brownley Trust, Walter

Greater Washington Educational Telecommunications Association ($20,000) see Kiplinger Foundation

Greater Washington Educational Telecommunications Association ($200,000) see Mobil Oil Corp.

Greater Washington Jewish Community Center ($100,000) see Kaplan Foundation, Charles I. and Mary

Greater Washington Research Center — Washington Metropolitan Area; to foster doctoral-level research on urban issues affecting the area ($100,000) see Meyer Foundation, Eugene and Agnes E.

Green Door — kitchen renovation and vocational equipment for the cafe in the clubhouse program for the recovering mentally ill ($50,000) see van Ameringen Foundation

Greenhouse Crisis Foundation ($10,000) see Levinson Foundation, Max and Anna

Greenpeace USA ($5,000) see Schoenbaum Family Foundation

Health Volunteers Overseas ($25,000) see Marriott Foundation, J. Willard

Healthy Babies Project — to support this program devoted to reducing the incidence of low birthweight and infant mortality ($50,000) see Federal Home Loan Mortgage Corp. (Freddie Mac)

Heritage Foundation ($100,000) see Aequus Institute

Heritage Foundation ($30,000) see Banbury Fund

Heritage Foundation ($156,000) see Carthage Foundation

Heritage Foundation ($140,000) see Coleman, Jr. Foundation, George E.

Heritage Foundation — conducts research and educational activities on major public policy ($150,000) see Coors Foundation, Adolph

Heritage Foundation ($1,400,000) see Davis Foundation, Shelby Cullom

Heritage Foundation ($50,000) see Grace & Co., W.R.

Heritage Foundation ($10,000) see Henderson Foundation

Heritage Foundation ($50,000) see JM Foundation

Heritage Foundation ($55,000) see McKenna Foundation, Philip M.

Heritage Foundation — program of public policy research ($15,000) see Montgomery Street Foundation

Heritage Foundation ($2,000) see Neese Family Foundation

Heritage Foundation — general operating support ($500,000) see Noble Foundation, Samuel Roberts

Heritage Foundation ($2,000) see Oxford Foundation

Heritage Foundation ($10,000) see Parsons - W.D. Charities, Vera Davis

Heritage Foundation ($2,000) see Pitt-Des Moines Inc.

Heritage Foundation ($10,000) see Roddis Foundation, Hamilton

Heritage Foundation ($55,000) see Roe Foundation

Heritage Foundation — espouse founding principles ($200,000) see Salvatori Foundation, Henry

Heritage Foundation ($650,000) see Scaife Foundation, Sarah

Heritage Foundation — healthcare reform project ($37,500) see Schultz Foundation

Heritage Foundation ($30,000) see Sunmark Capital Corp.

Heritage Foundation ($25,000) see Taylor Foundation, Ruth and Vernon

Heritage Foundation ($1,000) see True Oil Co.

Heritage Foundation ($50,000) see Van Andel Foundation, Jay and Betty

Heritage Foundation ($65,000) see Walker Educational and Charitable Foundation, Alex C.

Heritage Foundation ($5,000) see Williams Family Foundation

Heritage Foundation — to support the Bradley Resident Scholars for 1991-92 ($290,025) see Bradley Foundation, Lynde and Harry

Heritage Foundation — to support the Bradley Resident Scholars Program for 1992-93 ($265,076) see Bradley Foundation, Lynde and Harry

Heritage Foundation — continue sponsorship of Grover Hermann Fellow ($115,000) see Hermann Foundation, Grover

Heros ($15,000) see Dimick Foundation

Hida Educational Foundation ($5,000) see Midmark Corp.

High Frontier ($100,000) see Carthage Foundation

Higher Achievement Program (HAP) — HAP's six week academic summer enrichment program for highly motivated and talented low-income students in grades 5-8 ($7,500) see Strong Foundation, Hattie M.

Hirshhorn Museum ($75,000) see Greene Foundation, Jerome L.

Historically Black Research University Foundation ($20,000) see Alliant Techsystems

Holocaust Memorial Center ($8,500) see Imerman Memorial Foundation, Stanley

Holocaust Memorial Center ($50,000) see Maas Foundation, Benard L.

Holocaust Memorial Center ($10,000) see Maas Foundation, Benard L.

Holocaust Memorial Museum ($5,000) see Shapiro Fund, Albert

Holocaust Museum ($5,000) see Woodner Family Collection, Ian

Horizon Concerts ($15,000) see Chadwick Fund, Dorothy Jordan

Hospice ($15,000) see Brownley Trust, Walter

Hospice Council of Metropolitan Washington — hospital liaison program ($79,400) see Stewart Trust under the will of Mary E. Stewart, Alexander and Margaret

Hospital For Sick Children ($525,000) see Weinberg Foundation, Harry and Jeanette

Hospital for Sick Children — acquisition of hydrotherapy pool ($60,000) see Arcana Foundation

Hospital for Sick Children ($48,333) see Brownley Trust, Walter

Hospital for Sick Children ($2,500) see Rales and Ruth Rales Foundation, Norman R.

Hospital for Sick Children ($10,000) see Ross Foundation, Walter G.

Hospital for Sick Children ($125,000) see Shapiro, Inc.

Hospital for Sick Children — to support capital campaign for new, expanded facility ($75,000) see Graham Fund, Philip L.

Howard University see Eastman Kodak Co.

Howard University ($30,000) see Loughran Foundation, Mary and Daniel

Howard University ($100,000) see Technical Training Foundation

Howard University — scholarship award ($2,000) see Washington Post Co.

Howard University — scholarship award ($2,000) see Washington Post Co.

Howard University ($72,440) see Woodner Family Collection, Ian

Howard University ($46,750) see Woodner Family Collection, Ian

Howard University Hospital ($15,000) see Brownley Trust, Walter

Howard University — supports minority Ph.D. candidates preparing for careers in college and university teaching ($105,000) see Danforth Foundation

I Have a Dream Foundation ($2,508) see Freeman Foundation, Carl M.

ICMA ($7,000) see Seasongood Good Government Foundation, Murray and Agnes

ILSI Research Foundation ($50,000) see Hoffmann-La Roche

Independent Sector ($10,000) see Oakleaf Foundation

Institute for Alternative Journalism ($50,000) see New World Foundation

Institute for Educational Leadership ($21,660) see Glen Eagles Foundation

Institute for Educational Leadership ($150,000) see Metropolitan Life Insurance Co.

Institute for Educational Leadership ($30,000) see Ryder System

Institute for Illinois — operating ($25,000) see Sundstrand Corp.

Institute for International Economics ($125,000) see Keck, Jr. Foundation, William M.

Institute for International Economics ($5,000) see Thermo Electron Corp.

Institute for International Economics — to promote closer trade and economic relations among the United States and its neighbors in the Western Hemisphere

District of Columbia (cont.)

($50,000) see Tinker Foundation

Institute for Justice ($100,000) see Lambe Charitable Foundation, Claude R.

Institute for Justice — general ($50,000) see Lambe Charitable Foundation, Claude R.

Institute for Local Self-Reliance ($25,000) see HKH Foundation

Institute of Medicine/National Academy of Sciences ($30,000) see Pfizer

Institute for Mental Health Initiatives ($2,500) see Fuchsberg Family Foundation

Institute for Policy Studies ($35,000) see HKH Foundation

Institute for Policy Studies ($206,500) see Rubin Foundation, Samuel

Institute for Political Economy ($7,500) see Thirty-Five Twenty, Inc.

Institute for Public Policy Advocacy — development of institute's media advocacy leadership training and counseling program ($25,000) see Benton Foundation

Institute for the Release of Soviet Jewry ($16,500) see Gottesman Fund

Institute on Religion and Democracy ($150,000) see Randolph Foundation

Institute for the Study of Man ($48,500) see Pioneer Fund

Institute for Women's Policy Research ($4,000) see Vaughan Foundation, Rachael and Ben

Institute for Women's Policy Research — support for the Fund for Action Research ($25,000) see Norman Foundation

Institute of World Politics ($2,500) see Henry Foundation, Patrick

Institute for World Politics — teaching the founding principles ($25,000) see Salvatori Foundation, Henry

Insurance Industry AIDS Initiative see Capital Holding Corp.

Insurance Industry AIDS Initiative — operating fund ($7,500) see Ohio National Life Insurance Co.

Insure ($100,000) see Principal Financial Group

INSURE—ACLI AIDS Initiative ($1,000) see Uslico Corp.

Interfaith Conference of Metropolitan Washington ($5,000) see Hill-Snowdon Foundation

International Catholic Migration Commission — aid to central American refugee ($25,000) see Homeland Foundation

International Center — to send a citizens delegation to the Soviet Union to study conditions within the republics and Soviet foreign policy toward developing countries ($38,500) see Arca Foundation

International Conservation Policy Alliance Foundation ($20,000) see Krieble Foundation, Vernon K.

International Foundation ($75,000) see Solheim Foundation

International Foundation ($977,808) see Timmis Foundation, Michael & Nancy

International Foundation for the Survival and Development of Humanity — general support ($100,000) see Hammer Foundation, Armand

International Life Sciences Institute ($30,000) see Gerber Products Co.

International Life Sciences Institute ($19,912) see Lipton, Thomas J.

International Life Sciences Institute-Nutrition Foundation ($37,000) see Hershey Foods Corp.

International Life Sciences Institute — Nutrition Foundation ($21,000) see Life Investors Insurance Company of America

International Union for Conservation of Nature and Natural Resources-U.S. — a comprehensive review of the history of human impact on Antartica ($75,000) see Tinker Foundation

International Women's Forum ($80,000) see Federal Express Corp.

International Women's Media Foundation — year-round operation ($50,000) see Freedom Forum

Jamestown Foundation ($1,000) see Meyer Foundation, Alice Kleberg Reynolds

Jamestown Foundation ($2,000) see Smith Foundation, Gordon V. and Helen C.

Jamestown Foundation ($50,000) see Van Andel Foundation, Jay and Betty

Jamestown Foundation ($25,000) see Van Andel Foundation, Jay and Betty

Japan-America Student Conference see Marubeni America Corp.

Japan-American Student Conference ($1,500) see Kajima International, Inc.

Jewish Community Center ($25,000) see Gudelsky Family Foundation, Isadore and Bertha

Jewish Fund for Justice ($12,500) see New Prospect Foundation

Jewish Institute for National Security Affairs ($2,250) see Goldman Foundation, Aaron and Cecile

Jewish Institute for National Security Affairs ($3,500) see Henry Foundation, Patrick

Jewish Institute for National Security Affairs ($5,000) see Sequa Corp.

John F. Kennedy Center for the Performing Arts ($20,000) see Abramson Family Foundation

John F. Kennedy Center for the Performing Arts ($20,000) see Bender Foundation

John F. Kennedy Center for the Performing Arts ($132,050) see Botwinick-Wolfensohn Foundation

John F. Kennedy Center for the Performing Arts ($40,000) see CBS Inc.

John F. Kennedy Center for the Performing Arts ($50,000) see Chadwick Fund, Dorothy Jordan

John F. Kennedy Center for the Performing Arts ($52,500) see Folger Fund

John F. Kennedy Center for the Performing Arts ($13,524) see Gelman Foundation, Melvin and Estelle

John F. Kennedy Center for the Performing Arts ($20,000) see Giant Food

John F. Kennedy Center for the Performing Arts ($20,000) see Hechinger Co.

John F. Kennedy Center for the Performing Arts ($7,500) see Higginson Trust, Corina

John F. Kennedy Center for the Performing Arts ($4,000) see Jost Foundation, Charles and Mabel P.

John F. Kennedy Center for the Performing Arts ($3,000) see Matz Foundation — Edelman Division

John F. Kennedy Center for the Performing Arts ($15,000) see Mitsui & Co. (U.S.A.)

John F. Kennedy Center for the Performing Arts ($55,000) see Simon Charitable Trust, Esther

John F. Kennedy Center for the Performing Arts ($5,000) see Spiritus Gladius Foundation

John F. Kennedy Center for the Performing Arts ($2,220) see Truland Foundation

John F. Kennedy Center for the Performing Arts ($29,200) see Wasserman Foundation

John F. Kennedy Center for the Performing Arts — to help fund replacement and upgrading of the sound system in the Eisenhower Theatre ($100,000) see Graham Fund, Philip L.

John F. Kennedy Center for the Performing Arts — Trustees' Circle ($50,000) see Marriott Foundation, J. Willard

John F. Kennedy Memorial Library — sixth payment on 250,000 pledge ($25,000) see Hammer Foundation, Armand

John F. Kennedy Performing Arts Center ($5,000) see Harris Corp.

John Hopkins University — support for Chinese Studies ($25,000) see Jewett Foundation, George Frederick

Joint Center for Political and Economic Studies — general support for research, analysis, and dissemination activities on public policies affecting blacks in the United States ($2,000,000) see Ford Foundation

Jubilee Housing — low-income housing providers; water pipe replacement in three buildings ($104,672) see Arcana Foundation

Julie Gould Fund ($10,000) see Brady Foundation

Julie Gould Fund for Medical Research ($5,000) see Bostwick Foundation, Albert C.

Kennedy Center see Booz Allen & Hamilton

Kennedy Center ($500,000) see Cafritz Foundation, Morris and Gwendolyn

Kennedy Center ($20,000) see Farnsworth Trust, Charles A.

Kennedy Center Productions ($8,490) see Brody Foundation, Carolyn and Kenneth D.

Lab School of Washington ($15,000) see Daly Charitable Foundation Trust, Robert and Nancy

Lab School of Washington ($8,333) see Dweck Foundation, Samuel R.

Lab School of Washington ($20,000) see Fowler Memorial Foundation, John Edward

Lab School of Washington ($10,000) see Himmelfarb Foundation, Paul and Annetta

Lab School of Washington ($15,000) see Liberman Foundation, Bertha & Isaac

Land Trust Alliance — to expand its role and to increase the capacity of its service ($360,000) see Mellon Foundation, Richard King

Landon School ($11,500) see Kiplinger Foundation

Lawyer's Committee for Civil Rights ($15,000) see Deer Creek Foundation

Lawyer's Committee for Civil Rights ($15,000) see Weil, Gotshal & Manges Foundation

Lawyers' Committee for Civil Rights Under Law — Alien Rights Law Project ($60,000) see Scherman Foundation

Lawyers for the Republic ($50,000) see Cook Foundation

Leadership Washington ($7,500) see Higginson Trust, Corina

Legal Aid Society ($20,000) see Covington and Burling

Levine School of Music ($5,000) see Higginson Trust, Corina

Levine School of Music ($12,500) see Summerfield Foundation, Solon E.

Library of Congress ($237,500) see Engelhard Foundation, Charles

Library of Congress ($10,000) see Heineman Foundation for Research, Educational, Charitable, and Scientific Purposes

Library of Congress ($25,000) see Macmillan, Inc.

Library of Congress ($50,000) see Pickford Foundation, Mary

Library of Congress ($11,000) see Wouk Foundation, Abe

Library of Congress, James Madison National Council ($10,000) see Glanville Family Foundation

Library of Congress, James Madison National Council ($10,000) see Thornton Foundation, Flora L.

Library Theater ($5,000) see Higginson Trust, Corina

Life and Health Insurance Medical Research Fund ($5,000) see Ameritas Life Insurance Corp.

Life and Health Insurance Medical Research Fund ($250,000) see Nationwide Insurance Cos.

Life and Health Insurance Medical Research Fund — general operating ($100,000) see New York Life Insurance Co.

Life and Health Insurance Medical Research Fund ($1,000) see Uslico Corp.

Life and Health Insurance Medical Research Fund (ACLI) ($10,000) see Mutual of New York

Little Sisters of the Poor ($5,000) see Bloedorn Foundation, Walter A.

Little Sisters of Poor ($10,000) see McMahon Charitable Trust Fund, Father John J.

Local Initiatives Support Corporation ($25,000) see Hechinger Co.

Low-Income Housing Information Services — general operating support ($125,000) see Federal National Mortgage Assn., Fannie Mae

Luther Place Memorial Church — grant for food program for mentally ill women ($15,000) see Abell Foundation, Charles S.

Luther Place N Street Village ($9,000) see Bernstein Foundation, Diane and Norman

Luther Place N Street Village ($50,000) see Shapiro, Inc.

Luther Place Street Village Women's Shelters ($10,000) see Kapiloff Foundation, Leonard

Mainstream, Inc. ($31,243) see MCI Communications Corp.

Manic Depressive Illness Foundation ($150,000) see Dana Charitable Trust, Eleanor Naylor

MANNA — support for the capstone revolving loan fund ($70,000) see Meyer Foundation, Eugene and Agnes E.

Manna Community Development Corporation ($20,000) see Prince Trust, Abbie Norman

Marriott Foundation for People With Disabilities ($500,000) see Marriott Foundation, J. Willard

Marriott Foundation's "Bridges" program — to help initiate this program in the Los Angeles area, which arranges internships at local businesses for high school students with disabilities ($50,000) see Mitsubishi Electric America

Marshall Heights Community Development Organization — operating support for staff and the addition of a construction and office manager ($75,000) see Meyer Foundation, Eugene and Agnes E.

Martha's Table — educational after school program for homeless children ($7,500) see Strong Foundation, Hattie M.

Martha's Table ($10,000) see Willard Foundation, Helen Parker

McDonough School ($51,000) see Kiplinger Foundation

Medical Education for South African Blacks (MESAB) — to support a Bursary/Mentor Program that provides scholarships and counseling to black South Africans pursuing an education in health- related fields ($178,900) see IBM South Africa Projects Fund

Medical Research Fund, Washington, D.C. ($25,000) see Northwestern National Life Insurance Co.

Mentors ($5,000) see Higginson Trust, Corina

Meridian House International ($5,000) see Lea Foundation, Helen Sperry

Metropolitan Police Boys and Girls Clubs ($2,500) see Bloedorn Foundation, Walter A.

Metropolitan Washington Community AIDS Partnership ($25,000) see Glen Eagles Foundation

Metropolitan Washington Community AIDS Partnership ($58,000) see Hecht's

Metropolitan Washington Community AIDS Partnership — for AIDS services and education programs, a two-year grant ($300,000) see Cafritz Foundation, Morris and Gwendolyn

Middle East Institute ($2,000) see Sweatt Foundation, Harold W.

Middle East Research and Information Project ($4,000) see Carteh Foundation

Mineral Policy Center — to provide technical assistance through the Southwest Circuit Rider to communities affected by mining projects ($65,000) see Noyes Foundation, Jessie Smith

Mount Vernon College ($7,000) see Bay Branch Foundation

Mount Vernon College — educational ($20,000) see Dreyfus Foundation, Max and Victoria

Mount Vernon College — teachers salaries ($30,000) see Johnston Trust for Charitable and Educational Purposes, James M.

Ms. Foundation for Women ($50,000) see Levi Strauss & Co.

Museum of American Textile History ($175,000) see Fanwood Foundation

Museum of American Textile History ($10,000) see Hopedale Foundation

Museum Trustee Committee ($15,000) see Moore Memorial Foundation, James Starr

N.A.M.I. ($12,000) see Matz Foundation — Edelman Division

NAACP ($12,000) see Danner Foundation

NARAL Foundation ($5,000) see Duke Foundation, Doris

National Abortion Federation ($50,000) see Huber Foundation

National Abortion Rights Action League Foundation ($125,000) see Huber Foundation

National Abortion Rights Action League Foundation ($110,000) see Sunnen Foundation

National Abortion Rights League Foundation ($10,000) see Taubman Foundation, A. Alfred

National Academy of Science ($100,000) see Dow Chemical Co.

National Academy of Sciences — administration of minority doctoral and postdoctoral fellowship programs ($5,310,000) see Ford Foundation

National Academy of Sciences ($4,695,024) see Kellogg Foundation, W. K.

National Academy of Sciences ($55,000) see Klingenstein Fund, Esther A. and Joseph

National Academy of Sciences ($500,000) see Penzance Foundation

National Affairs ($100,000) see Carthage Foundation

National Affairs ($10,000) see Fox Foundation, Richard J.

National AIDS Network (NCAP) ($65,000) see Allstate Insurance Co.

National Alliance of Business ($111,437) see JCPenney Co.

National Alliance of Business, Washington, D.C. ($25,000) see Equitable Life Assurance Society of the U.S.

National Association of Black Journalists ($50,000) see Freedom Forum

National Association of Hispanic Journalists ($50,000) see Freedom Forum

National Association of Partners of Americas — support their program to address the needs of homeless children in Brazil ($300,200) see Jurzykowski Foundation, Alfred

National Association of Secondary School Principals — to provide a stronger emphasis on the day-to-day concerns and practices of principals ($116,000) see Danforth Foundation

National Association for the Southern Poor ($25,000) see Hillsdale Fund

National Cathedral School ($25,000) see Firestone Foundation, Roger S.

National Cathedral School ($20,000) see Hill-Snowdon Foundation

National Cathedral School ($25,000) see Manger and Audrey Cordero Plitt Trust, Clarence

National Catholic Educational Association ($157,500) see Doty Family Foundation

National Center for Clinical Infant Program ($25,000) see Pittway Corp.

National Center for Clinical Infant Programs — helping states improve child care for infants and toddlers ($75,000) see Foundation for Child Development

National Center for Neighborhood Enterprise ($100,000) see Allstate Insurance Co.

National Center-Neighborhood Enterprise ($100,000) see Sears, Roebuck and Co.

National Center for Neighborhood Enterprise (NCME) — to support a community developmental project for black South African community and business leaders ($400,000) see IBM South Africa Projects Fund

National Center for Neighborhood Enterprise — partial support for Neighborhood Capital Partners' program of loans to entrepreneurs in low income communities ($87,225) see Donner Foundation, William H.

National Center for Neighborhood Enterprise — to support the 1991/92 program activities ($225,000) see Bradley Foundation, Lynde and Harry

National Center for Neighborhood Enterprise — for the Yonkers-based, tenant-management program in public housing ($45,000) see Bodman Foundation

National Center for Policy Alternatives ($15,000) see Beldon II Fund

National Chamber Foundation ($10,000) see Durr-Fillauer Medical

National Chamber Foundation ($10,000) see Foote, Cone & Belding Communications

National Chamber Foundation ($35,000) see Krieble Foundation, Vernon K.

National Chamber Foundation ($25,000) see Reynolds Metals Co.

National Coalition of Hispanic Health and Human Services Organizations — to develop and implement community-based interventions that help Hispanic-Americans become effective health care consumers ($2,913,118) see Johnson Foundation, Robert Wood

National Commission Against Drunk Driving ($100) see Southland Corp.

National Commission for Economic Conversion and Disarmament ($25,000) see Mertz-Gilmore Foundation, Joyce

National Community AIDS Partnership — general operating ($50,000) see New York Life Insurance Co.

National Council on US-Arab Relations ($5,000) see Lea Foundation, Helen Sperry

National Crime Prevention Council ($100) see Southland Corp.

National Democratic Institute ($10,148) see Manilow Foundation, Nathan

National Endowment for Democracy ($25,000) see Freeman Charitable Trust, Samuel

National Endowment for the Humanities ($965,000) see Wallace-Reader's Digest Fund, DeWitt

National Family Planning and Reproductive Health Association ($30,000) see Sunnen Foundation

National Fish and Wildlife Foundation ($500,000) see Hofmann Co.

National Fish and Wildlife Foundation ($50,000) see Knapp Foundation

National Fish and Wildlife Foundation ($20,000) see Penney Foundation, James C.

National Fish and Wildlife Foundation ($52,500) see Trust for Mutual Understanding

National Fish and Wildlife Foundation ($25,000) see Weyerhaeuser Family Foundation

National Foundation for Improvement of Education — for implementation of the Learning Tomorrow program ($46,800) see NYNEX Corp.

National Foundation for Jewish Culture — for development of the Jewish Endowment for the Arts and Humanities ($110,000) see Cummings Foundation, Nathan

National Gallery of Art ($20,000) see Abramson Family Foundation

National Gallery of Art ($20,000) see Alsdorf Foundation

National Gallery of Art ($34,000) see Bell Atlantic Corp.

National Gallery of Art ($10,000) see Bernstein Foundation, Diane and Norman

National Gallery of Art ($1,000,000) see Cafritz Foundation, Morris and Gwendolyn

National Gallery of Art ($33,000) see Chadwick Fund, Dorothy Jordan

National Gallery of Art ($4,000) see Fein Foundation

National Gallery of Art — teachers institute ($14,330) see Folger Fund

National Gallery of Art ($310,000) see Frese Foundation, Arnold D.

National Gallery of Art ($500,000) see GTE Corp.

National Gallery of Art ($110,000) see Hall Charitable Trust, Evelyn A. J.

National Gallery of Art ($10,000) see Hazen Charitable Trust, Lita Annenberg

National Gallery of Art ($10,000) see Hooker Charitable Trust, Janet A.

National Gallery of Art ($4,000) see Hopkins Foundation, John Jay

National Gallery of Art ($152,000) see Kress Foundation, Samuel H.

National Gallery of Art ($30,000) see Lauder Foundation

National Gallery of Art — art collectors fund ($10,000) see Leighton-Oare Foundation

National Gallery of Art ($212,500) see Manoogian Foundation, Alex and Marie

National Gallery of Art ($50,000) see Manoogian Foundation, Alex and Marie

National Gallery of Art ($4,000) see McGregor Foundation, Thomas and Frances

National Gallery of Art — for endowment ($2,500,000) see Mellon Foundation, Andrew W.

National Gallery of Art ($20,000) see Moore Memorial Foundation, James Starr

National Gallery of Art ($10,000) see Ogden Foundation, Ralph E.

National Gallery of Art ($10,000) see PaineWebber

National Gallery of Art ($30,000) see Prince Trust, Abbie Norman

National Gallery of Art ($2,000) see Truland Foundation

National Gallery of Art ($10,000) see Vaughn, Jr. Foundation Fund, James M.

National Gallery of Art ($20,000) see W. W. W. Foundation

National Gallery of Art ($20,000) see W. W. W. Foundation

National Gallery of Art — in support of two Ittleson pre-doctoral fellowships in other than Western art; (final payment of a five-year grant) ($100,000) see Ittleson Foundation

National Gallery of Art — support of restoration of John Singer Sargent's "El Jaleo" and its subsequent exhibitions in Washington, D.C. and Boston, Massachusetts ($75,000) see NYNEX Corp.

National Gallery of Art — Paul Strand Exhibition ($250,000) see Southwestern Bell Corp.

National Gay and Lesbian Task Force Policy Institute — for the rights of lesbians and gays ($27,500) see Mertz-Gilmore Foundation, Joyce

National Geographic ($100,000) see Seaver Institute

National Geographic Education Foundation ($10,000) see Bloedorn Foundation, Walter A.

National Geographic Education Foundation ($50,000) see Westvaco Corp.

National Geographic Educational Foundation ($3,000) see Kautz Family Foundation

National Geographic Society ($236,500) see Kentland Foundation

National Geographic Society ($36,250) see Kentland Foundation

National Geographic Society ($36,250) see Kentland Foundation

National Geographic Society — Colorado geography education fund ($12,500) see Bonfils-Stanton Foundation

National Geographic Society Education Foundation ($20,000) see Chisholm Foundation

National Geographic Society Education Foundation ($200,000) see Gates Foundation

National Geographic Society Education Foundation ($17,000) see Kautz Family Foundation

National Governors' Association Foundation ($12,000) see Unilever United States

National Governors' Association (NGA) — to establish the new Kaiser Family Foundation Governors' Health Retreat Initiative ($415,000) see Kaiser Family Foundation, Henry J.

National Health/Education Consortium — Early Childhood Development ($100,000) see Honeywell

National Holocaust Museum ($10,000) see Stone Foundation, David S.

National Italian-American Foundation ($5,300) see Paulucci Family Foundation

National Italian-American Foundation ($1,800) see Paulucci Family Foundation

National Italian-American Foundation ($1,100) see Paulucci Family Foundation

National Italian-American Foundation ($1,000) see Paulucci Family Foundation

National Italian-American Foundation ($830) see Paulucci Family Foundation

National Italian-American Foundation ($373) see Paulucci Family Foundation

National Italian-American Foundation ($12,500) see Richmond Foundation, Frederick W.

National Italian-American Foundation ($12,500) see Richmond Foundation, Frederick W.

National Kidney Foundation — to fund an education and awareness program for physicians at four sites

Population/Environmental Balance ($10,000) see Shore Fund

Population Institute — program support ($100,000) see Allegheny Foundation

Population Institute — general fund ($11,400) see Armington Fund, Evenor

Population Institute ($28,000) see Harris Foundation, William H. and Mattie Wattis

Population Institute ($5,000) see Mott Charitable Trust/Spectemur Agendo, Stewart R.

Population Services International ($35,000) see Bergstrom Foundation, Erik E. and Edith H.

Population Services International ($16,000) see Westport Fund

Population Services International — program to reduce HIV/AIDS transmission among high-risk youth in Portland, Oregon ($400,000) see Kaiser Family Foundation, Henry J.

Potomac Institute — general support ($28,000) see Taconic Foundation

Presbyterian Home ($200) see Beitzell & Co.

Presidential Scholars Program ($2,500) see Piper Foundation, Minnie Stevens

President's Advisory Committee on the Arts ($10,000) see Keeler Fund, Miner S. and Mary Ann

Primary Movers Performance Company ($2,000) see Lazarus Charitable Trust, Helen and Charles

Prison Fellowship ($8,500) see C.I.O.S.

Prison Fellowship Ministries ($10,000) see Benfamil Charitable Trust

Prison Fellowship Ministries ($2,000) see Dupar Foundation

Prison Fellowship Ministries ($50,000) see M.E. Foundation

Prison Fellowship Ministries ($30,000) see M.E. Foundation

Prison Fellowship Ministries ($135,000) see Prince Corp.

Prison Fellowship Ministries ($50,000) see Timmis Foundation, Michael & Nancy

Prison Fellowship Ministries ($20,000) see Westwood Endowment

Prison Fellowship Ministries — Project Macedonia ($350,000) see Maclellan Foundation

Private Sector Initiatives — program development ($70,000) see Clover Foundation

Project on Military Procurement ($11,000) see Beidler Charitable Trust, Francis

Project Nishma — general support for their education programs regarding the peace process in Israel ($10,000) see Levinson Foundation, Max and Anna

Project Rainbow ($5,000) see Mullan Foundation, Thomas F. and Clementine L.

Protestant Episcopal Foundation ($5,000) see Coleman, Jr. Foundation, George E.

Providence Hospital ($15,000) see Brownley Trust, Walter

Providence Hospital — neonatal services ($40,000) see Stewart Trust under the will of Helen

S. Devore, Alexander and Margaret

Providence Hospital — cancer clinic ($90,000) see Stewart Trust under the will of Mary E. Stewart, Alexander and Margaret

Public Citizen — campaign contribution ($75,000) see Ira-Hiti Foundation for Deep Ecology

Public Citizen Foundation ($25,000) see HKH Foundation

Public Citizen Foundation — to examine fundraising practices of member of Congress and develop an educational campaign to promote public financing of congressional elections ($100,000) see Arca Foundation

Puerto Rico Disaster Relief Fund ($50,000) see ConAgra

Puerto Rico Disaster Relief Telethon ($5,000) see Rexham Inc.

Puerto Rico USA Foundation ($5,000) see Rexham Inc.

Rachael's Women Center — funding for cost of running the center for a year ($24,689) see Abell Foundation, Charles S.

Rails to Trails Conservancy ($20,000) see Tortuga Foundation

Reading is Fundamental ($5,400) see Crown Books Foundation, Inc.

Reading Is Fundamental ($310,000) see Chrysler Corp.

Reading Is Fundamental ($310,000) see Chrysler Corp.

Recording for the Blind ($15,000) see Aid Association for the Blind

Reed Cooke Neighborhood Association ($5,000) see Lea Foundation, Helen Sperry

Refugees International ($15,000) see Hasbro

Refugees International ($17,000) see Three Swallows Foundation

Religious Coalition for Abortion Rights ($75,000) see Sunnen Foundation

Research Center for Government Financial Management ($5,000) see Kellstadt Foundation

Resources for the Future ($10,000) see EG&G Inc.

Resources for the Future ($50,000) see Vetlesen Foundation, G. Unger

RFK Memorial — funds are being used to research, write and publish a report on the composition of incarcerated youth in the District of Columbia ($32,166) see Federal Home Loan Mortgage Corp. (Freddie Mac)

Richard Nixon Presidential Archives Foundation ($7,500) see Garvey Fund, Jean and Willard

Richard Nixon Presidential Archives Foundation ($5,000) see Ruan Foundation Trust, John

Robert F. Kennedy Memorial Foundation — Human Rights Award ($15,000) see Odell and Helen Pfeiffer Odell Fund, Robert Stewart

Ronald Reagan Foundation ($100,000) see Marriott Foundation, J. Willard

Ronald Reagan Library Foundation ($20,000) see Zilkha & Sons

Ronald Reagan Presidential Foundation ($2,100,000) see Annenberg Foundation

Ronald Reagan Presidential Foundation ($50,000) see Paramount Communications Inc.

Ronald Reagan Presidential Foundation and Library ($100,000) see Revlon

Ronald Reagan Presidential Foundation — 1990 pledge payments on three outstanding commitments ($140,000) see Hammer Foundation, Armand

Ronald Regan Presidential Foundation ($50,000) see Avon Products

St. Anslem's Abbey School ($5,110) see Truland Foundation

St. Gertrudes School — for mentally retarded ($50,000) see Abell Foundation, Charles S.

St. John's Child Development Center — summer autistic program ($42,000) see Stewart Trust under the will of Helen S. Devore, Alexander and Margaret

St. John's Child Development Center — to support the Facilitated Communication Project ($28,700) see Federal Home Loan Mortgage Corp. (Freddie Mac)

St. Patrick's Episcopal Day School ($25,000) see Prince Trust, Abbie Norman

Salvation Army see Capital Holding Corp.

Salvation Army ($125,000) see Casey Foundation, Eugene B.

Salvation Army — community service ($50,000) see Clark-Winchcole Foundation

Salvation Army ($10,000) see Willard Foundation, Helen Parker

Samaritan Inns — aid homeless ($50,000) see Clark-Winchcole Foundation

Sane/Freeze Education Fund ($5,000) see Carteh Foundation

SANE/FREEZE Education Fund ($30,000) see Rubin Foundation, Samuel

Sarafina for Ellington ($5,000) see Dart Group Corp.

Sarah's Circle ($5,000) see Appleby Trust, Scott B. and Annie P.

Sarah's Circle ($150,000) see Public Welfare Foundation

Sasha Bruce Youthwork — funds are supporting a new family preservation program ($41,515) see Federal Home Loan Mortgage Corp. (Freddie Mac)

Science Service (Westinghouse Science Talent Search) ($525,000) see Westinghouse Electric Corp.

Secretary of State ($2,000) see Rich Co., F.D.

Secretary of State of United States ($10,000) see Evans Foundation, T. M.

Secretary of State of the U.S. ($25,000) see Lauder Foundation

Secretary of State of United States ($26,500) see Legg Mason Inc.

Secretary of State of USA — diplomatic reception rooms ($25,000) see Folger Fund

Secretary of State of USA — diplomatic reception rooms

($12,000) see Goerlich Family Foundation

Selma M. Levine School of Music ($100,000) see Kiplinger Foundation

70001, Ltd. ($30,000) see MCI Communications Corp.

Shakespeare Theatre at the Folger Library ($235,000) see Cafritz Foundation, Morris and Gwendolyn

Shakespeare Theatre at the Folger Library — to jointly support, with the Washington Post, the 1992 Shakespeare Free For All ($75,000) see Graham Fund, Philip L.

SHARE Foundation — agricultural training school in El Salvador ($30,000) see Cudahy Fund, Patrick and Anna M.

Shrine Mont ($22,500) see Bloedorn Foundation, Walter A.

Sibley Memorial Hospital ($15,000) see Brownley Trust, Walter

Sidwell Friends School ($40,000) see Hechinger Co.

Sidwell Friends School ($8,740) see Lazarus Charitable Trust, Helen and Charles

Sidwell Friends School ($12,000) see Lea Foundation, Helen Sperry

Smithsonian Institute ($18,000) see Cleveland-Cliffs

Smithsonian Institute ($11,500) see Folger Fund

Smithsonian Institute/NMAA ($37,500) see Schwartz Foundation, David

Smithsonian Institution ($50,000) see Bell Atlantic Corp.

Smithsonian Institution ($10,000) see Field Foundation, Jamee and Marshall

Smithsonian Institution ($25,000) see Firestone Foundation, Roger S.

Smithsonian Institution — experimental gallery ($15,000) see Freed Foundation

Smithsonian Institution ($25,000) see Mott Fund, Ruth

Smithsonian Institution ($25,000) see NCR Corp.

Smithsonian Institution — environmental research center education building ($125,000) see Reed Foundation, Philip D.

Smithsonian Institution — new opportunities in animal health sciences fellowships ($60,000) see Reed Foundation, Philip D.

Smithsonian Institution ($4,000) see Stroud Foundation

Smithsonian Institution ($11,500) see Truland Foundation

Smithsonian National Museum of American History ($100,000) see Xerox Corp.

So Others Might Eat see Booz Allen & Hamilton

Society for the Advancement of Socioeconomics — conference March 1992 and summer workshop ($35,000) see Laurel Foundation

Society of the Cincinnati — museum support ($50,000) see Olmsted Foundation, George and Carol

Southern Africa Legal Services and Legal Education Project ($5,110) see Covington and Burling

Special Olympics ($7,500) see Mohasco Corp.

Student Conservation Association's Conservation Career Development Program ($50,000) see American Honda Motor Co.

Studio Theatre ($3,750) see Goldman Foundation, Aaron and Cecile

Supreme Court Historical Society ($4,000) see Bloedorn Foundation, Walter A.

Telecommunications Policy Research Conference — to continue the annual Telecommunications Policy Research Conference ($180,000) see Markle Foundation, John and Mary R.

Temple Sinai ($10,250) see Polinger Foundation, Howard and Geraldine

Textile Museum ($6,000) see Salgo Charitable Trust, Nicholas M.

Textile Museum ($7,000) see Speyer Foundation, Alexander C. and Tillie S.

Thrift Shop (Washington Antiques Show) ($15,000) see Mars Foundation

Tides Foundation ($25,000) see HKH Foundation

TLPJ Foundation ($10,000) see Hafif Family Foundation

Training — job training program for working poor ($20,000) see Abell Foundation, Charles S.

Trans Africa ($125,000) see Reebok International Ltd.

Travelers Aid Society ($5,060) see Gudelsky Family Foundation, Homer and Martha

Trial Lawyers for Public Justice ($12,000) see Fuchsberg Family Foundation, Abraham

Trial Lawyers for Public Justice ($8,000) see Fuchsberg Family Foundation, Abraham

Trial Layers for Public Justice ($80,000) see McIntosh Foundation

Trinity College ($87,000) see Rotterman Trust, Helen L. and Marie F.

21st Century Space Foundation ($10,000) see Rockwell Foundation

2691 Club ($10,000) see Crown Books Foundation, Inc.

Tyler/D.C. Vision Program ($6,000) see Aid Association for the Blind

Unicorn Projects-Roman City — to provide final funding for David Macaulay's film ($150,000) see Davis Foundations, Arthur Vining

United Cerebral Palsy Association ($20,000) see Coen Family Foundation, Charles S. and Mary

United Cerebral Palsy Associations "Tech Tots" Program — to establish libraries in five sites where parents of children with disabilities may borrow educational tools such as computers for use in helping to develop their children's physical, social, and cognitive skills ($45,000) see Mitsubishi Electric America

United Jewish Appeal Federation of Jewish Philanthropies ($40,000) see Himmelfarb Foundation, Paul and Annetta

United Jewish Appeal Federation of Jewish Philanthropies

District of Columbia (cont.)

($38,000) see Raskin Foundation, Hirsch and Braine

United Jewish Appeal-Federation of Jewish Philanthropies of Greater Washington, D.C. ($100,000) see Giant Food

United Jewish Appeal-Federation of Jewish Philanthropies of Greater Washington, D.C. ($50,000) see Giant Food

United Jewish Appeal-Federation of Jewish Philanthropies of Greater Washington, D.C. ($50,000) see Giant Food

United Service Organization ($5,000) see Swig Foundation

U.S. Association of Former Members of Congress — support for the activities of the Congressional Study Group on Germany ($170,000) see German Marshall Fund of the United States

U.S. Association of Former Members of Congress — to support activities of the Congressional Study Group on Germany ($170,000) see German Marshall Fund of the United States

United States Catholic Conference — dyslexia research program ($10,000) see Humphrey Foundation, Glenn & Gertrude

U.S. Department of State ($10,000) see Fribourg Foundation

U.S. English ($1,500) see Swensrud Charitable Trust, Sidney A.

U.S. Forest Service — Mount Shasta Ranger District; Everitt Memorial Highway picnic areas and meadow restoration ($142,700) see McConnell Foundation

United States Holocaust Memorial ($50,000) see Overseas Shipholding Group

United States Holocaust Memorial Council ($400,000) see Capital Fund Foundation

U.S. Holocaust Memorial Council ($10,000) see Cole Taylor Financial Group

United States Holocaust Memorial Council ($50,000) see Forest City Enterprises

U.S. Holocaust Memorial Council ($50,000) see Lauder Foundation

U.S. Holocaust Memorial Council ($3,000) see Livingston Foundation, Milton S. and Corinne N.

United States Holocaust Memorial Council ($50,000) see Loews Corp.

U.S. Holocaust Memorial Museum ($50,000) see Blum-Kovler Foundation

U.S. Holocaust Memorial Museum ($200,000) see Chrysler Corp.

United States Holocaust Memorial Museum ($5,000) see Cohn Family Foundation, Robert and Terri

U.S. Holocaust Memorial Museum ($7,000) see Regis Corp.

United States Holocaust Memorial Museum ($50,000) see Wasserman Foundation

United States Holocaust Memorial Museum ($12,000) see Wasserman Foundation, George

U.S. Holocaust Memorial Museum Campaign ($50,000) see Lauder Foundation

U.S. Holocaust Memorial Museum Campaign ($10,000) see Wouk Foundation, Abe

United States Holocaust Memorial Museum Campaign — endowment of The Cinema in the museum's Cultural and Conference Center in memory of Helena Rubinstein ($300,000) see Rubinstein Foundation, Helena

U.S. PIRG Education Fund — to examine links between campaign contributions from specific industries and opposition to renewal of the Clean Air Act and other environmental initiatives ($50,000) see Arca Foundation

U.S. Telecommunications Training Institute — program support ($35,000) see MCI Communications Corp.

United Way see Banner Life Insurance Co.

United Way ($10,000) see Bernstein Foundation, Diane and Norman

United Way of the National Capital Area — campaign support ($201,000) see Federal National Mortgage Assn., Fannie Mae

United Way of the National Capital Area ($114,804) see GEICO Corp.

United Way of National Capital Area ($175,000) see Giant Food

United Way (National Capital Area) ($145,000) see Hechinger Co.

United Way of the National Capital Area ($50,000) see MCI Communications Corp.

University of the District of Columbia — scholarship award ($2,000) see Washington Post Co.

University of the District of Columbia — Adult Education Peace Corps Fellows ($5,000) see Lea Foundation, Helen Sperry

US Business and Industrial Council ($2,750) see Media General, Inc.

US Department of State ($12,500) see Swig Foundation

US Department of State — Diplomatic Rooms Endowment Fund ($20,000) see Hopkins Foundation, John Jay

US Holocaust Memorial Museum ($250,000) see Abramson Family Foundation

US Holocaust Memorial Museum ($50,000) see Blaustein Foundation, Louis and Henrietta

US Holocaust Memorial Museum ($150,000) see Blum Foundation, Harry and Maribel G.

US Holocaust Memorial Museum ($10,000) see Blum Foundation, Lois and Irving

US Holocaust Memorial Museum ($94,000) see Carylon Foundation

US Holocaust Memorial Museum ($10,000) see Feinstein Foundation, Myer and Rosaline

US Holocaust Memorial Museum ($10,000) see Feinstein Foundation, Myer and Rosaline

US Holocaust Memorial Museum ($25,000) see Glen Eagles Foundation

US Holocaust Memorial Museum ($100,000) see Hassenfeld Foundation

US Holocaust Memorial Museum ($50,000) see Hecht-Levi Foundation

US Holocaust Memorial Museum ($20,000) see Kapiloff Foundation, Leonard

US Holocaust Memorial Museum ($20,000) see Kaplan Foundation, Charles I. and Mary

US Holocaust Memorial Museum ($80,000) see Lautenberg Foundation

US Holocaust Memorial Museum ($10,000) see Premier Dental Products Co.

US Holocaust Memorial Museum ($5,000) see Raskin Foundation, Hirsch and Braine

US Holocaust Memorial Museum ($20,000) see Rosenbloom Foundation, Ben and Esther

US Holocaust Memorial Museum ($10,000) see Ross Foundation, Lyn & George M.

US Holocaust Memorial Museum ($100,000) see Stern Foundation, Bernice and Milton

US Holocaust Memorial Museum ($50,000) see Swig Charity Foundation, Mae and Benjamin

US Holocaust Memorial Museum ($10,000) see Taube Family Foundation

US Holocaust Memorial Museum ($7,500) see Taube Family Foundation

US Holocaust Memorial Museum ($5,000) see Totsy Manufacturing Co.

US Holocaust Memorial Museum ($200,000) see Wilf Family Foundation

USSALEP ($7,000) see Wilbur-Ellis Co.

Video Action Fund — video focusing on the issues of access to drug and alcohol treatment by pregnant women ($50,000) see Kennedy, Jr. Foundation, Joseph P.

Visions ($12,000) see Summerfield Foundation, Solon E.

Visiting Nurse Association of the District of Columbia — care of cancer patients ($80,000) see Stewart Trust under the will of Mary E. Stewart, Alexander and Margaret

Volunteer Clearinghouse of D.C. — project for intern program for unemployed homeless women ($10,000) see Abell Foundation, Charles S.

Vote America Foundation ($5,000) see Ruan Foundation Trust, John

Washington AIDS Partnership — responding to the HIV/AIDS epidemic ($250,000) see Meyer Foundation, Eugene and Agnes E.

Washington Animal Rescue League ($10,000) see Dimick Foundation

Washington Ballet ($25,000) see Hechinger Co.

Washington Ballet ($7,500) see Higginson Trust, Corina

Washington Cathedral — bricks and mortar ($67,650) see Folger Fund

Washington Cathedral ($5,000) see Hopkins Foundation, John Jay

Washington Cathedral ($5,000) see Willard Foundation, Helen Parker

Washington Chamber Symphony ($7,500) see Neuberger Foundation, Roy R. and Marie S.

Washington Drama Society ($25,000) see Chadwick Fund, Dorothy Jordan

Washington Drama Society — Arena Stage Cultural Diversity Program ($25,000) see Glen Eagles Foundation

Washington Ear ($5,000) see Willard Foundation, Helen Parker

Washington Educational Telecommunication ($30,000) see Chadwick Fund, Dorothy Jordan

Washington Educational Television Association ($1,000) see Foundation for Middle East Peace

Washington Hebrew Congregation ($2,580) see Rales and Ruth Rales Foundation, Norman R.

Washington Hebrew Synagogue ($30,000) see Wasserman Foundation, George

Washington Home Hospice — hospice unit-care of cancer patients and national conference ($55,000) see Stewart Trust under the will of Mary E. Stewart, Alexander and Margaret

Washington Home and Hospice of Washington ($10,000) see Falk Medical Research Foundation, Dr. Ralph and Marian

Washington Hospital Center ($500) see Gross Foundation, Louis H.

Washington Hospital Center — care of cancer patients needy sick fund ($220,000) see Stewart Trust under the will of Mary E. Stewart, Alexander and Margaret

Washington Hospital Center — building fund ($25,000) see Winkler Foundation, Mark and Catherine

Washington Institute for Near East Policy ($11,910) see Blinken Foundation

Washington Institute for Near East Policy ($10,000) see Chais Family Foundation

Washington Institute for Near East Policy ($10,000) see Slant/Fin Corp.

Washington Institute for Near East Policy ($10,000) see Taub Foundation, Joseph and Arlene

Washington Institute for Near East Policy ($250) see Ushkow Foundation

Washington International School ($5,000) see Kent-Lucas Foundation

Washington Journalism Center ($70,100) see Kiplinger Foundation

Washington Lawyer Committee ($7,500) see Higginson Trust, Corina

Washington Legal Foundation ($125,000) see Carthage Foundation

Washington Legal Foundation ($2,000) see Fein Foundation

Washington Legal Foundation ($6,000) see Slaughter, Jr. Foundation, William E.

Washington Legal Foundation ($5,000) see Swim Foundation, Arthur L.

Washington National Eye Center ($50,000) see Aid Association for the Blind

Washington Office on Latin America — project support ($20,000) see Warsh-Mott Legacy

Washington Office on Latin America — to help shape a U.S. foreign policy that supports democratic development ($25,000) see Mertz-Gilmore Foundation, Joyce

Washington Opera ($17,000) see Dart Group Corp.

Washington Opera ($10,000) see Dimick Foundation

Washington Opera ($27,879) see Gelman Foundation, Melvin and Estelle

Washington Opera ($10,000) see Lehrman Foundation, Jacob and Charlotte

Washington Opera ($2,500) see Loewenberg Foundation

Washington Opera ($25,000) see O'Brien Foundation, Cornelius and Anna Cook

Washington Opera ($2,500) see Polinger Foundation, Howard and Geraldine

Washington Opera Endowment Fund ($2,000) see Crown Books Foundation, Inc.

Washington Opera — John F. Kennedy Center for Performing Arts ($253,000) see Fisher Foundation, Gramma

Washington Parent Group Fund — increased parental involvement in public schools and a youth anti-violence initiative ($110,000) see Federal National Mortgage Assn., Fannie Mae

Washington Peace Center ($7,500) see Wardlaw Fund, Gertrude and William C.

Washington Performing Arts Society ($20,000) see Dimick Foundation

Washington Performing Arts Society ($2,000) see Seidman Family Foundation

Washington Performing Arts Society ($5,000) see Uslico Corp.

Washington Project for the Arts ($5,000) see Best Products Co.

Washington Project for the Arts ($2,000) see Best Products Co.

Wesley Theological Seminary ($20,000) see Magee Christian Education Foundation

Wesley Theological Seminary ($13,000) see Smith Foundation, Gordon V. and Helen C.

WETA ($16,000) see Gudelsky Family Foundation, Homer and Martha

WETA ($40,000) see Hechinger Co.

WETA ($2,500) see Polinger Foundation, Howard and Geraldine

WETA-Baseball and American Lives — to help fund production of these two major educational series ($750,000) see Davis Foundations, Arthur Vining

WETA — public broadcasting; toward "Challenge to America" ($100,000) see Arcana Foundation

WETA Foundation — research and development of PBS documentary series ($150,000) see Culpeper Foundation, Charles E.

WETA Public Television ($60,000) see Town Creek Foundation

WETA Public TV DC ($35,000) see Circuit City Stores

WETA Television ($20,000) see Garvey Texas Foundation

WETA Television ($20,000) see Himmelfarb Foundation, Paul and Annetta

WETA Television ($75,000) see Marpat Foundation

WETA Television ($8,500) see McGregor Foundation, Thomas and Frances

WETA Television ($25,000) see Shapiro, Inc.

WETA Television ($80,500) see Smith Family Foundation, Charles E.

WETA-TV ($500,000) see Cafritz Foundation, Morris and Gwendolyn

WETA-TV — public broadcasting ($20,000) see Dreyfus Foundation, Max and Victoria

WETA-TV, The National Geographic Specials ($2,460,000) see Chevron Corp.

White House Endowment Fund ($5,000) see Priddy Foundation

White House Endowment Fund — permanent endowment for historical preservation of the public rooms ($250,000) see Tandy Foundation, Anne Burnett and Charles

White House Endowment Fund — towards the $25 million endowment fund ($100,000) see Hillman Foundation, Henry L.

Whitman-Walker Clinic ($14,647) see Aid Association for the Blind

Whitman-Walker Clinic ($10,000) see Bernstein Foundation, Diane and Norman

Whitman Walker Legal Services Project ($3,000) see Covington and Burling

Wilderness Society ($25,000) see Beneficia Foundation

Wilderness Society ($45,000) see Carolyn Foundation

Wilderness Society ($128,000) see Claiborne Art Ortenberg Foundation, Liz

Wilderness Society ($4,000) see G.A.G. Charitable Corporation

Wilderness Society ($25,000) see Glen Eagles Foundation

Wilderness Society ($9,500) see Harding Educational and Charitable Foundation

Wilderness Society ($95,000) see Kimmelman Foundation, Helen & Milton

Wilderness Society ($6,000) see Kingsley Foundation

Wilderness Society ($100,000) see Town Creek Foundation

Wilderness Society ($10,000) see Walker Educational and Charitable Foundation, Alex C.

Wilderness Society — a National Education campaign to preserve the Ancient Forests ($250,000) see Jones Foundation, W. Alton

Wildlife Management Institute ($24,000) see Wellman Foundation, S. K.

Wisconsin Project on Nuclear Arms Control — "Export

Control After the Cold War." A project to improve export controls on dual-use equipment ($250,000) see Jones Foundation, W. Alton

Witness for Peace ($5,000) see Cook Brothers Educational Fund

Women's Law and Public Policy Fellowship Program — to support Fellowship Program ($220,000) see Revson Foundation, Charles H.

Women's Legal Defense Fund ($40,000) see General Service Foundation

Women's Legal Defense Fund ($10,000) see Stern Family Fund

Women's Legal Defense Fund ($13,500) see Westport Fund

Woodrow Wilson International Center for Scholars ($100,000) see Archer-Daniels-Midland Co.

World Jewish Congress American Section ($5,000) see Jaydor Corp.

World Resources Institute ($50,000) see General Atlantic Partners L.P.

World Resources Institute ($50,000) see General Atlantic Partners L.P.

World Resources Institute — developing and promoting solutions to global warming ($300,000) see Jones Foundation, W. Alton

World Resources Institute — a forum for cooperation and exchange of ideas among representatives from North and South America ($75,000) see Tinker Foundation

World Resources Institute — in support of "The 2050 Project" ($3,000,000) see MacArthur Foundation, John D. and Catherine T.

World Resources Institute — for U.S.-Japan research on the transfer of environmental protection technology between developed and Third World countries ($150,000) see United States-Japan Foundation

World Wildlife Fund ($3,000) see Bailey Wildlife Foundation

World Wildlife Fund ($5,000) see Bluhdorn Charitable Trust, Charles G. and Yvette

World Wildlife Fund ($5,000) see Clark Charitable Trust

World Wildlife Fund ($50,000) see Cox, Jr. Foundation, James M.

World Wildlife Fund ($69,667) see Erpf Fund, Armand G.

World Wildlife Fund ($40,000) see Favrot Fund

World Wildlife Fund ($30,000) see Harriman Foundation, Mary W.

World Wildlife Fund ($141,000) see Homeland Foundation

World Wildlife Fund ($41,000) see Homeland Foundation

World Wildlife Fund ($20,000) see Island Foundation

World Wildlife Fund ($6,000) see Ix & Sons, Frank

World Wildlife Fund ($5,000) see Johnson Foundation, Howard

World Wildlife Fund ($116,175) see Liz Claiborne

World Wildlife Fund ($2,981) see Loomis House

World Wildlife Fund ($11,000) see Magowan Family Foundation

World Wildlife Fund ($8,100) see Mead Fund, Nelson

World Wildlife Fund ($100,000) see Phipps Foundation, Howard

World Wildlife Fund ($100) see Schneider Foundation, Robert E.

World Wildlife Fund — capital needs ($50,000) see Sequoia Foundation

World Wildlife Fund ($12,000) see Sewall Foundation, Elmina

World Wildlife Fund ($10,000) see Winona Corporation

World Wildlife Fund — Africa program ($10,000) see Davis Foundation, Edwin W. and Catherine M.

Worldwatch Institute ($80,000) see Noble Foundation, Edward John

Worldwatch Institute ($47,825) see Prickett Fund, Lynn R. and Karl E.

Worldwatch Institute — general budgetary support ($525,000) see Rockefeller Brothers Fund

Worldwatch Institute ($50,000) see Rockefeller Trust, Winthrop

YMCA ($5,000) see Willard Foundation, Helen Parker

Young Concert Artists of Washington ($10,000) see Dimick Foundation

Youth for Understanding Foreign Exchange School ($17,100) see Inland Container Corp.

Youth for Understanding International Exchange ($14,070) see Dexter Corp.

Youth for Understanding — 1991 Corporate Scholarship Program ($10,275) see Crum and Forster

Youth With A Mission ($140,000) see Timmis Foundation, Michael & Nancy

YWCA ($5,000) see Willard Foundation, Helen Parker

YWCA — for building repairs to the Phyllis Wheatley Center, a residence for low and moderate income women ($70,000) see Graham Fund, Philip L.

Florida

ABET ($3,000) see Quanex Corp.

Abilities of Florida ($20,000) see Jenkins Foundation, George W.

Abilities of Florida ($15,000) see Thomas Foundation, Dorothy

Academy of the Holy Names ($1,000) see Florida Steel Corp.

Actors Playhouse ($26,459) see Cohen Foundation, Manny and Ruthy

Adult Literacy League ($8,500) see Grable Foundation

Aid to Victims of Domestic Assault ($1,000) see Rosenberg Family Foundation, William

All Children's Hospital Foundation ($10,000) see Eckerd Corp., Jack

Alpha ($10,000) see Thomas Foundation, Dorothy

Alpha ($5,000) see Thomas Foundation, Dorothy

Alpha, "A Beginning" ($50,000) see Janirve Foundation

Alpha "A Beginning" of Tampa — family counseling early intervention program

($15,000) see Conn Memorial Foundation

Alzheimer's Association ($90,000) see Lattner Foundation, Forrest C.

Alzheimer's Care and Research Center ($20,000) see Florida Rock Industries

Alzheimer's Disease and Related Disorders Association ($10,000) see Reinhold Foundation, Paul E. and Ida Klare

Amelia Island Montessori School ($10,000) see Law Foundation, Robert O.

American Accounting Association ($41,379) see Ernst & Young

American Accounting Association ($218,764) see KPMG Peat Marwick

American Cancer Celeb. Bagging ($44,071) see Winn-Dixie Stores

American Cancer Society ($3,500) see Baker Foundation, George T.

American Cancer Society ($3,000) see Brown Charitable Trust, Peter D. and Dorothy S.

American Cancer Society ($5,100) see Falk Foundation, David

American Cancer Society ($500) see Garner Charitable Trust, James G.

American Cancer Society ($7,500) see Mastronardi Charitable Foundation, Charles A.

American Cancer Society ($6,000) see Stacy Foundation, Festus

American Cancer Society ($21,100) see Winn-Dixie Stores

American Cancer Society ($14,349) see Winn-Dixie Stores

American Cancer Society-Duval County ($60,043) see Winn-Dixie Stores

American Diabetes Association ($6,000) see Charitable Foundation of the Burns Family

American Diabetes Association of South Florida ($5,000) see Frankino Charitable Foundation, Samuel J. and Connie

American Friends of Yeshiva Aish Hatorah ($7,000) see Joselow Foundation

American Heart Association ($100) see Community Health Association

American Heart Association ($6,000) see Stacy Foundation, Festus

American Heart Association ($15,000) see Thoresen Foundation

American Institute of Polish Culture ($145,000) see Rosenstiel Foundation

American Lung Association ($100) see Briggs Family Foundation

American Red Cross ($3,000) see Baker Foundation, George T.

American Red Cross ($1,600) see Goerlich Family Foundation

American Red Cross see Michigan Mutual Insurance Corp.

American Red Cross (Greater Miami Chapter) — for emergency disaster relief

following Hurricane Andrew ($1,000,000) see Knight Foundation, John S. and James L.

America3 Foundation ($1,150,000) see Falcon Foundation

Americraft School ($21,000) see Ragen, Jr. Memorial Fund Trust No. 1, James M.

Angel of Mercy ($350) see Fiterman Charitable Foundation, Miles and Shirley

Ann Norton Sculpture Gardens ($25,000) see Chastain Charitable Foundation, Robert Lee and Thomas M.

Ann Norton Sculpture Gardens ($10,000) see Fuller Foundation

Anti-Defamation League ($12,000) see Wolfson Family Foundation

Anti-Defamation League ($12,500) see Yulman Trust, Morton and Helen

Arcadia Church of God ($10,000) see Morgan Foundation, Louie R. and Gertrude

Archbishop's Charity Drive ($5,000) see Mastronardi Charitable Foundation, Charles A.

Archdiocese of Miami ($10,000) see Abraham Foundation, Anthony R.

Archdiocese of Miami ($100,000) see Flatley Foundation

Arnold Palmer Hospital for Women and Children ($15,000) see Friends' Foundation Trust, A.

Arthritis Research Institute ($5,000) see Bickerton Charitable Trust, Lydia H.

Asolo Performing Arts Center ($13,898) see Beattie Foundation Trust, Cordelia Lee

Asolo Performing Arts Center ($100,000) see Ellis Foundation

Asolo Performing Arts Center ($11,000) see Keating Family Foundation

Asolo Performing Arts Center ($370) see MalCo Products Inc.

Auditory Verbal Institute ($10,000) see Griffin, Sr., Foundation, C. V.

Baptist Book Store ($838) see Poole & Kent Co.

Baptist Theological College ($10,000) see duPont Foundation, Alfred I.

Barry University ($355,000) see Andreas Foundation

Barry University ($2,000) see Baker Foundation, George T.

Barry University ($14,000) see Broad Foundation, Shepard

Barry University — general support ($57,000) see Dunspaugh-Dalton Foundation

Barry University ($30,000) see Garner Charitable Trust, James G.

Barry University ($30,000) see Garner Charitable Trust, James G.

Barry University ($5,000) see Jennings Foundation, Alma

Barry University ($10,000) see Mastronardi Charitable Foundation, Charles A.

Barry University ($2,000) see Meyer Foundation, Baron de Hirsch

Florida (cont.)

Barry University ($10,000) see Mosbacher, Jr. Foundation, Emil

Barry University School of Nursing ($36,000) see Hugoton Foundation

Bascom Palmer Eye Institute ($5,000) see Colt Foundation, James J.

Bascom Palmer Eye Institute ($1,000) see Friedland Family Foundation, Samuel

Bascom Palmer Eye Institute ($10,000) see Mastronardi Charitable Foundation, Charles A.

Bascom Palmer Eye Institute ($5,000) see Rahr Malting Co.

Bascom Palmer Eye Institute ($50,000) see Ross Foundation, Walter G.

Bascom Palmer Eye Institute ($5,000) see Smith 1963 Charitable Trust, Don McQueen

Bascom Palmer Eye Institute ($5,000) see Weinstein Foundation, Alex J.

Bay Medical Center ($50,000) see First Union Corp.

Beaks ($10,000) see River Branch Foundation

Benjamin Foundation ($12,660) see Hersey Foundation

Benjamin Foundation ($2,400) see Northern Star Foundation

Benjamin School ($2,000) see Sweatt Foundation, Harold W.

Bertha A. Bess Children's Center ($5,000) see Jennings Foundation, Alma

Beth Shalom ($10,000) see Cohen Foundation, Manny and Ruthy

Bethany Home ($15,000) see Harris Family Foundation, Hunt and Diane

Bethel Baptist Church ($1,200) see Union Manufacturing Co.

Bethesda Hospital Association — to fund a child day care center ($30,000) see Culpeper Memorial Foundation, Daphne Seybolt

Bethesda Hospital Association ($8,000) see Grimes Foundation

Bethesda Memorial Hospital ($25,000) see Bastien Memorial Foundation, John E. and Nellie J.

Bethesda by the Sea Church ($20,000) see Gronewaldt Foundation, Alice Busch

Bethune-Cookman College — to provide endowment challenge funding ($500,000) see Mott Foundation, Charles Stewart

Bible Alliance — religious ($1,340,000) see Aurora Foundation

Big Bend Hospice-Special Programs — rural program expansion ($50,000) see Frueauff Foundation, Charles A.

Billfish Foundation ($15,000) see Norcross Wildlife Foundation

Billfish Foundation ($10,000) see Stott Foundation, Robert L.

Bishop-Eaton School — scholarships ($10,000) see Jones Intercable, Inc.

B'nai B'rith Florida State Chapter ($5,000) see Woldenberg Foundation

Boat Company ($182,000) see McIntosh Foundation

Boca Raton Community Hospital ($2,500) see Dively Foundation, George S.

Boca Raton Community Hospital ($15,000) see Echlin Foundation

Boca Raton Community Hospital ($1,000) see Linnell Foundation

Boca Raton Community Hospital ($5,000) see Rales and Ruth Rales Foundation, Norman R.

Boca Raton Community Hospital ($66,190) see Volen Charitable Trust, Benjamin

Boca Raton Community Hospital Foundation ($5,000) see EIS Foundation

Boca Raton Community Hospital Foundation ($2,000) see Rukin Philanthropic Foundation, David and Eleanore

Boca Raton Museum ($1,000) see Linnell Foundation

Boca Raton Museum of Art — to offset increased overhead costs ($15,000) see Culpeper Memorial Foundation, Daphne Seybolt

Bolles School ($10,000) see Childress Foundation, Francis and Miranda

Bolles School ($50,000) see Davis Family - W.D. Charities, Tine W.

Bon Secours Hospital ($50,000) see Adams Foundation, Arthur F. and Alice E.

Boy Clubs of Central Florida ($2,000) see Leu Foundation, Harry P.

Boy Scouts of America ($100) see Community Health Association

Boy Scouts of America ($1,500) see Harris Foundation, John H. and Lucille

Boy Scouts of America ($42,150) see Jenkins Foundation, George W.

Boy Scouts of America ($31,000) see Jenkins Foundation, George W.

Boys Club of Broward County ($10,000) see Johnson Foundation, A. D.

Boys Club of Florida ($10,000) see Moore Foundation, Martha G.

Boys Club of Palm Beach County ($10,000) see Bastien Memorial Foundation, John E. and Nellie J.

Boys Club of Sarasota County ($5,000) see Schoenbaum Family Foundation

Boy's Clubs of Bay County ($2,000) see Gulf Power Co.

Boys Clubs of Broward County ($39,800) see Slaughter, Jr. Foundation, William E.

Boys Clubs of Miami ($2,500) see Weintraub Family Foundation, Joseph

Boys and Girls Club ($30,000) see Florida Rock Industries

Boys and Girls Club ($15,000) see Goodwin Foundation, Leo

Boys and Girls Club ($11,600) see Jones Intercable, Inc.

Boys and Girls Club ($20,000) see Walter Industries

Boys and Girls Club of Central Florida ($5,000) see Phillips Foundation, A. P.

Boys and Girls Clubs of Greater Tampa — special program ($25,000) see Conn Memorial Foundation

Boys and Girls Clubs of Greater Tampa — youth program

($15,000) see Conn Memorial Foundation

Braille Bible Foundation ($500) see Fibre Converters

Bread of Life Ministries ($8,000) see Briggs Family Foundation

Brevard Art Center and Museum ($8,955) see Harris Corp.

Brevard Symphony Orchestra ($7,665) see Harris Corp.

Broward Center for Performing Arts ($10,000) see Wells Foundation, Lillian S.

Broward Community College ($5,600) see Dettman Foundation, Leroy E.

Broward Community College ($20,000) see Wells Foundation, Lillian S.

Broward Community College Fund ($20,000) see Einstein Fund, Albert E. and Birdie W.

Broward Community Education Foundation ($5,000) see Buehler Foundation, Emil

Broward County Community Foundation ($5,000) see Einstein Fund, Albert E. and Birdie W.

Broward County Sherrifs Office ($100) see Amaturo Foundation

Broward Education Student Trust ($16,000) see Amaturo Foundation

Broward Performing Arts ($20,000) see Huizenga Family Foundation

Broward Performing Arts Center see Waste Management

Broward Performing Arts Foundation ($20,000) see Amaturo Foundation

Broward Performing Arts Foundation ($100,000) see Einstein Fund, Albert E. and Birdie W.

Broward Performing Arts Foundation ($8,000) see Halmos Foundation

Broward Sheriff's Office ($6,000) see Lipton Foundation

Brownville Church of God ($5,000) see Morgan Foundation, Louie R. and Gertrude

Calvary Baptist Church — religious ($111,000) see Aurora Foundation

Camillus House ($5,000) see Jennings Foundation, Alma

Campus Crusade for Christ ($4,206,246) see DeMoss Foundation, Arthur S.

Campus Crusade for Christ, International ($60,945) see First Fruit

Cardinal Newman High School ($151,000) see Lewis Foundation, Frank J.

Care-to-Share ($30,571) see Florida Power & Light Co.

Caribbean Conservation Fund ($2,500) see Truland Foundation

Catholic Charities ($3,000) see Walsh Charity Trust, Blanche M.

Catholic Charities of the Diocese of Palm Beach ($90,000) see Lewis Foundation, Frank J.

Center Against Spouse Abuse ($1,000) see Lauffer Trust, Charles A.

Center for the Arts — to support development activities and to provide a video film to be used as a development tool ($30,592) see Wahlstrom Foundation

Center for Family Services ($12,000) see Lost Tree Charitable Foundation

Center Foundation ($12,500) see Eckerd Corp., Jack

Central Florida Capital Funds ($10,000) see Friends' Foundation Trust, A.

Central Florida Capital Funds ($100,000) see Disney Co., Walt

Central Florida Capital Funds ($11,667) see Winn-Dixie Stores

Central Florida Children's Fund ($100,000) see Phillips Foundation, Dr. P.

Central Florida Young Men's Christian Association ($26,340) see Phillips Foundation, Dr. P.

Channel 2 ($14,500) see Mills Charitable Foundation, Henry L. and Kathryn

Chasaminade-Madonna College ($100) see Amaturo Foundation

Chi Chi Rodriguez Youth Foundation ($25,000) see Bastien Memorial Foundation, John E. and Nellie J.

Child Care Connection ($25,000) see Goodwin Foundation, Leo

Child Care Connection — statewide dissemination of parent services project ($36,148) see Mailman Family Foundation, A. L.

Child Care of Southwest Florida ($41,436) see United States Sugar Corp.

Child Care of Southwest Florida ($31,934) see United States Sugar Corp.

Child Development Center ($5,000) see Wilkof Foundation, Edward and Ruth

Child Guidance Center ($5,000) see Florida Rock Industries

Children's Cancer Caring Center ($5,000) see Crane Foundation, Raymond E. and Ellen F.

Children's Cancer Caring Center ($10,000) see Meyer Foundation, Baron de Hirsch

Children's Genetic Disease Research ($25,000) see Friedland Family Foundation, Samuel

Children's Haven Adult Center — playgroup equipment ($3,917) see Catlin Charitable Trust, Kathleen K.

Children's Haven of Clay County ($5,000) see Reinhold Foundation, Paul E. and Ida Klare

Children's Home ($6,276) see Falk Foundation, David

Children's Home ($5,000) see Thomas Foundation, Dorothy

Children's Home Society ($25,000) see Kennedy Family Foundation, Ethel and W. George

Children's Home Society Auxiliary ($2,100) see Baker Foundation, George T.

Children's Home Society of Florida ($3,500) see Halmos Foundation

Children's Home Society of Florida ($2,000) see Halmos Foundation

Children's Home Society of Florida ($5,641) see Lauffer Trust, Charles A.

Children's Home Society of Florida ($60,000) see Thomas Foundation, Dorothy

Children's Place/Connor's Nursery ($5,000) see Frankino Charitable Foundation, Samuel J. and Connie

Chipola Junior College — scholarship fund ($77,915) see McLendon Educational Fund, Violet H.

Chipola Junior College — scholarship fund ($77,915) see McLendon Educational Fund, Violet H.

Chopin Foundation of US ($60,000) see Rosenstiel Foundation

Christ the King Monastery ($7,000) see McMahon Charitable Trust Fund, Father John J.

Christian Medical Foundation International ($15,000) see Driehaus Foundation, Richard H.

Christian Service Center ($5,500) see Leu Foundation, Harry P.

Christmas Toy Shop Project ($500) see Isaly Klondike Co.

Church of Bethesda By The Sea ($20,000) see Halmos Foundation

Church of St. Brenden ($17,000) see Bickerton Charitable Trust, Lydia H.

Cities in Schools ($10,000) see Lost Tree Charitable Foundation

Citizens Scholarship Fund ($14,000) see Holmes Foundation

Citizens Scholarship Fund — scholarship support ($1,000) see Wahlstrom Foundation

City of Hope ($60,000) see Hoag Family Foundation, George

City Rescue Mission ($10,000) see Parsons - W.D. Charities, Vera Davis

City of Sarasota — development of a park ($100,000) see Selby and Marie Selby Foundation, William G.

Coalition for the Homeless ($5,200) see Greater Construction Corp. Charitable Foundation, Inc.

Coalition for the Homeless of Orlando ($28,000) see Overstreet Foundation

Coconut Grove Playhouse ($50,000) see Adams Foundation, Arthur F. and Alice E.

Coconut Grove Playhouse ($10,000) see Rosenberg Foundation, William J. and Tina

Coconut Grove Playhouse ($25,000) see Ryder System

Coconut Grove Playhouse State Theater of Florida ($15,000) see Rosenstiel Foundation

College of Boca Raton ($1,000,000) see Lynn Foundation, E. M.

College of Boca Raton ($500,000) see Lynn Foundation, E. M.

College of Boca Raton ($5,000) see Lynn Foundation, E. M.

College of Boca Raton ($283,573) see Pope Foundation, Lois B.

College of Boca Raton — Love Tree Project ($8,167) see Pope Foundation, Lois B.

College of Palm Beaches ($4,400) see Wiggins Memorial Trust, J. J.

Collier County Community Foundation ($50,000) see

Rollins Luetkemeyer Charitable Foundation

Community Christian Church ($500) see Garner Charitable Trust, James G.

Community Foundation of Greater Tampa ($40,500) see Beveridge Foundation, Frank Stanley

Community Foundation of Greater Tampa ($10,000) see Falk Foundation, David

Community Foundation of Greater Tampa ($25,000) see Saunders Foundation

Community Foundation of Sarasota County ($15,000) see Baird Foundation

Community Foundation of Sarasota County ($30,600) see Beveridge Foundation, Frank Stanley

Community Mobile Meals — purchase and renovation of new facility ($95,500) see Selby and Marie Selby Foundation, William G.

Community School of Naples ($17,360) see Smith 1963 Charitable Trust, Don McQueen

Community Television Foundation of South Florida, WPST ($45,000) see Hooker Charitable Trust, Janet A.

Concert Association of Greater Miami ($11,800) see Hooker Charitable Trust, Janet A.

Concert Association of Greater Miami ($25,000) see Mendel Foundation

Concert Association of Greater Miami ($11,300) see Mendel Foundation

Conservancy ($75,000) see Swensrud Charitable Trust, Sidney A.

Coral Ridge Ministries ($50) see Beitzell & Co.

Coral Ridge Ministries ($360,000) see DeVos Foundation, Richard and Helen

Coral Ridge Ministries — televised ministry program ($78,000) see Dow Foundation, Herbert H. and Barbara C.

Coral Ridge Ministries ($59,000) see Getsch Family Foundation Trust

Coral Ridge Ministries — televised ministry program ($5,000) see Maclellan Foundation, Robert L. and Kathrina H.

Coral Ridge Ministries ($35,000) see Van Andel Foundation, Jay and Betty

Coral Ridge Ministries, Coral Ridge Presbyterian Church ($8,000) see Stacy Foundation, Festus

Coral Ridge Presbyterian Church ($170,000) see DeVos Foundation, Richard and Helen

Coral Ridge Presbyterian Church ($64,308) see Huston Foundation

Council on Child Abuse ($5,000) see MacDonald Foundation, Marquis George

Council on Finance and Administration of the United Methodist Church — renovation of youth camp facility ($50,000) see Chatlos Foundation

Covenant House ($5,000) see Buehler Foundation, Emil

Covenant House ($20,000) see Goodwin Foundation, Leo

Crisis Line ($11,000) see Lost Tree Charitable Foundation

Crummer School Mentor Program ($1,000) see Greater Construction Corp. Charitable Foundation, Inc.

Cummer Gallery ($25,000) see Childress Foundation, Francis and Miranda

Cummer Gallery ($10,000) see Florida Rock Industries

Cummer Gallery of Art ($40,000) see duPont Foundation, Alfred I.

Cummer Museum Foundation ($50,000) see Williams Foundation, Edna Sproull

Cypress Village Alzheimer's Center ($40,000) see Davis Family - W.D. Charities, James E.

Cystic Fibrosis Foundation ($50,000) see Forchheimer Foundation

Dade Community Foundation ($10,000) see Dodge Foundation, P. L.

Dade Community Foundation — effort to rebuild affordable housing in South Dade's lowest income neighborhoods ($54,000) see Gap, The

Dade Public Education Fund ($5,000) see Dodge Foundation, P. L.

Dade Public Education Fund — Smarter Schools Program, Broward County ($187,956) see Citicorp

Dade Public Education Fund — Smarter Schools Program, Dade County ($187,956) see Citicorp

Daystar ($75,000) see Harding Foundation, Charles Stewart

Daytona Beach Community College ($7,700) see Fish Foundation, Bert

Deaf-Blind Children Centers — for a Senior Development Officer, Fundraising Consultant and Administrative Assistant ($66,000) see Bush Charitable Foundation, Edyth

Deaf Service Center ($7,500) see Jones Intercable, Inc.

Dermatology Foundation of Miami ($125,000) see Wallace Genetic Foundation

Desoto Memorial Hospital ($10,200) see Morgan Foundation, Louie R. and Gertrude

Diagnostic Center ($10,000) see River Branch Foundation

Diocese of Palm Beach ($242,500) see Lewis Foundation, Frank J.

Diocese of Palm Beach ($12,500) see Santa Maria Foundation

Diocese of Pensacola-Tallahassee — for a general evangelization program ($50,000) see Koch Foundation

Diocese of St. Petersburg Educational Appeal ($25,000) see Saint Gerard Foundation

Diocese of Venice in Florida — assist in office expenses and program development ($45,000) see Wilson Foundation, Hugh and Mary

Discovery Center ($50,000) see Florida Power & Light Co.

Discovery Center ($20,000) see Halmos Foundation

Divine Providence Food Bank ($5,000) see Thomas Foundation, Dorothy

Doral-Ryder Open Foundation — American Cancer Society ($5,000) see Zenkel Foundation

Dunedin Fine Art Center Facility Expansion ($500) see Isaly Klondike Co.

East Ridge Retirement Village ($2,500) see Garner Charitable Trust, James G.

Easter Seal Society ($2,500) see Garner Charitable Trust, James G.

Easter Seal Society ($1,000) see Kennedy Family Foundation, Ethel and W. George

Easter Seal Society ($1,000) see Kennedy Family Foundation, Ethel and W. George

Easter Seal Society ($10,000) see Ross Foundation, Walter G.

Eckerd College ($25,000) see Eckerd Corp., Jack

Eckerd College — annual fund support ($50,000) see Frueauff Foundation, Charles A.

Eckerd College ($2,500) see Hamel Family Charitable Trust, D. A.

Eckerd College ($25,000) see Poynter Fund

Eckerd College — purchase of database ($30,000) see Saunders Foundation

Eckerd College — to provide computer/peripheral equipment for an advanced writing laboratory or scientific computing facility and to upgrade general purpose laboratory ($55,000) see Bush Charitable Foundation, Edyth

Eckerd Family Youth Alternatives ($122,500) see Jenkins Foundation, George W.

Eckerd Family Youth Alternatives ($25,000) see Walter Industries

Edgewood Ranch Foundation ($5,000) see Phillips Foundation, A. P.

Education Partnership of Palm Beach County ($5,000) see Chastain Charitable Foundation, Robert Lee and Thomas M.

Edward W. Weidner Center for the Performing Arts ($4,000) see Blair Foundation, John

Edward Waters College President's Fund ($54,000) see Williams Foundation, Edna Sproull

El Hogar Projects ($5,000) see Clayton Fund

Elderly Interest Fund ($5,000) see Einstein Fund, Albert E. and Birdie W.

Elizabeth H. Faulk Foundation ($10,000) see Lynn Foundation, E. M.

Embry-Riddle Aeronautical University ($15,000) see Davis Family - W.D. Charities, Tine W.

Embry-Riddle Aeronautical University — scholarship fund ($1,200) see Gholston Trust, J. K.

Embry-Riddle Aeronautical University — toward construction of additional space and renovation of existing space for a Physical Science laboratory ($75,000) see Bush Charitable Foundation, Edyth

Embry-Riddle University ($14,000) see Dodge Foundation, P. L.

Encounters in Excellence ($10,000) see Rosenberg

Foundation, William J. and Tina

Environmental Learning Center ($10,000) see Holmes Foundation

Environmental Learning Center — to provide support in the establishment of a learning facility designed to create an informed electorate regarding environmental issues ($20,000) see Wahlstrom Foundation

Environmental Solutions International — to provide operational funding for the International Conservation and Environmental Projects ($85,000) see Hoover Foundation

Epilepsy Association of the Palm Beaches ($5,000) see Frankino Charitable Foundation, Samuel J. and Connie

Episcopal Diocese of Florida ($17,000) see Childress Foundation, Francis and Miranda

Episcopal Diocese of Florida and Bishop's Discretionary Fund — to support the Companion Project with Cuba program ($212,000) see duPont Fund, Jessie Ball

Episcopal High School ($5,000) see Reinhold Foundation, Paul E. and Ida Klare

Epworth Village — patient care at Susanna Wesley Health Center ($50,000) see Chatlos Foundation

Escot ($10,000) see Falk Foundation, David

Evangelism Explosion III ($4,500) see Getsch Family Foundation Trust

Everglades Nature Center at Flamingo Gardens ($5,000) see Wharton Trust, William P.

Eye Research Foundation ($25,000) see Davis Family - W.D. Charities, James E.

FACT ($30,000) see Saint Gerard Foundation

Faith Children's Home ($1,000) see Ellis Foundation

Faith Counseling Center — facility expansion ($50,000) see Frueauff Foundation, Charles A.

Federation of Allied Jewish Appeal ($94,000) see Brown Charitable Trust, Peter D. and Dorothy S.

Fillabelly ($1,250) see Harris Foundation, John H. and Lucille

Fine Arts Society ($2,000) see Harris Foundation, John H. and Lucille

First Baptist Church ($10,000) see Kelly Tractor Co.

First Baptist Church of Perrine ($14,212) see Dodge Foundation, P. L.

First Presbyterian Church ($20,000) see Bay Branch Foundation

First Presbyterian Church ($11,000) see Harper Foundation, Philip S.

First Presbyterian Church ($307,555) see Stacy Foundation, Festus

First United Methodist Church ($80,000) see Ellis Foundation

First United Methodist Church ($10,000) see Friends' Foundation Trust, A.

First United Methodist Church ($5,000) see Greater

Construction Corp. Charitable Foundation, Inc.

First United Methodist Church ($20,000) see Jenkins Foundation, George W.

Flagler College ($1,228,985) see Flagler Foundation

Flagler College ($400,000) see Kenan, Jr. Charitable Trust, William R.

Flagler College — to provide equipment for a radio control room, an audio production room, and hardware and software for a journalism lab ($75,000) see Bush Charitable Foundation, Edyth

Flagler Hospital — medical care of needy ($104,096) see Smith Benevolent Association, Buckingham

Florence Fuller Child Development ($5,000) see Lynn Foundation, E. M.

Florence Fuller Child Development Center ($50,000) see Stone Foundation, David S.

Florida A&M University ($50,000) see Deloitte & Touche

Florida A&M University ($100,000) see Edison Foundation, Harry

Florida A&M University ($10,000) see Navistar International Corp.

Florida A&M University ($39,750) see Ryder System

Florida A&M University ($3,600) see Wiggins Memorial Trust, J. J.

Florida Atlantic University ($1,120) see Rukin Philanthropic Foundation, David and Eleanore

Florida Atlantic University ($1,000) see Rukin Philanthropic Foundation, David and Eleanore

Florida Baptist Children's Home ($25,000) see Jenkins Foundation, George W.

Florida Chamber of Commerce ($5,000) see Gulf Power Co.

Florida Council on Economic Education ($1,000) see Florida Steel Corp.

Florida Council on Economic Education ($1,000) see Florida Steel Corp.

Florida Cystic Fibrosis ($10,000) see Johnson Foundation, A. D.

Florida Defenders of the Environment ($30,000) see Dunn Foundation, Elizabeth Ordway

Florida FFA Foundation — leadership program ($2,000) see Stuart Foundation, Edward C.

Florida Future Farmers of America Foundation ($7,500) see United States Sugar Corp.

Florida Government for the People Foundation ($25,000) see Chastain Charitable Foundation, Robert Lee and Thomas M.

Florida History Associates ($7,500) see Davis Family - W.D. Charities, James E.

Florida History Associates ($10,000) see Winn-Dixie Stores

Florida Horsemen's Benevolent Protection Association ($3,400) see Colt Foundation, James J.

Florida Hospice ($2,000) see Kennedy Family Foundation, Ethel and W. George

Florida (cont.)

Florida House ($1,000) see
Briggs Family Foundation

Florida Institute of Technology
— to develop a mechanical
evaluation test and analysis
system ($75,000) see Bush
Charitable Foundation, Edyth

Florida Institute of Technology
($50,000) see Janirve
Foundation

Florida International University
($63,334) see Hitachi

Florida International University
($10,000) see Rinker Materials
Corp.

Florida International University
($50,000) see Ryder System

Florida International University
($50,000) see Statler
Foundation

Florida International University
Foundation ($10,000) see
Meyer Foundation, Baron de
Hirsch

Florida Keys Educational
Foundation ($60,000) see
Beneficia Foundation

Florida Keys Land and Sea Trust
($7,000) see Eaton
Foundation, Cyrus

Florida Orchestra ($2,900) see
Bickerton Charitable Trust,
Lydia H.

Florida Orchestra ($100,000) see
English-Bonter- Mitchell
Foundation

Florida Orchestra ($5,100) see
Falk Foundation, David

Florida Orchestra ($100,000) see
GTE Corp.

Florida Orchestra ($25,000) see
Saunders Foundation

Florida Repertory Theatre
($5,000) see Fortin Foundation
of Florida

Florida Repertory Theatre
($12,474) see Howell
Foundation, Eric and Jessie

Florida Sheriff Boys Ranch
($5,000) see Cohen
Foundation, George M.

Florida Sheriffs Youth Ranch
Foundation — construction of
campus residence ($75,000)
see Selby and Marie Selby
Foundation, William G.

Florida Southern College
($10,000) see Grader
Foundation, K. W.

Florida Southern College
($94,255) see Jenkins
Foundation, George W.

Florida State University
($11,000) see Davis Family -
W.D. Charities, Tine W.

Florida State University
($237,000) see McIntosh
Foundation

Florida State University ($7,500)
see Rosenberg Foundation,
William J. and Tina

Florida State University — to
support preparation of a book,
BASIC ECONOMICS AND
THE WEALTH OF NATIONS
($18,191) see Earhart
Foundation

Florida State University
Foundation ($120,000) see
Centel Corp.

Florida State University
Foundation ($1,000) see
Kowalski Sausage Co.

Florida State University
Foundation ($60,000) see
Williams Family Foundation
of Georgia

Florida State University
Foundation ($10,000) see

Williams Family Foundation
of Georgia

Florida State University — to
support efforts of FSU and the
Florida Institute for Art
Education to develop a
comprehensive research and
development project for
student art assessment
($155,000) see duPont Fund,
Jessie Ball

Florida Studio Theater ($8,000)
see Appleby Trust, Scott B.
and Annie P.

Florida Symphonic Pops ($250)
see Linnell Foundation

Florida Symphony Orchestra
($5,000) see Phillips
Foundation, A. P.

Florida Tax Watch ($37,500) see
Davis Family - W.D. Charities,
James E.

Florida Tax Watch ($10,000) see
Winn-Dixie Stores

Florida Taxwatch ($25,015) see
Davis Family - W.D. Charities,
Tine W.

Florida Taxwatch ($7,500) see
United States Sugar Corp.

Florida Trust/Bonnet House —
historic preservation ($10,000)
see Pearce Foundation, Dr. M.
Lee

Florida West Coast Music
($5,000) see Wilkof
Foundation, Edward and Ruth

Florida West Coast Symphony
— scholarships ($30,000) see
Beattie Foundation Trust,
Cordelia Lee

Food Relief International
($4,000) see Dettman
Foundation, Leroy E.

Food Relief International
($4,000) see Dettman
Foundation, Leroy E.

Footlighters Foundation
($25,000) see Meyer
Foundation, Baron de Hirsch

Forerunner ($24,000) see
Generation Trust

Fort Lauderdale Philharmonic
Society ($25,000) see
Goodwin Foundation, Leo

Ft. Ogden Church of God
($5,000) see Morgan
Foundation, Louie R. and
Gertrude

Foundation for the Care and
Cure of Huntington's Disease
($5,000) see Stott Foundation,
Robert L.

Foundation for Leadership
Quality and Ethics Practice
($25,000) see Walter Industries

Foundation for the Malcolm
Baldrige National Quality
Award ($7,500) see Avon
Products

Foundation for the Malcolm
Baldrige National Quality
Award ($50,000) see Bechtel
Group

Foundation for the Malcolm
Baldrige National Quality
Award ($50,000) see Federal
Express Corp.

Foundation for Mental Health
($1,000) see Briggs Family
Foundation

Foundation for Mental Health
($1,500) see Swensrud
Charitable Trust, Sidney A.

Foundation for Mental Health
($10,000) see Wodecroft
Foundation

Friends of the Knotts Library
($11,610) see Felburn
Foundation

Friends of Lyric ($1,000) see
Blake Foundation, S. P.

Friends of Lyric ($18,000) see
Chastain Charitable
Foundation, Robert Lee and
Thomas M.

Friends of Research and
Psychiatry ($5,000) see Falk
Foundation, David

Friends of Riverside Theatre —
operational support ($1,000)
see Wahlstrom Foundation

Frostproof Methodist Church
($5,000) see Friends'
Foundation Trust, A.

Gator Boosters ($2,000) see
Metal Industries

Gator Boosters ($3,750) see
Phillips Foundation, A. P.

Gator Boosters ($5,000) see
Smith 1963 Charitable Trust,
Don McQueen

Geico Philanthropic Foundation
($30,000) see Goodwin
Foundation, Leo

Girl Scouts of America ($8,100)
see Cohen Foundation, George
M.

Girl Scouts of America
($25,000) see Kugelman
Foundation

Girl Scouts of America
($10,000) see Leu Foundation,
Harry P.

Girls Club of Lakeland
($31,000) see Jenkins
Foundation, George W.

Girls Incorporated ($300) see
MalCo Products Inc.

Glades County Sheriff
Department ($4,043) see
Wiggins Memorial Trust, J. J.

Glades County Youth Livestock
($6,350) see Wiggins
Memorial Trust, J. J.

Good Samaritan Foundation
($15,500) see Kohl
Foundation, Sidney

Good Samaritan Hospital
($10,000) see Strawbridge
Foundation of Pennsylvania II,
Margaret Dorrance

Good Samaritan Hospital
($1,000) see Tamarkin Co.

Goodwill Industries — training
center construction ($20,000)
see Catlin Charitable Trust,
Kathleen K.

Grace Lutheran Church ($2,000)
see Southern Furniture Co.

Gratitude House ($25,000) see
Fisher Foundation, Max M.
and Marjorie S.

Gratitude House ($15,000) see
Smithers Foundation,
Christopher D.

Greater Fort Lauderdale
Chamber Foundation
($20,000) see Huizenga
Family Foundation

Greater Miami Hebrew Academy
($5,000) see Pearce
Foundation, Dr. M. Lee

Greater Miami Jewish
Federation ($50,000) see
Applebaum Foundation

Greater Miami Jewish
Federation ($25,000) see
Broad Foundation, Shepard

Greater Miami Jewish
Federation ($1,030,135) see
Carnival Cruise Lines

Greater Miami Jewish
Federation ($10,000) see
Cohen Foundation, Manny and
Ruthy

Greater Miami Jewish
Federation ($45,000) see Geist
Foundation

Greater Miami Jewish
Federation ($128,278) see
Gerson Trust, B. Milfred

Greater Miami Jewish
Federation ($10,000) see
Grumbacher Foundation, M. S.

Greater Miami Jewish
Federation ($10,000) see
Herman Foundation, John and
Rose

Greater Miami Jewish
Federation ($43,000) see
Lipton Foundation

Greater Miami Jewish
Federation ($283,333) see
Mendel Foundation

Greater Miami Jewish
Federation ($43,300) see
Morgenstern Foundation,
Morris

Greater Miami Jewish
Federation ($375,000) see
Russell Memorial Foundation,
Robert

Greater Miami Jewish
Federation ($17,500) see Weil,
Gotshal & Manges Foundation

Greater Miami Jewish
Federation ($16,666) see
Yulman Trust, Morton and
Helen

Greater Miami Jewish
Federation ($15,000) see
Yulman Trust, Morton and
Helen

Greater Miami Jewish
Federation ($15,000) see
Yulman Trust, Morton and
Helen

Greater Miami Local Initiative
Support Corporation ($15,000)
see Dodge Foundation, P. L.

Greater Miami Opera ($305,000)
see Adams Foundation, Arthur
F. and Alice E.

Greater Miami Opera ($50,000)
see Ryder System

Greater Miami Opera
Association ($12,200) see
Gerson Trust, B. Milfred

Greater Miami Opera
Association ($10,000) see
Mastronardi Charitable
Foundation, Charles A.

Greater Miami Opera
Association ($3,020) see
Wiseheart Foundation

Greater Miami Opera
Association ($5,000) see
Woldenberg Foundation

Greek Orthodox Arch
Leadership ($10,000) see
Jaharis Family Foundation

Greek Orthodox Arch (Library
Tribute) ($9,000) see Jaharis
Family Foundation

Greek Orthodox Arch Telecom
Program ($10,000) see Jaharis
Family Foundation

Greek Orthodox Archdiocese
($29,000) see Jaharis Family
Foundation

Greenscape ($5,000) see Florida
Rock Industries

Grinnell-Harris Social Center
($875,000) see Harris
Foundation, John H. and
Lucille

Growing Together ($14,000) see
Lost Tree Charitable
Foundation

Gulf Coast Community College
Foundation ($10,000) see
duPont Foundation, Alfred I.

Gulf Coast Community College
Fund — scholarships ($3,000)
see Gulf Power Co.

Gulf Coast Jewish Family
Services ($1,000) see Metal
Industries

Gulf Stream School ($100,000)
see Lattner Foundation,
Forrest C.

Habilitation Center for
Handicapped ($5,000) see
Lynn Foundation, E. M.

Habitat for Humanity ($15,000)
see Houck Foundation, May K.

Habitat for Humanity ($10,000)
see Jones Intercable, Inc.

Habitat for Humanity Public
Charity — provide housing for
qualified residents of
Immokalle, FL ($5,000) see
Barstow Foundation

Hadassah ($350) see Shapiro
Fund, Albert

Haitian Refugee Center
($15,600) see Rosenberg
Foundation, William J. and
Tina

Handicapped Group Living
($25,000) see Jenkins
Foundation, George W.

Hanley-Hazelden Center at St.
Mary's, West Palm Beach
($3,000) see Iroquois Avenue
Foundation

Hanley Hazelden Foundation
($20,000) see Fisher
Foundation, Max M. and
Marjorie S.

Hanley Hazelden Foundation
($20,000) see Taubman
Foundation, A. Alfred

Hanley Hazelden Foundation
($6,000) see Vanneck-Bailey
Foundation

Harbor Branch Foundation
($25,000) see River Branch
Foundation

Harbor Branch Oceanographic
Institute — Marine Education
and Conference Center
($33,000) see Bay Branch
Foundation

Harbor City Volunteer
Ambulance Squad ($7,819)
see Harris Corp.

The Haven ($1,920) see Harris
Corp.

Haven ($10,000) see Mullan
Foundation, Thomas F. and
Clementine L.

Healthy Mothers/Healthy Babies
($10,000) see Lost Tree
Charitable Foundation

Hearing Research Institute
($10,000) see Mills Charitable
Foundation, Henry L. and
Kathryn

Heart Association of Greater
Miami ($5,000) see Greene
Foundation, Robert Z.

Heart of Florida United Way
($15,250) see Rinker Materials
Corp.

Helen Ellis Memorial Hospital
Auxiliary ($1,000) see Ellis
Foundation

Hendry County District School
Board ($25,000) see United
States Sugar Corp.

Heritage Baptist Church ($5,000)
see Morgan Foundation, Louie
R. and Gertrude

High School in Israel ($95,000)
see Russell Memorial
Foundation, Robert

Hillel School of Tampa ($5,000)
see Forbes Charitable Trust,
Herman

Hillsboro County Crisis Center
($20,000) see Jones Intercable,
Inc.

Hillsborough Educational
Partnership Foundation
($195,000) see GTE Corp.

Hillyer House, Florida Christian
Care Centers ($20,000) see
Reinhold Foundation, Paul E.
and Ida Klare

Hobe Sound Community Chest
— Child Care Center
($50,000) see Barra Foundation

Hole in the Wall Gang/South ($5,000) see Lynn Foundation, E. M.

Holmes Regional Medical Center ($5,250) see Harris Corp.

Holocaust Documentation and Education Center ($20,000) see Russell Memorial Foundation, Robert

Holy Cross Hospital ($5,000) see Mann Foundation, John Jay

Holy Cross Hospital Foundation ($5,000) see Amaturo Foundation

Home Association — back-up generator for elevator ($18,500) see Conn Memorial Foundation

Hope Haven ($4,000) see Schultz Foundation

Hope Rural School ($7,500) see Brunner Foundation, Fred J.

Hope Rural School ($5,000) see Chastain Charitable Foundation, Robert Lee and Thomas M.

Hospice ($15,000) see Culpeper Memorial Foundation, Daphne Seybolt

Hospice ($50,000) see Griffin, Sr., Foundation, C. V.

Hospice ($20,000) see Johnson Foundation, A. D.

Hospice ($750) see MacLeod Stewardship Foundation

Hospice ($25,000) see Terner Foundation

Hospice By-The-Sea ($13,000) see Bay Branch Foundation

Hospice Guild of Palm Beach ($50,000) see Gronewaldt Foundation, Alice Busch

Hospice Guild of Palm Beach ($7,000) see Strawbridge Foundation of Pennsylvania II, Margaret Dorrance

Hospice of Naples ($3,000) see May Mitchell Royal Foundation

Hospice of Northwest Florida ($5,000) see Kugelman Foundation

Hospice of Palm Beach — Love Tree Project ($8,166) see Pope Foundation, Lois B.

Hospice of Sarasota — build a hospice house in Venice ($100,000) see Selby and Marie Selby Foundation, William G.

Hospice by the Sea ($3,000) see Echlin Foundation

Hospice by the Sea — grief counseling ($8,879) see Innovating Worthy Projects Foundation

Hospice by the Sea ($2,000) see Rosenberg Family Foundation, William

Hubbard House ($5,000) see River Branch Foundation

Human Development Center of Pasco ($10,000) see Mills Charitable Foundation, Henry L. and Kathryn

Human Services Council ($1,000) see Greater Construction Corp. Charitable Foundation, Inc.

Humane Society of Manatee County ($20,000) see Bishop Trust for the SPCA of Manatee County, Florida, Lillian H.

Humane Society of Vero Beach ($5,500) see Triford Foundation

Hurricane Andrew Relief Efforts — donation of more than six million food service items see James River Corp. of Virginia

Immokalee Habitat for Humanity ($1,200) see MacLeod Stewardship Foundation

Independence ($15,000) see Mills Charitable Foundation, Henry L. and Kathryn

Independent Day School — expansion of school ($200,000) see Farish Fund, William Stamps

Indian River Hospital Foundation ($1,000) see Clark Charitable Foundation

Indian River Hospital Foundation ($10,000) see Hansen Memorial Foundation, Irving

Indian River Memorial Hospital — to provide opportunities for continuing education to nurses ($7,500) see Wahlstrom Foundation

Infants in Need ($10,000) see Mills Charitable Foundation, Henry L. and Kathryn

INSURE for Hurricane Andrew see Reliable Life Insurance Co.

Inter Varsity ($5,000) see Dodge Foundation, P. L.

International Billfish Foundation ($40,000) see Tyson Foods, Inc.

International Game Fish Association ($5,000) see Stott Foundation, Robert L.

Ivanhoe Foundation ($125,000) see Phillips Foundation, Dr. P.

J. Clifford Macdonald Center ($5,000) see Falk Foundation, David

Jacksonville Art Museum — to support institutional development ($200,000) see duPont Fund, Jessie Ball

Jacksonville Art Museum ($50,000) see River Branch Foundation

Jacksonville Community Foundation — miscellaneous ($12,636) see Barnett Banks

Jacksonville Jewish Center ($7,640) see Cohen Foundation, George M.

Jacksonville Jewish Federation ($50,300) see Cohen Foundation, George M.

Jacksonville Jewish Federation ($2,500) see Dubow Family Foundation

Jacksonville Jewish Federation ($75,000) see Wolfson Family Foundation

Jacksonville Museum of Arts and Sciences ($25,000) see River Branch Foundation

Jacksonville Public Library — endowment fund ($5,000) see Bound to Stay Bound Books Foundation

Jacksonville Public Schools Foundation ($500) see Bound to Stay Bound Books Foundation

Jacksonville Symphony Association ($42,855) see First Union Corp.

Jacksonville Symphony Orchestra ($5,000) see Dubow Family Foundation

Jacksonville Symphony Orchestra ($50,000) see Frankel Foundation

Jacksonville Symphony Orchestra ($5,100) see Schultz Foundation

Jacksonville University ($1,000) see Cohen Foundation, George M.

Jacksonville University ($100,000) see Davis Family - W.D. Charities, James E.

Jacksonville University ($50,000) see Kirbo Charitable Trust, Thomas M. and Irene B.

Jacksonville University ($227,287) see Parsons - W.D. Charities, Vera Davis

Jacksonville University ($32,000) see Williams Foundation, Edna Sproull

Jacksonville Zoological Society ($10,025) see Schultz Foundation

Jewish Association Residential Care ($5,000) see Rales and Ruth Rales Foundation, Norman R.

Jewish Community Alliance ($20,420) see Cohen Foundation, George M.

Jewish Community Alliance ($2,500) see Wolfson Family Foundation

Jewish Community Center ($20,000) see Appleman Foundation

Jewish Community Center ($500) see MalCo Products Inc.

Jewish Federation ($5,000) see Abrams Foundation, Benjamin and Elizabeth

Jewish Federation ($25,000) see Eder Foundation, Sidney and Arthur

Jewish Federation ($50,000) see Einstein Fund, Albert E. and Birdie W.

Jewish Federation ($45,000) see Ferkauf Foundation, Eugene and Estelle

Jewish Federation ($25,000) see Greater Construction Corp. Charitable Foundation, Inc.

Jewish Federation ($11,000) see Greater Construction Corp. Charitable Foundation, Inc.

Jewish Federation ($5,000) see Gurwin Foundation, J.

Jewish Federation ($7,500) see Guttag Foundation, Irwin and Marjorie

Jewish Federation ($55,000) see Hassenfeld Foundation

Jewish Federation ($24,625) see Koffler Family Foundation

Jewish Federation ($131,600) see Kohl Foundation, Sidney

Jewish Federation ($5,800) see Mandel Foundation, Jack N. and Lilyan

Jewish Federation ($15,000) see Mazer Foundation, Jacob and Ruth

Jewish Federation ($20,000) see Messing Foundation, Morris M. and Helen F.

Jewish Federation ($8,000) see Messing Foundation, Morris M. and Helen F.

Jewish Federation ($90,000) see Tamarkin Co.

Jewish Federation ($16,666) see Yulman Trust, Morton and Helen

Jewish Federation ($15,000) see Yulman Trust, Morton and Helen

Jewish Federation ($15,000) see Yulman Trust, Morton and Helen

Jewish Federation of Ft. Lauderdale ($3,500) see Oppenheimer Family Foundation

Jewish Federation of Greater Fort Lauderdale ($360,000) see Soref Foundation, Samuel M. Soref and Helene K.

Jewish Federation of Palm Beach ($125,000) see Fiterman Charitable Foundation, Miles and Shirley

Jewish Federation of Palm Beach ($25,000) see Strauss Foundation

Jewish Federation of Palm Beach County ($80,000) see Appleman Foundation

Jewish Federation of Palm Beach County ($1,000) see Berenson Charitable Foundation, Theodore W. and Evelyn

Jewish Federation of Palm Beach County ($15,000) see Dreitzer Foundation

Jewish Federation of Palm Beach County ($20,000) see Fisher Foundation, Max M. and Marjorie S.

Jewish Federation of Palm Beach County ($91,666) see Resnick Foundation, Jack and Pearl

Jewish Federation of Palm Beach County ($1,000) see Shapiro Fund, Albert

Jewish Federation of Palm Beach County ($50,000) see Simon Charitable Trust, Esther

Jewish Federation of Palm Beach County — $25,000 for Exodus Campaign and 500 for Hebrew Free Loan Society ($75,500) see Lowe Foundation, Joe and Emily

Jewish Federation of Palm County ($100,000) see Fisher Brothers

Jewish Federation of South Broward ($40,000) see Mailman Family Foundation, A. L.

Jewish Foundation for Southern Florida ($340) see Amdur Braude Riley, Inc.

Jewish Guild for the Blind ($200) see Shapiro Fund, Albert

Jewish Home for the Aged ($10,000) see Fein Foundation

Jewish Home for the Aged of Palm Beach County ($50,000) see Bauer Foundation, M. R.

John B. Stetson University ($75,000) see Bush Charitable Foundation, Edyth

John and Mable Ringling Museum of Art foundation — art program for senior citizens ($21,300) see Wilson Foundation, Hugh and Mary

John and Mable Ringling Museum of Art Foundation ($1,000) see Kasle Steel Corp.

John and Mable Ringling Museum of Art Foundation ($65,000) see Lannan Foundation

Joseph L. Morse Geriatric Center ($30,000) see Appleman Foundation

Joseph L. Morse Geriatric Center ($10,000) see Terner Foundation

Joseph L. Morse Geriatrics Center ($10,000) see Lazar Foundation

Joseph L. Morse Geriatrics Center ($3,000) see Tamarkin Co.

Junior Achievement ($10,000) see CIT Group Holdings

Junior Achievement ($17,000) see Florida Rock Industries

Junior Achievement ($400) see Isaly Klondike Co.

Junior Achievement ($500) see Wertheim Foundation, Dr. Herbert A.

Junior Achievement ($500) see Wertheim Foundation, Dr. Herbert A.

Junior Achievement of Orange County ($25,050) see Phillips Foundation, Dr. P.

Junior League of Ft. Lauderdale ($1,000) see Lipton Foundation

Junior Orange Bowl Committee ($5,000) see Rosenberg Foundation, William J. and Tina

Jupiter Hospital ($10,000) see Einstein Fund, Albert E. and Birdie W.

Jupiter Medical Center — cancer research ($400,000) see Milbank Foundation, Dunlevy

Jupiter Pre-School ($11,000) see Lost Tree Charitable Foundation

Key Chorale ($5,000) see Appleby Trust, Scott B. and Annie P.

Kidney Foundation of Central Florida ($10,000) see Ford III Memorial Foundation, Jefferson Lee

Kidney Foundation of Southern Florida ($5,000) see Greene Foundation, Robert Z.

Kidney Fund of South Florida ($3,000) see JJJ Foundation

Kids in Distress ($102,770) see Goodwin Foundation, Leo

Kids in Distress ($5,000) see Moore Foundation, Martha G.

Kids Fire House Museum ($200) see Isaly Klondike Co.

Kissimmee Osceola Chamber of Commerce ($2,000) see Greater Construction Corp. Charitable Foundation, Inc.

Kran's Centre for the Performing Arts see Bloomingdale's

Kravis Center for the Performing Arts ($10,000) see Appleman Foundation

Kravis Center for the Performing Arts ($10,000) see Dreitzer Foundation

Kravis Center for the Performing Arts ($27,500) see Einstein Fund, Albert E. and Birdie W.

Kravis Center for the Performing Arts ($30,000) see Florida Power & Light Co.

Kravis Center for the Performing Arts ($20,000) see Herndon Foundation

Kravis Center for the Performing Arts ($4,000) see Howell Foundation, Eric and Jessie

Kravis Center for the Performing Arts ($16,668) see Kohl Foundation, Sidney

Kravis Center for the Performing Arts ($80,000) see Levinson Foundation, Morris L.

Kravis Center for the Performing Arts ($50,000) see Pappas Charitable Foundation, Thomas Anthony

Kravis Center for the Performing Arts ($180,000) see Shapiro Foundation, Carl and Ruth

L.I.F.E., — treatment outcome program ($4,000) see Catlin Charitable Trust, Kathleen K.

Lake Sumter Community College ($20,000) see Griffin, Sr., Foundation, C. V.

Lakeland Boys Club ($25,600) see Jenkins Foundation, George W.

Latin American Mission ($6,000) see Combs Foundation, Earle M. and Virginia M.

Learn to Read of Northwest Florida ($6,000) see BCR Foundation

Learning Experience ($10,000) see Mills Charitable Foundation, Henry L. and Kathryn

Letters for Peace ($7,000) see Connemara Fund

Florida (cont.)

Lewis Jewish Community Center ($1,500) see Rukin Philanthropic Foundation, David and Eleanore

Life Concepts ($25,000) see Phillips Foundation, Dr. P.

Life is for Everyone ($5,000) see Schoenbaum Family Foundation

Life Is For Everyone — scholarship assistance for drug program ($10,000) see Wilson Foundation, Hugh and Mary

Ligonier Ministries ($25,000) see M.E. Foundation

Ligonier Ministries — operating funds ($175,000) see Maclellan Charitable Trust, R. J.

Little Flower Conference of St. Vincent dePaul Society ($12,000) see O'Neil Foundation, M. G.

Little Place ($6,200) see Hutcheson Foundation, Hazel Montague

Living with Loss ($11,000) see Reinhold Foundation, Paul E. and Ida Klare

Local Initiatives Support Corporation ($7,500) see Rosenberg Foundation, William J. and Tina

Logoi — training Hispanic pastors ($5,000) see Epaphroditus Foundation

Long Center ($2,580) see Bickerton Charitable Trust, Lydia H.

Lowry Park Zoological Society — construction of amphitheater ($50,000) see Saunders Foundation

Lutheran Social Services ($25,000) see Reinhold Foundation, Paul E. and Ida Klare

Mae Volen Senior Center ($574,950) see Volen Charitable Trust, Benjamin

Mana-Sota Lighthouse for the Blind ($5,000) see Schoenbaum Family Foundation

Manatee County Association for the Retarded — renovation of service center ($75,000) see Selby and Marie Selby Foundation, William G.

Manatee County Girls Club ($50,000) see Bishop Trust for the SPCA of Manatee County, Florida, Lillian H.

Manatee Day Care Service — community need ($30,000) see Aurora Foundation

Manatee River Youth Ranch — community need ($100,000) see Aurora Foundation

Manatee River Youth Ranch — construction of resident facility ($20,000) see Wilson Foundation, Hugh and Mary

Manatee Youth for Christ — religious ($60,000) see Aurora Foundation

Marathon Area Swim Association ($90,000) see Goldbach Foundation, Ray and Marie

Marathon High School ($37,000) see Goldbach Foundation, Ray and Marie

Marco Island YMCA ($10,000) see Smith 1963 Charitable Trust, Don McQueen

Marian Center for Retarded Children ($20,000) see Mastronardi Charitable Foundation, Charles A.

Marion Center Auxiliary ($3,000) see Baker Foundation, George T.

Martin Memorial Hospital ($10,000) see Hersey Foundation

Martin Memorial Hospital ($4,000) see Prentis Family Foundation, Meyer and Anna

Mary Alice Fortin Childcare Center Foundation ($12,131) see Fortin Foundation of Florida

Mary Alice Fortin Foundation ($250,000) see Fortin Foundation of Florida

Mary Help of Christians School ($10,000) see O'Toole Foundation, Theresa and Edward

Mary Queen of Universe Shrine ($5,000) see Mann Foundation, John Jay

Meals on Wheels ($100) see Community Health Association

Meals on Wheels ($2,500) see Phillips Foundation, A. P.

Mease Hospital and Clinic Foundation ($50,000) see Manning and Emma Austin Manning Foundation, James Hilton

Mease Hospital and Clinic Foundation ($25,000) see Manning and Emma Austin Manning Foundation, James Hilton

Mease Hospital Foundation ($1,000) see Isaly Klondike Co.

Medical Center at Ocean Reef ($100,000) see Ladish Family Foundation, Herman W.

Mental Health Association ($25,000) see Chastain Charitable Foundation, Robert Lee and Thomas M.

Methodist Medical Center ($10,000) see Davis Family - W.D. Charities, James E.

Metropolitan Fellowship of Churches ($8,563) see Dodge Foundation, P. L.

Metropolitan Ministries ($10,000) see Jones Intercable, Inc.

Metropolitan Ministries ($25,000) see Saunders Foundation

Metropolitan Ministries ($25,000) see Thomas Foundation, Dorothy

Miami Beach Housing Authority ($10,000) see Taylor Family Foundation, Jack

Miami Bridge see Home Depot

Miami BSOP ($22,800) see Taylor Family Foundation, Jack

Miami Children's Hospital see Bloomingdale's

Miami Children's Hospital ($28,000) see DeRoy Testamentary Foundation

Miami Children's Hospital ($5,000) see Weintraub Family Foundation, Joseph

Miami Children's Hospital Foundation ($11,000) see Abraham Foundation, Anthony R.

Miami Choral Society ($1,000) see Wiseheart Foundation

Miami Christian College — moving/upgrading of equipment ($52,450) see Chatlos Foundation

Miami City Ballet ($15,000) see Goodwin Foundation, Leo

Miami City Ballet ($10,000) see Mailman Foundation

Miami City Ballet ($1,270) see Wertheim Foundation, Dr. Herbert A.

Miami City Ballet ($1,270) see Wertheim Foundation, Dr. Herbert A.

Miami Dade Community College ($10,000) see Jennings Foundation, Alma

Miami-Dade Community College ($15,000) see Kettering Family Foundation

Miami-Dade Community College Foundation ($10,000) see Blank Family Foundation

Miami Dade Community College Foundation ($5,000) see Rosenberg Foundation, William J. and Tina

Miami Heart Institute ($5,800) see Baker Foundation, George T.

Miami Heart Institute ($10,000) see Bostwick Foundation, Albert C.

Miami Heart Institute ($11,570) see Broad Foundation, Shepard

Miami Heart Institute — nursing chair ($200,000) see Hugoton Foundation

Miami Heart Institute ($10,000) see Ross Foundation, Walter G.

Miami Heart Institute ($100,000) see Storer Foundation, George B.

Miami Heart Institute ($2,000) see Wilder Foundation

Miami Heart Institute — 1991 Campaign of Heart ($5,000) see Baker Foundation, George T.

Miami Jewish Federation ($5,000) see Stein Foundation, Louis

Miami Jewish Home and Hospital for the Aged ($10,000) see Friedland Family Foundation, Samuel

Miami Jewish Home and Hospital for the Aged ($95,824) see Gerson Trust, B. Milfred

Miami Jewish Home and Hospital for the Aged ($10,000) see Goldsmith Foundation

Miami Lighthouse for the Blind ($1,200) see Weintraub Family Foundation, Joseph

Miami Rescue Mission ($6,000) see Colt Foundation, James J.

Miami University ($50,000) see Souers Charitable Trust, Sidney W. and Sylvia N.

Miami University Deans Fund ($150,000) see Applebaum Foundation

Miami University Foundation ($208,243) see Mead Corp.

Miami University Gastro Department ($45,000) see Applebaum Foundation

Miami University Urology Department ($35,000) see Applebaum Foundation

Miami Valley Health Foundation ($25,000) see Philips Foundation, Jesse

Modern Talking Picture Service ($147,641) see Sears, Roebuck and Co.

Morikami ($10,000) see Grimes Foundation

Morse Geriatric Center — for the Alan Cummings Memorial Unit ($173,795) see Cummings Foundation, Nathan

Morton F. Plant Hospital Foundation ($6,750) see Bickerton Charitable Trust, Lydia H.

Morton Plant Hospital ($6,525) see Metal Industries

Morton Plant Hospital Foundation ($9,750) see Eckerd Corp., Jack

Mosaic ($5,000) see Cohen Foundation, George M.

Mosaic ($2,200) see Greater Construction Corp. Charitable Foundation, Inc.

Mosaic ($550) see MalCo Products Inc.

Mosaic ($2,500) see Wolfson Family Foundation

Mote Marine Foundation ($18,050) see Goldstein Foundation, Alfred and Ann

Mote Marine Foundation ($6,000) see Knox Family Foundation

Mote Marine Laboratory ($10,400) see Keating Family Foundation

Mote Marine Laboratory — equipment and cable linkage ($77,049) see Selby and Marie Selby Foundation, William G.

Museum of Art ($197,116) see Huizenga Family Foundation

Museum of Science ($25,000) see Dodge Foundation, P. L.

Museum of Science ($10,000) see Dodge Foundation, P. L.

Museum of Science ($30,000) see Florida Power & Light Co.

Museum of Science ($20,000) see Rosenberg Foundation, William J. and Tina

Museum of Science and History ($8,150) see Schultz Foundation

Museum Science and History ($20,000) see Winn-Dixie Stores

Museum of Science and Industry — construction of planetarium ($50,000) see Saunders Foundation

Mystic Seaport Museum ($3,000) see Blair Foundation, John

N.A.R.A.L. ($3,500) see Blair Foundation, John

NAACP Special Contribution Fund ($30,000) see Winn-Dixie Stores

Naples Community Hospital ($2,000) see Blair Foundation, John

Naples Community Hospital ($75,000) see Briggs Family Foundation

Naples Community Hospital ($1,000) see Harris Foundation, John H. and Lucille

Naples Community Hospital ($10,000) see Moore Foundation, C. F.

Naples Community Hospital ($75,000) see Norris Foundation, Dellora A. and Lester J.

Naples Community Hospital ($1,000) see Swensrud Charitable Trust, Sidney A.

Naples Community Hospital ($10,500) see Wallace Foundation, George R.

Naples Community Hospital ($100,000) see Whitaker Foundation

Naples/Marco Philharmonic ($135,000) see Whitaker Fund, Helen F.

Naples/Marco Philharmonic ($50,000) see Wodecroft Foundation

Naples Philharmonic Center — endowment fund ($5,000) see Barstow Foundation

National Benevolent Association of Christ ($100,000) see Kirbo Charitable Trust, Thomas M. and Irene B.

National Conference of Christians and Jews ($2,000) see Greater Construction Corp. Charitable Foundation, Inc.

National Council of Jewish Women ($12,000) see Gerson Trust, B. Milfred

National Foundation for Advancement in the Arts ($40,000) see Merck Family Fund

National Multiple Sclerosis Society ($5,000) see Brunner Foundation, Fred J.

National Multiple Sclerosis Society ($10,000) see Goldenberg Foundation, Max

National Music Foundation ($100,000) see Alpert Foundation, Herb

National Parkinson Foundation ($20,000) see Gerson Trust, B. Milfred

Nature Conservancy ($18,085) see Bailey Wildlife Foundation

Nature Conservancy ($74,000) see Perkins Charitable Foundation

Nature Conservancy ($5,000) see Schultz Foundation

Negative Population Growth ($3,500) see Blair Foundation, John

New Children's Hospital ($15,000) see Cohen Foundation, George M.

New College Foundation ($10,000) see Goldstein Foundation, Alfred and Ann

New College Foundation ($200,000) see PepsiCo

New College Foundation ($12,500) see Steigerwaldt Foundation, Donna Wolf

New College Foundation ($12,500) see Steigerwaldt Foundation, Donna Wolf

New College Foundation ($6,200) see Steigerwaldt Foundation, Donna Wolf

New Life Dwelling Place — to increase financial support for a shelter for single parent mothers and their abused children ($70,000) see Bush Charitable Foundation, Edyth

New Mount Zion Missionary Baptist Church ($20,000) see Hersey Foundation

New Pond Foundation ($6,000) see Holmes Foundation

New World Symphony — Lincoln Theatre ($50,000) see Dunspaugh-Dalton Foundation

Nich and Marc Buoniconti Fund ($1,000) see Weiss Foundation, Stephen and Suzanne

Nocatee Church of God ($5,000) see Morgan Foundation, Louie R. and Gertrude

North East Florida Institute for Science ($13,000) see River Branch Foundation

North Florida Educational Development Cooperation ($14,000) see Meyer Foundation, Bert and Mary

Norton Gallery and School of Art ($10,000) see Harris Foundation, J. Ira and Nicki

Nova University ($11,483) see Broad Foundation, Shepard

Nova University ($2,000) see Friedland Family Foundation, Samuel

Nova University ($10,000) see Gerard Foundation, Sumner

Nova University ($50,000) see Goodwin Foundation, Leo

Nova University — family center ($60,000) see Mailman Family Foundation, A. L.

Nova University ($3,600) see Wiggins Memorial Trust, J. J.

OCCA, Inc. — to provide support for artist fees ($81,100) see Bush Charitable Foundation, Edyth

Okaloosa-Walton Community College — scholarships ($5,000) see Gulf Power Co.

Old School Square Cultural Arts Center ($500,000) see Lattner Foundation, Forrest C.

Old Tavernier Town Association ($1,000) see Eaton Foundation, Cyrus

Opera Guild ($27,000) see Slaughter, Jr. Foundation, William E.

Opera Guild of Greater Miami ($64,000) see Hooker Charitable Trust, Janet A.

Orange County Public Schools ($37,650) see Phillips Foundation, Dr. P.

Orchid Ball Committee ($10,000) see Berry Foundation, Archie W. and Grace

Orlando Day Nursery ($25,000) see Magruder Foundation, Chesley G.

Orlando Junior Achievement ($10,000) see Martin Marietta Corp.

Orlando Museum of Art ($100,000) see Friends' Foundation Trust, A.

Orlando Museum of Art ($25,000) see Magruder Foundation, Chesley G.

Orlando Museum of Art ($51,000) see Phillips Foundation, Dr. P.

Orlando Opera Company ($4,200) see Farwell Foundation, Drusilla

Orlando Regional Medical Center ($25,000) see Magruder Foundation, Chesley G.

Orlando Regional Medical Center ($5,000) see Martin Marietta Corp.

Orlando Regional Medical Center ($75,000) see Disney Co., Walt

Orlando Regional Medical Center Foundation ($100,000) see Martin Foundation, Bert William

Orlando Regional Medical Center Foundation ($40,000) see Martin Foundation, Bert William

Orlando Regional Medical Center Foundation ($28,000) see Tippit Charitable Trust, C. Carlisle and Margaret M.

Orlando Science Center ($10,000) see Friends' Foundation Trust, A.

Orlando Science Center ($10,000) see Phillips Foundation, A. P.

Orlando Science Center ($53,100) see Phillips Foundation, Dr. P.

Orlando Union Rescue Mission ($11,200) see Overstreet Foundation

Ounce of Prevention Of Florida ($50,000) see Pittway Corp.

Out-of-Door Academy ($5,000) see Dart Foundation

Overtown Community Health Center ($7,500) see Cohen Foundation, Manny and Ruthy

PACT ($15,000) see Bickerton Charitable Trust, Lydia H.

Palm Beach Atlantic College ($500,000) see Rinker Materials Corp.

Palm Beach Atlantic University ($10,000) see Kelly Tractor Co.

Palm Beach Atlantic University ($10,000) see United States Sugar Corp.

Palm Beach Civic Center ($4,607) see Howell Foundation, Eric and Jessie

Palm Beach Community Chest ($10,000) see Falcon Foundation

Palm Beach Community Chest/United Way ($2,000) see Iroquois Avenue Foundation

Palm Beach Community Foundation ($10,000) see Fisher Foundation, Max M. and Marjorie S.

Palm Beach Community Foundation ($2,000) see Tamarkin Co.

Palm Beach County Center for the Arts ($25,000) see Cox Enterprises

Palm Beach County Community Foundation - AJ McIntosh Fund ($50,000) see McIntosh Foundation

Palm Beach County Home ($7,500) see Lost Tree Charitable Foundation

Palm Beach County Jewish Federation ($9,500) see Brown Charitable Trust, Peter D. and Dorothy S.

Palm Beach County Kidney Association ($10,000) see Lost Tree Charitable Foundation

Palm Beach Day School ($30,000) see Halmos Foundation

Palm Beach Day School ($7,120) see Messing Foundation, Morris M. and Helen F.

Palm Beach Day School ($10,000) see Strawbridge Foundation of Pennsylvania II, Margaret Dorrance

Palm Beach Day School — capital campaign ($125,000) see Wean Foundation, Raymond John

Palm Beach Day School — endowment fund ($125,000) see Wean Foundation, Raymond John

Palm Beach Day School — general fund ($75,000) see Wean Foundation, Raymond John

Palm Beach Festival ($10,000) see Chastain Charitable Foundation, Robert Lee and Thomas M.

Palm Beach Jewish Community Campus — general support ($100,000) see Lowe Foundation, Joe and Emily

Palm Beach Martin County Medical Center ($5,000) see Simpson Foundation, John M.

Palm Beach Opera ($2,500) see Abrams Foundation, Benjamin and Elizabeth

Palm Beach Opera ($3,500) see Chastain Charitable Foundation, Robert Lee and Thomas M.

Palm Beach Patrol Christmas Fund ($1,000) see Thorson Foundation

Palm Beaches Community College ($3,600) see Wiggins Memorial Trust, J. J.

Palmer Trinity School — general support ($85,500) see Dunspaugh-Dalton Foundation

Parent Resource Center of Dade County ($10,000) see Mills Charitable Foundation, Henry L. and Kathryn

Partnerships in Education Journal — for "100 Best for 1991-1992," a book which focuses on business role in education reform see Tenneco

Pass-It-On Ministries of South Florida ($10,500) see Mills Charitable Foundation, Henry L. and Kathryn

Payne Chapel — provide and expand services in Newtown and liquidate mortgage at Barnett Bank ($50,000) see Wilson Foundation, Hugh and Mary

Pediatric Pulmonary Research and Education Fund ($10,000) see Walter Industries

Pelican Island Audubon Society ($20,000) see Hopwood Charitable Trust, John M.

PEMH ($650) see Isaly Klondike Co.

Pensacola Federated Jewish Charities ($8,000) see Kugelman Foundation

Pensacola Historical Society — to fund a book on Pensacola history ($20,000) see Gulf Power Co.

Pensacola Junior College — fund drive for science center ($5,000) see Gulf Power Co.

Pensacola Museum of Arts Foundation ($5,250) see Kugelman Foundation

Performing Arts Center Pacers ($25,500) see Goodwin Foundation, Leo

Philharmonic Center for the Arts — endowment fund ($4,000) see Blair Foundation, John

Philharmonic Orchestra of Florida ($20,000) see Adams Foundation, Arthur F. and Alice E.

Philharmonic Orchestra of Florida ($75,000) see Hooker Charitable Trust, Janet A.

Pine Crest School ($5,000) see Dettman Foundation, Leroy E.

Pine Crest School ($10,000) see Johnson Foundation, A. D.

Pinellas County Arts Council ($1,500) see Isaly Klondike Co.

Pinellas County Education Foundation ($26,500) see Ellis Foundation

Pinellas County Education Foundation — Early Childhood Education Program ($102,000) see Honeywell

Pinellas County Jewish Day Care ($5,000) see Forbes Charitable Trust, Herman

Pines of Sarasota — assist in remodeling service center ($20,000) see Wilson Foundation, Hugh and Mary

Pines of Sarasota — day care center, Sarasota ($12,000) see Catlin Charitable Trust, Kathleen K.

Planned Parenthood ($6,000) see Blair Foundation, John

Planned Parenthood ($1,800) see Swensrud Charitable Trust, Sidney A.

Planned Parenthood Federation of America ($3,349) see Halmos Foundation

Planned Parenthood Federation of America ($11,000) see Strawbridge Foundation of

Pennsylvania II, Margaret Dorrance

Planned Parenthood of the Palm Beach Area ($10,000) see United States Sugar Corp.

Plymouth Congregational Church ($45,000) see Kennedy Family Foundation, Ethel and W. George

Police Athletic League ($5,000) see Florida Rock Industries

Polk Museum of Art ($25,000) see Cowles Charitable Trust

Pope John II Regional High School ($3,000) see Charitable Foundation of the Burns Family

Population Institute ($4,000) see Blair Foundation, John

Presbytery of St. Augustine ($50,000) see Williams Foundation, Edna Sproull

Preservation Foundation of Palm Beach ($5,000) see Falcon Foundation

Preservation Foundation of Palm Beach ($7,800) see Fortin Foundation of Florida

Preservation Foundation of Palm Beach ($10,000) see Fuller Foundation

Preservation Foundation of Palm Beach ($5,000) see Halmos Foundation

Preservation Foundation of Palm Beach ($11,000) see Harding Foundation, Charles Stewart

Preservation Foundation of Palm Beach ($6,500) see Hooker Charitable Trust, Janet A.

Prince Ministries ($20,000) see Generation Trust

Prison Crusade ($25,000) see Thomas Foundation, Dorothy

Project Return Florida ($10,000) see Schoenbaum Family Foundation

Providenciales Health Medical Clinic ($4,200) see Smith 1963 Charitable Trust, Don McQueen

Public Education Fund ($10,000) see Rosenberg Foundation, William J. and Tina

Queen of Peace Church — funds to be used for the partial construction of a church ($100,000) see Koch Foundation

Ransoh Everglades School ($13,385) see Gerson Trust, B. Milfred

Ranson Everglades School — for library ($25,000) see Mailman Foundation

Raymond F. Krairs Centers ($30,000) see Belfer Foundation

Recording for the Blind ($10,000) see Mills Charitable Foundation, Henry L. and Kathryn

Red Cross ($5,000) see Falcon Foundation

Reef Relief ($3,000) see Bailey Wildlife Foundation

Ringling Museum Foundation ($4,600) see Keating Family Foundation

Ringling School of Art and Design Library Association ($6,350) see Keating Family Foundation

River Garden Campus Development fund ($50,000) see Cohen Foundation, George M.

Riverhills Christian School — building of a library ($61,500) see Stein Foundation, Jules and Doris

Rivers of Living Water Ministries ($5,000) see Ebert Charitable Foundation, Horatio B.

Riverside Children's Theatre ($7,500) see Holmes Foundation

Riverside Youth Playhouse — to provide support in the establishment of a home for the Riverside Children's Theatre ($75,000) see Wahlstrom Foundation

Rollins College — for the environmental studies program ($60,000) see Baker Trust, George F.

Rollins College — capital fund drive and the environmental studies program ($50,000) see Baker Trust, George F.

Rollins College ($110,000) see Dexter Shoe Co.

Rollins College ($10,000) see Friends' Foundation Trust, A.

Rollins College ($5,500) see Genius Foundation, Elizabeth Morse

Rollins College ($4,500) see Harper Foundation, Philip S.

Rollins College ($2,000) see Kuehn Foundation

Rollins College ($65,000) see Marmot Foundation

Rollins College ($10,000) see Martin Foundation, Bert William

Ronald McDonald House ($10,000) see Falk Foundation, David

Ronald McDonald House of South Florida ($50,000) see Heckscher Foundation for Children

Rosentiel School of Marine and Atmospheric Science, University of Miami ($25,000) see Rosenstiel Foundation

Rotary Club of Tarpon Springs ($500) see Ellis Foundation

Royal Dames for Cancer Research — Goodwin Institute ($25,000) see Goodwin Foundation, Leo

Russell Home for Atypical Children ($30,000) see Phillips Foundation, Dr. P.

Safe Place and Rape Crisis Center ($5,200) see Keating Family Foundation

Safe Place and Rape Crisis Center of Sarasota — construction of 8-bedroom shelter ($100,000) see Selby and Marie Selby Foundation, William G.

Safe Place and Rape Crisis of Sarasota County ($10,000) see Houck Foundation, May K.

St. Andrew's School ($20,000) see Biddle Foundation, Margaret T.

St. Augustine Foundation ($31,977) see Flagler Foundation

St. Augustine School of the Arts ($10,000) see Lipton Foundation

St. Boniface Church ($4,500) see Knox Family Foundation

St. Cyrians Episcopal ($2,000) see Farwell Foundation, Drusilla

St. Edward's School ($10,000) see McDougall Charitable Trust, Ruth Camp

St. Francis Hospital ($60,000) see Mastronardi Charitable Foundation, Charles A.

St. Hagop Armenian Church ($25,000) see Mardigian Foundation

Florida (cont.)

St. James Episcopal Church — to support the establishment of the Christian Community Development Fund ($250,000) see duPont Fund, Jessie Ball

St. Johns Cathedral ($50,000) see Illges Memorial Foundation, A. and M. L.

St. Johns County Welfare Federation of St. Augustine — nursing care, medical care, emergency food and utilities for needy ($72,869) see Smith Benevolent Association, Buckingham

St. Johns River City Band — general support ($5,000) see Swisher Foundation, Carl S.

St. John's United Methodist Church — pre-school equipment ($5,000) see Harris Foundation, William H. and Mattie Wattis

St. Joseph's Catholic Church — for school purposes ($4,000) see Baker Foundation, George T.

St. Josephs Catholic Church ($11,000) see Mastronardi Charitable Foundation, Charles A.

St. Leo College ($20,000) see Walter Industries

St. Lucy's Church ($6,000) see Charitable Foundation of the Burns Family

St. Luke the Evangelist Catholic Church — funds to be used to underwrite a Catholic school program ($50,000) see Koch Foundation

St. Luke's Episcopal Church ($6,000) see Phillips Foundation, A. P.

St. Lukes Hospital ($10,000) see Reinhold Foundation, Paul E. and Ida Klare

St. Lukes Hospital Foundation — therapy equipment ($50,000) see Swisher Foundation, Carl S.

St. Marks Epis Day School — general support ($12,000) see Swisher Foundation, Carl S.

St. Mark's Episcopal School ($3,000) see Dettman Foundation, Leroy E.

St. Mary Catholic Church ($40,000) see Lewis Foundation, Frank J.

St. Marys Episcopal Church ($25,000) see River Branch Foundation

St. Marys Hospital ($50,000) see Appleman Foundation

St. Mary's Hospital ($25,000) see Hall Charitable Trust, Evelyn A. J.

St. Mary's Hospital ($109,000) see Lewis Foundation, Frank J.

St. Mary's Hospital ($1,000) see Tamarkin Co.

St. Marys Hospital Foundation ($25,000) see Schwartz Fund for Education and Health Research, Arnold and Marie

St. Marys Hospital Foundation ($5,000) see Shapiro Fund, Albert

St. Patricks Church ($16,000) see Ragen, Jr. Memorial Fund Trust No. 1, James M.

St. Paul Catholic Church ($5,000) see Morgan Foundation, Louie R. and Gertrude

St. Petersburg Museum of Fine Arts ($1,000) see Poynter Fund

St. Thomas Aquinas Foundation ($25,000) see Huizenga Family Foundation

St. Thomas Episcopal Church ($25,000) see Rockwell Foundation

St. Thomas University ($15,000) see Lynn Foundation, E. M.

St. Vincent Church/St. Peter's Catholic Church ($4,000) see Butler Foundation, J. Homer

Salvador Dali Museum ($250) see Hench Foundation, John C.

Salvation Army ($5,000) see Catlin Charitable Trust, Kathleen K.

Salvation Army ($1,000) see Cook Batson Foundation

Salvation Army ($57,505) see Harris Foundation, John H. and Lucille

Salvation Army ($15,000) see Stacy Foundation, Festus

Salvation Army — hungry fund ($5,000) see Swisher Foundation, Carl S.

Salvation Army ($10,000) see Walter Industries

Salvation Army ($10,000) see Walter Industries

San Antonio Boys Village — operations budget shortfall ($20,000) see Conn Memorial Foundation

Sarasota AIDS Support — benefit concert ($4,000) see Beattie Foundation Trust, Cordelia Lee

Sarasota AIDS Support — assist in resident facility expenses ($18,000) see Wilson Foundation, Hugh and Mary

Sarasota Ballet of Florida ($97,215) see Keating Family Foundation

Sarasota Ballet of Florida ($1,230) see MalCo Products Inc.

Sarasota Ballet Series — scholarships ($07) see Beattie Foundation Trust, Cordelia Lee

Sarasota Community Orchestra ($4,000) see Beattie Foundation Trust, Cordelia Lee

Sarasota County Public Schools Foundation — scholarships, field trips, equipment ($250,500) see Selby and Marie Selby Foundation, William G.

Sarasota County School Teacher Seminar ($2,502) see Dart Foundation

Sarasota County Twelfth Judicial Circuit ($11,245) see Wilson Foundation, Hugh and Mary

Sarasota Jewish Federation ($27,500) see Wilkof Foundation, Edward and Ruth

Sarasota-Manatee Jewish Federation ($14,500) see Foster Charitable Trust

Sarasota-Manatee Jewish Federation ($55,000) see Goldstein Foundation, Alfred and Ann

Sarasota-Manatee Jewish Federation ($15,000) see I. and L. Association

Sarasota-Manatee Jewish Federation ($1,000) see Kasle Steel Corp.

Sarasota-Manatee Jewish Federation ($5,000) see Keating Family Foundation

Sarasota-Manatee Jewish Federation ($11,250) see MalCo Products Inc.

Sarasota-Manatee Jewish Federation ($80,000) see Schoenbaum Family Foundation

Sarasota Memorial Hospital Foundation ($10,000) see Steigerwaldt Foundation, Donna Wolf

Sarasota Opera Association ($14,703) see Beattie Foundation Trust, Cordelia Lee

Sarasota Opera Association ($3,500) see Keating Family Foundation

Sarasota Opera Association ($14,000) see Steigerwaldt Foundation, Donna Wolf

School Board of Sarasota County ($11,345) see Beattie Foundation Trust, Cordelia Lee

School Board of Sarasota County — science fair, Selby tutorial ($178,154) see Selby and Marie Selby Foundation, William G.

Seacrest School ($1,600) see Smith 1963 Charitable Trust, Don McQueen

Seagull Industries for Disabled ($10,000) see Lost Tree Charitable Foundation

Self Reliance — apartments for the disabled ($15,000) see Thomas Foundation, Dorothy

Senior Friendship Center — senior friendship center building ($177,621) see Catlin Charitable Trust, Kathleen K.

Senior Society Planning Council ($1,900) see Sun Banks Inc.

Seventh Day Adventist Church ($5,000) see Morgan Foundation, Louie R. and Gertrude

Shelter for Abused Women ($8,000) see Briggs Family Foundation

Shriners Hospital for Crippled Children ($7,943) see Duncan Trust, James R.

Shriner's Hospital for Crippled Children ($31,386) see Kennedy Memorial Fund, Mark H.

Shriners Hospital for Crippled Children ($5,000) see Schmidt Charitable Foundation, William E.

Shriners Hospital for Crippled Children ($15,000) see Slusher Charitable Foundation, Roy W.

Shriners Hospital for Crippled Children ($10,000) see Trimble Family Foundation, Robert Mize and Isa White

Shriners Hospital for Crippled Children ($7,000) see Wolff Foundation, John M.

Society of Four Arts ($5,000) see Currey Foundation, Brownlee

Society of Four Arts ($10,000) see Fuller Foundation

Society of the Four Arts ($2,000) see Iroquois Avenue Foundation

Society of Four Arts ($15,000) see Magowan Family Foundation

Society of Four Arts ($12,000) see Moore Memorial Foundation, James Starr

Society of Four Arts ($10,000) see Strawbridge Foundation of Pennsylvania II, Margaret Dorrance

Society for the Prevention of Cruelty to Animals of Manatee County ($131,598) see Bishop Trust for the SPCA of Manatee County, Florida, Lillian H.

SOS Children's Village of Florida ($20,000) see Buehler Foundation, Emil

SOU Scholarship Foundation — scholarship fund ($5,000) see Swisher Foundation, Carl S.

South Brevard Women's Center ($3,949) see Harris Corp.

South Dade Jewish Community Center ($50,000) see Russell Memorial Foundation, Robert

South Florida Center for Theological Studies ($10,000) see Dodge Foundation, P. L.

South Florida Charitable Foundation ($1,000) see Gillett Foundation, Elesabeth Ingalls

South Florida Community College ($6,000) see Wiggins Memorial Trust, J. J.

South Florida Jail Ministries ($1,000) see Garner Charitable Trust, James G.

South Florida Museum and Bishop Planetarium ($121,764) see Bishop Trust for the SPCA of Manatee County, Florida, Lillian H.

South Florida Public Telecommunications ($3,500) see Chastain Charitable Foundation, Robert Lee and Thomas M.

South Miami Hospital ($25,000) see Marmot Foundation

South Palm Beach City Jewish Federation ($15,100) see Lasky Co.

South Palm Beach County Jewish Federation ($175,250) see Rales and Ruth Rales Foundation, Norman R.

South Palm Beach County Jewish Federation ($2,022) see Rukin Philanthropic Foundation, David and Eleanore

South Palm Beach Jewish Federation-Early Childhood Learing Center ($25,000) see Zale Foundation

Southeast Regional Office for Hispanic Affairs ($31,000) see Brencanda Foundation

Southeastern Guide Dogs ($25,000) see Bishop Trust for the SPCA of Manatee County, Florida, Lillian H.

Southeastern Guide Dogs — help construct 80 dog kennel ($10,000) see Wilson Foundation, Hugh and Mary

Southeastern University of the Health Sciences ($20,000) see Eckerd Corp., Jack

Southern Scholarship Foundation — operating endowment and construction of new scholarship house ($500,000) see Frueauff Foundation, Charles A.

Southern Scholarship Foundation ($5,000) see Rosenberg Foundation, William J. and Tina

Southern Scholarship Foundation — assist in scholarship house expenses ($5,000) see Wilson Foundation, Hugh and Mary

Southwest Florida Center for Independent Living ($10,000) see Foulds Trust, Claiborne F

Space Coast Science Center ($7,164) see Harris Corp.

Spanish Church of God ($5,000) see Morgan Foundation, Louie R. and Gertrude

Spanish Mission ($5,000) see Morgan Foundation, Louie R. and Gertrude

Step ($25,000) see Bastien Memorial Foundation, John E. and Nellie J.

Stetson University ($25,000) see McGraw Foundation, Donald C.

Stetson University ($120,000) see Rinker Materials Corp.

Sun Room Center ($15,000) see Mills Charitable Foundation, Henry L. and Kathryn

Sun System Development — Help Us Dream For a Cure Cancer Campaign ($50,000) see Chatlos Foundation

Suncoast Ronald McDonald House ($40,000) see Saunders Foundation

Sunrise Academy ($1,000) see Briggs Family Foundation

Tallahassee YMCA ($1,250) see Sun Banks Inc.

Talmudic University of Florida ($23,500) see Joselow Foundation

Tampa Bay Business Hall of Fame ($100,040) see Ellis Foundation

Tampa Bay Performing Arts Center ($5,000) see Bickerton Charitable Trust, Lydia H.

Tampa Bay Performing Arts Center ($10,000) see Eckerd Corp., Jack

Tampa Bay Performing Arts Center ($5,000) see Pyramid Foundation

Tampa Bay Performing Arts Center ($50,000) see Saunders Foundation

Tampa Bay Performing Arts Center ($100,000) see Walter Industries

Tampa Day Pre-School and Kindergarten ($10,000) see Jones Intercable, Inc.

Tampa Jesuit High School ($25,000) see Saint Gerard Foundation

Tampa Museum of Art ($15,000) see Jones Intercable, Inc.

Tampa Museum of Art ($5,000) see Pyramid Foundation

Tampa United Methodist Centers — child care services program ($20,000) see Conn Memorial Foundation

Tampa United Methodist Centers ($10,000) see Thomas Foundation, Dorothy

Tampa United Methodist Centers — SHARE Program ($15,000) see Jones Intercable, Inc.

Tarpon Springs Hospital Foundation ($200,000) see Ellis Foundation

Tarpon Springs Library ($1,000) see Ellis Foundation

Temple Beth-El ($38,600) see Rosenberg Family Foundation, William

Temple Beth-El ($66,190) see Volen Charitable Trust, Benjamin

Temple Beth Shalom ($52,594) see Gerson Trust, B. Milfred

Temple Beth Shalom ($2,490) see MalCo Products Inc.

Temple Emanu-el ($100,000) see Appleman Foundation

Temple Emanu-El ($43,600) see Gerson Trust, B. Milfred

Temple Israel ($15,000) see Hutcheson Foundation, Hazel Montague

Temple Israel of Miami ($100,000) see Gumenick Foundation, Nathan and Sophie

Thomas E. Whegham Trust ($1,000) see Kennedy Family Foundation, Ethel and W. George

Tibet Fund ($5,000) see Chastain Charitable Foundation, Robert Lee and Thomas M.

TMH Foundation — diabetes
center ($6,700) see Sun Banks
Inc.
TNC Florida Chapter ($150,000)
see Storer Foundation, George
B.
Town of Palm Beach ($12,000)
see Gillett Foundation,
Elesabeth Ingalls
Track Florida ($174,903) see
McIntosh Foundation
Trinity-By-The-Cove ($1,000)
see Briggs Family Foundation
Trinity College ($101,040) see
Lamb Foundation, Kirkland S.
and Rena B.
Trinity Episcopal School —
general support ($100,000) see
Dunspaugh-Dalton Foundation
Turnaround — adolescent drug
rehabilitation program
($1,000) see Stuart
Foundation, Edward C.
United Arts of Central Florida
($25,000) see Friends'
Foundation Trust, A.
United Arts of Central Florida
($100,000) see Phillips
Foundation, Dr. P.
United Arts of Central Florida
($100,000) see Disney Co.,
Walt
United Cerebral Palsy Broward
County ($37,000) see Wasie
Foundation
United Fund of Bay County
($3,960) see Gulf Power Co.
United Jewish Appeal
($141,666) see Resnick
Foundation, Jack and Pearl
United Jewish Association
Passage to Freedom
($100,000) see Appleman
Foundation
United Jewish Fund (State of
Israel Bonds) ($35,000) see
Price Foundation, Louis and
Harold
United Negro College Fund
($6,500) see Parsons - W.D.
Charities, Vera Davis
United Protestant Appeal Shelter
for the Homeless ($163,000)
see Kennedy Family
Foundation, Ethel and W.
George
United States Air Force ($5,000)
see Batchelor Foundation
United Way ($5,000) see
Childress Foundation, Francis
and Miranda
United Way ($15,000) see Cobb
Family Foundation
United Way ($10,000) see
Community Health Association
United Way ($2,000) see Dent
Family Foundation, Harry
United Way ($98,000) see
Florida Power & Light Co.
United Way ($87,500) see
Florida Power & Light Co.
United Way ($87,500) see
Florida Power & Light Co.
United Way ($87,500) see
Florida Power & Light Co.
United Way ($87,500) see
Florida Power & Light Co.
United Way ($55,000) see
Florida Power & Light Co.
United Way ($20,896) see
Florida Rock Industries
United Way ($13,125) see Folger
Fund
United Way ($10,000) see
Friends' Foundation Trust, A.
United Way ($500) see Genius
Foundation, Elizabeth Morse
United Way ($10,000) see
Halmos Foundation
United Way ($20,000) see
Jaharis Family Foundation

United Way ($5,125) see Kohl
Foundation, Sidney
United Way ($55,000) see Leu
Foundation, Harry P.
United Way ($10,000) see Leu
Foundation, Harry P.
United Way ($1,000) see Linnell
Foundation
United Way ($5,000) see Moore
Foundation, C. F.
United Way ($5,000) see Rales
and Ruth Rales Foundation,
Norman R.
United Way ($5,000) see Schultz
Foundation
United Way ($7,500) see Weil,
Gotshal & Manges Foundation
United Way ($5,500) see
Wolfson Family Foundation
United Way of Broward County
($19,050) see Rinker Materials
Corp.
United Way of Dade County
($340,000) see Federated
Department Stores and Allied
Stores Corp.
United Way of Dade County
($38,900) see Rinker Materials
Corp.
United Way of Dade County
($351,328) see Ryder System
United Way of Dade County
($175,671) see Ryder System
United Way of Dade County —
general purpose fund ($8,921)
see Walgreen Co.
United Way of Escambia County
— assist in campaign film
($10,000) see Gulf Power Co.
United Way of Greater Tampa
($137,268) see GTE Corp.
United Way of Manatee County
— community need ($50,000)
see Aurora Foundation
United Way Northeast Florida
($60,000) see First Union
Corp.
United Way of Northeast Florida
($60,000) see First Union
Corp.
United Way Northeast Florida
($50,000) see First Union
Corp.
United Way — 1991
campaign/Dade County
($30,000) see AMR Corp.
United Way of Orange County
($75,000) see Bush Charitable
Foundation, Edyth
United Way of Orange County
($133,000) see McDonnell
Douglas Corp.
United Way of Palm Beach
County ($15,450) see Rinker
Materials Corp.
United Way of Volusia County
— construction of a new
administrative/training facility
($100,000) see Bush
Charitable Foundation, Edyth
University Baptist ($5,000) see
Kelly Tractor Co.
University of Central Florida
($5,500) see Harper
Foundation, Philip S.
University of Central Florida
($37,178) see Magruder
Foundation, Chesley G.
University of Central Florida —
scholar chair in banking
($100,000) see Sun Banks Inc.
University of Central Florida
($7,950) see Wiggins
Memorial Trust, J. J.
University of Central Florida
Foundation ($10,000) see Leu
Foundation, Harry P.
University of Florida ($12,500)
see Broad Foundation, Shepard
University of Florida —
department of neurology

($75,000) see
Dunspaugh-Dalton Foundation
University of Florida ($10,000)
see duPont Foundation, Alfred
I.
University of Florida ($10,000)
see Eckerd Corp., Jack
University of Florida —
scholarships ($1,500) see
Erving Paper Mills
University of Florida ($2,000)
see Fortis Inc.
University of Florida ($20,250)
see Gerson Trust, B. Milfred
University of Florida ($8,000)
see Gloeckner Foundation,
Fred
University of Florida ($80,000)
see Hitachi
University of Florida ($50,000)
see Occidental Petroleum Corp.
University of Florida ($20,000)
see Phillips Foundation, A. P.
University of Florida ($17,000)
see Poinsettia Foundation,
Paul and Magdalena Ecke
University of Florida ($8,041)
see Reinhold Foundation, Paul
E. and Ida Klare
University of Florida ($100,000)
see Rinker Materials Corp.
University of Florida — nursing
($200,000) see Sutcliffe
Foundation, Walter and Louise
University of Florida —
Agrotechnologies Doctoral
Program ($15,912) see
Margoes Foundation
University of Florida College of
Medicine ($25,000) see
duPont Foundation, Alfred I.
University of Florida College of
Nursing ($50,000) see Kirbo
Charitable Trust, Thomas M.
and Irene B.
University of Florida College of
Pharmacy ($1,000) see Dubow
Family Foundation
University of Florida Foundation
($1,500) see Abrams
Foundation, Talbert and Leota
University of Florida Foundation
($15,000) see Childress
Foundation, Francis and
Miranda
University of Florida Foundation
— advanced seafood safety
and quality program
($200,000) see General Mills
University of Florida Foundation
($375,000) see Grader
Foundation, K. W.
University of Florida Foundation
($1,000) see Grass Family
Foundation
University of Florida Foundation
see Greenwood Mills
University of Florida Foundation
— capital campaign for
laboratory ($101,000) see
Honeywell
University of Florida Foundation
($2,000) see Smith 1963
Charitable Trust, Don
McQueen
University of Florida Foundation
— neurosurgery pediatrics
($100,000) see Swisher
Foundation, Carl S.
University of Florida Foundation
($120,000) see Wells
Foundation, Lillian S.
University of Florida Foundation
— addressing policy-relevant
topics of conservation and
development in Argentina and
Chile ($70,000) see Tinker
Foundation
University of Florida Foundation
— School of Medicine
($100,000) see Einstein Fund,
Albert E. and Birdie W.

University of Florida Research
Foundation — POG Data Base
($20,000) see Maxfield
Foundation
University of Miami ($2,000)
see Baker Foundation, George
T.
University of Miami — sexuality
education ($25,000) see Brush
Foundation
University of Miami ($31,200)
see Cobb Family Foundation
University of Miami ($30,000)
see Cobb Family Foundation
University of Miami ($16,000)
see Cobb Family Foundation
University of Miami ($10,000)
see Cobb Family Foundation
University of Miami ($3,020)
see Friedland Family
Foundation, Samuel
University of Miami ($6,000)
see Gerard Foundation, Sumner
University of Miami ($25,000)
see Gumenick Foundation,
Nathan and Sophie
University of Miami ($10,000)
see Gumenick Foundation,
Nathan and Sophie
University of Miami ($5,000)
see Gumenick Foundation,
Nathan and Sophie
University of Miami ($10,000)
see Harris Foundation, J. Ira
and Nicki
University of Miami ($50,000)
see Huizenga Family
Foundation
University of Miami ($50,000)
see Jennings Foundation, Alma
University of Miami ($10,000)
see Jennings Foundation, Alma
University of Miami ($400,000)
see Kennedy Family
Foundation, Ethel and W.
George
University of Miami ($1,000)
see Martini Foundation,
Nicholas
University of Miami ($10,000)
see Mostyn Foundation
University of Miami ($300,000)
see Pearce Foundation, Dr. M.
Lee
University of Miami ($100,000)
see Storer Foundation, George
B.
University of Miami ($100,000)
see Storer Foundation, George
B.
University of Miami ($100,000)
see Storer Foundation, George
B.
University of Miami ($8,356)
see Taylor Family Foundation,
Jack
University of Miami ($121,300)
see Weintraub Family
Foundation, Joseph
University of Miami ($2,700)
see Wertheim Foundation, Dr.
Herbert A.
University of Miami ($2,700)
see Wertheim Foundation, Dr.
Herbert A.
University of Miami Center for
Blood Diseases ($100) see
General Development Corp.
University of Miami — Marc
Boniconti fund ($10,000) see
Richardson Foundation, Frank
E. and Nancy M.
University of Miami McCoy
Scholarship Fund ($15,000)
see Mostyn Foundation
University of Miami Medical
School — endowment
($5,500,000) see Sylvester
Foundation, Harcourt M. and
Virginia W.
University of Miami — research,
equipment, education and

laboratory ($175,000) see
Hugoton Foundation
University of Miami School of
Law ($5,000) see Zarkin
Memorial Foundation, Charles
University of Miami School of
Medicine ($5,000) see
Gumenick Foundation, Nathan
and Sophie
University of Miami School of
Medicine, Department of
Immunology ($40,000) see
Jennings Foundation, Alma
University of North Florida
($43,464) see River Branch
Foundation
University of North Florida
Foundation — scholarship
fund American music
($10,000) see Swisher
Foundation, Carl S.
University of North Florida
Music Department ($7,500)
see Schultz Foundation
University Of Miami ($25,000)
see Pope Foundation, Lois B.
University of South Florida
($180,000) see Dana
Charitable Trust, Eleanor
Naylor
University of South Florida
($50,000) see Walter Industries
University of South Florida —
College of Medicine
($100,828) see Dana
Charitable Trust, Eleanor
Naylor
University of South Florida
Foundation ($100,000) see
Saunders Foundation
University of Tampa —
scholarship ($50,000) see
Conn Memorial Foundation
University of Tampa ($10,000)
see Falk Foundation, David
University of Tampa ($50,000)
see Saunders Foundation
University of West Florida
Foundation — scholarships
($5,000) see Gulf Power Co.
University of West Florida
Foundation ($30,000) see
Kugelman Foundation
Up with Downe Syndrome see
New York Mercantile
Exchange
UPARC Foundation ($5,500) see
Bickerton Charitable Trust,
Lydia H.
Uplift Assistance ($19,195) see
Lost Tree Charitable
Foundation
Valencia Community College
($5,000) see Phillips
Foundation, A. P.
Valencia Foundation ($6,000)
see Greater Construction Corp.
Charitable Foundation, Inc.
Van Wezel Foundation ($5,000)
see Wilkof Foundation,
Edward and Ruth
Venice Area Middle School PTA
($4,000) see Beattie
Foundation Trust, Cordelia Lee
Venice Area Mobile Meals —
Meals on Wheels ($5,000) see
Catlin Charitable Trust,
Kathleen K.
Venice Athletic Boosters —
athletic equipment ($5,000)
see Catlin Charitable Trust,
Kathleen K.
Venice High School —
chemistry lab computer
($5,000) see Catlin Charitable
Trust, Kathleen K.
Venice Symphony ($10,000) see
Beattie Foundation Trust,
Cordelia Lee
Very Special Arts/Sarasota
($3,000) see Beattie
Foundation Trust, Cordelia Lee

Florida (cont.)

Villas Maria Bon Secours ($3,000) see Broad Foundation, Shepard

Vircayans ($20,700) see Hooker Charitable Trust, Janet A.

Volunteers of America ($10,000) see Schultz Foundation

Warner Southern College ($15,000) see Community Hospital Foundation

Wayside House ($10,000) see Austin Memorial Foundation

Wayside House ($15,000) see Willits Foundation

Wayside House Fund ($10,000) see Ettinger Foundation

We Will Rebuild — to support rebuilding of South Dade County following Hurricane Andrew ($2,500,000) see Knight Foundation, John S. and James L.

WEDU Public Broadcasting ($6,600) see Falk Foundation, David

West Florida Child Care ($10,000) see BCR Foundation

WMFE-TV ($7,500) see Harper Foundation, Philip S.

Women's American ORT ($1,025) see MalCo Products Inc.

Women's American ORT ($10,200) see Rosenberg Foundation, Sunny and Abe

Womens Resource of Sarasota — building fund ($25,000) see Appleby Foundation

World Radio Missionary Fellowship — toward KVMV radio station facility ($30,000) see Crowell Trust, Henry P. and Susan C.

WPBT Communications Foundation ($2,500) see Rosenberg Family Foundation, William

WPBT Station 2 ($40) see Amdur Braude Riley, Inc.

WPBT — to purchase computers for its production of "The Nightly Business Report" ($210,000) see Digital Equipment Corp.

WPBT 2 ($1,100) see Wilder Foundation

Yankeetown Fire Department ($100) see Felburn Foundation

YMCA ($5,000) see Bishop Trust for the SPCA of Manatee County, Florida, Lillian H.

YMCA ($25,000) see Einstein Fund, Albert E. and Birdie W.

YMCA ($11,600) see Florida Rock Industries

YMCA ($3,620) see Houck Foundation, May K.

YMCA ($25,000) see Jones Intercable, Inc.

YMCA ($25,000) see Lynn Foundation, E. M.

YMCA ($25,000) see Magruder Foundation, Chesley G.

YMCA ($5,000) see Phillips Foundation, A. P.

YMCA ($20,000) see Walter Industries

YMCA ($50,000) see Williams Foundation, Edna Sproull

YMCA of Greater Pensacola — capital campaign ($4,000) see Gulf Power Co.

YMCA of the Palm Beaches ($13,200) see United States Sugar Corp.

YMCA-YMCO of Tampa and Hillsborough County — construction of new facility in

central Tampa ($50,000) see Conn Memorial Foundation

Young Life ($21,500) see River Branch Foundation

Young Life — general support ($3,000) see Swisher Foundation, Carl S.

Young Life ($50,000) see Williams Foundation, Edna Sproull

Young Life Urban — urban ministry program ($15,000) see Conn Memorial Foundation

Young Patronesses of the Opera ($4,000) see Kennedy Family Foundation, Ethel and W. George

Young Womens Residence ($5,640) see Lauffer Trust, Charles A.

Youth Haven ($1,500) see Briggs Family Foundation

Youth Haven ($1,000) see Harris Foundation, John H. and Lucille

Youth Leadership Jacksonville ($5,000) see Schultz Foundation

Youth for Renewal Fund ($20,000) see Jaharis Family Foundation

YWCA ($25,000) see Davis Family - W.D. Charities, James E.

YWCA ($5,641) see Lauffer Trust, Charles A.

Zoological Society of Florida ($1,000) see Frohring Foundation, Paul & Maxine

Georgia

Abraham Baldwin College ($1,200) see Gholston Trust, J. K.

Abraham Baldwin Foundation ($7,500) see Dorminy Foundation, John Henry

Abreu Fund of Metropolitan Atlanta Community Foundation ($13,500) see Abreu Charitable Trust u/w/o May P. Abreu, Francis I.

Advance Atlanta Speech School ($40,000) see Murphy Foundation, Katherine and John

Agape Village — Church of the Exceptional ($5,000) see Anderson Foundation, Peyton

Agnes Scott College ($4,300) see Dalton Foundation, Harry L.

Agnes Scott College ($10,000) see Love Foundation, Gay and Erskine

Agnes Scott College ($5,000) see Luchsinger Family Foundation

Ahavath Achim Congregation ($5,000) see Steinsapir Family Foundation, Julius L. and Libhie B.

Aid Atlanta ($10,000) see Atlanta Foundation

Albany Little Theatre ($16,667) see Haley Foundation, W. B.

Albany Museum of Art ($60,000) see Haley Foundation, W. B.

Albany Symphony ($1,250) see Haley Foundation, W. B.

Alexander Tharpe Fund ($2,500) see Union Manufacturing Co.

Alfred A. Davis Research Center ($350,000) see Raleigh Linen Service/National Distributing Co.

Alliance Theater Company ($10,000) see Glancy Foundation, Lenora and Alfred

Alliance Theater Company ($10,000) see Glancy Foundation, Lenora and Alfred

Alliance Theater Company ($20,000) see Moore Memorial Foundation, James Starr

Alliance Theater Company — capital grant ($50,000) see Tull Charitable Foundation

Alliance Theatre Company ($6,000) see Abreu Charitable Trust u/w/o May P. Abreu, Francis I.

Alliance Theatre Company — for endowment campaign ($10,000) see Loridans Foundation, Charles

Alliance Theatre Company ($25,000) see Woolley Foundation, Vasser

Alliance Theatre Company, Woodruff Arts Center ($250,000) see Campbell Foundation, J. Bulow

Alta (Downtown) Senior Services ($4,500) see Oxford Foundation

Alzheimer's Association, Atlanta, GA see SAFECO Corp.

Alzheimer's Disease and Related Disorders Association ($5,000) see Steiner Charitable Fund, Albert

American Cancer Society ($2,500) see Crawford & Co.

American Cancer Society ($17,000) see Georgia Health Foundation

American Cancer Society ($1,000) see Howell Fund

American Cancer Society ($23,180) see Wilson Foundation, Frances Wood

American Friends of IDI ($50,000) see Irmas Charitable Foundation, Audrey and Sydney

American Red Cross ($3,000) see Abreu Charitable Trust u/w/o May P. Abreu, Francis I.

American Red Cross ($4,600) see Porter Testamentary Trust, James Hyde

American Red Cross Metro Atlanta Chapter — capital grant ($50,000) see Tull Charitable Foundation

American Red Cross, Metropolitan Atlanta Chapter ($300,000) see Campbell Foundation, J. Bulow

AMI Hospital ($757,133) see Spalding Health Care Trust

Andrew College — scholarships ($6,000) see Baker Foundation, Clark and Ruby

Andrew College ($207,737) see Bradley-Turner Foundation

Andrew College ($5,000) see Haley Foundation, W. B.

Andrew College ($66,600) see Jinks Foundation, Ruth T.

Andrew College ($50,000) see Kirbo Charitable Trust, Thomas M. and Irene B.

Andrew College ($30,000) see Marshall Foundation, Mattie H.

Andrew College ($10,185) see McLendon Educational Fund, Violet H.

Andrew College ($47,000) see Pitts Foundation, William H. and Lula E.

Andrew College ($40,000) see Pitts Foundation, William H. and Lula E.

Andrew College ($33,000) see Pitts Foundation, William H. and Lula E.

Andrew College — renovation of Rhodes Hall ($250,000) see Evans Foundation, Lettie Pate

Anges Scott College ($5,000) see Marshall Foundation, Mattie H.

Archbold Foundation ($5,000) see Cherokee Foundation

Archbold Foundation ($12,500) see Williams Family Foundation of Georgia

Archbold Medical Center ($60,000) see Archbold Charitable Trust, Adrian and Jessie

Arthritis Foundation ($75,000) see Schering Trust for Arthritis Research, Margaret Harvey

Arthritis Foundation, Atlanta, GA see Kmart Corp.

Arts Center Foundation for Victory Theater ($35,000) see Cox, Jr. Foundation, James M.

Atlanta AIDS Fund, Metropolitan Atlanta Community Foundation ($30,000) see Woodward Fund-Atlanta, David, Helen, Marian

Atlanta Arts Alliance — annual support ($65,000) see Equifax

Atlanta Arts Alliance ($210,000) see Livingston Foundation

Atlanta Ballet ($20,000) see Courts Foundation

Atlanta Ballet ($50,000) see Gilbert, Jr. Charitable Trust, Price

Atlanta Ballet ($50,000) see Raleigh Linen Service/National Distributing Co.

Atlanta Ballet Company ($7,000) see Glancy Foundation, Lenora and Alfred

Atlanta Ballet Company ($5,000) see Howell Fund

Atlanta Ballet Company ($1,500) see Tomlinson Foundation, Kate and Elwyn

Atlanta Baptist Association ($5,000) see Patterson-Barclay Memorial Foundation

Atlanta Baptist Association for the Clark Howell-Techwood Baptist Center ($25,000) see Ragan Charitable Foundation, Carolyn King

Atlanta Baptist Church ($17,191) see Patterson-Barclay Memorial Foundation

Atlanta Botanical Garden ($25,000) see Cox Enterprises

Atlanta Botanical Garden ($10,000) see English Memorial Fund, Florence C. and H. L.

Atlanta Botanical Garden — special campaign ($12,500) see Equifax

Atlanta Botanical Garden ($16,666) see Gage Foundation, Philip and Irene Toll

Atlanta Botanical Garden ($25,000) see Georgia-Pacific Corp.

Atlanta Botanical Gardens — operating grant ($10,000) see Marshall Trust in Memory of Sanders McDaniel, Harriet McDaniel

Atlanta Botanical Gardens ($30,000) see Tomlinson Foundation, Kate and Elwyn

Atlanta Boys Club ($28,700) see Franklin Foundation, John and Mary

Atlanta Chamber of Commerce — final payment on a $150,000 pledge for the forward Atlanta campaign that

began in 1986 ($50,000) see Wachovia Bank of Georgia, N.A.

Atlanta Christian Church ($5,850) see Morrison Foundation, Harry W.

Atlanta Christian College ($12,825) see Delta Air Lines

Atlanta Executive Services Corps ($25,000) see Woodward Fund-Atlanta, David, Helen, Marian

Atlanta Heritage Row ($15,000) see Howell Fund

Atlanta Heritage Row ($5,000) see Howell Fund

Atlanta Heritage Row — operating grant ($16,666) see Trust Co. Bank

Atlanta Historical Center ($50,000) see Rich Foundation

Atlanta Historical Society ($2,500) see Abreu Charitable Trust u/w/o May P. Abreu, Francis I.

Atlanta Historical Society ($20,000) see Atlanta Foundation

Atlanta Historical Society ($500,000) see Campbell Foundation, J. Bulow

Atlanta Historical Society ($19,942) see Chatham Valley Foundation

Atlanta Historical Society ($33,333) see Cox, Jr. Foundation, James M.

Atlanta Historical Society ($12,500) see Exposition Foundation

Atlanta Historical Society ($25,000) see Franklin Foundation, John and Mary

Atlanta Historical Society — operating grant ($20,000) see Lanier Brothers Foundation

Atlanta Historical Society ($16,775) see Livingston Foundation

Atlanta Historical Society — operating grant ($6,250) see Marshall Trust in Memory of Sanders McDaniel, Harriet McDaniel

Atlanta Historical Society ($45,000) see Moore Memorial Foundation, James Starr

Atlanta Historical Society ($20,000) see Murphy Foundation, Katherine and John

Atlanta Historical Society ($5,000) see Parker, Jr. Foundation, William A.

Atlanta Historical Society ($50,000) see Robinson Foundation, J. Mack

Atlanta Historical Society ($10,000) see Tomlinson Foundation, Kate and Elwyn

Atlanta Historical Society — capital grant ($50,000) see Tull Charitable Foundation

Atlanta Historical Society ($25,000) see West Foundation

Atlanta Historical Society ($250,000) see Woodward Fund-Watertown, David, Helen, and Marian

Atlanta Historical Society ($20,000) see Zaban Foundation

Atlanta Historical Society — $15 million capital campaign for the Museum of Atlanta History ($5,000,000) see Woodruff Foundation, Robert W.

Atlanta Historical Society — to expand educational programs for school children and support the Education

Department ($100,000) see Coca-Cola Co.

Atlanta History Center ($15,000) see Livingston Foundation

Atlanta Hospital Hospitality House ($2,000) see Oxford Foundation

Atlanta Hospital Hospitality House ($5,000) see Waffle House, Inc.

Atlanta International School ($55,000) see Kimberly-Clark Corp.

Atlanta International School — capital grant ($50,000) see Tull Charitable Foundation

Atlanta International School ($20,000) see Woolley Foundation, Vasser

Atlanta Jewish Community Center ($50,000) see Raleigh Linen Service/National Distributing Co.

Atlanta Jewish Federation ($8,250) see Lubo Fund

Atlanta Jewish Federation ($545,000) see Raleigh Linen Service/National Distributing Co.

Atlanta Jewish Federation ($105,500) see Zaban Foundation

Atlanta Jewish Federation ($58,025) see Zaban Foundation

Atlanta Jewish Federation ($54,750) see Zaban Foundation

Atlanta Jewish Federation ($25,000) see Zaban Foundation

Atlanta Neighborhood Development Partnership — affordable housing and community revitalization public/private partnership ($100,000) see Federal National Mortgage Assn., Fannie Mae

Atlanta Opera ($10,000) see Exposition Foundation

Atlanta Outward Bound Center see Home Depot

Atlanta Photography Group ($2,200) see Lubo Fund

Atlanta Speech School ($30,000) see Wardlaw Fund, Gertrude and William C.

Atlanta Summer Olympics ($2,500) see Oxford Foundation

Atlanta Symphony Orchestra ($100,000) see Cox Enterprises

Atlanta Symphony Orchestra ($20,000) see Murphy Foundation, Katherine and John

Atlanta Symphony Orchestra — general support ($12,500) see RTM

Atlanta Symphony Orchestra ($30,000) see Woolley Foundation, Vasser

Atlanta University ($10,000) see Wilson Foundation, H. W.

Atlanta Urban League — capital grant ($100,000) see Tull Charitable Foundation

Atlanta Volunteer Lawyers ($7,500) see Livingston Foundation

Atlanta Zoo ($5,000) see Love Foundation, Gay and Erskine

Atlantic Historical Society ($7,000) see Patterson-Barclay Memorial Foundation

Auburn University see Greenwood Mills

Augusta Ballet ($2,000) see Ballet Makers

Augusta Public Library ($5,000) see Appleby Trust, Scott B. and Annie P.

Baptist Village ($244,962) see Beach Foundation Trust D for Baptist Village, Thomas N. and Mildred V.

Beat Leukemia Research — general support ($25,000) see RTM

Ben Franklin Academy ($25,000) see Murphy Foundation, Katherine and John

Ben Massell Dental Clinic ($7,500) see Steiner Charitable Fund, Albert

Beray College, Rome, GA see Kmart Corp.

Berry College ($1,000) see Dodson Foundation, James Glenwell and Clara May

Berry College ($5,156) see Ellsworth Trust, W. H.

Berry College ($24,500) see Florida Rock Industries

Berry College ($11,650) see Helms Foundation

Berry College ($5,000) see Hollis Foundation

Berry College ($50,000) see Kirbo Charitable Trust, Thomas M. and Irene B.

Berry College — operating grant ($5,000) see Marshall Trust in Memory of Sanders McDaniel, Harriet McDaniel

Berry College ($10,000) see Oxford Foundation

Berry College ($70,000) see Pittulloch Foundation

Berry College ($26,000) see Pittulloch Foundation

Berry College ($10,000) see Ratner Foundation, Milton M.

Berry College ($5,000) see Vale Foundation, Ruby R.

Berry College — automated circulation system and on-line catalog library ($50,000) see Hermann Foundation, Grover

Big Brothers and Big Sisters ($11,000) see RTM

Birdsong Nature Center ($100) see Roddenbery Co., Inc., W.B.

Black Youth and Business Program ($400) see Bibb Co.

Blair House Restoration Fund ($50,000) see Ross Foundation, Arthur

Boy Scouts of America ($21,000) see Arnold Fund

Boy Scouts of America ($6,528) see Cook Batson Foundation

Boy Scouts of America ($2,500) see Elkin Memorial Foundation, Neil Warren and William Simpson

Boy Scouts of America ($50,000) see Gilbert, Jr. Charitable Trust, Price

Boy Scouts of America ($2,025) see Gilman Paper Co.

Boy Scouts of America ($5,000) see Moore Foundation, Roy C.

Boy Scouts of America ($5,000) see Moore Foundation, Roy C.

Boy Scouts of America ($1,500) see Tomlinson Foundation, Kate and Elwyn

Boy Scouts of America ($25,000) see Wardlaw Fund, Gertrude and William C.

Boy Scouts of America ($27,500) see Watkins Christian Foundation

Boy Scouts of America ($15,000) see Woolley Foundation, Vasser

Boy Scouts of America — 3rd installment on capital campaign pledge of $45,000 ($10,000) see Wachovia Bank of Georgia, N.A.

Boy Scouts-NW Georgia Council ($7,800) see Inland Container Corp.

Boys Club of Albany ($1,500) see Haley Foundation, W. B.

Boys Club of America ($8,400) see Hodge Foundation

Boys Club of Macon ($5,000) see Porter Testamentary Trust, James Hyde

Boys Club of Rome ($5,000) see Negaunee Foundation

Boys and Girls Club ($50,000) see Gilbert, Jr. Charitable Trust, Price

Boys and Girls Club ($10,000) see Pittulloch Foundation

Boys and Girls Clubs of Metro Atlanta — final payment on capital campaign commitment ($56,875) see Harland Charitable Foundation, John and Wilhelmina D.

Boys and Girls Clubs of Metro Atlanta — program development ($400,000) see Whitehead Foundation, Joseph B.

Bradley Center ($691,793) see Bradley-Turner Foundation

Bradley Center ($5,000) see Schwob Foundation, Simon

Bradley Center ($50,000) see Synovus Financial Corp.

Bradley Center — $4.9 million capital campaign to build an adolescent residential treatment center and a multi-purpose activity center ($500,000) see Woodruff Foundation, Robert W.

Breakthru House ($5,000) see Churches Homes Foundation

Breakthru House ($7,000) see Patterson-Barclay Memorial Foundation

Brenau College ($30,000) see Jinks Foundation, Ruth T.

Brenau College ($10,000) see Moore Foundation, Roy C.

Brenau Visual Arts Center ($12,500) see Illges Foundation, John P. and Dorothy S.

Brewton-Parker College ($20,000) see Ragan Charitable Foundation, Carolyn King

Bridge Family Center of Atlanta ($5,000) see Gage Foundation, Philip and Irene Toll

Bridge Family Center of Atlanta — provide temporary shelter and therapy services to runaway and homeless youth ($500,000) see Whitehead Foundation, Joseph B.

Brookstone School ($400,400) see Bradley-Turner Foundation

Brookstone School ($10,000) see Hollis Foundation

Brookwood School ($9,500) see Cherokee Foundation

Brookwood School ($100,000) see Williams Family Foundation of Georgia

Brunswick First Baptist Church ($244,502) see Beach Foundation Trust for First Baptist Church, Thomas N. and Mildred V.

Brunswick Hospital ($245,449) see Beach Foundation Trust A for Brunswick Hospital, Thomas N. and Mildred V.

Butts Mehre Heritage Hall ($25,000) see Hill and Family Foundation, Walter Clay

Calhoun High School ($10,000) see Ratner Foundation, Milton M.

Callaway Educational Association — operations ($853,048) see Callaway Foundation

Callaway Gardens ($5,000) see Cook Batson Foundation

Callaway Gardens ($20,000) see Synovus Financial Corp.

Camp Best Friends 1990 — supporting camp best friends ($10,000) see Wachovia Bank of Georgia, N.A.

Camp Twin Lakes ($12,000) see English Memorial Fund, Florence C. and H. L.

Camp Twin Lakes ($10,000) see Gilbert, Jr. Charitable Trust, Price

Camp Twin Lakes — for camp development costs ($100,000) see Harland Charitable Foundation, John and Wilhelmina D.

Camp Twin Lakes ($4,500) see Lubo Fund

Cancer Society see Best Western International

Candler School of Theology ($41,000) see Illges Memorial Foundation, A. and M. L.

Canterbury Court ($10,000) see Courts Foundation

Carl Radcliff Dance Theatre ($20,000) see Rich Foundation

Carrie Steel Pitts Home ($5,000) see Herndon Foundation, Alonzo F. Herndon and Norris B.

Carter Center ($85,000) see Cox, Jr. Foundation, James M.

Carter Center ($25,000) see Golden Family Foundation

Carter Center ($22,000) see Livingston Foundation

Carter Center ($5,000) see Stokely, Jr. Foundation, William B.

Carter Center — in product donations of Abate larvacide ($2,000,000) see American Cyanamid Co.

Carter Center — the Carter Center Environmental Initiative ($200,000) see Jones Foundation, W. Alton

Carter Center for Human Rights ($50,000) see Reebok International Ltd.

Carter Presidential Center ($25,000) see Occidental Petroleum Corp.

Carter Presidential Center ($25,000) see 21 International Holdings

Carter Presidential Library ($50,000) see Kirbo Charitable Trust, Thomas M. and Irene B.

Carter Presidential Library ($25,000) see Zaban Foundation

Cathedral of Christ the King ($20,000) see Murphy Foundation, Katherine and John

Cathedral of St. Philip ($8,000) see Courts Foundation

Cathedral of St. Philip ($8,000) see Courts Foundation

Cathedral of St. Philip ($8,000) see Courts Foundation

Cathedral of St. Philip ($1,335) see Howell Fund

Cedars-Sinai Hospital ($200,000) see Raleigh Linen Service/National Distributing Co.

Center for Puppetry Arts ($3,300) see Lubo Fund

Center for Surgical Anatomy ($50,000) see Raleigh Linen Service/National Distributing Co.

Center for the Visually Impaired ($7,500) see Gage Foundation, Philip and Irene Toll

Center for the Visually Impaired Foundation ($5,000) see Kuse Foundation, James R.

Central Health Center — special project ($10,000) see Equifax

Central Health Center ($20,000) see Steiner Charitable Fund, Albert

Challenge Films ($3,000) see Churches Homes Foundation

Challenge Foundation ($10,000) see Arnold Fund

Challenged Child Program ($3,000) see Moore Foundation, Roy C.

Charis Community Housing of PCS Urban Ministries ($30,000) see Challenge Foundation

Chatham County Public Schools — financial assistance ($50,000) see Hodge Foundation

Chatham-Savannah Youth Futures Authority — New Futures Youth Initiative ($2,797,094) see Casey Foundation, Annie E.

Chickamauga City Schools ($19,824) see Jewell Memorial Foundation, Daniel Ashley and Irene Houston

Chickamauga City Schools — alumni association ($9,755) see Jewell Memorial Foundation, Daniel Ashley and Irene Houston

Chickamauga Public Library ($15,000) see Jewell Memorial Foundation, Daniel Ashley and Irene Houston

Children's Hospital/Medcen Foundation — purchase critical care beds ($8,000) see Porter Testamentary Trust, James Hyde

Christian Education Center ($2,000) see Moore Foundation, Roy C.

Church of the Apostles ($15,000) see McCarthy Foundation, John and Margaret

City of Atlanta Best Friends ($10,000) see English Memorial Fund, Florence C. and H. L.

City of Chickamauga Recreation Association ($5,000) see Jewell Memorial Foundation, Daniel Ashley and Irene Houston

City of LaGrange — legal mediation service ($47,452) see Callaway Foundation, Fuller E.

City of LaGrange and Troup County — Callaway Stadium Property ($1,222,000) see Callaway Foundation

Clark Atlanta University — scholarships ($7,000) see Baker Foundation, Clark and Ruby

Clark Atlanta University ($20,000) see Kuse Foundation, James R.

Clark Atlanta University — scholarships ($105,000) see Whitehead Foundation, Lettie Pate

Clark Atlanta University — to provide scholarships for MBA students at the School of Business ($50,000) see Sara Lee Corp.

Georgia (cont.)

Clark-Atlanta University — to support teacher education and to develop a School of Public and International Affairs ($300,000) see Coca-Cola Co.

Clayton State College ($25,000) see Delta Air Lines

Coastal Georgia Writing Project — financial assistance ($22,000) see Hodge Foundation

Colquitt United Methodist Church ($18,200) see Jinks Foundation, Ruth T.

Columbia Theological Seminary ($22,500) see Illges Memorial Foundation, A. and M. L.

Columbia Theological Seminary — for the John H. and Wilhelmina D. Harland Scholarship Fund ($35,000) see Harland Charitable Foundation, John and Wilhelmina D.

Columbus College ($1,000) see Beloco Foundation

Columbus College Foundation ($5,000) see Hollis Foundation

Columbus College Foundation ($30,000) see Illges Memorial Foundation, A. and M. L.

Columbus College Foundation ($31,000) see Schwob Foundation, Simon

Columbus Community Center ($12,500) see Synovus Financial Corp.

Columbus Medical Center ($10,000) see Elkin Memorial Foundation, Neil Warren and William Simpson

Columbus Medical Center ($50,000) see Synovus Financial Corp.

Columbus Museum ($250,000) see Bradley-Turner Foundation

Columbus Museum ($11,950) see Schwob Foundation, Simon

Columbus Museum ($16,000) see Synovus Financial Corp.

Columbus Museum of Art ($5,000) see Hollis Foundation

Columbus Symphony Orchestra ($12,000) see Schwob Foundation, Simon

Comer Cemetary Committee ($400) see Gholston Trust, J. K.

Comer Elementary School ($190,104) see Gholston Trust, J. K.

Committee Concerned for Children ($2,500) see Oxford Industries, Inc.

Community Action Center ($3,000) see Churches Homes Foundation

Community Concert Association ($20,000) see Arnold Fund

Corporation of Mercer University — complete tissue culture room ($30,000) see Porter Testamentary Trust, James Hyde

Covenant College ($150,000) see Benwood Foundation

Covenant College — matching grant ($36,000) see Brown Charitable Trust, Dora Maclellan

Covenant College — capital campaign ($438,000) see Maclellan Foundation

Coweta County School System — operating expenses ($55,000) see Georgia Power Co.

Cox Arboretum ($50,000) see Cox, Jr. Foundation, James M.

Crawford W. Long Hospital ($3,000) see Oxford Foundation

CURE — Emory Leukemia Research ($20,000) see Waffle House, Inc.

Cystic Fibrosis Foundation ($30,000) see Georgia Health Foundation

Decatur General Hospital Foundation ($10,000) see Gibson Foundation, E. L.

Decatur Orphans Home — general purposes ($6,000) see Baker Foundation, Clark and Ruby

Decatur Orphans Home — general purposes ($6,000) see Baker Foundation, Clark and Ruby

DeKalb Chamber Foundation — capital ($50,000) see Georgia Power Co.

DeKalb Community Council on Aging ($20,000) see Georgia Health Foundation

DeKalb Medical Center ($6,000) see Elkin Memorial Foundation, Neil Warren and William Simpson

Diabetes Association of Atlanta ($20,000) see Georgia Health Foundation

Downtown Atlanta Senior Services ($3,000) see Churches Homes Foundation

Eagle Ranch ($25,000) see Lee Foundation, Ray M. and Mary Elizabeth

Egleston Children's Hospital ($7,500) see Livingston Foundation

Elks Admore Children's Center ($4,000) see Tomlinson Foundation, Kate and Elwyn

Elks-Ardmore Childrens Home ($22,510) see Wilson Foundation, Frances Wood

Emmaus House ($2,500) see Abreu Charitable Trust u/w/o May P. Abreu, Francis I.

Emory-Egleston Children's Research Center ($3,000) see Parker, Jr. Foundation, William A.

Emory Geriatric Hospital ($5,000) see Schwob Foundation, Simon

Emory University ($102,068) see Bradley-Turner Foundation

Emory University ($1,000,000) see Campbell Foundation, J. Bulow

Emory University ($250,000) see Campbell Foundation, J. Bulow

Emory University ($20,000) see Community Enterprises

Emory University ($4,000) see Cook, Sr. Charitable Foundation, Kelly Gene

Emory University ($10,000) see Elkin Memorial Foundation, Neil Warren and William Simpson

Emory University — how children learn to resolve conflict in families ($173,978) see Grant Foundation, William T.

Emory University ($6,000) see Jinks Foundation, Ruth T.

Emory University — research and training in the field of immunodermatology ($32,700) see Kade Foundation, Max

Emory University — operating grant ($10,000) see Lanier Brothers Foundation

Emory University ($5,000) see Lebus Trust, Bertha

Emory University — scholar program ($50,000) see Mallinckrodt, Jr. Foundation, Edward

Emory University — operating grant ($10,000) see Marshall Trust in Memory of Sanders McDaniel, Harriet McDaniel

Emory University ($50,000) see NationsBank Corp.

Emory University ($12,500) see Parker, Jr. Foundation, William A.

Emory University ($40,000) see Pitts Foundation, William H. and Lula E.

Emory University ($80,000) see Pittulloch Foundation

Emory University ($40,000) see Ratner Foundation, Milton M.

Emory University ($75,000) see Rich Foundation

Emory University — scholarships ($245,000) see Whitehead Foundation, Lettie Pate

Emory University — for $00 million capital campaign ($5,000,000) see Woodruff Foundation, Robert W.

Emory University — $3 million capital campaign for The Aquinas Center ($500,000) see Woodruff Foundation, Robert W.

Emory University — persistent poverty of African-American male youth: a normative study of developmental transitions in high risk ($100,000) see Grant Foundation, William T.

Emory University Candler School of Theology ($5,000) see Magee Christian Education Foundation

Emory University — to continue and extend the work of the Carter Center Commission on Television Policy ($450,000) see Markle Foundation, John and Mary R.

Emory University/Crawford Long Hospital ($5,000) see Parker, Jr. Foundation, William A.

Emory University — collaborative training program in the humanities for faculty members from four-year liberal arts colleges and from Emory University ($151,000) see Dana Foundation, Charles A.

Emory University — Fraser Heart Center ($71,000) see Echlin Foundation

Emory University — sixth recipient of the Harry Frank Guggenheim Career Development Award for the research project entitled "The Role of Culture in the Early Evolution of Human Violence: A Crosscultural and Cross-disciplinary Study" ($35,000) see Guggenheim Foundation, Harry Frank

Emory University Hospital ($7,500) see Wardlaw Fund, Gertrude and William C.

Emory University Museum ($10,000) see Levy Foundation, Jerome

Emory University at Oxford ($35,000) see Arnold Fund

Emory University/Pediatrics ($20,849) see Georgia Health Foundation

Emory University, Robert W. Woodruff Health Sciences Center — to Alzheimer's

disease study ($415,000) see Digital Equipment Corp.

Emory University School of Medicine ($100,000) see Cox, Jr. Foundation, James M.

Emory University School of Medicine ($25,000) see Georgia-Pacific Corp.

Emory University School of Medicine — operating grant ($50,000) see Lanier Brothers Foundation

Emory University School of Medicine ($15,000) see Steiner Charitable Fund, Albert

Emory University School of Public Health — computer equipment for collaboration among AIDS researchers and clinicians ($490,000) see Digital Equipment Corp.

Emory University — to support the university's comprehensive campaign; specifically to provide funds for a challenge grant to match new or increased unrestricted giving ($325,000) see Coca-Cola Co.

Enoch Callaway Cancer Clinic — radiation therapy equipment ($750,795) see Callaway Foundation

Episcopal Church Home ($10,000) see Dodson Foundation, James Glenwell and Clara May

Epstein Solomon Schechter School ($5,000) see Steinsapir Family Foundation, Julius L. and Libhie B.

Epworth by the Sea ($23,900) see Jinks Foundation, Ruth T.

Exodus ($10,000) see Glancy Foundation, Lenora and Alfred

Exodus ($1,000) see McCarthy Foundation, John and Margaret

Exodus/Cities in Schools ($10,000) see Waffle House, Inc.

Families First ($10,000) see Hill and Family Foundation, Walter Clay

Family Counseling Center ($16,667) see Synovus Financial Corp.

Fargo Methodist Church ($1,100) see Williams Foundation, C. K.

FCS Urban Ministries ($5,000) see Noble Foundation, Vivian Bilby

Feed the Hungry ($7,500) see Waffle House, Inc.

Fernbank, Inc. — natural history facility project ($250,000) see Callaway Foundation

Fernbank, Inc. ($500,000) see Campbell Foundation, J. Bulow

Fernbank ($75,000) see Woodward Fund-Atlanta, David, Helen, Marian

Fernbank — toward $30 million campaign to build the Fernbank Museum of Natural History ($7,023,500) see Woodruff Foundation, Robert W.

Fernbank Museum of Natural History ($14,000) see English Memorial Fund, Florence C. and H. L.

Fernbank Museum of Natural History ($25,000) see Gage Foundation, Philip and Irene Toll

Fernbank Museum of Natural History ($20,000) see Murphy Foundation, Katherine and John

Fernbank Museum of Natural History ($15,000) see Pittulloch Foundation

Festival of Trees ($1,000) see Johnson, Lane, Space, Smith & Co., Inc.

First Baptist Church ($3,000) see Jinks Foundation, Ruth T.

First Baptist Church ($1,690) see Roddenbery Co., Inc., W.B.

First Congregational Church, United Church of Christ ($12,200) see Herndon Foundation, Alonzo F. Herndon and Norris B.

First Methodist Church Building Fund ($33,343) see Watkins Christian Foundation

First Presbyterian Church ($10,000) see Hill and Family Foundation, Walter Clay

First Presbyterian Church ($10,000) see Hill and Family Foundation, Walter Clay

First United Methodist Church ($5,000) see Marshall Foundation, Mattie H.

Ft. Valley State College ($200) see Bibb Co.

Ft. Valley State College — scholarship fund ($2,000) see Gholston Trust, J. K.

Foundation of the Holy Apostles ($10,000) see Courts Foundation

Foundation of Wesley Homes ($121,900) see Illges Memorial Foundation, A. and M. L.

Foundation of Wesley Woods ($5,000) see Pittulloch Foundation

Freewill Baptist Church — Trinity ($5,000) see Jinks Foundation, Ruth T.

Friends of Zoo Atlanta — operating grant ($7,500) see Marshall Trust in Memory of Sanders McDaniel, Harriet McDaniel

Fund for Southern Communities ($6,200) see Lubo Fund

Fuqua School of Business ($15,000) see Fuqua Foundation, J. B.

Gainesville College ($25,000) see Wrigley Co., Wm. Jr.

Galloway School — for endowment of the Eliot Galloway chair of mathematics ($50,000) see Loridans Foundation, Charles

Gate City Day Nursery Association ($200) see Herndon Foundation, Alonzo F. Herndon and Norris B.

General Board of Pensions — general purposes ($2,400) see Baker Foundation, Clark and Ruby

George E. Sims, Jr. Nursing Scholarship Fund, West Georgia Medical Center ($455,000) see Callaway Foundation, Fuller E.

George Walton Academy ($5,000) see West Foundation

Georgia Amateur Athletic Association ($25,000) see English Memorial Fund, Florence C. and H. L.

Georgia Amateur Athletic Association — operating grant ($15,000) see Marshall Trust in Memory of Sanders McDaniel, Harriet McDaniel

Georgia Amateur Athletic Foundation — special campaign ($75,000) see Equifax

Georgia Amateur Athletics ($5,000) see Crawford & Co.

Georgia Amateur Athletics Foundation ($20,000) see Atlanta Foundation

Georgia Amateur Athletics Foundation — final payment on a $150,000 pledge for the 1996 olympics ($50,000) see Wachovia Bank of Georgia, N.A.

Georgia Amateur Athletics Foundation — 1996 summer olympics ($75,000) see Wachovia Bank of Georgia, N.A.

Georgia Baptist Children's Home ($24,275) see Dodson Foundation, James Glenwell and Clara May

Georgia Baptist Children's Home and Family Ministries ($7,000) see Ragan Charitable Foundation, Carolyn King

Georgia Baptist Hospital ($10,000) see Waffle House, Inc.

Georgia Baptist Medical Center — charitable contribution ($10,000) see Wachovia Bank of Georgia, N.A.

Georgia Cities in Schools — statewide development of the Cities in Schools program ($750,000) see Whitehead Foundation, Joseph B.

Georgia College ($5,000) see Bibb Co.

Georgia College ($400) see Gholston Trust, J. K.

Georgia Council on Child Abuse ($1,500) see Churches Homes Foundation

Georgia Council on Child Abuse ($21,325) see Georgia Health Foundation

Georgia Council on Child Abuse ($7,600) see Livingston Foundation

Georgia Council on Child Abuse ($25,000) see McCamish Foundation

Georgia Council on Child Abuse ($8,643) see Waffle House, Inc.

Georgia Council on Economic Education ($2,500) see Bibb Co.

Georgia Council on Economic Education ($1,000) see Cook Batson Foundation

Georgia Department of Human Resources ($30,000) see Appleby Trust, Scott B. and Annie P.

Georgia Department of Human Services ($20,000) see Appleby Trust, Scott B. and Annie P.

Georgia District Wesleyan Methodist Church ($12,000) see Union Manufacturing Co.

Georgia Division of the Salvation Army ($400,000) see Campbell Foundation, J. Bulow

Georgia Easter Seal ($1,500) see Crawford & Co.

Georgia Foundation of Independent Colleges ($2,500) see Cook Batson Foundation

Georgia Foundation of Independent Colleges ($4,000) see Crawford & Co.

Georgia Foundation of Independent Colleges ($1,000) see Dillard Paper Co.

Georgia Foundation for Independent Colleges ($6,000) see Gregg-Graniteville Foundation

Georgia Foundation of Independent Colleges ($2,500) see Moore & Sons, B.C.

Georgia Foundation of Independent Colleges ($2,500) see Tomlinson Foundation, Kate and Elwyn

Georgia Foundation of Independent Colleges ($3,000) see Wehadkee Foundation

Georgia Foundation for Independent Colleges — for expansion of Georgia Foundation for Independent Colleges staff ($50,000) see Harland Charitable Foundation, John and Wilhelmina D.

Georgia Heart Association ($1,000) see Herndon Foundation, Alonzo F. Herndon and Norris B.

Georgia Industrial Home — renovation of cottage and school classroom equipment ($10,000) see Porter Testamentary Trust, James Hyde

Georgia Institute of Technology ($350,000) see BellSouth Corp.

Georgia Institute of Technology ($200,500) see Bradley-Turner Foundation

Georgia Institute of Technology — operating costs ($350,000) see Evans Foundation, Lettie Pate

Georgia Institute of Technology ($65,000) see Franklin Foundation, John and Mary

Georgia Institute of Technology ($4,669) see Texas Industries, Inc.

Georgia Lighthouse Foundation ($25,000) see Georgia Health Foundation

Georgia North Civitan Foundation ($20,000) see Wilson Foundation, Frances Wood

Georgia Peace Officer Standards and Training Council — Police Chaplain's Certification Course ($11,500) see Callaway Foundation, Fuller E.

Georgia Public Telecommunications ($1,000) see Beloco Foundation

Georgia Public Telecommunications Commission ($50,000) see Union Camp Corp.

Georgia Research Alliance — initial operating support for a new organization designed to leverage the combined research activity of Georgia's universities into broad-based economic development ($500,000) see Woodruff Foundation, Robert W.

Georgia Southern College ($35,000) see Chatham Valley Foundation

Georgia Southern College ($5,000) see Colonial Oil Industries, Inc.

Georgia Southwestern College ($5,000) see Marshall Foundation, Mattie H.

Georgia Special Olympics —financial assistance ($500) see Hodge Foundation

Georgia State Law School — for lecture series ($10,000) see Loridans Foundation, Charles

Georgia State University ($100,050) see Delta Air Lines

Georgia State University — scholarship fund ($40,000) see Franklin Foundation, John and Mary

Georgia State University ($25,000) see Pittulloch Foundation

Georgia State University — capital grant ($150,000) see Tull Charitable Foundation

Georgia State University College of Business Administration/Georgia State Foundation — to support Charles Loridans Scholars program in the College of Business ($15,000) see Loridans Foundation, Charles

Georgia State University Foundation ($10,500) see English Memorial Fund, Florence C. and H. L.

Georgia State University Foundation, Inner-city Athlete's ($5,000) see Marshall Trust in Memory of Sanders McDaniel, Harriet McDaniel

Georgia Student Educational Fund ($3,500) see Gilman Paper Co.

Georgia Tech ($16,000) see Community Enterprises

Georgia Tech Catholic Center ($5,500) see Taub Foundation, Joseph and Arlene

Georgia Tech Centennial Campaign ($5,000) see Mohasco Corp.

Georgia Tech Foundation ($15,000) see Arnold Fund

Georgia Tech Foundation ($15,000) see English Memorial Fund, Florence C. and H. L.

Georgia Tech Foundation — special campaign ($20,000) see Equifax

Georgia Tech Foundation ($5,000) see Fox Foundation, Richard J.

Georgia Tech Foundation ($50,000) see Gilbert, Jr. Charitable Trust, Price

Georgia Tech Foundation see Greenwood Mills

Georgia Tech Foundation — operating grant ($10,000) — Marshall Trust in Memory of Sanders McDaniel, Harriet McDaniel

Georgia Tech Foundation ($25,000) see NationsBank Corp.

Georgia Tech Foundation ($2,000) see Union Manufacturing Co.

Georgia Tech Foundation ($25,000) see Waffle House, Inc.

Georgia Tech Foundation ($1,000) see West Foundation

Georgia Tech Foundation — $3.3 million cost of property at 575 14th Street to house the Institute of Paper Science and Technology ($1,650,000) see Woodruff Foundation, Robert W.

Georgia Tech Foundation 40th Reunion ($20,000) see Love Foundation, Gay and Erskine

Georgia Tech Foundation — Vasser Woolley Chair in Chemistry ($30,000) see Woolley Foundation, Vasser

Georgia Tech — Love Chair ($25,000) see Waffle House, Inc.

Georgia Tech Theatre for the Arts ($1,000) see Beloco Foundation

Georgia Trust for Historic Preservation — to fund statewide revolving fund ($250,000) see Evans Foundation, Lettie Pate

Georgia Trust for Historic Preservation ($25,000) see Williams Family Foundation of Georgia

Georgia Trust for Historic Preservation ($25,000) see Williams Family Foundation of Georgia

Georgia Wildlife, Atlanta, GA see SAFECO Corp.

Georgia Wildlife Federation — capital ($50,000) see Georgia Power Co.

Georgia Youth Science and Technology Center — operating support ($200,000) see Evans Foundation, Lettie Pate

Georgia Youth Science and Technology Center — operating expenses ($150,000) see Georgia Power Co.

Girl Scout Council ($20,000) see Lane Memorial Foundation, Mills Bee

Girl Scout Council of Savannah — Foods project ($22,000) see Chatham Valley Foundation

Girls Club ($5,000) see Moore Foundation, Roy C.

Girls Club of Albany ($1,500) see Haley Foundation, W. B.

Glenn Memorial Methodist Church ($751,000) see Glenn Memorial Foundation, Wilbur Fisk

Good News Communication ($20,000) see Day Foundation, Cecil B.

Good Shepherd Riding Academy ($15,000) see Callaway Foundation, Fuller E.

Gospel Rescue Mission ($57,600) see Watkins Christian Foundation

Grady Memorial Hospital ($15,000) see Steiner Charitable Fund, Albert

Grant Park Family Health Center ($5,000) see Churches Homes Foundation

Grant Park Family Health Center ($5,000) see Steiner Charitable Fund, Albert

Gwinnett Community Center ($30,000) see Georgia Health Foundation

Gwinnett Senior Services, Lawrenceville, GA see SAFECO Corp.

Habitat For Humanity in Atlanta ($24,000) see NationsBank Corp.

Habitat for Humanity ($140) see Bruno Foundation, Angelo

Habitat for Humanity — operating support ($5,000) see Davis Foundation, Edwin W. and Catherine M.

Habitat for Humanity ($10,000) see English Memorial Fund, Florence C. and H. L.

Habitat for Humanity ($1,000) see Haley Foundation, W. B.

Habitat for Humanity International — building of low-income housing in six cities ($100,000) see Federal National Mortgage Assn., Fannie Mae

Habitat for Humanity — in 25 cities, including Atlanta, Dallas, Tampa, New Haven, and Knoxville see Home Depot

Haggai Institute ($25,000) see Bolten Charitable Foundation, John

Haggai Institute ($25,000) see Bolten Charitable Foundation, John

Haggai Institute ($10,000) see Bolten Charitable Foundation, John

Haggai Institute ($10,000) see Bolten Charitable Foundation, John

Haggai Institute ($10,000) see Bolten Charitable Foundation, John

Haggai Institute ($27,300) see C.I.O.S.

Haggai Institute ($10,000) see Maclellan Foundation, Robert L. and Kathrina H.

Haggai Institute ($175,200) see Meyer Family Foundation, Paul J.

Haggai Institute ($25,000) see Paulstan

Haggai Institute ($12,000) see Ware Foundation

Haggai Institute — organization to provide for Christian evangelization of Third World ($60,000) see Glaze Foundation, Robert and Ruth

Haggai Institute — training of 10 leaders ($91,000) see Chatlos Foundation

Hambrick Elementary School, Stone Mountain, GA see SAFECO Corp.

Harriett Tubman Museum and Cultural Museum ($8,000) see Porter Testamentary Trust, James Hyde

Health Champions ($75,000) see Raleigh Linen Service/National Distributing Co.

Heart Research Foundation ($6,100) see Oxford Industries, Inc.

Henrietta Egleston Hospital ($125,000) see Kirbo Charitable Trust, Thomas M. and Irene B.

Henrietta Egleston Hospital — capital expansion program ($2,500,000) see Whitehead Foundation, Joseph B.

Henrietta Egleston Hospital ($180,000) see Wilson Foundation, Frances Wood

Henrietta Egleston Hospital for Children ($150,000) see Woodward Fund-Atlanta, David, Helen, Marian

High Museum of Art ($10,000) see Exposition Foundation

High Museum of Art ($10,000) see Hill and Family Foundation, Walter Clay

High Museum of Art ($7,668) see Lubo Fund

High Museum of Art ($34,500) see Moore Memorial Foundation, James Starr

High Museum of Art ($412,000) see Raleigh Linen Service/National Distributing Co.

High Museum of Art ($10,000) see Robinson Foundation, J. Mack

High Museum of Art ($3,500) see West Foundation

Hillside ($10,000) see Hill and Family Foundation, Walter Clay

Hillside — capital grant ($60,000) see Tull Charitable Foundation

Hillside Specialty Psychiatric Hospital — for the new 20 bed residential unit ($50,000) see Harland Charitable Foundation, John and Wilhelmina D.

Historic Savannah ($1,000) see Colonial Oil Industries, Inc.

Historic Savannah Foundation — Memorial for H.B. Lane, Jr. ($5,000) see Lane Memorial Foundation, Mills Bee

Hodge Memorial Day Care Center — provide day care for

Georgia (cont.)

working mothers ($31,260) see Hodge Foundation

Holy Innocents Episcopal School ($24,955) see Abreu Charitable Trust u/w/o May P. Abreu, Francis I.

Holy Innocents Episcopal School ($24,937) see Abreu Charitable Trust u/w/o May P. Abreu, Francis I.

Hospice South ($20,000) see Patterson-Barclay Memorial Foundation

Howard Schools ($12,500) see Elkin Memorial Foundation, Neil Warren and William Simpson

Howard Schools — Phase II of the Campaign to Grow ($50,000) see Harland Charitable Foundation, John and Wilhelmina D.

Hughston Sports ($12,500) see Blount

Ichauway, Inc. — for establishment of Joseph W. Jones Ecological Research Center and general operating expenses ($1,000,000) see Woodruff Foundation, Robert W.

Ida Cason Callaway Foundation ($30,000) see Georgia-Pacific Corp.

In Touch Ministries ($50,000) see Prince Corp.

Independent Schools ($25,000) see West Foundation

Inman Park United Methodist Church ($46,000) see Illges Memorial Foundation, A. and M. L.

INSA ($5,000) see Exposition Foundation

INSA — International Service Association for Health; final payment on capital campaign commitment ($35,000) see Harland Charitable Foundation, John and Wilhelmina D.

Institute of Cultural Affairs ($26,667) see Osceola Foundation

Institute of Paper Science and Technology — scholarships ($81,000) see Consolidated Papers

Inter-Varsity Christian Fellowship ($28,200) see Brown Charitable Trust, Dora Maclellan

International Service for Health ($10,000) see Atlanta Foundation

J.D. Archbold Memorial Hospital ($10,000) see Love Foundation, George H. and Margaret McClintic

Jerusalem House ($4,000) see Exposition Foundation

Jewish Home for the Aged ($5,000) see Steiner Charitable Fund, Albert

Jewish Welfare Federation ($47,500) see Schwob Foundation, Simon

John Amos Cancer Center ($5,000) see Schwob Foundation, Simon

Joint Tech-Georgia Development Fund ($2,500) see Bibb Co.

Joint Tech-Georgia Development Fund ($2,500) see Cook Batson Foundation

Joint Tech-Georgia Development Fund ($6,000) see Jewell Memorial Foundation, Daniel Ashley and Irene Houston

Joint Tech-Georgia Development Fund ($12,000) see Lee Foundation, Ray M. and Mary Elizabeth

Joint Tech-Georgia Development Fund ($1,000) see Union Manufacturing Co.

Joint Tech-Georgia Development Fund ($4,000) see Wehadkee Foundation

Junior Achievement ($12,500) see Atlanta Foundation

Junior League of Savannah ($2,500) see Johnson, Lane, Space, Smith & Co., Inc.

Kiwanis Club of Covington ($7,500) see Arnold Fund

LaGrange Board of Education — foreign language lab equipment ($15,941) see Callaway Foundation, Fuller E.

LaGrange College — scholarships ($6,000) see Baker Foundation, Clark and Ruby

LaGrange College ($10,000) see Beloco Foundation

LaGrange College — property and improvements ($5,293,000) see Callaway Foundation

LaGrange College ($47,000) see Pitts Foundation, William H. and Lula E.

LaGrange College ($40,000) see Pitts Foundation, William H. and Lula E.

LaGrange College ($33,000) see Pitts Foundation, William H. and Lula E.

LaGrange College ($30,000) see Pitts Foundation, William H. and Lula E.

LaGrange College — research study of environmental conditions in Lake West Point ($43,000) see Callaway Foundation, Fuller E.

Lake Blackshear Regional Library ($5,000) see Marshall Foundation, Mattie H.

Lassiter High School ($20,000) see RTM

Leadership Georgia ($20,000) see NationsBank Corp.

Leadership Georgia ($25,000) see Pittulloch Foundation

Leading the Way International ($15,000) see Noble Foundation, Vivian Bilby

League of the Good Samaritan ($10,000) see Marshall Foundation, Mattie H.

Leukemia Society of America ($1,000) see Johnson, Lane, Space, Smith & Co., Inc.

Literacy Action ($15,000) see Atlanta Foundation

Literacy Action — annual support ($50,000) see Equifax

Literacy Action — to support the establishment of family literacy programs at eight Head Start sites in Atlanta, Georgia see United Parcel Service of America

Lovett School ($5,000) see Exposition Foundation

Lovett School ($5,000) see Oxford Foundation

Lovett School ($3,000) see West Foundation

Lowndes County Department of Family and Children Services Project ($79,400) see Levi Strauss & Co.

Lucas Theatre ($1,250) see Soling Family Foundation

Macon Arts Alliance — Bibb Institute for Arts in Education ($10,000) see Porter

Testamentary Trust, James Hyde

Macon Outreach Ministry ($7,500) see Porter Testamentary Trust, James Hyde

Macon Rescue Mission ($50,000) see Anderson Foundation, Peyton

Macon Rescue Mission — purchase kitchen equipment and renovate elevator ($25,000) see Porter Testamentary Trust, James Hyde

Macon Symphony ($3,000) see Bibb Co.

Mailbox Club Prison Ministries ($10,000) see McCarthy Foundation, John and Margaret

MAP International ($500) see Fibre Converters

MAP International ($10,000) see West Foundation

MAP International ($20,000) see Westwood Endowment

MAP International — endowment fund for Christian health care among the world's poor ($250,000) see Hermann Foundation, Grover

Maranatha Church of God ($43,500) see Watkins Christian Foundation

Marietta College see Brakeley, John Price Jones Inc.

Marist School ($40,000) see Gage Foundation, Philip and Irene Toll

Martin Luther King, Jr. Center for Nonviolent Social Change ($180,000) see BP America

Medcen Foundation ($50,000) see Grassmann Trust, E. J.

Medical College of Georgia — research facility project ($500,000) see Callaway Foundation

Medical College of Georgia — Alzheimer's disease project ($258,618) see Callaway Foundation

Medical College of Georgia Foundation — operating expenses ($50,000) see Georgia Power Co.

Medical Park Foundation ($20,000) see Russell Educational Foundation, Benjamin and Roberta

Mercer University ($7,000) see Alco Standard Corp.

Mercer University ($5,000) see Gilbert, Jr. Charitable Trust, Price

Mercer University ($5,000) see Imlay Foundation

Mercer University ($25,000) see NationsBank Corp.

Mercer University ($800) see Roddenbery Co., Inc., W.B.

Metro Atlanta Community ($20,000) see Day Foundation, Cecil B.

Metro Atlanta Foundation ($30,000) see Day Foundation, Cecil B.

Metro Boys Club of Columbus ($10,000) see Hollis Foundation

Metropolitan Atlanta Community Foundation — coordinate services to at-risk youth ($2,000,000) see Whitehead Foundation, Joseph B.

Metropolitan Atlanta Community Foundation — assess Georgia's health care system and shape public consensus on what values should guide ($500,000) see Whitehead Foundation, Joseph B.

Metropolitan Atlanta Community Foundation — fund for neighborhood planning in areas affected by construction of Olympic Venues ($500,000) see Whitehead Foundation, Joseph B.

Metropolitan Atlanta Community Foundation — Religious Liberty Teachers Education Program ($20,000) see Gilbert, Jr. Charitable Trust, Price

Middle Georgia Community Action Agency ($5,000) see Anderson Foundation, Peyton

Ministries to Women ($15,000) see Noble Foundation, Vivian Bilby

Mission Society for United Methodists ($1,000) see Parker Drilling Co.

Monroe Street United Methodist Church ($10,000) see Lee Foundation, Ray M. and Mary Elizabeth

Morehouse College ($10,000) see Herndon Foundation, Alonzo F. Herndon and Norris B.

Morehouse College — scholarships ($20,000) see Mifflin Memorial Fund, George H. and Jane A.

Morehouse College ($2,000) see New Orphan Asylum Scholarship Foundation

Morehouse School of Medicine ($30,000) see General Dynamics Corp.

Morehouse School of Medicine, Atlanta, GA ($16,600) see Cox Enterprises

Morehouse School of Medicine — support positions at Grady ($120,000) see Health 1st Foundation

Moriah Primitive Baptist Church ($7,600) see Gholston Trust, J. K.

Morris Brown College ($15,000) see Herndon Foundation, Alonzo F. Herndon and Norris B.

Morris Brown College — capital grant ($100,000) see Tull Charitable Foundation

Morris Brown College — to support faculty chair endowments and the Presidential Scholars Program for African-American students ($150,000) see Coca-Cola Co.

Mount Bethal Methodist Church ($10,000) see Patterson-Barclay Memorial Foundation

Mount DeSales Academy ($24,693) see Burke Foundation, Thomas C.

Mount Paran Church ($120,000) see Watkins Christian Foundation

Mount Paran Church of God ($10,000) see McCarthy Foundation, John and Margaret

Mount Vernon Christian Academy ($2,500) see Howell Fund

Mount Vernon Christian Academy ($15,000) see Ware Foundation

Mount Zion Baptist Church ($400) see Gholston Trust, J. K.

Museum of Atlanta History ($15,000) see Hill and Family Foundation, Walter Clay

Museum of the Sciences ($1,000) see Bibb Co.

National Black Women's Health Project ($2,600) see Lubo Fund

National Christian Foundation ($25,000) see Day Foundation, Cecil B.

National Coalition for Marine Conservation ($6,000) see Mostyn Foundation

National Science Center ($5,000) see Noland Co.

National Science Center for Communications and Electronics — capital commitment ($150,000) see CIGNA Corp.

National Science Center Foundation ($100,000) see Dow Chemical Co.

National Science Center Foundation ($20,000) see NationsBank Corp.

National Science Center Foundation ($150,000) see Xerox Corp.

National Science Foundation ($30,000) see Cray Research

Nature Conservancy — capital ($55,000) see Georgia Power Co.

Nell Hodgson Woodruff School of Nursing at Emory University ($25,000) see Support Systems International

New Savannah Science Museum ($10,000) see Chatham Valley Foundation

Newton City School System ($27,500) see Arnold Fund

Newton County Board of Education ($20,000) see Arnold Fund

Newton County United Fund ($5,000) see Arnold Fund

Nexus Contemporary Art Center ($26,500) see Massey Charitable Trust

North Atlanta Teen Center ($25,000) see Cox Enterprises

North Fulton Chamber of Commerce ($250) see Foundation for Advancement of Chiropractic Education

North Georgia Presbyterian Homes — for expansion of Presbyterian Village in Austell ($400,000) see Whitehead Foundation, Joseph B.

Northeast High School ($500) see Bibb Co.

Northside Hospital ($8,333) see National Service Industries

Northside Hospital Foundation ($7,500) see RTM

Northside Shepards Center ($5,000) see Churches Homes Foundation

Northside United Methodist Church ($6,000) see Tomlinson Foundation, Kate and Elwyn

Northwest Presbyterian Church ($37,500) see Illges Memorial Foundation, A. and M. L.

Oglethorpe University ($2,500) see Abreu Charitable Trust u/w/o May P. Abreu, Francis I.

Oglethorpe University ($15,100) see Delta Air Lines

Oglethorpe University — final payment on capital campaign commitment ($58,125) see Harland Charitable Foundation, John and Wilhelmina D.

Oglethorpe University ($5,000) see Preyer Fund, Mary Norris

Oglethorpe University ($50,000) see Rich Foundation

Oglethorpe University ($10,000) see Robinson Foundation, J. Mack

Oglethorpe University — operating grant ($15,000) see Trust Co. Bank

Oglethorpe University — renovation and expansion of main library to be named for the late Dr. Philip C. Weltner, former president of the University ($3,000,000) see Woodruff Foundation, Robert W.

Old Clinton Historical Society ($8,500) see Anderson Foundation, Peyton

Organization for the Enhancement of Public Education ($29,500) see GEICO Corp.

Our Lady of Perpetual Help Cancer Home ($7,500) see Gage Foundation, Philip and Irene Toll

Our Lady of Perpetual Help Cancer Home — care of aged women ($150,000) see Whitehead Foundation, Lettie Pate

Our Lady of Perpetual Hope Home ($17,000) see Steiner Charitable Fund, Albert

Oxford College, Emory University — scholarships ($6,000) see Baker Foundation, Clark and Ruby

Pace Academy ($5,000) see West Foundation

Pacelli High School ($5,000) see Schwob Foundation, Simon

Paideia School ($5,000) see Schultz Foundation

Paideia School — to institute beginning French classes in eighth grade ($12,000) see Rosenthal Foundation, Ida and William

Parent and Child Development Services ($6,000) see Colonial Oil Industries, Inc.

Parent and Child Development Services ($10,600) see Johnson, Lane, Space, Smith & Co., Inc.

Patrons of Music ($5,000) see Schwob Foundation, Simon

Peachtree Presbyterian Church ($1,000) see Parker, Jr. Foundation, William A.

Peter H Craig Elementary School ($6,000) see NutraSweet Co.

Piedmont College ($40,000) see Camp Younts Foundation

Piedmont College ($30,000) see Camp Younts Foundation

Piedmont Hospital ($10,000) see Dodson Foundation, James Glenwell and Clara May

Piedmont Hospital ($20,100) see Moore Memorial Foundation, James Starr

Piedmont Hospital ($75,000) see Murphy Foundation, Katherine and John

Piedmont Hospital Foundation — operating grant ($15,000) see Lanier Brothers Foundation

Presbyterian Homes — Presbyterian Village project ($50,000) see Callaway Foundation, Fuller E.

Professional Association of Georgia Educators ($25,000) see Lee Foundation, Ray M. and Mary Elizabeth

Project Reach ($2,500) see Bibb Co.

Protestant Radio and Television Center ($50,000) see Illges Memorial Foundation, A. and M. L.

Providence Christian Academy ($10,000) see Gage Foundation, Philip and Irene Toll

Providence Christian Academy ($16,024) see Overstreet Foundation

Public Museum of Historical Site ($199,989) see Herndon Foundation, Alonzo F. Herndon and Norris B.

Public TV Georgia ($35,000) see Circuit City Stores

Pure Praise Ministries ($23,568) see Watkins Christian Foundation

Radio Training Network (Purchase Stations) ($1,165,000) see Watkins Christian Foundation

Raoul Foundation American Lung Association ($10,000) see Wardlaw Fund, Gertrude and William C.

Real Life Ministries ($99,999) see Watkins Christian Foundation

Real Life Ministry (Air Time) ($75,139) see Watkins Christian Foundation

Red Cross ($15,000) see Patterson-Barclay Memorial Foundation

Reinhardt College — scholarships ($6,000) see Baker Foundation, Clark and Ruby

Reinhardt College ($3,000) see Moore Foundation, Roy C.

Resource Service Ministries ($7,000) see Courts Foundation

Richards Middle School see Ricoh Electronics Inc.

River House ($750) see Haley Foundation, W. B.

Robert Jones Memorial Scholarship Fund — Emory University ($10,000) see Imlay Foundation

Robert W. Woodruff Arts Center — for expenses in connection with long range facilities planning ($725,000) see Evans Foundation, Lettie Pate

Robert W. Woodruff Arts Center ($25,000) see Franklin Foundation, John and Mary

Robert W. Woodruff Arts Center ($125,000) see Georgia Power Co.

Robert W. Woodruff Arts Center — operating grant ($20,000) see Lanier Brothers Foundation

Robert W. Woodruff Arts Center ($50,000) see MCI Communications Corp.

Robert W. Woodruff Arts Center ($30,000) see MCI Communications Corp.

Robert W. Woodruff Arts Center — general support ($100,000) see Wachovia Bank of Georgia, N.A.

Robert W. Woodruff Arts Center ($35,000) see Woodward Fund-Atlanta, David, Helen, Marian

Robert W. Woodruff Arts Center ($10,000) see Woolley Foundation, Vasser

Roosevelt Warm Springs ($75,000) see Wilson Foundation, Frances Wood

Roosevelt Warm Springs Rehabilitation Development Fund — development cost for Camp Dream project ($300,000) see Callaway Foundation

Royce School ($5,000) see Johnson, Lane, Space, Smith & Co., Inc.

Rural Advancement Fund ($6,000) see Wardlaw Fund, Gertrude and William C.

RZIM ($141,000) see Paulstan

St. Andrews on the Marsh ($100,000) see Lane Memorial Foundation, Mills Bee

St. Catherine's Island Foundation — general support of its research and conservation programs ($434,400) see Noble Foundation, Edward John

St. Joseph Catholic Church ($25,309) see Burke Foundation, Thomas C.

St. Joseph Foundation ($10,000) see Gregg-Graniteville Foundation

St. Joseph's Hospital ($350,000) see Campbell Foundation, J. Bulow

St. Joseph's Hospital Foundation ($3,000) see Abreu Charitable Trust u/w/o May P. Abreu, Francis I.

St. Joseph's Hospital Foundation ($15,000) see Steiner Charitable Fund, Albert

St. Jude's House ($5,000) see Gage Foundation, Philip and Irene Toll

St. Luke Child Development Center ($58,850) see Synovus Financial Corp.

St. Luke United Methodist Church ($260,726) see Bradley-Turner Foundation

St. Luke's Economic Development Corporation — Employment Training Program (third of three) ($50,000) see Harland Charitable Foundation, John and Wilhelmina D.

St. Paul United Methodist Church ($39,000) see Illges Memorial Foundation, A. and M. L.

Salvation Army ($60,000) see Anderson Foundation, Peyton

Salvation Army ($11,900) see Cherokee Foundation

Salvation Army ($2,500) see Haley Foundation, W. B.

Salvation Army ($1,000) see McCarthy Foundation, John and Margaret

Salvation Army ($5,000) see Moore Foundation, Roy C.

Salvation Army — endowment fund ($109,200) see Murphy Foundation

Salvation Army ($1,000) see Parker, Jr. Foundation, William A.

Salvation Army School for Officers Training — officers training ($250,000) see Perot Foundation

Salvation Army — capital campaign for School for Officers' Training ($1,250,000) see Whitehead Foundation, Joseph B.

Savannah Ballet Theatre ($2,000) see Johnson, Lane, Space, Smith & Co., Inc.

Savannah Country Day School ($67,500) see Lane Memorial Foundation, Mills Bee

Savannah Country Day School Computer Program ($15,000) see Chatham Valley Foundation

Savannah Diocese ($12,500) see O'Neil Foundation, W.

Savannah Science Museum ($5,000) see Colonial Oil Industries, Inc.

Savannah Science Museum — financial assistance ($5,000) see Hodge Foundation

Savannah Science Museum ($2,500) see Johnson, Lane, Space, Smith & Co., Inc.

Savannah on Stage ($4,133) see Soling Family Foundation

Savannah State College — scholarship ($25,000) see Chatham Valley Foundation

Savannah Street Neighborhood ($5,000) see Churches Homes Foundation

Savannah Symphony ($20,000) see Chatham Valley Foundation

Savannah Symphony ($5,000) see Colonial Oil Industries, Inc.

Savannah Symphony ($3,500) see Johnson, Lane, Space, Smith & Co., Inc.

Save-a-Youth Wilderness Camp ($3,500) see Moore Foundation, Roy C.

Schenck School ($2,500) see Abreu Charitable Trust u/w/o May P. Abreu, Francis I.

Schenck School ($10,000) see Gilbert, Jr. Charitable Trust, Price

Schenck School ($2,000) see West Foundation

Science and Technology Museum of Atlanta ($75,000) see Cox Enterprises

Science and Technology Museum of Atlanta ($25,000) see Franklin Foundation, John and Mary

Science and Technology Museum of Atlanta — capital ($50,000) see Georgia Power Co.

Science and Technology Museum of Atlanta ($25,000) see Woolley Foundation, Vasser

Scottish Rite Children's Hospital ($10,000) see Dodson Foundation, James Glenwell and Clara May

Scottish Rite Children's Hospital ($125,000) see Kirbo Charitable Trust, Thomas M. and Irene B.

Scottish Rite Children's Hospital ($1,000) see Lauffer Trust, Charles A.

Scottish Rite Children's Hospital ($25,000) see Lee Foundation, Ray M. and Mary Elizabeth

Scottish Rite Children's Hospital ($53,500) see Livingston Foundation

Scottish Rite Children's Hospital ($5,000) see Marshall Foundation, Mattie H.

Scottish Rite Children's Hospital ($5,000) see Marshall Foundation, Mattie H.

Scottish Rite Children's Hospital ($15,000) see Wardlaw Fund, Gertrude and William C.

Scottish Rite Children's Hospital ($10,000) see Woolley Foundation, Vasser

Scottish Rite Children's Medical Center Foundation — capital grant ($75,000) see Tull Charitable Foundation

Scottish Rite Hospital for Crippled Children ($100,000) see Woodward Fund-Atlanta, David, Helen, Marian

Scottish Rite Medical Center ($32,500) see Wilson Foundation, Frances Wood

Second Harvest Food Bank — purchase food for needy ($5,000) see Hodge Foundation

Second Ponce De Leon Baptist Church ($35,000) see Ragan Charitable Foundation, Carolyn King

Second Ponce De Leon Baptist Church ($32,500) see Ragan Charitable Foundation, Carolyn King

Seminary Extension ($5,000) see Patterson-Barclay Memorial Foundation

Senior Citizens Services ($5,000) see Elkin Memorial Foundation, Neil Warren and William Simpson

Senior Citizens Services of Metropolitan Atlanta ($175,243) see Senior Citizens Foundation

Sheareth Israel Synagogue ($10,000) see Steinsapir Family Foundation, Julius L. and Libhie B.

Sheltering Arms ($2,000) see Crawford & Co.

Sheltering Arms ($5,000) see Dodson Foundation, James Glenwell and Clara May

Sheperd Spinal Center ($10,000) see Dodson Foundation, James Glenwell and Clara May

Sheperd Spinal Center ($10,000) see Gage Foundation, Philip and Irene Toll

Sheperd Spinal Center ($25,000) see Murphy Foundation, Katherine and John

Sheperd Spinal Center ($30,000) see RTM

Sheperd Spinal Center ($16,000) see Steiner Charitable Fund, Albert

Shepherd Center for Treatment of Spinal Injuries ($25,000) see Georgia-Pacific Corp.

Shepherd Spinal Center ($6,300) see Crawford & Co.

Shepherd Spinal Center ($5,000) see Elkin Memorial Foundation, Neil Warren and William Simpson

Shepherd Spinal Center ($110,000) see Fuqua Foundation, J. B.

Shepherd Spinal Center — operating grant ($10,000) see Lanier Brothers Foundation

Shepherd Spinal Center ($5,000) see Marshall Foundation, Mattie H.

Shepherd Spinal Center — operating grant ($5,000) see Marshall Trust in Memory of Sanders McDaniel, Harriet McDaniel

Shepherd Spinal Center ($5,000) see National Service Industries

Shepherd Spinal Center ($7,500) see Wardlaw Fund, Gertrude and William C.

Shepherd Spinal Center ($25,345) see Wilson Foundation, Frances Wood

Shepherd Spinal Clinic — operating grant ($15,000) see Trust Co. Bank

Sheppard Center ($37,500) see Illges Memorial Foundation, A. and M. L.

Shorter College — toward campaign to build an athletic complex ($250,000) see Evans Foundation, Lettie Pate

Shorter College ($10,000) see Patterson-Barclay Memorial Foundation

Shorter College ($10,000) see Ratner Foundation, Milton M.

Shorter College ($5,000) see Robinson Foundation, J. Mack

Shortoff Miss Baptist Church ($1,000) see Parker, Jr. Foundation, William A.

Smokerise Baptist Church ($50,000) see Watkins Christian Foundation

Georgia (cont.)

Sons of American Revolution ($8,000) see Patterson-Barclay Memorial Foundation

South Georgia Methodist Home for the Aging ($30,000) see Pitts Foundation, William H. and Lula E.

South Georgia Methodist Home for the Aging ($30,000) see Pitts Foundation, William H. and Lula E.

Southeastern Academy of Theater and Music ($15,000) see Atlanta Foundation

Southern Center for Human Rights ($250,000) see Public Welfare Foundation

Southern Center for International Studies ($29,000) see Livingston Foundation

Southern Center for International Studies ($50,000) see Woodward Fund-Watertown, David, Helen, and Marian

Southern Charitable Foundation ($10,800) see Vanneck-Bailey Foundation

Southern Christian Leadership ($1,000) see National Forge Co.

Southern College of Technology ($10,000) see ITT Rayonier

Southern Education Foundation ($910,000) see BellSouth Corp.

Southern Education Foundation — to strengthen libraries of leading private black colleges ($1,150,000) see Mellon Foundation, Andrew W.

Southern Prisoners' Defense Committee — to protect the rights of those confined in Southern prisons and jails ($280,000) see Clark Foundation, Edna McConnell

Southern Regional Council ($15,000) see Grant Foundation, Charles M. and Mary D.

Southern Regional Education Board ($600,000) see Kenan, Jr. Charitable Trust, William R.

Southern Tech Foundation ($3,035) see Oxford Industries, Inc.

Southern Tech Foundation ($3,035) see Oxford Industries, Inc.

Southwest Georgia Academy ($5,000) see Jinks Foundation, Ruth T.

Southwest Hospital and Medical Center — general support and research program to provide medical care to the indigent ($100,000) see Health 1st Foundation

Spelman College ($25,000) see Harvard Apparatus Foundation

Spelman College ($25,000) see Lang Foundation, Eugene M.

Spelman College — to support a mentoring program for at-risk African-American high school students in Atlanta public schools and to assist doctoral students financially ($150,000) see Coca-Cola Co.

Springer Opera House Arts Association ($137,500) see Bradley-Turner Foundation

Springer Society ($25,000) see Synovus Financial Corp.

State Botanical Garden of Georgia ($10,000) see Pittulloch Foundation

Study Hall at Emmaus House ($5,000) see Exposition Foundation

Sumter Humane Society ($5,000) see Marshall Foundation, Mattie H.

Teach for America — to help with a national teacher corps of top college graduates to teach in areas suffering from persisten teacher shortages by providing five TFA teachers in rural Georgia ($25,000) see Challenge Foundation

Telfair Academy ($1,000) see Johnson, Lane, Space, Smith & Co., Inc.

Temple Beth-El ($10,000) see Ratner Foundation, Milton M.

Temple Israel ($11,065) see Schwob Foundation, Simon

Thomas College ($2,000) see Cherokee Foundation

Thomas County Historical Society ($2,000) see Cherokee Foundation

Thomas County Humane Society ($2,000) see Cherokee Foundation

Thomasville Cultural Center ($6,750) see Cherokee Foundation

Thomasville Cultural Center ($27,000) see Williams Family Foundation of Georgia

Thomasville Cultural Center ($15,000) see Williams Family Foundation of Georgia

Thomasville Public Library ($6,250) see Cherokee Foundation

Tift County Foundation for Education Excellence ($5,000) see Dorminy Foundation, John Henry

Tift County Hospital Foundation ($6,800) see Dorminy Foundation, John Henry

Tift General Hospital ($2,500) see Dorminy Foundation, John Henry

Tommy Nobis Center ($25,000) see Rich Foundation

Tommy Nobis Center ($35,000) see Woodward Fund-Atlanta, David, Helen, Marian

Trinity Presbyterian Church ($7,500) see West Foundation

Trinity School ($4,000) see Howell Fund

Trinity School ($10,000) see Love Foundation, Gay and Erskine

Troup County — vacant land ($86,700) see Callaway Foundation, Fuller E.

Troup County Schools ($1,000) see Cook Batson Foundation

Troy State University ($13,500) see Simpson Foundation

Troy State University ($6,000) see Wiggins Memorial Trust, J. J.

Truett-McConnell College ($4,000) see Moore Foundation, Roy C.

Turner-Hodge-Young Community Center of Montgomery — financial assistance ($2,900) see Hodge Foundation

Underground Festival Development ($8,334) see National Service Industries

Union Mission ($5,000) see Hodge Foundation

United Funds ($200) see Joslyn Corp.

United Givers Fund of Rome and Floyd County ($42,140) see Inland Container Corp.

United Negro College Fund ($3,000) see Crawford & Co.

United Negro College Fund — annual support ($18,000) see Equifax

United Way ($4,370) see Arkwright-Boston Manufacturers Mutual

United Way ($25,000) see Atlanta Foundation

United Way ($6,000) see Bergner Co., P.A.

United Way ($35,800) see Cherokee Foundation

United Way ($46,000) see Crawford & Co.

United Way ($13,425) see Crown Central Petroleum Corp.

United Way ($7,579) see Crown Central Petroleum Corp.

United Way ($5,000) see Exposition Foundation

United Way ($5,640) see Federated Life Insurance Co.

United Way ($19,500) see Gilbert, Jr. Charitable Trust, Price

United Way ($22,132) see Gilman Paper Co.

United Way ($2,500) see Haley Foundation, W. B.

United Way ($2,500) see Howell Fund

United Way ($371) see Interstate National Corp.

United Way ($5,000) see Johnson, Lane, Space, Smith & Co., Inc.

United Way ($17,500) see Lanier Brothers Foundation

United Way ($20,000) see Lee Foundation, Ray M. and Mary Elizabeth

United Way ($4,000) see Lubo Fund

United Way ($5,000) see Marshall Trust in Memory of Sanders McDaniel, Harriet McDaniel

United Way ($2,500) see McCarthy Foundation, John and Margaret

United Way ($17,325) see National Service Industries

United Way ($17,325) see National Service Industries

United Way ($17,325) see National Service Industries

United Way ($17,325) see National Service Industries

United Way ($20,350) see Oxford Industries, Inc.

United Way ($9,600) see Oxford Industries, Inc.

United Way ($2,500) see Oxford Industries, Inc.

United Way ($10,000) see Ratner Foundation, Milton M.

United Way ($500) see SCT Yarns

United Way ($500) see SCT Yarns

United Way ($96,000) see Synovus Financial Corp.

United Way ($7,000) see Tomlinson Foundation, Kate and Elwyn

United Way ($1,500) see Wallace Computer Services

United Way ($20,000) see Wardlaw Fund, Gertrude and William C.

United Way ($30,000) see Woodward Fund-Watertown, David, Helen, and Marian

United Way of Atlanta ($24,200) see Inland Steel Industries

United Way of Atlanta ($175,000) see Rich Foundation

United Way of Central Georgia ($104,362) see GEICO Corp.

United Way of the Coastal Empire ($223,096) see Union Camp Corp.

United Way of Decatur and Macon County ($92,040) see Archer-Daniels-Midland Co.

United Way — 89/90 pledge ($482,000) see Wachovia Bank of Georgia, N.A.

United Way of Hall County ($56,600) see Wrigley Co., Wm. Jr.

United Way of Hall County — 1990 pledge ($6,000) see Wachovia Bank of Georgia, N.A.

United Way of Metro Atlanta ($600,000) see NationsBank Corp.

United Way of Metro Atlanta ($123,491) see Trust Co. Bank

United Way of Metro Atlanta — operating grant ($123,491) see Trust Co. Bank

United Way of Metro Atlanta — operating grant ($123,491) see Trust Co. Bank

United Way of Metro Atlanta — operating grant ($123,490) see Trust Co. Bank

United Way of Metro Atlanta — operating ($115,250) see Trust Co. Bank

United Way of Metropolitan Atlanta — annual support ($265,000) see Equifax

United Way of Metropolitan Atlanta ($330,600) see Federated Department Stores and Allied Stores Corp.

United Way of Metropolitan Atlanta ($184,000) see Georgia-Pacific Corp.

United Way of Metropolitan Atlanta ($112,218) see Mead Corp.

United Way of Metropolitan Atlanta ($105,000) see Norfolk Southern Corp.

United Way of Metropolitan Atlanta ($35,000) see Woodward Fund-Atlanta, David, Helen, Marian

United Way of Northeast Georgia ($13,750) see Reliance Electric Co.

United Way of Northwest Georgia — 1990 pledge ($18,000) see Wachovia Bank of Georgia, N.A.

University of Georgia ($2,000) see Arnold Fund

University of Georgia ($2,000) see Bibb Co.

University of Georgia ($200,500) see Bradley-Turner Foundation

University of Georgia ($12,500) see English Memorial Fund, Florence C. and H. L.

University of Georgia ($12,500) see English Memorial Fund, Florence C. and H. L.

University of Georgia — law scholarships ($25,000) see Franklin Foundation, John and Mary

University of Georgia — scholarship fund ($1,600) see Gholston Trust, J. K.

University of Georgia ($33,333) see Harris Foundation, James J. and Angelia M.

University of Georgia ($25,000) see Harris Foundation, James J. and Angelia M.

University of Georgia — capital campaign ($62,500) see Tull Charitable Foundation

University of Georgia — Child Competence, Parenting, and Family Transactions in Rural

Black Families ($333,000) see Spencer Foundation

University of Georgia College of Law ($50,000) see Kirbo Charitable Trust, Thomas M. and Irene B.

University of Georgia — Ed Rast Scholarship ($50,000) see Franklin Foundation, John and Mary

University of Georgia Foundation ($50,000) see Courts Foundation

University of Georgia Foundation — operating grant ($10,000) see Lanier Brothers Foundation

University of Georgia Foundation ($50,000) see NationsBank Corp.

University of Georgia School of Journalism ($300,000) see Cox, Jr. Foundation, James M.

University of Georgia School of Law ($50,000) see Woolley Foundation, Vasser

University of Georgia School of Law — for the Sibley lectureships ($7,603) see Loridans Foundation, Charles

University System of Georgia — to help improve public elementary and secondary education in Georgia through teacher training and development programs ($300,000) see Coca-Cola Co.

Upson County Hospital Trust Fund ($55,523) see Community Enterprises

Valdosta State College see Packaging Corporation of America

Valley United Fund ($4,000) see Cook Batson Foundation

Vanderbilt Club Scholarship Program ($7,500) see Oxford Foundation

Village Atlanta ($1,000) see Churches Homes Foundation

Village of St. Joseph ($15,000) see Georgia Health Foundation

Visiting Nurse Association ($600,000) see McCarthy Foundation, John and Margaret

Visiting Nurse Foundation ($30,000) see Georgia Health Foundation

Walk through the Bible ($24,000) see Christian Training Foundation

Walk through the Bible ($125,000) see Paulstan

Warren Memorial United Methodist Church ($3,000) see Herndon Foundation, Alonzo F. Herndon and Norris B.

Wayne County Literacy Coalition ($10,000) see ITT Rayonier

Wesley Community Centers of Savannah ($3,000) see Hodge Foundation

Wesley Homes ($12,000) see Elkin Memorial Foundation, Neil Warren and William Simpson

Wesley Homes — care of aged women ($550,000) see Whitehead Foundation, Lettie Pate

Wesley Homes ($200,000) see Wilson Foundation, Frances Wood

Wesley Woods ($50,000) see Cox, Jr. Foundation, James M.

Wesleyan College — scholarships ($6,000) see Baker Foundation, Clark and Ruby

Wesleyan College ($49,966) see Beloco Foundation

Wesleyan College ($45,000) see Beloco Foundation

Wesleyan College ($290,532) see Bradley-Turner Foundation

Wesleyan College ($18,000) see Porter Testamentary Trust, James Hyde

Wesleyan College — scholarship fund ($8,000) see Swisher Foundation, Carl S.

Wesleyan College — renovation of Banks Dormitory ($250,000) see Evans Foundation, Lettie Pate

West Georgia Medical Center — building renovation project ($861,380) see Callaway Foundation

West Georgia Medical Center — proposed "East Garden" at Florence Hand Home ($66,563) see Callaway Foundation, Fuller E.

Westminster Campaign ($25,000) see Love Foundation, Gay and Erskine

Westminster Schools ($13,000) see Fuqua Foundation, J. B.

Westminster Schools ($10,000) see Glancy Foundation, Lenora and Alfred

Westminster Schools — operating grant ($25,000) see Lanier Brothers Foundation

Westminster Schools ($10,000) see Parker, Jr. Foundation, William A.

Westminster Schools ($10,000) see Parker, Jr. Foundation, William A.

Widow's Home ($50,000) see Grant Foundation, Charles M. and Mary D.

Woodruff Arts Center ($25,000) see Atlanta Foundation

Woodruff Arts Center ($12,500) see Exposition Foundation

Woodruff Arts Center ($5,000) see Exposition Foundation

Woodruff Arts Center ($9,000) see Gilbert, Jr. Charitable Trust, Price

Woodruff Arts Center ($10,000) see Harland Co., John H.

Woodruff Arts Center ($25,000) see Hill and Family Foundation, Walter Clay

Woodruff Arts Center ($10,000) see Hill and Family Foundation, Walter Clay

Woodruff Arts Center ($6,000) see Howell Fund

Woodruff Arts Center — annual campaign ($25,000) see Lee Foundation, Ray M. and Mary Elizabeth

Woodruff Arts Center ($16,000) see Moore Memorial Foundation, James Starr

Woodruff Arts Center ($25,000) see Murphy Foundation, Katherine and John

Woodruff Arts Center ($12,000) see National Service Industries

Woodruff Arts Center ($115,000) see NationsBank Corp.

Woodruff Arts Center ($65,000) see Rich Foundation

Woodruff Arts Center — general support ($10,000) see RTM

Woodruff Arts Center ($7,000) see Tomlinson Foundation, Kate and Elwyn

Woodruff Arts Center ($100,000) see Trust Co. Bank

Woodruff Arts Center ($5,000) see Waffle House, Inc.

Woodruff Arts Center ($7,500) see Wardlaw Fund, Gertrude and William C.

Woodruff Arts Center ($5,000) see West Foundation

Woodruff Arts Center Renovation Campaign ($20,000) see Lee Foundation, Ray M. and Mary Elizabeth

Woodruff Arts Center Special Campaign ($5,000) see National Service Industries

Woodruff North ($10,000) see RTM

Woodruff (Robert W.) Arts Center ($293,909) see Ford Motor Co.

Woodward Academy — establish the Ben F. Johnson, III professorship of Woodward Academy ($100,000) see Loridans Foundation, Charles

Woodward North Academy ($15,000) see Burns Family Foundation

Yes Atlanta, Youth Experience Success ($5,500) see Livingston Foundation

YMCA ($15,000) see Cherokee Foundation

YMCA ($1,500) see Churches Homes Foundation

YMCA ($5,000) see Harland Co., John H.

YMCA ($2,500) see Herndon Foundation, Alonzo F. Herndon and Norris B.

YMCA ($50,000) see Kirbo Charitable Trust, Thomas M. and Irene B.

YMCA ($12,500) see Lee Foundation, Ray M. and Mary Elizabeth

YMCA ($21,250) see Synovus Financial Corp.

YMCA ($5,000) see Waffle House, Inc.

YMCA ($12,512) see Williams Family Foundation of Georgia

YMCA of Metropolitan Atlanta — special campaign ($12,500) see Equifax

YMCA of Metropolitan Atlanta — capital ($66,666) see Georgia Power Co.

YMCA of Metropolitan Atlanta — capital improvements at the Southwest, South DeKalb and Southeast Atlanta Branches ($1,500,000) see Whitehead Foundation, Joseph B.

Young Harris College ($1,000) see Alice Manufacturing Co.

Young Harris College — library ($20,000) see Appleby Foundation

Young Harris College — scholarships ($6,000) see Baker Foundation, Clark and Ruby

Young Harris College ($300,000) see Campbell Foundation, J. Bulow

Young Harris College ($33,000) see Harland Co., John H.

Young Harris College ($25,000) see Lee Foundation, Ray M. and Mary Elizabeth

Young Harris College ($650,000) see Wilson Foundation, Frances Wood

Young Harris College — for the new Center for Humanities and Social Studies ($50,000) see Harland Charitable Foundation, John and Wilhelmina D.

Young Harris College — Frank Malone Memorial fund ($35,000) see Franklin Foundation, John and Mary

Young Harris Development Campaign ($50,000) see Appleby Foundation

Zoo Atlanta ($25,000) see Cox Enterprises

Zoo Atlanta ($10,000) see Hill and Family Foundation, Walter Clay

Zoo Atlanta ($50,000) see Murphy Foundation, Katherine and John

Hawaii

Alaha United Way, Oahu — social welfare ($182,000) see First Hawaiian

Aloha United Way — campaign ($160,000) see Atherton Family Foundation

Aloha United Way ($116,000) see GTE Corp.

Aloha United Way ($116,000) see GTE Corp.

Aloha United Way ($3,500) see Servco Pacific

Aloha United Way — final payment on $186,000 pledge for 1990/91 campaign ($46,500) see BHP Pacific Resources

Aloha United Way — second quarterly payment on $186,000 pledge for 1990/91 campaign ($46,500) see BHP Pacific Resources

Aloha United Way — for third payment on $186,030 pledge for 1990/91 fund drive ($46,500) see BHP Pacific Resources

Aloha United Way — first payment on $136,000 pledge for 1991/92 campaign ($34,000) see BHP Pacific Resources

Aloha United Way — 1992 campaign ($68,000) see Castle Foundation, Samuel N. and Mary

Alternatives to Violence ($5,000) see Baldwin Memorial Foundation, Fred

American Red Cross ($4,000) see Brewer and Co., Ltd., C.

American Red Cross ($7,500) see Servco Pacific

American Red Cross ($1,250,000) see Weinberg Foundation, Harry and Jeanette

American Red Cross ($225,000) see Weinberg Foundation, Harry and Jeanette

Armed Services Special Education and Training Society — school for the handicapped see Nalco Chemical Co.

Asian/Pacific Foundation of Hawaii — toward completion of Eddie and Myrna Kamae's documentary ($10,000) see BHP Pacific Resources

Assets School ($50,000) see Brace Foundation, Donald C.

Assets School — second payment on $150,000 pledge for capital campaign ($50,000) see BHP Pacific Resources

Assets School — capital campaign: relocation and campus expansion ($100,000) see Castle Foundation, Samuel N. and Mary

ASSETS School for Gifted/Dyslexic Children — capital fund campaign ($36,667) see First Hawaiian

Associated Catholic Charities ($1,025,000) see Weinberg Foundation, Harry and Jeanette

Bernice P. Bishop Museum — publication of a book ($25,000) see Smith Horticultural Trust, Stanley

Bernice Pauahi Bishop Museum — Malacologist position ($30,000) see Cooke Foundation

Bishop Museum ($50,000) see Persis Corp.

Bishop Museum — capital improvement program ($10,000) see Watumull Fund, J.

Bishop Museum — operations of the planetarium and Neighbor Island starlab programs ($10,000) see BHP Pacific Resources

Bishop Museum Support Council ($10,000) see Persis Corp.

Boys and Girls Club ($10,000) see Persis Corp.

Catholic Charities ($5,000) see Baldwin Memorial Foundation, Fred

Chaminade University ($25,000) see Vidinha Charitable Trust, A. and E.

Chaminade University ($25,000) see Wilcox General Trust, George N.

Child and Family Service — group home for sexually abused girls ($35,000) see McInerny Foundation

Child and Family Services — quality innovative programs ($25,000) see First Hawaiian

Contemporary Arts Center — capital campaign ($60,000) see Castle Foundation, Samuel N. and Mary

Contemporary Museum ($25,000) see Bancorp Hawaii

Contemporary Museum — capital support ($100,000) see Cooke Foundation

Contemporary Museum ($10,000) see Watumull Fund, J.

Contemporary Museum ($50,000) see Weisman Art Foundation, Frederick R.

Contemporary Museum — renovating Spalding House ($50,000) see McInerny Foundation

Easter Seal Society ($19,300) see Vidinha Charitable Trust, A. and E.

Family Literacy Fund ($20,000) see Bancorp Hawaii

First Night Honolulu ($5,000) see Oceanic Cablevision Foundation

First Presbyterian Church ($5,000) see Brewer and Co., Ltd., C.

Friends of Foster Kids ($5,000) see Castle Trust, George P. and Ida Tenney

Girl Scouts of America ($3,000) see Castle Trust, George P. and Ida Tenney

Habilitat, Inc. ($50,000) see Castle Foundation, Harold K. L.

Hale Makua ($2,000) see Moore Foundation, O. L.

Hanahauoli School — scholarship fund ($5,000) see Watumull Fund, J.

Hawaii Advocates for Children and Youth ($15,000) see Castle Trust, George P. and Ida Tenney

Hawaii Baptist Academy ($20,000) see Bancorp Hawaii

Hawaii Baptist Academy ($5,000) see Brewer and Co., Ltd., C.

Hawaii Baptist Academy — building ($5,000) see Edwards Foundation, Jes

Hawaii Community Foundation — three-year support of its organizational development ($50,000) see Gerbode Foundation, Wallace Alexander

Hawaii Conference United Church/Christ — to build a community hall for the Hauula Congregational Church ($10,000) see Frear Eleemosynary Trust, Mary D. and Walter F.

Hawaii Food Bank ($20,000) see Bancorp Hawaii

Hawaii Foodbank — capital campaign for new warehouse ($25,000) see First Hawaiian

Hawaii Foodbank — capital drive fund ($50,000) see McInerny Foundation

Hawaii Island United Way ($10,000) see Frear Eleemosynary Trust, Mary D. and Walter F.

Hawaii Island United Way — 1991/92 campaign ($11,000) see BHP Pacific Resources

Hawaii Island Young Life ($2,000) see Castle Trust, George P. and Ida Tenney

Hawaii Lions Foundation/Eye Bank ($10,000) see May Mitchell Royal Foundation

Hawaii Literacy ($4,000) see Oceanic Cablevision Foundation

Hawaii Loa College ($200,000) see Castle Foundation, Harold K. L.

Hawaii Loa College — academic development and campus construction ($50,000) see First Hawaiian

Hawaii Loa College ($20,000) see Vidinha Charitable Trust, A. and E.

Hawaii Maritime Center ($15,000) see Persis Corp.

Hawaii Mental Health Clinic ($50,000) see Cox, Jr. Foundation, James M.

Hawaii Nature Center ($5,000) see Baldwin Memorial Foundation, Fred

Hawaii Pacific College ($20,000) see Bancorp Hawaii

Hawaii Pacific University — library renovation ($100,000) see Atherton Family Foundation

Hawaii Pacific University ($200,000) see Castle Foundation, Harold K. L.

Hawaii Pacific University — library renovation and construction ($70,000) see Castle Foundation, Samuel N. and Mary

Hawaii Pacific University ($5,000) see Wilcox Trust, S. W.

Hawaii Plantation Village ($10,000) see Persis Corp.

Hawaii Preparatory Academy — arts center and swimming pool ($105,000) see Atherton Family Foundation

Hawaii Preparatory Academy — capital campaign ($100,000) see Atherton Family Foundation

Hawaii Preparatory Academy ($50,000) see Castle Foundation, Harold K. L.

Hawaii Preparatory Academy ($10,000) see Persis Corp.

Hawaii Public Radio — capital fund drive ($50,000) see McInerny Foundation

Hawaii Public Radio ($7,500) see Oceanic Cablevision Foundation

Hawaii (cont.)

Hawaii Public Television ($2,000) see Moore Foundation, O. L.

Hawaii School for Girls — gym/student center complex ($100,000) see Cooke Foundation

Hawaii Theatre ($15,000) see Wilcox General Trust, George N.

Hawaii's Plantation Village — historical plantation village project ($40,000) see First Hawaiian

Hina Mauka ($25,000) see Bancorp Hawaii

Hina Mauka — residence for recovering alcoholics ($50,000) see McInerny Foundation

Hina Mauka ($10,000) see Wilcox General Trust, George N.

Historic Hawaii Foundation ($5,000) see Oceanic Cablevision Foundation

Holy Innocents' Episcopal Church ($10,000) see Moore Foundation, O. L.

Honolulu Academy of Arts — annual grant ($50,000) see Cooke Foundation

Honolulu Academy of Arts — Linekona renovations ($50,000) see Castle Foundation, Samuel N. and Mary

Honolulu Academy of Arts — restoration of the academy of art center at Linekona ($5,000) see Watumull Fund, J.

Honolulu Academy of Arts — Linekona School repair and improvements ($100,000) see Cooke Foundation

Honolulu Academy of Arts — renovate Linekona School ($50,000) see McInerny Foundation

Honolulu Symphony ($50,000) see Castle Foundation, Harold K. L.

Honolulu Symphony Orchestra ($2,125) see Servco Pacific

Honolulu Symphony Society — endowment fund ($25,000) see Cooke Foundation

Honolulu Theatre ($5,000) see Oceanic Cablevision Foundation

Hospice ($5,000) see Pettus, Jr. Foundation, James T.

Hospice Maui ($11,000) see Baldwin Memorial Foundation, Fred

Island School — capital campaign ($25,000) see Cooke Foundation

Island School — capital campaign ($25,000) see First Hawaiian

Island School — capital fund drive ($25,000) see Frear Eleemosynary Trust, Mary D. and Walter F.

Island School — capital fund frive ($32,500) see McInerny Foundation

Island School ($112,000) see Wilcox Trust, S. W.

Kahuku Hospital ($25,000) see Bancorp Hawaii

Kahuku Hospital ($15,000) see Frear Eleemosynary Trust, Mary D. and Walter F.

Kalihi-Palma Health Clinic ($5,000) see May Mitchell Royal Foundation

Kapiolani Medical Center ($2,000) see Servco Pacific

Kapiolani Medical Center — first payment on $30,000 pledge, payable over two years, for renovations of pediatric ICU and emergency room ($15,000) see BHP Pacific Resources

Kauai Community Players Children's Theater ($5,000) see Wilcox Trust, S. W.

Kauai Museum ($10,000) see Wilcox Trust, S. W.

Kauai Public Schools — donation of computer equipment for 13 public schools affected by Hurricane Iniki ($1,500,000) see IBM Corp.

Keeaumoka Street Congregation ($2,500) see Bell Trust

KHPR-Hawaii Public Radio — new site/program expansion ($50,000) see Cooke Foundation

Koloa Missionary Church ($21,500) see Vidinha Charitable Trust, A. and E.

La Pietra Hawaii School for Girls ($55,100) see Holy Land Charitable Trust

Lahaina Restoration Foundation ($6,000) see Moore Foundation, O. L.

Lahainaluna High School ($10,000) see Moore Foundation, O. L.

Learning Disabilities ($5,000) see Oceanic Cablevision Foundation

Learning Disabilities Association of Hawaii ($5,000) see Castle Trust, George P. and Ida Tenney

Lyman House Memorial Museum ($10,000) see Wilcox Trust, S. W.

Makawoo Union Church ($12,000) see Baldwin Memorial Foundation, Fred

Marimed Foundation ($10,000) see Baldwin Memorial Foundation, Fred

Maryknoll Schools — first payment on $45,000 pledge, payable over three years, for capital support ($15,000) see BHP Pacific Resources

Maui Community Arts and Cultural Center ($25,000) see Bancorp Hawaii

Maui Community Arts and Cultural Center ($10,000) see Brewer and Co., Ltd., C.

Maui Community Arts and Cultural Center — capital campaign ($33,333) see First Hawaiian

Maui Rehabilitation Center ($5,000) see Baldwin Memorial Foundation, Fred

Maui United Way ($10,000) see Frear Eleemosynary Trust, Mary D. and Walter F.

Moilili Community ($5,000) see Oceanic Cablevision Foundation

Montessori of Maui — construction of facility ($75,000) see Castle Foundation, Samuel N. and Mary

Muscular Dystrophy Association ($5,000) see Oceanic Cablevision Foundation

Na Pua O Kauai Island School ($100,000) see Atherton Family Foundation

Na Pua O Kauai-Island School — challenge grant ($50,000) see Castle Foundation, Samuel N. and Mary

National Tropical Botanical Garden ($11,000) see Magowan Family Foundation

Nature Conservancy ($50,000) see Weeden Foundation, Frank

Nature Conservancy of Hawaii ($50,000) see Homeland Foundation

Nature Conservancy of Hawaii — Islands of Life campaign ($400,000) see Cooke Foundation

Northern Hawaii Hospice ($4,000) see Simpson Foundation, John M.

Nui Nocau Visual Arts Center ($10,000) see Baldwin Memorial Foundation, Fred

Office of United Self Help ($15,000) see Vidinha Charitable Trust, A. and E.

Okinawan Cultural and Community Center ($25,000) see Bancorp Hawaii

Onizuka Memorial Committee — for the Ellison S. Onizuka Space Museum ($15,000) see Frear Eleemosynary Trust, Mary D. and Walter F.

Onizuka Memorial Committee — fund Onizuka space museum ($25,000) see First Hawaiian

P.E.F. Israel Endowment ($46,290) see Holy Land Charitable Trust

Pacific Institute of Chemical Dependency ($6,500) see Servco Pacific

Palama Settlement ($2,500) see Servco Pacific

Planned Parenthood ($3,500) see Pettus, Jr. Foundation, James T.

Planned Parenthood ($8,000) see Simpson Foundation, John M.

Punahou School — sesquicentennial campaign ($150,000) see Castle Foundation, Samuel N. and Mary

Punahou School — restoration historical campus buildings ($30,000) see First Hawaiian

Punahou School — scholarship program ($50,000) see McInerny Foundation

Punahou School ($25,000) see Persis Corp.

Rehabilitation Hospital — for replacing hospital roof ($15,000) see Frear Eleemosynary Trust, Mary D. and Walter F.

Rehabilitation Hospital Foundation ($7,809) see Brewer and Co., Ltd., C.

St. Andrews Cathedral ($56,724) see Hobart Memorial Fund, Marion W.

St. Christopher's Episcopal Church — capital improvements ($10,000) see Frear Eleemosynary Trust, Mary D. and Walter F.

St. Francis Hospital ($20,000) see Ernest & Julio Gallo Winery

St. Francis Medical Center ($5,000) see Oceanic Cablevision Foundation

St. Michael and All Angels — for the administration community building ($12,500) see Frear Eleemosynary Trust, Mary D. and Walter F.

Salvation Army ($7,000) see Castle Trust, George P. and Ida Tenney

Salvation Army ($39,500) see Wilcox General Trust, George N.

Salvation Army ($25,000) see Wilcox Trust, S. W.

Salvation Army ($5,000) see Wilcox Trust, S. W.

Salvation Army, Hawaii Division — support Woman's Way and Malama Makua ($30,500) see McInerny Foundation

Seabury Hall ($15,000) see Baldwin Memorial Foundation, Fred

Seabury Hall — matching grant ($500,000) see Castle Foundation, Harold K. L.

Seabury Hall — renovation of library ($200,000) see Castle Foundation, Samuel N. and Mary

Shriners Hospital for Crippled Children ($26,153) see May Mitchell Royal Foundation

State of Hawaii Department of Education ($10,000) see Castle Trust, George P. and Ida Tenney

State of Hawaii Department of Education ($1,254) see Castle Trust, George P. and Ida Tenney

State of Hawaii Department of Health ($25,000) see Vidinha Charitable Trust, A. and E.

State of Hawaii Department of Health ($16,500) see Vidinha Charitable Trust, A. and E.

Teen Challenge ($5,000) see Baldwin Memorial Foundation, Fred

Temple Emanu-El ($5,000) see Holy Land Charitable Trust

United Church of Christ ($20,000) see Vidinha Charitable Trust, A. and E.

United Way ($85,000) see Brewer and Co., Ltd., C.

United Way ($35,000) see Brewer and Co., Ltd., C.

United Way ($14,000) see Brewer and Co., Ltd., C.

United Way ($14,000) see Brewer and Co., Ltd., C.

United Way ($38,500) see Persis Corp.

United Way ($8,000) see Pettus, Jr. Foundation, James T.

University of Hawaii ($5,600) see Grant Thornton

University of Hawaii ($50,000) see Parvin Foundation, Albert

University of Hawaii ($67,550) see Vidinha Charitable Trust, A. and E.

University of Hawaii Community Colleges ($5,000) see Servco Pacific

University of Hawaii — electrical, biosynthetic and secretory characteristics in relation to morphogenesis of crustacean peptidergic neurons in culture ($42,924) see Whitehall Foundation

University of Hawaii Foundation ($3,000) see Brewer and Co., Ltd., C.

University of Hawaii Foundation — renewed support ($187,500) see Freedom Forum

University of Hawaii Foundation ($20,000) see Ranney Foundation, P. K.

University of Hawaii at Manda College of Business ($2,500) see Servco Pacific

University of Hawaii at Manoa ($63,000) see Pauley Foundation, Edwin W.

Waianae High School Peer Counseling Training Camp see HEI Inc.

Waikiki Health Center ($5,000) see Oceanic Cablevision Foundation

West Hawaii Support Council ($8,000) see Simpson Foundation, John M.

West Maui Taxpayers Association ($5,000) see Moore Foundation, O. L.

Wilcox Hospital ($50,000) see Wilcox General Trust, George N.

Wilcox Hospital Foundation ($25,000) see Bancorp Hawaii

Wilcox Hospital Foundation ($25,000) see Vidinha Charitable Trust, A. and E.

Wilcox Hospital Foundation ($25,000) see Wilcox Trust, S. W.

Winners Camp — scholarships ($9,500) see Wilcox Trust, S. W.

YMCA ($13,500) see Castle Trust, George P. and Ida Tenney

YMCA ($10,000) see Frear Eleemosynary Trust, Mary D. and Walter F.

YMCA ($12,000) see Wilcox Trust, S. W.

YMCA of Honolulu — capital campaign ($60,000) see Castle Foundation, Samuel N. and Mary

YMCA of Honolulu — construction of program center ($25,000) see Cooke Foundation

YMCA of Honolulu — capital drive fund ($50,000) see McInerny Foundation

Idaho

Adult and Child Development Center ($5,800) see Beckman Foundation, Leland D.

Alphonsus Foundation ($5,000) see Morrison Foundation, Harry W.

American Fest Ballet ($9,600) see Whittenberger Foundation, Claude R. and Ethel B.

Boise Art Museum ($20,000) see Cunningham Foundation, Laura Moore

Boise Art Museum ($30,000) see Morrison-Knudsen Corp.

Boise Neighborhood Housing Services — to expand a transitional housing program, to include longer-term housing and follow-up social services ($286,702) see Northwest Area Foundation

Boise Public Schools Education Foundation ($10,000) see Morrison-Knudsen Corp.

Boise State University ($36,000) see Cunningham Foundation, Laura Moore

Boise State University ($32,000) see Cunningham Foundation, Laura Moore

Boise State University ($3,850) see First Security Corp. (Salt Lake City, Utah)

Boise State University ($10,000) see Hemingway Foundation, Robert G.

Boise State University — scholarship fund ($11,600) see Morrison Foundation, Harry W.

Bonneville County Sheriff's Jeep Patrol ($11,645) see CHC Foundation

Caldwell Fine Arts ($5,500) see Whittenberger Foundation, Claude R. and Ethel B.

CART ($8,500) see CHC Foundation

Children's Village ($5,000) see Daugherty Foundation

Children's Voices ($7,128) see Whittenberger Foundation, Claude R. and Ethel B.

City of Boise ($190,000) see Morrison Foundation, Harry W.

City of Menan ($15,000) see CHC Foundation

City of Shelley ($19,850) see CHC Foundation

College of Idaho ($60,000) see Cunningham Foundation, Laura Moore

College of Idaho ($1,000) see Hemingway Foundation, Robert G.

College of Idaho — centennial clock ($95,000) see Morrison Foundation, Harry W.

College of Idaho — scholarship funds ($100,000) see Ore-Ida Foods, Inc.

College of Idaho ($41,000) see Whittenberger Foundation, Claude R. and Ethel B.

College of Southern Idaho ($20,000) see Helms Foundation

College of Southern Idaho ($25,000) see Whiting Foundation, Macauley and Helen Dow

Community Foundation ($35,000) see Daugherty Foundation

Community Hospital, Council, ID ($25,000) see Boise Cascade Corp.

Community School ($5,000) see McCrea Foundation

Crisis Hotline ($1,000) see Hemingway Foundation, Robert G.

Development Workshop Development Center — equipment purchases ($6,000) see Beckman Foundation, Leland D.

District 7 Health Department ($10,000) see CHC Foundation

Eastern Idaho Technical College ($4,000) see Beckman Foundation, Leland D.

Elks Rehabilitation Hospital ($141,109) see Daugherty Foundation

Epworth Village ($141,109) see Daugherty Foundation

Festival at Sandpoint ($5,000) see Johnston-Fix Foundation

First United Methodist Church — in memory of Edna M. Allen ($22,000) see Morrison Foundation, Harry W.

Gooding Memorial Hospital — mammography unit ($10,000) see Morrison Foundation, Harry W.

Hays Shelter Home — to provide short-term shelter and a home environment to youth needing emergency housing ($14,750) see Gannett Co.

Holy Rosary Memorial Hospital ($20,000) see Cunningham Foundation, Laura Moore

Hope House ($8,720) see Whittenberger Foundation, Claude R. and Ethel B.

Idaho Centennial Commission ($3,493) see Morrison Foundation, Harry W.

Idaho Citizens Network Research and Education ($15,000) see Beldon Fund

Idaho Community Foundation ($5,000) see Beckman Foundation, Leland D.

Idaho Community Foundation ($26,250) see Daugherty Foundation

Idaho Community Foundation ($20,000) see Whittenberger Foundation, Claude R. and Ethel B.

Idaho Community Foundation — partial support for operating costs during first three years, plus a matching grant for its endowment ($175,000) see Northwest Area Foundation

Idaho Elks Rehabilitation Hospital ($10,000) see Morrison-Knudsen Corp.

Idaho Falls Good Samaritan Center ($3,500) see Beckman Foundation, Leland D.

Idaho Falls Opera Theatre ($5,000) see Beckman Foundation, Leland D.

Idaho Falls Symphony Society ($5,000) see Beckman Foundation, Leland D.

Idaho Fish and Wildlife Foundation ($130,000) see Morrison-Knudsen Corp.

Idaho Foodbank Warehouse ($50,000) see Steele-Reese Foundation

Idaho Migrant Council ($53,997) see CHC Foundation

Idaho State University ($8,500) see EG&G Inc.

Idaho State University ($4,000) see First Security Corp. (Salt Lake City, Utah)

Idaho State University ($10,000) see Hemingway Foundation, Robert G.

Idaho State University Foundation ($10,000) see Beckman Foundation, Leland D.

Idaho State University Foundation ($31,493) see Gould Inc.

Idaho State University Foundation — student scholarships ($432,000) see Kasiska Family Foundation

Idaho State University Foundation — superconducting nuclear magnetic resonance spectrometer system ($68,600) see Kasiska Family Foundation

Idaho State University Foundation — planning funds for ISU Center for health research and treatment ($50,000) see Kasiska Family Foundation

Ketchum-Sun Valley Community School — scholarships ($50,000) see Cord Foundation, E. L.

KISU Friends of Channel 10 ($45,000) see CHC Foundation

Lewis-Clark State College 21st — target ($40,000) see Potlatch Corp.

McCall Memorial Hospital Fund ($15,000) see Dumke Foundation, Dr. Ezekiel R. and Edna Wattis

Menidoka Memorial Hospital ($15,000) see Cunningham Foundation, Laura Moore

Mercy House ($6,260) see Whittenberger Foundation, Claude R. and Ethel B.

Monastery of St. Gertrude — fire alarm system ($110,000) see Wiegand Foundation, E. L.

Moritz Community Hospital ($25,000) see Dula Educational and Charitable Foundation, Caleb C. and Julia W.

Multiple Sclerosis Society ($4,275) see Morrison Foundation, Harry W.

Nature Conservancy ($10,000) see Beckman Foundation, Leland D.

Northwest Children's Home ($18,000) see Daugherty Foundation

Northwest Nazarene College ($24,000) see Cunningham Foundation, Laura Moore

Northwest Resource Information Council ($12,000) see Harder Foundation

Nurturing Network ($22,000) see Arrillaga Foundation

Paintfest ($2,000) see Gould Inc.

Peregrine Fund ($15,000) see Burns Family Foundation

Peregrine Fund ($645,000) see Disney Family Foundation, Roy

Planned Parenthood Federation of America ($9,754) see CHC Foundation

Rotary Clubs ($35,004) see CHC Foundation

St. Joseph's RMC ($20,000) see Cunningham Foundation, Laura Moore

Satellite Development Center ($40,340) see CHC Foundation

School District 135 ($8,785) see Whittenberger Foundation, Claude R. and Ethel B.

School District 132 ($10,100) see Whittenberger Foundation, Claude R. and Ethel B.

Senior Citizens of Swan Valley ($3,500) see Beckman Foundation, Leland D.

Shriners Hospital ($141,109) see Daugherty Foundation

Shriners Hospital ($141,109) see Daugherty Foundation

State Department of Education ($20,000) see Whittenberger Foundation, Claude R. and Ethel B.

Steele Memorial Benefit Association ($80,000) see Steele-Reese Foundation

Teton Peals Council ($20,000) see Daugherty Foundation

Teton Valley Hospital ($20,000) see Cunningham Foundation, Laura Moore

TNC Idaho Chapter ($90,000) see Storer Foundation, George B.

United Way-Twin County — general ($45,000) see Potlatch Corp.

University of Idaho ($24,000) see Cunningham Foundation, Laura Moore

University of Idaho ($4,000) see First Security Corp. (Salt Lake City, Utah)

University of Idaho ($7,615) see Gloeckner Foundation, Fred

University of Idaho, Agriculture College ($13,000) see Harvest States Cooperative

University of Idaho Foundation ($30,611) see ASARCO

University of Idaho Foundation ($8,500) see EG&G Inc.

Wildlife Research Institute ($7,500) see DeVlieg Foundation, Charles

YMCA ($15,000) see Daugherty Foundation

YMCA ($3,500) see Morrison Foundation, Harry W.

Illinois

A. C. Buehler YMCA — partially fund capital campaign ($75,000) see Scholl Foundation, Dr.

A Safe Place/Lake County Crisis Center ($10,000) see IMCERA Group Inc.

ABC Club ($10,000) see Snite Foundation, Fred B.

Abraham Lincoln Centre see Waste Management

Abraham Lincoln Institute ($3,000) see House Educational Trust, Susan Cook

Academy for Mathematics and Science Teachers ($25,000) see Illinois Tool Works

Academy of the Sacred Heart ($1,000) see Thorson Foundation

Access Living — to produce a comprehensive curriculum guide to prepare high school and community college students for independent lives as adults ($36,000) see Mitsubishi Electric America

Account for Prisoners of War and Missing in Action ($2,250) see Rosenthal Foundation, Benjamin J.

ACT-SO ($10,000) see Chicago Sun-Times, Inc.

Ada McKinley Community Services ($7,500) see Rhoades Fund, Otto L. and Hazel E.

Adler Planetarium ($5,000) see Chicago Board of Trade

Adler Planetarium — general support see Nalco Chemical Co.

Adler Planetarium ($5,000) see Navistar International Corp.

Adler Planetarium see United Airlines

Adler Planetarium — development of a Research Center to provide adequate facilities for the Planetarium's History of Astronomy Collection, including rare books and antique scientific instruments ($100,000) see Field Foundation of Illinois

AFS-CMI Cast Metals Institute ($5,200) see Grede Foundries

Aid to Artisans ($5,000) see H. B. B. Foundation

AIDS Foundation of Chicago ($2,000) see Dunagan Foundation

AIDS Foundation of Chicago — expansion of grantmaking programs ($55,000) see Marshall Field's

AIDS Foundation of Chicago ($6,500) see Mirapaul Foundation

AIDS Foundation of Chicago ($2,500) see Russ Togs

Alamo Club ($2,500) see First National Bank & Trust Co. of Rockford

Alexian Brothers Medical Center see United Airlines

Alivio Medical Center — general support see Nalco Chemical Co.

Allendale School for the Blind ($16,750) see McGraw Foundation

Alliance for the Mentally Ill of Chicago ($2,500) see Schneider Foundation, Robert E.

Alzheimer's Association — research ($240,000) see Hermann Foundation, Grover

Alzheimer's Association ($75,000) see Lattner Foundation, Forrest C.

Alzheimer's Disease and Related Disorders Association ($10,000) see Boothroyd Foundation, Charles H. and Bertha L.

Alzheimer's Disease and Related Disorders Association ($5,000) see Brady Foundation

Alzheimer's Disease and Related Disorders Association ($5,000) see Claneil Foundation

Alzheimer's Disease and Related Disorders Association — general purpose ($10,000) see Echlin Foundation

Alzheimer's Disease and Related Disorders Association — continuing research ($30,000) see Kaufmann Foundation, Marion Esser

Alzheimer's Disease and Related Disorders Association ($10,000) see Kramer Foundation, C. L. C.

Alzheimer's Disease and Related Disorders Association — general purpose ($10,000) see Lederer Foundation, Francis L.

Alzheimer's Disease and Related Disorders Association ($500) see Mitchell Family Foundation, Bernard and Marjorie

Alzheimer's Disease and Related Disorders Association ($1,000) see Robin Family Foundation, Albert A.

Alzheimer's Disease and Related Disorders Association — general purpose ($10,000) see Stone Family Foundation, Jerome H.

Alzheimer's and Related Disorders Association ($3,250) see Stone Family Foundation, Norman H.

American Academy of Pediatrics ($20,000) see Disney Family Foundation, Roy

American Academy of Pediatrics — pediatric emergency CD-ROM development ($141,012) see Sega of America

American Bar Association — funding for conferences and workshops ($100,000) see Scholl Foundation, Dr.

American Bar Association Fund for Justice and Education see Atlantic Mutual Cos.

American Bar Association Fund for Justice and Education see West Publishing Co.

American Cancer Society ($15,000) see Staley, Jr. Foundation, A. E.

American College of Surgeons — FACS Memorial Research Career Development Award ($500,000) see Clowes Fund

American Commission for Keep ($5,000) see Thanksgiving Foundation

American Committee for Weizmann Institute ($210,000) see Feinberg Foundation, Joseph and Bessie

American Committee for the Weizmann Institute of Sciences ($2,500) see Berenson Charitable Foundation, Theodore and Evelyn

American Council of Pharmaceutical Education ($10,000) see Schwartz Fund for Education and Health Research, Arnold and Marie

American Diabetes Association ($2,500) see Interstate National Corp.

American Dietetic Association Foundation ($50,000) see Abbott Laboratories

American Floral Endowment ($15,650) see Poinsettia

Illinois (cont.)

Foundation, Paul and Magdalena Ecke

American Friends of Game Conservation ($5,000) see Sudix Foundation

American Friends of Israel Philharmonic Orchestra ($10,000) see Levin Foundation, Philip and Janice

American Friends of Israel Philharmonic Orchestra ($5,000) see Shapiro Family Foundation, Soretta and Henry

American Friends of Israel Philharmonic Orchestra ($25,000) see Solow Foundation

American Friends of Sanz Medical Center — Laniado Hospital ($25,100) see Shapiro Foundation, Charles and M. R.

American Fund for Dental Health ($48,250) see Dentsply International, Inc.

American Heart Association ($3,000) see Allyn Foundation

American Jewish Committee ($3,000) see Cole Taylor Financial Group

American Jewish Committee ($6,000) see Manilow Foundation, Nathan

American Judicature Society ($2,500) see Seasongood Good Government Foundation, Murray and Agnes

American Lung Association of DuPage and McHenry Counties — Camp Gottago for asthmatic children see Nalco Chemical Co.

American Medical Association Education and Research Foundation ($37,500) see Syntex Corp.

American Public Works Association see Waste Management

American Red Cross ($25,000) see Brach Foundation, Edwin I.

American Red Cross ($3,000) see Shirk Foundation, Russell and Betty

American Red Cross ($20,000) see Sprague Memorial Institute, Otho S. A.

American Society ($12,000) see Cox Charitable Trust, A. G.

American Society ($9,000) see Cox Charitable Trust, A. G.

American Society for Technion ($20,000) see Carylon Foundation

American Society for Technion ($200,000) see Feinberg Foundation, Joseph and Bessie

Americans United for Life ($1,485,000) see DeMoss Foundation, Arthur S.

Americans United for Life ($15,000) see Trust Funds

Amnesty International ($25,000) see CRI Charitable Trust

Amy E. Edgerton Foundation ($25,300) see Western Shade Cloth Charitable Foundation

Anshe Emet Synagogue ($6,415) see Berger Foundation, Albert E.

Anti-Drug Abuse Education Fund ($1,000) see Swift Co. Inc., John S.

Apollo Chorus ($2,500) see Huizenga Foundation, Jennie

Archdiocese of Chicago School Program ($200,000) see Coleman Foundation

Arden Shore Association ($15,000) see Kendall Foundation, George R.

Arrowhead Ranch ($100,000) see Deere & Co.

Arrowhead Ranch ($10,000) see Montgomery Elevator Co.

Art Institute ($5,000) see Chicago Board of Trade

Art Institute ($50,000) see Marshall Field's

Art Institute ($1,501,837) see Rice Foundation

Art Institute of Chicago ($7,500) see Amsted Industries

Art Institute of Chicago ($6,000) see Bergner Co., P.A.

Art Institute of Chicago ($7,500) see Blair and Co., William

Art Institute of Chicago ($10,000) see Boothroyd Foundation, Charles H. and Bertha L.

Art Institute of Chicago ($3,000) see Boulevard Bank, N.A.

Art Institute of Chicago ($3,000) see Boulevard Foundation

Art Institute of Chicago ($35,000) see Cheney Foundation, Elizabeth F.

Art Institute of Chicago ($15,100) see Davee Foundation

Art Institute of Chicago ($2,500) see Donnelley Foundation, Elliott and Ann

Art Institute of Chicago ($10,000) see Field Foundation, Jamee and Marshall

Art Institute of Chicago ($10,000) see Field Foundation, Jamee and Marshall

Art Institute of Chicago ($15,000) see Foote, Cone & Belding Communications

Art Institute of Chicago ($3,206) see Goldman Foundation, Morris and Rose

Art Institute of Chicago ($5,000) see H. B. B. Foundation

Art Institute of Chicago ($18,000) see Hales Charitable Fund

Art Institute of Chicago ($44,750) see Heller Foundation, Walter E.

Art Institute of Chicago ($15,000) see Illinois Tool Works

Art Institute of Chicago ($50,000) see Kemper Educational and Charitable Fund

Art Institute of Chicago ($10,000) see Knowles Foundation

Art Institute of Chicago — general purposes ($5,000) see Lederer Foundation, Francis L.

Art Institute of Chicago ($25,000) see Mayer Charitable Trust, Oscar G. & Elsa S.

Art Institute of Chicago ($110,000) see McCormick Foundation, Chauncey and Marion Deering

Art Institute of Chicago — museum support see Nalco Chemical Co.

Art Institute of Chicago ($15,000) see Northern Trust Co.

Art Institute of Chicago ($20,000) see Perkins Foundation, Edwin E.

Art Institute of Chicago ($500,000) see Regenstein Foundation

Art Institute of Chicago ($10,000) see Rhoades Fund, Otto L. and Hazel E.

Art Institute of Chicago ($150,000) see Robin Family Foundation, Albert A.

Art Institute of Chicago ($10,000) see Sang Foundation, Elsie O. and Philip D.

Art Institute of Chicago ($5,000) see Shapiro Family Foundation, Soretta and Henry

Art Institute of Chicago ($8,000) see Speyer Foundation, Alexander C. and Tillie S.

Art Institute of Chicago ($5,000) see Thoresen Foundation

Art Institute of Chicago see Waste Management

Art Institute of Chicago ($5,000) see Wood Foundation, Lester G.

Art Institute of Chicago — to endow the Sage Foundation Chair in Fashion Design ($65,000) see Sage Foundation

Art Institute of Chicago — first payment of a two-year, $200,000 grant for The New World ($135,000) see Sara Lee Corp.

Art Institute Michigan at Adams ($51,330) see Rothschild Foundation, Hulda B. and Maurice L.

Art League ($4,000) see Geneseo Foundation

Arthritis Foundation ($10,000) see Brunner Foundation, Fred J.

Arthritis Foundation ($30,900) see GSC Enterprises

Arthritis Foundation ($90,000) see Hagedorn Fund

Arts and Science Park ($25,750) see Smith Charitable Trust

Arts and Science Park ($1,500) see Warner Electric Brake & Clutch Co.

Arts and Science Park Capital Campaign ($9,375) see First National Bank & Trust Co. of Rockford

Associated Colleges of Illinois ($2,750) see Akzo America

Associated Colleges of Illinois ($5,000) see Allyn Foundation

Associated Colleges of Illinois see Banc One Illinois Corp.

Associated Colleges of Illinois ($5,000) see Brunner Foundation, Fred J.

Associated Colleges of Illinois ($25,000) see Centel Corp.

Associated Colleges of Illinois ($30,000) see DeSoto

Associated Colleges of Illinois see International Paper Co.

Associated Colleges of Illinois ($25,000) see McGraw Foundation

Associated Colleges of Illinois ($17,400) see Moorman Manufacturing Co.

Associated Colleges of Illinois ($10,000) see Pick, Jr. Fund, Albert

Associated Colleges of Illinois ($35,000) see Ward Foundation, A. Montgomery

Associated Colleges of Illinois ($30,000) see Willmott Foundation, Peter S.

Associated Colleges of Illinois — Millikin University ($25,000) see Staley Manufacturing Co., A.E.

Associated Talmud Torahs ($57,000) see Feinberg Foundation, Joseph and Bessie

Associated Talmud Torahs of Chicago ($100,000) see Goldman Foundation, Morris and Rose

Association of Colleges Illinois ($5,000) see Griswold Foundation, John C.

Association of Jewish Blind of Chicago ($40,000) see Shapiro Foundation, Charles and M. R.

Auditorium Theatre Council ($8,000) see Kaplan Foundation, Mayer and Morris

Augustana College ($800,000) see Carver Charitable Trust, Roy J.

Augustana College ($5,000) see Harris Family Foundation, Hunt and Diane

Augustana College ($20,000) see Plym Foundation

Augustinians ($70,000) see Warren Charite

Austin Career Education Center — adult education see Nalco Chemical Co.

Austin Special/West Side Mentally Retarded Children's Aid ($30,000) see Blowitz-Ridgeway Foundation

Auxiliary Board Art Institute of Chicago ($10,000) see Wenger Foundation, Henry L. and Consuelo S.

Back to God Hour ($15,000) see Artevel Foundation

Back to God Hour ($11,000) see Artevel Foundation

Back to God Hour ($5,000) see Huizenga Foundation, Jennie

Back to God Hour Religious Work ($25,000) see Tibstra Charitable Foundation, Thomas and Gertrude

Ballet Chicago see American Express Co.

Ballet Chicago ($5,000) see Boler Co.

Ballet Chicago ($10,000) see IMCERA Group Inc.

Ballet Chicago see United Airlines

Ballet Chicago — first payment of a two-year, $150,000 grant for the development of an original full-length ballet of Hansel and Gretel ($75,000) see Sara Lee Corp.

Barbara Olson School of Hope ($3,000) see Anderson Industries

Barbara Olson School of Hope ($20,000) see CLARCOR

Barbara Olson School of Hope ($3,333) see Elco Charitable Foundation

Barbara Olson School of Hope ($4,000) see Rockford Products Corp.

Barbara Olson School of Hope ($1,000) see Sjostrom & Sons

Barnabas Project ($10,700) see Frees Foundation

Barrington Area Arts Council — general purpose ($5,000) see Duchossois Industries

Barrington Youth Dance Ensemble — general purpose ($5,000) see Duchossois Industries

Belleville Area College Foundation see Illinois Power Co.

Ben May Institute — University Of Chicago ($139,500) see May Charitable Trust, Ben

Bensenville Home Society — foster parents program see Nalco Chemical Co.

Bernard Zell Anshe Emet Day School Endowment Fund — support early childhood center ($20,000) see Lederer Foundation, Francis L.

Bernard Zell Ashe Emet Day School ($21,000) see Levy Foundation, Charles and Ruth

Bethel New Life ($5,000) see Aigner

Bethel New Life ($60,000) see American National Bank & Trust Co. of Chicago

Bethel New Life ($10,000) see Boothroyd Foundation, Charles H. and Bertha L.

Bethel New Life — employment ($45,000) see Continental Bank N.A.

Bethel New Life ($15,000) see Northern Trust Co.

Bethlehem Center ($15,000) see Giles Foundation, Edward C.

Bethlehem Center ($15,000) see McGraw Foundation

Bethshan ($2,500) see Huizenga Foundation, Jennie

Better Boys Foundation — Nana's House ($10,000) see GATX Corp.

Better Government Association ($18,000) see Beidler Charitable Trust, Francis

Better Government Association ($7,000) see Blair and Co., William

Bible League ($9,000) see Tyndale House Foundation

Bible League ($6,000) see Word Investments

Big Brothers and Big Sisters ($2,000) see Aldeen Charity Trust, G. W.

Big Brothers and Big Sisters ($3,000) see Allyn Foundation

Big Brothers and Big Sisters ($2,136) see Foster and Gallagher

Big Brothers and Big Sisters ($500) see Interstate National Corp.

Big Shoulder Fund ($50,000) see Sears, Roebuck and Co.

Big Shoulders ($250,000) see McCormick Tribune Foundation, Robert R.

Big Shoulders Fund ($10,000) see Bere Foundation

Big Shoulders Fund ($10,000) see Best Foundation, Walter J. and Edith E.

Big Shoulders Fund ($100,000) see Brach Foundation, Helen

Big Shoulders Fund — education ($25,000) see Continental Bank N.A.

Big Shoulders Fund ($5,000) see Dower Foundation, Thomas W.

Big Shoulders Fund ($22,500) see Farley Industries

Big Shoulders Fund ($40,000) see Harris Trust & Savings Bank

Big Shoulders Fund ($100,000) see Mazza Foundation

Big Shoulders Fund ($100,000) see McIntosh Foundation

Big Shoulders Fund ($100,000) see Ryan Foundation, Patrick G. and Shirley W.

Big Shoulders Fund ($100,000) see Schmitt Foundation, Arthur J.

Big Shoulders Fund ($25,000) see Snite Foundation, Fred B.

Big Shoulders Fund see Waste Management

Big Shoulders Fund — for teacher training and staff development in inner city schools of the Archdiocese of Chicago ($100,000) see Fry Foundation, Lloyd A.

Black Hawk College ($120,000) see Deere & Co.

Blackburn College ($5,000) see Harris Family Foundation, Hunt and Diane

Blackburn College ($15,000) see House Educational Trust, Susan Cook

Blackburn College ($50,000) see Schmidt Charitable Foundation, William E.

Blackburn College ($10,000) see Schmidt Charitable Foundation, William E.

Blessing Hospital ($17,000) see Jackson Charitable Trust, Marion Gardner

Board of Jewish Education ($27,500) see Shapiro Foundation, Charles and M. R.

Board of Trustees of the University of Illinois — reneal of the Fellowship Program in the Social Sciences ($1,996,474) see Lilly Endowment

Bonaventure House — for expanded services ($50,000) see Fry Foundation, Lloyd A.

Bonaventure House — AIDS patients ($18,500) see Logan Foundation, E. J.

Bonaventure House — AIDS patients ($16,666) see Logan Foundation, E. J.

Boy Scouts of America ($200) see Barry Corp., R. G.

Boy Scouts of America ($5,000) see CBI Industries

Boy Scouts of America ($10,000) see Cooper Charitable Trust, Richard H.

Boy Scouts of America ($10,000) see Geneseo Foundation

Boy Scouts of America ($25,000) see Hoover Foundation, H. Earl

Boy Scouts of America ($6,500) see Hopper Memorial Foundation, Bertrand

Boy Scouts of America ($5,000) see Rockford Products Corp.

Boy Scouts of America ($1,500) see Russ Togs

Boy Scouts of America-Hoover Outdoor Education Center see Waste Management

Boys Club of America ($5,500) see Cole Taylor Financial Group

Boys Club of America ($1,000) see Wallace Computer Services

Boys and Girls Club ($35,000) see Camp and Bennet Humiston Trust, Apollos

Boys and Girls Club ($27,820) see Cooper Charitable Trust, Richard H.

Boys and Girls Club ($2,000) see Cooper Charitable Trust, Richard H.

Boys and Girls Club ($100) see LaSalle National Bank

Boys and Girls Club ($5,000) see Lehmann Foundation, Otto W.

Boys and Girls Club ($20,000) see Russell Charitable Foundation, Tom

Boys and Girls Club of Chicago ($111,750) see Crown Memorial, Arie and Ida

Boys and Girls Club of Sparta see Illinois Power Co.

Boys and Girls Clubs of America — legends and fans dinner; general purpose funds ($23,000) see Duchossois Industries

Boys and Girls Clubs of America Regional Service Center ($15,000) see NutraSweet Co.

Boys and Girls Clubs of Chicago — education ($30,000) see Continental Bank N.A.

Boys and Girls Clubs of Chicago ($250,000) see McCormick Tribune Foundation, Robert R.

Boys and Girls Clubs of Chicago see United Airlines

Boys and Girls Clubs of Chicago — support activities of Clubs ($95,000) see AON Corp.

Bradley University ($133,000) see Caterpillar

Bradley University ($95,250) see Caterpillar

Bradley University ($10,900) see First Chicago

Bradley University see International Paper Co.

Brain Research Foundation ($39,800) see Deuble Foundation, George H.

Brain Research Foundation ($60,000) see Sudix Foundation

Brain Research Foundation — for the Seed Grants Program ($75,000) see Fry Foundation, Lloyd A.

Brewster Academy ($2,500) see Stone Family Foundation, Norman H.

BroMenn Foundation ($100,000) see State Farm Mutual Automobile Insurance Co.

Brooks and Hope B. McCormick Foundation ($50,000) see McCormick Foundation, Chauncey and Marion Deering

Burnham Park Planning Board ($2,000) see Herald News

Business and Professional People for the Public Interest ($45,000) see New Prospect Foundation

Business and Professional People for the Public Interest ($10,000) see Petersen Foundation, Esper A.

Business and Professional People for the Public Interest — to develop new ways to implement outcomes in the Gautreaux litigation ($20,000) see Taconic Foundation

Cabdon Klesary League ($800) see Harrison Foundation, Fred G.

Cabrini Green Legal Aid Clinic ($10,000) see Montgomery Ward & Co.

Cabrino-Green Tutoring Program ($35,000) see Montgomery Ward & Co.

Cacosh ($3,000) see Mansfield Foundation, Albert and Anne

Cali in Chicago ($25,000) see National Center for Automated Information Retrieval

Calumet Area Family Fund see Waste Management

Camp Ability Foundation — general, charitable and educational purposes ($50,000) see Sage Foundation

Campaign for Medical Research ($150,000) see Galter Foundation

Canal Corridor Association — for completion and implementation of a strategic plan for a heritage park near Joliet, Illinois see USX Corp.

Cando ($5,000) see Chicago Sun-Times, Inc.

Car-A-Van ($1,000) see Atwood Foundation

Cardinal's Appeal ($25,000) see Gavin Foundation, James and Zita

Cardinal's Appeal ($25,000) see McIntosh Foundation

Cardinal's Big Shoulder's Fund — inner-city school program see United Airlines

CARE ($5,000) see Clark Charitable Trust

CARE ($10,000) see LeBrun Foundation

CARE ($15,791) see Miller Charitable Trust, Lewis N.

CARE ($13,000) see Overstreet Foundation

CARE ($33,000) see Peierls Foundation

CARE ($20,000) see Rolfs Foundation, Robert T.

CARE Philippines — ministry to poor in Manila ($3,000) see Epaphroditus Foundation

Carmel High School for Boys ($13,500) see Ragen, Jr. Memorial Fund Trust No. 1, James M.

Carnegie Public Library ($2,000) see Lumpkin Foundation

Cast Metals Institute ($33,500) see Harris Foundation, H. H.

Catholic Charities ($5,000) see Best Foundation, Walter J. and Edith E.

Catholic Charities ($15,000) see Bowyer Foundation, Ambrose and Gladys

Catholic Charities ($50,000) see Brach Foundation, Helen

Catholic Charities ($20,000) see Cuneo Foundation

Catholic Charities ($9,500) see Lapham-Hickey Steel Corp.

Catholic Charities ($5,000) see Lapham-Hickey Steel Corp.

Catholic Charities ($100,000) see Mazza Foundation

Catholic Charities ($10,000) see Merrion Foundation

Catholic Charities — Plainfield Disaster Fund ($8,000) see Material Service Corp.

Catholic Church Extension Society of the United States of America ($100,000) see Lewis Foundation, Frank J.

Catholic Community of Pilsen — general operating support ($15,000) see Wieboldt Foundation

Catholic Diocese of Spokane Campaign for Human Development ($5,000) see Lapham-Hickey Steel Corp.

Catholic Social Services ($500) see Elgin Sweeper Co.

Center of Chicago Historical Society ($10,000) see Prentice Foundation, Abra

Center City Limited Partnership — to provide bridge financing for low-income senior housing in Elgin ($350,000) see Retirement Research Foundation

Center for Community and Leadership Development — community organizing project ($10,000) see Wieboldt Foundation

Center for Development in Ministry ($18,500) see Morania Foundation

Center for Enriched Living ($1,000) see Fraida Foundation

Center for Ethics and Corporate Policy ($4,000) see Boulevard Bank, N.A.

Center for Ethics and Corporate Policy ($4,000) see Boulevard Foundation

Center for Ethics and Corporate Policy — support for a national conference in Chicago, "The Family, the Corporation and the Common Good" see Ameritech Corp.

Center for the Great Lakes — for upgrade of their development program ($150,000) see Joyce Foundation

Center for the Great Lakes — support for the Center to participate in the Great Lakes Information Network project see Ameritech Corp.

Center for Neighborhood Technology see Corroon & Black of Illinois

Center for Neighborhood Technology — general operating support ($15,000) see Wieboldt Foundation

Center for Sight and Hearing Impaired ($1,000) see Sjostrom & Sons

Centralia Public Library see Illinois Power Co.

Centro De Informacion Y Progression ($500) see Elgin Sweeper Co.

CGH Medical Center ($40,000) see Dillon Foundation

Chabad Youth Organization ($36,000) see El-An Foundation

Champaign Urbana Economic Development Corporation see Illinois Power Co.

Channel 11 ($10,000) see Comer Foundation

Channel 11 ($2,000) see Dick Family Foundation

Channel 11 ($7,000) see Donnelley Foundation, Elliott and Ann

Channel 11 ($500) see Lurie Family Foundation

Chicago Abused Women Coalition ($2,500) see Lurie Family Foundation

Chicago Academy of Sciences ($15,000) see Russell Charitable Foundation, Tom

Chicago Academy of Sciences — symposium was designed to review and integrate the rapidly growing volume of research on the behavioral and ecological diversity of chimpanzees ($10,000) see Wenner-Gren Foundation for Anthropological Research

Chicago Acorn — general operating support ($10,000) see Wieboldt Foundation

Chicago Action for Soviet Jewry ($5,000) see Relations Foundation

Chicago Area Project — Women for Economic Security, a welfare recipient-based initiative to train welfare-to-work reform advocates and spearhead a campaign to improve welfare and employment in Illinois ($45,000) see Woods Charitable Fund

Chicago Association of Neighborhood Development Organizations ($25,000) see Harris Trust & Savings Bank

Chicago Board of Education ($10,000) see Pick, Jr. Fund, Albert

Chicago Botanical Gardens ($10,000) see Butz Foundation

Chicago Botanical Gardens ($5,000) see Dennett Foundation, Marie G.

Chicago Boys Club ($5,500) see Western Shade Cloth Charitable Foundation

Chicago Celebrates Literacy ($500) see Mitchell Family Foundation, Bernard and Marjorie

Chicago Chapter Magen David Adom ($50,000) see Shapiro Foundation, Charles and M. R.

Chicago Child Care Society ($50,000) see Comer Foundation

Chicago Child Care Society ($12,000) see United Conveyor Corp.

Chicago Children's Museum ($15,000) see IMCERA Group Inc.

Chicago Children's Museum ($100) see LaSalle National Bank

Chicago Children's Museum — for a sponsorship of the new OAXACA Village exhibit which presented information about life in a rural Mexican town ($50,000) see Sara Lee Corp.

Chicago City Day School ($5,000) see Atwood Foundation

Chicago City Day School ($10,000) see Haffner Foundation

Chicago City Day School ($100,000) see Norris Foundation, Dellora A. and Lester J.

Chicago City Day School ($50,000) see Norris Foundation, Dellora A. and Lester J.

Chicago City Day School ($75,000) see Silver Spring Foundation

Chicago Coalition for the Homeless ($7,500) see Rhoades Fund, Otto L. and Hazel E.

Chicago Coalition for the Homeless — general support ($35,000) see Stone Foundation, W. Clement and Jessie V.

Chicago College of Osteo Medicine ($7,000) see Hook Drug

Chicago Commons Association — employment ($25,000) see Continental Bank N.A.

Chicago Commons Association ($3,125) see Hales Charitable Fund

Chicago Commons Association ($19,310) see Lurie Family Foundation

Chicago Commons Association ($10,000) see Pick, Jr. Fund, Albert

Chicago Commons Association — to develop the Chicago Manufacturing Institute ($150,000) see Joyce Foundation

Chicago Community Foundation — the McCormick Family Fund ($65,000) see McCormick Foundation, Chauncey and Marion Deering

Chicago Community Trust ($50,000) see Buchanan Family Foundation

Chicago Community Trust ($10,000) see Butler Family Foundation, George W. and Gladys S.

Chicago Community Trust ($77,000) see I and G Charitable Foundation

Chicago Council on Foreign Relations ($6,000) see Farley Industries

Chicago Council on Foreign Relations ($6,000) see Farley Industries

Chicago Council on Foreign Relations ($25,000) see Ryan

Illinois (cont.)

Foundation, Patrick G. and Shirley W.

Chicago Council on Foreign Relations ($2,000) see USG Corp.

Chicago Crime Commission see Amoco Corp.

Chicago Crime Commission ($3,000) see USG Corp.

Chicago Crusade of Mercy ($32,200) see Abbott Laboratories

Chicago Educational Television ($500,000) see Andreas Foundation

Chicago Educational Television Association/WTTW Channel 11 see Waste Management

Chicago Employment Service — training, placement, and long-term services for the hart-to-employ ($25,000) see Chicago Tribune Co.

Chicago Foundation for Education ($10,000) see NutraSweet Co.

Chicago Foundation for Education ($5,000) see Sudix Foundation

Chicago Foundation for Women ($5,000) see Forest Fund

Chicago Foundation for Women ($16,000) see Levy Foundation, Charles and Ruth

Chicago Hearing Society ($3,000) see Allyn Foundation

Chicago Historical Society ($50,000) see Cheney Foundation, Elizabeth F.

Chicago Historical Society — architectural photo archive ($20,000) see Graham Foundation for Advanced Studies in the Fine Arts

Chicago Historical Society ($5,000) see H. B. B. Foundation

Chicago Historical Society — support manuscript fund and library fund ($25,000) see Lederer Foundation, Francis L.

Chicago Historical Society ($50,000) see Regenstein Foundation

Chicago Historical Society ($500,000) see Rice Foundation

Chicago Historical Society ($2,750) see Thorson Foundation

Chicago Historical Society — for restoration work in Peter Caspar Butz Laboratory ($5,000) see Butz Foundation

Chicago Historical Society — final payment of a two-year, $150,000 grant to sponsor the exhibit A City Comes of Age: Chicago in the 1890s, and for general operating support ($85,000) see Sara Lee Corp.

Chicago Horticultural Society ($75,000) see Buchanan Family Foundation

Chicago Horticultural Society ($2,500) see Hales Charitable Fund

Chicago Horticultural Society — English Walled Garden ($10,250) see Norton Memorial Corporation, Geraldi

Chicago Horticulture Society ($20,000) see Donnelley Foundation, Gaylord and Dorothy

Chicago Horticulture Society ($10,000) see Haffner Foundation

Chicago Horticulture Society ($20,000) see Winona Corporation

Chicago House ($3,500) see Interstate National Corp.

Chicago House and Social Service Agency ($25,000) see Blowitz-Ridgeway Foundation

Chicago Housing Authority see Amoco Corp.

Chicago Initiative — gang intervention ($15,000) see GATX Corp.

Chicago Institute for Architecture and Urbanism ($350,000) see Skidmore, Owings & Merrill

Chicago Institute for Neurosurgery/Research ($20,000) see Perkins Foundation, Edwin E.

Chicago Institute of Urban Poverty ($15,000) see Sprague Memorial Institute, Otho S. A.

Chicago International Film Festival ($15,000) see Getz Foundation, Emma and Oscar

Chicago International Film Festival ($1,000) see Herald News

Chicago International Theatre Festival — 1990 Festival ($5,000) see Norton Memorial Corporation, Geraldi

Chicago Junior School ($120,000) see Katzenberger Foundation

Chicago Kent College of Law ($25,378) see Galvin Foundation, Robert W.

Chicago Library Foundation ($10,000) see Stone Container Corp.

Chicago Lighthouse for the Blind ($10,000) see Blum Foundation, Nathan and Emily S.

Chicago Maternity Center of Prentice Womens Hospital ($1,000) see Thorson Foundation

Chicago Metro History Fair ($50,400) see Borg-Warner Corp.

Chicago Metro History Fair ($15,000) see Russell Charitable Foundation, Tom

Chicago/Northern Illinois Multiple Sclerosis Society ($15,000) see Butz Foundation

Chicago Opera Theater ($8,000) see Getz Foundation, Emma and Oscar

Chicago Panel on Public School Policy and Finance — second payment of three-year $120,000 support for Monitoring School Reform in Chicago project ($40,000) see Woods Charitable Fund

Chicago Park District ($10,000) see Prentice Foundation, Abra

Chicago Public Art Group ($5,000) see Butz Foundation

Chicago Public Library ($200,000) see Blum Foundation, Harry and Maribel G.

Chicago Public Library — support to strengthen book collection ($25,000) see Kemper National Insurance Cos.

Chicago Public Library Foundation ($5,000) see Andersen Foundation, Arthur

Chicago Public Library Foundation — support for Adult New Reader Collection at the harold Washington Library Center ($50,000) see Chicago Tribune Co.

Chicago Public Schools ($65,000) see Michigan Bell Telephone Co.

Chicago Public Schools ($65,000) see Motorola

Chicago Public Schools/Crown Community Academy of Fine Arts ($22,500) see Material Service Corp.

Chicago Public Television ($5,000) see Forest Fund

Chicago Public Television, WTTW ($1,500) see Interstate National Corp.

Chicago Public Television WTTW ($3,500) see United Conveyor Corp.

Chicago Rehabilitation Center ($2,500) see Interstate National Corp.

Chicago State University Entrepreneurial Program ($100,000) see Coleman Foundation

Chicago Sunday Evening Club ($26,305) see Erickson Charitable Fund, Eben W.

Chicago Symphony ($50,000) see Shapiro Family Foundation, Soretta and Henry

Chicago Symphony Orchestra ($2,500) see Akzo America

Chicago Symphony Orchestra see Amoco Corp.

Chicago Symphony Orchestra ($3,000) see Boulevard Bank, N.A.

Chicago Symphony Orchestra ($3,000) see Boulevard Foundation

Chicago Symphony Orchestra ($5,000) see Chicago Board of Trade

Chicago Symphony Orchestra ($25,075) see Davee Foundation

Chicago Symphony Orchestra ($25,000) see Davee Foundation

Chicago Symphony Orchestra ($25,375) see Galvin Foundation, Robert W.

Chicago Symphony Orchestra ($15,500) see Hartmarx Corp.

Chicago Symphony Orchestra ($141,600) see Heller Foundation, Walter E.

Chicago Symphony Orchestra ($300,000) see Kraft General Foods

Chicago Symphony Orchestra ($50,000) see Marshall Field's

Chicago Symphony Orchestra ($25,000) see Seabury Foundation

Chicago Symphony Orchestra ($6,000) see United Conveyor Corp.

Chicago Symphony Orchestra ($25,000) see Ward Foundation, A. Montgomery

Chicago Symphony Orchestra see Waste Management

Chicago Symphony Orchestra ($5,000) see Wood Foundation, Lester G.

Chicago Symphony Orchestra/Lyric Opera Facilities Fund, Sara Lee Corporation — contribution to a capital campaign to raise funds for renovation of Orchestra Hall and the Lyric Opera House ($10,000,000) see MacArthur Foundation, John D. and Catherine T.

Chicago Symphony Orchestra Society ($80,000) see Frankel Foundation

Chicago Symphony Orchestra Society ($2,750) see Willmott Foundation, Peter S.

Chicago Theatre Group ($2,515) see Alsdorf Foundation

Chicago Theatre Group ($10,000) see Cheney Foundation, Elizabeth F.

Chicago Tribune Charities Christmas Fund ($5,000) see Rosenthal Foundation, Benjamin J.

Chicago Tribune Holiday Fund ($20,000) see Alexander Charitable Foundation

Chicago Tribune Holiday Fund ($500) see Lurie Family Foundation

Chicago United ($21,550) see Harris Trust & Savings Bank

Chicago United ($12,000) see Montgomery Ward & Co.

Chicago United ($22,550) see Pittway Corp.

Chicago United ($3,000) see USG Corp.

Chicago United — support for Family Learning Center ($25,000) see Chicago Tribune Co.

Chicago United — for 1991 member dues and two-year support for Hire the Future ($71,550) see Chicago Tribune Co.

Chicago Urban League see Booz Allen & Hamilton

Chicago Urban League ($4,000) see Ceco Corp.

Chicago Urban League ($3,000) see USG Corp.

Chicago Volunteer Legal Services Foundation ($10,000) see Boothroyd Foundation, Charles H. and Bertha L.

Chicago Youth Center ($10,000) see Griswold Foundation, John C.

Chicago Youth Centers ($19,000) see Barker Welfare Foundation

Chicago Youth Centers ($32,750) see Beidler Charitable Trust, Francis

Chicago Youth Centers ($5,000) see Chicago Sun-Times, Inc.

Chicago Youth Centers ($10,100) see Donnelley Foundation, Elliott and Ann

Chicago Youth Centers ($10,750) see Leo Burnett Co.

Chicago Youth Centers ($5,400) see Rosenthal Foundation, Benjamin J.

Chicago Youth Centers ($5,000) see Rosenthal Foundation, Benjamin J.

Chicago Zoological Society ($1,000) see Schiff, Hardin & Waite

Chicagoland Radio Information Service ($10,000) see Buehler Foundation, A. C.

Child Abuse Prevention Services ($5,000) see Mansfield Foundation, Albert and Anne

Child Abuse Prevention Services — support establishment of comprehensive, multi-program child abuse prevention sites ($10,000) see Lederer Foundation, Francis L.

Children's Heart Research Foundation ($4,000) see Cox Charitable Trust, A. G.

Children's Home and Aid Scoiety ($5,000) see Allyn Foundation

Children's Home and Aid Society ($10,000) see Best Foundation, Walter J. and Edith E.

Children's Home and Aid Society ($37,385) see Cooper Charitable Trust, Richard H.

Children's Home and Aid Society ($27,250) see Cuneo Foundation

Children's Home and Aid Society of Illinois ($10,700) see American National Bank & Trust Co. of Chicago

Children's Home and Aid Society of Illinois ($75,000) see McCormick Foundation, Chauncey and Marion Deering

Children's Home and Aid Society of Illinois ($20,000) see McGraw Foundation

Children's Home and Aid Society of Illinois ($100,000) see Ward Foundation, A. Montgomery

Children's Memorial Foundation ($20,225) see Donnelley Foundation, Elliott and Ann

Children's Memorial Foundation ($7,000) see Field Foundation, Jamee and Marshall

Children's Memorial Foundation ($2,000) see Kelly Foundation, T. Lloyd

Children's Memorial Foundation ($3,500) see Lurie Family Foundation

Children's Memorial Foundation ($35,000) see Siragusa Foundation

Children's Memorial Foundation ($1,000) see Thorson Foundation

Children's Memorial Hospital ($5,000) see Allyn Foundation

Children's Memorial Hospital ($25,000) see Best Foundation, Walter J. and Edith E.

Children's Memorial Hospital ($5,000) see Brach Foundation, Edwin I.

Children's Memorial Hospital ($191,100) see Buehler Foundation, A. C.

Children's Memorial Hospital ($3,000) see Dick Family Foundation

Children's Memorial Hospital ($5,000) see Eisenberg Foundation, George M.

Children's Memorial Hospital ($12,500) see Forest Fund

Children's Memorial Hospital ($20,000) see Galvin Foundation, Robert W.

Children's Memorial Hospital ($290,000) see Globe Corp.

Children's Memorial Hospital ($10,000) see Goldenberg Foundation, Max

Children's Memorial Hospital ($10,000) see H. B. B. Foundation

Children's Memorial Hospital ($3,000) see Material Service Corp.

Children's Memorial Hospital ($10,000) see McCrea Foundation

Children's Memorial Hospital ($10,000) see Pick, Jr. Fund, Albert

Children's Memorial Hospital ($10,000) see R. F. Foundation

Children's Memorial Hospital — general fund ($10,000) see Shaw Foundation, Arch W.

Children's Memorial Hospital ($100,000) see Shaw Foundation, Walden W. and Jean Young

Children's Memorial Hospital ($60,000) see Wells Foundation, Lillian S.

Children's Memorial Hospital of Chicago ($75,000) see Buchanan Family Foundation

Children's Memorial Medical Center ($5,000) see Lehmann Foundation, Otto W.

Children's Memorial Medical Center ($11,122) see Salwil Foundation

Children's Memorial Medical Center ($50,000) see Seabury Foundation

Children's Place — home for children with AIDS ($350,000) see Logan Foundation, E. J.

ChildServ ($30,000) see Blowitz-Ridgeway Foundation

Chinese American Service League ($300) see Florsheim Shoe Co.

Chinese American Service League — to develop a senior services department to provide social services, counseling and outreach to homebound Chinese elderly ($150,000) see Retirement Research Foundation

Christ Church of Oak Brook ($49,000) see Bere Foundation

Christ Episcopal Church ($3,000) see Butler Family Foundation, George W. and Gladys S.

Christian College Coalition ($10,000) see Bere Foundation

Christian Heritage Academy ($1,000) see Louis Foundation, Michael W.

Church of Holy Spirit ($2,500) see Butler Family Foundation, George W. and Gladys S.

Church of the Holy Spirit ($5,000) see Crane Foundation, Raymond E. and Ellen F.

Church of Holy Spirit ($8,870) see Salwil Foundation

Cicero, Berwyn, Stickney Interfaith Leadership Project — general operating support ($12,500) see Wieboldt Foundation

Citizens Information Services ($100) see LaSalle National Bank

Citizens Schools Committee ($57,500) see Borg-Warner Corp.

City of Chicago — community activities ($123,504) see Rosenbaum Foundation, Paul and Gabriella

City of Des Plaines Fire Department ($25,000) see Blowitz-Ridgeway Foundation

City of Des Plaines Police Department ($45,000) see Blowitz-Ridgeway Foundation

City in a Garden ($15,000) see Harris Trust & Savings Bank

City of Pontiac ($15,000) see Camp and Bennet Humiston Trust, Apollos

City of Sterling ($652,155) see Dillon Foundation

Civic Committee Foundation ($50,000) see Illinois Tool Works

Clarence Darrow Convention Center ($15,000) see Boothroyd Foundation, Charles H. and Bertha L.

Clay County Humane Society ($5,000) see Bishop Trust for the SPCA of Manatee County, Florida, Lillian H.

Clearbrook Center for Handicapped — funding for electrical upgrading and security at central facility ($80,000) see Scholl Foundation, Dr.

Clement and Jessie Stone Foundation ($9,900) see Pesch Family Foundation

Coalition of Limited Speaking Elderly — to support and expand the Coaliton's consortium of community-based ethnic agencies serving the elderly ($128,847) see Retirement Research Foundation

College of DuPage ($10,000) see Knowles Foundation

Columbia College — cultural activity ($175,150) see Rosenbaum Foundation, Paul and Gabriella

Columbus Cabrini Medical Center ($25,000) see Andersen Foundation, Arthur

Commercial Club Foundation — support for civic programs ($100,000) see AON Corp.

Commercial Club Foundation ($25,000) see Centel Corp.

Commercial Club Foundation ($50,000) see FMC Corp.

Commercial Club Foundation ($25,000) see Material Service Corp.

Commercial Club Foundation ($50,000) see Michigan Bell Telephone Co.

Commercial Club Foundation ($50,000) see Motorola

Commercial Club Foundation ($100,000) see Whitman Corp.

Community Chest ($5,000) see Geneseo Foundation

Community Child Care ($25,000) see Kendall Foundation, George R.

Community Church of Wilmette — capital and special program funds ($215,000) see Grainger Foundation

Community Crisis Center ($25,000) see Bersted Foundation

Community Crisis Center ($15,000) see Hoffer Plastics Corp.

Community Fund of Mount Pleasant ($2,000) see Ceco Corp.

Community Park District ($25,000) see Geneseo Foundation

Community Renewal Society ($7,500) see New Prospect Foundation

Community Response — volunteer program ($10,000) see GATX Corp.

Community Supportive Living Systems — general support ($40,000) see Stone Foundation, W. Clement and Jessie V.

Community Unit School District 5 ($79,492) see Dillon Foundation

Community Youth Creative Learning Experience ($8,000) see Montgomery Ward & Co.

Community Youth Creative Learning Experience ($150,000) see Square D Co.

Community Youth Creative Learning Experience (CYCLE) ($33,914) see Relations Foundation

Concordia College ($5,000) see Brunner Foundation, Fred J.

Condell Memorial Hospital ($20,000) see Cuneo Foundation

Congregation Beth Judea ($7,000) see Carylon Foundation

Congregational Church of Elmhurst ($2,000) see Hanson

Testamentary Charitable Trust, Anna Emery

Congregation Kol Ami ($6,350) see Stone Family Foundation, Norman H.

Conservative Baptist Foreign Mission Society ($19,100) see Tell Foundation

Copley Memorial Hospital ($6,300) see Copley Press

Cornerstone Christian School ($6,000) see Special People In Need

Corporate/Community Schools of America — pledge payment for educational programs ($75,000) see AON Corp.

Corporate/Community Schools of America — general support ($150,000) see Baxter International

Corporate/Community Schools of America ($100,000) see Blum-Kovler Foundation

Corporate/Community Schools of America ($50,000) see Driehaus Foundation, Richard H.

Corporate/Community Schools of America — general operating support ($15,000) see GATX Corp.

Corporate Community Schools of America ($33,000) see Quaker Oats Co.

Corporate/Community Schools of America ($30,000) see Whitman Corp.

Council for Jewish Elderly — senior social services ($323,037) see Rosenbaum Foundation, Paul and Gabriella

Council for Jewish Elderly ($5,000) see Sang Foundation, Elsie O. and Philip D.

Council for Jewish Elderly ($100,000) see Seid Foundation, Barre

Counseling Center of Lakeview ($500) see Lizzaro Family Foundation, Joseph

Cradle Society ($1,000) see Scherer Foundation, Karla

Creative Children's Academy ($60,000) see Logan Foundation, E. J.

Croatian Franciscan Fathers - Custody of the Holy Family of U.S. and Canada — to begin the reconstruction of Catholic churches destroyed by a civil war ($50,000) see Koch Foundation

Crulaler Clinic ($11,334) see AMCORE Bank, N.A. Rockford

Crusade of Mercy ($225,000) see Illinois Tool Works

Crusade of Mercy ($180,000) see Inland Steel Industries

Crusade of Mercy ($11,000) see Interstate National Corp.

Crusade of Mercy ($10,000) see Schiff, Hardin & Waite

Crusade of Mercy United Way ($135,000) see Borg-Warner Corp.

Crusader Clinic ($20,000) see CLARCOR

Crusader Clinic ($24,688) see Woodward Governor Co.

Cunningham Dance Foundation ($4,430) see Goldman Foundation, Morris and Rose

Cunningham Dance Foundation ($10,000) see Sheafer Charitable Trust, Emma A.

Currier Museum ($5,000) see H. B. B. Foundation

Cystic Fibrosis Foundation ($1,250) see Cole Taylor Financial Group

Cystic Fibrosis Foundation ($13,200) see Hopper Memorial Foundation, Bertrand

Daley Inaugural Committee Charitable Fund ($600) see Herald News

David and Alfred Smart Museum of Art ($109,750) see Smart Family Foundation

Dawn R. Schuman Institute for Jewish Learning ($1,000) see Linde Foundation, Ronald and Maxine

Day Care Action Council of Illinois — first payment to improve day care policies and child care provisions in Illinolis Department of Public Aid system ($39,000) see Woods Charitable Fund

De La Salle High School ($100,000) see Borg-Warner Corp.

De La Salle School ($10,000) see Snite Foundation, Fred B.

De Paul University — education ($31,300) see Continental Bank N.A.

Deborah's Place ($10,000) see CRI Charitable Trust

Decatur Advantage ($5,000) see Mueller Co.

Decatur Area Arts Council ($1,000) see Mueller Co.

Decatur Area Arts Council ($5,000) see Staley Manufacturing Co., A.E.

Decatur Area Children's Museum ($5,000) see Staley, Jr. Foundation, A. E.

Decatur Memorial Foundation ($12,500) see Staley Manufacturing Co., A.E.

Decatur Memorial Hospital ($74,250) see Staley, Jr. Foundation, A. E.

Decatur Parks Foundation ($1,000) see Mueller Co.

Deerfield Academy ($5,000) see Hay Foundation, John I.

DeKalb City Economic Development ($2,500) see Ideal Industries

DeKalb County Hospice ($3,000) see Ideal Industries

Delnor Community Hospital Foundation ($70,000) see Norris Foundation, Dellora A. and Lester J.

Delnor Community Hospital Foundation ($50,000) see Norris Foundation, Dellora A. and Lester J.

DePaul University ($25,000) see Bowyer Foundation, Ambrose and Gladys

DePaul University ($50,000) see Brach Foundation, Helen

DePaul University ($200,000) see Coleman Foundation

DePaul University ($12,365) see First Chicago

DePaul University ($5,000) see Harris Foundation, J. Ira and Nicki

DePaul University ($5,000) see Jaharis Family Foundation

DePaul University ($100,000) see Kellstadt Foundation

DePaul University — scholarships ($55,000) see Schmitt Foundation, Arthur J.

DePaul University — establish an expendable scholarship fund ($75,000) see Scholl Foundation, Dr.

DePaul University Blackstone Theatre — for Reading/Writing Chicago, a school improvement project in 10 inner-city schools

($62,000) see Fry Foundation, Lloyd A.

DePaul University Capital Project ($50,000) see Schmitt Foundation, Arthur J.

DePaul University College of Commerce ($7,500) see Vilter Manufacturing Corp.

DePaul University-College of Law ($12,190) see Mansfield Foundation, Albert and Anne

DePaul University School of Law — start-up expenses ($25,000) see Cudahy Fund, Patrick and Anna M.

DePaul University School of Music ($25,000) see Seid Foundation, Barre

DePaul University — Smarter Schools Program ($375,912) see Citicorp

DePaul University — Theater School ($5,000) see Linde Foundation, Ronald and Maxine

Designs for Change — second payment of $150,000 renewal grant for SCHOOLWATCH, a program of parent organizing, advocacy and technical assistance to local school counils, community groups and parents c ($50,000) see Woods Charitable Fund

Devereaux Foundation ($6,000) see Carylon Foundation

Diabetes Association of Greater Chicago ($4,000) see Cox Charitable Trust, A. G.

Ditka Foundation ($4,725) see Louis Foundation, Michael W.

Dr. Scholl College of Podiatric Medicine — funding for scholarship and museum project ($100,000) see Scholl Foundation, Dr.

Dr. School College ($20,000) see Swanson Foundation

Dominican Fathers ($20,000) see Merrion Foundation

Don Moyer Boys and Girls Club see Illinois Power Co.

Drug Free Rockford Partnership ($15,000) see CLARCOR

Ducks Unlimited ($5,000) see Beloco Foundation

Ducks Unlimited ($2,500) see Beloco Foundation

Ducks Unlimited ($2,975) see CRL Inc.

Ducks Unlimited ($20,000) see Davis Family - W.D. Charities, Tine W.

Ducks Unlimited ($7,000) see Hastings Trust

Ducks Unlimited ($75,000) see Knox Foundation, Seymour H.

Ducks Unlimited — general fund ($20,000) see Lakeside Foundation

Ducks Unlimited ($2,500) see Scott, Jr. Charitable Foundation, Walter

Ducks Unlimited ($6,000) see Tomlinson Foundation, Kate and Elwyn

Ducks Unlimited — Mackay Island Marship project ($96,875) see Knapp Foundation

Ducks Unlimited — Wildlife Conservation ($5,000) see Kleberg Foundation for Wildlife Conservation, Caesar

Duke Center for Living ($800) see Florsheim Shoe Co.

DuPage Easter Seal Treatment Center ($10,000) see Alexander Charitable Foundation

Dysautonomia ($10,000) see Galter Foundation

Illinois (cont.)

Dystonia ($22,000) see Relations Foundation

Dystonia Medical Research Foundation — general support ($20,000) see Fel-Pro Incorporated

Eagle Mount — "Professional Volunteers Through Professional Volunteer Training Efforts" ($500) see First Interstate Bancsystem of Montana

Eagles Mount ($12,000) see Special People In Need

Easter Seal Society ($10,000) see Aigner

Easter Seal Society ($5,000) see Rhoades Fund, Otto L. and Hazel E.

Eastern European Ecumenical Fund ($10,000) see Bere Foundation

Eastern Illinois University ($3,000) see Wyne Foundation

Eastern Illinois University School of Business ($3,000) see Hopper Memorial Foundation, Bertrand

ECC Foundation ($2,500) see Hoffer Plastics Corp.

Edison-McGraw Scholarship Program ($39,009) see McGraw Foundation

El Hogar Del Nino ($20,000) see NutraSweet Co.

El Valor ($5,000) see Chicago Sun-Times, Inc.

Elgin Academy ($10,000) see Rhoades Fund, Otto L. and Hazel E.

Elgin Community College ($1,000) see Elgin Sweeper Co.

Elgin High School — scholarships ($3,500) see Elgin Sweeper Co.

Elgin Symphony Orchestra ($3,450) see Hoffer Plastics Corp.

Eli Schulman Playground/Seneca Park Fund ($10,000) see Siragusa Foundation

Elim Christian School ($2,500) see Huizenga Foundation, Jennie

Elmhurst College ($500) see Lizzadro Family Foundation, Joseph

Elmhurst College ($10,000) see Siragusa Foundation

Emanuel Congregation — design, preparation, construction and installation of stained glass window ($38,000) see Lederer Foundation, Francis L.

Emergency Fund for Needy People ($2,500) see Mitchell Family Foundation, Bernard and Marjorie

Emergency Fund for Needy People ($40,460) see Stone Family Foundation, Norman H.

Endowment Fund of St. Johns United Methodist Church ($500) see Florsheim Shoe Co.

Envangelical Covenant Church of America Central Conference ($5,000) see Bjorkman Foundation

Episcopal Charities ($10,000) see Hoover Foundation, H. Earl

Episcopal Diocese ($5,000) see Hoover Foundation, H. Earl

Epstein Fine Arts Fund ($5,000) see Blum Foundation, Harry and Maribel G.

Erickson Institute ($3,000) see Brand Cos.

Erie Health Clinic ($10,000) see Simpson Foundation, John M.

Erikson Institute ($10,000) see Best Foundation, Walter J. and Edith E.

Erikson Institute ($40,000) see Shaw Foundation, Walden W. and Jean Young

Evaluation and Referral Services ($20,000) see Galvin Foundation, Robert W.

Evangelical Child and Family Services ($10,000) see Best Foundation, Walter J. and Edith E.

Evangelical Covenant Church — guesthouse ($31,500) see Young Foundation, Irvin L.

Evangelical Covenant Church of America ($10,000) see Bjorkman Foundation

Evangelical Covenant Church of America ($2,000) see Douglas Corp.

Evangelical Covenant Church of America — for missionary projects ($6,000) see Epaphroditus Foundation

Evangelical Covenant Church of America-Central Conference Camping Ministry ($7,000) see Bjorkman Foundation

Evangelical Covenant Church — housing, services, and AIDS protection ($26,500) see Young Foundation, Irvin L.

Evangelical Lutheran Church in America — study of theological education ($73,800) see Lutheran Brotherhood Foundation

Evanston Hospital ($100,000) see Allstate Insurance Co.

Evanston Hospital ($3,000) see Allyn Foundation

Evanston Hospital ($10,000) see Boothroyd Foundation, Charles H. and Bertha L.

Evanston Hospital — for arrhythmia research ($13,000) see Butz Foundation

Evanston Hospital ($220,000) see Crown Memorial, Arie and Ida

Evanston Hospital ($3,000) see Hales Charitable Fund

Evanston Hospital ($20,000) see Johnson Foundation, A. D.

Evanston Hospital ($10,000) see Winona Corporation

Evanston Hospital/Division of Behavioral and Development Pediatrics — support clinical services and research ($75,000) see AON Corp.

Executive Service Corporation of Chicago ($6,000) see Material Service Corp.

Executive Service Corps of Chicago ($10,000) see Morton International

Express-Ways Children's Museum ($8,000) see NutraSweet Co.

Expressways Children's Museum ($11,000) see Manilow Foundation, Nathan

Eye Research Foundation ($5,000) see Rhoades Fund, Otto L. and Hazel E.

Fairchild Tropical Garden ($10,000) see Kelly Tractor Co.

Faith, Hope and Charity Church — general support ($77,000) see Solo Cup Co.

Faith Lutheran Church ($25,000) see Petersen Foundation, Esper A.

Faith at Work ($3,000) see Bjorkman Foundation

Family Advocate ($3,333) see AMCORE Bank, N.A. Rockford

Family Advocate ($3,000) see Rockford Acromatics Products Co./Aircraft Gear Corp.

Family Builders of Adoption ($12,000) see Pesch Family Foundation

Family Focus ($3,000) see Brand Cos.

Family Focus ($77,100) see Pittway Corp.

Family Institute ($100,000) see Blum-Kovler Foundation

Family Institute of Chicago ($476,000) see McCormick Tribune Foundation, Robert R.

Family Resource Coalition ($25,000) see Daly Charitable Foundation Trust, Robert and Nancy

Family Service Agency of DeKalb ($20,000) see Bersted Foundation

Family Service of DuPage ($15,000) see Bersted Foundation

Family Service of South Lake County ($19,500) see IMCERA Group Inc.

Family Services Agency ($7,000) see Ideal Industries

Family Services and Community Mental Health Center ($35,000) see Bersted Foundation

Fenwick Scholarship and Development Fund ($5,000) see Brunner Foundation, Fred J.

Field Museum of Natural History ($2,000) see Alsdorf Foundation

Field Museum of Natural History — support for museum programs ($100,000) see AON Corp.

Field Museum of Natural History ($3,000) see Bergner Co., P.A.

Field Museum of Natural History ($2,500) see Boulevard Bank, N.A.

Field Museum of Natural History ($2,500) see Boulevard Foundation

Field Museum of Natural History ($25,000) see Cheney Foundation, Elizabeth F.

Field Museum of Natural History ($5,000) see Chicago Board of Trade

Field Museum of Natural History ($25,000) see Cooper Charitable Trust, Richard H.

Field Museum of Natural History ($10,050) see Donnelley Foundation, Elliott and Ann

Field Museum of Natural History ($50,500) see Field Foundation, Jamee and Marshall

Field Museum of Natural History — capital fund ($160,000) see Grainger Foundation

Field Museum of Natural History ($5,000) see H. B. B. Foundation

Field Museum of Natural History ($2,000) see Hales Charitable Fund

Field Museum of Natural History ($2,100) see Heller Foundation, Walter E.

Field Museum of Natural History ($20,000) see Lebus Trust, Bertha

Field Museum of Natural History ($25,000) see Mayer Charitable Trust, Oscar G. & Elsa S.

Field Museum of Natural History ($10,000) see Norton Memorial Corporation, Geraldi

Field Museum of Natural History ($600,000) see Regenstein Foundation

Field Museum of Natural History ($1,000,000) see Rice Foundation

Field Museum of Natural History ($3,500) see Thorson Foundation

Field Museum of Natural History ($10,000) see Winona Corporation

Field Museum of Natural History — for the establishment of the E. Leland Webber Research Fund ($250,000) see Field Foundation of Illinois

Fifth Epochal Fellowship ($35,000) see Hales Charitable Fund

First Baptist Church ($3,800) see Wyne Foundation

First Congregational Church ($5,000) see Wyne Foundation

First Presbyterian Church ($6,000) see Donnelley Foundation, Elliott and Ann

First Presbyterian Church ($3,000) see Hopper Memorial Foundation, Bertrand

First Presbyterian Church ($30,000) see Sudix Foundation

First Presbyterian Church of Chicago ($20,000) see Replogle Foundation, Luther I.

First Presbyterian Church of Evanston ($26,305) see Erickson Charitable Fund, Eben W.

Forest Bluff Montessori School ($1,000) see Mason Charitable Foundation

Foundation for Anesthesia Education and Research ($55,000) see Abbott Laboratories

Foundation for Chiropractic Education and Research ($1,000) see Iowa State Bank

Foundry Educational Foundation ($110) see Alhambra Foundry Co., Ltd.

Foundry Educational Foundation ($4,500) see Grede Foundries

Foundry Educational Foundation ($3,000) see North American Royalties

Foundry Educational Foundation ($3,000) see Wisconsin Centrifugal

Fox River Conservation Union of Nature Conservancy ($42,000) see Bersted Foundation

Fox Valley Family Center ($55,000) see Bersted Foundation

Francis W. Parker and the Latin School of Chicago — for operating support of High Jump, an academic program for disadvantaged seventh and eighth grade students in Chicago Public Schools ($100,000) see Fry Foundation, Lloyd A.

Franciscan Friars — for the education of seminarians and renovations of the major house of study ($40,000) see Koch Foundation

Franciscan Friars of Mary ($25,000) see Cuneo Foundation

Free Street Theater ($5,000) see Montgomery Ward & Co.

Friends of Fermilab ($3,000) see Forest Fund

Friends of Handicapped Riders ($2,500) see USG Corp.

Friends of Man ($2,000) see H. B. B. Foundation

Friends of St. Mary's Hospital Foundation — obstetrics department ($10,000) see Staley Manufacturing Co., A.E.

Fund for Community Redevelopment and Revitalization — in support of planning and program development related to the redevelopment of the Woodlawn and Kenwood-Oakland communities (over three years) ($1,200,000) see MacArthur Foundation, John D. and Catherine T.

Futures Unlimited ($5,000) see Camp and Bennet Humiston Trust, Apollos

Futures - Youth Vocational Outreach Foundation — for over two years for "Enter Here" career video series ($40,000) see Marshall Field's

G.W. Aldeen Fund for Missions ($53,000) see Aldeen Charity Trust, G. W.

Gastro-Intestinal Research Foundation ($11,000) see Getz Foundation, Emma and Oscar

Gastro-Intestinal Research Foundation ($2,500) see GSC Enterprises

Gastro-Intestinal Research Foundation ($10,000) see Mitchell Family Foundation, Bernard and Marjorie

General Medical Foundation ($20,000) see Perkins Foundation, Edwin E.

Gillespie Ministerial Alliance ($5,000) see Schmidt Charitable Foundation, William E.

GIRF ($10,500) see Stone Family Foundation, Norman H.

Girl Scouts of America ($10,200) see Smith Charitable Trust

Girl Scouts of Chicago ($1,000) see Rubin Family Fund, Cele H. and William B.

Girl Scouts-Rock River Valley Council — capital ($25,000) see Sundstrand Corp.

Glenkirk Foundation ($1,000) see CRL Inc.

Glenwood School for Boys ($3,500) see CBI Industries

Glenwood School for Boys ($26,305) see Erickson Charitable Fund, Eben W.

Glenwood School for Boys ($45,000) see Frankel Foundation

Glenwood School for Boys ($6,000) see Goldenberg Foundation, Max

Glenwood School for Boys ($20,000) see Inland Steel Industries

Glenwood School for Boys ($100) see LaSalle National Bank

Glenwood School for Boys ($50,000) see Square D Co.

Glenwood School for Boys ($2,500) see United Conveyor Corp.

Gonzaga Prep School — distinguished teachers program ($5,000) see Lapham-Hickey Steel Corp.

Good Samaritan Hospital ($1,000) see Bjorkman Foundation

Good Shepherd Church ($10,000) see Geneseo Foundation

Goodman Theater ($100) see LaSalle National Bank

Goodman Theatre ($7,000) see Manilow Foundation, Nathan

Goodman Theatre ($46,000) see Marshall Field's

Goodwill Industries ($2,500) see Foster and Gallagher

Goodwill Industries ($6,000) see Harper Foundation, Philip S.

Goodwill Industries ($9,000) see House Educational Trust, Susan Cook

Gordy Square Renovation ($2,000) see Comer Foundation

Grace Bible Church ($1,000) see GSC Enterprises

Grace Church of Hinsdale ($3,000) see Western Shade Cloth Charitable Foundation

Grace Episcopal Church ($3,900) see Borwell Charitable Foundation

Grace Episcopal Church ($16,000) see Dillon Foundation

Grant Hospital ($100,000) see CRI Charitable Trust

Grant Park Concert Society ($5,000) see Chicago Board of Trade

Greater Chicago Food Depository ($3,000) see Butler Family Foundation, George W. and Gladys S.

Greater Chicago Food Depository ($2,000) see Gavin Foundation, James and Zita

Greater Chicago Food Depository ($1,000) see Lurie Family Foundation

Greater Chicago Food Depository ($6,000) see Relations Foundation

Greater Chicago Food Depository — general fund ($10,000) see Shaw Foundation, Arch W.

Greenhouse Shelter ($2,000) see Lurie Family Foundation

Greenpeace ($20,000) see CRI Charitable Trust

Greenville College ($30,000) see Whitman Corp.

Greenwood School ($2,000) see Cooper Charitable Trust, Richard H.

H.O.M.E. ($6,000) see Replogle Foundation, Luther I.

Habitat for Humanity ($5,000) see Mansfield Foundation, Albert and Anne

Hadassah ($5,242) see Goldman Foundation, Morris and Rose

Hadassah Nursing Scholarship ($5,000) see Carylon Foundation

Hadley School for the Blind ($5,000) see Allyn Foundation

Hadley School for the Blind ($5,000) see Chicago Sun-Times, Inc.

Hadley School for the Blind ($10,000) see Katzenberger Foundation

Hadley School for the Blind ($10,000) see Pioneer Fund

Hadley School for the Blind ($50,000) see Seabury Foundation

Hales Franciscan High School — general operating expenses ($50,000) see Coleman Foundation

Hales Franciscan High School — renovation of gymnasium ($30,000) see Cudahy Fund, Patrick and Anna M.

Hammond-Henry Hospital ($4,760) see Geneseo Foundation

Harbert Community Covenant Church ($2,150) see Bjorkman Foundation

Harlen E. Moore Heart Research Foundation ($90,000) see Wallace Genetic Foundation

Health Research Group ($5,000) see Oppenheimer Family Foundation

Heart Association ($10,000) see Knowles Foundation

Heart of Illinois United Way ($450,000) see Caterpillar

Heart of Illinois United Way ($87,030) see Caterpillar

Heartland Institute ($6,000) see Sunmark Capital Corp.

Hebrew Cemetery Association ($4,000) see Geifman Family Foundation

Hebrew Theological College ($50,100) see Feinberg Foundation, Joseph and Bessie

Hebrew Theological College ($35,000) see Shapiro Foundation, Charles and M. R.

Hellenic Foundation ($7,500) see Replogle Foundation, Luther I.

Henry Meers Fund for Television Excellence ($1,000) see Willmott Foundation, Peter S.

Hephzibah Children's Association ($15,000) see Bowyer Foundation, Ambrose and Gladys

Herrin Area United Way ($1,700) see Harrison Foundation, Fred G.

Herrin Ball Park ($15,180) see Harrison Foundation, Fred G.

Herrin Chamber of Commerce ($10,000) see Harrison Foundation, Fred G.

Herrin Park Shelter ($10,650) see Harrison Foundation, Fred G.

Hesed House see Portec, Inc.

Highland Park Hospital — for the hospice program ($10,000) see Butz Foundation

Highland Park Hospital ($11,625) see Frank Fund, Zollie and Elaine

Highland Park Hospital ($5,000) see Hoover Foundation, H. Earl

Highland Park Hospital Foundation ($2,000) see Cole Taylor Financial Group

Hinsdale Community House ($15,400) see Bere Foundation

Hinsdale Evangelical Covenant Church ($1,500) see Bjorkman Foundation

Hinsdale Sanitarium and Hospital ($25,000) see Bowyer Foundation, Ambrose and Gladys

Holy Cross Monastery ($10,000) see Hoover Foundation, H. Earl

Holy Family Catholic Church ($5,000) see Schmidt Charitable Foundation, William E.

Holy Family Church ($58,500) see Cuneo Foundation

Holy Family Community — general fund ($10,000) see Shaw Foundation, Arch W.

Holy Family Lutheran Church School ($25,000) see Replogle Foundation, Luther I.

Homeless and Abused Children of Chicago ($500) see Florsheim Shoe Co.

Hoover Outdoor Education Center ($5,000) see Blair and Co., William

Horatio Alger Association ($20,000) see Fuqua Foundation, J. B.

Horizon Hospice ($3,000) see Kelly Foundation, T. Lloyd

Horizon Hospice Association ($7,500) see Mansfield Foundation, Albert and Anne

Hospice ($500) see Lizzadro Family Foundation, Joseph

Hospice ($35,000) see Logan Foundation, E. J.

Hospice ($35,000) see Logan Foundation, E. J.

Hospice ($34,785) see Logan Foundation, E. J.

Hospice ($10,000) see Shaw Foundation, Arch W.

Hospices of North Shore ($5,000) see Special People In Need

Hospital Research and Educational Trust — The Foster G. McGaw Prize ($160,300) see Baxter International

House of the Good Shepard ($5,500) see Western Shade Cloth Charitable Foundation

House of Good Shepherd ($23,352) see Blowitz-Ridgeway Foundation

House of Good Shepherd ($100,000) see Mazza Foundation

Housing Opportunities for Women — general support ($10,000) see Stone Foundation, W. Clement and Jessie V.

Howard Brown Memorial Clinic ($2,500) see Cooper Charitable Trust, Richard H.

Howard Brown Memorial Clinic — fund-raiser support; general funds ($13,000) see Duchossois Industries

Hubbard Street Dance Company ($15,000) see Cheney Foundation, Elizabeth F.

Hubbard Street Dance Company ($1,420) see Herald News

Hubbard Street Dance Company ($25,000) see Marshall Field's

Hull House ($6,000) see Blair and Co., William

Hull House ($10,000) see NutraSweet Co.

Hull House Association ($15,000) see Beidler Charitable Trust, Francis

Hull House — Meals-On-Wheels ($4,000) see Eisenberg Foundation, George M.

Human Relations Foundation/Chicago Com. Trust — pledge payment ($50,000) see AON Corp.

Humiston Woods Nature Center ($53,000) see Camp and Bennet Humiston Trust, Apollos

Hundred Club of Cook County ($5,000) see Lehmann Foundation, Otto W.

Hunger Connection ($2,000) see Elco Charitable Foundation

Hunger Connection ($12,600) see Woodward Governor Co.

Hunger Project ($3,800) see Cohn Family Foundation, Robert and Terri

Hyacinth Foundation ($10,000) see Ohl, Jr. Trust, George A.

Hyatt Foundation — Private Foundation ($382,000) see Pritzker Foundation

Illinois Agricultural Leadership Foundation ($6,000) see Moorman Manufacturing Co.

Illinois Audubon Society ($3,500) see House Educational Trust, Susan Cook

Illinois Benedictine College ($5,000) see American Society of Ephesus

Illinois Benedictine College ($50,000) see Andersen Foundation, Arthur

Illinois Benedictine College ($75,000) see Schmitt Foundation, Arthur J.

Illinois Chamber of Commerce ($1,000) see Florsheim Shoe Co.

Illinois Chamber Symphony ($3,000) see Garvey Kansas Foundation

Illinois Children's Home and Aid Society ($10,000) see Brach Foundation, Edwin I.

Illinois Children's Home and Aid Society ($50,000) see Seid Foundation, Barre

Illinois College ($24,000) see Monticello College Foundation

Illinois College of Optometry ($8,000) see Wildermuth Foundation, E. F.

Illinois Institute of Technology ($3,000) see Allyn Foundation

Illinois Institute of Technology ($11,000) see American National Bank & Trust Co. of Chicago

Illinois Institute of Technology ($30,000) see Amsted Industries

Illinois Institute of Technology ($3,500) see Chapin-May Foundation of Illinois

Illinois Institute of Technology ($3,500) see Chapin-May Foundation of Illinois

Illinois Institute of Technology ($5,000) see Cole Taylor Financial Group

Illinois Institute of Technology ($250,000) see Delany Charitable Trust, Beatrice P.

Illinois Institute of Technology ($250,000) see Delany Charitable Trust, Beatrice P.

Illinois Institute of Technology ($456,750) see Galvin Foundation, Robert W.

Illinois Institute of Technology ($1,000,000) see McCormick Tribune Foundation, Robert R.

Illinois Institute of Technology ($250,000) see McGraw Foundation

Illinois Institute of Technology ($3,000) see United Conveyor Corp.

Illinois Institute of Technology ($75,000) see Ward Foundation, A. Montgomery

Illinois Institute of Technology (Library) ($50,000) see Buchanan Family Foundation

Illinois Institute of Technology — for Project START ($50,000) see Fry Foundation, Lloyd A.

Illinois Math and Science Academy ($10,000) see Amsted Industries

Illinois Mathematics and Science Academy ($10,000) see Pick, Jr. Fund, Albert

Illinois Mathematics and Science Academy — to equip academy's video production lab ($50,000) see Toyota Motor Sales, U.S.A.

Illinois Mathematics and Science and Academy — to equip academy's video production ($50,000) see Toyota Motor Sales, U.S.A.

Illinois NARAL Fund ($2,000) see Brand Cos.

Illinois National Abortion Rights Action League Foundation ($7,000) see Beidler Charitable Trust, Francis

Illinois Pro-Choice Alliance ($2,500) see Forest Fund

Illinois Rehabilitation Association see Illinois Power Co.

Illinois State Foundation, Illinois State University ($10,125) see Shirk Foundation, Russell and Betty

Illinois State Historical Society ($17,500) see Kemper Educational and Charitable Fund

Illinois State Historical Society ($2,000) see Quincy Newspapers

Illinois State Museum Lockport Gallery — exhibition and catalogue about Chicago muralist John Warner Norton (1876-1934) ($10,000) see Graham Foundation for Advanced Studies in the Fine Arts

Illinois State Museum Society — women's internship ($10,500) see Monticello College Foundation

Illinois State University ($5,739) see Graphic Arts Show Co. Inc.

Illinois State University — presidential scholarship program ($150,000) see State Farm Mutual Automobile Insurance Co.

Illinois State University ($87,096) see State Farm Mutual Automobile Insurance Co.

Illinois State University-College of Business — support for endowed chair in insurance and financial services ($25,000) see Kemper National Insurance Cos.

Illinois Wesleyan University ($250,000) see Beckman Foundation, Arnold and Mabel

Illinois Wesleyan University see Illinois Power Co.

Illinois Wesleyan University ($30,000) see Model Foundation, Leo

Illinois Wesleyan University ($460,000) see Shirk Foundation, Russell and Betty

Illinois Wesleyan University ($10,000) see Siragusa Foundation

Illinois Wesleyan University — minority opportunity program ($50,395) see State Farm Mutual Automobile Insurance Co.

Illinois Wesleyan University — Interactive Learning Center ($50,000) see State Farm Mutual Automobile Insurance Co.

Immaculate Conception Church ($1,000) see Lizzadro Family Foundation, Joseph

Infant Jesus of Prague Parish — general, charitable, religious, and educational purposes ($50,000) see Sage Foundation

Ingalls Development Foundation-Ingalls Memorial Hospital — sponsor/fund-raiser ($7,500) see Duchossois Industries

Inland Architect Magazine — national direct-mail campaign seeking new subscribers ($10,000) see Graham

Illinois (cont.)

Foundation for Advanced Studies in the Fine Arts

Inner City Impact ($30,000) see Crowell Trust, Henry P. and Susan C.

Inner-City Impact — seminary training/Africian Nationalists ($5,000) see Epaphroditus Foundation

Inroads/Chicago ($10,000) see Brunswick Corp.

Institute of Charity ($5,000) see Childs Charitable Foundation, Roberta M.

Institute of Cultural Affairs ($8,400) see Jinks Foundation, Ruth T.

Institute for Human Relations ($37,500) see Camp and Bennet Humiston Trust, Apollos

Institute for Human Services ($3,000) see Simpson Foundation, John M.

Institute of Justice Ministries ($5,000) see Aigner

Institute for Philosophical Research ($54,167) see American National Bank & Trust Co. of Chicago

Institute for Philosophical Research ($5,000) see Hunt Foundation

Institute for Psychoanalysis ($600) see Baum Family Fund, Alvin H.

Institute for Psychoanalysis ($2,000) see Stone Family Foundation, Jerome H.

Intercultural Association ($20,000) see Merrion Foundation

Interfaith Organizing Project of Greater Chicago — general operating support ($15,000) see Wieboldt Foundation

International Food Service Executive Association ($40,425) see Statler Foundation

International Music Foundation ($10,000) see Davee Foundation

International Teams ($24,000) see Caddock Foundation

International Teams ($1,500) see Rixson Foundation, Oscar C.

Jayne Shover Easter Seals ($3,625) see Hoffer Plastics Corp.

Jewish Children's Bureau of Chicago — general operating support ($11,000) see Fel-Pro Incorporated

Jewish Community Center ($16,756) see Frank Fund, Zollie and Elaine

Jewish Council on Urban Affairs ($9,000) see Kaplan Foundation, Mayer and Morris

Jewish Council on Urban Affairs ($11,750) see New Prospect Foundation

Jewish Council for Youth Services ($3,835) see Goldman Foundation, Morris and Rose

Jewish Family and Children's Services ($500) see Baum Family Fund, Alvin H.

Jewish Federation ($5,000) see Robin Family Foundation, Albert A.

Jewish Federation of Chicago ($5,000) see Eisenberg Foundation, George M.

Jewish Federation of Metropolitan Chicago ($115,000) see Blum

Foundation, Nathan and Emily S.

Jewish Federation of Metropolitan Chicago ($1,000) see Goldberg Family Foundation, Milton D. and Madeline L.

Jewish Federation of Quad Cities ($15,000) see Geifman Family Foundation

Jewish United Fund ($26,562) see Aladdin Industries, Incorporated

Jewish United Fund ($5,000) see Baum Family Fund, Alvin H.

Jewish United Fund ($70,865) see Berger Foundation, Albert E.

Jewish United Fund ($30,500) see Blum Foundation, Nathan and Emily S.

Jewish United Fund ($22,375) see Carylon Foundation

Jewish United Fund ($127,500) see Cohn Family Foundation, Robert and Terri

Jewish United Fund ($9,000) see Cole Taylor Financial Group

Jewish United Fund ($140,000) see Crown Charitable Fund, Edward A.

Jewish United Fund ($124,760) see Feinberg Foundation, Joseph and Bessie

Jewish United Fund — for general support ($125,000) see Fel-Pro Incorporated

Jewish United Fund ($5,500) see Foster Charitable Trust

Jewish United Fund ($132,625) see Frank Fund, Zollie and Elaine

Jewish United Fund ($150,000) see Galter Foundation

Jewish United Fund ($5,000) see Getz Foundation, Emma and Oscar

Jewish United Fund ($113,000) see Harris Foundation, J. Ira and Nicki

Jewish United Fund ($37,000) see Harris Foundation, J. Ira and Nicki

Jewish United Fund ($9,000) see Hartmarx Corp.

Jewish United Fund ($21,500) see Heller Foundation, Walter E.

Jewish United Fund ($25,000) see Lederer Foundation, Francis L.

Jewish United Fund ($6,000) see Levitt Foundation, Richard S.

Jewish United Fund ($130,000) see Levy Foundation, Charles and Ruth

Jewish United Fund ($100,000) see Manilow Foundation, Nathan

Jewish United Fund ($10,000) see Mitchell Family Foundation, Bernard and Marjorie

Jewish United Fund ($9,000) see Oppenheimer Family Foundation

Jewish United Fund ($11,000) see Pick, Jr. Fund, Albert

Jewish United Fund — bond contribution ($500,000) see Pritzker Foundation

Jewish United Fund ($100,000) see Pritzker Foundation

Jewish United Fund ($88,000) see Relations Foundation

Jewish United Fund ($100,000) see Robin Family Foundation, Albert A.

Jewish United Fund ($75,000) see Sang Foundation, Elsie O. and Philip D.

Jewish United Fund ($50,000) see Seid Foundation, Barre

Jewish United Fund ($132,000) see Shapiro Family Foundation, Soretta and Henry

Jewish United Fund ($225,000) see Shapiro Foundation, Charles and M. R.

Jewish United Fund ($110,000) see Stern Foundation, Irvin

Jewish United Fund ($7,000) see Stone Family Foundation, Jerome H.

Jewish United Fund ($6,865) see Stone Family Foundation, Norman H.

Jewish United Fund of Chicago ($3,400) see Geifman Family Foundation

Jewish United Fund of Metropolitan Chicago ($60,000) see Bauer Foundation, M. R.

Jewish United Fund of Metropolitan Chicago ($200,000) see Blum Foundation, Harry and Maribel G.

Jewish United Fund of Metropolitan Chicago ($100,000) see Blum-Kovler Foundation

Jewish United Fund of Metropolitan Chicago ($369,333) see Stone Container Corp.

John G. Shedd Aquarium ($5,000) see Blair and Co., William

John G. Shedd Aquarium ($50,000) see Buehler Foundation, A. C.

John G. Shedd Aquarium ($10,000) see Heller Foundation, Walter E.

John G. Shedd Aquarium ($1,000) see Kearney Inc., A.T.

John G. Shedd Aquarium ($50,000) see Mason Charitable Foundation

John G. Shedd Aquarium ($40,000) see McCormick Foundation, Chauncey and Marion Deering

John G. Shedd Aquarium ($250,000) see Regenstein Foundation

John G. Shedd Aquarium ($500,000) see Rice Foundation

John G. Shedd Aquarium — campaign for Chicago Oceanarium ($5,000) see Norton Memorial Corporation, Geraldi

John Howard Association ($20,000) see Perkins Foundation, Edwin E.

John Marshall Law School ($50,000) see Borg-Warner Corp.

John Wood Community College Foundation ($12,000) see Moorman Manufacturing Co.

Joseph I. Kramer Foundation ($5,000) see Carylon Foundation

Josephinum High School ($50,000) see Brach Foundation, Helen

Jubilate Children's Choir ($2,500) see GSC Enterprises

Judge Abraham L. Marovitz Courtroom ($5,000) see Carylon Foundation

Judge Abraham Lincoln/Marovitz Courtroom Project ($5,000) see Cohn Family Foundation, Robert and Terri

Judson College ($650) see Arbie Mineral Feed Co.

Junior Achievement ($5,000) see Anderson Industries

Junior Achievement ($10,000) see Boler Co.

Junior Achievement ($2,200) see Elco Charitable Foundation

Junior Achievement ($7,000) see House Educational Trust, Susan Cook

Junior Achievement ($3,000) see Ideal Industries

Junior Achievement see Illinois Power Co.

Junior Achievement ($3,250) see Material Service Corp.

Junior Achievement ($400) see Sjostrom & Sons

Junior Achievement ($6,400) see Warner Electric Brake & Clutch Co.

Junior Achievement of Chicago ($25,000) see Centel Corp.

Junior Achievement of Chicago ($15,000) see Illinois Tool Works

Juvenile Diabetes Foundation ($100,500) see Galter Foundation

Juvenile Protection Association ($2,000) see Atwood Foundation

Kedvale Avenue Christian Reform Christian Education Church Education Fund ($15,000) see Tibstra Charitable Foundation, Thomas and Gertrude

Keith Country Day School ($9,350) see Rockford Acromatics Products Co./Aircraft Gear Corp.

Keith Country Day School ($14,600) see Smith Charitable Trust

KeKotek Center of Evanston ($20,000) see Kendall Foundation, George R.

Kellog School of Management at Northwestern ($1,000) see Lipton Foundation

Kemmerer Village ($3,000) see Hopper Memorial Foundation, Bertrand

Kendall College ($160,000) see Kendall Foundation, George R.

Kennedy School ($15,000) see McGraw Foundation

Keshet ($2,500) see Boulevard Foundation

Kewanee Economic Development Fund see Illinois Power Co.

Kidney Foundation ($2,600) see GSC Enterprises

King's College ($100,000) see Borg-Warner Corp.

Kishwaukee Valley Concert Bank ($300) see Sjostrom & Sons

Knights of Columbus ($1,125) see Warner Electric Brake & Clutch Co.

Knox College ($100,000) see Caterpillar

Knox College ($35,000) see Centel Corp.

Knox College ($13,000) see Dick Family Foundation

Knox College ($25,000) see Scripps Foundation, Ellen Browning

Knox College ($10,000) see Willmott Foundation, Peter S.

La Rabida Children's Hospital ($50,000) see Frankel Foundation

La Rabida Children's Hospital ($5,000) see Material Service Corp.

La Rabida Children's Hospital and Research Center ($25,000)

see Kemper Educational and Charitable Fund

LaGrange Memorial Treatment Pavilion ($20,000) see Russell Charitable Foundation, Tom

Lake Forest Academy ($10,000) see Blair and Co., William

Lake Forest Academy ($25,060) see CRL Inc.

Lake Forest College — toward language teaching laboratory ($116,000) see Culpeper Foundation, Charles E.

Lake Forest College ($50,000) see Day Family Foundation

Lake Forest College ($2,000) see Dick Family Foundation

Lake Forest College ($11,075) see Donnelley Foundation, Elliott and Ann

Lake Forest College ($10,000) see Johnson Foundation, A. D.

Lake Forest College ($24,000) see Johnson Foundation, Howard

Lake Forest College ($20,000) see Santa Fe Pacific Corp.

Lake Forest College ($25,000) see Schiff Foundation

Lake Forest College ($1,000) see Swift Co. Inc., John S.

Lake Forest College Endowment ($50,000) see Buchanan Family Foundation

Lake Forest College Scholarship Fund ($10,000) see Beidler Charitable Trust, Francis

Lake Forest College, Sheridan and College Roads ($5,000) see Alexander Foundation, Walter

Lake Forest Country Day School ($53,000) see Field Foundation, Jamee and Marshall

Lake Forest Country Day School ($1,000) see Mason Charitable Foundation

Lake Forest Country Day School ($11,000) see Salwil Foundation

Lake Forest Graduate School of Management ($5,000) see Butler Family Foundation, George W. and Gladys S.

Lake Forest Hospital ($10,000) see Alexander Charitable Foundation

Lake Forest Hospital ($75,000) see Buchanan Family Foundation

Lake Forest Hospital ($4,000) see Dick Family Foundation

Lake Forest Hospital ($5,000) see Salwil Foundation

Lake Forest Hospital ($20,000) see Sudix Foundation

Lake Forest Open Lands ($19,950) see Dick Family Foundation

Lake Forest Open Lands ($10,000) see Haffner Foundation

Lake Forest Symphony ($5,000) see Butler Family Foundation, George W. and Gladys S.

Lake Forest Symphony ($2,000) see CRL Inc.

Lake Region YMCA ($10,000) see Morton International

Lake Shore Drive Synagogue — building fund ($2,000) see Geifman Family Foundation

Lakefront Single Room Occupancy Corporation — general support ($5,000) see Stone Foundation, W. Clement and Jessie V.

Lambs ($5,000) see Blum Foundation, Harry and Maribel G.

Lambs ($5,000) see Rhoades Fund, Otto L. and Hazel E.

Lambs ($15,000) see Sudix Foundation

Lambs Farm ($50,000) see IMCERA Group Inc.

Lambs Farm ($330,000) see Regenstein Foundation

Langham Foundation ($5,000) see Combs Foundation, Earle M. and Virginia M.

LaRabida Children's Hospital ($12,000) see Best Foundation, Walter J. and Edith E.

LaRabida Children's Hospital ($5,000) see Chicago Sun-Times, Inc.

LaRabida Children's Hospital ($6,000) see Goldenberg Foundation, Max

LaRabida Children's Hospital and Research Center ($41,666) see Pick, Jr. Fund, Albert

Larkin High School — scholarships ($3,500) see Elgin Sweeper Co.

LaSalle Street Church — for missions ($4,000) see Epaphroditus Foundation

LaSalle Street Cycle ($56,647) see Kaplan Foundation, Mayer and Morris

Latin School of Chicago ($20,000) see Comer Foundation

Latin School of Chicago ($80,000) see Manger and Audrey Cordero Plitt Trust, Clarence

Laudholm Trust ($10,000) see Farley Industries

Lawndale Christian Health Center ($50,000) see Sprague Memorial Institute, Otho S. A.

Lawndale Community Church ($12,000) see Russell Charitable Foundation, Tom

Lawrence Hall ($20,000) see Hoover Foundation, H. Earl

Lawrence Hall Youth Services ($6,000) see Aigner

Leadership Council of Southwestern Illinois see Illinois Power Co.

Leadership for Quality Education ($16,667) see Stone Container Corp.

Legal Aid Bureau ($8,500) see Schiff, Hardin & Waite

Legal Assistance Foundation of Chicago — first payment of two-year $100,000 renewal grant restricted to costs of staff attorney to specialize in welfare-to-work policy issues in Illinois ($50,000) see Woods Charitable Fund

Les Turner ALS Foundation ($10,000) see Relations Foundation

Letters of Interest ($30,000) see Caddock Foundation

Leukemia Society of America ($1,000) see GSC Enterprises

Leukodystrophy Foundation ($2,000) see Jerome Foundation

Lewis and Clark Community College — scholarships for women ($11,000) see Monticello College Foundation

Lewis and Clark Community College ($10,000) see Webb Foundation

Lewis University Graduate School of Business ($1,500) see Kearney Inc., A.T.

Library of International Relations ($25,000) see Cooper Charitable Trust, Richard H.

Life Center on the Green ($500,000) see Galter Foundation

Lincoln Park Zoo ($5,000) see Chicago Board of Trade

Lincoln Park Zoological Society see Bloomingdale's

Lincoln Park Zoological Society ($55,000) see McCormick Foundation, Chauncey and Marion Deering

Lincoln Park Zoological Society ($20,000) see Prentice Foundation, Abra

Lincoln Park Zoological Society ($100,000) see Pritzker Foundation

Lincoln Park Zoological Society ($101,000) see Rice Foundation

Lincoln Park Zoological Society ($5,000) see Rosenthal Foundation, Benjamin J.

Lincoln Park Zoological Society — funding for three programs as requested ($76,000) see Scholl Foundation, Dr.

Lincoln Park Zoological Society — Koala Program ($20,000) see Thorson Foundation

Lincoln Park Zoological Society — support of the first phase of its Master Landscape Plan, relating the Zoo's horticultural and animal collections to enhance the zoo experience ($100,000) see Field Foundation of Illinois

Link Unlimited — pledge payment ($50,000) see AON Corp.

Link Unlimited ($29,000) see Gavin Foundation, James and Zita

Literary Council of Chicago ($1,375) see Schiff, Hardin & Waite

Little Brothers of the Poor ($10,000) see Simpson Foundation, John M.

Little City Foundation ($25,000) see Fraida Foundation

Little City Foundation ($20,000) see Galvin Foundation, Robert W.

Little Company of Mary Hospital ($10,750) see American National Bank & Trust Co. of Chicago

Little Company of Mary Hospital ($4,000) see Dower Foundation, Thomas W.

Little Sisters of Poor ($31,118) see Cuneo Foundation

Little Sisters of Poor ($1,000) see Gavin Foundation, James and Zita

Little Sisters of Poor ($125,000) see Mazza Foundation

Little Sisters of Poor ($100,000) see Mazza Foundation

Living Bibles ($18,750) see Bolten Charitable Foundation, John

Living Bibles ($18,750) see Bolten Charitable Foundation, John

Living Bibles ($18,750) see Bolten Charitable Foundation, John

Living Bibles ($18,750) see Bolten Charitable Foundation, John

Living Bibles International ($3,000) see Epaphroditus Foundation

Living Bibles International ($250,000) see Stranahan Foundation

Living Bibles International ($15,000) see Tell Foundation

Living Bibles International ($175,000) see Tyndale House Foundation

Living Bibles International ($75,000) see Tyndale House Foundation

Living Bibles International — for the Kiyombe Living New Testament ($30,000) see Crowell Trust, Henry P. and Susan C.

Living Desert Research ($10,000) see Hoover Foundation, H. Earl

Lizzadro Museum of Lapidary Art ($105,000) see Lizzadro Family Foundation, Joseph

Local Economic and Employment Development Council ($6,000) see Montgomery Ward & Co.

Local Initiatives Support Corporation — economic development ($30,000) see Continental Bank N.A.

Local Initiatives Support Corporation ($12,500) see Material Service Corp.

Local Initiatives Support Corporation ($20,000) see Northern Trust Co.

Local Initiatives Support Corporation — to expand Economic Development Initiative in Chicago ($50,000) see Chicago Tribune Co.

Logan Square Neighborhood Association — general operating support ($15,000) see Wieboldt Foundation

Lorene Replogle Counseling Center ($20,000) see Replogle Foundation, Luther I.

Louis A. Weiss Memorial Hospital ($2,000) see Blum Foundation, Harry and Maribel G.

Loyola Academy ($100,000) see Mazza Foundation

Loyola Academy ($25,000) see Ryan Foundation, Patrick G. and Shirley W.

Loyola University ($25,000) see Bowyer Foundation, Ambrose and Gladys

Loyola University ($5,000) see Cottrell Foundation

Loyola University ($15,000) see Eisenberg Foundation, George M.

Loyola University ($5,000) see Lapham-Hickey Steel Corp.

Loyola University ($10,000) see Lehmann Foundation, Otto W.

Loyola University ($75,000) see Schmitt Foundation, Arthur J.

Loyola University — scholarships ($55,000) see Schmitt Foundation, Arthur J.

Loyola University ($25,000) see Snite Foundation, Fred B.

Loyola University of Chicago ($75,000) see Brach Foundation, Helen

Loyola University-Chicago — preventive mental health programs for children and adolescents ($119,808) see Grant Foundation, William T.

Loyola University Medical Center ($10,000) see Brunner Foundation, Fred J.

Lutheran Child and Family Services ($40,000) see Schmidt Charitable Foundation, William E.

Lutheran Child and Family Services ($15,000) see Webb Foundation

Lutheran Church — Central Illinois District ($50,000) see

Werner Foundation, Clara and Spencer

Lutheran Congregation for Career Development ($5,000) see Aigner

Lutheran General Foundation ($1,000) see Pioneer Fund

Lutheran General Foundation ($10,000) see Siragusa Foundation

Lutheran General Hospital ($10,000) see Johnson Foundation, A. D.

Lutheran School of Theology ($2,000) see Chapin-May Foundation of Illinois

Lutheran School of Theology ($15,000) see Werner Foundation, Clara and Spencer

Lutheran Social Service of Illinois ($12,000) see Aigner

Lutheran Social Services of Illinois ($4,000) see Elgin Sweeper Co.

Lyric Opera of Chicago ($3,000) see Akzo America

Lyric Opera of Chicago — support for opera programs ($60,000) see AON Corp.

Lyric Opera of Chicago ($5,000) see Bergner Co., P.A.

Lyric Opera of Chicago ($5,000) see Chicago Board of Trade

Lyric Opera of Chicago ($200,000) see Crown Memorial, Arie and Ida

Lyric Opera of Chicago ($50,000) see Farley Industries

Lyric Opera of Chicago ($100,000) see Fisher Foundation, Gramma

Lyric Opera of Chicago ($9,022) see Frank Fund, Zollie and Elaine

Lyric Opera of Chicago ($115,000) see Frankel Foundation

Lyric Opera of Chicago ($20,000) see Galvin Foundation, Robert W.

Lyric Opera of Chicago ($4,687) see Goldman Foundation, Morris and Rose

Lyric Opera of Chicago ($5,000) see H. B. B. Foundation

Lyric Opera of Chicago ($80,000) see Heller Foundation, Walter E.

Lyric Opera of Chicago ($2,000) see Kearney Inc., A.T.

Lyric Opera of Chicago — educational programs ($25,000) see Kemper National Insurance Cos.

Lyric Opera of Chicago ($10,000) see Knowles Foundation

Lyric Opera of Chicago ($50,000) see Marshall Field's

Lyric Opera of Chicago ($25,000) see Mayer Charitable Trust, Oscar G. & Elsa S.

Lyric Opera of Chicago ($25,000) see Mitchell Family Foundation, Bernard and Marjorie

Lyric Opera of Chicago ($10,000) see Morton International

Lyric Opera of Chicago ($50,000) see Regenstein Foundation

Lyric Opera of Chicago ($50,000) see Ryan Foundation, Patrick G. and Shirley W.

Lyric Opera of Chicago ($12,500) see Searle & Co., G.D.

Lyric Opera of Chicago ($5,000) see Shapiro Family Foundation, Soretta and Henry

Lyric Opera of Chicago ($25,000) see Silver Spring Foundation

Lyric Opera of Chicago ($301,200) see Stern Foundation for the Arts, Richard J.

Lyric Opera of Chicago ($2,500) see Stone Family Foundation, Jerome H.

Lyric Opera of Chicago ($36,474) see Whitman Corp.

Lyric Opera of Chicago ($5,000) see Wurlitzer Foundation, Farny R.

Lyric Opera of Chicago — first payment of a two-year, $200,000 grant for sponsorship of Mefistofele and for operating support ($120,000) see Sara Lee Corp.

Lyric Opera Company ($50,000) see Thoresen Foundation

Lyric Opera — 1991-92 season support ($25,000) see AMR Corp.

Lyric Opera's Greater Opera Fund ($1,000) see Boler Co.

Macon County Heart Association ($8,750) see Staley, Jr. Foundation, A. E.

Make-A-Wish Foundation of Northern Illinois ($15,000) see Driehaus Foundation, Richard H.

Maram's ($5,000) see Rosenthal Foundation, Benjamin J.

March of Dimes ($15,000) see Chicago Sun-Times, Inc.

Marklund Children's Home ($25,000) see Bersted Foundation

Marmion Military Academy — general fund; scholarships ($50,000) see Bellamah Foundation, Dale J.

Mary Lawrence Chapter of the Jewish Children's Bureau ($600) see Mitchell Family Foundation, Bernard and Marjorie

Maryville Academy ($20,000) see Galter Foundation

Maryville Academy ($15,000) see Schneider Foundation, Robert E.

Maryville City of Youth ($9,500) see Blair and Co., William

Maryville City of Youth ($29,075) see Brunswick Corp.

Maryville City of Youth ($20,000) see Driehaus Foundation, Richard H.

Maryville City of Youth ($5,000) see Fraida Foundation

Maryville City of Youth ($5,000) see Hay Foundation, John I.

Mattoon Public Library ($5,000) see Lumpkin Foundation

Max McGraw Wildlife Foundation ($3,200) see Hoffer Plastics Corp.

Max McGraw Wildlife Foundation ($25,000) see McGraw Foundation

McCormick Theological Seminary ($5,000) see Chapin-May Foundation of Illinois

McCormick Theological Seminary ($26,305) see Erickson Charitable Fund, Eben W.

McCormick Theological Seminary ($25,659) see Hallett Charitable Trust

McCormick Theological Seminary ($25,658) see

Illinois (cont.)

Hallett Charitable Trust, Jessie F.

McCormick Theological Seminary ($20,000) see Replogle Foundation, Luther I.

McDermott Foundation ($1,000) see Baum Family Fund, Alvin H.

McDermott Foundation ($50,000) see Driehaus Foundation, Richard H.

McKendree College — scholarship ($10,000) see Monticello College Foundation

McKendree College ($15,000) see Schmidt Charitable Foundation, William E.

McLean County Illinois Historical Society ($300,000) see State Farm Mutual Automobile Insurance Co.

McLean County United Way ($86,500) see State Farm Mutual Automobile Insurance Co.

McLean County Youth Hockey ($4,000) see Shirk Foundation, Russell and Betty

Meadville Theological School ($2,000) see Chapin-May Foundation of Illinois

Memorial Medical Center ($10,000) see House Educational Trust, Susan Cook

Mendelssohn Club ($2,500) see AMCORE Bank, N.A. Rockford

Mental Health Association of Greater Chicago ($2,000) see Psychists

Mental Health Association in Illinois — fund-raisers support/underwriting ($34,700) see Duchossois Industries

Mercy Boys Home ($100,000) see Mazza Foundation

Mercy Foundation ($25,000) see Shaw Foundation, Walden W. and Jean Young

Mercy Hospital — support for medical center ($50,000) see AON Corp.

Mercy Hospital and Medical Center ($11,975) see American National Bank & Trust Co. of Chicago

Mercy Hospital and Medical Center ($54,000) see Bowyer Foundation, Ambrose and Gladys

Mercy Hospital and Medical Center ($50,000) see Buehler Foundation, A. C.

Merit Music Program ($8,000) see Replogle Foundation, Luther I.

Merit Music Program ($6,000) see Wurlitzer Foundation, Farny R.

Metro Chicago Youth for Christ — for missions ($5,000) see Epaphroditus Foundation

Metropolitan Chicago United Way/Crusade of Mercy ($200,000) see Quaker Oats Co.

Metropolitan Crusade of Mercy ($59,945) see DeSoto

Metropolitan Planning Council ($30,000) see Sprague Memorial Institute, Otho S. A.

Michael Reese Hospital and Medical Center ($15,000) see Blum Foundation, Nathan and Emily S.

Michael Reese Hospital and Medical Center ($128,325) see Rothschild Foundation, Hulda B. and Maurice L.

Mill ($3,334) see AMCORE Bank, N.A. Rockford

Mill ($2,000) see Elco Charitable Foundation

Mill ($3,333) see First National Bank & Trust Co. of Rockford

Mill ($2,000) see Rockford Products Corp.

The Mill — capital ($26,700) see Sundstrand Corp.

The Mill ($20,000) see Woodward Governor Co.

Millikin University ($50,000) see Griswold Foundation, John C.

Millikin University ($2,250) see Hopper Memorial Foundation, Bertrand

Millikin University ($3,175) see Mueller Co.

Millikin University ($80,750) see Staley, Jr. Foundation, A. E.

Miryam's House of Transition ($3,000) see Lapham-Hickey Steel Corp.

Misericordia ($6,000) see Chicago Board of Trade

Misericordia Heart of Mercy ($10,000) see Best Foundation, Walter J. and Edith E.

Misericordia Heart of Mercy ($200,000) see Coleman Foundation

Misericordia Heart of Mercy ($1,000) see Gavin Foundation, James and Zita

Misericordia Heart of Mercy ($10,000) see Petersen Foundation, Esper A.

Misericordia Heart of Mercy — general support ($50,000) see Solo Cup Co.

Misericordia Heart of Mercy — capital campaign; to partially cover the cost of construction of an Independent Living Apartment Complex for young adults with mild to moderate mental disabilities ($150,000) see Field Foundation of Illinois

Misericordia Home ($32,500) see Bowyer Foundation, Ambrose and Gladys

Misericordia Home ($100,000) see Brach Foundation, Helen

Misericordia Home ($20,000) see Dower Foundation, Thomas W.

Misericordia Home ($2,000) see Eisenberg Foundation, George M.

Misericordia Home ($100,000) see Mazza Foundation

Monmouth College ($100,000) see Wells Foundation, Franklin H. and Ruth L.

Moody Bible Institute ($4,000) see Christian Workers Foundation

Moody Bible Institute ($7,943) see Duncan Trust, James R.

Moody Bible Institute ($48,110) see Hallett Charitable Trust, Jessie F.

Moody Bible Institute ($500,000) see Solheim Foundation

Moody Bible Institute — George Sweeting Center Lecture Hall ($100,000) see Chatlos Foundation

Moody Bible Institute — Library Learning Resource Center ($750,000) see Crowell Trust, Henry P. and Susan C.

Moody Bible Institute Religious Work ($25,000) see Tibstra Charitable Foundation, Thomas and Gertrude

Morris Animal Foundation Digit Fund ($3,000) see Cox Charitable Trust, A. G.

Mount Carroll Fire Department ($1,200) see Anderson Industries

Mount Sinai Hospital Medical Center ($250,000) see Crown Memorial, Arie and Ida

Mount Sinai Hospital Medical Center — for capital improvements of its facility and acquisition of new medical equipment ($100,000) see Field Foundation of Illinois

Mount Sinai Hospital Medical Center ($250,000) see McCormick Tribune Foundation, Robert R.

Mundelein College ($75,000) see Brach Foundation, Helen

Mundelein College Chicago ($5,000) see Gellert Foundation, Celia Berta

Museum of Contemporary Art ($111,100) see Alsdorf Foundation

Museum of Contemporary Art ($75,000) see American National Bank & Trust Co. of Chicago

Museum of Contemporary Art ($50,000) see Barker Welfare Foundation

Museum of Contemporary Art ($4,105) see Berger Foundation, Albert E.

Museum of Contemporary Art ($5,400) see Cole Taylor Financial Group

Museum of Contemporary Art ($3,950) see Foster Charitable Trust

Museum of Contemporary Art ($3,700) see Goldman Foundation, Morris and Rose

Museum of Contemporary Art ($61,690) see Heller Foundation, Walter E.

Museum of Contemporary Art ($151,000) see Manilow Foundation, Nathan

Museum of Contemporary Art ($20,000) see Mitchell Family Foundation, Bernard and Marjorie

Museum of Contemporary Art ($67,125) see Pritzker Foundation

Museum of Contemporary Art ($4,660) see Stone Family Foundation, Jerome H.

Museum of Contemporary Art ($1,250) see Swift Co. Inc., John S.

Museum of Contemporary Art — first payment of a two-year, $250,000 grant to support the Museum's 25th anniversary exhibition, Art at the Armory: Occupied Territory, and for operating support ($135,000) see Sara Lee Corp.

Museum of Fine Arts ($2,500) see H. B. B. Foundation

Museum of Science and Industry ($2,500) see Alsdorf Foundation

Museum of Science and Industry ($7,500) see Blair and Co., William

Museum of Science and Industry ($6,000) see Chicago Board of Trade

Museum of Science and Industry ($5,000) see Hoover Foundation, H. Earl

Museum of Science and Industry ($25,000) see Lurie Foundation, Louis R.

Museum of Science and Industry ($100,000) see Morton International

Music of the Baroque ($2,500) see Forest Fund

Music Teachers National Association ($16,000) see Wurlitzer Foundation, Farny R.

NAED Education Foundation ($2,500) see Ideal Industries

NALL Association ($123,082) see GEICO Corp.

NALL Safety Association ($123,152) see GEICO Corp.

Naperville Heritage Society ($6,000) see Kelly Foundation, T. Lloyd

Naral Foundation ($12,500) see Levy Foundation, Charles and Ruth

Naral Foundation ($5,000) see Pettus Crowe Foundation

National Center for Effective Schools ($7,500) see Special People In Need

National College of Education ($5,000) see Chicago Sun-Times, Inc.

National College of Education ($36,390) see Cohn Family Foundation, Robert and Terri

National College of Education ($2,500) see Kearney Inc., A.T.

National College of Education ($100,000) see Ryan Foundation, Patrick G. and Shirley W.

National Committee for the Prevention of Child Abuse ($25,000) see Lederer Foundation, Francis L.

National Committee for the Prevention of Child Abuse ($266,568) see Pesch Family Foundation

National Conference of Christians and Jews ($5,250) see Material Service Corp.

National Fish and Wildlife Foundation — prairie farming program ($282,000) see Waterfowl Research Foundation

National Kidney Foundation ($10,000) see Brunner Foundation, Fred J.

National Lakotak Center ($25,000) see Quaker Oats Co.

National Lekotek Center ($5,000) see Aigner

National-Louis University — support for the classroom libraries program ($35,500) see Chicago Tribune Co.

National Louis University ($282,000) see Louis Foundation, Michael W.

National-Louis University-College of Management and Business — interim support for new business faculty ($25,000) see Kemper National Insurance Cos.

National-Louis University — for the Parent-School Community Reading Project ($50,000) see Fry Foundation, Lloyd A.

National Merit Scholarship ($10,900) see American Optical Corp.

National Merit Scholarship ($161,250) see Avon Products

National Merit Scholarship ($239,848) see Bristol-Myers Squibb Co.

National Merit Scholarship ($30,820) see Charities Foundation

National Merit Scholarship ($11,728) see Continental Grain Co.

National Merit Scholarship ($8,600) see Hubbell Inc.

National Merit Scholarship ($43,787) see National Starch & Chemical Corp.

National Merit Scholarship ($6,420) see Quanex Corp.

National Merit Scholarship ($7,250) see Robbins & Myers, Inc.

National Merit Scholarship ($41,135) see USG Corp.

National Merit Scholarship ($9,250) see Wolf Foundation, Benjamin and Fredora K.

National Merit Scholarship Corporation ($23,000) see Acushnet Co.

National Merit Scholarship Corporation ($14,920) see Alco Standard Corp.

National Merit Scholarship Corporation ($29,700) see AMETEK

National Merit Scholarship Corporation — scholarships ($25,330) see AMR Corp.

National Merit Scholarship Corporation ($56,199) see Armstrong World Industries Inc.

National Merit Scholarship Corporation ($25,740) see Armstrong World Industries Inc.

National Merit Scholarship Corporation ($3,630) see ASARCO

National Merit Scholarship Corporation — scholarship ($92,655) see Bemis Company

National Merit Scholarship Corporation ($29,250) see BFGoodrich

National Merit Scholarship Corporation ($13,340) see Blue Bell, Inc.

National Merit Scholarship Corporation ($7,365) see Central Soya Co.

National Merit Scholarship Corporation ($141,760) see CIGNA Corp.

National Merit Scholarship Corporation — scholarships ($33,790) see Consolidated Papers

National Merit Scholarship Corporation ($178,957) see Continental Corp.

National Merit Scholarship Corporation ($34,260) see Cooper Industries

National Merit Scholarship Corporation ($79,117) see Crum and Forster

National Merit Scholarship Corporation — scholarship fund ($53,630) see Deluxe Corp.

National Merit Scholarship Corporation ($22,313) see DeVlieg Foundation, Charles

National Merit Scholarship Corporation ($220,345) see Dow Jones & Co.

National Merit Scholarship Corporation ($94,840) see Dresser Industries

National Merit Scholarship Corporation ($37,745) see Dun & Bradstreet Corp.

National Merit Scholarship Corporation ($4,000) see Florida Steel Corp.

National Merit Scholarship Corporation ($37,220) see FMC Corp.

National Merit Scholarship Corporation ($28,860) see GenCorp

National Merit Scholarship Corporation ($244,182) see Georgia-Pacific Corp.

National Merit Scholarship Corporation ($114,425) see Georgia-Pacific Corp.

National Merit Scholarship Corporation ($114,956) see Gleason Memorial Fund

National Merit Scholarship Corporation ($96,120) see Harsco Corp.

National Merit Scholarship Corporation ($25,305) see Illinois Tool Works

National Merit Scholarship Corporation ($28,340) see Inland Steel Industries

National Merit Scholarship Corporation ($23,650) see Kennametal

National Merit Scholarship Corporation ($24,910) see Lehigh Portland Cement Co.

National Merit Scholarship Corporation ($27,315) see Lennox International, Inc.

National Merit Scholarship Corporation ($18,276) see Liberty Corp.

National Merit Scholarship Corporation ($46,580) see Life Investors Insurance Company of America

National Merit Scholarship Corporation ($50,290) see Lipton, Thomas J.

National Merit Scholarship Corporation ($110,900) see Lockheed Corp.

National Merit Scholarship Corporation ($62,145) see Loews Corp.

National Merit Scholarship Corporation ($39,872) see LTV Corp.

National Merit Scholarship Corporation ($98,095) see McGraw-Hill

National Merit Scholarship Corporation ($101,620) see McKesson Corp.

National Merit Scholarship Corporation ($87,285) see Michigan Bell Telephone Co.

National Merit Scholarship Corporation ($211,556) see Mobil Oil Corp.

National Merit Scholarship Corporation ($219,506) see Monsanto Co.

National Merit Scholarship Corporation ($87,285) see Motorola

National Merit Scholarship Corporation ($103,436) see Norfolk Southern Corp.

National Merit Scholarship Corporation ($43,830) see Occidental Petroleum Corp.

National Merit Scholarship Corporation ($49,390) see Paramount Communications Inc.

National Merit Scholarship Corporation ($56,040) see Payne Foundation, Frank E. and Seba B.

National Merit Scholarship Corporation ($850,630) see PepsiCo

National Merit Scholarship Corporation ($280,630) see PPG Industries

National Merit Scholarship Corporation ($80,413) see Quaker Oats Co.

National Merit Scholarship Corporation ($46,225) see Ralston Purina Co.

National Merit Scholarship Corporation ($99,803) see Santa Fe Pacific Corp.

National Merit Scholarship Corporation ($63,307) see Schering-Plough Corp.

National Merit Scholarship Corporation ($449,811) see State Farm Mutual Automobile Insurance Co.

National Merit Scholarship Corporation ($65,070) see Transamerica Corp.

National Merit Scholarship Corporation ($215,617) see Weyerhaeuser Co.

National Merit Scholarship — scholarship awards for children of Owens-Corning Foundation and subsidiary employees based upon National Merit standards plus administration fee ($5,750) see Owens-Corning Fiberglas Corp.

National Merit Scholarships — scholarship ($353,498) see RJR Nabisco Inc.

National Multiple Sclerosis Society ($1,500) see Kearney Inc., A.T.

National Safety Council ($500) see Akzo America

National Sigma Chi Foundation ($25,000) see Huntsman Foundation, Jon and Karen

National Society of Fund Raising Executives ($30) see Pesch Family Foundation

National Strategy Forum ($25,000) see Galvin Foundation, Robert W.

National Strategy Forum ($88,300) see Pritzker Foundation

National Strategy Forum ($25,000) see Ryan Foundation, Patrick G. and Shirley W.

National Training and Information Center ($75,000) see Allstate Insurance Co.

National Training and Information Center — participation in conference ($8,000) see Piton Foundation

Nature Conservancy ($1,000) see Atwood Foundation

Nature Conservancy ($5,000) see Haffner Foundation

Nature Conservancy ($20,000) see Wenger Foundation, Henry L. and Consuelo S.

Nature of Illinois Foundation ($10,000) see Donnelley Foundation, Gaylord and Dorothy

Neighborhood Boys Club ($15,000) see Sulzer Family Foundation

Neighborhood Housing Chicago ($5,000) see McVay Foundation

Neighborhood Housing Services ($3,000) see Boulevard Bank, N.A.

Neighborhood Housing Services ($3,000) see Boulevard Foundation

Neighborhood Housing Services of Chicago ($20,000) see Harris Trust & Savings Bank

Neighborhood Housing Services of Chicago ($20,000) see Northern Trust Co.

Neighborhood Housing Services of Chicago — low/moderate-income housing ($30,000) see Continental Bank N.A.

Neighborhood Housing Services of Chicago — (WLS-TV Special) ($70,000) see Allstate Insurance Co.

Neighborhood Institute ($20,000) see Harris Trust & Savings Bank

Neighborhood Institute ($20,000) see Industrial Bank of Japan Trust Co.

Neopolitan Lighthouse ($10,000) see CRI Charitable Trust

New American Theatre ($2,500) see Rockford Acromatics Products Co./Aircraft Gear Corp.

New Moms — general support ($8,000) see Stone Foundation, W. Clement and Jessie V.

Newberry Library ($25,000) see Allen-Heath Memorial Foundation

Newberry Library — for the endowment fund for the family history department ($15,000) see Allen-Heath Memorial Foundation

Newberry Library ($10,000) see Boothroyd Foundation, Charles H. and Bertha L.

Newberry Library ($9,000) see Haffner Foundation

Newberry Library ($250,000) see Regenstein Foundation

Newberry Library — Post Doctoral Fellowship for women ($12,500) see Monticello College Foundation

NHS Redevelopment Corporation — low/moderate-income housing ($125,000) see Continental Bank N.A.

NJATC Apprentice Program ($2,600) see Ideal Industries

North American Wildlife Foundation ($2,500) see Boulevard Bank, N.A.

North American Wildlife Foundation ($2,500) see Boulevard Foundation

North American Wildlife Foundation ($52,500) see Ingersoll Milling Machine Co.

North American Wildlife Foundation — wild mallard program ($175,000) see Waterfowl Research Foundation

North American Wildlife Foundation, Delta Station ($1,500) see Ingersoll Milling Machine Co.

North Avenue Day Nursery ($25,000) see Kemper Educational and Charitable Fund

North Avenue Day Nursery ($10,000) see Silver Spring Foundation

North Central College ($10,200) see Rockford Acromatics Products Co./Aircraft Gear Corp.

North Lakeside Cultural Center ($4,000) see Berger Foundation, Albert E.

North Park College ($7,000) see Bjorkman Foundation

North Park College ($3,000) see Douglas Corp.

North Park College ($10,000) see Sulzer Family Foundation

North Park College ($8,000) see Wurlitzer Foundation, Farny R.

North Park College and Theological Seminary ($4,000) see Chapin-May Foundation of Illinois

North Rockford Convalescent Home ($3,333) see AMCORE Bank, N.A. Rockford

North Rockford Convalescent Home ($3,150) see Rockford Acromatics Products Co./Aircraft Gear Corp.

North Shore Congregation Israel ($20,092) see Frank Fund, Zollie and Elaine

North Shore Friends of Multiple Sclerosis ($500) see Baum Family Fund, Alvin H.

Northeastern Illinois University — to continue its urban principal professional development program, Project Co-Lead ($115,000) see Joyce Foundation

Northern Baptist Theological Seminary ($650) see Arbie Mineral Feed Co.

Northern Baptist Theological Seminary ($5,124) see Combs Foundation, Earle M. and Virginia M.

Northern Illinois Blood Bank ($2,500) see Elco Charitable Foundation

Northern Illinois Blood Bank ($3,000) see Rockford Acromatics Products Co./Aircraft Gear Corp.

Northern Illinois Blood Bank ($2,000) see Rockford Products Corp.

Northern Illinois University ($75,000) see Square D Co.

Northfield Community Church ($2,650) see Keating Family Foundation

Northwest Home for the Aged ($35,000) see Eisenberg Foundation, George M.

Northwest Kidney Foundation ($3,000) see Cox Charitable Trust, A. G.

Northwest Medical Library ($1,895,995) see Galter Foundation

Northwest Memorial Hospital ($300,000) see Galter Foundation

Northwest Memorial Museum ($3,000) see Cox Charitable Trust, A. G.

Northwest Suburban Aid for the Retarded ($20,000) see Petersen Foundation, Esper A.

Northwest Suburban Council ($1,250) see CRL Inc.

Northwestern Illinois Special Olympics ($500) see Sjostrom & Sons

Northwestern Medical School ($30,000) see Prentice Foundation, Abra

Northwestern Memorial Foundation ($20,000) see Davee Foundation

Northwestern Memorial Foundation — general fund ($15,000) see Shaw Foundation, Arch W.

Northwestern Memorial Foundation — endowment fund ($10,000) see Shaw Foundation, Arch W.

Northwestern Memorial Foundation ($30,000) see Siragusa Foundation

Northwestern Memorial Foundation ($4,500) see Thorson Foundation

Northwestern Memorial Foundation ($35,000) see Wrigley Co., Wm. Jr.

Northwestern Memorial Hospital ($50,000) see Bere Foundation

Northwestern Memorial Hospital ($100,000) see Blum-Kovler Foundation

Northwestern Memorial Hospital ($2,000) see Dick Family Foundation

Northwestern Memorial Hospital ($136,000) see Frankel Foundation

Northwestern Memorial Hospital ($20,000) see Mayer Charitable Trust, Oscar G. & Elsa S.

Northwestern Memorial Hospital ($20,000) see Silver Spring Foundation

Northwestern Memorial Hospital (Prentice Hospital) ($75,000) see Buchanan Family Foundation

Northwestern Memorial Hospital — capital campaign to support the costs of expansion of Prentice Women's Hospital and Maternity Center ($100,000) see Field Foundation of Illinois

Northwestern Memorial Hospital — Wesley Pavilion ($20,000) see Silver Spring Foundation

Northwestern School ($12,250) see Schiff, Hardin & Waite

Northwestern University ($10,000) see Alexander Charitable Foundation

Northwestern University ($1,595) see Alsdorf Foundation

Northwestern University ($10,000) see Amsted Industries

Northwestern University ($3,464,826) see Annenberg Foundation

Northwestern University ($2,000) see Berkey Foundation, Peter

Northwestern University ($50,000) see Borg-Warner Corp.

Northwestern University ($2,500) see Boulevard Bank, N.A.

Northwestern University ($2,500) see Boulevard Foundation

Northwestern University ($1,000) see Bristol Savings Bank

Northwestern University ($400) see Chiquita Brands Co.

Northwestern University ($250,000) see Crown Charitable Fund, Edward A.

Northwestern University ($300,000) see Crown Memorial, Arie and Ida

Northwestern University ($10,000) see DeSoto

Northwestern University ($1,750,000) see Feinberg Foundation, Joseph and Bessie

Northwestern University ($23,615) see First Chicago

Northwestern University ($20,000) see Harris Foundation, J. Ira and Nicki

Northwestern University ($100,000) see I and G Charitable Foundation

Northwestern University ($70,056) see Inland Steel Industries

Northwestern University ($100,000) see Kellstadt Foundation

Northwestern University ($1,500) see Kelly Foundation, T. Lloyd

Northwestern University ($25,000) see Kemper Educational and Charitable Fund

Northwestern University ($20,000) see Knowles Foundation

Illinois (cont.)

Northwestern University ($35,000) see Lebus Trust, Bertha

Northwestern University ($525) see Leesona Corp.

Northwestern University ($7,500) see Lehmann Foundation, Otto W.

Northwestern University — endowed law school chair and research fund ($250,000) see Leighton-Oare Foundation

Northwestern University ($2,000) see Louis Foundation, Michael W.

Northwestern University ($20,000) see Mayer Charitable Trust, Oscar G. & Elsa S.

Northwestern University ($2,000,000) see McCormick Tribune Foundation, Robert R.

Northwestern University ($50,000) see Mitchell Family Foundation, Bernard and Marjorie

Northwestern University ($250,000) see Norris Foundation, Dellora A. and Lester J.

Northwestern University ($250,000) see Norris Foundation, Dellora A. and Lester J.

Northwestern University ($20,000) see Northern Trust Co.

Northwestern University ($12,832) see Rothschild Foundation, Hulda B. and Maurice L.

Northwestern University ($72,000) see Schneider Foundation, Robert E.

Northwestern University ($5,000) see Schneider Foundation, Robert E.

Northwestern University ($2,000) see Sehn Foundation

Northwestern University ($50,000) see Shapiro Family Foundation, Soretta and Henry

Northwestern University ($20,000) see Silver Spring Foundation

Northwestern University ($25,000) see Ward Foundation, A. Montgomery

Northwestern University ($25,000) see Ward Foundation, A. Montgomery

Northwestern University ($20,050) see Whitman Corp.

Northwestern University — capital campaign for $11.3 million to construct and equip a new building for its Institute of Modern Communications ($100,000) see Field Foundation of Illinois

Northwestern University Center on Aging ($367,500) see Buehler Foundation, A. C.

Northwestern University Dental School ($26,305) see Erickson Charitable Fund, Eben W.

Northwestern University Jewish Studies Program ($20,000) see Kaplan Foundation, Mayer and Morris

Northwestern University, Kellogg Graduate School of Management ($28,000) see Hartmarx Corp.

Northwestern University Kellogg School ($500,000) see Davee Foundation

Northwestern University (Kellogg School of Management) ($150,000) see Buchanan Family Foundation

Northwestern University Medical School ($60,000) see Bauer Foundation, M. R.

Northwestern University Medical School ($5,500) see Goldenberg Foundation, Max

Northwestern University Medical School ($175,000) see Sprague Memorial Institute, Otho S. A.

Northwestern University — Medill School of Journalism ($400,000) see McCormick Tribune Foundation, Robert R.

Northwestern University School of Law ($61,000) see Bauer Foundation, M. R.

Northwestern University School of Law ($7,820) see Mansfield Foundation, Albert and Anne

Northwestern University School of Law ($200,000) see Pritzker Foundation

Northwestern University School of Law ($10,000) see Siragusa Foundation

Northwestern University School of Management ($10,000) see Leo Burnett Co.

Northwestern University — "The Effects of Spatial and Skill Mismatches on Minority Employment" ($100,260) see Sage Foundation, Russell

Northwestern University-Transportation Center ($7,500) see American President Cos.

Oak Park and River Forest ($3,000) see Borwell Charitable Foundation

Oak Park Temple ($10,000) see Sang Foundation, Elsie O. and Philip D.

Oblate Media and Communications Corporation ($15,000) see Doty Family Foundation

Occupational Development Center ($2,000) see Shirk Foundation, Russell and Betty

Off the Street Club — offering teens a chance to earn $5-10 per week at the club by assisting with day care, arts and crafts and games ($4,000) see Gannett Co.

Off-the-Street Club ($5,000) see Boulevard Bank, N.A.

Off-the-Street Club ($5,000) see Boulevard Foundation

Off-the-Street Club ($15,425) see Foote, Cone & Belding Communications

Old St. Patrick's Church ($100,000) see Mazza Foundation

Old St. Patrick's Renaissance Campaign — general support ($50,000) see Solo Cup Co.

Old St. Patrick's School — Children at Crossroads Foundation ($75,000) see O'Shaughnessy Foundation, I. A.

Olin Sang Ruby Union Institute ($30,000) see Shapiro Foundation, Charles and M. R.

Olive Branch — toward building purchase ($30,000) see Crowell Trust, Henry P. and Susan C.

O'Neal School ($10,000) see Ceco Corp.

Operation Exodus ($10,000) see Sang Foundation, Elsie O. and Philip D.

Opportunities Industrialization ($2,500) see AMCORE Bank, N.A. Rockford

Opportunity ($10,000) see Bere Foundation

Opportunity International ($3,500) see Combs Foundation, Earle M. and Virginia M.

Opportunity International — business in underdeveloped countries ($25,000) see Logan Foundation, E. J.

Opportunity International — business in underdeveloped countries ($25,000) see Logan Foundation, E. J.

Opportunity International — creating jobs in Third World countries ($25,000) see Hoffman Foundation, Maximillian E. and Marion O.

Orchard Village ($5,000) see Aigner

Orchard Village ($6,000) see NutraSweet Co.

Orchestral Association ($10,000) see Amsted Industries

Orchestral Association ($50,000) see Bere Foundation

Orchestral Association ($30,000) see Cheney Foundation, Elizabeth F.

Orchestral Association ($45,300) see Cooper Charitable Trust, Richard H.

Orchestral Association ($25,000) see Farley Industries

Orchestral Association ($25,000) see Farley Industries

Orchestral Association ($7,011) see Frank Fund, Zollie and Elaine

Orchestral Association ($250,000) see McCormick Tribune Foundation, Robert R.

Orchestral Association ($75,000) see Regenstein Foundation

Orchestral Association ($51,330) see Rothschild Foundation, Hulda B. and Maurice L.

Orchestral Association ($5,000) see Sang Foundation, Elsie O. and Philip D.

Orchestral Association — funding for ensemble program outreach activities ($100,000) see Scholl Foundation, Dr.

Orchestral Association ($10,000) see Shapiro Family Foundation, Soretta and Henry

Orchestral Association, Chicago Symphony ($20,000) see Mayer Charitable Trust, Oscar G. & Elsa S.

Organization of the Northeast — general operating support ($15,000) see Wieboldt Foundation

Orr Community Academy — education ($42,500) see Continental Bank N.A.

Ounce of Prevention Fund ($3,000) see Brand Cos.

Ounce of Prevention Fund ($100,000) see Davis Family - W.D. Charities, Tine W.

Ounce of Prevention Fund ($25,000) see Northern Trust Co.

Ounce of Prevention Fund ($325,000) see Pittway Corp.

Ounce of Prevention Fund ($6,000) see Relations Foundation

Ounce of Prevention Fund - Beethoven Project ($15,000) see GATX Corp.

Our Lady of Lourdes Grade School ($2,500) see Sulzer Family Foundation

Our Lady of Perpetual Help Church ($40,000) see Rice Foundation

P. A. Peterson Home ($25,000) see Woodward Governor Co.

P.A. Peterson Home ($3,333) see AMCORE Bank, N.A. Rockford

P.A. Peterson Home ($500) see Sjostrom & Sons

Pacific Garden Mission ($26,305) see Erickson Charitable Fund, Eben W.

Page Conference Center ($5,000) see Hoover Foundation, H. Earl

Palatine Paramedics ($200) see Florsheim Shoe Co.

Park Ridge Center — to establish a Fellowship in Ethics, Values and The Meaning of Aging ($225,000) see Retirement Research Foundation

Park Shelter ($2,000) see Harrison Foundation, Fred G.

Park United Methodist Church ($2,000) see Shirk Foundation, Russell and Betty

Parkview Home-Rose Eisenberg Fund ($5,000) see Eisenberg Foundation, George M.

Paulina House Shelter ($30,000) see Driehaus Foundation, Richard H.

Peacock Camp ($5,000) see Allyn Foundation

Peacock Camp — camp for handicapped children ($34,128) see Logan Foundation, E. J.

Peacock Camp ($40,000) see Rice Foundation

Peacock Camp Crippled Child ($5,000) see Lehmann Foundation, Otto W.

Pediatric Rheumatology/RND Research ($10,000) see Levy Foundation, Charles and Ruth

People's Reinvestment and Development Effort ($12,000) see Harris Trust & Savings Bank

Peoria Symphony Orchestra ($2,230) see Foster and Gallagher

Performance Community ($1,000) see GSC Enterprises

Phi Delta Kappa ($2,500) see Anderson Industries

Physicians for Social Responsibility ($25,000) see CRI Charitable Trust

Pine Rest Christian Hospital Association ($30,000) see Van Andel Foundation, Jay and Betty

Planned Parenthood ($13,000) see Beidler Charitable Trust, Francis

Planned Parenthood ($10,000) see CRI Charitable Trust

Planned Parenthood ($5,000) see Forest Fund

Planned Parenthood ($9,000) see Kelly Foundation, T. Lloyd

Planned Parenthood ($15,000) see New Prospect Foundation

Planned Parenthood ($343,420) see Rosenbaum Foundation, Paul and Gabriella

Planned Parenthood ($20,000) see Silver Spring Foundation

Planned Parenthood Association ($500) see Herald News

Planned Parenthood Association, Chicago Area ($107,000) see Bauer Foundation, M. R.

Planned Parenthood Federation of America ($100,000) see Offield Family Foundation

Polio Plus ($5,000) see Fenton Foundation

Polio Plus/Rotary International ($14,344) see Mayer Foundation, James and Eva

Pontiac Alanon Club ($2,500) see Camp and Bennet Humiston Trust, Apollos

Pontiac Area Chamber of Commerce ($5,000) see Camp and Bennet Humiston Trust, Apollos

Pontiac Junior Baseball ($15,000) see Camp and Bennet Humiston Trust, Apollos

Pontiac Neediest Kids Fund ($3,000) see Camp and Bennet Humiston Trust, Apollos

Pontiac Township High School ($30,000) see Camp and Bennet Humiston Trust, Apollos

Pot of Gold Golf Classic ($500) see Pesch Family Foundation

Presbyterian Home — endowment fund ($150,000) see Grainger Foundation

Presbyterian Home ($4,500) see Louis Foundation, Michael W.

Presbyterian Home ($25,000) see Seabury Foundation

Presbyterian Home Evanston — for the Alzheimer's program ($10,000) see Butz Foundation

President's Fund ($2,000) see Baum Family Fund, Alvin H.

Prince of Peace United Methodist Church ($7,500) see Special People In Need

Principia College ($11,100) see Robinson Foundation

Pritzker Family Philanthropic Fund ($7,600,000) see Pritzker Foundation

Pro Bond Advocates ($2,000) see Mansfield Foundation, Albert and Anne

Pro Bono Advocates ($5,000) see Butler Family Foundation, George W. and Gladys S.

Profit Sharing Research Foundation ($8,333) see Harland Co., John H.

Profit Sharing Research Foundation ($25,000) see Woodward Governor Co.

Project Match ($2,500) see Mansfield Foundation, Albert and Anne

Project Team — providing vocational skills training and placement in the field of auto mechanics to economically disadvantaged youth and adults ($75,000) see Fel-Pro Incorporated

Prologue ($3,000) see Chicago Sun-Times, Inc.

Protecting All Children Together ($4,400) see Geneseo Foundation

Protestant Community Services ($5,000) see Aldeen Charity Trust, G. W.

Public Interest ($3,500) see Schiff, Hardin & Waite

Public Television ($12,000) see Rhoades Fund, Otto L. and Hazel E.

Quad City Civic Center Authority ($500,000) see Deere & Co.

Queen of Angels Grade School ($2,500) see Sulzer Family Foundation

Quincy College ($30,000) see Moorman Manufacturing Co.

Quincy College ($10,000) see Moorman Manufacturing Co.

Quincy College Music Department — equipment ($5,000) see Quincy Newspapers

Quincy Community Little Theatre and Designees ($3,952) see Quincy Newspapers

Quincy Park District — riverfront development ($10,000) see Quincy Newspapers

Rainbow House ($10,000) see CRI Charitable Trust

Rainbow House — general operating support ($15,000) see GATX Corp.

Rainbows for the Children ($1,000) see Pesch Family Foundation

Ravenswood Hospital Medical Center ($15,000) see Kemper Educational and Charitable Fund

Ravinia Festival ($40,000) see Frankel Foundation

Ravinia Festival ($50,000) see Marshall Field's

Ravinia Festival Association ($7,000) see Blair and Co., William

Ravinia Festival Association ($20,000) see Cheney Foundation, Elizabeth F.

Ravinia Festival Association ($2,000) see Donnelley Foundation, Elliott and Ann

Ravinia Festival Association ($2,850) see Hales Charitable Fund

Ravinia Festival Association ($10,000) see Johnson Foundation, A. D.

Ravinia Festival Association ($8,000) see Kaplan Foundation, Mayer and Morris

Ravinia Festival Association ($15,000) see Pick, Jr. Fund, Albert

Ravinia Festival Association ($25,000) see Snite Foundation, Fred B.

Ravinia Festival Association ($2,400) see Stone Family Foundation, Jerome H.

Ravinia Festival Association ($2,000) see Stone Family Foundation, Norman H.

Ravinia Festival Association ($3,000) see United Conveyor Corp.

Ravinia Festival Association ($3,000) see Wood Foundation, Lester G.

Ravinia Festival Young Artist Endowment Fund ($15,000) see Johnson Foundation, A. D.

Reading is Fundamental in Chicago ($4,500) see Blum Foundation, Nathan and Emily S.

Recording for the Blind ($20,000) see Rhoades Fund, Otto L. and Hazel E.

Rehabilitation Institute ($25,000) see Best Foundation, Walter J. and Edith E.

Rehabilitation Institute ($25,000) see Blowitz-Ridgeway Foundation

Rehabilitation Institute ($20,000) see Davee Foundation

Rehabilitation Institute ($2,000) see Dick Family Foundation

Rehabilitation Institute ($250,000) see Galter Foundation

Rehabilitation Institute ($50,000) see Galvin Foundation, Robert W.

Rehabilitation Institute ($7,500) see H. B. B. Foundation

Rehabilitation Institute ($3,000) see Lehmann Foundation, Otto W.

Rehabilitation Institute ($5,000) see Mason Charitable Foundation

Rehabilitation Institute ($143,000) see Prince Trust, Abbie Norman

Rehabilitation Institute ($25,000) see Seabury Foundation

Rehabilitation Institute ($2,000) see Simpson Foundation, John M.

Rehabilitation Institute of Chicago ($75,000) see Buchanan Family Foundation

Rehabilitation Institute of Chicago ($100,000) see Coleman Foundation

Rehabilitation Institute of Chicago ($100,000) see Rice Foundation

Rehabilitation Institute Foundation ($100,000) see Frankel Foundation

Rehabilitation Institute Foundation ($2,500) see Thorson Foundation

Renaissance Society ($100) see LaSalle National Bank

Renew Moline ($100,000) see Deere & Co.

Research and Education Fund of the AAE ($10,000) see Dentsply International, Inc.

Resource Center for Handicapped ($1,000) see Baum Family Fund, Alvin H.

Rest Haven of Chicago ($250,000) see Prince Corp.

Rest Haven Christian Services ($5,000) see Huizenga Foundation, Jennie

Richland Community College ($10,000) see Staley, Jr. Foundation, A. E.

Richland Community College — Staley Scholarships ($40,000) see Staley Manufacturing Co., A.E.

River Bend United Way ($75,000) see Olin Corp.

River Front Museum Park — capital ($500,000) see Sundstrand Corp.

Riverfront Museum Park ($10,000) see AMCORE Bank, N.A. Rockford

Riverfront Museum Park ($20,000) see Anderson Industries

Riverfront Museum Park ($50,000) see CLARCOR

Riverfront Museum Park ($5,000) see Elco Charitable Foundation

Riverfront Museum Park ($4,000) see Rockford Products Corp.

Robert B. Huff Scholarship Foundation ($1,500) see Louis Foundation, Michael W.

Robert Crown Center for Health Education ($10,000) see Alexander Charitable Foundation

Robert Lurie Endowment Fund ($1,025,000) see Lurie Family Foundation

Robert Morris College ($4,800) see USG Corp.

Rock County Opportunities Industrialization Center ($33,333) see Beloit Foundation

Rock Valley College ($4,700) see Anderson Industries

Rock Valley College Foundation ($5,300) see Rockford Acromatics Products Co./Aircraft Gear Corp.

Rockford Area Convention and Visitors Bureau ($9,700) see Smith Charitable Trust

Rockford College ($7,000) see AMCORE Bank, N.A. Rockford

Rockford College ($5,250) see Anderson Industries

Rockford College ($5,000) see Anderson Industries

Rockford College ($400,000) see CLARCOR

Rockford College ($12,500) see Dillon Foundation

Rockford College ($5,000) see Elco Charitable Foundation

Rockford College — capital fund ($5,000) see First National Bank & Trust Co. of Rockford

Rockford College — operating fund ($5,000) see First National Bank & Trust Co. of Rockford

Rockford College — pledge ($50,000) see R. F. Foundation

Rockford College ($5,000) see Rockford Products Corp.

Rockford College ($20,000) see Smith Charitable Trust

Rockford College ($2,000) see Starrett Co., L.S.

Rockford College — capital ($25,000) see Sundstrand Corp.

Rockford Institute ($30,000) see Ingersoll Milling Machine Co.

Rockford Institute — educational ($70,000) see Swim Foundation, Arthur L.

Rockford Institute ($35,000) see Vollrath Co.

Rockford Institute ($20,000) see Vollrath Co.

Rockford Institute ($15,000) see Vollrath Co.

Rockford Institute ($4,000) see Wilbur Foundation, Marguerite Eyer

Rockford Memorial Development Fund ($1,500) see Quality Metal Finishing Foundation

Rockford Memorial Hospital ($5,000) see Smith Charitable Trust

Rockford Museum Park ($10,000) see Atwood Foundation

Rockford Neighborhood Development ($4,000) see First National Bank & Trust Co. of Rockford

Rockford Park District ($2,500) see Anderson Industries

Rockford Public Schools Foundation ($2,500) see Sjostrom & Sons

Rockford Symphony Orchestra ($2,000) see First National Bank & Trust Co. of Rockford

Rockford Symphony Orchestra ($2,500) see Warner Electric Brake & Clutch Co.

Rockford Women's Club ($6,425) see Rockford Acromatics Products Co./Aircraft Gear Corp.

Roger Baldwin Foundation ($12,500) see New Prospect Foundation

Roger Baldwin Foundation ($47,960) see Schiff, Hardin & Waite

Roger Baldwin Foundation ($12,040) see Schiff, Hardin & Waite

Roger McCormick Foundation ($50,000) see McCormick Foundation, Chauncey and Marion Deering

Roman Catholic Diocese ($10,000) see Bickerton Charitable Trust, Lydia H.

Romanian Missionary Society ($25,000) see M.E. Foundation

Romanian Missionary Society ($10,000) see Tyndale House Foundation

Ronald McDonald Children's Charities ($1,600) see Gateway Apparel

Ronald McDonald House ($9,000) see Hartmarx Corp.

Roosevelt University ($50,000) see Centel Corp.

Roosevelt University — journalism workshop for high school minority schools ($53,600) see Chicago Tribune Co.

Roosevelt University ($10,000) see Goldenberg Foundation, Max

Roosevelt University ($60,000) see Harris Trust & Savings Bank

Roosevelt University ($25,000) see Heller Foundation, Walter E.

Roosevelt University ($15,000) see Kemper Educational and Charitable Fund

Roosevelt University ($100) see LaSalle National Bank

Roosevelt University ($150,000) see Robin Family Foundation, Albert A.

Roosevelt University ($100,000) see Seid Foundation, Barre

Roosevelt University ($28,000) see Solomon Foundation, Sarah M.

Roosevelt University — cost of installing a new electrical switch gear and construction of an electrical vault in its Auditorium Building ($200,000) see Field Foundation of Illinois

Rosary College ($66,667) see Borg-Warner Corp.

Rosary College ($66,323) see Regenstein Foundation

Rosary College ($30,000) see Snite Foundation, Fred B.

Rosecrance Center ($1,000) see Sjostrom & Sons

Rosecrane Memorial Home for Children ($5,050) see Smith Charitable Trust

Rotary Club — Chest Fund/One Foundation ($3,000) see Butler Family Foundation, George W. and Gladys S.

Roycemore School ($5,000) see GSC Enterprises

Rush-Presbyterian-St. Luke's Medical Center ($75,000) see Buchanan Family Foundation

Rush Presbyterian-St. Lukes Medical Center ($5,000) see Getz Foundation, Emma and Oscar

Rush Presbyterian-St. Lukes Medical Center ($4,000) see Hales Charitable Fund

Rush Presbyterian-St. Lukes Medical Center ($8,000) see Kelly Foundation, T. Lloyd

Rush-Presbyterian-St. Luke's Medical Center ($300,000) see McCormick Tribune Foundation, Robert R.

Rush Presbyterian — St. Lukes Medical Center ($175,000) see Sprague Memorial Institute, Otho S. A.

Rush-Presbyterian-St. Luke's Medical Center — in support of the medical care and daycare components of the Alzheimer's Disease Center ($200,000) see Field Foundation of Illinois

Rush Presbyterian-St. Lukes Medical Center — Bone

Marrow Research ($50,000) see Coleman Foundation

Rush-Presbyterian-St. Luke's Medical Center — improving patient-centered care through initiatives in nursing ($490,000) see Commonwealth Fund

Rush-Presbyterian-St. Luke's Medical Center — to create the Rush Medical College Community Service Initiative ($100,000) see Fry Foundation, Lloyd A.

Rush-Presbyterian-St. Luke's Medical Center — defray the costs and expenses incurred by St. Luke's Fashion Show ($100,000) see Sage Foundation

Rush Presbyterian St. Luke's Memorial Hospital ($20,500) see Borwell Charitable Foundation

Rush Presbyterian St. Luke's Memorial Hospital ($6,000) see Borwell Charitable Foundation

Rush Presbyterian St. Luke's Memorial Hospital ($13,500) see Carylon Foundation

Rush Presbyterian St. Luke's Memorial Hospital ($3,500) see Dick Family Foundation

Rush Presbyterian St. Luke's Memorial Hospital ($1,500) see Donnelley Foundation, Elliott and Ann

Rush Presbyterian St. Luke's Memorial Hospital ($5,000) see Harper Foundation, Philip S.

Rush Presbyterian St. Luke's Memorial Hospital ($8,000) see Winona Corporation

Rush University — College of Nursing; teaching endowment ($250,000) see Independence Foundation

Rush University — College of Nursing; scholarship and loan funds ($100,000) see Independence Foundation

Safer Foundation ($3,500) see Oppenheimer Family Foundation

St. Anthony Memorial Hospital ($5,000) see Lumpkin Foundation

St. Augustine Center ($11,000) see Western Shade Cloth Charitable Foundation

St. Augustine Center ($11,000) see Western Shade Cloth Charitable Foundation

St. Benedict High School ($3,500) see Sulzer Family Foundation

St. Charles Art and Music Festival ($11,800) see Garvey Kansas Foundation

St. Chrysostom Church ($10,000) see Prentice Foundation, Abra

St. Coletta's of Illinois ($20,000) see Ward Foundation, A. Montgomery

St. Colletta School ($10,000) see Best Foundation, Walter J. and Edith E.

St. Colletta School ($55,102) see Dower Foundation, Thomas W.

St. Edwards High School — scholarships ($3,500) see Elgin Sweeper Co.

St. Elizabeth Center ($4,000) see Elco Charitable Foundation

St. Elizabeth Community Center Capital Campaign ($3,000) see First National Bank & Trust Co. of Rockford

Illinois (cont.)

St. Frances Hospital ($5,000) see Lumpkin Foundation

St. Francis De Sales Church — Lake Geneva ($25,000) see Ryan Foundation, Patrick G. and Shirley W.

St. Francis Hospital ($15,000) see Steigerwaldt Foundation, Donna Wolf

St. Francis Hospital Foundation ($5,000) see Schmidt Charitable Foundation, William E.

St. Ignatius College Prep ($75,000) see Brach Foundation, Helen

St. Ignatius College Preparatory ($32,000) see Rice Foundation

St. Ignatius College Preparatory ($25,000) see Snite Foundation, Fred B.

St. Ignatius College Preparatory ($25,000) see Ward Foundation, A. Montgomery

St. Ignatius High School ($5,000) see Dower Foundation, Thomas W.

St. Johns Hospital School of Nursing ($10,000) see House Educational Trust, Susan Cook

St. Johns Military Academy ($1,300) see Goldberg Family Foundation, Milton D. and Madeline L.

St. Joseph Carondelet ($20,000) see McIntosh Foundation

St. Joseph Church ($30,000) see Cuneo Foundation

St. Joseph Health Care Foundation — general, charitable and educational purposes ($50,000) see Sage Foundation

St. Joseph's Home for the Elderly — to continue renovation ($200,000) see Retirement Research Foundation

St. Jude's Midwest ($1,575) see Foster and Gallagher

St. Leo High School ($4,000) see Dower Foundation, Thomas W.

St. Martin De Porres House of Hope ($20,000) see Driehaus Foundation, Richard H.

St. Martin de Porres House of Hope — general support ($42,000) see Stone Foundation, W. Clement and Jessie V.

St. Mary Hospital — communication system ($5,000) see Quincy Newspapers

St. Mary of Lake Seminary ($25,000) see Cuneo Foundation

St. Raphael Academy ($5,000) see Farley Industries

St. Scholastica High School — general support ($200,000) see Solo Cup Co.

St. Teresa Education Foundation ($20,000) see Staley Manufacturing Co., A.E.

St. Theresa Educational Foundation ($10,000) see Staley, Jr. Foundation, A. E.

St. Theresa Educational Foundation ($7,500) see Staley, Jr. Foundation, A. E.

St. Vincent Memorial Hospital ($5,000) see Lumpkin Foundation

St. Xavier College ($17,000) see Bowyer Foundation, Ambrose and Gladys

St. Xavier College ($50,000) see CRL Inc.

Saints Faith Hope and Charity ($5,000) see Caestecker Foundation, Charles and Marie

Saints Faith, Hope, and Charity Church ($20,000) see Ryan Foundation, Patrick G. and Shirley W.

Salvation Army ($27,385) see Bersted Foundation

Salvation Army ($10,000) see Brunner Foundation, Fred J.

Salvation Army ($8,000) see Cox Charitable Trust, A. G.

Salvation Army ($500) see Elgin Sweeper Co.

Salvation Army ($4,879) see Foster and Gallagher

Salvation Army ($6,500) see Hanson Testamentary Charitable Trust, Anna Emery

Salvation Army ($2,750) see Ideal Industries

Salvation Army ($25,000) see Kendall Foundation, George R.

Salvation Army ($25,000) see Kendall Foundation, George R.

Salvation Army ($100,000) see Mazza Foundation

Salvation Army ($100,000) see National Presto Industries

Salvation Army see Portec, Inc.

Salvation Army ($5,000) see Rhoades Fund, Otto L. and Hazel E.

Salvation Army ($2,000) see Rockford Products Corp.

Salvation Army ($1,500) see Rockford Products Corp.

Salvation Army ($50) see Schneider Foundation, Robert E.

Salvation Army ($2,500) see Sulzer Family Foundation

Sanbury Western Seminary ($10,000) see Hoover Foundation, H. Earl

Sangamon Valley Youth Symphony ($3,000) see House Educational Trust, Susan Cook

Sara Lee Foundation ($100,000) see Price Foundation, Louis and Harold

Sarah Bush Lincoln Health Center ($10,000) see Lumpkin Foundation

Sauk Valley Community College ($25,575) see Dillon Foundation

Scholarship and Guidance Association ($100) see Schneider Foundation, Robert E.

School of Art Institute ($12,350) see Manilow Foundation, Nathan

School of Art Institute ($50,000) see Seid Foundation, Barre

School of the Art Institute of Chicago ($30,000) see Siragusa Foundation

School of Social Service Administration — study: Family Responsive Policies in the Workplace ($46,022) see Fel-Pro Incorporated

Sculpture Chicago ($1,000) see Herald News

Sculpture School ($10,000) see Chicago Sun-Times, Inc.

Seabury-Western ($15,808) see Society for the Increase of the Ministry

Second Congregational Church ($5,600) see Smith Charitable Trust

Second Harvest — general unrestricted ($12,500) see Barstow Foundation

Second Harvest ($50,000) see Nabisco Foods Group

Senior Citizens of Christian County ($3,000) see Hopper Memorial Foundation, Bertrand

Sertoma Career Center ($5,000) see Dower Foundation, Thomas W.

Shakespeare Globe ($10,000) see Knowles Foundation

Shedd Aquarium — for construction of oceanarium ($1,000,000) see Kresge Foundation

Shedd Aquarium ($3,000) see Lehmann Foundation, Otto W.

Shedd Aquarium ($200,000) see Pritzker Foundation

Shelby County High School ($10,000) see Moore Foundation, O. L.

Shelby County Memorial Hospital ($2,500) see Lumpkin Foundation

Shore ($15,000) see Kendall Foundation, George R.

Shriners Hospital for Crippled Children ($8,000) see Cox Charitable Trust, A. G.

Silver Spring Foundation ($50,000) see McCormick Foundation, Chauncey and Marion Deering

Sisters of the Resurrection ($1,000) see Lizzadro Family Foundation, Joseph

Skip-A-Long Day Care Center ($20,000) see Harris Family Foundation, Hunt and Diane

Slavic Gospel Association ($914,069) see DeMoss Foundation, Arthur S.

Slavic Gospel Association ($5,000) see Kejr Foundation

Slavic Gospel Association ($25,000) see Paulstan

Slavic Gospel Association ($35,000) see Share Foundation

Slavic Gospel Association ($75,000) see Stewardship Foundation

Slavic Gospel Association — for Slavic missions ($5,000) see Epaphroditus Foundation

Slavic Gospel Association — video production for Soviet Union ($30,000) see Crowell Trust, Henry P. and Susan C.

Slavic Gospel Association — ministry needs in Soviet Union ($500,000) see Maclellan Charitable Trust, R. J.

SME-Manufacturing Engineering Education Foundation ($2,500) see Ingersoll Milling Machine Co.

Society of Jesus Chicago Province ($5,000) see Cottrell Foundation

South Central Community Service ($8,250) see Beidler Charitable Trust, Francis

South Elgin Little League ($5,125) see Hoffer Plastics Corp.

South Park Church ($150,000) see Tyndale House Foundation

South Park Church ($100,000) see Tyndale House Foundation

South Side Mission ($3,605) see Foster and Gallagher

Southern Human Services ($25,000) see NutraSweet Co.

Southern Illinois University Foundation ($10,000) see House Educational Trust, Susan Cook

Southwest Chicago Christian School Association Religious Education ($25,000) see Tibstra Charitable Foundation, Thomas and Gertrude

Sparta Community School District — to fund a Kindergarten Alternative Program ($36,366) see American Honda Motor Co.

Special Fund for 1991 LSC Elections — grants to community organizations ($25,000) see Wieboldt Foundation

Species Survival Commission — to study declining amphibian population ($60,000) see Fikes Foundation, Leland

Spertus College of Judaica ($21,215) see Levy Foundation, Charles and Ruth

Spertus College of Judaica ($10,000) see Relations Foundation

Spertus College of Judaica — Jewish culture and history education ($87,267) see Rosenbaum Foundation, Paul and Gabriella

Spokane Food Bank ($3,000) see Lapham-Hickey Steel Corp.

Springfield College in Illinois ($20,000) see House Educational Trust, Susan Cook

Stepenwolf Theatre ($50,000) see Frankel Foundation

Steppenwolf Theatre ($3,000) see Alsdorf Foundation

Steppenwolf Theatre ($10,000) see Cheney Foundation, Elizabeth F.

Steppenwolf Theatre ($72,500) see Herald News

Steppenwolf Theatre Company ($5,000) see Cohn Family Foundation, Robert and Terri

Steppenwolf Theatre Company ($2,500) see Forest Fund

Steppenwolf Theatre Company ($13,500) see IMCERA Group Inc.

Steppenwolf Theatre Company ($25,000) see Kemper Educational and Charitable Fund

Steppenwolf Theatre Company ($100) see LaSalle National Bank

Sterling Park District ($103,299) see Dillon Foundation

Sterling-Rock Falls Community Trust ($40,000) see Dillon Foundation

Sterling Schools Foundation ($164,858) see Dillon Foundation

Streator Township High School ($3,500) see Oakley Foundation, Hollie and Anna

Stritch School of Medicine ($19,000) see Cuneo Foundation

Sulzer Regional Library ($15,000) see Sulzer Family Foundation

Summit School ($2,500) see Hanson Testamentary Charitable Trust, Anna Emery

Sunset Home — elderly transportation ($2,500) see Quincy Newspapers

Survive Alive House ($125,000) see Allstate Insurance Co.

Swedish-American Hospital Foundation ($10,000) see Aldeen Charity Trust, G. W.

Swedish American Museum ($1,000) see Sulzer Family Foundation

Sycamore Education Foundation ($2,500) see Ideal Industries

Sycamore United Fund ($11,500) see Ideal Industries

Taylorville Community Schools ($56,708) see Hopper Memorial Foundation, Bertrand

Teach for America ($25,000) see Seid Foundation, Barre

TEAM ($3,200) see Combs Foundation, Earle M. and Virginia M.

TEAM ($40,000) see Crowell Trust, Henry P. and Susan C.

Teen Living Programs — support of Residential Program for Homeless Youth ($15,000) see GATX Corp.

Telshe Yeshiva ($76,860) see Feinberg Foundation, Joseph and Bessie

Temple Beth-El ($25,000) see Blowitz-Ridgeway Foundation

Temple Sholom ($384,000) see Shapiro Foundation, Charles and M. R.

Theosophical Society in America ($525,369) see Kern Foundation Trust

Think First Foundation — educational film for young people that discusses preventive measures for risk-taking behaviors that could lead to spinal cord and head injuries ($125,000) see Johnson & Johnson

Thresholds ($2,000) see Brand Cos.

Tidmarch Arts Foundation ($500) see Lizzadro Family Foundation, Joseph

Timothy Christian School ($125,000) see Anderson Foundation

Timothy Christian Schools ($110,000) see Huizenga Foundation, Jennie

Touchstone ($1,000) see Wilbur Foundation, Marguerite Eyer

Travelers Aid Society ($3,000) see Cox Charitable Trust, A. G.

Travelers and Immigrants Aid ($5,000) see Blair and Co., William

Travelers and Immigrants Aid ($5,000) see I and G Charitable Foundation

Travelers and Immigrants Aid ($100) see LaSalle National Bank

Travelers and Immigrants Aid — support human needs fund ($10,000) see Lederer Foundation, Francis L.

Travelers and Immigrants Aid ($30,000) see Sprague Memorial Institute, Otho S. A.

Travelers and Immigrants Aid of Chicago ($70,000) see Blum-Kovler Foundation

Tri-City Jewish Center ($50,000) see Geifman Family Foundation

Tri-City Jewish Center ($8,000) see Geifman Family Foundation

Tri-City Jewish Center ($7,000) see Geifman Family Foundation

Tri-County Humane Society ($5,000) see Wyne Foundation

Tri-County (Peoria) Urban League ($100,000) see Caterpillar

Tri County Urban League ($6,250) see Foster and Gallagher

Trinity Christian College ($1,100,000) see Huizenga Foundation, Jennie

Trinity Church of North Shore ($1,000) see Louis Foundation, Michael W.

Trinity College ($10,000) see Dexter Corp.

Trinity College ($26,305) see Erickson Charitable Fund, Eben W.

Trinity College ($20,000) see Santa Maria Foundation

Trinity College ($50,000) see Seymour and Troester Foundation

Trinity Episcopal Church ($1,422) see Smith Foundation, Gordon V. and Helen C.

Trinity Evangelical Divinity School ($25,000) see Aldeen Charity Trust, G. W.

Trinity United Presbyterian Church — scholarships ($75,000) see Gillespie Memorial Fund, Boynton

Trinity United Presbyterian Church — scholarships ($75,000) see Gillespie Memorial Fund, Boynton

Trout and Salmon Foundation ($2,000) see Donnelley Foundation, Elliott and Ann

Tuesday's Child ($5,000) see Harris Foundation, J. Ira and Nicki

Tuesday's Child ($5,000) see Perkins Foundation, Edwin E.

U of C for Emotional Disturbed Children ($5,000) see Stone Family Foundation, Norman H.

United Cerebral Palsy Association ($5,000) see Hopper Memorial Foundation, Bertrand

United Charities of Chicago ($57,500) see Blum Foundation, Nathan and Emily S.

United Charities of Chicago ($24,334) see Pick, Jr. Fund, Albert

United Charities of Chicago ($2,000) see Rosenthal Foundation, Benjamin J.

United Charities of Chicago ($20,000) see Ward Foundation, A. Montgomery

United Charities of Chicago ($5,000) see Wood Foundation, Lester G.

United Charities of Chicago — to develop the elder Mentors Project which will link senior adults with youth at risk of delinquent behavior ($135,650) see Retirement Research Foundation

United Community Fund ($100,000) see Material Service Corp.

United Fund ($1,200) see Eagle-Picher Industries

United Fund ($3,000) see Hopper Memorial Foundation, Bertrand

United Fund of Champaign County ($2,800) see Bergner Co., P.A.

United Fund of Decatur and Macon Counties ($79,000) see Caterpillar

United Funds ($28,000) see Joslyn Corp.

United Funds ($700) see Joslyn Corp.

United Negro College Fund ($5,000) see Ceco Corp.

United Negro College Fund ($2,500) see Forest Fund

United Negro College Fund ($80,000) see Kendall Foundation, George R.

United Negro College Fund ($6,000) see Moorman Manufacturing Co.

United Negro College Fund ($30,000) see Quaker Oats Co.

United Negro College Fund ($125,000) see Sears, Roebuck and Co.

United Negro College Fund ($5,000) see Wurlitzer Foundation, Farny R.

United States Olympic Committee — special program fund ($150,000) see Grainger Foundation

United Way ($30,000) see Amsted Industries

United Way ($13,485) see Arkwright-Boston Manufacturers Mutual

United Way ($185,000) see Bergner Co., P.A.

United Way ($2,700) see Bergner Co., P.A.

United Way ($57,500) see Blum Foundation, Nathan and Emily S.

United Way ($47,515) see Boulevard Foundation

United Way ($6,000) see Brach Foundation, Edwin I.

United Way ($3,000) see Brand Cos.

United Way ($12,000) see Butler Manufacturing Co.

United Way ($79,607) see CBI Industries

United Way ($6,808) see CBI Industries

United Way ($6,808) see CBI Industries

United Way ($16,500) see Ceco Corp.

United Way ($6,000) see Ceco Corp.

United Way ($3,000) see Ceco Corp.

United Way ($2,250) see Ceco Corp.

United Way ($2,000) see Ceco Corp.

United Way ($1,100) see Ceco Corp.

United Way ($17,000) see Cole Taylor Financial Group

United Way ($7,200) see Crane Fund for Widows and Children

United Way ($35,625) see DeKalb Genetics Corp.

United Way ($21,587) see DeKalb Genetics Corp.

United Way ($2,500) see Dick Family Foundation

United Way ($5,000) see Eisenberg Foundation, George M.

United Way ($42,000) see Elco Charitable Foundation

United Way ($15,000) see Elgin Sweeper Co.

United Way ($10,000) see Field Foundation, Jamee and Marshall

United Way ($34,000) see First National Bank & Trust Co. of Rockford

United Way ($1,000) see Florsheim Shoe Co.

United Way ($500) see Florsheim Shoe Co.

United Way ($20,729) see Foster and Gallagher

United Way ($14,000) see Frank Fund, Zollie and Elaine

United Way ($1,000) see Goodstein Family Foundation, David

United Way ($42,000) see Hoffer Plastics Corp.

United Way ($1,500) see Ingersoll Milling Machine Co.

United Way ($30,000) see Kearney Inc., A.T.

United Way ($75,000) see Navistar International Corp.

United Way ($52,500) see Navistar International Corp.

United Way ($15,000) see New Prospect Foundation

United Way ($22,445) see Outboard Marine Corp.

United Way ($500) see Robin Family Foundation, Albert A.

United Way see Rochester Midland Corp.

United Way ($40,000) see Rockford Products Corp.

United Way ($2,500) see Rosenthal Foundation, Benjamin J.

United Way ($51,330) see Rothschild Foundation, Hulda B. and Maurice L.

United Way ($5,000) see Sjostrom & Sons

United Way ($14,800) see Smith Charitable Trust

United Way ($62,500) see Staley, Jr. Foundation, A. E.

United Way ($6,087) see Stone Family Foundation, Norman H.

United Way ($2,000) see Swift Co. Inc., John S.

United Way ($3,000) see United Conveyor Corp.

United Way ($3,000) see United Conveyor Corp.

United Way ($8,000) see Wallace Computer Services

United Way ($7,500) see Wyne Foundation

United Way of Adams County ($69,985) see Moorman Manufacturing Co.

United Way of Chicago ($372,750) see Chicago Tribune Co.

United Way of Chicago ($69,000) see Whitman Corp.

United Way of Chicago/Crusade of Mercy — social welfare ($377,000) see Continental Bank N.A.

United Way/Crusade of Mercy ($300,000) see American National Bank & Trust Co. of Chicago

United Way Crusade of Mercy — support programs ($266,150) see AON Corp.

United Way/Crusade of Mercy — general support ($181,258) see Baxter International

United Way Crusade of Mercy ($68,448) see Borden

United Way Crusade of Mercy ($47,515) see Boulevard Bank, N.A.

United Way/Crusade of Mercy ($115,000) see Dun & Bradstreet Corp.

United Way/Crusade of Mercy — annual campaign ($50,000) see Fel-Pro Incorporated

United Way/Crusade of Mercy ($87,535) see FMC Corp.

United Way/Crusade of Mercy ($125,575) see Harris Trust & Savings Bank

United Way/Crusade of Mercy ($95,000) see Hartmarx Corp.

United Way/Crusade of Mercy ($20,000) see IMCERA Group Inc.

United Way Crusade of Mercy ($38,904) see Interco

United Way Crusade of Mercy ($15,000) see Kidder, Peabody & Co.

United Way/Crusade of Mercy ($644,000) see Kraft General Foods

United Way/Crusade of Mercy ($134,470) see Leo Burnett Co.

United Way Crusade of Mercy ($243,900) see Marshall Field's

United Way Crusade of Mercy ($224,182) see Montgomery Ward & Co.

United Way/Crusade of Mercy ($146,757) see Morton International

United Way/Crusade of Mercy ($275,000) see Motorola

United Way Crusade of Mercy ($57,500) see Nabisco Foods Group

United Way/Crusade of Mercy ($104,850) see Northern Trust Co.

United Way/Crusade of Mercy ($104,850) see Northern Trust Co.

United Way/Crusade of Mercy ($104,850) see Northern Trust Co.

United Way/Crusade of Mercy ($104,850) see Northern Trust Co.

United Way Crusade of Mercy ($100,108) see NutraSweet Co.

United Way/Crusade of Mercy ($25,000) see Reynolds Metals Co.

United Way/Crusade of Mercy ($175,805) see Santa Fe Pacific Corp.

United Way/Crusade of Mercy ($21,748) see Sherwin-Williams Co.

United Way/Crusade of Mercy ($25,282) see USG Corp.

United Way Crusade of Mercy ($81,900) see Wrigley Co., Wm. Jr.

United Way Crusade of Mercy ($81,900) see Wrigley Co., Wm. Jr.

United Way/Crusade of Mercy — corporate support for the Chicago metropolitan area's 1991 campaign ($348,000) see Sara Lee Corp.

United Way Crusade of Mercy, Chicago, IL ($125,000) see Searle & Co., G.D.

United Way of Decatur and Macon Counties — contribution ($33,000) see Bridgestone/ Firestone

United Way Elgin ($18,000) see Illinois Tool Works

United Way — Lake County ($400,000) see Abbott Laboratories

United Way of Lake County — general support ($181,258) see Baxter International

United Way of Lake County ($25,000) see IMCERA Group Inc.

United Way of Metropolitan Chicago ($330,000) see Allstate Insurance Co.

United Way of the Quad Cities Area ($67,500) see Aluminum Co. of America

United Way-Rockford — operating ($167,500) see Sundstrand Corp.

United Way-Rockford ($87,000) see Woodward Governor Co.

United Way Services ($5,000) see Atwood Foundation

University of Chicago ($55,000) see Bauer Foundation, M. R.

University of Chicago — diabetes research ($150,000) see Blum Foundation, Harry and Maribel G.

University of Chicago ($150,000) see Blum-Kovler Foundation

University of Chicago see Brakeley, John Price Jones Inc.

University of Chicago ($80,000) see Centel Corp.

University of Chicago ($1,000) see Chiquita Brands Co.

University of Chicago ($10,000) see DeSoto

University of Chicago ($91,450) see Donnelley Foundation, Gaylord and Dorothy

University of Chicago — to provide one graduate fellowship in economics ($22,750) see Earhart Foundation

University of Chicago ($32,853) see First Chicago

University of Chicago ($385,000) see Frankel Foundation

University of Chicago ($16,125) see Goldman Sachs & Co.

University of Chicago ($133,221) see Gund Foundation, George

University of Chicago ($75,000) see I and G Charitable Foundation

University of Chicago ($100,000) see Kellstadt Foundation

University of Chicago ($12,000) see Laerdal Foundation, Asmund S.

University of Chicago ($100) see LaSalle National Bank

University of Chicago — support medical scholarship ($20,000) see Lederer Foundation, Francis L.

University of Chicago ($3,000) see Lehmann Foundation, Otto W.

University of Chicago ($90,000) see Lurcy Charitable and Educational Trust, Georges

University of Chicago ($10,000) see Morton International

University of Chicago ($300,000) see Pioneer Fund

University of Chicago ($39,500) see Pittway Corp.

University of Chicago ($5,600) see Replogle Foundation, Luther I.

University of Chicago ($7,500) see Rosenthal Foundation, Richard and Hinda

University of Chicago ($51,330) see Rothschild Foundation, Hulda B. and Maurice L.

University of Chicago ($80,000) see Scaler Foundation

University of Chicago ($110,000) see Seid Foundation, Barre

University of Chicago ($5,000) see Shapiro Family Foundation, Soretta and Henry

University of Chicago ($100,000) see Shaw Foundation, Walden W. and Jean Young

University of Chicago ($10,000) see Siragusa Foundation

University of Chicago ($85,000) see Solomon Foundation, Sarah M.

University of Chicago ($25,000) see Ward Foundation, A. Montgomery

University of Chicago ($105,000) see Whiting Foundation, Mrs. Giles

University of Chicago Brain Research Institute ($10,000) see Boothroyd Foundation, Charles H. and Bertha L.

University of Chicago Burn Center ($33,000) see McGraw Foundation

University of Chicago Cancer Research Foundation ($5,000) see Lehmann Foundation, Otto W.

Allen County Fairgrounds ($10,000) see Journal Gazette Co.

Allen County Fairgrounds — construction ($15,000) see McMillen Foundation

Allen County/Ft. Wayne Historical Society ($65,000) see English-Bonter- Mitchell Foundation

Allen County-Fort Wayne Historical Society ($4,500) see Somers Foundation, Byron H.

Allen County 4-H ($1,500) see Flickinger Memorial Trust

Allen County League for the Blind ($8,528) see O'Connor Foundation, Magee

Allen County Public Library Foundation ($10,000) see Zollner Foundation

Allen County Public Library Foundation — fund the acquisition of the 1920 U.S. Census ($204,844) see Foellinger Foundation

American Camping Association ($20,000) see Lennox International, Inc.

American Cancer Society ($7,943) see Duncan Trust, James R.

American Cancer Society ($1,000) see Rieke Corp.

American College of Sports Medicine see Coors Brewing Co.

American Heart Association ($500) see Jasper Wood Products Co.

American Jewish Archives ($9,000) see Bronstein Foundation, Sol and Arlene

American Red Cross ($5,000) see Glick Foundation, Eugene and Marilyn

American Red Cross ($10,310) see Schust Foundation, Clarence L. and Edith B.

American Red Cross ($8,472) see Thrush-Thompson Foundation

Americanism Education Network — educational materials ($2,800) see Pennsylvania Dutch Co.

Anthony Wayne Services ($10,000) see Journal Gazette Co.

Arts United ($60,000) see Kuhne Foundation Trust, Charles

Arts United ($7,000) see Tokheim Corp.

Arts United of Greater Ft. Wayne ($49,883) see Central Soya Co.

Arts United of Greater Ft. Wayne ($110,000) see English-Bonter- Mitchell Foundation

Associated Colleges of Indiana ($210,000) see Anderson Foundation, John W.

Associated Colleges of Indiana ($75,000) see Arvin Industries

Associated Colleges of Indiana ($4,500) see Ayres Foundation, Inc.

Associated Colleges of Indiana ($21,000) see Central Soya Co.

Associated Colleges of Indiana ($14,000) see CTS Corp.

Associated Colleges of Indiana ($1,000) see DCB Corp.

Associated Colleges of Indiana ($70,000) see English-Bonter-Mitchell Foundation

Associated Colleges of Indiana ($31,000) see Ford Meter Box Co.

Associated Colleges of Indiana ($5,500) see Hook Drug

Associated Colleges of Indiana ($700) see Jasper Table Co.

Associated Colleges of Indiana ($1,200) see JOFCo., Inc.

Associated Colleges of Indiana ($25,000) see Jordan Foundation, Arthur

Associated Colleges of Indiana ($7,000) see Kilbourne Residuary Charitable Trust, E. H.

Associated Colleges of Indiana ($20,000) see Marathon Oil, Indiana Refining Division

Associated Colleges of Indiana see Northern Indiana Public Service Co.

Associated Colleges of Indiana ($5,000) see Old National Bank in Evansville

Associated Colleges of Indiana ($25,000) see Reilly Industries

Associated Colleges of Indiana ($10,000) see Thrush-Thompson Foundation

Associated Colleges of Indiana ($6,500) see Tokheim Corp.

Associated Colleges of Indiana — Lilly-Ball seminars $70,000, annual grant $100,000 ($170,000) see Ball Brothers Foundation

Associated Mennonite Biblical Seminaries ($10,000) see Schowalter Foundation

Association for a Loan Free Education — support of Next Step ($17,130) see Glick Foundation, Eugene and Marilyn

Association Retarded Citizens of Allen County — group home improvements ($10,000) see Raker Foundation, M. E.

Auburn Automotive Heritage ($5,000) see Frankino Charitable Foundation, Samuel J. and Connie

Auburn Automotive Heritage ($3,000) see Rieke Corp.

Ball Memorial Hospital Auxiliary ($400) see Maxon Charitable Foundation

Ball Memorial Hospital — Research Department ($40,000) see Ball Foundation, George and Frances

Ball State University ($10,000) see Central Newspapers, Inc.

Ball State University ($6,370) see Ontario Corp.

Ball State University ($4,025) see Tokheim Corp.

Ball State University — to support the Center for Integrating Technology in Teaching Science in the Indiana Academy ($60,000) see Toyota Motor Sales, U.S.A.

Ball State University Foundation — capital campaign ($1,031,225) see Ball Foundation, George and Frances

Ball State University Foundation ($1,000) see Excel Industries (Elkhart, Indiana)

Ball State University Foundation — Wings campaign ($900,000) see Ball Brothers Foundation

Baptist Homes of Indiana ($2,190) see Smock Foundation, Frank and Laura

Bartholomew Consolidated School Corporation — architect fees for expansion of Schmitt and Northside schools ($200,000) see Cummins Engine Co.

Bartholomew County — architect fees for new county jail ($60,000) see Cummins Engine Co.

Bartholomew County Area Hospice ($18,500) see Arvin Industries

Bartholomew County Hospital — support for architect fees for expansion ($100,000) see Cummins Engine Co.

Beaman Home ($9,500) see Saemann Foundation, Franklin I.

Benedictine Sisters of the Blessed Sacrament — religious ($87,000) see Domino's Pizza

Berne Community Chest ($1,500) see CTS Corp.

Bethany Presbyterian Church ($9,931) see Smock Foundation, Frank and Laura

Bethel College ($25,000) see Martin Foundation

Bethel College ($25,000) see Oliver Memorial Trust Foundation

Big Brothers and Big Sisters ($500) see Hand Industries

Big Brothers and Big Sisters ($500) see Indiana Desk Co.

Big Brothers and Big Sisters ($500) see Jasper Desk Co.

Big Brothers and Big Sisters ($500) see Rieke Corp.

Big Brothers and Big Sisters ($3,500) see Saemann Foundation, Franklin I.

Bishop Luers High School — academic success program ($10,000) see Raker Foundation, M. E.

Bishop Luers High School — scholarships ($10,000) see Raker Foundation, M. E.

Bloomington Symphony Society ($350) see Kajima International, Inc.

Boy Scouts of America ($5,000) see American General Finance

Boy Scouts of America ($1,000) see DCB Corp.

Boy Scouts of America ($500) see Indiana Desk Co.

Boy Scouts of America ($250) see Jasper Table Co.

Boy Scouts of America ($1,350) see Jasper Wood Products Co.

Boy Scouts of America ($8,045) see Kilbourne Residuary Charitable Trust, E. H.

Boy Scouts of America ($7,000) see Kimball International

Boy Scouts of America ($7,500) see Raker Foundation, M. E.

Boy Scouts of America ($7,500) see Zollner Foundation

Boys Club of America ($6,000) see Oakley Foundation, Hollie and Anna

Boys Club of Indianapolis — capital program ($250,000) see Lilly & Co., Eli

Boys and Girls Club ($25,000) see Griffith Foundation, W. C.

Boys and Girls Clubs of Indianapolis — capital campaign ($1,500,000) see Lilly Endowment

Boys and Girls Clubs of Northwest Indiana ($1,133,200) see Anderson Foundation, John W.

Boys and Girls Clubs of Porter County ($352,555) see Anderson Foundation, John W.

Boys Group Home ($250) see Jasper Desk Co.

Brian Bex Report — books for Freedom library ($2,250) see Pennsylvania Dutch Co.

Brownson Institute ($30,000) see Brady Foundation, W. H.

Building Public will to support Children's Education in Indiana — support children's education in Indiana ($2,900,000) see Lilly Endowment

Butler University ($5,000) see Ayres Foundation, Inc.

Butler University ($10,000) see Hook Drug

Butler University ($6,000) see Hook Drug

Butler University ($5,000) see Hook Drug

Butler University ($30,000) see Jordan Foundation, Arthur

Butler University ($22,050) see PSI Energy

Butler University ($16,000) see Reilly Industries

Butler University ($1,500) see Shirk Foundation, Russell and Betty

Butler University — four Hilton U. Brown awards ($6,000) see Central Newspapers, Inc.

Butler University — minority scholarship fund in memory of Robert A. Efroyomson ($250,000) see Moriah Fund

Calvary Presbyterian Church ($2,200) see Smock Foundation, Frank and Laura

Camp Awareness ($3,000) see Ford Meter Box Co.

Camp Good News ($500) see Hand Industries

Canco ($400) see Excel Industries (Elkhart, Indiana)

CANCO — "Holy Cross Associate" Program ($9,000) see Bowsher-Booher Foundation

Canterbury School — operating fund ($5,000) see Gabelli Foundation

Canterbury School — equipment ($17,000) see Somers Foundation, Byron H.

Carmel Lutheran Church ($11,100) see Thrush-Thompson Foundation

Carnegie Historic Landmarks ($2,000) see O'Brien Foundation, Cornelius and Anna Cook

Catholic Cemetery Association ($1,501) see Hutzell Foundation

Catholic Charities ($23,645) see Hutzell Foundation

Catholic Charities ($5,000) see Merrion Foundation

Catholic Diocese of Evansville ($18,000) see Habig Foundation, Arnold F.

Catholic Education Foundation ($8,000) see Duncan Trust, James R.

Catholic Education Foundation ($1,700) see National City Bank of Evansville

Cedar Lake Conference Grounds Religious Work ($35,000) see Tibstra Charitable Foundation, Thomas and Gertrude

Center for Attitudinal Healing of Indianapolis ($15,000) see Griffith Foundation, W. C.

Center for Christian Youth ($7,000) see Moore Foundation

Center for Leadership Development ($13,500) see Inland Container Corp.

Central High School ($10,000) see American General Finance

Central United School District ($13,675) see Dekko Foundation

Cerebral Palsy of Northwest Indiana ($100,000) see Anderson Foundation, John W.

Charleston Presbyterian Church ($4,223) see Smock Foundation, Frank and Laura

Children's Museum ($10,000) see Griffith Foundation, W. C.

Children's Museum ($10,000) see Jordan Foundation, Arthur

Children's Museum ($10,000) see Kimball International

Children's Museum ($20,000) see Reilly Industries

Christian Theological Seminary — endowment grant for faculty salaries ($50,000) see Irwin-Sweeney- Miller Foundation

Christmas in April ($10,000) see Bowsher-Booher Foundation

Circus City Festival ($17,110) see Thrush-Thompson Foundation

City of Columbus — architect fees for park renovation ($292,768) see Cummins Engine Co.

City of Columbus — support for expansion of Child Care Center ($60,000) see Cummins Engine Co.

City of Columbus Department of Parks and Recreation — support for maintenance of community cultural and activities center located in downtown area ($283,400) see Irwin-Sweeney- Miller Foundation

City of Columbus Department of Parks and Recreation — support for capital expenditure ($28,797) see Irwin-Sweeney-Miller Foundation

City of Garrett Parks ($1,000) see Rieke Corp.

Civic Foundation (Purdue University at IUSB) ($50,000) see South Bend Tribune

Clarksville Riverfront Foundation ($6,000) see Porter Paint Co.

Clay County Humane Society ($32,000) see Indiana Gas and Chemical Corp.

Cole County YMCA — challenge grant ($60,000) see Cole Foundation, Olive B.

Columbus Area Chamber Foundation — support for Columbus 2000 ($25,000) see Irwin-Sweeney- Miller Foundation

Columbus Child Care Center — capital grant for expansion of current facility ($30,000) see Irwin-Sweeney- Miller Foundation

Columbus Park Foundation/Heritage Fund Account ($525,000) see Arvin Industries

Combined Community Services ($15,000) see Saemann Foundation, Franklin I.

Commit Foundation ($26,667) see Arvin Industries

Community Foundation of Delaware County — unrestricted ($40,000) see Ball Foundation, George and Frances

Community Foundation Muncie/Delaware County ($65,000) see Ball Brothers Foundation

Community Harvest Food Bank — Nine County Food Program ($70,000) see Cole Foundation, Olive B.

Indiana (cont.)

Community Hospital Foundation ($10,000) see Griffith Foundation, W. C.

Community Hospitals Foundation — Indiana Regional Cancer Center Campaign ($25,000) see Clowes Fund

Community Improvement ($15,000) see Kuhne Foundation Trust, Charles

Concordia Theological Seminary ($4,000) see Woltman Foundation, B. M.

Concordia Theological Seminary ($3,000) see Woltman Foundation, B. M.

Concordia Theological Seminary ($3,000) see Woltman Foundation, B. M.

Corporation of Saint Marys College — science hall renovation ($150,000) see Leighton-Oare Foundation

Corporation of Saint Marys College — general purposes ($10,000) see Leighton-Oare Foundation

Crossroads ($10,000) see Journal Gazette Co.

Crossroads ($2,000) see Morrill Charitable Foundation

Crossroads — diagnostic/treatment center ($10,000) see Somers Foundation, Byron H.

Crossroads Rehabilitation Center ($63,333) see Brink Unitrust, Julia H.

Crossroads Rehabilitation Center ($15,000) see Griffith Foundation, W. C.

Culver Education Foundation — capital campaign ($100,000) see Duchossois Industries

Culver Education Foundation ($41,666) see Freeman Foundation, Ella West

Culver Education Foundation ($41,337) see Freeman Foundation, Ella West

Culver Educational Foundation ($500,000) see Batten Foundation

Culver Educational Foundation ($10,000) see Batten Foundation

Culver Educational Foundation ($5,000) see Falcon Foundation

Culver Educational Foundation ($1,500) see Goerlich Family Foundation

Culver Educational Foundation ($1,000) see Parker Drilling Co.

Culver Educational Foundation ($2,500) see Weatherwax Foundation

Culver Educational Foundation ($200,000) see Wenger Foundation, Henry L. and Consuelo S.

Culver Military Academy ($30,000) see Dickson Foundation

Culver Military Academy ($12,500) see Fuller Foundation

Culver Military Academy ($300,000) see Roberts Foundation

Culver Military Academy ($30,000) see Ruddick Corp.

Daughter of Charity ($10,000) see Koch Sons, George

DeKalb City Council on Aging ($6,000) see Rieke Corp.

DeKalb City Parent Group for Handicapped Children ($2,000) see Rieke Corp.

DeKalb County United Fund — operations campaign ($5,000) see JSJ Corp.

DeKalb Humane Society ($2,000) see Rieke Corp.

Delaware Advancement Corporation — Horizon '91 ($50,000) see Ball Foundation, George and Frances

DePauw University ($100,000) see Dow Jones & Co.

Depauw University ($102,000) see Frees Foundation

DePauw University ($27,600) see Pittway Corp.

Diocese of Fort Wayne-South Bend ($22,019) see Hutzell Foundation

Dubois County Easter Seal Society ($1,000) see Jasper Desk Co.

Earlham College ($25,000) see Cooper Industries

Earlham College ($1,000) see MidAmerica Radio Co.

East Enterprise Fire Department ($15,000) see Vevay-Switzerland County Foundation

East Noble Arts in Education ($11,000) see Dekko Foundation

East Noble School Corp — restructuring ($20,000) see Dekko Foundation

East Noble School Corp — Reading Is Fundamental program for grades K-8 ($11,500) see Dekko Foundation

East Wayne Street Center ($500) see Lassus Brothers Oil

East Wayne Street Center — inner-city program ($22,500) see McMillen Foundation

Eckhart Public Library ($3,000) see Rieke Corp.

Eisenhower Elementary School ($1,000) see Hand Industries

Eisenhower Memorial Scholarship Foundation ($5,000) see Thirty-Five Twenty, Inc.

Elkhart Civic Center Trust ($30,489) see Martin Foundation

Elkhart County Symphony ($90,000) see Martin Foundation

Elkhart General Hospital Foundation ($2,500) see Decio Foundation, Arthur J.

Embassy Theatre Foundation ($70,000) see English-Bonter-Mitchell Foundation

Emmanuel Community Church ($250,000) see Merillat Foundation, Orville D. and Ruth A.

Ensemble Music Society of Indianapolis ($8,000) see Winchester Foundation

Evangelical Baptist Mission ($2,000) see Hand Industries

Evansville Association for the Blind ($7,943) see Duncan Trust, James R.

Evansville Catholic High Schools ($10,000) see Koch Sons, George

Evansville Christian Life Center ($5,000) see American General Finance

Evansville Dance Theater ($25,000) see American General Finance

Evansville Jewish Community Council ($30,000) see

Bronstein Foundation, Sol and Arlene

Evansville Museum of Arts and Science ($10,000) see Crescent Plastics

Evansville Museum of Arts and Science ($5,000) see Crescent Plastics

Evansville Museum Arts and Sciences ($6,780) see Old National Bank in Evansville

Evansville Operation City Beautiful — sponsorship of recycling campaign see Ameritech Publishing

Evansville Philharmonic Orchestra ($7,500) see Crescent Plastics

Evansville Philharmonic Orchestra — annual fund ($3,000) see Crescent Plastics

Evansville Philharmonic Orchestra ($2,000) see National City Bank of Evansville

Evansville Protestant Home for the Aged ($7,943) see Duncan Trust, James R.

Evansville Zoological Society ($11,000) see Old National Bank in Evansville

Fairbanks Hospital — expand and renovate facility ($50,000) see Clowes Fund

Fairbanks Hospital ($3,000) see Marathon Oil, Indiana Refining Division

Fairbanks Hospital ($50,000) see Moore Foundation

Fairbanks Hospital ($10,000) see West Foundation

Ferdinand Community Center ($1,020) see Jasper Seating Co.

Festival Music Society of Indiana ($20,000) see Thirty-Five Twenty, Inc.

Festival Music Society of Indianapolis ($7,000) see Winchester Foundation

Fine Arts Foundation ($25,000) see Somers Foundation, Byron H.

First Presbyterian Church ($1,000) see Hand Industries

First Presbyterian Church ($500) see Jasper Wood Products Co.

First Presbyterian Church ($8,045) see Kilbourne Residuary Charitable Trust, E. H.

First Presbyterian Church ($15,500) see Smock Foundation, Frank and Laura

First Presbyterian Church of South Bend ($7,000) see Oliver Memorial Trust Foundation

First Presbyterian Church of South Bend — Bicentennial Fund ($25,000) see Leighton-Oare Foundation

Ft. Wayne Area Lifeline Homes ($3,500) see Morrill Charitable Foundation

Ft. Wayne Art Museum ($7,500) see Kuhne Foundation Trust, Charles

Ft. Wayne Community Foundation ($2,000) see Morrill Charitable Foundation

Fort Wayne Community Foundation ($45,310) see Schust Foundation, Clarence L. and Edith B.

Ft. Wayne Community Foundation — 1991-1992 services ($20,000) see Cole Foundation, Olive B.

Ft. Wayne Community Schools — at risk pilot program ($10,000) see Journal Gazette Co.

Ft. Wayne Fine Arts ($10,000) see Kilbourne Residuary Charitable Trust, E. H.

Fort Wayne Fine Arts Foundation ($7,000) see Tokheim Corp.

Fort Wayne Local Education Fund see Northern Indiana Public Service Co.

Ft. Wayne Museum of Art ($6,000) see Morrill Charitable Foundation

Fort Wayne Pace Program ($10,000) see McMillen Foundation

Ft. Wayne Park Foundation — grant for land acquisition ($190,000) see Foellinger Foundation

Ft. Wayne Parks and Recreation ($6,000) see Morrill Charitable Foundation

Ft. Wayne Philharmonic ($80,000) see English-Bonter-Mitchell Foundation

Ft. Wayne Philharmonic ($10,000) see Kuhne Foundation Trust, Charles

Ft. Wayne Philharmonic ($40,000) see Morrill Charitable Foundation

Fort Wayne Philharmonic ($25,000) see Somers Foundation, Byron H.

Ft. Wayne PTA Council ($10,000) see Kuhne Foundation Trust, Charles

Ft. Wayne Public Television ($5,000) see Kuhne Foundation Trust, Charles

Ft. Wayne Public Television ($8,015) see Zollner Foundation

Fort Wayne Urban Enterprise Association ($10,178) see Tokheim Corp.

Ft. Wayne Women's Bureau — capital grant ($147,370) see Foellinger Foundation

Ft. Wayne Zoological Society ($2,500) see O'Connor Foundation, Magee

Franciscan Mission Association Companion Office — install electricity and running water ($20,000) see Hackett Foundation

Franklin Retirement Home ($2,500) see Ayres Foundation, Inc.

Free Methodist Church ($600) see Hand Industries

French Lick Fire Department ($75,000) see Kimball International

Friends of the Arts ($1,000) see Indiana Desk Co.

Friends of the Arts ($1,000) see JOFCo., Inc.

Friends of the Helping Hands ($10,000) see Indiana Gas and Chemical Corp.

Gibault School for Boys ($25,000) see Indiana Gas and Chemical Corp.

Girl Scouts of America ($7,943) see Duncan Trust, James R.

Girl Scouts of America ($300) see Jasper Desk Co.

Goodwill Industries ($6,750) see Ayres Foundation, Inc.

Goodwill Industries ($12,500) see Bowsher-Booher Foundation

Goodwill Industries ($3,000) see First Source Corp.

Goodwill Industries ($15,000) see Griffith Foundation, W. C.

Goodwill Industries ($3,000) see Marathon Oil, Indiana Refining Division

Goodwill Industries of Michiana ($9,000) see Oliver Memorial Trust Foundation

Goshen College ($3,000) see CTS Corp.

Goshen College ($15,300) see Schowalter Foundation

Greater Fort Wayne Chamber of Commerce ($750) see Lassus Brothers Oil

H.W. McMillen Center for Health Education ($200,000) see McMillen Foundation

Habitat for Humanity ($15,000) see American General Finance

Habitat for Humanity ($10,000) see Koch Sons, George

Habitat for Humanity ($1,750) see Maxon Charitable Foundation

Hamilton Center ($2,000) see Oakley Foundation, Hollie and Anna

Hanover College ($4,000) see O'Brien Foundation, Cornelius and Anna Cook

Hanover College ($25,000) see Reilly Industries

Hanover College ($22,000) see Smock Foundation, Frank and Laura

Headwaters Park Commission — planning construction ($10,000) see McMillen Foundation

Heart Association ($511) see Lassus Brothers Oil

Heartline Pregnancy Care and Counseling ($10,000) see Saemann Foundation, Franklin I.

Heritage Fund of Bartholomew County ($125,000) see Irwin-Sweeney-Miller Foundation

Heritage Fund — multi-year commitment to capital campaign ($50,000) see Cummins Engine Co.

Hillel Foundation at Indiana University ($4,500) see Bronstein Foundation, Sol and Arlene

Historic Landmarks Foundation ($5,000) see Jordan Foundation, Arthur

Historic Landmarks Foundation ($2,000) see Jordan Foundation, Arthur

Historic Landmarks Foundation ($25,000) see O'Brien Foundation, Cornelius and Anna Cook

Holy Cross Foreign Missions ($500) see Tripifoods

Holy Family Catholic School ($17,000) see Habig Foundation, Arnold F.

Holy Family Catholic School ($600) see Jasper Table Co.

Holy Family Catholic School Foundation ($1,000) see Jasper Desk Co.

Holy Family Catholic School Foundation ($1,000) see Jasper Seating Co.

Holy Family Catholic School Foundation ($2,500) see Jasper Wood Products Co.

Holy Family Church ($150) see Jasper Table Co.

Holy Redeemer Catholic Church ($15,000) see Koch Sons, George

Homeless Center ($10,000) see First Source Corp.

Honeywell Foundation ($1,000,000) see Ford Meter Box Co.

Honeywell Foundation ($4,000) see Thrush-Thompson Foundation

Hoosier Alliance Against Drugs ($25,000) see PSI Energy

Huntingburg Foundation ($5,000) see Habig Foundation, Arnold F.

Huntington College ($5,000) see Durr-Fillauer Medical

Huntington College ($3,064,000) see Merillat Foundation, Orville D. and Ruth A.

Huntington College ($1,497,500) see Merillat Foundation, Orville D. and Ruth A.

Independent Council for Economic Education ($400) see Maxon Charitable Foundation

Indiana Chamber of Commerce ($5,000) see Ontario Corp.

Indiana Community Foundation Initiative — Indiana Community Foundation Initiative ($13,000,000) see Lilly Endowment

Indiana Demolay Foundation ($10,310) see Schust Foundation, Clarence L. and Edith B.

Indiana Family Health Council ($37,500) see Martin Foundation

Indiana Fiscal Policy Institute ($500) see Jasper Wood Products Co.

Indiana Institute of Technology ($10,056) see Kilbourne Residuary Charitable Trust, E. H.

Indiana Institute of Technology ($10,000) see Zollner Foundation

Indiana Legal Foundation ($500) see Indiana Desk Co.

Indiana Manufacturers Association Alliance ($51,600) see PSI Energy

Indiana Masonic Home Foundation ($10,310) see Schust Foundation, Clarence L. and Edith B.

Indiana Office for Campus Ministries ($6,000) see Kimball International

Indiana-Purdue Foundation — athletic scholarship grant ($176,096) see Foellinger Foundation

Indiana-Purdue University Foundation — land acquisition ($104,049) see Cole Foundation, Olive B.

Indiana-Purdue University Foundation ($1,000) see CTS Corp.

Indiana-Purdue University Foundation ($15,000) see Raker Foundation, M. E.

Indiana Repertory Theatre ($39,075) see PSI Energy

Indiana Special Olympics see Northern Indiana Public Service Co.

Indiana Sports Corporation ($25,000) see PSI Energy

Indiana State Symphony Society — attracting high caliber artists and expanding recording opportunities ($2,500,000) see Lilly Endowment

Indiana State University — to endow and develop the undergraduate insurance program ($100,000) see American United Life Insurance Co.

Indiana State University ($20,000) see Central Newspapers, Inc.

Indiana State University ($500) see Jasper Seating Co.

Indiana State University Foundation ($7,500) see Oakley Foundation, Hollie and Anna

Indiana University ($7,500) see Frank Fund, Zollie and Elaine

Indiana University ($15,000) see Hook Drug

Indiana University ($38,000) see Little Family Foundation

Indiana University ($6,000) see Moore Foundation

Indiana University ($49,837) see Raker Foundation, M. E.

Indiana University Foundation ($400,000) see Anderson Foundation, John W.

Indiana University Foundation ($130,000) see Dow Chemical Co.

Indiana University Foundation ($6,000) see First Source Corp.

Indiana University Foundation ($250,000) see Ford Meter Box Co.

Indiana University Foundation ($91,285) see Grassmann Trust, E. J.

Indiana University Foundation ($1,000) see Kowalski Sausage Co.

Indiana University Foundation ($10,000) see Leo Burnett Co.

Indiana University Foundation ($68,500) see Moore Foundation

Indiana University Foundation see Northern Indiana Public Service Co.

Indiana University Foundation ($15,000) see O'Brien Foundation, Cornelius and Anna Cook

Indiana University Foundation ($23,585) see PSI Energy

Indiana University Foundation ($16,000) see Thrush-Thompson Foundation

Indiana University Foundation ($17,500) see Union Foundation

Indiana University Foundation, Bloomington, IN ($20,000) see Dana Corp.

Indiana University Foundation — support for "Campaign for Indiana" designated for School of Music ($60,000) see Irwin-Sweeney-Miller Foundation

Indiana University Foundation — campaign for Indiana ($50,000) see Journal Gazette Co.

Indiana University Foundation — campaign for Indiana ($10,000) see Journal Gazette Co.

Indiana University Foundation — partial cost for theater building at IPFW ($300,000) see Foellinger Foundation

Indiana University Foundation — partial cost for theater building at IPFW ($300,000) see Foellinger Foundation

Indiana University Foundation — partial cost for theater building at IPFW ($300,000) see Foellinger Foundation

Indiana University Foundation — partial cost for theater building at IPFW ($300,000) see Foellinger Foundation

Indiana University Foundation — partial cost for theater building at IPFW ($300,000) see Foellinger Foundation

Indiana University Foundation/Library ($200,000) see Martin Foundation

Indiana University Foundation — Parkinsons Research ($40,000) see Arvin Industries

Indiana University Foundation — Roy W. Howard Seminar ($35,410) see Scripps Co., E.W.

Indiana University Foundation — center for Urban Policy and the Environment ($8,575,778) see Lilly Endowment

Indiana University — support of its Graduate Training and Teaching Program ($66,500) see Kade Foundation, Max

Indiana University — capital commitment to Herman B. Wells program ($100,000) see Cummins Engine Co.

Indiana University — two Kent Cooper Journalism Scholarships for men and two Sally Cooper Journalism Scholarships for women ($6,000) see Central Newspapers, Inc.

Indiana University at Kokomo ($10,000) see United Technologies, Automotive

Indiana University Northwest ($104,000) see Anderson Foundation, John W.

Indiana University-Purdue University at Ft. Wayne ($80,000) see English-Bonter-Mitchell Foundation

Indiana University — Purdue University at Ft. Wayne ($11,000) see Zollner Foundation

Indiana University School of Business ($2,500) see Kearney Inc., A.T.

Indiana Vocational Technical College ($10,000) see Zollner Foundation

Indiana Wesleyan University ($8,500) see Wurlitzer Foundation, Farny R.

Indiana Youth Institute — start-up support ($50,000) see Cummins Engine Co.

Indianapolis Art League ($15,000) see Griffith Foundation, W. C.

Indianapolis Ballet Theatre ($37,500) see Noyes, Jr. Memorial Foundation, Nicholas H.

Indianapolis Chamber of Commerce ($10,000) see Inland Container Corp.

Indianapolis Civic Theatre ($20,000) see Griffith Foundation, W. C.

Indianapolis Hebrew Congregation — current budget ($4,000) see Glick Foundation, Eugene and Marilyn

Indianapolis Museum of Art — annual maintenance ($80,000) see Clowes Fund

Indianapolis Museum of Art — antique fountain ($35,000) see Clowes Fund

Indianapolis Museum of Art ($7,500) see Jordan Foundation, Arthur

Indianapolis Museum of Art — capital program ($200,000) see Lilly & Co., Eli

Indianapolis Museum of Art — capital program ($175,000) see Lilly & Co., Eli

Indianapolis Museum of Art ($30,000) see Noyes, Jr. Memorial Foundation, Nicholas H.

Indianapolis Museum of Art ($12,500) see Stokely, Jr. Foundation, William B.

Indianapolis Museum of Art — funds for acquisition of Bertil Valliern "Calendarium" 1990 ($25,500) see Glick Foundation, Eugene and Marilyn

Indianapolis Museum of Art — funds for acquisition of Tom ($24,500) see Glick Foundation, Eugene and Marilyn

Indianapolis Neighborhood Housing Partnership — housing strategy implementation ($2,400,000) see Lilly Endowment

Indianapolis Opera ($5,000) see Ford Meter Box Co.

Indianapolis Symphony Orchestra ($30,000) see Noyes, Jr. Memorial Foundation, Nicholas H.

Indianapolis Symphony Orchestra ($35,000) see PSI Energy

Indianapolis Symphony Orchestra ($25,000) see Reilly Industries

Indianapolis Symphony Orchestra ($25,000) see Reilly Industries

Indianapolis Symphony Orchestra Foundation — capital/operating expense ($1,000,000) see Lilly & Co., Eli

Indianapolis Symphony Orchestra — Prelude to Greatness Endowment Campaign ($8,000) see Glick Foundation, Eugene and Marilyn

Indianapolis Zoo ($10,000) see Marathon Oil, Indiana Refining Division

Indianapolis Zoo Capital Campaign ($25,000) see Noyes, Jr. Memorial Foundation, Nicholas H.

Indianapolis Zoological Society ($5,000) see Ayres Foundation, Inc.

Indianapolis Zoological Society ($63,333) see Brink Unitrust, Julia H.

Indianapolis Zoological Society ($20,000) see Griffith Foundation, W. C.

Indianapolis Zoological Society ($20,000) see Hook Drug

Indianapolis Zoological Society ($5,000) see Jordan Foundation, Arthur

Indianapolis Zoological Society ($3,000,000) see Lilly Endowment

Indianapolis Zoological Society ($25,000) see Reilly Industries

Indianapolis Zoological Society — capital/operating expense ($260,000) see Lilly & Co., Eli

Insurance Education Foundation ($5,000) see Crum and Forster

Insurance Medical Research Fund — to provide medical scientist scholarship at Indiana University Medical School ($15,000) see American United Life Insurance Co.

InterCom ($200) see Hand Industries

Interfaith Citizens Organization — general operating support ($15,000) see Wieboldt Foundation

International Baseball Association ($8,500) see Louis Foundation, Michael W.

IPFW Scholarship Fund ($50,000) see Schust Foundation, Clarence L. and Edith B.

Ivy Tech ($100,000) see Martin Foundation

James Whitcomb Riley Hospital ($63,333) see Brink Unitrust, Julia H.

Jasper Band Parents ($500) see Indiana Desk Co.

Jasper Band Parents ($100) see Jasper Table Co.

Jasper Bank Parents — new uniforms ($300) see Jasper Desk Co.

Jasper Chamber of Commerce ($500) see Indiana Desk Co.

Jasper Jaycees ($500) see Jasper Wood Products Co.

Jasper Lions Club — "Skills for Adolescence" ($500) see Jasper Desk Co.

Jasper Lions Club — Skills for Adolescence ($500) see Jasper Seating Co.

Jasper Middle School ($500) see Jasper Wood Products Co.

Jasper Volunteer Fire Department ($4,000) see DCB Corp.

Jasper Volunteer Fire Department ($1,000) see Indiana Desk Co.

Jasper Volunteer Fire Department ($500) see Jasper Desk Co.

Jasper Volunteer Fire Department ($500) see Jasper Seating Co.

Jasper Volunteer Fire Department ($1,150) see Jasper Table Co.

Jasper Volunteer Fire Department ($1,000) see Jasper Wood Products Co.

Jasper Volunteer Fire Department ($3,500) see JOFCo., Inc.

Jasper Youth Baseball ($140) see Jasper Table Co.

Jefferson National Life Insurance ($50,112) see Meyer Family Foundation, Paul J.

Jewish Family and Children's Services ($35,000) see Glick Foundation, Eugene and Marilyn

Jewish Federation ($115,000) see Moriah Fund

JHS Athletic Department ($1,000) see DCB Corp.

Jordan College of Fine Arts of Butler University ($40,000) see Jordan Foundation, Arthur

Junior Achievement ($10,000) see Central Soya Co.

Junior Achievement ($2,750) see CTS Corp.

Junior Achievement ($300) see Excel Industries (Elkhart, Indiana)

Junior Achievement ($2,000) see First Source Corp.

Junior Achievement ($500) see Lassus Brothers Oil

Junior Achievement ($3,000) see Marathon Oil, Indiana Refining Division

Junior Achievement ($1,350) see Maxon Charitable Foundation

Junior Achievement ($22,000) see Morrill Charitable Foundation

Junior Achievement ($2,000) see O'Connor Foundation, Magee

Junior Achievement ($24,000) see Reilly Industries

Junior Achievement ($4,000) see South Bend Tribune

Junior Achievement ($3,425) see Tokheim Corp.

Junior Achievement ($8,400) see Zollner Foundation

Indiana (cont.)

Junior Achievement Premier Outreach — outreach program ($25,000) see McMillen Foundation

Katherine House Boys and Girls Clubs ($25,000) see Inland Steel Industries

KCH Foundation ($150) see Hand Industries

Kendallville Park and Recreation Department — land acquisition ($25,000) see Cole Foundation, Olive B.

Kosciusko County Theatre ($5,000) see Saemann Foundation, Franklin I.

LaGrange County Sewage District — feasibility study ($20,000) see Cole Foundation, Olive B.

Lake Area United Way ($154,500) see Anderson Foundation, John W.

Lake Area United Way ($365,000) see Inland Steel Industries

Lake Area United Way ($20,500) see Unilever United States

Lake County Association for Retarded ($47,500) see Griffin, Sr., Foundation, C. V.

LBO-Mad Anthony's ($1,020) see Lassus Brothers Oil

Life Leadership Development ($7,500) see Jordan Foundation, Arthur

Light House Mission ($7,500) see Indiana Gas and Chemical Corp.

Light House Mission ($2,000) see Oakley Foundation, Hollie and Anna

Lighthouse Mission — fulfillment of pledge ($5,000) see Glick Foundation, Eugene and Marilyn

Limberlost/Girl Scout Council ($38,440) see Martin Foundation

Lindenwood Historical Foundation — historic preservation ($25,000) see Somers Foundation, Byron H.

Little League Baseball Central Headquarter Development Fund - - - support of construction of Little League Headquarters ($7,505) see Glick Foundation, Eugene and Marilyn

Lockport Church ($750) see Hand Industries

Lutheran Hospital Foundation ($12,500) see Raker Foundation, M. E.

Lutheran Hospital Foundation ($13,310) see Schust Foundation, Clarence L. and Edith B.

Lutheran Social Services — facility renovation ($10,000) see McMillen Foundation

Lutheran Social Services ($25,000) see Schust Foundation, Clarence L. and Edith B.

Mad Anthony's ($360) see Lassus Brothers Oil

Madison Foundation ($300) see Excel Industries (Elkhart, Indiana)

Main Street United Methodist Church ($10,000) see Thrush-Thompson Foundation

Manchester College ($3,700) see Ford Meter Box Co.

Marian College ($500) see Jasper Seating Co.

Marian Heights Academy ($9,411) see Habig Foundation, Arnold F.

Marian High School Scholarship Fund ($6,500) see Decio Foundation, Arthur J.

Marion Heights Academy ($1,000) see DCB Corp.

Marion Heights Academy ($7,000) see Kimball International

Marion High School ($2,168) see MidAmerica Radio Co.

Masonic-Community Building Foundation ($35,000) see Ball Brothers Foundation

Matthew 25 Health Clinic ($3,500) see Morrill Charitable Foundation

McCray Memorial Hospital — EMS/VHF Radio/Communication System ($25,000) see Dekko Foundation

Media Indiana ($20,000) see West Foundation

Memorial Health Foundation — senior center building fund ($300,000) see Leighton-Oare Foundation

Memorial Health Foundation — "adolescent support and parenting" program ($10,000) see Bowsher-Booher Foundation

Memorial Hospital Auxiliary ($4,000) see Kimball International

Memorial Hospital Foundation ($200) see Jasper Table Co.

Mennonite Board of Education — program support ($10,000) see United Service Foundation

Mennonite Central Committee ($52,200) see Reynolds Foundation, Christopher

Mennonite Central Committee ($49,000) see Reynolds Foundation, Christopher

Mennonite Church ($9,500) see Schowalter Foundation

Mental Health Association ($500) see Excel Industries (Elkhart, Indiana)

Methodist Hospital — immunological study of retroviral antigens in Diabetic Human Placentae ($20,000) see Diabetes Research and Education Foundation

Michiana Public Broadcasting Corporation ($31,000) see Decio Foundation, Arthur J.

Minnetrista Cultural Foundation — operating ($1,145,745) see Ball Brothers Foundation

Minnetrista Cultural Foundation — capital expenditures ($226,909) see Ball Brothers Foundation

Minnetrista Cultural Foundation — collections ($39,096) see Ball Brothers Foundation

Minnetrista Cultural Foundation — Oakhurst Gardens ($512,298) see Ball Foundation, George and Frances

Monastery of St. Clair ($10,000) see Indiana Gas and Chemical Corp.

Muncie Area Career Center ($500) see Maxon Charitable Foundation

Muncie Children's Museum ($500) see Maxon Charitable Foundation

Muncie Clean City ($500) see Maxon Charitable Foundation

Muncie Symphony ($2,000) see Ontario Corp.

Muncie Symphony Orchestra ($800) see Maxon Charitable Foundation

National Consortium for Graduate Degrees for Minorities in Engineering ($50,000) see Michigan Bell Telephone Co.

National Consortium for Graduate Degrees for Minorities in Engineering ($50,000) see Motorola

National Institute for Trial Advocacy, Notre Dame Law School ($13,000) see Fuchsberg Family Foundation

Nature Conservancy — Waters of Life campaign ($20,000) see Cole Foundation, Olive B.

New American Schools Development Corporation ($344,230) see Arvin Industries

Noble County Community Foundation — establishing a community foundation ($150,000) see Cole Foundation, Olive B.

Noble County Community Foundation Corporation ($500,000) see Dekko Foundation

Noble County EMS — radios ($15,000) see Cole Foundation, Olive B.

North Manchester Community Foundation ($6,500) see Ford Meter Box Co.

North Manchester Community Foundation ($3,500) see Ford Meter Box Co.

North Side High School — foreign student program ($7,956) see McMillen Foundation

Northeast Dubois Little League ($500) see Indiana Desk Co.

Northeast Indiana Regional Association — funding ($46,642) see Cole Foundation, Olive B.

Northern Indiana Council #165 — "After School Scouting" Program ($11,000) see Bowsher-Booher Foundation

Northern Indiana Historical Foundation ($20,000) see First Source Corp.

Northern Indiana Historical Society — construction of new museum ($10,000) see Bowsher-Booher Foundation

Northern Indiana Historical Society — museum ($123,600) see Oliver Memorial Trust Foundation

Northern Indiana Historical Society ($5,000) see South Bend Tribune

Northern Indiana Historical Society — Connecting Galley ($200,000) see Leighton-Oare Foundation

Northwood Christian Church ($4,500) see Christian Workers Foundation

Northwood Christian Church (CAYBA) ($6,000) see Moore Foundation

Northwood Good Samaritan Nursing Home ($3,050) see Habig Foundation, Arnold F.

Notre Dame ($376,189) see Miles Inc.

Notre Dame University ($3,000) see Cottrell Foundation

Notre Dame University ($37,475) see Deloitte & Touche

Notre Dame University ($150) see Equimark Corp.

Notre Dame University ($9,818) see First Chicago

Notre Dame University ($10,000) see JOFCo., Inc.

Notre Dame University ($5,000) see Mathis-Pfohl Foundation

Notre Dame University ($100,000) see Murphy Foundation, John P.

Notre Dame University ($50,000) see Rolfs Foundation, Thomas J.

Notre Dame University ($264,351) see Wrape Family Charitable Trust

Notre Dame University — to support the mid-career faculty development program ($25,000) see Skaggs Foundation, L. J. and Mary C.

Oakland City College ($10,000) see Koch Sons, George

Otis Bowen Research Center, Indiana University Medical School ($100,000) see American United Life Insurance Co.

Overseas Council for Theological Education ($50,500) see First Fruit

Overseas Council for Theological Education and Missions — seminaries ($340,000) see Maclellan Foundation

Overseas Council for Theological Education and Missions — Evangelical Theological Seminary in Osijek, Yugoslavia ($200,000) see Maclellan Charitable Trust, R. J.

Park Tudor School ($10,000) see Ayres Foundation, Inc.

Parkview Foundation ($8,045) see Kilbourne Residuary Charitable Trust, E. H.

Parkview Foundation ($10,310) see Schust Foundation, Clarence L. and Edith B.

Parkview Hospital ($2,000) see First Source Corp.

Patoka Valley Center ($2,000) see JOFCo., Inc.

Peabody Retirement Community ($151,214) see Smock Foundation, Frank and Laura

Pleasant Run Children's Homes ($3,000) see Marathon Oil, Indiana Refining Division

Pleasant Run Children's Homes ($5,000) see West Foundation

Potawatomi Zoological Society ($5,000) see Oliver Memorial Trust Foundation

Precious Blood Church Picnic ($300) see Jasper Desk Co.

Presbyterian Church ($10,000) see Grigg-Lewis Trust

President Benjamin Harrison Foundation ($169,000) see Jordan Foundation, Arthur

Prince of Peace Lutheran Church ($10,000) see Saemann Foundation, Franklin I.

Project Future — economic development ($2,000) see Quincy Newspapers

Project Renew — computer needs ($15,000) see Raker Foundation, M. E.

Protestant Deaconess Hospital ($15,898) see Duncan Trust, James R.

Purdue Business Opportunity ($5,000) see Navistar International Corp.

Purdue Foundation ($45,500) see Hoffer Plastics Corp.

Purdue Foundation — Whistler Center for Carbohydrate Research ($75,000) see Staley Manufacturing Co., A.E.

Purdue University ($10,000) see Amsted Industries

Purdue University ($150,000) see Anderson Foundation, John W.

Purdue University ($100,000) see Bechtel, Jr. Foundation, S. D.

Purdue University ($5,000) see Caestecker Foundation, Charles and Marie

Purdue University ($10,625) see Central Newspapers, Inc.

Purdue University ($62,500) see Dow Corning Corp.

Purdue University ($836,440) see General Electric Co.

Purdue University ($8,000) see Gloeckner Foundation, Fred

Purdue University ($2,000) see Harris Foundation, H. H.

Purdue University ($234,000) see Intel Corp.

Purdue University ($500) see Jasper Seating Co.

Purdue University ($46,500) see NCR Corp.

Purdue University see Northern Indiana Public Service Co.

Purdue University ($5,000) see O'Brien Foundation, Cornelius and Anna Cook

Purdue University ($2,000) see Ontario Corp.

Purdue University ($15,000) see Pott Foundation, Robert and Elaine

Purdue University ($2,415) see Tokheim Corp.

Purdue University ($50,000) see Whirlpool Corp.

Purdue University Calumet ($150,000) see Anderson Foundation, John W.

Purdue University — Center for Manufacturing Management ($200,000) see Chrysler Corp.

Purdue University — support for a Center for Molecular Structure ($1,280,746) see Markey Charitable Trust, Lucille P.

Purdue University Foundation ($2,500) see Stans Foundation

Purdue University — Quality Undergraduate Education and Scientific Training ($20,000) see Dreyfus Foundation, Camille and Henry

Purdue University-West Lafayette ($26,250) see Inland Steel Industries

Reform Jewish Appeal ($30,000) see Bronstein Foundation, Sol and Arlene

Rehabilitation Center ($10,000) see American General Finance

Rehabilitation Center ($1,000) see DCB Corp.

Rehabilitation Center ($8,000) see Duncan Trust, James R.

Rehabilitation Center — capital campaign ($1,000) see Jasper Desk Co.

Rehabilitation Center ($500) see Jasper Seating Co.

Rehabilitation Center ($1,000) see Jasper Wood Products Co.

Rehabilitation Center ($35,000) see Koch Sons, George

Rehabilitation Center ($5,300) see National City Bank of Evansville

Rehabilitation Center ($16,300) see Old National Bank in Evansville

Rehabilitation Center Capital Campaign ($4,000) see Crescent Plastics

Reins of Life — site preparation to house horses ($15,000) see Bowsher-Booher Foundation

Reitz Memorial Catholic High School ($8,100) see Koch Sons, George

Renaissance-Fort Wayne Arts ($300) see Lassus Brothers Oil

Riley's Children's Hospital Fund ($250) see Jasper Seating Co.

Ripley County Health Coalition — materials, services ($10,000) see Tyson Fund

Ripley County Historical Society — equipment ($3,000) see Tyson Fund

Rose-Hulman Institute ($15,000) see Pott Foundation, Robert and Elaine

Rose-Hulman Institute of Technology ($25,000) see Indiana Gas and Chemical Corp.

Rose Hulman Institute of Technology ($10,000) see Oakley Foundation, Hollie and Anna

Rose-Hulman Institute of Technology ($2,000) see Stuart Foundation, Edward C.

Rose-Hulman Institute of Technology — for Delbert C. Staley/NYNEX Foundation Scholarships ($62,500) see NYNEX Corp.

Ruth Lilly Center for Health ($17,000) see Reilly Industries

Ruth Lilly Center for Health Education — to design and equip a multi-purpose teaching theater ($250,000) see American United Life Insurance Co.

Sacred Heart Home ($58,799) see Hutzell Foundation

Safe Sitter ($150,000) see Gerber Products Co.

St. Benedicts Church ($39,000) see Indiana Gas and Chemical Corp.

St. Elizabeth — refrigerator, ice maker, freezer ($590) see Lassus Brothers Oil

St. Francis College ($5,500) see Brooklyn Benevolent Society

St. Francis College ($10,056) see Kilbourne Residuary Charitable Trust, E. H.

St. Francis College — new athletic facility ($25,000) see McMillen Foundation

St. Francis College — endowment continuation ($3,000) see Tokheim Corp.

St. Francis College ($10,000) see Weatherhead Foundation

St. Francis College ($5,000) see Weatherhead Foundation

St. John the Baptist Catholic Church ($11,760) see Hutzell Foundation

St. Joseph Church ($1,000) see JOFCo., Inc.

St. Joseph Medical Center ($7,381) see Hutzell Foundation

St. Joseph Medical Center ($3,745) see Kilbourne Residuary Charitable Trust, E. H.

St. Joseph's Catholic Church ($13,850) see Habig Foundation, Arnold F.

St. Joseph's College ($27,000) see Lewis Foundation, Frank J.

St. Joseph's College ($22,000) see Whitman Corp.

St. Joseph's Hospital ($1,000) see DCB Corp.

St. Margaret's House — women's shelter ($12,000) see Bowsher-Booher Foundation

St. Mary-of-the-Woods College ($10,000) see Kimball International

St. Mary-of-the-Woods College ($10,000) see Kimball International

St. Mary of the Woods College ($2,500) see JOFCo., Inc.

St. Mary of Woods College ($2,500) see Oakley Foundation, Hollie and Anna

St. Mary's College ($10,000) see First Source Corp.

St. Marys College ($15,000) see Oliver Memorial Trust Foundation

St. Marys College ($25,000) see Ruffin Foundation, Peter B. & Adeline W.

St. Mary's College, Madeleva Society ($4,000) see Van Huffel Foundation, I. J.

St. Mary's Soup Kitchen ($500) see Lassus Brothers Oil

St. Meinrad Archabbey ($2,500) see DCB Corp.

St. Meinrad Archabbey ($25,000) see Habig Foundation, Arnold F.

St. Meinrad Archabbey ($200) see Jasper Table Co.

St. Meinrad Archabbey ($1,500) see National City Bank of Evansville

St. Meinrad Archabbey ($15,000) see Schneider Foundation Corp., Al J.

St. Meinrad Seminary ($1,500) see Indiana Desk Co.

St. Meinrad Seminary ($1,000) see Jasper Seating Co.

St. Meinrad Seminary ($2,000) see Jasper Wood Products Co.

St. Meinrad Seminary ($2,500) see JOFCo., Inc.

St. Meinrad Seminary ($25,000) see Kimball International

St. Patrick's Catholic School ($10,000) see Indiana Gas and Chemical Corp.

St. Richards School ($15,000) see Ayres Foundation, Inc.

St. Vincent Hospital Foundation ($5,000) see Marathon Oil, Indiana Refining Division

Salvation Army ($5,000) see Excel Industries (Elkhart, Indiana)

Salvation Army ($24,350) see PSI Energy

Samaritan Pastoral Center ($10,000) see Smock Foundation, Frank and Laura

Samaritan Shelter of Michigan City ($5,000) see Merrion Foundation

Sellersburg, Indiana — little league park ($25,000) see Ogle Foundation, Paul

Share Foundation ($5,000) see Merrion Foundation

Sisters of St. Benedict ($1,000) see DCB Corp.

Sisters of St. Benedict ($20,000) see Habig Foundation, Arnold F.

Sisters of St. Benedict ($2,000) see Marathon Oil, Indiana Refining Division

Sol Silver Ledge #24 of B'nai B'rith ($46,000) see Bronstein Foundation, Sol and Arlene

South Bend Heritage Foundation — "West Washington Homes" Project ($7,000) see Bowsher-Booher Foundation

South Bend Symphony ($6,000) see Oliver Memorial Trust Foundation

South Bend Symphony Orchestra ($5,000) see Decio Foundation, Arthur J.

Southern Ripley Life Squad — equipment ($31,751) see Tyson Fund

Southern Ripley Life Squad — building ($25,000) see Tyson Fund

Spain, Castile 15th/16th Century ($180,000) see Alsdorf Foundation

Stanley Clark School ($5,000) see Decio Foundation, Arthur J.

Stanley Clark School — general purposes ($20,000) see Leighton-Oare Foundation

Stanley Clark School ($5,000) see South Bend Tribune

Switzerland County — restore county courthouse ($500,000) see Ogle Foundation, Paul

Swope Art Gallery ($10,000) see Indiana Gas and Chemical Corp.

Tabernacle Presbyterian Church ($10,000) see Moore Foundation

Taylor University ($105,000) see English-Bonter- Mitchell Foundation

Temple Adath B'nai Israel ($78,000) see Bronstein Foundation, Sol and Arlene

Theater District ($20,000) see Koch Sons, George

Theatre District ($16,666) see American General Finance

34/WNIT TV ($1,000) see Excel Industries (Elkhart, Indiana)

Town of Patriot ($64,165) see Vevay-Switzerland County Foundation

Town of Versailles — sewer, water and equipment ($136,690) see Tyson Fund

Town of Vevay ($175,000) see Vevay-Switzerland County Foundation

Town of Vevay ($77,000) see Vevay-Switzerland County Foundation

Town of Vevay ($40,000) see Vevay-Switzerland County Foundation

Town of Vevay ($20,000) see Vevay-Switzerland County Foundation

Town of Vevay ($19,500) see Vevay-Switzerland County Foundation

Town of Vevay Library ($319,500) see Vevay-Switzerland County Foundation

Trade Winds Rehabilitation Center ($75,000) see Anderson Foundation, John W.

Tri Kappa of Warsaw ($15,000) see Saemann Foundation, Franklin I.

Tri-State University ($20,000) see Markey Charitable Fund, John C.

Tri-State University ($100,000) see Wells Foundation, Franklin H. and Ruth L.

Tri-State University ($30,500) see Zollner Foundation

Trinity English Lutheran Church ($20,619) see Schust Foundation, Clarence L. and Edith B.

Trinity Episcopal Church — education program ($1,429,964) see Lilly Endowment

Trustees of Purdue University ($400,000) see General Motors Corp.

Turnstone — equipment ($15,000) see Raker Foundation, M. E.

Tyson Library ($55,000) see Tyson Fund

Tyson United Methodist Church — repairs ($12,472) see Tyson Fund

Tyson United Methodist Church ($5,000) see Tyson Fund

Union Hospital Foundation ($20,750) see Oakley Foundation, Hollie and Anna

United Way — annual support ($65,000) see Ball Brothers Foundation

United Way ($50,000) see Central Soya Co.

United Way ($11,000) see Central Soya Co.

United Way ($5,400) see Crescent Plastics

United Way ($7,500) see CTS Corp.

United Way ($1,750) see CTS Corp.

United Way ($4,000) see Excel Industries (Elkhart, Indiana)

United Way ($46,000) see First Source Corp.

United Way ($11,750) see Glick Foundation, Eugene and Marilyn

United Way ($48,000) see Irwin-Sweeney- Miller Foundation

United Way ($35,000) see Journal Gazette Co.

United Way ($10,000) see Kilbourne Residuary Charitable Trust, E. H.

United Way ($18,850) see Koch Sons, George

United Way ($17,500) see Kuhne Foundation Trust, Charles

United Way ($1,000) see Lassus Brothers Oil

United Way ($38,000) see Marathon Oil, Indiana Refining Division

United Way ($20,000) see Marley Co.

United Way ($17,500) see Maxon Charitable Foundation

United Way ($1,100) see National By-Products

United Way ($13,488) see National City Bank of Evansville

United Way ($10,000) see Navistar International Corp.

United Way ($7,500) see Navistar International Corp.

United Way ($45,000) see Noyes, Jr. Memorial Foundation, Nicholas H.

United Way ($2,950) see Oakley Foundation, Hollie and Anna

United Way ($69,452) see Old National Bank in Evansville

United Way ($10,000) see Oliver Memorial Trust Foundation

United Way ($54,375) see PSI Energy

United Way ($11,050) see Quanex Corp.

United Way ($43,200) see Reilly Industries

United Way ($7,500) see Rieke Corp.

United Way see Rochester Midland Corp.

United Way ($33,633) see South Bend Tribune

United Way ($11,000) see South Bend Tribune

United Way ($1,000) see South Bend Tribune

United Way ($1,000) see South Bend Tribune

United Way ($20,195) see Thrush-Thompson Foundation

United Way ($77,056) see Tokheim Corp.

United Way ($50,000) see Zollner Foundation

United Way of Allen County — operating grant ($132,000) see Foellinger Foundation

United Way of Bartholomew County ($54,650) see Arvin Industries

United Way of Bartholomew County ($25,000) see Arvin Industries

United Way Bartholomew County ($305,840) see Cummins Engine Co.

United Way of Central Indiana ($41,000) see Inland Container Corp.

United Way-Central Indiana — community programs ($2,553,205) see Lilly & Co., Eli

United Way-Central Indiana — community programs ($2,204,770) see Lilly & Co., Eli

United Way of Central Indiana ($42,000) see National Starch & Chemical Corp.

United Way of Central Indiana ($16,600) see Universal Foods Corp.

United Way of Central Indiana — 1992 United Way Campaign ($3,750,000) see Lilly Endowment

United Way of Delaware County — unrestricted ($79,459) see Ball Foundation, George and Frances

United Way of Elkhart County ($70,000) see Miles Inc.

United Way of Elkhart County — to support the expanded implementation of its model critical thinking skills curriculum and new adult learner recruitment efforts see United Parcel Service of America

United Way-Greater Lafayette — community programs ($231,127) see Lilly & Co., Eli

United Way-Lafayette — community programs ($272,690) see Lilly & Co., Eli

United Way of Michigan City/Michigan Area ($16,000) see Hartmarx Corp.

United Way of Porter County ($25,000) see Inland Steel Industries

United Way-Southwestern Indiana ($80,000) see Whirlpool Corp.

United Way-Wabash Valley — community programs ($196,577) see Lilly & Co., Eli

United Way of Wayne County, Richmond, IN ($23,000) see Dana Corp.

University of Evansville ($5,000) see American General Finance

University of Evansville ($5,000) see Crescent Plastics

University of Evansville ($2,750) see Crescent Plastics

University of Evansville ($25,000) see Habig Foundation, Arnold F.

University of Evansville ($50,000) see Kuehn Foundation

University of Evansville ($10,525) see National City Bank of Evansville

Indiana (cont.)

University of Evansville ($24,150) see Old National Bank in Evansville

University of Evansville ($100,000) see Pott Foundation, Robert and Elaine

University of Indiana-Bloomington ($23,750) see Inland Steel Industries

University of Indianapolis ($3,500) see Ayres Foundation, Inc.

University of Notre Dame ($3,300) see Alsdorf Foundation

University of Notre Dame — restricted scholarship program ($20,000) see Beck Foundation, Elsie E. & Joseph W.

University of Notre Dame ($11,000) see Bowsher-Booher Foundation

University of Notre Dame ($50,000) see Bowyer Foundation, Ambrose and Gladys

University of Notre Dame — to support faculty development and minority graduate fellowships and undergraduate scholarships ($150,000) see Coca-Cola Co.

University of Notre Dame ($30,000) see Decio Foundation, Arthur J.

University of Notre Dame ($10,000) see Dower Foundation, Thomas W.

University of Notre Dame ($50,000) see Edison Fund, Charles

University of Notre Dame ($40,000) see Ernst & Young

University of Notre Dame ($35,972) see Ernst & Young

University of Notre Dame ($10,000) see Excel Industries (Elkhart, Indiana)

University of Notre Dame ($1,000) see Gateway Apparel

University of Notre Dame ($5,000) see Gavin Foundation, James and Zita

University of Notre Dame ($10,500) see Gore Family Memorial Foundation

University of Notre Dame ($145,000) see Grace & Co., W.R.

University of Notre Dame — fourth of five payments ($250,000) see Haggar Foundation

University of Notre Dame ($78,350) see Huisking Foundation

University of Notre Dame ($20,000) see Lapham-Hickey Steel Corp.

University of Notre Dame ($150,000) see Lewis Foundation, Frank J.

University of Notre Dame ($50,000) see Montgomery Elevator Co.

University of Notre Dame ($75,000) see Oliver Memorial Trust Foundation

University of Notre Dame ($1,000) see Ontario Corp.

University of Notre Dame ($15,000) see Pott Foundation, Robert and Elaine

University of Notre Dame ($400,000) see Ruffin Foundation, Peter B. & Adeline W.

University of Notre Dame ($30,000) see St. Mary's Catholic Foundation

University of Notre Dame — scholarship fund for chemistry ($10,000) see Sandoz Corp.

University of Notre Dame — endowment ($100,000) see Schmitt Foundation, Arthur J.

University of Notre Dame — scholarships ($55,000) see Schmitt Foundation, Arthur J.

University of Notre Dame ($15,000) see South Bend Tribune

University of Notre Dame ($7,000) see Van Huffel Foundation, I. J.

University of Notre Dame ($10,000) see Visciglia Foundation, Frank

University of Notre Dame ($10,000) see Warren Charite

University of Notre Dame ($10,000) see Western Southern Life Insurance Co.

University of Notre Dame ($6,000) see Wilsey Bennet Co.

University of Notre Dame, Athletic Endowment Fund — educational scholarships ($100,000) see Bellamah Foundation, Dale J.

University of Notre Dame Edward Frederick Sorin Society ($1,000) see Boler Co.

University of Notre Dame — Undergraduate Biological Sciences Education Program ($1,500,000) see Hughes Medical Institute, Howard

University of Notre Dame University Chapel Fund — educational improvements ($100,000) see Bellamah Foundation, Dale J.

University of Southern Indiana ($5,000) see American General Finance

University of Southern Indiana ($5,000) see Old National Bank in Evansville

University of Southern Indiana ($35,000) see Pott Foundation, Robert and Elaine

University of Southern Indiana Foundation ($4,500) see National City Bank of Evansville

University of Southern Indiana Foundation ($3,000) see National City Bank of Evansville

Valparaiso University ($3,500) see Fortis Inc.

Valparaiso University Association ($110,500) see Monsanto Co.

Vanderburgh County Society for Crippled Children and Adults ($15,898) see Duncan Trust, James R.

Versailles Fire Department — equipment ($15,000) see Tyson Fund

Versailles Senior Citizens — utilities, maintenance ($3,000) see Tyson Fund

Very Special Arts Indiana ($9,000) see Somers Foundation, Byron H.

Vincennes University ($1,000) see DCB Corp.

Vincennes University ($75,000) see Habig Foundation, Arnold F.

Vincennes University ($2,500) see JOFCo., Inc.

Vincennes University Foundation ($17,404) see Bierhaus Foundation

Vincennes University Jasper Foundation ($500) see Indiana Desk Co.

Vincennes University Jasper Foundation ($250) see Jasper Table Co.

Vincennes University Jasper Foundation ($7,500) see Kimball International

Volunteer Fire Department, Clay Township ($5,000) see Manville Corp.

Wabash College ($6,250) see Ayres Foundation, Inc.

Wabash College ($25,000) see Ball Brothers Foundation

Wabash College see Cosco, Inc.

Wabash College ($5,000) see Crescent Plastics

Wabash College — capital improvement project ($25,000) see Frohman Foundation, Sidney

Wabash College see National City Bank

Wabash College see Ulrich Chemical, Inc.

Wabash County United Fund ($15,000) see Ford Meter Box Co.

Wabash Valley Goodwill Industries ($5,100) see Oakley Foundation, Hollie and Anna

Wabash Valley Music Association ($5,000) see Ford Meter Box Co.

Washington Avenue Health Care Center ($5,000) see Old National Bank in Evansville

Washington House Treatment Center ($10,000) see Somers Foundation, Byron H.

WBNI-Public Radio ($3,500) see Morrill Charitable Foundation

Welborn Baptist Hospital ($3,000) see Crescent Plastics

Welborn Baptist Hospital ($2,500) see National City Bank of Evansville

Welborn Baptist Hospital ($6,500) see Old National Bank in Evansville

Wesley United Methodist Foundation ($10,000) see Shirk Foundation, Russell and Betty

Westminster Presbyterian Church ($9,865) see Smock Foundation, Frank and Laura

WFWA-Public Television ($3,500) see Morrill Charitable Foundation

Wildcat Recreation Association — build youth character ($256,812) see McMillen Foundation

Winchester Community High School ($1,500) see Winchester Foundation

Winchester Community Library ($15,000) see Winchester Foundation

WIPB TV ($1,000) see Maxon Charitable Foundation

WNIT-TV ($1,000) see CTS Corp.

YM/YWCA ($1,000) see Excel Industries (Elkhart, Indiana)

YMCA ($2,000) see Ayres Foundation, Inc.

YMCA ($20,000) see Central Soya Co.

YMCA ($5,000) see First Source Corp.

YMCA ($57,500) see Journal Gazette Co.

YMCA ($16,090) see Kilbourne Residuary Charitable Trust, E. H.

YMCA ($100,000) see Martin Foundation

YMCA ($50,000) see Martin Foundation

YMCA ($6,500) see Old National Bank in Evansville

YMCA ($30,000) see Saemann Foundation, Franklin I.

YMCA ($13,810) see Schust Foundation, Clarence L. and Edith B.

YMCA ($50,000) see Somers Foundation, Byron H.

YMCA ($5,000) see South Bend Tribune

YMCA ($28,740) see Thrush-Thompson Foundation

YMCA of Greater Fort Wayne ($65,000) see English-Bonter-Mitchell Foundation

YMCA of Muncie — renovation Camp Crosley House ($50,000) see Ball Brothers Foundation

Young Life ($42,000) see Moore Foundation

Young Life ($9,500) see Moore Foundation

Youth for Christ ($9,200) see Hand Industries

YWCA ($5,000) see American General Finance

YWCA ($20,000) see Central Soya Co.

YWCA ($5,000) see CTS Corp.

YWCA ($304,000) see Indiana Gas and Chemical Corp.

YWCA ($25,000) see Journal Gazette Co.

YWCA ($50,000) see Somers Foundation, Byron H.

YWCA ($6,000) see Tokheim Corp.

Iowa

Albrecht Acre ($1,500) see Spahn & Rose Lumber Co.

Alternative Living Environments ($25,000) see Mid-Iowa Health Foundation

American Cancer Society - Iowa Division — contribution toward cost of purchasing computer and personal typing systems for Iowa Division office, Central Area office, and South Central Area office ($34,170) see Maytag Family Foundation, Fred

American College Testing — scholarships for Children of Polaroid employees ($18,663) see Polaroid Corp.

American Diabetes Association ($1,000) see Guaranty Bank & Trust Co.

American Red Cross ($11,000) see Lee Endowment Foundation

American Red Cross ($4,310) see Lindstrom Foundation, Kinney

Area Substance Abuse Council ($2,000) see Gazette Co.

Bethel Mission ($5,000) see Vermeer Investment Company Foundation

B'nai B'rith Hillel Foundation ($8,000) see Levitt Foundation, Richard S.

Bonaparte First Response ($3,250) see Van Buren Foundation

Boy Scouts of America ($2,000) see Hanson Foundation

Boy Scouts of America ($500) see Harper Brush Works

Boy Scouts of America ($2,000) see IMT Insurance Co.

Boy Scouts of America ($18,967) see Lee Endowment Foundation

Boy Scouts of America ($35,000) see Lee Enterprises

Boys Club of America ($2,000) see Spahn & Rose Lumber Co.

Brenwood Lutheran Children's Home ($20,000) see Nestle U.S.A. Inc.

Buena Vista College ($4,000) see Citizens First National Bank

Buena Vista College — student loan fund ($50,000) see McElroy Trust, R. J.

Buena Vista College ($23,714) see Sherman Educational Fund, Mabel E.

Burlington Area Arts Council ($5,000) see Witte, Jr. Foundation, John H.

Burlington Area Catholic Schools ($10,000) see Witte, Jr. Foundation, John H.

Burlington High School ($75,000) see Witte, Jr. Foundation, John H.

Burlington Medical Center ($21,500) see Witte, Jr. Foundation, John H.

Burlington Medical Center ($5,000) see Witte, Jr. Foundation, John H.

Business Education Alliance ($3,500) see Ruan Foundation Trust, John

Caring Hearts Hospice ($3,600) see Hanson Foundation

Carroll County Hospice ($1,000) see Iowa Savings Bank

CASO ($25,000) see Adler Foundation Trust, Philip D. and Henrietta B.

Catholic Charities ($7,500) see Wahlert Foundation

Cedar Rapids Community Theatre Association — in support of capital campaign ($108,333) see Hall Foundation

Cedar Rapids Museum of Art — toward construction of a new museum ($543,000) see Hall Foundation

Cedar Rapids Museum of Art — for addition to house Lansansky collection ($200,000) see Hall Foundation

Cedar Rapids Symphony Orchestra see AEGON USA, Inc.

Cedar Rapids Symphony Orchestra ($3,000) see Gazette Co.

Cedar Rapids Symphony Orchestra — sponsor cultural events ($43,000) see IES Industries

Cedar Valley United Way — pledge commitment ($7,360) see Duchossois Industries

Center for Aging Services ($5,000) see Lee Enterprises

Central College ($250,000) see Kuyper Foundation, Peter H. and E. Lucille Gaass

Central College ($167,167) see Pella Corp.

Central College ($50,000) see Vermeer Manufacturing Co.

Central College — contribution - 4th installment on 1986 commitment toward cost of new student center ($150,000) see Maytag Family Foundation, Fred

Chemical Dependency Service of North Iowa ($10,000) see Lindstrom Foundation, Kinney

Chemical Dependency Services of North Iowa ($1,000) see Winnebago Industries, Inc.

Children's Square/USA ($750) see Scoular Co.

Christian Benevolent Association ($30,000) see Kuyper Foundation, Peter H. and E. Lucille Gaass

Church of Christ ($750) see Citizens First National Bank

Church Land Project — to promote sustainable agriculture by assisting church institutions to manage farmland owned by them ($70,000) see Noyes Foundation, Jessie Smith

Church and Life Lutheran ($1,500) see Jensen Construction Co.

City of Forest City ($2,000) see Hanson Foundation

City of Forest City ($1,000) see Winnebago Industries, Inc.

City of Keosauqua ($17,700) see Van Buren Foundation

City of Lorimor ($1,000) see Winnebago Industries, Inc.

City of Mason City ($22,000) see Lee Endowment Foundation

City of Muscatine ($400,000) see Carver Charitable Trust, Roy J.

Civic Center of Des Moines ($2,000) see Brenton Banks Inc.

Civic Center of Greater Des Moines ($1,000) see IMT Insurance Co.

Civic Center of Greater Des Moines ($1,000) see National By-Products

Civil Center of Greater Des Moines ($40,000) see Principal Financial Group

Clark Street House of Mercy ($5,000) see Hawley Foundation

Clarke College ($4,000) see Spahn & Rose Lumber Co.

Clear Lake Iowa — ball diamonds projects ($7,500) see Kinney-Lindstrom Foundation

Clear Lake Iowa — beautification projects ($4,000) see Kinney-Lindstrom Foundation

Coe College ($15,000) see Gazette Co.

Coe College — for renovation and expansion of library ($500,000) see Hall Foundation

Coe College — capital growth annual fund ($16,295) see IES Industries

Coe College — student loan fund ($50,000) see McElroy Trust, R. J.

Colo Iowa Library ($1,000) see Kinney-Lindstrom Foundation

Community Child Care Center ($1,000) see Harper Brush Works

Cornell College — endowment fund ($33,000) see Cowles Foundation, Gardner and Florence Call

Cornell College ($100) see Equimark Corp.

Cornell College — student loan fund ($50,000) see McElroy Trust, R. J.

Cornell College ($16,810) see Sherman Educational Fund, Mabel E.

Crossroads of Pella ($2,500) see Vermeer Manufacturing Co.

Danish Immigrant Museum ($12,000) see Jensen Construction Co.

Davenport Museum of Art ($17,500) see Adler Foundation Trust, Philip D. and Henrietta B.

Davenport Museum of Art — acquisition fund ($10,000) see Geifman Family Foundation

Davenport Public Library ($10,000) see Adler Foundation Trust, Philip D. and Henrietta B.

Davenport Public Library ($8,333) see Lee Enterprises

Deaf Missions ($50) see Fink Foundation

Des Moines Animal Rescue League ($500) see Brenton Banks Inc.

Des Moines Art Center ($300,000) see Blank Fund, Myron and Jacqueline

Des Moines Art Center ($1,200) see Brenton Banks Inc.

Des Moines Art Center — operating fund ($50,000) see Cowles Foundation, Gardner and Florence Call

Des Moines Art Center — contribution toward cost of Bruce Nauman sculpture "Animal Pyramid" ($100,000) see Maytag Family Foundation, Fred

Des Moines Ballet Association ($25,000) see Maytag Corp.

Des Moines Band Shelter ($2,500) see Iowa State Bank

Des Moines County Historical Society ($5,000) see Witte, Jr. Foundation, John H.

Des Moines Metro Opera — operating fund ($35,000) see Cowles Foundation, Gardner and Florence Call

Des Moines Metro Opera ($5,000) see Fisher Foundation, Gramma

Des Moines Metro Opera ($1,000) see IMT Insurance Co.

Des Moines Metro Opera ($1,000) see Iowa State Bank

Des Moines Metro Opera ($30,000) see Maytag Corp.

Des Moines Playhouse ($1,000) see IMT Insurance Co.

Des Moines Symphony — operating fund ($30,000) see Cowles Foundation, Gardner and Florence Call

Des Moines Symphony ($35,000) see Principal Financial Group

Des Moines Symphony Association ($30,000) see Maytag Corp.

Divine Word College Seminary ($2,000) see Kasal Charitable Trust, Father

Donna Reed Foundation for the Performing Arts — general scholarship funding ($1,000) see Pamida, Inc.

Dordt College ($3,333) see Demco Charitable Foundation

Dordt College — student loan fund ($50,000) see McElroy Trust, R. J.

Dordt College ($2,387) see Staley Foundation, Thomas F.

Dordt College ($25,000) see Vermeer Manufacturing Co.

Drake University ($50,000) see Bohen Foundation

Drake University — endowment fund ($700,000) see Cowles Foundation, Gardner and Florence Call

Drake University ($11,000) see Glazer Foundation, Madelyn L.

Drake University ($2,000) see Iowa State Bank

Drake University ($3,000) see Kellwood Co.

Drake University — construction of student center ($75,000) see Olmsted Foundation, George and Carol

Drake University ($200,000) see Principal Financial Group

Drake University ($35,000) see Principal Financial Group

Drake University Annual Fund ($5,000) see Lincoln Family Foundation

Drake University Crosby Scholars — pharmacy students ($24,000) see Mid-Iowa Health Foundation

Drake University Insurance Center — Kenneth W. Smith Memorial Fund ($50,000) see State Farm Mutual Automobile Insurance Co.

Dubuque Boys Club ($10,535) see McDonald Industries, Inc., A. Y.

Dubuque County Historical Society ($14,000) see Wahlert Foundation

Dubuque Historical Society ($3,000) see McDonald Industries, Inc., A. Y.

Dubuque Rescue Mission ($7,500) see Wahlert Foundation

Dubuque Symphony Orchestra ($1,500) see McDonald Industries, Inc., A. Y.

Easter Seal Society ($22,000) see Lee Endowment Foundation

Edmunson Art Foundation — photo catalog ($25,000) see Mapplethorpe Foundation, Robert

Emmaus Bible College ($3,000) see Rixson Foundation, Oscar C.

Emmaus Bible School ($52,000) see Caddock Foundation

Fairfield Community Fund ($2,000) see Harper Brush Works

Fairfield Community Schools ($1,000) see Harper Brush Works

Faith, Hope and Charity ($2,500) see Citizens First National Bank

Family Resources ($46,000) see Bechtel Charitable Remainder Uni-Trust, Marie H.

Farm Safety 4 Just Kids see Grinnell Mutual Reinsurance Co.

Field of Dreams ($500) see Citizens First National Bank

Fine Education Research Foundation ($70,000) see Maytag Corp.

Fine Foundation ($120,000) see Principal Financial Group

Finley Health Foundation ($5,000) see McDonald Industries, Inc., A. Y.

Finley Health Foundation ($2,500) see Wahlert Foundation

Finley Hospital ($2,500) see Spahn & Rose Lumber Co.

First Act Children's Theater ($150,000) see Lee Endowment Foundation

First Baptist Childcare Center ($5,000) see Hawley Foundation

First Baptist Church ($650) see Arbie Mineral Feed Co.

First Lutheran Church ($1,000) see Iowa State Bank

Fisher Community Center ($20,000) see Lennox International, Inc.

Forest City Fire Department ($1,000) see Winnebago Industries, Inc.

Forest City Hospital Auxilliary ($1,200) see Hanson Foundation

Forest City Neighborhood Food Bank ($2,000) see Hanson Foundation

Forest City Police Reserves ($2,000) see Hanson Foundation

Forest City United Fund ($1,500) see Winnebago Industries, Inc.

Foundation for Children's and Family Services — building fund ($50,000) see Cowles Foundation, Gardner and Florence Call

Foundation II ($5,000) see Gazette Co.

Friendly House ($100,000) see Adler Foundation Trust, Philip D. and Henrietta B.

Friendly House ($150,000) see Deere & Co.

Friends of Iowa Public Television ($1,000) see Iowa Savings Bank

Garst Educational Fund ($1,000) see Iowa Savings Bank

Gingerbread House ($600) see Citizens First National Bank

Girl Scouts of America ($500) see Harper Brush Works

Girl Scouts of America ($50,000) see Witte, Jr. Foundation, John H.

Grand View College — building expansion ($100,000) see Cowles Foundation, Gardner and Florence Call

Grand View College ($6,000) see Hawley Foundation

Grand View College ($5,000) see Iowa State Bank

Grant Wood Area Chapter American Red Cross ($200) see Guaranty Bank & Trust Co.

Greater Des Moines Foundation Forest Avenue Library — building fund ($50,000) see Cowles Foundation, Gardner and Florence Call

Grinnell College — operating fund ($250,000) see Cowles Foundation, Gardner and Florence Call

Grinnell College see Grinnell Mutual Reinsurance Co.

Grinnell College ($150,000) see Lennox International, Inc.

Grinnell College ($35,000) see United Conveyor Corp.

Grinnell College ($39,000) see Watson Foundation, Thomas J.

Grinnell Day Care see Grinnell Mutual Reinsurance Co.

Grinnell 2000 see Grinnell Mutual Reinsurance Co.

Grinnell Youth Softball/Baseball Association see Grinnell Mutual Reinsurance Co.

Grout Museum of History and Science — facility expansion ($50,000) see McElroy Trust, R. J.

Handicap Village ($20,000) see Lee Endowment Foundation

Harmony Athletic Boosters ($5,000) see Van Buren Foundation

Hawkeye Fund ($2,500) see Demco Charitable Foundation

Hawkeye Institute of Technology — black student scholarships and student loan fund ($75,000) see McElroy Trust, R. J.

HOME — housing for the needy ($1,500) see Waldinger Corp.

Homes of Oakridge ($50,000) see Principal Financial Group

Homes of Oakridge ($2,500) see Ruan Foundation Trust, John

Homes of Oakridge — building fund ($10,000) see Younkers, Inc.

Homes of Oakridge Human Services — equipment and furnishings ($20,000) see Mid-Iowa Health Foundation

Hoover Presidential Library Association — expansion of library ($200,000) see Hoover, Jr. Foundation, Margaret W. and Herbert

Hoover Presidential Library Association — biography project ($50,000) see Hoover, Jr. Foundation, Margaret W. and Herbert

Hoover Presidential Library Association — first installment toward Thirtieth Anniversary Fund Campaign ($34,000) see Maytag Family Foundation, Fred

Hope Haven ($10,000) see Demco Charitable Foundation

Hope Haven Area Development Center ($16,000) see Witte, Jr. Foundation, John H.

Horizons Unlimited of Palo Alto County — to purchase furnishing for two new group homes ($1,000) see Pamida, Inc.

Hospice of Central Iowa Foundation ($1,000) see IMT Insurance Co.

Hospice of Central Iowa Foundation ($1,000) see Iowa State Bank

I.S.U. Burroughs Wise Memorial in Animal Science ($2,120) see Iowa Savings Bank

Immanuel C.R.C ($6,350) see Vermeer Manufacturing Co.

Immanuel Reformed Church of Christ ($400) see Citizens First National Bank

Institute for Civil Justice see Grinnell Mutual Reinsurance Co.

Insurance Center Endowment Fund see Grinnell Mutual Reinsurance Co.

Insurance Education Foundation ($3,000) see IMT Insurance Co.

Iowa Children and Family Services ($6,000) see Hawley Foundation

Iowa Children and Family Services ($7,500) see National By-Products

Iowa Children's and Family Services ($5,000) see Blank Fund, Myron and Jacqueline

Iowa Children's and Family Services ($2,000) see IMT Insurance Co.

Iowa Children's and Family Services ($47,500) see Principal Financial Group

Iowa Children's and Family Services ($10,000) see Younkers, Inc.

Iowa College Foundation see Grinnell Mutual Reinsurance Co.

Iowa College Foundation ($200) see Guaranty Bank & Trust Co.

Iowa College Foundation ($1,000) see Harper Brush Works

Iowa College Foundation ($1,000) see Harper Foundation, Philip S.

Iowa (cont.)

Iowa College Foundation ($30,000) see HON Industries

Iowa College Foundation ($2,000) see IMT Insurance Co.

Iowa College Foundation ($1,000) see Iowa Savings Bank

Iowa College Foundation ($30,000) see Lindstrom Foundation, Kinney

Iowa College Foundation ($2,000) see Martin Marietta Aggregates

Iowa College Foundation ($50,000) see Maytag Corp.

Iowa College Foundation — contribution ($50,000) see Maytag Family Foundation, Fred

Iowa College Foundation ($2,500) see National By-Products

Iowa College Foundation ($15,000) see Pella Corp.

Iowa College Foundation ($50,000) see Principal Financial Group

Iowa College Foundation ($1,250) see Ruan Foundation Trust, John

Iowa College Foundation ($2,000) see Spahn & Rose Lumber Co.

Iowa Division United National Association ($4,000) see Glazer Foundation, Madelyn L.

Iowa Fellowship of Christian Athletes ($500) see Vermeer Investment Company Foundation

Iowa Games ($12,500) see Pella Corp.

Iowa Historical Museum Foundation ($20,000) see Maytag Corp.

Iowa Historical Museum Foundation — final installment on 1985 and 1987 commitments for building fund ($50,000) see Maytag Family Foundation, Fred

Iowa Jewish Home ($50,000) see Glazer Foundation, Madelyn L.

Iowa Methodist Medical Center — first installment on 1989 commitment for renewal of annual contribution for additional staffing for waiting area of ICU-CCU ($51,200) see Maytag Family Foundation, Fred

Iowa Natural Heritage Foundation ($25,000) see Bohen Foundation

Iowa Natural Heritage Foundation see Grinnell Mutual Reinsurance Co.

Iowa Natural Heritage Foundation ($750) see Iowa State Bank

Iowa Natural Heritage Foundation — internship program ($52,500) see McElroy Trust, R. J.

Iowa Natural Heritage Foundation ($31,582) see Pella Corp.

Iowa Osteopathic Education Foundation — health care ($20,000) see Waldinger Corp.

Iowa Osteopathic Education Foundation — health care ($18,500) see Waldinger Corp.

Iowa Peace Institute ($5,000) see Glazer Foundation, Madelyn L.

Iowa Peace Institute ($20,000) see Maytag Corp.

Iowa Public Television ($5,000) see Hawley Foundation

Iowa Public Television ($10,000) see Kuyper Foundation, Peter H. and E. Lucille Gaass

Iowa Public Television ($20,000) see Maytag Corp.

Iowa Scholarship Fund ($1,000) see Brenton Banks Inc.

Iowa Scholarship Fund ($2,500) see Wahlert Foundation

Iowa State University ($4,000) see Continental Grain Co.

Iowa State University ($75,000) see Frasch Foundation for Chemical Research (under the will of Elizabeth B. Frasch), Herman

Iowa State University — support staff position in music department ($10,000) see McDonald's Corp.

Iowa State University ($20,000) see Olin Corp.

Iowa State University Athletic Development ($1,000) see Iowa Savings Bank

Iowa State University Foundation, ISU ($60,000) see Aluminum Co. of America

Iowa State University Foundation — for Partnership for Prominence Campaign to create an endowed professorship in the Agronomy Department ($1,500,000) see Pioneer Hi-Bred International

Iowa State University — scholarship funding/support academic programs ($31,290) see IES Industries

Iowa State University Institute for Physical Research ($1,188,696) see Carver Charitable Trust, Roy J.

Iowa Wesleyan College ($12,500) see HON Industries

Jefferson County Agency on Aging ($1,000) see Harper Brush Works

Jewish Federation ($168,000) see Levitt Foundation, Richard S.

Jewish Federation of Des Moines ($75,000) see Blank Fund, Myron and Jacqueline

Jewish Federation of Des Moines ($50,000) see Blank Fund, Myron and Jacqueline

Jewish Federation of Des Moines ($25,000) see Blank Fund, Myron and Jacqueline

Jewish Federation of Des Moines ($18,000) see Blank Fund, Myron and Jacqueline

Jewish Federation of Des Moines ($62,525) see Glazer Foundation, Madelyn L.

Jewish Federation of Des Moines ($168,333) see Levitt Foundation

Jewish Federation of Des Moines ($4,500) see Tension Envelope Corp.

Junior Achievement ($8,000) see Harris Family Foundation, Hunt and Diane

Junior Achievement ($2,300) see McDonald Industries, Inc., A. Y.

KCMR — radio equipment ($4,000) see Kinney-Lindstrom Foundation

Kirkwood Community College Foundation ($7,000) see Gazette Co.

Kirkwood Community College Foundation — scholarship programs/support academic programs ($28,500) see IES Industries

Kirkwood Community Partners in Progress ($500) see Guaranty Bank & Trust Co.

KNWS Radio ($175) see Arbie Mineral Feed Co.

Kuemper Ball ($1,000) see Iowa Savings Bank

Lester Mulligan Park Expansion Project ($60,000) see Lee Endowment Foundation

Linn County Bankers for Playground Equipment ($2,500) see Guaranty Bank & Trust Co.

Listening Post ($100) see Arbie Mineral Feed Co.

Living History Farms — operating fund ($50,000) see Cowles Foundation, Gardner and Florence Call

Loras College ($10,000) see Mathis-Pfohl Foundation

Loras College ($5,000) see McDonald Industries, Inc., A. Y.

Loras College ($5,000) see Spahn & Rose Lumber Co.

Lorenz Recovery House ($5,000) see Blank Fund, Myron and Jacqueline

Luke Society ($50,000) see Vermeer Investment Company Foundation

Luther College ($2,054) see Bradish Trust, Norman C.

Luther College ($5,000) see Caestecker Foundation, Charles and Marie

Luther College ($3,000) see Getsch Family Foundation Trust

Luther College ($20,000) see Gudelsky Family Foundation, Homer and Martha

Luther College ($24,089) see Hallett Charitable Trust

Luther College ($16,036) see Hallett Charitable Trust, Jessie F.

Luther College ($15,000) see Whitman Corp.

Lutheran Social Services ($20,000) see Lee Endowment Foundation

Maharishi International University ($32,442) see Abramson Family Foundation

Main Street Grinnell see Grinnell Mutual Reinsurance Co.

Make-A-Wish Foundation ($10,000) see Gazette Co.

Mapleton Fall Creek Housing Development Corporation ($25,000) see Noyes, Jr. Memorial Foundation, Nicholas H.

Marriage Encounter Support Foundation ($270,135) see E and M Charities

Marriage Encounter Support Foundation ($173,869) see E and M Charities

Marriage Encounter Support Foundation ($147,804) see E and M Charities

Marriage Encounter Support Foundation ($87,910) see E and M Charities

Mason City ($14,000) see Lindstrom Foundation, Kinney

Mason City Iowa Beautification Project ($5,000) see Kinney-Lindstrom Foundation

Mason City, Iowa — 1991 beautification ($5,000) see Lindstrom Foundation, Kinney

Mason City MacNider Art Museum ($15,000) see Lindstrom Foundation, Kinney

Mayflower Homes — remodel/expansion program ($30,000) see JELD-WEN, Inc.

Mellinger Memorial Public Library ($25,000) see Mellinger Educational Foundation, Edward Arthur

Mental Health Center ($10,000) see Adler Foundation Trust, Philip D. and Henrietta B.

Mercy Health Center ($2,500) see Wahlert Foundation

Mercy Hospital ($12,500) see Donaldson Co.

Mercy Medical Center ($1,500) see Spahn & Rose Lumber Co.

Meth-Wick Retirement Community — for health center renovations ($125,000) see Hall Foundation

Methodist Manor ($600) see Citizens First National Bank

Metropolitan Cedar Rapids Library Foundation — toward construction of new library ($680,000) see Hall Foundation

Morningside College ($22,825) see Sherman Educational Fund, Mabel E.

Mount Mercy College — to construct a learning resources center ($320,000) see Hall Foundation

Mount Mercy College — construction of new library and support academic programs ($33,045) see IES Industries

Mount Mercy College — support for automated system in new library ($25,000) see Kemper National Insurance Cos.

Mount Mercy College ($50,000) see Square D Co.

Mt. Mercy College Library Campaign ($2,000) see Guaranty Bank & Trust Co.

Mt. Mercy College Project Access ($1,000) see Guaranty Bank & Trust Co.

Municipal Golf Course-City of Pella ($100,000) see Pella Corp.

Muscatine Community Schools ($18,000) see HON Industries

Muscatine YMCA-YWCA — Building Fund ($429,680) see Carver Charitable Trust, Roy J.

Mustard Seed International ($100) see Arbie Mineral Feed Co.

N. Iowa Area Community College ($4,034) see Lehigh Portland Cement Co.

Nature Conservancy - Iowa Chapter — first installment on 1989 commitment ($50,000) see Maytag Family Foundation, Fred

Navigators ($15,000) see Vermeer Manufacturing Co.

Nevada Iowa Library Building ($10,000) see Kinney-Lindstrom Foundation

New Hope Village ($10,000) see Iowa Savings Bank

New Hope Village ($13,550) see Pella Corp.

North Central Community School ($6,000) see Lindstrom Foundation, Kinney

North Central Regional Library ($17,100) see Lindstrom Foundation, Kinney

North Iowa Area Community College ($168,500) see Lee Endowment Foundation

North Iowa Vocational Center ($12,000) see Lee Endowment Foundation

Northwestern College ($27,000) see Demco Charitable Foundation

Oakridge Learning Center ($10,000) see Hawley Foundation

On With Life ($5,000) see Hawley Foundation

On With Life — facility for head injured adults ($25,000) see Mid-Iowa Health Foundation

Opera House ($25,000) see Vermeer Manufacturing Co.

Osage Community Chest ($2,000) see Wallace Computer Services

Our Primary Purpose ($10,000) see Blank Fund, Myron and Jacqueline

Our Savior Lutheran Church ($650) see Arbie Mineral Feed Co.

P.R.I.D.E. ($100) see Arbie Mineral Feed Co.

Palmer College of Chiropractic ($7,500) see Lee Enterprises

Palo Alto Community Health Care Foundation ($2,000) see SNC Manufacturing Co.

Pekin High School ($50) see Harper Brush Works

Pella Christian Grade School ($20,000) see Pella Corp.

Pella Christian Grade School ($35,200) see Vermeer Manufacturing Co.

Pella Christian High School ($10,000) see Kuyper Foundation, Peter H. and E. Lucille Gaass

Pella Christian High School ($5,000) see Vermeer Investment Company Foundation

Pella Christian High School ($19,576) see Vermeer Manufacturing Co.

Pella Community Day Care Center ($50,000) see Kuyper Foundation, Peter H. and E. Lucille Gaass

Pella Community Hospital ($20,000) see Pella Corp.

Pella Community Hospital ($50,000) see Vermeer Investment Company Foundation

Pella Historical Society ($10,000) see Kuyper Foundation, Peter H. and E. Lucille Gaass

Pella Historical Society ($25,000) see Vermeer Investment Company Foundation

Pella Opera House Commission ($25,000) see Pella Corp.

Pella Opera House Committee ($25,000) see Kuyper Foundation, Peter H. and E. Lucille Gaass

Pella Pine Rest ($5,000) see Vermeer Manufacturing Co.

Pioneer Museum and Historical Society Northern Iowa — printing costs history books ($6,140) see Kinney-Lindstrom Foundation

Planned Parenthood ($11,000) see Glazer Foundation, Madelyn L.

Planned Parenthood ($20,000) see Mid-Iowa Health Foundation

Planned Parenthood Federation of America ($30,000) see Buffett Foundation

Planned Parenthood Federation of America ($1,000) see Ruan Foundation Trust, John

Puckerbrush Days ($1,000) see Winnebago Industries, Inc.

Putnam Museum ($7,000) see Harris Family Foundation, Hunt and Diane

Quad Cities Symphony Orchestra Foundation ($25,000) see Harris Family Foundation, Hunt and Diane

Quad City Arts ($7,800) see Younkers, Inc.

Quad City Symphony Orchestra Trust ($10,000) see Adler Foundation Trust, Philip D. and Henrietta B.

Rejuvenate Davenport ($100,000) see Deere & Co.

River Park Center ($20,000) see HON Industries

Riverview Club ($2,500) see Van Buren Foundation

Robertelle Center ($5,000) see Hanson Foundation

Robertelle Center ($1,000) see Winnebago Industries, Inc.

Ruan/MS Charity Golf ($1,000) see Iowa Savings Bank

S.I.E.D.A. ($150) see Harper Brush Works

St. Ambrose University ($200,000) see Bechtel Charitable Remainder Uni-Trust, Marie H.

St. Ambrose University ($100,000) see Deere & Co.

St. Luke's Health Care Foundation — for construction of surgical intensive care and adolescent psychiatry ($100,000) see Hall Foundation

St. Lukes Hospital Foundation ($10,000) see Adler Foundation Trust, Philip D. and Henrietta B.

St. Mark's Lutheran Church ($400) see Citizens First National Bank

St. Mary's Catholic Church ($1,201) see Citizens First National Bank

Salvation Army ($35,000) see Bechtel Charitable Remainder Uni-Trust, Marie H.

Salvation Army ($200) see Harper Brush Works

Salvation Army ($15,000) see HON Industries

Scattergood Friends School Foundation — first installment contribution toward Scattergood Friends School endowment fund ($40,000) see Maytag Family Foundation, Fred

Science Center of Iowa ($75,000) see Bohen Foundation

Science Center of Iowa ($10,000) see Hawley Foundation

Science Center of Iowa ($2,500) see IMT Insurance Co.

Science Center of Iowa ($1,074) see Iowa State Bank

Science Center of Iowa ($10,000) see Levitt Foundation

Science Center of Iowa ($50,000) see Maytag Corp.

Science Center of Iowa ($10,000) see Younkers, Inc.

Scott County Family YMCA — capital campaign challenge matching grant ($50,000) see Bechtel Charitable Remainder Uni-Trust, Marie H.

Scott County Family YMCA — gang intervention program ($25,000) see Bechtel Charitable Remainder Uni-Trust, Marie H.

Scott County Family YMCA — project rebound ($23,490) see Bechtel Charitable Remainder Uni-Trust, Marie H.

Scott County Family YMCA — swimming pool ($16,433) see

Bechtel Charitable Remainder Uni-Trust, Marie H.

Settlement Services — chore services for elderly ($25,000) see Mid-Iowa Health Foundation

Sioux City Gospel Mission ($2,500) see Demco Charitable Foundation

Sioux City Iowa Library — grant ($50,000) see Kinney-Lindstrom Foundation

Siouxland Community Soup Kitchen ($2,500) see Quincy Newspapers

Smoother Sailing ($5,000) see Hawley Foundation

Smoother Sailing ($10,000) see Younkers, Inc.

Southeastern Community College ($10,000) see Witte, Jr. Foundation, John H.

Spiritual Frontiers Fellowship International ($6,000) see Ebert Charitable Foundation, Horatio B.

State of Iowa Historical Museum ($200,000) see Lindstrom Foundation, Kinney

State of Iowa Historical Museum Building ($200,000) see Kinney-Lindstrom Foundation

Stonehill Care Center ($2,000) see McDonald Industries, Inc., A. Y.

Stonehill Care Center ($12,000) see Wahlert Foundation

Storm Lake High School Academic Enrichment Program ($400) see Citizens First National Bank

Synod of the Heartland ($5,000) see Demco Charitable Foundation

Tabernacle Baptist Church ($10,000) see Demco Charitable Foundation

Tax Education Foundation ($70,000) see E and M Charities

Tax Education Support Organization ($354,820) see E and M Charities

Tax Education Support Organization ($320,015) see E and M Charities

Tax Education Support Organization ($100,039) see E and M Charities

Teikyo Westmar University ($10,225) see Sherman Educational Fund, Mabel E.

Temple B'nai Jeshurun ($6,038) see Glazer Foundation, Madelyn L.

Temple Emanu-el ($42,000) see Adler Foundation Trust, Philip D. and Henrietta B.

Theatre Cedar Rapids Building Corporation ($2,000) see Gazette Co.

Trinity College ($10,000) see Vermeer Investment Company Foundation

Trinity Episcopal Cathedral ($50,000) see Adler Foundation Trust, Philip D. and Henrietta B.

UMKC New Horizons ($8,000) see Tension Envelope Corp.

United Way ($6,000) see Blank Fund, Myron and Jacqueline

United Way ($23,400) see Gazette Co.

United Way ($75,764) see Glazer Foundation, Madelyn L.

United Way ($1,650) see Guaranty Bank & Trust Co.

United Way ($16,432) see IMT Insurance Co.

United Way ($6,000) see Iowa State Bank

United Way ($2,000) see Lamson & Sessions Co.

United Way ($2,800) see Lehigh Portland Cement Co.

United Way ($14,000) see Levitt Foundation

United Way ($10,000) see Levitt Foundation, Richard S.

United Way ($25,000) see Lindstrom Foundation, Kinney

United Way ($15,565) see McDonald Industries, Inc., A. Y.

United Way ($6,825) see National By-Products

United Way ($2,000) see National By-Products

United Way ($8,000) see Pitt-Des Moines Inc.

United Way see Rochester Midland Corp.

United Way ($2,500) see Ruan Foundation Trust, John

United Way ($6,300) see Spahn & Rose Lumber Co.

United Way ($2,875) see Tension Envelope Corp.

United Way ($2,000) see Wallace Computer Services

United Way ($33,000) see Witte, Jr. Foundation, John H.

United Way ($40,000) see Younkers, Inc.

United Way of Central Iowa — contribution ($55,000) see Bridgestone/Firestone

United Way of Central Iowa ($82,000) see Norwest Corp.

United Way of Central Iowa ($500,000) see Principal Financial Group

United Way East Central Iowa — community assistance ($88,000) see IES Industries

United Way of East Central Iowa ($58,000) see Quaker Oats Co.

United Way of East Central Iowa — for 1990 campaign ($125,000) see Hall Foundation

United Way of Eastern Iowa see AEGON USA, Inc.

United Way of Muscatine ($64,430) see HON Industries

United Way of Newton ($45,000) see Maytag Corp.

University of Dubuque ($12,500) see Dillon Foundation

University of Dubuque ($10,000) see McDonald Industries, Inc., A. Y.

University of Dubuque ($5,000) see Spahn & Rose Lumber Co.

University of Iowa ($47,500) see Copernicus Society of America

University of Iowa ($75,000) see Frasch Foundation for Chemical Research (under the will of Elizabeth B. Frasch), Herman

University of Iowa Business School see AEGON USA, Inc.

University of Iowa Foundation ($320,452) see Carver Charitable Trust, Roy J.

University of Iowa Foundation ($3,200) see Gazette Co.

University of Iowa Foundation ($4,000) see Glazer Foundation, Madelyn L.

University of Iowa Foundation ($25,500) see HON Industries

University of Iowa Foundation — scholarship funding ($31,500) see IES Industries

University of Iowa Foundation ($6,000) see Lee Enterprises

University of Iowa Foundation ($20,000) see Pella Corp.

University of Iowa Foundation ($100,000) see Square D Co.

University of Iowa Research Foundation ($1,000) see Gerlach Foundation

University of Northern Iowa see AEGON USA, Inc.

University of Northern Iowa — youth leadership studies ($200,000) see McElroy Trust, R. J.

University of Northern Iowa Foundation — scholarship funding ($26,500) see IES Industries

Van Buren County Agency on Aging ($5,000) see Van Buren Foundation

Van Buren County Agency on Aging ($2,000) see Van Buren Foundation

Van Buren County Courthouse ($92,081) see Van Buren Foundation

Van Buren County Memorial ($15,000) see Van Buren Foundation

Van Buren County Memorial Hospital ($2,000) see Van Buren Foundation

Van Buren High School ($2,772) see Van Buren Foundation

Variety Club ($7,000) see Blank Fund, Myron and Jacqueline

Variety Club ($9,300) see Glazer Foundation, Madelyn L.

Variety Club of Iowa ($3,000) see Gazette Co.

Variety Club of Iowa ($250) see Guaranty Bank & Trust Co.

Variety Club of Iowa ($2,600) see Ruan Foundation Trust, John

Variety Club of Iowa — support needed facilities, medical equipment and transportation services for ill, handicapped and underprivileged children ($13,500) see IES Industries

Very Special Arts — state of Iowa equipment ($1,545) see Kinney-Lindstrom Foundation

Veterans' Plaza Authority ($800,000) see HON Industries

Village Northwest ($10,000) see Demco Charitable Foundation

Visiting Nurse Association ($5,000) see Wahlert Foundation

Visiting Nurses Association ($25,000) see Adler Foundation Trust, Philip D. and Henrietta B.

Wahlert High School ($1,750) see Spahn & Rose Lumber Co.

Wahlert High School ($240,500) see Wahlert Foundation

Waldorf College ($2,500) see Hanson Foundation

Waldorf College ($2,000) see Winnebago Industries, Inc.

Wartburg College ($4,000) see Iowa Savings Bank

Wartburg College ($185,000) see Saemann Foundation, Franklin I.

Wartburg College ($10,000) see Schmidt Charitable Foundation, William E.

Wartburg College — Communications Center ($70,000) see McElroy Trust, R. J.

Wartburg Lutheran Home for the Aging ($3,500) see Faith Home Foundation

Wartburg Lutheran Services ($6,540) see Rauch Foundation

Wartburg Seminary ($5,000) see Wahlert Foundation

Waterloo Foundation for the Arts ($50,000) see Brennan Foundation, Robert E.

West Hancock Ambulance Service ($2,000) see Winnebago Industries, Inc.

Wittenmyer Youth Center ($10,000) see Harris Family Foundation, Hunt and Diane

Woden Commercial Club Park Department ($1,500) see Hanson Foundation

World Food Prize ($1,100,000) see Ruan Foundation Trust, John

YMCA ($1,000) see Guaranty Bank & Trust Co.

YMCA ($3,000) see Hanson Foundation

YMCA ($6,000) see Hawley Foundation

YMCA ($8,000) see Lee Enterprises

YMCA ($7,500) see Lee Enterprises

YMCA ($2,500) see Ruan Foundation Trust, John

YMCA ($2,000) see Winnebago Industries, Inc.

YMCA/YWCA Building Fund ($250,000) see HON Industries

Young Life ($2,000) see Faith Charitable Trust

Young Women's Resource Center — seminars and counseling sessions for pregnant and parenting young women ages 13-21, and a Young Dad's group ($7,976) see Gannett Co.

YWCA of Cedar Rapids and Linn County, Iowa — construction/renovation project/special projects ($17,000) see IES Industries

Kansas

Aboretum in City Park ($2,500) see Stauffer Communications

Agricultural Hall of Fame ($8,000) see Breidenthal Foundation, Willard J. and Mary G.

Allen-Lambe House Foundation — general ($100,000) see Lambe Charitable Foundation, Claude R.

American Cancer Society ($53,676) see Seaver Charitable Trust, Richard C.

American Red Cross ($100) see Bromley Residuary Trust, Guy I.

American Red Cross — disaster relief ($5,000) see Williams Charitable Trust, Mary Jo

American Society Cancer ($100) see Misco Industries

Andover Baptist Church ($4,000) see Oldham Little Church Foundation

Arthritis Foundation ($500) see Hesston Corp.

Arts Center of Topeka ($15,000) see Gault-Hussey Charitable Trust

Arts Center of Topeka ($10,000) see Security Benefit Life Insurance Co.

Association for Community Arts Agencies of Kansas ($750) see Ross Foundation

Association of Community Arts Councils of Kansas ($50,000) see Hansen Foundation, Dane G.

Audio Reader, University of Kansas ($9,500) see Rice Foundation, Ethel and Raymond F.

Babe Ruth Baseball Association of Liberal — youth activities ($15,129) see Baughman Foundation

Kansas (cont.)

Baker Arts Foundation — remodeling facilities ($30,000) see Baughman Foundation

Baker University ($10,000) see Bromley Residuary Trust, Guy I.

Baker University — building extension ($75,000) see Collins Foundation, George and Jennie

Baker University ($25,000) see Collins, Jr. Foundation, George Fulton

Baker University ($35,000) see Sunderland Foundation, Lester T.

Baker University FM Station ($2,850) see Stauffer Communications

Baker University — renovation of Jolliffe Hall ($50,000) see Collins, Jr. Foundation, George Fulton

Barton County Community College ($2,000) see Security State Bank

Beech Aircraft Scholarship Program ($32,500) see Beech Aircraft Corp.

Benedictine College — final payment to rebuild their traditional student base ($174,840) see Turner Charitable Trust, Courtney S.

Benedictine College — partial payment to rebuild their traditional student base ($42,160) see Turner Charitable Trust, Courtney S.

Bethany College ($35,000) see Mingenback Foundation, Julia J.

Bethany Medical Center ($10,000) see Breidenthal Foundation, Willard J. and Mary G.

Bethel College ($10,000) see Schowalter Foundation

Bethel College ($1,900) see Staley Foundation, Thomas F.

Bethel Home ($2,000) see Scroggins Foundation, Arthur E. and Cornelia C.

Board of Education USD #500 ($10,000) see Breidenthal Foundation, Willard J. and Mary G.

Botanica, The Wichita Gardens ($1,000) see Insurance Management Associates

Boy Scouts of America ($300) see Baehr Foundation, Louis W. and Dolpha

Boy Scouts of America ($5,000) see Bank IV

Boy Scouts of America ($3,800) see Bank IV

Boy Scouts of America ($20,000) see Baughman Foundation

Boy Scouts of America ($10,000) see Beech Aircraft Corp.

Boy Scouts of America ($500) see O'Connor Co.

Boys Club ($50) see Fink Foundation

Building Life Skills ($10,000) see Phillips Foundation, Waite and Genevieve

Butler Community College — help refurbish the Nixon Library and Student Center as part of $1.5 million gift to be disbursed over a period of years ($100,000) see Hubbard Foundation, R. Dee and Joan Dale

Butler Community College — R.D. Hubbard Scholarships

($8,000) see Hubbard Foundation, R. Dee and Joan Dale

Campaign Kansas — University of Kansas, general ($100,000) see O'Shaughnessy Foundation, I. A.

Capper Foundation ($13,250) see Gault-Hussey Charitable Trust

Capper Foundation ($5,000) see Security Benefit Life Insurance Co.

Capper Foundation for Crippled Children — Outreach Program ($16,333) see Bank IV

Capper Foundation Residence Hall ($5,000) see Stauffer Communications

Catholic Social Services ($500) see Security State Bank

Cedars Retirement Center ($30,000) see Mingenback Foundation, Julia J.

Center for the Improvement of Human Functioning ($1,089,526) see Garvey Trust, Olive White

Center for the Improvement of Human Functioning International ($62,500) see Garvey Fund, Jean and Willard

Chaflin Volunteer Fire Department ($2,000) see Security State Bank

Christian Worker's Fellowship Fund ($46,000) see Caddock Foundation

Church of God in Christ Mennonite ($10,500) see Schowalter Foundation

Church of God in Christ Mennonite ($10,000) see Schowalter Foundation

Church of God in Christ Mennonite ($7,500) see Schowalter Foundation

City of Dodge City Parks and Recreation ($4,000) see Scroggins Foundation, Arthur E. and Cornelia C.

City Haysville Pride Community ($28,000) see Vulcan Materials Co.

City of Hesston — Hesston Ambulance Department Rescue Unit ($500) see Hesston Corp.

City of Liberal — recreation department ($25,450) see Baughman Foundation

City of Logan ($225,000) see Hansen Foundation, Dane G.

City of Osborne ($15,000) see Seaver Charitable Trust, Richard C.

City of Salina Baseball Facility ($10,000) see Smoot Charitable Foundation

City of Wichita — Grillan Fund ($2,978) see Bloomfield Foundation, Sam and Rie

Colby University ($250) see Chiquita Brands Co.

Committee of 101 ($2,500) see Black & Veatch

Counseling and Growth center ($2,500) see Smoot Charitable Foundation

Crisis Hot Line Dial-Help ($2,500) see Smoot Charitable Foundation

Depot Restoration Project ($25,000) see Sunderland Foundation, Lester T.

Developmental Services of Northwest Kansas ($30,000) see Hansen Foundation, Dane G.

Dodge City Community College — daycare center ($1,500) see Scroggins Foundation, Arthur E. and Cornelia C.

Dodge City Community College — nursing scholarships ($1,500) see Scroggins Foundation, Arthur E. and Cornelia C.

Dodge City Head Start Project ($4,000) see Scroggins Foundation, Arthur E. and Cornelia C.

Dodge City Public Library ($3,000) see Scroggins Foundation, Arthur E. and Cornelia C.

Donnelly College ($10,000) see Breidenthal Foundation, Willard J. and Mary G.

Donnelly College ($5,000) see McGee Foundation

Doorstep ($3,000) see Gault-Hussey Charitable Trust

Douglas County Historical Society — museum support ($13,000) see Rice Foundation, Ethel and Raymond F.

Douglas County Visiting Nurses ($10,000) see Rice Foundation, Ethel and Raymond F.

Elyria Christian School — purchase building ($2,000) see Mingenback Foundation, Julia J.

Emergency Aid ($2,500) see Smoot Charitable Foundation

Emmaus House — aid to needy ($5,000) see Williams Charitable Trust, Mary Jo

Emporia Arts Council — feasibility study for the development of a community cultural center ($2,500) see Trusler Foundation

Emporia State University ($3,300) see Jellison Benevolent Society

Emporia State University Endowment — build a sports complex for use by university students and the community ($130,000) see Trusler Foundation

Emporia State University — for the Future Teacher's Academy, which brings 50 state high school students to the university for a week long workshop ($38,163) see Hubbard Foundation, R. Dee and Joan Dale

Episcopal Charities ($5,300) see Baird Charitable Trust, William Robert

Episcopal Social Services ($1,500) see DeVore Foundation

Family Charities Foundation ($169,000) see Fink Foundation

FHS Endowment Association Venture Fund ($1,500) see Ross Foundation

Finney County United Way ($10,000) see Williams Charitable Trust, Mary Jo

First Presbyterian Church ($11,450) see DeVore Foundation

First Presbyterian Church ($50) see Fink Foundation

FMSU Endowment Association ($53,676) see Seaver Charitable Trust, Richard C.

Ford County 4-H Foundations ($2,000) see Scroggins Foundation, Arthur E. and Cornelia C.

Fort Hays State University ($10,000) see Dreiling and Albina Dreiling Charitable Trust, Leo J.

Ft. Hays State University ($2,000) see Jellison Benevolent Society

Fort Hays State University Endowment Association ($3,000) see Dreiling and Albina Dreiling Charitable Trust, Leo J.

Ft. Hays State University — for the Hubbard Leadership Seminars for gifted students ($20,799) see Hubbard Foundation, R. Dee and Joan Dale

Fort Scott Community College Endowment ($12,000) see Baehr Foundation, Louis W. and Dolpha

Friends of Hospice ($125) see Fink Foundation

Friends of the Topeka Zoo ($11,000) see Security Benefit Life Insurance Co.

Friends University ($10,000) see Beech Aircraft Corp.

Friends University ($25,000) see Bloomfield Foundation, Sam and Rie

Friends University ($10,000) see Coleman Co.

Friends University — impact campaign ($30,000) see Fourth Financial Corp.

Friends University ($5,330) see Garvey Fund, Jean and Willard

Friends University ($296,805) see Garvey Fund, Olive White

Friends University ($50,000) see Graham Charitable Trust, William L.

Friends University ($1,000) see Insurance Management Associates

Friends University ($10,000) see Koch Industries

Friends University — Impact campaign ($20,000) see First National Bank in Wichita

Friends University — 2nd payment-five year-$100,000 pledge ($20,000) see Cessna Aircraft Co.

Friends of Wichita Art Museum ($1,000) see Insurance Management Associates

Frontier Army Museum ($35,000) see Santa Fe Pacific Corp.

Future Horizon for Homeless Children ($35,000) see Jones Foundation, Helen

Garden City Community College Endowment Association — establishment of a learning center and an endowed scholarship ($80,000) see Williams Charitable Trust, Mary Jo

Garden City Piano Teachers League ($1,000) see Williams Charitable Trust, Mary Jo

General Conference Mennonite Church ($10,000) see Schowalter Foundation

Gerard House ($6,000) see Garvey Trust, Olive White

Gillis Center — Kansas City Spirit Festival ($1,800) see Shughart, Thomson & Kilroy, P.C.

Girl Scouts of America ($200) see Fink Foundation

Girl Scouts of America ($5,000) see First National Bank in Wichita

Girl Scouts of America ($10,000) see Garvey Trust, Olive White

Girl Scouts of America ($5,000) see Trusler Foundation

Golden Belt Community Concert Association ($350) see Security State Bank

Great Bend Community Theatre Building Fund ($500) see Security State Bank

Greater Wichita Community Foundation — final payment-$100,000-five year pledge ($20,000) see Cessna Aircraft Co.

Halstead Hospital ($10,600) see Beech Aircraft Corp.

Hays Arts Council ($400) see Ross Foundation

Hays Community Assistance Center ($250) see Ross Foundation

Hays Medical Center ($50,000) see Dreiling and Albina Dreiling Charitable Trust, Leo J.

Hays Public Schools Foundation ($200) see Ross Foundation

Hesston College ($10,000) see Beech Aircraft Corp.

Historic Wichita ($1,000) see Insurance Management Associates

Historic Wichita — southern hotel restoration ($5,000) see Koch Industries

Historic Wichita ($6,025) see Ross Foundation

Hospice ($1,000) see Bloomfield Foundation, Sam and Rie

Hutchinson Community College — scholarships ($6,000) see Davis Foundation, James A. and Juliet L.

Independent School ($411,000) see Garvey Fund, Jean and Willard

Independent School ($90,000) see Garvey Fund, Jean and Willard

Institute of Logopedics ($6,000) see Coleman Co.

Institute of Logopedics ($500) see Hesston Corp.

Institute of Logopedics — Christmas card program ($5,000) see Koch Industries

Inter-Faith Inn ($6,000) see Coleman Co.

International Association of Jazz Educators ($25,000) see Alpert Foundation, Herb

Jewish Community Campus ($40,000) see Helzberg Foundation, Shirley and Barnett

Jewish Community Campus of Greater Kansas City ($40,000) see Block, H&R

Jewish Federation ($115,395) see Bloch Foundation, Henry W. and Marion H.

Johnson County Community College ($5,000) see Flarsheim Charitable Foundation, Louis and Elizabeth

Junior Achievement ($3,700) see Bank IV

Kansas Action for Children ($3,000) see Ross Foundation

Kansas Agriculture and Rural Leadership ($5,100) see Garvey Kansas Foundation

Kansas Bar Association — Bill of Rights ($5,000) see Stauffer Communications

Kansas Children's Receiving Home ($1,000) see Bromley Residuary Trust, Guy I.

Kansas City Kansas Neighborhood ($10,000) see Bromley Residuary Trust, Guy I.

Kansas City Public Television ($8,000) see Utilicorp United

Kansas Community College ($5,000) see IBP, Inc.

Kansas Cosmosphere ($500) see Misco Industries

Kansas Elks Training Center for the Handicapped ($5,000) see Garvey Kansas Foundation

Kansas Foodbank Warehouse — food for the needy at Christmas ($1,000) see O'Connor Co.

Kansas 4-H Foundation — capital funds drive; education building ($20,000) see Fourth Financial Corp.

Kansas Incorporated ($2,000) see Bartlett & Co.

Kansas Incorporated ($2,000) see Bartlett & Co.

Kansas Independent College Fund ($50,000) see Beech Aircraft Corp.

Kansas Independent College Fund ($2,500) see Black & Veatch

Kansas Independent College Fund ($10,000) see Gault-Hussey Charitable Trust

Kansas Independent College Fund ($5,000) see Marley Co.

Kansas Independent College Fund ($2,000) see Martin Marietta Aggregates

Kansas Independent College Fund ($2,500) see Nichols Co., J.C.

Kansas Independent College Fund ($20,000) see Santa Fe Pacific Corp.

Kansas Independent Colleges ($500) see Misco Industries

Kansas Masonic Foundation ($35,000) see Hansen Foundation, Dane G.

Kansas Newman College ($10,000) see Hedrick Foundation, Frank E.

Kansas Oil and Gas Museum ($500) see Insurance Management Associates

Kansas Oil and Gas Museum Foundation ($1,500) see Dreiling and Albina Dreiling Charitable Trust, Leo J.

Kansas Public Telecommunication Service ($500) see Hesston Corp.

Kansas Public Telecommunications Service — Sesame Street ($2,100) see Davis Foundation, James A. and Juliet L.

Kansas Special Olympics ($1,250) see DeVore Foundation

Kansas Special Olympics ($250) see O'Connor Co.

Kansas State University ($5,000) see Black & Veatch

Kansas State University ($2,000) see Black & Veatch

Kansas State University ($4,000) see Continental Grain Co.

Kansas State University ($5,000) see Davies Charitable Trust

Kansas State University ($19,050) see Jellison Benevolent Society

Kansas State University — research and training in the field of group theory and geometry ($32,050) see Kade Foundation, Max

Kansas State University ($50,000) see Ross Foundation

Kansas State University ($25,000) see Security Benefit Life Insurance Co.

Kansas State University ($250) see Security State Bank

Kansas State University — final payment on a $130,000 Hubbard Math project that helped more than 5,000 students and teachers learn to improve their math skills ($30,000) see Hubbard Foundation, R. Dee and Joan Dale

Kansas State University — Alfalfa management studies ($27,707) see Baughman Foundation

Kansas State University Foundation ($69,000) see Hansen Foundation, Dane G.

Kansas State University Foundation — Essential Edge campaign ($37,500) see First National Bank in Wichita

Kansas State University Foundation — Essential Edge campaign ($20,000) see Fourth Financial Corp.

Kansas University ($4,500) see Jellison Benevolent Society

Kansas University Audio Reader ($10,000) see Baehr Foundation, Louis W. and Dolpha

Kansas University — Campaign Kansas ($10,000) see Stauffer Communications

Kansas University Endowment Association ($60,000) see Baehr Foundation, Louis W. and Dolpha

Kansas University Endowment Association ($30,000) see Barrows Foundation, Geraldine and R. A.

Kansas University Endowment Association ($100) see Fink Foundation

Kansas University Endowment Association — financial support ($30,000) see Fourth Financial Corp.

Kansas University Endowment Association ($40,000) see Hansen Foundation, Dane G.

Kansas University Endowment Association — construction ($3,149,818) see Lied Foundation Trust

Kansas University Endowment Association ($58,000) see Phillips Petroleum Co.

Kansas University Endowment Association ($205,000) see Southwestern Bell Corp.

Kansas University Endowment Association ($20,000) see Summerfield Foundation, Solon E.

Kansas University Endowment Association ($250,000) see Ward Foundation, Louis L. and Adelaide C.

Kansas University Endowment Association — Art Museum ($8,000) see Breidenthal Foundation, Willard J. and Mary G.

Kansas University Endowment Association — support Campaign Kansas Medical Center Program ($50,000) see Turner Charitable Trust, Courtney S.

Kansas University Endowment Association, University of Kansas ($252,143) see Bohan Foundation, Ruth H.

Kansas University Endowment — Campaign Kansas Alumni Association ($33,333) see First National Bank in Wichita

Kansas University Endowment Fund ($7,500) see Kuehn Foundation

Kansas University Endowment — Rice Scholarships ($28,000) see Rice Foundation, Ethel and Raymond F.

Kansas University School of Social Welfare — social policy conference ($5,000) see Rhoden Charitable Foundation, Elmer C.

Kansas Wesleyan Foundation ($40,000) see Hansen Foundation, Dane G.

Kansas Wesleyan University ($85,000) see Smoot Charitable Foundation

Ketch ($5,200) see Garvey Trust, Olive White

KETCH Housing ($1,000) see DeVore Foundation

Kids After School ($2,000) see Davis Foundation, James A. and Juliet L.

KPTS Channel 8 ($300) see Insurance Management Associates

KPTS Channel 8 ($250) see Misco Industries

KSOF 91.1 FM ($100) see Misco Industries

Lakemary Center ($30,000) see Smith Foundation, Kenneth L. and Eva S.

Lakemary Endowment ($10,000) see Baehr Foundation, Louis W. and Dolpha

Land Institute ($50,000) see Austin Memorial Foundation

Land Institute — general support for their work on alternative agriculture methods ($10,000) see Levinson Foundation, Max and Anna

LAVTS Foundation — scholarships, assist equipment purchase ($30,000) see Baughman Foundation

Lawrence Arts Center ($11,000) see Rice Foundation, Ethel and Raymond F.

Lawrence United Fund ($7,600) see Rice Foundation, Ethel and Raymond F.

Let's Help ($300) see Fink Foundation

Liberal Memorial Library Foundation — computer equipment ($16,000) see Baughman Foundation

Living Land Foundation ($25,000) see Davis Foundation, James A. and Juliet L.

Living Land Foundation ($2,000) see Davis Foundation, James A. and Juliet L.

Manhattan Christian College ($1,000) see Jellison Benevolent Society

Mc Pherson Health Care Foundation — financial support ($20,000) see Fourth Financial Corp.

McPherson Arts Council ($500) see Mingenback Foundation, Julia J.

McPherson College — campus improvements ($50,000) see Mingenback Foundation, Julia J.

McPherson College ($300) see Mueller Co.

Meals on Wheels ($6,000) see Scroggins Foundation, Arthur E. and Cornelia C.

Meninger Foundation ($10,000) see Luce Charitable Trust, Theodore

Menninger Foundation ($4,000) see Bank IV

Menninger Foundation ($5,000) see Crane Foundation, Raymond E. and Ellen F.

Menninger Foundation — operating support ($10,000) see Davis Foundation, Edwin W. and Catherine M.

Menninger Foundation ($7,500) see Goerlich Family Foundation

Menninger Foundation ($2,600) see Goerlich Family Foundation

Menninger Foundation ($5,000) see Kunstadter Family Foundation, Albert

Menninger Foundation ($250,000) see Lattner Foundation, Forrest C.

Menninger Foundation ($5,000) see Lindsay Foundation

Menninger Foundation ($300) see Misco Industries

Menninger Foundation ($1,500) see Nash Foundation

Menninger Foundation ($25,000) see Security Benefit Life Insurance Co.

Menninger Foundation ($20,000) see Sooner Pipe & Supply Corp.

Menninger Foundation ($15,000) see Stauffer Communications

Menninger Foundation ($25,000) see Weyerhaeuser Memorial Foundation, Charles A.

Menninger Foundation — Seeley Fellows Program ($150,000) see Seeley Foundation

Menninger Foundation — Seeley Professorship in Psychiatry ($30,000) see Seeley Foundation

Menninger Foundation — Voluntary Controls Department ($5,000) see Seeley Foundation

Menninger Foundation — Voluntary Controls Department ($5,000) see Seeley Foundation

Mennonite Housing ($350) see Insurance Management Associates

Mennonite Housing Rehabilitation Service ($17,000) see Hedrick Foundation, Frank E.

Mental Health Association of South Central Kansas ($100,000) see Lattner Foundation, Forrest C.

Miami County Genealogy Society ($3,536) see Baehr Foundation, Louis W. and Dolpha

Miami County Recreation Commission ($22,500) see Baehr Foundation, Louis W. and Dolpha

Mobile Meals of Topeka ($2,500) see Gault-Hussey Charitable Trust

Model Block Program ($6,000) see Security Benefit Life Insurance Co.

Music Theater of Wichita ($500) see Insurance Management Associates

National Youth Leadership Council ($400) see Security State Bank

Occupational Center of Central Kansas ($4,000) see Smoot Charitable Foundation

Offender/Victim Ministries ($5,000) see Schowalter Foundation

Old Cowtown Museum ($6,000) see Coleman Co.

Old Cowtown — Pioneer drive ($5,000) see First National Bank in Wichita

Opera Kansas ($12,150) see Koch Industries

Operation Exodus ($25,000) see Bloch Foundation, Henry W. and Marion H.

Operation Holiday — help for families at Christmas ($1,000) see O'Connor Co.

Osborne County ($20,000) see Seaver Charitable Trust, Richard C.

Ottawa University ($50,000) see Ross Foundation

Paola Free Library ($27,405) see Baehr Foundation, Louis W. and Dolpha

Peter Marshall Golf Classic ($10,000) see Enright Foundation

Pittsburg State University ($2,750) see Harris Foundation, H. H.

Plymouth Congregational Church ($5,290) see Garvey Fund, Jean and Willard

Plymouth Congregational Church ($8,000) see Rice Foundation, Ethel and Raymond F.

Plymouth Congregational Church ($7,500) see Rice Foundation, Ethel and Raymond F.

Presbyterian Church (U.S.A.) — toward Hurricane Andrew relief services ($500,000) see McCune Foundation

Providence-St. Margaret Health Care Foundation ($10,000) see Breidenthal Foundation, Willard J. and Mary G.

Rainbows United ($10,000) see Garvey Trust, Olive White

Rainbows United ($11,200) see Hedrick Foundation, Frank E.

Rescue Mission ($4,000) see Stauffer Communications

Ronald McDonald House ($5,000) see Gault-Hussey Charitable Trust

Sacred Heart ($3,000) see Scroggins Foundation, Arthur E. and Cornelia C.

St. Anthony House ($2,000) see DeVore Foundation

St. Fidelis Church ($2,000) see Dreiling and Albina Dreiling Charitable Trust, Leo J.

St. Francis Centennial ($25,000) see Coleman Co.

St. Francis Endowment Association — Centennial campaign ($10,000) see First National Bank in Wichita

St. Francis Regional Medical Center — centennial campaign ($20,000) see Fourth Financial Corp.

St. John's Rest Home ($25,000) see Dreiling and Albina Dreiling Charitable Trust, Leo J.

St. Joseph Medical Center — Easy Street project ($5,000) see First National Bank in Wichita

St. Josephs Catholic Church ($1,000) see Bromley Residuary Trust, Guy I.

St. Josephs Catholic School — capital improvements ($50,000) see Mingenback Foundation, Julia J.

St. Josephs Catholic School — operating fund ($2,000) see Mingenback Foundation, Julia J.

Kansas (cont.)

St. Luke's Foundation — Lupus research ($50,651) see Coleman Co.

St. Mary College ($10,000) see Breidenthal Foundation, Willard J. and Mary G.

St. Mary College ($25,000) see Bromley Residuary Trust, Guy I.

St. Mary College ($10,000) see McGee Foundation

St. Mary of Plains ($4,000) see Scroggins Foundation, Arthur E. and Cornelia C.

St. Thomas Aquinas High School ($5,000) see Wornall Charitable Trust and Foundation, Kearney

Salgo Trust for Education ($141,509) see Salgo Charitable Trust, Nicholas M.

Salgo Trust for Education ($25,000) see Salgo Charitable Trust, Nicholas M.

Salgo Trust for Education ($3,702) see Salgo Charitable Trust, Nicholas M.

Salina Arts and Humanities Commission ($25,000) see Koch Industries

Salina Celtics ($3,000) see Smoot Charitable Foundation

Salvation Army ($1,610) see DeVore Foundation

Salvation Army ($10,000) see Garvey Fund, Jean and Willard

Salvation Army ($5,000) see Garvey Trust, Olive White

Salvation Army ($50,000) see Koch Charitable Foundation, Charles G.

Salvation Army ($7,500) see Rice Foundation, Ethel and Raymond F.

Salvation Army ($3,000) see Stauffer Communications

Salvation Army — aid to needy ($5,000) see Williams Charitable Trust, Mary Jo

Salvation Army — disaster relief ($5,000) see Williams Charitable Trust, Mary Jo

Sandzen Memorial Art Gallery — capital improvements ($1,000) see Mingenback Foundation, Julia J.

Sedgwick County Zoo ($3,000) see Insurance Management Associates

Sedgwick County Zoological Association ($25,000) see Beech Aircraft Corp.

Sedgwick County Zoological Society ($5,000) see Hedrick Foundation, Frank E.

Senior Citizens Christmas Telethon — aid to elderly ($1,000) see Williams Charitable Trust, Mary Jo

Senior Services ($10,000) see Hedrick Foundation, Frank E.

Seward County Community Development Foundation — scholarships ($102,925) see Baughman Foundation

Seward County Historical Society — operations ($15,000) see Baughman Foundation

Sister Ann Barton ($2,500) see Kasal Charitable Trust, Father

Sisters of St. Joseph — purchase an ambulance ($4,000) see Butler Foundation, J. Homer

Smith Center Public Schools — maintenance of the Miner and Loese Hubbard Scholarships ($7,000) see Hubbard

Foundation, R. Dee and Joan Dale

Spencer Museum of Art ($77,000) see Kemper Charitable Trust, William T.

Stafford County 4-H Council ($500) see Security State Bank

Stanley Elementary School ($250,000) see RJR Nabisco Inc.

Starkey Development Center — work activity building ($10,000) see First National Bank in Wichita

Sterling College ($2,000) see Jellison Benevolent Society

Stormont Vail Regional Medical Center ($12,500) see Gault-Hussey Charitable Trust

Temple Emanu-el ($1,100) see Bloomfield Foundation, Sam and Rie

Thomas More Prep — Marian High School ($82,285) see Dreiling and Albina Dreiling Charitable Trust, Leo J.

Topeka Community Foundation ($5,000) see Stauffer Communications

Topeka Rescue Mission ($5,750) see Security Benefit Life Insurance Co.

Topeka Zoological Foundation — General Fund ($10,000) see Bank IV

Training and Evaluation Center of Hutchinson ($3,000) see Davis Foundation, James A. and Juliet L.

Trees for Life — provides funding, management and expertise worldwide planting food bearing trees ($54,000) see Stein Foundation, Jules and Doris

United Fund ($1,700) see Baehr Foundation, Louis W. and Dolpha

United Methodist Urban Ministry of Wichita ($3,166) see Hedrick Foundation, Frank E.

United Presbyterian Fund ($1,000) see Jellison Benevolent Society

United Way ($50,000) see Bank IV

United Way ($113,000) see Beech Aircraft Corp.

United Way ($500) see Bromley Residuary Trust, Guy I.

United Way ($10,000) see Coleman Co.

United Way ($10,000) see Coleman Co.

United Way ($10,000) see Coleman Co.

United Way ($10,000) see Coleman Co.

United Way ($2,500) see DeVore Foundation

United Way ($50,250) see Eaton Corp.

United Way ($74,000) see First National Bank in Wichita

United Way ($10,000) see Gault-Hussey Charitable Trust

United Way ($5,000) see Insurance Management Associates

United Way ($1,600) see Misco Industries

United Way ($1,650) see National By-Products

United Way ($800) see O'Connor Co.

United Way ($34,000) see Security Benefit Life Insurance Co.

United Way ($30,000) see Smoot Charitable Foundation

United Way of Greater Topeka ($100,000) see Santa Fe Pacific Corp.

United Way of the Plain — 1st payment of $157,000 pledge ($39,250) see Cessna Aircraft Co.

United Way of the Plains — final payment-1990/91 pledge ($39,250) see Cessna Aircraft Co.

United Way of the Plains — 2nd payment-1990/91 pledge ($39,250) see Cessna Aircraft Co.

United Way of the Plains — 3rd installation-1990/91 pledge ($39,250) see Cessna Aircraft Co.

United Way of Topeka — financial support ($71,250) see Fourth Financial Corp.

United Way of Wichita and Sedgwick County — financial support ($100,000) see Fourth Financial Corp.

University of Health Sciences Foundation ($30,000) see Community Hospital Foundation

University of Kansas ($12,000) see Black & Veatch

University of Kansas ($3,000) see Black & Veatch

University of Kansas ($5,000) see Butler Manufacturing Co.

University of Kansas ($1,356) see Copolymer Rubber & Chemical Corp.

University of Kansas ($32,683) see Ernst & Young

University of Kansas ($147,100) see KPMG Peat Marwick

University of Kansas ($50,000) see Kress Foundation, Samuel H.

University of Kansas ($26,000) see Security Benefit Life Insurance Co.

University of Kansas ($50,000) see Sunderland Foundation, Lester T.

University of Kansas City Trustees ($2,500) see Black & Veatch

University of Kansas Endowment Association ($50,000) see Sprint

University of Kansas Endowment Fund — in support of strengthen nutrition education programs ($80,000) see Speas Memorial Trust, John W. and Effie E.

University Professors for Academic Order ($1,000) see Wilbur Foundation, Marguerite Eyer

USD 480 — court diversion program ($35,204) see Baughman Foundation

USD 428 Foundation ($250) see Security State Bank

USD 392 ($12,611) see Seaver Charitable Trust, Richard C.

USD #368 ($1,000) see Baehr Foundation, Louis W. and Dolpha

USD 253 — land donated for use in the construction of a new junior high school ($160,166) see Trusler Foundation

Venture House ($100,000) see Lattner Foundation, Forrest C.

Venture House — food and shelter for the homeless ($1,000) see O'Connor Co.

Venture House — food and shelter for the homeless ($1,000) see O'Connor Co.

Victory in the Valley ($3,050) see Hedrick Foundation, Frank E.

Village Presbyterian Church — renovation of pre-school facilities ($159,882) see Rhoden Charitable Foundation, Elmer C.

Village Presbyterian Church — radio broadcast series, 1991 ($9,880) see Rhoden Charitable Foundation, Elmer C.

Villages ($30,000) see Jones Foundation, Helen

Washburn Law Library ($2,500) see Stauffer Communications

Washburn University ($12,000) see Bank IV

Washburn University ($3,000) see Bank IV

Washburn University ($14,250) see Gault-Hussey Charitable Trust

Washburn University ($7,250) see Security Benefit Life Insurance Co.

Washburn University — endowment funds ($10,000) see Shughart, Thomson & Kilroy, P.C.

Wichita Area Girl Scouts ($10,000) see Hedrick Foundation, Frank E.

Wichita Art Association Center for the Arts ($10,000) see Garvey Kansas Foundation

Wichita Art Museum ($2,000) see Bloomfield Foundation, Sam and Rie

Wichita Center for the Arts ($136,815) see Koch Industries

Wichita Center for the Arts ($100,000) see Koch Industries

Wichita Center for the Arts ($14,020) see Koch Industries

Wichita Center for the Arts ($500) see O'Connor Co.

Wichita Center for the Arts ($3,000) see Ross Foundation

Wichita Children's Home ($5,025) see Hedrick Foundation, Frank E.

Wichita Children's Home ($500) see O'Connor Co.

Wichita Collegiate School ($4,000) see Grede Foundries

Wichita Collegiate School ($300,000) see Koch Charitable Foundation, Charles G.

Wichita Collegiate School ($90,000) see Lattner Foundation, Forrest C.

Wichita Crime Commission — crime prevention ($500) see O'Connor Co.

Wichita Institute for Clinical Research ($25,000) see Koch Industries

Wichita Sedgwich County Historic ($250) see Misco Industries

Wichita State University ($220,375) see Bloomfield Foundation, Sam and Rie

Wichita State University ($1,300) see DeVore Foundation

Wichita State University ($30,000) see First National Bank in Wichita

Wichita State University ($15,000) see Garvey Fund, Jean and Willard

Wichita State University ($50,000) see Graham Charitable Trust, William L.

Wichita State University ($9,000) see Koch Industries

Wichita State University ($500) see Security State Bank

Wichita State University Endowment Association — scholarships ($25,000) see Fourth Financial Corp.

Wichita State University Endowment Association — endowment fund ($20,000) see Fourth Financial Corp.

Wichita State University — Frank E. Hedrick Conference Room ($25,000) see Beech Aircraft Corp.

Wichita State University — Institute for Aviation Research ($50,000) see Beech Aircraft Corp.

Wichita Swim Club ($6,000) see Garvey Kansas Foundation

Wichita Symphony ($87,750) see Bloomfield Foundation, Sam and Rie

Wichita Symphony Society ($300) see Misco Industries

Wichita Symphony Society — last payment-$70,000 pledge ($17,000) see Cessna Aircraft Co.

Williams Educational Fund — scholarships ($10,000) see Rice Foundation, Ethel and Raymond F.

Williams Educational Fund ($10,000) see Ward Foundation, Louis L. and Adelaide C.

Women in the Arts ($3,000) see Garvey Trust, Olive White

Wyandotte House ($5,000) see Rhoden Charitable Foundation, Elmer C.

YMCA ($5,700) see Bank IV

YMCA ($5,000) see DeVore Foundation

YMCA ($5,000) see Gault-Hussey Charitable Trust

YMCA ($16,537) see Hedrick Foundation, Frank E.

YMCA ($18,200) see Jellison Benevolent Society

YMCA ($500) see Mingenback Foundation, Julia J.

YMCA ($200) see Misco Industries

YMCA ($173,544) see Smoot Charitable Foundation

YWCA ($12,770) see Garvey Kansas Foundation

YWCA ($25,000) see Smoot Charitable Foundation

Kentucky

Actors Theatre see PNC Bank

Actors Theatre of Louisville ($694,000) see Humana

Actors Theatre of Louisville ($85,000) see Shubert Foundation

Adath Jeshurun Congregation ($2,800) see Roth Foundation, Louis T.

Alice Lloyd College ($200,000) see Andersen Foundation

Alice Lloyd College ($250,000) see Brown Foundation, James Graham

Alice Lloyd College ($2,000) see Butler Family Foundation, George W. and Gladys S.

Alice Lloyd College ($10,000) see Campbell Foundation, Charles Talbot

Alice Lloyd College ($4,000) see Childs Charitable Foundation, Roberta M.

Alice Lloyd College ($8,078) see Ferre Revocable Trust, Joseph C.

Alice Lloyd College ($5,000) see Jephson Educational Trust No. 1

Alice Lloyd College ($100,000) see Mills Foundation, Ralph E.

American Heart Association see PNC Bank

American Red Cross ($20,000) see Brown Foundation, W. L. Lyons

Appalachia Science in the Public Interest — environmental studies ($54,500) see Hoffman Foundation, Maximillian E. and Marion O.

Appalshop/American Festival Project ($7,000) see Kentucky Foundation for Women

Artswatch ($3,300) see Kentucky Foundation for Women

Asbury College ($200,000) see Andersen Foundation

Asbury College ($21,500) see Edwards Foundation, O. P. and W. E.

Asbury College — scholarship ($16,350) see Froderman Foundation

Asbury College ($100,000) see Mills Foundation, Ralph E.

Asbury Methodist Home ($25,000) see Bastien Memorial Foundation, John E. and Nellie J.

Asbury Theological Seminary ($7,500) see Broadhurst Foundation

Asbury Theological Seminary ($1,000) see Jinks Foundation, Ruth T.

Asbury Theological Seminary — E. Stanley Jones School of Missions and Evangelism ($100,000) see Chatlos Foundation

Ballard High School/Effective Learning Project ($35,000) see Norton Foundation Inc.

Bank One Senior Classic ($4,000) see Greenebaum, Doll & McDonald

Bellarmine College ($5,000) see Bank of Louisville

Belle of Louisville ($8,000) see Blue Cross & Blue Shield of Kentucky Foundation

Belle of Louisville Operating Board ($350,000) see Brown Foundation, James Graham

Bellermine College ($66,000) see Brown Foundation, W. L. Lyons

Bellermine College ($15,000) see C. E. and S. Foundation

Berea College — capital campaign ($200,000) see Ball Foundation, George and Frances

Berea College — unrestricted ($50,000) see Ball Foundation, George and Frances

Berea College ($8,000) see Baumker Charitable Foundation, Elsie and Harry

Berea College ($4,300) see Bodenhamer Foundation

Berea College ($49,600) see Bonner Foundation, Corella and Bertram

Berea College ($42,320) see Bonner Foundation, Corella and Bertram

Berea College ($42,320) see Bonner Foundation, Corella and Bertram

Berea College ($36,800) see Bonner Foundation, Corella and Bertram

Berea College ($10,000) see Bradford Foundation, George and Ruth

Berea College ($4,000) see Childs Charitable Foundation, Roberta M.

Berea College ($35,000) see Ebert Charitable Foundation, Horatio B.

Berea College — library renovation ($50,000) see Frueauff Foundation, Charles A.

Berea College — entreprenuership development ($90,000) see Gheens Foundation

Berea College ($72,267) see Hallett Charitable Trust

Berea College ($48,110) see Hallett Charitable Trust

Berea College ($48,110) see Hallett Charitable Trust, Jessie F.

Berea College — nursing professorship ($5,000) see Johnson Foundation, Burdine

Berea College — nursing scholarship ($25,000) see Johnston Trust for Charitable and Educational Purposes, James M.

Berea College ($50,000) see Kendall Foundation, George R.

Berea College ($5,000) see Laub Foundation

Berea College ($5,000) see Lebus Trust, Bertha

Berea College ($100,000) see Mills Foundation, Ralph E.

Berea College ($2,000) see Moore Foundation, O. L.

Berea College ($25,000) see Moores Foundation, Harry C.

Berea College ($20,000) see Ross Foundation, Walter G.

Berea College ($95,028) see Second Foundation

Berea College ($22,500) see Sullivan Foundation, Algernon Sydney

Berea College — for Hutchins Library Acquisition Fund ($10,000) see Knapp Foundation

Bethany Bible Church ($500) see Houchens Foundation, Ervin G.

Bethany House — emergency assistance to rural poor ($4,000) see Walsh Charity Trust, Blanche M.

Black Achievers Program see PNC Bank

Blue Grass Community Action Agency ($7,500) see Brookdale Foundation

Bluegrass Tomorrow ($10,000) see Greenebaum, Doll & McDonald

Body Recall — geriatric care ($5,000) see Robinson Mountain Fund, E. O.

Bowling Green Association ($1,000) see Delacorte Fund, George

Boy Scouts of America ($51,666) see C. E. and S. Foundation

Boy Scouts of America ($10,895) see Schneider Foundation Corp., Al J.

Boy Scouts of America ($3,500) see Thomas Industries

Boyd County Board of Education ($75,000) see Ashland Oil

Boys Club of America ($1,825) see Houchens Foundation, Ervin G.

Brescia College ($10,000) see Yeager Charitable Trust, Lester E.

Broadway Baptist Church ($29,175) see Cooke Foundation Corporation, V. V.

Cabbage Patch Settlement House ($18,333) see C. E. and S. Foundation

Campaign for Greater Louisville see Capital Holding Corp.

Caney Creek Community Center — Alice Lloyd College; scholarship program ($572,856) see Berger Foundation, H.N. and Frances C.

Cardinal Hill Hospital ($5,000) see Parsons - W.D. Charities, Vera Davis

Carmel Manor ($117,567) see Cincinnati Foundation for the Aged

Catholic Services Appeal ($23,300) see Schneider Foundation Corp., Al J.

Cedar Lake Lodge ($10,000) see Schneider Foundation Corp., Al J.

Center for Leadership in School Reform — New Futures Project support ($1,135,721) see Casey Foundation, Annie E.

Center for Leadership in School Reform — continuation of 1988 grant to establish the Center in Louisville, Kentucky, and support its operation ($35,000) see Matsushita Electric Corp. of America

Center for Leadership in School Reform — continuation of 1988 grant to establish the Center in Louisville, Kentucky, and supports its operation ($35,000) see Matsushita Electric Corp. of America

Centre College ($110,000) see Ashland Oil

Centre College ($1,000,000) see Brown Foundation, James Graham

Centre College — entreprenuership development ($70,565) see Gheens Foundation

Centre College Annual Fund ($13,250) see Wunsch Foundation

Cerebral Palsy School of Louisville ($8,084) see Ferre Revocable Trust, Joseph C.

Chance School ($14,000) see Brown Foundation, W. L. Lyons

Chance School ($25,000) see Norton Foundation Inc.

Children's Home of Northern Kentucky ($7,000) see Russell Charitable Trust, Josephine S.

Christ Church United Methodist ($13,000) see Cooke Foundation Corporation, V. V.

Christian Appalachian Project ($10,000) see Von der Ahe Foundation

Christian Appalachian Project ($10,000) see Von der Ahe, Jr. Trust, Theodore Albert

Church of Redeemer ($500) see Houchens Foundation, Ervin G.

Church River School ($25,000) see Abercrombie Foundation

City of Hope see PNC Bank

Clark County Public Library see PNC Bank

Cumberland College ($25,000) see Arronson Foundation

Cumberland College — scholarship ($377,000) see Berger Foundation, H.N. and Frances C.

Cumberland College — expansion of existing library ($375,000) see Berger Foundation, H.N. and Frances C.

Cumberland College ($17,500) see Bissell Foundation, J. Walton

Cumberland College ($3,000) see Butler Family Foundation, George W. and Gladys S.

Cumberland College ($4,000) see Clark Charitable Trust

Cumberland College ($5,000) see Clayton Fund

Cumberland College ($10,000) see duPont Foundation, Alfred I.

Cumberland College ($5,000) see Garvey Trust, Olive White

Cumberland College ($10,000) see Goldenberg Foundation, Max

Cumberland College ($3,000) see Harcourt Foundation, Ellen Knowles

Cumberland College — to establish endowed scientific assistantship fund ($35,000) see Hearst Foundation

Cumberland College — crafts center ($1,000,000) see Herrick Foundation

Cumberland College — scientific equipment ($250,000) see Herrick Foundation

Cumberland College ($15,000) see Holmes Foundation

Cumberland College ($10,000) see Kellstadt Foundation

Cumberland College ($7,000) see Kilworth Charitable Foundation, Florence B.

Cumberland College ($100,000) see Mills Foundation, Ralph E.

Cumberland College ($25,000) see Oaklawn Foundation

Cumberland College ($5,000) see Oxford Foundation

Cumberland College ($3,500) see Ramlose Foundation, George A.

Cumberland College ($10,000) see Ratner Foundation, Milton M.

Cumberland College ($20,000) see Russell Charitable Foundation, Tom

Cumberland College ($5,000) see Soref Foundation, Samuel M. Soref and Helene K.

Cumberland College ($12,250) see Sullivan Foundation, Algernon Sydney

Cumberland College ($5,000) see Vale Foundation, Ruby R.

Cumberland College — acquiring building center for Appalachian enterprises ($200,000) see Hermann Foundation, Grover

Curriculum Resource Room ($20,000) see Norton Foundation Inc.

Dare to Care ($5,000) see Vogt Machine Co., Henry

David School — building program ($40,000) see Fohs Foundation

De Paul School ($14,000) see Brown Foundation, W. L. Lyons

DePaul School — expanding and updating the current facilities ($30,000) see Gheens Foundation

Diocese of Owensboro ($10,000) see Gore Family Memorial Foundation

Educational Foundation for Excellence ($23,334) see Koch Sons, George

Ephraim McDowell Cancer Research Foundation ($200,000) see Mills Foundation, Ralph E.

Family Place ($35,000) see Norton Foundation Inc.

Farnsley Moreman House ($200,000) see Humana

Federation of Appalachian Housing Enterprises ($20,000) see Penney Foundation, James C.

Federation of Appalachian Housing Enterprises — home loans ($5,000) see Robinson Mountain Fund, E. O.

Fellowship of Christian Athletes ($11,500) see Belk Stores

Fellowship of Christian Athletes ($500) see Cooke Foundation Corporation, V. V.

Fifteen Telecommunications ($8,000) see Glenmore Distilleries Co.

Fifteen Telecommunications ($1,750) see Roth Foundation, Louis T.

Forward Northern Kentucky — Tri-County Economic Development ($7,500) see Greenebaum, Doll & McDonald

Frontier Nursing Service ($3,000) see Cranshaw Corporation

Frontier Nursing Service — NEED and operating ($14,000) see Ireland Foundation

Fund for the Arts ($22,000) see Brown Foundation, W. L. Lyons

Fund for the Arts see Capital Holding Corp.

Fund for the Arts ($10,000) see Greenebaum, Doll & McDonald

Fund for Community Ministries ($1,500) see Cooke Foundation Corporation, V. V.

Georgetown College ($100,000) see Mills Foundation, Ralph E.

Girl Scouts of America ($750) see Houchens Foundation, Ervin G.

God's Pantry — food distribution ($5,000) see Robinson Mountain Fund, E. O.

Good News — United Methodist renewal and publications ($53,000) see E and M Charities

Good Shepherd Episcopal Church ($15,000) see Gross Charitable Trust, Walter L. and Nell R.

Grace Baptist Church ($7,008) see Houchens Foundation, Ervin G.

Grayson-Jockey Club Research Foundation — equine veterinary and genetics research ($2,206,140) see Kleberg, Jr. and Helen C. Kleberg Foundation, Robert J.

Greater Louisville Fund for the Arts ($36,000) see Bank of Louisville

Greater Louisville Fund for the Arts ($30,000) see Blue Cross & Blue Shield of Kentucky Foundation

Greater Louisville Fund for the Arts ($5,000) see Glenmore Distilleries Co.

Greater Louisville Fund for the Arts ($185,200) see Humana

Kentucky (cont.)

Greater Louisville Fund for the Arts ($500) see Levy's Lumber & Building Centers

Greenwood Park Church ($16,450) see Houchens Foundation, Ervin G.

Guston Missionary ($500) see Houchens Foundation, Ervin G.

Habitat for Humanity ($20,000) see Norton Foundation Inc.

Hayswood Home Health Services ($15,000) see Hayswood Foundation

Henderson County Educational Fund ($1,000) see Osborn Manufacturing Co.

Highland Presbyterian Church ($29,665) see C. E. and S. Foundation

Home of the Innocents ($5,000) see Vogt Machine Co., Henry

Hope Hill Children's Home ($15,000) see Trimble Family Foundation, Robert Mize and Isa White

Horse Cave Theater ($1,000) see Houchens Foundation, Ervin G.

Horse Cave Theater ($10,000) see Memton Fund

Hospice ($500) see Levy's Lumber & Building Centers

Hospice of Big Sandy ($50,000) see Steele-Reese Foundation

J.B. Speed Art ($10,000) see Weatherhead Foundation

Jefferson County Public Education Foundation ($98,000) see Vogt Machine Co., Henry

Jefferson County Public Education Fund ($11,600) see Bank of Louisville

Jefferson County Public Schools — continuing teacher education ($400,000) see Gheens Foundation

Jewish Hospital Foundation ($20,035) see Bank of Louisville

Jewish Hospital Foundation ($500) see Levy's Lumber & Building Centers

Jewish Hospital Foundation ($200,000) see Mills Foundation, Ralph E.

Jewish Hospital Foundation ($10,000) see Roth Foundation, Louis T.

Jewish Hospital Foundation ($3,600) see Thomas Industries

Junior Achievement ($5,000) see Vogt Machine Co., Henry

Keneseth Israel Congregation ($10,000) see Roth Foundation, Louis T.

Keneseth Israel Congregation ($4,500) see Roth Foundation, Louis T.

Kent School Endowment Fund ($20,000) see Brown Foundation, W. L. Lyons

Kentucky Alliance Against Racist and Political Repression ($8,000) see Ben & Jerry's Homemade

Kentucky Baptist Homes for Children ($26,000) see Cooke Foundation Corporation, V. V.

Kentucky Center for the Arts ($10,000) see Bank of Louisville

Kentucky Center for the Arts ($5,000) see Greenebaum, Doll & McDonald

Kentucky Council on Economic Education ($1,000) see Thomas Industries

Kentucky Educational Foundation ($2,500) see Porter Paint Co.

Kentucky Fair and Exposition Center ($33,200) see Schneider Foundation Corp., Al J.

Kentucky Harvest ($30,000) see Norton Foundation Inc.

Kentucky Independent College ($2,000) see Houchens Foundation, Ervin G.

Kentucky Independent College Fund ($1,000) see Thomas Industries

Kentucky Independent College Fund ($9,500) see Vogt Machine Co., Henry

Kentucky Lions Eye Foundation ($100) see Levy's Lumber & Building Centers

Kentucky Mountain Housing Development ($30,000) see Thompson Charitable Foundation

Kentucky Opera ($10,000) see Blue Cross & Blue Shield of Kentucky Foundation

Kentucky Opera see Capital Holding Corp.

Kentucky Opera ($125,000) see Humana

Kentucky Opera ($680) see Scheirich Co., H.J.

Kentucky School Reform Corporation ($100,000) see Ashland Oil

Kentucky Science and Technology Council ($365,203) see Brown Foundation, James Graham

Kentucky Special Olympics ($1,000) see Craigmyle Foundation

Kentucky United Methodist Foundation ($132,811) see LaViers Foundation, Harry and Maxie

Kentucky Valley Educational Cooperative ($50,000) see Steele-Reese Foundation

Kentucky Wesleyan College ($500,000) see Brown Foundation, James Graham

Kentucky Wesleyan College ($5,000) see Magee Christian Education Foundation

Kentucky Wesleyan College ($10,000) see Yeager Charitable Trust, Lester E.

King Solomon Baptist Church ($6,000) see Schneider Foundation Corp., Al J.

Lakeside Place ($875) see Cincinnati Foundation for the Aged

Leadership Kentucky ($3,000) see Blue Cross & Blue Shield of Kentucky Foundation

League of Women Voters ($100) see Levy's Lumber & Building Centers

Lee's Junior College ($135,000) see Mills Foundation, Ralph E.

Legal Aid Society ($6,400) see Greenebaum, Doll & McDonald

Leukemia Society of America ($5,000) see Blue Cross & Blue Shield of Kentucky Foundation

Lexington Arts and Cultural Council ($5,000) see Greenebaum, Doll & McDonald

Lexington Arts and Cultural Council ($2,500) see Greenebaum, Doll & McDonald

Lexington Arts and Cultural Council ($2,500) see

Greenebaum, Doll & McDonald

Lexington Bluegrass Chapter of the Alzheimers Disease and Related Disorders Association ($50,000) see Steele-Reese Foundation

Lexington-Fayette Urban County Government — Carnegie Literary Center; benefit of Carnegie Literacy Center ($200,000) see Farish Fund, William Stamps

Lexington School ($125,000) see Abercrombie Foundation

Lexington Theological Seminary — to help fund married student housing construction ($125,000) see Davis Foundations, Arthur Vining

Lindsey-Wilson College ($3,000) see Magee Christian Education Foundation

Louisville Astronomical Society ($25,000) see Perkin Fund

Louisville Ballet ($15,825) see Bank of Louisville

Louisville Ballet see Capital Holding Corp.

Louisville Civic Ventures — funds for final phase of the downtown development plan ($33,333) see Gheens Foundation

Louisville Civic Ventures — Planning Consultant ($33,333) see Gheens Foundation

Louisville Community Foundation ($14,226) see Scheirich Co., H.J.

Louisville Deaf Oral School ($4,000) see Blue Cross & Blue Shield of Kentucky Foundation

Louisville Development Foundation ($1,000) see Thomas Industries

Louisville Development Foundation — bring Presbyterian Church headquarters to Louisville ($60,000) see Gheens Foundation

Louisville Free Public Library ($14,794) see Norton Foundation Inc.

Louisville Free Public Library Foundation ($200,000) see C. E. and S. Foundation

Louisville Library see Capital Holding Corp.

Louisville Orchestra ($20,000) see Brown Foundation, W. L. Lyons

Louisville Orchestra see Capital Holding Corp.

Louisville Orchestra ($102,500) see Glenmore Distilleries Co.

Louisville Orchestra ($305,592) see Humana

Louisville Presbyterian Theological Seminary ($80,195) see C. E. and S. Foundation

Louisville Resource Conservation Council ($30,000) see Norton Foundation Inc.

Louisville Resource Conservation Council ($15,000) see Norton Foundation Inc.

Louisville Visual Arts Association ($8,500) see Kentucky Foundation for Women

Louisville Waterfront Development ($135,000) see Humana

Madonna Manor ($1,800) see Cincinnati Foundation for the Aged

March of Dimes ($750) see Thomas Industries

Metro United Way see Capital Holding Corp.

Metro United Way ($294,670) see Humana

Metro United Way ($3,000) see Thomas Industries

Metro United Way — to support the expanded implementation of its model workplace literacy curriculum and to provide training see United Parcel Service of America

Metro United Way, Louisville, KY ($12,000) see Blue Cross & Blue Shield of Kentucky Foundation

Metropolitan United Way ($31,000) see Reynolds Metals Co.

Midway College ($125,000) see Mills Foundation, Ralph E.

Midway College — scholarships ($5,000) see Robinson Mountain Fund, E. O.

Midway College ($50,000) see Steele-Reese Foundation

Morehead State University ($150,000) see Ashland Oil

Morehead State University — scholarships ($20,000) see Robinson Mountain Fund, E. O.

Morton Center ($25,000) see Norton Foundation Inc.

Murray State University ($10,000) see Briggs & Stratton Corp.

NAED Education Fund ($5,000) see Thomas Industries

National Center for Family Literacy — for training center project ($929,810) see Kenan, Jr. Charitable Trust, William R.

National Conference of Christians and Jews ($300) see Levy's Lumber & Building Centers

Northern Kentucky Easter Seals — hearing and air conditioning ($10,000) see Schmidlapp Trust No. 2, Jacob G.

Northside Free Will Baptist ($1,650) see Houchens Foundation, Ervin G.

Oliveros Foundation ($15,000) see Edwards Foundation, O. P. and W. E.

Oneida Baptist Institute ($1,000) see Cooke Foundation Corporation, V. V.

Owensboro Museum of Fine Art ($12,000) see Glenmore Distilleries Co.

Panco Youth Center ($10,000) see Robinson Mountain Fund, E. O.

Passionist Nuns of Owensville ($10,000) see Schneider Foundation Corp., Al J.

Patton Museum ($50,000) see General Dynamics Corp.

Phi Gamma Delta Educational Foundation ($1,000) see Bishop Foundation, Vernon and Doris

Pikesville College ($10,000) see Carnahan-Jackson Foundation

Pikeville College ($400,000) see Brown Foundation, James Graham

Pikeville College ($1,500) see Carbon Fuel Co.

Pikeville College ($35,000) see Newcombe Foundation, Charlotte W.

Pikeville College — scholarships ($10,000) see Robinson Mountain Fund, E. O.

Presbyterian Church ($50,750) see Richardson Fund, Mary Lynn

Presbyterian Church ($10,000) see Richardson Fund, Mary Lynn

Presbyterian Church ($56,800) see Scaler Foundation

Presbyterian Church (U.S.A.) — Somalia relief efforts ($5,000) see Trull Foundation

Progressive Productions ($3,300) see Kentucky Foundation for Women

Russell Independent Schools ($125,000) see Ashland Oil

St. Charles Nursing Home ($6,650) see Cincinnati Foundation for the Aged

St. Xavier High School ($8,000) see Bank of Louisville

Salvation Army ($200) see Levy's Lumber & Building Centers

Salvation Army ($2,000) see Scheirich Co., H.J.

Sarah Lawrence College ($50,000) see Ingalls Foundation, Louise H. and David S.

Scripture Memory Mountain Mission ($30,000) see Huston Foundation

Shakertown at Pleasant Hill Kentucky ($20,000) see Randleigh Foundation Trust

Shriners Hospital for Crippled Children ($5,000) see Carter Family Foundation

Sister Michaela ($12,029) see Schneider Foundation Corp., Al J.

Southern Baptist Theological Seminary ($60,000) see Cooke Foundation Corporation, V. V.

Southern Baptist Theological Seminary — campus center complex ($364,870) see Gheens Foundation

Southern Baptist Theological Seminary ($35,000) see Ragan Charitable Foundation, Carolyn King

Southern Baptist Theological Seminary ($32,500) see Ragan Charitable Foundation, Carolyn King

Southern Baptist Theological Seminary ($8,000) see Schneider Foundation Corp., Al J.

Spalding University — new design of general education component of higher education ($70,000) see Gheens Foundation

Speech Clinic — speech therapy for children ($20,000) see Robinson Mountain Fund, E. O.

Syncopated, Inc ($10,000) see Kentucky Foundation for Women

Theater Workshop of Louisville ($5,000) see Kentucky Foundation for Women

Thomas More College ($750,000) see Brown Foundation, James Graham

Thomas More College ($25,000) see Cincinnati Bell

Tom Browning Boys and Girls Club ($13,959) see Dayton Power and Light Co.

Transylvania University ($150,000) see Ashland Oil

Transylvania University ($200,000) see C. E. and S. Foundation

Transylvania University ($12,754) see Gardner

Charitable Foundation, Edith D.

Transylvania University — scholarships ($8,000) see Robinson Mountain Fund, E. O.

Triangle Foundation ($100,000) see Ashland Oil

Union College — scholarships ($20,000) see Robinson Mountain Fund, E. O.

Union College ($206,000) see Zemurray Foundation

Union College of Kentucky ($10,000) see Ratner Foundation, Milton M.

United Jewish Campaign ($48,334) see Levy's Lumber & Building Centers

United Jewish Campaign ($71,150) see Roth Foundation, Louis T.

United Way ($750) see Acme-Cleveland Corp.

United Way ($52,500) see Bank of Louisville

United Way ($10,000) see Brown Foundation, W. L. Lyons

United Way ($283,720) see General Electric Co.

United Way ($22,000) see Glenmore Distilleries Co.

United Way ($3,500) see Glenmore Distilleries Co.

United Way ($6,750) see Levy's Lumber & Building Centers

United Way ($3,700) see Osborn Manufacturing Co.

United Way ($11,700) see Roth Foundation, Louis T.

United Way ($2,500) see Scheirich Co., H.J.

United Way-Blue Grass ($25,607) see American Standard

United Way of Kentucky ($5,000) see Blue Cross & Blue Shield of Kentucky Foundation

United Way Metropolitan Louisville — general purpose fund ($7,158) see Walgreen Co.

United Way of Owensboro ($11,800) see HON Industries

University of Kentucky ($2,500) see Bird Inc.

University of Kentucky ($500) see Chiquita Brands Co.

University of Kentucky ($75,000) see Frasch Foundation for Chemical Research (under the will of Elizabeth B. Frasch), Herman

University of Kentucky ($250,000) see Humana

University of Kentucky ($10,000) see Lebus Trust, Bertha

University of Kentucky ($5,000) see Lebus Trust, Bertha

University of Kentucky — humanities book endowment ($10,000) see Randleigh Foundation Trust

University of Kentucky College of Business and Economics ($200,000) see Ashland Oil

University of Kentucky Community College ($5,000) see Thomas Industries

University of Kentucky-Community College System ($100,000) see Emerson Electric Co.

University of Kentucky — in new computer lab at the Medical Center library ($200,000) see Apple Computer

University of Louisville ($1,200) see Alro Steel Corp.

University of Louisville ($300,000) see BellSouth Corp.

University of Louisville ($5,550) see Greenebaum, Doll & McDonald

University of Louisville ($25,000) see Rodgers Foundation, Richard & Dorothy

University of Louisville — Department of Biology ($17,000) see Brown Foundation, W. L. Lyons

University of Louisville Foundation ($15,000) see Blue Cross & Blue Shield of Kentucky Foundation

University of Louisville Foundation ($13,000) see C. E. and S. Foundation

University of Louisville Quest for Excellence ($20,000) see Glenmore Distilleries Co.

Ursuline Pitt School ($100) see Levy's Lumber & Building Centers

Ursuline Sisters ($15,000) see Schneider Foundation Corp., Al J.

VA Medical Center — A Test for True Paracrine Interaction by the Measurement of Intra-Islet Interstitial Hormone Concentration ($20,000) see Diabetes Research and Education Foundation

Visiting Nurse Association of Louisville ($10,000) see Blue Cross & Blue Shield of Kentucky Foundation

Volunteers of America ($500) see Thomas Industries

Walnut Street Baptist Church ($40,000) see Cooke Foundation Corporation, V. V.

Wayside Christian Mission ($2,500) see Cooke Foundation Corporation, V. V.

Wayside Christian Mission ($4,000) see Glenmore Distilleries Co.

WKPC-TV ($15,250) see Bank of Louisville

Women Writers Conference ($20,000) see Kentucky Foundation for Women

YMCA ($2,500) see Cooke Foundation Corporation, V. V.

Louisiana

Agenda for Children ($10,000) see Keller Family Foundation

Agenda For Children ($30,462) see German Protestant Orphan Asylum Association

Alexandria Museum of Art ($15,000) see Coughlin-Saunders Foundation

Alton Ochsner Foundation — medical research ($2,000) see Pearce Foundation, Dr. M. Lee

Alton Ochsner Medical Foundation ($10,000) see Boh Brothers Construction Co.

Alton Ochsner Medical Foundation ($10,000) see Brown Foundation, Joe W. and Dorothy Dorsett

Alton Ochsner Medical Foundation ($200,000) see Freeman Foundation, Ella West

Alton Ochsner Medical Foundation ($75,000) see RosaMary Foundation

American Heart Association ($1,000) see Burton Foundation, William T. and Ethel Lewis

American Red Cross ($25,000) see Cabot Corp.

American Red Cross ($15,000) see Manville Corp.

Anti-Defamation League ($2,000) see Cahn Family Foundation

Anti-Defamation League ($5,000) see Goldring Family Foundation

Anti-Defamation League ($7,000) see Woldenberg Foundation

Archbishop Antoine Blanc Memorial ($134,622) see Azby Fund

Archbishop's Community Appeal ($25,000) see Booth-Bricker Fund

Archbishop's Community Appeal ($25,000) see Helis Foundation

Archbishop's Community Appeal ($5,000) see Keller Family Foundation

Archdiocese of New Orleans ($1,000) see Glazer Foundation, Jerome S.

Archives Commission ($17,200) see Young Foundation, H and B

Arthritis Foundation ($6,000) see Brown Foundation, Joe W. and Dorothy Dorsett

Arts Council of New Orleans ($26,250) see Azby Fund

Arts Council of New Orleans see Freeport-McMoRan

Arts Council of New Orleans ($45,000) see Zemurray Foundation

Ascension Fund ($3,000) see Ormet Corp.

Audubon Girl Scout Council ($3,000) see Pennington Foundation, Irene W. and C. B.

Audubon Institute ($100,000) see Aron Charitable Foundation, J.

Audubon Institute ($33,075) see Booth-Bricker Fund

Audubon Institute ($200,000) see RosaMary Foundation

Audubon Institute ($7,500) see Wisdom Foundation, Mary F.

Audubon Institute ($102,500) see Zemurray Foundation

Baton Rouge Alcohol and Drug Abuse Prevention Program see Freeport-McMoRan

Baton Rouge Campaign for Academic Distinction see Freeport-McMoRan

Baton Rouge Community Fund for the Arts see Freeport-McMoRan

Baton Rouge Earth Day see Freeport-McMoRan

Baton Rouge Marine Institute ($14,000) see German Protestant Orphan Asylum Association

Baton Rouge Public Radio ($1,560) see Copolymer Rubber & Chemical Corp.

Baton Rouge Symphony ($1,150) see Copolymer Rubber & Chemical Corp.

Biomedical Research Foundation ($13,500) see Poindexter Foundation

Biomedical Research Foundation ($30,000) see Powers Foundation

Biomedical Research Foundation ($5,000) see Premier Bank

Biomedical Research Foundation ($10,000) see Wheless Foundation

Boy Scouts of America ($2,000) see Burton Foundation, William T. and Ethel Lewis

Boy Scouts of America ($1,500) see Copolymer Rubber & Chemical Corp.

Boy Scouts of America ($400,000) see Pennington Foundation, Irene W. and C. B.

Boy Scouts of America ($5,000) see Pennington Foundation, Irene W. and C. B.

Boy Scouts of America ($28,000) see Powers Foundation

Boy Scouts of America ($2,750) see Wheless Foundation

Boy Scouts of America ($7,500) see Woolf Foundation, William C.

Boy Scouts of America ($6,000) see Zigler Foundation, Fred B. and Ruth B.

Boys and Girls Club ($83,000) see Coughlin-Saunders Foundation

Boys and Girls Club of Central Louisiana see International Paper Co.

Boys Hope ($10,000) see Wisdom Foundation, Mary F.

Cabot Hurricane Relief Fund ($48,000) see Cabot Corp.

Caddo Public Education Foundation ($7,500) see Community Coffee Co.

Calvary Baptist Church ($24,000) see Coughlin-Saunders Foundation

Camp Fire Council ($1,000) see Burton Foundation, William T. and Ethel Lewis

Catapult Campaign ($5,500) see Lakeside National Bank

Catholic High School ($5,000) see Pennington Foundation, Irene W. and C. B.

Cenla Pride ($10,000) see Coughlin-Saunders Foundation

Centenary College see Arkla

Centenary College — building fund ($10,000) see Poindexter Foundation

Centenary College ($35,650) see Wheless Foundation

Centenary College Choir ($2,500) see Poindexter Foundation

Centenary College of Louisiana — for the renovation of Jackson Hall on the campus ($195,000) see Frost Foundation

Centenary College of Louisiana — Mickle Hall of Science ($50,000) see Schlieder Educational Foundation, Edward G.

Children's Hospital ($2,000) see Cahn Family Foundation

Children's Hospital ($75,000) see Helis Foundation

Christ Church Retirement Home ($40,000) see Zemurray Foundation

Christian Service Program ($6,000) see Beaird Foundation, Charles T.

Christian Service Program ($2,500) see Poindexter Foundation

Ciapa (Centra de Investicacion y Adiestramiento Politico Administrativo) ($221,000) see Zemurray Foundation

City of Jennings ($10,000) see Zigler Foundation, Fred B. and Ruth B.

Clear Spring School Scholarship Endowment Fund ($5,000) see Beaird Foundation, Charles T.

Community Foundation of Shreveport ($40,000) see Beaird Foundation, Charles T.

Community Fund for the Arts ($4,250) see Copolymer Rubber & Chemical Corp.

Congregation Beth Israel ($3,700) see Glazer Foundation, Jerome S.

Contemporary Arts Center ($25,000) see Freeman Foundation, Ella West

Contemporary Arts Center ($1,000) see Freeman Foundation, Ella West

Contemporary Arts Center ($15,000) see Heymann-Wolf Foundation

Contemporary Arts Center ($50,000) see Lupin Foundation

Contemporary Arts Center ($25,000) see Lupin Foundation

Copolymer Merit Scholarship ($3,750) see Copolymer Rubber & Chemical Corp.

Council for a Better Louisiana ($300,000) see BellSouth Corp.

Covenant House ($20,000) see German Protestant Orphan Asylum Association

Covenant House ($5,000) see Woldenberg Foundation

Covenant House of New Orleans ($5,000) see Baird Charitable Trust, William Robert

De Louisiana Festival International ($5,000) see Forest Oil Corp.

Dillard University — to provide a $500,000 one-for-one endowment challenge ($500,000) see Mott Foundation, Charles Stewart

Dillard/Xavier Fund ($15,000) see Keller Family Foundation

Dwight D. Eisenhower Center for the Dwight D. Eisenhower Museum Program ($20,000) see Hobby Foundation

E. Baton Rouge Parish School System ($26,462) see Cook, Sr. Charitable Foundation, Kelly Gene

Eric Voeglin Institute ($25,000) see Vollrath Co.

Eye, Ear, Nose and Throat Hospital Foundation ($25,000) see Booth-Bricker Fund

Eye, Ear, Nose and Throat Hospital Foundation ($10,000) see German Protestant Orphan Asylum Association

Family of the Americas Foundation ($35,000) see Saint Gerard Foundation

Family Counseling Agency ($18,152) see German Protestant Orphan Asylum Association

Family Service of Greater New Orleans ($19,700) see German Protestant Orphan Asylum Association

First Baptist Church of Baton Rouge ($2,000) see Pennington Foundation, Irene W. and C. B.

First Presbyterian Church ($10,000) see Coughlin-Saunders Foundation

First Presbyterian Church ($5,000) see Woolf Foundation, William C.

First United Methodist Church ($10,000) see Coughlin-Saunders Foundation

First United Methodist Church of Lake Charles ($2,480) see Burton Foundation, William T. and Ethel Lewis

Louisiana (cont.)

Food Bank ($8,500) see Libby-Dufour Fund, Trustees of the

Friends of City Park ($25,000) see Booth-Bricker Fund

Friends of Louisiana State Museum ($5,115) see Beaird Foundation, Charles T.

Friends of the Zoo-Aquarium of the Americas ($100,000) see Shell Oil Co.

Girl Scouts of America ($5,000) see Brown Foundation, Joe W. and Dorothy Dorsett

Glen Oaks Retirement System — toward the construction and equipment costs associated with the expansion of the facilities and services ($40,000) see Frost Foundation

Glen Retirement System ($25,000) see Powers Foundation

Glen Retirement System ($5,000) see Woolf Foundation, William C.

Glen Retirement Village ($5,100) see Wheless Foundation

Governors Gifted Children ($18,000) see Brown Foundation, Joe W. and Dorothy Dorsett

Gradyer New Orleans Foundation ($20,000) see Baird Charitable Trust, William Robert

Greater New Orleans Foundation ($6,250) see Azby Fund

Greater New Orleans Foundation ($30,000) see Heymann Special Account, Mr. and Mrs. Jimmy

Greater New Orleans Foundation ($10,000) see Heymann-Wolf Foundation

Greater New Orleans Foundation ($550,000) see Zemurray Foundation

Greater New Orleans Regional Foundation ($62,500) see Reily & Co., William B.

Harold Keller Elementary ($5,309) see Cook, Sr. Charitable Foundation, Kelly Gene

Henning Memorial Methodist Church ($5,480) see Burton Foundation, William T. and Ethel Lewis

Hermann-Grima Preservation Center ($10,000) see Jones Family Foundation, Eugenie and Joseph

Holy Angels School ($2,500) see Poindexter Foundation

Hospice ($1,000) see Cahn Family Foundation

Isidore Newman School ($50,000) see Lupin Foundation

Isidore Newman School-Campaign for Newman ($10,000) see Jones Family Foundation, Eugenie and Joseph

Jennings High School ($9,000) see Zigler Foundation, Fred B. and Ruth B.

Jewish Children's Home ($10,000) see Cahn Family Foundation

Jewish Federation ($50,000) see Goldring Family Foundation

Jewish Federation ($1,042,500) see Woldenberg Foundation

Jewish Federation of New Orleans ($60,000) see Lupin Foundation

Jewish Welfare Federation ($5,000) see Glazer Foundation, Jerome S.

Jewish Welfare Fund ($50,000) see Cahn Family Foundation

Junior Achievement ($3,100) see Copolymer Rubber & Chemical Corp.

Junior Achievement ($500) see Ormet Corp.

Junior Achievement ($6,900) see Premier Bank

Junior Achievement ($51,000) see Reily & Co., William B.

Junior League of Shreveport ($5,000) see Premier Bank

L.E. Rebouin School ($5,000) see Boh Brothers Construction Co.

Lafayette Public Education Foundation ($7,500) see Community Coffee Co.

Lake End Park ($16,000) see Young Foundation, H and B

Lakewood Hospital ($12,500) see Young Foundation, H and B

Lighthouse for the Blind ($20,000) see Helis Foundation

Little Sisters of Poor ($5,000) see Keller Family Foundation

Little Sisters of Poor ($6,000) see Wisdom Foundation, Mary F.

Louis S. McGehee School ($6,350) see Libby-Dufour Fund, Trustees of the

Louisa McGehee School ($10,000) see Wisdom Foundation, Mary F.

Louisiana Archaeological Society, Delta Chapter ($5,000) see Azby Fund

Louisiana Boys and Girls Village ($6,000) see Zigler Foundation, Fred B. and Ruth B.

Louisiana Children's Museum ($10,000) see Keller Family Foundation

Louisiana College ($50,000) see Coughlin-Saunders Foundation

Louisiana Council on Economic Education ($2,500) see Poindexter Foundation

Louisiana Creative Scholars ($18,000) see Brown Foundation, Joe W. and Dorothy Dorsett

Louisiana Independent College Fund ($2,200) see Copolymer Rubber & Chemical Corp.

Louisiana Literacy Foundation — seed money grant for the development of a five-year plan including a marketplace-oriented feasibility study and short-term fundraising strategies and tactics ($50,000) see Frost Foundation

Louisiana Museum Foundation ($10,000) see Wisdom Foundation, Mary F.

Louisiana Nature and Science Center ($56,000) see Zemurray Foundation

Louisiana Philharmonic Society ($20,000) see Wisdom Foundation, Mary F.

Louisiana State University ($100,000) see Burlington Resources

Louisiana State University ($65,000) see Dow Chemical Co.

Louisiana State University — to purchase interactive video equipment ($65,476) see Fuld Health Trust, Helene

Louisiana State University ($3,000) see Glenn Foundation for Medical Research, Paul F.

Louisiana State University ($7,500) see Powers Foundation

Louisiana State University — functional organization of olfactory bulb circuits ($53,176) see Whitehall Foundation

Louisiana State University ($30,000) see Zigler Foundation, Fred B. and Ruth B.

Louisiana State University ($10,000) see Zigler Foundation, Fred B. and Ruth B.

Louisiana State University — scholarships for foreign students of East Indian ancestry ($6,000) see Watumull Fund, J.

Louisiana State University, Edward G. Schlieder Chair of Information Sciences ($120,000) see Schlieder Educational Foundation, Edward G.

Louisiana State University, Environmental Engineering ($200,000) see Texaco

Louisiana State University Foundation ($10,000) see Coughlin-Saunders Foundation

Louisiana State University Foundation ($2,500) see Poindexter Foundation

Louisiana State University, Pennington Biomedical Research Center ($50,000) see Schlieder Educational Foundation, Edward G.

Louisiana State University — alumni center (second of three payments) ($300,000) see ARCO

Louisiana State University, Stanley Scott Cancer Center of Excellence ($100,000) see Schlieder Educational Foundation, Edward G.

Loyola College Preparatory School ($10,000) see Woolf Foundation, William C.

Loyola University ($50,100) see Booth-Bricker Fund

Loyola University ($30,000) see DeSoto

Loyola University ($15,000) see Keller Family Foundation

Loyola University ($30,000) see Lupin Foundation

Loyola University ($30,000) see Lupin Foundation

Loyola University ($100,000) see Schlieder Educational Foundation, Edward G.

Loyola University — to equip and endow their Language Learning Resource Center ($25,000) see Frost Foundation

Lusher School ($10,000) see Wisdom Foundation, Mary F.

Lutheran Social Services of South ($10,000) see German Protestant Orphan Asylum Association

Magnolia Bible College ($25,000) see Frazier Foundation

Magnolia School ($5,000) see Boh Brothers Construction Co.

Magnolia School ($5,000) see Brown Foundation, Joe W. and Dorothy Dorsett

Magnolia School ($5,000) see Heymann Special Account, Mr. and Mrs. Jimmy

March of Dimes ($900) see Heymann-Wolf Foundation

Mary Bird Perkins Cancer Center ($10,000) see Copolymer Rubber & Chemical Corp.

Mayor's Foundation for Education ($4,750) see Azby Fund

McNeese State University ($62,203) see Zigler Foundation, Fred B. and Ruth B.

Mercy Academy ($7,000) see Libby-Dufour Fund, Trustees of the

Mercy Hospital ($60,000) see Booth-Bricker Fund

Metairie Park Country Day School ($50,000) see Reily & Co., William B.

Metairie Park Country Day School ($32,218) see Booth-Bricker Fund

Metairie Park Country Day School ($25,000) see Libby-Dufour Fund, Trustees of the

Metairie Park Country Day School ($25,000) see Libby-Dufour Fund, Trustees of the

Metairie Park Country Day School ($6,500) see Wisdom Foundation, Mary F.

Metropolitan Area Committee Education Foundation ($8,000) see Keller Family Foundation

Metropolitan Arts ($50,000) see Reily & Co., William B.

Metropolitan Arts Foundation ($10,000) see Woldenberg Foundation

Metropolitan Arts Fund ($12,000) see Boh Brothers Construction Co.

Metropolitan Crime Commission ($2,000) see Heymann-Wolf Foundation

Metrovision Partnership Foundation ($5,000) see Boh Brothers Construction Co.

Mia Casa FENIX Program ($5,000) see Beaird Foundation, Charles T.

Morgan City Auditorium ($12,302) see Young Foundation, H and B

Morgan City Garden Club ($10,000) see Young Foundation, H and B

Morgan City High School ($5,000) see Young Foundation, H and B

Morgan City Public Library ($10,000) see Young Foundation, H and B

Most Holy Name of Jesus Church ($8,250) see Azby Fund

Mothers Against Drugs ($5,000) see Wheless Foundation

Mothers Against Drugs ($5,000) see Woolf Foundation, William C.

National Council for Negro Women of Greater New Orleans ($18,750) see German Protestant Orphan Asylum Association

National Multiple Sclerosis Society ($10,000) see German Protestant Orphan Asylum Association

Nature Conservancy ($10,000) see Wisdom Foundation, Mary F.

Neighborhood Housing Services ($10,000) see Premier Bank

New Orleans Archdiocesan Cemeteries ($6,000) see Azby Fund

New Orleans Botanical Gardens ($12,000) see Jones Family Foundation, Eugenie and Joseph

New Orleans Center for Creative Arts ($30,000) see Lupin Foundation

New Orleans Council on Aging ($2,000) see Heymann Special Account, Mr. and Mrs. Jimmy

New Orleans Literary Festival ($2,000) see Heymann Special Account, Mr. and Mrs. Jimmy

New Orleans Museum of Art ($170,000) see Aron Charitable Foundation, J.

New Orleans Museum of Art ($4,000) see Boh Brothers Construction Co.

New Orleans Museum of Art ($100,000) see Booth-Bricker Fund

New Orleans Museum of Art ($2,500) see Cahn Family Foundation

New Orleans Museum of Art ($4,507) see Heymann Special Account, Mr. and Mrs. Jimmy

New Orleans Museum of Art ($10,000) see Heymann-Wolf Foundation

New Orleans Museum of Art ($10,000) see Jones Family Foundation, Eugenie and Joseph

New Orleans Museum of Art ($150,000) see RosaMary Foundation

New Orleans Museum of Art ($150,000) see RosaMary Foundation

New Orleans Museum of Art ($352,500) see Zemurray Foundation

New Orleans Philharmonic Symphony Society ($75,000) see RosaMary Foundation

New Orleans Police Department Reserve Division Benevolent Fund ($13,000) see Azby Fund

New Orleans Salvation Army ($25,000) see McDonough Foundation, Bernard

New Orleans Service Center ($8,500) see Keller Family Foundation

New Orleans Symphony ($50,000) see Lupin Foundation

New Orleans Symphony ($50,000) see Lupin Foundation

Nicholls State University ($5,000) see Brown Foundation, Joe W. and Dorothy Dorsett

Nicholls State University ($25,000) see Chatham Valley Foundation

Noel Memorial Methodist Church ($5,000) see Woolf Foundation, William C.

Orthodox Campus Ministry ($35,000) see Helis Foundation

Our Lady of Holy Cross College ($40,000) see Libby-Dufour Fund, Trustees of the

Our Lady of Holy Cross College — on-going programs ($100,000) see O'Neill Charitable Corporation, F. J.

Our Lady of Prompt Succor ($5,000) see Burton Foundation, William T. and Ethel Lewis

Our Lady Queen of Heaven School ($500) see Lakeside National Bank

Our Lady of Victory Catholic Church ($20,250) see Azby Fund

Parkway Partners ($20,000) see
Reily & Co., William B.

Planned Parenthood ($10,000)
see Libby-Dufour Fund,
Trustees of the

Planned Parenthood ($25,000)
see Reily & Co., William B.

Planned Parenthood Federation
of America ($5,000) see
Freeman Foundation, Ella West

Preservation Resource Center
($5,050) see Heymann Special
Account, Mr. and Mrs. Jimmy

Project Charlie ($63,765) see
Brown Foundation, Joe W. and
Dorothy Dorsett

Project Lazarus ($10,000) see
Wisdom Foundation, Mary F.

Ridgewood Preparatory School
($10,000) see Goldring Family
Foundation

Rutherford House ($3,500) see
Powers Foundation

St. Aloysius School ($30,000)
see Pennington Foundation,
Irene W. and C. B.

St. Augustine High School
($30,000) see Libby-Dufour
Fund, Trustees of the

St. Elizabeth's Children's House
($25,000) see Helis Foundation

St. Francis Cabrini Hospital
Foundation ($13,000) see
Coughlin-Saunders Foundation

St. Georges Episcopal School
($25,000) see Libby-Dufour
Fund, Trustees of the

St. James Episcopal Church
($5,000) see Pennington
Foundation, Irene W. and C. B.

St. James Historical Society —
permanent scholarship
endowment ($50,000) see
Stark Foundation, Nelda C.
and H. J. Lutcher

St. Jude Mission ($35,000) see
Helis Foundation

St. Mark's Episcopal Church
($13,300) see Wheless
Foundation

St. Mark's Foundation ($5,000)
see Woolf Foundation,
William C.

St. Mary Parish Police Jury
($76,921) see Williams
Foundation, Kemper and Leila

School of American Research
($50,000) see Zemurray
Foundation

Schumpert Medical Center
($25,000) see Sooner Pipe &
Supply Corp.

Second Harvesters ($20,000) see
Brown Foundation, Joe W. and
Dorothy Dorsett

Second Harvester's Food Bank
of Greater New Orleans
($25,000) see Helis Foundation

Shreveport Chamber Foundation
($12,500) see Premier Bank

Shreveport Chamber Foundation
for Educational Research
($7,500) see Powers
Foundation

Shreveport Landmark ($5,000)
see Beaird Foundation,
Charles T.

Shreveport Landmark ($3,800)
see Beaird Foundation,
Charles T.

Shreveport Little Theatre
($5,000) see Premier Bank

Shreveport Opera ($5,000) see
Premier Bank

Shreveport Regional Arts
($7,500) see Premier Bank

Shreveport Symphony ($25,000)
see Powers Foundation

Shreveport Symphony Orchestra
($6,000) see Poindexter
Foundation

Shreveport Symphony Orchestra
($5,000) see Poindexter
Foundation

Shreveport Symphony Orchestra
($15,000) see Premier Bank

Silliman Institute ($30,000) see
Pennington Foundation, Irene
W. and C. B.

Society for Coalition of Equity
Education ($20,000) see Reily
& Co., William B.

Society for the Prevention of
Cruelty to Animals ($1,500)
see Cahn Family Foundation

Southern Repertory Theater
($11,000) see Heymann-Wolf
Foundation

Southern University Foundation
($60,000) see Community
Coffee Co.

Southern University SEED
Program ($1,000) see
Copolymer Rubber &
Chemical Corp.

Southfield School ($5,000) see
Woolf Foundation, William C.

Swamp Garden ($97,666) see
Young Foundation, H and B

Tad Gormley Project ($14,000)
see Jones Family Foundation,
Eugenie and Joseph

Teen Challenge ($3,500) see
Poindexter Foundation

Temple Sinai ($6,000) see
Glazer Foundation, Jerome S.

Temple Sinai ($5,000) see
Goldring Family Foundation

Temple Sinai ($18,142) see
Heymann Special Account,
Mr. and Mrs. Jimmy

Times Picayune Doll and Toy
Fund ($5,156) see Ellsworth
Trust, W. H.

Touro Infirmary ($5,000) see
Goldring Family Foundation

Touro Infirmary ($50,425) see
Heymann Special Account,
Mr. and Mrs. Jimmy

Touro Infirmary ($10,000) see
Libby-Dufour Fund, Trustees
of the

Touro Infirmary ($51,000) see
Reily & Co., William B.

Touro Infirmary ($37,500) see
RosaMary Foundation

Touro Infirmary (Eye) ($63,500)
see Marriott Foundation, J.
Willard

Trinity Episcopal Church
($14,000) see Jones Family
Foundation, Eugenie and
Joseph

Tulane Medical Center ($10,000)
see Heymann-Wolf Foundation

Tulane University ($300,000) see
Aron Charitable Foundation, J.

Tulane University ($100,000) see
Aron Charitable Foundation, J.

Tulane University ($25,000) see
Boh Brothers Construction Co.

Tulane University ($100,000)
see Goldring Family
Foundation

Tulane University ($100,000)
see Goldring Family
Foundation

Tulane University ($25,000) see
Goldring Family Foundation

Tulane University ($7,075) see
Heymann Special Account,
Mr. and Mrs. Jimmy

Tulane University ($15,000) see
Heymann-Wolf Foundation

Tulane University ($10,000) see
Jones Family Foundation,
Eugenie and Joseph

Tulane University ($2,000) see
Kuehn Foundation

Tulane University ($15,000) see
Miller Foundation, Steve J.

Tulane University ($50,000) see
Reily & Co., William B.

Tulane University ($50,000) see
RosaMary Foundation

Tulane University ($25,000) see
Woldenberg Foundation

Tulane University ($415,000)
see Zemurray Foundation

Tulane University Department of
Anesthesiology ($100,000) see
Schlieder Educational
Foundation, Edward G.

Tulane University-Education
Reform in Louisiana ($87,975)
see Shell Oil Co.

Tulane University — Edward G.
Schlieder Chair in Medical
Oncology ($100,000) see
Schlieder Educational
Foundation, Edward G.

Tulane University — Edward G.
Schlieder Chair in Medical
Oncology ($35,500) see
Schlieder Educational
Foundation, Edward G.

Tulane University — James W.
Wilson Jr. Center ($100,000)
see Schlieder Educational
Foundation, Edward G.

Tulane University Medical
Center ($124,622) see Azby
Fund

Tulane University Medical
Center ($46,000) see Hayward
Foundation Charitable Trust,
John T. and Winifred

Tulane University Medical
Center ($25,000) see Iacocca
Foundation

Tulane University School of Law
Chair ($75,000) see Jones
Family Foundation, Eugenie
and Joseph

Turn of the Century House
($26,632) see Young
Foundation, H and B

United Negro College Fund
($10,000) see Glazer
Foundation, Jerome S.

United Way ($25,000) see Boh
Brothers Construction Co.

United Way ($10,000) see
Brown Foundation, Joe W. and
Dorothy Dorsett

United Way ($5,000) see Burton
Foundation, William T. and
Ethel Lewis

United Way ($15,000) see Cahn
Family Foundation

United Way ($211,000) see
Chevron Corp.

United Way ($14,000) see
Goldring Family Foundation

United Way ($80,000) see Helis
Foundation

United Way ($11,000) see
Heymann Special Account,
Mr. and Mrs. Jimmy

United Way ($17,000) see
Heymann-Wolf Foundation

United Way ($12,000) see Jacobs
Engineering Group

United Way ($20,000) see Jones
Family Foundation, Eugenie
and Joseph

United Way ($20,000) see Keller
Family Foundation

United Way ($2,200) see Ormet
Corp.

United Way ($50,000) see PPG
Industries

United Way ($5,900) see Texas
Industries, Inc.

United Way ($15,500) see
Wheless Foundation

United Way ($15,000) see
Woldenberg Foundation

United Way ($15,125) see Woolf
Foundation, William C.

United Way Campaign-Capital
Area ($243,600) see Exxon
Corp.

United Way for the Greater New
Orleans Area ($200,000) see
RosaMary Foundation

University of New Orleans
($4,000) see Heymann-Wolf
Foundation

University of New Orleans
($50,000) see RosaMary
Foundation

University of New Orleans —
Edward G. Schlieder Chair in
Engineering ($100,000) see
Schlieder Educational
Foundation, Edward G.

University of New Orleans
Foundation ($5,000) see Boh
Brothers Construction Co.

University of Southwestern
Louisiana ($22,500) see Zigler
Foundation, Fred B. and Ruth
B.

Volunteers of America ($15,000)
see Beaird Foundation,
Charles T.

Volunteers of America ($20,000)
see German Protestant Orphan
Asylum Association

Volunteers of America ($8,000)
see Powers Foundation

West Monroe Church of Christ
— missions ($30,000) see
Frazier Foundation

Willow Wood Home for the
Aged ($1,000) see Cahn
Family Foundation

Woman's Club ($5,000) see
Pennington Foundation, Irene
W. and C. B.

Xavier University ($51,000) see
Reily & Co., William B.

Xavier University of Louisiana
($50,000) see RosaMary
Foundation

YMCA ($5,000) see Beaird
Foundation, Charles T.

YMCA ($50,000) see
Booth-Bricker Fund

YMCA ($15,000) see
Coughlin-Saunders Foundation

YMCA ($5,000) see Eastover
Corp.

YMCA ($50,000) see
Pennington Foundation, Irene
W. and C. B.

YMCA ($10,000) see Powers
Foundation

YMCA ($3,100) see Wheless
Foundation

YMCA ($5,000) see Woolf
Foundation, William C.

Youth Enrichment Program
($4,745) see Powers
Foundation

Zigler Museum Foundation
($25,000) see Zigler
Foundation, Fred B. and Ruth
B.

Zigler Museum Foundation
($10,220) see Zigler
Foundation, Fred B. and Ruth
B.

Maine

Arcadia Wildlife Sanctuary
($500) see Hampden Papers

Asticou Terraces Trust —
support for endowment
($100,000) see Allegheny
Foundation

Bangor Outdoor Ice ($2,000) see
Webber Oil Co.

Bates College — scholarships
($60,000) see Ayling
Scholarship Foundation, Alice
S.

Bates College ($10,000) see
Braitmayer Foundation

Bates College — summer
research program for high
school teachers ($15,000) see
Dreyfus Foundation, Camille
and Henry

Bates College — endowment
fund for student research
($100,000) see Hoffman
Foundation, Maximillian E.
and Marion O.

Bates College ($63,000) see
Ladd Charitable Corporation,
Helen and George

Bates College ($28,000) see
Travelli Fund, Charles Irwin

Belgrade Regional Health Center
($12,500) see Dexter Shoe Co.

Birth Right Forces ($28,000) see
Sprague Educational and
Charitable Foundation, Seth

Birth Right Forces ($25,000) see
Sprague Educational and
Charitable Foundation, Seth

Boothbay Railway Village
($290,000) see McEvoy
Foundation, Mildred H.

Bowdoin College —
scholarships ($15,000) see
Ayling Scholarship
Foundation, Alice S.

Bowdoin College — grants
($250,000) see Balfour
Foundation, L. G.

Bowdoin College ($10,000) see
Braitmayer Foundation

Bowdoin College ($20,000) see
Cowles Charitable Trust

Bowdoin College ($10,000) see
Dexter Shoe Co.

Bowdoin College ($11,500) see
Doherty Charitable
Foundation, Henry L. and
Grace

Bowdoin College — library
wing ($760,000) see Hatch
Charitable Trust, Margaret
Milliken

Bowdoin College — science
library ($300,000) see Hatch
Charitable Trust, Margaret
Milliken

Bowdoin College ($2,500) see
Morgan Construction Co.

Bowdoin College ($50,000) see
Morris Foundation, William T.

Bowdoin College ($52,000) see
Travelli Fund, Charles Irwin

Brooksville Free Public Library
($15,000) see Vesper Corp.

Brownfield Community Church
($3,000) see Mulford Trust,
Clarence E.

Carrabassett Valley Academy
($50,000) see American
Foundation Corporation

Central Maine Healthcare
($5,000) see Shaw's
Supermarkets

Central Maine Indian Associate
see New England Telephone
Co.

Chewonki Foundation ($5,000)
see Plant Memorial Fund,
Henry B.

Children's Museum ($2,000) see
Gannett Publishing Co., Guy

Children's Museum of Maine —
capital funding to create a
permanent headquarters
($10,000) see Lindsay Trust,
Agnes M.

Children's Museum of Maine
($8,000) see Shaw's
Supermarkets

Children's Museum of Maine —
funded the development of an
exciting paper-related exhibit
see Scott Paper Co.

Christian Science Society
($2,500) see Mulford Trust,
Clarence E.

Maine (cont.)

Church of New Jerusalem ($4,250) see Mulford Trust, Clarence E.

Coastal Cancer Treatment ($5,000) see Gannett Publishing Co., Guy

Colby-Bates-Bowdoin Public Television ($15,000) see Davenport Trust Fund

Colby College — scholarships ($50,000) see Ayling Scholarship Foundation, Alice S.

Colby College ($10,000) see Braitmayer Foundation

Colby College ($50,000) see Dexter Shoe Co.

Colby College ($240,000) see Johnson Endeavor Foundation, Christian A.

Colby College ($20,000) see Oak Foundation U.S.A.

Colby College — dynamics of excited molecules in external fields ($35,830) see Research Corporation

Colby College ($25,000) see Texas Industries, Inc.

Colby College ($52,000) see Travelli Fund, Charles Irwin

Colby College ($5,000) see Williams Foundation, Arthur Ashley

Cold Spring Harbor Laboratory ($35,000) see Lounsbery Foundation, Richard

College of the Atlantic, Cobblestone Fund ($50,000) see Silver Spring Foundation

Community Schools ($11,400) see Davenport Trust Fund

Congregational Church of Boothbay Harbor ($30,000) see McEvoy Foundation, Mildred H.

Cumberland County Affordable Housing Venture ($50,000) see UNUM Corp.

Edythe Dyer Community Library ($2,000) see Webber Oil Co.

Elmhurst Association for Retarded Citizens ($15,200) see Davenport Trust Fund

Environmental and Economic Council of Maine ($2,500) see Key Bank of Maine

Family Planning Association — AIDS Education Program ($60,000) see UNUM Corp.

First Church of Nazarene ($6,180) see Davenport Trust Fund

Fort Western Museum ($5,000) see Key Bank of Maine

Fryeburg Academy ($170,540) see Mulford Trust, Clarence E.

Fryeburg Academy — Pequawket Valley Alternative School ($12,500) see Nellie Mae

Fryeburg Congregational Church ($9,500) see Mulford Trust, Clarence E.

Fryeburg Women's Library Club ($8,000) see Mulford Trust, Clarence E.

Good-Will Hinckley — capital improvements high school building ($75,000) see Gallagher Family Foundation, Lewis P.

Grand Banks Schooner Museum ($158,250) see McEvoy Foundation, Mildred H.

Greater Bangor Chamber of Commerce ($2,500) see Webber Oil Co.

Haystack Mountain School ($15,000) see Cheney Foundation, Elizabeth F.

Hebron Academy ($10,000) see Crane Fund for Widows and Children

Hebron Academy ($5,000) see Evans Foundation, T. M.

Hospice of Western Maine ($2,000) see Mulford Trust, Clarence E.

Hyde Foundation — to support establishment of demonstration schools ($75,000) see Donner Foundation, William H.

Isleboro Islands Trust ($5,000) see Bedminster Fund

Jackson Laboratory ($8,000) see Beck Foundation

Jackson Laboratory ($37,500) see Smith Foundation, Richard and Susan

Jackson Laboratory ($8,000) see South Waite Foundation

Jackson Laboratory ($6,000) see South Waite Foundation

Jackson Laboratory ($5,000) see Wheeler Foundation

John Baptist School ($5,000) see Webber Oil Co.

Kennebec Valley Medical School ($11,000) see Key Bank of Maine

Maine Aspirations Foundation — Community Compacts ($137,350) see UNUM Corp.

Maine Audubon Society see Bean, L.L.

Maine Audubon Society ($5,000) see Wharton Trust, William P.

Maine Audubon Society ($5,000) see Woodward Fund

Maine Audubon Society — support towards the Northwoods Coalition ($105,000) see Cox Charitable Trust, Jessie B.

Maine Central Institute ($4,000) see Webber Oil Co.

Maine Coast Heritage Trust ($5,000) see Comer Foundation

Maine Coast Heritage Trust ($50,000) see Ford Fund, Walter and Josephine

Maine Coast Heritage Trust ($2,000) see Milliken Foundation, Agnes G.

Maine Coast Heritage Trust ($10,000) see Sasco Foundation

Maine Coast Heritage Trust ($7,500) see Sewall Foundation, Elmina

Maine Coast Memorial Hospital ($5,000) see Key Bank of Maine

Maine Community Foundation ($95,000) see Bingham Second Betterment Fund, William

Maine Cytometry Research Institute ($15,000) see Davenport Trust Fund

Maine Development Foundation ($150,000) see Harriman Foundation, Gladys and Roland

Maine Maritime Academy ($100,000) see Bingham Second Betterment Fund, William

Maine Maritime Academy ($5,000) see Vesper Corp.

Maine Maritime Museum ($2,000) see Webber Oil Co.

Maine Medical Assessment ($25,000) see Bingham Second Betterment Fund, William

Maine Medical Center ($5,000) see Hunt Foundation

Maine Sea Coast Missionary Society ($5,000) see Milliken Foundation, Agnes G.

Marathon House ($1,000) see Gannett Publishing Co., Guy

Mercy Hospital ($5,000) see Hunt Foundation

Mid-Maine Medical Center ($3,000) see Gannett Publishing Co., Guy

Musker Power Club ($25,000) see Cook Foundation

National Academy of State Health Policy — expanding the use of managed care in Medicaid ($950,000) see Kaiser Family Foundation, Henry J.

Nature Conservancy ($15,000) see Whiting Foundation, Macauley and Helen Dow

New England Electric Railway Historical Society ($60,000) see O'Neil Foundation, Casey Albert T.

Northeast Harbor Library ($3,500) see Stroud Foundation

Our House of Maine ($7,500) see Hansen Memorial Foundation, Irving

Owls Head Transportation Museum ($1,000) see Key Bank of Maine

Parents Alternative to Latchkey — expanded before/after school care ($12,000) see Foundation for Seacoast Health

Parkview Memorial Hospital ($16,000) see Davenport Trust Fund

Parkview Memorial Hospital — ambulatory surgery and emergency ($101,275) see Hatch Charitable Trust, Margaret Milliken

Penobscot Marine Museum ($125,000) see Winona Corporation

Portland Museum of Art ($65,000) see UNUM Corp.

Portland Public Schools — Portland Partnership Program ($46,134) see UNUM Corp.

Portland Symphony Orchestra ($3,500) see Gannett Publishing Co., Guy

Regional Medical Center at Lubec ($25,000) see Bingham Second Betterment Fund, William

Riley School ($25,000) see Sprague Educational and Charitable Foundation, Seth

Riley School ($25,000) see Sprague Educational and Charitable Foundation, Seth

Robert R. Masterton Foundation ($5,000) see Gannett Publishing Co., Guy

Rockport Apprenticeshop ($30,000) see Sprague Educational and Charitable Foundation, Seth

Rockport Apprenticeshop ($30,000) see Sprague Educational and Charitable Foundation, Seth

S.A.I.L. ($25,000) see McGraw Foundation, Donald C.

St. Mary's Church ($7,500) see Davenport Trust Fund

Salvation Army ($14,000) see Davenport Trust Fund

School Administrative District ($9,200) see Mulford Trust, Clarence E.

Smith Cove Preservation Trust ($25,000) see Vesper Corp.

South Shore Health and Education Foundation ($50,000) see Killam Trust, Constance

South Shore Health and Education Foundation ($50,000) see Rodgers Trust, Elizabeth Killam

Spurwink School ($1,500) see Key Bank of Maine

Starlight Foundation Of Maine ($7,500) see Hansen Memorial Foundation, Irving

Strawberry Banke ($7,500) see French Foundation

Town of Brownfield ($3,700) see Mulford Trust, Clarence E.

Town of Fryeburg ($40,500) see Mulford Trust, Clarence E.

Town of Tremont ($5,000) see Milliken Foundation, Agnes G.

Town of Wayne ($43,945) see Ladd Charitable Corporation, Helen and George

United Way ($3,000) see Ansin Private Foundation, Ronald M.

United Way ($82,960) see Gannett Publishing Co., Guy

United Way ($7,000) see Key Bank of Maine

United Way ($35,000) see Shaw's Supermarkets

United Way of Greater Portland ($260,000) see UNUM Corp.

University of Maine — scholarships ($50,000) see Ayling Scholarship Foundation, Alice S.

University of Maine ($30,000) see Dexter Shoe Co.

University of Maine ($27,000) see Travelli Fund, Charles Irwin

University of Maine Cooperative Extension — to support a one-year demonstration "Waste Away" project to expand and test the effectiveness of a comprehensive mini-course on solid waste for upper elementary and junior high students in Maine schools ($16,000) see Island Foundation

University of Maine — third installment of a four-year, $150,000 grant for evaluation and expansion of a program to motivate personnel of elementary and secondary schools ($37,500) see Bingham Foundation, William

University of Maine at Orono ($18,450) see Davenport Trust Fund

University of Maine Pulp and Paper Foundation ($15,000) see Central National-Gottesman

University of Maine Pulp and Paper Foundation ($50,500) see Gilman Paper Co.

University of Southern Maine ($14,300) see Davenport Trust Fund

University of Southern Maine — Southern Maine Partnership ($233,418) see UNUM Corp.

Waterville Opera House Improvement ($1,500) see Gannett Publishing Co., Guy

Wayneflete School ($3,334) see Key Bank of Maine

Wilson Museum ($4,500) see Vesper Corp.

YMCA ($8,000) see Gannett Publishing Co., Guy

YMCA ($25,000) see McEvoy Foundation, Mildred H.

YMCA ($25,000) see Shaw's Supermarkets

YMCA ($7,000) see Webber Oil Co.

YMCA ($6,000) see Webber Oil Co.

YMCA ($1,000) see Webber Oil Co.

YMCA of Portland — capital campaign ($90,000) see UNUM Corp.

YWCA ($10,000) see Gannett Publishing Co., Guy

Maryland

Aberdeen Bible Church ($2,500) see Hobbs Foundation, Emmert

Academy of the Arts ($25,000) see Clark Charitable Foundation

Academy of Arts ($10,000) see Healy Family Foundation, M. A.

Accokeek Foundation — for pond renovation, purchase of scrubs, trees, plantings ($10,000) see Knapp Foundation

Accord Foundation ($65,550) see Ryan Family Charitable Foundation

Action for the Homeless ($25,000) see Knott Foundation, Marion I. and Henry J.

Advocates for Children and Youth ($120,000) see Straus Foundation, Aaron and Lillie

Advocates for Children and Youth — for improvements in the quality of public education in Baltimore ($90,000) see Goldseker Foundation of Maryland, Morris

Alvin Ailey Dance Theatre Foundation of Maryland ($10,000) see Rouse Co.

Alzheimers Disease Research ($4,000) see Amaturo Foundation

America College of Dentists Foundation ($5,000) see Stone Foundation, France

American Association of Colleges of Osteopathic Medicine ($150,000) see SmithKline Beecham

American Association of Colleges of Pharmacy ($350,000) see SmithKline Beecham

American Cancer Society ($800) see Clark Charitable Foundation

American Cancer Society ($500) see Hirschhorn Foundation, David and Barbara B.

American Council for Drug Education ($136,000) see Scaife Family Foundation

American Diabetes Association ($7,500) see Hobbs Foundation

American Diabetes Association ($7,500) see Hobbs Foundation, Emmert

American Diabetes Association ($3,000) see McCutchen Foundation

American Heart Association see Crestar Financial Corp.

American Heart Association ($2,000) see Poole & Kent Co.

American Horse Trials ($10,000) see Reinhold Foundation, Paul E. and Ida Klare

American Red Cross ($10,000) see Hoffberger Foundation

American Red Cross ($10,000) see PHH Corp.

American Technion Society ($105,000) see Slant/Fin Corp.

American Urological Association (UAU) Research Scholarship Fund ($22,000) see Bard, C. R.

America3 Foundation ($1,000) see Ingersoll Milling Machine Co.

Animal Welfare Society ($3,500) see Nathan Foundation

Anne Arundel County Public Schools — education award ($3,000) see Washington Post Co.

Anne Arundel General Hospital ($27,292) see Baldwin, Jr. Foundation, Summerfield

Anne Arundel Medical Center ($20,000) see Baldwin, Jr. Foundation, Summerfield

Anxiety Disorders Association of America — general support ($10,000) see Freed Foundation

Archdiocese for the Military Services, USA ($20,000) see Strake Foundation

Artscape ($2,000) see Mechanic Foundation, Morris A.

Asbury United Methodist Church ($125) see Hallowell Foundation

Asian Relief ($2,000) see Zock Endowment Trust

Aspen Institute — for the Pew Global Stewardship Initiative ($3,500,000) see Pew Charitable Trusts

Associated Black Charities — for an outside consulting group to study the central administration of the Baltimore City Public Schools ($120,000) see Abell Foundation, The

Associated Catholic Charities ($250,000) see Weinberg Foundation, Harry and Jeanette

Associated Jewish Charities ($30,000) see Rosenbloom Foundation, Ben and Esther

Associated Jewish Charities and Welfare ($749,868) see Blaustein Foundation, Jacob and Hilda

Associated Jewish Charities and Welfare Fund ($547,554) see Blaustein Foundation, Louis and Henrietta

Associated Jewish Charities and Welfare Fund ($50,000) see Hecht-Levi Foundation

Associated Jewish Charities and Welfare Fund ($2,080) see Lebovitz Fund

Associated Jewish Charities and Welfare Fund ($17,000) see Leidy Foundation, John J.

Associated Jewish Charities and Welfare Fund ($8,000) see Myers and Sons, D.

Associated Jewish Charities and Welfare Fund ($90,000) see Number Ten Foundation

Associated Jewish Charities and Welfare Fund ($353,500) see Rosenberg Foundation, Henry and Ruth Blaustein

Associated Jewish Charities and Welfare Fund ($110,000) see Shapiro Fund, Albert

Associated Jewish Charities and Welfare Fund ($16,666) see Shapiro Fund, Albert

Associated Jewish Charities and Welfare Fund ($1,121,500) see Straus Foundation, Aaron and Lillie

Associated Jewish Charities and Welfare Fund ($347,566) see Thalheimer Foundation, Alvin and Fanny Blaustein

Associated Jewish Charities and Welfare Fund ($49,000) see White Coffee Pot Family Inns

Associated Jewish Community Federation ($210,000) see Rosenbloom Foundation, Ben and Esther

Associated Jewish Community Federation of Baltimore ($100,000) see Meyerhoff Fund, Joseph

Associated Jewish Community Federation of Baltimore ($25,000) see Unger Foundation, Aber D.

Association of Baltimore Area Grantmakers ($1,500) see Unger Foundation, Aber D.

Association for Research in Vision and Ophthalmology — goodwill ($25,000) see Alcon Laboratories, Inc.

B.E.S.T. — scholarship for Black females ($3,000) see Egenton Home

B.U.I.L.D. ($10,000) see Rouse Co.

Bais Yaakou School for Girls ($5,000) see Pearlstone Foundation, Peggy Meyerhoff

BAISE ($10,000) see Macht Foundation, Morton and Sophia

Baldwin Memorial United Methodist Church ($4,000) see Weir Foundation Trust

Baltimore Arts Stabilization Project ($50,000) see Blaustein Foundation, Louis and Henrietta

Baltimore Center for Victims of Sexual Assault ($100) see Myers and Sons, D.

Baltimore City College Alumni Fund ($10,000) see Glazer Foundation, Jerome S.

Baltimore City Health Department ($4,514) see Leidy Foundation, John J.

Baltimore City Life Museum ($96,000) see Blaustein Foundation, Jacob and Hilda

Baltimore Commonwealth ($15,000) see Macht Foundation, Morton and Sophia

Baltimore Community Foundation ($60,000) see Baker, Jr. Memorial Fund, William G.

Baltimore Community Foundation ($32,610) see Baker, Jr. Memorial Fund, William G.

Baltimore Community Foundation ($25,000) see Blaustein Foundation, Louis and Henrietta

Baltimore Educational Scholarship Trust ($124,000) see France Foundation, Jacob and Annita

Baltimore Educational Scholarship Trust ($86,000) see Merrick Foundation, Robert G. and Anne M.

Baltimore Festival of Arts ($3,500) see Zamoiski Co.

Baltimore Goodwill Industries ($5,000) see Martin Marietta Corp.

Baltimore Goodwill Industries ($75) see Myers and Sons, D.

Baltimore Hebrew Congregation ($17,437) see Gordon Charitable Trust, Peggy and Yale

Baltimore Hebrew Congregation ($50,000) see Rosenberg Foundation, Henry and Ruth Blaustein

Baltimore Hebrew Congregation ($250,000) see Rosenthal-Statter Foundation

Baltimore Hebrew Congregation ($5,000) see Shapiro Fund, Albert

Baltimore Museum of Art ($62,500) see Blaustein

Foundation, Louis and Henrietta

Baltimore Museum of Art ($5,000) see Blum Foundation, Lois and Irving

Baltimore Museum of Art ($30,000) see Brown & Sons, Alex

Baltimore Museum of Art ($39,350) see First Maryland Bancorp

Baltimore Museum of Art ($20,000) see Gudelsky Family Foundation, Homer and Martha

Baltimore Museum of Art ($25,000) see Hoffberger Foundation

Baltimore Museum of Art ($2,100) see Legg Mason Inc.

Baltimore Museum of Art ($367,500) see MNC Financial

Baltimore Museum of Art ($100) see Myers and Sons, D.

Baltimore Museum of Art ($62,500) see Thalheimer Foundation, Alvin and Fanny Blaustein

Baltimore Museum of Art ($50,000) see USF&G Co.

Baltimore Museum of Art ($10,750) see Wunsch Foundation

Baltimore Museum of Art ($11,500) see Zamoiski Co.

Baltimore Museum of Industry — capital campaign ($50,000) see Baltimore Gas & Electric Co.

Baltimore Neighborhoods ($3,500) see Leidy Foundation, John J.

Baltimore Opera Company ($25,000) see Baker, Jr. Memorial Fund, William G.

Baltimore Opera Company ($4,500) see Campbell Foundation

Baltimore Opera Company ($52,421) see First Maryland Bancorp

Baltimore Opera Company ($7,720) see Kelly, Jr. Memorial Foundation, Ensign C. Markland

Baltimore Opera Company ($20,000) see Mechanic Foundation, Morris A.

Baltimore Opera Company ($50,000) see MNC Financial

Baltimore Opera Company ($100,000) see Procter & Gamble Cosmetic & Fragrance Products

Baltimore Reads ($20,000) see Baker, Jr. Memorial Fund, William G.

Baltimore Reads ($100,000) see Straus Foundation, Aaron and Lillie

Baltimore School for the Arts ($3,500) see Zamoiski Co.

Baltimore Symphony Orchestra see AEGON USA, Inc.

Baltimore Symphony Orchestra ($50,000) see Baker, Jr. Memorial Fund, William G.

Baltimore Symphony Orchestra ($20,000) see Baker, Jr. Memorial Fund, William G.

Baltimore Symphony Orchestra — annual fund ($50,000) see Baltimore Gas & Electric Co.

Baltimore Symphony Orchestra ($81,000) see Blaustein Foundation, Louis and Henrietta

Baltimore Symphony Orchestra — capital ($50,000) see Brown & Sons, Alex

Baltimore Symphony Orchestra ($2,500) see Campbell Foundation

Baltimore Symphony Orchestra ($45,000) see First Maryland Bancorp

Baltimore Symphony Orchestra ($32,167) see Gordon Charitable Trust, Peggy and Yale

Baltimore Symphony Orchestra ($100,000) see Hecht-Levi Foundation

Baltimore Symphony Orchestra ($25,000) see Hoffberger Foundation

Baltimore Symphony Orchestra ($31,184) see Kelly, Jr. Memorial Foundation, Ensign C. Markland

Baltimore Symphony Orchestra ($3,000) see Legg Mason Inc.

Baltimore Symphony Orchestra ($5,000) see Leidy Foundation, John J.

Baltimore Symphony Orchestra ($30,000) see Martin Marietta Corp.

Baltimore Symphony Orchestra ($2,000) see Mechanic Foundation, Morris A.

Baltimore Symphony Orchestra ($75,000) see Meyerhoff Fund, Joseph

Baltimore Symphony Orchestra ($50,000) see Meyerhoff Fund, Joseph

Baltimore Symphony Orchestra ($25,000) see Meyerhoff Fund, Joseph

Baltimore Symphony Orchestra ($75,000) see MNC Financial

Baltimore Symphony Orchestra ($1,500) see Number Ten Foundation

Baltimore Symphony Orchestra ($25,000) see PHH Corp.

Baltimore Symphony Orchestra ($7,000) see PHH Corp.

Baltimore Symphony Orchestra ($15,125) see Price Associates, T. Rowe

Baltimore Symphony Orchestra ($270,000) see Rosenberg Foundation, Henry and Ruth Blaustein

Baltimore Symphony Orchestra ($41,000) see Sheridan Foundation, Thomas B. and Elizabeth M.

Baltimore Symphony Orchestra ($18,000) see Thalheimer Foundation, Alvin and Fanny Blaustein

Baltimore Symphony Orchestra ($10,000) see Zamoiski Co.

Baltimore Theatre Project ($20,000) see Baker, Jr. Memorial Fund, William G.

Baltimore Zoo ($12,625) see Price Associates, T. Rowe

Baltimore Zoo Society ($20,000) see Brown & Sons, Alex

Baltimore Zoological Society ($42,500) see First Maryland Bancorp

Baltimore Zoological Society ($56,250) see MNC Financial

Baltimore Zoological Society ($27,500) see Procter & Gamble Cosmetic & Fragrance Products

Barnesville School ($10,000) see Truland Foundation

Basic Cancer Research Foundation ($50,000) see Hirschhorn Foundation, David and Barbara B.

Bender-Dosik Parenting Center of JCC of Greater Washington ($10,000) see Bender Foundation

Benedictine School Foundation — capital improvement ($160,000) see Solo Cup Co.

Beth Tfiloh Congregation ($5,000) see Rosenthal-Statter Foundation

Beth Tikvah Synagogue ($13,500) see Cohen Foundation, Manny and Ruthy

Bethesda Academy of Performing Arts ($6,000) see Stone Foundation, David S.

Bethesda Chevy Chase Rescue Squad ($100) see Beitzell & Co.

Bethesda General Hospital ($10,000) see Souers Charitable Trust, Sidney W. and Sylvia N.

Bethesda United Methodist Church ($5,600) see Smith Foundation, Gordon V. and Helen C.

Bethfilah Congregation ($8,000) see Number Ten Foundation

Big Brothers and Big Sisters ($750) see Loats Foundation

Board of Education ($15,000) see Chambers Development Co.

Boy Scouts of America see Banner Life Insurance Co.

Boy Scouts of America ($11,200) see Olmsted Foundation, George and Carol

Boy Scouts of America ($12,000) see Rosenberg Foundation, Henry and Ruth Blaustein

Boys and Girls Club ($38,495) see Hoffberger Foundation

Boys and Girls Club ($23,020) see Weir Foundation Trust

Boys Latin School — computer center ($50,000) see Hobbs Foundation

Boys Latin School ($50,000) see Hobbs Foundation, Emmert

Boys Latin School ($10,000) see Kelly, Jr. Memorial Foundation, Ensign C. Markland

Boys Latin School — upper school science facility, materials and instruction ($25,000) see Middendorf Foundation

Boys Latin School — lower/middle school computer center purchase equipment ($15,000) see Middendorf Foundation

Bradley Hills Presbyterian Church ($21,800) see Weir Foundation Trust

Browne Genetic Laboratory, Johns Hopkins School of Medicine ($25,000) see Blowitz-Ridgeway Foundation

Bryn Mawr School ($3,000) see Egenton Home

Bryn Mawr School ($50,000) see Ford Foundation, Edward E.

Bullis School ($13,000) see Abramson Family Foundation

Bullis School ($5,700) see Dart Group Corp.

C.E. Smith Jewish Day School ($200,000) see Smith Family Foundation, Charles E.

Cambridge Rescue Fire Company ($5,000) see Nathan Foundation

Camp Airy — Camp Louise Vacation Fund ($153,429) see Straus Foundation, Aaron and Lillie

Campaign for Our Children ($37,500) see USF&G Co.

Cancer Research Council ($50,000) see Wallace Genetic Foundation

Maryland (cont.)

Canterbury School ($10,000) see McCutchen Foundation

Capitol College ($50,000) see Gudelsky Family Foundation, Homer and Martha

Carnegie Institution of Washington, Department of Embryology ($24,500) see Childs Memorial Fund for Medical Research, Jane Coffin

Carnegie Institution of Washington, Department of Embryology ($24,500) see Childs Memorial Fund for Medical Research, Jane Coffin

Carole Haven Center ($36,290) see Ryan Family Charitable Foundation

Catholic Charities ($2,000) see Zamoiski Co.

Catholic Relief Services ($15,000) see Cottrell Foundation

Catholic Relief Services — emergency relief efforts ($5,000) see Greene Manufacturing Co.

Catholic Relief Services ($150,000) see Lewis Foundation, Frank J.

Catholic Relief Services ($1,000,000) see O'Neil Foundation, W.

Catholic Relief Services — to assist refugee Kurds in Mid-East to aid Bangledesh cyclone victims ($70,000) see Raskob Foundation for Catholic Activities

Catholic Youth Organization — youth programs ($30,000) see Clark-Winchcole Foundation

Center for the Handicapped ($50,000) see Gudelsky Family Foundation, Homer and Martha

Center Stage ($20,000) see Brown & Sons, Alex

Center Stage ($5,000) see Hecht-Levi Foundation

Center Stage ($10,000) see Pearlstone Foundation, Peggy Meyerhoff

Center Stage ($56,125) see Price Associates, T. Rowe

Center Stage ($215,000) see Procter & Gamble Cosmetic & Fragrance Products

Center Stage ($50,000) see Rollins Luetkemeyer Charitable Foundation

Center Stage ($16,000) see Unger Foundation, Aber D.

Center Stage ($35,000) see USF&G Co.

Central Scholarship Bureau ($1,235) see Number Ten Foundation

Chamber of Commerce ($6,000) see Nathan Foundation

Charles E. Smith Jewish Day School ($5,000) see Bernstein Foundation, Diane and Norman

Charles E. Smith Jewish Day School ($10,000) see Lehrman Foundation, Jacob and Charlotte

Chesapeake Bay Foundation ($20,000) see Bailey Wildlife Foundation

Chesapeake Bay Foundation ($10,000) see Baker Trust, Clayton

Chesapeake Bay Foundation ($500) see Bionetics Corp.

Chesapeake Bay Foundation ($22,000) see Carter Foundation, Beirne

Chesapeake Bay Foundation ($100,000) see Fair Play Foundation

Chesapeake Bay Foundation ($15,000) see McKnight Foundation, Sumner T.

Chesapeake Bay Foundation ($85,000) see Town Creek Foundation

Chesapeake Bay Maritime Museum ($50,000) see Kerr Fund, Grayce B.

Chesapeake Center ($30,000) see Ryan Family Charitable Foundation

Children's Cancer Foundation ($25,000) see Carvel Foundation, Thomas and Agnes

Children's Guild — facilities library ($5,000) see Hobbs Foundation

Children's Guild ($5,000) see Hobbs Foundation, Emmert

Children's Guild ($3,000) see Leidy Foundation, John J.

Chinese Language School of Baltimore ($300) see China Times Cultural Foundation

Chizuk Amund Congregation ($17,590) see Rosenbloom Foundation, Ben and Esther

Chizuk Amung Congregation ($10,000) see Lebovitz Fund

Choral Arts Society ($2,500) see Healy Family Foundation, M. A.

Christmas in April — start-up costs for project to repair houses for poor and elderly ($10,000) see Abell Foundation, Charles S.

Christmas in April — start-up costs for first Christmas in April project ($10,000) see Abell Foundation, Charles S.

Christopher Columbus Center ($25,000) see Baker, Jr. Memorial Fund, William G.

City of Hagerstown ($200,000) see Freeman Charitable Trust, Samuel

Coastal Hospice ($250) see Clark Charitable Foundation

CollegBound Foundation ($25,000) see Brown & Sons, Alex

College Bound Foundation ($25,000) see Crown Central Petroleum Corp.

College Bound Foundation ($40,000) see PHH Corp.

College-Bound Foundation ($25,000) see Rosenbloom Foundation, Ben and Esther

College Bound Foundation ($50,000) see USF&G Co.

College of Notre Dame ($30,000) see First Maryland Bancorp

College of Notre Dame of Maryland ($31,000) see Rouse Co.

College of Notre Dame of Maryland — toward establishment of a new International Center ($100,000) see Bryan Family Foundation, Kathleen Price and Joseph M.

CollegeBound Foundation ($60,000) see First Maryland Bancorp

CollegeBound Foundation ($100,000) see Procter & Gamble Cosmetic & Fragrance Products

Community Assistance Network — food for needy ($4,000) see Hobbs Foundation

Community Assistance Network ($3,000) see Hobbs Foundation, Emmert

Community Assistance Network ($5,000) see Leidy Foundation, John J.

Community Foundation of the Greater Baltimore Area ($20,000) see Rosenberg Foundation, Henry and Ruth Blaustein

Comprehensive Housing Assistance — three-year grant for a new program to address housing needs of elderly population ($75,000) see Goldseker Foundation of Maryland, Morris

Concerns of Police Survivors — awards to families of officers killed in the line of duty ($148,976) see Japanese American Agon Friendship League

Concert Artists of Baltimore ($5,750) see Gordon Charitable Trust, Peggy and Yale

Concert Artists of Baltimore ($15,000) see Rosenberg Foundation, Henry and Ruth Blaustein

Concert Society of Maryland ($20,000) see Freeman Foundation, Carl M.

Congregation Beth El of Montgomery County ($25,000) see Bender Foundation

Connelly School of the Holy Child — education ($30,000) see Clark-Winchcole Foundation

Connelly School of the Holy Child ($100,000) see McShain Charities, John

Connelly School of the Holy Child ($10,000) see O'Neil Foundation, W.

Coppin State College ($3,000) see Merit Oil Corp.

Corporation of St. Timothy's School ($18,500) see Ireland Foundation

Crossway Community — grant to assist high risk, low-income one parent families project ($10,000) see Abell Foundation, Charles S.

CU09-Performing Arts-Theatre-Center Stage ($97,500) see MNC Financial

CU10-Public Radio and Television — Maryland Public Broadcasting Foundation ($75,000) see MNC Financial

Cystic Fibrosis Foundation see Amoco Corp.

Cystic Fibrosis Foundation ($45,000) see Foundation for the Needs of Others

Cystic Fibrosis Foundation ($5,000) see Kelly, Jr. Memorial Foundation, Ensign C. Markland

Cystic Fibrosis Foundation ($2,500,000) see Richardson Foundation, Smith

Cystic Fibrosis Foundation ($500,000) see Richardson Foundation, Smith

Cystic Fibrosis Foundation ($2,000) see Uslico Corp.

Division of Catholic Schools ($300,000) see Knott Foundation, Marion I. and Henry J.

Dorchester County Commissioners ($5,100) see Nathan Foundation

Dorchester General Hospital ($17,000) see Nathan Foundation

Downtown Baltimore Children's Center ($2,860) see Egenton Home

Downtown Dance Company ($2,500) see Pearlstone Foundation, Peggy Meyerhoff

Ducks Unlimited, Baltimore Chapter ($5,200) see Mullan Foundation, Thomas F. and Clementine L.

Eastern Shore Land Conservancy ($25,000) see Healy Family Foundation, M. A.

Echo Hill Outdoor School ($60,000) see Merrick Foundation, Robert G. and Anne M.

Ed Block Courage Awards Foundation ($10,000) see Wilson Sanitarium for Children of Baltimore City, Thomas

Eldorado Brookview Volunteer Fire Department ($4,200) see Nathan Foundation

Enterprise Foundation ($35,000) see Baker Trust, Clayton

Enterprise Foundation ($20,000) see Batten Foundation

Enterprise Foundation — to support the development of four community life centers ($50,000) see Federal Home Loan Mortgage Corp. (Freddie Mac)

The Enterprise Foundation — technical assistance and capital campaign ($550,000) see Federal National Mortgage Assn., Fannie Mae

Enterprise Foundation — general operating support ($199,381) see MCJ Foundation

Enterprise Foundation ($12,500) see Salomon Foundation, Richard & Edna

Enterprise Foundation — general support ($20,000) see Taconic Foundation

Enterprise Foundation — to support a large-scale development of affordable housing in the District of Columbia ($100,000) see Graham Fund, Philip L.

Enterprise Foundation — to support predevelopment, acquisition, and other short-term loans for not-for-profit housing development projects and to help address the housing needs of the poor in dozens of American cities ($2,000,000) see MacArthur Foundation, John D. and Catherine T.

Environmental Action Foundation ($20,000) see Beldon Fund

Episcopal Social Ministries ($15,000) see Baker Trust, Clayton

Evergreen House Foundation ($20,000) see Rollins Luetkemeyer Charitable Foundation

Family and Children's Services of Central Maryland ($6,000) see Mullan Foundation, Thomas F. and Clementine L.

Family and Children's Society — unrestricted ($35,000) see Middendorf Foundation

Family Life Center ($2,250) see Loats Foundation

Foundation for Advanced Education in the Sciences ($10,300) see Glenn Foundation for Medical Research, Paul F.

Foundation for Advanced Education in the Sciences/

FAES ($10,000) see Gulton Foundation

Fr. Martin's Ashley — construct/furnish a medical wing in new building of inpatient treatment center for alcoholics/chemically-addicted ($50,000) see Raskob Foundation for Catholic Activities

Francis Scott Key Center ($750) see Loats Foundation

Frederick County Public Schools — education award ($2,000) see Washington Post Co.

Frederick County Services for the Hearing Impaired ($25,000) see Knott Foundation, Marion I. and Henry J.

Frederick County Youth Hot Line ($750) see Loats Foundation

Friends of Family ($30,000) see Baker Trust, Clayton

Friends School ($3,000) see Egenton Home

Fund for Educational Excellence ($10,000) see Baker Trust, Clayton

Fund for Educational Excellence ($30,000) see First Maryland Bancorp

Fund for Educational Excellence ($50,000) see Meyerhoff Fund, Joseph

Fund for Podiatry ($1,000) see Midmark Corp.

Garrison Forest School ($67,250) see France Foundation, Jacob and Annita

Garrison Forest School ($15,000) see Lightner Sams Foundation

Garrison Forest School ($58,750) see Merrick Foundation, Robert G. and Anne M.

Garrison Forest School ($15,000) see Rollins Luetkemeyer Charitable Foundation

Garrison Forest School ($50,500) see Sheridan Foundation, Thomas B. and Elizabeth M.

GBMC Foundation ($10,000) see PHH Corp.

Genesis Jobs ($1,000) see Legg Mason Inc.

George Williams Browne Molecular Genetic Facility ($10,000) see Wilson Sanitarium for Children of Baltimore City, Thomas

Gilman Capital Campaign ($10,000) see Campbell Foundation

Gilman School ($57,700) see France Foundation, Jacob and Annita

Gilman School ($145,000) see Merrick Foundation, Robert G. and Anne M.

Gilman School Scholarship Fund — to provide fund for financial support ($3,500) see Campbell Foundation

Girl Scouts of America ($16,667) see Pearlstone Foundation, Peggy Meyerhoff

Goucher College ($2,500) see Baldwin, Jr. Foundation, Summerfield

Goucher College ($8,000) see Polinger Foundation, Howard and Geraldine

Goucher College ($50,000) see Rollins Luetkemeyer Charitable Foundation

Goucher College Annual Giving Fund ($4,000) see Campbell Foundation

Govans Ecumenical Homes — for the establishment of Govans Ecumenical Development Coporation ($100,000) see Goldseker Foundation of Maryland, Morris

Governor's Commission Healthcare Policy ($2,500) see Unger Foundation, Aber D.

Greater Baltimore City CollegeBound Foundation ($187,500) see MNC Financial

Greater Baltimore Committee — in support of the regional High Technology Forum and Higher Education Program ($135,000) see Abell Foundation, The

Greater Baltimore Medical Center ($20,000) see Rouse Co.

Greater Washington Jewish Community Foundation ($35,000) see Cohen Foundation, Manny and Ruthy

Greater Washington Jewish Community Foundation ($5,000) see Dart Group Corp.

Greater Washington Jewish Community Foundation ($50,000) see Gelman Foundation, Melvin and Estelle

Greater Washington Jewish Community Foundation ($5,000) see Goldman Foundation, Aaron and Cecile

Greater Washington Jewish Community Foundation ($125,000) see Smith Family Foundation, Charles E.

Hadassah ($10,000) see Cohen Foundation, Manny and Ruthy

Hadassah Medical Institutions ($10,000) see Rosenthal-Statter Foundation

Hai Sinai Congregation ($17,437) see Gordon Charitable Trust, Peggy and Yale

Hammond Harwood House — capital fund campaign ($25,000) see Middendorf Foundation

Han Sinai Congregation ($2,036) see Number Ten Foundation

Har Sinai Congregation ($3,000) see Zamoiski Co.

Harbor Hospital ($2,000) see Zamoiski Co.

Hartley House ($750) see Loats Foundation

Harvey M. and Lyn P. Meyerhoff Fund — support of the associated Jewish charities ($80,000) see Meyerhoff Foundation, Lyn P.

Health Care ($5,000) see Campbell Foundation

Hearing and Speech Agency ($3,500) see Egenton Home

Hebrew Day Institute ($70,000) see Smith Family Foundation, Charles E.

Hebrew Home of Greater Washington ($12,750) see Dweck Foundation, Samuel R.

Hebrew Home of Greater Washington ($50,000) see Freeman Foundation, Carl M.

Hebrew Home of Greater Washington ($5,000) see Goldman Foundation, Aaron and Cecile

Hebrew Home of Greater Washington ($10,000) see Kapiloff Foundation, Leonard

Hebrew Home of Greater Washington ($30,000) see

Lehrman Foundation, Jacob and Charlotte

Hebrew Home of Greater Washington ($7,000) see Polinger Foundation, Howard and Geraldine

Hebrew Home of Greater Washington — Wasserman Renovation ($20,000) see Dweck Foundation, Samuel R.

Hebrew Home Ring Dedication ($26,000) see Dweck Foundation, Samuel R.

Historic Annapolis — capital campaign ($50,000) see Baltimore Gas & Electric Co.

Historic Annapolis Foundation ($5,000) see Mullan Foundation, Thomas F. and Clementine L.

Historical Society of Talbot County ($65,000) see Clark Charitable Foundation

Holton Arms School ($10,000) see Tauber Foundation

Hood College ($1,000) see Lauffer Trust, Charles A.

Hospice ($4,000) see Nathan Foundation

Hospice Caring ($25,000) see Fowler Memorial Foundation, John Edward

House of Ruth ($5,000) see Blum Foundation, Lois and Irving

House of Ruth ($5,000) see Blum Foundation, Lois and Irving

House of Ruth ($2,500) see Hobbs Foundation, Emmert

Howard County General Hospital — endowment fund ($8,333) see Giant Food

Independent College Fund of Maryland ($5,000) see Brown, Jr. Charitable Trust, Frank D.

Independent College Fund of Maryland ($20,000) see Crown Central Petroleum Corp.

Independent College Fund of Maryland ($12,000) see Price Associates, T. Rowe

Indigent Fund of Home Oncology Therapies ($10,000) see J. D. B. Fund

Information for the Partially Disabled — general support ($15,000) see Freed Foundation

Institute for Alternative Agriculture ($90,000) see Wallace Genetic Foundation

Institute for Energy and Environmental Research — project support ($15,000) see Warsh-Mott Legacy

International Cancer Alliance ($50,000) see Wallace Genetic Foundation

International Eye Foundation — Kwara State Blindness Prevention Program ($28,898) see River Blindness Foundation

Ivymount School — to help this school for learning disabled students build an operating endowment ($75,000) see Graham Fund, Philip L.

Ivymount School — funds cover the cost of tuition for the homebased services program for two identified at-risk infants ($40,000) see Federal Home Loan Mortgage Corp. (Freddie Mac)

Jemicy School ($500) see Gross Foundation, Louis H.

Jewish Community Center ($10,215) see Dweck Foundation, Samuel R.

Jewish Community Center ($8,000) see Polinger Foundation, Howard and Geraldine

Jewish Community Federation of Baltimore — continuing support for the Morris Goldseker Aid and Education Fund ($96,900) see Goldseker Foundation of Maryland, Morris

Jewish Council for the Aging ($5,500) see Polinger Foundation, Howard and Geraldine

Jewish Foundation for Group Homes ($10,000) see Himmelfarb Foundation, Paul and Annetta

Jewish Social Service Agency ($20,000) see Gudelsky Family Foundation, Isadore and Bertha

Jewish Social Service Agency ($50,000) see Shapiro, Inc.

Jewish Social Services ($13,471) see Gelman Foundation, Melvin and Estelle

Jewish Social Services Agency ($3,250) see Goldman Foundation, Aaron and Cecile

Jewish Social Services Agency ($6,000) see Polinger Foundation, Howard and Geraldine

JFK Institute ($10,000) see Rosenthal-Statter Foundation

John F. Kennedy Institute ($2,500) see Gross Foundation, Louis H.

John F. Kennedy Institute ($16,000) see Wilson Sanitarium for Children of Baltimore City, Thomas

John Hopkins University — investigator research ($50,000) see Mallinckrodt, Jr. Foundation, Edward

John Hopkins University — scholar program ($50,000) see Mallinckrodt, Jr. Foundation, Edward

Johns Hopkins CAAT ($35,000) see Barbour Foundation, Bernice

Johns Hopkins Hospital ($50,000) see Baldwin, Jr. Foundation, Summerfield

Johns Hopkins Hospital ($209,000) see Blaustein Foundation, Jacob and Hilda

Johns Hopkins Hospital ($37,000) see Blaustein Foundation, Louis and Henrietta

Johns Hopkins Hospital ($5,000) see Gross Foundation, Louis H.

Johns Hopkins Hospital ($10,000) see Mechanic Foundation, Morris A.

Johns Hopkins Hospital — toward the cost of purchasing an elutriator and cell separation and washing equipment ($183,235) see Rippel Foundation, Fannie E.

Johns Hopkins Hospital ($20,000) see Smith Charitable Fund, Eleanor Armstrong

Johns Hopkins Hospital ($7,500) see Thalheimer Foundation, Alvin and Fanny Blaustein

Johns Hopkins Hospital ($15,000) see Wilson Sanitarium for Children of Baltimore City, Thomas

Johns Hopkins Hospital ($15,000) see Wilson Sanitarium for Children of Baltimore City, Thomas

Johns Hopkins Hospital ($15,000) see Wilson Sanitarium for Children of Baltimore City, Thomas

Johns Hopkins Hospital Dementia Research ($3,000) see Weir Foundation Trust

Johns Hopkins Medical Center ($1,889) see Clark Charitable Foundation

Johns Hopkins Medical Center ($20,000) see Palisades Educational Foundation

Johns Hopkins Medical Center — Richard Starr Ross Fund ($20,000) see Palisades Educational Foundation

Johns Hopkins Medical Center School of Advanced Studies ($20,000) see Palisades Educational Foundation

Johns Hopkins Oncology Center ($22,500) see Preuss Foundation

Johns Hopkins Oncology Center ($22,500) see Preuss Foundation

Johns Hopkins University ($10,000) see Baldwin, Jr. Foundation, Summerfield

Johns Hopkins University ($10,000) see Blum Foundation, Lois and Irving

Johns Hopkins University ($55,000) see Brookdale Foundation

Johns Hopkins University ($115,604) see Educational Foundation of America

Johns Hopkins University ($50,000) see First Maryland Bancorp

Johns Hopkins University ($243,760) see France Foundation, Jacob and Annita

Johns Hopkins University ($26,455) see Gordon Charitable Trust, Peggy and Yale

Johns Hopkins University ($10,000) see Greenberg Foundation, Alan C.

Johns Hopkins University ($35) see Gross Foundation, Louis H.

Johns Hopkins University ($10,000) see Hecht-Levi Foundation

Johns Hopkins University ($17,000) see Hopkins Foundation, John Jay

Johns Hopkins University ($5,100) see Legg Mason Inc.

Johns Hopkins University — to support a center for macromolecular structure ($2,614,700) see Markey Charitable Trust, Lucille P.

Johns Hopkins University — computing applications competition to aid the disabled ($75,000) see MCI Communications Corp.

Johns Hopkins University ($180,000) see MNC Financial

Johns Hopkins University — educational ($100,000) see Olmsted Foundation, George and Carol

Johns Hopkins University ($25,000) see PHH Corp.

Johns Hopkins University ($90,000) see Pioneer Fund

Johns Hopkins University ($85,000) see Ramapo Trust

Johns Hopkins University ($10,000) see Roddis Foundation, Hamilton

Johns Hopkins University ($1,650,000) see SDB Foundation

Johns Hopkins University ($48,760) see SDB Foundation

Johns Hopkins University ($43,710) see SDB Foundation

Johns Hopkins University ($40,919) see Smithers Foundation, Christopher D.

Johns Hopkins University ($12,000) see Superior Tube Co.

Johns Hopkins University ($5,000) see Unger Foundation, Aber D.

Johns Hopkins University ($550,800) see Whitaker Foundation

Johns Hopkins University — support educational science programs ($77,295) see Whittier Foundation, L. K.

Johns Hopkins University ($23,693) see Zamoiski Co.

Johns Hopkins University ($6,950) see Zamoiski Co.

Johns Hopkins University/Baltimore International Festival — for staffing and related expenses in the fiscal planning and artistic development of an inaugural international arts festival ($200,000) see Abell Foundation, The

Johns Hopkins University — to sponsor a national competition to stimulate and discover computer-based solutions to help people with disabilities ($5,000) see NEC USA

Johns Hopkins University/CTY — public policy ($65,090) see Seaver Institute

Johns Hopkins University/CTY — Talent Search ($77,295) see Seaver Institute

Johns Hopkins University Department of Urology ($10,070) see Freygang Foundation, Walter Henry

Johns Hopkins University/Francis Scott Key Medical Center — for personnel and equipment to provide expanded outreach of Norplant contraceptive services ($100,000) see Abell Foundation, The

Johns Hopkins University — for the Goldseker Scholarship Fund, which in 1991 provided financial aid to 25 economically disadvantaged undergraduates from the Baltimore metropolitan area ($96,900) see Goldseker Foundation of Maryland, Morris

Johns Hopkins University Hospital ($10,000) see Spang & Co.

John's Hopkins University Medicine ($25,000) see Dreyfus Foundation, Jean and Louis

Johns Hopkins University Peabody Institute ($50,000) see Hecht-Levi Foundation

Johns Hopkins University Peabody Institute ($10,000) see Hecht-Levi Foundation

Johns Hopkins University School of Hygiene ($5,000) see Unger Foundation, Aber D.

Johns Hopkins University-School of Hygiene and Public Health ($165,000) see France Foundation, Jacob and Annita

Maryland (cont.)

Johns Hopkins University —
School of Hygiene and Public
Health ($135,000) see Merrick
Foundation, Robert G. and
Anne M.

Johns Hopkins University
School of Medicine ($25,000)
see Kapiloff Foundation,
Leonard

Johns Hopkins University
School of Medicine ($30,000)
see Kettering Family
Foundation

Johns Hopkins University
School of Medicine ($45,000)
see Pfeiffer Research
Foundation, Gustavus and
Louise

Johns Hopkins University
School of Medicine ($3,000)
see Rosenthal Foundation,
Benjamin J.

Johns Hopkins University
School of Medicine
($192,000) see Smith
Charitable Trust, W. W.

Johns Hopkins University
School of Medicine — to
endow a chair of
gynecological pathology
($285,842) see Telinde Trust,
Richard W.

Johns Hopkins University
School of Nursing —
scholarship in memory of
Leona B. Carpenter
($500,000) see Carpenter
Foundation, E. Rhodes and
Leona B.

Johns Hopkins University/Steve
Muller Endowment ($30,000)
see Brown & Sons, Alex

Johns Hopkins University —
Success for All Programs
($199,440) see Merrick
Foundation, Robert G. and
Anne M.

JSSA Home Health Care
Program ($10,000) see
Lehrman Foundation, Jacob
and Charlotte

Jubilee Baltimore ($2,000) see
Campbell Foundation

Junior Achievement of National
Capital Area ($35,000) see
Fowler Memorial Foundation,
John Edward

Junior Chamber of Commerce
($35,000) see Smith Family
Foundation, Charles E.

Kenedy Institute ($10,000) see
PHH Corp.

Kennedy Institute ($30,000) see
Hoffberger Foundation

Kent and Queen Anne's Hospital
— one-for-one matching grant
for a scholarship endowment
fund to enable nurses at the
hospital to pursue advanced
nursing degrees ($50,000) see
Bingham Foundation, William

Lacrosse Foundation ($5,000)
see Baldwin, Jr. Foundation,
Summerfield

Lacrosse Foundation ($10,000)
see Kelly, Jr. Memorial
Foundation, Ensign C.
Markland

Lady Maryland Foundation
($25,000) see Meyerhoff
Fund, Joseph

Lady Maryland Foundation
($24,400) see Wareheim
Foundation, E. C.

Lancer Boys Club ($10,000) see
Mechanic Foundation, Morris
A.

Landon School ($4,000) see
Barlow Family Foundation,
Milton A. and Gloria G.

Landon School ($20,000) see
Freeman Foundation, Carl M.

Landon School — teachers
salaries ($40,000) see
Johnston Trust for Charitable
and Educational Purposes,
James M.

Landon School ($8,000) see
McGregor Foundation,
Thomas and Frances

Laurel Armony Anderson
Murphy Community Center
($1,000) see Ames Department
Stores

League for Handicapped —
handicapped fitness center
($10,000) see Pearlstone
Foundation

League for Handicapped
($15,000) see Hobbs
Foundation, Emmert

Learning Independence ($2,000)
see Unger Foundation, Aber D.

Life Underwriter Training
Council Building Fund —
capital campaign for new
building ($35,000) see CM
Alliance Cos.

Life Underwriter Training
Council (LUTC) — insurance
education ($165,000) see
Prudential Insurance Co. of
America

Lifesongs 1991 ($1,000) see
White Coffee Pot Family Inns

Literacy Council of Montgomery
County ($100) see Beitzell &
Co.

Loyola College see AEGON
USA, Inc.

Loyola College ($6,000) see
Mullan Foundation, Thomas F.
and Clementine L.

Loyola College ($3,900) see
Sheridan Foundation, Thomas
B. and Elizabeth M.

Loyola College ($125,000) see
USF&G Co.

Loyola College in Maryland —
capital campaign ($300,000)
see Baltimore Gas & Electric
Co.

Lutheran Mission Society
($5,000) see Nathan
Foundation

Lutheran Mission Society of
Maryland ($15,000) see
Bastien Memorial Foundation,
John E. and Nellie J.

Lutheran Mission Society of
Maryland ($3,000) see
Egenton Home

Lyric Foundation ($10,000) see
Kelly, Jr. Memorial
Foundation, Ensign C.
Markland

Make-a-Wish Foundation see
Banner Life Insurance Co.

Make-A-Wish Foundation
($5,000) see Crown Books
Foundation, Inc.

MAOR ($87,000) see AVI CHAI
- A Philanthropic Foundation

Maryland Academy of Sciences
($35,000) see Crown Central
Petroleum Corp.

Maryland Academy of Sciences
($500) see Poole & Kent Co.

Maryland Association of
Non-Profit Organizations
($105,000) see Straus
Foundation, Aaron and Lillie

Maryland Association of
Nonprofit Organizations — for
start-up support for three years
($60,000) see Goldseker
Foundation of Maryland,
Morris

Maryland College of Art and
Design ($26,212) see
Gudelsky Family Foundation,
Homer and Martha

Maryland Committee for
Children — counseling project
for parents with children with
mental retardation and
developmental disabilities
($50,000) see Kennedy, Jr.
Foundation, Joseph P.

Maryland Committee for
Children ($100,000) see Straus
Foundation, Aaron and Lillie

Maryland Food Committee
($1,250) see Hirschhorn
Foundation, David and
Barbara B.

Maryland Food Committee
($20,000) see Pearlstone
Foundation, Peggy Meyerhoff

Maryland Food Committee —
for direct feeding at 124
emergency food centers and
soup kitchens ($130,000) see
Abell Foundation, The

Maryland Historical Society —
challenge grant ($100,000) see
Middendorf Foundation

Maryland Historical Society —
repairs and improvements
($12,500) see Middendorf
Foundation

Maryland Historical Society
($15,000) see Sheridan
Foundation, Thomas B. and
Elizabeth M.

Maryland Horsemen's Assistance
Fund ($25,000) see Jockey
Club Foundation

Maryland Horsemen's Assistance
Fund ($40,000) see Ryan
Family Charitable Foundation

Maryland Institute ($25,000) see
Thalheimer Foundation, Alvin
and Fanny Blaustein

Maryland Institute, College of
Art — capital campaign
($200,000) see Baltimore Gas
& Electric Co.

Maryland Institute College of
Art ($5,000) see Brown, Jr.
Charitable Trust, Frank D.

Maryland Institute, College of
Art ($120,000) see France
Foundation, Jacob and Annita

Maryland Institute College of
Art ($45,000) see Hoffberger
Foundation

Maryland Institute, College of
Art ($80,700) see Merrick
Foundation, Robert G. and
Anne M.

Maryland Institute, College of
Art ($85,500) see Procter &
Gamble Cosmetic & Fragrance
Products

Maryland Public Broadcasting
($15,000) see Mechanic
Foundation, Morris A.

Maryland Public Broadcasting
Foundation ($20,000) see
Gudelsky Family Foundation,
Homer and Martha

Maryland Public Broadcasting
Foundation — support of 1991
program ($40,000) see
Baltimore Gas & Electric Co.

Maryland School for the Blind
($400) see Legg Mason Inc.

Maryland School for the Blind
($12,000) see Wilson
Sanitarium for Children of
Baltimore City, Thomas

Maryland Science Center
($30,000) see Blaustein
Foundation, Louis and
Henrietta

Maryland Science Center
($58,000) see France
Foundation, Jacob and Annita

Maryland Sheriffs Boys Ranch
($750) see Loats Foundation

Maryland Sheriff's Youth Ranch
see Banner Life Insurance Co.

Maryland Special Olympics see
Banner Life Insurance Co.

Maryland Special Olympics
($50) see Myers and Sons, D.

Maryland State Department of
Education/Regional Teacher
Training Center — for the
establishment of the Regional
Teacher Training Center
($400,000) see Abell
Foundation, The

Maryvale Preparatory School
($25,000) see Sheridan
Foundation, Thomas B. and
Elizabeth M.

Mayors Advisor Committee
($5,000) see Pearlstone
Foundation, Peggy Meyerhoff

McDonogh School ($17,500) see
Campbell Foundation

McDonogh School ($4,500) see
Egenton Home

McDonogh School ($12,000) see
Mullan Foundation, Thomas F.
and Clementine L.

McDonogh School ($100,000)
see Rollins Luetkemeyer
Charitable Foundation

McDonogh School ($71,100) see
Rosenberg Foundation, Henry
and Ruth Blaustein

McKim Center ($3,500) see
Egenton Home

McLean School ($500) see
Barlow Family Foundation,
Milton A. and Gloria G.

Meals on Wheels ($10,000) see
Rouse Co.

Meals on Wheels ($3,550) see
Weir Foundation Trust

Meals on Wheels of Central
Maryland ($3,000) see
Number Ten Foundation

Meeting Place Foundation
($50,000) see Merrick
Foundation, Robert G. and
Anne M.

Meeting Place Foundation — for
matching grant ($50,000) see
Middendorf Foundation

MEGA (Maryland Economic
Growth Association) ($24,188)
see Crown Central Petroleum
Corp.

Memorial Hospital at Easton,
Maryland — final payment of
a $100,000, one-for-one
matching grant for endowment
of the Nick Rajacich Memorial
Scholarship Fund for the
Macqueen Gibbs Willis School
of Nursing ($50,000) see
Bingham Foundation, William

Mercy High School ($25,000)
see Sheridan Foundation,
Thomas B. and Elizabeth M.

Metropolitan Washington Ear
($26,000) see Aid Association
for the Blind

Midtown Churches — food for
homeless ($3,000) see Hobbs
Foundation

Mind-Brain Institute ($10,000)
see Rosenthal-Statter
Foundation

Ministry of Money ($50,000) see
Share Foundation

Mission Helpers of Sacred Heart
($13,500) see Gavin
Foundation, James and Zita

Montgomery County SPCA see
Banner Life Insurance Co.

Montgomery General Hospital
($10,000) see Gudelsky
Family Foundation, Isadore
and Bertha

Montgomery General Hospital
Health Foundation ($50,000)
see Freeman Foundation, Carl
M.

Montgomery Hospice Society
($500,000) see Casey
Foundation, Eugene B.

Montgomery Hospice Society
($157,775) see Casey
Foundation, Eugene B.

Morgan State University —
scholarship award ($2,500) see
Washington Post Co.

Morgan State University —
Center for Educating African
American Males ($150,000)
see Abell Foundation, The

Morgan State University — for
the Goldseker Fellows
Program, which in 1991
provided fellowships to 67
economically disadvantaged
graduate students from the
Baltimore metropolitan area
($96,900) see Goldseker
Foundation of Maryland,
Morris

Mount Washington Hospital
($10,000) see
Rosenthal-Statter Foundation

Mt. Washington Lacrosse Club
($2,500) see Baldwin, Jr.
Foundation, Summerfield

Mount Washington Pediatric
Hospital ($100) see Myers and
Sons, D.

Mount Washington Pediatric
Hospital ($5,000) see Unger
Foundation, Aber D.

Muslim Community School
($250,000) see Ala Vi
Foundation of New York

NAPA Education Foundation
($30,000) see Vulcan
Materials Co.

National Aquarium ($40,000) see
McKnight Foundation,
Sumner T.

National Aquarium ($12,500) see
PHH Corp.

National Aquarium in Baltimore
($130,000) see Blaustein
Foundation, Jacob and Hilda

National Aquarium in Baltimore
($36,000) see First Maryland
Bancorp

National Aquarium of Baltimore
($5,000) see Giant Food

National Aquarium in Baltimore
($12,000) see Price Associates,
T. Rowe

National Black Catholic
Congress — work shops for
training clergy, African
Ministries Program, lay
leaders ($30,000) see Raskob
Foundation for Catholic
Activities

National Center for Lead-Safe
Housing — start-up funding
for a national center for
lead-safe housing ($800,000)
see Federal National Mortgage
Assn., Fannie Mae

National Crime Prevention
Council — for continuing
partnership between the
Council and the Coalition of
Peninsula Organizations
($40,000) see Goldseker
Foundation of Maryland,
Morris

National Flag Day Foundation
($7,000) see Kelly, Jr.
Memorial Foundation, Ensign
C. Markland

National Flag Day Foundation
($15,000) see Rosenberg
Foundation, Henry and Ruth
Blaustein

National Foundation for
Infectious Diseases ($25,000)
see Thomas Memorial
Foundation, Theresa A.

National 4-H Council ($100,000)
see Deere & Co.

National Four-H Council ($105,000) see JCPenney Co.

National Four-H Council ($75,000) see Monsanto Co.

National Four-H Council ($51,000) see Unocal Corp.

National 4-H Council ($1,315,000) see Wallace-Reader's Digest Fund, DeWitt

National 4-H Council — Conservation of Natural Resources Program Sponsorship ($100,000) see Deere & Co.

National 4-H Educational Awards Program ($60,000) see Santa Fe Pacific Corp.

National Handicapped Sports and Recreation Association ($2,000) see Dickenson Foundation, Harriet Ford

National Institute Against Prejudice and Violence ($15,000) see Deer Creek Foundation

National Institute on Aging ($20,000) see Ridgefield Foundation

National Institutes of Health ($3,000) see McCutchen Foundation

National Institutes of Health ($31,750) see Whitney Foundation, Helen Hay

National Institutes of Health ($25,000) see Whitney Foundation, Helen Hay

National Library Week Legislative Day Committee ($100) see HarperCollins Publishers

National Museum of Dentistry ($5,000) see Dentsply International, Inc.

National Retinitis Pigmentosa Foundation ($142,202) see Chatlos Foundation

National Retinitis Pigmentosa Foundation ($431,071) see Gund Foundation, George

Ner Israel Rabbinical College ($10,800) see Belz Foundation

Ner Israel Rabbinical College ($10,250) see Fruchthandler Foundation, Alex and Ruth

Ner Israel Rabbinical College ($5,000) see Greene Foundation, David J.

Next Ice Age ($3,500) see Pearlstone Foundation, Peggy Meyerhoff

Norton Hospital ($50,000) see Ryan Family Charitable Foundation

Notre Dame Preparatory School — library construction ($400,000) see Knott Foundation, Marion I. and Henry J.

Notre Dame Preparatory School — library construction ($210,000) see Knott Foundation, Marion I. and Henry J.

Notre Dame Preparatory School — library construction ($111,294) see Knott Foundation, Marion I. and Henry J.

Notre Dame Preparatory School ($5,000) see Mullan Foundation, Thomas F. and Clementine L.

Notre Dame Preparatory School ($50,000) see Sheridan Foundation, Thomas B. and Elizabeth M.

Ohr Kodesh Congregation ($20,000) see Kapiloff Foundation, Leonard

Oldfields School ($25,000) see McBean Family Foundation

Open Gates — to establish Health Clinic on Washington Boulevard for needy ($250,000) see Middendorf Foundation

Operation Exodus ($2,000) see Bronstein Foundation, Soloman and Sylvia

Operation Exodus ($1,000,000) see Straus Foundation, Aaron and Lillie

Our Daily Bread ($12,500) see Rouse Co.

Pacific Basin Research Institute — support for the development of a market strategy for Vietnam ($75,000) see Donner Foundation, William H.

Park School ($7,000) see Hecht-Levi Foundation

Park School ($2,500) see Macht Foundation, Morton and Sophia

Park School ($75,000) see Meyerhoff Foundation, Lyn P.

Park School ($10,000) see Sheridan Foundation, Thomas B. and Elizabeth M.

Park School ($34,525) see Smith Foundation, Richard and Susan

Partners for Giving ($50,000) see Straus Foundation, Aaron and Lillie

Peabody Institute ($30,000) see Baker, Jr. Memorial Fund, William G.

Peabody Institute ($90,000) see Blaustein Foundation, Louis and Henrietta

Peabody Institute ($5,000) see DelMar Foundation, Charles

Peabody Institute ($57,457) see Gordon Charitable Trust, Peggy and Yale

Peabody Institute ($7,500) see Hobbs Foundation

Peabody Institute ($15,000) see Hobbs Foundation, Emmert

Peabody Institute ($1,000) see Legg Mason Inc.

Peabody Institute ($400,000) see Manger and Audrey Cordero Plitt Trust, Clarence

Peabody Institute ($75,000) see MNC Financial

Peabody Institute ($29,425) see Price Associates, T. Rowe

Peabody Institute ($20,000) see Thalheimer Foundation, Alvin and Fanny Blaustein

Peabody Institute ($19,000) see Unger Foundation, Aber D.

Peabody Institute ($50,000) see USF&G Co.

Peabody Institute of the City of Baltimore ($80,000) see Blaustein Foundation, Jacob and Hilda

PEF Israel Endowment Fund ($25,000) see Meyerhoff Fund, Joseph

People Encouraging People — facilities expansion ($10,000) see Hobbs Foundation

People Encouraging People ($10,000) see Hobbs Foundation, Emmert

People's Homesteading Group — for renovation of vacant houses in Baltimore for sale to very low-income families ($50,000) see Goldseker Foundation of Maryland, Morris

Planned Parenthood Federation of America ($10,000) see Baker Trust, Clayton

Planned Parenthood Federation of America ($10,000) see

Blum Foundation, Lois and Irving

Poolesville High School — wetlands ($10,000) see Toshiba America, Inc.

Pyramid Atlantic ($3,000) see Weir Foundation Trust

R P Foundation ($10,000) see Gund Foundation, Geoffrey

Raipe II ($25,000) see Hoffberger Foundation

RAISE ($10,000) see Macht Foundation, Morton and Sophia

Reginald S. Lourie Center for Infants and Small Children ($10,000) see Bender Foundation

Reginald S. Lourie Center for Infants and Young Children — diagnostic nursery project ($44,800) see Stewart Trust under the will of Helen S. Devore, Alexander and Margaret

Relay Improvement Association ($5,000) see Martin Marietta Corp.

Retirement for the Religious ($25,000) see Knott Foundation, Marion I. and Henry J.

Roland Park Country School ($4,500) see Egenton Home

Roland Park Police ($30,000) see Rollins Luetkemeyer Charitable Foundation

Roland Park Police ($25,000) see Rollins Luetkemeyer Charitable Foundation

RP Foundation ($5,000) see Goldenberg Foundation, Max

RP Foundation ($100) see Myers and Sons, D.

RP Foundation Fighting Blindness — intervention and prevention of this sight-destroying disorder afflicting the elderly ($50,000) see Cummings Memorial Fund Trust, Frances L. and Edwin L.

Rudolf Steiner Institute ($37,000) see Waldorf Educational Foundation

St. Ambrose Housing Aid Center ($40,000) see Ryan Family Charitable Foundation

St. Ann's Infant and Maternity Home — grant funds the salary of a consulting psychologist to work with children in residence ($45,361) see Federal Home Loan Mortgage Corp. (Freddie Mac)

St. Ann's Infant and Maternity Home — respite care program ($58,300) see Stewart Trust under the will of Helen S. Devore, Alexander and Margaret

St. Anthony of Padua Church ($5,000) see Macht Foundation, Morton and Sophia

St. Christopher's Church — building fund ($12,500) see Middendorf Foundation

St. Frances-Charles Hall High School ($20,000) see Sheridan Foundation, Thomas B. and Elizabeth M.

St. James School ($10,000) see Olmsted Foundation, George and Carol

St. Johns Literary Institution at Prospect Hall ($20,000) see Kentland Foundation

Saint John's at Prospect Hall ($30,000) see Knott Foundation, Marion I. and Henry J.

St. Joseph Hospital — capital campaign ($175,000) see Baltimore Gas & Electric Co.

St. Joseph Hospital Foundation ($2,500) see Macht Foundation, Morton and Sophia

St. Learning Center ($50,000) see Alpert Foundation, Herb

St. Mark United Presbyterian Church ($5,119) see Beitzell & Co.

Saint Martin's Catholic Community ($30,000) see Knott Foundation, Marion I. and Henry J.

St. Martins Church ($25,000) see Kentland Foundation

St. Martins School ($20,000) see Kentland Foundation

St. Mary's College ($5,000) see Macht Foundation, Morton and Sophia

St. Marys College of Maryland ($7,000) see Gordon Charitable Trust, Peggy and Yale

St. Mary's College of Maryland ($56,250) see Merrick Foundation, Robert G. and Anne M.

St. Mary's College of Maryland Foundation ($68,750) see France Foundation, Jacob and Annita

St. Mary's Seminary ($20,000) see Brown & Sons, Alex

St. Paul School ($23,015) see Price Associates, T. Rowe

St. Pauls School ($90,000) see Manger and Audrey Cordero Plitt Trust, Clarence

Saint Rose of Lima School ($34,000) see Knott Foundation, Marion I. and Henry J.

St. Timothy's School ($5,000) see Baldwin, Jr. Foundation, Summerfield

St. Timothy's School ($50,000) see Forbes

St. Timothys School ($25,000) see Kelly, Jr. Memorial Foundation, Ensign C. Markland

St. Timothy's School ($25,000) see Olsson Memorial Foundation, Elis

St. Vincent de Paul — facilities expansion ($5,000) see Hobbs Foundation

Saints Peter and Paul Parish — toward construction of a modular, 8-classroom building for the high school ($25,000) see Raskob Foundation for Catholic Activities

Salisbury State University ($4,000) see Lynch Scholarship Foundation, John B.

Salisbury State University ($40,000) see Nathan Foundation

Salisbury State University ($5,000) see Widgeon Foundation

Salvation Army ($10,000) see Hobbs Foundation

Salvation Army ($5,000) see Hobbs Foundation, Emmert

Salvation Army ($3,000) see Leidy Foundation, John J.

Salvation Army ($20,000) see Nathan Foundation

Salvation Army — food for the needy ($150,000) see Solo Cup Co.

Santa Claus Anonymous ($550) see Legg Mason Inc.

Santa Claus Anonymous ($100) see Myers and Sons, D.

Santa Maria Community Services ($10,000) see Dater Foundation, Charles H.

Save-A-Heart Foundation ($10,000) see Rosenthal-Statter Foundation

Search ($20,000) see Lamb Foundation, Kirkland S. and Rena B.

Second Genesis ($5,000) see Bender Foundation

Service to Youth Awards ($5,000) see Weir Foundation Trust

Severn Cross Roads Foundation ($9,423) see Baldwin, Jr. Foundation, Summerfield

Sexual Assault Recovery Center ($6,642) see Pearlstone Foundation, Peggy Meyerhoff

Sexual Assault Recovery Center ($12,000) see Wareheim Foundation, E. C.

Sheppard and Enoch Pratt ($500,000) see Weinberg Foundation, Harry and Jeanette

Sheppard Pratt Hospital — Step-Down Care Facility Support ($75,000) see Grable Foundation

Shrine for Crippled Children ($10,000) see Rosenthal-Statter Foundation

Sinai Hospital ($25,000) see Rosenbloom Foundation, Ben and Esther

Sinai Hospital ($500,000) see Rosenthal-Statter Foundation

Sinai Hospital ($15,000) see Rosenthal-Statter Foundation

SOAR ($223,750) see Loyola Foundation

Society for Autistic Children ($20,000) see Gudelsky Family Foundation, Isadore and Bertha

Society for the Prevention of Cruelty to Animals ($10,000) see Bishop Trust for the SPCA of Manatee County, Florida, Lillian H.

Society of Sponsors of United States Navy ($60,000) see Hooper Foundation, Elizabeth S.

South Baltimore Homeless Shelter ($10,000) see Baker Trust, Clayton

State of Israel Bond Office ($10,000) see Kapiloff Foundation, Leonard

State of Israel Bonds ($25,000) see Kapiloff Foundation, Leonard

State of Maryland — child welfare reform ($1,443,129) see Casey Foundation, Annie E.

Stella Maris Hospice ($10,100) see Mullan Foundation, Thomas F. and Clementine L.

Strathmore Hall Foundation ($25,000) see Shapiro, Inc.

Suburban Hospital — health care ($44,608) see Clark-Winchcole Foundation

Suburban Hospital ($75,000) see Shapiro, Inc.

Suburban Hospital — creation of Eugene B. Casey Center for Diagnostic Cardiology ($1,000,000) see Casey Foundation, Eugene B.

Temple Oheb Shalom ($65,388) see Gordon Charitable Trust, Peggy and Yale

Temple Oheb Shalom ($5,000) see Hecht-Levi Foundation

Temple Oheb Shalom ($13,180) see Number Ten Foundation

Theatre Project ($10,000) see Unger Foundation, Aber D.

Maryland (cont.)

Tissue Bank International ($10,000) see Mosher Foundation, Samuel B.

Tissue Banks International — matching grant to fund a portion of processing cost of eye research tissue ($25,000) see Kirchgessner Foundation, Karl

Torah Institute of Baltimore ($150) see Shapiro Fund, Albert

Towson State University ($6,200) see Mullan Foundation, Thomas F. and Clementine L.

Trappe Volunteer Fire Department ($5,000) see Darby Foundation

Treatment Learning Center ($10,000) see Freeman Foundation, Carl M.

Treatment and Learning Centers ($200) see Beitzell & Co.

Trinity Protestant Episcopal Church ($5,815) see Baldwin, Jr. Foundation, Summerfield

Union Memorial Hospital ($75,000) see Blaustein Foundation, Jacob and Hilda

Union Memorial Hospital ($12,500) see Blum Foundation, Lois and Irving

Union Memorial Hospital ($15,000) see Brown & Sons, Alex

Union Memorial Hospital ($16,668) see Rouse Co.

United Fund ($2,500) see Legg Mason Inc.

United Jewish Appeal Federation of Jewish Philanthropies ($100,000) see Bender Foundation

United Jewish Appeal Federation of Jewish Philanthropies ($185,000) see Bernstein Foundation, Diane and Norman

United Jewish Appeal Federation of Jewish Philanthropies ($200,000) see Cohen Foundation, Naomi and Nehemiah

United Jewish Appeal Federation of Jewish Philanthropies ($66,666) see Dweck Foundation, Samuel R.

United Jewish Appeal Federation of Jewish Philanthropies ($50,500) see Dweck Foundation, Samuel R.

United Jewish Appeal Federation of Jewish Philanthropies ($200,000) see Freeman Foundation, Carl M.

United Jewish Appeal Federation of Jewish Philanthropies ($50,000) see Freeman Foundation, Carl M.

United Jewish Appeal Federation of Jewish Philanthropies ($100,250) see Gelman Foundation, Melvin and Estelle

United Jewish Appeal Federation of Jewish Philanthropies ($25,000) see Goldman Foundation, Aaron and Cecile

United Jewish Appeal Federation of Jewish Philanthropies ($525,000) see Gudelsky Family Foundation, Isadore and Bertha

United Jewish Appeal Federation of Jewish Philanthropies ($105,000) see Kapiloff Foundation, Leonard

United Jewish Appeal Federation of Jewish Philanthropies ($65,000) see Kapiloff Foundation, Leonard

United Jewish Appeal Federation of Jewish Philanthropies ($35,000) see Kapiloff Foundation, Leonard

United Jewish Appeal Federation of Jewish Philanthropies ($499,000) see Kaplan Foundation, Charles I. and Mary

United Jewish Appeal Federation of Jewish Philanthropies ($250,000) see Lehrman Foundation, Jacob and Charlotte

United Jewish Appeal Federation of Jewish Philanthropies ($15,000) see Lehrman Foundation, Jacob and Charlotte

United Jewish Appeal Federation of Jewish Philanthropies ($142,336) see Levitt Foundation

United Jewish Appeal Federation of Jewish Philanthropies ($53,333) see Levitt Foundation, Richard S.

United Jewish Appeal Federation of Jewish Philanthropies ($50,000) see Shapiro, Inc.

United Jewish Appeal Federation of Jewish Philanthropies ($500,000) see Smith Family Foundation, Charles E.

United Jewish Appeal Federation of Jewish Philanthropies ($500,000) see Smith Family Foundation, Charles E.

United Jewish Appeal Federation of Jewish Philanthropies ($350,000) see Smith Family Foundation, Charles E.

United Jewish Appeal Federation of Jewish Philanthropies ($350,000) see Smith Family Foundation, Charles E.

United Jewish Appeal-Federation of Jewish Philanthropies of New York ($220,000) see Hechinger Co.

United States Holocaust Memorial Museum ($10,000) see Levin Foundation, Philip and Janice

United States Naval Academy ($26,667) see Grace & Co., W.R.

United States Naval Academy — Foreign Affairs Conference ($10,000) see Olmsted Foundation, George and Carol

United Way ($30,000) see Amsted Industries

United Way ($5,000) see Blum Foundation, Lois and Irving

United Way ($5,000) see Blum Foundation, Lois and Irving

United Way ($5,000) see Brown, Jr. Charitable Trust, Frank D.

United Way ($5,000) see Brown, Jr. Charitable Trust, Frank D.

United Way ($63,140) see Crown Central Petroleum Corp.

United Way ($4,000) see Handy & Harman

United Way ($4,000) see Handy & Harman

United Way ($11,000) see Heileman Brewing Co., Inc., G.

United Way ($38,215) see Hoffberger Foundation

United Way ($15,000) see Kiplinger Foundation

United Way ($4,200) see Lehigh Portland Cement Co.

United Way ($15,000) see Leidy Foundation, John J.

United Way ($900) see Myers and Sons, D.

United Way ($5,000) see Number Ten Foundation

United Way ($90,000) see PHH Corp.

United Way ($500) see Poole & Kent Co.

United Way ($70,000) see Price Associates, T. Rowe

United Way ($11,019) see Valspar Corp.

United Way ($10,000) see Zamoiski Co.

United Way of Central Maryland see AEGON USA, Inc.

United Way/Central Maryland ($20,000) see Armco Inc.

United Way of Central Maryland ($50,000) see Brown & Sons, Alex

United Way of Central Maryland ($200,000) see First Maryland Bancorp

United Way/Central Maryland ($635,000) see MNC Financial

United Way of Central Maryland ($161,760) see Procter & Gamble Cosmetic & Fragrance Products

United Way of Central Maryland ($50,000) see Straus Foundation, Aaron and Lillie

United Way Central Maryland ($14,000) see Unilever United States

United Way of Central Maryland ($330,403) see USF&G Co.

United Way of Central Maryland and Columbia ($375,000) see Westinghouse Electric Corp.

United Way of Central Maryland — to support the expanded implementation of its model computer-assisted instruction curriculum see United Parcel Service of America

United Way of Central Maryland — support of 1992 program ($686,000) see Baltimore Gas & Electric Co.

United Way of Lower Eastern Shore ($30,000) see Dresser Industries

University of Baltimore ($50,000) see Gordon Charitable Trust, Peggy and Yale

University of Baltimore ($33,333) see Hoffberger Foundation

University of Baltimore School of Law ($7,500) see Leidy Foundation, John J.

University Community Concerts ($4,000) see Polinger Foundation, Howard and Geraldine

University of Maryland ($45,750) see Ernst & Young

University of Maryland ($53,000) see Knapp Educational Fund

University of Maryland ($2,000) see Lebovitz Fund

University of Maryland ($30,000) see Loughran Foundation, Mary and Daniel

University of Maryland ($32,000) see Newcombe Foundation, Charlotte W.

University of Maryland ($5,000) see Poole & Kent Co.

University of Maryland ($100,000) see Procter & Gamble Cosmetic & Fragrance Products

University of Maryland ($10,000) see Wilson Foundation, H. W.

University of Maryland ($17,600) see Wilson Sanitarium for Children of Baltimore City, Thomas

University of Maryland ($12,500) see Wilson Sanitarium for Children of Baltimore City, Thomas

University of Maryland ($10,000) see Wilson Sanitarium for Children of Baltimore City, Thomas

University of Maryland — Anwar Sadat Chair ($2,500) see Freeman Foundation, Carl M.

University of Maryland at Baltimore Foundation ($100) see Myers and Sons, D.

University of Maryland at Baltimore Fund ($25,000) see Blum Foundation, Lois and Irving

University of Maryland (Baltimore) — School of Pharmacy ($5,000) see Giant Food

University of Maryland Foundation ($123,500) see France Foundation, Jacob and Annita

University of Maryland Foundation ($5,000) see Poole & Kent Co.

University of Maryland Foundation ($5,000) see Poole & Kent Co.

University of Maryland Foundation ($15,000) see Widgeon Foundation

University of Maryland Foundation — to establish the Center for Learning and Competitiveness ($835,160) see German Marshall Fund of the United States

University of Maryland Foundation — for the Mid-Atlantic Region Japan-in-the-Schools Program for precollege educators in the District of Columbia, Maryland, Virginia, and West Virginia ($218,536) see United States-Japan Foundation

University of Maryland Health Systems see AEGON USA, Inc.

University of Maryland School of Law ($20,000) see Macht Foundation, Morton and Sophia

University of Maryland — teaching, research, and use of total quality management principles ($1,400,000) see IBM Corp.

US Olympic Gymnastic Trials — Maryland '92 ($25,000) see Crown Central Petroleum Corp.

USF Constellation Foundation — special painting of ship ($25,000) see Kelly, Jr. Memorial Foundation, Ensign C. Markland

USNA Alumni Association ($4,000) see Miller-Mellor Association

Villa Julie College — capital campaign ($200,000) see Baltimore Gas & Electric Co.

Villa Julie College ($35,000) see Procter & Gamble Cosmetic & Fragrance Products

Villa Julie College ($10,000) see Rosenbloom Foundation, Ben and Esther

Villa Julie College ($37,500) see USF&G Co.

Volunteers for Medical Engineering — to increase the awareness of electronic home automation in order to permit independent living by people with disabilities ($40,000) see NEC USA

Volunteers for Medical Engineering ($100,000) see Straus Foundation, Aaron and Lillie

Volunteers for Visually Handicapped ($25,000) see Aid Association for the Blind

Walters Art Gallery ($25,000) see Baker, Jr. Memorial Fund, William G.

Walters Art Gallery ($40,000) see Blaustein Foundation, Louis and Henrietta

Walters Art Gallery ($10,000) see Brown, Jr. Charitable Trust, Frank D.

Walters Art Gallery — education ($12,500) see Kelly, Jr. Memorial Foundation, Ensign C. Markland

Walters Art Gallery ($3,000) see Leidy Foundation, John J.

Walters Art Gallery ($14,245) see Price Associates, T. Rowe

Walters Art Gallery ($9,500) see Weir Foundation Trust

Washington Charitable Fund ($2,500) see Weir Foundation Trust

Washington College ($675,000) see Casey Foundation, Eugene B.

Washington College ($500) see Legg Mason Inc.

Washington College — general ($5,000) see Upton Charitable Foundation, Lucy and Eleanor S.

Washington College ($5,000) see Widgeon Foundation

Washington Hebrew Congregation ($11,855) see Gelman Foundation, Melvin and Estelle

Washington Institute for Jewish Leadership Values ($6,000) see Goldman Foundation, Aaron and Cecile

Washington Theological Union ($50,000) see O'Toole Foundation, Theresa and Edward

Washington Theological Union ($50,000) see O'Toole Foundation, Theresa and Edward

Waverly Family Center ($4,500) see Egenton Home

West Nottingham Academy ($10,000) see Brown, Jr. Charitable Trust, Frank D.

Western Maryland College ($7,500) see Gordon Charitable Trust, Peggy and Yale

Western Maryland College — to support the partnership between Western Maryland College and the Western Maryland Interfaith Housing Development Corporation ($250,000) see duPont Fund, Jessie Ball

Wildfowl Trust of North America ($65,000) see Knapp Educational Fund

Wildfowl Trust of North America — maintenance of habitat for waterfowl and wildlife for educational purposes ($98,250) see Knapp Foundation

Wildlife Habitat Enhancement Council ($25,000) see Jackson Hole Preserve

Wilmer Ophthalmological Institute — goodwill ($25,000) see Alcon Laboratories, Inc.

Massachusetts (cont.)

Babson College ($5,000) see New England Foundation

Babson College ($200,000) see PepsiCo

Babson College — endowment fund ($50,000) see Wean Foundation, Raymond John

Banchetto Musicale ($35,000) see FMR Corp.

Banchetto Musicale ($750) see Harvard Musical Association

Banchetto Musicals ($3,000) see Poorvu Foundation, William and Lia

Baptist Home of Massachusetts ($40,000) see Farnsworth Trust, Charles A.

Barnstable County Deputy Sheriff's Association ($5,000) see Kelley and Elza Kelley Foundation, Edward Bangs

Baypath Senior Citizens ($42,135) see Farnsworth Trust, Charles A.

Baystate Health Systems ($25,000) see Dexter Charitable Fund, Eugene A.

Baystate Health Systems see Massachusetts Mutual Life Insurance Co.

Baystate Health Systems — Women and Infants Unit ($3,000) see Steiger Memorial Fund, Albert

Beacon Council ($25,000) see Ryder System

Bedford Athletic Association see Millipore Corp.

Bedford High School see Millipore Corp.

Bedford Youth Center see Millipore Corp.

Belleville Improvement Society ($10,000) see Arakelian Foundation, Mary Alice

Belleville Improvement Society ($10,000) see Arakelian Foundation, Mary Alice

Bement School — capital campaign ($10,000) see Olivetti Office USA, Inc.

Bentley College ($2,565) see Grant Thornton

Bentley College ($25,000) see Mardigian Foundation

Bentley College ($1,250) see Xtra Corp.

Bentley College — KIDS, Inc. ($15,000) see Nellie Mae

Berklee College of Music ($1,500) see Harvard Musical Association

Berkshire Country Day School ($55,000) see Country Curtains, Inc.

Berkshire Health System ($10,000) see Crane & Co.

Berkshire Medical Center ($60,000) see Country Curtains, Inc.

Berkshire Medical Center ($5,000) see Frelinghuysen Foundation

Berkshire Natural Resources ($15,000) see Crane & Co.

Berkshire Natural Resources Council — pledge ($25,000) see Country Curtains, Inc.

Berkshire Theatre Festival — pledge ($150,000) see Country Curtains, Inc.

Berkshire Theatre Festival ($12,500) see Frelinghuysen Foundation

Berkshire 21 Campaign ($25,000) see Country Curtains, Inc.

Berkshire United Way ($53,000) see Country Curtains, Inc.

Berwick Academy ($60,000) see Avis Inc.

Beth Israel Hospital ($101,100) see Berenson Charitable Foundation, Theodore W. and Evelyn

Beth Israel Hospital ($10,000) see Cole National Corp.

Beth Israel Hospital ($25,000) see Feldberg Family Foundation

Beth Israel Hospital ($8,000) see Gorin Foundation, Nehemiah

Beth Israel Hospital ($15,500) see King Trust, Charles A.

Beth Israel Hospital — operating support for their choose nursing in the nineties ($10,000) see Lindsay Trust, Agnes M.

Beth Israel Hospital ($5,100) see Morse Foundation, Richard P. and Claire W.

Beth Israel Hospital ($14,485) see Rabb Charitable Foundation, Sidney and Esther

Beth Israel Hospital ($14,485) see Rabb Charitable Trust, Sidney R.

Beth Israel Hospital ($50,000) see Reisman Charitable Trust, George C. and Evelyn R.

Beth Israel Hospital ($2,500) see Reisman Charitable Trust, George C. and Evelyn R.

Beth Israel Hospital ($1,000) see Reisman Charitable Trust, George C. and Evelyn R.

Beth Israel Hospital ($5,000) see Shapiro Fund, Albert

Beth Israel Hospital ($25,000) see Sherman Family Charitable Trust, George and Beatrice

Beth Israel Hospital ($12,000) see Simon Foundation, Sidney, Milton and Leoma

Beth Israel Hospital ($25,000) see TJX Cos.

Beth Israel Hospital — David J. Seder Fund ($500) see Baker Foundation, Solomon R. and Rebecca D.

Beth Israel Hospital — hospital directors task force, phase two ($303,300) see Commonwealth Fund

Beth Israel Hospital Vascular Research Fund ($10,000) see Reisman Charitable Trust, George C. and Evelyn R.

Better Homes Foundation ($10,000) see Henderson Foundation

Beverly Hospital ($6,800) see Winthrop Trust, Clara B.

Beverly School for the Deaf ($12,500) see Alden Trust, John W.

Big Brother Association of Boston ($35,000) see Harcourt General

Big Brother Association of Boston ($5,000) see Stride Rite Corp.

Big Brothers and Big Sisters ($5,000) see Fletcher Foundation

Big Brothers and Big Sisters ($10,000) see Russell Trust, Josephine G.

Big Brothers and Big Sisters ($12,000) see Stearns Trust, Artemas W.

Big Sister Association of Greater Boston ($2,000) see Fay Charitable Fund, Aubert J.

Big Sisters Association of Greater Boston ($5,000) see Fuller Foundation

Blackside/Civil Rights Project — toward production of a six

part series "The War on Poverty" ($160,000) see Surdna Foundation

Blessing Way Foundation ($50,000) see General Atlantic Partners L.P.

Boston Adult Literacy Fund ($30,000) see Merck Family Fund

Boston Against Drugs ($5,000) see Perini Corp.

Boston Aging Concerns ($50,000) see Charlesbank Homes

Boston Aging Concerns Young and Old United ($4,000) see Boynton Fund, John W.

Boston Aging Concerns Young and Old United ($12,000) see Sailors' Snug Harbor of Boston

Boston Aid to the Blind ($1,150) see Berenson Charitable Foundation, Theodore W. and Evelyn

Boston Aid to the Blind ($4,000) see Boston Fatherless and Widows Society

Boston Aid to the Blind ($6,000) see Gorin Foundation, Nehemiah

Boston Aid to the Blind ($10,000) see Horne Trust, Mabel

Boston Aid to the Blind ($7,000) see Pappas Charitable Foundation, Bessie

Boston Aid to the Blind ($10,000) see Yawkey Foundation II

Boston Area Educators for Social Responsibility ($2,000) see Foley, Hoag & Eliot

Boston Area Educators for Social Responsibility ($10,940) see Pierce Charitable Trust, Harold Whitworth

Boston Athenaeum ($35,000) see Rowland Foundation

Boston Ballet ($50,000) see Blanchard Foundation

Boston Ballet ($500) see Hagler Foundation, Jon L.

Boston Ballet ($50,000) see Little Family Foundation

Boston Ballet see Millipore Corp.

Boston Ballet ($500,000) see Peabody Foundation, Amelia

Boston Ballet Company ($3,000) see Ratshesky Foundation, A. C.

Boston Ballet — to support inner-city public school children ($35,000) see Hearst Foundation

Boston Biomedical Research Institute ($25,000) see Henderson Foundation

Boston Biomedical Research Institute see Millipore Corp.

Boston Biomedical Research Institute ($15,000) see Pierce Charitable Trust, Harold Whitworth

Boston Biomedical Research Institute — for Research Department ($300,000) see Peabody Charitable Fund, Amelia

Boston Center for Independent Living ($3,933) see Perini Foundation, Joseph

Boston Center for International Visitors ($5,000) see Lippitt Foundation, Katherine Kenyon

Boston Charities ($10,000) see Chase Trust, Alice P.

Boston Children's Hospital "A Volunteer Community for Everyone" Program — to train young people with disabilities to serve as volunteers, in the

process training parents, program directors, and others, with the goal of publishing a manual to be distributed nationwide ($40,000) see Mitsubishi Electric America

Boston Children's Services Association ($5,000) see Eaton Memorial Fund, Georgiana Goddard

Boston Chinese: Youth Essential Service — youth offenders ($20,000) see Shaw Foundation, Gardiner Howland

Boston City Hospital see Millipore Corp.

Boston City Lights ($1,000) see Eaton Memorial Fund, Georgiana Goddard

Boston College ($20,000) see Adams Trust, Charles E. and Caroline J.

Boston College ($30,000) see Demoulas Supermarkets

Boston College — minority scholarship fund ($5,000) see Devereaux Foundation

Boston College ($25,000) see Dexter Shoe Co.

Boston College ($100,000) see Flatley Foundation

Boston College — building fund ($25,000) see Gabelli Foundation

Boston College ($15,000) see Gerondelis Foundation

Boston College ($25,000) see Grace & Co., W.R.

Boston College ($7,500) see Grant Thornton

Boston College ($9,000) see Kellogg Foundation, J. C.

Boston College ($20,150) see M/A-COM, Inc.

Boston College ($50,000) see Morris Foundation, William T.

Boston College High School, Chestnut Hill ($1,000) see Burns Foundation

Boston College Law School ($12,500) see Xtra Corp.

Boston College Sports Center ($10,000) see Kraft Foundation

Boston College Tribute Dinner ($47,000) see Boisi Family Foundation

Boston College Tribute Dinner ($8,500) see Coles Family Foundation

Boston College Trustees ($100,000) see Andreas Foundation

Boston Community ($12,500) see Stoneman Charitable Foundation, Anne and David

Boston Community Schools Board see New England Telephone Co.

Boston Community Schools and Recreation Centers — general operating support ($15,000) see Island Foundation

Boston Conservatory of Music ($100) see Equimark Corp.

Boston Education Development Foundation, Boston Public Schools — integraged learning lab ($20,000) see Polaroid Corp.

Boston Education Foundation ($20,000) see Cabot Corp.

Boston Educational Development Fund ($74,000) see Bank of Boston Corp.

Boston Educational Development Fund ($74,000) see Bank of Boston Corp.

Boston Film-Video Foundation ($5,000) see Normandie Foundation

Boston Foundation Human Services — for the diversity

initiative ($50,000) see Riley Foundation, Mabel Louise

Boston Foundation-Human Services Personnel Collaborative — Diversity Initiative ($75,000) see Hyams Foundation

Boston Housing Partnership ($12,500) see Clipper Ship Foundation

Boston Kollel ($30,000) see Fruchthandler Foundation, Alex and Ruth

Boston Latin School ($5,000) see Seevak Family Foundation

Boston Latin School — for headmaster's fund ($25,000) see Mifflin Memorial Fund, George H. and Jane A.

Boston Lyric Opera ($100,000) see Day Foundation, Nancy Sayles

Boston Lyric Opera ($20,012) see Day Foundation, Nancy Sayles

Boston Memorial Medical Center ($5,000) see Leviton Manufacturing Co.

Boston Museum of Fine Arts ($500) see Hagler Foundation, Jon L.

Boston Museum of Science ($2,500) see Stride Rite Corp.

Boston Museum of Science ($1,000) see Xtra Corp.

Boston Natural Areas Fund ($15,562) see Chase Charity Foundation, Alfred E.

Boston Natural Areas Fund ($10,227) see Chase Charity Foundation, Alfred E.

Boston Natural Areas Fund ($37,500) see FMR Corp.

Boston Neighborhood Housing Service ($20,000) see Shawmut National Corp.

Boston Neighborhood Housing Services ($20,000) see Shawmut National Corp.

Boston Neighborhood Housing Services — Four Corners Public Safety Action Project ($40,000) see Hyams Foundation

Boston Neighborhood Housing Services/Mortgage Services Pilot Program ($25,000) see Shawmut National Corp.

Boston Neighborhood Ventures/Boston Youth Network ($5,000) see Foley, Hoag & Eliot

Boston Opera Association ($4,000) see Edmonds Foundation, Dean S.

Boston Opera Association ($2,000) see Edmonds Foundation, Dean S.

Boston Opera Theater ($10,000) see Day Foundation, Nancy Sayles

Boston Partners in Education ($15,000) see Clipper Ship Foundation

Boston Partners in Education ($12,000) see Lotus Development Corp.

Boston Partners in Education see Millipore Corp.

Boston Partner's In Education ($15,000) see Adams Trust, Charles E. and Caroline J.

Boston Plan ACCESS ($25,000) see Schrafft and Bertha E. Schrafft Charitable Trust, William E.

Boston Plan for Excellence ($12,500) see Eastern Enterprises

Boston Plan for Excellence in the Public Schools —

ACCESS Program ($25,000) see Nellie Mae

Boston Pops Orchestra ($5,000) see Yawkey Foundation II

Boston Post Road Stage ($5,000) see Hartman Foundation, Jesse and Dorothy

Boston Private Industry Council ($27,000) see Boston Edison Co.

Boston Schools Special Education ($5,000) see Hornblower Fund, Henry

Boston Symphony ($8,500) see M/A-COM, Inc.

Boston Symphony Orchestra ($5,100) see Arkwright-Boston Manufacturers Mutual

Boston Symphony Orchestra ($12,000) see Babson Foundation, Paul and Edith

Boston Symphony Orchestra ($5,000) see Barth Foundation, Theodore H.

Boston Symphony Orchestra ($5,000) see Clark Charitable Trust

Boston Symphony Orchestra — meeting room ($50,000) see Clowes Fund

Boston Symphony Orchestra — general ($28,650) see Country Curtains, Inc.

Boston Symphony Orchestra ($166,666) see Gould Foundation, Florence J.

Boston Symphony Orchestra ($10,000) see Killam Trust, Constance

Boston Symphony Orchestra ($6,000) see Little, Arthur D.

Boston Symphony Orchestra ($33,700) see Morse Foundation, Richard P. and Claire W.

Boston Symphony Orchestra see New England Telephone Co.

Boston Symphony Orchestra ($6,000) see Pappas Charitable Foundation, Bessie

Boston Symphony Orchestra ($12,500) see Rabb Charitable Foundation, Sidney and Esther

Boston Symphony Orchestra ($12,500) see Rabb Charitable Trust, Sidney R.

Boston Symphony Orchestra ($12,500) see Rabb Charitable Trust, Sidney R.

Boston Symphony Orchestra ($20,000) see Saltonstall Charitable Foundation, Richard

Boston Symphony Orchestra ($2,500) see Stare Fund

Boston Symphony Orchestra ($5,000) see Thermo Electron Corp.

Boston Symphony Orchestra ($28,000) see Webster Foundation, Edwin S.

Boston Symphony Orchestra 1992 Business Friend of Tanglewood ($20,000) see Country Curtains, Inc.

Boston University see Banner Life Insurance Co.

Boston University ($14,929) see Bruner Foundation

Boston University ($25,000) see Chase Trust, Alice P.

Boston University ($10,000) see Dibner Fund

Boston University ($6,000) see Fife Foundation, Elias and Bertha

Boston University ($28,000) see Gerondelis Foundation

Boston University ($5,000) see Manitou Foundation

Boston University ($3,000) see Merit Oil Corp.

Boston University ($25,000) see Pappas Charitable Foundation, Thomas Anthony

Boston University — brain-immune system interactions: mechanisms of immuno-suppression in stressed mice ($43,340) see Whitehall Foundation

Boston University-Chelsea School District — purchasing and installing an instructional computer laboratory in elementary school ($102,000) see Hayden Foundation, Charles

Boston University College of Communication ($35,000) see Sandoz Corp.

Boston University Health Policy Institute ($25,000) see Pearce Foundation, Dr. M. Lee

Boston University Human Resources Institute ($12,500) see Amsterdam Foundation, Jack and Mimi Leviton

Boston University — aid research towards a machine-based Igbo Dictionary, Owere and Wari, Nigeria ($12,000) see Wenner-Gren Foundation for Anthropological Research

Boston University Medical Center ($2,500) see New England Foundation

Boston University-Metcalf Center ($10,000) see Boston Edison Co.

Boston University School of Medicine ($8,800) see Ford III Memorial Foundation, Jefferson Lee

Boston University School of Medicine ($3,000) see Glenn Foundation for Medical Research, Paul F.

Boston University School of Medicine ($3,500) see Rubin Family Fund, Cele H. and William B.

Boston University School of Medicine ($25,000) see Sherman Family Charitable Trust, George and Beatrice

Boston University School of Medicine ($25,000) see Sherman Family Charitable Trust, George and Beatrice

Boston University School of Medicine ($200,000) see Whitaker Foundation

Boston University School of Medicine ($300,000) see Wolfson Foundation, Louis E.

Boston University School of Public Health ($10,000) see Horne Trust, Mabel

Boston University School of Public Health — national technical assistance project for substance abuse initiatives ($8,782,509) see Johnson Foundation, Robert Wood

Boston University School of Public Health ($35,000) see Sandoz Corp.

Boston Voyages in Learning ($6,300) see New England Biolabs Foundation

Boston Women's Health Book Collective ($2,750) see Rubin Family Fund, Cele H. and William B.

Boston YMCA ($10,000) see Boston Edison Co.

Bostonian Society Corporation ($20,000) see Webster Foundation, Edwin S.

Boston's University Hospital — "The Elders Living at Home Program" see Raytheon Co.

Boy Scouts of America ($7,000) see Acushnet Co.

Boy Scouts of America ($2,500) see Ansin Private Foundation, Ronald M.

Boy Scouts of America ($2,000) see Dennison Manufacturing Co.

Boy Scouts of America ($5,400) see Flatley Foundation

Boy Scouts of America ($5,000) see Fuller Foundation

Boy Scouts of America ($26,000) see Henderson Foundation

Boy Scouts of America ($10,467) see Massachusetts Charitable Mechanics Association

Boy Scouts of America ($5,000) see Perini Foundation, Joseph

Boy Scouts of America ($4,300) see Perini Foundation, Joseph

Boy Scouts of America-Greater Boston Council — renovation of their Scout Service Center ($100,000) see Hayden Foundation, Charles

Boys Club of America ($35,000) see Cambridge Mustard Seed Foundation

Boys Club of America ($25,000) see Dexter Charitable Fund, Eugene A.

Boys Club of America ($25,000) see Rogers Family Foundation

Boys Club of America ($5,000) see Stearns Trust, Artemas W.

Boys Club of America ($5,000) see Webster Charitable Foundation

Boys Club of Lynn ($15,000) see Benz Trust, Doris L.

Boys Club of Lynn ($5,000) see Eastern Bank Foundation

Boys and Girls Camps ($4,000) see Devonshire Associates

Boys and Girls Club ($20,000) see Adams Trust, Charles E. and Caroline J.

Boys and Girls Club ($6,500) see Childs Charitable Foundation, Roberta M.

Boys and Girls Club ($3,500) see Childs Charitable Foundation, Roberta M.

Boys and Girls Club ($60,000) see Devonshire Associates

Boys and Girls Club ($27,900) see Kraft Foundation

Boys and Girls Club ($25,000) see Parker Foundation, Theodore Edson

Boys and Girls Club ($20,000) see Schrafft and Bertha E. Schrafft Charitable Trust, William E.

Boys and Girls Club ($22,000) see Tupancy-Harris Foundation of 1986

Boys and Girls Club ($50,000) see Webster Foundation, Edwin S.

Boys and Girls Club ($20,000) see Yawkey Foundation II

Boys and Girls Club of Brockton see New England Telephone Co.

Boys and Girls Club of Greater Billerica — renovations and expansion of club facility ($10,000) see Lindsay Trust, Agnes M.

Boys and Girls Clubs of Boston ($50,000) see FMR Corp.

Boys and Girls Clubs of Boston ($2,500) see Stride Rite Corp.

Boys and Girls Clubs of Boston — construction of a new facility in Dorchester

($30,000) see State Street Bank & Trust Co.

Bradford College ($15,000) see Claneil Foundation

Bradford College ($300,000) see Johnson Fund, Edward C.

Bradford College ($5,000) see Kemper Foundation, Enid and Crosby

Bradford College — library automation project ($10,000) see Knapp Foundation

Bradford Library Building Fund ($10,000) see Witco Corp.

Braintree Work Center ($5,000) see Cowan Foundation Corporation, Lillian L. and Harry A.

Brandeis University ($2,467) see Carlyle & Co. Jewelers

Brandeis University ($17,000) see Crown Books Foundation, Inc.

Brandeis University ($10,000) see Dibner Fund

Brandeis University ($25,000) see Dingman Foundation, Michael D.

Brandeis University ($50,000) see Eder Foundation, Sidney and Arthur

Brandeis University ($10,000) see Erving Paper Mills

Brandeis University ($150,000) see Feldberg Family Foundation

Brandeis University ($15,000) see First Petroleum Corp.

Brandeis University ($1,131,275) see Ford Foundation, Joseph F. and Clara

Brandeis University ($100) see Fox Steel Co.

Brandeis University ($6,000) see Getz Foundation, Emma and Oscar

Brandeis University ($2,800) see Goldberg Family Foundation

Brandeis University ($5,000) see Goldberg Family Foundation, Milton D. and Madeline L.

Brandeis University ($2,000) see Greenspan Foundation

Brandeis University ($10,000) see Jaffe Foundation

Brandeis University ($1,000) see Jaydor Corp.

Brandeis University ($62,000) see Kraft Foundation

Brandeis University ($10,750) see Lemberg Foundation

Brandeis University ($500,000) see Mitrani Family Foundation

Brandeis University ($5,700) see Morris Foundation, Norman M.

Brandeis University ($100,000) see Phillips Family Foundation, Jay and Rose

Brandeis University ($5,000) see Pines Bridge Foundation

Brandeis University ($25,000) see Posnack Family Foundation of Hollywood

Brandeis University ($50,000) see Rubenstein Charitable Foundation, Lawrence J. and Anne

Brandeis University ($25,035) see Rukin Philanthropic Foundation, David and Eleanore

Brandeis University ($157,298) see Scheuer Family Foundation, S. H. and Helen R.

Brandeis University ($60,000) see Schwartz Foundation, David

Brandeis University ($80,000) see Shapiro Charity Fund, Abraham

Brandeis University ($104,000) see Shapiro Foundation, Carl and Ruth

Brandeis University ($50,000) see Sherman Family Charitable Trust, George and Beatrice

Brandeis University ($25,000) see Sherman Family Charitable Trust, George and Beatrice

Brandeis University ($10,000) see Sherman Family Charitable Trust, George and Beatrice

Brandeis University ($67,000) see Solomon Foundation, Sarah M.

Brandeis University ($5,025) see Steinberg Family Foundation, Meyer and Jean

Brandeis University ($10,000) see Stone Charitable Foundation

Brandeis University ($10,000) see Summerfield Foundation, Solon E.

Brandeis University ($57,565) see Volen Charitable Trust, Benjamin

Brandeis University ($15,125) see Wien Foundation, Lawrence A.

Brandeis University, Bigel Institute for Health Policy ($50,000) see Rosenstiel Foundation

Brandeis University — Heller Graduate School; to study role of siblings in care of their adult brother/sister with mental retardation ($52,500) see Kennedy, Jr. Foundation, Joseph P.

Brandeis University — to endow a visiting professorship in non-western and comparative studies ($200,000) see Columbia Foundation

Brandeis University — Rose Art Museum and continuing support of scholarship program in Fine Arts ($26,000) see Lowe Foundation, Joe and Emily

Brandeis University-Saul G. Cohen Fund for Research In Chemistry — capital campaign ($15,000) see Polaroid Corp.

Brandeis University — Undergraduate Biological Sciences Education Program ($1,400,000) see Hughes Medical Institute, Howard

Brandeis University's Heller School — Career Beginnings ($50,000) see Sun Microsystems

Bread and Roses ($5,500) see Stearns Trust, Artemas W.

Bread and Roses Heritage Committee ($16,910) see Stevens Foundation, Nathaniel and Elizabeth P.

Bridge ($7,500) see Pappas Charitable Foundation, Bessie

Bridge Over Troubled Waters ($15,000) see Flatley Foundation

Bridge Over Troubled Waters — purchase of new medical van ($10,000) see Lindsay Trust, Agnes M.

Bridge Over Troubled Waters ($7,500) see Stearns Charitable Foundation, Anna B.

Brigham and Women's Hospital ($15,000) see Cabot Family Charitable Trust

Massachusetts (cont.)

Brigham and Womens Hospital ($50,000) see Chase Trust, Alice P.

Brigham and Womens Hospital ($10,390) see Cowan Foundation Corporation, Lillian L. and Harry A.

Brigham and Women's Hospital ($10,000) see Gorin Foundation, Nehemiah

Brigham and Women's Hospital ($2,500) see Morse Foundation, Richard P. and Claire W.

Brigham and Womens Hospital ($90,000) see Peabody Foundation

Brigham and Women's Hospital ($40,000) see Saltonstall Charitable Foundation, Richard

Brigham and Women's Hospital ($5,000) see Weber Charities Corp., Frederick E.

Brigham and Women's Hospital — Cardiac Transplant Program ($12,500) see Rubenstein Charitable Foundation, Lawrence J. and Anne

Brigham and Women's Hospital Medical Foundation ($15,000) see King Trust, Charles A.

Brimmer and May School ($12,000) see Shapiro Foundation, Carl and Ruth

British American Education Foundation ($3,000) see Prouty Foundation, Olive Higgins

British American Education Foundation ($250) see Zarkin Memorial Foundation, Charles

Brooks School ($8,000) see Russell Trust, Josephine G.

Brooks School ($10,000) see Stearns Trust, Artemas W.

Brown University ($20,000) see Prudential-Bache Securities

Buckingham Browne and Nichols School ($100,000) see Watson Foundation, Thomas J.

Buckingham, Browne and Nicols School ($25,000) see Orchard Foundation

Bunker Hill Community College Fund Foundation ($25,000) see Blanchard Foundation

Bunker Hill Community College — Shooting for the Stars (Chelsea) ($15,000) see Nellie Mae

Burnham Walker Center ($5,000) see Ramlose Foundation, George A.

Business Friends of the Arts ($36,000) see American Saw & Manufacturing Co.

Business Friends of the Arts ($50,000) see Beveridge Foundation, Frank Stanley

Business Friends for the Arts ($15,000) see Steiger Memorial Fund, Albert

Business Fund for the Arts ($1,250) see Erving Paper Mills

C.P.S. ($9,617) see Massachusetts Charitable Mechanics Association

Cambodian Mutual Assistance Association ($5,000) see Dewing Foundation, Frances R.

Cambodian Mutual Assistance Association ($25,000) see Parker Foundation, Theodore Edson

Cambridge Camping Association ($4,000) see Dewing Foundation, Frances R.

Cambridge Camping Association ($5,000) see Weber Charities Corp., Frederick E.

Cambridge Center for Adult Education ($3,000) see Prouty Foundation, Olive Higgins

Cambridge College ($15,000) see Adams Trust, Charles E. and Caroline J.

Cambridge College ($25,000) see Blanchard Foundation

Cambridge College ($35,000) see Larsen Fund

Cambridge College ($3,000) see Osceola Foundation

Cambridge College ($50,000) see Peabody Foundation, Amelia

Cambridge College ($2,000) see Weiss Foundation, Stephen and Suzanne

Cambridge Committee of Elders ($4,000) see Boynton Fund, John W.

Cambridge Education ($5,000) see Bodenhamer Foundation

Cambridge Friends School ($5,000) see Fife Foundation, Elias and Bertha

Cambridge Fund for Housing the Homeless ($5,000) see Stride Rite Corp.

Cambridge Housing Authority ($25,000) see Eastern Enterprises

Cambridge Institute for Law and Justice ($4,000) see Childs Charitable Foundation, Roberta M.

Cambridge Institute for Law and Justice ($5,000) see Poorvu Foundation, William and Lia

Cambridge Partnership for Public Education ($2,500) see Stride Rite Corp.

Cambridge Police Mutual Aid Association ($300) see Index Technology Corp.

Cambridge School — scholarship assistance ($3,500) see Friendship Fund

Campaign for Norman Rockwell ($33,333) see Country Curtains, Inc.

Camps 89 ($1,000) see Cummings Properties Management, Inc.

Canine Unit Southbridge Police ($1,000) see Hyde Manufacturing Co.

Cape Ann Historical Association ($100,000) see Peabody Charitable Fund, Amelia

Cape Ann Historical Association ($75,000) see Plumsock Fund

Cape Cod Community College ($15,000) see Atlantic Foundation

Cape Cod Community College — educational ($15,000) see Dreyfus Foundation, Max and Victoria

Cape Cod Community College ($10,000) see Tupancy-Harris Foundation of 1986

Cape Cod Community College Education Foundation ($25,000) see Weezie Foundation

Cape Cod Community College Educational Foundation ($5,000) see Kelley and Elza Kelley Foundation, Edward Bangs

Cape Cod Hospital ($15,000) see Willits Foundation

Cape Cod Hospital Foundation ($16,667) see Kelley and Elza Kelley Foundation, Edward Bangs

Cardiac Surgical Research Fund of Brigham and Women's Hospital — Cardiac Transplant Project ($12,500) see Rubenstein Charitable Foundation, Lawrence J. and Anne

Cardinal Bernard Law ($10,200) see Sawyer Charitable Foundation

Cardinal Cushing School and Training ($1,000) see Xtra Corp.

Cardinal Cushing School and Training Center ($500) see Barry Corp., R. G.

Cardinal's Charity Fund ($15,000) see Orchard Foundation

Cardiology Research Trust of Massachusetts General Hospital ($2,000) see Rosenberg Family Foundation, William

CARE — preservation of global environment ($15,000) see Barstow Foundation

Careers For Later Years ($6,000) see Stearns Charitable Foundation, Anna B.

Carney Hospital ($15,000) see Globe Newspaper Co.

Carole Fund ($25,000) see Rubenstein Charitable Foundation, Lawrence J. and Anne

Carroll Center for the Blind ($4,000) see Boston Fatherless and Widows Society

Carroll Center for the Blind ($5,000) see Cowan Foundation Corporation, Lillian L. and Harry A.

Carroll Center for the Blind ($4,000) see Hornblower Fund, Henry

Carroll Center for the Blind ($15,100) see Sawyer Charitable Foundation

Carroll School ($5,000) see Higgins Foundation, Aldus C.

Casa Esperanza — to development of a recovery home for Latino substance abuse children ($10,000) see Lindsay Trust, Agnes M.

Catholic Charities ($30,000) see Birmingham Foundation

Catholic Charities ($10,000) see Home for Aged Men

Catholic Schools Foundation ($75,000) see Birmingham Foundation

Catholic Schools Foundation ($50,000) see FMR Corp.

Celebrity Series of Boston ($100,000) see Bank of Boston Corp.

Celebrity Series of Boston ($100,000) see Bank of Boston Corp.

Center for Arts Therapies ($5,000) see New England Biolabs Foundation

Center for Blood Research ($5,000) see Cohn Foundation, Peter A. and Elizabeth S.

Center for Common Security ($4,000) see Carteh Foundation

Center for Common Security ($4,000) see Carteh Foundation

Center for Middle East Studies — Harvard University ($500) see Foundation for Iranian Studies

Center for Nursing and Rehabilitation ($5,000) see Olive Bridge Fund

Center for the Performing Arts ($5,000) see Breyer Foundation

Center for the Performing Arts ($15,000) see Harrington Foundation, Francis A. and Jacquelyn H.

Center for the Study of Public Policy — for the Military Toxics Project which investigates practices fo the Department of Defense ($40,000) see Rockefeller Family Fund

Central Catholic High School ($10,000) see Stearns Trust, Artemas W.

Central Massachusetts Safe Energy Project ($8,000) see Ben & Jerry's Homemade

Central Massachusetts Safe Energy Project ($25,000) see Joukowsky Family Foundation

Centro Hispano de Chelsea ($17,500) see Lotus Development Corp.

Centro Panamericano-Ecuatorio ($20,000) see Stevens Foundation, Nathaniel and Elizabeth P.

Chabad House ($2,500) see Shapiro Charity Fund, Abraham

Chabad House of Greater Boston ($5,000) see Lipsky Foundation, Fred and Sarah

Channel 57 ($50,000) see Blake Foundation, S. P.

Channel 2 (WGBH) ($3,000) see Orchard Foundation

Charles River Industries ($9,585) see Massachusetts Charitable Mechanics Association

Charles River International Symposium ($2,200) see Charles River Laboratories

Charles River Medallion ($1,500) see Charles River Laboratories

Charles River Prize ($2,500) see Charles River Laboratories

Charles River School ($15,000) see Cabot-Saltonstall Charitable Trust

Charlton Memorial Hospital ($100,000) see Charlton, Jr. Charitable Trust, Earle P.

Chatham Hall ($11,000) see M/A-COM, Inc.

Chelsea Fire Department ($1,000) see Hargis Charitable Foundation, Estes H. and Florence Parker

Chelsea Human Services Collaborative ($63,750) see Clipper Ship Foundation

Chelsea School ($25,000) see Stone Foundation, David S.

Chelsea School Department ($150,000) see Harrington Trust, George

Chestnut Hill Benevolent Association ($25,000) see Wilson Foundation, Frances Wood

Children with Attentional Deficit Disorders ($1,500) see Wells Trust Fund, Fred W.

Children of Uniting Nations ($5,000) see Foley, Hoag & Eliot

Children's Campaign ($10,000) see Acushnet Co.

Children's Friend and Family Service Society ($25,000) see Sailors' Snug Harbor of Boston

Children's Friend and Family Service Society ($8,000) see Weber Charities Corp., Frederick E.

Children's Hospital ($50,000) see Blanchard Foundation

Children's Hospital ($10,000) see Cabot-Saltonstall Charitable Trust

Children's Hospital ($73,569) see Hood Foundation, Charles H.

Children's Hospital ($54,416) see Hood Foundation, Charles H.

Children's Hospital ($50,000) see Hood Foundation, Charles H.

Children's Hospital ($40,000) see Hood Foundation, Charles H.

Children's Hospital ($38,250) see Hood Foundation, Charles H.

Children's Hospital ($5,000) see Hornblower Fund, Henry

Children's Hospital ($15,000) see Horne Trust, Mabel

Children's Hospital ($50,000) see Merck Family Fund

Children's Hospital ($5,000) see New England Foundation

Children's Hospital ($100,000) see Pappas Charitable Foundation, Thomas Anthony

Children's Hospital ($100,000) see Peabody Foundation, Amelia

Children's Hospital see Raytheon Co.

Children's Hospital — cardiovascular surgical research ($50,000) see Rosenthal Foundation, Samuel

Children's Hospital — cerebral palsy clinic ($10,000) see Rosenthal Foundation, Samuel

Children's Hospital ($142,000) see Rubenstein Charitable Foundation, Lawrence J. and Anne

Children's Hospital ($20,000) see Schrafft and Bertha E. Schrafft Charitable Trust, William E.

Children's Hospital ($37,000) see Shawmut National Corp.

Children's Hospital ($101,500) see Smith Foundation, Richard and Susan

Children's Hospital of Boston ($1,000) see Totsy Manufacturing Co.

Children's Hospital — to study cause/effects relationship ($50,000) see Kennedy, Jr. Foundation, Joseph P.

Children's Hospital, Division of General Pediatrics — support a faculty development program that is designed to prepare young junior faculty to address the medical and social problems confronting children and their families ($258,135) see Dyson Foundation

Children's Hospital League ($1,500) see Shawmut Worcester County Bank, N.A.

Children's Hospital League, Boston, MA ($3,000) see Stride Rite Corp.

Children's Hospital Medical Center ($4,000) see Dell Foundation, Hazel

Children's Hospital Medical Center ($6,000) see Gorin Foundation, Nehemiah

Children's Hospital Medical Center ($25,000) see Hoffman Foundation, John Ernest

Children's Hospital Medical Center ($8,000) see Hopedale Foundation

Children's Hospital Medical Center ($21,500) see Kraft Foundation

Children's Hospital Medical Center ($152,500) see Peabody Foundation

Children's Hospital Medical Center ($25,000) see Shapiro Charity Fund, Abraham

Children's Hospital Medical
Center ($5,000) see Swensrud
Charitable Trust, Sidney A.
Children's Hospital Medical
Center ($16,700) see Tucker
Foundation, Marcia Brady
Children's Hospital Medical
Center ($5,000) see Weber
Charities Corp., Frederick E.
Children's Hospital Medical
Center ($15,000) see
Wodecroft Foundation
Children's Medical Center
($5,000) see Rabb Charitable
Foundation, Sidney and Esther
Children's Medical Center
($25,000) see Shapiro
Foundation, Carl and Ruth
Children's Medical Center — to
establish T. Berry Brazelton
chair in normal child
development ($75,000) see
Dodge Jones Foundation
Children's Museum ($10,000)
see Blanchard Foundation
Children's Museum see Great
Western Financial Corp.
Children's Museum — operating
expenses ($50,000) see Hyams
Foundation
Children's Museum ($10,000)
see Hyde Foundation, J. R.
Children's Museum ($20,000)
see Rubenstein Charitable
Foundation, Lawrence J. and
Anne
Children's Museum ($18,000)
see Stevens Foundation, Abbot
and Dorothy H.
Children's Museum, Boston
($206,000) see Engelhard
Foundation, Charles
Christ Memorial Church
($1,500) see Quabaug Corp.
Church of Convent Historic
Boston — capital campaign
($7,500) see Campbell and
Adah E. Hall Charity Fund,
Bushrod H.
Church of Covenant ($15,000)
see Horne Trust, Mabel
Church of Good Shepherd
($15,000) see Barth
Foundation, Theodore H.
Church of the Redeemer
($10,000) see New England
Foundation
Church of The Covenant
($15,000) see Globe
Newspaper Co.
Churchill School and Center
($20,000) see Frese
Foundation, Arnold D.
Churchill School and Center
($7,500) see Hobbs Charitable
Trust, John H.
Citizens Scholarship Foundation
($57,594) see Barnes Group
Citizens Scholarship Foundation
($57,593) see Barnes Group
Citizens' Scholarship Foundation
of America ($58,955) see
USF&G Co.
Citizen's Scholarship Foundation
of America ($56,115) see
USF&G Co.
City of Boston — restoration of
headstones at Central Burying
Ground on the Common
($2,340) see Henderson
Foundation, George B.
City of Fitchburg ($2,400) see
Ansin Private Foundation,
Ronald M.
City Mission Society ($4,000)
see Boston Fatherless and
Widows Society
City of Worcester ($60,528) see
Hoche-Scofield Foundation
City of Worcester ($53,723) see
Hoche-Scofield Foundation

City Year ($5,000) see Fuller
Foundation
City Year ($100,000) see General
Atlantic Partners L.P.
City Year ($166,166) see Reebok
International Ltd.
Clark School for the Deaf —
science education project
($10,000) see Knapp
Foundation
Clark University ($1,000) see
Acme-Cleveland Corp.
Clark University — scholarships
($50,000) see Ayling
Scholarship Foundation, Alice
S.
Clark University ($60,000) see
Ellsworth Foundation, Ruth H.
and Warren A.
Clark University ($42,000) see
Fuller Foundation, George F.
and Sybil H.
Clark University ($11,000) see
Harrington Foundation,
Francis A. and Jacquelyn H.
Clark University ($44,536) see
Higgins Foundation, Aldus C.
Clark University ($50,000) see
McEvoy Foundation, Mildred
H.
Clark University ($2,500) see
Morgan Construction Co.
Clark University ($30,000) see
Norton Co.
Clark University ($100,000) see
Stoddard Charitable Trust
Clark University ($28,000) see
Travelli Fund, Charles Irwin
Clark University ($10,000) see
Wyman-Gordon Co.
Clarke School for the Deaf
($10,000) see Dorr Foundation
Clarke School for the Deaf
($50,000) see Firestone, Jr.
Foundation, Harvey
Clarke School for the Deaf
($19,525) see Massachusetts
Charitable Mechanics
Association
Clarke School for the Deaf
($24,000) see McDonald
Foundation, J. M.
Clarke School for the Deaf
($400,000) see Oberkotter
Family Foundation
Clarke School for the Deaf
($5,000) see Pappas Charitable
Foundation, Bessie
Clarke School for the Deaf
($300,000) see Peabody
Foundation, Amelia
Clarke School for the Deaf
($30,000) see Scott
Foundation, Walter
CLASS ($5,000) see Stearns
Trust, Artemas W.
Coalition for a Better Acre
($30,000) see Parker
Foundation, Theodore Edson
Coalition for a Better Acre —
Hispanic Empowerment and
Leadership Program ($44,000)
see Sun Microsystems
College of Atlantic ($40,000) see
Merck Family Fund
College of Our Lady of the Elms
see Massachusetts Mutual Life
Insurance Co.
Collegiate School ($2,500) see
Foster Foundation, Joseph C.
and Esther
Combined Jewish Philanthropies
($50,000) see Berenson
Charitable Foundation,
Theodore W. and Evelyn
Combined Jewish Philanthropies
($50,000) see Erving Paper
Mills
Combined Jewish Philanthropies
($350,000) see Feldberg
Family Foundation

Combined Jewish Philanthropies
($200,000) see Feldberg
Family Foundation
Combined Jewish Philanthropies
($25,000) see Feldberg Family
Foundation
Combined Jewish Philanthropies
($20,000) see Filene
Foundation, Lincoln and
Therese
Combined Jewish Philanthropies
($279,325) see Ford
Foundation, Joseph F. and
Clara
Combined Jewish Philanthropies
($16,000) see Foster
Foundation, Joseph C. and
Esther
Combined Jewish Philanthropies
($7,000) see Galkin Charitable
Trust, Ira S. and Anna
Combined Jewish Philanthropies
($27,750) see Goldberg
Family Foundation
Combined Jewish Philanthropies
($10,575) see Goldberg
Family Foundation
Combined Jewish Philanthropies
($2,500) see Goldberg Family
Foundation
Combined Jewish Philanthropies
($35,000) see Gorin
Foundation, Nehemiah
Combined Jewish Philanthropies
($90,000) see Harcourt General
Combined Jewish Philanthropies
($49,300) see Kraft Foundation
Combined Jewish Philanthropies
($8,500) see Merit Oil Corp.
Combined Jewish Philanthropies
($73,000) see Morse
Foundation, Richard P. and
Claire W.
Combined Jewish Philanthropies
($40,000) see Olive Bridge
Fund
Combined Jewish Philanthropies
($10,000) see Pappas
Charitable Foundation, Bessie
Combined Jewish Philanthropies
($19,667) see Rabb Charitable
Foundation, Sidney and Esther
Combined Jewish Philanthropies
($10,000) see Rabb Charitable
Foundation, Sidney and Esther
Combined Jewish Philanthropies
($68,253) see Rabb Charitable
Trust, Sidney R.
Combined Jewish Philanthropies
($19,667) see Rabb Charitable
Trust, Sidney R.
Combined Jewish Philanthropies
($350,000) see Reisman
Charitable Trust, George C.
and Evelyn R.
Combined Jewish Philanthropies
($10,000) see Sawyer
Charitable Foundation
Combined Jewish Philanthropies
($145,000) see Shapiro
Charity Fund, Abraham
Combined Jewish Philanthropies
($235,000) see Shapiro
Foundation, Carl and Ruth
Combined Jewish Philanthropies
($50,000) see Shapiro
Foundation, Carl and Ruth
Combined Jewish Philanthropies
($50,000) see Sherman Family
Charitable Trust, George and
Beatrice
Combined Jewish Philanthropies
($320,000) see Smith
Foundation, Richard and Susan
Combined Jewish Philanthropies
($16,500) see Stoneman
Charitable Foundation, Anne
and David
Combined Jewish Philanthropies
($25,000) see TJX Cos.

Combined Jewish Philanthropies
($60,000) see Weston
Associates/R.C.M. Corp.
Combined Jewish Philanthropies
of Greater Boston ($10,000)
see Shaw's Supermarkets
Commitment to the Future
($5,000) see Shaw's
Supermarkets
Committee for Boston Public
Housing — Project FREE
(Franklin Residents' Efforts
for Equality) ($60,000) see
Hyams Foundation
Committee to End Rider
Homelessness — renovations
to Bishop Street boarding
House ($7,000) see Campbell
and Adah E. Hall Charity
Fund, Bushrod H.
Commonwealth of
Massachusetts Board of
Regents ($30,000) see Lindsay
Trust, Agnes M.
Commonwealth of
Massachusetts Department of
Social Services ($5,410) see
Weber Charities Corp.,
Frederick E.
Commonwealth School
($50,000) see Ford
Foundation, Edward E.
Community Council of Greater
Springfield ($7,000) see Heydt
Fund, Nan and Matilda
Community Educational Center
— assistance for immigrants,
refugees and school drop-outs
($7,500) see Campbell and
Adah E. Hall Charity Fund,
Bushrod H.
Community Foundation
($100,000) see Blake
Foundation, S. P.
Community Foundation of West
Massachusetts ($250,000) see
American Saw &
Manufacturing Co.
Community Foundation of
Western Massachusetts — to
develop philanthropic
resources ($65,000) see Cox
Charitable Trust, Jessie B.
Community Foundation of
Western Massachusetts see
Massachusetts Mutual Life
Insurance Co.
Community Foundation of
Western Massachusetts
($5,000) see Steiger Memorial
Fund, Albert
Community Health Foundation
($1,000) see Hampden Papers
Community Luther Church of
Enfield ($3,000) see Williams
Foundation, Arthur Ashley
Community Music Center
($5,000) see Eaton Memorial
Fund, Georgiana Goddard
Community Music Center
($1,500) see Harvard Musical
Association
Community Music Center — for
renovation and reconstruction
($50,000) see Riley
Foundation, Mabel Louise
Community Training and
Assistance Center — to
continue the Ledership of
School Reform initiative in
Camden, NJ, school district
($25,000) see Fund for New
Jersey
Community Workshops
($326,834) see Eaton
Memorial Fund, Georgiana
Goddard
Concord Antiquarian Society
($50,000) see FMR Corp.
Concord Area Trust for
Community Housing

($18,000) see Shaw's
Supermarkets
Concord Asabeth Adolescent
Services — general support
($3,000) see Cove Charitable
Trust
Concord Early Intervention
Program ($4,000) see GenRad
Concord Early Intervention
Program ($1,000) see GenRad
Concord Early Intervention
Program ($1,000) see GenRad
Concord Museum ($10,030) see
Eastern Enterprises
Concord Museum ($16,500) see
Pellegrino-Realmuto
Charitable Foundation
Concord Museum ($10,000) see
Smith Foundation, Richard
and Susan
Congregation Agudas Achim
($2,116) see Ansin Private
Foundation, Ronald M.
Congregation Agudus Achim
($1,000) see Foster
Foundation, Joseph C. and
Esther
Congregation Sons of Zion
($2,000) see Goldberg Family
Foundation, Israel and Matilda
Congregational Ahavas Achim
($10,000) see Arakelian
Foundation, Mary Alice
Conservation Law Foundation
($2,000) see Bright Charitable
Trust, Alexander H.
Conservation Law Foundation
($10,000) see
Cabot-Saltonstall Charitable
Trust
Conservation Law Foundation —
in support of a collaborative
project to participate in
hydropower relicensing
proceedings in New England
($75,000) see Cox Charitable
Trust, Jessie B.
Conservation Law Foundation of
New England ($50,000) see
Mertz-Gilmore Foundation,
Joyce
Conservation Law Foundation —
support New England
Groundfish Management
Project to encourage strong
conservation and rapid
implementation of measures to
allow recovery of depleted fish
stocks ($20,000) see Island
Foundation
Conservation Law Foundation of
New England — to expand
transportation planning,
advocacy and litigation
activities ($200,000) see
Surdna Foundation
Conservation Law Foundation —
"The Transportation Project"
($300,000) see Jones
Foundation, W. Alton
Cooley Dickinson Health Care
Corporation ($50,000) see
Beveridge Foundation, Frank
Stanley
Coolidge Center for
Environmental Leadership
($5,000) see Friendship Fund
Coolidge Center for
Environmental Leadership
($25,000) see Mifflin
Memorial Fund, George H.
and Jane A.
Cooperative Living of Newton
($20,000) see Farnsworth
Trust, Charles A.
COPE ($10,000) see Stearns
Charitable Foundation, Anna
B.
Corporation for Maintaining
Editorial Diversity in America
($75,000) see Coleman, Jr.
Foundation, George E.

Massachusetts (cont.)

Corporation for Public Management ($26,500) see Burden Foundation, Florence V.

Cotting School ($25,000) see Globe Newspaper Co.

Cotting School ($17,065) see Massachusetts Charitable Mechanics Association

Cotting School ($3,000) see Ramlose Foundation, George A.

Cotting School for Handicapped Children ($16,000) see Peabody Foundation

Country Roads — Armenian Project ($15,000) see Azadoutioun Foundation

Court Appointed Special Advocates ($5,000) see Fletcher Foundation

Crane Fund for Student Aid ($10,000) see Crane & Co.

Crane Fund for Student Aid ($10,000) see Crane & Co.

Cregg Neighborhood House Association ($5,000) see Eastern Bank Foundation

Crime and Justice Foundation — education initiative/criminal mediation ($27,000) see Shaw Foundation, Gardiner Howland

Crotched Mountain Foundation ($250,000) see Rowland Foundation

Curwin Childcare Center ($10,000) see Benz Trust, Doris L.

Cushing Academy ($25,000) see Wallace Foundation, George R.

Cushing Academy Trustees ($350,000) see Educational Foundation of America

Cushing House Museum ($15,000) see Arakelian Foundation, Mary Alice

Dana Farber Cancer Institute ($1,000) see Berkman Foundation, Louis and Sandra

Dana Farber Cancer Institute ($50,000) see Bleibtreu Foundation, Jacob

Dana Farber Cancer Institute ($2,000) see Decio Foundation, Arthur J.

Dana Farber Cancer Institute ($1,250) see Dynamet, Inc.

Dana Farber Cancer Institute ($10,000) see EG&G Inc.

Dana Farber Cancer Institute ($13,500) see King Trust, Charles A.

Dana-Farber Cancer Institute ($1,000,000) see Mayer Foundation, Louis B.

Dana Farber Cancer Institute ($50,000) see McGraw Foundation, Donald C.

Dana Farber Cancer Institute ($11,090) see Morse Foundation, Richard P. and Claire W.

Dana Farber Cancer Institute ($10,000) see Osborn Charitable Trust, Edward B.

Dana Farber Cancer Institute ($25,000) see Perini Corp.

Dana Farber Cancer Institute ($25,000) see Perini Foundation, Joseph

Dana Farber Cancer Institute ($100,000) see Rosenberg Family Foundation, William

Dana Farber Cancer Institute ($20,500) see Smith Foundation, Richard and Susan

Dana-Farber Cancer Institute, Department of Pediatrics — continuing support for research in pediatric hematologic and oncologic disease, with particular emphasis on bone marrow transplantation and engraftment ($200,000) see Dyson Foundation

Danbury Hospital ($1,000) see Fox Steel Co.

Dance Umbrella ($750) see Index Technology Corp.

Deaf Blind Contract Center ($9,950) see Memorial Foundation for the Blind

DeCordova Museum ($5,000) see Thermo Electron Corp.

Dedham Choral Society ($2,000) see Xtra Corp.

Deerfield Academy ($20,000) see Babson Foundation, Paul and Edith

Deerfield Academy ($10,000) see Field Foundation, Jamee and Marshall

Deerfield Academy ($6,000) see Mott Charitable Trust/Spectemur Agendo, Stewart R.

Deerfield Academy ($100,000) see Olin Foundation, Spencer T. and Ann W.

Delta Society ($50,000) see Donaldson Charitable Trust, Oliver S. and Jennie R.

Derno Street Plaque — commemorative plaque ($3,666) see Henderson Foundation, George B.

Diabetes Foundation Fund ($10,000) see Wyman-Gordon Co.

Diabetes Research Center of Massachusetts General Hospital ($3,000) see Rosenberg Family Foundation, William

Dibner Institute ($221,500) see Dibner Fund

Dimock Community Health Center ($15,000) see Clipper Ship Foundation

Dimock Community Health Center ($75,000) see FMR Corp.

Dimock Community Health Center ($15,000) see Globe Newspaper Co.

Dimock Community Health Center ($3,000) see Ratshesky Foundation, A. C.

Dimock Community Health Center — for the capital campaign ($50,000) see Riley Foundation, Mabel Louise

Dimock Community Health Center ($20,000) see Shaw Foundation, Gardiner Howland

Dimock Community Health Center — renovation of Goddard Building and construction of youth center ($50,000) see Riley Foundation, Mabel Louise

Dimock Community Health Center — offering comprehensive health, mental health services, vocational training facility for maternal health care for correctional facility inmates ($25,000) see State Street Bank & Trust Co.

Dimock Community Hospital ($15,000) see Stoneman Charitable Foundation, Anne and David

Diocese of Springfield ($50,000) see American Saw & Manufacturing Co.

Diocese of Worcester Bishops Fund ($5,000) see McCarthy Foundation, Michael W.

Discovery Museums — funds to purchase a new vortex machine ($10,000) see Little, Arthur D.

Discovery Museums see Raytheon Co.

Dorchester Youth Collaborative ($2,500) see Foley, Hoag & Eliot

Dorchester Youth Collaborative — inner city youth offenders ($17,500) see Shaw Foundation, Gardiner Howland

Dorothy Adler Geratric Assessment Center — for software and computer equipment to improve the care of pateints with Alzheimer's disease and to further reesearch into the disease ($150,000) see Digital Equipment Corp.

Douglas A. Thom Clinic For Children ($20,000) see Harrington Trust, George

Driscoll High School ($3,000) see Arkwright-Boston Manufacturers Mutual

Dudley Street Neighborhood ($15,000) see Stoneman Charitable Foundation, Anne and David

Dudley Street Neighborhood Initiative ($12,500) see Clipper Ship Foundation

Dudley Street Neighborhood Initiative — operations/"visionary" contribution ($55,000) see Riley Foundation, Mabel Louise

Dudley Street Neighborhood Initiative — executive search, operating support ($80,000) see Riley Foundation, Mabel Louise

Dynamy ($9,000) see Fletcher Foundation

Eaglebrook ($30,000) see Evans Foundation, Edward P.

Eaglebrook School ($20,000) see Comer Foundation

Earthwatch ($5,000) see Bayne Fund, Howard

Earthwatch ($20,000) see Cabot Family Charitable Trust

Earthwatch ($154,450) see Durfee Foundation

East Andover Village Preschool and Kindergarten ($3,000) see Williams Foundation, Arthur Ashley

East End House ($5,000) see Stearns Charitable Foundation, Anna B.

Easter Seal Society ($300) see Gear Motion

Education Development Center ($40,000) see Burden Foundation, Florence V.

Education Development Center — handbook on aggression ($30,000) see Mailman Family Foundation, A. L.

Elderlink ($10,000) see Sailors' Snug Harbor of Boston

Elderly Programs Serving North End Union ($10,000) see Bacon Trust, Charles F.

Eldershare ($7,000) see Cowan Foundation Corporation, Lillian L. and Harry A.

Elm Street Congregational Church ($2,000) see Hyde Manufacturing Co.

Emerge — counseling for male batterers ($17,500) see Shaw Foundation, Gardiner Howland

Emerson College — scholarships ($4,500) see Barker Foundation

Emerson College — for the Emerson Majestic Theatre ($100,000) see Getty Trust, J. Paul

Emerson Health Systems Hospital ($25,000) see GenRad

Emmanuel Gospel Center ($10,000) see Cove Charitable Trust

Endowment for Research in Human Biology ($1,043,752) see Seagram & Sons, Joseph E.

English Speaking Union ($4,000) see Winthrop Trust, Clara B.

Environmental Preservation Support Trust ($155,000) see Kendall Foundation, Henry P.

Episcopal Divinity School — program development ($50,000) see Stackpole-Hall Foundation

Executive Service Corps of New England ($5,000) see Higgins Foundation, Aldus C.

Eye Research Institute ($10,000) see Bay Branch Foundation

Eye Research Institute ($12,500) see Broadhurst Foundation

Eye Research Institute ($10,000) see Cabot-Saltonstall Charitable Trust

Eye Research Institute of Retina Foundation — retinal transplantation ($100,000) see Emerson Foundation, Fred L.

Facing History and Ourselves ($15,000) see Feldberg Family Foundation

Facing History and Ourselves ($1,000) see Foster Foundation, Joseph C. and Esther

Facing History and Ourselves ($35,000) see Kraft Foundation

Facing History and Ourselves ($2,500) see Poorvu Foundation, William and Lia

Facing History and Ourselves ($24,500) see Smith Foundation, Richard and Susan

Facing History and Ourselves ($30,000) see Zimmerman Family Foundation, Raymond

Facing History and Ourselves National Foundation ($5,000) see Kapor Family Foundation

Facing History and Ourselves National Foundation ($25,000) see Lazarus Charitable Trust, Helen and Charles

Facing History and Ourselves National Foundation ($4,000) see Rabb Charitable Foundation, Sidney and Esther

Fall River Jewish Community Council ($10,000) see Jaffe Foundation

Falmouth Hospital Association ($75,000) see Smith Foundation, Richard and Susan

Falmouth Hospital Foundation — laboratory information system ($50,000) see Clowes Fund

Falmouth Hospital Foundation ($10,000) see Kelley and Elza Kelley Foundation, Edward Bangs

Falmouth Hospital Foundation ($20,000) see Webster Foundation, Edwin S.

Falmouth Jewish Congregation ($10,000) see Rabb Charitable Foundation, Sidney and Esther

Family Center ($175,000) see Clark Foundation

Family Center ($7,500) see Geffen Foundation, David

Family Center ($5,000) see Hunt Foundation

Family to Family ($4,000) see Prouty Foundation, Olive Higgins

Family Service of Greater Boston ($20,000) see Schrafft and Bertha E. Schrafft Charitable Trust, William E.

Family Service of Greater Boston ($10,000) see Weber Charities Corp., Frederick E.

Family Services Association of Fall River ($50,000) see Charlton, Jr. Charitable Trust, Earle P.

Family Services of Greater Boston ($25,000) see Charlesbank Homes

Farm School ($3,000) see Prouty Foundation, Olive Higgins

Faulkner Sagoff Center, Faulkner Hospital ($5,000) see Bostwick Foundation, Albert C.

Federated Dorchester Neighborhood Houses ($20,000) see Farnsworth Trust, Charles A.

Federated Dorchester Neighborhood Houses ($35,000) see Harcourt General

Federated Dorchester Neighborhood Houses — operating expenses ($80,000) see Hyams Foundation

Federated Dorchester Neighborhood Houses ($20,000) see Schrafft and Bertha E. Schrafft Charitable Trust, William E.

Federation of Allied Jewish Appeal ($12,500) see Adams Trust, Charles E. and Caroline J.

Federation of Allied Jewish Appeal ($35,000) see Gorin Foundation, Nehemiah

Federation of Allied Jewish Appeal ($32,500) see Greenspan Foundation

Fenway Community Health Center ($10,000) see Boston Edison Co.

Fenway Middle College High School — to provide transitional operating support to allow the retention of a strategic planning group, the hiring of a Project Resources Coordinator and to underwrite a three-year evaluation to enhance the credibility of the program ($20,000) see Island Foundation

Fessenden School ($12,500) see Rosenthal Foundation, Samuel

Fidelity Investments Charitable Gift Fund ($3,000,000) see FMR Corp.

Fine Arts Work Center ($5,000) see Kelley and Elza Kelley Foundation, Edward Bangs

Fine Arts Work Center ($6,000) see Speyer Foundation, Alexander C. and Tillie S.

Fine Arts Work Center ($25,000) see Walker Foundation, Archie D. and Bertha H.

First Calvary Baptist Church ($35,000) see Stevens Foundation, Abbot and Dorothy H.

First Calvary Baptist Church ($5,000) see Webster Charitable Foundation

First Church of Christ Scientist ($150,000) see Katzenberger Foundation

First Church of Christ, Scientist ($5,000) see Moore Foundation, C. F.

First Church of Christ, Scientist ($26,000) see Robinson Foundation

First Congregational Church ($3,000) see Quabaug Corp.

First Congregational Church ($1,500) see Quabaug Corp.

First Parish Church of Framingham ($10,000) see Waters Foundation

First Parish Church of Newbury — installation of new backflow water valve ($3,200) see Bushee Foundation, Florence Evans

First Step Foundation ($1,500) see Hampden Papers

Fitchburg Art Museum ($26,000) see Wallace Foundation, George R.

Fitchburg Public Library ($20,750) see Wallace Foundation, George R.

Fitchburg State Art Museum ($1,000) see GenRad

Fitchburg State College ($12,500) see Wallace Foundation, George R.

Five Colleges — to support the New England Program for Teaching About Japan for precollege educators in Connecticut, Maine, Massachusetts, New Hampshire, Rhode Island, and Vermont ($145,541) see United States-Japan Foundation

5A Sports Program see Massachusetts Mutual Life Insurance Co.

Fogg Museum of Harvard University ($150,500) see Schimmel Foundation

Footlight Club — exterior renovation ($82,500) see Henderson Foundation, George B.

Forging Industry Educational and Research Foundation ($10,000) see Wyman-Gordon Co.

Forsyth Dental Center ($25,000) see Charlton, Jr. Charitable Trust, Earle P.

Framingham Court Mediation ($5,000) see Williams Foundation, Arthur Ashley

Framingham Court Mediation ($3,000) see Williams Foundation, Arthur Ashley

Framingham Union College ($7,500) see Perini Corp.

Framingham Union Hospital ($10,000) see TJX Cos.

Framingham Union Hospital Pledge ($7,500) see Perini Foundation, Joseph

Franklin County Agricultural Society ($4,851) see Wells Trust Fund, Fred W.

Franklin County Mediation Service — criminal mediation ($15,000) see Shaw Foundation, Gardiner Howland

Franklin Medical Center ($10,000) see Starrett Co., L.S.

Franklin Medical Center Capital Campaign (1989/1990) ($40,000) see Erving Paper Mills

Freedom from Chemical Dependency ($10,000) see Humane Society of the Commonwealth of Massachusetts

Freedom from Chemical Dependency Foundation — general fund ($5,000) see Stott Foundation, Louis L.

Freedom House ($10,000) see Sailors' Snug Harbor of Boston

Freedom House — Muriel S. Snowden Memorial Scholars Program Project REACH ($15,000) see Nellie Mae

French Library ($100,000) see Beaucourt Foundation

Friendly House ($2,100) see Morgan Construction Co.

Friends Academy ($20,000) see Plant Memorial Fund, Henry B.

Friends of Boston's Long Island Shelter ($15,000) see Clipper Ship Foundation

Friends of C.A.S.A. ($10,000) see Yawkey Foundation II

Friends of Dana Farber Cancer Institute ($1,000) see Reisman Charitable Trust, George C. and Evelyn R.

Friends of Harvard-Radcliffe ($2,500) see Horowitz Foundation, Gedale B. and Barbara S.

Friends of Holyoke Merry-Go-Round ($5,000) see Goldberg Family Foundation, Israel and Matilda

Friends of the Libraries of Boston University ($4,000) see Edmonds Foundation, Dean S.

Friends of Mount Auburn ($5,000) see Wharton Trust, William P.

Friends of Public Gardens — summer monument ($3,031) see Henderson Foundation, George B.

Fuller Museum of Art ($10,000) see Stone Charitable Foundation

G.W.A.R.C. ($8,895) see Massachusetts Charitable Mechanics Association

George School ($19,000) see Shoemaker Fund, Thomas H. and Mary Williams

George School — general support ($10,000) see Warsh-Mott Legacy

George School — Samuel S. Flug memorial scholarship fund ($50,000) see Martin & Deborah Flug Foundation

Gifford School ($15,000) see Clipper Ship Foundation

Gifford School ($7,000) see Cowan Foundation Corporation, Lillian L. and Harry A.

Girls', Inc. — capital/campaign ($125,000) see Alden Trust, George I.

Girls Club ($1,000) see Perpetual Benevolent Fund

Girls Club ($5,000) see Prouty Foundation, Olive Higgins

Girls Club ($10,000) see Rice Charitable Foundation, Albert W.

Girls Club of Lynn ($6,000) see Eastern Bank Foundation

Girls Incorporated ($25,000) see Ellsworth Foundation, Ruth H. and Warren A.

Girls of Lynn ($10,000) see Benz Trust, Doris L.

Glastonbeary Abbey ($10,000) see Flatley Foundation

Glen Urquhart School — scholarships ($30,000) see Mifflin Memorial Fund, George H. and Jane A.

Glen Urquhart School Playground ($15,000) see Good Samaritan

Gloucester Stage Company ($10,000) see New England Biolabs Foundation

Gordon College ($104,500) see Benfamil Charitable Trust

Gordon College ($5,000) see Fruehauf Foundation

Gordon College ($25,000) see Schrafft and Bertha E. Schrafft Charitable Trust, William E.

Gordon College ($429,625) see Stratford Foundation

Gordon Conwell Theological Seminary ($3,000) see Benfamil Charitable Trust

Gordon-Conwell Theological Seminary — to fund new library facilities ($125,000) see Davis Foundations, Arthur Vining

Gordon Conwell Theological Seminary ($10,000) see Fruehauf Foundation

Gordon-Conwell Theological Seminary ($184,331) see Stratford Foundation

Gordon Institute ($75,000) see Gordon Foundation

Governor Dunner Academy ($2,000) see O'Brien Foundation, James W.

Grandmother's Garden Trust Fund ($3,000) see Steiger Memorial Fund, Albert

Great Brook Valley Health Center — expansion ($2,500) see Mechanics Bank

Great Woods Institute ($27,500) see TJX Cos.

Greater Boston Adult Shelter Alliance ($20,000) see Clipper Ship Foundation

Greater Boston Business for Charity ($1,300) see Bird Inc.

Greater Boston Diabetes Society ($13,800) see Alden Trust, John W.

Greater Boston Legal Services ($5,000) see Eaton Memorial Fund, Georgiana Goddard

Greater Boston Legal Services ($25,000) see Farnsworth Trust, Charles A.

Greater Boston Legal Services ($10,000) see Sailors' Snug Harbor of Boston

Greater Boston Regional Youth Council ($2,000) see Foley, Hoag & Eliot

Greater Boston YMCA ($20,000) see Cabot Corp.

Greater Holyoke ($1,000) see Hampden Papers

Greater Holyoke Foundation ($25,000) see Occidental Petroleum Corp.

Greater Law Community Foundation ($35,500) see Stevens Foundation, Abbot and Dorothy H.

Greater Lawrence Community Foundation ($25,000) see Rogers Family Foundation

Greater Lawrence Community Foundation ($30,000) see Russell Trust, Josephine G.

Greater Lawrence Community Foundation — I Have A Dream ($55,301) see Webster Charitable Foundation

Greater Lynn Senior Service ($10,000) see Benz Trust, Doris L.

Greater New Bedford YMCA — Camp Massasoit improvement program ($15,000) see Lindsay Trust, Agnes M.

Greater Roxbury Neighborhood Authority ($15,000) see Lotus Development Corp.

Greater Trails Council #243, BSA ($1,500) see Erving Paper Mills

Greater Worcester Community Foundation ($5,000) see Mechanics Bank

Groton School ($55,000) see Caspersen Foundation for Aid to Health and Education, O. W.

Groton School ($5,000) see Coleman, Jr. Foundation, George E.

Groton School ($50,000) see Gund Foundation, Geoffrey

Groton School ($25,000) see McCormick Foundation, Chauncey and Marion Deering

Groton School ($1,000) see Stroud Foundation

Groton School, Library Renovation Fund ($25,000) see Silver Spring Foundation

Guide Dog Foundation for the Blind ($5,000) see Doyle Charitable Foundation

Guiding Eyes for the Blind ($5,000) see Doyle Charitable Foundation

Habitat for Humanity ($2,500) see Shawmut Worcester County Bank, N.A.

Hampshire College ($10,000) see Braitmayer Foundation

Hampshire College ($50,000) see Cohen Family Foundation, Saul Z. and Amy Scheuer

Hampshire College ($10,000) see Ettinger Foundation

Hampshire College ($15,000) see Globe Newspaper Co.

Hampshire College ($10,000) see Heydt Fund, Nan and Matilda

Hampshire College ($14,400) see Kendall Foundation, Henry P.

Hampshire College ($25,000) see Rubin Foundation, Samuel

Hampshire Country School ($1,000) see Cummings Properties Management, Inc.

Handel and Hayden Society ($45,000) see Nakamichi Foundation, E.

Handi Kids ($15,000) see Shapiro Charity Fund, Abraham

Harvard Business School ($50,000) see Charina Foundation

Harvard Business School ($4,000) see Continental Grain Co.

Harvard Business School ($50,000) see Dingman Foundation, Michael D.

Harvard Business School ($200,000) see Hobbs Charitable Trust, John H.

Harvard Business School ($2,500) see Rubin Family Fund, Cele H. and William B.

Harvard Business School — to support the Baxter Fellows program ($200,000) see Baxter International

Harvard Business School Fund ($10,000) see Batten Foundation

Harvard Business School Fund ($50,000) see Coles Family Foundation

Harvard Business School Fund ($10,000) see Gottesman Fund

Harvard Business School Fund ($10,000) see Hamel Family Charitable Trust, D. A.

Harvard Business School Fund ($50,000) see Hurford Foundation

Harvard Business School Fund ($1,500) see Liberty Hosiery Mills

Harvard Business School Fund ($6,500) see Schey Foundation

Harvard Business School Fund ($85,000) see Wollenberg Foundation

Harvard Class of 1927 ($25,000) see Ellison Foundation

Harvard Club ($6,912) see Hobbs Charitable Trust, John H.

Harvard College ($6,000) see Cameron Memorial Fund, Alpin J. and Alpin W.

Harvard College ($34,000) see Charina Foundation

Harvard College ($1,000) see Cole National Corp.

Harvard College ($35,000) see Fair Oaks Foundation, Inc.

Harvard College ($525,000) see Frese Foundation, Arnold D.

Harvard College ($25,000) see O'Neil Foundation, Cyril F. and Marie E.

Harvard College ($5,000) see O'Neil Foundation, Cyril F. and Marie E.

Harvard College ($84,941) see Pellegrino-Realmuto Charitable Foundation

Harvard College ($10,000) see Rollins Luetkemeyer Charitable Foundation

Harvard College Class Fund ($25,000) see Cabot-Saltonstall Charitable Trust

Harvard College Countway Library ($2,000) see Stare Fund

Harvard College Department of Human Nutrition ($20,000) see Stare Fund

Harvard College Fund ($20,500) see Goodman Family Foundation

Harvard College Fund ($5,000) see Hamel Family Charitable Trust, D. A.

Harvard College Fund ($10,000) see Hobbs Charitable Trust, John H.

Harvard College Fund ($20,000) see I. and L. Association

Harvard College Fund ($10,000) see Ix & Sons, Frank

Harvard College Fund ($10,000) see Mathis-Pfohl Foundation

Harvard College Fund — scholarship fund ($10,000) see Milbank Foundation, Dunlevy

Harvard College Fund ($25,000) see Model Foundation, Leo

Harvard College Fund — scholarships ($15,000) see Norton Memorial Corporation, Geraldi

Harvard College Fund ($100,000) see Orchard Foundation

Harvard College Fund ($10,000) see Pellegrino-Realmuto Charitable Foundation

Harvard College Fund ($15,000) see Weston Associates/R.C.M. Corp.

Harvard College Fund ($12,500) see Westport Fund

Harvard College Fund ($35,000) see Wyss Foundation

Harvard College Fund ($35,000) see Wyss Foundation

Harvard College — Library ($250,000) see Littauer Foundation, Lucius N.

Harvard College — Library ($250,000) see Littauer Foundation, Lucius N.

Harvard College of Public Health ($5,000) see Stare Fund

Harvard Crimson Trust II ($125,000) see Gordon/Rousmaniere/Roberts Fund

Harvard Crimson Trust II ($50,000) see Normandie Foundation

Harvard Dental School ($50,000) see Pappas Charitable Foundation, Thomas Anthony

Massachusetts (cont.)

Harvard Graduate School of Business Administration ($35,000) see Fair Oaks Foundation, Inc.

Harvard Graduate School of Education ($262,500) see Hobbs Charitable Trust, John H.

Harvard Institute of International Development ($127,250) see Reynolds Foundation, Christopher

Harvard Institute of International Development ($80,000) see Reynolds Foundation, Christopher

Harvard Institute of International Development ($61,868) see Reynolds Foundation, Christopher

Harvard Institute of International Development ($61,867) see Reynolds Foundation, Christopher

Harvard Institute for International Development — support or field research conducted by a network of scientists to develop sustainable management practices for Southeast Asian forests with biodiversity ($77,500) see Merck Fund, John

Harvard Institute of Rehabilitation ($3,500) see Goodman Memorial Foundation, Joseph C. and Clare F.

Harvard Law School ($25,000) see Beneficial Corp.

Harvard Law School ($25,000) see Burns Foundation

Harvard Law School ($5,000) see Cameron Memorial Fund, Alpin J. and Alpin W.

Harvard Law School ($10,000) see Clark Family Charitable Trust, Andrew L.

Harvard Law School ($100,000) see Cohen Family Foundation, Saul Z. and Amy Scheuer

Harvard Law School ($27,435) see Covington and Burling

Harvard Law School ($15,000) see Harding Educational and Charitable Foundation

Harvard Law School ($10,000) see Mathis-Pfohl Foundation

Harvard Law School Campaign Fund ($50,000) see Berkman Charitable Trust, Allen H. and Selma W.

Harvard Law School Foundation ($50,000) see Green Fund

Harvard Law School Fund ($35,000) see Fair Oaks Foundation, Inc.

Harvard Law School Fund ($7,500) see Mathis-Pfohl Foundation

Harvard Law School Fund ($10,000) see Seevak Family Foundation

Harvard Law School — Harvard Law School Fund ($55,500) see Stein Foundation, Jules and Doris

Harvard/Massachusetts Institute of Technology Division of Health ($20,000) see Lemberg Foundation

Harvard/Massachusetts Institute of Technology Health and Science ($5,000) see Humane Society of the Commonwealth of Massachusetts

Harvard Medical Center ($200,000) see I. and L. Association

Harvard Medical Center ($125,000) see Overseas Shipholding Group

Harvard Medical School ($105,651) see Adams Trust, Charles E. and Caroline J.

Harvard Medical School — to support research in virology and immunology ($250,000) see Baxter International

Harvard Medical School ($500,000) see Dana Charitable Trust, Eleanor Naylor

Harvard Medical School ($1,000,000) see Dorot Foundation

Harvard Medical School — towards the teaching and research fund ($5,000) see Fish Foundation, Vain and Harry

Harvard Medical School — to support a program in molecular and cellular basis of development ($1,236,000) see Markey Charitable Trust, Lucille P.

Harvard Medical School ($25,000) see Masco Corp.

Harvard Medical School ($463,000) see Merck & Co.

Harvard Medical School ($5,000) see Rabb Charitable Trust, Sidney R.

Harvard Medical School ($16,000) see Tai and Co., J. T.

Harvard Medical School ($250,000) see Warner-Lambert Co.

Harvard Medical School ($25,000) see Whitney Foundation, Helen Hay

Harvard Medical School ($25,000) see Whitney Foundation, Helen Hay

Harvard Medical School — support medical science graduate fellowships ($83,333) see Whittier Foundation, L. K.

Harvard Medical School ($50,000) see Wilf Family Foundation

Harvard Medical School ($300,000) see Wolfson Foundation, Louis E.

Harvard Medical School and Medical Foundation ($14,500) see King Trust, Charles A.

Harvard Radcliffe Hillel ($110,000) see Olive Bridge Fund

Harvard-Radcliffe Parents Fund ($2,500) see Rubin Family Fund, Cele H. and William B.

Harvard Scholarship Fund ($20,000) see Bastien Memorial Foundation, John E. and Nellie J.

Harvard School ($5,000) see Sprague, Jr. Foundation, Caryll M. and Norman F.

Harvard School of Medicine — support of pre-doctoral and post-doctoral fellowships in biological chemistry and molecular pharmacology ($500,000) see Merck & Co.

Harvard School for Public Health ($250,000) see Gordon/Rousmaniere/Roberts Fund

Harvard School of Public Health ($500,000) see Monell Foundation, Ambrose

Harvard School for Public Health ($30,000) see Morris Foundation, Margaret T.

Harvard School of Public Health ($16,500) see Pines Bridge Foundation

Harvard University ($20,000) see Barker Foundation, J. M. R.

Harvard University — undergraduate fund ($5,000) see Bedminster Fund

Harvard University ($300,000) see Berenson Charitable Foundation, Theodore W. and Evelyn

Harvard University ($4,100) see Bird Inc.

Harvard University ($7,500) see Brown Foundation, George Warren

Harvard University — programs on the role and organization of the military in a democratic society ($752,000) see Carnegie Corporation of New York

Harvard University ($15,000) see Chadwick Fund, Dorothy Jordan

Harvard University — academic assistance ($98,900) see Chiles Foundation

Harvard University ($4,000) see Cook, Sr. Charitable Foundation, Kelly Gene

Harvard University ($45,000) see Dively Foundation, George S.

Harvard University ($100,000) see Edison Foundation, Harry

Harvard University ($1,000) see Ellis Fund

Harvard University ($7,500) see Field Foundation, Jamee and Marshall

Harvard University ($74,287) see Filene Foundation, Lincoln and Therese

Harvard University ($27,955) see First Chicago

Harvard University ($935) see Floyd Family Foundation

Harvard University ($20,000) see Forest Oil Corp.

Harvard University ($13,194) see Foulds Trust, Claiborne F

Harvard University — endowment fund ($250,000) see Freed Foundation

Harvard University ($309,185) see General Electric Co.

Harvard University ($14,000) see Gerondelis Foundation

Harvard University — for internships ($140,000) see Getty Trust, J. Paul

Harvard University ($22,975) see Goldman Sachs & Co.

Harvard University ($9,900) see Goldman Sachs & Co.

Harvard University ($600,000) see Gordon/Rousmaniere/Roberts Fund

Harvard University ($2,000) see Gutman Foundation, Edna and Monroe C.

Harvard University ($10,000) see Halmos Foundation

Harvard University ($10,000) see Harrison Foundation Trust, Francena T.

Harvard University ($10,000) see Hornblower Fund, Henry

Harvard University ($5,000) see Hunt Foundation

Harvard University ($1,000) see Jellison Benevolent Society

Harvard University ($25,000) see Kent Foundation, Ada Howe

Harvard University ($50,000) see Kress Foundation, Samuel H.

Harvard University ($10,000) see Lebus Trust, Bertha

Harvard University ($255,000) see Lehman Foundation, Robert

Harvard University ($10,000) see Lieberman Enterprises

Harvard University — medical research ($115,000) see Lowenstein Foundation, Leon

Harvard University ($61,825) see Lurcy Charitable and Educational Trust, Georges

Harvard University ($5,300) see MacDonald Foundation, James A.

Harvard University ($7,500) see Mark IV Industries

Harvard University — medical research ($600,000) see Mathers Charitable Foundation, G. Harold and Leila Y.

Harvard University — to apply elliptic curves to dense packing of spheres ($500,000) see Packard Foundation, David and Lucile

Harvard University ($165,059) see Pellegrino-Realmuto Charitable Foundation

Harvard University ($150,000) see Pforzheimer Foundation, Carl and Lily

Harvard University ($5,000) see Ramlose Foundation, George A.

Harvard University ($11,000) see Richardson Foundation, Frank E. and Nancy M.

Harvard University ($325,000) see Rubin Family Fund, Cele H. and William B.

Harvard University ($2,500) see Rubin Family Fund, Cele H. and William B.

Harvard University ($5,000) see Ryan Foundation, Nina M.

Harvard University ($25,897) see Salomon

Harvard University ($30,000) see Sperry Fund

Harvard University ($30,000) see Sperry Fund

Harvard University ($5,000) see Stroud Foundation

Harvard University — academic tournament ($4,000) see Stuart Foundation, Edward C.

Harvard University ($25,000) see Taub Foundation, Henry and Marilyn

Harvard University ($545,040) see Wexner Foundation

Harvard University ($175,000) see Whiting Foundation, Mrs. Giles

Harvard University ($25,375) see Whitney Foundation, Helen Hay

Harvard University ($25,000) see Whitney Foundation, Helen Hay

Harvard University ($92,000) see Wiener Foundation, Malcolm Hewitt

Harvard University — single parent scholarship fund ($100,000) see Winkler Foundation, Mark and Catherine

Harvard University ($37,500) see Zale Foundation

Harvard University ($5,000) see Ziegler Foundation for the Blind, E. Matilda

Harvard University Art Museum ($400,000) see Bafflin Foundation

Harvard University — Brigham and Womens Hospital ($30,000) see Abbott Laboratories

Harvard University Business School ($25,000) see Cole National Corp.

Harvard University Business School ($1,500) see Donaldson, Lufkin & Jenrette

Harvard University Business School — matching gifts ($2,000) see Mechanics Bank

Harvard University Business School Fund ($5,000) see Devereaux Foundation

Harvard University Business School Fund ($10,500) see Titan Industrial Co.

Harvard University, Center for International Affairs — to establish the John M. Olin Institute for Strategic Studies ($405,475) see Olin Foundation, John M.

Harvard University Center for Study of World Religion ($15,000) see Kent Foundation, Ada Howe

Harvard University — Chapel and School of Government ($16,500) see Folger Fund

Harvard University and Colleges ($189,304) see Rowland Foundation

Harvard University David Woods Kemper Memorial Fund ($10,000) see Kemper Memorial Foundation, David Woods

Harvard University, Department of Biochemistry and Molecular Biology ($25,250) see Childs Memorial Fund for Medical Research, Jane Coffin

Harvard University, Department of Biochemistry and Molecular Biology ($24,500) see Childs Memorial Fund for Medical Research, Jane Coffin

Harvard University Divinity School ($13,000) see Palmer Fund, Francis Asbury

Harvard University — perception and control of acoustic images in echo-locating bats ($58,146) see Whitehall Foundation

Harvard University — "Experiments on Distributed Choice" ($100,000) see Sage Foundation, Russell

Harvard University Extension Course ($78,212) see Lowell Institute, Trustees of the

Harvard University — Full Professorship in Russian/Soviet Studies at the Faculty of Arts and Sciences ($250,000) see Baker Trust, George F.

Harvard University-Graduate — support of the new fitness and recreational sports facility ($200,000) see Baker Trust, George F.

Harvard University-Graduate School or Business Administration ($50,000) see Wachtell, Lipton, Rosen & Katz

Harvard University — for Harvard Project Zero to design and implement Project Co-Arts ($150,000) see Cummings Foundation, Nathan

Harvard University John F. Kennedy School of Government ($100,000) see Appleman Foundation

Harvard University Law School — defray student loan expense ($7,000) see Friendship Fund

Harvard University — Law School ($65,000) see Winston

Foundation, Norman and Rosita

Harvard University Law School-Criminal Justice Institute — clinical program ($15,000) see Shaw Foundation, Gardiner Howland

Harvard University Law School Fund — scholarship fund ($100,000) see Milbank Foundation, Dunlevy

Harvard University Law School Fund — scholarship fund ($10,000) see Milbank Foundation, Dunlevy

Harvard University Library ($36,333) see Larsen Fund

Harvard University Library ($50,000) see Phipps Foundation, Howard

Harvard University — Loeb Fellowship ($6,000) see Osceola Foundation

Harvard University Medical Center — for Division of Medical Ethics ($187,000) see DeCamp Foundation, Ira W.

Harvard University Medical School ($30,000) see Allen Foundation, Rita

Harvard University Medical School ($155,000) see Brookdale Foundation

Harvard University Medical School — fellowship program for research training of physicians in neuroscience ($172,200) see Dana Foundation, Charles A.

Harvard University Medical School ($5,000) see Rabb Charitable Foundation, Sidney and Esther

Harvard University Medical School ($120,000) see Ramapo Trust

Harvard University Middle East Institute ($12,500) see Jaffe Foundation

Harvard University — to support the program activities of the Olin Institute for Strategic Studies ($225,000) see Bradley Foundation, Lynde and Harry

Harvard University — Phillips Brooks House Association ($5,000) see AHS Foundation

Harvard University President and Fellows ($101,611) see Kapor Family Foundation

Harvard University — Samuel S. Flug scholarship fund ($10,000) see Martin & Deborah Flug Foundation

Harvard University Scholarship Program, Cambridge, MA ($67,550) see Stride Rite Corp.

Harvard University School of Medicine ($40,000) see Pfeiffer Research Foundation, Gustavus and Louise

Harvard University School of Public Health ($300,000) see Goldsmith Foundation, Horace W.

Harvard University School of Public Health ($30,000) see Mayer Charitable Trust, Oscar G. & Elsa S.

Harvard University School of Public Health — international health training program ($50,000) see Spunk Fund

Harvard University Semitic Museum ($325,000) see Levy Foundation, Jerome

Harvard University Semitic Museum ($10,000) see Levy Foundation, Jerome

Harvard University — Smithsonian Center

Astrophysics ($40,000) see Perkin Fund

Harvard University — to establish the Wiktor Weintraub Lectureship in Polish literature ($25,000) see Jurzykowski Foundation, Alfred

Harvard University — Writing Development and Instruction in the English-writing World ($300,000) see Spencer Foundation

Harvard University's John F. Kennedy School of Government ($21,000) see Johnson & Johnson

Haywood Hospital ($5,000) see Shawmut Worcester County Bank, N.A.

HBS Fund 1991 ($50,000) see Brody Foundation, Carolyn and Kenneth D.

Health Agricultural Society ($800) see Wells Trust Fund, Fred W.

Hearing Dog Program ($15,000) see Peabody Foundation

Hebrew College ($83,800) see Ford Foundation, Joseph F. and Clara

Hebrew College ($40,000) see Stone Charitable Foundation

Hebrew Rehabilitation Center for the Aged ($2,700) see Goldberg Family Foundation

Hebrew Rehabilitation Center for the Aged ($6,000) see Gorin Foundation, Nehemiah

Hebrew Rehabilitation Center for the Aged ($20,000) see Lipsky Foundation, Fred and Sarah

Hebrew Rehabilitation Center for the Aged ($6,667) see Rabb Charitable Trust, Sidney R.

Hebrew Rehabilitation Center for the Aged ($1,000) see Reisman Charitable Trust, George C. and Evelyn R.

Helping Hands ($15,100) see Stern Foundation, Bernice and Milton

Helping Hands Simian Aides ($5,000) see Childs Charitable Foundation, Roberta M.

Higgins Armory Museum ($10,000) see Hoche-Scofield Foundation

Higgins Armory Museum ($10,000) see Hoche-Scofield Foundation

Higgins Armory Museum — capital: repairs/renovations ($75,000) see Alden Trust, George I.

Historic Deerfield — purchase of additional computer equipment ($25,000) see Hyde and Watson Foundation

Historic Deerfield ($10,000) see Vanderbilt Trust, R. T.

Historical Society of Old Newbury — for continued support of their intern program ($1,000) see Bushee Foundation, Florence Evans

Holy Cross College ($10,000) see Perini Corp.

Holy Cross College ($15,000) see Perini Foundation, Joseph

Holy Family Hospital ($40,000) see Russell Trust, Josephine G.

Holy Family Hospital ($30,000) see Stearns Trust, Artemas W.

Holy Family Hospital ($25,000) see Stevens Foundation, Abbot and Dorothy H.

Holy Family Hospital and Medical Center ($25,000) see Rogers Family Foundation

Holy Family Hospital and Medical Center ($32,000) see Stevens Foundation, Nathaniel and Elizabeth P.

Holy Trinity Greek Orthodox Church ($200,000) see Demoulas Supermarkets

Holyoke Chapter of Hadassah ($2,000) see Goldberg Family Foundation, Israel and Matilda

Holyoke-Chicopee Area Health Resources ($1,005) see Goldberg Family Foundation, Israel and Matilda

Holyoke Hebrew School ($1,000) see Goldberg Family Foundation, Israel and Matilda

Holyoke Hospital — capital fund ($1,500) see Totsy Manufacturing Co.

Holyoke United Jewish Appeal ($40,000) see Goldberg Family Foundation, Israel and Matilda

Holyoke United Jewish Appeal ($10,000) see Goldberg Family Foundation, Israel and Matilda

Homeowner's Rehab ($20,000) see Charlesbank Homes

Hospice ($10,000) see Wells Trust Fund, Fred W.

Hospice of Boston ($5,000) see Boynton Fund, John W.

Hospice of Cambridge ($25,000) see Farnsworth Trust, Charles A.

Hospice Care of Nantucket ($6,000) see Tupancy-Harris Foundation of 1986

House of Hope ($10,000) see Stevens Foundation, Nathaniel and Elizabeth P.

House of Seven Gables ($40,350) see Plumsock Fund

Hull Public Schools — in support of planning retreats, curriculum development, professional training and development and consultants to aid teachers incorporating an environmental theme into Hull High School ($20,000) see Island Foundation

Human Services Personnel Collaborative-Diversity Initiative/Boston Foundation ($40,000) see Globe Newspaper Co.

Huntington Theatre ($75,000) see Peabody Foundation, Amelia

Huntington Theatre Company ($20,000) see Cabot-Saltonstall Charitable Trust

Ideals Associated ($157,500) see Waters Foundation

Immaculate Conception Church ($2,000) see Fay Charitable Fund, Aubert J.

Immaculate Conception College ($10,000) see M/A-COM, Inc.

Immaculate Conception School ($2,000) see Fay Charitable Fund, Aubert J.

Impact II ($51,500) see Reebok International Ltd.

In Fact ($10,000) see Valentine Foundation, Lawson

Indian Hill Arts see New England Business Service

Individual Research Project — entitled "Chronicles of Subversion: A Study of the Italian Anarchist Movement in America" ($32,100) see Guggenheim Foundation, Harry Frank

Infact ($20,000) see List Foundation, Albert A.

Infectious Diseases Society of America ($113,685) see Burroughs Wellcome Co.

Infectious Diseases Society of America ($90,000) see Burroughs Wellcome Co.

Inquilinos Boricuas en Accion ($35,000) see Blanchard Foundation

Inquilinos Boricuas en Accion ($4,000) see Foley, Hoag & Eliot

Inquilinos Boricuas en Accion ($12,000) see Sailors' Snug Harbor of Boston

Institute for Biospheric Research ($41,600) see Waters Foundation

Institute of Contemporary Art ($35,000) see Lannan Foundation

Institute for Foreign Policy Analysis ($370,000) see Scaife Foundation, Sarah

Institute Mental Health Initiatives ($2,500) see Poorvu Foundation, William and Lia

J.J. Burns Library ($150,000) see Burns Foundation

Jacob's Pillow Dance Festival ($2,500) see Ballet Makers

Jacobs Pillow Dance Festival ($100,000) see Trust for Mutual Understanding

Jamaica Plain Neighborhood House — renovation ($5,000) see Henderson Foundation, George B.

Jeremiah's Hospice ($1,500) see Mechanics Bank

Jeremiah's Inn — renovation ($5,000) see Fletcher Foundation

Jesuits of Holy Cross College — for new porch Casa Maria ($2,000) see Mechanics Bank

Jewish Community Center ($40,000) see Rubenstein Charitable Foundation, Lawrence J. and Anne

Jewish Community Center ($20,000) see Rubenstein Charitable Foundation, Lawrence J. and Anne

Jewish Family and Children's Services ($42,000) see Stone Charitable Foundation

Jewish Federation ($10,000) see Shapiro Foundation, Carl and Ruth

Jewish Federation ($17,000) see Stoneman Charitable Foundation, Anne and David

Jewish Memorial Hospital ($5,000) see Feldberg Family Foundation

Jewish National Fund ($37,600) see Kraft Foundation

Jewish Vocational Services ($10,000) see Chase Charity Foundation, Alfred E.

Jimmy Fund ($200) see Amdur Braude Riley, Inc.

Joan Shorenstein Barone Foundation for Harvard ($50,000) see Gilman Foundation, Howard

Jobs for Youth ($3,000) see Boynton Fund, John W.

Jobs for Youth ($1,500) see Devonshire Associates

Jobs for Youth ($20,000) see Schrafft and Bertha E. Schrafft Charitable Trust, William E.

John F. Kennedy Library Foundation ($2,000) see Ansin Private Foundation, Ronald M.

John F. Kennedy School of Government ($330,000) see Getty Foundation, Ann and Gordon

John Woodman Higgens Armory ($6,650) see Morgan Construction Co.

John Woodman Higgins Armory Museum ($40,000) see Fuller Foundation, George F. and Sybil H.

Joint Program in Neonatology ($35,000) see Peabody Foundation

Joslin Diabetes Center ($60,000) see Adler Foundation

Joslin Diabetes Center ($100,200) see Blum-Kovler Foundation

Joslin Diabetes Center ($5,000) see Cox Foundation

Joslin Diabetes Center ($705,000) see Hood Foundation, Charles H.

Joslin Diabetes Center ($75,000) see Iacocca Foundation

Joslin Diabetes Center ($1,500,000) see Peabody Foundation, Amelia

Joslin Diabetes Center — general fund ($15,000) see Shaw Foundation, Arch W.

Joslin Diabetes Center ($1,000) see Wolfson Family Foundation

Joslin Diabetes Center — Autoimmunity in Offspring of Mothers versus Fathers with Type I Diabetes ($20,000) see Diabetes Research and Education Foundation

Joslin Diabetes Foundation ($10,000) see Blackmer Foundation, Henry M.

Joslin Diabetes Foundation — in support of the start-up costs of Joslin's new research section on Islet Cell Transportation and Cell Biology ($75,000) see Cox Charitable Trust, Jessie B.

Judge Baker Children's Center ($5,000) see Goldberg Family Foundation, Israel and Matilda

Judge Baker Children's Center ($7,500) see Stearns Charitable Foundation, Anna B.

Junior Achievement ($6,000) see Acushnet Co.

Junior Achievement ($1,500) see Bird Inc.

Junior Achievement ($4,000) see Crapo Charitable Foundation, Henry H.

Junior Achievement see Massachusetts Mutual Life Insurance Co.

Junior Achievement ($1,000) see Quabaug Corp.

Kedaly Center of America ($100,000) see Rowland Foundation

Kendall Whaling Museum ($801,019) see Kendall Foundation, Henry P.

Kennedy Donovan Center ($3,000) see Hornblower Fund, Henry

Kennedy School of Government, Harvard University ($75,000) see Edison Fund, Charles

Knight Science Journalism Fellowship ($7,500) see Media General, Inc.

Knights of Don Orione ($25,250) see Sawyer Charitable Foundation

La Alianza Hispana ($20,000) see Farnsworth Trust, Charles A.

La Alianza Hispana ($10,000) see Horne Trust, Mabel

La Alianza Hispana ($3,000) see Ratshesky Foundation, A. C.

Massachusetts (cont.)

La Alianza Hispana ($12,000) see Sailors' Snug Harbor of Boston

La Salette Missions ($5,000) see Butler Foundation, J. Homer

Laboure Center ($10,000) see Bacon Trust, Charles F.

Laboure Center ($15,000) see Birmingham Foundation

Lahey Clinic Foundation ($125,000) see Bonner Foundation, Corella and Bertram

Lahey Clinic Foundation ($350,000) see Dana Charitable Trust, Eleanor Naylor

Lahey Clinic Foundation ($15,000) see Jost Foundation, Charles and Mabel P.

Lahey Clinic Foundation ($7,500) see Orchard Foundation

Lahey Clinic Foundation ($86,000) see Peabody Foundation, Amelia

Lahey Clinic Foundation ($25,000) see Rogers Family Foundation

Lahey Clinic Medical Center ($5,000) see Barker Foundation

Lahey Clinic Medical Center ($120,000) see Dana Charitable Trust, Eleanor Naylor

Lasell College — annual giving ($10,000) see Saunders Charitable Foundation, Helen M.

Lasell College — challenge grant ($6,125) see Saunders Charitable Foundation, Helen M.

Law Boys Club ($20,000) see Stevens Foundation, Abbot and Dorothy H.

Lawrence Boys Club ($15,000) see McCarthy Memorial Trust Fund, Catherine

Lawrence Boys Club ($25,000) see Stevens Foundation, Nathaniel and Elizabeth P.

Lawrence General Hospital ($66,700) see Russell Trust, Josephine G.

Lawrence General Hospital ($30,000) see Stearns Trust, Artemas W.

Lawrence General Hospital Capital Campaign ($5,000) see Webster Charitable Foundation

Lawrence General Hospital Foundation ($25,000) see Rogers Family Foundation

Lawrence Neighborhood Housing Services ($4,000) see Webster Charitable Foundation

Lawrence Public Library ($6,500) see McCarthy Memorial Trust Fund, Catherine

Lawrence Public Library ($10,500) see Russell Trust, Josephine G.

Lawrence Youth Commission — adult leadership development program ($31,471) see Sun Microsystems

Lena Park Community Development Corporation — renovation of baseball field ($2,644) see Henderson Foundation, George B.

Lena Park Community Development Corporation — operating expenses ($70,000) see Hyams Foundation

Lena Park Community Development Corporation — developing an expanded

library/reading program also Family Impact Project which brings social services to the residents of affordable housing units they manage ($25,000) see State Street Bank & Trust Co.

Leonard Morse Hospital ($50,000) see Weezie Foundation

Lesley College ($1,000) see Cole National Corp.

Lesson One Associates ($10,000) see Chase Charity Foundation, Alfred E.

Levine Associates — for fundraising training to be offered to Manchester and Amherst organizations ($17,000) see Bean Foundation, Norwin S. and Elizabeth N.

Lexington Christian Academy ($8,000) see Benfamil Charitable Trust

Lighthouse Hospice Association — support to purchase computer ($3,000) see Cove Charitable Trust

Lighthouse Preservation ($15,000) see Cabot-Saltonstall Charitable Trust

Little Brothers/Friends of Elderly ($5,000) see Boston Fatherless and Widows Society

Little Sisters of Poor ($10,000) see Sawyer Charitable Foundation

Living Church Foundation ($5,500) see Roddis Foundation, Hamilton

Living Church Foundation ($2,000) see Wheeler Foundation, Wilmot

Living in Dorchester ($30,000) see Charlesbank Homes

Living Here Tomorrow — sponsorship ($2,500) see Mechanics Bank

Local Initiative Support Corporation ($12,500) see Clipper Ship Foundation

Local Initiatives Support Corporation — general support ($15,000) see Polaroid Corp.

Longy School of Music ($25,000) see Chase Trust, Alice P.

Longy School of Music ($1,500) see Harvard Musical Association

Longy School of Music ($10,000) see Poorvu Foundation, William and Lia

Longy School of Music ($1,500) see Poorvu Foundation, William and Lia

Longyear Historical Society ($15,000) see Aequus Institute

Lowell Boys Club Association ($3,000) see Fay Charitable Fund, Aubert J.

Lowell General Hospital — pledge ($250,000) see Demoulas Supermarkets

Lowell General Hospital ($4,000) see Fay Charitable Fund, Aubert J.

Lowell General Hospital ($10,000) see Stevens Foundation, Nathaniel and Elizabeth P.

Lowell General Hospital Intensive Care ($50,000) see Demoulas Supermarkets

Lowell Girls Club ($2,000) see Fay Charitable Fund, Aubert J.

Lowell Institute School of Massachusetts Institute of Technology — lecture series

($280,978) see Lowell Institute, Trustees of the

Lowell Institute School of Massachusetts Institute of Technology ($50,000) see Lowell Institute, Trustees of the

Lowell Plan ($40,000) see Parker Foundation, Theodore Edson

Lowell University ($625) see Technical Training Foundation

Lower Columbia Head Start — playground surfacing and storage ($30,000) see Wollenberg Foundation

Lutheran Home — repairs ($2,500) see Mechanics Bank

Lutheran Nursing Home ($10,000) see Home for Aged Men

Lynn Business Education Foundation ($10,000) see Eastern Bank Foundation

Lynn English High School ($30,000) see O'Brien Foundation, James W.

Lynn Historical Society ($8,250) see Eastern Bank Foundation

Lynn Shelter ($15,000) see Chase Trust, Alice P.

Lyric Stage Company of Boston ($30,000) see Johnson Fund, Edward C.

Maimonides School ($3,000) see Lipsky Foundation, Fred and Sarah

Malden Hebrew School ($5,000) see Lipsky Foundation, Fred and Sarah

Malden Hospital ($15,000) see Chase Trust, Alice P.

Manadnock Children's Museum ($10,000) see Chadwick Fund, Dorothy Jordan

Management Sciences for Health Population Program — for an experimental project to increase the rates of contraceptive use in three developing countries ($570,000) see Hewlett Foundation, William and Flora

Manchester Public Library ($4,000) see Quaker Hill Foundation

Manomet Bird Observatory ($25,000) see Dorr Foundation

Manomet Bird Observatory ($100,000) see Peabody Charitable Fund, Amelia

Marine Biological Laboratory — education program ($35,000) see Clowes Fund

Marine Biological Laboratory — fellowships and park ($6,000) see Friendship Fund

Marine Biological Laboratory ($12,000) see Harvard Apparatus Foundation

Marine Biological Laboratory Fellowship ($165,674) see Grass Foundation

Marine Biological Laboratory Leech Course ($6,000) see Grass Foundation

Marine Biological Laboratory Neural Systems and Behavior Summer Course ($35,000) see Grass Foundation

Marine Biological Laboratory Summer Neurobiology Courses ($20,000) see Grass Foundation

Marshfield Public Schools ($7,820) see Phillips Trust, Edwin

Martha's Vineyard Hospital ($5,000) see Johnson Foundation, Howard

Martha's Vineyard Hospital ($61,746) see Luce Charitable Foundation, Stephen C.

Mary C. Wheel Wright Museum ($10,000) see Cabot-Saltonstall Charitable Trust

Mason Square Development Corporation see Massachusetts Mutual Life Insurance Co.

Masonic Education and Charity Trust ($61,746) see Luce Charitable Foundation, Stephen C.

Mass General Hospital ($5,000) see Perini Foundation, Joseph

Massachusetts Advanced Studies Program of Milton Academy — Merrimack Valley Initiative ($30,300) see Sun Microsystems

Massachusetts Association for the Blind ($5,000) see Cowan Foundation Corporation, Lillian L. and Harry A.

Massachusetts Association for the Blind ($79,583) see Memorial Foundation for the Blind

Massachusetts Audubon Society ($3,100) see Bailey Wildlife Foundation

Massachusetts Audubon Society ($1,500) see Bright Charitable Trust, Alexander H.

Massachusetts Audubon Society ($5,000) see Clark Charitable Trust

Massachusetts Audubon Society ($10,000) see Day Foundation, Nancy Sayles

Massachusetts Audubon Society — for new computer system to set up statewide computer network and to manage its membership and donor base ($185,000) see Digital Equipment Corp.

Massachusetts Audubon Society ($5,000) see French Foundation

Massachusetts Audubon Society ($10,000) see Hoche-Scofield Foundation

Massachusetts Audubon Society ($10,000) see Hoche-Scofield Foundation

Massachusetts Audubon Society — for land acquisition for wildlife sanctuary protection ($10,000) see Knapp Foundation

Massachusetts Audubon Society — for interns project ($25,000) see Mifflin Memorial Fund, George H. and Jane A.

Massachusetts Audubon Society ($100,000) see South Branch Foundation

Massachusetts Audubon Society ($3,000) see Wharton Trust, William P.

Massachusetts Citizens Against the Death Penalty — general operating support of a full-time director and part time support staff person to continue education activities and advocacy to oppose the potential reinstatement of the death penalty in Massachusetts ($20,000) see Island Foundation

Massachusetts Civil Liberties Foundation ($20,000) see Kapor Family Foundation

Massachusetts Committee For Children and Youth ($10,000) see Stearns Charitable Foundation, Anna B.

Massachusetts Corporation for Educational Telecommunications (MCET) — science program for young children ($10,000) see Little, Arthur D.

Massachusetts Easter Seal Society ($15,000) see TJX Cos.

Massachusetts Elders ($20,000) see Bacon Trust, Charles F.

Massachusetts Eye and Ear Infirmary ($1,000) see Devonshire Associates

Massachusetts Eye and Ear Infirmary ($15,000) see Dingman Foundation, Michael D.

Massachusetts Eye and Ear Infirmary ($50,000) see Hood Foundation, Charles H.

Massachusetts Eye and Ear Infirmary ($20,000) see Pappas Charitable Foundation, Bessie

Massachusetts Eye and Ear Infirmary ($300,000) see Peabody Charitable Fund, Amelia

Massachusetts 4-H Club ($30,000) see Saltonstall Charitable Foundation, Richard

Massachusetts General Hospital ($50,000) see American Saw & Manufacturing Co.

Massachusetts General Hospital ($3,000) see Arkwright-Boston Manufacturers Mutual

Massachusetts General Hospital ($20,000) see Birmingham Foundation

Massachusetts General Hospital ($50,000) see Charlton, Jr. Charitable Trust, Earle P.

Massachusetts General Hospital ($25,000) see Cox Foundation

Massachusetts General Hospital — capital drive ($10,000) see Cox Foundation

Massachusetts General Hospital ($200,000) see Demoulas Supermarkets

Massachusetts General Hospital ($6,000) see Dennison Manufacturing Co.

Massachusetts General Hospital ($10,000) see EG&G Inc.

Massachusetts General Hospital ($1,500,000) see Ellison Foundation

Massachusetts General Hospital ($17,000) see First Petroleum Corp.

Massachusetts General Hospital ($5,000) see GenRad

Massachusetts General Hospital ($20,000) see Gerondelis Foundation

Massachusetts General Hospital ($20,000) see Good Samaritan

Massachusetts General Hospital ($6,000) see Gorin Foundation, Nehemiah

Massachusetts General Hospital ($8,000) see Hopedale Foundation

Massachusetts General Hospital ($20,000) see Horne Trust, Mabel

Massachusetts General Hospital ($20,000) see Jaffe Foundation

Massachusetts General Hospital ($15,500) see King Trust, Charles A.

Massachusetts General Hospital ($15,500) see King Trust, Charles A.

Massachusetts General Hospital ($14,500) see King Trust, Charles A.

Massachusetts General Hospital ($14,500) see King Trust, Charles A.

Massachusetts General Hospital ($50,000) see Levy Foundation, June Rockwell

Massachusetts General Hospital ($382,500) see Merck & Co.

Massachusetts General Hospital ($200,000) see Monell Foundation, Ambrose

Massachusetts General Hospital ($7,500) see New England Foundation

Massachusetts General Hospital ($75,000) see Pappas Charitable Foundation, Thomas Anthony

Massachusetts General Hospital ($65,000) see Pappas Charitable Foundation, Thomas Anthony

Massachusetts General Hospital ($25,000) see Pappas Charitable Foundation, Thomas Anthony

Massachusetts General Hospital ($44,644) see Peabody Foundation

Massachusetts General Hospital ($5,000) see Perini Corp.

Massachusetts General Hospital — capital campaign ($25,000) see Polaroid Corp.

Massachusetts General Hospital ($147,797) see Rowland Foundation

Massachusetts General Hospital ($43,295) see Rubenstein Charitable Foundation, Lawrence J. and Anne

Massachusetts General Hospital ($25,000) see Saltonstall Charitable Foundation, Richard

Massachusetts General Hospital ($20,000) see Shawmut National Corp.

Massachusetts General Hospital ($16,668) see Smith Foundation, Richard and Susan

Massachusetts General Hospital — support emergency room facilities ($30,000) see State Street Bank & Trust Co.

Massachusetts General Hospital ($10,000) see Thermo Electron Corp.

Massachusetts General Hospital ($40,000) see Webster Foundation, Edwin S.

Massachusetts General Hospital ($15,000) see Weight Watchers International

Massachusetts General Hospital ($50,000) see Yawkey Foundation II

Massachusetts General Hospital Cancer Center ($50,000) see Hood Foundation, Charles H.

Massachusetts General Hospital — for construction of the Merck Medical Oncology Wing ($1,000,000) see Merck & Co.

Massachusetts General Hospital — multi-drug resistance in cancer patients ($99,594) see Mallinckrodt, Jr. Foundation, Edward

Massachusetts Health Research Institute ($10,000) see Peabody Foundation

Massachusetts Health Research Institute — technical assistance and direction for the Community Health Leadership Recognition Program ($3,515,839) see Johnson Foundation, Robert Wood

Massachusetts Historical Society ($4,200) see Winthrop Trust, Clara B.

Massachusetts Human Services Coalition ($3,500) see Foley, Hoag & Eliot

Massachusetts Indian Scholarship Association ($12,000) see Claneil Foundation

Massachusetts Institute of Technology ($10,000) see Abroms Charitable Foundation

Massachusetts Institute of Technology ($10,000) see Acushnet Co.

Massachusetts Institute of Technology ($105,651) see Adams Trust, Charles E. and Caroline J.

Massachusetts Institute of Technology ($30,000) see Allen Foundation, Rita

Massachusetts Institute of Technology ($750,000) see AMAX

Massachusetts Institute of Technology ($269,517) see American Telephone & Telegraph Co.

Massachusetts Institute of Technology ($4,320) see Arkwright-Boston Manufacturers Mutual

Massachusetts Institute of Technology — scholarships ($200,000) see Balfour Foundation, L. G.

Massachusetts Institute of Technology ($100,000) see Bechtel, Jr. Foundation, S. D.

Massachusetts Institute of Technology ($10,000) see Belz Foundation

Massachusetts Institute of Technology ($158,539) see Bozzone Family Foundation

Massachusetts Institute of Technology ($140,000) see BP America

Massachusetts Institute of Technology ($140,000) see Dibner Fund

Massachusetts Institute of Technology ($100,000) see Dow Foundation, Herbert H. and Barbara C.

Massachusetts Institute of Technology ($82,439) see Edgerton Foundation, Harold E.

Massachusetts Institute of Technology ($5,000) see Edmonds Foundation, Dean S.

Massachusetts Institute of Technology — unrestricted operating grant ($500,000) see General Motors Corp.

Massachusetts Institute of Technology ($15,000) see Gudelsky Family Foundation, Isadore and Bertha

Massachusetts Institute of Technology ($930,478) see Hewlett-Packard Co.

Massachusetts Institute of Technology ($50,000) see Killam Trust, Constance

Massachusetts Institute of Technology ($13,500) see King Trust, Charles A.

Massachusetts Institute of Technology ($13,500) see King Trust, Charles A.

Massachusetts Institute of Technology ($10,000) see Klingler Foundation, Helen and Charles

Massachusetts Institute of Technology ($5,000) see Kunstadter Family Foundation, Albert

Massachusetts Institute of Technology ($5,000) see Kunstadter Family Foundation, Albert

Massachusetts Institute of Technology ($20,000) see

Levinson Foundation, Max and Anna

Massachusetts Institute of Technology — excellence awards ($50,000) see Lockheed Corp.

Massachusetts Institute of Technology ($30,350) see Lurcy Charitable and Educational Trust, Georges

Massachusetts Institute of Technology ($25,000) see Lyons Foundation

Massachusetts Institute of Technology ($5,150) see M/A-COM, Inc.

Massachusetts Institute of Technology ($3,000) see Macht Foundation, Morton and Sophia

Massachusetts Institute of Technology ($6,750) see Miller Memorial Trust, George Lee

Massachusetts Institute of Technology ($6,064) see Miller Memorial Trust, George Lee

Massachusetts Institute of Technology ($100,000) see Orchard Foundation

Massachusetts Institute of Technology ($25,000) see Pappas Charitable Foundation, Thomas Anthony

Massachusetts Institute of Technology ($50,000) see Pinewood Foundation

Massachusetts Institute of Technology ($87,281) see River Road Charitable Corporation

Massachusetts Institute of Technology ($50,000) see Rodgers Trust, Elizabeth Killam

Massachusetts Institute of Technology — research ($79,000) see Rosenbaum Foundation, Paul and Gabriella

Massachusetts Institute of Technology ($10,000) see Schott Foundation

Massachusetts Institute of Technology ($150,000) see Seaver Institute

Massachusetts Institute of Technology ($10,000) see Shea Foundation, Edmund and Mary

Massachusetts Institute of Technology ($5,000) see Sifco Industries Inc.

Massachusetts Institute of Technology — support for a new program for the study of the pharmaceutical industry ($803,950) see Sloan Foundation, Alfred P.

Massachusetts Institute of Technology — scientific research ($50,000) see State Street Bank & Trust Co.

Massachusetts Institute of Technology — academic tournament ($3,500) see Stuart Foundation, Edward C.

Massachusetts Institute of Technology ($300,000) see Tang Foundation

Massachusetts Institute of Technology ($5,000) see Thermo Electron Corp.

Massachusetts Institute of Technology ($40,000) see Waters Foundation

Massachusetts Institute of Technology ($3,000) see Wheless Foundation

Massachusetts Institute of Technology ($25,000) see

Whitney Foundation, Helen Hay

Massachusetts Institute of Technology, Chemical Engineering Department ($100,000) see Texaco

Massachusetts Institute of Technology — support of the Defense and Arms Control Studies Program ($1,350,000) see Carnegie Corporation of New York

Massachusetts Institute of Technology, Department of Biology ($25,083) see Childs Memorial Fund for Medical Research, Jane Coffin

Massachusetts Institute of Technology, Department of Biology ($24,786) see Childs Memorial Fund for Medical Research, Jane Coffin

Massachusetts Institute of Technology — Leaders for Manufacturing ($250,000) see Intel Corp.

Massachusetts Institute of Technology — support of a three year study of the automobile industry at MIT, through its Center for Technology, Policy and Industrial Development ($687,000) see Sloan Foundation, Alfred P.

Massachusetts Institute of Technology — to study the electronic properties of nanometer-sized crystallites ($500,000) see Packard Foundation, David and Lucile

Massachusetts Institute of Technology/New England Science Teachers ($15,000) see Little, Arthur D.

Massachusetts Institute of Technology — for the Ralph M. Parsons Graduate Fellowships ($500,000) see Parsons Foundation, Ralph M.

Massachusetts Institute of Technology — support for a program of research and education to further understand and improve U.S. industrial performance ($926,814) see Sloan Foundation, Alfred P.

Massachusetts Job Training ($100,000) see Norton Co.

Massachusetts Job Training ($5,450) see Shawmut Worcester County Bank, N.A.

Massachusetts Land League ($4,000) see Wharton Trust, William P.

Massachusetts Maritime ($18,500) see Woman's Seamen's Friend Society of Connecticut

Massachusetts Parents Anonymous ($5,754) see Cowan Foundation Corporation, Lillian L. and Harry A.

Massachusetts Senior Action Council ($3,500) see Boynton Fund, John W.

Massachusetts Senior Action Council ($10,000) see Sailors' Snug Harbor of Boston

Massachusetts Society for Medical Research ($5,000) see Harvard Apparatus Foundation

Massachusetts SPCA ($15,500) see Sewall Foundation, Elmina

Massachusetts SPCA — Angel Memorial Hospital ($50,000) see Doyle Charitable Foundation

Massachusetts Taxpayers Foundation ($10,000) see Cabot Family Charitable Trust

MCCM Foundation ($20,000) see McEvoy Foundation, Mildred H.

McLean Hospital ($10,000) see Rabb Charitable Trust, Sidney R.

Meadowbrook School ($10,000) see Devonshire Associates

MECC Child Care Program ($5,000) see Webster Charitable Foundation

Mechanics Hall ($15,000) see Harrington Foundation, Francis A. and Jacquelyn H.

Mechanics Hall ($5,000) see Prouty Foundation, Olive Higgins

Mechanics Hall ($5,000) see Rice Charitable Foundation, Albert W.

Medical Foundation — postdoctoral biomedical research fellowships ($48,000) see Campbell and Adah E. Hall Charity Fund, Bushrod H.

Medical Foundation ($128,854) see Farnsworth Trust, Charles A.

Medical Foundation ($29,000) see Harcourt General

Medical Foundation ($50,000) see Levy Foundation, June Rockwell

Medicine in the Public Interest, Boston, MA ($20,000) see Searle & Co., G.D.

Memorial Hospital — Kidney Dialysis Unit ($761) see Memorial Foundation for the Blind

Merrimack Valley Catholic Charities ($2,000) see Fay Charitable Fund, Aubert J.

Merrimack College ($25,000) see McCarthy Memorial Trust Fund, Catherine

Merrimack College ($140,000) see O'Brien Foundation, James W.

Merrimack College ($50,000) see Stevens Foundation, Abbot and Dorothy H.

Merrimack College ($5,825) see Technical Training Foundation

Merrimack College Scholarship Program ($25,000) see Rogers Family Foundation

Merrimack Repertory Theatre ($35,000) see Parker Foundation, Theodore Edson

Merrimack River Watershed see New England Business Service

Merrimack River Watershed Council ($7,000) see French Foundation

Merrimack River Watershed Council ($4,000) see Wharton Trust, William P.

Merrimack Valley Catholic Charities — emergency food program ($3,500) see Walsh Charity Trust, Blanche M.

Merrimack Valley Housing Partnership ($25,000) see Parker Foundation, Theodore Edson

Merrimack Valley United Fund ($15,000) see Arakelian Foundation, Mary Alice

Merrimack Valley United Fund ($13,312) see M/A-COM, Inc.

Merrimack Valley United Fund ($31,500) see Rogers Family Foundation

Merrimack Valley United Fund ($15,000) see Russell Trust, Josephine G.

Merrimack Valley United Fund ($20,000) see Stearns Trust, Artemas W.

Massachusetts (cont.)

Merrimack Valley United Fund ($20,000) see Webster Charitable Foundation

Metropolitan Boston Housing Partnership — expansion of tenant involvement initiative of the Partnership ($70,000) see State Street Bank & Trust Co.

Metropolitan District Commission — restoration of statues by the Hatch Shell ($2,500) see Henderson Foundation, George B.

MFA Boston ($25,000) see Pellegrino-Realmuto Charitable Foundation

MGH Institution/Health Professions ($25,000) see Stevens Foundation, Abbot and Dorothy H.

Middlesex Community College ($25,000) see Parker Foundation, Theodore Edson

Milford Salvation Army ($5,000) see Hopedale Foundation

Milford-Whitinsville Regional Hospital ($55,000) see Hopedale Foundation

Milton Academy ($64,000) see Jockey Hollow Foundation

Milton Academy ($60,000) see Little Family Foundation

Milton Academy see Metropolitan Bank & Trust Co.

Milton Academy ($20,000) see Orchard Foundation

Milton Academy ($5,000) see Perini Corp.

Milton Academy ($2,000) see Prouty Foundation, Olive Higgins

Milton Academy — headmaster's discretionary fund ($10,000) see Devonwood Foundation

Milton Hospital ($154,295) see Pierce Charitable Trust, Harold Whitworth

Minuteman Home Care ($2,500) see GenRad

Miss Hall's School ($23,000) see Janssen Foundation, Henry

Miss Hall's School ($5,200) see Erpf Fund, Armand G.

Miss Hall's School ($20,000) see Leonhardt Foundation, Dorothea L.

Miss Hall's School ($45,000) see Leonhardt Foundation, Frederick H.

Miss Hall's School ($25,000) see Mars Foundation

Miss Hall's School ($50,000) see Perkins Charitable Foundation

Miss Hall's School ($1,898) see Scherer Foundation, Karla

Miss Hall's School — capital/new construction ($50,000) see Alden Trust, George I.

Mohawk Valley Medical Center ($2,000) see Wells Trust Fund, Fred W.

Morgan Memorial ($17,000) see Boston Fatherless and Widows Society

Morgan Memorial ($11,000) see Charlton, Jr. Charitable Trust, Earle P.

Morgan Memorial ($30,000) see Ellison Foundation

Mother Church First Church of Christ Scientist ($10,000) see Bair Memorial Trust, Charles M.

Mothers Against Drunk Drivers ($20,000) see Flatley Foundation

Mothers Against Drunk Driving ($3,000) see Arkelian Foundation, Ben H. and Gladys

Mount Auburn Hospital ($10,000) see Little, Arthur D.

Mount Auburn Hospital ($50,000) see Pappas Charitable Foundation, Thomas Anthony

Mount Auburn Hospital ($5,000) see Prouty Foundation, Olive Higgins

Mount Auburn Hospital Foundation ($100,000) see Rowland Foundation

Mount Holyoke College — general charitable contribution ($25,000) see Carter-Wallace

Mount Holyoke College ($25,000) see DeRoy Testamentary Foundation

Mount Holyoke College ($7,070) see Freygang Foundation, Walter Henry

Mount Holyoke College ($5,900) see Soling Family Foundation

Mount Holyoke College ($25,000) see Wallace Foundation, George R.

Mount Holyoke College — capital: repairs/renovations ($50,000) see Alden Trust, George I.

MSPCC-Cape Cod ($10,000) see Wallace Foundation, George R.

Multiple Sclerosis see Best Western International

Muscular Dystrophy Research Fund ($10,000) see Allen Brothers Foundation

Muse ($8,000) see Boston Fatherless and Widows Society

Museum of Afro-American History see Raytheon Co.

Museum for American Textile History ($10,000) see Quaker Hill Foundation

Museum of American Textile History ($100,000) see Stevens Foundation, Nathaniel and Elizabeth P.

Museum of Fine Arts ($100,000) see Blanchard Foundation

Museum of Fine Arts ($106,000) see Dingman Foundation, Michael D.

Museum of Fine Arts ($2,500) see Dorminy Foundation, John Henry

Museum of Fine Arts ($10,000) see Falcon Foundation

Museum of Fine Arts ($10,000) see French Foundation

Museum of Fine Arts ($17,000) see Haffner Foundation

Museum of Fine Arts ($25,000) see Harcourt General

Museum of Fine Arts ($3,000) see Hornblower Fund, Henry

Museum of Fine Arts ($41,220) see Johnson Fund, Edward C.

Museum of Fine Arts ($25,100) see Morse Foundation, Richard P. and Claire W.

Museum of Fine Arts ($15,000) see Pellegrino-Realmuto Charitable Foundation

Museum of Fine Arts ($3,000) see Thermo Electron Corp.

Museum of Fine Arts Boston ($17,500) see Dammann Fund

Museum of Science ($15,000) see Adams Trust, Charles E. and Caroline J.

Museum of Science ($75,000) see Blanchard Foundation

Museum of Science ($12,500) see Boston Edison Co.

Museum of Science ($50,000) see Cabot Corp.

Museum of Science ($15,000) see Eastern Enterprises

Museum of Science ($28,000) see Edgerton Foundation, Harold E.

Museum of Science ($8,000) see Goldberg Family Foundation

Museum of Science ($4,000) see Hornblower Fund, Henry

Museum of Science ($5,000) see Pappas Charitable Foundation, Bessie

Museum of Science ($100,000) see Pierce Charitable Trust, Harold Whitworth

Museum of Science ($25,000) see Saltonstall Charitable Foundation, Richard

Museum of Science ($10,000) see Shaw's Supermarkets

Museum of Science ($10,000) see Thermo Electron Corp.

Museum of Science ($45,000) see Webster Foundation, Edwin S.

Museum of Textile History ($10,000) see Rogers Family Foundation

My Brother's Table ($25,000) see Benz Trust, Doris L.

N.E. Medical Center ($30,000) see Peabody Foundation

N.F. Conservatory — handicapped access renovations for Jordan Hall ($50,000) see Riley Foundation, Mabel Louise

Naismith Basketball Hall of Fame ($25,000) see Zollner Foundation

Nantucket AIDS Network ($12,000) see Tupancy-Harris Foundation of 1986

Nantucket Boys and Girls Club ($45,000) see Weezie Foundation

Nantucket Chamber Music Center ($3,000) see Frank Foundation, Ernest and Elfriede

Nantucket College Hospital ($38,000) see Tupancy-Harris Foundation of 1986

Nantucket Conservation Foundation ($16,000) see Larsen Fund

Nantucket Conservation Foundation ($24,000) see Osceola Foundation

Nantucket Conservation Foundation ($193,087) see Tupancy-Harris Foundation of 1986

Nantucket Cottage Hospital — endowment fund ($10,000) see Cox Foundation

Nantucket Cottage Hospital ($20,000) see Day Foundation, Nancy Sayles

Nantucket Cottage Hospital ($20,000) see Heinz Family Foundation

Nantucket Cottage Hospital ($61,000) see Jockey Hollow Foundation

Nantucket Cottage Hospital ($5,000) see Monadnock Paper Mills

Nantucket Cottage Hospital ($10,000) see Osceola Foundation

Nantucket Cottage Hospital — endowment fund ($10,000) see Seidman Family Foundation

Nantucket Cottage Hospital ($5,000) see Willard Foundation, Helen Parker

Nantucket Historical Association — capital support ($120,000) see Allegheny Foundation

Nantucket Historical Association ($100,909) see Tupancy-Harris Foundation of 1986

Nantucket Maria Mitchell Association ($35,000) see Perkin Fund

Nantucket Marra Mitchell Association ($10,000) see Tupancy-Harris Foundation of 1986

Nantucket Shellfish and Marine Department ($41,575) see Atlantic Foundation

Nashoba Community Hospital see New England Business Service

Nashua River Watershed see New England Business Service

National Aeronautics Association ($3,000) see Edmonds Foundation, Dean S.

National Association for Armenian Studies and Research ($50,000) see Mardigian Foundation

National Braille Press ($11,059) see Massachusetts Charitable Mechanics Association

National Bureau of Economic Research — to support comparative research on the treatment of renal disease in Canada and the United States ($64,537) see Donner Foundation, William H.

National Bureau of Economic Research — to support the John M. Olin Fellowship Program in Economics, 1991 ($276,000) see Olin Foundation, John M.

National Bureau of Economic Research — "The Intergenerational Mobility of Immigrants" ($99,047) see Sage Foundation, Russell

National Coalition of Advocates for Students (NCAS) — support a project that identifies and educates parent and community groups as advocates for comprehensive school reform ($50,000) see Hazen Foundation, Edward W.

National Fund for Medical Education ($35,000) see Wollenberg Foundation

National Plastics Center and Museum ($25,000) see Hoffer Plastics Corp.

National Society of Colonial Dames of American in the Commonwealth of Massachusetts ($20,000) see Dula Educational and Charitable Foundation, Caleb C. and Julia W.

National Spinal Cord Foundation ($500) see Cummings Properties Management, Inc.

National Tay-Sachs and Allied Diseases Association ($5,000) see Kaplun Foundation, Morris J. and Betty

National Toxic Campaign Fund ($30,000) see New World Foundation

National Toxic Campaign Fund/Environmental Justice Program ($50,000) see New World Foundation

National Toxics Campaign Fund ($70,000) see Azadoutioun Foundation

National Toxics Campaign Fund ($35,000) see HKH Foundation

National Toxics Campaign Fund ($5,000) see New England Biolabs Foundation

National Toxics Campaign Fund — to promote grassroots organizing ($150,000) see

Schumann Foundation, Florence and John

National Toxics Campaign Fund ($30,000) see Tortuga Foundation

Nativity Boston ($10,000) see Flatley Foundation

Nature Conservancy ($66,441) see Stearns Charitable Foundation, Anna B.

Nauset Workshop ($5,000) see Kelley and Elza Kelley Foundation, Edward Bangs

Nauset Workshop ($8,412) see Massachusetts Charitable Mechanics Association

New Bedford Child and Family Services ($5,000) see Crapo Charitable Foundation, Henry H.

New Bedford Child and Family Services ($40,000) see Sailors' Snug Harbor of Boston

New Bedford Whaling Museum ($10,000) see Plant Memorial Fund, Henry B.

New Bedford Women's Center — support for battered women ($5,000) see Cove Charitable Trust

New Bedford Women's Center ($2,000) see Stride Rite Corp.

New England Aquarium ($18,000) see Eastern Enterprises

New England Aquarium, Boston, MA ($2,500) see Stride Rite Corp.

New England Association of Schools and Colleges — School/College Collaboration Starter Kit ($15,000) see Nellie Mae

New England College Fund ($1,500) see Hyde Manufacturing Co.

New England Colleges Fund ($3,250) see Arkwright-Boston Manufacturers Mutual

New England Colleges Fund ($14,000) see Hopedale Foundation

New England Colleges Fund ($7,500) see Kidder, Peabody & Co.

New England Colleges Fund see New England Business Service

New England Colleges Fund ($17,500) see Schrafft and Bertha E. Schrafft Charitable Trust, William E.

New England Colleges Fund ($4,000) see Wiremold Co.

New England Conservatory of Music ($20,000) see Babson Foundation, Paul and Edith

New England Conservatory of Music ($25,000) see Day Foundation, Nancy Sayles

New England Conservatory of Music ($11,000) see Day Foundation, Nancy Sayles

New England Conservatory of Music ($16,000) see Firan Foundation

New England Conservatory of Music ($16,000) see Firestone, Jr. Foundation, Harvey

New England Conservatory of Music ($140,000) see FMR Corp.

New England Conservatory of Music ($1,500) see Harvard Musical Association

New England Conservatory of Music ($50,000) see Perkin Fund

New England Conservatory of Music ($25,000) see Phillips Foundation, Ellis L.

New England Conservatory of Music ($40,000) see Pierce

Charitable Trust, Harold Whitworth

New England Conservatory of Music ($4,000) see Rabb Charitable Foundation, Sidney and Esther

New England Conservatory of Music ($3,500) see Ratshesky Foundation, A. C.

New England Conservatory of Music ($15,000) see Stare Fund

New England Conservatory of Music ($5,000) see Stare Fund

New England Conservatory of Music ($1,250) see Stare Fund

New England Conservatory of Music ($25,000) see Webster Foundation, Edwin S.

New England Conservatory of Music ($4,200) see Winthrop Trust, Clara B.

New England Deaconess Hospital ($1,000) see Berkman Foundation, Louis and Sandra

New England Deaconess Hospital ($5,000) see Hunt Foundation

New England Deaconess Hospital ($5,000) see Weber Charities Corp., Frederick E.

New England Deaconess Hospital — donation for AIDS research facility ($91,301) see Mapplethorpe Foundation, Robert

New England Deaconess Hospital — toward the cost of purchasing core equipment for the hospital's Laboratory of Cancer Biology ($200,000) see Rippel Foundation, Fannie E.

New England Foundation for the Arts ($20,000) see Norton Co.

New England Foundation for the Arts ($884,000) see Wallace Reader's Digest Fund, Lila

New England Hasidic Center ($30,000) see Joselow Foundation

New England Historic Genealogical Society ($12,500) see Phillips Foundation, Ellis L.

New England Historical Genealogical Center ($20,000) see Henderson Foundation

New England Kurn Hattin Homes ($41,000) see Bissell Foundation, J. Walton

New England Learning Center for Women in Transition ($5,000) see Wells Trust Fund, Fred W.

New England Legal Foundation ($1,000) see Brown & Sharpe Manufacturing Co.

New England for Little Wanderers ($10,000) see Sawyer Charitable Foundation

New England Medical Center ($25,000) see Alden Trust, John W.

New England Medical Center ($15,000) see Boston Edison Co.

New England Medical Center ($20,000) see Dexter Shoe Co.

New England Medical Center ($137,675) see Ford Foundation, Joseph F. and Clara

New England Medical Center ($6,000) see Gerondelis Foundation

New England Medical Center ($53,054) see Hood Foundation, Charles H.

New England Medical Center ($5,000) see Morse

Foundation, Richard P. and Claire W.

New England Medical Center ($40,000) see Saltonstall Charitable Foundation, Richard

New England Medical Center Hospital — research and training in the field of cytokine biology ($31,400) see Kade Foundation, Max

New England Medical Center Hospitals ($13,400) see Weight Watchers International

New England Philharmonic ($750) see Harvard Musical Association

New England School of Law ($7,500) see Crapo Charitable Foundation, Henry H.

New England Science Center ($15,000) see Ellsworth Foundation, Ruth H. and Warren A.

New England Science Center ($100,000) see Harrington Foundation, Francis A. and Jacquelyn H.

New England Science Center ($25,000) see Harrington Foundation, Francis A. and Jacquelyn H.

New England Science Center ($25,000) see McEvoy Foundation, Mildred H.

New England Science Center ($15,000) see McEvoy Foundation, Mildred H.

New England Science Center ($20,000) see Rice Charitable Foundation, Albert W.

New England Science Center ($150,000) see Stoddard Charitable Trust

New England Science Center — equipment: acquisition/repair/upkeep ($100,000) see Alden Trust, George I.

New England Sinai Hospital ($10,000) see Gorin Foundation, Nehemiah

New England Sinai Hospital ($10,000) see Home for Aged Men

New England Sinai Hospital ($10,000) see Home for Aged Men

New England Small Farm Institute ($25,000) see Sacharuna Foundation

New Israel Fund ($60,000) see Stone Charitable Foundation

Newton Court Program ($5,000) see Perpetual Benevolent Fund

Newton Public Schools ($5,000) see Dewing Foundation, Frances R.

Newton Wellesley Hospital ($5,000) see Feldberg Family Foundation

Newton Wellesley Hospital ($8,000) see Gorin Foundation, Nehemiah

Nichols College ($223,000) see American Saw & Manufacturing Co.

Nichols College ($14,000) see Cranston Print Works

Nichols College ($40,000) see Fuller Foundation, George F. and Sybil H.

Nichols College ($27,000) see Hyde Manufacturing Co.

Nichols College ($75,000) see Stoddard Charitable Trust

Nichols College — capital/new construction ($75,000) see Alden Trust, George I.

Norman Rockwell Campaign ($10,000) see Richmond Foundation, Frederick W.

Norman Rockwell Museum — general ($20,560) see Country Curtains, Inc.

Norman Rockwell Museum ($10,000) see Prentice Foundation, Abra

Norman Rockwell Museum ($25,000) see Sandusky International Inc.

North Adams Community Development Corp. ($5,000) see Willmott Foundation, Peter S.

North American Indian Center of Boston ($15,000) see Knistrom Foundation, Fanny and Svante

North Andover High School ($2,000) see O'Brien Foundation, James W.

North Atlantic Ballet ($5,000) see New England Biolabs Foundation

North Bennet School ($17,379) see Massachusetts Charitable Mechanics Association

North Brookfield Ambulance Squad ($1,000) see Quabaug Corp.

North End Union — building improvement program ($50,000) see Riley Foundation, Mabel Louise

North Essex Development and Action Council — treatment and prevention of substance abusers ($20,000) see Schultz Foundation

North Shore Community College ($20,000) see Benz Trust, Doris L.

North Suffolk Mental Health Association — support a community-based youth development organization ($25,000) see Hazen Foundation, Edward W.

Northampton Community College — to assist in building a conference and training center ($20,000) see Laros Foundation, R. K.

Northampton Consortium ($7,500) see Brace Foundation, Donald C.

Northeast Document Conservation Center — for internships ($107,000) see Getty Trust, J. Paul

Northeast Document Conservation Center ($25,000) see Stevens Foundation, Abbot and Dorothy H.

Northeast Medical Center ($42,850) see Devonshire Associates

Northeast Medical Center ($50,000) see Shapiro Charity Fund, Abraham

Northeastern University ($3,000) see American Optical Corp.

Northeastern University ($2,750) see Bird Inc.

Northeastern University ($18,100) see Boston Edison Co.

Northeastern University ($12,000) see Dennison Manufacturing Co.

Northeastern University ($279,325) see Ford Foundation, Joseph F. and Clara

Northeastern University ($50,000) see Gillette Co.

Northeastern University ($50,000) see Henderson Foundation

Northeastern University ($200,000) see Peabody Charitable Fund, Amelia

Northeastern University ($50,000) see Rabb Charitable Trust, Sidney R.

Northeastern University ($25,000) see Rabb Charitable Trust, Sidney R.

Northeastern University ($250,000) see Reebok International Ltd.

Northeastern University ($50,000) see Shawmut National Corp.

Northeastern University ($80,000) see Travelli Fund, Charles Irwin

Northeastern University ($25,000) see Waters Foundation

Northeastern University, Boston, MA ($2,500) see Stride Rite Corp.

Northeastern University — participation in the Century Fund campaign ($40,000) see State Street Bank & Trust Co.

Northfield Mount Hermon ($2,000) see Blake Foundation, S. P.

Northfield Mount Hermon ($15,000) see Stevens Foundation, Nathaniel and Elizabeth P.

Northfield Mount Hermon School ($27,500) see Beveridge Foundation, Frank Stanley

Northfield Mount Hermon School ($20,000) see Snow Foundation, John Ben

Notre Dame Academy — capital: repairs/renovations ($100,000) see Alden Trust, George I.

Notre Dame Montessori School ($5,000) see Cowan Foundation Corporation, Lillian L. and Harry A.

Nuestra Comunidad Development Corporation — for a community organizer and half-time secretary ($53,000) see Riley Foundation, Mabel Louise

NUVA ($20,000) see Charlesbank Homes

Odwin Learning Center ($5,000) see Pappas Charitable Foundation, Bessie

Old Colony Charitable Fund ($344,000) see Rubin Family Fund, Cele H. and William B.

Old Sturbridge Village ($3,000) see Arakelian Foundation, Mary Alice

Old Sturbridge Village ($3,500) see Hyde Manufacturing Co.

Old Sturbridge Village ($25,000) see Rice Charitable Foundation, Albert W.

Olympus High School ($5,000) see Poorvu Foundation, William and Lia

On Orione Home ($10,000) see Home for Aged Men

Opportunity Workshops ($25,000) see Arakelian Foundation, Mary Alice

Orange Scholarship Association ($3,000) see Starrett Co., L.S.

Organizing and Leadership Training Center ($40,000) see Hyams Foundation

Our Lady of the Elms ($35,000) see American Saw & Manufacturing Co.

Overseas Development Council ($1,000) see Hagler Foundation, Jon L.

OxFam America ($100,000) see Homeland Foundation

Oxfam-America ($42,500) see Model Foundation, Leo

Oxfam-America ($100,000) see Moriah Fund

Oxfam-America ($10,000) see Von der Ahe, Jr. Trust, Theodore Albert

Oxfam America — assistance to Kurdish refugees ($25,000) see Cudahy Fund, Patrick and Anna M.

Oxfam America — Papaturro Resettlement Project in El Salvador ($40,000) see Cudahy Fund, Patrick and Anna M.

Pair Foods ($5,000) see Williams Foundation, Arthur Ashley

Para Tours ($5,000) see Boston Fatherless and Widows Society

Parents and Children's Services ($20,000) see Adams Trust, Charles E. and Caroline J.

Parents and Childrens Services ($5,000) see Eaton Memorial Fund, Georgiana Goddard

Park School ($13,829) see New England Foundation

Parkinsons Disease Foundation ($3,000) see Prouty Foundation, Olive Higgins

Partners for Disabled Youth ($5,000) see Cowan Foundation Corporation, Lillian L. and Harry A.

Partners for Disabled Youth — a mentor program that pairs disabled youth and adults ($25,000) see Mitsubishi Electric America

Paski's Out on the Town ($3,750) see Memorial Foundation for the Blind

Pathfinder Fund ($2,000) see Stare Fund

Pathfinder International — expanded reproductive health services ($11,500) see Brush Foundation

Pathfinder International ($15,000) see Campbell and Adah E. Hall Charity Fund, Bushrod H.

Peabody Museum of Salem ($8,000) see Eastern Bank Foundation

Peabody Museum of Salem ($739,486) see Johnson Fund, Edward C.

Peabody Museum of Salem ($100,000) see Rodgers Trust, Elizabeth Killam

Peabody Museum of Salem ($6,000) see Winthrop Trust, Clara B.

People's Task Force ($10,000) see Chase Trust, Alice P.

Perkins School for the Blind ($5,000) see Cox Foundation

Perkins School for the Blind ($7,070) see Freygang Foundation, Walter Henry

Perkins School for the Blind ($3,058,604) see Hilton Foundation, Conrad N.

Perkins School for the Blind — equipment ($74,000) see Littlefield Memorial Trust, Ida Ballou

Phillips Academy ($10,000) see Burns Family Foundation

Phillips Academy ($75,000) see Gelb Foundation, Lawrence M.

Phillips Academy ($42,142) see Gelb Foundation, Lawrence M.

Phillips Academy ($25,000) see Gelb Foundation, Lawrence M.

Phillips Academy ($335,000) see Israel Foundation, A. Cremieux

Phillips Academy ($128,600) see Israel Foundation, A. Cremieux

Massachusetts (cont.)

Phillips Academy ($30,000) see Manger and Audrey Cordero Plitt Trust, Clarence

Phillips Academy ($100,000) see Phipps Foundation, Howard

Phillips Academy ($10,000) see Russell Trust, Josephine G.

Phillips Academy ($20,000) see Winona Corporation

Phillips Academy — Andover Alumni and capital ($18,000) see Ireland Foundation

Phillips Academy — capital campaign to renovate George Washington Hall ($34,000) see Prospect Hill Foundation

Phillips Andover School — annual fund ($1,000) see Olivetti Office USA, Inc.

Phillips Brooks House Association ($25,000) see Cabot Family Charitable Trust

Phillips Brooks House Association ($4,500) see Dewing Foundation, Frances R.

Phillipston Youth Center ($25,000) see Starrett Co., L.S.

Photographic Resource Center ($10,000) see LEF Foundation

Photographic Resource Center — exhibition program ($15,000) see Polaroid Corp.

Pike School ($10,000) see Pellegrino-Realmuto Charitable Foundation

Pine Manor College ($5,000) see Abercrombie Foundation

Pine Manor College ($10,000) see Elkins, Jr. Foundation, Margaret and James A.

Pine Manor College ($65,000) see Ellison Foundation

Pine Manor College ($25,000) see Ellsworth Foundation, Ruth H. and Warren A.

Pine Manor College ($15,000) see Markey Charitable Fund, John C.

Pine Manor College ($5,000) see Paulucci Family Foundation

Pine Manor College ($45,000) see Plumsock Fund

Pine Manor College ($25,000) see Stevens Foundation, Abbot and Dorothy H.

Pine Manor College — Endowment Senior Faculty Professorship ($150,000) see Wean Foundation, Raymond John

Pine Street Inn ($15,000) see Charlesbank Homes

Pine Street Inn ($4,000) see Childs Charitable Foundation, Roberta M.

Pine Street Inn — for lodging houses ($20,000) see Mifflin Memorial Fund, George H. and Jane A.

Pioneer Institute ($5,000) see Kendall Foundation, Henry P.

Pioneer Valley United Way ($29,800) see Shawmut National Corp.

Planned Parenthood Federation of America ($10,000) see Campbell and Adah E. Hall Charity Fund, Bushrod H.

Planned Parenthood Federation of America — national assistance family planning ($100,000) see Johnson Fund, Edward C.

Planned Parenthood Federation of America ($5,000) see Ratshesky Foundation, A. C.

Planned Parenthood Federation of America ($12,000) see

Stearns Charitable Foundation, Anna B.

Planned Parenthood Federation of America ($10,000) see Waters Foundation

Plimoth Plantation ($25,000) see Devonshire Associates

Plimoth Plantation ($4,000) see Hornblower Fund, Henry

Plimoth Plantation ($100,000) see Peabody Charitable Fund, Amelia

Plymouth Bay Girl Scout Council ($7,000) see Acushnet Co.

Plymouth Bay Girl Scout Council ($5,000) see Kelley and Elza Kelley Foundation, Edward Bangs

Plymouth Church ($12,500) see Cobb Family Foundation

Plymouth Church ($10,600) see Cobb Family Foundation

Plymouth Plantation ($377,196) see Davis Foundation, Shelby Cullom

Plymouth State College ($10,000) see Benz Trust, Doris L.

Plymouth State College — music department ($15,000) see Smyth Trust, Marion C.

Plymouth State College Cultural Arts Center ($10,000) see Putnam Foundation

Political Research Associates ($112,500) see Chicago Resource Center

Pope John XXIII ($1,000) see Xtra Corp.

Por Christo ($25,000) see Yawkey Foundation II

Presbyterian Church ($12,000) see Stoneman Charitable Foundation, Anne and David

Preservation Institute: Nantucket ($58,317) see Osceola Foundation

President and Fellows of Harvard College — final payment on scholarship fund pledge ($33,000) see Bemis Company

Prevent Blindness ($2,000) see KSM Foundation

Pro Arte Chamber Orchestra ($750) see Harvard Musical Association

Project Bread Walk for Hunger ($150,000) see Smith Foundation, Richard and Susan

Project Coach, New Bedford Juvenile Offender Program ($20,000) see Shaw Foundation, Gardiner Howland

Project Hope ($5,000) see Bird Inc.

Project Hope ($6,000) see Gerondelis Foundation

Project Hope ($1,200) see Weiss Fund, Clara

Project Nishma ($15,000) see Stone Charitable Foundation

Project Place ($5,000) see Cowan Foundation Corporation, Lillian L. and Harry A.

Project Save ($10,000) see Azadoutioun Foundation

Project Step ($1,500) see Harvard Musical Association

Project Triangle ($10,000) see Fuller Foundation

Provincetown Art Association ($7,000) see Speyer Foundation, Alexander C. and Tillie S.

Pulpit Harbor Foundation ($50,000) see Cabot-Saltonstall Charitable Trust

Quebec-Labrador Foundation — endowment fund ($50,000) see Baker Trust, George F.

Quebec Labrador Foundation ($25,000) see Sharp Foundation

Quincy Community Little Theatre ($20,000) see Jackson Charitable Trust, Marion Gardner

Quincy School Community Council ($25,000) see Harcourt General

Quincy Society of Fine Arts ($15,000) see Jackson Charitable Trust, Marion Gardner

Radcliffe College ($171,995) see Green Fund

Recording for the Blind ($1,500) see Bird Inc.

Recruiting New Teachers — nationwide minority teacher recruiting initiative ($125,000) see Prudential Insurance Co. of America

Recuperative Center ($2,500) see Shapiro Charity Fund, Abraham

Recuperative Center ($10,000) see Shapiro Foundation, Carl and Ruth

Recuperative Center Committee ($1,000) see Reisman Charitable Trust, George C. and Evelyn R.

Recuperative Center Committee ($1,000) see Reisman Charitable Trust, George C. and Evelyn R.

Respond ($23,762) see Hoffman Foundation, John Ernest

Responsibility ($20,460) see Phillips Trust, Edwin

Retarded Citizens ($70,000) see Phillips Trust, Edwin

Retarded Citizens ($69,300) see Phillips Trust, Edwin

Revels ($500) see Index Technology Corp.

Revels ($4,000) see Lea Foundation, Helen Sperry

Robert and Jane Cizik Endowment-Harvard Business School ($312,500) see Cooper Industries

Robert Saver Hale Camping Reservation ($1,000) see Hagler Foundation, Jon L.

Robert W. White School ($30,000) see Hoffman Foundation, Marion O. and Maximilian

ROCA ($15,000) see Cabot Family Charitable Trust

Rofeh Inc ($39,000) see Jesselson Foundation

Roman Catholic Bishop ($5,527) see Luce Charitable Foundation, Stephen C.

Ronald McDonald House ($3,500) see Steiger Memorial Fund, Albert

Rosie's Place ($18,000) see Sawyer Charitable Foundation

Roxbury Comprehensive Community Health Center ($1,350) see Lipton Foundation

Roxbury Multi-Service Center — Project RIGHT (Rebuild and Improve Grove Hall Together) ($60,000) see Hyams Foundation

Rudolf Steiner School ($40,000) see Lennox International, Inc.

Sacred Heart Trust Fund ($10,000) see O'Neil Foundation, M. G.

Sail Boston 1992 — co-sponsorship of the tall ships in bicentennial celebration

($50,000) see State Street Bank & Trust Co.

St. Charles School ($1,000) see Cummings Properties Management, Inc.

St. Elizabeth's Hospital Social Services Department ($5,000) see Weber Charities Corp., Frederick E.

St. John Church — restoration of tower ($52,500) see Henderson Foundation, George B.

St. Johns Foundation ($5,000) see Fay Charitable Fund, Aubert J.

St. Joseph Church ($1,500) see Quabaug Corp.

St. Joseph Hospital ($150,000) see Demoulas Supermarkets

St. Joseph Manor Nursing Home ($10,000) see Home for Aged Men

Saint Joseph's Abbey ($100,000) see East Foundation, Sarita Kenedy

St. Josephs Hospital ($5,000) see Fay Charitable Fund, Aubert J.

St. Luke's Capital Drive ($50,000) see Acushnet Co.

St. Luke's Hospital ($12,500) see Acushnet Co.

St. Mark's School ($5,000) see Frelinghuysen Foundation

St. Mark's School ($50,000) see Weezie Foundation

Saint Mary's Church ($100,000) see East Foundation, Sarita Kenedy

St. Mary's High School ($24,000) see O'Brien Foundation, James W.

St. Patrick's Church ($8,500) see Huisking Foundation

St. Patricks School — social studies materials ($3,000) see Walsh Charity Trust, Blanche M.

St. Paul A.M.E. ($25,000) see Charlesbank Homes

St. Peters Church ($10,000) see McGraw Foundation, Donald C.

St. Vincent de Paul Society — operating ($6,000) see Walsh Charity Trust, Blanche M.

Salem Community Corporation ($150,000) see Stoddard Charitable Trust

Salem Fraternity Boy's Club ($5,000) see Eastern Bank Foundation

Salem Hospital ($20,000) see Chase Charity Foundation, Alfred E.

Salem Hospital Century Fund ($5,000) see Eastern Bank Foundation

Salem State College ($90,000) see Teagle Foundation

Salem State College — to purchase interactive video and CAI equipment ($60,000) see Fuld Health Trust, Helene

Salvation Army ($17,000) see Boston Fatherless and Widows Society

Salvation Army ($12,250) see Henderson Foundation

Salvation Army ($25,000) see Hoffman Foundation, John Ernest

Salvation Army ($13,200) see Sawyer Charitable Foundation

Samaritans ($15,008) see Harrington Trust, George

Samaritans ($7,500) see Stearns Charitable Foundation, Anna B.

Sanders Fund ($122,588) see Sanders Trust, Charles

Sandwich Senior Resources ($50,000) see Benz Trust, Doris L.

Sankaty Head Foundation ($10,000) see Cox Foundation

Santa's Kitchen Project Break ($10,000) see Flatley Foundation

Satelife ($20,000) see Masco Corp.

SatelLife — support their "Access to Medical Information" project for Poland ($30,000) see Jurzykowski Foundation, Alfred

Save the Bay ($42,000) see Donaldson Charitable Trust, Oliver S. and Jennie R.

Save the Bay ($10,000) see McBean Charitable Trust, Alletta Morris

School for Field Studies ($200,000) see Andreas Foundation

Scientific Imaging Systems ($20,000) see Hofheinz Fund

Scientific Imaging Systems ($10,000) see Hofheinz Fund

Sea Education Association ($25,000) see Doherty Charitable Foundation, Henry L. and Grace

Sea Education Association ($60,000) see FMR Corp.

Sea Education Association ($50,000) see Penzance Foundation

Sea Education Association ($10,000) see Plant Memorial Fund, Henry B.

Sea Education Association ($100,000) see Watson Foundation, Thomas J.

Sea Education Association — refit the "Westward" ($50,000) see Clowes Fund

Second Helping Program ($10,000) see Yawkey Foundation II

Second Home ($25,000) see Charlesbank Homes

Shady Hill Alumni Annual Fund ($38,689) see Little Family Foundation

Shadyhill School ($5,000) see AKC Fund

Shaloh House — Milton and Stoughton ($6,000) see Lipsky Foundation, Fred and Sarah

Shawangunk Conservancy ($3,000) see Frank Foundation, Ernest and Elfriede

Shawmut Bank Caring Tree Program ($15,000) see Shawmut Worcester County Bank, N.A.

Sherborn Rural Land Foundation ($50,000) see Saltonstall Charitable Foundation, Richard

Sheriff's Meadow Foundation ($20,000) see Stott Foundation, Louis L.

Shriners Burns Institute ($5,000) see Barker Foundation

Shriners Burns Institute ($4,000) see Hornblower Fund, Henry

Shriners Burns Institute ($11,000) see Sawyer Charitable Foundation

Shriners Hospital for Crippled Children ($8,000) see Jost Foundation, Charles and Mabel P.

Simmons College — scholarships ($50,000) see Ayling Scholarship Foundation, Alice S.

Simmons College see Seiler Corp.

Simmons Rock College ($10,000) see Henderson Foundation

Simon's Rock of Bard College ($25,000) see Sharp Foundation

Sister Constantine/Helen Church ($50,000) see Demoulas Supermarkets

Sisters of Charity of Nazareth Provincial House — operating/ESL ($3,000) see Walsh Charity Trust, Blanche M.

Sisters of St. Anne Bethany Convent ($20,000) see Hanson Testamentary Charitable Trust, Anna Emery

Small Friends ($18,000) see Tupancy-Harris Foundation of 1986

Smith College ($5,000) see AKC Fund

Smith College ($10,000) see Braitmayer Foundation

Smith College ($100,000) see Carlson Cos.

Smith College ($1,000) see Charter Manufacturing Co.

Smith College ($1,000) see Chiquita Brands Co.

Smith College ($100,000) see Gordon/Rousmaniere/Roberts Fund

Smith College ($1,000) see Hobbs Charitable Trust, John H.

Smith College ($20,000) see Janssen Foundation, Henry

Smith College ($72,000) see Julia R. and Estelle L. Foundation

Smith College ($25,000) see Kent Foundation, Ada Howe

Smith College ($15,000) see Lilly Foundation, Richard Coyle

Smith College ($5,000) see Rauch Foundation

Smith College ($5,000) see Smith Charitable Fund, Eleanor Armstrong

Smith College ($11,000) see Southways Foundation

Smith College ($5,000) see Tension Envelope Corp.

Smith College ($3,000) see Tension Envelope Corp.

Smith College ($10,000) see Tippit Charitable Trust, C. Carlisle and Margaret M.

Smith College ($25,000) see Vale Foundation, Ruby R.

Smith College ($10,000) see Williams Foundation, C. K.

Smith College — education ($505,000) see Young Foundation, Robert R.

Smith College — for Ada Comstock Scholarship ($6,000) see Fisher Foundation

Smith College Alumni Fund ($5,000) see Orchard Foundation

Smith College Alumni Fund ($30,000) see Winona Corporation

Smith College Department of Religion ($20,000) see Kent Foundation, Ada Howe

Smith College — for the Smith College Museum of Art Capital Campaign for an endowment for acquisitions ($50,000) see Columbia Foundation

Social Action Ministries — general support ($10,000) see Cove Charitable Trust

Social Justice for Women ($40,000) see Burden Foundation, Florence V.

Social Justice for Women ($10,000) see Horne Trust, Mabel

Social Justice for Women ($20,000) see Shaw Foundation, Gardiner Howland

Social Justice for Women — Neil J. Houston House (residential treatment program) ($10,000) see Campbell and Adah E. Hall Charity Fund, Bushrod H.

Society of Analytical Chemists ($15,000) see Waters Foundation

Society of the Cincinnati of New Hampshire ($12,500) see Vesper Corp.

Society of Jesus of New England ($75,000) see O'Neil Foundation, W.

Society for the Preservation of New England Antiquities ($10,000) see Mifflin Memorial Fund, George H. and Jane A.

Society of the Protestant Episcopal Church ($50,000) see Chase Trust, Alice P.

Sojourner House ($15,000) see Charlesbank Homes

Somerville Cambridge Elder Services ($25,000) see Farnsworth Trust, Charles A.

South Boston Neighborhood House — operating expenses ($38,000) see Hyams Foundation

South Church — Andover ($18,000) see Stevens Foundation, Abbot and Dorothy H.

South Congregational Church ($22,000) see Webster Charitable Foundation

South End Historical Society — Mackery School; landscaping Winter Garden along Montgomery Street ($10,000) see Henderson Foundation, George B.

South Shore Baptist Church ($30,750) see Benfamil Charitable Trust

South Shore Natural Science Center ($20,000) see Shaw's Supermarkets

South Yarmouth Library Association ($5,000) see Kelley and Elza Kelley Foundation, Edward Bangs

Southeastern Massachusetts University ($3,200) see United Merchants & Manufacturers

Southern Area Jewish Community Center ($5,000) see Feldberg Family Foundation

Spaulding Rehabilitation Hospital ($5,000) see Charlton, Jr. Charitable Trust, Earle P.

Spaulding Rehabilitation Hospital ($100,000) see Ellison Foundation

Special Education Technology Resource Center — Equal Access program, which uses specialized software and teaching techniques to mainstream children with disabilities into full participation in regular elementary school cases ($30,000) see Mitsubishi Electric America

Spectrum House ($5,000) see Fletcher Foundation

SPNEA Boston ($10,000) see Pellegrino-Realmuto Charitable Foundation

Springfield Central Business District see Massachusetts Mutual Life Insurance Co.

Springfield College ($1,000) see Blake Foundation, S. P.

Springfield College — academic assistance ($2,000) see Cove Charitable Trust

Springfield College ($180,000) see Dodge Foundation, Cleveland H.

Springfield College see Massachusetts Mutual Life Insurance Co.

Springfield College ($721) see York Barbell Co.

Springfield Day Nursery ($10,000) see Dexter Charitable Fund, Eugene A.

Springfield Employment Resource Center ($15,000) see Dexter Charitable Fund, Eugene A.

Springfield Library and Museum ($1,000) see Blake Foundation, S. P.

Springfield Neighborhood Housing Services see Massachusetts Mutual Life Insurance Co.

Springfield Symphony Orchestra ($1,000) see Blake Foundation, S. P.

Stagewest ($115,000) see Blake Foundation, S. P.

Stagewest ($2,500) see Steiger Memorial Fund, Albert

Stanley Park of Westfield ($665,000) see Beveridge Foundation, Frank Stanley

Starlight Foundation ($5,000) see Weiss Foundation, William E.

State Legislative Leaders Foundation ($15,000) see Unilever United States

Steppingstone Foundation ($11,500) see Bachmann Foundation

Steppingstone Foundation ($25,000) see Simon Charitable Trust, Esther

Steppingstone Foundation ($10,000) see Stoneman Charitable Foundation, Anne and David

Stonehill College ($10,000) see Home for Aged Men

Stoneleigh Burnham School ($20,000) see Wallace Foundation, George R.

Sturdy Memorial Foundation — grant ($130,000) see Balfour Foundation, L. G.

Sturgis Library ($2,000) see Harris Foundation, John H. and Lucille

Suffolk University ($15,000) see Horne Trust, Mabel

Suffolk University ($7,000) see New England Biolabs Foundation

Suffolk University of Law ($2,000) see O'Brien Foundation, James W.

Survival Education Fund ($45,500) see Agape Foundation

Swarthmore College ($10,000) see Eastern Enterprises

Tafts College ($50,000) see Rowland Foundation

Talking Book Library ($28,000) see Memorial Foundation for the Blind

Talking Information Center ($2,500) see Crapo Charitable Foundation, Henry H.

Tanglewood Music Center ($7,000) see Crane & Co.

Tanglewood Music Center ($6,000) see Frelinghuysen Foundation

Technion ($20,000) see Kaplan Foundation, Rita J. and Stanley H.

Teens As Community ($10,000) see Stoneman Charitable Foundation, Anne and David

Teens as Community Action ($7,000) see New England Biolabs Foundation

Temple Israel ($2,000) see Erving Paper Mills

Temple Israel ($4,000) see Rabb Charitable Foundation, Sidney and Esther

Thayer Academy ($5,000) see Hornblower Fund, Henry

Thayer Academy ($150,000) see Peabody Charitable Fund, Amelia

Third Century Campaign ($15,000) see Perini Foundation, Joseph

Thomas More College — general ($160,000) see Homeland Foundation

Thompson Island City Bound Program ($40,000) see Boston Edison Co.

Thompson Island Outward Bound ($300,000) see Penzance Foundation

Thompson Island Outward Bound ($40,000) see Penzance Foundation

Thompson Island Outward Bound ($17,385) see Penzance Foundation

Thompson Island Outward Bound Education Center — support general operations and experimental outdoor education programs for inner city Boston youth ($25,000) see Island Foundation

Thompson Island Outward Bound Educational Centre ($15,000) see Humane Society of the Commonwealth of Massachusetts

Thoreau Society — institutional development ($7,500) see Phillips Foundation, Ellis L.

Tobey Health Systems ($11,000) see Stone Charitable Foundation

Tobey Hospital — annual fund ($28,000) see Cove Charitable Trust

Tower Hill Botanic Garden — cost of building visitors and education center ($15,000) see Lindsay Trust, Agnes M.

Town of Belmont ($20,000) see Pappas Charitable Foundation, Bessie

Town of Florida ($500) see Christodora

Town of Hopedale ($20,000) see Hopedale Foundation

Town of Manchester-by-the-Sea ($5,000) see Winthrop Trust, Clara B.

Town of Southbridge ($5,000) see American Optical Corp.

Tracing History and Ourselves — inner-city project ($30,000) see Mailman Family Foundation, A. L.

Trinity College ($150,000) see Waters Foundation

Trinity Episcopal Church of Topsfield ($5,000) see Vingo Trust II

Trinity Episcopal Church of Topsfield ($5,000) see Vingo Trust II

Trinity Pulpit Trust ($5,000) see Triford Foundation

Trustees of Christ Methodist Church ($5,527) see Luce Charitable Foundation, Stephen C.

Trustees of Christian Science Society ($5,527) see Luce Charitable Foundation, Stephen C.

Trustees for Deerfield Academy ($25,000) see Meyer Foundation

Trustees of First Baptist Church ($5,527) see Luce Charitable Foundation, Stephen C.

Trustees of Friends Academy ($7,000) see Crapo Charitable Foundation, Henry H.

Trustees of Grace Episcopal Church ($5,527) see Luce Charitable Foundation, Stephen C.

Trustees of Hampshire College ($175,000) see Educational Foundation of America

Trustees of Health and Hospitals ($10,000) see Horne Trust, Mabel

Trustees of Health and Hospitals ($60,467) see Noonan Memorial Fund under the will of Frank Noonan, Deborah Munroe

Trustees of Health and Hospitals ($59,324) see Noonan Memorial Fund under the will of Frank Noonan, Deborah Munroe

Trustees of Health and Hospitals ($55,824) see Noonan Memorial Fund under the will of Frank Noonan, Deborah Munroe

Trustees of Health and Hospitals ($55,824) see Noonan Memorial Fund under the will of Frank Noonan, Deborah Munroe

Trustees of Health and Hospitals ($49,013) see Noonan Memorial Fund under the will of Frank Noonan, Deborah Munroe

Trustees of Health and Hospitals of the City of Boston ($1,630,450) see Kellogg Foundation, W. K.

Trustees of Martha's Vineyard Hebrew Center ($5,527) see Luce Charitable Foundation, Stephen C.

Trustees of Phillips Academy ($15,000) see Israel Foundation, A. Cremieux

Trustees of Reservations — capital campaign ($40,000) see Butler Family Foundation, Patrick and Aimee

Trustees of Reservations ($10,000) see Chase Trust, Alice P.

Trustees of Reservations ($25,000) see Devonshire Associates

Trustees of Reservations — conservation of landscape ($12,500) see Folger Fund

Trustees of Reservations ($3,500) see Haffner Foundation

Trustees of Reservations ($5,000) see Killam Trust, Constance

Trustees of Reservations ($3,500) see Orchard Foundation

Trustees of Reservations ($25,000) see Pierce Charitable Trust, Harold Whitworth

Massachusetts (cont.)

Trustees of Reservations ($40,000) see Saltonstall Charitable Foundation, Richard

Trustees of Reservations ($75,000) see Stoddard Charitable Trust

Trustees of Reservations ($2,626,380) see Vingo Trust II

Trustees of Reservations ($4,500) see Winthrop Trust, Clara B.

Trustees of Tufts College ($35,000) see Ames Charitable Trust, Harriett

Trustees of Tufts College, Boston, MA ($31,500) see Searle & Co., G.D.

Trustees, Vineyard Haven Public Library ($61,746) see Luce Charitable Foundation, Stephen C.

Trustees of W.M. Crane Community House ($13,000) see Crane & Co.

Trustees of W.M. Crane Community House ($10,000) see Crane & Co.

Trustees of W.M. Crane Community House ($10,000) see Crane & Co.

Tufts Center for Urban Studies ($30,000) see Goldberg Family Foundation

Tufts College ($20,000) see First Petroleum Corp.

Tufts College ($10,000) see M/A-COM, Inc.

Tufts Society of Fellows (1989/1990) ($20,000) see Erving Paper Mills

Tufts University — scholarships ($200,000) see Balfour Foundation, L. G.

Tufts University ($15,000) see Dennison Manufacturing Co.

Tufts University ($60,000) see Devonshire Associates

Tufts University ($50,000) see Doyle Charitable Foundation

Tufts University ($25,050) see Erpf Fund, Armand G.

Tufts University ($60,000) see Gerondelis Foundation

Tufts University — cost of renovating and equipping their new undergraduate chemical engineering laboratory ($100,000) see Hayden Foundation, Charles

Tufts University ($4,500) see Higgins Foundation, Aldus C.

Tufts University ($38,933) see Kevorkian Fund, Hagop

Tufts University ($50,000) see Loews Corp.

Tufts University — central nervous system ($70,000) see Mallinckrodt, Jr. Foundation, Edward

Tufts University ($10,000) see McGregor Foundation, Thomas and Frances

Tufts University ($2,404,000) see Olin Foundation, F. W.

Tufts University ($50,000) see Pappas Charitable Foundation, Thomas Anthony

Tufts University ($10,000) see Pellegrino-Realmuto Charitable Foundation

Tufts University ($55,000) see Porter Foundation, Mrs. Cheever

Tufts University ($56,000) see Travelli Fund, Charles Irwin

Tufts University Fletcher School of Law and Diplomacy ($75,000) see Banyan Tree Foundation

Tufts University Lincoln Filene Center ($25,000) see Filene Foundation, Lincoln and Therese

Tufts University Medical School ($40,000) see Jaharis Family Foundation

Tufts University Medical School — to support research in pathogenesis and treatment of osteosarcoma (human and canine) ($55,876) see Greenwall Foundation

Tufts University — 1989 Medical Science Scholar ($108,000) see Culpeper Foundation, Charles E.

Tufts University School of Dental Medicine ($30,670) see Peabody Foundation

Tufts University School of Medicine ($25,000) see Terner Foundation

Tufts University School of Medicine ($300,000) see Wolfson Foundation, Louis E.

Tufts University School of Veterinary Medicine ($5,000) see Childs Charitable Foundation, Roberta M.

Tufts Veterinarian School ($6,000) see Bailey Wildlife Foundation

21st Century Foundation ($46,500) see Donaldson Charitable Trust, Oliver S. and Jennie R.

Two/Ten International Footwear Foundation ($2,000) see Ansin Private Foundation, Ronald M.

Two/Ten National Foundation Charity Trust ($1,000) see Quabaug Corp.

Union of Concerned Scientists ($100,000) see Kendall Foundation, Henry P.

Unitarian Universalist Association ($10,000) see Cassett Foundation, Louis N.

Unitarian Universalist Society ($5,527) see Luce Charitable Foundation, Stephen C.

United Cerebral Palsy Association ($8,391) see Massachusetts Charitable Mechanics Association

United Church of Christ ($15,000) see Blanchard Foundation

United Fund ($12,000) see Cranston Print Works

United Jewish Appeal Federation of Jewish Philanthropies ($40,000) see Fair Oaks Foundation, Inc.

United Negro College Fund ($5,000) see Perini Corp.

United Negro College Fund ($15,000) see Pierce Charitable Trust, Harold Whitworth

United Negro College Fund ($25,000) see Webster Foundation, Edwin S.

United South End Settlement Houses ($4,000) see Ratshesky Foundation, A. C.

United South End Settlements — operating expenses ($63,000) see Hyams Foundation

United Way ($58,750) see Acushnet Co.

United Way ($1,500) see Ansin Private Foundation, Ronald M.

United Way ($41,865) see Arkwright-Boston Manufacturers Mutual

United Way ($4,800) see Arkwright-Boston Manufacturers Mutual

United Way ($7,000) see Barnes Group

United Way ($7,000) see Barnes Group

United Way ($10,000) see Benz Trust, Doris L.

United Way ($3,000) see Berenson Charitable Foundation, Theodore W. and Evelyn

United Way ($5,000) see Boynton Fund, John W.

United Way ($20,000) see Cabot-Saltonstall Charitable Trust

United Way ($58,500) see Crane & Co.

United Way ($37,500) see Crapo Charitable Foundation, Henry H.

United Way ($50,000) see Dennison Manufacturing Co.

United Way ($20,000) see Dennison Manufacturing Co.

United Way ($12,500) see Dexter Charitable Fund, Eugene A.

United Way ($32,000) see Eastern Bank Foundation

United Way ($10,000) see EG&G Inc.

United Way ($5,000) see Erving Paper Mills

United Way ($3,000) see Fletcher Foundation

United Way ($869) see Gear Motion

United Way ($375,000) see General Electric Co.

United Way ($10,000) see Goldberg Family Foundation

United Way ($500) see Hagler Foundation, Jon L.

United Way ($18,000) see Hampden Papers

United Way ($15,500) see Justus Trust, Edith C.

United Way ($6,562) see Kelley and Elza Kelley Foundation, Edward Bangs

United Way ($13,091) see M/A-COM, Inc.

United Way ($29,700) see Mechanics Bank

United Way ($60,000) see Morgan Construction Co.

United Way ($3,500) see Motter Printing Press Co.

United Way ($30,000) see Parker Foundation, Theodore Edson

United Way ($5,000) see Perini Foundation, Joseph

United Way ($10,000) see Reisman Charitable Trust, George C. and Evelyn R.

United Way ($25,000) see Rice Charitable Foundation, Albert W.

United Way ($40,000) see Saltonstall Charitable Foundation, Richard

United Way ($5,050) see Sawyer Charitable Foundation

United Way ($80,000) see Schrafft and Bertha E. Schrafft Charitable Trust, William E.

United Way ($4,000) see Shapiro Charity Fund, Abraham

United Way ($20,000) see Shaw Foundation, Gardiner Howland

United Way ($22,010) see Starrett Co., L.S.

United Way ($42,000) see Steiger Memorial Fund, Albert

United Way ($4,000) see Thermo Electron Corp.

United Way ($6,500) see United Merchants & Manufacturers

United Way ($15,000) see Weber Charities Corp., Frederick E.

United Way ($50,000) see Webster Foundation, Edwin S.

United Way ($2,100) see White Construction Co.

United Way ($187,500) see Wyman-Gordon Co.

United Way ($12,941) see Wyman-Gordon Co.

United Way ($10,553) see Wyman-Gordon Co.

United Way ($1,000) see Xtra Corp.

United Way of Central Massachusetts ($137,373) see Fuller Foundation, George F. and Sybil H.

United Way of Central Massachusetts ($240,000) see Norton Co.

United Way of Central Massachusetts ($26,250) see Textron

United Way of Eastern New England ($12,452) see Gillette Co.

United Way of Eastern New England ($424,733) see Shawmut National Corp.

United Way of Eastern New England ($79,500) see Shaw's Supermarkets

United Way of Eastern New England ($26,800) see TJX Cos.

United Way of Eastern New England — general purpose fund ($9,049) see Walgreen Co.

United Way of Eastern New England-Attleboro ($55,000) see Texas Instruments

United Way of Massachusetts Bay ($400,000) see Boston Edison Co.

United Way of Massachusetts Bay ($105,468) see Eastern Enterprises

United Way of Massachusetts Bay ($315,000) see Globe Newspaper Co.

United Way of Massachusetts Bay ($16,000) see Kidder, Peabody & Co.

United Way of Massachusetts Bay ($1,500) see Lippitt Foundation, Katherine Kenyon

United Way of Massachusetts Bay/Child Care Initiative ($30,000) see Globe Newspaper Co.

United Way of Massachusetts Bay — annual corporate gift for 1991 ($530,000) see State Street Bank & Trust Co.

United Way of North Central Massachusetts see New England Business Service

United Way of Pioneer Valley ($220,000) see American Saw & Manufacturing Co.

United Way of Pioneer Valley ($35,000) see Dow Jones & Co.

United Way of Pioneer Valley ($166,980) see Monsanto Co.

United Way of Pioneer Valley ($31,616) see Westvaco Corp.

United Way of Worcester ($80,000) see Shawmut National Corp.

United Ways of Eastern New England ($105,000) see GTE Corp.

United Ways of New England — corporate support for 1992 ($35,000) see Little, Arthur D.

University Christian Movement ($10,000) see Wallace Foundation, George R.

University Hospital ($6,000) see Roehl Foundation

University Hospital ($15,000) see Sailors' Snug Harbor of Boston

University of Lowell ($4,250) see Barker Foundation

University of Lowell Research Foundation ($30,000) see Parker Foundation, Theodore Edson

University of Massachusetts ($1,000) see American Optical Corp.

University of Massachusetts ($159,460) see Educational Foundation of America

University of Massachusetts ($33,334) see GenCorp

University of Massachusetts ($7,600) see Gloeckner Foundation, Fred

University of Massachusetts ($3,600) see Goldberg Family Foundation, Israel and Matilda

University of Massachusetts ($10,000) see Hopedale Foundation

University of Massachusetts/Boston — John I. Taylor and William Davis Taylor Scholars Program ($125,000) see Globe Newspaper Co.

University of Massachusetts/Boston — John I. Taylor and William Davis Taylor Scholars Program ($125,000) see Globe Newspaper Co.

University of Massachusetts at Boston — Urban Scholars Program ($20,000) see Nellie Mae

University of Massachusetts Foundation — endowment of scholarship funds ($100,000) see Litton Industries

University of Massachusetts Foundation — urban scholars program ($15,000) see Polaroid Corp.

University of Massachusetts — aid biocultural research on food storage options among the Hopi, Arizona ($10,000) see Wenner-Gren Foundation for Anthropological Research

University of Massachusetts Medical Center ($16,500) see Memorial Foundation for the Blind

University School of Public Health ($1,500) see Index Technology Corp.

Urban Health Project ($2,900) see Humane Society of the Commonwealth of Massachusetts

Urban League of Springfield see Massachusetts Mutual Life Insurance Co.

US Rugby Football Foundation ($2,300) see Dell Foundation, Hazel

Valley Land Fund ($2,000) see Steiger Memorial Fund, Albert

Valley Programs ($3,250) see Boynton Fund, John W.

Very Special Arts ($5,000) see Boynton Fund, John W.

Very Special Arts Massachusetts ($10,000) see Straus Foundation, Philip A. and Lynn

Vess Chigas Memorial Foundation ($100,000) see Demoulas Supermarkets

Visions ($5,000) see Foley, Hoag & Eliot

Visiting Nurse Association ($6,000) see Hopedale Foundation

Visiting Nurse Association — Cancer Care ($20,000) see Rubenstein Charitable Foundation, Lawrence J. and Anne

Visiting Nurse Foundation ($10,000) see McGraw Foundation, Donald C.

Visiting Nurses Association ($10,000) see Quaker Hill Foundation

Visiting Nurses Association ($5,000) see Ramlose Foundation, George A.

Visiting Nurses Association ($5,000) see Wells Trust Fund, Fred W.

Visiting Nurses Association of Boston ($10,000) see Boston Fatherless and Widows Society

Wales Home ($5,000) see Home for Aged Men

Walnut Hill School ($55,000) see Wallace Foundation, George R.

Wang Center ($75,000) see Blanchard Foundation

Wang Center ($2,500) see Ratshesky Foundation, A. C.

Wang Center ($15,000) see Shapiro Foundation, Carl and Ruth

Wang Center for the Performing Arts ($12,000) see Boston Edison Co.

Wang Center for the Performing Arts ($5,000) see Cox Foundation

Wang Center for Performing Arts ($50,000) see Harcourt General

Wang Center for the Performing Arts ($100,000) see Peabody Foundation, Amelia

Wang Center for the Performing Arts ($20,000) see TJX Cos.

WBUR, National Public Radio ($5,000) see Hagler Foundation, Jon L.

WBUR-90 ($200) see Index Technology Corp.

We the People 2000 ($75,000) see Bell Atlantic Corp.

Wediko Children's Services ($60,000) see Harrington Trust, George

Wediko Children's Services — short-term residential diagnostic/treatment program for seriously disturbed children ($73,195) see van Ameringen Foundation

Wellesley College ($2,000) see Bodine Corp.

Wellesley College — general support ($20,000) see Collins Foundation, Carr P.

Wellesley College ($45,000) see Collins Foundation, James M.

Wellesley College ($25,000) see Cowles Charitable Trust

Wellesley College — endowment fund ($56,000) see Cowles Foundation, William H.

Wellesley College — endowment fund ($30,000) see Favrot Fund

Wellesley College ($10,000) see Hanson Testamentary Charitable Trust, Anna Emery

Wellesley College ($205,000) see Hess Foundation

Wellesley College ($25,000) see Hughes Memorial Foundation, Charles Evans

Wellesley College ($5,000) see Kelly Foundation, T. Lloyd

Wellesley College ($25,000) see Kentucky Foundation for Women

Wellesley College ($10,000) see Kopf Foundation

Wellesley College ($25,000) see Kopf Foundation, Elizabeth Christy

Wellesley College — for renovation and expansion of science center ($1,000,000) see Kresge Foundation

Wellesley College ($1,500) see Lebovitz Fund

Wellesley College ($15,000) see Lumpkin Foundation

Wellesley College ($10,000) see Morse Foundation, Richard P. and Claire W.

Wellesley College ($260,000) see Newhouse Foundation, Samuel I.

Wellesley College ($20,000) see Shapiro Foundation, Carl and Ruth

Wellesley College ($30,000) see Sperry Fund

Wellesley College ($72,857) see Van Nuys Foundation, I. N. and Susanna H.

Wellesley College ($4,000) see Wilson Foundation, John and Nevils

Wellesley College ($48,000) see Zimmermann Fund, Marie and John

Wellesley College, Durant Society ($40,000) see New England Foundation

Wellesley College Office of Resources ($7,500) see Wood Foundation of Chambersburg, PA

Wellesley College Office of Resources ($7,500) see Wood Foundation of Chambersburg, PA

Wellness Community Organization of Boston ($7,000) see Waters Foundation

Wellspring Land Trust ($20,000) see Charlesbank Homes

Wellspring Land Trust ($115,000) see Oak Foundation U.S.A.

Wentworth Institute of Technology ($2,000) see Dennison Manufacturing Co.

Wentworth Institute of Technology ($7,500) see EG&G Inc.

Wesson Women and Infants Unit ($100,000) see American Saw & Manufacturing Co.

Western Massachusetts Food Bank ($1,500) see Wells Trust Fund, Fred W.

Weston School of Theology ($25,000) see Doty Family Foundation

Weston School of Theology ($10,000) see Doty Family Foundation

WGBH ($38,035) see GenRad

WGBH ($5,000) see Hagler Foundation, Jon L.

WGBH ($595) see Index Technology Corp.

WGBH ($180,423) see Nakamichi Foundation, E.

WGBH Education Foundation — support for PBS "The Health Quarterly" television series ($10,189,229) see Johnson Foundation, Robert Wood

WGBH Educational Foundation ($10,000) see Axe-Houghton Foundation

WGBH Educational Foundation ($2,500) see Goldberg Family Foundation

WGBH Educational Foundation ($10,000) see Higgins Foundation, Aldus C.

WGBH Educational Foundation ($7,000) see Hopedale Foundation

WGBH Educational Foundation ($200,000) see Lowell Institute, Trustees of the

WGBH Educational Foundation ($2,130) see Morgan Construction Co.

WGBH Educational Foundation ($2,500) see Morse Foundation, Richard P. and Claire W.

WGBH Educational Foundation ($20,000) see Pierce Charitable Trust, Harold Whitworth

WGBH Educational Foundation ($2,500) see Rosenberg Family Foundation, William

WGBH Educational Foundation ($34,500) see Saltonstall Charitable Foundation, Richard

WGBH Educational Foundation ($25,000) see Solow Foundation, Sheldon H.

WGBH Educational Foundation ($7,000) see Winthrop Trust, Clara B.

WGBH Educational Foundation ($37,500) see Wrigley Co., Wm. Jr.

WGBH Educational Foundation — support for a four-part television series on competitiveness ($1,000,000) see Sloan Foundation, Alfred P.

WGBH-Long Ago and Far Away — to provide capstone funding for season III of this children's series ($140,000) see Davis Foundations, Arthur Vining

WGBH Public Broadcasting ($100,000) see Rowland Foundation

WGBH Radio ($15,000) see Arakelian Foundation, Mary Alice

WGBN Television ($15,000) see Arakelian Foundation, Mary Alice

WGBY-TV Channel 57 ($3,500) see Steiger Memorial Fund, Albert

Wheaton College ($2,500) see Benfamil Charitable Trust

Wheaton College ($66,000) see McCune Charitable Trust, John R.

Wheaton College ($5,000) see Obernauer Foundation

Wheelock College ($16,000) see Higgins Foundation, Aldus C.

Wheelock College — new visions in career development ($25,000) see Mailman Family Foundation, A. L.

Whellock Family Theatre ($5,200) see New England Biolabs Foundation

Whitaker Health Sciences Fund ($1,650,000) see Whitaker Foundation

Whitehead Institute ($30,000) see Allen Foundation, Rita

WICN ($5,000) see Fletcher Foundation

WICN — Audio Journal ($35,000) see Memorial Foundation for the Blind

Wilbraham Monson Academy ($137,000) see Blake Foundation, S. P.

William H. Harris Foundation — medical research ($10,000) see Rosenberg Family Foundation, William

Williams College ($25,000) see Archbold Charitable Trust, Adrian and Jessie

Williams College ($25,000) see Bobst Foundation, Elmer and Mamdouha

Williams College — capital campaign ($50,000) see Crestlea Foundation

Williams College ($25,000) see Eckman Charitable Foundation, Samuel and Rae

Williams College ($15,000) see Essel Foundation

Williams College ($6,000) see Essick Foundation

Williams College ($650) see Interstate Packaging Co.

Williams College ($20,000) see Kraft Foundation

Williams College ($50,000) see Lehman Foundation, Edith and Herbert

Williams College ($2,500) see Lehman Foundation, Edith and Herbert

Williams College ($313,200) see Pasadena Area Residential Aid

Williams College ($22,400) see Perkins Charitable Foundation

Williams College ($150,000) see Wallach Foundation, Miriam G. and Ira D.

Williams College ($130,000) see Willmott Foundation, Peter S.

Williamstown Regional Art Conservation Laboratory — for internships ($95,000) see Getty Trust, J. Paul

Wilson Community ($15,000) see Stoneman Charitable Foundation, Anne and David

Winchester Hospital ($5,000) see Cummings Properties Management, Inc.

Winchester Photographic Exhibit (Griffin) ($25,000) see Schrafft and Bertha E. Schrafft Charitable Trust, William E.

Winchester Scholarship Foundation ($1,000) see Cummings Properties Management, Inc.

Windrush Farm Therapeutic Equitation ($500) see Index Technology Corp.

Winsor School ($7,000) see Winthrop Trust, Clara B.

Woburn Council of Social Concern ($1,000) see Cummings Properties Management, Inc.

Women for Economic Justice ($5,000) see Azadoutioun Foundation

Women in Theater ($20,000) see Kentucky Foundation for Women

Womens Action for Nuclear Disarmament Education ($4,000) see Carteh Foundation

Women's Educational and Industrial Union ($6,000) see Boston Fatherless and Widows Society

Woodlands Mountain Institute — general fund ($35,000) see Mifflin Memorial Fund, George H. and Jane A.

Woods Hole Marine Biology Laboratory ($250,000) see Vetlesen Foundation, G. Unger

Woods Hole Oceanographic Institute ($37,200) see Devonshire Associates

Woods Hole Oceanographic Institute ($5,000) see Kelley and Elza Kelley Foundation, Edward Bangs

Woods Hole Oceanographic Institute ($400,000) see Vetlesen Foundation, G. Unger

Woods Hole Oceanographic Institution ($62,800) see Donaldson Charitable Trust, Oliver S. and Jennie R.

Woods Hole Public Library — renovation ($50,000) see Clowes Fund

Woods Hole Research Center ($25,000) see Schiff Foundation, Dorothy

Worcester Academy ($2,000) see Hyde Manufacturing Co.

Worcester Academy ($20,000) see Rice Charitable Foundation, Albert W.

Worcester Art Museum ($10,000) see Doyle Charitable Foundation

Worcester Art Museum ($65,000) see Fuller Foundation, George F. and Sybil H.

Worcester Art Museum ($65,528) see Hoche-Scofield Foundation

Worcester Art Museum ($53,723) see Hoche-Scofield Foundation

Worcester Art Museum ($12,538) see Morgan Construction Co.

Worcester Art Museum ($25,000) see Norton Co.

Worcester Art Museum ($300,000) see Stoddard Charitable Trust

Worcester Association of Retarded Children ($1,500) see Gear Motion

Worcester Center for Crafts — for renovations in the exhibition gallery ($1,500) see Nash Foundation

Worcester Center for Performing ($5,000) see Prouty Foundation, Olive Higgins

Worcester Children's Friend Society ($25,000) see Ellsworth Foundation, Ruth H. and Warren A.

Worcester Children's Friend Society ($15,125) see White Construction Co.

Worcester Common Ground Piedmont Co-op ($10,000) see Shawmut Worcester County Bank, N.A.

Worcester Consortium for Higher Education — Worcester Early Awareness Program ($15,000) see Nellie Mae

Worcester Country Music Association ($60,528) see Hoche-Scofield Foundation

Worcester County Horticultural Society ($5,570) see Morgan Construction Co.

Worcester County Horticultural Society ($1,000) see Quabaug Corp.

Worcester County Horticultural Society — development of visitor center and library ($30,000) see Smith Horticultural Trust, Stanley

Worcester County Horticultural Society ($100,000) see Stoddard Charitable Trust

Worcester County Music Association ($53,723) see Hoche-Scofield Foundation

Worcester Foothills Theatre ($51,547) see Fuller Foundation, George F. and Sybil H.

Worcester Foothills Theatre Company ($20,000) see Harrington Foundation, Francis A. and Jacquelyn H.

Worcester Forum Theatre Ensemble ($2,500) see Shawmut Worcester County Bank, N.A.

Worcester Foundation for Experimental Biology ($25,000) see Ellsworth Foundation, Ruth H. and Warren A.

Massachusetts (cont.)

Worcester Foundation for Experimental Biology ($20,000) see Harrington Foundation, Francis A. and Jacquelyn H.

Worcester Foundation for Experimental Biology — medical research ($265,000) see Mathers Charitable Foundation, G. Harold and Leila Y.

Worcester Foundation for Experimental Biology — toward contraceptive research for males ($84,000) see Noble Foundation, Edward John

Worcester Foundation for Experimental Biology ($10,000) see Wyman-Gordon Co.

Worcester Girls Club ($75,000) see Stoddard Charitable Trust

Worcester Historical Museum ($20,000) see Ellsworth Foundation, Ruth H. and Warren A.

Worcester Historical Museum ($15,000) see Fletcher Foundation

Worcester Historical Museum ($40,000) see Rice Charitable Foundation, Albert W.

Worcester Historical Museum ($10,000) see Wyman-Gordon Co.

Worcester Horticultural Society ($10,000) see Rice Charitable Foundation, Albert W.

Worcester Municipal Research Bureau ($2,500) see Morgan Construction Co.

Worcester Polytechnic Institute ($1,000) see American Optical Corp.

Worcester Polytechnic Institute ($50,000) see Ellsworth Foundation, Ruth H. and Warren A.

Worcester Polytechnic Institute ($140,000) see Fuller Foundation, George F. and Sybil H.

Worcester Polytechnic Institute ($20,000) see Harrington Foundation, Francis A. and Jacquelyn H.

Worcester Polytechnic Institute ($6,000) see Hyde Manufacturing Co.

Worcester Polytechnic Institute ($7,634) see Morgan Construction Co.

Worcester Polytechnic Institute ($35,000) see Norton Co.

Worcester Polytechnic Institute ($1,000) see Quabaug Corp.

Worcester Polytechnic Institute ($15,000) see Starrett Co., L.S.

Worcester Polytechnic Institute ($325,000) see Stoddard Charitable Trust

Worcester Polytechnic Institute ($18,295) see Wyman-Gordon Co.

Worcester Polytechnic Institute ($10,000) see Wyman-Gordon Co.

Worcester Square Area Neighborhood Association — black granite basis for fountain ($20,000) see Henderson Foundation, George B.

Worcester Vocational High School ($10,000) see Higgins Foundation, Aldus C.

World Society for the Protection of Animals ($25,000) see Baker Foundation, Elinor Patterson

World Society for the Protection of Animals ($2,000) see Bright Charitable Trust, Alexander H.

YMCA ($10,000) see Acushnet Co.

YMCA ($15,000) see Adams Trust, Charles E. and Caroline J.

YMCA ($12,500) see Alden Trust, John W.

YMCA ($50,000) see American Saw & Manufacturing Co.

YMCA ($5,000) see Arkwright-Boston Manufacturers Mutual

YMCA ($50,000) see Charlton, Jr. Charitable Trust, Earle P.

YMCA ($25,000) see Chase Charity Foundation, Alfred E.

YMCA ($25,000) see Chase Charity Foundation, Alfred E.

YMCA ($15,000) see Chase Charity Foundation, Alfred E.

YMCA ($15,000) see Chase Charity Foundation, Alfred E.

YMCA ($15,000) see Chase Trust, Alice P.

YMCA ($8,000) see Crapo Charitable Foundation, Henry H.

YMCA ($1,000) see Cummings Properties Management, Inc.

YMCA ($100,000) see Donaldson Charitable Trust, Oliver S. and Jennie R.

YMCA ($10,000) see Eastern Bank Foundation

YMCA ($20,000) see Ellsworth Foundation, Ruth H. and Warren A.

YMCA ($15,000) see Harrington Foundation, Francis A. and Jacquelyn H.

YMCA ($30,000) see Harris Foundation, John H. and Lucille

YMCA ($15,000) see Home for Aged Men

YMCA ($15,000) see Home for Aged Men

YMCA ($10,000) see Horne Trust, Mabel

YMCA ($15,000) see Hyde Manufacturing Co.

YMCA ($500) see Index Technology Corp.

YMCA ($2,000) see Mechanics Bank

YMCA ($25,000) see Rogers Family Foundation

YMCA ($10,000) see Russell Trust, Josephine G.

YMCA ($10,000) see Stearns Trust, Artemas W.

YMCA ($47,000) see Webster Charitable Foundation

YMCA ($5,000) see Webster Charitable Foundation

YMCA of Central Massachusetts — operating support ($77,000) see Alden Trust, George I.

YMCA of Central Massachusetts — capital/new construction ($500,000) see Alden Trust, George I.

YMCA of Greater Worcester ($10,000) see Norton Co.

You ($5,000) see Fletcher Foundation

YOU — new program ($1,000) see Mechanics Bank

Young Audiences of Massachusetts ($1,000) see Harvard Musical Association

Youth Build Boston ($10,000) see Chase Charity Foundation, Alfred E.

Youth Build Boston ($17,000) see Lotus Development Corp.

Youth Build Boston — takes inner-city youth and teaches them trade skills through the rehabilitation of affordable housing units in their neighborhoods ($30,000) see State Street Bank & Trust Co.

Youth Enrichment Services ($5,000) see Fuller Foundation

Youthbuild Boston — for unemployed youth ($75,000) see Riley Foundation, Mabel Louise

Youthbuild Boston ($10,000) see Stoneman Charitable Foundation, Anne and David

YWCA ($5,000) see Higgins Foundation, Aldus C.

YWCA ($35,000) see Parker Foundation, Theodore Edson

YWCA ($12,500) see Rice Charitable Foundation, Albert W.

YWCA ($10,000) see Russell Trust, Josephine G.

YWCA ($15,000) see Stevens Foundation, Nathaniel and Elizabeth P.

YWCA of Central Massachusetts ($50,000) see Fuller Foundation, George F. and Sybil H.

YWCA of Central Massachusetts ($100,000) see Stoddard Charitable Trust

YWCA of Central Massachusetts — capital: repairs/renovations ($75,000) see Alden Trust, George I.

YWCA of Greater Lawrence — YWCA Study Center ($35,000) see Sun Microsystems

Zeiterion Theatre ($10,000) see Crapo Charitable Foundation, Henry H.

Zoryan Institute ($25,000) see Simone Foundation

Michigan

Abuse/Neglect ($13,857) see Delano Foundation, Mignon Sherwood

Academy of Scared Heart ($12,500) see Sehn Foundation

Acton Institute ($40,000) see Chicago Resource Center

Acton Institute ($40,000) see Chicago Resource Center

Akiva Hebrew Day School ($15,000) see Rohlik Foundation, Sigmund and Sophie

Albion College — scholarship fund ($44,223) see Bentley Foundation, Alvin M.

Albion College ($70,000) see Dow Chemical Co.

Albion College ($30,000) see Dresser Industries

Albion College ($10,000) see Loutit Foundation

Albion College ($10,000) see McIntyre Foundation, C. S. and Marion F.

Albion College ($20,000) see Sebastian Foundation

Albion College — for the Dow Recreation and Wellness Center construction and renovation program ($500,000) see Dow Foundation, Herbert H. and Grace A.

Albion College — Kresge Gymnasium Renovation ($5,000) see Norton Memorial Corporation, Geraldi

All Saints Episcopal Church — renovations and operations ($5,000) see Ransom Fidelity Company

Allegan County 4-H Clubs ($15,000) see Delano Foundation, Mignon Sherwood

Allegan Dollars for Scholars ($6,000) see Delano Foundation, Mignon Sherwood

Alliance-Economic Alliance of Michigan ($5,000) see Handleman Co.

Allied Jewish Campaign ($20,000) see Borman's

Allied Jewish Campaign ($80,300) see Mandell Foundation, Samuel P.

Alma College ($14,000) see Besser Foundation

Alma College ($50,000) see Dow Corning Corp.

Alma College — support for operations ($7,000) see JSJ Corp.

Alma College ($33,333) see McIntyre Foundation, C. S. and Marion F.

Alma College ($33,000) see Research Corporation

Alma College — complete renovation of the Dow Science Center ($600,000) see Dow Foundation, Herbert H. and Grace A.

Alpena Community College ($24,000) see Besser Foundation

Alpena Community College — Fred Johnson Memorial ($10,000) see Besser Foundation

Alpena Target 2000 ($10,000) see Besser Foundation

Alzheimer's Disease and Related Disorders Association ($5,000) see Ramlose Foundation, George A.

American Cancer Society ($1,490) see Alro Steel Corp.

American Cancer Society ($5,000) see Bray Charitable Trust, Viola E.

American Cancer Society, Kalamazoo County Unit — for office improvements and new equipment see Gilmore Foundation, Irving S.

American Diabetes Foundation ($3,000) see Bierlein Family Foundation

American Red Cross ($5,000) see Batts Foundation

American Red Cross — caseworker salaries ($25,000) see Dalton Foundation, Dorothy U.

American Red Cross ($1,000) see Fibre Converters

American Red Cross ($1,000) see Grand Rapids Label Co.

American Red Cross ($7,500) see Ransom Fidelity Company

American Red Cross ($25,000) see Sebastian Foundation

American Red Cross ($7,500) see Wege Foundation

American Red Cross ($5,000) see Whiting Memorial Foundation, Henry and Harriet

Andrews University ($7,000) see Tiscornia Foundation

Ann Arbor Housing Bureau for Seniors ($100) see Robertson Brothers

Anna Freud Foundation ($1,000) see Awrey Bakeries

Apple Farm Arts and Music Center ($32,200) see Bergen Foundation, Frank and Lydia

Applied Technology Center ($20,000) see Batts Foundation

Aquinas College ($10,000) see Baldwin Foundation

Aquinas College ($1,000) see Perpetual Benevolent Fund

Aquinas College ($1,000) see Perpetual Benevolent Fund

Aquinas College ($1,000) see Perpetual Benevolent Fund

Aquinas Junior College ($1,800) see Perpetual Benevolent Fund

Aquinas Junior College ($1,000) see Perpetual Benevolent Fund

Aquinas Junior College ($1,000) see Perpetual Benevolent Fund

Archdiocese of Detroit ($5,000) see Seymour and Troester Foundation

Armenian Apostolic Society ($50,000) see Manoogian Foundation, Alex and Marie

Armenian Apostolic Society ($55,000) see Mardigian Foundation

Armenian Congregational Church ($20,000) see Mardigian Foundation

Armenian General Benevolent Union ($750) see Federal Screw Works

Arnold Center ($2,500) see Dow Fund, Alden and Vada

Arthritis Foundation ($1,000) see Kasle Steel Corp.

Arthritis Foundation ($10,000) see Westerman Foundation, Samuel L.

Artran ($5,000) see DeRoy Foundation, Helen L.

Arts Council of Greater Grand Rapids ($1,000) see Grand Rapids Label Co.

Arts Council of Greater Kalamazoo — to assist in the implementation of the Community Cultural Plan see Gilmore Foundation, Irving S.

Association for Retired Citizens of Ottawa County ($25,000) see Loutit Foundation

Attic Theatre ($15,000) see Kaufman Memorial Trust, Chaim, Fanny, Louis, Benjamin, and Anne Florence

Automotive Hall of Fame ($5,000) see Whalley Charitable Trust

Automotive Hall of Fame Scholarship Fund ($5,000) see Echlin Foundation

Bach Festival Society — operational expenses see Gilmore Foundation, Irving S.

Bais Chabad of Farmington Hills ($5,000) see Herman Foundation, John and Rose

Ballet Michigan Ensemble — to provide emergency funding for heating system repair see Gilmore Foundation, Irving S.

Baptist Haiti Mission — for Haiti missions ($5,000) see Epaphroditus Foundation

Battle Creek Area Urban League ($15,000) see Miller Foundation

Battle Creek Community Foundation ($625,000) see Kellogg's

Battle Creek Community Foundation ($33,333) see Miller Foundation

Battle Creek Health System ($15,000) see Miller Foundation

Battle Creek Public Schools ($110,000) see Miller Foundation

Bay Area Community Foundation — operating expenses ($42,780) see Kantzler Foundation

Bay Area Community Foundation — operating

expenses ($14,000) see
Kantzler Foundation

Bay City Public Schools —
school closure study ($11,500)
see Kantzler Foundation

Bay Cliff Health Camp ($3,500)
see Kaufman Endowment
Fund, Louis G.

Beaumont Foundation ($6,000)
see Barton-Malow Co.

Beaumont Foundation ($5,000)
see DeVlieg Foundation,
Charles

Beaumont Foundation ($2,000)
see Erb Lumber Co.

Beaumont Foundation ($10,000)
see Handleman Co.

Beaumont Foundation ($10,000)
see Wilson Trust, Lula C.

Beaumont Hospital ($4,000) see
Prentis Family Foundation,
Meyer and Anna

Beginning Experience ($30,000)
see Deseranno Educational
Foundation

Berrien County Intermediate
School District ($50,000) see
Whirlpool Corp.

Bethany Christian Services
($5,000) see Artevel
Foundation

Bethany Christian Services
($7,000) see Caldwell
Foundation, Hardwick

Bethany Christian Services
($5,000) see Cook Charitable
Foundation

Bethany Christian Services
($5,000) see Dexter Industries

Bethany Christian Services
($104,295) see Word
Investments

Bethesda-By-The-Sea Church
($6,000) see Meek Foundation

Bharatiya Temple of Flint
($11,250) see India Foundation

Big Brothers and Big Sisters
($6,000) see Bishop Charitable
Trust, A. G.

Big Brothers and Big Sisters
($3,000) see Dow Fund, Alden
and Vada

Big Brothers and Big Sisters
($2,150) see Monroe Auto
Equipment Co.

Big Brothers and Big Sisters of
Greater Kalamazoo — to
purchase equipment at the
Howard Street facility see
Gilmore Foundation, Irving S.

Bishop Hafey Heritage Fund
($1,000) see Fabri-Kal Corp.

Bixby Community Health
Foundation ($200,000) see
Merillat Foundation, Orville
D. and Ruth A.

Blodgett/St. Mary's MRI —
MRI equipment ($200,000)
see Wege Foundation

Blue Lake Public Radio ($7,700)
see SPX Corp.

Blue Water Child Guidance
Clinic ($3,000) see Whiting
Memorial Foundation, Henry
and Harriet

Board of Education of the City
of Detroit — summer program
($20,000) see Holden Fund,
James and Lynelle

Bon Secours Hospital ($12,500)
see Zimmerman Foundation,
Mary and George Herbert

Boy Scouts see Michigan Mutual
Insurance Corp.

Boy Scouts of America ($4,125)
see Bierlein Family Foundation

Boy Scouts of America ($5,000)
see DeRoy Foundation, Helen
L.

Boy Scouts of America
($17,500) see Shapero

Foundation, Nate S. and Ruth
B.

Boy Scouts of America
($10,000) see Shelden Fund,
Elizabeth, Allan and Warren

Boy Scouts of America ($1,500)
see Weatherwax Foundation

Boy Scouts of America ($3,500)
see Whiting Memorial
Foundation, Henry and Harriet

Boy Scouts of America
($10,000) see Whitney Fund,
David M.

Boy Scouts of America,
Southwest Michigan Council
— to support a new scouting
program on Kalamazoo's north
side see Gilmore Foundation,
Irving S.

Boys and Girls Club ($250) see
Alro Steel Corp.

Boys and Girls Club ($10,911)
see Boutell Memorial Fund,
Arnold and Gertrude

Boys and Girls Club ($6,500) see
DeVlieg Foundation, Charles

Boys and Girls Club ($2,500) see
Farwell Foundation, Drusilla

Boys and Girls Club ($20,250)
see Greater Lansing
Foundation

Boys and Girls Club ($60,000)
see Holden Fund, James and
Lynelle

Boys and Girls Club ($12,880)
see Kantzler Foundation

Boys and Girls Club ($10,000)
see Kantzler Foundation

Boys and Girls Club ($36,025)
see Slaughter, Jr. Foundation,
William E.

Boys and Girls Club ($100) see
Volkswagen of America, Inc.

Boys and Girls Club ($15,000)
see Whitney Fund, David M.

Boys and Girls Club ($5,000) see
Wilson Trust, Lula C.

Boys and Girls Club of
Kalamazoo — to support a
renovation and expansion
project see Gilmore
Foundation, Irving S.

Boys and Girls Club of
Kalamazoo ($35,000) see
Upjohn Co.

Boys and Girls Club of
Kalamazoo — to support the
boys and girls' participating
arts program see Gilmore
Foundation, Irving S.

Boys and Girls Club of
Southeastern Michigan —
capital ($40,000) see Wilson
Fund, Matilda R.

Boys Hope ($10,600) see
Earl-Beth Foundation

Boysville of Michigan —
building trades program
($5,000) see Bauervic
Foundation, Charles M.

Boysville of Michigan —
building trades program
($5,000) see Bauervic-Paisley
Foundation

Boysville of Michigan —
purchase of vehicle ($15,000)
see Besser Foundation

Boysville of Michigan — St.
Joseph Hall Fund ($5,000) see
Vollbrecht Foundation,
Frederick A.

Brandywine High School —
Washington, D.C. student trip
($2,400) see Hunter
Foundation, Edward and Irma

Brighton Hospital ($1,000) see
Awrey Bakeries

Business Education Alliance,
Detroit, MI see Kmart Corp.

Butterworth Foundation —
Dorothy Gerber Endowment

Fund ($25,000) see Gerber
Products Co.

Butterworth Hospital
($1,042,800) see DeVos
Foundation, Richard and Helen

C.R.C. World Literature
Ministries ($5,000) see Artevel
Foundation

C.R.C. World Relief Committee
($15,000) see Artevel
Foundation

Cadillac/Rel ($8,350) see Kysor
Industrial Corp.

Calhoun County Adult Day Care
($50,000) see Kellogg's

Calvin College ($10,000) see
Artevel Foundation

Calvin College ($1,000) see
Dexter Industries

Calvin College ($20,000) see
Westerman Foundation,
Samuel L.

Calvin College and Seminary
Religious Work ($15,000) see
Tibstra Charitable Foundation,
Thomas and Gertrude

Calvin Theological Seminary
($5,000) see Artevel
Foundation

Campaign for St. Gregorys
Abbey ($2,500) see Decio
Foundation, Arthur J.

Capital Area Humane Society
($15,000) see Baker
Foundation, Elinor Patterson

Capital Area Humane Society
($21,000) see Greater Lansing
Foundation

Capital Area Humane Society
($8,500) see Ransom Fidelity
Company

Capital Region Community
Foundation ($20,000) see
Greater Lansing Foundation

Capitol Region Community
Foundation ($25,000) see
Thoman Foundation, W. B.
and Candace

Capuchin Community Center
($5,200) see Slaughter, Jr.
Foundation, William E.

Capuchin Community Center
($10,000) see Westerman
Foundation, Samuel L.

Capuchin Community Center
($10,000) see Whitney Fund,
David M.

Capuchin Community Center
($7,000) see Zimmerman
Foundation, Mary and George
Herbert

Capuchin Community Center
Soup Kitchen ($3,000) see
Seymour and Troester
Foundation

Capuchin Mission ($1,000) see
Atalanta/Sosnoff Capital Corp.

Care Area ($5,000) see Borwell
Charitable Foundation

Caregivers — "Parents Plus"
($280,000) see Skillman
Foundation

CARP ($21,000) see Fisher
Foundation, Max M. and
Marjorie S.

Cascades Humane Society
($2,500) see Weatherwax
Foundation

Catch ($30,000) see Domino's
Pizza

Cathedral Church of St. Paul
($25,000) see Earl-Beth
Foundation

Cathedral Church of St. Paul
($401,441) see Green
Charitable Trust, Leslie H. and
Edith C.

Cathedral School — building
renovation and expansion
($100,000) see
Hudson-Webber Foundation

Catherine McAuley Health
Center ($10,000) see Taubman
Foundation, A. Alfred

Catherine McAuley Health
Center (Systems) —
(outpatient Oncology
Treatment Facility) ($250,000)
see Towsley Foundation, Harry
A. and Margaret D.

Catholic Family Services
($10,000) see Vicksburg
Foundation

Catholic Services Appeal
($10,000) see Sehn Foundation

Catholic Services Appeal
($10,000) see Vlasic
Foundation

CEDC ($20,000) see Tiscornia
Foundation

Center for Creative Studies
($25,000) see Ford Fund,
Benson and Edith

Center for Creative Studies
($245,000) see Ford Fund,
Eleanor and Edsel

Center for Creative Studies
($200,350) see Ford Fund,
Walter and Josephine

Center for Creative Studies —
operating expenses ($31,000)
see Wilson Fund, Matilda R.

Center for Environmental Study
($50,394) see Wege Foundation

Center for Gerontology
($20,000) see Whiting
Foundation

Center Hall of Fame ($1,000) see
Ewald Foundation, H. T.

Center for Women in Transition
($15,000) see Delano
Foundation, Mignon Sherwood

Central Business District
Foundation — downtown
master lighting plan ($25,000)
see American Natural
Resources Co.

Central Michigan ($4,300) see
Kysor Industrial Corp.

Central Michigan University see
Coors Brewing Co.

Central Michigan University
($30,000) see Gerstacker
Foundation, Rollin M.

Central Michigan University
($40,000) see Strosacker
Foundation, Charles J.

CEO Council ($3,000) see Todd
Co., A.M.

Cereal City Development
Corporation ($2,200,000) see
Kellogg Foundation, W. K.

Chelsea Education Foundation
($500) see Federal Screw
Works

Child Abuse and Neglect
Council County of Oakland
($5,000) see Wilson Trust,
Lula C.

Child Evangelism Fellowship
($5,000) see Christian Workers
Foundation

Child and Family Services —
operating expenses ($28,000)
see Besser Foundation

Child and Family Services of
Western Michigan ($8,000)
see Delano Foundation,
Mignon Sherwood

Child Welfare Society ($5,000)
see Bishop Charitable Trust,
A. G.

Children's Center ($12,659) see
Earl-Beth Foundation

Children's Center ($5,000) see
Shelden Fund, Elizabeth, Allan
and Warren

Children's Center of Wayne
County ($35,000) see Ford
Fund, Benson and Edith

Children's Center of Wayne
County ($10,000) see
Handleman Co.

Children's Center of Wayne
County — building renovation
($150,000) see
Hudson-Webber Foundation

Children's Home of Detroit
($25,000) see Ford Fund,
Benson and Edith

Children's Home of Detroit
($12,000) see Ford Fund,
William and Martha

Children's Homes of Judson
Center ($7,000) see DeVlieg
Foundation, Charles

Children's Hospital Medical
Center ($5,000) see Imerman
Memorial Foundation, Stanley

Children's Hospital Medical
Center ($10,000) see Ratner
Foundation, Milton M.

Children's Hospital Medical
Center ($12,500) see Shelden
Fund, Elizabeth, Allan and
Warren

Children's Hospital Medical
Center ($5,000) see Vollbrecht
Foundation, Frederick A.

Children's Hospital Medical
Center ($3,000) see
Zimmerman Foundation, Mary
and George Herbert

Children's Hospital of Michigan
($5,000) see Barton-Malow Co.

Children's Hospital of Michigan
($20,000) see Ford Fund,
Benson and Edith

Children's Hospital of Michigan
($25,250) see Ford Fund,
Walter and Josephine

Children's Hospital of Michigan
— for medical research
($5,000) see Lincoln Health
Care Foundation

Children's Hospital of Michigan
($15,000) see Masco Corp.

Children's Hospital of Michigan
($15,000) see Masco Corp.

Children's Hospital of Michigan
($7,000) see Padnos Iron &
Metal Co., Louis

Children's Hospital of Michigan,
Detroit, MI see Kmart Corp.

Children's Hospital of Michigan
— New Century Project
($250,000) see
Hudson-Webber Foundation

Children's Museum ($5,000) see
Bishop Charitable Trust, A. G.

Children's Museum Friends
($9,600) see Shiffman
Foundation

Children's Play School —
(Preschool Education)
($150,000) see Towsley
Foundation, Harry A. and
Margaret D.

Chinese Association of Great
Kalamazoo ($500) see China
Times Cultural Foundation

Christian Family Foundation
($2,380,000) see Merillat
Foundation, Orville D. and
Ruth A.

Christian Reformed Work
Missions Religious Work
($20,000) see Tibstra
Charitable Foundation,
Thomas and Gertrude

Christian Reformed World
Mission ($10,000) see Artevel
Foundation

Christian Reformed World Relief
Committee ($5,000) see
Huizenga Foundation, Jennie

Christian Schools International
($5,000) see Vermeer
Investment Company
Foundation

Citizens Research Council of
Michigan ($30,000) see
Earhart Foundation

Michigan (cont.)

City of Allegan ($8,000) see Delano Foundation, Mignon Sherwood

City of Allegan ($6,000) see Delano Foundation, Mignon Sherwood

City of Battle Creek — sports promotion ($20,000) see Miller Foundation

City of Battle Creek — Bailey Stadium ($200,000) see Miller Foundation

City of Bay City — city parking lot/airport landscaping ($15,000) see Kantzler Foundation

City of Flint Mayor's Office on Aging and Handicapped ($6,000) see Bishop Charitable Trust, A. G.

City of Grand Haven ($318,540) see Loutit Foundation

City of Holland Historic Depot ($250,000) see Padnos Iron & Metal Co., Louis

City of Jackson ($46,000) see Hurst Foundation

City of Kalamazoo — to support the city's after-school Fine Arts Skill Enhancement Program for targeted middle school students see Gilmore Foundation, Irving S.

City of Marquette — city band ($2,000) see Kaufman Endowment Fund, Louis G.

City of Marquette — junior hockey ($15,000) see Kaufman Endowment Fund, Louis G.

City of Marquette Police Department — DARE program ($1,000) see Kaufman Endowment Fund, Louis G.

City of Midland-Riverside Place ($200,300) see Strosacker Foundation, Charles J.

City of Niles — roof repair of Chamber of Commerce ($6,000) see Hunter Foundation, Edward and Irma

City Rescue Mission ($6,500) see Wickson-Link Memorial Foundation

City of Saginaw — rent expense ($6,000) see Eddy Family Memorial Fund, C. K.

City of Saginaw — Eddy Band ($69,195) see Eddy Family Memorial Fund, C. K.

City of St. Clair ($5,000) see Moore Foundation, C. F.

City of Saline ($50,000) see R&B Tool Co.

City of Zeeland ($5,000) see Batts Foundation

Civic Auditorium Trustee Corporation — special project ($60,000) see Dalton Foundation, Dorothy U.

CLAL ($37,240) see Borman's

Coalition on Temporary Shelter — Essential Service program ($150,000) see McGregor Fund

Coalition on Temporary Shelters (COTS) ($10,000) see Earl-Beth Foundation

Community Economic Development Corp ($50,000) see Upton Foundation, Frederick S.

Community Economic Development Corporation ($980,000) see Whirlpool Corp.

Community Economic Development Corporation ($107,214) see Whirlpool Corp.

Community Foundation of Greater Flint ($70,000) see Harding Foundation, Charles Stewart

Community Foundation of Greater Flint — to provide ongoing endowment challenge funding ($900,000) see Mott Foundation, Charles Stewart

Community Foundation of Monroe County ($6,000) see McIntyre Foundation, B. D. and Jane E.

Community Foundation of Monroe County see Michigan Gas Utilities

Community Foundation of Monroe County ($2,500) see Monroe Auto Equipment Co.

Community Foundation of Southeast Michigan ($25,000) see Holley Foundation

Community Foundation for Southeast Michigan ($20,000) see Masco Corp.

Community Foundation for Southeast Michigan — Van Dusen Endowment Challenge program for select human service agencies ($500,000) see McGregor Fund

Community Foundation of Southeastern Michigan ($20,000) see Ford Fund, William and Martha

Community Foundation of Southeastern Michigan — to establish endowment program ($3,278,400) see Kresge Foundation

Community Foundation for Southeastern Michigan — neighborhood initiative ($25,000) see Michigan Consolidated Gas Co.

Community Foundation for Southeastern Michigan ($50,000) see NBD Bank

Community Foundation for Southeastern Michigan ($5,000) see Shelden Fund, Elizabeth, Allan and Warren

Community House Association ($30,000) see Americana Foundation

Community House Association ($10,000) see Vollbrecht Foundation, Frederick A.

Community Services of Oakland ($5,000) see Wilson Trust, Lula C.

Concerned Citizens for the Arts in Michigan ($1,500) see Perry Drug Stores

Concerned Citizens for the Arts in Michigan ($1,500) see Perry Drug Stores

Congregation Shaarey Zedek ($8,250) see Shiffman Foundation

Conservancy ($20,000) see Moore Foundation, C. F.

Construction Innovation Forum ($250) see Barton-Malow Co.

Cottage Hospital of Grosse Pointe ($35,000) see Ford Fund, Benson and Edith

Cottage Hospital — obstetrics unit; improvements at Pierson Clinic ($125,000) see McGregor Fund

Council of Michigan Foundation ($780) see McIntyre Foundation, C. S. and Marion F.

Council of Michigan Foundations ($780) see McIntyre Foundation, B. D. and Jane E.

Council of Orthodox Rabbi ($12,745) see Borman's

Cranbrook Academy of Art ($1,200) see Farwell Foundation, Drusilla

Cranbrook Challenge ($50,000) see Masco Corp.

Cranbrook Educational Community ($2,500) see Kowalski Sausage Co.

Cranbrook Educational Community ($25,000) see Wenger Foundation, Henry L. and Consuelo S.

Cranbrook Institute — capital campaign ($20,000) see Consumers Power Co.

Cranbrook Institute of Science ($1,000) see Erb Lumber Co.

Cranbrook Institute of Science ($1,000) see Kowalski Sausage Co.

Created for Caring ($22,500) see Kantzler Foundation

Crooked Tree Arts Council ($100,000) see Offield Family Foundation

Crossroads ($35,000) see Whitney Fund, David M.

DARE ($5,000) see Monroe Auto Equipment Co.

DARE-Monroe County Sheriff's Department ($5,000) see Monroe Auto Equipment Co.

Davenport Schools ($50,000) see Davenport Foundation, M. E.

David Reece Fund ($40,000) see Strosacker Foundation, Charles J.

David Reece Memorial Fund ($40,000) see Gerstacker Foundation, Rollin M.

Dearborn Community Arts Council ($4,888) see Cablevision of Michigan

Dearborn Private Parochial Schools — Binble Quiz Program ($320) see Cablevision of Michigan

Dearborn Public Schools ($21,906) see Cablevision of Michigan

Delano Clinic — program support ($88,000) see Dalton Foundation, Dorothy U.

Delano Clinic — start-up costs ($110,000) see Dalton Foundation, Dorothy U.

DeTour Area Chamber of Commerce ($15,000) see Wenger Foundation, Henry L. and Consuelo S.

DeTour School ($75,000) see Wenger Foundation, Henry L. and Consuelo S.

Detroit Association of Phi Beta Kappa — operating expenses ($25,500) see Wilson Fund, Matilda R.

Detroit College of Law ($15,000) see Federal-Mogul Corp.

Detroit College of Law ($1,000) see Kowalski Sausage Co.

Detroit Country Day School ($5,000) see Barton-Malow Co.

Detroit Country Day School ($20,000) see Honigman Foundation

Detroit Country Day School ($5,000) see Prentis Family Foundation, Meyer and Anna

Detroit Economic Growth ($250) see Federal Screw Works

Detroit Educational Television Foundation ($31,500) see Ford II Fund, Henry

Detroit Educational Television Foundation — Channel 56 ($52,500) see NBD Bank

Detroit Historical Society see Michigan Mutual Insurance Corp.

Detroit Institute of Arts ($1,000) see Erb Lumber Co.

Detroit Institute of Arts ($300) see Federal Screw Works

Detroit Institute of Arts ($12,600) see Fisher Foundation, Max M. and Marjorie S.

Detroit Institute of Arts ($80,000) see Ford Fund, Eleanor and Edsel

Detroit Institute of Arts ($10,000) see Kaufman Memorial Trust, Chaim, Fanny, Louis, Benjamin, and Anne Florence

Detroit Institute of Arts see Kmart Corp.

Detroit Institute of Arts ($75,000) see Masco Corp.

Detroit Institute of the Arts see Michigan Mutual Insurance Corp.

Detroit Institute of Arts ($1,000) see Scherer Foundation, Karla

Detroit Institute of Arts ($4,230) see Shapero Foundation, Nate S. and Ruth B.

Detroit Institute of Arts — operating support for Founders Society ($25,000) see American Natural Resources Co.

Detroit Institute of Arts-Founders Society ($100,000) see Ford II Fund, Henry

Detroit Institute of Arts Founders Society ($29,000) see Handleman Co.

Detroit Institute of Arts-Founders Society ($112,000) see Manoogian Foundation, Alex and Marie

Detroit Institute of Arts — Founders Society; operational support ($100,000) see McGregor Fund

Detroit Institute of Arts-Founders Society — Second Century Campaign ($30,000) see American Natural Resources Co.

Detroit Institute for Children ($400) see Federal Screw Works

Detroit Institute for Children ($9,000) see Ford Fund, Walter and Josephine

Detroit Institute for Children ($50,000) see Ford II Fund, Henry

Detroit Province of the Society of Jesus ($1,000,000) see O'Neill Charitable Corporation, F. J.

Detroit Public Library — capital ($56,371) see Wilson Fund, Matilda R.

Detroit Renaissance Foundation ($36,000) see Domino's Pizza

Detroit Renaissance Foundation ($12,000) see Federal-Mogul Corp.

Detroit Renaissance Foundation ($12,000) see Federal-Mogul Corp.

Detroit Renaissance Foundation ($12,000) see Federal-Mogul Corp.

Detroit Renaissance Foundation ($500) see Federal Screw Works

Detroit Renaissance Foundation ($150,000) see NBD Bank

Detroit Renaissance Foundation — Detroit Strategic Plan support ($60,000) see American Natural Resources Co.

Detroit Renaissance Foundation — Detroit Strategic Plan

Detroit Institute of Arts ($1,000) see Erb Lumber Co.

($60,000) see Michigan Consolidated Gas Co.

Detroit Rescue Mission — renovation of Genesis II women's shelter ($100,000) see McGregor Fund

Detroit Science Center ($1,000) see Kowalski Sausage Co.

Detroit Symphony Orchestra — special grants program ($60,000) see American Natural Resources Co.

Detroit Symphony Orchestra — operating support ($35,000) see American Natural Resources Co.

Detroit Symphony Orchestra ($2,350) see Farwell Foundation, Drusilla

Detroit Symphony Orchestra ($85,000) see Handleman Co.

Detroit Symphony Orchestra ($250) see Kasle Steel Corp.

Detroit Symphony Orchestra see Michigan Mutual Insurance Corp.

Detroit Symphony Orchestra ($70,000) see NBD Bank

Detroit Symphony Orchestra ($12,000) see Perry Drug Stores

Detroit Symphony Orchestra ($4,000) see Perry Drug Stores

Detroit Symphony Orchestra ($1,500) see Rohlik Foundation, Sigmund and Sophie

Detroit Symphony Orchestra ($1,000) see Scherer Foundation, Karla

Detroit Symphony Orchestra ($23,000) see Shapero Foundation, Nate S. and Ruth B.

Detroit Symphony Orchestra ($15,000) see Shelden Fund, Elizabeth, Allan and Warren

Detroit Symphony Orchestra ($2,000) see Vlasic Foundation

Detroit Symphony Orchestra ($100) see Volkswagen of America, Inc.

Detroit Symphony Orchestra ($66,000) see Whitney Fund, David M.

Detroit Symphony Orchestra Hall ($200,000) see Chrysler Corp.

Detroit Symphony Orchestra Hall ($200,000) see Chrysler Corp.

Detroit Symphony Orchestra Hall ($50,000) see Detroit Edison Co.

Detroit Symphony Orchestra Hall ($35,000) see Detroit Edison Co.

Detroit Symphony Orchestra Hall ($15,000) see Federal-Mogul Corp.

Detroit Symphony Orchestra Hall — operational support ($150,000) see McGregor Fund

Detroit Symphony Orchestra Hall — general ($20,000) see Michigan Consolidated Gas Co.

Detroit Symphony Orchestra Hall — extraordinary operating support ($300,000) see Skillman Foundation

Detroit Temple of International Society for Krishna ($1,250) see India Foundation

Detroit Zoological Society ($10,000) see Borman's

Detroit Zoological Society ($1,000) see Ewald Foundation, H. T.

Detroit Zoological Society ($20,000) see Ford Fund, Benson and Edith

Michigan (cont.)

Guest House ($10,000) see Driehaus Foundation, Richard H.

Guest House ($400) see Robertson Brothers

Guest House ($6,000) see Sehn Foundation

Guest House ($3,000) see Zimmerman Foundation, Mary and George Herbert

Guiding Light Mission ($10,000) see Sebastian Foundation

Gull Lake Bible and Missionary Conference ($75,000) see Miller Charitable Foundation, C. John and Reva

Habitat for Humanity ($30,000) see Boutell Memorial Fund, Arnold and Gertrude

Hamilton Family Health Center ($16,000) see Bray Charitable Trust, Viola E.

Happendance ($5,000) see Thoman Foundation, W. B. and Candace

Harper-Grace Hospitals ($5,000) see Barton-Malow Co.

Harper-Grace Hospitals ($40,000) see Hess Charitable Trust, Myrtle E. and William C.

Harper-Grace Hospitals — Cardiology program ($250,000) see Hudson-Webber Foundation

Harper Hospital ($25,000) see Kellogg's

Hart County Historical Society ($3,000) see Monroe Auto Equipment Co.

Heat and Warmth Fund also known as Thaw Fund — emergency heating assistance for low-income households ($200,000) see Skillman Foundation

Henry Ford Community College ($500) see Cablevision of Michigan

Henry Ford Community College ($50,000) see Ford II Fund, Henry

Henry Ford Health System ($10,000) see Vlasic Foundation

Henry Ford Health System — construction of Critical Care Pavilion ($100,000) see McGregor Fund

Henry Ford Health Systems ($2,250) see Awrey Bakeries

Henry Ford Heart and Vascular ($25,000) see Masco Corp.

Henry Ford Hospital ($26,500) see Firestone, Jr. Foundation, Harvey

Henry Ford Hospital ($100,000) see Ford Fund, Benson and Edith

Henry Ford Hospital ($59,500) see Ford Fund, Walter and Josephine

Henry Ford Hospital ($225,500) see Ford Fund, William and Martha

Henry Ford Hospital ($100,000) see Ford II Fund, Henry

Henry Ford Hospital ($65,000) see Holden Fund, James and Lynelle

Henry Ford Hospital ($35,000) see Holden Fund, James and Lynelle

Henry Ford Hospital — community cholesterol program at Heart and Vascular Institute ($5,000) see Shelden Fund, Elizabeth, Allan and Warren

Henry Ford Museum ($11,000) see Levy Foundation, Edward C.

Henry Ford Museum and Greenfield Village ($5,000) see Bauervic Foundation, Charles M.

Henry Ford Museum and Greenfield Village see Loomis-Sayles & Co.

Henry Ford Museum and Greenfield Village see Thor Industries, Inc.

Herrick Memorial Health Care Center ($500,000) see Herrick Foundation

Herrick Memorial Hospital — new office building ($1,300,000) see Herrick Foundation

High/Scope Educational Research Foundation ($25,000) see Nordson Corp.

High Scope Educational Research Foundation — operating expenses ($40,000) see Wilson Fund, Matilda R.

Highfields — new building ($10,000) see Ransom Fidelity Company

Hillel Day School ($15,000) see Rohlik Foundation, Sigmund and Sophie

Hillsdale college — ultracentrifuge ($10,000) see Ransom Fidelity Company

Hillsdale College — unrestricted ($40,000) see Ball Foundation, George and Frances

Hillsdale College ($12,500) see Bargman Foundation, Theodore and Mina

Hillsdale College ($25,000) see Bauervic Foundation, Charles M.

Hillsdale College ($10,000) see Beal Foundation

Hillsdale College ($5,000) see Boler Co.

Hillsdale College ($5,000) see Curran Foundation

Hillsdale College ($50,000) see Ellwood Foundation

Hillsdale College ($1,000) see Gaisman Foundation, Catherine and Henry J.

Hillsdale College ($20,000) see Generation Trust

Hillsdale College ($2,500) see Henry Foundation, Patrick

Hillsdale College ($25,000) see Holden Fund, James and Lynelle

Hillsdale College ($1,500) see Ingersoll Milling Machine Co.

Hillsdale College ($26,000) see McIntyre Foundation, B. D. and Jane E.

Hillsdale College — scholarship fund ($50,000) see Nason Foundation

Hillsdale College ($100,000) see Philips Foundation, Jesse

Hillsdale College ($15,000) see Phillipps Foundation

Hillsdale College — create college chair in traditional values ($150,000) see Salvatori Foundation, Henry

Hillsdale College — health education and sports complex ($25,000) see Simpson Industries

Hillsdale College ($225,000) see Stranahan Foundation

Hillsdale College ($20,000) see Swim Foundation, Arthur L.

Hillsdale College ($6,000) see Triford Foundation

Hillsdale College ($5,600) see Triford Foundation

Hillsdale College ($5,000) see V and V Foundation

Hillsdale College — operating expenses ($60,000) see Wilson Fund, Matilda R.

Hillsdale College ($10,000) see Winchester Foundation

Hillsdale College ($5,000) see Wurlitzer Foundation, Farny R.

Hillsdale College ($1,000) see Youth Foundation

Hillsdale College — support the Center for Constructive Alternatives ($105,000) see Coors Foundation, Adolph

Hillsdale College — to the GAR Scholarship Fund ($150,000) see GAR Foundation

Hillsdale College — to defray construction costs of the Sage Center for Cultural and Performing Arts ($450,000) see Sage Foundation

Hillsdale College — construction costs of the Sage Center for Cultural and Performing Arts ($100,000) see Sage Foundation

Hillsdale County Community Foundation ($145,550) see Simpson Foundation

Hindu Temple ($6,000) see India Foundation

Historical Society Mason County ($2,500) see Great Lakes Casting Corp.

Holland Area Arts Council ($2,500) see Padnos Iron & Metal Co., Louis

Holland Area Arts Council ($75,000) see Prince Manufacturing, Inc.

Holland Christian ($56,000) see Prince Corp.

Holland Christian ($100,700) see Prince Manufacturing, Inc.

Holland Community Foundation ($100,000) see Prince Manufacturing, Inc.

Holland Home ($400,000) see DeVos Foundation, Richard and Helen

Holocaust Memorial Center ($1,100) see Honigman Foundation

Home Health ($6,900) see Kysor Industrial Corp.

Home Health Education Service ($480) see Fibre Converters

Home Non-Profit Housing Corporation ($1,000) see McIntyre Foundation, B. D. and Jane E.

Homeopathic Pharmocopoea Convention of United States ($6,500) see Bauervic Foundation, Charles M.

Honey Creek Christian Homes ($10,000) see Cook Charitable Foundation

Hope College ($5,000) see Batts Foundation

Hope College ($150,000) see Cook Charitable Foundation

Hope College — kinetics data acquisition and analysis system for the undergraduate physical chemistry laboratory ($20,000) see Dreyfus Foundation, Camille and Henry

Hope College ($200,000) see Prince Manufacturing, Inc.

Hospice of Greater Grand Rapids ($7,600) see Keeler Fund, Miner S. and Mary Ann

Hospice of Michigan ($5,050) see Ransom Fidelity Company

Hospice of Naples ($10,000) see Moore Foundation, C. F.

Hot Line to God — human services ($15,000) see La-Z-Boy Chair Co.

Hoyt Public Library ($15,000) see Eddy Family Memorial Fund, C. K.

Hunger Action Coalition — emergency assistance for food providers ($300,000) see Skillman Foundation

Hutzel Hospital — Kresge Eye Institute ($150,000) see Hudson-Webber Foundation

Hutzel Hospital/Kresge Eye Institute ($10,000) see Taubman Foundation, A. Alfred

Hydra ($5,000) see Monroe Auto Equipment Co.

Impressions 5 Museum ($5,000) see Dart Foundation

Industrial Technology Institute ($2,200,000) see Kellogg Foundation, W. K.

Industrial Technology Institute (ITI) — science and technology center dedicated to research and development of flexible factory automation processes and activities in support of manufacturing improvement ($1,428,000) see Dow Foundation, Herbert H. and Grace A.

Ingham County Humane Society ($12,628) see Greater Lansing Foundation

Ingham Intermediate School District ($35,000) see Dart Foundation

Ingham Intermediate School District ($45,000) see Thoman Foundation, W. B. and Candace

Inner City Christian Federation ($10,000) see Sebastian Foundation

INSIGHT ($30,000) see Bishop Charitable Trust, A. G.

Insight ($5,000) see Bray Charitable Trust, Viola E.

Insight Recovery Center ($9,800) see Wilson Trust, Lula C.

Institute in Basic Life Principles ($20,000) see Bauervic Foundation, Charles M.

Interlochen Arts Academy ($5,000) see Wurlitzer Foundation, Farny R.

Interlochen Center for the Arts ($27,500) see DeRoy Testamentary Foundation

Interlochen Center for the Arts ($2,500) see Dexter Industries

Interlochen Center for the Arts ($100,000) see Dow Foundation, Herbert H. and Barbara C.

Interlochen Center for the Arts ($140,240) see Emerson Electric Co.

Interlochen Center for the Arts ($35,000) see Greater Lansing Foundation

Interlochen Center for the Arts ($5,000) see Kysor Industrial Corp.

Interlochen Center for the Arts ($5,000) see Kysor Industrial Corp.

Interlochen Center for the Arts ($10,000) see Monticello College Foundation

Interlochen Center for the Arts ($1,000) see Scherer Foundation, Karla

Interlochen Center for the Arts ($1,000) see Simpson Industries

Interlochen Center for the Arts ($60,000) see Upton Foundation, Frederick S.

Interlochen Center for the Arts — capital ($62,500) see Wilson Fund, Matilda R.

International Aid ($25,000) see Young Foundation, Irvin L.

International Foundation for Homeopathy ($2,500) see Bauervic Foundation, Charles M.

International Service Society ($2,500) see India Foundation

International Youth Foundation ($3,197,246) see Kellogg Foundation, W. K.

Irish Hills Girl Scout ($12,500) see Hurst Foundation

Itasca Heart Project ($47,031) see Blue Cross and Blue Shield of Minnesota Foundation Inc.

Jackson Community College ($2,000) see Eagle-Picher Industries

Jackson Community College — tech training equipment ($10,000) see Simpson Industries

Jackson Community Foundation — program support ($30,000) see Consumers Power Co.

Jackson Community Foundation ($80,000) see Hurst Foundation

Jackson Community Foundation ($26,317) see Hurst Foundation

Jackson County ($15,000) see Hurst Foundation

Jackson Little League ($250) see Alro Steel Corp.

Jain Society of Greater Detroit ($7,602) see India Foundation

James E. Wickson Memorial Library ($7,000) see Wickson-Link Memorial Foundation

Japhet School ($25,000) see Chamberlin Foundation, Gerald W.

Japhet School ($5,000) see Harding Foundation, Charles Stewart

JARC ($10,000) see Borman's

Jewish Community Center ($90,804) see Gershenson Foundation, Charles H.

Jewish Community Center for Metropolitan Detroit ($50,000) see DeRoy Testamentary Foundation

Jewish Community Fund ($60,000) see Padnos Iron & Metal Co., Louis

Jewish Home for the Aging ($20,000) see Mitchell Family Foundation, Edward D. and Anna

Jewish National Fund ($2,500) see Honigman Foundation

Jewish National Fund ($45,000) see Imerman Memorial Foundation, Stanley

Jewish National Fund ($2,000) see Perry Drug Stores

Jewish Policy Center ($15,000) see Borman's

Jewish Welfare Federation ($180,000) see Handleman Co.

Jewish Welfare Foundation ($35,000) see Fisher Foundation, Max M. and Marjorie S.

Jewish Welfare Organization of Detroit ($1,020,000) see Taubman Foundation, A. Alfred

John F. Kennedy Library Corps ($1,000) see Meek Foundation

John George Home ($7,500) see Hurst Foundation

John George Home ($2,000) see Weatherwax Foundation

Joy of Jesus ($74,500) see Timmis Foundation, Michael & Nancy

Junior Achievement ($1,000) see Abrams Foundation, Talbert and Leota

Junior Achievement see Michigan Mutual Insurance Corp.

Junior Achievement ($2,750) see Monroe Auto Equipment Co.

Junior Achievement ($5,000) see SPX Corp.

Junior Achievement of SE Michigan ($4,000) see Tomkins Industries, Inc.

Junior League of Saginaw Festival of Trees ($2,000) see Bierlein Family Foundation

Juvenile Diabetes Foundation ($1,000) see Awrey Bakeries

Juvenile Diabetes Foundation ($2,500) see Kaufman Memorial Trust, Chaim, Fanny, Louis, Benjamin, and Anne Florence

Kahil Gibran Centennial ($2,500) see Simone Foundation

Kal-Haven Trail ($1,000) see Fabri-Kal Corp.

Kalamazoo Alcohol and Drug Abuse ($30,000) see Upjohn Foundation, Harold and Grace

Kalamazoo Center for Independent Living see First of America Bank Corp.

Kalamazoo Child Guidance Clinic— capital campaign ($75,000) see Dalton Foundation, Dorothy U.

Kalamazoo Christian Schools ($5,000) see Monroe-Brown Foundation

Kalamazoo College ($13,000) see Monroe-Brown Foundation

Kalamazoo College ($60,500) see Strosacker Foundation, Charles J.

Kalamazoo College ($4,000) see Vicksburg Foundation

Kalamazoo College — building of the Dow Science Center ($1,000,000) see Dow Foundation, Herbert H. and Grace A.

Kalamazoo College — heavy-atom effect on reactions of imidogen with small hydrocarbons in cryogenic rare gas matrices ($33,500) see Research Corporation

Kalamazoo Consultation Center ($2,000) see Todd Co., A.M.

Kalamazoo Consultation Center ($27,500) see Upjohn Co.

Kalamazoo Foundation ($5,000) see Todd Co., A.M.

Kalamazoo Foundation ($25,000) see Upjohn Foundation, Harold and Grace

Kalamazoo Foundation ($5,000) see Vicksburg Foundation

Kalamazoo Foundation-Arcadia Creek Project ($50,000) see Upjohn Foundation, Harold and Grace

Kalamazoo Foundation Excellence in Education Program ($50,000) see Monroe-Brown Foundation

Kalamazoo Foundation Public Education Fund ($155,383) see Monroe-Brown Foundation

Kalamazoo Institute of Arts ($30,000) see Upjohn Co.

Kalamazoo Jr. Girls Organization ($2,000) see Monroe-Brown Foundation

Kalamazoo Natural Center ($10,000) see Americana Foundation

Kalamazoo Neighborhood Housing Service ($1,000) see Fabri-Kal Corp.

Kalamazoo New Museum see First of America Bank Corp.

Kalamazoo Public Schools ($30,000) see Upjohn Foundation, Harold and Grace

Kalamazoo Public Schools ($30,000) see Upjohn Foundation, Harold and Grace

Kalamazoo Science Foundation ($1,000) see Meek Foundation

Kalamazoo Symphony ($25,000) see Upjohn Co.

Kalamazoo Valley Community College — new museum ($200,000) see Dalton Foundation, Dorothy U.

Kalamazoo Valley Community College ($50,000) see Upjohn Foundation, Harold and Grace

Kalamazoo Valley Community College — Foundation for the New Museum ($2,750,000) see Gilmore Foundation, Irving S.

Kellogg Community College ($2,495,000) see Kellogg Foundation, W. K.

Kellogg Community College ($10,000) see Miller Foundation

Kendall College of Art and Design ($2,000) see Dexter Industries

Kensington Academy — new computers for the lower school ($25,000) see Bauervic-Paisley Foundation

Kent Intermediate School District — start up funding for Instructional Delivery System ($125,000) see Steelcase

Kershaw City Fine Arts Center ($39,000) see Upton Foundation, Frederick S.

Kiwanis ($1,045) see Cablevision of Michigan

Klavon Kids ($750) see Alro Steel Corp.

Klavon Memorial Trust ($500) see Alro Steel Corp.

Kresge Eye Institute ($10,000) see May Mitchell Royal Foundation

Kresge Eye Institute, Wayne State University — goodwill ($10,000) see Alcon Laboratories, Inc.

KVCC Foundation ($422,500) see Upjohn Co.

LaGrave Avenue Christian Reformed Church ($163,000) see DeVos Foundation, Richard and Helen

Lake Michigan College ($250,000) see Mendel Foundation

Lake Michigan College Educational Foundation ($50,000) see Upton Foundation, Frederick S.

Lake Michigan College, Mendel Center ($10,000) see Tiscornia Foundation

Lake Shore Public Schools — technical and career education academy program ($369,000) see Skillman Foundation

Lake Vacation Camp ($1,000) see Meek Foundation

Lansing Community College Architectural Studies ($1,500) see Abrams Foundation, Talbert and Leota

Lawrence Technological University ($12,000) see Bauervic Foundation, Charles M.

LCC Foundation — scholarships ($11,850) see Greater Lansing Foundation

Leader Dogs for the Blind ($1,500) see Honigman Foundation

Leader Dogs for the Blind ($6,500) see May Mitchell Royal Foundation

Leader Dogs for the Blind ($20,000) see Westerman Foundation, Samuel L.

Leelanau Center for Education ($1,500) see Weatherwax Foundation

Leelanau Conservancy ($6,000) see Harper Foundation, Philip S.

Legatus ($300,002) see Domino's Pizza

Leila Arboretum Society ($25,000) see Miller Foundation

Leukemia Society of America ($100) see Robertson Brothers

Library of Michigan see First of America Bank Corp.

Library of Michigan Foundation ($15,000) see Abrams Foundation, Talbert and Leota

Life Action Ministries ($117,110) see DeMoss Foundation, Arthur S.

Life Worker Project ($20,000) see Deseranno Educational Foundation

LISC-Kalamazoo ($100,000) see Upjohn Co.

Little Sisters of Poor ($2,250) see Zimmerman Foundation, Mary and George Herbert

Little Traverse Conservancy — for acquisition of property ($25,000) see H.C.S. Foundation

Little Traverse Conservancy ($100,000) see Offield Family Foundation

Livonia Heart Fund ($1,500) see Awrey Bakeries

Livonia Symphony Orchestra ($1,000) see Awrey Bakeries

Lourdes ($25,000) see Hess Charitable Trust, Myrtle E. and William C.

Ludington Area Foundation ($4,697) see Great Lakes Casting Corp.

Lukes Episcopal Church ($1,000) see Meek Foundation

Lumen Christi High School ($2,000) see Weatherwax Foundation

Lumen Christi School ($30,000) see Hurst Foundation

Lutheran High School Association ($170,800) see Burchfield Foundation, Charles E.

Lutheran High School Association ($2,000) see Chamberlin Foundation, Gerald W.

Lutheran Homes of Michigan ($7,000) see McIntyre Foundation, C. S. and Marion F.

M.L. Prentis Comprehensive Cancer Center of Metropolitan Detroit ($50,000) see Prentis Family Foundation, Meyer and Anna

Madonna College ($72,000) see Deseranno Educational Foundation

Madonna College — for a joint faculty development project ($16,000) see Matsushita Electric Corp. of America

Make-A-Wish Foundation ($4,000) see Honigman Foundation

Managers of the Roman Catholic Orphan's Asylums —

operating ($3,500) see Walsh Charity Trust, Blanche M.

Manistee County Youth Center see Packaging Corporation of America

Manor House Foundation ($400) see Eagle-Picher Industries

March of Dimes ($1,500) see Sehn Foundation

Mariner's Inn ($5,000) see Kaufman Memorial Trust, Chaim, Fanny, Louis, Benjamin, and Anne Florence

Marquette Area Public Schools — computer program ($50,000) see Kaufman Endowment Fund, Louis G.

Marquette Area Public Schools — senior high school awards ($34,000) see Kaufman Endowment Fund, Louis G.

Marquette Area Public Schools — planetarium project ($8,175) see Kaufman Endowment Fund, Louis G.

Marquette Area Public Schools — middle school awards ($7,000) see Kaufman Endowment Fund, Louis G.

Marquette Area Public Schools — middle school incentive program ($2,000) see Kaufman Endowment Fund, Louis G.

Marquette County Historical Society — developing kits ($1,000) see Kaufman Endowment Fund, Louis G.

Mary Free Bed Hospital and Rehabilitation Center ($20,000) see Keeler Fund, Miner S. and Mary Ann

Mary Free Bed Hospital and Rehabilitation Center — funding to create Biomotion Analysis Laboratory to aid persons with impaired mobility ($100,000) see Steelcase

Marygrove College ($100) see Ameribank

Marygrove College ($40,000) see Detroit Edison Co.

MCHS Infant Mortality Project ($10,000) see DeRoy Foundation, Helen L.

Meadow Montessori School ($20,000) see McIntyre Foundation, C. S. and Marion F.

Meals on Wheels — meals for homebound ($1,800) see Hunter Foundation, Edward and Irma

Mental Health Association ($5,000) see Whiting Memorial Foundation, Henry and Harriet

Mental Health Association ($5,000) see Whiting Memorial Foundation, Henry and Harriet

Mercy College ($10,000) see Borman's

Mercy College of Detroit ($10,000) see Hess Charitable Trust, Myrtle E. and William C.

Mercy College of Detroit — to defray expenses in connection with the renovation of the Student/Conference Center ($100,000) see Sage Foundation

Mercy Memorial Health Foundation ($25,000) see Tiscornia Foundation

Mercy Memorial Hospital Foundation — health ($35,000) see La-Z-Boy Chair Co.

Mercy Memorial Hospital Foundation ($5,000) see McIntyre Foundation, B. D. and Jane E.

Mercy Memorial Hospital Foundation ($5,000) see Monroe Auto Equipment Co.

Mercy Respite Center ($1,500) see Grand Rapids Label Co.

Mercy Respite Center ($7,000) see Keeler Fund, Miner S. and Mary Ann

Metropolitan Center for High Technology — general ($15,000) see Michigan Consolidated Gas Co.

Michigan Art Train ($500) see Awrey Bakeries

Michigan Association of Children's Alliances ($600) see Dart Foundation

Michigan Cancer Foundation ($400) see Alro Steel Corp.

Michigan Cancer Foundation ($2,000) see Awrey Bakeries

Michigan Cancer Foundation ($5,025) see Honigman Foundation

Michigan Cancer Foundation ($1,000) see Kasle Steel Corp.

Michigan Cancer Foundation ($20,000) see Levy Foundation, Edward C.

Michigan Cancer Foundation — for the study of an immortal line of normal, human breast epithelial cells ($104,292) see Pardee Foundation, Elsa U.

Michigan Christian Homes ($50,000) see Miller Charitable Foundation, C. John and Reva

Michigan Colleges Foundation ($25,000) see DeVlieg Foundation, Charles

Michigan Colleges Foundation ($1,000) see Federal Screw Works

Michigan Colleges Foundation ($20,000) see Loutit Foundation

Michigan Colleges Foundation ($6,000) see Tiscornia Foundation

Michigan Colleges Foundation ($50,000) see Upjohn Co.

Michigan Council of Foundations ($250) see Bentley Foundation, Alvin M.

Michigan Dyslexia Initiative ($50,000) see Abrams Foundation, Talbert and Leota

Michigan Dyslexia Institute ($40,000) see Thoman Foundation, W. B. and Candace

Michigan Environmental Council ($11,000) see Harder Foundation

Michigan Eye Bank ($10,000) see Westerman Foundation, Samuel L.

Michigan Family Forum ($53,000) see Prince Corp.

Michigan Family Forum ($75,000) see Prince Manufacturing, Inc.

Michigan 4-H Foundation ($350,000) see Americana Foundation

Michigan 4-H Foundation ($43,000) see Americana Foundation

Michigan 4-H Fund ($500) see McIntyre Foundation, C. S. and Marion F.

Michigan Harvest Gathering Food Bank ($5,000) see Levy Foundation, Edward C.

Michigan Health Care Education and Research Foundation — health insurance program for uninsured Michigan children

Michigan (cont.)

($250,000) see Skillman Foundation

Michigan Humane Society ($25,000) see Ford Fund, Benson and Edith

Michigan Jewish Sports Hall of Fame ($1,000) see Ewald Foundation, H. T.

Michigan Jewish Sports Hall of Fame ($10,000) see Maas Foundation, Benard L.

Michigan Maritime Museum — capital campaign ($15,000) see Consumers Power Co.

Michigan Metro Girl Scouts ($6,500) see Scherer Foundation, Karla

Michigan Molecular Institute ($100,000) see Dow Corning Corp.

Michigan Molecular Institute (MMI) — operating and capital expenses ($600,000) see Dow Foundation, Herbert H. and Grace A.

Michigan New Detroit Fund Pledge ($18,000) see Federal-Mogul Corp.

Michigan Opera Theatre ($500) see Barton-Malow Co.

Michigan Opera Theatre ($5,000) see Prentis Family Foundation, Meyer and Anna

Michigan Opera Theatre ($14,100) see Westerman Foundation, Samuel L.

Michigan Opera Theatre ($10,000) see Whitney Fund, David M.

Michigan Parkinson Foundation ($1,000) see Awrey Bakeries

Michigan Parkinson Foundation ($12,353) see Borman's

Michigan Partnership for New Education see Scott Paper Co.

Michigan SHE ($10,000) see Kysor Industrial Corp.

Michigan State Chamber Foundation ($500) see Barton-Malow Co.

Michigan State University ($5,000) see Abrams Foundation, Talbert and Leota

Michigan State University ($1,000) see Americana Foundation

Michigan State University ($400,000) see Chrysler Corp.

Michigan State University ($20,000) see DeVlieg Foundation, Charles

Michigan State University ($150,000) see Dow Chemical Co.

Michigan State University ($50,000) see Dow Corning Corp.

Michigan State University ($312,500) see Ford Motor Co.

Michigan State University ($312,500) see Ford Motor Co.

Michigan State University — capital campaign ($500,000) see General Motors Corp.

Michigan State University ($100,000) see Gerber Products Co.

Michigan State University ($100,000) see Gerstacker Foundation, Rollin M.

Michigan State University ($8,000) see Gloeckner Foundation, Fred

Michigan State University ($1,569,783) see Kellogg Foundation, W. K.

Michigan State University ($32,000) see Poinsettia

Foundation, Paul and Magdalena Ecke

Michigan State University ($4,000) see Quaker Chemical Corp.

Michigan State University — practices of teaching and learning authentic mathematics for understanding in school ($345,000) see Spencer Foundation

Michigan State University — Alumni Distinguished Scholarships ($10,000) see Baldwin Foundation

Michigan State University — Capital Fund Drive ($20,000) see Baldwin Foundation

Michigan State University — (College of Natural Sciences-Center for Science and Mathematics Teachers) ($100,000) see Towsley Foundation, Harry A. and Margaret D.

Michigan State University — to fund science courses/workshops for elementary teachers in Michigan ($66,700) see Toyota Motor Sales, U.S.A.

Michigan State University — to endow a Knight Chair in Journalism ($1,000,000) see Knight Foundation, John S. and James L.

Michigan State University Mildred Erickson Fellowship — reactivate students ($5,000) see Ransom Fidelity Company

Michigan State University Scholarship ($950) see Robertson Brothers

Michigan Tech/Century II Campaign ($20,000) see Cleveland-Cliffs

Michigan Tech Fund ($1,500) see Abrams Foundation, Talbert and Leota

Michigan Tech Fund ($13,000) see Brunswick Corp.

Michigan Tech Fund ($50,000) see Dow Corning Corp.

Michigan Tech Fund — metallurgical engineering program ($12,500) see Ladish Co.

Michigan Technological University ($3,845) see Caestecker Foundation, Charles and Marie

Michigan Technological University ($15,000) see DeVlieg Foundation, Charles

Michigan Technological University ($3,950) see Harris Foundation, H. H.

Michigan Technological University ($4,000) see Van Evera Foundation, Dewitt Caroline

Michigan Technological University ($25,000) see Walker Foundation, L. C. and Margaret

Michigan Thanksgiving Day Parade Foundation ($1,000) see Perry Drug Stores

Michigan Thanksgiving Day Parade Foundation ($2,150) see Shapero Foundation, Nate S. and Ruth B.

Michigan Thanksgiving Foundation ($250) see Federal Screw Works

Michigan Thanksgiving Parade Foundation — general ($25,000) see Michigan Consolidated Gas Co.

Michigan Visiting Nurse Service for Christian Scientists

($5,000) see Harding Foundation, Charles Stewart

Michigan Youth in Government ($2,500) see Dow Fund, Alden and Vada

Mid Michigan Alliance — to assist in the control and cure of cancer through the program of the Cancer Treatment Committee of Clare, Gladwin, and Bay County ($355,000) see Pardee Foundation, Elsa U.

Mid Michigan Regional Medical Center ($5,000) see May Mitchell Royal Foundation

Midland Center for the Arts ($2,000) see Bierlein Family Foundation

Midland Center for the Arts — "Friends of Center" Annual Fund Drive ($5,000) see Dow Foundation, Herbert H. and Barbara C.

Midland Center for the Arts — on-going general support ($1,568,000) see Dow Foundation, Herbert H. and Grace A.

Midland Community Center ($150,000) see Dow Corning Corp.

Midland Community Center ($4,400) see Dow Fund, Alden and Vada

Midland Community Center ($232,000) see Gerstacker Foundation, Rollin M.

Midland Community Center ($100,000) see Strosacker Foundation, Charles J.

Midland County Child Protection Council ($2,500) see Dow Fund, Alden and Vada

Midland County Probate Court ($15,000) see Dow Foundation, Herbert H. and Barbara C.

Midland Explorers Boosters — fastpitch program ($5,000) see Dow Foundation, Herbert H. and Barbara C.

Midland Foundation ($1,241,000) see Gerstacker Foundation, Rollin M.

Midland Foundation ($31,200) see Strosacker Foundation, Charles J.

Midland Foundation — a Kellogg challenge grant will expose young people to an experience in philanthropy and volunteerism ($300,000) see Dow Foundation, Herbert H. and Grace A.

Midland Foundation — Washington Woods III Project ($16,500) see Barstow Foundation

Midland Public Schools — grant for a Science Resources Center for elementary school students can have an exciting hands-on learning experience with scientific concepts and materials ($300,000) see Dow Foundation, Herbert H. and Grace A.

MidMichigan Regional Medical Center — to build the hospital's Neuroscience Institute which serves citizens who have medical problems related to the nervous system ($1,500,000) see Dow Foundation, Herbert H. and Grace A.

Mission Chapels Foundation — religious ($75,000) see Domino's Pizza

Model High School ($250,000) see RJR Nabisco Inc.

Monastery of the Blessed Sacrament ($20,000) see Hess

Charitable Trust, Myrtle E. and William C.

Monroe County Challenge Cup see Michigan Gas Utilities

Monroe County Chamber of Commerce see Michigan Gas Utilities

Monroe County Ducks Unlimited see Michigan Gas Utilities

Monroe County Historical Society ($5,000) see McIntyre Foundation, B. D. and Jane E.

Monroe County Industrial Development Corporation see Michigan Gas Utilities

Monroe Family YMCA — human services ($30,000) see La-Z-Boy Chair Co.

Monroe Public Schools — education ($35,000) see La-Z-Boy Chair Co.

Mott Community College ($10,000) see Bray Charitable Trust, Viola E.

Municipal Construction Task Force ($20,000) see Loutit Foundation

Munson Medical Center ($110,892) see Keeney Trust, Hattie Hannah

Music Hall Center for the Performing Arts — building restoration ($150,000) see Hudson-Webber Foundation

Muskegon County Catholic ($8,333) see SPX Corp.

Muskegon County Community Foundation ($10,000) see Brunswick Corp.

National Bio Diversity Institute ($5,000) see Wege Foundation

National Board for Professional Teaching Standards — support ($1,000,000) see Carnegie Corporation of New York

National Center for Community Education — to plan, coordinate and conduct a comprehensive national community education leadership training program ($600,000) see Mott Foundation, Charles Stewart

National Center for Effective Schools Research and Development ($354,475) see Olin Foundation, Spencer T. and Ann W.

National Center for Homeopathy ($10,000) see Bauervic Foundation, Charles M.

National Conference of Christians and Jews ($2,000) see Perry Drug Stores

National Conference of Christians and Jews ($3,800) see Prentis Family Foundation, Meyer and Anna

National Council on Alcoholism ($14,900) see Greater Lansing Foundation

National Council of Jewish Women ($12,245) see DeRoy Foundation, Helen L.

Nature Conservancy ($500) see Lizzadro Family Foundation, Joseph

Nature Way Association ($13,700) see Greater Lansing Foundation

Nature Way Association ($14,400) see Ransom Fidelity Company

Navy League of the United States, Oakland County ($26,250) see Slaughter, Jr. Foundation, William E.

Nazareth College ($60,000) see Deseranno Educational Foundation

Neighborhood Club ($1,000) see Chamberlin Foundation, Gerald W.

Neutrophic Research Fund ($191,300) see Tauber Foundation

New College Foundation ($500) see Kasle Steel Corp.

New Detroit — general ($55,000) see Michigan Consolidated Gas Co.

New Detroit Fund — unrestricted operating grant ($333,000) see General Motors Corp.

New Horizons of Oakland County ($10,000) see Wilson Trust, Lula C.

New Paths ($35,000) see Whiting Foundation

New Perspective Center ($20,000) see Boutell Memorial Fund, Arnold and Gertrude

New Vic Supper Theatre ($10,000) see Harding Foundation, Charles Stewart

Newaygo County Area Vocational Center ($110,000) see Gerber Products Co.

Niles Community Schools — Washington, D.C. student trip ($3,512) see Hunter Foundation, Edward and Irma

Niles Y Family Center ($5,000) see Plym Foundation

North Michigan Hospital Foundation ($37,000) see Wenger Foundation, Henry L. and Consuelo S.

North Oakland SCAMP Funding Corporation ($3,000) see Vollbrecht Foundation, Frederick A.

North Ohio Conference Church of the United Brethren Church ($922,676) see Merillat Foundation, Orville D. and Ruth A.

North Ohio Conference Church of the United Brethren Church ($125,000) see Merillat Foundation, Orville D. and Ruth A.

Northeast Michigan Community Foundation ($200,000) see Besser Foundation

Northern High School ($2,475) see Vlasic Foundation

Northern Michigan Hospital Foundation ($5,000) see Batts Foundation

Northern Michigan Hospital Foundation ($6,000) see Triford Foundation

Northwestern Michigan College ($20,421) see Oleson Foundation

Northwood Institute ($5,000) see Bauervic Foundation, Charles M.

Northwood Institute ($300,000) see DeVos Foundation, Richard and Helen

Northwood Institute ($5,000) see Dow Fund, Alden and Vada

Northwood Institute ($29,000) see Phillipps Foundation

Northwood Institute ($15,000) see Whiting Foundation, Macauley and Helen Dow

O.A.R. ($150,000) see Prince Corp.

Oakland Community College Foundation ($3,000) see Vollbrecht Foundation, Frederick A.

Oakland County Special Olympics ($250) see Ewald Foundation, H. T.

Oakland County Special Olympics ($2,000) see Vlasic Foundation

Oakland Family Services ($25,592) see DeRoy Testamentary Foundation

Oakland Family Services — special needs programs ($12,000) see Earl-Beth Foundation

Oakland Family Services — preventive services program ($15,000) see Vollbrecht Foundation, Frederick A.

Oakland Family Services ($7,500) see Wilson Trust, Lula C.

Oakland Literacy Council ($3,000) see Vollbrecht Foundation, Frederick A.

Oakland University — capital ($415,291) see Wilson Fund, Matilda R.

Oakland University — sponsorship of Business Forum see Ameritech Publishing

Oakland University — Department of Chemistry ($25,000) see Holden Fund, James and Lynelle

Oakland University Meadow Brook ($7,500) see Wilson Trust, Lula C.

OIC of Oakland County ($5,000) see Wilson Trust, Lula C.

Okemos Education Foundation ($58,824) see Dart Foundation

Okemos Education Foundation ($7,500) see Dart Foundation

Old Newsboys Good Fellow Fund ($2,500) see Slaughter, Jr. Foundation, William E.

Oleson Island ($131) see Oleson Foundation

Olivet College ($10,000) see Thoman Foundation, W. B. and Candace

Olivet College/Conservatory of Music ($50,000) see Upton Foundation, Frederick S.

Olivet College/Library Fund ($51,000) see Upton Foundation, Frederick S.

Onaway Camp Trust ($200) see Ewald Foundation, H. T.

Opera Company of Mid-Michigan ($2,500) see Thoman Foundation, W. B. and Candace

Opera Grand Rapids ($40,000) see Van Andel Foundation, Jay and Betty

Opera Grand Rapids ($20,000) see Van Andel Foundation, Jay and Betty

Operation Independence ($10,000) see Borman's

Opportunities Industrialization Center of Saginaw ($24,000) see Morley Brothers Foundation

Opportunity Industrial Center ($16,000) see Wickson-Link Memorial Foundation

Optometric Institute and Clinic ($10,000) see Westerman Foundation, Samuel L.

Orchard Lake Schools ($40,000) see Hess Charitable Trust, Myrtle E. and William C.

Orchards Children's Services ($11,000) see Bargman Foundation, Theodore and Mina

Orchards Children's Services ($11,000) see Imerman Memorial Foundation, Stanley

Our Lady of Providence Center ($40,000) see Hess Charitable Trust, Myrtle E. and William C.

Our Lady of Sorrows Church ($55,000) see Deseranno Educational Foundation

Our Lady of Victory ($30,000) see Deseranno Educational Foundation

Owatonna Foundation ($12,000) see SPX Corp.

Owosso Historical Commission ($100) see Bentley Foundation, Alvin M.

Paper Technology Foundation — 1991 Scholarship Fund ($3,500) see Sandoz Corp.

Parade Company ($5,000) see Handleman Co.

Parchment Library ($1,000) see Fabri-Kal Corp.

Pardee Cancer Treatment Fund of Midland — to assist in the control and cure of cancer through the program of the Cancer Treatment Committee ($200,000) see Pardee Foundation, Elsa U.

Parent Action ($50,500) see Levy Foundation, Charles and Ruth

Paul Oliver Memorial Hospital ($42,000) see Seabury Foundation

Peace Development Fund ($12,000) see Shiffman Foundation

Petoskey Music Boosters ($5,000) see Slaughter, Jr. Foundation, William E.

Pewabic Society ($7,500) see Kaufman Memorial Trust, Chaim, Fanny, Louis, Benjamin, and Anne Florence

Pewabic Society ($4,000) see Triford Foundation

Pharmaceutical Manufacturers Association Foundation ($200,000) see Bristol-Myers Squibb Co.

Philadelphia Society ($2,000) see Curran Foundation

Philadelphia Society ($6,500) see Thirty-Five Twenty, Inc.

Philippine American ($2,000) see Farwell Foundation, Drusilla

Pine Rest Christian Hospital ($27,000) see Jaqua Foundation

Pine Rest Christian Hospital — capital campaign ($5,000) see JSJ Corp.

Piney Woods Country Life School ($5,000) see Appleby Trust, Scott B. and Annie P.

Pistons Palace Foundation ($300) see Ewald Foundation, H. T.

Pit and Balcony ($29,136) see Boutell Memorial Fund, Arnold and Gertrude

Planned Parenthood ($2,000) see Padnos Iron & Metal Co., Louis

Planned Parenthood Federation of America ($5,000) see Batts Foundation

Planned Parenthood Federation of America ($17,030) see Earl-Beth Foundation

Planned Parenthood Federation of America ($15,000) see Kaufman Memorial Trust, Chaim, Fanny, Louis, Benjamin, and Anne Florence

Planned Parenthood Federation of America ($100,000) see Offield Family Foundation

Planned Parenthood Federation of America ($7,500) see Tiscornia Foundation

Plymouth Congregational Church ($12,767) see Greater Lansing Foundation

Pontiac Area Lighthouse ($10,000) see Hess Charitable Trust, Myrtle E. and William C.

Pope John Paul II Cultural Foundation — religious ($66,672) see Domino's Pizza

Porter Hills Presbyterian Village ($12,500) see Batts Foundation

Porter Hills Presbyterian Village ($5,000) see Ramlose Foundation, George A.

Porter Hills Presbyterian Village ($25,000) see Sebastian Foundation

Pride Place ($2,500) see Todd Co., A.M.

Providence Hospital Foundation ($100,000) see DeRoy Testamentary Foundation

Providence Hospital Foundation ($10,000) see Sehn Foundation

Providence Hospital Foundation — Pastoral Care Department ($3,000) see Bauervic-Paisley Foundation

Public Broadcasting ($100,000) see Offield Family Foundation

Public Museum Building Fund ($10,000) see Keeler Fund, Miner S. and Mary Ann

Public Museum Building Fund ($5,000) see Wolverine World Wide, Inc.

Public Museum Foundation ($8,333) see Grand Rapids Label Co.

Public Museum Foundation ($500,000) see Van Andel Foundation, Jay and Betty

Radio Bible Class ($8,500) see C.I.O.S.

Recordings for Recovery — general unrestricted contribution ($2,000) see Barstow Foundation

Red Cross Capital Campaign ($4,000) see Triford Foundation

Reformed Bible College ($5,000) see Artevel Foundation

Reformed Bible College ($25,000) see Van Andel Foundation, Jay and Betty

Reformed Bible College ($5,000) see Vermeer Investment Company Foundation

Reformed Bible College Religious Education ($20,000) see Tibstra Charitable Foundation, Thomas and Gertrude

Rehabilitation Institute ($5,000) see Shiffman Foundation

Rest Haven ($100,000) see Prince Manufacturing, Inc.

Richland Bible Church ($41,565) see Miller Charitable Foundation, C. John and Reva

Right Place Program ($1,000) see Grand Rapids Label Co.

River Raisin Center for the Arts ($3,500) see McIntyre Foundation, B. D. and Jane E.

Rivers Edge Environmental ($10,000) see Wege Foundation

Riverside Place — new apartment complex for senior citizens ($1,000,000) see Dow Foundation, Herbert H. and Grace A.

Rockford High School ($1,500) see Wolverine World Wide, Inc.

Rollins Fund ($5,000) see Vlasic Foundation

Ronald McDonald House ($5,000) see Bray Charitable Trust, Viola E.

Rose City Soccer ($10,000) see Hurst Foundation

Rose Hill Center — sponsorship of computer department see Ameritech Publishing

Rose Hill Center ($10,000) see Levy Foundation, Edward C.

Rose Hill Center ($5,000) see Vlasic Foundation

Rotary Club of Lansing Foundation ($2,000) see Abrams Foundation, Talbert and Leota

Rudolf Steiner Centre ($11,500) see Waldorf Educational Foundation

Saginaires ($10,000) see Morley Brothers Foundation

Saginaw Art Museum ($10,000) see Mather and William Gwinn Mather Fund, Elizabeth Ring

Saginaw Business Incubator ($15,000) see Morley Brothers Foundation

Saginaw Community Foundation ($10,000) see Wickson-Link Memorial Foundation

Saginaw County Chamber of Commerce ($5,000) see Bierlein Family Foundation

Saginaw County Historical Society ($12,000) see Morley Brothers Foundation

Saginaw County Youth Protection Council ($18,500) see Wickson-Link Memorial Foundation

Saginaw General Hospital ($5,000) see Bierlein Family Foundation

Saginaw General Hospital — endoscopy equipment ($35,000) see Mills Fund, Frances Goll

Saginaw General Hospital Foundation — endoscopy equipment and refurbishing ($100,000) see Wickes Foundation, Harvey Randall

Saginaw Symphony Association ($30,000) see Boutell Memorial Fund, Arnold and Gertrude

Saginaw Township-H. R. Wickes Recreation Complex — land development ($100,000) see Wickes Foundation, Harvey Randall

Saginaw Township Soccer Association ($3,800) see Bierlein Family Foundation

Saginaw Township Soccer Association — construction of soccer complex ($100,000) see Mills Fund, Frances Goll

Saginaw Township Soccer Association — soccer fields ($100,000) see Wickes Foundation, Harvey Randall

Saginaw Township Soccer Association ($10,000) see Wickson-Link Memorial Foundation

Saginaw Valley Blood Program ($5,000) see May Mitchell Royal Foundation

Saginaw Valley State University ($50,000) see Boutell Memorial Fund, Arnold and Gertrude

Saginaw Valley State University ($7,500) see May Mitchell Royal Foundation

Saginaw Valley State University ($75,000) see Strosacker Foundation, Charles J.

Saginaw Valley State University Foundation ($20,667) see Morley Brothers Foundation

Saginaw Valley State University Foundation — conference

center ($50,000) see Wickes Foundation, Harvey Randall

Saginaw Valley State University Foundation — expansion of Valley Library Consortium ($128,511) see Wickes Foundation, Harvey Randall

Saginaw Valley Zoological Society ($20,000) see Morley Brothers Foundation

Saginaw Valley Zoological Society — new entrance to the Saginaw zoo ($88,400) see Wickes Foundation, Harvey Randall

Saginaw Zoological Society ($10,000) see Wickson-Link Memorial Foundation

St. Andrews School ($5,000) see Baldwin Foundation

St. Augustine Catholic Church ($1,000) see Kowalski Sausage Co.

St. Cecilia Music Society ($10,000) see Dexter Industries

St. Cecilia Music Society ($10,000) see Wege Foundation

St. Clair Community Foundation ($11,000) see Whiting Memorial Foundation, Henry and Harriet

St. Edwards College ($50,000) see Plym Foundation

St. Francis Hospital ($1,600) see Atalanta/Sosnoff Capital Corp.

St. Hugo Completion Fund ($70,000) see Vlasic Foundation

St. Hugo of Hills ($2,500) see Farwell Foundation, Drusilla

St. Hugo of the Hills Church ($100,000) see Iacocca Foundation

St. Hugo of the Hills Church ($14,100) see Sehn Foundation

St. John's Armenian Church ($28,050) see Manoogian Foundation, Alex and Marie

St. John's Home ($10,000) see Cook Charitable Foundation

St. Johns Home ($1,000) see Grand Rapids Label Co.

St. Johns Hospital and Medical Center — for patient care fund ($10,000) see Lincoln Health Care Foundation

St. Joseph Hospital ($15,000) see Hess Charitable Trust, Myrtle E. and William C.

St. Joseph Mercy Hospital ($23,637) see May Mitchell Royal Foundation

St. Joseph Sport Scholarship ($3,000) see Messick Charitable Trust, Harry F.

St. Lawrence Hospital and Health Care Services — for renovation ($5,000) see Ransom Fidelity Company

St. Lorenz Building Fund ($8,300) see Wickson-Link Memorial Foundation

St. Luke's Hospital ($25,000) see Boutell Memorial Fund, Arnold and Gertrude

St. Luke's Hospital Foundation ($4,000) see Bierlein Family Foundation

St. Martha's Episcopal Church ($127,272) see Ford Fund, Eleanor and Edsel

St. Mary Catholic Central High School — operating capital ($5,000) see Bauervic-Paisley Foundation

St. Mary's Hospital Foundation ($25,000) see Morley Brothers Foundation

St. Marys Medical Center — medical equipment ($25,000) see Eddy Family Memorial Fund, C. K.

Michigan (cont.)

St. Mary's Preparatory — funds to purchase eight classroom doors and 100 lockers ($12,040) see Bauervic-Paisley Foundation

St. Monica School ($10,000) see Deseranno Educational Foundation

St. Patricks Church ($85,000) see Hess Charitable Trust, Myrtle E. and William C.

St. Paul's Church ($11,200) see Zimmerman Foundation, Mary and George Herbert

St. Pauls Episcopal Church ($6,000) see Bishop Charitable Trust, A. G.

St. Paul's Episcopal Church ($30,000) see Whiting Foundation

St. Paul's Lutheran Church ($2,000) see Farwell Foundation, Drusilla

St. Peters Home for Boys ($106,788) see Green Charitable Trust, Leslie H. and Edith C.

St. Peter's Home for Boys ($20,000) see Whitney Fund, David M.

St. Vincent de Paul ($10,000) see Whiting Memorial Foundation, Henry and Harriet

St. Vincent de Paul Society ($2,650) see Zimmerman Foundation, Mary and George Herbert

St. Vincent and Sarah Fisher Center — emergency shelter and infant mortality program ($250,000) see Skillman Foundation

St. Vincent Sarah Fisher Home — residences ($25,050) see Earl-Beth Foundation

Saline Community Hospital ($10,000) see R&B Tool Co.

Saline Library ($5,000) see R&B Tool Co.

Salvation Army ($1,000) see Awrey Bakeries

Salvation Army ($20,000) see Baldwin Foundation

Salvation Army ($4,000) see Dart Foundation

Salvation Army ($500) see Fibre Converters

Salvation Army ($50,000) see Ford II Fund, Henry

Salvation Army ($2,500) see McIntyre Foundation, B. D. and Jane E.

Salvation Army ($1,180) see McIntyre Foundation, C. S. and Marion F.

Salvation Army ($16,000) see Morley Brothers Foundation

Salvation Army ($10,000) see Ransom Fidelity Company

Salvation Army ($2,000) see Rohlik Foundation, Sigmund and Sophie

Salvation Army ($7,000) see Shelden Fund, Elizabeth, Allan and Warren

Salvation Army ($3,000) see Todd Co., A.M.

Salvation Army ($10,500) see Westerman Foundation, Samuel L.

Salvation Army — renovations ($50,000) see Wickes Foundation, Harvey Randall

Salvation Army — capital ($100,000) see Wilson Fund, Matilda R.

Salvation Army — Christmas food baskets ($2,000) see

Hunter Foundation, Edward and Irma

Sarett Nature Center ($5,000) see Tiscornia Foundation

School District of the City of Royal Oak — curriculum design and career awareness program ($286,000) see Skillman Foundation

Schoolcraft Community Library ($10,000) see Vicksburg Foundation

Servant Ministries ($202,150) see Timmis Foundation, Michael & Nancy

Share Our Strength ($5,000) see DeRoy Foundation, Helen L.

Shelter ($15,000) see Besser Foundation

Shelter ($15,000) see Besser Foundation

Shelter House ($12,000) see Dow Fund, Alden and Vada

Shiawassee Adult Literacy Association ($700) see Bentley Foundation, Alvin M.

Shiawassee County Courthouse Preservation ($5,000) see Bentley Foundation, Alvin M.

Siena Heights College ($5,000) see Bauervic-Paisley Foundation

Siena Heights College ($500,000) see Merillat Foundation, Orville D. and Ruth A.

Sinai Hospital ($90,803) see Gershenson Foundation, Charles H.

Sisters, Servants of Immaculate Heart of Mary — for electric beds and a medication cart in health care center ($6,200) see Bauervic-Paisley Foundation

SMCC Capital Campaign ($10,000) see Monroe Auto Equipment Co.

Society of Manufacturing Engineers Foundation ($1,000) see Nelson Industries, Inc.

Society for the Propagation of the Faith ($10,000) see Mex-Am Cultural Foundation

South Central Education Association ($2,880) see Weatherwax Foundation

South Lyon Fire Department ($5,000) see Quanex Corp.

Southeastern Minnesota Initiative ($10,000) see SPX Corp.

Southwest Detroit Hospital — for education program, diabetic and hypertension ($5,000) see Lincoln Health Care Foundation

Southwest Michigan Council #270 ($500) see Fibre Converters

Southwest Michigan Symphony Orchestra ($35,900) see Upton Foundation, Frederick S.

Specific Language Disability Center ($2,500) see Monroe-Brown Foundation

Specific Language Disability Center ($1,000) see Todd Co., A.M.

Spring Arbor College — remodeling gymnasium ($250,000) see Herrick Foundation

Spring Arbor College ($250,000) see Merillat Foundation, Orville D. and Ruth A.

Starr Commonwealth ($15,000) see Baldwin Foundation

Starr Commonwealth Schools ($2,500) see Abrams Foundation, Talbert and Leota

Starr Commonwealth Schools ($10,000) see Dow Fund, Alden and Vada

Starr Commonwealth Schools, Albion Campus — (health, physical education and recreation center) ($100,000) see Towsley Foundation, Harry A. and Margaret D.

Substance Abuse Council of Battle Creek ($25,000) see Kellogg's

Sunshine Networks ($35,000) see Miller Charitable Foundation, C. John and Reva

Suomi College ($4,000) see Roddis Foundation, Hamilton

Superior Radio Network ($5,000) see Grotto Foundation

SWMI Symphony Orchestra ($3,500) see Tiscornia Foundation

Talbot Farm — general purposes ($60,000) see Leighton-Oare Foundation

Taproot Community Education Center ($6,500) see Shiffman Foundation

Tau Beta Camp ($1,000) see Chamberlin Foundation, Gerald W.

Teach Michigan Educational Fund ($5,000) see Honigman Foundation

Teamster Rank and File Education, Legal Defense Foundation ($30,000) see New World Foundation

Teen Ranch ($7,000) see Salwil Foundation

Teen Ranch ($7,000) see Whiting Memorial Foundation, Henry and Harriet

Temple Beth-El ($90,804) see Gershenson Foundation, Charles H.

Temple Beth-El ($10,000) see Prentis Family Foundation, Meyer and Anna

Temple Beth-El ($40,160) see Shapero Foundation, Nate S. and Ruth B.

Temple Israel Detroit ($18,770) see Herman Foundation, John and Rose

Temple New Tamid ($4,200) see Herman Foundation, John and Rose

Three Rivers Area Foundation ($750) see Fibre Converters

Tip of the Mitt Watershed Council ($63,507) see Harder Foundation

Traffic Safety Association of Michigan ($2,000) see Farwell Foundation, Drusilla

Transitions-Building Tomorrows Campaign ($1,500) see Grand Rapids Label Co.

Travelers Aid Society ($2,000) see Kaufman Memorial Trust, Chaim, Fanny, Louis, Benjamin, and Anne Florence

Tri-Cities Area United Fund ($14,500) see Loutit Foundation

Tri-Cities Ministries Counseling Service — support for operations ($4,000) see JSJ Corp.

Tri-Cities United Fund — operations campaign ($35,000) see JSJ Corp.

Tri-County Youth for Christ ($3,000) see Bierlein Family Foundation

Trinity Episcopal Church ($24,124) see McIntyre Foundation, B. D. and Jane E.

Trinity Lutheran Church — other ($20,000) see La-Z-Boy Chair Co.

Tynedale College ($50,000) see Lamb Foundation, Kirkland S. and Rena B.

Unitarian-Universalist Church — operating expenses ($500) see Hooper Handling

United Arts Council ($15,000) see Miller Foundation

United Community Services ($5,000) see Shiffman Foundation

United Foundation ($5,000) see Erb Lumber Co.

United Foundation ($12,000) see Fruehauf Foundation

United Foundation ($58,650) see NBD Bank

United Foundation ($1,500) see Zimmerman Foundation, Mary and George Herbert

United Foundation, Detroit, MI ($16,128) see Dana Corp.

United Foundation Urban Fund ($145,000) see NBD Bank

United Foundation Urban Progress Fund ($375) see United Technologies, Automotive

United Foundation Vanguard Program ($10,000) see Holley Foundation

United Jewish Appeal Federation ($340,000) see Borman's

United Jewish Appeal Federation of Jewish Philanthropies ($400,000) see Levy Foundation, Edward C.

United Jewish Charities ($13,500) see Kaufman Memorial Trust, Chaim, Fanny, Louis, Benjamin, and Anne Florence

United Jewish Charities ($2,000) see Shapero Foundation, Nate S. and Ruth B.

United Methodist Community House ($5,000) see Cook Charitable Foundation

United Methodist Community House ($5,000) see Seidman Family Foundation

United Negro College Fund ($1,500) see Rohlik Foundation, Sigmund and Sophie

United States Ski Education Foundation Hall of Fame ($12,000) see Cleveland-Cliffs

United Way ($2,000) see Abrams Foundation, Talbert and Leota

United Way ($2,225) see Alro Steel Corp.

United Way ($750) see Barton-Malow Co.

United Way ($10,000) see Batts Foundation

United Way ($5,000) see Bentley Foundation, Alvin M.

United Way ($33,600) see Besser Foundation

United Way ($3,575) see Bierlein Family Foundation

United Way ($47,500) see Boutell Memorial Fund, Arnold and Gertrude

United Way ($12,000) see Bray Charitable Trust, Viola E.

United Way ($8,000) see DeRoy Foundation, Helen L.

United Way ($3,000) see Dexter Industries

United Way ($5,000) see Dow Foundation, Herbert H. and Barbara C.

United Way ($41,763) see Eaton Corp.

United Way ($40,900) see Eaton Corp.

United Way ($42,500) see Eddy Family Memorial Fund, C. K.

United Way ($12,500) see Eddy Family Memorial Fund, C. K.

United Way ($8,695) see Fabri-Kal Corp.

United Way ($8,440) see Fabri-Kal Corp.

United Way ($7,326) see Fabri-Kal Corp.

United Way ($1,000) see Federal Screw Works

United Way ($27,000) see Ford Fund, William and Martha

United Way ($2,000) see Giddings & Lewis

United Way ($17,000) see Grand Rapids Label Co.

United Way ($19,400) see Greater Lansing Foundation

United Way ($50,500) see Handleman Co.

United Way ($25,000) see Holden Fund, James and Lynelle

United Way ($21,000) see Holden Fund, James and Lynelle

United Way ($8,000) see Hunter Foundation, Edward and Irma

United Way ($15,000) see Kantzler Foundation

United Way ($15,000) see Kantzler Foundation

United Way ($8,967) see Kantzler Foundation

United Way ($3,000) see Kasle Steel Corp.

United Way ($10,000) see Keeler Fund, Miner S. and Mary Ann

United Way ($12,000) see Kysor Industrial Corp.

United Way ($6,600) see Kysor Industrial Corp.

United Way ($6,500) see Kysor Industrial Corp.

United Way ($4,000) see Kysor Industrial Corp.

United Way ($2,000) see Meek Foundation

United Way ($33,865) see Miller Foundation

United Way ($3,315) see Perry Drug Stores

United Way ($3,800) see Quanex Corp.

United Way ($1,000) see Robertson Brothers

United Way ($50,000) see Sebastian Foundation

United Way ($5,000) see Shapero Foundation, Nate S. and Ruth B.

United Way ($90,000) see Shelden Fund, Elizabeth, Allan and Warren

United Way ($5,000) see Shiffman Foundation

United Way ($37,000) see SPX Corp.

United Way ($34,748) see SPX Corp.

United Way ($6,064) see SPX Corp.

United Way ($8,400) see Texas Industries, Inc.

United Way ($7,700) see Todd Co., A.M.

United Way ($8,000) see Vicksburg Foundation

United Way ($5,000) see Vlasic Foundation

United Way ($12,750) see Whiting Foundation

United Way ($4,000) see Whiting Memorial Foundation, Henry and Harriet

United Way ($6,050) see Wickson-Link Memorial Foundation

United Way, Genesee and Lapeer counties — unrestricted

operating grant ($580,000) see General Motors Corp.

United Way Genesee/Lapeeer County — program support ($13,000) see Consumers Power Co.

United Way Jackson County — program support ($30,000) see Consumers Power Co.

United Way of Jackson County — program support ($15,000) see Consumers Power Co.

United Way of Jackson County — program support ($15,000) see Consumers Power Co.

United Way of Jackson County ($29,950) see TRINOVA Corp.

United Way of Kent County — general ($30,000) see Michigan Consolidated Gas Co.

United Way of Kent County — 1992 Campaign ($375,000) see Steelcase

United Way of Midland County ($105,500) see Gerstacker Foundation, Rollin M.

United Way of Midland County ($277,500) see Strosacker Foundation, Charles J.

United Way of Monroe County ($102,000) see Detroit Edison Co.

United Way of Monroe County — human services ($32,550) see La-Z-Boy Chair Co.

United Way of Muskegon County ($12,000) see Brunswick Corp.

United Way, Oakland County — unrestricted operating grant ($309,750) see General Motors Corp.

United Way of Pontiac ($51,000) see NBD Bank

United Way of Saginaw County — operations ($35,500) see Wickes Foundation, Harvey Randall

United Way of St. Clair County ($81,000) see Detroit Edison Co.

United Way of SE Michigan — Torch Drive for affiliated agencies ($160,000) see Hudson-Webber Foundation

United Way for Southeastern Michigan — corporate pledge ($77,220) see American Natural Resources Co.

United Way of Southeastern Michigan — program support ($24,757) see Consumers Power Co.

United Way of Southeastern Michigan — program support ($12,379) see Consumers Power Co.

United Way of Southeastern Michigan — program support ($12,378) see Consumers Power Co.

United Way for Southeastern Michigan ($159,000) see Detroit Edison Co.

United Way for Southeastern Michigan ($159,000) see Detroit Edison Co.

United Way for Southeastern Michigan ($159,000) see Detroit Edison Co.

United Way for Southeastern Michigan ($159,000) see Detroit Edison Co.

United Way for Southeastern Michigan ($159,000) see Detroit Edison Co.

United Way for Southeastern Michigan ($30,000) see Ford Fund, Walter and Josephine

United Way for Southeastern Michigan ($60,000) see Ford II Fund, Henry

United Way for Southeastern Michigan ($650,000) see Ford Motor Co.

United Way for Southeastern Michigan ($650,000) see Ford Motor Co.

United Way for Southeastern Michigan ($17,000) see Graco

United Way, Southeastern Michigan — unrestricted operating grant ($785,250) see General Motors Corp.

United Way of Southeastern Michigan — general ($135,750) see Michigan Consolidated Gas Co.

United Way of Southeastern Michigan ($540,000) see NBD Bank

United Way for Southeastern Michigan — New Detroit Fund ($29,300) see American Natural Resources Co.

University Cultural Center ($5,000) see Kaufman Memorial Trust, Chaim, Fanny, Louis, Benjamin, and Anne Florence

University Cultural Center Association, David MacKenzie House, Wayne State University — Cultural Center master plan ($100,000) see Hudson-Webber Foundation

University of Detroit ($45,000) see Detroit Edison Co.

University of Detroit ($10,000) see Seymour and Troester Foundation

University of Detroit Jesuit High School and Academy ($10,000) see Seymour and Troester Foundation

University of Detroit Mercy ($10,000) see DeRoy Foundation, Helen L.

University Liggett School ($2,000) see Chamberlin Foundation, Gerald W.

University Liggett School ($245,000) see Ford Fund, Eleanor and Edsel

University Liggett School ($20,000) see Ford Fund, William and Martha

University Liggett School ($200,000) see Ford II Fund, Henry

University Liggett School ($15,000) see Fruehauf Foundation

University Liggett School ($30,000) see Glancy Foundation, Lenora and Alfred

University Liggett School ($50,000) see Manoogian Foundation, Alex and Marie

University Liggett School ($5,000) see Scherer Foundation, Karla

University Liggett School — annual fund, endowment ($30,000) see Shelden Fund, Elizabeth, Allan and Warren

University of Michigan ($10,000) see Baldwin Foundation

University of Michigan — law school faculty research endowment ($500,000) see Benedum Foundation, Claude Worthington

University of Michigan — scholarship ($69,041) see Bentley Foundation, Alvin M.

University of Michigan ($1,000) see Bishop Foundation, Vernon and Doris

University of Michigan — juvenile justice reform

($729,666) see Casey Foundation, Annie E.

University of Michigan ($50,000) see CBS Inc.

University of Michigan ($10,000) see Chernow Trust for the Benefit of Charity Dated 3/13/75, Michael

University of Michigan ($21,000) see DeVlieg Foundation, Charles

University of Michigan — educational ($122,000) see Domino's Pizza

University of Michigan ($150,000) see Dow Chemical Co.

University of Michigan ($100,000) see Dow Chemical Co.

University of Michigan ($10,000) see Earl-Beth Foundation

University of Michigan ($90,803) see Gershenson Foundation, Charles H.

University of Michigan ($110,000) see Gerstacker Foundation, Rollin M.

University of Michigan ($10,000) see Helzberg Foundation, Shirley and Barnett

University of Michigan ($69,058) see Honigman Foundation

University of Michigan ($40,000) see Jameson Foundation, J. W. and Ida M.

University of Michigan ($4,300) see Johnson Foundation, Barbara P.

University of Michigan — for construction and addition to chemistry building ($2,500,000) see Kresge Foundation

University of Michigan — student aid ($15,000) see Lincoln Health Care Foundation

University of Michigan ($15,000) see Link Foundation

University of Michigan — excellence ($100,000) see Lockheed Corp.

University of Michigan ($66,975) see Lurie Family Foundation

University of Michigan ($76,000) see Mardigian Foundation

University of Michigan ($10,368) see Margoes Foundation

University of Michigan ($2,500) see National Service Industries

University of Michigan ($1,000) see Perry Drug Stores

University of Michigan ($15,000) see Schlink Foundation, Albert G. and Olive H.

University of Michigan ($20,000) see Stern Foundation, Irvin

University of Michigan ($40,000) see Upjohn Foundation, Harold and Grace

University of Michigan ($110,000) see Whirlpool Corp.

University of Michigan ($78,000) see Whiting Foundation

University of Michigan ($16,000) see Whitman Corp.

University of Michigan — gold course restoration fund ($20,000) see Whitney Fund, David M.

University of Michigan ($35,000) see Zenkel Foundation

University of Michigan-Athletic Department-Center of Champions — (replacement sports facility) ($100,000) see Towsley Foundation, Harry A. and Margaret D.

University of Michigan — Capital Fund Drive ($20,000) see Baldwin Foundation

University of Michigan Center for Champions ($100,000) see Monroe-Brown Foundation

University of Michigan Center of Champions Facility ($22,500) see Upton Foundation, Frederick S.

University of Michigan-Center for the Education of Women — scholarship fund (endowment) ($250,000) see Towsley Foundation, Harry A. and Margaret D.

University of Michigan Clements Library ($5,000) see Monroe-Brown Foundation

University of Michigan, College of Pharmacy ($95,000) see Schering-Plough Corp.

University of Michigan — to purchase computer-assisted instruction equipment ($78,782) see Fuld Health Trust, Helene

University of Michigan, Department of Communication — to complete endowments for three journalism fellowships ($875,000) see Knight Foundation, John S. and James L.

University of Michigan Engineering School ($7,000) see Monroe-Brown Foundation

University of Michigan — for graduate fellowships in the Environmental and Water Resources Engineering Department ($150,000) see Parsons Foundation, Ralph M.

University of Michigan at Flint ($15,000) see Bishop Charitable Trust, A. G.

University of Michigan at Flint ($25,000) see Bray Charitable Trust, Viola E.

University of Michigan-Flint — capital campaign for library construction ($2,900,000) see Mott Foundation, Charles Stewart

University of Michigan-Flint — to redevelop the former Water Street Pavilion for use by the University of Michigan-Flint as a student center ($1,900,000) see Mott Foundation, Charles Stewart

University of Michigan Institute for Humanities ($5,000) see Furth Foundation

University of Michigan Law School ($25,000) see Bargman Foundation, Theodore and Mina

University of Michigan Law School ($25,000) see Imerman Memorial Foundation, Stanley

University of Michigan Law School Fund ($6,550) see Dekalb Energy Co.

University of Michigan Mathematics Department ($20,000) see Keeler Fund, Miner S. and Mary Ann

University of Michigan Medical Center ($5,000) see Cohen Foundation, Wilfred P.

University of Michigan — for students working on projects

in the Operations Management 610 courses to cover travel and expenses ($2,000) see Owens-Corning Fiberglas Corp.

University of Michigan — Project on Student Success ($28,000) see Dreyfus Foundation, Camille and Henry

University of Michigan School of Medicine — scholarship fund ($90,000) see Mette Foundation

University of Michigan School of Natural Resources ($20,170) see Sussman Fund, Edna Bailey

University of Michigan — first year of six-year pledge/Environmental Journalism Fellows ($10,925) see Scripps Co., E.W.

US National Ski Hall of Fame and Museum — building fund ($2,000) see Pamida, Inc.

Vaishnava Center for Enlightenment ($71,000) see India Foundation

Very Special Arts/Allegan County ($5,000) see Delano Foundation, Mignon Sherwood

Vicksburg Community Library ($8,929) see Vicksburg Foundation

Vicksburg Community Library ($5,000) see Vicksburg Foundation

Vicksburg Community Schools ($25,000) see Vicksburg Foundation

Vicksburg School Foundation ($7,500) see Vicksburg Foundation

Village of Vicksburg ($93,890) see Vicksburg Foundation

Visiting Nurses see First of America Bank Corp.

Visiting Nurses Association ($25,000) see Eddy Family Memorial Fund, C. K.

Visiting Nurses Association ($10,000) see Wickson-Link Memorial Foundation

Visiting Nurses Association of Saginaw ($40,000) see Morley Brothers Foundation

Vista Maria-Sisters of the Good Shepherd ($15,000) see Deseranno Educational Foundation

Volunteer Impact — sponsorship of Volunteer-A-Thon see Ameritech Publishing

Walker Cisler Endowment ($10,000) see Cleveland-Cliffs

Walsh College ($5,000) see Bauervic-Paisley Foundation

Walsh College ($25,000) see Earl-Beth Foundation

Walsh College of Accountancy and Business Administration — capital campaign ($30,000) see Vollbrecht Foundation, Frederick A.

Walsh College of Accountancy and Business Administration ($10,000) see Vollbrecht Foundation, Frederick A.

Washington Heights Community Ministries ($25,000) see Kellogg's

Washtenaw Community College ($3,000) see R&B Tool Co.

Washtenaw United Way ($51,884) see Johnson Controls

Waterford Township Department of Recreation ($25,000) see Hess Charitable Trust, Myrtle E. and William C.

Wayne State University ($20,000) see DeVlieg Foundation, Charles

Michigan (cont.)

Wayne State University ($250,000) see Ford Motor Co.

Wayne State University ($90,804) see Gershenson Foundation, Charles H.

Wayne State University ($5,500) see Kowalski Sausage Co.

Wayne State University — clinical research building ($5,000) see Shelden Fund, Elizabeth, Allan and Warren

Wayne State University — Elliman Research Building instrumentation ($100,000) see Hudson-Webber Foundation

Wayne State University — Faculty Research Awards program ($36,000) see American Natural Resources Co.

Wayne State University — for reservation of student housing in Freiburg ($150,000) see Kade Foundation, Max

Wayne State University McGregor Memorial Conference Building — extraordinary maintenance and capital improvements ($125,000) see McGregor Fund

Wayne State University-University Cultural Center Association — David Mackenzie House ($25,000) see Ford Fund, Walter and Josephine

West Michigan Environmental Action Council ($9,000) see Keeler Fund, Miner S. and Mary Ann

West Michigan Public Broadcasting — support for capital campaign to expand and improve public radio and television stations ($100,000) see Steelcase

West Midland Community Center — endowment fund ($25,000) see Barstow Foundation

West Shore Community College ($1,000) see Great Lakes Casting Corp.

West Shore Symphony ($15,000) see SPX Corp.

Western Michigan Public Broadcasting see First of America Bank Corp.

Western Michigan Ronald McDonald House ($1,000) see Grand Rapids Label Co.

Western Michigan University see First of America Bank Corp.

Western Michigan University ($13,500) see Kowalski Sausage Co.

Western Michigan University Foundation ($35,000) see Monroe-Brown Foundation

Western Michigan University Foundation ($25,000) see Upjohn Foundation, Harold and Grace

Western St. Joseph County Community Chest ($2,300) see Fibre Converters

Whaley Children's Center ($5,000) see Harding Foundation, Charles Stewart

Whaley Children's Center ($15,000) see Whiting Foundation

Whaley Memorial Foundation for Whaley Children's Center ($8,333) see Bishop Charitable Trust, A. G.

Whistlestop Park Association ($2,000) see Weatherwax Foundation

WIAA Interlochen ($3,000) see Borwell Charitable Foundation

William Beaumont Hospital ($50,000) see DeRoy Testamentary Foundation

William Booth Hospital — for patient care fund ($5,000) see Lincoln Health Care Foundation

Wings of Hope Hospice ($10,000) see Delano Foundation, Mignon Sherwood

Wolverine Council Boy Scouts of America see Michigan Gas Utilities

Women's Resource Center of Northern Michigan ($100,000) see Offield Family Foundation

World Home Bible League ($15,000) see Tibstra Charitable Foundation, Thomas and Gertrude

Worldwide Christian Schools ($10,000) see Richardson Fund, Mary Lynn

WTVA/Channel 56 ($2,000) see Farwell Foundation, Drusilla

WTVS Channel 56 ($20,000) see Masco Corp.

WTVS/Channel 56, Detroit Public Television ($11,000) see Whitney Fund, David M.

Y Center ($1,000) see Weatherwax Foundation

Y Center of Battle Creek ($99,370) see Kellogg's

Y Family Christian Association ($20,000) see SPX Corp.

Yeshiva Gedolah Ateres Mordechi ($5,000) see Prentis Family Foundation, Meyer and Anna

YMCA ($500) see Barton-Malow Co.

YMCA ($33,333) see Bishop Charitable Trust, A. G.

YMCA ($11,640) see Bishop Charitable Trust, A. G.

YMCA ($50,000) see Cook Charitable Foundation

YMCA ($200,000) see Dalton Foundation, Dorothy U.

YMCA ($10,887) see Eddy Family Memorial Fund, C. K.

YMCA ($15,000) see Holley Foundation

YMCA ($10,000) see Holley Foundation

YMCA ($66,667) see Hunter Foundation, Edward and Irma

YMCA ($4,800) see JSJ Corp.

YMCA ($100) see Kasle Steel Corp.

YMCA ($1,000) see McIntyre Foundation, B. D. and Jane E.

YMCA ($1,000) see Meek Foundation

YMCA ($500) see Meek Foundation

YMCA ($11,000) see Sebastian Foundation

YMCA ($50,200) see Upton Foundation, Frederick S.

YMCA ($5,000) see Whiting Memorial Foundation, Henry and Harriet

YWCA — sexual assault program ($35,000) see Dalton Foundation, Dorothy U.

YWCA ($15,000) see Sebastian Foundation

YWCA ($12,000) see Tiscornia Foundation

YWCA ($2,500) see Todd Co., A.M.

YWCA ($100,000) see Upjohn Co.

YWCA ($25,000) see Upjohn Foundation, Harold and Grace

YWCA, Grand Rapids — funding for building

renovation and creation of Grand Rapids Center for Women ($200,000) see Steelcase

YWCA — 2000 campaign ($100,000) see Dalton Foundation, Dorothy U.

Minnesota

A Chance to Grow see American Express Co.

Abbott Northwestern ($5,000) see Sweatt Foundation, Harold W.

Abbott Northwestern Foundation ($260,000) see Chadwick Foundation

Abbott-Northwestern Hospital — capital see Cargill

Abbott Northwestern Hospital ($30,000) see Carolyn Foundation

Abbott Northwestern Hospital ($33,000) see Meadowood Foundation

Abbott Northwestern Hospital — Piper Cancer Institute ($50,000) see Medtronic

Abbott Northwestern Hospital — Virginia Piper Cancer Institute ($250,000) see General Mills

ABC of Edina Foundation see Jostens

Academy of Holy Angels ($5,000) see Quinlan Foundation, Elizabeth C.

Accessibility ($100,000) see Groves & Sons Co., S.J.

Accessible Space ($5,000) see Beim Foundation

Accessible Space — for equipment and a transportation van to assist physically disabled adults see USX Corp.

Adath Jeshurun Congregation ($100,000) see Phillips Family Foundation, Jay and Rose

Adath Jeshurun Synagogue — building fund ($150,000) see Phillips Family Foundation, Jay and Rose

Advantage Minnesota see First Bank System

African American Film Festival see Piper Jaffray Cos.

Albert Northwestern Hospital — Piper Cancer Center ($10,000) see Marbrook Foundation

Aliveness Project ($10,000) see Beim Foundation

Alpha Center for Public/Private Initiatives ($50,000) see Whitehead Foundation

Alpha Center for Public/Private Initiatives ($50,000) see Whitehead Foundation

Alpha Center for Public/Private Initiatives — support to advance the growth of for-profit businesses that deliver social services at lower cost than government see Ameritech Corp.

American Association of Cereal Chemists Scholarship Endowment Fund ($18,000) see Staley Manufacturing Co., A.E.

American Cancer Society ($40,000) see Andersen Foundation, Hugh J.

American Cancer Society ($500) see Fiterman Charitable Foundation, Miles and Shirley

American Chestnut Foundation — general support ($25,000) see Laurel Foundation

American Indian Opportunities Industrialization Center ($10,000) see Grotto Foundation

American Indian Opportunities Industrialization Center ($25,000) see Mardag Foundation

American Museum of Wildlife ($5,000) see Red Wing Shoe Co.

American Public Radio — to support coverage of business and economic news and issues from Japan through American Public Radio's weeknightly series, Marketplace ($146,391) see United States-Japan Foundation

American Red Cross ($10,000) see McKnight Foundation, Sumner T.

American Red Cross ($5,000) see Nash Foundation

American Red Cross ($148,418) see 3M Co.

American Red Cross, Greater Minneapolis Area Chapter ($30,000) see Andersen Foundation, Hugh J.

American Red Cross - St. Paul ($12,000) see Minnesota Mutual Life Insurance Co.

American Swedish Institute ($10,000) see Carlson Cos.

Animal Allies Humane Society — Duluth ($5,000) see Beim Foundation

Anoka Wesleyan Church ($4,000) see Oldham Little Church Foundation

Anti-Defamation League ($1,000) see Liberty Diversified Industries Inc.

Apple Tree Dental — general operating support see Cargill

Aquinas High School ($7,000) see Hiawatha Education Foundation

Archdiocesan AIDS Ministry ($5,000) see Sexton Foundation

Archdiocesan AIDS Ministry Program ($1,000) see Quinlan Foundation, Elizabeth C.

Archdiocese of St. Paul and Minneapolis — for the 1990 Annual Catholic Appeal ($10,000) see Butler Family Foundation, Patrick and Aimee

Arthritis Foundation ($15,000) see Lieberman Enterprises

Artspace Projects see First Bank System

Association for Retarded Citizens ($20,000) see O'Brien Foundation, Alice M.

Augsburg College — scholarships ($131,720) see Alliss Educational Foundation, Charles and Ellora

Augsburg College ($75,000) see Groves & Sons Co., S.J.

Augsburg College — American Indian student scholarships see Cargill

Austin Community College — to aid in providing scholarships to students ($1,000) see Independent Financial Corp.

Austin Community College, Booster Club ($500) see Independent Financial Corp.

AVTC ($15,000) see Hartz Foundation

Basilica of St. Mary ($5,000) see Beim Foundation

Bell Museum ($25,000) see Schott Foundation

Bemidji High School ($1,000) see Neilson Foundation, George W.

Bethany Lutheran College — capital drive ($33,000) see Mankato Citizens Telephone Co.

Bethany Ministry to International ($5,000) see Kejr Foundation

Bethel College and Seminary ($72,267) see Hallett Charitable Trust

Bethel College and Seminary ($48,110) see Hallett Charitable Trust

Bethel College and Seminary ($48,110) see Hallett Charitable Trust, Jessie F.

Better Business Bureau of Minnesota — general operating support see Cargill

Big Brothers and Big Sisters ($5,000) see Beim Foundation

Big Brothers/Big Sisters — Child Abuse Prevention Program see Cargill

Big Brothers and Sisters of Minneapolis see Piper Jaffray Cos.

Billy Graham Evangelistic Association ($10,000) see Benfamil Charitable Trust

Billy Graham Evangelistic Association ($268,100) see Berry Foundation, Lowell

Billy Graham Evangelistic Association ($5,000) see Christian Workers Foundation

Billy Graham Evangelistic Association ($20,000) see Fruehauf Foundation

Billy Graham Evangelistic Association ($2,000) see Moore & Sons, B.C.

Billy Graham Evangelistic Association ($6,000) see Ryan Foundation, David Claude

Billy Graham Evangelistic Association ($1,000) see Youth Foundation

Biomedical Research Institute ($5,000) see Thorpe Foundation, James R.

Bishop of Winona ($5,000) see Kasal Charitable Trust, Father

Blake School ($20,500) see Southways Foundation

Blake Schools ($151,000) see Chadwick Foundation

Blake Schools — capital fund drive ($10,000) see Marbrook Foundation

Blandin Foundation ($666,425) see Blandin Foundation

Blandin Foundation ($378,000) see Blandin Foundation

Blandin Foundation ($352,000) see Blandin Foundation

Blandin Foundation ($250,000) see Blandin Foundation

Bloomington Art Center see Jostens

Bloomington Community Foundation see First Bank System

Bloomington Fine Arts Council/Anne Frank Exhibit see Piper Jaffray Cos.

Blue Earth County Historical Society ($20,000) see Gray Charitable Trust, Mary S.

Blue Earth County Historical Society ($1,440) see Gray Charitable Trust, Mary S.

Boy Scouts of America ($8,500) see Cherne Foundation, Albert W.

Boy Scouts of America ($250) see Liberty Diversified Industries Inc.

Boy Scouts of America ($100,000) see Phipps Foundation, William H.

Boy Scouts of America ($13,000) see Tozer Foundation

Boy Scouts of America-Indianhead Council ($67,500) see Andersen Corp.

Boy Scouts Viking Council — program support ($10,000) see International Multifoods Corp.

Boys and Girls Club ($10,000) see O'Neil Foundation, Casey Albert T.

Boys and Girls Club ($100,000) see Phillips Family Foundation, Jay and Rose

Boys and Girls Club of St. Paul ($50,000) see Andersen Foundation, Hugh J.

Boys and Girls Club of St. Paul see Jostens

Boys and Girls Club of St. Paul ($50,000) see Mardag Foundation

Breck School ($10,000) see Cherne Foundation, Albert W.

Breck School ($3,000) see Fiterman Charitable Foundation, Miles and Shirley

Breck School ($30,000) see Larsen Fund

Breck School ($25,000) see Meadowood Foundation

Breck School — private-public school collaborative for hands-on science for students of similar and different ages ($60,000) see Medtronic

Bridge for Runaway Youth — general operating support see Cargill

Business Economics Education Foundation ($5,000) see Dain Bosworth/Inter- Regional Financial Group

Business Economics Education Foundation see Jostens

Camp Sunrise see First Bank System

Camp Sunrise ($92,334) see Northern States Power Co.

Camphill Village Minnesota see Piper Jaffray Cos.

Carleton College see American Tobacco Co.

Carleton College see Ayco Corp.

Carleton College ($600) see Bradish Trust, Norman C.

Carleton College ($10,000) see Getsch Family Foundation Trust

Carleton College ($15,250) see Grossman Foundation, N. Bud

Carleton College ($400,000) see Hulings Foundation, Mary Andersen

Carleton College ($2,000) see Lebovitz Fund

Carleton College ($5,000) see Moore Foundation, O. L.

Carleton College see Security Life Insurance Co. of America

Carleton College ($10,000) see Wallin Foundation

Carleton College — (Chair in Biology) ($141,375) see Towsley Foundation, Harry A. and Margaret D.

Carlson School of Management ($5,000) see Dain Bosworth/Inter- Regional Financial Group

Carlton Amateur Hockey Association — purchase equipment ($1,000) see Pamida, Inc.

Carondelet Health Care Foundation see Piper Jaffray Cos.

Catholic Charities ($10,000) see Butler Family Foundation, Patrick and Aimee

Catholic Charities ($50,000) see Northern States Power Co.

Catholic Charities ($15,000) see O'Neil Foundation, Casey Albert T.

Catholic Charities ($1,000) see Quinlan Foundation, Elizabeth C.

Catholic Charities/Dorothy Day — renovation of Center, which serves the homeless in downtown St. Paul ($200,000) see Saint Paul Cos.

Catholic Services for the Elderly — capital campaign ($25,000) see Butler Family Foundation, Patrick and Aimee

Catholic Services for the Elderly — start-up costs ($25,000) see Edwards Memorial Trust

Cenacle ($5,000) see Kennedy Foundation, Ethel

Cenacle ($5,000) see Kennedy Foundation, Quentin J.

Cenacle ($3,000) see Quinlan Foundation, Elizabeth C.

Centennial Auditorium — capital ($7,500) see International Multifoods Corp.

Center for Arts Criticism — general support ($77,713) see Jerome Foundation

Center for Biomedical Ethics ($3,000) see Lieberman Enterprises

Center for Global Education ($2,000) see Sexton Foundation

Center State ($10,000) see McKnight Foundation, Sumner T.

Central Minnesota Community Foundation ($5,000) see Dain Bosworth/Inter- Regional Financial Group

Central Minnesota Initiative Fund ($3,932,105) see McKnight Foundation

Central Seminary ($22,000) see Christian Training Foundation

Charities Review Council of Minnesota see Jostens

Chart/Wedco ($16,000) see Chadwick Foundation

Children's Bible Club ($10,000) see McVay Foundation

Children's Cancer Research Fund ($10,000) see Thorpe Foundation, James R.

Children's Home Society of Minnesota ($2,500) see Bauervic Foundation, Peggy

Children's Home Society of Minnesota ($50,000) see Carlson Cos.

Children's Home Society of Minnesota ($500) see Liberty Diversified Industries Inc.

Children's Home Society of Minnesota ($10,000) see Pearson Foundation, E. M.

Children's Home Society of Minnesota — Waiting American Child Program see Cargill

Children's Hospital ($16,000) see Meadowood Foundation

Children's Hospital Association — one year pilot program ($20,000) see Edwards Memorial Trust

Children's Hospital of Minneapolis see Amoco Corp.

Children's Hospital, St. Paul ($46,000) see Andersen Foundation, Hugh J.

Children's Miracle Network ($1,470,433) see Wal-Mart Stores

Children's Miracle Network ($106,354) see Wal-Mart Stores

Children's Miracle Network ($55,260) see Wal-Mart Stores

Children's Museum — capital ($250,000) see General Mills

Children's Museum see Piper Jaffray Cos.

Children's Museum — capital campaign support to relocate in downtown St. Paul ($333,000) see Saint Paul Cos.

Children's Theatre — family theatre guides see Cargill

Children's Theatre Company and School — to sponsor a production ($60,000) see IDS Financial Services

Child's Play Theatre Company see Jostens

Christian College Consortium — to help fund a faculty development program ($125,000) see Davis Foundations, Arthur Vining

Church of St. Nicholas ($14,295) see Wasie Foundation

Citizens Scholarship of America ($12,127) see Mankato Citizens Telephone Co.

Citizens Scholarship Foundation ($71,440) see Mohasco Corp.

Citizens Scholarship Foundation ($83,826) see Norwest Corp.

Citizens' Scholarship Foundation of America ($310,000) see Allstate Insurance Co.

Citizens Scholarship Foundation of America ($14,200) see Bardes Corp.

Citizens' Scholarship Foundation of America — vocational scholarship awards ($22,550) see Bemis Company

Citizen's Scholarship Foundation of America ($356,530) see Chrysler Corp.

Citizens' Scholarship Foundation of America see First Bank System

Citizens Scholarship Foundation of America ($53,750) see GEICO Corp.

Citizens' Scholarship Foundation of America ($275,958) see General Electric Co.

Citizens' Scholarship Foundation of America ($98,245) see Iacocca Foundation

Citizens' Scholarship Foundation of America ($57,500) see Illinois Tool Works

Citizens' Scholarship Foundation of America see Jostens

Citizen's Scholarship Foundation of America — scholarship fund ($10,000) see MDU Resources Group, Inc.

Citizens Scholarship Foundation of America ($20,620) see Northwestern National Life Insurance Co.

Citizens Scholarship Foundation of America ($72,200) see Pillsbury Co.

Citizens Scholarship Foundation of America ($6,000) see Tennant Co.

Citizens' Scholarship Foundation of America ($92,100) see Unocal Corp.

Citizens Scholarship Foundation of America ($112,030) see Weyerhaeuser Co.

Citizens Scholarship Foundation of America ($30,970) see Wisconsin Power & Light Co.

Citizens' Scholarship Foundation of America — Fluor Daniel Engineering Scholarship Program and the Fluor Daniel Engineering Scholarship Program for Women and Minorities ($203,490) see Fluor Corp.

Citizens' Scholarship Foundation of America — for the Fluor Foundation Scholarship Program for children of Fluor employees ($258,508) see Fluor Corp.

Citizens' Scholarship Foundation of America — scholarship program for the children of employees of HCA and its affiliates ($196,055) see Hospital Corp. of America

Citizens' Scholarship Foundation of America — 1992 scholarship awards for the First Interstate Scholarship Program ($37,500) see First Interstate Bank of California

Citizens Scholarship Foundation of America/Pathways ($137,189) see Metropolitan Life Insurance Co.

Citizens' Scholarship Foundation of America — post-high school scholarships for children of General Mills employees ($169,550) see General Mills

Citizens Scholarship Foundation of America, St. Peter, MN — company-sponsored employee scholarships ($31,080) see Searle & Co., G.D.

Citizens Scholarship Foundation of America — support of The Baxter Foundation Scholarship program ($271,682) see Baxter International

Citizens Scholarship Foundation of America — providing 270 merit-based scholarships in United States and Canada to students pursuing training in automotive technology ($154,235) see Fel-Pro Incorporated

Citizen's Scholarships-Foundation of America ($189,460) see CIGNA Corp.

City of Lake City — window replacements in City Hall ($12,000) see O'Neil Foundation, Casey Albert T.

City of Minneapolis — enable hard-to-employ young people to gain work experience through internships and employment ($425,000) see McKnight Foundation

Cloquet Community Memorial Hospital Foundation — replace hospital equipment ($1,000) see Pamida, Inc.

Cloquet Community Memorial Hospital Foundation — target ($30,000) see Potlatch Corp.

CLUES, Chicanos Latinos Unidos en Servicio — for the operations of this mental health program that serves the Hispanic community ($45,000) see Bremer Foundation, Otto

Coffee House Press see First Bank System

College of St. Benedict — scholarships ($118,270) see Alliss Educational Foundation, Charles and Ellora

College of St. Benedict ($5,000) see Warner Foundation, Lee and Rose

College of St. Benedicts ($18,000) see Sexton Foundation

College of St. Catherine ($350,000) see Bush Foundation

College of St. Catherine — capital campaign ($150,000) see Butler Family Foundation, Patrick and Aimee

College of St. Catherine — capital fund ($50,000) see Deluxe Corp.

College of St. Catherine — capital fund ($50,000) see Deluxe Corp.

College of St. Scholastica ($412,500) see Bush Foundation

College of St. Scholastica ($2,000) see Kasal Charitable Trust, Father

College of St. Scholastica — target ($25,000) see Potlatch Corp.

College of St. Scholastica ($4,000) see Van Evera Foundation, Dewitt Caroline

College of St. Scholastica ($5,000) see Warner Foundation, Lee and Rose

College of St. Scholastica — loans for low-income Registered Nursing and Physical Therapy students ($50,000) see Ordean Foundation

College of St. Tarego ($87,933) see Hiawatha Education Foundation

College of St. Thomas ($300,070) see Business Incentives

College of St. Thomas ($43,500) see McNeely Foundation

College of St. Thomas ($20,000) see Quinlan Foundation, Elizabeth C.

College of St. Thomas ($8,350) see Tennant Co.

College of St. Thomas ($10,000) see Valspar Corp.

College of St. Thomas, St. Paul, MN ($20,000) see Northwestern National Life Insurance Co.

Community Clinic Consortium — community health fund see Cargill

Community Clinic Consortium — general ($21,000) see Edwards Memorial Trust

Community Clinic Consortium, St. Paul, MN ($13,000) see Northwestern National Life Insurance Co.

Compas ($34,222) see Steele Foundation

Concordia College ($48,178) see Hallett Charitable Trust

Concordia College ($32,074) see Hallett Charitable Trust

Concordia College ($32,073) see Hallett Charitable Trust, Jessie F.

Concordia College ($10,000) see Pearson Foundation, E. M.

Concordia College ($3,105) see Staley Foundation, Thomas F.

Concordia College - Moorhead — scholarships ($169,420) see Alliss Educational Foundation, Charles and Ellora

Concordia Language Village ($15,000) see Cherne Foundation, Albert W.

Convent of the Visitation ($5,000) see O'Brien Foundation, Alice M.

Cooperative Older Adult Ministry ($3,000) see AHS Foundation

Cotton High School ($566,236) see Hiawatha Education Foundation

Courage Center ($22,200) see Alliant Techsystems

Courage Center ($100,000) see Andersen Corp.

Courage Center ($2,200) see Federated Life Insurance Co.

Minnesota (cont.)

Courage Center ($1,000) see Groves & Sons Co., S.J.

Courage Center ($100,000) see Mardag Foundation

Courage Center ($5,000) see McVay Foundation

Courage Center ($20,000) see O'Brien Foundation, Alice M.

Courage Center ($6,000) see Onan Family Foundation

Courage Center ($105,000) see Phipps Foundation, William H.

Courage Center ($6,500) see Special People In Need

Courage Center ($15,000) see Tozer Foundation

Courage Center — handi-ham program ($20,000) see O'Neil Foundation, Casey Albert T.

Crown Ministries ($7,000) see Salwil Foundation

Dakota — programs to help disadvantaged people achieve independence ($3,000) see Blue Cross and Blue Shield of Minnesota Foundation Inc.

Dakota Area Referral and Transportation for Seniors — for the capital campaign ($100,000) see Bigelow Foundation, F. R.

Dale Warland Singers — emerging composers program ($33,661) see Jerome Foundation

De La Salle High School — skills lab program ($9,500) see Wasie Foundation

DeLaSalle High School ($5,000) see Onan Family Foundation

District 77 Outcome Based Education ($1,600) see Mankato Citizens Telephone Co.

Dr. Knight Science and Technology Magnet Elementary School ($1,000) see Weyerhaeuser Memorial Foundation, Charles A.

Domestic Violence Center ($11,000) see Rahr Malting Co.

Dorothy Day Center ($1,500) see McNeely Foundation

Downtown Council ($10,000) see TCF Banking & Savings, FSB

Duluth Community Action Program — emergency fuel-assistance for low-income households ($200,000) see Ordean Foundation

Duluth Community Health Center — health care services for low-income people ($52,000) see Ordean Foundation

Duluth Hunger Coalition — soup kitchen, food shelf, Duluth Food and Nutrition Council and Community Garden Program ($50,000) see Ordean Foundation

Duluth Public TV ($5,000) see Beim Foundation

Duluth-Superior Community Foundation ($15,000) see Beim Foundation

Duluth Technical College — scholarships for low-income ($31,200) see Ordean Foundation

Dunwoody Industrial Institute — third and final payment on pledge ($18,000) see Bemis Company

Dunwoody Institute ($5,000) see Thorpe Foundation, James R.

Edwards Endowment United Hospital Foundation ($4,000)

see Lilly Foundation, Richard Coyle

Employee Assistance ($3,600) see CENEX

Episcopal Diocese of Minnesota — building fund, Collegeville ($56,963) see Athwin Foundation

F. R. Bigelow Foundation — the Children, Families and Community Initiative ($146,315) see Bigelow Foundation, F. R.

Family Housing Fund of Minneapolis and St. Paul — provide affordable rental housing for low-income families ($500,000) see Saint Paul Cos.

Family Housing Fund of Minneapolis and St. Paul — to assist the development of affordable housing for low-income people in St. Paul ($60,000) see Bremer Foundation, Otto

Family Service — to support the Gay and Lesbian Counseling service, a mental health program for residents of Ramsey, Dakota, and Washington County ($30,000) see Bremer Foundation, Otto

Family Service of St. Croix Area — building campaign ($10,000) see Phipps Foundation, William H.

Family Service of St. Croix Area ($6,350) see Tozer Foundation

Father Martin's Ashley-Building Fund ($10,000) see McKnight Foundation, Sumner T.

Federation of Jewish Services ($16,600) see Lebovitz Fund

First Baptist Church ($16,000) see Kejr Foundation

Forest Resource Center ($215,000) see Blandin Foundation

Freshwater Biological Research Foundation ($5,000) see Rodman Foundation

Freshwater Foundation ($15,000) see Athwin Foundation

Freshwater Foundation ($10,000) see Onan Family Foundation

Friends of Minneapolis Public Library — planetarium see Cargill

Friends of the St. Paul Public Library ($25,000) see Mardag Foundation

Gillette Children's Hospital ($205,000) see Andersen Foundation

Girl Scouts of America ($80,000) see Phipps Foundation, William H.

Glen Avon Presbyterian Church ($500) see Paulucci Family Foundation

Goodhue County Historical Society ($50,000) see Red Wing Shoe Co.

Gospel Temple ($29,000) see Hersey Foundation

Gospel Temple ($21,100) see Northern Star Foundation

Grace Church of Edina ($7,500) see Douglas Corp.

Graw House of Minneapolis — residence for AIDS patients ($10,000) see Pax Christi Foundation

Great North American History Theatre ($30,000) see Andersen Foundation, Hugh J.

Great River Homes ($10,000) see O'Neil Foundation, Casey Albert T.

Greater Minneapolis Food Bank ($5,000) see SIT Investment Associates, Inc.

Greater Minneapolis Girl Scout Council ($25,000) see Graco

Greater Minneapolis Girl Scout Council ($15,000) see Graco

Groves Learning Center ($82,764) see Groves & Sons Co., S.J.

Groves Learning Center ($7,000) see Schott Foundation

Groves Learning Center ($5,000) see Thorpe Foundation, James R.

Gustavus Adolphus — capital fund ($50,000) see Hubbard Milling Co.

Gustavus Adolphus ($7,000) see Hubbard Milling Co.

Gustavus Adolphus College — scholarships ($140,790) see Alliss Educational Foundation, Charles and Ellora

Gustavus Adolphus College ($2,500) see Douglas Corp.

Gustavus Adolphus College ($1,380,000) see Olin Foundation, F. W.

Guthrie Annual Fund ($6,500) see Levitt Foundation

Guthrie Endowment ($20,000) see Levitt Foundation

Guthrie Endowment (Guthrie Theatre Foundation) ($15,000) see Levitt Foundation, Richard S.

Guthrie Theater — capital campaign ($20,000) see Bemis Company

Guthrie Theater ($5,000) see Dain Bosworth/Inter- Regional Financial Group

Guthrie Theater ($25,000) see Grossman Foundation, N. Bud

Guthrie Theater ($21,500) see Regis Corp.

Guthrie Theater ($15,000) see Southways Foundation

Guthrie Theater ($10,000) see Southways Foundation

Guthrie Theater ($4,500) see Tennant Co.

Guthrie Theater Foundation — endow and renovate the theater ($1,000,000) see Bush Foundation

Guthrie Theatre — for grant and endowment support for nationally acclaimed theatre ($112,000) see Ecolab

Guthrie Theatre — to sponsor a publication ($20,000) see IDS Financial Services

Guthrie Theatre ($6,500) see Lilly Foundation, Richard Coyle

Guthrie Theatre ($100,000) see Pillsbury Co.

Guthrie Theatre Foundation ($50,000) see Andersen Foundation, Hugh J.

Guthrie Theatre Foundation — general support and capital grant ($125,000) see Honeywell

Habitat for Humanity ($25,000) see Pax Christi Foundation

Hamline University ($50,000) see Rodman Foundation

Hamline University School of Law ($10,000) see Business Incentives

Hamline University School of Law ($6,700) see Grotto Foundation

Harriet Tubman Women's Shelter, Inc. see Bloomingdale's

Hazelden — general support ($50,000) see Solo Cup Co.

Hazelden Foundation ($5,000) see Gilman, Jr. Foundation, Sondra and Charles

Hazelden Foundation ($10,000) see Grotto Foundation

Hazelden Foundation ($50,000) see O'Brien Foundation, Alice M.

Hazelden Foundation ($10,000) see O'Brien Foundation, Alice M.

Hazelden Foundation ($80,900) see Offield Family Foundation

Hazelden Foundation — financial assistance ($25,000) see Edwards Memorial Trust

Health Futures Institute — support of health education advertisements and general operating support ($49,000) see Medtronic

Hearing Dog Program of Minnesota ($5,000) see Beim Foundation

Hennepin Avenue Methodist Church ($10,000) see Onan Family Foundation

Hennepin Avenue Methodist Church ($6,000) see Onan Family Foundation

Hennepin County Library Foundation — bookmobile service ($50,000) see Cowles Media Co.

Herzl Camp ($4,000) see Heilicher Foundation, Menahem

Herzl Camp Association ($10,000) see Fingerhut Family Foundation

Herzl Camp Association ($2,500) see Liberty Diversified Industries Inc.

Honeywell/Alliant Techsystems/Medtronic Academies ($17,000) see Alliant Techsystems

Hospital House ($6,000) see Business Incentives

Hospitality House — preventive treatment ($10,000) see O'Neil Foundation, Casey Albert T.

Hospitality House ($5,000) see Rahr Malting Co.

House of Hope Presbyterian Church ($72,976) see Weyerhaeuser Memorial Foundation, Charles A.

Illusion Theater ($10,000) see TCF Banking & Savings, FSB

Incarnation House ($7,500) see SIT Investment Associates, Inc.

Independent School District #704-Proctor — community center for youth and senior citizens ($35,000) see Ordean Foundation

Indianhead Council Boy Scouts of America ($10,000) see Pearson Foundation, E. M.

Institute of Agriculture Trade — Fair Trade campaign ($50,000) see Ira-Hiti Foundation for Deep Ecology

Institute for Agriculture and Trade Policy — support for the Citizen's Campaign on Trade Action Plan ($25,000) see Norman Foundation

Institute of Social ($6,250) see TCF Banking & Savings, FSB

Institute for Trade and Agricultural Policy ($40,000) see HKH Foundation

Intermedia Arts — 1990 and 1991 Installation Arts Commissioning Programs ($33,000) see Jerome Foundation

International Special Olympic Games ($10,000) see Wasie Foundation

International Special Olympic Games — 1991 games ($15,000) see O'Neil Foundation, Casey Albert T.

International Special Olympics — general support and special pledge ($142,931) see Honeywell

International Special Olympics ($1,000) see Liberty Diversified Industries Inc.

James Ford Bell Museum, International Falls, MN — finnish wood sculpture exhibit ($16,000) see Boise Cascade Corp.

Janesville High School ($2,500) see Johnson Co., E. F.

Jehovah Evangelical Lutheran Church ($32,000) see Pearson Foundation, E. M.

Jerome Foundation — New York City Film/Video Program ($156,493) see Jerome Foundation

Jerome Foundation — Travel and Study Grant Program ($103,211) see Jerome Foundation

Jessie F. Hallett Memorial Library ($175,390) see Hallett Charitable Trust

Jessie F. Hallett Memorial Library ($25,000) see Van Evera Foundation, Dewitt Caroline

Jewish Community Center ($1,000) see Heilicher Foundation, Menahem

Jewish Community Center ($1,000) see Heilicher Foundation, Menahem

Jewish Community Center Early Childhood Center ($750) see Heilicher Foundation, Menahem

Joint Ministry Project ($25,000) see Needmor Fund

Junior Achievement ($4,700) see Blue Cross and Blue Shield of Minnesota Foundation Inc.

Junior Achievement ($10,000) see Dain Bosworth/Inter-Regional Financial Group

Junior Achievement — general operating ($5,350) see International Multifoods Corp.

Junior Achievement ($6,500) see Minnesota Mutual Life Insurance Co.

Junior Achievement ($9,075) see Phipps Foundation, William H.

Junior Achievement of Twin Cities ($6,500) see Donaldson Co.

Kanabec City Historical Society ($9,000) see McVay Foundation

KBPR/FM ($1,500) see Van Evera Foundation, Dewitt Caroline

Kooch-Itasca Action Council — toward the construction of a new building for the Head Start early childhood education program ($100,000) see Bremer Foundation, Otto

KTCA ($7,000) see Red Wing Shoe Co.

KTCA-TV ($29,000) see Andersen Corp.

KTCA 2/KTCI 17 — annual program ($15,000) see O'Neil Foundation, Casey Albert T.

Ladew Topiary Gardens ($10,000) see McKnight Foundation, Sumner T.

Lake Superior Big Top Chautauqua ($95,000) see

Hulings Foundation, Mary Andersen

Lakeview Memorial Hospital ($25,000) see Saint Croix Foundation

Lakeview Memorial Hospital ($10,000) see Tozer Foundation

Landmark Center ($5,000) see Minnesota Mutual Life Insurance Co.

Learning Disabilities Association ($77,000) see Andersen Foundation, Hugh J.

Leo A. Hoffman Center — capital campaign for new treatment center ($25,000) see Edwards Memorial Trust

Listening House of St. Paul ($5,000) see Wasie Foundation

Little Brothers Friends of the Elderly ($5,000) see Wasie Foundation

Loaves and Fishes ($1,000) see Hooper Handling

Local Initiatives Support Corporation — to improve the physical, economic, and social conditions of older, distressed neighborhoods in St. Paul ($225,000) see Northwest Area Foundation

Loft ($7,500) see Thorpe Foundation, James R.

Loring-Nicollet-Bethlehem Community Center ($10,000) see Cherne Foundation, Albert W.

Loring-Nicollet-Bethlehem Community Center ($4,000) see SIT Investment Associates, Inc.

Lourdes High School ($139,400) see Hiawatha Education Foundation

Luther Haven Nursing Home ($8,000) see Pearson Foundation, E. M.

Luther Northwestern Theological Seminary — reformation library ($120,000) see Lutheran Brotherhood Foundation

Luther Northwestern Theological Seminary — model advocacy and mentoring program ($50,000) see Lutheran Brotherhood Foundation

Lutheran Church of Redeemer ($15,000) see AHS Foundation

Lutheran Social Service/Duluth — to provide medical, dental and optical assistance to low-income people ($145,800) see Ordean Foundation

Lutheran Social Service of Minnesota — capital campaign ($346,000) see Bush Foundation

Macalester College ($36,113) see Bradish Trust, Norman C.

Macalester College ($10,000) see Gray Charitable Trust, Mary S.

Macalester College ($25,000) see Littauer Foundation, Lucius N.

Macalester College — library building fund ($10,000) see Marbrook Foundation

Macalester College ($25,000) see Mercy, Jr. Foundation, Sue and Eugene

Macalester College ($25,000) see Weyerhaeuser Foundation, Frederick and Margaret L.

Macalester College ($20,000) see Weyerhaeuser Foundation, Frederick and Margaret L.

Macalester College — continued support of the Foundation Professorship in Economics

and for renovation of Carnegie Hall ($100,000) see Bigelow Foundation, F. R.

Madeline Island Music Camp ($50,000) see Hulings Foundation, Mary Andersen

Madonna College ($1,000) see Bauervic Foundation, Peggy

Madonna College ($5,500) see Shapero Foundation, Nate S. and Ruth B.

Mankato High Potential ($4,826) see Hubbard Milling Co.

Mankato State University ($7,000) see Hubbard Milling Co.

Mankato State University Foundation ($10,000) see Johnson Co., E. F.

Mankato State University Foundation — scholarships ($20,000) see Mankato Citizens Telephone Co.

Mankato United Fund ($8,500) see Hubbard Milling Co.

Mary and Jackson Burke Foundation — acquisition ($110,000) see Griggs and Mary Griggs Burke Foundation, Mary Livingston

Mary and Jackson burke Foundation — administration ($150,000) see Griggs and Mary Griggs Burke Foundation, Mary Livingston

Mayo Clinic ($50,000) see Griffin, Sr., Foundation, C. V.

Mayo Clinic ($50,000) see Griffin, Sr., Foundation, C. V.

Mayo Clinic ($25,000) see Philips Foundation, Jesse

Mayo Clinic ($200,000) see Phillips Family Foundation, Jay and Rose

Mayo Clinic ($50,000) see Weintraub Family Foundation, Joseph

Mayo Clinic Foundation ($10,000) see Klingler Foundation, Helen and Charles

Mayo Foundation ($250,000) see Andersen Foundation

Mayo Foundation ($85,000) see Borchard Foundation, Albert and Elaine

Mayo Foundation ($50,000) see Borchard Foundation, Albert and Elaine

Mayo Foundation ($20,000) see Chadwick Foundation

Mayo Foundation — equipment fund ($100,000) see Grainger Foundation

Mayo Foundation ($5,000) see Heller Foundation, Walter E.

Mayo Foundation — general purposes ($150,000) see Leighton-Oare Foundation

Mayo Foundation ($530,337) see Parsons - W.D. Charities, Vera Davis

Mayo Foundation — medical school scholarships ($10,000) see Phillips Family Foundation, L. E.

Mayo Foundation — medical education and research ($2,500) see Quincy Newspapers

Mayo Foundation ($11,000) see Roddis Foundation, Hamilton

Mayo Foundation ($10,000) see Salomon Foundation, Richard & Edna

Mayo Foundation ($100,000) see Taylor Family Foundation, Jack

Mayo Foundation ($25,401) see Walker Foundation, L. C. and Margaret

Mayo Foundation — general ($15,000) see Wehr Foundation, Todd

Mayo Foundation for Medical Research ($25,000) see Adler Foundation

Mayo Foundation for Medical Research ($75,000) see Bonner Foundation, Corella and Bertram

Mayo Foundation for Medical Research ($75,000) see Bonner Foundation, Corella and Bertram

Mayo Foundation for Medical Research ($150,000) see Davis Family - W.D. Charities, James E.

Mayo Foundation for Medical Research ($20,000) see Dodson Foundation, James Glenwell and Clara May

Mayo Foundation for Medical Research ($20,000) see Hartz Foundation

Mayo Foundation for Medical Research ($25,000) see Knowles Foundation

Mayo Foundation for Medical Research ($75,000) see Ladish Family Foundation, Herman W.

Mayo Foundation for Medical Research ($50,000) see Mayer Charitable Trust, Oscar G. & Elsa S.

Mayo Foundation for Medical Research ($500) see Parker Drilling Co.

Mayo Foundation for Medical Research ($1,000) see Plym Foundation

Mayo Foundation for Medical Research ($5,000) see Puett Foundation, Nelson

Mayo Foundation for Medical Research ($3,000) see Sang Foundation, Elsie O. and Philip D.

Mayo Foundation for Medical Research ($20,000) see Zarrow Foundation, Anne and Henry

Mayo Foundation Section of Dermatology — medical research in dermatology; general purposes ($20,000) see Kieckhefer Foundation, J. W.

Mayo Medical School ($12,500) see Taylor Family Foundation, Jack

Mcalester College ($20,000) see Weatherhead Foundation

McKnight Endowment Fund for Neuroscience — awards programs supporting research in neuroscience ($1,839,000) see McKnight Foundation

Meadowbrook/Oakland University ($500) see Kasle Steel Corp.

Mennepin Avenue United Methodist Church ($5,102) see Carlson Cos.

Mennepin Avenue United Methodist Church ($4,783) see Carlson Cos.

Merriam Park Community Center ($5,000) see Rodman Foundation

Merriam Park Community Center ($25,000) see Weyerhaeuser Foundation, Frederick and Margaret L.

Merrick Community Center ($1,500) see McNeely Foundation

Mesabi Family Y ($262,000) see Blandin Foundation

Messiah Willard Day Care Center — Northside Family Connection Way to Grow

program ($187,750) see General Mills

Metropolitan State University — student stipends program ($20,000) see IDS Financial Services

Milestone Growth Fund ($58,000) see Norwest Corp.

Minneapolis Board of Education ($130,000) see Regis Corp.

Minneapolis Children's Foundation — capital for hospital expansion project ($250,000) see General Mills

Minneapolis Children's Foundation — capital campaign ($12,000) see Marbrook Foundation

Minneapolis Children's Foundation ($100,000) see Oakleaf Foundation

Minneapolis Children's Medical Center ($50,000) see Carolyn Foundation

Minneapolis Children's Medical Foundation ($115,000) see Chadwick Foundation

Minneapolis College of Art and Design — annual fund ($27,000) see Athwin Foundation

Minneapolis College of Art and Design — Jerome Artists Fellowship Program ($57,000) see Jerome Foundation

Minneapolis Crisis Nursery ($5,000) see Wasie Foundation

Minneapolis Federation for Jewish Service ($200,000) see Phillips Family Foundation, Jay and Rose

Minneapolis Federation for Jewish Services ($450,070) see Fingerhut Family Foundation

Minneapolis Federation for Jewish Services ($50,000) see Fingerhut Family Foundation

Minneapolis Federation for Jewish Services ($10,000) see Fingerhut Family Foundation

Minneapolis Federation for Jewish Services ($25,000) see Heilicher Foundation, Menahem

Minneapolis Federation for Jewish Services ($25,000) see Heilicher Foundation, Menahem

Minneapolis Federation for Jewish Services ($263,358) see Levitt Foundation

Minneapolis Federation for Jewish Services ($165,833) see Levitt Foundation, Richard S.

Minneapolis Federation for Jewish Services ($170,600) see Liberty Diversified Industries Inc.

Minneapolis Federation for Jewish Services ($50,000) see Lieberman Enterprises

Minneapolis Federation of Jewish Services ($357,000) see Regis Corp.

Minneapolis Foundation — research ($70,000) see North Star Research Foundation

Minneapolis Foundation ($10,000) see SIT Investment Associates, Inc.

Minneapolis Institute of Art ($5,000) see Donaldson Co.

Minneapolis Institute of Art ($60,000) see Driscoll Foundation

Minneapolis Institute of Art — general operating ($6,000) see International Multifoods Corp.

Minneapolis Institute of Art ($25,045) see Levitt Foundation, Richard S.

Minneapolis Institute of Art ($10,000) see Lieberman Enterprises

Minneapolis Institute of Arts — completion of building and renewal ($500,000) see Athwin Foundation

Minneapolis Institute of Arts — capital campaign ($200,000) see Butler Family Foundation, Patrick and Aimee

Minneapolis Institute of Arts ($100,000) see Carolyn Foundation

Minneapolis Institute of Arts — month sponsorship program ($30,000) see IDS Financial Services

Minneapolis Institute of Arts ($29,600) see Levitt Foundation

Minneapolis Institute of Arts — capital campaign ($20,000) see Marbrook Foundation

Minneapolis Institute of Arts ($50,000) see Norwest Corp.

Minneapolis Institute of Arts ($65,000) see Pillsbury Co.

Minneapolis Institute of Arts ($3,000) see SIT Investment Associates, Inc.

Minneapolis Institute of Arts ($50,000) see Southways Foundation

Minneapolis Institute of Arts ($137,000) see 3M Co.

Minneapolis Institute of Arts ($10,000) see Valspar Corp.

Minneapolis Institute of the Arts ($3,500) see Wallin Foundation

Minneapolis Institute of Arts ($50,000) see Weyerhaeuser Foundation, Frederick and Margaret L.

Minneapolis Institute of Arts — bridge fund/education division $250,000 pledge ($60,000) see Northern States Power Co.

Minneapolis Institute of Arts — New Beginnings campaign ($100,000) see Cowles Media Co.

Minneapolis Institute of Arts — for major art museum in the Twin Cities ($11,500) see Ecolab

Minneapolis Public Schools ($25,000) see Cray Research

Minneapolis Public Schools - Roosevelt High School — support of Health Magnet program ($51,680) see Medtronic

Minneapolis Rotary Community Service ($5,000) see Neilson Foundation, George W.

Minneapolis/St. Paul Family Housing Fund ($25,000) see Pax Christi Foundation

Minneapolis/St. Paul Family Housing Fund — support for the development of affordable housing for low- and moderate-income families ($1,000,000) see McKnight Foundation

Minneapolis/St. Paul Family Housing Fund — to enable moderate-income homeowners to avoid foreclosure by providing financial counseling and emergency financial assistance on case management basis ($330,000) see Northwest Area Foundation

Minneapolis Society for the Blind ($16,036) see Hallett Charitable Trust, Jessie F.

Minnesota (cont.)

Minneapolis Society for the Blind ($2,500) see Nash Foundation

Minneapolis Society of Fine Arts ($13,333) see Lilly Foundation, Richard Coyle

Minneapolis Society of Fine Arts ($5,000) see Lilly Foundation, Richard Coyle

Minneapolis Society of Fine Arts ($33,000) see Meadowood Foundation

Minneapolis Society of Fine Arts ($1,500) see Nash Foundation

Minneapolis Society of Fine Arts — New Beginning's Campaign ($250,000) see General Mills

Minneapolis United Way ($111,000) see Donaldson Co.

Minnehaha Academy ($10,000) see Carlson Cos.

Minnehana Academy ($5,000) see Douglas Corp.

Minnepolis Society of Fine Art ($5,000) see Lieberman Enterprises

Minnesota Agricultural Interpretive Center ($5,000) see Johnson Co., E. F.

Minnesota AIDS Funding Consortium, Minneapolis, MN ($25,000) see Northwestern National Life Insurance Co.

Minnesota AIDS Project — to provide services to those affected by Aids, and educate the public ($3,000) see Blue Cross and Blue Shield of Minnesota Foundation Inc.

Minnesota Astronomical Society ($20,000) see Onan Family Foundation

Minnesota Chamber Foundation ($600) see Liberty Diversified Industries Inc.

Minnesota Chorale ($15,000) see Quaker Hill Foundation

Minnesota Coalition of Health ($11,600) see Blue Cross and Blue Shield of Minnesota Foundation Inc.

Minnesota Community College — scholarships ($250,000) see Alliss Educational Foundation, Charles and Ellora

Minnesota Composers Forum — Composers Commissioning Program ($35,000) see Jerome Foundation

Minnesota Conservatory of the Performing Arts ($5,000) see Nash Foundation

Minnesota Conservatory of Performing Arts ($20,000) see Weyerhaeuser Memorial Foundation, Charles A.

Minnesota Council on Foundations ($1,200) see Fuller Co., H.B.

Minnesota Council on Foundations ($710) see Neilson Foundation, George W.

Minnesota Council on Foundations ($200) see Oakleaf Foundation

Minnesota Council of Nonprofits ($1,000) see Oakleaf Foundation

Minnesota Council of Nonprofits — to continue the Nonprofit Internship Program which provides opportunities for students to explore careers and gain experience in the sector ($365,175) see Bremer Foundation, Otto

Minnesota Cultural Center ($1,500) see Ontario Corp.

Minnesota Dance Alliance — Dancer Pool and Sponsor Pool programs ($32,000) see Jerome Foundation

Minnesota Diversified Industries ($500,000) see Blandin Foundation

Minnesota Festival of Music ($5,000) see Bauervic Foundation, Peggy

Minnesota Food Shelves ($7,500) see Caring and Sharing Foundation

Minnesota FoodShare ($58,000) see Alliant Techsystems

Minnesota Head Injury Foundation ($10,000) see Meadowood Foundation

Minnesota Historical Society ($250,000) see Andersen Foundation

Minnesota Historical Society ($40,000) see Carolyn Foundation

Minnesota Historical Society — capital campaign ($20,000) see Marbrook Foundation

Minnesota Historical Society ($25,000) see Mardag Foundation

Minnesota Historical Society ($10,000) see O'Brien Foundation, Alice M.

Minnesota Historical Society ($10,000) see Saint Croix Foundation

Minnesota Historical Society ($200,000) see 3M Co.

Minnesota Historical Society ($20,000) see Weyerhaeuser Foundation, Frederick and Margaret L.

Minnesota Independent School Fund — scholarships ($240,000) see Alliss Educational Foundation, Charles and Ellora

Minnesota Independent School Fund ($17,500) see Graco

Minnesota Independent School Fund ($5,000) see Thorpe Foundation, James R.

Minnesota Indian Women's Resource Center — shelter ($25,000) see Pax Christi Foundation

Minnesota Jobs with Peace ($9,000) see Ben & Jerry's Homemade

Minnesota Landmarks ($30,000) see Hersey Foundation

Minnesota Landscape Arboretum Foundation ($25,000) see Weyerhaeuser Foundation, Frederick and Margaret L.

Minnesota Literacy Council — Family Literacy Project/State Hotline ($50,000) see Cowles Media Co.

Minnesota Medical Foundation ($50,000) see Eddy Foundation

Minnesota Medical Foundation ($50,000) see Groves & Sons Co., S.J.

Minnesota Medical Foundation — Unversity of Minnesota Cancer Center ($50,000) see Medtronic

Minnesota Meeting ($5,000) see TCF Banking & Savings, FSB

Minnesota Opera ($203,000) see Andersen Foundation

Minnesota Opera — for professional vocal music theatre company ($12,000) see Ecolab

Minnesota Opera ($1,100) see Fuller Co., H.B.

Minnesota Opera — capital and general operating ($16,500) see International Multifoods Corp.

Minnesota Opera ($5,000) see Rahr Malting Co.

Minnesota Opera ($5,000) see Saint Croix Foundation

Minnesota Opera ($8,500) see Tennant Co.

Minnesota Opera ($10,000) see Valspar Corp.

Minnesota Opera Center — annual support and capital campaign ($100,000) see Honeywell

Minnesota Opera Company ($117,000) see Hulings Foundation, Mary Andersen

Minnesota Opera Company — for the Endowment and Capital Campaign ($100,000) see Bigelow Foundation, F. R.

Minnesota Opera — development of Minnesota Opera Center ($40,000) see Cowles Media Co.

Minnesota Opera-Suite 20 — capital campaign ($50,000) see Bemis Company

Minnesota Orchestra ($7,132) see Grossman Foundation, N. Bud

Minnesota Orchestra ($1,200) see Heilicher Foundation, Menahem

Minnesota Orchestra ($5,000) see Lieberman Enterprises

Minnesota Orchestra Guaranty ($16,500) see Grossman Foundation, N. Bud

Minnesota Orchestral Association ($2,500) see Bauervic Foundation, Peggy

Minnesota Orchestral Association ($5,000) see Carlson Cos.

Minnesota Orchestral Association ($2,500) see Fingerhut Family Foundation

Minnesota Orchestral Association ($2,500) see Groves & Sons Co., S.J.

Minnesota Orchestral Association ($20,500) see Hubbard Broadcasting

Minnesota Orchestral Association — cultural sponsorship ($55,000) see IDS Financial Services

Minnesota Orchestral Association — general operating ($7,500) see International Multifoods Corp.

Minnesota Orchestral Association ($67,500) see Pillsbury Co.

Minnesota Orchestral Association ($2,500) see Regis Corp.

Minnesota Orchestral Association ($10,000) see Saint Croix Foundation

Minnesota Orchestral Association ($5,000) see SIT Investment Associates, Inc.

Minnesota Orchestral Association ($5,500) see Tennant Co.

Minnesota Orchestral Association ($20,000) see Tozer Foundation

Minnesota Orchestral Association ($5,000) see Wasie Foundation

Minnesota Orchestral Association, Minneapolis, MN ($35,000) see Northwestern National Life Insurance Co.

Minnesota Orchestral Association — New Dimension II ($50,000) see Hubbard Broadcasting

Minnesota Orchestral Association — New

Dimensions II ($15,000) see Marbrook Foundation

Minnesota Outward Bound ($2,000) see McNeely Foundation

Minnesota Private College Foundation ($1,500) see Mankato Citizens Telephone Co.

Minnesota Private College Fund — financial aid for students ($2,000) see Blue Cross and Blue Shield of Minnesota Foundation Inc.

Minnesota Private College Fund ($7,500) see Dain Bosworth/Inter- Regional Financial Group

Minnesota Private College Fund — college support ($75,300) see Deluxe Corp.

Minnesota Private College Fund ($11,000) see Donaldson Co.

Minnesota Private College Fund ($4,200) see Federated Life Insurance Co.

Minnesota Private College Fund ($2,000) see Fuller Co., H.B.

Minnesota Private College Fund ($25,000) see Graco

Minnesota Private College Fund ($25,000) see Graco

Minnesota Private College Fund ($7,200) see Hubbard Milling Co.

Minnesota Private College Fund — campaign for private colleges ($35,000) see IDS Financial Services

Minnesota Private College Fund — general operating ($10,000) see International Multifoods Corp.

Minnesota Private College Fund ($4,000) see Johnson Co., E. F.

Minnesota Private College Fund ($2,200) see McNeely Foundation

Minnesota Private College Fund ($15,000) see Minnesota Mutual Life Insurance Co.

Minnesota Private College Fund ($75,000) see Northern States Power Co.

Minnesota Private College Fund ($27,500) see Northwestern National Life Insurance Co.

Minnesota Private College Fund ($62,500) see Pillsbury Co.

Minnesota Private College Fund ($6,000) see Quinlan Foundation, Elizabeth C.

Minnesota Private College Fund ($12,500) see Rahr Malting Co.

Minnesota Private College Fund ($6,500) see Red Wing Shoe Co.

Minnesota Private College Fund ($9,000) see Saint Croix Foundation

Minnesota Private College Fund ($9,000) see Tennant Co.

Minnesota Private College Fund ($20,000) see Thorpe Foundation, James R.

Minnesota Private College Fund — scholarships for 15 minority students in science ($45,000) see Medtronic

Minnesota Private College Fund — for the 15-member colleges of MPCF ($12,000) see Ecolab

Minnesota Private College Research Foundation ($519,600) see Blandin Foundation

Minnesota Private Colleges ($17,500) see TCF Banking & Savings, FSB

Minnesota Public Radio — for public radio production and

programming ($10,000) see Ecolab

Minnesota Public Radio ($55,000) see Hulings Foundation, Mary Andersen

Minnesota Public Radio ($1,000) see Quinlan Foundation, Elizabeth C.

Minnesota Public Radio ($7,500) see Thorpe Foundation, James R.

Minnesota Public Radio — broadcasts of the 1992/93 season of Minnesota Orchestra and St. Paul Chamber Orchestra ($40,000) see Fuller Co., H.B.

Minnesota Public Radio Station Construction ($20,000) see Hartz Foundation

Minnesota Public Radio — support for the 25th Anniversary Campaign for equipment replacement ($250,000) see Saint Paul Cos.

Minnesota Rural Organizing Project ($25,000) see Needmor Fund

Minnesota Smoke Free — self help programs to help individuals quit smoking ($5,000) see Blue Cross and Blue Shield of Minnesota Foundation Inc.

Minnesota Society for Crippled Children ($10,000) see Gray Charitable Trust, Mary S.

Minnesota State University System — scholarships ($505,310) see Alliss Educational Foundation, Charles and Ellora

Minnesota Vietnam Veterans Memorial ($5,000) see Thorpe Foundation, James R.

Minnesota Vo-tech Trust Association ($65,000) see Northern States Power Co.

Minnesota Wellspring ($250) see BMC Industries

Minnesota Woman's Fund ($10,000) see Grossman Foundation, N. Bud

Minnesota Women's Fund ($20,000) see Cherne Foundation, Albert W.

Minnesota Zoo Foundation ($157,000) see Chadwick Foundation

Minnesota Zoological Garden ($1,250) see Nash Foundation

Minnetonka Community Church ($16,000) see Kejr Foundation

Moorhead State University — boron based polymers and ceramic precursors via the coupling of borane clusters with diborylalkanes ($35,000) see Research Corporation

Mounds Midway Foundation ($7,667) see McNeely Foundation

Mounds Park Academy — capital campaign ($175,000) see Bigelow Foundation, F. R.

Mount Olivet Lutheran Church of Plymouth ($25,000) see Onan Family Foundation

Naeve Health Care Foundation ($10,000) see Kasal Charitable Trust, Father

National Ataxia Foundation ($2,000) see Andersen Foundation, Arthur

National Ataxia Foundation ($1,000) see Fibre Converters

National Childhood Grief Institute ($10,000) see Driscoll Foundation

National Conference of Christians and Jews ($500) see

Liberty Diversified Industries Inc.

National Network Women's Funds ($8,000) see Hunt Alternatives Fund, Helen

National Retiree Volunteer Center ($25,000) see Illinois Tool Works

Nature Conservancy ($10,000) see Marbrook Foundation

Nature Conservancy ($5,000) see O'Brien Foundation, Alice M.

Nature Conservancy ($5,000) see Schott Foundation

Nature Conservancy, Minnesota Chapter ($50,000) see Hulings Foundation, Mary Andersen

Neighborhood House — to support the Afterschool Clubs and other youth activities ($40,000) see Bremer Foundation, Otto

Neighborhood Involvement Program (NIP) — apply toward mortgage ($100,000) see Athwin Foundation

Neighborhood Involvement Program (NIP) — adolescent pregnancy prevention ($19,793) see Athwin Foundation

New Connections Programs ($5,000) see Walker Foundation, Archie D. and Bertha H.

New Richland/Hartland High School ($2,500) see Johnson Co., E. F.

North Central Baptist Church ($22,000) see Hersey Foundation

North Central Baptist Church ($33,000) see Northern Star Foundation

North Memorial Medical Center ($9,000) see Onan Family Foundation

Northeastern Minnesota Initiative Fund ($3,354,662) see McKnight Foundation

Northside Residents Redevelopment Council — social help ($10,000) see Pax Christi Foundation

Northwest Minnesota Initiative Fund ($3,732,019) see McKnight Foundation

Northwest Minnesota Initiative Fund ($90,000) see Neilson Foundation, George W.

Northwest Minnesota Initiative Fund ($32,000) see Neilson Foundation, George W.

Northwest Minnesota Initiative Fund ($2,000) see Neilson Foundation, George W.

Northwestern Chiropractic College ($40,000) see Foundation for Advancement of Chiropractic Education

Northwestern Chiropractic College — research ($40,000) see Foundation for Advancement of Chiropractic Education

Northwestern College ($20,000) see Cherne Foundation, Albert W.

Object for Pride in Living — capital campaign for affordable housing for low-income families ($12,500) see Butler Family Foundation, Patrick and Aimee

1991 International Special Olympics Games ($5,000) see Dain Bosworth/Inter- Regional Financial Group

Order of St. Benedict for St. John's Abbey and Preparatory School — racial minorities

($30,000) see O'Neil Foundation, Casey Albert T.

Ordway Music Theater — capital fund ($25,000) see Bemis Company

Ordway Music Theater ($25,000) see Saint Croix Foundation

Ordway Music Theatre ($400,000) see Andersen Foundation

Ordway Music Theatre — finance replacement of the theatrical lighting system ($250,000) see Bigelow Foundation, F. R.

Ordway Music Theatre ($285,000) see 3M Co.

Ordway Music Theatre ($20,000) see Tozer Foundation

Ordway Music Theatre ($20,000) see Weyerhaeuser Foundation, Frederick and Margaret L.

Our Fair Carousel ($5,000) see O'Brien Foundation, Alice M.

Palmer Foundation — scholarships ($22,000) see Hubbard Milling Co.

Park Nicollet Medical Foundation ($50,000) see Schott Foundation

Pathfinders — programs to improve children's health ($5,000) see Blue Cross and Blue Shield of Minnesota Foundation Inc.

Patrick Henry High School ($11,800) see TCF Banking & Savings, FSB

Patrick Henry High School ($11,800) see TCF Banking & Savings, FSB

Patrick Henry High School ($11,000) see TCF Banking & Savings, FSB

Patrick Henry High School ($10,000) see TCF Banking & Savings, FSB

Phillips Eye Institute ($10,000) see Carlson Cos.

Phillips Eye Institute ($100,000) see Phillips Family Foundation, Jay and Rose

Phoenix Residence — adults with developmental disabilities ($25,000) see Edwards Memorial Trust

Pillsbury United Neighborhood Services ($10,000) see Cherne Foundation, Albert W.

Pillsbury United Neighborhood Services — Fund Way to Grow program in Camden area ($37,500) see Medtronic

Planned Parenthood ($20,000) see Meadowood Foundation

Planned Parenthood ($5,000) see Neilson Foundation, George W.

Planned Parenthood ($50,000) see Oakleaf Foundation

Planned Parenthood Federation of America ($10,500) see Lilly Foundation, Richard Coyle

Planned Parenthood of Minnesota — capital campaign ($100,000) see Cowles Media Co.

Planned Parenthood of Minnesota ($20,000) see Gray Charitable Trust, Mary S.

Planned Parenthood of Minnesota ($1,800) see Wallin Foundation

Playwrights' Center — Jerome Fellowship program for emerging playwrights and Midwest Playlabs ($65,000) see Jerome Foundation

Plymouth Music Series ($50,000) see Hulings Foundation, Mary Andersen

Prairie Creek Community School ($10,000) see Cartinhour Foundation

Prairie Creek Community School ($4,500) see Cartinhour Foundation

Prairie Creek Community School ($30,000) see Woods-Greer Foundation

Presbyterian Homes of Minnesota — expansion of community program ($25,000) see Edwards Memorial Trust

Presbyterian Homes of Minnesota ($4,000) see Wallin Foundation

Presbyterian Homes of Minnesota ($50,000) see Weyerhaeuser Foundation, Frederick and Margaret L.

Pro-Choice Resources ($68,540) see Hersey Foundation

Project for Pride in Living ($50,000) see Northern States Power Co.

Project for Pride in Living — shelter ($10,000) see Pax Christi Foundation

Project for Pride in Living ($85,000) see Pillsbury Co.

Queen of Peace Hospital — health inv. program ($25,000) see Athwin Foundation

R.C. Community Center ($3,334) see Hubbard Milling Co.

Rebuild Resources ($15,000) see Driscoll Foundation

Rebuild Resources ($10,000) see Saint Croix Foundation

Red Cross — St. Paul area ($10,000) see Pearson Foundation, E. M.

Red Wing Arts Association ($10,000) see Red Wing Shoe Co.

Red Wing School District #256, Environmental Learning Center ($170,000) see Red Wing Shoe Co.

Refugee and Immigrant Resource Center ($7,000) see Grotto Foundation

Regents of the University of Minnesota ($25,000) see Mardag Foundation

Resources for Child Caring ($10,000) see Saint Croix Foundation

Rise ($5,000) see Wasie Foundation

Roberta Mann Ray Foundation — civic ($120,000) see Mann Foundation, Ted

Roberta Mann Ray Foundation — civic ($100,000) see Mann Foundation, Ted

St. Cloud State University ($1,000) see Regis Corp.

St. Croix Area United Way ($50,000) see Andersen Corp.

St. Croix Valley Youth Center ($50,000) see Hubbard Broadcasting

St. David School ($2,000) see Sweatt Foundation, Harold W.

St. David's School for Child Development ($5,000) see Thorpe Foundation, James R.

St. James Academy ($33,333) see McKnight Foundation, Sumner T.

St. John's Preparatory School ($5,000) see Grotto Foundation

St. John's Preparatory School ($25,000) see Van Evera Foundation, Dewitt Caroline

St. John's University ($500,000) see Bush Foundation

St. Johns University ($1,000) see Warner Foundation, Lee and Rose

St. Joseph Home for Children — shelter for abused children ($15,000) see Pax Christi Foundation

St. Joseph Hospital ($100) see Bauervic Foundation, Peggy

St. Mary's College ($10,000) see Hiawatha Education Foundation

St. Mary's College ($15,000) see News & Observer Publishing Co.

St. Mary's College of Minnesota ($15,000) see Bowyer Foundation, Ambrose and Gladys

St. Mercy's School ($6,000) see Hiawatha Education Foundation

St. Olaf Catholic Church ($10,000) see Quinlan Foundation, Elizabeth C.

St. Olaf College — scholarships ($184,610) see Alliss Educational Foundation, Charles and Ellora

St. Olaf College — scholarship ($6,000) see Petteys Memorial Foundation, Jack

St. Paul Academy and Summit School ($10,000) see Lilly Foundation, Richard Coyle

St. Paul American Indian Center ($10,000) see Hersey Foundation

St. Paul Chamber ($15,000) see Grossman Foundation, N. Bud

St. Paul Chamber Orchestra ($6,000) see Bolz Family Foundation, Eugenie Mayer

St. Paul Chamber Orchestra ($4,000) see Fuller Co., H.B.

St. Paul Chamber Orchestra ($60,000) see Hulings Foundation, Mary Andersen

St. Paul Chamber Orchestra ($1,500) see McNeely Foundation

St. Paul Chamber Orchestra ($12,500) see Minnesota Mutual Life Insurance Co.

St. Paul Chamber Orchestra ($260,000) see 3M Co.

St. Paul Chamber Orchestra ($15,000) see Tozer Foundation

St. Paul Chamber Orchestra — bridge fund $350,000 pledge ($50,000) see Northern States Power Co.

St. Paul Chamber Orchestra — endowment/bridge fund campaign ($50,000) see Cowles Media Co.

St. Paul Chamber Orchestra — endowment/bridge campaign support ($200,000) see Saint Paul Cos.

St. Paul Chamber Orchestra — for St. Paul-based chamber orchestra ($47,500) see Ecolab

St. Paul Foundation — operating budget ($100,000) see Bigelow Foundation, F. R.

St. Paul Foundation ($50,000) see Mardag Foundation

St. Paul Seminary ($10,000) see Quinlan Foundation, Elizabeth C.

St. Paul Union Gospel Mission — pledge ($20,000) see Andersen Corp.

St. Peter and Paul School ($3,500) see Sexton Foundation

St. Stanislaus Church ($41,422) see Hiawatha Education Foundation

St. Thomas Christ Learn ($10,000) see Grossman Foundation, N. Bud

Salvation Army ($10,000) see Beim Foundation

Salvation Army — capital ($6,000) see International Multifoods Corp.

Salvation Army ($5,000) see Minnesota Mutual Life Insurance Co.

Salvation Army Heart Share Program St. Paul ($50,000) see Northern States Power Co.

Salvation Army — purchase building for Thrift Store and transitional housing program ($45,000) see Ordean Foundation

Schubert Club ($1,000) see Weyerhaeuser Memorial Foundation, Charles A.

Science Museum ($4,000) see Red Wing Shoe Co.

Science Museum of Minnesota — payment pledge ($50,000) see Bemis Company

Science Museum of Minnesota — support dinosaur exhibit ($89,500) see Cowles Media Co.

Science Museum of Minnesota ($9,500) see Hubbard Broadcasting

Science Museum of Minnesota — capital and general operating ($15,000) see International Multifoods Corp.

Science Museum of Minnesota ($100,000) see Mardag Foundation

Science Museum of Minnesota ($25,000) see Mardag Foundation

Science Museum of Minnesota ($17,000) see Minnesota Mutual Life Insurance Co.

Science Museum of Minnesota ($10,000) see O'Brien Foundation, Alice M.

Science Museum of Minnesota ($8,000) see Pearson Foundation, E. M.

Science Museum of Minnesota ($25,000) see Rodman Foundation

Science Museum of Minnesota — bridge fund ($300,000) see Saint Paul Cos.

Science Museum of Minnesota ($355,000) see 3M Co.

Science Museum of Minnesota ($200,000) see Warner Foundation, Lee and Rose

Science Museum of Minnesota — for local museum organized to exhibit, study, and interpret science ($15,500) see Ecolab

Scottish Rite Foundation of Duluth ($5,000) see Eddy Foundation

Selby Area Community Development Corporation ($10,000) see Pax Christi Foundation

Senior Resources ($4,000) see Grotto Foundation

Senior Resources ($4,200) see Tennant Co.

Seward Cooperative Child Care Center ($10,000) see Horncrest Foundation

Shalom Home West — Campus for the Elderly ($50,000) see Fingerhut Family Foundation

Sharing and Caring Hands — feeding and clothing ($25,000) see Pax Christi Foundation

Minnesota (cont.)

Sharing and Caring Hands ($5,000) see Tennant Co.

Shattuck-St. Mary's Schools ($100,000) see Hulings Foundation, Mary Andersen

Skills 2000 ($10,000) see Cherne Foundation, Albert W.

Sons of Jacob Synagogue ($5,000) see Higgins Foundation, Aldus C.

South St. Paul Public Schools ($600) see BMC Industries

Southeastern Minnesota Initiative Fund ($4,129,467) see McKnight Foundation

Southwest Minnesota Initiative Fund ($3,682,362) see McKnight Foundation

SPRC ($5,000) see Grotto Foundation

Stassen Center ($5,000) see Carlson Cos.

Stevens Community Mental Health ($15,000) see Kunkel Foundation, John Crain

Stillwater Area Schools ($10,000) see Hubbard Broadcasting

Stillwater School District ($10,000) see Tozer Foundation

T.B. Sheldon Auditorium ($34,600) see Red Wing Shoe Co.

Taste Nation ($2,000) see Bauervic Foundation, Peggy

Teenage Child Care Center ($5,000) see Mankato Citizens Telephone Co.

Temple Israel ($5,200) see Regis Corp.

Theatre de la Jenue Lune ($100,000) see Oakleaf Foundation

Thief River Falls Golf Course ($25,000) see Hartz Foundation

Thief River Falls Swimming Pool Project ($10,000) see Hartz Foundation

Twin Cities Neighborhood ($20,000) see TCF Banking & Savings, FSB

Twin Cities Opera Guild ($300) see Bauervic Foundation, Peggy

Twin Cities Public Television ($16,500) see Donaldson Co.

Twin Cities Public Television ($4,000) see Grotto Foundation

Twin Cities Public Television ($1,500) see Nash Foundation

Twin Cities Public Television ($14,560) see Onan Family Foundation

Twin Cities Public Television ($12,500) see Pearson Foundation, E. M.

Twin Cities Public Television ($24,000) see Schott Foundation

Twin Cities Public Television ($1,403,940) see 3M Co.

Twin Cities Public Television/KTCA ($26,000) see Wasie Foundation

Twin Cities Public Television-KTCA — support for additional programs for Minnesota Century ($451,270) see Saint Paul Cos.

Twin Cities Public Television — for St. Paul-based public television programming ($35,000) see Ecolab

Twin Cities Public TV — programming ($12,000) see International Multifoods Corp.

Twin City Area Educational Television ($4,000) see Best Products Co.

Twin City Institute for Talented Youth ($5,000) see Neilson Foundation, George W.

Union Gospel Mission Association ($2,100) see Rodman Foundation

Union Gospel Mission Association of St. Paul ($37,500) see Mardag Foundation

United Arts — provide support for small cultural organizations ($1,200) see Blue Cross and Blue Shield of Minnesota Foundation Inc.

United Arts ($1,500) see Fuller Co., H.B.

United Arts ($8,500) see Minnesota Mutual Life Insurance Co.

United Arts Landmark Center ($10,000) see Horncrest Foundation

United Arts — to produce multi-cultural training tools using the arts as vehicles for both understanding and expressing diversity ($153,514) see Saint Paul Cos.

United Cerebral Palsy — apartment complex for adults with physical disabilities ($56,000) see Ordean Foundation

United Hospital — capital campaign ($17,000) see Driscoll Foundation

United Hospital — expand emergency room ($50,000) see Edwards Memorial Trust

United Hospital ($15,000) see Saint Croix Foundation

United Hospital Foundation — United Nineties Campaign ($16,750) see Rodman Foundation

United Hospitals Foundation ($100,000) see Andersen Foundation, Hugh J.

United Jewish Appeal Federation of Jewish Philanthropies ($12,500) see Paulucci Family Foundation

United Negro College Fund ($1,000) see Faith Charitable Trust

United Negro College Fund ($2,000) see Neilson Foundation, George W.

United Negro College Fund ($8,500) see Tozer Foundation

U.S. Swedish Fund for International Research ($10,000) see Carlson Cos.

United Way ($195,632) see Blue Cross and Blue Shield of Minnesota Foundation Inc.

United Way ($1,498) see BMC Industries

United Way ($1,454) see BMC Industries

United Way ($1,454) see BMC Industries

United Way ($1,410) see BMC Industries

United Way ($1,000) see Business Incentives

United Way ($3,000) see CTS Corp.

United Way ($67,760) see Dain Bosworth/Inter- Regional Financial Group

United Way ($15,000) see Driscoll Foundation

United Way ($50,000) see Edwards Memorial Trust

United Way ($45,000) see Edwards Memorial Trust

United Way ($2,520) see Federated Life Insurance Co.

United Way ($11,500) see Grossman Foundation, N. Bud

United Way ($10,000) see Harvest States Cooperative

United Way ($1,200) see Heilicher Foundation, Menahem

United Way ($1,200) see Heilicher Foundation, Menahem

United Way ($6,000) see Johnson Co., E. F.

United Way ($6,000) see Levitt Foundation, Richard S.

United Way ($14,250) see Liberty Diversified Industries Inc.

United Way ($55,000) see Lieberman Enterprises

United Way ($12,050) see Lieberman Enterprises

United Way ($18,000) see Lilly Foundation, Richard Coyle

United Way ($11,380) see Mankato Citizens Telephone Co.

United Way ($10,000) see Marbrook Foundation

United Way ($10,610) see McNeely Foundation

United Way ($9,539) see McNeely Foundation

United Way ($7,764) see McNeely Foundation

United Way ($5,000) see McVay Foundation

United Way ($175,750) see Minnesota Mutual Life Insurance Co.

United Way ($60,000) see Minnesota Mutual Life Insurance Co.

United Way ($5,000) see Neilson Foundation, George W.

United Way ($15,000) see Onan Family Foundation

United Way ($6,000) see Quinlan Foundation, Elizabeth C.

United Way ($7,000) see Rahr Malting Co.

United Way ($11,500) see Red Wing Shoe Co.

United Way ($6,000) see Regis Corp.

United Way ($6,600) see Rodman Foundation

United Way ($20,200) see Saint Croix Foundation

United Way ($3,200) see Sifco Industries Inc.

United Way ($32,000) see Southways Foundation

United Way ($3,000) see Sweatt Foundation, Harold W.

United Way ($27,600) see Tennant Co.

United Way ($51,420) see Tozer Foundation

United Way ($13,250) see Valspar Corp.

United Way ($13,250) see Valspar Corp.

United Way ($13,250) see Valspar Corp.

United Way ($13,250) see Valspar Corp.

United Way ($1,000) see Weyerhaeuser Memorial Foundation, Charles A.

United Way ($20,000) see White Consolidated Industries

United Way of Minneapolis ($10,000) see Donaldson Co.

United Way of Minneapolis ($320,000) see IDS Financial Services

United Way of Minneapolis ($473,400) see Northern States Power Co.

United Way of Minneapolis ($180,300) see Northwestern National Life Insurance Co.

United Way Minneapolis ($353,500) see Norwest Corp.

United Way Minneapolis ($353,500) see Norwest Corp.

United Way of Minneapolis ($430,000) see Pillsbury Co.

United Way of Minneapolis Area ($205,000) see Alliant Techsystems

United Way of Minneapolis Area ($38,000) see Bemis Company

United Way of Minneapolis Area — general operating support ($196,428) see Cowles Media Co.

United Way of Minneapolis Area ($38,560) see FMC Corp.

United Way of Minneapolis Area ($350,000) see Graco

United Way of Minneapolis Area — a challenge to encourage new contributors ($395,000) see McKnight Foundation

United Way of Minneapolis Area — for annual support ($282,700) see US WEST

United Way of Minneapolis Area Learning Readiness Fund ($20,000) see Alliant Techsystems

United Way of Minneapolis Area — Phillips TLC Project New Vistas ($200,000) see Honeywell

United Way of St. Paul ($310,105) see Northern States Power Co.

United Way of St. Paul ($60,000) see Norwest Corp.

United Way of St. Paul ($201,794) see 3M Co.

United Way of the St. Paul Area ($45,000) see Burlington Northern Inc.

United Way of the St. Paul Area — capital campaign ($35,000) see Cowles Media Co.

United Way of the St. Paul Area — capital fund ($70,000) see Deluxe Corp.

United Way of the St. Paul Area — capital fund ($7,500) see Fuller Co., H.B.

United Way of the St. Paul Area — annual campaign ($30,000) see Griggs and Mary Griggs Burke Foundation, Mary Livingston

United Way of St. Paul Area — capital campaign ($10,000) see Hubbard Broadcasting

United Way of the St. Paul Area — operating support ($369,825) see Saint Paul Cos.

United Way of the St. Paul Area — capital campaign ($188,000) see Saint Paul Cos.

United Way of St. Paul Area ($1,088,000) see 3M Co.

United Way of the St. Paul Area — for planning to enable federated campaign/agencies work to increase access/effectiveness human services to communities of color by implementing a pluralism vision statement ($45,000) see Bremer Foundation, Otto

United Way of the St. Paul Area — Challenge Match Program ($160,000) see Bigelow Foundation, F. R.

United Way of St. Paul Area — to support the continuation of work with community based

agencies on the use of technology and the development of multi-cultural family literacy programs see United Parcel Service of America

United Way of the St. Paul Area — 1989 capital campaign ($125,000) see Bigelow Foundation, F. R.

United Way of the St. Paul Area — 1990 annual campaign ($202,700) see Bigelow Foundation, F. R.

University of Minneapolis Children's Cancer Research Fund ($6,000) see Dain Bosworth/Inter- Regional Financial Group

University of Minnesota — scholarships ($343,630) see Alliss Educational Foundation, Charles and Ellora

University of Minnesota ($351) see BMC Industries

University of Minnesota ($75,000) see Frasch Foundation for Chemical Research (under the will of Elizabeth B. Frasch), Herman

University of Minnesota ($1,000) see Liberty Diversified Industries Inc.

University of Minnesota ($10,000) see Meadowood Foundation

University of Minnesota ($200,000) see Phillips Family Foundation, Jay and Rose

University of Minnesota ($105,000) see Pioneer Fund

University of Minnesota ($8,548) see Regis Corp.

University of Minnesota — to test effectiveness and applicability of structural process for assessing the values and preferences of older long term care clients ($278,201) see Retirement Research Foundation

University of Minnesota ($12,832) see Rothschild Foundation, Hulda B. and Maurice L.

University of Minnesota ($6,400) see Schott Foundation

University of Minnesota ($49,827) see Tuohy Foundation, Alice Tweed

University of Minnesota — final installment of a grant of $500,000, payable in five equal installments in 1987-91, inclusive, to assist in the creation of a Center for Interdisciplinary Studies in Distribution/Logistics in the Carlson School of Management ($100,000) see Union Pacific Corp.

University of Minnesota Academic Writing Center — capital fund ($100,000) see Deluxe Corp.

University of Minnesota Academic Writing Center — capital fund ($100,000) see Deluxe Corp.

University of Minnesota — Andersen Chair in corporate responsibility ($143,000) see Fuller Co., H.B.

University of Minnesota Art Museum ($120,000) see Walker Foundation, Archie D. and Bertha H.

University of Minnesota — Assessment of Quality of Life Following Pancreas Transplant ($20,000) see Diabetes Research and Education Foundation

University of Minnesota — Bakken Chair in Biomedical Engineering ($350,000) see Medtronic

University of Minnesota — Cancer Research Center ($750,000) see Andersen Foundation

University of Minnesota Compass Institute ($30,000) see Perkins Foundation, Edwin E.

University of Minnesota Conflict and Change Center ($30,000) see Weyerhaeuser Family Foundation

University of Minnesota Continuing Education and Extension Division ($5,000) see Grotto Foundation

University of Minnesota, Department of Civil and Mineral Engineering ($25,000) see Schlumberger Ltd.

University of Minnesota Department of School of Journalism and Mass Communication for Media and Social Studies ($80,000) see China Times Cultural Foundation

University of Minnesota-Duluth ($26,000) see Eddy Foundation

University of Minnesota-Duluth ($15,000) see Eddy Foundation

University of Minnesota Foundation ($30,350) see Cray Research

University of Minnesota Foundation — civic ($500,000) see Mann Foundation, Ted

University of Minnesota Foundation ($85,000) see Norwest Corp.

University of Minnesota Foundation ($106,669) see Pillsbury Co.

University of Minnesota Foundation ($15,000) see Schott Foundation

University of Minnesota Foundation — commitment to Focus ($500,000) see Honeywell

University of Minnesota Foundation Hubert H. Humphrey Institute of Public Affairs — to redesign the Regional Issues Forum into the State and Local Policy Center ($177,589) see Northwest Area Foundation

University of Minnesota-Hubert Humphrey Institute ($50,000) see Archer-Daniels-Midland Co.

University of Minnesota Institute of Agriculture ($13,000) see Harvest States Cooperative

University of Minnesota Institute on Community Integration "Yes I Can" Program — for two years, to develop positive peer support for disabled youth ($74,000) see Mitsubishi Electric America

University of Minnesota Law School ($11,270) see Mansfield Foundation, Albert and Anne

University of Minnesota — support for a mid-career management training program for school principals, assistant principals, and teacher-leaders 1989 grant ($478,550) see Bush Foundation

University of Minnesota, Minneapolis, MN ($67,500) see Northwestern National Life Insurance Co.

University of Minnesota — Natural Resources Research Institute ($260,000) see Blandin Foundation

University of Minnesota — 1992 grant ($452,924) see Bush Foundation

University of Minnesota Project Technology Power ($29,800) see Alliant Techsystems

University of Minnesota — for scholarships, curriculum development and deans' recognition of outstanding faculty research ($10,500) see Ecolab

University of Minnesota — School of Journalism ($6,000) see Hubbard Broadcasting

University of Minnesota School of Management — educational program ($45,000) see IDS Financial Services

University of Minnesota School of Public Health — to examine rural health care services ($145,662) see Northwest Area Foundation

University of Minnesota — Tel Aviv Research ($25,000) see Lieberman Enterprises

University of Minnesota — for the University Art Museum's new building ($25,000) see Butler Family Foundation, Patrick and Aimee

University of St. Thomas — scholarships ($268,180) see Alliss Educational Foundation, Charles and Ellora

University of St. Thomas — capital campaign ($25,000) see Butler Family Foundation, Patrick and Aimee

University of St. Thomas — final payment on matching challenge grant pledge ($160,000) see O'Shaughnessy Foundation, I. A.

University of St. Thomas — pledge to "cap off" library fund drive ($375,000) see O'Shaughnessy Foundation, I. A.

University Way of Minneapolis Area — general support ($264,000) see Medtronic

UNUM Employee Scholarship Program — Citizens' Scholarship Foundation of America ($44,000) see UNUM Corp.

Vail Place ($10,375) see Grossman Foundation, N. Bud

Vail Place ($6,500) see McVay Foundation

VEAP ($1,086) see Business Incentives

Vinland National Center ($6,000) see Walker Foundation, Archie D. and Bertha H.

Walker Art Center see ADC Telecommunications

Walker Art Center see Alliance Capital Management Corp.

Walker Art Center see American Linen Supply Co.

Walker Art Center — capital campaign ($25,000) see Bemis Company

Walker Art Center see Bio-Medicus, Inc.

Walker Art Center — to support its endowment ($425,000) see Bush Foundation

Walker Art Center — capital fund drive ($50,000) see Cowles Media Co.

Walker Art Center see Faribault Foods

Walker Art Center — capital campaign ($400,000) see General Mills

Walker Art Center ($203,150) see Grossman Foundation, N. Bud

Walker Art Center ($6,000) see Hubbard Broadcasting

Walker Art Center see Korn/Ferry International

Walker Art Center ($21,000) see Levitt Foundation

Walker Art Center ($65,500) see Lilly Foundation, Richard Coyle

Walker Art Center ($1,200,000) see Oakleaf Foundation

Walker Art Center see Onan Corp.

Walker Art Center see Polaris Industries, LP

Walker Art Center ($72,000) see Regis Corp.

Walker Art Center see Rosemount, Inc.

Walker Art Center ($7,500) see SIT Investment Associates, Inc.

Walker Art Center ($16,150) see Southways Foundation

Walker Art Center ($10,000) see Southways Foundation

Walker Art Center ($5,100) see Tennant Co.

Walker Art Center ($100,000) see Walker Foundation, Archie D. and Bertha H.

Walker Art Center — emerging artists' commissions for the Sculpture Garden ($35,000) see Jerome Foundation

Walker Art Center — "Free Thursdays" program ($30,000) see IDS Financial Services

Walker Center — Minneapolis Sculpture Garden ($15,000) see Marbrook Foundation

Walker Methodist Residence ($40,000) see Gray Charitable Trust, Mary S.

Wanda Gag House Association ($2,500) see Obernauer Foundation

Waseca Arts Council ($2,500) see Johnson Co., E. F.

Waseca High School ($2,500) see Johnson Co., E. F.

Waseca High School ($2,500) see Johnson Co., E. F.

Waseca School District (IDS #829) ($7,500) see Johnson Co., E. F.

Washburn Child Guidance Center ($10,000) see Dain Bosworth/Inter- Regional Financial Group

WCTS — FM ($12,000) see Christian Training Foundation

West Central Minnesota Initiative Fund ($3,527,409) see McKnight Foundation

Westminster Corporation ($25,000) see Pax Christi Foundation

Westminster Presbyterian Church ($14,000) see Chadwick Foundation

Wilderness Inquiry ($2,500) see Sexton Foundation

Winona Area Catholic Schools ($18,063) see Hiawatha Education Foundation

Winona State University Foundation ($66,496) see Hiawatha Education Foundation

Wolf Ridge Environmental Learning Center ($300,000) see Blandin Foundation

Women's Association of Minnesota Orchestra — Twin Cities Chapter of Young Audiences; concerts in St. Paul Public Schools ($15,000) see Davis Foundation, Edwin W. and Catherine M.

Women's Coalition — shelter and outreach services for victims of domestic abuse ($35,000) see Ordean Foundation

WomenVenture ($10,000) see Friedman Family Foundation

YMCA ($36,300) see Mankato Citizens Telephone Co.

YMCA ($7,500) see Mankato Citizens Telephone Co.

YMCA ($100,000) see Meadowood Foundation

YMCA ($8,400) see Red Wing Shoe Co.

YMCA ($4,500) see Rodman Foundation

Young Life ($3,000) see Northern Star Foundation

Youth Forum ($19,225) see Northern Star Foundation

Youth Leadership — operating support ($10,000) see Davis Foundation, Edwin W. and Catherine M.

YWCA, Minneapolis, MN ($21,000) see Northwestern National Life Insurance Co.

Mississippi

Agricola Elementary see Mississippi Power Co.

American Family Association — to support the Biblical ethic of decency in American Society with emphasis on TV and other media ($20,000) see Templeton Foundation, John

Baddour Memorial Center ($29,000) see Community Foundation

Baddour Memorial Center ($1,000) see Feild Co-Operative Association

Ballet Mississippi ($10,572) see Deposit Guaranty National Bank

Bayou View Junior High School see International Paper Co.

Bayou View Junior High School see Mississippi Power Co.

Belhaven College ($14,000) see Deposit Guaranty National Bank

Board of Trustees of State Institutions of Higher Learning — operating support first year of Mississippi Teacher Corps ($30,500) see Hardin Foundation, Phil

Board of Trustees of State Institutions of Higher Learning — support for Project 95 ($50,000) see Hardin Foundation, Phil

Boy Scouts of America ($3,500) see Baird Charitable Trust, William Robert

Boy Scouts of America ($5,000) see Community Foundation

Boy Scouts of America ($1,750) see Mohasco Corp.

Carroll County Tornado Disaster Relief Fund ($25,000) see United States Sugar Corp.

Cedar Lake Christian Academy see Mississippi Power Co.

Center for Family Education ($45,000) see Feild Co-Operative Association

Center for International Security and Strategic Studies ($30,000) see Weyerhaeuser Family Foundation

Central Elementary see Mississippi Power Co.

Chapel Hill Methodist Church ($24,716) see Cook, Sr. Charitable Foundation, Kelly Gene

Children's Hospital for AIDS ($2,500) see Feild Co-Operative Association

Children's Hospital — AIDS project ($63,132) see Walker Foundation, W. E.

Christian Mission Concern ($113,927) see C.I.O.S.

City of New Albany ($3,000) see Mohasco Corp.

Clay County Association for Retarded Children — to complete construction of a building to house the Association's educational programs ($33,500) see Hardin Foundation, Phil

Clinton Arrow Baseball Booster Club ($5,000) see Manville Corp.

Collins High School see Mississippi Power Co.

Columbia School District see Mississippi Power Co.

Community Food Bank ($5,000) see Luckyday Foundation

Community Foundation of East Mississippi — support East Mississippi Center for Educational Development at Mississippi State University ($34,490) see Hardin Foundation, Phil

Community Foundation of East Mississippi — support East Mississippi Center for Educational Development's model computerized academic and career counselling program ($30,000) see Hardin Foundation, Phil

Community Foundation of East Mississippi — support East Mississippi Center for Educational Development's Math Solution Project ($69,000) see Hardin Foundation, Phil

Cystic Fibrosis Foundation ($2,000) see Feild Co-Operative Association

Delta Health Center ($20,000) see Grant Foundation, Charles M. and Mary D.

Diocese of Mississippi — Gray Center Assembly Building ($50,000) see Walker Foundation, W. E.

Diocese of Mississippi — Gray Center Chapel ($100,000) see Walker Foundation, W. E.

East Central Elementary School see Mississippi Power Co.

East Central Technology Student Association see Mississippi Power Co.

Eastlawn Elementary see Mississippi Power Co.

Ecumenical Health Care Organization ($50,000) see Walker Foundation, W. E.

Episcopal Diocese of Mississippi ($50,000) see Chisholm Foundation

Foundation for the Mid-South ($10,000) see Deposit Guaranty National Bank

Foundation of Mid-South ($10,000) see McRae Foundation

Foundation for the Mid-South — in support of the Delta Enterprise Corporation ($2,800,000) see Pew Charitable Trusts

Foundation for the Mid-South — in support of the Delta Workforce Alliance

Mississippi (cont.)

($3,800,000) see Pew Charitable Trusts

Foundation for Public Broadcasting ($2,500) see Feild Co-Operative Association

Foundation for Public Broadcasting in Mississippi — partial support production of Mississippi Masters Series ($30,000) see Hardin Foundation, Phil

French Camp Academy ($25,000) see Cook, Sr. Charitable Foundation, Kelly Gene

French Camp Academy ($1,000) see Feild Co-Operative Association

Friends of Walter Anderson ($10,000) see Freeman Foundation, Ella West

Galloway Memorial United Methodist Church ($175,000) see McRae Foundation

Galloway Memorial United Methodist Church ($10,000) see McRae Foundation

George County Schools see Mississippi Power Co.

Global Outreach — mission work ($5,000) see Edwards Foundation, Jes

Goodwill Industries of Mississippi ($100,000) see National Presto Industries

Greater Jackson Youth Services Corporation ($15,000) see McRae Foundation

Habitat for Humanity ($3,000) see Baird Charitable Trust, William Robert

Highlands Hospital ($10,000) see Eastover Corp.

Hillsaps College Centennial Fund ($5,000) see Eastover Corp.

Hinds Community College ($25,000) see Vicksburg Hospital Medical Foundation

Holmes Community College ($100,000) see Cook, Sr. Charitable Foundation, Kelly Gene

Institute for Technology Development ($18,750) see First Mississippi Corp.

Itawamba Junior College ($6,660) see Mohasco Corp.

Jackson Public Library — education ($3,500) see Smith, Jr. Foundation, M. W.

Jackson Public Schools ($12,000) see Eastover Corp.

Jackson Public Schools ($4,000) see Eastover Corp.

Jackson State University ($5,000) see Eastover Corp.

Jubilee Jam 1990 ($5,000) see Eastover Corp.

Junior Achievement of Mississippi — for support rural expansion of Applied Economics Program during the period 1990- 1993 ($30,000) see Hardin Foundation, Phil

Literary Olympiad ($10,000) see Feild Co-Operative Association

Loas ($25,000) see Grant Foundation, Charles M. and Mary D.

Love Soup Kitchen ($12,500) see Baird Charitable Trust, William Robert

Magnolia Speech School ($2,000) see Feild Co-Operative Association

MCCSA — South Harbor Shelter ($4,000) see Baird Charitable Trust, William Robert

McLean Foundation ($1,105,043) see Walker Foundation, W. E.

Mendenhall Ministries ($15,000) see McRae Foundation

Metropolitan Jackson Mississippi Boys Club ($178,495) see Hay Foundation, John I.

Mid South Foundation see Arkla

Millsaps College ($50,000) see Chisholm Foundation

Millsaps College ($5,000) see Luckyday Foundation

Millsaps College ($23,000) see McRae Foundation

Millsaps College ($100,000) see Vicksburg Hospital Medical Foundation

Millsaps College — scholarships, chair in business administration ($121,000) see Cook, Sr. Charitable Foundation, Kelly Gene

Millsaps College — renovations of Sullivan-Harrell Hall ($50,000) see Frueauff Foundation, Charles A.

Mississippi Animal Rescue League ($12,000) see Baker Foundation, Elinor Patterson

Mississippi Ballet International ($8,750) see Eastover Corp.

Mississippi Baptist Foundation ($9,820) see First Mississippi Corp.

Mississippi Baptist Hospital ($5,156) see Ellsworth Trust, W. H.

Mississippi Baptist Medical Center Life Endowment Program ($10,000) see Deposit Guaranty National Bank

Mississippi Baptist Mission ($32,912) see Deposit Guaranty National Bank

Mississippi College ($50,000) see Community Foundation

Mississippi College ($50,000) see Vicksburg Hospital Medical Foundation

Mississippi Forward Foundation — to provide start up support for a new youth organization to stimulate academic success among Mississippi Delta Youth ($20,000) see Hazen Foundation, Edward W.

Mississippi Foundation of Independent Colleges ($2,000) see Eastover Corp.

Mississippi Pharmacy Foundation ($5,000) see Durr-Fillauer Medical

Mississippi School of Chinese ($300) see China Times Cultural Foundation

Mississippi State University ($22,500) see Chisholm Foundation

Mississippi State University, Cobb Institute of Archaeology ($65,300) see Dorot Foundation

Mississippi State University — scholarships, chair in engineering ($467,942) see Cook, Sr. Charitable Foundation, Kelly Gene

Mississippi Symphony Orchestra ($5,000) see Eastover Corp.

Mississippi Symphony Orchestra ($10,000) see McRae Foundation

Mustard Seed ($1,000) see Feild Co-Operative Association

Nature Conservancy ($10,000) see Walker Wildlife Conservation Foundation

Neighborhood Housing Service ($70,543) see Deposit Guaranty National Bank

Oxford University School ($2,500) see Frohring Foundation, Paul & Maxine

Parents for Public Schools ($15,000) see Grant Foundation, Charles M. and Mary D.

Parents for Public Schools ($15,000) see McRae Foundation

Pasagoula School District ($10,000) see First Mississippi Corp.

Public Education Forum ($20,000) see Deposit Guaranty National Bank

Public Education Forum of Mississippi ($300,000) see BellSouth Corp.

Reformed Theological Seminary ($10,000) see Community Foundation

Reformed Theological Seminary ($50,000) see Hopewell Foundation

Reformed Theological Seminary — operating funds ($200,000) see Maclellan Foundation

Reformed Theological Seminary ($30,000) see Maclellan Foundation, Robert L. and Kathrina H.

Reformed Theological Seminary — Orlando, Florida campus ($200,000) see Maclellan Foundation

Rush Hospital/Newton — health ($50,000) see La-Z-Boy Chair Co.

Rust College — gift ($10,000) see Atkinson Foundation

Rust College ($20,000) see Chisholm Foundation

Rust College — challenge grant for capital fund ($20,000) see Conn Memorial Foundation

Rust College ($5,000) see Luckyday Foundation

St. Andrews Episcopal Church ($44,357) see Luckyday Foundation

St. Andrews School — teacher's salaries ($100,000) see Walker Foundation, W. E.

St. Michaels Farm for Boys ($9,000) see Baird Charitable Trust, William Robert

St. Vincent de Paul ($5,000) see Baird Charitable Trust, William Robert

Scholarship Program ($25,500) see First Mississippi Corp.

Soil Conservancy Service ($200) see Walker Wildlife Conservation Foundation

State Institute of Higher Learning ($25,000) see Vicksburg Hospital Medical Foundation

Tougaloo College ($10,000) see Deposit Guaranty National Bank

Tougaloo College ($250,000) see Herzog Foundation, Carl J.

Tougaloo College ($125,000) see Joukowsky Family Foundation

Tougaloo College ($10,000) see Luckyday Foundation

Tougaloo College ($10,000) see McRae Foundation

Trinity Episcopal School for Ministry ($50,000) see Walker Foundation, W. E.

United Givers Fund of Forrest County ($36,371) see Georgia-Pacific Corp.

United Way ($135,872) see Deposit Guaranty National Bank

United Way ($2,200) see Mohasco Corp.

United Way of the Capital Area ($16,460) see TRINOVA Corp.

University of Mississippi ($7,603) see First Mississippi Corp.

University of Mississippi ($30,000) see Jones Foundation, Montfort Jones and Allie Brown

University of Mississippi ($50,000) see Schillig Trust, Ottilie

University of Mississippi ($143,000) see Vicksburg Hospital Medical Foundation

University of Mississippi ($1,000) see Willmott Foundation, Peter S.

University of Mississippi — scholarships, chair in journalism ($121,086) see Cook, Sr. Charitable Foundation, Kelly Gene

University of Mississippi/School of Pharmacy ($10,000) see Eckerd Corp., Jack

University Press of Mississippi — for the National Endowment for the Humanities challenge grant ($35,000) see Hardin Foundation, Phil

University of Southern Mississippi ($250,000) see Schillig Trust, Ottilie

University of Southern Mississippi Foundation — endowment of scholarship funds ($75,000) see Litton Industries

University of Southern Mississippi Foundation — to endow the Charles W. Moorman Alumni Distinguished Professorship in the Humanities ($62,500) see Hardin Foundation, Phil

USA International Ballet Competition ($12,500) see Deposit Guaranty National Bank

Vicksburg Patient Education ($30,000) see Vicksburg Hospital Medical Foundation

Voice of Calvary ($16,000) see McRae Foundation

Walker Education Enrichment Foundation ($295,000) see Walker Foundation, W. E.

Wesley House ($28,000) see Baird Charitable Trust, William Robert

Yazoo City Library ($1,000) see Feild Co-Operative Association

Young People in Action Ministry — operating expenses ($60,000) see Swalm Foundation

Missouri

A.L.O.T. ($1,000) see Missouri Farmers Association

AACSB ($345,533) see KPMG Peat Marwick

Adolescent Resources — support health track coalition ($30,000) see Speas Foundation, Victor E.

Adolescent Resources Corporation — support of health track ($109,144) see Speas Memorial Trust, John W. and Effie E.

AFRAS see Reliable Life Insurance Co.

Agape House of Springfield ($5,000) see Slusher Charitable Foundation, Roy W.

Agent Scholarship Awards ($231,279) see Shelter Mutual Insurance Co.

All Saints School — use of facility for 8 computer courses ($500) see Pendergast-Weyer Foundation

All Stars Community Outreach for Christ ($30,000) see Share Foundation

American Baptist Assembly ($4,000) see Clarke Trust, John

American Cancer Society ($25,000) see Barrows Foundation, Geraldine and R. A.

American Cancer Society ($3,000) see Shoenberg Foundation

American Diabetes Association — summer camp program, selected research projects and educational scholarships ($100,000) see Bellamah Foundation, Dale J.

American Polled Hereford Foundation ($1,500) see Shughart, Thomson & Kilroy, P.C.

American Red Cross ($1,000) see ACF Industries, Inc.

American Royal ($167,000) see Kemper Charitable Trust, William T.

American Royal Association ($10,000) see Barrows Foundation, Geraldine and R. A.

American Royal Association ($10,000) see Breidenthal Foundation, Willard J. and Mary G.

American Royal Association ($13,000) see Butler Manufacturing Co.

American Royal Association — capital support for new arena complex ($700,000) see Hall Family Foundations

American Royal Association ($249,542) see Kemper Foundation, William T.

American Royal Association ($105,443) see Kemper Foundation, William T.

American Royal Association ($90,717) see Kemper Foundation, William T.

American Royal Association ($5,000) see McGee Foundation

American Royal Association ($2,000) see Shughart, Thomson & Kilroy, P.C.

American Royal Association ($40,000) see Sprint

American Royal Association ($40,000) see Sunderland Foundation, Lester T.

American Royal Association ($86,000) see Wornall Charitable Trust and Foundation, Kearney

American Society for Technion ($12,500) see Lopata Foundation, Stanley and Lucy

American Youth Foundation ($125,000) see Ralston Purina Co.

American Youth Foundation ($10,000) see Woods Foundation, James H.

American Youth Foundation — student leadership and educational programs for adults who work in the Youth Leadership Compact Programs ($110,000) see Danforth Foundation

Americanism Foundation ($7,500) see Phillipps Foundation

Missouri (cont.)

Culver Stockton College ($50,000) see Moorman Manufacturing Co.

Culver-Stockton College ($50,000) see Morris Foundation, William T.

David M. Danneger Memorial Scholarship Fund ($6,000) see Fabick Tractor Co., John

De LaSalle ($3,000) see Forster-Powers Charitable Trust

Deaf Services ($2,200) see Gateway Apparel

DeKalb County Extension Office ($3,585) see Messick Charitable Trust, Harry F.

Diabetes Association of Greater St. Louis ($1,500) see Gateway Apparel

Diabetes Foundation ($10,000) see Slusher Charitable Foundation, Roy W.

Diabetes Foundation ($2,500) see Wolff Shoe Co.

Diocese of Jefferson City ($62,400) see Orscheln Co.

Diocese of Kansas City — St. Joseph ($25,000) see McGee Foundation

Diocese of Kansas City — St. Joseph ($4,000) see Miller-Mellor Association

Dog Museum ($110,250) see Dobson Foundation

Dog Museum ($97,000) see Hooker Charitable Trust, Janet A.

Don Bosco Community Center ($100,000) see Kemper Charitable Lead Trust, William T.

Doulos Ministries ($10,000) see Herschend Family Foundation

Drury College ($2,087,000) see Olin Foundation, F. W.

Drury College ($25,000) see Sunderland Foundation, Lester T.

Duolos Ministries ($2,000) see Bowers Foundation

Duolos Ministries ($1,000) see Bowers Foundation

Ecumenical Housing Production Corporation ($10,000) see Horncrest Foundation

Edgewood Children's Center ($20,000) see Gaylord Foundation, Clifford Willard

Edgewood Children's Center ($29,000) see Green Foundation, Allen P. and Josephine B.

Edgewood Children's Center ($4,000) see Pettus, Jr. Foundation, James T.

Education Incorporated ($25,000) see Kemper Charitable Trust, William T.

Epworth Children's Home ($10,000) see Fuller Foundation, C. G.

Epworth Children's Home ($20,000) see Stupp Foundation, Norman J.

Evangel College ($50,000) see RTM

Even Start Program see Reliable Life Insurance Co.

Excellence in Education Fund ($50,400) see Orscheln Co.

Excelsior Springs Medical Center — for expansion of out-patient addition ($50,000) see Speas Memorial Trust, John W. and Effie E.

Eye Research Foundation ($1,000) see Missouri Farmers Association

Fair Acres Family Y ($10,000) see Titus Foundation, C. W.

Farmington Annual Fund ($1,000) see Columbia Terminals Co.

Fellowship of Christian Athletes — bus transportation ($2,500) see Collins Foundation, George and Jennie

Fellowship of Christian Athletes — transportation ($2,500) see Collins, Jr. Foundation, George Fulton

Fellowship of Christian Athletes ($98,000) see DeMoss Foundation, Arthur S.

Fellowship of Christian Athletes ($20,000) see Fowler Memorial Foundation, John Edward

FFA General Fund ($5,000) see Missouri Farmers Association

First Community Church ($101,000) see Tamko Asphalt Products

Focus on the Family ($15,000) see Herschend Family Foundation

Folly Theater ($7,180) see Flarsheim Charitable Foundation, Louis and Elizabeth

Fontbonne College ($5,000) see Brown Foundation, George Warren

Fontbonne College ($5,000) see Edison Foundation, Irving and Beatrice C.

Fontbonne College ($10,000) see Garvey Memorial Foundation, Edward Chase

Forest Park Forever ($15,000) see Keller Family Foundation

Forest Park Forever ($10,125) see Messing Family Charitable Foundation

Forsyth School — promotion of education ($15,000) see Love Charitable Foundation, John Allan

4-H General Fund ($2,250) see Missouri Farmers Association

Francis Child Development Center ($400,000) see Francis Families Foundation

Freeman Hospital —- building fund ($80,000) see Titus Foundation, C. W.

Friends of Chamber Music ($6,666) see Kemper Memorial Foundation, David Woods

Friends of Chamber Music ($3,100) see Miller-Mellor Association

Friends of Chamber Music ($1,250) see Shughart, Thomson & Kilroy, P.C.

Friends of Chamber Music — underwrite their 1991 piano recital series ($35,000) see Turner Charitable Trust, Courtney S.

Friends of Historic Booneville ($5,000) see Kemper Foundation, Enid and Crosby

Full Employment Council — summer jobs for youth ($200,000) see Hallmark Cards

Full Employment Council ($30,213) see Sprint

Genesis Schools ($35,000) see Cowden Foundation, Louetta M.

Gillis Home ($1,000) see Ward Foundation, Louis L. and Adelaide C.

Girls Club of St. Louis ($10,000) see Roblee Foundation, Joseph H. and Florence A.

Girls Club of St. Louis ($10,000) see Webb Foundation

Girls Town of Missouri ($1,500) see Missouri Farmers Association

Golden Apple ($7,500) see Levy Foundation, Charles and Ruth

Good Shepherd Manor ($10,000) see Enright Foundation

Grace Hill Settlement House ($30,000) see Pott Foundation, Herman T. and Phenie R.

Grace and Holy Trinity Cathedral ($200,000) see Kemper Foundation, William T.

Grand Center ($700,000) see Southwestern Bell Corp.

Grand Center ($100,000) see Whitaker Charitable Foundation, Lyndon C.

Grand Center (The New Performing Arts Center) ($25,000) see Laclede Gas Co.

Greater Kansas City Community Foundation ($12,500) see Kemper Memorial Foundation, David Woods

Greater Kansas City Community Foundation ($7,000) see Nichols Co., J.C.

Greater Kansas City Community Foundation ($20,000) see Oppenstein Brothers Foundation

Greater Kansas City Community Foundation — assist funding a comprehensive health clinic ($75,000) see Speas Foundation, Victor E.

Greater Kansas City Community Foundation ($10,000) see Garvey Memorial Foundation, Edward Chase

Greater Kansas City Community Foundation and Affiliated Trusts — support for Ewing Kauffman Book Fund ($300,000) see Hall Family Foundations

Greater Kansas City Community Foundation — Kauffman Book Fund Pledge ($20,000) see Sosland Foundation

Greater Kansas City Community Foundation — Take Part ($50,000) see Sosland Foundation

Greater Kansas City Foundation Marketing Study ($22,000) see Yellow Corp.

Greater Kansas City Sports Commission ($10,000) see Block, H&R

Greater Kansas Community Foundation ($30,000) see Sunderland Foundation, Lester T.

Groves Learning Center ($30,000) see Cherne Foundation, Albert W.

Habitat for Humanity ($2,000) see Lowenstein Brothers Foundation

Harry C. McCray Senior Endowed Football Scholarship ($1,000) see McCray Lumber Co.

Harvesters ($10,000) see Block, H&R

Harvesters ($9,000) see Enright Foundation

Harvesters ($2,000) see Forster-Powers Charitable Trust

Harvesters ($5,000) see Marley Co.

Harvesters — Kansas City Harvest Program ($20,000) see Loose Trust, Carrie J.

Health Fair ($3,000) see Rhoden Charitable Foundation, Elmer C.

Health Track Fund — ARC ($50,000) see Loose Trust, Carrie J.

Heart of America United Way — first and second quarter installments on pledge ($63,100) see Boatmen's Bancshares

Heart of America United Way ($775,000) see Hallmark Cards

Heart of America United Way ($20,000) see Oppenstein Brothers Foundation

Heart of America United Way ($20,000) see Oppenstein Brothers Foundation

Heart of America United Way ($180,000) see Sprint

Heart of America United Way ($60,000) see Union Pacific Corp.

Heartland Institute of Missouri ($10,000) see Tamko Asphalt Products

Heartland Presbytery of the Presbyterian Church ($20,000) see Green Foundation, Allen P. and Josephine B.

Heartlight ($6,725) see Herschend Family Foundation

Henry County Youth Services ($5,000) see Geneseo Foundation

Hickory Joint Baptist ($5,000) see Oldham Little Church Foundation

Hope ($5,600) see Horncrest Foundation

Hospice ($10,000) see Southern Furniture Co.

Hugh O'Brian Youth Foundation ($10,000) see Young & Rubicam

Humana Society of Missouri ($35,000) see Dula Educational and Charitable Foundation, Caleb C. and Julia W.

I am Third ($25,382) see Herschend Family Foundation

I'm Friend Foundation ($39,559) see Share Foundation

I'm Third Foundation ($10,000) see Bowers Foundation

I'm Third Foundation ($90,367) see Share Foundation

Immaculate Conception School — use of facility for eight computer training courses ($500) see Pendergast-Weyer Foundation

Independence Center ($25,000) see Green Foundation, Allen P. and Josephine B.

Independence Center ($5,000) see Love Charitable Foundation, John Allan

INROADS ($4,600) see Butler Manufacturing Co.

Inroads Pre Collegiate Program ($19,909) see Loose Trust, Carrie J.

Inter-Varsity Camp ($12,800) see Herschend Family Foundation

J.C.C.A. ($5,000) see Wolff Shoe Co.

J.V.L. Housing ($4,500) see Pettus, Jr. Foundation, James T.

JCCA Campaign ($5,000) see Sachs Fund

JCCA Samp Sabra ($5,000) see Sachs Fund

Jewish Center for the Aged ($1,100) see Kahn Memorial Trust

Jewish Community Center ($10,000) see Bromley Residuary Trust, Guy I.

Jewish Community Center ($50,000) see Edison Foundation, Harry

Jewish Community Center ($7,000) see Graybar Electric Co.

Jewish Community Center ($15,000) see Lowenstein Brothers Foundation

Jewish Community Center ($8,000) see Orchard Corp. of America.

Jewish Community Foundation — fund for Jewish education ($50,000) see Sosland Foundation

Jewish Family and Children's Services ($3,200) see Kahn Memorial Trust

Jewish Federation ($40,246) see Edison Foundation, Irving and Beatrice C.

Jewish Federation ($60,000) see Helzberg Foundation, Shirley and Barnett

Jewish Federation ($40,000) see Helzberg Foundation, Shirley and Barnett

Jewish Federation ($25,000) see Interco

Jewish Federation ($49,000) see Lopata Foundation, Stanley and Lucy

Jewish Federation ($7,500) see Lopata Foundation, Stanley and Lucy

Jewish Federation ($112,409) see Lowenstein Brothers Foundation

Jewish Federation ($94,158) see Millstone Foundation

Jewish Federation ($66,667) see Millstone Foundation

Jewish Federation ($50,000) see Sachs Fund

Jewish Federation ($368,069) see Sosland Foundation

Jewish Federation of Greater Kansas City ($40,000) see Oppenstein Brothers Foundation

Jewish Federation of Greater Kansas City ($40,000) see Oppenstein Brothers Foundation

Jewish Federation of Kansas City ($30,094) see Tension Envelope Corp.

Jewish Federation of Kansas City ($30,094) see Tension Envelope Corp.

Jewish Federation — Operation E ($107,334) see Sosland Foundation

Jewish Federation of St. Louis ($190,000) see Block Family Charitable Trust, Ephraim

Jewish Federation of St. Louis ($16,000) see Brown Group

Jewish Federation of St. Louis — unspecified operating funds ($33,333) see CPI Corp.

Jewish Federation of St. Louis ($93,000) see Edison Foundation, Harry

Jewish Federation of St. Louis ($8,800) see Gateway Apparel

Jewish Federation of St. Louis ($13,000) see Kahn Memorial Trust

Jewish Federation of St. Louis — operating expenses ($7,000) see Laclede Gas Co.

Jewish Federation of St. Louis ($5,389) see Messing Family Charitable Foundation

Jewish Federation of St. Louis ($15,000) see Shoenberg Foundation

Jewish Federation of St. Louis ($50,000) see Wolff Shoe Co.

Jewish Federation of St. Louis — to provide aid to indigent Jewish people ($190,000) see Block Family Foundation, Emphraim

Jewish Hospital of St. Louis ($1,550) see Edison

Foundation, Irving and Beatrice C.

Jewish Hospital of St. Louis ($17,850) see Kahn Memorial Trust

Jewish Hospital of St. Louis ($15,000) see Olin Charitable Trust, John M.

Jewish Hospital of St. Louis ($100,000) see Shoenberg Foundation

Jewish Vocational Service ($10,000) see Cowden Foundation, Louetta M.

Jewish Vocational Services ($10,000) see Lowenstein Brothers Foundation

John Burroughs School ($100,000) see Edison Foundation, Harry

John Burroughs School ($3,400) see Edison Foundation, Irving and Beatrice C.

John M. Olin School of Business ($10,000) see Kautz Family Foundation

John M. Olin School of Business, Washington University ($15,000) see Kellwood Co.

Johnson County Community College Foundation ($6,000) see Black & Veatch

Joplin Family Y ($676) see Steadley Memorial Trust, Kent D. and Mary L.

Judevine Center for Autistic Children, St. Louis, MO see SAFECO Corp.

Junior Achievement ($1,500) see ACF Industries, Inc.

Junior Achievement ($1,000) see Bartlett & Co.

Junior Achievement — operating expenses ($5,750) see Laclede Gas Co.

Junior Achievement of Mississippi Valley ($5,000) see Pet

K.C.M.S. Together We Can ($2,500) see Southern Furniture Co.

Kairos Community Service ($5,000) see Southern Furniture Co.

Kansas City Art Institute ($7,500) see Barrows Foundation, Geraldine and R. A.

Kansas City Art Institute ($112,000) see Hallmark Cards

Kansas City Art Institute ($1,038,391) see Kemper Charitable Trust, William T.

Kansas City Art Institute ($6,039) see Kemper Foundation, Enid and Crosby

Kansas City Art Institute ($250,000) see Kemper Foundation, William T.

Kansas City Art Institute ($250,000) see Kemper Foundation, William T.

Kansas City Art Institute ($30,000) see Reynolds Foundation, J. B.

Kansas City Art Institute ($50,000) see Stern Foundation for the Arts, Richard J.

Kansas City Association for the Blind — for purchase of plastic blow molding equipment ($50,000) see Speas Foundation, Victor E.

Kansas City Chamber Soloists ($3,745) see Flarsheim Charitable Foundation, Louis and Elizabeth

Kansas City Community Foundation Palestine Missionary Church, Kansas

City ($150,000) see Kemper Charitable Lead Trust, William T.

Kansas City Consensus ($140,000) see Hallmark Cards

Kansas City Eye Bank ($5,000) see Kauffman Foundation, Muriel McBrien

Kansas City Foundation of Chamber Music ($50,000) see Kemper Charitable Lead Trust, William T.

Kansas City Friends of Alvin Ailey ($30,568) see Loose Trust, Carrie J.

Kansas City Friends of Alvin Ailey ($7,850) see Loose Trust, Harry Wilson

Kansas City Friends of Alvin Ailey ($2,100) see Shughart, Thomson & Kilroy, P.C.

Kansas City Lyric Opera ($14,500) see Kauffman Foundation, Muriel McBrien

Kansas City Metropolitan Bar Association ($15,000) see Shughart, Thomson & Kilroy, P.C.

Kansas City Museum ($10,000) see Kuehn Foundation

Kansas City Museum ($100,000) see Sprint

Kansas City Neighborhood Alliance ($1,000) see Shughart, Thomson & Kilroy, P.C.

Kansas City Public Television ($75,000) see Francis Families Foundation

Kansas City Public Television ($35,000) see Sprint

Kansas City Public Television — capital campaign over five years ($100,000) see Yellow Corp.

Kansas City Public Television — general operations ($15,000) see Yellow Corp.

Kansas City Regional Council for Higher Education ($10,000) see Block, H&R

Kansas City Rescue Mission ($30,000) see Sunderland Foundation, Lester T.

Kansas City Symphony ($10,000) see Block, H&R

Kansas City Symphony ($157,000) see Hallmark Cards

Kansas City Symphony ($10,000) see Kemper Memorial Foundation, David Woods

Kansas City Symphony ($75,000) see Sprint

Kansas City Symphony ($194,000) see Yellow Corp.

Kansas Symphony ($50,000) see Stern Foundation for the Arts, Richard J.

KCMC Child Development Corporation — new start ($100,000) see Loose Trust, Carrie J.

KCPT Channel 19 — capital campaign ($50,000) see Turner Charitable Trust, Courtney S.

KCPT Public Television ($6,000) see Marley Co.

KCUR-FM Public Radio ($55,000) see Francis Families Foundation

Kemper Military School and College ($50,000) see Kemper Charitable Trust, William T.

KETC Channel Nine ($60,000) see Ralston Purina Co.

KETC Channel 9 ($15,000) see Stupp Foundation, Norman J.

Khilath Israel Synagogue ($38,361) see Share Foundation

Kidsplace ($10,000) see Roblee Foundation, Joseph H. and Florence A.

Kirksville College — Osteopathic Medicine ($166,280) see Rosenwald Family Fund, William

Kirksville Newman Center ($10,000) see Orscheln Co.

Knights of Columbus ($20,000) see Voelkerding Charitable Trust, Walter and Jean

Landmark Editions Literary Scholarships — funds to help students with literary and artistic abilities with college expenses ($9,408) see Hubbard Foundation, R. Dee and Joan Dale

Landmark Legal Foundation ($25,000) see Cain Foundation, Gordon and Mary

Landmark Legal Foundation ($5,000) see Nichols Co., J.C.

Learning Exchange ($55,000) see Francis Families Foundation

Learning Exchange — operating support and capital campaign ($180,000) see Hallmark Cards

Learning Exchange ($305,000) see Sprint

Learning Exchange — support for the Great Expectations program ($265,501) see Hall Family Foundations

Leukemia Society of America ($1,550) see Shughart, Thomson & Kilroy, P.C.

Liberty Community Center ($7,000) see Kemper Charitable Lead Trust, William T.

Life Action Ministries ($50,000) see Share Foundation

Life Skills Foundation — computer system ($4,000) see Norman Foundation, Andrew

Lights of the Jewish Special Needs Society ($6,000) see Kahn Memorial Trust

Lindenwood College ($10,000) see Brown Foundation, George Warren

Little Sisters of Poor ($7,000) see Enright Foundation

Little Sisters of Poor ($7,500) see Miller-Mellor Association

Lives Under Construction Boys Ranch ($9,000) see Herschend Family Foundation

Llamba Association ($2,000) see Forster-Powers Charitable Trust

Logos High School ($12,500) see Gaylord Foundation, Clifford Willard

Logos High School ($1,000) see Lopata Foundation, Stanley and Lucy

Logos High School ($5,000) see Pettus, Jr. Foundation, James T.

LOGOS School ($19,500) see Pillsbury Foundation

Lutheran Church ($200,000) see Comer Foundation

Lyric Opera ($30,000) see Yellow Corp.

Lyric Opera of Kansas City ($25,000) see Kauffman Foundation, Muriel McBrien

Lyric Opera of Kansas City ($59,000) see Sprint

Lyric Opera of Kansas City — assistance to purchase and partially rehabilitate the Lyric Theatre ($750,000) see Hall Family Foundations

Lyric Opera of Kansas City — general support for program; performance subsidy

($125,000) see Stein Foundation, Jules and Doris

Lyric Theater ($2,000) see Bartlett & Co.

Main Street Corridor Development ($5,000) see Flarsheim Charitable Foundation, Louis and Elizabeth

Marillac Center for Children ($25,000) see Oppenstein Brothers Foundation

Mark Twain Home Foundation ($5,000) see Pet

Mark Twain Summer Institute ($10,000) see Garvey Memorial Foundation, Edward Chase

Mary Institute ($1,000) see Columbia Terminals Co.

Mary Institute ($2,500) see Dunagan Foundation

Mary Institute ($17,500) see Messing Family Charitable Foundation

Mary Institute ($11,250) see Stupp Brothers Bridge & Iron Co.

Mary Institute — a contribution to the school's capital campaign ($300,000) see McDonnell Foundation, James S.

Maryland Heights Church of Christ — missions ($30,000) see Frazier Foundation

Maryville College ($7,500) see Brown Foundation, George Warren

Maryville College ($5,000) see Kellwood Co.

Maryville College ($131,100) see Monsanto Co.

Maryville University ($10,000) see Sachs Fund

Matthews-Dickey Boys Club ($25,000) see Gaylord Foundation, Clifford Willard

Matthews-Dickey Girls Program ($10,000) see Olin Charitable Trust, John M.

McDonnell Douglas Scholarship Foundation ($217,101) see McDonnell Douglas Corp.

Memorah Medical Center Foundation ($5,840) see Helzberg Foundation, Shirley and Barnett

Memorial Home ($20,000) see Jordan and Ettie A. Jordan Charitable Foundation, Mary Ranken

Menorah Medical Center — to renovate and furnish their new mother/baby unit ($79,000) see Speas Memorial Trust, John W. and Effie E.

Mental Health Association ($2,000) see Pitzman Fund

Metro Theatre Company ($8,357) see Horncrest Foundation

Metropolitan Community College ($50,000) see Francis Families Foundation

Metropolitan Community Colleges — talent ($50,000) see Loose Trust, Carrie J.

Metropolitan Lutheran Ministry ($25,000) see Loose Trust, Carrie J.

Metropolitan Lutheran Ministry ($20,000) see Oppenstein Brothers Foundation

Mid America Arts Alliance — general support grant ($25,000) see Stark Foundation, Nelda C. and H. J. Lutcher

Mid-America Assistance Coalition ($7,500) see Flarsheim Charitable

Foundation, Louis and Elizabeth

Mid Continent Council of Girl Scouts — capital campaign ($35,000) see Turner Charitable Trust, Courtney S.

Midwest Bioethics Center ($5,000) see Kemper Foundation, Enid and Crosby

Midwest Christian Counseling ($7,500) see Wornall Charitable Trust and Foundation, Kearney

Missionaries of Charity ($2,500) see Louis Foundation, Michael W.

Missouri Baptist Children's Home ($42,500) see Pillsbury Foundation

Missouri Botanical Garden ($60,000) see Boatmen's Bancshares

Missouri Botanical Garden ($79,000) see Claiborne Art Ortenberg Foundation, Liz

Missouri Botanical Garden ($1,000) see Columbia Terminals Co.

Missouri Botanical Garden ($10,000) see Commerce Bancshares, Inc.

Missouri Botanical Garden ($40,000) see Dula Educational and Charitable Foundation, Caleb C. and Julia W.

Missouri Botanical Garden ($150,000) see Emerson Electric Co.

Missouri Botanical Garden ($10,000) see Garvey Memorial Foundation, Edward Chase

Missouri Botanical Garden ($60,000) see General Dynamics Corp.

Missouri Botanical Garden ($5,000) see Grant Charitable Trust, Elberth R. and Gladys F.

Missouri Botanical Garden ($10,000) see Graybar Electric Co.

Missouri Botanical Garden ($35,000) see Interco

Missouri Botanical Garden ($100,000) see Jordan and Ettie A. Jordan Charitable Foundation, Mary Ranken

Missouri Botanical Garden ($1,000) see Lopata Foundation, Stanley and Lucy

Missouri Botanical Garden ($5,000) see Love Charitable Foundation, John Allan

Missouri Botanical Garden ($30,000) see Mercantile Bancorp

Missouri Botanical Garden ($100,000) see Olin Foundation, Spencer T. and Ann W.

Missouri Botanical Garden ($25,000) see Pott Foundation, Herman T. and Phenie R.

Missouri Botanical Garden ($10,000) see Sachs Fund

Missouri Botanical Garden ($121,000) see Shoenberg Foundation

Missouri Botanical Garden ($19,000) see Smith Horticultural Trust, Stanley

Missouri Botanical Garden ($15,000) see Souers Charitable Trust, Sidney W. and Sylvia N.

Missouri Botanical Garden ($200,000) see Southwestern Bell Corp.

Missouri Botanical Garden ($55,000) see Stupp Foundation, Norman J.

Missouri (cont.)

Missouri Botanical Garden Japanese Fest ($80,000) see Coleman Foundation

Missouri Citizens For Life Education Fund ($8,000) see Orscheln Co.

Missouri College Fund ($6,000) see Kemper Memorial Foundation, David Woods

Missouri Colleges, Inc. see Reliable Life Insurance Co.

Missouri Colleges Fund ($2,500) see Black & Veatch

Missouri Colleges Fund ($5,000) see Brown Foundation, George Warren

Missouri Colleges Fund ($5,000) see Marley Co.

Missouri Colleges Fund ($2,500) see Nichols Co., J.C.

Missouri Colleges Fund ($6,000) see Utilicorp United

Missouri Girls Town Foundation ($30,000) see Pott Foundation, Herman T. and Phenie R.

Missouri Historical Society ($10,000) see Shoenberg Foundation

Missouri Religious Coalition for Abortion Rights ($45,000) see Sunnen Foundation

Missouri Repertory Theatre ($21,670) see Butler Manufacturing Co.

Missouri Repertory Theatre ($75,000) see Francis Families Foundation

Missouri Repertory Theatre ($200,000) see Hallmark Cards

Missouri Repertory Theatre ($30,000) see Kauffman Foundation, Muriel McBrien

Missouri Repertory Theatre ($50,000) see Kemper Charitable Lead Trust, William T.

Missouri Repertory Theatre ($30,000) see Turner Charitable Trust, Courtney S.

Missouri Repertory Theatre ($12,500) see Wornall Charitable Trust and Foundation, Kearney

Missouri Repertory Theatre ($15,000) see Yellow Corp.

Missouri Southern State College — to purchase A-V and NAL equipment; classroom renovation ($74,411) see Fuld Health Trust, Helene

Missouri Western State College ($25,000) see Kemper Charitable Trust, William T.

Missouri Young Farmers ($5,000) see Missouri Farmers Association

Moolah Temple Shrine Circus ($100) see Wolff Shoe Co.

Most Precious Blood School — national telecommunications networking of computer lab to databases ($3,700) see Pendergast-Weyer Foundation

MRMC Foundation ($5,500) see Orscheln Co.

Multiple Sclerosis Society ($1,250) see Lopata Foundation, Stanley and Lucy

Multiple Sclerosis Society, St. Louis, MO ($10,000) see General American Life Insurance Co.

Muny Grantors Fund see Reliable Life Insurance Co.

National Benevolent Association — building fund ($50,000) see Beasley Foundation, Theodore and Beulah

National Bowling Hall of Fame and Museum ($25,000) see Brunswick Corp.

National Cancer Institute ($5,000) see Bloch Foundation, Henry W. and Marion H.

National Cancer Institute ($5,000) see Bloch Foundation, Henry W. and Marion H.

National Conference of Christians and Jews ($1,250) see Lowenstein Brothers Foundation

National Council on Alcoholism ($6,000) see Pitzman Fund

National Federation TARGET Program ($109,855) see Carter Foundation, Amon G.

National Kidney Foundation ($2,000) see Conwood Co. L.P.

National Kidney Foundation ($2,500) see Wolff Shoe Co.

Nature Conservancy ($1,200) see Gateway Apparel

Nature Conservancy — general support for program; preserving threatened species and ecosystems; land conservation in Missouri ($62,000) see Stein Foundation, Jules and Doris

Nazareth Home ($5,000) see Enright Foundation

Neighborhood Ecumenical Witness Services ($50,000) see Cowden Foundation, Louetta M.

Neighborhood Housing Services ($10,000) see Commerce Bancshares, Inc.

Nelson Art Gallery ($100,000) see Ward Foundation, Louis L. and Adelaide C.

Nelson-Atkins Museum of Art ($25,000) see Block, H&R

Nelson-Atkins Museum of Art ($50,000) see Butler Manufacturing Co.

Nelson-Atkins Museum of Art ($100,000) see Francis Families Foundation

Nelson-Atkins Museum of Art ($36,000) see Kemper Foundation, Enid and Crosby

Nelson Atkins Museum of Art ($10,000) see Kemper Memorial Foundation, David Woods

Nelson Atkins Museum of Art — to underwrite 1990 Spring Impressionism Exhibit ($135,500) see Turner Charitable Trust, Courtney S.

Nelson Gallery Acquisition Funding ($193,825) see Yellow Corp.

Nelson Gallery of Art — museum continuity ($37,500) see Yellow Corp.

Nelson Gallery Foundation ($2,500) see Bartlett & Co.

Nelson Gallery Foundation ($2,500) see Bartlett & Co.

Nelson Gallery Foundation ($750) see Bartlett & Co.

Nelson Gallery Foundation ($100,000) see Hallmark Cards

Nelson Gallery Foundation ($50,000) see Kemper Foundation, William T.

Nelson Gallery Foundation ($3,750) see Miller-Mellor Association

Nelson Gallery Foundation ($5,000) see Owen Industries, Inc.

Nelson Gallery Foundation ($15,000) see Randa

Nelson Gallery Foundation ($25,000) see Sosland Foundation

Nelson Gallery Foundation ($2,500) see Tension Envelope Corp.

Nelson Gallery Foundation ($5,000) see Utilicorp United

Nelson Gallery Foundation ($11,000) see Westport Fund

Neosho United Fund — human services ($11,048) see La-Z-Boy Chair Co.

Network for Educational Development ($10,000) see Brown Group

Nevada Area Economic Development Commission ($5,000) see Moss Charitable Trust, Finis M.

Nevada Public Library ($4,000) see Moss Charitable Trust, Finis M.

Nevada R-5 Schools ($1,000) see Moss Charitable Trust, Finis M.

Nevada Shrine Club Transportation Fund for Crippled Children ($2,000) see Moss Charitable Trust, Finis M.

New City Schools ($2,000) see Pitzman Fund

New Directions Education Fund ($30,000) see Pearlstone Foundation, Peggy Meyerhoff

New Israel Fund ($2,000) see Lowenstein Brothers Foundation

New Reform Temple ($5,150) see Bloch Foundation, Henry W. and Marion H.

North Side Team Ministry ($17,430) see Pillsbury Foundation

Northwest Missouri Industries ($2,500) see Morgan Charitable Residual Trust, W. and E.

Northwest Missouri Industries ($2,500) see Morgan Charitable Residual Trust, W. and E.

Northwest Missouri State University ($1,000) see Kelly Tractor Co.

Notre Dame High School ($2,300) see Pendergast-Weyer Foundation

Notre Dame High School ($250) see Pendergast-Weyer Foundation

Oakland City College ($10,000) see Webb Foundation

Opera Theater of St. Louis ($1,000) see Orchard Corp. of America.

Opera Theatre of St. Louis ($50,000) see Driscoll Foundation

Opera Theatre of St. Louis ($10,000) see Garvey Memorial Foundation, Edward Chase

Opera Theatre of St. Louis ($75,000) see Whitaker Charitable Foundation, Lyndon C.

Opera Theatre of St. Louis ($50,000) see Whitaker Charitable Foundation, Lyndon C.

Operation Brightside ($10,000) see Roblee Foundation, Joseph H. and Florence A.

Operation Brightside ($2,500) see Vogt Machine Co., Henry

Operation Discovery School — replacement of playground ($30,200) see Rhoden Charitable Foundation, Elmer C.

Our Lady's Montessori School ($5,000) see Forster-Powers Charitable Trust

Ozanam Home for Boys ($15,000) see Loose Trust, Harry Wilson

Ozanam Home for Boys — support joint special consultation team program unit ($71,000) see Speas Foundation, Victor E.

Ozark Christian Counseling — start-up costs new counseling center ($14,900) see Slusher Charitable Foundation, Roy W.

Ozark Medical Center — Alzheimers building fund ($25,000) see Shaw Foundation, Arch W.

Ozark Medical Center — Alzheimers building fund ($25,000) see Shaw Foundation, Arch W.

Paraquad ($30,000) see Green Foundation, Allen P. and Josephine B.

Paraquad ($5,000) see Pettus, Jr. Foundation, James T.

Paraquad ($35,000) see Whitaker Charitable Foundation, Lyndon C.

Pembroke Hill School ($50,000) see Francis Families Foundation

Pembroke Hill School ($15,000) see Helzberg Foundation, Shirley and Barnett

Pembroke Hill School ($5,800) see Helzberg Foundation, Shirley and Barnett

Pembroke Hill School ($30,000) see Kemper Charitable Trust, William T.

Pembroke Hill School — library endowment ($10,000) see Kemper Memorial Foundation, David Woods

Pembroke Hill School — scholarships ($75,000) see Powell Family Foundation

Pembroke School ($5,000) see Westport Fund

Pets for Life ($500) see McCray Lumber Co.

Philadelphia High School Academics ($5,000) see Pet

Planned Parenthood ($48,000) see Kelly Foundation, T. Lloyd

Planned Parenthood ($4,000) see Pettus, Jr. Foundation, James T.

Planned Parenthood Federation of America ($8,000) see Breidenthal Foundation, Willard J. and Mary G.

Planned Parenthood Federation of America — national assistance family planning ($30,000) see Oppenstein Brothers Foundation

Planned Parenthood Federation of America ($5,000) see Pitzman Fund

Planned Parenthood Federation of America ($8,000) see Westport Fund

Planned Parenthood - St. Louis ($75,000) see Sunnen Foundation

Powell Gardens ($35,000) see Flarsheim Charitable Foundation, Louis and Elizabeth

Powell Gardens — operating ($72,700) see Powell Family Foundation

Powell Gardens — operating ($68,000) see Powell Family Foundation

Powell Gardens — operating ($67,400) see Powell Family Foundation

Powell Gardens — operating ($65,400) see Powell Family Foundation

Powell Gardens — operating ($64,500) see Powell Family Foundation

Powell Gardens — Perennial Garden ($150,000) see Powell Family Foundation

Powell Gardens — Perennial Garden ($100,000) see Powell Family Foundation

Powell Gardens Project ($500) see Bartlett & Co.

Powell Symphony Hall ($10,000) see Garvey Memorial Foundation, Edward Chase

Presser Hall Preservation Society ($25,000) see Green Foundation, Allen P. and Josephine B.

Principia ($5,000) see Wolff Foundation, John M.

Principia Corporation ($1,000) see Chamberlin Foundation, Gerald W.

Principia Corporation ($122,000) see Harding Foundation, Charles Stewart

Principia Corporation ($3,000) see Moore Foundation, C. F.

Principia Corporation ($4,500) see Slaughter, Jr. Foundation, William E.

Principle Foundation ($10,000) see Aequus Institute

Principle Foundation — operations ($90,000) see Powell Family Foundation

Public TV 19 ($17,850) see Kemper Charitable Lead Trust, William T.

Ranken-Jordan Home ($6,000) see Group Health Plan Inc.

Ranken-Jordan Home for Convalescent Crippled Children ($50,000) see Jordan and Ettie A. Jordan Charitable Foundation, Mary Ranken

Ranken Technical College — operating expenses ($5,000) see Laclede Gas Co.

Ranken Technical Institute ($3,000) see ACF Industries, Inc.

Ranken Technical Institute ($5,000) see Brown Foundation, George Warren

Ranken Technical Institute ($5,000) see Fabick Tractor Co., John

Red Cross ($5,000) see Ward Foundation, Louis L. and Adelaide C.

Renaissance West ($50,000) see Cowden Foundation, Louetta M.

Renaissance West ($50,000) see Oppenstein Brothers Foundation

Repertory Theatre ($1,000) see Interstate Packaging Co.

Repertory Theatre of St. Louis ($25,000) see Jordan and Ettie A. Jordan Charitable Foundation, Mary Ranken

Research Foundation — in support of research project involving implantable insulin pumps ($92,000) see Speas Memorial Trust, John W. and Effie E.

Research Medical Center ($250,000) see Kemper Foundation, William T.

Research Medical Center ($20,000) see Reynolds Foundation, J. B.

ReStart, Inc. — capital support for relocation and expansion of facility for homeless

($400,000) see Hall Family Foundations

Restart ($30,000) see Oppenstein Brothers Foundation

Richard Cabot Clinic ($5,000) see Forster-Powers Charitable Trust

Rockhurst College ($10,000) see Breidenthal Foundation, Willard J. and Mary G.

Rockhurst College ($1,000,000) see Mabee Foundation, J. E. and L. E.

Rockhurst College ($20,000) see Marley Co.

Rockhurst College ($50,000) see McGee Foundation

Rockhurst College ($2,000) see Nichols Co., J.C.

Rockhurst College ($25,000) see Reynolds Foundation, J. B.

Rockhurst College — support of revolving loan fund for accelerated nursing degree options ($50,000) see Speas Foundation, Victor E.

Rockhurst High School ($125,000) see Forster-Powers Charitable Fund

Rockhurst High School ($25,000) see McGee Foundation

Rose Brooks Center ($20,600) see Kemper Charitable Lead Trust, William T.

Rossman School — unrestricted gift ($25,000) see Enterprise Rent-A-Car Co.

Royal Night of Fashion ($1,000) see Ward Foundation, Louis L. and Adelaide C.

St. Ajus Church ($64,557) see Orscheln Co.

St. Catherine Laboure Church ($5,000) see Fabick Tractor Co., John

St. Elizabeth Church ($5,200) see Enright Foundation

St. Francis Borgia Regional High School ($10,000) see Voelkerding Charitable Trust, Walter and Jean

Saint Francis Hospital see New England Business Service

St. Francis Xavier Church ($4,000) see Forster-Powers Charitable Trust

St. Johns Mercy Medical Center ($3,000) see Edison Foundation, Irving and Beatrice C.

St. Joseph Greater United Way ($33,025) see Quaker Oats Co.

St. Joseph Health Center Foundation — for construction of new community center for health education ($75,000) see Speas Memorial Trust, John W. and Effie E.

St. Joseph School District ($20,000) see Messick Charitable Trust, Harry F.

St. Louis Archdiocese School System ($80,000) see Union Electric Co.

St. Louis Area Council Boy Scouts of America ($114,000) see Anheuser-Busch Cos.

St. Louis Area Food Bank ($5,000) see Wolff Foundation, John M.

St. Louis Art Museum ($50,000) see Jordan and Ettie A. Jordan Charitable Foundation, Mary Ranken

St. Louis Art Museum — promotion of arts ($5,000) see Love Charitable Foundation, John Allan

St. Louis Art Museum ($21,000) see Orchard Corp. of America.

St. Louis Art Museum ($50,000) see Pulitzer Publishing Co.

St. Louis Art Museum ($101,500) see Shoenberg Foundation

St. Louis Art Museum ($20,000) see Stupp Foundation, Norman J.

St. Louis Art Museum ($5,000) see Swift Co. Inc., John S.

St. Louis Association for Retarded Citizens — for the alleviation of disease ($10,000) see Love Charitable Foundation, John Allan

St. Louis Association for Retarded Citizens — capital campaign-Childgarden ($25,000) see CPI Corp.

St. Louis Childrens Hospital ($1,300) see Edison Foundation, Irving and Beatrice C.

St. Louis Children's Hospital ($250,000) see Lattner Foundation, Forrest C.

St. Louis Childrens Hospital ($20,000) see Souers Charitable Trust, Sidney W. and Sylvia N.

St. Louis Children's Hospital ($25,000) see Stupp Foundation, Norman J.

St. Louis Children's Hospital ($200,000) see Union Electric Co.

St. Louis Community Foundation ($25,000) see Mercantile Bancorp

St. Louis Conservatory for the Arts ($5,000) see Norman Foundation, Andrew

St. Louis Conservatory and School for the Arts ($13,000) see Monticello College Foundation

St. Louis Conservatory and School for the Arts ($12,000) see Orchard Corp. of America.

St. Louis Country Day School ($11,500) see Stupp Brothers Bridge & Iron Co.

St. Louis Country Day School ($650) see Wolff Shoe Co.

St. Louis Effort for AIDS ($5,000) see Roblee Foundation, Joseph H. and Florence A.

St. Louis Institute of Virology ($10,000) see General American Life Insurance Co.

St. Louis Mercantile Library Association ($40,000) see Pott Foundation, Herman T. and Phenie R.

St. Louis Mercantile Library Association ($30,000) see Pott Foundation, Herman T. and Phenie R.

St. Louis Mercantile Library Association ($8,200) see Stupp Brothers Bridge & Iron Co.

St. Louis Psychoanalytic Institute ($150,000) see Edison Foundation, Harry

St. Louis School of Medicine ($39,760) see Group Health Plan Inc.

St. Louis Science Center ($400,000) see Anheuser-Busch Cos.

St. Louis Science Center — unspecified operating funds ($30,000) see CPI Corp.

St. Louis Science Center ($50,000) see Edison Foundation, Harry

St. Louis Science Center — unrestricted gift ($25,000) see Enterprise Rent-A-Car Co.

St. Louis Science Center ($50,000) see Lopata Foundation, Stanley and Lucy

St. Louis Science Center ($200,000) see May Department Stores Co.

St. Louis Science Center ($200,000) see May Department Stores Co.

St. Louis Science Center ($500,000) see McDonnell Douglas Corp.

St. Louis Science Center ($2,000) see Pitzman Fund

St. Louis Science Center ($200,000) see Ralston Purina Co.

St. Louis Science Center ($10,000) see Sachs Fund

St. Louis Science Center ($300,000) see Southwestern Bell Corp.

St. Louis Science Center ($30,000) see Stupp Foundation, Norman J.

St. Louis Science Center ($250,000) see Union Electric Co.

St. Louis Science Center Foundation ($87,500) see Boatmen's Bancshares

St. Louis Science Center Foundation ($10,000) see Fabick Tractor Co., John

St. Louis Science Center Foundation ($16,667) see Graybar Electric Co.

St. Louis Science Center Foundation ($16,666) see Graybar Electric Co.

St. Louis Science Center Foundation ($25,000) see Pet

St. Louis Society for Crippled Children ($2,000) see Pitzman Fund

St. Louis Symphony — unspecified operating funds ($22,500) see CPI Corp.

St. Louis Symphony ($125,000) see Emerson Electric Co.

St. Louis Symphony ($100,000) see Emerson Electric Co.

St. Louis Symphony — unrestricted gift ($25,000) see Enterprise Rent-A-Car Co.

St. Louis Symphony ($50,000) see General Dynamics Corp.

St. Louis Symphony see Mallinckrodt Specialty Chemicals Co.

St. Louis Symphony — commitment to excellence endowment ($175,000) see McDonnell Douglas Corp.

St. Louis Symphony ($2,000) see Orchard Corp. of America.

St. Louis Symphony ($6,000) see Sachs Fund

St. Louis Symphony Orchestra ($10,000) see Garvey Memorial Foundation, Edward Chase

St. Louis Symphony Orchestra ($20,000) see Gaylord Foundation, Clifford Willard

St. Louis Symphony Orchestra ($11,000) see General American Life Insurance Co.

St. Louis Symphony Orchestra ($17,500) see Graybar Electric Co.

St. Louis Symphony Orchestra ($30,000) see Interco

St. Louis Symphony Orchestra ($50,000) see Mercantile Bancorp

St. Louis Symphony Orchestra ($50,000) see Whitaker Charitable Foundation, Lyndon C.

St. Louis Symphony Orchestra ($40,000) see Whitaker Charitable Foundation, Lyndon C.

St. Louis Symphony Orchestra ($200) see Wolff Shoe Co.

St. Louis Symphony Society ($50,000) see Boatmen's Bancshares

St. Louis Symphony Society ($10,844) see Brown Group

St. Louis Symphony Society ($1,150) see Gateway Apparel

St. Louis Symphony Society ($100,000) see Jordan and Ettie A. Jordan Charitable Foundation, Mary Ranken

St. Louis Symphony Society — operating expenses ($35,000) see Laclede Gas Co.

St. Louis Symphony Society ($50,000) see Pulitzer Publishing Co.

St. Louis Symphony Society ($50,000) see Pulitzer Publishing Co.

St. Louis University ($9,000) see Allendale Mutual Insurance Co.

St. Louis University ($300,000) see Anheuser-Busch Cos.

St. Louis University ($200,000) see Emerson Electric Co.

St. Louis University ($50,000) see Gaylord Foundation, Clifford Willard

St. Louis University ($10,000) see JOFCo., Inc.

St. Louis University ($25,000) see Jordan and Ettie A. Jordan Charitable Foundation, Mary Ranken

St. Louis University — endowment fund ($10,000) see Kellwood Co.

St. Louis University ($6,000) see Kellwood Co.

St. Louis University — operating expenses ($20,250) see Laclede Gas Co.

St. Louis University — scholarship for medical students ($27,560) see Van Schaick Scholarship Fund, Nellie

St. Louis University ($10,000) see Wolff Foundation, John M.

St. Louis University ($105,743) see Wrape Family Charitable Trust

St. Louis University (Arts and Science) ($15,000) see Webb Foundation

St. Louis University Hospital Cardiology Division ($100,000) see Lichtenstein Foundation, David B.

St. Louis University — Matching Gift Program ($6,495) see Laclede Gas Co.

St. Louis University Mercantile Endowment Graduate Fellowship ($50,000) see Mercantile Bancorp

St. Louis University School of Business and Administration ($139,000) see McDonnell Douglas Corp.

St. Louis University School of Nursing ($10,000) see Group Health Plan Inc.

St. Louis Variety Club ($1,000) see Lopata Foundation, Stanley and Lucy

St. Louis Zoo ($5,000) see Fabick Tractor Co., John

St. Louis Zoo ($5,000) see Graybar Electric Co.

St. Louis Zoo Association ($7,700) see Stupp Brothers Bridge & Iron Co.

St. Louis Zoological Park ($50,000) see Boatmen's Bancshares

St. Louis Zoological Park — unspecified operating funds ($10,000) see CPI Corp.

St. Louis Zoological Park ($50,000) see Interco

St. Louis Zoological Society ($300,000) see Southwestern Bell Co.

St. Luke's Hospital ($20,000) see Brown Group

St. Lukes Hospital ($5,000) see Olin Charitable Trust, John M.

St. Luke's Hospital ($50,000) see Smith Foundation, Kenneth L. and Eva S.

St. Lukes Hospital ($20,000) see Souers Charitable Trust, Sidney W. and Sylvia N.

St. Luke's Hospital ($5,000) see Wornall Charitable Trust and Foundation, Kearney

St. Lukes Hospital Capital Fund ($15,000) see Nichols Co., J.C.

St. Lukes Hospital Electrophysiologic Program ($10,000) see Kemper Memorial Foundation, David Woods

St. Luke's Hospital Foundation ($30,000) see Bloch Foundation, Henry W. and Marion H.

St. Lukes Hospital Foundation ($50,000) see Cowden Foundation, Louetta M.

St. Luke's Hospital Foundation — to establish a geriatric assessment program ($100,000) see Speas Memorial Trust, John W. and Effie E.

St. Luke's Hospital Foundation — urologic oncology fellowship program ($55,000) see Stowers Foundation

St. Patrick Center Food Program ($10,000) see Fabick Tractor Co., John

St. Vincent de Paul Church ($12,000) see Voelkerding Charitable Trust, Walter and Jean

St. Wenceslaus Church ($5,000) see Fabick Tractor Co., John

Salvation Army ($60,000) see Boatmen's Bancshares

Salvation Army — unspecified operating funds ($21,875) see CPI Corp.

Salvation Army ($120,000) see Emerson Electric Co.

Salvation Army ($7,000) see Enright Foundation

Salvation Army ($10,000) see Graybar Electric Co.

Salvation Army ($2,000) see Graybar Electric Co.

Salvation Army ($6,000) see Love Charitable Foundation, John Allan

Salvation Army ($3,500) see Moss Charitable Trust, Finis M.

Salvation Army ($2,500) see Nichols Co., J.C.

Salvation Army ($50,000) see Pet

Salvation Army ($20,000) see Webb Foundation

Salvation Army ($7,000) see Westport Fund

Salvation Army ($10,000) see Whitney Fund, David M.

Salvation Army ($25,000) see Wolff Foundation, John M.

Salvation Army Hope Center ($30,000) see Pott Foundation, Herman T. and Phenie R.

Missouri (cont.)

Salvation Army of Kansas City — capital campaign ($30,000) see Sosland Foundation

Salvation Army — renovation of Linwood Center ($1,500,000) see Hall Family Foundations

Salvation Army-St. Louis ($250,000) see Union Electric Co.

Salvation Army, St. Louis, MO ($8,000) see General American Life Insurance Co.

Samuel U. Rodgers Community Health Center — in support of development of comprehensive eye center ($80,000) see Speas Memorial Trust, John W. and Effie E.

Savannah R-III School District ($2,250) see Messick Charitable Trust, Harry F.

Scholarship Foundation of St. Louis ($50,000) see Edison Foundation, Harry

School of Ozarks ($10,000) see Campbell Foundation, Charles Talbot

School of the Ozarks ($2,000) see Swift Co. Inc., John S.

Second Presbyterian Church ($25,000) see Jordan and Ettie A. Jordan Charitable Foundation, Mary Ranken

Seton Family Center ($2,000) see Forster-Powers Charitable Trust

Shalom Geriatric ($1,000) see Lowenstein Brothers Foundation

Sharenet Association — support of Phase II of telecommunications system ($39,250) see Speas Foundation, Victor E.

Shepherd's Center ($2,000) see Forster-Powers Charitable Trust

Shepherd's Centers of America — to continue development of Shepherd's Centers nationwide ($135,000) see Retirement Research Foundation

Shrine of St. Patrick ($90,000) see Fabick Tractor Co., John

Sister Cities Association of Greater Kansas City ($30,000) see Sprint

Sister City Association ($1,000) see Bartlett & Co.

Sixth Church of Christian Scientists ($5,000) see Kemper Foundation, Enid and Crosby

Skaggs Community Hospital — building fund ($20,000) see Slusher Charitable Foundation, Roy W.

SLICAH ($2,000) see Messing Family Charitable Foundation

Society for the Preservation of John Wornall House Museum ($25,000) see Wornall Charitable Trust and Foundation, Kearney

Society of St. Mary (Marianists) ($12,000) see Doty Family Foundation

Soulard Association for Family Services ($2,000) see Pitzman Fund

Soulard Association for Family Services ($2,000) see Pitzman Fund

Southeast Missouri State University ($7,500) see Brown Foundation, George Warren

Southside Womens Center ($1,085) see Horncrest Foundation

Southwest Baptist University ($15,000) see Plaster Foundation, Robert W.

Southwest Baptist University ($100,000) see Share Foundation

Southwest Missouri State University Foundation ($500,000) see Plaster Foundation, Robert W.

Spelman Memorial Hospital — to establish older adult memory assessment program ($60,000) see Speas Memorial Trust, John W. and Effie E.

Spofford Home ($20,000) see Barrows Foundation, Geraldine and R. A.

Spofford Home ($25,000) see Smith Foundation, Kenneth L. and Eva S.

Springfield Victory Mission — capital improvements ($26,176) see Slusher Charitable Foundation, Roy W.

Stages Production Company ($1,000) see Vaughn, Jr. Foundation Fund, James M.

State Ballet of Missouri ($16,000) see Bloch Foundation, Henry W. and Marion H.

State Ballet of Missouri ($14,820) see Block, H&R

State Ballet of Missouri ($25,000) see Kauffman Foundation, Muriel McBrien

State Ballet of Missouri ($5,000) see Kauffman Foundation, Muriel McBrien

State Ballet of Missouri ($25,000) see Yellow Corp.

State Historical Society of Missouri ($12,500) see Gaylord Foundation, Clifford Willard

State of St. Louis Foundation ($7,500) see Stupp Brothers Bridge & Iron Co.

Stephens College ($5,000) see Johnston-Hanson Foundation

Stephens College — continuation of performing arts grants ($30,000) see Pendergast-Weyer Foundation

Stephens College ($97,500) see Pillsbury Foundation

Stephens College ($3,500) see Shelter Mutual Insurance Co.

Stephens College — continuation and expansion of computer training for Catholic teachers ($95,000) see Pendergast-Weyer Foundation

Strongly Oriented for Action ($5,000) see Roblee Foundation, Joseph H. and Florence A.

Students in Free Enterprise ($120,000) see Wal-Mart Stores

Supreme Court of Missouri Historical Society ($12,500) see Gaylord Foundation, Clifford Willard

Swope Parkway Health Center ($10,000) see Loose Trust, Harry Wilson

Tablerock Christian Associates ($18,000) see Herschend Family Foundation

Teen Challenge of Ozarks — capital improvements ($42,600) see Slusher Charitable Foundation, Roy W.

Temple B'nai Jehudah ($10,000) see Helzberg Foundation, Shirley and Barnett

Temples B'nai Jehuda ($20,000) see Helzberg Foundation, Shirley and Barnett

Third Baptist Church ($77,000) see Pillsbury Foundation

Thomas Jefferson School ($29,000) see Miller Foundation, Steve J.

Tower Grove Park ($12,500) see Gaylord Foundation, Clifford Willard

Tower Grove Park ($15,900) see Stupp Brothers Bridge & Iron Co.

Triple "A" ($5,000) see Love Charitable Foundation, John Allan

Truman Medical Center Foundation ($15,000) see Barrows Foundation, Geraldine and R. A.

Truman Medical Center Foundation ($16,000) see Sosland Foundation

Truman Medical Center —Kansas City P.A.C.T. program to address pregnancy and substance abuse ($266,865) see Hall Family Foundations

Truman Medical Center — support of nursing services Manpower Development Program ($42,000) see Speas Foundation, Victor E.

UAHC ARZA ($1,000) see Lowenstein Brothers Foundation

UMKC Advocacy Program ($6,000) see Shughart, Thomson & Kilroy, P.C.

Unicorn Theater ($5,000) see Flarsheim Charitable Foundation, Louis and Elizabeth

Unicorn Theatre ($30,000) see Kemper Foundation, Enid and Crosby

Unicorn Theatre ($500) see McCray Lumber Co.

United Cerebral Palsey ($2,750) see Messick Charitable Trust, Harry F.

United Community Funds of Vernon County ($2,500) see Moss Charitable Trust, Finis M.

United Nations Association ($5,000) see Roblee Foundation, Joseph H. and Florence A.

United Way ($10,000) see Bloch Foundation, Henry W. and Marion H.

United Way ($58,000) see Butler Manufacturing Co.

United Way ($30,750) see Commerce Bancshares, Inc.

United Way ($30,750) see Commerce Bancshares, Inc.

United Way ($30,750) see Commerce Bancshares, Inc.

United Way ($19,000) see Commerce Bancshares, Inc.

United Way ($19,000) see Commerce Bancshares, Inc.

United Way ($19,000) see Commerce Bancshares, Inc.

United Way ($12,500) see Commerce Bancshares, Inc.

United Way ($10,500) see Commerce Bancshares, Inc.

United Way ($406,262) see Edison Brothers Stores

United Way ($13,000) see Edison Foundation, Irving and Beatrice C.

United Way ($7,500) see Fabick Tractor Co., John

United Way ($6,921) see First Financial Bank FSB

United Way ($15,000) see Gateway Apparel

United Way ($15,000) see Graybar Electric Co.

United Way ($5,000) see Hamilton Foundation, Florence P.

United Way ($7,500) see Heileman Brewing Co., Inc., G.

United Way ($12,000) see Helzberg Foundation, Shirley and Barnett

United Way ($20,000) see Kellwood Co.

United Way ($10,000) see Kemper Memorial Foundation, David Woods

United Way ($25,000) see Loose Trust, Harry Wilson

United Way ($8,000) see Lopata Foundation, Stanley and Lucy

United Way ($89,705) see Marley Co.

United Way ($5,000) see MDU Resources Group, Inc.

United Way ($1,100) see National By-Products

United Way ($27,585) see Nichols Co., J.C.

United Way ($10,000) see Olin Charitable Trust, John M.

United Way ($13,000) see Sachs Fund

United Way ($28,000) see Shoenberg Foundation

United Way ($47,000) see Stupp Brothers Bridge & Iron Co.

United Way ($3,000) see Swift Co. Inc., John S.

United Way ($20,000) see Tension Envelope Corp.

United Way ($20,000) see Tension Envelope Corp.

United Way ($30,000) see Wornall Charitable Trust and Foundation, Kearney

United Way of Greater St. Louis ($875,000) see Anheuser-Busch Cos.

United Way of Greater St. Louis ($125,000) see Boatmen's Bancshares

United Way of Greater St. Louis ($125,000) see Boatmen's Bancshares

United Way of Greater St. Louis ($125,000) see Boatmen's Bancshares

United Way of Greater St. Louis ($25,000) see Brown Group

United Way of Greater St. Louis ($25,000) see Brown Group

United Way of Greater St. Louis ($25,000) see Brown Group

United Way of Greater St. Louis ($25,000) see Brown Group

United Way of Greater St. Louis ($25,000) see Brown Group

United Way of Greater St. Louis ($28,665) see Cooper Industries

United Way of Greater St. Louis — unspecified operating funds ($76,527) see CPI Corp.

United Way Greater St. Louis — annual giving ($45,294) see Enterprise Rent-A-Car Co.

United Way of Greater St. Louis ($33,781) see General American Life Insurance Co.

United Way of Greater St. Louis ($50,000) see General Dynamics Corp.

United Way of Greater St. Louis ($50,000) see Interco

United Way of Greater St. Louis ($50,000) see Interco

United Way of Greater St. Louis ($807,289) see McDonnell Douglas Corp.

United Way of Greater St. Louis ($807,289) see McDonnell Douglas Corp.

United Way of Greater St. Louis ($117,896) see Mercantile Bancorp

United Way of Greater St. Louis ($117,896) see Mercantile Bancorp

United Way of Greater St. Louis ($117,896) see Mercantile Bancorp

United Way of Greater St. Louis ($117,896) see Mercantile Bancorp

United Way of Greater St. Louis ($1,320,000) see Monsanto Co.

United Way of Greater St. Louis ($95,000) see Pet

United Way of Greater St. Louis ($22,000) see Pott Foundation, Herman T. and Phenie R.

United Way of Greater St. Louis ($90,500) see Pulitzer Publishing Co.

United Way of Greater St. Louis ($195,000) see Ralston Purina Co.

United Way of Greater St. Louis ($195,000) see Ralston Purina Co.

United Way of Greater St. Louis ($195,000) see Ralston Purina Co.

United Way of Greater St. Louis ($180,000) see Ralston Purina Co.

United Way of Greater St. Louis ($130,000) see Union Pacific Corp.

United Way of Greater St. Louis ($16,050) see Universal Foods Corp.

United Way Greater St. Louis — general purpose fund ($9,620) see Walgreen Co.

United Way of Greater St. Louis — contributions to over 100 charitable organizations through United Way ($233,937) see Laclede Gas Co.

United Way of St. Joseph ($20,000) see Messick Charitable Trust, Harry F.

United Way-St. Louis ($770,000) see Union Electric Co.

United Way of St. Louis and St. Louis County ($750,000) see Emerson Electric Co.

University of Kansas/University of Missouri Kansas City — to support the establishment of a biological and biomedical center for research on the diseases and treatment of the aging population ($392,500) see Marion Merrell Dow

University of Missouri ($500,000) see Anheuser-Busch Cos.

University of Missouri ($3,000) see Black & Veatch

University of Missouri ($48,140) see Bloch Foundation, Henry W. and Marion H.

University of Missouri ($10,000) see Garvey Memorial Foundation, Edward Chase

University of Missouri ($75,000) see General Dynamics Corp.

University of Missouri ($4,500) see Harris Foundation, H. H.

University of Missouri ($61,000) see JCPenney Co.

University of Missouri ($50,000) see Jordan and Ettie A. Jordan Charitable Foundation, Mary Ranken

University of Missouri ($5,800) see Messing Family Charitable Foundation

University of Missouri ($25,000) see Olin Corp.

University of Missouri ($16,000) see Pulitzer Publishing Co.

University of Missouri ($6,989,261) see Reynolds Foundation, Donald W.

University of Missouri ($7,500) see Roblee Foundation, Joseph H. and Florence A.

University of Missouri Arthritis Center ($25,000) see Orscheln Co.

University of Missouri Arthritis Center ($25,000) see Reynolds Foundation, J. B.

University of Missouri College of Business ($13,000) see Shelter Mutual Insurance Co.

University of Missouri at Columbia ($50,000) see Bromley Residuary Trust, Guy I.

University of Missouri at Columbia ($47,715) see Flarsheim Charitable Foundation, Louis and Elizabeth

University of Missouri at Columbia ($50,000) see Kemper Foundation, William T.

University of Missouri — Columbia ($200,000) see Southwestern Bell Corp.

University of Missouri-Columbia Minority Engineering Program ($150,000) see Union Electric Co.

University of Missouri, Columbia, MO ($7,000) see General American Life Insurance Co.

University of Missouri Columbia Veterinary School ($10,000) see Missouri Farmers Association

University of Missouri — CPI Youth Employment Program ($30,000) see CPI Corp.

University of Missouri Kansas City ($1,000) see Bartlett & Co.

University of Missouri, Kansas City ($133,200) see Block, H&R

University of Missouri at Kansas City ($50,000) see Kemper Foundation, William T.

University of Missouri at Kansas City ($50,000) see Sunderland Foundation, Lester T.

University of Missouri at Kansas City — to acquire computers and support equipment at Block Business School ($100,000) see Turner Charitable Trust, Courtney S.

University of Missouri, Kansas City Life Sciences ($50,000) see Francis Families Foundation

University of Missouri Nodaway County Extension ($2,250) see Messick Charitable Trust, Harry F.

University of Missouri-Rolla ($30,150) see ASARCO

University of Missouri-Rolla ($5,000) see USG Corp.

University of Missouri-St. Louis see Mallinckrodt Specialty Chemicals Co.

University of Missouri-St. Louis/Bridge Program ($125,000) see Monsanto Co.

University of Missouri School of Forestry — building fund ($15,000) see Shaw Foundation, Arch W.

University of Missouri School of Medicine ($25,000) see Green

Foundation, Allen P. and Josephine B.

University of Missouri — Thomas Jefferson Library ($166,666) see McDonnell Douglas Corp.

University of Missouri Veterinary School ($25,000) see Green Foundation, Allen P. and Josephine B.

Univesity of Missouri Andrew County Extension — to buy equipment for youth at-risk program ($1,945) see Messick Charitable Trust, Harry F.

Univesity of Missouri Holt County Extension ($2,250) see Messick Charitable Trust, Harry F.

Urban League of St. Louis see Reliable Life Insurance Co.

US Business School in Prague ($200,000) see Anheuser-Busch Cos.

V. P. Foundation — unrestricted gift ($25,000) see Enterprise Rent-A-Car Co.

Vernon County Ambulance District ($17,187) see Moss Charitable Trust, Finis M.

Very Special Arts of Missouri ($9,500) see Lichtenstein Foundation, David B.

Victorian Carthage ($50,000) see Steadley Memorial Trust, Kent D. and Mary L.

Washington University ($425,000) see Anheuser-Busch Cos.

Washington University ($200,000) see Boatmen's Bancshares

Washington University ($80,000) see Brown Group

Washington University ($50,000) see Edison Foundation, Harry

Washington University ($90,000) see Gaylord Foundation, Clifford Willard

Washington University ($100,000) see Interco

Washington University ($75,000) see Jordan and Ettie A. Jordan Charitable Foundation, Mary Ranken

Washington University ($1,000) see Kahn Memorial Trust

Washington University — operating expenses ($30,000) see Laclede Gas Co.

Washington University ($50,000) see Lopata Foundation, Stanley and Lucy

Washington University — sepsis research ($60,000) see Mallinckrodt, Jr. Foundation, Edward

Washington University ($20,000) see Marx Foundation, Virginia & Leonard

Washington University ($250,000) see May Department Stores Co.

Washington University ($500,000) see McDonnell Foundation, James S.

Washington University ($60,000) see Mercantile Bancorp

Washington University ($2,000) see Messing Family Charitable Foundation

Washington University ($30,000) see Pott Foundation, Herman T. and Phenie R.

Washington University ($30,000) see Pott Foundation, Herman T. and Phenie R.

Washington University ($500,000) see Ralston Purina Co.

Washington University ($56,000) see Sachs Fund

Washington University ($100,000) see Souers Charitable Trust, Sidney W. and Sylvia N.

Washington University ($100,000) see Souers Charitable Trust, Sidney W. and Sylvia N.

Washington University ($200,000) see Southwestern Bell Corp.

Washington University ($41,500) see Stupp Brothers Bridge & Iron Co.

Washington University ($93,333) see Stupp Foundation, Norman J.

Washington University ($110,000) see Union Electric Co.

Washington University ($150,000) see Whitaker Charitable Foundation, Lyndon C.

Washington University ($50,000) see Whitaker Charitable Foundation, Lyndon C.

Washington University Department of Dermatology, ($1,000) see Swift Co. Inc., John S.

Washington University, Endowed Scholarship Fund — promotion of education ($10,000) see Love Charitable Foundation, John Allan

Washington University — Founders Scholarship 1989 ($25,000) see CPI Corp.

Washington University, Graduate School of Business Administration — to establish the John M. Olin Graduate School of Business Administration ($3,398,460) see Olin Foundation, John M.

Washington University, John M. Olin School of Business ($30,000) see Olin Charitable Trust, John M.

Washington University — support for the new Natural Sciences Building ($500,000) see McDonnell Foundation, James S.

Washington University — Olin Fellowship ($160,000) see Monticello College Foundation

Washington University School of Business ($20,000) see Webb Foundation

Washington University School of Business and Administration ($5,250) see Kellwood Co.

Washington University School of Fine Arts ($5,520) see Kellwood Co.

Washington University School of Medicine ($75,000) see Macy, Jr. Foundation, Josiah

Washington University School of Medicine ($50,000) see Orchard Corp. of America.

Washington University School of Medicine — support for the Center for Cellular and Molecular Neurobiology ($1,000,000) see McDonnell Foundation, James S.

Washington University School of Medicine — Fellowship support and administrative costs ($234,152) see McDonnell Foundation, James S.

Washington University School of Social Work ($20,099) see Group Health Plan Inc.

Washington University — Spencer T. and Ann W. Olin Medical Scientist Fellowship Program ($1,500,000) see Olin

Foundation, Spencer T. and Ann W.

Washington University — Undergraduate Biological Sciences Education Program ($1,700,000) see Hughes Medical Institute, Howard

Washington Universtiy ($300,000) see General Dynamics Corp.

Webster Groves Day Care see Reliable Life Insurance Co.

Webster University ($12,000) see Brown Foundation, George Warren

Webster University ($12,500) see Garvey Memorial Foundation, Edward Chase

Webster University ($26,800) see Gaylord Foundation, Clifford Willard

Webster University ($10,000) see General American Life Insurance Co.

Webster University ($200,000) see Grant Charitable Trust, Elberth R. and Gladys F.

Webster University ($1,000,000) see Mabee Foundation, J. E. and L. E.

Webster University ($24,650) see Messing Family Charitable Foundation

Webster University see Reliable Life Insurance Co.

Westminster College — scholarships for women ($15,000) see Monticello College Foundation

Whitfield School ($4,000) see Columbia Terminals Co.

Whitfield School ($35,000) see Dula Educational and Charitable Foundation, Caleb C. and Julia W.

Whitfield School for Scholarships ($25,000) see Pott Foundation, Herman T. and Phenie R.

William Jewell College ($10,000) see Kelly Tractor Co.

William Jewell College ($340,859) see Pillsbury Foundation

William Jewell College ($30,690) see Share Foundation

William Jewell College — scientific teaching equipment ($50,000) see Speas Foundation, Victor E.

William Jewell College — continued support for the Oxbridge Center of Excellence ($1,000,000) see Hall Family Foundations

Womens Christian Association — Central Management ($30,000) see Loose Trust, Carrie J.

Women's Self Help Center ($2,000) see Orchard Corp. of America.

Woodhaven ($1,500) see Missouri Farmers Association

Woodhaven Learning Center ($1,500) see Shelter Mutual Insurance Co.

Wyandotte House ($20,000) see Kemper Charitable Trust, William T.

YMCA ($1,100) see ACF Industries, Inc.

YMCA ($13,584) see Bromley Residuary Trust, Guy I.

YMCA ($5,000) see Brown Foundation, George Warren

YMCA ($3,000) see Kellwood Co.

YMCA ($4,000) see Kuehn Foundation

YMCA ($28,000) see Stupp Foundation, Norman J.

YMCA of Greater St. Louis see Mallinckrodt Specialty Chemicals Co.

YMCA of Greater St. Louis ($7,000) see Pet

YMCA of the Ozarks ($50,000) see Sunnen Foundation

YMCA of the Ozarks ($75,000) see Union Electric Co.

Young Life ($25,000) see Herschend Family Foundation

Young Life ($10,000) see Herschend Family Foundation

Young Life ($20,000) see Slusher Charitable Foundation, Roy W.

Youth Symphony Association ($500) see Sealright Co., Inc.

Montana

Alberta Bair Theater ($5,000) see Lee Enterprises

Americas Hand in Hand — Honduras project, capital improvement ($42,500) see Gallagher Family Foundation, Lewis P.

Big Horn County Memorial Hospital ($30,807) see Knowles Charitable Memorial Trust, Gladys E.

Billings Area Catholic Education Trust ($15,000) see Fortin Foundation of Florida

Billings Council of the National Committee for Child Abuse — to reduce inappropriate, violent behaviors in children ($1,500) see First Interstate Bancsystem of Montana

Billings Masonic Center Association ($100,000) see Fortin Foundation of Florida

Billings Studio Theatre — underwrite performance ($12,000) see Buck Foundation, Carol Franc

Browning High School ($950) see Heisey Foundation

Butte Family YMCA ($15,000) see Montana Power Co.

Carroll College ($11,000) see Haynes Foundation

Carroll College ($25,000) see Jaharis Family Foundation

Carroll College ($20,000) see Montana Power Co.

College of Great Falls ($26,000) see Heisey Foundation

Columbus Hospital ($10,000) see Montana Power Co.

Craighead Wildlife-Wildlands Institute ($205,000) see Engelhard Foundation, Charles

Cut Bank High School ($600) see Heisey Foundation

Deaconess Medical Center ($400,000) see Bair Memorial Trust, Charles M.

Eastern Montana College ($11,000) see Haynes Foundation

Emerson Cultural Center ($45,000) see Taylor Foundation, Ruth and Vernon

First Church of Christ Scientist ($15,000) see Bair Memorial Trust, Charles M.

Foundation for Research on Economics and the Environment ($8,000) see Thirty-Five Twenty, Inc.

Friends of the Wild Swan ($60,000) see Banbury Fund

Great Falls School — Charles M. Russell High School ($3,750) see Heisey Foundation

Montana (cont.)

Great Falls School — Great Falls High School ($4,150) see Heisey Foundation

Greater Yellowstone Coalition ($50,000) see Claiborne Art Ortenberg Foundation, Liz

Greater Yellowstone Coalition ($30,000) see Jackson Hole Preserve

Greater Yellowstone Coalition ($25,000) see Ohrstrom Foundation

Greater Yellowstone Coalition ($6,000) see Special People In Need

Headwater Academy ($26,000) see Richardson Fund, Grace

Helena Film Society ($10,000) see Buck Foundation, Carol Franc

Helena Film Society see SAFECO Corp.

Heritage Acres Nursing Home ($30,807) see Knowles Charitable Memorial Trust, Gladys E.

Make-A-Wish Foundation of Montana — provide tip to Disneyland for 7-year old leukemia patient and family ($1,500) see First Interstate Bancsystem of Montana

Montana College of Mineral Science Technology ($11,700) see Heisey Foundation

Montana College of Mineral Sciences and Technology ($11,000) see Haynes Foundation

Montana 4-H Foundation ($50,000) see Taylor Foundation, Ruth and Vernon

Montana Historical Society ($16,667) see Montana Power Co.

Montana Land Reliance ($50,000) see Wenger Foundation, Henry L. and Consuelo S.

Montana State University ($11,000) see Haynes Foundation

Montana State University ($32,500) see Heisey Foundation

Montana State University Agriculture College ($13,000) see Harvest States Cooperative

Montana Tech Foundation ($40,800) see ASARCO

Montana Tech Foundation ($30,000) see Montana Power Co.

Montana Tech Foundation ($35,000) see Phelps Dodge Corp.

Montana Wilderness Association — organizing activities ($15,000) see Beldon Fund

Mountain View Hospital ($1,000) see Ward Foundation, Louis L. and Adelaide C.

Mountain View Memorial Hospital ($200,000) see Bair Memorial Trust, Charles M.

Museum of the Rockies ($15,000) see Montana Power Co.

Museum of the Rockies ($66,100) see Taylor Foundation, Ruth and Vernon

Northern Montana College ($11,000) see Haynes Foundation

Northern Montana College ($9,100) see Heisey Foundation

Northern Plains Resource Council ($10,000) see Beldon II Fund

Political Economy Research Center ($20,000) see Koch Charitable Foundation, Charles G.

Rocky Mountain College ($9,850) see Knowles Charitable Memorial Trust, Gladys E.

St. James Community Hospital ($25,000) see Montana Power Co.

St. Labre Indian School ($1,000) see Rasmussen Foundation

St. Lukes Episcopal Church ($30,807) see Knowles Charitable Memorial Trust, Gladys E.

St. Philips Episcopal Church ($7,500) see Borwell Charitable Foundation

United Way ($3,500) see MDU Resources Group, Inc.

United Way Billings ($11,793) see Montana Power Co.

United Way Missoula ($12,594) see Montana Power Co.

United Way - Silver Bow County ($39,030) see Montana Power Co.

University of Montana ($11,000) see Haynes Foundation

University of Montana ($32,500) see Heisey Foundation

Western Montana College ($5,200) see Heisey Foundation

Wheatland Memorial Hospital ($200,000) see Bair Memorial Trust, Charles M.

Wildlife Program ($30,212) see Davis Family - W.D. Charities, James E.

Yellowstone Boys Ranch ($9,866) see Knowles Charitable Memorial Trust, Gladys E.

Zoo Montana ($25,000) see Lee Enterprises

Nebraska

Agate Fossil Beds National Monument Visitors Center — construction of visitors center ($100,000) see Hitchcock Foundation, Gilbert M. and Martha H.

Ak-Sar-Ben Youth Foundation ($10,000) see Owen Industries, Inc.

Ak-Sar-Ben Youth Foundation ($3,340) see Scoular Co.

Aksarben Agricultural Youth Foundation see Norwest Bank Nebraska

Alternative Worksite ($5,000) see Millard Charitable Trust, Adah K.

American Diabetes Association ($3,000) see Giger Foundation, Paul and Oscar

American Red Cross see Norwest Bank Nebraska

Bellevue College — construction of humanities center ($25,000) see Hitchcock Foundation, Gilbert M. and Martha H.

Bellevue College ($25,000) see Kiewit Sons, Peter

Bellevue College see Norwest Bank Nebraska

Bellevue College ($15,000) see Owen Industries, Inc.

Bellevue College ($25,000) see Sunderland Foundation, Lester T.

Bellevue College Foundation ($25,000) see Scoular Co.

Benedictine Mission House ($10,000) see Goldbach Foundation, Ray and Marie

Bishop Clarkson Memorial Hospital ($100,000) see Criss Memorial Foundation, Dr. C.C. and Mabel L.

Boy Scouts of America ($49,180) see ConAgra

Boy Scouts of America ($2,000) see Giger Foundation, Paul and Oscar

Boy Scouts of America ($25,000) see Millard Charitable Trust, Adah K.

Boy Scouts of America see Norwest Bank Nebraska

Boy Scouts of America ($15,000) see Quivey-Bay State Foundation

Boy Scouts of America ($3,603) see Scoular Co.

Boy Scouts of America ($25,000) see Storz Foundation, Robert Herman

Boy Scouts of America ($10,000) see Valmont Industries

Boy Scouts of America, Mid America Council ($100,000) see Kiewit Sons, Peter

Boy Scouts of America — Mid America Council; constructing a new, winterized dining hall facility ($550,000) see Kiewit Foundation, Peter

Boys Club of America ($1,000) see Scoular Co.

Boys and Girls Club ($1,500) see Scott, Jr. Charitable Foundation, Walter

Boystown National Institute see Norwest Bank Nebraska

Bremer Community Center ($11,000) see Farr Trust, Frank M. and Alice M.

Bright Lights ($25,000) see Rogers Foundation

Brownell-Talbot School ($10,000) see Pamida, Inc.

Brownell-Talbot School ($6,500) see Scott, Jr. Charitable Foundation, Walter

Bryan Memorial Hospital — Excel 60 Program ($5,000) see Ameritas Life Insurance Corp.

Buford Foundation ($18,000) see Lightner Sams Foundation

Bureau of Jewish Education ($10,000) see Livingston Foundation, Milton S. and Corinne N.

Camp Fire Girls ($10,000) see Quivey-Bay State Foundation

Camp Fire Pioneer Council see Norwest Bank Nebraska

Canotrum Foundation ($1,000) see Giger Foundation, Paul and Oscar

Capital Area Humane Society ($10,000) see Rogers Foundation

Central Community College Foundation see Norwest Bank Nebraska

Central Nebraska Goodwill ($2,250) see Reynolds Foundation, Edgar

Chadron State Foundation ($10,000) see Quivey-Bay State Foundation

Chappell Senior Citizens ($12,000) see Buckley Trust, Thomas D.

Children's Memorial Hospital ($2,100) see Faith Charitable Trust

Children's Memorial Hospital Foundation ($150,000) see Criss Memorial Foundation, Dr. C.C. and Mabel L.

Christian Record Braille Foundation ($273) see Shelter Mutual Insurance Co.

Christian Urban Education Service ($2,000) see Faith Charitable Trust

Christian Urban Education Service ($10,000) see Lozier Foundation

Christian Urban Education Service ($15,000) see Millard Charitable Trust, Adah K.

City of Chappell — ambulance payment ($39,000) see Buckley Trust, Thomas D.

City of Chappell — ambulance chassis purchase ($17,550) see Buckley Trust, Thomas D.

City of Omaha Public Library Foundation — to purchase equipment and software ($228,442) see Kiewit Foundation, Peter

Clarkson Hospital Fashion Production ($2,700) see Storz Foundation, Robert Herman

College Park at Grand Island ($30,000) see ConAgra

College Park Grand Island Foundation ($166,700) see Reynolds Foundation, Edgar

College of St. Mary ($6,450) see Baer Foundation, Alan and Marcia

College of St. Mary ($50,000) see Criss Memorial Foundation, Dr. C.C. and Mabel L.

College of St. Mary ($30,000) see Kiewit Sons, Peter

College of Saint Mary see Norwest Bank Nebraska

College of St. Mary ($11,040) see Scoular Co.

College of St. Mary ($16,167) see Valmont Industries

College of St. Mary Foundation ($50,000) see ConAgra

Community College Foundation see Norwest Bank Nebraska

Community Concerts see Norwest Bank Nebraska

Countryside Community Church ($35,000) see Scott, Jr. Charitable Foundation, Walter

Creighton Preparatory School ($31,100) see Baer Foundation, Alan and Marcia

Creighton Preparatory School — construction of facilities ($150,000) see Criss Memorial Foundation, Dr. C.C. and Mabel L.

Creighton Preparatory School ($5,000) see Hamilton Foundation, Florence P.

Creighton University — endowment fund ($1,350,000) see Criss Memorial Foundation, Dr. C.C. and Mabel L.

Creighton University — gymnasium addition ($320,000) see Criss Memorial Foundation, Dr. C.C. and Mabel L.

Creighton University — athletic department ($60,000) see Criss Memorial Foundation, Dr. C.C. and Mabel L.

Creighton University ($25,000) see Lozier Foundation

Creighton University ($10,000) see Pamida, Inc.

Creighton University ($25,000) see Valmont Industries

Creighton University Foundation ($150,175) see ConAgra

Creighton University — construction of Hitchcock writing and design laboratory ($50,000) see Hitchcock Foundation, Gilbert M. and Martha H.

Creighton University Jesuit Community ($15,000) see Baer Foundation, Alan and Marcia

Creighton University School of Law ($3,250) see Lane Foundation, Winthrop and Frances

Dana College — construction of journalism facility ($20,000) see Hitchcock Foundation, Gilbert M. and Martha H.

Dana College ($40,000) see Kiewit Sons, Peter

Dana College — for health science scholarships ($5,000) see Lincoln Health Care Foundation

Dana College Add Campaign ($10,000) see Valmont Industries

Doane College ($15,000) see Cooper Foundation

Dodar County 4-H Society ($2,500) see Keene Trust, Hazel R.

Dodar County Historical Society ($3,500) see Keene Trust, Hazel R.

Domestic Abuse Crisis Center ($5,000) see Keene Trust, Hazel R.

Douglas County, Nebraska — to acquire land and prepare it for use as a park facility in the Riverfront Development District ($500,000) see Kiewit Foundation, Peter

Duel County Treasurer — construct new exhibit building ($42,000) see Buckley Trust, Thomas D.

Eastern Nebraska Office on Aging ($70,000) see ConAgra

Edmonson Youth Development ($500) see Scoular Co.

Emmy Gifford Theater ($1,000) see Giger Foundation, Paul and Oscar

Eugene T. Mahoney State Park ($10,000) see Valmont Industries

Father Flanagan's Boys Home — general operating support ($500,916) see MCJ Foundation

Father Flanagan's Boys Home ($25,000) see Ritter Foundation, May Ellen and Gerald

Federated Churches ($5,132) see Quivey-Bay State Foundation

Fellowship of Christian Athletes ($660) see Scoular Co.

First Plymouth Church ($12,000) see Abel Construction Co.

Fontenelle Forect ($500) see Scoular Co.

Fontenelle Forest ($2,500) see Storz Foundation, Robert Herman

Food Bank — to change the food bank's warehousing ability to take advantage of more donated frozen food ($20,000) see Hitchcock Foundation, Gilbert M. and Martha H.

Foundation of the Jewish Federation — scholarship fund ($10,000) see Livingston Foundation, Milton S. and Corinne N.

Foundation of the Jewish Federation ($8,750) see Livingston Foundation, Milton S. and Corinne N.

Fremont Area Community Foundation ($10,000) see Keene Trust, Hazel R.

Friends of Scouting ($1,000) see Faith Charitable Trust

Girl Scouts of America ($16,670) see Lozier Foundation

Girls Incorporated ($45,000) see Lozier Foundation

Hastings College ($7,500) see Stone Foundation

Hastings College Foundation ($125,000) see Kiewit Sons, Peter

Hastings College Foundation ($12,500) see Owen Industries, Inc.

Health Fair ($5,000) see Giger Foundation, Paul and Oscar

Henry Doorly Zoo ($45,000) see Enron Corp.

Heritage-Joslyn Foundation ($200,000) see Kiewit Sons, Peter

Heritage Joslyn Foundation ($200,000) see Lozier Foundation

Heritage-Joslyn Foundation — to partially fund the cost of collection acquisition at Joslyn Art Museum and improvements to the physical plant at the Western Heritage Museum ($2,000,000) see Kiewit Foundation, Peter

Highland Hills Baptist ($4,500) see Oldham Little Church Foundation

Jewish Federation ($4,950) see Baer Foundation, Alan and Marcia

Jewish Federation ($10,000) see Livingston Foundation, Milton S. and Corinne N.

Jewish Federation of Omaha ($100,000) see Livingston Foundation, Milton S. and Corinne N.

Jewish Federation of Omaha — ADL CRC Committee ($5,000) see Livingston Foundation, Milton S. and Corinne N.

Joslyn Art Museum ($31,000) see Baer Foundation, Alan and Marcia

Joslyn Art Museum ($15,000) see Millard Charitable Trust, Adah K.

Joslyn Art Museum ($500) see Scoular Co.

Joslyn Liberal Arts Society ($35,950) see Enron Corp.

Joslyn Liberal Arts Society ($35,950) see Enron Corp.

Joslyn Liberal Arts Society ($15,000) see Scott, Jr. Charitable Foundation, Walter

Julesburg School District Re-1 — computer networking system ($10,000) see Buckley Trust, Thomas D.

League of Human Dignity ($10,000) see Lincoln Family Foundation

Lewellen Wesleyan Church ($15,000) see Buckley Trust, Thomas D.

Lighthouse ($10,000) see Cooper Foundation

Lincoln Action Program ($10,000) see Cooper Foundation

Lincoln Action Program ($1,300) see Lincoln Family Foundation

Lincoln/Lancaster County Senior Center Foundation ($16,000) see Cooper Foundation

Lincoln Midget Football League ($16,000) see Cooper Foundation

Lincoln Symphony Orchestra Association ($20,000) see Rogers Foundation

Lincoln YWCA ($62,862) see Cooper Foundation

Low Income Ministry ($15,000) see Keene Trust, Hazel R.

Madonna Centers ($10,000) see Abel Construction Co.

Madonna Centers ($5,000) see Ameritas Life Insurance Corp.

Madonna Foundation ($2,000) see Lincoln Family Foundation

Madonna Foundation ($30,000) see Rogers Foundation

Make-A-Wish Foundation ($5,000) see Baer Foundation, Alan and Marcia

Memorial Foundation ($18,000) see Farr Trust, Frank M. and Alice M.

Memorial Hospital of Dodar County ($10,000) see Keene Trust, Hazel R.

Memorial Hospital and Home ($25,000) see Buckley Trust, Thomas D.

Midland Lutheran College ($65,000) see Keene Trust, Hazel R.

Midland Lutheran College ($11,666) see Valmont Industries

Miller Memorial Nursing Home — for a generator ($25,000) see Buckley Trust, Thomas D.

Musical Concert Series ($3,000) see Giger Foundation, Paul and Oscar

National Contact Lenses Examiners ($2,500) see Lane Foundation, Winthrop and Frances

Nebraska Academy of Sciences ($2,500) see Lincoln Family Foundation

Nebraska Community College Scholarship Fund ($10,000) see Quivey-Bay State Foundation

Nebraska Game and Parks ($26,740) see Giger Foundation, Paul and Oscar

Nebraska Game and Parks Foundation — fund construction of lodge facility at Eugene Mahoney State Park ($391,127) see Kiewit Foundation, Peter

Nebraska Games and Parks ($37,500) see ConAgra

Nebraska General Hospital ($10,000) see Quivey-Bay State Foundation

Nebraska Independent College Foundation ($10,000) see Quivey-Bay State Foundation

Nebraska Jewish Historical Society ($2,000) see Livingston Foundation, Milton S. and Corinne N.

Nebraska State Bar Foundation ($3,000) see Lane Foundation, Winthrop and Frances

Nebraska Wesleyan Presbyterian Society ($1,000) see Faith Charitable Trust

Nebraska Wesleyan University ($23,000) see Abel Construction Co.

Nebraska Wesleyan University ($25,000) see Ameritas Life Insurance Corp.

Nebraska Wesleyan University ($20,000) see Lincoln Family Foundation

Nebraska Wesleyan University — science education program ($10,000) see Sandoz Corp.

Nebraska Youth Leadership Center ($50,000) see Farr Trust, Frank M. and Alice M.

Omaha Ballet ($2,000) see Scott, Jr. Charitable Foundation, Walter

Omaha Ballet Society ($5,000) see Baer Foundation, Alan and Marcia

Omaha Children's Museum ($250,000) see Kiewit Sons, Peter

Omaha Children's Museum ($25,000) see Lozier Foundation

Omaha Children's Museum ($5,000) see Owen Industries, Inc.

Omaha Community Playhouse ($50,000) see Hitchcock Foundation, Gilbert M. and Martha H.

Omaha Community Playhouse ($160,736) see Storz Foundation, Robert Herman

Omaha Community Playhouse ($15,000) see Younkers, Inc.

Omaha Community Playhouse Foundation ($5,000) see Owen Industries, Inc.

Omaha Home for Boys ($5,500) see Kingsley Foundation

Omaha Symphony Association — support the chamber orchestra ($25,000) see Hitchcock Foundation, Gilbert M. and Martha H.

Omaha Symphony Association ($6,000) see Scott, Jr. Charitable Foundation, Walter

Omaha Zoological Foundation ($104,000) see Scott, Jr. Charitable Foundation, Walter

Omaha Zoological Society — construction ($229,932) see Lied Foundation Trust

Opera Omaha ($7,500) see Giger Foundation, Paul and Oscar

OPS Special Olympics ($2,000) see Pamida, Inc.

Pembroke Hill School ($5,000) see Owen Industries, Inc.

Planned Parenthood ($10,000) see Millard Charitable Trust, Adah K.

Planned Parenthood Federation of America ($21,000) see Lozier Foundation

Presbyterian Bicentennial Fund ($24,000) see Faith Charitable Trust

Presbyterian Ministries ($3,500) see Giger Foundation, Paul and Oscar

Progress ($3,000) see Storz Foundation, Robert Herman

Quality Living ($6,140) see Faith Charitable Trust

Quality Living ($25,000) see Kiewit Sons, Peter

Radio Talking Book Services — replacement of studio recorders ($15,000) see Hitchcock Foundation, Gilbert M. and Martha H.

Regional West Medical Center ($25,000) see Buckley Trust, Thomas D.

Ridar Cemetery Association ($5,000) see Keene Trust, Hazel R.

River City Roundup ($1,000) see Physicians Mutual Insurance

Riverside Zoological Society ($3,000) see Quivey-Bay State Foundation

Roncalli High School ($5,200) see Baer Foundation, Alan and Marcia

Roncalli High School ($1,000) see Physicians Mutual Insurance

Rural Fire District No. 2 Big Springs — fire truck purchase ($25,000) see Buckley Trust, Thomas D.

Sacred Heart School ($15,131) see Lozier Foundation

Salvation Army ($250,000) see Lozier Foundation

Salvation Army ($900) see Physicians Mutual Insurance

Senior Health Foundation ($35,125) see Lozier Foundation

Shakespeare on the Green ($750) see Physicians Mutual Insurance

Siena Francis House ($1,000) see Physicians Mutual Insurance

Sniffles ($10,000) see Rogers Foundation

Tabitha Foundation ($8,333) see Ameritas Life Insurance Corp.

Tabitha Home ($25,000) see Lincoln Family Foundation

Temple Israel ($6,400) see Baer Foundation, Alan and Marcia

Temple Israel ($75,989) see Livingston Foundation, Milton S. and Corinne N.

Trinity Cathedral ($10,531) see Storz Foundation, Robert Herman

Union College ($14,000) see Cooper Foundation

United Arts Omaha ($100,000) see ConAgra

United Arts of Omaha ($36,667) see Criss Memorial Foundation, Dr. C.C. and Mabel L.

United Arts Omaha ($100,000) see Kiewit Sons, Peter

United Arts of Omaha ($50,000) see Norwest Corp.

United Arts of Omaha ($12,000) see Owen Industries, Inc.

United Arts of Omaha ($24,000) see Valmont Industries

United Arts Omaha — final installment of a grant of $345,000, payable in three installments in 1989-91, inclusive, to provide continued support to this organization and the 30+ Omaha area arts group it supports ($115,000) see Union Pacific Corp.

United Arts Omaha — support of United Arts Omaha-1990 ($600,000) see Kiewit Foundation, Peter

United Catholic Social Services ($5,000) see Physicians Mutual Insurance

United Cerebral Palsy Association ($2,500) see Physicians Mutual Insurance

United Methodist Community Center ($31,000) see ConAgra

United Ministries of Northeast Nebraska ($9,400) see Millard Charitable Trust, Adah K.

United Way ($12,548) see Abel Construction Co.

United Way ($12,547) see Abel Construction Co.

United Way ($27,025) see Ameritas Life Insurance Corp.

United Way ($122,411) see Buffett Foundation

United Way ($14,750) see Cooper Foundation

United Way — general operations ($27,000) see Monfort Charitable Foundation

United Way ($5,000) see Monroe Auto Equipment Co.

United Way ($2,000) see National By-Products

United Way ($31,400) see Physicians Mutual Insurance

United Way ($625) see Physicians Mutual Insurance

United Way ($3,500) see Quivey-Bay State Foundation

United Way see Rochester Midland Corp.

United Way ($10,000) see Scott, Jr. Charitable Foundation, Walter

United Way ($22,000) see Storz Foundation, Robert Herman

United Way ($55,000) see Valmont Industries

United Way ($10,000) see Younkers, Inc.

United Way of the Midlands ($98,875) see ConAgra

United Way of the Midlands ($19,435) see TRINOVA Corp.

United Way of the Midlands ($225,000) see Union Pacific Corp.

United Way of the Midlands — for annual support ($280,390) see US WEST

United Way of the Midlands — Youth at Risk Program ($579,332) see Kiewit Foundation, Peter

University of Nebraska ($1,000) see Storz Foundation, Robert Herman

University of Nebraska College of Nursing ($90,000) see Teagle Foundation

University of Nebraska Foundation ($15,500) see Abel Construction Co.

University of Nebraska Foundation ($12,500) see Abel Construction Co.

University of Nebraska Foundation — building fund ($5,000) see Abel Construction Co.

University of Nebraska Foundation ($25,000) see Ameritas Life Insurance Corp.

University of Nebraska Foundation — building fund ($20,000) see Ameritas Life Insurance Corp.

University of Nebraska Foundation — building fund ($12,500) see Ameritas Life Insurance Corp.

University of Nebraska Foundation ($10,000) see Ameritas Life Insurance Corp.

University of Nebraska Foundation ($4,050) see Baer Foundation, Alan and Marcia

University of Nebraska Foundation ($114,050) see Cooper Foundation

University of Nebraska Foundation ($27,200) see Cooper Foundation

University of Nebraska Foundation ($100,000) see Criss Memorial Foundation, Dr. C.C. and Mabel L.

University of Nebraska Foundation — research initiative ($100,000) see Criss Memorial Foundation, Dr. C.C. and Mabel L.

University of Nebraska Foundation ($25,000) see Lincoln Family Foundation

University of Nebraska Foundation ($50,000) see McGraw-Hill

University of Nebraska Foundation ($2,000) see Reynolds Foundation, Edgar

University of Nebraska Foundation ($2,000) see Scott, Jr. Charitable Foundation, Walter

University of Nebraska Foundation — sixth payment of ten-year $1,000,000 grant for land acquisition, building construction costs and landscaping costs for Lied

Nebraska (cont.)

Performing Arts Center ($100,000) see Woods Charitable Fund
University of Nebraska — performance fund for Lied Center ($453,914) see Lied Foundation Trust
University of Nebraska at Lincoln ($6,100) see Grant Thornton
University of Nebraska at Lincoln College of Law ($5,000) see Lane Foundation, Winthrop and Frances
University of Nebraska Lincoln Foothold Facilities Fund ($10,000) see Valmont Industries
University of Nebraska at Omaha — Maverick Club — athletic fund ($2,000) see Pamida, Inc.
University of Nebraska Press ($35,000) see Rogers Foundation
Volunteers Intervening for Equity ($1,500) see Millard Charitable Trust, Adah K.
Western Heritage Museum ($50,000) see Hitchcock Foundation, Gilbert M. and Martha H.
Westhills Presbyterian Church ($19,000) see Faith Charitable Trust
Winthrop and Frances Lane Foundation ($3,250) see Lane Foundation, Winthrop and Frances
World Herald Good Fellows ($1,000) see Giger Foundation, Paul and Oscar
YMCA ($7,500) see Abel Construction Co.
YMCA ($25,000) see Hitchcock Foundation, Gilbert M. and Martha H.
YMCA ($5,000) see Keene Trust, Hazel R.
YMCA ($10,000) see Lincoln Family Foundation
YMCA ($10,000) see Lincoln Family Foundation
YMCA ($5,000) see Owen Industries, Inc.
YMCA ($900) see Physicians Mutual Insurance
YMCA ($15,000) see Quivey-Bay State Foundation
YMCA ($10,000) see Rogers Foundation
YWCA ($10,000) see Rogers Foundation
Zoofair ($6,000) see Owen Industries, Inc.
Zoofair VIII ($10,500) see Valmont Industries

Nevada

Adopt-A-Family ($5,000) see Southwest Gas Corp.
American Animal Assistance ($28,000) see Hawkins Foundation, Robert Z.
Boys and Girls Club ($205,618) see Lied Foundation Trust
Boys and Girls Club ($200,000) see Lied Foundation Trust
Boys Town USA ($20,000) see Reynolds Foundation, Donald W.
Brewery Arts Center ($5,000) see Southwest Gas Corp.
Children's Cabinet — bedroom equipment for shelter ($31,397) see Redfield Foundation, Nell J.
Children's Inn of Greater Las Vegas (Ronald McDonald House) — funds for capital building program ($100,000) see Webb Foundation, Del E.
Citizens Alert ($3,500) see Carteh Foundation
Community Food Bank ($6,000) see Southwest Gas Corp.
Diocese of Reno-Las Vegas ($10,000) see O'Toole Foundation, Theresa and Edward
Eagle Valley Children's Home — respite care program ($30,000) see Thompson Charitable Foundation, Marion G.
Eagle Valley Children's Home — general ($25,000) see Thompson Charitable Foundation, Marion G.
Food Bank of Northern Nevada ($10,000) see Redfield Foundation, Nell J.
Friends of Washoe County Library — purchase new books, equipment ($38,700) see Cord Foundation, E. L.
Iona College ($402,412) see Connelly Foundation
KUNR FM ($30,000) see Hawkins Foundation, Robert Z.
Lake Tahoe Public Television ($9,000) see Buck Foundation, Carol Franc
Las Vegas Symphony Orchestra ($6,500) see Southwest Gas Corp.
Lied Institute for Real Estate Studies, University of Nevada, Las Vegas — endowment ($592,691) see Lied Foundation Trust
Lied Institute for Real Estate Studies, University of Nevada, Las Vegas — established program ($500,000) see Lied Foundation Trust
Meadows School ($30,000) see Reynolds Foundation, Donald W.
Meadows School ($1,500,000) see SDB Foundation
Meadows School ($100,000) see SDB Foundation
Meadows School ($45,000) see SDB Foundation
Music at St. John's ($10,000) see Mostyn Foundation
National Council of Juvenile and Family Court Judges — construction of new educational building ($150,000) see Cord Foundation, E. L.
National Council of Juvenile and Family Court Judges ($356,183) see Hilton Foundation, Conrad N.
National Judicial College ($5,000) see Porsche Cars North America, Inc.
National Judicial College — library equipment ($100,000) see Wiegand Foundation, E. L.
Nevada Museum of Art — general support ($75,000) see Wiegand Foundation, E. L.
Nevada Opera — underwrite opera ($35,000) see Buck Foundation, Carol Franc
Nevada Opera Association ($500) see Porsche Cars North America, Inc.
Northern Nevada Center for Independent Living — therapy ($25,000) see Redfield Foundation, Nell J.
Northern Nevada Community College see Alltel/Western Region
Northern Nevada Community College ($50,000) see Snow Memorial Trust, John Ben
Northern Nevada Community College — help fund completion of phase II building ($50,000) see Cord Foundation, E. L.
Opportunity Village ($250,000) see Lincy Foundation
Our Lady of Snows School — tuition assistance program ($44,000) see Thompson Charitable Foundation, Marion G.
Our Lady of Snows School — heating and air conditioning system ($23,000) see Thompson Charitable Foundation, Marion G.
Our Lady of Snows School ($20,000) see Thompson Charitable Foundation, Marion G.
Our Lady of Snows School — general ($18,000) see Thompson Charitable Foundation, Marion G.
Rebel Golf Foundation — golf foundation scholarship fund ($293,562) see Lied Foundation Trust
Reno Chamber Orchestra ($5,000) see Buck Foundation, Carol Franc
Reno Philharmonic ($15,000) see Buck Foundation, Carol Franc
Reno Philharmonic ($10,000) see Porsche Cars North America, Inc.
Reno/Tahoe Organizing Committee ($2,500) see Porsche Cars North America, Inc.
Roman Catholic Diocese of Reno-Las Vegas — chapel furnishings ($102,000) see Wiegand Foundation, E. L.
St. Judes Ranch ($9,600) see SDB Foundation
St. Mary's Hospital ($24,393) see Hawkins Foundation, Robert Z.
St. Marys Regional Medical Center — cardiac monitors ($25,000) see Redfield Foundation, Nell J.
St. Rose Dominican Hospital — operating room equipment ($100,000) see Wiegand Foundation, E. L.
St. Vincents Emergency Services — food ($10,000) see Redfield Foundation, Nell J.
Salvation Army ($6,350) see Southwest Gas Corp.
Shepherd House ($10,000) see Seid Foundation, Barre
Sierra Arts Foundation ($1,000) see Porsche Cars North America, Inc.
Sierra Nevada College — fine arts gallery endowment ($5,000) see Harris Foundation, William H. and Mattie Wattis
Sierra Nevada College ($17,500) see Hawkins Foundation, Robert Z.
Sierra Nevada Red Cross ($82,563) see Saturno Foundation
Special Recreation Services — camp program ($13,000) see Redfield Foundation, Nell J.
Trinity Episcopal Church ($61,284) see Hawkins Foundation, Robert Z.
Truckee Meadows Boys and Girls Club — fund building renovation project ($100,000) see Cord Foundation, E. L.
Truckee Meadows Boys and Girls Club ($75,486) see Hawkins Foundation, Robert Z.
Truckee Meadows Community College — technical building fund ($25,000) see Thompson Charitable Foundation, Marion G.
United Way ($3,000) see Quanex Corp.
United Way ($60,408) see Southwest Gas Corp.
University Medical Center of Southern Nevada Foundation ($1,000,000) see Lincy Foundation
University of Nevada — construct experimental theater ($50,000) see Redfield Foundation, Nell J.
University of Nevada Department of Speech Pathology — equipment ($23,350) see Redfield Foundation, Nell J.
University of Nevada Foundation ($1,300) see Porsche Cars North America, Inc.
University of Nevada Las Vegas ($25,000) see EG&G Inc.
University of Nevada at Las Vegas ($1,500,000) see Newmont Mining Corp.
University of Nevada Las Vegas Foundation ($29,225) see Southwest Gas Corp.
University of Nevada Press ($500) see Porsche Cars North America, Inc.
University of Nevada Reno — scholarship fund ($25,000) see Thompson Charitable Foundation, Marion G.
University of Nevada-Reno Foundation ($11,000) see AMAX
University of Nevada Reno School of Engineering ($20,000) see Hawkins Foundation, Robert Z.
University of Nevada Students Aid Fund — Mackey stadium expansion ($200,000) see Lied Foundation Trust
UNR Foundation-College of Agriculture — experimental sheep project equipment ($350,000) see Wiegand Foundation, E. L.
Vitality Center ($20,000) see Hawkins Foundation, Robert Z.
Vitality Center ($20,000) see Hawkins Foundation, Robert Z.
Washoe County Parks and Recreation ($500,000) see May Foundation, Wilbur
Washoe Medical Foundation ($20,000) see Porsche Cars North America, Inc.
YMCA ($30,000) see Hawkins Foundation, Robert Z.
YWCA ($19,600) see Redfield Foundation, Nell J.

New Hampshire

A Safe Place ($2,500) see Hamel Family Charitable Trust, D. A.
A Safe Place ($4,630) see Quaker Hill Foundation
Adult Learning Center ($25,000) see Nashua Trust Co.
Advance Fund for the 90s ($1,500) see Monadnock Paper Mills
Alice Peck Day Memorial Hospital ($5,000) see Pettus, Jr. Foundation, James T.
American Cancer Society ($16,650) see Bartsch Memorial Trust, Ruth
American Diabetes Association ($25,000) see Paramount Communications Inc.
American Red Cross — leasing financial assistance ($17,280) see Foundation for Seacoast Health
American Red Cross ($5,000) see Nashua Trust Co.
American Red Cross ($10,000) see Putnam Foundation
Andy's Summer Playhouse see Millipore Corp.
Antioch New England Graduate School ($33,000) see Waldorf Educational Foundation
Apple Hill Center for Chamber Music ($100) see First NH Banks, Inc.
Audubon Society of New Hampshire ($3,000) see Wharton Trust, William P.
Berwick Academy — pledge payment ($60,000) see Avis Inc.
Boy Scouts of America ($20,000) see Hunt Foundation, Samuel P.
Boys and Girls Club ($7,000) see Nashua Trust Co.
Boys and Girls Club ($3,000) see Nashua Trust Co.
Boys and Girls Club ($10,000) see Rogers Family Foundation
Boys and Girls Club ($23,500) see Smith Charitable Foundation, Lou and Lutza
Burr and Burton Annual Fund ($1,000) see Wallace Computer Services
Canaan Fire Department — equipping a van with rescue equipment ($1,500) see Mascoma Savings Bank
Caregivers ($4,000) see Swift Memorial Health Care Foundation
Catholic Charities ($5,000) see Nashua Trust Co.
Catholic Medical Center — to support endowment of the Health Baby Fund ($25,000) see Bean Foundation, Norwin S. and Elizabeth N.
Cedarcrest Construction Campaign ($8,000) see Kingsbury Corp.
Cedarcrest Construction Campaign ($10,000) see Putnam Foundation
Central New Hampshire Community Mental Health ($500) see First NH Banks, Inc.
Channel 11 ($10,000) see Cogswell Benevolent Trust
Channel 11 ($100) see Page Belting Co.
Channel 11 ($15,000) see Putnam Foundation
Child and Family Services ($5,000) see Jameson Trust, Oleonda
Child and Family Services of New Hampshire ($14,000) see Hunt Foundation, Samuel P.
Child and Family Services of New Hampshire see New England Telephone Co.
Child Health Services — to support the purchase and renovation of the clinic site ($25,000) see Bean Foundation, Norwin S. and Elizabeth N.
Child Health Services ($2,859) see Greenspan Foundation

Christa McAuliffe Sabbatical Fund ($10,000) see Flatley Foundation

Citizens Scholarship Foundation of America ($25,000) see Hechinger Co.

Citizens Scholarship Foundation of America ($25,000) see Hechinger Co.

Colby-Sawyer College ($35,000) see Lindsay Trust, Agnes M.

Colby-Sawyer College — Olivetti Series ($10,000) see Olivetti Office USA, Inc.

Community Caregivers ($45,000) see Eastman Foundation, Alexander

Community Council ($6,114) see Barker Foundation

Community Council/Senior Citizens ($24,570) see Foundation for Seacoast Health

Community Hospice ($12,000) see Nashua Trust Co.

Concord Area Boys and Girls Club ($5,000) see First NH Banks, Inc.

Concord Area Trust for Community Housing ($50) see First NH Banks, Inc.

Concord Area Trust for Community Housing ($5,000) see Jameson Trust, Oleonda

Connecticut River Watch Program — laboratory equipment and supplies involving collecting and analyzing water samples by students, teachers and volunteers ($1,000) see Mascoma Savings Bank

Court Appointed Special Advocates of New Hampshire — general operating support in 1991 ($20,000) see Bean Foundation, Norwin S. and Elizabeth N.

Crotched Mountain Community Care — Alzheimer project ($25,000) see Smith Charitable Foundation, Lou and Lutza

Crotched Mountain Foundation ($5,775) see Monadnock Paper Mills

Daniel Webster Council — explorers music post #934 ($11,100) see Smyth Trust, Marion C.

Dartmouth College ($6,000) see Allendale Mutual Insurance Co.

Dartmouth College ($26,755) see Alperin/Hirsch Family Foundation

Dartmouth College ($3,250) see ASARCO

Dartmouth College ($1,500,000) see Borwell Charitable Foundation

Dartmouth College — introduction of modern computational methods into the chemistry major curriculum ($20,000) see Dreyfus Foundation, Camille and Henry

Dartmouth College ($11,400) see Eastern Enterprises

Dartmouth College — construction of chemistry building ($1,750,000) see Fairchild Foundation, Sherman

Dartmouth College ($50,200) see Farallon Foundation

Dartmouth College ($10,000) see Fife Foundation, Elias and Bertha

Dartmouth College ($20,000) see Frese Foundation, Arnold D.

Dartmouth College ($14,675) see Goldman Sachs & Co.

Dartmouth College ($50,000) see Gruss Petroleum Corp.

Dartmouth College ($7,400) see Harper Foundation, Philip S.

Dartmouth College ($15,000) see Janssen Foundation, Henry

Dartmouth College — for a cooperative and educational research program ($1,500,000) see Kiewit Foundation, Peter

Dartmouth College ($10,000) see Leo Burnett Co.

Dartmouth College ($10,000) see Lilly Foundation, Richard Coyle

Dartmouth College ($14,100) see Mellam Family Foundation

Dartmouth College ($50,000) see Pillsbury Co.

Dartmouth College ($10,000) see Randa

Dartmouth College see Raytheon Co.

Dartmouth College ($25,000) see Vale Foundation, Ruby R.

Dartmouth College ($5,000) see Zenkel Foundation

Dartmouth College Alumni Fund ($10,000) see Borwell Charitable Foundation

Dartmouth College — Full Circle Program; comprehensive plan for Native American student retention ($155,000) see General Mills

Dartmouth College Fund ($5,000) see Amsterdam Foundation, Jack and Mimi Leviton

Dartmouth-Hitchcock Medical Center ($10,000) see Ford III Memorial Foundation, Jefferson Lee

Dartmouth-Hitchcock Medical Center ($1,000) see Greenspan Foundation

Dartmouth-Hitchcock Medical Center ($8,000) see Kingsbury Corp.

Dartmouth-Hitchcock Medical Center ($5,000) see Knox Family Foundation

Dartmouth-Hitchcock Medical Center ($10,000) see Putnam Foundation

Dartmouth-Hitchcock Medical Center — to establish the C. V. Starr Center for Magnetic Resonance Imaging ($500,000) see Starr Foundation

Dartmouth Medical School — support of construction of new medical center ($100,000) see DeCamp Foundation, Ira W.

Dartmouth Medical School ($250,000) see Delany Charitable Trust, Beatrice P.

Dartmouth Medical School — general ($250,000) see Delany Charitable Trust, Beatrice P.

Dartmouth Medical School — general ($250,000) see Delany Charitable Trust, Beatrice P.

Dartmouth Medical School ($731,046) see Hartford Foundation, John A.

Dartmouth Medical School ($31,300) see Zimmermann Fund, Marie and John

Dartmouth Medical School Charitable — general ($250,000) see Delany Charitable Trust, Beatrice P.

Dartmouth Medical School — support for medical research project "Receptor-Mediated Induction and Suppression of Collagenase Synthesis" ($30,626) see RGK Foundation

Dartmouth Parents Fund ($15,000) see Ryan

Foundation, Patrick G. and Shirley W.

Derry Visiting Nurses ($19,274) see Eastman Foundation, Alexander

Derryfield School — music department ($13,000) see Smyth Trust, Marion C.

Easter Seal Foundation of New Hampshire and Vermont ($50,000) see Cogswell Benevolent Trust

Easter Seal Society ($15,000) see Bean Foundation, Norwin S. and Elizabeth N.

Easter Seal Society ($40,000) see Hunt Foundation, Samuel P.

Easter Seal Society ($20,000) see Smith Charitable Foundation, Lou and Lutza

Easter Seals ($7,711) see Eastman Foundation, Alexander

Ellyct Hospital ($15,000) see Hunt Foundation, Samuel P.

Exeter Hospital — general operating support ($100,000) see Avis Inc.

Foundation for Inspiration and Recognition of Science and Technology — to inspire children to study science and to recognize heroes of science and industry ($50,000) see NYNEX Corp.

4-H Foundation of New Hampshire ($250) see First NH Banks, Inc.

Friends of Manchester Trees ($4,200) see Winthrop Trust, Clara B.

Friends Program ($10,000) see Cogswell Benevolent Trust

Friends Program ($13,000) see Smith Charitable Foundation, Lou and Lutza

Gibson Center for Senior Services ($7,500) see Mostyn Foundation

Grand Monadnock Arts Council ($5,000) see Kingsbury Corp.

Granite State Public Library ($25,000) see Hunt Foundation, Samuel P.

Greater Derry Prenatal Services ($43,750) see Eastman Foundation, Alexander

Hampstead Conservation Commission ($5,000) see French Foundation

Harris Center for Conservation Education ($975) see Monadnock Paper Mills

Havenwood/Heritage Heights — aquatic therapy program ($10,000) see Cogswell Benevolent Trust

Holderness School — general endowment ($20,000) see Olivetti Office USA, Inc.

Holderness School ($9,500) see Webber Oil Co.

Hollis Elementary School — computers, software, training ($10,000) see Barnes Foundation

Hood Museum of Art ($15,000) see Cramer Foundation

Jewish Center Torah Society ($2,400) see Greenspan Foundation

Jewish Federation ($15,000) see Greenspan Foundation

Keene Public Library ($10,000) see Putnam Foundation

Keene State College — scholarships ($51,000) see Ayling Scholarship Foundation, Alice S.

Keene State College — scholarships ($6,000) see Smyth Trust, Marion C.

Keene State College ($47,000) see Travelli Fund, Charles Irwin

Keene Teen Center ($5,000) see Kingsbury Corp.

Lebanon College — endowment fund for community college ($5,000) see Mascoma Savings Bank

Lebanon College — endowment campaign ($10,000) see Phillips Foundation, Ellis L.

Liberty Township Trustees ($5,000) see Massie Trust, David Meade

Lions Camp Pride ($4,292) see Barker Foundation

Londonderry Fire Department ($21,200) see Eastman Foundation, Alexander

MacDowell Colony ($20,000) see Coleman, Jr. Foundation, George E.

MacDowell Colony ($100) see HarperCollins Publishers

MacDowell Colony ($30,000) see Heyward Memorial Fund, DuBose and Dorothy

MacDowell Colony ($25,000) see Heyward Memorial Fund, DuBose and Dorothy

MacDowell Colony ($5,000) see Monadnock Paper Mills

MacDowell Colony ($50,000) see Putnam Foundation

MacDowell Colony ($50,000) see Putnam Foundation

Manchester Historical Center ($10,000) see Hunt Foundation, Samuel P.

Manchester Institute of Arts and Sciences — for capital improvements ($20,000) see Bean Foundation, Norwin S. and Elizabeth N.

Manchester Institute of Arts and Sciences ($1,100) see Greenspan Foundation

Manchester Institute of Arts and Sciences ($20,000) see Hunt Foundation, Samuel P.

Mascoma Area Health Services ($3,500) see Brundage Charitable, Scientific, and Wildlife Conservation Foundation, Charles E. and Edna T.

Mayhew Program — general support for troubled boys to build self worth and give them a running start toward useful and rewarding adult lives ($1,500) see Mascoma Savings Bank

Mayhew Program — equipment and reconstruct facility ($35,000) see Smith Charitable Foundation, Lou and Lutza

Meals on Wheels ($10,070) see Freygang Foundation, Walter Henry

Meriden Fire Department — materials to create a training room ($1,500) see Mascoma Savings Bank

MHMN Building Fund — hospital relocation project ($15,000) see Mascoma Savings Bank

Milford Town Hall Auditorium Restoration Corporation ($7,500) see Nashua Trust Co.

Monadnock Community Hospital see New England Business Service

Monadnock Music — Lend an Ear Program ($10,000) see Putnam Foundation

Montshire Museum of Science Endowment Fund ($5,000) see Brundage Charitable, Scientific, and Wildlife Conservation Foundation, Charles E. and Edna T.

Mount Washington Observatory ($100,000) see Brooks Foundation, Gladys

Nashua Pastoral Care ($10,000) see Nashua Trust Co.

Nashua Soup Kitchen ($6,000) see Barker Foundation

Nature Conservancy ($5,000) see French Foundation

Nature Conservancy ($3,000) see Kingsbury Corp.

New England College — equipment for computer center ($350,000) see Digital Equipment Corp.

New England Colleges Fund ($11,290) see Putnam Foundation

New England Frontier Camps — capital improvements challenge grant ($32,000) see Gallagher Family Foundation, Lewis P.

New Hampshire Alliance for Children and Youth — support of Access to Care, a three-year project to improve the health of low-income children ($60,000) see Cox Charitable Trust, Jessie B.

New Hampshire Alliance for Effective School — to support participation by the Parker-Varney School in the School Improvement Program ($22,090) see Bean Foundation, Norwin S. and Elizabeth N.

New Hampshire Art Association ($600) see Genius Foundation, Elizabeth Morse

New Hampshire Charitable Association ($10,070) see Greenspan Foundation

New Hampshire Charitable Foundation — general operating support ($100,000) see Avis Inc.

New Hampshire Charitable Foundation — pledge payment ($100,000) see Avis Inc.

New Hampshire Charitable Foundation — pledge payment ($100,000) see Avis Inc.

New Hampshire Charitable Foundation — pledge payment ($100,000) see Avis Inc.

New Hampshire Charitable Foundation — pledge payment ($100,000) see Avis Inc.

New Hampshire Charitable Fund ($174,857) see Benz Trust, Doris L.

New Hampshire Charitable Fund ($16,750) see Eastman Foundation, Alexander

New Hampshire Charitable Fund ($20,000) see Jameson Trust, Oleonda

New Hampshire Charitable Fund ($7,500) see Jameson Trust, Oleonda

New Hampshire Charitable Fund ($226,843) see Switzer Foundation

New Hampshire Charitable Fund — for services to affiliated trusts, other grantmakers and nonprofit organizations ($24,850) see Bean Foundation, Norwin S. and Elizabeth N.

New Hampshire College — computers for graphic and design lab ($10,990) see Cogswell Benevolent Trust

New Hampshire (cont.)

New Hampshire Community Loan Fund ($3,000) see Friendship Fund

New Hampshire Community Loan Fund ($10,000) see Hunt Foundation, Samuel P.

New Hampshire Community Loan Fund ($8,000) see Phillips Foundation, Ellis L.

New Hampshire Community Loan Fund — permanent capital ($50,000) see Smith Charitable Foundation, Lou and Lutza

New Hampshire Community Loan Fund — to support the Manchester housing program ($17,500) see Bean Foundation, Norwin S. and Elizabeth N.

New Hampshire Easter Seal Society ($3,100) see Barker Foundation

New Hampshire Historical Society ($8,000) see Jameson Trust, Oleonda

New Hampshire Humane Society ($16,650) see Bartsch Memorial Trust, Ruth

New Hampshire Humanities Council — financial management ($15,000) see Phillips Foundation, Ellis L.

New Hampshire Land Trust — preservation of land ($5,000) see Mascoma Savings Bank

New Hampshire Loan Fund — renovations ($10,000) see Cogswell Benevolent Trust

New Hampshire Music Festival ($10,500) see Smyth Trust, Marion C.

New Hampshire Odd Fellows Home ($7,500) see First NH Banks, Inc.

New Hampshire Public Television ($15,000) see Fuller Foundation

New Hampshire Public Television ($10,500) see Smyth Trust, Marion C.

New Hampshire Symphony Orchestra ($250) see First NH Banks, Inc.

New Hampshire Symphony Orchestra ($1,280) see Greenspan Foundation

New Hampshire Symphony Orchestra ($10,000) see Smyth Trust, Marion C.

New Hampshire Technical College at Manchester ($4,000) see Barker Foundation

New Hampton School ($100,000) see McEvoy Foundation, Mildred H.

Norris Cotton Cancer Center ($7,000) see Jameson Trust, Oleonda

Northern New Hampshire Foundation ($295,000) see Stearns Charitable Foundation, Anna B.

Parkland Medical Center ($21,000) see Eastman Foundation, Alexander

Phillips Exeter Academy ($5,000) see Beck Foundation

Phillips Exeter Academy — boathouse renovation ($200,000) see Coors Foundation, Adolph

Phillips Exeter Academy ($596,573) see Ellis Fund

Phillips Exeter Academy ($2,000) see Ewald Foundation, H. T.

Phillips Exeter Academy ($1,000) see Goldie-Anna Charitable Trust

Phillips Exeter Academy — observatory project ($330,000) see Grainger Foundation

Phillips Exeter Academy ($100,000) see Heinz Family Foundation

Phillips Exeter Academy ($10,500) see Ingersoll Milling Machine Co.

Phillips Exeter Academy ($1,000,000) see JFM Foundation

Phillips Exeter Academy ($18,500) see Kennedy Foundation, Ethel

Phillips Exeter Academy ($6,000) see Laub Foundation

Phillips Exeter Academy ($5,000) see Porter Foundation, Mrs. Cheever

Phillips Exeter Academy — capital needs ($55,000) see Sequoia Foundation

Portsmouth Housing Authority — respite care program ($65,000) see Foundation for Seacoast Health

Portsmouth Regional Visiting Nurses — elder medical day care project ($56,000) see Foundation for Seacoast Health

Portsmouth Regional Visiting Nurses Association ($5,000) see Fuller Foundation

Portsmouth Regional Visiting Nurses Association ($10,000) see Knistrom Foundation, Fanny and Svante

Portsmouth School Department — clipper health center ($105,091) see Foundation for Seacoast Health

Proctor Academy ($10,000) see Courts Foundation

Proctor Academy ($10,000) see Day Family Foundation

Proctor Academy ($208,000) see Hobbs Charitable Trust, John H.

Proctor Academy ($2,000) see Hyde Manufacturing Co.

Proctor Academy ($500,000) see Johnson Fund, Edward C.

Proctor Academy ($7,000) see Ladd Charitable Corporation, Helen and George

Proctor Academy ($2,000) see Wheeler Foundation, Wilmot

Rockingham Community Land Trust ($10,000) see Thompson Trust, Thomas

Rockingham County Community Action — leasing financial assistance ($35,000) see Foundation for Seacoast Health

Rockingham Memorial Hospital ($7,500) see Banta Corp.

Rockingham Visiting Nurses ($18,000) see Eastman Foundation, Alexander

St. Anselm College ($250) see Chiquita Brands Co.

St. Anselm College ($20,000) see Hunt Foundation, Samuel P.

St. Anselm College — for Geisel Library pledge ($10,000) see Cogswell Benevolent Trust

St. Anselm's College — music department ($10,000) see Smyth Trust, Marion C.

St. Pauls School ($8,000) see Jameson Trust, Oleonda

St. Paul's School ($250) see Page Belting Co.

St. Paul's School ($20,000) see Southways Foundation

Salvation Army ($5,000) see Jameson Trust, Oleonda

Science Center of New Hampshire at Squam Lakes ($10,000) see Hunt Foundation, Samuel P.

Seacoast Mental Health Center — new heights program ($99,449) see Foundation for Seacoast Health

Seacoast Mental Health Center — evaluation report ($13,408) see Foundation for Seacoast Health

Seacoast Science Center — build new facility ($50,000) see Smith Charitable Foundation, Lou and Lutza

Sharon Arts Center ($1,500) see Monadnock Paper Mills

Society of Preservation of New Hampshire Forests ($10,000) see French Foundation

Society for the Protection of New Hampshire Forests ($7,500) see Jameson Trust, Oleonda

Soup Kitchen ($10,000) see Nashua Trust Co.

State of New Hampshire ($50) see First NH Banks, Inc.

State of New Hampshire Certificate of Revival ($75) see First NH Banks, Inc.

Student Conservation Association — publication of earth work ($25,000) see Vidda Foundation

Student Conservation Association — Conservation Career Development Program identifies youth in high school and college and guides them through college graduation into conservation careers ($50,000) see Ittleson Foundation

Sunshine Soup Kitchen ($20,000) see Eastman Foundation, Alexander

Thayer Junior/Senior High School — for "Here, Thayer and Everywhere" program see Melville Corp.

Trust for New Hampshire Lands ($50,000) see Rowland Foundation

Twin State Housing Trust — low cost housing ($1,000) see Mascoma Savings Bank

United Way ($100) see Burndy Corp.

United Way ($100) see Burndy Corp.

United Way ($28,000) see Cogswell Benevolent Trust

United Way ($20,000) see First NH Banks, Inc.

United Way ($22,500) see Jameson Trust, Oleonda

United Way ($6,881) see Kingsbury Corp.

United Way ($6,881) see Kingsbury Corp.

United Way ($6,615) see Kingsbury Corp.

United Way ($3,881) see Kingsbury Corp.

United Way ($4,000) see Nashua Trust Co.

United Way ($18,000) see New Hampshire Ball Bearings

United Way ($5,000) see New Hampshire Ball Bearings

United Way ($1,700) see Page Belting Co.

United Way ($50,000) see Smith Charitable Foundation, Lou and Lutza

United Way of Greater Nashua ($40,000) see Fleet Financial Group

United Way of Merrimack Valley ($22,823) see Bard, C. R.

University of New Hampshire ($7,750) see Barker Foundation

University of New Hampshire ($5,000) see Dewing Foundation, Frances R.

University of New Hampshire ($20,000) see Mellen Foundation

University of New Hampshire — music department ($30,000) see Smyth Trust, Marion C.

University of New Hampshire — scholarships ($28,000) see Smyth Trust, Marion C.

Upper Room ($21,000) see Eastman Foundation, Alexander

Upper Valley Community Land Trust ($3,000) see Brundage Charitable, Scientific, and Wildlife Conservation Foundation, Charles E. and Edna T.

Upper Valley Humane Society — toward construction of new building ($3,000) see Mascoma Savings Bank

Upper Valley Land Trust — endowment fund ($3,000) see Friendship Fund

Upper Valley Support Group — parent support network ($15,000) see Smith Charitable Foundation, Lou and Lutza

VNA of Manchester and Southern New Hampshire — to support the capital campaign for expansion of the child care facility, contingent on other contributions totaling $350,000 ($50,000) see Bean Foundation, Norwin S. and Elizabeth N.

Weeks Memorial Hospital ($50,000) see Norris Foundation, Dellora A. and Lester J.

WEVO — capital campaign ($33,333) see Smith Charitable Foundation, Lou and Lutza

Wolfeboro Area Children's Center — aid for maintenance of services of social worker ($10,000) see Vernon Fund, Miles Hodsdon

Wolfeboro Area Children's Center — aid for operating expenses ($5,000) see Vernon Fund, Miles Hodsdon

Women's Resource Center — leasing financial assistance ($19,710) see Foundation for Seacoast Health

YMCA ($100,000) see Cogswell Benevolent Trust

YMCA ($2,500) see Kingsbury Corp.

New Jersey

A.A. Schwartz Memorial Library ($9,000) see Schwartz Foundation, Arnold A.

A.C.O. Building Program ($10,000) see Fox Foundation, Richard J.

ABWE ($66,100) see Miller Charitable Foundation, C. John and Reva

Adirondack Conservation Council ($4,000) see Knox Family Foundation

AGBU ($31,325) see Mardigian Foundation

Amelior Charitable Fund ($75,000) see Boisi Family Foundation

American Cancer Society ($300) see Charitable Foundation of the Burns Family

American Cancer Society ($5,000) see Havens Foundation, O. W.

American Cancer Society ($500) see Zock Endowment Trust

American Foundation for Pharmaceutical Education ($100,700) see Burroughs Wellcome Co.

American Gastroenterology Association ($53,800) see Fiterman Charitable Foundation, Miles and Shirley

American Heart Association ($5,000) see Havens Foundation, O. W.

American Jewish Committee ($5,000) see Litwin Foundation

American Leprosy Missions ($20,000) see Palisades Educational Foundation

American Paralysis Association — general charitable contribution ($28,500) see Carter-Wallace

American Red Cross ($5,000) see Havens Foundation, O. W.

Andover United Methodist Church ($500) see Caspersen Foundation for Aid to Health and Education, O. W.

ARC Union County ($26,995) see Snyder Foundation, Harold B. and Dorothy A.

Archdiocese of Newark ($200,000) see Brennan Foundation, Robert E.

Archdiocese of Newark ($10,000) see CIT Group Holdings

Archdiocese of Newark ($1,085,000) see Connelly Foundation

Archdiocese of Newark ($200,000) see Hess Foundation

Archdiocese of Newark ($50,000) see Kennedy Foundation, Quentin J.

Archdiocese of Newark ($25,000) see St. Mary's Catholic Foundation

Archway Programs — child assistance ($30,000) see Innovating Worthy Projects Foundation

Archway Schools ($60,000) see Innovating Worthy Projects Foundation

Armenian General Benevolent Union ($275) see Alro Steel Corp.

Armenian General Benevolent Union ($448,563) see Simone Foundation

Armenian General Benevolent Union ($9,950) see Simone Foundation

Armenian General Benevolent Union of America ($1,097,675) see Manoogian Foundation, Alex and Marie

Armenian Missionary Association ($99,000) see Philibosian Foundation, Stephen

Art Museum at Princeton University ($58,333) see Sharp Foundation

Arthritis Foundation ($7,100) see Peierls Foundation

Arts Council of the Essex Area ($5,000) see Mulford Foundation, Vincent

ARTS FOR EVERYKID see Johnson & Johnson

Arts Foundation of New Jersey ($20,000) see Bergen Foundation, Frank and Lydia

Asbury Park Public Library — improvements ($9,865) see

McMurray-Bennnett
Foundation

Associated Alumnae of Douglass
College — Center for Global
Issues ($25,000) see Lowe
Foundation, Joe and Emily

Association of New Jersey
Environmental Commissions
— to support its Freshwater
Wetlands Education Project to
build public support and
educate local environmental
officials ($25,000) see Fund
for New Jersey

Atlantic City Day Nursery
($15,000) see Scholler
Foundation

Augustinian Recollect
Monastery St. Cloud ($5,000)
see Pendergast-Weyer
Foundation

Babyland Nursery — child care
provider that the foundation
has supported since 1971
($80,000) see Schumann Fund
for New Jersey

Barnert Hospital Foundation
($65,000) see Van Houten
Charitable Trust

Bayshore Youth and Family
Services ($10,000) see Borden
Memorial Foundation, Mary
Owen

Bender Memorial Academy
($3,600) see Charitable
Foundation of the Burns
Family

Bergen Community College
Foundation — building fund
($25,000) see Buehler
Foundation, Emil

Bernards Area Scholarship
Assistance ($36,250) see
Jockey Hollow Foundation

Beth Israel Hospital see Valley
National Bancorp

Beth Midrash Govaha ($33,000)
see Lupin Foundation

Beth Midrash Govoha ($20,000)
see Parnes Foundation, E. H.

Black People's Unity Movement
— an economic development
force in Camden ($130,000)
see Campbell Soup Co.

Blair Academy — special
($50,000) see Turrell Fund

B'nai B'rith Hillel
Counselorship ($800) see
Abrams Foundation

Boy Scouts of America
($25,000) see Brennan
Foundation, Robert E.

Boy Scouts of America
($10,250) see Rosenthal
Foundation, Ida and William

Boy Scouts of
America-Hudson-Hamilton
Council — to purchase and
renovate their Council Service
Center ($150,000) see Hayden
Foundation, Charles

Boys and Girls Club ($26,400)
see Brady Foundation

Boys and Girls Club ($10,000)
see Darby Foundation

Boys and Girls Club ($725) see
Jaydor Corp.

Boys and Girls Club ($1,000) see
KSM Foundation

Boys and Girls Club ($100) see
Martini Foundation, Nicholas

Boys and Girls Club ($20,000)
see Schenck Fund, L. P.

Boys & Girls Club see Valley
National Bancorp

Boys and Girls Clubs of Newark
($50,000) see Sandy Hill
Foundation

Boys and Girls Clubs of Newark
— general program ($65,000)
see Turrell Fund

Boys and Girls Clubs of Newark
— general operating support
($100,000) see Victoria
Foundation

Brundage Park Playhouse
($4,000) see Brundage
Charitable, Scientific, and
Wildlife Conservation
Foundation, Charles E. and
Edna T.

Caldwell College — scholarship
Program ($12,500) see
Palisades Educational
Foundation

Camden Area Players ($2,500)
see Gilman and
Gonzalez-Falla Theatre
Foundation

Camden County Council of Girl
Scouts — renovation and
expansion ($50,000) see
Campbell Soup Co.

Camden Military College
($6,000) see Scurry
Foundation, D. L.

Camp Nejeda Foundation
($10,000) see Caspersen
Foundation for Aid to Health
and Education, O. W.

Campaign for Princeton Day
School ($150,000) see
Harriman Foundation, Gladys
and Roland

Campbell Summer Program —
provides wholesome activities
for youth in Camden through
existing organizations and
programs ($175,000) see
Campbell Soup Co.

Cancer Care Center ($1,000) see
KSM Foundation

Cancer Care of New Jersey
($9,200) see CIT Group
Holdings

CATA: El Comite de Apoyo a los
Trabajadores Agricolas
($20,000) see Needmor Fund

Catholic Community Services —
supports emergency shelters
for homeless mothers and
children in Newark ($40,000)
see Schumann Fund for New
Jersey

Center for Analysis of Public
Issues — operations ($50,000)
see Fund for New Jersey

Center for Educational
Advancement ($25,000) see
Large Foundation

Center for Energy and
Environmental Studies —
Princeton University;
"Program on Energy
Technology Assessment and
Energy Policy Analysis:
Energy Strategies for
Sustainable Development"
($200,000) see Jones
Foundation, W. Alton

Center for Help in Time of Loss
($9,500) see Mutual of New
York

Center for Non-Profit
Corporations — 1991
operations ($25,000) see Fund
for New Jersey

Center of Theological Inquiry
($40,000) see Blum
Foundation, Edith C.

Center for Theological Inquiry
($10,000) see Weyerhaeuser
Foundation, Frederick and
Margaret L.

Central Presbyterian Church
($2,000) see Donaldson,
Lufkin & Jenrette

Central Presbyterian Church —
purchase and installation of a
new sanctuary pipe organ
($25,000) see Hyde and
Watson Foundation

Centrastate Medical Center
($17,000) see Dell Foundation,
Hazel

Cerebral Palsy Association
($8,000) see Snyder
Foundation, Harold B. and
Dorothy A.

Chad School ($42,000) see
Schumann Fund for New
Jersey

Chamber Symphony of Princeton
($12,660) see Bergen
Foundation, Frank and Lydia

Charill Services ($10,070) see
Freygang Foundation, Walter
Henry

Chemocare ($5,000) see
Beneficial Corp.

Children's Aid and Adoption
Society ($16,000) see Orange
Orphan Society

Children's Home Society
($10,000) see Kerney
Foundation, James

Children's Hospital of New
Jersey Pediatric Sickle Cell
Anemia Research Account
($31,000) see Hoffmann-La
Roche

Children's Institute — program
and computer lab text books
($10,000) see Kern
Foundation, Ilma

Children's Institute ($13,300)
see Orange Orphan Society

Children's Specialized Hospital
($20,000) see Ohl, Jr. Trust,
George A.

Chilton Hospital Foundation
($1,000) see Spiro Foundation,
Donald W.

Christian Missions in Many
Lands ($24,000) see Caddock
Foundation

Christmas in April ($10,313) see
Kerney Foundation, James

Christmas in April ($5,070) see
Kerney Foundation, James

Church of Good Shepherd
($20,000) see O'Toole
Foundation, Theresa and
Edward

Church of Good Shepherd
($10,000) see O'Toole
Foundation, Theresa and
Edward

Church of Many Lands
($10,000) see McCarthy
Foundation, John and Margaret

Citizens Committee on
Biomedical Ethics — to
participate in a six-state
initiative of the Public Agenda
Foundation to educate the
public on cost and quality
issues in health care and to
discuss various systemic
reforms ($25,000) see Fund
for New Jersey

Clarence Dillon Public Library
($30,000) see Brady
Foundation

Clifton Memorial Library
($5,000) see Martini
Foundation, Nicholas

Cokesbury United Methodist
Church ($5,000) see Harris
Brothers Foundation

College Scholarship Service
($63,157) see Chesapeake
Corp.

Colonial Symphony ($5,000) see
Klipstein Foundation, Ernest
Christian

Columbia University ($3,000)
see Fortis Inc.

Community Care Association
($25,000) see Large
Foundation

Community Center for Mental
Health ($40,000) see Schenck
Fund, L. P.

Community Center for Mental
Health ($40,000) see Schenck
Fund, L. P.

Community Church of Smoke
Rise ($755) see Spiro
Foundation, Donald W.

Community Day Nursery
($17,600) see Orange Orphan
Society

Community Foundation of New
Jersey ($20,000) see
Hoffmann-La Roche

Community Nursing Services
($10,000) see Rutgers
Community Health Foundation

Congregation Brothers of Israel
($7,000) see Abrams
Foundation

Convent ($8,117) see Kavanagh
Foundation, T. James

Cooperative Business Assistance
Corporation — to provide
loans and technical advice to
Camden businesses with fewer
than 25 employees ($30,000)
see Campbell Soup Co.

Corielle Institute for Medical
Research ($39,997) see
Scholler Foundation

Corner House Foundation
($50,000) see Johnson
Foundation, Willard T. C.

Covenant House ($35,000) see
Grassmann Trust, E. J.

Covenant House ($14,000) see
Union Foundation

CPC Mental Health Services
($100,000) see Brooks
Foundation, Gladys

Crawford House ($65,000) see
Winslow Foundation

Daughters of Israel Geriatric
Center — for cultural
programs ($15,000) see
Alexander Foundation, Joseph

Daughters of Miriam Center for
the Aged ($25,000) see
Schamach Foundation, Milton

Deborah Hospital ($5,000) see
Colt Foundation, James J.

Deborah Hospital ($132,860) see
Patterson and Clara Guthrie
Patterson Trust, Robert Leet

Deborah Hospital Foundation
($30,000) see Berkowitz
Family Foundation, Louis

Deborah Hospital Foundation —
equipment for sleep studies
($5,000) see Catlin Charitable
Trust, Kathleen K.

Deborah Hospital Foundation
($7,500) see Schamach
Foundation, Milton

Deborah Hospital Foundation
($37,743) see Snyder
Foundation, Harold B. and
Dorothy A.

Deborah Hospital
Foundation-Jackson Chapter
($10,000) see Havens
Foundation, O. W.

Delbarton School ($110,000) see
Engelhard Foundation, Charles

Delbarton School ($22,000) see
Thanksgiving Foundation

Developmental Learning
Systems Foundation ($80,000)
see Palisades Educational
Foundation

Dominican Sisters of Divine
Providence ($75,000) see East
Foundation, Sarita Kenedy

Dow Jones Newspaper Fund
($350,000) see Dow Jones &
Co.

Drew University ($10,000) see
Beneficial Corp.

Drew University ($10,000) see
Read Foundation, Charles L.

Drew University ($69,108) see
Schering-Plough Corp.

Dwight Morrow High School
($224,912) see RJR Nabisco
Inc.

Easter Seal Society ($10,000)
see Ohl, Jr. Trust, George A.

Eastern Christian Children's
Retreat see Valley National
Bancorp

Eastern Economic Association
($10,000) see PHH Corp.

Edison Community College
($12,000) see Wiggins
Memorial Trust, J. J.

Edison Festival of Lights
($50,045) see Foulds Trust,
Claiborne F

Edison Sheltered Workshop
($6,000) see Schwartz
Foundation, Arnold A.

Edison State College ($500) see
French Oil Mill Machinery Co.

Education Law Center —
operational support ($40,000)
see Fund for New Jersey

Education Law Center — equal
educational opportunity
project ($30,000) see Norman
Foundation

Educational Information and
Resource Center — training
program ($58,500) see Turrell
Fund

Educational Testing Service
($69,375) see Allendale
Mutual Insurance Co.

Educational Testing Service
($33,500) see Textron

Educational Testing Service —
for the 1992 Cafritz Teacher
Fellowship Awards and
expenses ($150,000) see
Cafritz Foundation, Morris
and Gwendolyn

Electronic Information and
Education Service of New
Jersey ($4,000) see Brundage
Charitable, Scientific, and
Wildlife Conservation
Foundation, Charles E. and
Edna T.

Elizabeth General Medical
Center Foundation ($165,000)
see Grassmann Trust, E. J.

Elizabeth General Medical
Center Foundation ($2,000)
see Psychists

Elizabeth General Medical
Center Foundation ($42,000)
see Union Foundation

Elizabethport Presbyterian
Center ($15,000) see Snyder
Foundation, Harold B. and
Dorothy A.

EMS Squad see Suburban
Propane

EMS Squad see Suburban
Propane

Englewood Public Library
($10,000) see Schenck Fund,
L. P.

Epiphany House ($5,000) see
Duke Foundation, Doris

Episcopal Ministries of Bergen
Hill ($3,000) see Read
Foundation, Charles L.

Essex County College (For:
Training) — toward Training,
operating costs ($100,000) see
Victoria Foundation

Fairleigh Dickinson University
($25,000) see Hoechst
Celanese Corp.

Fairleigh Dickinson University
($68,030) see Schering-Plough
Corp.

Fairleigh Dickinson University
— research on Blackspot
Disease of roses ($25,000) see
Vidda Foundation

Fairleigh Dickinson University
— Engineering and Science

New Jersey (cont.)

Building ($100,000) see AlliedSignal

Fairliegh Dickinson University ($25,000) see Pope Foundation

Fairmount United Methodist Church ($5,000) see Harris Brothers Foundation

Family Planning Services of Cumberland and Gloucester ($10,000) see Rutgers Community Health Foundation

Family Service Bureau of Newark ($10,000) see Ohl, Jr. Trust, George A.

Family Service and Child Guidance Center ($45,500) see Orange Orphan Society

Family Services and Child Guidance Center ($5,000) see Seevak Family Foundation

Far Hills Country Day School ($4,000) see Darby Foundation

Far Hills Country Day School ($50,000) see Forbes

Far Hills Country Day School ($5,000) see Klipstein Foundation, Ernest Christian

Federation of Allied Jewish Appeal ($170) see Kellmer Co., Jack

Felician College ($35,000) see Link, Jr. Foundation, George

Festival CF Music ($15,000) see Bergen Foundation, Frank and Lydia

Financial Executives Research Foundation ($1,000) see Mohasco Corp.

First Christian Church ($7,500) see Stacy Foundation, Festus

Fish, Inc. — Dunellen Area; expansion of its facilities ($25,000) see Hyde and Watson Foundation

Flemington-Raritan First Aid and Rescue Squad ($15,000) see Large Foundation

Food and Water ($5,000) see Sacharuna Foundation

Foundation for Independent Higher Education — Independent College Fund of New Jersey ($230,000) see American Telephone & Telegraph Co.

Foundation for Student Communication ($3,800) see Scherer Foundation, Karla

Foundation of University of Medicine and Dentistry ($100,025) see Schering-Plough Corp.

Foundation of University of Medicine and Dentistry ($86,512) see Schultz Foundation

Foundation of University of Medicine and Dentistry ($50,000) see Schultz Foundation

Foundation of University of Medicine and Dentistry ($50,514) see Van Houten Charitable Trust

Foundation of University of Medicine and Dentistry of New Jersey — capital campaign ($100,000) see AlliedSignal

Foundation of the University of Medicine and Dentistry of New Jersey ($46,666) see Hoffmann-La Roche

Foundation of the University of Medicine and Dentistry of New Jersey — to train day care providers to identify the developmental needs of preschool children ($30,000)

see Schumann Fund for New Jersey

Friends of Israel ($5,000) see Morris Charitable Foundation, E. A.

Friends of Yad Sarah ($1,000) see Abrams Foundation

Friendship House ($35,000) see Schenck Fund, L. P.

G.E.A. ($10,000) see Caspersen Foundation for Aid to Health and Education, O. W.

Garden State Cancer Center ($40,000) see Edison Fund, Charles

Georgian Court College ($7,000) see Havens Foundation, O. W.

Gill/St. Bernard's School — alteration and modernization of its Chapel building ($30,000) see Hyde and Watson Foundation

Gladstone Equestrian Association ($5,000) see Brady Foundation

Glassboro State College ($23,000) see SICO Foundation

Good Counsel — to support a catechesis and Bible study program ($40,000) see Koch Foundation

Greater Newark Christmas Fund, 1990 ($3,500) see Brundage Charitable, Scientific, and Wildlife Conservation Foundation, Charles E. and Edna T.

Greater Newark Christmas Fund, 1990 — general ($5,000) see Upton Charitable Foundation, Lucy and Eleanor S.

Green Hill Memorial Center — general ($7,500) see Upton Charitable Foundation, Lucy and Eleanor S.

Groton School Annual Fund ($400,000) see Getty Foundation, Ann and Gordon

Habitat for Humanity ($20,000) see Snyder Foundation, Harold B. and Dorothy A.

Hackensack Medical Center Foundation ($32,500) see Link, Jr. Foundation, George

Hackensack Medical Center Foundation ($25,400) see Schamach Foundation, Milton

Hackensack Medical Foundation ($5,000) see Flemm Foundation, John J.

Harbor Branch Oceanographic Institution ($3,107,313) see Atlantic Foundation

Harbor Branch Oceanographic Institution ($29,281) see Link Foundation

Helene Fuld School of Nursing of Camden County — scholarships ($206,250) see Fuld Health Trust, Helene

Help for Unclaimed Dogs — animal protection ($3,000) see South Branch Foundation

Hemophilia Association of New Jersey ($1,000) see Kajima International, Inc.

Henry H. Kessler Foundation ($50,000) see Day Family Foundation

Henry H. Kessler Foundation ($10,070) see Freygang Foundation, Walter Henry

Henry H. Kessler Foundation ($5,000) see Jones Fund, Blanche and George

Henry H. Kessler Foundation ($30,000) see Link, Jr. Foundation, George

Highland Foundation ($5,000) see Brady Foundation

Hillel Yeshiva ($3,000) see N've Shalom Foundation

Hispanic/American Chamber of Commerce see Valley National Bancorp

Holy Name Hospital ($25,000) see Schenck Fund, L. P.

Hospice of Morris County ($1,000) see Spiro Foundation, Donald W.

Hospital Center at Orange ($83,000) see Edison Fund, Charles

Hospital Center at Orange ($30,000) see Orange Orphan Society

House of the Good Shepherd — general ($7,500) see Upton Charitable Foundation, Lucy and Eleanor S.

House of the Holy Comforter — general ($7,500) see Upton Charitable Foundation, Lucy and Eleanor S.

Housing New Jersey — to publish the monthly "Housing New Jersey" magazine on affordable housing ($35,000) see Fund for New Jersey

Humana Foundation Scholarship Program ($200,000) see Humana

Hunterdon Art Center — preservation and promotion of art ($11,500) see South Branch Foundation

Hunterdon County Historical Society ($10,000) see Large Foundation

Hunterdon Hospice ($17,500) see Large Foundation

Hunterdon Medical Center Foundation ($20,000) see Beneficial Corp.

Hunterdon Medical Center Foundation ($4,000) see Harris Brothers Foundation

Hunterdon Medical Center Foundation ($80,000) see Large Foundation

Huntington's Disease Society of America, New Jersey Chapter ($10,000) see Rutgers Community Health Foundation

Immaculate Conception Cathedral ($10,000) see O'Neil Foundation, W.

Independent College Fund of New Jersey — general charitable contribution ($25,000) see Carter-Wallace

Independent College Fund of New Jersey ($100,000) see Hoffmann-La Roche

Independent College Fund of New Jersey — general support and urban initiative program ($133,000) see Prudential Insurance Co. of America

Independent College Fund of New Jersey — Project Success ($20,000) see Crum and Forster

Inner-City Scholarship Fund ($5,000) see Kellogg Foundation, Peter and Cynthia K.

Institute for Advanced Studies ($350,000) see Monell Foundation, Ambrose

Institute for Advanced Study ($400,000) see Botwinick-Wolfensohn Foundation

Institute for Advanced Study ($144,000) see Seaver Institute

Interdenominational Outreach Choir — transportation ($10,000) see Innovating Worthy Projects Foundation

Interfaith Care Givers ($4,000) see Concord Chemical Co.

Interfaith Care Givers ($25,000) see Ware Foundation

International Institute of Ne Jersey — toenable the institute to continue to coordinate the activities of th statewide New Jersey Immigration Policy Network in 1992 ($30,000) see Fund for New Jersey

International Mahavir Jain Mission ($5,000) see India Foundation

International Research and Exchange Board ($50,000) see Kress Foundation, Samuel H.

International Research and Exchanges Board — a project on ethnic conflict in Eastern Europe ($1,200,000) see Carnegie Corporation of New York

Intersearch Institute — toward the cost of the operations, drug development and research program expenses ($500,000) see Rippel Foundation, Fannie E.

Isaiah House — general ($5,000) see Upton Charitable Foundation, Lucy and Eleanor S.

Isles ($15,000) see Borden Memorial Foundation, Mary Owen

Isles ($20,000) see Kerney Foundation, James

Isles — to support the Wood Steet housing project ($25,000) see Fund for New Jersey

Israel Emergency Fund ($15,279) see Mattus Foundation, Reuben and Rose

JCC Camp Scholarship Fund ($300) see Kellmer Co., Jack

Jersey Shore Audubon ($2,500) see Kajima International, Inc.

Jersey Shore Medical Center ($2,500) see McMurray-Bennnett Foundation

Jersey Shore Medical Center ($1,000) see Zock Endowment Trust

Jersey Shore Medical Foundation ($28,500) see Brennan Foundation, Robert E.

Jewish Community Center ($1,000) see Abrams Foundation

Jewish Community Center on the Palisades ($15,100) see Taub Foundation, Henry and Marilyn

Jewish Community Foundation of Metrowest ($5,000) see Jaydor Corp.

Jewish Community Foundation of MetroWest New Jersey ($27,500) see Hirschhorn Foundation, David and Barbara B.

Jewish Educational Center ($260,120) see Wilf Family Foundation

Jewish Family Services ($100) see Martini Foundation, Nicholas

Jewish Federation ($10,000) see Federation Foundation of Greater Philadelphia

Jewish Federation ($145,000) see Garfinkle Family Foundation

Jewish Federation ($80,000) see Kaufman Foundation, Henry & Elaine

Jewish Federation ($35,000) see Kaufman Foundation, Henry & Elaine

Jewish Federation ($30,000) see Kaufman Foundation, Henry & Elaine

Jewish Federation ($10,000) see Muller Foundation, C. John and Josephine

Jewish Federation of Mercer ($2,000) see Homasote Co.

Jewish Federation of Mercer and Bucks County ($30,800) see Abrams Foundation

Jewish Federation of South New Jersey ($5,000) see Schwartz and Robert Schwartz Foundation, Bernard

John F. Kennedy Medical Center ($50,000) see Revlon

Johnson Atelier and Technical Institute of Sculpture ($300,000) see Atlantic Foundation

Joseph H. Firth Youth Center ($11,250) see Wade Endowment Fund, Elizabeth Firth

Joseph H. Firth Youth Center ($11,250) see Wade Endowment Fund, Elizabeth Firth

Joseph H. Firth Youth Center ($11,250) see Wade Endowment Fund, Elizabeth Firth

Joseph H. Firth Youth Center ($11,250) see Wade Endowment Fund, Elizabeth Firth

Joyce and Steward Johnson Foundation ($7,000) see Atlantic Foundation

June Opera Festival of New Jersey ($5,000) see Valentine Foundation, Lawson

Kent Place School ($7,000) see Harris Brothers Foundation

Kent Place School ($50,000) see McGraw Foundation, Donald C.

Kent Place School — general operating support ($125,005) see MCJ Foundation

Kent Place School ($15,000) see Union Foundation

Kent Place School — initial costs for the construction of a new Primary School building ($30,000) see Hyde and Watson Foundation

Kids of North Jersey ($32,220) see Liz Claiborne

Kilbarchan Home for Children ($16,666) see Jaqua Foundation

Kimball Medical Center Foundation ($12,000) see Havens Foundation, O. W.

La Casa De Don Pedro — general operating support ($200,000) see Victoria Foundation

Lakeland Emergency Squad ($2,500) see Caspersen Foundation for Aid to Health and Education, O. W.

Lawrence Fire Company ($150) see Goodall Rubber Co.

Lawrenceville School — annual giving ($6,000) see Bardes Corp.

Lawrenceville School ($5,000) see Dobson Foundation

Lawrenceville School ($5,000) see Globe Corp.

Lawrenceville School ($200,000) see Kirby Foundation, F. M.

Lawrenceville School ($50,000) see Noyes, Jr. Memorial Foundation, Nicholas H.

Lawrenceville School Camp ($5,000) see Kerney Foundation, James

Lebanon United Methodist Church ($5,000) see Harris Brothers Foundation

Liberty Science Center — for development of educational programs ($100,000) see Dodge Foundation, Geraldine R.

Liberty Science Center ($145,000) see Nabisco Foods Group

Liberty Science Center ($20,000) see Thomas & Betts Corp.

Liberty Science Center — five-year pledge ($290,000) see Johnson & Johnson

Liberty Science Center and Hall of Technology ($100,000) see AMAX

Liberty Science Center and Hall of Technology ($250,000) see Johnson Foundation, Willard T. C.

Liberty Science Center and Hall of Technology ($100,000) see Schering-Plough Corp.

Liberty Science Center and Hall of Technology ($300,000) see Warner-Lambert Co.

Liberty Science Center and Hall of Technology — toward the Victoria Environmental Education Center ($100,000) see Victoria Foundation

Little Sisters of Poor ($15,000) see Monaghan Charitable Trust, Rose

Lubo Opera Company ($6,500) see Brundage Charitable, Scientific, and Wildlife Conservation Foundation, Charles E. and Edna T.

Lunch Break — general fund ($1,000) see McMurray-Bennnett Foundation

Manasquan First Aid ($1,000) see Zock Endowment Trust

Manasquan Police Department ($1,800) see Dell Foundation, Hazel

March of Dimes ($50) see Martini Foundation, Nicholas

Maris Stella Church ($3,500) see Kavanagh Foundation, T. James

Market Street Mission ($5,000) see Harris Brothers Foundation

Martin House Community for Justice ($10,000) see Kerney Foundation, James

Massachusetts Forestry Association ($3,500) see Wharton Trust, William P.

Massachusetts association of Health Boards — publish a legal handbook ($2,000) see Cove Charitable Trust

Mathematica Policy Research — evaluation of ACHIEVE, a program to increase the number of graduates of an African American high school in Memphis, TN who are prepared to enter college programs in health ($434,831) see Kaiser Family Foundation, Henry J.

Mathematica Policy Research — an observational study of parent-child behavior within the Teen Parent Demonstration ($95,921) see Foundation for Child Development

Matheny School ($6,000) see Havens Foundation, O. W.

Matheny School ($60,000) see Jockey Hollow Foundation

Matheny School ($7,500) see Schwartz Foundation, Arnold A.

Matheny School ($150,000) see South Branch Foundation

Matheny School ($20,000) see Thomas & Betts Corp.

Matheny School and Hospital ($10,000) see Willits Foundation

McCarter Theater ($10,000) see Bunbury Company

MCOSS — general fund ($750) see McMurray-Bennnett Foundation

Meadow Lakes Christmas Fund ($2,000) see Williams Foundation, C. K.

Medical Center at Princeton ($20,000) see McGraw Foundation, Curtis W.

Medical Center at Princeton — capital fund ($150,000) see Reed Foundation, Philip D.

Mercer Council on Alcoholism ($10,000) see Hamel Family Charitable Trust, D. A.

Mercer Council on Alcoholism ($8,957) see Kerney Foundation, James

Metropolitan Area Youth for Christ ($13,000) see Three Swallows Foundation

Mid-Bergen Community Mental Health Center ($12,000) see Buehler Foundation, Emil

Monmouth Arts Center — general fund ($2,000) see McMurray-Bennnett Foundation

Monmouth College ($15,000) see Charina Foundation

Monmouth College ($5,000) see Kautz Family Foundation

Monmouth College — ethics chair ($55,000) see McMurray-Bennnett Foundation

Monmouth College ($10,000) see McMurray-Bennnett Foundation

Monmouth College ($25,000) see Murdy Foundation

Monmouth County Heart Association ($1,000) see Zock Endowment Trust

Monmouth Health Care Foundation ($26,580) see Borden Memorial Foundation, Mary Owen

Monmouth Health Care Foundation ($22,000) see Terner Foundation

Monmouth Memorial Medical Center ($200,000) see Hess Foundation

Monmouth Opera Guild — general fund ($1,000) see McMurray-Bennnett Foundation

Montclair State College Foundation ($10,000) see Mulford Foundation, Vincent

Morristown-Beard School ($30,000) see Kellogg Foundation, Peter and Cynthia K.

Morristown-Beard School ($2,500) see Kellogg Foundation, Peter and Cynthia K.

Morristown Beard School-Anderson Endowment — general operating support ($101,234) see MCJ Foundation

Morristown Memorial Health Foundation ($10,000) see Brady Foundation

Morristown Memorial Health Foundation ($25,000) see Caspersen Foundation for Aid to Health and Education, O. W.

Morristown Memorial Health Foundation ($12,000) see Crum and Forster

Morristown Memorial Health Foundation ($10,000) see Frelinghuysen Foundation

Morristown Memorial Health Foundation ($3,000) see Jones Fund, Blanche and George

Morristown Memorial Health Foundation ($12,500) see Oaklawn Foundation

Morristown Memorial Health Foundation ($50,000) see Simon Foundation, William E. and Carol G.

Morristown Memorial Health Foundation — Era of Excellence Campaign ($200,000) see AlliedSignal

Morristown Memorial Hospital ($100,000) see Forbes

Morristown Memorial Hospital ($60,000) see Hutchins Foundation, Mary J.

Morristown Memorial Hospital ($25,000) see Jockey Hollow Foundation

Morristown Memorial Hospital ($50,000) see Nabisco Foods Group

Morristown Memorial Hospital ($50,150) see Schering-Plough Corp.

Morristown Memorial Hospital ($225,000) see Warner-Lambert Co.

Morristown Memorial Hospital ($15,000) see Willits Foundation

Morristown Neighborhood House ($45,000) see Jockey Hollow Foundation

Mount St. Mary Academy ($14,000) see Union Foundation

Mrs. Wilson's ($10,000) see Willits Foundation

Muhlenberg Foundation ($55,000) see Grassmann Trust, E. J.

Muhlenberg Foundation ($20,504) see Snyder Foundation, Harold B. and Dorothy A.

Muhlenberg Regional Medical Center ($370,000) see Fanwood Foundation

Muhlenberg Regional Medical Center ($4,000) see Harris Brothers Foundation

Muhlenberg Regional Medical Center ($17,100) see Schwartz Foundation, Arnold A.

Muhlenberg Regional Medical Center ($13,000) see Union Foundation

Nassau Foundation — support to remodel a residence for university students ($20,000) see Clover Foundation

National Association of Scholars — general operating support ($300,000) see Scaife Foundation, Sarah

National Committee for Preventing Child Abuse ($25,000) see McDonald Foundation, J. M.

Nature Conservancy ($5,000) see Beneficial Corp.

Nature Conservancy ($90,000) see Grassmann Trust, E. J.

Nature Conservancy ($125,000) see South Branch Foundation

Nature Conservancy ($17,000) see Union Foundation

New Community Corporation ($50,000) see Sandy Hill Foundation

New Community Corporation — operating and expansion funds for the Employment Center ($380,000) see Victoria Foundation

New Community Corporation — provide summer employment for Newark youth and fund a publication describing the organization's 25-year history ($105,000) see Prudential Insurance Co. of America

New Community Corporation — to purchase and renovate the 201 Bergen Street facility ($400,000) see Victoria Foundation

New Jersey Academy for Aquatic Sciences — revitalization of the Camden waterfront; a challenge component to spur the rapid development ($250,000) see Campbell Soup Co.

New Jersey Association on Correction ($10,000) see Rutgers Community Health Foundation

New Jersey Association for the Deaf & Blind see New York Mercantile Exchange

New Jersey Association for Retarded Citizens, Morris Unit ($13,000) see Knistrom Foundation, Fanny and Svante

New Jersey Audubon Society ($43,750) see Barbour Foundation, Bernice

New Jersey Ballet ($3,100) see Brady Foundation

New Jersey Business/Industry/Science/Edu cation Consortium ($12,000) see Unilever United States

New Jersey Center for Visual Arts ($2,500) see Fortis Inc.

New Jersey Chamber Music Society ($15,000) see Bergen Foundation, Frank and Lydia

New Jersey Conservation Fund ($2,500) see Gerard Foundation, Sumner

New Jersey Cystic Fibrosis ($2,500) see Kajima International, Inc.

New Jersey Future — to provide public input to a state land-use plan and to join forces with three other nonprofit groups to coordinate their efforts to promote its final adoption ($40,000) see Fund for New Jersey

New Jersey Historical Society — campaign for stability ($15,000) see Day Family Foundation

New Jersey Historical Society — purchase of equipment and furnishings ($29,460) see Hyde and Watson Foundation

New Jersey Historical Society ($1,000) see KSM Foundation

New Jersey Historical Society ($20,000) see South Branch Foundation

New Jersey Historical Society ($100,000) see Whitehead Foundation

New Jersey HLA Registry ($5,000) see Kopf Foundation, Elizabeth Christy

New Jersey HLA Registry ($35,000) see Van Houten Charitable Trust

New Jersey Institute of Technology ($5,350) see ASARCO

New Jersey Institute of Technology ($100) see Leesona Corp.

New Jersey Institute of Technology — general operating support ($200,000) see MCJ Foundation

New Jersey Museum of Agriculture ($5,000) see Agway

New Jersey Opera Festival ($250,000) see Johnson Foundation, Willard T. C.

New Jersey Performing Arts Center ($200,000) see Hess Foundation

New Jersey Performing Arts Center — general operating support ($254,794) see MCJ Foundation

New Jersey Performing Arts Center — general operating support ($251,813) see MCJ Foundation

New Jersey Performing Arts Center ($335,000) see Newhouse Foundation, Samuel I.

New Jersey Performing Arts Center — supporting the establishment and construction of the new Multi-Purpose Cultural Center in Newark, NJ ($1,000,000) see Merck & Co.

New Jersey Performing Arts Center at Newark Corporation — new arts center construction ($130,000) see Prudential Insurance Co. of America

New Jersey Performing Arts Center — payable over five years. $1 million be used for leveraging; as a challenge grant to the newly created statewide Attorney's Campaign ($500,000) see Victoria Foundation

New Jersey Press Association — scholarships ($1,258) see McMurray-Bennnett Foundation

New Jersey Science Tech Center Liberty Science Center ($50,000) see Dun & Bradstreet Corp.

New Jersey Shakespeare Festival ($10,000) see Beneficial Corp.

New Jersey State Museum ($5,500) see Kerney Foundation, James

New Jersey Symphony Orchestra ($6,000) see Brundage Charitable, Scientific, and Wildlife Conservation Foundation, Charles E. and Edna T.

New Jersey Symphony Orchestra ($7,500) see CIT Group Holdings

New Jersey Symphony Orchestra ($25,000) see Hoechst Celanese Corp.

New Jersey Symphony Orchestra ($8,000) see Mulford Foundation, Vincent

New Jersey Symphony Orchestra — general ($50,000) see Upton Charitable Foundation, Lucy and Eleanor S.

New Jersey Symphony Orchestra — establishment of and enhancement of an "Independence Initiative Fund" ($50,000) see Hyde and Watson Foundation

New Jersey Vietnam Veterans Memorial Committee ($250,000) see Schering-Plough Corp.

New Jersey Youth Symphony ($10,000) see Bergen Foundation, Frank and Lydia

New Prospect — to improve and promote the publication The American Prospect ($150,000) see Schumann Foundation, Florence and John

New Vernon Volunteer Fire Department ($2,500) see Klipstein Foundation, Ernest Christian

New Jersey (cont.)

Newark Abbey ($191,851) see Brennan Foundation, Robert E.

Newark Academy ($10,000) see Clapp Charitable and Educational Trust, George H.

Newark Beth Israel Medical Center ($1,500) see Delacorte Fund, George

Newark Beth Israel Medical Center ($25,000) see Jaqua Foundation

Newark Boys Chorus School ($5,000) see Brady Foundation

Newark Boys and Girls Club ($8,500) see Schloss & Co., Marcus

Newark Community School of Arts ($20,000) see Bergen Foundation, Frank and Lydia

Newark Museum ($6,000) see Brundage Charitable, Scientific, and Wildlife Conservation Foundation, Charles E. and Edna T.

Newark Museum ($35,000) see Day Family Foundation

Newark Museum — for support of exhibition development costs ($120,000) see Dodge Foundation, Geraldine R.

Newark Museum ($7,500) see Ohl, Jr. Trust, George A.

Newark Museum — an emergency grant to help meet current budget deficit ($100,000) see Victoria Foundation

Newark Public Library — to renovate the North End branch library and toward the position of coordinator ($139,000) see Victoria Foundation

Newark Renaissance House — residential youth program ($65,000) see Turrell Fund

Newton Memorial Hospital ($5,000) see Quincy Newspapers

North Ward Center — continuing support ($50,000) see Schumann Fund for New Jersey

Nurses Registry of Plainfield ($10,000) see Fanwood Foundation

Occupational Center of Essex County ($8,000) see Luce Charitable Trust, Theodore

Occupational Center of Essex County ($15,000) see Ohl, Jr. Trust, George A.

Ocean County Unit of Retarded Citizens ($6,000) see Havens Foundation, O. W.

Odyssey of the Mind — to provide scholarships to high school seniors who are participants in the national OM competition in creative problem solving ($50,000) see American Honda Motor Co.

Oldwick Fire Company ($1,000) see Klipstein Foundation, Ernest Christian

One to One Foundation ($50,000) see Boisi Family Foundation

1991 Waterloo Festival School of Music ($25,000) see Bergen Foundation, Frank and Lydia

Opera Music Theatre International ($3,000) see Bedminster Fund

Opera Music Theatre International ($11,500) see Wyne Foundation

Orange Neighborhood House ($6,500) see Ohl, Jr. Trust, George A.

Orange Neighborhood House ($15,000) see Orange Orphan Society

Our Lady of Lourdes Medical Center — Nursery Unit modernization ($35,000) see Campbell Soup Co.

Our Lady of Mount Carmel Church ($125) see Martini Foundation, Nicholas

Outside Cuba Symposium ($10,000) see Cintas Foundation

Overlook Hospital ($15,000) see Willits Foundation

Overlook Hospital — $15,000 general charitable contribution, $10,000 pledge ($25,000) see Carter-Wallace

Overlook Hospital Foundation ($30,000) see Bard, C. R.

Overlook Hospital Foundation ($80,000) see Grassmann Trust, E. J.

Overlook Hospital Foundation ($5,000) see Read Foundation, Charles L.

Overlook Hospital Foundation ($17,000) see Union Foundation

Partnership of New Jersey ($10,000) see CIT Group Holdings

Partnership for New Jersey, Early Childhood Facilities Fund — create a financial intermediary to expand and improve child-care facilities ($200,000) see Prudential Insurance Co. of America

Pascack Valley Hospital ($7,168) see Holzer Memorial Foundation, Richard H.

Pascack Valley Hospital Foundation ($7,500) see Schamach Foundation, Milton

Pascack Valley Meals on Wheels ($10,070) see Freygang Foundation, Walter Henry

Passaic Valley Hospital Foundation ($1,000) see Kajima International, Inc.

Passport Award for Staying in School (PASS) see Valley National Bancorp

Paterson Alumni Association ($30,500) see Taub Foundation, Henry and Marilyn

Paterson Alumni Association ($20,505) see Taub Foundation, Joseph and Arlene

Paterson Police Athletic League ($150) see Martini Foundation, Nicholas

Peddie School ($100,000) see Beneficial Corp.

Peddie School ($10,000) see Bunbury Company

Pennington First Aid Squad ($100) see Homasote Co.

Philanthropic Fund of Jewish Community Foundation ($98,925) see Sagamore Foundation

Pingry School ($25,000) see Bunbury Company

Pingry School — scholarships ($10,000) see Vernon Fund, Miles Hodsdon

Plainfield Symphony ($2,500) see McCutchen Foundation

Planned Parenthood of Bergen County ($10,000) see Rutgers Community Health Foundation

Planned Parenthood Federation of America ($10,500) see Schenck Fund, L. P.

Planned Parenthood Federation of America — national assistance family planning ($50,000) see Schultz Foundation

Port Richmond High School ($10,000) see Anderson Foundation

Pottersville Volunteer Fire Company ($2,000) see Darby Foundation

Presbyterian Church ($12,000) see Willits Foundation

Presbyterian Church ($6,000) see Willits Foundation

Princeton in Asia ($5,000) see Kajima International, Inc.

Princeton Ballet Society ($25,000) see McGraw Foundation, Curtis W.

Princeton-Blairstown Center ($10,000) see Borden Memorial Foundation, Mary Owen

Princeton Center for Leadership Training ($10,500) see Ohl, Jr. Trust, George A.

Princeton Center for Leadership Training ($142,480) see Sears, Roebuck and Co.

Princeton Center for Leadership Training — Jersey City peer leadership project ($48,000) see Turrell Fund

Princeton Center for Leadership Training-Peer Group Connection — to support a program in five states that prepares high school seniors to serve as role models for younger students ($139,000) see Coca-Cola Co.

Princeton Day School ($20,000) see McGraw Foundation, Curtis W.

Princeton Dollars for Scholars ($2,000) see Wedum Foundation

Princeton Friends School ($20,000) see McGraw Foundation, Curtis W.

Princeton Graduate Fellowship ($10,000) see Weston Associates/R.C.M. Corp.

Princeton Theological Seminary ($13,000) see Palmer Fund, Francis Asbury

Princeton Theological Seminary ($4,000) see Schautz Foundation, Walter L.

Princeton Theological Seminary ($3,000) see Shattuck Charitable Trust, S. F.

Princeton Theological Seminary ($11,417) see Snyder Foundation, Harold B. and Dorothy A.

Princeton Theological Seminary ($10,000) see Warwick Foundation

Princeton University ($30,000) see Allen Foundation, Rita

Princeton University ($100) see Beitzell & Co.

Princeton University ($41,500) see Botwinick- Wolfensohn Foundation

Princeton University see Brakeley, John Price Jones Inc.

Princeton University ($25,000) see Carvel Foundation, Thomas and Agnes

Princeton University ($25,000) see Cohn Foundation, Peter A. and Elizabeth S.

Princeton University — endowment ($250,000) see Devonwood Foundation

Princeton University ($50,000) see Firestone Foundation, Roger S.

Princeton University ($50,000) see General Atlantic Partners L.P.

Princeton University ($12,000) see Glancy Foundation, Lenora and Alfred

Princeton University ($2,500) see Goldie-Anna Charitable Trust

Princeton University ($9,543) see Goldman Sachs & Co.

Princeton University ($10,000) see I and G Charitable Foundation

Princeton University ($1,500) see Klipstein Foundation, Ernest Christian

Princeton University ($11,000) see Love Foundation, George H. and Margaret McClintic

Princeton University ($500,000) see Lowenstein Foundation, Leon

Princeton University ($10,000) see Memton Fund

Princeton University — to support research on energy efficiency technologies and alternatives to fossil fuels and nuclear power ($75,000) see Merck Fund, John

Princeton University ($5,000) see Mulford Foundation, Vincent

Princeton University ($73,000) see Parvin Foundation, Albert

Princeton University ($21,180) see Salomon

Princeton University ($1,000) see Schiff, Hardin & Waite

Princeton University ($46,705) see Schoonmaker J-Sewkly Valley Hospital Trust

Princeton University — blood brain barrier research ($100,000) see Schultz Foundation

Princeton University ($100,000) see Seaver Institute

Princeton University — academic tournament ($1,000) see Stuart Foundation, Edward C.

Princeton University ($25,000) see Walker Foundation, L. C. and Margaret

Princeton University ($10,000) see Warwick Foundation

Princeton University ($10,000) see Warwick Foundation

Princeton University ($225,000) see Weinberg Foundation, John L.

Princeton University ($217,500) see Whiting Foundation, Mrs. Giles

Princeton University Department of East Asian Studies ($50,000) see China Times Cultural Foundation

Princeton University — scholarships for foreign students of East Indian ancestry ($6,000) see Watumull Fund, J.

Princeton University — for Ira W. DeCamp university professorship endowment ($300,000) see DeCamp Foundation, Ira W.

Princeton University-Nadelmann ($327,300) see Smart Family Foundation

Princeton University — renewed support for Phase II of the Human Information Processing Group ($512,500) see McDonnell Foundation, James S.

Princeton University — conference focused on ritual, performing arts, plastic arts, and literary composition in Bali ($10,000) see Wenner-Gren Foundation for Anthropological Research

Princeton University School of Engineering ($30,000) see New-Land Foundation

Princeton University — in support of the University's annual giving campaign ($100,000) see Hillman Foundation, Henry L.

Princeton University — Upton Fellowship Program ($96,560) see Upton Charitable Foundation, Lucy and Eleanor S.

Professional Secretaries ($100) see Homasote Co.

Protestant Community Center — general support; to fund a full time Education Coordinator ($101,000) see Victoria Foundation

Purnell School ($25,000) see Cox Foundation

Rabbinical College of America ($50,000) see Wilf Family Foundation

Race Track Chaplaincy ($15,000) see Jockey Club Foundation

Raptor Trust ($3,000) see Bailey Wildlife Foundation

Recording for the Blind ($500) see Scherer Foundation, Karla

Recording for the Blind ($5,000) see Ziegler Foundation for the Blind, E. Matilda

Recording for the Blind — Anne T. Macdonald Center ($10,000) see Clayton Fund

Recording for the Blind — to establish electronic text programs which will provide PC-compatible disks of science and math textbooks for use by print-disabled students ($30,000) see NEC USA

Recording for the Blind — to provide tape-recorded textbooks to blind and other print- disabled individuals residing in North Carolina ($25,000) see Glaxo

Recording for the Blind — Vision for the Future Fund Drive ($100,000) see Herrick Foundation

Renew ($100,000) see Brencanda Foundation

Rescue Mission of Trenton ($10,000) see Borden Memorial Foundation, Mary Owen

Rescue Mission of Trenton ($15,000) see Kerney Foundation, James

Respiratory Health Assocaition see Valley National Bancorp

Richard G. Rosenthal YM-YWHA of Northern Westchester ($528,200) see Rosenthal Foundation, Richard and Lois

Richard Nixon Presidential Archives Foundation ($50,000) see Hooker Charitable Trust, Janet A.

Rider College (Holocaust Resource Center) ($1,000) see Abrams Foundation

Rolling Hills Girl Scout Council ($3,000) see Klipstein Foundation, Ernest Christian

Rolling Hills Girl Scout Council ($15,500) see Large Foundation

Rolling Hills Girl Scout Council ($13,000) see Thomas & Betts Corp.

Roman Catholic Archbishop of Newark ($250,000) see Murphy Foundation, Dan

Rona Stern Staut Hematology/Oncology

Foundation ($10,000) see
Hansen Memorial Foundation,
Irving

Rumson Country Day School —
alteration and modernization
of its facilities ($50,000) see
Hyde and Watson Foundation

Rutgers Foundation ($10,000)
see Terner Foundation

Rutgers Preparatory School
($1,000) see Klipstein
Foundation, Ernest Christian

Rutgers University see Brakeley,
John Price Jones Inc.

Rutgers University ($7,000) see
Christodora

Rutgers University ($7,500) see
CIT Group Holdings

Rutgers University ($15,000) see
Katzenberger Foundation

Rutgers University ($41,000) see
Levin Foundation, Philip and
Janice

Rutgers University ($20,000) see
Life Investors Insurance
Company of America

Rutgers University ($20,000) see
Lipton, Thomas J.

Rutgers University ($5,000) see
Manville Corp.

Rutgers University — general
operating support ($100,495)
see MCJ Foundation

Rutgers University ($74,693) see
Randolph Foundation

Rutgers University —
scholarships ($600) see Red
Devil

Rutgers University —
scholarships ($600) see Red
Devil

Rutgers University —
scholarships ($600) see Red
Devil

Rutgers University —
scholarships ($600) see Red
Devil

Rutgers University ($20,000) see
Robinson Fund, Maurice R.

Rutgers University ($20,000) see
Robinson Fund, Maurice R.

Rutgers University ($250,000)
see Warner-Lambert Co.

Rutgers University-Camden
Campus — primarily for
scholarships and faculty
support ($225,000) see
Campbell Soup Co.

Rutgers University College of
Pharmacy ($50,000) see
Lipton, Thomas J.

Rutgers University Foundation
($40,000) see National Starch
& Chemical Corp.

Rutgers University Foundation
($40,000) see National Starch
& Chemical Corp.

Rutgers University Foundation
($14,000) see Thomas & Betts
Corp.

Rutgers University Foundation,
Department of Biological
Sciences — supports efforts to
restore native plant
communities on capped
landfills in the Meadowlands
($32,111) see Schumann Fund
for New Jersey

Rutgers University Foundation
— urban services project of
New Jersey network for family
life education ($15,000) see
Freed Foundation

Rutgers University Foundation
— Thomas Edison Papers
($15,000) see Upton
Charitable Foundation, Lucy
and Eleanor S.

Rutgers University — Win
Project ($50,000) see Bell
Atlantic Corp.

S.I.M International Sudan
Interior Mission ($18,000) see
Kejr Foundation

Sacred Heart Church ($10,000)
see Kerney Foundation, James

St. Anthony's High School —
athletic department ($75) see
Martini Foundation, Nicholas

St. Barnabas Trustee Campaign
($10,000) see CIT Group
Holdings

St. Benedicts Prep ($20,000) see
Sandy Hill Foundation

St. Benedicts Preparatory School
— general ($16,500) see Beck
Foundation, Elsie E. & Joseph
W.

St. Benedict's Preparatory
School ($169,174) see
Brennan Foundation, Robert E.

St. Benedict's Preparatory
School ($40,000) see
Grassmann Trust, E. J.

St. Bernards School ($5,000) see
Willits Foundation

St. Clares-Riverside Foundation
Project 2000 ($50,000) see
Nabisco Foods Group

St. Elizabeth Hospital
($125,000) see Grassmann
Trust, E. J.

St. Elizabeth Hospital ($20,000)
see Prange Co., H. C.

St. Elizabeth Hospital ($28,000)
see Union Foundation

St. Elizabeth Hospital
Foundation ($10,000) see
Thomas & Betts Corp.

St. Francis Hospital ($103,000)
see Link, Jr. Foundation,
George

St. Joseph's Hospital and
Medical Center ($9,250) see
Schamach Foundation, Milton

St. Peter's College ($30,000) see
Van Houten Charitable Trust

St. Peter's Medical Center
($40,000) see Link, Jr.
Foundation, George

St. Peter's Preparatory ($54,000)
see Link, Jr. Foundation,
George

St. Stephens Armenian Church
($2,500) see Simone
Foundation

St. Vincent Academy ($45,000)
see Grassmann Trust, E. J.

St. Vincents Academy — general
($30,000) see Beck
Foundation, Elsie E. & Joseph
W.

Salvation Army ($3,000) see
Brundage Charitable,
Scientific, and Wildlife
Conservation Foundation,
Charles E. and Edna T.

Salvation Army ($9,000) see
Havens Foundation, O. W.

Salvation Army ($2,000) see
Zock Endowment Trust

Salvation Army — children's
and youth services ($75,000)
see Turrell Fund

Sea Girt Library ($150,000) see
Zock Endowment Trust

Seeing Eye ($200,000) see Kirby
Foundation, F. M.

Seeing Eye — Wallace S. Jones
Memorial Fund ($25,000) see
International Foundation

Seton Hall Pre ($25,000) see
Sandy Hill Foundation

Seton Hall Prep — general
($23,500) see Beck
Foundation, Elsie E. & Joseph
W.

Seton Hall Prep ($50,000) see
Sandy Hill Foundation

Seton Hall University ($28,925)
see Brennan Foundation,
Robert E.

Seton Hall University ($1,000)
see KSM Foundation

Seton Hall University ($10,000)
see Meyer Memorial
Foundation, Aaron and Rachel

Seton Hall University ($5,000)
see Roche Relief Foundation,
Edward and Ellen

Seton Hall University ($210,000)
see Sandy Hill Foundation

Seton Hall University-Peter
Rodino Chair Law School
($200,000) see
Warner-Lambert Co.

Seton Hall University —
restricted, maintenance of
Beck Hall ($10,000) see Beck
Foundation, Elsie E. & Joseph
W.

Sisters of Mercy of New Jersey
($5,000) see McCutchen
Foundation

Sisters of Mercy of New Jersey
($5,000) see McCutchen
Foundation

Sisters of Mercy of New Jersey
($25,000) see Snite
Foundation, Fred B.

Social Services Federation
($125,128) see Schenck Fund,
L. P.

Somerset Hills Community
Chest ($5,000) see
Thanksgiving Foundation

Somerset Home for Temporarily
Displaced Children ($5,000)
see Schwartz Foundation,
Arnold A.

Somerset Medical Center
($10,000) see Duke
Foundation, Doris

Somerset Medical Center
($15,000) see Fanwood
Foundation

Somerset Medical Center
($10,000) see Harris Brothers
Foundation

Somerset Medical Center ($600)
see Red Devil

Somerset Medical Center
($5,000) see Schwartz
Foundation, Arnold A.

Somerset Medical Center
($12,000) see Thomas & Betts
Corp.

Somerset Valley YMCA
($17,000) see Thomas & Betts
Corp.

South Bergen Mental Health
Center ($9,200) see Mutual of
New York

Stevens Institute of Technology
($30,140) see Freygang
Foundation, Walter Henry

Stevens Institute of Technology
($30,000) see Shepherd
Foundation

Stevens Institute of Technology
($15,250) see Snyder
Foundation, Harold B. and
Dorothy A.

Stevens Institute of Technology
($11,675) see Snyder
Foundation, Harold B. and
Dorothy A.

Stevens Institute of Technology
($30,000) see Unilever United
States

Stockton State College ($22,500)
see SICO Foundation

Summer Educational
Opportunity Awards — for
grants to each of 24 teachers in
Morris County high schools to
enable them to pursue summer
educational opportunities
($125,000) see Dodge
Foundation, Geraldine R.

Summit Speech School — to
enable hearing impaired
children to communicate
effectively using speech

($100,000) see Cummings
Memorial Fund Trust, Frances
L. and Edwin L.

Tekeyan Cultural Association
($181,000) see Manoogian
Foundation, Alex and Marie

Temple B'nai Abraham ($3,412)
see Jaydor Corp.

Temple Sinai ($32,485) see Taub
Foundation, Henry and Marilyn

Textile Research Institute
($72,500) see Milliken & Co.

Tomorrow's Children ($5,000)
see Daily News

Tomorrow's Children Fund see
Valley National Bancorp

Trustees of Princeton University
($50,000) see Bunbury
Company

Turning Point ($15,000) see
McGraw Foundation, Donald
C.

Unified Vailsburg Services
Organziation — grass-roots
community organization
provides Meals-on-Wheels,
senior citizen services, youth
and day care programs, and
neighborhood housing
development ($45,000) see
Schumann Fund for New
Jersey

Union Hospital Foundation
($25,000) see Snyder
Foundation, Harold B. and
Dorothy A.

Union Hospital Foundation for
Happiness ($50,000) see
Simon Foundation, William E.
and Carol G.

United Family and Children's
Society ($6,000) see Harris
Brothers Foundation

United Jewish Appeal of Bergen
County — general support
($50,000) see Lowe
Foundation, Joe and Emily

United Jewish Appeal Federation
of Jewish Philanthropies
($50,000) see Garfinkle
Family Foundation

United Jewish Appeal Federation
of Jewish Philanthropies
($67,500) see Seevak Family
Foundation

United Jewish Appeal Federation
of Jewish Philanthropies
($10,000) see Seevak Family
Foundation

United Jewish Appeal Federation
of Jewish Philanthropies
($10,000) see Seevak Family
Foundation

United Jewish Community of
Bergen County ($5,000) see
Greene Foundation, David J.

United Jewish Community of
Bergen County ($989,366) see
Taub Foundation, Henry and
Marilyn

United States Equestrian Team
($1,000) see Saul Foundation,
Joseph E. & Norma G.

United Way ($1,000) see Abrams
Foundation

United Way ($2,000) see Brand
Cos.

United Way ($28,750) see Coltec
Industries

United Way ($10,880) see Coltec
Industries

United Way ($2,000) see Darby
Foundation

United Way ($68) see Goodall
Rubber Co.

United Way ($8,000) see Hamel
Family Charitable Trust, D. A.

United Way ($50,000) see Life
Investors Insurance Company
of America

United Way ($3,000) see
Maneely Fund

United Way ($4,000) see
Mulford Foundation, Vincent

United Way ($1,600) see United
Merchants & Manufacturers

United Way of Bergen ($52,500)
see Lipton, Thomas J.

United Way — Bergen County
($30,000) see Nabisco Foods
Group

United Way-Gergen County
($55,000) see Sony Corp. of
America

United Way of Morris County
($160,000) see Kirby
Foundation, F. M.

United Way — Morris County
($170,000) see Nabisco Foods
Group

United Way, Morris County
($300,000) see
Warner-Lambert Co.

United Way-Princeton Area
Communities ($40,000) see
Dow Jones & Co.

United Way of Somerset County
($149,000) see National Starch
& Chemical Corp.

United Way of Union County
($28,072) see Bard, C. R.

United Way of Union County
($328,950) see Merck & Co.

United Way - Union County
($12,000) see Thomas & Betts
Corp.

University of Medicine and
Dentistry — Environmental
and Occupation Health
Sciences Institute ($25,000)
see Sandoz Corp.

University of Medicine and
Dentistry Foundation
($200,000) see
Warner-Lambert Co.

University of Medicine and
Dentistry of New Jersey
($20,000) see Sinsheimer
Fund, Alexandrine and
Alexander L.

University of Medicine and
Dentistry of New Jersey —
special projects ($62,500) see
Turrell Fund

University of Medicine and
Dentistry of New Jersey
($5,000) see Willits Foundation

Upper Raritan Watershed
Association ($10,000) see
Cape Branch Foundation

Valley Hospital ($25,000) see
Jaqua Foundation

Valley Hospital Foundation
($7,500) see Schamach
Foundation, Milton

Valley Settlement House
($17,600) see Orange Orphan
Society

Van Ost Institute for Family
Living ($5,000) see Kennedy
Foundation, Quentin J.

Van Ost Institute for Family
Living ($20,000) see Schenck
Fund, L. P.

Vietnam Veterans Memorial
Fund ($600) see Homasote Co.

Visiting Health and Supportive
Services ($24,000) see Large
Foundation

Waterloo Foundation for the Arts
($150,000) see Beneficial
Corp.

Waterloo Foundation for the Arts
($25,000) see Bergen
Foundation, Frank and Lydia

Waterloo Foundation for the Arts
($60,000) see Caspersen
Foundation for Aid to Health
and Education, O. W.

Wayne General Hospital
($12,500) see Meyer Memorial
Foundation, Aaron and Rachel

New Jersey (cont.)

Wayne General Hospital ($8,000) see Schamach Foundation, Milton

West Hudson Hospital see Valley National Bancorp

West Jersey Health System — underwrote the cost of nurseries in largest obstetrics program ($60,000) see Campbell Soup Co.

West Orange Community House ($17,600) see Orange Orphan Society

West Trenton Volunteer Fire Company ($1,000) see Homasote Co.

Westfield Symphony ($10,000) see Bergen Foundation, Frank and Lydia

Westminster Choir College — toward general operations and educational programs ($500,000) see Hillman Foundation

Westminster Choir College ($20,000) see Valentine Foundation, Lawson

Westminster Church Choir ($5,000) see Love Foundation, George H. and Margaret McClintic

Windham Foundation ($12,500) see Bunbury Company

Womens Crisis Center ($20,000) see Large Foundation

Woodrow Wilson National Fellowship Foundation ($2,400) see Falk Medical Fund, Maurice

Woodrow Wilson National Fellowship Foundation — program in public policy and international affairs ($200,000) see Reed Foundation, Philip D.

Woodrow Wilson National Fellowship Foundation ($927,620) see Wallace-Reader's Digest Fund, DeWitt

Woodrow Wilson National Fellowship Foundation — for Mellon Fellowships in the Humanities program ($5,600,000) see Mellon Foundation, Andrew W.

Woodrow Wilson School of Public and International Affairs, Council on New Jersey Affairs — multi-year grant ($111,000) see Schumann Fund for New Jersey

Yearly Meeting Friends Home ($50,000) see McCutchen Foundation

YM-YMaa of North Jersey see Valley National Bancorp

YMCA ($10,000) see Brady Foundation

YMCA ($20,000) see Day Family Foundation

YMCA ($10,000) see Day Family Foundation

YMCA ($5,000) see Harris Brothers Foundation

YMCA ($10,000) see Havens Foundation, O. W.

YMCA ($12,500) see Large Foundation

YMCA ($15,000) see Ohl, Jr. Trust, George A.

YMCA ($38,700) see Orange Orphan Society

YMCA ($8,333) see Smeal Foundation, Mary Jean & Frank P.

YMCA of Eastern Union County — completion of improvements to its existing facilities ($30,000) see Hyde and Watson Foundation

YMCA-Oranges, Maplewood, West Essex and Sussex county, New Jersey ($75,000) see Turrell Fund

Youth Consultation Services ($45,000) see Schenck Fund, L. P.

YWCA ($2,000) see Concord Chemical Co.

YWCA ($23,700) see Orange Orphan Society

New Mexico

Alamogordo Civic Auditorium ($34,000) see National Presto Industries

Albuquerque Museum ($12,273) see Weisman Art Foundation, Frederick R.

Albuquerque Museum Foundation ($10,000) see Public Service Co. of New Mexico

American Diabetes Association, New Mexico Affiliate — summer camp program ($50,000) see Bellamah Foundation, Dale J.

Amigos Bravos ($2,500) see Healy Family Foundation, M. A.

Animal Alliance — program to reduce dog/cat populations, educate rural people in humane animal care, and train local veterinarians and graduate students in modern medical and surgical techniques ($40,000) see Frost Foundation

Archaeological Conservancy ($20,000) see Driscoll Foundation

Armand Hammer United World College of the American West ($1,800,000) see Hammer United World College Trust, Armand

Boys and Girls Club of Hobbs ($128,000) see Maddox Foundation, J. F.

Carlsbad Association of Retarded Citizens ($100,000) see Maddox Foundation, J. F.

Carrie Tingley Hospital Foundation — Spencer Cerebral Palsy Clinic ($55,000) see Bancroft, Jr. Foundation, Hugh

Casa Esperanza ($15,000) see Public Service Co. of New Mexico

Casa Experanza — general support ($50,000) see Solo Cup Co.

Chaparral Home and Adoption Services ($7,500) see Burns Family Foundation

College of Santa Fe ($1,000,000) see Mabee Foundation, J. E. and L. E.

College of the Southwest ($79,818) see Maddox Foundation, J. F.

Cystic Fibrosis Foundation ($10,000) see Oxnard Foundation

Daughters of Charity of Canossa, Casa Angelica Foundation — care of mentally retarded ($104,296) see Bellamah Foundation, Dale J.

Eastern New Mexico University ($5,000) see Public Service Co. of New Mexico

First United Methodist Church ($51,000) see Maddox Foundation, J. F.

Four Corners Interstate MESA Jamboree ($50,000) see American Honda Motor Co.

Futures for Children ($1,500) see Chanin Family Foundation, Paul R.

Girl Scouts of America ($10,000) see Cogswell Benevolent Trust

Guidance Center of Lea County ($264,750) see Maddox Foundation, J. F.

Hokoji ($5,000) see Healy Family Foundation, M. A.

Hubbard Museum, Anne C. Stradling Museum of the Horse — toward renovation of the old Chaparral Convention Center, home for Anne Stradling's collection of horse-related artifacts ($2,930,000) see Hubbard Foundation, R. Dee and Joan Dale

Institute of American Indian Arts ($50,000) see Healy Family Foundation, M. A.

KRWG FM Radio and TV ($3,000) see Huthsteiner Fine Arts Trust

La Compania de Teatro de Albuquerque ($5,000) see Public Service Co. of New Mexico

Lighthawk ($4,500) see Harris Foundation, William H. and Mattie Wattis

Lighthawk see Patagonia

Little Brothers of Good Shepherd ($275,000) see Murphy Foundation, Dan

Lovington Municipal Schools ($758,300) see Maddox Foundation, J. F.

Monastery of Christ in the Desert ($25,000) see Louis Foundation, Michael W.

Mount Light Center ($2,500) see Healy Family Foundation, M. A.

Museum New Mexico ($26,500) see Herzstein Charitable Foundation, Albert and Ethel

Museum of New Mexico Foundation ($2,000) see Miller-Mellor Association

New Mexico Boys and Girls Ranch ($30,000) see Bancroft, Jr. Foundation, Hugh

New Mexico Boys and Girls Ranch ($7,500) see Burns Family Foundation

New Mexico Boys and Girls Ranch Foundation ($151,000) see Maddox Foundation, J. F.

New Mexico Boys Ranch and Girls Ranch ($25,000) see Kerr Foundation

New Mexico Christian Children's Home — building construction ($100,000) see Doss Foundation, M. S.

New Mexico Christian Children's Home ($118,350) see Maddox Foundation, J. F.

New Mexico Community Foundation — to assist in developing church preservation plans ($25,000) see Skaggs Foundation, L. J. and Mary C.

New Mexico Highlands University Foundation ($9,000) see Public Service Co. of New Mexico

New Mexico MESA ($33,333) see American Honda Motor Co.

New Mexico Military Institute ($107,800) see Kerr Foundation

New Mexico Military Institute — scholarships and centennial projects ($50,000) see Rockwell Fund

New Mexico Museum of Natural History Foundation ($25,000) see Phillips Foundation, Waite and Genevieve

New Mexico School for the Visually Handicapped ($2,500) see Goldie-Anna Charitable Trust

New Mexico Symphony Orchestra ($100,000) see Bancroft, Jr. Foundation, Hugh

New Mexico Symphony Orchestra ($52,500) see Leonhardt Foundation, Frederick H.

New Mexico Tech Presidents Club ($10,000) see Phillips Foundation, Waite and Genevieve

Philmont Scout Ranch ($51,637) see Phillips Foundation, Waite and Genevieve

Presbyterian Health Care Foundation ($20,000) see Phillips Foundation, Waite and Genevieve

Project Lighthawk ($10,000) see Sacharuna Foundation

Roadrunners Recycling ($10,000) see Healy Family Foundation, M. A.

St. Bonaventure Catholic Indian Mission — four-wheel drive ($6,000) see Butler Foundation, J. Homer

St. Catherine's Church ($100,000) see O'Toole Foundation, Theresa and Edward

St. Elizabeth Shelter ($15,000) see Wardle Family Foundation

St. Francis Cathedral — elderly ministry ($10,000) see Hankamer Foundation, Curtis and Doris K.

Saint Joseph's Hospital — purchase of hospital equipment ($100,000) see Bellamah Foundation, Dale J.

Saint Joseph's Hospital — nursing scholarships ($50,000) see Bellamah Foundation, Dale J.

St. Pauls Catholic Missions — van ($21,368) see Hackett Foundation

Santa Fe Chamber Music Festival — 1991 O'Keefe posters ($30,000) see Driscoll Foundation

Santa Fe Institute — systems research ($20,000) see Maxfield Foundation

Santa Fe Institute ($12,000) see Walker Educational and Charitable Foundation, Alex C.

Santa Fe Mountain Center ($5,000) see Westport Fund

Santa Fe Opera ($3,000) see Cranshaw Corporation

Santa Fe Opera ($50,000) see Stieren Foundation, Arthur T. and Jane J.

Santa Fe Opera ($15,000) see Thornton Foundation, Flora L.

Santa Fe Opera Foundation ($50,000) see Stieren Foundation, Arthur T. and Jane J.

Santa Fe Opera — general production grant for Strauss' Capriccio for 1993 season ($75,000) see Skaggs Foundation, L. J. and Mary C.

Santa Fe Partners in Education ($10,000) see Public Service Co. of New Mexico

Santa Fe Watercolor Society ($21,500) see Hubbard

Foundation, R. Dee and Joan Dale

School of American Research ($260,000) see Weatherhead Foundation

Society of Our Lady of the Most Holy Trinity ($1,500) see Kasal Charitable Trust, Father

Southwest Research and Information Center — oil and gas wastes ($15,000) see Beldon Fund

Southwest Research and Information Center — for work on issues pertaining to the Department of Energy's nuclear weapons production facilities ($35,000) see Rockefeller Family Fund

Taso County Economic Development Corporation — community organizer and operating support for Costilla Arts and Crafts Cooperative ($22,390) see Levinson Foundation, Max and Anna

Taso County Economic Development Corporation — Creation of small business and employment opportunities for low-income minority residents of Taso County ($15,000) see Levinson Foundation, Max and Anna

University of New Mexico ($302,910) see Herzstein Charitable Foundation, Albert and Ethel

University of New Mexico ($77,712) see Levi Strauss & Co.

University of New Mexico — scholar program ($60,000) see Mallinckrodt, Jr. Foundation, Edward

University of New Mexico ($38,985) see Oxnard Foundation

University of New Mexico ($250,000) see Sunwest Bank of Albuquerque, N.A.

University of New Mexico Foundation ($5,100) see Public Service Co. of New Mexico

Visiting Nurses Association ($12,000) see McKee Foundation, Robert E. and Evelyn

Wagon Mound Public Schools — art, science, and library department ($1,500) see Seidman Family Foundation

Water Lines ($7,500) see Wardle Family Foundation

Western New Mexico University ($5,000) see Public Service Co. of New Mexico

Youth Development ($11,400) see Public Service Co. of New Mexico

New York

A. J. Muste Memorial Institute ($23,000) see Rubin Foundation, Samuel

A. O. Fox Memorial Hospital ($100,000) see Dewar Foundation

A.F. Moschant Ohal ($15,000) see Hidary Foundation, Jacob

A.O. Fox Memorial Hospital ($25,000) see Warren and Beatrice W. Blanding Foundation, Riley J. and Lillian N.

A.O. Fox Memorial Hospital Chaplaincy Program ($6,000) see Warren and Beatrice W. Blanding Foundation, Riley J. and Lillian N.

New York (cont.)

Alvin Ailey Dance Theatre Foundation ($150,000) see Brody Foundation, Carolyn and Kenneth D.

Alzheimers Association see MBIA, Inc.

Alzheimer's Disease and Related Disorders Association ($1,000) see Baldwin Foundation, David M. and Barbara

Alzheimer's Disease and Related Disorders Association ($50,000) see Cohen Foundation, Wilfred P.

Alzheimer's Disease and Related Disorders Association ($15,000) see Cornell Trust, Peter C.

Alzheimer's Disease and Related Disorders Association ($8,500) see Israel Foundation, A. Cremieux

Alzheimer's Disease and Related Disorders Association — continuing research ($20,000) see Kaufmann Foundation, Marion Esser

Alzheimer's Disease and Related Disorders Association ($11,000) see Meyer Memorial Foundation, Aaron and Rachel

Alzheimer's Disease and Related Disorders Association ($25,000) see Miller Fund, Kathryn and Gilbert

Alzheimer's Disease and Related Disorders Association ($10,000) see Seevak Family Foundation

American Academy of Achievement ($10,000) see Greenberg Foundation, Alan C.

American Academy of Achievement ($25,000) see Mattus Foundation, Reuben and Rose

American Academy of Dramatic Arts ($25,000) see Freeman Charitable Trust, Samuel

American Academy in Rome ($48,000) see Kress Foundation, Samuel H.

American Academy in Rome ($35,000) see Lehman Foundation, Robert

American Academy in Rome ($17,600) see Replogle Foundation, Luther I.

American Assembly ($50,000) see Harriman Foundation, Mary W.

American Assembly — "The Cities and the Nations" ($100,000) see Citicorp

American Associates of Ben Gurion University ($20,000) see Benenson Foundation, Frances and Benjamin

American Associates of Ben Gurion University ($100,000) see Feinberg Foundation, Joseph and Bessie

American Associates of Ben Gurion University ($150,000) see Fohs Foundation

American Associates of Ben Gurion University ($5,000) see Gulton Foundation

American Associates of Ben Gurion University — agricultural research project ($280,000) see Moriah Fund

American Associates of Ben Gurion University ($1,000) see Poorvu Foundation, William and Lia

American Associates of Ben Gurion University — agricultural research project

($60,000) see Posnack Family Foundation of Hollywood

American Associates of Ben Gurion University ($10,000) see Smithers Foundation, Christopher D.

American Associates of Ben Gurion University ($10,000) see Spingold Foundation, Nate B. and Frances

American Associates of Ben Gurion University ($5,000) see Steinberg Family Foundation, Meyer and Jean

American Associates, Ben Gurion University of the Negev ($750,000) see Blaustein Foundation, Jacob and Hilda

American Associates of Ben Gurion University of the Negev ($500,000) see Mitrani Family Foundation

American Associates of Ben Gurion University of the Negev ($500,000) see Mitrani Family Foundation

American Associates of the Royal National Theatre ($10,000) see Matz Foundation — Edelman Division

American Association for Bikur Cholim Hospital ($60,000) see Cohen Foundation, Naomi and Nehemiah

American Association for Bikur Cholim Hospital Jerusalem ($100,000) see Morgenstern Foundation, Morris

American Association International Center-University Teaching of Jewish Civilization ($5,000) see Sang Foundation, Elsie O. and Philip D.

American Ballet Theater ($10,000) see Osborn Charitable Trust, Edward B.

American Ballet Theater ($10,000) see Picower Foundation, Jeffrey M. and Barbara

American Ballet Theater ($10,000) see Randleigh Foundation Trust

American Ballet Theater ($40,000) see Rigler-Deutsch Foundation

American Ballet Theater — artist direction of 890 Fire Bird ($25,000) see Homeland Foundation

American Ballet Theatre ($25,000) see Capital Cities/ABC

American Ballet Theatre ($100,000) see Dana Charitable Trust, Eleanor Naylor

American Ballet Theatre ($6,000) see Kingsley Foundation

American Ballet Theatre ($50,000) see Mendel Foundation

American Ballet Theatre ($80,000) see Shubert Foundation

American Ballet Theatre ($7,500) see Werblow Charitable Trust, Nina W.

American Ballet Theatre, New York, NY ($100,000) see Equitable Life Assurance Society of the U.S.

American Baptist Home Mission ($15,750) see Clark Charitable Trust, Frank E.

American Baptist Home Mission Society ($17,500) see Clark Charitable Trust, Frank E.

American Cancer Society ($1,000) see Berry Foundation, Archie W. and Grace

American Cancer Society ($7,500) see Bluhdorn Charitable Trust, Charles G. and Yvette

American Cancer Society ($5,500) see Colt Foundation, James J.

American Cancer Society ($50) see Community Health Association

American Cancer Society ($10,000) see DCNY Corp.

American Cancer Society ($10,000) see EG&G Inc.

American Cancer Society ($7,500) see Ernest & Julio Gallo Winery

American Cancer Society ($500) see Erteszek Foundation

American Cancer Society ($10,000) see Ford III Memorial Foundation, Jefferson Lee

American Cancer Society ($16,000) see Grader Foundation, K. W.

American Cancer Society ($2,000) see Hovnanian Foundation, Hirair and Anna

American Cancer Society ($975) see Jaydor Corp.

American Cancer Society ($5,000) see Key Food Stores Cooperative Inc.

American Cancer Society ($5,000) see MacDonald Foundation, James A.

American Cancer Society see New York Mercantile Exchange

American Cancer Society ($5,000) see Ottenstein Family Foundation

American Cancer Society ($10,000) see Phillips Charitable Trust, Dr. and Mrs. Arthur William

American Cancer Society ($5,212) see Rankin and Elizabeth Forbes Rankin Trust, William

American Cancer Society ($4,754) see Rankin and Elizabeth Forbes Rankin Trust, William

American Cancer Society ($2,000) see Shea Foundation

American Cancer Society — Dreamball - "Look Good...Feel Better Program" ($15,000) see International Flavors & Fragrances

American Civil Liberties Union — immigrant rights project ($30,000) see Norman Foundation

American Civil Liberties Union Foundation ($10,000) see Armington Fund, Evenor

American Civil Liberties Union Foundation ($25,000) see Brody Foundation, Carolyn and Kenneth D.

American Civil Liberties Union Foundation ($10,000) see Brush Foundation

American Civil Liberties Union Foundation ($25,000) see Bydale Foundation

American Civil Liberties Union Foundation ($25,000) see Cabot Family Charitable Trust

American Civil Liberties Union Foundation ($4,500) see Candlesticks Inc.

American Civil Liberties Union Foundation ($5,000) see Cow Hollow Foundation

American Civil Liberties Union Foundation ($100,000) see Educational Foundation of America

American Civil Liberties Union Foundation ($30,000) see Glen Eagles Foundation

American Civil Liberties Union Foundation ($120,000) see Huber Foundation

American Civil Liberties Union Foundation ($50,000) see Kapor Family Foundation

American Civil Liberties Union Foundation ($20,000) see MacArthur Foundation, J. Roderick

American Civil Liberties Union Foundation ($10,000) see Mott Charitable Trust/Spectemur Agendo, Stewart R.

American Civil Liberties Union Foundation ($26,000) see Norman Foundation, Andrew

American Civil Liberties Union Foundation ($20,000) see Normandie Foundation

American Civil Liberties Union Foundation ($5,000) see Schecter Private Foundation, Aaron and Martha

American Civil Liberties Union Foundation ($75,000) see Scherman Foundation

American Civil Liberties Union Foundation — reproductive freedom project ($75,000) see Scherman Foundation

American Civil Liberties Union Foundation ($30,000) see Tortuga Foundation

American Civil Liberties Union Foundation — to support the Arts Censorship Project ($100,000) see Cummings Foundation, Nathan

American Civil Liberties Union Foundation — continuing support of Reproductive Freedom Project ($15,000) see Lowe Foundation, Joe and Emily

American Civil Liberties Union — women's rights project ($25,000) see Norman Foundation

American Committee for Shaare Zedek Hospital ($36,500) see Burns Foundation, Jacob

American Committee for Shaare Zedek Hospital ($185,000) see Forchheimer Foundation

American Committee for Shaare Zedek Hospital ($10,000) see Posnack Family Foundation of Hollywood

American Committee for Shaare Zedek Hospital ($6,000) see Propp Sons Fund, Morris and Anna

American Committee for Shaare Zedek Hospital ($2,500) see Rohlik Foundation, Sigmund and Sophie

American Committee for Shaare Zedek Hospital in Jerusalem ($64,820) see Jesselson Foundation

American Committee for the Tel Aviv Foundation ($20,000) see Macmillan, Inc.

American Committee for the Tel Aviv Foundation ($50,000) see Rudin Foundation, Samuel and May

American Committee for the Tel Aviv Foundation ($20,000) see Steinhardt Foundation, Judy and Michael

American Committee on United States/Soviet Relations

($15,000) see Bydale Foundation

American Committee for the Weizmann Institute ($25,000) see Abramson Family Foundation

American Committee for the Weizmann Institute ($5,000) see Bender Foundation

American Committee for the Weizmann Institute ($5,000) see Bennett Foundation, Carl and Dorothy

American Committee for the Weizmann Institute ($35,000) see Gulton Foundation

American Committee for the Weizmann Institute ($40,000) see Levy Foundation, Betty and Norman F.

American Committee for the Weizmann Institute ($25,000) see McGonagle Foundation, Dextra Baldwin

American Committee for the Weizmann Institute ($25,000) see Newman Assistance Fund, Jerome A. and Estelle R.

American Committee for the Weizmann Institute ($40,000) see Raskin Foundation, Hirsch and Braine

American Committee for the Weizmann Institute ($5,000) see Rohlik Foundation, Sigmund and Sophie

American Committee for Weizmann Institute ($25,000) see Shapiro Foundation, Charles and M. R.

American Committee for the Weizmann Institute ($65,000) see Stone Charitable Foundation

American Committee for the Weizmann Institute of Science ($2,000) see Broad Foundation, Shepard

American Committee for the Weizmann Institute of Science ($250,000) see Crown Memorial, Arie and Ida

American Committee for the Weizmann Institute of Science ($200) see Florsheim Shoe Co.

American Committee for the Weizmann Institute of Science ($1,000) see Herald News

American Committee for the Weizmann Institute of Science ($2,500,000) see Kimmelman Foundation, Helen & Milton

American Committee for the Weizmann Institute of Science ($10,000) see Kimmelman Foundation, Helen & Milton

American Committee for the Weizmann Institute of Sciences ($2,000) see Berger Foundation, Albert E.

American Committee for the Weizmann Institute of Sciences ($45,000) see Dweck Foundation, Samuel R.

American Committee for the Weizmann Institute of Sciences ($7,000) see Getz Foundation, Emma and Oscar

American Committee for the Weizmann Institute of Sciences ($61,551) see Weinstein Foundation, J.

American Composers Orchestra ($5,000) see Commerce Clearing House

American Composers Orchestra ($10,000) see Foundation for the Needs of Others

American Composers Orchestra ($2,500) see Goodman Family Foundation

American Composers Orchestra ($7,000) see Paul and C. Michael Paul Foundation, Josephine Bay

American Conservation Association ($2,000,000) see Jackson Hole Preserve

American Council for the Arts — support to improve management and communications skills for arts organizations see Ameritech Corp.

American Council of Drug Education ($26,500) see Cheatham Foundation, Owen

American Council on Germany ($3,000) see Gruss Petroleum Corp.

American Council on Germany ($10,000) see Hunt Foundation, Roy A.

American Council of Learned Societies ($62,500) see Reynolds Foundation, Christopher

American Council for Nationalities Service ($20,000) see MacArthur Foundation, J. Roderick

American Council on Science and Health ($35,000) see Gerstacker Foundation, Rollin M.

American Council on Science and Health see Millipore Corp.

American Council on Science and Health — general support see Nalco Chemical Co.

American Council on Science and Health, New York, NY — to assist in the completion of a series of new programs ($15,000) see Searle & Co., G.D.

American Craft Council ($76,460) see Chazen Foundation

American Craft Council — operating fund ($20,000) see Dow Foundation, Herbert H. and Barbara C.

American Craft Museum ($35,000) see Glickenhaus & Co.

American Diabetes Association ($1,000) see Key Bank of Maine

American Diabetes Association ($50,000) see Pincus Family Fund

American Diabetes Association ($35,000) see Schlink Foundation, Albert G. and Olive H.

American Diabetes Association ($10,000) see Schlink Foundation, Albert G. and Olive H.

American Documentary ($20,000) see MacArthur Foundation, J. Roderick

American Dominican Nuns of Fatima ($12,000) see Morania Foundation

American Express Foundation — funds for nationwide distribution ($540,000) see IDS Financial Services

American Federation for Aging Research ($25,000) see Bedminster Fund

American Federation for Aging Research ($2,500) see Brace Foundation, Donald C.

American Federation for Aging Research ($50,000) see Glenn Foundation for Medical Research, Paul F.

American Federation for Aging Research — research in the field of the aging ($50,000)

see Kaufmann Foundation, Marion Esser

American Federation for Aging Research ($100) see Kobacker Co.

American Federation for Aging Research ($100,000) see Loeb Foundation, Frances and John L.

American Federation for Aging Research — Creative Investigator Grants-Administrative Grant ($115,000) see AlliedSignal

American Federation of Arts ($3,500) see Schloss & Co., Marcus

American Foundation on Aging Research (AFAR) ($25,000) see Smeal Foundation, Mary Jean & Frank P.

American Foundation for AIDS Research ($20,000) see Bluhdorn Charitable Trust, Charles G. and Yvette

American Foundation for AIDS Research ($83,333) see Chartwell Foundation

American Foundation for AIDS Research ($5,000) see Dammann Fund

American Foundation for AIDS Research ($15,000) see Duke Foundation, Doris

American Foundation for AIDS Research ($15,000) see Eckman Charitable Foundation, Samuel and Rae

American Foundation for AIDS Research ($20,000) see Greenville Foundation

American Foundation for AIDS Research ($25,000) see Hughes Memorial Foundation, Charles Evans

American Foundation for AIDS Research ($10,000) see Larsen Fund

American Foundation for AIDS Research ($5,000) see Pyramid Foundation

American Foundation for AIDS Research ($28,000) see Schaffer Foundation, Michael & Helen

American Foundation for AIDS Research ($25,000) see Schiff Foundation, Dorothy

American Foundation for AIDS Research ($30,000) see Sulzberger Foundation

American Foundation for AIDS Research ($25,000) see Turner Fund, Ruth

American Foundation for AIDS Research ($12,000) see Winston Research Foundation, Harry

American Foundation for AIDS Research — donation to AIDS research ($212,750) see Mapplethorpe Foundation, Robert

American Foundation for the Blind ($6,250) see Beasley Foundation, Theodore and Beulah

American Foundation for the Blind ($10,000) see Rogers Foundation, Mary Stuart

American Foundation for the Blind ($11,000) see Simon Foundation, Sidney, Milton and Leoma

American Foundation for Boys Town of Jerusalem ($7,850) see Stern Family Foundation, Harry

American Friends of the Alliance Israelite Universelle ($50,000) see David-Weill Foundation, Michel

American Friends of Assaf Harofe Medical Center — third payment of $100,000 pledge ($25,000) see Hammer Foundation, Armand

American Friends of Assaf Harofeh Hospital ($112,000) see Milken Family Medical Foundation

American Friends of Assaf Harofeh Hospital ($56,000) see Milken Foundation, L. and S.

American Friends of Ateret Cohanim ($507,500) see Moskowitz Foundation, Irving I.

American Friends of Bet El Yeshiva Center ($21,500) see Lowenstein Foundation, William P. and Marie R.

American Friends of Bet El Yeshiva Center ($135,000) see Moskowitz Foundation, Irving I.

American Friends of Beth Hatefusoth ($15,000) see Columbia Savings Charitable Foundation

American Friends of Beth Hatefusoth ($5,000) see Nelco Sewing Machine Sales Corp.

American Friends of Bezel Academy ($100,000) see Cohen Foundation, Naomi and Nehemiah

American Friends of B'nei Akiva Yeshivas ($55,000) see Moskowitz Foundation, Irving I.

American Friends of Boys Town ($5,000) see Forbes Charitable Trust, Herman

American Friends of Elins Sourasky Tel Aviv Medical Center ($16,667) see Mitchell Family Foundation, Edward D. and Anna

American Friends of Haifa University ($12,400) see Spingold Foundation, Nate B. and Frances

American Friends of Hebrew University ($11,000) see Abrams Foundation, Benjamin and Elizabeth

American Friends of Hebrew University ($165,000) see Belfer Foundation

American Friends of the Hebrew University ($15,100) see Berger Foundation, Albert E.

American Friends of Hebrew University ($10,000) see Bernstein & Co., Sanford C.

American Friends of the Hebrew University ($30,000) see de Hirsch Fund, Baron

American Friends of the Hebrew University ($5,000) see Domino of California

American Friends of Hebrew University ($38,100) see Dorot Foundation

American Friends of the Hebrew University ($10,000) see Dweck Foundation, Samuel R.

American Friends of the Hebrew University ($25,000) see Ernest & Julio Gallo Winery

American Friends of the Hebrew University ($125,700) see Ford Foundation, Joseph F. and Clara

American Friends Hebrew University ($10,000) see Gurwin Foundation, J.

American Friends of Hebrew University ($2,000) see Gussman Foundation, Herbert and Roseline

American Friends of Hebrew University ($5,000) see Horowitz Foundation, Gedale B. and Barbara S.

American Friends of Hebrew University ($5,000) see Imerman Memorial Foundation, Stanley

American Friends of Hebrew University ($5,000) see Kohl Foundation, Sidney

American Friends of the Hebrew University ($5,000) see Matz Foundation — Edelman Division

American Friends of Hebrew University ($25,000) see Millstone Foundation

American Friends of Hebrew University ($25,000) see Millstone Foundation

American Friends of Hebrew University ($25,000) see Millstone Foundation

American Friends of Hebrew University ($25,000) see Millstone Foundation

American Friends of Hebrew University ($500,000) see Mitrani Family Foundation

American Friends of Hebrew University ($310,600) see Raleigh Linen Service/National Distributing Co.

American Friends of Hebrew University ($5,500) see Raskin Foundation, Hirsch and Braine

American Friends of Hebrew University ($20,000) see Schamach Foundation, Milton

American Friends of Hebrew University ($50,000) see Shapiro Charity Fund, Abraham

American Friends of Hebrew University ($5,000) see Shapiro Family Foundation, Soretta and Henry

American Friends of Hebrew University ($333,333) see Smith Family Foundation, Charles E.

American Friends of Hebrew University ($10,000) see Stone Charitable Foundation

American Friends of Hebrew University ($30,000) see Taub Foundation, Henry and Marilyn

American Friends of the Hebrew University ($5,000) see Taube Family Foundation

American Friends of Hebrew University ($100,000) see Winston Foundation, Norman and Rosita

American Friends of Hebrew University ($25,000) see Wolens Foundation, Kalman and Ida

American Friends of Hebrew University Department of Immunology ($10,000) see Harris Foundation, J. Ira and Nicki

American Friends Israel Museum ($15,000) see Bravmann Foundation, Ludwig

American Friends of Israel Museum ($25,000) see Cohen Foundation, Naomi and Nehemiah

American Friends of Israel Museum ($50,000) see de Rothschild Foundation, Edmond

American Friends of Israel Museum ($25,000) see Fairchild Corp.

American Friends of Israel Museum ($10,000) see

Feinstein Foundation, Myer and Rosaline

American Friends of Israel Museum ($7,000) see Fink Foundation

American Friends of Israel Museum ($2,000) see Fiterman Charitable Foundation, Miles and Shirley

American Friends of Israel Museum ($9,500) see Hillman Family Foundation, Alex

American Friends of Israel Museum ($12,500) see Honigman Foundation

American Friends of Israel Museum ($48,915) see Kevorkian Fund, Hagop

American Friends of Israel Museum ($4,000) see Propp Sons Fund, Morris and Anna

American Friends of Israel Museum ($30,000) see Rosen Foundation, Joseph

American Friends of Israel Museum ($1,250) see Schapiro Fund, M. A.

American Friends of Israel Museum ($200,000) see Skirball Foundation

American Friends of Israel Museum ($239,550) see Steinhardt Foundation, Judy and Michael

American Friends of Israel Museum ($75,000) see 21 International Holdings

American Friends of the Israel Museum ($29,900) see Weinstein Foundation, J.

American Friends of the Israel Philharmonic ($25,000) see Hammer Foundation, Armand

American Friends of Israel Philharmonic Orchestra ($5,000) see Getz Foundation, Emma and Oscar

American Friends of Israel Philharmonic Orchestra ($1,000) see Robin Family Foundation, Albert A.

American Friends of Israel Philharmonic Orchestra ($7,000) see Steinberg Family Foundation, Meyer and Jean

American Friends Jerusalem College of Technology ($15,000) see Jaqua Foundation

American Friends Karem B'Yav ($15,000) see Friedman Brothers Foundation

American Friends of Marha Hatch ($15,000) see Hidary Foundation, Jacob

American Friends Migdal Ohr ($18,000) see Eckman Charitable Foundation, Samuel and Rae

American Friends of National Galleries of Scotland ($67,720) see Heinz Foundation, Drue

American Friends of the National Gallery London ($1,666,667) see Annenberg Foundation

American Friends of National Portrait Gallery Foundation ($840,000) see Heinz Foundation, Drue

American Friends of Neot Kedumin ($33,000) see Greenberg Foundation, Alan C.

American Friends of Open University of Israel ($3,500) see Bronstein Foundation, Soloman and Sylvia

American Friends of Open University of Israel ($5,000) see Fink Foundation

New York (cont.)

American Friends of Open University of Israel ($50,000) see Rochlin Foundation, Abraham and Sonia

American Friends for Oxford ($50,000) see Burns Foundation, Jacob

American Friends of Philharmonic Orchestra ($1,650) see Gruss Charitable Foundation, Emanuel and Riane

American Friends Rab Kol Torah ($10,000) see Stern Foundation, Max

American Friends Service Committee ($7,000) see Abelard Foundation

American Friends Service Committee ($5,000) see Berlin Charitable Fund, Irving

American Friends Service Committee ($10,000) see McCutchen Foundation

American Friends Service Committee ($10,000) see Mulligan Charitable Trust, Mary S.

American Friends Service Committee ($10,000) see Mulligan Charitable Trust, Mary S.

American Friends Service Committee ($10,000) see Mulligan Charitable Trust, Mary S.

American Friends Service Committee ($10,000) see Mulligan Charitable Trust, Mary S.

American Friends Service Committee ($10,000) see Mulligan Charitable Trust, Mary S.

American Friends of Shalom Hartman Institute ($25,000) see Berrie Foundation, Russell

American Friends of Shvut Ami ($13,000) see Bravmann Foundation, Ludwig

American Friends Shvut Ami ($12,000) see Bravmann Foundation, Ludwig

American Friends of Tel Aviv Museum of Art — Rov V. and Niuta Titus Endowment Fund ($100,000) see Rubinstein Foundation, Helena

American Friends of Tel Aviv University ($30,000) see Fribourg Foundation

American Friends of Tel Aviv University ($123,000) see Gulton Foundation

American Friends of Tel Aviv University ($10,000) see Kaplun Foundation, Morris J. and Betty

American Friends of Tel Aviv University ($500,000) see Mitrani Family Foundation

American Friends of Tel Aviv University ($75,000) see Rochlin Foundation, Abraham and Sonia

American Friends of The Israel Museum ($325,000) see Rose Foundation, Billy

American Friends of Winchester Cathedral ($100,000) see Gordon/Rousmaniere/Roberts Fund

American Friends of Yeshiva ($5,000) see Mattus Foundation, Reuben and Rose

American Friends of Yeshivat B'nai Akiva ($57,000) see Ehrman Foundation, Fred and Susan

American Friends Yeshivat Shilo ($7,500) see Mattus Foundation, Reuben and Rose

American Friends of Zichron ($10,000) see Lipton Foundation

American Friends of Zvi La'Tzadik Chasidei Breslov ($5,000) see Lowenstein Foundation, William P. and Marie R.

American Gathering of Jewish Holocaust Survivors ($25,000) see Atran Foundation

American Heart Association ($16,650) see Bartsch Memorial Trust, Ruth

American Heart Association ($100,000) see Laerdal Foundation, Asmund S.

American Heart Association ($60,000) see Laerdal Foundation, Asmund S.

American Heart Association ($2,000) see Laerdal Foundation, Asmund S.

American Heart Association ($5,212) see Rankin and Elizabeth Forbes Rankin Trust, William

American Heart Association ($4,754) see Rankin and Elizabeth Forbes Rankin Trust, William

American Hospital of Paris — $10,000 general charitable contribution, $20,000 pledge ($30,000) see Carter-Wallace

American Hospital of Paris Foundation ($333,333) see Gould Foundation, Florence J.

American Hospital of Paris Foundation — pledge-French Designers Showhouse ($25,000) see International Flavors & Fragrances

American Humane Association ($32,852) see Killough Trust, Walter H. D.

American Indian College Fund — operating support and advertising campaign ($339,599) see US WEST

American Institute of Chemical Engineers-New York see du Pont de Nemours & Co., E. I.

American Israel Cultural Foundation ($3,200) see Grass Family Foundation

American-Israel Cultural Foundation ($25,000) see Levin Foundation, Philip and Janice

American Israel Culture Foundation ($2,500) see Matz Foundation — Edelman Division

American Italian Foundation for Cancer Research ($20,000) see Bohen Foundation

American Jewish College ($27,500) see Stern Memorial Trust, Sidney

American Jewish Committee ($15,300) see Alperin/Hirsch Family Foundation

American Jewish Committee ($70,000) see Appleman Foundation

American Jewish Committee ($15,750) see Bachmann Foundation

American Jewish Committee ($25,500) see Berkman Charitable Trust, Allen H. and Selma W.

American Jewish Committee ($192,500) see Blaustein Foundation, Jacob and Hilda

American Jewish Committee ($5,000) see Cedars-Sinai Medical Center Section D Fund

American Jewish Committee ($10,000) see Central National-Gottesman

American Jewish Committee ($5,000) see Chais Family Foundation

American Jewish Committee ($6,000) see Cohn Foundation, Peter A. and Elizabeth S.

American Jewish Committee ($2,275) see Coleman Foundation

American Jewish Committee ($3,000) see Cottrell Foundation

American Jewish Committee ($500) see Foster Foundation, Joseph C. and Esther

American Jewish Committee ($45,000) see Fox Foundation, Richard J.

American Jewish Committee ($10,000) see Friedman Foundation, Stephen and Barbara

American Jewish Committee ($1,000) see Ginsberg Family Foundation, Moses

American Jewish Committee ($10,000) see Glazer Foundation, Jerome S.

American Jewish Committee ($1,000) see Goldberg Family Foundation, Milton D. and Madeline L.

American Jewish Committee ($2,000) see Goldberger Foundation, Edward and Marjorie

American Jewish Committee ($65,000) see Greenberg Foundation, Alan C.

American Jewish Committee ($46,250) see Greene Foundation, Jerome L.

American Jewish Committee ($3,000) see Handleman Co.

American Jewish Committee ($10,000) see Jacobson & Sons, Benjamin

American Jewish Committee ($750) see Jaydor Corp.

American Jewish Committee ($250) see Kasle Steel Corp.

American Jewish Committee ($9,000) see Kohl Foundation, Sidney

American Jewish Committee ($5,000) see Loewenberg Foundation

American Jewish Committee ($4,000) see Lubo Fund

American Jewish Committee ($4,000) see Lubo Fund

American Jewish Committee ($15,000) see Mailman Foundation

American Jewish Committee ($5,000) see Messing Foundation, Morris M. and Helen F.

American Jewish Committee ($5,000) see Meyer Fund, Milton and Sophie

American Jewish Committee ($2,000) see Morse Foundation, Richard P. and Claire W.

American Jewish Committee ($5,000) see Nathan Berkman & Co.

American Jewish Committee ($27,500) see Newman Assistance Fund, Jerome A. and Estelle R.

American Jewish Committee ($5,000) see Olive Bridge Fund

American Jewish Committee ($31,000) see Philadelphia Industries

American Jewish Committee ($5,600) see Robin Family Foundation, Albert A.

American Jewish Committee ($30,000) see Rosenwald Family Fund, William

American Jewish Committee ($12,000) see Ross Foundation, Lyn & George M.

American Jewish Committee ($43,500) see Sequa Corp.

American Jewish Committee ($5,000) see Sequa Corp.

American Jewish Committee ($5,000) see Sheinberg Foundation, Eric P.

American Jewish Committee ($3,000) see Shiffman Foundation

American Jewish Committee ($11,000) see Simon Foundation, Sidney, Milton and Leoma

American Jewish Committee ($11,500) see Stern Family Foundation, Harry

American Jewish Committee ($20,000) see Taubman Foundation, A. Alfred

American Jewish Congress ($25,000) see Chanin Family Foundation, Paul R.

American Jewish Congress ($3,500) see Guttag Foundation, Irwin and Marjorie

American Jewish Congress ($1,000) see Loewenberg Foundation

American Jewish Congress ($10,000) see Manilow Foundation, Nathan

American Jewish Congress ($17,000) see Rudin Foundation

American Jewish Congress ($13,350) see Stein Foundation, Joseph F.

American Jewish Congress ($5,000) see Zenkel Foundation

American Jewish Friends of Ungvar ($15,000) see Wilf Family Foundation

American Jewish Joint Distribution Committee ($25,000) see de Hirsch Fund, Baron

American Jewish Joint Distribution Committee ($20,000) see de Hirsch Fund, Baron

American Jewish Joint Distribution Committee ($5,500) see Flemm Foundation, John J.

American Jewish Joint Distribution Committee ($81,717) see Hassenfeld Foundation

American Jewish World Service ($8,000) see I and G Charitable Foundation

American Jewish World Service ($100,000) see Phillips-Van Heusen Corp.

American Jewish World Services ($500) see Hirschhorn Foundation, David and Barbara B.

American Labor Education Center — for National Coalition of Educational Activists (NCEA) ($25,000) see Hazen Foundation, Edward W.

American Lung Association ($5,000) see Rice Family Foundation, Jacob and Sophie

American Lung Association — education program vs tuberculosis spread in Brooklyn ($61,000) see

Parshelsky Foundation, Moses L.

American Museum-Hayden Planetarium — modernization of their Hall of Sun, improvement of the quality of sound in the Sky Theater, and modernization of three classrooms ($117,377) see Hayden Foundation, Charles

American Museum of Moving Image ($30,000) see Levy Foundation, Edward C.

American Museum of Natural History ($2,000) see Allen Foundation, Frances

American Museum of Natural History see American Express Co.

American Museum of Natural History ($310,000) see Barker Foundation, J. M. R.

American Museum of Natural History see Bloomingdale's

American Museum of Natural History ($150,000) see Booth Ferris Foundation

American Museum of Natural History ($15,120) see Christodora

American Museum of Natural History ($50,000) see Dodge Foundation, Cleveland H.

American Museum of Natural History ($500,000) see Exxon Corp.

American Museum of Natural History ($535,360) see Golden Family Foundation

American Museum of Natural History ($520,000) see Harriman Foundation, Gladys and Roland

American Museum of Natural History ($25,000) see McKenna Foundation, Katherine Mabis

American Museum of Natural History ($50,000) see McKenna Foundation, Philip M.

American Museum of Natural History ($1,000) see Mitsui & Co. (U.S.A.)

American Museum of Natural History see Morgan Stanley & Co.

American Museum of Natural History — toward renovation of dinosaur and late mammal exhibition halls ($150,000) see Noble Foundation, Edward John

American Museum of Natural History ($450,000) see Phipps Foundation, Howard

American Museum of Natural History — the restoration of murals ($50,000) see Prospect Hill Foundation

American Museum of Natural History ($40,000) see Ross Foundation, Arthur

American Museum of Natural History ($35,000) see Snow Memorial Trust, John Ben

American Museum of Natural History ($25,000) see Thorne Foundation

American Museum of Natural History — endowment for the Department of Education ($250,000) see Hearst Foundation, William Randolph

American Museum of Natural History, New York, NY ($50,000) see Chemical Bank

American Museum of Natural History — for archaeological research project/St. Catherine's Island, Georgia

($159,096) see Noble
Foundation, Edward John
American Museum of Natural
History — support of a
world-class "Global Warming
Exhibit" ($100,000) see
Dodge Foundation, Geraldine
R.
American Music Center ($5,000)
see Oakleaf Foundation
American Music Center —
support for the 1993 Live
Music for Dance program
($200,000) see Cary
Charitable Trust, Mary Flagler
American Music Center —
support for the 1992 Live
Music for Dance program
($185,000) see Cary
Charitable Trust, Mary Flagler
American ORT Federation
($10,000) see FAB Industries
American ORT Federation
($10,000) see Feil Foundation,
Louis and Gertrude
American ORT Federation
($5,000) see Imerman
Memorial Foundation, Stanley
American ORT Federation
($10,000) see Levy
Foundation, Betty and Norman
F.
American ORT Federation
($10,000) see Ridgefield
Foundation
American ORT Federation
($14,000) see Rosen
Foundation, Joseph
American ORT Federation
($6,000) see Silverman
Foundation, Marty and
Dorothy
American Paralysis Association
($20,500) see Baldwin
Foundation, David M. and
Barbara
American Parkinson Disease
Association ($5,000) see
Frank Foundation, Ernest and
Elfriede
American Parkinson's Disease
Association ($3,000) see Rabb
Foundation, Harry W.
American Parkinson's Disease
Association ($5,000) see
Saemann Foundation, Franklin
I.
American Place Theater ($7,500)
see Durst Foundation
American Red Cross ($15,900)
see Abrams Foundation
American Red Cross ($1,000)
see Baker & Baker
American Red Cross ($20,000)
see Carvel Foundation,
Thomas and Agnes
American Red Cross ($5,000)
see Cawsey Trust
American Red Cross ($2,000)
see DCNY Corp.
American Red Cross ($1,000)
see Delacorte Fund, George
American Red Cross ($5,156)
see Ellsworth Trust, W. H.
American Red Cross ($2,000)
see Erteszek Foundation
American Red Cross ($7,000)
see Essick Foundation
American Red Cross ($10,000)
see Foundation for the Needs
of Others
American Red Cross ($37,000)
see Gifford Charitable
Corporation, Rosamond
American Red Cross ($5,000)
see Grigg-Lewis Trust
American Red Cross ($500) see
Hirschhorn Foundation, David
and Barbara B.
American Red Cross see
Michigan Mutual Insurance
Corp.

American Red Cross ($12,500)
see Mitchell Family
Foundation, Edward D. and
Anna
American Red Cross ($5,212)
see Rankin and Elizabeth
Forbes Rankin Trust, William
American Red Cross ($4,754)
see Rankin and Elizabeth
Forbes Rankin Trust, William
American Red Cross ($10,000)
see Rudin Foundation
American Red Cross ($6,500)
see Schwartz Foundation,
Arnold A.
American Red Cross ($1,000)
see Sealright Co., Inc.
American Red Cross ($2,000)
see Simone Foundation
American Red Cross ($1,000)
see Wolfson Family
Foundation
American Red Cross ($10,000)
see Woman's Seamen's Friend
Society of Connecticut
American School of Classical
Studies ($70,000) see
Williams Foundation, C. K.
American School of Classical
Studies in Athens ($61,000)
see Replogle Foundation,
Luther I.
American School of Oriental
Research ($5,000) see
Coleman, Jr. Foundation,
George E.
American Sephardic Federation
($20,000) see Amado
Foundation, Maurice
American Sephardic Federation
($10,000) see Levy
Foundation, Hyman Jebb
American Sephardic Federation
($5,000) see Levy Foundation,
Hyman Jebb
American Society for the
Prevention of Cruelty to
Animals ($3,000) see Gerard
Foundation, Sumner
American Society of Protection
of Nature in Israel ($25,000)
see Dorot Foundation
American Society of Protection
of Nature in Israel ($11,250)
see Gottesman Fund
American Society for Technion
($36,250) see Bargman
Foundation, Theodore and
Mina
American Society for Technion
($51,000) see Berrie
Foundation, Russell
American Society for Technion
($1,000) see Eder Foundation,
Sidney and Arthur
American Society for Technion
($35,000) see Factor Family
Foundation, Max
American Society for Technion
($2,500) see Feintech
Foundation
American Society for Technion
($15,000) see Fife Foundation,
Elias and Bertha
American Society for Technion
($5,000) see Fireman
Charitable Foundation, Paul
and Phyllis
American Society for Technion
($10,000) see Fischbach
Foundation
American Society for Technion
($5,000) see Fischbach
Foundation
American Society for Technion
($5,000) see Fischbach
Foundation
American Society for Technion
($40,000) see Fohs Foundation
American Society for Technion
($50,000) see Forchheimer
Foundation

American Society for Technion
($630,010) see Goodstein
Family Foundation, David
American Society for Technion
($18,000) see Hebrew
Technical Institute
American Society for Technion
($15,000) see Herzstein
Charitable Foundation, Albert
and Ethel
American Society for Technion
($12,750) see Imerman
Memorial Foundation, Stanley
American Society for Technion
($100,000) see Jurodin Fund
American Society for Technion
($25,000) see Lurcy
Charitable and Educational
Trust, Georges
American Society for Technion
($25,000) see Maas
Foundation, Benard L.
American Society for Technion
($25,000) see Maas
Foundation, Benard L.
American Society for Technion
($7,000) see Mazer
Foundation, Jacob and Ruth
American Society for Technion
($20,000) see Millstone
Foundation
American Society for Technion
($23,800) see Mitchell Family
Foundation, Edward D. and
Anna
American Society for Technion
($45,000) see Posnack Family
Foundation of Hollywood
American Society for Technion
($200,000) see Rogow Birken
Foundation
American Society for Technion
($15,000) see Rohlik
Foundation, Sigmund and
Sophie
American Society for Technion
($50,000) see Schaffer
Foundation, Michael & Helen
American Society for Technion
($35,000) see Sherman Family
Charitable Trust, George and
Beatrice
American Society for Technion
($45,000) see Swig Charity
Foundation, Mae and Benjamin
American Society for Technion
($75,000) see Taub
Foundation, Henry and Marilyn
American Society for Technion
($25,000) see Taubman
Foundation, Herman P. and
Sophia
American Society for Technion
($15,000) see Walker
Educational and Charitable
Foundation, Alex C.
American Society for Technion
($25,000) see Wolens
Foundation, Kalman and Ida
American Society for Technion
($100) see Wolff Shoe Co.
American Society for Technion
($7,500) see Wunsch
Foundation
American Society for
Technion-Israel Institute of
Technology ($250,000) see
Crown Memorial, Arie and Ida
American Society for
Technion-Israel Institute of
Technology ($250,000) see
Crown Memorial, Arie and Ida
American Society for Yad
Vashem ($37,800) see Belfer
Foundation
American Suicide Foundation
($1,000) see Levy Foundation,
Betty and Norman F.
American Theatre Wing
($25,000) see Rose
Foundation, Billy

American Theological Institute
($25,000) see Fogel
Foundation, Shalom and
Rebecca
American Theological Institute
($50,000) see Newbrook
Charitable Foundation
American Theological Institute
($10,000) see Newbrook
Charitable Foundation
American Trust for Oxford
University ($25,000) see
Milbank Foundation, Dunlevy
American Trust for Oxford
University ($20,000) see Reed
Foundation
American University of Beirut
($50,000) see Atlantic
Foundation of New York
American University of Beirut
($200,000) see Bobst
Foundation, Elmer and
Mamdouha
American University of Beirut
($25,000) see Dodge
Foundation, Cleveland H.
American University in Cairo
($25,000) see Ingalls
Foundation, Louise H. and
David S.
American University in Cairo
($20,000) see Weyerhaeuser
Foundation, Frederick and
Margaret L.
American Women's Economic
Development Corporation
($25,000) see Equitable Life
Assurance Society of the U.S.
American Women's Economic
Development Corporation
($50,000) see Whitehead
Foundation
American Women's Hadassah
($40,000) see Novotny
Charitable Trust, Yetta Deitch
American Women's ORT
($1,000) see Chait Memorial
Foundation, Sara
American Women's ORT
($10,000) see Novotny
Charitable Trust, Yetta Deitch
Americans for A Safe Israel
($52,500) see Moskowitz
Foundation, Irving I.
Americans for Peace Now
($25,000) see Bydale
Foundation
Americans for Peace Now
($100,000) see Cohen
Foundation, Naomi and
Nehemiah
Americans for Peace Now
($15,000) see Cohen
Foundation, Wilfred P.
Americans for Peace Now
($4,125) see Foundation for
Middle East Peace
Americans for Peace Now
($500) see Foundation for
Middle East Peace
Americans for Peace Now
($15,000) see Levinson
Foundation, Max and Anna
Americans for Peace Now
($2,500) see Schecter Private
Foundation, Aaron and Martha
Americans for Peace Now
($15,000) see Stone Charitable
Foundation
Americans for Peace Now
($5,000) see Warner Fund,
Albert and Bessie
Americans for Peace Now
($14,000) see Westport Fund
Americans for a Safe Israel
($25,000) see Mattus
Foundation, Reuben and Rose
America's Future ($12,000) see
Durell Foundation, George
Edward
America's Future ($3,500) see
Phillipps Foundation

Americas Society ($50,000) see
Milstein Family Foundation
Americas Society — support of a
two-part public affairs
program focused on transitions
in Latin America ($107,000)
see Tinker Foundation
Amgotsophic Lateral Sclerosis
Society ($5,000) see Chait
Memorial Foundation, Sara
AMIT ($5,000) see Fink
Foundation
Amit Women ($3,800) see
Flemm Foundation, John J.
Amnesty International ($15,000)
see Davee Foundation
Amnesty International ($2,000)
see G.A.G. Charitable
Corporation
Amnesty International ($10,000)
see Von der Ahe Foundation
Amnesty International ($25,000)
see Wiener Foundation,
Malcolm Hewitt
Amnesty International of U.S.A.
— unrestricted grant ($10,000)
see Davis Foundation, Edwin
W. and Catherine M.
Amos Tuck Graduate School
($25,000) see First Boston
Amsterdam Memorial Hospital
($60,000) see Arkell Hall
Foundation
Anderson School see Bank of
New York
Andrew Glover Youth Program
($12,563) see Mandeville
Foundation
Andrew Oliver Trust ($49,000)
see Coleman, Jr. Foundation,
George E.
Angel Guardian Home ($15,560)
see Mertz Foundation, Martha
ANHD ($300) see Consumer
Farmer Foundation
Animal Medical Center
($20,000) see Barbour
Foundation, Bernice
Animal Medical Center
($25,500) see Bobst
Foundation, Elmer and
Mamdouha
Animal Medical Center
($25,000) see Hoffman
Foundation, Marion O. and
Maximilian
Animal Medical Center ($5,000)
see Porter Foundation, Mrs.
Cheever
Animal Medical Center ($5,000)
see Schiff Foundation
Animal Medical College
($25,000) see Jaqua
Foundation
Animal Recovery and
Rehabilitation Fund ($5,100)
see Flemm Foundation, John J.
Anna Freud Foundation
($35,000) see Cohen Family
Foundation, Saul Z. and Amy
Scheuer
Anthony L. Jordan Health Center
($25,000) see Wilson
Foundation, Marie C. and
Joseph C.
Anti-Defamation League
($110,000) see Andreas
Foundation
Anti-Defamation League
($50,000) see
Archer-Daniels-Midland Co.
Anti-Defamation League
($5,000) see Baker & Baker
Anti-Defamation League
($10,000) see Bernstein & Co.,
Sanford C.
Anti-Defamation League
($2,500) see Brody
Foundation, Frances
Anti-Defamation League
($1,000) see Brody
Foundation, Frances

New York (cont.)

Anti-Defamation League ($1,000) see Chais Family Foundation

Anti-Defamation League ($2,800) see Eder Foundation, Sidney and Arthur

Anti-Defamation League ($2,000) see Erving Paper Mills

Anti-Defamation League ($2,000) see Fingerhut Family Foundation

Anti-Defamation League ($50,000) see Fireman Charitable Foundation, Paul and Phyllis

Anti-Defamation League ($7,000) see First Petroleum Corp.

Anti-Defamation League ($10,000) see Ginsberg Family Foundation, Moses

Anti-Defamation League ($1,000) see Goldberg Family Foundation, Milton D. and Madeline L.

Anti-Defamation League ($10,050) see Goldberger Foundation, Edward and Marjorie

Anti-Defamation League ($850) see Goldstein Foundation, Leslie and Roslyn

Anti-Defamation League ($5,000) see Gumenick Foundation, Nathan and Sophie

Anti-Defamation League ($325) see Interstate Packaging Co.

Anti-Defamation League ($1,000) see Jaydor Corp.

Anti-Defamation League ($5,000) see Kline Foundation, Charles and Figa

Anti-Defamation League ($5,000) see Kohl Foundation, Sidney

Anti-Defamation League ($1,000) see KSM Foundation

Anti-Defamation League ($10,250) see Levy Foundation, Charles and Ruth

Anti-Defamation League ($3,000) see Ottenstein Family Foundation

Anti-Defamation League ($5,000) see Pesch Family Foundation

Anti-Defamation League ($100,000) see Phillips Family Foundation, Jay and Rose

Anti-Defamation League ($10,000) see Ridgefield Foundation

Anti-Defamation League ($10,000) see Rudin Foundation

Anti-Defamation League ($1,000) see Saul Foundation, Joseph E. & Norma G.

Anti-Defamation League ($10,000) see Sequa Corp.

Anti-Defamation League ($22,000) see Slant/Fin Corp.

Anti-Defamation League ($12,030) see Steinberg Family Foundation, Meyer and Jean

Anti-Defamation League ($100,000) see Steinhardt Foundation, Judy and Michael

Anti-Defamation League ($10,000) see Tauber Foundation

Anti-Defamation League ($380) see Ushkow Foundation

Anti-Defamation League ($10,000) see Waldbaum Family Foundation, I.

Anti-Defamation League ($81,000) see Weston Associates/R.C.M. Corp.

Anti-Defamation League ($10,000) see Winston Research Foundation, Harry

Anti-Defamation League of B'nai B'rith ($20,000) see Amado Foundation, Maurice

Anti-Defamation League of B'nai B'rith ($73,500) see Belfer Foundation

Anti-Defamation League of B'nai B'rith ($4,000) see Brenner Foundation

Anti-Defamation League of B'nai B'rith ($665,500) see Capital Fund Foundation

Anti-Defamation League of B'nai B'rith ($11,500) see Forest City Enterprises

Anti-Defamation League of B'nai B'rith ($4,000) see Kepco, Inc.

Anti-Defamation League of B'nai B'rith ($30,300) see Rosenbloom Foundation, Ben and Esther

Anti-Defemation League ($31,000) see Litwin Foundation

Aperture Foundation ($25,000) see Warhol Foundation for the Visual Arts, Andy

Apoleto Festival USA ($23,000) see Harkness Foundation, William Hale

Appeal of Conscience Foundation ($3,800) see Propp Sons Fund, Morris and Anna

Appleby Foundation ($10,000) see Neuberger Foundation, Roy R. and Marie S.

Archbishop of New York ($25,000) see Hugoton Foundation

Archdiocese of New York ($10,000) see Abraham Foundation, Anthony R.

Archdiocese of New York ($262,500) see Capital Fund Foundation

Archdiocese of New York ($300,000) see Center for Educational Programs

Archdiocese of New York ($25,000) see Doty Family Foundation

Archdiocese of New York — school endowment campaign ($50,000) see Joyce Foundation, John M. and Mary A.

Archdiocese of New York ($166,667) see Simon Foundation, William E. and Carol G.

Archdiocese of New York — leadership gift to the "Learning for Life Campaign" - third of four annual payments toward $1,000,000 pledge ($250,000) see Altman Foundation

Archdiocese of New York/Partnership for Quality Education ($250,339) see Archbold Charitable Trust, Adrian and Jessie

Architectural League of New York ($25,000) see Warhol Foundation for the Visual Arts, Andy

Architectural League of New York — exhibition of the work of Italian architect, Renzo Piano ($10,000) see Graham Foundation for Advanced Studies in the Fine Arts

Archives of American Art ($5,500) see Shapero

Foundation, Nate S. and Ruth B.

Arden Hill Hospital see Bank of New York

Ariel American Friends of Midrasha ($2,500) see Fischel Foundation, Harry and Jane

Armitage Foundation ($65,000) see Leonhardt Foundation, Dorothea L.

Arnold and Marie Schwartz College of Pharmacy and Health Sciences ($102,450) see Schwartz Fund for Education and Health Research, Arnold and Marie

Arnot Art Museum ($500) see Hilliard Corp.

Art Awareness ($25,000) see Warhol Foundation for the Visual Arts, Andy

Art Resources ($10,000) see Sheafer Charitable Trust, Emma A.

Arthritis Foundation ($10,000) see Ettinger Foundation

Arthritis Foundation ($5,000) see Mastronardi Charitable Foundation, Charles A.

Arthritis Foundation-New York Chapter see Freeport-McMoRan

Arthur Ross Gallery of Art ($62,911) see Ross Foundation, Arthur

Artists Space ($25,000) see Cowles Charitable Trust

Artists Space ($10,255) see Leonhardt Foundation, Dorothea L.

Arts Council ($10,000) see Goldome F.S.B

Arts International ($903,506) see Wallace Reader's Digest Fund, Lila

Artsconnection — School Newspaper Project ($10,000) see Daily News

Asbury First United Methodist — operating funds ($8,000) see Gleason Works

Asia Society ($28,533) see Erpf Fund, Armand G.

Asia Society ($25,000) see Flagler Co.

Asia Society ($10,000) see Gerschel Foundation, Patrick A.

Asia Society — annual fund ($50,000) see Griggs and Mary Griggs Burke Foundation, Mary Livingston

Asia Society ($5,000) see Hazen Charitable Trust, Lita Annenberg

Asia Society ($5,000) see Ogden Foundation, Ralph E.

Asia Society ($42,541) see Ross Foundation, Arthur

Asia Society ($50,000) see Simon Foundation, William E. and Carol G.

Asia Society ($50,000) see Warhol Foundation for the Visual Arts, Andy

Asia Society ($100,000) see Whitehead Foundation

Asian Americans for Equality see Bank of New York

Asian Americans for Equality ($100,000) see Bleibtreu Foundation, Jacob

Asian Cultural Council — toward general operating expenses ($540,000) see Rockefeller Brothers Fund

ASNE Foundation — to promote and encourage a wholesome community life ($20,000) see Landmark Communications

Asphalt Green ($12,500) see Barker Welfare Foundation

Asphalt Green ($300,000) see Gordon/Rousmaniere/Roberts Fund

Asphalt Green ($445,000) see Murphy Charitable Fund, George E. and Annette Cross

Aspira of New York see Morgan Stanley & Co.

Associated Alumni of Vassar College ($5,000) see Normandie Foundation

Associated Blind ($5,212) see Rankin and Elizabeth Forbes Rankin Trust, William

Associated Blind ($4,754) see Rankin and Elizabeth Forbes Rankin Trust, William

Association to Benefit Children ($20,000) see Disney Family Foundation, Roy

Association to Benefit Children ($25,000) see Frelinghuysen Foundation

Association to Benefit Children ($15,000) see Kenworthy - Sarah H. Swift Foundation, Marion E.

Association for Religion and Intelligent Life ($5,000) see Woods-Greer Foundation

Association for Retarded Children ($4,000) see Eisenberg Foundation, George M.

Association for Retarded Children ($17,000) see Fisher Brothers

Association for Retarded Citizens ($5,000) see Utica National Insurance Group

Association for Voluntary Sterilization — operating budget ($30,000) see duPont Foundation, Chichester

Association for Voluntary Surgical Contraception ($32,355) see Bergstrom Foundation, Erik E. and Edith H.

Association for Voluntary Surgical Contraception ($3,000) see Swensrud Charitable Trust, Sidney A.

Association for Voluntary Surgical Contraception — to initiate or continue programs in Latin America and sub-Saharan Africa ($500,000) see Hewlett Foundation, William and Flora

Association for Volunteer Sterilization ($350) see Genius Foundation, Elizabeth Morse

Astor Home for Children — general support ($25,000) see Astor Foundation, Vincent

Astor Home for Children — little red schoolhouse ($50,000) see Homeland Foundation

Ateret Torah ($66,014) see Bag Bazaar, Ltd.

Atlantic Beach Synagogue ($1,000) see Gruss Charitable Foundation, Emanuel and Riane

Atlantic Legal Foundation ($75,000) see Randolph Foundation

Atlantic Salmon Foundation ($6,750) see Walker Wildlife Conservation Foundation

Atonement Friars ($6,000) see Trimble Family Foundation, Robert Mize and Isa White

Auburn Memorial Hospital ($3,000) see Cayuga Foundation

Auburn Memorial Hospital — capital campaign ($250,000) see Emerson Foundation, Fred L.

Auburn Memorial Hospital ($5,114) see Everett Charitable Trust

Auburn Memorial Hospital ($3,000) see Everett Charitable Trust

Aurora Free Library Association ($4,000) see Cayuga Foundation

Aurora Pre-school Center ($5,000) see Cayuga Foundation

Auxilliary to Bellvue Hospital see New York Mercantile Exchange

B.C. Pops ($7,500) see Klee Foundation, Conrad and Virginia

Backstretch Employee Assistance Team ($5,000) see Strawbridge Foundation of Pennsylvania I, Margaret Dorrance

Bailey Arboretum, Friends of Nassau County ($15,000) see Vanneck-Bailey Foundation

Bailey-Delavan Community Services ($5,000) see Goodyear Foundation, Josephine

Bais Yaakov D'Chassidei Gur ($52,907) see Fishoff Family Foundation

Ballet Theater Foundation ($100,000) see Koch Charitable Trust, David H.

Ballet Theater Foundation ($100,000) see Koch Charitable Trust, David H.

Ballet Theater Foundation ($12,500) see Rubin Foundation, Rob E. & Judith O.

Ballet Theater Foundation ($15,000) see Stern Foundation, Gustav and Irene

Ballet Theatre Foundation ($10,000) see Garfinkle Family Foundation

Ballet Theatre Foundation ($154,679) see Gilman Foundation, Howard

Ballet Theatre Foundation ($34,834) see Green Fund

Ballet Theatre Foundation ($125,000) see L and L Foundation

Ballet Theatre Foundation ($25,000) see Piankova Foundation, Tatiana

Ballet Theatre Foundation ($15,000) see Wade Endowment Fund, Elizabeth Firth

Bank Street College ($25,000) see Atlantic Foundation of New York

Bank Street College of Education ($8,500) see Bruner Foundation

Bank Street College of Education ($7,000) see Coleman Foundation

Bank Street College of Education ($25,000) see Dreyfus Foundation, Jean and Louis

Bank Street College of Education ($20,000) see Hughes Memorial Foundation, Charles Evans

Bank Street College of Education ($30,000) see Love Foundation, George H. and Margaret McClintic

Bank Street College of Education ($100,000) see Pforzheimer Foundation, Carl and Lily

Bank Street College of Education ($10,000) see Young & Rubicam

Bank Street College of Education — includes first payment of $150,000 grant for the Leadership Continuum and first payment of $100,000 capital grant ($110,000) see J.P. Morgan & Co.

Bank Street College of Education — production and field-test planning of Early Childhood Curriculum Materials Package ($100,000) see NYNEX Corp.

Baptist Home of Brooklyn ($2,000) see Rauch Foundation

Bar-Ilan University ($5,000) see Abrams Foundation, Benjamin and Elizabeth

Bar-Ilan University ($10,500) see Bargman Foundation, Theodore and Mina

Bar-Ilan University ($25,000) see Belfer Foundation

Bar-Ilan University ($25,000) see Blackman Foundation, Aaron and Marie

Bar-Ilan University ($20,000) see Dorot Foundation

Bar-Ilan University ($10,500) see Imerman Memorial Foundation, Stanley

Bar Ilan University ($26,100) see Jesselson Foundation

Bar-Ilan University ($10,000) see Kaplun Foundation, Morris J. and Betty

Bar-Ilan University ($10,000) see Maas Foundation, Benard L.

Bar-Ilan University ($500,000) see Mitrani Family Foundation

Bar-Ilan University ($40,000) see Plitt Southern Theatres

Bar-Ilan University ($50,000) see Posnack Family Foundation of Hollywood

Bar-Ilan University ($25,000) see Resnick Foundation, Jack and Pearl

Bar-Ilan University ($20,000) see Rohlik Foundation, Sigmund and Sophie

Bar-Ilan University ($150,000) see Shapell Foundation, Nathan and Lilly

Bar-Ilan University ($5,000) see Waldbaum Family Foundation, I.

Bar-Ilan University ($10,000) see Wouk Foundation, Abe

Bar-Ilan University — for the Emanuel Rackman Law Center ($50,000) see Alexander Foundation, Joseph

Bard College ($10,000) see Helms Foundation

Bard College ($20,000) see Henderson Foundation

Bard College ($100,000) see Johnson Endeavor Foundation, Christian A.

Bard College ($25,000) see Lang Foundation, Eugene M.

Bard College ($10,000) see Levy Foundation, Jerome

Bard College — to enable The Institute for Writing and Thinking to initiate a two-year professional developemnt program for teachers in NYC public schools, with Bank Street College (two years, $26,775/year) ($53,550) see Greenwall Foundation

Barge Music ($5,000) see Paul and C. Michael Paul Foundation, Josephine Bay

Barnard College ($6,000) see Abraham Foundation

Barnard College — toward one million dollar campaign

($205,000) see Bedminster Fund

Barnard College ($5,000) see Berlin Charitable Fund, Irving

Barnard College ($122,085) see Bristol-Myers Squibb Co.

Barnard College ($44,000) see Golden Family Foundation

Barnard College ($150,000) see Horowitz Foundation, Gedale B. and Barbara S.

Barnard College ($100,000) see Jurodin Fund

Barnard College — building fund ($5,000) see Kingsley Foundation

Barnard College ($25,000) see Lang Foundation, Eugene M.

Barnard College ($35,000) see Mnuchin Foundation

Barnard College ($81,000) see Overbrook Foundation

Barnard College — scholarship endowment ($100,000) see Rosenthal Foundation, Ida and William

Barnard College ($10,000) see Summerfield Foundation, Solon E.

Barnard College Development Fund ($10,000) see Gulton Foundation

Barton Youth Services-Edwin Gould Foundation for Children — renovation of dormitory units at their facility in Spring Valley, NY ($100,000) see Hayden Foundation, Charles

Baruch College ($15,000) see Rosenberg Foundation, Sunny and Abe

Bassett Hospital ($15,000) see Arkell Hall Foundation

Bausch and Lomb Center ($2,250) see Harris Foundation, H. H.

Bay Ridge Day Nursery ($3,000) see Goodman Memorial Foundation, Joseph C. and Clare F.

Bayith Lapleitot ($17,000) see Rosen Foundation, Joseph

Bay's Hope ($14,500) see O'Sullivan Children Foundation

BCC Foundation ($17,500) see Hoyt Foundation, Stewart W. and Willma C.

Beautification Committee ($32,000) see Taylor Foundation, Fred and Harriett

Bedford Stuyvesant Restoration Corporation see Bank of New York

Beekman Downtown Hospital ($10,000) see DCNY Corp.

Beekman Downtown Hospital ($5,000) see Kellogg Foundation, J. C.

Beirut University College — for library endowment ($500,000) see McCune Foundation

Beit Issie Shapiro Foundation ($6,000) see Pearlstone Foundation, Peggy Meyerhoff

Bellevue Hospital Auxiliary ($5,000) see Milliken Foundation, Agnes G.

Bellevue Hospital Center — renewed support for research into the pathogenesis and management of hypothermia and hyperthermia in emergency ward patients ($270,075) see Diamond Foundation, Aaron

Bellevue Hospital Center ($5,000) see Foerderer Foundation, Percival E. and Ethel Brown

Bement School ($15,000) see Gutman Foundation, Edna and Monroe C.

Ben Gurion University ($5,000) see United Togs Inc.

Ben Gurion University of Negev ($1,500) see Cedars-Sinai Medical Center Section D Fund

Ben Gurion University of Negev ($25,000) see Loeb Foundation, Frances and John L.

Ben-Gurion University of Negev ($25,000) see Russell Memorial Foundation, Robert

Benedictine Health Foundation ($25,000) see Kingston Foundation

Benedictine Health Foundation ($3,000) see Lehigh Portland Cement Co.

Benedictine Hospital ($20,000) see Rice Family Foundation, Jacob and Sophie

Berkeley Carroll School ($50,000) see Ford Foundation, Edward E.

Berwick Boys Foundation — to assist in its educational program ($7,500) see Loewy Family Foundation

Bet Torah ($5,000) see Goldie-Anna Charitable Trust

Betances Health Unit — expansion of primary care services ($35,000) see Hearst Foundation

Beth Israel Foundation ($11,000) see Ginsberg Family Foundation, Moses

Beth Israel Foundation ($120,000) see McGonagle Foundation, Dextra Baldwin

Beth Israel Foundation ($10,000) see Mercy, Jr. Foundation, Sue and Eugene

Beth Israel Hospice ($25,000) see Reicher Foundation, Anne & Harry J.

Beth Israel Medical Center ($10,000) see Feil Foundation, Louis and Gertrude

Beth Israel Medical Center ($50,000) see Forchheimer Foundation

Beth Israel Medical Center ($5,000) see Lautenberg Foundation

Beth Israel Medical Center ($20,000) see Mercy, Jr. Foundation, Sue and Eugene

Beth Israel Medical Center ($50,000) see Peabody Foundation, Amelia

Beth Israel Medical Center ($5,000) see Stony Wold Herbert Fund

Beth Israel Medical Center ($7,500) see Werblow Charitable Trust, Nina W.

Beth Israel Medical Center — towards the construction, renovation and furnishing of the Samuel's Planetree Model Hospital Unit ($100,000) see Samuels Foundation, Fan Fox and Leslie R.

Beth Israel Medical Center Foundation — medical research ($50,000) see Overseas Shipholding Group

Beth Israel Medical Center Foundation ($35,000) see Overseas Shipholding Group

Beth Israel Medical Center Foundation — Peter Kruger Clinic ($50,000) see Overseas Shipholding Group

Beth Medrash Govoha of America ($10,000) see Sapirstein-Stone-Weiss Foundation

Beth Medresh ($15,500) see FAB Industries

Beth Rivka Building Fund ($24,000) see Fishoff Family Foundation

Beth Shalom Foundation ($750) see Baker & Baker

Beth Torah Congregation ($5,000) see Sutton Foundation

Better Business Bureau of Metropolitan New York see Bank of New York

Bexley Hall ($5,628) see Society for the Increase of the Ministry

Big Apple Circus ($19,000) see Normandie Foundation

Big Apple Circus ($15,000) see Silverweed Foundation

Big Apple Circus ($50,000) see Slifka Foundation, Alan B.

Big Apple Circus ($10,000) see Slifka Foundation, Joseph and Sylvia

Big Brothers and Big Sisters ($50,000) see Boisi Family Foundation

Big Brothers and Big Sisters ($10,000) see St. Faith's House Foundation

Binding Together see Morgan Stanley & Co.

Binghamton Area Girls Softball Association ($15,912) see Hoyt Foundation, Stewart W. and Willma C.

Bishop Annual Appeal ($10,000) see O'Sullivan Children Foundation

Black Leadership Commission on AIDS — general operating ($50,000) see New York Life Insurance Co.

Black Rock Forest Preserve ($75,000) see Golden Family Foundation

Blenheim Foundation ($10,000) see Taubman Foundation, A. Alfred

Blessed Sacrament Roman Catholic Church ($100) see Hendrickson Brothers

Blue Card ($2,500) see Number Ten Foundation

Blue Earth County Historical Society ($20,000) see Mankato Citizens Telephone Co.

Blythedale Children's Hospital ($28,500) see Weiler Foundation, Theodore & Renee

BMCF Antiques Show and Sale ($500) see Baker & Baker

B'nai B'rith ($135,000) see Seagram & Sons, Joseph E.

B'nai B'rith Hill Foundations and Counselorships ($25,000) see Burns Foundation, Jacob

B'nai Jeshurin Temple ($10,000) see Slifka Foundation, Joseph and Sylvia

Bnos Rochel ($200) see MacAndrews & Forbes Holdings

Board of Cooperative Educational Services-Southern Westchester — educational/vocational training ($15,000) see Dreyfus Foundation, Max and Victoria

Board of Education-City of Buffalo — purchase of computers/software for high school ($30,160) see Wendt Foundation, Margaret L.

Board of Jewish Education ($50,000) see AVI CHAI - A Philanthropic Foundation

Board of Jewish Education of Greater New York ($5,000) see Mandel Foundation, Morton and Barbara

Bob Lanier Center for Education, Physical and Cultural Development ($12,000) see Western New York Foundation

Bobover Yeshivah B'nai Zion ($50,000) see Zacharia Foundation, Isaac Herman

Boquet River Association ($1,000) see Crary Foundation, Bruce L.

Borough of Manhattan College — financial support to students in need of support ($20,000) see Lincoln Fund

Borough of Manhattan Community College see Coors Brewing Co.

Bowne House Historical Society ($4,000) see Kepco, Inc.

Boy Scouts of America ($3,000) see American Welding & Manufacturing Co.

Boy Scouts of America ($750) see Central National-Gottesman

Boy Scouts of America — camp improvements ($25,000) see Corning Incorporated

Boy Scouts of America ($40,000) see Dewar Foundation

Boy Scouts of America ($4,000) see Everett Charitable Trust

Boy Scouts of America ($2,100) see Fein Foundation

Boy Scouts of America see Genesco

Boy Scouts of America ($25,000) see Gifford Charitable Corporation, Rosamond

Boy Scouts of America ($5,000) see Jacobson & Sons, Benjamin

Boy Scouts of America ($10,000) see Kellogg Foundation, J. C.

Boy Scouts of America ($15,000) see Kingston Foundation

Boy Scouts of America ($5,000) see Liberman Foundation, Bertha & Isaac

Boy Scouts of America ($12,500) see Rubin Foundation, Rob E. & Judith O.

Boy Scouts of America ($5,400) see Russ Togs

Boy Scouts of America ($8,000) see Schiff Foundation

Boy Scouts of America ($5,000) see Schiff Foundation

Boy Scouts of America ($50,000) see Sheldon Foundation, Ralph C.

Boy Scouts of America ($10,000) see Smeal Foundation, Mary Jean & Frank P.

Boy Scouts of America ($2,000) see United Merchants & Manufacturers

Boy Scouts of America ($100,000) see Whitehead Foundation

Boy Scouts of America ($5,000) see Winston Research Foundation, Harry

Boy Scouts of America — completion of the modernization of the water system at Camp Alpine ($150,000) see Hayden Foundation, Charles

Boyce Thompson Institute ($3,000) see Curtice-Burns Foods

Boys Brotherhood ($7,500) see Perley Fund, Victor E.

New York (cont.)

Boys Brotherhood Republic ($35,000) see Baier Foundation, Marie

Boys Choir of Harlem — for general, operating support ($21,666) see Achelis Foundation

Boys Club of America ($50,000) see Andreas Foundation

Boys Club of America ($27,500) see Avon Products

Boys Club of America ($10,000) see Bloedorn Foundation, Walter A.

Boys Club of America ($10,000) see Broccoli Charitable Foundation, Dana and Albert R.

Boys Club of America ($50,000) see Ford Fund, William and Martha

Boys Club of America ($25,000) see Gelb Foundation, Lawrence M.

Boys Club of America ($10,000) see Gelb Foundation, Lawrence M.

Boys Club of America ($1,000) see Goldberger Foundation, Edward and Marjorie

Boys Club of America ($25,000) see Griffis Foundation

Boys Club of America ($15,000) see Johnson Foundation, Willard T. C.

Boys Club of America ($5,000) see Krimendahl II Foundation, H. Frederick

Boys Club of America ($10,000) see Oaklawn Foundation

Boys Club of America ($13,750) see Osborn Charitable Trust, Edward B.

Boys Club of Harlem — summer music institute program at Skidmore College ($15,000) see Blum Foundation, Edna F.

Boy's Club of New York ($50,000) see Ford Foundation, Edward E.

Boys Club of New York ($35,000) see Harriman Foundation, Mary W.

Boys' Club of New York ($2,000) see Iroquois Avenue Foundation

Boys Club of New York ($25,000) see McDonald Foundation, J. M.

Boys' Club of New York see Morgan Stanley & Co.

Boys Clubs of America New York — general support ($22,500) see Sonat

Boys and Girls Club ($1,000) see Barlow Family Foundation, Milton A. and Gloria G.

Boys and Girls Club ($4,500) see Bedminster Fund

Boys and Girls Club ($25,000) see Bobst Foundation, Elmer and Mamdouha

Boys and Girls Club ($10,000) see Cornell Trust, Peter C.

Boys and Girls Club ($30,000) see Heineman Foundation for Research, Educational, Charitable, and Scientific Purposes

Boys and Girls Club ($28,320) see Meyer Family Foundation, Paul J.

Boys and Girls Club ($20,000) see Sharp Foundation, Evelyn

Boys and Girls Club ($6,000) see Steinberg Family Foundation, Meyer and Jean

Boys and Girls Club ($10,650) see Thorne Foundation

Boys and Girls Club of America — public housing programs ($1,425,000) see Casey Foundation, Annie E.

Boys and Girls Clubs ($50,000) see Pfizer

Boys and Girls Clubs of America see Arkla

Boys and Girls Clubs of America ($250,000) see JM Foundation

Boys and Girls Clubs of Buffalo — safety-related renovations to the five locations ($35,000) see Wendt Foundation, Margaret L.

Boys Harbor ($15,000) see McIntosh Foundation

Boys Harbor ($40,000) see Ross Foundation, Arthur

Boys Harbor ($100) see Saul Foundation, Joseph E. & Norma G.

Boys Harbor/Girls Harbor of Houston ($2,500) see Holmes Foundation

Boys Hope ($5,000) see Roche Relief Foundation, Edward and Ellen

Boys Town of Italy ($5,000) see Handleman Co.

Boys Town of Italy ($3,700) see Key Food Stores Cooperative Inc.

Boys Town of Italy ($150) see Martini Foundation, Nicholas

Boys Town of Jerusalem ($50,000) see Berrie Foundation, Russell

Boys Town of Jerusalem ($10,000) see Ridgefield Foundation

Brearley School ($5,000) see Israel Foundation, A. Cremieux

Brearley School ($100,000) see Johnson Endeavor Foundation, Christian A.

Brearley School ($5,000) see Joselow Foundation

Brearley School ($2,000) see Lehman Foundation, Edith and Herbert

Brearley School ($10,000) see Milliken Foundation, Agnes G.

Brearley School ($25,000) see Zarkin Memorial Foundation, Charles

Brearly School ($70,250) see Gruss Petroleum Corp.

Breslov World Center ($2,300) see Lowenstein Foundation, William P. and Marie R.

Brick Church ($12,000) see Brody Foundation, Carolyn and Kenneth D.

Brick Hawkins Dance Foundation ($5,000) see Titan Industrial Co.

Brick Presbyterian Church ($1,000) see Griswold Foundation, John C.

Brick Presbyterian Church — public welfare ($10,000) see Young Foundation, Robert R.

British American Arts Association (US) ($1,950,200) see Heinz Foundation, Drue

British Schools and Universities Foundation ($75,000) see Heinz Foundation, Drue

Broad Jump Prep for Prep ($1,500) see Beir Foundation

Broad Jump Prep for Prep ($10,000) see Crane Fund for Widows and Children

Broad Jump Prep for Prep ($20,000) see Thanksgiving Foundation

Bronx Community College — financial aid to students in need of support ($20,000) see Lincoln Fund

Bronx Community College Department of Nursing — scholarships ($45,000) see Rudin Foundation, Louis and Rachel

Bronx Educational Services ($20,000) see Lavanburg-Corner House

Bronx Educational Services — support for teaching salaries and adult literacy program ($20,000) see Lincoln Fund

Bronx-House Emanuel Camps ($5,000) see Cohn Foundation, Peter A. and Elizabeth S.

Bronx-Lebanon Hospital Center New Directions Fund — to help establish a comprehensive Pediatric AIDS Treatment Center ($100,000) see Altman Foundation

Bronx Municipal Hospital Auxiliary ($100,000) see Kaplan Fund, J. M.

Bronx Museum of the Arts ($13,500) see Mex-Am Cultural Foundation

Brookdale Center ($15,000) see Eckman Charitable Foundation, Samuel and Rae

Brookdale Center on Aging of Hunter College ($15,000) see Dreyfus Foundation, Jean and Louis

Brookdale Hospital and Medical Center ($30,000) see Parshelsky Foundation, Moses L.

Brookings Institute ($125,000) see Zilkha & Sons

Brooklyn Academy of Music ($25,000) see Dow Jones & Co.

Brooklyn Academy of Music ($20,000) see Harkness Ballet Foundation

Brooklyn Academy of Music ($41,000) see Harkness Foundation, William Hale

Brooklyn Academy of Music ($24,569) see Hillman Family Foundation, Alex

Brooklyn Academy of Music ($31,200) see Leonhardt Foundation, Dorothea L.

Brooklyn Academy of Music ($10,000) see Sharp Foundation, Evelyn

Brooklyn Academy of Music ($5,000,000) see Wallace Reader's Digest Fund, Lila

Brooklyn Academy of Music — support of Opera/Music Theater 1992-1994 ($75,000) see Samuels Foundation, Fan Fox and Leslie R.

Brooklyn Botanic Garden ($5,000) see Culver Foundation, Constans

Brooklyn Botanic Garden see Morgan Stanley & Co.

Brooklyn Botanic Garden ($300,000) see Steinhardt Foundation, Judy and Michael

Brooklyn Botanic Garden ($10,000) see Vanneck-Bailey Foundation

Brooklyn Botanic Garden Corporation ($45,000) see Uris Brothers Foundation

Brooklyn Botanical Garden ($5,000) see Barth Foundation, Theodore H.

Brooklyn Bureau of Community Service see Bank of New York

Brooklyn Bureau of Community Services ($4,750) see Brooklyn Benevolent Society

Brooklyn Children's Museum ($100) see Contempo Communications

Brooklyn Childrens' Museum — support after-school and community programs ($30,000) see Pinkerton Foundation

Brooklyn Ecumenical Cooperative ($5,000) see Culver Foundation, Constans

Brooklyn Historical Society — for improvements to collection storage system ($5,000) see Bay Foundation

Brooklyn Historical Society see Morgan Stanley & Co.

Brooklyn Hospital ($30,000) see Hutchins Foundation, Mary J.

Brooklyn In Touch Information Center see Morgan Stanley & Co.

Brooklyn Mosque ($330,000) see Ala Vi Foundation of New York

Brooklyn Museum ($500,000) see Cantor Foundation, Iris and B. Gerald

Brooklyn Museum ($52,500) see Gilman Foundation, Howard

Brooklyn Museum ($650,000) see Hillman Family Foundation, Alex

Brooklyn Museum ($9,994) see Kevorkian Fund, Hagop

Brooklyn Museum ($5,000) see Kidder, Peabody & Co.

Brooklyn Museum ($10,000) see Smeal Foundation, Mary Jean & Frank P.

Brooklyn Museum ($13,250) see Wunsch Foundation

Brooklyn Museum ($25,000) see Zuckerberg Foundation, Roy J.

Brooklyn Philharmonic ($3,500) see Goldie-Anna Charitable Trust

Brooklyn Public Library ($5,938) see Tuch Foundation, Michael

Brooklyn Society for the Prevention of Cruelty to Children — to expand existing group home for girls ($50,000) see St. Giles Foundation

Brooklyn in Touch Information Center ($25,000) see Bowne Foundation, Robert

Brooklyn in Touch Information Center ($20,000) see Snyder Fund, Valentine Perry

Brooklyn United Methodist Church Home ($5,500) see Faith Home Foundation

Brooks School ($30,000) see Greentree Foundation

Brookville Reformed Church ($10,000) see Kopf Foundation, Elizabeth Christy

Brookville Reformed Church ($3,000) see Rauch Foundation

Broome County Arts Council ($57,500) see Hoyt Foundation, Stewart W. and Willma C.

Broome County Arts Council ($17,000) see Klee Foundation, Conrad and Virginia

Broome County Child Development Council ($18,000) see Hoyt Foundation, Stewart W. and Willma C.

Broome County College — capital ($22,500) see Klee Foundation, Conrad and Virginia

Brown Sports Foundation ($1,000) see Stuart Foundation

Brunswick Prep School ($6,000) see Messing Foundation, Morris M. and Helen F.

Brunswick Prep School ($35,000) see Oaklawn Foundation

Bryant Park Restoration Corporation ($195,000) see Pinewood Foundation

Bryant Park Restoration Corporation ($50,000) see Wallach Foundation, Miriam G. and Ira D.

B'Tselam Israel Information Center ($20,000) see Bydale Foundation

Buffalo and Erie County Historical Society — resource center ($20,000) see Baird Foundation

Buffalo Fine Arts Academy ($18,400) see Goldome F.S.B

Buffalo Fine Arts Academy ($205,600) see Knox Foundation, Seymour H.

Buffalo General Hospital ($39,145) see Cummings Foundation, James K.

Buffalo General Hospital ($65,000) see Julia R. and Estelle L. Foundation

Buffalo Guitar Quartet — operating expenses ($100) see Hooper Handling

Buffalo Medical Foundation ($20,000) see Baird Foundation

Buffalo Philharmonic Orchestra ($45,000) see Cornell Trust, Peter C.

Buffalo Philharmonic Orchestra ($45,000) see Cornell Trust, Peter C.

Buffalo Philharmonic Orchestra ($30,000) see Goldome F.S.B

Buffalo Philharmonic Orchestra ($6,500) see Hooper Handling

Buffalo Philharmonic Orchestra ($7,000) see Mark IV Industries

Buffalo Philharmonic Orchestra ($10,000) see Rich Products Corp.

Buffalo Philharmonic Orchestra Society — annual fund drive ($130,000) see Baird Foundation, Cameron

Buffalo Philharmonic Orchestra Society — endowment campaign ($75,000) see Baird Foundation, Cameron

Buffalo Seminary — scholarships ($30,000) see Baird Foundation, Cameron

Buffalo State College Foundation — for internships ($250,000) see Getty Trust, J. Paul

Bulletin of Asia Institute ($1,000) see Foundation for Iranian Studies

Burden Center for the Aged ($3,500) see Litwin Foundation

Burke Rehabilitation Center ($3,000) see Glenn Foundation for Medical Research, Paul F.

Burke Rehabilitation Center ($80,000) see Langeloth Foundation, Jacob and Valeria

Burke Rehabilitation Center ($25,000) see Webster Foundation, Edwin S.

Bushwick Community Service Society — support for a community-based coordinatior of children's services ($100,000) see Foundation for Child Development

Business Committee for the Arts see Johnson & Johnson

Business Council for the United Nations ($3,000) see United Merchants & Manufacturers

Business Executives for National Security ($10,000) see Phillips-Van Heusen Corp.

C. and L. Feil Cornell Scholarship Fund ($25,000) see Feil Foundation, Louis and Gertrude

C.H.I. Manhattan ($50,000) see Lounsbery Foundation, Richard

C-Media ($15,000) see Vollrath Co.

Cabrini Medical Center ($50,000) see Morris Foundation, William T.

Calhoun School — capital campaign ($200,000) see Beir Foundation

Calhoun School ($2,500) see Beir Foundation

Calvary Fund — for scholarship fund ($5,000) see Stott Foundation, Louis L.

Calvary Hospital — endowment fund ($50,000) see Hearst Foundation, William Randolph

Calvary Hospital ($19,000) see Nias Foundation, Henry

Calvary Hospital ($10,000) see Rice Family Foundation, Jacob and Sophie

Camelot Family Foundation see New York Mercantile Exchange

Camp Fire of Buffalo and Erie County ($4,000) see Children's Foundation of Erie County

Camp Good Days, Special Times ($600) see Gear Motion

Camp Isabella Freedman ($42,000) see Abrons Foundation, Louis and Anne

Camp Isabella Freedman of Connecticut ($155,908) see Scheuer Family Foundation, S. H. and Helen R.

Camp School of Holy Childhood — capital campaign ($25,000) see Davenport-Hatch Foundation

Camp Shelter Island ($7,500) see Palmer-Fry Memorial Trust, Lily

Camp Sloane ($6,000) see Palmer-Fry Memorial Trust, Lily

Camp Vacamas Association ($30,000) see Dreitzer Foundation

Camp Vacamas Association ($16,500) see Forbes Charitable Trust, Herman

Camp Vacamas Association ($16,000) see Forbes Charitable Trust, Herman

Camp Vacamas Association ($10,000) see Parshelsky Foundation, Moses L.

Camp Washington ($6,500) see Palmer-Fry Memorial Trust, Lily

Camp Wethersfield — operational expenses ($72,000) see Homeland Foundation

Campaign for Carnegie Hall ($30,000) see Kimmelman Foundation, Helen & Milton

Canajoharie Central School ($50,000) see Arkell Hall Foundation

Canajoharie Library and Art Gallery ($200,000) see Arkell Hall Foundation

Canajoharie Youth Center ($20,000) see Arkell Hall Foundation

Cancer Prevention Research Institute ($10,000) see McGonagle Foundation, Dextra Baldwin

Cancer Research Institute ($50,000) see Freeman Charitable Trust, Samuel

Cancer Research Institute ($50,000) see Freeman Charitable Trust, Samuel

Cancer Research Institute ($7,500) see Geist Foundation

Cancer Research Institute ($50,000) see Herzog Foundation, Carl J.

Cancer Research Institute ($25,000) see Jacobson & Sons, Benjamin

Cancer Research Institute ($8,000) see Simpson Foundation

Cancer Research Institute (CRI) ($100,000) see Cummings Memorial Fund Trust, Frances L. and Edwin L.

Cancer Research Institute — Kirby Foundation Fellowship to name the Clinical Research Program ($210,000) see Kirby Foundation, F. M.

Canisius College ($10,000) see Cottrell Foundation

Canisius College ($25,000) see Goldome F.S.B

Canisius College ($105,000) see Julia R. and Estelle L. Foundation

Canisius College ($10,000) see Mark IV Industries

Canisius College ($50,000) see Palisano Foundation, Vincent and Harriet

Canisius College ($6,000) see Palisano Foundation, Vincent and Harriet

Canisius College ($5,000) see Rich Products Corp.

Canisius High School ($2,500) see Tripifoods

Capital Area Community Health Plan — patient-centered care in managed care group practice programs, phase two ($250,000) see Commonwealth Fund

Caramoor ($15,000) see Icahn Foundation, Carl C.

Caramoor Arts Center ($5,000) see Williams Foundation, C. K.

Cardinal Hayes Home for Children ($115,000) see Millbrook Tribute Garden

Cardinal's Archdiocesan Appeal ($25,000) see Joyce Foundation, John M. and Mary A.

Cardinal's Committee for the Laity ($5,000) see Mann Foundation, John Jay

Cardinal's Committee of the Laity ($15,000) see Prudential-Bache Securities

Cardinal's Committee for the Laity ($25,000) see Rice Family Foundation, Jacob and Sophie

Cardinal's Committee of the Laity on Wall Street ($25,000) see Salomon

CARE ($5,000) see Bluhdorn Charitable Trust, Charles G. and Yvette

CARE ($200) see Gross Foundation, Louis H.

CARE ($500) see Hirschhorn Foundation, David and Barbara B.

CARE ($2,981) see Loomis House

CARE ($100,000) see Penzance Foundation

Care Worldwide ($15,000) see Frees Foundation

Carl C. Icahn Program Child Abuse ($70,000) see Icahn Foundation, Carl C.

Carmelite Monastery of Rochester ($50,000) see Link, Jr. Foundation, George

Carmelites of Mary Immaculate ($7,500) see Butler Foundation, J. Homer

Carnegie Corporation of New York — for the Carnegie Commission on science, technology, and government ($2,500,000) see Carnegie Corporation of New York

Carnegie Corporation of New York — for the Carnegie Council on adolescent development ($1,500,000) see Carnegie Corporation of New York

Carnegie Council on Ethics ($10,000) see Phillips-Van Heusen Corp.

Carnegie Council on Ethics ($10,000) see Phillips-Van Heusen Corp.

Carnegie Council on Ethics ($10,000) see See Foundation, Charles

Carnegie Council on Ethics and International Affairs — to support the third year of the consultative group on U.S.-Japan economic cooperation in the Philippines ($185,636) see United States-Japan Foundation

Carnegie Hall ($50,000) see Heckscher Foundation for Children

Carnegie Hall see Morgan Stanley & Co.

Carnegie Hall ($17,882) see Morse, Jr. Foundation, Enid and Lester S.

Carnegie Hall — capital campaign ($42,000) see Paramount Communications Inc.

Carnegie Hall ($300,000) see Primerica Corp.

Carnegie Hall ($90,000) see Revlon

Carnegie Hall ($50,000) see Rigler-Deutsch Foundation

Carnegie Hall ($50,000) see Rose Foundation, Billy

Carnegie Hall Society ($35,000) see Baier Foundation, Marie

Carnegie Hall Society ($147,450) see Botwinick-Wolfensohn Foundation

Carnegie Hall Society ($10,000) see Holzer Memorial Foundation, Richard H.

Carnegie Hall Society ($5,000) see Kramer Foundation, C. L. C.

Carnegie Hall Society ($10,000) see Odyssey Partners

Carnegie Hall Society ($10,000) see Phillips-Van Heusen Corp.

Carnegie Hall Society ($50,000) see Rohatyn Foundation, Felix and Elizabeth

Carnegie Hall Society ($10,000) see Rohatyn Foundation, Felix and Elizabeth

Carnegie Hall Society ($25,000) see Weiler Foundation, Theodore & Renee

Carnegie Hall Society Centennial ($100,000) see New York Times Co.

Casetlani Art Museum Niagara University ($10,000) see Bernstein & Co., Sanford C.

Casita Maria — providing Outreach to homebound elderly in East Harlem ($30,000) see New York Foundation

Casita Maria Settlement House ($25,000) see Freeman Charitable Trust, Samuel

Catalyst see Booz Allen & Hamilton

Catalyst see United Airlines

Cathedral Church of St. John the Devine — to expand their Stoneyard Institute's urban job training program ($120,000) see Kaplan Fund, J. M.

Cathedral Church of St. Thomas the Apostle ($8,000) see Foundation for the Needs of Others

Cathedral of St. John the Devine ($5,000) see Manitou Foundation

Cathedral of St. John the Divine ($1,000) see Adams Memorial Fund, Emma J.

Cathedral of St. John the Divine ($1,000) see Adams Memorial Fund, Emma J.

Cathedral of St. John the Divine ($7,500) see Berlin Charitable Fund, Irving

Cathedral of St. John the Divine ($50,000) see Ross Foundation, Arthur

Cathedral of St. John Divine — religious ($5,000) see Young Foundation, Robert R.

Cathedral of St. John The Divine — to underwrite the salary of the Reverend Cecily Broderick y Guerra ($35,000) see Hunt Alternatives Fund

Catholic Big Sisters ($3,000) see Charitable Foundation of the Burns Family

Catholic Big Sisters ($5,000) see O'Neil Foundation, Cyril F. and Marie E.

Catholic Charities ($15,000) see Biddle Foundation, Margaret T.

Catholic Charities ($50,000) see Bobst Foundation, Elmer and Mamdouha

Catholic Charities ($20,992) see Goldome F.S.B

Catholic Charities — food pantry ($2,000) see Joy Family Foundation

Catholic Charities ($30,000) see Joyce Foundation, John M. and Mary A.

Catholic Charities ($10,000) see Lavanburg-Corner House

Catholic Charities ($25,000) see Noble Charitable Trust, John L. and Ethel G.

Catholic Charities ($5,000) see O'Neil Foundation, Cyril F. and Marie E.

Catholic Charities ($5,000) see Rice Family Foundation, Jacob and Sophie

Catholic Charities ($15,000) see Turner Fund, Ruth

Catholic Charities Appeal ($105,000) see Julia R. and Estelle L. Foundation

Catholic Charities of Archdiocese of New York ($25,000) see Badgeley Residuary Charitable Trust, Rose M.

Catholic Charities — Diocese of Brooklyn ($50,000) see Goldman Foundation, Herman

Catholic Charities — Inner City Scholarship Fund ($20,000) see Nias Foundation, Henry

Catholic Home Bureau ($25,100) see Mertz Foundation, Martha

Catholic Home Bureau ($47,500) see O'Sullivan Children Foundation

Catholic Home Bureau — to support the Maternity Birthcare Program ($100,000) see Altman Foundation

Catholic Institute of the Food Industry ($1,200) see Key Food Stores Cooperative Inc.

Catholic Medical Center of Brooklyn and Queens see Merrill Lynch & Co.

Catholic Medical Mission Board ($10,000) see Goldbach Foundation, Ray and Marie

Catholic Union of Sick in America (CUSA) ($60,100) see Brunner Foundation, Robert

Catholic Youth Organization of the Archdiocese of New York ($47,600) see Grace & Co., W.R.

Catholics United for the Faith ($15,000) see Drum Foundation

Catholics United for the Faith ($20,000) see Joyce Foundation, John M. and Mary A.

Catskill Center for Conservation and Development ($21,477) see Erpf Fund, Armand G.

Catskill Flyfishing Center ($6,000) see Kellogg Foundation, Peter and Cynthia K.

Catskill Forest Association — firewood processing program ($121,296) see O'Connor Foundation, A. Lindsay and Olive B.

Cayuga County Arts Council ($3,000) see Everett Charitable Trust

Cayuga County Community College — scholarship fund ($6,000) see Allyn Foundation

Cayuga County Community College Foundation — general endowment fund ($100,000) see Emerson Foundation, Fred L.

Cayuga County Health Association — building program for meals on wheels quarters ($12,500) see Allyn Foundation

Cayuga Nature Center ($7,500) see Delavan Foundation, Nelson B.

Cazenovia College ($10,000) see Chapman Charitable Corporation, Howard and Bess

Cazenovia College ($7,000) see Chapman Charitable Corporation, Howard and Bess

Cazenovia College ($5,000) see Mather Fund, Richard

CD ($58,333) see Zilkha & Sons

CDS International ($21,700) see Miles Inc.

Center on Addiction and Substance Abuse ($6,000,000) see Johnson Foundation, Robert Wood

Center on Addiction and Substance Abuse ($50,000) see Primerica Corp.

Center on Addiction and Substance Abuse at Columbia University — drug-abuse prevention efforts for Newark youth ($105,000) see Prudential Insurance Co. of America

Center on Addiction and Substance Abuse at Columbia University — general support of research, demonstration and public information projects ($50,000) see Hearst Foundation, William Randolph

Center for African Art ($91,200) see Benenson Foundation, Frances and Benjamin

Center for African Art ($27,400) see Gulton Foundation

Center for African Art ($10,000) see Mnuchin Foundation

New York (cont.)

Center for African Art ($40,000) see Solow Foundation

Center for Anti-Violence Education ($10,000) see Hunt Alternatives Fund, Helen

Center for Catholic Lay Leadership Formation — to develop a lay catechetical leadership core for South Bronx and Harlem ($50,000) see Koch Foundation

Center for Children and Families ($4,000) see Kepco, Inc.

Center for Collaborative Education — for parent involvement programs in alternative public schools ($15,000) see Bay Foundation

Center for Collaborative Education ($41,000) see Bruner Foundation

Center for Collaborative Education ($50,000) see Uris Brothers Foundation

Center for Collaborative Education — to support Central Park East Secondary School's administrative expenses, internes, and consultants for the school year 1990-91 ($20,000) see Matsushita Electric Corp. of America

Center for Collaborative Education — to support Central Park East Secondary School's administrative expenses, internes, and consultants for the school year 1990-91 ($5,000) see Matsushita Electric Corp. of America

Center for Constitutional Rights ($20,000) see Boehm Foundation

Center for Constitutional Rights ($10,000) see Boehm Foundation

Center for Constitutional Rights ($3,500) see Carteh Foundation

Center for Constitutional Rights ($20,000) see MacArthur Foundation, J. Roderick

Center for Constitutional Rights ($20,000) see MacArthur Foundation, J. Roderick

Center for Constitutional Rights ($50,000) see Rubin Foundation, Samuel

Center for Constitutional Rights ($10,000) see Warner Fund, Albert and Bessie

Center for Constitutional Rights — Anti-Bias Violence Project ($25,000) see Norman Foundation

Center for Constitutional Rights — for the Reproductive Rights and Women's Rights Litigation project ($20,000) see Hunt Alternatives Fund

Center for Democratic Renewal ($15,000) see Bydale Foundation

Center for Educational Option — continuing program of teaching elementary school level ($20,000) see Lincoln Fund

Center for Family Life ($10,000) see Silverweed Foundation

Center for Governmental Research ($90,000) see Gleason Memorial Fund

Center for Intergenerational Reading — for Literacy Through Love; New York City Technical College; parents who read to their children at home ($20,000) see Hunt Alternatives Fund

Center for Preventive Psychiatry ($25,000) see Oppenheimer and Flora Oppenheimer Haas Trust, Leo

Center for Public Resources ($4,000) see Covington and Burling

Center for Public Resources ($4,000) see Donovan, Leisure, Newton & Irvine

Center for Religion, Ethics, and Society Policy ($10,000) see Delavan Foundation, Nelson B.

Center for Religion, Ethics, and Society Policy ($5,000) see Delavan Foundation, Nelson B.

Center for Research on Institutions and Social Policy ($5,000) see Macht Foundation, Morton and Sophia

Center for Retina Research ($4,000) see Kaplun Foundation, Morris J. and Betty

Center School — for minority teaching interns ($6,000) see Bay Foundation

Center for Science in the Public Interest ($3,000) see Ogden Foundation, Ralph E.

Central Nassau Services ($15,000) see Lennox International, Inc.

Central New York Community Foundation Greater Pulaski Fund ($50,000) see Snow Memorial Trust, John Ben

Central New York Community Fund ($25,000) see Mather Fund, Richard

Central Park Conservancy ($5,000) see Abrams Foundation, Benjamin and Elizabeth

Central Park Conservancy ($5,000) see Barth Foundation, Theodore H.

Central Park Conservancy ($5,000) see Cayuga Foundation

Central Park Conservancy ($11,650) see Foote, Cone & Belding Communications

Central Park Conservancy ($250,000) see Gilder Foundation

Central Park Conservancy ($27,750) see Golden Family Foundation

Central Park Conservancy ($50,000) see Hall Charitable Trust, Evelyn A. J.

Central Park Conservancy ($30,000) see Hall Charitable Trust, Evelyn A. J.

Central Park Conservancy ($5,000) see Johnson Foundation, Howard

Central Park Conservancy ($30,000) see McConnell Foundation, Neil A.

Central Park Conservancy see Merrill Lynch & Co.

Central Park Conservancy see Morgan Stanley & Co.

Central Park Conservancy ($50,000) see Moses Fund, Henry and Lucy

Central Park Conservancy ($80,000) see New York Times Co.

Central Park Conservancy ($10,000) see Osborn Charitable Trust, Edward B.

Central Park Conservancy — special project ($25,000) see Pfizer

Central Park Conservancy — program support ($383,333) see RJR Nabisco Inc.

Central Park Conservancy ($109,318) see Ross Foundation, Arthur

Central Park Conservancy ($10,000) see Sasco Foundation

Central Park Conservancy ($10,000) see Sheinberg Foundation, Eric P.

Central Park Conservancy ($15,000) see Tucker Foundation, Marcia Brady

Central Park Conservancy ($15,000) see United States Trust Co. of New York

Central Park Conservancy Honor of Jim Evans ($70,000) see Gilder Foundation

Central Park Conservancy — Shakespeare Gardener ($25,000) see Griggs and Mary Griggs Burke Foundation, Mary Livingston

Central Park Conservancy — start-up funding for the "Nature's Classroom" program see New Street Capital Corp.

Central Rabbinical Seminary ($25,000) see Fogel Foundation, Shalom and Rebecca

Central School District #1 — Recycling Program ($35,000) see Snow Foundation, John Ben

Central Suffolk Hospital ($3,000) see Fish Foundation, Vain and Harry

Central Synagogue ($2,965) see Beir Foundation

Central Synagogue ($150) see Ginsberg Family Foundation, Moses

Centurion Foundation ($50,000) see Ames Charitable Trust, Harriett

Cerebral Palsy Center for the Disabled ($15,000) see Fleet Bank of New York

Chai Lifeline ($7,000) see Gruber Research Foundation, Lila

CHAMAH ($7,500) see Mazer Foundation, Jacob and Ruth

CHAMAH ($25,000) see Meyerhoff Fund, Joseph

CHAMAH ($3,500) see Propp Sons Fund, Morris and Anna

Channel 13 ($200) see Contempo Communications

Channel 13 ($1,000) see Hillman Family Foundation, Alex

Channel 13 ($15,000) see Kern Foundation, Ilma

Channel Thirteen ($18,000) see Rodgers Foundation, Richard & Dorothy

Channel 13 ($5,000) see Sasco Foundation

Chapin Home for the Aging ($2,500) see Faith Home Foundation

Chapin School — expansion of facilities ($50,000) see Baker Trust, George F.

Charter Seventy Seven ($36,000) see Trust for Mutual Understanding

Chase Manhattan Foundation ($320,000) see Chase Manhattan Bank, N.A.

Chase Manhattan Foundation Scholarship Program ($91,473) see Chase Manhattan Bank, N.A.

Chautauqua Area Girl Scout Council ($50,000) see Hultquist Foundation

Chautauqua Fire Department ($10,000) see Carnahan-Jackson Foundation

Chautauqua Institute ($10,000) see Darrah Charitable Trust, Jessie Smith

Chautauqua Institution ($120,000) see Carnahan-Jackson Foundation

Chautauqua Institution ($25,000) see Hultquist Foundation

Chautauqua Institution ($55,000) see Sheldon Foundation, Ralph C.

Chautauqua Lake Association ($54,650) see Sheldon Foundation, Ralph C.

Chautauqua Striders ($12,000) see Hultquist Foundation

Chemotherapy Foundation ($3,000) see Lazarus Charitable Trust, Helen and Charles

Chemotherapy Foundation ($40,000) see Tai and Co., J. T.

Chemung County Area Community Foundation ($4,000) see Anderson Foundation

Chemung County Historical Society ($4,700) see Hilliard Corp.

Chemung Valley Arts Council ($10,000) see Taylor Foundation, Fred and Harriett

Child Adoption Service of Children Aid Society ($8,000) see Luce Charitable Trust, Theodore

Child Care ($100,000) see Booth Ferris Foundation

Child Care — evaluation of homeless ($30,000) see Mailman Family Foundation, A. L.

Child Care, Inc. ($37,000) see Primerica Corp.

Child Care Action Campaign ($40,000) see Primerica Corp.

Child and Family Services ($7,500) see Children's Foundation of Erie County

Child and Family Services ($5,000) see Goodyear Foundation, Josephine

Childhope Foundation — support "PROJICA A collaborative Project to Protect the Rights of Children and Youth in Brazil" ($30,000) see Jurzykowski Foundation, Alfred

Children of Alcoholics Foundation ($50,000) see Primerica Corp.

Children of Alcoholics Foundation ($5,000) see Sequa Corp.

Children's Aid Society ($200,000) see Clark Foundation

Children's Aid Society ($25,000) see Hagedorn Fund

Children's Aid Society ($30,000) see Moore Foundation, Edward S.

Children's Aid Society ($6,000) see Palmer-Fry Memorial Trust, Lily

Children's Aid Society ($100,560) see Stern Foundation, Bernice and Milton

Children's Aid Society — support an Adolescent Sexuality and Pregnancy Prevention training program for 15 New York City community-based social service agencies ($25,000) see Guttman Foundation, Stella and Charles

Children's Aid Society Alvin Ailey/CAS Comp Dance Theatre ($23,000) see Blum Foundation, Edna F.

Children's Aid Society — for the Career Readiness and Summer Teen Employment Programs ($75,000) see Bodman Foundation

Children's Annex ($5,000) see Agape Foundation

Children's Arts and Sciences Workshop ($4,000) see Davis Foundation, Simon and Annie

Children's Blood Foundation ($2,000) see Berkowitz Family Foundation, Louis

Children's Blood Foundation — AIDS research and ongoing support of clinic ($60,000) see Rubinstein Foundation, Helena

Children's Defense Fund ($10,000) see Cohen Foundation, Wilfred P.

Children's Defense Fund — includes second payment of $75,000 capital grant, $40,000 for general support, and $10,000 for the New York City "Leave No Child Behind" campaign ($75,000) see J.P. Morgan & Co.

Children's Diabetes Foundation ($5,000) see I. and L. Association

Children's Emergency Holiday Fund ($8,200) see Gould Foundation for Children, Edwin

Children's Harbor ($150,000) see Russell Educational Foundation, Benjamin and Roberta

Children's Health Fund ($10,000) see PaineWebber

Children's Health Fund ($10,000) see United States Trust Co. of New York

Children's Heart Fund ($10,000) see Bastien Memorial Foundation, John E. and Nellie J.

Children's Heart Fund ($2,500) see Getsch Family Foundation Trust

Children's Heart Hospital ($25,000) see Carvel Foundation, Thomas and Agnes

Children's Hospital ($25,000) see Cornell Trust, Peter C.

Children's Hospital ($18,000) see Goldome F.S.B

Children's Hospital ($25,000) see Goodyear Foundation, Josephine

Children's Hospital ($30,300) see Knox Foundation, Seymour H.

Children's Hospital ($20,000) see Mark IV Industries

Children's Hospital of Buffalo ($106,323) see Cummings Foundation, James H.

Children's Hospital of Buffalo — enhanced support services, services of high risk infants ($28,500) see Joy Family Foundation

Children's Hospital Medical Center ($5,000) see Grigg-Lewis Trust

Children's House ($25,000) see Silverburgh Foundation, Grace, George & Judith

Children's Immunology Research Fund ($10,000) see Turner Fund, Ruth

Children's Museum of Manhattan ($27,500) see Berrie Foundation, Russell

Children's Museum of Manhattan ($16,667) see Macmillan, Inc.

Children's Museum of Manhattan ($16,666) see Solow Foundation

Children's Museum of Manhattan ($16,668) see Stern Foundation, Leonard N.

Children's Museum of Manhattan ($10,000) see United States Trust Co. of New York

Children's Museum of Manhattan ($2,000) see Weiss Foundation, Stephen and Suzanne

Children's Rescue Fund ($25,000) see Icahn Foundation, Carl C.

Children's Rescue Fund ($25,000) see Paramount Communications Inc.

Children's Rights Project ACLUF ($50,000) see Icahn Foundation, Carl C.

Children's Storefront ($15,000) see Dreyfus Foundation, Jean and Louis

Children's Storefront ($10,000) see Gould Foundation for Children, Edwin

Children's Storefront ($2,000) see Iroquois Avenue Foundation

Children's Storefront — toward salary of counselor for graduates of school ($15,000) see Lincoln Fund

Children's Storefront ($20,000) see Mellam Family Foundation

Children's Storefront ($15,000) see Menil Foundation

Children's Television Workshop — "Square One TV" sponsorship ($710,000) see Intel Corp.

Children's Torah Foundation ($10,000) see Icahn Foundation, Carl C.

Children's Torah Foundation ($1,000) see Melohn Foundation

Children's Village ($20,000) see St. Faith's House Foundation

Children's Village — to meet a Kresge Foundation Challenge grant toward a capital campaign ($35,000) see Hearst Foundation

Chinese Bible Church ($15,000) see Tai and Co., J. T.

Chinese Institute in America ($20,000) see Tai and Co., J. T.

Chinese Staff and Workers Association — to enable workers to advance their rights in the workplace and community ($25,000) see Norman Foundation

Christ Church ($20,000) see Gronewaldt Foundation, Alice Busch

Christ Church ($6,000) see MacDonald Foundation, James A.

Christ Church and Holy Family ($1,062) see Killough Trust, Walter H. D.

Christ Community Alliance Church ($15,000) see M.E. Foundation

Christ Hospital ($6,000) see Switzer Foundation

Christian Heralds Children's Home ($16,036) see Hallett Charitable Trust, Jessie F.

Christian Missionary Alliance — in support of outreach program to the needy and disadvantaged ($3,000) see

Fish Foundation, Vain and Harry

Church and Friary of St. Francis of Assisi ($100,000) see Link, Jr. Foundation, George

Church of Heavenly Rest ($25,000) see Vidda Foundation

Church of Holy Trinity ($5,000) see Memton Fund

Church of Holy Trinity ($5,000) see Stott Foundation, Robert L.

Church in New York ($10,000) see Tai and Co., J. T.

Church of St. Luke in the Fields ($2,500) see Kautz Family Foundation

Church of St. Rose of Lima — 1991 Ford Club Wagon ($19,450) see Hackett Foundation

Churchill School ($25,000) see Neu Foundation, Hugo and Doris

Churchill School and Center ($75,000) see Brooks Foundation, Gladys

Chusid Torah Center ($20,000) see Fuchsberg Family Foundation, Abraham

Chusid Torah Center ($12,500) see Fuchsberg Family Foundation, Abraham

Circle Repertory Company ($12,500) see Witco Corp.

Circle in the Square ($10,000) see Sheafer Charitable Trust, Emma A.

Circle in the Square ($5,000) see Spiritus Gladius Foundation

Circle in the Square Theatre ($3,000) see Wyne Foundation

Circle in the Square Theatre — for partial support of Production of Search and Destroy ($5,000) see Axe-Houghton Foundation

Citizen Exchange Council ($25,000) see Weyerhaeuser Family Foundation

Citizens Budget Commission ($9,000) see Durst Foundation

Citizens Budget Commission ($3,000) see Odyssey Partners

Citizens Budget Commission ($40,000) see Smeal Foundation, Mary Jean & Frank P.

Citizens Budget Commission ($40,000) see Smeal Foundation, Mary Jean & Frank P.

Citizens Committee for the Children of New York ($10,000) see Dreitzer Foundation

Citizens Committee for Children of New York City ($10,000) see Reicher Foundation, Anne & Harry J.

Citizens Committee for New York City ($50,000) see Guggenheim Foundation, Daniel and Florence

Citizens Committee for New York City ($30,000) see Merck Family Fund

Citizens Committee for New York City — general program ($10,000) see Paley Foundation, William S.

Citizens Committee for New York City — demonstration program to reduce youth involvement in drug trafficking ($40,000) see Pinkerton Foundation

Citizens Committee for New York City ($15,000) see Stern Foundation, Irvin

Citizens Committee for New York City — for the 1991-92

Neighborhood Environmental Action Awards program ($125,000) see Cary Charitable Trust, Mary Flagler

Citizens Committee for New York City — support for the 1992-93 Neighborhood Environmental Action Awards program ($125,000) see Cary Charitable Trust, Mary Flagler

Citizens Crime Commission of New York ($10,000) see Rudin Foundation

Citizens Exchange Council ($71,360) see Gilman Foundation, Howard

Citizens Hose Company ($20,000) see Taylor Foundation, Fred and Harriett

City Center ($25,750) see Harkness Ballet Foundation

City Center ($12,000) see Harkness Foundation, William Hale

City Center ($3,500) see Schloss & Co., Marcus

City College of the City University of New York ($100,000) see Goldman Foundation, Herman

City College-CUNY ($150,000) see Pforzheimer Foundation, Carl and Lily

City College Simon H. Rifkind Center ($100,000) see Winston Foundation, Norman and Rosita

City Harvest ($5,000) see Barth Foundation, Theodore H.

City Harvest ($1,000) see Donaldson, Lufkin & Jenrette

City Harvest ($50,000) see Goldman Charitable Trust, Sol

City Harvest ($10,000) see New York Stock Exchange

City Harvest ($25,000) see Rhodebeck Charitable Trust

City of Jamestown ($167,000) see Sheldon Foundation, Ralph C.

City Meals on Wheels see Bloomingdale's

City Meals on Wheels ($5,000) see Kern Foundation, Ilma

City of New York Department of Cultural Affairs ($40,000) see Primerica Corp.

City Opera ($5,000) see Holzer Memorial Foundation, Richard H.

City Parks Foundation ($50,000) see Heckscher Foundation for Children

City Parks Foundation ($12,500) see Stern Foundation, Leonard N.

City Parks Foundation ($1,267,830) see Wallace Reader's Digest Fund, Lila

City Parks Foundation ($15,000) see Weininger Foundation, Richard and Gertrude

City University Community School ($77,223) see Bruner Foundation

City University of New York ($5,000) see Gould Foundation for Children, Edwin

City University of New York — an institute on disability studies ($50,000) see Kennedy, Jr. Foundation, Joseph P.

City University of New York ($10,000) see Wenner-Gren Foundation for Anthropological Research

City University of New York Graduate Center — aid field research on international uses of scientific models for the

acquisition of immunodeficiency, Rio de Janeiro, Brazil ($10,000) see Wenner-Gren Foundation for Anthropological Research

City University of New York Graduate School ($9,100) see Durst Foundation

City University of New York Law School at Queens College — Dean's Discretionary Fund ($15,000) see Boehm Foundation

City University of New York, Office of Academic Affairs — implementation of minority teacher recruitment and retention program ($249,856) see Diamond Foundation, Aaron

City University of New York, Office of Academic Affairs: Chancellor's Minority Graduate Scholars Program — the Pipeline program ($250,000) see Diamond Foundation, Aaron

City University of New York Research Foundation ($85,400) see Bowne Foundation, Robert

Civil Justice Fund ($10,000) see Fuchsberg Family Foundation, Abraham

CLAL ($5,000) see Bravmann Foundation, Ludwig

CLAL ($8,750) see Odyssey Partners

CLAL ($4,000) see Steinberg Family Foundation, Meyer and Jean

Clarkson Center for Human Services ($15,000) see Children's Foundation of Erie County

Clarkson University see Eastman Kodak Co.

Clarkson University ($2,500) see General Railway Signal Corp.

Clarkson University ($66,000) see Gleason Memorial Fund

Clarkson University ($25,000) see Kent Foundation, Ada Howe

Clarkson University ($15,000) see Snow Foundation, John Ben

Clarkson University — Cheel Campus Center Project ($125,000) see Emerson Foundation, Fred L.

Clarkson University — William C. Decker-Corning Scholars program ($25,000) see Corning Incorporated

Clear Pool Camp ($5,156) see Ellsworth Trust, W. H.

Clear Pool Camp ($55,000) see Moore Foundation, Edward S.

Clear Pool Camp ($50,000) see Moore Foundation, Edward S.

Clear Pool Camp ($10,000) see New York Stock Exchange

Clear Pool/District #16 ($10,000) see Gould Foundation for Children, Edwin

Clear View School ($10,000) see St. Faith's House Foundation

Clearpool School — model year-round school program ($64,000) see Sega of America

Clemens Center for the Performing Arts ($12,500) see Anderson Foundation

Clemens Center for the Performing Arts ($2,500) see Hilliard Corp.

Clifton Springs Hospital and Clinic — cancer center construction ($30,000) see Davenport-Hatch Foundation

Clubhouse of Suffolk — public welfare ($10,000) see Young Foundation, Robert R.

Coalition for the Homeless ($3,500) see Candlesticks Inc.

Cobleskill Agricultural and Technical College Foundation — scholarships ($15,000) see O'Connor Foundation, A. Lindsay and Olive B.

CODESH ($75,000) see Smith Fund, George D.

Cold Spring Harbor Laboratory ($30,000) see Allen Foundation, Rita

Cold Spring Harbor Laboratory ($125,000) see Banbury Fund

Cold Spring Harbor Laboratory ($75,000) see Banbury Fund

Cold Spring Harbor Laboratory ($25,000) see Chait Memorial Foundation, Sara

Cold Spring Harbor Laboratory — for neuro science center ($100,000) see DeCamp Foundation, Ira W.

Cold Spring Harbor Laboratory — building fund ($645,313) see Dolan Family Foundation

Cold Spring Harbor Laboratory — building fund ($247,500) see Dolan Family Foundation

Cold Spring Harbor Laboratory ($15,000) see Grass Foundation

Cold Spring Harbor Laboratory ($250,000) see Harriman Foundation, Gladys and Roland

Cold Spring Harbor Laboratory ($333,333) see Hazen Charitable Trust, Lita Annenberg

Cold Spring Harbor Laboratory ($50,000) see Hoffmann-La Roche

Cold Spring Harbor Laboratory — postgraduate program ($60,000) see Klingenstein Fund, Esther A. and Joseph

Cold Spring Harbor Laboratory — medical research ($342,667) see Mathers Charitable Foundation, G. Harold and Leila Y.

Cold Spring Harbor Laboratory — cancer research ($15,000) see Maxfield Foundation

Cold Spring Harbor Laboratory ($50,000) see Mellam Family Foundation

Cold Spring Harbor Laboratory ($25,000) see Nichols Foundation

Cold Spring Harbor Laboratory ($50,000) see Weezie Foundation

Cold Spring Harbor Laboratory ($35,000) see Westvaco Corp.

Cold Spring Harbor Laboratory — toward the cost of purchasing certain equipment for the Laboratory's new Bio-Technology Center ($250,000) see Rippel Foundation, Fannie E.

Cold Spring Harbor Laboratory — for renovation of the McClintock Laboratory ($100,000) see J.P. Morgan & Co.

Cold Spring Harbor Laboratory — to establish an endowed chair for the director of the W. M. Keck Structural Biology Laboratory see Keck Foundation, W. M.

Colgate University ($14,000) see Baird Foundation

Colgate University ($35,000) see Banfi Vintners

Colgate University ($48,000) see Banyan Tree Foundation

New York (cont.)

Colgate University ($10,000) see Branta Foundation

Colgate University ($25,000) see Dewar Foundation

Colgate University ($10,000) see Greene Foundation, David J.

Colgate University ($10,000) see Slifka Foundation, Joseph and Sylvia

College Board ($4,236,000) see Wallace-Reader's Digest Fund, DeWitt

College Careers ($5,000) see Kern Foundation, Ilma

College Careers see MBIA, Inc.

College Careers — part-time penitentiary counselor ($15,000) see Kern Foundation, Ilma

College of City of New York ($41,000) see Boehm Foundation

College of City of New York ($35,000) see Boehm Foundation

College of City of New York ($30,000) see Boehm Foundation

College of City of New York ($30,000) see Boehm Foundation

College Entrance Examination Board — for Hispanic scholar awards program ($1,000,000) see Mellon Foundation, Andrew W.

College Foundation ($20,000) see Yeager Charitable Trust, Lester E.

College for Human Services ($10,000) see Gould Foundation for Children, Edwin

College for Human Services ($10,000) see Joselow Foundation

College of Insurance — third payment of a three year pledge ($30,000) see Crum and Forster

College of Insurance ($100,000) see Metropolitan Life Insurance Co.

College of Mount St. Vincent ($155,000) see Grace & Co., W.R.

College of New Rochelle ($667) see Gilbane Foundation, Thomas and William

College of New Rochelle ($10,800) see Glickenhaus & Co.

College of Physicians and Surgeons ($20,000) see Dreyfus Foundation, Jean and Louis

College of Physicians and Surgeons ($75,300) see Edison Fund, Charles

College of Physicians and Surgeons — Alzheimer's Disease ($15,000) see Dreyfus Foundation, Jean and Louis

College of Physicians and Surgeons — Cancer ($15,000) see Dreyfus Foundation, Jean and Louis

College of Physicians and Surgeons of Columbia University — for hearing affiliated research ($225,000) see Capita Charitable Trust, Emil

College of Physicians and Surgeons of Columbia University — markers of early blood vessel injury research project ($60,000) see Schultz Foundation

College of Physicians and Surgeons of Columbia University — purchase of PCR machine ($20,000) see Schultz Foundation

College of Staten Island ($10,000) see Kettering Family Foundation

Collegiate School ($50,000) see Friedman Foundation, Stephen and Barbara

Collegiate School ($13,500) see Rubin Foundation, Rob E. & Judith O.

Collegiate School ($5,000) see Sharp Foundation, Charles S. and Ruth C.

Colonial Dames ($10,000) see Hyde Foundation, J. R.

Columbia Business School ($50,000) see Avis Inc.

Columbia Business School ($5,000) see Fair Oaks Foundation, Inc.

Columbia College ($2,500) see Baker & Baker

Columbia College ($25,000) see Blum Foundation, Edith C.

Columbia College ($2,500) see Davis Foundation, Simon and Annie

Columbia College see Greenwood Mills

Columbia College ($52,000) see Kraft Foundation

Columbia College ($50,000) see Newman Assistance Fund, Jerome A. and Estelle R.

Columbia College ($5,000) see Rice Family Foundation, Jacob and Sophie

Columbia College ($5,000) see Scurry Foundation, D. L.

Columbia College ($10,000) see Summerfield Foundation, Solon E.

Columbia College Fund ($1,500) see Ehrman Foundation, Fred and Susan

Columbia College Fund ($8,000) see Horowitz Foundation, Gedale B. and Barbara S.

Columbia College — addition to J. Henry Esser Scholarship Fund ($100,000) see Kaufmann Foundation, Marion Esser

Columbia College of Physicians and Surgeons ($30,000) see Sulzberger Foundation

Columbia Grammar and Prep School ($5,100) see Abrams Foundation, Benjamin and Elizabeth

Columbia Grammar and Prep School ($25,000) see Pincus Family Fund

Columbia Grammar and Preparatory School ($25,000) see Solow Foundation

Columbia Grammar School ($30,000) see AMETEK

Columbia Jewish Welfare Association ($75,000) see Baker & Baker

Columbia Law School ($100,000) see Blum Foundation, Edith C.

Columbia Law School ($5,000) see Fair Oaks Foundation, Inc.

Columbia Law School ($25,000) see Pines Bridge Foundation

Columbia Law School Fund ($100,000) see Horowitz Foundation, Gedale B. and Barbara S.

Columbia Museum ($20,000) see Baker & Baker

Columbia Presbyterian, Edwards, Harkness Eye Institute ($250,000) see Beinecke Foundation

Columbia Presbyterian Hospital ($10,000) see Cranshaw Corporation

Columbia Presbyterian Hospital — for the continuation of research and study of growth plate ($100,000) see St. Giles Foundation

Columbia-Presbyterian Medical Center ($25,000) see Allen Foundation, Frances

Columbia-Presbyterian Medical Center — cancer research ($235,000) see Hettinger Foundation

Columbia-Presbyterian Medical Center ($10,000) see Killough Trust, Walter H. D.

Columbia Presbyterian Medical Center ($10,000) see Simon Foundation, Sidney, Milton and Leoma

Columbia-Presbyterian Medical Center — aid for research in oral diseases and viral infections of the mouth ($10,000) see Vernon Fund, Miles Hodsdon

Columbia Presbyterian Medical Center — $5,000 general charitable contribution, $10,000 annual dinner, $10,000 Department of Medicine ($25,000) see Carter-Wallace

Columbia Presbyterian Medical Center, Clinical Oncology Fund ($10,000) see Straus Foundation, Martha Washington Straus and Harry H.

Columbia Presbyterian Medical Center Fund — hospital renovation and expansion ($100,000) see Farish Fund, William Stamps

Columbia-Presbyterian Medical Center Fund ($20,000) see Life Investors Insurance Company of America

Columbia Presbyterian Medical Center Fund — Edward S. Harkness Eye Institute ($125,000) see Bedminster Fund

Columbia-Presbyterian Medical Center, New York, NY ($50,000) see Chemical Bank

Columbia Presbyterian Otolarncology ($15,000) see Kingsley Foundation

Columbia Theological Seminary ($140,000) see Smith Charities, John

Columbia Univeristy — for the Encyclopaedia Iranica ($200,000) see Getty Trust, J. Paul

Columbia University ($120,000) see Banbury Fund

Columbia University ($100,000) see Booth Ferris Foundation

Columbia University ($250,000) see Botwinick-Wolfensohn Foundation

Columbia University ($50,000) see Branta Foundation

Columbia University ($25,000) see Bugher Foundation

Columbia University ($7,000) see Burnham Donor Fund, Alfred G.

Columbia University ($7,000) see China Times Cultural Foundation

Columbia University ($4,500) see China Times Cultural Foundation

Columbia University ($10,000) see Craigmyle Foundation

Columbia University ($24,000) see Crane Fund for Widows and Children

Columbia University ($1,000,000) see Delacorte Fund, George

Columbia University — nursing school and medical school operations ($10,000) see Devonwood Foundation

Columbia University ($20,000) see Diabetes Research and Education Foundation

Columbia University ($100,000) see Essel Foundation

Columbia University ($2,000) see Essel Foundation

Columbia University ($10,000) see Fair Oaks Foundation, Inc.

Columbia University ($25,000) see Gabelli Foundation

Columbia University ($25,000) see Gelb Foundation, Lawrence M.

Columbia University ($10,200) see Goldman Sachs & Co.

Columbia University ($10,000) see Hansen Memorial Foundation, Irving

Columbia University ($195,000) see Harriman Foundation, Gladys and Roland

Columbia University ($600,000) see Hatch Charitable Trust, Margaret Milliken

Columbia University ($500,000) see Hatch Charitable Trust, Margaret Milliken

Columbia University ($100,000) see Hatch Charitable Trust, Margaret Milliken

Columbia University ($32,500) see Hebrew Technical Institute

Columbia University ($125,000) see Helis Foundation

Columbia University ($30,000) see Heyward Memorial Fund, DuBose and Dorothy

Columbia University ($19,326) see Killough Trust, Walter H. D.

Columbia University ($52,272) see Lurcy Charitable and Educational Trust, Georges

Columbia University ($50,000) see MCA

Columbia University ($300,000) see Milken Institute for Job and Capital Formation

Columbia University ($10,000) see Miller Fund, Kathryn and Gilbert

Columbia University — neurology ($500,000) see Moses Fund, Henry and Lucy

Columbia University ($6,000) see Olivetti Office USA, Inc.

Columbia University — to study quasar clustering at very large distances ($500,000) see Packard Foundation, David and Lucile

Columbia University ($104,167) see Patterson and Clara Guthrie Patterson Trust, Robert Leet

Columbia University ($400,000) see Pincus Family Fund

Columbia University ($50,000) see Pulitzer Publishing Co.

Columbia University ($150,000) see Rudin Foundation, Samuel and May

Columbia University ($7,000) see Schamach Foundation, Milton

Columbia University ($288,000) see Seagram & Sons, Joseph E.

Columbia University ($64,772) see Sinsheimer Fund, Alexandrine and Alexander L.

Columbia University ($85,645) see Spunk Fund

Columbia University ($10,000) see Stony Wold Herbert Fund

Columbia University ($72,065) see Tai and Co., J. T.

Columbia University ($500,000) see Vetlesen Foundation, G. Unger

Columbia University ($25,000) see Vetlesen Foundation, G. Unger

Columbia University ($500,000) see Vidda Foundation

Columbia University ($250,000) see Warner-Lambert Co.

Columbia University ($350,000) see Weatherhead Foundation

Columbia University ($10,000) see Weil, Gotshal & Manges Foundation

Columbia University ($340,000) see Whiting Foundation, Mrs. Giles

Columbia University ($26,000) see Wiener Foundation, Malcolm Hewitt

Columbia University ($35,000) see Wilson Foundation, H. W.

Columbia University — support of the Charles H. Revson Fellows Program ($238,000) see Revson Foundation, Charles H.

Columbia University in the City of New York ($35,200) see Atran Foundation

Columbia University in the City of New York/School of Law — a new professorship in international environmental law ($320,000) see Prospect Hill Foundation

Columbia University College of Physicians — medical equipment ($150,000) see Hugoton Foundation

Columbia University College of Physicians and Surgeons ($44,727) see Hatch Charitable Trust, Margaret Milliken

Columbia University College of Physicians and Surgeons ($25,000) see Jockey Hollow Foundation

Columbia University, College of Physicians and Surgeons — for medical schools to improve the basic science education and clinical training of medical students ($2,501,497) see Johnson Foundation, Robert Wood

Columbia University College of Physicians and Surgeons ($12,500) see Klosk Fund, Louis and Rose

Columbia University College of Physicians and Surgeons ($12,500) see Klosk Fund, Louis and Rose

Columbia University College of Physicians and Surgeons ($25,000) see Perkin Fund

Columbia University College of Physicians and Surgeons — medical scholarships ($75,000) see Rudin Foundation, Louis and Rachel

Columbia University College of Physicians and Surgeons ($20,000) see Slaughter Foundation, Charles

Columbia University College of Physicians and Surgeons ($20,000) see Straus Foundation, Martha Washington Straus and Harry H.

Columbia University College of Physicians and Surgeons

New York (cont.)

Consumer-Farmer Foundation ($16,000) see United States Trust Co. of New York

Consumers Union ($1,000) see Ansin Private Foundation, Ronald M.

Convent of Sacred Heart ($25,000) see Joyce Foundation, John M. and Mary A.

Convent of Sacred Heart ($5,000) see Komes Foundation

Cooper-Hewitt Museum — exhibition and guide to Donald Deskey Archive ($10,000) see Graham Foundation for Advanced Studies in the Fine Arts

Cooper Union ($50,000) see Lehman Foundation, Robert

Cooper Union for the Advancement of Science ($40,000) see Hebrew Technical Institute

Cooper Union for the Advancement of Science ($3,000) see Lehman Foundation, Edith and Herbert

Cooper Union for the Advancement of Science ($25,000) see Loeb Foundation, Frances and John L.

Cooper Union for the Advancement of Science and Art ($12,500) see United States Trust Co. of New York

Cooper Union for the Advancement of Science and Art — to create an Infrastructure Institute to advocate, design and teach solutions to New York City's transportation program ($175,000) see Surdna Foundation

Coordination in Development ($25,000) see Weyerhaeuser Family Foundation

Cornell Associates, Cornell University ($2,000) see Campbell Foundation

Cornell Cooperative Extension — preservation project ($25,000) see Homeland Foundation

Cornell Cooperative Extension Suffolk County — to support a parent education program ($45,000) see Cummings Memorial Fund Trust, Frances L. and Edwin L.

Cornell Law School ($10,000) see Weinstein Foundation, Alex J.

Cornell Medical Center — for cancer research ($5,000) see Lincoln Health Care Foundation

Cornell Medical Center ($3,000) see Morris Foundation, Norman M.

Cornell School of Hotel Administration ($15,000) see Banfi Vintners

Cornell University — engineering building renovation ($20,000) see Air Products & Chemicals

Cornell University ($20,000) see Arkell Hall Foundation

Cornell University ($10,000) see Banta Corp.

Cornell University ($16,666) see Charina Foundation

Cornell University — endowment of professorship in engineering ($300,000) see Charter Manufacturing Co.

Cornell University ($250) see Chiquita Brands Co.

Cornell University ($5,000) see Delavan Foundation, Nelson B.

Cornell University see Eastman Kodak Co.

Cornell University ($500,000) see Emerson Electric Co.

Cornell University ($125,000) see Fair Oaks Foundation, Inc.

Cornell University ($2,500) see Fox Steel Co.

Cornell University ($38,000) see Friedman Foundation, Stephen and Barbara

Cornell University ($34,000) see Gerschel Foundation, Patrick A.

Cornell University ($7,500) see Gloeckner Foundation, Fred

Cornell University ($300,000) see Goldsmith Foundation, Horace W.

Cornell University ($120,120) see Gussman Foundation, Herbert and Roseline

Cornell University ($833,303) see Hewlett-Packard Co.

Cornell University ($50,000) see Hirschl Trust for Charitable Purposes, Irma T.

Cornell University ($30,000) see Holt Foundation, William Knox

Cornell University ($7,500) see Holzer Memorial Foundation, Richard H.

Cornell University ($15,000) see Jaqua Foundation

Cornell University ($25,000) see Kent Foundation, Ada Howe

Cornell University ($25,000) see Kent Foundation, Ada Howe

Cornell University ($19,391) see Lindner Foundation, Fay J.

Cornell University ($3,100) see Lynch Scholarship Foundation, John B.

Cornell University ($5,000) see Newman Assistance Fund, Jerome A. and Estelle R.

Cornell University ($5,000) see Obernauer Foundation

Cornell University — renovation ($25,000) see Phillips Foundation, Ellis L.

Cornell University ($4,000) see Quaker Chemical Corp.

Cornell University ($43,060) see Ritter Foundation

Cornell University ($454,764) see Schwartz Foundation, David

Cornell University ($25,000) see Seneca Foods Corp.

Cornell University ($5,000) see Seneca Foods Corp.

Cornell University ($35,000) see Snow Memorial Trust, John Ben

Cornell University ($360,000) see Statler Foundation

Cornell University — first installment of a $333,333 two for one challenge grant ($125,000) see Calder Foundation, Louis

Cornell University — establishment and endowment of the Charles H. Dyson Professorship inManagement at he Johnson School of Management to honor Charles H. Dyson's 80th birthday in 1989 ($300,000) see Dyson Foundation

Cornell University-Department of Chemistry ($40,000) see Johnson & Son, S.C.

Cornell University — James Baker Institute ($10,000) see

Bostwick Foundation, Albert C.

Cornell University Law School Scholarship ($4,000) see Donovan, Leisure, Newton & Irvine

Cornell University — provide funding for the Leslie R. Severinghaus research room, the new centerpiece of the University Library's Asian collection ($300,000) see Luce Foundation, Henry

Cornell University Medical Center ($25,000) see Blum Foundation, Edith C.

Cornell University Medical Center ($10,000) see Duke Foundation, Doris

Cornell University Medical Center ($20,000) see Hughes Memorial Foundation, Charles Evans

Cornell University Medical Center ($64,772) see Sinsheimer Fund, Alexandrine and Alexander L.

Cornell University Medical Center ($9,000) see Werblow Charitable Trust, Nina W.

Cornell University Medical Center ($110,700) see Zimmermann Fund, Marie and John

Cornell University Medical Center Cardiovascular Center ($5,000) see Piankova Foundation, Tatiana

Cornell University Medical Center — New York Hospital ($20,000) see Blum Foundation, Edith C.

Cornell University Medical College ($20,000) see Bostwick Foundation, Albert C.

Cornell University Medical College ($35,000) see Feil Foundation, Louis and Gertrude

Cornell University Medical College ($12,500) see Klosk Fund, Louis and Rose

Cornell University Medical College ($10,000) see L and L Foundation

Cornell University Medical College ($5,000) see Lasdon Foundation

Cornell University Medical College — medical scholarships ($45,000) see Rudin Foundation, Louis and Rachel

Cornell University Medical College ($12,000) see Tai and Co., J. T.

Cornell University Medical College Biomedical Research ($100,000) see Winston Foundation, Norman and Rosita

Cornell University Medical College Departments of Ophthalmology and Pediatrics — funding for the establishment of the Margaret M. Dyson Vision Research Insititute of New York Hospital- Cornell Medical Center which is concentrating initially on retinal research ($1,500,000) see Dyson Foundation

Cornell University Medical College — scholarships for NYC residencies ($41,000) see Rudin Foundation, Louis and Rachel

Cornell University Ornithology Lab ($3,308) see Howell Foundation, Eric and Jessie

Cornell University/School of Hotel Administration ($100,000) see Loews Corp.

Cornell University, Space Sciences Building ($75,000) see Norris Foundation, Kenneth T. and Eileen L.

Cornell University — Spencer T. and Ann W. Olin Graduate Fellowship Program ($1,500,000) see Olin Foundation, Spencer T. and Ann W.

Cornell University Veterinary School ($10,000) see Porter Foundation, Mrs. Cheever

Cornell University — to endow the directorship of the Writing in the Majors Program in the John S. Knight Writing Program ($620,921) see Knight Foundation, John S. and James L.

Corning City School District — curriculum enrichment ($43,000) see Corning Incorporated

Corning Hospital — renovation project ($125,000) see Corning Incorporated

Coro Foundation ($25,000) see 21 International Holdings

Corporation for Maintaining Editorial Diversity in Boston, MA ($15,000) see Burns Foundation

Corporation for Supportive Housing — financial and technical support to create housing for people who need special support services; (first payment of a $100,000 grant) ($50,000) see Ittleson Foundation

Corporation of Yaddo — operational support ($1,000) see Wahlstrom Foundation

Corporation for Youth Energy Corps — loan converted to grant ($25,000) see Taconic Foundation

Council for Aid to Education see General Signal Corp.

Council for Aid to Education ($15,000) see Industrial Bank of Japan Trust Co.

Council on Economic Priorities ($5,000) see Natural Heritage Foundation

Council on Economic Priorities ($10,000) see Wilson Foundation, Marie C. and Joseph C.

Council on the Environment New York City ($1,000) see Abraham Foundation

Council on the Environment of New York City ($200,000) see Abrons Foundation, Louis and Anne

Council on the Environment of New York City ($64,500) see Sulzberger Foundation

Council on Foreign Relations ($3,000) see Goodman Family Foundation

Council on Foreign Relations ($2,500) see Gruss Petroleum Corp.

Council on Foreign Relations ($25,000) see Harriman Foundation, Mary W.

Council on Foreign Relations ($30,000) see Hurford Foundation

Council on Foreign Relations ($62,000) see Wiener Foundation, Malcolm Hewitt

Council on Foreign Relations ($7,500) see Young & Rubicam

Council on Foreign Relations — Philip D. Reed Senior

Fellowship in Science and Technology ($308,500) see Reed Foundation, Philip D.

Council on Foreign Relations — to examine and define the developing post-Cold War agenda for relations between the United States and Latin America ($100,000) see Tinker Foundation

Council on Jewish Poverty ($25,000) see Lavanburg-Corner House

Council of Literary Magazines and Presses ($979,809) see Wallace Reader's Digest Fund, Lila

Council of New York Law Associates (now Lawyers' Alliance) — in support of the Community Development Legal Assistance Center program ($20,000) see Taconic Foundation

Council of Senior Centers and Services of New York City ($1,000) see Leibovitz Foundation, Morris P.

Counseling and Human Development Center ($5,000) see Roche Relief Foundation, Edward and Ellen

County of Omonga ($43,300) see Gifford Charitable Corporation, Rosamond

Cove Foundation ($50,000) see Comer Foundation

Covenant House ($20,000) see Biddle Foundation, Margaret T.

Covenant House ($5,000) see Coles Family Foundation

Covenant House — crisis care program ($25,000) see Cudahy Fund, Patrick and Anna M.

Covenant House ($15,000) see Davis Foundation, Simon and Annie

Covenant House ($5,000) see DCNY Corp.

Covenant House ($1,200) see Doherty Charitable Foundation, Henry L. and Grace

Covenant House ($100,000) see First Boston

Covenant House ($15,000) see Hettinger Foundation

Covenant House ($25,000) see Hoffman Foundation, Marion O. and Maximilian

Covenant House ($10,000) see Kennedy Foundation, Ethel

Covenant House ($21,600) see Kennedy Foundation, Quentin J.

Covenant House ($8,000) see Luce Charitable Trust, Theodore

Covenant House ($10,000) see Monroe Foundation (1976), J. Edgar

Covenant House ($10,000) see New York Stock Exchange

Covenant House ($25,000) see Palisades Educational Foundation

Covenant House ($2,500) see Rice Family Foundation, Jacob and Sophie

Covenant House ($15,000) see Ruffin Foundation, Peter B. & Adeline W.

Covenant House ($25,000) see Schieffelin Residuary Trust, Sarah I.

Covenant House ($10,000) see Trimble Family Foundation, Robert Mize and Isa White

Covenant House ($1,000) see Youth Foundation

Creative Alternatives of New York ($100,000) see Simon Charitable Trust, Esther

Creative Arts Rehabilitation Center ($30,000) see Model Foundation, Leo

Creative Education Foundation — for operating support ($4,000) see Fisher Foundation

Creative Glass Center of America ($8,150) see Chazen Foundation

Crime Victims Assistance Center ($10,130) see Hoyt Foundation, Stewart W. and Willma C.

Crohns Colitis Foundation of America ($15,000) see Ohl, Jr. Trust, George A.

Crouse Irving Memorial Foundation ($500) see De Lima Co., Paul

Cultural Council Foundation ($40,000) see Connemara Fund

Cumberland College ($165,000) see Johnson Endeavor Foundation, Christian A.

CWS/Crop ($1,500) see Hartzell Industries, Inc.

Cystic Fibrosis Foundation ($13,000) see Fay's Incorporated

Cystic Fibrosis Foundation ($75,955) see Frankel Foundation, George and Elizabeth F.

Cystic Fibrosis Foundation see Merrill Lynch & Co.

Cystic Fibrosis Foundation ($15,650) see O'Sullivan Children Foundation

Cystic Fibrosis Foundation ($160,000) see Weinberg Foundation, John L.

Cystic Fibrosis Foundation ($1,000) see Weiss Foundation, Stephen and Suzanne

D.C. Women's Council on AIDS ($5,000) see Pettus Crowe Foundation

D.R. Reed Speech Center ($10,000) see St. Faith's House Foundation

Daemon College — library equipment ($12,000) see Palisano Foundation, Vincent and Harriet

Dahesh Museum — museum rental facility ($575,000) see Dahesh Museum

Daisy Child Development Center ($11,000) see Boehm Foundation

Dalton School ($300,000) see Goldsmith Foundation, Horace W.

Dalton School ($10,000) see Gurwin Foundation, J.

Dalton School ($21,744) see Lazarus Charitable Trust, Helen and Charles

Dalton School ($21,000) see Ritter Foundation

Dalton School ($20,000) see Rosenberg Foundation, Sunny and Abe

Dalton School ($62,000) see Steinhardt Foundation, Judy and Michael

Damien-Dutton Society for Leprosy Aid ($5,000) see Butler Foundation, J. Homer

Damon Runyon/Walter Winchell Cancer Fund — cancer research ($10,000) see Hettinger Foundation

Dance Theater of Harlem ($100) see Contempo Communications

Dance Theatre Foundation ($12,500) see Harkness Foundation, William Hale

Danish Home for the Aged ($4,500) see Faith Home Foundation

Daughters of British Empire ($1,000) see Adams Memorial Fund, Emma J.

Day Care Center of Oswego ($15,000) see Truman Foundation, Mildred Faulkner

Day School ($5,000) see Rosenwald Family Fund, William

Daytop Village ($100,000) see Smeal Foundation, Mary Jean & Frank P.

Daytop Village ($75,000) see Whitehead Foundation

Daytop Village Foundation ($6,000) see Olivetti Office USA, Inc.

Daytop Village Foundation — grant for Daytop/Dallas "Just Say, Yes" campaign ($60,000) see Halliburton Co.

Deafness Research Foundation ($100,000) see AlliedSignal

Deafness Research Foundation — reasearch for hearing loss in elderly ($50,000) see Hermann Foundation, Grover

Deafness Research Foundation ($218,418) see Oberkotter Family Foundation

Deafness Research Foundation ($10,000) see Scott Foundation, Walter

Deal Sephardic Bikur Holim ($24,252) see Bag Bazaar, Ltd.

Deemen College ($55,000) see Julia R. and Estelle L. Foundation

Deja Vu Dance Theatre ($10,000) see Sheafer Charitable Trust, Emma A.

Delaware County Planning Board — TPAS programs ($46,725) see O'Connor Foundation, A. Lindsay and Olive B.

Delaware County Planning Board — TPAS Programs ($15,575) see O'Connor Foundation, A. Lindsay and Olive B.

Department of Urology — Cancer Research ($10,000) see Tai and Co., J. T.

Depot Theater ($500) see Crary Foundation, Bruce L.

Design Industry Foundation For AIDS ($2,500) see GSC Enterprises

DIA Center for the Arts — construction of a glass pavilion by artist Dan Graham ($10,000) see Graham Foundation for Advanced Studies in the Fine Arts

Diller-Quaile School of Music ($6,000) see Goodman Family Foundation

Dimitri House ($2,000) see General Railway Signal Corp.

Diocese of Armenian Church ($50,000) see Mardigian Foundation

Diocese of the Armenian Church of America ($5,000) see Simone Foundation

Diocese of Brooklyn (Catholic) ($17,500) see Clark Charitable Trust, Frank E.

Diocese of Brooklyn (Catholic) ($15,750) see Clark Charitable Trust, Frank E.

Diocese of Brooklyn Department of Education "Prosper" Program ($7,500) see Brooklyn Benevolent Society

Diocese of Rockville Center ($45,000) see Link, Jr. Foundation, George

Direct Marketing Foundation ($25,000) see Reader's Digest Association

Disability Awareness ($3,500) see AHS Foundation

Disarm Education Fund — demonstration of new low-cost video production techniques for public television broadcast ($2,500) see Benton Foundation

Discovery Center ($1,000) see Gear Motion

Discovery Fund ($56,300) see Cantor Foundation, Iris and B. Gerald

Discovery Fund ($50,000) see Cantor Foundation, Iris and B. Gerald

Dobbs Ferry Hospital ($6,000) see Akzo America

Doctor Amy and James Research Fund ($5,000) see Jacobson & Sons, Benjamin

Dome Project ($25,000) see Bowne Foundation, Robert

Dome Project ($50,000) see Edwards Foundation, O. P. and W. E.

Dominican Sisters Family Health Services ($15,000) see Morania Foundation

Dominican Sisters of Sick Poor ($11,000) see Luce Charitable Trust, Theodore

Donald R. Reed Speech Center — for partial support of Pediatric Otitis Media Education and Identification Program ($8,000) see Axe-Houghton Foundation

The Door ($30,000) see Cohn Foundation, Herman and Terese

The Door — supplementary general support for reorganization and development efforts ($500,000) see Diamond Foundation, Aaron

The Door ($5,000) see Tuch Foundation, Michael

The Door — to provide health, vocational, recreational, and educational aid to children and young adults ($34,700) see Washington Square Fund

The Door — Unity High School ($200,000) see Citicorp

Dorot ($800) see Zacharia Foundation, Isaac Herman

Dover Fund ($75,000) see Pincus Family Fund

Dowling College ($6,000) see DelMar Foundation, Charles

Down Syndrome Adoption Exchange — placement of Down Syndrome babies and children for adoption ($40,000) see Kennedy, Jr. Foundation, Joseph P.

Downtown Community Television Center ($25,000) see Rubin Foundation, Samuel

Drawing Center ($10,000) see Kimmelman Foundation, Helen & Milton

Drawing Center ($100,000) see Lehman Foundation, Robert

Drum Thwacket Foundation ($5,000) see Kellogg Foundation, J. C.

Duononga Pastoral Counseling ($50,000) see Gifford Charitable Corporation, Rosamond

Dutchess Day School ($200,000) see Millbrook Tribute Garden

Dutchess Land Conservancy ($25,000) see Millbrook Tribute Garden

Dwelling Place ($4,800) see Adams Memorial Fund, Emma J.

D'Youville College ($100,000) see Julia R. and Estelle L. Foundation

D'Youville College ($3,500) see Palisano Foundation, Vincent and Harriet

E. S. Harkness Eye Institute of Columbia-Presbyterian University ($10,000) see Milbank Foundation, Dunlevy

E B Jermyn Lodge #2, Scranton Fraternal Order of Police ($35,000) see Golub Corp.

Early Steps ($10,000) see Zarkin Memorial Foundation, Charles

Earthview Foundation ($90,000) see Wallach Foundation, Miriam G. and Ira D.

East Brooklyn Churches Sponsoring Committee — support a parent organizing project to improve public schools ($25,000) see Hazen Foundation, Edward W.

East Brooklyn Congregations — for a community-based neighborhood improvement coalition in East Brooklyn ($30,000) see New York Foundation

East Harlem Block Nursery ($15,000) see Lavanburg-Corner House

East Harlem Employment Service ($473,722) see Clark Foundation

East Harlem Employment Service — Project Strive; to meet the Clark Foundation's challenge grant ($25,000) see Achelis Foundation

East Harlem Tutorial Program ($12,000) see Bernstein & Co., Sanford C.

East Side International Community Center ($1,000) see Weiss Foundation, Stephen and Suzanne

East Side Settlement House ($2,000) see Adams Memorial Fund, Emma J.

East Side Settlement House ($5,000) see Griffis Foundation

East West Management Institute ($145,000) see Open Society Fund

Eastern Long Island Hospital ($25,000) see Cowles Charitable Trust

Eastman Dental Center ($2,500) see Bausch & Lomb

Eastman School ($100,000) see Orchard Corp. of America.

Eastman School of Music ($2,000) see Jellison Benevolent Society

Eastman School of Music ($10,000) see Mulligan Charitable Trust, Mary S.

Echo Hills ($10,000) see St. Faith's House Foundation

Edna McConnell Clark Foundation — to continue support for a Foundation-administered program for the dissemination of information about issues within the Foundation's program areas and for communications assistance to grantees ($275,000) see Clark Foundation, Edna McConnell

Education Resources Group — for evaluation and documentation of middle grades reform initiatives in the five Foundation-assisted urban school systems ($302,000) see Clark Foundation, Edna McConnell

Educational Alliance ($15,000) see Fourjay Foundation

Educational Alliance ($25,000) see Guttag Foundation, Irwin and Marjorie

Educational Alliance — general support ($35,000) see Guttman Foundation, Stella and Charles

Educational Alliance ($25,000) see Guttman Foundation, Stella and Charles

Educational Alliance ($47,350) see Kaufmann Foundation, Henry

Educational Alliance ($20,000) see Lee Foundation, James T.

Educational Alliance ($7,500) see Perley Fund, Victor E.

Educational Alliance ($76,000) see Rosenberg Foundation, Sunny and Abe

Educational Alliance ($28,200) see Solow Foundation

Educational Alliance ($5,000) see Tuch Foundation, Michael

Educational Alliance Homeless Residence Program ($25,000) see Nias Foundation, Henry

Educational Broadcasting ($100,000) see Burns Foundation, Jacob

Educational Broadcasting ($50,000) see Fein Foundation

Educational Broadcasting ($125,000) see Greene Foundation, Jerome L.

Educational Broadcasting ($45,480) see Schaffer Foundation, Michael & Helen

Educational Broadcasting ($12,000) see Simon Foundation, Sidney, Milton and Leoma

Educational Broadcasting ($10,000) see Solow Foundation, Sheldon H.

Educational Broadcasting Company ($200,000) see Monell Foundation, Ambrose

Educational Broadcasting Corporation ($10,000) see Barth Foundation, Theodore H.

Educational Broadcasting Corporation/Adam Smith ($1,500,000) see Metropolitan Life Insurance Co.

Educational Broadcasting Corporation/Channel 13 WNET — toward Channel 13's capital campaign ($150,000) see Astor Foundation, Vincent

Educational Broadcasting Corporation Thirteen ($217,925) see Liz Claiborne

Educational Broadcasting Corps ($150,000) see Bristol-Myers Squibb Co.

Educational Foundation for the Fashion Institute ($31,500) see Liz Claiborne

Educational Fund ($10,000) see Thorne Foundation

Educational Testing Services ($27,500) see Bruner Foundation

Educational Video Center ($18,000) see Bowne Foundation, Robert

Educational Video Center ($6,000) see Christodora

Educational Video Center ($40,000) see Cohn Foundation, Herman and Terese

Edwin Gould Academy ($61,870) see Gould

New York (cont.)

Foundation for Children, Edwin

Effective Parenting Information for Children ($100,000) see Julia R. and Estelle L. Foundation

Effective Parenting Information for Children — program for targeted high-risk parents of infants and toddlers ($47,300) see Wendt Foundation, Margaret L.

Eger Lutheran Homes ($5,000) see Faith Home Foundation

Eighth Church of Christ ($10,000) see Richardson Foundation, Frank E. and Nancy M.

Eisner Family Fund ($5,097,587) see Dammann Fund

Elaine Kaufman Cultural Center ($350,000) see Kaufman Foundation, Henry & Elaine

Elders Share the Arts ($100,000) see Bingham Trust, The

Eldridge Street Project ($60,000) see Dorot Foundation

Eldridge Street Project ($25,000) see Silverweed Foundation

Eldridge Street Project ($5,000) see Slifka Foundation, Joseph and Sylvia

Eldridge Street Project — toward renovation of the Eldridge Street Synagogue ($25,000) see Astor Foundation, Vincent

Eldridge Street Synagogue ($35,000) see Ross Foundation, Arthur

Elementary School Center ($195,000) see Johnson Endeavor Foundation, Christian A.

Elie Wiesel Humanitarian Foundation ($12,500) see Wilf Family Foundation

Elizabethtown Community Hospital ($1,000) see Crary Foundation, Bruce L.

Ellis Hospital Foundation ($25,000) see Schaffer Foundation, H.

Elmcrest Children's Center ($75,000) see Gifford Charitable Corporation, Rosamond

Elmira College — building restoration ($25,000) see Corning Incorporated

Elmira College ($5,000) see Stein Foundation, Louis

Elmira Symphony and Choral Society — 1991-92 concert season ($5,000) see Anderson Foundation

Elmwood Frankin School ($25,000) see Knox Foundation, Seymour H.

Elmwood Franklin School ($16,000) see Baird Foundation

Elmwood-Franklin School ($9,500) see Western New York Foundation

Emanu-El Midtown YM-YWHA ($5,000) see Menschel Foundation, Robert and Joyce

Emanu-El Midtown YM-YWHA ($25,000) see Oppenheimer and Flora Oppenheimer Haas Trust, Leo

Emek Hebrew Academy ($47,000) see Friedman Brothers Foundation

Emergency Shelter ($50,000) see Rudin Foundation, Samuel and May

Emma Willard School ($15,000) see Oshkosh B'Gosh

Emmaus House ($50,000) see Ryan Family Charitable Foundation

Emmaus House — Study Hall ($10,000) see Atlanta Foundation

Emmaus House Study Hall ($5,000) see Elkin Memorial Foundation, Neil Warren and William Simpson

Empire State Food and Agricultural Institute ($5,000) see Agway

Emunah Women of America ($3,000) see Chernow Trust for the Benefit of Charity Dated 3/13/75, Michael

Emunah Women of America ($1,000) see Marcus Brothers Textiles Inc.

En Garde Arts ($10,000) see Sheafer Charitable Trust, Emma A.

Endowment for the Neurosciences ($63,000) see Three Swallows Foundation

English Speaking Union ($20,000) see Greentree Foundation

Enter — to provide monies for the direct expenses of operating a shelter ($11,000) see Washington Square Fund

Enterprise Foundation ($30,000) see Coles Family Foundation

Enterprise Foundation — low-cost housing in New York City ($50,000) see New York Times Co.

Enterprises Foundation ($25,000) see Bleibtreu Foundation, Jacob

Environmental Defense Fund ($25,000) see Beneficia Foundation

Environmental Defense Fund ($25,000) see Carter Foundation, Beirne

Environmental Defense Fund ($35,000) see Colburn Fund

Environmental Defense Fund ($100,000) see Dodge Foundation, Geraldine R.

Environmental Defense Fund ($4,000) see Flemm Foundation, John J.

Environmental Defense Fund ($5,000) see French Foundation

Environmental Defense Fund ($20,000) see Gleason Foundation, James

Environmental Defense Fund ($50,000) see Heineman Foundation for Research, Educational, Charitable, and Scientific Purposes

Environmental Defense Fund — for air quality program to reduce fossil fuel combustion through market incentives ($250,000) see Joyce Foundation

Environmental Defense Fund ($6,000) see Kingsley Foundation

Environmental Defense Fund ($10,000) see Magowan Family Foundation

Environmental Defense Fund ($10,000) see PaineWebber

Environmental Defense Fund ($20,000) see Penney Foundation, James C.

Environmental Defense Fund ($50,000) see Phipps Foundation, Howard

Environmental Defense Fund ($5,000) see Prairie Foundation

Environmental Defense Fund ($200,000) see Public Welfare Foundation

Environmental Defense Fund ($300,000) see Surdna Foundation

Environmental Defense Fund — waste reduction ($35,000) see True North Foundation

Environmental Defense Fund — support for Environmental Defense Fund's Atmospheric Program ($200,000) see Jones Foundation, W. Alton

Environmental Defense Fund — for research, policy and education activities of the biotechnology program ($125,000) see Joyce Foundation

Environmental Defense Fund — third-year payment of a five-year, $1,000,000 grant for a program to identify and promote means to reduce climate change and the depletion of ozone ($200,000) see Bingham Foundation, William

Episcopal Church Foundation ($10,000) see Culver Foundation, Constans

Episcopal Church Home — construction project ($100,000) see Wendt Foundation, Margaret L.

Episcopal Diocese of Western New York ($40,000) see Cornell Trust, Peter C.

Episcopal Diocese of Western New York ($20,000) see Cornell Trust, Peter C.

Episcopal Mission Society ($7,000) see Luce Charitable Trust, Theodore

Equestrian Order of Holy Sepulchur of Jerusalem ($10,350) see Gaisman Foundation, Catherine and Henry J.

Erie Canal Museum ($25,000) see Gifford Charitable Corporation, Rosamond

Erie Community College ($5,500) see Harris Foundation, H. H.

Erie Community College Newman Center ($1,000) see Joy Family Foundation

Erie County Medical Center ($26,620) see Cummings Foundation, James H.

Erie County Sheriff's Department — computer aided dispatch and emergency management system ($45,000) see Wendt Foundation, Margaret L.

ERPF Catskill Cultural Center ($20,700) see Erpf Fund, Armand G.

ESAC ($7,000) see Fife Foundation, Elias and Bertha

Essay Contest ($21,227) see Kaplun Foundation, Morris J. and Betty

Essex County Historical Society ($1,000) see Crary Foundation, Bruce L.

Ethical Culture Schools — Joseph A. Coleman scholarship fund and capital campaign ($10,000) see Rosenthal Foundation, Ida and William

Ethical-Fieldston Fund ($5,000) see Loewenberg Foundation

Ethical-Fieldstone Fund ($25,000) see Gruss Petroleum Corp.

Ethical-Fieldstone Fund ($15,000) see Neuberger Foundation, Roy R. and Marie S.

Ethical-Fieldstone Fund ($5,000) see Orchard Foundation

Ethical-Fieldstone Fund ($30,000) see Silverweed Foundation

Etz Chaim of Kew Garden Hills ($1,500) see Fischel Foundation, Harry and Jane

Etzion Foundation ($10,000) see Gruber Research Foundation, Lila

Etzion Foundation ($30,000) see Jesselson Foundation

Everson Museum of Art ($500) see De Lima Co., Paul

Everson Museum Foundation ($50,000) see Mather Fund, Richard

Executive Council on Foreign Diplomats ($20,000) see Fuqua Foundation, J. B.

Executive Council on Foreign Diplomats ($20,000) see Whitman Corp.

Eye Bank for Sight Restoration ($5,000) see Manning and Emma Austin Manning Foundation, James Hilton

Eye Bank for Sight Restoration ($10,000) see Steinbach Fund, Ruth and Milton

Eye Bank for Sighthood ($2,000) see Fife Foundation, Elias and Bertha

Ezra Lemarpeh Association ($10,000) see Stern Foundation, Bernice and Milton

Ezras Chaim ($1,000) see Fischel Foundation, Harry and Jane

F.I.R.S.T. ($112,800) see Dammann Fund

F.M.C.C. ($20,000) see Arkell Hall Foundation

Face University ($40,000) see Gottesman Fund

Fairfield University ($20,000) see Hagedorn Fund

Fairness and Accuracy in Reporting ($10,000) see Rubin Foundation, Samuel

Fairness and Accuracy in Reporting (FAIR) — support for the Women's Meida Watch Project ($25,000) see Norman Foundation

Fairview Public Library ($25,000) see Allen-Heath Memorial Foundation

Fairview Public Library — library building and development funds ($25,000) see Allen-Heath Memorial Foundation

Families and Work Institute — family child care quality study ($30,000) see Mailman Family Foundation, A. L.

Families and Work Institute ($50,000) see Primerica Corp.

Family and Children's Services ($18,500) see Truman Foundation, Mildred Faulkner

Family Counseling Service ($25,000) see Cowles Charitable Trust

Family Dynamics ($5,000) see Plant Memorial Fund, Henry B.

Family Dynamics — to support services to New York children in danger of abuse or neglect ($15,000) see Washington Square Fund

Family Planning Center — educational health care ($10,000) see Allyn Foundation

Family Recovery Center — for general operation support ($2,000) see Fisher Foundation

Family Rosary ($10,000) see O'Neil Foundation, W.

Family Service Association — general operating fund ($10,000) see Dolan Family Foundation

Family Service Association of Nassau County — annual giving for underprivileged families ($200,000) see Farish Fund, William Stamps

Family Service Association of Nassau County ($42,000) see Lindner Foundation, Fay J.

Family Service of Greater Utica ($5,000) see Utica National Insurance Group

Farber Institute ($2,500) see Guttag Foundation, Irwin and Marjorie

Farm School ($5,664) see Paul and C. Michael Paul Foundation, Josephine Bay

Fashion Group Foundation ($42,586) see Claiborne Art Ortenberg Foundation, Liz

Fashion Institute of Technology ($20,000) see Phillips-Van Heusen Corp.

Federated Protestant Charities ($20,000) see Hagedorn Fund

Federation Employment and Guidance Service ($30,000) see de Hirsch Fund, Baron

Federation of Handicapped ($25,000) see Nias Foundation, Henry

Federation of Jewish Agencies of Atlantic County ($6,500) see Jaydor Corp.

Federation of Jewish Philanthropies ($7,500) see Berlin Charitable Fund, Irving

Federation of Jewish Philanthropies ($100,000) see Charina Foundation

Federation of Jewish Philanthropies ($25,000) see Charina Foundation

Federation of Jewish Philanthropies ($260,000) see Golden Family Foundation

Federation of Jewish Philanthropies ($100,000) see Marx Foundation, Virginia & Leonard

Federation of Jewish Philanthropies ($20,000) see McGonagle Foundation, Dextra Baldwin

Federation of Jewish Philanthropies ($10,000) see Zilkha & Sons

Federation of Jewish Philanthropies of New York ($15,000) see Turner Fund, Ruth

Federation of Jewish Philanthropies — United Jewish Appeal ($50,000) see Uris Brothers Foundation

Federation for Protestant Welfare ($136,150) see de Kay Foundation

Federation of Protestant Welfare Agencies ($25,000) see Badgeley Residuary Charitable Trust, Rose M.

Federation of Protestant Welfare Agencies ($5,500) see Thanksgiving Foundation

Federation of Protestant Welfare Agencies — for support of FPWA's core programs ($100,000) see Altman Foundation

Feedback Production ($5,000) see Chait Memorial Foundation, Sara

Felician College ($8,500) see Switzer Foundation

Fellowship Center ($35,000) see Archbold Charitable Trust, Adrian and Jessie

New York (cont.)

Friends of Yeshiva Harav Amiel ($15,000) see Stern Foundation, Max

Frontier Fund ($10,000) see Essel Foundation

Frost Valley ($10,000) see PaineWebber

Frost Valley YMCA ($35,000) see Snow Memorial Trust, John Ben

Fund for Aging Services ($10,000) see Huntsman Foundation, Jon and Karen

Fund for Aging Services ($30,000) see Johnson Foundation, Willard T. C.

Fund for Aging Services ($15,000) see Stern Foundation, Leonard N.

Fund for Architecture and the Environment — for their Special Projects Fund ($150,000) see Kaplan Fund, J. M.

Fund for Blood and Cancer Research ($10,000) see Hansen Memorial Foundation, Irving

Fund for the City of New York ($150,000) see Booth Ferris Foundation

Fund for the City of New York — general support ($3,000,000) see Ford Foundation

Fund for the City of New York ($2,815,000) see Wallace-Reader's Digest Fund, DeWitt

Fund for the City of New York — for exchange between officals and urban experts from three large metropolitan areas in the U.S. and their counterparts in Japan ($242,002) see United States-Japan Foundation

Fund for Free Expression/Human Rights Watch ($105,000) see Overbrook Foundation

Fund for Free Expression — continuing support for their six Human Rights Watch Committees ($175,000) see Kaplan Fund, J. M.

Fund for Jewish Education ($100,000) see Tisch Foundation

Fund for Modern Courts ($25,000) see Blum Foundation, Edith C.

Fund for Modern Courts ($5,000) see Kaye, Scholer, Fierman, Hays & Handler

Fund for New York City Education ($50,000) see Rohatyn Foundation, Felix and Elizabeth

Fund for New York City Public Education ($100,000) see Bankers Trust Co.

Fund for New York City Public Education — to purchase and install new integrated computer systems ($135,000) see Hayden Foundation, Charles

Fund for New York City Public Education ($75,000) see Heckscher Foundation for Children

Fund for the New York City Public Education ($50,000) see Industrial Bank of Japan Trust Co.

Fund for New York City Public Education ($30,000) see Lavanburg-Corner House

Fund for New York City Public Education ($200,000) see Lowenstein Foundation, Leon

Fund for New York City Public Education — continued support for a model conflict resolution and peer mediation program ($300,000) see Rockefeller Brothers Fund

Fund for New York City Public Education ($25,000) see Stern Foundation, Leonard N.

Fund for New York City Public Education ($925,000) see Wallace-Reader's Digest Fund, DeWitt

Fund for New York City Public Education — for CAL II Program ($120,000) see Chase Manhattan Bank, N.A.

Fund for New York City Public Education — renewed support for 30 middle school math and science teachers in Brooklyn to participate in the Professional Exchange Program in 1991/92 ($30,000) see Greenwall Foundation

Fund for Peace — general support ($65,000) see Compton Foundation

Fund for Public Schools ($42,500) see Primerica Corp.

Fund for Public Schools — first payment of $500,000 grant for the Professional Development Laboratory Program ($250,000) see J.P. Morgan & Co.

Fund for Reform Judaism ($10,000) see Daniel Foundation, Gerard and Ruth

Funders Concerned About AIDS ($2,500) see Pettus Crowe Foundation

Funding Exchange ($15,000) see Boehm Foundation

Funding Exchange ($50,000) see List Foundation, Albert A.

Funding Exchange ($30,000) see Schecter Private Foundation, Aaron and Martha

Funding Exchange ($50,000) see Warner Fund, Albert and Bessie

Funding Exchange ($30,000) see Warner Fund, Albert and Bessie

Funding Exchange — for funding documentaries ($105,000) see Women's Project Foundation

Funding Exchange National Community Funds ($25,000) see Horncrest Foundation

GAIA Leadership Project ($25,000) see Joukowsky Family Foundation

Gar Reichman Foundation ($25,000) see Altschul Foundation

Garden City Congregational Church ($4,500) see Belmont Metals

Garden Club of America ($2,000) see Hales Charitable Fund

Garden Club of America ($45,000) see McIntosh Foundation

Garden Club of America ($10,000) see Strawbridge Foundation of Pennsylvania II, Margaret Dorrance

Garden Conservancy ($16,000) see Mather and William Gwinn Mather Fund, Elizabeth Ring

Garment Industry Day Care Center of China ($27,000) see Liz Claiborne

Garment Industry Day Care Center of China ($700) see United Togs Inc.

Gates County Flag GIA- Wagner College ($5,625) see Spiro Foundation, Donald W.

Gateway to Higher Education — to support the junior high school program whose goal is to increase the number of minority students preparing for careers in medicine, engineering or science ($90,000) see Greenwall Foundation

Gay Men's Health Crisis — cut volunteer turnover substantially by initiating grief and healing workshops for volunteers and staff ($40,000) see Ittleson Foundation

Gay Mens Health Crisis ($150,000) see Loews Corp.

Gay Men's Health Crisis ($80,000) see Rudin Foundation, Samuel and May

Gay Men's Health Crisis ($65,000) see Rudin Foundation, Samuel and May

Gay Men's Health Crisis ($151,000) see Tisch Foundation

Gay Men's Health Crisis ($75,000) see Wiener Foundation, Malcolm Hewitt

General Buffalo Foundation ($24,475) see Goode Trust, Mae Stone

General Buffalo Foundation ($12,238) see Goode Trust, Mae Stone

General Buffalo Foundation ($12,238) see Goode Trust, Mae Stone

General Motors Cancer Research Foundation — foundation grant ($2,000,000) see General Motors Corp.

General Theological Seminary ($30,000) see Hunt Trust for Episcopal Charitable Institutions, Virginia

General Theological Seminary ($10,000) see Mostyn Foundation

General Theological Seminary ($13,000) see Palmer Fund, Francis Asbury

Genesee Hospital ($150,000) see Pluta Family Foundation

Genesis Foundation ($20,000) see Bender Foundation

Geneva B. Scruggs Community Health Care Center ($125,000) see Public Welfare Foundation

George Junior Republic ($10,000) see New York Stock Exchange

Geriatric Research Montefiore Hospital ($50,000) see Klau Foundation, David W. and Sadie

German Society ($55,000) see Baier Foundation, Marie

Gesher ($5,000) see Geist Foundation

Geva Theatre ($2,500) see Curtice-Burns Foods

Geva Theatre ($1,500) see General Railway Signal Corp.

Gimmel Foundation ($20,000) see Amado Foundation, Maurice

Girl Scout Council ($10,000) see Western New York Foundation

Girl Scouts — construction of new program and service center ($250,000) see Gebbie Foundation

Girl Scouts of America — improvements to program centers ($25,000) see Corning Incorporated

Girl Scouts of America ($15,000) see Darrah Charitable Trust, Jessie Smith

Girl Scouts of America ($1,000) see Goldberger Foundation, Edward and Marjorie

Girl Scouts of America ($5,000) see Grigg-Lewis Trust

Girl Scouts of America ($1,500) see Hilliard Corp.

Girl Scouts of America ($50,000) see Phipps Foundation, Howard

Girl Scouts Indian Hill Council — Scout Executive ($20,000) see O'Connor Foundation, A. Lindsay and Olive B.

Girls Incorporated — Toshiba Traveling SMART program ($17,688) see Toshiba America, Inc.

Givat Haziva Educational Foundation ($100,000) see Cohen Foundation, Naomi and Nehemiah

Glen Cove Boys and Girls Club ($10,000) see Craigmyle Foundation

Glimmerglass Opera ($200,000) see Clark Foundation

Glimmerglass Opera Theater ($10,000) see Lippitt Foundation, Katherine Kenyon

Goddard Riverside Children ($50,000) see 21 International Holdings

Goddard-Riverside Community Center ($15,000) see Barker Welfare Foundation

Goddard-Riverside Community Center ($6,000) see Palmer-Fry Memorial Trust, Lily

Goddard Riverside Community Center ($28,800) see Uris Brothers Foundation

God's Love We Deliver ($30,000) see Johnson Charitable Trust, Keith Wold

God's Love We Deliver ($10,000) see PaineWebber

God's Love We Deliver — toward expanding a food delivery program to women with AIDS and their children ($5,000) see Gannett Co.

Golda Meir Association ($10,000) see Glazer Foundation, Jerome S.

Golda Meir Association ($5,000) see Polinsky-Rivkin Family Foundation

Golden Horseshoe of Metropolitan Opera, Metropolitan Opera Association ($60,000) see Colburn Fund

Good Samaritan Health Center ($10,000) see Allen Foundation, Frances

Good Shepherd Services — family case management in a school setting ($85,000) see Foundation for Child Development

Good Shepherd Services ($15,000) see Lavanburg-Corner House

Good Shepherd Services — an alternative high school program ($30,000) see Pinkerton Foundation

Goodwill Industries — support of their Building Better Lives capital campaign ($200,000) see Calder Foundation, Louis

Governor's Commission on Women ($30,000) see Paul and C. Michael Paul Foundation, Josephine Bay

Governors Committee on Scholastic Achievement ($6,000) see Gruss Petroleum Corp.

Governors Committee on Scholastic Achievement ($25,000) see PaineWebber

Grace United Methodist Church ($1,500) see Hendrickson Brothers

Grace United Methodist Church ($16,025) see Willmott Foundation, Fred & Floy

Graduate School Cornell University ($22,473) see Sussman Fund, Edna Bailey

Graham-Windham — rebuilding of one of their cottages ($250,000) see Hayden Foundation, Charles

Graham-Windham ($18,500) see Mertz Foundation, Martha

Grand Street Settlement — to establish endowment ($150,000) see Cummings Memorial Fund Trust, Frances L. and Edwin L.

Grand Street Settlement ($60,000) see Rhodebeck Charitable Trust

Grayson-Jockey Club Research Foundation ($9,100) see Dobson Foundation

Greater Buffalo Athletic Corporation — support of the World University Games Buffalo '93 ($50,000) see Wendt Foundation, Margaret L.

Greater Buffalo Development Foundation — annual fund drive ($40,000) see Baird Foundation, Cameron

Greater Buffalo Development Foundation ($7,500) see Mark IV Industries

Greater Buffalo Development Foundation ($25,000) see Rich Products Corp.

Greater Buffalo Divinity Foundation ($25,000) see Goldome F.S.B

Greater New York Council on Religion ($5,000) see Stern Foundation, Max

Greater New York Ophthalmology Clinical — goodwill ($15,000) see Alcon Laboratories, Inc.

Greek Orthodox Archdiocese ($200,000) see Demoulas Supermarkets

Green Meadow Waldorf School ($6,500) see Waldorf Educational Foundation

Green Vale School ($5,000) see Johnson Foundation, Howard

Greenburgh 11 Union Free ($25,000) see Carvel Foundation, Thomas and Agnes

Greenfield Review Literary Center — for North American native writers' festival and educational outreach ($10,000) see Bay Foundation

Greenhouse Crisis Foundation ($30,000) see Bydale Foundation

Greenpark Foundation — Paley Park ($150,000) see Paley Foundation, William S.

Greenport United Methodist Church ($100) see Hendrickson Brothers

Greenwich Hospital Association ($5,000) see Spiegel Family Foundation, Jerry and Emily

Greenwich House ($3,000) see Allen Foundation, Frances

Greenwich House ($1,000) see Loeb Partners Corp.

Greenwich House ($20,000) see Perley Fund, Victor E.

Greenwich House ($25,000) see Weiler Foundation, Theodore & Renee

Grenville Baker Boys and Girls Club ($10,000) see Craigmyle Foundation

Group 1 Acting ($20,000) see Moore Memorial Foundation, James Starr

Guggenheim Museum ($20,000) see Cheatham Foundation, Owen

Guide Dog Foundation for the Blind ($12,000) see Ragen, Jr. Memorial Fund Trust No. 1, James M.

Guide Dog Foundation for the Blind ($5,000) see Ritter Foundation

Guiding Eyes for the Blind ($500) see Cohen Foundation, George M.

Guiding Eyes for the Blind ($10,000) see Steinbach Fund, Ruth and Milton

Guild for Exceptional Children ($7,500) see Goodman Memorial Foundation, Joseph C. and Clare F.

Guild for Exceptional Children ($50,000) see Mastronardi Charitable Foundation, Charles A.

Guild Hall ($1,000) see Spiritus Gladius Foundation

Guild of St. Francis ($12,135) see O'Sullivan Children Foundation

Gurion Jewish Geriatric Center ($12,000) see Gruber Research Foundation, Lila

Gurrin Jewish Center ($50,000) see Feil Foundation, Louis and Gertrude

Gurwin Jewish Geriatric Center ($85,000) see Lindner Foundation, Fay J.

Gurwin Jewish Geriatric Center ($25,000) see Waldbaum Family Foundation, I.

Gush Emunim ($200,000) see Block Family Charitable Trust, Ephraim

Gush Emunim — to provide aid to indigent Jewish people ($200,000) see Block Family Foundation, Emphraim

Habitat for Humanity ($1,000) see Hilliard Corp.

Habitat for Humanity — transitional housing ($5,000) see Joy Family Foundation

Habitat for Humanity ($5,000) see Manville Corp.

Habitat for Humanity ($20,000) see United States Trust Co. of New York

Hackley School — for professional development programs ($25,000) see Fohs Foundation

Hadassah ($100,000) see Federation Foundation of Greater Philadelphia

Hadassah ($5,000) see Goldstein Foundation, Leslie and Roslyn

Hadassah ($630,010) see Goodstein Family Foundation, David

Hadassah ($20,000) see Goodstein Foundation

Hadassah ($50,000) see Guggenheim Foundation, Daniel and Florence

Hadassah ($15,000) see Himmelfarb Foundation, Paul and Annetta

Hadassah ($20,000) see Innovating Worthy Projects Foundation

Hadassah ($12,800) see Price Foundation, Louis and Harold

Hadassah ($11,000) see Rosenbloom Foundation, Ben and Esther

Hadassah ($150,000) see Taper Foundation, Mark

Hadassah Hospital ($10,000) see Fink Foundation

Hadassah Hospital ($5,000) see Raskin Foundation, Hirsch and Braine

Hadassah Hospital Medical Organization ($11,000) see Simon Foundation, Sidney, Milton and Leoma

Hadassah Israel Education Service ($16,333) see Blinken Foundation

Hadassah Medical Organization ($10,000) see Gussman Foundation, Herbert and Roseline

Hadassah Medical Relief ($250,000) see Roth Foundation

Hadassah, The Women's Zionist Organization of America ($1,299,727) see Taper Foundation, S. Mark

Hadassah University Hospital ($83,800) see Ford Foundation, Joseph F. and Clara

Hadassh/Women's Zionist Organization of America — second payment of $60,000 pledge ($20,000) see Lowe Foundation, Joe and Emily

Hairy Cell Leukemia Foundation ($10,000) see Cohen Foundation, Wilfred P.

Hale Makua ($15,000) see Mellam Family Foundation

Hale Makua ($15,000) see Mellam Family Foundation

Hallel Institute ($20,000) see Morania Foundation

Hamilton College ($20,000) see Arkell Hall Foundation

Hamilton College ($50,000) see Brooks Foundation, Gladys

Hamilton College ($15,000) see CIT Group Holdings

Hamilton College ($34,000) see Dewar Foundation

Hamilton College — scholarship endowment ($100,000) see Emerson Foundation, Fred L.

Hamilton College — state distributions and energy transfer in ligands ejected by photolysis of organometallic compounds ($33,100) see Research Corporation

Hamilton College ($5,000) see Zlinkoff Fund for Medical Research and Education, Sergei S.

Hamilton College — Joseph Drown Loan Fund ($200,000) see Drown Foundation, Joseph

Hamilton College Scholarship Fund ($14,000) see Kennedy Foundation, Ethel

Hand House — for community development activities ($9,533) see Crary Foundation, Bruce L.

Handgun Control ($3,000) see Candlesticks Inc.

Handicap International — physical therapist/nurse in Thailand ($64,800) see Spunk Fund

Handicap International — physical therapist/nurse in Thailand ($48,000) see Spunk Fund

Handicapped Scouting ($5,000) see Winston Research Foundation, Harry

Hanford Mills Museum ($26,973) see O'Connor

Foundation, A. Lindsay and Olive B.

Hanford Mills Museum — salaries, accounting insurance ($64,795) see O'Connor Foundation, A. Lindsay and Olive B.

Hangar Theatre ($10,000) see Delavan Foundation, Nelson B.

Harkness Space Grant Program ($15,000) see Harkness Ballet Foundation

Harlem School of the Arts see Oki America Inc.

Harlem School of Arts ($7,000) see Sharp Foundation, Evelyn

Harley School ($15,000) see Wilson Foundation, Elaine P. and Richard U.

Harold Schneiderman Memorial Fund ($1,000) see Associated Food Stores

Harpischord Music Society ($13,000) see Stroud Foundation

Harry Fishel Institute ($258,000) see Fischel Foundation, Harry and Jane

Hartley House ($25,000) see Meyer Foundation

Hartley House ($20,000) see Perley Fund, Victor E.

Hartwick College ($125,000) see Dewar Foundation

Hartwick College — capital campaign ($100,000) see Emerson Foundation, Fred L.

Hartwick College ($25,000) see McDonald Foundation, J. M.

Hartwick College ($50,000) see Morris Foundation, William T.

Hartwick College ($20,000) see Warren and Beatrice W. Blanding Foundation, Riley J. and Lillian N.

Hartwick College ($100,000) see Wilber National Bank

Hastings Center ($20,000) see Pettus Crowe Foundation

Health Research — Roswell Park Memorial Institute — for the study of parameters that induce T-cell-mediated recognition of mammary adenocarcinomas by syngeneic C3Hf/He Mice; for the study of metastasis genes in ovarian carcinoma; for the study of endogenous retroviral sequ ($216,634) see Pardee Foundation, Elsa U.

Health Research, RPCI Division ($37,500) see Three Swallows Foundation

Health Science Center State ($20,000) see Sinsheimer Fund, Alexandrine and Alexander L.

Heart Fund ($25,000) see Allen Foundation, Frances

Heart Research Foundation ($2,400) see Russ Togs

Heart Rosaneh Foundation of Mount Sinai ($50,000) see Chait Memorial Foundation, Sara

Hebrew Arts School ($500,000) see Moses Fund, Henry and Lucy

Hebrew Free Loan Society ($12,000) see Durst Foundation

Hebrew Fund ($50,000) see Mattus Foundation, Reuben and Rose

Hebrew Home for the Aged at Riverdale ($50,000) see Hirschl Trust for Charitable Purposes, Irma T.

Hebrew Home for the Aged at Riverdale ($200,000) see Kaufmann Foundation, Henry

Hebrew Home for the Aged in Riverdale ($5,000) see Klosk Fund, Louis and Rose

Hebrew Home for the Aged at Riverdale ($13,000) see Morris Foundation, Norman M.

Hebrew Home for the Aged at Riverdale ($5,000) see Odyssey Partners

Hebrew Home for the Aged at Riverdale — in support of renovation and expansion project ($500,000) see Starr Foundation

Hebrew Institute ($1,000) see Marcus Brothers Textiles Inc.

Hebrew Institute of Riverdale ($1,000) see Marcus Brothers Textiles Inc.

Hechel Synagogue ($1,000) see Marcus Brothers Textiles Inc.

Helen Hayes Hospital ($30,000) see Scott Foundation, Walter

Helene Fuld School of Nursing North General Hospital — scholarships ($187,500) see Fuld Health Trust, Helene

Help the Children Foundation ($115,000) see Icahn Foundation, Carl C.

Help the Poor Foundation ($5,000) see Gateway Apparel

Help and Reconstruction ($10,000) see Ridgefield Foundation

Hemophilia Center of Western New York ($3,000) see Children's Foundation of Erie County

Henry Street Settlement ($265,550) see Abrons Foundation, Louis and Anne

Henry Street Settlement ($5,000) see Amsterdam Foundation, Jack and Mimi Leviton

Henry Street Settlement — good companions program ($20,000) see Blum Foundation, Edna F.

Henry Street Settlement ($10,000) see Dreitzer Foundation

Henry Street Settlement — capital campaign ($25,000) see Guttman Foundation, Stella and Charles

Henry Street Settlement ($100,000) see Kaufmann Foundation, Henry

Henry Street Settlement ($30,500) see Lehman Foundation, Edith and Herbert

Henry Street Settlement ($20,000) see Penney Foundation, James C.

Herbert E. Hawkes Fund — scholarships ($50,000) see Hugoton Foundation

Heritage Synagogue of Westchester ($4,300) see Nelco Sewing Machine Sales Corp.

Hewlett East Rockaway Jewish Center ($4,295) see Associated Food Stores

HIAS ($50,000) see Rochlin Foundation, Abraham and Sonia

HID Research and Development Foundation ($2,500) see Morris Foundation, Norman M.

Highbridge Community Housing Development Fund Corporation ($15,000) see Kenworthy - Sarah H. Swift Foundation, Marion E.

Highbridge Community Life Center ($20,000) see Bowne Foundation, Robert

Highland Hospital Foundation ($5,000) see Curtice-Burns Foods

Highland Hospital Foundation — memorial to J. Wallace Ely ($40,000) see Davenport-Hatch Foundation

Hilbert College — computers ($19,625) see Palisano Foundation, Vincent and Harriet

Hillcrest Jewish Center ($24,500) see Ferkauf Foundation, Eugene and Estelle

Hillcrest Jewish Center ($80,000) see Stein Foundation, Joseph F.

Hillside Children's Center see Eastman Kodak Co.

Hillside Children's Center — to help construct a new educational building and renovate the existing child welfare and mental health treatment facility ($35,000) see Jones Foundation, Daisy Marquis

Hineni Heritage Center ($10,400) see Mattus Foundation, Reuben and Rose

HIOBS ($10,000) see Kellogg Foundation, J. C.

Hispanic Federation of New York City — to strengthen the Hispanic organizational network ($40,000) see Cummings Memorial Fund Trust, Frances L. and Edwin L.

Historic Hudson Valley — toward an endowed fund for education programs ($50,000) see Astor Foundation, Vincent

Historic Hudson Valley ($500,000) see Jackson Hole Preserve

Historic Hudson Valley ($10,000) see Levy Foundation, Jerome

Historic Hudson Valley ($10,000) see Richardson Foundation, Frank E. and Nancy M.

Historic Hudson Valley ($30,000) see Schwartz Foundation, David

Historic Hudson Valley ($50,000) see Warhol Foundation for the Visual Arts, Andy

HJD Research and Development Foundation ($15,000) see Neu Foundation, Hugo and Doris

Hobart and William Smith Colleges ($100,000) see Olin Foundation, Spencer T. and Ann W.

Hobart and William Smith Colleges ($16,750) see Rosenberg Foundation, Henry and Ruth Blaustein

Hobart and William Smith Colleges ($15,000) see Schloss & Co., Marcus

Hobart and William Smith Colleges ($10,000) see Schloss & Co., Marcus

Hofstra University ($50,000) see Lindner Foundation, Fay J.

Hofstra University ($5,000) see Roche Relief Foundation, Edward and Ellen

Hofstra University ($15,000) see Slant/Fin Corp.

Hofstra University ($2,000) see Ushkow Foundation

Hofstra University School of Law ($15,250) see Spiegel Family Foundation, Jerry and Emily

Holocaust Publications ($20,000) see Slant/Fin Corp.

Holy Apostles Soup Kitchen ($50,000) see Rhodebeck Charitable Trust

New York (cont.)

Holy Name of Mary Roman Catholic Church ($100) see Hendrickson Brothers

Home for Contemporary Theater and Art ($12,000) see Geffen Foundation, David

Homes for the Homeless ($32,000) see Stern Foundation, Leonard N.

Homes for the Homeless Summer Camp ($100,000) see Stern Foundation, Leonard N.

Homestead ($141,533) see Faulkner Trust, Marianne Gaillard

Hope for Bereaved ($40,000) see Gifford Charitable Corporation, Rosamond

Hope Program ($20,000) see Snyder Fund, Valentine Perry

Horace Mann-Barnard School ($7,500) see Charina Foundation

Horticultural Society of New York ($5,000) see Commerce Clearing House

Horticultural Society of New York ($5,000) see Vesper Corp.

Hospice ($10,000) see Western New York Foundation

Hospice Buffalo ($10,000) see Goodyear Foundation, Josephine

Hospice Buffalo ($100,000) see Julia R. and Estelle L. Foundation

Hospital Authority of Albany ($5,000) see Olin Charitable Trust, John M.

Hospital for Joint Diseases and Medical Center ($27,975) see Harkness Ballet Foundation

Hospital for Joint Diseases and Medical Center ($2,000) see Morris Foundation, Norman M.

Hospital for Joint Diseases and Medical Center ($600,000) see Reicher Foundation, Anne & Harry J.

Hospital for Joint Diseases and Medical Center ($10,000) see Weininger Foundation, Richard and Gertrude

Hospital for Joint Diseases and Medical Center ($100,000) see Witco Corp.

Hospital for Joint Diseases Orthopaedic Institute — toward construction of the Samuels Urgent Care Center ($220,000) see Samuels Foundation, Fan Fox and Leslie R.

Hospital for Joint Diseases Orthopedic Institute ($10,000) see Aeroflex Foundation

Hospital for Joint Diseases Orthopedic Institute ($10,000) see Aeroflex Foundation

Hospital for Joint Diseases Orthopedic Institute ($3,000) see Goodman Memorial Foundation, Joseph C. and Clare F.

Hospital for Joint Diseases Orthopedic Institute ($25,171) see Harkness Foundation, William Hale

Hospital for Joint Diseases Orthopedic Institute ($75,000) see Langeloth Foundation, Jacob and Valeria

Hospital for Joint Diseases Orthopedic Institute ($25,000) see Levee Charitable Trust, Polly Annenberg

Hospital for Special Surgery ($12,500) see Appleman Foundation

Hospital for Special Surgery ($10,000) see Charina Foundation

Hospital for Special Surgery ($250,000) see Clark Foundation

Hospital for Special Surgery ($5,000) see Donaldson, Lufkin & Jenrette

Hospital for Special Surgery ($10,000) see Fortin Foundation of Florida

Hospital for Special Surgery ($35,000) see Frese Foundation, Arnold D.

Hospital for Special Surgery ($25,000) see Frohlich Charitable Trust, Ludwig W.

Hospital for Special Surgery ($350,000) see Goldsmith Foundation, Horace W.

Hospital for Special Surgery — equipment ($50,000) see Hugoton Foundation

Hospital for Special Surgery ($4,000) see Jost Foundation, Charles and Mabel P.

Hospital for Special Surgery — in support of research activities ($25,000) see Kieckhefer Foundation, J. W.

Hospital for Special Surgery — support research activities ($75,000) see Morris Foundation, Margaret T.

Hospital for Special Surgery ($9,200) see Mosbacher, Jr. Foundation, Emil

Hospital for Special Surgery ($35,000) see Oxnard Foundation

Hospital for Special Surgery ($40,000) see Pope Foundation

Hospital for Special Surgery ($43,333) see Zilkha & Sons

Hospital for Special Surgery Fund ($50,000) see JM Foundation

Hotel/Motel Association ($194,195) see Statler Foundation

Houghton College ($13,000) see Palmer Fund, Francis Asbury

Housing Action Council ($10,000) see St. Faith's House Foundation

Hudson Guild ($20,000) see Perley Fund, Victor E.

Hudson Guild ($6,000) see Straus Foundation, Philip A. and Lynn

Hudson Guild ($1,100) see Stuart Foundation

Hudson Memorial Hospital ($50,000) see Andersen Foundation, Hugh J.

Hudson River Film and Video ($5,000) see Commerce Clearing House

Hudson Valley Health Systems Agency ($5,500) see Westchester Health Fund

Hudson Valley Philharmonic — for annual support ($45,000) see McCann Foundation

Human Life Foundation ($10,000) see Burkitt Foundation

Human Resources Center ($33,334) see Heckscher Foundation for Children

Human Resources Center ($140,000) see Oberkotter Family Foundation

Human Resources Center ($100,000) see Weezie Foundation

Human Rights Watch — general support ($500,000) see Diamond Foundation, Aaron

Human Rights Watch ($5,000) see Sheinberg Foundation, Eric P.

Hunter College ($6,000) see Halloran Foundation, Mary P. Dolciani

Hunter College ($45,000) see Lang Foundation, Eugene M.

Hunter College ($27,000) see Newcombe Foundation, Charlotte W.

Hunter College/Brookdale Center on Aging ($350,000) see Ramapo Trust

Hunter College, Brookdale Center on Aging ($25,000) see Rhodebeck Charitable Trust

Hunter College Scholarship Fund ($4,500) see Abeles Foundation, Joseph and Sophia

Huntington Coalition for the Homeless ($5,000) see Foerderer Foundation, Percival E. and Ethel Brown

Huntington Townwide Fund ($14,000) see Porter Foundation, Mrs. Cheever

Hurlbut Memorial Community Church ($15,000) see Carnahan-Jackson Foundation

Hurricane Allen St. Lucia Rebuilding Fund ($300,000) see Hess Foundation

Hurricane Allen St. Lucia Rebuilding Fund ($25,000) see Pitt-Des Moines Inc.

I Have a Dream Foundation ($51,000) see Benenson Foundation, Frances and Benjamin

I Have a Dream Foundation ($25,112) see Lang Foundation, Eugene M.

I Have a Dream Foundation ($44,100) see Ritter Foundation

ICD-International Center for the Disabled ($347,500) see JM Foundation

ICD International Center for the Disabled ($100,000) see Langeloth Foundation, Jacob and Valeria

ICD International Center for the Disabled — for the 75th Anniversary Campaign ($100,000) see Bodman Foundation

ICD International Center for the Disabled — for the 75th Anniversary Campaign and to meet a J. M. Foundation challenge award ($30,000) see Achelis Foundation

ICD Rehabilitation and Research Center ($25,000) see Lee Foundation, James T.

ICP ($18,000) see Hillman Family Foundation, Alex

Illuminating Engineering Society ($9,167) see Guth Lighting Co.

IMPACT II — New York, Chicago, and Los Angeles ($46,300) see Industrial Bank of Japan Trust Co.

In Touch Networks ($2,000) see Fein Foundation

In-Touch Networks ($17,500) see Lee Foundation, James T.

Incarnation Parish ($4,000) see Vanderbilt Trust, R. T.

Independent College Fund of New York — scholarships ($15,000) see Allyn Foundation

Independent College Fund of New York — general charitable contribution ($25,000) see Carter-Wallace

Independent College Fund of New York ($80,000) see Taylor Foundation, Fred and Harriett

Independent Curators — exhibit catalog ($20,000) see Mapplethorpe Foundation, Robert

Independent Curators Incorporated — support of exhibition and catalogue Eternal Metaphors: New Art from Italy ($7,000) see Rosenthal Foundation, Ida and William

Independent Production Fund ($5,000) see Blum Foundation, Harry and Maribel G.

Independent Production Fund ($81,000) see Blum-Kovler Foundation

Independent Production Fund ($30,000) see Deer Creek Foundation

Independent Production Fund ($6,000) see MacDonald Foundation, Marquis George

Independent Production Fund — for "EARTH: A USER'S GUIDE", an eight-part PBS series; (first payment of a three-year $70,000 grant) ($47,000) see Ittleson Foundation

Independent Production Fund — to support the Voices of the Electorate project ($220,000) see Schumann Foundation, Florence and John

Indian Hills Council ($10,000) see Klee Foundation, Conrad and Virginia

Indian Youth of America ($20,000) see Gould Foundation for Children, Edwin

Individual Research Project — entitled "The Dynamics of Political Violence, The Recent Irish Experience" ($30,000) see Guggenheim Foundation, Harry Frank

Industrial Management Council of Rochester see Eastman Kodak Co.

Infanta Montessori ($2,000) see Cranshaw Corporation

INFORM ($60,000) see Clark Foundation, Robert Sterling

Inform ($72,000) see Millbrook Tribute Garden

Inform ($20,000) see Penney Foundation, James C.

Inner Circle ($2,800) see Goodman Family Foundation

Inner-City Scholarship Fund ($20,000) see Belding Heminway Co.

Inner-City Scholarship Fund — for the endowment drive ($60,000) see Bodman Foundation

Inner City Scholarship Fund ($2,000) see Coleman Foundation

Inner City Scholarship Fund ($15,000) see Coles Family Foundation

Inner City Scholarship Fund ($5,000) see Donovan, Leisure, Newton & Irvine

Inner City Scholarship Fund ($50,000) see Ellison Foundation

Inner-City Scholarship Fund ($125,000) see Heinz Co., H.J.

Inner-City Scholarship Fund — scholarships to minority students ($25,000) see Homeland Foundation

Inner-City Scholarship Fund ($5,000) see Russ Togs

Inner-City Scholarship Fund ($25,000) see Weinberg Foundation, John L.

Inner-City Scholarship Fund — for the current endowment drive for the 79 member schools ($25,000) see Achelis Foundation

Institute for Advanced Strategic and Political Studies ($15,000) see Burns Foundation, Jacob

Institute for Advanced Strategic and Political Studies ($5,000) see Ehrman Foundation, Fred and Susan

Institute for Advanced Strategic and Political Studies ($1,000) see Marcus Brothers Textiles Inc.

Institute for the Advancement of Education in Jaffa ($25,000) see Russell Memorial Foundation, Robert

Institute for the Advancement of Education in Jaffa ($50,000) see Schwartz and Robert Schwartz Foundation, Bernard

Institute of Biomedical Ethics ($5,000) see Pettus Crowe Foundation

Institute for Contemporary Art ($10,000) see Titan Industrial Co.

Institute for Contemporary Art ($5,000) see Titan Industrial Co.

Institute for East-West Security Studies see Blackstone Group LP

Institute for East-West Security Studies ($45,000) see Salomon Foundation, Richard & Edna

Institute for East/West Security Studies ($25,000) see Weyerhaeuser Family Foundation

Institute/East-West Studies — toward 1992 budget ($50,000) see Arcana Foundation

Institute for Eastwest Studies — general budgetary support ($600,000) see Rockefeller Brothers Fund

Institute of Ecosystem Studies ($50,000) see Millbrook Tribute Garden

Institute of Fine Arts ($110,000) see Wiener Foundation, Malcolm Hewitt

Institute of Fine Arts of New York University ($128,265) see Lehman Foundation, Robert

Institute of Fine Arts, New York University — fellowship for outstanding first-year student ($10,000) see Rosenthal Foundation, Ida and William

Institute of Human Relations ($2,500) see Schapiro Fund, M. A.

Institute of Intern Education ($250,000) see Hoffman Foundation, Marion O. and Maximilian

Institute of International Education see Bonner & Moore Associates

Institute of International Education — contribution ($37,126) see Bridgestone/ Firestone

Institute of International Education ($30,930) see Bridgestone/ Firestone

Institute of International Education see Brown & Root, Inc.

Institute of International Education see First Colorado Bank & Trust, N.A.

Institute of International Education see Grace Petroleum Corp.

Institute on International Education ($100,000) see Kaufman Foundation, Henry & Elaine

Institute of International Education see Kemper Securities Inc.

Institute of International Education see Keystone International

Institute for International Education ($5,000) see Kunstadter Family Foundation, Albert

Institute of International Education ($50,000) see Mex-Am Cultural Foundation

Institute of International Education see Omega World Travel

Institute for Literacy Studies ($1,029,000) see Wallace-Reader's Digest Fund, DeWitt

Institute of Neurological Science ($10,000) see Massey Foundation, Jack C.

Institute for Policy Studies ($40,000) see Bydale Foundation

Institute for Policy Studies ($25,000) see Mott Fund, Ruth

Institute for Policy Studies ($15,000) see Warner Fund, Albert and Bessie

Institute for Policy Studies ($10,000) see Warner Fund, Albert and Bessie

Institute of Public Administration ($100,000) see Pforzheimer Foundation, Carl and Lily

Institute of Public Administration — to support exchange between American and Japanese public works professionals ($162,461) see United States-Japan Foundation

Institute for Public Affairs ($10,000) see Warner Fund, Albert and Bessie

Institute on Religion and Public Life — to support general program activities ($350,000) see Bradley Foundation, Lynde and Harry

Institute for Research in Hypnosis ($40,000) see Ames Charitable Trust, Harriett

Institute of Semitic Studies ($56,500) see Blum Foundation, Edith C.

Institute for Social Justice ($10,000) see Abelard Foundation

Insurance Education Council of New York — sponsorship dues 1990-91 ($10,000) see Crum and Forster

Interfaith Hunger Appeal ($50,000) see Banfi Vintners

Interfaith Hunger Appeal ($1,250) see Hirschhorn Foundation, David and Barbara B.

International Art of Jazz ($5,000) see Bayne Fund, Howard

International Cancer Education Fund ($600,000) see Bobst Foundation, Elmer and Mamdouha

International Center for the Disabled ($5,000) see Roche Relief Foundation, Edward and Ellen

International Center for the Disabled ($5,000) see Roche Relief Foundation, Edward and Ellen

International Center for the Disabled ($15,000) see Sharp Foundation

International Center for the Disabled ($5,000) see Woodland Foundation

International Center for Hearing and Speech Research — equipment for research ($30,000) see Davenport-Hatch Foundation

International Center for Hearing and Speech Research/Rochester Institute of Technology ($250,000) see Oberkotter Family Foundation

International Center for Integrative Studies — to assist The Door in making the transition to an independent organization and overcoming a major financial deficit ($500,000) see Mott Foundation, Charles Stewart

International Center for Integrative Studies, (The Door) — support of The Door's Counseling Center, which offers free services to at-risk adolescents from off the streets ($50,000) see van Ameringen Foundation

International Center for Intergrative Studies ($5,000) see Tuch Foundation, Michael

International Center of Photography ($10,000) see Levin Foundation, Philip and Janice

International Center of Photography — exhibit catalog ($12,500) see Mapplethorpe Foundation, Robert

International Center of Photography ($4,000) see Rosenwald Family Fund, William

International Center of Photography ($25,000) see Zenkel Foundation

International Center of Photography — Student Admission Program ($15,000) see Lowe Foundation, Joe and Emily

International Center of Syracuse ($6,500) see Mather Fund, Richard

International College ($10,000) see Sweatt Foundation, Harold W.

International Council of MOMA ($5,000) see Alsdorf Foundation

International Council of Religious Education ($4,000) see Chapin-May Foundation of Illinois

International Festival of the Arts ($25,000) see Wien Foundation, Lawrence A.

International Festival Society ($18,500) see Colburn Fund

International Film Seminars — Museum of Modern Art ($35,000) see Pinewood Foundation

International Friends of London Literary ($100,000) see Heinz Foundation, Drue

International Heart of Variety ($308,000) see Capital Fund Foundation

International House ($50,000) see Dodge Foundation, Cleveland H.

International House ($20,000) see Frohlich Charitable Trust, Ludwig W.

International Institute for the Arts ($10,000) see Kauffman Foundation, Muriel McBrien

International Institute of Rural Reconstruction — to support an expansion of the institute's work in sustainable agriculture ($210,000) see Rockefeller Brothers Fund

International League — Jewish ($15,000) see Belding Heminway Co.

International Management Center ($202,500) see Open Society Fund

International Ministries ($12,000) see Christian Training Foundation

International Museum of Photography see Eastman Kodak Co.

International Museum of Photography ($55,000) see Edgerton Foundation, Harold E.

International Museum of Photography ($20,000) see Wilson Foundation, Marie C. and Joseph C.

International Narcotic Enforcement Officers Association — awards to families of officers killed in the line of duty ($30,000) see Japanese American Agon Friendship League

International Peace Academy ($180,000) see Educational Foundation of America

International Peace Academy ($40,000) see Wallach Foundation, Miriam G. and Ira D.

International Rescue Committee ($2,000) see Cottrell Foundation

International Rescue Committee — operating support ($30,000) see Davis Foundation, Edwin W. and Catherine M.

International Rescue Committee ($500,000) see Johnson Foundation, Barbara P.

International Rescue Committee ($27,500) see LeBrun Foundation

International Rescue Committee ($5,000) see Normandie Foundation

International Rescue Committee ($8,500) see Ogden Foundation, Ralph E.

International Rescue Committee ($10,700) see Peierls Foundation

International Rescue Committee ($20,000) see Rolfs Foundation, Robert T.

International Rescue Committee ($500) see Spiro Foundation, Donald W.

International Rescue Committee ($10,000) see Thanksgiving Foundation

International Rescue Committee ($30,000) see Westwood Endowment

International Rescue Committee ($100,000) see Whitehead Foundation

International Rescue Committee — for emergency relief for the Kurds ($25,000) see Achelis Foundation

International Rescue Committee — women's training and housing ($44,892) see Spunk Fund

International Rescue Committee — women's agricultural project ($41,631) see Spunk Fund

International Research and Exchange Board — toward support ($1,600,000) see Carnegie Corporation of New York

International Scripture Center ($12,000) see Bydale Foundation

International Sephardic Education Foundation ($19,700) see Gindi Associates Foundation

International Sephardic Education Foundation ($10,000) see Weininger Foundation, Richard and Gertrude

International Sephardic Educational Foundation ($31,000) see Gitano Group

International Society for Arts, Sciences and Technology ($75,000) see Macmillan, Inc.

International Society for Arts, Sciences, and Technology ($50,000) see Macmillan, Inc.

International Voluntary Services ($35,000) see General Service Foundation

International Women's Health Coalition — general support ($10,000) see Campbell and Adah E. Hall Charity Fund, Bushrod H.

International Women's Health Coalition — for reproductive health activities in Latin America ($30,000) see Prospect Hill Foundation

Interns for Peace ($2,000) see Garfinkle Family Foundation

Interns for Peace ($25,000) see Meyerhoff Fund, Joseph

Interracial Council for Business Opportunity ($35,478) see Borden

Interschool Orchestras of New York ($25,000) see Vidda Foundation

Inwood House — toward salary of teen choice counselor ($20,000) see Lincoln Fund

Inwood House ($20,000) see McDonald Foundation, J. M.

Inwood House ($62,300) see Mertz Foundation, Martha

Inwood House — to support an outreach service to counsel and guide teenagers in local high schools before problems develop ($7,500) see Washington Square Fund

Iona College — endowment funding ($50,000) see Badgeley Residuary Charitable Trust, Rose M.

Iona College ($9,600) see Crane Fund for Widows and Children

Iona College ($5,000) see Joyce Foundation, John M. and Mary A.

Iona College ($20,000) see Lee Foundation, James T.

Iona College — first installment of a $250,000 two for one challenge grant ($100,000) see Calder Foundation, Louis

Iona Preparatory School ($5,000) see Joyce Foundation, John M. and Mary A.

Iona Senior Services ($25,000) see Marpat Foundation

Irish American Partnership ($101,500) see Banfi Vintners

Irish Educational Development (Maynooth) ($250,000) see Leavey Foundation, Thomas and Dorothy

Irvington Institute for Medical Research ($6,000) see Oestreicher Foundation, Sylvan and Ann

Islamic Seminary ($95,000) see Ala Vi Foundation of New York

Israel Cancer Research ($20,000) see Bennett Foundation, Carl and Dorothy

Israel Cancer Research ($2,000) see Livingston Foundation, Milton S. and Corinne N.

Israel Congregation ($300) see Amdur Braude Riley, Inc.

Israel Education Fund ($100,000) see Chais Family Foundation

Israel Heritage ($20,000) see Belding Heminway Co.

Israel Heritage ($5,000) see Goldie-Anna Charitable Trust

Israel Heritage/Moreshet Israel ($100,000) see Wasserman Foundation

Israel Institute of Technology ($500,000) see Mitrani Family Foundation

Israel Tennis Center Associates ($156,000) see Eisenberg Foundation, Ben B. and Joyce E.

Israel Tennis Centers Association ($5,000) see Altschul Foundation

Israel Tennis Centers Association ($1,800) see Goldberg Family Foundation, Israel and Matilda

Israel Tennis Centers Association ($6,000) see Lasky Co.

Israel Tennis Centers Association ($6,000) see Oppenheimer Family Foundation

Israel Tennis Centers Association ($5,400) see Stone Foundation, David S.

Israel Tennis Fund ($1,800) see Associated Food Stores

Israeli Endowment Fund ($5,000) see Altschul Foundation

Issacs Center ($10,000) see Adams Memorial Fund, Emma J.

Ithaca College — scholarship assistance ($9,000) see Cove Charitable Trust

Ithaca College — endowment scholarship ($100,000) see Emerson Foundation, Fred L.

J. Gurwin Foundation ($5,000) see Spiegel Family Foundation, Jerry and Emily

J. K. Miller Memorial Fund ($10,000) see Key Food Stores Cooperative Inc.

J. L. Morse Geriatric Center ($15,000) see Kramer Foundation

Jackie Robinson Foundation ($80,000) see Chesebrough-Pond's

Jackie Robinson Foundation ($5,625) see Fisher Brothers

Jacob D. Fuchsberg Law Center ($5,000) see Fuchsberg Family Foundation

James Investment Research ($6,451) see Hartzell Industries, Inc.

James Prendergast Library Association ($12,035) see Carnahan-Jackson Foundation

James Prendergast Library Association ($9,690) see Darrah Charitable Trust, Jessie Smith

James Prendergast Library Association ($49,422) see Hultquist Foundation

Jamestown Audubon Society ($45,000) see Carnahan-Jackson Foundation

Jamestown Audubon Society ($5,000) see Darrah Charitable Trust, Jessie Smith

New York (cont.)

Jamestown Audubon Society — capital campaign ($125,000) see Gebbie Foundation

Jamestown Audubon Society ($75,000) see Sheldon Foundation, Ralph C.

Jamestown Community College — matching grant ($200,000) see Gebbie Foundation

Jamestown Community College ($300,000) see Hultquist Foundation

Jamestown Community College ($140,000) see Sheldon Foundation, Ralph C.

Jamestown Concert Association ($9,000) see Hultquist Foundation

Japan Society — general support ($20,000) see Collins Foundation, Carr P.

Japan Society — to support the Commission on U.S.-Japan Relations for the 21st Century ($200,000) see United States-Japan Foundation

Japanese Chamber of Commerce see Marubeni America Corp.

JASA ($35,000) see Green Fund

Jean Cocteau Repertory — for partial support of production of Mary Stuart in a new translation ($5,000) see Axe-Houghton Foundation

Jericho Project — for a van to be used for transportation between Jericho's three residences ($25,000) see Astor Foundation, Vincent

Jerry Finkelstein Cancer Foundation ($1,000) see Marcus Brothers Textiles Inc.

Jerusalem College of Technology ($13,333) see United Togs Inc.

Jerusalem Foundation ($401,000) see Blaustein Foundation, Jacob and Hilda

Jerusalem Foundation ($15,000) see Blinken Foundation

Jerusalem Foundation ($55,000) see Botwinick-Wolfensohn Foundation

Jerusalem Foundation ($200,000) see Cohen Foundation, Naomi and Nehemiah

Jerusalem Foundation ($5,000) see Cole Taylor Financial Group

Jerusalem Foundation ($25,000) see Feldman Foundation

Jerusalem Foundation ($25,000) see Feldman Foundation

Jerusalem Foundation ($10,000) see Fellner Memorial Foundation, Leopold and Clara M.

Jerusalem Foundation ($5,000) see Fink Foundation

Jerusalem Foundation ($20,450) see Friedland Family Foundation, Samuel

Jerusalem Foundation ($370,000) see Goldsmith Foundation, Horace W.

Jerusalem Foundation ($5,000) see Goldstein Foundation, Alfred and Ann

Jerusalem Foundation ($250,000) see Greenberg Foundation, Alan C.

Jerusalem Foundation ($154,137) see Hassenfeld Foundation

Jerusalem Foundation ($25,000) see Loeb Foundation, Frances and John L.

Jerusalem Foundation ($251,000) see Model Foundation, Leo

Jerusalem Foundation ($50,000) see Polinsky-Rivkin Family Foundation

Jerusalem Foundation ($10,000) see Ridgefield Foundation

Jerusalem Foundation ($2,500) see Rittenhouse Foundation

Jerusalem Foundation ($100,000) see Rochlin Foundation, Abraham and Sonia

Jerusalem Foundation ($50,000) see Rose Foundation, Billy

Jerusalem Foundation ($30,000) see Rosenberg Foundation, Sunny and Abe

Jerusalem Foundation ($50,000) see Schwartz Foundation, David

Jerusalem Foundation ($25,000) see Spingold Foundation, Nate B. and Frances

Jerusalem Foundation ($204,000) see Wasserman Foundation

Jerusalem Foundation ($100,000) see Witco Corp.

Jerusalem Foundation Endowment Fund ($1,000) see FAB Industries

Jerusalem Foundation Endowment Fund ($800) see Foundation for Middle East Peace

Jerusalem Foundation Endowment Fund ($10,000) see Harris Foundation, J. Ira and Nicki

Jerusalem Foundation — support an educational exchange program between Jewish and Arab high school students ($33,000) see Guttman Foundation, Stella and Charles

Jesuit Program for Living and Learning of New York ($7,500) see Brooklyn Benevolent Society

Jewish Agency ($50,000) see Morgenstern Foundation, Morris

Jewish Association for Services for the Aged ($300,000) see Kaufmann Foundation, Henry

Jewish Association for Services for the Aged ($13,500) see Kevorkian Fund, Hagop

Jewish Association for Services to the Aged ($25,000) see Nias Foundation, Henry

Jewish Association for Services for the Aged ($157,294) see Scheuer Family Foundation, S. H. and Helen R.

Jewish Board of Family and Children's Services ($5,000) see Beir Foundation

Jewish Board of Family and Children's Services ($2,200) see Daniel Foundation, Gerard and Ruth

Jewish Board of Family and Children's Services ($102,500) see Kaufmann Foundation, Henry

Jewish Board of Family and Children's Services ($10,000) see Lee Foundation, James T.

Jewish Board of Family and Children's Services ($24,975) see Marx Foundation, Virginia & Leonard

Jewish Board of Family and Children's Services ($45,000) see Oppenheimer and Flora Oppenheimer Haas Trust, Leo

Jewish Braille Institute of America ($10,000) see

Ferkauf Foundation, Eugene and Estelle

Jewish Braille Institute of America ($10,500) see Gudelsky Family Foundation, Isadore and Bertha

Jewish Braille Institute of America ($20,000) see Oppenheimer and Flora Oppenheimer Haas Trust, Leo

Jewish Braille Institute of America ($11,000) see Parshelsky Foundation, Moses L.

Jewish Center ($2,060) see House of Gross

Jewish Center ($30,000) see Stern Foundation, Max

Jewish Center ($20,000) see Stern Foundation, Max

Jewish Center of Atlantic Beach ($175) see Falk Foundation, Michael David

Jewish Center of Hamptons ($5,000) see Rosenwald Family Fund, William

Jewish Center Torah Society ($15,000) see Propp Sons Fund, Morris and Anna

Jewish Child Care Association ($5,000) see Olive Bridge Fund

Jewish Child Care Association ($30,000) see Oppenheimer and Flora Oppenheimer Haas Trust, Leo

Jewish Communal Fund ($80,000) see Falk Foundation, Michael David

Jewish Communal Fund ($246,000) see Gruss Charitable and Educational Foundation, Oscar and Regina

Jewish Communal Fund ($200,000) see Gruss Charitable Foundation, Emanuel and Riane

Jewish Communal Fund of New York ($40,000) see Loewenberg Foundation

Jewish Community Center ($25,000) see Chait Memorial Foundation, Sara

Jewish Community Center ($2,000) see Fischbach Foundation

Jewish Community Center ($1,311) see Fuchsberg Family Foundation

Jewish Community Center ($30,000) see Hoyt Foundation, Stewart W. and Willma C.

Jewish Community Center ($83,850) see Kaplen Foundation

Jewish Community Center ($5,000) see Odyssey Partners

Jewish Community Center ($30,000) see Schaffer Foundation, H.

Jewish Community Center of Fulton County ($10,000) see Littauer Foundation, Lucius N.

Jewish Community Center of Upper West Side ($7,500) see Geist Foundation

Jewish Community Centers Association of North America ($255,800) see Capital Fund Foundation

Jewish Community Day School ($4,600) see Fireman Charitable Foundation, Paul and Phyllis

Jewish Community House of Bensonhurst ($25,000) see de Hirsch Fund, Baron

Jewish Community Relations Council ($5,000) see Guttag Foundation, Irwin and Marjorie

Jewish Community Relations Council ($5,000) see Odyssey Partners

Jewish Diabetes Foundation ($11,150) see Greenberg Foundation, Alan C.

Jewish Family Service ($20,000) see Statler Foundation

Jewish Federation ($5,000) see FAB Industries

Jewish Federation ($5,000) see Kramer Foundation

Jewish Federation ($5,000) see Kramer Foundation

Jewish Fund for Justice ($5,000) see Thalheimer Foundation, Alvin and Fanny Blaustein

Jewish Geriatric Center ($3,500) see Frankel Foundation, George and Elizabeth F.

Jewish Guild for the Blind ($12,500) see Eckman Charitable Foundation, Samuel and Rae

Jewish Guild for the Blind ($25,000) see Golden Family Foundation

Jewish Guild for the Blind ($50,000) see Hirschl Trust for Charitable Purposes, Irma T.

Jewish Guild for the Blind ($60,000) see Kramer Foundation, C. L. C.

Jewish Guild for the Blind ($141,000) see Newman Assistance Fund, Jerome A. and Estelle R.

Jewish Guild for the Blind ($25,000) see Olive Bridge Fund

Jewish Guild for the Blind ($25,000) see Olive Bridge Fund

Jewish Guild for the Blind ($15,000) see Straus Foundation, Martha Washington Straus and Harry H.

Jewish Guild for the Blind ($500) see Weiss Foundation, Stephen and Suzanne

Jewish Guild for the Blind ($3,000) see Zacharia Foundation, Isaac Herman

Jewish Home for the Aged ($12,000) see Alperin/Hirsch Family Foundation

Jewish Home for the Aged ($50,000) see Kaplen Foundation

Jewish Home for the Aged ($14,686) see Lender Family Foundation

Jewish Home for the Aged ($10,000) see Meyer Fund, Milton and Sophie

Jewish Home for the Elderly ($21,000) see Goldstein Foundation, Leslie and Roslyn

Jewish Home and Hospital for Aged — intervention and evaluation of physically restrained nursing home residents ($824,000) see Commonwealth Fund

Jewish Home and Hospital for the Aged ($25,000) see Nias Foundation, Henry

Jewish Home and Hospital for the Aged ($150,000) see Saul Foundation, Joseph E. & Norma G.

Jewish Home and Hospital for the Aged ($2,500) see Spingold Foundation, Nate B. and Frances

Jewish Labor Committee ($80,000) see Atran Foundation

Jewish Media Fund — to support further development, testing, and distribution of the Jewish Heritage Video Collection

($300,000) see Revson Foundation, Charles H.

Jewish Media Fund — for the second phase of development of Jewish Heritage Video Collection ($250,000) see Revson Foundation, Charles H.

Jewish Museum ($827,972) see Dorot Foundation

Jewish Museum ($50,750) see Horowitz Foundation, Gedale B. and Barbara S.

Jewish Museum ($50,000) see Kaplan Foundation, Rita J. and Stanley H.

Jewish Museum ($100,000) see Kaufman Foundation, Henry & Elaine

Jewish Museum ($10,000) see Kaufman Foundation, Henry & Elaine

Jewish Museum ($1,000) see Levy Foundation, Betty and Norman F.

Jewish Museum — general support ($180,000) see Lowe Foundation, Joe and Emily

Jewish Museum ($120,000) see Milstein Family Foundation

Jewish Museum — support library ($25,000) see Morris Foundation, Margaret T.

Jewish Museum ($6,000) see Morse, Jr. Foundation, Enid and Lester S.

Jewish Museum ($60,000) see Rodgers Foundation, Richard & Dorothy

Jewish Museum ($8,500) see Ross Foundation, Lyn & George M.

Jewish Museum ($1,505,000) see Scheuer Family Foundation, S. H. and Helen R.

Jewish Museum ($5,000) see Schimmel Foundation

Jewish Museum ($10,000) see Sequa Corp.

Jewish Museum ($5,000) see Sequa Corp.

Jewish Museum ($250,000) see Skirball Foundation

Jewish Museum ($115,000) see Tisch Foundation

Jewish Museum ($70,000) see Zuckerberg Foundation, Roy J.

Jewish National Fund ($35,000) see Bargman Foundation, Theodore and Mina

Jewish National Fund ($1,000) see Brody Foundation, Frances

Jewish National Fund ($5,000) see Flemm Foundation, John J.

Jewish National Fund ($1,300) see Key Food Stores Cooperative Inc.

Jewish National Fund ($5,000) see Novotny Charitable Trust, Yetta Deitch

Jewish National Fund ($5,000) see Sang Foundation, Elsie O. and Philip D.

Jewish National Fund — 1991 Tree of Life Award ($3,000) see Giant Food

Jewish Theologian Seminary ($25,750) see Belfer Foundation

Jewish Theological Seminary ($9,750) see Alperin/Hirsch Family Foundation

Jewish Theological Seminary ($22,500) see Amado Foundation, Maurice

Jewish Theological Seminary ($1,000) see Barry Corp., R. G.

Jewish Theological Seminary ($6,500) see Bronstein Foundation, Soloman and Sylvia

Jewish Theological Seminary ($50,000) see Feinberg Foundation, Joseph and Bessie

Jewish Theological Seminary ($75,750) see Holtzmann Foundation, Jacob L. and Lillian

Jewish Theological Seminary ($20,750) see Levy Foundation, Betty and Norman F.

Jewish Theological Seminary ($5,000) see Pyramid Foundation

Jewish Theological Seminary ($10,000) see Shapiro Family Foundation, Soretta and Henry

Jewish Theological Seminary ($50,000) see Sosland Foundation

Jewish Theological Seminary ($11,750) see Stein Foundation, Joseph F.

Jewish Theological Seminary ($5,000) see Stein Foundation, Louis

Jewish Theological Seminary ($5,500) see Steinberg Family Foundation, Meyer and Jean

Jewish Theological Seminary ($21,900) see Stern Family Foundation, Harry

Jewish Theological Seminary ($324,556) see Wexner Foundation

Jewish Theological Seminary of America ($5,000) see Bernstein Foundation, Diane and Norman

Jewish Theological Seminary of America ($83,800) see Ford Foundation, Joseph F. and Clara

Jewish Theological Seminary of America ($12,500) see Friedland Family Foundation, Samuel

Jewish Theological Seminary of America ($102,000) see Jurodin Fund

Jewish Theological Seminary of America ($2,500) see Nelco Sewing Machine Sales Corp.

Jewish Theological Seminary of America ($140,000) see Winston Foundation, Norman and Rosita

Jewish Welfare Board Associates ($1,550) see Nelco Sewing Machine Sales Corp.

Jewish Welfare Federation ($10,000) see Bargman Foundation, Theodore and Mina

Jewish Youth Movement ($5,000) see Litwin Foundation

Jobs for Youth ($2,500) see Duke Foundation, Doris

Jobs for Youth — support for youth leadership program ($30,000) see Lincoln Fund

Jobs for Youth ($20,000) see Silverburgh Foundation, Grace, George & Judith

Jobs for Youth ($8,200) see Young & Rubicam

Jockey Club Foundation ($5,000) see Dobson Foundation

Joffery Ballet ($13,750) see Harkness Ballet Foundation

Joffrey Ballet ($100,000) see Beinecke Foundation

Joffrey Ballet ($3,500) see Berger Foundation, Albert E.

Joffrey Ballet ($100,000) see Booth Ferris Foundation

Joffrey Ballet ($31,000) see Harkness Foundation, William Hale

Joffrey Ballet ($450,409) see Levy Foundation, Charles and Ruth

Joffrey Ballet ($5,000) see Osborn Charitable Trust, Edward B.

Joffrey Ballet ($529,999) see Rigler-Deutsch Foundation

Joffrey Ballet ($5,000) see Wade Endowment Fund, Elizabeth Firth

Joffrey Ballet ($2,500) see Wheeler Foundation, Wilmot

Joffrey Ballet, New York, NY ($25,000) see Equitable Life Assurance Society of the U.S.

John B. Pierce Foundation ($10,000) see Kingsley Foundation

John F. Kennedy School of Government ($5,000) see I. and L. Association

John Sloan Memorial Foundation ($5,000) see Lasdon Foundation

Joint Council on Economic Education ($500) see Central National-Gottesman

Joint Council on Economic Education ($3,000) see Multimedia, Inc.

Joint Council on Economic Education ($117,000) see Sears, Roebuck and Co.

Joint Distribution Committee ($250,000) see Rochlin Foundation, Abraham and Sonia

Joseph Bulova School — general support ($480,000) see Bulova Fund

Joyce Theater ($2,500) see Ballet Makers

Joyce Theater ($1,100,000) see Wallace Reader's Digest Fund, Lila

Juilliard School ($10,000) see Katzenberger Foundation

Juilliard School — for the dormitory project ($400,000) see Noble Foundation, Edward John

Juilliard School ($6,000) see Ogden Foundation, Ralph E.

Juilliard School ($133,600) see Seaver Institute

Juilliard School ($192,500) see Sharp Foundation

Juilliard School ($30,000) see Berlin Charitable Fund, Irving

Juilliard School ($50,000) see Cohen Family Foundation, Saul Z. and Amy Scheuer

Juilliard School ($25,000) see Cohen Family Foundation, Saul Z. and Amy Scheuer

Juilliard School ($25,000) see Cohen Family Foundation, Saul Z. and Amy Scheuer

Juilliard School — student fellowship program ($414,816) see Gluck Foundation, Maxwell H.

Juilliard School ($381,250) see Greene Foundation, Jerome L.

Juilliard School ($10,000) see Heyward Memorial Fund, DuBose and Dorothy

Juilliard School ($1,000) see Loeb Partners Corp.

Juilliard School ($20,000) see Rodgers Foundation, Richard & Dorothy

Juilliard School ($21,000) see Sharp Foundation, Evelyn

Juilliard School ($50,000) see South Branch Foundation

Juilliard School — funding for the Dorothy Richard Starling Chair for violin studies

($336,000) see Starling Foundation, Dorothy Richard

Junior Achievement ($800) see Gear Motion

Junior Achievement see Home Depot

Junior Achievement ($1,000) see Leucadia National Corp.

Junior Achievement ($28,000) see New York Stock Exchange

Junior Achievement ($5,000) see Willmott Foundation, Fred & Floy

Junior Achievement of New York ($15,000) see Dun & Bradstreet Corp.

Junior Achievement of WNY ($4,000) see Joy Family Foundation

Juvenile Diabetes see New York Mercantile Exchange

Juvenile Diabetes Foundation ($2,500) see Doherty Charitable Foundation, Henry L. and Grace

Juvenile Diabetes Foundation ($2,500) see Eder Foundation, Sidney and Arthur

Juvenile Diabetes Foundation ($10,000) see Fisher Brothers

Juvenile Diabetes Foundation ($5,000) see Goodman Memorial Foundation, Joseph C. and Clare F.

Juvenile Diabetes Foundation ($37,500) see Lender Family Foundation

Juvenile Diabetes Foundation ($10,000) see Lichtenstein Foundation, David B.

Juvenile Diabetes Foundation ($25,000) see Life Investors Insurance Company of America

Juvenile Diabetes Foundation ($25,000) see Lipton, Thomas J.

Juvenile Diabetes Foundation ($10,000) see Picower Foundation, Jeffrey M. and Barbara

Juvenile Diabetes Foundation ($35,000) see Saltz Foundation, Gary

Juvenile Diabetes Foundation International ($50,000) see Wrigley Co., Wm. Jr.

Juvenile Diabetes Fund ($10,000) see Fischbach Foundation

Juvenile Diabetes International ($25,000) see Johnson Foundation, A. D.

Kahel Adath Yeshurun ($1,500) see House of Gross

Karen Horney Clinic ($10,000) see Reicher Foundation, Anne & Harry J.

Katonah Art Gallery ($5,000) see Rosenthal Foundation, Ida and William

Katonah Art Gallery ($15,000) see Tucker Foundation, Marcia Brady

Katonah Museum see MBIA, Inc.

Katonah Museum of Art ($25,000) see Dreyfus Foundation, Jean and Louis

Kenmore Mercy Hospital ($75,000) see Julia R. and Estelle L. Foundation

Kennedy Center 100 Circle ($100,000) see Macmillan, Inc.

Kent Schools Community Playground ($5,000) see Weinstein Foundation, J.

Keren Menachem ($9,000) see Propp Sons Fund, Morris and Anna

Keuka College — capital campaign ($300,000) see Ball Foundation, George and Frances

Keuka College — centennial campaign ($200,000) see Emerson Foundation, Fred L.

Keuka College ($50,000) see Jephson Educational Trust No. 1

Keuka College ($23,949) see Jephson Educational Trust No. 1

Keuka College ($15,000) see Lightner Sams Foundation

Keuka College ($5,000) see Seneca Foods Corp.

Keuka College ($15,000) see Snow Foundation, John Ben

Kids Adjusting Through Support — expand group programs for children and families in which a member has a life-threatening illness or has died, and for the special needs of foster families ($30,000) see Jones Foundation, Daisy Marquis

Kids Escaping Drugs — construct facility ($25,000) see Western New York Foundation

Kings Point Challenge ($50,000) see Bauer Foundation, M. R.

Kings Point Challenge ($75,000) see Overseas Shipholding Group

Kingsbrook Jewish Medical Center ($25,000) see Parshelsky Foundation, Moses L.

Kingsbrook Jewish Medical Center ($10,000) see Parshelsky Foundation, Moses L.

Kingston Area Library ($14,000) see Kingston Foundation

Kingston Boys Club ($21,750) see Kingston Foundation

Kingston Hospital 2nd Century ($20,000) see Kingston Foundation

Kips Bay Boys and Girls Club — outreach projects ($25,000) see Badgeley Residuary Charitable Trust, Rose M.

Kip's Bay Boys and Girls Club ($15,000) see McConnell Foundation, Neil A.

Kips Bay Boys and Girls Club — cost of emergency repairs, resurfacing their outdoor courts and installation of a ceiling in their gamesroom area ($101,624) see Hayden Foundation, Charles

Kirkside of Roxbury — maintenance contingency ($25,000) see O'Connor Foundation, A. Lindsay and Olive B.

Kiryat Ungvar Synagogue ($10,000) see Tauber Foundation

Knesset Yenudo Building Fund ($500) see Wasserman Foundation, George

Knightsbridge Heights Community Center ($75,000) see Stern Foundation, Bernice and Milton

Kolel Shohrei Hachomoth ($20,000) see Fogel Foundation, Shalom and Rebecca

Kolelut Rabbe Meir Bahal Hanes Sephardic ($5,000) see Gindi Associates Foundation

Kollel Bnei Yeshivot ($10,000) see Sutton Foundation

Kollel New La'Brohom ($100,000) see Kest Family Foundation, Sol and Clara

Kosciuszko Foundation — Polish scholarships/grants program ($120,000) see

Jurzykowski Foundation, Alfred

Laban Bartenieff Institute for Movement Studies ($6,000) see Bay Branch Foundation

Laban Bartenieff Institute for Movement Studies ($50,000) see Vidda Foundation

Labor Community Strategy Center ($10,000) see Abelard Foundation

Ladies Auxiliary of Adas Yereim ($250) see Melohn Foundation

Ladies Auxiliary, Niagara Falls Memorial Medical Center ($200) see Tripifoods

Lafayette Escadrille Memorial ($15,000) see Bismarck Charitable Trust, Mona

Lake Carmel Fire Department ($1,000) see Weinstein Foundation, J.

Lake Placid Center for the Arts ($1,000) see Crary Foundation, Bruce L.

Lambda Legal Defense and Education Fund — for the rights of lesbians, gays and people with HIV and AIDS ($35,000) see Mertz-Gilmore Foundation, Joyce

Landmark Society of Western New York — capital building fund ($30,000) see Davenport-Hatch Foundation

Larchmont Public Library — expansion fund ($20,000) see Coles Family Foundation

Larchmont Temple ($10,000) see Ritter Foundation

Latinos for a Better New York ($10,000) see Daily News

Lautenberg Center for General and Tumor Immunology ($1,000) see KSM Foundation

Lawyers Committee for Civil Rights Under Law ($6,000) see Kaye, Scholer, Fierman, Hays & Handler

Lawyers Committee for Human Rights ($5,000) see Covington and Burling

Lawyers Committee for Human Rights ($75,000) see General Service Foundation

Lawyers Committee for Human Rights ($20,000) see 21 International Holdings

Lawyers Committee on Nuclear Policy ($15,000) see Rubin Foundation, Samuel

Le Moyne College — to endow student-aid funds for over a five year period ($500,000) see UST

Lead Program in Business — business development for disadvantaged and minority youths ($30,000) see MCI Communications Corp.

League of Women Voters ($1,000) see Ohio Savings Bank

Learning Foundation see MBIA, Inc.

Learning to Read Through the Arts ($100,826) see Gilman Foundation, Howard

Legal Aid Society ($50,000) see Abrons Foundation, Louis and Anne

Legal Aid Society ($5,000) see Continental Grain Co.

Legal Aid Society ($55,550) see Donovan, Leisure, Newton & Irvine

Legal Aid Society ($135,000) see Kaye, Scholer, Fierman, Hays & Handler

Legal Aid Society ($80,000) see Scherman Foundation

Little Orchestra Society ($104,000) see Johnson Endeavor Foundation, Christian A.

Little Orchestra Society ($67,922) see Smart Family Foundation

Little Sisters of Poor ($16,900) see Doty Family Foundation

LMK Middle School ($25,000) see Doherty Charitable Foundation, Henry L. and Grace

Local Education Initiatives ($35,000) see Reader's Digest Association

Local Initiatives Support Corporation ($125,000) see Bankers Trust Co.

Local Initiatives Support Corporation ($200,000) see Continental Corp.

Local Initiatives Support Corporation ($25,000) see Levy Foundation, June Rockwell

Local Initiatives Support Corporation ($100,000) see Uris Brothers Foundation

Local Initiatives Support Corporation and Child Care — for technical assistance to 12-15 community development organizations ($500,000) see Surdna Foundation

Local Initiatives Support Corporation — to help Community Development Corporations alleviate South Dade County's low-income housing shortage in the wake of Hurricane Andrew ($1,500,000) see MacArthur Foundation, John D. and Catherine T.

Local Initiatives Support Corporation-National — affordable single-family homeownership programs ($150,000) see Federal National Mortgage Assn., Fannie Mae

Local Initiatives Support Corporation — Round IV capital campaign ($6,500) see Hunt Manufacturing Co.

Local United Ways ($650,940) see Metropolitan Life Insurance Co.

Lockport Senior Citizens Center ($50,000) see Grigg-Lewis Trust

Lockwood Matthews Mansion Museum ($5,500) see Kingsley Foundation

Long Beach Memorial Hospital ($75,000) see Goldman Foundation, Herman

Long Beach Memorial Hospital ($75,000) see Goldman Foundation, Herman

Long Beach Memorial Hospital ($5,000) see Key Food Stores Cooperative Inc.

Long Island Biological Association ($3,000) see Foerderer Foundation, Percival E. and Ethel Brown

Long Island Hearing and Speech Society ($20,000) see Jaqua Foundation

Long Island Heart Council ($1,000) see Key Food Stores Cooperative Inc.

Long Island Jewish Hospital ($25,000) see Bleibtreu Foundation, Jacob

Long Island Jewish Hospital ($25,700) see Slant/Fin Corp.

Long Island Jewish Hospital Medical Center ($25,000) see Brennan Foundation, Robert E.

Long Island Jewish Hospital Medical Center ($25,000) see Brennan Foundation, Robert E.

Long Island Jewish Medical Center ($50,000) see Ames Charitable Trust, Harriett

Long Island Jewish Medical Center see Bloomingdale's

Long Island Jewish Medical Center ($2,500) see FAB Industries

Long Island Jewish Medical Center ($50,000) see Goldman Foundation, Herman

Long Island Jewish Medical Center ($100,000) see Horowitz Foundation, Gedale B. and Barbara S.

Long Island Jewish Medical Center ($100,000) see Lowenstein Foundation, Leon

Long Island Jewish Medical Center ($25,000) see Oppenheimer and Flora Oppenheimer Haas Trust, Leo

Long Island Jewish Medical Center ($100,000) see Pyramid Foundation

Long Island Jewish Medical Center ($75,000) see Spingold Foundation, Nate B. and Frances

Long Island Jewish Medical Center ($100,000) see Zuckerberg Foundation, Roy J.

Long Island Jewish Medical Center ($25,000) see Zuckerberg Foundation, Roy J.

Long Island Jewish Medical Center — to establish a Geriatric Assessment Team ($98,875) see Samuels Foundation, Fan Fox and Leslie R.

Long Island Jewish Medical Center — toward founding a Regional Neonatal Satellite Program ($110,000) see Samuels Foundation, Fan Fox and Leslie R.

Long Island Sound Keeper Fund ($3,800) see Woman's Seamen's Friend Society of Connecticut

Long Island Stage ($25,000) see Leviton Manufacturing Co.

Long Island University ($12,000) see Lindner Foundation, Fay J.

Long Island University ($3,000) see Merit Oil Corp.

Long Island University ($10,000) see Schwartz Fund for Education and Health Research, Arnold and Marie

Long Island University ($6,000) see Weinstein Foundation, Alex J.

Long Island University College of Pharmacy ($25,000) see Lasdon Foundation

Long Island University College of Pharmacy ($25,000) see Lasdon Foundation

Longview-Niagara Day Care Center ($7,000) see Children's Foundation of Erie County

Louise Adelia Read Memorial Library ($11,500) see Read Foundation, Charles L.

Louise Wise Services ($25,000) see Kenworthy - Sarah H. Swift Foundation, Marion E.

Louise Wise Services ($31,000) see Mertz Foundation, Martha

Lourdes Hospital ($5,000) see Raymond Corp.

Lourdes Hospital Foundation ($60,000) see Dickenson Foundation, Harriet Ford

Lower East Side Catholic Area Conference — construction expenses ($60,000) see Rhodebeck Charitable Trust

Lower East Side Community School — social worker for the Parent-Pupil School-Based Support Team ($60,000) see van Ameringen Foundation

Lower East Side Mutual Housing Association — in general support ($20,000) see Taconic Foundation

Lower East Side Tenement Museum ($12,500) see Jacobson & Sons, Benjamin

Lower Manhattan Cultural Council ($63,820) see Continental Corp.

Lown Cardiovascular Research Foundation ($12,500) see Belding Heminway Co.

Lubavitch Center ($54,000) see Revlon

Lubavitch of the East End ($10,000) see MacAndrews & Forbes Holdings

Lubavitch Youth Organization ($6,000) see Kaplun Foundation, Morris J. and Betty

Lucille Ball Festival of New Comedy ($50,000) see Sheldon Foundation, Ralph C.

Lupus Foundation of America ($5,000) see Fingerhut Family Foundation

Lupus Foundation of America ($10,000) see Lastfogel Foundation, Abe and Frances

Lupus Foundation of America ($7,000) see Lipsky Foundation, Fred and Sarah

Lupus Foundation of America ($1,050) see Rales and Ruth Rales Foundation, Norman R.

Lutheran Church of Our Saviour ($100) see Hendrickson Brothers

Lutheran Home for the Aging ($3,000) see Read Foundation, Charles L.

Lutheran Social Services ($34,459) see Hultquist Foundation

Lyford Cay Foundation ($100,000) see Little Family Foundation

M and M Stern Foundation ($20,000) see Stern Foundation, Bernice and Milton

Mablebrook School ($10,000) see Ferkauf Foundation, Eugene and Estelle

Machane Sva Rotzohn ($100,000) see Kest Family Foundation, Sol and Clara

Machne Israel ($65,250) see El-An Foundation

Machne Israel ($22,500) see Joselow Foundation

Machne Israel ($56,000) see MacAndrews & Forbes Holdings

Machne Israel ($215,000) see Revlon

Macula Foundation ($10,000) see Dreitzer Foundation

Madison Square Boys and Girls Club — to support the development of comprehensive youth services in Brooklyn by expanding the days and hours of clubhouse operation ($50,000) see Cummings Memorial Fund Trust, Frances L. and Edwin L.

Madison Square Boys and Girls Club — for Flatbush clubhouse ($100,000) see Pinkerton Foundation

Madison Square Girls and Boys Club ($30,000) see Capital Cities/ABC

Madonna Manor — day room for alzheimer patients ($3,000) see Walsh Charity Trust, Blanche M.

Magan David Yumor ($25,000) see Hidary Foundation, Jacob

Magan Osurd Yeshiva ($25,000) see Hidary Foundation, Jacob

Magen David Yeshiva ($29,000) see Gitano Group

Magen David Yeshiva ($10,000) see N've Shalom Foundation

Magen David Yeshiva ($8,000) see Sutton Foundation

Magen David Yeshivah ($58,200) see Gindi Associates Foundation

Magen Israel ($21,095) see Gitano Group

Maimonides Medical Center ($2,000) see Parthenon Sportswear

Maimonides Relief Center ($25,000) see Newbrook Charitable Foundation

Main Street Child Care ($19,400) see Soling Family Foundation

Make-a-Wish Foundation ($5,000) see Silverburgh Foundation, Grace, George & Judith

Malta Human Services Foundation ($100,000) see Grace & Co., W.R.

Manhattan College ($90,000) see Archbold Charitable Trust, Adrian and Jessie

Manhattan College ($10,000) see Switzer Foundation

Manhattan Country School ($30,000) see Greentree Foundation

Manhattan Day School ($300) see Fischel Foundation, Harry and Jane

Manhattan Day School ($6,000) see House of Gross

Manhattan Eye and Ear ($20,000) see Thorne Foundation

Manhattan Institute ($15,000) see Oaklawn Foundation

Manhattan Institute for Cancer Research ($50,000) see Brooks Foundation, Gladys

Manhattan Institute General Hospital ($60,000) see Gilder Foundation

Manhattan Institute for Policy Research ($25,000) see Davis Foundation, Shelby Cullom

Manhattan Institute for Policy Research, New York, NY see SAFECO Corp.

Manhattan Institute for Policy Research — to establish a new project on "privatization", the contracting out of municipal functions to competitive private organizations ($102,500) see Kaplan Fund, J. M.

Manhattan School of Music ($15,000) see Borden Memorial Foundation, Mary Owen

Manhattan School of Music ($9,950) see Greenfield Foundation, Albert M.

Manhattan School of Music ($5,000) see Jephson Educational Trust No. 1

Manhattan Theater ($20,000) see Kaplen Foundation

Manhattan Theatre Club ($29,800) see Aeroflex Foundation

Manhattan Theatre Club ($15,000) see Coles Family Foundation

Manhattan Theatre Club ($120,000) see Shubert Foundation

Manhattan Theatre Club ($50,000) see Simon Charitable Trust, Esther

Manhattanville College ($9,833) see Morse, Jr. Foundation, Enid and Lester S.

Manhattanville College ($200,000) see PepsiCo

Manhattanville College ($100,000) see Simon Foundation, William E. and Carol G.

Manice Education Center ($65,393) see Christodora

Mannes College of Music ($18,000) see Mather and William Gwinn Mather Fund, Elizabeth Ring

Mannes College of Music ($19,285) see Osceola Foundation

Manpower Demonstration Research Corporation — youth apprenticeship ($300,000) see Commonwealth Fund

Manpower Demonstration Research Corporation — observational research within the JOBS and New Chance evaluations ($125,000) see Foundation for Child Development

Mansion House ($2,500) see Chapman Charitable Corporation, Howard and Bess

Maplebrook School ($20,000) see Statler Foundation

Marien-Heim of Brooklyn ($5,000) see Faith Home Foundation

Marine Environmental Research ($65,000) see Stroud Foundation

Marion A. Buckley School of Nursing ($25,000) see Zlinkoff Fund for Medical Research and Education, Sergei S.

Marist College — for new baseball field ($467,986) see McCann Foundation

Marist College — for athletic fields ($71,312) see McCann Foundation

Marist College — for scholarships ($50,000) see McCann Foundation

Marist College — construction of the Dyson Center to house the college's Business, Social and Behavioral Sciences, Public Policy and Administration departments to commemorate Charles H. Dyson's 80th birthday ($500,000) see Dyson Foundation

Maritime/Outdoor Education ($15,775) see Gould Foundation for Children, Edwin

Markle Foundation (Election Project '92) — to support Cable News Network's "Democracy in America" series ($315,000) see Markle Foundation, John and Mary R.

Markle Foundation (Henry Geller, Markle Fellow) — to conduct research and policy studies on issues in telecommunications

New York (cont.)

($165,000) see Markle Foundation, John and Mary R.

Markle Foundation (Markle Commission on the Media and the Electorate Follow-Up) — to conduct research on the 1992 Presidential election ($327,000) see Markle Foundation, John and Mary R.

Markle Foundation (Political Advertising Study) — to conduct a benchmark study on political advertising ($140,000) see Markle Foundation, John and Mary R.

Markle Foundation (Public Education Project) — to continue the planning and implementation of public education programs ($131,000) see Markle Foundation, John and Mary R.

Markos L'inyonei Chinuch ($5,000) see Lowenstein Foundation, William P. and Marie R.

Martha Graham Center for Contemporary Dance ($15,000) see Harkness Foundation, William Hale

Martha Graham Center for Dance ($15,000) see Firestone Foundation, Roger S.

Marty Lyon's Foundation ($1,000) see Donaldson, Lufkin & Jenrette

Mary E. Seymour Memorial Free Library ($5,000) see Darrah Charitable Trust, Jessie Smith

Mary Imogene Bassett Hospital ($167,000) see Clark Foundation

Mary Imogene Bassett Hospital ($300,000) see Gronewaldt Foundation, Alice Busch

Maryknoll Fathers ($10,000) see Goldbach Foundation, Ray and Marie

Maryknoll Fathers ($14,500) see Rotterman Trust, Helen L. and Marie F.

Maryknoll Fathers and Brothers ($7,000) see Butler Foundation, J. Homer

Maryknoll Fathers and Brothers — Sisters of St. John the Baptist — Zambia, Africa ($4,000) see Butler Foundation, J. Homer

Maryknoll Missionaries ($3,000) see Geneva Foundation

Maryknoll Sisters ($7,250) see Rotterman Trust, Helen L. and Marie F.

Maryknoll Sisters — support of programs in Guatemala, Phillipines, Tanzania and Taiwan ($88,000) see Cudahy Fund, Patrick and Anna M.

Maryknoll Sisters of St. Dominic ($12,000) see Von der Ahe Foundation

Maryknoll Sisters of St. Dominic ($8,000) see Von der Ahe, Jr. Trust, Theodore Albert

Marymount Manhattan College ($40,000) see Donaldson Charitable Trust, Oliver S. and Jennie R.

Marymount Manhattan College ($100,000) see Freeman Charitable Trust, Samuel

Marymount Manhattan College ($50,000) see Freeman Charitable Trust, Samuel

Marymount Manhattan College — provided start-up funding for a program to allow women who were formerly on public assistance to earn a college

degree and a certificate as a Teacher for Developmentally Disabled students see New Street Capital Corp.

Masters School ($3,000) see Shattuck Charitable Trust, S. F.

Masters School Annual Fund ($5,000) see Shore Fund

McGill University Department of Chemistry ($25,000) see Krieble Foundation, Vernon K.

Mcoss ($10,000) see Jacobson & Sons, Benjamin

MCOSS Nursing Services ($12,500) see Borden Memorial Foundation, Mary Owen

Meals-on-Wheels ($10,000) see Osborn Charitable Trust, Edward B.

Meals on Wheels ($4,275) see Anderson Foundation

Meals on Wheels ($1,000) see Chapman Charitable Corporation, Howard and Bess

Medaille College ($12,000) see Palisano Foundation, Vincent and Harriet

Medical Development for Israel ($35,000) see Belfer Foundation

Medical Development for Israel ($65,000) see Gudelsky Family Foundation, Isadore and Bertha

Medical Development for Israel ($6,000) see Kaplun Foundation, Morris J. and Betty

Medical Development for Israel ($100,000) see Mitchell Family Foundation, Edward D. and Anna

Medical Development for Israel ($20,000) see Price Foundation, Louis and Harold

Medical Foundation of Buffalo ($17,000) see Goode Trust, Mae Stone

Medical Foundation of Buffalo ($5,000) see Grigg-Lewis Trust

Meet the Composer ($10,000) see Sheafer Charitable Trust, Emma A.

Memorial Art Gallery ($2,000) see Curtice-Burns Foods

Memorial Art Gallery ($25,000) see Wilson Foundation, Elaine P. and Richard U.

Memorial Hospital/Sloan-Kettering Cancer Center ($70,000) see Langeloth Foundation, Jacob and Valeria

Memorial Sloan-Kettering ($2,000) see Iroquois Avenue Foundation

Memorial Sloan-Kettering Cancer Center — for cancer research ($25,000) see Alexander Foundation, Joseph

Memorial Sloan-Kettering Cancer Center ($25,000) see AMETEK

Memorial Sloan-Kettering Cancer Center ($20,000) see Beneficial Corp.

Memorial Sloan-Kettering Cancer Center ($25,000) see Bobst Foundation, Elmer and Mamdouha

Memorial Sloan-Kettering Cancer Center ($30,000) see Carvel Foundation, Thomas and Agnes

Memorial Sloan-Kettering Cancer Center ($30,000) see Clark Family Charitable Trust, Andrew L.

Memorial Sloan-Kettering Cancer Center ($5,000) see

Cohn Foundation, Peter A. and Elizabeth S.

Memorial Sloan-Kettering Cancer Center ($5,000) see Crane Foundation, Raymond E. and Ellen F.

Memorial Sloan-Kettering Cancer Center ($100,000) see Donaldson Charitable Trust, Oliver S. and Jennie R.

Memorial Sloan-Kettering Cancer Center ($3,000) see EIS Foundation

Memorial Sloan-Kettering Cancer Center ($100,000) see Forbes

Memorial Sloan-Kettering Cancer Center ($11,000) see Fribourg Foundation

Memorial Sloan-Kettering Cancer Center ($125,000) see Gelb Foundation, Lawrence M.

Memorial Sloan-Kettering Cancer Center ($100,000) see Gordon/Rousmaniere/Roberts Fund

Memorial Sloan-Kettering Cancer Center ($25,000) see Griffith Foundation, W. C.

Memorial Sloan-Kettering Cancer Center ($400,750) see Hall Charitable Trust, Evelyn A. J.

Memorial Sloan-Kettering Cancer Center ($2,000) see Hartzell Industries, Inc.

Memorial Sloan Kettering Cancer Center ($83,187) see Heckscher Foundation for Children

Memorial Sloan-Kettering Cancer Center ($5,500) see Herman Foundation, John and Rose

Memorial Sloan-Kettering Cancer Center ($20,000) see Heyward Memorial Fund, DuBose and Dorothy

Memorial Sloan-Kettering Cancer Center ($20,000) see Jurodin Fund

Memorial Sloan-Kettering Cancer Center ($10,000) see Kennedy Foundation, Ethel

Memorial Sloan-Kettering Cancer Center ($10,000) see Kennedy Foundation, John R.

Memorial Sloan-Kettering Cancer Center — to establish a fund to support structural biology research programs ($6,000,435) see Kleberg, Jr. and Helen C. Kleberg Foundation, Robert J.

Memorial Sloan-Kettering Cancer Center ($500,000) see Koch Charitable Trust, David H.

Memorial Sloan-Kettering Cancer Center ($1,000) see Kuhns Investment Co.

Memorial Sloan-Kettering Cancer Center ($5,000) see Lasdon Foundation

Memorial Sloan-Kettering Cancer Center ($50,000) see Lauder Foundation

Memorial Sloan-Kettering Cancer Center ($10,000) see Lazar Foundation

Memorial Sloan-Kettering Cancer Center ($20,000) see Lee Foundation, James T.

Memorial Sloan-Kettering Cancer Center ($5,000) see Leonhardt Foundation, Frederick H.

Memorial Sloan-Kettering Cancer Center ($75,000) see McIntosh Foundation

Memorial Sloan-Kettering Cancer Center ($12,000) see Middendorf Foundation

Memorial Sloan-Kettering Cancer Center ($255,000) see Milken Family Medical Foundation

Memorial Sloan-Kettering Cancer Center ($7,500) see Oestreicher Foundation, Sylvan and Ann

Memorial Sloan-Kettering Cancer Center ($20,000) see Osborn Charitable Trust, Edward B.

Memorial Sloan-Kettering Cancer Center ($25,000) see PaineWebber

Memorial Sloan-Kettering Cancer Center ($5,000) see Picower Foundation, Jeffrey M. and Barbara

Memorial Sloan-Kettering Cancer Center ($2,000) see Psychists

Memorial Sloan-Kettering Cancer Center ($93,821) see Ramapo Trust

Memorial Sloan-Kettering Cancer Center ($12,500) see Rohatyn Foundation, Felix and Elizabeth

Memorial Sloan-Kettering Cancer Center ($215,000) see Rudin Foundation, Samuel and May

Memorial Sloan-Kettering Cancer Center ($75,000) see Rudin Foundation, Samuel and May

Memorial Sloan-Kettering Cancer Center ($25,000) see Schaffer Foundation, Michael & Helen

Memorial Sloan-Kettering Cancer Center ($25,000) see Schiff Foundation, Dorothy

Memorial Sloan-Kettering Cancer Center — for cancer research ($62,082) see Schultz Foundation

Memorial Sloan-Kettering Cancer Center ($275,000) see Stern Foundation, Bernice and Milton

Memorial Sloan-Kettering Cancer Center ($75,000) see Stern Foundation, Gustav and Irene

Memorial Sloan-Kettering Cancer Center ($25,000) see Stern Foundation, Gustav and Irene

Memorial Sloan-Kettering Cancer Center ($18,000) see Stern Foundation, Gustav and Irene

Memorial Sloan-Kettering Cancer Center ($17,000) see Strawbridge Foundation of Pennsylvania I, Margaret Dorrance

Memorial Sloan-Kettering Cancer Center ($10,000) see Strawbridge Foundation of Pennsylvania II, Margaret Dorrance

Memorial Sloan-Kettering Cancer Center ($25,000) see Swanson Foundation

Memorial Sloan-Kettering Cancer Center — capital campaign ($1,200,000) see Tandy Foundation, Anne Burnett and Charles

Memorial Sloan-Kettering Cancer Center ($35,000) see Taubman Foundation, A. Alfred

Memorial Sloan-Kettering Cancer Center ($5,000) see

Trimble Family Foundation, Robert Mize and Isa White

Memorial Sloan-Kettering Cancer Center ($25,000) see Upton Charitable Foundation, Lucy and Eleanor S.

Memorial Sloan-Kettering Cancer Center ($10,000) see Weinberg, Jr. Foundation, Sidney J.

Memorial Sloan-Kettering Cancer Center ($50,000) see Wells Foundation, Lillian S.

Memorial Sloan-Kettering Cancer Center — biomedical research ($100,000) see Winston Foundation, Norman and Rosita

Memorial Sloan-Kettering Cancer Center ($280) see Wolff Shoe Co.

Memorial Sloan-Kettering Cancer Center ($8,180) see Wolfson Family Foundation

Memorial Sloan Kettering Cancer Center ($5,000) see Zilkha & Sons

Memorial Sloan-Kettering Cancer Society ($150,000) see Texaco

Memorial Sloan-Kettering Hospital — breast cancer research ($250,000) see International Flavors & Fragrances

Memorial Sloon Kettering see Brakeley, John Price Jones Inc.

Mental Health Association in Essex County ($9,000) see Ben & Jerry's Homemade

Mental Health Institution ($2,500) see Fuchsberg Family Foundation

Mental Health Law Project ($25,000) see Rhodebeck Charitable Trust

Mental Illness Foundation ($1,500) see Kearney Inc., A.T.

Merry-Go-Round Playhouse ($4,000) see Everett Charitable Trust

Mesifta Bais Yisroel ($125,360) see Fishoff Family Foundation

Mesifta Rabbi Chaim Berlin ($18,360) see Fishoff Family Foundation

Mesorah Heritage Foundation ($900,000) see Schottenstein Foundation, Jerome & Saul

Methodist Church ($6,684) see Surrena Memorial Fund, Harry and Thelma

Metro New York Coordinating Council on Jewish Poverty ($10,000) see Odyssey Partners

Metropolitan Council on Jewish Poverty ($5,000) see Garfinkle Family Foundation

Metropolitan Jewish Geriatric Center ($5,000) see Greene Foundation, Robert Z.

Metropolitan Jewish Geriatric Center ($27,500) see Parshelsky Foundation, Moses L.

Metropolitan Jewish Geriatric Center ($333,000) see Scheuer Family Foundation, S. H. and Helen R.

Metropolitan Museum of Art ($6,500) see Abeles Foundation, Joseph and Sophia

Metropolitan Museum of Art ($2,000,000) see Annenberg Foundation

Metropolitan Museum of Art ($6,000) see Bayne Fund, Howard

Metropolitan Museum of Art ($120,000) see Burchfield Foundation, Charles E.

Metropolitan Museum of Art ($3,000) see Cohn Foundation, Peter A. and Elizabeth S.

Metropolitan Museum of Art ($5,000) see Coltec Industries

Metropolitan Museum of Art ($1,000,000) see Coral Reef Foundation

Metropolitan Museum of Art ($5,000) see Culver Foundation, Constans

Metropolitan Museum of Art ($50,000) see Dingman Foundation, Michael D.

Metropolitan Museum of Art ($3,665) see Dobson Foundation

Metropolitan Museum of Art ($11,400) see Eckman Charitable Foundation, Samuel and Rae

Metropolitan Museum of Art ($182,125) see Engelhard Foundation, Charles

Metropolitan Museum of Art ($50,500) see Erpf Fund, Armand G.

Metropolitan Museum of Art ($9,000) see Evans Foundation, T. M.

Metropolitan Museum of Art — objects conservation center ($1,250,000) see Fairchild Foundation, Sherman

Metropolitan Museum of Art — paintings conservation chairmanship ($300,000) see Fairchild Foundation, Sherman

Metropolitan Museum of Art ($2,000) see Fein Foundation

Metropolitan Museum of Art ($3,000) see Fortis Inc.

Metropolitan Museum of Art ($50,000) see Frelinghuysen Foundation

Metropolitan Museum of Art ($902,168) see Gould Foundation, Florence J.

Metropolitan Museum of Art ($42,500) see Hall Charitable Trust, Evelyn A. J.

Metropolitan Museum of Art — general support of donee ($250,000) see Hammer Foundation, Armand

Metropolitan Museum of Art ($30,000) see Hazen Charitable Trust, Lita Annenberg

Metropolitan Museum of Art ($1,500) see Hillman Family Foundation, Alex

Metropolitan Museum of Art ($30,000) see Hoechst Celanese Corp.

Metropolitan Museum of Art ($5,000) see Holzer Memorial Foundation, Richard H.

Metropolitan Museum of Art ($2,500) see Kearney Inc., A.T.

Metropolitan Museum of Art ($290,500) see Kevorkian Fund, Hagop

Metropolitan Museum of Art ($500,000) see Kimmelman Foundation, Helen & Milton

Metropolitan Museum of Art ($3,755) see Krimendahl II Foundation, H. Frederick

Metropolitan Museum of Art ($3,730) see Krimendahl II Foundation, H. Frederick

Metropolitan Museum of Art — pursuant to agreement ($586,153) see Lehman Foundation, Robert

Metropolitan Museum of Art — other ($525,203) see Lehman Foundation, Robert

Metropolitan Museum of Art ($73,759) see Levy Foundation, Jerome

Metropolitan Museum of Art ($55,170) see Levy Foundation, Jerome

Metropolitan Museum of Art ($5,000) see Liberman Foundation, Bertha & Isaac

Metropolitan Museum of Art ($5,000) see Marx Foundation, Virginia & Leonard

Metropolitan Museum of Art ($15,000) see Menschel Foundation, Robert and Joyce

Metropolitan Museum of Art ($4,000) see Menschel Foundation, Robert and Joyce

Metropolitan Museum of Art ($15,000) see Mex-Am Cultural Foundation

Metropolitan Museum of Art ($2,000) see Mitsui & Co. (U.S.A.)

Metropolitan Museum of Art ($8,500) see Morse, Jr. Foundation, Enid and Lester S.

Metropolitan Museum of Art ($20,000) see Neuberger Foundation, Roy R. and Marie S.

Metropolitan Museum of Art ($215,860) see Overbrook Foundation

Metropolitan Museum of Art ($533,169) see Richardson Foundation, Frank E. and Nancy M.

Metropolitan Museum of Art ($72,600) see Richmond Foundation, Frederick W.

Metropolitan Museum of Art ($32,800) see Rosen Foundation, Joseph

Metropolitan Museum of Art ($30,900) see Rosenstiel Foundation

Metropolitan Museum of Art ($1,600) see Roth Foundation, Louis T.

Metropolitan Museum of Art ($35,000) see Rowland Foundation

Metropolitan Museum of Art ($210) see Ryan Foundation, Nina M.

Metropolitan Museum of Art ($5,000) see Schiff Foundation

Metropolitan Museum of Art ($34,500) see Schwartz Foundation, David

Metropolitan Museum of Art ($1,077,360) see Sharp Foundation

Metropolitan Museum of Art ($6,000) see Sheinberg Foundation, Eric P.

Metropolitan Museum of Art ($300) see Soling Family Foundation

Metropolitan Museum of Art ($5,000) see Steinberg Family Foundation, Meyer and Jean

Metropolitan Museum of Art ($77,150) see Sulzberger Foundation

Metropolitan Museum of Art ($52,500) see Thorne Foundation

Metropolitan Museum of Art ($1,000,000) see Tisch Foundation

Metropolitan Museum of Art — department of paintings conservation ($35,000) see Vidda Foundation

Metropolitan Museum of Art ($7,000) see Werblow Charitable Trust, Nina W.

Metropolitan Museum of Art ($94,500) see Wiener Foundation, Malcolm Hewitt

Metropolitan Museum of Art ($10,000) see Zenkel Foundation

Metropolitan Museum of Art — in support of C. V. Starr Conservatorship in Asian Art at The Met ($875,000) see Starr Foundation

Metropolitan Museum of Art — Corporate Patron Program ($50,000) see New York Times Co.

Metropolitan Museum of Art — toward the purchase of a landscape painting by Peter Paul Rubens ($100,000) see Astor Foundation, Vincent

Metropolitan Museum of Art — Rembrandt Gallery ($30,000) see Corning Incorporated

Metropolitan Museum of Art — to support an exhibition and catalogue on "Stuart Davis, American Painter"; further support for the exhibition, "American Rococo, 1750-1775: Elegance in Ornament" ($150,000) see Luce Foundation, Henry

Metropolitan Museum of Modern Art — general operating ($25,000) see Griggs and Mary Griggs Burke Foundation, Mary Livingston

Metropolitan New York Coordinating Council on Jewish Poverty ($100,000) see Kaufmann Foundation, Henry

Metropolitan New York SYNOD Lutheran Church of America ($17,750) see Clark Charitable Trust, Frank E.

Metropolitan Opera ($70,000) see Abrons Foundation, Louis and Anne

Metropolitan Opera ($55,000) see Baier Foundation, Marie

Metropolitan Opera ($3,500) see Davis Foundation, Simon and Annie

Metropolitan Opera ($2,000) see Fischbach Foundation

Metropolitan Opera ($5,175) see Frank Foundation, Ernest and Elfriede

Metropolitan Opera ($41,500) see Green Fund

Metropolitan Opera ($2,500) see Gruss Charitable Foundation, Emanuel and Riane

Metropolitan Opera ($33,333) see Holzer Memorial Foundation, Richard H.

Metropolitan Opera ($25,000) see Kaplan Foundation, Rita J. and Stanley H.

Metropolitan Opera ($6,000) see Mathis-Pfohl Foundation

Metropolitan Opera ($7,000) see Pyramid Foundation

Metropolitan Opera ($10,000) see Seaver Charitable Trust, Richard C.

Metropolitan Opera ($196,200) see Tobin Foundation

Metropolitan Opera ($1,500) see Weiss Foundation, Stephen and Suzanne

Metropolitan Opera ($52,683) see Zilkha & Sons

Metropolitan Opera Association ($4,555) see Abeles Foundation, Joseph and Sophia

Metropolitan Opera Association — annual fund drive ($50,000) see Baird Foundation, Cameron

Metropolitan Opera Association ($200,000) see Bankers Trust Co.

Metropolitan Opera Association ($61,000) see Barker Welfare Foundation

Metropolitan Opera Association ($8,000) see Beir Foundation

Metropolitan Opera Association ($20,000) see Berlin Charitable Fund, Irving

Metropolitan Opera Association ($66,000) see Blum Foundation, Edith C.

Metropolitan Opera Association ($47,500) see Botwinick-Wolfensohn Foundation

Metropolitan Opera Association ($7,500) see Brotman Foundation of California

Metropolitan Opera Association ($57,000) see Burns Foundation, Jacob

Metropolitan Opera Association ($10,250) see Chazen Foundation

Metropolitan Opera Association — telecasts of four operas ($250,000) see Culpeper Foundation, Charles E.

Metropolitan Opera Association ($5,000) see Culver Foundation, Constans

Metropolitan Opera Association ($8,000) see Daniel Foundation, Gerard and Ruth

Metropolitan Opera Association ($10,000) see Dobson Foundation

Metropolitan Opera Association ($500,000) see Dyson Foundation

Metropolitan Opera Association ($10,000) see Eckman Charitable Foundation, Samuel and Rae

Metropolitan Opera Association ($10,000) see Evans Foundation, T. M.

Metropolitan Opera Association ($34,000) see Frohlich Charitable Trust, Ludwig W.

Metropolitan Opera Association ($15,000) see Frohlich Charitable Trust, Ludwig W.

Metropolitan Opera Association ($200,000) see Getty Foundation, Ann and Gordon

Metropolitan Opera Association ($50,000) see Gilman Foundation, Howard

Metropolitan Opera Association ($250,000) see Goldsmith Foundation, Horace W.

Metropolitan Opera Association ($30,000) see Harrison Foundation Trust, Francena T.

Metropolitan Opera Association ($20,000) see Heyward Memorial Fund, DuBose and Dorothy

Metropolitan Opera Association ($3,500) see Horowitz Foundation, Gedale B. and Barbara S.

Metropolitan Opera Association ($10,000) see Icahn Foundation, Carl C.

Metropolitan Opera Association ($90,000) see Ireland Foundation

Metropolitan Opera Association ($25,000) see J C S Foundation

Metropolitan Opera Association ($3,500) see Kern Foundation, Ilma

Metropolitan Opera Association ($35,000) see Kimmelman Foundation, Helen & Milton

Metropolitan Opera Association ($2,000) see Klipstein Foundation, Ernest Christian

Metropolitan Opera Association ($8,500) see L and L Foundation

Metropolitan Opera Association ($43,500) see Lang Foundation, Eugene M.

Metropolitan Opera Association ($7,000) see Litwin Foundation

Metropolitan Opera Association ($2,500) see Martin Family Fund

Metropolitan Opera Association ($25,000) see Miller Fund, Kathryn and Gilbert

Metropolitan Opera Association ($50,000) see Mnuchin Foundation

Metropolitan Opera Association ($6,000) see Mnuchin Foundation

Metropolitan Opera Association ($350,000) see Monell Foundation, Ambrose

Metropolitan Opera Association ($250,000) see Morris Foundation, William T.

Metropolitan Opera Association ($10,000) see Pearce Foundation, Dr. M. Lee

Metropolitan Opera Association ($6,500) see Piankova Foundation, Tatiana

Metropolitan Opera Association ($10,000) see Richardson Charitable Trust, Anne S.

Metropolitan Opera Association ($7,000) see Richardson Foundation, Frank E. and Nancy M.

Metropolitan Opera Association ($40,000) see Rose Foundation, Billy

Metropolitan Opera Association ($13,500) see Rosen Foundation, Joseph

Metropolitan Opera Association ($33,333) see Sharp Foundation

Metropolitan Opera Association ($5,000) see Stuart Foundation

Metropolitan Opera Association ($500,000) see Texaco

Metropolitan Opera Association ($7,000) see Werblow Charitable Trust, Nina W.

Metropolitan Opera Association — for the Carlos Moseley Music Pavillion ($100,000) see Samuels Foundation, Fan Fox and Leslie R.

Metropolitan Opera Company ($5,000) see Cole Foundation, Robert H. and Monica H.

Metropolitan Opera Guild — underwrite the student season - programs for school children ($30,000) see Badgeley Residuary Charitable Trust, Rose M.

Metropolitan Opera Guild ($7,250) see Richardson Foundation, Frank E. and Nancy M.

Metropolitan Opera Guild ($17,185) see Spiegel Family Foundation, Jerry and Emily

Metropolitan Opera — Lincoln Center ($350,000) see Fisher Foundation, Gramma

Michael Chekhov Studio ($15,000) see Greentree Foundation

Michael Wolk Heart Foundation ($10,000) see Slifka Foundation, Joseph and Sylvia

Mid-Hudson Civic Center — for debt reduction ($136,210) see McCann Foundation

Mid-Hudson Civic Center — for capital repairs ($60,797) see McCann Foundation

Mid-Manhattan Center ($10,000) see Richardson Charitable Trust, Anne S.

Midtown Lifelink ($10,000) see Odyssey Partners

Mifal Leman Yerushalaim ($10,000) see Newbrook Charitable Foundation

New York (cont.)

Mifall Hachesey ($36,000) see Fogel Foundation, Shalom and Rebecca

Milbank Memorial Fund ($11,750) see Memton Fund

Milbank Memorial Fund ($11,750) see Memton Fund

Milbank Memorial Fund ($11,750) see Memton Fund

Milbank Memorial Fund ($11,750) see Memton Fund

Millard Fillmore Hospital ($20,000) see Cornell Trust, Peter C.

Millard Fillmore Hospital ($125,000) see Cummings Foundation, James H.

Millard Fillmore Hospital ($10,450) see Goode Trust, Mae Stone

Millard Fillmore — MS Tissue Preservation Project ($20,000) see Baird Foundation

Millard Filmore Hospital ($100,000) see Dent Family Foundation, Harry

Millard Filmore Hospital ($100,000) see Dent Family Foundation, Harry

Millbrook Free Library ($25,000) see Millbrook Tribute Garden

Millbrook School ($5,000) see Commerce Clearing House

Millbrook School ($2,000) see Darby Foundation

Millbrook School ($153,300) see Hettinger Foundation

Millbrook School ($90,000) see Millbrook Tribute Garden

Millbrook School ($3,000) see Xtra Corp.

Mind Builders Creative Arts Center ($15,000) see Snyder Fund, Valentine Perry

Minds for History ($1,000) see Zacharia Foundation, Isaac Herman

Mirer Yeshiva ($500) see Gruss Charitable and Educational Foundation, Oscar and Regina

Miriam Foundation ($16,667) see Millstone Foundation

Miriam Hospital ($5,000) see Leviton Manufacturing Co.

Mission Metro ($125,000) see DeMoss Foundation, Arthur S.

Missionaries of Charity ($1,002,000) see Andreas Foundation

Missionaries of Charity ($10,000) see Bozzone Family Foundation

Missionaries of Charity ($100,000) see McIntosh Foundation

Missionaries of Charity ($75,000) see McIntosh Foundation

Missionary Sisters of Charity ($10,000) see Trimble Family Foundation, Robert Mize and Isa White

Momentum Project — consolidation and enhancement of basic program ($10,000) see Blum Foundation, Edna F.

Monday Afternoon Club ($24,000) see Hoyt Foundation, Stewart W. and Willma C.

Monroe Community College Foundation — construct child care center ($30,000) see Davenport-Hatch Foundation

Monroe Development Center ($1,958) see General Railway Signal Corp.

Montclair Kimberly Academy ($5,000) see Kramer Foundation

Montefiore Foundation ($10,000) see Taub Foundation, Joseph and Arlene

Montefiore Hospital and Medical Center — to support a surgical research fellow ($40,000) see Hearst Foundation

Montefiore Medical Center ($2,000) see Abraham Foundation

Montefiore Medical Center ($10,000) see Glickenhaus & Co.

Montefiore Medical Center ($10,000) see Glickenhaus & Co.

Montefiore Medical Center ($14,000) see Greene Foundation, Jerome L.

Montefiore Medical Center ($100,000) see Gutman Foundation, Edna and Monroe C.

Montefiore Medical Center ($200,000) see Klau Foundation, David W. and Sadie

Montefiore Medical Center ($50,000) see Mailman Family Foundation, A. L.

Montefiore Medical Center ($100,000) see Manning and Emma Austin Manning Foundation, James Hilton

Montefiore Medical Center ($5,000) see Menschel Foundation, Robert and Joyce

Montefiore Medical Center ($100,000) see Pincus Family Fund

Montefiore Medical Center ($50,000) see Sapirstein-Stone-Weiss Foundation

Montefiore Medical Center — renewed support for the study of infants born to AIDS-infected mothers who are also intravenous drug users ($306,328) see Diamond Foundation, Aaron

Montefiore Womens Center — support for child development specialist to establish program for children of minority women participating in the Center's AIDS-related counseling programs ($20,000) see Rosenthal Foundation, Ida and William

Morality in Media ($5,000) see Donnelly Foundation, Mary J.

Morality in Media ($25,000) see St. Mary's Catholic Foundation

Moreshet Israel ($5,000) see Fribourg Foundation

Moreshet Israel ($12,500) see Millstone Foundation

Moreshet Israel ($25,000) see Schapiro Fund, M. A.

Moreshet Israel ($50,000) see Wallach Foundation, Miriam G. and Ira D.

Moriah School ($5,000) see Flemm Foundation, John J.

Mosdoa Spinka International ($100,000) see Kest Family Foundation, Sol and Clara

Mosdos Bobov ($25,000) see Zacharia Foundation, Isaac Herman

Mount Carmel Church — for capital improvements ($51,060) see McCann Foundation

Mount St. Mary's Hospital ($19,915) see Goode Trust, Mae Stone

Mount St. Ursula Speech Center — educational remediation ($30,000) see Pinkerton Foundation

Mt. Sinai Hospital — orthopaedics department — equipment restoration ($35,000) see Hugoton Foundation

Mount Sinai Hospital ($100,000) see Langeloth Foundation, Jacob and Valeria

Mount Sinai Hospital ($25,000) see Levee Charitable Trust, Polly Annenberg

Mount Sinai Hospital ($10,000) see Maas Foundation, Benard L.

Mount Sinai Hospital ($50,000) see Simon Charitable Trust, Esther

Mount Sinai Hospital ($523,100) see Tisch Foundation

Mount Sinai Hospital and Medical Center ($12,000) see Parthenon Sportswear

Mount Sinai Hospital-Polychemia Vera Study Group ($30,200) see List Foundation, Albert A.

Mount Sinai Medical Center ($75,000) see Ames Charitable Trust, Harriett

Mount Sinai Medical Center ($10,000) see Amsterdam Foundation, Jack and Mimi Leviton

Mount Sinai Medical Center ($10,000) see Amsterdam Foundation, Jack and Mimi Leviton

Mount Sinai Medical Center ($90,000) see Bachmann Foundation

Mount Sinai Medical Center ($5,000) see Beck Foundation

Mount Sinai Medical Center ($15,000) see Blank Family Foundation

Mount Sinai Medical Center ($10,000) see Blank Family Foundation

Mount Sinai Medical Center ($63,200) see Brookdale Foundation

Mount Sinai Medical Center ($50,000) see Cohn Foundation, Herman and Terese

Mt. Sinai Medical Center ($5,000) see Cohn Foundation, Peter A. and Elizabeth S.

Mount Sinai Medical Center ($30,000) see Cole National Corp.

Mount Sinai Medical Center ($9,100) see Dammann Fund

Mount Sinai Medical Center ($10,000) see Ford III Memorial Foundation, Jefferson Lee

Mount Sinai Medical Center ($150,000) see Gaisman Foundation, Catherine and Henry J.

Mount Sinai Medical Center ($150,000) see Gaisman Foundation, Catherine and Henry J.

Mount Sinai Medical Center ($12,700) see Golden Family Foundation

Mount Sinai Medical Center ($250,000) see Goldsmith Foundation, Horace W.

Mount Sinai Medical Center ($164,158) see Gould Foundation, Florence J.

Mount Sinai Medical Center ($118,000) see Green Fund

Mount Sinai Medical Center ($100,000) see Hazen

Charitable Trust, Lita Annenberg

Mount Sinai Medical Center ($100,000) see Heckscher Foundation for Children

Mount Sinai Medical Center ($500) see Heilicher Foundation, Menahem

Mount Sinai Medical Center ($191,075) see Hess Foundation

Mount Sinai Medical Center ($7,500) see Israel Foundation, A. Cremieux

Mount Sinai Medical Center ($100,000) see Klau Foundation, David W. and Sadie

Mount Sinai Medical Center ($50,000) see Kramer Foundation, C. L. C.

Mount Sinai Medical Center ($50,000) see Levy Foundation, Betty and Norman F.

Mount Sinai Medical Center ($50,000) see Liberman Foundation, Bertha & Isaac

Mount Sinai Medical Center — capital ($250,000) see Lowenstein Foundation, Leon

Mount Sinai Medical Center ($30,000) see Manilow Foundation, Nathan

Mount Sinai Medical Center ($10,000) see Mendel Foundation

Mount Sinai Medical Center ($3,300) see Meyer Foundation, Baron de Hirsch

Mount Sinai Medical Center ($500,000) see Moses Fund, Henry and Lucy

Mount Sinai Medical Center ($25,000) see Neu Foundation, Hugo and Doris

Mount Sinai Medical Center ($304,000) see Pforzheimer Foundation, Carl and Lily

Mount Sinai Medical Center ($15,000) see Price Foundation, Louis and Harold

Mount Sinai Medical Center ($178,369) see Ramapo Trust

Mount Sinai Medical Center — toward the cost of purchasing major equipment to be used in cancer research ($192,100) see Rippel Foundation, Fannie E.

Mount Sinai Medical Center ($3,000) see Rosenthal Foundation, Richard and Hinda

Mt. Sinai Medical Center ($10,000) see Sheinberg Foundation, Eric P.

Mt. Sinai Medical Center ($6,300) see Stony Wold Herbert Fund

Mount Sinai Medical Center ($25,000) see Sulzberger Foundation

Mt. Sinai Medical Center ($100,000) see Swanson Foundation

Mount Sinai Medical Center ($15,000) see Turner Fund, Ruth

Mount Sinai Medical Center ($10,000) see Turner Fund, Ruth

Mount Sinai Medical Center ($1,000) see United Togs Inc.

Mount Sinai Medical Center ($50,000) see Zarkin Memorial Foundation, Charles

Mount Sinai Medical Center Foundation ($32,788) see Gerson Trust, B. Milfred

Mt. Sinai Medical Center — Gus and Janet Levy Library Fund ($20,000) see Sheinberg Foundation, Eric P.

Mount Sinai Medical Center — infection-permissive immunization with influenza virus neuraminidase ($212,084) see Diamond Foundation, Aaron

Mt. Sinai Medical Center, Mt. Sinai Medical School ($25,000) see Nias Foundation, Henry

Mount Sinai Medical Center — for the Nathan Cummings Atrium ($400,000) see Cummings Foundation, Nathan

Mount Sinai Medical Center, New York, NY ($25,000) see Chemical Bank

Mount Sinai Medical Center (Oncology) ($250,000) see Hess Foundation

Mount Sinai Medical Foundation ($81,200) see Taylor Family Foundation, Jack

Mount Sinai School of Medicine ($16,000) see Dammann Fund

Mount Sinai School of Medicine ($250,000) see Macy, Jr. Foundation, Josiah

Mount Sinai School of Medicine ($20,000) see Sinsheimer Fund, Alexandrine and Alexander L.

Mount Sinai School of Medicine — functional role of peptidergic feedback regulation of neurotransmitter release ($47,140) see Whitehall Foundation

Mt. Sinai School of Medicine ($30,000) see Witco Corp.

Mountainside Hospital ($9,500) see Switzer Foundation

Ms. Foundation for Women ($50,000) see General Service Foundation

Ms. Foundation for Women ($95,000) see Model Foundation, Leo

Ms. Foundation for Women — for incest related projects and violence in families ($160,000) see Women's Project Foundation

Ms. Foundation for Women — for a donor-advised fund ($75,000) see Hunt Alternatives Fund

Ms. Foundation for Women — Reproductive Rights Coalition Fund, which provides financial support and technical assistance to reproductive rights groups ($50,000) see Rockefeller Family Fund

Ms. Foundation for Women — to develop and solidify state level coalitions working to safeguard reproductive rights (USA) ($60,000) see Noyes Foundation, Jessie Smith

Multiple Sclerosis Society ($20,300) see Berkey Foundation, Peter

Multiple Sclerosis Society ($25,000) see Berkowitz Family Foundation, Louis

Multiple Sclerosis Society ($10,000) see Buehler Foundation, Emil

Multiple Sclerosis Society ($10,000) see Durst Foundation

Multiple Sclerosis Society ($41,250) see First Petroleum Corp.

Multiple Sclerosis Society ($15,000) see Musson Charitable Foundation, R. C. and Katharine M.

Multiple Sclerosis Society ($3,000) see Plankenhorn Foundation, Harry

New York (cont.)

National Coalition for the Homeless ($10,000) see Levy Foundation, Jerome

National Coalition for the Homeless ($10,000) see Neu Foundation, Hugo and Doris

National Committee of US-China Relations ($50,000) see Bechtel, Jr. Foundation, S. D.

National Conference of Christians and Jews ($2,000) see Berger Foundation, Albert E.

National Conference of Christians and Jews ($1,000) see Carlyle & Co. Jewelers

National Conference of Christians and Jews ($2,000) see Kimball Co., Miles

National Conference of Christians and Jews ($10,500) see Meyer Foundation, Baron de Hirsch

National Conference of Christians and Jews ($7,500) see Millard Charitable Trust, Adah K.

National Conference of Christians and Jews ($1,000) see Storz Foundation, Robert Herman

National Conference of Christians and Jews ($2,500) see Thermo Electron Corp.

National Conference of Synagogue Youth of the Union of Orthodox Jewish Congregations of America ($60,000) see Goldman Foundation, Herman

National Council on Alcoholism ($30,000) see McGovern Fund for the Behavioral Sciences

National Council on Alcoholism ($10,000) see McGraw Foundation, Donald C.

National Council on Alcoholism ($10,000) see Montgomery Street Foundation

National Council on Alcoholism ($250,000) see Smithers Foundation, Christopher D.

National Council of Jewish Women ($7,000) see Cahn Family Foundation

National Council of Jewish Women ($25,000) see DeRoy Testamentary Foundation

National Council of Jewish Women ($3,000) see Frank Foundation, Ernest and Elfriede

National Council of Jewish Women ($10,000) see Wolens Foundation, Kalman and Ida

National Council of Young Israel ($100,000) see Moskowitz Foundation, Irving I.

National Cystic Fibrosis ($25,000) see Hirschl Trust for Charitable Purposes, Irma T.

National Dance Institute ($3,500) see G.A.G. Charitable Corporation

National Dance Institute ($900) see Monadnock Paper Mills

National Dance Institute ($3,500) see Schwartz Foundation, Bernard Lee

National Dance Institute ($8,000) see Sharp Foundation, Evelyn

National Foundation Depressive Illness ($2,800) see Lazarus Charitable Trust, Helen and Charles

National Foundation for Facial Reconstruction ($30,000) see Thorne Foundation

National Foundation for the History of Chemistry ($25,000) see Witco Corp.

National Foundation for Ileitis and Colitis ($66,000) see Bowles and Robert Bowles Memorial Fund, Ethel Wilson

National Foundation for Ileitis and Colitis ($25,000) see Levee Charitable Trust, Polly Annenberg

National Foundation for Ileitis and Colitis ($11,000) see Lichtenstein Foundation, David B.

National Foundation for Ileitis and Colitis ($10,000) see Weil, Gotshal & Manges Foundation

National Foundation for Jewish Culture ($35,000) see Dorot Foundation

National Foundation for Jewish Culture ($25,000) see Littauer Foundation, Lucius N.

National Gay and Lesbian Task Force ($1,000) see Pettus Crowe Foundation

National Hemophilia Foundation ($2,000) see Andersen Foundation, Arthur

National Jewish Center for Learning and Leadership ($6,500) see Mnuchin Foundation

National Jewish Community Relations Advisory Council ($2,700) see Goldman Foundation, Aaron and Cecile

National Jewish Outreach Program ($32,000) see AVI CHAI - A Philanthropic Foundation

National Jewish Outreach Program ($15,000) see Ehrman Foundation, Fred and Susan

National Jewish Research Center ($10,000) see Gudelsky Family Foundation, Isadore and Bertha

National Kidney Disease Foundation ($35,000) see Goldman Charitable Trust, Sol

National Kidney Foundation ($250) see Spiro Foundation, Donald W.

National Lawyers Guild ($5,000) see Warner Fund, Albert and Bessie

National Leukemia Foundation ($25) see Falk Foundation, Michael David

National Maritime Historical Society ($25,000) see McGraw Foundation, Donald C.

National Medical Fellowships — to provide medical fellowship to minority students ($18,000) see Lincoln Fund

National Minority Business Council ($9,600) see Mitsui & Co. (U.S.A.)

National Missions of the United Presbyterian Church ($16,036) see Hallett Charitable Trust, Jessie F.

National Multiple Sclerosis see New York Mercantile Exchange

National Multiple Sclerosis Society ($5,000) see Goldman Charitable Trust, Sol

National Multiple Sclerosis Society ($15,000) see Icahn Foundation, Carl C.

National Multiple Sclerosis Society ($5,000) see Schloss & Co., Marcus

National Museum of American Jewish History ($15,000) see Littauer Foundation, Lucius N.

National Museum of Dance ($5,000) see Dobson Foundation

National Museum of Dance ($100,000) see Freeman Charitable Trust, Samuel

National Museum of Racing ($8,600) see Dobson Foundation

National Pastoral Life Center ($90,000) see Brencanda Foundation

National Playwrights Conference Endowment ($10,000) see I. and L. Association

National Public Radio ($25,000) see Smith Fund, George D.

National Resources Defense Council — to support the Energy and Transportation Project ($200,000) see Cummings Foundation, Nathan

National Retinitis Pigmentosa Foundation ($65,000) see Milken Family Medical Foundation

National Review Institute ($26,500) see Cook Foundation

National Review Institute ($20,000) see Vollrath Co.

National Soaring Museum ($500) see Hilliard Corp.

National Soccer Hall of Fame ($66,500) see Dewar Foundation

National Society for Hebrew Day Schools ($100,300) see Morgenstern Foundation, Morris

National Society to Prevent Blindness ($10,000) see Steinbach Fund, Ruth and Milton

National Survival Education Fund ($19,500) see Agape Foundation

National Technical Institute for Deaf — Rochester Institute of Technology, to bring more hearing-impaired youngsters into the mainstream ($45,000) see NYNEX Corp.

National Tennis Foundation and Hall of Fame ($5,500) see Kent-Lucas Foundation

National Theater Network ($2,500) see Spiritus Gladius Foundation

National Urban League ($15,000) see Chesebrough-Pond's

National Urban League ($2,000) see Gould Inc.

National Urban League ($30,000) see Hoechst Celanese Corp.

National Urban League ($250,000) see IBM South Africa Projects Fund

National Urban League ($80,000) see Reebok International Ltd.

National Urban League ($14,000) see Unilever United States

National Urban League ($10,000) see Zenkel Foundation

National Victims Center ($10,000) see Mnuchin Foundation

National Wildlife Federation ($30,000) see Schieffelin Residuary Trust, Sarah I.

National Women's Law Center ($2,500) see Pettus Crowe Foundation

Nativity Mission Center ($33,550) see Edison Fund, Charles

Nativity Mission Center — general support and

scholarships ($40,000) see Pinkerton Foundation

Natural Resource Defense Council ($51,000) see Overbrook Foundation

Natural Resources Defense Council ($100,000) see Beinecke Foundation

Natural Resources Defense Council ($2,500) see Bright Charitable Trust, Alexander H.

Natural Resources Defense Council ($25,000) see Bydale Foundation

Natural Resources Defense Council ($20,000) see Crocker Trust, Mary A.

Natural Resources Defense Council ($10,000) see Deer Creek Foundation

Natural Resources Defense Council ($30,000) see Dunn Foundation, Elizabeth Ordway

Natural Resources Defense Council ($45,000) see Favrot Fund

Natural Resources Defense Council ($7,500) see Field Foundation, Jamee and Marshall

Natural Resources Defense Council ($100,000) see Frelinghuysen Foundation

Natural Resources Defense Council ($25,000) see Glen Eagles Foundation

Natural Resources Defense Council ($100,000) see Homeland Foundation

Natural Resources Defense Council ($50,000) see Hughes Memorial Foundation, Charles Evans

Natural Resources Defense Council ($200,000) see Kaplan Fund, J. M.

Natural Resources Defense Council ($5,000) see Ladd Charitable Corporation, Helen and George

Natural Resources Defense Council ($25,000) see Larsen Fund

Natural Resources Defense Council ($25,000) see Mott Fund, Ruth

Natural Resources Defense Council ($3,000) see Oppenheimer Family Foundation

Natural Resources Defense Council ($20,000) see Penney Foundation, James C.

Natural Resources Defense Council ($250,000) see Public Welfare Foundation

Natural Resources Defense Council ($70,000) see Scherman Foundation

Natural Resources Defense Council ($50,000) see Steele-Reese Foundation

Natural Resources Defense Council ($20,000) see True North Foundation

Natural Resources Defense Council ($65,000) see Trust for Mutual Understanding

Natural Resources Defense Council ($75,000) see Wallace Genetic Foundation

Natural Resources Defense Council ($50,000) see Weeden Foundation, Frank

Natural Resources Defense Council — ozone protection plan ($25,000) see Winkler Foundation, Mark and Catherine

Natural Resources Defense Council — energy and transportation - Columbia

River Basin/Salmon ($150,000) see Bullitt Foundation

Natural Resources Defense Council — Nuclear Program ($400,000) see Jones Foundation, W. Alton

Natural Resources Defense Council — NW energy project ($15,000) see Tucker Charitable Trust, Rose E.

Natural Resources Defense Council — forestry program, Chernobyl project ($75,000) see duPont Foundation, Chichester

Natural Resources Defense Council — second-year payment of a three-year, $750,000 grant for operation and endowment of an environmental conflict negotiation program ($250,000) see Bingham Foundation, William

Natural Resources Defense Council — revise the legal framework for United States nuclear non-proliferation policy; to strengthen the 1972 Clean Water Act ($30,000) see Prospect Hill Foundation

Nature Conservancy — for the preservation of the maritime grasslands and heathlands ($30,000) see Achelis Foundation

Nature Conservancy ($10,000) see Bayne Fund, Howard

Nature Conservancy ($70,000) see Model Foundation, Leo

Nature Conservancy ($5,000) see Sasco Foundation

Nature Conservancy ($10,000) see Schieffelin Residuary Trust, Sarah I.

Nazareth College of Rochester — endowed scholarship fund ($35,000) see Hearst Foundation

NCCJ — First Time/Last Time ($5,000) see Goodyear Foundation, Josephine

Near East Foundation ($40,000) see Dodge Foundation, Cleveland H.

Neco Foundation ($10,000) see O'Sullivan Children Foundation

Neighborhood Center of Utica ($4,654) see Utica National Insurance Group

Neighborhood Coalition for Shelter — expansion of work program professional assistant ($47,555) see Kern Foundation, Ilma

Neighborhood Coalition for Shelter ($1,500) see Salgo Charitable Trust, Nicholas M.

Neighborhood HOPE ($14,450) see Wilson Foundation, Marie C. and Joseph C.

Neighborhood Housing Services of New York ($50,000) see Industrial Bank of Japan Trust Co.

Neighborhood Legal Services — hotline for low income clients ($20,000) see Western New York Foundation

Neighborhood Preservation of New York ($30,000) see Green Fund

Neve Yerushalaim ($1,000) see Rubin Family Fund, Cele H. and William B.

New Alternatives for Children ($7,000) see Dammann Fund

New Community Cinema ($150,000) see Hoffman

Index to Grant Recipient by State

New York (cont.)

New York Experimental Glass Workshop ($100,000) see Pforzheimer Foundation, Carl and Lily

New York Eye and Ear Infirmary ($7,500) see Klosk Fund, Louis and Rose

New York Eye and Ear Infirmary ($35,000) see Nichols Foundation

New York Federation for the Arts/Leo Dratfield Endowment — to advance appreciation and recognition of independent films and videos ($2,500) see Benton Foundation

New York Fellowship ($44,000) see Three Swallows Foundation

New York Festival of Arts ($10,000) see Greene Foundation, Jerome L.

New York Foundation for the Arts ($1,000) see Ballet Makers

New York Foundation for the Arts — general operating fund ($144,950) see Stein Foundation, Jules and Doris

New York Foundation Nursing Home ($15,000) see Frank Foundation, Ernest and Elfriede

New York Foundation for Senior Citizens ($5,000) see Leucadia National Corp.

New York Foundling Hospital ($12,500) see Davis Foundation, Simon and Annie

New York Foundling Hospital ($15,000) see Ferkauf Foundation, Eugene and Estelle

New York Foundling Hospital ($84,596) see Hirschl Trust for Charitable Purposes, Irma T.

New York Graduate School of Public Service ($25,000) see Zlinkoff Fund for Medical Research and Education, Sergei S.

New York Hall of Science ($17,500) see Hebrew Technical Institute

New York Hall of Science ($62,500) see Hitachi

New York Hall of Science — renewed support for an Explainer Coordinator of the Science Teacher Career Ladder, and in-service teacher training for "Starlab II" ($30,000) see Greenwall Foundation

New York Heart Association ($30,000) see Mellam Family Foundation

New York Historical Society ($20,000) see Equitable Life Assurance Society of the U.S.

New York Historical Society ($250,000) see Harriman Foundation, Gladys and Roland

New York Historical Society ($45,000) see Milbank Foundation, Dunlevy

New York Historical Society ($40,000) see Milbank Foundation, Dunlevy

New York Historical Society ($110,000) see Wien Foundation, Lawrence A.

New York Historical Society — Cataloging and preserving Society archives ($100,000) see Dana Foundation, Charles A.

New York Historical Society — in support of New Study/Storage Center for the Permanent Collections

($500,000) see Starr Foundation

New York Holocaust Memorial Commission ($100,000) see Stern Foundation, Max

New York Hospital ($15,000) see Archbold Charitable Trust, Adrian and Jessie

New York Hospital ($1,000,000) see Greentree Foundation

New York Hospital ($500,000) see Harriman Foundation, Gladys and Roland

New York Hospital ($25,000) see Lazarus Charitable Trust, Helen and Charles

New York Hospital ($20,000) see Ridgefield Foundation

New York Hospital ($10,000) see Stott Foundation, Robert L.

New York Hospital ($225,000) see Weinberg Foundation, John L.

New York Hospital, Cornell ($32,000) see Lounsbery Foundation, Richard

New York Hospital Cornell Medical Center ($10,000) see Baker Foundation, Solomon R. and Rebecca D.

New York Hospital-Cornell Medical Center — support research in the field of hormones and their effects on brain function ($50,000) see Baker Trust, George F.

New York Hospital — Cornell Medical Center ($22,500) see Banfi Vintners

New York Hospital Cornell Medical Center ($20,500) see Barth Foundation, Theodore H.

New York Hospital — Cornell Medical Center ($11,000) see Belding Heminway Co.

New York Hospital-Cornell Medical Center ($500,000) see David-Weill Foundation, Michel

New York Hospital-Cornell Medical Center ($16,650) see Fribourg Foundation

New York Hospital Cornell Medical Center ($25,000) see Frohlich Charitable Trust, Ludwig W.

New York Hospital-Cornell Medical Center ($20,000) see Frohlich Charitable Trust, Ludwig W.

New York Hospital-Cornell Medical Center ($2,000) see Gerard Foundation, Sumner

New York Hospital-Cornell Medical Center ($3,500) see Goldie-Anna Charitable Trust

New York Hospital-Cornell Medical Center ($30,000) see Lasdon Foundation

New York Hospital-Cornell Medical Center ($5,000) see Lasdon Foundation

New York Hospital-Cornell Medical Center ($5,000) see Piankova Foundation, Tatiana

New York Hospital Cornell Medical Center ($20,000) see Rosenwald Family Fund, William

New York Hospital Cornell Medical Center ($150,000) see St. Giles Foundation

New York Hospital Cornell Medical Center ($25,000) see Stony Wold Herbert Fund

New York Hospital-Cornell Medical Center ($41,250) see Wallach Foundation, Miriam G. and Ira D.

New York Hospital Cornell Medical Center ($15,000) see Weight Watchers International

New York Hospital-Cornell Medical Center ($7,000) see Werblow Charitable Trust, Nina W.

New York Hospital Cornell Medical Center ($60,000) see Wiener Foundation, Malcolm Hewitt

New York Hospital-Cornell Medical Center — medical research ($30,000) see Young Foundation, Robert R.

New York Hospital/Cornell Medical Center — $15,000 general charitable contribution, $10,000 Gala, $1,000 Journal ad ($26,000) see Carter-Wallace

New York Hospital-Cornell Medical Center — the final installment of a $200,000 grant ($100,000) see Calder Foundation, Louis

New York Hospital-Cornell Medical Center — Clinical Research Fellowship Program ($45,344) see Pinewood Foundation

New York Hospital-Cornell Medical Center — Department of Plastic Surgery ($50,000) see Pinewood Foundation

New York Hospital-Cornell Medical Center — Division of Endocrinology and Metabolism ($133,333) see Pinewood Foundation

New York Hospital-Cornell Medical Center — for the Dr. Mary Allen Engle Division of Pediatric Cardiology ($65,000) see Badgeley Residuary Charitable Trust, Rose M.

New York Hospital-Cornell Medical Center Fund ($50,000) see Ames Charitable Trust, Harriett

New York Hospital Cornell Medical Center Fund ($700,000) see Penzance Foundation

New York Hospital — for joint program in molecular neuroscience by Department of Neurology and Psychiatry ($125,000) see DeCamp Foundation, Ira W.

New York Hospital Department of Social Work ($35,000) see Rodgers Foundation, Richard & Dorothy

New York Hospital — in support of its Major Modernization Campaign ($6,250,000) see Starr Foundation

New York Hospital Major Modernization Campaign ($200,000) see Weinberg Foundation, John L.

New York Hospital/Womens Endowment Fund ($25,000) see Collins & Aikman Holdings Corp.

New York Hundred Neediest Cases ($100,000) see Klau Foundation, David W. and Sadie

New York Infirmary ($10,000) see Kellogg Foundation, J. C.

New York Infirmary ($5,000) see Porter Foundation, Mrs. Cheever

New York Infirmary Beekman Downtown Hospital ($40,000) see Hutchins Foundation, Mary J.

New York Infirmary/Beekman Downtown Hospital ($10,000) see New York Stock Exchange

New York Infirmary Beekman Downtown Hospital ($20,000) see Prudential-Bache Securities

New York Institute for Special Education ($5,000) see Steinbach Fund, Ruth and Milton

New York Interface Development Project for Professional Development Laboratory School Project ($15,000) see Snyder Fund, Valentine Perry

New York International Festival of Arts ($10,000) see Atlantic Foundation

New York International Festival of the Arts ($150,000) see New York Times Co.

New York International Festival of Arts ($134,000) see Rudin Foundation, Samuel and May

New York Junior Tennis League ($20,000) see Benenson Foundation, Frances and Benjamin

New York Junior Tennis League ($22,428) see Kaplen Foundation

New York Junior Tennis League ($6,520) see Krimendahl II Foundation, H. Frederick

New York Landmarks Conservancy ($7,070) see Durst Foundation

New York Landmarks Conservancy ($10,000) see MacDonald Foundation, James A.

New York Landmarks Conservancy — for re-granting through their Sacred Sites and Properties Fund to allow religious institutions around New York State to preserve their landmark buildings ($110,000) see Kaplan Fund, J. M.

New York Law School ($20,000) see Hagedorn Fund

New York Law School ($25,000) see Scott Foundation, Walter

New York Law School ($57,500) see Snow Memorial Trust, John Ben

New York Lawn and Garden ($5,000) see Agway

New York Lawyers for the Public Interest ($6,000) see Kaye, Scholer, Fierman, Hays & Handler

New York League for the Hard of Hearing ($15,000) see AMAX

New York League for the Hard of Hearing ($10,000) see Borden Memorial Foundation, Mary Owen

New York League for the Hard of Hearing ($15,000) see Driehaus Foundation, Richard H.

New York League for the Hard of Hearing ($2,000) see Leucadia National Corp.

New York League for Hard of Hearing ($25,000) see Nias Foundation, Henry

New York League for the Hard of Hearing ($25,000) see Vidda Foundation

New York Library for the Blind ($500) see Adler Foundation

New York Lighthouse for the Blind ($5,000) see Daily News

New York Lung Association ($3,000) see Stony Wold Herbert Fund

New York Medical Center ($30,000) see Chait Memorial Foundation, Sara

New York Medical Center ($40,000) see Joyce Foundation, John M. and Mary A.

New York Medical College ($12,500) see Amsterdam Foundation, Jack and Mimi Leviton

New York Medical College ($3,500) see Amsterdam Foundation, Jack and Mimi Leviton

New York Medical College ($3,500) see Gaisman Foundation, Catherine and Henry J.

New York Medical College ($16,666) see Mosbacher, Jr. Foundation, Emil

New York Medical College ($14,850) see Smithers Foundation, Christopher D.

New York Medical College — toward the capital campaign for New York Medical College ($100,000) see Altman Foundation

New York Medical College — fellowship program for visiting Polish scientists and pathologists at the College's Department of Pathology ($40,000) see Jurzykowski Foundation, Alfred

New York Open Center ($10,000) see Richardson Charitable Trust, Anne S.

New York Philanthropic League ($10,000) see Parshelsky Foundation, Moses L.

New York Philharmonic ($2,725) see Abrams Foundation, Benjamin and Elizabeth

New York Philharmonic ($35,000) see Baier Foundation, Marie

New York Philharmonic ($12,500) see Blinken Foundation

New York Philharmonic ($6,000) see Harrison Foundation Trust, Francena T.

New York Philharmonic ($3,000) see Israel Foundation, A. Cremieux

New York Philharmonic ($92,000) see Krimendahl II Foundation, H. Frederick

New York Philharmonic ($25,890) see Krimendahl II Foundation, H. Frederick

New York Philharmonic ($30,000) see Pfizer

New York Philharmonic ($5,000) see Ryan Foundation, Nina M.

New York Philharmonic ($60,000) see Whitaker Fund, Helen F.

New York Philharmonic — capital campaign; general support ($85,000) see Prospect Hill Foundation

New York Philharmonic Society ($6,800) see Brody Foundation, Carolyn and Kenneth D.

New York Philharmonic Society ($9,307) see Greene Foundation, David J.

New York Philharmonic Society ($92,000) see Levin Foundation, Philip and Janice

New York Philharmonic Society ($25,000) see O'Neil Foundation, Cyril F. and Marie E.

New York Philharmonic — Young People's Concerts ($50,000) see Rose Foundation, Billy

New York Public Library ($10,000) see AKC Fund

New York Public Library ($25,000) see Allen Brothers Foundation

New York Public Library ($7,000) see Bayne Fund, Howard

New York Public Library ($50,000) see Benenson Foundation, Frances and Benjamin

New York Public Library ($12,500) see Blinken Foundation

New York Public Library see Bloomingdale's

New York Public Library — open hours and page program ($15,000) see Blum Foundation, Edna F.

New York Public Library — for care of the collections ($45,000) see Bodman Foundation

New York Public Library ($40,000) see CBS Inc.

New York Public Library ($15,000) see Charina Foundation

New York Public Library ($55,000) see Chemical Bank

New York Public Library ($5,000) see Cohn Foundation, Peter A. and Elizabeth S.

New York Public Library ($6,000) see Coltec Industries

New York Public Library ($100,000) see Continental Corp.

New York Public Library — book cataloging project ($500,000) see Diamond Foundation, Aaron

New York Public Library ($1,036,000) see Engelhard Foundation, Charles

New York Public Library ($10,000) see Erpf Fund, Armand G.

New York Public Library ($20,000) see First Boston

New York Public Library ($22,000) see Hagedorn Fund

New York Public Library ($100) see HarperCollins Publishers

New York Public Library ($20,000) see Hebrew Technical Institute

New York Public Library ($50,000) see Heckscher Foundation for Children

New York Public Library ($3,500) see Kaye, Scholer, Fierman, Hays & Handler

New York Public Library ($20,000) see Larsen Fund

New York Public Library ($25,000) see Liberman Foundation, Bertha & Isaac

New York Public Library ($100,000) see Loews Corp.

New York Public Library ($5,500) see MacDonald Foundation, James A.

New York Public Library ($75,000) see Macmillan, Inc.

New York Public Library ($25,000) see MCA

New York Public Library ($55,000) see McGraw-Hill

New York Public Library ($15,000) see Mellam Family Foundation

New York Public Library ($5,000) see Menschel Foundation, Robert and Joyce

New York Public Library ($16,666) see Miller Fund, Kathryn and Gilbert

New York Public Library ($5,000) see Mitsui & Co. (U.S.A.)

New York Public Library ($390,000) see Newhouse Foundation, Samuel I.

New York Public Library ($25,000) see PaineWebber

New York Public Library — general program ($30,000) see Paley Foundation, William S.

New York Public Library ($17,029) see Prudential-Bache Securities

New York Public Library ($17,028) see Prudential-Bache Securities

New York Public Library ($25,000) see Rodgers Foundation, Richard & Dorothy

New York Public Library ($50,000) see Rohatyn Foundation, Felix and Elizabeth

New York Public Library ($20,000) see Rohatyn Foundation, Felix and Elizabeth

New York Public Library ($200,000) see Salomon Foundation, Richard & Edna

New York Public Library — book fund for branch libraries ($100,000) see Scherman Foundation

New York Public Library — general support ($100,000) see Scherman Foundation

New York Public Library ($20,000) see Schieffelin Residuary Trust, Sarah I.

New York Public Library ($25,000) see Schiff Foundation, Dorothy

New York Public Library — manuscript department ($25,000) see Schiff Foundation, Dorothy

New York Public Library ($200,000) see Seagram & Sons, Joseph E.

New York Public Library ($10,000) see Sheinberg Foundation, Eric P.

New York Public Library ($25,000) see Solow Foundation

New York Public Library ($15,000) see Steinbach Fund, Ruth and Milton

New York Public Library ($166,666) see Stern Foundation, Leonard N.

New York Public Library ($25,000) see Sulzberger Foundation

New York Public Library ($127,000) see Uris Brothers Foundation

New York Public Library ($1,367,000) see Wallace-Reader's Digest Fund, DeWitt

New York Public Library ($25,000) see Wien Foundation, Lawrence A.

New York Public Library ($15,000) see Zlinkoff Fund for Medical Research and Education, Sergei S.

New York Public Library — for the cataloguing of art-related materials ($224,000) see Getty Trust, J. Paul

New York Public Library Astor, Lenox and Tilden Foundation ($35,000) see Simon Charitable Trust, Esther

New York Public Library, Astor, Lenox and Tilden Foundations — $10,000,000 toward The Campaign for the Library ($1,428,571) see Astor Foundation, Vincent

New York Public Library — for CATNYP System at the Science, Industry and Business Library ($100,000) see Chase Manhattan Bank, N.A.

New York Public Library — for an exhibition celebrating the life and work of George Balanchine ($100,000) see Samuels Foundation, Fan Fox and Leslie R.

New York Public Library — Oriental Division ($25,000) see Griggs and Mary Griggs Burke Foundation, Mary Livingston

New York Public Library, Schomburg Center — program support ($230,046) see RJR Nabisco Inc.

New York Regional Association of Grantmakers ($13,000) see Roche Relief Foundation, Edward and Ellen

New York Regional Association of Grantmakers — 1991 membership ($650) see Sandoz Corp.

New York School of Drawing ($7,000) see Speyer Foundation, Alexander C. and Tillie S.

New York Services for the Handicapped ($500) see Newbrook Charitable Foundation

New York Shakespeare Festival ($25,000) see Delacorte Fund, George

New York Shakespeare Festival ($3,000) see Schneiderman Foundation, Roberta and Irwin

New York Shakespeare Festival ($200,000) see Shubert Foundation

New York Shakespeare Festival ($75,000) see Stein Foundation, Jules and Doris

New York Shakespeare Festival ($25,000) see Taub Foundation, Henry and Marilyn

New York Shakespeare Festival — Estelle R. Newman Theatre ($16,000) see Newman Assistance Fund, Jerome A. and Estelle R.

New York Shakespeare Festival — for the upcoming production of John Ford's 'Tis Pity She's a Whore ($75,000) see Samuels Foundation, Fan Fox and Leslie R.

New York Sports Museum ($6,000) see Kopf Foundation

New York State Agricultural Child Care Program ($25,600) see Statler Foundation

New York State Agricultural Experiment ($38,830) see Weeden Foundation, Frank

New York State Coalition Against Domestic Violence ($2,500) see Candlesticks Inc.

New York State Coalition for Children ($10,000) see Gould Foundation for Children, Edwin

New York State Council of Churches ($25,000) see Straus Foundation, Philip A. and Lynn

New York State Historical Association ($400,000) see Clark Foundation

New York State Museum ($18,300) see Wunsch Foundation

New York State Sheriffs Association — operating funds ($50) see Gleason Works

New York State Task Force on Life and the Law — to support research on advance directives, Tracy E. Miller, J.D., Principal Investigator

($50,000) see Greenwall Foundation

New York Studio School of Drawing, Painting and Sculpture ($45,000) see Plumsock Fund

New York Theater ($25,000) see Leonhardt Foundation, Dorothea L.

New York Theatre ($15,000) see Blount

New York Theatre ($16,000) see Cheatham Foundation, Owen

New York Theatre ($2,000) see Gilman and Gonzalez-Falla Theatre Foundation

New York Theatre ($50,000) see Rose Foundation, Billy

New York Theatre ($13,600) see Rudin Foundation

New York Theological Seminary ($6,000) see MacDonald Foundation, James A.

New York Theological Seminary Fund ($30,000) see Moore Foundation, Edward S.

New York Times Neediest Cases ($55,000) see Hutchins Foundation, Mary J.

New York Times Neediest Cases Fund ($15,000) see Goodman Family Foundation

New York Times Neediest Cases Fund ($125,000) see Johnson Foundation, Willard T. C.

New York Times Neediest Cases Fund ($8,500) see MacDonald Foundation, James A.

New York Times Neediest Cases Fund ($20,000) see Mellam Family Foundation

New York Times Neediest Cases Fund ($5,000) see Sequa Corp.

New York University ($10,000) see Allen Foundation, Frances

New York University ($40,000) see Benenson Foundation, Frances and Benjamin

New York University ($5,000) see Berkowitz Family Foundation, Louis

New York University ($5,000) see Berkowitz Family Foundation, Louis

New York University ($200,000) see Bobst Foundation, Elmer and Mamdouha

New York University ($6,000) see Gerondelis Foundation

New York University — for internships ($250,000) see Getty Trust, J. Paul

New York University ($15,000) see Hebrew Technical Institute

New York University ($50,000) see Hirschl Trust for Charitable Purposes, Irma T.

New York University ($30,000) see Katzenberger Foundation

New York University ($229,006) see Kaufman Foundation, Henry & Elaine

New York University ($24,000) see Liberman Foundation, Bertha & Isaac

New York University ($180,000) see Loeb Foundation, Frances and John L.

New York University ($4,000) see Loewenberg Foundation

New York University ($5,000) see Mandel Foundation, Joseph and Florence

New York University ($26,600) see Matz Foundation — Edelman Division

New York University ($10,000) see Matz Foundation — Edelman Division

New York University — general operating support ($400,150) see MCJ Foundation

New York University ($5,000) see McNutt Charitable Trust, Amy Shelton

New York University — disabled program ($200,000) see Moses Fund, Henry and Lucy

New York University ($39,000) see Newcombe Foundation, Charlotte W.

New York University ($5,000) see Ogden Foundation, Ralph E.

New York University — to study how bulk properties of matter arise from microscopic laws of nature ($500,000) see Packard Foundation, David and Lucile

New York University — for the development of a vaccine to human malignant melanoma ($130,000) see Pardee Foundation, Elsa U.

New York University ($50,000) see Pincus Family Fund

New York University ($204,000) see Scheuer Family Foundation, S. H. and Helen R.

New York University ($156,000) see Schwartz Fund for Education and Health Research, Arnold and Marie

New York University ($500,000) see Skirball Foundation

New York University ($108,150) see Tai and Co., J. T.

New York University ($15,000) see United States Trust Co. of New York

New York University ($5,000) see Whitehead Charitable Foundation

New York University — first payment of $150,000 grant for the Reading Recovery Program ($75,000) see J.P. Morgan & Co.

New York University Building Fund ($25,000) see Weiler Foundation, Theodore & Renee

New York University — Cherkasky Chair ($200,000) see Moses Fund, Henry and Lucy

New York University — fund to study Cognitive Decline of Elderly ($15,000) see Werblow Charitable Trust, Nina W.

New York University Conservation Center ($32,636) see Hebrew Technical Institute

New York University Department of Psychology ($25,000) see Manning and Emma Austin Manning Foundation, James Hilton

New York University Department of Psychology ($7,500) see Manning and Emma Austin Manning Foundation, James Hilton

New York University — Gerstenberg Chair ($15,000) see Palisades Educational Foundation

New York University Graduate School ($5,000) see Goodman Memorial Foundation, Joseph C. and Clare F.

New York University Graduate School ($10,000) see Gutman Foundation, Edna and Monroe C.

New York University — Hagop Kevorkiam Center ($61,066) see Kevorkian Fund, Hagop

New York University — Inquiries in Cultural

New York (cont.)

Psychology ($350,000) see Spencer Foundation

New York University — Institute of Fine Arts; endowment of faculty chair ($300,000) see Fairchild Foundation, Sherman

New York University Institute of Fine Arts ($269,691) see Kevorkian Fund, Hagop

New York University Medical center ($7,348) see Wunsch Foundation

New York University Medical Center ($25,000) see Abeles Foundation, Joseph and Sophia

New York University Medical Center ($20,000) see Abeles Foundation, Joseph and Sophia

New York University Medical Center ($5,000) see Abeles Foundation, Joseph and Sophia

New York University Medical Center ($150,000) see Bleibtreu Foundation, Jacob

New York University Medical Center ($25,000) see Bobst Foundation, Elmer and Mamdouha

New York University Medical Center ($100,000) see Capital Cities/ABC

New York University Medical Center ($50,000) see Coleman Foundation

New York University Medical Center ($50,000) see David-Weill Foundation, Michel

New York University Medical Center ($80,000) see Evans Foundation, T. M.

New York University Medical Center ($185,000) see Gilman Foundation, Howard

New York University Medical Center ($100,000) see Gruss Charitable Foundation, Emanuel and Riane

New York University Medical Center ($20,000) see I. and L. Association

New York University Medical Center ($20,000) see Jurodin Fund

New York University Medical Center ($100,000) see Kaplan Foundation, Rita J. and Stanley H.

New York University Medical Center ($31,500) see Kenworthy - Sarah H. Swift Foundation, Marion E.

New York University Medical Center ($20,000) see Lee Foundation, James T.

New York University Medical Center ($50,000) see Levin Foundation, Philip and Janice

New York University Medical Center ($100,000) see MacAndrews & Forbes Holdings

New York University Medical Center ($5,000) see Newman Assistance Fund, Jerome A. and Estelle R.

New York University Medical Center ($5,000) see Ogden Foundation, Ralph E.

New York University Medical Center ($195,000) see Pope Foundation

New York University Medical Center ($10,000) see Rosenberg Foundation, Sunny and Abe

New York University Medical Center ($51,000) see Schaffer Foundation, Michael & Helen

New York University Medical Center ($3,500) see Weinstein Foundation, Alex J.

New York University Medical Center, Department of Obstetrics and Gynecology — establishment of clinic and research program for postmenopausal women ($104,000) see Rubinstein Foundation, Helena

New York University Medical Center — support of Dr. Wade Park's research program on pediatric AIDS ($100,000) see Calder Foundation, Louis

New York University Medical Center — purchase of equipment to enhance its Interactive Video-Computer courseware project ($30,000) see Hyde and Watson Foundation

New York University Medical Center — Whitlow, M.D. ($108,000) see Culpeper Foundation, Charles E.

New York University Network East-West Women ($5,000) see Pettus Crowe Foundation

New York University Nursing Division of the School of Education, Health, Nursing and the Arts Professions — scholarships ($55,000) see Rudin Foundation, Louis and Rachel

New York University Para-Educator Center for Young Adults ($44,074) see Pinkerton Foundation

New York University Research Center ($30,000) see Kenworthy - Sarah H. Swift Foundation, Marion E.

New York University School of Business ($1,250) see Ellis Fund

New York University School of Law ($50,000) see Snow Memorial Trust, John Ben

New York University School of Law — to support 50 internships in public interest law ($220,000) see Revson Foundation, Charles H.

New York University School of Medicine ($125,000) see Oberkotter Family Foundation

New York University School of Medicine — medical scholarships ($65,000) see Rudin Foundation, Louis and Rachel

New York University School of Medicine ($64,772) see Sinsheimer Fund, Alexandrine and Alexander L.

New York University School of Social Work Building Fund ($25,000) see Seevak Family Foundation

New York University Stern School of Business and Public Administration ($50,000) see Snow Memorial Trust, John Ben

New York University Student Art Center Lounge ($30,000) see Rosenberg Foundation, Sunny and Abe

New York University Theater Program ($2,000) see Contempo Communications

New York University-Tisch School of the Arts ($775,000) see Tisch Foundation

New York University — support of the Urban Research Center ($275,000) see Revson Foundation, Charles H.

New York Urban Coalition ($4,000) see Fife Foundation, Elias and Bertha

New York Women's Foundation — for the endowment fund ($50,000) see Hunt Alternatives Fund

New York Women's Foundation ($10,000) see Seevak Family Foundation

New York Youth at Risk — to provide an intensive intervention experience combined with follow-up support in order to produce a breakthrough in the lives of youth "at risk" see New Street Capital Corp.

New York Youth Symphony ($15,000) see Chadwick Fund, Dorothy Jordan

New York Youth Symphony ($5,000) see McCutchen Foundation

New York Zoological Society ($3,000) see Bailey Wildlife Foundation

New York Zoological Society ($25,000) see Barker Welfare Foundation

New York Zoological Society — for support for a field veterinarian ($60,000) see Bay Foundation

New York Zoological Society ($20,000) see Beneficia Foundation

New York Zoological Society ($7,330) see Christodora

New York Zoological Society ($75,000) see Erpf Fund, Armand G.

New York Zoological Society ($5,000) see Fein Foundation

New York Zoological Society ($30,000) see Hoffmann-La Roche

New York Zoological Society ($1,000) see Iroquois Avenue Foundation

New York Zoological Society ($3,000) see Johnson Charitable Trust, Keith Wold

New York Zoological Society ($35,340) see Liz Claiborne

New York Zoological Society ($25,000) see McBean Family Foundation

New York Zoological Society ($25,000) see Model Foundation, Leo

New York Zoological Society ($25,000) see Nichols Foundation

New York Zoological Society ($50,000) see Perkin Fund

New York Zoological Society ($450,000) see Phipps Foundation, Howard

New York Zoological Society ($100,000) see Schiff Foundation

New York Zoological Society ($8,000) see Schiff Foundation

New York Zoological Society ($5,000) see Sheinberg Foundation, Eric P.

New York Zoological Society ($9,000) see Simon Foundation, Sidney, Milton and Leoma

New York Zoological Society ($52,250) see Thorne Foundation

New York Zoological Society ($50,000) see Tortuga Foundation

New York Zoological Society ($10,000) see Vanderbilt Trust, R. T.

New York Zoological Society ($50,000) see Zarkin Memorial Foundation, Charles

New York Zoological Society — for the Center for Ecological Education at the Bronx Zoo ($170,000) see Bodman Foundation

New York Zoological Society — to endow the Crisis Fund for Vanishing Wildlife ($50,000) see Prospect Hill Foundation

New York Zoological Society — Super Science Day ($10,918) see Toshiba America, Inc.

New York Zoological Society — for the Wildlife Crisis Campaign ($45,000) see Achelis Foundation

New York Zoological Society — for the Wildlife Survival Center on St. Catherine's Island, Georgia ($359,000) see Noble Foundation, Edward John

New York Zoological Society — women's committee ($10,000) see Evans Foundation, Edward P.

Newton Community Service Center ($5,000) see Fife Foundation, Elias and Bertha

Niagara Frontier Vocational Rehabilitation Center — equipment ($15,000) see Western New York Foundation

Nickolois/Louis Foundation for the Dance ($10,000) see Magowan Family Foundation

Night Kitchen/A National Children's Theater ($35,000) see Plumsock Fund

Nightingale Bamford School ($10,000) see Axe-Houghton Foundation

Nightingale Bamford School ($11,000) see Charina Foundation

Nightingale Bamford School ($100,000) see Joukowsky Family Foundation

Nightingale Bamford School ($15,000) see Picower Foundation, Jeffrey M. and Barbara

Nightingale Bamford School ($10,000) see Picower Foundation, Jeffrey M. and Barbara

Nightingale Bamford School ($25,000) see Randleigh Foundation Trust

Nightingale Bamford School ($100,000) see Revlon

Nine for the Nineties ($15,000) see Golub Corp.

92nd Street Y ($50,000) see Friedman Foundation, Stephen and Barbara

92nd Street Y ($12,500) see Harkness Ballet Foundation

92nd Street Y ($15,000) see Miller Fund, Kathryn and Gilbert

92nd Street Y ($18,000) see Weininger Foundation, Richard and Gertrude

92nd Street YM/YWHA ($5,600) see Guttag Foundation, Irwin and Marjorie

92nd Street YM and YWHA ($10,500) see Lazarus Charitable Trust, Helen and Charles

92nd Street YM/YWHA ($90,000) see Liberman Foundation, Bertha & Isaac

92nd Street YM/YWHA ($25,000) see Oppenheimer and Flora Oppenheimer Haas Trust, Leo

92nd Street YM/YWHA ($50,000) see Rubin Foundation, Rob E. & Judith O.

92nd Street YM and YWHA ($20,000) see Stern Foundation, Max

92nd Street YMHA ($100,000) see Sequa Corp.

NMF Research Fund ($10,000) see Loewenberg Foundation

Nonprofit Facilities Fund ($900,000) see Wallace-Reader's Digest Fund, DeWitt

Norman Foundation ($15,000) see Loeb Partners Corp.

Norman Howard School ($13,500) see Bennett Foundation, Carl and Dorothy

Norman Williams Public Library ($2,000) see Pettus Crowe Foundation

North Adirondack Parenthood ($700) see Crary Foundation, Bruce L.

North American College ($5,000) see Kasal Charitable Trust, Father

North American Conference on Ethiopian Jewery ($2,000) see Litwin Foundation

North American Conference on Ethiopian Jewry — to bring Ethiopian Jews to Israel and resettlement and cultural preservation programs in Israel ($20,000) see Fel-Pro Incorporated

North American Friends of Kafka Center ($10,000) see Cohen Foundation, Wilfred P.

North Carolina School of the Arts — for Recognition ($500,000) see Kenan, Jr. Charitable Trust, William R.

North General Hospital ($25,000) see McIntosh Foundation

North General Hospital-Helen Fuld School of Nursing — scholarships ($66,000) see Rudin Foundation, Louis and Rachel

North Nassau Mental Health Center ($4,500) see Kepco, Inc.

North Presbyterian Church ($4,000) see Joy Family Foundation

North Shore Child and Family Guidance ($22,500) see Ada Foundation, Julius

North Shore Child and Family Guidance ($1,000) see Linus Foundation

North Shore Child and Family Guidance ($100) see Ushkow Foundation

North Shore Synagogue ($25,000) see Spingold Foundation, Nate B. and Frances

North Shore Synagogue ($2,400) see Weinstein Foundation, Alex J.

North Shore University ($5,000) see Gurwin Foundation, J.

North Shore University ($100,000) see Kopf Foundation

North Shore University ($100,000) see Kopf Foundation, Elizabeth Christy

North Shore University Hospital ($20,000) see Banfi Vintners

North Shore University Hospital ($20,600) see Belding Heminway Co.

North Shore University Hospital ($1,050) see Belmont Metals

North Shore University Hospital ($50,000) see Chernow Trust for the Benefit of Charity Dated 3/13/75, Michael

North Shore University Hospital ($100,000) see Cohen Foundation, Wilfred P.

North Shore University Hospital ($5,000) see Fife Foundation, Elias and Bertha

North Shore University Hospital ($51,400) see Greene Foundation, David J.

North Shore University Hospital ($4,000) see Gurwin Foundation, J.

North Shore University Hospital ($8,000) see Harding Educational and Charitable Foundation

North Shore University Hospital — health care services for women and children at risk ($250,000) see Hearst Foundation, William Randolph

North Shore University Hospital ($33,334) see Heckscher Foundation for Children

North Shore University Hospital ($20,000) see Leviton Manufacturing Co.

North Shore University Hospital ($15,000) see Lindner Foundation, Fay J.

North Shore University Hospital ($2,500) see Saul Foundation, Joseph E. & Norma G.

North Shore University Hospital ($450) see Ushkow Foundation

North Shore University Hospital at Glen Cove ($40,000) see Craigmyle Foundation

North Shore University Hospital — to purchase a Tecan Robotic Cell Harvester and Genevision Multiscanning System ($130,000) see St. Giles Foundation

North Shore YM YWHA ($12,225) see Gruber Research Foundation, Lila

North Star Fund ($1,435,000) see Common Giving Fund

North Star Fund ($375,000) see Common Giving Fund

Northeastern Association of the Blind at Albany ($25,000) see Schaffer Foundation, H.

Northern Dutchess Hospital ($100,000) see Thompson Trust, Thomas

Northern Oswego County Health Services ($8,000) see Snow Foundation, John Ben

Northern Westchester Council of the Arts see MBIA, Inc.

Northgate Parkinson Fund ($89,000) see Randolph Foundation

Northside Center for Child Development — to support an educational and emotional support program for children aged 2-7 ($15,000) see Washington Square Fund

Norwegian Christian Home and Health Center ($5,000) see Faith Home Foundation

Norwegian Seaman's Church ($50,000) see Vetlesen Foundation, G. Unger

Norwegian Seamens Church ($19,500) see Paul and C. Michael Paul Foundation, Josephine Bay

Notre Dame High School ($15,000) see Wilson Foundation, Marie C. and Joseph C.

N'Ve Eretz ($1,000) see N've Shalom Foundation

NYBAC Convention Promotion and Services Fund ($100,000) see Rubin Foundation, Rob E. & Judith O.

NYSES Bicentennial Foundation ($25,000) see Jacobson & Sons, Benjamin

Occupational Training Program — towards salary of development officer ($25,000) see Lincoln Fund

Ohab Zedek ($25,000) see AVI CHAI - A Philanthropic Foundation

OHEL Children's Home and Family Services ($4,000) see Kaplun Foundation, Morris J. and Betty

Ohr Chadash ($108,000) see Bag Bazaar, Ltd.

Ohr Ha Chaiam ($8,000) see Bag Bazaar, Ltd.

Ohr Someyach ($10,000) see Stein Foundation, Joseph F.

Ohr Torah ($25,000) see Stern Foundation, Gustav and Irene

Ohr Torah ($5,000) see Stern Foundation, Gustav and Irene

Ohr Torah Institute for Israel ($250,000) see Applebaum Foundation

Ohr Torah Institution ($10,000) see Ehrman Foundation, Fred and Susan

Ohr Torah Institution ($2,000) see Marcus Brothers Textiles Inc.

OHR Torah Institutions of Israel ($36,000) see Jesselson Foundation

Ohr Torah Institutions of Israel ($15,000) see Parthenon Sportswear

Old Westbury Gardens ($50,000) see Phipps Foundation, Howard

Old Westbury School of the Holy Child — general operating fund ($228,895) see Dolan Family Foundation

Old Westbury School of the Holy Child ($114,050) see O'Sullivan Children Foundation

Olivet Baptist Church ($100) see Hendrickson Brothers

On With Life ($10,000) see Rich Products Corp.

On Your Mark Program ($13,000) see Chait Memorial Foundation, Sara

One Percent For Peace ($17,500) see Ben & Jerry's Homemade

One Percent for Peace ($27,333) see Ben & Jerry's Homemade

One Percent for Peace ($20,667) see Ben & Jerry's Homemade

One Percent for Peace ($8,800) see Ben & Jerry's Homemade

One Seventy One Cedar — glass-making studio ($44,600) see Corning Incorporated

Oneida Area Arts Council ($1,500) see Chapman Charitable Corporation, Howard and Bess

Oneida County Historical Society ($5,000) see Utica National Insurance Group

Oneida County Industrial Development Corporation ($25,000) see Fleet Bank of New York

Oneida United Way ($2,000) see Chapman Charitable Corporation, Howard and Bess

Onondaga Community College Foundation ($1,000) see Gear Motion

Onondaga Council on Alcoholism and Drug

Addiction ($10,000) see Fay's Incorporated

Onondaga Council on Alcoholism and Drug Addiction ($8,500) see Fay's Incorporated

Onondaga Council on Alcoholism and Drug Addiction ($7,000) see Fay's Incorporated

Onondaga County Special Olympics ($10,000) see Fay's Incorporated

Open Housing Center ($2,250) see Spingold Foundation, Nate B. and Frances

Open Space Institute ($170,000) see Beinecke Foundation

Open Space Institute ($5,000) see Hettinger Foundation

Open Space Institute ($10,000) see Normandie Foundation

Open Space Institute ($10,000) see Titan Industrial Co.

Opera America ($17,083) see Sullivan Musical Foundation, William Matheus

Opera Orchestra of New York ($2,500) see Pines Bridge Foundation

Operation Exodus ($25,000) see Altschul Foundation

Operation Exodus ($100,000) see Benenson Foundation, Frances and Benjamin

Operation Exodus ($12,000) see Beren Foundation, Robert M.

Operation Exodus ($16,000) see EIS Foundation

Operation Exodus ($4,000) see Fisher Foundation, Max M. and Marjorie S.

Operation Exodus ($46,000) see Friedman Brothers Foundation

Operation Exodus ($6,000) see Gruber Research Foundation, Lila

Operation Exodus ($100,000) see Kohl Charitable Foundation, Allen D.

Operation Exodus ($10,000) see Levine Family Foundation, Hyman

Operation Exodus ($5,000) see Menschel Foundation, Robert and Joyce

Operation Exodus ($5,000) see National Metal & Steel

Operation Exodus ($6,000) see Schloss & Co., Marcus

Operation Independence ($20,000) see Taub Foundation, Henry and Marilyn

Operation Sail New York ($50,000) see Frese Foundation, Arnold D.

Operation Welcome Home ($50,000) see Revlon

Operation Welcome Home-NYC ($25,000) see Paramount Communications Inc.

Ophthalmological Foundation of America ($25,000) see Bostwick Foundation, Albert C.

Opportunities for Otsego ($25,000) see Dewar Foundation

Opportunity Foundation — organization to combat homelessness and joblessness among the urban poor ($50,000) see Baker Trust, George F.

Or Hachaim ($50,000) see Hidary Foundation, Jacob

Or Hachaim ($15,000) see Hidary Foundation, Jacob

Or Hachaim ($15,000) see Hidary Foundation, Jacob

Orenreich Foundation for the Advancement of Science ($6,000) see Gruber Research Foundation, Lila

Original Ballets Foundation ($10,000) see Kunstadter Family Foundation, Albert

Orpheus Chamber Orchestra ($10,000) see Sheafer Charitable Trust, Emma A.

ORT American Federation ($1,000) see Gruss Charitable and Educational Foundation, Oscar and Regina

Ossining Child Care Center ($10,000) see St. Faith's House Foundation

Ossining Open Door ($6,000) see Burnham Donor Fund, Alfred G.

Ossining Open Door ($10,000) see St. Faith's House Foundation

Ostego County Conservation Association ($100,000) see Gronewaldt Foundation, Alice Busch

Our Lady of Grace Church ($7,000) see Huisking Foundation

Our Lady of Solace Parish — repair roof of parish school ($100,000) see Raskob Foundation for Catholic Activities

Outward Bound ($25,000) see Bowne Foundation, Robert

Outward Bound ($30,000) see Fanwood Foundation

Outward Bound ($1,000) see Quality Metal Finishing Foundation

Outward Bound ($5,000) see Schiff Foundation

Overlook Hospital ($50,000) see Hutchins Foundation, Mary J.

Ozar Hatorah ($21,200) see Bag Bazaar, Ltd.

Ozar Hatorah ($50,000) see N've Shalom Foundation

P.E.F. Israel Development Fund ($5,000) see Gruss Charitable Foundation, Emanuel and Riane

P.E.F. Israel Endowment Fund ($25,000) see Levy Foundation, Jerome

P.E.F. Israel Endowment Fund ($425,000) see Rochlin Foundation, Abraham and Sonia

P.E.F. Israel Endowment Fund ($13,000) see Rosenbloom Foundation, Ben and Esther

P.E.F. Israel Endowment Funds ($19,250) see Stern Family Foundation, Harry

P.E.P. Israel Endowment Funds ($831,000) see Capital Fund Foundation

P.S. 40 Manhattan ($10,342) see Dorr Foundation

Pace University ($140,000) see Goldstein Foundation, Alfred and Ann

Pace University ($3,000) see Handy & Harman

Pace University ($310,000) see Pforzheimer Foundation, Carl and Lily

Pace University ($8,000) see Switzer Foundation

Pace University Environmental Center ($10,000) see Burnham Donor Fund, Alfred G.

Pace University — Schaeberle Chair of Accounting ($50,000) see Nabisco Foods Group

Pan American Center ($10,000) see Rosenwald Family Fund, William

Pan Asian Repertory Theatre — cultural program ($7,205) see Kohler Co.

Paralyzed Veterans of America ($5,000) see Jackson Mills

Parents Place ($5,000) see Straus Foundation, Philip A. and Lynn

Parish Campaign ($25,000) see Gaisman Foundation, Catherine and Henry J.

Park Avenue Methodist Church ($3,000) see Allen Foundation, Frances

Park Avenue Methodist Church ($2,500) see Douglas Corp.

Park Avenue Synagogue ($1,805) see Gruss Charitable and Educational Foundation, Oscar and Regina

Park Avenue Synagogue ($150,000) see Hess Foundation

Park Avenue Synagogue ($10,525) see Lemberg Foundation

Park Avenue Synagogue ($1,950) see Nelco Sewing Machine Sales Corp.

Park Avenue Synagogue ($6,005) see Steinberg Family Foundation, Meyer and Jean

Park Avenue Synagogue ($4,760) see Weinstein Foundation, J.

Park East Day School ($10,000) see Wilf Family Foundation

Park East Synagogue ($7,000) see Fribourg Foundation

Park East Synagogue ($5,500) see Greene Foundation, David J.

Park Foundation — support charitable activities ($195,000) see Kennedy, Jr. Foundation, Joseph P.

Parker Institute for Geriatric Care ($40,000) see Lindner Foundation, Fay J.

Parks Council ($10,000) see J C S Foundation

Parks Council ($21,980) see Wien Foundation, Lawrence A.

Parks Council — Urban Conservation Corp ($55,000) see Scherman Foundation

Parot Yarif Foundation ($16,000) see Hidary Foundation, Jacob

Parrish Art Museum ($25,000) see Cowles Charitable Trust

Parrish Art Museum ($5,000) see Krimendahl II Foundation, H. Frederick

Parsons School of Design ($173,591) see Bluhdorn Charitable Trust, Charles G. and Yvette

Partnership for a Drug-Free America — media campaign to reduce demand for illegal drugs ($3,000,000) see Johnson Foundation, Robert Wood

Partnership for a Drug Free America — California initiative ($100,000) see Drown Foundation, Joseph

Partnership for the Homeless ($15,000) see Dreitzer Foundation

Partnership for the Homeless ($10,000) see Kidder, Peabody & Co.

Partnership for the Homeless — employment coordinator ($64,732) see Rhodebeck Charitable Trust

Partnership for the Homeless ($7,500) see Weiss Foundation, William E.

Partnership for Homeless — homeless AIDS supportive

New York (cont.)

housing program ($9,000) see Blum Foundation, Edna F.

Partnership for Homeless — Project Domicile - support services for relocated families ($11,000) see Blum Foundation, Edna F.

Partnership for Quality ($150,000) see Bristol-Myers Squibb Co.

Partnership for Quality Education ($39,150) see Benenson Foundation, Frances and Benjamin

Partnership for Quality Education — final payment of a three for one challenge grant ($125,000) see Calder Foundation, Louis

Partnership of Quality Education ($100,000) see Warren Foundation, William K.

Paruer Jewish Geriatric ($5,000) see FAB Industries

Patronato Beneficio Oriental U.S. ($3,000) see Gillett Foundation, Elesabeth Ingalls

Paul Taylor Dance Foundation ($50,000) see Simon Charitable Trust, Esther

Pauline Oliveros Foundation ($24,000) see Foundation for the Needs of Others

PCDC (Philips House) ($5,000) see Brody Foundation, Carolyn and Kenneth D.

Peachtown Elementary School ($4,000) see Cayuga Foundation

Pearl S. Buck Foundation ($5,000) see Bayne Fund, Howard

Peconic Land Trust ($50,000) see Greve Foundation, William and Mary

Peconic Land Trust ($25,000) see Lauder Foundation

Peconic Land Trust ($25,000) see Lauder Foundation

Pediatric Aids Foundation ($1,000) see Herald News

Pediatric AIDS Foundation ($10,000) see Johnson Foundation, Willard T. C.

Pediatric Orthopaedic Society of North America — support field of pediatric orthopaedics ($25,000) see St. Giles Foundation

Peekskill Community Hospital ($65,000) see Langeloth Foundation, Jacob and Valeria

Peekskill Community Hospital Foundation ($6,587) see Killough Trust, Walter H. D.

PEF Israel Endowment Fund ($5,000) see Fink Foundation

PEF Israel Endowment Fund ($4,600) see Flemm Foundation, John J.

PEF Israel Endowment Fund ($100,000) see Fraida Foundation

PEF Israel Endowment Fund ($50,000) see Meyer Foundation

PEF Israel Endowment Fund ($100,000) see Morgenstern Foundation, Morris

PEF Israel Endowment Fund ($133,500) see Moskowitz Foundation, Irving I.

PEF Israel Endowment Fund ($18,000) see Posnack Family Foundation of Hollywood

PEF Israel Endowment Fund ($15,000) see Rosen Foundation, Joseph

PEF Israel Endowment Fund ($52,500) see Steinhardt Foundation, Judy and Michael

PEF-Israel Endowment Funds ($132,400) see Jesselson Foundation

Pen American Center ($500) see Simon Foundation, Jennifer Jones

Peninsula Counseling Center ($20,000) see Oppenheimer and Flora Oppenheimer Haas Trust, Leo

People for the American Way — to support art space ($11,500) see Mapplethorpe Foundation, Robert

Peoples Reinvestment and Development Effort-PRIDE ($12,500) see Stern Foundation, Irvin

Performing Artservices ($13,500) see Foundation for the Needs of Others

Phelps Memorial Hospital Center ($100,000) see Davis Foundation, Shelby Cullom

Phelps Pre-Natal Clinic ($10,000) see St. Faith's House Foundation

Philharmonic Symphony Society ($350,000) see Monell Foundation, Ambrose

Philharmonic Symphony Society of New York ($20,000) see Culver Foundation, Constans

Philharmonic Symphony Society of New York ($25,000) see Miller Fund, Kathryn and Gilbert

Philips Beth Israel School of Nursing ($100,000) see Hillman Family Foundation, Alex

Phipps Community Development Corporation ($40,155) see Industrial Bank of Japan Trust Co.

Phipps Community Development Corporation ($5,000) see Kautz Family Foundation

Phipps Community Development Corporation — general purposes ($20,000) see Morris Foundation, Margaret T.

Phoenix House ($5,000) see Abraham Foundation

Phoenix House ($50,000) see Geffen Foundation, David

Phoenix House ($5,500) see Lasdon Foundation

Phoenix House Development Fund ($3,000) see Candlesticks Inc.

Phoenix House Development Fund ($50,000) see Weezie Foundation

Phoenix House Foundation — the Belle Terre property in South Kortright, NY ($200,000) see Bodman Foundation

Phoenix House Foundation — for the purchase of a new young-adult- and adolescent-treatment facility ($100,000) see Achelis Foundation

Phoenix House — in honor of Nancy S. Ittleson ($100,000) see Ittleson Foundation

Pierpoint Morgan Library ($250,000) see Gilder Foundation

Pierpoint Morgan Library — toward a courtyard to connect the library complex on 36th Street and Madison Avenue with the Morgan Mansion on 37th Street ($150,000) see Astor Foundation, Vincent

Pierpont Morgan Library — to help build an endowment for public programming ($100,000) see Altman Foundation

Pierpont Morgan Library — toward endowment ($2,500,000) see Arcana Foundation

Pierpont Morgan Library ($200,000) see Dula Educational and Charitable Foundation, Caleb C. and Julia W.

Pierpont Morgan Library ($500) see Ellis Fund

Pierpont Morgan Library ($500,000) see Heinz Foundation, Drue

Pierpont Morgan Library ($135,000) see Pforzheimer Foundation, Carl and Lily

Pierpont Morgan Library ($50,000) see Phipps Foundation, Howard

Pierpont Morgan Library ($100,000) see Thorne Foundation

Pierpont Morgan Library ($10,000) see Vaughn, Jr. Foundation Fund, James M.

Pierpont Morgan Library ($100,000) see Vetlesen Foundation, G. Unger

Pierpont Morgan Library ($5,000) see Whiting Foundation, Mrs. Giles

Pierpont Morgan Library — exhibition Armenian manuscripts ($50,000) see Arcana Foundation

Pierpont Morgan Library — to support a landmark treasures exhibition in celebration of the completion of the library's major expansion and renovation ($150,000) see Luce Foundation, Henry

Pierpont Morgan Library — funding for the position of cataloguer of rare books and materials, given in memory of Franklin H. Kissner, co-founder of the Dyson-Kissner-Moran Corporation ($120,000) see Dyson Foundation

Pierpont Morgan Library — capital campaign for New Garden Court/Expansion of Library ($20,000) see International Flavors & Fragrances

Pilsudski Institute of America — document storage and retrieval system for copying their archival collections ($30,000) see Jurzykowski Foundation, Alfred

Planned Parenthood ($35,500) see Bleibtreu Foundation, Jacob

Planned Parenthood — adolescent pregnancy impact program ($15,000) see Blum Foundation, Edna F.

Planned Parenthood ($500) see Hirschhorn Foundation, David and Barbara B.

Planned Parenthood ($13,500) see Salomon Foundation, Richard & Edna

Planned Parenthood ($20,000) see Stott Foundation, Louis L.

Planned Parenthood ($5,000) see Straus Foundation, Philip A. and Lynn

Planned Parenthood ($20,000) see Weil, Gotshal & Manges Foundation

Planned Parenthood Federation of America ($12,500) see Allyn Foundation

Planned Parenthood Federation of America ($5,000) see Anderson Foundation

Planned Parenthood Federation of America — national assistance family planning ($40,000) see Baird Foundation, Cameron

Planned Parenthood Federation of America — international assistance family planning ($35,000) see Baird Foundation, Cameron

Planned Parenthood Federation of America ($4,100) see Belmont Metals

Planned Parenthood Federation of America ($15,000) see Blinken Foundation

Planned Parenthood Federation of America ($100,000) see Buffett Foundation

Planned Parenthood Federation of America ($25,000) see Chait Memorial Foundation, Sara

Planned Parenthood Federation of America ($10,000) see Children's Foundation of Erie County

Planned Parenthood Federation of America ($100,000) see Clark Foundation, Robert Sterling

Planned Parenthood Federation of America ($50,000) see Cohen Family Foundation, Saul Z. and Amy Scheuer

Planned Parenthood Federation of America ($700) see Crary Foundation, Bruce L.

Planned Parenthood Federation of America ($150,000) see Dodge Foundation, Geraldine R.

Planned Parenthood Federation of America ($5,000) see Durst Foundation

Planned Parenthood Federation of America ($108,000) see Foundation for the Needs of Others

Planned Parenthood Federation of America ($35,650) see Greene Foundation, Jerome L.

Planned Parenthood Federation of America ($2,000) see Hilliard Corp.

Planned Parenthood Federation of America ($25,000) see HKH Foundation

Planned Parenthood Federation of America ($225,000) see Huber Foundation

Planned Parenthood Federation of America ($1,000) see Ingersoll Milling Machine Co.

Planned Parenthood Federation of America ($50,000) see Johnson Foundation, Willard T. C.

Planned Parenthood Federation of America ($100,000) see Kenworthy - Sarah H. Swift Foundation, Marion E.

Planned Parenthood Federation of America ($10,000) see Marx Foundation, Virginia & Leonard

Planned Parenthood Federation of America ($4,000) see Mazer Foundation, Jacob and Ruth

Planned Parenthood Federation of America — national assistance family planning ($100,000) see Merck Family Fund

Planned Parenthood Federation of America — to support litigation in state and federal courts on behalf of reproductive rights ($75,000) see Merck Fund, John

Planned Parenthood Federation of America ($20,000) see Penney Foundation, James C.

Planned Parenthood Federation of America ($5,000) see Plant Memorial Fund, Henry B.

Planned Parenthood Federation of America ($50,000) see Reed Foundation, Philip D.

Planned Parenthood Federation of America ($10,000) see Schiff Foundation, Dorothy

Planned Parenthood Federation of America ($10,000) see Schiff Foundation, Dorothy

Planned Parenthood Federation of America ($8,500) see Schiro Fund

Planned Parenthood Federation of America ($20,000) see Sharp Foundation, Evelyn

Planned Parenthood Federation of America — national assistance family planning ($75,000) see Smith Fund, George D.

Planned Parenthood Federation of America — general support ($500,000) see Steele Foundation, Harry and Grace

Planned Parenthood Federation of America ($50,000) see True North Foundation

Planned Parenthood Federation of America ($70,000) see Vanderbilt Trust, R. T.

Planned Parenthood Federation of America ($11,500) see Vanderbilt Trust, R. T.

Planned Parenthood Federation of America ($5,000) see Vanderbilt Trust, R. T.

Planned Parenthood Federation of America ($35,000) see Zlinkoff Fund for Medical Research and Education, Sergei S.

Planned Parenthood Federation of America — New York City ($50,000) see Compton Foundation

Planned Parenthood of New York City ($100,000) see Clark Foundation, Robert Sterling

Planned Parenthood of New York City ($75,000) see Klingenstein Fund, Esther A. and Joseph

Planned Parenthood of New York City ($227,750) see Overbrook Foundation

Planned Parenthood of New York City ($50,000) see Pinewood Foundation

Planned Parenthood of New York City — toward pregnancy prevention services and public education ($40,000) see Prospect Hill Foundation

Planned Parenthood of New York City ($35,000) see Schneiderman Foundation, Roberta and Irwin

Planned Parenthood of New York — for the Hub Center located in the South Bronx, New York ($75,000) see Noble Foundation, Edward John

Play Schools Association ($25,000) see Lehman Foundation, Edith and Herbert

Play Schools Association ($12,000) see Simon Foundation, Sidney, Milton and Leoma

Playing to Win ($50,000) see General Atlantic Partners L.P.

Playing to Win ($15,000) see Snyder Fund, Valentine Perry

Playing to Win ($15,000) see United States Trust Co. of New York

Playing to Win — renewed funding for a second year of MathTech, a collaboration between community-based technology center and teachers, students, and parents in New York City public schools ($42,000) see Greenwall Foundation

Plays for Living ($21,000) see Marx Foundation, Virginia & Leonard

Playwrights Horizons ($62,000) see Rubin Foundation, Rob E. & Judith O.

Playwrights Horizons ($47,060) see Rubin Foundation, Rob E. & Judith O.

Playwrights Horizons ($10,000) see Sheafer Charitable Trust, Emma A.

Playwrights Horizons ($80,000) see Shubert Foundation

Playwrights Horizons — for partial support of New Theatre Wing series in 1991-1992 ($7,500) see Axe-Houghton Foundation

Pleasant Valley Cemetery ($20,000) see Taylor Foundation, Fred and Harriett

Poetry Works ($10,000) see Magowan Family Foundation

Poets House — for partial support of "Axe-Houghton" Poetry Tape Archive ($5,000) see Axe-Houghton Foundation

Poets and Writers ($40,000) see Banyan Tree Foundation

Poets & Writers ($2,000) see Whiting Foundation, Mrs. Giles

Police Athletic League ($69,015) see Botwinick- Wolfensohn Foundation

Police Athletic League ($500,000) see Fisher Brothers

Police Athletic League ($50,000) see Forbes

Police Athletic League ($50,000) see Forbes

Police Athletic League ($8,000) see Palmer-Fry Memorial Trust, Lily

Police Athletic League ($10,200) see Schwartz Fund for Education and Health Research, Arnold and Marie

Police Athletic League — capital campaign ($25,000) see Sheinberg Foundation, Eric P.

Police Athletic League ($10,000) see Sheinberg Foundation, Eric P.

Polo Museum and Hall of Fame ($50,000) see Knox Foundation, Seymour H.

Polytechnic Preparatory Country Day School ($5,000) see Matz Foundation — Edelman Division

Polytechnic University ($175,000) see Dibner Fund

Polytechnic University ($2,000) see Handy & Harman

Polytechnic University — endowment of scholarship funds ($100,000) see Litton Industries

Polytechnic University — for faculty renewal in materials science and engineering ($100,000) see Teagle Foundation

Polytechnic University ($60,000) see Wunsch Foundation

Polytechnic University — to equip and furnish laboratories in its new Center for Advanced Technology in Telecommunications ($250,000) see NYNEX Corp.

Population Communications International ($10,000) see Dunagan Foundation

Population Communications International ($3,000) see Swensrud Charitable Trust, Sidney A.

Population Communications International ($51,000) see Weeden Foundation, Frank

Population Communications International ($25,000) see Weyerhaeuser Family Foundation

Population Council ($79,125) see Bergstrom Foundation, Erik E. and Edith H.

Population Council ($50,000) see Compton Foundation

Population Council — for social science research ($900,000) see Mellon Foundation, Andrew W.

Population Council — to conduct acceptability studies of RU486 among users of the abortifacient in China ($91,000) see Merck Fund, John

Practical Bible Training School — Alice E. Chatlos Library upkeep, maintenance and expansion ($50,000) see Chatlos Foundation

Prague Mozart Foundation ($50,000) see Colburn Fund

Pratt Institute ($9,000) see Switzer Foundation

Pratt Institute Center for Community and Environmental Development ($15,000) see Penney Foundation, James C.

Prep for Prep ($5,000) see Gruss Petroleum Corp.

Prep for Prep ($30,000) see Hettinger Foundation

Prep for Prep ($6,338) see Morse, Jr. Foundation, Enid and Lester S.

Prep for Prep ($15,000) see Oaklawn Foundation

Prep for Prep ($10,000) see Odyssey Partners

Prep for Prep ($15,000) see Picower Foundation, Jeffrey M. and Barbara

Prep for Prep ($10,000) see Picower Foundation, Jeffrey M. and Barbara

Prep for Prep ($2,500) see Schneiderman Foundation, Roberta and Irwin

Prep for Prep ($25,000) see Zarkin Memorial Foundation, Charles

Prep for Prep — prepares intellectually gifted inner-city children of color for admission to and successful graduation from leading "prep" schools see New Street Capital Corp.

Presbyterian Homes of Western New York ($15,000) see Grigg-Lewis Trust

Presbyterian Hospital ($100,000) see Langeloth Foundation, Jacob and Valeria

Presbyterian Hospital ($20,000) see Rohatyn Foundation, Felix and Elizabeth

Presbyterian Hospital ($20,000) see Vanneck-Bailey Foundation

Presbyterian Hospital ($250,000) see Weinberg, Jr. Foundation, Sidney J.

Presbyterian Hospital ($25,000) see Weinberg, Jr. Foundation, Sidney J.

Presbyterian Hospital in the City of New York ($500,000) see Penzance Foundation

Presbyterian Hospital — in support of the Day Hospital of the Division of Pediatric Hematology/Oncology ($100,000) see Chase Manhattan Bank, N.A.

Presbyterian Hospital Foundation ($25,000) see Giles Foundation, Edward C.

Presbyterian Hospital Foundation ($15,000) see Stella D'Oro Biscuit Co.

Presbytery of New York ($17,750) see Clark Charitable Trust, Frank E.

Presbytery of New York ($15,750) see Clark Charitable Trust, Frank E.

Preservation League of New York State ($7,500) see MacDonald Foundation, James A.

Preservation League of New York State ($15,000) see Reed Foundation

Preservation League of New York State — for their technical assistance center, and for their New York State Gazetteer project, a publication about New York State ($150,000) see Kaplan Fund, J. M.

Preventive Medicine Institute — toward the cost of equipping PMI/Strang's new clinic and of purchasing a gas chromatography/mass spectrometry machine ($250,000) see Rippel Foundation, Fannie E.

Price Institute for Entrepreneurial Studies ($1,011,300) see Price Foundation, Louis and Harold

Princess Grace Foundation ($3,000) see Titan Industrial Co.

Princeton University ($100,000) see Johnson Endeavor Foundation, Christian A.

Professional Children's School ($5,000) see Frank Foundation, Ernest and Elfriede

Professional Children's School ($5,000) see Frank Foundation, Ernest and Elfriede

Professional Children's School ($5,000) see Statter Foundation, Amy Plant

Professional Engineers Society ($1,500) see General Railway Signal Corp.

Project Impact ($20,000) see Hunt Alternatives Fund, Helen

Project Interchange ($5,000) see Raskin Foundation, Hirsch and Braine

Project Orbis ($75,000) see Banbury Fund

Project Orbis — program ($15,000) see Littlefield Memorial Trust, Ida Ballou

Project Reach Youth ($18,000) see Bowne Foundation, Robert

Propsect Park Environmental Center ($6,800) see Christodora

Protestant Episcopal Church ($12,000) see Hersey Foundation

Providence Rest Foundation ($152,500) see Pope Foundation

Providence-St. Mel School ($12,000) see Stern Foundation, Irvin

PS1 ($10,000) see Brody Foundation, Carolyn and Kenneth D.

Psychoanalytic Research and Development Fund ($33,000) see Overseas Shipholding Group

Public Affairs Television — in support of the public television cultural and public affairs productions of Bill Moyers (over three years) ($1,500,000) see MacArthur Foundation, John D. and Catherine T.

Public Agenda Foundation ($125,500) see Bohen Foundation

Public Citizen Fund ($2,500) see Fuchsberg Family Foundation, Abraham

Public Education Association ($1,000) see Schneiderman Foundation, Roberta and Irwin

Public Education Association — general support ($25,000) see Taconic Foundation

Public Health Research Institute — molecular disruption of the life cycle of the HIV virus ($217,500) see Diamond Foundation, Aaron

Public Policy Institute ($25,000) see Manilow Foundation, Nathan

Pulaski Baptist Church ($35,000) see Snow Memorial Trust, John Ben

Purchase College Foundation ($15,000) see Benenson Foundation, Frances and Benjamin

Purchase College Foundation ($50,000) see Loeb Foundation, Frances and John L.

Purchase College Foundation ($50,000) see McGonagle Foundation, Dextra Baldwin

Purchase College Foundation ($200,000) see PepsiCo

Purchase College Foundation — R.R. Neuberger Endowment Fund ($250,000) see Neuberger Foundation, Roy R. and Marie S.

Putnam Association for Retarded Citizens ($1,350) see Weinstein Foundation, J.

Putnam County Humane Society ($1,250) see Weinstein Foundation, J.

Queens Child Guidance Center — help families achieve successful adoptions of troubled foster children who have no hope of being reunited with their birth families ($40,000) see Cummings Memorial Fund Trust, Frances L. and Edwin L.

Queens Citizens Organization — multi-issue citizen organizing project ($35,000) see New York Foundation

Queens College Foundation ($1,000) see Central National-Gottesman

Queens College Foundation ($4,500) see Kepco, Inc.

Queens College Foundation ($10,000) see Schwartz Fund for Education and Health Research, Arnold and Marie

Rabbi Isaac Elchanan Theological Seminary

($10,000) see Propp Sons Fund, Morris and Anna

Rabbi Isaak Elehanan Theological Seminars ($20,000) see Nelco Sewing Machine Sales Corp.

Rabbi Jacob Joseph School ($50,000) see Applebaum Foundation

Rabbinical Seminary of Israel ($20,000) see Newbrook Charitable Foundation

Race Track Chaplaincy of America ($101,254) see Ryan Family Charitable Foundation

Ragosin Institute ($6,000) see Rosenwald Family Fund, William

Ramapo Anchorage Camp ($27,000) see Uris Brothers Foundation

Ramaz Academy ($1,500) see Fischel Foundation, Harry and Jane

Ramaz Scholarship Fund ($1,500) see Ehrman Foundation, Fred and Susan

Ramaz School ($43,068) see Associated Food Stores

Ramaz School ($5,100) see Stern Family Foundation, Harry

Ramaz 21 Century Fund ($100,000) see Applebaum Foundation

Randolph Children's Home ($10,000) see Hultquist Foundation

Raoul Wallenberg Committee ($10,500) see Greenberg Foundation, Alan C.

Reading Reform Foundation ($25,000) see Gottesman Fund

Realty Foundation of New York ($2,000) see Baldwin Foundation, David M. and Barbara

Realty Foundation of New York ($11,000) see Levy Foundation, Betty and Norman F.

Recording for the Blind ($8,000) see Luce Charitable Trust, Theodore

Recording for the Blind ($5,000) see Statter Foundation, Amy Plant

Recording for the Blind ($20,000) see Turner Fund, Ruth

Red Cross ($100,000) see Gleason Memorial Fund

Red Magen David ($1,000) see Gruss Charitable and Educational Foundation, Oscar and Regina

Reformed Church in America ($50,000) see Kuyper Foundation, Peter H. and E. Lucille Gaass

Reg Lenna Civic Center ($5,000) see Darrah Charitable Trust, Jessie Smith

Reg Lenna Civic Center ($20,000) see Hultquist Foundation

Reg Lenna Civic Center — Lucille Ball Festival of New Comedy ($150,000) see Gebbie Foundation

Regents of the University of New York ($100,000) see Cantor Foundation, Iris and B. Gerald

Regional Plan Association ($10,000) see CIT Group Holdings

Regis High School — to establish a scholarship endowment fund ($50,000) see Sage Foundation

Relief Committee of General Jewish Workers Union of

New York (cont.)

Foundation, Theresa and Edward

St. Vincents Hospital and Medical Center of New York ($111,000) see Ritter Foundation, May Ellen and Gerald

St. Vincent's Hospital and Medical Center of New York — to support the design and development of a comprehensive strategic plan for St. Vincent's ($200,000) see Altman Foundation

St. Vincent's Hospital and Medical Center of New York — support St. Vincent's commitment to care for the poor ($100,000) see Cummings Memorial Fund Trust, Frances L. and Edwin L.

St. Vincent's Hospital School of Nursing — scholarships ($75,000) see Rudin Foundation, Louis and Rachel

St. Vincent's School of Nursing ($10,000) see Switzer Foundation

St. Vincents Services — 20 washers and dryers, developmental toys and video equipment ($18,500) see Hackett Foundation

Salanter Akiba Riverdale Academy ($125,650) see Jesselson Foundation

Salmon River Fine Arts Center ($15,000) see Snow Foundation, John Ben

Salvation Army ($15,000) see Bargman Foundation, Theodore and Mina

Salvation Army ($5,000) see Bluhdorn Charitable Trust, Charles G. and Yvette

Salvation Army ($20,000) see Bowne Foundation, Robert

Salvation Army ($7,000) see Children's Foundation of Erie County

Salvation Army ($2,500) see De Lima Co., Paul

Salvation Army ($27,500) see Decio Foundation, Arthur J.

Salvation Army ($6,000) see Ebert Charitable Foundation, Horatio B.

Salvation Army ($5,156) see Ellsworth Trust, W. H.

Salvation Army ($250) see Gear Motion

Salvation Army ($10,000) see Hettinger Foundation

Salvation Army ($10,000) see Mark IV Industries

Salvation Army ($5,212) see Rankin and Elizabeth Forbes Rankin Trust, William

Salvation Army ($4,754) see Rankin and Elizabeth Forbes Rankin Trust, William

Salvation Army ($10,000) see Richardson Charitable Trust, Anne S.

Salvation Army ($13,000) see Roche Relief Foundation, Edward and Ellen

Salvation Army ($15,000) see Ruffin Foundation, Peter B. & Adeline W.

Salvation Army ($5,000) see Sequa Corp.

Salvation Army ($29,000) see Spiro Foundation, Donald W.

Salvation Army ($7,000) see Statter Foundation, Amy Plant

Salvation Army ($15,000) see Wasily Family Foundation

Salvation Army of Greater New York — to establish the Mary

R. Williams Memorial Endowment which will assist cadets from the New York Division with the cost of attending its officers' training school ($100,000) see Teagle Foundation

Sam Waxman Cancer Research Foundation ($6,200) see Mazer Foundation, Jacob and Ruth

Samaritan Hospital Foundation ($15,307) see Robison Foundation, Ellis H. and Doris B.

Samaritan Institute of Keene Valley ($15,000) see Holley Foundation

Samuel Field YM/YWHA ($6,000) see Spingold Foundation, Nate B. and Frances

Samuel Waxman Cancer Research Foundation ($1,500) see Goldstein Foundation, Leslie and Roslyn

Samuel Waxman Cancer Research Foundation ($16,000) see Weiler Foundation, Theodore & Renee

Sanctuary for Animals ($5,000) see Bright Charitable Trust, Alexander H.

Sane Education Fund ($17,500) see Cohn Foundation, Herman and Terese

SAR Academy ($18,000) see Bravmann Foundation, Ludwig

Sarah Lawrence College ($100,000) see Cohen Family Foundation, Saul Z. and Amy Scheuer

Sarah Lawrence College ($23,750) see Donnelley Foundation, Gaylord and Dorothy

Sarah Lawrence College — general operating ($25,000) see Griggs and Mary Griggs Burke Foundation, Mary Livingston

Sarah Lawrence College ($25,000) see Horncrest Foundation

Sarah Lawrence College ($100,000) see Olin Foundation, F. W.

Sarah Lawrence College — endowment fund ($10,000) see Smith Family Foundation, Theda Clark

Sarah Lawrence College ($2,000) see Stroud Foundation

Sarah Lawrence College ($100,000) see Thalheimer Foundation, Alvin and Fanny Blaustein

Sarah Lawrence College ($25,000) see Woodland Foundation

Sarah Lawrence College ($6,000) see Woodland Foundation

Saratoga Hospital Foundation ($500) see Firan Foundation

Saratoga Hospital Foundation ($100,000) see Greentree Foundation

Saratoga Performing Arts Center ($58,060) see Dobson Foundation

Saratoga Performing Arts Center — to support endowment and operating funds ($6,750) see Wahlstrom Foundation

Satya Narayah Mandir ($50,000) see Watumull Fund, J.

Save the Children see Asgrow Seed Co.

Save the Children ($749) see Contempo Communications

Save the Children see Oppenheimer Management Corp.

Save the Children see Pro-line Corp.

Save the Children ($1,176) see Spiro Foundation, Donald W.

Save the Children ($43,968) see TJX Cos.

Save the Children ($39,552) see TJX Cos.

SCAN New York — general support for a community-sponsored recreational, cultural, and educational facility in the South Bronx ($35,000) see New York Foundation

SCAN New York Volunteer Parent Aides Association ($27,174) see Uris Brothers Foundation

Scarsdale Council of Parent/Teacher Association ($1,176) see Cohn Foundation, Herman and Terese

Scarsdale School District ($31,550) see Liz Claiborne

Schenectady Museum Association ($25,000) see Schaffer Foundation, H.

Scholarship Program ($1,701) see Leucadia National Corp.

Scholarship and Welfare Fund of New Alumni Association ($25,000) see Goodman Memorial Foundation, Joseph C. and Clare F.

Schomburg Center ($100,000) see Avon Products

School of American Ballet ($8,500) see Levin Foundation, Philip and Janice

School of American Ballet ($100,000) see Pincus Family Fund

School of Living ($7,500) see Paul and C. Michael Paul Foundation, Josephine Bay

Schweinfurth Memorial Center ($3,000) see Everett Charitable Trust

Scientists' Institute for Public Information ($75,000) see Klingenstein Fund, Esther A. and Joseph

Scotia-Glenville Central Schools ($20,000) see Golub Corp.

Sdei Chemed Children's Village ($265,000) see Davis Foundation, Simon and Annie

Seamen's Church Institute of New York and New Jersey ($60,000) see Goldman Foundation, Herman

Second Stage ($75,000) see Greve Foundation, William and Mary

Seeing Eye ($10,000) see Steinbach Fund, Ruth and Milton

Self Help Community Services ($65,000) see Model Foundation, Leo

Seneca Center ($10,000) see Chazen Foundation

Seneca Falls Historical Society ($7,500) see Delavan Foundation, Nelson B.

Seneca Neighborhood Center ($5,000) see Kennedy Foundation, Ethel

Seneca Neighborhood Center ($2,000) see Perley Fund, Victor E.

Seneca Park Zoo Society ($70,000) see Gleason Memorial Fund

Seneca Zoological Society — staff position ($30,000) see Wilson Foundation, Elaine P. and Richard U.

Senior Citizens Center of Schenectady County ($50,000) see Schaffer Foundation, H.

Seniors Resource Center ($4,000) see Paul and C. Michael Paul Foundation, Josephine Bay

Sephardic Bikur Cholim ($13,000) see N've Shalom Foundation

Sephardic Bikur Holim ($10,000) see Parthenon Sportswear

Sephardic Bikur Holim & Maozlaebyon ($6,000) see Gindi Associates Foundation

Sephardic Home for the Aged ($50) see Amdur Braude Riley, Inc.

Sephardic Home for the Aged ($2,400) see Russ Togs

Sephardic Home for the Aged ($5,000) see Zacharia Foundation, Isaac Herman

Sephardic Mikvah Israel ($15,000) see Bag Bazaar, Ltd.

Sephardic Temple ($3,075) see United Togs Inc.

Sephardic Temple ($5,500) see Zacharia Foundation, Isaac Herman

Servants of Relief for Incurable Cancer ($22,500) see Lee Foundation, James T.

Servants for Relief for Incurable Cancer ($15,000) see Wasily Family Foundation

Seton Foundation for Learning — the second installment of a three for one challenge grant ($100,000) see Calder Foundation, Louis

Seton Foundation for Learning — to help build an endowment for this model educational program for mildly retarded and/or learning disabled children ($100,000) see Altman Foundation

Seton Hall Preparatory School ($10,000) see Clark Family Charitable Trust, Andrew L.

Seton Hall University ($10,000) see Clark Family Charitable Trust, Andrew L.

Settlement Housing Fund ($100,000) see Reicher Foundation, Anne & Harry J.

Seventh Avenue Windsor Place Community Association — to support the operations of a community hotline ($5,000) see Washington Square Fund

77th Avenue/Windsor Place Community Association of Brooklyn ($1,000) see Adams Memorial Fund, Emma J.

Shaare Zion Congregation ($11,120) see Bag Bazaar, Ltd.

Shaarei Torah Institute of Rockland ($7,000) see Lowenstein Foundation, William P. and Marie R.

Shaarey Zedeck Synagogue ($750) see Zacharia Foundation, Isaac Herman

Shafer Nadec Trust ($5,000) see Fuchsberg Family Foundation, Abraham

Shakespeare Globe Center ($60,000) see Hanson Testamentary Charitable Trust, Anna Emery

Sharon Hospital Foundation ($150,000) see Delacorte Fund, George

Shea's Buffalo Center for the Performing Arts — market development ($13,000) see Western New York Foundation

Shechen Tennyi Vargneling ($10,000) see Sacharuna Foundation

Sheltering Arms Children's Service ($5,000) see Roche Relief Foundation, Edward and Ellen

Sheltering Arms Children's Service ($25,000) see Thanksgiving Foundation

Shephardic Community ($5,200) see Sutton Foundation

Sherrae Torah High School ($10,000) see Sutton Foundation

Shetilei Zetim ($5,200) see Sutton Foundation

Shirak Foundation ($30,000) see Mardigian Foundation

Shorefront YMHA/YWHA of Brighton/Manhattan Beach ($15,000) see de Hirsch Fund, Baron

Shuba Israel ($20,000) see Bag Bazaar, Ltd.

Sid Jacobson North Shore YMHA and YWHA ($7,600) see United Togs Inc.

Sid Jacobson North Shore YWCA ($10,000) see Spingold Foundation, Nate B. and Frances

Siena College ($25,000) see Dewar Foundation

Siena College ($16,500) see Fleet Bank of New York

Siena College ($50,000) see Schaffer Foundation, H.

Siena College ($10,000) see Warren and Beatrice W. Blanding Foundation, Riley J. and Lillian N.

Sienna Foundation ($50,000) see East Foundation, Sarita Kenedy

Sigmund Freud Archives ($90,000) see New-Land Foundation

Sigmund Freud Archives ($50,000) see New-Land Foundation

Sigmund Freud Archives ($40,000) see New-Land Foundation

Sigmund Freud Archives ($40,000) see New-Land Foundation

Sinai Academy ($24,000) see AVI CHAI - A Philanthropic Foundation

Sinai Heritage Fund ($5,000) see Associated Food Stores

Sinai Special Needs Institute ($20,000) see Lawrence Foundation, Alice

Single Parent Resource Center ($2,500) see Fuchsberg Family Foundation

Sisters of Mercy ($2,000) see Kasal Charitable Trust, Father

Sisters of St. Joseph ($1,000) see Loeb Partners Corp.

SKI Hematopoietic Cell Kinetics ($25,000) see Bostwick Foundation, Albert C.

Skidmore College ($5,000) see Baldwin Foundation, David M. and Barbara

Skidmore College ($132,000) see Filene Foundation, Lincoln and Therese

Skidmore College ($6,000) see Jephson Educational Trust No. 1

Skidmore College ($5,000) see Kopf Foundation

Skidmore College ($45,000) see Ladd Charitable Corporation, Helen and George

Skidmore College ($2,000) see Psychists

Skidmore College — parents fund, alumni fund, and riding program ($15,000) see Freed Foundation

Skin Cancer Foundation — continuing funding for research into vaccine to prevent malignant melanoma ($60,000) see Badgeley Residuary Charitable Trust, Rose M.

Skin Disease Society ($85,000) see Archbold Charitable Trust, Adrian and Jessie

Skowhegan School of Painting and Sculpture ($15,000) see Firestone Foundation, Roger S.

Skowhegan School of Painting and Sculpture ($30,000) see L and L Foundation

Skowhegan School of Painting and Sculpture ($16,000) see Piankova Foundation, Tatiana

Skowhegan School of Painting and Sculpture ($63,000) see Simon Charitable Trust, Esther

Sloan-Kettering Institute for Cancer Research ($10,000) see Olin Charitable Trust, John M.

Social Science Research Council — for program of dissertation fellowships for foreign area research ($2,500,000) see Mellon Foundation, Andrew W.

Social Science Research Council — for interdisciplinary research on the underclass ($500,000) see Rockefeller Foundation

Social Science Research Council — "Neighborhood and Family Influences on the Development of Poor Urban Children and Adolescents" ($190,290) see Sage Foundation, Russell

Social Science Research Council — provide support for the SSRC/ACLS predissertation fellowship program ($2,187,410) see Ford Foundation

Society of the Holy Child Jesus ($175,000) see McShain Charities, John

Society of Memorial Sloan-Kettering Cancer Center ($50,000) see Perkin Fund

Society of Memorial Sloan-Kettering Crisis Center ($2,500) see Ritter Foundation, May Ellen and Gerald

Society of the New York Hospital ($25,000) see Sprague Educational and Charitable Foundation, Seth

Society of the New York Hospital ($20,000) see Sprague Educational and Charitable Foundation, Seth

Society for the Preservation of Long Island Antiquities ($5,000) see Schiff Foundation

Society for the Prevention of Cruelty to Animals ($8,000) see Turner Fund, Ruth

Society for the Promotion of Jewish Education ($50,000) see Jesselson Foundation

Society for the Propagation of Faith ($2,000) see Gavin Foundation, James and Zita

Society for the Propagation of Faith ($15,000) see Joyce Foundation, John M. and Mary A.

Society for the Propagation of Faith ($175,000) see Morania Foundation

Society for the Propagation of the Faith — funds to be used

for the education of seminarians in Africa and Asia ($200,000) see Koch Foundation

Society of the Propogation of Faith ($3,400) see Bozzone Family Foundation

Solaris Dance Theatre ($4,000) see Truland Foundation

Solid Waste Management Foundation ($277,400) see Dart Foundation

Solomon Guggenheim Museum ($50,000) see Sharp Foundation, Evelyn

Solomon R. Guggenheim Foundation — contribution for Guggenheim Museum expansion ($100,000) see Guggenheim Foundation, Harry Frank

Solomon R. Guggenheim Museum — international directors council ($25,000) see Cox Foundation

Solomon R. Guggenheim Museum ($2,500) see Fuller Foundation

Solomon R. Guggenheim Museum ($100,000) see Saul Foundation, Joseph E. & Norma G.

Solomon R. Guggenheim Museum ($108,000) see Sharp Foundation

Solomon R. Guggenheim Museum ($25,000) see Terner Foundation

Solomon Schechter School ($7,500) see Beren Foundation, Robert M.

Solomon Schechter School ($8,000) see Fuchsberg Family Foundation

SOS Shelter ($10,000) see Truman Foundation, Mildred Faulkner

South Bronx 2000 ($60,000) see Rhodebeck Charitable Trust

South Bronx 2000 — to fund the stabilization and expansion of environmental and housing enterprises ($225,000) see Surdna Foundation

South Bronx 2000 Local Development ($2,000) see Candlesticks Inc.

South Bronx 2000 Local Development ($20,000) see Penney Foundation, James C.

South Bronx 2000 Local Development ($200) see Spiritus Gladius Foundation

South Bronx 2000 Local Development Corporation — general support ($20,000) see Taconic Foundation

South Hampton Hospital ($10,000) see Olin Charitable Trust, John M.

South Street Seaport ($309,375) see Aron Charitable Foundation, J.

South Street Seaport Museum ($100,000) see Aron Charitable Foundation, J.

South Street Seaport Museum ($100,000) see Aron Charitable Foundation, J.

South Street Seaport Museum ($100,000) see Aron Charitable Foundation, J.

South Street Seaport Museum ($79,082) see Aron Charitable Foundation, J.

South Street Seaport Museum ($10,000) see Day Family Foundation

South Street Seaport Museum ($100,000) see Macy, Jr. Foundation, Josiah

South Street Seaport Museum ($11,250) see Prudential-Bache Securities

South Street Seaport Museum — annual operations ($225,000) see Timken Foundation of Canton

Southampton Hospital ($12,500) see Fanwood Foundation

Southampton Hospital ($2,250) see Iroquois Avenue Foundation

Southampton Hospital ($8,000) see L and L Foundation

Southampton Hospital ($8,000) see Warner Fund, Albert and Bessie

Southern Educational Communications Association — support for firing line ($35,000) see Laurel Foundation

Southern Tier Community Food Bank ($1,000) see Hilliard Corp.

Southside Hospital ($6,000) see Read Foundation, Charles L.

Southside United Housing Development Fund Corporation (Los Sures) ($55,000) see Bankers Trust Co.

Spanish Institute — for art ($15,000) see Mapplethorpe Foundation, Robert

SPCA ($10,000) see Baird Foundation

SPCA ($10,000) see Goodyear Foundation, Josephine

Special Children's Center ($3,750) see Howell Foundation, Eric and Jessie

Special Needs Center ($50,000) see Noble Charitable Trust, John L. and Ethel G.

Special Olympics see Marubeni America Corp.

Speech and Hearing Institute of International Center for the Disabled ($25,000) see Nias Foundation, Henry

Spence-Chapin Services to Family and Children ($25,000) see Boisi Family Foundation

Spence-Chapin Services to Family and Children ($8,000) see Stony Wold Herbert Fund

Spence School ($68,000) see Bachmann Foundation

Spence School ($2,000) see Hobbs Charitable Trust, John H.

Stanley Issacs Neighborhood ($5,000) see Perley Fund, Victor E.

Starlight Foundation see Best Western International

State Communities Aid Association ($60,000) see Weezie Foundation

State of New York ($15,097) see Gund Foundation

State University of Buffalo ($100,000) see Burchfield Foundation, Charles E.

State University of Leiden ($50,000) see Lounsbery Foundation, Richard

State University of New York ($10,000) see Mark IV Industries

State University of New York ($20,000) see Sinsheimer Fund, Alexandrine and Alexander L.

State University of New York ($20,000) see Sinsheimer Fund, Alexandrine and Alexander L.

State University of New York — genetic analysis of developmental plasticity in

insects ($46,003) see Whitehall Foundation

State University of New York-Binghamton (Jewish Studies) ($15,000) see Littauer Foundation, Lucius N.

State University of New York-Binghamton — Undergraduate Biological Sciences Education Program ($1,500,000) see Hughes Medical Institute, Howard

State University of New York-Buffalo ($92,500) see Burroughs Wellcome Co.

State University of New York College of Environmental Science and Forestry ($32,553) see Sussman Fund, Edna Bailey

State University of New York — effect of glucose-related changes in hypothalamic GABAergic Activity on feeding behavior ($42,902) see Whitehall Foundation

State University of New York Health Science Center — eye research ($20,000) see Allyn Foundation

State University of New York Purchase ($14,098) see Harkness Foundation, William Hale

State University of New York at Purchase — for capital campaign see Melville Corp.

State University of New York Research Foundation ($35,000) see Foster-Davis Foundation

State University of New York Research Foundation ($10,000) see Pritchard Charitable Trust, William E. and Maude S.

State University of New York School of Management ($5,000) see Straus Foundation, Martha Washington Straus and Harry H.

State University of New York at Stony Brook ($15,000) see Weight Watchers International

Steele Memorial Library ($20,000) see Anderson Foundation

Stella and Charles Guttman Breast Diagnostic Institute ($25,000) see Guttman Foundation, Stella and Charles

Stella Niagara — hearing loop ($5,100) see Joy Family Foundation

Stephen Wise Free Synagogue ($50,000) see Reicher Foundation, Anne & Harry J.

Stonwin Medical Conference ($47,805) see Winston Research Foundation, Harry

Stony Brook Foundation-State University of New York ($90,000) see Rosenbaum Foundation, Paul and Gabriella

Stony Brook School ($10,000) see Mack Foundation, J. S.

Stony Brook University Foundation ($25,000) see Rosenberg Foundation, Sunny and Abe

Storm King Art Center ($15,000) see Hazen Charitable Trust, Lita Annenberg

Storm King Art Center ($3,000) see Loewenberg Foundation

Storm King Art Center ($919,841) see Ogden Foundation, Ralph E.

Storm King School ($15,000) see Ogden Foundation, Ralph E.

Strang Cancer Prevention Center-James E. Olson Fund ($200,000) see American Telephone & Telegraph Co.

Strang Clinic ($13,000) see Chait Memorial Foundation, Sara

Strong Memorial Hospital ($100,000) see Pluta Family Foundation

Strong Museum ($1,000) see Bausch & Lomb

Student Sponsor Partnership ($5,000) see Allen Foundation, Frances

Student/Sponsor Partnership ($9,230) see Goldman Sachs & Co.

Studio in School ($10,000) see Gund Foundation, Geoffrey

Studio in a School ($50,000) see Warhol Foundation for the Visual Arts, Andy

Studio in a School Association ($50,000) see Atlantic Foundation of New York

Studio in a School Association ($37,200) see Greve Foundation, William and Mary

Studio in a School Association — toward establishment of program in an additional school ($25,000) see Morris Foundation, Margaret T.

Study Hall at Emmaus House ($25,000) see Howell Fund

Suburban Adult Services — support for public information program ($2,500) see Fisher Foundation

Summit Speech School ($25,000) see Levy Foundation, Betty and Norman F.

Sunnyside Community Services ($15,000) see Snyder Fund, Valentine Perry

Surdna Foundation/CCRP-Multi Funders Account ($75,000) see Uris Brothers Foundation

Surprise Lake Camp ($40,000) see Kaufmann Foundation, Henry

Susquehana Society for the Prevention of Cruelty to Animals ($100,000) see Gronewaldt Foundation, Alice Busch

Sutton Place Synagogue ($18,000) see Kaplan Foundation, Rita J. and Stanley H.

Swedish Home for the Aged ($3,500) see Faith Home Foundation

Sy Symm School of Business ($25,000) see Phillips-Van Heusen Corp.

Syracuse Cancer Research Institute ($15,000) see Fuller Foundation

Syracuse Cancer Research Institute ($10,000) see Stein Foundation, Joseph F.

Syracuse Opera ($6,500) see Mather Fund, Richard

Syracuse Pulp and Paper Foundation ($4,000) see Central National-Gottesman

Syracuse Salvation Army — building fund ($10,000) see Allyn Foundation

Syracuse Stage ($750) see De Lima Co., Paul

Syracuse Stage ($5,000) see Mather Fund, Richard

Syracuse Symphony Orchestra ($25,000) see Mather Fund, Richard

Syracuse University ($10,000) see Allyn Foundation

New York (cont.)

Syracuse University ($1,000) see American Optical Corp.

Syracuse University ($5,000) see Cove Charitable Trust

Syracuse University ($3,000) see De Lima Co., Paul

Syracuse University ($2,000) see De Lima Co., Paul

Syracuse University ($50,000) see Gifford Charitable Corporation, Rosamond

Syracuse University ($533,000) see Goldstein Foundation, Alfred and Ann

Syracuse University ($4,000) see Guttag Foundation, Irwin and Marjorie

Syracuse University ($2,000) see Klipstein Foundation, Ernest Christian

Syracuse University ($50,000) see Lender Family Foundation

Syracuse University ($5,000) see Martin Family Fund

Syracuse University ($125,000) see Mead Foundation, Giles W. and Elise G.

Syracuse University ($60,000) see Nason Foundation

Syracuse University ($250,000) see Newhouse Foundation, Samuel I.

Syracuse University ($15,000) see Snow Foundation, John Ben

Syracuse University ($15,000) see Snow Foundation, John Ben

Syracuse University ($15,000) see Snow Foundation, John Ben

Syracuse University ($395) see Soling Family Foundation

Syracuse University — to endow the Remembrance Scholarships ($75,000) see Scholl Foundation, Dr.

Syracuse University Society of Fellows ($5,000) see Menschel Foundation, Robert and Joyce

Tabor Academy ($10,000) see Fireman Charitable Foundation, Paul and Phyllis

Tabor Academy ($5,000) see O'Neil Foundation, Cyril F. and Marie E.

Talmud Torah Bnei Shimon Yisadel ($10,800) see Hudson Neckwear

Talmudic College ($25,860) see Applebaum Foundation

Tchaikovsky Chamber Orchestra ($10,000) see Ferkauf Foundation, Eugene and Estelle

Tcherepin Society ($1,000) see Loeb Partners Corp.

Teach for America ($300,000) see BellSouth Corp.

Teach for America ($75,000) see General Atlantic Partners L.P.

Teach for America — for operating support and curriculum development ($750,000) see Knight Foundation, John S. and James L.

Teach for America ($50,000) see O'Donnell Foundation

Teach for America — general support ($100,000) see Reed Foundation, Philip A.

Teach for America ($50,000) see Union Carbide Corp.

Teach for America — to support the expansion of the New York City program of placing new corps members in the public schools to teach in

under-resourced urban and rural schools ($50,000) see Cummings Memorial Fund Trust, Frances L. and Edwin L.

Teach for America — to fund national teacher recruitment, training and placement program ($200,000) see Toyota Motor Sales, U.S.A.

Teach for America — to fund national teacher recruitment, training and placement program ($100,000) see Toyota Motor Sales, U.S.A.

Teachers College ($36,000) see Gottesman Fund

Teachers College, J.L. Weinberg Fellowship ($25,000) see Weinberg Foundation, John L.

Teachers and Writers Collaborative ($75,000) see Steele-Reese Foundation

Teamwork Foundation ($50,000) see Revlon

Tel Aviv Foundation ($5,000) see Morris Foundation, Norman M.

Temple Beth Adovah ($1,380) see Fireman Charitable Foundation, Paul and Phyllis

Temple Beth Am ($1,500) see Contempo Communications

Temple Beth El ($1,610) see Abraham Foundation

Temple Beth-El ($15,000) see Cohen Foundation, Wilfred P.

Temple Beth El ($6,100) see Greene Foundation, David J.

Temple Beth-El ($20,000) see Spiegel Family Foundation, Jerry and Emily

Temple Beth El of Great Neck ($42,686) see Bass and Edythe and Sol G. Atlas Fund, Sandra Atlas

Temple Beth Elohim ($2,000) see Fireman Charitable Foundation, Paul and Phyllis

Temple Beth Shalom ($3,000) see Kepco, Inc.

Temple Beth Shalom ($1,000) see Weinstein Foundation, J.

Temple B'nai B'rith ($2,900) see Daniel Foundation, Gerard and Ruth

Temple B'nai Shalom ($128,000) see Mendel Foundation

Temple Emanu-El ($22,000) see Alperin/Hirsch Family Foundation

Temple Emanu-El ($50,000) see Chapin Foundation of Myrtle Beach, South Carolina

Temple Emanu-el ($12,100) see Friedland Family Foundation, Samuel

Temple Emanu-El ($50,000) see Zarkin Memorial Foundation, Charles

Temple Emanuel ($4,250) see Mazer Foundation, Jacob and Ruth

Temple Gates of Heaven ($100,000) see Schaffer Foundation, H.

Temple Israel ($12,450) see Guttag Foundation, Irwin and Marjorie

Temple Israel ($50,000) see Milstein Family Foundation

Temple Israel Center ($10,368) see Stein Foundation, Joseph F.

Temple Israel of Great Neck ($10,000) see Slant/Fin Corp.

Temple Shalom ($150) see Contempo Communications

Temple Sharay Tefola ($10,000) see Altschul Foundation

Temple Sholom ($2,170) see Morris Foundation, Norman M.

Temple Sholom ($4,256) see Spiegel Family Foundation, Jerry and Emily

Temple of Understanding ($10,000) see Connemara Fund

Theater for the New City Foundation ($50,000) see Vidda Foundation

Theatre at Storm King ($37,500) see Hoffman Foundation, Marion O. and Maximilian

Third Church of Christ ($22,500) see Culver Foundation, Constans

Thirteen ($25,000) see Thorne Foundation

Thirteen ($600) see United Togs Inc.

Threshold Center for Alternative Youth Service ($12,500) see Mulligan Charitable Trust, Mary S.

Thresholds ($25,000) see Stern Foundation, Irvin

Tibet Fund ($35,000) see New Cycle Foundation

Tibet Fund ($40,000) see Sacharuna Foundation

Tikva Layeled ($180) see Melohn Foundation

Tioga County Squad Captains Association ($10,513) see Truman Foundation, Mildred Faulkner

Tioga County Squad Captains Association ($10,303) see Truman Foundation, Mildred Faulkner

Tioga Opportunities Program ($15,346) see Truman Foundation, Mildred Faulkner

Tisch Hospital ($2,000,000) see Tisch Foundation

Tisch School of the Arts of New York University ($12,000) see Wyne Foundation

Tomchei Torah Institute ($25,000) see Newbrook Charitable Foundation

Tomchei Torah Institute ($10,000) see Newbrook Charitable Foundation

Tompkins Wetland Community ($10,000) see Truman Foundation, Mildred Faulkner

Tora Temiman ($50,000) see Bag Bazaar, Ltd.

Torah Academy for Girls ($25,000) see Fogel Foundation, Shalom and Rebecca

Torah Education in Israel ($4,000) see Wouk Foundation, Abe

Torah Institute ($85,000) see Morgenstern Foundation, Morris

Torah or Seminart ($5,000) see Lowenstein Foundation, William P. and Marie R.

Torah Umesorah ($53,000) see AVI CHAI - A Philanthropic Foundation

Toras Emes Hebrew Academy ($22,000) see Friedman Brothers Foundation

Tourette Syndrome Association ($1,000) see Goldman Charitable Trust, Sol

Tourette Syndrome Association — in support of the permanent research fund ($15,000) see Kieckhefer Foundation, J. W.

Town Club Foundation ($2,100) see Nelco Sewing Machine Sales Corp.

Town Club Foundation ($5,400) see Rosenberg Foundation, Sunny and Abe

Town Club Foundation ($12,000) see Wouk Foundation, Abe

Town and Village Synagogue ($4,000) see Davis Foundation, Simon and Annie

Townsend Harris Alumni Association ($20,000) see Nias Foundation, Henry

TRAILS ($20,000) see Hoffman Foundation, Marion O. and Maximilian

Transactional Records Access Clearinghouse ($30,000) see Deer Creek Foundation

Tri-Cities Opera ($50,000) see Hoyt Foundation, Stewart W. and Willma C.

Tri-County United Way ($21,861) see Bard, C. R.

Tri-Valley YMCA ($73,333) see Chapman Charitable Corporation, Howard and Bess

Trickle Up Program ($32,000) see Joselow Foundation

Trinity Episcopal Church ($3,500) see Belmont Metals

Trinity Fund ($5,000) see Obernauer Foundation

Trinity Memorial Church ($22,500) see Klee Foundation, Conrad and Virginia

Trinity Parish ($5,000) see Sasco Foundation

Trocaire College — computers ($20,000) see Palisano Foundation, Vincent and Harriet

Trotting Horse Museum ($9,000) see Sheppard Foundation, Lawrence B.

Troy Rehabilitation and Improvement Program ($50,000) see Howard and Bush Foundation

Troy Rehabilitation and Improvement Program — for benefit of bridge coalition ($30,711) see Howard and Bush Foundation

Trudeau Institute ($75,000) see Donaldson Charitable Trust, Oliver S. and Jennie R.

Trudeau Institute ($10,000) see Richardson Charitable Trust, Anne S.

Trumansburg Conservatory of Fine Arts ($6,000) see Delavan Foundation, Nelson B.

Trust and Agency Fund Hancock Central School ($23,000) see Read Foundation, Charles L.

Trust for Public Land — open space ($250,000) see Bullitt Foundation

Trust for Public Land see Oki America Inc.

Trust for Public Land — establishment of permanent community open space in conjunction with housing projects in the South Bronx ($20,000) see New York Foundation

Trustees of Columbia University in the City of New York ($150,000) see Ames Charitable Trust, Harriett

Trustees of Columbia University in the City of New York ($25,000) see Hall Charitable Trust, Evelyn A. J.

Trustees of Columbia University in the City of New York Columbia University Community Services-The Rio — for social and mental-health services to formerly homeless families in residence at The Rio in Washington Heights ($53,689) see van Ameringen Foundation

Trustees of Columbia University — support activities

designated to bring Portuguese and Brazilian issues to the attention of the public ($50,000) see Tinker Foundation

Trustees of the Estate ($15,750) see Clark Charitable Trust, Frank E.

Tuftonboro Free Library Building Fund ($85,000) see Hamel Family Charitable Trust, D. A.

Turtle Bay Music School ($100,000) see Gordon/Rousmaniere/Roberts Fund

Tuxedo Park School — Capital Campaign ($150,000) see Harriman Foundation, Gladys and Roland

U. A. P. C. ($10,000) see Kingston Foundation

U. A. R. C. ($15,000) see Kingston Foundation

U. C. C. C. ($15,000) see Kingston Foundation

U.S.O. of Metropolitan New York ($5,000) see Piankova Foundation, Tatiana

UAHC ($4,000) see Roth Family Foundation

UNA of the USA ($234,000) see Ross Foundation, Arthur

Under One Roof ($10,000) see Sheafer Charitable Trust, Emma A.

UNICEF ($200) see Gross Foundation, Louis H.

UNICEF ($1,000) see Matthews International Corp.

UNICEF ($25,000) see Schaffer Foundation, Michael & Helen

Union of American Hebrew Congregations ($5,000) see Bronstein Foundation, Sol and Arlene

Union College ($10,500) see Vanneck-Bailey Foundation

Union College Annual Fund ($10,000) see Yulman Trust, Morton and Helen

Union College — restore/renovate gymnasium ($250,000) see Herrick Foundation

Union of Orthodox Jewish Congregation ($100,000) see El-An Foundation

Union of Orthodox Jewish Congregations of America/Orthodox Congregation ($5,972) see Stern Family Foundation, Harry

Union Settlement Association — special project ($57,600) see New York Life Insurance Co.

Union Settlement Association ($20,000) see Snyder Fund, Valentine Perry

Union Theological Seminary ($35,000) see Hagedorn Fund

Union Theological Seminary — renovation of Hastings Hall ($250,000) see Fairchild Foundation, Sherman

United Arts Fund of Mohawk Valley ($3,500) see Utica National Insurance Group

United Bobov International ($150,000) see Kest Family Foundation, Sol and Clara

United Cerebral Palsy Association ($36,200) see Belding Heminway Co.

United Cerebral Palsy Association ($5,000) see Bradford & Co., J.C.

United Cerebral Palsy Association ($4,000) see Broad Foundation, Shepard

United Cerebral Palsy Association ($25,000) see Broccoli Charitable Foundation, Dana and Albert R.

United Cerebral Palsy Association ($2,000) see Central National-Gottesman

United Cerebral Palsy Association ($30,000) see Cohen Foundation, Wilfred P.

United Cerebral Palsy Association ($1,500) see Delacorte Fund, George

United Cerebral Palsy Association ($7,500) see Feil Foundation, Louis and Gertrude

United Cerebral Palsy Association ($20,000) see Goodman Memorial Foundation, Joseph C. and Clare F.

United Cerebral Palsy Association ($10,000) see Greene Foundation, David J.

United Cerebral Palsy Association ($4,000) see Greene Foundation, Robert Z.

United Cerebral Palsy Association ($15,919) see I. and L. Association

United Cerebral Palsy Association ($6,000) see Key Food Stores Cooperative Inc.

United Cerebral Palsy Association ($100,000) see Life Investors Insurance Company of America

United Cerebral Palsy Association ($150,000) see Lindner Foundation, Fay J.

United Cerebral Palsy Association ($1,500) see Morris Foundation, Norman M.

United Cerebral Palsy Association ($7,300) see Oestreicher Foundation, Sylvan and Ann

United Cerebral Palsy Association ($54,000) see Rudin Foundation

United Cerebral Palsy Association ($10,000) see Ruffin Foundation, Peter B. & Adeline W.

United Cerebral Palsy Association of Nassau County ($10,200) see Belding Heminway Co.

United Cerebral Palsy of New York City ($70,000) see Ames Charitable Trust, Harriet

United Church of Christ — project support ($20,000) see Warsh-Mott Legacy

United Community Services of Chemung County ($5,000) see Anderson Foundation

United Fund ($12,000) see Cranston Print Works

United Health Services ($12,500) see Dickenson Foundation, Harriet Ford

United Health Services ($750,000) see Hartford Foundation, John A.

United Health Services ($50,000) see Klee Foundation, Conrad and Virginia

United Health Services ($20,000) see Truman Foundation, Mildred Faulkner

United Hebrew Geriatric Center ($5,000) see Kramer Foundation

United Help ($50,000) see Forchheimer Foundation

United Hospital ($5,000) see Fischbach Foundation

United Hospital Fund — first payment of $150,000 grant for the Primary Care Development Program ($75,000) see J.P. Morgan & Co.

United Hospital of Portchester ($50,150) see Adler Foundation

United Hospital of Portchester ($1,000) see Central National-Gottesman

United Hospital of Portchester ($8,000) see Statter Foundation, Amy Plant

United Hospital of Portchester ($2,000) see United Merchants & Manufacturers

United Jewish Appeal ($400,000) see Fisher Brothers

United Jewish Appeal ($100,000) see Resnick Foundation, Jack and Pearl

United Jewish Appeal ($1,200,000) see Revlon

United Jewish Appeal ($10,000) see Silverburgh Foundation, Grace, George & Judith

United Jewish Appeal ($50,000) see Weinberg Foundation, John L.

United Jewish Appeal Federation ($710,000) see Abrons Foundation, Louis and Anne

United Jewish Appeal Federation ($25,000) see Belding Heminway Co.

United Jewish Appeal Federation ($36,000) see Belfer Foundation

United Jewish Appeal Federation ($40,000) see Bernstein & Co., Sanford C.

United Jewish Appeal Federation ($50,000) see Chanin Family Foundation, Paul R.

United Jewish Appeal Federation ($33,000) see Cranston Print Works

United Jewish Appeal Federation ($130,000) see Essel Foundation

United Jewish Appeal Federation ($20,000) see Essel Foundation

United Jewish Appeal Federation ($50,000) see Fairchild Corp.

United Jewish Appeal Federation ($50,000) see Forbes

United Jewish Appeal Federation ($10,000) see Geffen Foundation, David

United Jewish Appeal Federation ($51,500) see Glickenhaus & Co.

United Jewish Appeal Federation ($60,000) see Jurodin Fund

United Jewish Appeal Federation ($25,000) see Kaplan Foundation, Rita J. and Stanley H.

United Jewish Appeal Federation ($70,000) see Klau Foundation, David W. and Sadie

United Jewish Appeal Federation ($175,000) see Leviton Manufacturing Co.

United Jewish Appeal Federation ($100,000) see Leviton Manufacturing Co.

United Jewish Appeal Federation ($50,000) see Leviton Manufacturing Co.

United Jewish Appeal Federation ($625,000) see Loews Corp.

United Jewish Appeal Federation ($814,100) see Rosenwald Family Fund, William

United Jewish Appeal Federation ($150,000) see Schwartz Foundation, David

United Jewish Appeal Federation — fund for programs for the aged ($1,862,500) see

Silverman Foundation, Marty and Dorothy

United Jewish Appeal Federation ($20,080) see Taub Foundation, Henry and Marilyn

United Jewish Appeal Federation ($628,413) see Tisch Foundation

United Jewish Appeal Federation ($110,000) see Witco Corp.

United Jewish Appeal Federation Campaign ($333,667) see Seagram & Sons, Joseph E.

United Jewish Appeal Federation of Jewish Philanthropies ($5,000) see Abeles Foundation, Joseph and Sophia

United Jewish Appeal Federation of Jewish Philanthropies ($35,000) see Alperin/Hirsch Family Foundation

United Jewish Appeal Federation of Jewish Philanthropies ($25,000) see Altschul Foundation

United Jewish Appeal Federation of Jewish Philanthropies ($50,000) see Amsterdam Foundation, Jack and Mimi Leviton

United Jewish Appeal Federation of Jewish Philanthropies ($15,000) see Associated Food Stores

United Jewish Appeal Federation of Jewish Philanthropies ($55,500) see Bachmann Foundation

United Jewish Appeal Federation of Jewish Philanthropies ($25,000) see Badgeley Residuary Charitable Trust, Rose M.

United Jewish Appeal Federation of Jewish Philanthropies ($15,000) see Bank of Louisville

United Jewish Appeal Federation of Jewish Philanthropies ($12,500) see Beir Foundation

United Jewish Appeal Federation of Jewish Philanthropies ($20,000) see Beren Foundation, Robert M.

United Jewish Appeal Federation of Jewish Philanthropies ($25,000) see Bleibtreu Foundation, Jacob

United Jewish Appeal Federation of Jewish Philanthropies ($301,000) see Botwinick-Wolfensohn Foundation

United Jewish Appeal Federation of Jewish Philanthropies ($74,000) see Bravmann Foundation, Ludwig

United Jewish Appeal Federation of Jewish Philanthropies ($50,000) see Bravmann Foundation, Ludwig

United Jewish Appeal Federation of Jewish Philanthropies ($15,000) see Bravmann Foundation, Ludwig

United Jewish Appeal Federation of Jewish Philanthropies ($55,000) see Brenner Foundation

United Jewish Appeal Federation of Jewish Philanthropies ($15,000) see Brody Foundation, Frances

United Jewish Appeal Federation of Jewish Philanthropies ($11,800) see Brody Foundation, Frances

United Jewish Appeal Federation of Jewish Philanthropies ($50,000) see Burns Foundation, Jacob

United Jewish Appeal Federation of Jewish Philanthropies

($63,000) see Caplan Charity Foundation, Julius H.

United Jewish Appeal Federation of Jewish Philanthropies ($50,000) see Chazen Foundation

United Jewish Appeal Federation of Jewish Philanthropies ($32,500) see Coleman Foundation

United Jewish Appeal Federation of Jewish Philanthropies ($564) see Contempo Communications

United Jewish Appeal Federation of Jewish Philanthropies ($4,000) see Crown Books Foundation, Inc.

United Jewish Appeal Federation of Jewish Philanthropies ($7,200) see Daniel Foundation, Gerard and Ruth

United Jewish Appeal Federation of Jewish Philanthropies ($150,000) see David-Weill Foundation, Michel

United Jewish Appeal Federation of Jewish Philanthropies ($35,000) see Davis Foundation, Simon and Annie

United Jewish Appeal Federation of Jewish Philanthropies ($30,000) see de Hirsch Fund, Baron

United Jewish Appeal Federation of Jewish Philanthropies ($22,500) see de Hirsch Fund, Baron

United Jewish Appeal Federation of Jewish Philanthropies ($10,000) see Dreitzer Foundation

United Jewish Appeal Federation of Jewish Philanthropies ($220,000) see Durst Foundation

United Jewish Appeal Federation of Jewish Philanthropies ($100,000) see Durst Foundation

United Jewish Appeal Federation of Jewish Philanthropies ($10,000) see Eckman Charitable Foundation, Samuel and Rae

United Jewish Appeal Federation of Jewish Philanthropies ($10,018) see Ehrman Foundation, Fred and Susan

United Jewish Appeal Federation of Jewish Philanthropies ($20,000) see EIS Foundation

United Jewish Appeal Federation of Jewish Philanthropies ($33,333) see FAB Industries

United Jewish Appeal Federation of Jewish Philanthropies ($25,000) see Federation Foundation of Greater Philadelphia

United Jewish Appeal Federation of Jewish Philanthropies ($30,000) see Feil Foundation, Louis and Gertrude

United Jewish Appeal Federation of Jewish Philanthropies ($15,000) see Feil Foundation, Louis and Gertrude

United Jewish Appeal Federation of Jewish Philanthropies ($100,250) see Fife Foundation, Elias and Bertha

United Jewish Appeal Federation of Jewish Philanthropies ($10,000) see Fischbach Foundation

United Jewish Appeal Federation of Jewish Philanthropies ($5,000) see Fischbach Foundation

United Jewish Appeal Federation of Jewish Philanthropies

($500,000) see Forchheimer Foundation

United Jewish Appeal Federation of Jewish Philanthropies ($200,000) see Forchheimer Foundation

United Jewish Appeal Federation of Jewish Philanthropies ($22,500) see Frankel Foundation, George and Elizabeth F.

United Jewish Appeal Federation of Jewish Philanthropies ($50,000) see Friedman Foundation, Stephen and Barbara

United Jewish Appeal Federation of Jewish Philanthropies ($35,000) see Friedman Foundation, Stephen and Barbara

United Jewish Appeal Federation of Jewish Philanthropies ($56,000) see Fuchsberg Family Foundation

United Jewish Appeal Federation of Jewish Philanthropies ($50,000) see Fuchsberg Family Foundation

United Jewish Appeal Federation of Jewish Philanthropies ($50,000) see Fuchsberg Family Foundation, Abraham

United Jewish Appeal Federation of Jewish Philanthropies ($66,000) see Geist Foundation

United Jewish Appeal Federation of Jewish Philanthropies ($15,000) see Geist Foundation

United Jewish Appeal Federation of Jewish Philanthropies ($7,500) see Geist Foundation

United Jewish Appeal Federation of Jewish Philanthropies ($5,200) see Geist Foundation

United Jewish Appeal Federation of Jewish Philanthropies ($85,000) see Gindi Associates Foundation

United Jewish Appeal Federation of Jewish Philanthropies ($210,000) see Ginsberg Family Foundation, Moses

United Jewish Appeal Federation of Jewish Philanthropies ($15,000) see Ginsberg Family Foundation, Moses

United Jewish Appeal Federation of Jewish Philanthropies ($2,500) see Goldberg Family Foundation

United Jewish Appeal Federation of Jewish Philanthropies ($7,500) see Goldberger Foundation, Edward and Marjorie

United Jewish Appeal Federation of Jewish Philanthropies ($35,200) see Goldstein Foundation, Leslie and Roslyn

United Jewish Appeal Federation of Jewish Philanthropies ($630,010) see Goodstein Family Foundation, David

United Jewish Appeal Federation of Jewish Philanthropies ($934,590) see Greenberg Foundation, Alan C.

United Jewish Appeal Federation of Jewish Philanthropies ($55,950) see Greene Foundation, David J.

United Jewish Appeal Federation of Jewish Philanthropies ($75,000) see Greene Foundation, Jerome L.

United Jewish Appeal Federation of Jewish Philanthropies ($57,000) see Greene Foundation, Robert Z.

United Jewish Appeal Federation of Jewish Philanthropies

New York (cont.)

($18,100) see Gruber Research Foundation, Lila

United Jewish Appeal Federation of Jewish Philanthropies ($20,000) see Gruss Charitable and Educational Foundation, Oscar and Regina

United Jewish Appeal Federation of Jewish Philanthropies ($40,000) see Guggenheim Foundation, Daniel and Florence

United Jewish Appeal Federation of Jewish Philanthropies ($246,000) see Gurwin Foundation, J.

United Jewish Appeal Federation of Jewish Philanthropies ($39,125) see Guttag Foundation, Irwin and Marjorie

United Jewish Appeal Federation of Jewish Philanthropies ($300,000) see Guttman Foundation, Stella and Charles

United Jewish Appeal Federation of Jewish Philanthropies ($100,000) see Guttman Foundation, Stella and Charles

United Jewish Appeal Federation of Jewish Philanthropies ($13,000) see Hartman Foundation, Jesse and Dorothy

United Jewish Appeal Federation of Jewish Philanthropies ($77,000) see Hassenfeld Foundation

United Jewish Appeal Federation of Jewish Philanthropies ($15,500) see Herman Foundation, John and Rose

United Jewish Appeal Federation of Jewish Philanthropies ($15,000) see Hidary Foundation, Jacob

United Jewish Appeal Federation of Jewish Philanthropies ($35,000) see Hirschl Trust for Charitable Purposes, Irma T.

United Jewish Appeal Federation of Jewish Philanthropies ($70,000) see Holtzmann Foundation, Jacob L. and Lillian

United Jewish Appeal Federation of Jewish Philanthropies ($220,000) see Horowitz Foundation, Gedale B. and Barbara S.

United Jewish Appeal Federation of Jewish Philanthropies ($1,000) see House of Gross

United Jewish Appeal Federation of Jewish Philanthropies ($34,000) see Jaydor Corp.

United Jewish Appeal Federation of Jewish Philanthropies ($50,000) see Kaplen Foundation

United Jewish Appeal Federation of Jewish Philanthropies ($10,000) see Kaplen Foundation

United Jewish Appeal Federation of Jewish Philanthropies ($4,000) see Kepco, Inc.

United Jewish Appeal Federation of Jewish Philanthropies ($69,000) see Key Food Stores Cooperative Inc.

United Jewish Appeal Federation of Jewish Philanthropies ($100,000) see Kimmelman Foundation, Helen & Milton

United Jewish Appeal Federation of Jewish Philanthropies ($8,000) see Klosk Fund, Louis and Rose

United Jewish Appeal Federation of Jewish Philanthropies

($7,000) see Klosk Fund, Louis and Rose

United Jewish Appeal Federation of Jewish Philanthropies ($6,000) see Klosk Fund, Louis and Rose

United Jewish Appeal Federation of Jewish Philanthropies ($300,000) see Kohl Charitable Foundation, Allen D.

United Jewish Appeal Federation of Jewish Philanthropies ($20,000) see Kramer Foundation

United Jewish Appeal Federation of Jewish Philanthropies ($10,000) see Kramer Foundation

United Jewish Appeal Federation of Jewish Philanthropies ($10,000) see Kramer Foundation

United Jewish Appeal Federation of Jewish Philanthropies ($50,000) see Kramer Foundation, C. L. C.

United Jewish Appeal Federation of Jewish Philanthropies ($11,500) see Lasdon Foundation

United Jewish Appeal Federation of Jewish Philanthropies ($77,200) see Lasky Co.

United Jewish Appeal Federation of Jewish Philanthropies ($25,000) see Lasky Co.

United Jewish Appeal Federation of Jewish Philanthropies ($25,000) see Lavanburg-Corner House

United Jewish Appeal Federation of Jewish Philanthropies ($50,000) see Lawrence Foundation, Alice

United Jewish Appeal Federation of Jewish Philanthropies ($15,000) see Lawrence Foundation, Alice

United Jewish Appeal Federation of Jewish Philanthropies ($75,000) see Lazar Foundation

United Jewish Appeal Federation of Jewish Philanthropies ($10,000) see Lazar Foundation

United Jewish Appeal Federation of Jewish Philanthropies ($15,000) see Lazarus Charitable Trust, Helen and Charles

United Jewish Appeal Federation of Jewish Philanthropies ($207,525) see Lemberg Foundation

United Jewish Appeal Federation of Jewish Philanthropies ($9,000) see Leucadia National Corp.

United Jewish Appeal Federation of Jewish Philanthropies ($142,500) see Levin Foundation, Philip and Janice

United Jewish Appeal Federation of Jewish Philanthropies ($26,000) see Levinson Foundation, Morris L.

United Jewish Appeal Federation of Jewish Philanthropies ($100,000) see Levy Foundation, Betty and Norman F.

United Jewish Appeal Federation of Jewish Philanthropies ($10,000) see Liberman Foundation, Bertha & Isaac

United Jewish Appeal Federation of Jewish Philanthropies ($75,000) see Loeb Foundation, Frances and John L.

United Jewish Appeal Federation of Jewish Philanthropies ($50,000) see Loeb Foundation, Frances and John L.

United Jewish Appeal Federation of Jewish Philanthropies ($110,000) see Mailman Foundation

United Jewish Appeal Federation of Jewish Philanthropies ($360) see MalCo Products Inc.

United Jewish Appeal Federation of Jewish Philanthropies ($150,000) see Mendel Foundation

United Jewish Appeal Federation of Jewish Philanthropies ($50,000) see Mercy, Jr. Foundation, Sue and Eugene

United Jewish Appeal Federation of Jewish Philanthropies ($11,000) see Merit Oil Corp.

United Jewish Appeal Federation of Jewish Philanthropies ($25,000) see Miller Fund, Kathryn and Gilbert

United Jewish Appeal Federation of Jewish Philanthropies ($805,000) see Milstein Family Foundation

United Jewish Appeal Federation of Jewish Philanthropies ($75,000) see Mnuchin Foundation

United Jewish Appeal Federation of Jewish Philanthropies ($25,000) see Mnuchin Foundation

United Jewish Appeal Federation of Jewish Philanthropies ($7,800) see Mnuchin Foundation

United Jewish Appeal Federation of Jewish Philanthropies ($123,700) see Morgenstern Foundation, Morris

United Jewish Appeal Federation of Jewish Philanthropies ($8,100) see Morse, Jr. Foundation, Enid and Lester S.

United Jewish Appeal Federation of Jewish Philanthropies ($5,000) see National Metal & Steel

United Jewish Appeal Federation of Jewish Philanthropies ($80,000) see Neu Foundation, Hugo and Doris

United Jewish Appeal Federation of Jewish Philanthropies ($30,000) see Neu Foundation, Hugo and Doris

United Jewish Appeal Federation of Jewish Philanthropies ($11,000) see Neu Foundation, Hugo and Doris

United Jewish Appeal Federation of Jewish Philanthropies ($50,000) see Neuberger Foundation, Roy R. and Marie S.

United Jewish Appeal Federation of Jewish Philanthropies ($15,000) see Neuberger Foundation, Roy R. and Marie S.

United Jewish Appeal Federation of Jewish Philanthropies ($150,000) see Newman Assistance Fund, Jerome A. and Estelle R.

United Jewish Appeal Federation of Jewish Philanthropies ($25,000) see N've Shalom Foundation

United Jewish Appeal Federation of Jewish Philanthropies ($15,000) see N've Shalom Foundation

United Jewish Appeal Federation of Jewish Philanthropies ($10,000) see N've Shalom Foundation

United Jewish Appeal Federation of Jewish Philanthropies ($80,000) see Oppenheimer and Flora Oppenheimer Haas Trust, Leo

United Jewish Appeal Federation of Jewish Philanthropies ($30,000) see Oppenheimer and Flora Oppenheimer Haas Trust, Leo

United Jewish Appeal Federation of Jewish Philanthropies ($15,000) see Ottenstein Family Foundation

United Jewish Appeal Federation of Jewish Philanthropies ($15,000) see Parthenon Sportswear

United Jewish Appeal Federation of Jewish Philanthropies ($25,000) see Picower Foundation, Jeffrey M. and Barbara

United Jewish Appeal Federation of Jewish Philanthropies ($30,000) see Pincus Family Fund

United Jewish Appeal Federation of Jewish Philanthropies ($77,000) see Propp Sons Fund, Morris and Anna

United Jewish Appeal Federation of Jewish Philanthropies ($5,000) see Pyramid Foundation

United Jewish Appeal Federation of Jewish Philanthropies ($45,400) see Ritter Foundation

United Jewish Appeal Federation of Jewish Philanthropies ($75,000) see Rodgers Foundation, Richard & Dorothy

United Jewish Appeal Federation of Jewish Philanthropies ($10,000) see Rosen Foundation, Joseph

United Jewish Appeal Federation of Jewish Philanthropies ($236,000) see Rosenberg Foundation, Sunny and Abe

United Jewish Appeal Federation of Jewish Philanthropies ($500,000) see Rudin Foundation

United Jewish Appeal Federation of Jewish Philanthropies ($10,000) see Russ Togs

United Jewish Appeal Federation of Jewish Philanthropies ($35,000) see Schaffer Foundation, H.

United Jewish Appeal Federation of Jewish Philanthropies ($50,000) see Schaffer Foundation, Michael & Helen

United Jewish Appeal Federation of Jewish Philanthropies ($50,000) see Silverweed Foundation

United Jewish Appeal Federation of Jewish Philanthropies ($10,000) see Simon Foundation, Sidney, Milton and Leoma

United Jewish Appeal Federation of Jewish Philanthropies ($33,000) see Slifka Foundation, Alan B.

United Jewish Appeal Federation of Jewish Philanthropies ($25,000) see Slifka Foundation, Alan B.

United Jewish Appeal Federation of Jewish Philanthropies ($60,000) see Slifka Foundation, Joseph and Sylvia

United Jewish Appeal Federation of Jewish Philanthropies ($60,000) see Slifka Foundation, Joseph and Sylvia

United Jewish Appeal Federation of Jewish Philanthropies ($15,050) see Spiegel Family Foundation, Jerry and Emily

United Jewish Appeal Federation of Jewish Philanthropies ($268,160) see Stein Foundation, Joseph F.

United Jewish Appeal Federation of Jewish Philanthropies ($531,362) see Steinberg Family Foundation, Meyer and Jean

United Jewish Appeal Federation of Jewish Philanthropies ($354,025) see Steinhardt Foundation, Judy and Michael

United Jewish Appeal Federation of Jewish Philanthropies ($50,000) see Stern Foundation, Gustav and Irene

United Jewish Appeal Federation of Jewish Philanthropies ($18,000) see Stern Foundation, Gustav and Irene

United Jewish Appeal Federation of Jewish Philanthropies ($50,000) see Stern Foundation, Irvin

United Jewish Appeal Federation of Jewish Philanthropies ($17,000) see Stern Foundation, Irvin

United Jewish Appeal Federation of Jewish Philanthropies ($150,000) see Stern Foundation, Leonard N.

United Jewish Appeal Federation of Jewish Philanthropies ($10,000) see Straus Foundation, Martha Washington Straus and Harry H.

United Jewish Appeal Federation of Jewish Philanthropies ($5,000) see Stuart Foundation

United Jewish Appeal Federation of Jewish Philanthropies ($7,500) see Sutton Foundation

United Jewish Appeal Federation of Jewish Philanthropies ($158,115) see Taub Foundation, Joseph and Arlene

United Jewish Appeal Federation of Jewish Philanthropies ($12,100) see Terner Foundation

United Jewish Appeal Federation of Jewish Philanthropies ($10,000) see Titan Industrial Co.

United Jewish Appeal Federation of Jewish Philanthropies ($7,000) see Titan Industrial Co.

United Jewish Appeal Federation of Jewish Philanthropies ($10,000) see Tuch Foundation, Michael

United Jewish Appeal Federation of Jewish Philanthropies ($5,000) see Tuch Foundation, Michael

United Jewish Appeal Federation of Jewish Philanthropies ($5,000) see United Merchants & Manufacturers

United Jewish Appeal Federation of Jewish Philanthropies ($600) see United Togs Inc.

United Jewish Appeal Federation of Jewish Philanthropies ($60,000) see Waldbaum Family Foundation, I.

United Jewish Appeal Federation of Jewish Philanthropies ($36,000) see Waldbaum Family Foundation, I.

United Jewish Appeal Federation of Jewish Philanthropies ($15,000) see Waldbaum Family Foundation, I.

United Jewish Appeal Federation of Jewish Philanthropies ($6,000) see Waldbaum Family Foundation, I.

United Jewish Appeal Federation of Jewish Philanthropies ($500,000) see Weil, Gotshal & Manges Foundation

United Jewish Appeal Federation of Jewish Philanthropies ($91,500) see Weiler Foundation, Theodore & Renee

United Jewish Appeal Federation of Jewish Philanthropies ($25,000) see Werblow Charitable Trust, Nina W.

United Jewish Appeal Federation of Jewish Philanthropies ($20,000) see Wien Foundation, Lawrence A.

United Jewish Appeal Federation of Jewish Philanthropies ($25,000) see Zarkin Memorial Foundation, Charles

United Jewish Appeal Federation of Jewish Philanthropies ($50,000) see Zenkel Foundation

United Jewish Appeal Federation of Jewish Philanthropies ($30,000) see Zuckerberg Foundation, Roy J.

United Jewish Appeal-Federation of Jewish Philanthropies of New York — for general support ($100,000) see Altman Foundation

United Jewish Appeal-Federation of Jewish Philanthropies of New York ($5,000,000) see Annenberg Foundation

United Jewish Appeal - Federation of Jewish Philanthropies of New York ($135,000) see Aron Charitable Foundation, J.

United Jewish Appeal - Federation of Jewish Philanthropies of New York ($1,500) see Gilman Paper Co.

United Jewish Appeal - Federation of Jewish Philanthropies of New York ($150,000) see Goldman Foundation, Herman

United Jewish Appeal-Federation of Jewish Philanthropies of New York ($270,946) see Green Fund

United Jewish Appeal - Federation of Jewish Philanthropies of New York ($35,000) see Hall Charitable Trust, Evelyn A. J.

United Jewish Appeal - Federation of Jewish Philanthropies of New York ($50,000) see Hazen Charitable Trust, Lita Annenberg

United Jewish Appeal-Federation of Jewish Philanthropies of New York ($125,000) see Littauer Foundation, Lucius N.

United Jewish Appeal - Federation of Jewish Philanthropies of New York — general support ($75,000) see Lowe Foundation, Joe and Emily

United Jewish Appeal - Federation of Jewish Philanthropies of New York ($125,000) see Moses Fund, Henry and Lucy

United Jewish Appeal - Federation of Jewish Philanthropies of New York

($370,000) see Newhouse Foundation, Samuel I.

United Jewish Appeal-Federation of Jewish Philanthropies of New York ($40,000) see Overseas Shipholding Group

United Jewish Appeal-Federation of Jewish Philanthropies of New York — general support ($242,000) see Rubinstein Foundation, Helena

United Jewish Appeal-Federation of Jewish Philanthropies of New York ($100,000) see Salomon

United Jewish Appeal Federation of Jewish Philanthropies of New York ($663,411) see Scheuer Family Foundation, S. H. and Helen R.

United Jewish Appeal-Federation of Jewish Philanthropies of New York ($39,445) see Slant/Fin Corp.

United Jewish Appeal-Federation of Jewish Philanthropies of New York ($1,500,000) see Wachtell, Lipton, Rosen & Katz

United Jewish Appeal - Federation of Jewish Philanthropies of New York — Federation of Jewish Philanthropies ($75,000) see Scherman Foundation

United Jewish Appeal - Federation of Jewish Philanthropies of New York — Operation Exodus ($334,500) see Newhouse Foundation, Samuel I.

United Jewish Appeal Federation of Jewish Philanthropies of New York — Operation Exodus ($40,000) see Overseas Shipholding Group

United Jewish Appeal-Federation of Jewish Philanthropies of New York — Operation Exodus ($1,000,000) see Tisch Foundation

United Jewish Appeal - Federation of Jewish Philanthropies of New York — United Jewish Appeal ($55,000) see Scherman Foundation

United Jewish Appeal Federation of New York ($100,000) see Gottesman Fund

United Jewish Appeal Federation of New York ($424,350) see Wilf Family Foundation

United Jewish Appeal Overseas Affairs Division ($50,000) see Atran Foundation

United Jewish Appeal Overseas Affairs Division ($50,000) see Atran Foundation

United Jewish Appeal Passage to Freedom ($5,000) see Schoenbaum Family Foundation

United Jewish Campaign ($50,000) see Rukin Philanthropic Foundation, David and Eleanore

United Jewish Campaign Project Exodus ($17,000) see Holzer Memorial Foundation, Richard H.

United Jewish Federation of Northeastern New York ($40,000) see Golub Corp.

United Jewish Federation of Northeastern New York ($35,000) see Golub Corp.

United Jewish Federation of Northeastern New York ($35,000) see Golub Corp.

United Jewish Federation of Northeastern New York ($35,000) see Golub Corp.

United Jewish Federation of Northeastern New York ($35,000) see Golub Corp.

United Jewish Federation of Northeastern New York ($11,905) see Golub Corp.

United Jewish Federation of Northeastern New York ($11,905) see Golub Corp.

United Jewish Fund ($108,000) see Cantor Foundation, Iris and B. Gerald

United Jewish Fund ($7,500) see Leviton Manufacturing Co.

United Jewish Fund ($443,333) see Mitchell Family Foundation, Edward D. and Anna

United Jewish Welfare Fund ($25,000) see Friedman Brothers Foundation

United Jewish Y's of Long Island ($6,200) see Spiegel Family Foundation, Jerry and Emily

United Methodist City ($15,750) see Clark Charitable Trust, Frank E.

United Methodist Society ($17,750) see Clark Charitable Trust, Frank E.

United Munkalser Yeshiva ($25,000) see Fogel Foundation, Shalom and Rebecca

United Nations Association ($40,000) see Branta Foundation

United Nations Association ($250,000) see Gerschel Foundation, Patrick A.

United Nations Association ($10,000) see Gerschel Foundation, Patrick A.

United Nations Association ($60,000) see Richardson Foundation, Frank E. and Nancy M.

United Nations Association ($20,625) see Weyerhaeuser Family Foundation

United Nations Association of the USA — for US-Japan dialogue on regional crisis management and the United Nations ($140,000) see United States-Japan Foundation

United Negro College Fund ($22,000) see Allyn Foundation

United Negro College Fund ($25,000) see AMAX

United Negro College Fund ($5,150,000) see Annenberg Foundation

United Negro College Fund ($3,750) see Bausch & Lomb

United Negro College Fund see Booz Allen & Hamilton

United Negro College Fund ($105,500) see Borden

United Negro College Fund ($5,000) see Brown, Jr. Charitable Trust, Frank D.

United Negro College Fund — general charitable contribution ($50,000) see Carter-Wallace

United Negro College Fund ($40,000) see CBS Inc.

United Negro College Fund ($24,000) see Crane Fund for Widows and Children

United Negro College Fund ($2,000) see Davey Tree Expert Co.

United Negro College Fund ($13,485) see Delta Air Lines

United Negro College Fund ($250) see Federal Screw Works

United Negro College Fund ($15,000) see Firestone Foundation, Roger S.

United Negro College Fund — capital campaign ($250,000) see General Mills

United Negro College Fund — special project grant ($307,500) see General Motors Corp.

United Negro College Fund ($5,000) see Goodman Family Foundation

United Negro College Fund — capital and annual support ($120,000) see Hallmark Cards

United Negro College Fund ($50,000) see Keck, Jr. Foundation, William M.

United Negro College Fund ($20,000) see Mellam Family Foundation

United Negro College Fund ($225,300) see Newhouse Foundation, Samuel I.

United Negro College Fund ($200,000) see PepsiCo

United Negro College Fund ($25,800) see Reader's Digest Association

United Negro College Fund ($15,000) see Ruffin Foundation, Peter B. & Adeline W.

United Negro College Fund ($150,000) see Seagram & Sons, Joseph E.

United Negro College Fund ($400,000) see Texaco

United Negro College Fund — operating grant ($18,000) see Trust Co. Bank

United Negro College Fund ($200,000) see Warner-Lambert Co.

United Negro College Fund ($27,500) see Wrigley Co., Wm. Jr.

United Negro College Fund — Campaign 2000: An Investment in america's future ($250,000) see Citicorp

United Negro College Fund — to establish Campaign 2000, a scholarship assistance program for students in Los Angeles County ($100,000) see Times Mirror Co.

United Negro College Fund, New York, NY ($80,000) see Equitable Life Assurance Society of the U.S.

United Negro College Fund, New York, NY ($10,000) see General American Life Insurance Co.

United Negro College Fund — Project ($640,000) see American Telephone & Telegraph Co.

United Neighborhood Houses of New York ($15,000) see Snyder Fund, Valentine Perry

U.S. Committee for UNICEF — Watson Water Project and Aid to Orphaned Children in Romania ($25,000) see Barstow Foundation

U.S. Wheel Chair Sports Fund ($7,000) see Luce Charitable Trust, Theodore

United Way ($1,000) see Acme United Corp.

United Way ($51,300) see Agway

United Way ($15,000) see Anderson Foundation

United Way ($2,200) see Baker & Baker

United Way ($10,000) see Barnes Group

United Way ($30,000) see Carnahan-Jackson Foundation

United Way ($10,000) see Coles Family Foundation

United Way ($33,000) see Cornell Trust, Peter C.

United Way ($18,000) see Crane Fund for Widows and Children

United Way ($75,000) see Daily News

United Way ($1,500) see Daniel Foundation, Gerard and Ruth

United Way ($22,000) see Darrah Charitable Trust, Jessie Smith

United Way ($45,000) see Davenport-Hatch Foundation

United Way ($10,000) see DCNY Corp.

United Way ($1,000) see De Lima Co., Paul

United Way ($8,000) see Dent Family Foundation, Harry

United Way ($43,647) see Everett Charitable Trust

United Way ($100) see Falk Foundation, Michael David

United Way ($10,700) see Fay's Incorporated

United Way ($10,500) see Fay's Incorporated

United Way ($5,000) see Fay's Incorporated

United Way ($4,500) see Fay's Incorporated

United Way ($3,150) see Fein Foundation

United Way ($2,500) see Fireman Charitable Foundation, Paul and Phyllis

United Way ($2,189) see Gear Motion

United Way ($986) see Gear Motion

United Way ($24,000) see General Railway Signal Corp.

United Way ($89,900) see Gifford Charitable Corporation, Rosamond

United Way ($260,000) see Gleason Memorial Fund

United Way ($154,000) see Goldome F.S.B

United Way ($6,500) see Goldome F.S.B

United Way ($15,000) see Goodyear Foundation, Josephine

United Way ($10,000) see Greenberg Foundation, Alan C.

United Way ($26,100) see Handy & Harman

United Way ($8,500) see Hilliard Corp.

United Way ($70,000) see Hirschl Trust for Charitable Purposes, Irma T.

United Way ($14,500) see Hultquist Foundation

United Way ($55,000) see Hutchins Foundation, Mary J.

United Way ($35) see Interstate National Corp.

United Way ($20,000) see Jurodin Fund

United Way ($70,000) see Kaye, Scholer, Fierman, Hays & Handler

United Way ($10,000) see Kingston Foundation

United Way ($89,000) see Klee Foundation, Conrad and Virginia

United Way ($2,500) see Lehman Foundation, Edith and Herbert

United Way ($1,000) see Link Foundation

United Way ($1,000) see Loeb Partners Corp.

United Way ($17,600) see Mark IV Industries

United Way ($7,500) see Marx Foundation, Virginia & Leonard

New York (cont.)

United Way ($5,250) see Mather Fund, Richard

United Way ($10,000) see McCarthy Charities

United Way ($6,930) see Merit Oil Corp.

United Way ($35,000) see Mitchell Family Foundation, Edward D. and Anna

United Way ($7,500) see Monarch Machine Tool Co.

United Way ($164,212) see New York Stock Exchange

United Way see Oki America Inc.

United Way ($4,250) see Rich Products Corp.

United Way ($4,250) see Rich Products Corp.

United Way ($4,250) see Rich Products Corp.

United Way see Rochester Midland Corp.

United Way ($75,000) see Schaffer Foundation, H.

United Way ($63,000) see Sheldon Foundation, Ralph C.

United Way ($2,700) see Standard Register Co.

United Way ($1,638) see Stuart Foundation

United Way ($25,000) see Susquehanna Investment Group

United Way ($55,000) see Utica National Insurance Group

United Way ($13,000) see Wilson Foundation, Elaine P. and Richard U.

United Way ($109,177) see Young & Rubicam

United Way ($33,697) see Young & Rubicam

United Way of Buffalo and Erie County ($20,500) see Arvin Industries

United Way of Buffalo and Erie County ($450,625) see Bristol-Myers Squibb Co.

United Way of Buffalo and Erie County ($26,000) see Cummings Foundation, James H.

United Way of Buffalo and Erie County ($90,000) see Fleet Financial Group

United Way of Buffalo and Erie County ($14,450) see Hartmarx Corp.

United Way of Buffalo and Erie County ($105,000) see Julia R. and Estelle L. Foundation

United Way of Buffalo and Erie County ($33,000) see Knox Foundation, Seymour H.

United Way of Buffalo and Erie County ($60,000) see Quaker Oats Co.

United Way of Buffalo and Erie County — annual grant ($46,000) see Wendt Foundation, Margaret L.

United Way of Cayuga County — annual support ($122,676) see Emerson Foundation, Fred L.

United Way of Central New York ($47,619) see Cooper Industries

United Way (Central New York) ($106,255) see Mutual of New York

United Way — Crusade of Mercy ($100,000) see Commerce Clearing House

United Way of Greater Rochester ($58,000) see Fleet Financial Group

United Way of Greater Rochester — annual campaign ($125,000) see Freedom Forum

United Way of Greater Rochester ($23,250) see Hartmarx Corp.

United Way of Greater Rochester ($150,000) see Mobil Oil Corp.

United Way of Greater Rochester — for Housing Programs and Programs for the Homeless ($104,250) see Chase Manhattan Bank, N.A.

United Way of Long Island ($45,000) see Fleet Financial Group

United Way of Long Island ($58,684) see GEICO Corp.

United Way of New York City ($394,197) see Center for Educational Programs

United Way of New York City ($33,000) see Commerce Clearing House

United Way of New York City ($8,500) see Fisher Brothers

United Way of New York City ($139,358) see Kidder, Peabody & Co.

United Way of New York City ($60,000) see Milliken & Co.

United Way of New York City ($50,000) see United States Trust Co. of New York

United Way of Northeastern New York ($250,000) see Fleet Bank of New York

United Way of Northeastern New York ($22,500) see Norton Co.

United Way of Schenectady County ($18,000) see Fleet Bank of New York

United Way of Southeastern Steuben County — general program support ($213,150) see Corning Incorporated

United Way of Southern Chautauqua County — toward 1991 campaign ($200,000) see Gebbie Foundation

United Way of Syracuse ($25,000) see Susquehanna-Pfaltzgraff Co.

United Way of Tri-State ($445,000) see AlliedSignal

United Way of Tri-State ($25,000) see AMAX

United Way-Tri-State ($24,073) see American Standard

United Way of Tri-State ($100,000) see CBS Inc.

United Way of Tri-State ($1,100,000) see Chase Manhattan Bank, N.A.

United Way of Tri-State ($189,000) see Continental Corp.

United Way of Tri-State — annual contribution ($25,000) see Crum and Forster

United Way of Tri-State ($55,000) see Dow Jones & Co.

United Way of Tri-State ($220,714) see Dun & Bradstreet Corp.

United Way of Tri-State ($67,900) see Dun & Bradstreet Corp.

United Way of Tri-State ($25,000) see Dun & Bradstreet Corp.

United Way of Tri-State ($140,000) see Federated Department Stores and Allied Stores Corp.

United Way of Tri-State ($125,000) see First Boston

United Way of Tri-State ($329,600) see GTE Corp.

United Way of Tri-State ($50,000) see International Flavors & Fragrances

United Way of Tri-State ($170,000) see McGraw-Hill

United Way of Tri-State ($150,000) see Mobil Oil Corp.

United Way (Tri-State) ($102,445) see Mutual of New York

United Way of Tri-State — general operating ($400,000) see New York Life Insurance Co.

United Way of Tri-State ($83,176) see Olin Corp.

United Way of Tri State ($200,000) see Prudential-Bache Securities

United Way of Tri State ($92,000) see Prudential-Bache Securities

United Way of Tri-State ($107,500) see Salomon

United Way of Tri-State ($35,000) see Unilever United States

United Way of Tri-State ($70,107) see Westvaco Corp.

United Way of Tri-State ($436,000) see Xerox Corp.

United Way of Tri-State ($436,000) see Xerox Corp.

United Way Tri-State Challenge ($80,000) see McGraw-Hill

United Way Tri State New York — annual giving ($12,904) see Enterprise Rent-A-Car Co.

United Way of Westchester ($284,354) see PepsiCo

United Ways of New York City ($20,000) see Avon Products

Unity College ($5,000) see Woodward Fund

University of Albany ($2,500) see Oxford Industries, Inc.

University at Albany Fund ($12,500) see Yulman Trust, Morton and Helen

University of Albany Fund ($12,500) see Yulman Trust, Morton and Helen

University at Buffalo ($24,500) see Goode Trust, Mae Stone

University at Buffalo ($12,944) see Goode Trust, Mae Stone

University of Buffalo ($25,000) see Statler Foundation

University at Buffalo Foundation ($90,000) see Cornell Trust, Peter C.

University at Buffalo Foundation ($150,000) see Cummings Foundation, James H.

University of Buffalo Foundation ($152,000) see Knox Foundation, Seymour H.

University at Buffalo Foundation ($10,000) see LeBrun Foundation

University of Buffalo Foundation ($30,000) see Quaker Oats Co.

University of Buffalo Foundation ($100,000) see Rich Products Corp.

University of Cape Town Fund ($15,000) see Palisades Educational Foundation

University of Rochester ($17,500) see Cheney Foundation, Elizabeth F.

University of Rochester ($50,000) see Cohen Family Foundation, Saul Z. and Amy Scheuer

University of Rochester — nurse fellowship ($333,430) see Commonwealth Fund

University of Rochester ($65,000) see Drown Foundation, Joseph

University of Rochester ($4,500) see Essick Foundation

University of Rochester — tuition support ($5,000) see Friendship Fund

University of Rochester ($275,000) see Gleason Memorial Fund

University of Rochester ($21,250) see Goode Trust, Mae Stone

University of Rochester ($115,000) see Link Foundation

University of Rochester ($11,000) see Orchard Corp. of America.

University of Rochester ($10,000) see Ritter Foundation

University of Rochester ($100,000) see Simon Foundation, William E. and Carol G.

University of Rochester ($100,000) see Simon Foundation, William E. and Carol G.

University of Rochester ($100,000) see Simon Foundation, William E. and Carol G.

University of Rochester ($100,000) see Simon Foundation, William E. and Carol G.

University of Rochester ($100,000) see Simon Foundation, William E. and Carol G.

University of Rochester ($100,000) see Simon Foundation, William E. and Carol G.

University of Rochester — posterior parahippocampal gyrus ($44,632) see Whitehall Foundation

University of Rochester ($10,000) see Willmott Foundation, Fred & Floy

University of Rochester ($78,554) see Wilson Foundation, Elaine P. and Richard U.

University of Rochester ($21,446) see Wilson Foundation, Elaine P. and Richard U.

University of Rochester ($1,000,000) see Xerox Corp.

University of Rochester Medical Center ($33,000) see Adler Foundation

University of Rochester Medical Center — to support interest in special education law and social policy and special education reform ($53,502) see Kennedy, Jr. Foundation, Joseph P.

University of Rochester Pain Treatment Center ($3,000) see Curtice-Burns Foods

University of Rochester School of Medicine ($21,250) see Goode Trust, Mae Stone

University of Rochester, School of Medicine and Dentistry — for medical schools to improve the basic science education and clinical training of medical students ($2,499,501) see Johnson Foundation, Robert Wood

University of Rochester — School of Nursing; teaching endowment ($250,000) see Independence Foundation

University of Rochester — "Ventures in Chemistry"; teaching around a theme ($20,250) see Dreyfus Foundation, Camille and Henry

University of Rochester, William E. Simon Graduate School of Business Administration — to support the John M. Olin Institute for the Study of Economic Policy and Markets ($506,460) see Olin Foundation, John M.

University of Southern California School of Medicine ($1,000) see Baker & Baker

Upper Hudson Planned Parenthood ($20,500) see Howard and Bush Foundation

Upstate New York Synod, ELCA — conference center ($50,000) see Wendt Foundation, Margaret L.

Urban Foundation, New York, NY ($25,000) see Chemical Bank

Urban Foundation (USA) ($60,000) see SmithKline Beecham

Urban Homesteading Assistance Board ($15,000) see Industrial Bank of Japan Trust Co.

Urban League see General Signal Corp.

US Catholic Conference ($54,000) see Bowne Foundation, Robert

US Committee Sports for Israel ($30,000) see FAB Industries

US Committee for UNICEF ($140,000) see Banyan Tree Foundation

US Committee for UNICEF ($50,000) see Levy Foundation, Edward C.

US Committee for UNICEF ($25,000) see Nabisco Foods Group

USA Foundation ($20,833) see Icahn Foundation, Carl C.

USC of Metropolitan New York ($10,000) see L and L Foundation

Usdan Center for the Performing Arts ($6,350) see Morse, Jr. Foundation, Enid and Lester S.

Usdan Center for the Performing Arts ($5,000) see Schloss & Co., Marcus

Usdan Center for the Performing Arts ($7,500) see Titan Industrial Co.

Valley Hospital Foundation ($5,000) see Avon Products

Valley Torah High School Center ($35,000) see Friedman Brothers Foundation

Vassar College ($200,000) see Kautz Family Foundation

Vassar College ($131,000) see Lehman Foundation, Robert

Vassar College ($100,000) see Mars Foundation

Vassar College ($25,000) see Straus Foundation, Philip A. and Lynn

Vassar College ($6,000) see Westport Fund

Vassar College ($37,500) see Woodward Fund-Watertown, David, Helen, and Marian

Vassar College, Ford Scholars Program ($50,000) see Weinberg Foundation, John L.

Vassar College — Koopman Scholarship ($25,000) see Koopman Fund

Venture Fund Diocese of New York ($7,000) see Mulford Foundation, Vincent

Vera Institute of Justice/Housing and Services — to produce permanent housing for homeless families and individuals; (second payment

of a two-year $100,000 grant)
($50,000) see Ittleson
Foundation
Versailles Foundation ($15,000)
see Hooker Charitable Trust,
Janet A.
Village of Canajoharie ($35,000)
see Arkell Hall Foundation
Village of Cayuga ($9,000) see
Cayuga Foundation
Village of Hobart — rebuilding
sewer system ($400,000) see
O'Connor Foundation, A.
Lindsay and Olive B.
Village of Millbrook ($56,000)
see Millbrook Tribute Garden
Village Nursing Home ($75,000)
see Noble Charitable Trust,
John L. and Ethel G.
Village of Owego ($35,000) see
Truman Foundation, Mildred
Faulkner
Village of Youngstown — full
service recreation department
building ($5,000) see Joy
Family Foundation
Vishwa Hindu Parishad of
America ($50,000) see
Watumull Fund, J.
Visions ($25,000) see Blum
Foundation, Edna F.
Visions — endowment
($100,000) see Kern
Foundation, Ilma
Visions Services ($71,012) see
Ramapo Trust
VISIONS/Services for the Blind
and Visually Impaired
($17,500) see Parshelsky
Foundation, Moses L.
Visiting Nurse Association of
Oyster Bay ($1,000) see
Pritchard Charitable Trust,
William E. and Maude S.
Visiting Nurse Service ($60,000)
see Hirschl Trust for
Charitable Purposes, Irma T.
Visiting Nurse Service of New
York ($12,500) see
Frelinghuysen Foundation
Visiting Nurse Service of
Westchester ($20,000) see
Mellam Family Foundation
VITA ($5,000) see Paul and C.
Michael Paul Foundation,
Josephine Bay
Vitam Center ($2,700) see
Weinstein Foundation, Alex J.
Vocational Foundation — job
training program for high-risk
youth ($40,000) see Pinkerton
Foundation
Volunteer Center ($2,000) see
Mason Charitable Foundation
Volunteer Consulting Group
($39,000) see Atlantic
Foundation of New York
Volunteer Lawyers for the Arts
($15,000) see Reed Foundation
VVS Dollars for Scholars
($2,000) see Chapman
Charitable Corporation,
Howard and Bess
W. W. Norton and Company —
History of Philadelphia
($30,925) see Barra Foundation
W.F. Albright Institute of
Archaeological Research
($1,000) see Abraham
Foundation
Wadhams Free Library ($500)
see Crary Foundation, Bruce L.
Wagner College ($30,000) see
Baier Foundation, Marie
Wagner College ($25,000) see
McDonald Foundation, J. M.
Wagner College ($7,000) see
Switzer Foundation
Waldorf Institute of Spring
Valley ($60,000) see Waldorf
Educational Foundation

Waldorf School of Garden City
($200,000) see Waldorf
Educational Foundation
Wall Street Synagogue
($542,825) see Cantor
Foundation, Iris and B. Gerald
Waterford Institute ($200,000)
see Zilkha & Sons
Waterford Institute — to place
its computer-training program
in the New York City school
system ($25,000) see Achelis
Foundation
Wave Hill ($25,000) see Dodge
Foundation, Cleveland H.
Wave Hill ($25,000) see Dodge
Foundation, Cleveland H.
WCA Hospital ($250,000) see
Sheldon Foundation, Ralph C.
WCA Hospital — renovations to
old General Hospital
($250,000) see Gebbie
Foundation
WCNY ($3,625) see Fay's
Incorporated
WCNY Capital Development
Program ($4,000) see Agway
WCNY — CDP ($1,000) see De
Lima Co., Paul
WCNY-TV/24 Classic FM
($25,000) see McDonald
Foundation, J. M.
We Care About New York
($60,000) see Atlantic
Foundation of New York
We Care About New York
($5,000) see Bartsch Memorial
Trust, Ruth
We Care About New York
($25,000) see Chemical Bank
Weizmann Institute of Science
($10,000) see Altschul
Foundation
Weizmann Institute of Science
($27,000) see Carylon
Foundation
Weizmann Institute of Science
($50,000) see Goldman
Foundation, Morris and Rose
Weizmann Institute of Science
($100,000) see Heineman
Foundation for Research,
Educational, Charitable, and
Scientific Purposes
Weizmann Institute of Science
($15,000) see Himmelfarb
Foundation, Paul and Annetta
Weizmann Institute of Science,
American Committee —
Helena Rubinstein
Postdoctoral Fellowship in
Biomedical Sciences and
Cancer Research ($83,333) see
Rubinstein Foundation, Helena
Wells College ($4,000) see
Cayuga Foundation
Wells College ($15,000) see
Janssen Foundation, Henry
Wells College ($25,000) see
Kent Foundation, Ada Howe
Wells College ($20,000) see
Rauch Foundation
Werther Research Foundation
($12,500) see Jacobson &
Sons, Benjamin
West Side Institutional
Synagogue ($12,500) see
Davis Foundation, Simon and
Annie
West Side Institutional
Synagogue ($2,000) see
Fischel Foundation, Harry and
Jane
West Side International
Synagogue ($10,000) see
Gruber Research Foundation,
Lila
West Side Rowing Club — for
piling ($10,000) see Baird
Foundation
West Side YMCA ($500) see
Gilman Paper Co.

Westchester Association of
Retarded Citizens ($30,000)
see Frese Foundation, Arnold
D.
Westchester Clubman see MBIA,
Inc.
Westchester Community College
($20,000) see Marx
Foundation, Virginia &
Leonard
Westchester Community College
Foundation ($5,525) see
Abeles Foundation, Joseph
and Sophia
Westchester Community
Opportunity Program
($25,000) see
Lavanburg-Corner House
Westchester Day School
($9,300) see Propp Sons Fund,
Morris and Anna
Westchester Education Coalition
($50,000) see Reader's Digest
Association
Westchester Education Coalition
— in this latest grant, covering
a 3-year period, school
principals for encouraged to
assess special problems and
needs of their schools
($54,000) see NYNEX Corp.
Westchester Exceptional
Children's School see MBIA,
Inc.
Westchester Jewish Center
($17,100) see Stein
Foundation, Joseph F.
Westchester Land Trust
($25,000) see Dorr Foundation
Westchester Reform Temple
($3,625) see Frankel
Foundation, George and
Elizabeth F.
Westchester Symphony
Orchestra ($1,500) see
Fuchsberg Family Foundation
Westchester Symphony
Orchestra ($1,000) see
Gutman Foundation, Edna and
Monroe C.
Western Hall Heritage
Foundation ($25,000) see
Alexander Foundation, Joseph
Western New York Heritage
Institute — funding for
teacher's seminar, textbook
project and summer
cooperative program ($30,000)
see Wendt Foundation,
Margaret L.
Western New York Scholarship
Awards Committee ($83,750)
see Statler Foundation
Westhampton Cultural
Consortium ($15,000) see
Brace Foundation, Donald C.
Westhampton Writers Festival
($5,000) see Brace
Foundation, Donald C.
Westin School ($2,000) see
Fireman Charitable
Foundation, Paul and Phyllis
Westminster Presbyterian
Church ($10,229) see Everett
Charitable Trust
Westmoreland Sanctuary
($56,250) see Frick
Foundation, Helen Clay
Westside Cluster of Centers and
Settlements ($100) see
HarperCollins Publishers
Westwood Hall Hebrew Home
($77,500) see Gindi Associates
Foundation
White Plains Hospital Center
($25,000) see Noble
Charitable Trust, John L. and
Ethel G.
White Plains Hospital Medical
Center ($2,000) see Frankel
Foundation, George and
Elizabeth F.

White Plains Hospital Medical
Center ($77,619) see Milstein
Family Foundation
White Plains Hospital Medical
Center ($152,500) see Morris
Foundation, Norman M.
White Plains Hospital Medical
Center ($25,000) see Straus
Foundation, Martha
Washington Straus and Harry
H.
White Plains Hospital Medical
Center ($1,000) see Stuart
Foundation
White Plains School District
($30,000) see Reader's Digest
Association
Whitney Museum of American
Art ($91,500) see Bohen
Foundation
Whitney Museum of American
Art see Conde Nast
Publications, Inc.
Whitney Museum of American
Art ($1,000) see Cramer
Foundation
Whitney Museum of American
Art ($6,000) see Erpf Fund,
Armand G.
Whitney Museum of American
Art ($25,000) see Gilman, Jr.
Foundation, Sondra and
Charles
Whitney Museum of American
Art ($25,000) see Gilman, Jr.
Foundation, Sondra and
Charles
Whitney Museum of American
Art see Heffernan & Co.
Whitney Museum of American
Art ($30,000) see Kaufman
Foundation, Henry & Elaine
Whitney Museum of American
Art ($25,000) see Kaufman
Foundation, Henry & Elaine
Whitney Museum of American
Art ($25,000) see Kettering
Family Foundation
Whitney Museum of American
Art ($20,000) see L. L. W. W.
Foundation
Whitney Museum of American
Art ($27,320) see Lemberg
Foundation
Whitney Museum of American
Art ($50,133) see Leonhardt
Foundation, Dorothea L.
Whitney Museum of American
Art ($190,000) see Mnuchin
Foundation
Whitney Museum of American
Art ($25,000) see Rosenstiel
Foundation
Whitney Museum of American
Art — fellowship endowment
and annual fellowships
($100,000) see Rubinstein
Foundation, Helena
Whitney Museum of American
Art ($10,000) see Thendara
Foundation
Whitney Museum of American
Art ($50,000) see Weisman
Art Foundation, Frederick R.
Whitney Museum of American
Art ($11,000) see Werblow
Charitable Trust, Nina W.
Whitney Museum of American
Art — presents and supports
20th century American art
($25,000) see International
Flavors & Fragrances
Whitney National Committee
($4,000) see DiRosa
Foundation, Rene and Veronica
Whittier Institute ($15,000) see
Cox Foundation
Wildlife Conservation ($25,000)
see Ogilvy & Mather
Worldwide
Wildlife Conservation
International ($413,100) see

Claiborne Art Ortenberg
Foundation, Liz
Wildwood ($5,000) see
Rebsamen Companies, Inc.
Williamstown Advocate ($135)
see Soling Family Foundation
Williamstown Community
($200) see Soling Family
Foundation
Williamstown Theatre Festival
($1,070) see Soling Family
Foundation
Willing Helpers Home ($6,000)
see Knox Family Foundation
Wilson Center ($25,000) see
Greentree Foundation
Wilson Commencement Park
($896,707) see Wilson
Foundation, Marie C. and
Joseph C.
Wilson Commencement Park
($82,500) see Wilson
Foundation, Marie C. and
Joseph C.
Wilson Commencement Park —
the Family Learning Center, a
transitional housing and
support program for
single-parent families
($50,000) see Jones
Foundation, Daisy Marquis
Wilson Free Library ($5,000) see
Grigg-Lewis Trust
Wilson Free Library — renovate
library ($23,000) see Western
New York Foundation
Windward School ($15,000) see
Connemara Fund
Winston Churchill Foundation
— operating fund ($10,000)
see Gabelli Foundation
Winston Churchill Foundation
($10,000) see Gerschel
Foundation, Patrick A.
Winston Foundation for World
Peace ($186,000) see Wiener
Foundation, Malcolm Hewitt
Winston Preparatory School
($40,000) see Simon
Charitable Trust, Esther
Winthrop University Hospital
($100,000) see Brooks
Foundation, Gladys
WIZA — Women's International
Zionist Organization ($25,600)
see Moskowitz Foundation,
Irving I.
WMHT ($79,469) see Robison
Foundation, Ellis H. and Doris
B.
WNED Communicating the
Future — building fund
($10,000) see Baird Foundation
WNED-TV ($12,500) see
Western New York Foundation
WNET ($10,000) see Levin
Foundation, Philip and Janice
WNET Channel 13 ($20,000) see
Carvel Foundation, Thomas
and Agnes
WNET Thirteen ($15,000) see
Gulton Foundation
WNET Thirteen ($23,000) see
Lemberg Foundation
WNET Thirteen ($1,000) see
Loeb Partners Corp.
WNET Thirteen ($5,000) see
Marx Foundation, Virginia &
Leonard
WNET Thirteen ($365,000) see
Rohatyn Foundation, Felix and
Elizabeth
WNET Thirteen ($25,000) see
Rubin Foundation, Rob E. &
Judith O.
WNET Thirteen ($38,077) see
Sharp Foundation, Evelyn
WNET Thirteen ($1,500) see
Spiritus Gladius Foundation
WNET Thirteen ($50,000) see
Williams Foundation, C. K.

New York (cont.)

WNET/Thirteen — year-round sponsorship of children's television programming ($200,000) see Rubinstein Foundation, Helena

WNY Public Broadcasting ($5,000) see Mark IV Industries

WNYC ($20,000) see Heyward Memorial Fund, DuBose and Dorothy

WNYC Foundation ($32,000) see Loews Corp.

Women In Need — special project ($52,194) see New York Life Insurance Co.

Women In Need — to support a family therapist program ($21,000) see Washington Square Fund

Women on the Job ($5,000) see Silverburgh Foundation, Grace, George & Judith

Women in Need ($29,000) see Abraham Foundation

Women in Need ($25,000) see Bowne Foundation, Robert

Women in Need ($35,000) see McIntosh Foundation

Women in Need ($10,000) see Richardson Charitable Trust, Anne S.

Women in Need ($12,500) see Snyder Fund, Valentine Perry

Women USA Fund — to support Latin, Central American and Caribbean women in their efforts to develop action and policies to protect the environment ($70,000) see Noyes Foundation, Jessie Smith

Womens American ORT ($1,275) see Goldstein Foundation, Alfred and Ann

Womens American ORT ($2,000) see Greene Foundation, Robert Z.

Womens American ORT ($35,000) see Weinstein Foundation, Alex J.

Women's Branch UOJCA ($2,250) see Fischel Foundation, Harry and Jane

Women's Health Network ($10,000) see Pettus Crowe Foundation

Womens Housing Corporation ($165) see Consumer Farmer Foundation

Women's League for Israel ($5,000) see Klosk Fund, Louis and Rose

Women's League for Israel ($5,000) see Klosk Fund, Louis and Rose

Womens League for Israel ($2,100) see Weinstein Foundation, J.

Woods Schools ($40,000) see Cowles Charitable Trust

Woodstock Area Council on the Aging ($25,000) see Faulkner Trust, Marianne Gaillard

Woodstock Community Recreation Center ($95,160) see Faulkner Trust, Marianne Gaillard

Woodstock Theological Center ($10,000) see Richardson Charitable Trust, Anne S.

Word of Life Fellowship — capital improvements ($40,000) see Gallagher Family Foundation, Lewis P.

Workshop for Business ($7,700) see Gould Foundation for Children, Edwin

World Jewish Congress ($12,500) see Goldring Family Foundation

World Jewish Congress ($12,500) see Woldenberg Foundation

World Jewish Congress-American Section ($1,000,000) see Seagram & Sons, Joseph E.

World Monuments Fund ($2,500) see Hobbs Charitable Trust, John H.

World Monuments Fund ($150,000) see Kress Foundation, Samuel H.

World Monuments Fund ($50,000) see Kress Foundation, Samuel H.

World Monuments Fund ($50,000) see Kress Foundation, Samuel H.

World Monuments Fund ($50,000) see L. L. W. W. Foundation

World Monuments Fund ($5,000) see Ogden Foundation, Ralph E.

World Monuments Fund — support the city center in Puebla, Mexico ($50,000) see L. L. W. W. Foundation

World Music Institute ($50,500) see Foundation for the Needs of Others

World Policy Institute ($55,000) see Wallach Foundation, Miriam G. and Ira D.

World Rehabilitation Fund ($5,000) see Culver Foundation, Constans

World Rehabilitation Fund ($15,000) see Frohlich Charitable Trust, Ludwig W.

World Rehabilitation Fund ($5,000) see Stott Foundation, Robert L.

World Union ($1,500) see Grass Family Foundation

World Union For Progressive Judaism ($15,000) see Reicher Foundation, Anne & Harry J.

World Union for Progressive Judaism ($5,000) see Bronstein Foundation, Sol and Arlene

World Union for Progressive Judaism ($184,890) see Daniel Foundation, Gerard and Ruth

World Union for Progressive Judaism ($5,000) see Padnos Iron & Metal Co., Louis

World Union for Progressive Judaism — to promote religious pluralism, youth and community development, and special services in the former Soviet Union ($20,000) see Fel-Pro Incorporated

Worldwide Documentaries ($2,000) see Falk Medical Fund, Maurice

WPA Theatre — for partial support of production of Bella, Belle of Byelorussia ($5,000) see Axe-Houghton Foundation

Writers and Books ($250,000) see Gleason Memorial Fund

Writing to Read Program — education assistance for deprived racial groups in south Africa ($1,660,330) see IBM South Africa Projects Fund

WSKG ($12,500) see Truman Foundation, Mildred Faulkner

WXXI Broadcasting Council — support for programs the Foundation express areas of interest ($33,000) see Jones Foundation, Daisy Marquis

WXXI Broadcasting Council — to support the WXXI capital campaign ($45,000) see Jones Foundation, Daisy Marquis

WXXI Public Broadcasting Council — 24-hour reading service ($1,000) see Houck Foundation, May K.

WXXI Television ($22,500) see Loewy Family Foundation

Wyndham Lawn Home for Children ($10,000) see Grigg-Lewis Trust

Wyoming Conference Home — capital ($12,500) see Klee Foundation, Conrad and Virginia

Yad Tikva ($17,000) see Saltz Foundation, Gary

Yakirei Yerushalaim ($5,200) see Sutton Foundation

Yard ($55,000) see Newman Assistance Fund, Jerome A. and Estelle R.

Yavneh Hebrew Academy ($37,000) see Friedman Brothers Foundation

Yeshiva Aberek Torah ($2,000) see N've Shalom Foundation

Yeshiva Ateres Yisroel ($10,000) see Neuberger Foundation, Roy R. and Marie S.

Yeshiva Beer Hagola ($1,000) see Gruss Charitable and Educational Foundation, Oscar and Regina

Yeshiva Beth Shearim ($10,000) see Wilf Family Foundation

Yeshiva Boyan Rishin ($12,100) see Fishoff Family Foundation

Yeshiva Chasan Sofer ($1,000) see Hudson Neckwear

Yeshiva Chasen Sofer ($12,680) see Fishoff Family Foundation

Yeshiva Chatan Sofer ($1,500) see Hudson Neckwear

Yeshiva Darchel Torah ($10,500) see Stern Family Foundation, Harry

Yeshiva Elementary School ($60,000) see Applebaum Foundation

Yeshiva of Flatbush ($13,552) see Bag Bazaar, Ltd.

Yeshiva Gedolah High ($28,000) see Friedman Brothers Foundation

Yeshiva Ihrei Yosep ($50,000) see Fogel Foundation, Shalom and Rebecca

Yeshiva Imrei Yossef ($300,000) see Kest Family Foundation, Sol and Clara

Yeshiva Kehilath ($15,000) see Sutton Foundation

Yeshiva Ketana of Manhattan ($1,000) see House of Gross

Yeshiva Limudei Hashem ($25,000) see Lawrence Foundation, Alice

Yeshiva Mesifta Ohr Yisroel ($8,625) see Fishoff Family Foundation

Yeshiva Ohr Torah ($25,000) see Ehrman Foundation, Fred and Susan

Yeshiva Ohr Yisroel ($5,400) see Hudson Neckwear

Yeshiva Prospect Park ($14,500) see Fishoff Family Foundation

Yeshiva Samson Raphael Hirsch ($1,470) see House of Gross

Yeshiva Shaarei Torah ($1,250) see House of Gross

Yeshiva Sharmt ($12,000) see Hidary Foundation, Jacob

Yeshiva Torah Vodnath and Mesivta ($5,000) see Wouk Foundation, Abe

Yeshiva Torah Yodaath ($1,500) see Hudson Neckwear

Yeshiva Torath Emeth Academy ($28,000) see Friedman Brothers Foundation

Yeshiva Tov V'Chesed ($10,000) see Newbrook Charitable Foundation

Yeshiva University ($25,000) see Arronson Foundation

Yeshiva University ($250,000) see Beinecke Foundation

Yeshiva University ($50,000) see Belz Foundation

Yeshiva University ($50,000) see Bennett Foundation, Carl and Dorothy

Yeshiva University ($5,000) see Beren Foundation, Robert M.

Yeshiva University ($73,000) see Berkowitz Family Foundation, Louis

Yeshiva University ($30,000) see Berrie Foundation, Russell

Yeshiva University ($25,000) see Bravmann Foundation, Ludwig

Yeshiva University ($211,000) see Burns Foundation, Jacob

Yeshiva University ($10,000) see Ehrman Foundation, Fred and Susan

Yeshiva University ($15,000) see FAB Industries

Yeshiva University ($50,000) see Feil Foundation, Louis and Gertrude

Yeshiva University ($25,000) see Fischel Foundation, Harry and Jane

Yeshiva University ($50,000) see Forchheimer Foundation

Yeshiva University ($500) see Gilman Paper Co.

Yeshiva University ($10,000) see Gordon Foundation

Yeshiva University ($100,000) see Gruber Research Foundation, Lila

Yeshiva University ($150,000) see Icahn Foundation, Carl C.

Yeshiva University ($5,000) see Jacoby Foundation, Lela Beren and Norman

Yeshiva University ($241,950) see Jesselson Foundation

Yeshiva University ($25,000) see Lautenberg Foundation

Yeshiva University ($100,000) see Lawrence Foundation, Alice

Yeshiva University ($5,000) see Mandel Foundation, Joseph and Florence

Yeshiva University ($500,000) see Mitrani Family Foundation

Yeshiva University ($2,000) see Nelco Sewing Machine Sales Corp.

Yeshiva University ($8,000) see Propp Sons Fund, Morris and Anna

Yeshiva University ($255,000) see Ramapo Trust

Yeshiva University ($1,140,000) see Resnick Foundation, Jack and Pearl

Yeshiva University ($73,000) see Sapirstein-Stone-Weiss Foundation

Yeshiva University ($3,000) see Schloss & Co., Marcus

Yeshiva University ($3,000) see Schloss & Co., Marcus

Yeshiva University ($156,500) see Wexner Foundation

Yeshiva University ($250,000) see Wilf Family Foundation

Yeshiva University-Albert Einstein College of Medicine — medical scholarships ($85,000) see Rudin Foundation, Louis and Rachel

Yeshiva University High School ($57,500) see Friedman Brothers Foundation

Yeshiva University High School ($20,000) see Lawrence Foundation, Alice

Yeshiva University — for Joseph Alexander Library at Yeshiva High School for Boys ($50,000) see Alexander Foundation, Joseph

Yeshiva University Library ($65,000) see Jesselson Foundation

Yeshiva University Scholars Program ($125,000) see Stern Foundation, Max

Yeshiva University Scholars Program ($125,000) see Stern Foundation, Max

Yeshiva University — Stern College ($10,000) see Stern Foundation, Max

Yeshiva Viznitz D'Khal T.C. ($36,000) see Fogel Foundation, Shalom and Rebecca

Yeshivah Gedolah Ohr Hatorah ($180) see Melohn Foundation

Yeshivas Mesifta Tiferes Shulim Nadvorne ($10,000) see Fishoff Family Foundation

Yeshivat Torath Emet Academy ($100,000) see Kest Family Foundation, Sol and Clara

Yeshivath Kol Yaakov ($880) see Melohn Foundation

Yeshivath Spinka ($100,000) see Kest Family Foundation, Sol and Clara

Yeshivoth Har Etzion ($500) see United Togs Inc.

Yeshivoth Spinka ($25,000) see Fogel Foundation, Shalom and Rebecca

YIVO Institute for Jewish Research ($60,000) see Atran Foundation

YIVO Institute for Jewish Research ($60,000) see Atran Foundation

Yivo Institute for Jewish Research ($39,670) see Kaufmann Foundation, Henry

YM-YWHA ($10,000) see Abraham Foundation

YM/YWHA ($5,000) see Axe-Houghton Foundation

YM/YWHA ($30,000) see Cohen Family Foundation, Saul Z. and Amy Scheuer

YM-YWHA of the Bronx and Riverdale ($100,000) see Moses Fund, Henry and Lucy

YM and YWHA of Mid-Westchester ($10,000) see Frankel Foundation, George and Elizabeth F.

YM and YWHA-92nd Street ($510,228) see Tisch Foundation

YM-YWHA of Northern Westchester — building fund ($10,000) see Harris Foundation, J. Ira and Nicki

YMCA ($25,000) see Carnahan-Jackson Foundation

YMCA ($5,000) see Colt Foundation, James J.

YMCA ($20,000) see Darrah Charitable Trust, Jessie Smith

YMCA ($10,000) see Doherty Charitable Foundation, Henry L. and Grace

YMCA ($5,156) see Ellsworth Trust, W. H.

YMCA ($5,114) see Everett Charitable Trust

YMCA ($5,000) see Goldome F.S.B

YMCA ($35,000) see Goodman Memorial Foundation, Joseph C. and Clare F.

YMCA see Home Depot

YMCA ($5,000) see Kepco, Inc.

YMCA ($2,000) see Key Bank of Maine

YMCA ($25,000) see Kingston Foundation

YMCA ($15,000) see Klee Foundation, Conrad and Virginia

YMCA ($16,000) see Monarch Machine Tool Co.

YMCA ($10,000) see Olive Bridge Fund

YMCA ($8,000) see Palmer-Fry Memorial Trust, Lily

YMCA ($5,000) see Pyramid Foundation

YMCA ($2,000) see Raskin Foundation, Hirsch and Braine

YMCA ($10,000) see Roblee Foundation, Joseph H. and Florence A.

YMCA ($25,000) see Rodgers Foundation, Richard & Dorothy

YMCA ($250,000) see Sheldon Foundation, Ralph C.

YMCA ($19,350) see Steinhardt Foundation, Judy and Michael

YMCA of Greater New York ($25,000) see Equitable Life Assurance Society of the U.S.

YMCA of Greater New York — special project ($125,000) see New York Life Insurance Co.

YMCA of Greater New York — capital campaign ($50,000) see Pfizer

Yonkers Youth Connection ($10,000) see St. Faith's House Foundation

Yorkville Community Kitchen ($50,000) see Bleibtreu Foundation, Jacob

Yorkville Community Pantry ($10,000) see PaineWebber

Young Adult Institute and Workshop ($6,000) see Commerce Clearing House

Young Adult Institute and Workshop ($15,000) see McGonagle Foundation, Dextra Baldwin

Young Audiences ($5,000) see Abrams Foundation, Benjamin and Elizabeth

Young Audiences ($41,000) see Fribourg Foundation

Young Audiences ($15,000) see Fribourg Foundation

Young Audiences ($100,000) see Hoffman Foundation, Marion O. and Maximilian

Young Audiences ($10,000) see Morse, Jr. Foundation, Enid and Lester S.

Young Audiences of Western New York — operating expenses ($4,000) see Hooper Handling

Young Concert Artists ($5,500) see Wheeler Foundation

Young Concert Artists ($100,000) see Whitaker Fund, Helen F.

Young Israel ($2,100) see Key Food Stores Cooperative Inc.

Young Women's Christian Association ($15,000) see Wasily Family Foundation

Youth Counseling League ($10,000) see L and L Foundation

Youth Counseling League ($5,000) see Piankova Foundation, Tatiana

Youth Counseling League ($10,700) see Schiff Foundation

Youth Counseling League ($10,000) see Washington Square Fund

Youth Counseling League ($35,000) see Weezie Foundation

Youth Service League ($5,000) see Berkowitz Family Foundation, Louis

Youth Town of Israel ($16,667) see Mitchell Family Foundation, Edward D. and Anna

Youth Towns of Israel ($62,500) see Mattus Foundation, Reuben and Rose

Youth for Understanding see Oki America Inc.

YWCA ($5,000) see Goodyear Foundation, Josephine

YWCA ($150,000) see Gordon/Rousmaniere/Roberts Fund

YWCA ($10,000) see Grigg-Lewis Trust

YWCA ($14,500) see Mertz Foundation, Martha

YWCA ($6,000) see Palmer-Fry Memorial Trust, Lily

YWCA ($50,000) see Penney Foundation, James C.

YWCA ($10,000) see Richardson Charitable Trust, Anne S.

YWCA ($6,000) see Young & Rubicam

YWCA of the City of New York ($100,000) see Dodge Foundation, Cleveland H.

YWCA of the City of New York — Young Fathers Program ($50,000) see Pinkerton Foundation

YWCA of Rochester and Monroe County — to help start up the Women's Resource Center ($30,000) see Jones Foundation, Daisy Marquis

Zeta Psi Educational Foundation — education ($5,000) see Holt Foundation, William Knox

Zionist Organization of America ($7,200) see Caplan Charity Foundation, Julius H.

Zionist Organization of America ($5,000) see Mattus Foundation, Reuben and Rose

Zionist Organization of America ($5,000) see Wasserman Foundation, George

Zionist Organization of America ($21,500) see Wolens Foundation, Kalman and Ida

North Carolina

Aery Mitchell Yancey Regional Library ($1,000) see McClure Educational and Development Fund, James G. K.

Africa Evangelical Fellowship ($25,000) see Crowell Trust, Henry P. and Susan C.

African Medical Mission ($10,000) see Lacy Foundation

African Medical Missions — medical training ($40,000) see International Foundation

Afro-American Culture Center ($5,000) see Radiator Specialty Co.

Agricultural Resources Center — for the Pesticide Education Project ($40,000) see Babcock Foundation, Mary Reynolds

AIDS Council ($15,000) see Glenn Foundation, Carrie C. & Lena V.

Aids Service Agency of Orange County — toward start-up of a facility to provide housing and support services for homeless people from North Carolina living with AIDS ($50,000) see Bryan Family Foundation, Kathleen Price and Joseph M.

Alamance County Arts Council ($1,500) see Liberty Hosiery Mills

Alcoholics Home ($1,000) see Thomas Built Buses L.P.

Allen Chapel AME Zion Church ($100) see Morgan Trust for Charity, Religion, and Education

Alzheimers Association of Western North Carolina ($20,000) see Lane Charitable Trust, Melvin R.

Alzheimer's Disease and Related Disorders Association ($4,000) see Ginter Foundation, Karl and Anna

American Association for Gifted Children — Duke University; 141 Presidential Scholars ($160,524) see Dodge Foundation, Geraldine R.

American Association of Obstetricians and Gynecologists Foundation ($87,500) see Burroughs Wellcome Co.

American Children's Home ($5,000) see Whitener Foundation

American Dance Festival ($10,000) see Devonwood Foundation

American Dance Festival ($95,500) see Trust for Mutual Understanding

American Red Cross ($14,460) see Lance, Inc.

American Social Health Association ($15,000) see Overlake Foundation

Amethyst ($20,000) see Dickson Foundation

Amethyst Foundation ($25,000) see Close Foundation

Amethyst Foundation ($10,000) see Giles Foundation, Edward C.

Amethyst Foundation ($3,000) see Rexham Inc.

Amethyst Foundation ($20,000) see Ruddick Corp.

Amethyst Treatment Center ($6,250) see Hemby Foundation, Alex

Andean Rural Health Care ($10,000) see Richardson Fund, Mary Lynn

Andrews Wildlife Rehabilitation Clinic ($10,800) see Felburn Foundation

Annie Penn Memorial Hospital — for a construction program ($200,000) see Duke Endowment

Appalachian State University ($10,000) see Burlington Industries

Appalachian State University, Appalachian Summer ($35,000) see Broyhill Family Foundation

Art Council ($7,500) see Shelton Cos.

Art School ($1,000) see Love Foundation, Martha and Spencer

Art and Science Council ($500) see BarclaysAmerican Corp.

Arts Council ($2,500) see Dillard Paper Co.

Arts Council for Davidson County ($10,000) see

Thomasville Furniture Industries

Arts and Science Council ($22,000) see BarclaysAmerican Corp.

Arts and Science Council ($10,000) see Lance, Inc.

Arts and Science Council ($26,100) see Radiator Specialty Co.

Arts and Science Council ($10,000) see United Dominion Industries

Arts and Science Council of Charlotte ($81,000) see First Union Corp.

Ashe County Performing Arts Building Committee ($8,000) see Thomasville Furniture Industries

Asheville School ($30,000) see Hillsdale Fund

Asheville School ($15,600) see Perkins Charitable Foundation

Asheville School Building Fund ($5,000) see Crane Foundation, Raymond E. and Ellen F.

Ashland University — establish a Burton D. Morgan Chair ($25,000) see Morgan Foundation, Burton D.

Association for the Benefit of Child Development — for the ABCD Preschool Child/Parent Resource Centers Program ($150,000) see Babcock Foundation, Mary Reynolds

Autism Society of North Carolina ($40,000) see Fletcher Foundation, A. J.

Baptist Children's Homes of North Carolina ($47,682) see Carter Charitable Trust, Wilbur Lee

Bayboro Baptist Church ($250) see Perry-Griffin Foundation

Bayboro Methodist ($250) see Perry-Griffin Foundation

Bayleaf Baptist Church — building fund ($35,000) see Palin Foundation

Bayleaf Church ($63,975) see Palin Foundation

Bellamy Mansion ($25,000) see Hillsdale Fund

Belmont Abbey College ($60,000) see Janirve Foundation

Belmont Abbey College ($41,500) see Stowe, Jr. Foundation, Robert Lee

Belmont Community Organization ($6,660) see Stowe, Jr. Foundation, Robert Lee

Bennett College ($3,000) see New Orphan Asylum Scholarship Foundation

Bennett College — to provide one-for-one endowment-challenge grant ($500,000) see Mott Foundation, Charles Stewart

Bethesda Presbyterian Church ($10,000) see Campbell Foundation, Ruth and Henry

Bible Pentecostal Church ($100) see Morgan Trust for Charity, Religion, and Education

Bible Tabernacle ($4,500) see Dauch Foundation, William

Black Mountain Pairing Project ($1,000) see McClure Educational and Development Fund, James G. K.

Black Mountain Pairing Project ($1,000) see McClure Educational and Development Fund, James G. K.

Blue ridge Community Health Services ($50,000) see

Cummings Foundation, James H.

Blue Ridge Assembly ($2,000) see Dillard Paper Co.

Blue Ridge Teachers Network ($2,000) see McClure Educational and Development Fund, James G. K.

Blue Ridge Technical College ($25,000) see Cummings Foundation, James H.

Blumenthal Jewish Home ($20,000) see Brenner Foundation

Blumenthal Jewish Home ($5,000) see Weininger Foundation, Richard and Gertrude

Botanical Garden Foundation ($12,169) see Radiator Specialty Co.

Bounce Back for Homeless ($5,000) see Royal Group Inc.

Bowman Gray School of Medicine — to develop a model geriatrics curriculum for medical students and resident physicians ($45,000) see Fullerton Foundation

Bowman Gray School of Medicine ($10,000) see Gilmer-Smith Foundation

Bowman Gray School of Medicine ($5,000) see Goody's Manufacturing Corp.

Bowman Gray School of Medicine — for construction and renovations ($1,000,000) see Kresge Foundation

Bowman Gray School of Medicine — cancer center ($15,000) see Lacy Foundation

Bowman Gray School of Medicine — capital campaign ($900,000) see RJR Nabisco Inc.

Bowman Gray School of Medicine — scholarships ($85,000) see Whitehead Foundation, Lettie Pate

Boy Scouts of America ($1,000) see Burress, J.W.

Boy Scouts of America ($500) see Classic Leather

Boy Scouts of America ($3,500) see Liberty Hosiery Mills

Boy Scouts of America ($6,000) see North Carolina Foam Foundation

Boy Scouts of America ($30,000) see Parsons - W.D. Charities, Vera Davis

Boy Scouts of America ($3,500) see Rexham Inc.

Boy Scouts of America ($2,000) see Starrett Co., L.S.

Boy Scouts of America ($2,000) see Thomas Built Buses L.P.

Boy Scouts of America ($10,000) see Whitener Foundation

Boys Club of Rocky Mount ($5,000) see Standard Products Co.

Boys and Girls Club ($2,500) see Thomas Built Buses L.P.

Boys and Girls Homes of North Carolina ($500) see Bossong Hosiery Mills

Brenner Children's Hospital ($5,075) see Goody's Manufacturing Corp.

Brenner Children's Hospital ($5,000) see Lacy Foundation

Brevard College ($5,000) see Moore & Sons, B.C.

Brevard Music Center ($3,000) see Rauch Foundation

Brigade Boys Club ($15,000) see Davis Charitable Foundation, Champion McDowell

North Carolina (cont.)

Buffalo Springs Missionary Church ($100) see Morgan Trust for Charity, Religion, and Education

Burlington Educational Foundation ($2,500) see Liberty Hosiery Mills

Cabarrus County Schools ($150,000) see Cannon Foundation

Cabarrus Memorial Hospital ($800,000) see Cannon Foundation

Cabarrus Memorial Hospital ($430,000) see Cannon Foundation

Caldwell Community College ($31,666) see Coffey Foundation

Caldwell Community College — economic development ($10,000) see La-Z-Boy Chair Co.

Caldwell County Hospice ($26,500) see Broyhill Family Foundation

Caldwell County United Way ($43,000) see Interco

Caldwell House ($3,000) see Coffey Foundation

Caldwell Residential Services ($5,000) see Coffey Foundation

Calvary Baptist Church ($5,000) see Nanney Foundation, Charles and Irene

Calvary Church ($923,541) see DeMoss Foundation, Arthur S.

Campbell University ($100,000) see Booth Ferris Foundation

Campbell University ($5,000) see Taylor Foundation

Cannon Hospital ($7,500) see Bay Branch Foundation

Cannon Memorial YMCA and Community Center ($250,000) see Cannon Foundation

Cannon YMCA ($20,000) see Fieldcrest Cannon

Cape Fear Community College — to establish additional allied health services ($922,400) see Reynolds Charitable Trust, Kate B.

Cape Fear Hospital Endowment ($15,000) see Davis Charitable Foundation, Champion McDowell

Caramore Community ($2,500) see Wellons Foundation

Carolina Community Project ($4,000) see Carteh Foundation

Carolina Day School ($50,000) see Ford Foundation, Edward E.

Carolina New Life Church ($100) see Morgan Trust for Charity, Religion, and Education

Carolina Raptor Center ($3,000) see Bailey Wildlife Foundation

Carolina Symphony ($2,500) see Martin Marietta Aggregates

Carolinas Medical Center — trauma ($125,000) see Hemby Foundation, Alex

Carteret County General Hospital Corporation ($150,000) see Duke Endowment

Catawba College ($22,000) see Hurley Foundation, J. F.

Catawba College ($20,000) see Whitener Foundation

Catawba College ($6,000) see Whitener Foundation

Caudale Cemetery ($5,000) see Davis Charitable Foundation, Champion McDowell

Celebration North Carolina ($83,333) see Duke Power Co.

Celebration North Carolina/Charlotte Salute ($2,500) see BarclaysAmerican Corp.

Center for Community Self-Help — to expand the center's technical and financial assistance to business and housing projects ($1,500,000) see MacArthur Foundation, John D. and Catherine T.

Center for Creative Leadership — for land acquisition and construction of conference facility ($750,000) see El Pomar Foundation

Center for Creative Leadership ($1,600,000) see Richardson Foundation, Smith

Center for Creative Leadership ($1,000,000) see Richardson Foundation, Smith

Center for Independent Living ($500) see Trion

Center for Research on Population Control ($20,000) see Zlinkoff Fund for Medical Research and Education, Sergei S.

Center for Rural Affairs ($75,000) see Austin Memorial Foundation

Central Baptist Association ($5,000) see Whitener Foundation

Central Piedmont Community College ($20,000) see Dickson Foundation

Central Piedmont Community College ($20,000) see Ruddick Corp.

Chapel Hill Training Outreach Program ($17,481) see Wareheim Foundation, E. C.

Charles A. Cannon, Jr. Memorial Hospital ($200,000) see Cannon Foundation

Charles A. Cannon Memorial Hospital ($20,000) see Blackmer Foundation, Henry M.

Charles A. Cannon Memorial Hospital ($20,000) see Blackmer Foundation, Henry M.

Charles McCrary School ($1,500) see Acme-McCrary Corp.

Charlotte Chamber Foundation — town clock ($500) see BarclaysAmerican Corp.

Charlotte Country Day School — general campaign ($50,000) see Belk Stores

Charlotte Country Day School ($6,250) see Charitable Foundation of the Burns Family

Charlotte Country Day School ($43,100) see Dalton Foundation, Harry L.

Charlotte Country Day School ($50,000) see Dickson Foundation

Charlotte Country Day School — capital campaign ($115,000) see Foothills Foundation

Charlotte Country Day School ($50,000) see Harris Foundation, James J. and Angelia M.

Charlotte Country Day School ($50,000) see Ruddick Corp.

Charlotte Country Day School ($5,000) see Shenandoah Foundation

Charlotte County Day School ($10,000) see Hogan Foundation, Royal Barney

Charlotte Homeless Shelter ($25,000) see Giles Foundation, Edward C.

Charlotte Housing Authority ($5,000) see Ginter Foundation, Karl and Anna

Charlotte-Mecklenburg Hospital ($125,000) see Van Every Foundation, Philip L.

Charlotte-Mecklenburg Hospital ($125,000) see Van Every Foundation, Philip L.

Charlotte Mecklenburg Schools ($2,000) see Martin Marietta Aggregates

Charlotte Symphony ($27,500) see Pepsi-Cola Bottling Co. of Charlotte

Charlotte Symphony ($17,343) see Radiator Specialty Co.

Charlotte Symphony Orchestra — annual fund and radiothon 90 ($10,000) see Foothills Foundation

Charlotte World Affairs Council ($1,500) see BarclaysAmerican Corp.

Child Care Task Force ($5,000) see Royal Group Inc.

Children's Home Society ($70,000) see Ebert Charitable Foundation, Horatio B.

Children's Home Society of North Carolina ($15,000) see Whitener Foundation

Children's Miracle Network ($10,000) see Pepsi-Cola Bottling Co. of Charlotte

Children's Theatre of Charlotte ($1,000) see Love Foundation, Martha and Spencer

Chowan College ($50,000) see Camp Younts Foundation

Chowan College ($23,750) see Campbell Foundation, Ruth and Henry

Chowan College — to equip a series of laboratories and work stations ($40,000) see Fletcher Foundation, A. J.

Christian Coalition ($550) see Wellons Foundation

Christian Lay Ministries ($25,000) see Generation Trust

Church of the Good Shepherd ($1,000) see Davis Charitable Foundation, Champion McDowell

Church in the Pines ($10,000) see Morgan Trust for Charity, Religion, and Education

Cities in Schools ($7,500) see Ginter Foundation, Karl and Anna

City of Fayetteville Police Department — to support judo program ($3,200) see Rogers Charitable Trust, Florence

City of Thomasville ($15,000) see Finch Foundation, Thomas Austin

City of Winston Salem ($20,000) see Hanes Foundation, John W. and Anna H.

Clemson University — to move a demonstration project in Custom Implant Design out of laboratory into clinical use ($100,000) see Fullerton Foundation

Clemson University Foundation ($100,000) see Duke Power Co.

Cleveland Community College School of Nursing ($10,000) see Dover Foundation

Cleveland Memorial Hospital — to construct a new patient care tower ($175,000) see Duke Endowment

Cleveland Memorial Library ($12,500) see Dover Foundation

Cleveland Psychosocial Services ($15,000) see Lane Charitable Trust, Melvin R.

Coalition for Freedom ($2,500) see Henry Foundation, Patrick

Coalition for Freedom ($35,000) see Pioneer Fund

College Scholarship Service ($9,082) see Cone Mills Corp.

Community General Hospital ($25,000) see Finch Foundation, Doak

Community General Hospital of Thomasville ($20,000) see Finch Foundation, Thomas Austin

Community General Hospital of Thomasville ($15,000) see Finch Foundation, Thomas Austin

Community General Hospital of Thomasville ($25,000) see Thomasville Furniture Industries

Community School of Arts ($5,000) see Ginter Foundation, Karl and Anna

Concerned Citizens of Tillery ($20,000) see Needmor Fund

Connie Maxwell Children's Home ($15,894) see Carter Charitable Trust, Wilbur Lee

Consolidated YMCA ($66,960) see Fieldcrest Cannon

Corinth Reformed United Church of Christ ($25,000) see Abernethy Testamentary Charitable Trust, Maye Morrison

Cornelia Hiton Davis Health Care Center ($342,500) see Davis Charitable Foundation, Champion McDowell

Cornerstone Christian Center ($1,500) see Nanney Foundation, Charles and Irene

County of Hoke — to establish a community-based primary health care center ($320,000) see Reynolds Charitable Trust, Kate B.

CP and L for Project Share ($1,000) see Trion

CPCC ($5,000) see Royal Group Inc.

CPCC Campaign for Excellence ($5,000) see BarclaysAmerican Corp.

CPCC Foundation ($5,000) see Rexham Inc.

Crisis Assistance Ministry ($62,510) see Duke Power Co.

Crisis Assistance Ministry ($54,351) see Duke Power Co.

Crisis Assistance Ministry ($20,000) see Ginter Foundation, Karl and Anna

Crisis Assistance Ministry ($18,000) see Glenn Foundation, Carrie C. & Lena V.

Crisis Assistance Ministry ($1,500) see Nanney Foundation, Charles and Irene

Crisis Assistance Ministry ($5,000) see Preyer Fund, Mary Norris

Crisis Control — Good Samaritan Soup Kitchen ($5,000) see Brenner Foundation

Crisis Control Ministry ($15,000) see Lacy Foundation

Crosby Fund-Winston-Salem Foundation ($50,000) see Wachovia Bank & Trust Co., N.A.

Crossnore School ($25,586) see Willard Helping Fund, Cecilia Young

Crossroads of North Carolina ($1,500) see Akzo America

Currituck County High School ($40,000) see Knapp Educational Fund

Davidson College ($1,300) see Acme-McCrary Corp.

Davidson College ($6,000) see Allendale Mutual Insurance Co.

Davidson College ($3,000) see Bossong Hosiery Mills

Davidson College ($500,000) see Campbell Foundation, J. Bulow

Davidson College ($6,000) see Coffey Foundation

Davidson College — educational purposes ($2,100,000) see Duke Endowment

Davidson College ($25,000) see Harris Foundation, James J. and Angelia M.

Davidson College ($20,000) see Hemby Foundation, Alex

Davidson College ($250,000) see Smith Charities, John

Davidson College ($50,000) see Steele-Reese Foundation

Davidson College ($20,000) see Stowe, Jr. Foundation, Robert Lee

Davidson College ($68,651) see Stuart Foundation, Edward C.

Davidson College ($10,000) see Ukrop's Super Markets, Inc.

Davidson College — Baker Sports Arena ($10,000) see Hemby Foundation, Alex

Davidson College — to expand the university's computer network ($162,000) see Digital Equipment Corp.

Davidson County Arts Council ($5,000) see Finch Foundation, Doak

Davidson County Library Foundation ($33,500) see Finch Foundation, Thomas Austin

Davidson County Library Foundation ($25,000) see Finch Foundation, Thomas Austin

Davidson County Library Foundation ($20,000) see Thomasville Furniture Industries

Davis Community Hospital ($24,100) see Davis Hospital Foundation

Delancey Street North Carolina ($2,500) see Dillard Paper Co.

Department of Human Resources Division of Vocational Rehabilitation Services ($50,000) see Janirve Foundation

Discovery Place ($10,871) see Glenn Foundation, Carrie C. & Lena V.

Discovery Place ($10,000) see Royal Group Inc.

Discovery Place Capital Campaign ($5,000) see Rexham Inc.

District Memorial Hospital of Southwestern North Carolina ($9,995) see Ferebee Endowment, Percy O.

District Memorial Mission Hospital of Southwestern North Carolina ($15,250) see Ferebee Endowment, Percy O.

Dover Baptist Church ($17,000) see Dover Foundation

DOVIA ($1,000) see McClure Educational and Development Fund, James G. K.

North Carolina (cont.)

Gardner Webb College — Dover scholarships ($15,000) see Dover Foundation

Gaston Comprehensive Day Center ($10,500) see Lane Charitable Trust, Melvin R.

Gaston-Lincoln Library ($12,000) see Glenn Foundation, Carrie C. & Lena V.

Gaston Skills ($10,000) see Glenn Foundation, Carrie C. & Lena V.

Gateway Community Development Corporation — operating support for three years ($150,000) see Reynolds Foundation, Z. Smith

Gertrude Smith Historical House ($23,662) see Gilmer-Smith Foundation

Gideons ($125) see Wellons Foundation

Girl Scouts of America ($3,000) see Acme-McCrary Corp.

Givens Estate ($75,000) see Janirve Foundation

Glad Tidings ($12,120) see Christian Training Foundation

Goals ($2,500) see Jewell Memorial Foundation, Daniel Ashley and Irene Houston

Goldsboro City Schools ($1,932) see Bryan Foundation, James E. and Mary Z.

Goldsboro High School — scholarship fund ($12,000) see Bryan Foundation, James E. and Mary Z.

Goodwill Industries ($3,500) see Stewards Fund

Gospel Tabernacle ($11,275) see Wellons Foundation

Governor's Institute on Alcohol and Substance Abuse — comprehensive curriculum on alcohol and other drugs at each of the four medical schools ($887,479) see Reynolds Charitable Trust, Kate B.

Grace Reformed United Church of Christ ($25,000) see Abernethy Testamentary Charitable Trust, Maye Morrison

Graham Community College ($2,000) see Hexcel Corp.

Graham County ($15,000) see Ferebee Endowment, Percy O.

Grandfather Home for Children ($3,000) see Coffey Foundation

Grandfather Home for Children ($25,586) see Willard Helping Fund, Cecilia Young

Grassroots Leadership — support a project to link a youth initiative with a grassroots community organizing project in three rural South Carolina counties ($25,000) see Hazen Foundation, Edward W.

Greensboro College ($1,500) see Liberty Hosiery Mills

Greensboro College — library renovation ($16,666) see Sternberger Foundation, Sigmund

Greensboro Community Arts Council Capital Fund — to promote and encourage a wholesome community life ($20,000) see Landmark Communications

Greensboro Day School ($8,000) see Jackson Mills

Greensboro Historical Museum ($5,250) see Weaver Foundation

Greensboro Independent School ($25,000) see Hillsdale Fund

Greensboro Music Academy ($4,000) see Love Foundation, Martha and Spencer

Greensboro Music Academy Foundation ($1,500) see Halstead Foundation

Greensboro Public Schools ($10,000) see Richardson Fund, Mary Lynn

Greensboro Urban Ministry — toward establishment of a comprehensive facility ($1,000,000) see Bryan Family Foundation, Kathleen Price and Joseph M.

Greensboro Urban Ministry ($16,667) see Covington Foundation, Marion Stedman

Greensboro Urban Ministry ($2,500) see Halstead Foundation

Greensboro Urban Ministry ($5,000) see Preyer Fund, Mary Norris

Greensboro Urban Ministry ($14,000) see Richardson Fund, Mary Lynn

Greensboro Urban Ministry ($15,000) see Sternberger Foundation, Sigmund

Greensboro Urban Ministry ($100,000) see Weaver Foundation

Guildford College ($10,000) see Blue Bell, Inc.

Guildord Battleground ($100,000) see Sternberger Foundation, Sigmund

Guilford College ($5,000) see Dillard Paper Co.

Guilford College ($2,000) see Love Foundation, Martha and Spencer

Guilford College — for the first Distinguished Visiting Professorship program ($300,000) see Bryan Family Foundation, Kathleen Price and Joseph M.

Guilford County School System — for new educational equipment ($75,000) see Bryan Family Foundation, Kathleen Price and Joseph M.

Gum Creek Presbyterian Church ($3,000) see Morgan Trust for Charity, Religion, and Education

Habitat for Humanity ($4,000) see Halstead Foundation

Habitat for Humanity ($10,000) see Nanney Foundation, Charles and Irene

Habitat for Humanity ($3,000) see Ramlose Foundation, George A.

Habitat for Humanity ($45,000) see Stewards Fund

Habitat for Humanity ($10,000) see Stewards Fund

Habitat for Humanity of Thomasville ($5,000) see Thomasville Furniture Industries

Hale High School ($50,000) see Palin Foundation

Halifax Court Day Care ($5,000) see Stewards Fund

Health Adventure ($5,000) see Ferebee Endowment, Percy O.

Health Adventure ($2,000) see McClure Educational and Development Fund, James G. K.

Health Adventure ($1,500) see McClure Educational and Development Fund, James G. K.

Hebron Colony and Grace Home ($5,000) see Taylor Foundation

Heineman Foundation ($50,000) see Lance, Inc.

Henderbed Street Foundation — operations ($45,000) see Kenan Family Foundation

Henderson County Council on Aging ($16,800) see Lane Charitable Trust, Melvin R.

Henderson County Sheltered Workshop ($25,000) see Lane Charitable Trust, Melvin R.

Hezekiah Alexander Foundation ($500) see BarclaysAmerican Corp.

High Hope of Hickory ($2,000) see Classic Leather

High Point Arts Council ($3,000) see Thomas Built Buses L.P.

High Point College ($2,500) see Dillard Paper Co.

High Point College ($150,000) see Shelton Cos.

High Point College ($2,000) see Thomas Built Buses L.P.

Historic Preservation Foundation ($25,000) see Covington Foundation, Marion Stedman

Historic Preservation Foundation ($25,000) see Covington Foundation, Marion Stedman

Historic Salisbury Foundation ($15,000) see Hurley Foundation, J. F.

Hobbton High School — scholarship fund ($15,000) see Bryan Foundation, James E. and Mary Z.

Hollis College ($150) see Marsh Furniture Co.

Holy Angels — toward establishment of three intermediate-care residential facilities ($50,000) see Bryan Family Foundation, Kathleen Price and Joseph M.

Holy Angels Nursery ($25,000) see Giles Foundation, Edward C.

Homeowner's Model Experiment — toward endowment of a lease-purchase program ($50,000) see Bryan Family Foundation, Kathleen Price and Joseph M.

Horatio Alger Association ($5,000) see Burress, J.W.

Hospice ($7,500) see Davis Charitable Foundation, Champion McDowell

Hospice ($10,000) see Dillard Paper Co.

Hospice ($2,500) see Stewards Fund

Hospice of Gaston County ($18,500) see Glenn Foundation, Carrie C. & Lena V.

Hospice at Greensboro ($13,000) see Weaver Foundation

Hospice of Surry County ($6,500) see North Carolina Foam Foundation

Hospice of Wake County ($10,000) see Cheatham Foundation, Owen

Hospitality House ($10,000) see Davis Charitable Foundation, Champion McDowell

Hospitality House of the Boone Area — for child care coordinator as a full time staff member ($5,500) see Butz Foundation

Hudson River Sloop Clearwater ($5,000) see Preyer Fund, Mary Norris

Human Kindness Foundation ($5,000) see Hunt Foundation

Hurley Park ($37,814) see Hurley Foundation, J. F.

I.P.A.S. — general programs support ($10,000) see Campbell and Adah E. Hall Charity Fund, Bushrod H.

Indepedent College Fund of North Carolina ($20,000) see Cone Mills Corp.

Independent College Fund of North Carolina ($1,500) see Acme-McCrary Corp.

Independent College Fund of North Carolina ($1,000) see Dillard Paper Co.

Independent College Fund of North Carolina ($113,500) see Duke Power Co.

Independent College Fund of North Carolina ($1,680) see Florida Steel Corp.

Independent College Fund of North Carolina ($4,000) see Goody's Manufacturing Corp.

Independent College Fund of North Carolina ($25,000) see Lance, Inc.

Independent College Fund of North Carolina ($5,500) see Martin Marietta Aggregates

Independent College Fund of North Carolina ($6,000) see Thomas Built Buses L.P.

Independent College Fund of North Carolina ($2,500) see Trion

Independent College Fund of North Carolina ($12,500) see Universal Leaf Tobacco Co.

Independent College Fund of North Carolina ($45,000) see Wachovia Bank & Trust Co., N.A.

Industrial Opportunities ($5,000) see Ferebee Endowment, Percy O.

Industrial Opportunities ($23,600) see Lane Charitable Trust, Melvin R.

Inner City Scholarship Fund ($4,000) see Acme-McCrary Corp.

Institute for Servant Leadership ($7,500) see Mostyn Foundation

Institute for Southern Studies ($10,000) see Beldon II Fund

International House ($2,000) see BarclaysAmerican Corp.

International House ($5,000) see Ginter Foundation, Karl and Anna

International Projects Assistance Services ($51,530) see Bergstrom Foundation, Erik E. and Edith H.

International Projects Assistance Services — training and service delivery ($10,000) see Brush Foundation

International Projects Assistance Services — continued support ($750,000) see Steele Foundation, Harry and Grace

Isothermal Community College Foundation ($100,000) see Stonecutter Mills Corp.

J. Wise Fund ($1,000) see Burress, J.W.

Jesse Helms Center, Wingate College ($2,500) see Henry Foundation, Patrick

Jewish National Fund ($1,200) see Lowe's Cos.

John C. Campbell Folk School ($10,000) see Ferebee Endowment, Percy O.

Johnson C. Smith University — educational purposes ($1,700,000) see Duke Endowment

Johnson C. Smith University — for the capital campaign ($1,000,000) see Knight Foundation, John S. and James L.

Johnson C. Smith University ($10,000) see Rexham Inc.

Johnston County Education Foundation ($25,000) see Holding Foundation, Robert P.

Judge Gaston House Restoration — partial repair of roof ($15,100) see Kellenberger Historical Foundation, May Gordon Latham

Jungle Aviation and Radio Service International ($12,000) see Kejr Foundation

Junior Achievement ($300) see Classic Leather

Junior Achievement ($11,500) see Lance, Inc.

Junior Achievement see Michigan Mutual Insurance Corp.

Junior League ($5,000) see Halstead Foundation

Kershaw Fire Department ($1,500) see Moore & Sons, B.C.

Kings Mountain School District ($1,250) see Foote Mineral Co.

Kings Mountain United Fund ($500) see Foote Mineral Co.

Knight Foundation Commission on Intercollegiate Athletics — for operating funds for an independent national commission ($631,678) see Knight Foundation, John S. and James L.

Lausanne Committee on World Evangelism ($31,000) see Huston Foundation

Lausanne Committee for World Evangelization ($40,000) see First Fruit

Lausanne Committee for World Evangelization — operating funds ($100,000) see Maclellan Charitable Trust, R. J.

Leadership Winston-Salem ($4,000) see Brenner Foundation

Lee County Alzheimer's Disease Support Group ($500) see Trion

Lee County Emergency Food Pantry ($1,000) see Trion

Lees-McRae College ($6,000) see Anderson Foundation, Robert C. and Sadie G.

Lees-McRae College ($102,500) see Broyhill Family Foundation

Lees-McRae College ($5,000) see Coffey Foundation

Lees-McRae College ($15,000) see Glenn Foundation, Carrie C. & Lena V.

Lees-McRae College ($25,586) see Willard Helping Fund, Cecilia Young

Leighton Ford Foundation ($25,000) see Dalton Foundation, Harry L.

Leighton Ford Ministries ($5,000) see Christian Workers Foundation

Lenior-Rhyne College ($9,780) see Classic Leather

Lenoir County Educational Foundation ($2,000) see Harvey Foundation, Felix

Lenoir-Rhyne College ($150,000) see Cannon Foundation

Lenoir-Rhyne College ($25,000) see Dickson Foundation

Lenoir-Rhyne College ($40,000) see First Union Corp.

Lenoir-Rhyne College ($10,000) see M/A-COM, Inc.

Lenoir Rhyne College ($25,000) see Ruddick Corp.

Lenoir Rhyne College ($9,375) see Willard Helping Fund, Cecilia Young

Liberty United Methodist Church ($3,067) see Liberty Hosiery Mills

Life After Cancer ($15,000) see Appleby Foundation

Lineberger Comprehensive Cancer Center ($5,000) see Stowe, Jr. Foundation, Robert Lee

Lineberger Comprehensive Cancer Center ($10,000) see Titmus Foundation

Lineberger Comprehensive Cancer Center ($10,000) see Titmus Foundation

Links Adolescent Services ($10,000) see Weaver Foundation

Links Adolescent Services Foundation ($5,000) see Dillard Paper Co.

Links Adolescent Services Foundation ($25,000) see Sternberger Foundation, Sigmund

Livingstone College ($15,000) see Hurley Foundation, J. F.

Long-McRae College ($50,000) see Cain Foundation, Gordon and Mary

Louisburg College ($20,000) see News & Observer Publishing Co.

Lubavitch of North Carolina ($12,300) see Radiator Specialty Co.

Lutheran Family Services ($10,000) see Richardson Fund, Mary Lynn

Lutheran Retirement Ministries ($6,000) see Liberty Hosiery Mills

Macon County Public Library ($15,000) see Ferebee Endowment, Percy O.

Macon County Public Library ($5,000) see Ferebee Endowment, Percy O.

Main Street Baptist Church ($5,000) see Stonecutter Mills Corp.

Mars Hill College ($30,200) see Broyhill Family Foundation

Mars Hill College ($150,000) see Cannon Foundation

Mars Hill College ($75,000) see Janirve Foundation

Mars Hill College ($1,100) see Lowe's Cos.

Mars Hill College ($51,000) see Nanney Foundation, Charles and Irene

Maryfield Nursing Home ($3,000) see Love Foundation, Martha and Spencer

McColl Main Street United Methodist Church ($100) see Morgan Trust for Charity, Religion, and Education

McPherson Foundation ($1,000) see Kenan Family Foundation

MDC ($25,000) see Grant Foundation, Charles M. and Mary D.

Mecklenburg County Council ($1,000) see Love Foundation, Martha and Spencer

Mecklenburg County Health Department ($50,000) see Van Every Foundation, Philip L.

Medical Center ($20,000) see Shelton Cos.

Medical Center of Boman-Gray School of Medicine ($100,000) see Janirve Foundation

Medical Center — Brenner Children's Hospital ($572,000) see Brenner Foundation

Medical Foundation of East Carolina University ($1,000) see Trion

Medical Foundation of North Carolina ($50,000) see Dover Foundation

Memorial Mission Medical Center — for heart care and clinical laboratory needs ($83,000) see Fullerton Foundation

Memorial United Methodist Church ($50,000) see Finch Foundation, Doak

Memorial United Methodist Church ($25,000) see Finch Foundation, Doak

Memorial United Methodist Church ($58,500) see Finch Foundation, Thomas Austin

Memorial United Methodist Church ($24,750) see Finch Foundation, Thomas Austin

Memorial United Methodist Church ($15,000) see Finch Foundation, Thomas Austin

Mental Health Association of Forsyth County ($7,000) see Lacy Foundation

Mercy Fund ($2,000) see Rexham Inc.

Meredith College ($9,180) see Bryan Foundation, James E. and Mary Z.

Meredith College ($75,000) see Fletcher Foundation, A. J.

Meredith College ($100,000) see Palin Foundation

Methodist College — microscopes and steam scrubber washer ($8,574) see Rogers Charitable Trust, Florence

Methodist College — purchase of human anatomy model ($3,725) see Rogers Charitable Trust, Florence

Methodist College — equipment in communications department ($3,200) see Rogers Charitable Trust, Florence

Mitchell Community College ($6,165) see Davis Hospital Foundation

Monkey Island Education Project — for environmental improvements for education center ($10,000) see Knapp Foundation

Montreat-Anderson College ($83,750) see Anderson Foundation, Robert C. and Sadie G.

Moore County Children's Center ($3,000) see Finch Foundation, Doak

Motherhead, Inc. — for the Baby Ready program ($45,000) see Babcock Foundation, Mary Reynolds

Motor Racing Outreach ($4,000) see Goody's Manufacturing Corp.

Mount Olive African Methodist ($65,000) see Chapin Foundation of Myrtle Beach, South Carolina

Mount Olive College — toward establishment of an endowed scholarship fund ($75,000) see Bryan Family Foundation, Kathleen Price and Joseph M.

Mount Olive College ($40,000) see Bryan Foundation, James E. and Mary Z.

Mount Olive College ($26,325) see Harvey Foundation, Felix

Mount Olive College ($4,773) see Holding Foundation, Robert P.

Mount Olive College ($5,000) see Wellons Foundation

Mountain Home Nursing Home ($3,000) see Ferebee Endowment, Percy O.

Mountain Retreat Association — for lodge addition at the Presbyterian conference center ($150,000) see Reynolds Foundation, Richard S.

Museum of the New South — campaign fund ($35,000) see Belk Stores

Museum of the New South ($9,000) see Radiator Specialty Co.

Myers Park Presbyterian Church ($4,000) see Dalton Foundation, Harry L.

Myers Park Presbyterian Church ($62,500) see Hemby Foundation, Alex

NAACP ($10,000) see Preyer Fund, Mary Norris

National Association for Minority Trustees in Higher Education ($5,000) see Kenan Family Foundation

National Fund for Medical Education — health care education ($8,000) see Allyn Foundation

National Humanities Center ($10,000) see Devonwood Foundation

National Humanities Center ($15,000) see Donnelley Foundation, Gaylord and Dorothy

National Humanities Center ($2,250,000) see Mellon Foundation, Andrew W.

Natural Science Center — drug and nutrition exhibits ($50,000) see Sternberger Foundation, Sigmund

Natural Science Center of Greensboro ($10,000) see Covington Foundation, Marion Stedman

Natural Science Center of Greensboro ($5,000) see Preyer Fund, Mary Norris

Natural Science Center of Greensboro — toward start-up of a satellite storefront science museum ($100,000) see Bryan Family Foundation, Kathleen Price and Joseph M.

Nature Science Center ($1,667) see Brenner Foundation

Nature Science Center ($3,583) see Goody's Manufacturing Corp.

Nature Science Center ($25,000) see Lane Memorial Foundation, Mills Bee

Nature Science Center ($10,000) see Shelton Cos.

Nazareth Children's Home ($25,000) see Hurley Foundation, J. F.

Newton-Conover City Schools ($500) see Classic Leather

North Carolina A&T State University ($125,000) see Square D Co.

North Carolina A&T University ($45,000) see Deloitte & Touche

North Carolina A&T University Foundation ($7,947) see Holding Foundation, Robert P.

North Carolina A&T University Foundation ($10,000) see Weaver Foundation

North Carolina Agricultural and Technical State University

($91,000) see Teagle Foundation

North Carolina Association of Community Development Corporation ($37,500) see Wachovia Bank & Trust Co., N.A.

North Carolina Association of Community Development Corporations — operational support for two years to assist the Association in better serving member Community Development Corporations and to stabilize its operations ($125,000) see Reynolds Foundation, Z. Smith

North Carolina Baptist Hospitals — operating funds ($31,755) see Carter Charitable Trust, Wilbur Lee

North Carolina Blumenthal Center for Performing Arts ($10,000) see Dalton Foundation, Harry L.

North Carolina Blumenthal Center for Performing Arts ($30,000) see Harris Foundation, James J. and Angelia M.

North Carolina Center for Nonprofit Organizations — for "Self-Help for North Carolina Nonprofits" ($70,000) see Babcock Foundation, Mary Reynolds

North Carolina Child Advocacy Institute — to improve the quality and expand the quantity of child care in North Carolina ($89,167) see Glaxo

North Carolina Community College Foundation ($2,500) see Lowe's Cos.

North Carolina Community Foundation ($132,500) see Bryan Foundation, James E. and Mary Z.

North Carolina Dance Theater ($5,000) see Foote, Cone & Belding Communications

North Carolina Dance Theatre ($6,000) see Stowe, Jr. Foundation, Robert Lee

North Carolina Education Fund ($1,000) see Royal Group Inc.

North Carolina Environmental Defense Fund ($100) see Felburn Foundation

North Carolina Foundation for Alternative Health Programs — to develop prepaid managed mental health services for children ($326,443) see Reynolds Charitable Trust, Kate B.

North Carolina Foundation of Church-Related Colleges ($2,500) see Moore & Sons, B.C.

North Carolina Institute of Justice — operational support for the North Carolina Center on Crime and Punishment to work for criminal justice reform and crime prevention ($155,000) see Reynolds Foundation, Z. Smith

North Carolina Institute of Political Leadership ($5,000) see Preyer Fund, Mary Norris

North Carolina Museum of Art — operating activity ($5,000) see Foothills Foundation

North Carolina Museum of History ($50,000) see News & Observer Publishing Co.

North Carolina Museum of History — Museum of Cape Fear ($18,000) see Rogers Charitable Trust, Florence

North Carolina Museum of Life and Science — purchase of

van ($12,500) see Durham Merchants Association Charitable Foundation

North Carolina Nature Conservancy ($25,000) see Hillsdale Fund

North Carolina Newspapers First Amendment Foundation ($43,327) see News & Observer Publishing Co.

North Carolina Performing Arts Center ($20,000) see BarclaysAmerican Corp.

North Carolina Performing Arts Center ($50,000) see. Dickson Foundation

North Carolina Performing Arts Center ($50,000) see First Union Corp.

North Carolina Performing Arts Center — educational and cultural growth ($20,000) see Foothills Foundation

North Carolina Performing Arts Center ($30,000) see Harris Foundation, James J. and Angelia M.

North Carolina Performing Arts Center ($50,000) see Hoechst Celanese Corp.

North Carolina Performing Arts Center ($30,000) see Lance, Inc.

North Carolina Performing Arts Center ($25,000) see Pepsi-Cola Bottling Co. of Charlotte

North Carolina Performing Arts Center ($50,000) see Ruddick Corp.

North Carolina Performing Arts Center ($5,000) see Stevens Foundation, John T.

North Carolina Poetry Society — for two day poetry festival - Duke 1991 ($5,000) see Durham Merchants Association Charitable Foundation

North Carolina Public Television Foundation ($10,000) see Radiator Specialty Co.

North Carolina Public TV ($10,000) see Glenn Foundation, Carrie C. & Lena V.

North Carolina Pulp and Paper Foundation ($5,000) see Gilman Paper Co.

North Carolina School of Arts Foundation ($100,000) see Hanes Foundation, John W. and Anna H.

North Carolina School of Arts Foundation ($15,000) see Hanes Foundation, John W. and Anna H.

North Carolina School of Science and Mathematics — pilot project with the ultimate goal of restructuring science teaching throughout North Carolina ($168,685) see Glaxo

North Carolina School of Science and Mathematics — to initiate the Rural Schools Laboratory Science Initiative ($200,000) see Bryan Family Foundation, Kathleen Price and Joseph M.

North Carolina Shakespeare Festival ($4,000) see Whitener Foundation

North Carolina State Student Aid Association ($3,000) see Coffey Foundation

North Carolina State University ($25,000) see Dover Foundation

North Carolina State University ($67,000) see Finley Foundation, A. E.

North Carolina (cont.)

North Carolina State University ($75,000) see Frasch Foundation for Chemical Research (under the will of Elizabeth B. Frasch), Herman

North Carolina State University see Greenwood Mills

North Carolina State University — to develop computer facility for climatic research ($1,900,000) see IBM Corp.

North Carolina State University — to research selective cleavage of nucleic acids ($500,000) see Packard Foundation, David and Lucile

North Carolina State University ($7,500) see Seasongood Good Government Foundation, Murray and Agnes

North Carolina State University ($5,000) see Taylor Foundation

North Carolina State University ($100,000) see Wachovia Bank & Trust Co., N.A.

North Carolina State University Foundation ($10,000) see Holding Foundation, Robert P.

North Carolina State University — to spread a piloted educational program for family caregivers of the dependent elderly to all 100 counties and the Cherokee Reservation in North Carolina ($61,100) see Glaxo

North Carolina State University — Pulp and Paper Foundation ($25,000) see Union Camp Corp.

North Carolina State University — Pulp and Paper Science Technology scholarship program ($10,000) see Sandoz Corp.

North Carolina State Veterinary School ($10,000) see Glenn Foundation, Carrie C. & Lena V.

North Carolina Symphony ($25,000) see Covington Foundation, Marion Stedman

North Carolina Textile Foundation ($25,000) see Burlington Industries

North Carolina Textile Foundation ($10,000) see Cone Mills Corp.

North Carolina Textile Foundation ($26,000) see Fieldcrest Cannon

North Carolina Textile Foundation ($50,000) see Hoechst Celanese Corp.

North Carolina Tobacco Foundation ($13,000) see Universal Leaf Tobacco Co.

North Carolina Veterinary Medical Foundation ($15,000) see Randleigh Foundation Trust

North Carolina Wesleyan College ($5,000) see Burlington Industries

North Carolina-West Virginia Community Action Nutrition Program ($5,000) see Brown Family Foundation, John Mathew Gay

North Carolina Zoological Society ($4,250) see Acme-McCrary Corp.

North Carolina Zoological Society ($1,000) see BarclaysAmerican Corp.

North Carolina Zoological Society ($10,000) see Covington Foundation, Marion Stedman

North Carolina Zoological Society ($5,000) see Lowe's Cos.

North Carolina Zoological Society ($1,000) see Trion

Northampton Memorial Hospital ($72,000) see Finley Foundation, A. E.

Northern Hospital of Surry ($7,000) see North Carolina Foam Foundation

Northside Baptist Church ($38,167) see Christian Training Foundation

Northwest Christian Church ($2,000) see Harvey Foundation, Felix

Oakdale Cemetery — restoration fund ($10,000) see Kenan Family Foundation

Old Colony Players ($500) see Valdese Manufacturing Co., Inc.

Old Salem ($50,000) see Hanes Foundation, John W. and Anna H.

Old Wilkes ($2,500) see Lowe's Cos.

Operation Santa Claus ($150) see Felburn Foundation

Operation Smile International ($10,000) see Richardson Fund, Mary Lynn

Orange County Literacy Council — operations support ($10,000) see Kenan Family Foundation

Organization for Tropical Studies ($44,500) see General Service Foundation

Pack Place Education Arts and Science Center ($100,000) see Janirve Foundation

Pack Place Education Arts and Science Center ($30,000) see Wachovia Bank & Trust Co., N.A.

Peace College ($3,500) see Anderson Foundation, Robert C. and Sadie G.

Peace College ($35,000) see Finley Foundation, A. E.

Peace College ($42,000) see Fletcher Foundation, A. J.

Pembroke State University ($5,000) see Burlington Industries

Penick Memorial Home — care of aged women ($150,000) see Whitehead Foundation, Lettie Pate

Penland School of Crafts ($100,000) see Janirve Foundation

People for the American Way in North Carolina — for the North Carolina Students Teach and Reach program ($70,000) see Babcock Foundation, Mary Reynolds

Pepperland Farm Camp ($12,500) see McGregor Foundation, Thomas and Frances

Performing Arts Center ($25,000) see Royal Group Inc.

Pfeiffer College ($150,000) see Cannon Foundation

Piedmont Educational Foundation ($600) see Classic Leather

Piedmont Pizazz ($1,000) see Carlyle & Co. Jewelers

Piedmont School ($3,000) see Thomas Built Buses L.P.

Planned Parenthood ($14,000) see Kelly Foundation, T. Lloyd

Planned Parenthood Federation of America ($4,000) see Ginter Foundation, Karl and Anna

Poe Center for Health Education ($100,000) see Palin Foundation

Population Planning Associates ($181,000) see International Fund for Health and Family Planning

Presbyterian Homes ($10,000) see Palin Foundation

Presbyterian Hospital ($50,000) see Van Every Foundation, Philip L.

Presbyterian Hospital Foundation — Carolinas Heart Institute ($100,000) see Belk Stores

Presbyterian Intercommunity Hospital Foundation ($47,500) see Baker Foundation, R. C.

Prison Fellowship USA ($5,000) see Preyer Fund, Mary Norris

Progressive Missionary Baptist Association ($100) see Morgan Trust for Charity, Religion, and Education

Project Uplift ($120,000) see Weaver Foundation

Project Uplift — to measure the effectiveness of computer learning for low-income children, enhance school readiness, introduce children to problem-solving techniques, and reinforce self-esteem ($18,790) see Glaxo

Providence Day School ($10,000) see Hemby Foundation, Alex

Public School Forum of North Carolina — general operational support to continue the Forum's role as a change agent and consensus builder around education policy and practices in North Carolina ($125,000) see Reynolds Foundation, Z. Smith

Queen Street United Methodist Church ($4,750) see Harvey Foundation, Felix

Queens College ($20,000) see Anderson Foundation, Robert C. and Sadie G.

Queens College ($10,000) see Dalton Foundation, Harry L.

Queens College ($25,000) see Dickson Foundation

Queens College ($100,000) see Duke Power Co.

Queens College ($25,000) see Ellis Foundation

Queens College ($20,000) see Ginter Foundation, Karl and Anna

Queens College ($50,000) see Harris Foundation, James J. and Angelia M.

Queens College ($25,000) see Harris Foundation, James J. and Angelia M.

Queens College ($10,000) see Hemby Foundation, Alex

Queens College ($250,000) see Livingstone Charitable Foundation, Betty J. and J. Stanley

Queens College ($15,000) see Royal Group Inc.

Queens College ($25,000) see Ruddick Corp.

Queens College Library ($10,000) see Dalton Foundation, Harry L.

Raleigh Rescue Mission ($5,000) see Stewards Fund

Randolph Arts Guild ($10,000) see Covington Foundation, Marion Stedman

Randolph Hospital ($20,000) see Acme-McCrary Corp.

Randolph Hospital ($3,000) see Bossong Hosiery Mills

Randolph Hospital — to construct a major addition to the hospital ($175,000) see Duke Endowment

Ravenscroft School ($15,000) see Bryan Foundation, James E. and Mary Z.

Ravenscroft School ($140,000) see Finley Foundation, A. E.

Rebound ($13,500) see Christian Training Foundation

Reeves Community Center ($6,000) see North Carolina Foam Foundation

Reeves Community Center ($5,000) see Starrett Co., L.S.

Reformed Lutheran Church ($2,500) see Burress, J.W.

Renaissance Campaign ($10,000) see Blue Bell, Inc.

Renaissance Campaign-United Way ($25,000) see Cone Mills Corp.

Reynolda House ($33,334) see Hanes Foundation, John W. and Anna H.

Reynolda House ($30,000) see Hillsdale Fund

Reynolda House Museum of American Art ($3,000) see Love Foundation, Martha and Spencer

Reynolda House Museum of American Art ($2,000) see Lowe's Cos.

Reynolda House — general operational support for three years for the Museum of American Art ($150,000) see Reynolds Foundation, Z. Smith

Reynolda House Museum of American Art ($7,000) see Thomasville Furniture Industries

Richmond County Health Department ($40,000) see Cole Foundation

Robert Smith Park ($9,708) see Gilmer-Smith Foundation

Rocky Mount/Edgecombe Community Development Corporation — operational support for three years to develop and maintain key core staff positions ($150,000) see Reynolds Foundation, Z. Smith

Rosman Elementary ($250,000) see RJR Nabisco Inc.

Rowan County United Fund ($8,000) see Cone Mills Corp.

Rowan Public Library ($62,000) see Hurley Foundation, J. F.

St. Albans Psychiatric Hospital ($15,000) see Dover Foundation

St. Andrews Presbyterian College ($10,000) see Anderson Foundation, Robert C. and Sadie G.

St. Andrews Presbyterian College ($125,000) see Cannon Foundation

St. Andrews Presbyterian College ($10,000) see McDougall Charitable Trust, Ruth Camp

St. Andrews Presbyterian College ($315,000) see Morgan Trust for Charity, Religion, and Education

St. Andrew's School — support to enhance the school's math and science program ($100,000) see Steelcase

St. Augustine's College ($75,000) see Wachovia Bank & Trust Co., N.A.

St. Augustine's College — Student Activities Health Center ($25,000) see Good Samaritan

St. Catherine's School ($8,000) see Holding Foundation, Robert P.

St. John's Museum of Art — to support general art education exhibit program, school tour program, docent program and studio art classes ($50,000) see Glaxo

St. Marys AME Zion Church ($600) see Morgan Trust for Charity, Religion, and Education

St. Mary's College ($1,000) see Classic Leather

Salisbury City Schools ($20,000) see Hurley Foundation, J. F.

Salvation Army ($1,000) see Acme-McCrary Corp.

Salvation Army ($5,000) see Finch Foundation, Doak

Salvation Army ($2,600) see Harvey Foundation, Felix

Salvation Army ($5,000) see Nanney Foundation, Charles and Irene

Salvation Army ($6,000) see North Carolina Foam Foundation

Salvation Army ($3,145) see Rogers Charitable Trust, Florence

Salvation Army ($10,000) see Stewards Fund

Salvation Army ($3,500) see Thomas Built Buses L.P.

Samaritan's Purse ($40,000) see M.E. Foundation

Sampson Technical College ($1,000) see Mohasco Corp.

San-Lee Humane ($1,000) see Trion

Sand Hills Little Theater ($7,800) see Finch Foundation, Doak

Sandhills Children's Center ($20,000) see Cole Foundation

Sandhills Community College ($2,000) see Trion

Schiele Museum of Natural History and Planetarium ($30,000) see Belk Stores

Science Museum of Charlotte ($20,000) see Radiator Specialty Co.

Science Museums of Charlotte ($10,000) see Dixie Yarns, Inc.

Science Museums of Charlotte ($10,000) see Ginter Foundation, Karl and Anna

Science Museums of Charlotte ($15,000) see Pepsi-Cola Bottling Co. of Charlotte

Science Museums of Charlotte ($5,835) see Stowe, Jr. Foundation, Robert Lee

Sea Level Fire and Rescue Squad ($5,000) see Taylor Foundation

Semiconductor Research Corporation ($2,875,000) see Intel Corp.

Shelter Home of Caldwell County ($4,000) see Coffey Foundation

Shepherd's Table Soup Kitchen ($26,000) see Hillsdale Fund

Shriners Hospital ($5,000) see Coffey Foundation

SIM ($149,207) see Westwood Endowment

SIM USA ($30,000) see Crowell Trust, Henry P. and Susan C.

Society for the History of Technology ($10,000) see Dibner Fund

Southeastern Baptist Theological Seminary ($31,788) see Carter Charitable Trust, Wilbur Lee

Southeastern Center for Contemporary Art —

exhibition ($54,000) see Lannan Foundation

Southern Environmental Law Center — operational support for the North Carolina office of the Law Center ($150,000) see Reynolds Foundation, Z. Smith

Southmountain Children's Home ($5,000) see Stonecutter Mills Corp.

Spencer Baptist Church ($5,000) see Stonecutter Mills Corp.

Spindale Elementary School ($7,000) see Stonecutter Mills Corp.

Spindale First United Methodist Church ($10,000) see Stonecutter Mills Corp.

Spirit Square ($10,000) see Royal Group Inc.

Stanly Memorial Hospital ($25,000) see Collins & Aikman Holdings Corp.

Sudan Interior Mission ($5,000) see Demco Charitable Foundation

Sudan Interior Mission ($26,305) see Erickson Charitable Fund, Eben W.

Surry Arts Council ($2,000) see Gilmer-Smith Foundation

Surry County Health Foundation ($6,000) see North Carolina Foam Foundation

Swain County Hospital ($10,000) see Ferebee Endowment, Percy O.

Tammy Lynn Center — building fund ($16,666) see Palin Foundation

Tammy Lynn Center ($15,000) see Stewards Fund

Tammy Lynn Memorial Foundation ($50,000) see Fletcher Foundation, A. J.

Tanglewood Park Foundation — to develop a new winter light show to help the Park achieve economic self-sufficiency ($150,000) see Reynolds Foundation, Z. Smith

Thomasville Library Fund ($125,000) see Finch Foundation, Doak

Thomasvillle City Schools ($20,000) see Finch Foundation, Doak

To Life ($11,000) see Pepsi-Cola Bottling Co. of Charlotte

Tom Haggai and Association Foundation ($25,000) see Tripifoods

Tommorrow's America Foundation ($101,100) see Broyhill Family Foundation

Town of LaGrange Public Library ($5,000) see Harvey Foundation, Felix

Trans World Radio ($10,000) see Caddock Foundation

Triad United Methodist Home — care of aged women ($125,000) see Whitehead Foundation, Lettie Pate

Triangle Opera Theatre — 1991 Street Opera ($10,000) see Biddle Foundation, Mary Duke

Trinity Avenue Presbyterian Church ($3,000) see Devonwood Foundation

Trinity Center ($20,000) see Hanes Foundation, John W. and Anna H.

Tryon Palace Commission ($41,346) see Kellenberger Historical Foundation, May Gordon Latham

Tryon Palace Commission ($29,349) see Kellenberger Historical Foundation, May Gordon Latham

Tryon Palace Commission ($23,872) see Kellenberger Historical Foundation, May Gordon Latham

Tryon Palace Commission ($15,670) see Kellenberger Historical Foundation, May Gordon Latham

Tryon Palace Commission ($14,621) see Kellenberger Historical Foundation, May Gordon Latham

Tryon Palace Commission ($13,048) see Kellenberger Historical Foundation, May Gordon Latham

Tryon Palace Commission ($11,749) see Kellenberger Historical Foundation, May Gordon Latham

Tryon Palace Commission ($10,702) see Kellenberger Historical Foundation, May Gordon Latham

Tryon Palace Commission ($1,000) see Kellenberger Historical Foundation, May Gordon Latham

United Appeal of Greater Greensboro ($2,300) see Bossong Hosiery Mills

United Appeal of Rutherford ($22,000) see Cone Mills Corp.

United Arts Council ($20,000) see Sternberger Foundation, Sigmund

United Arts Council of Greensboro ($12,000) see Blue Bell, Inc.

United Arts Council of North Carolina ($17,000) see Cone Mills Corp.

United Cerebral Palsy Association ($15,000) see Whitener Foundation

United Fund ($12,000) see Cranston Print Works

United Fund ($199,909) see Fieldcrest Cannon

United Fund ($16,000) see North Carolina Foam Foundation

United Fund ($1,015) see Trion

United Negro College Fund ($12,500) see Lance, Inc.

United Way ($750) see Acme-Cleveland Corp.

United Way ($750) see Acme-Cleveland Corp.

United Way ($14,750) see Acme-McCrary Corp.

United Way ($2,100) see Acme United Corp.

United Way ($10,000) see Blue Bell, Inc.

United Way ($10,000) see Blue Bell, Inc.

United Way ($10,000) see Blue Bell, Inc.

United Way ($10,000) see Blue Bell, Inc.

United Way ($10,582) see Carlyle & Co. Jewelers

United Way ($3,500) see Dalton Foundation, Harry L.

United Way ($10,000) see Devonwood Foundation

United Way ($16,500) see Dover Foundation

United Way ($10,000) see Ginter Foundation, Karl and Anna

United Way ($5,000) see Goody's Manufacturing Corp.

United Way ($2,500) see Halstead Foundation

United Way ($84,700) see Lance, Inc.

United Way ($2,400) see Martin Marietta Aggregates

United Way ($25,000) see Nanney Foundation, Charles and Irene

United Way ($9,313) see Outboard Marine Corp.

United Way ($7,919) see Outboard Marine Corp.

United Way ($3,750) see Pepsi-Cola Bottling Co. of Charlotte

United Way ($30,842) see Rexham Inc.

United Way ($30,000) see Shelton Cos.

United Way ($20,000) see United Dominion Industries

United Way ($2,000) see Wallace Computer Services

United Way ($10,000) see Weaver Foundation

United Way of Central Carolinas ($53,000) see Duke Power Co.

United Way of Central Carolinas ($250,000) see First Union Corp.

United Way of Forsyth County ($20,200) see AMP

United Way of Forsyth County ($44,729) see Johnson Controls

United Way of Gaston County ($37,500) see Dixie Yarns, Inc.

United Way of Greater Greensboro ($16,900) see AMP

United Way Greater Greensboro ($50,000) see Cone Mills Corp.

United Way of Greater Greensboro ($50,000) see Cone Mills Corp.

United Way of Greensboro — to promote and encourage a wholesome community life ($31,200) see Landmark Communications

United Way of Iredell County ($9,260) see Hunt Manufacturing Co.

United Way of Wake County ($56,250) see News & Observer Publishing Co.

University of North Carolina ($6,145) see Akzo America

University of North Carolina — business building fund ($250,000) see Belk Stores

University of North Carolina ($1,400) see Bossong Hosiery Mills

University of North Carolina ($26,075) see Deloitte & Touche

University of North Carolina ($25,695) see Deloitte & Touche

University of North Carolina ($25,000) see Doherty Charitable Foundation, Henry L. and Grace

University of North Carolina ($4,000) see Edmonds Foundation, Dean S.

University of North Carolina ($12,500) see Herzog Foundation, Carl J.

University of North Carolina — in multimedia computer equipment to improve access to library resources ($1,000,000) see IBM Corp.

University of North Carolina ($103,950) see KPMG Peat Marwick

University of North Carolina ($87,000) see Lurcy Charitable and Educational Trust, Georges

University of North Carolina — quality criteria in family child care ($29,624) see Mailman Family Foundation, A. L.

University of North Carolina ($30,000) see Sperry Fund

University of North Carolina ($31,000) see Wal-Mart Stores

University of North Carolina — scholarships ($124,000) see Whitehead Foundation, Lettie Pate

University of North Carolina at Chapel Hill ($6,000) see Allendale Mutual Insurance Co.

University of North Carolina-Chapel Hill ($17,405) see Burlington Industries

University of North Carolina at Chapel Hill ($1,000) see Burress, J.W.

University of North Carolina at Chapel Hill ($65,000) see Finley Foundation, A. E.

University of North Carolina at Chapel Hill ($20,000) see Goody's Manufacturing Corp.

University of North Carolina at Chapel Hill ($166,667) see Hanes Foundation, John W. and Anna H.

University of North Carolina at Chapel Hill ($25,000) see Harris Foundation, James J. and Angelia M.

University of North Carolina at Chapel Hill ($15,000) see Harvey Foundation, Felix

University of North Carolina at Chapel Hill ($7,810) see Holding Foundation, Robert P.

University of North Carolina at Chapel Hill — undergraduate scholarship ($680,000) see Johnston Trust for Charitable and Educational Purposes, James M.

University of North Carolina at Chapel Hill — nursing scholarship ($260,000) see Johnston Trust for Charitable and Educational Purposes, James M.

University of North Carolina at Chapel Hill — budget ($190,899) see Johnston Trust for Charitable and Educational Purposes, James M.

University of North Carolina at Chapel Hill ($4,000) see Liberty Hosiery Mills

University of North Carolina at Chapel Hill ($10,000) see McGregor Foundation, Thomas and Frances

University of North Carolina at Chapel Hill ($10,000) see Pepsi-Cola Bottling Co. of Charlotte

University of North Carolina at Chapel Hill ($7,000) see Pepsi-Cola Bottling Co. of Charlotte

University of North Carolina at Chapel Hill ($4,000) see Pepsi-Cola Bottling Co. of Charlotte

University of North Carolina at Chapel Hill ($153,533) see Richardson Foundation, Smith

University of North Carolina at Chapel Hill — a gift of computer equipment for programs in the AIDS Neurological Center ($166,000) see Digital Equipment Corp.

University of North Carolina-Chapel Hill — to initiate a B.S.N. program ($368,578) see Reynolds Charitable Trust, Kate B.

University of North Carolina at Chapel Hill — for Bicentennial Campaign ($1,000,000) see Kenan, Jr. Charitable Trust, William R.

University of North Carolina-Chapel Hill — Environmental Resource Project - for "Finding Common Ground: Toward a Sustainable North Carolina" ($150,000) see Babcock Foundation, Mary Reynolds

University of North Carolina-Chapel Hill School of Education Foundation — for Child Development and Family Studies Planning ($60,000) see Babcock Foundation, Mary Reynolds

University of North Carolina-Chapel Hill School of Medicine ($500,000) see Burroughs Wellcome Co.

University of North Carolina Charlotte ($100,000) see Duke Power Co.

University of North Carolina Charlotte ($50,000) see Giles Foundation, Edward C.

University of North Carolina Charlotte ($66,600) see Hemby Foundation, Alex

University of North Carolina Charlotte ($10,000) see Hemby Foundation, Alex

University of North Carolina at Charlotte ($4,640) see Holding Foundation, Robert P.

University of North Carolina at Charlotte ($125,000) see Livingstone Charitable Foundation, Betty J. and J. Stanley

University of North Carolina Charlotte ($1,000) see Love Foundation, Martha and Spencer

University of North Carolina Charlotte ($11,500) see Randleigh Foundation Trust

University of North Carolina Charlotte ($25,000) see Royal Group Inc.

University of North Carolina Charlotte Foundation ($20,000) see Lance, Inc.

University of North Carolina at Charlotte Foundation ($10,000) see Stowe, Jr. Foundation, Robert Lee

University of North Carolina — Clinical Center for the Study of Development and Learning ($193,488) see Dodge Foundation, Geraldine R.

University of North Carolina Educational Foundation ($10,542) see Harvey Foundation, Felix

University of North Carolina Educational Foundation ($10,000) see Whitener Foundation

University of North Carolina Educational Foundation ($6,000) see Whitener Foundation

University of North Carolina — to provide technical assistance to the five Foundation-assisted urban school systems implementing middle grades reform ($335,153) see Clark Foundation, Edna McConnell

University of North Carolina at Greensboro ($65,500) see Weaver Foundation

University of North Carolina — for support of the Katharine Smith Reynolds Scholarships for 1992-93 ($125,000) see Reynolds Foundation, Z. Smith

University of North Carolina Medical Foundation ($10,000) see Gilmer-Smith Foundation

North Carolina (cont.)

University of North Carolina Pharmacy Foundation ($12,500) see Goody's Manufacturing Corp.

University of North Carolina School of Business ($5,000) see Harvey Foundation, Felix

University of North Carolina School of Social Works ($25,000) see Sternberger Foundation, Sigmund

University of North Carolina — Strands Project ($119,829) see Smart Family Foundation

University of North Carolina at Wilmington ($50,000) see Fletcher Foundation, A. J.

University of North Carolina at Wilmington ($5,000) see Kenan Family Foundation

University of North Carolina Writers in Residence Program ($20,000) see News & Observer Publishing Co.

Uplift ($7,500) see Preyer Fund, Mary Norris

Urban Ministries ($3,000) see Stewards Fund

Vance H. Havner Scholarship Fund ($2,500) see Morris Charitable Foundation, E. A.

Wake County AIDS Service Agency ($10,000) see Preyer Fund, Mary Norris

Wake Forest University ($2,000) see Belmont Metals

Wake Forest University ($50,000) see Boswell Foundation, James G.

Wake Forest University ($100,000) see Broyhill Family Foundation

Wake Forest University ($2,500) see Burress, J.W.

Wake Forest University ($10,000) see McDougall Charitable Trust, Ruth Camp

Wake Forest University ($1,000) see Nanney Foundation, Charles and Irene

Wake Forest University — athletic department ($35,000) see Palin Foundation

Wake Forest University — general fund ($12,000) see Palin Foundation

Wake Forest University ($25,000) see Prickett Fund, Lynn R. and Karl E.

Wake Forest University ($100,000) see Shelton Cos.

Wake Forest University ($50,000) see Ware Foundation

Wake Forest University — Deacon Club ($2,250) see Brenner Foundation

Wake Forest University — to provide a three-year, merit-based scholarship to selected students in the School of Law ($61,900) see Fletcher Foundation, A. J.

Warren Wilson College ($3,000) see Anderson Foundation, Robert C. and Sadie G.

Warren Wilson College ($7,000) see Bierhaus Foundation

Warren Wilson College ($50,000) see Broyhill Family Foundation

Warren Wilson College — scholarship fund ($1,200) see Gholston Trust, J. K.

Warren Wilson College ($2,500) see McClure Educational and Development Fund, James G. K.

Warren Wilson College — to provide professional

opportunities for faculty members ($1,800,000) see Mellon Foundation, Andrew W.

Warren Wilson College ($5,000) see Stonecutter Mills Corp.

Warren Wilson College ($13,500) see Sullivan Foundation, Algernon Sydney

Watauga County Hospital ($5,000) see Shattuck Charitable Trust, S. F.

Wayne Country Day School ($50,500) see Bryan Foundation, James E. and Mary Z.

Wayne Country Day School ($25,000) see Bryan Foundation, James E. and Mary Z.

Wayne Memorial Hospital — to establish an intermediate care nursery ($473,402) see Reynolds Charitable Trust, Kate B.

Well-Spring Retirement Community ($148,000) see Weaver Foundation

Wells Spring Capital Retirement Center ($5,000) see Halstead Foundation

Westchester Academy ($40,000) see Finch Foundation, Thomas Austin

Westchester Academy ($19,402) see Finch Foundation, Thomas Austin

Western Carolina University ($6,036) see Cranston Print Works

Western Carolina University Speech and Hearing ($1,000) see Pearce Foundation, Dr. M. Lee

Western North Carolina Regional Child Abuse Center ($22,000) see Lane Charitable Trust, Melvin R.

Western North Carolina Visual Rehabilitation Center ($75,000) see Janirve Foundation

White Memorial Presbyterian Church ($35,000) see Finley Foundation, A. E.

Wilkes Developmental Daily School ($5,000) see Lowe's Cos.

Wilkes Regional Medical Center — to develop integrated primary health care services for the county ($1,127,671) see Reynolds Charitable Trust, Kate B.

William R. Kenan, Jr. Fund — to assist mortgage loan liquidation ($500,000) see Kenan, Jr. Charitable Trust, William R.

William R. Kenan, Jr. Fund — for Endowment Fund ($6,000,000) see Kenan, Jr. Charitable Trust, William R.

Wing Haven Foundation ($2,900) see Pepsi-Cola Bottling Co. of Charlotte

Wingate College ($200,000) see Cannon Foundation

Wingate College — in support of a major new center for historical and educational research ($100,000) see Fletcher Foundation, A. J.

Wingate College ($5,000) see Moore & Sons, B.C.

Winston-Salem Business and Technology Center ($56,200) see Wachovia Bank & Trust Co., N.A.

Winston-Salem Foundation ($6,000) see Alco Standard Corp.

Winston-Salem Rescue Squad ($2,500) see Brenner Foundation

Winston-Salem State University ($50,000) see Hanes Foundation, John W. and Anna H.

Winston-Salem State University ($55,500) see Shelton Cos.

Woodhill School ($10,300) see Glenn Foundation, Carrie C. & Lena V.

WUNC Radio ($17,000) see News & Observer Publishing Co.

Yadkin Valley Economic Group ($3,000) see Gilmer-Smith Foundation

YMCA ($6,000) see Acme-McCrary Corp.

YMCA ($3,000) see Bossong Hosiery Mills

YMCA ($2,500) see Burress, J.W.

YMCA ($3,000) see Classic Leather

YMCA ($1,850) see Classic Leather

YMCA ($10,000) see Dillard Paper Co.

YMCA ($15,000) see Finch Foundation, Doak

YMCA ($59,750) see Finley Foundation, A. E.

YMCA ($50,000) see Hanes Foundation, John W. and Anna H.

YMCA ($41,666) see Harris Foundation, James J. and Angelia M.

YMCA ($10,000) see Hemby Foundation, Alex

YMCA ($35,000) see Hurley Foundation, J. F.

YMCA ($17,000) see Hurley Foundation, J. F.

YMCA ($10,000) see Hurley Foundation, J. F.

YMCA ($10,000) see Lowe's Cos.

YMCA ($10,000) see Nanney Foundation, Charles and Irene

YMCA ($3,000) see Rexham Inc.

YMCA ($9,300) see Rogers Charitable Trust, Florence

YMCA ($25,000) see Sternberger Foundation, Sigmund

YMCA ($2,500) see Thomas Built Buses L.P.

YMCA ($2,000) see Thomas Built Buses L.P.

YMCA ($18,000) see Thomasville Furniture Industries

YMCA ($15,000) see Thomasville Furniture Industries

YMCA ($10,000) see Thomasville Furniture Industries

YMCA ($5,779) see Thomasville Furniture Industries

YMCA of Hendersonville ($18,000) see Lane Charitable Trust, Melvin R.

YMCA, Iredell — for capital campaign ($15,000) see Hunt Manufacturing Co.

YMCA-Raleigh ($24,500) see News & Observer Publishing Co.

Yokefellow Service Center ($6,000) see Coffey Foundation

Yorefellow Ministry ($5,000) see North Carolina Foam Foundation

Youth for Christ ($200) see Wellons Foundation

YWCA ($5,000) see Royal Group Inc.

North Dakota

American Red Cross Mid-Dakota Chapter see First Bank System

Arena — building project ($4,000) see MDU Resources Group, Inc.

Bismarck Junior College — scholarship program ($2,400) see CENEX

Bismarck-Mandan Orchestral Association — artistic personnel stipend budget for 1990-91 Concert Season with 2 children's' concerts ($6,000) see Leach Foundation, Tom & Frances

Bismarck State College see Piper Jaffray Cos.

Bismarck State College Foundation — endowment fund ($4,000) see MDU Resources Group, Inc.

Bismarck State College Foundation — scholarship program for academic, performing arts, and journalism ($10,000) see Leach Foundation, Tom & Frances

Dakota Zoological Society ($5,000) see Leach Foundation, Tom & Frances

Dickinson State College ($1,500) see True Oil Co.

Evangelical Lutheran Church — Preaching Deacons Program ($61,518) see Lutheran Brotherhood Foundation

Eventide Foundation — assistance with construction and related expenses for Alzheimer Unit at Eventide Nursing Home ($10,000) see Stern Family Foundation, Alex

Friends of North Dakota Museum of Art — construction of art museum and sculpture garden ($10,000) see Myra Foundation

Friends of the North Dakota Museum of Art — to stabilize the financial base of the Museum ($140,008) see Northwest Area Foundation

Grace Lutheran School — matching grant to assist in purchase of a new school bus ($10,000) see Stern Family Foundation, Alex

Grand Forks County Historical Society — trees and landscaping ($11,200) see Myra Foundation

Greater Grand Forks Community Theatre — live stage productions ($8,000) see Myra Foundation

Greater Grand Forks Senior Citizens Association — kitchen and bath room improvements ($7,297) see Myra Foundation

Greater Grand Forks Symphony Association — symphony concerts ($12,000) see Myra Foundation

Heartview Foundation ($1,000) see Holley Foundation

Home on the Range for Boys ($7,500) see Leach Foundation, Tom & Frances

Hospice ($10,000) see Stern Family Foundation, Alex

Jamestown College — Tom and Frances Leach Scholarship Fund for needy and worthy students ($15,000) see Leach Foundation, Tom & Frances

Jamestown Hospital Foundation ($50,000) see Burlington Northern Inc.

Jamestown Presbyterian College ($32,074) see Hallett Charitable Trust

Jamestown Presbyterian College ($32,073) see Hallett Charitable Trust, Jessie F.

Lisbon Public School District — to install a wooden floor in the new community gymnasium ($40,000) see Bremer Foundation, Otto

Listen Drop-In Center — computer system and other improvements ($9,129) see Myra Foundation

Medical Center Rehabilitation Hospital Foundation — Child Evaluation Treatment Program (CETP) has financial assistance for families with at-risk kids ($20,000) see Leach Foundation, Tom & Frances

Moorehead State University Foundation — honors apprenticeship program ($10,000) see Stern Family Foundation, Alex

North Dakota Boys Ranch ($115,000) see Voelkerding Charitable Trust, Walter and Jean

North Dakota Consensus Council — to reorganize government at all levels in North Dakota ($200,000) see Northwest Area Foundation

North Dakota State School of Science — scholarship program ($5,500) see CENEX

North Dakota State University — scholarship program ($4,500) see CENEX

North Dakota State University Foundation — fourth installment on five-year grant of $150,000, equipment for Biotechnical Center ($30,000) see Stern Family Foundation, Alex

North Dakota State University Harvest Bowl ($13,000) see Harvest States Cooperative

Northern Crops Institute ($25,000) see Harvest States Cooperative

Prairie Public Television ($10,000) see Harvest States Cooperative

Prairie Public Television — program support/local programming ($10,000) see Stern Family Foundation, Alex

Railroad Museum of Minot ($50,000) see Burlington Northern Inc.

Red River Valley Gymnastics — gymnastics equipment ($12,000) see Myra Foundation

St. Lukes Foundation — first installment on a five-year grant of $250,000 designated for the Roger Maris Cancer Center ($50,000) see Stern Family Foundation, Alex

Salvation Army ($10,000) see Leach Foundation, Tom & Frances

School of Hope — pre-school center with specialized care for multi-handicapped youth ($10,000) see Leach Foundation, Tom & Frances

Shanley High School — purchase of computer related equipment ($10,000) see Stern Family Foundation, Alex

Share House of Fargo and Moorehead — assistance with

salary costs of an addiction counselor for Share House ($10,000) see Stern Family Foundation, Alex

Shelter for Homeless — renovation of shelter ($12,000) see Myra Foundation

State of North Dakota — child welfare reform ($776,640) see Casey Foundation, Annie E.

United Way ($10,500) see Leach Foundation, Tom & Frances

United Way ($8,625) see MDU Resources Group, Inc.

University of Mary ($20,000) see MDU Resources Group, Inc.

University of Mary — Tom and Frances Leach Scholarship Fund for worthy, needy students ($45,000) see Leach Foundation, Tom & Frances

University of North Dakota — scholarships ($27,000) see Myra Foundation

University of North Dakota Center for Innovation and Business Development ($7,500) see Nash Foundation

University of North Dakota Foundation — scholarships ($10,000) see Bay Branch Foundation

West River Health Services Foundation ($5,000) see MDU Resources Group, Inc.

YMCA ($25,000) see Myra Foundation

YMCA ($10,000) see Stern Family Foundation, Alex

Ohio

Accord Associates ($3,000) see AHS Foundation

Achievement Center for Children ($20,000) see Second Foundation

Adaith Israel Congregation ($2,500) see Glazer Foundation, Jerome S.

Adolescent Clinic/Division of Adolescent Medicine — for postponing sexual involvement ($10,000) see Jergens Foundation, Andrew

Adriel School ($6,000) see Grimes Foundation

Agnon School ($2,000) see Kangesser Foundation, Robert E., Harry A., and M. Sylvia

Agnon School ($2,500) see MalCo Products Inc.

Agnon School ($5,000) see Ohio Savings Bank

Agudas Achim Congregation ($70,000) see El-An Foundation

Aid Associates for Lutherans ($5,000) see Markey Charitable Fund, John C.

AIDS Volunteers of Cincinnati ($10,000) see Thendara Foundation

AIR ($5,000) see Seasongood Good Government Foundation, Murray and Agnes

Aish Hatorah ($1,000) see Barry Corp., R. G.

Aish Hatorah ($159,375) see Schottenstein Foundation, Jerome & Saul

Akron Area YMCA ($28,233) see BFGoodrich

Akron Art Museum — toward the endowment fund and toward operating funds ($100,000) see GAR Foundation

Akron Art Museum ($10,000) see Mirapaul Foundation

Akron Baptist Temple ($10,000) see Musson Charitable Foundation, R. C. and Katharine M.

Akron Children's Hospital see General Tire Inc.

Akron City Hospital ($125,000) see Corbin Foundation, Mary S. and David C.

Akron City Hospital ($20,000) see McFawn Trust No. 2, Lois Sisler

Akron City Hospital ($10,000) see Musson Charitable Foundation, R. C. and Katharine M.

Akron General Development Foundation ($20,500) see Calhoun Charitable Trust, Kenneth

Akron Jewish Community Federation ($40,000) see Mirapaul Foundation

Akron Pregnancy Services ($10,000) see O'Neil Foundation, W.

Akron Symphony see General Tire Inc.

Akron University ($70,000) see BFGoodrich

Akron University (Polymer Center) ($55,000) see Rubbermaid

Alcoholic Clinic ($1,500) see American Welding & Manufacturing Co.

Alcoholic Clinic of Youngstown ($21,668) see Beeghly Fund, Leon A.

Alcoholism Services of Cleveland ($8,000) see South Waite Foundation

Alcoholism Services of Cleveland — for second year support of the Addiction Intervention and Rehabilitation Services project at the Department of Human Services for families cited for child abuse ($30,000) see Bruening Foundation, Eva L. and Joseph M.

All-American Soap Box Derby see General Tire Inc.

Alliance for the Mentally Ill of Metropolitan Cleveland — one-for-one matching grant for management and development of this public education and family support organization for the mentally ill ($30,000) see Bingham Foundation, William

American Cancer Society ($1,200) see American Welding & Manufacturing Co.

American Cancer Society ($2,500) see Dively Foundation, George S.

American Cancer Society ($5,000) see LDI Charitable Foundation

American Cancer Society ($15,792) see Miller Charitable Trust, Lewis N.

American Cancer Society ($2,000) see Motch Corp.

American Cancer Society ($725) see Ormet Corp.

American Cancer Society ($1,000) see Schey Foundation

American Ceramic Society ($10,000) see Norton Co.

American Civil Liberties Union Foundation ($10,000) see Gerson Family Foundation, Benjamin J.

American Civil Liberties Union of Ohio Foundation ($17,000) see Forest City Enterprises

American Committee for the Tel Aviv Foundation ($10,000) see Mandel Foundation, Jack N. and Lilyan

American Diabetes Association ($1,000) see Motch Corp.

American Friends of Hebrew University — two pretenure fellowships and dormitory refurbishment ($175,000) see Moriah Fund

American Friends of Israel Museum ($10,000) see Mandel Foundation, Morton and Barbara

American Friends of Oxford Center ($1,000) see Mandel Foundation, Joseph and Florence

American Heart Association ($1,400) see Kuhns Investment Co.

American Heart Association ($1,000) see Motch Corp.

American Heart Association see Seaway Food Town

American Jewish Committee ($1,000) see Mandel Foundation, Joseph and Florence

American Jewish Congress ($5,000) see Mandel Foundation, Jack N. and Lilyan

American Legion Post 165 ($10,000) see Huffy Corp.

American Music Scholarship Association ($5,000) see Ramlose Foundation, George A.

American Music Scholarship Association ($10,000) see Robison Foundation, Ellis H. and Doris B.

American National Red Cross ($6,000) see Ferro Corp.

American National Red Cross ($3,000) see Pollock Company Foundation, William B.

American Red Cross ($3,333) see Commercial Intertech Corp.

American Red Cross — capital campaign ($83,000) see Eaton Corp.

American Red Cross ($1,000) see Eyman Trust, Jesse

American Red Cross ($6,500) see LDI Charitable Foundation

American Red Cross ($3,000) see McDonald & Co. Securities

American Red Cross ($30,000) see Moores Foundation, Harry C.

American Red Cross ($9,000) see Murch Foundation

American Red Cross ($40,000) see Nestle U.S.A. Inc.

American Red Cross ($50,000) see Second Foundation

American Red Cross ($21,000) see Sherwin-Williams Co.

American Red Cross ($5,000) see Standard Products Co.

American's Future Trees Foundation ($500) see Oglebay Norton Co.

Ameriflora ($2,000) see Lancaster Colony

Amherst Historical Society — capital operations ($110,846) see Nord Family Foundation

Andrew College — scholarship fund ($27,499) see McLendon Educational Fund, Violet H.

Andrews School ($5,000) see Hershey Foundation

Anti-Defamation League ($2,000) see Mandel Foundation, Jack N. and Lilyan

Anti-Defamation League of B'nai B'rith ($25,000) see Columbus Dispatch Printing Co.

Antioch College ($15,000) see Cowles Foundation, William H.

Antioch College ($4,000) see Shwayder Foundation, Fay

Art Fowler Ministries — challenge grant, Evangelism project ($50,000) see Gallagher Family Foundation, Lewis P.

Arthritis Foundation ($15,792) see Miller Charitable Trust, Lewis N.

Arts Center Foundation ($100,000) see Beerman Foundation

Arts Center Foundation ($8,000) see Duriron Co., Inc.

Arts Center Foundation ($10,000) see Huffy Corp.

Arts Center Foundation ($20,000) see Orleton Trust Fund

Arts Center Foundation ($100,000) see Reynolds & Reynolds Co.

Arts Center Foundation ($20,000) see Tait Foundation, Frank M.

Arts Center Foundation ($19,000) see Tait Foundation, Frank M.

Arts Center Foundation — renovation of Victory Theatre ($1,000,000) see Kettering Fund

Arts Dayton ($1,250) see Amcast Industrial Corp.

Arts Dayton ($26,675) see Beerman Foundation

Arts Dayton ($17,500) see Berry Foundation, Loren M.

Arts Dayton ($4,000) see Duriron Co., Inc.

Arts Dayton ($300) see French Oil Mill Machinery Co.

Arts Dayton ($30,000) see Iddings Benevolent Trust

Arts Dayton — general support ($235,000) see Kettering Fund

Arts Dayton ($101,850) see Mead Corp.

Arts Dayton ($40,000) see Orleton Trust Fund

Arts Dayton ($17,500) see Reynolds & Reynolds Co.

Arts Dayton ($15,000) see Reynolds & Reynolds Co.

Arts Dayton ($4,000) see Standard Register Co.

Arts Etc. ($5,000) see Eaton Foundation, Cyrus

Artsdayton ($10,000) see Dayton Power and Light Co.

ARTSDAYTON ($75,000) see NCR Corp.

Ash International Metals Park ($1,000) see American Welding & Manufacturing Co.

Ashland College ($15,000) see Eyman Trust, Jesse

Ashland College ($1,000) see Park National Bank

Ashland Symphony Orchestra Association ($4,500) see Young Foundation, Hugo H. and Mabel B.

Ashland University ($6,000) see Tremco Inc.

Ashland University ($6,000) see Tremco Inc.

Ashland University — for computer hardware and support of the Business and Student Dialogue Program see USX Corp.

Association for Children for Enforcement of Support ($25,000) see Mott Fund, Ruth

Athens Area Hospice ($10,000) see O'Bleness Foundation, Charles G.

Athens Area Technical Institute ($25,000) see Reliance Electric Co.

Atlantic Foundation ($24,000) see Parker-Hannifin Corp.

Aultman Hospital Development Fund ($6,751) see Miller Memorial Trust, George Lee

Aultman Hospital Development Fund ($6,604) see Miller Memorial Trust, George Lee

Bainbridge Volunteer Fire Department — lifesaving ($5,000) see Massie Trust, David Meade

Baldwin-Wallace College ($30,000) see Beeghly Fund, Leon A.

Baldwin-Wallace College ($20,000) see Codrington Charitable Foundation, George W.

Baldwin-Wallace College ($25,000) see Ernsthausen Charitable Foundation, John F. and Doris E.

Baldwin-Wallace College ($1,000) see Hauserman, Inc.

Baldwin-Wallace College — student scholarships ($23,000) see Huntington Fund for Education, John

Baldwin-Wallace College ($25,000) see Kulas Foundation

Baldwin-Wallace College see Lubrizol Corp.

Baldwin-Wallace College ($50,000) see M.T.D. Products

Baldwin-Wallace College ($35,000) see Mellen Foundation

Baldwin-Wallace College ($35,464) see Ritter Charitable Trust, George W. & Mary F.

Baldwin-Wallace College ($7,020) see Standard Products Co.

Baldwin-Wallace College ($41,000) see Strosacker Foundation, Charles J.

Ballet Met ($2,000) see Jasam Foundation

Ballet Met ($10,000) see Wildermuth Foundation, E. F.

Ballet Metropolitan ($40,000) see National City Corp.

Ballet Metropolitan, Columbus, OH see Battelle

Baptist Mid Mission ($361,780) see Christian Training Foundation

Baptist World Mission ($39,670) see Christian Training Foundation

Battelle Institute ($30,343) see Graphic Arts Show Co. Inc.

Beaumont School ($5,000) see Mill-Rose Co.

Beaumont School — faculty endowment fund ($100,000) see O'Neill Charitable Corporation, F. J.

Beck Center for the Cultural Arts ($2,700) see Hershey Foundation

Bellefaire/Jewish Children's Bureau ($10,000) see Sapirstein-Stone-Weiss Foundation

Bellefaire Jewish Children's Bureau ($40,000) see Treuhaft Foundation

Bellefaire-Jewish Children's Bureau ($15,000) see Wellman Foundation, S. K.

Bellflower Center for the Prevention of Child Abuse

Ohio (cont.)

($2,838) see LDI Charitable
Foundation
Bellflower Center for Prevention
of Child Abuse ($2,800) see
Ohio Savings Bank
Bellflower Center for Prevention
of Child Abuse ($20,000) see
Second Foundation
Bethany House of Hospitality
($2,500) see Giddings & Lewis
Bethesda Hospital ($184,635)
see Taylor Trust, Lydia M.
Betsey Mills Club ($5,000) see
Fenton Foundation
Betty Jane Memorial
Rehabilitation Center
($30,000) see National
Machinery Co.
Bexley United Methodist Church
($25,000) see English
Foundation, Walter and Marian
Bexley United Methodist Church
($35,000) see Moores
Foundation, Harry C.
Bible Believers of Lima
($166,000) see Dauch
Foundation, William
Bible Institute ($100,000) see
Paulstan
Bible Literature International
($2,500) see Hartzell
Industries, Inc.
Big Brothers and Big Sisters
($15,000) see Ohio Valley
Foundation
Blessed Sacrament Church
($30,000) see Snyder
Foundation, Frost and Margaret
Blessed Sacrament Church
($5,000) see Van Huffel
Foundation, I. J.
Blossom Music Center see
General Tire Inc.
Blossom Music Center
Endowment ($8,000) see
Ritchie Memorial Foundation,
Charles E. and Mabel M.
Blue Chip Campaign ($35,000)
see Cincinnati Bell
Blue Chip Campaign ($10,000)
see Cincinnati Milacron
Blue Chips Campaign ($3,000)
see XTEK Inc.
B'nai B'rith Hillel Foundation
($15,000) see Beerman
Foundation
Boardman Rotary Foundation
Program ($10,000) see
Crandall Memorial
Foundation, J. Ford
Bob Hipple Laboratory ($2,000)
see Hartzell Industries, Inc.
Bowling Green State University
see Amoco Corp.
Bowling Green State University
see du Pont de Nemours &
Co., E. I.
Bowling Green State University
($10,750) see Markey
Charitable Fund, John C.
Bowling Green State University
($11,000) see Schlink
Foundation, Albert G. and
Olive H.
Bowling Green State University
Scholarship ($5,000) see Love
Foundation, Gay and Erskine
Bowling Green State University
— Social Philosophy and
Policy Center ($200,000) see
Stranahan Foundation
Boy Scouts — capital campaign
($75,000) see Schmidlapp
Trust No. 1, Jacob G.
Boy Scouts of America ($2,000)
see American Aggregates Corp.
Boy Scouts of America ($500)
see Dively Foundation, George
S.

Boy Scouts of America ($6,000)
see Eagle-Picher Industries
Boy Scouts of America ($2,250)
see Edwards Industries
Boy Scouts of America
($26,000) see Emery
Memorial, Thomas J.
Boy Scouts of America ($3,000)
see English Foundation,
Walter and Marian
Boy Scouts of America ($5,000)
see Hoover Fund-Trust, W.
Henry
Boy Scouts of America
($35,378) see Kling Trust,
Louise
Boy Scouts of America ($1,600)
see Kuhns Investment Co.
Boy Scouts of America ($3,334)
see Lamson & Sessions Co.
Boy Scouts of America ($960)
see Mill-Rose Co.
Boy Scouts of America ($1,000)
see Oglebay Norton Co.
Boy Scouts of America
($10,000) see Ohio Valley
Foundation
Boy Scouts of America ($2,500)
see Peterloon Foundation
Boy Scouts of America ($6,000)
see Ritchie Memorial
Foundation, Charles E. and
Mabel M.
Boy Scouts of America
($10,000) see Rupp
Foundation, Fran and Warren
Boy Scouts of America
($10,000) see Smith, Jr.
Charitable Trust, Jack J.
Boy Scouts of America
($37,500) see Star Bank, N.A.
Boy Scouts of America ($4,000)
see Young Foundation, Hugo
H. and Mabel B.
Boy Scouts of America-Central
Ohio Council ($26,285) see
Borden
Boy Scouts of America — Dan
Beard Council ($35,000) see
Cincinnati Bell
Boy Scouts of America, Dayton,
OH ($20,000) see Cox
Enterprises
Boy Scouts/Girl Scouts see
General Tire Inc.
Boys Club of America ($20,000)
see Kramer Foundation, Louise
Boys and Girls Club ($100,000)
see Beerman Foundation
Boys and Girls Club ($10,000)
see Charities Foundation
Boys and Girls Club ($3,000)
see Danis Industries
Boys and Girls Club ($4,000) see
Finnegan Foundation, John D.
Boys and Girls Club ($8,000) see
Huffy Corp.
Boys and Girls Club ($21,000)
see Iddings Benevolent Trust
Boys and Girls Club ($40,000)
see Miniger Memorial
Foundation, Clement O.
Boys and Girls Club ($5,000) see
Stone Foundation, France
Boys and Girls Club ($25,000)
see Tait Foundation, Frank M.
Boys Hope ($11,000) see
Charities Foundation
Boys Hope ($5,750) see Ritchie
Memorial Foundation, Charles
E. and Mabel M.
Breckenridge Retirement
Community ($25,000) see
Murch Foundation
Brethren Church ($5,000) see
Eyman Trust, Jesse
Brighten Your Future ($5,000)
see Childs Charitable
Foundation, Roberta M.

Brinkhaven Ministries — to the
capital campaign ($100,000)
see GAR Foundation
Broadway United Methodist
Church ($30,000) see Austin
Memorial Foundation
Bryan Public Library ($5,000)
see Markey Charitable Fund,
John C.
Buckeye Boys Ranch ($1,000)
see Electric Power Equipment
Co.
Buckeye Boys Ranch ($3,500)
see English Foundation,
Walter and Marian
Buckeye Boys Ranch ($7,500)
see Wildermuth Foundation, E.
F.
Buckeye Boys Ranch ($10,000)
see Yassenoff Foundation, Leo
Bucyrus Area United Way
($26,000) see Timken Co.
Builders Exchange Foundation
Fund ($3,000) see Edwards
Industries
Building Bridges ($10,000) see
Iddings Benevolent Trust
Building Bridges ($2,000) see
Mead Fund, Nelson
Butler Institute of American Art
($3,000) see Commercial
Intertech Corp.
Butler Institute of American Art
($25,000) see Kilcawley Fund,
William H.
Butler Institute of American Art
— sponsorship of parent/child
workshop see Ameritech
Publishing
Calvert High School ($25,000)
see National Machinery Co.
Camp Ho-Mita-Koda ($2,000)
see Frohring Foundation,
William O. and Gertrude Lewis
Camping and Education
Foundation ($60,000) see
Woods Foundation, James H.
Cancer Hotline ($5,000) see
Mandel Foundation, Joseph
and Florence
Canfield United Methodist
Church ($10,000) see
Kilcawley Fund, William H.
Canton Art Institute — to be
applied toward the endowment
fund ($100,000) see GAR
Foundation
Canton Scholarship Foundation
($35,000) see Deuble
Foundation, George H.
Canton Scholarship Foundation
— for scholarships ($156,250)
see Hoover Foundation
Canton Scholarship Foundation
— scholarship fund
($625,000) see Timken
Foundation of Canton
Canton Symphony ($4,313) see
Wilkof Foundation, Edward
and Ruth
Canton Symphony Orchestra —
support for ensemble program
($15,000) see Fisher
Foundation
Capital Square Renovation
($15,000) see Dayton Power
and Light Co.
Capital University ($19,000) see
Mellen Foundation
Capitol Square Renovation
Foundation ($20,000) see
Columbus Dispatch Printing
Co.
Cardinal Stritch High School
($151,500) see Brencanda
Foundation
Carmelite Monastery ($25,000)
see O'Neill Foundation,
William J. and Dorothy K.
Carpenter-Briggs Radiation
Therapy Center ($10,000) see
Wodecroft Foundation

Case Alumni Association
($10,000) see Grader
Foundation, K. W.
Case Alumni Association
($10,000) see Knudsen
Charitable Foundation, Earl
Case Alumni Association
($6,250) see Tremco Inc.
Case Associates Program
($10,000) see Standard
Products Co.
Case Western Reserve —
Herbert Henry Dow
Distinguished Professorship
($200,000) see Towsley
Foundation, Harry A. and
Margaret D.
Case Western Reserve University
($1,300) see Acme-Cleveland
Corp.
Case Western Reserve University
($50,000) see Barstow
Foundation
Case Western Reserve University
($5,000) see Bicknell Fund
Case Western Reserve University
($5,000) see Blair Foundation,
John
Case Western Reserve University
($276,000) see BP America
Case Western Reserve University
($20,000) see Britton Fund
Case Western Reserve University
($127,200) see Centerior
Energy Corp.
Case Western Reserve University
($25,000) see Codrington
Charitable Foundation, George
W.
Case Western Reserve University
($6,000) see Common Wealth
Trust
Case Western Reserve University
— capital ($100,000) see
Consolidated Natural Gas Co.
Case Western Reserve University
— operating ($100,000) see
Consolidated Natural Gas Co.
Case Western Reserve University
($12,500) see Dentsply
International, Inc.
Case Western Reserve University
($633,000) see Dively
Foundation, George S.
Case Western Reserve University
($125,000) see Dow Chemical
Co.
Case Western Reserve University
($10,000) see Ferro Corp.
Case Western Reserve University
($17,500) see Fox Charitable
Foundation, Harry K. & Emma
R.
Case Western Reserve University
($3,000) see Glenn Foundation
for Medical Research, Paul F.
Case Western Reserve University
($4,565) see Gould Inc.
Case Western Reserve University
($2,000,000) see Gund
Foundation, George
Case Western Reserve University
($179,408) see Gund
Foundation, George
Case Western Reserve University
($4,000) see Haskell Fund
Case Western Reserve University
($10,000) see Hauserman, Inc.
Case Western Reserve University
— student scholarships
($420,700) see Huntington
Fund for Education, John
Case Western Reserve University
($56,500) see Ireland
Foundation
Case Western Reserve University
— for organic synthesis
laboratories in a new
macromolecular science
building see Keck Foundation,
W. M.

Case Western Reserve University
($25,000) see Lincoln Electric
Co.
Case Western Reserve University
see Lubrizol Corp.
Case Western Reserve University
— scholar program ($60,000)
see Mallinckrodt, Jr.
Foundation, Edward
Case Western Reserve University
($100,000) see Mellen
Foundation
Case Western Reserve University
($1,500) see Motch Corp.
Case Western Reserve University
($57,143) see National City
Corp.
Case Western Reserve University
($326,971) see 1525
Foundation
Case Western Reserve University
($116,099) see Premier
Industrial Corp.
Case Western Reserve University
($50,000) see Prentiss
Foundation, Elisabeth
Severance
Case Western Reserve University
($60,000) see Reliance
Electric Co.
Case Western Reserve University
($30,000) see Reliance
Electric Co.
Case Western Reserve University
($447,343) see Second
Foundation
Case Western Reserve University
($40,000) see Treuhaft
Foundation
Case Western Reserve University
($5,000) see V and V
Foundation
Case Western Reserve University
($910,000) see Weatherhead
Foundation
Case Western Reserve University
($400,000) see Weatherhead
Foundation
Case Western Reserve University
($15,000) see Wellman
Foundation, S. K.
Case Western Reserve University
($10,000) see Wenner-Gren
Foundation for
Anthropological Research
Case Western Reserve University
— support to endow the
Ameritech Chair in Regional
Economics. see Ameritech
Corp.
Case Western Reserve
University, Department of
Medicine ($250,000) see
Prentiss Foundation, Elisabeth
Severance
Case Western Reserve University
Health Careers Enhancement
Program ($15,000) see White
Consolidated Industries
Case Western Reserve University
— Kelvin Smith Library
($1,000,000) see Smith
Foundation, Kelvin and
Eleanor
Case Western Reserve University
— Parent, Teacher, and Peer
Partnership to enhance Health
Education ($37,250) see
Jennings Foundation, Martha
Holden
Case Western Reserve University
— Polymer Environmental
Research ($250,000) see BP
America
Case Western Reserve University
— nursing program,
construction of science
building ($250,000) see
Fairchild Foundation, Sherman
Case Western Reserve
University, School of

Medicine ($10,000) see Sherwin-Williams Co.

Case Western Reserve University School of Medicine, University Hospitals of Cleveland ($25,000) see Prentiss Foundation, Elisabeth Severance

Case Western Reserve University Weatherhead School ($42,857) see National City Corp.

Case Western Reserve University — Weatherhead School of Management ($15,000) see Lincoln Electric Co.

Catholic Charities Corporation — general purpose ($82,500) see O'Neill Charitable Corporation, F. J.

Catholic Charities — for the 1991 annual campaign ($45,000) see Bruening Foundation, Eva L. and Joseph M.

Catholic Diocese of Youngstown ($4,000) see Van Huffel Foundation, I. J.

Catholic Service League of Summit County ($5,000) see Ritchie Memorial Foundation, Charles E. and Mabel M.

Catholic Social Services ($5,000) see Danis Industries

Catholic Social Services ($3,000) see Minster Machine Co.

Cedarville College ($123,500) see Miller Charitable Foundation, C. John and Reva

Cedarville College — scholarship endowment College of Nursing ($200,000) see Gallagher Family Foundation, Lewis P.

Celina Combined Charities ($31,000) see Huffy Corp.

Center for Individual and Family Services ($42,000) see Sterkel Trust, Justine

Center for Mediation of Disputes ($25,000) see Seasongood Good Government Foundation, Murray and Agnes

Center for New Directions ($4,000) see English Foundation, Walter and Marian

Center of Science and Industry, Columbus, OH see Battelle

Central Catholic High School ($17,668) see Andersons Management Corp.

Central Catholic High School — for the conversion of two lecture classrooms into laboratory facilities for Biology and Chemistry ($60,000) see Hoover Foundation

Central City Ministries ($10,000) see Andersons Management Corp.

Central College Presbyterian Church ($2,500) see Shafer Foundation, Richard H. and Ann

Central Ohio Diabetes Association ($25,000) see Moores Foundation, Harry C.

Central Ohio Radio Reading Service ($2,500) see Shafer Foundation, Richard H. and Ann

Central School of Practical Nursing — student scholarships ($28,700) see Huntington Fund for Education, John

Central School of Practical Nursing ($20,000) see Prentiss Foundation, Elisabeth Severance

Champion County EDC ($8,000) see Grimes Foundation

Champion County Teen Center ($4,000) see Grimes Foundation

Charity Newsies ($1,000) see Electric Power Equipment Co.

CHCS ($51,000) see Paulstan

Cherry Street Mission ($4,000) see Baumker Charitable Foundation, Elsie and Harry

Child Guidance Center ($10,000) see Fox Charitable Foundation, Harry K. & Emma R.

Child Guidance Center ($80,000) see Gerson Family Foundation, Benjamin J.

Child Guidance Center — building addition ($20,000) see Mather Charitable Trust, S. Livingston

Childhood League ($5,000) see Edwards Industries

Childhood League ($20,000) see Jasam Foundation

Childhood League Center ($5,000) see English Foundation, Walter and Marian

Children's Defense Fund ($6,000) see Gerson Family Foundation, Benjamin J.

Children's Dental Clinic ($3,050) see Montgomery Foundation

Children's Home ($35,378) see Kling Trust, Louise

Children's Hospital ($125,000) see Corbin Foundation, Mary S. and David C.

Children's Hospital ($50,000) see Emery Memorial, Thomas J.

Children's Hospital ($1,000) see Jarson-Stanley and Mickey Kaplan Foundation, Isaac & Esther

Children's Hospital ($10,000) see Musson Charitable Foundation, R. C. and Katharine M.

Children's Hospital ($20,000) see Schiff Foundation, John J. and Mary R.

Children's Hospital ($10,000) see Shafer Foundation, Richard H. and Ann

Children's Hospital Foundation ($10,000) see Westerman Foundation, Samuel L.

Children's Hospital Foundation ($206,776) see Wexner Foundation

Children's Hospital Foundation, Columbus, OH see Battelle

Children's Hospital Medical Center ($10,000) see Dater Foundation, Charles H.

Children's Hospital Medical Center ($5,000) see Griswold Foundation, John C.

Children's Hospital Medical Center ($240,000) see Mayerson Foundation, Manuel D. and Rhoda

Children's Hospital Medical Center ($35,000) see Mayerson Foundation, Manuel D. and Rhoda

Children's Hospital Medical Center ($30,000) see McFawn Trust No. 2, Lois Sisler

Children's Hospital Medical Center ($30,000) see McFawn Trust No. 2, Lois Sisler

Children's Hospital Medical Center ($5,000) see Robison Foundation, Ellis H. and Doris B.

Children's Hospital Medical Center ($113,972) see

Schmidlapp Trust No. 1, Jacob G.

Children's Hospital Medical Center ($23,250) see Smith, Jr. Charitable Trust, Jack J.

Children's Hospital Medical Center/W.S. Rowe Division ($118,286) see Schmidlapp Trust No. 1, Jacob G.

Children's Hospital Medical Center/W.S. Rowe Division — pediatric grant ($65,000) see Schmidlapp Trust No. 1, Jacob G.

Children's Medical Center ($100,250) see Beerman Foundation

Choral Arts Performing Society ($3,000) see Frohring Foundation, William O. and Gertrude Lewis

Christian Family Outreach ($9,000) see Calhoun Charitable Trust, Kenneth

Church of Redeemer ($5,000) see Robison Foundation, Ellis H. and Doris B.

Church Women United ($2,000) see Eyman Trust, Jesse

Cincinnati Area Senior Services ($25,000) see Ohio Valley Foundation

Cincinnati Art Museum ($2,000) see Gradison & Co.

Cincinnati Art Museum ($400,000) see Procter & Gamble Co.

Cincinnati Art Museum ($192,888) see Schiff Foundation, John J. and Mary R.

Cincinnati Art Museum ($25,000) see Thendara Foundation

Cincinnati Art Museum for restoration of Damascus Room ($15,000) see Jergens Foundation, Andrew

Cincinnati Association for the Blind ($250) see Hayfields Foundation

Cincinnati Association for the Blind ($5,000) see Peterloon Foundation

Cincinnati Association for the Blind ($10,000) see Smith, Jr. Charitable Trust, Jack J.

Cincinnati Ballet — for lightening system ($7,000) see Alms Trust, Eleanora

Cincinnati Ballet ($2,000) see Gradison & Co.

Cincinnati Ballet ($20,000) see Jarson-Stanley and Mickey Kaplan Foundation, Isaac & Esther

Cincinnati Ballet Company — challenge grant to assist with funding of performance ($45,000) see Corbett Foundation

Cincinnati Contemporary Center ($25,000) see Mapplethorpe Foundation, Robert

Cincinnati Educational Initiatives ($585,400) see Procter & Gamble Co.

Cincinnati Fine Arts Fund ($125,000) see American Financial Corp.

Cincinnati Fine Arts Fund ($5,000) see Eagle-Picher Industries

Cincinnati Fine Arts Fund ($5,750) see Powell Co., William

Cincinnati Fine Arts Fund ($2,750) see Powell Co., William

Cincinnati Hills Christian Academy ($15,000) see

Semple Foundation, Louise Taft

Cincinnati Historical Society ($15,000) see Ohio Valley Foundation

Cincinnati Institute of Fine Art ($8,000) see Anderson Foundation, William P.

Cincinnati Institute of Fine Arts ($121,299) see Federated Department Stores and Allied Stores Corp.

Cincinnati Institute of Fine Arts — for 1990 campaign ($15,000) see Jergens Foundation, Andrew

Cincinnati Museum Center Foundation ($19,886) see Seasongood Good Government Foundation, Murray and Agnes

Cincinnati Music Festival Association — May Festival's Carnegie Hall performance ($28,000) see Corbett Foundation

Cincinnati Music Hall Association ($5,000) see Bardes Corp.

Cincinnati Music Hall Association ($30,000) see Emery Memorial, Thomas J.

Cincinnati-Ohio Arts Center ($715,000) see Procter & Gamble Co.

Cincinnati Opera ($15,000) see Semple Foundation, Louise Taft

Cincinnati Playhouse in the Park ($5,000) see Jarson-Stanley and Mickey Kaplan Foundation, Isaac & Esther

Cincinnati Salvation Army ($25,672) see Epp Fund B Charitable Trust, Otto C.

Cincinnati Scholarship Foundation — scholarship awards ($80,000) see Gardner Foundation

Cincinnati Symphony Orchestra ($7,500) see Dater Foundation, Charles H.

Cincinnati Symphony Orchestra ($8,500) see Gradison & Co.

Cincinnati Symphony Orchestra ($3,500) see Hayfields Foundation

Cincinnati Tech College ($4,681) see New Orphan Asylum Scholarship Foundation

Cincinnati Youth Collaboration — start-up program ($100,000) see Schmidlapp Trust No. 1, Jacob G.

Cincinnati Youth Collaborative ($900) see Cincinnati Enquirer

Cincinnati Youth Collaborative ($15,000) see Cincinnati Milacron

Cincinnati Youth Collaborative ($125,000) see Federated Department Stores and Allied Stores Corp.

Cincinnati Youth Collaborative ($5,000) see Gross Charitable Trust, Walter L. and Nell R.

Cincinnati Youth Collaborative — operating fund ($10,000) see Ohio National Life Insurance Co.

Cincinnati Youth Collaborative ($3,000) see Seasongood Good Government Foundation, Murray and Agnes

Cincinnati Youth Collaborative ($16,000) see Star Bank, N.A.

Cincinnati Youth Collaborative ($35,000) see Western Southern Life Insurance Co.

Cincinnati Youth Collaborative — for Taft and McKinley pre-

schools ($15,000) see Jergens Foundation, Andrew

Cincinnati Youth Symphony see SAFECO Corp.

Cincinnati Zoo ($8,500) see Anderson Foundation, William P.

Cincinnati Zoo ($8,000) see Anderson Foundation, William P.

Cincinnati Zoo ($75,000) see Cincinnati Bell

Cincinnati Zoo ($25,000) see Cincinnati Milacron

Cincinnati Zoo and Botanical Garden ($15,100) see Bardes Corp.

Cincinnati Zoo and Botanical Garden ($9,000) see Dater Foundation, Charles H.

Cincinnati Zoo and Botanical Garden ($2,417) see Gradison & Co.

Cincinnati Zoo and Botanical Garden ($10,000) see Russell Charitable Trust, Josephine S.

Cincinnati Zoo and Botany Garden ($10,000) see Western Southern Life Insurance Co.

Cincinnati Zoo — funding of primate exhibit, portion of capital campaign ($500,000) see Kettering Fund

CitiFest ($4,500) see Blade Communications

Citifest see Seaway Food Town

Citizens League for Nursing — student scholarships ($13,000) see Huntington Fund for Education, John

City of Amherst — building ($83,000) see Nord Family Foundation

City Club of Cleveland ($1,000) see Common Wealth Trust

City of Columbus ($6,000) see Lancaster Colony

City of Columbus Parks and Recreation Department — Cultural Arts Center ($3,000) see English Foundation, Walter and Marian

City of Crestline ($7,000) see Common Wealth Trust

City of Kettering ($100,000) see Mead Corp.

City of Kettering ($5,000) see Robbins & Myers, Inc.

City of Kettering — Lincoln Park ($8,000) see Amcast Industrial Corp.

City Mission ($20,000) see Codrington Charitable Foundation, George W.

City Mission ($142,020) see M.T.D. Products

City of Nelsonville ($14,970) see Baird Brothers Co.

City of Tiffin — Community Pool Project ($30,000) see National Machinery Co.

City of Urbana Tree Planting ($4,000) see Grimes Foundation

City of Washington — Eyman Park ($2,000) see Eyman Trust, Jesse

City Young Mothers Educational Development Program — support for program of counseling, education, and health care for school age parents and pregnant teens ($23,000) see Irwin-Sweeney-Miller Foundation

Civic Development Corporation of Ashtabula — Ashtabula County Interactive Television Network ($45,000) see Jennings Foundation, Martha Holden

Ohio (cont.)

Civic Theatre see General Tire Inc.

Clark and Champaign Counties ($11,100) see Robbins & Myers, Inc.

Clark Civic Center ($10,000) see Robbins & Myers, Inc.

Clark Memorial Home Association ($90,000) see Baker Charitable Foundation, Jessie Foos

Clark State Community College-Clark County Civic Center ($25,000) see Cooper Industries

Cleanland, Ohio ($18,250) see Premier Industrial Corp.

Cleveland Academy of Finance ($5,000) see McDonald & Co. Securities

Cleveland Artists Foundation ($10,000) see Frankino Charitable Foundation, Samuel J. and Connie

Cleveland Ballet ($10,000) see Codrington Charitable Foundation, George W.

Cleveland Ballet ($12,000) see Ferro Corp.

Cleveland Ballet ($60,000) see Kulas Foundation

Cleveland Ballet see Lubrizol Corp.

Cleveland Ballet ($15,000) see McDonald & Co. Securities

Cleveland Ballet ($100,000) see Murphy Foundation, John P.

Cleveland Ballet ($90,000) see Reinberger Foundation

Cleveland Ballet ($10,587) see Schey Foundation

Cleveland Ballet ($5,525) see Stocker Foundation

Cleveland Ballet — Nutcracker Sponsorship ($40,000) see Eaton Corp.

Cleveland Bureau of Jewish Education ($5,000) see Hershey Foundation

Cleveland Capital Foundation — capital ($20,000) see Cleveland-Cliffs

Cleveland Center for Contemporary Art ($12,500) see Kangesser Foundation, Robert E., Harry A., and M. Sylvia

Cleveland Center for Contemporary Art ($25,000) see Progressive Corp.

Cleveland Center for Economic Education ($3,000) see Dively Foundation, George S.

Cleveland Center of Research in Child Development ($2,000) see Frohring Foundation, William O. and Gertrude Lewis

Cleveland Central Catholic High School Endowment Fund ($25,000) see Saint Gerard Foundation

Cleveland Central Catholic High School — on-going programs ($100,000) see O'Neill Charitable Corporation, F. J.

Cleveland Children's Museum ($6,000) see Hershey Foundation

Cleveland Children's Museum see Lubrizol Corp.

Cleveland Clinic Foundation ($20,000) see Federal-Mogul Corp.

Cleveland Clinic Foundation ($24,250) see Forest City Enterprises

Cleveland Clinic Foundation ($200,000) see Lennon Foundation, Fred A.

Cleveland Clinic Foundation ($2,600) see Mandel Foundation, Jack N. and Lilyan

Cleveland Clinic Foundation ($25,000) see McFawn Trust No. 2, Lois Sisler

Cleveland Clinic Foundation ($200,000) see Mellen Foundation

Cleveland Clinic Foundation ($5,000) see Minster Machine Co.

Cleveland Clinic Foundation ($12,500) see Moore Foundation, Martha G.

Cleveland Clinic Foundation ($50,000) see Murphy Foundation, John P.

Cleveland Clinic Foundation ($160,000) see National City Corp.

Cleveland Clinic Foundation ($75,000) see Ohio Bell Telephone Co.

Cleveland Clinic Foundation ($250,000) see Prentiss Foundation, Elisabeth Severance

Cleveland Clinic Foundation ($10,000) see Ranney Foundation, P. K.

Cleveland Clinic Foundation ($100,000) see Reinberger Foundation

Cleveland Clinic Foundation — medical research ($50,000) see Rosenthal Foundation, Samuel

Cleveland Clinic Foundation ($20,000) see Rubbermaid

Cleveland Clinic Foundation ($50,000) see Scott and Fetzer Co.

Cleveland Clinic Foundation ($50,000) see Scott and Fetzer Co.

Cleveland Clinic Foundation ($2,000) see Sifco Industries Inc.

Cleveland Clinic Foundation ($7,000) see South Waite Foundation

Cleveland Clinic Foundation — capital campaign ($250,000) see Timken Foundation of Canton

Cleveland Clinic Foundation ($25,000) see Tippit Charitable Trust, C. Carlisle and Margaret M.

Cleveland Clinic Foundation-de Windt Family Cancer Research Lab ($100,000) see Eaton Corp.

Cleveland College of Jewish Studies ($2,500) see Mandel Foundation, Jack N. and Lilyan

Cleveland College of Jewish Studies — teacher training in Jewish education ($50,000) see Rosenthal Foundation, Samuel

Cleveland Development Foundation ($20,000) see Cole National Corp.

Cleveland Development Foundation ($1,000) see Oglebay Norton Co.

Cleveland Development Foundation Inner-City School Fund ($10,000) see Ferro Corp.

Cleveland Development Foundation/Inner-City School Fund ($16,000) see Sherwin-Williams Co.

Cleveland Engineering Society ($550) see Motch Corp.

Cleveland Eye Bank ($10,000) see Murch Foundation

Cleveland Eye Bank ($15,000) see Wellman Foundation, S. K.

Cleveland Foundation ($100,000) see Lincoln Electric Co.

Cleveland Foundation ($50,000) see Ranney Foundation, P. K.

Cleveland Foundation — support for program implementation activities of the teaching leadership consortium of Ohio ($2,000,000) see Ford Foundation

Cleveland Health Education ($5,000) see South Waite Foundation

Cleveland Health Education Museum ($25,000) see Frohring Foundation, Paul & Maxine

Cleveland Health Education Museum ($10,000) see Ranney Foundation, P. K.

Cleveland Health Education Museum ($25,000) see South Waite Foundation

Cleveland Health Museum and Educational Center ($15,000) see Hankins Foundation

Cleveland Hearing and Speech Center ($3,000) see Frohring Foundation, William O. and Gertrude Lewis

Cleveland Initiative for Education — scholarship in escrow ($486,500) see BP America

Cleveland Initiative for Education ($154,800) see Gund Foundation, George

Cleveland Initiative for Education ($20,000) see LTV Corp.

Cleveland Initiative for Education ($15,000) see McDonald & Co. Securities

Cleveland Initiative for Education ($50,000) see Premier Industrial Corp.

Cleveland Initiative for Education ($200,000) see Progressive Corp.

Cleveland Initiative for Education ($35,000) see Standard Products Co.

Cleveland Initiative for Education ($20,000) see White Consolidated Industries

Cleveland Initiative for Education — payment on a $1.2 million pledge to support innovative educational programs in the Cleveland public schools ($240,000) see TRW Corp.

Cleveland Initiative for Education Campaign ($30,000) see Centerior Energy Corp.

Cleveland, Initiative for Education (CIE) ($40,000) see Parker-Hannifin Corp.

Cleveland Initiative for Education (Roundtable) ($15,000) see Cleveland-Cliffs

Cleveland Initiative for Education Roundtable ($44,392) see National City Corp.

Cleveland Institute of Art ($33,150) see American Foundation Corporation

Cleveland Institute of Art ($3,000) see Frohring Foundation, William O. and Gertrude Lewis

Cleveland Institute of Art — student scholarships ($50,000) see Huntington Fund for Education, John

Cleveland Institute of Art ($3,000) see Mather Charitable Trust, S. Livingston

Cleveland Institute of Art ($70,000) see Reinberger Foundation

Cleveland Institute of Art ($15,000) see Wellman Foundation, S. K.

Cleveland Institute of Music ($8,333) see Calhoun Charitable Trust, Kenneth

Cleveland Institute of Music ($6,000) see Ferro Corp.

Cleveland Institute of Music ($25,500) see Kulas Foundation

Cleveland Institute of Music — violin scholarships ($75,000) see Smith Foundation, Kelvin and Eleanor

Cleveland Institute of Music for Case Western Reserve University ($115,000) see Kulas Foundation

Cleveland Medical Library Association ($20,000) see Prentiss Foundation, Elisabeth Severance

Cleveland Museum ($30,000) see BFGoodrich

Cleveland Museum of Art ($3,375) see Kangesser Foundation, Robert E., Harry A., and M. Sylvia

Cleveland Museum of Art ($1,000) see Mandel Foundation, Joseph and Florence

Cleveland Museum of Art ($5,000) see Mandel Foundation, Morton and Barbara

Cleveland Museum of Art — art exhibit ($225,000) see Smith Foundation, Kelvin and Eleanor

Cleveland Museum of Art — Archival Project ($5,000) see Mather Charitable Trust, S. Livingston

Cleveland Museum of Natural History ($45,194) see American Foundation Corporation

Cleveland Museum of Natural History ($6,000) see Hankins Foundation

Cleveland Museum of Natural History — new wing ($77,833) see Ingalls Foundation, Louise H. and David S.

Cleveland Museum of Natural History ($10,000) see Ireland Foundation

Cleveland Museum of Natural History ($45,000) see Murch Foundation

Cleveland Museum of Natural History ($25,000) see Ranney Foundation, P. K.

Cleveland Museum of Natural History ($66,000) see Reinberger Foundation

Cleveland Museum of Natural History ($15,000) see Robbins & Myers, Inc.

Cleveland Museum of Natural History ($254,098) see Second Foundation

Cleveland Museum of Natural History ($12,500) see Sherwin-Williams Co.

Cleveland Museum of Natural History ($15,000) see Wellman Foundation, S. K.

Cleveland Music School Settlement ($40,000) see Kulas Foundation

Cleveland Music School Settlement ($20,000) see Treuhaft Foundation

Cleveland Music School Settlement ($5,000) see White Consolidated Industries

Cleveland Opera ($25,000) see BFGoodrich

Cleveland Opera ($7,500) see Eaton Foundation, Cyrus

Cleveland Opera ($50,000) see Murphy Foundation, John P.

Cleveland Opera ($100,000) see Reinberger Foundation

Cleveland Orchestra ($35,000) see BFGoodrich

Cleveland Orchestra ($10,000) see Frohring Foundation, William O. and Gertrude Lewis

Cleveland Orchestra ($3,000) see Gould Inc.

Cleveland Orchestra ($30,000) see McFawn Trust No. 2, Lois Sisler

Cleveland Orchestra ($400) see Motch Corp.

Cleveland Orchestra ($10,000) see Scott and Fetzer Co.

Cleveland Orchestra ($25,000) see White Consolidated Industries

Cleveland Orchestra ($5,950) see Wilkof Foundation, Edward and Ruth

Cleveland Orchestra Severance Hall ($10,000) see M.T.D. Products

Cleveland Play House ($10,000) see Ferro Corp.

Cleveland Play House ($2,500) see Hauserman, Inc.

Cleveland Play House ($50,000) see Ohio Bell Telephone Co.

Cleveland Play House ($50,000) see Treuhaft Foundation

Cleveland Playhouse — theater campaign ($20,000) see Andrews Foundation

Cleveland Playhouse ($1,000) see Eaton Foundation, Cyrus

Cleveland Playhouse ($10,000) see Gerson Family Foundation, Benjamin J.

Cleveland Playhouse ($7,000) see Hankins Foundation

Cleveland Playhouse ($16,250) see Mandel Foundation, Jack N. and Lilyan

Cleveland Playhouse ($400) see Motch Corp.

Cleveland Playhouse ($25,000) see Premier Industrial Corp.

Cleveland Public Schools/Scholarship-In-Escrow-Program ($10,000) see Sherwin-Williams Co.

Cleveland Recycling Center ($25,000) see 1525 Foundation

Cleveland Recycling Center ($25,000) see Second Foundation

Cleveland Scholarship Program ($3,000) see Frohring Foundation, William O. and Gertrude Lewis

Cleveland Scholarship Programs ($150,000) see Gund Foundation, George

Cleveland Scholarship Programs ($5,200) see Haskell Fund

Cleveland Scholarship Programs — student scholarships ($226,500) see Huntington Fund for Education, John

Cleveland Scholarship Programs ($17,000) see Perkins Charitable Foundation

Cleveland Scholarships Programs — assistance program ($150,000) see Nord Family Foundation

Cleveland Sight Center ($75,000) see Storer Foundation, George B.

Cleveland Sight Center — for start-up operating support for the Low Vision Clinic ($30,000) see Bruening Foundation, Eva L. and Joseph M.

Cleveland Skilled Industries ($2,500) see Smith Charitable Fund, Eleanor Armstrong

Cleveland Society for the Blind — computerization ($50,445) see Smith Foundation, Kelvin and Eleanor

Cleveland State University ($30,000) see Mellen Foundation

Cleveland State University-Advanced Manufacturing Center ($25,000) see Parker-Hannifin Corp.

Cleveland State University Development Foundation ($75,000) see Dively Foundation, George S.

Cleveland Tenants Organization ($10,000) see Gerson Family Foundation, Benjamin J.

Cleveland Tomorrow ($30,000) see Centerior Energy Corp.

Cleveland Tomorrow ($14,000) see Forest City Enterprises

Cleveland Tomorrow ($200,000) see Newhouse Foundation, Samuel I.

Cleveland Tomorrow ($30,000) see Parker-Hannifin Corp.

Cleveland Tomorrow ($25,000) see Scott and Fetzer Co.

Cleveland Tomorrow ($30,000) see Sherwin-Williams Co.

Cleveland UNCF Foundation ($3,000) see Mather Charitable Trust, S. Livingston

Cleveland Women Incorporated — templum house ($5,000) see AHS Foundation

Cleveland Works ($10,000) see Fox Charitable Foundation, Harry K. & Emma R.

Cleveland Works ($10,000) see Gerson Family Foundation, Benjamin J.

Cleveland Zoological ($525) see Schey Foundation

Clovernook Home for the Blind ($500) see Hayfields Foundation

Co-op Fiscal Services — start-up funding ($7,500) see Alms Trust, Eleanora

College of Mt. St. Joseph ($1,000) see Eagle-Picher Industries

College of Mt. St. Joseph ($500) see XTEK Inc.

College of Wooster ($5,000) see DelMar Foundation, Charles

College of Wooster ($10,000) see Pick Charitable Trust, Melitta S.

College of Wooster ($50,000) see Powers Higher Educational Fund, Edward W. and Alice R.

College of Wooster ($175,000) see Rubbermaid

College of Wooster ($25,000) see Smucker Co., J.M.

College of Wooster — Henry Luce III Hall ($20,000) see Grable Foundation

Collier County Conservancy ($10,000) see Wodecroft Foundation

Columbus Academy ($15,000) see Gross Charitable Trust, Walter L. and Nell R.

Columbus Academy ($100,000) see Reinberger Foundation

Columbus Academy Building Campaign ($2,000) see Electric Power Equipment Co.

Columbus Academy — Fund for Tomorrow ($20,000) see Columbus Dispatch Printing Co.

Columbus America — corporate pledge for economic development see Ameritech Publishing

Columbus Area Chamber of Commerce ($250) see Barry Corp., R. G.

Columbus Cancer Clinic ($500) see Kobacker Co.

Columbus College of Art and Design ($5,000) see Edwards Industries

Columbus College of Art and Design ($29,625) see Gerlach Foundation

Columbus College of Art and Design ($100,000) see Nationwide Insurance Cos.

Columbus Commission on Ethics and Values see Battelle

Columbus Education Endowment see Battelle

Columbus Foundation ($10,000) see Block, H&R

Columbus Foundation ($29,250) see Gerlach Foundation

Columbus Foundation ($2,500) see Lancaster Colony

Columbus Foundation — Trilogy ($200,000) see Columbus Dispatch Printing Co.

Columbus Foundation - Trilogy ($125,000) see Federated Department Stores and Allied Stores Corp.

Columbus Jewish Federation ($375,120) see El-An Foundation

Columbus Jewish Foundation ($20,000) see Yassenoff Foundation, Leo

Columbus Jewish Home for the Aged ($40,850) see Schottenstein Foundation, Jerome & Saul

Columbus Literary Council ($1,000) see Electric Power Equipment Co.

Columbus Montessori School ($500) see Kobacker Co.

Columbus Museum of Art see Battelle

Columbus Museum of Art ($80,000) see Burchfield Foundation, Charles E.

Columbus Museum of Art ($15,150) see Gerlach Foundation

Columbus Public Schools ($50,000) see Ohio Bell Telephone Co.

Columbus Public Schools — Know I Can Program see Battelle

Columbus Quincentennial Jubilee Commission see Battelle

Columbus School for Girls ($20,000) see Columbus Dispatch Printing Co.

Columbus Symphony Orchestra see Battelle

Columbus Symphony Orchestra ($3,000) see English Foundation, Walter and Marian

Columbus Symphony Orchestra ($283,000) see Nationwide Insurance Cos.

Columbus Torah Academy ($64,240) see El-An Foundation

Columbus Torah School ($250,000) see Schottenstein Foundation, Jerome & Saul

Columbus Zoo ($5,000) see Schlinger Foundation

Community Action Commission of Fayette County ($3,000) see Eyman Trust, Jesse

Community Christian Church ($35,000) see Hoover Fund-Trust, W. Henry

Community Christian Church ($20,000) see Hoover Fund-Trust, W. Henry

Community Christian Church ($3,000) see Hoover Fund-Trust, W. Henry

Community Foundation of Greater Lorain County — strengthen public school endowment funds ($400,000) see Nord Family Foundation

Community Foundation of Greater Lorain County — beautification efforts ($71,000) see Nord Family Foundation

Community Foundation of Greater Lorain County ($118,500) see Nordson Corp.

Community Foundation of Greater Lorain County ($6,500) see Stocker Foundation

Community Foundation of Greater Lorain County ($5,500) see Stocker Foundation

Congregation Levi Yitzchok ($7,000) see Mandel Foundation, Jack N. and Lilyan

Congregation Ohev Tzedek ($4,137) see Schermer Charitable Trust, Frances

Contemporary Arts Center ($10,000) see Schiff Foundation, John J. and Mary R.

Contemporary Arts Center ($5,000) see Thendara Foundation

Corinne Dolan Alzheimer's Center ($100,000) see Frohring Foundation, William O. and Gertrude Lewis

Corning Institute for Education and Research ($26,000) see American Foundation Corporation

Cornucopia — to purchase the initial inventory of a natural foods store serving as an employment training program for the developmentally disabled ($30,000) see Bingham Foundation, William

Cornucopia ($40,000) see 1525 Foundation

Corporate Matching Gift-White Consolidated Industries, Inc. Foundation ($18,411) see White Consolidated Industries

Coshocton City and County Park District — recreation facilities ($40,000) see Montgomery Foundation

Coshocton County Emergency Medical Service — equipment ($2,300) see Montgomery Foundation

Coshocton County Memorial Hospital — building program ($15,000) see Montgomery Foundation

Coshocton Foundation ($1,000) see Lancaster Colony

Coshocton Foundation ($3,665) see Montgomery Foundation

Council for a Beautiful Israel ($16,000) see Mandel Foundation, Morton and Barbara

Council on Child Abuse ($5,000) see Dater Foundation, Charles H.

Council on Child Abuse of Southwestern Ohio ($22,000) see Mayerson Foundation, Manuel D. and Rhoda

Council on Domestic Violence ($33,000) see Gerstacker Foundation, Rollin M.

Council of Jewish Federation ($7,000) see Mandel Foundation, Morton and Barbara

Councils of Religion ($16,000) see Monarch Machine Tool Co.

Courage Center Swimming Pool ($1,150,000) see Andersen Foundation

Crandall Medical Center ($60,000) see Crandall Memorial Foundation, J. Ford

Creative Living Endowment Fund — Mac Henny Memorial ($25,000) see Benua Foundation

Crisis Care House of Transportation ($10,000) see Van Wert County Foundation

CSC Industries Foundation ($20,000) see Copperweld Steel Co.

Cultural Center for the Arts ($6,350) see Wilkof Foundation, Edward and Ruth

Cummings Zucker Center ($5,000) see Stone Foundation, France

Cuyahoga Valley Christian Academy — capital improvements ($30,000) see Gallagher Family Foundation, Lewis P.

CVCA ($62,500) see Paulstan

Dakota Center ($15,000) see Kramer Foundation, Louise

Dan Beard Council ($25,000) see Cincinnati Milacron

Darke County Arts Center ($59,853) see American Aggregates Corp.

Darke County Center for Arts ($1,500) see Midmark Corp.

Darke County Center for Arts ($1,500) see Midmark Corp.

Darke County Historical Society ($100) see American Aggregates Corp.

Dayton Area Chamber of Commerce ($5,000) see Amcast Industrial Corp.

Dayton Art Institute ($750) see Amcast Industrial Corp.

Dayton Art Institute ($2,200) see Midmark Corp.

Dayton Art Institute ($10,000) see Orleton Trust Fund

Dayton Art Institute ($27,000) see Reynolds & Reynolds Co.

Dayton Art Institute ($10,000) see Tait Foundation, Frank M.

Dayton Ballet Association ($3,000) see Robbins & Myers, Inc.

Dayton Boys/Girls Club ($100,000) see Dayton Power and Light Co.

Dayton Boys/Girls Club — general support ($153,000) see Kettering Fund

Dayton Boys and Girls Club ($125,000) see Mead Corp.

Dayton Boys and Girls Club ($102,000) see Philips Foundation, Jesse

Dayton Christian School ($5,000) see Bauervic Foundation, Charles M.

Dayton Christian School ($17,500) see Kramer Foundation, Louise

Dayton Christian School ($6,000) see Kramer Foundation, Louise

Dayton Foundation ($10,000) see Berry Foundation, Loren M.

Dayton Foundation ($5,000) see Danis Industries

Dayton Foundation ($120,500) see Mead Corp.

Dayton Foundation ($10,000) see Mead Fund, Nelson

Dayton Foundation ($10,000) see Orleton Trust Fund

Dayton Foundation ($50,000) see Philips Foundation, Jesse

Dayton Foundation ($10,000) see Tait Foundation, Frank M.

Dayton Foundation — Annie E. Casey Foundation Challenge ($15,000) see Dayton Power and Light Co.

Dayton Foundation — New Futures Fund ($20,000) see Reynolds & Reynolds Co.

Dayton Foundation — New Futures Youth Initiative ($2,253,620) see Casey Foundation, Annie E.

Dayton Home — health care ($5,000) see Kutz Foundation, Milton and Hattie

Dayton Masonic Blood Bank ($10,404) see Iddings Benevolent Trust

Dayton Montgomery County Scholarship Fund ($160,000) see Tomkins Industries, Inc.

Dayton Museum of Natural History ($10,000) see Berry Foundation, Loren M.

Dayton Museum of Natural History ($30,000) see Danis Industries

Dayton Museum of Natural History ($20,000) see Dayton Power and Light Co.

Dayton Museum of Natural History ($6,000) see Duriron Co., Inc.

Dayton Museum of Natural History ($104,000) see NCR Corp.

Dayton Museum of Natural History ($265,000) see Philips Foundation, Jesse

Dayton Museum of Natural History ($80,000) see Reynolds & Reynolds Co.

Dayton Museum of Natural History ($5,000) see Robbins & Myers, Inc.

Dayton Museum of Natural History ($20,000) see Tait Foundation, Frank M.

Dayton Museum of Natural History ($20,000) see Tait Foundation, Frank M.

Dayton Opera ($13,000) see Dayton Power and Light Co.

Dayton Opera ($10,000) see Tait Foundation, Frank M.

Dayton Philharmonic ($12,500) see Berry Foundation, Loren M.

Dayton Philharmonic ($12,500) see Berry Foundation, Loren M.

Dayton Philharmonic Orchestra ($10,000) see Huffy Corp.

Dayton Philharmonic Orchestra Association ($3,500) see Danis Industries

Dayton Philharmonic Women's Association — for underwriting the printing of Show House program book ($7,500) see H.C.S. Foundation

Dayton Society of Natural History ($10,000) see Orleton Trust Fund

Deaconess Hospital ($30,000) see Schiff Foundation, John J. and Mary R.

Ohio (cont.)

Defiance College ($6,000) see Baumker Charitable Foundation, Elsie and Harry

Defiance College ($5,000) see Manville Corp.

Defiance College ($13,000) see Palmer Fund, Francis Asbury

Delta Gamma Foundation ($1,500) see Group Health Plan Inc.

Delta Gamma Foundation ($1,000) see Metal Industries

Denison University — general ($8,000) see Beck Foundation, Elsie E. & Joseph W.

Denison University ($20,000) see Carnahan-Jackson Foundation

Denison University ($122,348) see Jasam Foundation

Denison University ($100,000) see Olin Foundation, F. W.

DePaul School ($10,000) see Vogt Machine Co., Henry

Development Fund — amphitheater ($50,000) see Evans Foundation, Thomas J.

Diocese of Cleveland ($100,000) see O'Neill Foundation, William J. and Dorothy K.

Doctors Hospital of Nelsonville ($35,000) see Baird Brothers Co.

Dominican Community Services ($50,000) see Jergens Foundation, Andrew

Dorothy Love Retirement Community ($15,000) see Hartzell Industries, Inc.

Dover City Schools ($27,745) see Reeves Foundation

Dover Historical Society ($50,000) see Reeves Foundation

Down Syndrome Center ($5,000) see Dater Foundation, Charles H.

Dublin Schools ($10,000) see Honda of America Manufacturing, Inc.

Dunlap Memorial Hospital ($33,334) see Smucker Co., J.M.

Dyke College — student scholarships ($59,500) see Huntington Fund for Education, John

East Cleveland City Schools ($10,000) see Gerson Family Foundation, Benjamin J.

Easter Seal Society ($1,000) see Edwards Industries

Easter Seals see Seaway Food Town

Echoing Hills Village — main lodge building project ($10,100) see Montgomery Foundation

Education and Public Improvement Foundation ($6,500) see Duriron Co., Inc.

Educational Enhancement Partnership — for implementation of program ($128,000) see Hoover Foundation

Educational Television ($7,000) see Tremco Inc.

Educational Television Association of Metropolitan Cleveland ($25,000) see Codrington Charitable Foundation, George W.

El Centro de Servicios Sociales ($22,000) see Nordson Corp.

Elder High School — for computers ($15,000) see Alms Trust, Eleanora

Electrical Contracting Foundation ($10,000) see Electric Power Equipment Co.

Eliza Bryant Center ($1,000) see Hauserman, Inc.

Eliza Bryant Center — for second year funding for the Adult Day Care program ($40,000) see Bruening Foundation, Eva L. and Joseph M.

Eliza Jennings Group ($60,000) see Ranney Foundation, P. K.

Elmdale Grange — restroom facilities ($5,000) see Massie Trust, David Meade

Elyria Family YMCA — boiler replacement ($70,000) see Nordson Corp.

Elyria Memorial Hospital — support of program ($5,000) see Ross Corp.

Elyria Methodist Home ($25,000) see Ernsthausen Charitable Foundation, John F. and Doris E.

Elyria Public Library ($15,791) see Miller Charitable Trust, Lewis N.

Emery Center ($2,042) see Jarson-Stanley and Mickey Kaplan Foundation, Isaac & Esther

Epilepsy Foundation ($4,530) see LDI Charitable Foundation

Epilepsy Foundation see Seaway Food Town

Fairhill Institute for the Elderly — for phase I of the Adult Day Care program payable over two years ($80,000) see Bruening Foundation, Eva L. and Joseph M.

Fairlawn West ($10,000) see Musson Charitable Foundation, R. C. and Katharine M.

Fairmont Montessori Association ($5,000) see AHS Foundation

Fairmount Presbyterian Church, Cleveland Heights ($6,000) see Tippit Charitable Trust, C. Carlisle and Margaret M.

Fairmount Theater of Deaf ($6,000) see Eaton Foundation, Cyrus

Fairview General Hospital ($20,000) see M.T.D. Products

Fairview General Hospital ($1,000) see Weiss Fund, Clara

Faith Mission ($25,000) see Hillsdale Fund

Faith Mission ($15,000) see Yassenoff Foundation, Leo

Fairview General Hospital — to purchase interactive video and CAI equipment ($63,604) see Fuld Health Trust, Helene

Family Services Association of Lorain ($5,510) see Stocker Foundation

Family Violence Project — Talbert House and YWCA ($50,000) see Mayerson Foundation, Manuel D. and Rhoda

Fayette County Department of Services ($3,000) see Eyman Trust, Jesse

Fayette County Senior Nutrition Program ($3,000) see Eyman Trust, Jesse

Fellowship of Christian Athletes ($4,000) see Tomkins Industries, Inc.

Financial Accounting Foundation ($1,200) see Minster Machine Co.

Fine Arts Fund ($6,000) see Bardes Corp.

Fine Arts Fund ($37,000) see Cincinnati Bell

Fine Arts Fund ($44,000) see Cincinnati Milacron

Fine Arts Fund — annual contribution ($50,000) see Fifth Third Bancorp

Fine Arts Fund ($5,000) see Gradison & Co.

Fine Arts Fund — operating fund ($11,000) see Ohio National Life Insurance Co.

Fine Arts Fund ($5,000) see Ohio Valley Foundation

Fine Arts Fund ($8,500) see Peterloon Foundation

Fine Arts Fund ($277,500) see Procter & Gamble Co.

Fine Arts Fund ($60,500) see Semple Foundation, Louise Taft

Fine Arts Fund ($35,000) see Star Bank, N.A.

Fine Arts Fund ($15,000) see Thendara Foundation

Fine Arts Fund ($10,500) see XTEK Inc.

Fine Arts Fund — 1990 annual campaign ($6,500) see Alms Trust, Eleanora

Firelands Community Hospital Fund — to purchase equipment for Firelands Community Hospital ($25,000) see Frohman Foundation, Sidney

First Baptist Church ($8,085) see Miller Memorial Trust, George Lee

First Church of Christ ($5,000) see Smucker Co., J.M.

First Presbyterian Church ($13,900) see Baird Brothers Co.

First Presbyterian Church ($11,000) see Kilcawley Fund, William H.

First Presbyterian Church ($10,000) see True Trust, Henry A.

First Presbyterian Church ($5,000) see Van Huffel Foundation, I. J.

First Step ($10,000) see National Machinery Co.

First United Methodist Church ($36,000) see Ernsthausen Charitable Foundation, John F. and Doris E.

Flower Hospital ($10,186) see Ritter Charitable Trust, George W. & Mary F.

Flower Memorial Hospital ($2,000) see Goerlich Family Foundation

4-H Clubs ($12,000) see Monarch Machine Tool Co.

Frances Payne Bolton School of Nursing ($22,000) see Perkins Charitable Foundation

Franciscan Mission Service ($10,000) see O'Neill Foundation, William J. and Dorothy K.

Franciscan University of Steubenville — educational ($181,725) see Domino's Pizza

Franciscan University of Steubenville ($150,000) see Williams Charitable Trust, John C.

Frankfort Presbyterian Church — roof for church ($5,000) see Massie Trust, David Meade

Franklin County Board of Education ($1,000) see Kobacker Co.

Franklin University ($50,000) see Moores Foundation, Harry C.

Franklin University ($201,000) see Nationwide Insurance Cos.

Fred Hutchinson Cancer Research ($20,000) see Foster Foundation

Fred Hutchinson Cancer Research Center ($100,000) see Forest Foundation

Free Medical Clinic of Cleveland ($22,000) see Britton Fund

Free Medical Clinic of Cleveland ($3,000) see Haskell Fund

Free Medical Clinic of Cleveland ($500) see Osborn Manufacturing Co.

Free Store/Food Bank — operating fund ($2,500) see Ohio National Life Insurance Co.

Freestore/Foodbank ($20,000) see Mayerson Foundation, Manuel D. and Rhoda

Freestore/Foodbank ($2,500) see Peterloon Foundation

Friendly Center ($5,000) see Baumker Charitable Foundation, Elsie and Harry

Friendly Center ($5,000) see Stone Foundation, France

Friends of Cornell School ($1,000) see Park National Bank

Friends of Jesus ($100) see Arbie Mineral Feed Co.

Friends of Kirtland ($6,000) see Mill-Rose Co.

Friends of the Library ($500) see Midmark Corp.

Friends of Plum Street Temple ($60,000) see Mayerson Foundation, Manuel D. and Rhoda

Friends of Project: LEARN ($2,500) see Lamson & Sessions Co.

Friends of the School for Creative and Performing Arts — capital improvements ($15,700) see Corbett Foundation

Friends of Shakers ($7,000) see Tremco Inc.

Friends of WOSU ($1,500) see Shafer Foundation, Richard H. and Ann

Fund for Independent Schools ($5,000) see Eagle-Picher Industries

Furnace Street Mission ($23,000) see Calhoun Charitable Trust, Kenneth

Future Farmers of America see General Tire Inc.

Garden Center of Greater Cleveland ($3,000) see V and V Foundation

Geauga Park District — Heron Rookery ($5,000) see Mather Charitable Trust, S. Livingston

Gifts for Relief of Poverty ($37,235) see Beerman Foundation

Gilmour Academy ($20,000) see Andrews Foundation

Gilmour Academy ($6,000) see Laub Foundation

Gilmour Academy ($50,000) see Murphy Foundation, John P.

Gilmour Academy ($50,000) see O'Neill Foundation, William J. and Dorothy K.

Girl Scouts of America ($10,000) see Andrews Foundation

Girl Scouts of America ($35,378) see Kling Trust, Louise

Girl Scouts of America ($750) see Minster Machine Co.

Girl Scouts of America ($25,000) see Sandusky International Inc.

Girl Scouts of America ($50,000) see Treuhaft Foundation

Gish Film Theatre ($20,000) see Pickford Foundation, Mary

Gladden Community Center ($25,500) see Yassenoff Foundation, Leo

Gladden Community House ($10,000) see Benua Foundation

Glenmont ($229,000) see 1525 Foundation

Glenmont Home of Christian Scientists ($5,000) see Lancaster Colony

Golden Age Centers ($1,000) see Frohring Foundation, Paul & Maxine

Good Samaritan Hospital ($1,650) see Gradison & Co.

Good Samaritan Hospital — for their cardiac arrhythmia mapping system ($25,000) see H.C.S. Foundation

Goodrich Gannett Center ($350) see Osborn Manufacturing Co.

Goodwill Industries ($12,000) see Crandall Memorial Foundation, J. Ford

Goodwill Industries ($15,000) see Iddings Benevolent Trust

Goodwill Industries ($10,000) see Kilcawley Fund, William H.

Goodwill Industries ($5,000) see Kramer Foundation, Louise

Goodwill Industries ($20,000) see M.T.D. Products

Goodwill Industries ($15,000) see Orleton Trust Fund

Goodwill Industries ($2,500) see Pollock Company Foundation, William B.

Goodwill Industries ($10,000) see Sandusky International Inc.

Goodwill Industries ($1,000) see Weiss Fund, Clara

Goodwill Industries of Central Ohio ($50,000) see Moores Foundation, Harry C.

Goodwill Industries of Dayton ($30,000) see Cox Enterprises

Grady Home ($5,000) see Stone Foundation, France

Grant Hospital ($45,000) see Moores Foundation, Harry C.

Granville Library ($10,000) see Evans Foundation, Thomas J.

Great Lakes Historical Society ($25,000) see Mather and William Gwinn Mather Fund, Elizabeth Ring

Great Lakes Historical Society ($10,000) see Mather Charitable Trust, S. Livingston

Great Lakes Historical Society ($5,000) see Oglebay Norton Co.

Great Lakes Museum ($959,734) see Gund Foundation, George

Great Lakes Theater Festival ($8,000) see AHS Foundation

Great Lakes Theater Festival ($1,000) see Eaton Foundation, Cyrus

Great Lakes Theater Festival ($60,000) see Kulas Foundation

Great Lakes Theater Festival ($50,000) see Murphy Foundation, John P.

Great Lakes Theater Festival, Cleveland, OH ($50,000) see Progressive Corp.

Great Lakes Theater Festival — support for the Festival's Student Education program ($30,000) see Jennings Foundation, Martha Holden

Great Lakes Theatre ($2,500) see Schey Foundation

Great Lakes Theatre Festival ($10,000) see Andrews Foundation

Great Lakes Theatre Festival ($2,000) see Sears Family Foundation

Great Lakes Theatre Festival ($55,000) see Smith Foundation, Kelvin and Eleanor

Greater Akron Musical Association ($13,500) see Calhoun Charitable Trust, Kenneth

Greater Canton Amateur Sports Hall of Fame ($2,000) see Flowers Charitable Trust, Albert W. and Edith V.

Greater Cincinnati Center for Economic Education ($500) see XTEK Inc.

Greater Cincinnati Chamber of Commerce — Blue Chip campaign ($30,000) see Star Bank, N.A.

Greater Cincinnati Foundation ($15,000) see Griswold Foundation, John C.

Greater Cincinnati Foundation ($15,000) see Gross Charitable Trust, Walter L. and Nell R.

Greater Cincinnati Foundation ($5,000) see Jarson-Stanley and Mickey Kaplan Foundation, Isaac & Esther

Greater Cincinnati for Matching Funds ($10,000) see Smith, Jr. Charitable Trust, Jack J.

Greater Cincinnati Scholarship Association Fund ($2,500) see Gradison & Co.

Greater Cleveland Camping Alliance ($10,000) see Codrington Charitable Foundation, George W.

Greater Cleveland Committee on Hunger ($20,000) see Codrington Charitable Foundation, George W.

Greater Cleveland Growth Association ($2,000) see Hauserman, Inc.

Greater Cleveland Interfaith Council ($22,000) see Britton Fund

Greater Cleveland Round Table ($12,500) see Forest City Enterprises

Greater Cleveland Roundtable ($5,000) see Bicknell Fund

Greater Cleveland Roundtable ($30,000) see Forest City Enterprises

Greater Dayton Public Television ($7,500) see Berry Foundation, Loren M.

Greater Dayton Public TV ($12,012) see Dayton Power and Light Co.

Greater Erie County Marketing Group ($5,000) see Sandusky International Inc.

Habitat for Humanity ($10,000) see Corbin Foundation, Mary S. and David C.

Habitat for Humanity ($10,000) see Ernsthausen Charitable Foundation, John F. and Doris E.

Habitat for Humanity ($20,000) see Rupp Foundation, Fran and Warren

Hale Farm and Village ($5,000) see Bicknell Fund

Hale Farm and Village ($25,000) see Corbin Foundation, Mary S. and David C.

Hale Farm and Village ($62,500) see GenCorp

Hale Farm and Village ($5,000) see Hershey Foundation

Hale Farm and Village ($10,000) see McAlonan Trust, John A.

Hale Farm and Village ($50,000) see 1525 Foundation

Hale Farm and Village ($10,000) see Ritchie Memorial Foundation, Charles E. and Mabel M.

Hale Farm and Village — fireplace at gatehouse ($30,000) see Smith Foundation, Kelvin and Eleanor

Hale Farm and Village ($15,000) see Wellman Foundation, S. K.

Hale Farm and Village Western Reserve Historical Society — to be used to finish non-public areas in the Gatehouse ($140,000) see GAR Foundation

Halom House ($25,000) see Reicher Foundation, Anne & Harry J.

Hamilton County Department of Human Services ($10,000) see Rice Foundation, Helen Steiner

Hamilton County O.E.S. Home ($4,320) see Cincinnati Foundation for the Aged

Hamilton County SPCA ($500) see Hayfields Foundation

Hanna Perkins School ($10,000) see Calhoun Charitable Trust, Kenneth

Hannah Perkins School ($25,000) see Andrews Foundation

Harding Evans Foundation ($20,000) see Schottenstein Foundation, Jerome & Saul

Harvest for Hunger ($17,500) see Rosenthal Foundation, Samuel

Hathaway Brown School ($102,000) see American Foundation Corporation

Hathaway Brown School ($100,000) see Frohring Foundation, Paul & Maxine

Hathaway Brown School ($12,000) see Hankins Foundation

Hathaway Brown School ($25,000) see Humphrey Fund, George M. and Pamela S.

Hathaway Brown School ($6,000) see Laub Foundation

Hathaway Brown School ($25) see Mather and William Gwinn Mather Fund, Elizabeth Ring

Hathaway Brown School — capital campaign ($16,667) see Rosenthal Foundation, Samuel

Hathaway Brown School — capital campaign ($150,000) see Smith Foundation, Kelvin and Eleanor

Hathaway Brown School ($25,000) see V and V Foundation

Haven of Rest see General Tire Inc.

Haven of Rest ($29,217) see Musson Charitable Foundation, R. C. and Katharine M.

Haven of Rest Ministries ($10,000) see Corbin Foundation, Mary S. and David C.

Haven of Rest Ministries ($10,000) see McAlonan Trust, John A.

Hawken School ($5,000) see Bicknell Fund

Hawken School — capital campaign ($25,000) see Gries Charity Fund, Lucile and Robert H.

Hawken School ($6,000) see Laub Foundation

Hawken School ($50,000) see Mather and William Gwinn Mather Fund, Elizabeth Ring

Hawken School — alumni fund, capital and endowment ($15,100) see Ireland Foundation

Haymarket Peoples Fund ($10,000) see Schecter Private Foundation, Aaron and Martha

Haymarket Peoples Fund ($7,000) see Schecter Private Foundation, Aaron and Martha

Head and Neck Medicine and Surgery Foundation ($40,000) see Smith Charitable Fund, Eleanor Armstrong

Health Education Center ($10,000) see McAlonan Trust, John A.

Health Hill Hospital ($15,000) see Perkins Charitable Foundation

Health Initiative — toward primary health care needs of medically indigent ($20,000) see H.C.S. Foundation

Hearing and Speech Center ($10,000) see Gries Charity Fund, Lucile and Robert H.

Heather Hill ($100,000) see American Foundation Corporation

Heather Hill ($1,000) see Frohring Foundation, Paul & Maxine

Heather Hill ($2,500) see Hershey Foundation

Heather Hill — hospital expansion ($75,000) see Ingalls Foundation, Louise H. and David S.

Heather Hill ($25,000) see O'Neill Foundation, William J. and Dorothy K.

Heather Hill ($16,000) see Perkins Charitable Foundation

Heather Hill Hospital — capital fund ($1,000) see Oglebay Norton Co.

Hebrew Academy of Cleveland ($20,000) see Forest City Enterprises

Hebrew Academy of Cleveland ($3,000) see Kangesser Foundation, Robert E., Harry A., and M. Sylvia

Hebrew Academy of Cleveland ($800) see Ohio Savings Bank

Hebrew Academy of Cleveland ($357,895) see Sapirstein-Stone-Weiss Foundation

Hebrew Union College ($50,000) see Beerman Foundation

Hebrew Union College ($25,000) see Berkman Charitable Trust, Allen H. and Selma W.

Hebrew Union College ($70,000) see Blaustein Foundation, Jacob and Hilda

Hebrew Union College ($5,000) see Daniel Foundation, Gerard and Ruth

Hebrew Union College ($107,450) see Feintech Foundation

Hebrew Union College ($12,500) see Hess Charitable Foundation, Ronne and Donald

Hebrew Union College ($50,500) see Kevorkian Fund, Hagop

Hebrew Union College ($200,000) see Klau Foundation, David W. and Sadie

Hebrew Union College ($50,000) see Klau Foundation, David W. and Sadie

Hebrew Union College ($50,000) see Klau Foundation, David W. and Sadie

Hebrew Union College ($25,000) see Lurie Foundation, Louis R.

Hebrew Union College ($2,000,000) see Skirball Foundation

Hebrew Union College ($1,000,000) see Skirball Foundation

Hebrew Union College ($1,000,000) see Skirball Foundation

Hebrew Union College ($1,000,000) see Skirball Foundation

Hebrew Union College ($100,000) see Smart Family Foundation

Hebrew Union College ($15,000) see Star Bank, N.A.

Hebrew Union College ($37,150) see Steinhardt Foundation, Judy and Michael

Hebrew Union College ($30,000) see Swig Charity Foundation, Mae and Benjamin

Hebrew Union College — fellowships ($435,972) see Wexner Foundation

Hebrew Union College ($300) see XTEK Inc.

Hebrew Union College ($10,000) see Zimmerman Family Foundation, Raymond

Hebrew Union College Archaeology ($2,500) see Levine Family Foundation, Hyman

Hebrew Union College Institute of Religion ($250,000) see Skirball Foundation

Hebrew Union College Jewish Institute of Religion ($235,999) see Berkman Charitable Trust, Allen H. and Selma W.

Hebrew Union College Jewish Institute of Religion ($100,500) see Bronstein Foundation, Sol and Arlene

Hebrew Union College Jewish Institute of Religion ($3,500) see Fellner Memorial Foundation, Leopold and Clara M.

Hebrew Union College Jewish Institute of Religion ($99,000) see Forchheimer Foundation

Hebrew Union College Jewish Institute of Religion ($25,500) see Mayerson Foundation, Manuel D. and Rhoda

Hebrew Union College Jewish Institute of Religion ($33,333) see Millstone Foundation

Hebrew Union College Jewish Institute of Religion ($10,000) see Reicher Foundation, Anne & Harry J.

Hebrew Union College Jewish Institute Religion ($85,000) see Shapiro Foundation, Charles and M. R.

Hebrew Union College Skirball Museum ($5,000) see Bronstein Foundation, Sol and Arlene

Heidelberg College ($30,000) see Beeghly Fund, Leon A.

Heidelberg College ($15,792) see Miller Charitable Trust, Lewis N.

Heidelberg College ($50,000) see National Machinery Co.

Heidelberg College ($7,850) see Osceola Foundation

Heilel Foundation ($34,633) see Yassenoff Foundation, Leo

Heimlich Medical Center ($10,000) see Griswold Foundation, John C.

Heinzerling Foundation ($100,000) see Moores Foundation, Harry C.

Henry H. Stambaugh Auditorium Association — rental for five Monday musical club concerts ($3,750) see Beecher Foundation, Florence Simon

Henry H. Stombough Auditorium Association — capital fund ($40,000) see Watson Foundation, Walter E. and Caroline H.

Heritage Center ($10,000) see Anderson Foundation, William P.

Heritage Center ($10,000) see Anderson Foundation, William P.

Hershey Montessori School ($10,000) see Hershey Foundation

Highland Presbyterian Church ($1,100) see Schey Foundation

Hillside Trust ($100) see Hayfields Foundation

Hipple Cancer Research Center ($600) see French Oil Mill Machinery Co.

Hipple Cancer Research Center ($450) see French Oil Mill Machinery Co.

Hipple Cancer Research Center ($2,600) see Kuhns Investment Co.

Hiram College ($20,000) see Austin Memorial Foundation

Hiram College ($5,000) see Dively Foundation, George S.

Hiram College ($25,000) see Frohring Foundation, Paul & Maxine

Hiram College ($10,000) see Frohring Foundation, Paul & Maxine

Hiram College ($3,035) see Gould Inc.

Hiram House ($7,500) see Mather Charitable Trust, S. Livingston

Historic Southwest Ohio — reconstruction of Sharon Woods Village ($15,000) see Schmidlapp Trust No. 2, Jacob G.

Hitchcock Center for Women — for consolidation of all the agency's chemical dependency treatment programs at the former St. Mary Seminary building payable over three years ($60,000) see Bruening Foundation, Eva L. and Joseph M.

Hitchcock Center for Women — to become self-supporting ($100,000) see O'Neill Charitable Corporation, F. J.

Hitchcock House ($10,000) see Andrews Foundation

Hocking Valley Museum ($2,831) see Baird Brothers Co.

Hocking Valley Scenic RR ($84,312) see Baird Brothers Co.

Holden Arboretum ($189,956) see American Foundation Corporation

Ohio (cont.)

Holly Hills Baseball Association ($5,000) see Flowers Charitable Trust, Albert W. and Edith V.

Holy Angels School ($16,500) see Monarch Machine Tool Co.

Holy Family Cancer Home ($15,000) see Britton Fund

HOME Communication Channel ($20,000) see Russell Charitable Foundation, Tom

Home Health Care ($20,000) see Wellman Foundation, S. K.

Hope Lutheran Church ($1,250) see Goerlich Family Foundation

Hospice ($1,000) see American Aggregates Corp.

Hospice Care of Southwestern Ohio ($25,000) see Emery Memorial, Thomas J.

Hospice of Dayton ($17,000) see Cox Enterprises

Hospice of Dayton ($25,000) see Reynolds & Reynolds Co.

Hospice of Wayne County ($2,000) see Weiss Fund, Clara

Hotchkiss School ($3,250) see Mead Fund, Nelson

House of Tradition ($147,875) see El-An Foundation

Hoxworth Blood Center ($1,000) see Eagle-Picher Industries

Hoxworth Blood Center — capital fund for new building ($3,250) see Ohio National Life Insurance Co.

Hudson Presbyterian Church — for organ fund ($16,300) see Morgan Foundation, Burton D.

Hudson School District Foundation — college scholarship ($25,000) see Gallagher Family Foundation, Lewis P.

Human Life Center ($15,000) see Trust Funds

Humane Society of Dayton ($20,000) see Berry Foundation, Loren M.

Hunger Task Force ($3,000) see Osborn Manufacturing Co.

Hunger Task Force Cleveland ($3,000) see Haskell Fund

Huron Road Hospital ($8,000) see Murch Foundation

I Know I Can ($10,000) see Columbus Dispatch Printing Co.

IBFI Foundation ($35,000) see Reynolds & Reynolds Co.

Images, Images, Images ($10,000) see Schiff Foundation, John J. and Mary R.

Indian Hill Church ($6,000) see Gross Charitable Trust, Walter L. and Nell R.

Industrial Information Institute ($3,900) see Commercial Intertech Corp.

Inner-City Scholarship Fund ($25,000) see Salomon

Inner City School Fund ($10,000) see Cleveland-Cliffs

Inner City School Fund ($3,000) see McDonald & Co. Securities

Inner City School Fund ($50,000) see Murphy Foundation, John P.

Inner City School Fund ($3,000) see Sifco Industries Inc.

Institute of Pathology — Alzheimer's Research ($35,000) see Britton Fund

Interchurch Council ($10,000) see Fox Charitable Foundation, Harry K. & Emma R.

Interfaith Home Maintenance Service — maintenance service for senior and low income homeowners ($3,000) see Beecher Foundation, Florence Simon

Interfaith Home Maintenance Service ($9,000) see Crandall Memorial Foundation, J. Ford

International Family Center of Union County ($5,134) see Honda of America Manufacturing, Inc.

International Friendship Center of Logan County ($4,000) see Honda of America Manufacturing, Inc.

Interval Brotherhood Home ($9,203) see McAlonan Trust, John A.

Jefferson Patterson Society ($2,200) see Midmark Corp.

Jewish Community Center ($20,000) see Sapirstein-Stone-Weiss Foundation

Jewish Community Center Association ($15,100) see Mandel Foundation, Morton and Barbara

Jewish Community Complex ($50,000) see Beerman Foundation

Jewish Community Council ($16,000) see Berkman Foundation, Louis and Sandra

Jewish Community Federation ($100,000) see Cole National Corp.

Jewish Community Federation ($18,000) see Fox Charitable Foundation, Harry K. & Emma R.

Jewish Community Federation ($20,000) see Gries Charity Fund, Lucile and Robert H.

Jewish Community Federation ($165,000) see Kangesser Foundation, Robert E., Harry A., and M. Sylvia

Jewish Community Federation ($25,000) see Kangesser Foundation, Robert E., Harry A., and M. Sylvia

Jewish Community Federation ($166,667) see Mandel Foundation, Jack N. and Lilyan

Jewish Community Federation ($266,667) see Mandel Foundation, Joseph and Florence

Jewish Community Federation ($172,266) see Mandel Foundation, Morton and Barbara

Jewish Community Federation ($4,500) see Ohio Savings Bank

Jewish Community Federation ($750,000) see Premier Industrial Corp.

Jewish Community Federation ($315,000) see Rosenthal Foundation, Samuel

Jewish Community Federation ($600,000) see Sapirstein-Stone-Weiss Foundation

Jewish Community Federation ($13,050) see Shiffman Foundation

Jewish Community Federation ($260,000) see Treuhaft Foundation

Jewish Community Federation of Cleveland ($50,000) see Tranzonic Cos.

Jewish Community Federation of Cleveland ($25,000) see Tranzonic Cos.

Jewish Community Federation of Cleveland ($25,000) see Tranzonic Cos.

Jewish Community Federation of Cleveland ($25,000) see Tranzonic Cos.

Jewish Community Federation of Cleveland ($25,000) see Tranzonic Cos.

Jewish Community Federation of Cleveland ($20,000) see Tranzonic Cos.

Jewish Community Federation of Cleveland ($20,000) see Tranzonic Cos.

Jewish Community Federation of Cleveland ($20,000) see Tranzonic Cos.

Jewish Community Federation of Cleveland ($20,000) see Tranzonic Cos.

Jewish Community Federation of Cleveland ($20,000) see Tranzonic Cos.

Jewish Community Relations Council ($1,000) see Jarson-Stanley and Mickey Kaplan Foundation, Isaac & Esther

Jewish Federation ($345,000) see Beerman Foundation

Jewish Federation ($5,000) see Blade Communications

Jewish Federation ($75,000) see Jarson-Stanley and Mickey Kaplan Foundation, Isaac & Esther

Jewish Federation ($100,000) see Mayerson Foundation, Manuel D. and Rhoda

Jewish Federation ($78,000) see Mayerson Foundation, Manuel D. and Rhoda

Jewish Federation ($4,000) see Roth Foundation, Louis T.

Jewish Federation ($5,000) see Schermer Charitable Trust, Frances

Jewish Federation of Greater Dayton ($140,000) see Philips Foundation, Jesse

Jewish Hospital ($10,000) see Jarson-Stanley and Mickey Kaplan Foundation, Isaac & Esther

Jewish Hospital of Cincinnati ($40,000) see Smith, Jr. Charitable Trust, Jack J.

Jewish Hospital of Cincinnati ($30,000) see Smith, Jr. Charitable Trust, Jack J.

Jewish National Fund ($2,000) see Mandel Foundation, Joseph and Florence

Jewish National Fund of Cleveland ($1,000) see Ohio Savings Bank

Jewish Vocational Service ($5,000) see Goldenberg Foundation, Max

Jewish Vocational Services ($10,000) see Rice Foundation, Helen Steiner

Jewish Welfare Fund ($150,000) see American Financial Corp.

John Carroll University ($1,000) see Acme-Cleveland Corp.

John Carroll University ($25,000) see Andrews Foundation

John Carroll University ($6,000) see Ferro Corp.

John Carroll University — student scholarships ($69,000) see Huntington Fund for Education, John

John Carroll University ($100,000) see Mellen Foundation

John Carroll University ($1,500) see Motch Corp.

John Carroll University ($1,000) see Oglebay Norton Co.

John Carroll University — capital fund ($28,572) see Parker-Hannifin Corp.

John Carroll University ($3,000) see Sifco Industries Inc.

John Carroll University ($17,025) see Standard Products Co.

John Carroll University ($10,000) see White Consolidated Industries

John Carroll University — toward construction of Dining and Conference Addition ($500,000) see H.C.S. Foundation

John Carroll University Hobert M. Ginn Institute ($3,000) see Lamson & Sessions Co.

John Carroll University President's Forum ($5,000) see Boler Co.

John Carroll University, (School of Business) ($25,000) see Sherwin-Williams Co.

John F. Kennedy High School ($7,000) see Van Huffel Foundation, I. J.

Johnson County Education Fund — pre-college matching gifts ($114,341) see Eaton Corp.

Joint Township District Memorial Hospital ($17,000) see Huffy Corp.

Joint Township District Memorial Hospital ($5,000) see Minster Machine Co.

Joy Outdoor Education Center ($10,000) see Anderson Foundation, William P.

Joy Outdoor Education Center ($5,000) see Thendara Foundation

Judean Hills Foundation ($50,000) see Hassenfeld Foundation

Judson Retirement Community ($70,000) see Reinberger Foundation

Judson Retirement Community ($15,000) see Treuhaft Foundation

Judson Retirement Community — for the Bruening Health Care Center ($150,000) see Bruening Foundation, Eva L. and Joseph M.

Junior Achievement ($2,000) see Amcast Industrial Corp.

Junior Achievement ($350) see American Aggregates Corp.

Junior Achievement ($750) see Belden Brick Co., Inc.

Junior Achievement ($11,000) see Charities Foundation

Junior Achievement ($2,500) see Commercial Intertech Corp.

Junior Achievement ($8,500) see Evans Foundation, Thomas J.

Junior Achievement ($2,100) see Goerlich Family Foundation

Junior Achievement ($5,000) see Massie Trust, David Meade

Junior Achievement ($15,000) see Miniger Memorial Foundation, Clement O.

Junior Achievement ($200) see Motch Corp.

Junior Achievement of Dayton ($4,000) see Tomkins Industries, Inc.

Junior Achievement of Northwestern Ohio ($14,000) see TRINOVA Corp.

Junior Achievement of Northwestern Ohio, Toledo, OH ($25,000) see Dana Corp.

Junior Achievement Stark County ($20,000) see Timken Co.

Junior Fair Building Committee — new building project ($5,000) see Montgomery Foundation

Junior League of Cleveland ($3,000) see Sears Family Foundation

Junior League of Columbus — Kelton House ($5,000) see English Foundation, Walter and Marian

Karamu House ($40,000) see Nordson Corp.

Keep America Beautiful ($25,000) see Charities Foundation

Kennedy Heights Nursery School — for facility expansion ($25,000) see Jergens Foundation, Andrew

Kent Social Services ($2,500) see Davey Tree Expert Co.

Kent State University ($3,470) see Gould Inc.

Kent State University ($50,000) see Murphy Foundation, John P.

Kent State University ($7,500) see Schermer Charitable Trust, Frances

Kent State University ($2,500) see Schermer Charitable Trust, Frances

Kent State University Foundation ($10,000) see Corbin Foundation, Mary S. and David C.

Kenyon College ($2,000) see Blade Communications

Kenyon College ($15,350) see First Chicago

Kenyon College ($10,000) see Mather and William Gwinn Mather Fund, Elizabeth Ring

Kenyon College — general operating support ($100,495) see MCJ Foundation

Kenyon College ($6,500) see V and V Foundation

Kenyon College — Asia study ($150,000) see Storer Foundation, George B.

Kettering Mohican Area Medical Center ($82,812) see Young Foundation, Hugo H. and Mabel B.

Kettering Parks Foundation ($20,000) see NCR Corp.

Kids Helping Kids ($5,000) see Ohio Valley Foundation

Kings Academy ($10,000) see Generation Trust

Kingswood Center ($140,000) see Lippitt Foundation, Katherine Kenyon

Klondike Horse Center Association ($1,000) see American Welding & Manufacturing Co.

Knights of Columbus ($1,000) see Minster Machine Co.

Lake Avenue Church of Christ ($15,791) see Miller Charitable Trust, Lewis N.

Lake Catholic High School ($5,000) see Mill-Rose Co.

Lake Erie College ($10,000) see Andrews Foundation

Lake Erie College ($50,000) see Kilcawley Fund, William H.

Lake Erie College — debt retirement ($25,000) see Lincoln Electric Co.

Lake Erie College — operating fund ($25,000) see Lincoln Electric Co.

Lake Erie College ($800) see Mill-Rose Co.

Lake Erie College ($24,000) see Murch Foundation

Lake Erie College ($50,000) see Powers Higher Educational Fund, Edward W. and Alice R.

Lake Erie College — scholarship fund ($20,000) see Ritchie Memorial Foundation, Charles E. and Mabel M.

Lake Erie College — Equestrian Center ($26,000) see Humphrey Fund, George M. and Pamela S.

Lake Erie Nature and Science Center ($10,000) see Fox Charitable Foundation, Harry K. & Emma R.

Lake Ridge Academy ($6,000) see Laub Foundation

Lake Ridge Academy ($2,500) see Weiss Fund, Clara

Lakewood Hospital ($10,000) see White Consolidated Industries

Lakewood Hospital Foundation ($3,000) see LDI Charitable Foundation

Lakewood Little Theatre ($50,000) see Kulas Foundation

LaSalle High School — capital campaign ($12,500) see Alms Trust, Eleanora

Laurel School — general and centennial fund ($23,000) see Ireland Foundation

Laurel School ($6,000) see Laub Foundation

Laurel School ($9,000) see Murch Foundation

Laurel School ($10,900) see Tippit Charitable Trust, C. Carlisle and Margaret M.

Law Enforcement Foundation ($10,000) see Andrews Foundation

Law Enforcement Foundation ($10,000) see Bicknell Fund

Law Enforcement Foundation ($2,500) see Lancaster Colony

Lawrence County Education Foundation ($25,000) see Tomkins Industries, Inc.

Leadership Lorain County ($20,000) see Nordson Corp.

Leadership Lorain County ($6,500) see Ross Corp.

LEADS ($5,000) see Evans Foundation, Thomas J.

Learning Directory Grant — publication of 1990 Learning directory ($500) see Ross Corp.

Lee Street Presbyterian Church ($6,000) see True Trust, Henry A.

Legacy of Catholic Learning ($50,000) see Columbus Dispatch Printing Co.

Legal Aid Society ($5,000) see Peterloon Foundation

Legal Aid Society ($10,000) see Stocker Foundation

Lehman High Development Fund ($15,000) see Monarch Machine Tool Co.

Leipsic United Methodist Church ($21,500) see Edwards Foundation, O. P. and W. E.

Leo Yassenoff Jewish Center ($250) see Kobacker Co.

Leonard Morse Hospital ($15,000) see Anderson Foundation, William P.

Library Association of Sandusky — to upgrade its computer equipment ($18,232) see Frohman Foundation, Sidney

Licking Memorial Hospital ($2,500) see Park National Bank

Lifecare Alliance ($155,000) see Nationwide Insurance Cos.

Lima Rescue Home ($1,500) see Flickinger Memorial Trust

Lincoln Park Amphitheater ($5,000) see Danis Industries

Linden School — education program ($73,772) see Nord Family Foundation

Literacy Initiative of Central Ohio/Challenge 2000 ($20,000) see Columbus Dispatch Printing Co.

Lithapolis Cemetery — operating funds ($3,000) see Wagnalls Memorial

Lithapolis Community Projects — general support ($12,956) see Wagnalls Memorial

Little Sisters of Poor ($10,000) see McMahon Charitable Trust Fund, Father John J.

Living Arrangements for the Developmentally Disabled (L.A.D.D.) ($7,500) see Russell Charitable Trust, Josephine S.

Llanfair Terrace ($33,960) see Cincinnati Foundation for the Aged

Local Initiatives Support Corporation ($10,000) see Blade Communications

Londonville Agricultural Society ($3,500) see Young Foundation, Hugo H. and Mabel B.

Londonville Swim Team Boosters ($3,702) see Young Foundation, Hugo H. and Mabel B.

Lonnie Henthorn Memorial Fund ($2,000) see Ormet Corp.

Look Up to Cleveland ($1,000) see Ohio Savings Bank

Lorain County Animal Protective League ($15,792) see Miller Charitable Trust, Lewis N.

Lorain County Community College ($150,000) see Nord Family Foundation

Lorain County Community College — public service internship program ($97,015) see Nord Family Foundation

Lorain County Community College ($50,000) see Nordson Corp.

Lorain County Community College ($20,000) see Stocker Foundation

Lorain County Community College Women's Link ($5,000) see Rice Foundation, Helen Steiner

Lorain County Community College Womens Link — support ($3,000) see Ross Corp.

Lorain County FREE NET ($30,000) see Nordson Corp.

Lorain County Habitat for Humanity ($25,000) see Nordson Corp.

Lorain County Historical Society ($15,791) see Miller Charitable Trust, Lewis N.

Lord of Life Lutheran Church ($2,500) see Frohring Foundation, William O. and Gertrude Lewis

Loudonville Fire Department ($22,157) see Young Foundation, Hugo H. and Mabel B.

Loudonville-Perrysville Scholarship Fund ($4,000) see Young Foundation, Hugo H. and Mabel B.

Loudonville-Perrysville School ($35,185) see Young Foundation, Hugo H. and Mabel B.

Lourdes College ($10,000) see McMaster Foundation, Harold and Helen

Lower Price Hill Community School ($10,000) see Rice Foundation, Helen Steiner

Lower Price Hill Schools ($2,840) see Peterloon Foundation

Lutheran Employment Awareness Program ($24,000) see 1525 Foundation

Lutheran High School Association ($60,000) see M.T.D. Products

Lutheran Medical Center ($20,000) see M.T.D. Products

Lutheran Medical Center Foundation — for renovation to create new pre-admission testing area payable over two years ($50,000) see Bruening Foundation, Eva L. and Joseph M.

Lutheran Metro Minority Association ($10,000) see Fox Charitable Foundation, Harry K. & Emma R.

Luventure Place see General Tire Inc.

Mad River Valley Ambulance Service ($10,000) see Ranney Foundation, P. K.

Mahoning Lodge 339 B'nai B'rith ($11,000) see Schermer Charitable Trust, Frances

Mahoning Valley Economic Development Council ($10,000) see Pollock Company Foundation, William B.

Mahoning Valley Historical Society — Phase II of renovation ($10,000) see Beecher Foundation, Florence Simon

Majestic Theater ($25,000) see Massie Trust, David Meade

Make-A-Wish Foundation ($4,000) see Cayuga Foundation

Make-A-Wish Foundation ($2,400) see LDI Charitable Foundation

Malachi House ($2,500) see LDI Charitable Foundation

Malone College ($350) see Belden Brick Co., Inc.

Malone College — operating funds ($107,500) see Hoover Foundation

Malone College ($16,000) see Timken Co.

Mansfield Christian Education Center ($1,040,986) see Larsh Foundation Charitable Trust

Mansfield Symphony Society ($50,000) see Rupp Foundation, Fran and Warren

Mansfield Symphony Society ($1,000) see Sterkel Trust, Justine

Maranatha Baptist Church ($4,500) see Oldham Little Church Foundation

March of Dimes ($5,000) see Copperweld Steel Co.

March of Dimes see Seaway Food Town

Marietta College ($15,000) see Benua Foundation

Marietta College ($10,000) see Fenton Foundation

Marietta College ($4,125) see Gould Inc.

Marietta College — Minority Student Program ($20,000) see McDonough Foundation, Bernard

Marietta Memorial Hospital ($20,000) see Fenton Foundation

Marion Junior Service Guild ($5,000) see True Trust, Henry A.

Marotta Montessori Schools of Cleveland ($10,000) see Gerson Family Foundation, Benjamin J.

Marotta Montessori Schools of Cleveland ($3,000) see Hershey Foundation

Marotta Montessori Schools of Cleveland ($3,000) see Mather Charitable Trust, S. Livingston

Martha K. Lottman Philanthropy Fund ($50,000) see Klein Fund, Nathan J.

Mary Scott Nursing Center — general support ($15,000) see Kettering Fund

Masonic Toledo Trust ($10,000) see Andersons Management Corp.

McCord Junior High School-Odyssey of the Mind — K-12 grant; travel expenses for junior high school girls who were competing in a creative thinking competition in the World finals in Knoxville, Tennessee ($1,000) see Owens-Corning Fiberglas Corp.

McLean Hospital ($10,000) see Mandel Foundation, Morton and Barbara

Medical Center Hospital Volunteer Advisory Council ($9,755) see Massie Trust, David Meade

Medical College of Ohio Foundation ($121,000) see Stone Foundation, France

Medical College of Ohio Foundation ($400,000) see Stranahan Foundation

Medical College of Ohio at Toledo ($15,000) see Frohman Foundation, Sidney

Mennonite Central Committee ($5,000) see Schowalter Foundation

Mercy Hospital of Tiffin ($10,000) see National Machinery Co.

Meridia Euclid Hospital — capital/development fund ($20,000) see Lincoln Electric Co.

Methodist Theological School in Ohio ($30,000) see Beeghly Fund, Leon A.

Methodist Theological School in Ohio ($5,000) see Magee Christian Education Foundation

Metro Health Foundation ($500) see Ohio Savings Bank

Metro Health Foundation ($10,000) see Second Foundation

Metrohealth Clement Center ($205,000) see Gund Foundation, George

Miami of Piqua Ohio ($6,000) see Hartzell Industries, Inc.

Miami Purchase Association for Hamilton ($10,000) see Anderson Foundation, William P.

Miami University ($25,000) see NCR Corp.

Miami University ($3,500) see New Orphan Asylum Scholarship Foundation

Miami University ($25,000) see Smucker Co., J.M.

Miami University ($78,370) see Star Bank, N.A.

Miami University — Prodesse Society ($20,000) see Gross Charitable Trust, Walter L. and Nell R.

Miami Valley Health Foundation ($5,000) see Amcast Industrial Corp.

Miami Valley Regional Planning Commission — ISUS Project ($12,500) see Iddings Benevolent Trust

Miami Valley School ($20,000) see Beerman Foundation

Miami Valley School ($25,000) see Mead Fund, Nelson

Miami Valley School ($2,100) see Mead Fund, Nelson

Michigan Area Growth Foundation ($30,000) see Young Foundation, Hugo H. and Mabel B.

Midview Local School District — challenge grant ($11,400) see Ross Corp.

Mildred Bayer Health Clinic for Homeless ($5,000) see Baumker Charitable Foundation, Elsie and Harry

Mill Creek Child Development Center ($10,000) see Finnegan Foundation, John D.

Mill Creek Park ($5,000) see Pollock Company Foundation, William B.

Millcreek Child Development Center ($10,000) see Kilcawley Fund, William H.

Millcreek Childcare Center ($2,000) see Debartolo Foundation, Marie P.

Minster Cub Scouts ($750) see Minster Machine Co.

Minster High School Scholarship Fund ($1,000) see Minster Machine Co.

Mobile Meals ($10,070) see Freygang Foundation, Walter Henry

Mobile Meals ($10,000) see McAlonan Trust, John A.

Mobile Meals on Marion County ($5,000) see True Trust, Henry A.

Mobile Meals of Toledo ($16,000) see Dana Corp.

Monday Musical Club ($10,000) see Kilcawley Fund, William H.

Monday Musical Club — 1990 programs ($5,000) see Watson Foundation, Walter E. and Caroline H.

Monroe Adult Craft Organization ($4,000) see Ormet Corp.

Montefiore Home ($10,000) see Fox Charitable Foundation, Harry K. & Emma R.

Montefiore Home ($5,000) see Gries Charity Fund, Lucile and Robert H.

Montefiore Home ($12,000) see Kangesser Foundation, Robert E., Harry A., and M. Sylvia

Montefiore Home ($50,000) see Rosenthal Foundation, Samuel

Montefiore Home ($33,333) see Treuhaft Foundation

Montessori Development Partnerships ($25,000) see Hershey Foundation

Montgomery County Community Action Agency ($15,000) see Iddings Benevolent Trust

Montifiore Home ($83,333) see Premier Industrial Corp.

Mt. Auburn Health Center — operating fund ($5,000) see Ohio National Life Insurance Co.

Mount Sinai Medical Center ($19,000) see LTV Corp.

Mt. Union College ($40,000) see Beeghly Fund, Leon A.

Ohio (cont.)

Mount Union College ($6,000) see Jasam Foundation

Mount Union College ($50,000) see Powers Higher Educational Fund, Edward W. and Alice R.

Mount Vernon YMCA — renovation of facility ($15,000) see JELD-WEN, Inc.

Museum Center ($20,000) see Rice Foundation, Helen Steiner

Museum Center at Cincinnati Union Terminal ($30,000) see Semple Foundation, Louise Taft

Museum Center at Cincinnati Union Terminal ($20,000) see Star Bank, N.A.

Museum Center Foundation ($15,000) see Dater Foundation, Charles H.

Museum Center Foundation — capital campaign ($40,000) see Fifth Third Bancorp

Museum Center Foundation ($12,500) see Smith, Jr. Charitable Trust, Jack J.

Museum Center at Union Terminal ($100,010) see American Financial Corp.

Museum Center at Union Terminal ($100,000) see American Financial Corp.

Museum of Natural History ($25,000) see Sears Family Foundation

Music Hall Association ($10,000) see Ohio Valley Foundation

Music School Settlement ($25,000) see Gries Charity Fund, Lucile and Robert H.

Music School Settlement ($5,000) see Sears Family Foundation

Musical Art Association ($15,000) see Forest City Enterprises

Musical Arts Association ($6,000) see Calhoun Charitable Trust, Kenneth

Musical Arts Association ($41,935) see Centerior Energy Corp.

Musical Arts Association ($10,000) see Codrington Charitable Foundation, George W.

Musical Arts Association ($5,000) see Gund Foundation, Geoffrey

Musical Arts Association ($100,000) see Kulas Foundation

Musical Arts Association ($12,000) see Mather and William Gwinn Mather Fund, Elizabeth Ring

Musical Arts Association ($20,000) see Mellen Foundation

Musical Arts Association ($1,400) see Mill-Rose Co.

Musical Arts Association ($85,000) see Murphy Foundation, John P.

Musical Arts Association ($3,000) see Oglebay Norton Co.

Musical Arts Association ($83,000) see Ohio Bell Telephone Co.

Musical Arts Association ($75,000) see Reinberger Foundation

Musical Arts Association ($12,000) see Sherwin-Williams Co.

Musical Arts Association ($10,000) see Smith Charitable Fund, Eleanor Armstrong

Musical Arts Association — artistic initiative ($150,000) see Smith Foundation, Kelvin and Eleanor

Musical Arts Association ($100,000) see Smith Foundation, Kelvin and Eleanor

Musical Arts Association ($35,000) see Standard Products Co.

Musical Arts Association — Blossom Music Center ($6,000) see Morgan Foundation, Burton D.

Musical Arts Association — Cleveland orchestra ($51,600) see Eaton Corp.

Musical Arts Association - Cleveland Orchestra — student educational concerts ($30,000) see Jennings Foundation, Martha Holden

Musical Arts Association — Cleveland Orchestra; student educational concerts ($30,000) see Jennings Foundation, Martha Holden

Musical Arts Association — to provide general support for the Cleveland Orchestra and payment on $400,000 deficit reduction pledge ($117,500) see TRW Corp.

Musical Arts Association — support of Cleveland Orchestra 75th Anniversary Campaign ($335,000) see BP America

Musical Arts Association — 1991-92 support for Youth Orchestra ($60,000) see Jennings Foundation, Martha Holden

Musical Arts Association — 75th anniversary ($30,000) see Ingalls Foundation, Louise H. and David S.

Musical Arts Association — Youth Orchestra support 1990-91 ($30,000) see Jennings Foundation, Martha Holden

Muskigum College ($35,000) see Mack Foundation, J. S.

Muskingum College — renovation ($5,000) see Montgomery Foundation

National Aviation Hall of Fame ($100,000) see NCR Corp.

National Child Safety Council ($1,000) see Minster Machine Co.

National Coalition Against Pornography — operating fund ($60,000) see Dow Foundation, Herbert H. and Barbara C.

National Coallition Against Pornography ($417,802) see DeMoss Foundation, Arthur S.

National Conference of Christians and Jews ($1,450) see Gradison & Co.

National Conference of Christians and Jews ($2,000) see Mandel Foundation, Jack N. and Lilyan

National Conference of Christians and Jews ($300) see XTEK Inc.

National Council of Jewish Women ($14,000) see Mandel Foundation, Morton and Barbara

National Family Service see Seaway Food Town

National Invention Center ($30,000) see BFGoodrich

National Invention Center ($30,000) see BFGoodrich

National Invention Center ($20,000) see McFawn Trust No. 2, Lois Sisler

National Invention Center ($10,000) see Ritchie Memorial Foundation, Charles E. and Mabel M.

National Merit Scholarship Program ($28,910) see Parker-Hannifin Corp.

National Society to Prevent Blindness — Ohio Affiliate - general support ($14,000) see Kettering Fund

Nature Conservancy ($25,000) see Benua Foundation

Nature Conservancy ($1,500) see Davey Tree Expert Co.

Nature Conservancy ($5,350) see Mead Fund, Nelson

Nature Conservancy ($20,000) see Rupp Foundation, Fran and Warren

Nature Conservancy ($8,333) see Sears Family Foundation

Nature Conservancy ($5,000) see South Waite Foundation

Nature Conservancy ($5,000) see South Waite Foundation

Nautical Arts Association/Cleveland Orchestra ($7,500) see Hankins Foundation

Neighborhood House Association of Lorain ($5,000) see Rice Foundation, Helen Steiner

Neighborhood Improvement Foundation of Toledo ($45,500) see Dana Corp.

Neighborhood Ministries ($20,000) see Crandall Memorial Foundation, J. Ford

Neighborhood Progress ($500,000) see BP America

Neighborhood Progress ($1,200,000) see Gund Foundation, George

Neighborhood Progress ($125,000) see Premier Industrial Corp.

Nelsonville Athletic Department ($5,000) see Baird Brothers Co.

Nelsonville-York School ($982) see Baird Brothers Co.

New Cleveland Campaign ($3,750) see McDonald & Co. Securities

New Cleveland Opera ($48,987) see Kulas Foundation

New Directions ($5,000) see Hankins Foundation

New Futures Fund ($10,000) see Kramer Foundation, Louise

New Life Youth Services — for transitional loan ($10,000) see Alms Trust, Eleanora

New Philadelphia Fire Department ($26,857) see Reeves Foundation

New Philadelphia Quaker Club ($18,462) see Reeves Foundation

New School ($14,000) see Anderson Foundation, William P.

Newark Catholic Foundation ($5,000) see Park National Bank

Newark City Schools — Newark High School entrance ($92,676) see Evans Foundation, Thomas J.

Newman Baptist Church ($8,975) see Miller Memorial Trust, George Lee

Newman Center ($3,000) see Pollock Company Foundation, William B.

NIFTI ($10,000) see Miniger Memorial Foundation, Clement O.

9 to 5, Working Women Education Fund — to help increase grassroots activism of working women on issues such as pregnancy and maternity benefits, sexual harassment, and family and medical leave ($30,000) see Rockefeller Family Fund

Noren Circle Trinity Baptist Church ($3,000) see True Trust, Henry A.

North Canton Medical Center — new facility ($250,000) see Timken Foundation of Canton

North Canton Medical Foundation ($108,484) see Reeves Foundation

North Canton Memorial Fund — stadium project ($150,000) see Hoover Foundation

North Canton Public Library Association — purchase new computer hardware/software ($134,202) see Hoover Foundation

North Coast Harbor ($260,000) see Gund Foundation, George

North Toledo Community House ($14,000) see Dana Corp.

Northcoast Harbor ($1,000) see Ohio Savings Bank

Northcoast Harvest ($10,000) see Fox Charitable Foundation, Harry K. & Emma R.

Northern Ohio Fine Arts ($60,000) see American Foundation Corporation

Northwest/Canal Fulton Baseball Association ($3,000) see Flowers Charitable Trust, Albert W. and Edith V.

Northwest Jackson Soccer League ($3,000) see Flowers Charitable Trust, Albert W. and Edith V.

Northwestern Ohio Community Action ($1,000) see Flickinger Memorial Trust

Norwalk City School District ($50,000) see Ernsthausen Charitable Foundation, John F. and Doris E.

Notre Dame Cathedral Latin School ($25,000) see Saint Gerard Foundation

Notre Dame College — student scholarships ($41,800) see Huntington Fund for Education, John

Notre Dame College Ohio ($1,000) see Acme-Cleveland Corp.

Notre Dame College of Ohio ($2,500) see Hauserman, Inc.

Notre Dame Elementary School ($2,000) see OsCo. Industries

Oberlin College ($128,000) see BP America

Oberlin College — to endow the purchase of scientific equipment for teaching and research ($150,000) see GAR Foundation

Oberline College ($20,000) see Knudsen Charitable Foundation, Earl

Oblate Sisters SHJ ($2,000) see Tamarkin Co.

Obleness Hospital ($25,000) see O'Bleness Foundation, Charles G.

Oceanic Institute ($10,000) see Ranney Foundation, P. K.

Ofeg ($20,000) see Sapirstein-Stone-Weiss Foundation

Ohio Academy of Science, Columbus, OH see Battelle

Ohio Ballet ($3,300) see Mirapaul Foundation

Ohio Ballet — operating support ($1,000) see Morgan Foundation, Burton D.

Ohio Boys Town ($25,000) see Nordson Corp.

Ohio Business Week Foundation ($2,000) see Park National Bank

Ohio Cancer Foundation ($100,500) see Borden

Ohio Center for the Arts ($100,000) see Star Bank, N.A.

Ohio Chamber Orchestra ($4,000) see Eaton Foundation, Cyrus

Ohio Council on Economic Development ($500) see French Oil Mill Machinery Co.

Ohio Department of Education/Division of Inservice Education ($150,000) see Ohio Bell Telephone Co.

Ohio Department of Natural Resources — Old Woman Creek ($15,000) see Benua Foundation

Ohio Dominican College ($4,000) see Park National Bank

Ohio Foundation of Independent Colleges ($3,000) see Acme-Cleveland Corp.

Ohio Foundation of Independent Colleges ($1,000) see Amcast Industrial Corp.

Ohio Foundation of Independent Colleges ($3,500) see American Aggregates Corp.

Ohio Foundation of Independent Colleges ($2,000) see American Welding & Manufacturing Co.

Ohio Foundation of Independent Colleges ($10,000) see Andersons Management Corp.

Ohio Foundation of Independent Colleges ($7,500) see Avon Products

Ohio Foundation of Independent Colleges ($250) see Barry Corp., R. G.

Ohio Foundation of Independent Colleges ($1,850) see Belden Brick Co., Inc.

Ohio Foundation of Independent Colleges ($7,500) see Central Soya Co.

Ohio Foundation of Independent Colleges ($9,000) see Commercial Intertech Corp.

Ohio Foundation of Independent Colleges ($2,000) see Davey Tree Expert Co.

Ohio Foundation of Independent Colleges ($9,000) see Ernsthausen Charitable Foundation, John F. and Doris E.

Ohio Foundation of Independent Colleges ($8,000) see Ferro Corp.

Ohio Foundation of Independent Colleges ($500) see French Oil Mill Machinery Co.

Ohio Foundation of Independent Colleges ($12,500) see Hankins Foundation

Ohio Foundation of Independent Colleges ($1,850) see Hauserman, Inc.

Ohio Foundation of Independent Colleges ($36,000) see Honda of America Manufacturing, Inc.

Ohio Foundation of Independent Colleges ($1,500) see Kuhns Investment Co.

Ohio Foundation of Independent Colleges ($70,000) see Lincoln Electric Co.

Ohio Foundation of Independent Colleges ($6,000) see McDonald & Co. Securities

Ohio Foundation of Independent Colleges ($3,500) see Midmark Corp.

Ohio Foundation of Independent Colleges ($12,000) see Miniger Memorial Foundation, Clement O.

Ohio Foundation of Independent Colleges ($1,500) see Minster Machine Co.

Ohio Foundation of Independent Colleges ($50,000) see Moores Foundation, Harry C.

Ohio Foundation of Independent Colleges ($3,000) see Oglebay Norton Co.

Ohio Foundation of Independent Colleges ($125,000) see Ohio Bell Telephone Co.

Ohio Foundation of Independent Colleges ($3,000) see Pollock Company Foundation, William B.

Ohio Foundation of Independent Colleges ($10,000) see Reeves Foundation

Ohio Foundation of Independent Colleges ($6,000) see Robbins & Myers, Inc.

Ohio Foundation of Independent Colleges ($41,500) see Rubbermaid

Ohio Foundation of Independent Colleges ($2,500) see Sifco Industries Inc.

Ohio Foundation Independent Colleges ($40,000) see Timken Co.

Ohio Foundation of Independent Colleges — challenge funds ($500,000) see Timken Foundation of Canton

Ohio Foundation of Independent Colleges ($8,000) see Tremco Inc.

Ohio Foundation of Independent Colleges ($15,000) see TRINOVA Corp.

Ohio 4-H Foundation — general support ($50,000) see Kettering Fund

Ohio Northern University — equipment purchase ($20,000) see Community Hospital Foundation

Ohio State ($20,000) see Nestle U.S.A. Inc.

Ohio State Bar Association ($10,186) see Ritter Charitable Trust, George W. & Mary F.

Ohio State Development Fund ($40,000) see Edwards Industries

Ohio State Fair Fine Arts Exhibition ($100) see Kobacker Co.

Ohio State University ($30,000) see Abramson Family Foundation

Ohio State University ($55,000) see Barnett Charitable Foundation, Lawrence and Isabel

Ohio State University ($25,000) see Barnett Charitable Foundation, Lawrence and Isabel

Ohio State University ($6,000) see Barnett Charitable Foundation, Lawrence and Isabel

Ohio State University ($15,000) see Benua Foundation

Ohio State University ($4,000) see Continental Grain Co.

Ohio State University ($5,000) see Duriron Co., Inc.

Ohio State University ($2,500) see Flickinger Memorial Trust

Ohio State University ($315,000) see Ford Motor Co.

Ohio State University ($75,000) see Frasch Foundation for Chemical Research (under the will of Elizabeth B. Frasch), Herman

Ohio State University ($17,245) see Gerlach Foundation

Ohio State University ($67,720) see Gleason Memorial Fund

Ohio State University — donation of computer equipment ($537,000) see IBM Corp.

Ohio State University ($3,330) see New Orphan Asylum Scholarship Foundation

Ohio State University ($6,000) see Park National Bank

Ohio State University ($150,000) see Randolph Foundation

Ohio State University ($25,000) see Schiff Foundation, John J. and Mary R.

Ohio State University — agriculture ($10,000) see Smucker Co., J.M.

Ohio State University ($50,000) see Wildermuth Foundation, E. F.

Ohio State University College of Arts ($10,000) see Yassenoff Foundation, Leo

Ohio State University — Department of Food Science and Technology ($38,000) see Abbott Laboratories

Ohio State University — donated equipment for the Department of Opthamology ($57,900) see Storz Instrument Co.

Ohio State University Department of Orthopedic Surgery ($12,500) see Benua Foundation

Ohio State University Development Fund ($107,100) see El-An Foundation

Ohio State University Development Fund ($12,000) see Electric Power Equipment Co.

Ohio State University Development Fund ($50,000) see National City Corp.

Ohio State University Development Fund ($30,000) see Shafer Foundation, Richard H. and Ann

Ohio State University Development Fund ($140,000) see Yassenoff Foundation, Leo

Ohio State University Development Fund-College of Agriculture ($115,000) see Nationwide Insurance Cos.

Ohio State University — Epidermal Growth Factor and Insulin Receptor Expression in Placentae from Pregnancies Complicated by Maternal Diabetes Mellitus ($20,000) see Diabetes Research and Education Foundation

Ohio State University — for the study of type I and type II interleukin 1 (IL-1) receptors; for the study of topographic vaccine against HTLV-I infection; for the study of dietary fat as a promotor of mammary tumorigenesis in MMTV/v-Ha-ras transgenic mice ($167,083) see Pardee Foundation, Elsa U.

Ohio State University Law School ($10,000) see Benua Foundation

Ohio State University — Leo Yassenoff Chair ($30,000) see Yassenoff Foundation, Leo

Ohio University see Banner Life Insurance Co.

Ohio University ($33,330) see New Orphan Asylum Scholarship Foundation

Ohio University ($35,714) see O'Bleness Foundation, Charles G.

Ohio University ($80,000) see Ohio Bell Telephone Co.

Ohio University ($34,219) see Schey Foundation

Ohio University College of Engineering and Technology ($25,000) see AMETEK

Ohio State University-College of Engineering and Technology ($100,000) see Cooper Industries

Ohio University Foundation see Cincom Systems, Inc.

Ohio University Foundation see Kolene Corp.

Ohio University Foundation see Messenger Publishing Co.

Ohio University Foundation — Midwest Newspaper Workshop for Minorities ($10,000) see Scripps Co., E.W.

Ohio University Fund ($2,000) see Electric Power Equipment Co.

Ohio University Fund — ninth year of ten-year pledge/E.W. Scripps endowment program ($75,000) see Scripps Co., E.W.

Ohio Wesleyan see Brakeley, John Price Jones Inc.

Ohio Wesleyan University ($30,000) see Beeghly Fund, Leon A.

Ohio Wesleyan University ($25,000) see Deuble Foundation, George H.

Ohio Wesleyan University ($400,000) see Smith Foundation, Gordon V. and Helen C.

Ohio Wesleyan University ($12,328) see Smith Foundation, Gordon V. and Helen C.

Old Trail School ($7,500) see Calhoun Charitable Trust, Kenneth

1990/1991 Jennings Scholar Lecture Program ($46,167) see Jennings Foundation, Martha Holden

1990/1991 Jennings Scholar Lecture Program ($42,400) see Jennings Foundation, Martha Holden

1992 Corporation ($31,000) see Columbus Dispatch Printing Co.

Opera Columbus ($2,000) see Barry Corp., R. G.

Opera Columbus ($2,500) see Gerlach Foundation

Opera Columbus ($2,000) see Jasam Foundation

Operation Exodus ($200,000) see El-An Foundation

Operation Exodus — charter plane for Russian Jewish immigrants ($100,000) see Mayerson Foundation, Manuel D. and Rhoda

Options, Inc. — K-12 grant to a youth counseling and drug prevention agency for early identification and counseling of at risk children in Metro

Toledo public schools ($10,000) see Owens-Corning Fiberglas Corp.

Options for "Starting Early" program, Toledo, OH ($97,973) see Dana Corp.

Orrville Boys and Girls ($5,500) see Smucker Co., J.M.

Otterbein College ($300,000) see Nationwide Insurance Cos.

Otterbein College ($10,000) see Shafer Foundation, Richard H. and Ann

Otterbein College ($90,000) see Teagle Foundation

Our Lady of Elms School ($10,000) see McAlonan Trust, John A.

Our Lady of Elms — 65th Anniversary Fund ($11,000) see O'Neil Foundation, M. G.

Our Lady of Mt. Carmel Church ($11,000) see Debartolo Foundation, Marie P.

Our Lady of Perpetual Help Church — toward asbestos removal, furnace and air conditioning repairs ($50,000) see H.C.S. Foundation

Palace Cultural Arts Association ($10,000) see True Trust, Henry A.

Palace Theatre ($30,000) see Flowers Charitable Trust, Albert W. and Edith V.

Parents of Murdered Children ($7,500) see Berry Foundation, Loren M.

Park Vista Foundation — annual life care fund ($3,500) see Watson Foundation, Walter E. and Caroline H.

Park Vista Presbyterian Home — life care fund ($6,000) see Beecher Foundation, Florence Simon

Park Vista Presbyterian Home ($12,000) see Finnegan Foundation, John D.

Parkview Place ($50,000) see Sandusky International Inc.

Parmadale Children's Home ($5,000) see LDI Charitable Foundation

Peaslee Neighborhood Center — for Clark Academy day care ($10,000) see Jergens Foundation, Andrew

Perry Panther Cubs Midget Football ($2,000) see Flowers Charitable Trust, Albert W. and Edith V.

Phillips-Osborne School ($5,000) see Hershey Foundation

Phillips Osborne School ($50,000) see Humphrey Fund, George M. and Pamela S.

Pilot Dogs ($2,250) see Shafer Foundation, Richard H. and Ann

Pioneer Historical Society ($5,000) see Taylor Trust, Lydia M.

Piqua Area United Fund ($2,470) see French Oil Mill Machinery Co.

Planned Parenthood ($1,000) see Frohring Foundation, Paul & Maxine

Planned Parenthood ($2,000) see Lippitt Foundation, Katherine Kenyon

Planned Parenthood ($5,500) see Morse, Jr. Foundation, Enid and Lester S.

Planned Parenthood ($24,000) see Treuhaft Foundation

Planned Parenthood of Akron ($5,000) see Mirapaul Foundation

Planned Parenthood of Cleveland ($8,251) see Tippit Charitable Trust, C. Carlisle and Margaret M.

Planned Parenthood Federation of America ($7,500) see Anderson Foundation, William P.

Planned Parenthood Federation of America ($4,000) see Baumker Charitable Foundation, Elsie and Harry

Planned Parenthood Federation of America ($5,000) see Beecher Foundation, Florence Simon

Planned Parenthood Federation of America ($5,000) see Berry Foundation, Loren M.

Planned Parenthood Federation of America ($25,000) see Deuble Foundation, George H.

Planned Parenthood Federation of America ($2,000) see Edwards Industries

Planned Parenthood Federation of America ($12,000) see Hayfields Foundation

Planned Parenthood Federation of America ($20,000) see Iddings Benevolent Trust

Planned Parenthood Federation of America ($2,000) see Klein Fund, Nathan J.

Planned Parenthood Federation of America ($5,000) see Mather Charitable Trust, S. Livingston

Planned Parenthood Federation of America ($20,000) see Orleton Trust Fund

Planned Parenthood Federation of America ($10,000) see Pollock Company Foundation, William B.

Planned Parenthood Federation of America ($10,000) see Rupp Foundation, Fran and Warren

Planned Parenthood Federation of America ($3,000) see Sears Family Foundation

Planned Parenthood Federation of America ($3,000) see Sears Family Foundation

Planned Parenthood of Miami Valley — continued support ($30,000) see Kettering Fund

Players Theatre of Columbus ($1,500) see Kobacker Co.

Playhouse Square ($500) see Schey Foundation

Playhouse Square Center ($10,000) see Codrington Charitable Foundation, George W.

Playhouse Square Center ($2,000) see Lamson & Sessions Co.

Playhouse Square Foundation ($15,000) see Acme-Cleveland Corp.

Playhouse Square Foundation ($5,000) see Hankins Foundation

Playhouse Square Foundation ($25,000) see Kulas Foundation

Playhouse Square Foundation ($10,000) see Lincoln Electric Co.

Playhouse Square Foundation ($10,000) see Scott and Fetzer Co.

Playhouse Square Foundation ($10,000) see Scott and Fetzer Co.

Plymouth Church Foundation ($40,000) see Dively Foundation, George S.

Poinciana Chapel ($5,000) see Bardes Corp.

Ohio (cont.)

Police Athletic League ($5,000) see Eyman Trust, Jesse

Police Athletic League ($500) see Osborn Manufacturing Co.

Portage Area Senior Services ($1,500) see Davey Tree Expert Co.

Practical Family Living — for additional office space ($10,000) see Alms Trust, Eleanora

Presbyterian Hospital ($25,000) see Mandel Foundation, Morton and Barbara

Presiding Bishops Fund ($15,000) see Mead Fund, Nelson

Project Learn ($2,000) see Frohring Foundation, Paul & Maxine

Project Learn ($500) see Osborn Manufacturing Co.

Promusica ($1,250) see Lancaster Colony

Prospect House ($5,000) see Gross Charitable Trust, Walter L. and Nell R.

Providence House ($30,100) see Saint Gerard Foundation

Psychiatric Professional Services ($2,400) see Jarson-Stanley and Mickey Kaplan Foundation, Isaac & Esther

Public Broadcasting Foundation of Northwest Ohio ($4,200) see Blade Communications

Public Broadcasting Foundation of Northwest Ohio ($165,000) see Stranahan Foundation

Public Broadcasting WPTD Channel 16 ($3,000) see Kuhns Investment Co.

Public Library of Cincinnati ($20,000) see Dater Foundation, Charles H.

Pump House — improvements/ceiling ($25,000) see Massie Trust, David Meade

Quest International ($120,000) see Moore Foundation

Rabbinical College of Telshe ($2,500) see Kangesser Foundation, Robert E., Harry A., and M. Sylvia

Radio Reading Services ($10,000) see Ohio Valley Foundation

Rainbow Babies and Children's Hospital ($20,000) see Humphrey Fund, George M. and Pamela S.

Rainbow Kids Cards ($7,248) see Tippit Charitable Trust, C. Carlisle and Margaret M.

Raintree Pediatric Development Center ($22,380) see Sterkel Trust, Justine

Read for Literacy ($15,000) see Blade Communications

Recreation Unlimited ($1,000) see Lancaster Colony

Recreation Unlimited ($1,500) see Shafer Foundation, Richard H. and Ann

Red Cross ($1,200) see Kuhns Investment Co.

Rehabilitation Services of North Central Ohio ($59,380) see Sterkel Trust, Justine

Renaissance Theatre ($2,100,000) see Rupp Foundation, Fran and Warren

Rescue Mission of Mahoning Valley ($18,240) see Crandall Memorial Foundation, J. Ford

Rescue Missions — capital campaign ($25,000) see

Watson Foundation, Walter E. and Caroline H.

Richland Carousel Park ($5,000) see Park National Bank

Richland Corousel Park ($100,000) see Lippitt Foundation, Katherine Kenyon

Richland Country Children Services ($2,000) see Sterkel Trust, Justine

Richland Pregnancy Services ($2,500) see Sterkel Trust, Justine

Rio Grande University (President's Home) ($6,000) see Robbins & Myers, Inc.

Ritter Library Board of Trustees ($25,465) see Ritter Charitable Trust, George W. & Mary F.

Ritz Theatre for the Performing Arts ($20,050) see National Machinery Co.

River View Local School District — day care center ($11,000) see Montgomery Foundation

Riverside Foundation for Riverside Hospital ($10,186) see Ritter Charitable Trust, George W. & Mary F.

Riverside Methodist Hospital ($50,000) see Moores Foundation, Harry C.

Riverside Methodist Hospital Foundation ($1,100) see Edwards Industries

Rock n' Roll Hall of Fame ($10,000) see Cleveland-Cliffs

Rock and Roll Hall of Fame ($5,000) see McDonald & Co. Securities

Rock and Roll Hall of Fame and Museum ($7,000) see Ferro Corp.

Ronald McDonald House ($3,500) see LDI Charitable Foundation

Ronald McDonald House ($1,440) see Mandel Foundation, Joseph and Florence

Ronald McDonald House ($6,000) see Mill-Rose Co.

Roscoe Village Foundation — restoration of historic area ($670,355) see Montgomery Foundation

Rosemont Center ($10,000) see English Foundation, Walter and Marian

Ross County Juvenile Court ($10,763) see Massie Trust, David Meade

Rutherford B. Hayes Presidential Center — to maintain the Charles C. Frohman Collection and to help pay operating expenses ($20,000) see Frohman Foundation, Sidney

St. Albert the Great Church ($6,000) see Leonardt Foundation

St. Alexis Hospital ($1,500) see Motch Corp.

St. Alexis Hospital Medical Center ($4,000) see Ebert Charitable Foundation, Horatio B.

St. Alexis Hospital Medical Center ($1,668) see Hauserman, Inc.

St. Anthonys Hospital ($10,000) see Shafer Foundation, Richard H. and Ann

St. Augustine Corporation Improvement Account — capital improvement ($500,000) see O'Neill Charitable Corporation, F. J.

St. Augustine Corporation — for the relocation of St. Augustine Nursing Care Manor to the

former St. John Hospital building payable over eight years ($800,000) see Bruening Foundation, Eva L. and Joseph M.

St. Augustine Manor ($25,000) see O'Neill Foundation, William J. and Dorothy K.

St. Charles Catholic Church ($12,000) see Debartolo Foundation, Marie P.

St. Charles Preparatory School Scholarship Fund ($10,000) see Benua Foundation

St. Dominic's Church ($7,000) see Debartolo Foundation, Marie P.

St. Edward High School — to update primary health care needs of medically indigent ($13,936) see H.C.S. Foundation

St. Edward High School — student endowment fund ($150,000) see O'Neill Charitable Corporation, F. J.

St. Edward Home ($10,000) see McAlonan Trust, John A.

St. Elizabeth Hospital Medical Center ($10,000) see Beecher Foundation, Florence Simon

St. Elizabeth Hospital Medical Center ($5,000) see Commercial Intertech Corp.

St. Elizabeth Hospital Medical Center ($50,000) see Finnegan Foundation, John D.

St. Francis Rehabilitation Hospital — to purchase new rehabilitation equipment ($20,000) see Frohman Foundation, Sidney

St. Francis Rehabilitation Hospital ($26,000) see Schlink Foundation, Albert G. and Olive H.

St. Francis Seraph School ($10,000) see Smith, Jr. Charitable Trust, Jack J.

St. Ignatius High School ($1,000) see Hauserman, Inc.

St. Ignatius High School ($5,000) see McMahon Charitable Trust Fund, Father John J.

St. Ignatius High School ($2,000) see Mill-Rose Co.

St. Joan of Arc/Parish, Toledo ($14,760) see Andersons Management Corp.

St. John's Episcopal Church ($5,200) see Robison Foundation, Ellis H. and Doris B.

Saint John's Social Center ($20,000) see Semple Foundation, Louise Taft

St. Joseph Home ($30,000) see Emery Memorial, Thomas J.

St. Joseph Home — for capital campaign ($15,000) see Jergens Foundation, Andrew

Saint Joseph Home ($20,000) see Semple Foundation, Louise Taft

St. Joseph Home ($10,000) see Smith, Jr. Charitable Trust, Jack J.

St. Joseph Infant and Maternity Home — toward capital campaign ($250,000) see H.C.S. Foundation

St. Joseph Infant and Maternity Home — capital campaign ($50,000) see Schmidlapp Trust No. 1, Jacob G.

St. Joseph Riverside Development Fund ($2,300) see American Welding & Manufacturing Co.

St. Joseph Riverside Hospital ($20,100) see Van Huffel Foundation, I. J.

St. Louisville Athletic Park ($5,000) see Evans Foundation, Thomas J.

St. Luke Hospital ($30,000) see Prentiss Foundation, Elisabeth Severance

St. Luke Hospital Association ($1,050,630) see Prentiss Foundation, Elisabeth Severance

St. Luke's Hospital Foundation ($5,000) see Stone Foundation, France

St. Marks Christian Fellowship Church of God — for construction of outreach center ($15,000) see Jergens Foundation, Andrew

St. Mary of the Hills ($1,800) see Baird Brothers Co.

St. Mary-Joseph Home ($10,000) see O'Neil Foundation, M. G.

St. Mary Middle School ($5,000) see Van Huffel Foundation, I. J.

St. Mary-of-the-Woods College ($50,000) see O'Neill Foundation, William J. and Dorothy K.

St. Mary of Wood College — support ($25,000) see Froderman Foundation

St. Mary's Central Catholic High School — computer fund ($5,000) see Sandusky International Inc.

St. Mary's Church ($14,400) see O'Neil Foundation, M. G.

St. Patrick School — window replacement ($4,000) see Beecher Foundation, Florence Simon

St. Patrick's Church ($16,000) see Crandall Memorial Foundation, J. Ford

St. Patricks Historic Church ($10,000) see Stone Foundation, France

St. Paul High School ($50,000) see Ernsthausen Charitable Foundation, John F. and Doris E.

St. Paul's Episcopal Church ($53,067) see Kling Trust, Louise

St. Paul's Episcopal Church ($10,000) see True Trust, Henry A.

St. Rita School for the Deaf ($15,000) see Rice Foundation, Helen Steiner

St. Theresa Home ($14,580) see Cincinnati Foundation for the Aged

St. Vincent Charity Hospital ($50,000) see Murphy Foundation, John P.

St. Vincent Charity Hospital ($10,000) see Schlink Foundation, Albert G. and Olive H.

St. Vincent Hotel ($15,000) see Kramer Foundation, Louise

St. Vincent de Paul Society ($18,000) see O'Neil Foundation, M. G.

St. Vincent-St. Mary High School ($10,200) see O'Neil Foundation, M. G.

St. Vincents Childrens Center ($2,000) see Kobacker Co.

St. Vincent's Hotel ($10,000) see Iddings Benevolent Trust

St. Xavier High School ($25,000) see Emery Memorial, Thomas J.

St. Xavier High School — capital campaign ($150,000)

see Schmidlapp Trust No. 1, Jacob G.

Salvation Army ($5,000) see Baumker Charitable Foundation, Elsie and Harry

Salvation Army ($7,000) see Bicknell Fund

Salvation Army ($5,000) see Bicknell Fund

Salvation Army ($11,000) see Britton Fund

Salvation Army — building fund ($7,000) see Copperweld Steel Co.

Salvation Army ($10,700) see Edwards Foundation, O. P. and W. E.

Salvation Army ($29,000) see Eyman Trust, Jesse

Salvation Army — capital campaign ($40,000) see Fifth Third Bancorp

Salvation Army ($1,000) see French Oil Mill Machinery Co.

Salvation Army ($5,000) see Hartzell Industries, Inc.

Salvation Army ($200) see Hayfields Foundation

Salvation Army ($10,000) see Kramer Foundation, Louise

Salvation Army ($12,500) see M.T.D. Products

Salvation Army ($1,000) see Martin Foundation, Bert William

Salvation Army ($12,720) see Massie Trust, David Meade

Salvation Army ($15,792) see Miller Charitable Trust, Lewis N.

Salvation Army ($10,000) see Monarch Machine Tool Co.

Salvation Army ($550) see Osborn Manufacturing Co.

Salvation Army ($15,000) see Ranney Foundation, P. K.

Salvation Army ($66,667) see Reinberger Foundation

Salvation Army ($8,334) see Smucker Co., J.M.

Sandusky Board of Education ($57,180) see Frohman Foundation, Sidney

Sandusky City School — Gazebo Public Address System ($10,338) see Sandusky International Inc.

Sandusky State Theatre — restoration fund ($9,000) see Sandusky International Inc.

School for Creative and Performing Arts ($500) see XTEK Inc.

School of Fine Arts ($11,000) see Murch Foundation

Sea Research Foundation ($133,333) see Smith Foundation, Kelvin and Eleanor

Sea Research Foundation ($180,000) see Smith 1980 Charitable Trust, Kelvin

Self-Help Center ($14,762) see Reeves Foundation

Service for the Aging ($19,536) see Ernsthausen Charitable Foundation, John F. and Doris E.

Seven Hills Neighborhood Houses ($10,000) see Cincinnati Milacron

Seven Hills Neighborhood Houses ($25,000) see Semple Foundation, Louise Taft

Seven Hills School ($15,000) see O'Brien Foundation, Cornelius and Anna Cook

Seven Hills School ($5,000) see Peterloon Foundation

Seven Hills School — capital campaign ($50,000) see

Schmidlapp Trust No. 1, Jacob G.

Seven Hills Schools ($12,500) see Bardes Corp.

Seven Hills Schools ($25,000) see Semple Foundation, Louise Taft

Seven Hills Schools ($20,000) see Tucker Foundation, Marcia Brady

Shaker Lakes Regional Nature Center ($2,500) see Lamson & Sessions Co.

Shaker Lakes Regional Nature Center ($7,000) see Sears Family Foundation

Shaker Schools Foundation ($5,000) see Tippit Charitable Trust, C. Carlisle and Margaret M.

Shelby County Scholarship ($6,000) see Monarch Machine Tool Co.

Shiloh Baptist Church — Par-excellence school ($25,000) see Evans Foundation, Thomas J.

Shoes for Kids ($300) see Osborn Manufacturing Co.

Shriners Hospital for Crippled Children ($20,134) see Ritter Charitable Trust, George W. & Mary F.

Sight Center ($13,000) see Humphrey Fund, George M. and Pamela S.

Sight Center ($13,000) see Miniger Memorial Foundation, Clement O.

Sight Center ($32,000) see Schlink Foundation, Albert G. and Olive H.

Sinclair Community College ($20,000) see Iddings Benevolent Trust

Sisters of Notre Dame de Mamur ($30,000) see Brencanda Foundation

Sisters of Notre Dame de Mamur ($15,000) see Ohio Valley Foundation

Sisters of St. Francis ($1,500) see Tripifoods

Social Philosophy and Policy Center Foundation — to appoint a Visiting Scholar ($17,500) see Earhart Foundation

Social Philosophy and Policy Foundation — general operating support ($250,000) see Scaife Foundation, Sarah

Society Fox Rehabilitation ($1,000) see Mill-Rose Co.

Southern Ohio Museum and Cultural Center ($1,500) see OsCo. Industries

Southwest Licking Local School District ($1,000) see Evans Foundation, Thomas J.

Southwest Ohio Easter Seals — for air conditioner ($10,000) see Alms Trust, Eleanora

Special Wish Foundation ($1,000) see Shafer Foundation, Richard H. and Ann

Spire Foundation ($500) see XTEK Inc.

Springer Educational Fund ($26,600) see Hayfields Foundation

Springer School ($8,300) see Dater Foundation, Charles H.

Springfield Foundation ($24,362) see Baker Charitable Foundation, Jessie Foos

Stan Hywet and Gardens ($10,000) see McAlonan Trust, John A.

Stark County District Library ($20,000) see Double Foundation, George H.

Stark County Foundation ($63,665) see Double Foundation, George H.

Stark County Foundation ($50,000) see Double Foundation, George H.

Stark County Foundation — education enhancement partnership ($580,000) see Timken Foundation of Canton

Stark County Historical Society ($8,974) see Miller Memorial Trust, George Lee

Stark County Historical Society ($8,086) see Miller Memorial Trust, George Lee

Stark County Treasurer (Courthouse) — funds for renovation ($213,935) see Hoover Foundation

Stark Development Board ($20,000) see Double Foundation, George H.

Stark Development Board ($5,000) see Flowers Charitable Trust, Albert W. and Edith V.

Stark Development Board — operating expenses ($500,000) see Timken Foundation of Canton

Stark Wilderness Center ($100) see Belden Brick Co., Inc.

Starr Commonwealth Schools ($10,700) see Edwards Foundation, O. P. and W. E.

State of Ohio/Department of Health ($390,000) see Aetna Life & Casualty Co.

Stengel-True Museum ($15,000) see True Trust, Henry A.

Stepping Stones ($1,500) see Hayfields Foundation

Suburban Temple — for draperies and chairs for the Gries Library ($5,675) see Gries Charity Fund, Lucile and Robert H.

Summit Country Day School ($30,000) see Emery Memorial, Thomas J.

Summit County Historical Society of Akron ($22,000) see Calhoun Charitable Trust, Kenneth

Suring Community Child Care Center ($35,000) see Huffy Corp.

Tabor House ($15,000) see Andrews Foundation

Taft Museum ($43,500) see Emery Memorial, Thomas J.

Taft Museum — Artist in Residence Program ($6,000) see Ohio National Life Insurance Co.

Tallmadge City Schools — for acquisition of computer hardware and software and related training costs for expansion of the Lighthouse Project ($600,000) see GAR Foundation

Tallmadge High School ($6,000) see Ritchie Memorial Foundation, Charles E. and Mabel M.

Taylor Road Synagogue ($28,000) see AVI CHAI - A Philanthropic Foundation

Teays Valley-Amanda Clearcreek School Districts ($77,500) see Hosler Memorial Educational Fund, Dr. R. S.

Temple Israel ($2,750) see Klein Fund, Nathan J.

Temple Israel ($100) see Kobacker Co.

Temple Israel ($1,500) see Tamarkin Co.

Temple Israel ($1,500) see Tamarkin Co.

Therapeutic Riding Center ($10,000) see O'Neill Foundation, William J. and Dorothy K.

Thurber House ($3,000) see Gerlach Foundation

Timken Mercy Medical Center ($6,750) see Miller Memorial Trust, George Lee

Timken Mercy Medical Center ($6,064) see Miller Memorial Trust, George Lee

Toledo Christian Schools ($10,000) see McMaster Foundation, Harold and Helen

Toledo Classic ($10,000) see Charities Foundation

Toledo Community Jewish Fund ($10,000) see Stone Foundation, David S.

Toledo Hearing and Speech Center ($4,000) see Baumker Charitable Foundation, Elsie and Harry

Toledo Hospital ($38,198) see Ritter Charitable Trust, George W. & Mary F.

Toledo Hospital ($250,000) see Stranahan Foundation

Toledo Lodge Masons of Ohio ($1,993) see Ritter Charitable Trust, George W. & Mary F.

Toledo Museum of Art ($16,768) see Andersons Management Corp.

Toledo Museum of Art ($5,000) see Baumker Charitable Foundation, Elsie and Harry

Toledo Museum of Art ($20,000) see Blade Communications

Toledo Museum of Art ($10,000) see Goerlich Family Foundation

Toledo Museum of Art ($28,841) see McMaster Foundation, Harold and Helen

Toledo Museum of Art ($20,000) see Miniger Memorial Foundation, Clement O.

Toledo Museum of Art see Seaway Food Town

Toledo Museum of Art ($22,000) see Stone Foundation, France

Toledo Museum of Art ($10,000) see TRINOVA Corp.

Toledo Museum of Art ($10,000) see TRINOVA Corp.

Toledo Museum of Art — first payment of a multi-year commitment to capital program expansion for a new art school building ($16,700) see Owens-Corning Fiberglas Corp.

Toledo Opera ($10,000) see Miniger Memorial Foundation, Clement O.

Toledo Opera see Seaway Food Town

Toledo Opera — to Toledo Opera for their Broadway play series ($23,000) see Owens-Corning Fiberglas Corp.

Toledo Orchestra Association ($30,950) see Andersons Management Corp.

Toledo Orchestra Association ($60,000) see Charities Foundation

Toledo Red Cross ($10,000) see United Technologies, Automotive

Toledo Repertoire Theatre see Seaway Food Town

Toledo Society for the Blind ($12,050) see Goerlich Family Foundation

Toledo Symphony ($27,500) see Blade Communications

Toledo Symphony ($20,000) see Miniger Memorial Foundation, Clement O.

Toledo Symphony Orchestra ($7,500) see Baumker Charitable Foundation, Elsie and Harry

Toys for Tots see Seaway Food Town

Trilogy ($170,000) see Nationwide Insurance Cos.

Trilogy Fund ($50,000) see Yassenoff Foundation, Leo

TRILOGY Fund of the Columbus Foundation ($60,000) see Borden

Trilogy Fund of the Columbus Foundation ($191,666) see El-An Foundation

Trilogy Fund of the Columbus Foundation ($100,000) see Reinberger Foundation

Trinity Lutheran Church ($30,000) see Musson Charitable Foundation, R. C. and Katharine M.

Trinity Methodist Church ($69,000) see Beeghly Fund, Leon A.

Trinity United Church of Christ ($25,000) see Double Foundation, George H.

Trinity United Methodist Vision 2000 ($55,000) see Jasam Foundation

Trumbull County Catholic School ($10,000) see Van Huffel Foundation, I. J.

Trumbull Memorial Hospital ($5,000) see Van Huffel Foundation, I. J.

Tuscampus City Council of Churches ($25,000) see Reeves Foundation

Tuscampus-Kent State University ($28,565) see Reeves Foundation

Tuslan Baseball Association ($3,000) see Flowers Charitable Trust, Albert W. and Edith V.

Twin Towers, Home on College Hill ($21,500) see Edwards Foundation, O. P. and W. E.

Union Terminal Trust Fund ($12,500) see Bardes Corp.

Union Terminal Trust Fund ($15,000) see Russell Charitable Trust, Josephine S.

United Appeal ($15,000) see Powell Co., William

United Appeal ($7,500) see Powell Co., William

United Appeal/Community Chest-Red Cross of Cincinnati Area ($8,500) see Corbett Foundation

United Appeal of Kings Mountain ($3,800) see Commercial Intertech Corp.

United Arts Fund ($1,750) see Belden Brick Co., Inc.

United Arts Fund ($25,000) see News & Observer Publishing Co.

United Arts Fund ($33,500) see Timken Co.

United Cerebral Palsy Association ($7,500) see Corbin Foundation, Mary S. and David C.

United Community Fund Knox County ($21,800) see JELD-WEN, Inc.

United Fund of Ross County/Chillicothe ($53,130) see PACCAR

United Funds ($4,500) see Joslyn Corp.

United Jewish Appeal Federation of Jewish Philanthropies ($10,000) see Schermer Charitable Trust, Frances

United Leukodystrophy Foundation ($5,000) see Mandel Foundation, Joseph and Florence

United Methodist Church West Ohio Conference ($21,500) see Edwards Foundation, O. P. and W. E.

United Methodist Community Center ($35,000) see Beeghly Fund, Leon A.

United Methodist Community Center ($20,000) see Crandall Memorial Foundation, J. Ford

United Methodist Community Center ($12,000) see Finnegan Foundation, John D.

United Negro College Fund ($15,000) see Britton Fund

United Theological Seminary ($40,000) see Gross Charitable Trust, Walter L. and Nell R.

United Way ($1,000) see Acme-Cleveland Corp.

United Way ($6,500) see Alms Trust, Eleanora

United Way ($8,000) see Amcast Industrial Corp.

United Way ($389,524) see American Financial Corp.

United Way ($282,000) see American Financial Corp.

United Way ($22,500) see American Welding & Manufacturing Co.

United Way ($21,500) see Bardes Corp.

United Way ($15,000) see Barnes Group

United Way ($500) see Barry Corp., R. G.

United Way ($8,000) see Beecher Foundation, Florence Simon

United Way ($70,000) see Beeghly Fund, Leon A.

United Way ($6,500) see Belden Brick Co., Inc.

United Way ($4,600) see Belden Brick Co., Inc.

United Way ($500) see Belden Brick Co., Inc.

United Way ($1,275) see Bergner Co., P.A.

United Way ($200,000) see Berry Foundation, Loren M.

United Way ($30,000) see Bicknell Fund

United Way ($45,000) see Blade Communications

United Way ($68,000) see Britton Fund

United Way ($300,000) see Charities Foundation

United Way ($32,900) see Cincinnati Enquirer

United Way ($32,900) see Cincinnati Enquirer

United Way — fund drive ($39,878) see Cleveland-Cliffs

United Way ($57,000) see Codrington Charitable Foundation, George W.

United Way ($30,000) see Cole National Corp.

United Way ($50,000) see Copperweld Steel Co.

United Way ($10,800) see Crane Fund for Widows and Children

United Way ($15,000) see Danis Industries

United Way ($19,235) see Davey Tree Expert Co.

United Way ($22,000) see Double Foundation, George H.

United Way ($34,000) see Duriron Co., Inc.

Ohio (cont.)

United Way ($34,000) see Duriron Co., Inc.

United Way ($396,710) see Eaton Corp.

United Way ($137,000) see Edwards Industries

United Way ($3,000) see Electric Power Equipment Co.

United Way ($3,000) see Electric Power Equipment Co.

United Way ($55,000) see Emery Memorial, Thomas J.

United Way ($16,175) see English Foundation, Walter and Marian

United Way ($55,000) see Ernsthausen Charitable Foundation, John F. and Doris E.

United Way ($3,000) see Fenton Foundation

United Way — annual contribution ($56,950) see Fifth Third Bancorp

United Way — annual contribution ($56,950) see Fifth Third Bancorp

United Way — annual contribution ($56,950) see Fifth Third Bancorp

United Way — annual contribution ($53,350) see Fifth Third Bancorp

United Way ($6,500) see Fox Charitable Foundation, Harry K. & Emma R.

United Way ($9,800) see Frohman Foundation, Sidney

United Way ($2,020) see Garvey Kansas Foundation

United Way ($500,000) see General Electric Co.

United Way ($300,000) see General Electric Co.

United Way ($3,719) see Gerlach Foundation

United Way ($20,000) see Gradison & Co.

United Way ($11,000) see Gries Charity Fund, Lucile and Robert H.

United Way ($10,000) see Gross Charitable Trust, Walter L. and Nell R.

United Way — toward annual campaign ($10,000) see H.C.S. Foundation

United Way ($30,000) see Hankins Foundation

United Way ($5,000) see Haskell Fund

United Way ($10,000) see Hook Drug

United Way ($130,600) see Hoover Foundation

United Way ($60,000) see Hoover Foundation

United Way ($10,000) see Hoover Fund-Trust, W. Henry

United Way ($20,000) see Huffy Corp.

United Way ($10,000) see Huffy Corp.

United Way ($31,000) see Humphrey Fund, George M. and Pamela S.

United Way ($40,000) see Ireland Foundation

United Way ($30,000) see Jergens Foundation, Andrew

United Way ($2,500) see Kangesser Foundation, Robert E., Harry A., and M. Sylvia

United Way ($3,500) see Klein Fund, Nathan J.

United Way ($2,800) see Kuhns Investment Co.

United Way ($5,250) see Lamson & Sessions Co.

United Way ($5,250) see Lamson & Sessions Co.

United Way ($5,250) see Lamson & Sessions Co.

United Way ($1,800) see Lancaster Colony

United Way ($1,000) see Lancaster Colony

United Way ($21,200) see LDI Charitable Foundation

United Way ($30,000) see Mather Charitable Trust, S. Livingston

United Way ($25,875) see McDonald & Co. Securities

United Way ($19,200) see McFawn Trust No. 2, Lois Sisler

United Way ($10,500) see Mead Fund, Nelson

United Way ($7,500) see Mill-Rose Co.

United Way ($11,000) see Monarch Machine Tool Co.

United Way ($30,000) see Musson Charitable Foundation, R. C. and Katharine M.

United Way ($28,500) see National Machinery Co.

United Way ($946,731) see NCR Corp.

United Way ($30,000) see Oglebay Norton Co.

United Way ($66,250) see Ohio National Life Insurance Co.

United Way ($10,000) see O'Neil Foundation, M. G.

United Way ($51,000) see Orleton Trust Fund

United Way ($10,000) see OsCo. Industries

United Way ($10,000) see OsCo. Industries

United Way ($34,000) see Park National Bank

United Way ($8,000) see Peterloon Foundation

United Way ($3,000) see Pollock Company Foundation, William B.

United Way ($253,750) see Reynolds & Reynolds Co.

United Way ($8,000) see Ritchie Memorial Foundation, Charies E. and Mabel M.

United Way ($11,000) see Sandusky International Inc.

United Way ($25,000) see Sapirstein-Stone-Weiss Foundation

United Way ($6,720) see Schey Foundation

United Way ($1,000) see Schey Foundation

United Way — contribution ($60,000) see Schmidlapp Trust No. 1, Jacob G.

United Way ($5,000) see Scott and Fetzer Co.

United Way ($10,000) see Sears Family Foundation

United Way ($56,400) see Semple Foundation, Louise Taft

United Way ($2,500) see Sifco Industries Inc.

United Way ($5,000) see Smith Charitable Fund, Eleanor Armstrong

United Way ($12,000) see South Waite Foundation

United Way ($14,050) see Standard Products Co.

United Way ($225,000) see Star Bank, N.A.

United Way ($19,000) see Tait Foundation, Frank M.

United Way ($97,380) see Tomkins Industries, Inc.

United Way ($23,750) see Tranzonic Cos.

United Way ($73,000) see Tremco Inc.

United Way ($18,423) see Tremco Inc.

United Way ($7,528) see Tremco Inc.

United Way ($35,000) see Treuhaft Foundation

United Way ($7,500) see True Trust, Henry A.

United Way ($358,210) see TRW Corp.

United Way ($1,000) see Wallace Computer Services

United Way ($30,000) see Watson Foundation, Walter E. and Caroline H.

United Way ($78,000) see White Consolidated Industries

United Way ($2,000) see Wolverine World Wide, Inc.

United Way ($30,000) see XTEK Inc.

United Way-Ashtabula County ($32,000) see Centerior Energy Corp.

United Way of Central Stark County ($230,000) see Timken Co.

United Way of Cincinnati ($200,000) see Cincinnati Milacron

United Way of Cincinnati ($109,046) see Federated Department Stores and Allied Stores Corp.

United Way of Cincinnati ($100,066) see Federated Department Stores and Allied Stores Corp.

United Way of Cleveland — corporate pledge ($1,435,085) see BP America

United Way of Cleveland ($25,000) see Nestle U.S.A. Inc.

United Way/Corporate ($350,000) see Parker-Hannifin Corp.

United Way of Dayton ($97,600) see National City Corp.

United Way of Dayton Area ($196,640) see Mead Corp.

United Way of Franklin County ($14,060) see Andersons Management Corp.

United Way of Franklin County ($165,750) see Borden

United Way of Franklin County ($322,000) see Columbus Dispatch Printing Co.

United Way of Franklin County ($122,500) see Federated Department Stores and Allied Stores Corp.

United Way-Franklin County ($286,926) see National City Corp.

United Way of Franklin County ($1,746,707) see Nationwide Insurance Cos.

United Way of Franklin County ($45,475) see Ohio Bell Telephone Co.

United Way of Greater Cleveland ($28,750) see Reliance Electric Co.

United Way of Greater Cleveland ($28,750) see Reliance Electric Co.

United Way of Greater Cleveland ($28,750) see Reliance Electric Co.

United Way of the Greater Dayton Area ($21,300) see Arvin Industries

United Way-Greater Toledo ($79,500) see Centerior Energy Corp.

United Way of Greater Toledo ($178,000) see Dana Corp.

United Way Greater Toledo — annual contribution ($25,375) see Fifth Third Bancorp

United Way Greater Toledo — annual contribution ($25,375) see Fifth Third Bancorp

United Way of Greater Toledo ($500,000) see Stranahan Foundation

United Way-Lake County ($38,500) see Centerior Energy Corp.

United Way Mansfield ($2,000) see Lippitt Foundation, Katherine Kenyon

United Way-Montgomery, Greene and Preble Counties ($190,000) see Dayton Power and Light Co.

United Way Services — operating ($75,000) see Consolidated Natural Gas Co.

United Way Services — operating ($75,000) see Consolidated Natural Gas Co.

United Way Services — operating ($75,000) see Consolidated Natural Gas Co.

United Way Services ($202,500) see Forest City Enterprises

United Way Services ($10,000) see Frankino Charitable Foundation, Samuel J. and Connie

United Way Services ($26,250) see LTV Corp.

United Way Services ($26,250) see LTV Corp.

United Way Services ($549,656) see National City Corp.

United Way Services ($131,250) see Ohio Bell Telephone Co.

United Way Services ($131,250) see Ohio Bell Telephone Co.

United Way Services ($45,000) see Pittway Corp.

United Way Services ($159,400) see Sherwin-Williams Co.

United Way Services ($15,000) see Tippit Charitable Trust, C. Carlisle and Margaret M.

United Way Services of Greater Cleveland ($115,000) see Lincoln Electric Co.

United Way-Shelby County ($78,000) see Aluminum Co. of America

United Way of Summit County — charitable contribution ($37,500) see Bridgestone/ Firestone

United Way of Summit County — contribution ($37,500) see Bridgestone/ Firestone

United Way of Summit County — contribution ($37,500) see Bridgestone/ Firestone

United Way Summit County ($37,500) see Bridgestone/ Firestone

United Way-Summit County ($52,500) see GenCorp

United Way of Summit County ($11,000) see Norton Co.

United Way of Summit County — to assist in general operations plus $30,000 toward the current shortfall ($200,000) see GAR Foundation

United Way of Toledo ($211,500) see Andersons Management Corp.

United Way-Toledo ($79,500) see Centerior Energy Corp.

United Way-Toledo ($100,000) see National City Corp.

United Way of Van Wert County ($15,040) see TRINOVA Corp.

United Way of Wooster ($32,500) see Rubbermaid

United Way of Wooster ($32,500) see Rubbermaid

United Way of Wooster ($32,500) see Rubbermaid

United Way of Wooster ($32,500) see Rubbermaid

University of Akron ($50,000) see McFawn Trust No. 2, Lois Sisler

University of Akron ($17,000) see Mirapaul Foundation

University of Akron ($15,000) see Ritchie Memorial Foundation, Charies E. and Mabel M.

University of Akron Development Foundation — for the maintenance endowment fund ($250,000) see GAR Foundation

University of Akron Foundation ($8,500) see Calhoun Charitable Trust, Kenneth

University of Akron-Musson Chair ($85,000) see Musson Charitable Foundation, R. C. and Katharine M.

University of Cincinnati ($10,000) see Boothroyd Foundation, Charles H. and Bertha L.

University of Cincinnati — capital improvements ($160,000) see Corbett Foundation

University of Cincinnati — challenge grant ($45,000) see Corbett Foundation

University of Cincinnati ($1,548) see Corbett Foundation

University of Cincinnati ($19,600) see New Orphan Asylum Scholarship Foundation

University of Cincinnati ($1,000) see Powell Co., William

University of Cincinnati, College of Conservation of Music — funding for the Dorothy Richard Starling Chair for Violin Studies ($91,000) see Starling Foundation, Dorothy Richard

University of Cincinnati-College of Engineering ($30,300) see Cincinnati Milacron

University of Cincinnati Continum ($60,000) see Cincinnati Bell

University of Cincinnati Foundation ($181,500) see American Financial Corp.

University of Cincinnati Foundation ($25,000) see Kautz Family Foundation

University of Cincinnati Foundation ($2,000) see Schiff Foundation, John J. and Mary R.

University of Cincinnati Foundation ($7,000) see Seasongood Good Government Foundation, Murray and Agnes

University Circle ($539,611) see Mather and William Gwinn Mather Fund, Elizabeth Ring

University Circle ($100,000) see 1525 Foundation

University Circle ($50,000) see Second Foundation

University Circle ($1,000) see Smith Charitable Fund, Eleanor Armstrong

University of Dayton — in computer software that will provide researchers and students with ability to design computer chips ($6,400,000) see Cadence Design Systems

University of Dayton ($35,500) see Kramer Foundation, Louise

University of Dayton ($25,000) see Leonardt Foundation

University of Dayton ($28,724) see NCR Corp.

University of Dayton ($100,000) see Reynolds & Reynolds Co.

University of Dayton ($5,000) see Seymour and Troester Foundation

University of Findley ($250,000) see Second Foundation

University Hospitals — general fund ($15,000) see Armington Fund, Evenor

University Hospitals of Cleveland ($15,000) see Frohman Foundation, Sidney

University Hospitals of Cleveland ($60,000) see GenCorp

University Hospitals of Cleveland ($60,000) see GenCorp

University Hospitals of Cleveland ($749,606) see Hartford Foundation, John A.

University Hospitals of Cleveland ($5,000) see Haskell Fund

University Hospitals of Cleveland ($25,000) see Humphrey Fund, George M. and Pamela S.

University Hospitals of Cleveland ($25,000) see Humphrey Fund, George M. and Pamela S.

University Hospitals of Cleveland ($2,500) see Kangesser Foundation, Robert E., Harry A., and M. Sylvia

University Hospitals of Cleveland ($8,000) see Murch Foundation

University Hospitals of Cleveland ($40,000) see Perkins Charitable Foundation

University Hospitals of Cleveland ($390,708) see Prentiss Foundation, Elisabeth Severance

University Hospitals of Cleveland ($2,000) see Smith Charitable Fund, Eleanor Armstrong

University Hospitals of Cleveland ($8,000) see Standard Products Co.

University Hospitals — David S. Ingalls Neurological Institute Alzheimer's Research ($84,000) see Ingalls Foundation, Louise H. and David S.

University School ($25,000) see Cleveland-Cliffs

University School ($25,000) see Davis Foundation, Joe C.

University School ($1,500) see Eaton Foundation, Cyrus

University School ($6,000) see Laub Foundation

University School ($1,000) see Ohio Savings Bank

University School ($250,000) see O'Neil Foundation, Cyril F. and Marie E.

University School ($15,000) see O'Neil Foundation, Cyril F. and Marie E.

University School ($20,000) see Ranney Foundation, P. K.

University School ($13,850) see Tippit Charitable Trust, C. Carlisle and Margaret M.

University School ($5,000) see V and V Foundation

University School ($24,000) see Wellman Foundation, S. K.

University School/Huntington Valley ($25,000) see Parker-Hannifin Corp.

University School Library ($33,300) see Kilroy Foundation, William S. and Lora Jean

University School — Wean Faculty Development Fund ($150,000) see Wean Foundation, Raymond John

University of Steubenville ($11,000) see Berkman Foundation, Louis and Sandra

University of Toledo ($38,443) see Andersons Management Corp.

University of Toledo ($200) see Leesona Corp.

University of Toledo Corporation ($8,500) see Blade Communications

University of Toledo — donation of computer equipment for National Center for Tooling and Precision Components ($1,000,000) see IBM Corp.

Upside of Downs ($500) see Cole National Corp.

Urban Community School ($10,000) see O'Neill Foundation, William J. and Dorothy K.

Urbana City Schools ($15,000) see Grimes Foundation

Urbana Fire Department ($15,000) see Grimes Foundation

Urbana Fire Department ($8,000) see Grimes Foundation

Urbana University ($50,000) see Grimes Foundation

Urbana University ($2,000) see Hartzell Industries, Inc.

Ursuline College — student scholarships ($67,800) see Huntington Fund for Education, John

Ursuline College ($5,000) see Laub Foundation

Ursuline College ($120,000) see Lennon Foundation, Fred A.

Ursuline Nuns — St. Angela Center ($1,000,000) see O'Neill Charitable Corporation, F. J.

Ursuline Sisters Motherhouse ($25,000) see Finnegan Foundation, John D.

Ursuline Sisters Motherhouse ($20,000) see Kilcawley Fund, William H.

Ursuline Wellness Center ($15,000) see O'Neill Foundation, William J. and Dorothy K.

US Committee for UNICEF ($5,000) see Scott and Fetzer Co.

USS Constitution Museum ($15,000) see Mifflin Memorial Fund, George H. and Jane A.

Van Wert City Schools ($16,914) see Van Wert County Foundation

Van Wert City Schools ($6,600) see Van Wert County Foundation

Van Wert Civic Theater ($10,000) see Van Wert County Foundation

Van Wert Community Concerts ($7,000) see Van Wert County Foundation

Van Wert County Foundation ($50,531) see Flickinger Memorial Trust

Van Wert County YMCA ($10,000) see TRINOVA Corp.

Van Wert Extension Service ($9,500) see Van Wert County Foundation

Van Wert Historical Society ($10,000) see Van Wert County Foundation

Vascon Center of Central Ohio ($10,500) see Yassenoff Foundation, Leo

Victim Assistance ($10,000) see Corbin Foundation, Mary S. and David C.

Victim Assistance ($15,000) see Musson Charitable Foundation, R. C. and Katharine M.

Victim Assistance Program ($10,000) see McAlonan Trust, John A.

Victoria Theatre Association ($10,000) see Orleton Trust Fund

Victoria Theatre Association ($10,000) see Tait Foundation, Frank M.

Village of Leipsic ($21,500) see Edwards Foundation, O. P. and W. E.

Visiting Nurse Service ($10,000) see Corbin Foundation, Mary S. and David C.

Vocational Guidance Services ($10,000) see Austin Memorial Foundation

Vocational Guidance Services ($20,000) see Gries Charity Fund, Lucile and Robert H.

Vocational Guidance Services ($13,000) see Murch Foundation

Vocational Guidance Services — renovations ($75,000) see Nord Family Foundation

Vocational Guidance Services ($164,746) see 1525 Foundation

Vocational Guidance Services ($50,000) see Sears Family Foundation

Vocational Guidance Services ($10,026) see Stocker Foundation

Vocational Guidance Services — toward start-up funds for a Janitorial Training and Placement Program for disadvantaged youth ($22,000) see H.C.S. Foundation

Vocational Guidence Services ($12,000) see Humphrey Fund, George M. and Pamela S.

W.G. Nord Community Mental Health Center — capital campaign ($150,000) see Nord Family Foundation

Walnut Hills High School ($20,000) see Ohio Valley Foundation

Walsh College ($5,000) see Belden Brick Co., Inc.

Walsh College ($400) see Belden Brick Co., Inc.

Walsh College Annual Drive ($800) see Hoover Fund-Trust, W. Henry

Walsh Jesuit High School ($10,000) see McAlonan Trust, John A.

Warren City School Recreation Department ($1,000) see American Welding & Manufacturing Co.

Wassenburg Art Center ($54,100) see Van Wert County Foundation

Wassenburg Art Center ($53,131) see Van Wert County Foundation

Waynesboro Baseball Association ($3,000) see Flowers Charitable Trust, Albert W. and Edith V.

WCET ($10,000) see Dater Foundation, Charles H.

WCET ($30,025) see Jarson-Stanley and Mickey Kaplan Foundation, Isaac & Esther

WCET ($2,500) see Peterloon Foundation

WCET ($10,000) see Russell Charitable Trust, Josephine S.

WCET ($34,750) see Schmidlapp Trust No. 2, Jacob G.

WDPR-FM 89.5 ($100) see American Aggregates Corp.

Weathervane — physical facility improvements ($30,000) see Evans Foundation, Thomas J.

Weathervane Playhouse ($3,000) see Park National Bank

WECO ($15,000) see Tremco Inc.

Wellness Community of Greater Cincinnati — furnishings, office equipment and kitchen supplies ($50,000) see Corbett Foundation

Wesley Hall ($21,500) see Edwards Foundation, O. P. and W. E.

Wesley Hall ($15,000) see Rice Foundation, Helen Steiner

Wesleyan Church ($2,620) see Baird Brothers Co.

West Holmes School ($49,139) see Young Foundation, Hugo H. and Mabel B.

West Park Retirement Community ($57,485) see Cincinnati Foundation for the Aged

Western Reserve Academy ($42,100) see American Foundation Corporation

Western Reserve Academy ($5,000) see Bicknell Fund

Western Reserve Academy ($2,500) see Cole National Corp.

Western Reserve Academy ($6,000) see Laub Foundation

Western Reserve Academy ($2,500) see Lippitt Foundation, Katherine Kenyon

Western Reserve Academy — to help complete the James L. Knight Fine Arts Center ($1,000,000) see Knight Foundation, John S. and James L.

Western Reserve Care System ($5,000) see Commercial Intertech Corp.

Western Reserve Care System — general purposes ($50,316) see Watson Foundation, Walter E. and Caroline H.

Western Reserve Historical Society ($194,663) see Common Wealth Trust

Western Reserve Historical Society ($500) see Eaton Foundation, Cyrus

Western Reserve Historical Society ($112,000) see Lennon Foundation, Fred A.

Western Reserve Historical Society ($15,000) see McFawn Trust No. 2, Lois Sisler

Western Reserve Historical Society ($543,750) see Nason Foundation

Western Reserve Historical Society ($500,000) see Nason Foundation

Western Reserve Historical Society ($25,000) see Snyder Charitable Fund, W. P.

Western Reserve Historical Society — payment on $475,000 grant to help expand the Crawford Auto Museum ($125,000) see TRW Corp.

Wexner Center for the Arts ($1,000) see Gerlach Foundation

Wexner Heritage Foundation — educaitonal seminar ($500,000) see Wexner Foundation

Wexner Heritage Foundation — educational seminar ($500,000) see Wexner Foundation

Wexner Heritage Foundation — educational seminar ($500,000) see Wexner Foundation

Wexner Heritage Foundation — educational seminar ($250,000) see Wexner Foundation

Wexner Heritage Foundation — educational seminar ($100,000) see Wexner Foundation

WGUC — capital improvements ($33,100) see Corbett Foundation

WGUC ($400) see Hayfields Foundation

Wilberforce University ($122,000) see Abrons Foundation, Louis and Anne

Wilberforce University — scholarship program ($13,194) see Dayton Power and Light Co.

Wilberforce University ($125,000) see Pforzheimer Foundation, Carl and Lily

Wilda ($20,000) see Rupp Foundation, Fran and Warren

Wildlife Conservation Fund ($2,500) see Robinson Foundation

Willard Hospital ($37,500) see M.T.D. Products

Willoughby Fine Arts Association ($8,000) see South Waite Foundation

WKSU Kent State University ($20,000) see Mirapaul Foundation

Womanlife ($12,500) see Kramer Foundation, Louise

Womanline ($5,150) see Danis Industries

Womanline ($2,000) see Standard Register Co.

Women's Community Fund ($10,000) see Gerson Family Foundation, Benjamin J.

Women's Community Fund — for Renewal Program ($11,000) see Women's Project Foundation

Womens Research and Development Center — school project ($10,000) see Russell Charitable Trust, Josephine S.

WomenSafe ($5,000) see Frohring Foundation, William O. and Gertrude Lewis

Wooster College — building fund ($50,000) see Ebert Charitable Foundation, Horatio B.

Wooster College — president's fund ($10,000) see Ebert Charitable Foundation, Horatio B.

Wooster Community Hospital ($250,000) see Rubbermaid

Wooster Community Hospital ($13,334) see Smucker Co., J.M.

Work and Rehabilitation Centers ($3,500) see Peterloon Foundation

Boy Scouts of America ($10,000) see Kirkpatrick Foundation

Boy Scouts of America ($10,000) see Kirkpatrick Foundation

Boy Scouts of America ($50,000) see Oklahoman Foundation

Boy Scouts of America ($10,000) see Share Trust, Charles Morton

Boy Scouts of America ($30,000) see Zink Foundation, John Steele

Boy Scouts of America-Black Beaver Council ($55,000) see McCasland Foundation

Boys Club of America ($25,000) see Puterbaugh Foundation

Boys and Girls Club ($50,000) see Lyon Foundation

Bristow Community Center ($1,000) see Jones Foundation, Montfort Jones and Allie Brown

Bristow Day Camp ($2,000) see Jones Foundation, Montfort Jones and Allie Brown

Bristow Memorial Hospital ($9,000) see Jones Foundation, Montfort Jones and Allie Brown

Bristow Ministerial Alliance ($3,360) see Jones Foundation, Montfort Jones and Allie Brown

Bristow Park and Recreation ($26,000) see Jones Foundation, Montfort Jones and Allie Brown

Bristow Public Library ($3,000) see Jones Foundation, Montfort Jones and Allie Brown

Bristow Public Schools ($6,838) see Jones Foundation, Montfort Jones and Allie Brown

Cameron Foundation ($10,000) see Harris Foundation

Cameron University — scholarships ($109,500) see McMahon Foundation

Cameron University Foundation ($96,000) see McCasland Foundation

Carter County Historical and Genealogical Society ($10,000) see Goddard Foundation, Charles B.

Casady School ($4,000) see McGee Foundation

Cascia Hall ($13,000) see Warren Charite

Cascia Hall School ($2,000) see Hamilton Foundation, Florence P.

Catholic Charities ($12,500) see Zarrow Foundation, Anne and Henry

Catholic Social Ministries ($10,000) see Brand Foundation, C. Harold and Constance

Central Oklahoma Economic Development District ($10,000) see Wood Charitable Trust, W. P.

Central State University ($10,000) see Parman Foundation, Robert A.

Chapman Institute of Medical Genetics ($215,000) see Chapman Charitable Trust, H. A. and Mary K.

Charles B. Goddard Center ($12,000) see Merrick Foundation

Cherokee Strip Museum Association ($50,000) see Share Trust, Charles Morton

Children's Day Nursery — window replacement ($656) see Collins Foundation, George and Jennie

Children's Center ($10,000) see Brand Foundation, C. Harold and Constance

Childrens Day Nursery ($20,000) see Warren Foundation, William K.

Children's Medical Center ($250,000) see Chapman Charitable Trust, H. A. and Mary K.

Children's Medical Center ($25,000) see Kaiser Foundation, Betty E. and George B.

Children's Medical Research ($5,000) see Brand Foundation, C. Harold and Constance

Children's Medical Research ($25,000) see Oklahoman Foundation

Christ Church ($17,722) see Downs Perpetual Charitable Trust, Ellason

Christ the King Church ($85,000) see Warren Charite

Citizen CPR-Critical Link ($50,000) see Warren Foundation, William K.

City of Alva ($75,000) see Share Trust, Charles Morton

City of Alva — capital improvements ($30,000) see Share Trust, Charles Morton

City of Alva ($14,000) see Share Trust, Charles Morton

City of Lawton — renovate McMahon Auditorium, landscape E. T. Park ($184,609) see McMahon Foundation

City of Tulsa ($50,000) see Chapman Charitable Trust, H. A. and Mary K.

City of Tulsa — park property acquisition ($1,000,000) see Helmerich Foundation

City of Tulsa-Riverside Park Project ($100,000) see Bovaird Foundation, Mervin

City of Tulsa — War on Drugs Program ($100,000) see Bovaird Foundation, Mervin

Coffee Creek Riding Center — to construct an indoor riding hall for inclement weather for free therapeutic horseback classes ($35,000) see Kerr Foundation, Robert S. and Grayce B.

Comanche County Fairgrounds Trust Authority — building grant ($440,500) see McMahon Foundation

Community Activities of Ardmore ($10,000) see Goddard Foundation, Charles B.

Community Development Support Association — to implement the Parents As Teachers Program in Oklahoma ($30,000) see Kerr Foundation, Robert S. and Grayce B.

Congregation B'nai Emunah ($9,667) see Kaiser Foundation, Betty E. and George B.

Congregational B'Nai Emman Endowment Fund ($250,000) see Sooner Pipe & Supply Corp.

Cookson Hills Christian School ($25,000) see Walton Family Foundation

Crohns and Colitis Foundation ($25,000) see Bernsen

Foundation, Grace and Franklin

Crohn's and Colitis Foundation of America ($51,000) see Sooner Pipe & Supply Corp.

Daily Living Center ($10,000) see Wegener Foundation, Herman and Mary

Deaconess Hospital ($15,000) see Wegener Foundation, Herman and Mary

Deaconess Hospital Foundation ($2,000) see National City Bank of Evansville

Diocese of Tulsa ($46,624) see Warren Foundation, William K.

Duncan Public Schools ($69,238) see McCasland Foundation

Duncan Rescue Mission ($32,553) see McCasland Foundation

Eastern Oklahoma Chapter of Arthritis Foundation ($5,000) see Collins, Jr. Foundation, George Fulton

Eastern Oklahoma State College ($32,500) see Grimes Foundation, Otha H.

Eastern Oklahoma State College ($25,000) see Puterbaugh Foundation

Epworth United Methodist Church — new organ fund ($1,000) see Collins Foundation, George and Jennie

Epworth United Methodist Church — new organ fund ($1,000) see Collins, Jr. Foundation, George Fulton

Family and Children's Service ($5,000) see Cuesta Foundation

First Baptist Church ($563,050) see Young Foundation, R. A.

First Presbyterian Helping Hand ($30,000) see Bernsen Foundation, Grace and Franklin

First United Methodist Church ($90,000) see Parker Drilling Co.

First United Methodist Church ($61,000) see Parker Drilling Co.

First United Methodist Church ($10,900) see Parker Drilling Co.

Five Civilized Tribes Museum ($7,500) see Cornerstone Foundation of Northeastern Wisconsin

Gateway to Drug Prevention ($23,400) see Wood Charitable Trust, W. P.

Gilcrease Museum Association ($13,000) see Campbell Foundation

Glen Foundation ($10,000) see Noble Foundation, Vivian Bilby

Goodland Presbyterian Children's Home — home for disturbed boys ($5,000) see Early Foundation

Goodland Presbyterian Children's Home ($10,000) see Puterbaugh Foundation

Goodwill Industries of Tulsa ($27,000) see Sooner Pipe & Supply Corp.

Grand Lake Mental Health ($3,216) see Harmon Foundation, Pearl M. and Julia J.

Great Plains Area Vo-Tech Foundation — scholarships ($40,720) see McMahon Foundation

Greater Ardmore Scholarship Foundation ($55,707) see Merrick Foundation

Green Country Village ($140,000) see Lyon Foundation

Hardy Murphy Coliseum Authority ($20,000) see Goddard Foundation, Charles B.

Heritage Hall ($25,000) see Kirkpatrick Foundation

Heritage Hall School — books and supplies ($5,000) see Rapp Foundation, Robert Glenn

Hillcrest Medical Center Foundation ($5,000) see Kaiser Foundation, Betty E. and George B.

Historical and Genealogical Society of Carter County — contribution to the permanent endowment ($211,426) see Noble Foundation, Samuel Roberts

Holland Hall Fine and Performing Arts Center ($10,000) see Cuesta Foundation

Holland Hall School ($8,000) see Broadhurst Foundation

Holland Hall School ($100,000) see Chapman Charitable Trust, H. A. and Mary K.

Holland Hall School ($20,000) see Sooner Pipe & Supply Corp.

Holland Hall School — Financial Aid ($50,000) see Chapman Charitable Trust, H. A. and Mary K.

Indian Nations Council — building fund ($50,000) see Helmerich Foundation

Jane Brooks School for Deaf — dormitory mortgage ($5,000) see Rapp Foundation, Robert Glenn

Jane Philips Medical Center ($2,852) see Harmon Foundation, Pearl M. and Julia J.

Jane Philips Medical Center ($2,852) see Harmon Foundation, Pearl M. and Julia J.

Jasmine Moran Children's Museum ($25,000) see Kerr Foundation, Robert S. and Grayce B.

Jesus House — challenge grant to assist in the purchase and renovation of housing for the homeless ($30,000) see Kerr Foundation, Robert S. and Grayce B.

Jewish Federation ($12,000) see Taubman Foundation, Herman P. and Sophia

Jewish Federation of Greater East Bay — East Bay fire fund ($25,000) see Goldman Fund, Richard and Rhoda

Jewish Federation Operation ($12,500) see Kaiser Foundation, Betty E. and George B.

Jewish Federation of Tulsa ($4,500) see Kaiser Foundation, Betty E. and George B.

Jewish Health Center ($25,000) see Kaiser Foundation, Betty E. and George B.

John 3:16 Mission ($6,000) see Zarrow Foundation, Anne and Henry

John Zink Foundation ($620,000) see Zink Foundation, John Steele

Junior Achievement ($11,000) see Collins Foundation, George and Jennie

Junior League of Tulsa — building expansion ($75,000) see Helmerich Foundation

Kanchi/Arts and Humanities Council ($5,000) see Harmon Foundation, Pearl M. and Julia J.

Lake Hefner Trails ($10,000) see American Fidelity Corp.

Langston University ($25,000) see Central & South West Services

Last Frontier Council ($12,383) see American Fidelity Corp.

Lawton Philharmonic Society — music competition ($25,000) see McMahon Foundation

Legion Park — park improvement ($5,000) see Beatty Trust, Cordelia Lunceford

Little Flower Church ($1,000) see Brand Foundation, C. Harold and Constance

Little Light House — building expansion ($50,000) see Helmerich Foundation

Little Light House ($10,000) see Zarrow Foundation, Anne and Henry

McAlester Alcoholism Council ($5,000) see Puterbaugh Foundation

McAlester Economic Development Authority ($15,000) see Puterbaugh Foundation

Mental Health Association in Oklahoma County ($20,150) see Kirkpatrick Foundation

Mercy Health Center ($250,000) see Brand Foundation, C. Harold and Constance

Mercy Hospice — staff training ($3,000) see Rapp Foundation, Robert Glenn

Mercy Hospital ($15,000) see Wegener Foundation, Herman and Mary

Midwest/Del City Schools ($10,000) see Wegener Foundation, Herman and Mary

Mount St. Mary School — endowment funding ($5,000) see Rapp Foundation, Robert Glenn

Museum of Plains ($15,000) see Share Trust, Charles Morton

Muskogee Community Concert Association ($1,000) see Cornerstone Foundation of Northeastern Wisconsin

Mutual Girls Club — building fund — construction ($100,000) see Lyon Foundation

National Cowboy Hall of Fame ($10,035) see American Fidelity Corp.

National Cowboy Hall of Fame ($20,000) see Boatmen's First National Bank of Oklahoma

National Cowboy Hall of Fame and Western Heritage ($25,000) see Kerr Foundation, Robert S. and Grayce B.

National Cowboy Hall of Fame and Western Heritage Center — support for office of development ($100,000) see Noble Foundation, Samuel Roberts

National Cowboy Hall of Fame and Western Heritage Center ($50,000) see Oklahoma Gas & Electric Co.

National Multiple Sclerosis Society ($600) see Parker Drilling Co.

Nature Conservancy - Oklahoma Chapter see Arkla

Oklahoma (cont.)

Nature Conservancy — support purchase of land for the Tallgrass Prairie Preserve, a pre-settlement tallgrass prairie in northeastern Oklahoma ($125,000) see Kerr Foundation, Robert S. and Grayce B.

Neighborhood Services Organization ($10,000) see Kirkpatrick Foundation

Norman Public School Foundation ($60,000) see Sarkeys Foundation

Northeastern State University — College of Optometry ($10,750) see Bright Family Foundation

Northern Oklahoma Youth Services ($3,500) see Beatty Trust, Cordelia Lunceford

Oak Hall Alphabetic Phonics Program ($15,000) see Goddard Foundation, Charles B.

Oklahoma Arts Institute ($5,000) see Central & South West Services

Oklahoma Arts Institute ($60,000) see Zarrow Foundation, Anne and Henry

Oklahoma Baptist University ($77,695) see Phillips Petroleum Co.

Oklahoma Baptist University ($17,200) see Wood Charitable Trust, W. P.

Oklahoma Centennial Sports ($16,667) see American Fidelity Corp.

Oklahoma Christian College — equipment for laboratories ($4,000) see Rapp Foundation, Robert Glenn

Oklahoma Christian University — faculty development endowment fund ($50,000) see Frueauff Foundation, Charles A.

Oklahoma Christian University ($10,000) see Wegener Foundation, Herman and Mary

Oklahoma Christian University of Science and Arts ($75,000) see Boatmen's First National Bank of Oklahoma

Oklahoma Christian University of Science and Arts — capital campaign ($25,000) see Boatmen's First National Bank of Oklahoma

Oklahoma Christian University of Science and Arts ($56,385) see Oklahoma Gas & Electric Co.

Oklahoma Christian University of Science and Arts ($60,000) see Oklahoman Foundation

Oklahoma City Art Museum ($12,000) see Kirkpatrick Foundation

Oklahoma City Art Museum ($5,400) see Young Foundation, R. A.

Oklahoma City Chamber of Commerce — Science and Mathematics School ($15,000) see Boatmen's First National Bank of Oklahoma

Oklahoma City Church of Christ — missions ($33,750) see Frazier Foundation

Oklahoma City Community Foundation ($707,000) see Kirkpatrick Foundation

Oklahoma City Economic Development Foundation ($30,000) see Oklahoma Gas & Electric Co.

Oklahoma City Economic Development Foundation ($30,000) see Oklahoman Foundation

Oklahoma City Food Bank ($10,000) see Harris Foundation

Oklahoma City Metro Alliance for Safer Cities ($10,000) see Kirkpatrick Foundation

Oklahoma City Philharmonic Orchestra ($10,000) see Harris Foundation

Oklahoma City Public Schools Foundation ($18,000) see Kirkpatrick Foundation

Oklahoma City University — scholarship ($10,000) see Community Hospital Foundation

Oklahoma City University ($115,000) see Kerr Foundation

Oklahoma City University ($35,475) see Oklahoma Gas & Electric Co.

Oklahoma City University ($50,000) see Parman Foundation, Robert A.

Oklahoma City University ($10,000) see Wegener Foundation, Herman and Mary

Oklahoma City University — Angie Smith Chapel Endowment ($25,000) see Harris Foundation

Oklahoma City University — Harris Hall Renovation ($50,000) see Harris Foundation

Oklahoma City University School of Law — Sumners scholarship endowment ($407,679) see Sumners Foundation, Hatton W.

Oklahoma City Zoological Trust — underwrite exhibit ($16,380) see Harris Foundation

Oklahoma Educational Television ($75,000) see Phillips Petroleum Co.

Oklahoma Foundation for Excellence ($7,500) see Occidental Oil & Gas Corp.

Oklahoma Medical Research — library ($4,000) see Rapp Foundation, Robert Glenn

Oklahoma Medical Research — Fleming Scholars program ($3,000) see Rapp Foundation, Robert Glenn

Oklahoma Medical Research Foundation ($30,000) see Boatmen's First National Bank of Oklahoma

Oklahoma Medical Research Foundation ($200,000) see Chapman Charitable Trust, H. A. and Mary K.

Oklahoma Medical Research Foundation ($25,000) see Kerr Fund, Grayce B.

Oklahoma Medical Research Foundation ($15,000) see Parman Foundation, Robert A.

Oklahoma Medical Research Foundation ($20,000) see Warren Charite

Oklahoma Medical Research Foundation ($5,000) see Zarrow Foundation, Anne and Henry

Oklahoma Pharmacy Heritage Foundation ($20,000) see Share Trust, Charles Morton

Oklahoma Philharmonic Society ($11,449) see American Fidelity Corp.

Oklahoma School of Science and Mathematics ($10,000) see American Fidelity Corp.

Oklahoma School of Science and Mathematics ($30,000) see Kimberly-Clark Corp.

Oklahoma Sinfonia ($5,000) see Cuesta Foundation

Oklahoma State Foundation ($25,000) see Warren Charite

Oklahoma State University ($50,000) see Boatmen's First National Bank of Oklahoma

Oklahoma State University ($43,697) see Deloitte & Touche

Oklahoma State University ($43,672) see Deloitte & Touche

Oklahoma State University ($35,000) see Fourjay Foundation

Oklahoma State University ($5,200) see Grant Thornton

Oklahoma State University ($32,500) see Grimes Foundation, Otha H.

Oklahoma State University ($50,000) see Parman Foundation, Robert A.

Oklahoma State University ($8,123) see Technical Foundation of America

Oklahoma State University Center for Laser Research ($100,000) see Chapman Charitable Trust, H. A. and Mary K.

Oklahoma State University Endowment Fund ($31,250) see Reynolds Foundation, Donald W.

Oklahoma State University Foundation ($32,500) see Halliburton Co.

Oklahoma State University Foundation ($46,168) see Kerr Foundation

Oklahoma State University Foundation ($111,500) see McCasland Foundation

Oklahoma State University Foundation ($17,000) see Merrick Foundation

Oklahoma State University Foundation ($72,235) see Oklahoma Gas & Electric Co.

Oklahoma State University Foundation ($90,250) see Phillips Petroleum Co.

Oklahoma State University Foundation ($50,000) see Puterbaugh Foundation

Oklahoma State University Foundation ($33,334) see Williams Cos.

Oklahoma State University Foundation ($8,500) see Young Foundation, R. A.

Oklahoma State University — Undergraduate Biological Sciences Education Program ($2,000,000) see Hughes Medical Institute, Howard

Oklahoma University ($2,614) see Young Foundation, R. A.

Oklahoma University Foundation ($10,000) see Campbell Foundation

Oklahoma University Foundation ($111,500) see McCasland Foundation

Oklahoma University Foundation ($10,000) see Merrick Foundation

Oklahoma University Foundation — Health Science Center Fellowships ($25,000) see Harris Foundation

Oklahoma University Geological Survey ($10,000) see Merrick Foundation

Oklahoma Vocational Technical Foundation ($32,500) see Grimes Foundation, Otha H.

Operation Aware — drug prevention program ($5,000) see Collins Foundation, George and Jennie

Operation Aware — drug abuse programs ($5,000) see Collins, Jr. Foundation, George Fulton

Operation Aware of Oklahoma ($35,200) see Kerr Foundation

Oral Roberts University ($53,597) see Campbell Foundation

Oral Roberts University ($1,500) see Davey Tree Expert Co.

Oral Roberts University ($250) see Wellons Foundation

Park Friends ($37,500) see Central & South West Services

Park Friends ($2,500) see Kaiser Foundation, Betty E. and George B.

Park Friends ($10,000) see Occidental Oil & Gas Corp.

Park Friends ($10,000) see Occidental Oil & Gas Corp.

Park Friends ($110,000) see Zink Foundation, John Steele

Park Friends — first year of two-year commitment ($50,000) see AMR Corp.

Pauls Valley Community Education ($50,000) see McCasland Foundation

Percussive Arts Society — building ($272,297) see McMahon Foundation

Philbrook Art Center ($100,000) see Bernsen Foundation, Grace and Franklin

Philbrook Art Center ($27,400) see Gussman Foundation, Herbert and Roseline

Philbrook Art Center ($27,400) see Gussman Foundation, Herbert and Roseline

Philbrook Art Museum ($13,500) see Campbell Foundation

Philbrook Museum of Art — building expansion ($250,000) see Helmerich Foundation

Philbrook Museum of Art — building fund ($20,000) see Occidental Oil & Gas Corp.

Philbrook Museum of Art ($176,800) see Phillips Foundation, Waite and Genevieve

Philbrook Museum of Art ($173,867) see Zink Foundation, John Steele

Phillips Graduate Seminary ($5,000) see Broadhurst Foundation

Phillips University ($150,000) see Chapman Charitable Trust, H. A. and Mary K.

Phillips University ($12,500) see Harris Foundation

Phillips University ($50,000) see Parman Foundation, Robert A.

Phillips University ($84,000) see Sarkeys Foundation

Phillips University ($83,000) see Sarkeys Foundation

Pittsburgh County Youth Shelter — deprived children support ($6,000) see Puterbaugh Foundation

Planned Parenthood ($10,000) see Cuesta Foundation

Planned Parenthood Federation of America ($5,100) see Gussman Foundation, Herbert and Roseline

Planned Parenthood Federation of America ($20,000) see McGee Foundation

Pott County Historical Society ($6,500) see Wood Charitable Trust, W. P.

Pott County Telecom Corporation ($17,200) see Wood Charitable Trust, W. P.

Pottawatomie County Telecommunications ($50,000) see Kerr Fund, Grayce B.

Project Get Together ($11,500) see Sooner Pipe & Supply Corp.

Putnam City Schools ($10,000) see Wegener Foundation, Herman and Mary

Rainbow Fleet ($12,000) see Parman Foundation, Robert A.

Resonance ($10,000) see Campbell Foundation

Resonance ($26,000) see Kerr Fund, Grayce B.

Resonance ($60,500) see Zink Foundation, John Steele

Ronald McDonald House ($50,000) see Zink Foundation, John Steele

S.E. Baptist Church ($2,500) see Harmon Foundation, Pearl M. and Julia J.

St. Anthony Hospital ($15,000) see Wegener Foundation, Herman and Mary

St. Gregory's College — satellite dish and video camera recorder ($3,800) see Rapp Foundation, Robert Glenn

St. Gregory's Abbey ($1,000) see Brand Foundation, C. Harold and Constance

St. Gregory's Abbey ($72,000) see Wood Charitable Trust, W. P.

St. John Medical Center — medical equipment ($25,000) see Hugoton Foundation

St. John Medical Center Foundation ($5,000) see Cuesta Foundation

St. John Medical Center Foundation ($30,000) see Williams Cos.

St. Johns Medical Center Foundation ($2,050) see Gussman Foundation, Herbert and Roseline

St. Mary's School ($10,000) see Warren Charite

St. Simeons ($50,000) see McCasland Foundation

St. Simeon's ($35,000) see Zink Foundation, John Steele

St. Simeon's Episcopal Home ($1,000,000) see Mabee Foundation, J. E. and L. E.

St. Simeon's Episcopal Home — facility renovation and expansion ($150,000) see Noble Foundation, Samuel Roberts

Salvation Army ($4,000) see Collins Foundation, George and Jennie

Salvation Army ($5,000) see Cuesta Foundation

Salvation Army ($1,000) see Kaiser Foundation, Betty E. and George B.

Salvation Army ($10,000) see Merrick Foundation

Salvation Army ($5,000) see Mulford Foundation, Vincent

Salvation Army ($10,000) see Oklahoman Foundation

Salvation Army ($25,000) see Parman Foundation, Robert A.

Salvation Army ($5,000) see Young Foundation, R. A.

Salvation Army ($10,000) see Zarrow Foundation, Anne and Henry

Sapulpa Public School Foundation ($2,500) see Collins, Jr. Foundation, George Fulton

Scottish Rite Foundation ($30,000) see McCasland Foundation

Simmons Center Foundation ($160,000) see McCasland Foundation

Simmons Center Foundation — Convention Center construction ($83,333) see Noble Foundation, Samuel Roberts

Simmons Center Foundation — Halliburton Atrium ($100,000) see Halliburton Co.

South Central Sheltered Workshop ($25,000) see Wood Charitable Trust, W. P.

South Community Hospital ($15,000) see Wegener Foundation, Herman and Mary

Southern Nazarene University ($7,500) see Broadhurst Foundation

Southern Nazarene University ($50,000) see Parman Foundation, Robert A.

Southern Nazarene University ($2,807) see Staley Foundation, Thomas F.

Southern Oklahoma Ambulance Service ($10,000) see Merrick Foundation

Southwest Youth/Family Services ($45,000) see Kerr Foundation, Robert S. and Grayce B.

Sutton Avian Research Center — operational costs ($15,000) see Lyon Foundation

Temple Baptist Church ($4,800) see Oldham Little Church Foundation

10-33 Emergency C.B. Team ($4,800) see Harmon Foundation, Pearl M. and Julia J.

Tender Loving Care, Ronald McDonald House — building program ($10,000) see Titus Foundation, C. W.

Thomas Gilcrease Museum see Apache Corp.

Thomas Gilcrease Museum ($10,000) see Occidental Oil & Gas Corp.

Thomas Gilcrease Museum ($10,000) see Warren Charite

Thomas Gilcrease Museum Association ($51,000) see Williams Cos.

Thrive Program ($50,000) see Sumners Foundation, Hatton W.

TLC, Tulsa Ronald McDonald House ($75,000) see Bovaird Foundation, Mervin

Town and Country School ($25,000) see Bernsen Foundation, Grace and Franklin

Town and Country School ($10,000) see Broadhurst Foundation

Town and Country School ($10,000) see Sooner Pipe & Supply Corp.

Town and Country School ($10,000) see Zarrow Foundation, Anne and Henry

Town of Fletcher — recreational park grant ($50,000) see McMahon Foundation

Trinity Episcopal Church ($60,000) see Mulford Foundation, Vincent

Tulsa Area United Way ($10,000) see Kaiser Foundation, Betty E. and George B.

Tulsa Area United Way ($125,065) see McDonnell Douglas Corp.

Tulsa Area United Way ($95,000) see Occidental Oil & Gas Corp.

Tulsa Area United Way ($510,463) see Williams Cos.

Tulsa Ballet Company ($150,000) see Bernsen Foundation, Grace and Franklin

Tulsa Ballet Theatre see Apache Corp.

Tulsa Ballet Theatre ($5,000) see Campbell Foundation

Tulsa Ballet Theatre ($5,000) see Harmon Foundation, Pearl M. and Julia J.

Tulsa Ballet Theatre — operations ($30,000) see Helmerich Foundation

Tulsa Ballet Theatre ($70,000) see Williams Cos.

Tulsa Ballet Theatre ($176,667) see Zink Foundation, John Steele

Tulsa Ballet Theatre, Education Program — school program ($10,000) see Occidental Oil & Gas Corp.

Tulsa Boys Home ($15,000) see Titus Foundation, C. W.

Tulsa Center for Physically Limited ($45,000) see Zarrow Foundation, Anne and Henry

Tulsa Chamber of Commerce ($10,000) see Warren Charite

Tulsa Garden Center — renovation ($60,000) see Helmerich Foundation

Tulsa Heart/Growing Healthy ($30,000) see Fourjay Foundation

Tulsa Jewish Federation ($751,000) see Gussman Foundation, Herbert and Roseline

Tulsa Jewish Retirement and Health Care Center ($2,500) see Kaiser Foundation, Betty E. and George B.

Tulsa Library Trust — building fund ($502,994) see Helmerich Foundation

Tulsa Literacy Coalition ($3,000) see Harmon Foundation, Pearl M. and Julia J.

Tulsa Meals on Wheels ($23,000) see Zarrow Foundation, Anne and Henry

Tulsa Metropolitan Ministry ($45,000) see Bernsen Foundation, Grace and Franklin

Tulsa Metropolitan Ministry ($10,000) see Noble Foundation, Vivian Bilby

Tulsa Metropolitan Ministry ($31,000) see Warren Foundation, William K.

Tulsa Opera ($35,000) see Bernsen Foundation, Grace and Franklin

Tulsa Opera ($7,500) see Campbell Foundation

Tulsa Opera ($5,000) see Harmon Foundation, Pearl M. and Julia J.

Tulsa Opera — operations ($30,000) see Helmerich Foundation

Tulsa Performing Arts Center Trust ($30,000) see Williams Cos.

Tulsa Philharmonic ($8,000) see Campbell Foundation

Tulsa Philharmonic — operations ($30,000) see Helmerich Foundation

Tulsa Philharmonic Society ($11,000) see Cuesta Foundation

Tulsa Ronald McDonald House ($5,000) see Cuesta Foundation

Tulsa Speech and Hearing Association — building fund ($25,000) see Titus Foundation, C. W.

Tulsa University ($2,600) see Gussman Foundation, Herbert and Roseline

Tulsa University ($46,500) see Zink Foundation, John Steele

Tulsa Zoo ($80,000) see Bernsen Foundation, Grace and Franklin

Tulsa Zoo Development ($41,666) see Williams Cos.

Tulsa Zoo Friends — expansion program ($5,000) see Collins Foundation, George and Jennie

Tulsa Zoo Friends ($5,000) see Collins, Jr. Foundation, George Fulton

United Fund ($12,000) see Merrick Foundation

United Methodist Cooperative Ministries — case management ($1,000) see Collins Foundation, George and Jennie

United Methodist Cooperative Ministries ($1,000) see Collins, Jr. Foundation, George Fulton

United Way ($37,541) see American Fidelity Corp.

United Way ($71,000) see Boatmen's First National Bank of Oklahoma

United Way ($3,042) see CBI Industries

United Way ($10,000) see Davis Foundation, Ken W.

United Way ($13,820) see General Accident Insurance Co. of America

United Way ($500) see Hadson Corp.

United Way ($2,500) see Hamilton Foundation, Florence P.

United Way ($5,000) see Mulford Foundation, Vincent

United Way ($3,500) see National Center for Automated Information Retrieval

United Way ($22,475) see Oklahoman Foundation

United Way ($10,000) see Parker Drilling Co.

United Way ($8,132) see Puterbaugh Foundation

United Way ($25,000) see Titus Foundation, C. W.

United Way ($25,000) see Titus Foundation, C. W.

United Way ($25,000) see Wood Charitable Trust, W. P.

United Way ($3,990) see Young Foundation, R. A.

United Way ($40,000) see Zink Foundation, John Steele

United Way of Lawton — annual contribution ($62,500) see McMahon Foundation

United Way of Oklahoma City ($8,000) see Occidental Oil & Gas Corp.

United Way — 1991 annual campaign drive ($108,000) see AMR Corp.

University of Oklahoma ($5,000) see Bass Foundation, Harry

University of Oklahoma ($200,000) see Upjohn Co.

University of Oklahoma Foundation ($60,000) see Boatmen's First National Bank of Oklahoma

University of Oklahoma Foundation — pledge to cover financing of the education and research center ($20,000) see Boatmen's First National Bank of Oklahoma

University of Oklahoma Foundation ($49,922) see Halliburton Co.

University of Oklahoma Foundation ($115,000) see Kerr Foundation

University of Oklahoma Foundation ($46,795) see Kerr Foundation

University of Oklahoma Foundation ($50,000) see McCormick Foundation, Chauncey and Marion Deering

University of Oklahoma Foundation ($36,575) see Oklahoma Gas & Electric Co.

University of Oklahoma Foundation ($83,800) see Phillips Petroleum Co.

University of Oklahoma Foundation ($63,148) see Phillips Petroleum Co.

University of Oklahoma Foundation ($40,000) see Puterbaugh Foundation

University of Oklahoma Foundation ($230,000) see Sarkeys Foundation

University of Oklahoma Foundation ($18,600) see Sooner Pipe & Supply Corp.

University of Oklahoma Foundation ($10,000) see Webb Educational and Charitable Trust, Torrey H. and Dorothy K.

University of Oklahoma Foundation ($33,334) see Williams Cos.

University of Oklahoma Foundation — College of Business Administration projects ($527,987) see Noble Foundation, Samuel Roberts

University of Oklahoma Health Science Center — to provide funds to purchase books and journals fundamental to the medical library collection and advance computer information ($25,000) see Kerr Foundation, Robert S. and Grayce B.

University of Oklahoma — Petroleum and Geological Engineering ($60,000) see Unocal Corp.

University of Oklahoma School of Meteorology ($37,500) see Kerr Fund, Grayce B.

University of Tulsa ($110,000) see Bernsen Foundation, Grace and Franklin

University of Tulsa — scholarships ($395,371) see Bovaird Foundation, Mervin

University of Tulsa ($53,597) see Campbell Foundation

University of Tulsa ($75,000) see Chapman Charitable Trust, H. A. and Mary K.

University of Tulsa ($10,000) see Cuesta Foundation

University of Tulsa ($25,000) see Fourjay Foundation

University of Tulsa ($250,000) see Sarkeys Foundation

University of Tulsa/Environmental Engineering ($50,000) see Bovaird Foundation, Mervin

University of Tulsa Foundation ($15,000) see Cuesta Foundation

University of Tulsa Foundation ($66,100) see Phillips Petroleum Co.

Variety Health Center ($25,000) see Kerr Fund, Grayce B.

Washington County Association for Retarded Citizens — assist purchase of group home ($40,000) see Lyon Foundation

Washington/Nowata County Outreach Nutrition — purchase and install freezer ($15,000) see Lyon Foundation

Wentworth Institute of Technology ($3,990) see Young Foundation, R. A.

Western Kay Literacy Council ($1,500) see Beatty Trust, Cordelia Lunceford

Westminister Day School ($150,000) see Kerr Foundation, Robert S. and Grayce B.

Westminister Church ($13,500) see American Fidelity Corp.

William K. Warren Medical Research Center ($5,000,000) see Warren Foundation, William K.

Woods County Commission, District #2 ($35,000) see Share Trust, Charles Morton

Work Activity Center ($25,000) see Parman Foundation, Robert A.

World Neighbors — support family planning activities ($12,500) see Brush Foundation

World Neighbors ($35,000) see General Service Foundation

World Neighbors ($60,000) see Martin Foundation

World Neighbors ($25,000) see West Foundation

Wright Christian Academy ($15,000) see Titus Foundation, C. W.

YMCA ($25,000) see Harris Foundation

YMCA ($12,500) see Merrick Foundation

YMCA ($12,000) see Merrick Foundation

YMCA ($10,000) see Oklahoma Foundation

YMCA ($25,000) see Titus Foundation, C. W.

YMCA ($27,500) see Williams Cos.

YMCA ($50,000) see Wood Charitable Trust, W. P.

YMCA ($25,453) see Young Foundation, R. A.

YMCA, Metro Tulsa ($15,000) see Occidental Oil & Gas Corp.

Youth and Family Center ($50,000) see Wood Charitable Trust, W. P.

YWCA ($20,000) see Oklahoman Foundation

Oregon

Ainsworth School ($5,000) see McCrea Foundation

Albina Ministerial Alliance — neighborhood connections ($10,000) see Templeton Foundation, Herbert A.

American Heart Association ($1,000) see Corvallis Clinic

American Hellenic Educational Center ($10,000) see Pappas Charitable Foundation, Bessie

American Red Cross ($500) see Pioneer Trust Bank, NA

Oregon (cont.)

Archdiocese of Portland ($36,000) see Frank Family Foundation, A. J.

Art in Public Places ($25,000) see Bend Millwork Systems

Assistance League of Eugene — towards the Operation School Bell Program ($10,000) see Barker Foundation, Donald R.

Assistance League of Salem ($1,200) see Pioneer Trust Bank, NA

Augustana Lutheran Church — peer support network ($10,000) see Templeton Foundation, Herbert A.

B'nai B'rith Summer Camp ($6,000) see Friendly Rosenthal Foundation

Battered Person's Advocacy ($5,000) see Hunt Charitable Trust, C. Giles

Beaverton School District #48 — home-school project ($10,000) see Templeton Foundation, Herbert A.

Beaverton United School District ($6,000) see Brenner Foundation, Mervyn

Bend, Lapine School District — teaching awards ($23,000) see Bend Millwork Systems

Bend Metro Parks and Recreation District — McKay House ($22,705) see Bend Millwork Systems

Benton Hospice ($1,500) see Corvallis Clinic

Black United Fund ($5,000) see Portland General Electric Co.

Boy Scouts of America ($10,000) see Higgins Charitable Trust, Lorene Sails

Boy Scouts of America ($5,000) see Templeton Foundation, Herbert A.

Boy Scouts of America ($12,500) see Wessinger Foundation

Boy Scouts of America ($5,474) see Woodard Family Foundation

Boy Scouts of America, Columbia Pacific Council — Butte Creek Cub Scout Camp ($200,000) see Collins Foundation

Boy Scouts of America — Columbia Pacific Council; to develop a Cub Scout camp at Scouter's Mountain ($500,000) see Meyer Memorial Trust

Boyle Endowment School ($2,500) see Bend Millwork Systems

Boys and Girls Aid Society ($10,000) see Clark Foundation

Boys and Girls Aid Society ($20,000) see Wessinger Foundation

Boys and Girls Aid Society of Oregon ($5,000) see McCrea Foundation

Boys and Girls Club of Lebanon ($30,000) see Georgia-Pacific Corp.

Boys and Girls Club, Salem, OR ($30,000) see Boise Cascade Corp.

Catholic Near East Welfare Association ($16,740) see Abraham Foundation, Anthony R.

Catlin Gabel School ($10,000) see Clark Foundation

Catlin Gable School ($25,000) see Wessinger Foundation

Chemeketa Foundation ($16,081) see Higgins Charitable Trust, Lorene Sails

Circle of Life Educational ($3,000) see Friendly Rosenthal Foundation

City of Klamath Falls — Foreign Trade Zone application ($28,700) see JELD-WEN, Inc.

Coalition for Kids ($19,100) see Carpenter Foundation

COCC Foundation ($5,000) see Bend Millwork Systems

Columbia Christian College ($2,500) see Stephens Foundation Trust

Columbia River Maritime Museum ($5,000) see Wessinger Foundation

Committed Partners for Youth — to be used for operating support for the Challenge Course ($15,000) see Barker Foundation, Donald R.

Community Health Center ($13,500) see Carpenter Foundation

Community Outreach ($1,000) see Corvallis Clinic

Community Theatre ($10,000) see Bend Millwork Systems

Concordia College — new science education facilities ($500,000) see Murdock Charitable Trust, M. J.

Confederated Tribes of the Umatilla Indian Reservation — for the construction of the Umatilla Indian Reservation Interpretive Institute ($500,000) see Meyer Memorial Trust

Crater High School ($14,000) see Carpenter Foundation

DePaul Center ($8,000) see Wheeler Foundation

Deschutes Citizens ($2,000) see Bend Millwork Systems

Dogs for the Deaf, Central Point, OR see SAFECO Corp.

Ecotrust Conservation International ($25,000) see Mead Foundation, Giles W. and Elise G.

Ecumenical Ministries of Oregon ($5,000) see Templeton Foundation, Herbert A.

Emanuel Medical Center Foundation ($15,000) see Jackson Foundation

Emanuel Medical Center Foundation — LINAC Photon Scalpel ($100,000) see Collins Foundation

Emerald Kidsports — second installment of 3-year pledge for "Wellness in Sports" program ($9,750) see Barker Foundation, Donald R.

Eugene Mission — finance phase 11 of building expansion ($75,000) see Cord Foundation, E. L.

First Church of Christ, Scientist ($11,391) see Higgins Charitable Trust, Lorene Sails

First Presbyterian Church ($1,025) see Woodard Family Foundation

Fish ($1,000) see Corvallis Clinic

Friendly House — Community Center ($100,000) see Collins Foundation

Friends of Pioneer Cemetery ($1,000) see Pioneer Trust Bank, NA

Friends of Zoo ($10,000) see Mentor Graphics

George Fox College ($20,000) see Higgins Charitable Trust, Lorene Sails

George Fox College ($10,000) see Jackson Foundation

George Fox College — to construct a new science building ($500,000) see Meyer Memorial Trust

George Fox College — new science building ($1,500,000) see Murdock Charitable Trust, M. J.

George Fox College ($14,000) see Wheeler Foundation

Gilbert House Children Museum ($1,000) see Pioneer Trust Bank, NA

Good Samaritan Foundation — net income from this trust is to be paid quarterly to be used to support the hospital's nursing education program and for acquisition of medical equipment ($583,247) see Peterson Memorial Fund, Chris and Mary L.

Good Samaritan Hospital ($100,000) see Autzen Foundation

Good Samaritan Hospital ($3,334) see Corvallis Clinic

Good Samaritan Hospital ($16,338) see Failing Fund, Henry

Good Samaritan Hospital ($25,000) see Zlinkoff Fund for Medical Research and Education, Sergei S.

Grace Center ($1,500) see Corvallis Clinic

The Grotto ($50,000) see Louisiana Land & Exploration Co.

The Grotto ($50,000) see Louisiana-Pacific Corp.

Habitat for Humanity ($10,000) see Bend Millwork Systems

Heart Institute at St. Vincent Hospital ($100,000) see Louisiana Land & Exploration Co.

Heart Institute at St. Vincent Hospital ($100,000) see Louisiana-Pacific Corp.

High Desert Museum — building construction and general operating support ($311,800) see Chiles Foundation

High Desert Museum ($25,000) see Higgins Charitable Trust, Lorene Sails

High Desert Museum ($30,000) see Louisiana Land & Exploration Co.

High Desert Museum ($30,000) see Louisiana-Pacific Corp.

HIV Day Center Ecumenical ($20,000) see Greenville Foundation

Home Gardening Project ($5,000) see Autzen Foundation

House of Umoja ($100,000) see Nike Inc.

I Have A Dream — for at-risk, low-income children of Martin Luther King Elementary School in Northeast Portland ($50,000) see Challenge Foundation

Integral Youth Services — purchase of permanent building ($20,000) see JELD-WEN, Inc.

Jerome D. Gregoire Scholarship ($10,000) see ITT Rayonier

Jesuit High School ($25,000) see Autzen Foundation

Jesuit High School ($8,000) see Wheeler Foundation

Jewish Family and Children's Services ($25,000) see Friendly Rosenthal Foundation

Jewish Federation ($7,000) see Friendly Rosenthal Foundation

KBPS ($10,000) see Higgins Charitable Trust, Lorene Sails

Klamath Kid Center — mortgage payment ($15,000) see JELD-WEN, Inc.

Lambert House Adult Care ($2,000) see Friendly Rosenthal Foundation

Lewis and Clark College — scholarships ($30,000) see Tucker Charitable Trust, Rose E.

Lewis and Clark College — student scholarships ($25,000) see Tucker Charitable Trust, Rose E.

Lewis and Clark College ($12,500) see Wessinger Foundation

Lewis and Clark College ($9,000) see Wheeler Foundation

Lewis and Clark College ($20,000) see Woodard Family Foundation

Linfield College ($13,750) see Day Foundation, Willametta K.

Linfield College ($25,000) see Gilmore Foundation, William G.

Linfield College — health/PE complex ($230,000) see Roseburg Forest Products Co.

Linfield College — for the renovation of Riley Hall, the campus center ($875,000) see Meyer Memorial Trust

Linfield College — renovation of Riley Hall ($15,000) see Tucker Charitable Trust, Rose E.

Linfield President's Discrete Fund ($15,000) see Ford Foundation, Kenneth W.

Low Income Families Emergency Center — to help clothing recovery center and to produce a video promoting center's mission ($30,000) see Challenge Foundation

Marylhurst College ($20,205) see First Interstate Bank of Oregon

Marylhurst College ($15,000) see Wheeler Foundation

Marylhurst College — science equipment ($73,000) see Wiegand Foundation, E. L.

Marylhurst College — Student Services project ($400,000) see Collins Foundation

Mercy Corps International ($2,500) see S.G. Foundation

Mid-Columbia Health Foundation — Planetree Health Resource Center ($35,000) see Hearst Foundation

Mid Valley Children's Guild ($1,000) see Pioneer Trust Bank, NA

Middle Oregon Historical Society ($5,000) see Portland General Electric Co.

Mighty Oaks ($1,000) see Corvallis Clinic

Mittleman Jewish Community Center ($23,500) see Friendly Rosenthal Foundation

Mobility International ($12,000) see Ferkauf Foundation, Eugene and Estelle

Mother Church ($15,000) see Higgins Charitable Trust, Lorene Sails

Mount Angel Abbey ($10,000) see Frank Family Foundation, A. J.

Multnomah County Department of Human Resources

($14,475) see Collins Medical Trust

Multnomah County Library — to purchase books about Japan (in honor of opening a Portland office) ($5,000) see Bank of Tokyo Trust Co.

Multnomah County Public Library ($34,717) see Failing Fund, Henry

National Business Education Alliance ($20,910) see Mercantile Bancorp

National Environmental Education Development ($30,000) see Woodard Family Foundation

Nature Conservancy ($25,000) see Carpenter Foundation

Nature Conservancy ($10,000) see Wessinger Foundation

North UMPQUA Bible Fellowship ($45,000) see Caddock Foundation

Old Mill School ($4,000) see Corvallis Clinic

OMSI ($35,000) see Mentor Graphics

OMSI ($5,000) see OCRI Foundation

OMSI — new complex ($150,000) see Roseburg Forest Products Co.

1000 Friends of Oregon — open space ($100,000) see Bullitt Foundation

One Thousand Friends of Oregon — computer system ($25,000) see Tucker Charitable Trust, Rose E.

1000 Friends of Oregon — to partially fund a land use/transportation project that would find alternatives to the Western Bypass Freeway plan for Portland and apply the lessons nationally ($160,000) see Surdna Foundation

Oregon Acupuncture Association — general fund ($4,000) see Stott Foundation, Louis L.

Oregon Art Institute ($16,338) see Failing Fund, Henry

Oregon Aviation Museum ($2,000) see Woodard Family Foundation

Oregon Ballet Theatre ($25,000) see Louisiana Land & Exploration Co.

Oregon Ballet Theatre ($25,000) see Louisiana-Pacific Corp.

Oregon Ballet Theatre ($10,000) see Mentor Graphics

Oregon Coast Aquarium ($10,000) see Autzen Foundation

Oregon Coast Aquarium ($25,000) see Gilmore Foundation, William G.

Oregon Community Foundation ($100,000) see Woodard Family Foundation

Oregon Environmental Council ($58,105) see Harder Foundation

Oregon Environmental Council — clean air project ($20,000) see True North Foundation

Oregon Episcopal School ($16,338) see Failing Fund, Henry

Oregon Graduate Institute ($24,000) see Clark Foundation

Oregon Graduate Institute of Science and Technology ($10,000) see Jackson Foundation

Oregon Graduate Institute of Science and Technology — Biochemical Technology Center ($100,000) see Collins Foundation

Oregon Health Sciences University ($92,500) see Burroughs Wellcome Co.

Oregon Health Sciences University ($25,000) see Higgins Charitable Trust, Lorene Sails

Oregon Health Sciences University — for audio-visual telecommunications equipment to broadcast educational programs to nursing students ($536,000) see Meyer Memorial Trust

Oregon Health Sciences University Foundation ($12,500) see Collins Medical Trust

Oregon Health Sciences University Foundation — Dr. Lester T. Jones Chair Department of Ophthalmology ($100,000) see Collins Foundation

Oregon Historical Society ($10,000) see Clark Foundation

Oregon Historical Society ($17,500) see Wheeler Foundation

Oregon Independent College Foundation — for operating support at the eight member colleges ($10,000) see Barker Foundation, Donald R.

Oregon Independent College Foundation ($85,000) see First Interstate Bank of Oregon

Oregon Independent College Foundation ($4,500) see General Accident Insurance Co. of America

Oregon Independent College Foundation ($50,000) see Marriott Foundation, J. Willard

Oregon Independent College Foundation — for operating support at the eight member colleges ($5,000) see Mentor Graphics

Oregon Independent College Foundation ($46,000) see PacifiCorp

Oregon Independent College Foundation ($78,600) see Portland General Electric Co.

Oregon Independent College Foundation ($100,000) see Roseburg Forest Products Co.

Oregon Independent College Foundation ($80,000) see Tektronix

Oregon Independent College Fund see Nike Inc.

Oregon Independent Colleges Foundation ($25,000) see Ford Foundation, Kenneth W.

Oregon Independent Colleges Foundation ($4,000) see Woodard Family Foundation

Oregon Legal Services — for a matching grant to raise funds from Oregon attorneys for legal aid services ($750,000) see Meyer Memorial Trust

Oregon Museum of Science and Industries ($105,000) see Louisiana Land & Exploration Co.

Oregon Museum of Science and Industries ($105,000) see Louisiana-Pacific Corp.

Oregon Museum of Science and Industry ($20,000) see Clark Foundation

Oregon Museum of Science and Industry see Corroon & Black of Oregon

Oregon Museum of Science and Industry ($22,750) see First Interstate Bank of Oregon

Oregon Museum of Science and Industry ($25,000) see

Gilmore Foundation, William G.

Oregon Museum of Science and Industry see Key Bank of Oregon

Oregon Museum of Science and Industry ($25,000) see Northwest Publishing Co. — Portland

Oregon Museum of Science and Industry ($25,000) see Portland Food Products Co.

Oregon Museum of Science and Industry ($100,000) see Precision Castparts Corp.

Oregon Museum of Science and Industry ($20,000) see Seafirst Corp.

Oregon Museum of Science and Industry ($45,000) see Tektronix

Oregon Museum of Science and Industry ($25,000) see Tektronix

Oregon Museum of Science and Industry ($6,500) see Templeton Foundation, Herbert A.

Oregon Museum of Science and Industry — capital campaign ($15,000) see Tucker Charitable Trust, Rose E.

Oregon Museum of Science and Industry see United Grocers, Inc.

Oregon Museum of Science and Industry ($15,000) see Wessinger Foundation

Oregon Museum of Science and Industry ($30,000) see Wollenberg Foundation

Oregon Museum of Science and Industry — construct Early Childhood Center at new OMSI location ($150,000) see Collins Foundation

Oregon Museum of Science and Industry — purchase equipment and refurbish facilities for Spaceflight Academy ($29,250) see Cheney Foundation, Ben B.

Oregon Natural Resource Council — general support for Concerned Citizens for Responsible Mining and their work on the issue of cyanide heap leach mining ($15,000) see Levinson Foundation, Max and Anna

Oregon Natural Resources Council — support for Endangered Salmon, Eastside Ancient Forests campaigns ($17,000) see Levinson Foundation, Max and Anna

Oregon Public Broadcasting ($34,000) see First Interstate Bank of Oregon

Oregon Public Broadcasting ($15,000) see Mentor Graphics

Oregon Public Broadcasting ($6,500) see OCRI Foundation

Oregon Public Broadcasting ($1,000) see Pioneer Trust Bank, NA

Oregon Public Broadcasting ($2,000) see Wyss Foundation

Oregon Rivers Council — towards start-up costs for the McKenzie Watershed Council ($10,000) see Barker Foundation, Donald R.

Oregon Shakespeare Festival ($22,500) see Carpenter Foundation

Oregon Shakespeare Festival ($12,500) see Carpenter Foundation

Oregon Shakespeare Festival ($5,000) see Dalton Foundation, Harry L.

Oregon Shakespeare Festival — capital campaign ($15,000) see Montgomery Street Foundation

Oregon Shakespeare Festival ($10,000) see Portland General Electric Co.

Oregon Shakespeare Festival ($25,000) see Wessinger Foundation

Oregon Shakespeare Festival ($25,000) see Portland Food Products Co.

Oregon Shakespeare Festival — to underwrite production of Shakespeare's Cymbeline to be presented at the 1993 Festival ($25,000) see Skaggs Foundation, L. J. and Mary C.

Oregon Shakespearean Association see US Bancorp

Oregon State University ($10,000) see Associated Foundations

Oregon State University ($58,100) see Autzen Foundation

Oregon State University ($12,500) see Blount

Oregon State University ($12,500) see Blount

Oregon State University ($3,750) see CENEX

Oregon State University ($25,000) see Clark Foundation

Oregon State University ($13,000) see Harvest States Cooperative

Oregon State University ($5,200) see Mentor Graphics

Oregon State University ($100,000) see Tektronix

Oregon State University ($28,803) see Tektronix

Oregon State University ($250,000) see Valley Foundation, Wayne and Gladys

Oregon State University, Department of Mechanical Engineering ($25,000) see Schlumberger Ltd.

Oregon State University Foundation — accounting development fund ($5,000) see Brenner Foundation, Mervyn

Oregon State University Foundation — academic assistance and equipment ($110,500) see Chiles Foundation

Oregon State University Foundation ($19,097) see First Interstate Bank of Oregon

Oregon State University Foundation ($1,000) see Kuse Foundation, James R.

Oregon State University, School of Pharmacy ($5,000) see Long Foundation, J.M.

Oregon Symphony ($10,000) see Higgins Charitable Trust, Lorene Sails

Oregon Symphony Association ($132,500) see Chiles Foundation

Oregon Symphony Association ($10,000) see Mentor Graphics

Oregon Symphony Association ($5,000) see Portland General Electric Co.

Oregon Trail Foundation ($5,000) see Portland General Electric Co.

Our New Beginnings ($2,000) see Friendly Rosenthal Foundation

Outside In — support for teen parents education and pregnancy programs for homeless youth in Portland ($20,390) see Challenge Foundation

Own Town Clinic ($3,000) see Friendly Rosenthal Foundation

Pacific Institute for Natural Sciences — for the development of a new natural history museum ($1,000,000) see Meyer Memorial Trust

Pacific University ($25,000) see Wessinger Foundation

Pacific University — Science Education Center ($200,000) see Collins Foundation

Parry Center for Children ($16,338) see Failing Fund, Henry

Parry Center for Children — for the Imani Women's Support Project ($30,000) see Challenge Foundation

Phoenix School ($17,000) see Ford Foundation, Kenneth W.

Phoenix School — operating funds ($20,000) see Roseburg Forest Products Co.

Phoenix School of Roseburg ($10,000) see Hunt Charitable Trust, C. Giles

Portland Center ($23,483) see Gunderson Trust, Helen Paulson

Portland Children's Museum ($7,600) see Woodard Family Foundation

Portland Opera ($50,000) see Buck Foundation, Carol Franc

Portland Opera Association ($10,000) see Jackson Foundation

Portland State University ($7,000) see Autzen Foundation

Portland State University ($45,000) see Higgins Charitable Trust, Lorene Sails

Portland State University ($8,125) see Mentor Graphics

Portland State University ($141,200) see Tektronix

Portland State University ($96,182) see Tektronix

Portland State University — honors program and faculty development ($29,000) see Tucker Charitable Trust, Rose E.

Portland State University Foundation ($5,000) see Portland General Electric Co.

Portland State University Foundation ($30,000) see Tektronix

Project Literacy Umpqua Region ($5,000) see Hunt Charitable Trust, C. Giles

Providence Hospital — assist in equipping a cardiac catheterization lab ($50,000) see Cheney Foundation, Ben B.

Providence Medical Foundation — general building construction ($216,900) see Chiles Foundation

Providence Milwaukee Hospital — angiodynograph system ($85,000) see Wiegand Foundation, E. L.

Raphael House ($1,500) see Wasserman Foundation, George

Redmond City Pledge ($5,000) see Bend Millwork Systems

Reed College ($10,000) see Roth Family Foundation

Reed College — new science building, Hewlitt Foundation Challenge, endowment, and annual fund ($650,000) see Wollenberg Foundation

Reed College — for the construction of a new state-of-the-art chemistry building ($1,000,000) see Meyer Memorial Trust

Reed Institute DBA Reed College — new chemistry building ($500,000) see Murdock Charitable Trust, M. J.

Robinson Jewish Home ($30,000) see Friendly Rosenthal Foundation

Safari Game Search Foundation ($7,500) see Hunt Charitable Trust, C. Giles

Safe Haven Home — assist in meeting ($25,000) see Roseburg Forest Products Co.

St. Francis Conference ($1,000) see Pioneer Trust Bank, NA

St. Mary's Academy of Portland — for building restoration ($1,500,000) see Meyer Memorial Trust

St. Patrick's Church ($6,000) see Autzen Foundation

St. Vincent ($40,000) see Tektronix

St. Vincent Hospital ($16,338) see Failing Fund, Henry

St. Vincent Medical Foundation ($119,000) see Chiles Foundation

St. Vincent Medical Foundation — capital campaign to expand medical facilities ($20,000) see Montgomery Street Foundation

St. Vincent Medical Foundation — center of Excellence in Laser Medicine and Surgery ($200,000) see Collins Foundation

Salmon and Trout Enhancement Program, OR ($25,000) see Boise Cascade Corp.

Salvation Army ($6,000) see Ford Foundation, Kenneth W.

Salvation Army ($6,000) see Templeton Foundation, Herbert A.

Salvation Army ($20,000) see Wessinger Foundation

Saturday Academy — to expand outreach ($50,000) see Challenge Foundation

Self Enhancement (AMA) — for a SEI counselor ($30,000) see Challenge Foundation

Shakespeare Festival of Oregon ($3,250) see Farallon Foundation

Shangri-La Corporation ($1,000) see Todd Co., A.M.

Shriners Hospital for Crippled Children ($10,000) see Barker Foundation, Donald R.

Sisters of Holy Names of Jesus and Mary ($12,000) see Wheeler Foundation

Sisters of St. Mary ($10,000) see Frank Family Foundation, A. J.

SOSC ($20,000) see Carpenter Foundation

South Empqua Historical Society ($5,000) see Hunt Charitable Trust, C. Giles

Southern Oregon Public Television ($15,000) see Carpenter Foundation

Sutherlin Park and Recreation ($10,200) see Hunt Charitable Trust, C. Giles

Tel-Med ($1,400) see Corvallis Clinic

Tri-County Youth Services Consortium ($5,000) see Templeton Foundation, Herbert A.

Trinity Episcopal Church ($23,483) see Gunderson Trust, Helen Paulson

Tucker-Maxon Oral School ($23,483) see Gunderson Trust, Helen Paulson

Oregon (cont.)

Tucker-Maxon Oral School — current program ($18,000) see Tucker Charitable Trust, Rose E.

Umpqua Community College ($18,500) see Ford Foundation, Kenneth W.

Umpqua Community College ($6,319) see Hunt Charitable Trust, C. Giles

Umpqua Community College ($75,000) see Roseburg Forest Products Co.

Umpqua Literacy and Life Skills ($5,000) see Hunt Charitable Trust, C. Giles

Umpqua Valley Christian School ($15,643) see Roseburg Forest Products Co.

Union Gospel Mission ($1,000) see Pioneer Trust Bank, NA

United Way ($18,000) see Barker Foundation, Donald R.

United Way ($5,000) see Bend Millwork Systems

United Way ($13,000) see Carpenter Foundation

United Way ($17,000) see Corvallis Clinic

United Way ($25,500) see Ford Foundation, Kenneth W.

United Way ($6,500) see Ford Foundation, Kenneth W.

United Way ($5,500) see Ford Foundation, Kenneth W.

United Way ($22,000) see General Accident Insurance Co. of America

United Way ($18,000) see Heileman Brewing Co., Inc., G.

United Way ($1,500) see Pioneer Trust Bank, NA

United Way ($15,000) see Templeton Foundation, Herbert A.

United Way ($2,750) see Woodard Family Foundation

United Way of the Columbia Willamette ($360,000) see First Interstate Bank of Oregon

United Way of the Columbia-Willamette ($70,125) see PacifiCorp

United Way of the Columbia-Willamette ($52,500) see PacifiCorp

United Way of the Columbia-Willamette ($52,500) see PacifiCorp

United Way of the Columbia-Willamette ($52,500) see PacifiCorp

United Way of the Columbia-Willamette ($52,500) see PacifiCorp

United Way Columbia-Willamette — for annual support ($323,242) see US WEST

United Way of Columbia/Willamette — 1990 campaign ($20,000) see Tucker Charitable Trust, Rose E.

United Way of Douglas County ($29,000) see Roseburg Forest Products Co.

United Way of Klamath Basin ($42,800) see JELD-WEN, Inc.

United Way of Lane County ($25,085) see First Interstate Bank of Oregon

University of Oregon ($16,338) see Failing Fund, Henry

University of Oregon Development Fund — second installment of 3-year pledge for the media room at the Len

Casanova Athletic Center ($11,000) see Barker Foundation, Donald R.

University of Oregon Foundation ($114,600) see Autzen Foundation

University of Oregon Foundation — academic assistance and equipment ($112,000) see Chiles Foundation

University of Oregon Foundation ($19,004) see First Interstate Bank of Oregon

University of Oregon Fund ($500) see Bohemia Inc.

University of Oregon Scholarship Fund ($30,500) see Bohemia Inc.

University of Portland — academic assistance and equipment ($359,450) see Chiles Foundation

University of Portland ($35,000) see Clark Foundation

University of Portland ($4,000) see Frank Family Foundation, A. J.

University of Portland ($302,795) see Louisiana Land & Exploration Co.

University of Portland ($302,795) see Louisiana-Pacific Corp.

University of Portland — for a two-part symposium of education reform ($21,000) see Challenge Foundation

Western Biomedical Research Institute ($112,427) see Hoover, Jr. Foundation, Margaret W. and Herbert

Western Evangelical Seminary — expansion of the Institute for Christian Leadership ($884,500) see Murdock Charitable Trust, M. J.

Western Evangelical Seminary — New Directions in Theological Education ($1,450,000) see Murdock Charitable Trust, M. J.

Willamette University — for instructional technology and library resources that strengthen the university ($1,000,000) see Meyer Memorial Trust

Willamette University ($25,000) see Tucker Charitable Trust, Rose E.

Willamette University — T. W. Collins Legal Center ($300,000) see Collins Foundation

Willamette Valley Law Project/Pineros Y Campesinos Unidos del Noroeste ($30,000) see New World Foundation

Willamette View Manor ($16,338) see Failing Fund, Henry

William Temple House ($2,000) see Friendly Rosenthal Foundation

Winston/Dillard Fire Department ($6,385) see Ford Foundation, Kenneth W.

Winston Training School ($25,000) see Roseburg Forest Products Co.

World Forestry Center ($100,000) see Louisiana Land & Exploration Co.

World Forestry Center ($100,000) see Louisiana-Pacific Corp.

World Forestry Center ($8,000) see Wheeler Foundation

YMCA ($5,000) see Autzen Foundation

YMCA ($15,000) see Carpenter Foundation

YMCA ($8,000) see Ford Foundation, Kenneth W.

YMCA ($5,000) see Hunt Charitable Trust, C. Giles

YMCA School for Homeless Children — to begin a school for pre-kindergarten through elementary aged children of homeless families in Portland ($30,000) see Challenge Foundation

Yoncalla Parks and Recreation ($10,000) see Hunt Charitable Trust, C. Giles

Youth With a Mission ($5,000) see Tell Foundation

YWCA ($2,500) see Pioneer Trust Bank, NA

YWCA ($7,500) see Templeton Foundation, Herbert A.

Pennsylvania

A.C. Chemical People ($250) see Lebanon Mutual Insurance Co.

A Child's Haven ($20,000) see Piedmont Health Care Foundation

Abington Friends School — van purchase ($21,000) see Scholler Foundation

Abington Memorial Hospital ($15,000) see Muller Foundation, C. John and Josephine

Abington Memorial Hospital ($10,000) see Muller Foundation, C. John and Josephine

Abington Memorial Hospital ($30,000) see Roth Foundation

Abington Memorial Hospital ($1,000) see SPS Technologies

Abraxas Foundation ($200,000) see Eden Hall Foundation

Academy of Music ($50,000) see Huston Foundation

Academy of Music ($5,000) see Rittenhouse Foundation

Academy of Music ($5,000) see Tasty Baking Co.

Academy of Music of Philadelphia see Meridian Bancorp

Academy of Natural Science ($50,000) see Arcadia Foundation

Academy of Natural Sciences ($10,000) see Hooper Foundation, Elizabeth S.

Academy of Natural Sciences — for construction of multipurpose building ($750,000) see Kresge Foundation

Academy of Natural Sciences ($50,000) see Marpat Foundation

Academy of Natural Sciences ($25,000) see McLean Contributionship

Academy of Natural Sciences ($25,000) see 1957 Charity Trust

Academy of Natural Sciences ($10,000) see Rouse Co.

Academy of Natural Sciences ($120,000) see Stroud Foundation

Academy of Natural Sciences ($5,500) see Tasty Baking Co.

Academy of Natural Sciences — to support the Ludwick Institute Programs ($35,000) see Ludwick Institute

Academy of Natural Sciences of Philadelphia — for the Courtyard Building, a new educational facility at the academy ($50,000) see Cox Charitable Trust, Jessie B.

Academy of Natural Sciences of Philadelphia — Forest Resource Information System: a database on wood for designers and woodworkers ($200,000) see Jones Foundation, W. Alton

Academy of New Church ($493,526) see Glencairn Foundation

Academy of Vocal Arts ($25,500) see Arronson Foundation

Academy of Vocal Arts ($15,000) see Garrigues Trust, Edwin B.

Academy of Vocal Arts ($45,000) see Superior Tube Co.

ACES ($10,000) see Kunkel Foundation, John Crain

ACORN Housing Corporation — national homeownership counseling program ($100,000) see Federal National Mortgage Assn., Fannie Mae

Action-Housing ($36,250) see Pittsburgh Child Guidance Foundation

ACTION-Housing ($140,000) see Scaife Family Foundation

Adams Memorial Library ($10,000) see Kennametal

Adelphoi ($33,170) see Kennametal

Adelphoi ($50,000) see McKenna Foundation, Katherine Mabis

Adelphoi, Inc. — Latrobe Community Children's Center ($300,000) see Timken Foundation of Canton

Adoption Center of Delaware Valley ($2,000) see Emergency Aid of Pennsylvania Foundation

Agricultural and Industrial Museum ($250) see General Machine Works

Akiba Hebrew Academy ($300) see Conston Corp.

Akiba Hebrew Academy ($13,000) see Premier Dental Products Co.

Akiba Hebrew Hearing ($800) see Pennsylvania Knitted Outerwear Manufacturing Association

Albert Einstein Foundation ($2,000) see Premier Dental Products Co.

Albert Einstein Medical Center Auxiliary ($2,500) see Korman Family Foundation, Hyman

Albert Gallatin School District ($1,575) see Eberly Foundation

Albright College ($25,000) see Wyomissing Foundation

All Saints Unitarian Church ($7,500) see Cassett Foundation, Louis N.

Allegheny Ballet Company ($2,000) see Ballet Makers

Allegheny College ($2,200) see Dynamet, Inc.

Allegheny College ($300,000) see Eden Hall Foundation

Allegheny College ($50,000) see Phillips Charitable Trust, Dr. and Mrs. Arthur William

Allegheny College ($21,000) see Tippens Foundation

Allegheny Conference on Community Development ($15,000) see Aristech Chemical Corp.

Allegheny Conference of Community Development ($20,000) see Chambers Development Co.

Allegheny Conference on Community Development ($22,000) see Giant Eagle

Allegheny Conference on Community Development — towards continuing operations and programs ($25,000) see Hillman Foundation, Henry L.

Allegheny Conference of Community Development ($20,000) see Mine Safety Appliances Co.

Allegheny Conference on Community Development ($30,000) see Pittsburgh National Bank

Allegheny County Bar Foundation — for computer hardware/software for its pro bono legal services program see USX Corp.

Allegheny Foundation ($1,000) see Copperweld Corp.

Allegheny Health Services ($15,000) see Snyder Charitable Fund, W. P.

Allegheny Health Services, Mobile Mammogram Unit ($50,000) see PPG Industries

Allegheny Mountain Health Systems ($25,000) see Justus Trust, Edith C.

Allegheny Mountain Health Systems ($25,000) see Phillips Charitable Trust, Dr. and Mrs. Arthur William

Allegheny Trails Council ($20,000) see Allegheny Ludlum Corp.

Allegheny Trails Council ($5,000) see Pitt-Des Moines Inc.

Allegheny Trails Council ($25,000) see Tippens Foundation

Allegheny Valley Hospital ($30,000) see Allegheny Ludlum Corp.

Allegheny Valley School ($60,000) see Jennings Foundation, Mary Hillman

Allegheny Valley School ($100,000) see Polk Foundation

Allegheny Valley School ($60,000) see Polk Foundation

Allegheny West Foundation — summer career exploration program for disadvantaged students ($7,250) see Hunt Manufacturing Co.

Allentown Art Museum see Meridian Bancorp

Allentown Art Museum — to provide exhibits entitled America Worked Representing 1990 ($20,000) see Rider-Pool Foundation

Allentown College — to provide funding for a scholars program for nursing students ($10,000) see Rider-Pool Foundation

Allentown College — scholarship aid ($50,000) see Trexler Trust, Harry C.

Allentown Public Library — debt reduction ($70,000) see Trexler Trust, Harry C.

Allentown School District — to provide funding for the mini grant program ($59,401) see Rider-Pool Foundation

Allied Jewish Appeal ($14,500) see Strouse, Greenberg & Co.

Alpha House — for the re-entry program ($26,000) see Staunton Farm Foundation

ALS and Neuromuscular Research Center ($34,594) see Hedco Foundation

ALS and Neuromuscular Research Center ($30,000) see Hedco Foundation

ALS and Neuromuscular Research Center ($30,000) see Hedco Foundation

ALS and Neuromuscular Research Center ($100,000) see Muller Foundation, C. John and Josephine

ALS and Neuromuscular Research Center ($2,500) see Muller Foundation, C. John and Josephine

Alvernia College see Meridian Bancorp

Alzheimer's Association of Greater Philadelphia — research support ($100,000) see Independence Foundation

Alzheimer's Disease and Related Disorders Association ($5,000) see Cassett Foundation, Louis N.

Alzheimer's Disease and Related Disorders Association ($1,000) see Millstein Charitable Foundation

Alzheimer's Disease and Related Disorders Association ($3,000) see Patterson Charitable Fund, W. I.

American Association of Botanic Gardens and Arboreta — payroll ($20,300) see Smith Horticultural Trust, Stanley

American Baptist ($100,000) see American Financial Corp.

American Cancer Society ($15,000) see Clapp Charitable and Educational Trust, George H.

American Cancer Society ($135) see Conston Corp.

American Cancer Society ($1,000) see Freeport Brick Co.

American Cancer Society ($100) see General Machine Works

American Cancer Society ($556) see Goodall Rubber Co.

American Cancer Society ($300) see Kellmer Co., Jack

American Cancer Society ($8,000) see Sheppard Foundation, Lawrence B.

American College ($75,000) see Travelers Cos.

American College — ACE Program ($36,600) see Mutual of New York

American College, Bryn Mawr, PA ($10,000) see General American Life Insurance Co.

American College of Physicians ($3,658) see Rosenthal Foundation, Richard and Hinda

American College of Physicians — enhancing the physician's role in patient-centered care, phase two ($362,500) see Commonwealth Fund

American Diabetes Association ($250) see Ormet Corp.

American Field Service ($2,000) see Federated Life Insurance Co.

American Friends ($100,000) see Belfer Foundation

American Friends Service Committee — annual fund drive ($35,000) see Baird Foundation, Cameron

American Friends Service Committee ($3,500) see G.A.G. Charitable Corporation

American Friends Service Committee ($15,000) see Horncrest Foundation

American Friends Service Committee ($5,000) see Knox Family Foundation

American Friends Service Committee ($10,000) see McCutchen Foundation

American Friends Service Committee ($78,666) see Reynolds Foundation, Christopher

American Heart Association ($5,000) see Alco Standard Corp.

American Heart Association ($5,000) see McCormick Trust, Anne

American Heart Association ($10,000) see Phillips Charitable Trust, Dr. and Mrs. Arthur William

American Heart Association ($5,000) see Wildermuth Foundation, E. F.

American Heart Association ($20,000) see Wood-Claeyssens Foundation

American Institute for Voice and Ear Research ($195,000) see Oberkotter Family Foundation

American Ireland Fund ($5,000) see Perini Corp.

American Jewish Committee ($100) see Klein Charitable Foundation, Raymond

American Philosophical Society ($60,000) see Watson Foundation, Thomas J.

American Red Cross ($2,500) see Asplundh Foundation

American Red Cross ($1,000) see McCormick Trust, Anne

American Red Cross ($7,946) see Piedmont Health Care Foundation

American Red Cross ($7,000) see Sheppard Foundation, Lawrence B.

American Red Cross ($1,000) see SPS Technologies

American Red Cross ($10,000) see Tippens Foundation

American Red Cross ($15,000) see Wells Foundation, Franklin H. and Ruth L.

American Red Cross-Lehigh Valley Chapter — capital campaign ($25,000) see Air Products & Chemicals

American Rescue Workers ($22,500) see Plankenhorn Foundation, Harry

American Swedish Historical Museum ($35,000) see Arronson Foundation

Andrew Kaul Memorial Hospital — unrestricted ($27,280) see Stackpole-Hall Foundation

Annenberg Center for Communication Arts and Sciences —Japanese kite-making workshop at International Children's Festival. ($3,500) see Subaru of America Inc.

Annie Haalenbake Ross Library — operating expenses ($5,000) see Piper Foundation

Annville Free Library ($5,000) see Lebanon Mutual Insurance Co.

Anti-Defamation League of B'nai B'rith see Meridian Bancorp

Apfelbaum-Fisher Periodontal Associates ($2,900) see Hambay Foundation, James T.

ARC Allegheny County ($209,000) see Trees Charitable Trust, Edith L.

ARC Allegheny County ($30,000) see Weisbrod Foundation Trust Dept., Robert and Mary

ARC Allegheny Foundation ($35,000) see Massey Charitable Trust

ARC Westmoreland Chapter ($64,443) see Trees Charitable Trust, Edith L.

Archdiocese of Philadelphia ($1,147,500) see Connelly Foundation

Archdiocese of Philadelphia ($196,755) see Ellis Grant and Scholarship Fund, Charles E.

Archdiocese of Philadelphia ($93,500) see Ellis Grant and Scholarship Fund, Charles E.

Archdiocese of Philadelphia ($75,695) see Ellis Grant and Scholarship Fund, Charles E.

Arden Theater Company ($2,000) see Groome Beatty Trust, Helen D.

Armstrong County Memorial Hospital ($1,000) see Freeport Brick Co.

Arsenal Family and Children's Center — for therapy for emotionally deprived children ($33,000) see Staunton Farm Foundation

Art Association of Harrisburg ($3,000) see McCormick Trust, Anne

ARTREACH see American Express Co.

Arts Council of Erie see International Paper Co.

Ashlands Trusts Helping Hand ($20,000) see Reidler Foundation

Aspira ($4,000) see Douty Foundation

Associated United Way of Pennsylvania and New Jersey ($62,500) see Elf Atochem North America

Associated United Way of Pennsylvania and New Jersey ($62,500) see Elf Atochem North America

Associated United Way of Pennsylvania and New Jersey ($62,500) see Elf Atochem North America

Associated United Ways of Pennsylvania and New Jersey ($500,000) see SmithKline Beecham

Association for Retarded Citizens Allegheny Foundation ($2,500) see Patterson Charitable Fund, W. I.

Association for Retarded Citizens Camp ($1,745) see Hambay Foundation, James T.

Athenaeum of Philadelphia — capital campaign ($100,000) see Barra Foundation

Atwater Kent Museum ($40,000) see Kent-Lucas Foundation

Audubon Society of Western Pennsylvania ($5,000) see Grable Foundation

Aurora Club ($1,000) see Grass Family Foundation

Avington Memorial Hospital, Avington, PA see Rhone-Poulenc Rorer

Bach Choir of Bethlehem ($5,000) see South Branch Foundation

Balch Institute ($1,500) see Rittenhouse Foundation

Baldwin School ($50,000) see Ford Foundation, Edward E.

Ball Pavillion ($12,000) see Roddis Foundation, Hamilton

Ballet Guild of Lehigh Valley ($1,000) see Baker Foundation, Dexter F. and Dorothy H.

BAND ($5,000) see Quaker Hill Foundation

Barnett Transplant Institute ($5,000) see Cassett Foundation, Louis N.

Beaver College ($25,000) see Fourjay Foundation

Beaver College ($66,400) see Rumbaugh Foundation, J. H. and F. H.

Beaver College ($1,025) see SPS Technologies

Beaver College — Kuch Athletic Center ($25,000) see Barra Foundation

Bebashi ($6,000) see Corestates Bank

Beech Corporation — to support the non-business activities of the Cecil B. Moore Avenue Business Association ($2,723,000) see Penn Foundation, William

Berean Educational Advisory Council ($5,000) see Fox Foundation, Richard J.

Berks Community Television ($4,000) see Oberlaender Foundation, Gustav

Berks Festival ($15,000) see Carpenter Technology Corp.

Berks Teen Talk Line ($1,000) see Penn Savings Bank, a division of Sovereign Bank Bank of Princeton, a division of Sovereign Bank

Beth Hamedresh Synagogue ($2,500) see Morris Charitable Trust, Charles M.

Beth Shalom — program support ($4,000) see United Service Foundation

Beth Shalom Congregation ($8,700) see Federation Foundation of Greater Philadelphia

Beth Shalom Foundation ($50) see Klein Charitable Foundation, Raymond

Bethel Park Historical Society ($10,000) see Knudsen Charitable Foundation, Earl

Bethesda Mission ($10,000) see Harsco Corp.

Betsy Ross House Foundation ($6,800) see Kent-Lucas Foundation

Better Homes — construct 15 rental units for low-income families with children ($25,000) see Grundy Foundation

Better Housing for Chester ($20,000) see Smith Memorial Fund, Ethel Sergeant Clark

Bible Study Hour ($5,000) see C.I.O.S.

Biblical Theological Seminary ($1,000) see Rixson Foundation, Oscar C.

Big Brothers and Big Sisters ($10,000) see Campbell Foundation, Charles Talbot

Big Brothers and Big Sisters ($10,000) see Grable Foundation

Big Brothers and Big Sisters ($5,000) see Knudsen Charitable Foundation, Earl

Big Sisters of Philadelphia ($3,500) see Wurts Memorial, Henrietta Tower

Blind Relief Fund ($5,000) see Tasty Baking Co.

BLOCS ($10,000) see General Accident Insurance Co. of America

Bloomsburg University ($179,385) see Smith Golden Rule Trust Fund, Fred G.

Bloomsburg University — to purchase interactive video, A-V and CAI equipment

($101,332) see Fuld Health Trust, Helene

Blossburg Borough ($5,000) see Packer Foundation, Horace B.

B'nai B'rith ($83) see Kellmer Co., Jack

B'nai Israel Congregation ($5,000) see Steinsapir Family Foundation, Julius L. and Libhie B.

B'nai Israel Synagogue ($2,500) see Morris Charitable Trust, Charles M.

Bob Prince Charities ($15,333) see Dynamet, Inc.

Bonaventure School ($10,000) see Kelley Foundation, Kate M.

Borough of Bristol — construct neighborhood parking lots ($30,000) see Grundy Foundation

Borough of Sligo ($10,000) see Eccles Foundation, Ralph M. and Ella M.

Borough of Wellsboro ($11,500) see Packer Foundation, Horace B.

Borough of Westfield ($5,000) see Packer Foundation, Horace B.

Boy Scouts of America ($72,500) see Bishop Foundation, Vernon and Doris

Boy Scouts of America ($125) see Charitable Fund

Boy Scouts of America ($6,000) see Corestates Bank

Boy Scouts of America ($50,000) see Firestone Foundation, Roger S.

Boy Scouts of America ($27,000) see Mengle Foundation, Glenn and Ruth

Boy Scouts of America ($25,000) see Mengle Foundation, Glenn and Ruth

Boy Scouts of America ($20,000) see Mengle Foundation, Glenn and Ruth

Boy Scouts of America ($10,000) see Safeguard Scientifics Foundation

Boy Scouts of America ($9,341) see Schoonmaker J-Sewkly Valley Hospital Trust

Boy Scouts of America-Bucktail Council — unrestricted ($27,280) see Stackpole-Hall Foundation

Boys Club of America ($5,000) see Steinman Foundation, James Hale

Boys Club of Harrisburg ($10,000) see Hall Foundation

Boys Club of Scranton ($25,672) see Epp Fund B Charitable Trust, Otto C.

Boys and Girls Club ($20,000) see Chesebrough-Pond's

Boys and Girls Club ($10,000) see Crawford Estate, E. R.

Boys and Girls Club ($10,000) see High Foundation

Boys and Girls Club ($5,000) see Kline Foundation, Charles and Figa

Boys and Girls Club ($25,000) see Laurel Foundation

Boys and Girls Club ($40,000) see Miller Charitable Foundation, Howard E. and Nell E.

Boys and Girls Club ($1,750) see Rittenhouse Foundation

Boys and Girls Club ($5,080) see Schautz Foundation, Walter L.

Boys and Girls Club ($5,000) see Williams Foundation, C. K.

Boys Town of Jerusalem ($105,000) see Federation

Pennsylvania (cont.)

Foundation of Greater Philadelphia

Braddock General Hospital ($27,000) see Gibson Foundation, Addison H.

Bradford Area Public Library ($50,000) see Dresser Industries

Bradford Area Public Library ($9,500) see Forest Oil Corp.

Bradford County Regional Arts Center see International Paper Co.

Bradford Hospital ($10,000) see Forest Oil Corp.

Brandywine Conservancy ($200,000) see Carthage Foundation

Brandywine Conservancy — environmental management handbook ($59,000) see Crystal Trust

Brandywine Conservancy — environmental management program ($50,000) see duPont Foundation, Chichester

Brandywine Conservancy ($200,000) see Good Samaritan

Brandywine Conservancy ($15,000) see 1957 Charity Trust

Brandywine Conservancy ($200,000) see Scaife Foundation, Sarah

Brandywine Conservancy — capital campaign ($100,000) see Welfare Foundation

Brandywine Conservancy Brandywine River Museum ($10,000) see Strawbridge Foundation of Pennsylvania I, Margaret Dorrance

Brandywine Conservancy — purchase of N. C. Wyeth painting ($150,000) see Allegheny Foundation

Brandywine Conservancy — Third Decade Fund Campaign ($300,000) see Allegheny Foundation

Brandywine Health Services ($15,000) see Claneil Foundation

Brandywine Museum ($14,670) see Philibosian Foundation, Stephen

Brandywine YMCA ($41,500) see Lukens

Bristol Riverside Theatre — core support operating grant ($50,000) see Grundy Foundation

Brookside Park ($8,140) see York Barbell Co.

BRSI- Beaumont Fund ($25,000) see Lovett Foundation

Bryn Athyn Church of New Jerusalem ($120,000) see Asplundh Foundation

Bryn Athyn Church of New Jerusalem ($33,000) see Asplundh Foundation

Bryn Athyn Church of New Jerusalem ($3,500) see Asplundh Foundation

Bryn Athyn Church of New Jerusalem ($2,500) see Asplundh Foundation

Bryn Athyn Church of New Jerusalem ($100,000) see Glencairn Foundation

Bryn Athyn Fire Company Building Fund ($10,000) see Asplundh Foundation

Bryn Mawr College ($10,000) see Littauer Foundation, Lucius N.

Bryn Mawr College ($5,000) see Memton Fund

Bryn Mawr College see Meridian Bancorp

Bryn Mawr College ($50,000) see Milliken Foundation, Agnes G.

Bryn Mawr College ($250,000) see Neuberger Foundation, Roy R. and Marie S.

Bryn Mawr College ($10,000) see Orchard Corp. of America.

Bryn Mawr College ($295,000) see Schwartz Foundation, Bernard Lee

Bryn Mawr College ($30,000) see Sperry Fund

Bryn Mawr College — for research ($5,000) see Stott Foundation, Louis L.

Bryn Mawr College ($10,000) see Summerfield Foundation, Solon E.

Bryn Mawr College ($10,000) see Warwick Foundation

Bryn Mawr College ($50,000) see Whiting Foundation, Mrs. Giles

Bryn Mawr College — for the Art and Archaeology Library ($100,000) see Mars Foundation

Bryn Mawr Fire Company ($500) see Dietrich Foundation, William B.

Bryn Mawr Hospital ($25,000) see Breyer Foundation

Bryn Mawr Hospital ($25,000) see Breyer Foundation

Bryn Mawr Hospital ($2,500) see Colket Foundation, Ethel D.

Bryn Mawr Hospital — computer equipment ($50,000) see McLean Contributionship

Bryn Mawr Hospital ($90,000) see Superior Tube Co.

Bryn Mawr Hospital Foundation ($200,000) see Hooper Foundation, Elizabeth S.

Bryn Mawr Presbyterian Church ($5,000) see Foerderer Foundation, Percival E. and Ethel Brown

Bryn Mawr Rehabilitation Hospital ($25,000) see 1957 Charity Trust

Bucknell University ($25,000) see Day Foundation, Willametta K.

Bucknell University ($10,000) see Fowler Memorial Foundation, John Edward

Bucknell University ($38,400) see Freas Foundation

Bucknell University ($10,000) see Freas Foundation

Bucknell University ($4,000) see Jephson Educational Trust No. 1

Bucknell University — to purchase an nuclear magnetic resonance spectrometer see Keck Foundation, W. M.

Bucknell University — for construction of chemistry building and renovation of science building ($800,000) see Kresge Foundation

Bucks County Community College Foundation — purchase vocational/technical equipment ($25,000) see Grundy Foundation

Bucks County Conservancy — repairs for ALDIE mansion ($25,000) see Grundy Foundation

Bucks County Historical Society ($10,000) see Warwick Foundation

Bucks County Housing Authority — housing for elderly in Tullytown, PA

($55,000) see Grundy Foundation

Buhl Farm Trust ($150,000) see Charitable Fund

Buhl Farm Trust ($25,000) see Sharon Steel Corp.

Bunker Challenge ($3,000) see Edgewater Steel Corp.

Burgettstown Area School District — renovations to the Burgettstown Community Park ($30,000) see Hillman Foundation, Henry L.

Burn Foundation ($400) see Foote Mineral Co.

Burnside Plantation — developing living history farm ($10,000) see Laros Foundation, R. K.

Business Volunteers for the Arts ($1,000) see Subaru of America Inc.

Butler County Community College ($35,000) see Armco Inc.

Butler Memorial Hospital ($25,000) see Armco Inc.

Byrn Mawr College — scholarship fund ($25,000) see Fohs Foundation

C. E. D.-Eastman School of Music ($1,000) see Eberly Foundation

C.A.R.E. Center ($5,000) see Coen Family Foundation, Charles S. and Mary

California Center ($10,000) see Snee-Reinhardt Charitable Foundation

California University of Pennsylvania Foundation ($1,500) see Eberly Foundation

Calvary Episcopal Church ($20,000) see Love Foundation, George H. and Margaret McClintic

Calvary Episcopal Church — towards $2 million capital campaign ($50,000) see Hillman Foundation, Henry L.

Calvary Episcopal Church — towards the Celebrate 1991 program ($25,000) see Hillman Foundation, Henry L.

Cambria Free Library ($4,000) see Waters Charitable Trust, Robert S.

Camp Hebron — equipment fund ($24,974) see United Service Foundation

Camp Hebron — equipment fund ($18,843) see United Service Foundation

Camp Kiwanis for Underprivileged Children ($5,000) see Plankenhorn Foundation, Harry

Camp Ramah ($20,000) see Beren Foundation, Robert M.

Camp Ramah ($10,000) see Beren Foundation, Robert M.

Camp Ramah in the Poconos ($25,218) see Stern Family Foundation, Harry

Camp Shikellimay YMCA — resident camp ($4,500) see Hambay Foundation, James T.

Camphill Foundation ($4,000) see Schautz Foundation, Walter L.

Camphill Soltane Grant ($250,000) see Watson Foundation, Thomas J.

Cancer Support Network — therapeutic programs for survivors ($3,000) see Patterson Charitable Fund, W. I.

Cancer Support Network ($25,000) see Shore Fund

Canterbury Place ($12,500) see Snyder Charitable Fund, W. P.

Cantor and Ziegler Orthodontic, Ltd. ($5,985) see Hambay Foundation, James T.

Capital Area Health Foundation ($20,000) see AMP

Capital Area Health Foundation ($25,000) see Kunkel Foundation, John Crain

Capital Health Products ($1,275) see Hambay Foundation, James T.

Capitolo Cowboys ($2,000) see Emergency Aid of Pennsylvania Foundation

CARE ($50,000) see Pine Tree Foundation

Carlisle Early Education Center see Meridian Bancorp

Carlisle Hospital — medical care ($1,726) see Hambay Foundation, James T.

Carlow College ($10,000) see Aristech Chemical Corp.

Carlow College ($63,000) see Donnelly Foundation, Mary J.

Carlow College — toward expansion of biology department ($50,000) see Hillman Foundation

The Carnegie ($50,000) see Allegheny Ludlum Corp.

The Carnegie ($300,000) see Aluminum Co. of America

Carnegie ($25,000) see Aristech Chemical Corp.

Carnegie ($50,000) see Berkman Charitable Trust, Allen H. and Selma W.

Carnegie ($1,000) see Edgewater Steel Corp.

Carnegie ($1,000) see Foster Co., L.B.

Carnegie — second century fund ($33,333) see Giant Eagle

The Carnegie — for various projects ($365,000) see Hillman Foundation

The Carnegie — to purchase mineral specimens and gemstones ($64,850) see Hillman Foundation

The Carnegie ($35,000) see Hunt Foundation, Roy A.

The Carnegie ($25,000) see Hunt Foundation, Roy A.

Carnegie ($7,500) see Knudsen Charitable Foundation, Earl

The Carnegie ($50,000) see Mellon Bank Corp.

The Carnegie ($50,000) see Mine Safety Appliances Co.

The Carnegie ($94,750) see Pittsburgh National Bank

The Carnegie — second century fund ($1,000,000) see Scaife Family Foundation

Carnegie ($25,000) see Snee-Reinhardt Charitable Foundation

The Carnegie ($50,000) see Snyder Charitable Fund, W. P.

Carnegie ($10,000) see Tippens Foundation

The Carnegie ($25,000) see Vesuvius Charitable Foundation

Carnegie ($200,000) see Waters Charitable Trust, Robert S.

Carnegie Free Library ($40,000) see Crawford Estate, E. R.

Carnegie Institute ($10,000) see Dynamet, Inc.

Carnegie Institute — capital campaign ($1,500,000) see Heinz Endowment, Howard

Carnegie Institute — for construction of science center ($850,000) see Kresge Foundation

Carnegie Institute — supplement to the Benedum Educational

Resources Endowment to support public educational programs in the Museum of Natural History ($1,000,000) see Benedum Foundation, Claude Worthington

Carnegie Institute — Museum of Art ($105,000) see Hillman Foundation, Henry L.

Carnegie Institute Second Century Fund ($4,000) see Pitt-Des Moines Inc.

Carnegie Library of Homestead — sewer and ramp project - for repair of the sewer system and installation of ramps for handicapped persons ($30,000) see Buhl Foundation

Carnegie Library of Homestead — for renovations see USX Corp.

Carnegie Library of Pittsburgh see Calgon Corp.

Carnegie Library of Pittsburgh see Neville Chemical Co.

Carnegie Mellon University ($200,000) see Aluminum Co. of America

Carnegie-Mellon University ($12,500) see Aristech Chemical Corp.

Carnegie Mellon University — in computer software to assist engineering students to design electronic circuits ($36,000,000) see Cadence Design Systems

Carnegie-Mellon University ($20,000) see Coen Family Foundation, Charles S. and Mary

Carnegie-Mellon University — capital ($125,000) see Consolidated Natural Gas Co.

Carnegie-Mellon University — operating ($125,000) see Consolidated Natural Gas Co.

Carnegie-Mellon University — operating ($100,000) see Consolidated Natural Gas Co.

Carnegie-Mellon University see du Pont de Nemours & Co., E. I.

Carnegie-Mellon University ($60) see Equimark Corp.

Carnegie-Mellon University ($20,000) see First Boston

Carnegie-Mellon University ($20,000) see Fitz-Gibbon Charitable Trust

Carnegie-Mellon University ($26,138) see Graphic Arts Show Co. Inc.

Carnegie-Mellon University ($112,706) see Grobstein Charitable Trust No. 2, Ethel

Carnegie-Mellon University ($100,000) see Hunt Foundation, Roy A.

Carnegie-Mellon University ($50,000) see Hunt Foundation, Roy A.

Carnegie-Mellon University ($50,000) see Hunt Foundation, Roy A.

Carnegie Mellon University — to develop technology to make recycling easier ($1,900,000) see IBM Corp.

Carnegie-Mellon University ($15,000) see Kettering Family Foundation

Carnegie Mellon University see Lubrizol Corp.

Carnegie-Mellon University ($80,000) see Mellon Bank Corp.

Carnegie-Mellon University ($60,000) see Pittsburgh National Bank

Carnegie-Mellon University ($15,000) see Schlumberger Ltd.

Carnegie-Mellon University ($24,500) see Snyder Charitable Fund, W. P.

Carnegie-Mellon University ($11,000) see Speyer Foundation, Alexander C. and Tillie S.

Carnegie-Mellon University ($6,000) see Vesuvius Charitable Foundation

Carnegie-Mellon University — to establish a joint Center for Computational Biology with the University of Pittsburgh see Keck Foundation, W. M.

Carnegie Mellon University — support of the development of the Merck Laboratory for freshman Chemistry ($500,000) see Merck & Co.

Carnegie-Mellon University — University Center ($150,000) see Wean Foundation, Raymond John

Carnegie Museum ($900,000) see Heinz Foundation, Drue

Carnegie Museum ($37,500) see Hopwood Charitable Trust, John M.

Carnegie Museum ($1,500) see Starling Foundation, Dorothy Richard

Carnegie Museum of Art ($11,850) see Speyer Foundation, Alexander C. and Tillie S.

Carnegie — support Powdermill ($37,000) see Laurel Foundation

Carnegie Science Center ($33,000) see Edison Fund, Charles

Carnegie Science Center ($100,000) see PPG Industries

Carnegie Second Century Fund The Carnegie ($100,000) see Jennings Foundation, Mary Hillman

Carnigie Mellon University ($666,000) see Intel Corp.

Caron Foundation ($500) see Lebanon Mutual Insurance Co.

Caron Foundation Capital Fund Campaign ($2,500) see Penn Savings Bank, a division of Sovereign Bank Bank of Princeton, a division of Sovereign Bank

Catholic Charities ($1,000) see Goldman Foundation, William

Catholic Charities ($20,000) see J. D. B. Fund

Catholic Crusade for the Future ($10,000) see Kelley Foundation, Kate M.

Catholic Diocese of Allentown Scholarship Fund ($45,000) see Stabler Foundation, Donald B. and Dorothy L.

Catholic Diocese of Harrisburg Scholarship Fund ($45,000) see Stabler Foundation, Donald B. and Dorothy L.

Catholic Diocese of Pittsburgh ($100,000) see Chambers Development Co.

Catholic Youth Association ($10,000) see Kelley Foundation, Kate M.

CCFA ($100) see Kellmer Co., Jack

Cedar Crest College ($50,000) see Arcadia Foundation

Cedar Crest College ($15,000) see Kline Foundation, Charles and Figa

Cedar Crest College — to provide funding for a pool scholars program for nursing

students ($10,000) see Rider-Pool Foundation

Cedar Crest College — scholarships ($75,000) see Trexler Trust, Harry C.

Celian Heights School ($100,000) see Trees Charitable Trust, Edith L.

Centennial Campaign for Mercersburg ($40,000) see Grumbacher Foundation, M. S.

Center for American Jewish History/Temple University ($12,500) see Philadelphia Industries

Center for Assessment and Policy Development ($6,540,000) see Pew Charitable Trusts

Center for Autistic Children ($6,000) see Binswanger Co.

Center for Early Childhood Services ($4,000) see Wurts Memorial, Henrietta Tower

Center in the Park ($31,705) see Scholler Foundation

Center for Responsible Funding ($3,015) see Quaker Hill Foundation

Central Bucks Family YMCA — acquire a 7.5 acre tract of land adjacent to its present facilities ($50,000) see Grundy Foundation

Central Catholic High School ($10,000) see Kelley Foundation, Kate M.

Central Pennsylvania Business School ($2,500) see Smith Golden Rule Trust Fund, Fred G.

Central Philadelphia Development Corporation ($5,000) see PMA Industries

Chadds Ford Historical Society ($25,000) see Fair Play Foundation

Chambersburg Hospital Health Services ($25,000) see Wood Foundation of Chambersburg, PA

Chapel of Four Chaplains ($400) see Kellmer Co., Jack

Chatham College ($3,615) see McFeely-Rogers Foundation

Chester County Historical Society ($20,000) see Claneil Foundation

Chester Education Foundation ($10,000) see Smith Memorial Fund, Ethel Sergeant Clark

Chester Education Foundation Summer Training and Employment Program see Scott Paper Co.

Chestnut Hill College ($50,000) see McShain Charities, John

Chestnut Hill Historical Society ($3,000) see Groome Beatty Trust, Helen D.

Chestnut Hill Hospital — seminars in cardiology ($5,100) see Kynett Memorial Foundation, Edna G.

Chestnut Hill Hospital ($10,000) see Smith Foundation

Cheyney University ($25,000) see SICO Foundation

Children's Fund ($100) see Action Industries, Inc.

Children's Home of Pittsburgh ($10,000) see Hunt Foundation, Roy A.

Children's Home of Reading see Meridian Bancorp

Children's Home of York ($2,500) see Hall Foundation

Children's Hospital ($15,000) see Snee-Reinhardt Charitable Foundation

Children's Hospital ($1,342) see Spang & Co.

Children's Hospital Foundation ($5,000) see Binswanger Co.

Children's Hospital Foundation ($12,500) see 1957 Charity Trust

Children's Hospital Foundation ($2,500,000) see Pew Charitable Trusts

Children's Hospital Foundation ($6,000) see Strawbridge Foundation of Pennsylvania II, Margaret Dorrance

Children's Hospital Medical Center ($20,000) see Clapp Charitable and Educational Trust, George H.

Children's Hospital Medical Center ($1,000) see Edgewater Steel Corp.

Children's Hospital Medical Center ($20,000) see Firestone Foundation, Roger S.

Children's Hospital Medical Center ($17,000) see Scholler Foundation

Children's Hospital Medical Center ($200,000) see Shore Fund

Children's Hospital Medical Center ($25,000) see Smith Foundation

Children's Hospital of Philadelphia see Amoco Corp.

Children's Hospital of Philadelphia — Evaluation of a Home Based Program for children at Risk for Poor Diabetic Control ($19,864) see Diabetes Research and Education Foundation

Children's Hospital of Pittsburgh ($5,000) see Heileman Brewing Co., Inc., G.

Children's Hospital of Pittsburgh ($20,000) see Mine Safety Appliances Co.

Children's Hospital of Pittsburgh — for the Family Advocate program ($35,000) see Staunton Farm Foundation

Children's House ($4,000) see Maneely Fund

Christian Home ($4,000) see Waters Charitable Trust, Robert S.

Christian and Missionary Alliance Church ($2,000) see Peters Foundation, Charles F.

Christy Park United Methodist ($2,000) see Peters Foundation, Charles F.

Church Farm School ($2,000) see Bishop Foundation, Vernon and Doris

Church Farm School ($1,500) see Dietrich Foundation, William B.

Church Farm School ($10,000) see Strawbridge Foundation of Pennsylvania II, Margaret Dorrance

Church Farm School ($1,000) see Zock Endowment Trust

Church of St. James the Less ($13,000) see Beck Foundation

Church of St. James the Less ($3,000) see Dobson Foundation

Citizens Crime Commission see Berwind Corp.

Citizens Crime Commission of Delaware Valley ($3,000) see SPS Technologies

Citizens Library ($12,500) see Coen Family Foundation, Charles S. and Mary

Citizen's Library ($10,000) see Snee-Reinhardt Charitable Foundation

Citizens Library Association of Western Pennsylvania

($30,000) see Hopwood Charitable Trust, John M.

City of Allentown — improve/extend/maintain parks ($625,811) see Trexler Trust, Harry C.

City of Bethlehem — 250th anniversary ($50,000) see Laros Foundation, R. K.

City of Franklin ($6,500) see Justus Trust, Edith C.

City of Pittsburgh/County of Allegheny/United Way of Allegheny County — summer youth community service project - to provide engaging occupations for young people in Allegheny County ($75,000) see Buhl Foundation

City of Sharon Desquicentennial ($1,000) see Sharon Steel Corp.

City Theatre Company — support for capital campaign ($25,000) see Laurel Foundation

City Theatre Company ($20,000) see Miller Charitable Foundation, Howard E. and Nell E.

City Theatre Company ($14,000) see Snee-Reinhardt Charitable Foundation

City Theatre Company ($25,000) see Weisbrod Foundation Trust Dept., Robert and Mary

City of Warren ($16,420) see Betts Industries

Civic Light Opera ($2,000) see Dynamet, Inc.

Civic Light Opera ($12,000) see Rockwell Foundation

Clairton High School — scholarships see USX Corp.

Clarion University Foundation ($1,265) see Eccles Foundation, Ralph M. and Ella M.

Clarion University Foundation ($100,000) see Phillips Charitable Trust, Dr. and Mrs. Arthur William

Clarion University of Pennsylvania ($20,000) see Wilson Foundation, H. W.

Clarke County Parks and Recreation ($30,000) see Kentland Foundation

Clay Studio ($5,000) see Bartol Foundation, Stockton Rush

Claysburg-Kimmel High School ($65,000) see Dively Foundation, George S.

Clayton Corporation ($1,755,000) see Frick Foundation, Helen Clay

Clayton Corporation ($46,716) see Frick Foundation, Helen Clay

Clearview Terrace II ($10,000) see Sheppard Foundation, Lawrence B.

Cleona Fire Company, No. 1 ($250) see Lebanon Mutual Insurance Co.

Clinton County Historical Society — aviation museum ($3,000) see Piper Foundation

Clinton County United Way — current operating expenses ($10,000) see Piper Foundation

Coalition for Christian Outreach ($15,000) see Finley Charitable Trust, J. B.

Coalition for Christian Outreach ($6,000) see Hulme Charitable Foundation, Milton G.

Coalition for Christian Outreach ($7,500) see Mack Foundation, J. S.

Coalition for Christian Outreach ($40,000) see Miller

Charitable Foundation, Howard E. and Nell E.

Coatesville Day Care Center ($19,071) see Lukens

Coatesville Pediatric Center ($20,000) see Lukens

Coatesville Recreation Department ($26,100) see Lukens

Coatesville Summer Enrichment Program ($88,102) see Lukens

Coatesville YWCA ($51,880) see Lukens

College Misericordia ($5,000) see Sordoni Foundation

College Misericordia — unrestricted ($15,000) see Beck Foundation, Elsie E. & Joseph W.

College Misericordia ($75) see Leesona Corp.

Collegiate Museum of Art ($55,000) see Sordoni Foundation

Colonial Pennsylvania Plantation ($10,000) see Smith Memorial Fund, Ethel Sergeant Clark

Committee for Economic Growth ($5,000) see Sordoni Foundation

Committee of Seventy ($5,000) see Philadelphia Industries

Commonwealth Foundation ($10,000) see Kennametal

Commonwealth Foundation ($25,000) see PMA Industries

Commonwealth Foundation for Public Policy Alternatives ($60,000) see McKenna Foundation, Philip M.

Community Accountants ($20,000) see Fels Fund, Samuel S.

Community Alliance Church ($3,000) see Peters Foundation, Charles F.

Community Arts Center of Cambria County ($2,000) see Glosser Foundation, David A.

Community Care Health Care Services ($5,000) see National Forge Co.

Community College of Allegheny County ($50,000) see Crawford Estate, E. R.

Community General Osteopathic Hospital ($5,000) see Grass Family Foundation

Community Hospital of Lancaster ($7,500) see Crels Foundation

Community Nursing Service of Clinton County — community nursing service for needy persons requiring home health care ($2,500) see Piper Foundation

Community Progress Council ($500) see York Barbell Co.

Community Services of Venango County ($22,000) see Justus Trust, Edith C.

Community Women Foundation Project ($15,000) see Pine Tree Foundation

Community Women's Education Program ($5,000) see Douty Foundation

Conamough Valley Hospital ($4,000) see Waters Charitable Trust, Robert S.

Concordia Evangelical Lutheran Church ($2,000) see Peters Foundation, Charles F.

Conestoga House Foundation ($293,374) see Steinman Foundation, James Hale

Conewange Township Police Department ($2,280) see Betts Industries

Pennsylvania (cont.)

Congregation Adath Jeshurun ($11,014) see Klein Charitable Foundation, Raymond

Congregation Adath Jeshurun ($5,000) see Novotny Charitable Trust, Yetta Deitch

Congregation Adath Jeshurun ($5,475) see Stern Family Foundation, Harry

Congregation Beth Ann Israel ($2,150) see Roth Foundation, Louis T.

Congregation Beth Israel ($3,972) see Caplan Charity Foundation, Julius H.

Congregation Emanu-El Israel ($750) see Millstein Charitable Foundation

Congregation Emanuel ($3,075) see Millstein Charitable Foundation

Congregation Kenseth Israel ($26,500) see Kline Foundation, Charles and Figa

Congregation Or Shalom ($5,000) see Premier Dental Products Co.

Congregation Rodelph Shalom ($5,000) see Cassett Foundation, Louis N.

Congregation Sons of Israel ($18,000) see Kline Foundation, Charles and Figa

Conservancy ($50,000) see Shore Fund

Conservative Baptist Seminary of East ($10,000) see Benfamil Charitable Trust

Consortium for Health Information and Library Sciences ($37,500) see Measey Foundation, Benjamin and Mary Siddons

Contributors to the Pennsylvania Hospital Mill Creek School/The Institute of Pennsylvania Hospital — school for emotionally-disturbed adolescents ($50,000) see van Ameringen Foundation

Cort Center — riding activities for the handicapped ($2,000) see Laros Foundation, R. K.

Council for Court Excellence ($75,000) see Good Samaritan

Council for Public Education ($16,687) see Wells Foundation, Franklin H. and Ruth L.

County of Venango ($4,688) see Justus Trust, Edith C.

Creative Artists Network ($5,000) see Dietrich Foundation, William B.

Crime Prevention Association of Philadelphia ($20,000) see Schwartz and Robert Schwartz Foundation, Bernard

Crisis Addition Recovery and Education Center ($5,100) see Pittsburgh Child Guidance Foundation

Crispus Attacks ($10,000) see Hamilton Bank

Crispus Attucks Association ($33,334) see Grumbacher Foundation, M. S.

Crispus Attucks Association ($1,000) see Motter Printing Press Co.

Crispus Attucks Community Cantor ($10,500) see York Barbell Co.

Cumberland County Coalition for Shelter — Safe Harbour ($17,500) see Wells Foundation, Franklin H. and Ruth L.

Curtis Institute of Music ($65,000) see Garrigues Trust, Edwin B.

Curtis Institute of Music ($3,000) see Jephson Educational Trust No. 1

Curtis Institute of Music ($10,350) see Rock Foundation, Milton and Shirley

Cystic Fibrosis Foundation ($500) see Action Industries, Inc.

Cystic Fibrosis Foundation ($2,500) see Korman Family Foundation, Hyman

Cystic Fibrosis Foundation ($6,000) see Lebovitz Fund

Cystic Fibrosis Foundation ($500) see Safeguard Scientifics Foundation

D. Arron Parkinson's Disease Foundation ($5,000) see Binswanger Co.

D. T. Watson Rehabilitation Services ($75,000) see McCune Charitable Trust, John R.

D.T. Watson Rehabilitation Services ($2,000) see Foster Co., L.B.

D.T. Watson Rehabilitation Services ($50,000) see Massey Charitable Trust

D.T. Watson Rehabilitation Services ($7,500) see Pittsburgh Child Guidance Foundation

D.T. Watson Rehabilitation Services ($20,000) see Weisbrod Foundation Trust Dept., Robert and Mary

David Mahoney Institute of Neurological Sciences ($500,000) see Dana Charitable Trust, Eleanor Naylor

Decision House ($8,784) see Justus Trust, Edith C.

Decision House ($25,000) see Phillips Charitable Trust, Dr. and Mrs. Arthur William

Delandre Community College ($600) see Pennsylvania Knitted Outerwear Manufacturing Association

Delaware Valley Citizens Council for Clean Air ($16,000) see Fels Fund, Samuel S.

Delaware Valley College ($4,000) see Kavanagh Foundation, T. James

Delaware Valley College ($56,000) see Mandell Foundation, Samuel P.

Delco Blind/Sight Center ($25,000) see Smith Memorial Fund, Ethel Sergeant Clark

Delone Catholic High School ($20,000) see Sheppard Foundation, Lawrence B.

DePaul Institute ($10,000) see Kelley Foundation, Kate M.

Devereux Foundation ($250,000) see Delany Charitable Trust, Beatrice P.

Devereux Foundation — general ($250,000) see Delany Charitable Trust, Beatrice P.

Devereux Foundation — general ($250,000) see Delany Charitable Trust, Beatrice P.

Devereux Foundation — general ($250,000) see Delany Charitable Trust, Beatrice P.

Devereux Foundation ($100,000) see Hooper Foundation, Elizabeth S.

Devereux Foundation ($30,000) see Hooper Foundation, Elizabeth S.

Devereux Foundation ($5,000) see Perini Corp.

Dickinson College ($50,000) see Kline Foundation, Josiah W. and Bessie H.

Dickinson College — alpha, beta-dehydropeptides as building blocks for efficient peptide modification ($36,500) see Research Corporation

Dickinson School of Law ($40,000) see Vale Foundation, Ruby R.

Dignity Housing Youth Services ($5,000) see Rosenberg Foundation, Alexis

Diocese of Bethlehem ($75,000) see Payne Foundation, Frank E. and Seba B.

Diocese of Bethlehem ($50,000) see Payne Foundation, Frank E. and Seba B.

Diocese of Greensburg — campaign for secondary schools ($100,000) see Allegheny Foundation

Diocese of Harrisburg ($200,000) see St. Mary's Catholic Foundation

Divine Providence Hospital ($27,000) see Gibson Foundation, Addison H.

Divine Providence Hospital ($1,000) see LamCo. Communications

Dock Woods see Harleysville Mutual Insurance Co.

Domestic Abuse Project of Delaware County ($2,000) see Emergency Aid of Pennsylvania Foundation

Domestic Abuse Project of Delaware County ($3,000) see Groome Beatty Trust, Helen D.

Domestic Abuse Project of Delaware County ($25,000) see Smith Memorial Fund, Ethel Sergeant Clark

Douglass Elementary School ($16,233) see Seybert Institution for Poor Boys and Girls, Adam and Maria Sarah

Doylestown Hospital ($2,500) see SPS Technologies

Doylestown Hospital ($5,000) see Warwick Foundation

Drexel University ($5,900) see Lynch Scholarship Foundation, John B.

Drexel University ($46,849) see Rosenbaum Foundation, Paul and Gabriella

Drexel University ($50,000) see Ross Foundation, Lyn & George M.

Drexel University — to support the Intelligent Manufacturing Processing and Quality Technologies Program ($40,000) see Fluor Corp.

Drexel University — Minority Engineering Consortium Program ($25,000) see Air Products & Chemicals

Drueding Center ($205,000) see Drueding Foundation

Drueding Center Project Rainbow ($2,000) see Emergency Aid of Pennsylvania Foundation

DuBois Regional Medical Center ($69,050) see Mengle Foundation, Glenn and Ruth

Duquesne University ($80,000) see Aluminum Co. of America

Duquesne University ($10,000) see Aristech Chemical Corp.

Duquesne University ($200,000) see Chambers Development Co.

Duquesne University ($20,000) see Donnelly Foundation, Mary J.

Duquesne University ($110,000) see Heinz Co., H.J.

Duquesne University ($150,000) see Humana

Duquesne University ($10,000) see Kelley Foundation, Kate M.

Duquesne University ($50,000) see Pittsburgh National Bank

Duquesne University ($5,000) see Steinsapir Family Foundation, Julius L. and Libhie B.

Duquesne University — for School of Business and Administration and endowment fund for book acquisition ($100,000) see Hillman Foundation

Duquesne University — to support growth and development of major programs within the School of Music ($200,000) see Heinz Endowment, Vira I.

Eagles Fly for Leukemia ($8,500) see Philadelphia Industries

Eagles Fly for Leukemia ($15,000) see PMA Industries

Earth Day 1990 ($5,000) see Heinz Family Foundation

East End Cooperative Ministry ($6,500) see Hulme Charitable Foundation, Milton G.

East End Cooperative Ministry — to support the Life Learning Curriculum in a summer day camp program for children ages 5 to 16 in the East End of Pittsburgh ($5,000) see Pittsburgh Child Guidance Foundation

East Liberty Development — support for Capital Campaign for Regent Theatre ($30,000) see Laurel Foundation

East Liberty Development — further community/civic relationships ($2,500) see Matthews International Corp.

East Whiteland Volunteer Fire Association ($1,200) see Foote Mineral Co.

Easter Seal Society ($1,840) see Muller Foundation, C. John and Josephine

Easter Seal Society ($15,000) see 1957 Charity Trust

Easter Seal Society — to support children who have severely impaired siblings and to train staff to conduct support groups for these children ($7,500) see Pittsburgh Child Guidance Foundation

Easter Seal Society ($5,000) see Rosenberg Foundation, Alexis

Easter Seal Society ($5,000) see Spang & Co.

Easter Seals Building Campaign see Harleysville Mutual Insurance Co.

Eastern College — to complete a bibliography of research by scientists on spiritual subjects ($24,600) see Templeton Foundation, John

Easton Pennsylvania Hospital ($25,000) see Williams Foundation, C. K.

Eccles-Lesher Memorial Library Association ($62,560) see Eccles Foundation, Ralph M. and Ella M.

Ecole Francaise Internationale de Philadelphia ($10,000) see CertainTeed Corp.

Edgewater Psychiatric Center ($15,000) see Wells Foundation, Franklin H. and Ruth L.

Education Center at D. T. Watson Rehabilitation Hospital — to construct a new school building ($500,000) see Mellon Foundation, Richard King

Education Law Center — supports the Equal Educational Opportunity Project which strives to achieve parity in per-pupil spending throughout New Jersey public schools ($40,000) see Schumann Fund for New Jersey

Education for Parenting ($5,000) see Wurts Memorial, Henrietta Tower

Education for Patenting ($5,000) see Rosenberg Foundation, Alexis

Eisenhower Exchange Fellowships — Philip D. Reed Fellowship ($250,000) see Reed Foundation, Philip D.

Eleanor Bower Agency ($3,000) see Plankenhorn Foundation, Harry

Elizabeth College ($40,000) see Armstrong World Industries Inc.

Elizabethtown College ($150,000) see High Foundation

Elizabethtown College ($50,000) see Kline Foundation, Josiah W. and Bessie H.

Elizabethtown College Library Fund ($40,000) see Stabler Foundation, Donald B. and Dorothy L.

Elk County Christian High School ($248,814) see St. Mary's Catholic Foundation

Elk County Christian High School ($60,000) see St. Mary's Catholic Foundation

Elk County Development Foundation Loan Fund — community economic development ($150,000) see Stackpole-Hall Foundation

Ellis School ($5,000) see Shore Fund

Ellis School ($3,500) see Waters Charitable Trust, Robert S.

Elwyn Institute ($7,000) see Borkee Hagley Foundation

Elwyn Institute ($20,000) see Mandell Foundation, Samuel P.

Elwyn Institute ($13,250) see Widgeon Foundation

Emergency Aid ($55,000) see Plankenhorn Foundation, Harry

Emergency Outreach — purchase apartment building for transitional housing ($25,000) see Grundy Foundation

Enterprise and Education Foundation ($3,000) see Bozzone Family Foundation

Enterprise and Education Foundation ($800) see Lockhart Iron & Steel Co.

Ephrata Community Hospital Foundation ($15,000) see Crels Foundation

Ephrata Mennonite School ($5,000) see Crels Foundation

Episcopal Church Farm School ($12,722) see Downs Perpetual Charitable Trust, Ellason

Episcopal Community Services ($5,000) see Wurts Memorial, Henrietta Tower

Episcopal Community Services — Student Aid Program Fund ($5,000) see Ludwick Institute

Episcopal Diocese of Northwest Pennsylvania — unrestricted ($68,202) see Stackpole-Hall Foundation

Episcopal Diocese of Pennsylvania ($10,000) see Steinman Foundation, James Hale

Episcopal Hospital ($30,000) see Roth Foundation

Epworth Foundation ($500) see Isaly Klondike Co.

Esperanza Health Services ($40,000) see Huston Foundation

Evangelical School of Theology ($1,000) see Bishop Foundation, Vernon and Doris

Extra Mile Education Foundation ($125,000) see Eden Hall Foundation

Extra Mile Education Foundation ($20,000) see Giant Eagle

Extra Mile Education Foundation ($100,000) see Heinz Co., H.J.

Extra Mile Education Foundation ($20,000) see Mellon Bank Corp.

Extra Mile Education Foundation ($20,000) see Tippens Foundation

Extra Mile Education Foundation ($100,000) see Westinghouse Electric Corp.

Extra Mile Education Foundation — to support the operation of inner-city Catholic elementary schools ($600,000) see Heinz Endowment, Howard

Extra-Mile Foundation — scholarship fund for inner-city elementary schools ($200,000) see Scaife Family Foundation

Eye and Ear Institute ($100,000) see Campbell Foundation, Charles Talbot

Eye and Ear Institute of Pittsburgh ($50,000) see Jennings Foundation, Mary Hillman

F.H. Buhl Club ($540) see Charitable Fund

Fairmount Rest Home ($7,500) see Crels Foundation

Falling Spring Greenway — preservation of Falling Spring Creek ($5,881) see Wood Foundation of Chambersburg, PA

Family Communication ($225,000) see Sears, Roebuck and Co.

Family Counseling Center of Greenville ($2,800) see Piedmont Health Care Foundation

Family Health Council of Western Pennsylvania ($78,000) see Jewish Healthcare Foundation of Pittsburgh

Family House ($15,000) see Wardle Family Foundation

Family Intervention Center of Children's Hospital ($50,000) see Jewish Healthcare Foundation of Pittsburgh

Family Life Institute ($10,000) see Plankenhorn Foundation, Harry

Family Resources ($7,000) see Hulme Charitable Foundation, Milton G.

Family Service and Children's Aid Society ($31,500) see Justus Trust, Edith C.

Family Service of Philadelphia — "Learning to Grow" program ($10,000) see Hunt Manufacturing Co.

Family Services of Warren County ($8,500) see Betts Industries

Family Social Services ($5,000) see Waters Charitable Trust, Robert S.

Farrell/Wheatland Little League ($500) see Sharon Steel Corp.

Federated Allied Jewish Appeal ($101,000) see Schwartz and Robert Schwartz Foundation, Bernard

Federated Allied Jewish Appeal ($100,000) see Schwartz and Robert Schwartz Foundation, Bernard

Federation of Allied Jewish Agencies ($100,000) see Arronson Foundation

Federation of Allied Jewish Agencies ($350) see Conston Corp.

Federation of Allied Jewish Agencies ($3,500) see Greene Foundation, Robert Z.

Federation of Allied Jewish Agencies ($10,900) see Groome Beatty Trust, Helen D.

Federation of Allied Jewish Agencies ($40,000) see Philadelphia Industries

Federation of Allied Jewish Appeal ($87,625) see Binswanger Co.

Federation of Allied Jewish Appeal ($10,000) see Cassett Foundation, Louis N.

Federation of Allied Jewish Appeal ($12,000) see Conston Corp.

Federation of Allied Jewish Appeal ($469,458) see Federation Foundation of Greater Philadelphia

Federation of Allied Jewish Appeal ($305,000) see Feinstein Foundation, Myer and Rosaline

Federation of Allied Jewish Appeal ($250,000) see Fox Foundation, Richard J.

Federation of Allied Jewish Appeal ($10,500) see Goldman Foundation, William

Federation of Allied Jewish Appeal ($5,000) see Greenfield Foundation, Albert M.

Federation of Allied Jewish Appeal ($200,000) see Korman Family Foundation, Hyman

Federation of Allied Jewish Appeal ($5,000) see Novotny Charitable Trust, Yetta Deitch

Federation Allied Jewish Appeal ($85,000) see Premier Dental Products Co.

Federation of Allied Jewish Appeal ($160,000) see Snider Foundation

Federation of Independent School Alumnae ($1,000) see Edgewater Steel Corp.

Federation of Jewish Agencies — FJA Operation Exodus ($66,000) see Premier Dental Products Co.

Federation of Jewish Agencies of Greater Philadelphia ($135,000) see Levee Charitable Trust, Polly Annenberg

Federation of Jewish Agencies of Greater Philadelphia ($166,935) see Schwartz and Robert Schwartz Foundation, Bernard

Federation of Jewish Philanthropies ($141,453) see Bronstein Foundation, Soloman and Sylvia

Federation of Jewish Philanthropies ($30,000) see Caplan Charity Foundation, Julius H.

Federation of Jewish Philanthropies ($122,473) see Klein Charitable Foundation, Raymond

First United Methodist Church ($3,000) see Peters Foundation, Charles F.

FJA Project Renewal ($15,200) see Federation Foundation of Greater Philadelphia

Forbes Health Foundation ($27,000) see Gibson Foundation, Addison H.

Forbes Health Foundation ($10,000) see Rockwell Foundation

Foreign Policy Research Institute ($40,000) see Hooper Foundation, Elizabeth S.

Foreign Policy Research Institute ($12,500) see Snider Foundation

Ft. Mifflin ($10,000) see Corestates Bank

Foundation for Independant College ($2,500) see McCormick Trust, Anne

Foundation of Independent Colleges ($6,000) see Vesuvius Charitable Foundation

Foundation for Independent Colleges of Pennsylvania ($6,000) see General Accident Insurance Co. of America

Foundation for Independent Colleges of Pennsylvania ($14,500) see Harsco Corp.

Foundation for Independent Colleges of Pennsylvania ($400) see Isaly Klondike Co.

Foundation of Independent Colleges of Pennsylvania ($22,000) see Kennametal

Foundation for Independent Colleges of Pennsylvania ($2,500) see Pitt-Des Moines Inc.

Foundation of the Lancaster Chamber ($35,000) see Armstrong World Industries Inc.

Foundation at Paoli ($1,000) see Safeguard Scientifics Foundation

Foundation for the Reading Public Museum and Art Gallery ($25,000) see Wyomissing Foundation

Four-H Livestock Scholarship ($500) see Eberly Foundation

Fourth of July Homecoming Committee ($100) see Pottstown Mercury

Fox Chase Cancer Center ($22,000) see AMETEK

Fox Chase Cancer Center ($55,000) see Binswanger Co.

Fox Chase Cancer Center ($15,000) see Cassett Foundation, Louis N.

Fox Chase Cancer Center ($10,000) see Iacocca Foundation

Fox Chase Cancer Center — support new outpatient care facility ($25,000) see McLean Contributionship

Fox Chase Cancer Center ($160,000) see Oberkotter Family Foundation

Fox Chase Cancer Center ($155) see Reedman Car-Truck World Center

Fox Chase Cancer Center ($25,000) see Scholler Foundation

Fox Chase Cancer Center ($15,000) see Smith Foundation

Fox Chase Cancer Institute ($26,323) see Roth Foundation

Foxview Manor ($10,000) see Phillips Charitable Trust, Dr. and Mrs. Arthur William

Frankford Hospital ($30,000) see Roth Foundation

Frankford Hospital ($15,091) see Scholler Foundation

Franklin Area School District ($3,250) see Eccles Foundation, Ralph M. and Ella M.

Franklin Civic Operetta Association ($14,000) see Justus Trust, Edith C.

Franklin Institute ($8,333) see Alco Standard Corp.

Franklin Institute ($50,000) see Arcadia Foundation

Franklin Institute see Berwind Corp.

Franklin Institute ($50,000) see CertainTeed Corp.

Franklin Institute ($8,000) see Claneil Foundation

Franklin Institute ($5,000) see Colket Foundation, Ethel D.

Franklin Institute ($100,000) see Dietrich Foundation, William B.

Franklin Institute ($50,000) see Greenfield Foundation, Albert M.

Franklin Institute ($250,850) see Mandell Foundation, Samuel P.

Franklin Institute — exhibits and programs ($10,000) see 1957 Charity Trust

Franklin Institute ($10,000) see Philadelphia Industries

Franklin Institute — to support scientific work of institute ($10,000) see PQ Corp.

Franklin Institute ($4,000) see Quaker Chemical Corp.

Franklin Institute ($4,000) see Rock Foundation, Milton and Shirley

Franklin Institute ($39,000) see Safeguard Scientifics Foundation

Franklin Institute ($5,000) see SPS Technologies

Franklin Institute ($5,000) see Tasty Baking Co.

Franklin Institute ($20,000) see West Co.

Franklin Institute — capital campaign pledge for the Futures Center ($15,000) see Hunt Manufacturing Co.

Franklin Institute — three year grant toward Futures Center capital campaign ($8,333) see Subaru of America Inc.

Franklin Institute Futures Center ($20,000) see West Co.

Franklin Institute — Futures Center Campaign ($20,000) see Air Products & Chemicals

Franklin and Marshall College ($17,821) see Hamilton Bank

Franklin and Marshall College ($35,000) see Kunkel Foundation, John Crain

Franklin and Marshall College ($1,000) see Lauffer Trust, Charles A.

Franklin and Marshall College Bicentennial ($50,000) see Armstrong World Industries Inc.

Franklin and Marshall Science Library ($25,000) see

Armstrong World Industries Inc.

Free Library of Philadelphia ($4,000) see Rittenhouse Foundation

Freedom Foundation at Valley Forge ($5,000) see Monroe Foundation (1976), J. Edgar

Freedom Foundation at Valley Forge ($1,000) see Youth Foundation

Freedom Theater ($3,000) see Corestates Bank

Freedoms Foundation ($15,000) see Firestone Foundation, Roger S.

Freedoms Foundation at Valley Forge ($300,100) see Lennon Foundation, Fred A.

Freeport Area Meals on Wheels ($2,000) see Freeport Brick Co.

Freeport Community Park Corporation ($39,000) see Freeport Brick Co.

Freeport Pennsylvania Area Library ($1,000) see Freeport Brick Co.

Freeport Volunteer Fire Department ($1,000) see Freeport Brick Co.

Friends of Als ($1,000) see Pennsylvania Knitted Outerwear Manufacturing Association

Friends General Conference ($28,000) see Shoemaker Fund, Thomas H. and Mary Williams

Friends of Historic Rittenhouse Town ($5,000) see Corestates Bank

Friends of Moss Rehabilitation ($500) see Rock Foundation, Milton and Shirley

Friends of Rittenhouse Square ($1,000) see Gershman Foundation, Joel

Friends of Samuel Paley Day Care Center ($1,064) see Gershman Foundation, Joel

Friends of Scouting ($2,500) see Bozzone Family Foundation

Friends World Committee for Consultation ($33,000) see Shoemaker Fund, Thomas H. and Mary Williams

Friendship House ($10,000) see Schautz Foundation, Walter L.

Fulton County Crime Solvers ($100) see Lebanon Mutual Insurance Co.

Fund for the International Exchange of Scientific and Cultural Information ($16,000) see Klein Charitable Foundation, Raymond

Gannon University — faculty and curriculum development in business ($25,000) see Kemper National Insurance Cos.

Gateway Rehabilitation Center ($1,000) see Edgewater Steel Corp.

Gateway Rehabilitation Center ($7,500) see Knudsen Charitable Foundation, Earl

Gateway Rehabilitation Center — addictive diseases treatment ($2,500) see Patterson Charitable Fund, W. I.

Gateway Rehabilitation Center ($50,000) see Shore Fund

Gateway Rehabilitation Centers ($30,000) see Jennings Foundation, Mary Hillman

Geisinger Foundation ($20,000) see Mars Foundation

Geisinger Foundation ($5,000) see Reidler Foundation

Geisinger Foundation ($60,000) see Sordoni Foundation

Pennsylvania (cont.)

Geisinger Medical School ($850) see Smith Golden Rule Trust Fund, Fred G.

General Church of New Jerusalem ($12,000) see Asplundh Foundation

General Church of the New Jerusalem ($33,000) see Harder Foundation

Geneva College — operating ($100,000) see Consolidated Natural Gas Co.

German Society of Pennsylvania ($100,000) see Muller Foundation, C. John and Josephine

Germantown Academy ($2,000) see Copernicus Society of America

Germantown Academy Program ($28,610) see Seybert Institution for Poor Boys and Girls, Adam and Maria Sarah

Germantown Friends ($35,000) see Ellis Grant and Scholarship Fund, Charles E.

Germantown Friends School ($5,000) see Rosenberg Foundation, Alexis

Gesu School — funding for their pre-kindergarten and kindergarten programs see New Street Capital Corp.

Gettysburg College ($50,000) see Kline Foundation, Josiah W. and Bessie H.

Gettysburg Lutheran Theological Seminary ($8,300) see Aigner

Girl Scouts of America ($250) see Eccles Foundation, Ralph M. and Ella M.

Girl Scouts of America ($5,000) see Spang & Co.

Girls, Inc. ($1,000) see McCormick Trust, Anne

Girls Club of Allentown ($3,000) see Lehigh Portland Cement Co.

Girls Club of Allentown — to provide funding for support and personal costs and evaluation of the program ($24,400) see Rider-Pool Foundation

Girls Club of Allentown — debt reduction ($49,727) see Trexler Trust, Harry C.

Girls Club of Lancaster ($40,000) see Steinman Foundation, John Frederick

Glaucoma Services Foundation to Prevent Blindness ($5,000) see Cameron Memorial Fund, Alpin J. and Alpin W.

Glaucoma Services Foundation to Prevent Blindness ($23,500) see Scholler Foundation

Glencairn Museum — carriage restoration and museum restoration ($53,390) see Glencairn Foundation

Golden Cradle ($500) see Lizzadro Family Foundation, Joseph

Golden Slipper Club ($255) see Kellmer Co., Jack

Good Samaritan Hospital ($50,300) see Caplan Charity Foundation, Julius H.

Good Shepherd Home — vocational success building ($25,000) see Air Products & Chemicals

Goodwill Industries ($26,000) see AMP

Goodwill Industries ($50,000) see Campbell Foundation, Charles Talbot

Goodwill Industries ($46,922) see Hambay Foundation, James T.

Goodwill Industries ($7,500) see Knudsen Charitable Foundation, Earl

Goodwill Industries ($15,000) see McCormick Trust, Anne

Goodwill Industries ($20,000) see Miller Charitable Foundation, Howard E. and Nell E.

Goodwill Industries ($35,000) see Snyder Charitable Fund, W. P.

Goodwill Industries ($56,937) see Trees Charitable Trust, Edith L.

Goodwill Industries of Central Pennsylvania ($23,000) see Harsco Corp.

Goodwill Industries of Central Pennsylvania ($41,000) see Hershey Foods Corp.

Goodwill Industries of Pittsburgh ($24,000) see McKee Poor Fund, Virginia A.

Grace Episcopal Church — unrestricted ($88,663) see Stackpole-Hall Foundation

Graduate Hospital ($277,000) see Smith Charitable Trust, W. W.

Grand View Hospital see Harleysville Mutual Insurance Co.

Grand View Hospital Capital Campaign ($20,000) see AMETEK

Grantmakers of Western Pennsylvania ($300) see Copperweld Corp.

Graphic Arts Technical Foundation ($174,615) see Graphic Arts Show Co. Inc.

Gratz College ($200) see Kellmer Co., Jack

Great Meadows Arts and Heritage ($500) see Eberly Foundation

Greater Harrisburg Youth for Christ ($15,000) see Wells Foundation, Franklin H. and Ruth L.

Greater Hazelton Historical Society ($500) see Fabri-Kal Corp.

Greater Latrobe School District ($5,070) see McFeely-Rogers Foundation

Greater Philadelphia Federation of Settlements ($351,664) see Penn Foundation, William

Greater Philadelphia First Corporation — to provide corporate leadership and coordinated support for programs that benefit Greater Philadelphia ($118,000) see CIGNA Corp.

Greater Philadelphia First Foundation — educational and economic development programs ($67,500) see Hunt Manufacturing Co.

Greater Philadelphia Women's Medical Fund ($10,000) see Seybert Institution for Poor Boys and Girls, Adam and Maria Sarah

Greater Pittsburgh Community Food Bank ($10,000) see Murphy Co., G.C.

Greater Pittsburgh Food Bank ($6,000) see Hulme Charitable Foundation, Milton G.

Greater Pittsburgh Guild for the Blind ($25,000) see Campbell Foundation, Charles Talbot

Greater Pittsburgh Guild for the Blind ($5,000) see Donnelly Foundation, Mary J.

Greater Pittsburgh Guild for the Blind ($27,000) see Gibson Foundation, Addison H.

Greater Pittsburgh Guild for the Blind ($8,600) see Vesuvius Charitable Foundation

Greater Pittsburgh Guild for the Blind ($100,000) see Weisbrod Foundation Trust Dept., Robert and Mary

Greater Pittsburgh Guild for the Blind Low Vision Clinic ($60,000) see PPG Industries

Greater Pittsburgh Literacy Council — literacy ($10,000) see Scripps Co., E.W.

Greater Pittsburgh Literacy Council ($5,000) see Vesuvius Charitable Foundation

Green Free Library ($4,000) see Packer Foundation, Horace B.

Green Home ($11,500) see Packer Foundation, Horace B.

Greensburg Garden and Civic Center ($112,000) see McKenna Foundation, Katherine Mabis

Greensburg Garden and Civic Center ($3,000) see Millstein Charitable Foundation

Greensburg Garden and Civic Center — Palace Theater ($50,000) see McKenna Foundation, Katherine Mabis

Greenville Council for the Prevention of Teenage Pregnancy ($10,525) see Piedmont Health Care Foundation

Greenville Technical College ($22,000) see Piedmont Health Care Foundation

Gretna Productions ($12,500) see Bishop Foundation, Vernon and Doris

Grier Foundation ($19,171) see Knox Family Foundation

Grove City College ($9,000) see Curran Foundation

Grove City College ($200,000) see Eden Hall Foundation

Grove City College ($125) see Leesona Corp.

Grove City College ($50,000) see Phillips Charitable Trust, Dr. and Mrs. Arthur William

Gwynedd Mercy College ($75,000) see Fourjay Foundation

Habitat for Humanity ($5,455) see CertainTeed Corp.

Habitat for Humanity ($25,000) see Kunkel Foundation, John Crain

Habitat for Humanity ($12,500) see Steinman Foundation, John Frederick

Habitat for Humanity ($30,000) see United Service Foundation

Hadassah Jewish Museum ($365) see Klein Charitable Foundation, Raymond

Hahneman University ($45,760) see Measey Foundation, Benjamin and Mary Siddons

Hahnemann Medical Faculty Fund ($10,000) see Frankino Charitable Foundation, Samuel J. and Connie

Hahnemann University — for grants ($3,000) see Groome Beatty Trust, Helen D.

Hahnemann University ($100,000) see Levee Charitable Trust, Polly Annenberg

Hahnemann University — for grants ($11,000) see Pearce Foundation, Dr. M. Lee

Hahnemann University ($30,000) see Snider Foundation

Hahnemann University Hospital see Berwind Corp.

Hannah House-U-Help ($2,000) see Emergency Aid of Pennsylvania Foundation

Hanover Area Historical Society ($7,000) see Sheppard Foundation, Lawrence B.

Har Zion ($2,850) see Premier Dental Products Co.

Har Zion Yom Kippur Mr M ($2,000) see Premier Dental Products Co.

HARB — Adult ($15,000) see Steinman Foundation, John Frederick

Harcum Junior College ($2,500) see Goldman Foundation, William

Harmar Township Volunteer Fire Company No. 1 ($200) see Action Industries, Inc.

Harmarville Affiliates — for construction and renovation of main facility ($50,000) see Hillman Foundation

Harmarville Foundation ($30,000) see Jennings Foundation, Mary Hillman

Harmarville Foundation ($2,000) see Lockhart Iron & Steel Co.

Harmarville Rehabilitation Center ($27,000) see Gibson Foundation, Addison H.

Harrisburg Academy ($9,000) see Grass Family Foundation

Harrisburg Academy ($50,000) see Kunkel Foundation, John Crain

Harrisburg Area Community College ($50,000) see Stabler Foundation, Donald B. and Dorothy L.

Harrisburg Area Community College ($100,000) see Whitaker Foundation

Harrisburg Area Community College, John N. Hall Technology Center ($40,000) see Hall Foundation

Harrisburg Cemetary Association ($1,000) see McCormick Trust, Anne

Harrisburg Diocese ($100,000) see Brencanda Foundation

Harrisburg Parks Partnership ($2,500) see Hall Foundation

Harrisburg School District ($20,000) see Wells Foundation, Franklin H. and Ruth L.

Harrisburg Symphony Association ($4,000) see Hall Foundation

Harrisburg Symphony Association ($3,500) see McCormick Trust, Anne

Harvest ($100,000) see DeMoss Foundation, Arthur S.

Haverford College ($1,250) see Gilman Paper Co.

Haverford College see Greenwood Mills

Haverford College ($50,000) see Hurford Foundation

Haverford College ($39,000) see Watson Foundation, Thomas J.

Haverford College ($375,000) see Whitehead Foundation

Haverford College — 300 MHz NMR spectrometer for undergraduate education and research ($25,000) see Dreyfus Foundation, Camille and Henry

Hawk Mountain Sanctuary Association ($25,000) see Wyomissing Foundation

Hawthordem Literary Institute ($5,000,000) see Heinz Foundation, Drue

Hawthornden Literary Institute ($600,000) see Heinz Foundation, Drue

Hazleton Area Public Library ($3,000) see Reidler Foundation

Health Education Center ($100,000) see Caterpillar

Health Education Center ($100,000) see Caterpillar

Health Education Center ($5,600) see Foster Charitable Trust

Health Education Center — for the revolving fund ($750,000) see McCune Foundation

Henry C. Frick Educational Commission ($30,000) see Frick Foundation, Helen Clay

Heritage Center of Lancaster ($7,500) see High Foundation

Heritage Center of Lancaster ($16,125) see Steinman Foundation, James Hale

Hershey Foods Corporation Scholarship Program ($78,000) see Hershey Foods Corp.

Hershey Medical Center ($25,000) see Kline Foundation, Josiah W. and Bessie H.

Hershey's National Track and Field Youth Program ($894,628) see Hershey Foods Corp.

Historic Sugartown ($15,000) see Kent-Lucas Foundation

Historic York ($5,000) see Freas Foundation

Historic York ($100) see General Machine Works

Historic York ($12,000) see Susquehanna Investment Group

Historic York ($12,000) see Susquehanna-Pfaltzgraff Co.

Historical Society of Pennsylvania — history camp ($5,000) see Ludwick Institute

Historical Society of Trappe ($20,000) see Superior Tube Co.

Historical Society of Western Pennsylvania ($10,000) see Campbell Foundation, Charles Talbot

Historical Society of Western Pennsylvania ($10,000) see Hunt Foundation, Roy A.

Historical Society of Western Pennsylvania — to renovate a former ice house building near Pittsburgh's downtown Convention Center ($500,000) see Mellon Foundation, Richard King

Historical York of York County ($500) see General Machine Works

Holy Annunciation Monastery — construction of a new chapel ($3,000) see Kavanagh Foundation, T. James

Holy Redeemer Hospital ($5,000) see SPS Technologies

Holy Redeemer Hospital and Medical Center ($10,000) see Smith Foundation

Holy Spirit Hospital ($20,000) see AMP

Hope Lodge Historical Center, Ft. Washington, PA see Rhone-Poulenc Rorer

Horizon Homes ($5,000) see Finley Charitable Trust, J. B.

Horning Mennonite Church ($38,000) see Crels Foundation

Hospital of University of Pennsylvania — medical ($99,000) see Measey

Foundation, Benjamin and Mary Siddons

Hospital of University of Pennsylvania — surgery ($99,000) see Measey Foundation, Benjamin and Mary Siddons

Housing Opportunities — to recapitalize the organization's second mortgage revolving loan fund ($275,000) see Heinz Endowment, Vira I.

Housing Opportunities — operating support/revolving loan fund ($150,000) see Scaife Family Foundation

Howard H. Steel Orthopedic Foundation ($50,000) see Berry Foundation, Archie W. and Grace

Howard H. Steel Orthopedic Foundation ($10,000) see Berry Foundation, Archie W. and Grace

Hoyt Institute of Fine Arts ($52,500) see Giant Eagle

Hunter Elementary School ($16,080) see Seybert Institution for Poor Boys and Girls, Adam and Maria Sarah

Immaculata College ($25,000) see Arcadia Foundation

Immaculata College ($30,000) see Sandy Hill Foundation

Immaculate Heart of Mary ($5,000) see Berry Foundation, Archie W. and Grace

Immaculate Heart of Mary Church ($10,000) see O'Neil Foundation, W.

Immanuel Church of New Jerusalem ($6,000) see Asplundh Foundation

Independence for Dogs — newsletter and trained dog ($15,229) see Innovating Worthy Projects Foundation

Independence Hall Preservation ($2,000) see Emergency Aid of Pennsylvania Foundation

Indian Creek Foundation see Harleysville Mutual Insurance Co.

Indiana County Historical Society ($3,500) see Mack Foundation, J. S.

Indiana University of Pennsylvania ($60) see Equimark Corp.

Indiana University of Pennsylvania ($6,000) see Mack Foundation, J. S.

Indochinese American Council ($2,000) see Emergency Aid of Pennsylvania Foundation

INROADS ($25,600) see Armstrong World Industries Inc.

Institute for Cancer and Blood Diseases at Hahnemann University ($25,000) see Levee Charitable Trust, Polly Annenberg

Institute of Contemporary Art ($1,900) see Gershman Foundation, Joel

Institute of Contemporary Art — Engelhard Award ($172,538) see Engelhard Foundation, Charles

Institute for Experimental Psychiatry Research Foundation — a clinical study of the effects of hypnosis on children in pain with sickle-cell disease ($50,707) see van Ameringen Foundation

Intercollegiate Studies Institute ($100,000) see Aequus Institute

Intercollegiate Studies Institute ($27,000) see Coleman, Jr. Foundation, George E.

Intercollegiate Studies Institute ($20,000) see Curran Foundation

Intercollegiate Studies Institute ($17,500) see Earhart Foundation

Intercollegiate Studies Institute ($60,000) see McKenna Foundation, Philip M.

Intercollegiate Studies Institute ($75,000) see Roe Foundation

Intercollegiate Studies Institute ($200,000) see Scaife Foundation, Sarah

Intercollegiate Studies Institute ($5,000) see Western Shade Cloth Charitable Foundation

Intercollegiate Studies Institute ($20,000) see Wilbur Foundation, Marguerite Eyer

Intercollegiate Studies Institute ($5,000) see Winchester Foundation

Intercollegiate Studies Institute — for the Richard M. Weaver Fellowship Program ($32,500) see Earhart Foundation

International Centre for Diffraction Data — crystallography scholarship fund ($5,000) see Dow Foundation, Herbert H. and Barbara C.

International House see Berwind Corp.

International House of Philadelphia ($4,000) see Quaker Chemical Corp.

International Management and Development Institute ($15,000) see CertainTeed Corp.

International Service Fellowship ($15,000) see Kent Foundation, Ada Howe

Irene Stacy Community Mental Health ($20,000) see Stacy Foundation, Festus

Italian American War Veterans ($120) see Copperweld Corp.

James Buchanan Foundation ($3,500) see Steinman Foundation, James Hale

Jameson Memorial Hospital ($75,000) see Hoyt Foundation

Jamestown Community College ($5,260) see Betts Industries

Jarrettown First Ward Latter Day Saints ($2,500) see Hallowell Foundation

Jefferson Medical College ($40,000) see Pfeiffer Research Foundation, Gustavus and Louise

Jefferson Medical College of Thomas Jefferson University ($65,540) see Measey Foundation, Benjamin and Mary Siddons

Jesuit Community Mission Fund ($12,000) see Morania Foundation

Jesus Good Shepherd Church ($10,000) see Murphy Co., G.C.

Jewish Community Center ($7,500) see Action Industries, Inc.

Jewish Community Center ($2,500) see Bronstein Foundation, Soloman and Sylvia

Jewish Community Center ($10,000) see Conston Corp.

Jewish Community Center ($5,000) see Gershman Foundation, Joel

Jewish Community Center ($155,000) see Kaufmann Foundation, Henry

Jewish Community Center ($57,300) see Kline Foundation, Charles and Figa

Jewish Community Center ($2,000) see Motter Printing Press Co.

Jewish Community Center ($20,000) see Weiler Foundation, Theodore & Renee

Jewish Community Center Klein Branches ($5,420) see Klein Charitable Foundation, Raymond

Jewish Day School of Allentown ($29,325) see Kline Foundation, Charles and Figa

Jewish Family and Children's Services ($29,200) see Binswanger Co.

Jewish Family and Children's Services ($7,000) see Merit Oil Corp.

Jewish Family Services — guardianship program ($12,000) see Innovating Worthy Projects Foundation

Jewish Family Services ($4,500) see Lebovitz Fund

Jewish Federation ($20,196) see Federation Foundation of Greater Philadelphia

Jewish Federation ($300,000) see Kline Foundation, Charles and Figa

Jewish Federation ($100,330) see Merit Oil Corp.

Jewish Federation ($250,000) see Ross Foundation, Lyn & George M.

Jewish Federation of Allentown ($11,000) see Lebovitz Fund

Jewish Federation of Philadelphia ($325) see Kellmer Co., Jack

Jewish Home of Greater Harrisburg ($5,357) see Grumbacher Foundation, M. S.

Jewish Home and Hospital for Aged D.B.A. Riverview Center for Jewish Seniors ($236,000) see Morris Charitable Trust, Charles M.

Jewish Memorial Fund ($400) see Pennsylvania Knitted Outerwear Manufacturing Association

Jewish National Fund ($33,333) see Giant Eagle

Jewish National Fund ($4,000) see Premier Dental Products Co.

Jewish National Fund ($1,250) see Tamarkin Co.

John Bartram Association — for children's educational program ($5,000) see Ludwick Institute

John Paul II Foundation ($69,350) see Copernicus Society of America

Johnson Technical Institute ($10,000) see Schautz Foundation, Walter L.

Johnstown Central High School ($2,000) see Glosser Foundation, David A.

Johnstown Symphony Orchestra ($1,700) see Glosser Foundation, David A.

Juniata College ($30,000) see Beeghly Fund, Leon A.

Junior Achievement ($8,000) see Aristech Chemical Corp.

Junior Achievement ($330) see Charitable Fund

Junior Achievement ($501) see Foster Co., L.B.

Junior Achievement ($100) see General Machine Works

Junior Achievement ($750) see Sharon Steel Corp.

Juvenile Diabetes Foundation ($10,000) see Tasty Baking Co.

Juvenile Law Center of Philadelphia ($16,050) see Fels Fund, Samuel S.

Juvenile Law Center — will develop a system of transitional/discharge programs for children with severe emotional problems ($35,000) see Ittleson Foundation

Kardon Institute of Music for Handicapped ($20,000) see Arronson Foundation

Kearsley-Christ Church Hospital ($12,500) see Smith Foundation

Kenmore Association ($6,091) see Schoonmaker J-Sewkly Valley Hospital Trust

Kennedy Christian High School ($5,000) see Kavanagh Foundation, T. James

Keystone Sports Foundation ($22,000) see Hall Foundation

Kimberton Waldorf School ($12,000) see Waldorf Educational Foundation

Kirby Center ($5,000) see MacDonald Foundation, Marquis George

Kirby, The F. M. Center for the Performing Arts — restoration of front doors; general operating expenses; reduction of mortgage; endowment ($200,000) see Kirby Foundation, F. M.

Kiski School ($15,000) see McFeely-Rogers Foundation

Kops for Kids ($1,250) see Foster Co., L.B.

Kress Society, Allentown Art Museum ($2,500) see Baker Foundation, Dexter F. and Dorothy H.

Kutztown University ($46,000) see SICO Foundation

La Roche College — Library Automation - to support retrospective conversion and a CD-ROM system and introduction of an interactive on-line system will follow ($150,000) see Buhl Foundation

La Salle College High School ($1,004,850) see Connelly Foundation

Lady Keystone Open ($200,000) see Hershey Foods Corp.

Lafayette College ($1,000) see Donaldson, Lufkin & Jenrette

Lafayette College ($25,000) see Jaqua Foundation

Lafayette College ($600,000) see Kirby Foundation, F. M.

Lafayette College ($66,399) see Rumbaugh Foundation, J. H. and F. H.

Lakenau Hospital ($5,000) see Lovett Foundation

Lakeside Youth Service ($2,000) see Emergency Aid of Pennsylvania Foundation

Lancaster Bible College ($5,000) see Crels Foundation

Lancaster Bible College ($25,000) see Steinman Foundation, John Frederick

Lancaster Celebration 250 ($10,000) see Hamilton Bank

Lancaster Cleft Palate Clinic — towards $3 million Golden Anniversary campaign ($25,000) see Hillman Foundation, Henry L.

Lancaster Farmland Trust ($50,000) see Oxford Foundation

Lancaster Foundation for Education and Enrichment ($2,500) see Steinman Foundation, James Hale

Lancaster General Hospital ($15,000) see Crels Foundation

Lancaster Mennonite High School ($30,000) see High Foundation

Lancaster Mennonite High School ($12,500) see Steinman Foundation, John Frederick

Lancaster Public Library ($1,500) see Penn Savings Bank, a division of Sovereign Bank Bank of Princeton, a division of Sovereign Bank

Lancaster Summer Arts ($2,000) see Steinman Foundation, James Hale

Lancaster Summer Arts Festival ($1,500) see Penn Savings Bank, a division of Sovereign Bank Bank of Princeton, a division of Sovereign Bank

Lancaster Theological Seminary ($25,000) see Steinman Foundation, John Frederick

Lankenau Medical Research Center — support a new research building ($50,000) see McLean Contributionship

LaRobe College — building program ($150,000) see Eden Hall Foundation

LaRoche College ($30,000) see Hopwood Charitable Trust, John M.

LaRoche College ($3,000) see Pitt-Des Moines Inc.

LaSalle University ($25,000) see Mandell Foundation, Samuel P.

Latrobe Area Hospital — toward the construction of the medical tower ($500,000) see McCune Foundation

Latrobe Area Hospital ($100,000) see McFeely-Rogers Foundation

Latrobe Area Hospital ($100,000) see McKenna Foundation, Katherine Mabis

Latrobe Foundation ($10,000) see Kennametal

Latrobe Presbyterian Church ($77,000) see McFeely-Rogers Foundation

Laughlin Children's Center ($7,500) see Finley Charitable Trust, J. B.

Learning Club — to provide funding for underwriting the quality control element of the program ($20,000) see Rider-Pool Foundation

Lebanon County Historical Society ($100) see Lebanon Mutual Insurance Co.

Lebanon Valley College ($3,000) see Bishop Foundation, Vernon and Doris

Lebanon Valley College ($80,000) see Kline Foundation, Josiah W. and Bessie H.

Lebanon Valley College ($2,000) see Lebanon Mutual Insurance Co.

Lebanon Valley College ($100,000) see Whitaker Foundation

Lebanon Valley Educational Partnership ($1,000) see Lebanon Mutual Insurance Co.

Lehigh County Conference of Churches — Alliance Hall project ($100,000) see Trexler Trust, Harry C.

Lehigh County Senior Citizens — to provide support for the creation of a financial

Pennsylvania (cont.)

development office ($45,000) see Rider-Pool Foundation

Lehigh University ($5,710) see Belmont Metals

Lehigh University ($10,000) see Charities Foundation

Lehigh University ($18,750) see Frankel Foundation, George and Elizabeth F.

Lehigh University ($200,000) see Iacocca Foundation

Lehigh University ($15,000) see Janssen Foundation, Henry

Lehigh University ($55,000) see Mercy, Jr. Foundation, Sue and Eugene

Lehigh University ($20,000) see Neu Foundation, Hugo and Doris

Lehigh University ($2,000) see Reedman Car-Truck World Center

Lehigh University ($6,500) see Reidler Foundation

Lehigh University ($210,000) see Sandy Hill Foundation

Lehigh University ($6,000) see Sheridan Foundation, Thomas B. and Elizabeth M.

Lehigh University ($50,000) see Snyder Charitable Fund, W. P.

Lehigh University ($10,000) see Weinstein Foundation, Alex J.

Lehigh University ($25,000) see Wyomissing Foundation

Lehigh University Center of Jewish Studies ($7,500) see Kline Foundation, Charles and Figa

Lehigh University-Iacocca Institute ($300,000) see Chrysler Corp.

Lehigh University — to establish and endow Robert D. Rodale Faculty Chair in Writing ($1,000,000) see Rodale Press

Lehigh University Scholarship Fund ($50,000) see Stabler Foundation, Donald B. and Dorothy L.

Lehigh University — development of an integrated chemical science/math/technology program for K-12 teachers ($20,000) see Dreyfus Foundation, Camille and Henry

Lehigh Valley Chamber Orchestra ($10,000) see Baker Foundation, Dexter F. and Dorothy H.

Lehigh Valley Easter Seals ($10,000) see Shaffer Family Charitable Trust

Lehigh Valley Telecommunications — underwriting MacNeil/Lehrer and Scholastic Scrimmage ($14,500) see Air Products & Chemicals

Leukemia Society of America ($300) see Action Industries, Inc.

Leukemia Society of America ($15,000) see Chambers Development Co.

Leukemia Society of America ($200) see General Machine Works

Leukemia Society of America ($10,000) see Kelley Foundation, Kate M.

Liberty VFW ($5,800) see Packer Foundation, Horace B.

Library of the College of Physicians of Philadelphia ($100,000) see Independence Foundation

Lincoln University ($5,000) see General Accident Insurance Co. of America

Linda Creed Foundation ($150) see Kellmer Co., Jack

Little Sisters of Poor ($10,000) see Kelley Foundation, Kate M.

Little Sisters of Poor ($10,000) see McMahon Charitable Trust Fund, Father John J.

Local Initiatives Support Corporation ($10,000) see Douty Foundation

Local Initiatives Support Corporation ($10,000) see 1957 Charity Trust

Lock Haven UMCA — operating expenses ($10,000) see Piper Foundation

Lock Haven University Foundation— presidential scholarships ($5,000) see Piper Foundation

Longwood Gardens — project expenditures ($4,562,000) see Longwood Foundation

Louise Child Care — Pittsburgh Child Care Institute toddler rooms - to underwrite the cost of toddler rooms in a new child care center on the South Side of Pittsburgh ($50,000) see Buhl Foundation

Lower Marion Counseling Services ($1,000) see Goldman Foundation, William

Luddington Library ($5,000) see Lovett Foundation

Luddington Public Library ($5,000) see Lovett Foundation

Lupus Foundation of America ($15,000) see Clapp Charitable and Educational Trust, George H.

Lutheran Social Services ($5,000) see Susquehanna-Pfaltzgraff Co.

Lutheran Welfare Center — dental care unit ($5,000) see Reidler Foundation

Lycoming College ($1,250) see LamCo. Communications

Lycoming County Association for the Blind ($80,000) see Plankenhorn Foundation, Harry

Lyons Foundation of Philadelphia ($25) see Klein Charitable Foundation, Raymond

Magee Rehabilitation Hospital ($2,500) see Philadelphia Industries

Magee Women's Hospital ($27,000) see Hopwood Charitable Trust, John M.

Main Line Reform Temple ($10,200) see Conston Corp.

Main Line Reform Temple ($23,000) see Ross Foundation, Lyn & George M.

Malvern Preparatory School ($5,000) see Kavanagh Foundation, T. James

Malvern Preparatory School ($25,000) see Maneely Fund

Malvern Preparatory School ($2,500) see Maneely Fund

Manchester Youth Development ($91,000) see McCune Charitable Trust, John R.

Manchester Youth Development Center ($25,000) see Weisbrod Foundation Trust Dept., Robert and Mary

Manchester Youth Development Center (Formerly Bidwell Education, Music and Recreation Center) — expansion of programs - supported development programs offering afterschool

ed support for children North Side of Pittsburgh ($50,000) see Buhl Foundation

Mann Music Center ($3,360) see Maneely Fund

Mann Music Center ($3,360) see Maneely Fund

Mansfield Library ($5,495) see Packer Foundation, Horace B.

Marble Public Library ($10,000) see Smith Memorial Fund, Ethel Sergeant Clark

March of Dimes ($10,299) see CertainTeed Corp.

March of Dimes ($70,400) see Corestates Bank

March of Dimes ($2,500) see Corestates Bank

March of Dimes ($1,348) see Foster Co., L.B.

Maria Joseph Manor ($25,000) see Gavin Foundation, James and Zita

Maria Joseph Manor — general support ($50,000) see Solo Cup Co.

Marquis Society ($10,000) see Williams Foundation, C. K.

Martha Lloyd Community Services — sprinkler and air conditioning systems/motor vehicle ($58,000) see Trees Charitable Trust, Edith L.

Marwood College ($5,500) see Bickerton Charitable Trust, Lydia H.

Mary and Alexander Laughlin Children's Center ($15,000) see Snyder Charitable Fund, W. P.

Marywood College ($5,000) see Sordoni Foundation

Maternity Care Coalition of Greater Philadelphia ($25,000) see Fels Fund, Samuel S.

Maternity Care Coalition of Greater Philadelphia ($10,000) see Seybert Institution for Poor Boys and Girls, Adam and Maria Sarah

Mayford Boys Football Club ($1,000) see Berkman Foundation, Louis and Sandra

McKeesport Heritage Center ($25,000) see Crawford Estate, E. R.

McKeesport Heritage Center ($5,000) see Murphy Co., G.C.

McKeesport Hospital ($27,000) see Gibson Foundation, Addison H.

McKeesport Hospital ($5,000) see Peters Foundation, Charles F.

McKeesport Hospital Foundation ($25,000) see Crawford Estate, E. R.

Meals on Wheels ($25,000) see Crawford Estate, E. R.

Meals on Wheels ($10,000) see Laros Foundation, R. K.

Meals on Wheels ($100,000) see Payne Foundation, Frank E. and Seba B.

MEDA ($5,000) see United Service Foundation

Media-Providence Friends School ($25,000) see Smith Memorial Fund, Ethel Sergeant Clark

Medical College of Pennsylvania ($3,000) see Glenn Foundation for Medical Research, Paul F.

Medical College of Pennsylvania ($2,500) see Gulton Foundation

Medical College of Pennsylvania — to start the Schizophrenic Diagnostic and Referral Center ($50,000) see van Ameringen Foundation

Medical Missionary Sisters ($7,250) see Rotterman Trust, Helen L. and Marie F.

Mel Blount Youth Home of Washington County — capital support ($175,000) see Scaife Family Foundation

Melmark Charitable Foundation ($50,000) see Nason Foundation

Melmark Home ($10,000) see duPont Foundation, Alfred I.

Melmark Home ($15,000) see 1957 Charity Trust

Memorial Health Systems Corporation ($1,000) see Motter Printing Press Co.

Mendelssohn Choir of Pittsburgh ($13,500) see Mine Safety Appliances Co.

Mengle Memorial Library ($20,000) see Mengle Foundation, Glenn and Ruth

Menno Haven ($10,000) see Wood Foundation of Chambersburg, PA

Mental Health Association in Westmoreland County — for external advocacy services ($40,000) see Staunton Farm Foundation

Mercersburg Academy ($1,500) see Andersen Foundation, Arthur

Mercersburg Academy ($50,000) see Janssen Foundation, Henry

Mercersburg Academy ($66,400) see Rumbaugh Foundation, J. H. and F. H.

Mercersburg Academy ($8,000) see Western Shade Cloth Charitable Foundation

Mercersburg Academy ($10,000) see Wood Foundation of Chambersburg, PA

Mercersburg Academy — scholarship ($10,400) see York Barbell Co.

Mercersburg Academy — William Irvine Society ($3,000) see Grumbacher Foundation, M. S.

Mercy Catholic Medical Center ($500,625) see Connelly Foundation

Mercy Catholic Medical Center — ventilator ($20,000) see Scholler Foundation

Mercy Catholic Medical Center ($25,000) see Superior Tube Co.

Mercy Hospital ($4,000) see Waters Charitable Trust, Robert S.

Mercy Hospital Foundation ($6,500) see Donnelly Foundation, Mary J.

Merion Mercy Academy ($25,200) see Ellis Grant and Scholarship Fund, Charles E.

Messiah College ($20,000) see High Foundation

Messiah College ($70,000) see Kline Foundation, Josiah W. and Bessie H.

Messiah College ($100,000) see Whitaker Foundation

Messiah College Scholarship Fund ($50,000) see Stabler Foundation, Donald B. and Dorothy L.

Methodist Hospital ($31,800) see Roth Foundation

Methodist Hospital of Philadelphia ($10,000) see Lovett Foundation

Metro Arts ($30,000) see Kunkel Foundation, John Crain

Metropolitan Career Center ($5,000) see Wurts Memorial, Henrietta Tower

Metropolitan Collegiate Center, Germantown, PA see Rhone-Poulenc Rorer

Miley House — to support and develop the orchard hills campus and house an acute care psychiatric facility for children ($25,000) see Rider-Pool Foundation

Millbrook Playhouse— operating expenses ($4,000) see Piper Foundation

Millersville University ($4,000) see Quaker Chemical Corp.

Millersville University ($105,000) see SICO Foundation

Milton S. Hershey Medical Center ($5,000) see McCormick Trust, Anne

Milton S. Hershey Medical Center ($242,000) see Smith Charitable Trust, W. W.

Milton S. Hershey Medical Center — establish a professorship in the name of Dr. Bernard B. Brodie ($30,000) see Glaxo

Miriam Hospital Foundation ($50,000) see Hasbro

Miryams — adolescent rehabilitation ($5,000) see Donnelly Foundation, Mary J.

Miryam's ($2,000) see Falk Medical Fund, Maurice

MMI ($4,000) see Reidler Foundation

Mogan David Association Armdi ($40,000) see Premier Dental Products Co.

Mom's House ($20,000) see Miller Charitable Foundation, Howard E. and Nell E.

Mon Valley Tri-State Network ($2,500) see Eberly Foundation

Mon-Yough Chamber Foundation ($10,000) see Murphy Co., G.C.

Mon Yough Human Services — for the program for Angora Gardens ($80,000) see Staunton Farm Foundation

Monastery of Bethlehem ($10,000) see Santa Maria Foundation

Monell Chemical Senses Center ($500,000) see Monell Foundation, Ambrose

Monell Chemical Senses Center — ongoing sponsor's fee; research mechanisms of taste ($25,000) see International Flavors & Fragrances

Montgomery County Association for the Blind ($2,000) see Groome Beatty Trust, Helen D.

Montgomery County OIC ($5,000) see Douty Foundation

Montgomery Health Foundation ($4,000) see Quaker Chemical Corp.

Moore College of Art and Design ($100,000) see Paley Foundation, Goldie

Moore College of Art and Design ($25,000) see Perkins Memorial Foundation, George W.

Moravian College — athletic complex ($20,000) see Laros Foundation, R. K.

Moravian College ($1,200,000) see Payne Foundation, Frank E. and Seba B.

Moravian College ($400,000) see Reeves Foundation

Moravian Manor ($60,000) see Steinman Foundation, John Frederick

Moravian Theological Seminary — to help fund the library expansion ($125,000) see

Davis Foundations, Arthur Vining

Moss Rehabilitation ($500) see Safeguard Scientifics Foundation

Moss Rehabilitation Center ($50,000) see Aronson Foundation

Moss Rehabilitation Center ($50,000) see Levee Charitable Trust, Polly Annenberg

Mount Ararat Activity Center ($125,000) see Aluminum Co. of America

Mt. Lebanon Baptist Church ($10,000) see Knudsen Charitable Foundation, Earl

Mount Olivet Cemetery Association ($8,000) see Sheppard Foundation, Lawrence B.

Mt. St. Joseph Academy ($26,500) see Ellis Grant and Scholarship Fund, Charles E.

Mountour Trail Council ($250) see Copperweld Corp.

Movement Theater International ($3,000) see Groome Beatty Trust, Helen D.

MPC Corporation — partial support for the initial funding of a center for the study of the steel industry ($800,000) see Sloan Foundation, Alfred P.

Muhlenberg College — scholarships ($600) see Red Devil

Muhlenberg College — debt reduction ($100,000) see Trexler Trust, Harry C.

Muhlenberg College, Music and Drama ($3,000) see Baker Foundation, Dexter F. and Dorothy H.

Muhlenberg College, Summer Theater ($2,000) see Baker Foundation, Dexter F. and Dorothy H.

Music Group ($1,600) see Philadelphia Industries

Naaman Center — program support ($10,000) see United Service Foundation

National Foundation for Ileitis and Colitis ($25,000) see Levee Charitable Trust, Polly Annenberg

National Junior Tennis League ($7,500) see Reynolds Foundation, Eleanor T.

National Multiple Sclerosis Chapter ($15,000) see Clapp Charitable and Educational Trust, George H.

National Museum of American Jewish History ($20,000) see Boisi Family Foundation

National Museum of American Jewish History ($2,500) see Bronstein Foundation, Soloman and Sylvia

National Museum of American Jewish History ($2,500) see Feinstein Foundation, Myer and Rosaline

National Museum of American Jewish History ($1,000) see Gershman Foundation, Joel

National Museum of American Jewish History ($19,250) see Mandell Foundation, Samuel P.

National Museum of American Jewish History ($20,000) see Ross Foundation, Lyn & George M.

National Museum of American Jewish History ($11,500) see Snider Foundation

National Poetry Series ($18,342) see Copernicus Society of America

Natural Lands Trust ($3,000) see Groome Beatty Trust, Helen D.

Natural Lands Trust — land conservation and preservation ($595,560) see J. D. B. Fund

Nature Conservancy ($50,000) see McLean Contributionship

Nazareth Academy ($42,900) see Ellis Grant and Scholarship Fund, Charles E.

Nazareth Hospital ($1,020,000) see Connelly Foundation

Neffsville Mennonite Church ($38,333) see High Foundation

Negro Educational Emergency Drive (NEED) — follow-up study of past NEED recipients ($31,300) see Buhl Foundation

Neighborhood Housing Services ($1,000) see Penn Savings Bank, a division of Sovereign Bank Bank of Princeton, a division of Sovereign Bank

Neshaminy Warwick Presbyterian Church ($8,000) see Warwick Foundation

New Castle Christian Academy ($21,000) see Hoyt Foundation

New Jewish Community Center ($15,000) see Foster Charitable Trust

New Meadow Run School ($5,000) see Coen Family Foundation, Charles S. and Mary

North Catholic High School ($10,000) see Kelley Foundation, Kate M.

North Hills Passavant ($15,000) see Finley Charitable Trust, J. B.

North Hills Passavant Hospital — construction ($300,000) see Eden Hall Foundation

North Hills Passavant Hospital Foundation ($27,000) see Gibson Foundation, Addison H.

North Penn Hospital see Harleysville Mutual Insurance Co.

North Penn YMCA see Harleysville Mutual Insurance Co.

Northeast Pennsylvania Philharmonic ($5,000) see Sordoni Foundation

Northeastern Christian Junior College ($11,000) see Kiplinger Foundation

Northeastern Hospital ($30,000) see Mandell Foundation, Samuel P.

Northeastern Hospital of Philadelphia ($30,000) see Roth Foundation

Notre Dame Church — to assist parish youth with retreats, help fund social outreach and general expenses of running the church ($5,000) see Kavanagh Foundation, T. James

Oakland Catholic High School ($10,000) see Donnelly Foundation, Mary J.

Oakmont's Boulevard Project ($2,000) see Edgewater Steel Corp.

Ohio Valley General Hospital ($27,000) see Gibson Foundation, Addison H.

Ohio Valley General Hospital ($25,000) see Snee-Reinhardt Charitable Foundation

Oil City Area Health Center Foundation ($11,500) see Justus Trust, Edith C.

Oil City Economic Development Corporation ($60,000) see Justus Trust, Edith C.

Old Bedford Village ($10,000) see Whalley Charitable Trust

Olivet Covenant Presbyterian Church ($35,780) see Muller Foundation, C. John and Josephine

One to One: Citizen ($8,500) see Finley Charitable Trust, J. B.

One to One Citizen Advocacy ($2,000) see Falk Medical Fund, Maurice

Operation Exodus ($50,000) see Feinstein Foundation, Myer and Rosaline

Options for Aging ($5,000) see Dietrich Foundation, William B.

Orr Compassionate Care Center ($25,000) see McFeely-Rogers Foundation

Osterhout Free Library ($5,000) see Sordoni Foundation

Our Mother of Good Council Church ($10,000) see Lovett Foundation

Outreach South Hills ($5,000) see Murphy Co., G.C.

Overseas Mission Fellowship — missionary ($30,000) see Aurora Foundation

Oxford Area Civic Association ($35,000) see Oxford Foundation

Oxford Area School District ($50,000) see Oxford Foundation

Oxford Presbyterian Church ($50,000) see Oxford Foundation

PAAR ($5,000) see Shore Fund

Palace Theatre ($40,000) see Kennametal

Palmer R. Chitester Fund ($50,000) see Koch Charitable Foundation, Charles G.

Palmer R. Chitester Fund ($50,000) see Koch Charitable Foundation, Charles G.

Paoli Memorial Hospital ($2,500) see Colket Foundation, Ethel D.

Paoli Memorial Hospital ($50,000) see 1957 Charity Trust

Paoli Memorial Hospital ($15,000) see Superior Tube Co.

Papal Foundation ($33,000) see Booth-Bricker Fund

Papal Foundation ($40,000) see Brennan Foundation, Robert E.

Papal Foundation ($50,000) see Copernicus Society of America

Papal Foundation — religious ($100,000) see Domino's Pizza

Papal Foundation ($25,000) see Komes Foundation

Papal Foundation ($100,000) see McCarthy Foundation, Michael W.

Papal Foundation ($100,000) see McIntosh Foundation

Papal Foundation ($1,043,400) see Murphy Foundation, Dan

Papal Foundation ($250,000) see Sehn Foundation

Parent and Child Guidance Center ($1,000) see Foster Co., L.B.

Parents Union for Public Schools ($2,500) see Groome Beatty Trust, Helen D.

Parents Union for Public Schools in Philadelphia ($20,000) see Fels Fund, Samuel S.

Parish Resource Center ($15,000) see Steinman Foundation, John Frederick

Partners of Youth ($5,000) see Schautz Foundation, Walter L.

PATHS/PRISM, Philadelphia Partnership for Education ($2,400,000) see Pew Charitable Trusts

Pendle Hill ($24,000) see Shoemaker Fund, Thomas H. and Mary Williams

Penn Foundation for Mental Health — construction of apartment building for persons with chronic mental illness ($25,000) see Grundy Foundation

Penn Laurel Girl Scout Council ($5,000) see York Barbell Co.

Penn State University ($10,910) see Hamilton Bank

Penn State York Campaign ($8,000) see Susquehanna-Pfaltzgraff Co.

Penn's Southwest Association ($60,000) see Pittsburgh National Bank

Penn's Southwest Association ($35,000) see PPG Industries

Pennsylvania DUI Association see Harleysville Mutual Insurance Co.

Pennsylvania Academy of the Fine Arts ($50,000) see Arcadia Foundation

Pennsylvania Academy of the Fine Arts — program support and capital campaign ($262,500) see ARCO Chemical

Pennsylvania Academy of Fine Arts ($7,500) see Cameron Memorial Fund, Alpin J. and Alpin W.

Pennsylvania Academy of the Fine Arts ($75,000) see Claneil Foundation

Pennsylvania Academy of Fine Arts ($15,000) see Federation Foundation of Greater Philadelphia

Pennsylvania Academy of Fine Arts ($6,200) see Klein Charitable Foundation, Raymond

Pennsylvania Academy of the Fine Arts ($32,055) see Mandell Foundation, Samuel P.

Pennsylvania Academy of Fine Arts ($43,000) see Ross Foundation, Lyn & George M.

Pennsylvania Academy of Fine Arts ($15,000) see Smith Foundation

Pennsylvania Academy of the Fine Arts ($80,000) see SmithKline Beecham

Pennsylvania Academy of Fine Arts ($30,000) see Warwick Foundation

Pennsylvania Ballet ($5,000) see Bartol Foundation, Stockton Rush

Pennsylvania Ballet Association ($20,000) see Fels Fund, Samuel S.

Pennsylvania Ballet Association ($105,000) see Rock Foundation, Milton and Shirley

Pennsylvania Ballet Association ($5,000) see Tasty Baking Co.

Pennsylvania Catholic Conference — research/publicity to raise awareness of value and quality of Catholic education and parental choice in education ($100,000) see Raskob Foundation for Catholic Activities

Pennsylvania Chamber/Business/Industry ($20,000) see Armco Inc.

Pennsylvania College of Optometry ($35,000) see Wildermuth Foundation, E. F.

Pennsylvania College of Technology ($5,000) see Packer Foundation, Horace B.

Pennsylvania College of Technology ($3,418) see Smith Golden Rule Trust Fund, Fred G.

Pennsylvania Council on Economic Education ($500) see Safeguard Scientifics Foundation

Pennsylvania Department of Higher Education — "Philadelphia Parents as Teachers" see Scott Paper Co.

Pennsylvania Economic League ($420) see Charitable Fund

Pennsylvania Economic League ($550) see Edgewater Steel Corp.

Pennsylvania Economic League ($700) see Spang & Co.

Pennsylvania Engineering Foundation ($1,500) see York Barbell Co.

Pennsylvania Free Enterprise Week ($7,500) see PMA Industries

Pennsylvania Higher Education Assistance Agency ($18,313) see Wells Foundation, Franklin H. and Ruth L.

Pennsylvania Historical Society ($2,000) see Breyer Foundation

Pennsylvania Horticultural Society ($13,000) see Strawbridge Foundation of Pennsylvania II, Margaret Dorrance

Pennsylvania Horticultural Society ($5,000) see Widgeon Foundation

Pennsylvania Horticultural Society — a four-year grant for an urban tree planting project ($302,061) see Penn Foundation, William

Pennsylvania Hospital ($150,000) see Betz Foundation Trust, Theodora B.

Pennsylvania Hospital ($25,000) see Kynett Memorial Foundation, Edna G.

Pennsylvania Hospital ($43,100) see Scholler Foundation

Pennsylvania Hospital ($10,000) see Smith Foundation

Pennsylvania Humanities Council Film Project ($10,000) see Snee-Reinhardt Charitable Foundation

Pennsylvania Institute for Service Learning ($4,000) see Douty Foundation

Pennsylvania School of Art and Design ($4,000) see High Foundation

Pennsylvania School of Arts ($25,000) see Steinman Foundation, John Frederick

Pennsylvania Stage Company ($32,000) see Air Products & Chemicals

Pennsylvania Stage Company — underwriting grant ($17,000) see Air Products & Chemicals

Pennsylvania Stage Company ($1,000) see Baker Foundation, Dexter F. and Dorothy H.

Pennsylvania State McKeesport Campus ($5,000) see Murphy Co., G.C.

Pennsylvania State Police Camp Cadet ($1,000) see Freeport Brick Co.

Pennsylvania State University ($75,000) see Aluminum Co. of America

Pennsylvania State University ($37,533) see AMP

Pennsylvania (cont.)

Pennsylvania State University ($50,000) see Borg-Warner Corp.

Pennsylvania State University ($54,712) see Brookdale Foundation

Pennsylvania State University ($3,000) see Caplan Charity Foundation, Julius H.

Pennsylvania State University ($30,000) see Carpenter Technology Corp.

Pennsylvania State University ($1,000) see Clark Charitable Foundation

Pennsylvania State University ($50,000) see Crawford Estate, E. R.

Pennsylvania State University ($1,200) see Dekalb Energy Co.

Pennsylvania State University ($460) see Equimark Corp.

Pennsylvania State University ($1,000) see Fabri-Kal Corp.

Pennsylvania State University ($6,000) see Fisher Foundation

Pennsylvania State University ($10,000) see Gloeckner Foundation, Fred

Pennsylvania State University ($75,000) see Grumbacher Foundation, M. S.

Pennsylvania State University ($150,000) see Heinz Co., H.J.

Pennsylvania State University ($4,000) see Hexcel Corp.

Pennsylvania State University ($10,000) see Kunkel Foundation, John Crain

Pennsylvania State University ($30,000) see Mellon Bank Corp.

Pennsylvania State University ($3,000) see Motter Printing Press Co.

Pennsylvania State University ($29,000) see Newcombe Foundation, Charlotte W.

Pennsylvania State University ($10,000) see Oberlaender Foundation, Gustav

Pennsylvania State University — to investigate the dynamics of icefields and glaciers ($500,000) see Packard Foundation, David and Lucile

Pennsylvania State University ($1,500) see Penn Savings Bank, a division of Sovereign Bank Bank of Princeton, a division of Sovereign Bank

Pennsylvania State University — college of engineering fund ($3,000) see Pennsylvania Dutch Co.

Pennsylvania State University ($5,000) see Peters Foundation, Charles F.

Pennsylvania State University ($36,901) see Pfeiffer Research Foundation, Gustavus and Louise

Pennsylvania State University ($10,000) see Picower Foundation, Jeffrey M. and Barbara

Pennsylvania State University ($30,000) see Pittsburgh National Bank

Pennsylvania State University ($2,500) see PMA Industries

Pennsylvania State University ($44,000) see Poinsettia Foundation, Paul and Magdalena Ecke

Pennsylvania State University ($20,000) see Pulitzer Publishing Co.

Pennsylvania State University ($24,000) see Rockwell Foundation

Pennsylvania State University ($5,200) see Schautz Foundation, Walter L.

Pennsylvania State University ($10,060) see Smeal Foundation, Mary Jean & Frank P.

Pennsylvania State University ($100,000) see Westinghouse Electric Corp.

Pennsylvania State University ($100,000) see Whitaker Foundation

Pennsylvania State University ($50,000) see Wyomissing Foundation

Pennsylvania State University — Ceramic Science and Engineering Faculty Fellowship ($25,000) see Corning Incorporated

Pennsylvania State University — DuBois Campus ($25,000) see Mengle Foundation, Glenn and Ruth

Pennsylvania State University — for the purchase of electric-powered van to be used in solar energy research ($25,000) see Pennsylvania Power & Light

Pennsylvania State University at Harrisburg ($100,000) see Whitaker Foundation

Pennsylvania State University — for establishing a Max Kade Center ($350,000) see Kade Foundation, Max

Pennsylvania State University-School of Education ($120,000) see Hershey Foods Corp.

Pennsylvania State University School of Forest Resources ($570) see Sussman Fund, Edna Bailey

Pennsylvania State University — York Campaign ($10,000) see Dentsply International, Inc.

Pennsylvania State York Campaign ($8,000) see Susquehanna Investment Group

Pennsylvania Young Playwrights Festival ($5,000) see Bartol Foundation, Stockton Rush

Pennsylvania Youth Theater ($2,500) see Baker Foundation, Dexter F. and Dorothy H.

Pennsylvanians for Effective Government Education Committee — internships ($37,000) see McKenna Foundation, Philip M.

Pennypack Watershed Association ($139,500) see Beneficia Foundation

Penobscot Respiratory ($5,300) see Potts Memorial Foundation

People Library of Lower Burrell ($5,000) see Bozzone Family Foundation

Peoples Library-Lower Burrell Campaign ($20,000) see Allegheny Ludlum Corp.

People's Light and Theater Company ($50,000) see Arcadia Foundation

Peoples Light and Theater Company ($5,000) see Bartol Foundation, Stockton Rush

Pharmacists Against Drug Abuse see Rhone-Poulenc Rorer

Philabundance — Emergency Food Project ($5,000) see Seybert Institution for Poor Boys and Girls, Adam and Maria Sarah

Philadelphia Art Alliance ($3,000) see Corestates Bank

Philadelphia Ballet see Berwind Corp.

Philadelphia Biomedical Research ($2,000) see Berry Foundation, Archie W. and Grace

Philadelphia Center for Community Corrections ($75,575) see Friedland Family Foundation, Samuel

Philadelphia Children's Network ($4,000) see Douty Foundation

Philadelphia College of Pharmacy ($900) see Pennsylvania Knitted Outerwear Manufacturing Association

Philadelphia College Pharmacy ($20,000) see West Co.

Philadelphia College Pharmacy ($20,000) see West Co.

Philadelphia College of Pharmacy and Science — over five years ($50,000) see Thrift Drug, Inc.

Philadelphia College of Pharmacy and Science — over five years ($75,000) see U.S. Healthcare, Inc.

Philadelphia College of Pharmacy and Science — Humanities Project ($72,916) see Barra Foundation

Philadelphia College of Textile and Science ($50,000) see Burlington Industries

Philadelphia College of Textiles and Sciences ($1,300) see Pennsylvania Knitted Outerwear Manufacturing Association

Philadelphia Dance Alliance ($5,000) see Bartol Foundation, Stockton Rush

Philadelphia Drama Guild ($5,000) see Corestates Bank

Philadelphia Festival Theater ($5,000) see Bartol Foundation, Stockton Rush

Philadelphia Festival Theatre for New Plays ($25,000) see Arcadia Foundation

Philadelphia Foundation — to help establish a community development corporation support program to increase affordable housing ($1,000,000) see Penn Foundation, William

Philadelphia Futures ($5,000) see Rosenberg Foundation, Alexis

Philadelphia Geriatric Center ($1,000) see Gershman Foundation, Joel

Philadelphia Geriatric Center ($10,000) see Novotny Charitable Trust, Yetta Deitch

Philadelphia Geriatric Center ($10,000) see Snider Foundation

Philadelphia High School Academies — to provide academic and occupational training that transitions youth from school to employment see New Street Capital Corp.

Philadelphia Historic Preservation Corporation — in support of a technical assistance and regrant program for historic house museums located in the five-county region of Southeastern Pennsylvania ($2,635,000) see Pew Charitable Trusts

Philadelphia Maritime Museum ($10,000) see Hooper Foundation, Elizabeth S.

Philadelphia Museum of Art — program support and capital campaign ($52,500) see ARCO Chemical

Philadelphia Museum of Art ($5,000) see Asplundh Foundation

Philadelphia Museum of Art ($50,000) see Bell Atlantic Corp.

Philadelphia Museum of Art ($150,000) see Bohen Foundation

Philadelphia Museum of Art ($6,000) see Breyer Foundation

Philadelphia Museum of Art ($2,000) see Breyer Foundation

Philadelphia Museum of Art ($5,100) see CertainTeed Corp.

Philadelphia Museum of Art ($10,000) see Colket Foundation, Ethel D.

Philadelphia Museum of Art ($4,500) see Colket Foundation, Ethel D.

Philadelphia Museum of Art ($100,000) see Elf Atochem North America

Philadelphia Museum of Art ($40,000) see Elf Atochem North America

Philadelphia Museum of Art ($10,000) see Gershman Foundation, Joel

Philadelphia Museum of Art see Harleysville Mutual Insurance Co.

Philadelphia Museum of Art ($7,000) see Quaker Chemical Corp.

Philadelphia Museum of Art ($1,000) see Schwartz and Robert Schwartz Foundation, Bernard

Philadelphia Museum of Art ($10,000) see Snider Foundation

Philadelphia Museum of Art ($5,000) see Subaru of America Inc.

Philadelphia Museum of Art ($5,000) see Tasty Baking Co.

Philadelphia Museum of Art ($2,000,000) see Wallace Reader's Digest Fund, Lila

Philadelphia Museum of Art — acquisition fund for drawings, photographs and prints ($26,500) see Hunt Manufacturing Co.

Philadelphia Museum of Art — to fund general operating expenses and capital support for the Museum's Publication Department ($190,000) see CIGNA Corp.

Philadelphia Museum of Art — a six-year, $1-million grant ($225,000) see Campbell Soup Co.

Philadelphia Museum of Art — Tuffts Highboy ($198,000) see Barra Foundation

Philadelphia Music Foundation ($500) see Greene Foundation, Robert Z.

Philadelphia OIC ($1,000) see Safeguard Scientifics Foundation

Philadelphia Orchestra — capital campaign ($156,250) see Bell Atlantic Corp.

Philadelphia Orchestra ($25,000) see Beneficia Foundation

Philadelphia Orchestra see Berwind Corp.

Philadelphia Orchestra see Bloomingdale's

Philadelphia Orchestra ($52,583) see Eastern Foundry Co.

Philadelphia Orchestra ($50,000) see Elf Atochem North America

Philadelphia Orchestra ($50,000) see Elf Atochem North America

Philadelphia Orchestra ($37,000) see Elf Atochem North America

Philadelphia Orchestra ($50,000) see Huston Foundation

Philadelphia Orchestra ($60,000) see Nakamichi Foundation, E.

Philadelphia Orchestra ($5,000) see Rock Foundation, Milton and Shirley

Philadelphia Orchestra ($10,000) see Ross Foundation, Lyn & George M.

Philadelphia Orchestra ($5,000) see SPS Technologies

Philadelphia Orchestra Association ($9,000) see Cassett Foundation, Louis N.

Philadelphia Orchestra Association ($7,500) see Rittenhouse Foundation

Philadelphia Orchestra Association ($200,000) see SmithKline Beecham

Philadelphia Orchestra Association ($8,000) see Subaru of America Inc.

Philadelphia Orchestra Association — a three-year grant toward a new concert hall ($1,000,000) see Penn Foundation, William

Philadelphia Orchestra — children's concerts ($4,000) see Quaker Chemical Corp.

Philadelphia Orchestra — orchestra's proposed new hall and funding for the Academy of Music's Annual Ball ($505,240) see CIGNA Corp.

Philadelphia Psychiatric ($7,500) see Caplan Charity Foundation, Julius H.

Philadelphia Psychiatric Center ($1,000) see Strouse, Greenberg & Co.

Philadelphia Ranger Corps — a three-year grant to continue the Philadelphia Ranger Corps program ($3,000,000) see Penn Foundation, William

Philadelphia Refugee Service Center ($4,000) see Wurts Memorial, Henrietta Tower

Philadelphia Scholars Fund ($100,000) see Pine Tree Foundation

Philadelphia School District see Scott Paper Co.

Philadelphia Schools Collaborative ($7,820,000) see Pew Charitable Trusts

Philadelphia Schools Collaborative Fund ($6,000) see General Accident Insurance Co. of America

Philadelphia Senior Center ($3,500) see Douty Foundation

Philadelphia Senior Center — to help fund roof repairs ($40,000) see McLean Contributionship

Philadelphia Society ($6,000) see Coleman, Jr. Foundation, George E.

Philadelphia Society for Services to Children ($5,000) see Rosenberg Foundation, Alexis

Philadelphia Society for Services to Children — Kids 'N Kin Program ($6,000) see Seybert Institution for Poor Boys and Girls, Adam and Maria Sarah

Philadelphia Task Force ($21,000) see Dietrich Foundation, William B.

Pennsylvania (cont.)

($1,000) see Motter Printing Press Co.

Rehabilitation Institute ($100,000) see Heinz Foundation, Drue

Rehabilitation Institute ($50,000) see Shore Fund

Rehabilitation Institute ($10,000) see Tippens Foundation

Rehabilitation Institute of Pittsburgh — building addition program ($183,000) see Eden Hall Foundation

Rehabilitation Institute of Pittsburgh — for renovation and expansion of facilities and parking garage ($75,000) see Hillman Foundation

Rehabilitation Institute of Pittsburgh ($30,000) see Jennings Foundation, Mary Hillman

Rehabilitation Institute of Pittsburgh — handicapped children ($2,000) see Patterson Charitable Fund, W. I.

Rehabilitation Institute of Pittsburgh ($25,000) see Vesuvius Charitable Foundation

Rehabilitation Institute of Pittsburgh — for the capital funding drive, Miracles in Progress ($250,000) see Heinz Endowment, Vira I.

Renaissance Center — to evaluate a new program whose purpose is to develop parenting skills in mentally ill parents of young children ($4,965) see Pittsburgh Child Guidance Foundation

Rev. Paul Bradley Fund ($10,000) see Kelley Foundation, Kate M.

Rhoads School/ARCO Chemical Partnership — school restructuring ($77,000) see ARCO Chemical

Ridgway Area School District — Votech educaton feasibility study ($29,251) see Stackpole-Hall Foundation

Rimersburg Borough ($20,000) see Eccles Foundation, Ralph M. and Ella M.

Rimersburg Medical Center ($19,673) see Eccles Foundation, Ralph M. and Ella M.

Rivers Center for Independent Living Foundation ($30,000) see Massey Charitable Trust

Riverside Center for Jewish Seniors ($5,000) see Steinsapir Family Foundation, Julius L. and Libhie B.

Riverview Children's Center ($25,000) see Rockwell Foundation

Robert Morris College ($75,000) see Massey Charitable Trust

Robert Packer Hospital ($1,000) see LamCo. Communications

Rodale Institute ($5,488) see Copernicus Society of America

Rodef Shalom ($10,000) see Speyer Foundation, Alexander C. and Tillie S.

Rodef Shalom Congregation ($50,000) see Berkman Charitable Trust, Allen H. and Selma W.

Rodef Shalom Congregation ($2,500) see Obernauer Foundation

Rodef Shalom Restoration Fund ($20,000) see Berkman Foundation, Louis and Sandra

Rodef Shalom Temple Restoration Campaign ($25,000) see Foster Charitable Trust

Roman Catholic High School ($4,000) see Maneely Fund

Roper Mountain Science Center Association ($20,000) see Piedmont Health Care Foundation

Rosebach Museum and Library ($3,000) see Klein Charitable Foundation, Raymond

Rosemont College ($10,000) see Donnelly Foundation, Mary J.

Rosemont College ($5,000) see Ix & Sons, Frank

Rosemont College ($200,000) see McShain Charities, John

Rosemont College ($73,480) see McShain Charities, John

Rosemont College ($4,000) see Quaker Chemical Corp.

Roxborough Memorial Hospital ($30,000) see Roth Foundation

Ruffed Grouse Society ($1,000) see Holley Foundation

Sacred Heart Church and School ($23,950) see St. Mary's Catholic Foundation

Sain Vincent Archabbey ($20,000) see McFeely-Rogers Foundation

St. Agnes Episcopal Church — unrestricted ($27,280) see Stackpole-Hall Foundation

St. Alban's Episcopal Church ($6,000) see Kavanagh Foundation, T. James

St. Anthonys Center ($500) see LamCo. Communications

St. Anthony's School — expressive therapies ($42,612) see Trees Charitable Trust, Edith L.

St. Barnabas Free Home ($3,900) see Mack Foundation, J. S.

St. Barnabas Medical Center — for the relocation and modernization of the Elizabeth DeCamp McInerny Burn Center ($100,000) see DeCamp Foundation, Ira W.

St. Basil Academy ($35,400) see Ellis Grant and Scholarship Fund, Charles E.

St. Benedict's Church ($20,000) see Muller Foundation, C. John and Josephine

St. Bonaventure University ($4,000) see Holtzmann Foundation, Jacob L. and Lillian

St. Bonaventure University ($10,000) see Mark IV Industries

St. Charles Borromeo Seminary ($4,650) see General Accident Insurance Co. of America

St. Christopher's Hospital for Children ($25,000) see Smith Foundation

St. Clair Hospital Foundation ($25,000) see Hopwood Charitable Trust, John M.

St. Davids Episcopal Church ($5,000) see Strawbridge Foundation of Pennsylvania I, Margaret Dorrance

St. Edmund's Academy ($26,500) see Hunt Foundation, Roy A.

St. Francis Hospital ($80,000) see Berry Foundation, Archie W. and Grace

St. Francis Women's Hospital ($5,430) see Piedmont Health Care Foundation

St. Francis Xavier Church — used to improve the church property and aid in the

expense of education in school ($8,500) see Kavanagh Foundation, T. James

St. Gabriel's System ($5,000) see Wurts Memorial, Henrietta Tower

St. Hugh Catholic School — Fine Arts Program ($8,000) see Seybert Institution for Poor Boys and Girls, Adam and Maria Sarah

St. Ignatius Nursing Home — to fund the installation of smoke detectors ($32,000) see McLean Contributionship

St. James Church ($2,500) see Steinman Foundation, James Hale

St. Joseph Church ($30,000) see St. Mary's Catholic Foundation

St. Joseph Hospital ($20,000) see Crels Foundation

St. Joseph's Hospital ($25,000) see Wyomissing Foundation

St. Joseph's Hospital Capital Campaign ($5,000) see Oberlaender Foundation, Gustav

St. Joseph's Prep ($3,910) see General Accident Insurance Co. of America

St. Joseph's Preparatory School ($4,140) see SPS Technologies

St. Joseph's Preparatory School ($125,000) see Superior Tube Co.

St. Joseph's School ($10,000) see Kavanagh Foundation, T. James

St. Josephs University ($250) see Chiquita Brands Co.

St. Joseph's University ($9,000) see Lynch Scholarship Foundation, John B.

St. Joseph's University ($700,000) see McShain Charities, John

St. Joseph's University ($5,000) see Rosenberg Foundation, Alexis

St. Joseph's University ($75,000) see Superior Tube Co.

St. Lukes Hospital ($100,000) see Payne Foundation, Frank E. and Seba B.

St. Margaret Mary's Church ($10,000) see Bozzone Family Foundation

St. Margaret Memorial Hospital ($25,000) see Mine Safety Appliances Co.

St. Margaret Memorial Hospital — to help endow the medical director's chair of the Family Practice Residency Program ($500,000) see Mellon Foundation, Richard King

St. Margaret Memorial Hospital Foundation ($75,000) see McCune Charitable Trust, John R.

St. Margaret Memorial Hospital Foundation ($10,000) see Tippens Foundation

St. Margaret's Memorial Hospital Foundation ($500) see Edgewater Steel Corp.

St. Mark's Evangelical Lutheran Church ($66,265) see Rudy, Jr. Trust, George B.

St. Marys Parochial School ($32,300) see St. Mary's Catholic Foundation

St. Patrick's Catholic Church — building fund ($3,000) see Pennsylvania Dutch Co.

St. Peters Child Development ($150,000) see Trees Charitable Trust, Edith L.

St. Rose of Lima Church ($6,000) see J. D. B. Fund

St. Stephens Church ($18,680) see Schoonmaker J-Sewkly Valley Hospital Trust

St. Vincent College ($54,030) see Kennametal

St. Vincent College ($9,500) see McFeely-Rogers Foundation

Saint Vincent College ($50,000) see McKenna Foundation, Katherine Mabis

Saint Vincent College ($50,000) see McKenna Foundation, Philip M.

St. Vincent de Paul Church ($8,000) see Sheppard Foundation, Lawrence B.

Salem Lutheran Church ($10,000) see Zock Endowment Trust

Salem Lutheran Church ($1,000) see Zock Endowment Trust

Salisbury School District — to provide funding for the mini grant program ($39,714) see Rider-Pool Foundation

SALT ($25,000) see Bingham Second Betterment Fund, William

Saltworks — for the prevention/intervention program on sexual abuse ($25,000) see Staunton Farm Foundation

Salvation Army ($25,000) see Allegheny Ludlum Corp.

Salvation Army ($21,000) see Crawford Estate, E. R.

Salvation Army ($2,000) see Dynamet, Inc.

Salvation Army ($286) see Foster Co., L.B.

Salvation Army ($10,000) see Hulme Charitable Foundation, Milton G.

Salvation Army ($4,300) see Kent-Lucas Foundation

Salvation Army ($5,000) see Murphy Co., G.C.

Salvation Army ($5,000) see Patterson Charitable Fund, W. I.

Salvation Army ($4,000) see Peters Foundation, Charles F.

Salvation Army ($50,000) see Pine Tree Foundation

Salvation Army ($1,000) see Piper Foundation

Salvation Army ($22,500) see Plankenhorn Foundation, Harry

Salvation Army ($5,000) see Plankenhorn Foundation, Harry

Salvation Army ($66,264) see Rudy, Jr. Trust, George B.

Salvation Army ($5,500) see Schautz Foundation, Walter L.

Salvation Army ($20,000) see Tippens Foundation

Salvation Army ($20,000) see Wood Foundation of Chambersburg, PA

Salvation Army Western Pennsylvania Division — toward relocation, renovation and endowment projects ($1,500,000) see McCune Foundation

Santa Cruz Mission ($50,000) see Ryan Family Charitable Foundation

Sassafras Corporation — a three-year grant for operating costs of the Arts Bank on South Broad Street ($2,535,750) see Penn Foundation, William

Scenic River Days '89 ($7,500) see Penn Savings Bank, a division of Sovereign Bank Bank of Princeton, a division of Sovereign Bank

Scholarship Trust ($10,000) see Glosser Foundation, David A.

School for Blind Children ($1,000) see Spang & Co.

School District of Philadelphia — student aid program fund ($16,000) see Ludwick Institute

Schuylkill Center ($305,250) see J. D. B. Fund

Schuylkill Center — to help relocate and expand Teachers Resource Center ($50,000) see McLean Contributionship

Schuylkill River Greenway Association ($25,000) see Wyomissing Foundation

Scranton Little Sisters of the Poor ($200,000) see Weinberg Foundation, Harry and Jeanette

Second Century Fund ($25,000) see Berkman Charitable Trust, Allen H. and Selma W.

Second Mile ($10,000) see Richardson Charitable Trust, Anne S.

Security on Campus ($2,000) see Maneely Fund

Self-Help Group Network ($2,080) see Falk Medical Fund, Maurice

Seton Hill College ($40,000) see McFeely-Rogers Foundation

Seven Dolors Roman Catholic Church ($7,500) see J. D. B. Fund

Sewickley Academy ($15,000) see Clapp Charitable and Educational Trust, George H.

Sewickley Academy ($25,000) see Simmons Family Foundation, R. P.

Sewickley Academy ($3,000) see Simmons Family Foundation, R. P.

Sewickley Academy ($15,000) see Snyder Charitable Fund, W. P.

Sewickley Valley Hospital ($20,000) see Clapp Charitable and Educational Trust, George H.

Sewickley Valley Hospital ($46,705) see Schoonmaker J-Sewkly Valley Hospital Trust

Sewickley Valley Hospital ($5,000) see Simmons Family Foundation, R. P.

Shady Lane School ($25,000) see Love Foundation, George H. and Margaret McClintic

Shady Side Academy ($3,500) see Waters Charitable Trust, Robert S.

Shadyside Academy ($13,500) see Hulme Charitable Foundation, Milton G.

Shadyside Academy ($5,000) see Tippens Foundation

Shadyside Hospital ($9,341) see Schoonmaker J-Sewkly Valley Hospital Trust

Shadyside Hospital Foundation ($48,800) see Hopwood Charitable Trust, John M.

Shadyside Hospital Foundation ($15,000) see Hulme Charitable Foundation, Milton G.

Shadyside Presbyterian Church ($15,000) see Hulme Charitable Foundation, Milton G.

Shalom Center ($50,000) see List Foundation, Albert A.

Shalom Center ($40,000) see List Foundation, Albert A.

Shalom Center ($25,000) see List Foundation, Albert A.

Shalom Center ($12,000) see List Foundation, Albert A.

Sharon Regional Health System — expansion ($160,000) see Eden Hall Foundation

Sharon Rotary ($50) see Charitable Fund

Shefa Fund ($40,000) see List Foundation, Albert A.

Shefa Fund — for planning and development, and for general operating support of the Jewish Healing Center ($170,000) see Cummings Foundation, Nathan

Sherwood Hall ($60,000) see Hershey Foods Corp.

Shippensburg University ($10,000) see Kunkel Foundation, John Crain

Shippensburg University ($66,000) see SICO Foundation

Shippensburg University Foundation ($25,000) see Wood Foundation of Chambersburg, PA

Shriners Hospital for Crippled Children ($10,070) see Freygang Foundation, Walter Henry

Sisters of Holy Spirit — nursing home expansion ($10,000) see Snee-Reinhardt Charitable Foundation

Sisters, Servants of Immaculate Heart of Mary ($20,000) see O'Neil Foundation, M. G.

Sisters, Servants of the Immaculate Heart of Mary ($10,000) see Seymour and Troester Foundation

Smithfield United Church ($25,000) see Weisbrod Foundation Trust Dept., Robert and Mary

Society for the Preservation of the Duquesne Heights Incline ($4,393) see Patterson Charitable Fund, W. I.

Sol C. Snider Entrepreneurial Center ($100,000) see Snider Foundation

Soldiers and Sailors Memorial Hospital ($6,500) see Packer Foundation, Horace B.

Soli Deo Gloria ($15,000) see Finley Charitable Trust, J. B.

Solomon and Sylvia Bronstein Scholarship Fund of Har Zion Temple ($8,000) see Bronstein Foundation, Soloman and Sylvia

South Hills Health System ($27,000) see Gibson Foundation, Addison H.

South Hills Interfaith Ministries — for a one year extension of the Morgan Project program ($33,000) see Staunton Farm Foundation

South Side Hospital ($27,000) see Gibson Foundation, Addison H.

South Street Dance Company ($5,000) see Bartol Foundation, Stockton Rush

Southeast DELCO School District — general support ($62,000) see ARCO Chemical

Southeast Neighborhood Center ($100,000) see Payne Foundation, Frank E. and Seba B.

Southern Alleghenies Museum of Art ($2,000) see Glosser Foundation, David A.

Southern Alleghenies Museum of Art ($3,000) see Polk Foundation

Southern Alleghenies Museum of Art ($4,000) see Waters Charitable Trust, Robert S.

Southern Chester County Medical Center ($100,000) see Oxford Foundation

Southern Chester County YMCA ($105,000) see Oxford Foundation

Southern Clarion County Development Corporation ($4,130) see Eccles Foundation, Ralph M. and Ella M.

Southwest Community Enrichment Program Project ($4,000) see Wurts Memorial, Henrietta Tower

Southwest Services ($3,000) see Vesuvius Charitable Foundation

Spanish Mennonite Church — program support ($3,000) see United Service Foundation

Specola Vaticana ($20,000) see Copernicus Society of America

Speech Hearing and Learning Center ($22,000) see Piedmont Health Care Foundation

SPIN (Special People In Northeast) ($10,000) see Muller Foundation, C. John and Josephine

Spina Bifida Association of West Pennsylvania ($20,000) see Weisbrod Foundation Trust Dept., Robert and Mary

Spina Bifida Association of Western Pennsylvania — for construction of transitional living program facility ($50,000) see Hillman Foundation

Spina Bifida Association of Western Pennsylvania ($30,000) see Hopwood Charitable Trust, John M.

Spina Bifida Association of Western Pennsylvania ($62,500) see Massey Charitable Trust

Spina Bifida Association of Western Pennsylvania — camp program ($2,500) see Patterson Charitable Fund, W. I.

Spiritual Frontiers Fellowship International ($4,000) see Ebert Charitable Foundation, Horatio B.

Springetts Fire Company ($1,000) see Motter Printing Press Co.

Statement of Principle Support ($6,000) see Donaldson Co.

Strand-Capitol Performing Arts Center ($4,600) see Freas Foundation

Strand-Capitol Performing Arts Center ($400) see General Machine Works

Strand-Capitol Performing Arts Center ($30,000) see Grumbacher Foundation, M. S.

Strand-Capitol Performing Arts Center ($35,000) see Susquehanna Investment Group

Strand-Capitol Performing Arts Center ($26,500) see Weiler Foundation, Theodore & Renee

Strand-Capitol Performing Arts Center Capital Campaign ($4,000) see Motter Printing Press Co.

Struthers Presbyterian Church ($15,000) see Murphy Co., G.C.

Students Against Drunk Driving (SADD) see Harleysville Mutual Insurance Co.

Supportive Child/Adult Network ($5,000) see Rosenberg Foundation, Alexis

Susquehanna University ($11,000) see Harding Educational and Charitable Foundation

Susquehanna University ($50,000) see Kline Foundation, Josiah W. and Bessie H.

Susquehanna University ($10,000) see Reidler Foundation

Susquehanna University — Fisher Science Hall ($20,000) see Stabler Foundation, Donald B. and Dorothy L.

Swarthmore College ($25,000) see Garrigues Trust, Edwin B.

Swarthmore College ($550,100) see Lang Foundation, Eugene M.

Swarthmore College ($137,500) see Oxford Foundation

Swarthmore College/Foundation ($20,000) see Stern Memorial Trust, Sidney

Sweetwater Art Center ($10,000) see Rockwell Foundation

Sweetwater Art Center ($5,000) see Simmons Family Foundation, R. P.

Talmudical Yeshiva ($5,000) see Korman Family Foundation, Hyman

Talmudical Yeshiva of Philadelphia ($225,000) see Morgenstern Foundation, Morris

Teen Haven ($10,000) see J. D. B. Fund

Teen Pregnancy Childcare Training Program ($10,768) see Wardle Family Foundation

Temple Adath Israel ($2,000) see Schwartz and Robert Schwartz Foundation, Bernard

Temple Beth-El ($10,000) see Kline Foundation, Charles and Figa

Temple Beth Zion ($4,000) see Rittenhouse Foundation

Temple B'nai Israel ($3,000) see Peters Foundation, Charles F.

Temple Shalom ($11,350) see Korman Family Foundation, Hyman

Temple University ($8,000) see Claneil Foundation

Temple University ($25,000) see Feinstein Foundation, Myer and Rosaline

Temple University ($100,000) see Fox Foundation, Richard J.

Temple University ($25,000) see Garrigues Trust, Edwin B.

Temple University ($15,000) see Jaqua Foundation

Temple University ($32,000) see Newcombe Foundation, Charlotte W.

Temple University ($5,000) see Rosenberg Foundation, Alexis

Temple University ($210,000) see Smith Charitable Trust, W. W.

Temple University ($500,000) see SmithKline Beecham

Temple University — support cardiac electro-physiological program ($50,000) see McLean Contributionship

Temple University, Fels Research Institute for Cancer ($250,000) see Fels Fund, Samuel S.

Temple University — a four-year grant for an infant mortality reduction program in high-risk neighborhoods ($1,200,558) see Penn Foundation, William

Temple University Institute on Aging — Center for Intergenerational Learning

($28,900) see Burden Foundation, Florence V.

Temple University School of Medicine ($53,380) see Measey Foundation, Benjamin and Mary Siddons

Temple University School of Medicine ($233,000) see Smith Charitable Trust, W. W.

Tenek University ($800) see Pennsylvania Knitted Outerwear Manufacturing Association

Thiel College ($50,000) see Powers Higher Educational Fund, Edward W. and Alice R.

Thiel College — automation and advanced information technology for the Langenheim Memorial Library - to support the library automation component of a campus-wide on-line telecommunications and info system ($186,230) see Buhl Foundation

Thomas Jefferson University ($286,200) see Foerderer Foundation, Percival E. and Ethel Brown

Thomas Jefferson University ($50,000) see Foerderer Foundation, Percival E. and Ethel Brown

Thomas Jefferson University ($5,000) see Foerderer Foundation, Percival E. and Ethel Brown

Thomas Jefferson University ($4,000) see Foerderer Foundation, Percival E. and Ethel Brown

Thomas Jefferson University — to develop computer software for use by family practitioners in heart disease screening ($35,000) see Kynett Memorial Foundation, Edna G.

Thomas Jefferson University — cardiology symposium seminars ($10,000) see Kynett Memorial Foundation, Edna G.

Thomas Jefferson University ($50,000) see McLean Contributionship

Thomas Jefferson University — toward the cost of purchasing certain equipment for a new cardiology research laboratory ($200,000) see Rippel Foundation, Fannie E.

Thomas Jefferson University, Philadelphia, PA — to underwrite a rheumatology lab ($15,000) see Searle & Co., G.D.

Three Rivers Adoption Council — to provide counseling and support services to foster and adoptive families in crisis ($3,000) see Pittsburgh Child Guidance Foundation

Three Rivers Center for Independent Living — renovation ($2,500) see Patterson Charitable Fund, W. I.

Three Rivers Rowing Association — to support the third year of a year-around Youth Rowing Program for children ages 10 to 16 from inner-city neighborhoods ($50,328) see Pittsburgh Child Guidance Foundation

Three Rivers Shakespeare Festival ($15,000) see Chambers Development Co.

Three Rivers Young Peoples Orchestras ($20,000) see Campbell Foundation, Charles Talbot

Three Rivers Youth — for the program for renovating and upgrading the intensive treatment unit ($75,000) see Staunton Farm Foundation

Tonto Rim Baptist Camp ($6,000) see Tell Foundation

Torah Academy ($3,000) see Fingerhut Family Foundation

Torah Academy ($3,000) see Fingerhut Family Foundation

Torah Academy of Greater Philadelphia ($7,410) see Stern Family Foundation, Harry

Touchstone Center for Crafts ($5,000) see Grable Foundation

Treatment Trends ($15,000) see Rider-Pool Foundation

Tree of Life Congregation ($750) see Millstein Charitable Foundation

Trevor's Campaign ($5,000) see Kent-Lucas Foundation

Tri-County Easter Seal Scoeity ($43,973) see Hambay Foundation, James T.

Tri-County United Way ($29,224) see Hamilton Bank

Trinity Cathedral — towards $1.5 million Community Campaign ($25,000) see Hillman Foundation, Henry L.

Trinity High School — development fund ($5,000) see Pennsylvania Dutch Co.

Trinity Lutheran Church ($20,000) see Reidler Foundation

Trinity Playgroup ($1,000) see Bronstein Foundation, Soloman and Sylvia

Trustees of Struthers Library Building ($3,132) see Betts Industries

Trustees of University of Pennsylvania ($250,000) see Measey Foundation, Benjamin and Mary Siddons

Trustees of the University of Pennsylvania — Bolton Center ($5,000) see Strawbridge Foundation of Pennsylvania I, Margaret Dorrance

Trustees of University of Pennsylvania — Department of Medicine ($250,000) see Barra Foundation

Trustees of the University of Pennsylvania, Fels Center ($125,000) see Fels Fund, Samuel S.

Trustees of the University of Pennsylvania, Fels Center ($100,000) see Fels Fund, Samuel S.

Try Again Homes ($10,000) see Coen Family Foundation, Charles S. and Mary

Try Again Homes ($25,000) see Weisbrod Foundation Trust Dept., Robert and Mary

Tylenol Kids ($5,000) see PMA Industries

Ukrainian Technological Society C.C.R.F. ($10,000) see Campbell Foundation, Charles Talbot

Union School District ($10,420) see Eccles Foundation, Ralph M. and Ella M.

United Cerebral Palsy ($12,500) see Dynamet, Inc.

United Cerebral Palsy ($8,750) see Hambay Foundation, James T.

United Cerebral Palsy Association ($25,000) see Cassett Foundation, Louis N.

United Cerebral Palsy of Western Pennsylvania

Pennsylvania (cont.)

($30,000) see Hopwood Charitable Trust, John M.

United Community Independence Programs ($25,000) see Phillips Charitable Trust, Dr. and Mrs. Arthur William

United Fund ($40,000) see Steinman Foundation, James Hale

United Fund ($38,500) see Steinman Foundation, John Frederick

United Fund ($18,491) see Superior Tube Co.

United Funds ($105,000) see Carpenter Technology Corp.

United Jewish Appeal Federation of Jewish Philanthropies ($125,000) see Action Industries, Inc.

United Jewish Appeal Federation of Jewish Philanthropies ($16,667) see Berkman Charitable Trust, Allen H. and Selma W.

United Jewish Appeal Federation of Jewish Philanthropies ($7,500) see Berkman Foundation, Louis and Sandra

United Jewish Appeal Federation of Jewish Philanthropies ($100,000) see Foster Charitable Trust

United Jewish Appeal Federation of Jewish Philanthropies ($62,500) see Foster Charitable Trust

United Jewish Appeal Federation of Jewish Philanthropies ($70,000) see Glosser Foundation, David A.

United Jewish Appeal Federation of Jewish Philanthropies ($10,000) see Glosser Foundation, David A.

United Jewish Appeal Federation of Jewish Philanthropies ($4,000) see Glosser Foundation, David A.

United Jewish Appeal Federation of Jewish Philanthropies ($300,000) see Grass Family Foundation

United Jewish Appeal Federation of Jewish Philanthropies ($4,461) see Grumbacher Foundation, M. S.

United Jewish Appeal Federation of Jewish Philanthropies ($3,000) see Millstein Charitable Foundation

United Jewish Appeal Federation of Jewish Philanthropies ($2,500) see Millstein Charitable Foundation

United Jewish Appeal Federation of Jewish Philanthropies ($13,100) see Speyer Foundation, Alexander C. and Tillie S.

United Jewish Appeal Federation of Jewish Philanthropies ($4,000) see Steinsapir Family Foundation, Julius L. and Libhie B.

United Jewish Appeal Federation of Jewish Philanthropies ($3,200) see Steinsapir Family Foundation, Julius L. and Libhie B.

United Jewish Community ($5,000) see Grass Family Foundation

United Jewish Federation ($217,000) see Jewish Healthcare Foundation of Pittsburgh

United Jewish Federation ($138,500) see Jewish Healthcare Foundation of Pittsburgh

United Methodist Church ($1,500) see Eccles Foundation, Ralph M. and Ella M.

United Ministries ($5,000) see Piedmont Health Care Foundation

United Negro College Fund ($1,000) see Matthews International Corp.

United Presbyterian Home for Children ($75,000) see Wardle Family Foundation

United Rehabilitation Services ($2,500) see Sordoni Foundation

United States Committee — Sports for Israel ($100) see Wasserman Foundation, George

United Way ($5,000) see ACF Industries, Inc.

United Way ($21,000) see Action Industries, Inc.

United Way ($23,538) see Alco Standard Corp.

United Way ($5,200) see Alco Standard Corp.

United Way ($50,000) see Aristech Chemical Corp.

United Way ($10,000) see Berkman Charitable Trust, Allen H. and Selma W.

United Way ($10,000) see Berkman Charitable Trust, Allen H. and Selma W.

United Way ($9,150) see Betts Industries

United Way ($52,000) see Binswanger Co.

United Way ($14,000) see Bozzone Family Foundation

United Way ($2,000) see Brand Cos.

United Way ($11,000) see Breyer Foundation

United Way ($100) see Burndy Corp.

United Way ($5,000) see Caplan Charity Foundation, Julius H.

United Way ($55,691) see CertainTeed Corp.

United Way ($13,229) see CertainTeed Corp.

United Way ($48,226) see Chambers Development Co.

United Way ($30,500) see Clapp Charitable and Educational Trust, George H.

United Way ($4,000) see Colket Foundation, Ethel D.

United Way ($24,000) see Conston Corp.

United Way ($15,000) see Crels Foundation

United Way ($17,250) see Dentsply International, Inc.

United Way ($3,200) see Dynamet, Inc.

United Way — yearly campaign ($150,000) see Eden Hall Foundation

United Way ($15,000) see Edgewater Steel Corp.

United Way ($25,000) see Fair Oaks Foundation, Inc.

United Way ($46,000) see Feinstein Foundation, Myer and Rosaline

United Way ($13,500) see Foster Charitable Trust

United Way ($9,000) see Foster Co., L.B.

United Way ($33,000) see Fox Foundation, Richard J.

United Way ($1,000) see Freeport Brick Co.

United Way ($223,436) see General Accident Insurance Co. of America

United Way ($235,000) see General Electric Co.

United Way ($500) see General Machine Works

United Way ($65,000) see Gershman Foundation, Joel

United Way ($1,600) see Glosser Foundation, David A.

United Way ($57,575) see Hamilton Bank

United Way ($38,547) see Hamilton Bank

United Way ($38,418) see Hamilton Bank

United Way ($15,540) see Hamilton Bank

United Way ($2,800) see Handy & Harman

United Way ($11,000) see Heileman Brewing Co., Inc., G.

United Way ($159) see Interstate National Corp.

United Way ($20,000) see J. D. B. Fund

United Way ($88,500) see Janssen Foundation, Henry

United Way ($28,000) see Kennametal

United Way ($5,000) see Korman Family Foundation, Hyman

United Way ($2,000) see Lebanon Mutual Insurance Co.

United Way ($6,500) see Lehigh Portland Cement Co.

United Way ($10,000) see Love Foundation, George H. and Margaret McClintic

United Way ($10,000) see Lovett Foundation

United Way ($3,300) see Mack Foundation, J. S.

United Way ($11,000) see Maneely Fund

United Way ($31,203) see Matthews International Corp.

United Way ($2,500) see Matthews International Corp.

United Way ($30,000) see McKee Poor Fund, Virginia A.

United Way ($16,600) see Merit Oil Corp.

United Way ($10,000) see Motter Printing Press Co.

United Way ($34,000) see National Forge Co.

United Way ($5,500) see Oberlaender Foundation, Gustav

United Way ($5,500) see Oberlaender Foundation, Gustav

United Way ($5,500) see Oberlaender Foundation, Gustav

United Way ($5,500) see Oberlaender Foundation, Gustav

United Way ($5,200) see Penn Savings Bank, a division of Sovereign Bank Bank of Princeton, a division of Sovereign Bank

United Way ($3,000) see Penn Savings Bank, a division of Sovereign Bank Bank of Princeton, a division of Sovereign Bank

United Way ($5,000) see Philadelphia Industries

United Way ($6,000) see Pitt-Des Moines Inc.

United Way ($4,000) see Rittenhouse Foundation

United Way ($10,000) see Rock Foundation, Milton and Shirley

United Way ($11,000) see Ross Foundation, Lyn & George M.

United Way ($4,250) see Schautz Foundation, Walter L.

United Way ($46,705) see Schoonmaker J-Sewkly Valley Hospital Trust

United Way ($8,000) see Schoonmaker J-Sewkly Valley Hospital Trust

United Way ($10,000) see Schwartz and Robert Schwartz Foundation, Bernard

United Way ($25,000) see Simmons Family Foundation, R. P.

United Way ($20,000) see Spang & Co.

United Way ($8,000) see Speyer Foundation, Alexander C. and Tillie S.

United Way ($63,000) see SPS Technologies

United Way ($10,000) see Stabler Foundation, Donald B. and Dorothy L.

United Way ($44,000) see Susquehanna Investment Group

United Way ($7,300) see Tasty Baking Co.

United Way ($25,000) see Tippens Foundation

United Way ($11,496) see Valspar Corp.

United Way ($5,000) see Vesuvius Charitable Foundation

United Way ($10,000) see Wardle Family Foundation

United Way ($5,000) see Wardle Family Foundation

United Way ($6,000) see Warwick Foundation

United Way ($26,000) see West Co.

United Way ($13,752) see West Co.

United Way ($7,260) see White Consolidated Industries

United Way ($74,500) see Wyomissing Foundation

United Way of Adams County ($35,000) see Susquehanna-Pfaltzgraff Co.

United Way of Allegheny County — to help purchase and equip this new human service center ($500,000) see Mellon Foundation, Richard King

United Way of Allegheny County ($15,000) see Morris Charitable Trust, Charles M.

United Way of Beaver County ($45,000) see ARCO Chemical

United Way of Boyertown ($24,780) see Cabot Corp.

United Way — Bradford Area ($27,500) see Dresser Industries

United Way of Bucks County — annual fund drive ($95,000) see Grundy Foundation

United Way of Butler County ($11,000) see Mine Safety Appliances Co.

United Way of the Capital Region ($110,500) see AMP

United Way of the Capital Region ($140,448) see Hershey Foods Corp.

United Way of Chester County ($76,915) see Lukens

United Way of Lackawanna County — annual contribution ($10,000) see Duchossois Industries

United Way of Lancaster County ($390,000) see Armstrong World Industries Inc.

United Way of Lebanon County ($61,400) see Hershey Foods Corp.

United Way - North Penn ($10,000) see Thomas & Betts Corp.

United Way of Southeastern Pennsylvania ($200,000) see ARCO Chemical

United Way of Southeastern Pennsylvania — campaign ($727,630) see CIGNA Corp.

United Way of Southeastern Pennsylvania ($13,700) see Dun & Bradstreet Corp.

United Way of Southeastern Pennsylvania ($34,200) see FMC Corp.

United Way of Southeastern Pennsylvania ($10,000) see Hunt Manufacturing Co.

United Way of Southeastern Pennsylvania ($10,500) see Kidder, Peabody & Co.

United Way of Southeastern Pennsylvania ($15,015) see Lukens

United Way of Southeastern Pennsylvania — for the 1992 campaign ($415,766) see Penn Foundation, William

United Way of Southwestern Pennsylvania ($346,792) see Allegheny Ludlum Corp.

United Way of Southwestern Pennsylvania ($460,000) see Heinz Co., H.J.

United Way of Southwestern Pennsylvania ($125,000) see Mellon Bank Corp.

United Way of Southwestern Pennsylvania ($125,000) see Mellon Bank Corp.

United Way of Southwestern Pennsylvania ($125,000) see Mellon Bank Corp.

United Way of Southwestern Pennsylvania ($125,000) see Mellon Bank Corp.

United Way of Southwestern Pennsylvania ($112,500) see Mine Safety Appliances Co.

United Way of Southwestern Pennsylvania ($550,000) see Pittsburgh National Bank

United Way, Southwestern Pennsylvania ($440,000) see PPG Industries

United Way of Southwestern Pennsylvania ($1,000,000) see Westinghouse Electric Corp.

United Way of Westmoreland County ($22,000) see Timken Co.

United Way of Wyoming Valley ($30,250) see Nabisco Foods Group

United Way of York County ($44,000) see Susquehanna-Pfaltzgraff Co.

University of the Arts — capital campaign ($100,000) see Arronson Foundation

University of Arts ($25,000) see Gershman Foundation, Joel

University of Arts ($100,000) see Greenfield Foundation, Albert M.

University of the Arts — for capital campaign ($20,000) see Hunt Manufacturing Co.

University of the Arts ($5,000) see Safeguard Scientifics Foundation

University of the Arts ($5,000) see Safeguard Scientifics Foundation

University of the Arts — for the installation of security gates on the Arts Bank Theater ($422,000) see Penn Foundation, William

YMCA ($30,000) see Kline Foundation, Josiah W. and Bessie H.

YMCA ($10,000) see Knudsen Charitable Foundation, Earl

YMCA ($1,000) see LamCo. Communications

YMCA ($1,500) see Lockhart Iron & Steel Co.

YMCA ($14,550) see Mack Foundation, J. S.

YMCA ($100,000) see McKenna Foundation, Katherine Mabis

YMCA ($30,398) see Mengle Foundation, Glenn and Ruth

YMCA ($22,000) see Mengle Foundation, Glenn and Ruth

YMCA ($22,000) see Mengle Foundation, Glenn and Ruth

YMCA ($15,000) see Murphy Co., G.C.

YMCA ($5,000) see Oberlaender Foundation, Gustav

YMCA ($2,800) see Pennsylvania Dutch Co.

YMCA ($3,000) see Peters Foundation, Charles F.

YMCA ($50,000) see Phillips Charitable Trust, Dr. and Mrs. Arthur William

YMCA ($8,000) see Piedmont Health Care Foundation

YMCA ($10,000) see Plankenhorn Foundation, Harry

YMCA ($5,000) see Rosenberg Foundation, Alexis

YMCA ($66,264) see Rudy, Jr. Trust, George B.

YMCA ($25,000) see Sheppard Foundation, Lawrence B.

YMCA ($37,500) see West Co.

YMCA ($5,741) see York Barbell Co.

YMCA ($4,000) see York Barbell Co.

YMCA-Allegheny Valley ($22,500) see Allegheny Ludlum Corp.

YMCA-Capital Campaign ($20,000) see AMP

YMCA, Philadelphia, PA see Rhone-Poulenc Rorer

YMCA Youth and Government ($1,000) see McCormick Trust, Anne

Yokefellow Center ($200) see LamCo. Communications

York Area Chamber of Commerce ($1,000) see Motter Printing Press Co.

York Catholic High School — development program ($5,000) see Susquehanna Investment Group

York City 250th Anniversary Celebration ($10,000) see Susquehanna Investment Group

York City 250th Anniversary Celebration ($10,000) see Susquehanna-Pfaltzgraff Co.

York College of Pennsylvania ($25,000) see Frazier Foundation

York College of Pennsylvania ($3,000) see Grumbacher Foundation, M. S.

York College of Pennsylvania ($66,265) see Rudy, Jr. Trust, George B.

York College of Pennsylvania ($1,000) see York Barbell Co.

York County Farmland Trust ($5,000) see Susquehanna Investment Group

York County Farmland Trust ($5,000) see Susquehanna-Pfaltzgraff Co.

York Hospital ($5,000) see Freas Foundation

York Hospital ($2,000) see Grumbacher Foundation, M. S.

York Hospital ($15,000) see Hamilton Bank

York Hospital ($20,000) see Susquehanna Investment Group

York Hospital Building Fund ($500) see General Machine Works

York Hospital Building Fund ($5,000) see Pennsylvania Dutch Co.

York Hospital — Century Project ($20,000) see Susquehanna-Pfaltzgraff Co.

York Hospital Dental Clinic ($5,000) see Dentsply International, Inc.

York Hospital Foundation ($25,000) see Dentsply International, Inc.

York House Hospice — cabinets and equipment ($5,000) see Freas Foundation

York Place ($20,403) see Close Foundation

York Theatre Company ($2,000) see Gilman and Gonzalez-Falla Theatre Foundation

Youth Guidance ($1,500) see Lockhart Iron & Steel Co.

Youth Guidance ($30,000) see Miller Charitable Foundation, Howard E. and Nell E.

Youth Home of Mel Blount ($75,000) see Aluminum Co. of America

Youth Opportunities Unlimited ($20,000) see Grable Foundation

Youth Opportunities Unlimited ($7,500) see Pittsburgh Child Guidance Foundation

YWCA ($20,000) see Crawford Estate, E. R.

YWCA ($2,000) see Falk Medical Fund, Maurice

YWCA ($200) see General Machine Works

YWCA ($7,000) see McKee Poor Fund, Virginia A.

YWCA ($5,000) see Pennsylvania Dutch Co.

YWCA ($5,000) see Susquehanna Investment Group

YWCA ($25,000) see Wells Foundation, Franklin H. and Ruth L.

YWCA — Child Care Center ($5,000) see Susquehanna-Pfaltzgraff Co.

Zionist Organization of America ($800) see Novotny Charitable Trust, Yetta Deitch

Zoar Home — renovation ($1,000) see Matthews International Corp.

Zoological Society ($8,334) see Alco Standard Corp.

Zoological Society see Berwind Corp.

Zoological Society ($5,000) see Binswanger Co.

Zoological Society ($10,000) see Hooper Foundation, Elizabeth S.

Zoological Society ($18,000) see Ludwick Institute

Zoological Society ($20,000) see Snee-Reinhardt Charitable Foundation

Zoological Society of Philadelphia ($5,000) see Subaru of America Inc.

Zoological Society of Philadelphia — Carnivore Exhibit ($50,000) see Barra Foundation

Puerto Rico

Fondos Unidos de Puerto Rico ($38,100) see Abbott Laboratories

Puerto Rico Community Foundation ($30,000) see Abbott Laboratories

Rhode Island

American Baptist Churches of Rhode Island ($7,030) see Clarke Trust, John

American Friends of Israel Philharmonic Orchestra ($35,000) see Jaffe Foundation

Attleboro Scholarship Foundation ($800) see Attleboro Pawtucket Savings Bank

Block Island Conservancy ($5,000) see Barth Foundation, Theodore H.

Boy Scouts of America ($350) see Attleboro Pawtucket Savings Bank

Boy Scouts of America ($5,500) see Johnstone and H. Earle Kimball Foundation, Phyllis Kimball

Boy Scouts of America — Narragansett Council ($324,974) see Champlin Foundations

Boys and Girls Club of Newport — public welfare ($30,000) see Young Foundation, Robert R.

Boys and Girls Club of Pawtucket ($258,291) see Champlin Foundations

Bradford Jonnycake Center ($10,000) see Kimball Foundation, Horace A. Kimball and S. Ella

Brick Market Foundation ($125,000) see McBean Charitable Trust, Alletta Morris

Brown University ($5,000) see Beir Foundation

Brown University ($2,000) see Belmont Metals

Brown University ($175,000) see Beneficial Corp.

Brown University ($3,000) see Berger Foundation, Albert E.

Brown University ($10,000) see Braitmayer Foundation

Brown University ($647,500) see Champlin Foundations

Brown University ($140,000) see Crown Memorial, Arie and Ida

Brown University ($10,000) see Doherty Charitable Foundation, Henry L. and Grace

Brown University ($28,500) see Dorot Foundation

Brown University — modern spectroscopy laboratory ($20,000) see Dreyfus Foundation, Camille and Henry

Brown University — scholarship aid ($5,000) see Fish Foundation, Vain and Harry

Brown University ($50,000) see Forbes

Brown University ($50,000) see Frese Foundation, Arnold D.

Brown University ($10,000) see Fruehauf Foundation

Brown University ($360,000) see Genesis Foundation

Brown University ($103,400) see Gilbane Foundation, Thomas and William

Brown University ($20,150) see Goldberger Foundation, Edward and Marjorie

Brown University ($25,000) see Haffenreffer Family Fund

Brown University ($9,625) see Haffenreffer Family Fund

Brown University ($9,625) see Haffenreffer Family Fund

Brown University ($9,625) see Haffenreffer Family Fund

Brown University ($9,625) see Haffenreffer Family Fund

Brown University ($16,000) see Hassenfeld Foundation

Brown University ($25,000) see Hughes Memorial Foundation, Charles Evans

Brown University ($85,000) see Jaffe Foundation

Brown University ($449,627) see Joukowsky Family Foundation

Brown University ($25,000) see Levy Foundation, June Rockwell

Brown University ($500) see Loeb Partners Corp.

Brown University ($60,000) see Michigan Bell Telephone Co.

Brown University ($60,000) see Motorola

Brown University ($4,700) see Oxford Industries, Inc.

Brown University ($60,000) see Salomon Foundation, Richard & Edna

Brown University ($30,000) see Sperry Fund

Brown University ($84,448) see Stuart Foundation

Brown University ($10,000) see Summerfield Foundation, Solon E.

Brown University ($25,000) see Terner Foundation

Brown University ($40,000) see Textron

Brown University — program in medicine ($10,000) see Zlinkoff Fund for Medical Research and Education, Sergei S.

Brown University — to strengthen and expand the environmental studies program at Brown University; (first payment of a five-year $2,000,000 grant) ($400,000) see Ittleson Foundation

Brown University — to augment the C. V. Starr National Service Fellowship at Brown ($1,000,000) see Starr Foundation

Brown University — Center for Population Training and Research ($52,000) see Compton Foundation

Brown University — Coalition of Essential Schools ($180,000) see Gates Foundation

Brown University — the Compton Fellowship Program supports university Ph.D. candidates preparing for careers in college and university teaching ($105,000) see Danforth Foundation

Brown University Drama Department ($20,000) see Randleigh Foundation Trust

Brown University Medical School ($10,000) see Citizens Bank

Brown University — Providence Public Schools Science Initiative see New England Telephone Co.

Bryant College ($5,000) see Koffler Family Foundation

Bryant College ($350) see Leesona Corp.

Camp Davis ($10,000) see Kimball Foundation, Horace A. Kimball and S. Ella

Camp Ruggles — towards camperships ($15,000) see Johnstone and H. Earle Kimball Foundation, Phyllis Kimball

Catholic Charities ($1,500) see Attleboro Pawtucket Savings Bank

Chariho Westerly Animal Rescue League ($10,000) see Kimball Foundation, Horace A. Kimball and S. Ella

Child and Family Services of Newport County ($25,000) see Johnstone and H. Earle Kimball Foundation, Phyllis Kimball

Coalition of Essential Schools ($50,000) see Circuit City Stores

Dorcas Place ($15,000) see Kimball Foundation, Horace A. Kimball and S. Ella

Dorcas Place ($1,000) see Nortek, Inc.

Episcopal Charities Fund of Rhode Island ($550) see Attleboro Pawtucket Savings Bank

Franklin Pierce College Scholarship Fund ($5,000) see Galkin Charitable Trust, Ira S. and Anna

Friends of Waterfront ($10,000) see McBean Charitable Trust, Alletta Morris

General Federation of Women's Clubs ($79,200) see Allstate Insurance Co.

Gordon School — construction ($15,000) see Littlefield Memorial Trust, Ida Ballou

Health Center of South County ($25,000) see Johnstone and H. Earle Kimball Foundation, Phyllis Kimball

Health Center of South County — towards payment of fund consultants ($10,000) see Johnstone and H. Earle Kimball Foundation, Phyllis Kimball

Home Health Services of Rhode Island — education program ($10,000) see Littlefield Memorial Trust, Ida Ballou

Hubbard Regional Hospital ($10,000) see Cranston Print Works

In-Sight ($10,000) see Kimball Foundation, Horace A. Kimball and S. Ella

International House of Rhode Island — toward fire code repairs ($5,000) see Johnstone and H. Earle Kimball Foundation, Phyllis Kimball

International Institute of Rhode Island ($30,000) see Providence Journal Company

Jacobs Pillow ($35,800) see Jaffe Foundation

Jesse M. Smith Memorial Library ($26,500) see Levy Foundation, June Rockwell

Jewish Federation ($25,000) see Alperin/Hirsch Family Foundation

Jewish Federation ($50,000) see Galkin Charitable Trust, Ira S. and Anna

Jewish Federation ($10,000) see Galkin Charitable Trust, Ira S. and Anna

Jewish Federation ($583,000) see Hassenfeld Foundation

Jewish Federation ($181,050) see Koffler Family Foundation

Jewish Home for the Aged ($6,608) see Koffler Family Foundation

Bowers-Rodgers Home ($500) see County Bank

Bowers-Rogers Home ($25,000) see Abney Foundation

Boy Scouts of America ($3,000) see Alice Manufacturing Co.

Boys Home of South ($4,000) see Scurry Foundation, D. L.

Buena Vista Elementary School ($1,195) see Bannon Foundation

Buffalo Baptist Church ($5,000) see Stevens Foundation, John T.

Carolina Art Association ($13,500) see Donnelley Foundation, Gaylord and Dorothy

Carolina Children's Home ($1,000) see Budweiser of Columbia

Carolina Christian Ministries ($25,000) see Bailey Foundation

Carolina Youth Development Center ($62,477) see Evening Post Publishing Co.

Carolina Youth Symphony ($250) see Builder Marts of America

Catholic Charities ($25,968) see Evening Post Publishing Co.

Center for Performing Arts ($10,000) see Builder Marts of America

Center for the Performing Arts — cultural/performing arts ($20,000) see Dreyfus Foundation, Max and Victoria

Center Place — operating fund ($5,000) see South Carolina Electric & Gas Co.

Central Carolina Community Foundation ($3,000) see Budweiser of Columbia

Central Wesleyan College ($4,295) see Fuller Foundation, C. G.

Charles Lea Center ($50,000) see Milliken & Co.

Charleston Museum ($250) see Porsche Cars North America, Inc.

Charleston Southern University ($12,500) see Evening Post Publishing Co.

Charleston Symphony Orchestra ($10,000) see Evening Post Publishing Co.

Charleston Symphony Orchestra ($7,500) see Ramlose Foundation, George A.

Charleston Symphony Orchestra ($10,000) see W. W. W. Foundation

Charlotte Latin School ($4,000) see Arkwright Foundation

Cherokee Children's Home — endowment fund ($100,000) see Fullerton Foundation

Cherokee County Family YMCA — to establish a health education program in Cherokee County ($52,876) see Fullerton Foundation

Cherokee County School District — support four projects to enhance quality of education ($387,027) see Timken Foundation of Canton

Christ Church ($4,000) see Arkwright Foundation

Christ School ($3,500) see Bailey Foundation

Christian Heritage Congregational Holiness Church ($10,000) see Gregg-Graniteville Foundation

The Citadel ($250,000) see Daniel Foundation of Alabama

Citadel in Charleston, SC ($25,000) see Lane Memorial Foundation, Mills Bee

Cities in Schools of Charleston ($5,000) see Evening Post Publishing Co.

City of Abbeville — building fund ($5,000) see South Carolina Electric & Gas Co.

City of Charleston ($20,000) see Heyward Memorial Fund, DuBose and Dorothy

City of Orangeburg Parks Division ($3,800) see Horne Foundation, Dick

Claflin College ($100,000) see Abney Foundation

Claflin College — honors program scholarship endowment ($5,000) see South Carolina Electric & Gas Co.

Clemson IPTAY Club ($5,200) see Stowe, Jr. Foundation, Robert Lee

Clemson University ($15,000) see Abney Foundation

Clemson University ($25,000) see Bannon Foundation

Clemson University ($23,700) see Budweiser of Columbia

Clemson University ($31,000) see Close Foundation

Clemson University ($100,000) see Fluor Corp.

Clemson University — capital ($55,000) see Georgia Power Co.

Clemson University ($210,000) see Grace & Co., W.R.

Clemson University see Greenwood Mills

Clemson University ($4,500) see Inman Mills

Clemson University — scholarships ($6,250) see Jackson Mills

Clemson University — scholarships ($5,000) see Jackson Mills

Clemson University ($15,000) see Reliance Electric Co.

Clemson University ($15,000) see Reliance Electric Co.

Clemson University Foundation ($50,000) see Gregg-Graniteville Foundation

Clemson University Foundation ($95,000) see Hopewell Foundation

Clemson University Foundation ($20,000) see Liberty Corp.

Clinton Chapel African Methodist Episcopal Church ($6,700) see Stevens Foundation, John T.

Coker College ($100,000) see Sonoco Products Co.

College of Charleston ($2,000) see Bradford & Co., J.C.

College of Charleston ($3,000) see DelMar Foundation, Charles

Columbia Bible College ($4,000) see Simpson Foundation

Columbia Bible College and Seminary — educational ($60,000) see Aurora Foundation

Columbia Bible College and Seminary ($10,000) see Morris Charitable Foundation, E. A.

Columbia College — purchase of 3 IBM PC II computers for the H. Drake Edens Library ($10,000) see Knapp Foundation

Columbia Urban League ($1,000) see Budweiser of Columbia

Community Foundation Child Care Project ($5,000) see Builder Marts of America

Community Foundation of Greater Greenville ($25,000) see Symmes Foundation, F. W.

Community Foundation for Public Housing ($100,000) see Smith Charities, John

Connie Maxwell Children's Home ($4,000) see Scurry Foundation, D. L.

Converse College ($15,000) see Abney Foundation

Converse College ($8,250) see Arkwright Foundation

Converse College — centennial campaign ($5,000) see Arkwright Foundation

Converse College ($6,000) see Inman Mills

Converse College ($5,000) see Jephson Educational Trust No. 1

Converse College — scholarship fund ($100,000) see Maclellan Charitable Trust, R. J.

Converse College ($162,500) see Romill Foundation

Converse College ($11,000) see Simpson Foundation

Conway Hospital Foundation — annual funding raising ($5,000) see South Carolina Electric & Gas Co.

Council on Aging of the Midlands ($3,000) see Fuller Foundation, C. G.

Crossroads Baptist Church ($5,000) see Stevens Foundation, John T.

Darlington County School Anti-Drug ($37,846) see Sonoco Products Co.

Darlington County School District ($27,000) see Sonoco Products Co.

Darlington County School System ($42,975) see Sonoco Products Co.

Eastside Improvement Society ($10,000) see Romill Foundation

Edgefield County Council — rural fire departments improvements ($5,000) see South Carolina Electric & Gas Co.

Elliott White Springs Memorial Hospital — radiology equipment ($150,000) see Springs Foundation

Enoree Church of God ($5,600) see Inman Mills

Episcopal Church of Advent ($9,650) see Arkwright Foundation

Episcopal Church of Advent ($12,606) see Romill Foundation

Epworth Children's Home ($100,000) see Bock Charitable Trust, George W.

Erskine College — scholarship program ($240,455) see Stuart Foundation, Edward C.

Erskine College ($12,250) see Sullivan Foundation, Algernon Sydney

Erskine Theological Seminary ($20,000) see Grader Foundation, K. W.

ETV Endowment of South Carolina ($150,000) see Carthage Foundation

ETV Endowment of South Carolina ($5,000) see Evening Post Publishing Co.

ETV Endowment of South Carolina — support for a six-part television series on the contribution and social impact

of engineering ($1,000,000) see Sloan Foundation, Alfred P.

Family Counseling Center ($25,000) see Smith Charities, John

Family YMCA of Greenwood — assist with cost of new facility ($60,000) see Self Foundation

First Presbyterian Church ($5,000) see Hopewell Foundation

Florence-Darlington Technical College ($3,000) see South Carolina Electric & Gas Co.

Fourth Presbyterian Church ($8,000) see Simpson Foundation

Free Congress and Education Foundation ($50,000) see Romill Foundation

Friends of the Arts ($5,000) see Inman Mills

Fullerton Medical Scholarship Program ($140,000) see Fullerton Foundation

Furman University ($20,000) see Bannon Foundation

Furman University ($10,000) see Belk Stores

Furman University ($12,735) see Delta Air Lines

Furman University — educational purposes ($2,100,000) see Duke Endowment

Furman University — scholarships ($3,750) see Jackson Mills

Furman University ($15,000) see Multimedia, Inc.

Furman University ($5,000) see Scurry Foundation, D. L.

Furman University ($15,000) see Simpson Foundation

Furman University ($50,000) see Smith Charities, John

Furman University ($12,250) see Sullivan Foundation, Algernon Sydney

Furman University ($100,000) see Symmes Foundation, F. W.

Furman University — new approaches to macromolecule/ligand binding analysis using capillary electrophoresis ($34,600) see Research Corporation

Furman University — assist with cost of math/computer science building in honor of Dick Riley ($50,000) see Self Foundation

Governor's School for the Arts ($1,150) see Horne Foundation, Dick

Greenville Center for Performing Arts ($10,000) see Cincinnati Milacron

Greenville County Library ($1,500) see Bannon Foundation

Greenville County Library ($50,000) see Symmes Foundation, F. W.

Greenville Habitat for Humanity ($22,000) see Reliance Electric Co.

Greenville Literacy Association ($1,500) see Bannon Foundation

Greenville Literacy Association ($10,000) see Symmes Foundation, F. W.

Greenville Performing Arts ($50,000) see Liberty Corp.

Greenville Symphony Orchestra ($500) see Builder Marts of America

Greenville Technical College ($10,000) see Bannon Foundation

Greenville Technical College ($500) see Builder Marts of America

Greenville Technical College ($5,000) see Scurry Foundation, D. L.

Greenville Urban League ($3,000) see Multimedia, Inc.

Greenwood Community Theatre ($1,000) see County Bank

Greenwood Genetic Center — cost of architectural and engineering drawings and related documents re establishing a Research Institute ($50,000) see Self Foundation

Greenwood Methodist Home ($12,500) see Gregg-Graniteville Foundation

Greenwood Methodist Home — assist with cost of rehabilitating the Health Center ($150,000) see Self Foundation

Gregg Park Civic Center ($342,682) see Gregg-Graniteville Foundation

Harold Jennings Foundation ($4,500) see Simpson Foundation

Hartsville Downtown Development ($16,668) see Sonoco Products Co.

Hartsville United Way ($52,000) see Sonoco Products Co.

Hartsville YMCA ($20,000) see Sonoco Products Co.

Health Science Foundation ($20,000) see Stevens Foundation, John T.

Highlands Hospital ($50,000) see Abney Foundation

Historic Charleston Foundation ($10,000) see Taubman Foundation, A. Alfred

Hitchcock Rehabilitation Center — building fund ($5,000) see South Carolina Electric & Gas Co.

Hospital Foundation ($10,025) see County Bank

Independent Colleges and Universities of South Carolina — conduit for grant to Erskine College to assist with Campus Master Plan for computers ($66,667) see Self Foundation

Inman Youth Association ($8,020) see Inman Mills

Institute of Textile Technology ($4,000) see Inman Mills

IPTAY ($1,000) see County Bank

Kershaw County Humane Society ($25,000) see Upton Foundation, Frederick S.

Kershaw Methodist Church ($8,000) see Stevens Foundation, John T.

Kershaw Second Baptist Church ($5,800) see Stevens Foundation, John T.

Kid's Fair (Jewish Community Center) ($7,500) see Evening Post Publishing Co.

Lancaster County Healthy Mothers/Healthy Babies Coalition ($50,000) see Springs Foundation

Lancaster County Library ($13,937) see Stevens Foundation, John T.

Lancaster County Recreation Commission ($20,000) see Springs Foundation

Lander College ($100,000) see Abney Foundation

Lander College ($1,000) see Budweiser of Columbia

Lander Foundation ($2,050) see County Bank

South Carolina (cont.)

Lander University Foundation — for establishing an electronic campus ($300,000) see Self Foundation

Leroy Springs and Company — operation/maintenance ($775,000) see Springs Foundation

Leroy Springs and Company — Springmaid Beach $4 Million Project ($355,050) see Springs Foundation

Limestone College ($30,000) see Milliken & Co.

Limestone College ($5,000) see Oshkosh Truck Corp.

Limestone College — renovate Montgomery Classroom Building ($250,000) see Timken Foundation of Canton

Lowcountry Open Land Trust ($10,000) see Evening Post Publishing Co.

Meals on Wheels ($50,000) see Smith Charities, John

Medical University of South Carolina ($6,500) see JJJ Foundation

Medical University of South Carolina ($10,000) see Multimedia, Inc.

Medical University of South Carolina — support for scleroderma research ($85,000) see RGK Foundation

Medical University of South Carolina ($90,000) see Teagle Foundation

Medical University of South Carolina — capital campaign ($25,000) see Westvaco Corp.

Miracle Hill Ministries ($50,000) see Symmes Foundation, F. W.

Mobile Meal Service of Spartanburg County ($13,500) see Inman Mills

Museum Association ($1,000) see Builder Marts of America

Museum of York County ($36,826) see Stans Foundation

Nancy Fulwood Hospital — Pakistan orthopaedic project ($12,500) see Stuart Foundation, Edward C.

National Audubon Society ($10,000) see Beidler Charitable Trust, Francis

Newberry College ($1,000) see Budweiser of Columbia

Newberry College ($10,000) see Gregg-Graniteville Foundation

Newberry College ($5,000) see Reinhold Foundation, Paul E. and Ida Klare

North Greenville College ($5,500) see Scurry Foundation, D. L.

Oliver Gospel Mission ($5,000) see Fuller Foundation, C. G.

Orangeburg League of Arts ($1,050) see Horne Foundation, Dick

Orangeburg Nature Trail ($1,627) see Horne Foundation, Dick

Orangeburg Teen Center ($6,260) see Horne Foundation, Dick

Osbourne Senior High School ($2,500) see Bannon Foundation

Palmetto Partnership — Teen Institute for Alcohol and Drug Abuse ($2,500) see South Carolina Electric & Gas Co.

Peace Center ($1,000) see Builder Marts of America

Peace Center ($250,000) see Symmes Foundation, F. W.

Pendleton Place ($20,000) see Smith Charities, John

Phyllis Wheatley Association ($22,000) see Symmes Foundation, F. W.

Piedmont Agency on Aging ($1,000) see County Bank

Piedmont Technical College ($3,100) see County Bank

Presbyterian College ($25,000) see Bailey Foundation

Presbyterian College ($2,800) see Bailey Foundation

Presbyterian College ($6,000) see Belk Stores

Presbyterian College ($5,156) see Ellsworth Trust, W. H.

Presbyterian College see Greenwood Mills

Presbyterian College ($5,500) see Simpson Foundation

Presbyterian College ($136,450) see Smith Charities, John

Richland County Health Department — health facility equipment ($12,500) see South Carolina Electric & Gas Co.

Roper Mountain Center ($20,000) see Liberty Corp.

Rosewood House of Recovery ($88,000) see Symmes Foundation, F. W.

Rural Health Services ($40,000) see Huber Foundation

St. Eugene Community Hospital ($4,000) see Mohasco Corp.

St. Frances Hospital ($50,000) see Smith Charities, John

Salvation Army ($1,500) see Bannon Foundation

Samaritan's Purse ($10,000) see Simpson Foundation

School Assistance Programs — Chester County Department of Education ($20,277) see Springs Foundation

School Assistance Programs — Lancaster County School District ($29,745) see Springs Foundation

Sister Marietta Elementary School ($1,012) see Bannon Foundation

South Carolina Council on Economic Education ($2,500) see Standard Products Co.

South Carolina Educational Television ($32,500) see Close Foundation

South Carolina Federation of Blind ($600) see Budweiser of Columbia

South Carolina Festival of Flowers ($500) see County Bank

South Carolina Foundation of Charitable Contributions ($5,000) see Alice Manufacturing Co.

South Carolina Foundation of Independent Colleges ($1,000) see County Bank

South Carolina Foundation of Independent Colleges ($56,750) see Duke Power Co.

South Carolina Foundation of Independent Colleges ($15,000) see Gregg-Graniteville Foundation

South Carolina Foundation of Independent Colleges ($25,000) see Lance, Inc.

South Carolina Foundation of Independent Colleges ($2,500) see Moore & Sons, B.C.

South Carolina Foundation of Independent Colleges ($2,500) see Multimedia, Inc.

South Carolina Foundation of Independent Colleges — general support ($60,000) see Self Foundation

South Carolina Foundation of Independent Colleges ($25,000) see Springs Foundation

South Carolina Foundation of Independent Colleges — conduit for four Virginia Turner Self Scholarships at Converse College ($59,177) see Self Foundation

South Carolina Governor's School For the Arts ($12,500) see Symmes Foundation, F. W.

South Carolina Historical Society ($12,000) see Donnelley Foundation, Gaylord and Dorothy

South Carolina Independent College Fund ($100,000) see Sonoco Products Co.

South Carolina Independent Colleges ($20,000) see Liberty Corp.

South Carolina Music Teachers ($3,000) see DelMar Foundation, Charles

South Carolina Policy Council ($52,500) see Roe Foundation

South Carolina School Science and Math ($21,635) see Liberty Corp.

South Carolina State College ($75,000) see Abney Foundation

South Carolina State Museum ($25,000) see Union Camp Corp.

South Carolina Waterfowl Foundation ($5,000) see Griswold Foundation, John C.

South Carolina Wildlife Association ($5,000) see Scurry Foundation, D. L.

Spartanburg Conservation Endowment ($5,000) see Jackson Mills

Spartanburg County Arts ($5,000) see Inman Mills

Spartanburg Day School ($15,000) see Arkwright Foundation

Spartanburg Day School ($17,000) see Inman Mills

Spartanburg Day School ($5,000) see Milliken Foundation, Agnes G.

Spartanburg Day School ($107,657) see Romill Foundation

Spartanburg Little Theater ($5,750) see Arkwright Foundation

Spartanburg Methodist College ($30,000) see Milliken & Co.

Spoleto Festival U.S.A. — exhibition ($50,000) see Lannan Foundation

Spoleto Festival USA ($15,000) see Donnelley Foundation, Gaylord and Dorothy

Spoleto Festival, USA ($10,000) see Heyward Memorial Fund, DuBose and Dorothy

Spoleto Festival USA ($10,000) see Sharp Foundation

Spoleto Festival USA ($5,000) see Simpson Foundation

Tara Hall — public school operations ($20,000) see Yawkey Foundation II

Town of Edgefield — downtown development ($5,000) see South Carolina Electric & Gas Co.

Town of Kershaw — fire truck ($25,000) see Springs Foundation

Town of Kershaw ($29,600) see Stevens Foundation, John T.

Tri-County Tec College ($100,000) see Abney Foundation

Tri-County Technical College — medical laboratory technology equipment ($54,972) see Self Foundation

Trident Community Foundation ($50,000) see Woodward Fund-Watertown, David, Helen, and Marian

United Funds ($4,000) see Joslyn Corp.

United Way ($5,791) see Arkwright Foundation

United Way ($4,791) see Arkwright Foundation

United Way ($1,200) see Budweiser of Columbia

United Way ($47,200) see Builder Marts of America

United Way ($20,000) see Cole Foundation

United Way ($3,792) see County Bank

United Way ($46,000) see Liberty Corp.

United Way ($11,525) see Liberty Corp.

United Way ($8,935) see Liberty Corp.

United Way ($7,500) see Marley Co.

United Way ($17,500) see Romill Foundation

United Way ($10,000) see Symmes Foundation, F. W.

United Way Cherokee County ($18,500) see Timken Co.

United Way of Greenwood County ($93,600) see Monsanto Co.

United Way of Lancaster County ($20,000) see Springs Foundation

United Way of the Midlands ($32,000) see Union Camp Corp.

Unity Baptist Church ($18,000) see Stevens Foundation, John T.

University of Edinburgh ($8,000) see G.A.G. Charitable Corporation

University of South Carolina ($100,000) see Alice Manufacturing Co.

University of South Carolina ($600,000) see BellSouth Corp.

University of South Carolina ($50,000) see Brookdale Foundation

University of South Carolina ($4,500) see Budweiser of Columbia

University of South Carolina ($50,000) see Donaldson Charitable Trust, Oliver S. and Jennie R.

University of South Carolina — scholarships ($7,500) see Jackson Mills

University of South Carolina ($20,000) see Manning and Emma Austin Manning Foundation, James Hilton

University of South Carolina at Aiken ($20,000) see Gregg-Graniteville Foundation

University of South Carolina Business Partnership Foundation ($30,000) see Close Foundation

University of South Carolina Business School ($5,000) see Multimedia, Inc.

University of South Carolina — support current capital campaign to complete the computerization project of Mary Black School of Nursing ($50,000) see Fullerton Foundation

University of Southern California School of Medicine — support a rural primary care education project in Winsboro, SC ($117,000) see Fullerton Foundation

Voorhees College ($60,000) see Abney Foundation

Wallace Thompson Hospital ($10,000) see Dodson Foundation, James Glenwell and Clara May

Ware Shoals School ($25,000) see Abney Foundation

Wofford College ($50,000) see Close Foundation

Wofford College ($10,000) see Liberty Corp.

Wofford College ($9,000) see Romill Foundation

YMCA ($66,000) see Bailey Foundation

York Technical College — child development center ($40,000) see Close Foundation

York Technical College ($25,000) see Close Foundation

York Technical College — Anne S. Close Library ($25,000) see Close Foundation

York Technical College Foundation ($25,000) see Hopewell Foundation

Youth Enrichment Adventures ($10,600) see W. W. W. Foundation

YWCA ($5,000) see Builder Marts of America

South Dakota

Aberdeen Area Career Planning Center ($1,000) see Hatterscheidt Foundation

Black Hills Regional Eye Institute Foundation see First Bank System

Black Hills State College ($750) see True Oil Co.

Boys and Girls Club ($5,000) see Hatterscheidt Foundation

Children's Inn ($5,000) see Sioux Steel Co.

Custer Battlefield Preservation Committee ($100,000) see Muth Foundation, Peter and Mary

Dacotah Prairie Museum ($2,694) see Hatterscheidt Foundation

Farm Subsidy ($12,000) see Trust Funds

First Baptist Church ($5,500) see Sioux Steel Co.

Lutheran Social Services ($1,000) see Sioux Steel Co.

McCrossan Boys Ranch ($1,000) see Sioux Steel Co.

Mitchell School District No. 17-2 — Science, Technology and Society Out-Reach Program ($9,969) see Toshiba America, Inc.

Mount Rushmore Memorial Society ($25,000) see Lee Enterprises

Mount Rushmore National Memorial Society — supplemental support toward construction ($225,000) see Freedom Forum

North American Baptist Seminary ($3,000) see Sioux Steel Co.

North Plains Hospice ($3,000) see Hatterscheidt Foundation

Oglala Lakota College ($6,000) see I and G Charitable Foundation

Oglala Lakota College ($48,000) see Plumsock Fund

O'Gorman High School Foundation ($750) see Sioux Steel Co.

Presentation College — endowment fund ($3,000) see Hatterscheidt Foundation

Roncalli Foundation ($4,000) see Hatterscheidt Foundation

St. Josephs Indian School ($250,000) see Summerlee Foundation

Salvation Army ($2,500) see Hatterscheidt Foundation

Sinte Gleska College ($8,000) see Beck Foundation

Sioux Falls Youth Hockey ($4,000) see Sioux Steel Co.

South Dakota Community Foundation — endowment fund for Economic Development ($5,000) see MDU Resources Group, Inc.

South Dakota Special Olympics ($1,000) see Hatterscheidt Foundation

South Dakota State University ($72,600) see Briggs Family Foundation

South Dakota State University ($3,750) see CENEX

South Dakota State University ($18,000) see Harvest States Cooperative

United Way ($7,350) see Hatterscheidt Foundation

United Way ($5,700) see Sioux Steel Co.

United Way Sioux Empire ($51,906) see Norwest Corp.

University of South Dakota — lanthanide to ligand energy transfer in a molecular beam ($32,984) see Research Corporation

Watertown Memorial Hospital — health and welfare ($10,000) see Menasha Corp.

YMCA ($6,000) see Hatterscheidt Foundation

YMCA ($58,624) see Sioux Steel Co.

YMCA ($1,000) see Sioux Steel Co.

Tennessee

Africian Christian YDS Trust ($20,000) see Brown Charitable Trust, Dora Maclellan

Agape ($3,300) see Foster Charitable Foundation, M. Stratton

Agape ($9,150) see Stephens Foundation Trust

Akioa School ($500) see Interstate Packaging Co.

Aland Club ($20,000) see Davis Foundation, Joe C.

Alexis de Tocqueville Society ($12,500) see Currey Foundation, Brownlee

Alive Hospice ($20,000) see Washington Foundation

Alive Hospice Building ($10,000) see Currey Foundation, Brownlee

Allied Arts Fund ($16,000) see AMP

Allied Arts Fund of Greater Chattanooga ($12,000) see Dixie Yarns, Inc.

Allied Arts Fund of Greater Chattanooga ($25,000) see Sulzberger Foundation

Allied Arts Fund of Greater Chattanooga ($7,000) see Woods-Greer Foundation

Allied Arts of Greater Chattanooga ($275,000) see Benwood Foundation

American Diabetes Association ($5,000) see Foster Charitable Foundation, M. Stratton

American Israel Public Affairs Commission ($6,000) see Zimmerman Family Foundation, Raymond

American Society for Technion ($1,000) see Wurzburg, Inc.

Anesthesia — cancer treatment ($1,677) see Hurlbut Memorial Fund, Orion L. and Emma S.

Apostolic Ark ($5,000) see Dauch Foundation, William

Appalachian Counseling Center ($4,000) see Massengill-DeFriece Foundation

Appalachian Girl Scout Council ($10,000) see Massengill-DeFriece Foundation

Arts Council of Knoxville ($500) see Toms Foundation

Associates in Diagnostic Radiology — cancer treatment ($1,315) see Hurlbut Memorial Fund, Orion L. and Emma S.

Associates in Ear, Nose, Throat, Head and Neck Surgery — cancer treatment ($3,054) see Hurlbut Memorial Fund, Orion L. and Emma S.

Associates in Pathology — cancer treatment ($5,654) see Hurlbut Memorial Fund, Orion L. and Emma S.

B'nai B'rith Home and Hospital Building Fund ($5,000) see Wurzburg, Inc.

Baddour Memorial Center ($10,000) see Briggs Foundation, T. W.

Baptist Hospital Foundation ($4,000) see Kelly Tractor Co.

Baron Hirch Congregation ($44,688) see Belz Foundation

Baylor School ($353,000) see Benwood Foundation

Baylor School ($10,000) see Dixie Yarns, Inc.

Baylor School ($20,000) see North American Royalties

Baylor School — for Hedges Library ($299,675) see Tonya Memorial Foundation

Belmont College ($200,000) see Andersen Foundation

Belmont College ($50,000) see Davis Foundation, Joe C.

Belmont College ($25,000) see Davis Foundation, Joe C.

Belmont College ($1,000) see Elkin Memorial Foundation, Neil Warren and William Simpson

Belmont College ($225,000) see Massey Charitable Trust

Belmont College ($100,000) see Massey Foundation, Jack C.

Belmont College ($30,000) see Washington Foundation

Belmont College School of Biblical Studies ($2,667) see Foster Charitable Foundation, M. Stratton

Ben Haden Evangelistic Association ($20,000) see Maclellan Foundation, Robert L. and Kathrina H.

Benton Hall ($5,000) see Foster Charitable Foundation, M. Stratton

Bethel Bible School ($2,000) see Cartinhour Foundation

Big Brothers of Nashville see SAFECO Corp.

Bill Wilkerson Association ($6,000) see Ansley Foundation, Dantzler Bond

BIMI ($76,165) see Christian Training Foundation

Blair School of Music for Youth Symphony ($25,000) see Potter Foundation, Justin and Valere

Blount Mansion Association ($5,000) see Cole Foundation, Robert H. and Monica H.

B'nai B'rith Home and Hospital for the Aged ($18,000) see Forchheimer Memorial Foundation Trust, Louise and Josie

Boy Scouts of America see Genesco

Boy Scouts of America ($6,500) see Schadt Foundation

Boy Scouts of America ($5,000) see Schilling Motors

Boy Scouts of America ($1,500) see Toms Foundation

Boys Club of Memphis ($25,000) see Federal Express Corp.

Boys Club of Memphis ($1,000) see Willmott Foundation, Peter S.

Boys and Girls Club see Nike Inc.

Bridge Builders ($15,000) see Briggs Foundation, T. W.

Bright School ($10,000) see North American Royalties

Bristol Regional Counseling Center ($30,000) see Massengill-DeFriece Foundation

Bristol Regional Rehabilitation Center ($5,000) see Massengill-DeFriece Foundation

Bristol Regional Rehabilitation Center see Raytheon Co.

Bristol Regional Rehabilitation Center ($50,000) see SmithKline Beecham

Bryan College ($2,500) see Morris Charitable Foundation, E. A.

Carson Newman College ($1,000) see Weiss Foundation, Stephen and Suzanne

Catholic Charities ($25,000) see Davis Foundation, Joe C.

Cedar Springs Presbyterian ($4,500) see 1939 Foundation

Cell Therapy Research Foundation ($180,000) see Andreas Foundation

Chambliss Emergency Shelter — for general purposes ($10,000) see Westend Foundation

Chattanooga Bible Institute ($30,000) see Brown Charitable Trust, Dora Maclellan

Chattanooga Bible Institute — Unity Theological Center ($20,000) see Brown Charitable Trust, Dora Maclellan

Chattanooga Boys Club ($10,000) see SCT Yarns

Chattanooga Boys Club ($500) see SCT Yarns

Chattanooga Christian School — operating funds ($350,000) see Maclellan Charitable Trust, R. J.

Chattanooga Christian School ($40,000) see Maclellan Foundation, Robert L. and Kathrina H.

Chattanooga Christian School Association — scholarship fund ($15,000) see Brown Charitable Trust, Dora Maclellan

Chattanooga Nature Center ($2,000) see Jewell Memorial Foundation, Daniel Ashley and Irene Houston

Chattanooga Neighborhood Enterprise — general support ($1,000,000) see Lyndhurst Foundation

Chattanooga School for the Arts and Sciences — for school equipment fund ($5,000) see Westend Foundation

Chattanooga Service — cancer treatment ($2,300) see Hurlbut Memorial Fund, Orion L. and Emma S.

Chattanooga Symphony and Opera Association ($25,000) see Sulzberger Foundation

Chattanooga Venture — operations ($1,000,000) see Lyndhurst Foundation

Cheekwood ($10,000) see Zimmerman Family Foundation, Raymond

Cheekwood — Swan Ball ($10,000) see Massey Foundation, Jack C.

Children's Museum of Memphis — exhibits endowment ($100,000) see Van Vleet Foundation

Children's Advocacy Center of Sullivan County ($10,000) see Massengill-DeFriece Foundation

Children's Family House ($500) see Toms Foundation

Children's Home ($12,500) see Caldwell Foundation, Hardwick

Children's Home ($25,000) see Maclellan Foundation, Robert L. and Kathrina H.

Christ United Methodist Church ($5,000) see Schilling Motors

Christ United Methodist Church ($20,000) see Washington Foundation

Christian Brothers College ($2,500) see Conwood Co. L.P.

Christian Brothers College ($2,400) see Wurzburg, Inc.

Church of the Good Shepherd ($4,000) see Hutcheson Foundation, Hazel Montague

Church Health Center ($38,000) see Briggs Foundation, T. W.

Church Health Center ($10,000) see Hyde Foundation, J. R.

City Ballet ($5,000) see Cole Foundation, Robert H. and Monica H.

City of Chattanooga-Memorial Auditorium ($117,000) see Benwood Foundation

City of Chattanooga — renovation of Memorial Auditorium ($167,000) see Tonya Memorial Foundation

Clay County Board of Education ($25,000) see Reader's Digest Association

CMBC ($51,000) see Miller Charitable Foundation, C. John and Reva

Cole Neuroscience Foundation ($15,000) see Cole Foundation, Robert H. and Monica H.

Community Foundation of Greater Memphis ($8,000) see Schadt Foundation

Community Helpers — prescription drugs for the indigent ($90,000) see Christy-Houston Foundation

Conference for Christians and Jews ($1,000) see Wurzburg, Inc.

Cotton Foundation ($1,000) see Beloco Foundation

Covenant College ($10,000) see Caldwell Foundation, Hardwick

Covenant College ($5,000) see Cartinhour Foundation

Covenant College ($100,000) see Maclellan Foundation, Robert L. and Kathrina H.

Covenant College ($35,000) see Maclellan Foundation, Robert L. and Kathrina H.

Covenant College ($3,188) see Staley Foundation, Thomas F.

Creative Discovery Museum — general support ($1,000,000) see Lyndhurst Foundation

Crippled Children's Hospital ($8,000) see Brinkley Foundation

Crittenden County Hospital ($15,000) see Brinkley Foundation

Cumberland Museum ($5,000) see Aladdin Industries, Incorporated

Cumberland Museum ($1,000) see Currey Foundation, Brownlee

Cumberland Museum ($100,000) see Potter Foundation, Justin and Valere

Cumberland Science Museum — Toshiba scholarship days ($20,000) see Toshiba America, Inc.

Cumberland Valley Girl Scout Council ($1,000) see Currey Foundation, Brownlee

Cumberland Valley Girl Scout Council ($5,000) see Foster Charitable Foundation, M. Stratton

Cumberland Valley Girls Scouts ($4,500) see Aladdin Industries, Incorporated

David Lipscomb College ($35,000) see Potter Foundation, Justin and Valere

David Lipscomb University ($10,500) see Stephens Foundation Trust

David Lipscomb University ($60,000) see Washington Foundation

Dixon Gallery ($50,000) see Plough Foundation

Dixon Gallery and Gardens ($20,000) see Adams Foundation, Arthur F. and Alice E.

Dixon Gallery and Gardens ($10,000) see Briggs Foundation, T. W.

Dixon Gallery and Gardens ($3,000) see Brinkley Foundation

Dixon Gallery and Gardens ($2,500) see Conwood Co. L.P.

Dixon Gallery and Gardens ($5,000) see Schilling Motors

Dixon Gallery and Gardens, Memphis, TN ($40,000) see Federal Express Corp.

Dogwood Arts Festival ($5,000) see Martin Marietta Corp.

Downtown Memphis Ministry ($9,400) see Briggs Foundation, T. W.

Drug Abuse Resistance Education Program — salary and training expenses; police officer ($20,000) see Christy-Houston Foundation

East Tennessee Community Foundation ($5,000) see Cole Foundation, Robert H. and Monica H.

Tennessee (cont.)

East Tennessee Foundation ($25,000) see Stokely, Jr. Foundation, William B.

East Tennessee Foundation — Youth risk ($50,000) see 1939 Foundation

Empty Stocking Fund ($200) see Toms Foundation

Enterprise Fund of Greater Chattanooga ($329,668) see Tonya Memorial Foundation

Erlanger Medical Center — cancer treatment ($388,135) see Hurlbut Memorial Fund, Orion L. and Emma S.

Fannie Battle Day Home ($10,000) see Ansley Foundation, Dantzler Bond

Fellowship of Christian Athletes ($5,000) see Schilling Motors

First Presbyterian Church ($10,000) see Foster Charitable Foundation, M. Stratton

Fisk University ($20,000) see Danner Foundation

Fisk University ($10,000) see Werthan Foundation

Fisk University — toward renovation of the Talley-Brady Science Building ($50,000) see Hospital Corp. of America

Fit Kids ($5,000) see Massengill-DeFriece Foundation

Franklin Road Academy ($50,144) see Danner Foundation

Franklin Road Academy Minority Scholarship ($13,035) see Danner Foundation

Friends of Linebaugh Library — computer system catalogue and card file function ($70,000) see Christy-Houston Foundation

Gideons International ($6,638) see Tell Foundation

Girl Scouts see Genesco

Girl Scouts of America ($8,000) see Ansley Foundation, Dantzler Bond

Girl Scouts of America ($5,000) see Werthan Foundation

Girls Club of Knoxville ($500) see Toms Foundation

Girls Incorporated ($5,000) see Massengill-DeFriece Foundation

Girls Incorporated of Chattanooga ($5,000) see Hutcheson Foundation, Hazel Montague

Girls Preparatory School ($330,000) see Benwood Foundation

Girls Preparatory School ($20,000) see Caldwell Foundation, Hardwick

Girls Preparatory School ($15,000) see Cartinhour Foundation

Girls Preparatory School — capital campaign ($62,500) see Dixie Yarns, Inc.

Girls Preparatory School — annual fund ($10,000) see Dixie Yarns, Inc.

Girls Preparatory School ($20,000) see North American Royalties

Girls Preparatory School — endowment ($416,000) see Tonya Memorial Foundation

Girls Preparatory School — for the sustaining fund ($5,000) see Westend Foundation

Girls Preparatory School — Bible and Counseling Program ($29,995) see Brown Charitable Trust, Dora Maclellan

Habitat for Humanity ($5,000) see Maclellan Foundation, Robert L. and Kathrina H.

Habitat for Humanity ($2,000) see 1939 Foundation

Hampton Classic Horse Show ($10,000) see Currey Foundation, Brownlee

Hampton Classic Horse Show ($23,000) see Currey Foundation, Brownlee

Harding Academy ($20,000) see Danner Foundation

Harpeth Hall School ($750,000) see Massey Foundation, Jack C.

Harwood Day Training Center ($10,000) see Brinkley Foundation

Helen Ross McNabb Foundation — youth center ($100,000) see Thompson Charitable Foundation

Heska Amuna Congregation ($1,500) see Glazer Foundation, Jerome S.

Highlander Research and Education Center — to protect groundwater from industrial pollution and waste disposal in Appalachia and the Southeast ($60,000) see Noyes Foundation, Jessie Smith

Hillsboro Church of Christ ($7,250) see Stephens Foundation Trust

Hiwassee College — student center ($25,000) see Magic Chef

Holcomb Medical Research Institute ($10,000) see Massey Foundation, Jack C.

Hope House ($10,000) see Frankino Charitable Foundation, Samuel J. and Connie

Hutchinson School ($11,000) see Schadt Foundation

Hutchison School ($20,000) see Brinkley Foundation

Idlewild Presbyterian Church ($25,428) see Schilling Motors

Independent College Fund ($5,200) see Conwood Co. L.P.

Inner-City Ministries — operating budget ($35,000) see Brown Charitable Trust, Dora Maclellan

INROADS see Genesco

International Steeplechase Group ($20,000) see Strawbridge Foundation of Pennsylvania I, Margaret Dorrance

Jewish Federation ($141,750) see Werthan Foundation

Jewish Federation ($91,750) see Werthan Foundation

Jewish Federation ($50,000) see Werthan Foundation

Jewish Federation of Nashville ($8,675) see Interstate Packaging Co.

Junior Achievement ($2,000) see Bradford & Co., J.C.

Junior Achievement ($5,000) see Conwood Co. L.P.

Junior Achievement see Genesco

Junior Achievement ($25,000) see Tonya Memorial Foundation

Junior Achievement ($10,000) see Washington Foundation

Just Organized Neighborhoods Area Headquarters ($32,000) see New World Foundation

Katrina Overall McDonald Memorial ($20,000) see Warren Foundation, William K.

Kimsey Radiology, P.C. — cancer treatment ($22,357) see Hurlbut Memorial Fund, Orion L. and Emma S.

Knoxville Art Museum ($5,000) see Cole Foundation, Robert H. and Monica H.

Knoxville Museum of Art ($40,000) see Stokely, Jr. Foundation, William B.

Knoxville Opera Company ($5,000) see Cole Foundation, Robert H. and Monica H.

Knoxville Opera Company ($250) see Toms Foundation

Knoxville Symphony ($150,000) see Thompson Charitable Foundation

Knoxville Symphony Orchestra ($10,000) see Stokely, Jr. Foundation, William B.

Knoxville Zoological Park ($750) see Toms Foundation

Lake Shore Home for Aged ($12,500) see Washington Foundation

Lakeshore Home ($7,500) see Stephens Foundation Trust

Lambuth College ($25,000) see Hyde Foundation, J. R.

Lane College Center ($5,000) see Florida Steel Corp.

Lausanne School Foundation ($15,273) see Adams Foundation, Arthur F. and Alice E.

Lebonheur Children's Hospital ($6,000) see Brinkley Foundation

LeBonheur Children's Hospital ($7,500) see Schadt Foundation

Les Passe Rehabilitation Hospital ($23,287) see Adams Foundation, Arthur F. and Alice E.

Lincoln Memorial University ($100,000) see Mills Foundation, Ralph E.

Lincoln Memorial University ($16,000) see Sullivan Foundation, Algernon Sydney

Linebaugh Library — payment of set aside for building ($1,471,200) see Christy-Houston Foundation

Literacy Academy of Bristol Lab ($2,860) see Massengill-DeFriece Foundation

Little League Baseball ($50,000) see Stokely, Jr. Foundation, William B.

Little Theatre of Chattanooga — capital campaign ($500,000) see Lyndhurst Foundation

Lonsdale Day Care Center ($2,000) see Florida Steel Corp.

Love Worth Finding ($25,000) see Schilling Motors

March of Dimes ($100) see Schneider Foundation, Robert E.

Martha O'Bryan Center ($2,000) see Foster Charitable Foundation, M. Stratton

Martin Luther King Boulevard Community Development Corporation — to fund Bessie Smith Hall ($65,000) see Tonya Memorial Foundation

Maryville College ($5,000) see Cole Foundation, Robert H. and Monica H.

Maryville College ($2,000) see 1939 Foundation

Maryville College ($3,000) see Shattuck Charitable Trust, S. F.

Maryville College ($50,000) see Thompson Charitable Foundation

Maryville College ($5,000) see Wilson Foundation, John and Nevils

McCallie School ($620,000) see Benwood Foundation

McCallie School ($60,000) see Caldwell Foundation, Hardwick

McCallie School ($85,000) see Dickson Foundation

McCallie School ($7,000) see Dorminy Foundation, John Henry

McCallie School ($10,000) see Jewell Memorial Foundation, Daniel Ashley and Irene Houston

McCallie School — capital program ($250,000) see Maclellan Charitable Trust, R. J.

McCallie School ($20,000) see North American Royalties

McCallie School ($85,000) see Ruddick Corp.

McCallie School ($300,000) see Tonya Memorial Foundation

McCallie School — for general purposes ($5,000) see Westend Foundation

McKendree Methodist Church ($15,000) see Ansley Foundation, Dantzler Bond

Meharry Medical Center ($30,000) see Potter Foundation, Justin and Valere

Meharry Medical College ($75,000) see Compton Foundation

Meharry Medical College ($15,000) see Davee Foundation

Meharry Medical College ($20,000) see Green Foundation, Allen P. and Josephine B.

Meharry Medical College — scholarship ($15,000) see Kern Foundation, Ilma

Meharry Medical College ($268,370) see Kraft General Foods

Meharry Medical College ($268,370) see Kraft General Foods

Meharry Medical College ($30,000) see Moore Foundation, Edward S.

Meharry Medical College ($12,000) see Shattuck Charitable Trust, S. F.

Meharry Medical College ($75,000) see Wollenberg Foundation

Memphis Arts Council ($6,000) see Belz Foundation

Memphis Arts Council ($3,000) see Conwood Co. L.P.

Memphis Arts Council ($107,000) see Federal Express Corp.

Memphis Ballet ($75,000) see Hyde Foundation, J. R.

Memphis Botanical Garden Foundation ($10,000) see Goldsmith Foundation

Memphis Brooks Museum of Art ($25,000) see Austin Memorial Foundation

Memphis Community Television Foundation — WKNO ($5,500) see Lowenstein Foundation, William P. and Marie R.

Memphis Food Bank ($2,000) see Wurzburg, Inc.

Memphis Hebrew Academy ($43,250) see Belz Foundation

Memphis Interfaith Association ($11,000) see Brinkley Foundation

Memphis Jewish Community Center ($20,000) see Belz Foundation

Memphis Jewish Community Center ($55,500) see Lowenstein Foundation, William P. and Marie R.

Memphis Jewish Community Center ($100,000) see Plough Foundation

Memphis Jewish Federation ($100,000) see Belz Foundation

Memphis Jewish Federation ($50,250) see Goldsmith Foundation

Memphis Jewish Federation ($19,625) see Goldsmith Foundation

Memphis Jewish Federation ($7,700) see Goldsmith Foundation

Memphis Jewish Federation ($7,125) see Goldsmith Foundation

Memphis Jewish Federation ($21,000) see Lowenstein Foundation, William P. and Marie R.

Memphis Jewish Federation ($250,000) see Plough Foundation

Memphis Jewish Federation ($28,500) see Wurzburg, Inc.

Memphis Jewish Federation Operation Exodus ($7,700) see Goldsmith Foundation

Memphis Jewish Home — formerly B'nai B'rith ($250,000) see Plough Foundation

Memphis Junior League ($20,000) see Briggs Foundation, T. W.

Memphis Orchestral Society ($10,000) see Belz Foundation

Memphis Orchestral Society ($15,000) see Brinkley Foundation

Memphis Orchestral Society ($62,500) see Plough Foundation

Memphis Partners see Nike Inc.

Memphis Pink Palace Museum ($20,000) see Austin Memorial Foundation

Memphis Pink Palace Museum ($10,000) see Briggs Foundation, T. W.

Memphis Rotary Foundation ($7,000) see Wurzburg, Inc.

Memphis State University ($5,000) see Schilling Motors

Memphis State University — scholarships ($60,100) see Van Vleet Foundation

Memphis Symphony Orchestra ($25,000) see Schilling Motors

Memphis University School ($6,000) see Brinkley Foundation

Memphis University School ($50,000) see Hyde Foundation, J. R.

Memphis University School ($30,000) see Hyde Foundation, J. R.

Memphis University School ($13,000) see Hyde Foundation, J. R.

Memphis University School ($21,000) see Schadt Foundation

Memphis University School ($25,000) see Willmott Foundation, Peter S.

Memphis Zoo ($30,000) see Briggs Foundation, T. W.

Memphis Zoo ($5,000) see Wurzburg, Inc.

Memphis Zoological Society ($5,000) see Goldsmith Foundation

Mental Health Association of Nashville ($8,000) see Ansley Foundation, Dantzler Bond

Metropolitan Interfaith Association ($5,000) see Schadt Foundation

Mid-America Seminary ($3,500) see Schilling Motors

Mid Cumberland Human Resource Agency — elderly nutrition program ($12,560) see Christy-Houston Foundation

Mid-South Hunger Coalition, Memphis, TN ($40,000) see Federal Express Corp.

Middle Tennessee Medical Center — magnetic resonance imaging unit ($975,000) see Christy-Houston Foundation

Middle Tennessee Medical Center — final payment for expansion ($180,000) see Christy-Houston Foundation

Middle Tennessee Medical Center — health professions library ($180,000) see Christy-Houston Foundation

Middle Tennessee State University ($25,000) see Danner Foundation

Middle Tennessee State University ($32,283) see Ernst & Young

MIFA ($3,000) see Conwood Co. L.P.

Milligan College — to support the development of a Bachelor of Science in Nursing degree program ($180,000) see duPont Fund, Jessie Ball

Montgomery Bell Academy ($25,000) see Davis Foundation, Joe C.

Murci Home for Retarded ($10,000) see Washington Foundation

Nashville Adult Literacy Council — to help hire a part-time evaluator ($2,500) see Gannett Co.

Nashville Ballet ($5,000) see Aladdin Industries, Incorporated

Nashville Ballet ($8,333) see Bradford & Co., J.C.

Nashville Ballet ($5,000) see Currey Foundation, Brownlee

Nashville Ballet — general support for the 1991-92 season ($60,000) see Hospital Corp. of America

Nashville Ballet — general support for the 1992-93 season ($60,000) see Hospital Corp. of America

Nashville Bar Association ($6,000) see Ansley Foundation, Dantzler Bond

Nashville Institute for the Arts — summer session offering arts education to teachers and principals ($75,000) see Hospital Corp. of America

Nashville Opera ($5,000) see Aladdin Industries, Incorporated

Nashville School of Law ($7,000) see Ansley Foundation, Dantzler Bond

Nashville Symphony — general purpose ($25,000) see AMR Corp.

Nashville Symphony ($10,000) see Bradford & Co., J.C.

Nashville Symphony ($20,000) see Danner Foundation

Nashville Symphony ($16,000) see Zimmerman Family Foundation, Raymond

Nashville Symphony Association ($8,500) see Werthan Foundation

Nashville Symphony Association — underwriting for summer concerts in Centennial Park in summer 1993, with the balance going to general support ($75,000) see Hospital Corp. of America

Nashville Tennis Association ($12,000) see Davis Foundation, Joe C.

Nashville Union Rescue Mission ($2,500) see Aladdin Industries, Incorporated

National Jewish Center for Learning and Leadership ($26,000) see Friedman Foundation, Stephen and Barbara

National Jewish Center for Learning and Leadership ($10,000) see Zimmerman Family Foundation, Raymond

NCSL Host Committee ($20,000) see Aladdin Industries, Incorporated

Neighborhood Christian Center ($10,000) see Briggs Foundation, T. W.

New Heritage Ministries ($8,000) see Ansley Foundation, Dantzler Bond

Northside Neighborhood House — for capital funds campaign ($5,000) see Westend Foundation

Opera Memphis ($25,000) see Adams Foundation, Arthur F. and Alice E.

Outlook Nashville ($6,000) see Ansley Foundation, Dantzler Bond

Owen Graduate School of Business ($1,000) see Currey Foundation, Brownlee

P.E.A.C.E. ($2,500) see Aladdin Industries, Incorporated

Pallottine Fathers ($2,000) see Kasal Charitable Trust, Father

Parkinson Support Group Fund ($10,000) see Stott Foundation, Robert L.

PENCIL Foundation see Genesco

PENCIL Foundation — 1992 HCA Teacher Awards ($70,000) see Hospital Corp. of America

Piedmont Adopt-A-School ($1,000) see SCT Yarns

Piedmont Adopt-A-School ($1,000) see SCT Yarns

Planned Parenthood ($40,000) see Massey Foundation, Jack C.

Plaza Ambulatory Care — cancer treatment ($20,877) see Hurlbut Memorial Fund, Orion L. and Emma S.

Plaza Cancer Treatment Center — cancer treatment ($1,083) see Hurlbut Memorial Fund, Orion L. and Emma S.

Prizewinner Community Initiatives Program ($147,833) see Lyndhurst Foundation

Project Pencil ($2,500) see Werthan Foundation

Public Education Foundation ($20,000) see Caldwell Foundation, Hardwick

Public Education Foundation — for general purposes ($10,000) see Westend Foundation

Recovery Residences of Nashville ($2,500) see Foster Charitable Foundation, M. Stratton

Reflection Riding ($5,000) see Hutcheson Foundation, Hazel Montague

Rhodes College ($5,000) see Conwood Co. L.P.

Rhodes College ($20,000) see Hyde Foundation, J. R.

Rhodes College ($55,000) see Plough Foundation

River City Company ($100,000) see Tonya Memorial Foundation

River City Company — partial payment for planning work on Riverwalk ($35,950) see Tonya Memorial Foundation

RiverCity Company ($500,000) see Lyndhurst Foundation

RiverCity Company — third installment of $200,000 pledge ($50,000) see Westend Foundation

RiverCity Company — endowment of Miller Plaza ($500,000) see Lyndhurst Foundation

Rotary Club of Bristol ($3,000) see Massengill-DeFriece Foundation

Rural Hill Congregation ($8,400) see Bell Trust

Rutherford County Department of Health — building in the Smyrna area ($20,000) see Christy-Houston Foundation

SAHC Stan A. Murray Memorial Fund ($1,000) see Felburn Foundation

St. Andrews ($5,000) see Woods-Greer Foundation

St. Andrews School and Sewanee Military Academy ($5,000) see Cartinhour Foundation

St. Andrews - Sewanee — final payment of three-year pledge ($5,000) see Westend Foundation

St. Jude Children's Research Hospital ($225,008) see Abraham Foundation, Anthony R.

St. Jude Children's Research Hospital ($10,000) see Brinkley Foundation

St. Jude Children's Research Hospital ($10,000) see Ford III Memorial Foundation, Jefferson Lee

St. Jude Children's Research Hospital ($10,300) see Goody's Manufacturing Corp.

St. Jude Children's Research Hospital ($3,000) see JJJ Foundation

St. Jude Childrens Research Hospital ($20,000) see Schilling Motors

St. Jude Childrens Research Hospital ($18,000) see Tibstra Charitable Foundation, Thomas and Gertrude

St. Jude Childrens Research Hospital ($5,000) see Trimble Family Foundation, Robert Mize and Isa White

St. Jude Children's Research Hospital ($1,000) see Wurzburg, Inc.

St. Jude Children's Research Hospital, Memphis, TN ($200,000) see Federal Express Corp.

St. Jude UTCHS ($50,000) see Belz Foundation

St. Jude's Children's Hospital ($10,000) see Bergner Co., P.A.

St. Mary's Episcopal School ($50,000) see Willmott Foundation, Peter S.

Salvation Army — comprehensive family resource center ($1,295,000) see Christy-Houston Foundation

Salvation Army ($3,535) see 1939 Foundation

Salvation Army, Memphis, TN ($25,000) see Federal Express Corp.

Senior Citizens ($9,500) see Massey Foundation, Jack C.

Show Jumping Hall of Fame ($5,000) see Currey Foundation, Brownlee

Siskin Memorial Foundation ($300,000) see Benwood Foundation

Siskin Memorial Foundation ($20,000) see Caldwell Foundation, Hardwick

Siskin Memorial Foundation ($10,000) see Jewell Memorial Foundation, Daniel Ashley and Irene Houston

Siskin Memorial Foundation ($7,000) see North American Royalties

Siskin Memorial Foundation ($5,000) see Woods-Greer Foundation

SPECK/USA — printing press operation to supply textbooks to schools ($25,000) see International Foundation

Tanasi Girl Scout Council ($500) see Toms Foundation

Teen Challenge ($33,500) see Brown Charitable Trust, Dora Maclellan

Temple ($24,299) see Zimmerman Family Foundation, Raymond

Temple Israel ($2,000) see Wurzburg, Inc.

Tennessee Aquarium ($20,000) see Caldwell Foundation, Hardwick

Tennessee Aquarium ($43,750) see Dixie Yarns, Inc.

Tennessee Aquarium ($23,000) see Hutcheson Foundation, Hazel Montague

Tennessee Aquarium ($25,000) see North American Royalties

Tennessee Aquarium ($40,000) see Sulzberger Foundation

Tennessee Aquarium Fund — aquarium fund ($507,625) see Tonya Memorial Foundation

Tennessee Baptist Convention ($14,300) see C.I.O.S.

Tennessee Environmental Council ($10,000) see Beldon II Fund

Tennessee Foundation of Independent Colleges ($3,500) see Tomkins Industries, Inc.

Tennessee Foundation of Independent Colleges Foundation see Genesco

Tennessee Historical Society ($5,000) see Leu Foundation

Tennessee Performing Arts Center ($25,000) see Danner Foundation

Tennessee Performing Arts Center ($5,015) see Zimmerman Family Foundation, Raymond

Tennessee River Gorge Trust ($125,000) see Benwood Foundation

Tennessee River Gorge Trust ($10,000) see Caldwell Foundation, Hardwick

Tennessee State Museum ($5,000) see Bradford & Co., J.C.

Tennessee State Museum Foundation ($2,500) see

Aladdin Industries, Incorporated

Tennessee State University ($2,000) see New Orphan Asylum Scholarship Foundation

Tennessee Tech College of Business ($5,000) see Duriron Co., Inc.

Thompson Cancer Center ($2,500) see Toms Foundation

Thompson Cancer Survival Center — purchase of MRI equipment ($3,380,000) see Thompson Charitable Foundation

TPAC Foundation ($5,000) see Aladdin Industries, Incorporated

Traveller's Rest Historic House Museum ($40,000) see Potter Foundation, Justin and Valere

Turning Point Ministries — operating funds ($165,000) see Maclellan Charitable Trust, R. J.

United Negro College Fund see Nike Inc.

United Way ($50,000) see Ansley Foundation, Dantzler Bond

United Way ($10,500) see Briggs Foundation, T. W.

United Way ($10,000) see Cole Foundation, Robert H. and Monica H.

United Way ($21,500) see Conwood Co. L.P.

United Way ($10,000) see Davis Foundation, Joe C.

United Way ($6,000) see Duriron Co., Inc.

United Way ($13,000) see Goldsmith Foundation

United Way ($2,500) see Jewell Memorial Foundation, Daniel Ashley and Irene Houston

United Way ($6,328) see Lawyers Title Foundation

United Way ($15,000) see Maclellan Foundation, Robert L. and Kathrina H.

United Way ($10,000) see Massey Foundation, Jack C.

United Way ($10,000) see Massey Foundation, Jack C.

United Way ($46,700) see North American Royalties

United Way ($6,000) see Schadt Foundation

United Way ($2,000) see SCT Yarns

United Way ($1,500) see SCT Yarns

United Way ($1,500) see SCT Yarns

United Way ($500) see SCT Yarns

United Way ($10,000) see Stokely, Jr. Foundation, William B.

United Way ($4,500) see Thalhimer Brothers Inc.

United Way ($50,000) see Washington Foundation

United Way ($10,000) see Werthan Foundation

United Way ($8,000) see Westend Foundation

United Way ($12,100) see Zimmerman Family Foundation, Raymond

United Way-Clarksville ($87,582) see American Standard

United Way of Greater Chattanooga ($50,000) see Dixie Yarns, Inc.

United Way of Greater Memphis — general purpose fund ($7,972) see Walgreen Co.

Texas (cont.)

Believe in Me ($2,500) see Henry Foundation, Patrick

Bell Company Society Fund for Crippled Children ($15,000) see Wilson Public Trust, Ralph

Ben Richey Boys Ranch — dorm construction ($140,000) see Doss Foundation, M. S.

Ben Taub General Hospital ($2,000) see Taub Foundation

Bess Harris Jones Fund of United Methodist Church — endowment fund ($25,000) see Cockrell Foundation

Bethania Regional Health Center ($10,000) see White Foundation, Erle and Emma

Bethphage of Dallas ($5,000) see Sharp Foundation, Charles S. and Ruth C.

Bethune Day Care Nursery School ($10,000) see Corpus Christi Exploration Co.

Better Business Bureau see Apache Corp.

Bexar County Women's Center ($5,000) see Walthall Perpetual Charitable Trust, Marjorie T.

Big Bend Regional Medical Center ($50,000) see Roberts Foundation, Dora

Big Brothers and Big Sisters ($10,000) see Halff Foundation, G. A. C.

Big Brothers and Big Sisters ($18,200) see Luttrell Trust

Big Brothers and Sisters of Wichita County ($5,000) see Bridwell Foundation, J. S.

Big Spring State Hospital Volunteer Advisory Council ($2,500) see Priddy Foundation

Big Spring YMCA ($500,000) see Roberts Foundation, Dora

Big Spring YMCA ($66,573) see Roberts Foundation, Dora

Bill Glass Evangelistic Association — prison ministry ($10,000) see Edwards Foundation, Jes

Bill Glass Evangelistic Association ($30,000) see Share Foundation

Birdwell Elementary School and PTA ($1,250) see Rogers Foundation

Black Evangelistic Enterprises ($20,000) see Lamb Foundation, Kirkland S. and Rena B.

Black Evangelistic Enterprises ($22,750) see Owen Trust, B. B.

Blessed Sacrament Academy ($5,000) see Burkitt Foundation

Blooming Grove Independent School District ($500) see Hofstetter Trust, Bessie

B'nai B'rith Foundation of US ($1,150) see Weiner Foundation

Botanical Research Institute — general support ($430,455) see Bass Foundation

Boy Scouts of America see Apache Corp.

Boy Scouts of America ($1,000) see Bass Foundation, Harry

Boy Scouts of America ($26,000) see Brown Foundation, M. K.

Boy Scouts of America ($90,100) see Clements Foundation

Boy Scouts of America ($41,550) see Clements Foundation

Boy Scouts of America ($2,500) see Cook Foundation, Loring

Boy Scouts of America ($30,000) see Elkins Foundation, J. A. and Isabel M.

Boy Scouts of America ($30,000) see FINA, Inc.

Boy Scouts of America ($25,000) see Hachar Charitable Trust, D. D.

Boy Scouts of America ($5,000) see Hervey Foundation

Boy Scouts of America ($30,000) see Jones Foundation, Helen

Boy Scouts of America ($6,000) see Luse Foundation, W. P. and Bulah

Boy Scouts of America ($46,000) see Meyer Family Foundation, Paul J.

Boy Scouts of America ($5,000) see Perkins Foundation, Joe and Lois

Boy Scouts of America ($3,000) see Semmes Foundation

Boy Scouts of America ($15,000) see Seymour Foundation, W. L. and Louise E.

Boy Scouts of America ($15,000) see Swalm Foundation

Boy Scouts of America ($1,662,000) see Wallace-Reader's Digest Fund, DeWitt

Boy Scouts of America — Buffalo Trail Council; building acquisition and renovation, dining hall renovation ($132,000) see Abell-Hanger Foundation

Boy Scouts of America — for matching endowment and Friends of Scouting campaign ($285,000) see Cockrell Foundation

Boy Scouts of America — Sam Houston Area Council ($36,000) see Strake Foundation

Boy Scouts of America Sam Houston Area Council ($11,863) see Texas Commerce Bank Houston, N.A.

Boys Club of America ($15,000) see Mayor Foundation, Oliver Dewey

Boys Club of America ($58,883) see Meyer Family Foundation, Paul J.

Boys Club of America ($1,837) see Waggoner Foundation, E. Paul and Helen Buck

Boys Country of Houston ($65,000) see Ellwood Foundation

Boys and Girls Club ($200) see Gordon Foundation, Meyer and Ida

Boys and Girls Club ($45,000) see Hachar Charitable Trust, D. D.

Boys and Girls Club ($25,000) see Hervey Foundation

Boys and Girls Club ($6,000) see Luse Foundation, W. P. and Bulah

Boys and Girls Club ($2,500) see Munson Foundation, W. B.

Boys and Girls Club ($5,000) see Owsley Foundation, Alvin and Lucy

Boys and Girls Club ($100) see Southland Corp.

Boys and Girls Club ($7,000) see Waggoner Foundation, E. Paul and Helen Buck

Boys and Girls Club of Beeville — for operating expenses ($10,000) see Dougherty, Jr. Foundation, James R.

Boys and Girls Club of Galveston ($20,000) see Kempner Fund, Harris and Eliza

Boys and Girls Clubs ($31,000) see Fleming Foundation

Boys and Girls Clubs of Greater Dallas — capital funds for new facility in North Cliff ($50,000) see Contran Corp.

Boys and Girls Clubs of Greater Dallas-Turnkey Branch ($241,000) see Hoblitzelle Foundation

Boys Haven of America ($35,000) see Steinhagen Benevolent Trust, B. A. and Elinor

Brady Presbyterian Church ($10,000) see White Trust, G. R.

Branksome Hall ($4,416) see LBJ Family Foundation

Brazosport Health Foundation — cancer therapy center see Nalco Chemical Co.

Bread Basket Ministries ($10,000) see Falk Medical Research Foundation, Dr. Ralph and Marian

Briarwood-Brookwood ($35,000) see West Texas Corp., J. M.

Briarwood School ($5,000) see Lowe Foundation

Bridge Association ($5,000) see Fifth Avenue Foundation

Bridge Center for Contemporary Art — learning disability program for children ($8,000) see Seymour Foundation, W. L. and Louise E.

Bridge Children's Advocacy Center — operating expenses ($10,000) see Craig Foundation, J. Paul

Bridges School ($1,500) see Hervey Foundation

Bridges School — dyslexic program ($5,000) see Seymour Foundation, W. L. and Louise E.

Broadway Baptist Church ($50,000) see Fleming Foundation

Broadway Baptist Church — elderly ministry ($7,000) see Hankamer Foundation, Curtis and Doris K.

Broadway Baptist Church ($70,000) see Walsh Foundation

Brooks County Area Volunteer Emergency Response Team ($50,000) see Rachal Foundation, Ed

Brooks County Hospital Recreational Community Fund ($5,935) see Rachal Foundation, Ed

Brooks County Independent School District ($40,000) see Rachal Foundation, Ed

Brookwood Community — endowment fund ($50,000) see Cockrell Foundation

Brookwood Community — home for dysfunctional adult ($100,000) see Farish Fund, William Stamps

Brookwood Community ($1,225) see Taub Foundation

Brookwood Community Volunteers ($12,000) see Duncan Foundation, Lillian H. and C. W.

Brookwood Community Volunteers ($12,000) see Duncan Foundation, Lillian H. and C. W.

Brown Trail Congregation — school of preaching ($6,000) see Bell Trust

Buckner Baptist Benevolences — dorm renovation ($78,200) see Doss Foundation, M. S.

Buckner Baptist Church ($50,000) see Morris Foundation

C.A.M. International ($4,000) see Kejr Foundation

Cabbages and Kings ($5,000) see Geifman Family Foundation

Caesar Klegerg Wildlife Institute ($5,000) see Robinson Foundation

Cain Center — repairs to civic center ($310,000) see Cain Foundation, Effie and Wofford

Cain Center — operation of civic center ($124,650) see Cain Foundation, Effie and Wofford

Calhoun County Emergency Medical Service — to purchase a Rescue Truck-First Responder Unit ($55,000) see Johnson Foundation, M. G. and Lillie A.

Calvary Road Baptist ($4,300) see Oldham Little Church Foundation

Camp Fire Campaign for Children ($25,000) see Davidson Family Charitable Foundation

Camp Fire Council of North Texas ($5,000) see Priddy Foundation

Campaign for Healthier Babies ($10,000) see Duncan Foundation, Lillian H. and C. W.

Cancer Research and Therapy ($20,000) see Koehler Foundation, Marcia and Otto

Cancer Therapy and Research ($10,000) see Halff Foundation, G. A. C.

Cancer Therapy and Research Foundation of South Texas ($12,000) see Burnham Donor Fund, Alfred G.

Cancer Therapy and Research Foundation of South Texas ($3,000) see Ferguson Family Foundation, Kittie and Rugeley

Cancer Therapy and Research Foundation of South Texas ($20,000) see Zachry Co., H. B.

Capital Area Food Bank — vehicle purchase ($7,000) see Priddy Foundation

Capital Area Radiation and Research Foundation ($10,000) see West Texas Corp., J. M.

Caritas of Austin ($5,000) see Veritas Foundation

Caritas of Waco ($100) see Ward Co., Joe L.

Carrizo Springs Consolidated Independent School District ($5,000) see West Foundation, Neva and Wesley

Carver Community Center ($2,750) see Tobin Foundation

CASA — child advocacy ($10,000) see Seymour Foundation, W. L. and Louise E.

Casa de Amigos ($30,000) see Fasken Foundation

CASA De Esperanza ($15,000) see Lyons Foundation

Casa De Esperanza ($10,000) see Smith Foundation, Julia and Albert

Casa Manana ($5,000) see Tandy Foundation, David L.

Casa de Proyacto Libertad ($4,500) see Carteh Foundation

Cassata Learning Center ($25,000) see Morris Foundation

Cathedral Church of St. John ($31,000) see Tobin Foundation

Cathedral High School ($45,000) see Birmingham Foundation

Cathedral High School ($5,000) see Burkitt Foundation

Catholic Charities ($20,000) see Dishman Charitable Foundation Trust, H. E. and Kate

Catholic Charities ($9,500) see Orleans Trust, Carrie S.

Catholic Charities ($20,000) see Steinhagen Benevolent Trust, B. A. and Elinor

Catholic Foundation ($1,000) see Bordeaux Foundation

CBA Foundation ($100) see Luttrell Trust

Cenikor Foundation ($5,000) see Edwards Foundation, Jes

Center for Battered Women ($3,500) see Henry Foundation, Patrick

Center for Battered Women — Shelter Fund ($10,000) see Clayton Fund

Center for Housing Resources ($16,000) see Redman Foundation

Center for Housing Resources ($25,000) see Temple-Inland

Center for Human Nutrition, Southwestern Medical Center, Dallas ($1,000) see Bordeaux Foundation

Center Incorporated — mortgage retirement and co-compliance renovation of properties used for housing and rehabilitation of low-income and indigent substance abusers, building purchase ($20,000) see Swalm Foundation

Center for Non-Profit Management see Centex Corp.

Center for Nonprofit Management ($35,000) see King Foundation, Carl B. and Florence E.

Center for the Retarded ($10,000) see Rienzi Foundation

Center for the Retarded ($34,000) see Turner Charitable Foundation

Central American Mission International ($10,000) see Ukrop's Super Markets, Inc.

Central Texas Zoological and Botanical Society ($2,590) see Lux Trust, Dr. Konrad and Clara

Challenge ($10,000) see Lard Trust, Mary Potishman

Challenger Center for Space Science Education ($1,000) see Taub Foundation

Cherokee Civic Theatre ($5,000) see Pineywoods Foundation

Child Abuse Prevention Center ($10,000) see Abercrombie Foundation

Child Advocate ($10,000) see Abercrombie Foundation

Child Advocates see Compaq Computer Corp.

Child Advocates ($25,000) see Favrot Fund

Child Advocates of Houston ($15,000) see Lyons Foundation

Child Care Partnership ($14,000) see Redman Foundation

Child Crisis Center ($5,000) see Cimarron Foundation

Child Crisis Center ($2,000) see Hervey Foundation

Child Crisis Center of El Paso ($18,167) see McKee Foundation, Robert E. and Evelyn

Child Study Center ($25,000) see Brown and C. A. Lupton Foundation, T. J.

Child Study Center — building fund ($245,000) see Carter Foundation, Amon G.

Child Study Center ($35,000) see Crump Fund, Joe and Jessie

Child Study Center — renovate family center ($50,000) see Davidson Family Charitable Foundation

Child Study Center ($10,000) see Davis Foundation, Ken W.

Child Study Center ($2,500) see Fifth Avenue Foundation

Child Study Center ($30,000) see Fort Worth Star Telegram

Child Study Center ($20,100) see Garvey Texas Foundation

Child Study Center ($17,500) see Luttrell Trust

Child Study Center ($50,000) see Morris Foundation

Child Study Center ($60,000) see Scott Foundation, William E.

Child Study Center ($15,000) see Waggoner Charitable Trust, Crystelle

Child Study Center ($9,000) see Weaver Foundation, Gil and Dody

Child Study Center — support Bright Futures Campaign to fund expansion of facilities ($250,000) see Richardson Foundation, Sid W.

Child Study Center — operating expenses; capital campaign ($150,000) see Tandy Foundation, Anne Burnett and Charles

Childrens Aid Society of West Texas ($5,000) see Bridwell Foundation, J. S.

Children's Cancer Fund ($10,000) see White Foundation, Erle and Emma

Children's Fund ($2,500) see West Foundation, Neva and Wesley

Children's Home of Lubbock — building addition ($63,085) see Doss Foundation, M. S.

Children's Medical Center see Centex Corp.

Childrens Medical Center ($50,000) see Constantin Foundation

Children's Medical Center — expansion and renovation ($100,000) see Fikes Foundation, Leland

Children's Medical Center ($50,000) see Goddard Foundation, Charles B.

Children's Medical Center — capital fund ($5,000) see Jonsson Foundation

Children's Medical Center ($10,000) see Stemmons Foundation

Children's Medical Center of Dallas see Merrill Lynch & Co.

Children's Medical Center of Dallas ($200,000) see Moss Heart Trust, Harry S.

Children's Medical Center Foundation — building fund ($6,250) see Beasley Foundation, Theodore and Beulah

Children's Medical Foundation — first annual payment of $150,000 ($50,000) see Green Foundation

Children's Medical Foundation — Diamond Jubilee Development Program-five year grant for renovation and expansion of Children's Medical Center ($50,000) see Contran Corp.

Children's Medical Foundation of Texas ($3,500) see Orleans Trust, Carrie S.

Children's Medical Foundation of Texas — building fund ($300,590) see Seay Charitable Trust, Sarah M. and Charles E.

Children's Medical Foundation of Texas ($34,000) see Zale Foundation, William and Sylvia

Children's Museum — capital campaign ($150,000) see Fondren Foundation

Children's Museum ($25,000) see McGovern Fund for the Behavioral Sciences

Children's Museum ($10,000) see Rienzi Foundation

Children's Museum ($10,200) see Scurlock Foundation

Childrens Museum — to fund the Environmental Gallery in the new museum facility ($300,000) see Meadows Foundation

Children's Museum of Houston — museum programs ($100,000) see Farish Fund, William Stamps

Children's Museum of Houston — capital campaign ($8,333) see First Interstate Bank of Texas, N.A.

Children's Museum of Houston ($14,535) see Texas Commerce Bank Houston, N.A.

Children's Museum of Houston — for construction of a new building see USX Corp.

Children's Museum of Houston — capital campaign, Take a Giant Step ($500,000) see Cullen Foundation

Children's Museum of Houston — toward construction of the Mary Gibbs Jones Building ($1,000,000) see Houston Endowment

Children's Presbyterian Health-Care Center — ropes course, flagpoles, lighting ($35,445) see Seay Charitable Trust, Sarah M. and Charles E.

Children's Rehabilitation Center — remodel center's facilities ($164,329) see Carpenter Foundation, E. Rhodes and Leona B.

Children's Rehabilitation Center — expand center's facilities ($120,050) see Carpenter Foundation, E. Rhodes and Leona B.

Chinquapin School ($5,000) see Clayton Fund

Chinquapin School — scholarship fund ($10,000) see Creel Foundation

Chinquapin School ($50,000) see Herzstein Charitable Foundation, Albert and Ethel

Chinquapin School ($10,800) see Klein Fund, Nathan J.

Chinquapin School ($3,000) see Lowe Foundation

Chinquapin School ($16,800) see Lyons Foundation

Chinquapin School ($1,000) see Mason Charitable Foundation

Christ Episcopal Church ($7,000) see Ferguson Family Foundation, Kittie and Rugeley

Christ Episcopal Church ($41,916) see Morrison Trust, Louise L.

Christ Episcopal Church ($25,000) see Semmes Foundation

Christ Episcopal Church ($10,000) see Walthall Perpetual Charitable Trust, Marjorie T.

Christ King Catholic Church ($10,000) see Bordeaux Foundation

Christ the King Church ($27,000) see Haggar Foundation

Christ the King Lutheran Church ($3,000) see Woltman Foundation, B. M.

Christ the King School — mothers club ($25,000) see Haggar Foundation

Christ The Good Shepherd ($26,200) see Cameron Foundation, Harry S. and Isabel C.

ChristChurch Cathedral ($15,000) see Hamman Foundation, George and Mary Josephine

Christian Church Division of Higher Education ($50,000) see Beasley Foundation, Theodore and Beulah

Christian Farms ($15,000) see Wilson Public Trust, Ralph

Christian Leadership Center ($50,000) see Lamb Foundation, Kirkland S. and Rena B.

Christian Medical and Dental Society — to support their training module ($44,745) see Templeton Foundation, John

Christian Medical and Dental Society — to support Phase I bibliography ($23,360) see Templeton Foundation, John

Christian Mission Concerns ($20,000) see Meyer Family Foundation, Paul J.

Christmas in April ($25,000) see Cauthorn Charitable Trust, John and Mildred

Christmas In April see Reliable Life Insurance Co.

Christ's Kitchen ($30,000) see South Texas Charitable Foundation

Church of Good Shepherd — operating fund ($31,445) see Cauthorn Charitable Trust, John and Mildred

Circle T. Girl Scout Council ($10,000) see Lard Trust, Mary Potishman

Cistercian Preparatory School ($15,000) see Belo Corp., A.H.

City of Abilene — to fund Redbud Park development costs ($215,771) see Dodge Jones Foundation

City of Allen, Texas — for construction of the new Allen Civic Center ($60,000) see McDermott Foundation, Eugene

City of Beeville — to purchase the City of Beeville Emergency Medical Service a Type III Ambulance ($52,500) see Johnson Foundation, M. G. and Lillie A.

City of Big Spring ($50,000) see Roberts Foundation, Dora

City/County Drug and Alcohol Abuse Center ($12,000) see

Franklin Charitable Trust, Ershel

City of Dallas ($250,000) see Mobil Oil Corp.

City of Diboll ($249,868) see Temple-Inland

City of Edna — to purchase a Frazier Ambulance unit ($82,437) see Johnson Foundation, M. G. and Lillie A.

City of El Paso/Community and Human Development ($50,000) see Levi Strauss & Co.

City of Falfurrias ($35,000) see Rachal Foundation, Ed

City of Ft. Worth/Burnett Park — support of maintenance and landscaping of Burnett Park ($456,617) see Tandy Foundation, Anne Burnett and Charles

City of Graham — memorial auditorium ($30,000) see Bertha Foundation

City of Jasper ($75,000) see Temple-Inland

City of Kyle ($10,000) see Johnson Foundation, Burdine

City of Laredo Fire Department ($75,000) see Hachar Charitable Trust, D. D.

City of Lufkin ($7,500) see Pineywoods Foundation

City of Lufkin ($7,500) see Pineywoods Foundation

City of Lufkin ($7,500) see Pineywoods Foundation

City of Lufkin — Jones Park improvements ($255,500) see Temple Foundation, T. L. L.

City of Lufkin — Phase I and Phase II/recycling program ($252,425) see Temple Foundation, T. L. L.

City of Midland Swim Team ($5,000) see Davis Foundation, Ken W.

City of Midland Swim Team ($35,000) see King Foundation, Carl B. and Florence E.

City of Midland Swim Team ($10,000) see West Texas Corp., J. M.

City of Midland Swim Team — expand and renovate the Swim Center and Fund the Utility and Maintenance Trust ($500,000) see Abell-Hanger Foundation

City of Mineola ($30,000) see Meredith Foundation

City of Pineland ($25,075) see Temple-Inland

City of Vernon ($1,000) see Waggoner Foundation, E. Paul and Helen Buck

City of Wharton Emergency Medical Service — for the purchase of an ambulance ($50,000) see Johnson Foundation, M. G. and Lillie A.

Clarendon College Foundation ($10,000) see Brown Foundation, M. K.

Clean Pampa ($5,000) see Brown Foundation, M. K.

Coastal Bend Youth City ($12,000) see Behmann Brothers Foundation

Coastal Bend Youth City ($40,000) see King Ranch

College of Saint Thomas More ($2,500) see Piper Foundation, Minnie Stevens

Common Ground ($10,000) see Redman Foundation

Communities Foundation — for Jubilee Dallas for celebrating 150 years ($50,000) see

McDermott Foundation, Eugene

Communities Foundation of Texas ($10,000) see Moncrief Foundation, William A. and Elizabeth B.

Communities Foundation of Texas ($165,000) see Priddy Foundation

Communities in Schools see Compaq Computer Corp.

Communities in Schools ($10,000) see Corpus Christi Exploration Co.

Communities in Schools ($15,000) see Haas Foundation, Paul and Mary

Community Daycare Center ($5,000) see Brown Foundation, M. K.

Community Foundation of Metropolitan Tarrant County ($17,200) see Scott Foundation, William E.

Community Guidance Center ($10,000) see Halff Foundation, G. A. C.

Community Guidance Center ($5,000) see Walthall Perpetual Charitable Trust, Marjorie T.

Community Partners ($10,000) see Belo Corp., A.H.

Community and Senior Services ($15,000) see Fasken Foundation

Community Services ($5,000) see Wolens Foundation, Kalman and Ida

Concordia Lutheran Church ($19,000) see Southern Furniture Co.

Concordia Lutheran College ($3,500) see Hugg Trust, Leoia W. and Charles H.

Concordia Lutheran College — for construction costs ($100,000) see Johnson Foundation, M. G. and Lillie A.

Concordia Lutheran College ($32,700) see Woltman Foundation, B. M.

Concordia Lutheran College ($2,500) see Woltman Foundation, B. M.

Confederate Air Force ($5,000) see Brown Foundation, M. K.

Congregation Agudas Achim ($35,500) see Wolens Foundation, Kalman and Ida

Congregation Beth Israel ($15,000) see Lewis Foundation, Lillian Kaiser

Congregation Beth Yeshurun ($1,554) see Weiner Foundation

Congregation Emanuel ($21,855) see Klein Fund, Nathan J.

Congregation Shearith Israel ($20,000) see Feldman Foundation

Congregation Sherith Israel ($20,000) see Zale Foundation, William and Sylvia

Contemporary Art Museum of Houston ($5,000) see Vaughn, Jr. Foundation Fund, James M.

Contemporary Arts Association of Houston ($62,000) see Lannan Foundation

Contemporary Arts Museum ($5,000) see Menil Foundation

Contemporary Arts Museum ($5,450) see Owsley Foundation, Alvin and Lucy

Contemporary Arts Museum ($5,000) see Vale-Asche Foundation

Texas (cont.)

Converse Area Public Library ($2,500) see Piper Foundation, Minnie Stevens

Cook Fort Worth Children's Medical Center ($36,500) see Alexander Foundation, Robert D. and Catherine R.

Cook Fort Worth Children's Medical Center ($9,000) see Weaver Foundation, Gil and Dody

Cook Ft. Worth Children's Hospital ($13,468) see Fort Worth Star Telegram

Cook-Ft. Worth Children's Medical Center — cardiac catheterization lab ($200,000) see Bass Foundation

Cook-Ft. Worth Children's Medical Center ($10,000) see Edwards Foundation, Jes

Cook-Fort Worth Children's Medical Center ($1,500) see JMK-A M Micallef Charitable Foundation

Cook-Ft. Worth Children's Medical Center — provide assistance in the completion of the fifth floor of the facility ($500,000) see Richardson Foundation, Sid W.

Cooper Institute for Aerobics Research ($10,000) see Tyler Corp.

Corpus Christi Academy — new library ($300,000) see Kenedy Memorial Foundation, John G. and Marie Stella

Corpus Christi Academy ($250,000) see Kenedy Memorial Foundation, John G. and Marie Stella

Corpus Christi Academy — new library ($239,000) see Kenedy Memorial Foundation, John G. and Marie Stella

Corpus Christi Catholic School ($5,000) see Burkitt Foundation

Corpus Christi Christian Ministries ($10,000) see Behmann Brothers Foundation

Corpus Christi Church ($2,500) see Shea Foundation, Edmund and Mary

Corpus Christi Metro Ministries ($8,500) see Behmann Brothers Foundation

Corpus Christi Metro Ministries ($15,000) see Corpus Christi Exploration Co.

Corpus Christi State University ($41,106) see Haas Foundation, Paul and Mary

Corpus Christi State University Foundation ($10,000) see Corpus Christi Exploration Co.

Corsicana Independent School District ($25,000) see Wolens Foundation, Kalman and Ida

Corsicana-Navarro County Health Department ($28,500) see Hofstetter Trust, Bessie

Cougar Valley ($300,000) see Tandy Corp.

Council for Chemical Research — operating support ($30,000) see Air Products & Chemicals

Council for National Policy ($5,000) see Puett Foundation, Nelson

Council for National Policy ($5,000) see Puett Foundation, Nelson

County of Refugio ($10,000) see O'Connor Foundation, Kathryn

Covenant House ($125,000) see South Texas Charitable Foundation

Covenant House — for Medical Director's position ($30,000) see Cockrell Foundation

Covenant House of Texas — emergency shelter, food and medical care ($5,500) see Kayser Foundation

Cowboy Artists of America Museum ($500) see Parker Drilling Co.

Cowboy Artists of America Museum ($1,000) see Wiseheart Foundation

Creative Learning Center — education in South Dallas, quality academics salaries ($50,000) see Hillcrest Foundation

Crime Stoppers of Houston — aid in solving crimes ($3,000) see Kayser Foundation

Cristercian Preparatory School ($5,000) see Haggerty Foundation

Crosbyton Clinic — for equipment ($28,657) see South Plains Foundation

Crystal Charity Ball ($20,000) see Chilton Foundation Trust

Crystal Charity Ball ($10,000) see Clements Foundation

Crystal Charity Ball ($2,000) see Tyler Corp.

Crystal Charity Ball — beneficiaries: Dallas Child Guidance Clinic, foster Child Advocate Services Dallas School ($80,000) see Contran Corp.

Cultural Activities Center ($15,000) see Wilson Public Trust, Ralph

Cultural Arts Council see American Telephone & Telegraph Co./Dallas Region

Cypress-Fairbanks Independent School District — Biotechnology ($18,128) see Toshiba America, Inc.

Czech Educational Foundation of Texas — non-restricted ($197,390) see Birch Foundation, Stephen and Mary

D.A. Camera ($5,000) see Vaughn, Jr. Foundation Fund, James M.

Da Camera Society ($8,000) see Menil Foundation

Dallas Aboretum and Botanical Society ($10,000) see Moss Foundation, Harry S.

Dallas Ambassadors Forum see American Telephone & Telegraph Co./Dallas Region

Dallas Baptist University — general support ($250,000) see Collins Foundation, Carr P.

Dallas Baptist University ($750,000) see Mabee Foundation, J. E. and L. E.

Dallas Baptist University — toward construction of a new student center ($250,000) see Meadows Foundation

Dallas Baptist University ($2,834) see Staley Foundation, Thomas F.

Dallas Baptist University — final payment of 1991 commitment for construction of Mahler Student Center ($50,000) see Hillcrest Foundation

Dallas Black Chamber of Commerce see American Telephone & Telegraph Co./Dallas Region

Dallas Black Dance Theatre see American Telephone & Telegraph Co./Dallas Region

Dallas Black Dance Theatre — general purpose ($25,000) see AMR Corp.

Dallas Boys & Girls Club see Centex Corp.

Dallas Can! Academy ($10,000) see Bosque Foundation

Dallas Child Guidance ($200,000) see Gill Foundation, Pauline Allen

Dallas Child Guidance Clinic ($50,000) see Constantin Foundation

Dallas Child Guidance Clinic ($10,000) see Goddard Foundation, Charles B.

Dallas Child Guidance Clinic ($130,000) see Hoblitzelle Foundation

Dallas Child Guidance Clinic — for new facility ($50,000) see McDermott Foundation, Eugene

Dallas Children's Advocacy Center — general support ($175,000) see Collins Foundation, Carr P.

Dallas Children's Advocacy Center — purchase medical services building for child abuse victims ($50,000) see Hillcrest Foundation

Dallas Children's Advocacy Center ($5,000) see Hunt Alternatives Fund, Helen

Dallas Commision for International Affairs see American Telephone & Telegraph Co./Dallas Region

Dallas Council on World Affairs ($1,000) see Bass Foundation, Harry

Dallas County Adult Literacy Council ($100) see Southland Corp.

Dallas County Community College District ($100) see Southland Corp.

Dallas County Community College District Foundation ($15,000) see Chilton Foundation Trust

Dallas County Heritage Society ($16,666) see Clements Foundation

Dallas County Heritage Society — for Quarter Century Endowment Fund ($50,000) see McDermott Foundation, Eugene

Dallas Foundation ($5,000) see Gill Foundation, Pauline Allen

Dallas Foundation ($67,333) see King Foundation, Carl B. and Florence E.

Dallas Foundation ($25,000) see Redman Foundation

Dallas Foundation Committee for Excellence in Education ($10,000) see Zale Foundation, William and Sylvia

Dallas Foundation for Health, Education and Research ($250,000) see O'Donnell Foundation

Dallas Habitat for Humanity, East Garrett Park Neighborhood — community revitalization, house construction for low income families ($50,000) see Hillcrest Foundation

Dallas Hispanic Chamber of Commerce see American Telephone & Telegraph Co./Dallas Region

Dallas Historical Society ($20,000) see King Foundation, Carl B. and Florence E.

Dallas Historical Society — conditional grant to mount Catherine the Great exhibit ($50,000) see Fikes Foundation, Leland

Dallas Home for Jewish Aged ($24,000) see Feldman Foundation

Dallas Home for Jewish Aged ($12,000) see Florence Foundation

Dallas Home for Jewish Aged ($40,000) see Taubman Foundation, Herman P. and Sophia

Dallas Home for Jewish Aged ($25,000) see Wolens Foundation, Kalman and Ida

Dallas Institute of Humanities and Culture ($31,000) see Moss Foundation, Harry S.

Dallas Institute for Humanities and Culture for Dallas VISION ($50,000) see Belo Corp., A.H.

Dallas Jewish Coalition for Homeless ($20,000) see Florence Foundation

Dallas Lighthouse for the Blind ($6,000) see Luse Foundation, W. P. and Bulah

Dallas Medical Resource Foundation Fountain Place — FACILIS, medical referral program of health resources ($50,000) see Hillcrest Foundation

Dallas Memorial Center for Holocaust Studies ($3,000) see Belo Corp., A.H.

Dallas Morning News Charities ($30,000) see Owen Trust, B. B.

Dallas Museum of Art — building fund ($45,000) see Bass Foundation, Harry

Dallas Museum of Art ($5,000) see Bass Foundation, Harry

Dallas Museum of Art see Centex Corp.

Dallas Museum of Art ($10,000) see Collins Foundation, James M.

Dallas Museum of Art ($10,000) see Collins Foundation, James M.

Dallas Museum of Art ($100,000) see Cook Foundation

Dallas Museum of Art — general operating fund ($25,000) see Green Foundation

Dallas Museum of Art ($82,000) see Haggerty Foundation

Dallas Museum of Art ($250,000) see JFM Foundation

Dallas Museum of Art — for the endowed directors chair ($500,000) see McDermott Foundation, Eugene

Dallas Museum of Art — for textile collection ($50,000) see McDermott Foundation, Eugene

Dallas Museum of Art ($17,907) see Moss Foundation, Harry S.

Dallas Museum of Art ($1,250,000) see O'Donnell Foundation

Dallas Museum of Art ($52,800) see Owsley Foundation, Alvin and Lucy

Dallas Museum of Art ($30,500) see Perkins Foundation, Joe and Lois

Dallas Museum of Art ($30,000) see Seay Charitable Trust, Sarah M. and Charles E.

Dallas Museum of Art ($100) see Southland Corp.

Dallas Museum of Art ($5,000) see Texas Industries, Inc.

Dallas Museum of Art ($5,000) see Tyler Corp.

Dallas Museum of Art ($2,300) see Tyler Corp.

Dallas Museum of Art — toward construction of the new Hamon Wing, specifically for the A. H. Meadows Pre-Columbian Galleries ($1,500,000) see Meadows Foundation

Dallas Museum of Arts see American Telephone & Telegraph Co./Dallas Region

Dallas Museum of Natural History ($50,000) see Constantin Foundation

Dallas Museum of Natural History ($30,000) see Goddard Foundation, Charles B.

Dallas Museum of Natural History see Recognition Equipment

Dallas Museum of Natural History Association — for facility and exhibit improvements ($450,000) see Meadows Foundation

Dallas Opera ($105,000) see Chadwick Foundation

Dallas Opera ($2,000) see Early Foundation

Dallas Opera ($15,000) see FINA, Inc.

Dallas Opera ($15,000) see FINA, Inc.

Dallas Opera ($60,000) see Fisher Foundation, Gramma

Dallas Opera ($100,000) see Kimberly-Clark Corp.

Dallas Opera ($8,300) see Mary Kay Foundation

Dallas Opera ($10,000) see Moss Foundation, Harry S.

Dallas Opera ($10,000) see Stemmons Foundation

Dallas Opera — Patron/Annual Fundraising for Operating Expenses ($5,000) see National Gypsum Co.

Dallas Park Foundation ($25,000) see King Foundation, Carl B. and Florence E.

Dallas Public Library — to purchase books on Japan's history and culture and travel guides (in honor opening a Dallas agency) ($10,000) see Bank of Tokyo Trust Co.

Dallas Services for Visually Impaired Children ($20,000) see Bosque Foundation

Dallas Summer Musicals ($25,000) see Plitt Southern Theatres

Dallas Symphony see Recognition Equipment

Dallas Symphony Association see Centex Corp.

Dallas Symphony Association ($300,000) see Exxon Corp.

Dallas Symphony Association ($50,000) see Green Foundation

Dallas Symphony Association ($175,000) see JCPenney Co.

Dallas Symphony Association ($175,000) see JCPenney Co.

Dallas Symphony Association ($10,000) see Jonsson Foundation

Dallas Symphony Association ($181,000) see Kahn Dallas Symphony Foundation, Louise W. and Edmund J.

Dallas Symphony Association — for concert hall ($150,000) see McDermott Foundation, Eugene

Dallas Symphony Association — annual support ($3,000) see National Gypsum Co.

Dallas Symphony Association ($10,000) see Stemmons Foundation

Dallas Theater Company ($50,000) see Cook Foundation

Dallas Theological Seminary ($11,000) see Helms Foundation

Dallas Theological Seminary ($29,650) see Lamb Foundation, Kirkland S. and Rena B.

Dallas Theological Seminary ($10,000) see Morris Charitable Foundation, E. A.

Dallas Theological Seminary ($22,500) see Owen Trust, B. B.

Dallas Theological Seminary ($1,000) see Rixson Foundation, Oscar C.

Dallas Theological Seminary ($1,000,000) see Solheim Foundation

Dallas Women's Foundation see Centex Corp.

Dallas Women's Foundation — to meet the special needs of women and girls in the Dallas community ($30,000) see Hunt Alternatives Fund

Dallas Zoological Society ($47,000) see Cook Foundation

Dance Umbrella ($29,950) see Little Family Foundation

Danforth Youth Collaborative — youth program ($5,000) see Seymour Foundation, W. L. and Louise E.

Daughters of Charity Centro San Vicente ($2,000) see Cimarron Foundation

Daughters of the Republic of Texas Library ($21,000) see Summerlee Foundation

Davey O'Brien Educational and Charitable Trust ($25,000) see Scott Foundation, William E.

Daytop Village Foundation ($30,000) see Texas Instruments

Del Mar College ($65,667) see Haas Foundation, Paul and Mary

Del Mar College of Corpus Christi ($7,500) see Behmann Brothers Foundation

Delpelchin Children's Center ($5,000) see Lewis Foundation, Lillian Kaiser

Delta Gamma Foundation ($1,000) see Alexander Foundation, Robert D. and Catherine R.

Denison Community — renovation ($50,000) see Smith and W. Aubrey Smith Charitable Foundation, Clara Blackford

Denison Community Foundation ($10,000) see Munson Foundation, W. B.

Denison Performing Arts ($7,000) see Munson Foundation, W. B.

Denison Public Library ($95,355) see Munson Foundation, W. B.

Denton Baptist Association — expand facilities ($25,000) see Davidson Family Charitable Foundation

Denton City Clinic ($6,000) see Sexton Foundation

DePelchin Children's Center ($5,000) see Bowers Foundation

DePelchin Children's Center ($10,000) see Turner Charitable Foundation

DePelchin Children's Center ($25,000) see Wolff Memorial Foundation, Pauline Sterne

Depelchin Children's Center Cullen Bayou Place ($10,000) see Texas Commerce Bank Houston, N.A.

DePelchin Children's Center — for emergency shelter for Youth Opportunities Unlimited ($250,000) see George Foundation

Development Office for Inner City Catholic School ($5,000) see Burkitt Foundation

Developmental Disabilities Center — general operations ($50,000) see Davidson Family Charitable Foundation

Diboll Booster Club ($45,000) see Temple-Inland

Diocese of Corpus Christi ($944,950) see Kenedy Memorial Foundation, John G. and Marie Stella

Diocese of Corpus Christi ($228,463) see Kenedy Memorial Foundation, John G. and Marie Stella

Diocese of Corpus Christi ($195,160) see Kenedy Memorial Foundation, John G. and Marie Stella

Diocese of Galveston ($117,000) see Cameron Foundation, Harry S. and Isabel C.

Diocese of Galveston-Houston ($28,500) see Strake Foundation

Diocese of Victoria ($100,000) see O'Connor Foundation, Kathryn

Discovery Center (Amarillo Foundation for Health and Science Education) ($10,000) see Anderson Charitable Trust, Josephine

Doctors Nursing Center ($36,300) see Bordeaux Foundation

Dominican Order of Catholic Church ($5,000) see Leonardt Foundation

Dora Roberts Rehabilitation Center ($136,030) see Roberts Foundation, Dora

Dorothy Shaw Bell Choir ($262,000) see Fleming Foundation

Dougherty Historical Foundation — for operating expenses ($10,000) see Dougherty, Jr. Foundation, James R.

Dougherty Historical Foundation — for operating expenses ($10,000) see Dougherty, Jr. Foundation, James R.

Downtown Dallas Family Shelter ($30,000) see Kimberly-Clark Corp.

East Dallas Community School ($10,000) see Gill Foundation, Pauline Allen

East Dallas Community School ($7,500) see Glaze Foundation, Robert and Ruth

East Dallas Cooperative Parish ($8,000) see Sharp Foundation, Charles S. and Ruth C.

East Seal Society for Children and Adults ($100,000) see Crump Fund, Joe and Jessie

East Texas Baptist University ($5,000) see Armstrong Foundation

East Texas Baptist University ($15,000) see Central & South West Services

East Texas Baptist University ($3,000) see Heath Foundation, Ed and Mary

East Texas Baptist University ($20,000) see McMillan, Jr. Foundation, Bruce

East Texas Baptist University ($256,300) see Rogers Foundation

East Texas Health Center ($8,000) see Griffin Foundation, Rosa May

East Texas State University — scholarships ($21,000) see Mayor Foundation, Oliver Dewey

East Texas Treatment Center ($20,000) see Griffin Foundation, Rosa May

East Texas Treatment Center ($20,000) see McMillan, Jr. Foundation, Bruce

Easter Seal Society of Dallas ($200,000) see Sturgis Charitable and Educational Trust, Roy and Christine

Eastern European Missions ($12,200) see Stephens Foundation Trust

Eastern European Seminary ($112,000) see First Fruit

Ebenezer Child Development Center — purchase of vans ($51,850) see Wright Foundation, Lola

Edna Gladney Center ($20,000) see Bryce Memorial Fund, William and Catherine

Edna Gladney Center — foundation assisting young women, children and adoptive parents ($10,000) see Martin & Deborah Flug Foundation

Educational Opportunities ($5,000) see Gill Foundation, Pauline Allen

El Campo Medical Foundation — to purchase radiology equipment ($160,000) see Johnson Foundation, M. G. and Lillie A.

El Paso Art Association — art shows and awards ($7,000) see Huthsteiner Fine Arts Trust

El Paso Cancer Treatment Center ($50,000) see McKee Foundation, Robert E. and Evelyn

El Paso Community Foundation — crippled children ($148,234) see Dues Charitable Foundation, Cesle C. and Mamie

El Paso Community Foundation ($100,000) see Hervey Foundation

El Paso Community Foundation — to be distributed exclusively for the benefit of crippled children ($179,000) see Hightower Foundation, Walter

El Paso East Side Library Branch ($1,500) see Huthsteiner Fine Arts Trust

El Paso Pro Musica ($2,000) see Huthsteiner Fine Arts Trust

El Paso Rehabilitation Center ($10,000) see McKee Foundation, Robert E. and Evelyn

El Paso Rehabilitation Center ($5,000) see Seymour Foundation, W. L. and Louise E.

El Paso Shelter for Battered Women ($7,500) see McKee Foundation, Robert E. and Evelyn

El Paso Symphony ($22,500) see Huthsteiner Fine Arts Trust

El Paso's Centro Medico Del Valle — to improve maternal and child health care services for their local communities ($30,000) see Johnson & Johnson

Elf Louise ($15,000) see Overlake Foundation

Emergency Animal Relief Fund ($19,844) see Summerlee Foundation

Emmanuel Church of God in Christ ($13,000) see Chilton Foundation Trust

Emmanuel Lutheran Church ($3,000) see Woltman Foundation, B. M.

End Hunger ($3,000) see Rienzi Foundation

Endow a Child — School for deaf children ($20,000) see Duncan Foundation, Lillian H. and C. W.

Ennis Independent School District ($81,000) see O'Donnell Foundation

Enterprise Foundation — working capital-Dallas affordable housing ($10,000) see First Interstate Bank of Texas, N.A.

Epiphany Episcopal Day School ($25,000) see King Ranch

Epiphany School Education Foundation ($33,000) see King Ranch

Episcopal Church of Good Shepherd ($10,000) see Gill Foundation, Pauline Allen

Episcopal Church of the Holy Trinity ($10,000) see Wilson Foundation, John and Nevils

Episcopal High School — scholarship fund ($25,000) see Creel Foundation

Episcopal High School — debt retirement ($200,000) see Farish Fund, William Stamps

Episcopal High School — capital campaign ($25,000) see Fish Foundation, Ray C.

Episcopal High School — reduction of indebtedness ($250,000) see Fondren Foundation

Episcopal High School ($25,000) see Lyons Foundation

Episcopal High School — toward the Fine Arts Center ($1,000,000) see Brown Foundation

Episcopal School of Dallas ($100,000) see Cook Foundation

Episcopal School of Dallas ($5,000) see Gill Foundation, Pauline Allen

Episcopal Theological Seminary ($10,157) see Society for the Increase of the Ministry

EXCAPE (Exchange Club Center for the Prevention of Child Abuse) — intervene in child abuse ($27,000) see Favrot Fund

Executive Service Corps ($23,000) see Kaplan Foundation, Mayer and Morris

F. W. Cook Children's Medical Center ($10,000) see Keith Foundation Trust, Ben E.

Family Gateway ($4,750) see Orleans Trust, Carrie S.

Family Outreach ($5,500) see Owsley Foundation, Alvin and Lucy

Family Place ($10,000) see Florence Foundation

Family Place ($8,075) see Orleans Trust, Carrie S.

Family Service Center — scholarship for art therapy

program for abused children ($10,000) see Swalm Foundation

Fay School — funding for preschool ($150,000) see Fondren Foundation

Fay School ($10,000) see West Texas Corp., J. M.

Fellowship of Christian Athletes ($15,000) see Chilton Foundation Trust

Fellowship of Christian Athletes ($1,250) see JMK-A M Micallef Charitable Foundation

Fellowship of Christian Athletes ($10,000) see Kilroy Foundation, William S. and Lora Jean

Fellowship of Christian Athletes, Greater Dallas Chapter — Tom Landry FCA Open Golf Tournament ($100,000) see Contran Corp.

First Baptist Church ($88,500) see Fair Foundation, R. W.

First Baptist Church ($7,500) see Heath Foundation, Ed and Mary

First Baptist Church ($23,375) see McMillan, Jr. Foundation, Bruce

First Baptist Church of Jacinto City ($15,000) see Community Hospital Foundation

First Baptist Church of Woodway ($356,500) see Meyer Family Foundation, Paul J.

First Christian Church ($3,000) see Heath Foundation, Ed and Mary

First Christian Church ($1,300) see Luttrell Trust

First English Lutheran Church Cancer Aid Fund ($10,000) see Overlake Foundation

First Presbyterian Church — donation of land ($126,000) see Abell-Hanger Foundation

First Presbyterian Church ($5,000) see Bryce Memorial Fund, William and Catherine

First Presbyterian Church ($23,800) see Cook Foundation, Loring

First Presbyterian Church ($27,644) see Franklin Charitable Trust, Ershel

First Presbyterian Church ($10,000) see Franklin Charitable Trust, Ershel

First Presbyterian Church ($11,205) see Griffin Foundation, Rosa May

First Presbyterian Church ($10,000) see Griffin Foundation, Rosa May

First Presbyterian Church — dental clinic ($24,900) see Hawn Foundation

First Presbyterian Church ($2,000) see Heath Foundation, Ed and Mary

First Presbyterian Church ($55,600) see Luchsinger Family Foundation

First Presbyterian Church ($2,500) see Piper Foundation, Minnie Stevens

First Presbyterian Church ($13,000) see Vaughn Foundation

First Presbyterian Church ($70,000) see Wilson Foundation, John and Nevils

First Step of Wichita Falls ($50,000) see Bridwell Foundation, J. S.

First Step of Wichita Falls ($25,000) see Perkins Foundation, Joe and Lois

Texas (cont.)

First Step of Wichita Falls ($50,000) see Priddy Foundation

First Texas Council of Camp Fire ($20,000) see Fort Worth Star Telegram

First Texas Council of Camp Fire ($25,000) see Pangburn Foundation

First Texas Council of Camp Fire ($30,000) see Scott Foundation, William E.

First Texas Council of Camp Fire Girls ($2,500) see Edwards Foundation, Jes

First United Methodist Church — general support ($200,000) see Bass Foundation

First United Methodist Church ($10,000) see Fuller Foundation

First United Methodist Church ($20,000) see McMillan, Jr. Foundation, Bruce

First United Methodist Church ($100,884) see Morris Foundation

First United Methodist Church ($1,000) see Parker Drilling Co.

First United Methodist Church ($926) see Perkins-Prothro Foundation

First United Methodist Church ($3,000) see Potts and Sibley Foundation

First United Methodist Church ($50,000) see Rachal Foundation, Ed

Floral Heights United Methodist Church — food pantry ($20,000) see White Foundation, Erle and Emma

Food Bank of Corpus Christi ($10,000) see Corpus Christi Exploration Co.

Food Bank of Greater Tarrant County ($10,000) see Falk Medical Research Foundation, Dr. Ralph and Marian

Food Bank of Greater Tarrant County ($20,000) see Lard Trust, Mary Potishman

Food Bank of Greater Tarrant County ($10,000) see Weaver Foundation, Gil and Dody

Food Bank of Tarrant County ($10,000) see Brown and C. A. Lupton Foundation, T. J.

Food Pantry ($5,000) see Luchsinger Family Foundation

Fort Bend County Fair Association ($3,700) see Quanex Corp.

Ft. Bend County Museum Association — to develop and implement public programs at The George Ranch Historical Park ($150,000) see George Foundation

Ft. Bend Family Health Center — Family Practice Residency Program ($174,307) see George Foundation

Ft. Bend Independent School District — scholarships ($58,500) see George Foundation

Fort Bend Senior Citizens — to support The Homemaker, home delivered meals and transportation programs ($50,000) see George Foundation

Ft. Bend Womens Center ($30,000) see Moores Foundation

Fort Griffin Fandangle ($125) see Ward Co., Joe L.

Fort Worth Art Association for Modern Art ($25,000) see Brown and C. A. Lupton Foundation, T. J.

Ft. Worth Arts Association — general support ($200,000) see Bass Foundation

Fort Worth Ballet ($2,000) see Alexander Foundation, Robert D. and Catherine R.

Fort Worth Ballet ($12,500) see Lard Trust, Mary Potishman

Fort Worth Ballet ($25,000) see Maddox Trust, Web

Fort Worth Ballet ($20,000) see Scott Foundation, William E.

Fort Worth Ballet Association ($15,000) see Brown and C. A. Lupton Foundation, T. J.

Fort Worth Ballet Association ($7,500) see Keith Foundation Trust, Ben E.

Fort Worth Ballet Association ($50,000) see Pangburn Foundation

Fort Worth Ballet Association ($50,000) see Pangburn Foundation

Fort Worth Ballet Association ($10,000) see Walsh Foundation

Fort Worth Botanic Garden ($160,972) see Fuller Foundation

Ft. Worth Country Day — building fund ($500,000) see Carter Foundation, Amon G.

Fort Worth Country Day School — general support ($200,000) see Bass Foundation

Fort Worth Country Day School ($3,000) see Childress Foundation, Francis and Miranda

Ft. Worth Country Day School ($160,000) see Fleming Foundation

Fort Worth Country Day School ($25,000) see Maddox Trust, Web

Ft. Worth Country Day School — support faculty trust ($516,232) see Richardson Foundation, Sid W.

Ft. Worth Country Day School — support Capital and Endowment Campaign ($500,000) see Richardson Foundation, Sid W.

Ft. Worth Culture District ($165,750) see Carter Foundation, Amon G.

Ft. Worth Independent School District — support Keystone project ($205,000) see Richardson Foundation, Sid W.

Ft. Worth Modern Art Museum Association — general operating expenses ($285,000) see Tandy Foundation, Anne Burnett and Charles

Fort Worth Museum of Science and History ($2,400) see Alexander Foundation, Robert D. and Catherine R.

Fort Worth Museum of Science and History — general support ($200,000) see Bass Foundation

Ft. Worth Museum of Science and History ($25,000) see Burlington Northern Inc.

Fort Worth Museum of Science and History ($2,500) see Fifth Avenue Foundation

Fort Worth Museum of Science and History ($4,000) see Tandy Foundation, David L.

Fort Worth Opera Association ($2,500) see Fifth Avenue Foundation

Fort Worth Opera Association ($15,000) see Lard Trust, Mary Potishman

Fort Worth Opera Association ($15,000) see Pangburn Foundation

Fort Worth Opera Association ($10,000) see Walsh Foundation

Fort Worth Symphony Orchestra ($50,000) see Brown and C. A. Lupton Foundation, T. J.

Fort Worth Symphony Orchestra Association — general support ($200,000) see Bass Foundation

Ft. Worth Symphony Orchestra Association ($25,000) see Burlington Northern Inc.

Fort Worth Symphony Orchestra Association ($5,000) see Fifth Avenue Foundation

Fort Worth Symphony Orchestra Association ($16,600) see Garvey Texas Foundation

Fort Worth Symphony Orchestra Association ($75,000) see Lard Trust, Mary Potishman

Fort Worth Symphony Orchestra Association ($25,000) see Maddox Trust, Web

Fort Worth Symphony Orchestra Association ($50,000) see Pangburn Foundation

Fort Worth Symphony Orchestra Association ($12,000) see Pangburn Foundation

Fort Worth Symphony Orchestra Association ($4,000) see Tandy Foundation, David L.

Fort Worth Symphony Orchestra Association ($19,000) see Walsh Foundation

Ft. Worth Symphony Orchestra Association — support 91-92 concert season ($274,377) see Richardson Foundation, Sid W.

Ft. Worth Symphony — 3rd-year of five-year commitment ($25,000) see AMR Corp.

Fort Worth Theatre ($10,000) see Walsh Foundation

Fort Worth Zoological Association — general support ($200,000) see Bass Foundation

Fort Worth Zoological Association — general support ($100,000) see Brown and C. A. Lupton Foundation, T. J.

Fort Worth Zoological Association ($25,000) see Maddox Trust, Web

Fort Worth Zoological Association ($30,000) see Pangburn Foundation

Fort Worth Zoological Association ($100,000) see Scott Foundation, William E.

Ft. Worth Zoological Association — capital campaign ($1,000,000) see Tandy Foundation, Anne Burnett and Charles

Ft. Worth Zoological Association — support completion of construction of World of Primates exhibit ($300,000) see Richardson Foundation, Sid W.

Fort Worth Zoological Association — support construction of World of Primates Exhibit ($1,250,000) see Bass Foundation

Ft. Worth Zoological Society — building fund ($260,000) see Carter Foundation, Amon G.

Forth Worth Opera ($11,000) see Waggoner Charitable Trust, Crystelle

Foundation for Interfaith ($5,000) see Steinhagen Benevolent Trust, B. A. and Elinor

Foundation for Jones Hall — restoration and maintenance ($1,000,000) see Houston Endowment

Foundation for the Museum of Medical Science ($5,000) see Robinson Foundation

Foundation for the Retarded ($25,000) see Elkins Foundation, J. A. and Isabel M.

Foundation for the Retarded ($65,000) see Ellwood Foundation

Foundation for the Retarded — building campaign ($50,000) see Fish Foundation, Ray C.

Foundation for the Retarded ($20,000) see Lyons Foundation

Foundation for the Retarded — Willow River Farms project ($265,000) see Temple Foundation, T. L. L.

Free Market Foundation ($42,000) see Lightner Sams Foundation

Freedom Center ($25,000) see Klein Fund, Nathan J.

Friends of the Bourne Public Library ($4,000) see Willard Helping Fund, Cecilia Young

Friends of Dallas Public Library — general support of programs and services ($3,000) see National Gypsum Co.

Friends of Ronald McDonald House ($20,000) see Clayton Fund

Fund for Excellence in Education in the DISD — School Reward Fund ($150,000) see Fikes Foundation, Leland

Funding Information Center ($1,000) see Meyer Foundation, Alice Kleberg Reynolds

Galleria Chamber see Apache Corp.

Galveston College — baseball program ($270,238) see Moody Foundation

Galveston College — men's baseball and women's volleyball ($289,740) see Moody Foundation

Galveston County Jewish Welfare Association ($37,000) see Kempner Fund, Harris and Eliza

Galveston Historical Foundation ($40,000) see Cameron Foundation, Harry S. and Isabel C.

Galveston Historical Foundation ($5,000) see Commerce Clearing House

Galveston Historical Foundation ($42,082) see Kempner Fund, Harris and Eliza

Galveston Historical Foundation ($32,082) see Kempner Fund, Harris and Eliza

Galveston Historical Foundation ($7,500) see Knox, Sr., and Pearl Wallis Knox Charitable Foundation, Robert W.

Galveston Historical Foundation — endowment fund ($1,000,000) see Moody Foundation

Galveston Historical Foundation — for various maintenance and equipment needs of the Historical Foundation, the Strand Street Theatre, and the Galveston Arts Center

($300,000) see Meadows Foundation

Galveston Historical Foundation — Rainbow Row development ($25,000) see Favrot Fund

Galveston Historical Society ($500,000) see Wortham Foundation

Galveston Symphony ($1,000) see Northen, Mary Moody

Garland Independent School District ($10,000) see Belo Corp., A.H.

General Land Office ($15,000) see Haas Foundation, Paul and Mary

Genesis Womens Shelter (Shelter Ministries of Dallas) ($10,000) see Falk Medical Research Foundation, Dr. Ralph and Marian

Gethsemane Foundation ($10,000) see Aequus Institute

Gib Lewis Charity Classic — cancer research ($3,000) see National Gypsum Co.

Gilbert and Sullivan Society of Houston ($7,850) see Lewis Foundation, Lillian Kaiser

Girl Scouts of America ($12,500) see Brown Foundation, M. K.

Girl Scouts of America ($5,000) see Collins Foundation, James M.

Girl Scouts of America ($2,000) see Cook Foundation, Loring

Girls Club ($41,725) see Perkins Foundation, Joe and Lois

Girlstown USA ($176,639) see Harrington Foundation, Don and Sybil

Gladney Center ($35,500) see Fair Foundation, R. W.

Gladney Center ($10,000) see Lard Trust, Mary Potishman

Glenwood Methodist Church ($50,000) see Fair Foundation, R. W.

Glenwood United Methodist Church ($3,000) see Heath Foundation, Ed and Mary

Good Neighbor Health Care Center ($10,000) see Klein Fund, Nathan J.

Good Samaritan Center ($10,000) see Halff Foundation, G. A. C.

Good Samaritan Foundation ($10,000) see Bowers Foundation

Good Samaritan Foundation ($100,500) see Cain Foundation, Gordon and Mary

Good Samaritan Foundation ($1,050) see Hay Foundation, John I.

Good Samaritan Foundation ($15,000) see Smith Foundation, Bob and Vivian

Good Samaritan Foundation — nursing scholarships ($23,000) see Turner Charitable Foundation

Goodfellow Fund ($750) see Luttrell Trust

Goodfellows ($5,000) see Gordon Foundation, Meyer and Ida

Goodwill Industries ($5,000) see Belo Corp., A.H.

Goodwill Industries ($15,000) see Chilton Foundation Trust

Goodwill Industries ($10,000) see Collins Foundation, James M.

Goodwill Industries ($10,000) see Halff Foundation, G. A. C.

Goodwill Industries ($10,934) see Knox, Sr., and Pearl Wallis Knox Charitable Foundation, Robert W.

Goodwill Industries of Houston ($15,000) see Dunn Research Foundation, John S.

Grace Evangelical Society ($42,000) see Caddock Foundation

Grace Presbyterian Village ($15,000) see Griffin Foundation, Rosa May

Graham Community Campus — computer ($2,683) see Bertha Foundation

Graham General Hospital — long range planning ($25,000) see Bertha Foundation

Graham General Hospital — nursing scholarships ($12,430) see Bertha Foundation

Graham Independent School District — alternative school program ($25,000) see Bertha Foundation

Graham Independent School District — operating ($25,000) see Bertha Foundation

Graham Independent School District — computers/software ($3,622) see Bertha Foundation

Graham Independent School District — masters/mini-grant ($3,550) see Bertha Foundation

Graham Public Library — building fund ($50,000) see Bertha Foundation

Grand 1894 Opera House ($25,000) see Kempner Fund, Harris and Eliza

Grand 1894 Opera House ($20,000) see Kempner Fund, Harris and Eliza

Grandparents Outreach ($15,000) see Zachry Co., H. B.

Grayson County College — lab learning center ($62,265) see Smith and W. Aubrey Smith Charitable Foundation, Clara Blackford

Grayson County College — nursing program ($25,270) see Smith and W. Aubrey Smith Charitable Foundation, Clara Blackford

Grayson County College Nursing Program — expand nursing program ($44,670) see Mayor Foundation, Oliver Dewey

Grayson County Crisis Center — capital expenses ($25,000) see Smith and W. Aubrey Smith Charitable Foundation, Clara Blackford

Grayson County Rehabilitation Center — aquatic program ($15,000) see Mayor Foundation, Oliver Dewey

Grayson County Rehabilitation Center — computer network ($53,500) see Smith and W. Aubrey Smith Charitable Foundation, Clara Blackford

Greater Dallas Community of Churches ($10,000) see Haggerty Foundation

Greater Dallas Community of Churches — to promote ecumenical spirit of cooperation among various Dallas churches and which operates a Christian ministry to city jails ($5,000) see Glaze Foundation, Robert and Ruth

Greater Houston Coalition for Education Excellence ($25,000) see Cain Foundation, Gordon and Mary

Greater Houston Partnership ($5,000) see Weiner Foundation

Greenhill School ($84,700) see Zale Foundation

Gregg Home for the Aged ($10,000) see Griffin Foundation, Rosa May

Growing Up in Arlington ($2,000) see Morris Foundation

Guadalupe-Parkway Neighborhood Center — building addition ($50,000) see Doss Foundation, M. S.

Gulf Coast Regional Blood Center — toward building expansion ($1,000,000) see Houston Endowment

Hamlet ($5,000) see Dishman Charitable Foundation Trust, H. E. and Kate

Happy Hill Farm — scholarships ($2,500) see Edwards Foundation, Jes

Happy Hill Farm ($15,000) see Garvey Texas Foundation

Happy Hill Farm ($5,000) see Tandy Foundation, David L.

Harbourview Care Center — research laboratory ($263,727) see Moody Foundation

Hardin Simmons University ($73,399) see Mayer Foundation, James and Eva

Harrington Cancer Center ($1,766,390) see Harrington Foundation, Don and Sybil

Harrington Discovery Center ($353,278) see Harrington Foundation, Don and Sybil

Harrington Discovery Center ($15,500) see Phillips Foundation, Waite and Genevieve

Harris County Emergency Corps ($19,000) see Vale-Asche Foundation

Harris County Heritage Society ($263,000) see Wortham Foundation

Harris County Psychiatric Center ($5,000) see Vale-Asche Foundation

Harris Hospital H-E-B ($5,000) see Davis Foundation, Ken W.

Harris Hospital-Methodist — assist with establishment of Outpatient Surgery Center ($500,000) see Richardson Foundation, Sid W.

Harris Methodist Health System ($15,000) see Weaver Foundation, Gil and Dody

Hays Consolidated Independent School District ($25,000) see Johnson Foundation, Burdine

Head Start of Greater Dallas ($216,600) see Texas Instruments

Heard Natural Science Museum ($5,000) see Owen Trust, B. B.

Heart of Texas Hospice ($15,000) see Stocker Foundation

Hendrick Medical Center — to establish the Women's Health Center donated property ($166,394) see Dodge Jones Foundation

Heritage Museum of Big Spring ($105,500) see Roberts Foundation, Dora

Hermann Eye Center ($190,000) see Dunn Research Foundation, John S.

Hermann Eye Fund — pediatric ophthalmology professorship ($35,000) see Rockwell Fund

Hermann Eye Fund ($10,000) see West Texas Corp., J. M.

Hermann Hospital ($30,000) see Ellwood Foundation

Hidalgo County Historical Museum ($2,100) see Cook Foundation, Loring

High Frontier Ranch — building construction ($84,507) see Doss Foundation, M. S.

High Plains Baptist Hospital ($85,000) see Mayer Foundation, James and Eva

High Sky Children's Ranch ($10,000) see Beal Foundation

High Sky Children's Ranch ($65,000) see Fasken Foundation

High Sky Girls Ranch ($3,500) see Thagard Foundation

Highland Congregation — Harvest Campaign in Mexico ($8,000) see Bell Trust

Highland Congregation — Ukraine TV/Radio Programs ($25,000) see Bell Trust

Highland Park Baptist Church ($25,000) see Griffin Foundation, Rosa May

Highland Park Methodist Church ($10,000) see Bass Foundation, Harry

Highland Park Presbyterian Church ($60,000) see Hawn Foundation

Highland Park Presbyterian Church ($10,500) see Seay Charitable Trust, Sarah M. and Charles E.

Highland Park Presbyterian Church Day School ($17,125) see Seay Charitable Trust, Sarah M. and Charles E.

Highland Park United Methodist Church ($6,000) see Collins Co.

Hill Country Youth Ranch — lighting project ($25,000) see Fish Foundation, Ray C.

Hill Country Youth Ranch — campground headquarters ($40,000) see Turner Charitable Foundation

Hill School of Ft. Worth — building program ($100,000) see Carter Foundation, Amon G.

Hill School of Fort Worth ($10,000) see Waggoner Charitable Trust, Crystelle

Hillcrest Baptist Medical Center ($63,469) see Lux Trust, Dr. Konrad and Clara

Hills School ($5,000) see JMK-A M Micallef Charitable Foundation

HISA ($10,000) see Moores Foundation

Hispanic Association of Colleges and Universities ($130,539) see Sears, Roebuck and Co.

Historic Waco ($100) see Ward Co., Joe L.

HIV/AIDS Housing Center — for operating expenses or for the purchase of a dwelling ($25,000) see Dougherty, Jr. Foundation, James R.

HIV/AIDS Housing Center — for operating expenses of The Passage for one year ($10,000) see Dougherty, Jr. Foundation, James R.

HIV Housing Center ($15,000) see Haas Foundation, Paul and Mary

Hockaday School ($14,000) see Chadwick Foundation

Hockaday School ($10,000) see Clements Foundation

Hockaday School ($100,000) see Luse Foundation, W. P. and Bulah

Hockaday School ($5,000) see Moss Foundation, Harry S.

Holly Hall ($10,250) see Rienzi Foundation

Holly Hall Building Fund ($50,000) see Turner Charitable Foundation

Homeless Intervention ($50,000) see Moores Foundation

Hope Christian Reformed Church ($10,000) see Frankino Charitable Foundation, Samuel J. and Connie

Hope of South Texas ($10,400) see Overlake Foundation

Hospice ($300,000) see Wortham Foundation

Hospice of El Paso ($12,000) see McKee Foundation, Robert E. and Evelyn

Hospice of Lufkin ($3,500) see Pineywoods Foundation

Hospice of Midland ($25,000) see Fasken Foundation

Hospice of the Plains ($5,720) see Mayer Foundation, James and Eva

Hospice of South Texas ($50,000) see O'Connor Foundation, Kathryn

Hospice at the Texas Medical Center — capital campaign ($200,000) see Cullen Foundation

Hospice at Texas Medical Center ($50,000) see Elkins, Jr. Foundation, Margaret and James A.

Hospice at the Texas Medical Center ($25,000) see Strake Foundation

Hospice at The Texas Medical Center — toward construction of a new patient-care facility and chapel ($300,000) see Meadows Foundation

Hospice of Wichita Falls ($2,500) see Bridwell Foundation, J. S.

House of Cornelius ($31,000) see Seymour Foundation, W. L. and Louise E.

Houston Achievement Place ($3,000) see Lewis Foundation, Lillian Kaiser

Houston Arboretum and Botanical Society — operating funds ($5,000) see Johnson Foundation, Burdine

Houston Arboretum and Botanical Society ($10,000) see Murfee Endowment, Kathryn

Houston Area Womens Center — general operating support ($15,000) see Butler Family Foundation, Patrick and Aimee

Houston Area Women's Center ($15,000) see Frees Foundation

Houston Area Women's Center ($15,000) see Frees Foundation

Houston Ballet — activities ($10,000) see First Interstate Bank of Texas, N.A.

Houston Ballet ($500,000) see Wortham Foundation

Houston Ballet Foundation ($15,000) see Duncan Foundation, Lillian H. and C. W.

Houston Ballet Foundation ($10,000) see Hofheinz Foundation, Irene Cafcalas

Houston Ballet Foundation ($25,000) see Humphreys Foundation

Houston Ballet Foundation ($100,000) see Kilroy Foundation, William S. and Lora Jean

Houston Ballet Foundation ($5,000) see Kilroy Foundation, William S. and Lora Jean

Houston Ballet Foundation ($11,400) see Owsley Foundation, Alvin and Lucy

Houston Ballet Foundation ($10,400) see Texas Commerce Bank Houston, N.A.

Houston Ballet Foundation ($10,000) see Turner Charitable Foundation

Houston Baptist University ($50,000) see Dunn Research Foundation, John S.

Houston Baptist University Auxiliary — scholarship fund ($10,000) see Community Hospital Foundation

Houston Church of Christ, Garden Oaks — missions ($222,500) see Frazier Foundation

Houston Church of Christ, Memorial Drive — missions ($100,000) see Frazier Foundation

Houston Citizens Chamber of Commerce ($10,250) see Texas Commerce Bank Houston, N.A.

Houston Committee for Private Sector Initiatives ($30,000) see Texas Commerce Bank Houston, N.A.

Houston Convention Fund ($25,000) see McGovern Fund for the Behavioral Sciences

Houston Council on Alcohol and Drug Abuse see Compaq Computer Corp.

Houston Ear Research Foundation ($100,000) see Dunn Research Foundation, John S.

Houston Ear Research Foundation ($10,000) see Smith Foundation, Julia and Albert

Houston Food Bank ($1,000) see McCullough Foundation, Ralph H. and Ruth J.

Houston-Galveston Area Food Bank — construction and renovation of existing facility ($50,000) see Rockwell Fund

Houston-Galveston Psychoanalytic Institute ($75,000) see West Foundation, Neva and Wesley

Houston Grand Opera ($202,000) see Anderson Foundation, M. D.

Houston Grand Opera ($62,500) see Buck Foundation, Carol Franc

Houston Grand Opera ($60,000) see Enron Corp.

Houston Grand Opera — performances ($10,000) see First Interstate Bank of Texas, N.A.

Houston Grand Opera ($21,000) see Hobby Foundation

Houston Grand Opera ($5,000) see Lewis Foundation, Lillian Kaiser

Houston Grand Opera ($50,000) see Turner Charitable Foundation

Houston Grand Opera ($10,000) see Winston Research Foundation, Harry

Houston Grand Opera ($240,000) see Wortham Foundation

Houston Grand Opera ($200,000) see Wortham Foundation

Houston Grand Opera — underwrite production of Annie Get Your Gun ($25,000) see Stark Foundation, Nelda C. and H. J. Lutcher

Texas (cont.)

Houston Grand Opera Association ($45,000) see Humphreys Foundation

Houston Grand Opera Association ($20,000) see Tobin Foundation

Houston Grand Opera Association ($15,000) see West Texas Corp., J. M.

Houston Grand Opera Association — toward the Wortham move, new works and the endowment ($1,010,278) see Brown Foundation

Houston Grand Opera — underwrite production of My Fair Lady ($25,000) see Stark Foundation, Nelda C. and H. J. Lutcher

Houston Hospice ($600,000) see Herzstein Charitable Foundation, Albert and Ethel

Houston Hospice — general operating ($6,000) see Swalm Foundation

Houston Host Committee Fund — for construction cost inside the Astrodome for GOP national convention ($250,000) see Tenneco

Houston Independent School District ($6,000) see Owsley Foundation, Alvin and Lucy

Houston International Festival see American Telephone & Telegraph Co./Dallas Region

Houston International Fund ($15,000) see Elkins, Jr. Foundation, Margaret and James A.

Houston International Theater School ($5,000) see Lewis Foundation, Lillian Kaiser

Houston Livestock Show and Rodeo — scholarship funds ($18,000) see First Interstate Bank of Texas, N.A.

Houston Livestock Show and Rodeo ($20,000) see Quanex Corp.

Houston Livestock Show and Rodeo ($8,000) see Quanex Corp.

Houston Metropolitan Ministries, Meals on Wheels — elderly ministry ($15,000) see Hankamer Foundation, Curtis and Doris K.

Houston Museum ($6,500) see Wilder Foundation

Houston Museum of Fine Arts ($100,000) see Anderson Foundation, M. D.

Houston Museum of Natural Science — toward the capital campaign ($1,000,000) see Brown Foundation

Houston Museum of Natural Science ($100,000) see Burlington Resources

Houston Museum of Natural Science ($65,000) see Hamman Foundation, George and Mary Josephine

Houston Museum of Natural Science ($10,000) see Murfee Endowment, Kathryn

Houston Museum of Natural Science ($500,000) see Wortham Foundation

Houston Museum of Natural Science — Face of the Future II campaign ($927,500) see Cockrell Foundation

Houston Museum of Natural Science — Phase II: Face of Future Campaign ($50,000) see Cain Foundation, Gordon and Mary

Houston Museum of Natural Science — to assist in construction of The George Observatory ($176,666) see George Foundation

Houston Public Library ($300,500) see Hobby Foundation

Houston Public Library — toward increased automation and enhancement of the collection ($1,000,000) see Houston Endowment

Houston Public Library — enhancement campaign ($2,000) see Kayser Foundation

Houston Read Commission ($250) see West Foundation, Neva and Wesley

Houston School for Deaf Children ($10,000) see Clayton Fund

Houston School for Deaf Children ($100,000) see Dunn Research Foundation, John S.

Houston School for Deaf Children ($10,000) see Vale-Asche Foundation

Houston School for Deaf Children — faculty development/psychologist and research consultants ($40,000) see Rockwell Fund

Houston SPCA ($18,000) see McCrea Foundation

Houston Symphony — activities ($10,800) see First Interstate Bank of Texas, N.A.

Houston Symphony ($5,000) see Rienzi Foundation

Houston Symphony Capital Campaign ($50,000) see Belo Corp., A.H.

Houston Symphony Orchestra ($20,000) see Hamman Foundation, George and Mary Josephine

Houston Symphony Society — toward the permanent endowment fund ($1,000,000) see Brown Foundation

Houston Symphony Society ($100,000) see Shell Oil Co.

Houston Symphony Society ($750,000) see Wortham Foundation

Howard County Junior College ($210,000) see Roberts Foundation, Dora

Howard Payne University — to construct university center ($85,000) see Dodge Jones Foundation

Howard Payne University ($750,000) see Mabee Foundation, J. E. and L. E.

Howard Payne University — student center building ($100,000) see Sumners Foundation, Hatton W.

Hugs of Galveston for Ronald McDonald House ($5,000) see Northen, Mary Moody

Humane Society of Bexar County ($5,000) see Walthall Perpetual Charitable Trust, Marjorie T.

Humane Society of North Texas ($35,500) see Moncrief Foundation, William A. and Elizabeth B.

Humanities Research Center, University of Texas ($30,000) see Mayer Foundation, Louis B.

Hundred Club of Houston ($25,000) see Smith Foundation, Bob and Vivian

Hyde Park Baptist Church ($7,500) see Veritas Foundation

I Have A Dream — Children's Home ($30,000) see Cain Foundation, Gordon and Mary

Immaculate Conception Church ($44,500) see Cameron Foundation, Harry S. and Isabel C.

Independent College Fund ($5,000) see Parsons - W.D. Charities, Vera Davis

Ingram Fire Department ($750) see Wilson Foundation, John and Nevils

Institute for Aerobics Research ($29,250) see King Foundation, Carl B. and Florence E.

Institute of Aerobics Research ($2,000) see Rales and Ruth Rales Foundation, Norman R.

Institute for Geophysics ($75,000) see Vetlesen Foundation, G. Unger

Institute of International Education ($82,893) see Reynolds Foundation, Christopher

Institute of International Education ($3,050) see Taub Foundation

Institute of Nautical Archaeology Foundation ($25,000) see Nason Foundation

Institute for Rehabilitation and Research Foundation ($20,000) see Baker Foundation, R. C.

Institute for Rehabilitation and Research Foundation ($10,000) see Brochsteins Inc.

Institute for Rehabilitation and Research Foundation ($22,000) see Strake Foundation

Institute of Religion ($10,000) see Elkins, Jr. Foundation, Margaret and James A.

Institute of Religion ($10,000) see Murfee Endowment, Kathryn

Institute of Religion ($10,000) see Turner Charitable Foundation

Institute of Texas Cultures ($1,000) see Meyer Foundation, Alice Kleberg Reynolds

Intercultura ($50,000) see Brown and C. A. Lupton Foundation, T. J.

InterCultura ($5,000) see Fifth Avenue Foundation

Intercultura ($25,000) see Maddox Trust, Web

Intercultural Development Research Association-Coca-Cola Valued Youth Program - - to support and replicate a program that enlists at-risk Hispanic middle schoolers to tutor young children ($345,000) see Coca-Cola Co.

Interfaith Ministries ($5,000) see Perkins Foundation, Joe and Lois

Interfaith Ministries ($14,000) see White Foundation, Erle and Emma

Interfaith Ministries ($6,800) see Wilson Foundation, John and Nevils

International Association for Learning Disabilities — scholarship fund ($10,000) see Creel Foundation

International Center — to serve information and assistance to people of all nations; help them be assimilated in the community ($8,000) see Early Foundation

International Oleander Society ($10,000) see Knox, Sr., and Pearl Wallis Knox Charitable Foundation, Robert W.

Inwood Baptist ($25,000) see Herzstein Charitable Foundation, Albert and Ethel

Irving Community Hospital ($10,000) see Falk Medical Research Foundation, Dr. Ralph and Marian

Irving Hospital Foundation ($25,000) see Bosque Foundation

Irving Medical Center see Recognition Equipment

Irving Opera see Recognition Equipment

Irving Symphony see Recognition Equipment

Irving YMCA see Recognition Equipment

ITD Cerebral Palsy of Tarrant County ($2,000) see Morris Foundation

James Dick Foundation for the Performing Arts — building fund ($75,300) see Johnson Foundation, Burdine

James Dick Foundation for the Performing Arts ($2,500) see Piper Foundation, Minnie Stevens

James Dick Foundation for the Performing Arts ($35,000) see Wright Foundation, Lola

Jeanette Smith Crowley Lung Fund ($200) see Luttrell Trust

Jesuit College Preparatory School ($30,000) see Haggar Foundation

Jesuit High School ($130,000) see Hoblitzelle Foundation

Jewel Charity Ball ($5,000) see Fifth Avenue Foundation

Jewel Charity Ball ($10,000) see Waggoner Charitable Trust, Crystelle

Jewel Charity Ball ($25,000) see Walsh Foundation

Jewish Community Center ($10,000) see Hofheinz Foundation, Irene Cafcalas

Jewish Community Center ($7,750) see Weiner Foundation

Jewish Community Center ($161,836) see Wolff Memorial Foundation, Pauline Sterne

Jewish Community Center ($12,000) see Zale Foundation, William and Sylvia

Jewish Family Services ($5,000) see Brochsteins Inc.

Jewish Family Services ($19,115) see Klein Fund, Nathan J.

Jewish Family Services ($70,000) see Wolff Memorial Foundation, Pauline Sterne

Jewish Family Services ($10,000) see Zale Foundation, William and Sylvia

Jewish Federation ($10,000) see Brochsteins Inc.

Jewish Federation ($155,000) see Gordon Foundation, Meyer and Ida

Jewish Federation ($350,100) see Weiner Foundation

Jewish Federation ($16,666) see Wolens Foundation, Kalman and Ida

Jewish Federation ($50,000) see Zale Foundation, William and Sylvia

Jewish Federation ($50,000) see Zale Foundation, William and Sylvia

Jewish Federation ($33,000) see Zale Foundation, William and Sylvia

Jewish Federation of Greater Dallas ($444,000) see Feldman Foundation

Jewish Federation of Greater Dallas ($300,000) see Feldman Foundation

Jewish Federation of Greater Dallas ($90,000) see Feldman Foundation

Jewish Federation of Greater Dallas ($35,000) see Feldman Foundation

Jewish Federation of Greater Dallas — United Jewish Appeal ($300,000) see Feldman Foundation

Jewish Geriatric Center ($350,000) see Wolff Memorial Foundation, Pauline Sterne

John Cooper School ($10,000) see Elkins Foundation, J. A. and Isabel M.

John Cooper School ($20,000) see West Texas Corp., J. M.

John Peter Smith Hospital ($6,666) see Keith Foundation Trust, Ben E.

John Peter Smith Hospital ($10,000) see Moncrief Foundation, William A. and Elizabeth B.

Jordan School — memorial endowment fund ($200,000) see Fondren Foundation

Jordan School — retirement of debt ($106,100) see Fondren Foundation

Jubilee Dallas ($20,000) see Hawn Foundation

Jubilee Dallas ($2,500) see Moss Foundation, Harry S.

Juliette Fower Homes ($17,000) see Florence Foundation

Junior Achievement ($10,000) see Beal Foundation

Junior Achievement see Michigan Mutual Insurance Corp.

Junior Achievement ($3,500) see Munson Foundation, W. B.

Junior Achievement ($4,000) see National Gypsum Co.

Junior Achievement ($100) see Southland Corp.

Junior Achievement ($4,000) see Tandy Foundation, David L.

Junior Achievement-Dallas ($25,000) see Texas Instruments

Junior Achievement of Tarrant County — goodwill ($16,500) see Alcon Laboratories, Inc.

Junior League of Dallas ($12,000) see Chilton Foundation Trust

Junior League of Dallas ($5,000) see Clements Foundation

Junior League of Dallas ($15,000) see Falk Medical Research Foundation, Dr. Ralph and Marian

Junior League of Waco ($200) see Ward Co., Joe L.

Justin Paul Foundation — developmental disabilities and other programs ($80,000) see Cain Foundation, Effie and Wofford

Juvenile Court Volunteers ($15,340) see Mason Charitable Foundation

Juvenile Diabetes Foundation see Compaq Computer Corp.

Juvenile Diabetes Foundation ($40,000) see Luse Foundation, W. P. and Bulah

Karl Folkers Foundation for Biomedical and Clinical Research — research ($25,000) see Wright Foundation, Lola

KCOS TV ($500) see Luttrell Trust

KEDT Public Television ($1,000) see Sams Foundation, Earl C.

KEDT TV ($25,000) see Behmann Brothers Foundation

KEDT TV ($33,000) see King Ranch

Kelsey Seybold Clinic ($20,000) see Crump Fund, Joe and Jessie

Kelsey Seybold Clinic ($45,000) see Smith Foundation, Bob and Vivian

Kelsey Seybold Clinic ($15,000) see Smith Foundation, Bob and Vivian

Kent School — scholarships for needy dyslexic students ($10,000) see Swalm Foundation

KERA ($5,000) see Fifth Avenue Foundation

KERA ($15,000) see Florence Foundation

KERA ($15,000) see Pangburn Foundation

KERA ($60) see Ward Co., Joe L.

KERA Public TV Dallas ($25,000) see Circuit City Stores

Kerens Public Schools ($500) see Hofstetter Trust, Bessie

Kidsville ($35,000) see Mayer Foundation, James and Eva

Kilgore College ($8,000) see Griffin Foundation, Rosa May

Kilgore Independent School District ($13,346) see Griffin Foundation, Rosa May

Kimble Hospital ($5,000) see McNutt Charitable Trust, Amy Shelton

Kings Manor Methodist Home — operating expenses ($10,000) see Craig Foundation, J. Paul

Kinkaid School — scholarship fund ($10,000) see Creel Foundation

Kinkaid School ($10,000) see Elkins Foundation, J. A. and Isabel M.

Kinkaid School — operating activity ($2,500) see Foothills Foundation

Kinkaid School ($20,000) see Hofheinz Foundation, Irene Cafcalas

Kinkaid School — endowment fund ($15,000) see Johnson Foundation, Burdine

Kinkaid School — computer purchase ($50,000) see Kilroy Foundation, William S. and Lora Jean

Kinkaid School — computer purchase ($25,000) see Kilroy Foundation, William S. and Lora Jean

Kinkaid School ($12,500) see West Texas Corp., J. M.

Kinkaid School ($2,000) see Wilder Foundation

Kleberg County Sheriff's Department — drug abuse education and prevention in schools ($40,000) see Kleberg, Jr. and Helen C. Kleberg Foundation, Robert J.

KLRN — Alamo Public Telecommunications Council ($5,000) see Meyer Foundation, Alice Kleberg Reynolds

KLRN TV 9 ($2,500) see Piper Foundation, Minnie Stevens

Komen Foundation ($25,000) see Kimberly-Clark Corp.

KPAC FM- Public Radio ($2,500) see Ferguson Family Foundation, Kittie and Rugeley

KUHF - 88.7FM see Apache Corp.

Kuht Association for Community Television ($25,000) see Mason Charitable Foundation

KUHT-TV Public Television see Compaq Computer Corp.

La Casas ($10,000) see Koehler Foundation, Marcia and Otto

La Mujer Obrera Program ($2,000) see Vaughan Foundation, Rachael and Ben

LaCasas Foundation ($5,000) see McNutt Charitable Trust, Amy Shelton

Lake Country Playhouse ($52,500) see Meredith Foundation

Lakehill Preparatory School ($100,000) see Hoblitzelle Foundation

Lamar University ($6,000) see Humphreys Foundation

Lamplighter School ($100,000) see Cook Foundation

Laredo Junior College Nursing Program ($28,870) see Hachar Charitable Trust, D. D.

Laredo Philharmonic Orchestra ($3,300) see Hachar Charitable Trust, D. D.

Laredo Public Library ($28,808) see Hachar Charitable Trust, D. D.

Law Focused Education — teachers training seminars ($75,000) see Sumners Foundation, Hatton W.

Law School Foundation ($6,000) see Kayser Foundation

LBJ Foundation ($30,000) see King Foundation, Carl B. and Florence E.

LBJ Library ($5,000) see LBJ Family Foundation

LBJ School of Public Affairs ($15,000) see Hobby Foundation

LBJ School of Public Affairs ($6,000) see LBJ Family Foundation

League of Women Voters of Texas — general operating costs ($2,500) see National Gypsum Co.

Lena Pope Home ($11,000) see Weaver Foundation, Gil and Dody

Leo Beck Education Center Foundation ($2,500) see Garfinkle Family Foundation

Letot Center ($49,000) see Owen Trust, B. B.

Letot Center Capital Camp ($5,000) see Perkins-Prothro Foundation

Letot Center Capital Foundation — first of two annual payments ($25,000) see Green Foundation

LeTourneau College ($4,420) see Gibson Foundation, E. L.

Liberation Community ($5,000) see Davis Foundation, Ken W.

Life Flight ($2,500) see Rienzi Foundation

Lift ($15,500) see Zale Foundation

Lighthouse for the Blind — living skills ($30,000) see Seymour Foundation, W. L. and Louise E.

Littlest Wiseman ($130,000) see Fleming Foundation

Lon Morris College ($36,500) see Fair Foundation, R. W.

Lon Morris College ($6,000) see Humphreys Foundation

Lon Morris College ($10,000) see Murfee Endowment, Kathryn

Lon Morris College ($48,300) see Scurlock Foundation

Lone Star Ballet ($10,000) see Anderson Charitable Trust, Josephine

Lone Star Ballet ($10,000) see Anderson Charitable Trust, Josephine

Lone Star Ballet ($10,000) see Anderson Charitable Trust, Josephine

Lone Star Historical Drama Association — production and operating expenses ($600,000) see Moody Foundation

Loring Cook Foundation Scholarship Fund ($9,000) see Cook Foundation, Loring

Los Nino's International Adoption Center ($10,000) see Wardle Family Foundation

Love/Joy Ministries ($13,612) see Frees Foundation

Lovers Lane Methodist ($10,400) see Gill Foundation, Pauline Allen

Lubbock General Hospital — William Gordon lectures ($25,000) see South Plains Foundation

Lubbock International Cultural Center ($25,000) see Jones Foundation, Helen

Lubbock Methodist Hospital ($50,000) see Roberts Foundation, Dora

Lubbock Regional Mental Health Mental Retardation Adolescent Drug and Alcohol ($10,000) see Franklin Charitable Trust, Ershel

Lubbock Shared Homes ($15,000) see Jones Foundation, Helen

Luchoo Ministries ($20,000) see Boeckmann Charitable Foundation

Lutheran High School ($85,000) see Hoblitzelle Foundation

Lutheran High School Association ($121,000) see Woltman Foundation, B. M.

Lutheran Outdoor Ministry ($5,400) see Woltman Foundation, B. M.

M. D. Anderson Cancer Center — International Bone Marrow Transplantation Center ($123,333) see Cockrell Foundation

M.D. Anderson Cancer Center — cancer research ($50,000) see Hankamer Foundation, Curtis and Doris K.

M.D. Anderson Cancer Center ($35,000) see Hobby Foundation

M.D. Anderson Cancer Center ($58,000) see Smith and W. Aubrey Smith Charitable Foundation, Clara Blackford

M.D. Anderson Cancer Center ($12,500) see Zaban Foundation

M.D. Anderson Cancer Research Center ($25,000) see McMillan, Jr. Foundation, Bruce

M.D. Anderson Hospital ($20,000) see Biddle Foundation, Margaret T.

M.D. Anderson Hospital ($5,000) see Brochsteins Inc.

M.D. Anderson Hospital ($30,000) see Ellwood Foundation

M.D. Anderson Hospital ($12,700) see Scurlock Foundation

M.D. Anderson Hospital Park ($5,000) see Rienzi Foundation

M.D. Anderson Hospital and Tumor Center ($10,000) see Phillips Foundation, Waite and Genevieve

Main Street Theater ($5,000) see Murfee Endowment, Kathryn

Make-A-Wish Foundation ($20,000) see Overlake Foundation

Manned Space Flight Education Foundation ($100,000) see Enron Corp.

Manned Space Flight Foundation ($15,000) see Hofheinz Foundation, Irene Cafcalas

Marble Falls Fire Department ($1,000) see Gould Inc.

March of Dimes ($35,000) see Crump Fund, Joe and Jessie

March of Dimes ($15,000) see Keith Foundation Trust, Ben E.

Marine Military Academy ($25,000) see Fish Foundation, Vain and Harry

Market Square Park Project ($2,500) see Belo Corp., A.H.

Mars Hill Productions ($20,000) see Bowers Foundation

Mars Hill Productions ($30,000) see Ware Foundation

Martin Luther King, Jr. Community Center ($8,550) see Orleans Trust, Carrie S.

Marywood/Marywood Maternity and Adoption Service — for the "Teens at Risk: Getting Essentials Together" program ($10,000) see Dougherty, Jr. Foundation, James R.

Masonic Home and School ($1,000) see Waggoner Foundation, E. Paul and Helen Buck

Mayfest ($13,000) see Keith Foundation Trust, Ben E.

McAllen International Museum ($3,100) see Cook Foundation, Loring

McFaddin Ward House ($749,517) see Ward Heritage Foundation, Mamie McFaddin

McGovern Fund for the Behavioral Sciences — contribution ($2,430,000) see McGovern Foundation, John P.

McLennan Community College Foundation ($25,255) see Kimberly-Clark Corp.

McMurry University ($76,500) see Maddox Foundation, J. F.

McNay Art Museum — auditorium project ($200,000) see Semmes Foundation

McNay Art Museum ($6,608) see Semmes Foundation

McNay Art Museum ($50,000) see Tobin Foundation

Meals on Wheels — operating expenses ($10,000) see Craig Foundation, J. Paul

Meals on Wheels ($750) see Luttrell Trust

Meals on Wheels ($30,000) see South Texas Charitable Foundation

Meals on Wheels ($5,000) see Tandy Foundation, David L.

Meals on Wheels ($10,000) see Waggoner Charitable Trust, Crystelle

Meals on Wheels ($15,000) see Weaver Foundation, Gil and Dody

Medical Benevolence Foundation ($15,000) see Lacy Foundation

Memorial Care Systems ($30,000) see Ellwood Foundation

Memorial Hall High School ($29,500) see Cameron Foundation, Harry S. and Isabel C.

Memorial Medical Center of East Texas — Magnetic Resonance Image facility ($1,410,149) see Temple Foundation, T. L. L.

Memorial Medical Center of East Texas — Stewart Blood Center; Lufkin Branch ($476,120) see Temple Foundation, T. L. L.

Menil Collection ($10,000) see Lowe Foundation

Menil Collection ($50,000) see Weisman Art Foundation, Frederick R.

Menil Collection — toward the $35 million endowment ($1,000,000) see Brown Foundation

Menil Foundation ($100,000) see Scaler Foundation

Menlo College ($5,000) see Vaughn, Jr. Foundation Fund, James M.

Mental Health Association ($5,000) see Bass Foundation, Harry

Mental Health Association of Houston and Harris County — for publishing a manual to assist the clergy in understanding mental health issues and community resources ($16,500) see Swalm Foundation

Methodist Bread Basket ($20,000) see Redman Foundation

Methodist Home — dorm renovations ($51,500) see Doss Foundation, M. S.

Methodist Home ($4,000) see Meredith Foundation

Methodist Hospital — medical equipment ($75,000) see Doss Foundation, M. S.

Methodist Hospital ($30,000) see Ellwood Foundation

Methodist Hospital ($250,000) see Forest Lawn Foundation

Methodist Hospital ($25,000) see Hobby Foundation

Methodist Hospital Foundation ($1,250,000) see Dunn Research Foundation, John S.

Methodist Hospital Foundation ($25,000) see Ferguson Family Foundation, Kittie and Rugeley

Methodist Hospital Foundation — pavillion renovation ($420,000) see Fondren Foundation

Methodist Hospital Foundation ($5,000) see Murfee Endowment, Kathryn

Methodist Medical Center — final payment on 1991 commitment for special care nursery ($100,000) see Hillcrest Foundation

Methodist Mission Home of San Antonio ($5,000) see Perkins-Prothro Foundation

Methodist Retirement Services — construction of retirement facility ($1,693,000) see Temple Foundation, T. L. L.

MHMR Services of Texoma ($2,500) see Munson Foundation, W. B.

Midland Cerebral Palsy ($75,000) see Fasken Foundation

Texas (cont.)

Midland Cerebral Palsy Center ($100,000) see Crump Fund, Joe and Jessie

Midland Cerebral Palsy Treatment — general operations ($40,000) see Davidson Family Charitable Foundation

Midland College ($443,934) see Abell-Hanger Foundation

Midland Junior College ($50,000) see Beal Foundation

Midland Memorial Foundation ($50,000) see Forest Oil Corp.

Midland-Odessa Symphony and Chorale ($5,000) see Potts and Sibley Foundation

Midland Presbyterian Homes — construction of an Alzheimers Unit at the Manor Park Facility ($320,000) see Abell-Hanger Foundation

Midland Soup Kitchen ($14,000) see Beal Foundation

Midwestern State University ($600,000) see Bridwell Foundation, J. S.

Midwestern State University ($100,000) see Bridwell Foundation, J. S.

Midwestern State University ($7,720) see Perkins Foundation, Joe and Lois

Midwestern State University ($100,000) see Perkins-Prothro Foundation

Midwestern State University ($6,250) see Priddy Foundation

Midwestern State University ($15,000) see Waggoner Foundation, E. Paul and Helen Buck

Midwestern State University ($50,000) see West Foundation

Midwestern State University ($20,000) see West Foundation

Midwestern State University ($25,000) see White Foundation, Erle and Emma

Mildred Independent School District ($1,000) see Hofstetter Trust, Bessie

Miller Outdoor Theater ($10,000) see Knox, Sr., and Pearl Wallis Knox Charitable Foundation, Robert W.

Mineola Civic Center ($113,600) see Meredith Foundation

Mineola ISA ($105,500) see Meredith Foundation

Mineola Library ($81,097) see Meredith Foundation

Mineola Youth Foundation ($40,390) see Meredith Foundation

Minnie Hexter Milk Fund ($4,750) see Orleans Trust, Carrie S.

Miracle Farm ($1,000) see McCullough Foundation, Ralph H. and Ruth J.

Missionary Society of Oblate Fathers of Texas — first installment on grant to provide endowment funds ($100,000) see O'Shaughnessy Foundation, I. A.

Modern Art Museum of Fort Worth ($25,000) see Maddox Trust, Web

Monastery of St. Clare ($10,000) see O'Connor Foundation, Kathryn

Moody Gardens — equipment ($2,455,240) see Moody Foundation

Moody Gardens — expansion of greenhouse ($365,000) see Moody Foundation

Moody Scholars Program — scholarship ($300,000) see Moody Foundation

Morrison Family Foundation ($50,000) see Semmes Foundation

Mothers Against Drunk Driving — for MADD Student Library ($5,000) see Subaru of America Inc.

Mount Calvary Luthern Church — building fund ($10,000) see White Trust, G. R.

Multiple Sclerosis — Dallas Chapter ($25,000) see Hawn Foundation

Muscular Dystrophy Association ($100) see Ormet Corp.

Museum Association ($10,000) see Ferguson Family Foundation, Kittie and Rugeley

Museum of Fine Arts ($5,000) see Brochsteins Inc.

Museum of Fine Arts ($11,000) see Duncan Foundation, Lillian H. and C. W.

Museum of Fine Arts ($10,000) see Duncan Foundation, Lillian H. and C. W.

Museum of Fine Arts ($41,000) see Glanville Family Foundation

Museum of Fine Arts ($260,000) see Hobby Foundation

Museum of Fine Arts ($5,000) see Hofheinz Foundation, Irene Cafcalas

Museum of Fine Arts ($2,500) see Kayser Foundation

Museum of Fine Arts ($33,000) see Kilroy Foundation, William S. and Lora Jean

Museum of Fine Arts ($9,200) see Kilroy Foundation, William S. and Lora Jean

Museum of Fine Arts ($5,000) see Murfee Endowment, Kathryn

Museum of Fine Arts ($10,450) see Scurlock Foundation

Museum of Fine Arts ($50,000) see Smith Foundation, Bob and Vivian

Museum of Fine Arts ($2,300) see Taub Foundation

Museum of Fine Arts ($10,000) see Vaughn, Jr. Foundation Fund, James M.

Museum of Fine Arts ($6,500) see Vaughn, Jr. Foundation Fund, James M.

Museum of Fine Arts — Gala Ball ($5,000) see Menil Foundation

Museum of Fine Arts, Houston — continuation of the matching grant for the endowment ($1,615,000) see Brown Foundation

Museum of Fine Arts, Houston — general operating funds ($19,000) see Fish Foundation, Ray C.

Museum of Fine Arts of Houston — Bayou Bend capital campaign ($120,000) see Farish Fund, William Stamps

Museum of Science and History ($25,000) see Maddox Trust, Web

Museum of Science and History ($20,000) see Scott Foundation, William E.

Museum of Southwest ($20,000) see West Texas Corp., J. M.

Museums of Abilene — to support the costs of permanent exhibits ($100,000) see Dodge Jones Foundation

Music Festival at Roundtop — for general funding, advancement of listening

pleasure of violin ($15,000) see Starling Foundation, Dorothy Richard

National Center for Employment of Disabled ($25,150) see Seymour Foundation, W. L. and Louise E.

National Center for Policy Analysis — pro-free enterprise ($15,000) see JELD-WEN, Inc.

National Center for Political Analysis ($10,000) see Armstrong Foundation

National Center for Political Analysis ($1,500) see Meyer Foundation, Alice Kleberg Reynolds

National Children's Eye Care Foundation ($1,000) see Alexander Foundation, Robert D. and Catherine R.

National Conference of Christians and Jews ($465) see Gordon Foundation, Meyer and Ida

National Conference of Christians and Jews ($2,500) see Weiner Foundation

National Endowment for the Humanities — Institute of Nautical Archaeology ($25,000) see JFM Foundation

National Endowment for Liberty ($40,000) see Durell Foundation, George Edward

National Museum of Communications ($20,000) see Chilton Foundation Trust

National Vitiligo Foundation — operating expenses ($5,000) see Swalm Foundation

National Wildflower Research Center — capital campaign to construct new facilities ($35,000) see Kleberg, Jr. and Helen C. Kleberg Foundation, Robert J.

National Wildflower Research Center — for new building and endowment ($100,000) see McDermott Foundation, Eugene

National Wildflower Research Center ($25,000) see Perkins-Prothro Foundation

National Wildflower Research Center ($6,000) see Veritas Foundation

Native Plant Society of Texas ($6,500) see McNutt Charitable Trust, Amy Shelton

Nature Conservancy ($52,000) see Weeden Foundation, Frank

Nature Conservancy of Texas — conservation ($25,000) see Fish Foundation, Ray C.

Navarro College ($98,000) see Caston Foundation, M. C. and Mattie

Navarro College ($1,000) see Hofstetter Trust, Bessie

Navarro County United Fund ($24,000) see Hofstetter Trust, Bessie

Nazareth Academy ($25,000) see O'Connor Foundation, Kathryn

Neighborhood Center ($15,000) see Herzstein Charitable Foundation, Albert and Ethel

Neighborhood Centers — acquisition; human services facility ($500,000) see Cullen Foundation

Neighbors United for Quality Education — establish pilot program for teacher training and early childhood education ($244,850) see Perot Foundation

Neuhaus Education Center ($13,000) see Scurlock Foundation

New Age Hospice of Houston ($15,000) see Luchsinger Family Foundation

New Black Ministry Lutheran Church ($3,000) see Woltman Foundation, B. M.

New Covenant Church ($140,000) see Rachal Foundation, Ed

New Foundation ($72,000) see Texas Commerce Bank Houston, N.A.

New Horizons Ranch ($12,000) see C.I.O.S.

NFL Alumni ($5,000) see Davis Foundation, Ken W.

Nolan Ryan Historical Foundation ($25,000) see Hofheinz Foundation, Irene Cafcalas

North Amarillo Church of Christ ($8,000) see Anderson Charitable Trust, Josephine

North Central Texas Medical Foundation ($6,800) see Wilson Foundation, John and Nevils

North Street Congregation — Yellow House Campus Ministry ($3,600) see Bell Trust

North Texas Leukemia Society see Recognition Equipment

North Texas Public Broadcasting ($140,000) see King Foundation, Carl B. and Florence E.

North Texas Public Broadcasting ($10,000) see Mary Kay Foundation

North Texas Public Broadcasting ($10,000) see Owen Trust, B. B.

North Texas Public Broadcasting ($15,000) see Pangburn Foundation

North Texas Public Broadcasting ($5,000) see Tandy Foundation, David L.

North Texas Rehabilitation Center ($25,000) see Perkins-Prothro Foundation

North Texas Rehabilitation Center ($25,000) see White Foundation, Erle and Emma

Northwood Institute — sports and fitness center construction ($75,000) see Cain Foundation, Effie and Wofford

Northwood Institute ($200,000) see O'Donnell Foundation

Notre Dame of Dallas Schools — for development fund ($25,000) see Green Foundation

Notre Dame of Dallas Schools ($10,000) see Haggerty Foundation

Notre Dame of Dallas Schools ($5,000) see Tyler Corp.

Oak Cliff Development Corporation ($5,000) see Moss Foundation, Harry S.

Oakridge School ($7,000) see Keith Foundation Trust, Ben E.

Open Arms ($1,300) see JMK-A M Micallef Charitable Foundation

Open Door Mission — facilities, new construction ($30,000) see McCullough Foundation, Ralph H. and Ruth J.

Operation Exodus ($200,000) see Zale Foundation

Operation Life ($5,000) see Owsley Foundation, Alvin and Lucy

Opportunities Foundation of Texas ($965,000) see McGovern Fund for the Behavioral Sciences

Opportunity Plan ($10,000) see Anderson Charitable Trust, Josephine

Orange County United Fund ($2,000) see Brand Cos.

Our Friend's Place ($5,000) see Falk Medical Research Foundation, Dr. Ralph and Marian

Our Lady of Victory Cathedral ($25,000) see Overlake Foundation

Our Lady of Victory Cathedral ($240,000) see South Texas Charitable Foundation

Our Lady of Victory Cathedral TV Fund ($40,000) see South Texas Charitable Foundation

Our Lady of Victory Parish Education Endowment Fund ($25,000) see South Texas Charitable Foundation

Our Lady of Victory School ($25,000) see O'Connor Foundation, Kathryn

P.O.I.N.T ($11,300) see Mary Kay Foundation

Palmer Drug Abuse Program ($8,500) see Behmann Brothers Foundation

Palmer Drug Abuse Program ($25,000) see Fasken Foundation

Palmer Drug Abuse Program ($25,000) see King Ranch

Palmer Drug Abuse Program ($6,000) see Koehler Foundation, Marcia and Otto

Palmer Drug Abuse Program ($28,000) see Overlake Foundation

Palmer Drug Abuse Program ($1,000) see Sams Foundation, Earl C.

Palmer Drug Abuse Program — providing rehabilitation programs to substance abusers ($4,900) see Swalm Foundation

Palmer Drug Abuse Program — operating capital in Milford ($8,000) see Bauervic-Paisley Foundation

Palmer Memorial Church ($1,500) see Vaughn, Jr. Foundation Fund, James M.

Pan American University Foundation ($2,000) see Cook Foundation, Loring

PanAmerican Presbyterian School — school to educate Mexican- American students in high school ($5,000) see Early Foundation

Panhandle Plains Historical Society ($88,319) see Harrington Foundation, Don and Sybil

Paramount Theatre — restoration ($26,000) see Wright Foundation, Lola

Pardee Cancer Treatment Association of Greater Brazosport — for a program supporting the cure and control of cancer ($200,000) see Pardee Foundation, Elsa U.

Parent Services Center ($500) see Rogers Foundation

Paris Educational Foundation ($30,000) see Fasken Foundation

Parish School ($28,000) see Hamman Foundation, George and Mary Josephine

Parish School ($50,500) see Herzstein Charitable Foundation, Albert and Ethel

Park Cities Baptist Church — promoting Christian Gospel ($61,000) see Glaze Foundation, Robert and Ruth

Park People ($2,000) see Mason Charitable Foundation

Park People ($1,250) see Taub Foundation

Parker County Crime Commission ($1,000) see JMK-A M Micallef Charitable Foundation

Parkland Foundation ($10,000) see Stemmons Foundation

Parkland Foundation ($10,000) see Zale Foundation, William and Sylvia

Passage House ($63,582) see Sams Foundation, Earl C.

Pastoral Counseling Center ($5,000) see Perkins-Prothro Foundation

Pastoral Counseling Center ($6,800) see Wilson Foundation, John and Nevils

PATH ($91,500) see Buffett Foundation

PATH ($1,500) see Rogers Foundation

Path ($10,000) see Vaughn Foundation

Patrons and Friends of Moody Mansion and Museum ($4,000) see Northen, Mary Moody

Patrons of McNay ($5,000) see Ferguson Family Foundation, Kittie and Rugeley

Paul Quinn College — building fund ($150,000) see Carter Foundation, Amon G.

Paul Quinn College — scholarship ($2,800) see Mayborn Foundation, Frank W.

Peaceable Kingdom Retreat for Children — nature trail ($200,000) see Mayborn Foundation, Frank W.

Perkins School of Theology ($50,000) see Clements Foundation

Perkins School of Theology — to help fund a chair endowment in Old Testament Studies ($125,000) see Davis Foundations, Arthur Vining

Permian Basin CAPP ($5,000) see Lowe Foundation

Permian Basin Food Bank ($110,526) see Abell-Hanger Foundation

Permian Basin Petroleum Museum ($25,000) see Davidson Family Charitable Foundation

Permian Basin Petroleum Museum ($5,000) see Potts and Sibley Foundation

Permian Basin Petroleum Museum Hall of Fame ($5,000) see Dunagan Foundation

Permian Basin Petroleum Museum, Library and Hall of Fame ($252,025) see Abell-Hanger Foundation

Permian Honor Scholarship Foundation ($104,750) see Dunagan Foundation

Pinecrest Retirement ($20,000) see Pineywoods Foundation

Piper Professors Program ($25,000) see Piper Foundation, Minnie Stevens

Piper Scholars Program ($182,500) see Piper Foundation, Minnie Stevens

Plainview Education Partnership ($10,000) see Mayer Foundation, James and Eva

Planned Parenthood Center of Houston — new center ($110,000) see Farish Fund, William Stamps

Planned Parenthood Federation of America ($77,745) see Buffett Foundation

Planned Parenthood Federation of America ($2,400) see Dunagan Foundation

Planned Parenthood Federation of America ($23,070) see Frees Foundation

Planned Parenthood Federation of America ($10,000) see Halff Foundation, G. A. C.

Planned Parenthood Federation of America — national assistance family planning ($15,000) see Hamman Foundation, George and Mary Josephine

Planned Parenthood Federation of America — national assistance family planning ($47,500) see Johnson Foundation, Burdine

Planned Parenthood Federation of America — national assistance family planning ($15,000) see Johnson Foundation, Burdine

Planned Parenthood Federation of America ($11,500) see King Ranch

Planned Parenthood Federation of America ($11,000) see Owsley Foundation, Alvin and Lucy

Planned Parenthood Federation of America ($11,000) see Waggoner Charitable Trust, Crystelle

Playgrounds Unlimited ($1,000) see Alexander Foundation, Robert D. and Catherine R.

Polk Street Methodist Church — operating expenses ($23,750) see Craig Foundation, J. Paul

Pollard Memorial Methodist ($36,000) see Fair Foundation, R. W.

Polly Ryon Memorial Hospital — land for hospital parking lot ($91,671) see George Foundation

Port Lavaca Volunteer Fire Department — to purchase a rescue boat and equipment ($55,000) see Johnson Foundation, M. G. and Lillie A.

Post Oak School ($16,666) see Abercrombie Foundation

Prairie View A&M University — excellence award ($50,000) see Lockheed Corp.

Presbyterian Children's Home ($15,000) see Bryce Memorial Fund, William and Catherine

Presbyterian Children's Home — operating expenses ($5,000) see Craig Foundation, J. Paul

Presbyterian Children's Home ($5,000) see Meyer Foundation, Alice Kleberg Reynolds

Presbyterian Children's Home and Service Agency — operating fund ($47,167) see Cauthorn Charitable Trust, John and Mildred

Presbyterian Children's Services of Synod of Sun ($25,000) see Hofstetter Trust, Bessie

Presbyterian Healthcare Foundation ($50,000) see Green Foundation

Presbyterian Healthcare Foundation ($50,000) see Hawn Foundation

Presbyterian Home for Children — funds to remodel Union Cottage ($130,000) see Harrington Foundation, Don and Sybil

Presbyterian Manor ($11,800) see Wilson Foundation, John and Nevils

Presbyterian Night Shelter ($5,000) see Tandy Foundation, David L.

Presbyterian Night Shelter ($8,000) see Weaver Foundation, Gil and Dody

Presbyterian Pan American School — support of programs ($5,000) see Trull Foundation

Preston Hollow Presbyterian Church — a church dedicated to mission of Jesus in the world ($7,575) see Early Foundation

Priests of Holy Cross ($10,000) see Merrion Foundation

Private Sector Initiatives — balance of existing pledge ($15,000) see First Interstate Bank of Texas, N.A.

Project Any Baby Can ($25,000) see Klein Fund, Nathan J.

Project Homes ($55,955) see Puett Foundation, Nelson

Project Homes ($52,250) see Puett Foundation, Nelson

Project Homes ($42,750) see Puett Foundation, Nelson

Project Homes ($35,150) see Puett Foundation, Nelson

Project Homes ($21,780) see Puett Foundation, Nelson

Prostate Cancer Research ($2,500) see Fuller Foundation

Providence Hospital ($63,469) see Lux Trust, Dr. Konrad and Clara

Proyecto Adelanti ($10,000) see Sexton Foundation

Public Communication Foundation for North Texas ($9,300) see Garvey Texas Foundation

Public Radio ($5,000) see Tobin Foundation

Quality of Life, Adopt A School ($9,000) see Mary Kay Foundation

R. D. Alexander Scholarship Fund Junior Achievement — goodwill ($10,000) see Alcon Laboratories, Inc.

Railroad and Pioneer Museum — general fund ($250) see Mayborn Foundation, Frank W.

Ralph Wilson Youth Club ($150,000) see Wilson Public Trust, Ralph

Ramparts ($5,000) see Walthall Perpetual Charitable Trust, Marjorie T.

Red River Railroad Museum ($5,000) see Munson Foundation, W. B.

Red River Valley Museum ($8,745) see Waggoner Foundation, E. Paul and Helen Buck

Refugio Del Rio Grande ($3,400) see Vaughan Foundation, Rachael and Ben

Regional East Texas Food Bank ($10,000) see Vaughn Foundation

Restart ($2,000) see Moss Foundation, Harry S.

Restart Corporation ($2,000) see Tyler Corp.

Retina Foundation of SW ($5,000) see Wolens Foundation, Kalman and Ida

Retina Research Foundation ($5,000) see Elkins Foundation, J. A. and Isabel M.

Retina Research Foundation — award of merit in retina research ($70,000) see Kayser Foundation

Retina Research Foundation ($80,000) see Murfee Endowment, Kathryn

Retina Research Foundation — retina research ($5,000) see Stark Foundation, Nelda C. and H. J. Lutcher

Rice University ($200,000) see Abercrombie Foundation

Rice University ($225,000) see Anderson Foundation, M. D.

Rice University ($50,000) see Bowers Foundation

Rice University ($53,333) see Glanville Family Foundation

Rice University ($10,000) see Lewis Foundation, Lillian Kaiser

Rice University ($150,000) see Shell Oil Co.

Rice University ($25,000) see Starling Foundation, Dorothy Richard

Rice University ($1,000) see Vaughn, Jr. Foundation Fund, James M.

Rice University — biomedical-biosciences building ($50,000) see Cain Foundation, Gordon and Mary

Rice University — grant for renovation of Engineering ($50,000) see Halliburton Co.

Rice University — Institute for Arts ($114,239) see Menil Foundation

Rice University — model science lab; faculty support; lecture series ($35,000) see Rockwell Fund

Rice University — McAgy fund ($10,000) see Menil Foundation

Rice University School of Architecture ($10,000) see Brochsteins Inc.

Richardson Medical Center ($100) see Southland Corp.

Ridgelea Christian Church ($10,000) see Moncrief Foundation, William A. and Elizabeth B.

Rio Grande Bible Institute ($5,000) see Morris Charitable Foundation, E. A.

Rio Grande Food Bank ($9,245) see Cimarron Foundation

Rio Grande Food Bank ($10,000) see Hervey Foundation

Rio Grande Radiation Treatment and Cancer Research Foundation ($3,100) see Cook Foundation, Loring

Ripley House ($30,000) see Frees Foundation

River Blindness Foundation ($2,112,500) see Moores Foundation

River Blindness Foundation ($16,010) see Moores Foundation

Roberts County, Texas Museum ($5,000) see Brown Foundation, M. K.

Rochelle Baptist Church — building fund ($10,000) see White Trust, G. R.

Rochelle Volunteer Fire Department — truck purchase ($17,281) see White Trust, G. R.

Ronald McDonald House see Apache Corp.

Rosalind Kress Haley Library ($2,500) see Henry Foundation, Patrick

Rosenberg Library ($30,000) see Kempner Fund, Harris and Eliza

Rosenberg Library ($10,000) see Knox, Sr., and Pearl Wallis

Knox Charitable Foundation, Robert W.

Rotary Club of Graham — scholarship ($3,000) see Bertha Foundation

Rotary Club of Houston Foundation — toward a housing facility for patients ($2,000,000) see Houston Endowment

Rotary Club of Houston Foundation ($5,000) see Knox, Sr., and Pearl Wallis Knox Charitable Foundation, Robert W.

Rotary Polio-Plus ($5,000) see Dunagan Foundation

Rural South Texas Development Corporation ($50,000) see Rachal Foundation, Ed

Sacred Heart Catholic Church ($37,000) see Rachal Foundation, Ed

St. Agnes Academy — academic scholarships ($70,000) see Rockwell Fund

St. Andrews Day School ($35,000) see Phillips Foundation, Waite and Genevieve

St. Andrew's Episcopal Church ($10,000) see Anderson Charitable Trust, Josephine

St. Andrew's Episcopal Church ($7,500) see Anderson Charitable Trust, Josephine

St. Andrews Episcopal School ($50,000) see Meyer Foundation, Alice Kleberg Reynolds

St. Anne's Church ($53,000) see Cameron Foundation, Harry S. and Isabel C.

St. Anthony School ($11,687) see Haggerty Foundation

St. Anthony's School ($10,000) see Sexton Foundation

St. Augustine School ($27,700) see Saint Gerard Foundation

St. Clements School ($25,000) see Cimarron Foundation

St. Dennis Church ($45,870) see O'Connor Foundation, Kathryn

St. Edward's University — to help fund the campaign to improve catalog access and circulation in the library ($10,000) see Dougherty, Jr. Foundation, James R.

St. Edward's University ($4,000) see Hugg Trust, Leoia W. and Charles H.

St. Edward's University — library automation project ($25,000) see Wright Foundation, Lola

St. Edward's University — support for Center for Teaching Excellence ($100,000) see RGK Foundation

St. Elizabeth Hospital ($15,000) see Steinhagen Benevolent Trust, B. A. and Elinor

St. Francis Charities ($14,000) see Cameron Foundation, Harry S. and Isabel C.

St. Francis Nursing Home ($6,000) see Koehler Foundation, Marcia and Otto

St. Francis Nursing Home ($5,000) see McNutt Charitable Trust, Amy Shelton

St. James School — non-restricted ($40,000) see Birch Foundation, Stephen and Mary

St. John the Divine Episcopal Church ($25,000) see Hamman Foundation, George and Mary Josephine

Texas (cont.)

St. John's Episcopal Church ($10,000) see Weaver Foundation, Gil and Dody

St. John's School ($25,000) see Hobby Foundation

St. Joseph Foundation ($15,000) see Turner Charitable Foundation

St. Joseph High School ($50,000) see O'Connor Foundation, Kathryn

St. Joseph Hospital Foundation ($30,000) see Ellwood Foundation

St. Joseph Hospital Foundation ($115,000) see Strake Foundation

St. Joseph's Catholic Church — elderly ministry ($15,000) see Hankamer Foundation, Curtis and Doris K.

St. Joseph's Hospital Foundation ($25,000) see Lyons Foundation

St. Jude's Home ($5,000) see Walthall Perpetual Charitable Trust, Marjorie T.

St. Lukes Episcopal Hospital ($30,000) see Ellwood Foundation

St. Luke's Episcopal Hospital ($25,000) see Ford Fund, William and Martha

St. Luke's Episcopal Hospital — respiratory division ($25,000) see McCullough Foundation, Ralph H. and Ruth J.

St. Luke's Episcopal Hospital ($100,000) see Shell Oil Co.

St. Luke's Episcopal Hospital ($25,000) see Smith Foundation, Bob and Vivian

St. Mark's School of Texas ($98,597) see Hoblitzelle Foundation

Saint Mary's — computer lab ($49,450) see Brackenridge Foundation, George W.

St. Mary's Episcopal Church ($100,000) see Roberts Foundation, Dora

St. Mary's Hall — education ($120,000) see Holt Foundation, William Knox

St. Mary's Hall ($85,000) see Taylor Foundation, Ruth and Vernon

St. Mary's University ($10,000) see Koehler Foundation, Marcia and Otto

St. Mary's University ($36,000) see McNutt Charitable Trust, Amy Shelton

St. Mary's University ($36,500) see Zachry Co., H. B.

St. Matthews Episcopal Church ($6,000) see Brown Foundation, M. K.

St. Michael and All Angels Church ($25,000) see Clements Foundation

St. Michael and All Angels Church — capital expansion ($250,000) see Fikes Foundation, Leland

St. Michaels Academy ($25,100) see Saint Gerard Foundation

St. Paul Medical Center ($50,000) see Mary Kay Foundation

St. Paul Medical Center — fund raising campaign ($4,000) see National Gypsum Co.

St. Paul's United Methodist Church ($80,000) see Murfee Endowment, Kathryn

St. Phillip Neri School ($5,000) see Burkitt Foundation

St. Phillips of Jesus Community Health Center ($6,986) see Morrison Trust, Louise L.

St. Stephen's Episcopal School — building and operating funds ($57,500) see Johnson Foundation, Burdine

St. Stephen's Episcopal School — construction and renovations ($500,000) see Temple Foundation, T. L. L.

St. Stephen's School — building and operating fund ($497,856) see Johnson Foundation, Burdine

St. Thomas of Canterbury School ($1,000) see Kajima International, Inc.

St. Thomas High School ($10,000) see Burkitt Foundation

St. Vincent De Paul Society — Seton Fund ($18,500) see Cameron Foundation, Harry S. and Isabel C.

St. Vincent de Paul Church ($25,000) see Strake Foundation

Salesmanship Club ($1,400) see Bordeaux Foundation

Salesmanship Club of Dallas ($18,500) see Lard Trust, Mary Potishman

Salvation Army — general support ($20,100) see Collins Foundation, Carr P.

Salvation Army ($10,000) see Fort Worth Star Telegram

Salvation Army ($5,000) see Knox, Sr., and Pearl Wallis Knox Charitable Foundation, Robert W.

Salvation Army ($5,000) see LBJ Family Foundation

Salvation Army ($9,500) see Orleans Trust, Carrie S.

Salvation Army ($122,750) see Owen Trust, B. B.

Salvation Army ($50,000) see Roberts Foundation, Dora

Salvation Army ($1,000) see Rogers Foundation

Salvation Army ($27,500) see Sharp Foundation, Charles S. and Ruth C.

Salvation Army ($7,500) see Veritas Foundation

Salvation Army ($100) see Ward Co., Joe L.

Salvation Army ($3,500) see Weir Foundation Trust

Salvation Army ($50,000) see Wright Foundation, Lola

Salvation Army, Camp Hoblitzelle — construct, renovate, improve and expand camp facilities ($175,000) see Hillcrest Foundation

Salvation Army Home for Girls — equipment for residential center ($15,000) see Kleberg, Jr. and Helen C. Kleberg Foundation, Robert J.

Salvation Army - Houston Command ($15,000) see Texas Commerce Bank Houston, N.A.

Sam Houston State University — toward endowment fund and continuing education program ($1,000,000) see Houston Endowment

Sam Houston State University ($7,000) see Humphreys Foundation

San Antonio Academy ($20,000) see King Ranch

San Antonio Academy Huntress Memorial ($75,000) see Brackenridge Foundation, George W.

San Antonio Alliance for Education ($208,000) see Meyer Foundation, Alice Kleberg Reynolds

San Antonio Art Institute ($10,000) see Halff Foundation, G. A. C.

San Antonio Art League ($10,000) see Koehler Foundation, Marcia and Otto

San Antonio Art League ($4,000) see McNutt Charitable Trust, Amy Shelton

San Antonio College Nursing School ($10,000) see Walthall Perpetual Charitable Trust, Marjorie T.

San Antonio Council on Alcohol and Drug Abuse ($10,000) see Halff Foundation, G. A. C.

San Antonio Festival — tickets for students ($15,000) see Brackenridge Foundation, George W.

San Antonio Festival — performance of "La Perichole" ($150,000) see Halsell Foundation, Ewing

San Antonio Food Bank — equipment replacement for nutrition services ($20,000) see Kleberg, Jr. and Helen C. Kleberg Foundation, Robert J.

San Antonio Independent School District — support 3-year project with Gamma Phi Boule at S.H. Gates Elementary School ($20,000) see Brackenridge Foundation, George W.

San Antonio Independent School District — tickets to the Witte Museum and the Museum of Art ($30,000) see Brackenridge Foundation, George W.

San Antonio Museum of Art ($25,000) see Schwartz Fund for Education and Health Research, Arnold and Marie

San Antonio Museum Association — additional endowment antiquities curator ($150,000) see Halsell Foundation, Ewing

San Antonio Museum Association ($8,830) see Koehler Foundation, Marcia and Otto

San Antonio Museum Association ($5,000) see Walthall Perpetual Charitable Trust, Marjorie T.

San Antonio Museum Association ($14,130) see Weisman Art Foundation, Frederick R.

San Antonio Museum Association ($5,000) see Willard Helping Fund, Cecilia Young

San Antonio Public Library Foundation ($2,500) see Tobin Foundation

San Antonio State Hospital — contribution toward day care drop-in center project ($50,000) see Halsell Foundation, Ewing

San Antonio Symphony ($2,500) see Piper Foundation, Minnie Stevens

San Antonio Symphony ($6,000) see Tobin Foundation

San Antonio Symphony ($30,000) see Zachry Co., H. B.

San Antonio Zoological Society — tickets for students ($19,900) see Brackenridge Foundation, George W.

San Antonio Zoological Society ($5,000) see Walthall Perpetual Charitable Trust, Marjorie T.

San Houston State University ($7,000) see Armstrong Foundation

San Jacinto Methodist Hospital ($250,000) see Dunn Research Foundation, John S.

San Jacinto Museum of History ($90,000) see Summerlee Foundation

San Jacinto Museum of History ($41,000) see Summerlee Foundation

San Jacinto Museum of History Association ($60,000) see Strake Foundation

San Rayburn Library ($5,000) see LBJ Family Foundation

Sands Art Center ($3,200) see Dunagan Foundation

Santa Margarita Parish — construction of a new church parish hall ($200,000) see Kenedy Memorial Foundation, John G. and Marie Stella

Santa's Helpers ($3,000) see Gordon Foundation, Meyer and Ida

Sara Robert French Home ($7,500) see Koehler Foundation, Marcia and Otto

Sarah Roberts French Home ($6,986) see Morrison Trust, Louise L.

Save Our Children ($1,000) see Moss Foundation, Harry S.

Schreiner College ($2,000) see Cook Foundation, Loring

Schreiner College ($50,000) see Fasken Foundation

Schreiner College ($5,000) see McNutt Charitable Trust, Amy Shelton

Schreiner College — a four-year Presbyterian college ($5,000) see Early Foundation

Schreiner College — Sumners scholarship endowment ($201,554) see Sumners Foundation, Hatton W.

Schreiner College — Weir Building renovation/library refurbishing/scholarships ($105,000) see Fish Foundation, Ray C.

Science Spectrum ($25,000) see Jones Foundation, Helen

Science Spectrum ($100,000) see Maddox Foundation, J. F.

Scott and White Memorial Hospital ($25,000) see Goddard Foundation, Charles B.

Scott and White Memorial Hospital ($1,500,000) see Mabee Foundation, J. E. and L. E.

Scott and White Memorial Hospital ($40,000) see Oxnard Foundation

Scott and White Memorial Hospital — Fastrac CT Scanner ($500,000) see Noble Foundation, Samuel Roberts

Second Baptist School Fund ($10,000) see Scurlock Foundation

Selco/Roosevelt ISD, Slaton — drug abuse prevention ($10,300) see South Plains Foundation

Self Help for African People ($5,000) see Hofheinz Foundation, Irene Cafcalas

Senior Citizens Center ($6,000) see White Foundation, Erle and Emma

Senior Citizens of Greater Dallas ($5,000) see Florence Foundation

Senior Citizens Service ($2,000) see Morris Foundation

Senior Citizens Service of North Texas ($5,000) see Priddy Foundation

Senior Citizens of Tarrant County ($10,000) see Fort Worth Star Telegram

Service of Emergency ($5,000) see West Foundation, Neva and Wesley

Service of Emergency aid Resource Center for the Homeless ($5,000) see West Foundation, Neva and Wesley

Seton Fund of the Daughters of Charity of St. Vincent de Paul — to help the Manos de Christo dental clinic hire a part-time dentist and full-time dental assistant ($11,000) see Dougherty, Jr. Foundation, James R.

Seton Fund (Hospital) ($3,000) see Potts and Sibley Foundation

Seven Acres Geriatric Center ($5,000) see Brochsteins Inc.

Seven Acres Geriatric Center ($1,075) see Weiner Foundation

Seymour Hospital Foundation ($10,000) see Phillips Foundation, Waite and Genevieve

Shakespeare in the Park ($3,000) see Fifth Avenue Foundation

Shalom Center ($76,000) see Cameron Foundation, Harry S. and Isabel C.

Shelter Ministries ($15,000) see Mary Kay Foundation

Shelter Ministries ($16,000) see Redman Foundation

Shelter Ministries ($12,500) see Stemmons Foundation

Sheltering Arms ($3,800) see Gordon Foundation, Meyer and Ida

Sheltering Arms ($5,000) see Knox, Sr., and Pearl Wallis Knox Charitable Foundation, Robert W.

Shepherd Ministries ($60,000) see Solheim Foundation

Sherman Preservation League — C.S. Roberts Home ($16,203) see Mayor Foundation, Oliver Dewey

Sherwood Myrtie Foster Home for Children — building construction ($175,000) see Doss Foundation, M. S.

Shriner's Hospital For Crippled Children — pledged contribution ($10,000) see First Interstate Bank of Texas, N.A.

Sibley Environmental Learning Center ($3,000) see Potts and Sibley Foundation

Sin Fronteras Organizing Project ($8,000) see Ben & Jerry's Homemade

Sister Cities ($15,000) see Maddox Trust, Web

Sister of the Incarnate Word ($144,000) see Warren Foundation, William K.

Sisters of St. Marys ($7,000) see Sexton Foundation

Society for the Performing Arts ($4,000) see Hofheinz Foundation, Irene Cafcalas

Society for the Performing Arts ($9,000) see Humphreys Foundation

Society for the Performing Arts ($4,500) see Taub Foundation

Society for the Prevention of Cruelty to Animals see Recognition Equipment

Society for the Prevention of Cruelty to Animals ($40,000) see Summerlee Foundation

Soldiers for Jesus ($2,500) see Heath Foundation, Ed and Mary

Some Other Place ($10,000) see Steinhagen Benevolent Trust, B. A. and Elinor

Sonora High School ($12,000) see Cauthorn Charitable Trust, John and Mildred

South Texas Alcohol and Drug Rehabilitation Center ($60,000) see Rachal Foundation, Ed

South Texas Art Council ($8,000) see Steinhagen Benevolent Trust, B. A. and Elinor

South Texas Art Council ($8,000) see Steinhagen Benevolent Trust, B. A. and Elinor

South Texas College of Law — renovation of the library and instructional building ($1,000,000) see Houston Endowment

South Texas College of Law ($10,000) see O'Quinn Foundation, John M. and Nancy C.

South Texas College of Law — furnishing two new conference rooms ($50,000) see Rockwell Fund

South Texas Emergency Corps ($3,000) see Sams Foundation, Earl C.

South Texas Primate Observation ($13,000) see Summerlee Foundation

South Texas Primate Observatory ($13,000) see Luster Family Foundation

South Texas Public Broadcasting System ($22,765) see Haas Foundation, Paul and Mary

Southeast Texas Hospice — hospice care for 45 days ($2,500) see Stark Foundation, Nelda C. and H. J. Lutcher

Southern Bible Training School ($5,000) see Morris Charitable Foundation, E. A.

Southern Methodist University ($10,000) see Central & South West Services

Southern Methodist University ($75,000) see Clements Foundation

Southern Methodist University — general support ($33,000) see Collins Foundation, Carr P.

Southern Methodist University ($285,000) see Fondren Foundation

Southern Methodist University ($10,000) see Glaze Foundation, Robert and Ruth

Southern Methodist University ($350,000) see Hawn Foundation

Southern Methodist University ($150,000) see Hoblitzelle Foundation

Southern Methodist University ($30,000) see Jones Foundation, Montfort Jones and Allie Brown

Southern Methodist University ($33,000) see Killson Educational Foundation, Winifred and B. A.

Southern Methodist University ($15,000) see Oaklawn Foundation

Southern Methodist University ($10,000) see Scurlock Foundation

Southern Methodist University — undergraduate scholarships ($36,000) see Sumners Foundation, Hatton W.

Southern Methodist University ($50,000) see Taubman Foundation, Herman P. and Sophia

Southern Methodist University ($10,000) see Weil, Gotshal & Manges Foundation

Southern Methodist University ($80,000) see Wilder Foundation

Southern Methodist University, Meadows School of the Arts — to supplement current endowment earnings to fund events related to the awarding of the A. H. Meadows Award for Excellence in the Arts ($300,000) see Meadows Foundation

Southern Methodist University School of Law — first of two payments on 1992 commitment to renovate the Underwood Law Library ($125,000) see Hillcrest Foundation

Southern Methodist University School of Law — Sumners scholarship endowment ($100,809) see Sumners Foundation, Hatton W.

Southern Methodist University — Synthesis of Polycyclics by the Tandem Addition-Rearrangement Aryne Reaction see Welch Foundation, Robert A.

Southern Methodist University Treaty Verification Conference ($15,000) see Macmillan, Inc.

Southwest Alternate Media Project ($10,000) see Menil Foundation

Southwest Family Institute ($6,000) see Luse Foundation, W. P. and Bulah

Southwest Foundation ($5,000) see Forest Oil Corp.

Southwest Foundation for Biomedical Research ($10,000) see Ferguson Family Foundation, Kittie and Rugeley

Southwest Foundation for Biomedical Research — support molecular retrovirology biologist ($65,000) see Halsell Foundation, Ewing

Southwest Foundation for Biomedical Research — Golden Circle ($10,000) see Ferguson Family Foundation, Kittie and Rugeley

Southwest Medical Center ($5,000) see Dunagan Foundation

Southwest Medical Center ($6,584,742) see Mobility Foundation

Southwest Medical Foundation ($50,000) see Hawn Foundation

Southwest Neuropsychiatric Institute ($5,000) see Veritas Foundation

Southwest Texas State University ($10,000) see Azadoutioun Foundation

Southwest Texas State University ($8,000) see Hugg Trust, Leoia W. and Charles H.

Southwestern Baptist Seminary ($12,000) see C.I.O.S.

Southwestern Baptist Theological Seminary — building fund ($150,000) see Carter Foundation, Amon G.

Southwestern Baptist Theological Seminary ($11,000) see Glaze Foundation, Robert and Ruth

Southwestern Law Enforcement Institute ($2,500) see Piper Foundation, Minnie Stevens

Southwestern Medical Center — Mobility Research and Assessment Laboratory (Gait Lab) ($164,020) see Mobility Foundation

Southwestern Medical Foundation ($100,000) see Collins Foundation, James M.

Southwestern Medical Foundation — sustentation campaign ($75,000) see Green Foundation

Southwestern Medical Foundation Karl and Esther Hobliotzelle Fund/Children's Medical Center ($100,000) see Hoblitzelle Foundation

Southwestern Medical School of University of Texas at Dallas — establish two chairs in child psychiatry ($500,000) see Seay Charitable Trust, Sarah M. and Charles E.

Southwestern University — continuation of the matching grant for the endowment ($1,321,795) see Brown Foundation

Southwestern University ($10,000) see Duncan Foundation, Lillian H. and C. W.

Southwestern University ($10,000) see Garvey Texas Foundation

Southwestern University ($8,875) see Hugg Trust, Leoia W. and Charles H.

Southwestern University ($33,000) see Killson Educational Foundation, Winifred and B. A.

Southwestern University ($10,000) see Murfee Endowment, Kathryn

Southwestern University ($11,500) see Perkins Foundation, Joe and Lois

Southwestern University — renovation and expansion, fine arts creation, central campus mall ($300,000) see Cullen Foundation

Southwestern University — partial funding of Tower library ($25,000) see Wright Foundation, Lola

Space Center Houston ($750,000) see Wortham Foundation

Sparks Houston Park Board ($5,000) see Knox, Sr., and Pearl Wallis Knox Charitable Foundation, Robert W.

SPCA of Houston ($12,500) see Lyons Foundation

SPCA of Texas ($10,000) see Stemmons Foundation

Special Camps for Special Kids ($125,000) see Andersen Foundation, Arthur

Special Camps for Special Kids ($10,000) see Haggerty Foundation

Special Camps for Special Kids ($50,000) see King Foundation, Carl B. and Florence E.

Special Camps for Special Kids ($5,000) see Overlake Foundation

Special Camps for Special Kids ($25,000) see Smith Foundation, Bob and Vivian

Spohn Hospital ($50,000) see South Texas Charitable Foundation

Spohn Kleberg Memorial Hospital ($50,000) see King Ranch

Spohn-Kleberg Memorial Hospital — ambulance and radiology equipment ($683,106) see Kleberg, Jr. and Helen C. Kleberg Foundation, Robert J.

Star of Hope — transitional living centers ($50,000) see Cockrell Foundation

Star of Hope ($25,000) see Luchsinger Family Foundation

Starr County Historical Foundation — to purchase a historic inn ($437,500) see Meadows Foundation

Stars for Children ($15,000) see Moncrief Foundation, William A. and Elizabeth B.

State of Texas, Department of Mental Health and Mental Retardation — land for construction of a Behavior Treatment and Training Center ($93,849) see George Foundation

Stehlin Foundation — cancer research ($30,000) see Hankamer Foundation, Curtis and Doris K.

Stehlin Foundation for Cancer Research — cancer research ($50,000) see Fish Foundation, Ray C.

Stella Link Redevelopment Association — land acquisition and develop deteriorated neighborhood ($50,000) see Rockwell Fund

Step Foundation ($21,500) see Lightner Sams Foundation

STEP Foundation — STEP-Strategies to Elevate People is intended to inspire, encourage, and assist ghetto dwellers ($31,375) see Glaze Foundation, Robert and Ruth

Stew Pot Kitchen (Community Ministries, First Presbyterian Church) ($15,000) see Falk Medical Research Foundation, Dr. Ralph and Marian

Stewart Blood Center ($10,000) see Pineywoods Foundation

Strake Jesuit College Preparatory ($15,000) see Lyons Foundation

Suicide Crisis Center see Centex Corp.

Suicide and Crisis Center ($10,000) see Luse Foundation, W. P. and Bulah

Sul Ross State University ($8,000) see Armstrong Foundation

Sul Ross State University ($3,000) see Potts and Sibley Foundation

Sundry-School and Churches ($50,600) see Perkins Foundation, Joe and Lois

Sunshine Kids ($2,500) see Robinson Foundation

Susan G. Komen Breast Cancer Foundation ($25,000) see Mary Kay Foundation

Susan G. Komen Foundation ($5,000) see Lowe Foundation

Susan G. Komen Foundation — breast cancer research ($5,000) see National Gypsum Co.

Sylvania Baptist Church ($2,000) see Heath Foundation, Ed and Mary

Symphony League of Fort Worth ($16,000) see Keith Foundation Trust, Ben E.

Symphony Society of San Antonio ($6,500) see Koehler Foundation, Marcia and Otto

Symphony Society of San Antonio ($5,000) see Willard Helping Fund, Cecilia Young

Synod of the Sun, Bicentennial Fund — for enlarging missions of church ($5,000) see Early Foundation

Tamu Development Foundation ($78,050) see Phillips Petroleum Co.

TAMU Development Foundation — Rice Research Program ($10,000) see Trull Foundation

Tarleton State College — scholarships ($13,000) see Mayor Foundation, Oliver Dewey

Tarleton State University ($8,000) see Armstrong Foundation

Tarleton State University ($5,000) see Moncrief Foundation, William A. and Elizabeth B.

Tarrant Council on Alcoholism ($10,000) see Fort Worth Star Telegram

Tarrant Council on Alcoholism ($3,000) see Morris Foundation

Tarrant County Hospital District ($10,000) see Weaver Foundation, Gil and Dody

Tarrant County United Way ($31,250) see Textron

Tarrant County United Way ($31,250) see Textron

Tarrant County United Way ($31,250) see Textron

Tarrant County United Way ($31,250) see Textron

Teen Challenge of Grayson County — transportation ($23,876) see Smith and W. Aubrey Smith Charitable Foundation, Clara Blackford

Teens Off the Street ($8,000) see Wilson Public Trust, Ralph

Temple Civic Theatre ($10,000) see Wilson Public Trust, Ralph

Temple Emanuel ($15,000) see Florence Foundation

Temple Shalom ($60,000) see Zale Foundation

Tennis A.C.E., Ingram ($75,000) see Turner Charitable Foundation

Texans United Education Fund ($5,000) see Azadoutioun Foundation

Texarkana Special Education Center ($2,500) see Kohl Charities, Herbert H.

Texas A&I University ($10,000) see Corpus Christi Exploration Co.

Texas A&I University ($150,000) see Rachal Foundation, Ed

Texas A&I University — research ($40,000) see West Foundation, Neva and Wesley

Texas A&I University — Wildlife Conservation ($325,000) see Kleberg Foundation for Wildlife Conservation, Caesar

Texas A&M Agricultural Extension Service ($42,500) see Behmann Brothers Foundation

Texas A&M Development Center ($100,000) see Fasken Foundation

Texas (cont.)

Texas A&M Development Fund ($20,000) see Smith Foundation, Bob and Vivian

Texas A&M Research and Extension ($42,500) see Behmann Brothers Foundation

Texas A & M Research Foundation ($18,500) see Robinson Foundation

Texas A&M Student Loan Fund ($63,631) see White Trust, G. R.

Texas A&M University — dormitory expansion ($500,000) see Cain Foundation, Effie and Wofford

Texas A&M University — park construction ($75,000) see Cain Foundation, Effie and Wofford

Texas A&M University ($5,280) see Central & South West Services

Texas A&M University ($24,280) see Haas Foundation, Paul and Mary

Texas A&M University ($100,000) see Hagler Foundation, Jon L.

Texas A&M University ($18,750) see Hugg Trust, Leoia W. and Charles H.

Texas A & M University ($6,000) see Hutcheson Foundation, Hazel Montague

Texas A & M University ($1,500) see JMK-A M Micallef Charitable Foundation

Texas A & M University ($5,000) see Love Foundation, Gay and Erskine

Texas A&M University ($50,000) see Luse Foundation, W. P. and Bulah

Texas A & M University ($50,000) see McMillan, Jr. Foundation, Bruce

Texas A&M University ($2,321) see Northen, Mary Moody

Texas A&M University ($48,854) see Technical Foundation of America

Texas A&M University ($14,015) see Technical Foundation of America

Texas A&M University ($119,116) see Temple-Inland

Texas A&M University ($160,750) see Terry Foundation

Texas A&M University ($50,000) see Waggoner Foundation, E. Paul and Helen Buck

Texas A&M University ($54,000) see Wal-Mart Stores

Texas A&M University ($200,000) see West Foundation, Neva and Wesley

Texas A&M University — Chemisorption and Growth on Semiconductor Surfaces see Welch Foundation, Robert A.

Texas A&M University — Dating & Chemical Characterization of Rock Paintings see Welch Foundation, Robert A.

Texas A&M University Department of Agriculture Economics ($19,600) see White Trust, G. R.

Texas A&M University Development Foundation ($75,000) see Burlington Resources

Texas A&M University Development Foundation — construction of large animal veterinary isolation unit ($1,459,242) see Kleberg, Jr. and Helen C. Kleberg Foundation, Robert J.

Texas A&M University Development Foundation-Institute of Biosciences and Technology; Corporate-GEO ($200,000) see Shell Oil Co.

Texas A&M University Development Foundation — support International Center for Bat Research and Education ($500,000) see Richardson Foundation, Sid W.

Texas A&M University — Interactions of a Flavin Monooxygenase with the Flavin Substrate see Welch Foundation, Robert A.

Texas A&M University — Ligand Control of Reactivity in Organometallic Chemistry see Welch Foundation, Robert A.

Texas A&M University — On the Kinetics of Certain Electrode Reactions see Welch Foundation, Robert A.

Texas A&M University, Petroleum Engineering Department ($106,400) see Texaco

Texas A&M University — Photochemically Triggered 1,4-Diyl Formation: Design and Applications see Welch Foundation, Robert A.

Texas A&M University — Technology ($38,231) see Halliburton Co.

Texas A&M University Veterinary Medical Center ($13,000) see Community Hospital Foundation

Texas A&M University — Wildlife Conservation ($250,000) see Kleberg Foundation for Wildlife Conservation, Caesar

Texas Agricultural Experiment Station ($25,000) see Overlake Foundation

Texas Aquatics ($15,000) see Burns Family Foundation

Texas Baptist Childrens Home — passenger van ($20,000) see Edwards Foundation, Jes

Texas Baptist Men ($10,000) see White Trust, G. R.

Texas Boys Choir ($26,000) see Fleming Foundation

Texas Boys Choir ($10,500) see Waggoner Charitable Trust, Crystelle

Texas Boys Choir ($10,000) see Walsh Foundation

Texas Business Hall of Fame — scholarship ($500) see Mayborn Foundation, Frank W.

Texas Center for Policy Studies — to protect water quality and the environment in the Texas/Mexico border region ($60,000) see Noyes Foundation, Jessie Smith

Texas Children's Hospital ($5,000) see Brochsteins Inc.

Texas Children's Hospital — pediatric support services ($2,000,000) see Brown Foundation

Texas Children's Hospital ($250,000) see Cain Foundation, Gordon and Mary

Texas Children's Hospital — defray cost of construction ($600,000) see Cullen Foundation

Texas Childrens Hospital — capital improvements program ($100,000) see George Foundation

Texas Children's Hospital ($300,000) see Gordon Foundation, Meyer and Ida

Texas Children's Hospital ($7,500) see McCrea Foundation

Texas Children's Hospital ($5,000) see O'Quinn Foundation, John M. and Nancy C.

Texas Children's Hospital ($1,250) see Powell Co., William

Texas Children's Hospital ($50,000) see Scurlock Foundation

Texas Children's Hospital ($60,000) see Smith Foundation, Bob and Vivian

Texas Children's Hospital ($100,000) see Texaco

Texas Children's Hospital — capital campaign ($250,000) see West Foundation, Neva and Wesley

Texas Children's Hospital ($10,000) see Wolff Memorial Foundation, Pauline Sterne

Texas Chiropractic College ($15,000) see Foundation for Advancement of Chiropractic Education

Texas Christian University ($2,500) see Alexander Foundation, Robert D. and Catherine R.

Texas Christian University ($13,000) see Armstrong Foundation

Texas Christian University — operating fund ($22,000) see Beasley Foundation, Theodore and Beulah

Texas Christian University — student union renovation ($12,500) see Beasley Foundation, Theodore and Beulah

Texas Christian University ($672,500) see Brown and C. A. Lupton Foundation, T. J.

Texas Christian University ($75,000) see Bryce Memorial Fund, William and Catherine

Texas Christian University ($92,000) see Fleming Foundation

Texas Christian University ($12,000) see Fort Worth Star Telegram

Texas Christian University ($5,000) see Glaze Foundation, Robert and Ruth

Texas Christian University ($10,000) see Keith Foundation Trust, Ben E.

Texas Christian University ($135,000) see Lard Trust, Mary Potishman

Texas Christian University ($20,000) see McMillan, Jr. Foundation, Bruce

Texas Christian University ($36,500) see Moncrief Foundation, William A. and Elizabeth B.

Texas Christian University ($16,000) see Pangburn Foundation

Texas Christian University — purchase equipment for science departments ($250,000) see Richardson Foundation, Sid W.

Texas Christian University ($7,000) see Tandy Foundation, David L.

Texas Christian University ($200,000) see Waggoner Foundation, E. Paul and Helen Buck

Texas Christian University ($15,000) see Walsh Foundation

Texas Christian University — final installment of a grant of $240,000, payable in four equal installments in 1988-91, inclusive, to help establish an Academic Services Center that will offer writing enhancement programs and academic advising to students ($60,000) see Union Pacific Corp.

Texas Christian University — Burnett Ranches Endowed Professorship ($650,000) see Tandy Foundation, Anne Burnett and Charles

Texas Christian University — support new recital hall to be added to the Ed Landreth Auditorium ($500,000) see Bass Foundation

Texas Christian University Ranch Management ($1,050,000) see Rockefeller Trust, Winthrop

Texas Christian University — Ranch Management Program ($20,000) see White Trust, G. R.

Texas Christian University — to endow The Frost Foundation Lectureship for Global Issues ($35,000) see Frost Foundation

Texas College of Osteopathy ($25,000) see Community Hospital Foundation

Texas Department of Human Services ($4,600) see Orleans Trust, Carrie S.

Texas Energy Museum ($10,000) see Dishman Charitable Foundation Trust, H. E. and Kate

Texas Energy Museum ($50,000) see Steinhagen Benevolent Trust, B. A. and Elinor

Texas Energy Museum Foundation — renovation expense ($10,000) see Stark Foundation, Nelda C. and H. J. Lutcher

Texas Engineering Foundation ($64,000) see O'Donnell Foundation

Texas Foundation for Conservative Studies — general support ($59,500) see Collins Foundation, Carr P.

Texas Foundation for Visually Impaired Children ($100) see Southland Corp.

Texas Heart Institute ($100,000) see Ford Fund, William and Martha

Texas Heart Institute — Cardiovascular Surgical Research program ($100,000) see Cockrell Foundation

Texas Heart Institute Foundation — cardiovascular research ($25,000) see Fish Foundation, Ray C.

Texas Independent College Fund ($5,000) see Moncrief Foundation, William A. and Elizabeth B.

Texas Independent College Fund ($179,500) see Southwestern Bell Corp.

Texas Institute for Rehabilitation and Research ($500,000) see Dunn Research Foundation, John S.

Texas Institute for Rehabilitation Research — handicap programs ($5,000) see Kayser Foundation

Texas Interfaith Education Fund ($25,000) see Needmor Fund

Texas Interscholastic League Foundation ($143,800) see Abell-Hanger Foundation

Texas Interscholastic League Foundation — scholarship program ($143,600) see Stark Foundation, Nelda C. and H. J. Lutcher

Texas Interscholastic League Fund ($10,000) see Owen Trust, B. B.

Texas Interscholastic League Fund ($8,000) see Stemmons Foundation

Texas Lions League — building renovation ($75,700) see Doss Foundation, M. S.

Texas Lutheran College ($2,000) see Hexcel Corp.

Texas Lutheran College ($2,250) see Hugg Trust, Leoia W. and Charles H.

Texas Lutheran College — to build a new dining hall ($100,000) see Johnson Foundation, M. G. and Lillie A.

Texas Lutheran College ($850,000) see Mabee Foundation, J. E. and L. E.

Texas Marketing Education Foundation ($100) see Gordon Foundation, Meyer and Ida

Texas Medical Center ($220,000) see Anderson Foundation, M. D.

Texas Medical Center — land purchase ($150,000) see Cockrell Foundation

Texas Medical Center — acquisition of properties ($210,000) see Fondren Foundation

Texas Medical Center ($2,288,006) see Wortham Foundation

Texas Military Institute ($27,944) see Morrison Trust, Louise L.

Texas Military Institute ($50,000) see Semmes Foundation

Texas Nature Conservancy ($5,000) see Brochsteins Inc.

Texas Nature Conservancy ($3,000) see Potts and Sibley Foundation

Texas Parks and Wildlife Foundation — to plan and develop a project to interpret Texas' Spanish Colonial ranching heritage ($500,000) see Meadows Foundation

Texas Scottish Rite Hospital ($15,000) see Hawn Foundation

Texas Scottish Rite Hospital ($25,000) see Luttrell Trust

Texas Scottish Rite Hospital ($25,000) see Seay Charitable Trust, Sarah M. and Charles E.

Texas Society to Prevent Blindness ($10,000) see Fort Worth Star Telegram

Texas and Southwestern Cattle Raisers Foundation ($25,000) see White Trust, G. R.

Texas Special Olympics — Special Olympics aquatics ($1,400) see South Plains Foundation

Texas State Aquarium ($25,000) see Central & South West Services

Texas State Aquarium ($25,000) see Corpus Christi Exploration Co.

Texas State Aquarium ($15,000) see McNutt Charitable Trust, Amy Shelton

Texas State Aquarium ($70,000) see Sams Foundation, Earl C.

Texas State Aquarium Association ($10,000) see Meyer Foundation, Alice Kleberg Reynolds

Texas State Aquarium — Wildlife Conservation ($25,000) see Kleberg Foundation for Wildlife Conservation, Caesar

Texas State Historical Association ($5,000) see Priddy Foundation

Texas State Technical Institute ($30,000) see Ryder System

Texas Tech Research Foundation ($20,000) see Central & South West Services

Texas Tech University ($100,000) see Burlington Resources

Texas Tech University — professorship ($21,000) see Franklin Charitable Trust, Ershel

Texas Tech University — allied health ($18,000) see Franklin Charitable Trust, Ershel

Texas Tech University — alcohol treatment ($15,000) see Franklin Charitable Trust, Ershel

Texas Tech University ($150,000) see GTE Corp.

Texas Tech University ($1,500) see Hugg Trust, Leoia W. and Charles H.

Texas Tech University ($6,000) see Mayborn Foundation, Frank W.

Texas Tech University ($6,000) see Mayborn Foundation, Frank W.

Texas Tech University — fellowship in psychology ($4,000) see South Plains Foundation

Texas Tech University ($15,000) see Thornton Foundation

Texas Tech University College of Education ($35,000) see Jones Foundation, Helen

Texas Tech University, Department of Psychology — risk taking adolescents/young adults ($4,000) see South Plains Foundation

Texas Tech University Foundation — funding of two professorships ($50,000) see Rockwell Fund

Texas Tech University Health ($9,900) see Monroe Foundation (1976), J. Edgar

Texas Tech University Health Science Center — endogenous digitalis ($11,650) see South Plains Foundation

Texas Tech University Health Science Center ($9,550) see South Plains Foundation

Texas Tech University Museum African Collection — construction ($30,000) see Jones Foundation, Helen

Texas Tech University Museum for African Collection — African art ($50,000) see Jones Foundation, Helen

Texas Tech University Press — print programs ($16,666) see Jones Foundation, Helen

Texas Tech University — W. T. Campbell scholarship ($25,000) see South Plains Foundation

Texas Technical University — to research growing cotton fibers without plants ($75,000) see Dodge Jones Foundation

Texas Wesleyan University — Sumners scholars program ($55,000) see Sumners Foundation, Hatton W.

Texas Works Together — construction ($50,000) see McGovern Fund for the Behavioral Sciences

Texas Works Together — construction ($50,000) see McGovern Fund for the Behavioral Sciences

Texoma Concert Association ($2,500) see Munson Foundation, W. B.

Texoma Medical Center ($193,632) see Munson Foundation, W. B.

Texoma Medical Center — ICU ($400,000) see Smith and W. Aubrey Smith Charitable Foundation, Clara Blackford

Texoma Medical Center — Reba's Ranch House ($61,500) see Mayor Foundation, Oliver Dewey

Texoma Medical Foundation — fund drive ($250,000) see Smith and W. Aubrey Smith Charitable Foundation, Clara Blackford

Theatre Under the Stars ($75,000) see Burlington Resources

Theatre Under the Stars ($95,000) see Humphreys Foundation

Timberlawn Foundation ($10,000) see Andersen Foundation, Arthur

Timberlawn Psychiatric Foundation ($15,000) see Florence Foundation

Tommy Paul Memorial Fund ($500) see Rogers Foundation

Transitional Learning Center — endowment ($32,652,000) see Moody Foundation

Transitional Learning Community, Galveston Institute of Human Communication, Speech Physiology Lab — clinical and research missions ($329,749) see Moody Foundation

Transplant Resources and Services Center, University of Texas Health Science Center at Dallas — for coalition on organ and tissue donor awareness ($50,000) see Green Foundation

Tree for Houston ($3,000) see Elkins, Jr. Foundation, Margaret and James A.

Trees of Hope Festival see Apache Corp.

Tri County Senior Nutrition Project — capital assets ($20,000) see Mayor Foundation, Oliver Dewey

Trinity Christian Academy ($20,000) see Chilton Foundation Trust

Trinity Church Endowment ($1,000) see McCullough Foundation, Ralph H. and Ruth J.

Trinity Episcopal Church ($5,000) see Rienzi Foundation

Trinity Episcopal School ($10,000) see O'Connor Foundation, Kathryn

Trinity Ministries ($30,000) see Haggerty Foundation

Trinity River Mission ($13,500) see Redman Foundation

Trinity School ($10,000) see Prairie Foundation

Trinity School of Midland ($65,000) see Beal Foundation

Trinity School of Midland ($15,000) see Beal Foundation

Trinity Terrance ($190,665) see Stonestreet Trust, Eusebia S.

Trinity University ($3,815) see Bowers Foundation

Trinity University ($2,500) see Bowers Foundation

Trinity University ($2,020) see Bowers Foundation

Trinity University — teacher training ($100,000) see Brackenridge Foundation, George W.

Trinity University — affirmative action ($69,890) see Brackenridge Foundation, George W.

Trinity University — urban studies ($25,000) see Brackenridge Foundation, George W.

Trinity University — scholarship fund ($55,000) see Hearst Foundation, William Randolph

Trinity University ($24,000) see Koehler Foundation, Marcia and Otto

Trinity University ($1,000) see Wilson Foundation, John and Nevils

Trinity University — educational improvement project and reserve for consultants, Hawthorne Elementary ($220,100) see Halsell Foundation, Ewing

Trinity Valley School ($15,000) see Fleming Foundation

Trinity Valley School ($25,000) see Maddox Trust, Web

TSTO Development Foundation ($25,000) see Zachry Co., H. B.

TVKEDTFM ($10,000) see Corpus Christi Exploration Co.

TWU ($20,000) see Bryce Memorial Fund, William and Catherine

Tyler Baseball ($10,000) see Vaughn Foundation

Tyler Economics Development Council ($97,000) see Fair Foundation, R. W.

Tyler Independent School District ($15,000) see Vaughn Foundation

Tyler Junior College ($16,300) see Vaughn Foundation

Tyler Junior League ($750) see Rogers Foundation

Tyler Metropolitan YMCA ($76,000) see Fair Foundation, R. W.

Tyler Museum of Art ($700) see Rogers Foundation

Tyler Rose Museum ($2,500) see Heath Foundation, Ed and Mary

U.S.O. South Texas — for the Capital Development Program ($10,000) see Dougherty, Jr. Foundation, James R.

Union Gospel Mission ($15,000) see Falk Medical Research Foundation, Dr. Ralph and Marian

Union Gospel Mission ($2,000) see Morris Foundation

United Community Services of Port Arthur ($16,754) see FINA, Inc.

United Community Services of Port Arthur ($16,754) see FINA, Inc.

United Community Services of Port Arthur ($16,754) see FINA, Inc.

United Day School ($41,200) see Hachar Charitable Trust, D. D.

United Fund ($30,000) see Wright Foundation, Lola

United Fund of Austin and Travis County ($57,000) see Motorola

United Jewish Appeal Federation of Jewish Philanthropies ($20,000) see Smith Foundation, Bob and Vivian

United Jewish Campaign ($25,000) see Herzstein Charitable Foundation, Albert and Ethel

United Jewish Campaign ($382,050) see Levit Family Foundation, Joe

United Jewish Campaign ($25,000) see Weil, Gotshal & Manges Foundation

United Negro College Fund ($13,000) see Chilton Foundation Trust

United Negro College Fund ($1,000) see Gordon Foundation, Meyer and Ida

United Negro College Fund ($25,500) see Hobby Foundation

United Negro College Fund ($100,000) see JCPenney Co.

United Negro College Fund ($5,000) see Luchsinger Family Foundation

United Negro College Fund ($1,000) see Meyer Foundation, Alice Kleberg Reynolds

United Presbyterian — endowment fund ($38,000) see Franklin Charitable Trust, Ershel

United Way ($78,000) see Beal Foundation

United Way ($32,000) see Beal Foundation

United Way ($7,500) see Behmann Brothers Foundation

United Way ($6,000) see Bergner Co., P.A.

United Way ($12,860) see Brown Foundation, M. K.

United Way ($34,591) see CBI Industries

United Way ($250,000) see Chevron Corp.

United Way ($15,000) see Chilton Foundation Trust

United Way ($10,000) see Clements Foundation

United Way ($10,500) see Collins Foundation, Carr P.

United Way ($10,000) see Collins Foundation, James M.

United Way ($65,000) see Constantin Foundation

United Way ($2,000) see Cook Foundation, Loring

United Way ($15,000) see Corpus Christi Exploration Co.

United Way ($44,969) see Crown Central Petroleum Corp.

United Way ($30,000) see Davis Foundation, Ken W.

United Way ($5,000) see Davis Foundation, Ken W.

United Way ($3,360) see Dishman Charitable Foundation Trust, H. E. and Kate

United Way ($50,000) see Fasken Foundation

United Way ($31,980) see FINA, Inc.

United Way ($31,980) see FINA, Inc.

United Way ($31,980) see FINA, Inc.

United Way ($10,000) see Foothills Foundation

United Way ($10,000) see Gill Foundation, Pauline Allen

United Way ($12,500) see Green Foundation

United Way ($25,000) see Haas Foundation, Paul and Mary

United Way ($36,000) see Haggerty Foundation

United Way ($25,000) see Halff Foundation, G. A. C.

United Way ($26,200) see Hawn Foundation

United Way ($2,000) see Heath Foundation, Ed and Mary

United Way ($25,000) see Heileman Brewing Co., Inc., G.

United Way ($3,000) see Hervey Foundation

United Way ($12,000) see IBP, Inc.

United Way ($588) see Interstate National Corp.

United Way ($6,250) see Jacobs Engineering Group

United Way ($3,000) see JSJ Corp.

United Way ($11,500) see Keith Foundation Trust, Ben E.

United Way ($15,000) see Luchsinger Family Foundation

United Way ($25,000) see McGovern Fund for the Behavioral Sciences

United Way ($32,000) see McKee Foundation, Robert E. and Evelyn

United Way ($25,000) see McNutt Charitable Trust, Amy Shelton

United Way ($2,000) see Meredith Foundation

United Way ($2,000) see Morris Foundation

United Way ($6,986) see Morrison Trust, Louise L.

United Way ($6,986) see Morrison Trust, Louise L.

United Way ($5,000) see Munson Foundation, W. B.

United Way ($23,000) see National Gypsum Co.

United Way ($1,500) see Nelco Sewing Machine Sales Corp.

United Way ($25,000) see Prairie Foundation

United Way ($9,327) see Quanex Corp.

United Way see Recognition Equipment

United Way ($6,000) see Rienzi Foundation

United Way ($13,500) see Scott Foundation, William E.

United Way ($10,000) see Scurlock Foundation

United Way ($10,000) see Semmes Foundation

United Way ($25,000) see Stemmons Foundation

United Way ($100,202) see Temple-Inland

United Way ($18,300) see Texas Industries, Inc.

United Way ($12,750) see Texas Industries, Inc.

United Way ($7,600) see Texas Industries, Inc.

United Way ($5,875) see Texas Industries, Inc.

United Way ($37,500) see Tobin Foundation

United Way ($2,000) see Tyler Corp.

United Way ($3,650) see Weiner Foundation

United Way ($10,000) see Zale Foundation, William and Sylvia

Texas (cont.)

United Way of Amarillo — 1991 net income distribution ($176,639) see Harrington Foundation, Don and Sybil

United Way of Austin-Capital ($25,000) see Texas Instruments

United Way Campaign-Metropolitan Dallas ($250,000) see Exxon Corp.

United Way Campaign-Texas Gulf Coast ($1,759,100) see Exxon Corp.

United Way of Dallas ($10,000) see Bordeaux Foundation

United Way-Dallas ($160,000) see May Department Stores Co.

United Way of Denton County ($69,520) see PACCAR

United Way of El Paso County ($135,000) see Burlington Resources

United Way of El Paso County ($50,000) see Levi Strauss & Co.

United Way of Grayson County ($40,000) see Texas Instruments

United Way of Greater Wichita Falls ($12,500) see Bridwell Foundation, J. S.

United Way of Gulf Coast — operating ($27,125) see Simpson Investment Co.

United Way of Metro Dallas ($225,000) see Mobil Oil Corp.

United Way of Metro Dallas ($14,750) see Zale Foundation

United Way of Metropolitan Dallas ($60,415) see GEICO Corp.

United Way of Metropolitan Dallas ($36,800) see Kimberly-Clark Corp.

United Way of Metropolitan Dallas ($17,171) see LTV Corp.

United Way of Metropolitan Dallas ($17,169) see LTV Corp.

United Way of Metropolitan Dallas ($347,207) see PepsiCo

United Way of Metropolitan Dallas ($450,000) see Texas Instruments

United Way of Metropolitan Dallas ($93,000) see Xerox Corp.

United Way of Metropolitan Dallas — 1992 campaign ($52,387) see Fikes Foundation, Leland

United Way of Metropolitan Tarrant County ($30,000) see Burlington Northern Inc.

United Way-Metropolitan Tarrant County ($216,000) see Carter Foundation, Amon G.

United Way of Metropolitan Tarrant County — annual campaign ($40,000) see Davidson Family Charitable Foundation

United Way of Metropolitan Tarrant County ($100,000) see Union Pacific Corp.

United Way of Metropolitan Tarrant County/Tarrant County Housing Partnership ($250,000) see Tandy Foundation, Anne Burnett and Charles

United Way of Midland ($45,000) see Davidson Family Charitable Foundation

United Way of Midland ($82,700) see Enron Corp.

United Way of Midland — general operating support and matching grant for the 1991 campaign ($273,093) see Abell-Hanger Foundation

United Way — 1991 combined Dallas-Ft. Worth campaign ($175,000) see AMR Corp.

United Way of San Antonio and Bexar Company — eastside outreach project ($30,000) see Davidson Family Charitable Foundation

United Way of Texas Gulf Coast ($46,460) see ARCO Chemical

United Way of the Texas Gulf Coast ($60,000) see Bechtel Group

United Way of the Texas Gulf Coast ($33,197) see Cooper Industries

United Way of the Texas Gulf Coast ($32,542) see Cooper Industries

United Way of the Texas Gulf Coast ($27,063) see Cooper Industries

United Way of Texas Gulf Coast ($30,000) see Dresser Industries

United Way of Texas Gulf Coast ($452,564) see Enron Corp.

United Way of the Texas Gulf Coast — to support annual operating budget ($68,000) see George Foundation

United Way of the Texas Gulf Coast ($405,000) see Texas Commerce Bank Houston, N.A.

United Way of the Texas Gulf Coast ($27,000) see Texas Instruments

United Way of the Texas Gulf Coast — general purpose fund ($22,144) see Walgreen Co.

United Way of the Texas Gulf Coast — 1991 general campaign ($225,000) see Cullen Foundation

United Way of the Texas Gulf Coast — 1991 annual campaign ($50,000) see Rockwell Fund

University Christian Church ($25,000) see Alexander Foundation, Robert D. and Catherine R.

University of Dallas ($250,000) see Constantin Foundation

University of Dallas ($200,000) see Constantin Foundation

University of Dallas ($200,000) see Constantin Foundation

University of Dallas — second of three payments ($50,000) see Haggar Foundation

University of Dallas ($1,500) see Hillman Family Foundation, Alex

University of Dallas ($15,500) see Saint Gerard Foundation

University of Dallas ($5,000) see Texas Industries, Inc.

University of Dallas — Rome program ($50,000) see Haggar Foundation

University of Houston ($15,000) see Durfee Foundation

University of Houston ($60,000) see First Interstate Bank of Texas, N.A.

University of Houston ($845,000) see Moores Foundation

University of Houston ($139,300) see Moores Foundation

University of Houston — funding for scholarships for violin students ($10,000) see Starling Foundation, Dorothy Richard

University of Houston — Conrad N. Hilton College of Hotel and Restaurant Management ($2,187,500) see Hilton Foundation, Conrad N.

University of Houston/Department of Drama ($15,000) see Lewis Foundation, Lillian Kaiser

University of Houston — establishment of the Jesse H. Jones Business Leadership Development Program ($1,333,333) see Houston Endowment

University of Houston Law Center ($37,500) see O'Quinn Foundation, John M. and Nancy C.

University of Houston Law Foundation ($2,500) see Hofheinz Foundation, Irene Cafcalas

University of Houston Law Foundation — support Moot Court Term fund ($5,000) see Kayser Foundation

University of Houston — Lillie and Roy Cullen endowment ($6,000,000) see Cullen Foundation

University of Houston System — grant for Creative Partnerships campaign ($50,000) see Halliburton Co.

University of Mary Hardin — Baylor ($5,000) see Lux Trust, Dr. Konrad and Clara

University Medical Center — 3rd-year payment on five-year commitment ($50,000) see AMR Corp.

University of North Texas ($3,900) see Grant Thornton

University of North Texas ($3,000) see Mayborn Foundation, Frank W.

University of North Texas Foundation ($70,000) see Haggar Foundation

University of North Texas Foundation — scholarships ($68,000) see Haggar Foundation

University of St. Thomas ($10,000) see Burkitt Foundation

University of St. Thomas ($5,000) see Burkitt Foundation

University of St. Thomas — defray cost of science building construction ($400,000) see Cullen Foundation

University of St. Thomas ($50,000) see Graco

University of St. Thomas ($75,000) see Lyons Foundation

University of St. Thomas ($30,000) see Strake Foundation

University of St. Thomas — education, science lab ($30,000) see Hankamer Foundation, Curtis and Doris K.

University of Texas ($10,000) see Central & South West Services

University of Texas ($50,800) see Fair Foundation, R. W.

University of Texas ($12,000) see Goldwyn Foundation, Samuel

University of Texas — endow chair for distinguished professor in biology ($500,000) see Halsell Foundation, Ewing

University of Texas ($101,000) see Herzog Foundation, Carl J.

University of Texas — research and training in the field of skin cancer immunology ($32,700) see Kade Foundation, Max

University of Texas ($193,318) see KPMG Peat Marwick

University of Texas ($5,500) see Miller-Mellor Association

University of Texas ($27,950) see Owsley Foundation, Alvin and Lucy

University of Texas ($43,466) see Temple-Inland

University of Texas — scholarships ($279,086) see Terry Foundation

University of Texas ($15,000) see Vanneck-Bailey Foundation

University of Texas ($31,000) see Wal-Mart Stores

University of Texas ($12,500) see Wunsch Foundation

University of Texas at Arlington ($14,100) see Armstrong Foundation

University of Texas at Arlington ($34,000) see Texas Instruments

University of Texas at Austin ($21,000) see Baker Foundation, R. C.

University of Texas at Austin ($30,000) see Bosque Foundation

University of Texas at Austin — athletic chair endowment ($33,000) see Cain Foundation, Effie and Wofford

University of Texas at Austin ($25,000) see Cameron Foundation, Harry S. and Isabel C.

University of Texas — Austin ($25,000) see Dresser Industries

University of Texas at Austin ($15,000) see Eckerd Corp., Jack

University of Texas at Austin ($500) see Foundation for Iranian Studies

University of Texas at Austin ($12,500) see Grant Thornton

University of Texas at Austin ($16,965) see Haas Foundation, Paul and Mary

University of Texas at Austin ($30,500) see Hugg Trust, Leoia W. and Charles H.

University of Texas-Austin ($662,000) see Intel Corp.

University of Texas at Austin — endowment of theatre ($250,000) see McCullough Foundation, Ralph H. and Ruth J.

University of Texas at Austin ($6,200) see Moncrief Foundation, William A. and Elizabeth B.

University of Texas Austin ($650,000) see O'Donnell Foundation

University of Texas at Austin ($394,450) see Perkins-Prothro Foundation

University of Texas at Austin ($5,000) see Potts and Sibley Foundation

University of Texas at Austin ($66,666) see Seay Charitable Trust, Sarah M. and Charles E.

University of Texas at Austin ($20,700) see Seay Charitable Trust, Sarah M. and Charles E.

University of Texas at Austin ($150,000) see Shell Oil Co.

University of Texas at Austin — engineering education excellence ($521,260) see Temple Foundation, T. L. L.

University of Texas at Austin — support for research on the history and potential of black American entrepreneurs ($54,655) see Donner Foundation, William H.

University of Texas at Austin, Center for Research on Communication Technology and Society — support for telecommunications forum "The Coming Intelligent Network" ($37,325) see RGK Foundation

University of Texas at Austin — Clark field improvements ($50,000) see Cain Foundation, Effie and Wofford

University of Texas at Austin — supports minority Ph.D. candidates preparing for careers in college and university teaching ($105,000) see Danforth Foundation

University of Texas, Austin, Population Research Center — support of research in or on developing countries and for foreign student training ($650,000) see Hewlett Foundation, William and Flora

University of Texas at Austin School of Law ($200,000) see Anderson Foundation, M. D.

University of Texas at Austin — "The Home Economics of Single Parent Households" ($182,321) see Sage Foundation, Russell

University of Texas Cancer Center ($25,000) see Adler Foundation

University of Texas — for study of marker potential of transforming growth factor alpha in breast and colon carcinomas; for study of vascular targeting: a new approach to the therapy of solid tumors ($102,443) see Pardee Foundation, Elsa U.

University of Texas Century Club ($13,650) see Perkins Foundation, Joe and Lois

University of Texas College of Business Administration ($13,925) see King Ranch

University of Texas at Dallas ($100,000) see Hoblitzelle Foundation

University of Texas at Dallas ($4,000) see Leonhardt Foundation, Frederick H.

University of Texas at Dallas ($4,000) see Potts and Sibley Foundation

University of Texas at Dallas ($33,000) see Redman Foundation

University of Texas at Dallas ($25,000) see Texas Instruments

University of Texas at Dallas ($20,000) see Tyler Corp.

University of Texas at Dallas ($31,000) see Zale Foundation

University of Texas at Dallas — Caruth Chair School of Management; final payment on commitment ($150,000) see Hillcrest Foundation

University of Texas at Dallas — for remodeling of McDermott Library ($66,000) see McDermott Foundation, Eugene

University of Texas Dental Branch ($200,000) see Anderson Foundation, M. D.

University of Texas at El Paso ($75,000) see Burlington Resources

University of Texas at El Paso ($8,500) see Hervey Foundation

University of Texas at El Paso — music department ($16,000) see Huthsteiner Fine Arts Trust

University of Texas-El Paso ($1,850,671) see Kellogg Foundation, W. K.

University of Texas at El Paso — to support an investigation into the contamination of ground water from agricultural irrigation with sewage ($50,000) see Tinker Foundation

University of Texas — Engineering Foundation Scholarship Fund ($1,025,000) see Cockrell Foundation

University of Texas Health Center ($10,500) see Vaughn Foundation

University of Texas Health — Dallas ($20,000) see Cimarron Foundation

University of Texas Health Science Center — nursing scholarship ($25,000) see Brackenridge Foundation, George W.

University of Texas Health Science Center ($130,000) see Cain Foundation, Gordon and Mary

University of Texas Health Science Center ($17,585) see Dunn Research Foundation, John S.

University of Texas Health Science Center — vasoactive peptides in renal transplant ($5,000) see South Plains Foundation

University of Texas Health Science Center-Houston ($150,000) see Anderson Foundation, M. D.

University of Texas Health Science Center at Houston ($75,000) see Ellwood Foundation

University of Texas Health Science Center San Antonio — medical research ($262,325) see Mathers Charitable Foundation, G. Harold and Leila Y.

University of Texas Health Science Center at San Antonio ($15,000) see West Texas Corp., J. M.

University of Texas Health Science Center at San Antonio, Department of Medicine — support for medical research project "Antibodies to Retroviral Proteins in Autoimmunity" ($81,000) see RGK Foundation

University of Texas — J.J. Pickle Scholarship Program ($25,000) see Zachry Co., H. B.

University of Texas Law School ($75,000) see White Trust, G. R.

University of Texas Law School Foundation ($50,000) see Hobby Foundation

University of Texas M. D. Anderson Cancer Center ($600,000) see Exxon Corp.

University of Texas M. D. Anderson Cancer Center — toward the cost of a comprehensive chemoprevention research program on the study of cancers of the lung, head, neck and esophagus ($200,000) see Rippel Foundation, Fannie E.

University of Texas-M.D. Anderson Cancer Center ($838,497) see Dunn Research Foundation, John S.

University of Texas Marine Science — Wildlife Conservation ($20,000) see Kleberg Foundation for Wildlife Conservation, Caesar

University of Texas — mathematics/statistics lab ($50,000) see MCI Communications Corp.

University of Texas — McDonald Observatory ($25,000) see Zachry Co., H. B.

University of Texas Medical Branch — student scholarship fund ($7,500) see McGovern Foundation, John P.

University of Texas Medical Branch ($10,000) see O'Connor Foundation, Kathryn

University of Texas Medical Branch at Galveston ($18,000) see Vaughn Foundation

University of Texas Medical Branch at Galveston — Magnetocencephaolographic Study of Reorganization of Brain Foundation in Recover from Aphasia ($40,692) see Mobility Foundation

University of Texas Medical Branch Galveston Science and Engineering Fair ($500) see Northen, Mary Moody

University of Texas — 1991 Medical Science Scholar ($108,000) see Culpeper Foundation, Charles E.

University of Texas Press ($70,000) see Plumsock Fund

University of Texas at San Antonio ($15,390) see Haas Foundation, Paul and Mary

University of Texas at San Antonio ($64,000) see Zachry Co., H. B.

University of Texas School of Law ($25,000) see Brown and C. A. Lupton Foundation, T. J.

University of Texas School of Law ($25,000) see Seay Charitable Trust, Sarah M. and Charles E.

University of Texas School of Nursing ($15,000) see Veritas Foundation

University of Texas Southwestern Medical Center ($150,000) see Biological Humanics Foundation

University of Texas Southwestern Medical Center ($33,358) see Biological Humanics Foundation

University of Texas Southwestern Medical Center ($16,000) see Biological Humanics Foundation

University of Texas Southwestern Medical Center ($100,000) see Bordeaux Foundation

University of Texas Southwestern Medical Center — research ($360,000) see Fikes Foundation, Leland

University of Texas Southwestern Medical Center — molecular cardiology research ($300,000) see Fikes Foundation, Leland

University of Texas Southwestern Medical Center — research ($75,000) see Fikes Foundation, Leland

University of Texas Southwestern Medical Center — research ($64,922) see Fikes Foundation, Leland

University of Texas Southwestern Medical Center ($6,200,000) see O'Donnell Foundation

University of Texas-Southwestern Medical Center at Dallas ($500,000) see Bosque Foundation

University of Texas Southwestern Medical Center at Dallas ($300,000) see Contran Corp.

University of Texas Southwestern Medical Center at Dallas ($300,000) see Contran Corp.

University of Texas Southwestern Medical Center at Dallas ($26,730) see Halliburton Co.

University of Texas Southwestern Medical Center at Dallas — medical research ($343,750) see Perot Foundation

University of Texas Southwestern Medical Center at Dallas — medical research ($325,000) see Perot Foundation

University of Texas Southwestern Medical Center at Dallas — medical research ($325,000) see Perot Foundation

University of Texas Southwestern Medical Center at Dallas — medical research ($287,500) see Perot Foundation

University of Texas Southwestern Medical Center at Dallas — medical research ($192,000) see Perot Foundation

University of Texas Southwestern Medical Center at Dallas — medical research ($192,000) see Perot Foundation

University of Texas Southwestern Medical Center at Dallas — medical research ($192,000) see Perot Foundation

University of Texas Southwestern Medical Center at Dallas — medical research ($143,875) see Perot Foundation

University of Texas Southwestern Medical Center at Dallas — four distinguished chairs at the Simmons Comprehensive Cancer Center ($300,000) see Contran Corp.

University of Texas Southwestern Medical Center at Dallas — four distinguished chairs at the Simmons Comprehensive Cancer Center ($300,000) see Contran Corp.

University of Texas Southwestern Medical School ($850,000) see Moss Heart Trust, Harry S.

University of Texas Southwestern Medical School ($22,000) see Redman Foundation

University of Texas System Cancer Center — to establish a fund to provide support for innovative cancer research ($6,327,369) see Kleberg, Jr. and Helen C. Kleberg Foundation, Robert J.

University of Texas System Cancer Center/M.D. Anderson Hospital and Tumor Institute ($1,000,000) see Kimberly-Clark Corp.

University of Texas System — M. D. Anderson Cancer Center; Golden Jubilee campaign ($1,000,000) see Temple Foundation, T. L. L.

University of Texas at Tyler ($2,000) see Heath Foundation, Ed and Mary

University of Texas at Tyler ($3,000) see Mayborn Foundation, Frank W.

Ursuline Academy ($10,000) see Green Foundation

Ursuline Academy ($29,313) see Haggerty Foundation

Ursuline Academy — sound system ($10,000) see Schmidlapp Trust No. 2, Jacob G.

Ursuline Academy of Dallas ($3,000) see Tyler Corp.

USO, South Texas ($7,500) see Behmann Brothers Foundation

UT Southwestern Medical Center ($250,000) see Zale Foundation

UTMB ($31,250) see Kempner Fund, Harris and Eliza

UTMB/Jeane B. Kempner Scholarship/Fellowship Program ($65,000) see Kempner Fund, Harris and Eliza

UTMB/Jeane B. Kempner Scholarship/Fellowship Program ($60,000) see Kempner Fund, Harris and Eliza

Valley Players ($10,000) see Humphreys Foundation

Valley Zoological Society ($160,000) see Lightner Sams Foundation

Valley Zoological Society ($76,000) see Sams Foundation, Earl C.

Van Cliburn Foundation ($4,000) see Fuller Foundation

Van Cliburn Foundation ($11,500) see Garvey Texas Foundation

Van Cliburn Foundation ($25,000) see Maddox Trust, Web

Van Cliburn Piano Competition ($6,500) see Walsh Foundation

Variety Club Houston — general fund ($5,000) see Foothills Foundation

Vaughn House ($3,500) see Veritas Foundation

Vernon Regional Junior College ($5,000) see Waggoner Foundation, E. Paul and Helen Buck

Vernon Regional Junior College ($15,000) see White Foundation, Erle and Emma

Victim's Outreach see Centex Corp.

Victoria College ($50,000) see South Texas Charitable Foundation

Victoria Preservation ($20,000) see South Texas Charitable Foundation

Visiting Nurse Association ($16,667) see Beasley Foundation, Theodore and Beulah

Visiting Nurse Association ($5,000) see Davis Foundation, Ken W.

Visiting Nurse Association ($100,000) see Haggerty Foundation

Visiting Nurse Association — for new facilities ($60,000) see McDermott Foundation, Eugene

Visiting Nurse Association ($12,000) see McKee Foundation, Robert E. and Evelyn

Visiting Nurse Association — capital campaign to purchase building to house operations and Meals on Wheels kitchen ($100,000) see Contran Corp.

Visiting Nurses Association ($1,000) see Bordeaux Foundation

Visiting Nurses Association ($100,000) see Constantin Foundation

Visiting Nurses Association ($25,000) see Moss Heart Trust, Harry S.

Visiting Nurses Association ($50,000) see Sharp Foundation, Charles S. and Ruth C.

Visiting Nurses Association of Texas ($29,450) see Orleans Trust, Carrie S.

Vogel Alcove ($25,000) see Zale Foundation

Volunteer Center — points of light partnership ($50,000) see McGovern Fund for the Behavioral Sciences

Volunteer Center — Points of Light Partnership ($25,000) see McGovern Foundation, John P.

Volunteer Service Council for Wichita Falls State Hospital ($5,000) see Priddy Foundation

Waco Christian School ($175,925) see Meyer Family Foundation, Paul J.

Walter H. Hightower Foundation — for the New Mexico Boys Ranch ($35,209) see Hightower Foundation, Walter

Waterview Congregation — Grenada Medical Mission ($5,000) see Bell Trust

Weatherford Business Alliance ($10,000) see JMK-A M Micallef Charitable Foundation

Wee Care Child Care Center ($150,000) see Mayer Foundation, James and Eva

Wellway Center — drug abuse program ($10,000) see Beasley Foundation, Theodore and Beulah

Wesley Community Center — operating expenses ($15,000) see Craig Foundation, J. Paul

Wesley Rankin Community Center ($17,000) see Redman Foundation

West Dallas Multipurpose Center ($4,000) see Orleans Trust, Carrie S.

West Jefferson County Volunteers ($28,600) see Dishman Charitable Foundation Trust, H. E. and Kate

West Side Lions Youth Activity ($8,500) see Armstrong Foundation

West Side Optimist Club ($200) see Luttrell Trust

West Texas Boys Ranch ($3,500) see Thagard Foundation

West Texas Rehabilitation Center — to expand and renovate facilities and replace equipment ($250,000) see Dodge Jones Foundation

Westminster Presbyterian Church ($30,000) see Hofstetter Trust, Bessie

Wheatley High School — donation of weight room equipment see Tenneco

Texas *(cont.)*

Wichita Falls Area Food Bank ($5,000) see Bridwell Foundation, J. S.

Wichita Falls District, First United Methodist Church ($1,000) see Perkins-Prothro Foundation

Wichita Falls Faith Mission ($5,000) see Bridwell Foundation, J. S.

Wichita Falls Hospice ($40,000) see White Foundation, Erle and Emma

Wichita Falls Hospice Trust ($100,000) see Perkins-Prothro Foundation

Wichita Falls Independent School District ($153,168) see West Foundation

Wichita Falls Independent School District ($25,000) see West Foundation

Wilbarger County Welfare ($5,000) see Waggoner Foundation, E. Paul and Helen Buck

William Marsh Rice University — continuation of the matching grant for the endowment ($2,645,000) see Brown Foundation

William Marsh Rice University — toward construction of the George R. Brown Hall and the Alice Pratt Brown Hall ($1,000,000) see Brown Foundation

Willow River Farms ($5,000) see Lowe Foundation

Willow Springs Baptist Church ($12,000) see Griffin Foundation, Rosa May

Wilson N. Jones Hospital — nursing program ($25,000) see Mayor Foundation, Oliver Dewey

Winston School ($5,000) see Jonsson Foundation

Woman's Forum Trust Fund ($10,000) see White Foundation, Erle and Emma

Women's Christian Home ($5,000) see Lowe Foundation

Women's Crisis Center ($10,000) see Overlake Foundation

Womens Haven ($3,000) see Edwards Foundation, Jes

Women's Haven of Tarrant County ($5,000) see Tandy Foundation, David L.

Woodlands Center for the Performing Arts — sponsorship of the Cynthia Woods Mitchell Pavilion-music of Andrew Lloyd Weber and Cole Porter ($20,000) see First Interstate Bank of Texas, N.A.

World Affairs Council of San Antonio ($16,000) see Zachry Co., H. B.

World Bible School ($7,500) see Stephens Foundation Trust

World Christian Broadcasting ($7,900) see Stephens Foundation Trust

World Hunger Relief — development ($5,000) see Edwards Foundation, Jes

YMCA ($100,000) see Beasley Foundation, Theodore and Beulah

YMCA ($125,000) see Belo Corp., A.H.

YMCA ($250,000) see Bosque Foundation

YMCA ($5,000) see Craig Foundation, J. Paul

YMCA ($25,000) see Duncan Foundation, Lillian H. and C. W.

YMCA ($20,000) see FINA, Inc.

YMCA ($115,000) see Fort Worth Star Telegram

YMCA ($5,000) see Hervey Foundation

YMCA ($1,000) see Hofstetter Trust, Bessie

YMCA ($5,000) see Jonsson Foundation

YMCA ($5,000) see Keith Foundation Trust, Ben E.

YMCA ($100,000) see McCune Charitable Trust, John R.

YMCA ($7,000) see McKee Foundation, Robert E. and Evelyn

YMCA ($7,000) see McKee Foundation, Robert E. and Evelyn

YMCA ($100,000) see Moss Heart Trust, Harry S.

YMCA ($10,000) see Owen Trust, B. B.

YMCA ($7,500) see Semmes Foundation

YMCA ($20,000) see Seymour Foundation, W. L. and Louise E.

YMCA ($3,000) see Steinhagen Benevolent Trust, B. A. and Elinor

YMCA ($10,500) see Stemmons Foundation

YMCA ($11,000) see Waggoner Charitable Trust, Crystelle

YMCA ($500) see Ward Co., Joe L.

YMCA of Abilene — to construct a second facility at Redbud Park ($275,000) see Dodge Jones Foundation

YMCA Camp Grady Spruce ($100,000) see Constantin Foundation

YMCA-East Branch ($21,000) see Bridwell Foundation, J. S.

YMCA of Greater El Paso ($100,000) see Burlington Resources

YMCA Greater Houston Area ($30,700) see Baker Foundation, R. C.

YMCA of the Greater Houston Area ($80,000) see Enron Corp.

YMCA of Metropolitan Dallas ($125,000) see Hoblitzelle Foundation

YMCA of Metropolitan Dallas ($100,000) see JCPenney Co.

YMCA of Metropolitan Dallas ($200,000) see Sturgis Charitable and Educational Trust, Roy and Christine

YMCA of Metropolitan Dallas — gift to the 21st Century Campaign, to complete funding for a new child care center, and for facility refurbishments ($252,950) see Meadows Foundation

YMCA of San Antonio — construction education classroom at Camp Flaming Arrow ($65,000) see Halsell Foundation, Ewing

Young Audiences ($10,000) see Stemmons Foundation

Young Audiences of Houston ($5,000) see Humphreys Foundation

Young Life — operating expenses ($5,000) see Craig Foundation, J. Paul

Young Life ($2,500) see Dishman Charitable Foundation Trust, H. E. and Kate

Young Life ($19,625) see Meyer Family Foundation, Paul J.

Young Life ($2,500) see Steinhagen Benevolent Trust, B. A. and Elinor

Youth Alternatives ($10,000) see Halff Foundation, G. A. C.

Youth Home of Victoria — to create shelter to handle any level of care ($100,000) see Johnson Foundation, M. G. and Lillie A.

Youth Young Adult Fellowship ($29,000) see Temple-Inland

YWAM-Mercy Ships ($50,000) see Biddle Foundation, Margaret T.

YWCA ($10,000) see Beasley Foundation, Theodore and Beulah

YWCA — for renovation and construction ($312,500) see Hall Foundation

YWCA ($20,000) see Waggoner Charitable Trust, Crystelle

YWCA ($11,000) see Weaver Foundation, Gil and Dody

YWCA of Metropolitan Dallas ($50) see Bordeaux Foundation

Zachary Scott Theatre Center — two performances of "A Christmas Carol" ($3,500) see Trull Foundation

Zale Lipshy Hospital ($200,000) see Gill Foundation, Pauline Allen

Zale Lipsny University Hospital ($10,000) see Winston Research Foundation, Harry

Zoo Friends of Houston — Wildlife Conservation ($5,000) see Kleberg Foundation for Wildlife Conservation, Caesar

Zoological Society ($50,000) see Ferguson Family Foundation, Kittie and Rugeley

Zoological Society ($2,500) see Moss Foundation, Harry S.

Zoological Society of Houston ($117,000) see Lowe Foundation

Utah

Air Force Heritage Foundation of Utah ($75,000) see Browning Charitable Foundation, Val A.

American Indian Services ($14,000) see Callister Foundation, Paul Q.

Ballet West ($10,000) see Caine Charitable Foundation, Marie Eccles

Ballet West ($6,000) see Dee Foundation, Annie Taylor

Ballet West ($40,000) see Eccles Foundation, Marriner S.

Ballet West ($7,500) see Michael Foundation, Herbert I. and Elsa B.

Ballet West — to fund live Utah Symphony music for Ballet West performances ($250,000) see Eccles Foundation, George S. and Dolores Dore

Benson Institute — farmer assistance ($135,000) see Swim Foundation, Arthur L.

Boy Scouts of America ($500) see Huntsman Foundation, Jon and Karen

Boys and Girls Clubs of Greater Salt Lake ($37,000) see Eccles Foundation, Marriner S.

Brigham Young University ($205,000) see Barlow Family Foundation, Milton A. and Gloria G.

Brigham Young University ($100,000) see Burns Foundation, Fritz B.

Brigham Young University ($5,700) see First Security Corp. (Salt Lake City, Utah)

Brigham Young University ($3,000) see Grant Thornton

Brigham Young University ($549,812) see Hewlett-Packard Co.

Brigham Young University — scholarship fund ($25,000) see Kingsley Foundation, Lewis A.

Brigham Young University ($10,000) see Reynolds Foundation, Donald W.

Brigham Young University ($2,000) see Sargent Foundation, Newell B.

Brigham Young University ($25,000) see Sunmark Capital Corp.

Brigham Young University ($10,000) see Wilson Foundation, H. W.

Brigham Young University Cancer Research Center ($36,000) see Bireley Foundation

Brigham Young University-Marriott School of Management — curriculum development ($25,000) see Kemper National Insurance Cos.

Capitol Arts Alliance — to restore the historic Capitol Theatre in Logan, Utah ($2,000,000) see Eccles Foundation, George S. and Dolores Dore

Cathedral of Madeleine ($10,000) see Bamberger and John Ernest Bamberger Memorial Foundation, Ruth Eleanor

Cathedral of the Madeleine ($10,000) see Huntsman Foundation, Jon and Karen

Catholic Evangelization Committee ($8,000) see Price Foundation, Lucien B. and Katherine E.

Center for Women and Children in Crisis ($25,000) see Bireley Foundation

Children and Youth Services, Utah Boys Ranch ($5,000) see Michael Foundation, Herbert I. and Elsa B.

Children's Aid Society of Utah ($4,000) see Dee Foundation, Annie Taylor

Children's Center ($20,000) see Bireley Foundation

Church of Jesus Christ Latter Day Saints ($25,000) see Barlow Family Foundation, Milton A. and Gloria G.

Church of Jesus Christ Latter Day Saints ($25,000) see Woods Foundation, James H.

Church of Latter Day Saints ($187,500) see Peery Foundation

City of Salt Lake ($100,000) see PacifiCorp

City of Salt Lake ($50,000) see PacifiCorp

College of Eastern Utah ($1,675) see First Security Corp. (Salt Lake City, Utah)

Community Connection of Ogden ($10,000) see Dee Foundation, Lawrence T. and Janet T.

Community Services ($3,000) see Callister Foundation, Paul Q.

Corporation of Presiding Bishop ($155,000) see Swim Foundation, Arthur L.

Cottonwood Alta View Health Care Foundation — third installment of a grant of $300,000, payable in five equal installments in 1989-93, inclusive, to construct a building and therapy pool for the Back Institute/Work Hardening Program at Cottonwood Hospital ($60,000) see Union Pacific Corp.

Deseret International — medical care ($5,000) see Swim Foundation, Arthur L.

Diocese of Sale Lake City ($15,000) see Price Foundation, Lucien B. and Katherine E.

Dixie College ($15,000) see Barlow Family Foundation, Milton A. and Gloria G.

Dixie College ($75,000) see Browning Charitable Foundation, Val A.

Dixie College ($3,000) see Callister Foundation, Paul Q.

Enable ($26,000) see Swanson Family Foundation, Dr. W.C.

Faith Baptist Church ($4,500) see Oldham Little Church Foundation

FARMS ($1,000) see Wilbur Foundation, Marguerite Eyer

Festival of American West ($5,000) see Browning Charitable Foundation, Val A.

Hansen Planetarium ($20,000) see Dumke Foundation, Dr. Ezekiel R. and Edna Wattis

Heritage Society — genealogical research ($6,000) see Swim Foundation, Arthur L.

Holy Cross Hospital — funding for acquisition of neonatal intensive care equipment ($61,778) see Eccles Charitable Foundation, Willard L.

Holy Cross Hospital ($50,000) see Eccles Foundation, Marriner S.

Holy Cross Hospital see Packaging Corporation of America

Holy Cross Hospital Foundation ($10,000) see Moore Foundation, Martha G.

Holy Cross Hospital Foundation — Diabetes Research ($30,000) see Margolis Charitable Foundation for Medical Research, Ben B. and Iris M.

Holy Cross Hospital Nurse Refresher Course ($15,639) see Bamberger and John Ernest Bamberger Memorial Foundation, Ruth Eleanor

Hospice of Northern Utah — funding for full time nurse ($40,000) see Eccles Charitable Foundation, Willard L.

Judge Memorial Catholic High School — to improve, renovate and expand the chemistry, physics and language laboratories ($265,000) see Eccles Foundation, George S. and Dolores Dore

Judge Memorial High School ($10,000) see Bamberger and John Ernest Bamberger Memorial Foundation, Ruth Eleanor

Judge Memorial High School ($17,000) see Price

Foundation, Lucien B. and Katherine E.

KUED Channel 7 ($10,000) see Caine Charitable Foundation, Marie Eccles

Latter-Day Saints Church ($110,000) see Callister Foundation, Paul Q.

Latter Day Saints Church Trust Scholarship ($50,000) see Marriott Foundation, J. Willard

Latter Day Saints Hospital-Deseret Foundation ($50,000) see Eccles Foundation, Marriner S.

LDS Business College — capital improvements ($30,000) see Swim Foundation, Arthur L.

Lowell Bennion Community Service Center ($20,000) see Borchard Foundation, Albert and Elaine

McKay-Dee Hospital Foundation ($100,000) see Dee Foundation, Lawrence T. and Janet T.

McKay-Dee Hospital Foundation ($55,000) see Stewart Educational Foundation, Donnell B. and Elizabeth Dee Shaw

Nature Conservancy ($10,000) see Dee Foundation, Lawrence T. and Janet T.

Notre Dame School ($10,000) see Price Foundation, Lucien B. and Katherine E.

Ogden Arts Commission ($7,500) see Dumke Foundation, Dr. Ezekiel R. and Edna Wattis

Ogden Discovery Center ($10,000) see Stewart Educational Foundation, Donnell B. and Elizabeth Dee Shaw

Ogden Nature Center ($5,000) see Dee Foundation, Annie Taylor

Ogden Nature Center ($2,000) see Stewart Educational Foundation, Donnell B. and Elizabeth Dee Shaw

Ogden School Foundation ($46,000) see Swanson Family Foundation, Dr. W.C.

Ogden Surgical Society ($15,000) see Dumke Foundation, Dr. Ezekiel R. and Edna Wattis

Ogden Surgical Society ($1,000) see Dumke Foundation, Dr. Ezekiel R. and Edna Wattis

Ogden Symphony Ballet Association ($25,050) see Browning Charitable Foundation, Val A.

Ogden Symphony Ballet Association ($7,500) see Dee Foundation, Lawrence T. and Janet T.

Ogden Symphony Ballet Foundation ($10,000) see Stewart Educational Foundation, Donnell B. and Elizabeth Dee Shaw

Ogden Union Station ($5,000) see Dee Foundation, Lawrence T. and Janet T.

Ogden Weber AVC Foundation ($1,000) see Stewart Educational Foundation, Donnell B. and Elizabeth Dee Shaw

Park City Christian Fellowship Church ($15,000) see McCarthy Foundation, John and Margaret

Planned Parenthood Federation of America ($5,000) see Dee Foundation, Lawrence T. and Janet T.

Planned Parenthood Federation of America ($2,500) see Dumke Foundation, Dr. Ezekiel R. and Edna Wattis

Planned Parenthood Federation of America ($4,500) see Harris Foundation, William H. and Mattie Wattis

Planned Parenthood-Utah ($50,000) see Eccles Foundation, Marriner S.

Primary Children's Hospital ($1,000) see Callister Foundation, Paul Q.

Primary Children's Hospital ($25,000) see Margolis Charitable Foundation for Medical Research, Ben B. and Iris M.

Primary Children's Hospital ($1,500) see Sargent Foundation, Newell B.

Primary Children's Hospital ($40,000) see Swanson Family Foundation, Dr. W.C.

Primary Children's Medical Center ($30,500) see Eccles Foundation, Marriner S.

Primary Children's Medical Center Foundation — funding for 30 bed Medical/Surgical Unit for infants ($75,000) see Eccles Charitable Foundation, Willard L.

Primary Children's Medical Center in Salt Lake City — to help build a new hospital serving the Intermountain West ($25,000) see Boise Cascade Corp.

Repertory Dance Theatre ($5,000) see Dee Foundation, Lawrence T. and Janet T.

Ririe Woodbury Dance Company ($4,000) see Dee Foundation, Annie Taylor

Roy Historical Foundation ($100,000) see Swanson Family Foundation, Dr. W.C.

Rural Health Care Foundation — rural health care ($100,000) see Swim Foundation, Arthur L.

St. Anne's Center ($50,000) see Browning Charitable Foundation, Val A.

St. Annes Center ($90,000) see Swanson Family Foundation, Dr. W.C.

St. Benedict's Foundation ($38,000) see Browning Charitable Foundation, Val A.

St. Benedict's Foundation — acquisition of equipment for Willard L. Eccles Eye Center ($101,450) see Eccles Charitable Foundation, Willard L.

St. Mark's School ($3,000) see Van Evera Foundation, Dewitt Caroline

St. Peters School ($25,000) see Swanson Family Foundation, Dr. W.C.

Salt Lake City Community College ($5,000) see Callister Foundation, Paul Q.

Salt Lake Olympic Organizing Committee ($50,000) see Bechtel Group

Salvation Army ($5,000) see Michael Foundation, Herbert I. and Elsa B.

Shriners Hospital ($5,000) see Bamberger and John Ernest Bamberger Memorial Foundation, Ruth Eleanor

Shriners Hospital ($1,000) see Callister Foundation, Paul Q.

Snow College Scholarship ($10,000) see Peery Foundation

South Utah University ($2,000) see Callister Foundation, Paul Q.

Southern Utah State College ($1,675) see First Security Corp. (Salt Lake City, Utah)

Southern Utah Wilderness Alliance — finance intern program ($4,000) see Harris Foundation, William H. and Mattie Wattis

Sundance Institute for Film and Television ($10,000) see Spiritus Gladius Foundation

Travelers Aid Society ($20,000) see Borchard Foundation, Albert and Elaine

Unicorn Theatre ($25,210) see Caine Charitable Foundation, Marie Eccles

Union Station Foundation ($1,000) see Stewart Educational Foundation, Donnell B. and Elizabeth Dee Shaw

United Way of the Great Salt Lake Area ($126,424) see PacifiCorp

University of Utah ($133,986) see Bugher Foundation

University of Utah ($3,750) see Dee Foundation, Annie Taylor

University of Utah ($47,500) see Dee Foundation, Lawrence T. and Janet T.

University of Utah ($47,500) see Dumke Foundation, Dr. Ezekiel R. and Edna Wattis

University of Utah ($25,000) see Dumke Foundation, Dr. Ezekiel R. and Edna Wattis

University of Utah ($8,547) see Dumke Foundation, Dr. Ezekiel R. and Edna Wattis

University of Utah ($3,000) see Dumke Foundation, Dr. Ezekiel R. and Edna Wattis

University of Utah — for department of opthalmology ($62,500) see Eccles Charitable Foundation, Willard L.

University of Utah ($5,700) see First Security Corp. (Salt Lake City, Utah)

University of Utah ($10,000) see Harris Foundation, William H. and Mattie Wattis

University of Utah ($10,000) see Huntsman Foundation, Jon and Karen

University of Utah ($15,000) see Kingsley Foundation, Lewis A.

University of Utah ($30,000) see Margolis Charitable Foundation for Medical Research, Ben B. and Iris M.

University of Utah ($15,000) see Margolis Charitable Foundation for Medical Research, Ben B. and Iris M.

University of Utah ($15,000) see Margolis Charitable Foundation for Medical Research, Ben B. and Iris M.

University of Utah ($15,000) see Margolis Charitable Foundation for Medical Research, Ben B. and Iris M.

University of Utah ($5,000) see Margolis Charitable Foundation for Medical Research, Ben B. and Iris M.

University of Utah ($80,000) see Smith Fund, George D.

University of Utah, Artistic Support in Oponeer Theatre Company ($10,000) see Michael Foundation, Herbert I. and Elsa B.

University of Utah — to purchase of Beckman DU-70 spectrophotometer ($10,000) see Michael Foundation, Herbert I. and Elsa B.

University of Utah College of Law Library ($10,000) see Michael Foundation, Herbert I. and Elsa B.

University of Utah, Department of Biology ($26,000) see Childs Memorial Fund for Medical Research, Jane Coffin

University of Utah — Department of Dance; to support the American Dance Festival West ($200,000) see Eccles Foundation, George S. and Dolores Dore

University of Utah — Department of Human Genetics; to support general programs, fellowships and visiting scholars ($700,000) see Eccles Foundation, George S. and Dolores Dore

University of Utah — Department of Ophthalmology; to establish the Center of Excellence in Ophthalmic Education ($500,000) see Eccles Foundation, George S. and Dolores Dore

University of Utah — funding for development of DWA Diagnostic Laboratory ($112,850) see Eccles Charitable Foundation, Willard L.

University of Utah, Facility Items, Broadcast Center ($5,000) see Michael Foundation, Herbert I. and Elsa B.

University of Utah (GARN Institute) ($50,000) see Columbia Savings Charitable Foundation

University of Utah Health Services — for the eye center ($100,000) see Eccles Charitable Foundation, Willard L.

University of Utah — funding for development of an in-vitro testing of newborn/infant/pediatric artificial heart ($76,095) see Eccles Charitable Foundation, Willard L.

University of Utah — KUED-Channel 7 ($40,000) see Eccles Foundation, Marriner S.

University of Utah — Law Library Endowment Fund ($10,000) see Michael Foundation, Herbert I. and Elsa B.

University of Utah Medical Center Development Fund — diabetes research ($125,000) see Treadwell Foundation, Nora Eccles

University of Utah, MESA/MEP Program Upgrade, scholarships ($7,500) see Michael Foundation, Herbert I. and Elsa B.

University of Utah N.E. Harrison Cardiovascular Research and Training Institute — cardiovascular electrophy ($800,000) see Treadwell Foundation, Nora Eccles

University of Utah N.E. Harrison Cardiovascular Research and Training Institute — biochemistry ($200,000) see Treadwell Foundation, Nora Eccles

University of Utah N.E. Harrison Cardiovascular Research and Training Institute — cardiovascular flow ($200,000) see Treadwell Foundation, Nora Eccles

University of Utah N.E. Harrison Cardiovascular Research and Training Institute — cardiovascular pharm ($200,000) see Treadwell Foundation, Nora Eccles

University of Utah N.E. Harrison Cardiovascular Research and Training Institute — cardio-electric mapping ($125,000) see Treadwell Foundation, Nora Eccles

University of Utah — Utah Museum of Fine Arts ($100,000) see Eccles Foundation, Marriner S.

University of Utal Medical Center — arthritis research ($125,000) see Treadwell Foundation, Nora Eccles

Utah Bible Mission ($25,000) see Lamb Foundation, Kirkland S. and Rena B.

Utah Council of Blind ($5,000) see Bamberger and John Ernest Bamberger Memorial Foundation, Ruth Eleanor

Utah Department of Health — for support of the baby your baby program ($125,000) see Eccles Charitable Foundation, Willard L.

Utah Downs Syndrome Foundation ($5,000) see Stewart Educational Foundation, Donnell B. and Elizabeth Dee Shaw

Utah FolkLife Center ($10,000) see Falcon Foundation

Utah Girl Scout Council ($2,000) see Dee Foundation, Annie Taylor

Utah Girl Scout Council ($20,000) see Stewart Educational Foundation, Donnell B. and Elizabeth Dee Shaw

Utah Girl Scout Council ($25,000) see Swanson Family Foundation, Dr. W.C.

Utah Heritage Foundation ($2,500) see Dee Foundation, Annie Taylor

Utah Museum of Natural History ($4,250) see Dee Foundation, Lawrence T. and Janet T.

Utah North Mission 2000 ($5,000) see Stewart Educational Foundation, Donnell B. and Elizabeth Dee Shaw

Utah Olympic Organizing Committee ($10,000) see Dee Foundation, Lawrence T. and Janet T.

Utah Sports Authority ($200,000) see Browning Charitable Foundation, Val A.

Utah State University ($70,000) see Caine Charitable Foundation, Marie Eccles

Utah State University ($32,000) see Caine Charitable Foundation, Marie Eccles

Utah State University ($21,000) see Caine Charitable Foundation, Marie Eccles

Utah State University ($20,000) see Caine Charitable Foundation, Marie Eccles

Utah State University ($16,000) see Caine Charitable Foundation, Marie Eccles

Utah State University ($15,000) see Caine Charitable Foundation, Marie Eccles

Utah State University ($12,700) see Caine Charitable Foundation, Marie Eccles

Utah (cont.)

Utah State University ($1,000) see Callister Foundation, Paul Q.

Utah State University — funding for research of relationship between iron in asbestos and cancer ($98,320) see Eccles Charitable Foundation, Willard L.

Utah State University ($5,700) see First Security Corp. (Salt Lake City, Utah)

Utah State University ($15,000) see Gore Family Memorial Foundation

Utah State University College of Engineering ($2,400) see Bourns, Inc.

Utah State University — to support the "Festival of the American West" ($10,000) see Quest for Truth Foundation

Utah State University — research and support for the publication of book entitled "Yellowstone: Ecological Malpractice." ($39,800) see Quest for Truth Foundation

Utah Symphony — general support ($300,000) see Eccles Foundation, George S. and Dolores Dore

Utah Symphony ($50,000) see Eccles Foundation, Marriner S.

Utah Symphony — to support the Audience Development Program ($250,000) see Eccles Foundation, George S. and Dolores Dore

Utah Symphony Society ($10,000) see Michael Foundation, Herbert I. and Elsa B.

Utah Technical College Foundation at Provo ($100,000) see Browning Charitable Foundation, Val A.

Utah Valley Community College ($5,000) see Bamberger and John Ernest Bamberger Memorial Foundation, Ruth Eleanor

Utah Valley Community College ($2,200) see Callister Foundation, Paul Q.

UTE Distribution Corporation — operating expenses ($20,000) see Piper Foundation

Valley Bible Church ($4,500) see Oldham Little Church Foundation

Wasatch Academy ($15,000) see Bamberger and John Ernest Bamberger Memorial Foundation, Ruth Eleanor

Waterford Institute ($200,000) see Rohatyn Foundation, Felix and Elizabeth

Waterford Institute — support of a model program to introduce Waterford Institute's integrated instructional computer system to the New York City public schools ($150,000) see Revson Foundation, Charles H.

Webber State University ($2,500) see Bourns, Inc.

Weber/Morgan Child Abuse ($2,500) see Dee Foundation, Annie Taylor

Weber School Foundation ($300,000) see Swanson Family Foundation, Dr. W.C.

Weber State College ($5,700) see First Security Corp. (Salt Lake City, Utah)

Weber State College ($100,000) see Shaw Charitable Trust, Mary Elizabeth Dee

Weber State University ($2,500) see Bourns, Inc.

Weber State University ($38,000) see Browning Charitable Foundation, Val A.

Weber State University ($15,000) see Dee Foundation, Annie Taylor

Weber State University ($53,000) see Stewart Educational Foundation, Donnell B. and Elizabeth Dee Shaw

Westminster College ($25,000) see Bamberger and John Ernest Bamberger Memorial Foundation, Ruth Eleanor

Westminster College — to provide scholarships for entering freshmen ($240,000) see Eccles Foundation, George S. and Dolores Dore

Westminster College ($50,000) see Eccles Foundation, Marriner S.

Westminster College — general support for the nursing program ($100,000) see Hospital Corp. of America

Westminster College ($4,000) see Van Evera Foundation, Dewitt Caroline

YMCA ($5,000) see Bamberger and John Ernest Bamberger Memorial Foundation, Ruth Eleanor

Your Community Foundation ($26,000) see Swanson Family Foundation, Dr. W.C.

YWCA ($5,000) see Bamberger and John Ernest Bamberger Memorial Foundation, Ruth Eleanor

YWCA ($20,000) see Bireley Foundation

Vermont

Addison Northeast Supervisory Union — to support school district's initiative to provide technical support to teachers ($25,000) see Bay Foundation

Bennington College ($30,000) see Harriman Foundation, Mary W.

Bennington College ($105,000) see Hartman Foundation, Jesse and Dorothy

Bennington College ($11,500) see Lemberg Foundation

Bennington College — summer scholars program see New England Telephone Co.

Bennington College ($25,000) see Newman Assistance Fund, Jerome A. and Estelle R.

Bennington College ($25,000) see Scott Fund, Olin

Bennington College ($10,000) see Summerfield Foundation, Solon E.

Bennington College Corporation ($30,500) see Rosenberg Foundation, Henry and Ruth Blaustein

Brattleboro Memorial Hospital ($50,000) see Thompson Trust, Thomas

Brattleboro Mutual Aid Association ($35,000) see Thompson Trust, Thomas

Burlington Youth Employment Program see New England Telephone Co.

Champlain College ($25,000) see Merchants Bancshares

Community College of Vermont ($25,000) see Scott Fund, Olin

Critical Languages and Area Studies Consortium — toward Japanese language programs

and general support ($150,800) see Culpeper Foundation, Charles E.

Daniel Clark Foundation ($50,000) see Pinewood Foundation

Diocese of Vermont ($85,500) see Hunt Trust for Episcopal Charitable Institutions, Virginia

Experiment in International Living ($25,000) see Bunbury Company

Family Place — start up costs ($10,000) see Phillips Foundation, Ellis L.

Farm and Wilderness — for camperships ($20,000) see Fohs Foundation

Governor's Institute of Vermont ($2,800) see Christodora

Grafton Fire Department ($15,000) see Bunbury Company

Greater Brattleboro Teen Community ($10,000) see Thompson Trust, Thomas

King Street Youth Fund ($5,000) see Merchants Bancshares

Marlboro College ($100,000) see Johnson Endeavor Foundation, Christian A.

Mental Health Services of S.E. Vermont ($10,000) see Thompson Trust, Thomas

Middlebury College ($333,334) see C. E. and S. Foundation

Middlebury College ($25,000) see Kent Foundation, Ada Howe

Middlebury College ($20,000) see Nason Foundation

Middlebury College ($51,000) see Travelli Fund, Charles Irwin

Montshire Museum of Science — pre-school science center ($15,000) see Phillips Foundation, Ellis L.

N.E. Kurn Hatin Home ($5,500) see Merchants Bancshares

New Beginnings Womens Support Network ($5,000) see Walker Foundation, Archie D. and Bertha H.

Planned Parenthood ($25,000) see Lintilhac Foundation

Planned Parenthood of Northern New England ($45,000) see Huber Foundation

Preservation Trust of Vermont ($8,000) see Thompson Trust, Thomas

Proctor Elementary School ($37,460) see Proctor Trust, Mortimer R.

Proctor Elementary School Playground ($47,251) see Proctor Trust, Mortimer R.

Proctor Free Library ($5,128) see Proctor Trust, Mortimer R.

Proctor School System ($34,511) see Proctor Trust, Mortimer R.

Proctor School System Youth League ($8,982) see Proctor Trust, Mortimer R.

Putland Central Supervisory Union ($8,000) see Proctor Trust, Mortimer R.

Putney Cares ($10,000) see Thompson Trust, Thomas

Putney School ($1,500) see Lippitt Foundation, Katherine Kenyon

Putney School ($30,000) see New Cycle Foundation

Rhinebeck Community Center ($20,004) see Thompson Trust, Thomas

Rice Cathedral Annual Fund ($4,500) see Merchants Bancshares

River Watch Network ($35,000) see General Service Foundation

St. Dominic's Catholic Church ($10,353) see Proctor Trust, Mortimer R.

St. Johnsbury Academy — special ($50,000) see Turrell Fund

St. Paul Lutheran Church ($3,700) see Proctor Trust, Mortimer R.

Shelburne Farms ($150,000) see Bettingen Corporation, Burton G.

Shelburne Farms Resources — Centennial Campaign — to support the conservation of Shelburne Farms and its educational programs in natural resources ($166,667) see Lintilhac Foundation

Shelburne Museum ($10,000) see Bostwick Foundation, Albert C.

Smokey House Project — general support ($265,000) see Taconic Foundation

Southern Vermont College ($50,000) see Scott Fund, Olin

Spectrum ($5,000) see McCarthy Memorial Trust Fund, Catherine

Spring Lake Ranch ($24,000) see O'Neil Foundation, M. G.

Stern Center for Language and Learning ($100,500) see Stern Foundation, Bernice and Milton

Third Century, Vermont ($25,000) see Merchants Bancshares

Town of Proctor ($39,839) see Proctor Trust, Mortimer R.

Trinity College of Vermont — Small School Institute ($26,025) see Phillips Foundation, Ellis L.

Union Church of Proctor ($6,108) see Proctor Trust, Mortimer R.

United Way ($13,000) see Merchants Bancshares

University of Vermont — scholarships ($47,700) see Ayling Scholarship Foundation, Alice S.

University of Vermont ($388,694) see Grant Foundation, William T.

University of Vermont ($57,500) see Holzer Memorial Foundation, Richard H.

University of Vermont ($5,000) see Mattus Foundation, Reuben and Rose

University of Vermont ($5,000) see Merchants Bancshares

University of Vermont ($200,000) see Sandy Hill Foundation

University of Vermont ($25,000) see Sandy Hill Foundation

University of Vermont ($52,875) see Travelli Fund, Charles Irwin

University of Vermont ($42,000) see Vanneck-Bailey Foundation

University of Vermont — "ABC"- Midwifery Program and Claire Lintilhac Alternative Birthing Center, Medical Center Hospital of Vermont ($142,000) see Lintilhac Foundation

University of Vermont College of Medicine — scholarships ($15,000) see Bay Branch Foundation

University of Vermont Department of Botany — to support the Dr. James Marvin

Memorial Lecture Series which is to provide funds over a ten year period, for the payment and remuneration of guest lecturers in the Botanical and related fields ($10,000) see Lintilhac Foundation

University of Vermont Department of Geology — to support the department of Geology Visiting Lecture Series at the University of Vermont ($10,000) see Lintilhac Foundation

University of Vermont — to support the George W. Merck Environmental Scholars Program ($75,000) see Merck Fund, John

University of Vermont Graduate College — for the establishment of the Lake Champlain Research Fund ($10,000) see Lintilhac Foundation

University of Vermont Metropolitan Health Medical Center ($7,500) see Weight Watchers International

University of Vermont School of Nature Resources — to purchase and provide maintenance support for the research vessel used in the Lake Champlain studies ($20,000) see Lintilhac Foundation

University of Vermont School of Nature Resources — to establish the Lake Champlain Biological Monitoring Program; a program to monitor and assess the status of the Lake Champlain ecosystem ($100,000) see Lintilhac Foundation

Upper Valley Habitat for Humanity — low income housing ($2,000) see Mascoma Savings Bank

Vermont health Care Information Consortium ($735,500) see Hartford Foundation, John A.

Vermont Child Care Center ($6,000) see French Foundation

Vermont Community Loan Funds ($5,000) see Merchants Bancshares

Vermont Council on the Arts — development of a state-wide arts portfolio assessment in Vermont ($70,000) see Cox Charitable Trust, Jessie B.

Vermont Handicapped Ski and Sports Association ($5,000) see Scott Foundation, Walter

Vermont Institute of Natural Science ($10,000) see Barker Foundation, J. M. R.

Vermont Land Trust — continued support of a matching fund for purchasing development rights to preserve Vermont farm land ($250,000) see Merck Fund, John

Vermont Natural Resources Council — to create a Vermont River Action Network ($85,000) see Cox Charitable Trust, Jessie B.

Vermont Public Interest Research Fund ($10,000) see Beldon II Fund

Vermont Public Radio — to continue to support Vermont Public Radio's news and public affairs program; "Switchboard" ($21,447) see Lintilhac Foundation

Vermont Respite House ($10,000) see Merchants Bancshares

Vermont State Colleges ($20,000) see Lindsay Trust, Agnes M.

Vermont Studio School ($10,000) see South Branch Foundation

Vermont Warmth Support Program ($5,000) see Merchants Bancshares

Visiting Nurses Association ($15,000) see Lintilhac Foundation

Windham Foundation ($12,500) see Bunbury Company

Windham Foundation ($12,500) see Bunbury Company

Windham Foundation ($12,500) see Bunbury Company

Winston L. Prouty Center ($18,000) see Thompson Trust, Thomas

Woodbury College ($2,000) see Seidman Family Foundation

Virgin Islands

J.R. O'Neal Arboretum Society — landscaping and planting ($23,000) see Smith Horticultural Trust, Stanley

Virginia

Abingdon Community Park see Crestar Financial Corp.

Abingdon Volunteer Fire Company — equipment ($11,100) see Treakle Foundation, J. Edwin

Achievement Center ($9,000) see Thurman Charitable Foundation for Children, Edgar A.

Alexandria Hospital see Crestar Financial Corp.

Alexandria Library ($15,000) see Bryant Foundation

Alive ($7,000) see Ivakota Association

ALIVE/Christ Church ($3,000) see Hopkins Foundation, John Jay

Altavista Area Chamber of Commerce ($750) see Lane Co., Inc.

Altavista Chamber of Commerce ($1,000) see English Foundation, W. C.

Altavista Presbyterian Church ($742) see English Foundation, W. C.

American Cancer Society see Crestar Financial Corp.

American Cancer Society ($25,000) see Thomas Memorial Foundation, Theresa A.

American Cancer Society ($2,500) see Truland Foundation

American Cancer Society-Harrisonburg see Crestar Financial Corp.

American Diabetes Association ($100,000) see AlliedSignal

American Diabetes Association National Center ($142,000) see NutraSweet Co.

American Friends of Cambridge University ($82,000) see Donnelley Foundation, Gaylord and Dorothy

American Friends of Cambridge University ($5,000) see Kent-Lucas Foundation

American Friends of Cambridge University ($5,000) see Kent-Lucas Foundation

American Friends of Cambridge University ($10,000) see Richmond Foundation, Frederick W.

American Frontier Culture Foundation ($30,000) see Carter Foundation, Beirne

American Frontier Culture Foundation ($7,500) see Thanksgiving Foundation

American Home Economics Association ($98,912) see Whirlpool Corp.

American Press Institute — support of four Ted Scripps Fellows ($20,000) see Scripps Co., E.W.

American Red Cross—Arlington Chapter ($3,500) see Uslico Corp.

American Red Cross — Gulf Crisis Fund ($312,792) see General Motors Corp.

American Red Cross - Roanoke Chapter see Shenandoah Life Insurance Co.

American Spectator Educational Foundation ($9,000) see Thirty-Five Twenty, Inc.

American Trust for Agriculture in Poland see American Express Co.

American Trust for Agriculture in Poland ($30,000) see Atlantic Foundation of New York

AMF/Signet Open of Virginia ($43,500) see Universal Leaf Tobacco Co.

Animal Industry Foundation ($10,000) see Moorman Manufacturing Co.

APSO ($5,000) see Mostyn Foundation

Arlington Arts Center ($20,000) see Glen Eagles Foundation

Arlington County Department of Human Services ($13,863) see Washington Forrest Foundation

Arlington Food Assistance Center ($16,794) see Washington Forrest Foundation

Arlington Historical Society — historical magazine ($3,300) see Olmsted Foundation, George and Carol

Arlington Hospital Foundation ($2,000) see Uslico Corp.

Arlington Hospital Foundation — Cardiac Catherization Lab ($7,500) see Washington Forrest Foundation

Arlington Housing Corporation ($2,500) see Uslico Corp.

Arlington Public Schools — education award ($2,100) see Washington Post Co.

Arlington Symphony—Ballston Pops '92 ($1,000) see Uslico Corp.

Arlington United Methodist Church ($18,500) see Washington Forrest Foundation

Arts Council of Richmond — annual fund drive ($4,500) see Best Products Co.

Arts Council of Richmond ($500) see Robertshaw Controls Co.

Arts Council of Richmond ($2,300) see Thalhimer, Jr. and Family Foundation, William B.

ASHOKA ($78,000) see General Atlantic Partners L.P.

Ashoka — in support of its program of fellowships to public service entrepreneurs in ten countries in Asia, Africa and the Americas (over three years) ($1,000,000) see MacArthur Foundation, John D. and Catherine T.

Association for the Preservation of Virginia Antiquities ($6,000) see Gray Foundation, Garland

Association of State and Territorial Health Officials see Coors Brewing Co.

Association of University Programs in Health Administration ($30,000) see Abbott Laboratories

Atlas Economic Research Foundation ($100,000) see Pioneer Fund

Atlas Economic Research Foundation ($176,500) see Richardson Foundation, Smith

Atlas Economic Research Foundation ($10,000) see Sunmark Capital Corp.

Averett College ($1,000) see Dan River, Inc.

Averett College ($1,000) see English Foundation, W. C.

Averett College ($2,900) see Staley Foundation, Thomas F.

Averette College, Danville, VA ($13,644) see Bustard Charitable Permanent Trust Fund, Elizabeth and James

Battelle Memorial Institute — a case study evaluation of the Foundation's Community Health Promotion Grant Program in the South ($322,932) see Kaiser Family Foundation, Henry J.

Better Hearing Institute ($10,000) see Knowles Foundation

Blue Ridge Area Food Bank — new refrigerated truck ($50,000) see Cabell III and Maude Morgan Cabell Foundation, Robert G.

Blue Ridge Hospice see United Airlines

Blue Ridge School ($12,844) see Hunter Trust, Emily S. and Coleman A.

Blue Ridge School — for the Haptic program ($10,000) see Butz Foundation

Bluefield College — construction of new science facility ($75,000) see Cabell III and Maude Morgan Cabell Foundation, Robert G.

Boone and Crockett Club ($15,000) see McCrea Foundation

Boy Scouts of America ($17,440) see Camp Foundation

Boy Scouts of America ($10,000) see Gray Foundation, Garland

Boy Scouts of America ($2,000) see Lawrence Foundation, Lind

Boy Scouts of America ($10,000) see Thurman Charitable Foundation for Children, Edgar A.

Boys Club of America ($5,000) see Luck Stone

Boys and Girls Club ($40,000) see Wareheim Foundation, E. C.

Boys Home ($12,844) see Hunter Trust, Emily S. and Coleman A.

Boys Home ($20,000) see Morgan and Samuel Tate Morgan, Jr. Foundation, Marietta McNeil

Broadwater Academy ($37,500) see Finley Foundation, A. E.

Business Consortium for Arts Support ($8,820) see Campbell Foundation, Ruth and Henry

Business Consortium for Arts Support see Crestar Financial Corp.

Business Consortium for Arts Support — to promote and encourage a wholesome community life ($39,360) see Landmark Communications

Business Consortium for Arts Support ($15,750) see Norfolk Shipbuilding & Drydock Corp.

Business Consortium for Arts Support ($58,000) see North Shore Foundation

Business Consortium for Arts Support ($58,000) see North Shore Foundation

C.R.O.S.S. — special campaign ($10,000) see Wood Foundation of Chambersburg, PA

Cambridge Baptist Church ($3,333) see Lawrence Foundation, Lind

Camp Holiday Trails ($12,500) see Himmelfarb Foundation, Paul and Annetta

Camp Virginia Jaycees ($5,000) see Lacy Foundation

Campagna Center ($7,000) see Ivakota Association

Cancer Research Foundation of America — education program ($15,000) see Dreyfus Foundation, Max and Victoria

Cape Henry Collegiate School ($10,000) see Taylor Foundation

Capital Area Agency on Aging ($12,000) see Memorial Foundation for Children

Capital Area Assembly ($10,000) see Wheat First Securites

Carfields Childs Memorial Fund ($21,000) see Memorial Foundation for Children

Carpenter Center for the Performing Arts ($250) see Robertshaw Controls Co.

Carpenter Center for the Performing Arts ($6,000) see Thalhimer and Family Foundation, Charles G.

Carpenter Museum ($13,422) see Gray Foundation, Garland

Carpenter Shelter ($7,500) see Washington Forrest Foundation

Carpenter's Lodging ($5,000) see Ivakota Association

Carpenter's Shelter for the Homeless ($5,000) see Ivakota Association

Catholic Charities ($37,000) see Brencanda Foundation

Center for Aged and Visually Handicapped — general budget ($5,000) see Smith Trust, May and Stanley

Center for Foreign Journalists ($20,000) see Dow Jones & Co.

Center for Judicial Studies ($4,500) see Wilbur Foundation, Marguerite Eyer

Center for the Study of Market Processes ($33,100) see Koch Charitable Foundation, Charles G.

Central Fidelity Bank — general purpose ($150,000) see Central Fidelity Banks, Inc.

Central Virginia Community College Education Foundation ($1,000) see Lane Co., Inc.

Central Virginia Education Television see Crestar Financial Corp.

Central Virginia Foodbank ($23,500) see Morgan and Samuel Tate Morgan, Jr. Foundation, Marietta McNeil

Chatham Hall ($10,000) see Ford Fund, Walter and Josephine

Chatham Hall ($10,000) see Statter Foundation, Amy Plant

Chelonia Institute ($25,000) see Truland Foundation

Chesapeake Volunteers in Youth Services ($24,000) see Wareheim Foundation, E. C.

Chesterfield County Museum ($2,000) see Lawrence Foundation, Lind

Chesterfield Historical Society ($15,000) see Jeffress Memorial Trust, Elizabeth G.

Child Development Center of Northern Virginia — care/treatment of sick or handicapped children ($60,000) see Stewart Trust under the will of Helen S. Devore, Alexander and Margaret

Children Incorporated ($147,000) see Philibosian Foundation, Stephen

Children's Center ($10,000) see Campbell Foundation, Ruth and Henry

Children's Hospital ($12,844) see Hunter Trust, Emily S. and Coleman A.

Children's Hospital of the King's Daughters ($33,600) see Beazley Foundation

Children's Hospital Medical Center ($10,000) see Wareheim Foundation, E. C.

Children's Medical Center ($1,000) see Noland Co.

Christ Church ($20,000) see Hopkins Foundation, John Jay

Christ the Church Fund ($5,000) see Fabick Tractor Co., John

Christchurch School ($15,000) see Olsson Memorial Foundation, Elis

Christchurch School — scholarships ($10,000) see Washington Forrest Foundation

Christian Aid Mission ($9,650) see Lane Foundation, Minnie and Bernard

Christian Children's Fund ($50,000) see Edouard Foundation

Christopher Newport College ($500) see Bionetics Corp.

Christopher Newport College ($5,000) see Gray Foundation, Garland

Christopher Newport College ($2,100) see Hastings Trust

Christopher Newport College — Japanese Tea House project ($5,750) see Noland Co.

CHROME ($500) see Bionetics Corp.

Chrysler Museum ($5,000) see Menschel Foundation, Robert and Joyce

Chrysler Museum ($75,000) see Norfolk Southern Corp.

Church of Good Shepherd ($29,000) see North Shore Foundation

Church of Resurrection — Danny Chitwood Early Learning Institute ($10,000) see Fowler Memorial Foundation, John Edward

Citizens Clearinghouse for Hazardous Waste — environmental concerns ($25,000) see Hoffman Foundation, Maximillian E. and Marion O.

Citizens Clearinghouse for Hazardous Waste, Arlington, VA ($7,500) see Beldon II Fund

Citizen's Clearinghouse for Hazardous Wastes ($30,000) see New World Foundation

City of Franklin ($96,300) see Camp Foundation

Virginia (cont.)

City of Franklin ($119,500) see Campbell Foundation, Ruth and Henry

City of Norfolk ($10,000) see Goodman & Company

City of Portsmouth — Parks and Recreation; Youth Against Drugs summer day camps and the pre-teen enrichment program ($50,000) see Frederick Foundation

City of Portsmouth Public Schools — relocation of the Public Schools Planetarium to the new Children's Museum ($79,167) see Frederick Foundation

City Rescue Mission of Roanoke ($12,000) see Thurman Charitable Foundation for Children, Edgar A.

City of Richmond ($12,000) see Cole Trust, Quincy

Clarke County Parks and Recreation ($25,000) see Kentland Foundation

Clean Sites ($30,000) see Olin Corp.

Clean Sites ($25,000) see Syntex Corp.

Close Up Foundation ($30,000) see Burlington Northern Inc.

Coal Pit Learning Center ($12,000) see Memorial Foundation for Children

College of William and Mary see Amoco Corp.

College of William and Mary ($18,000) see Chesapeake Corp.

College of William and Mary — conferences and cultural events ($500,000) see Evans Foundation, Lettie Pate

College of William and Mary ($15,000) see Fitz-Gibbon Charitable Trust

College of William and Mary ($50,000) see Gumenick Foundation, Nathan and Sophie

College of William and Mary ($10,000) see Hooper Foundation, Elizabeth S.

College of William and Mary ($40,724) see Jeffress Memorial Trust, Thomas F. and Kate Miller

College of William and Mary ($25,000) see Morgan and Samuel Tate Morgan, Jr. Foundation, Marietta McNeil

College of William and Mary ($60,000) see Reynolds Metals Co.

College of William and Mary — development fund ($20,000) see Wheat First Securites

College of William and Mary — Carol Veazey Titmus Endowment ($10,000) see Titmus Foundation

Collegiate ($3,000) see Estes Foundation

Collegiate Schools ($25,000) see Cole Trust, Quincy

Collegiate Schools ($70,000) see Herndon Foundation

Collegiate Schools ($12,844) see Hunter Trust, Emily S. and Coleman A.

Collegiate Schools ($5,000) see McCrea Foundation

Collegiate Schools — for capital campaign ($100,000) see Reynolds Foundation, Richard S.

Collegiate Schools ($50,500) see Thalhimer, Jr. and Family Foundation, William B.

Collegiate Schools, North Mooreland Road ($5,000) see Gottwald Foundation

Colonial Williamsburg ($5,500) see Beck Foundation

Colonial Williamsburg Foundation ($2,500,000) see Annenberg Foundation

Colonial Williamsburg Foundation ($25,000) see Flagler Foundation

Colonial Williamsburg Foundation ($2,000) see Old Dominion Box Co.

Colonial Williamsburg Foundation ($1,000,000) see Rockefeller Trust, Winthrop

Colonial Williamsburg Foundation ($2,500) see Uvas Foundation

Colonial Williamsburg Foundation — preparation of an interpretive program relating to urban history in Colonial America ($30,000) see Skaggs Foundation, L. J. and Mary C.

Colonial Williamsburg Foundation — Raleigh Tavern Society ($3,500) see Hopkins Foundation, John Jay

Colonial Williamsburg Foundation, Williamsburg, VA ($10,000) see New England Foundation

Congregation Beth Ahabah ($1,070) see Thalhimer, Jr. and Family Foundation, William B.

Conservation Council of Virginia ($30,000) see Hillsdale Fund

Conservation Council of Virginia ($5,000) see Sacharuna Foundation

Conservation Fund ($50,000) see Gilder Foundation

Conservation Fund ($25,000) see Norcross Wildlife Foundation

Conservation Fund ($57,500) see Sacharuna Foundation

Conservation Fund ($25,000) see Weyerhaeuser Family Foundation

Conservation Fund — American Greenways Program ($100,000) see Good Samaritan

Conservative Caucus Research Analysis and Education Foundation ($25,000) see Milliken & Co.

Core Knowledge Foundation — for "A K-4 Content-Based Empowerment Initiative in Mississippi" ($45,000) see Babcock Foundation, Mary Reynolds

Corps of Engineers Historical Foundation ($5,000) see Perini Corp.

County of Pulaski — construction of arena ($12,000) see Richardson Benevolent Foundation, C. E.

Cousteau Society ($47,825) see Prickett Fund, Lynn R. and Karl E.

Cross-Over Ministry — purchase and renovation of medical center building ($50,000) see Cabell III and Maude Morgan Cabell Foundation, Robert G.

Cross Over Ministry ($10,000) see Carter Foundation, Beirne

Cross-Over Ministry ($5,000) see Media General, Inc.

Cross-Over Ministry ($20,000) see Morgan and Samuel Tate Morgan, Jr. Foundation, Marietta McNeil

Cross-Over Ministry ($15,000) see Scott Foundation, William R., John G., and Emma

Cystic Fibrosis see Best Western International

Daily Bread ($2,467) see Harris Corp.

Dan Daniel Memorial Park ($5,000) see Dan River, Inc.

Danville Community College, Danville, VA ($13,324) see Bustard Charitable Permanent Trust Fund, Elizabeth and James

Danville Life Saving and First Aid Crew, Danville, VA ($13,644) see Bustard Charitable Permanent Trust Fund, Elizabeth and James

Darden Graduate Business School/University of Virginia ($10,000) see Batten Foundation

DCA: Medical Care for Children Project — funds provide medical care for the children of the working poor ($50,000) see Federal Home Loan Mortgage Corp. (Freddie Mac)

Deerfield Fire and Rescue ($1,000) see Foote Mineral Co.

Department of Public Health — City of Portsmouth ($165,459) see Beazley Foundation

DePaul Health Foundation ($25,000) see North Shore Foundation

DePaul Hospital ($10,000) see Goodman & Company

DePaul Hospital ($10,000) see Norfolk Shipbuilding & Drydock Corp.

Desert Storm Homecoming Celebration Committee ($5,000) see Noland Co.

Diabetes Institute Foundation ($30,000) see Morgan and Samuel Tate Morgan, Jr. Foundation, Marietta McNeil

Didlake ($5,000) see Ivakota Association

Diocese of Richmond ($33,124) see McMahon Charitable Trust Fund, Father John J.

Diocese of Southern Virginia ($30,000) see North Shore Foundation

Eastern Mennonite College — purchase of science center equipment ($50,000) see Cabell III and Maude Morgan Cabell Foundation, Robert G.

Eastern Mennonite College ($20,000) see High Foundation

Eastern Virginia Medical Association ($8,000) see Fitz-Gibbon Charitable Trust

Eastern Virginia Medical School ($104,089) see Jeffress Memorial Trust, Thomas F. and Kate Miller

Elk Hill Farm ($50,000) see Carter Foundation, Beirne

Elk Hill Farm ($12,000) see Flagler Foundation

Elk Hill Farm ($33,333) see Lawrence Foundation, Lind

Elk Hill Farm ($13,500) see Memorial Foundation for Children

Elk Hill Farm — for swimming pool ($50,000) see Reynolds Foundation, Richard S.

Elk Hill Farm ($20,000) see Scott Foundation, William R., John G., and Emma

Elk Hill Farm ($16,666) see Thomas Memorial Foundation, Theresa A.

Elms Foundation ($38,000) see Camp Younts Foundation

Elms Foundation ($38,000) see Camp Younts Foundation

Elms Foundation ($30,000) see Campbell Foundation, Ruth and Henry

Emergency Shelter — renovation of shelter ($100,000) see Cabell III and Maude Morgan Cabell Foundation, Robert G.

Emergency Shelter ($20,000) see Cole Trust, Quincy

Emergency Shelter ($8,000) see Metropolitan Health Foundation

Emergency Shelter ($4,000) see Thalhimer Brothers Inc.

Emory and Henry College ($11,923) see Jeffress Memorial Trust, Thomas F. and Kate Miller

Emory and Henry College ($35,000) see Morgan and Samuel Tate Morgan, Jr. Foundation, Marietta McNeil

End Baptist Church ($10,700) see Titmus Foundation

Endependence Center ($69,424) see Beazley Foundation

Endowment Association of William and Mary College ($20,000) see Charities Foundation

Episcopal Church of the Epiphany, Fund for Foreign Mission, Danville, VA ($13,644) see Bustard Charitable Permanent Trust Fund, Elizabeth and James

Episcopal Church of Redeemers ($10,833) see Lawrence Foundation, Lind

Episcopal High School ($100,000) see Olsson Memorial Foundation, Elis

Episcopal High School — establishment of Mastership in English Composition ($300,000) see Evans Foundation, Lettie Pate

Fairfax Bar Association — legal aid fund ($50,000) see Winkler Foundation, Mark and Catherine

Fairfax County Public Schools ($3,600) see Washington Post Co.

Fairfax County Public Schools Education Foundation ($165,000) see Mobil Oil Corp.

Faith Christian Academy ($51,000) see English Foundation, W. C.

Faith Home, Blairs, VA ($6,822) see Bustard Charitable Permanent Trust Fund, Elizabeth and James

Family and Children's Service ($5,000) see Seay Memorial Trust, George and Effie

Family Resource Center ($10,000) see Seay Memorial Trust, George and Effie

Family Service of Roanoke Valley ($11,000) see Thurman Charitable Foundation for Children, Edgar A.

Ferrum College ($15,000) see Easley Trust, Andrew H. and Anne O.

Ferrum College — student scholarship assistance ($4,000) see Richardson Benevolent Foundation, C. E.

Ferrum College ($10,000) see Slemp Foundation

Fieldale Community Center ($24,000) see Fieldcrest Cannon

FINCA — family income community solidarity ($25,000) see International Foundation

Fine Arts Center for the New River Valley — building repairs ($5,000) see Richardson Benevolent Foundation, C. E.

First Baptist Maintenance Trust ($10,000) see Estes Foundation

First Nations Development Institute ($10,000) see Friedman Family Foundation

First Nations Financial Project ($25,000) see New World Foundation

First Nations Financial Project — for Native American marketing program ($15,000) see Bay Foundation

Fishburne Military School — Beazley Scholarship program ($40,000) see Frederick Foundation

Flight Safety Foundation — aviation safety research project ($15,000) see Friendship Fund

Flight Safety Foundation, Arlington, VA ($50,000) see Federal Express Corp.

Flint Hill School ($10,000) see Washington Forrest Foundation

Food for the Hungry ($45,590) see Lane Foundation, Minnie and Bernard

Fork Union Military Academy ($4,000) see Estes Foundation

Forward Hampton Roads — general purpose ($20,000) see Central Fidelity Banks, Inc.

Foundation for Chiropractic Education and Research ($285,000) see Foundation for Advancement of Chiropractic Education

Foundation Endowment ($9,500) see Moore Foundation

Foundation for Endowment ($2,500) see Swensrud Charitable Trust, Sidney A.

Foundation for Evangelism ($30,000) see Lane Foundation, Minnie and Bernard

Foundation for Exceptional Children ($10,000) see Ernest & Julio Gallo Winery

Foundation for Exceptional Children — for a program that trains corporate volunteers and retirees to serve as mentors to help disabled youth prepare for and find employment ($40,000) see Mitsubishi Electric America

Foundation for Exceptional Children ($130,000) see Shell Oil Co.

Foundation for Roanoke Valley see Shenandoah Life Insurance Co.

Foxcroft School ($20,000) see AKC Fund

Foxcroft School ($50,000) see Firestone, Jr. Foundation, Harvey

Foxcroft School ($1,000) see Foerderer Foundation, Percival E. and Ethel Brown

Foxcroft School ($25,000) see McGraw Foundation, Curtis W.

Foxcroft School ($2,600) see Psychists

Foxcroft School ($10,000) see Rollins Luetkemeyer Charitable Foundation

Franklin Area United Way ($31,822) see Union Camp Corp.

Free Clinic of Central Virginia ($50,000) see Easley Trust, Andrew H. and Anne O.

Free Medical Clinic of Northern Shenandoah Valley — Dr.

Monford D. Custer
Endowment Fund ($100,000)
see Gallagher Family
Foundation, Lewis P.

Friends Association for Children
($6,650) see Seay Memorial
Trust, George and Effie

Friends of the Capital Children
Museum ($5,000) see Dart
Group Corp.

Friends of Mathews Memorial
Library — painting, blinds,
equipment ($10,650) see
Treakle Foundation, J. Edwin

Garth Newell Music Center
($25,000) see Jeffress
Memorial Trust, Elizabeth G.

Gateway Homes of Greater
Richmond ($10,000) see
Carter Foundation, Beirne

George C. Marshall Research
Foundation — operating fund
($5,000) see Gottwald
Foundation

George Mason University
($28,053) see Jeffress
Memorial Trust, Thomas F.
and Kate Miller

George Mason University
($250,000) see Koch
Charitable Foundation,
Charles G.

George Mason University —
single parent scholarship fund
($100,000) see Winkler
Foundation, Mark and
Catherine

George Mason University
Department of Economics
($20,000) see Krieble
Foundation, Vernon K.

George Mason University
Foundation ($25,000) see
Earhart Foundation

George Mason University Law
and Economic Center
($10,000) see Walker
Educational and Charitable
Foundation, Alex C.

Gloucester Library Endowment
Foundation ($10,650) see
Treakle Foundation, J. Edwin

Gloucester Volunteer Fire and
Rescue Squad ($22,200) see
Treakle Foundation, J. Edwin

Goochland Fellowship and
Family Service ($8,200) see
Seay Memorial Trust, George
and Effie

Good Neighbor Village
($17,500) see Chesapeake
Corp.

Good Neighbor Village ($5,000)
see Estes Foundation

Good News Tape Ministry
($30,000) see M.E. Foundation

Goodwin House ($15,000) see
Washington Forrest Foundation

Grace House ($17,500) see
Memorial Foundation for
Children

Greater Richmond Community
Foundation ($15,000) see
Gray Foundation, Garland

Greater Richmond Informed
Parents ($9,600) see Seay
Memorial Trust, George and
Effie

Greenvale Nursery School
($12,000) see Thurman
Charitable Foundation for
Children, Edgar A.

Gretna High School PAT
($1,000) see Lane Co., Inc.

Habitat for Humanity ($30,000)
see Carter Foundation, Beirne

Habitat for Humanity ($25,000)
see Easley Trust, Andrew H.
and Anne O.

Hampden-Sydney College
($25,000) see Centel Corp.

Hampden Sydney College
($20,000) see Easley Trust,
Andrew H. and Anne O.

Hampden-Sydney College
($30,000) see Huston
Foundation

Hampden-Sydney College
($500,000) see Kenan, Jr.
Charitable Trust, William R.

Hampden-Sydney College
($1,650) see Lawyers Title
Foundation

Hampden-Sydney College
($13,250) see Sullivan
Foundation, Algernon Sydney

Hampton Institute ($5,000) see
Hopkins Foundation, John Jay

Hampton Metro Annual Fund
($500) see Bionetics Corp.

Hampton University ($35,000)
see Morgan and Samuel Tate
Morgan, Jr. Foundation,
Marietta McNeil

Hampton University ($90,000)
see Teagle Foundation

Hanover Tavern Foundation —
restoration of tavern ($50,000)
see Cabell III and Maude
Morgan Cabell Foundation,
Robert G.

Hargrave Military Academy
($36,500) see Finley
Foundation, A. E.

Help and Emergency Response
— general operations
($54,000) see Frederick
Foundation

Hillsdale Review ($2,000) see
Wilbur Foundation,
Marguerite Eyer

Historic Petersburg Foundation
— restoration Battersea
Plantation ($100,000) see
Cabell III and Maude Morgan
Cabell Foundation, Robert G.

Hollins College ($6,000) see
Arkwright Foundation

Hollins College ($25,000) see
Batten Foundation

Hollins College ($11,000) see
Dorminy Foundation, John
Henry

Hollins College ($30,000) see
Scott Foundation, William R.,
John G., and Emma

Holy Cross Abbey ($20,000) see
Kentland Foundation

Hopkins House Associates
($6,000) see Ivakota
Association

Horatio Alger Association
($100,000) see Louisiana Land
& Exploration Co.

Horatio Alger Association
($100,000) see
Louisiana-Pacific Corp.

Horatio Alger Scholarship Fund
($10,000) see Mary Kay
Foundation

Horatio Alger Scholarship Fund
($10,000) see Mary Kay
Foundation

Hospice of Northern Virginia —
care of cancer patients
($55,000) see Stewart Trust
under the will of Mary E.
Stewart, Alexander and
Margaret

Hospice for Northern Virginia
($500) see Uslico Corp.

Hotel of the Good Shepard
($15,000) see Lane Charitable
Trust, Melvin R.

Howard and Georgeanna Jones
Institute ($50,000) see
Goodman & Company

Human Growth Foundation
($20,000) see Himmelfarb
Foundation, Paul and Annetta

Hurt Volunteer Fire Department
($500) see Lane Co., Inc.

ICF, Inc. — development of the
Americans Over 55 at Work
Program ($250,000) see
Commonwealth Fund

Individual Research Project,
Smithsonian Institution
Conservation and Research
Center — entitled
"Physiological and Behavior
Ecological Determinants of
Female Aggression in Yellow
Baboons" ($33,740) see
Guggenheim Foundation,
Harry Frank

Innisfree ($25,000) see Jeffress
Memorial Trust, Elizabeth G.

Institute of Early American
History and Culture — partial
support for producing "Mary
Silliman's War" for television
($52,000) see Donner
Foundation, William H.

Institute for Humane Studies
($10,000) see Durell
Foundation, George Edward

Institute for Humane Studies
($2,500) see Garvey Kansas
Foundation

Institute for Humane Studies
($250,000) see Koch
Charitable Trust, David H.

Institute for Humane Studies
($10,000) see Tamko Asphalt
Products

Institute for Humane Studies
($20,000) see Winchester
Foundation

Institute for Humane
Studies-George Mason
University ($5,000) see Curran
Foundation

Institute for Humane Studies
George Mason University —
professional program
($103,000) see Lambe
Charitable Foundation, Claude
R.

Institute for Humane Studies
George Mason University —
Lambe Fellowship Program
($250,000) see Lambe
Charitable Foundation, Claude
R.

Institute of Textile Technology
($110,000) see Milliken & Co.

Institute for Workplace Learning
— for Technology and the
Organization of Work Project
($113,000) see Joyce
Foundation

Insurance Institute for Highway
Safety ($44,000) see GEICO
Corp.

International Fellowship
($168,255) see Timmis
Foundation, Michael & Nancy

International Foundation
($102,920) see Three
Swallows Foundation

Irvington Baptist Church — to
support the establishment of
Church Resource Services
($500,000) see duPont Fund,
Jessie Ball

Izaak Walton League of America
($4,000) see Seasongood Good
Government Foundation,
Murray and Agnes

J. Sargeant Reynolds
Community College ($27,000)
see Metropolitan Health
Foundation

J. Sargeant Reynolds
Community College Education
Foundation ($1,168) see
Metropolitan Health
Foundation

Jackson-Feild Homes ($25,000)
see Titmus Foundation

Jackson-Feild Homes ($25,000)
see Titmus Foundation

Jackson Field Home ($2,500) see
Lawrence Foundation, Lind

James Madison Foundation
($5,000) see Estes Foundation

James Madison University
($13,740) see Jeffress
Memorial Trust, Thomas F.
and Kate Miller

James Madison University
($2,000) see Lawyers Title
Foundation

James Madison University
($3,100) see Lynch
Scholarship Foundation, John
B.

James Madison University
($19,353) see Technical
Foundation of America

James Madison University
($5,000) see Thalhimer and
Family Foundation, Charles G.

James Madison University
($5,000) see Thalhimer
Brothers Inc.

James Madison University
($10,000) see Universal Leaf
Tobacco Co.

James Madison University
($20,000) see Wheat First
Securites

Jamestown 4-H Center ($10,000)
see Widgeon Foundation

Jamestown-Yorktown ($2,000)
see Hastings Trust

Jamestown/Yorktown
Foundation ($6,000) see Gray
Foundation, Garland

Jefferson Center Foundation see
Shenandoah Life Insurance Co.

Jefferson Poplar Forest Fund
($9,000) see Lane Co., Inc.

Jewish Community Center
($4,000) see Media General,
Inc.

Jewish Community Federation
($95,000) see Circuit City
Stores

Jewish Community Federation
($70,000) see Thalhimer and
Family Foundation, Charles G.

Jewish Community Federation
($70,000) see Thalhimer
Brothers Inc.

Jewish Community Federation
($1,710) see Thalhimer, Jr. and
Family Foundation, William B.

John Marshall Foundation
($2,500) see Media General,
Inc.

John Marshall Foundation —
restoration of John Marshall
House ($50,000) see Cabell III
and Maude Morgan Cabell
Foundation, Robert G.

John Tyler Community College
($10,000) see Metropolitan
Health Foundation

John Tyler Community College
($9,000) see Metropolitan
Health Foundation

Joy Ranch — vehicle to
transport children ($3,500) see
Richardson Benevolent
Foundation, C. E.

Joy Ranch Christian School of
Hillsville, Hillsville, VA
($6,822) see Bustard
Charitable Permanent Trust
Fund, Elizabeth and James

Julian Stanley Wise Foundation
see Shenandoah Life Insurance
Co.

Junior Engineering Technical
Society — to expand a high
school design competition to
develop devices to serve
society, especially the disabled
($35,000) see NEC USA

Junior League of Norfolk and
Virginia Beach ($27,100) see
Wareheim Foundation, E. C.

Kenmore Association ($40,000)
see Ingalls Foundation, Louise
H. and David S.

Kenmore Association ($35,000)
see Scott Foundation, William
R., John G., and Emma

Kilmarnock-Lancaster County
Volunteer Rescue Squad
($25,000) see Thomas
Memorial Foundation, Theresa
A.

Lane Memorial Methodist
Church ($16,447) see Lane
Foundation, Minnie and
Bernard

Leadership Institute ($10,000)
see Noble Foundation, Vivian
Bilby

Leadership Institute ($10,000)
see Roe Foundation

Leadership Institute ($20,000)
see Romill Foundation

Leadership Institute ($10,000)
see Walker Educational and
Charitable Foundation, Alex C.

Lee County Public School
($50,000) see Slemp
Foundation

Lee County Public School
($7,000) see Slemp Foundation

Legacy International Youth
Program ($3,500) see
Goldman Foundation, Aaron
and Cecile

Lewis Ginter Botanical Garden
($50,000) see Jeffress
Memorial Trust, Elizabeth G.

Lewis Ginter Botanical Gardens
— Flagler Garden ($743,823)
see Flagler Foundation

Life Learning Center ($2,500)
see Faith Charitable Trust

Linton Hall School ($20,000) see
Washington Forrest Foundation

Lion's Club Fund for the Blind,
Danville, VA ($13,644) see
Bustard Charitable Permanent
Trust Fund, Elizabeth and
James

Literacy Council of Metro
Richmond ($9,800) see Seay
Memorial Trust, George and
Effie

Literacy South — to support
"learner centered literacy"
instructor training and model
site development in three
Southeastern states see United
Parcel Service of America

Little River Foundation
($206,000) see Ohrstrom
Foundation

Little River Foundation
($124,000) see Ohrstrom
Foundation

Little Sisters of Poor ($10,000)
see McMahon Charitable Trust
Fund, Father John J.

Lombardi Cancer Research
Center ($10,000) see Dimick
Foundation

Lonesome Pine Regional Library
($7,062) see Slemp Foundation

Longwood College ($15,000) see
Fuqua Foundation, J. B.

Loudoun Association for
Retarded Citizens (LARC)
($159,794) see Harrison and
Conrad Memorial Trust

Lower James River Association
($4,000) see Friendship Fund

Lynchburg College ($15,000) see
Easley Trust, Andrew H. and
Anne O.

Lynchburg College ($15,000) see
McMillan, Jr. Foundation,
Bruce

Lynchburg College ($20,000) see
Old Dominion Box Co.

Lynchburg College ($5,000) see
Plym Foundation

Virginia (cont.)

Lynchburg College ($5,000) see Straus Foundation, Martha Washington Straus and Harry H.

Lynchburg College ($5,000) see V and V Foundation

Lynchburg Fine Arts Center ($20,000) see Easley Trust, Andrew H. and Anne O.

Lynchburg Fine Arts Center ($500) see Old Dominion Box Co.

Lynchburg Museum System ($28,300) see Easley Trust, Andrew H. and Anne O.

Madeira School ($350,000) see Payne Foundation, Frank E. and Seba B.

Madeira School ($31,000) see Perkins Charitable Foundation

Madeira School ($135,000) see Taylor Foundation, Ruth and Vernon

Maderia ($2,500) see Sweatt Foundation, Harold W.

Maderia School ($30,000) see Prince Trust, Abbie Norman

Mariners Museum ($11,000) see Norfolk Shipbuilding & Drydock Corp.

Marrow Foundation ($50,000) see Contran Corp.

Marshall-Wythe School of Law Foundation ($85,000) see Beazley Foundation

Mary Baldwin College — support for program in health care and ministry ($174,600) see Carpenter Foundation, E. Rhodes and Leona B.

Mary Baldwin College ($15,000) see Fitz-Gibbon Charitable Trust

Mary Baldwin College ($16,000) see Sullivan Foundation, Algernon Sydney

Marymont Foundation ($41,575) see Carter Foundation, Beirne

Marymont Foundation ($1,500) see Robertshaw Controls Co.

Marymount School ($15,000) see Cole Trust, Quincy

Marymount University ($25,000) see Jeffress Memorial Trust, Elizabeth G.

Massanutten Military Academy ($12,844) see Hunter Trust, Emily S. and Coleman A.

Mathcounts Foundation ($80,152) see Cray Research

Mathews Memorial Library, Friends of ($10,650) see Treakle Foundation, J. Edwin

Mathews Volunteer Fire Department ($11,100) see Treakle Foundation, J. Edwin

Mathews Volunteer Rescue Squad ($11,100) see Treakle Foundation, J. Edwin

Mathews Volunteer Rescue Squad — toward replacement of chassis for ambulance ($11,100) see Treakle Foundation, J. Edwin

Medical College of Hampton Roads Foundation ($50,000) see Batten Foundation

Medical College of Virginia — for chair of neurosurgery ($200,000) see Reynolds Foundation, Richard S.

Medical College of Virginia — for neurosurgery research lab support ($100,000) see Reynolds Foundation, Richard S.

Medical College of Virginia Foundation ($13,700) see

Metropolitan Health Foundation

Medical College of Virginia Foundation ($5,000) see Metropolitan Health Foundation

Medical College of Virginia Foundation ($20,000) see Olsson Memorial Foundation, Elis

Medical College of Virginia Foundation — Virginia Commonwealth University ($250,000) see Thomas Memorial Foundation, Theresa A.

Metropolitan Area Resource Clearinghouse ($20,000) see Scott Foundation, William R., John G., and Emma

Metropolitan Foundation ($5,000) see Media General, Inc.

Metropolitan Foundation ($2,000) see Noland Co.

Metropolitan Foundation ($2,000) see Noland Co.

Metropolitan Richmond Chamber of Commerce ($5,000) see Thalhimer and Family Foundation, Charles G.

MHS Student Aid Fund ($10,000) see Lacy Foundation

Middleburg City College Foundation ($6,000) see Visciglia Foundation, Frank

Minority Youth Appreciation Society ($15,000) see Memorial Foundation for Children

Monelison Fire Department ($500) see Old Dominion Box Co.

Monticello ($100,000) see Ray Foundation

Mount Vernon Ladies Association of Union ($28,000) see Herndon Foundation

Mountain Empire Community College Education Foundation ($10,000) see Slemp Foundation

Museum of the Confederacy ($25,000) see Cole Trust, Quincy

Museum of the Confederacy ($6,500) see Seay Memorial Trust, George and Effie

Nansemond-Suffolk Academy ($10,000) see Gray Foundation, Garland

National Alliance for the Mentally Ill ($3,000) see Agape Foundation

National Association of Elementary School Principals Foundation ($25,000) see Cray Research

National Association of Secondary School Principals — scholarships ($200,000) see Balfour Foundation, L. G.

National Captioning Institute ($10,000) see R. F. Foundation

National Center for Clinical Infant Programs ($220,000) see Richardson Foundation, Smith

National Center for Missing and Exploited Children — assist in search for missing children ($2,500) see Rosenberg Family Foundation, William

National Council for Better Education ($5,000) see Noble Foundation, Vivian Bilby

National Future Homemakers of America Foundation ($5,000) see Pet

National Law Enforcement Officers Memorial Fund

($10,000) see Cornerstone Foundation of Northeastern Wisconsin

National Maritime Center Foundation ($20,000) see Norfolk Shipbuilding & Drydock Corp.

National Multiple Sclerosis Society ($1,000) see Lawyers Title Foundation

National Right to Work Legal Defense Foundation ($5,000) see Florida Steel Corp.

National Right to Work Legal Defense Foundation ($1,000) see Lane Co., Inc.

National Right to Work Legal Defense Foundation ($27,600) see Pillsbury Foundation

National Right to Work Legal Defense Foundation ($10,000) see Stockham Valves & Fittings

National Right to Work Legal Defense Foundation ($30,000) see Sunderland Foundation, Lester T.

National Right to Work Legal Defense Foundation ($50,000) see Sunmark Capital Corp.

National Right to Work Legal Defense Foundation ($10,000) see Tamko Asphalt Products

National Right to Work Legal Defense Foundation ($15,000) see West Foundation

National Right to Work Legal Defense Fund ($15,000) see Davis Foundation, Shelby Cullom

National Right to Work Legal Defense Fund ($7,000) see North Carolina Foam Foundation

National Right to Work Legal Defense Fund ($2,000) see Pitt-Des Moines Inc.

National Right to Work Legal Defense Fund ($10,000) see Stonecutter Mills Corp.

National Right to Work Legal Defense Fund ($100,000) see Swim Foundation, Arthur L.

National Society of Colonial Dames of American in the State of Connecticut ($5,000) see Beloco Foundation

National Society of Colonial Dames of American in the State of Connecticut ($12,135) see Sewall Foundation, Elmina

Nature Conservancy — open space ($150,000) see Bullitt Foundation

Nature Conservancy ($200,000) see Cape Branch Foundation

Nature Conservancy ($225,750) see Castle Foundation, Harold K. L.

Nature Conservancy ($12,500) see Chadwick Foundation

Nature Conservancy ($249,500) see Claiborne Art Ortenberg Foundation, Liz

Nature Conservancy ($10,000) see Harder Foundation

Nature Conservancy ($5,000) see Hastings Trust

Nature Conservancy ($10,000) see Hopkins Foundation, John Jay

Nature Conservancy ($25,000) see Hughes Memorial Foundation, Charles Evans

Nature Conservancy ($100,000) see Joselow Foundation

Nature Conservancy ($130,000) see Lennox International, Inc.

Nature Conservancy ($12,000) see Mars Foundation

Nature Conservancy ($50,000) see McKnight Foundation, Sumner T.

Nature Conservancy ($5,000) see MDU Resources Group, Inc.

Nature Conservancy ($50,000) see Meadowood Foundation

Nature Conservancy ($15,000) see Meadowood Foundation

Nature Conservancy ($148,500) see Merck Family Fund

Nature Conservancy ($220,000) see Moriah Fund

Nature Conservancy ($55,000) see Nason Foundation

Nature Conservancy ($225,000) see Olin Foundation, Spencer T. and Ann W.

Nature Conservancy ($25,000) see Schlumberger Ltd.

Nature Conservancy ($15,000) see Wellman Foundation, S. K.

Nature Conservancy ($10,000) see Winona Corporation

Nature Conservancy — to protect critical Atlantic coastal ecosystems ($442,500) see Cary Charitable Trust, Mary Flagler

Nature Conservancy — supports the "Campaign for the Delaware," a four-state initiative to protect the Delaware River Basin ($50,000) see Schumann Fund for New Jersey

Nature Conservancy Fund ($50,000) see Schlinger Foundation

Nature Conservancy — support of the development of its Pacific Program ($100,000) see Gerbode Foundation, Wallace Alexander

Nauticus, National Maritime Center ($75,000) see Norfolk Southern Corp.

Naval Academy Model Museum — Class of '51 ($75,000) see Hooper Foundation, Elizabeth S.

New American Schools Development Corporation ($1,000,000) see American Telephone & Telegraph Co.

New American Schools Development Corporation ($800,000) see BellSouth Corp.

New Community High School ($12,000) see Flagler Foundation

New Community School ($18,000) see Cole Trust, Quincy

New Community School ($50,000) see Massey Foundation

New Land Samaritan Inns ($30,592) see Easley Trust, Andrew H. and Anne O.

New River Community College Educational Foundation — expand library ($10,000) see Richardson Benevolent Foundation, C. E.

New Virginia Review ($15,000) see Jeffress Memorial Trust, Elizabeth G.

Norfolk Academy ($25,000) see Batten Foundation

Norfolk Christian School ($6,000) see Taylor Foundation

Norfolk Senior Center ($4,000) see Goodman & Company

Northern Virginia Community College — construct community center ($5,000) see Olmsted Foundation, George and Carol

Northwest Child Development Center ($12,000) see Thurman

Charitable Foundation for Children, Edgar A.

Old Dominion University — donation of mainframe ($6,000,000) see IBM Corp.

Old Dominion University ($13,816) see Jeffress Memorial Trust, Thomas F. and Kate Miller

Old Dominion University — research and training in the field of computational gas discharge physics ($31,150) see Kade Foundation, Max

Old Dominion University — eminent scholars professorship and expansion of the Child Study Center ($60,000) see Frederick Foundation

Old Dominion University Educational Foundation ($10,000) see Batten Foundation

Old Dominion University Intercollegiate ($6,000) see Taylor Foundation

Old Dominion University-Spong Professorship — to promote and encourage a wholesome community life ($20,000) see Landmark Communications

Old Time Gospel Hour ($5,000) see Fruehauf Foundation

Operation Smile see MBIA, Inc.

Operation Smile ($20,000) see North Shore Foundation

Operation Smile ($20,500) see Rosenstiel Foundation

Operation Smile ($1,150) see Smith Foundation, Gordon V. and Helen C.

Operation Smile International ($10,000) see Goodman & Company

Operation Smile International — medical team to Viet Nam ($10,000) see Innovating Worthy Projects Foundation

Packaging Education Foundation ($5,000) see Martin Foundation, Bert William

Patrick Henry Boys Plantation ($500) see Lane Co., Inc.

Patrick Henry Memorial Foundation ($83,629) see Casey Foundation, Eugene B.

Physicians for Peace ($35,000) see McIntosh Foundation

Physicians for Peace ($20,000) see Sweatt Foundation, Harold W.

Piedmont Environmental Council — operating budget ($40,000) see duPont Foundation, Chichester

Piedmont Environmental Council ($25,000) see Prince Trust, Abbie Norman

Pioneers ($15,000) see Tasty Baking Co.

Planned Parenthood Federation of America ($10,000) see Thurman Charitable Foundation for Children, Edgar A.

Poplar Springs Baptist Church ($10,000) see Ukrop's Super Markets, Inc.

Portsmouth Central YMCA — Capital campaign ($80,000) see Beazley Foundation

Portsmouth General Hospital — scholarship-loan program for qualified but financially disadvantaged students ($30,000) see Frederick Foundation

Portsmouth Public Schools — scholarships ($30,000) see Beazley Foundation

Potomac School ($165,000) see Engelhard Foundation, Charles

Powell Valley Primary School ($50,000) see Slemp Foundation

Powhatan School ($20,000) see Scott Foundation, William R., John G., and Emma

Powhatan School ($2,500) see Weiss Fund, Clara

Presbyterian Home and Family Services ($50,000) see Easley Trust, Andrew H. and Anne O.

Presbyterian School of Christian Education ($53,500) see Board of Trustees of the Prichard School

Presbyterian School of Christian Education — to train men and women for ministry in the church ($20,000) see Early Foundation

Presbyterian School of Christian Education ($15,000) see Richardson Fund, Mary Lynn

Prestwould Foundation ($20,000) see Morgan and Samuel Tate Morgan, Jr. Foundation, Marietta McNeil

Prestwould Foundation — restoration of Prestwould foundation ($50,000) see Cabell III and Maude Morgan Cabell Foundation, Robert G.

Prince William County Public Schools — education award ($2,100) see Washington Post Co.

Prison Fellowship ($46,500) see Berry Foundation, Lowell

Prison Fellowship International ($600,000) see DeMoss Foundation, Arthur S.

Pro-Art Association ($20,000) see Slemp Foundation

Project Hope ($2,000) see Shattuck Charitable Trust, S. F.

Project Hope-Health Sciences Education Center ($32,500) see Hoffmann-La Roche

Protestant Episcopal Theological Seminary ($37,500) see Olsson Memorial Foundation, Elis

Protestant Episcopal Theological Seminary, Alexandria, VA ($13,644) see Bustard Charitable Permanent Trust Fund, Elizabeth and James

Protestant Episcopal Theological Seminary in Virginia — toward campaign to build a new Academic Center ($500,000) see Evans Foundation, Lettie Pate

Radford University ($14,820) see Helms Foundation

Radford University Foundation — student scholarship assistance ($5,000) see Richardson Benevolent Foundation, C. E.

Randolph Macon Academy ($1,000) see Beitzell & Co.

Randolph-Macon Academy ($250,000) see Manger and Audrey Cordero Plitt Trust, Clarence

Randolph-Macon College ($25,000) see Centel Corp.

Randolph-Macon College ($10,000) see Estes Foundation

Randolph-Macon College ($250,000) see Manger and Audrey Cordero Plitt Trust, Clarence

Randolph-Macon College ($14,750) see Sullivan Foundation, Algernon Sydney

Randolph-Macon Woman's College — scholarships for needy students ($50,000) see Maier Foundation, Sarah Pauline

Randolph-Macon Woman's College ($250,000) see Manger and Audrey Cordero Plitt Trust, Clarence

Randolph-Macon Woman's College ($2,000,000) see Thoresen Foundation

Randolph-Macon Women's College ($10,000) see Old Dominion Box Co.

Randolph-Macon Women's College — establish the Eugene B. Casey Honor Scholarship Fund ($50,000) see Casey Foundation, Eugene B.

Rappahannock CASA Program ($15,000) see Wareheim Foundation, E. C.

Rectors and Visitors of the University of Virginia — promotion of education ($20,000) see Love Charitable Foundation, John Allan

Regent University ($15,000) see Rockwell Foundation

Retreat Hospital ($12,844) see Hunter Trust, Emily S. and Coleman A.

Richmond Ballet ($2,000) see Best Products Co.

Richmond Ballet ($25,000) see Cole Trust, Quincy

Richmond Ballet ($12,000) see Flagler Foundation

Richmond Ballet ($500) see Robertshaw Controls Co.

Richmond Ballet — defray costs of 1991-1992 operations ($150,000) see Carpenter Foundation, E. Rhodes and Leona B.

Richmond Cerebral Palsy Center ($25,000) see Cole Trust, Quincy

Richmond Cerebral Palsy Center ($12,844) see Hunter Trust, Emily S. and Coleman A.

Richmond Cerebral Palsy Center ($12,000) see Metropolitan Health Foundation

Richmond Chaplaincy Service ($7,000) see Seay Memorial Trust, George and Effie

Richmond Children's Museum ($1,000) see Best Products Co.

Richmond Children's Museum — for operating expenses ($40,000) see Reynolds Foundation, Richard S.

Richmond Children's Museum ($500) see Robertshaw Controls Co.

Richmond Community Senior Center ($15,000) see Scott Foundation, William R., John G., and Emma

Richmond Forum ($5,000) see Media General, Inc.

Richmond Forum ($5,000) see Thalhimer, Jr. and Family Foundation, William B.

Richmond Metropolitan Chamber of Commerce ($5,000) see Thalhimer Brothers Inc.

Richmond Renaissance — general purpose ($33,334) see Central Fidelity Banks, Inc.

Richmond Renaissance ($29,000) see Chesapeake Corp.

Richmond Renaissance ($11,000) see Universal Leaf Tobacco Co.

Richmond Symphony ($2,000) see Best Products Co.

Richmond Symphony — general purpose ($15,000) see Central Fidelity Banks, Inc.

Richmond Symphony ($12,500) see Herndon Foundation

Richmond Symphony ($500) see Robertshaw Controls Co.

Richmond Symphony ($15,000) see Thalhimer and Family Foundation, Charles G.

Richmond Symphony ($15,000) see Thalhimer Brothers Inc.

Richmond Symphony ($2,400) see Thalhimer, Jr. and Family Foundation, William B.

Richmond Symphony — support for 1991-92 season ($100,000) see Carpenter Foundation, E. Rhodes and Leona B.

Richmond Symphony — support for 1991-1992 season ($120,000) see Carpenter Foundation, E. Rhodes and Leona B.

Richmond Technical Schools ($5,250) see Metropolitan Health Foundation

The River Foundation see Shenandoah Life Insurance Co.

River Foundation ($10,000) see Wheat First Securites

River Road United Methodist Church ($21,030) see Estes Foundation

River Road United Methodist Church ($6,000) see Estes Foundation

River Road United Methodist Church ($4,000) see Estes Foundation

River Road United Methodist Church ($2,958) see Estes Foundation

Roanoke College — faculty development ($20,000) see Cabell III and Maude Morgan Cabell Foundation, Robert G.

Roanoke College ($25,000) see Cook Foundation, Louella

Roanoke College ($10,000) see Courts Foundation

Roanoke College ($10,000) see Gage Foundation, Philip and Irene Toll

Roanoke College Library see Shenandoah Life Insurance Co.

Roanoke College — fund the Richardson Bibliographic classroom ($20,000) see Richardson Benevolent Foundation, C. E.

Robert E. Lee Memorial Association ($50,000) see Dula Educational and Charitable Foundation, Caleb C. and Julia W.

St. Agnes School ($5,000) see Cartinhour Foundation

St. Agnes School ($5,000) see Woods-Greer Foundation

St. Anne's Belfield School ($100,000) see Ray Foundation

St. Catherine's School ($5,000) see Hastings Trust

St. Charles Health Council — capital improvements ($8,303) see Thomas Memorial Foundation, Theresa A.

St. Christopher's School Foundation ($5,000) see Gottwald Foundation

St. Christopher's School Foundation ($75,000) see Massey Foundation

St. Francis Home ($5,000) see McMahon Charitable Trust Fund, Father John J.

St. John's Episcopal Church ($188,500) see Carter Foundation, Beirne

St. John's Episcopal Church ($12,000) see Thurman Charitable Foundation for Children, Edgar A.

St. Joseph's Villa — Flagler Home ($345,014) see Flagler Foundation

St. Margaret's School ($25,000) see Chesapeake Corp.

St. Margarets School ($25,000) see Morgan and Samuel Tate Morgan, Jr. Foundation, Marietta McNeil

St. Margaret's School ($20,000) see Olsson Memorial Foundation, Elis

St. Mary's Health Care Foundation — for Bon Secours Health Center campaign ($100,000) see Reynolds Foundation, Richard S.

St. Marys Hospital Foundation ($50,000) see Thalhimer, Jr. and Family Foundation, William B.

St. Paul's Episcopal Church ($80,000) see Massey Foundation

Salvation Army — street feeding program and unsolicited grant ($36,600) see Frederick Foundation

Salvation Army ($7,300) see Ivakota Association

Salvation Army ($7,000) see Ivakota Association

Salvation Army ($10,000) see Thurman Charitable Foundation for Children, Edgar A.

Save Our Schools Campaign — advocating against cutbacks in the public school budget ($25,000) see New York Foundation

SCAN ($1,200) see O'Connor Foundation, Magee

Second Baptist Church ($28,825) see Titmus Foundation

Senior Center of Richmond ($8,000) see Metropolitan Health Foundation

Senior Citizens Employment and Services of Alexandria ($7,000) see Ivakota Association

Seven Hills School ($500) see Lane Co., Inc.

Seven Hills School ($15,000) see Wodecroft Foundation

Sheltered Workshop ($10,078) see Lane Foundation, Minnie and Bernard

Sheltering Arms Hospital ($10,000) see O'Bleness Foundation, Charles G.

Sheltering Arms Rehabilitation Hospital ($12,844) see Hunter Trust, Emily S. and Coleman A.

Shenandoah College and Conservatory ($5,000) see Jephson Educational Trust No. 1

Shenandoah College and Conservatory ($22,475) see Osborn Charitable Trust, Edward B.

Shenandoah University ($100,000) see Bryant Foundation

Shenandoah University ($15,000) see Durell Foundation, George Edward

Shenandoah University ($25,000) see Morgan and Samuel Tate Morgan, Jr. Foundation, Marietta McNeil

Shenandoah University ($10,000) see Wheat First Securites

Shenandoah University Library ($25,000) see Scott Foundation, William R., John G., and Emma

Shenandoah University — capital improvement Smith Library ($25,000) see

Gallagher Family Foundation, Lewis P.

Shining Mountain School — scholarship fund ($30,000) see Winkler Foundation, Mark and Catherine

Sister Cities International ($35,000) see Reader's Digest Association

Sky Ranch Foundation see Bacardi Imports

Smith Mountain Lake 4-H Center ($1,700) see Lane Co., Inc.

Smith Mountain Lake 4-H Center ($5,000) see Old Dominion Box Co.

Society of Automotive Engineers' VISION 200 Program ($400,000) see Rockwell International Corp.

Society of St. Andrew ($15,000) see Lane Foundation, Minnie and Bernard

Society of St. Andrew ($10,000) see Three Swallows Foundation

Southampton Academy ($66,250) see Campbell Foundation, Ruth and Henry

Southampton County ($30,000) see Camp Foundation

Southampton County ($42,000) see Campbell Foundation, Ruth and Henry

Southampton County, Virginia ($27,500) see Camp Younts Foundation

Southampton Memorial Hospital ($19,000) see Camp Foundation

Southeast 4-H Educational Center ($31,000) see Camp Foundation

Southeast 4-H Educational Center ($53,000) see Gray Foundation, Garland

Southeastern 4-H Educational ($42,500) see McDougall Charitable Trust, Ruth Camp

Southern Environmental Law Center ($30,000) see Hillsdale Fund

Southern Environmental Law Center — in support of the Center's work to protect coastal wetlands and barrier islands of the Atlantic and Gulf Coast states ($70,000) see Cary Charitable Trust, Mary Flagler

Southern Seminary College — dormitory renovations ($5,000) see Richardson Benevolent Foundation, C. E.

SPARC ($10,000) see Memorial Foundation for Children

SPCA ($8,000) see Universal Leaf Tobacco Co.

Special Olympics ($50) see Schneider Foundation, Robert E.

SRC Housing Richmond ($7,500) see Universal Leaf Tobacco Co.

Steward School Foundation ($25,000) see Herndon Foundation

Stuart Hall ($10,000) see Fitz-Gibbon Charitable Trust

Stuart Hall School ($10,000) see Scott Foundation, William R., John G., and Emma

Student Aid Foundation of Virginia, University of Virginia ($1,000) see Taylor Foundation

Sunnyside Presbyterian Home ($25,000) see Lacy Foundation

Sweet Briar College — scholarship endowment

Virginia (cont.)

($100,000) see Frueauff Foundation, Charles A.

Sweet Briar College ($100,000) see O'Neill Charitable Corporation, F. J.

Sweetbriar College ($5,000) see Charitable Foundation of the Burns Family

Sweetbriar College ($15,000) see Easley Trust, Andrew H. and Anne O.

Sweetbriar College ($4,350) see Perkins Foundation, Joe and Lois

Tazewell County Public School System ($205,000) see Shott, Jr. Foundation, Hugh I.

Theatre IV ($102,000) see Flagler Foundation

Theatre IV ($15,000) see Memorial Foundation for Children

Theatre IV ($500) see Robertshaw Controls Co.

Theatre IV ($5,000) see Thalhimer and Family Foundation, Charles G.

Theatre IV, Empire Theatre — general purpose ($14,750) see Central Fidelity Banks, Inc.

Theatre Virginia ($1,500) see Robertshaw Controls Co.

Theatre Virginia ($1,295) see Thalhimer, Jr. and Family Foundation, William B.

Theological Seminary ($34,000) see Society for the Increase of the Ministry

Theological Seminary ($20,410) see Society for the Increase of the Ministry

Tidewater Academy ($30,000) see Gray Foundation, Garland

Tidewater AIDS Crisis ($1,000) see Goodman & Company

Tidewater Child Care Association — one year mortgage payment on planned building purchase ($44,000) see Frederick Foundation

Tidewater Community College ($25,000) see Wareheim Foundation, E. C.

Tidewater Scholarship Foundation ($75,000) see Beazley Foundation

Town of Altavista, Staunton River Park ($25,000) see Lane Foundation, Minnie and Bernard

Travelers Aid Society ($7,500) see Seay Memorial Trust, George and Effie

Treasurer of Virginia Department of Conservation ($200,000) see Slemp Foundation

Trout Unlimited — support for federal fisheries program ($7,000) see Fisher Foundation

Uncle Billy's Day Committee ($600) see Lane Co., Inc.

Union Mission — furnishings in new senior citizen's cottage and repairs to heating and hot water system ($35,000) see Frederick Foundation

Union Theological Seminary ($10,000) see Board of Trustees of the Prichard School

Union Theological Seminary ($15,000) see Jeffress Memorial Trust, Elizabeth G.

United Offering Fund of Women of the Episcopal Church of the Epiphany, Danville, VA ($6,822) see Bustard Charitable Permanent Trust Fund, Elizabeth and James

U.S. Armored Forces Monument Fund — monument fund

($10,000) see Duchossois Industries

United Way ($1,600) see Bionetics Corp.

United Way ($22,500) see Fair Oaks Foundation, Inc.

United Way ($5,000) see Gottwald Foundation

United Way ($10,000) see Herndon Foundation

United Way ($12,844) see Hunter Trust, Emily S. and Coleman A.

United Way ($5,000) see Media General, Inc.

United Way ($10,988) see Noland Co.

United Way ($6,000) see Taylor Foundation

United Way ($35,000) see Thalhimer and Family Foundation, Charles G.

United Way ($35,000) see Thalhimer Brothers Inc.

United Way ($30,033) see Ukrop's Super Markets, Inc.

United Way of America — expenses related to the organization's search for a new chief executive officer ($111,033) see Hospital Corp. of America

United Way of America — to support a second round of local United Way challenge grants to build the capacity of literacy efforts in up to 13 communities see United Parcel Service of America

United Way of Central Virginia — general purpose ($35,000) see Central Fidelity Banks, Inc.

United Way of Greater Richmond — general purpose ($74,737) see Central Fidelity Banks, Inc.

United Way of Greater Richmond ($80,000) see Reynolds Metals Co.

United Way of Greater Richmond ($35,000) see Universal Leaf Tobacco Co.

United Way of Greater Richmond ($32,400) see Westvaco Corp.

United Way International ($63,000) see Aluminum Co. of America

United Way of the National Capital Area ($250,000) see Mobil Oil Corp.

United Way of Roanoke Valley — to promote and encourage a wholesome community life ($36,000) see Landmark Communications

United Way of Roanoke Valley ($105,000) see Norfolk Southern Corp.

United Way Services ($30,750) see Circuit City Stores

United Way of South Hampton Roads ($20,000) see Batten Foundation

United Way-South Hampton Roads — general purpose ($33,626) see Central Fidelity Banks, Inc.

United Way of South Hampton Roads — to promote and encourage a wholesome community life ($123,000) see Landmark Communications

United Way of South Hampton Roads ($105,000) see Norfolk Southern Corp.

United Way of South Hampton Roads, Building Fund — to promote and encourage a wholesome community life ($50,000) see Landmark Communications

United Way-Virginia Peninsula — general purpose ($12,550) see Central Fidelity Banks, Inc.

University of Richmond ($30,000) see Cole Trust, Quincy

University of Richmond ($10,000) see Gottwald Foundation

University of Richmond ($12,000) see Herndon Foundation

University of Richmond ($100,000) see Massey Foundation

University of Richmond ($20,000) see McCrea Foundation

University of Richmond — building fund ($7,500) see Treakle Foundation, J. Edwin

University of Richmond — soccer scholarship fund ($14,560) see Ukrop's Super Markets, Inc.

University of Richmond ($10,000) see Universal Leaf Tobacco Co.

University of Richmond ($15,000) see Wheat First Securites

University of Richmond ($10,000) see Widgeon Foundation

University of Richmond — for the Butz Foundation scholarship ($5,000) see Butz Foundation

University of Virginia — scholarships ($200,000) see Balfour Foundation, L. G.

University of Virginia ($2,500) see Bannon Foundation

University of Virginia ($20,000) see Brown Foundation, W. L. Lyons

University of Virginia ($30,000) see Chesapeake Corp.

University of Virginia ($4,000) see Dettman Foundation, Leroy E.

University of Virginia ($4,000) see Dettman Foundation, Leroy E.

University of Virginia ($1,500) see Dettman Foundation, Leroy E.

University of Virginia ($33,258) see Huston Foundation

University of Virginia ($386,059) see Jeffress Memorial Trust, Thomas F. and Kate Miller

University of Virginia — to support a center for the study of molecular mechanisms of cell signalling processes ($1,266,900) see Markey Charitable Trust, Lucille P.

University of Virginia ($100,000) see Massey Foundation

University of Virginia ($90,000) see Massey Foundation

University of Virginia ($59,000) see McDougall Charitable Trust, Ruth Camp

University of Virginia ($200,000) see PepsiCo

University of Virginia ($7,500) see Rosenthal Foundation, Richard and Hinda

University of Virginia ($100,000) see Ruffin Foundation, Peter B. & Adeline W.

University of Virginia — health sciences center ($35,000) see Sandoz Corp.

University of Virginia ($12,500) see Ukrop's Super Markets, Inc.

University of Virginia — building program ($20,000) see Wheat First Securites

University of Virginia Alumni Association ($10,000) see Uvas Foundation

University of Virginia Auxiliary Service ($50,000) see Bryant Foundation

University of Virginia Blue Ridge Hospital ($70,000) see Massey Foundation

University of Virginia Football Support Facility ($17,000) see Olsson Memorial Foundation, Elis

University of Virginia Fund ($50,000) see Camp Foundation

University of Virginia Fund ($5,000) see Cassett Foundation, Louis N.

University of Virginia Fund ($10,000) see Fitz-Gibbon Charitable Trust

University of Virginia Fund ($5,000) see Fitz-Gibbon Charitable Trust

University of Virginia Fund — general scholarship ($90,000) see Whitehead Foundation, Lettie Pate

University of Virginia, Graduate Business — to promote and encourage a wholesome community life ($25,000) see Landmark Communications

University of Virginia Health Science — for research in urology ($25,000) see Alexander Foundation, Joseph

University of Virginia Health Sciences Center — nursing fellowship ($250,000) see Thomas Memorial Foundation, Theresa A.

University of Virginia — Jefferson Scholars ($25,000) see Loughran Foundation, Mary and Daniel

University of Virginia Law School ($25,000) see Bryant Foundation

University of Virginia Law School Foundation — security law ($300,000) see Scaife Foundation, Sarah

University of Virginia Law School Foundation — to support the John M. Olin Program in Law and Economics ($212,500) see Olin Foundation, John M.

University of Virginia Medical School ($5,000) see AKC Fund

University of Virginia School of Law ($10,000) see Fortis Inc.

University of Virginia School of Law ($66,664) see Reed Foundation

University of Virginia Student Aid Foundation ($10,000) see Bowen Foundation, Ethel N.

Urban League of Hampton Roads ($10,000) see Norfolk Shipbuilding & Drydock Corp.

Valentine Museum ($1,000) see Best Products Co.

Valentine Museum — capital improvements ($6,000) see Ukrop's Super Markets, Inc.

Valentine Museum ($20,000) see Wheat First Securites

VCU Fund School of Social Work ($50,000) see Circuit City Stores

Virginia Air and Space Museum ($15,000) see Bionetics Corp.

Virginia Baptist Children's Home ($12,500) see Thurman Charitable Foundation for Children, Edgar A.

Virginia Beach Foundation ($5,000) see Fitz-Gibbon Charitable Trust

Virginia Beach Public Library ($25,000) see Goodman & Company

Virginia Center for the Creative Arts ($500) see Old Dominion Box Co.

Virginia College Fund ($50,000) see Beazley Foundation

Virginia College Fund ($12,844) see Hunter Trust, Emily S. and Coleman A.

Virginia College Fund ($12,500) see Mars Foundation

Virginia College Fund ($10,000) see McDougall Charitable Trust, Ruth Camp

Virginia College Fund ($7,500) see Washington Forrest Foundation

Virginia Commonwealth University ($1,700) see Dan River, Inc.

Virginia Commonwealth University ($345,475) see Jeffress Memorial Trust, Thomas F. and Kate Miller

Virginia Commonwealth University ($130,000) see Lawrence Foundation, Lind

Virginia Commonwealth University ($15,000) see Lawrence Foundation, Lind

Virginia Commonwealth University ($2,000) see Lawyers Title Foundation

Virginia Commonwealth University ($20,416) see Reynolds Metals Co.

Virginia Commonwealth University ($5,000) see Thalhimer and Family Foundation, Charles G.

Virginia Commonwealth University ($5,000) see Thalhimer and Family Foundation, Charles G.

Virginia Commonwealth University ($6,000) see Ukrop's Super Markets, Inc.

Virginia Commonwealth University ($5,000) see Widgeon Foundation

Virginia Commonwealth University/Medical College of Virginia ($330,000) see Massey Foundation

Virginia Commonwealth University Special Fund Raising Campaign ($5,000) see Thalhimer Brothers Inc.

Virginia Commonwealth University — Thalhimer Family Fund ($5,000) see Thalhimer Brothers Inc.

Virginia Coop Extension Service ($6,000) see Slemp Foundation

Virginia Crime Prevention Association — for the Crime Prevention Journal for Children ($600) see Bionetics Corp.

Virginia Foundation for Architecture ($5,000) see Fitz-Gibbon Charitable Trust

Virginia Foundation for Independent Colleges ($60,000) see Beazley Foundation

Virginia Foundation for Independent Colleges ($31,000) see Camp Foundation

Virginia Foundation for Independent Colleges — general purpose ($18,500) see Central Fidelity Banks, Inc.

Virginia Foundation for Independent Colleges

($22,500) see Chesapeake Corp.

Virginia Foundation for Independent Colleges ($10,000) see Gottwald Foundation

Virginia Foundation for Independent Colleges ($3,000) see Lawyers Title Foundation

Virginia Foundation for Independent Colleges ($15,000) see Mars Foundation

Virginia Foundation for Independent Colleges ($30,000) see McDougall Charitable Trust, Ruth Camp

Virginia Foundation for Independent Colleges ($5,000) see Noland Co.

Virginia Foundation for Independent Colleges ($8,000) see Norfolk Shipbuilding & Drydock Co.

Virginia Foundation for Independent Colleges ($100,000) see Norfolk Southern Corp.

Virginia Foundation for Independent Colleges ($70,000) see North Shore Foundation

Virginia Foundation for Independent Colleges ($1,500) see Old Dominion Box Co.

Virginia Foundation of Independent Colleges ($21,000) see Reynolds Metals Co.

Virginia Foundation for Independent Colleges ($5,000) see Richardson Benevolent Foundation, C. E.

Virginia Foundation for Independent Colleges ($6,000) see Thalhimer and Family Foundation, Charles G.

Virginia Foundation for Independent Colleges ($6,000) see Thalhimer Brothers Inc.

Virginia Foundation for Independent Colleges ($5,000) see Ukrop's Super Markets, Inc.

Virginia Foundation of Independent Colleges ($10,000) see Universal Leaf Tobacco Co.

Virginia Historical Society ($20,000) see Camp Foundation

Virginia Historical Society ($15,000) see Gray Foundation, Garland

Virginia Historical Society ($30,000) see Jeffress Memorial Trust, Elizabeth G.

Virginia Historical Society ($5,000) see Luck Stone

Virginia Historical Society ($20,000) see McDougall Charitable Trust, Ruth Camp

Virginia Historical Society ($13,500) see Memorial Foundation for Children

Virginia Historical Society ($7,500) see Norfolk Shipbuilding & Drydock Corp.

Virginia Historical Society ($50,000) see Olsson Memorial Foundation, Elis

Virginia Historical Society ($10,000) see Thalhimer, Jr. and Family Foundation, William B.

Virginia Historical Society ($15,000) see Titmus Foundation

Virginia Historical Society Fifth Century Fund ($15,000) see Titmus Foundation

Virginia Home for Boys in Richmond ($30,000) see Flagler Foundation

Virginia Home for Boys in Richmond — shareholder society ($3,000) see Gottwald Foundation

Virginia Institute of Marine Science ($20,000) see Chesapeake Corp.

Virginia Institute of Marine Science ($17,163) see Jeffress Memorial Trust, Thomas F. and Kate Miller

Virginia Intermont College ($32,000) see Massengill-DeFriece Foundation

Virginia Intermont College — handicapped program ($15,500) see Reynolds Foundation, Eleanor T.

Virginia Intermont College ($3,200) see Staley Foundation, Thomas F.

Virginia Mennonite Retirement Community, Inc ($25,000) see Jeffress Memorial Trust, Elizabeth G.

Virginia Military Institute ($25,000) see Camp Younts Foundation

Virginia Military Institute ($100) see Leesona Corp.

Virginia Military Institute — endowment ($20,000) see Wheat First Securites

Virginia Military Institute Foundation ($25,000) see Camp Younts Foundation

Virginia Military Institute Foundation ($25,000) see Camp Younts Foundation

Virginia Military Institute Foundation ($300,000) see Gottwald Foundation

Virginia Military Institute Foundation ($13,000) see Gottwald Foundation

Virginia Military Institute Foundation ($15,000) see Jeffress Memorial Trust, Elizabeth G.

Virginia Muesem of Transportation see Shenandoah Life Insurance Co.

Virginia Museum Foundation ($10,000) see Best Products Co.

Virginia Museum Foundation ($20,000) see Camp Foundation

Virginia Museum Foundation — endowment for decorative arts ($200,000) see Reynolds Foundation, Richard S.

Virginia Museum Foundation ($1,000) see Robertshaw Controls Co.

Virginia Museum Foundation ($3,450) see Thalhimer, Jr. and Family Foundation, William B.

Virginia Museum Foundation — endowment for American Art ($150,000) see Gottwald Foundation

Virginia Museum Foundation — support for program in Himalayan exhibitions ($101,700) see Carpenter Foundation, E. Rhodes and Leona B.

Virginia Museum Foundation — underwrite purchase of 20 Nepalese and Tibetan art objects ($250,000) see Carpenter Foundation, E. Rhodes and Leona B.

Virginia Opera ($23,000) see McDougall Charitable Trust, Ruth Camp

Virginia Opera ($50,000) see Norfolk Shipbuilding & Drydock Corp.

Virginia Opera ($75,000) see Norfolk Southern Corp.

Virginia Opera ($75,000) see North Shore Foundation

Virginia Polytechnic Institute ($50,000) see Beazley Foundation

Virginia Polytechnic Institute ($50,000) see GenCorp

Virginia Polytechnic Institute and State University ($40,000) see Greve Foundation, William and Mary

Virginia Polytechnic Institute and State University ($174,938) see Jeffress Memorial Trust, Thomas F. and Kate Miller

Virginia Polytechnic Institute and State University — research and training in the field of equine gastroenterology ($32,700) see Kade Foundation, Max

Virginia Polytechnic Institute and State University ($5,000) see Love Foundation, Gay and Erskine

Virginia Polytechnic Institute and State University ($4,500) see Lynch Scholarship Foundation, John B.

Virginia Polytechnic Institute and State University ($50,000) see Massey Foundation

Virginia Polytechnic Institute and State University ($25,000) see Reynolds Metals Co.

Virginia Polytechnic Institute and State University ($10,000) see Schott Foundation

Virginia Polytechnic Institute and State University ($36,500) see Sussman Fund, Edna Bailey

Virginia Polytechnic Institute and State University ($7,500) see White Construction Co.

Virginia Polytechnic Institute and State University — to support the establishment of an Adult Day Care Center ($208,000) see duPont Fund, Jessie Ball

Virginia Polytechnic Institute and State University for Department of Animal Science (Morven Park) ($15,000) see Ohrstrom Foundation

Virginia Polytechnic Institute and State University for the Middleburg Equine Research Station ($25,000) see Ohrstrom Foundation

Virginia Scholarship Fund ($1,500) see Dettman Foundation, Leroy E.

Virginia School of Arts ($12,000) see Cheatham Foundation, Owen

Virginia Special Olympics see Booz Allen & Hamilton

Virginia Stage Company ($75,000) see Norfolk Southern Corp.

Virginia Student Aid Foundation ($6,000) see Hastings Trust

Virginia Student Aid Foundation ($3,500) see Noland Co.

Virginia Tech Foundation — for renovations at the continuing education center and Reynolds Homestead ($220,000) see Reynolds Foundation, Richard S.

Virginia Tech Foundation—Tommorow's Teachers Program see Shenandoah Life Insurance Co.

Virginia Theological Seminary ($5,000) see Woods-Greer Foundation

Virginia Union University ($25,000) see Cole Trust, Quincy

Virginia United Methodist Conference ($10,000) see Lane Foundation, Minnie and Bernard

Virginia Wesleyan College ($10,000) see Norfolk Shipbuilding & Drydock Corp.

Virginia Wesleyan College Annual Fund — to promote and encourage a wholesome community life ($52,000) see Landmark Communications

Virginia Wesleyan College — fourth payment on pledge and honorarium for Dr. Lambuth Clarke ($75,000) see Frederick Foundation

Virginia Zoological Park ($500) see Bionetics Corp.

Visiting Nurse Association of Northern Virginia — care of cancer patients ($80,000) see Stewart Trust under the will of Mary E. Stewart, Alexander and Margaret

Volunteer Emergency Families for Children ($2,000) see Lawrence Foundation, Lind

Volunteer — National Center ($11,000) see Garvey Fund, Jean and Willard

Washington and Lee Law School ($4,305) see Kilmartin Industries

Washington and Lee University — scholarship ($11,000) see Franklin Charitable Trust, Ershel

Washington & Lee University see Greenwood Mills

Washington and Lee University ($100,000) see Herndon Foundation

Washington and Lee University ($10,000) see Jones Family Foundation, Eugenie and Joseph

Washington and Lee University ($30,000) see Loughran Foundation, Mary and Daniel

Washington and Lee University ($4,000) see Media General, Inc.

Washington and Lee University — addition for law school ($7,500) see Treakle Foundation, J. Edwin

Washington and Lee University ($50,000) see Williams Family Foundation of Georgia

Washington Strategy Seminar ($125,000) see Randolph Foundation

West End Christian School — tuition support ($5,000) see Friendship Fund

West Point Literacy Club ($20,000) see Olsson Memorial Foundation, Elis

West Point Volunteer Fire Department ($15,000) see Chesapeake Corp.

Western Virginia Foundatin for Arts & Sciences see Shenandoah Life Insurance Co.

Western Virginia Foundation for the Arts and Sciences ($40,275) see Carter Foundation, Beirne

Westminster-Canterbury Foundation — fellowship endowment ($100,000) see Thomas Memorial Foundation, Theresa A.

Westminster-Canterbury Foundation — care of aged

women ($145,000) see Whitehead Foundation, Lettie Pate

WHRO Capital Campaign ($10,000) see Norfolk Shipbuilding & Drydock Corp.

WHRO Public Broadcasting ($20,000) see North Shore Foundation

WHRO-TV, Channel 15 ($2,400) see Bionetics Corp.

Wilderness Conservancy ($10,000) see Northen, Mary Moody

William and Mary Athletic Education Foundation ($26,635) see Ukrop's Super Markets, Inc.

William and Mary College ($100,000) see Herndon Foundation

William and Mary Tennis Endowment ($100,000) see Bryant Foundation

Winchester Shelter for Abused Spouses, VA ($25,000) see Luchsinger Family Foundation

Winkler Botanical Preserve — general funding ($130,000) see Winkler Foundation, Mark and Catherine

Wolf Trap ($5,000) see Fairchild Corp.

Wolf Trap Foundation see Booz Allen & Hamilton

Wolf Trap Foundation ($100,000) see Filene Foundation, Lincoln and Therese

Wolf Trap Foundation ($25,000) see Filene Foundation, Lincoln and Therese

Wolf Trap Foundation ($12,500) see Filene Foundation, Lincoln and Therese

Wolf Trap Foundation ($7,500) see Higginson Trust, Corina

Women in Community Service ($5,000) see DeRoy Foundation, Helen L.

Woodberry Forest School ($15,000) see Fitz-Gibbon Charitable Trust

Woodberry Forest School ($610,512) see Kenan, Jr. Charitable Trust, William R.

Woodberry Forest School ($5,000) see Osceola Foundation

Woodberry Forest School ($200,000) see Ruffin Foundation, Peter B. & Adeline W.

Woodberry Forest School ($45,000) see Sprague Educational and Charitable Foundation, Seth

Woodway Volunteer Fire Department ($15,000) see Slemp Foundation

YMCA ($40,600) see Camp Foundation

YMCA ($13,000) see Campbell Foundation, Ruth and Henry

YMCA ($25,000) see Lacy Foundation

YMCA ($44,900) see Lane Foundation, Minnie and Bernard

YMCA ($7,307) see Noland Co.

YMCA ($5,000) see Richardson Benevolent Foundation, C. E.

YMCA ($15,000) see Titmus Foundation

YMCA ($112,109) see United Co.

YMCA ($30,300) see Wareheim Foundation, E. C.

YMCA of Roanoke Valley see Shenandoah Life Insurance Co.

Virginia (cont.)

Young America's Foundation ($2,500) see Bannan Foundation, Arline and Thomas J.

Young America's Foundation — college lecture series ($25,000) see Salvatori Foundation, Henry

Young America's Foundation ($5,000) see Wilbur Foundation, Marguerite Eyer

YWCA ($25,000) see Memorial Foundation for Children

YWCA ($10,000) see Seay Memorial Trust, George and Effie

Washington

Aberdeen Little League ($78,822) see Bishop Foundation, E. K. and Lillian F.

AIDS Housing of Washington see Boeing Co.

Allegro ($6,750) see Washington Trust Bank

Allegro-Baroque and Beyond ($2,500) see Wasmer Foundation

Altrusa Club ($1,050) see Welch Testamentary Trust, George T.

American Cancer Society ($3,000) see Dupar Foundation

American Cancer Society ($1,200) see Shemanski Testamentary Trust, Tillie and Alfred

American Leadership Forum ($45,000) see New Horizon Foundation

American Red Cross ($3,000) see Lassen Foundation, Irving A.

American Red Cross ($20,000) see McEachern Charitable Trust, D. V. & Ida J.

American Red Cross ($15,000) see New Horizon Foundation

Annie Wright School ($50,000) see Ford Foundation, Edward E.

Annie Wright School ($8,500) see New Horizon Foundation

Applied Technology Training Center see Boeing Co.

Arbor Fund ($3,542,072) see Bloedel Foundation

Arboretum Foundation see Boeing Co.

Archdiocesan Housing Authority ($15,000) see Fuchs Foundation, Gottfried & Mary

Archdiocese of Seattle ($25,000) see Lewis Foundation, Frank J.

Archdiocese of Seattle ($50,000) see Snyder Foundation, Frost and Margaret

Architecture and Children ($5,000) see Archibald Charitable Foundation, Norman

Arthritis Foundation ($25,000) see Lockwood Foundation, Byron W. and Alice L.

Artist Trust ($20,000) see New Horizon Foundation

Asian Plaza Youth Foundation — scholarships ($5,000) see Kawabe Memorial Fund

Associated Ministries ($14,000) see Kilworth Charitable Foundation, Florence B.

Atlantic Street Center Early Childhood Project see Boeing Co.

AVIS ($50,000) see Murray Foundation

Bainbridge Alliance Church ($1,000) see Bloedel Foundation

Bainbridge Christian Assembly ($1,000) see Bloedel Foundation

Bainbridge First Baptist Church ($1,000) see Bloedel Foundation

Bainbridge Foundation ($1,800) see Bloedel Foundation

Ballet Tacoma ($2,000) see Ballet Makers

BASH ($13,076) see New Horizon Foundation

Battle Ground High School ($1,000) see Haas Foundation, Saul and Dayee G.

Behavioral Sciences Institute — to support training, quality assurance, and communications activities to assist in expanding the use of the Homebuilders model of family preservation ($625,000) see Clark Foundation, Edna McConnell

Bellarmine Preparatory School ($32,000) see Snyder Foundation, Frost and Margaret

Bellevue Botanical Garden Society — building expansion ($30,000) see Smith Horticultural Trust, Stanley

Ben B. Cheney Scholarship Program — provide college scholarships to students from Pierce County high schools ($37,500) see Cheney Foundation, Ben B.

Bennington College Corporation ($60,000) see Valentine Foundation, Lawson

Bethany Lutheran Church ($1,000) see Bloedel Foundation

Bethel School District ($5,000) see New Horizon Foundation

Big Brothers and Big Sisters ($7,500) see Cawsey Trust

Big Brothers and Big Sisters ($2,000) see Lassen Foundation, Irving A.

Big Brothers and Big Sisters ($9,750) see New Horizon Foundation

Black Dollar Days Task Force ($20,000) see Needmor Fund

Blue Mountain Area Foundation ($3,650) see Welch Testamentary Trust, George T.

Bob Hope Fund ($12,000) see Anderson Foundation

Boy Scouts of America ($25,000) see McEachern Charitable Trust, D. V. & Ida J.

Boy Scouts of America ($12,500) see PemCo. Corp.

Boyer Children's Clinic ($25,000) see Medina Foundation

Boyer Clinic and Preschool ($3,000) see Anderson Foundation

Boys and Girls Club ($35,000) see Forest Foundation

Boys and Girls Club ($10,000) see Kilworth Charitable Trust, William

Boys and Girls Club ($5,000) see Murray Foundation

Boys and Girls Club ($35,000) see New Horizon Foundation

Boys and Girls Club ($10,000) see PemCo. Corp.

Boys Village ($5,000) see Glaser Foundation

Bread of Life Mission ($2,500) see Cook Foundation, Louella

Bread of Life Mission ($30,000) see Medina Foundation

Bread of Life Mission Association ($5,000) see Fales Foundation Trust

Broadway Theater District ($10,000) see Kilworth Charitable Foundation, Florence B.

Broadway Theatre District ($20,000) see Murray Foundation

Bush School ($6,500) see Gilmore Foundation, Earl B.

Bush School ($10,000) see Wyman Youth Trust

Camp Brotherhood ($50,000) see PemCo. Corp.

Camp Brotherhood ($2,000) see Shemanski Testamentary Trust, Tillie and Alfred

Campaign for Puget Sound ($10,000) see Harder Foundation

Campbell Charitable Foundation ($50,000) see Cawsey Trust

Campfire ($5,000) see Kilworth Charitable Trust, William

Campfire of Snohomish County ($10,915) see PemCo. Corp.

Capital Area Youth Symphony ($2,000) see Dupar Foundation

Carnegie Art Center ($1,780) see Welch Testamentary Trust, George T.

Caroline Kline Galland Home ($3,000) see Shemanski Testamentary Trust, Tillie and Alfred

Cathedral of St. John the Evangelist ($19,000) see Leuthold Foundation

Catherine Booth House — lease payments on new facility ($20,500) see Hemingway Foundation, Robert G.

Catholic Bishop of Spokane ($206,900) see Guse Endowment Trust, Frank J. and Adelaide

Catholic Community Center ($10,000) see Univar Corp.

Catholic Community Services ($10,000) see Cook Foundation, Louella

Catholic Community Services ($3,000) see Dupar Foundation

Catholic Community Services ($12,000) see Fales Foundation Trust

Catholic Community Services ($25,000) see Forest Foundation

Catholic Community Services ($5,000) see Glaser Foundation

Catholic Community Services ($15,000) see PemCo. Corp.

Catholic Community Services Sacred Heart Shelter ($7,500) see Fales Foundation Trust

Catholic Community Services, Seattle/King County ($82,500) see Norcliffe Fund

Catholic Fund — tuition assistance ($20,000) see Fuchs Foundation, Gottfried & Mary

Central DuPage Hospital ($2,000) see Psychists

Central Washington University ($15,000) see Petrie Trust, Lorene M.

Central Youth and Family Services ($25,000) see Horizons Foundation

Central Youth and Family Services ($25,000) see McEachern Charitable Trust, D. V. & Ida J.

Centrum ($5,000) see Bishop Foundation, E. K. and Lillian F.

Charles Wright Academy ($50,000) see Murray Foundation

Chelan County Public Hospital ($57,855) see Wells Foundation, A. Z.

Chelan County Public Hospital ($47,440) see Wells Foundation, A. Z.

Childhaven ($65,000) see Foster Foundation

Childhaven ($150,000) see Glaser Foundation

Children Activity Museum ($22,225) see Petrie Trust, Lorene M.

Children's Home Society ($5,200) see Stubblefield, Estate of Joseph L.

Children's Home Society ($1,575) see Welch Testamentary Trust, George T.

Children's Hospital ($35,000) see Foster Foundation

Children's Hospital Foundation ($25,000) see Bishop Foundation, E. K. and Lillian F.

Children's Hospital Foundation ($25,000) see Seafirst Corp.

Children's Hospital Foundation ($4,000) see Wyman Youth Trust

Children's Industrial Home ($8,000) see Kilworth Charitable Trust, William

Children's Museum of Tacoma — capital ($32,000) see Simpson Investment Co.

Children's Trust Foundation ($15,000) see Ray Foundation

Chrystos ($35,000) see Lannan Foundation

Citizens Against Domestic Abuse ($7,500) see Arise Charitable Trust

City of Lacey ($5,000) see Lassen Foundation, Irving A.

City of Sumner — complete the Daffodil Valley Sports Complex ($50,000) see Cheney Foundation, Ben B.

City of Vancouver ($25,000) see Burlington Northern Inc.

Clallam-Jefferson County Community Action ($8,000) see ITT Rayonier

Clark State Community College ($28,125) see Navistar International Corp.

Clymer Foundation ($30,000) see Kreielsheimer Foundation Trust

Clymer Museum ($75,000) see Petrie Trust, Lorene M.

Clymer Museum of Western Art ($10,000) see PemCo. Corp.

Community Alcohol and Drug Services ($5,000) see Archibald Charitable Foundation, Norman

Community College District 15 ($23,955) see Wells Foundation, A. Z.

Community Colleges of Spokane ($16,000) see Washington Trust Bank

Community Youth Services ($5,000) see Lassen Foundation, Irving A.

Conzaga University — support of the University Center for Information Technology ($25,000) see Jewett Foundation, George Frederick

Cornish College of the Arts — scholarships; books and supplies ($265,958) see Kreielsheimer Foundation Trust

Cornish Institute ($9,333) see Merrill Foundation, R. D.

Corporate Council for the Arts ($17,500) see First Interstate Bank NW Region

Corporate Council for the Arts ($100,000) see PACCAR

Corporate Council of Arts ($10,000) see Univar Corp.

Corporate Council for the Arts ($20,000) see Washington Mutual Savings Bank

Corporate Council for the Arts ($95,000) see Weyerhaeuser Co.

Corporation of the Archdiocese of Seattle ($93,000) see Norcliffe Fund

Cowiche Canyon Conservancy ($3,000) see Petrie Trust, Lorene M.

Crisis Clinic of Thurston and Mason Counties ($2,800) see Olympia Brewing Co.

Crista Ministries — world concern ($75,000) see Stewardship Foundation

Cystic Fibrosis Foundation ($5,000) see Thurston Charitable Foundation

DESC ($20,000) see Foster Foundation

Discovery Lodge Campaign ($10,000) see Cawsey Trust

District 17 Community College Foundation ($6,200) see Wasmer Foundation

Dominican Outreach Foundation ($40,000) see Leuthold Foundation

Downtown Emergency Services ($5,000) see Cook Foundation, Louella

Eagle Harbor Congregational Church ($1,000) see Bloedel Foundation

Eastern Washington Historical Society ($4,000) see Wasmer Foundation

Eastern Washington Museum ($450,000) see Cowles Foundation, Harriet Cheney

Eastside Domestic Violence ($5,000) see Wharton Foundation

Educare Center ($2,200) see Welch Testamentary Trust, George T.

Episcopal Diocese of Spokane ($5,500) see Johnston-Fix Foundation

Episcopal Diocese of Spokane ($5,000) see Johnston-Hanson Foundation

Episcopal Diocese of Spokane — maintenance fund ($5,000) see Johnston-Hanson Foundation

Evergreen Counseling Center ($7,500) see ITT Rayonier

Family Counseling ($5,000) see Murray Foundation

Family Services — rehabilitation program for low-income stroke survivors ($35,000) see Hearst Foundation

Fauntleroy Center ($20,000) see Bishop Foundation, E. K. and Lillian F.

First Avenue Service Center ($12,500) see Fales Foundation Trust

First Presbyterian Church ($4,000) see Cawsey Trust

First Presbyterian Church ($10,000) see Lockwood Foundation, Byron W. and Alice L.

Food Lifeline ($5,000) see Kawabe Memorial Fund

Food Lifeline ($15,000) see McEachern Charitable Trust, D. V. & Ida J.

Forest Ridge Convent ($15,000) see Geneva Foundation

45th Street Community Clinic — obstetrics program ($5,000) see Fales Foundation Trust

Foundation for Community Initiatives ($52,760) see Medina Foundation

Fred Hutchinson Cancer Research ($2,000) see See Foundation, Charles

Fred Hutchinson Cancer Research Center — core equipment for structural biology program ($700,000) see Murdock Charitable Trust, M. J.

Fred Hutchinson Cancer Research Center ($20,000) see Seafirst Corp.

Fred Hutchinson Cancer Research Center ($1,200) see Shemanski Testamentary Trust, Tillie and Alfred

Fred Hutchinson Cancer Research Center ($25,000) see Skinner Corp.

Fred Hutchinson Cancer Research Center, Department of Genetics ($25,958) see Childs Memorial Fund for Medical Research, Jane Coffin

Fred Hutchinson Cancer Research Center — support the publication of the Scientific Report and other papers as may benefit from the Scientific Community and inform the General Public of research in process at the Center ($60,000) see Quest for Truth Foundation

Fremont Public Association ($20,000) see Fales Foundation Trust

Friends of the Earth ($10,000) see Horizons Foundation

Friends of Lakewold Fund ($2,000) see Bloedel Foundation

Full Gospel Mission — youth summer camp ($4,000) see Wasmer Foundation

Full Gospel Mission for All Nations ($12,300) see Leuthold Foundation

Future Leaders of America ($10,000) see Wharton Foundation

Giraffe Project ($5,000) see Hunt Foundation

Gonzaga Preparatory School — educational ($20,000) see Dreyfus Foundation, Max and Victoria

Gonzaga University ($25,000) see Burlington Northern Inc.

Gonzaga University — scholarship funds ($150,000) see Comstock Foundation

Gonzaga University ($12,250) see Johnston-Fix Foundation

Gonzaga University ($16,000) see Johnston-Hanson Foundation

Gonzaga University ($4,400) see Johnston-Hanson Foundation

Gonzaga University ($250,000) see Kreielsheimer Foundation Trust

Gonzaga University — engineering building fund ($12,500) see Washington Trust Bank

Gonzaga University, Spokane, WA — to establish a regional library ($250,000) see Boise Cascade Corp.

Good Samaritan Hospital ($5,000) see Kilworth Charitable Trust, William

Good Samaritan Outreach Services — senior day care ($15,000) see Fuchs Foundation, Gottfried & Mary

Goodwill Games — a multicultural athletic competition see Puget Sound Power & Light Co.

Grant County Public Hospital District Number 1 ($57,855) see Wells Foundation, A. Z.

Grant County Public Hospital District Number 3 ($57,855) see Wells Foundation, A. Z.

Grant County Public Hospital District Number 2 ($57,855) see Wells Foundation, A. Z.

Greater Japanese Cultural Committee — scholarship ($3,000) see Kawabe Memorial Fund

Greater Tacoma Community Center ($43,500) see Forest Foundation

Greater Tacoma Community Foundation ($295,000) see Weyerhaeuser Co.

Greater Tacoma Community Foundation — Broadway Theatre — capital ($66,667) see Simpson Investment Co.

Habitat for Humanity ($7,000) see Johnston-Hanson Foundation

Hearing, Speech, and Deafness Center ($15,000) see Glaser Foundation

Hearing Speech and Deafness Center ($10,000) see Lockwood Foundation, Byron W. and Alice L.

Helping Hand of South Whidbey ($9,166) see Arise Charitable Trust

Heritage College — library and learning center ($500,000) see Murdock Charitable Trust, M. J.

Heritage College ($50,000) see Petrie Trust, Lorene M.

Heritage College ($25,000) see Seafirst Corp.

Heritage College ($15,000) see Skinner Corp.

Heritage College ($13,000) see Washington Mutual Savings Bank

Holy Family of Jesus Cambodian Episcopal Church ($27,500) see Forest Foundation

Holy Names Music Center ($3,500) see Wasmer Foundation

HOPE ($3,000) see Arise Charitable Trust

Hope Heart Foundation ($10,000) see Lockwood Foundation, Byron W. and Alice L.

Hospice of Spokane ($3,000) see Lapham-Hickey Steel Corp.

Hospital District Number Four of Okanogan County ($71,060) see Wells Foundation, A. Z.

Hudson Bay's High School ($1,500) see Haas Foundation, Saul and Dayee G.

Immanuel Presbyterian Church ($7,500) see Kilworth Charitable Foundation, Florence B.

Independent Colleges of Washington ($5,000) see Anderson Foundation

Independent Colleges of Washington ($35,000) see First Interstate Bank NW Region

Independent Colleges of Washington ($70,000) see PACCAR

Independent Colleges of Washington ($15,000) see PemCo. Corp.

Independent Colleges of Washington see Puget Sound Power & Light Co.

Independent Colleges of Washington ($20,000) see Washington Mutual Savings Bank

Independent Colleges of Washington ($55,000) see Wollenberg Foundation

Inglewood Residence Services ($3,000) see See Foundation, Charles

Inland Empire Girl Scout Council ($10,000) see Leuthold Foundation

Inland Empire Public Lands Council see Patagonia

Inland Northwest Community Foundation ($12,750) see Washington Trust Bank

Interfaith Center ($20,000) see New Horizon Foundation

Intiman Theatre — living history program ($18,000) see Nesholm Family Foundation

ISSACHAR ($125,000) see Stewardship Foundation

Japan American Society — scholarships ($4,000) see Kawabe Memorial Fund

Jewish Community Center ($3,000) see Shemanski Testamentary Trust, Tillie and Alfred

Jewish Federation ($3,100) see Shemanski Testamentary Trust, Tillie and Alfred

Joel E. Ferris High School ($3,000) see Haas Foundation, Saul and Dayee G.

Joel E. Ferris High School ($2,200) see Haas Foundation, Saul and Dayee G.

Junior Achievement ($2,500) see Dupar Foundation

Junior Achievement ($15,000) see PemCo. Corp.

Junior Achievement see Puget Sound Power & Light Co.

Kawabe Memorial House ($2,000) see Kawabe Memorial Fund

KCTS Association ($12,500) see Skinner Corp.

KCTS Channel 9 ($10,000) see Thurston Charitable Foundation

Kennedy High School ($10,000) see PemCo. Corp.

King High School ($1,000) see Haas Foundation, Saul and Dayee G.

KPBX Spokane Public Radio ($7,500) see Leuthold Foundation

L.I.S.C. ($35,700) see Medina Foundation

Lakeside School ($3,500) see Haas Foundation, Saul and Dayee G.

Lakeside School ($5,000) see Wyman Youth Trust

Lakeside School Alumni Fund ($7,000) see Wyman Youth Trust

Laughing Horse Summer Theater ($7,508) see Petrie Trust, Lorene M.

Legal Aid for Washington Foundation ($51,000) see Hemingway Foundation, Robert G.

Lewis and Clark High School ($4,000) see Haas Foundation, Saul and Dayee G.

Life Skills ($10,000) see Bishop Foundation, E. K. and Lillian F.

Life Skills ($4,000) see Glaser Foundation

Longview Public Schools — head start program at St. Helens Elementary School ($30,000) see Wollenberg Foundation

Loschky, Marquardt and Nesholm — Seattle Concert Hall design ($36,000) see Kreielsheimer Foundation Trust

Love ($8,000) see Thurston Charitable Foundation

Luther Child Center ($5,000) see Cawsey Trust

Lutheran Compass Center ($2,500) see Cook Foundation, Louella

Make-A-Wish Foundation ($10,225) see Hemingway Foundation, Robert G.

Market Foundation ($15,000) see Horizons Foundation

Martin Luther King Housing Development Association — assist with the purchase and renovation of 30 rental houses ($50,000) see Cheney Foundation, Ben B.

Mary Bridge Children's Hospital ($15,000) see Fuchs Foundation, Gottfried & Mary

Mary Bridge Children's Hospital ($8,333) see Merrill Foundation, R. D.

Mary Bridge Children's Hospital ($5,000) see Murray Foundation

Mason County Senior Activities Association — operating ($30,325) see Simpson Investment Co.

Medical Foundation Harborview Medical Center ($1,200) see Shemanski Testamentary Trust, Tillie and Alfred

Medina Children's Service ($20,000) see Wharton Foundation

Mercer Island School District — Phase II Cognitive Studies for Educational Practice ($184,268) see McDonnell Foundation, James S.

Metro Catholic Broadcasting ($10,000) see Clark Foundation

Middle East Media ($20,000) see M.E. Foundation

Middle East Media ($15,000) see Tyndale House Foundation

Millionaire Club ($2,500) see Cook Foundation, Louella

Multicare Center ($7,000) see Kilworth Charitable Trust, William

Multicare Medical Center ($4,500) see Kilworth Charitable Foundation, Florence B.

Multiple Sclerosis Society ($1,200) see Shemanski Testamentary Trust, Tillie and Alfred

Museum of Flight ($15,000) see Archibald Charitable Foundation, Norman

Museum of Flight ($11,000) see Lockwood Foundation, Byron W. and Alice L.

Museum of Flight ($15,000) see McEachern Charitable Trust, D. V. & Ida J.

Mustard Seed Neighborhood Center ($6,000) see Bishop Foundation, E. K. and Lillian F.

Nature Conservancy ($5,000) see Univar Corp.

New Horizon Foundation — unrestricted grant ($2,692,000) see Sequoia Foundation

New Horizons for Learning ($5,000) see Wyman Youth Trust

New Horizons Ministries ($10,500) see Wharton Foundation

Nikkei Concerns ($150,000) see Ishiyama Foundation

Nikkei Concerns — nursing home ($10,000) see Kawabe Memorial Fund

North Central High School ($1,200) see Haas Foundation, Saul and Dayee G.

North Thurston School District ($4,000) see Lassen Foundation, Irving A.

Northwest Center for the Retarded ($26,175) see McEachern Charitable Trust, D. V. & Ida J.

Northwest Community Center Association ($10,000) see Leuthold Foundation

Northwest Congregation ($24,000) see Bell Trust

Northwest Harvest ($20,000) see Foster Foundation

Northwest Mediation Service ($10,000) see Wharton Foundation

Northwest Public Affairs Network ($15,000) see Deer Creek Foundation

Northwest Public Affairs Network ($10,000) see Deer Creek Foundation

Northwest School for Hearing Impaired ($78,600) see Medina Foundation

Northwest School for Hearing-Impaired Children ($15,000) see Skinner Corp.

Northwest Trek — construct bear exhibit and educational complex ($50,000) see Cheney Foundation, Ben B.

Northwest Trek Foundation ($35,000) see Forest Foundation

Northwest Youth Services ($5,000) see Glaser Foundation

NRIC/Save Our Wild Salmon — Columbia River Basin/Salmon ($100,000) see Bullitt Foundation

NW School Hearing Impaired Children ($7,000) see Kilworth Charitable Foundation, Florence B.

Office of Rural and Farmworker Housing — to develop a revolving loan fund for financing the predevelopment costs related to farm worker housing development ($500,000) see Northwest Area Foundation

Okanogan County Public Hospital District Number 3 ($57,855) see Wells Foundation, A. Z.

Okanogan-Douglas County Hospital District Number 1 ($57,855) see Wells Foundation, A. Z.

1000 Friends of Washington — open space ($100,000) see Bullitt Foundation

1224 South I Street ($1,217) see New Horizon Foundation

Overlake Hospital Foundation ($100,000) see PACCAR

Overlake Hospital Foundation ($6,000) see Thurston Charitable Foundation

Overlake Hospital Foundation ($20,000) see Wyman Youth Trust

Washington (cont.)

Oysterville Foundation ($6,000) see Thurston Charitable Foundation

P.A.C.T. ($25,000) see Vollrath Co.

Pacific Arts Center ($5,000) see Wyman Youth Trust

Pacific Lutheran University ($3,000) see Anderson Foundation

Pacific Lutheran University ($25,000) see Forest Foundation

Pacific Lutheran University ($15,000) see Fuchs Foundation, Gottfried & Mary

Pacific Lutheran University ($7,000) see Kilworth Charitable Foundation, Florence B.

Pacific Lutheran University ($10,000) see Kilworth Charitable Trust, William

Pacific Lutheran University ($15,000) see Murray Foundation

Pacific Lutheran University — capital needs ($50,000) see Sequoia Foundation

Pacific Lutheran University ($5,000) see Stubblefield, Estate of Joseph L.

Pacific Lutheran University — acquire an energy dispersive X-ray spectrometer ($35,000) see Cheney Foundation, Ben B.

Pacific Northwest Association of Independent Schools ($33,000) see McEachern Charitable Trust, D. V. & Ida J.

Pacific Northwest Ballet ($20,000) see Persis Corp.

Pacific Northwest Ballet ($40,000) see Seafirst Corp.

Pacific Northwest Ballet ($10,100) see Thurston Charitable Foundation

Pacific Northwest Ballet ($5,000) see Wyman Youth Trust

Pacific Northwest Ballet — phase III construction ($350,000) see Kreielsheimer Foundation Trust

Pacific Northwest Ballet — artistic fees and translator for "Pepita" ($10,000) see Nesholm Family Foundation

Pacific Northwest Research Foundation ($100,000) see Lockwood Foundation, Byron W. and Alice L.

Pacific Northwest Research Foundation — to support a study of the impact of pollution of Puget Sound ($50,000) see Quest for Truth Foundation

Pacific Science Center ($25,000) see Seafirst Corp.

Pacific Science Center Foundation — technology exhibit ($400,000) see Murdock Charitable Trust, M. J.

Pan Terra Alternative ($1,500) see Haas Foundation, Saul and Dayee G.

Pathways for Women ($15,000) see Cawsey Trust

People for Puget Sound ($15,000) see Horizons Foundation

People for Puget Sound — Puget Sound and Strait of Georgia ($100,000) see Bullitt Foundation

Peregrine Fund, Yakima, WA ($15,000) see Boise Cascade Corp.

Phoenix Country Day School ($35,500) see Wharton Foundation

Pierce County Association of Catholic Educators ($20,000) see Fuchs Foundation, Gottfried & Mary

Pierce County Deanery ($15,000) see Fuchs Foundation, Gottfried & Mary

Pike Market Medical Center ($15,000) see Glaser Foundation

Pike Market Medical Clinic ($20,000) see Foster Foundation

Pioneer Farm Museum — restore the activities cabin ($29,000) see Cheney Foundation, Ben B.

Planet Earth Foundation ($25,000) see Norcliffe Fund

Planned Parenthood Federation of America ($750) see Arise Charitable Trust

Planned Parenthood Federation of America ($25,000) see Foster Foundation

Planned Parenthood Federation of America ($3,000) see Shwayder Foundation, Fay

Planned Parenthood Federation of America ($1,500) see Welch Testamentary Trust, George T.

Planned Parenthood of Seattle ($25,000) see Horizons Foundation

Poncho ($8,000) see Thurston Charitable Foundation

Program for Appropriate Technology in Health — support for the International Task Force on Hepatitis B Immunization ($1,000,000) see McDonnell Foundation, James S.

Program for Appropriate Technology in Health — support of family planning-related activities ($1,050,000) see Hewlett Foundation, William and Flora

Program for Early Parent Support ($25,000) see Horizons Foundation

Project Read of Walla Walla ($3,750) see Welch Testamentary Trust, George T.

Prosthetics Research Foundation ($80,000) see Hemingway Foundation, Robert G.

Prosthetics Research Foundation ($35,000) see Herzog Foundation, Carl J.

Protestant Espicopal Churches and Dioceses of United States — capital ($35,000) see Simpson Investment Co.

Providence Foundation of Seattle ($12,400) see Wharton Foundation

Radio Help Program — makes Puget Power vehicles a ready resource from which to make emergency calls for help see Puget Sound Power & Light Co.

Resource Center for the Handicapped ($35,000) see Medina Foundation

Ruth Dykeman Children's Center ($50,000) see Medina Foundation

Ruth Dykeman Children's Foundation ($9,000) see Thurston Charitable Foundation

Ryther Child Center ($35,000) see McEachern Charitable Trust, D. V. & Ida J.

Safe Streets Campaign — capital ($35,000) see Simpson Investment Co.

St. Elizabeth Medical Center ($100,000) see Petrie Trust, Lorene M.

St. George's School — capital campaign ($50,000) see Jewett Foundation, George Frederick

St. George's School ($17,500) see Johnston-Fix Foundation

St. George's School ($25,600) see Leuthold Foundation

St. George's School ($69,167) see Washington Trust Bank

St. James Cathedral Grade School ($166,666) see PACCAR

St. Joseph Hospital — expand the emergency medical services center ($100,000) see Cheney Foundation, Ben B.

St. Joseph's Hospital ($5,000) see Kilworth Charitable Trust, William

St. Martins College ($8,000) see Clark Foundation

St. Martin's College — pavilion improvements ($20,000) see Fuchs Foundation, Gottfried & Mary

St. Marys Episcopal Church ($5,000) see Merrill Foundation, R. D.

St. Peter Health Foundation ($3,000) see Olympia Brewing Co.

St. Peter's Hospital Foundation ($4,000) see Gavin Foundation, James and Zita

Salvation Army ($15,000) see Anderson Foundation

Salvation Army ($2,500) see Cook Foundation, Louella

Salvation Army ($10,000) see Lassen Foundation, Irving A.

Salvation Army ($12,000) see Leuthold Foundation

San Juan Community Theatre Group ($116,314) see Confidence Foundation

Seafirst Scholarships ($161,478) see Seafirst Corp.

Seattle Art Museum ($31,250) see Lockwood Foundation, Byron W. and Alice L.

Seattle Art Museum ($4,375) see Merrill Foundation, R. D.

Seattle Art Museum ($143,850) see Norcliffe Fund

Seattle Art Museum ($15,000) see Thurston Charitable Foundation

Seattle Art Museum ($10,000) see Univar Corp.

Seattle Art Museum ($40,540) see Washington Mutual Savings Bank

Seattle Art Museum — support of the Downtown Museum Capital Campaign ($25,000) see Jewett Foundation, George Frederick

Seattle Art Museum Foundation ($200,000) see Kreielsheimer Foundation Trust

Seattle Art Museum — Weyerhaeuser Gallery ($5,000) see Rodman Foundation

Seattle Arts Stabilization Fund ($21,000) see Seafirst Corp.

Seattle Betsuin Buddhist Temple ($10,500) see Kawabe Memorial Fund

Seattle Catholic Community Services ($40,000) see Brencanda Foundation

Seattle Center Foundation — summer program ($75,000) see Kreielsheimer Foundation Trust

Seattle Central Community College Foundation ($10,000) see Ray Foundation

Seattle Children's Theater ($25,000) see First Interstate Bank NW Region

Seattle Children's Theater ($14,063) see McCaw Foundation

Seattle Children's Theatre ($6,250) see Bishop Foundation, E. K. and Lillian F.

Seattle Emergency Housing Service ($15,000) see Fales Foundation Trust

Seattle Goodwill Games ($2,000) see Dupar Foundation

Seattle Goodwill Games Organizing Committee ($35,250) see Norcliffe Fund

Seattle Habitat for Humanity ($30,000) see Medina Foundation

Seattle Housing Resource Group ($30,000) see Foster Foundation

Seattle Indian Shelter — emergency shelter ($8,000) see Fales Foundation Trust

Seattle Kidney Center ($8,000) see Lassen Foundation, Irving A.

Seattle Opera ($13,375) see McCaw Foundation

Seattle Opera Association ($12,000) see Archibald Charitable Foundation, Norman

Seattle Opera Association ($120,000) see Kreielsheimer Foundation Trust

Seattle Opera Association ($2,000) see Merrill Foundation, R. D.

Seattle Opera Association ($35,000) see Nesholm Family Foundation

Seattle Pacific University ($25,000) see First Interstate Bank NW Region

Seattle Pacific University ($5,000) see Stubblefield, Estate of Joseph L.

Seattle Public Library ($25,000) see Nesholm Family Foundation

Seattle Repertory Theater ($8,000) see Fales Foundation Trust

Seattle Repertory Theatre ($2,000) see Merrill Foundation, R. D.

Seattle Repertory Theatre ($15,000) see Skinner Corp.

Seattle Symphony ($6,000) see Archibald Charitable Foundation, Norman

Seattle Symphony ($4,219) see McCaw Foundation

Seattle Symphony ($50,000) see Nakamichi Foundation, E.

Seattle Symphony Orchestra ($2,000) see Merrill Foundation, R. D.

Seattle Symphony Orchestra ($35,000) see Nesholm Family Foundation

Seattle Symphony — consultation services; concert hall ($10,000) see Kreielsheimer Foundation Trust

Seattle University ($7,500) see Cook Foundation, Louella

Seattle University ($3,000) see Dupar Foundation

Seattle University — literacy tutoring project ($15,000) see Nesholm Family Foundation

Seattle University ($48,462) see Snyder Foundation, Frost and Margaret

Seattle University ($20,000) see Univar Corp.

Seattle University ($5,000) see Wharton Foundation

Seattle University Honors Program for the Humanities ($10,000) see Lockwood Foundation, Byron W. and Alice L.

Seattle Youth Investment ($30,000) see Nesholm Family Foundation

Seattle Youth Investment — planning, implementation of educational projects ($30,000) see Nesholm Family Foundation

Seattle Zoological Society ($16,666) see Skinner Corp.

Senior Services of Seattle ($5,000) see Glaser Foundation

Senior Services of Seattle-King County ($5,500) see Archibald Charitable Foundation, Norman

Senior Services for South Sound ($2,500) see Lassen Foundation, Irving A.

Sentinal Group ($30,000) see Westwood Endowment

Skagit Valley College ($2,730) see Arise Charitable Trust

South Whidbey Children's Center ($20,500) see Arise Charitable Trust

Spokane Art School ($5,282) see Johnston-Fix Foundation

Spokane Art School — tuition assistance ($10,000) see Wasmer Foundation

Spokane Care Center (Formerly Spokane Alcoholism Care Service, Inc.) — building grant ($22,000) see Comstock Foundation

Spokane Chamber Music Association — guest artist program ($2,500) see Wasmer Foundation

Spokane Civic Theater ($5,000) see Johnston-Fix Foundation

Spokane Food Bank ($7,550) see Leuthold Foundation

Spokane Food Bank — food distribution ($17,500) see Wasmer Foundation

Spokane Food Bank — quality control equipment and Repack Project ($31,121) see Comstock Foundation

Spokane Guilds' School — building grant ($15,000) see Comstock Foundation

Spokane Inland Northwest Community Foundation — music fund ($35,000) see Wasmer Foundation

Spokane Symphony — instruments and office equipment ($20,000) see Comstock Foundation

Spokane Symphony ($20,076) see Washington Trust Bank

Spokane Symphony — endowment fund ($20,000) see Washington Trust Bank

Spokane Symphony Endowment ($17,250) see Johnston-Fix Foundation

Spokane Symphony Society ($10,000) see Leuthold Foundation

Spokane Symphony Society ($5,000) see Wasmer Foundation

Spokane Symphony Society — support of the Endowment Campaign ($40,000) see Jewett Foundation, George Frederick

Spokesman-Review — Christmas Fund ($10,000) see Washington Trust Bank

Tacoma Actors Guild ($35,000) see Forest Foundation

Tacoma Actors Guild ($2,500) see Merrill Foundation, R. D.

Tacoma Art Museum ($35,000) see Forest Foundation

Tacoma Art Museum ($5,000) see Murray Foundation

Tacoma Art Museum ($10,000) see Univar Corp.

Tacoma Community College ($9,000) see Kilworth Charitable Trust, William

Tacoma Goodwill Industries ($5,000) see Archibald Charitable Foundation, Norman

Tacoma Rescue Mission — furnish Jefferson Apartments for low-income housing ($30,000) see Cheney Foundation, Ben B.

Tacoma Symphony ($8,500) see Kilworth Charitable Foundation, Florence B.

Tacoma Technical High School ($1,700) see Haas Foundation, Saul and Dayee G.

Tacoma YMCA ($20,000) see First Interstate Bank NW Region

Tacoma Zoological Society ($5,000) see Univar Corp.

Transitional Resources ($14,000) see Horizons Foundation

Union Gospel Mission ($5,000) see Archibald Charitable Foundation, Norman

Union Gospel Mission ($10,000) see Bishop Foundation, E. K. and Lillian F.

Union Gospel Mission ($2,500) see Cook Foundation, Louella

Union Gospel Mission ($15,000) see Glaser Foundation

Union Gospel Mission ($20,000) see Lockwood Foundation, Byron W. and Alice L.

Union Gospel Mission ($35,000) see Medina Foundation

United Funds ($500) see Joslyn Corp.

United Way ($1,500) see Bloedel Foundation

United Way ($6,000) see Cawsey Trust

United Way ($4,500) see Dupar Foundation

United Way ($35,000) see Foster Foundation

United Way ($5,000) see Haffner Foundation

United Way ($21,440) see ITT Rayonier

United Way ($20,000) see ITT Rayonier

United Way ($8,000) see ITT Rayonier

United Way ($12,000) see Kilworth Charitable Foundation, Florence B.

United Way ($9,000) see Kilworth Charitable Trust, William

United Way ($12,000) see Lassen Foundation, Irving A.

United Way ($2,000) see Merrill Foundation, R. D.

United Way ($30,250) see PemCo. Corp.

United Way ($2,000) see See Foundation, Charles

United Way ($4,700) see Shemanski Testamentary Trust, Tillie and Alfred

United Way ($7,500) see Stubblefield, Estate of Joseph L.

United Way ($20,000) see Univar Corp.

United Way ($5,000) see Univar Corp.

United Way ($69,250) see Washington Trust Bank

United Way of Benton and Franklin Counties ($117,000) see Westinghouse Electric Corp.

United Way of King County ($24,000) see Alliant Techsystems

United Way of King County ($120,000) see Federated Department Stores and Allied Stores Corp.

United Way of King County ($175,500) see First Interstate Bank NW Region

United Way of King County ($353,388) see PACCAR

United Way of King County — operating ($57,240) see Simpson Investment Co.

United Way of King County ($30,185) see Skinner Corp.

United Way of King County ($21,352) see Skinner Corp.

United Way of King County — operating ($22,000) see Sundstrand Corp.

United Way-King County ($107,775) see Washington Mutual Savings Bank

United Way of King County ($124,968) see Weyerhaeuser Co.

United Way of King County — for annual support and KidsPlace ($594,500) see US WEST

United Way of Mason County — operating ($26,000) see Simpson Investment Co.

United Way of Pierce County ($55,000) see First Interstate Bank NW Region

United Way of Pierce County ($134,032) see Weyerhaeuser Co.

United Way of Pierce County ($100,000) see Weyerhaeuser Co.

United Way of Snohomish County ($20,500) see Alliant Techsystems

United Way of Snohomish County ($35,500) see First Interstate Bank NW Region

United Way-Spokane ($17,000) see Washington Mutual Savings Bank

United Way of Spokane County ($26,000) see First Interstate Bank NW Region

United Way of Spokane County — general support ($22,000) see Jewett Foundation, George Frederick

United Way of Tacoma/Pierce County — operating ($26,050) see Simpson Investment Co.

United Way of Yakima County ($13,900) see JELD-WEN, Inc.

United Ways of Washington, Seattle-Tacoma-Olympia ($554,910) see Seafirst Corp.

University Hospital ($5,000) see Statter Foundation, Amy Plant

University Preparatory Academy ($12,500) see Dupar Foundation

University Preparatory Academy ($70,044) see Norcliffe Fund

University Presbyterian Church ($20,000) see Wharton Foundation

University of Puget Sound ($10,000) see Kilworth Charitable Foundation, Florence B.

University of Puget Sound ($30,000) see Kilworth Charitable Trust, William

University of Puget Sound ($10,000) see Rodman Foundation

University of Puget Sound ($20,600) see Washington Mutual Savings Bank

University of Washington — research on eye anatomy and disease ($90,193) see Bishop Foundation

University of Washington — equipment and salary support ($30,000) see Flintridge Foundation

University of Washington ($400,000) see Ford Motor Co.

University of Washington ($500,000) see Foster Foundation

University of Washington — to purchase electronic classroom equipment ($100,000) see Fuld Health Trust, Helene

University of Washington ($5,000) see Haffner Foundation

University of Washington ($294,000) see Intel Corp.

University of Washington ($95,000) see Laerdal Foundation, Asmund S.

University of Washington ($100,000) see Lockwood Foundation, Byron W. and Alice L.

University of Washington ($100,000) see Lucas Cancer Foundation, Richard M.

University of Washington — to support a molecular medicine center ($1,229,800) see Markey Charitable Trust, Lucille P.

University of Washington ($18,000) see Ragen, Jr. Memorial Fund Trust No. 1, James M.

University of Washington ($2,125) see Servco Pacific

University of Washington ($15,000) see Weight Watchers International

University of Washington ($517,139) see Whitaker Foundation

University of Washington — single parent scholarship fund ($100,000) see Winkler Foundation, Mark and Catherine

University of Washington ($5,000) see Wyman Youth Trust

University of Washington — the Campaign ($50,000) see Skinner Corp.

University of Washington — instrumentation for the Center for Biomolecular Structure ($940,700) see Murdock Charitable Trust, M. J.

University of Washington Center for Streamside Studies ($10,000) see ITT Rayonier

University of Washington College of Forestry Resources, Seattle, WA — Pulp and Paper Program ($500,000) see Boise Cascade Corp.

University of Washington Department of Urology ($280,000) see Allen Foundation for Medical Research, Paul G.

University of Washington — to support evaluation of novel approaches for the prevention of diabetes, Ake Lernmark, Ph.D., Principal Investigator ($94,371) see Greenwall Foundation

University of Washington — support of the "Merck Distinguished Fellowship Program" in School of Medicine ($350,000) see Merck & Co.

University of Washington — to support the research project "Our Changing Atmosphere" ($33,063) see Quest for Truth Foundation

University of Washington School of Medicine — research and training program in human health risks from environmental chemical exposures ($223,000) see Dana Foundation, Charles A.

University of Washington School of Medicine — to salvage, strengthen, and expand primary health care services ($200,000) see Northwest Area Foundation

University of Washington School of Pharmacy ($92,500) see Burroughs Wellcome Co.

University of Washington — to support the School of Social Work's development of a master's-level concentration in family preservation ($295,000) see Clark Foundation, Edna McConnell

University of Washington — first of a two-year $500,000 grant to develop educational uses for virtual reality technology ($250,000) see US WEST

US Ski Education Foundation ($5,000) see Thurston Charitable Foundation

Vashon Children's Center ($5,000) see Dupar Foundation

Virginia Mason Medical Foundation ($13,400) see Murray Foundation

Virginia Mason Medical Foundation ($50,000) see Norcliffe Fund

Virginia Mason Medical Foundation ($20,000) see See Foundation, Charles

Visiting Nurse Services ($5,000) see Kawabe Memorial Fund

Visiting Nurses Service ($8,000) see Archibald Charitable Foundation, Norman

Volunteers of America ($30,000) see Cawsey Trust

Volunteers of America ($7,500) see Cawsey Trust

Volunteers of America ($15,000) see Phelps, Inc.

Walla Walla College ($10,000) see Stubblefield, Estate of Joseph L.

Walla Walla Community College ($20,000) see Welch Testamentary Trust, George T.

Walla Walla Community Hospice ($11,000) see Stubblefield, Estate of Joseph L.

Walla Walla Dance ($2,315) see Welch Testamentary Trust, George T.

Walla Walla Symphony Guild ($5,000) see Stubblefield, Estate of Joseph L.

Washington Environmental Council — salary support ($27,950) see Flintridge Foundation

Washington Literacy ($5,000) see Fales Foundation Trust

Washington Pulp and Paper Foundation ($30,000) see Wollenberg Foundation

Washington State Council Alcoholism/Drug Dependency

($35,000) see Medina Foundation

Washington State NARAL Foundation ($16,000) see Horizons Foundation

Washington State University ($5,000) see Autzen Foundation

Washington State University ($3,750) see CENEX

Washington State University see Eldec Corp.

Washington State University see Federated American Insurance

Washington State University ($13,000) see Harvest States Cooperative

Washington State University ($25,000) see Louisiana-Pacific Corp.

Washington State University ($10,000) see Washington Trust Bank

Washington State University Foundation see Bartell Drug Co.

Washington State University Foundation see Insurance Systems, Inc.

Washington State University Foundation see Kice Industries, Inc.

Washington State University Foundation see MicroSim Corp.

Washington State University Foundation see Oregon Mutual Insurance Co.

Washington State University Foundation see OSF International, Inc.

Washington State University Foundation see Pickering Industries

Washington State University — Undergraduate Biological Sciences Education Program ($1,500,000) see Hughes Medical Institute, Howard

Washington University — to support a center for the study of the molecular biology of human disease ($1,876,000) see Markey Charitable Trust, Lucille P.

Washington Women's Employment and Education ($20,000) see Fuchs Foundation, Gottfried & Mary

Washington Women's Employment and Education ($15,000) see Fuchs Foundation, Gottfried & Mary

Whitman College — scholarship funds ($150,000) see Comstock Foundation

Whitman College ($8,500) see Johnston-Fix Foundation

Whitman College ($7,500) see Johnston-Hanson Foundation

Whitman College ($81,250) see Steele-Reese Foundation

Whitman College ($15,000) see Stubblefield, Estate of Joseph L.

Whitworth College — scholarship funds ($150,000) see Comstock Foundation

Whitworth College ($1,000,000) see Cowles Foundation, Harriet Cheney

Whitworth College ($8,500) see Johnston-Fix Foundation

Whitworth College ($8,500) see Johnston-Hanson Foundation

Whitworth College ($75,000) see Stewardship Foundation

Wildwood Park Project ($4,000) see Welch Testamentary Trust, George T.

Wink Luke Museum ($5,000) see Kawabe Memorial Fund

University of Charleston
($17,000) see Daywood
Foundation

University of Charleston
($17,000) see Daywood
Foundation

University of Charleston — for
general fundraising challenge
to alumni, and for endowment
challenge ($400,000) see
Maier Foundation, Sarah
Pauline

Victorian Wheeling Foundation
($23,000) see Weiss
Foundation, William E.

West Virginia Business
Foundation ($5,000) see Shott,
Jr. Foundation, Hugh I.

West Virginia Department of
Health and Human Resources
— development of maternal
and infant health initiative
($158,300) see Benedum
Foundation, Claude
Worthington

West Virginia Education Fund
($25,000) see Maier
Foundation, Sarah Pauline

West Virginia Education Fund —
support staffing, volunteer
training, and related expenses
for the existing "READ
ALOUD West Virginia"
Program and expand the
program statewide ($289,385)
see Benedum Foundation,
Claude Worthington

West Virginia Foundation for
Independent Colleges
($25,000) see Carbon Fuel Co.

West Virginia Foundation for
Independent Colleges ($5,500)
see Fenton Foundation

West Virginia Foundation for
Independent Colleges —
grants for nine private colleges
($50,000) see Maier
Foundation, Sarah Pauline

West Virginia Foundation for
Independent Colleges ($500)
see Oglebay Norton Co.

West Virginia Foundation for
Independent Colleges
($23,500) see One Valley
Bank, N.A.

West Virginia Health Care
Planning Commission —
community education
component of planning
commission ($160,000) see
Benedum Foundation, Claude
Worthington

West Virginia Lions Sight
Conservation Foundation
($59,283) see Teubert
Charitable Trust, James H. and
Alice

West Virginia Roundtable
Foundation ($5,000) see Shott,
Jr. Foundation, Hugh I.

West Virginia School for the
Deaf and Blind ($10,000) see
Teubert Charitable Trust,
James H. and Alice

West Virginia Symphony —
opera production ($57,000)
see Clay Foundation

West Virginia Symphony — to
establish string quartet
endowment ($100,000) see
Maier Foundation, Sarah
Pauline

West Virginia Symphony
Orchestra ($21,000) see
Jacobson Foundation, Bernard
H. and Blanche E.

West Virginia University
($3,891) see Carter Family
Foundation

West Virginia University —
donation of computer
equipment ($537,000) see
IBM Corp.

West Virginia University —
toward the cost of purchasing
equipment for the cancer
research laboratories
($250,000) see Rippel
Foundation, Fannie E.

West Virginia University —
Cancer Center ($3,000) see
One Valley Bank, N.A.

West Virginia University College
of Law ($23,396) see Maier
Foundation, Sarah Pauline

West Virginia University
Foundation — geriatrics clinic
($15,000) see Brown Family
Foundation, John Mathew Gay

West Virginia University
Foundation — needy students
($5,000) see Brown Family
Foundation, John Mathew Gay

West Virginia University
Foundation ($15,000) see
Jacobson Foundation, Bernard
H. and Blanche E.

West Virginia University
Foundation ($175,000) see
Schoenbaum Family
Foundation

West Virginia University
Foundation ($100,000) see
Shott, Jr. Foundation, Hugh I.

West Virginia University
Foundation — Klingberg
Center ($20,000) see Brown
Family Foundation, John
Mathew Gay

West Virginia University
Foundation Point Chair — to
establish endowed chair at
West Virginia University
Medical Center ($250,000) see
Maier Foundation, Sarah
Pauline

West Virginia University
Foundation — Preventicare
health program ($50,000) see
Clay Foundation

West Virginia University
Foundation — continuation of
project to re-examine
standards and reform teacher
education ($483,792) see
Benedum Foundation, Claude
Worthington

West Virginia Wesleyan College
— for endowment of student
financial aid on a need basis
($750,000) see McCune
Foundation

West Virginia Wesleyan College
($2,000) see One Valley Bank,
N.A.

Wetzel County Hospital ($500)
see Ormet Corp.

Wheeling College ($15,000) see
Mellen Foundation

Wheeling Health Right ($4,800)
see Chambers Memorial,
James B.

Wheeling Hospital ($5,000) see
Chambers Memorial, James B.

Wheeling Jesuit College
($35,000) see Donnelly
Foundation, Mary J.

Wheeling Jesuit College
($100,000) see McShain
Charities, John

Wheeling Park Commission
($75,000) see Chambers
Memorial, James B.

Wheeling Park Commission
($31,386) see Kennedy
Memorial Fund, Mark H.

Women's Health Center
($26,200) see Jacobson
Foundation, Bernard H. and
Blanche E.

Womens Resource Center —
Comprehensive Service
Council ($3,000) see Carter
Family Foundation

Woodlands Institute — for
scholars academy and college
bound counseling ($50,000)
see Maier Foundation, Sarah
Pauline

Woodlands Mountain Institute —
program support ($100,000)
see Sequoia Foundation

YMCA ($12,700) see Chambers
Memorial, James B.

YMCA ($31,386) see Kennedy
Memorial Fund, Mark H.

YMCA ($15,000) see
McDonough Foundation,
Bernard

YMCA ($18,500) see One Valley
Bank, N.A.

YMCA ($11,045) see Teubert
Charitable Trust, James H. and
Alice

Wisconsin

A.R.C. Campaign Housing Start
($25,000) see Ziemann
Foundation

Alpha Pi Alliance for
Preservation of Historic Places
($6,667) see Anderson
Industries

Alverno College ($50,000) see
Badger Meter, Inc.

Alverno College — provide
funds needed for tuition
assistance and scholarships
($5,000) see Blue Cross and
Blue Shield United of
Wisconsin Foundation

Alverno College see First Bank
System

Alverno College ($5,000) see
Monaghan Charitable Trust,
Rose

Alverno College ($20,000) see
Ross Memorial Foundation,
Will

Alverno College — to redesign
instruction/assessment
practices in Milwaukee public
schools ($125,000) see Joyce
Foundation

Amanda the Panda ($6,500) see
Wagner Foundation, Ltd., R. H.

American Associates Ben Gurion
University ($5,000) see
Domino of California

American Baptist Assembly
($71,500) see Pillsbury
Foundation

American Bishops Overseas
Appeal ($5,000) see Goldbach
Foundation, Ray and Marie

American Cancer Center
($25,000) see Helfaer
Foundation, Evan and Marion

American Cancer Society
($25,000) see Ladish Family
Foundation, Herman W.

American Cancer Society
($4,600) see Vilter
Manufacturing Corp.

American Cancer Society
($4,000) see Vilter
Manufacturing Corp.

American Cancer Society ($600)
see Wigwam Mills

American Heart Association
($500) see Wigwam Mills

American Players Theater
($15,000) see Wisconsin
Power & Light Co.

American Players Theatre —
general operating support
($5,000) see Blue Cross and
Blue Shield United of
Wisconsin Foundation

American Players Theatre
($10,000) see Bolz Family
Foundation, Eugenie Mayer

American Players Theatre
($10,000) see CUNA Mutual
Insurance Group

American Public Library
Foundation ($20,000) see
Mielke Family Foundation

American Red Cross ($2,000)
see Cleary Foundation

American Red Cross ($20,000)
see Diabetes Research and
Education Foundation

Americanism Foundation —
educational materials ($2,000)
see Pennsylvania Dutch Co.

Americanism Foundation —
educational materials ($2,000)
see Pennsylvania Dutch Co.

Appleton Area School District
($7,000) see Mielke Family
Foundation

Arbor Vitae Voluntary Fire
Department ($1,000) see
Pukall Lumber

Arthritis Foundation ($1,000)
see Pfister and Vogel Tanning
Co.

Arthritis Foundation ($2,500)
see Rolfs Foundation, Robert
T.

Arthritis Foundation of
Wisconsin ($15,000) see
Reinhart Institutional Foods

Associates for University of
Wisconsin ($500) see Castle
Industries

Attic Angels Association
($25,000) see Rennebohm
Foundation, Oscar

Bad River Band of Lake
Superior Chippewa Indians —
to build a youth sports and
culture center ($75,000) see
Bremer Foundation, Otto

Badger Association of the Blind
— Low Vision Education
Program ($40,000) see
McBeath Foundation, Faye

Battle Creek Community
Foundation ($10,000) see
Furth Foundation

Bellin College of Nursing
($3,000) see Wood
Foundation, Lester G.

Beloit Catholic High School —
capital improvements
($28,334) see Beloit
Foundation

Beloit Catholic High School
($3,200) see Warner Electric
Brake & Clutch Co.

Beloit College — library
($150,000) see Beloit
Foundation

Beloit College ($20,884) see
Bradish Trust, Norman C.

Beloit College ($100,000) see
Coleman Foundation

Beloit College — capital grant
($25,000) see Consolidated
Papers

Beloit College ($50,000) see
Janesville Foundation

Beloit College ($50,000) see
Mayer Charitable Trust, Oscar
G. & Elsa S.

Beloit College ($20,000) see
Neese Family Foundation

Beloit College ($30,000) see
Sperry Fund

Beloit College ($10,000) see
Warner Electric Brake &
Clutch Co.

Beloit College — capital
($250,000) see Wilson Fund,
Matilda R.

Beloit College — Help Yourself
Program ($100,000) see Beloit
Foundation

Beloit College — continuation of
W. M. Keck Foundation
Twelve-College Geology
Consortium see Keck
Foundation, W. M.

Beloit Historical Society
($15,000) see Neese Family
Foundation

Beloit Jamesville Symphony
Orchestra ($1,125) see Warner
Electric Brake & Clutch Co.

Beloit Memorial Hospital
($10,000) see Coltec Industries

Beloit 2000 Development
Corporation ($10,000) see
Coltec Industries

Beloit 2000 Development
Corporation ($50,000) see
Neese Family Foundation

Ben R. Lawton Center for
Research and Education
($10,000) see Goldbach
Foundation, Ray and Marie

Berlin Memorial Hospital
($5,000) see Caestecker
Foundation, Charles and Marie

Best Friends of Neenah-Menasha
($10,000) see Smith Family
Foundation, Theda Clark

Bethesda Lutheran Home
($2,400) see Business
Incentives

Bethesda Lutheran Home —
remodeling project ($10,000)
see Schoenleber Foundation

Big Brothers and Big Sisters
($500) see DEC International,
Inc.

Big Red Club — University of
Wisconsin Athletic Foundation
($1,080) see Nelson Industries,
Inc.

Blessed Sacrament Endowment
Fund ($25,000) see Reinhart
Institutional Foods

Blood Center ($25,000) see
Helfaer Foundation, Evan and
Marion

Blood Center ($50,000) see
Marshall & Ilsley Bank

Blood Center Research Center
— health care ($100,000) see
Schroeder Foundation, Walter

Blood Center of SE Wisconsin
($4,000) see Charter
Manufacturing Co.

Blood Center of Southeastern
Wisconsin ($12,000) see Rolfs
Foundation, Thomas J.

Blood Center of Southeastern
Wisconsin ($20,000) see Ross
Memorial Foundation, Will

Blood Center of Southeastern
Wisconsin ($50,000) see
Ziegler Foundation

Blood Center of Southeastern
Wisconsin Research and
Education — capital campaign
($20,000) see Humphrey
Foundation, Glenn & Gertrude

Blood Center of Southwestern
Wisconsin ($15,000) see
Pollybill Foundation

Boy Scouts of America
($175,000) see Alexander
Foundation, Judd S.

Boy Scouts of America ($600)
see Brillion Iron Works

Boy Scouts of America ($500)
see DEC International, Inc.

Boy Scouts of America ($4,000)
see Northwestern National
Insurance Group

Boy Scouts of America ($2,500)
see Oshkosh Truck Corp.

Boy Scouts of America ($7,000)
see Sentry Insurance Co.

Boy Scouts of America ($5,000)
see Wauwatosa Savings &
Loan Association

Boy Scouts of America ($5,000)
see Wauwatosa Savings &
Loan Association

Boy Scouts of America ($300)
see Wigwam Mills

Boys Baseball ($43,500) see
Janesville Foundation

Wisconsin (cont.)

Boys and Girls Brigade ($10,000) see Shattuck Charitable Trust, S. F.

Boys and Girls Club ($5,000) see Blue Cross and Blue Shield United of Wisconsin Foundation

Boys and Girls Club ($2,600) see Cleary Foundation

Boys and Girls Club ($25,000) see Helfaer Foundation, Evan and Marion

Boys and Girls Club ($5,000) see Lindsay Foundation

Boys and Girls Club ($1,500) see Rite-Hite Corp.

Boys and Girls Club ($4,000) see SNC Manufacturing Co.

Boys and Girls Club ($25,000) see Walter Family Trust, Byron L.

Boys and Girls Club ($5,000) see Wehr Foundation, Todd

Boys and Girls Club of Greater Milwaukee — Computer Education Program ($29,700) see McBeath Foundation, Faye

Boys and Girls Club of Milwaukee — in support of the capitol campaign Mission Possible ($10,000) see Smith Corp., A.O.

Briarpatch — crisis intervention, run-away counseling and crisis phone line ($10,000) see Cremer Foundation

Bridge of Green Bay ($25,000) see Walter Family Trust, Byron L.

Brillion City Community Drive ($1,200) see Brillion Iron Works

Brillion City Community Drive ($1,500) see Endries Fastener & Supply Co.

Brillion High School ($107,925) see Peters Foundation, R. D. and Linda

Brillion Housing Authority ($30,000) see Peters Foundation, R. D. and Linda

Brookfield Academy ($5,500) see Grede Foundries

Brown Deer Scholarship Fund see First Bank System

C. A. S. I ($7,000) see Mielke Family Foundation

Cable Natural History Museum — building fund ($70,000) see Griggs and Mary Griggs Burke Foundation, Mary Livingston

Cable Natural History Museum — general operating ($60,000) see Griggs and Mary Griggs Burke Foundation, Mary Livingston

Calvary Lutheran Church ($2,500) see Pukall Lumber

Camp Evergreen ($15,000) see Prange Co., H. C.

Camp Five Museum Foundation ($18,000) see Roddis Foundation, Hamilton

Camp Manito-Wish ($80,000) see Pasadena Area Residential Aid

Camp St. Croix — lodge remodeling ($7,500) see Phipps Foundation, William H.

Cap Services — Family Crisis Center ($15,000) see Sentry Insurance Co.

Capitol Civic Centre ($500) see Formrite Tube Co.

Cardinal Stritch College ($5,000) see Kohl Charities, Herbert H.

Cardinal Stritch College ($25,000) see Monaghan Charitable Trust, Rose

Cardinal Stritch College — educational ($50,000) see Schroeder Foundation, Walter

Cardinal Stritch College — general ($10,000) see Wehr Foundation, Todd

Cardinal Stritch Jubilee ($1,000) see Wagner Manufacturing Co., E. R.

Caring Community — leadership development ($55,000) see Lutheran Brotherhood Foundation

Carroll College — building program ($5,000) see First Financial Bank FSB

Carroll College ($1,500) see Godfrey Co.

Carroll College — scholarship and endowment fund ($10,000) see Humphrey Foundation, Glenn & Gertrude

Carroll College ($60,000) see Stackner Family Foundation

Carroll College Art Building ($100,000) see Pollybill Foundation

Carthage College ($5,000) see I and G Charitable Foundation

Carthage College — capital campaign ($250,000) see Siebert Lutheran Foundation

Carthage College — capital campaign ($75,000) see Siebert Lutheran Foundation

Carthage College ($5,000) see Steigerwaldt Foundation, Donna Wolf

Carthage College ($5,000) see Steigerwaldt Foundation, Donna Wolf

Catholic League ($2,000) see Monaghan Charitable Trust, Rose

Catholic Social Services ($2,000) see Taylor Charitable Trust, Jack DeLoss

Cedar Lake Home Campus ($10,000) see Rolfs Foundation, Thomas J.

Center for Blind and Visually Impaired Children ($10,000) see Demmer Foundation, Edward U.

Center for Blind and Visually Impaired Children ($2,500) see Park Bank

Center for Community Concern — general fund ($1,000) see Greene Manufacturing Co.

Center for Deaf-Blind Persons ($2,500) see Ziemann Foundation

Center of Performing Arts ($25,000) see Prange Co., H. C.

Central City Catholic Schools — building improvements ($25,000) see Cudahy Fund, Patrick and Anna M.

Centre for the Performing Arts Fund ($30,000) see Walter Family Trust, Byron L.

Centre for the Performing Arts in Green Bay ($50,000) see Kress Foundation, George

Channel 10/36 ($7,200) see Briggs & Stratton Corp.

Channel 10/36 ($16,590) see Time Insurance Co.

Channel 10/36 ($10,000) see Time Insurance Co.

Channel 10/36 Friends ($40,000) see Demmer Foundation, Edward U.

Channel 10/36 Friends ($10,000) see Marquette Electronics

Channel 10/36 Friends ($3,100) see Northwestern National Insurance Group

Channel 10/36 Friends ($4,000) see Ziemann Foundation

Channel 10-TV ($30,000) see National Presto Industries

Channels 10/36 ($5,000) see Wauwatosa Savings & Loan Association

Children's Hospital ($20,000) see Badger Meter, Inc.

Children's Hospital ($5,000) see Neenah Foundry Co.

Children's Hospital ($5,620) see U.S. Oil/Schmidt Family Foundation, Inc.

Children's Hospital Foundation ($10,000) see Klingler Foundation, Helen and Charles

Children's Hospital Foundation ($25,000) see Reinhart Institutional Foods

Children's Hospital Medical Center ($25,000) see Ladish Family Foundation, Herman W.

Children's Hospital Medical Center ($2,500) see Wagner Foundation, Ltd., R. H.

Children's Hospital of Milwaukee ($15,000) see Northwestern National Insurance Group

Children's Hospital of Wisconsin ($5,000) see Banta Corp.

Children's Hospital of Wisconsin ($20,000) see Bucyrus-Erie

Children's Hospital of Wisconsin ($50,000) see Clark Family Foundation, Emory T.

Children's Hospital of Wisconsin — building fund ($25,000) see Firstar Bank Milwaukee NA

Children's Hospital of Wisconsin ($40,000) see Johnson & Son, S.C.

Children's Hospital of Wisconsin ($2,000) see Kimball Co., Miles

Children's Hospital of Wisconsin ($50,000) see Marshall & Ilsley Bank

Children's Hospital of Wisconsin ($25,000) see Universal Foods Corp.

Children's Hospital of Wisconsin ($8,000) see Wagner Manufacturing Co., E. R.

Children's Hospital of Wisconsin — general ($50,000) see Wehr Foundation, Todd

Children's Hospital of Wisconsin ($20,000) see WICOR, Inc.

Children's Hospital of Wisconsin ($70,000) see Wisconsin Energy Corp.

Children's Hospital of Wisconsin — to aid in the purchase of an Echocardiograph Machine ($20,000) see Smith Corp., A.O.

Children's Hospital of Wisconsin — for the bereavement counselor in the Pediatric Hospice Bereavement Program ($15,000) see Birnschein Foundation, Alvin and Marion

Children's Outing Association — speech therapy program ($10,000) see Birnschein Foundation, Alvin and Marion

Children's Outing Association — capital campaign for a new facility ($30,000) see Cudahy Fund, Patrick and Anna M.

Children's Outing Association ($2,500) see Ziemann Foundation

Children's Service Society ($1,000) see Rite-Hite Corp.

Children's Service Society of Wisconsin ($2,000) see Taylor Charitable Trust, Jack DeLoss

Children's Theater of Madison ($1,000) see Steinhauer Charitable Foundation

Chippewa Falls Area Unified School District ($234,961) see Cray Research

Christian League for the Handicapped ($26,305) see Erickson Charitable Fund, Eben W.

Church of the Helping Hand ($500) see DEC International, Inc.

Church of Resurrection ($5,000) see Roehl Foundation

Church of Resurrection ($5,000) see Roehl Foundation

Citizen Advocacy ($2,200) see Ziegler Foundation

City of Abbotsford ($9,000) see Christensen Charitable and Religious Foundation, L. C.

City of Brillion ($70,000) see Peters Foundation, R. D. and Linda

City of Jamesville ($30,000) see Janesville Foundation

City of La Crosse ($14,307) see Stry Foundation, Paul E.

City Libraries ($10,369) see Outboard Marine Corp.

City of Lodi — library fund ($1,666) see DEC International, Inc.

City of Madison ($711,000) see Bolz Family Foundation, Eugenie Mayer

City of Madison Parks Division ($75,000) see Rennebohm Foundation, Oscar

City of Menasha ($10,000) see Neenah Foundry Co.

City of Mosinee ($45,000) see Alexander Foundation, Judd S.

City of Neenah — Anderson Sculpture Riverside Park ($10,000) see Shattuck Charitable Trust, S. F.

City of Shell Lake — Arrasmith Library ($17,500) see Reinhart Institutional Foods

City of South Milwaukee ($20,000) see Bucyrus-Erie

City of Tomah Parks and Recreation ($8,000) see Andres Charitable Trust, Frank G.

City of Tomah Parks and Recreation ($5,000) see Andres Charitable Trust, Frank G.

City of Tomah Public Works — purchase 128 new flags ($3,209) see Andres Charitable Trust, Frank G.

City of Wisconsin Rapids — park ($50,000) see Consolidated Papers

Coalition of Wisconsin Aging ($2,000) see Kimball Co., Miles

Columbia Foundation ($3,043) see Evinrude Foundation, Ralph

Columbia Hospital ($50,000) see Marshall & Ilsley Bank

Columbia Hospital ($3,000) see Park Bank

Columbia Hospital ($100,000) see Pollybill Foundation

Columbia Hospital — health care ($50,000) see Schroeder Foundation, Walter

Columbia Hospital ($20,000) see Universal Foods Corp.

Columbia Hospital Building Fund ($50,000) see Helfaer Foundation, Evan and Marion

Community Action ($13,000) see Phipps Foundation, William H.

Community Advocates — partial funding for the Family Transitional Living Program ($10,000) see Birnschein Foundation, Alvin and Marion

Community Assembly of God ($500) see Brillion Iron Works

Community Care Organization of Milwaukee — Adult Day Health Center ($50,000) see McBeath Foundation, Faye

Community Church ($1,000) see Pukall Lumber

Community Core Group ($1,000) see Wigwam Mills

Community Foundation of the Fox ($40,011) see Mielke Family Foundation

Community Foundation of the Fox Valley Region ($6,000) see Alexander Foundation, Walter

Community Foundation for the Region ($19,470) see U.S. Oil/Schmidt Family Foundation, Inc.

Concordia College — "Toward the 21st Century Capital Campaign" ($10,000) see Humphrey Foundation, Glenn & Gertrude

Concordia University ($12,500) see Birnschein Foundation, Alvin and Marion

Concordia University ($25,000) see Schoenleber Foundation

Concordia University — capital campaign ($200,000) see Siebert Lutheran Foundation

Concordia University ($5,000) see Wurlitzer Foundation, Farny R.

Congregation Emanu-El ($161,738) see Peck Foundation, Milton and Lillian

Congregation Emanuel ($100,000) see Rubenstein Foundation, Philip

Congregation Shalom ($5,000) see Rubenstein Foundation, Philip

Connecticut Association of Independent Schools ($2,500) see Saunders Charitable Foundation, Helen M.

Cudahy High School ($12,000) see Ladish Co.

Curative Foundation ($12,500) see Krause Foundation, Charles A.

Deerfield Food Pantry ($1,500) see Taylor Charitable Trust, Jack DeLoss

Delavan Darien UWAY ($15,412) see WICOR, Inc.

Department of Ophthalmology ($25,000) see Reinhart Institutional Foods

DePaul Foundation — Mission of Hope ($5,000) see Time Insurance Co.

Diocesan Mission — Dominican Republic, St. Al's Parish ($5,000) see U.S. Oil/Schmidt Family Foundation, Inc.

Diocese of La Crosse ($10,000) see Goldbach Foundation, Ray and Marie

Diocese of La Crosse ($25,000) see Reinhart Institutional Foods

Divine Savior ($5,000) see Monaghan Charitable Trust, Rose

Door County Auditorium Funding corporation ($25,000) see Kress Foundation, George

Door County Memorial Hospital Foundation ($100,000) see Peterson Foundation, Fred J.

Downtown Rotary ($3,000) see Taylor Charitable Trust, Jack DeLoss

Ducks Unlimited ($564) see Pukall Lumber

EAA Aviation Foundation ($25,000) see Clark Family Foundation, Emory T.

EAA Aviation Foundation ($125,000) see Ray Foundation

EAA Aviation Foundation ($30,000) see Ray Foundation

EAA Aviation Foundation ($10,000) see Ray Foundation

EAA Aviation Foundation ($30,000) see Robinson Foundation

EAA Aviation Foundation ($16,667) see SNC Manufacturing Co.

EAA Aviation Foundation ($17,000) see Witco Corp.

Easter Seal Society ($500) see DEC International, Inc.

Easter Seal Society ($2,000) see Northwestern National Insurance Group

Easter Seal Society of Wisconsin ($100,000) see Rennebohm Foundation, Oscar

Eau Claire Fire Department — water safety and rescue program ($10,000) see Phillips Family Foundation, L. E.

Edgewood College ($470,000) see Rennebohm Foundation, Oscar

Edgewood College ($1,000) see Steinhauer Charitable Foundation

Edgewood College — general ($80,000) see Wehr Foundation, Todd

Elmbrook Memorial Hospital ($25,000) see Ladish Family Foundation, Herman W.

Elmore Foundation — new dining room in the Health Care Center to be named the Glenn Humphrey Dining Hall ($25,000) see Humphrey Foundation, Glenn & Gertrude

Experimental Aircraft Association ($3,000) see Rolfs Foundation, Thomas J.

Eye Bank Association of America ($14,000) see Woodward Governor Co.

Faith Evangelical Free ($4200) see Oldham Little Church Foundation

Faith United Methodist Church ($4,000) see Brillion Iron Works

Faith United Methodist Church ($3,000) see Peters Foundation, R. D. and Linda

Family Center ($10,000) see CUNA Mutual Insurance Group

Family Centers ($2,500) see Madison Gas & Electric Co.

Family Enhancement ($25,000) see Rennebohm Foundation, Oscar

Family Service — building ($20,000) see Bassett Foundation, Norman

Family Service — assist with facility purchase ($7,500) see Cremer Foundation

Family Service ($7,000) see CUNA Mutual Insurance Group

Family Service of Milwaukee ($5,000) see Lindsay Foundation

Family Services ($50,000) see Rennebohm Foundation, Oscar

First Presbyterian Church ($3,000) see Cleary Foundation

Florentine Opera Company — cultural ($75,000) see Schroeder Foundation, Walter

Florentine Opera of Milwaukee ($11,000) see Marquette Electronics

Fond du Lac Blue Line Club ($1,000) see Castle Industries

Fort Atkinson Memorial Hospital Foundation ($50,000) see Ladish Family Foundation, Herman W.

Forward Wisconsin — operating support ($30,000) see American Natural Resources Co.

Foundation for Economic Education ($250) see Formrite Tube Co.

Fox River Area Girl Scout Council ($9,500) see Alexander Foundation, Walter

Fox River Area Girl Scout Council ($5,000) see Banta Corp.

Fox Valley Chapter of Juvenile Diabetes ($100) see Endries Fastener & Supply Co.

Fox Valley Technical College Foundation ($250) see Endries Fastener & Supply Co.

Fox Valley Technical College Foundation ($10,000) see Kimball Co., Miles

Fox Valley Technical Institute Foundation ($1,750) see SNC Manufacturing Co.

Fox Valley Unites — health and welfare ($20,000) see Menasha Corp.

Fox Valley Unites ($10,000) see Banta Corp.

Friends of Clintonville Library — to help furnish new library with shelves and furniture ($100) see Pamida, Inc.

Friends of Fond du Lac Public Library ($15,000) see Brunswick Corp.

Friends of the Museum — membership ($20,000) see Krause Foundation, Charles A.

Friends of the Museum ($25,000) see Pollybill Foundation

Friends of Museum ($40,000) see Stackner Family Foundation

Friends of Old World Wisconsin ($10,000) see Demmer Foundation, Edward U.

Friends of Schlitz Audubon Center ($1,750) see Rite-Hite Corp.

Friends of WHA-TV ($20,000) see National Presto Industries

Froedtert Memorial Lutheran Hospital, The Ambulatory Care Center ($100,000) see Helfaer Foundation, Evan and Marion

Full Shelf Pantry ($2,500) see Rolfs Foundation, Robert T.

Future Farmers of America ($3,000) see Curtice-Burns Foods

Future Farmers of America ($39,500) see Santa Fe Pacific Corp.

Future Neenah Development Corporation ($15,000) see Neenah Foundry Co.

Geneva Lake Sailing School ($6,000) see Ingersoll Milling Machine Co.

Gibraltar School AODA ($3,000) see Peterson Foundation, Fred J.

Girl Scouts of America ($10,000) see Cleary Foundation

Girl Scouts of America ($105) see Endries Fastener & Supply Co.

Girl Scouts of America ($10,000) see Humphrey Foundation, Glenn & Gertrude

Good Samaritan Health Care Center Foundation ($5,600) see Wausau Paper Mills Co.

Goodrich Hockey Boosters ($500) see Castle Industries

Goodwill Industries ($10,000) see Badger Meter, Inc.

Goodwill Industries ($2,000) see Christensen Charitable and Religious Foundation, L. C.

Goodwill Industries of Milwaukee ($5,000) see Lindsay Foundation

Grace Christian Center ($1,000) see Castle Industries

Grace Christian Center ($500) see Castle Industries

Grace Christian Center ($500) see Castle Industries

Grace Episcopal Church ($19,000) see Bolz Family Foundation, Eugenie Mayer

Grand Opera House Foundation ($5,000) see Oshkosh Truck Corp.

Grand Opera House Foundation ($1,100) see SNC Manufacturing Co.

Grand Opera House Fund ($7,500) see Oshkosh B'Gosh

Great Circus Parade ($50,000) see Helfaer Foundation, Evan and Marion

Great Lakes Hemophilia Foundation ($3,000) see Evinrude Foundation, Ralph

Greater Milwaukee Committee for Community Development ($1,610) see Rite-Hite Corp.

Greater Milwaukee Education Trust — budget support ($5,000) see Blue Cross and Blue Shield United of Wisconsin Foundation

Greater Milwaukee Education Trust ($5,000) see Time Insurance Co.

Greater Milwaukee Open ($2,100) see Wauwatosa Savings & Loan Association

Green Bay Packers/NFL ($25,000) see Lipton, Thomas J.

Gunderson Medical ($500) see Lizzadro Family Foundation, Joseph

Gunderson Medical Foundation ($10,100) see Cleary Foundation

Habitat for Humanity ($14,000) see Alexander Foundation, Judd S.

Happy Puppy ($10,000) see Western Shade Cloth Charitable Foundation

Harambee School Development Corporation ($2,000) see Park Bank

Health Care Network — volunteer health care ($1,000) see Greene Manufacturing Co.

Herb Kohl Educational Foundation ($100,000) see Kohl Charities, Herbert H.

Heritage Hill Foundation ($12,000) see Kress Foundation, George

Heritage Hill Foundation ($30,000) see Walter Family Trust, Byron L.

Heritage Hill Foundation ($3,000) see Wood Foundation, Lester G.

Heritage Hill State Park Foundation ($20,000) see Wisconsin Public Service Corp.

Heritage Hill State Park Foundation ($20,000) see Wisconsin Public Service Corp.

Historic Sites Foundation ($5,000) see Hay Foundation, John I.

Historic Sites Foundation ($4,000) see Northwestern National Insurance Group

Historic Sites Foundation ($7,100) see Thorson Foundation

Historic Sites Foundation — support of 1990 circus parade, civic event ($2,000) see Vilter Manufacturing Corp.

Holiday Home ($40,000) see Hanson Testamentary Charitable Trust, Anna Emery

Holy Communion Lutheran Church ($1,800) see Christensen Charitable and Religious Foundation, L. C.

House of Peace ($5,000) see Monaghan Charitable Trust, Rose

Howard Young Medical Center ($7,500) see Pukall Lumber

Hudson Memorial Medical Center — construction on clinic ($100,000) see Phipps Foundation, William H.

Hudson Senior High School — scholarships ($17,000) see Phipps Foundation, William H.

Hunger Task Force of Milwaukee ($5,000) see Pieper Electric

Ice Age Park and Trail ($10,000) see Vollrath Co.

Indiana University ($5,000) see First Source Corp.

INROADS ($7,500) see Badger Meter, Inc.

Inroads/Wisconsin ($59,000) see Beloit Foundation

Inroads/Wisconsin ($29,500) see Beloit Foundation

INROADS/Wisconsin ($55,000) see Johnson & Son, S.C.

Inter-Varsity Christian Fellowship ($32,000) see Huston Foundation

Inter-Varsity Christian Fellowship ($5,000) see Madison Gas & Electric Co.

Inter-Varsity Christian Fellowship ($25,000) see Solheim Foundation

Inter-Varsity Christian Fellowship of United States of America ($7,500) see Noble Foundation, Vivian Bilby

Inter-Varsity (Urbana '90) ($2,500) see Cook Charitable Foundation

International Crane Foundation ($25,000) see Donnelley Foundation, Gaylord and Dorothy

International Crane Foundation ($31,000) see Johnson & Son, S.C.

Janesville School District ($25,000) see Janesville Foundation

Jeffrey Fitzmaurice Fund ($1,000) see Nelson Industries, Inc.

Jewish Community Federation ($30,000) see Rubenstein Foundation, Philip

Jewish Community Fund ($5,000) see Herman Foundation, John and Rose

John Michael Kohler Arts Center ($3,500) see Wigwam Mills

Junior Achievement ($5,000) see Blue Cross and Blue Shield United of Wisconsin Foundation

Junior Achievement of Southeastern Wisconsin — in support of the pacesetter campaign ($10,000) see Smith Corp., A.O.

Kemper Center ($10,000) see Steigerwaldt Foundation, Donna Wolf

Kenosha Jewish Welfare Fund ($7,500) see I and G Charitable Foundation

Kettle Moraine YMCA ($35,000) see Ziegler Foundation

Kettle Moraine YMCA ($2,000) see Ziegler Foundation

Kiddies Camp Corporation ($5,600) see Wigwam Mills

Ko-Thi Dance Company ($3,000) see Evinrude Foundation, Ralph

L. E. Phillips Boy Scout Camp Trust — trust capital for benefit of boy scout camp ($20,000) see Phillips Family Foundation, L. E.

L. E. Phillips Memorial Public Library — building remodeling ($24,260) see Phillips Family Foundation, L. E.

La Crosse Area United Fund — operations campaign ($5,000) see JSJ Corp.

Lake Geneva Charitable Sailing Trust — Olympic Entry ($20,000) see Stackner Family Foundation

Lakefront Festival of the Arts ($2,500) see Godfrey Co.

Lakeland College — annual fund ($25,000) see Brotz Family Foundation, Frank G.

Lakeland College — international business project ($25,000) see Brotz Family Foundation, Frank G.

Lakeland College ($200,000) see Herrick Foundation

Lakeland College ($100,000) see Herrick Foundation

Lakeland College ($125,000) see Kimberly-Clark Corp.

Lakeland College ($2,800) see Wigwam Mills

Lakeside Players ($10,000) see Steigerwaldt Foundation, Donna Wolf

Lawrence University ($5,000) see Alexander Foundation, Walter

Lawrence University ($5,000) see Banta Corp.

Lawrence University ($50,000) see Barstow Foundation

Lawrence University ($500) see Castle Industries

Lawrence University ($25,000) see CUNA Mutual Insurance Group

Lawrence University ($75,000) see Mielke Family Foundation

Lawrence University ($10,000) see Neenah Foundry Co.

Lawrence University ($5,000) see Oshkosh Truck Corp.

Lawrence University ($10,000) see Wehr Foundation, Todd

Lawrence University of Wisconsin ($8,000) see Banc One Wisconsin Corp.

Leigh-Yawkey-Woodson Art Museum ($1,500) see Greenheck Fan Corp.

Leigh Yawkey Woodson Art Museum — general operations ($100,000) see Woodson Foundation, Aytchmonde

Leigh Yawkey Woodson Art Museum — general operations ($75,000) see Woodson Foundation, Aytchmonde

Wisconsin (cont.)

Leigh Yawkey Woodson Art Museum — collections acquisitions ($21,000) see Woodson Foundation, Aytchmonde

Leigh Yawkey Woodson Art Museum — collections acquisitions ($19,600) see Woodson Foundation, Aytchmonde

Leigh Yawkey Woodson Art Museum — office equipment ($7,085) see Woodson Foundation, Aytchmonde

Leigh Yawkey Woodson Art Museum — communications services office ($5,117) see Woodson Foundation, Aytchmonde

Leigh Yawkey Woodson Art Museum — collections acquisitions ($1,503) see Woodson Foundation, Aytchmonde

Leigh Yawkey Woodson Art Museum — hygrothermograph ($417) see Woodson Foundation, Aytchmonde

Leigh Yawkey Woodson Art Museum — office equipment, software ($1,697) see Woodson Foundation, Aytchmonde

Leukemia Society of America ($10,000) see Blue Cross and Blue Shield United of Wisconsin Foundation

Literacy Service ($10,000) see Brady Foundation, W. H.

Literacy Service ($2,500) see Ziemann Foundation

Lodi Womens Club Free Library ($2,500) see Madison Gas & Electric Co.

Lombardi Cancer Society ($1,800) see Rite-Hite Corp.

Lourdes Academy ($20,000) see Oshkosh Truck Corp.

Lutheran Church ($5,000) see Monaghan Charitable Trust, Rose

Lutheran Church of the Redeemer ($5,137) see Donaldson, Lufkin & Jenrette

Lutheran Counseling and Family Services — family life education program ($15,000) see Birnschein Foundation, Alvin and Marion

Lutheran Hospital Foundation ($2,000) see First Financial Bank FSB

Lutheran Hospital Foundation ($50,000) see Journal Gazette Co.

MADD ($200) see Endries Fastener & Supply Co.

Madison Art Center ($14,400) see Bassett Foundation, Norman

Madison Art Center ($5,000) see Bolz Family Foundation, Eugenie Mayer

Madison Art Center ($500) see DEC International, Inc.

Madison Art Center ($8,225) see Prange Co., H. C.

Madison Art Center ($15,000) see Smith Family Foundation, Theda Clark

Madison Art Center ($1,000) see Steinhauer Charitable Foundation

Madison Art Center Building Fund ($100,000) see Bolz Family Foundation, Eugenie Mayer

Madison Avenue Presbyterian Church ($10,000) see Tai and Co., J. T.

Madison Boys Choir ($1,000) see Steinhauer Charitable Foundation

Madison Center for Educational Affairs ($30,000) see McConnell Foundation, Neil A.

Madison Center for Educational Affairs ($25,000) see McConnell Foundation, Neil A.

Madison Civic Center ($15,000) see Evjue Foundation

Madison Civic Center ($5,000) see Steinhauer Charitable Foundation

Madison Civic Center ($1,000) see Steinhauer Charitable Foundation

Madison Civic Center Endowment Fund — program support ($10,000) see Madison Gas & Electric Co.

Madison Civic Music Association ($25,000) see Bassett Foundation, Norman

Madison Civic Music Association ($6,000) see Bolz Family Foundation, Eugenie Mayer

Madison Civic Music Association ($2,000) see Madison Gas & Electric Co.

Madison Community Foundation — Bassett Fund ($302,969) see Bassett Foundation, Norman

Madison Festival of the Lakes ($1,500) see Steinhauer Charitable Foundation

Madison Urban League — YES scholarship ($15,000) see Wisconsin Power & Light Co.

Madison Urban League — YES scholarship ($12,000) see Wisconsin Power & Light Co.

Make-A-Wish Foundation ($1,000) see Pfister and Vogel Tanning Co.

Manitowa County Humane Society ($100) see Formrite Tube Co.

Manitowa Maritime Museum ($200) see Formrite Tube Co.

Maple Dale/Indian Hill School ($14,210) see Rite-Hite Corp.

Marathon County Historical Society — support historical preservation ($1,000) see Greenheck Fan Corp.

Marian College ($1,000) see Castle Industries

Marian Housing ($10,000) see Christensen Charitable and Religious Foundation, L. C.

Marilyn O'Brien Fund ($1,000) see Ziemann Foundation

Marquette University ($6,676) see Abraham Foundation, Anthony R.

Marquette University see Benefit Trust Life Insurance Co.

Marquette University ($17,100) see Bucyrus-Erie

Marquette University — unrestricted ($32,500) see Consolidated Papers

Marquette University — scholarships ($24,079) see Evinrude Foundation, Ralph

Marquette University ($6,496) see Evinrude Foundation, Ralph

Marquette University ($200,000) see Humphrey Foundation, Glenn & Gertrude

Marquette University ($40,000) see Janesville Foundation

Marquette University ($100,000) see Johnson Controls

Marquette University ($10,000) see Klingler Foundation, Helen and Charles

Marquette University — business administration ($10,000) see Ladish Co.

Marquette University ($100,000) see Ladish Family Foundation, Herman W.

Marquette University see Lappin Electric Co.

Marquette University ($10,000) see Marquette Electronics

Marquette University ($50,000) see Marshall & Ilsley Bank

Marquette University see Maynard Steel Casting Co.

Marquette University see McGill Manufacturing Co.

Marquette University ($365,000) see Monaghan Charitable Trust, Rose

Marquette University see National Manufacturing Co.

Marquette University see New York Marine & General Insurance Co.

Marquette University see Pegasus Gold Corp.

Marquette University — endowment ($100,000) see Schmitt Foundation, Arthur J.

Marquette University — scholarships ($55,000) see Schmitt Foundation, Arthur J.

Marquette University — in support of an engineering school renovation project ($15,000) see Smith Corp., A.O.

Marquette University ($12,500) see Wehr Foundation, Todd

Marquette University ($50,000) see WICOR, Inc.

Marquette University ($100,000) see Wisconsin Energy Corp.

Marquette University ($22,000) see Wisconsin Public Service Corp.

Marquette University ($10,580) see Wrape Family Charitable Trust

Marquette University — endowments/capital programs ($30,000) see Firstar Bank Milwaukee NA

Marquette University — Helfaer Tennis Stadium and Recreation Center ($35,000) see Helfaer Foundation, Evan and Marion

Marquette University School of Dentistry ($25,000) see Helfaer Foundation, Evan and Marion

Marquette University The Campaign for Marquette Beliefs and Actions ($50,000) see Helfaer Foundation, Evan and Marion

Marshfield Medical Foundation ($15,000) see Miller Foundation, Steve J.

Marshfield Medical Research Foundation ($5,000) see Sentry Insurance Co.

Martin Luther Preparatory School ($5,000) see Roehl Foundation

Masonic Village on the Square — capital campaign for construction of 66-69 independent apartment units and community center ($200,000) see Humphrey Foundation, Glenn & Gertrude

MATC Foundation — assistance to keep students in school ($10,000) see Cremer Foundation

McDevco ($83,050) see Alexander Foundation, Judd S.

McDevco ($5,263) see Wausau Paper Mills Co.

McFarland Food Pantry ($1,500) see Taylor Charitable Trust, Jack DeLoss

Medical College of Milwaukee — educational ($50,000) see Schroeder Foundation, Walter

Medical College of Wisconsin ($5,000) see Banta Corp.

Medical College of Wisconsin ($50,000) see Clark Family Foundation, Emory T.

Medical College of Wisconsin — building construction ($20,000) see Firstar Bank Milwaukee NA

Medical College of Wisconsin ($60,000) see Johnson Controls

Medical College of Wisconsin ($20,000) see Kettering Family Foundation

Medical College of Wisconsin ($40,000) see Ladish Family Foundation, Herman W.

Medical College of Wisconsin ($10,000) see Marcus Corp.

Medical College of Wisconsin ($5,000) see Park Bank

Medical College of Wisconsin ($2,000) see Park Bank

Medical College of Wisconsin ($25,000) see Ross Memorial Foundation, Will

Medical College of Wisconsin ($20,000) see WICOR, Inc.

Medical College of Wisconsin ($50,000) see Wisconsin Energy Corp.

Medical College of Wisconsin ($7,500) see Ziemann Foundation

Medical College of Wisconsin — in support of medical education, teaching and research ($20,000) see Smith Corp., A.O.

Melvin S. Cohen Trust F/B/O — trust principal for the benefit of Minneapolis Federation for Jewish Service ($1,935,000) see Phillips Family Foundation, L. E.

Mercy Medical Center Foundation ($7,500) see SNC Manufacturing Co.

Meriter Foundation ($30,000) see Evjue Foundation

Meriter Hospital ($26,000) see Rennebohm Foundation, Oscar

Messmer High School ($10,040) see Evinrude Foundation, Ralph

Messmer High School — for the "right brain/left brain" learning environment ($5,600) see Birnschein Foundation, Alvin and Marion

Meta House ($25,000) see Demmer Foundation, Edward U.

Methodist Manor ($99,000) see Clark Family Foundation, Emory T.

Methodist Manor Health Care Center ($5,000) see Godfrey Co.

Methodist Manor Health Center ($26,000) see Stackner Family Foundation

Milwaukee Art Museum ($8,000) see Briggs & Stratton Corp.

Milwaukee Art Museum ($1,000) see Charter Manufacturing Co.

Milwaukee Art Museum ($20,000) see Demmer Foundation, Edward U.

Milwaukee Art Museum ($3,300) see Kohl Charities, Herbert H.

Milwaukee Art Museum ($20,000) see Kohler Co.

Milwaukee Art Museum ($20,000) see Kohler Foundation

Milwaukee Art Museum — exhibition ($40,000) see Lannan Foundation

Milwaukee Art Museum ($5,240) see Northwestern National Insurance Group

Milwaukee Art Museum ($50,000) see Pick Charitable Trust, Melitta S.

Milwaukee Art Museum ($1,500) see Rite-Hite Corp.

Milwaukee Art Museum ($17,000) see Stackner Family Foundation

Milwaukee Art Museum ($10,000) see Time Insurance Co.

Milwaukee Art Museum ($1,200) see Wagner Manufacturing Co., E. R.

Milwaukee Ballet ($13,750) see Marquette Electronics

Milwaukee Career Cooperative — toward the start-up operating funds to assure the effective, stable establishment of the new Cooperative divisions ($20,000) see Schoenleber Foundation

Milwaukee County Historical Society ($15,000) see Brady Foundation, W. H.

Milwaukee County Historical Society — for funding of an assistant curator for the library ($22,149) see Schoenleber Foundation

Milwaukee Foundation ($15,000) see Evinrude Foundation, Ralph

Milwaukee Foundation ($2,500) see Kohl Charities, Herbert H.

Milwaukee Foundation ($20,000) see Universal Foods Corp.

Milwaukee Foundation ($60,000) see Wisconsin Energy Corp.

Milwaukee Heart Research ($4,000) see Rubenstein Foundation, Philip

Milwaukee Heart Research Foundation ($10,000) see Kimball Co., Miles

Milwaukee Institute of Art and Design ($25,000) see Pick Charitable Trust, Melitta S.

Milwaukee Institute of Art and Design ($50,000) see Pollybill Foundation

Milwaukee Institute of Art and Design — to aid in the purchase and renovation of the terminal building ($15,000) see Smith Corp., A.O.

Milwaukee Jewish Community ($20,000) see Rubenstein Foundation, Philip

Milwaukee Jewish Day School ($160,000) see Rubenstein Foundation, Philip

Milwaukee Jewish Federation ($30,000) see Kohl Charitable Foundation, Allen D.

Milwaukee Jewish Federation ($65,000) see Kohl Foundation, Sidney

Milwaukee Jewish Federation ($30,000) see Kohl Foundation, Sidney

Milwaukee Jewish Federation ($100,000) see Peck Foundation, Milton and Lillian

Milwaukee Jewish Federation ($1,081,000) see Rubenstein Foundation, Philip

Milwaukee Jewish Home ($25,000) see Rubenstein Foundation, Philip

Milwaukee Jewish Home Foundation ($200,000) see Rubenstein Foundation, Philip

Milwaukee Protestant Home ($2,000) see Pick Charitable Trust, Melitta S.

Milwaukee Public Library Foundation — donation for educational computer software see Ameritech Publishing

Milwaukee Public Library Foundation — for the improvements to the Humanities Library ($15,000) see Schoenleber Foundation

Milwaukee Public Museum — noncash contribution ($95,656) see Kohler Co.

Milwaukee Public Museum ($45,000) see Kohler Foundation

Milwaukee Public Museum see Packaging Corporation of America

Milwaukee Redevelopment Corporation ($10,000) see Briggs & Stratton Corp.

Milwaukee Redevelopment Corporation ($5,000) see Park Bank

Milwaukee Redevelopment Corporation ($10,000) see Time Insurance Co.

Milwaukee Repertory Theater — capital campaign ($30,000) see Firstar Bank Milwaukee NA

Milwaukee Repertory Theater ($150,000) see Stackner Family Foundation

Milwaukee Repertory Theater ($4,000) see Wagner Manufacturing Co., E. R.

Milwaukee Rescue Mission ($10,000) see Demmer Foundation, Edward U.

Milwaukee Rescue Mission ($1,000) see Pfister and Vogel Tanning Co.

Milwaukee Resuce Mission ($5,000) see Lindsay Foundation

Milwaukee School of Engineering ($10,000) see Badger Meter, Inc.

Milwaukee School of Engineering — endowment of scholarships for students enrolled in the biomedical engineering program ($5,000) see Birnschein Foundation, Alvin and Marion

Milwaukee School of Engineering ($10,000) see Brady Foundation, W. H.

Milwaukee School of Engineering ($10,000) see Briggs & Stratton Corp.

Milwaukee School of Engineering ($23,225) see Bucyrus-Erie

Milwaukee School of Engineering ($5,000) see Caestecker Foundation, Charles and Marie

Milwaukee School of Engineering ($25,000) see Clark Family Foundation, Emory T.

Milwaukee School of Engineering ($15,000) see Demmer Foundation, Edward U.

Milwaukee School of Engineering ($6,000) see Grede Foundries

Milwaukee School of Engineering ($6,000) see Grede Foundries

Milwaukee School of Engineering ($5,000) see Greenheck Fan Corp.

Milwaukee School of Engineering — annual scholarship fund in mechanical engineering ($10,000) see Humphrey Foundation, Glenn & Gertrude

Milwaukee School of Engineering — scholarships ($10,000) see Ladish Co.

Milwaukee School of Engineering ($50,000) see Marshall & Ilsley Bank

Milwaukee School of Engineering ($100,000) see Peters Foundation, R. D. and Linda

Milwaukee School of Engineering ($6,000) see Rolfs Foundation, Robert T.

Milwaukee School of Engineering — toward the endowment of a scholarship for outstanding students ($15,000) see Schoenleber Foundation

Milwaukee School of Engineering ($3,000) see United Conveyor Corp.

Milwaukee School of Engineering ($3,000) see Warner Electric Brake & Clutch Co.

Milwaukee Symphony Friends ($10,000) see Rolfs Foundation, Robert T.

Milwaukee Symphony Orchestra ($17,500) see Krause Foundation, Charles A.

Milwaukee Symphony Orchestra ($10,000) see Marcus Corp.

Milwaukee Symphony Orchestra ($39,760) see Marquette Electronics

Milwaukee Symphony Orchestra ($150,000) see Pollybill Foundation

Milwaukee Symphony Orchestra — Arts in Community Education Program ($35,000) see McBeath Foundation, Faye

Milwaukee Theatre Festival ($12,500) see Marquette Electronics

Milwaukee World Festival — strengthen resources in community ($5,000) see Blue Cross and Blue Shield United of Wisconsin Foundation

Milwaukee World Festival ($5,000) see Kohl Charitable Foundation, Allen D.

Milwaukee World Festival ($100,000) see Marcus Corp.

Milwaukee World Festival ($8,000) see Rite-Hite Corp.

Milwaukee Zoological Society ($2,500) see Ziegler Foundation

Monroe County Crime Stoppers — education training ($13,570) see Andres Charitable Trust, Frank G.

Montessori School of Waukesha ($17,000) see Stackner Family Foundation

Mosinee School System — scholarships ($2,800) see Mosinee Paper Corp.

Mount Mary College ($32,500) see Helfaer Foundation, Evan and Marion

Mount Mary College ($27,000) see Monaghan Charitable Trust, Rose

Mount Mary College ($6,000) see Rolfs Foundation, Thomas J.

Mount Scenario College ($9,000) see Alexander Foundation, Walter

MPC Endowment, Ltd ($2,000) see Vilter Manufacturing Corp.

MSOE Milwaukee School of Engineering ($5,000) see Wagner Manufacturing Co., E. R.

Museum of Science, Economics and Technology — cultural ($50,000) see Schroeder Foundation, Walter

Museum of Science, Economics & Technology — general ($156,000) see Wehr Foundation, Todd

Muskegon Metropolitan Partnership for New Education see Scott Paper Co.

N. W. T. C. Scholarship Fund ($3,000) see Wood Foundation, Lester G.

Nashotah House ($10,000) see Neenah Foundry Co.

Nashotah House ($2,000) see Wagner Manufacturing Co., E. R.

Nashotah House Campaign — Vision in Action ($25,000) see Pollybill Foundation

National Future Farmers of America Foundation ($4,000) see Agway

National Future Farmers of America Foundation ($17,900) see Briggs & Stratton Corp.

National Future Farmers of America Foundation ($23,478) see Butler Manufacturing Co.

National Future Farmers of America Foundation ($250) see Endries Fastener & Supply Co.

National Future Farmers of America Foundation ($43,000) see Wal-Mart Stores

National Future Farmers Foundation ($7,500) see Moorman Manufacturing Co.

National PFA Foundation ($4,500) see Poinsettia Foundation, Paul and Magdalena Ecke

Navarino Nature Center ($11,000) see Mielke Family Foundation

Neenah Historical Society ($15,000) see Smith Family Foundation, Theda Clark

Neighborhood Home of Milwaukee ($5,000) see Lindsay Foundation

Neighborhood House of Milwaukee ($4,000) see Wagner Manufacturing Co., E. R.

Neighborhood House of Milwaukee ($1,000) see Wagner Manufacturing Co., E. R.

Neighborhood Housing Services ($3,000) see First Financial Bank FSB

Neighborhood Housing Services ($2,000) see Park Bank

Neighborhood Housing Services ($2,750) see Wauwatosa Savings & Loan Association

Neighborhood Housing Services ($2,500) see Wauwatosa Savings & Loan Association

Neville Public Museum ($1,000) see Cornerstone Foundation of Northeastern Wisconsin

New Day Shelter — to support the operations of this shelter and counseling service for victims of domestic violence ($45,000) see Bremer Foundation, Otto

New Ventures of Wisconsin — for costs to recruit and train advocates ($5,000) see Cremer Foundation

NEWIST — Babies with AIDS project ($30,000) see Walter Family Trust, Byron L.

Newman High School ($10,000) see Goldbach Foundation, Ray and Marie

Next Door Foundation ($20,000) see Ross Memorial Foundation, Will

Next Door Foundation — capital project ($100,000) see Siebert Lutheran Foundation

Next Door Foundation — capital project ($100,000) see Siebert Lutheran Foundation

Next Door Foundation ($2,000) see Wauwatosa Savings & Loan Association

Next Door Foundation — renovation of Helwig community center ($100,000) see Siebert Lutheran Foundation

Northland College ($50,000) see Hulings Foundation, Mary Andersen

Northland College ($20,000) see Peters Foundation, R. D. and Linda

Northland College ($1,000) see Pukall Lumber

Northland College ($40,000) see Van Evera Foundation, Dewitt Caroline

Northland College — 5th and final installment on 1986 commitment toward Endowment and Peder Madsen Work-Study Program ($100,000) see Maytag Family Foundation, Fred

Northwestern Preparatory School ($10,000) see Roehl Foundation

NWTC Foundation ($5,000) see Peterson Foundation, Fred J.

Oak Creek Community Center ($5,000) see Wauwatosa Savings & Loan Association

Oak Creek/Franklin Scholarship Fund ($2,000) see Wauwatosa Savings & Loan Association

Oakwood Village ($50,000) see Rennebohm Foundation, Oscar

Olbrich Botanical Garden — fountain and garden ($20,000) see Bassett Foundation, Norman

Olbrich Botanical Society ($20,000) see Evjue Foundation

Olbrich Botanical Society ($4,000) see Madison Gas & Electric Co.

Olin, Sang, Ruby Institute Camp ($145,000) see Sang Foundation, Elsie O. and Philip D.

115 Club ($5,000) see Peterson Foundation, Fred J.

Operation Fresh Start — assist with purchasing tools, equipment ($2,500) see Cremer Foundation

Opportunity Development Center ($5,750) see Miller Foundation, Steve J.

Opportunity Development Centers ($17,000) see Alexander Charitable Foundation

Oshkosh Area United Way ($11,500) see Kimball Co., Miles

Oshkosh Area United Way ($45,000) see Oshkosh B'Gosh

Oshkosh Big Brothers and Big Sisters ($2,500) see Oshkosh Truck Corp.

Oshkosh Public Museum ($5,000) see Kimball Co., Miles

Our House in Milwaukee — support for Ronald McDonald House, for families of hospitalized children ($2,000) see Vilter Manufacturing Corp.

Our Lady of Charity Family Program ($25,000) see Walter Family Trust, Byron L.

Overflowing Cup — homeless a/c and heating units ($25,000) see Beloit Foundation

Paine Art Center and Arboretum ($17,500) see Oshkosh B'Gosh

Paine Art Center and Arboretum ($2,500) see Oshkosh Truck Corp.

Parents Anonymous of Greater Milwaukee ($16,430) see Bucyrus-Erie

Park People ($10,000) see Ross Memorial Foundation, Will

Parker Memorial Scholarship ($6,000) see Janesville Foundation

Peace United Church of Christ ($4,000) see Brillion Iron Works

Penfield Children's Center ($10,000) see Demmer Foundation, Edward U.

Penfield Children's Center ($5,000) see Kohl Charities, Herbert H.

Penfield Children's Center ($3,000) see Park Bank

Penfield Children's Center ($2,500) see Ziemann Foundation

PEO Education Fund ($3,000) see Banta Corp.

Phipps Center for the Arts ($80,000) see Andersen Foundation, Hugh J.

Phipps Center for the Arts ($133,000) see Phipps Foundation, William H.

Planned Parenthood ($5,500) see Charter Manufacturing Co.

Planned Parenthood ($2,000) see Pfister and Vogel Tanning Co.

Planned Parenthood ($25,000) see Pollybill Foundation

Planned Parenthood ($20,000) see Ross Memorial Foundation, Will

Project Bridges ($6,000) see Mielke Family Foundation

Province of St. Joseph ($10,000) see Goldbach Foundation, Ray and Marie

Racine Alcohol Patrol ($2,500) see Greene Manufacturing Co.

Racine Area Soccer Association ($70,000) see Johnson & Son, S.C.

Racine Area United Way — annual fund ($9,091) see Greene Manufacturing Co.

Racine Area United Way ($36,500) see Wisconsin Energy Corp.

Racine Arts Council ($1,500) see Christensen Charitable and Religious Foundation, L. C.

Racine County Area Foundation — Project 3000 Christmas baskets ($1,000) see Greene Manufacturing Co.

Racine Lutheran High School ($3,000) see Christensen Charitable and Religious Foundation, L. C.

Racine Public Library ($21,000) see Christensen Charitable and Religious Foundation, L. C.

Racine Symphony ($4,000) see Christensen Charitable and Religious Foundation, L. C.

Racine Zoological Society ($100,000) see Johnson & Son, S.C.

Wisconsin (cont.)

Rahr Foundation Scholarship Fund ($50,573) see Rahr Malting Co.

Rawhide Boys Ranch ($250,000) see Kimberly-Clark Corp.

Rawhide Boys Ranch ($7,500) see Sentry Insurance Co.

RCHS ($250,000) see Jeffris Family Foundation

Reforestation Camp ($10,000) see Kress Foundation, George

Regional Domestic Abuse ($3,400) see SNC Manufacturing Co.

Rehabilitation Center Lakeland Council ($1,000) see Pukall Lumber

Rescue Squad ($7,500) see Jeffris Family Foundation

Retarded Citizens ($10,000) see Badger Meter, Inc.

Ripon College ($15,000) see Caestecker Foundation, Charles and Marie

Ripon College ($10,000) see Moore Foundation, O. L.

Ripon College ($15,000) see Neenah Foundry Co.

Ripon College ($30,000) see Oshkosh B'Gosh

Ripon College ($20,000) see Oshkosh B'Gosh

Ripon Memorial Hospital ($300,000) see Caestecker Foundation, Charles and Marie

Ripon Memorial Hospital ($5,000) see Caestecker Foundation, Charles and Marie

Riveredge Nature Center ($50,000) see Marshall & Ilsley Bank

Riveredge Nature Center ($12,500) see Pollybill Foundation

Riveredge Nature Center — educational ($50,000) see Schroeder Foundation, Walter

Riveredge Nature Center ($50,000) see Wisconsin Energy Corp.

Riveredge Nature Center ($40,000) see Ziegler Foundation

Riverview Hospital ($18,000) see Alexander Charitable Foundation

Rock County ($3,000) see Warner Electric Brake & Clutch Co.

Rock County Historical Society ($6,000) see Janesville Foundation

Rock Valley Community Corrections — substance abuse facility ($25,000) see Beloit Foundation

Rolfs Educational Foundation ($12,750) see Rolfs Foundation, Thomas J.

Ronald McDonald House of Madison ($25,000) see Evjue Foundation

Rosalie Manor — families united to prevent teen pregnancy program ($10,000) see Birnschein Foundation, Alvin and Marion

Rotary Scholarship ($3,000) see Peterson Foundation, Fred J.

Rx for Reading ($1,112,523) see Riordan Foundation

Rx for Reading in Wisconsin ($10,000) see Badger Meter, Inc.

Rx for Reading in Wisconsin ($25,000) see Marquette Electronics

Rx for Reading in Wisconsin ($20,000) see Universal Foods Corp.

Sacred Heart School of Theology — field education program ($5,000) see Birnschein Foundation, Alvin and Marion

St. Albans Episcopal Church ($13,750) see Roddis Foundation, Hamilton

St. Bartholomew Lutheran Church ($4,000) see Brillion Iron Works

St. Bartholomew Lutheran Church ($4,000) see Peters Foundation, R. D. and Linda

St. Catherine's — capital fund drive ($1,000) see Greene Manufacturing Co.

St. Catherine's Infirmary — OBRA requirements, re: nursing assistance certification and registration ($500) see Greene Manufacturing Co.

St. Coletta School ($25,000) see Ladish Family Foundation, Herman W.

St. Colettas School ($30,000) see Ziemann Foundation

St. Elizabeth Hospital Foundation ($3,000) see U.S. Oil/Schmidt Family Foundation, Inc.

St. Elizabeth Hospital Foundation ($3,000) see U.S. Oil/Schmidt Family Foundation, Inc.

St. Francis Children's Activity Center — concern for youth ($50,000) see Schroeder Foundation, Walter

St. Francis Children's Center ($5,000) see Kohl Charities, Herbert H.

St. Francis Foundation ($15,000) see Reinhart Institutional Foods

St. John United Church of Christ ($10,000) see Rogers Foundation

St. John's Military Academy Foundation ($25,000) see Noble Foundation, Vivian Bilby

St. Joseph of the Capuchin Order — St. Benedict the Morr Loaves and Fishes Meal Program ($20,000) see Birnschein Foundation, Alvin and Marion

St. Joseph's Community Hospital ($62,000) see Rolfs Foundation, Robert T.

St. Joseph's Community Hospital ($37,500) see Ziegler Foundation

St. Joseph's Hospital — window replacement ($8,500) see Phillips Family Foundation, L. E.

St. Josephs Hospital — for medical care and treatment ($10,000) see Vilter Manufacturing Corp.

St. Luke's Medical Center ($50,000) see Marshall & Ilsley Bank

St. Margaret's Episcopal Church ($4,500) see Bolz Family Foundation, Eugenie Mayer

St. Mary's Catholic Church ($4,000) see Brillion Iron Works

St. Marys Catholic Church ($15,000) see Peters Foundation, R. D. and Linda

St. Mary's Home ($200) see Formrite Tube Co.

St. Mary's Hospital — cardiac capers ($500) see Greene Manufacturing Co.

St. Mary's Hospital ($25,000) see Walter Family Trust, Byron L.

St. Marys Hospital Foundation ($2,000) see First Financial Bank FSB

St. Mary's Hospital Foundation ($12,500) see Wausau Paper Mills Co.

St. Marys Hospital Medical Center ($15,000) see Evjue Foundation

St. Marys Parish ($27,600) see McCarthy Memorial Trust Fund, Catherine

St. Matthew's Evangelical Lutheran Church ($6,500) see Roehl Foundation

St. Norbert College ($50,000) see Clark Family Foundation, Emory T.

St. Norbert College ($100,000) see Cornerstone Foundation of Northeastern Wisconsin

St. Norbert College ($20,000) see Kress Foundation, George

St. Norbert College ($1,000) see Schreiber Foods, Inc.

St. Norbert College ($32,000) see Walter Family Trust, Byron L.

St. Norbert College ($32,000) see Walter Family Trust, Byron L.

St. Norbert College ($25,000) see Wisconsin Public Service Corp.

St. Norbert College ($1,000) see Ziemann Foundation

St. Paul Episcopal Church ($10,000) see Klingler Foundation, Helen and Charles

St. Paul Home ($25,000) see U.S. Oil/Schmidt Family Foundation, Inc.

St. Paul's Evangelical Lutheran Church ($6,500) see Roehl Foundation

St. Peter and Paul School — computer fund ($4,000) see Peterson Foundation, Fred J.

St. Vincent Hospital ($10,000) see Kress Foundation, George

St. Vincent Hospital ($20,000) see Wisconsin Public Service Corp.

St. Vincent Hospital ($20,000) see Wisconsin Public Service Corp.

St. Vincent de Paul Society ($10,000) see Rolfs Foundation, Thomas J.

St. Vincents Hospital ($3,000) see Mosinee Paper Corp.

Salvadorian Mission Warehouse ($4,000) see Rolfs Foundation, Thomas J.

Salvation Army ($3,000) see Bolz Family Foundation, Eugenie Mayer

Salvation Army ($200) see Brillion Iron Works

Salvation Army ($5,000) see Cleary Foundation

Salvation Army ($2,620) see Cleary Foundation

Salvation Army ($100) see Formrite Tube Co.

Salvation Army ($5,000) see Pick Charitable Trust, Melitta S.

Salvation Army ($3,000) see Taylor Charitable Trust, Jack DeLoss

Salvation Army ($5,000) see Wood Foundation, Lester G.

Salvation Army — for after-school program ($5,575) see Cremer Foundation

Salvatorian Mission Warehouse ($25,000) see U.S.

Oil/Schmidt Family Foundation, Inc.

Schoenstatt Sister of Mary Province House ($10,000) see Klingler Foundation, Helen and Charles

Scholarships, Inc. ($8,400) see Cornerstone Foundation of Northeastern Wisconsin

School District of Marinette — Project Success see Scott Paper Co.

School Sisters of St. Francis ($2,000) see Kasal Charitable Trust, Father

School Sisters of St. Francis ($10,000) see O'Neil Foundation, W.

School Sisters of St. Francis — furniture and equipment, ($6,531) see Hackett Foundation

Science, Economics and Technology Center ($25,000) see Briggs & Stratton Corp.

Science, Economics and Technology Center ($10,000) see Briggs & Stratton Corp.

Second Harvesters of Wisconsin ($15,000) see Ross Memorial Foundation, Will

Seton Health Care Foundation ($1,000) see Pfister and Vogel Tanning Co.

Shamrock Healthcare — for increased staffing of 24/hr. on-call program ($11,500) see Cremer Foundation

Shanano County Arts Council ($13,177) see Mielke Family Foundation

Sheboygan Area United Way ($6,000) see Wigwam Mills

Sheboygan Arts Foundation ($15,000) see Brotz Family Foundation, Frank G.

Sheboygan Arts Foundation — capital improvements ($400,000) see Kohler Co.

Sheboygan Arts Foundation ($200,000) see Kohler Foundation

Sheboygan Arts Foundation ($44,914) see Kohler Foundation

Sheboygan Country Fair Association — Chapel ($25,000) see Brotz Family Foundation, Frank G.

Sheboygan Symphony Orchestra ($300) see Wigwam Mills

Sienna Center — adult learning program ($500) see Greene Manufacturing Co.

Sinai Samaritan Medical Center ($50,000) see Clark Family Foundation, Emory T.

Sinai Samaritan Medical Center — in support of the Commitment for Tomorrow program ($16,000) see Smith Corp., A.O.

Sisters of Charity ($2,500) see Godfrey Co.

Sisters of St. Francis of Holy Cross ($5,000) see U.S. Oil/Schmidt Family Foundation, Inc.

Sixteenth Street Community Health Center — building expansion ($29,500) see Cudahy Fund, Patrick and Anna M.

Skylight Opera Theatre ($10,000) see Demmer Foundation, Edward U.

South Milwaukee Police Department ($20,823) see Bucyrus-Erie

South Milwaukee School District ($65,125) see Bucyrus-Erie

State Historical Society of Wisconsin ($10,447) see Kohler Co.

State of Wisconsin ($18,000) see Peters Foundation, R. D. and Linda

Stateline United Givers Fund ($25,250) see Neese Family Foundation

Stoughton Syteende Mai Run ($1,000) see Nelson Industries, Inc.

Sturgeon Bay Rotary Club ($3,100) see Peterson Foundation, Fred J.

Tellurian Community — program on drugs and alcohol ($15,000) see Bassett Foundation, Norman

Tomah Area Ambulance — rescue equipment and protective gear ($15,800) see Andres Charitable Trust, Frank G.

Tomah Area School District — landscaping ball fields ($9,000) see Andres Charitable Trust, Frank G.

Tomah Area School District — playground equipment for Camp Douglas ($5,000) see Andres Charitable Trust, Frank G.

Tomah Memorial Hospital ($30,000) see Andres Charitable Trust, Frank G.

Tomah Police Department — DARE program ($12,536) see Andres Charitable Trust, Frank G.

Tomah Public Library — on-line computer catalog ($7,890) see Andres Charitable Trust, Frank G.

Town of Arbor Vitae ($1,500) see Pukall Lumber

Town of LaPointe, Wisconsin Fire Department ($10,000) see Rogers Foundation

Trees for Tomorrow ($15,000) see Kress Foundation, George

Trees for Tomorrow ($2,000) see Mosinee Paper Corp.

Trees for Tomorrow ($4,000) see Prange Co., H. C.

Trees for Tomorrow ($6,660) see Wausau Paper Mills Co.

Trees for Tomorrow ($20,000) see Wisconsin Public Service Corp.

Trees for Tomorrow 21st Century Campaign ($1,000) see Greenheck Fan Corp.

Trinity Evangelical Lutheran Church ($4,000) see Brillion Iron Works

Trinity Evangelical Lutheran Church ($11,000) see Peters Foundation, R. D. and Linda

Trinity Lutheran Church ($500) see Pukall Lumber

Trinity Memorial Hospital ($40,000) see Ladish Family Foundation, Herman W.

Trinity Memorial Hospital Foundation ($45,000) see Ladish Co.

Two Rivers Junior Ramblers ($100) see Formrite Tube Co.

United Cerebral Palsy Association ($2,500) see Kohl Charities, Herbert H.

United Community Center — for the new Italian Community Center ($10,000) see Humphrey Foundation, Glenn & Gertrude

United Lutheran Program for the Aging — social services ($50,000) see Schroeder Foundation, Walter

United Lutheran Program for Aging — building needs ($100,000) see Siebert Lutheran Foundation

United Lutheran Program for Aging — capital improvement campaign ($100,000) see Siebert Lutheran Foundation

United Lutheran Program for Aging — daycare, health services and worship center ($100,000) see Siebert Lutheran Foundation

United Methodist Church of Port Edwards ($33,702) see Alexander Charitable Foundation

United Negro College Fund ($10,000) see Rolfs Foundation, Robert T.

United Performing Arts Fund ($80,000) see Briggs & Stratton Corp.

United Performing Arts Fund ($46,130) see Bucyrus-Erie

United Performing Arts Fund ($5,000) see Charter Manufacturing Co.

United Performing Arts Fund ($18,000) see Demmer Foundation, Edward U.

United Performing Arts Fund ($6,000) see Evinrude Foundation, Ralph

United Performing Arts Fund — operating expense ($95,000) see Firstar Bank Milwaukee NA

United Performing Arts Fund ($225,000) see Johnson Controls

United Performing Arts Fund ($3,300) see Kohl Charities, Herbert H.

United Performing Arts Fund ($15,000) see Krause Foundation, Charles A.

United Performing Arts Fund ($26,780) see Northwestern National Insurance Group

United Performing Arts Fund ($3,500) see Park Bank

United Performing Arts Fund ($1,000) see Pfister and Vogel Tanning Co.

United Performing Arts Fund ($50,000) see Pick Charitable Trust, Melitta S.

United Performing Arts Fund ($2,500) see Pieper Electric

United Performing Arts Fund ($2,000) see Rite-Hite Corp.

United Performing Arts Fund ($7,000) see Rolfs Foundation, Robert T.

United Performing Arts Fund — to assist in meeting the operating expenses of the performing arts organizations ($35,000) see Smith Corp., A.O.

United Performing Arts Fund ($15,000) see Time Insurance Co.

United Performing Arts Fund ($16,000) see Universal Foods Corp.

United Performing Arts Fund ($40,000) see WICOR, Inc.

United Performing Arts Fund ($35,000) see WICOR, Inc.

United Performing Arts Fund ($245,000) see Wisconsin Energy Corp.

United Performing Arts Fund ($3,000) see Ziegler Foundation

United Way ($8,000) see Amsted Industries

United Way ($7,634) see Autotrol Corp.

United Way ($8,000) see Badger Meter, Inc.

United Way ($12,500) see Bassett Foundation, Norman

United Way ($60,000) see Beloit Foundation

United Way ($48,300) see Blue Cross and Blue Shield United of Wisconsin Foundation

United Way ($200,000) see Briggs & Stratton Corp.

United Way ($500) see Castle Industries

United Way ($5,700) see Charter Manufacturing Co.

United Way ($20,068) see Cleary Foundation

United Way ($20,000) see Coltec Industries

United Way ($162,000) see CUNA Mutual Insurance Group

United Way ($11,000) see CUNA Mutual Insurance Group

United Way ($13,500) see DEC International, Inc.

United Way ($108,500) see Eaton Corp.

United Way ($15,094) see First Financial Bank FSB

United Way ($5,773) see First Financial Bank FSB

United Way ($850) see Formrite Tube Co.

United Way ($300) see Formrite Tube Co.

United Way ($30,000) see Giddings & Lewis

United Way ($11,500) see Godfrey Co.

United Way ($11,000) see Godfrey Co.

United Way ($15,000) see Grede Foundries

United Way ($3,000) see Grede Foundries

United Way ($7,400) see Handy & Harman

United Way ($70,100) see Heileman Brewing Co., Inc., G.

United Way ($5,000) see Heileman Brewing Co., Inc., G.

United Way ($60,000) see Janesville Foundation

United Way ($8,600) see Janesville Foundation

United Way ($3,500) see Kohl Charities, Herbert H.

United Way ($38,000) see Kress Foundation, George

United Way ($50,000) see Madison Gas & Electric Co.

United Way ($20,000) see Marquette Electronics

United Way ($11,000) see Mosinee Paper Corp.

United Way ($3,000) see Mosinee Paper Corp.

United Way ($31,200) see Neenah Foundry Co.

United Way ($4,000) see Nelson Industries, Inc.

United Way ($44,500) see Northwestern National Insurance Group

United Way ($21,002) see Outboard Marine Corp.

United Way ($17,000) see Park Bank

United Way ($6,000) see Pieper Electric

United Way ($2,500) see Pitt-Des Moines Inc.

United Way ($4,000) see Rite-Hite Corp.

United Way ($60,000) see Ross Memorial Foundation, Will

United Way ($1,450) see Rubenstein Foundation, Philip

United Way ($95,000) see Sentry Insurance Co.

United Way ($7,787) see SNC Manufacturing Co.

United Way ($4,500) see Taylor Charitable Trust, Jack DeLoss

United Way ($121,451) see Time Insurance Co.

United Way ($16,397) see Time Insurance Co.

United Way ($20,000) see Vilter Manufacturing Corp.

United Way ($8,500) see Wagner Manufacturing Co., E. R.

United Way ($15,750) see Warner Electric Brake & Clutch Co.

United Way ($35,655) see Wausau Paper Mills Co.

United Way ($20,000) see Wausau Paper Mills Co.

United Way ($32,875) see WICOR, Inc.

United Way ($32,875) see WICOR, Inc.

United Way ($31,878) see WICOR, Inc.

United Way ($24,710) see WICOR, Inc.

United Way of Benton County ($11,516) see Oshkosh B'Gosh

United Way of Brown County ($70,500) see Wisconsin Public Service Corp.

United Way of Brown County ($66,500) see Wisconsin Public Service Corp.

United Way of Dane County ($15,000) see Banc One Wisconsin Corp.

United Way, Dane County ($10,500) see Banc One Wisconsin Corp.

United Way of Dane County — general purpose fund ($17,716) see Walgreen Co.

United Way of Dane County ($61,900) see Wisconsin Power & Light Co.

United Way of Eau Claire — operating funds ($15,000) see Phillips Family Foundation, L. E.

United Way of Greater Milwaukee ($103,495) see Bucyrus-Erie

United Way of Greater Milwaukee ($109,750) see Johnson Controls

United Way of Greater Milwaukee ($101,105) see Johnson Controls

United Way of Greater Milwaukee ($101,105) see Johnson Controls

United Way of Greater Milwaukee ($101,103) see Johnson Controls

United Way of Greater Milwaukee ($10,000) see Klingler Foundation, Helen and Charles

United Way of Greater Milwaukee ($32,600) see Marshall Field's

United Way of Greater Milwaukee ($210,000) see Smith Corp., A.O.

United Way of Greater Milwaukee ($68,850) see Universal Foods Corp.

United Way of Greater Milwaukee — general purpose fund ($9,338) see Walgreen Co.

United Way of Greater Milwaukee ($600,000) see Wisconsin Energy Corp.

United Way of Greater Milwaukee — '89 pledge ($274,500) see Firstar Bank Milwaukee NA

United Way-Kenosha County ($200,000) see Chrysler Corp.

United Way-LaCrosse ($97,017) see American Standard

United Way of Madison see New England Business Service

United Way-Milwaukee — operating ($33,000) see Sundstrand Corp.

United Way of Neenah-Menasha ($20,150) see Chesapeake Corp.

United Way of Neenah-Menasha — health and welfare ($5,600) see Menasha Corp.

United Way, Portage County ($6,025) see Banc One Wisconsin Corp.

United Way of Portage County — unrestricted ($26,800) see Consolidated Papers

United Way-Portage County ($27,000) see Woodward Governor Co.

United Way of South Wood County — unrestricted ($115,500) see Consolidated Papers

United Way of South Wood County ($40,568) see Georgia-Pacific Corp.

United Way of Washington County ($8,100) see Banc One Wisconsin Corp.

United Way of Waukesha ($45,000) see Dresser Industries

University Arboretum, Friends of — center for new student development ($15,000) see Evjue Foundation

University Arboretum, Friends of — Chancellor's scholarships for undergraduate minority and disadvantaged students ($25,000) see Evjue Foundation

University Arboretum, Friends of — Evjue, William T. Endowed ($100,000) see Evjue Foundation

University Arboretum, Friends of — exchange program with Moscow State University ($27,600) see Evjue Foundation

University Arboretum, Friends of — Summer Institute for Teachers of Minority Science Students ($14,400) see Evjue Foundation

University Lake School ($5,000) see Roehl Foundation

University Lake School ($60,000) see Stackner Family Foundation

University Lake School ($60,000) see Stackner Family Foundation

University Lake School Special Programs ($5,000) see Roehl Foundation

University School ($51,500) see Marshall & Ilsley Bank

University School of Milwaukee ($10,000) see Klingler Foundation, Helen and Charles

University School of Milwaukee Wisconsin ($1,000) see Charter Manufacturing Co.

University of Wisconsin ($125,000) see Beinecke Foundation

University of Wisconsin ($15,200) see Brunswick Corp.

University of Wisconsin — scholarship program ($2,250) see CENEX

University of Wisconsin ($7,100) see Cleary Foundation

University of Wisconsin ($100,000) see Cornerstone Foundation of Northeastern Wisconsin

University of Wisconsin ($7,750) see Gloeckner Foundation, Fred

University of Wisconsin ($5,000) see Grede Foundries

University of Wisconsin ($6,000) see Hanson Testamentary Charitable Trust, Anna Emery

University of Wisconsin ($3,450) see Harris Foundation, H. H.

University of Wisconsin ($16,000) see Herzog Foundation, Carl J.

University of Wisconsin — scholarship ($16,824) see Kohler Co.

University of Wisconsin — graduate school ($11,900) see Kohler Co.

University of Wisconsin ($8,000) see Ladish Co.

University of Wisconsin ($63) see Leesona Corp.

University of Wisconsin ($17,500) see Life Investors Insurance Company of America

University of Wisconsin ($17,000) see Lipton, Thomas J.

University of Wisconsin ($10,000) see Pott Foundation, Robert and Elaine

University of Wisconsin ($25,000) see Reinhart Institutional Foods

University of Wisconsin ($1,000) see Schreiber Foods, Inc.

University of Wisconsin ($66,593) see Sears, Roebuck and Co.

University of Wisconsin ($2,000) see Seneca Foods Corp.

University of Wisconsin ($30,000) see Smith Family Foundation, Theda Clark

University of Wisconsin ($10,000) see Wausau Paper Mills Co.

University of Wisconsin ($23,350) see Wisconsin Public Service Corp.

University of Wisconsin — Agriculture and Life Sciences ($10,000) see Miller Foundation, Steve J.

University of Wisconsin, Center for Performing Arts ($1,000,000) see AEC Trust

University Wisconsin Cooperative Studies — scholarship program ($2,250) see CENEX

University of Wisconsin Department of Wild Life Ecology ($17,000) see McGraw Foundation

University of Wisconsin Eau Claire Foundation — visiting professorship ($32,500) see Phillips Family Foundation, L. E.

University of Wisconsin Eau Claire Foundation — internship program ($17,500) see Phillips Family Foundation, L. E.

University of Wisconsin — to fund a traveling science experience, "The Great White Wave Machine" ($30,000) see American Honda Motor Co.

Wisconsin (cont.)

University of Wisconsin Foundation ($75,000) see Dow Chemical Co.

University of Wisconsin Foundation ($1,200) see Giddings & Lewis

University of Wisconsin Foundation — special program ($2,938,938) see Grainger Foundation

University of Wisconsin Foundation ($1,000) see Greenheck Fan Corp.

University of Wisconsin Foundation ($1,000) see J C S Foundation

University of Wisconsin Foundation — minority scholarships ($5,160) see Madison Gas & Electric Co.

University of Wisconsin Foundation ($50,000) see Mayer Charitable Trust, Oscar G. & Elsa S.

University of Wisconsin Foundation ($359,500) see Rennebohm Foundation, Oscar

University of Wisconsin Foundation ($40,000) see Rochlin Foundation, Abraham and Sonia

University of Wisconsin Foundation ($12,000) see Roddis Foundation, Hamilton

University of Wisconsin Foundation ($131,542) see Surgical Science Foundation for Research and Development

University of Wisconsin Foundation ($120,000) see Surgical Science Foundation for Research and Development

University of Wisconsin Foundation — Felber Scholarships ($60,344) see Madison Gas & Electric Co.

University of Wisconsin Foundation-Madison — capital campaign ($43,000) see Firstar Bank Milwaukee NA

University of Wisconsin Foundation — toward the Schoenleber Freshmen Seminary Fund ($25,000) see Schoenleber Foundation

University of Wisconsin Foundation — toward the endowment of the Schoenleber Scholarship Fund ($50,000) see Schoenleber Foundation

University of Wisconsin, Graduate School ($12,100) see Kohler Foundation

University of Wisconsin at Green Bay Performing Arts Center ($50,000) see Wood Foundation, Lester G.

University of Wisconsin — La Crosse Foundation ($97,670) see Stry Foundation, Paul E.

University of Wisconsin, Laboratory of Molecular Biology ($25,266) see Childs Memorial Fund for Medical Research, Jane Coffin

University of Wisconsin Law School — Minority Scholarship Fund ($15,000) see Smith Family Foundation, Theda Clark

University of Wisconsin—LPS Endowment ($100,000) see Uslico Corp.

University of Wisconsin — Lymnology, Basset chair ($16,000) see Bassett Foundation, Norman

University of Wisconsin Madison ($33,750) see CUNA Mutual Insurance Group

University of Wisconsin-Madison ($555,130) see Hewlett-Packard Co.

University of Wisconsin-Madison ($520,538) see Hewlett-Packard Co.

University of Wisconsin-Madison ($80,000) see Wisconsin Energy Corp.

University of Wisconsin Madison Medical School ($10,000) see Ross Memorial Foundation, Will

University of Wisconsin Madison School of Business ($10,000) see Mosinee Paper Corp.

University of Wisconsin Madison School of Business ($10,000) see Nelson Industries, Inc.

University of Wisconsin-Milwaukee ($40,000) see Wisconsin Energy Corp.

University of Wisconsin Milwaukee Business Administration ($10,000) see Marcus Corp.

University of Wisconsin-Milwaukee — Center for Teacher Education; for collaborative model project to restructure teacher roles in four Milwaukee public schools ($113,707) see Joyce Foundation

University of Wisconsin-Oshkosh ($5,000) see Kimball Co., Miles

University of Wisconsin-Oshkosh ($5,000) see Kimball Co., Miles

University of Wisconsin-Oshkosh Foundation ($25,000) see Oshkosh Truck Corp.

University of Wisconsin-Oshkosh Foundation — Business Administration College ($25,000) see Oshkosh B'Gosh

University of Wisconsin — Platteville Foundation ($3,500) see Giddings & Lewis

University of Wisconsin School of Business ($50,000) see CUNA Mutual Insurance Group

University of Wisconsin School of Business ($6,000) see CUNA Mutual Insurance Group

University of Wisconsin-Sheboygan County Foundation ($15,000) see Brotz Family Foundation, Frank G.

University of Wisconsin — children of children of the '60's at adolescence: a longitudinal study of drug use and sex typing ($126,008) see Grant Foundation, William T.

University of Wisconsin-STCUT ($20,000) see National Presto Industries

University of Wisconsin Stevens Point Foundation ($50,000) see Sentry Insurance Co.

University of Wisconsin Stevens Point Foundation ($3,890) see Sentry Insurance Co.

UPAF ($3,000) see Godfrey Co.

UPAF ($25,901) see Marquette Electronics

UPAF ($50,000) see Ross Memorial Foundation, Will

Urban Day School ($10,000) see Badger Meter, Inc.

UW-O Foundation — for education and research programs in business ($5,000) see Vilter Manufacturing Corp.

UWF-Big Red Club ($1,500) see DEC International, Inc.

UWMC Foundation ($1,500) see Greenheck Fan Corp.

Vernon Memorial Hospital Foundation ($1,000) see Nelson Industries, Inc.

Very Special Arts — arts opportunities for disabled children ($8,000) see Cremer Foundation

Vietnam Veterans ($1,760) see Godfrey Co.

Village Church ($11,000) see Combs Foundation, Earle M. and Virginia M.

Village of Plover Library Fund ($5,000) see Sentry Insurance Co.

Visiting Nurse Foundation ($2,600) see Curtice-Burns Foods

Viterbo College ($7,500) see Hiawatha Education Foundation

Viterbo College ($35,000) see Reinhart Institutional Foods

Viterbo College — general ($100,000) see Wehr Foundation, Todd

Voluntary Action Center — Merrill Center start up ($37,600) see Beloit Foundation

Volunteer Services for the Visually Handicapped ($10,000) see Schoenleber Foundation

Washington County Campus Foundation ($3,000) see Rolfs Foundation, Thomas J.

Watertown Memorial Hospital ($2,000) see First Financial Bank FSB

Waukesha Memorial Hospital ($2,000) see Wisconsin Centrifugal

Waukesha Memorial Hospital Foundation ($1,200) see Godfrey Co.

Wausau Area Community Foundation ($80,000) see Alexander Foundation, Judd S.

Wausau Area Community Foundation ($54,725) see Alexander Foundation, Judd S.

Wausau Area Community Foundation ($50,000) see Alexander Foundation, Judd S.

Wausau Area Community Foundation ($6,000) see Alexander Foundation, Walter

Wausau Area Community Foundation ($10,000) see Greenheck Fan Corp.

Wausau Area Community Foundation ($19,500) see Wausau Paper Mills Co.

Wausau Area Hmong Mutual Association ($71,632) see Alexander Foundation, Judd S.

Wausau Area Performing Arts Foundation — building fund ($10,000) see Mosinee Paper Corp.

Wausau Area Performing Arts Foundation ($2,000) see Mosinee Paper Corp.

Wausau Area Performing Arts Foundation ($1,000) see Pukall Lumber

Wausau Canoe and Kayak Corporation ($5,000) see Wausau Paper Mills Co.

Wausau Hospitals ($50,000) see Alexander Foundation, Judd S.

Wausau Kayak/Canoe Corporation ($20,985) see Alexander Foundation, Judd S.

Wauwatosa Economic Development Corporation ($4,000) see Wauwatosa Savings & Loan Association

Wayland Academy ($5,000) see Alexander Foundation, Walter

Wayland Academy ($500) see Chiquita Brands Co.

Wayland Academy ($15,000) see Neenah Foundry Co.

Wayland Academy ($12,000) see Oshkosh B'Gosh

WEMI ($1,885) see Endries Fastener & Supply Co.

West Bend Gallery of the Arts ($15,000) see Ziegler Foundation

West Bend Gallery of Fine Arts ($15,000) see Ziegler Foundation

West Bend Memorial Foundation ($58,000) see Pick Charitable Trust, Melitta S.

West Bend Memorial Foundation ($50,000) see Pick Charitable Trust, Melitta S.

West Bend Memorial Foundation ($45,000) see Pick Charitable Trust, Melitta S.

West Bend Memorial Foundation ($43,000) see Pick Charitable Trust, Melitta S.

West Madison Little League — lights ($16,200) see Bassett Foundation, Norman

Westby Coon Prairie Lutheran Church ($5,000) see Roehl Foundation

Whitefish Bay ($1,200) see Wagner Manufacturing Co., E. R.

Wilderness Fellowship ($8,000) see Pearson Foundation, E. M.

Wildlife Sanctuary ($10,000) see Kress Foundation, George

Winnebagoland Council of Campfire ($1,000) see SNC Manufacturing Co.

Wisconsin Academy of Adaptive Learning — scholarship assistance ($4,000) see Cremer Foundation

Wisconsin Chamber Orchestra ($1,000) see DEC International, Inc.

Wisconsin Coalition for Alternatives in Education/Rethinking Schools ($27,000) see New World Foundation

Wisconsin Conservatory of Music ($5,000) see Northwestern National Insurance Group

Wisconsin Conservatory of Music ($3,200) see Pfister and Vogel Tanning Co.

Wisconsin Economic Education Council ($250) see Endries Fastener & Supply Co.

Wisconsin Economic Educational Council ($2,500) see Oshkosh Truck Corp.

Wisconsin Educational Television ($6,500) see Mielke Family Foundation

Wisconsin Electric Power Electronic Consortium ($7,500) see Schott Foundation

Wisconsin Eye Bank ($18,000) see Woodward Governor Co.

Wisconsin Foundation of Independent Colleges ($7,500) see Banta Corp.

Wisconsin Foundation of Independent Colleges ($5,000)

see Bolz Family Foundation, Eugenie Mayer

Wisconsin Foundation of Independent Colleges — scholarships ($45,000) see Consolidated Papers

Wisconsin Foundation of Independent Colleges — scholarships ($45,000) see Consolidated Papers

Wisconsin Foundation of Independent Colleges ($1,750) see Endries Fastener & Supply Co.

Wisconsin Foundation of Independent Colleges ($7,500) see Giddings & Lewis

Wisconsin Foundation of Independent Colleges ($7,500) see Janesville Foundation

Wisconsin Foundation of Independent Colleges ($15,000) see Ladish Co.

Wisconsin Foundation of Independent Colleges ($2,200) see Mosinee Paper Corp.

Wisconsin Foundation of Independent Colleges ($2,250) see Nelson Industries, Inc.

Wisconsin Foundation of Independent Colleges ($3,000) see Northwestern National Insurance Group

Wisconsin Foundation of Independent Colleges ($6,500) see Oshkosh Truck Corp.

Wisconsin Foundation of Independent Colleges ($3,000) see Peterson Foundation, Fred J.

Wisconsin Foundation of Independent Colleges ($4,500) see Rahr Malting Co.

Wisconsin Foundation of Independent Colleges ($15,000) see Rolfs Foundation, Thomas J.

Wisconsin Foundation of Independent Colleges ($25,000) see Sentry Insurance Co.

Wisconsin Foundation of Independent Colleges ($2,500) see SNC Manufacturing Co.

Wisconsin Foundation of Independent Colleges ($6,000) see Time Insurance Co.

Wisconsin Foundation for Vocational, Technical and Adult Education — research to help determine future skill needs of Wisconsin employers ($5,000) see Blue Cross and Blue Shield United of Wisconsin Foundation

Wisconsin 4-H Foundation ($25,000) see Brotz Family Foundation, Frank G.

Wisconsin Heritages ($2,000) see Pfister and Vogel Tanning Co.

Wisconsin Historical Foundation ($1,000) see Nelson Industries, Inc.

Wisconsin Historical Foundation ($5,000) see Roddis Foundation, Hamilton

Wisconsin Historical Foundation ($97,000) see Silver Spring Foundation

Wisconsin Lutheran College — for the funding of five presidential scholarship annually over a period of five years ($10,000) see Schoenleber Foundation

Wisconsin Lutheran College — construction of recreation center ($100,000) see Siebert Lutheran Foundation

Wisconsin Nordic Sports Foundation ($1,000) see Nelson Industries, Inc.

Wisconsin Policy Research Institute ($15,000) see Cornerstone Foundation of Northeastern Wisconsin

Wisconsin Public Broadcasting ($4,500) see Brillion Iron Works

Wisconsin Public Broadcasting ($12,000) see Oshkosh B'Gosh

Wisconsin Public Broadcasting ($4,000) see Peterson Foundation, Fred J.

Wisconsin Public Broadcasting Foundation ($11,000) see Alexander Foundation, Walter

Wisconsin Public Broadcasting Foundation — underwrite ($27,000) see Consolidated Papers

Wisconsin Public Broadcasting Foundation — education ($7,500) see Menasha Corp.

Wisconsin Public Broadcasting Foundation — education ($7,500) see Menasha Corp.

Wisconsin Public Radio ($3,600) see Mielke Family Foundation

Wisconsin Rapids Chamber of Commerce ($1,000) see Prange Co., H. C.

Wisconsin Right to Life ($4,000) see Evinrude Foundation, Ralph

Wisconsin Special Olympics ($1,800) see DEC International, Inc.

Wisconsin Sports Authority ($5,000) see Cleary Foundation

Wisconsin State Historical Society ($5,000) see Banta Corp.

Wisconsin Taxpayer Alliance ($64,500) see Rennebohm Foundation, Oscar

Wisconsin Taxpayers Alliance ($2,000) see Cornerstone Foundation of Northeastern Wisconsin

Wisconsin Union Theater — performance ($10,000) see Bassett Foundation, Norman

Wisconsin Vietnam Veterans' Memorial Project — Vietnam memorial construction ($10,000) see Phillips Family Foundation, L. E.

WMC Foundation ($400) see Endries Fastener & Supply Co.

Woodland Dunes ($200) see Formrite Tube Co.

Woodland Girl Scout Council ($7,000) see Sentry Insurance Co.

Xavier High School ($5,000) see U.S. Oil/Schmidt Family Foundation, Inc.

YMCA ($339,701) see Alexander Charitable Foundation

YMCA ($12,000) see Alexander Foundation, Walter

YMCA ($5,000) see Alexander Foundation, Walter

YMCA ($7,000) see Blue Cross and Blue Shield United of Wisconsin Foundation

YMCA ($500) see Castle Industries

YMCA ($9,000) see Christensen Charitable and Religious Foundation, L. C.

YMCA ($9,000) see Christensen Charitable and Religious Foundation, L. C.

YMCA ($3,000) see Cremer Foundation

YMCA ($10,000) see First Financial Bank FSB

YMCA ($5,000) see First Financial Bank FSB

YMCA ($4,000) see Grede Foundries

YMCA ($7,000) see Greenheck Fan Corp.

YMCA ($20,000) see Kress Foundation, George

YMCA ($12,000) see Ladish Co.

YMCA ($12,000) see Ladish Co.

YMCA ($5,100) see Miller Foundation, Steve J.

YMCA ($4,000) see Mosinee Paper Corp.

YMCA ($15,000) see Neenah Foundry Co.

YMCA ($3,000) see Peterson Foundation, Fred J.

YMCA ($22,500) see Prange Co., H. C.

YMCA ($90,000) see Rolfs Foundation, Robert T.

YMCA ($21,000) see Shattuck Charitable Trust, S. F.

YMCA ($3,000) see U.S. Oil/Schmidt Family Foundation, Inc.

YMCA ($24,200) see Wausau Paper Mills Co.

YMCA ($2,600) see Wigwam Mills

YMCA Building Fund ($20,000) see Bucyrus-Erie

YMCA Covenant with Tomorrow — building fund ($30,000) see Firstar Bank Milwaukee NA

YWCA ($10,000) see CUNA Mutual Insurance Group

YWCA ($6,000) see Madison Gas & Electric Co.

YWCA ($20,000) see Walter Family Trust, Byron L.

YWCA ($3,000) see Wood Foundation, Lester G.

Zoological Society ($15,000) see Badger Meter, Inc.

Zoological Society ($60,000) see Stackner Family Foundation

Zoological Society of Milwaukee — capital campaign ($25,000) see Firstar Bank Milwaukee NA

Zoological Society of Milwaukee county ($10,500) see Krause Foundation, Charles A.

Zoological Society of Milwaukee County ($29,250) see Marquette Electronics

Zoological Society of Milwaukee County ($50,000) see Marshall & Ilsley Bank

Zoological Society of Milwaukee County ($100,000) see Peck Foundation, Milton and Lillian

Zoological Society of Milwaukee County — cultural ($60,000) see Schroeder Foundation, Walter

Zoological Society of Milwaukee County — general ($50,000) see Wehr Foundation, Todd

Zoological Society of Milwaukee County — to maintain membership with the Platypus Society ($32,500) see Smith Corp., A.O.

Wyoming

Big Horn Mountain Foundation — grant for first conference ($25,000) see Halliburton Co.

Big Horne Equestrian Center ($5,000) see Charitable Foundation of the Burns Family

Blue Envelope Fund ($10,000) see Kamps Memorial Foundation, Gertrude

Boys and Girls Club ($45,497) see Kamps Memorial Foundation, Gertrude

Buffalo Bill Historical Center ($125,000) see Browning Charitable Foundation, Val A.

Buffalo Bill Historical Center ($10,000) see Ray Foundation

Buffalo Bill Historical Center ($32,500) see Weiss Foundation, William E.

Buffalo Bill Historical Center — to complete funding of the Museum's $6.4 million capital campaign ($1,000,000) see Woodruff Foundation, Robert W.

Buffalo Bill Historical Society ($20,000) see Duncan Foundation, Lillian H. and C. W.

Buffalo Bill Memorial Association ($25,000) see Olin Corp.

Buffalo Bill Memorial Association — stock residence upkeep ($30,000) see Stock Foundation, Paul

Buffalo Bill Memorial Association ($45,000) see Weiss Foundation, William E.

Buffalo Bill Memorial Association ($18,470) see Woods Foundation, James H.

Buffalo Bill Memorial Association — Cody Firearms museum ($25,000) see Stock Foundation, Paul

Buffalo Bill Memorial Association — Jack Richards Photo Collection ($6,259) see Stock Foundation, Paul

Caring Center ($10,000) see Kamps Memorial Foundation, Gertrude

Caring Program for Children ($5,000) see Tonkin Foundation, Tom and Helen

Casper Community College ($2,000) see Sargent Foundation, Newell B.

Casper Legion Baseball ($10,000) see Kamps Memorial Foundation, Gertrude

Cathedral Home for Children ($20,000) see Nason Foundation

Cathedral Home for Children ($10,000) see Stock Foundation, Paul

Central Wyoming Rescue Mission ($1,500) see Sargent Foundation, Newell B.

Cheyenne Artist Guild see Public Service Co. of Colorado

Children's Center ($31,999) see Surrena Memorial Fund, Harry and Thelma

Children's Center ($27,200) see Surrena Memorial Fund, Harry and Thelma

Children's Center ($25,000) see Surrena Memorial Fund, Harry and Thelma

Children's Dental Fund ($5,000) see Tonkin Foundation, Tom and Helen

Church of St. Anthony — equipment and supplies, Seton House ($22,330) see Hackett Foundation

City of Worland ($5,810) see Sargent Foundation, Newell B.

Community Recreation Foundation ($4,000) see Tonkin Foundation, Tom and Helen

Crook County School District No. 1 ($1,000) see Stock Foundation, Paul

Crusade for Family Prayer ($200,000) see East Foundation, Sarita Kenedy

Friends of Washakie County Museum ($5,000) see Sargent Foundation, Newell B.

Gottsche Foundation ($5,000) see Stock Foundation, Paul

Grand Teton Music Festival ($5,000) see Goodman Family Foundation

Grand Teton Music Festival ($65,000) see Lightner Sams Foundation

Grand Teton Natural History Association ($10,000) see Armington Fund, Evenor

Handicapped Education and Referral Systems ($11,228) see Tonkin Foundation, Tom and Helen

Hearing Education and Referral Service ($8,564) see Tonkin Foundation, Tom and Helen

Hearing Education and Rehabilitation Service ($14,615) see Tonkin Foundation, Tom and Helen

HIRES ($4,720) see Tonkin Foundation, Tom and Helen

Holy Cross Center ($15,000) see Goodstein Foundation

Jackson Christian Association ($25,000) see Lightner Sams Foundation

Jackson Hole Alliance ($30,000) see Jackson Hole Preserve

Jackson Hole Land Trust ($50,000) see Jackson Hole Preserve

Jackson Hole Land Trust ($30,000) see Jackson Hole Preserve

Lions Club ($5,000) see Kamps Memorial Foundation, Gertrude

Memorial Hospital of Sheridan County — construct a new outpatient surgical suite and remodel the radiographic and clinical laboratory areas ($250,000) see Kiewit Foundation, Peter

Mercer House ($7,000) see Kamps Memorial Foundation, Gertrude

Mother Seton Housing ($10,000) see Goodstein Foundation

Mother Seton Housing ($1,000) see True Oil Co.

National Outdoor Leadership School ($10,000) see McGregor Foundation, Thomas and Frances

Northern Wyoming Community College ($1,000) see Bryan Foundation, Dodd and Dorothy L.

Northwest College — scholarships ($30,000) see Stock Foundation, Paul

Northwest Community College ($1,500) see Sargent Foundation, Newell B.

Northwest Community College ($1,000) see Sargent Foundation, Newell B.

Nutrition and Child Development ($3,900) see

Tonkin Foundation, Tom and Helen

Park County Search and Rescue ($5,000) see Stock Foundation, Paul

Rawlins Day Care Center ($4,128) see Tonkin Foundation, Tom and Helen

St. John's Hospital ($10,000) see Bostwick Foundation, Albert C.

St. Joseph Orphanage ($10,000) see Kamps Memorial Foundation, Gertrude

Special Friends of Rawlins ($4,000) see Tonkin Foundation, Tom and Helen

Special Olympics ($6,000) see Kamps Memorial Foundation, Gertrude

SPOE Grand Lodge ($30,865) see Kamps Memorial Foundation, Gertrude

Sublette County Historical Society ($73,750) see Taylor Foundation, Ruth and Vernon

Sublette County Retirement Center ($73,750) see Taylor Foundation, Ruth and Vernon

Teton Science School ($5,000) see Hill-Snowdon Foundation

Teton Science School ($25,000) see Weiss Foundation, William E.

TNC-Wyoming Chapter ($80,000) see Storer Foundation, George B.

United Way ($18,386) see True Oil Co.

United Way of Campbell County ($11,000) see AMAX

University of Wyoming ($25,000) see AMAX

University of Wyoming ($2,000) see Sargent Foundation, Newell B.

University of Wyoming ($1,000) see Sargent Foundation, Newell B.

University of Wyoming ($56,000) see Stock Foundation, Paul

University of Wyoming ($4,500) see True Oil Co.

University of Wyoming ($10,000) see Weiss Foundation, William E.

University of Wyoming ($10,000) see Wolf Foundation, Melvin and Elaine

University of Wyoming — Department of Animal Science ($11,400) see Animal Assistance Foundation

Weston County Memorial Hospital Foundation ($1,000) see True Oil Co.

Wildlife of American West Museum ($5,000) see Weiss Foundation, William E.

WYO Theatre ($6,000) see Charitable Foundation of the Burns Family

Wyoming Elks Association ($12,000) see Kamps Memorial Foundation, Gertrude

Wyoming Nature Conservancy ($25,000) see Healy Family Foundation, M. A.

Wyoming Nature Conservancy ($35,000) see Rupp Foundation, Fran and Warren

Wyoming State 4-H Foundation ($1,250) see True Oil Co.

YMCA ($147,378) see Whitney Benefits

International

Australia

Big Brothers and Big Sisters ($15,000) see Newman's Own
Child Abuse Prevention ($25,000) see Newman's Own
Children's Hospital Fund ($23,000) see Newman's Own
Children's Leukemia and Cancer ($24,000) see Newman's Own
Open Family Foundation ($15,000) see Newman's Own
Royal Blind Society ($25,000) see Newman's Own
St. Marks Community Center ($15,000) see Newman's Own
Shephard Center for the Deaf ($25,000) see Newman's Own
Spastic Society of Victoria ($25,000) see Newman's Own

Belgium

Commission for Educational Exchange Foundation for Scientific Research and Educational Exchange ($4,000) see Covington and Burling
Maison de L'Enfant Jesus ($210,000) see Brunner Foundation, Robert

Belize

Belize ($53,282) see Wagner Foundation, Ltd., R. H.
Diocese of Belize ($15,000) see Loyola Foundation

Bermuda

Bermuda Biological Station for Research ($33,000) see Foster-Davis Foundation
Genetic Research Trust ($325,200) see Winston Research Foundation, Harry

Brazil

Church of Latter Day Saints ($10,000) see Peery Foundation

Bulgaria

Operation Society Fund ($1,217,960) see Open Society Fund

Canada

Assumption Catholic Church ($10,000) see Trust Funds
Camosum College ($2,000) see Davey Tree Expert Co.
Camp Oochigeas ($20,000) see Newman's Own
Canada Department of External Affairs — gift of art work to Canadian government ($7,000) see Amway Corp.
Canadian Equestrian Team ($17,500) see Firan Foundation
Capstone Ministry Association ($42,500) see Dauch Foundation, William

Lake of the Woods Hospital ($150,000) see Boise Cascade Corp.
McGill University ($35,000) see Ala Vi Foundation of New York
McMaster University — to support Clinical Epidemiology and Training Center ($638,000) see Rockefeller Foundation
Meakaz Hatorah ($5,000) see N've Shalom Foundation
Montreal General Hospital ($30,000) see Blowitz-Ridgeway Foundation
Quebec-Labrador Foundation ($8,000) see Colket Foundation, Ethel D.
University of Western Ontario ($50,063) see Pioneer Fund
World Leisure and Recreation Association ($20,000) see National Forge Co.

People's Republic of China

Beijing Medical University — support various projects ($210,000) see China Medical Board of New York
China Medical University — programs in emergency medicine ($211,240) see China Medical Board of New York
Hunan Medical University Sun-Yat Sen University — support joint programs on nasopharyngeal cancer and fellowships ($215,000) see China Medical Board of New York
Lingnan College ($50,000) see Lingnan Foundation
Lingnan College ($17,000) see Lingnan Foundation
Shanghai Medical University — support Public Health Administration and Management ($220,000) see China Medical Board of New York
Sun Yat-Sen University of Medical Sciences — program in behavioral medicine ($215,000) see China Medical Board of New York
West China University — support various projects ($420,000) see China Medical Board of New York
Xi'an Medical University — program in medical education ($350,000) see China Medical Board of New York
Zhejiang Medical University — program in cancer screening ($275,000) see China Medical Board of New York
Zhongshan University ($51,000) see Lingnan Foundation
Zhongshan University ($29,000) see Lingnan Foundation
Zhongshan University ($22,600) see Lingnan Foundation

Zhongshan University ($15,900) see Lingnan Foundation

Czech Republic

Central European University ($1,099,774) see Open Society Fund

England

ABC Language School ($77,850) see ARCO Chemical
Balliol College ($25,000) see River Road Charitable Corporation
Centre for Research into Communist Economies ($6,500) see Thirty-Five Twenty, Inc.
Family in Trust Appeal ($100,000) see Wiener Foundation, Malcolm Hewitt
Living Streams Foundation ($20,000) see Generation Trust
London Symphony Orchestra ($85,000) see Gilman Foundation, Howard
Marie Stopes International ($500,000) see International Fund for Health and Family Planning
Mission Rainforest — land in Pinalito, Argentina ($81,525) see Ira-Hiti Foundation for Deep Ecology
Open University, Oxford ($5,000) see Glenn Foundation for Medical Research, Paul F.
Royal College of General Practitioners Research Unit — part of five-year grant to support study of the effects of hormones on postmenopausal subjects ($20,000) see Searle & Co., G.D.
Royal National Institute for the Blind ($38,875) see Taubman Foundation, A. Alfred
Salisbury Review ($2,500) see Wilbur Foundation, Marguerite Eyer

France

Alliance Israelite Universelle ($121,290) see de Rothschild Foundation, Edmond
American Aid Society — meet operating expenses ($500) see Bismarck Charitable Trust, Mona
American Hospital in Paris ($250,000) see David-Weill Foundation, Michel
American Hospital in Paris ($10,000) see Scaler Foundation
American Library in Paris ($35,000) see Berlin Charitable Fund, Irving
American Library in Paris — purchase books ($3,000) see Bismarck Charitable Trust, Mona

American Library in Paris ($50,000) see Scaler Foundation
Appel Unifie Juif de France ($121,940) see de Rothschild Foundation, Edmond
Association Auxilium ($113,257) see Eaton Foundation, Edwin M. and Gertrude S.
Association du Foeyer de l'Institution ($25,000) see Whittell Trust for Disabled Veterans of Foreign Wars, Elia
ASUNOR ($40,000) see Whittell Trust for Disabled Veterans of Foreign Wars, Elia
Centre de Documentation Juive Contemporaine ($50,000) see de Rothschild Foundation, Edmond
European Institute of Business Administration (INSEAD) — general support ($12,500) see Little, Arthur D.
Foundation De France — Legion d'Honneur ($20,000) see Whittell Trust for Disabled Veterans of Foreign Wars, Elia
Foundation pour la Jeunesse Francaise ($622,344) see de Rothschild Foundation, Edmond
Foundation Ophtalmologique ($57,411) see de Rothschild Foundation, Edmond
La Fondation pour le developpement ($291,073) see de Rothschild Foundation, Edmond
La Fondation de France — "ARS Gratia Vitae" project ($1,586,673) see Scaler Foundation
Lacoste School of the Arts in France ($10,000) see Piankova Foundation, Tatiana
L'Office National des Anciens Cobbattan et Vitimes deGuerre ($40,000) see Whittell Trust for Disabled Veterans of Foreign Wars, Elia
Maison du Foyer Rural ($18,895) see de Dampierre Memorial Foundation, Marie C.
Maison des Sciences de l'Homme Public ($80,000) see Scaler Foundation
Mona Bismarck Foundation — conduct exhibit, and meet part of operating expenses ($601,177) see Bismarck Charitable Trust, Mona
Playground School Reime ($45,795) see ARCO Chemical
Union de Aveugles de Guerre ($20,000) see Whittell Trust for Disabled Veterans of Foreign Wars, Elia
Union National Des Combattants ($30,000) see Whittell Trust for Disabled Veterans of Foreign Wars, Elia

Germany

Bonn House ($58,000) see Timmis Foundation, Michael & Nancy
Intercessors International ($30,000) see Generation Trust
Islamische Wissenchaftliche Akademie ($65,000) see Ala Vi Foundation of New York
Max Planck Institute for Psychiatric — pioneering basic research in the identification, purification, and molecular cloning of brain derived neurotrophic factor ($26,090) see American Foundation

Ghana

Diocese of Kumasi ($14,500) see Loyola Foundation

Greece

Aegean School — scholarship for Italy session ($3,000) see Olivetti Office USA, Inc.
American College of Greece ($10,000) see Demos Foundation, N.
American Farm School ($3,000) see DelMar Foundation, Charles
American Farm School ($20,000) see Demos Foundation, N.
American Farm School ($10,000) see Foster-Davis Foundation
American Farm School ($6,500) see Sofia American Schools
American Farm School ($5,300) see Sofia American Schools
Anatolia College ($25,000) see Demos Foundation, N.
Anatolia College ($25,000) see Sofia American Schools
Anatolia College ($9,000) see Sofia American Schools
Athens College ($11,000) see Demos Foundation, N.
Centre D'Estudes D'Asie Meneure ($11,250) see Demos Foundation, N.
Gennadius Library, American School of Classical Studies ($14,000) see Demos Foundation, N.
Kefalonia Orphanage ($5,000) see Demos Foundation, N.
Patriarchal Institute for Patriotic Studies ($10,000) see Demos Foundation, N.
Social Work Foundation ($15,000) see Demos Foundation, N.
Spastics Society ($45,000) see Demos Foundation, N.

Guatemala

Center for Regional Meso-American Investigations ($182,000) see Plumsock Fund

Honduras

Catholic Church ($40,000) see Timmis Foundation, Michael & Nancy

Hong Kong

Chinese University of Hong Kong ($26,000) see Lingnan Foundation

Raimondi College ($1,300) see Eaton Foundation, Edwin M. and Gertrude S.

University of Hong Kong — scholarships for scholarship funding ($7,800) see Van Schaick Scholarship Fund, Nellie

Hungary

Consultrade ($750,000) see Soros Foundation-Hungary

East-West Management Institute Foundation ($100,000) see Soros Foundation-Hungary

Free Trade Union Foundation ($100,000) see Soros Foundation-Hungary

HAS-Soros Foundation Secretariat ($362,244) see Soros Foundation-Hungary

Kisvallaklozo's Orszagos Szovestsege ($250,000) see Soros Foundation-Hungary

National Szechenyi Library ($216,645) see Soros Foundation-Hungary

Student Advising Center ($146,341) see Soros Foundation-Hungary

University of Budapest ($63,544) see Salgo Charitable Trust, Nicholas M.

University of Texas Summer Travel ($100,000) see Soros Foundation-Hungary

India

Jesuit Jamshedpur Missions ($14,567) see Loyola Foundation

Iran

Red Crescent of Iran ($100,000) see Ala Vi Foundation of New York

Ireland

Shrine of Our Lady ($1,000) see Berkman Foundation, Louis and Sandra

Israel

Ahli Arab Hospital ($5,000) see Jerusalem Fund for Education and Community Development

Arab Women's Union ($2,500) see Jerusalem Fund for Education and Community Development

Beit Sahour Health Care Cooperative ($10,000) see Jerusalem Fund for Education and Community Development

Boys Town ($250,000) see Soref Foundation, Samuel M. Soref and Helene K.

Boys Town Jerusalem ($30,000) see Applebaum Foundation

Challenge/Etgar ($500) see Foundation for Middle East Peace

Four Homes of Mercy ($5,000) see Jerusalem Fund for Education and Community Development

Hadassah ($100,000) see Hoffberger Foundation

Hebrew University ($150,000) see Goldie-Anna Charitable Trust

Howard Gilman Israel Cultural Foundation ($120,000) see Gilman Foundation, Howard

Individual Research Project — entitled "Thawra to Infitada: The Domestication of Arab Rebellion in Palestine. Mastering Techniques of Resistance and Repression through Alternating Structures of Violence, 1936 - present" ($32,000) see Guggenheim Foundation, Harry Frank

Israel Academy of Sciences — to support the Basic Research Fund ($1,000,000) see Revson Foundation, Charles H.

Israel Museum ($66,430) see Dorot Foundation

Israel Museum ($143,529) see Wallach Foundation, Miriam G. and Ira D.

Israeli Society for Coastal and Sand Vegetation ($15,000) see Smith Horticultural Trust, Stanley

Keren Aviad — Israel TV Series ($45,000) see AVI CHAI - A Philanthropic Foundation

Kohl Children's Museum ($10,000) see Kohl Foundation, Sidney

Mental Health Center ($10,000) see Jerusalem Fund for Education and Community Development

Mesifta of Rabbi Yochanan ($4,000) see Lowenstein Foundation, William P. and Marie R.

Palestinian Counseling Center ($5,000) see Jerusalem Fund for Education and Community Development

Palestinian Women's Union ($10,000) see Jerusalem Fund for Education and Community Development

Patient's Friends Society ($5,000) see Jerusalem Fund for Education and Community Development

Public Committee Against Torture ($500) see Foundation for Middle East Peace

State of Israel ($25,000) see Frank Fund, Zollie and Elaine

State of Israel ($200,000) see Greenberg Foundation, Alan C.

Tel Aviv University ($6,500) see Fellner Memorial Foundation, Leopold and Clara M.

Tel Aviv University ($5,000) see Garfinkle Family Foundation

Tel Aviv University ($5,000) see Stein Foundation, Louis

Weizmann Institute of Science — cellular and molecular correlates of a gustatory memory engram: acquired gustatory representations in the rat ($44,000) see Whitehall Foundation

Young Women's Moslem Association ($5,000) see Jerusalem Fund for Education and Community Development

Italy

Boys Town of Italy ($5,000) see Kennedy Family Foundation, Ethel and W. George

Boystown of Italy ($5,000) see Mann Foundation, John Jay

Economic Prefecture for the Holy See ($100,000) see Doty Family Foundation

Gregorian University Foundation ($25,000) see Loyola Foundation

Pope John Paul II Cultural Foundation, Vatican ($1,000,000) see Connelly Foundation

Vatican Museums — mosaic restoration, conference and publication of book ($123,500) see Homeland Foundation

Verona Fathers — Sons of the Sacred Heart ($30,000) see Stella D'Oro Biscuit Co.

Verona Fathers — Sons of the Sacred Heart ($30,000) see Stella D'Oro Biscuit Co.

Verona Fathers — Sons of the Sacred Heart ($3,100) see Stella D'Oro Biscuit Co.

Japan

International University of Japan ($14,814) see Ishiyama Foundation

Kenya

Day Star University ($1,000) see Rixson Foundation, Oscar C.

Franciscan Sisters ($2,000) see Tripifoods

International Council for Research in Agroforestry ($541,000) see Rockefeller Foundation

Republic of Korea

Bible Church of Korea ($4,000) see Dauch Foundation, William

Lao People's Democratic Republic

University of Health Sciences — fellowship ($263,000) see China Medical Board of New York

Lesotho

Bible Believers of Malawi ($4,000) see Dauch Foundation, William

Diocese of Leribe ($34,000) see Genesis Foundation

Lesotho/Ireland Technical ($56,786) see Genesis Foundation

Luxembourg

Christ Saviour Church St. ($15,000) see Loyola Foundation

Marshall Islands

Queen of Peace Mission ($2,000) see Jerome Foundation

Mexico

Escuela Femenina de Montefalco — educational programs for girls from rural farm areas ($12,000) see Clover Foundation

Salvation Army ($26,500) see Frees Foundation

San Miguel Educational Foundation ($25,000) see Cabot Family Charitable Trust

New Zealand

Eastwood Hill Arboretum — construction of a building

($31,000) see Smith Horticultural Trust, Stanley

Peru

Individual Research Project — entitled "History as a Police Report: The Impact of Cocaine Trafficking on Peru" ($34,900) see Guggenheim Foundation, Harry Frank

Philippines

International Rice Research Institute — research ($700,000) see Rockefeller Foundation

Jerome Foundation ($55,131) see Jerome Foundation

Tabernacle of Living God ($12,500) see Dauch Foundation, William

Poland

Commission of Education on Alcohol and Drug Dependency ($125,000) see Open Society Fund

Stefan Batory Foundation ($1,475,974) see Open Society Fund

Puerto Rico

School Sisters of Notre Dame in the Region of Puerto Rico ($5,000) see Halloran Foundation, Mary P. Dolciani

United Way ($1,000) see Wolverine World Wide, Inc.

Romania

Knights of Malta ($15,000) see Loyola Foundation

Open Society Fund ($759,999) see Open Society Fund

Romania Libera ($151,268) see Open Society Fund

Scotland

Clan Donald Lands Trust ($126,787) see Glencoe Foundation

Clan Donald Lands Trust ($49,350) see Glencoe Foundation

Clan Donald Lands Trust ($37,673) see Glencoe Foundation

Clan Donald Lands Trust ($24,675) see Glencoe Foundation

Clan Donald Lands Trust ($17,683) see Glencoe Foundation

Clan Donald Lands Trust ($14,024) see Glencoe Foundation

Glasgow University Department of Archaeology ($13,050) see Durfee Foundation

National Trust for Scotland ($8,225) see Glencoe Foundation

Republic of South Africa

Career Centre — to help the implementation of a computerized information system to better counsel black South African high school students ($78,780) see IBM South Africa Projects Fund

Grassroots Educare Trust ($36,284) see Genesis Foundation

Holy Trinity High School ($29,500) see Genesis Foundation

Langayde School ($40,006) see Genesis Foundation

Legal Resources Centre (LRC) — to help fund the LRC centers in South Africa which provide free legal assistance to blacks ($89,475) see IBM South Africa Projects Fund

Nottingham Road Farm School ($30,000) see Genesis Foundation

READ Education ($33,808) see Genesis Foundation

St. John Bosco College ($26,363) see Genesis Foundation

St. Mark's College ($25,531) see Genesis Foundation

Small Home Builders Loan Fund — to assist small home building contractors in black areas by arranging financing for approved black building contractors ($191,638) see IBM South Africa Projects Fund

Spoken Word ($18,000) see Dauch Foundation, William

Teacher Opportunity Programmes (TOPS) — to help sponsor teacher and principal training efforts to upgrade job skills and qualifications ($62,180) see IBM South Africa Projects Fund

Technikon Witwatersrand — to help establish a training program and center for underprivileged black South Africans ($183,508) see IBM South Africa Projects Fund

Spain

Association of Espanola de Eusenanja Biblica ($15,000) see M.E. Foundation

Sri Lanka

International Irrigation Management Institute — for irrigation agencies in Bangladesh ($500,000) see Rockefeller Foundation

Sweden

Vagnharad Filadelfia Church ($70,000) see Generation Trust

Switzerland

Pecusa for Emmanuel Church ($3,000) see Bloedel Foundation

University of Zurich — fourth recipient of the Harry Frank Guggenheim Career Development Award for research project ($35,000) see Guggenheim Foundation, Harry Frank

World Health Organization — to monitor health and safety of Norplant contraceptive method ($700,000) see Rockefeller Foundation

Thailand

Chulalongkorn University — support Public Health Administration and Management ($600,000) see China Medical Board of New York

Turkey

American Hospital of Istanbul ($15,000) see Sofia American Schools

American Hospital of Istanbul School of Nursing ($5,000) see Sofia American Schools

Robert College of Istanbul ($7,000) see Dorr Foundation

Robert College of Istanbul ($19,000) see Sofia American Schools

Robert College of Istanbul ($3,050) see Sofia American Schools

United Kingdom

Save the Children see Booz Allen & Hamilton

Uruguay

Diocese of Salto ($17,000) see Loyola Foundation

Venezuela

A.C. Centro Medico Docente La Trinidad — general purposes ($44,992) see Vollmer Foundation

Academia Nacional de Medicina — support for Venezuelan Medical programs ($124,389) see Vollmer Foundation

Archdiocese of Caracas — general purposes ($8,224) see Vollmer Foundation

Asociacion Venezolana de Conciertos — general

purposes ($169,646) see Vollmer Foundation

Dividendo Voluntario para la Comunidad — construction and support rural schools ($230,757) see Vollmer Foundation

Fundacion Palmar Banco del Orinoco — capital grant ($7,458,867) see Vollmer Foundation

Instituto de Estudios Superiores de Administracion — general purposes of graduate school of Business Administration ($16,447) see Vollmer Foundation

Sociedad de Proteccion Benefica y Social, Sol. Santa Maria Micaela, Calle F. Urb. Vista

Alegre — general purposes ($46,711) see Vollmer Foundation

Universidad Catolica Andres Bello — general purposes ($145,908) see Vollmer Foundation

Universidad Catolica del Tachira — general purposes ($49,342) see Vollmer Foundation

Virgin Islands of the United States

British Virgin Island National Parks Trust ($15,000) see Jackson Hole Preserve

Caribbean Institute on Alcoholism ($25,000) see

Smithers Foundation, Christopher D.

Council on Alcoholism St. Thomas/St. Johns ($10,000) see O'Brien Foundation, Alice M.

Zambia

Intercessors for Zambia ($20,000) see Generation Trust

Master Index to Corporations and Foundations

American Telephone & Telegraph Co./Los Angeles Region, 82

American Telephone & Telegraph Co./New Jersey Region, 82

American Telephone & Telegraph Co./New York City Region, 83

American Telephone & Telegraph Co./New York Region, 83

American Telephone & Telegraph Co./San Francisco Region, 83

American Telephone & Telegraph Co./Washington, DC, Region, 83

American Tobacco Co., 83

American Trading & Production Corp., 83

American United Life Insurance Co., 83

American Water Works Co., Inc., 84

American Welding & Manufacturing Co., 84

American Welding & Manufacturing Co. Foundation, 84

Americana Foundation, 85

Amerigas, 85

Ameritas Charitable Foundation, 85

Ameritas Life Insurance Corp., 85

Ameritech Corp., 86

Ameritech Development, 87

Ameritech Foundation, 86

Ameritech Information Systems, 87

Ameritech International, 87

Ameritech Mobile Communications, 87

Ameritech Publishing, 88

Ameritech Services, 88

Ameron, Inc., 89

Ames Charitable Trust, Harriett, 89

Ames Department Stores, 89

Ames Foundation, Inc., 89

AMETEK, 90

AMETEK Foundation, 90

Amev Foundation, 949

Amfac/JMB Hawaii, 91

Amgen Foundation, 91

Amgen, Inc., 91

Amoco Corp., 91

Amoco Foundation, 91

Amoskeag Co., 93

AMP, 93

AMP Foundation, 93

Ampacet Corp., 93

Ampco-Pittsburgh Foundation, 845

AMR Corp., 94

AMR/American Airlines Foundation, 94

Amsco International, 94

AmSouth Bancorporation, 95

Amstar Corp., 95

Amsted Industries, 95

Amsted Industries Foundation, 95

Amsterdam Foundation, Jack and Mimi Leviton, 96

Amway Corp., 96

Amway Environmental Foundation, 96

Anacomp, Inc., 96

Anadarko Petroleum Corp., 97

Analog Devices, 97

Analogic Corp., 97

Anchor Fasteners, 97

Anchor Glass Container Corp., 98

Andal Corp., 98

Andalusia Health Services, 98

Andersen Corp., 98

Andersen Foundation, 99

Andersen Foundation, Arthur, 99

Andersen Foundation, Hugh J., 100

Anderson Charitable Trust, Josephine, 100

Anderson Foundation, 101

Anderson Foundation, John W., 101

Anderson Foundation, M. D., 102

Anderson Foundation, Marion & John E., 10

Anderson Foundation, Peyton, 103

Anderson Foundation, Robert C. and Sadie G., 103

Anderson Foundation, William P., 103

Anderson Industries, 104

Anderson Industries Charitable Foundation, 104

Andersons Management Corp., 104

Andreas Foundation, 105

Andres Charitable Trust, Frank G., 105

Andrew Corp., 106

Andrews Foundation, 106

Angeles Corp., 106

Angelica Corp., 106

Anheuser-Busch Cos., 107

Anheuser-Busch Foundation/Anheuser-Busch Charitable Trust, 107

Animal Assistance Foundation, 107

Ann & Hope, 108

Annenberg Foundation, 108

ANR Coal Company, 824

ANR Foundation, 75

Anschutz Family Foundation, 109

Ansin Private Foundation, Ronald M., 110

Ansley Foundation, Dantzler Bond, 110

Anthony Co., C.R., 111

AON Corp., 111

AON Foundation, 111

APAC Inc., 112

Apache Corp., 112

Apex Oil Co., 113

APL Corp., 113

Apogee Enterprises Inc., 113

Apollo Computer Inc., 113

Apple and Eve, 113

Apple Bank for Savings, 113

Apple Computer, 113

Applebaum Foundation, 114

Appleby Foundation, 115

Appleby Trust, Scott B. and Annie P., 115

Appleman Foundation, 115

Appleton Papers, 116

Applied Energy Services, 116

Applied Power Foundation, 116

Applied Power, Inc., 116

APS Foundation, 127

APV Crepaco Inc., 116

ARA Services, 117

Arakelian Foundation, Mary Alice, 117

Arata Brothers Trust, 117

Aratex Services, 117

Arbie Mineral Feed Co., 118

Arbor Acres Farm, Inc., 118

Arca Foundation, 118

Arcadia Foundation, 119

Arcana Foundation, 120

Arcata Corp., 120

Arcata Graphics Co., 120

Arch Mineral Corp., 121

Archbold Charitable Trust, Adrian and Jessie, 121

Archbold Expeditions, 121

Archer-Daniels-Midland Co., 121

Archer-Daniels-Midland Foundation, 121

Archibald Charitable Foundation, Norman, 122

ARCO, 123

ARCO Chemical, 124

ARCO Foundation, 123

Arden Group, Inc., 125

Arell Foundation, 125

Argonaut Group, 125

Argyros Foundation, 125

Arise Charitable Trust, 126

Arison Foundation, 442

Aristech Chemical Corp., 126

Aristech Foundation, 126

Arizona Public Service Co., 127

Arizona Supermarkets/Q-Fresh Markets, 127

Arkansas Best Corp., 128

Arkansas Power & Light Co., 128

Arkelian Foundation, Ben H. and Gladys, 128

Arkell Hall Foundation, 129

Arkla, 129

Arkwright Foundation, 130

Arkwright-Boston Manufacturers Mutual, 130

Armbrust Chain Co., 130

Armbrust Foundation, 130

Armco Foundation, 131

Armco Inc., 131

Armco Steel Co., 132

Armco Steel Co. Foundation, 132

Brody Foundation, Carolyn and Kenneth D., 361

Brody Foundation, Frances, 361

Bromley Residuary Trust, Guy I., 361

Bronfman Foundation, Samuel, 2401

Bronstein Foundation, Sol and Arlene, 362

Bronstein Foundation, Soloman and Sylvia, 362

Brookdale Foundation, 362

Brooke Group Ltd., 363

Brooklyn Benevolent Society, 363

Brooklyn Union Gas Co., 363

Brooks Brothers, 364

Brooks Fashion Stores Inc., 364

Brooks Foundation, Gladys, 364

Brother International Corp., 364

Brotman Foundation of California, 365

Brotz Family Foundation, Frank G., 365

Brown & Associates, Clayton, 366

Brown & Root, Inc., 372

Brown & Sharpe Foundation, 372

Brown & Sharpe Manufacturing Co., 372

Brown & Sons Charitable Foundation, Alex, 372

Brown & Sons, Alex, 372

Brown & Williamson Tobacco Corp., 373

Brown and C. A. Lupton Foundation, T. J., 365

Brown Brothers Harriman & Co., 366

Brown Brothers Harriman & Co. Undergraduate Fund, 366

Brown Charitable Trust, Dora Maclellan, 366

Brown Charitable Trust, Peter D. and Dorothy S., 367

Brown Family Foundation, John Mathew Gay, 367

Brown Foundation, 368

Brown Foundation, Clayton, 366

Brown Foundation, George Warren, 368

Brown Foundation, James Graham, 369

Brown Foundation, Joe W. and Dorothy Dorsett, 370

Brown Foundation, M. K., 370

Brown Foundation, W. L. Lyons, 370

Brown Group, 371

Brown Group Incorporated Charitable Trust, 371

Brown Inc., John, 371

Brown Inc., Tom, 373

Brown Shoe Co., 372

Brown, Jr. Charitable Trust, Frank D., 372

Brown-Forman Corp., 367

Browning, 374

Browning Charitable Foundation, Val A., 374

Browning Masonic Memorial Fund, Otis Avery, 375

Browning-Ferris Industries, 374

Brownley Trust, Walter, 375

Broyhill Family Foundation, 375

Bruening Foundation, Eva L. and Joseph M., 376

Brundage Charitable, Scientific, and Wildlife Conservation Foundation, Charles E. and Edna T., 376

Bruner Foundation, 377

Brunetti Charitable Trust, Dionigi, 377

Brunner Foundation, Fred J., 377

Brunner Foundation, Robert, 378

Bruno Charitable Foundation, Joseph S., 378

Bruno Foundation, Angelo, 378

Bruno's Inc., 378

Brunswick Corp., 379

Brunswick Foundation, 379

Brush Foundation, 379

Brush Wellman Inc., 380

Bryan Family Foundation, Kathleen Price and Joseph M., 380

Bryan Foods, 381

Bryan Foundation, Dodd and Dorothy L., 381

Bryan Foundation, James E. and Mary Z., 381

Bryant Foundation, 382

Bryce Memorial Fund, William and Catherine, 382

Bryn Mawr Trust Co., 382

BT Foundation, 195

BTL Foundation, 254

Buchalter, Nemer, Fields, & Younger, 382

Buchalter, Nemer, Fields, Chrystie & Younger Charitable Foundation, 382

Buchanan Family Foundation, 383

Buck Foundation, Carol Franc, 383

Buckley Trust, Thomas D., 384

Bucyrus-Erie, 384

Bucyrus-Erie Foundation, 384

Budd Co., 385

Budweiser of Columbia, 385

Budweiser of the Carolinas Foundation, 385

Buehler Foundation, A. C., 385

Buehler Foundation, Emil, 386

Buell Foundation, Temple Hoyne, 386

Buffalo Color Corp., 387

Buffalo Forge Co., 387

Buffett Foundation, 387

Bugher Foundation, 387

Buhl Family Foundation, 388

Buhl Foundation, 388

Builder Marts of America, 389

Builderway Foundation, 389

Bull Foundation, Henry W., 390

Bull HN Information Systems Inc., 390

Bullitt Foundation, 390

Bulova Fund, 391

Bumble Bee Seafoods Inc., 391

Bunbury Company, 391

Burchfield Foundation, Charles E., 392

Burden Foundation, Florence V., 392

Burdines, 393

Burger King Corp., 394

Burgess Trust, Ralph L. and Florence R., 394

Burke Foundation, Thomas C., 394

Burkitt Foundation, 394

Burlington Air Express Inc., 395

Burlington Industries, 395

Burlington Industries Foundation, 395

Burlington Northern Foundation, 396

Burlington Northern Inc., 396

Burlington Resources, 396

Burlington Resources Foundation, 396

Burnand Medical and Educational Foundation, Alphonse A., 397

Burndy Corp., 398

Burnett Construction Co., 398

Burnham Donor Fund, Alfred G., 398

Burnham Foundation, 399

Burns Family Foundation, 399

Burns Foundation, 399

Burns Foundation, Fritz B., 399

Burns Foundation, Jacob, 400

Burns International, 400

Burns International Foundation, 400

Burress Foundation, J.W., 401

Burress, J.W., 401

Burron Medical, 401

Burroughs Educational Fund, N. R., 401

Burroughs Wellcome Co., 401

Burroughs Wellcome Fund, 401

Burton Foundation, William T. and Ethel Lewis, 403

Bush Charitable Foundation, Edyth, 403

Bush Family Foundation, Peter W., 404

Bush Foundation, 404

Bush-D.D. Nusbaum Foundation, M.G., 2383

Bushee Foundation, Florence Evans, 405

Business Incentives, 406

Business Incentives Foundation, 406

Business Men's Assurance Co. of America, 406

Business Records Corp., 406

Bustard Charitable Permanent Trust Fund, Elizabeth and James, 407

Butler Family Foundation, George W. and Gladys S., 407

Butler Family Foundation, Patrick and Aimee, 407

Butler Foundation, Alice, 408

Butler Foundation, J. Homer, 408

Master Index to Corporations and Foundations

Cole Taylor Financial Group Foundation, 552

Cole Trust, Quincy, 552

Coleman Charitable Trust, 552

Coleman Co., 552

Coleman Foundation, 553

Coleman Scholarship Trust, Lillian R., 554

Coleman, Jr. Foundation, George E., 554

Coles Family Foundation, 554

Colgan Scholarship Fund, James W., 555

Colgate-Palmolive Co., 555

Colket Foundation, Ethel D., 555

Collins & Aikman Corp., 555

Collins & Aikman Holdings Corp., 556

Collins & Aikman Holdings Foundation, 556

Collins Co., 556

Collins Food International Foundation, 2465

Collins Foundation, 556

Collins Foundation, Carr P., 557

Collins Foundation, George and Jennie, 558

Collins Foundation, James M., 558

Collins Foundation, Joseph, 558

Collins Medical Trust, 559

Collins, Jr. Foundation, George Fulton, 559

Collins-McDonald Trust Fund, 559

Colonial Foundation, 560

Colonial Life & Accident Insurance Co., 560

Colonial Oil Industries, Inc., 560

Colonial Parking, 560

Colonial Penn Group, Inc., 561

Colonial Stores, 561

Colonial Stores Foundation, 561

Colorado Interstate Gas Co., 561

Colorado National Bankshares, 561

Colorado State Bank Foundation, 562

Colorado State Bank of Denver, 562

Colorado Trust, 562

Colt Foundation, James J., 563

Colt Industries Charitable Foundation, 563

Coltec Industries, 563

Coltec Industries Charitable Foundation, 563

Columbia Foundation, 564

Columbia Gas Distribution Cos., 565

Columbia Savings & Loan Association, 565

Columbia Savings Charitable Foundation, 565

Columbia Terminals Co., 565

Columbia Terminals Co. Charitable Trust, 565

Columbus Dispatch Printing Co., 566

Columbus Foundation, 1606

Columbus Life Insurance Co., 566

Columbus Southern Power Co., 566

Combs Foundation, Earle M. and Virginia M., 567

Comcast Corp., 567

Comer Foundation, 567568

Comerica, 568

Cominco American Inc., 569

Commerce Bancshares, Inc., 569

Commerce Clearing House, 569

Commerce Foundation, 569

Commercial Bank, 570

Commercial Bank Foundation, 570

Commercial Credit Co., 570

Commercial Federal Corp., 570

Commercial Intertech Corp., 571

Commercial Intertech Foundation, 571

Commercial Metals Co., 571

Commerzbank AG, New York, 572

Commodore International Ltd., 572

Common Giving Fund, 572

Common Wealth Trust, 572

Commonwealth Edison Co., 572

Commonwealth Energy System, 573

Commonwealth Fund, 573

Commonwealth Industries Corp., 574

Commonwealth Life Insurance Co., 575

Communications Satellite Corp. (COMSAT), 575

Community Coffee Co., 575

Community Coffee Co., Inc. Foundation, 575

Community Cooperative Development Foundation, 575

Community Enterprises, 576

Community Foundation, 576

Community Health Association, 576

Community Hospital Foundation, 576

Community Mutual Insurance Co., 577

Community National Bank & Trust Co. of New York, 577

Community Psychiatric Centers, 577

Compaq Computer Corp., 577

Compaq Computer Foundation, 577

Comprecare Foundation, 578

Comprehensive Care Corp., 578

Compton Foundation, 578

Computer Associates International, 579

Computer Sciences Corp., 579

Comstock Foundation, 580

ConAgra, 580

ConAgra Foundation, 580

Conair, Inc., 581

Concord Chemical Co., 581

Concord Fabrics, Inc., 581

Concord Foundation, 581

Conde Nast Publications, Inc., 582

Cone Automatic Machine Co. Charitable Foundation, 582

Cone Mills Corp., 582

Cone-Blanchard Machine Co., 582

Confidence Foundation, 583

Conn Memorial Foundation, 583

Connecticut Energy Foundation, Inc., 584

Connecticut General Corp., 584

Connecticut Mutual Life Foundation, 539

Connecticut Natural Gas Corp., 584

Connecticut Savings Bank, 584

Connell Foundation, Michael J., 584

Connell LP, 585

Connell Rice & Sugar Co., 585

Connelly Foundation, 585

Connemara Fund, 586

Conner Peripherals, 586

Conoco Inc., 586

Consol Energy Inc., 587

Consolidated Edison Co. of New York Inc., 587

Consolidated Electrical Distributors, 587

Consolidated Freightways, 587

Consolidated Natural Gas Co., 587

Consolidated Natural Gas Co. Foundation, 587

Consolidated Papers, 588

Consolidated Papers Foundation, 588

Consolidated Rail Corp. (Conrail), 589

Constantin Foundation, 589

Constar International Inc., 590

Conston Corp., 590

Conston Foundation, 590

Consumer Farmer Foundation, 590

Consumers Power Co., 591

Consumers Power Foundation, 591

Contel Federal Systems, 591

Contempo Communications, 592

Contempo Communications Foundation for the Arts, Inc., 592

Continental Airlines, 592

Continental Airlines Foundation, 592

Continental Bancorp, Inc., 592

Continental Bank Foundation, 592

Continental Bank N.A., 592

Continental Can Co., 593

Continental Corp., 594

Continental Corp. Foundation, 594

Continental Divide Electric Co-op, 595

Continental Divide Electric Education Foundation, 595

Continental Grain Co., 595

Continental Grain Foundation, 595

Continental Wingate Co., Inc., 595

Contran Corp., 596

Contraves USA, 596

Control Data Corp., 597

Conway Scholarship Foundation, Carle C., 593

Conwood Co. L.P., 597

Cook & Co., Frederic W., 598

Cook Batson Foundation, 597

Cook Brothers Educational Fund, 598

Cook Charitable Foundation, 598

Cook Family Trust, 598

Cook Foundation, 598

Cook Foundation, Loring, 599

Cook Foundation, Louella, 599

Cook Inlet Region, 599

Cook, Sr. Charitable Foundation, Kelly Gene, 600

Cooke Foundation, 600

Cooke Foundation Corporation, V. V., 601

Cookson America, 601

Cooper Charitable Trust, Richard H., 601

Cooper Foundation, 602

Cooper Industries, 602

Cooper Industries Foundation, 480602

Cooper Oil Tool, 603

Cooper Tire & Rubber Co., 603

Cooper Tire & Rubber Foundation, 603

Cooper Wood Products, 604

Cooper Wood Products Foundation, 604

Coopers & Lybrand, 604

Coopers & Lybrand Foundation, 604

CooperVision, Inc., 604

Coors Brewing Co., 604

Coors Foundation, Adolph, 605

Copeland Corp., 606

Copernicus Society of America, 606

Copley Foundation, James S., 607

Copley Press, 607

Copolymer Foundation, 608

Copolymer Rubber & Chemical Corp., 608

Copperweld Corp., 608

Copperweld Foundation, 608

Copperweld Steel Co., 608

Copperweld Steel Co.'s Warren Employees' Trust, 608

Coral Reef Foundation, 609

Corbett Foundation, 609

Corbin Foundation, Mary S. and David C., 610

Cord Foundation, E. L., 610

Corestates Bank, 610

Corestates Foundation, 610

Corke Educational Trust, Hubert and Alice, 611

Cornelius O'Brien Foundation, 2000

Cornell Trust, Peter C., 611

Cornerstone Foundation of Northeastern Wisconsin, 611

Corning Incorporated, 612

Corning Incorporated Foundation, 612

Cornnuts, Inc., 613

Corporate Printing Co., 613

Corpus Christi Exploration Co., 613

Corpus Christi Exploration Co. Foundation, 613

Corroon & Black of Illinois, 614

Corroon & Black of Oregon, 614

Corvallis Clinic, 614

Corvallis Clinic Foundation, 614

Cosco, Inc., 614

Cosden Trust f/b/o the University of Arizona College of Medicine, Curtis C., 614

Cosmair, Inc., 614

Costain Holdings Inc., 615

Cotter & Co., 615

Cottrell Foundation, 615

Coughlin-Saunders Foundation, 615

Coulter Corp., 616

Country Cos., 616

Country Curtains, Inc., 616

Countrymark Cooperative, 617

County Bank, 617

County Bank Foundation, 617

Courier Corp., 617

Courier-Journal & Louisville Times, 617

Courtaulds Fibers Inc., 618

Courts Foundation, 618

Cove Charitable Trust, 618

Covington and Burling, 619

Covington and Burling Foundation, 619

Covington Foundation, Marion Stedman, 619

Cow Hollow Foundation, 620

Cowan Foundation Corporation, Lillian L. and Harry A., 620

Cowden Foundation, Louetta M., 620

Cowell Foundation, S. H., 621

Cowles Charitable Trust, 621

Cowles Foundation, Gardner and Florence Call, 622

Cowles Foundation, Harriet Cheney, 623

Cowles Foundation, William H., 623

Cowles Media Co., 623

Cowles Media Foundation, 623

Cox Charitable Trust, A. G., 624

Cox Charitable Trust, Jessie B., 625

Cox Charitable Trust, Opal G., 626

Cox Enterprises, 626

Cox Foundation, 627

Cox Foundation of Georgia, James M., 626

Cox Foundation, James M., 627

Cox, Jr. Foundation, James M., 627

CP&L Foundation, 443

CPC International, 628

CPI Corp., 628

CPI Philanthropic Trust, 628

CR Industries, 629

Craig Foundation, E. L., 2620

Craig Foundation, J. Paul, 629

Craigmyle Foundation, 630

Crail-Johnson Foundation, 630

Cralle Foundation, 630

Cramer Foundation, 630

Crandall Memorial Foundation, J. Ford, 631

Crane & Co., 631

Crane & Co. Fund, 631

Crane Co., 631

Crane Foundation, Raymond E. and Ellen F., 632

Crane Fund, 631

Crane Fund for Widows and Children, 632

Cranshaw Corporation, 632

Cranston Foundation, 633

Cranston Print Works, 633

Crapo Charitable Foundation, Henry H., 633

Crappiethon USA/American Outdoors, Inc., 633

Crary Foundation, Bruce L., 634

Crawford & Co., 634

Crawford & Co. Foundation, 634

Crawford Estate, E. R., 634

Cray Research, 635

Cray Research Foundation, 635

CRC Evans Pipeline International, Inc., 635

Crean Foundation, 635

Credit Agricole, 636

Credit Suisse, 636

Creditanstalt- Bankverein, New York, 636

Credithrift Financial - Richard E. Meier Foundation, Inc., 70

Creel Foundation, 636

Crels Foundation, 637

Cremer Foundation, 637

Crescent Plastics, 638

Crescent Plastics Foundation, 638

Crestar Financial Corp., 638

Crestar Food Products, Inc., 639

Crestar Foundation, 638

Crestlea Foundation, 639

CRI Charitable Trust, 639

Criss Memorial Foundation, Dr. C.C. and Mabel L., 640

CRL Inc., 640

Crocker Trust, Mary A., 640

Croft Metal Products Educational Trust Fund, 641

Croft Metals, 641

Crompton & Knowles Corp., 641

Cross Co., A.T., 641

Crossland Savings FSB, 641

D

De Lima Co., Paul, 689
De Lima Foundation, Paul, 689
de Rothschild Foundation, Edmond, 690
Dean Foods Co., 690
Dean Foods, Jimmy, 690
Dean Witter Discover, 690
Dearborn Cable Communications Fund, 412
DeBartolo Corp., Edward J., 691
Debartolo Foundation, Marie P., 691
DeBlois Oil Co., 691
DEC International, Inc., 691
DEC International- Albrecht Foundation, 691
DeCamp Foundation, Ira W., 692
Decio Foundation, Arthur J., 692
Decision Data Computer Corp., 693
Dee Foundation, Annie Taylor, 693
Dee Foundation, Lawrence T. and Janet T., 693
Deer Creek Foundation, 694
Deer Valley Farm, 694
Deere & Co., 694
Deere Foundation, John, 694
Dekalb Energy Co., 695
Dekalb Energy Foundation, 695
DeKalb Foundation, 695
DeKalb Genetics Corp., 695
DeKalb Genetics Foundation, 695
Dekko Foundation, 696
Del Monte Foods, 696
Delacorte Fund, George, 696
Delano Foundation, Mignon Sherwood, 697
Delany Charitable Trust, Beatrice P., 697
Delavan Foundation, Nelson B., 698
Delaware North Cos., 698
Delco Electronics Corp., 698
Delhi Gas Pipeline Co., 698
Dell Foundation, Hazel, 698
Dellwood Foods, Inc., 699
DelMar Foundation, Charles, 699
Delmarva Power & Light Co., 699
Deloitte & Touche, 700
Deloitte & Touche Foundation, 700
Deloitte Haskins & Sells Foundation, 700
Delta Air Lines, 700
Delta Air Lines Foundation, 700
Delta Tau Delta Educational Fund, 701
Delta Woodside Industries, 701
Deltona Corp., 701
Deluxe Corp., 702
Deluxe Corp. Foundation, 702
Demco Charitable Foundation, 702
Demmer Foundation, Edward U., 703
Demos Foundation, N., 703
DeMoss Foundation, Arthur S., 703
Demoulas Foundation, 704

Demoulas Supermarkets, 704
Dennett Foundation, Marie G., 704
Dennison Foundation, 705
Dennison Manufacturing Co., 705
Dent Family Foundation, Harry, 705
Dentsply International Foundation, 705
Dentsply International, Inc., 705
Dentsu, Inc., NY, 706
Deposit Guaranty Foundation, 706
Deposit Guaranty National Bank, 706
DeRoy Foundation, Helen L., 707
DeRoy Testamentary Foundation, 707
Deseranno Educational Foundation, 708
DeSoto, 708
DeSoto Foundation, 708
Detroit Edison Co., 708
Detroit Edison Foundation, 708
Dettman Foundation, Leroy E., 709
Deuble Foundation, George H., 710
Deutsch Co., 710
Deutsch Foundation, 710
Deutsche Bank AG, 711
Development Dimensions International, 711
Devereaux Foundation, 711
DeVlieg Foundation, Charles, 711
Devon Group, 712
Devonshire Associates, 712
Devonwood Foundation, 712
DeVore Foundation, 712
DeVos Foundation, Richard and Helen, 713
Dewar Foundation, 713
Dewar, A.W.G., 713
Dewing Foundation, Frances R., 714
Dewitt Van Evera Foundation, 2758
Dexter Charitable Fund, Eugene A., 714
Dexter Co., 714
Dexter Corp., 714
Dexter Corp. Foundation, 714
Dexter Industries, 715
Dexter Industries Charitable Trust, 715
Dexter Shoe Co., 715
DFS Group Limited, 716
DHL Airways Inc., 716
Diabetes Research and Education Foundation, 716
Dial Corp., 717
Dial Corporation Fund, 717
Diamond Foundation, Aaron, 717
Diamond Shamrock, 719
Diamond State Telephone Co., 719
Diamond Walnut Growers, 719
Diasonics, Inc., 720
Dibner Fund, 720
Dibrell Brothers, Inc., 720
Dick Corp., 721
Dick Family Foundation, 721

Dickenson Foundation, Harriet Ford, 721
Dickey-John Corp., 721
Dickson Foundation, 7212326
Didier Taylor Refractories Corp., 722
Diebold, Inc., 722
Diederich Educational Trust Fund, John T. and Ada, 722
Diener Foundation, Frank C., 722
Dietrich Foundation, 723
Dietrich Foundation, William B., 723
Difco Laboratories, 723
Digicon, 723
Digital Communications Associates, Inc., 723
Digital Equipment Corp., 723
Digital Sciences Corp., 724
Dillard Department Stores, Inc., 724
Dillard Fund, 724
Dillard Paper Co., 724
Dillon Foundation, 725
Dillons Super Markets, 725
Dime Savings Bank of New York, 725
Dimeo Construction Co., 726
Dimick Foundation, 726
Dingman Foundation, Michael D., 726
DiRosa Foundation, Rene and Veronica, 727
Discount Corp. of New York Charitable Foundation, 688
Discovery Channel/Cable Education Network, 727
Dishman Charitable Foundation Trust, H. E. and Kate, 727
Disney Co. Foundation, Walt, 2795
Disney Co., Walt, 2795
Disney Family Foundation, Roy, 727
Dively Foundation, George S., 728
Diversified Industries, Inc., 728
Dixie Yarns Foundation, 728
Dixie Yarns, Inc., 728
Dixie-Portland Flour Mills, 728
DNP (America), Inc., 729
Dobson Foundation, 729
Dodge Foundation, Cleveland H., 730
Dodge Foundation, Geraldine R., 730
Dodge Foundation, P. L., 731
Dodge Jones Foundation, 732
Dodson Foundation, James Glenwell and Clara May, 732
Doelger Charitable Trust, Thelma, 733
Doheny Foundation, Carrie Estelle, 733
Doherty Charitable Foundation, Henry L. and Grace, 734
Dolan Family Foundation, 734
Dole Food Company, Inc., 735
Dole Fresh Vegetables, 735
Dollar Dry Dock Bank, 735
Dollar General Corp., 735

Equimark Charitable Foundation, 827
Equimark Corp., 827
Equitable Foundation, 828
Equitable Life Assurance Society of the U.S., 828
Equitable Resources, 829
Equitable Variable Life Insurance Co., 829
Erb Foundation, 829
Erb Lumber Co., 829
Erickson Charitable Fund, Eben W., 830
Ernest & Julio Gallo Winery, 830
Ernst & Young, 830
Ernst & Young Foundation, 830
Ernsthausen Charitable Foundation, John F. and Doris E., 831
Erpf Fund, Armand G., 831
Erteszek Foundation, 832
Erving Paper Mills, 832
Essel Foundation, 832
Esselte Pendaflex Corp., 833
Essick Foundation, 833
Esterline Technologies Corp., 833
Estes Foundation, 833
ETCO Inc., 834
Ethyl Corp., 834
Ettinger Foundation, 835
Eureka Co., 835
European American Bank, 835
Evans Foundation, Edward P., 836
Evans Foundation, Lettie Pate, 836
Evans Foundation, T. M., 837
Evans Foundation, Thomas J., 837
Evening Post Publishing Co., 838
Everest & Jennings International, 838
Everett Charitable Trust, 838
Evinrude Foundation, Ralph, 839
Evjue Foundation, 839
Ewald Foundation, H. T., 839
Excel Corp., 840
Excel Industries (Elkhart, Indiana), 840
Excel Industries Charitable Foundation, 840
Exchange Bank, 840
Exchange Bank Foundation, 840
Exposition Foundation, 841
Exxon Corp., 841
Exxon Education Foundation, 841
Eyman Trust, Jesse, 842

F

FAB Industries, 842
Fabick Charitable Trust, 843
Fabick Tractor Co., John, 843
Fabri-Kal Corp., 843
Fabri-Kal Foundation, 843
Factor Family Foundation, Max, 844

Factory Mutual Engineering Corp., 844
Fahrney Education Foundation, 844
Failing Fund, Henry, 844
Fair Foundation, R. W., 845
Fair Oaks Foundation, Inc., 845
Fair Play Foundation, 846
Fairchild Corp., 846
Fairchild Foundation, Sherman, 847
Fairchild Industries Foundation, 846
Fairey Educational Fund, Kittie M., 847
Fairfield Communities, Inc., 847
Fairfield Foundation, Freeman E., 848
Fairfield-Meeker Charitable Trust, Freeman E., 848
Fairview Foundation, 848
Faith Charitable Trust, 849
Faith Home Foundation, 849
Falcon Foundation, 849
Fales Foundation Trust, 850
Falk Foundation, David, 850
Falk Foundation, Elizabeth M., 850
Falk Foundation, Michael David, 851
Falk Medical Fund, Maurice, 851
Falk Medical Research Foundation, Dr. Ralph and Marian, 851
Famous Amos Chocolate Chip Cookie Co., 852
Fantastic Foods, 852
Fanuc U.S.A. Corp., 852
Fanwood Foundation, 852
Far West Financial Corp., 852
Farallon Foundation, 853
Farber Foundation, 2117
Faribault Foods, 853
Farish Fund, William Stamps, 853
Farley Foundation, William F., 854
Farley Industries, 854
Farm & Home Savings Association, 854
Farm Credit Banks of Springfield, 854
Farm Fresh Inc. (Norfolk, Virginia), 854
Farmers & Mechanics Bank, 855
Farmers Group Safety Foundation, 855
Farmers Group, Inc., 855
Farmland Industries, Inc., 855
Farmstead Foods, 855
Farnsworth Trust, Charles A., 856
Farr Trust, Frank M. and Alice M., 856
Farwell Foundation, Drusilla, 856
Fashion Bar, 857
Fasken Foundation, 857
Fast Food Merchandisers, 857
Faulkner Trust, Marianne Gaillard, 857
Favrot Fund, 858
Fay Charitable Fund, Aubert J., 858
Fay S. Carter Foundation, 2450
Fay's Foundation, Inc., 858
Fay's Incorporated, 858
FDL Foods/Dubuque Packing Co., 859

Fearn International, Inc., 859
Fedco, Inc., 859
Fedders Corp., 859
Federal Express Corp., 859
Federal Home Loan Mortgage Corp. (Freddie Mac), 860
Federal National Mortgage Assn. Foundation, 862
Federal National Mortgage Assn., Fannie Mae, 862
Federal Paper Board Co., 863
Federal Screw Works, 863
Federal Screw Works Foundation, 863
Federal-Mogul Corp., 861
Federal-Mogul Corp. Charitable Trust Fund, 861
Federated American Insurance, 863
Federated Department Stores and Allied Stores Corp., 863
Federated Life Insurance Co., 864
Federated Life Insurance Foundation, 864
Federation Foundation of Greater Philadelphia, 865
Feil Foundation, Louis and Gertrude, 865
Feild Co-Operative Association, 866
Fein Foundation, 866
Feinberg Foundation, Joseph and Bessie, 866
Feinstein Foundation, Myer and Rosaline, 867
Feintech Foundation, 867
Fel-Pro Incorporated, 867
Fel-Pro/ Mecklenburger Foundation, 867
Felburn Foundation, 868
Feldberg Family Foundation, 868
Feldman Foundation, 869
Felix G. Rohatyn Foundation, 2300
Fellner Memorial Foundation, Leopold and Clara M., 869
Fels Fund, Samuel S., 870
Female Association of Philadelphia, 870
Femino Foundation, 870
Fenton Foundation, 871
Ferebee Endowment, Percy O., 871
Ferguson Family Foundation, Kittie and Rugeley, 872
Ferkauf Foundation, Eugene and Estelle, 872
Ferranti Tech, 872
Ferre Revocable Trust, Joseph C., 872
Ferrell Cos., 873
Ferriday Fund Charitable Trust, 873
Ferro Corp., 873
Ferro Foundation, 873
Fiat U.S.A., Inc., 874
Fibre Converters, 874
Fibre Converters Foundation, 874
Fidelity Bank, 874

Fraser Paper Ltd., 967

Frazier Foundation, 967

Frear Eleemosynary Trust, Mary D. and Walter F., 968

Freas Foundation, 968

Freddie Mac Foundation, 860

Frederick Foundation, 969

Frederick R. Weisman Collection, 2833

Freed Foundation, 969

Freedom Forum, 970

Freedom Newspapers Inc., 971

Freeman Charitable Trust, Samuel, 971

Freeman Foundation, Carl M., 972

Freeman Foundation, Ella West, 972

Freeport Brick Co., 973

Freeport Brick Co. Charitable Trust, 973

Freeport-McMoRan, 973

Frees Foundation, 974

Freightliner Corp., 974

Frelinghuysen Foundation, 974

French Foundation, 975

French Oil Mill Machinery Co., 975

French Oil Mill Machinery Co. Charitable Trust, 975

Frese Foundation, Arnold D., 975

Frey Trust f/b/o YMCA, Harry D., 976

Freygang Foundation, Walter Henry, 976

Fribourg Foundation, 976

Frick Educational Commission, Henry C., 977

Frick Foundation, Helen Clay, 977

Friedland Family Foundation, Samuel, 978

Friedman Bag Co., 978

Friedman Brothers Foundation, 978

Friedman Family Foundation, 978

Friedman Foundation, Stephen and Barbara, 979

Friendly Ice Cream Corp., 979

Friendly Rosenthal Foundation, 979

Friends' Foundation Trust, A., 980

Friendship Fund, 980

Friona Industries L.P., 980

Frisch Foundation, 980

Frisch's Restaurants Inc., 980

Frito-Lay, 981

Fritz Cos., 981

Froderman Foundation, 981

Frohlich Charitable Trust, Ludwig W., 981

Frohman Foundation, Sidney, 982

Frohring Foundation, Paul & Maxine, 982

Frohring Foundation, William O. and Gertrude Lewis, 983

Fromm Scholarship Trust, Walter and Mabel, 983

Frontier Oil & Refining Co., 983

Frost Foundation, 983

Frost National Bank, 984

Frozfruit Corp., 984

Fru-Con Construction Corp., 984

Fruchthandler Foundation, Alex and Ruth, 985

Frueauff Foundation, Charles A., 985

Fruehauf Foundation, 985

Fruit of the Loom, Inc., 986

Frumkes Foundation, Alana and Lewis, 986

Fry Foundation, Lloyd A., 986

Fuchs Foundation, Gottfried & Mary, 987

Fuchsberg Family Foundation, 988

Fuchsherg Family Foundation, Abraham, 988

Fujitsu America, Inc., 988

Fujitsu Systems of America, Inc., 989

Fulbright and Monroe L. Swyers Foundation, James H., 989

Fuld Health Trust, Helene, 989

Fuller Co. Foundation, H.B., 990

Fuller Co., H.B., 990

Fuller Foundation, 991

Fuller Foundation, C. G., 991

Fuller Foundation, George F. and Sybil H., 992

Fullerton Foundation, 992

Fullerton Metals Co., 993

Fullerton Metals Foundation, 993

Fund for New Jersey, 993

Funderburke & Associates, 994

Fuqua Foundation, J. B., 994

Fuqua Industries, Inc., 995

Furr's Supermarkets, 995

Furth Foundation, 995

Fusenot Charity Foundation, Georges and Germaine, 996

G

G.A.G. Charitable Corporation, 996

G.P.G. Foundation, 996

Gabelli Foundation, 997

GAF Corp., 997

Gage Foundation, Philip and Irene Toll, 997

Gahagen Charitable Trust, Zella J., 997

Gaisman Foundation, Catherine and Henry J., 998

Galileo Electro-Optics Corp., 998

Galkin Charitable Trust, Ira S. and Anna, 998

Gallagher Family Foundation, Lewis P., 998

Gallo Foundation, 830

Gallo Foundation, Ernest, 999

Gallo Foundation, Julio R., 999

Galter Foundation, 1000

Galvin Foundation, Robert W., 1000

Gann Charitable Foundation, Joseph and Rae, 1000

Gannett Co., 1000

Gannett Foundation, 970

Gannett Foundation, Guy P., 1001

Gannett Publishing Co., Guy, 1001

Gap Foundation, 1002

Gap, The, 1002

GAR Foundation, 1003

Garden Foundation, Allan C. and Lelia J., 1004

Gardiner Savings Institution FSB, 1004

Gardiner Scholarship Foundation, 1004

Gardner Charitable Foundation, Edith D., 1004

Gardner Foundation, 1004

Garfinkle Family Foundation, 1004

Garland Foundation, John Jewett and H. Chandler, 1005

Garner Charitable Trust, James G., 1005

Garrigues Trust, Edwin B., 1005

Garvey Fund, Jean and Willard, 1006

Garvey Kansas Foundation, 1006

Garvey Memorial Foundation, Edward Chase, 1006

Garvey Texas Foundation, 1007

Garvey Trust, Olive White, 1007

Gast Manufacturing Corp., 1008

Gates Corp., 1008

Gates Foundation, 1008

Gateway Apparel, 1009

Gateway Apparel Charitable Foundation, 1009

GATX Corp., 1009

Gault-Hussey Charitable Trust, 1010

Gavin Foundation, James and Zita, 1011

Gaylord Container Corp., 1011

Gaylord Foundation, Clifford Willard, 1011

Gazette Co., 1011

Gazette Foundation, 1011

GCA Corp., 1012

GE Foundations, 1022

Gear Motion, 1012

Gear Motions Foundation, 1012

Gebbie Foundation, 1012

Geffen Foundation, David, 1013

GEICO Corp., 1013

GEICO Philanthropic Foundation, 1013

Geifman Family Foundation, 1014

Geist Foundation, 1015

Gelb Foundation, Lawrence M., 1015

Gelco Foundation, 333

Gellert Foundation, Carl, 1016

Gellert Foundation, Celia Berta, 1016

Gellert Foundation, Fred, 1016

Gelman Foundation, Melvin and Estelle, 1017

GenCorp, 1017
GenCorp Foundation, 1017
Genentech, 1018
Genentech Foundation for Biomedical
　Sciences, 1018
Genentech Research Foundation, 1018
General Accident Charitable Trust, 1018
General Accident Insurance Co. of
　America, 1018
General American Charitable Foundation,
　1019
General American Life Insurance Co.,
　1019
General Atlantic Partners Foundation &
　Veronese Foundation, 1020
General Atlantic Partners L.P., 1020
General Color Co., 1020
General Development Corp., 1020
General Development Corp. Foundation,
　1020
General Dynamics Corp., 1021
General Educational Fund, 1021
General Electric Co., 1022
General Housewares Corp., 1023
General Machine Works, 1023
General Machine Works Foundation, 1023
General Mills, 1023
General Mills Foundation, 1023
General Motors Corp., 1025
General Motors Foundation, 1025
General Public Utilities Corp., 1026
General Railway Signal Corp., 1026
General Railway Signal Foundation, 1026
General Reinsurance Corp., 1027
General Service Foundation, 1027
General Signal Corp., 1028
General Steel Fabricators, 1028
General Steel Fabricators College
　Scholarship Foundation, 1028
General Tire Inc., 1029
Generation Trust, 1029
Genesco, 1030
Geneseo Foundation, 1030
Genesis Foundation, 1030
Genetics Institute, 1031
Geneva Foundation, 1031
Genius Foundation, Elizabeth Morse, 1031
GenRad, 1031
GenRad Foundation, 1031
Gensler Jr. & Associates, M. Arthur, 1032
Genuine Parts Co., 1032
George B. Quatman Foundation, 79
George Foundation, 1032
George Norton Foundation, 1988
George P. Davenport Trust Fund, 676
Georgia Gulf Corp., 1033
Georgia Health Foundation, 1033
Georgia Pork Producers Association, 1034

Georgia Power Co., 1034
Georgia Power Foundation, 1034
Georgia Scientific and Technical Research
　Foundation, 1035
Georgia-Pacific Corp., 1033
Georgia-Pacific Foundation, 1033
Gerald David Neuman Foundation, 1955
Gerard Foundation, Sumner, 1036
Gerber Cos. Foundation, 1036
Gerber Products Co., 1036
Gerbode Foundation, Wallace Alexander,
　1037
Gerlach Foundation, 1037
German Marshall Fund of the United
　States, 1038
German Protestant Orphan Asylum
　Association, 1039
Gerondelis Foundation, 1040
Gerschel Foundation, Patrick A., 1040
Gershenson Foundation, Charles H., 1040
Gershman Foundation, Joel, 1040
Gerson Family Foundation, Benjamin J.,
　1041
Gerson Trust, B. Milfred, 1041
Gerstacker Foundation, Rollin M., 1041
Getsch Family Foundation Trust, 1042
Getty Foundation, Ann and Gordon, 1042
Getty Trust, J. Paul, 1043
Getz Foundation, Emma and Oscar, 1044
Gheens Foundation, 1044
Ghidotti Foundation, William and Marian,
　1045
Gholston Trust, J. K., 1045
Giant Eagle, 1046
Giant Eagle Foundation, 1046
Giant Food, 1046
Giant Food Foundation, 1046
Giant Food Stores, 1047
Gibson Foundation, Addison H., 1047
Gibson Foundation, E. L., 1048
Giddings & Lewis, 1048
Giddings & Lewis Foundation, 1048
Gifford Charitable Corporation,
　Rosamond, 1049
Giger Foundation, Paul and Oscar, 1049
Gilbane Building Co., 1049
Gilbane Foundation, Thomas and
　William, 1050
Gilbert Associates, Inc., 1050
Gilbert, Jr. Charitable Trust, Price, 1050
Gilder Foundation, 1051
Gildred Foundation, 1051
Giles Foundation, Edward C., 1051
Gill Foundation, Pauline Allen, 1052
Gillespie Memorial Fund, Boynton, 1052
Gillett Foundation, Elesabeth Ingalls, 1052
Gillette Charitable and Educational
　Foundation, 1052

Gillette Co., 1052
Gilman and Gonzalez-Falla Theatre
　Foundation, 1053
Gilman Foundation, Howard, 1053
Gilman Investment Co., 1054
Gilman Paper Co., 1054
Gilman Paper Co. Foundation, 1054
Gilman, Jr. Foundation, Sondra and
　Charles, 1054
Gilmer-Smith Foundation, 1055
Gilmore Foundation, Earl B., 1055
Gilmore Foundation, Irving S., 1055
Gilmore Foundation, William G., 1056
Gindi Associates Foundation, 1056
Ginsberg Family Foundation, Moses, 1057
Ginter Foundation, Karl and Anna, 1057
Girard Foundation, 1057
Gitano Foundation, 1057
Gitano Group, 1057
Givenchy, Inc., 1058
Glancy Foundation, Lenora and Alfred,
　1058
Glanville Family Foundation, 1059
Glaser Foundation, 1059
Glatfelter Co., P.H., 1059
Glaxo, 1060
Glaxo Foundation, 1060
Glaze Foundation, Robert and Ruth, 1061
Glazer Foundation, Jerome S., 1061
Glazer Foundation, Madelyn L., 1061
Gleason Foundation, James, 1062
Gleason Foundation, Katherine, 1062
Gleason Memorial Fund, 1063
Gleason Works, 1063
Gleason Works Foundation, 1063
Glen Eagles Foundation, 1063
Glencairn Foundation, 1064
Glencoe Foundation, 1064
Glendale Federal Bank, 1064
Glendorn Foundation, 946
Glenmede Trust Corp., 1065
Glenmore Distilleries Co., 1065
Glenmore Foundation, 1065
Glenn Foundation for Medical Research,
　Paul F., 1066
Glenn Foundation, Carrie C. & Lena V.,
　1065
Glenn Memorial Foundation, Wilbur Fisk,
　1066
Glick Foundation, Eugene and Marilyn,
　1066
Glickenhaus & Co., 1066
Glickenhaus Foundation, 1066
Glidden Co., 1067
Global Van Lines, 1067
Globe Corp., 1067
Globe Foundation, 1067
Globe Newspaper Co., 1068

Hales Foundation, William M., 1156
Haley Foundation, W. B., 1156
Halff Foundation, G. A. C., 1157
Hall & Co. Inc., Frank B., 1158
Hall Charitable Trust, Evelyn A. J., 1157
Hall Family Foundations, 1158
Hall Financial Group, 1159
Hall Foundation, 1159
Hallberg Foundation, E. L. and R. F., 1160
Hallett Charitable Trust, 1160
Hallett Charitable Trust, Jessie F., 1161
Halliburton Co., 1161
Halliburton Foundation, 1161
Hallmark Cards, 1162
Hallmark Corporate Foundation, 1162
Halloran Foundation, Mary P. Dolciani, 1163
Hallowell Foundation, 1163
Halmos Foundation, 1163
Halsell Foundation, Ewing, 1164
Halsell Foundation, O. L., 1164
Halstead Foundation, 1165
Hambay Foundation, James T., 1165
Hamel Family Charitable Trust, D. A., 1165
Hamilton Bank, 1165
Hamilton Bank Foundation, 1165
Hamilton Foundation, Florence P., 1166
Hamilton Oil Corp., 1167
Hamman Foundation, George and Mary Josephine, 1167
Hammer Foundation, Armand, 1168
Hammer United World College Trust, Armand, 1168
Hammill Foundation, Donald D., 1168
Hammond Foundation, 1169
Hammond Machinery, 1169
Hampden Papers, 1169
Hampden Papers Co. Trust, 1169
Hampton Casting Division, 1169
Hampton Industries, 1169
Hancock Foundation, Luke B., 1169
Hand Industries, 1170
Hand Industries Foundation, 1170
Handleman Charitable Foundation, 1170
Handleman Co., 1170
Handy & Harman, 1171
Handy & Harman Foundation, 1171
Hanes Foundation, John W. and Anna H., 1171
Hang Seng Bank, 1172
Hankamer Foundation, Curtis and Doris K., 1172
Hankins Foundation, 1173
Hanley Family Foundation, 1173
Hanna Co. Foundation, M.A., 1173
Hanna Co., M.A., 1173
Hannon Foundation, William H., 1174

Hanover Insurance Co., 1174
Hansen Foundation, Dane G., 1174
Hansen Memorial Foundation, Irving, 1175
Hanson Foundation, 1175
Hanson Office Products, 1175
Hanson Testamentary Charitable Trust, Anna Emery, 1176
Harbert Corp., 1176
HarCo. Drug, 1176
HarCo. Foundation, 1176
Harcourt Brace Jovanovich, 1176
Harcourt Foundation, Ellen Knowles, 1177
Harcourt General, 1177
Harcourt General Charitable Foundation, 1177
Harden Foundation, 1178
Harder Foundation, 1179
Hardin Foundation, Phil, 1179
Harding Educational and Charitable Foundation, 1180
Harding Foundation, Charles Stewart, 1181
Hargis Charitable Foundation, Estes H. and Florence Parker, 1181
Hariri Foundation, 1181
Harkness Ballet Foundation, 1182
Harkness Foundation, William Hale, 1182
Harland Charitable Foundation, John and Wilhelmina D., 1182
Harland Co. Foundation, John H., 1183
Harland Co., John H., 1183
Harley-Davidson, Inc., 1183
Harleysville Mutual Insurance Co., 1184
Harman Foundation, Reed L. and Nan H., 1184
Harmon Foundation, Pearl M. and Julia J., 1184
Harnischfeger Foundation, 1185
Harper Brush Works, 1185
Harper Brush Works Foundation, 1185
Harper Foundation, Philip S., 1185
Harper Group, 1185
HarperCollins Publishers, 1186
Harrah's Hotels & Casinos, 1186
Harriman Foundation, Gladys and Roland, 1186
Harriman Foundation, Mary W., 1187
Harrington Charitable Trust, Charles J., 1187
Harrington Foundation, Don and Sybil, 1187
Harrington Foundation, Francis A. and Jacquelyn H., 1188
Harrington Trust, George, 1188
Harris Bank Foundation, 1193
Harris Brothers Foundation, 1189
Harris Corp., 1189

Harris Family Charitable Foundation, 1191
Harris Family Foundation, Hunt and Diane, 1190
Harris Foundation, 1189
Harris Foundation, H. H., 1190
Harris Foundation, J. Ira and Nicki, 1191
Harris Foundation, James J. and Angelia M., 1191
Harris Foundation, John H. and Lucille, 1191
Harris Foundation, William H. and Mattie Wattis, 1192
Harris Stores, Paul, 1192
Harris Trust & Savings Bank, 1193
Harris-Teeter Super Markets, 1192
Harrison and Conrad Memorial Trust, 1193
Harrison Foundation Trust, Francena T., 1194
Harrison Foundation, Fred G., 1194
Harsco Corp., 1194
Harsco Corp. Fund, 1194
Harte-Hanks Communications, Inc., 1195
Harte-Hanks Media Development Foundation, 1195
Hartford Courant Foundation, 1195
Hartford Foundation, John A., 1196
Hartford Steam Boiler Inspection & Insurance Co., 1197
Hartman Foundation, Jesse and Dorothy, 1197
Hartmarx Charitable Foundation, 1197
Hartmarx Corp., 1197
Hartz Foundation, 1198
Hartz Mountain Corp., 1198
Hartzell Industries, Inc., 1198
Hartzell-Norris Charitable Trust, 1198
Harvard Apparatus Foundation, 1199
Harvard Industries, 1199
Harvard Interiors Manufacturing Co., 1199
Harvard Musical Association, 1199
Harvest States Cooperative, 1200
Harvest States Foundation, 1200
Harvey Foundation, Felix, 1200
Hasbro, 1201
Hasbro Charitable Trust, 1201
Haskell Fund, 1201
Hassenfeld Foundation, 1202
Hastings Trust, 1202
Hatch Charitable Trust, Margaret Milliken, 1202
Hatterscheidt Foundation, 1203
Hauser Foundation, 1203
Hauserman Charitable Trust Fund, 1203
Hauserman, Inc., 1203
Hauss-Helms Foundation, 1204
Haven Charitable Foundation, Nina, 1204

Havens Foundation, O. W., 1204
Haverty Furniture Cos., Inc., 1204
Hawaii National Bank, 1204
Hawaii National Foundation, 1204
Hawaiian Telephone Co., 1205
Hawkeye Bancorporation, 1205
Hawkeye Bancorporation Charitable Trust, 1205
Hawkins Foundation, Robert Z., 1205
Hawley Foundation, 1205
Hawn Foundation, 1206
Haworth, Inc., 1206
Hay Foundation, John I., 1206
Hayden Foundation, Charles, 1207
Hayden Foundation, William R. and Virginia, 1208
Hayden Recreation Center, Josiah Willard, 1208
Hayes Albion Industries, 1208
Hayfields Foundation, 1208
Haynes Foundation, 1209
Haynes Foundation, John Randolph and Dora, 1209
Hayswood Foundation, 1210
Hayward Foundation Charitable Trust, John T. and Winifred, 1210
Hazeltine Corp., 1210
Hazen Charitable Trust, Lita Annenberg, 1210
Hazen Foundation, Edward W., 1211
HCA Foundation, 1289
HCB Contractors, 1212
Health 1st Foundation, 1212
Healy Family Foundation, M. A., 1212
Hearst Corp., 1212
Hearst Foundation, 1212
Hearst Foundation, William Randolph, 1214
Heath Foundation, Ed and Mary, 1215
Hebrew Technical Institute, 1215
Hechinger Co., 1216
Hechinger Foundation, 1216
Hecht's, 1217
Hecht-Levi Foundation, 1216
Heckscher Foundation for Children, 1217
Hecla Mining Co., 1218
Hecla Mining Co. Foundation, 1218
Hedco Foundation, 1218
Hedrick Foundation, Frank E., 1218
Heed Ophthalmic Foundation, 1219
Heffernan & Co., 1219
Heginbotham Trust, Will E., 1219
HEI Charitable Foundation, 1219
HEI Inc., 1219
Heil Co., 1220
Heileman Brewing Co., Inc., G., 1220
Heileman Old Style Foundation, 1220
Heilicher Foundation, Menahem, 1221

Heilig-Meyers Co., 1221
Hein-Werner Corp., 1221
Heineman Foundation for Research, Educational, Charitable, and Scientific Purposes, 1221
Heinz Co. Foundation, H.J., 1222
Heinz Co., H.J., 1222
Heinz Endowment, Howard, 1223
Heinz Endowment, Vira I., 1223
Heinz Family Foundation, 1224
Heinz Foundation, 2034
Heinz Foundation, Drue, 1225
Heisey Foundation, 1225
Helena Chemical Co., 1225
Helfaer Foundation, Evan and Marion, 1225
Helis Foundation, 1226
Heller Financial, 1226
Heller Foundation, Walter E., 1227
Helmerich & Payne Inc., 1228
Helmerich Foundation, 1227
Helms Foundation, 1228
Helzberg Foundation, Shirley and Barnett, 1228
Hemby Foundation, Alex, 1228
Hemingway Foundation, Robert G., 1229
Hench Foundation, John C., 1229
Henderson Foundation, 1229
Henderson Foundation, George B., 1230
Hendrickson Brothers, 1230
Hendrickson Brothers Foundation, 1230
Henkel Corp., 1230
Henkel-Harris Co., Inc., 1231
Henredon Furniture Industries, 1231
Henry Foundation, 1231
Henry Foundation, Patrick, 1231
Herald News, 1232
Herald Newspapers Foundation, 1232
Herbst Foundation, 1232
Hercules Inc., 1232
Heritage Foundation, 1233
Heritage Pullman Bank & Trust, 1233
Heritage Pullman Bank Charitable Foundation, 1233
Heritage Travel Inc./Thomas Cook Travel, 1233
Herman Foundation, John and Rose, 1233
Hermann Foundation, Grover, 1233
Herndon Foundation, 1234
Herndon Foundation, Alonzo F. Herndon and Norris B., 1235
Herr Foods, 1235
Herrick Foundation, 12352634
Herschend Family Foundation, 1236
Hersey Foundation, 1236
Hershey Entertainment & Resort Co., 1236

Hershey Foods Corp., 1237
Hershey Foods Corp. Fund, 1237
Hershey Foundation, 1237
Hertz Foundation, Fannie and John, 1238
Hervey Foundation, 1238
Herzog Foundation, Carl J., 1239
Herzstein Charitable Foundation, Albert and Ethel, 1239
Hess Charitable Foundation, Ronne and Donald, 1239
Hess Charitable Trust, Myrtle E. and William C., 1240
Hess Foundation, 1240
Hesston Corp., 1240
Hesston Foundation, 1240
Hettinger Foundation, 1241
Heublein, 1241
Heublein Foundation, 1241
Hewit Family Foundation, 1242
Hewlett Foundation, William and Flora, 1242
Hewlett-Packard Co., 1244
Hewlett-Packard Co. Foundation, 1244
Hexcel Corp., 1245
Hexcel Foundation, 1245
Heydt Fund, Nan and Matilda, 1245
Heymann Special Account, Mr. and Mrs. Jimmy, 1245
Heymann-Wolf Foundation, 1246
Heyward Memorial Fund, DuBose and Dorothy, 1246
Hiawatha Education Foundation, 1246
Hibernia Corp., 1247
Hickory Tech Corp. Foundation, 1687
Hidary Foundation, Jacob, 1247
Higgins Charitable Trust, Lorene Sails, 1247
Higgins Foundation, Aldus C., 1248
Higginson Trust, Corina, 1248
High Foundation, 1248
High Meadow Foundation, 6161292
Higher Education Publications, 1249
Hightower Foundation, Walter, 1249
Hill and Family Foundation, Walter Clay, 1249
Hill Crest Foundation, 1249
Hill Foundation, 1250
Hill-Snowdon Foundation, 1250
Hillcrest Foundation, 1250
Hillenbrand Industries, 1251
Hilliard Corp., 1251
Hilliard Foundation, 1251
Hillman Co., 1252
Hillman Family Foundation, Alex, 1252
Hillman Foundation, 1252
Hillman Foundation, Henry L., 1253
Hills Department Stores, Inc., 1254
Hills Fund, Edward E., 1254

Hubbard Foundation, R. Dee and Joan Dale, 1300

Hubbard Milling Co., 1300

Hubbell Foundation, Harvey, 1301

Hubbell Inc., 1301

Huber Corp., J.M., 1301

Huber Foundation, 1302

Huber, Hunt & Nichols, 1302

Huck International Inc., 1302

Hudson Charitable Foundation, 1303

Hudson Foods, 1302

Hudson Jewellers, J.B., 1303

Hudson Neckwear, 1303

Hudson's, 1304

Hudson-Webber Foundation, 1303

Huffington Foundation, 1305

Huffy Corp., 1305

Huffy Foundation, Inc., 1305

Hugg Trust, Leoia W. and Charles H., 1305

Hughes Aircraft Co., 1306

Hughes Charitable Trust, Mabel Y., 1306

Hughes Medical Institute, Howard, 1306

Hughes Memorial Foundation, Charles Evans, 1308

Hughes Supply, Inc., 1309

Hugoton Foundation, 1309

Huisking Foundation, 1309

Huizenga Family Foundation, 1310

Huizenga Foundation, Jennie, 1310

Hulings Foundation, Mary Andersen, 1310

Hulme Charitable Foundation, Milton G., 1311

Hultquist Foundation, 1311

Humana, 1311

Humana Foundation, 1311

Humane Society of the Commonwealth of Massachusetts, 1313

Hume Foundation, Jaquelin, 1313

Humphrey Foundation, Glenn & Gertrude, 1314

Humphrey Fund, George M. and Pamela S., 1314

Humphreys Foundation, 1314

Hunnicutt Foundation, H. P. and Anne S., 1315

Hunt Alternatives Fund, 1315

Hunt Alternatives Fund, Helen, 1316

Hunt Charitable Trust, C. Giles, 1316

Hunt Chemical Corp., Phillip A., 1316

Hunt Foundation, 1316

Hunt Foundation, Roy A., 1317

Hunt Foundation, Samuel P., 1317

Hunt Manufacturing Co., 1318

Hunt Manufacturing Co. Foundation, 1318

Hunt Oil Co., 1319

Hunt Transport Services, J.B., 1319

Hunt Trust for Episcopal Charitable Institutions, Virginia, 1319

Hunter Foundation, Edward and Irma, 1319

Hunter Trust, A. V., 1320

Hunter Trust, Emily S. and Coleman A., 1320

Huntington Bancshares Inc., 1321

Huntington Fund for Education, John, 1321

Huntsman Foundation, Jon and Karen, 1321

Hurford Foundation, 1322

Hurlbut Memorial Fund, Orion L. and Emma S., 1322

Hurley Foundation, Ed E. and Gladys, 1322

Hurley Foundation, J. F., 1322

Hurst Foundation, 1323

Huston Charitable Trust, Stewart, 1323

Huston Foundation, 1323

Hutcheson Foundation, Hazel Montague, 1324

Hutchins Foundation, Mary J., 1324

Huthsteiner Fine Arts Trust, 1324

Hutzell Foundation, 1325

Hy-Vee Food Stores, 1325

Hyams Foundation, 1325

Hyde and Watson Foundation, 1326

Hyde Foundation, 1327

Hyde Foundation, J. R., 1327

Hyde Manufacturing Co., 1327

Hyde, Jr. Scholarship Fund, J.R., 1327

Hydraulic Co., 1328

Hyman Construction Co., George, 1328

Hyster-Yale, 1328

Hyundai Motor America, 1328

I

I and G Charitable Foundation, 1329

I Have A Dream Foundation - Los Angeles, 1329

I. and L. Association, 1329

Iacocca Foundation, 1329

IBJ Foundation, 1346

IBM Corp., 1330

IBM South Africa Projects Fund, 1331

IBP Foundation, Inc., The, 1331

IBP, Inc., 1331

Icahn Foundation, Carl C., 1332

ICC Industries, 1332

ICH Corp., 1332

ICI Americas, 1333

Icon Systems & Software, 1333

Ida J. McEachern Charitable Trust, 1756

Iddings Benevolent Trust, 1333

Ideal Industries, 1334

Ideal Industries Foundation, 1334

IDEX Corp., 1334

IDS Financial Services, 1334

IES Industries, 1335

IES Industries Charitable Foundation, 1335

IFF Foundation, 1356

Illges Foundation, John P. and Dorothy S., 1336

Illges Memorial Foundation, A. and M. L., 1336

Illinois Bell, 1337

Illinois Central Railroad Co., 1337

Illinois Cereal Mills, 1337

Illinois Consolidated Telephone Co., 1337

Illinois Power Co., 1337

Illinois Tool Works, 1338

Illinois Tool Works Foundation, 1338

Imagine Foods, 1339

IMCERA Foundation and Pitman-Moore Community Partnership Program, 1339

IMCERA Group Inc., 1339

Imerman Memorial Foundation, Stanley, 1340

Imlay Foundation, 1340

IMO Industries Inc., 1340

Imperial Bancorp, 1341

Imperial Bank Foundation, 1341

Imperial Corp. of America, 1341

Imperial Electric, 1341

Imperial Electric Foundation, 1341

Imperial Holly Corp., 1341

IMS America Ltd., 1341

IMT Co. Charitable Trust, 1342

IMT Insurance Co., 1342

In His Name, 1342

Inco Alloys International, 1342

Independence Foundation, 1342

Independent Bankshares, 1343

Independent Financial Corp., 1343

Independent Financial Corp. Charitable Trust, 1343

Index Technology Corp., 1343

Index Technology Foundation, 1343

India Foundation, 1344

Indiana Bell Telephone Co., 1344

Indiana Chemical Trust, 1345

Indiana Desk Co., 1345

Indiana Desk Foundation, 1345

Indiana Gas and Chemical Corp., 1345

Indiana Gas Co., 1345

Indiana Insurance Cos., 1346

Indianapolis Newspapers, Inc., 1346

Indianapolis Water Co., 1346

Industrial Bank of Japan Trust Co., 1346

Industrial Risk Insurers, 1347

J

Jasper Office Furniture Foundation, 1405
Jasper Seating Co., 1387
Jasper Seating Foundation, 1387
Jasper Table Co., 1388
Jasper Table Co. Foundation, 1388
Jasper Wood Products Co., 1388
Jasper Wood Products Co. Foundation, 1388
Jaydor Corp., 1389
JCPenney Co., 1389
JCPenney Co. Fund, 1389
Jeffers Memorial Fund, Michael, 1390
Jefferson Endowment Fund, John Percival and Mary C., 1390
Jefferson Smurfit Corp., 1391
Jefferson-Pilot, 1390
Jefferson-Pilot Communications, 1390
Jeffress Memorial Trust, Elizabeth G., 1391
Jeffress Memorial Trust, Thomas F. and Kate Miller, 1391
Jeffries & Co., 1392
Jeffris Family Foundation, 1392
JELD-WEN Foundation, 1392
JELD-WEN, Inc., 1392
Jellison Benevolent Society, 1393
Jenkins Foundation, 2196
Jenkins Foundation, George W., 1393
Jennings Foundation, Alma, 1393
Jennings Foundation, Martha Holden, 1394
Jennings Foundation, Mary Hillman, 1395
Jensen Construction Co., 1395
Jensen Foundation, 1395
Jephson Educational Trust No. 1, 1396
Jephson Educational Trust No. 2, 1396
Jeppesen Sanderson, 1396
Jergens Foundation, Andrew, 1396
Jerome Foundation, 1397
Jerry Spiegel Foundation, 2520
Jersey Central Power & Light Co., 1398
Jerusalem Fund for Education and Community Development, 1398
Jesselson Foundation, 1399
Jessie Ball duPont Religious, Charitable and Educational Fund, 771
Jessop Steel Co., 1399
Jewell Memorial Foundation, Daniel Ashley and Irene Houston, 1399
Jewett Foundation, George Frederick, 1400
Jewish Foundation for Education of Women, 1401
Jewish Healthcare Foundation of Pittsburgh, 1401
JFM Foundation, 1402
Jim Beam Brands Co., 1402
Jim Walter Corp. Foundation, 2796

Jinks Foundation, Ruth T., 1402
JJJ Foundation, 1403
JM Foundation, 1403
JMK-A M Micallef Charitable Foundation, 1404
Jochum-Moll Foundation, 1663
Jockey Club Foundation, 1404
Jockey Hollow Foundation, 1404
Jockey International, 1405
JOFCo., Inc., 1405
John Hancock Mutual Life Insurance Co., 1405
Johnson & Higgins, 1415
Johnson & Johnson, 1416
Johnson & Johnson Family of Cos. Contribution Fund, 1416
Johnson & Son, S.C., 1417
Johnson Charitable Trust, Keith Wold, 1406
Johnson Co. Foundation, E. F., 1406
Johnson Co., E. F., 1406
Johnson Controls, 1407
Johnson Controls Foundation, 1407
Johnson Day Trust, Carl and Virginia, 1408
Johnson Educational and Benevolent Trust, Dexter G., 1408
Johnson Endeavor Foundation, Christian A., 1408
Johnson Foundation, 1409
Johnson Foundation, A. D., 1409
Johnson Foundation, Barbara P., 1409
Johnson Foundation, Burdine, 1409
Johnson Foundation, Helen K. and Arthur E., 1410
Johnson Foundation, Howard, 1410
Johnson Foundation, M. G. and Lillie A., 1411
Johnson Foundation, Robert Wood, 1411
Johnson Foundation, Walter S., 1413
Johnson Foundation, Willard T. C., 1414
Johnson Fund, Edward C., 1414
Johnson Inc., Axel, 1406
Johnson Matthey Investments, 1417
Johnson's Wax Fund, 1417
Johnson, Lane, Space, Smith & Co., Inc., 1417
Johnson, Lane, Space, Smith Foundation, Inc., 1417
Johnston Trust for Charitable and Educational Purposes, James M., 1418
Johnston-Fix Foundation, 1418
Johnston-Hanson Foundation, 1418
Johnstone and H. Earle Kimball Foundation, Phyllis Kimball, 1419
Jones and Bessie D. Phelps Foundation, Cyrus W. and Amy F., 1419

Jones Charitable Trust, Harvey and Bernice, 1420
Jones Construction Co., J.A., 1420
Jones Family Foundation, Eugenie and Joseph, 1421
Jones Foundation, Daisy Marquis, 1421
Jones Foundation, Fletcher, 1422
Jones Foundation, Harvey and Bernice, 1423
Jones Foundation, Helen, 1423
Jones Foundation, Montfort Jones and Allie Brown, 1424
Jones Foundation, W. Alton, 1424
Jones Foundation, Walter S. and Evan C., 1425
Jones Fund, Blanche and George, 1425
Jones Fund, Paul L., 1425
Jones Intercable Tampa Trust, 1426
Jones Intercable, Inc., 1426
Jonsson Foundation, 1426
Jordan and Ettie A. Jordan Charitable Foundation, Mary Ranken, 1426
Jordan Charitable Trust, Martha Annie, 1427
Jordan Foundation, Arthur, 1427
Jorgensen Co., Earle M., 1428
Joselow Foundation, 1428
Josephson International Inc., 1428
Joslin-Needham Family Foundation, 1428
Joslyn Corp., 1429
Joslyn Foundation, 1429
Joslyn Foundation, Marcellus I., 1429
Jost Foundation, Charles and Mabel P., 1429
Jostens, 1430
Jostens Foundation, 1430
Joukowsky Family Foundation, 1431
Journal Communications, 1431
Journal Gazette Co., 1431
Journal Gazette Foundation, 1431
Joy Family Foundation, 1432
Joyce Foundation, 1432
Joyce Foundation, John M. and Mary A., 1433
JSJ Corp., 1434
JSJ Foundation, 1434
JTB Cultural Exchange Corp., 1434
JTB International, Inc., 1434
Julia Foundation, Laura, 1434
Julia R. and Estelle L. Foundation, 1434
Julius & Ray Charlestein Foundation, 2170
Jupiter Industries, Inc., 1435
Jurodin Fund, 1435
Jurzykowski Foundation, Alfred, 1436
Justin Industries, Inc., 1436
Justus Trust, Edith C., 1436

K

Law Foundation, Robert O., 1569
Lawrence Foundation, 433
Lawrence Foundation, Alice, 1569
Lawrence Foundation, Lind, 1570
Lawson Products, Inc., 1570
Lawyers Co-operative Publishing Co., 1570
Lawyers Title Foundation, 1570
Layne Foundation, 1570
Lazar Foundation, 1571
Lazard Freres & Co., 1571
Lazarus Charitable Trust, Helen and Charles, 1571
LBJ Family Foundation, 1571
LDB Corp., 1572
LDI Charitable Foundation, 1572
Lea Country Electric Education Foundation, 1572
Lea County Electric Co-op, 1572
Lea Foundation, Helen Sperry, 1572
Leach Foundation, Tom & Frances, 1573
Leader Foundation, 1573
Learjet Inc., 1573
LeaRonal, Inc., 1573
Leaseway Transportation Corp., 1574
Leavey Foundation, Thomas and Dorothy, 1574
Lebanon Mutual Foundation, 1574
Lebanon Mutual Insurance Co., 1574
Lebovitz Fund, 1575
LeBrun Foundation, 1575
Lebus Trust, Bertha, 1575
Lechmere, 1576
Lederer Foundation, Francis L., 1576
Ledler Corp., 1576
Ledwith Charitable Trust Bank, Mary B., 1576
Lee Apparel Co., 1576
Lee Endowment Foundation, 1576
Lee Enterprises, 1577
Lee Foundation, 1577
Lee Foundation, James T., 1577
Lee Foundation, Ray M. and Mary Elizabeth, 1578
Leesona Charitable Foundation, 1578
Leesona Corp., 1578
LEF Foundation, 1579
Legg & Co. Foundation, 1579
Legg Mason Inc., 1579
Leggett & Platt, Inc., 1579
Lehigh Portland Cement Charitable Trust, 1579
Lehigh Portland Cement Co., 1579
Lehigh Press, Inc., 1580
Lehman Foundation, Edith and Herbert, 1580
Lehman Foundation, Robert, 1580
Lehmann Foundation, Otto W., 1581

Lehrman Foundation, Jacob and Charlotte, 1581
Leibovitz Foundation, Morris P., 1582
Leidy Foundation, John J., 1582
Leighton-Oare Foundation, 1582
Lemberg Foundation, 1583
Lender Family Foundation, 1583
Lender's Bagel Bakery, 1584
Lennar Corp., 1584
Lennon Foundation, Fred A., 1584
Lennox Foundation, 1584
Lennox International, Inc., 1584
Leo Burnett Co., 1585
Leo Burnett Co. Charitable Foundation, 1585
Leonardt Foundation, 1585
Leonhardt Foundation, Dorothea L., 1586
Leonhardt Foundation, Frederick H., 1586
Lesher Foundation, Margaret and Irvin, 1586
Leslie Fay Cos., Inc., 1586
Leu Foundation, 1587
Leu Foundation, Harry P., 1587
Leucadia Foundation, 1587
Leucadia National Corp., 1587
Leuthold Foundation, 1588
Levee Charitable Trust, Polly Annenberg, 1588
Levi Strauss & Co., 1589
Levi Strauss Foundation, 1589
Levin Foundation, Philip and Janice, 1590
Levine Family Foundation, Hyman, 1590
Levinson Foundation, Max and Anna, 1590
Levinson Foundation, Morris L., 1591
Levinson's, Inc., 1591
Levit Family Foundation, Joe, 1591
Leviton Foundation New York, 1591
Leviton Manufacturing Co., 1591
Levitt Foundation, 1592
Levitt Foundation, Richard S., 1592
Levy Circulating Co., Charles, 1592
Levy Co., Edward C., 1593
Levy Foundation, Achille, 187
Levy Foundation, Betty and Norman F., 1593
Levy Foundation, Charles and Ruth, 1593
Levy Foundation, Edward C., 1594
Levy Foundation, Hyman Jebb, 1594
Levy Foundation, Jerome, 1594
Levy Foundation, June Rockwell, 1595
Levy's Lumber & Building Centers, 1595
Levy's Lumber & Building Centers Foundation, 1595
Levy-Markus Foundation, 1595
Lewis Foundation, Frank J., 1596
Lewis Foundation, Lillian Kaiser, 1596
Lewis Homes of California, 1596

Libbey-Owens Ford Co., 1597
Libby-Dufour Fund, Trustees of the, 1597
Liberman Foundation, Bertha & Isaac, 1597
Liberty Corp., 1597
Liberty Corp. Foundation, 1597
Liberty Diversified Industries Inc., 1598
Liberty Glass Co., 1599
Liberty Hosiery Mills, 1599
Liberty Hosiery Mills Foundation, 1599
Liberty Mutual Insurance Group/Boston, 1599
Liberty National Bank, 1599
Library Association of Warehouse Point, 1600
Lichtenstein Foundation, David B., 1600
Lieberman Enterprises, 1600
Lieberman-Okinow Foundation, 1600
Lied Foundation Trust, 1601
Life Insurance Co. of Georgia, 1601
Life Investors Insurance Company of America, 1602
Life Sciences Research Foundation, 1602
Lightner Sams Foundation, 1603
Lilly & Co. Foundation, Eli, 1603
Lilly & Co., Eli, 1603
Lilly Endowment, 1604
Lilly Foundation, Richard Coyle, 1605
LIN Broadcasting Corp., 1606
Lincoln Electric Co., 1606
Lincoln Electric Foundation Trust, 1606
Lincoln Family Foundation, 1607
Lincoln Fund, 1607
Lincoln Health Care Foundation, 1607
Lincoln National Corp., 1608
Lincoln Property Co., 1609
Lincoln Telecommunications Co., 1609
Lincoln-Lane Foundation, 1608
Lincolnshire, 1609
Lincy Foundation, 1609
Linde Foundation, Ronald and Maxine, 1610
Lindner Foundation, Fay J., 1610
Lindsay Foundation, 1611
Lindsay Student Aid Fund, Franklin, 1611
Lindsay Trust, Agnes M., 1611
Lindstrom Foundation, Kinney, 1612
Lingnan Foundation, 1612
Link Foundation, 1612
Link, Jr. Foundation, George, 1613
Linn-Henley Charitable Trust, 1613
Linnell Foundation, 1613
Lintilhac Foundation, 1614
Linus Foundation, 1614
Lionel Corp., 1614
Lipchitz Foundation, Jacques and Yulla, 1615

M

M. E. G. Foundation, 1662
M.D.C. Holdings, 1663
M.E. Foundation, 1663
M.T.D. Products, 1663
M/A-COM Charitable Foundation, 1662
M/A-COM, Inc., 1662
M/A/R/C Inc., 1662
Maas Foundation, Benard L., 1664
Mabee Foundation, J. E. and L. E., 1664
MacAndrews & Forbes Foundation, 1665
MacAndrews & Forbes Holdings, 1665
MacArthur Foundation, J. Roderick, 1666
MacArthur Foundation, John D. and
   Catherine T., 1666
MacCurdy Salisbury Educational
   Foundation, 1668
MacDonald Foundation, James A., 1668
MacDonald Foundation, Marquis George,
   1669
Macht Foundation, Morton and Sophia,
   1669
Mack Foundation, J. S., 1669
MacKall and Evanina Evans Bell
   MacKall Trust, Paul, 1670
MacKenzie Foundation, 1670
MacLean-Fogg Co., 1670
Maclellan Charitable Trust, R. J., 1671
Maclellan Foundation, 1671
Maclellan Foundation, Robert L. and
   Kathrina H., 1672
MacLeod Stewardship Foundation, 1672
Macmillan Foundation, 1672
Macmillan, Inc., 1672
Macom-Venitz, 1673
Macy & Co., R.H., 1673
Macy, Jr. Foundation, Josiah, 1674
Maddox Foundation, J. F., 1675
Maddox Trust, Web, 1676
Madison Gas & Electric Co., 1676
Madison Gas & Electric Foundation, 1676
Madison Mutual Insurance Co., 1676
Magee Carpet Co., 1677
Magee Christian Education Foundation,
   1677
Magic Chef, 1677
Magic Chef Foundation, 1677
Magma Copper Co., 1677
Magnatek, 1678
Magowan Family Foundation, 1678
Magruder Foundation, Chesley G., 1678
Maguire Oil Co., 1679
Maguire Thomas Partners, 1679
Mahadh Foundation, 1310
Maier Foundation, Sarah Pauline, 1679
Mailman Family Foundation, A. L., 1679
Mailman Foundation, 1680

Makita U.S.A., Inc., 1680
MalCo Charitable Foundation, 1681
MalCo Products Inc., 1681
Malden Mills Industries, 1681
Mallinckrodt Specialty Chemicals, 1682
Mallinckrodt, Jr. Foundation, Edward,
   1681
Mamiye Brothers, 1683
Mamiye Foundation, 1683
Management Compensation
   Group/Dulworth Inc., 1683
Manat Foundation, 1683
Mandel Foundation, Jack N. and Lilyan,
   1683
Mandel Foundation, Joseph and Florence,
   1684
Mandel Foundation, Morton and Barbara,
   1684
Mandell Foundation, Samuel P., 1684
Mandeville Foundation, 1685
Maneely Fund, 1685
Manger and Audrey Cordero Plitt Trust,
   Clarence, 1685
Manilow Foundation, Nathan, 1686
Manitou Foundation, 1686
Manitowoc Co., 1686
Mankato Citizens Telephone Co., 1687
Mankato Citizens Telephone Co.
   Foundation, 1687
Mann Foundation, John Jay, 1687
Mann Foundation, Ted, 1687
Manning and Emma Austin Manning
   Foundation, James Hilton, 1688
Manoogian Foundation, Alex and Marie,
   1688
Manor Care, 1689
Manpower, Inc., 1689
Mansfield Foundation, Albert and Anne,
   1689
Manufacturers Life Insurance Co. of
   America, 1689
Manufacturers National Bank of Detroit,
   1690
Manville Corp., 1690
Manville Fund, 1690
Mapco Inc., 1691
Mapplethorpe Foundation, Robert, 1691
Marathon Cheese Corp., 1692
Marathon Oil, Indiana Refining Division,
   1692
Marbrook Foundation, 1692
Marcade Group, Inc., 1693
Marcus Brothers Textiles Inc., 1693
Marcus Corp., 1693
Marcus Corp. Foundation, 1693
Marcus Foundation, 1693
Mardag Foundation, 1694
Mardigian Foundation, 1694
Margoes Foundation, 1695

Margolis Charitable Foundation for
   Medical Research, Ben B. and Iris M.,
   1695
Marguerite N. and Thomas L. Williams,
   Jr., Foundation, 2887
Margulf Foundation, 1709
Marian W. Ottley Trust-Watertown, 2916
Mariani Nut Co., 1695
Mariani Nut Co. Foundation, 1695
Marine Midland Banks, 1696
Marinette Marine Corp., 1696
Marinette Marine Foundation, 1696
Marion Fabrics, 1696
Marion Merrell Dow, 1696
Marion Merrell Dow Foundation, 1696
Maritz Inc., 1697
Mark Controls Corp., 1697
Mark IV Industries, 1697
Mark IV Industries Foundation, 1697
Markem Corp., 1698
Markey Charitable Fund, John C., 1698
Markey Charitable Trust, Lucille P., 1698
Markle Foundation, John and Mary R.,
   1700
Marks Family Foundation, 1701
Marley Co., 1701
Marley Fund, 1701
Marmon Group, Inc., 1701
Marmot Foundation, 1702
Marpat Foundation, 1702
Marquette Electronics, 1702
Marquette Electronics Foundation, 1702
Marriott Corp., 1703
Marriott Foundation, J. Willard, 1703
Mars Foundation, 1704
Mars, Inc., 1704
Marsh & McLennan Cos., 1705
Marsh Foundation, 1705
Marsh Furniture Co., 1705
Marsh Supermarkets, Inc., 1705
Marshall & Ilsley Bank, 1707
Marshall & Ilsley Foundation, 1707
Marshall Field's, 1706
Marshall Foundation, 1706
Marshall Foundation, Mattie H., 1707
Marshall Fund, 1707
Marshall Trust in Memory of Sanders
   McDaniel, Harriet McDaniel, 1708
Marshalls Inc., 1709
Marshburn Foundation, 1709
Martin & Deborah Flug Foundation, 1709
Martin Family Fund, 1710
Martin Foundation, 1710
Martin Foundation, Bert William, 1710
Martin Foundation, Della, 1711
Martin Marietta Aggregates, 1711
Martin Marietta Corp., 1711
Martin Marietta Corp. Foundation, 1711

Martin Marietta Philanthropic Trust, 1711

Martin-Brower Co., The, 1709

Martini Foundation, Nicholas, 1712

Marubeni America Corp., 1713

Marx Foundation, Virginia & Leonard, 1713

Mary Kay Cosmetics, 1713

Mary Kay Foundation, 1713

Maryland Casualty Co., 1714

Masco Corp., 1714

Masco Corp. Charitable Trust, 1714

Mascoma Savings Bank, 1715

Mascoma Savings Bank Foundation, 1715

Masland & Sons, C.H., 1715

Mason Charitable Foundation, 1715

Masonite Corp., 1715

Mass Merchandisers, Inc., 1715

Massachusetts Charitable Mechanics Association, 1716

Massachusetts Mutual Life Insurance Co., 1716

Massengill-DeFriece Foundation, 1717

Masserini Charitable Trust, Maurice J., 1717

Massey Charitable Trust, 1717

Massey Foundation, 1718

Massey Foundation, Jack C., 1718

Massie Trust, David Meade, 1719

Mast Drug Co., 1719

Mastronardi Charitable Foundation, Charles A., 1719

Matchbox Toys (USA) Ltd., 1719

Material Service Corp., 1720

Material Service Foundation, 1720

Mather and William Gwinn Mather Fund, Elizabeth Ring, 1720

Mather Charitable Trust, S. Livingston, 1721

Mather Fund, Richard, 1721

Mathers Charitable Foundation, G. Harold and Leila Y., 1721

Mathis-Pfohl Foundation, 1722

Matlock Foundation, 2462

Matson Navigation Co., 1722

Matsushita Electric Corp. of America, 1722

Matsushita Foundation, 1722

Mattel, 1723

Mattel Foundation, 1723

Matthews and Co. Educational and Charitable Trust, James H., 1724

Matthews International Corp., 1724

Mattus Foundation, Reuben and Rose, 1725

Matz Foundation — Edelman Division, 1725

Mauger Insurance Co., 1725

Mauger Insurance Fund, 1725

Mautz Paint Co., 1726

Mautz Paint Foundation, 1726

Max Charitable Foundation, 1726

Maxfield Foundation, 1726

Maxicare Health Plans, 1726

Maxon Charitable Foundation, 1727

Maxtor Corp., 1727

Maxus Energy Corp., 1727

May Charitable Trust, Ben, 1727

May Department Stores Co., 1728

May Foundation, Wilbur, 1728

May Mitchell Royal Foundation, 1729

May Stores Foundation, 880

Mayacamas Corp., 1729

Mayborn Foundation, Frank W., 1729

Mayer Charitable Trust, Oscar G. & Elsa S., 1730

Mayer Foods Corp., Oscar, 1730

Mayer Foundation, James and Eva, 1731

Mayer Foundation, Louis B., 1731

Mayerson Foundation, Manuel D. and Rhoda, 1732

Mayfair Super Markets, 1732

Mayflower Group, 1732

Maynard Steel Casting Co., 1732

Mayne Nickless, 1732

Mayor Foundation, Oliver Dewey, 1732

Mays, Inc., J.W., 1733

Maytag Corp., 1733

Maytag Corp. Foundation, 1733

Maytag Family Foundation, Fred, 1734

Mazda Motor of America, 1734

Mazer Foundation, Jacob and Ruth, 1735

Mazza Foundation, 1735

MBIA, Inc., 1735

MCA, 1736

MCA Foundation, 1736

McAlister Charitable Foundation, Harold, 1737

McAlonan Trust, John A., 1737

McAshan Foundation, 1737

McBean Charitable Trust, Alletta Morris, 1737

McBean Family Foundation, 1738

McBeath Foundation, Faye, 1738

McBride & Son Associates, 1739

McBride Charitable Foundation, Joseph & Elsie, 1739

McCamish Foundation, 1739

McCann Foundation, 1740

McCarthy Charities, 1740

McCarthy Foundation, John and Margaret, 1741

McCarthy Foundation, Michael W., 1741

McCarthy Memorial Trust Fund, Catherine, 1741

McCasland Foundation, 1741

McCaw Cellular Communications, 1742

McCaw Foundation, 1742

McClure Educational and Development Fund, James G. K., 1743

McConnell Foundation, 1743

McConnell Foundation, Neil A., 1744

McCormick & Co., 1744

McCormick Foundation, Chauncey and Marion Deering, 1745

McCormick Tribune Foundation, Robert R., 1745

McCormick Trust, Anne, 1746

McCourtney Trust, Flora S., 1747

McCray Charitable Foundation, 1747

McCray Lumber Co., 1747

McCrea Foundation, 1747

McCrory Corp., 1747

McCullough Foundation, Ralph H. and Ruth J., 1748

McCune Charitable Trust, John R., 1748

McCune Foundation, 1749

McCutchen Foundation, 1749

McDermott, 1750

McDermott Foundation, Eugene, 1750

McDevitt Street Bovis Inc., 1751

McDonald & Co. Securities, 1751

McDonald & Co. Securities Foundation, 1751

McDonald Foundation, J. M., 1751

McDonald Foundation, Tillie and Tom, 1752

McDonald Industries, Inc., A. Y., 1752

McDonald Manufacturing Co. Charitable Foundation, A. Y., 1752

McDonald's Corp., 1752

McDonnell Douglas Corp., 1753

McDonnell Douglas Corp.-West, 1754

McDonnell Douglas Employee's Community Fund-West, 1754

McDonnell Douglas Foundation, 1753

McDonnell Foundation, James S., 1755

McDonough Foundation, Bernard, 1755

McDougall Charitable Trust, Ruth Camp, 1756

McEachern Charitable Trust, D. V. & Ida J., 1756

McElroy Trust, R. J., 1757

McEvoy Foundation, Mildred H., 1757

McFarland Charitable Foundation, 1758

McFawn Trust No. 2, Lois Sisler, 1758

McFeely-Rogers Foundation, 1758

McGee Foundation, 1759

McGill Manufacturing Co., 1759

McGonagle Foundation, Dextra Baldwin, 1760

McGovern Foundation, John P., 1760

McGovern Fund for the Behavioral Sciences, 1760

McGraw Foundation, 1761

McGraw Foundation, Curtis W., 1761

McGraw Foundation, Donald C., 1762

McGraw-Hill, 1762
McGraw-Hill Foundation, 1762
McGregor Foundation, Thomas and Frances, 1763
McGregor Fund, 1763
MCI Communications Corp., 1765
MCI Foundation, 1765
McIlhenny and Sons Corp, 1765
McInerny Foundation, 1765
McIntire Educational Fund, John, 1766
McIntosh Foundation, 1767
McIntyre Foundation, B. D. and Jane E., 1768
McIntyre Foundation, C. S. and Marion F., 1768
MCJ Foundation, 1768
McKaig Foundation, Lalitta Nash, 1769
McKee Foundation, Robert E. and Evelyn, 1769
McKee Poor Fund, Virginia A., 1770
McKenna Foundation, Katherine Mabis, 1770
McKenna Foundation, Philip M., 1771
McKenzie Family Foundation, Richard, 1771
McKesson Corp., 1771
McKesson Foundation, 1771
McKinsey & Co., 1772
McKnight Foundation, 1772
McKnight Foundation, Sumner T., 1773
McLean Contributionship, 1773
McLendon Educational Fund, Violet H., 1774
McLouth Steel-An Employee Owned Co., 1774
McMahon Charitable Trust Fund, Father John J., 1774
McMahon Foundation, 1775
McMannis and A. Haskell McMannis Educational Fund, William J., 1775
McMaster Foundation, Harold and Helen, 1775
McMillan Foundation, D. W., 1776
McMillan, Jr. Foundation, Bruce, 1776
McMillen Foundation, 1776
McMurray-Bennnett Foundation, 1777
McNeely Foundation, 1777
McNeil Consumer Products, 1777
McNeil, Jr. Charitable Trust, Robert L., 1777
McNutt Charitable Trust, Amy Shelton, 1778
McRae Foundation, 1778
McShain Charities, John, 1778
McVay Foundation, 1779
McWane Foundation, 1779
McWane Inc., 1779
MDU Resources Foundation, 1779

MDU Resources Group, Inc., 1779
Mead Corp., 1780
Mead Corp. Foundation, 1780
Mead Foundation, Giles W. and Elise G., 1781
Mead Fund, Nelson, 1781
Meadowood Foundation, 1782
Meadows Foundation, 1782
Mearl Corp., 1783
Mearl Foundation, 1783
Measey Foundation, Benjamin and Mary Siddons, 1783
Measurex Corp., 1784
Mebane Packaging Corp., 1784
Mechanic Foundation, Morris A., 1784
Mechanics Bank, 1785
Mechanics Bank Foundation, 1785
Medalist Industries, Inc., 1785
Medford Corp., 1785
Media General Foundation, 1785
Media General, Inc., 1785
Medina Foundation, 1786
Medtronic, 1786
Medtronic Foundation, 1786
Meek Foundation, 1788
Meenan Oil Co., Inc., 1788
MEI Diversified, Inc., 1788
Meijer Inc., 1788
Meland Outreach, 1788
Melitta North America Inc., 1789
Mellam Family Foundation, 1789
Mellen Foundation, 1789
Mellinger Educational Foundation, Edward Arthur, 1790
Mellon Bank (East) Foundation, 1793
Mellon Bank Corp., 1790
Mellon Bank Foundation, 1790
Mellon Foundation, Andrew W., 1791
Mellon Foundation, Richard King, 1792
Mellon PSFS, 1793
Mellon Stuart Construction Inc., 1794
Melohn Foundation, 1794
Melville Corp., 1794
Memorex Telex Corp., 1794
Memorial Baptist Church Trust, 2256
Memorial Foundation for Children, 1795
Memorial Foundation for the Blind, 1795
Memorial Homes for the Blind, 1795
Memphis Light Gas & Water Division, 1795
Memton Fund, 1796
Menahem Heilicher Charitable Foundation, 1221
Menasha Corp., 1796
Menasha Corporate Foundation, 1796
Mendel Foundation, 1797
Mengle Foundation, Glenn and Ruth, 1797
Menil Foundation, 1797

Mennen Co., 1798
Menschel Foundation, Robert and Joyce, 1798
Mentor Graphics, 1798
Mentor Graphics Foundation, 1798
Mercantile Bancorp, 1799
Mercantile Bank Co. Charitable Trust, 1799
Mercantile Bankshares Corp., 1800
Mercantile Stores Co., 1800
Mercedes-Benz of North America, Inc., 1800
Mercer, William M., 1800
Merchants Bancshares, 1800
Merchants Bank Foundation, 1800
Merck & Co., 1801
Merck Co. Foundation, 1801
Merck Family Fund, 1802
Merck Fund, John, 1803
Merck Human Health Division, 1803
Mercury Aircraft, 1804
Mercury Aircraft Foundation, 1804
Mercy, Jr. Foundation, Sue and Eugene, 1804
Meredith Corp., 1804
Meredith Foundation, 1805
Mericos Foundation, 1805
Meridian Bancorp, 1806
Meridian Foundation, 1806
Meridian Insurance Group Inc., 1807
Meridien Hotels, 1807
Merillat Foundation, Orville D. and Ruth A., 1807
Merit Gasoline Foundation, 1807
Merit Oil Corp., 1807
Meritor Financial Group, 1808
Merkley Charitable Trust, 1808
Merlo Foundation, Harry A., 1808
Merrick Foundation, 1808
Merrick Foundation, Robert G. and Anne M., 1809
Merrill Corp., 1809
Merrill Foundation, R. D., 1809
Merrill Lynch & Co., 1810
Merrill Lynch & Co. Foundation, 1810
Merrion Foundation, 1811
Merry-Go-Round Enterprises, Inc., 1811
Mertz Foundation, Martha, 1811
Mertz-Gilmore Foundation, Joyce, 1811
Mervyn's, 1812
Mesa Inc., 1812
Meserve Memorial Fund, Albert and Helen, 1813
Messenger Publishing Co., 1813
Messick Charitable Trust, Harry F., 1813
Messing Family Charitable Foundation, 1813

Messing Foundation, Morris M. and
    Helen F., 1814
Metal Industries, 1814
Metal Industries Foundation, 1814
Metallgesellschaft Corp., 1814
Metallurg, Inc., 1815
Metromail Corp., 1815
Metromedia Co., 1815
Metropolitan Bank & Trust Co., 1815
Metropolitan Health Council of
    Indianapolis, 1815
Metropolitan Health Foundation, 1815
Metropolitan Life Foundation, 1816
Metropolitan Life Insurance Co., 1816
Metropolitan Theatres Corp., 1817
Metropolitan Theatres Foundation, 1817
Metroquip, 1817
Mette Foundation, 1817
Mettler Instrument Corp., 1817
Mex-Am Cultural Foundation, 1818
Meyer Family Foundation, Paul J., 1818
Meyer Foundation, 1818
Meyer Foundation, Alice Kleberg
    Reynolds, 1818
Meyer Foundation, Baron de Hirsch, 1819
Meyer Foundation, Bert and Mary, 1819
Meyer Foundation, Eugene and Agnes E.,
    1820
Meyer Foundation, George C., 1821
Meyer Foundation, Robert R., 1821
Meyer Fund, Milton and Sophie, 1822
Meyer Memorial Foundation, Aaron and
    Rachel, 1822
Meyer Memorial Trust, 1823
Meyer Steinberg Foundation, 2553
Meyer, Inc., Fred, 1822
Meyer-Ceco Foundation, 464
Meyerhoff Foundation, Lyn P., 1824
Meyerhoff Fund, Joseph, 1824
MFA Foundation, 1852
MGIC Investment Corp., 1824
Miami Corp., 1825
Michael Foundation, Herbert I. and Elsa
    B., 1825
Michael-Walters Industries, 1825
Michael-Walters Industries Foundation,
    1825
Michaels Scholarship Fund, Frank J., 1826
MichCon Foundation, 1827
Michelin North America, 1826
Michigan Bell Telephone Co., 1826
Michigan Consolidated Gas Co., 1827
Michigan Gas Utilities, 1827
Michigan Health Care & Research
    Foundation, 305
Michigan Mutual Insurance Corp., 1828
Michigan National Corp., 1828
Michigan Wheel Corp., 1828

Microdot, Inc., 1828
MicroSim Corp., 1829
Microsoft Corp., 1829
Mid-America Dairymen, 1829
Mid-Continent Supply Co., 1829
Mid-Iowa Health Foundation, 1830
Mida Foundation, 1830
MidAmerica Radio Co., 1830
Midas International Corp., 1830
MidCon Corp., 1830
Middendorf Foundation, 1831
Middle South Utilities, 1831
Middlesex Mutual Assurance Co., 1831
Middleton Fund, Kate Kinloch, 1831
Midland Co., 1831
Midland Montagu, 1832
Midland Mutual Life Insurance Co., 1832
Midlantic Banks, Inc., 1832
Midmark Corp., 1832
Midmark Foundation, 1832
Midway Airlines, 1832
Midwest Gas Co., 1833
Midwest Resources, 1833
Mielke Family Foundation, 1833
Mifflin Memorial Fund, George H. and
    Jane A., 1834
Milbank Foundation, Dunlevy, 1834
Miles Inc., 1834
Miles Inc. Foundation, 1834
Miles Inc., Diagnostic Division, 1835
Miles Inc., Pharmaceutical Division, 1835
Milken Family Foundation, 436
Milken Family Medical Foundation, 1835
Milken Foundation, L. and S., 1836
Milken Institute for Job and Capital
    Formation, 1836
Mill-Rose Co., 1836
Mill-Rose Foundation, 1836
Millard Charitable Trust, Adah K., 1837
Millbrook Tribute Garden, 1837
Miller & Co., 1839
Miller Brewing Co., 1837
Miller Brewing Company/California, 1838
Miller Brewing Company/Georgia, 1838
Miller Brewing Company/New York, 1838
Miller Brewing Company/North Carolina,
    1838
Miller Brewing Company/Ohio, 1838
Miller Brewing Company/Texas, 1838
Miller Charitable Foundation, C. John and
    Reva, 1838
Miller Charitable Foundation, Howard E.
    and Nell E., 1839
Miller Charitable Trust, Lewis N., 1839
Miller Foundation, 1840
Miller Foundation, Earl B. and Loraine
    H., 1840
Miller Foundation, Steve J., 1840

Miller Fund, Kathryn and Gilbert, 1841
Miller Inc., Herman, 1841
Miller Memorial Trust, George Lee, 1841
Miller-Mellor Association, 1841
Millhollon Educational Trust Estate,
    Nettie, 1842
Milliken & Co., 1842
Milliken Foundation, 1842
Milliken Foundation, Agnes G., 1843
Million Memorial Park Trust, E. C., 1843
Millipore Corp., 1843
Millipore Foundation, 1843
Millis Foundation, James H. and Jesse E.,
    1844
Mills Charitable Foundation, Henry L.
    and Kathryn, 1844
Mills Foundation, Ralph E., 1844
Mills Fund, Frances Goll, 1844
Millstein Charitable Foundation, 1845
Millstone Foundation, 1845
Milstein Family Foundation, 1845
Milton Bradley Co., 1846
Milton Gordon Foundation, 1846
Milwaukee Golf Development Co., 1846
Mine Safety Appliances Co., 1846
Mine Safety Appliances Co. Charitable
    Trust, 1846
Mineral Trust, 1847
Mingenback Foundation, Julia J., 1847
Miniger Memorial Foundation, Clement
    O., 1847
Minnegasco, 1848
Minnesota Foundation, 1848
Minnesota Mutual Foundation, 1849
Minnesota Mutual Life Insurance Co.,
    1849
Minnesota Power & Light Co., 1849
Minnetrista Cultural Foundation, 1850
Minolta Corp., 1850
Minster Machine Co., 1850
Minster Machine Co. Foundation, 1850
Mirage Casino-Hotel, 1850
Mirapaul Foundation, 1851
Misco Charitable Trust, 1851
Misco Industries, 1851
Mississippi Chemical Corp., 1851
Mississippi Power & Light Co., 1852
Mississippi Power Co., 1851
Mississippi Power Foundation, 1851
Missouri Farmers Association, 1852
Missouri Public Service, 1853
Mitchell Energy & Development Corp.,
    1853
Mitchell Family Foundation, Bernard and
    Marjorie, 1853
Mitchell Family Foundation, Edward D.
    and Anna, 1854
Mitchell Foundation, 1854

Mitchell, Jr. Trust, Oscar, 1855
Mitrani Family Foundation, 1855
Mitre Corp., 1855
Mitsubishi Electric America, 1855
Mitsubishi Electric America Foundation, 1855
Mitsubishi Heavy Industries America, 1857
Mitsubishi International Corp., 1857
Mitsubishi Kasei America, 1857
Mitsubishi Motor Sales of America, Inc., 1857
Mitsubishi Semiconductor America, Inc. Funds, 1858
Mitsui & Co. (U.S.A.), 1858
Mitsui USA Foundation, 1858
MNC Financial, 1859
MNC Financial Foundation, 1859
Mnuchin Foundation, 1859
Mobil Foundation, 1860
Mobil Oil Corp., 1860
Mobility Foundation, 1861
Model Foundation, Leo, 1861
Modern Maid Food Products, Inc., 1861
Modglin Family Foundation, 1861
Mohasco Corp., 1862
Mohasco Memorial Fund, 1862
Molex, Inc., 1862
Monadnock Paper Mills, 1862
Monaghan Charitable Trust, Rose, 1862
Monarch Machine Tool Co., 1863
Monarch Machine Tool Co. Foundation, 1863
Moncrief Foundation, William A. and Elizabeth B., 1863
Monell Foundation, Ambrose, 1863
Monfort Charitable Foundation, 1864
Monfort of Colorado, Inc., 1864
Monroe Auto Equipment Co., 1865
Monroe Auto Equipment Foundation Trust, 1865
Monroe Foundation (1976), J. Edgar, 1865
Monroe-Brown Foundation, 1865
Monsanto Co., 1866
Monsanto Fund, 1866
Montana Power Co., 1867
Monterey Bay Aquarium Foundation, 1868
Montgomery Elevator Co., 1868
Montgomery Elevator Co. Charitable Trust, 1868
Montgomery Foundation, 1868
Montgomery Street Foundation, 1868
Montgomery Ward & Co., 1869
Montgomery Ward Foundation, 1869
Monticello College Foundation, 1870
Moody Foundation, 1870
Moog Automotive, Inc., 1871

Moog, Inc., 1871
Mooney Chemicals, 1871
Moore & Co., Benjamin, 1872
Moore & Sons Foundation, B.C., 1876
Moore & Sons, B.C., 1876
Moore Business Forms, Inc., 1872
Moore Charitable Foundation, Marjorie, 1872
Moore Educational Foundation, Benjamine, 1872
Moore Family Foundation, 1872
Moore Foundation, 1873
Moore Foundation, Alfred, 1379
Moore Foundation, C. F., 1873
Moore Foundation, Edward S., 1873
Moore Foundation, Martha G., 1874
Moore Foundation, O. L., 1874
Moore Foundation, Roy C., 1875
Moore McCormack Resources, 1875
Moore Medical Corp., 1875
Moore Memorial Foundation, James Starr, 1875
Moore, Costello & Hart, 1872
Moores Foundation, 1876
Moores Foundation, Harry C., 1876
Moorman Co. Fund, 1877
Moorman Manufacturing Co., 1877
Moosehead Manufacturing Co., 1877
Moosehead Manufacturing Co. Trust, 1877
Mor-Flo Industries, Inc., 1878
Morania Foundation, 1878
Morehead Foundation, John Motley, 1878
Morgan and Samuel Tate Morgan, Jr. Foundation, Marietta McNeil, 1878
Morgan Charitable Residual Trust, W. and E., 1879
Morgan City Fund, 2931
Morgan Construction Co., 1879
Morgan Foundation, Burton D., 1879
Morgan Foundation, Louie R. and Gertrude, 1880
Morgan Stanley & Co., 1880
Morgan Stanley Foundation, 1880
Morgan Trust for Charity, Religion, and Education, 1881
Morgan-Worcester, Inc., 1879
Morgenstern Foundation, Morris, 1881
Moriah Fund, 1882
Morley Brothers Foundation, 1882
MorningStar Foods, 1882
Morrill Charitable Foundation, 1883
Morris Charitable Foundation, E. A., 1883
Morris Charitable Trust, Charles M., 1883
Morris Foundation, 1884
Morris Foundation, Margaret T., 1884
Morris Foundation, Norman M., 1884

Morris Foundation, William T., 1885
Morris Joseloff Foundation, 1524
Morrison Charitable Trust, Pauline A. and George R., 1885
Morrison Foundation, Harry W., 1886
Morrison Knudsen Corp. Foundation Inc., 1886
Morrison Trust, Louise L., 1887
Morrison, Inc., 1885
Morrison-Knudsen Corp., 1886
Morristown Casting Support Division, 1887
Morse Foundation, Richard P. and Claire W., 1887
Morse Shoe, Inc., 1888
Morse, Jr. Foundation, Enid and Lester S., 1887
Morse-Diesel International, 1887
Mortenson Co., M.A., 1888
Morton International, 1888
Morton Memorial Fund, Mark, 1889
Mosbacher, Jr. Foundation, Emil, 1889
Moses Fund, Henry and Lucy, 1889
Mosher Foundation, Samuel B., 1890
Mosinee Paper Corp., 1890
Mosinee Paper Corp. Foundation, 1890
Moskowitz Foundation, Irving I., 1891
Moss Charitable Trust, Finis M., 1891
Moss Foundation, 1892
Moss Foundation, Harry S., 1892
Moss Heart Trust, Harry S., 1892
Mostazafan Foundation of New York, 30
Mostyn Foundation, 1892
Motch Corp., 1893
Motch Corp. Foundation, 1893
Motorola, 1893
Motorola Foundation, 1893
Mott Charitable Trust/Spectemur Agendo, Stewart R., 1894
Mott Foundation, Charles Stewart, 1895
Mott Fund, Ruth, 1896
Motter Foundation, 1896
Motter Printing Press Co., 1896
Mount Vernon Mills, 1897
Mount Vernon Mills Foundation, 1897
MPB Corp., 1897
MPCo/Entech Foundation, 1867
Mrs. Fields Children's Health Foundation, 1897
Mrs. Fields, Inc., 1897
MSI Insurance, 1898
MSI Insurance Foundation, 1898
MTS Systems Corp., 1898
Mueller Co., 1898
Mueller Co. Foundation, 1898
Mulcahy Foundation, 1898
Mulford Foundation, Vincent, 1899
Mulford Trust, Clarence E., 1899

Mullan Foundation, Thomas F. and Clementine L., 1899
Mullen Foundation, J. K., 1900
Muller Foundation, 1900
Muller Foundation, C. John and Josephine, 1900
Mulligan Charitable Trust, Mary S., 1901
Multimedia Foundation, 1901
Multimedia, Inc., 1901
Munger Foundation, Alfred C., 1902
Munsingwear, Inc., 1902
Munson Foundation, W. B., 1902
Murata Erie North America, 1902
Murch Foundation, 1903
Murdock Charitable Trust, M. J., 1903
Murdock Development Co., 1904
Murdy Foundation, 1904
Murfee Endowment, Kathryn, 1904
Murphey Foundation, Lluella Morey, 1904
Murphy Charitable Fund, George E. and Annette Cross, 1905
Murphy Co. Foundation, G.C., 1905
Murphy Co., G.C., 1905
Murphy Foundation, 1905
Murphy Foundation, Dan, 1906
Murphy Foundation, John P., 1906
Murphy Foundation, Katherine and John, 1907
Murphy Oil Corp., 1907
Murray Foundation, 1908
Murray Ohio Manufacturing Co., 1908
Murray, Jr. Foundation, John P., 1908
Musson Charitable Foundation, R. C. and Katharine M., 1908
Muth Foundation, Peter and Mary, 1909
Mutual of America Life, 1909
Mutual of New York, 1909
Mutual of New York Foundation, 1909
Mutual of Omaha Insurance Co., 1910
Mutual Savings Life Insurance Co., 1910
Mutual Service Life Insurance Cos., 1910
Myers and Sons, D., 1910
Myra Foundation, 1910

N

N've Shalom Foundation, 1995
Nabisco Foods Group, 1911
Nabisco Foundation Trust, 1911
NACCO Industries, 1911
Nakamichi Foundation, E., 1912
Nalco Chemical Co., 1912
Nalco Foundation, 1912
Nancy Reynolds Bagley Foundation, 118
Nanney Foundation, Charles and Irene, 1913
Napier Co., 1913

Nash Foundation, 1914
Nash-Finch Co., 1913
Nashua Trust Co., 1914
Nashua Trust Co. Foundation, 1914
Nason Foundation, 1914
Nathan Berkman & Co., 1915
Nathan Foundation, 1915
National Broadcasting Co., Inc., 1915
National By-Products, 1915
National By-Products Foundation, 1915
National Car Rental System, Inc., 1916
National Center for Automated Information Retrieval, 1916
National City Bank, 1916
National City Bank of Evansville, 1917
National City Bank of Evansville Foundation, 1917
National City Bank of Indiana, 1917
National City Bank, Columbus, 1916
National City Corp., 1918
National City Corporation Charitable Foundation Trust, 1918
National Computer Systems, 1918
National Convenience Stores, Inc., 1919
National Data Corp., 1919
National Distributing Co., Inc., 1919
National Dollar Stores, Ltd., 1919
National Forge Co., 1919
National Forge Foundation, 1919
National Fuel Gas Co., 1920
National Gypsum Co., 1920
National Gypsum Foundation, 1920
National Life Charitable Trust, 1921
National Life of Vermont, 1921
National Machinery Co., 1921
National Machinery Foundation, 1921
National Manufacturing Co., 1922
National Medical Enterprises, 1922
National Metal & Steel, 1923
National Metal & Steel Foundation, 1923
National Presto Industries, 1923
National Pro-Am Youth Fund, 1924
National Semiconductor Corp., 1924
National Service Foundation, 1924
National Service Industries, 1924
National Spinning Co., 1925
National Standard Co., 1925
National Standard Foundation, 1925
National Starch & Chemical Corp., 1925
National Starch & Chemical Foundation, 1925
National Steel, 1926
National Travelers Life Co., 1926
National Travelers Life Co. Charitable Trust, 1926
National Westminster Bank New Jersey, 1926

Nationale-Nederlanden North America Corp., 1927
NationsBank Corp., 1927
NationsBank Texas, 1928
Nationwide Insurance Cos., 1928
Nationwide Insurance Foundation, 1928
Natural Heritage Foundation, 1929
Naurison Scholarship Fund, James Z., 1929
Navajo Refining Co., 1930
Navarro County Educational Foundation, 1930
Navistar Foundation, 1930
Navistar International Corp., 1930
NBD Bank, 1931
NBD Bank, N.A., 1931
NBD Charitable Trust, 1931
NBD Genesee Bank, 1932
NBD Genesee Bank Charitable Trust, 1932
NCH Corp., 1933
NCR Corp., 1933
NCR Foundation, 1933
NEBS Foundation, 1942
NEC Electronics, Inc., 1933
NEC Foundation of America, 1934
NEC Technologies, Inc., 1934
NEC USA, 1934
Needmor Fund, 1935
Neenah Foundry Co., 1935
Neenah Foundry Foundation, 1935
Neese Family Foundation, 1936
Negaunee Foundation, 1936
Neilson Foundation, George W., 1936
Neiman Marcus, 1937
Nelco Foundation, 1937
Nelco Sewing Machine Sales Corp., 1937
Nellie Mae, 1937
Nellie Mae Fund for Education, 1937
Nelson Foundation, Florence, 1938
Nelson Industries, Inc., 1938
Nepera Inc., 1938
Nerco, Inc., 1938
Nesholm Family Foundation, 1939
Nestle U.S.A. Inc., 1939
Nestle USA Foundation, 1939
Neu Foundation, Hugo and Doris, 1940
Neuberger Foundation, Roy R. and Marie S., 1940
Neutrogena Corp., 1940
Nevada Power Co., 1941
Neville Chemical Co., 1941
New & Sons, Hugo, 1947
New Balance Athletic Shoe, 1941
New Cycle Foundation, 1941
New England Aircraft Products Co., 1941
New England Biolabs Foundation, 1941
New England Business Service, 1942

New England Electric System, 1942
New England Foundation, 1942
New England Grocer Supply, 1942
New England Mutual Life Insurance Co., 1943
New England Telephone Co., 1943
New Hampshire Ball Bearings, 1944
New Hampshire Ball Bearings Foundation, 1944
New Horizon Foundation, 1944
New Jersey Bell Telephone Company, 1944
New Jersey Manufacturers Insurance Co., 1945
New Jersey National Bank, 1945
New Jersey Resources Corp., 1945
New Milford Savings Bank Foundation, 1958
New Orphan Asylum Scholarship Foundation, 1946
New Penn Motor Express, 1946
New Prospect Foundation, 1947
New Street Capital Corp., 1947
New Street Foundation, 1947
New Valley, 1948
New World Foundation, 1948
New York Foundation, 1949
New York Life Foundation, 1950
New York Life Insurance Co., 1950
New York Marine & General Insurance Co., 1951
New York Mercantile Exchange, 1951
New York Post Corp., 1951
New York Racing Association, 1951
New York State Electric & Gas Corp., 1951
New York Stock Exchange, 1952
New York Stock Exchange Foundation, 1952
New York Telephone Co., 1952
New York Times Co., 1953
New York Times Co. Foundation, 1953
New-Land Foundation, 1945
Newberg Scholarship Trust, Gust K., 2097
Newbrook Charitable Foundation, 1955
Newcombe Foundation, Charlotte W., 1955
Newell Co., 1956
Newhall Foundation, Henry Mayo, 1956
Newhall Land & Farming Co., 1956
Newhouse Foundation, Samuel I., 1957
Newhouse Publication Corp., 1957
Newman Assistance Fund, Jerome A. and Estelle R., 1957
Newman Charitable Trust, Calvin M. and Raquel H., 1958
Newman's Own, 1958
Newman's Own Foundation, 1958
Newmil Bancorp, 1958

Newmont Mining Corp., 1959
Newport News Shipbuilding & Dry Dock Co., 1959
News & Observer Publishing Co., 1960
News America Publishing Inc., 1959
Newsweek, Inc., 1960
Niagara Mohawk Power Corp., 1960
Nias Foundation, Henry, 1961
NIBCO Inc., 1961
Nichimen America, Inc., 1961
Nichols Co. Charitable Trust, 1962
Nichols Co., J.C., 1962
Nichols Farmhouse, 1962
Nichols Foundation, 1962
Nicol Scholarship Foundation, Helen Kavanagh, 1962
Nicor, Inc., 1963
Nielsen Co., A.C., 1963
Nike Inc., 1963
Nippon Life Insurance Co., 1963
Nirenberg Family Charitable Foundation, 1964
Nissan Foundation, 1964
Nissan Motor Corp. in U.S.A., 1964
NMB (USA) Inc., 1964
NMC Foundation, 1922
NMC Projects, 1938
Noble Affiliates, Inc., 1964
Noble Charitable Trust, John L. and Ethel G., 1964
Noble Foundation, Edward John, 1965
Noble Foundation, Samuel Roberts, 1966
Noble Foundation, Vivian Bilby, 1966
Noland Co., 1967
Noland Co. Foundation, 1967
Noll Foundation, 1967
Nomura Securities International, 1967
Noonan Memorial Fund under the will of Frank Noonan, Deborah
Munroe, 1967
Norcliffe Fund, 1968
Norcross Wildlife Foundation, 1968
Nord Family Foundation, 1969
Nordson Corp., 1969
Nordson Corporation Foundation, 1969
Nordstrom, Inc., 1970
Norfolk Shipbuilding & Drydock Corp., 1970
Norfolk Shipbuilding & Drydock Corp. Charitable Trust, 1970
Norfolk Southern Corp., 1971
Norfolk Southern Foundation, 1971
Norgren Foundation, Carl A., 1972
Norman Foundation, 1972
Norman Foundation, Andrew, 1973
Norman Foundation, Summers A., 1974
Norman/Nethercutt Foundation, Merle, 1974

Normandie Foundation, 1974
Norris Foundation, Dellora A. and Lester J., 1974
Norris Foundation, Kenneth T. and Eileen L., 1975
Nortek, Inc., 1975
North American Coal Corp., 1976
North American Life & Casualty Co., 1976
North American Philips Corp., 1976
North American Philips Foundation, 1976
North American Reinsurance Corp., 1977
North American Royalties, 1977
North American Royalties Welfare Fund, 1977
North Carolina Foam Foundation, 1977
North Face, The, 1978
North Shore Foundation, 1978
North Star Research Foundation, 1978
North Star Steel Co., 1978
North Star Universal Inc., 1978
Northeast Savings, FA, 1978
Northeast Utilities, 1979
Northen, Mary Moody, 1979
Northern Engraving Corp., 1980
Northern Illinois Gas Co., 1980
Northern Indiana Fuel & Light Co., 1980
Northern Indiana Fuel & Light Co. Fund & Trust, 1980
Northern Indiana Public Service Co., 1980
Northern Star Foundation, 1981
Northern States Power Co., 1981
Northern Telecom Inc., 1982
Northern Trust Co., 1982
Northern Trust Co. Charitable Trust, 1982
Northern Virginia Natural Gas, 1983
NorthPark National Bank, 1983
Northrop Corp., 1983
Northwest Airlines, Inc., 1984
Northwest Area Foundation, 1984
Northwest Natural Gas Co., 1985
Northwest Pipeline Corp., 1986
Northwest Publishing Co. — Portland, 1986
Northwestern Golf Co., 1986
Northwestern National Insurance Foundation, 1986
Northwestern National Insurance Group, 1986
Northwestern National Life Foundation, 1986
Northwestern National Life Insurance Co., 1986
Northwestern Steel & Wire Co., 1987
Norton & Co., W.W., 1988
Norton Co., 1987
Norton Co. Foundation, 1987
Norton Foundation Inc., 1988

Norton Memorial Corporation, Geraldi, 1989

Norton Simon Inc., 1989

Norwest Bank Nebraska, 1989

Norwest Corp., 1990

Norwest Foundation, 1990

Novell Inc., 1991

Novotny Charitable Trust, Yetta Deitch, 1991

Noxell Foundation, 2184

Noyes Foundation, Jessie Smith, 1991

Noyes, Jr. Memorial Foundation, Nicholas H., 1993

NRC, Inc., 1993

Nucor Corp., 1993

Nucor Foundation, 1993

NUI Corp., 1994

Number Ten Foundation, 1994

NuTone Inc., 1994

NutraSweet Co., 1994

NutraSweet Co. Charitable Trust, 1994

Nutri/System Inc., 1995

Nuveen & Co., Inc., John, 1995

NVF Co., 1995

NYMEX Charitable Foundation, 1951

NYNEX Corp., 1996

NYNEX Foundation, 1996

O

O'Bleness Foundation, Charles G., 2000

O'Brien Foundation, Alice M., 2000

O'Brien Foundation, Cornelius and Anna Cook, 2000

O'Brien Foundation, James W., 2001

O'Connor Co., 2003

O'Connor Co.-Piller Foundation, 2003

O'Connor Foundation, A. Lindsay and Olive B., 2003

O'Connor Foundation, Kathryn, 2004

O'Connor Foundation, Magee, 2004

O'Donnell Foundation, 2006

O'Fallon Trust, Martin J. and Mary Anne, 2007

O'Neil Foundation, Casey Albert T., 2026

O'Neil Foundation, Cyril F. and Marie E., 2027

O'Neil Foundation, M. G., 2027

O'Neil Foundation, W., 2027

O'Neill Charitable Corporation, F. J., 2028

O'Neill Foundation, William J. and Dorothy K., 2028

O'Quinn Foundation, John M. and Nancy C., 2031

O'Shaughnessy Foundation, I. A., 2038

O'Sullivan Children Foundation, 2041

O'Sullivan Corp., 2041

O'Toole Foundation, Theresa and Edward, 2041

Oak Foundation U.S.A., 1997

Oak Hall Foundation, 1997

Oak Hall, Inc., 1997

Oak Industries, 1997

Oakite Products, 1997

Oaklawn Foundation, 1997

Oakleaf Foundation, 1998

Oakley Foundation, Hollie and Anna, 1998

Oakley-Lindsay Foundation of Quincy Newspapers & Quincy Broadcasting Co., 2205

Obayashi America Corp., 1998

Oberkotter Family Foundation, 1999

Oberlaender Foundation, Gustav, 1999

Obernauer Foundation, 1999

Occidental Oil & Gas Charitable Foundation, 2001

Occidental Oil & Gas Corp., 2001

Occidental Petroleum Charitable Foundation, 2002

Occidental Petroleum Corp., 2002

Ocean Spray Cranberries, 2002

Oceanic Cablevision Foundation, 2003

OCRI Foundation, 2005

Odell and Helen Pfeiffer Odell Fund, Robert Stewart, 2005

Odessa Trading Co., 2005

Odessa Trading Co. Educational Trust, 2005

Odyssey Partners, 2006

Odyssey Partners Foundation, 2006

Oestreicher Foundation, Sylvan and Ann, 2006

Offield Family Foundation, 2007

Offshore Logistics, 2008

Ogden College Fund, 2008

Ogden Corp., 2008

Ogden Foundation, Ralph E., 2008

Ogilvy & Mather Worldwide, 2009

Ogilvy Foundation, 2009

Ogle Foundation, Paul, 2009

Oglebay Norton Co., 2009

Oglebay Norton Foundation, 2009

Ohio Bell Foundation, 2010

Ohio Bell Telephone Co., 2010

Ohio Casualty Corp., 2011

Ohio Citizens Bank, 2011

Ohio Citizens Bank Minority Scholarship Trust Fund, 2011

Ohio Edison Corp., 2011

Ohio National Foundation, 2011

Ohio National Life Insurance Co., 2011

Ohio Road Paving Co., 2012

Ohio Savings Bank, 2012

Ohio Savings Charitable Foundation, 2012

Ohio Valley Foundation, 2012

Ohl, Jr. Trust, George A., 2013

Ohrstrom Foundation, 2013

Oki America Inc., 2014

Oklahoma Gas & Electric Co., 2014

Oklahoma Gas & Electric Co. Foundation, 2014

Oklahoman Foundation, 2015

Okonite Co., 2015

Old American Insurance Co., 2015

Old Dominion Box Co., 2015

Old Dominion Box Co. Foundation, 2015

Old Kent Bank & Trust Co., 2016

Old National Bank Charitable Trust, 2016

Old National Bank in Evansville, 2016

Old Republic International Corp., 2016

Oldham Little Church Foundation, 2017

Oleson Foundation, 2017

Olin Charitable Trust, John M., 2017

Olin Corp., 2018

Olin Corp. Charitable Trust, 2018

Olin Foundation, F. W., 2018

Olin Foundation, John M., 2019

Olin Foundation, Spencer T. and Ann W., 2020

Olive Bridge Fund, 2021

Oliver Memorial Trust Foundation, 2021

Olivetti Foundation, 2022

Olivetti Office USA, Inc., 2022

Olmsted Foundation, George and Carol, 2022

Olsson Memorial Foundation, Elis, 2023

Olsten Corp., 2023

Olympia Brewing Co., 2023

Olympia Brewing Co. Employees Beneficial Trust, 2023

Olympus Corp., 2024

Omaha National Bank Charitable Trust, 908

OMC Foundation, 2042

Omega World Travel, 2024

OMNI Construction, 2024

Onan Corp., 2024

Onan Family Foundation, 2024

One Valley Bank Foundation, 2025

One Valley Bank, N.A., 2025

Oneida Ltd., 2026

ONEOK Inc., 2029

Ontario Corp., 2029

Ontario Corporation Foundation, 2029

Open Society Fund, 2029

Openaka Corp., 2030

Oppenheimer & Co., Inc., 2030

Oppenheimer and Flora Oppenheimer Haas Trust, Leo, 2030

Oppenheimer Family Foundation, 2030

Oppenheimer Management Corp., 2031

Oppenstein Brothers Foundation, 2031

Physicians Mutual Insurance Co. Foundation, 2126

Piankova Foundation, Tatiana, 2127

Pic 'N' Save Corp., 2127

Pick Charitable Trust, Melitta S., 2127

Pick, Jr. Fund, Albert, 2127

Picker International, 2128

Pickering Industries, 2128

Pickett and Hatcher Educational Fund, 2128

Pickford Foundation, Mary, 2129

Picower Foundation, Jeffrey M. and Barbara, 2129

Piedmont Health Care Foundation, 2129

Piedmont Natural Gas Co., Inc., 2130

Pieper Electric, 2130

Pieperpower Foundation, 2130

Pier 1 Imports, Inc., 2130

Pierce Charitable Trust, Harold Whitworth, 2130

Piggly Wiggly Southern, 2131

Piggly Wiggly Southern Foundation, 2131

Pilgrim Foundation, 2131

Pilgrim Industries, 2131

Pilgrim's Pride Corp., 2131

Pillsbury Co., 2131

Pillsbury Foundation, 2132

Pilot Trust, 2132

Pincus Family Fund, 2133

Pine Tree Foundation, 2133

Pines Bridge Foundation, 2133

Pinewood Foundation, 2134

Pineywoods Foundation, 2134

Pinkerton Foundation, 2135

Pinkerton Tobacco Co., 2135

Pioneer Concrete of America Inc., 2136

Pioneer Electronics (USA) Inc., 2136

Pioneer Fund, 2136

Pioneer Group, 2137

Pioneer Hi-Bred International, 2137

Pioneer Trust Bank, NA, 2138

Pioneer Trust Bank, NA, Foundation, 2138

Piper Foundation, 2138

Piper Foundation, Minnie Stevens, 2138

Piper Jaffray Cos., 2139

Pirelli Armstrong Foundation, 2139

Pirelli Armstrong Tire Corp., 2139

Pitney Bowes, 2140

Piton Foundation, 2140

Pitt-Des Moines Inc., 2141

Pitts Foundation, William H. and Lula E., 2141

Pittsburgh & Midway Coal Mining Co., 2142

Pittsburgh Child Guidance Foundation, 2142

Pittsburgh National Bank, 2142

Pittsburgh National Bank Foundation, 2142

Pittsburgh-Des Moines Inc. Charitable Trust, 2141

Pittston Co., 2143

Pittulloch Foundation, 2143

Pittway Corp., 2144

Pittway Corp. Charitable Foundation, 2144

Pitzman Fund, 2144

Pizza Hut, 2145

PK Lumber Co., 2145

Placid Oil Co., 2145

Plankenhorn Foundation, Harry, 2145

Planning Research Corp., 2145

Plant Memorial Fund, Henry B., 2146

Plante & Moran, CPAs, 2146

Plantronics, Inc., 2146

Plaster Foundation, Robert W., 2146

Plastics Engineering Co., 2146

Playboy Enterprises, Inc., 2147

Playboy Foundation, 2147

Plitt Southern Theatres, 2147

Plitt Southern Theatres, Inc., Employees Fund, 2147

Plough Foundation, 2148

Plumsock Fund, 2148

Pluta Family Foundation, 2148

Ply-Gem Industries, Inc., 2149

Plym Foundation, 2149

PMA Foundation, 2149

PMA Industries, 2149

PMC Inc., 2149

PMI Food Equipment Group Inc., 2150

PNC Bank, 2150

PNM Foundation, 2193

Pogo Producing Co., 2151

Poindexter Foundation, 2151

Poinsettia Foundation, Paul and Magdalena Ecke, 2151

Polaris Industries, LP, 2151

Polaroid Corp., 2151

Polaroid Foundation, 2151

Polinger Foundation, Howard and Geraldine, 2153

Polinsky-Rivkin Family Foundation, 2153

Polk & Co., R.L., 2153

Polk Foundation, 2153

Pollock Company Foundation, William B., 2154

Pollock-Krasner Foundation, 2154

Pollybill Foundation, 2154

Polychrome Corp., 2155

Poncin Scholarship Fund, 2155

Ponderosa, Inc., 2155

Pool Energy Services Co., 2155

Poole & Kent Co., 2156

Poole and Kent Foundation, 2156

Poole Equipment Co., Gregory, 2155

Poorvu Foundation, William and Lia, 2156

Pope & Talbot, Inc., 2157

Pope Family Foundation, Blanche & Edker, 2156

Pope Foundation, 2156

Pope Foundation, Lois B., 2157

Porsche Cars North America, Inc., 2157

Porsche Foundation, 2157

Portec, Inc., 2158

Porter Foundation, Mrs. Cheever, 2158

Porter Paint Co., 2158

Porter Paint Foundation, 2158

Porter Testamentary Trust, James Hyde, 2158

Portland Food Products Co., 2159

Portland General Electric Co., 2159

Portsmouth General Hospital Foundation, 2159

Portsmouth Hospital Foundation, 956

Posey Trust, Addison, 2160

Posnack Family Foundation of Hollywood, 2160

Post & Courier Foundation, 838

Post Foundation of D.C., Marjorie Merriweather, 2160

Potlatch Corp., 2161

Potlatch Foundation for Higher Education/Potlatch Foundation II, 2161

Potomac Edison Co., 2161

Potomac Electric Power Co., 2162

Potomac Foundation, 223

Pott Foundation, Herman T. and Phenie R., 2162

Pott Foundation, Robert and Elaine, 2163

Potter Foundation, Justin and Valere, 2163

Potts and Sibley Foundation, 2163

Potts Memorial Foundation, 2164

Pottstown Mercury, 2164

Pottstown Mercury Foundation, 2164

Powell Co. Foundation, William, 2164

Powell Co., William, 2164

Powell Family Foundation, 2165

Powell Foundation, Charles Lee, 2165

Powers Foundation, 2166

Powers Higher Educational Fund, Edward W. and Alice R., 2166

Poynter Fund, 2166

PPG Industries, 2166

PPG Industries Foundation, 2166

PQ Corp., 2167

PQ Corp. Foundation, 2167

Prairie Foundation, 2168

Prange Co. Fund, H. C., 2168

Prange Co., H. C., 2168

Pratt & Lambert, Inc., 2168

Pratt Memorial Fund, 2168

Precision Castparts Corp., 2169
Precision Rubber Products, 2169
Precision Rubber Products Foundation, 2169
Preferred Risk Mutual Insurance Co., 2169
Preformed Line Products Co., 2169
Premark International, 2170
Premier Bank, 2170
Premier Bank Lafayette, 2170
Premier Bank of South Louisiana, 2170
Premier Dental Products Co., 2170
Premier Foundation, 2170
Premier Industrial Corp., 2171
Premier Industrial Foundation, 2171
Prentice Foundation, Abra, 2172
Prentis Family Foundation, Meyer and Anna, 2172
Prentiss Foundation, Elisabeth Severance, 2172
Presley Cos., 2173
Presser Foundation, 2173
Presto Foundation, 1923
Preston Trucking Co., Inc., 2174
Preston Trust, Evelyn W., 2174
Preuss Foundation, 2174
Preyer Fund, Mary Norris, 2174
PRI Foundation, 276
Price Associates Foundation, T. Rowe, 2175
Price Associates, T. Rowe, 2175
Price Company, 2176
Price Educational Foundation, Herschel C., 2176
Price Foundation, Louis and Harold, 2176
Price Foundation, Lucien B. and Katherine E., 2176
Price Waterhouse Foundation, 2177
Price Waterhouse-U.S., 2177
Prickett Fund, Lynn R. and Karl E., 2177
Priddy Foundation, 2178
Primark Corp., 2178
Prime Computer, Inc., 2178
Primerica Corp., 2178
Primerica Financial Services, 2179
Primerica Foundation, 2178
PriMerit F.S.B., 2179
Prince Corp., 2180
Prince Foundation, 2180
Prince Manufacturing, Inc., 2180
Prince Trust, Abbie Norman, 2180
Principal Financial Group, 2181
Principal Financial Group Foundation, 2181
Printpack, Inc., 2181
Pritchard Charitable Trust, William E. and Maude S., 2182
Pritzker Foundation, 2182
Pro-line Corp., 2183

Procter & Gamble Co., 2183
Procter & Gamble Cosmetic & Fragrance Products, 2184
Procter & Gamble Fund, 2183
Procter & Gamble/Noxell Foundation, 2184
Proctor Trust, Mortimer R., 2184
Producers Livestock Marketing Association, 2185
Progressive Corp., 2185
Promus Cos., 2185
Property Capital Trust, 2186
Propp Sons Fund, Morris and Anna, 2186
Prospect Hill Foundation, 2186
Protherapy of America, 2187
Prouty Foundation, Olive Higgins, 2187
Providence Energy Corp., 2188
Providence Journal Charitable Foundation, 2188
Providence Journal Company, 2188
Provident Life & Accident Insurance Co., 2189
Provident Mutual Life Insurance Co. of Philadelphia, 2189
Provigo Corp. Inc., 2189
Prudential Foundation, 2190
Prudential Insurance Co. of America, 2190
Prudential Securities Foundation, 2190
Prudential-Bache Securities, 2190
PSI Energy, 2192
PSI Foundation, 2192
Psychists, 2192
Public Service Co. of Colorado, 2193
Public Service Co. of New Mexico, 2193
Public Service Co. of Oklahoma, 2194
Public Service Electric & Gas Co., 2194
Public Welfare Foundation, 2195
Publicker Industries, Inc., 2196
Publix Supermarkets, 2196
Puett Foundation, Nelson, 2196
Puget Sound National Bank, 2196
Puget Sound Power & Light Co., 2196
Pukall Lumber, 2197
Pukall Lumber Foundation, 2197
Pulitzer Publishing Co., 2198
Pulitzer Publishing Co. Foundation, 2198
Pullman Educational Foundation, George M., 2198
Puterbaugh Foundation, 2199
Putnam Foundation, 2199
Putnam Prize Fund for the Promotion of Scholarship, William Lowell, 2200
Pyramid Foundation, 2200
Pyramid Technology Corp., 2200

Q

Qantas Airways Ltd., 2200
Quabaug Corp., 2200
Quabaug Corp. Charitable Foundation, 2200
Quad City Osteopathic Foundation, 2201
Quaker Chemical Corp., 2201
Quaker Chemical Foundation, 2201
Quaker Hill Foundation, 2202
Quaker Oats Co., 2202
Quaker Oats Foundation, 2202
Quaker State Corp., 2203
Quality Inn International, 2203
Quality Metal Finishing Foundation, 2203
Quanex Corp., 2204
Quanex Foundation, 2204
Quantum Chemical Corp., 2204
Quebecor Printing (USA) Inc., 2205
Quest for Truth Foundation, 2205
Questar Corp., 2205
Quincy Newspapers, 2205
Quinlan Foundation, Elizabeth C., 2206
Quivey-Bay State Foundation, 2206

R

R&B Tool Co., 2207
R. Dee Hubbard Foundation, 1300
R. F. Foundation, 2207
R. L. Stowe Mills Inc., 2207
R. P. Foundation, 2207
Rabb Charitable Foundation, Sidney and Esther, 2208
Rabb Charitable Trust, Sidney R., 2208
Rabb Foundation, Harry W., 2209
Racal-Milgo, 2209
Racetrac Petroleum, 2209
Rachal Foundation, Ed, 2209
Radiator Specialty Co., 2210
Radin Foundation, 2210
Ragan Charitable Foundation, Carolyn King, 2211
Ragen, Jr. Memorial Fund Trust No. 1, James M., 2211
Rahr Foundation, 2211
Rahr Malting Co., 2211
Rainwater Charitable Foundation, 2212
Raker Foundation, M. E., 2212
Raleigh Linen Service/National Distributing Co., 2212
Rales and Ruth Rales Foundation, Norman R., 2212
Raley's, 2213
Ralston Purina Co., 2213
Ralston Purina Trust Fund, 2213

Ramapo Trust, 2214
Ramlose Foundation, George A., 2215
Ranco, Inc., 2215
Rand McNally and Co., 2215
Rand McNally Foundation, 2215
Rand-Whitney Packaging-Delmar Corp., 2215
Randa, 2215
Randleigh Foundation Trust, 2216
Randolph Foundation, 2216
Random House Inc., 2217
Rangeley Educational Trust, 2217
Rankin and Elizabeth Forbes Rankin Trust, William, 2217
Ranney Foundation, P. K., 2217
Ransburg Corp., 2218
Ransom Fidelity Company, 2218
Raper Foundation, Tom, 2218
Rapp Foundation, Robert Glenn, 2218
Raskin Foundation, Hirsch and Braine, 2219
Raskob Foundation for Catholic Activities, 2219
Raskob Foundation, Bill, 2219
Rasmussen Foundation, 2220
Ratner Foundation, Milton M., 2221
Ratshesky Foundation, A. C., 2221
Rauch Foundation, 2221
Ravenswood Aluminum Corp., 2222
Ray Foundation, 2222
Raychem Corp., 2222
Raymark Corp., 2222
Raymond Corp., 2222
Raymond Educational Foundation, 2223
Raymond Foundation, 2222
Rayovac Corp., 2223
Raytheon Co., 2224
Raytheon Engineers & Constructors, 2224
RB&W Corp., 2225
Read Foundation, Charles L., 2225
Reade Industrial Fund, 2225
Reader's Digest Association, 2225
Reader's Digest Foundation, 2225
Reading & Bates Corp., 2226
Reasoner, Davis & Fox, 2226
Rebsamen Companies, Inc., 2226
Rebsamen Fund, 2226
Reckitt & Colman, 2227
Recognition Equipment, 2227
Red Devil, 2227
Red Devil Foundation, 2227
Red Food Stores, Inc., 2228
Red Wing Shoe Co., 2228
Red Wing Shoe Co. Foundation, 2228
Redfield Foundation, Nell J., 2228
Redies Foundation, Edward F., 2207
Redlands Federal Bank, 2229
Redman Foundation, 2229

Redman Industries, 2229
Reebok Foundation, 2229
Reebok International Ltd., 2229
Reed Foundation, 2230
Reed Foundation, Philip D., 2231
Reed Publishing USA, 2231
Reedman Car-Truck World Center, 2231
Reedman FCS Foundation, 2231
Reell Precision Manufacturing, 2231
Reeves Foundation, 2232
Reflection Riding, 2232
Reflector Hardware Corp., 2232
Regenstein Foundation, 2232
Reginald Brothers Wurzburg Foundation, 2923
Regis Corp., 2233
Regis Foundation, 2233
REI-Recreational Equipment, Inc., 2233
Reich & Tang L.P., 2234
Reicher Foundation, Anne & Harry J., 2234
Reichhold Chemicals, Inc., 2234
Reidler Foundation, 2235
Reilly Foundation, 2235
Reilly Industries, 2235
Reily & Co., William B., 2236
Reily Foundation, 2236
Reinberger Foundation, 2236
Reinghardt Foundation, Albert, 2237
Reinhart Family Foundation, D.B., 2237
Reinhart Institutional Foods, 2237
Reinhold Foundation, Paul E. and Ida Klare, 2237
Reisman Charitable Trust, George C. and Evelyn R., 2238
Reiss Coal Co. Scholarship Fund Trust, C., 2238
Reiss Coal Co., C., 2238
Relations Foundation, 2238
Reliable Life Insurance Co., 2239
Reliance Electric Co., 2239
Reliance Electric Co. Charitable, Scientific & Educational Trust, 2239
Reliance Group Holdings, Inc., 2240
Reliance Insurance Cos., 2240
Remmele Engineering, Inc., 2240
Rennebohm Foundation, Oscar, 2240
Renner Foundation, 2241
Rennie Scholarship Fund, Waldo E., 2241
Replogle Foundation, Luther I., 2241
Republic Automotive Parts, Inc., 2241
Republic Engineered Steels, 2242
Republic Financial Services, Inc., 2242
Republic New York Corp., 2242
Research Corporation, 2242
Research Institute of America, 2244
Research-Cottrell Inc., 2244
Resnick Foundation, Jack and Pearl, 2244

Restaurant Associates, Inc., 2244
Retirement Research Foundation, 2244
Reviva Labs, 2246
Revlon, 2246
Revlon Foundation, 2246
Revson Foundation, Charles H., 2246
Rexene Products Co., 2247
Rexford Fund, 2375
Rexham Corp. Foundation, 2248
Rexham Inc., 2248
Reynolds & Reynolds Co., 2254
Reynolds & Reynolds Company Foundation, 2254
Reynolds Charitable Trust, Kate B., 2248
Reynolds Foundation, Christopher, 2249
Reynolds Foundation, Donald W., 2249
Reynolds Foundation, Edgar, 2250
Reynolds Foundation, Eleanor T., 2250
Reynolds Foundation, J. B., 2251
Reynolds Foundation, Richard S., 2251
Reynolds Foundation, Z. Smith, 2252
Reynolds Metals Co., 2253
Reynolds Metals Co. Foundation, 2253
RGK Foundation, 2255
Rhoades Fund, Otto L. and Hazel E., 2256
Rhode Island Hospital Trust, 2256
Rhode Island Hospital Trust National Bank, 2256
Rhodebeck Charitable Trust, 2256
Rhoden Charitable Foundation, Elmer C., 2257
Rhone-Poulenc Inc., 2257
Rhone-Poulenc Rorer, 2257
Rice Charitable Foundation, Albert W., 2258
Rice Family Foundation, Jacob and Sophie, 2258
Rice Foundation, 2258
Rice Foundation, Ethel and Raymond F., 2259
Rice Foundation, Helen Steiner, 2259
Riceland Foods, Inc., 2260
Rich Co., F.D., 2260
Rich Foundation, 2260
Rich Foundation, Inc., 2260
Rich Products Corp., 2260
Richardson Benevolent Foundation, C. E., 2261
Richardson Charitable Trust, Anne S., 2261
Richardson County Bank and Trust Co., 2262
Richardson County Bank and Trust Co. Centennial Trust, 2262
Richardson Foundation, Frank E. and Nancy M., 2262
Richardson Foundation, Sid W., 2262
Richardson Foundation, Smith, 2263

Rosenwald Family Fund, William, 2313
Ross Corp., 2313
Ross Foundation, 23132314
Ross Foundation, Arthur, 2315
Ross Foundation, Lyn & George M., 2315
Ross Foundation, Walter G., 2316
Ross Laboratories, 2316
Ross Memorial Foundation, Will, 2316
Ross, Johnston & Kersting, 2316
Roswell Messing, Jr., Charitable
   Foundation, 1813
Roth Family Foundation, 2317
Roth Foundation, 2317
Roth Foundation, Louis T., 2317
Rothschild Foundation, Hulda B. and
   Maurice L., 2318
Rotterman Trust, Helen L. and Marie F.,
   2318
Rouge Steel Co., 2318
Roundy's Inc., 2318
Rouse Co., 2319
Rouse Co. Foundation, 2319
Rowan Cos., Inc., 2319
Rowland Foundation, 2319
Royal Crown Cos., Inc., 2320
Royal Group Inc., 2320
Royal Insurance Co. of America, 2321
Royal Insurance Foundation, 2320
Royston Manufacturing Corp., 2321
RPM, Inc., 2321
RSR Corp., 2321
RTM, 2321
RTM Foundation, 2321
Ruan Foundation Trust, John, 2322
Rubbermaid, 2322
Rubbermaid Foundation, 2322
Rubenstein Charitable Foundation,
   Lawrence J. and Anne, 2323
Rubenstein Foundation, Philip, 2323
Rubin Family Fund, Cele H. and William
   B., 2323
Rubin Foundation, Rob E. & Judith O.,
   2324
Rubin Foundation, Samuel, 2324
Rubinstein Foundation, Helena, 2325
Ruddick Corp., 2326
Rudin Foundation, 2326
Rudin Foundation, Louis and Rachel,
   2327
Rudin Foundation, Samuel and May, 2327
Rudy, Jr. Trust, George B., 2328
Ruffin Foundation, Peter B. & Adeline
   W., 2328
Rukin Philanthropic Foundation, David
   and Eleanore, 2328
Rumbaugh Foundation, J. H. and F. H.,
   2329
Rupp Foundation, Fran and Warren, 2329

Russ Togs, 2329
Russ Togs Foundation, 2329
Russell Charitable Foundation, Tom, 2330
Russell Charitable Trust, Josephine S.,
   2330
Russell Corp., 2330
Russell Educational Foundation,
   Benjamin and Roberta, 2330
Russell Foundation, 2330
Russell Memorial Foundation, Robert,
   2331
Russell Trust, Josephine G., 2331
Rust International Corp., 2332
Rust-Oleum Corp., 2332
Rutgers Community Health Foundation,
   2332
Rutledge Charity, Edward, 2332
Ryan Family Charitable Foundation, 2332
Ryan Foundation, David Claude, 2333
Ryan Foundation, Nina M., 2333
Ryan Foundation, Patrick G. and Shirley
   W., 2333
Ryder System, 2334
Ryder System Charitable Foundation,
   2334
Rykoff & Co., S.E., 2335
Ryland Group, 2335

S

S & H Foundation, 2519
S.G. Foundation, 2335
S.T.J. Group, Inc., 2335
Saab Cars USA, Inc., 2335
Sacharuna Foundation, 2335
Sachs Electric Corp., 2336
Sachs Foundation, 2336
Sachs Fund, 2336
Saemann Foundation, Franklin I., 2337
SAFECO Corp., 2337
Safeguard Scientifics Foundation, 2338
Safety-Kleen Corp., 2338
Safeway, Inc., 2338
Sagamore Foundation, 2338
Sage Foundation, 2339
Sage Foundation, Russell, 2339
Sailors' Snug Harbor of Boston, 2340
Saint Croix Foundation, 2341
Saint Gerard Foundation, 2342
Saint Johnsbury Trucking Co., 2343
Saint Paul Cos., 2343
Saks Fifth Ave., 2344
Salem Lutheran Foundation, 1277
Salem News Publishing Co., 2344
Salgo Charitable Trust, Nicholas M., 2344
Salomon, 2345
Salomon Foundation, 2345

Salomon Foundation, Richard & Edna,
   2345
Saltonstall Charitable Foundation,
   Richard, 2346
Saltz Foundation, Gary, 2346
Salvatori Foundation, Henry, 2346
Salwil Foundation, 2347
Sammons Enterprises, 2347
Sammons Foundation, 2347
Sams Foundation, Earl C., 2347
Samsung America Inc., 2347
Samuels Foundation, Fan Fox and Leslie
   R., 2348
San Diego Gas & Electric, 2348
San Diego Trust & Savings Bank, 2349
San Francisco Federal Savings & Loan
   Association, 2349
Sanders Trust, Charles, 2349
Sandia National Laboratories, 2349
Sandoz Corp., 2349
Sandoz Foundation Am, 2349
Sandusky International Foundation, 2350
Sandusky International Inc., 2350
Sandy Foundation, George H., 2350
Sandy Hill Foundation, 2351
Sang Foundation, Elsie O. and Philip D.,
   2351
Sanguinetti Foundation, Annunziata, 2352
Santa Fe International Corp., 2352
Santa Fe Pacific Corp., 2352
Santa Fe Pacific Foundation, 2352
Santa Maria Foundation, 2353
Sanwa Bank Ltd. New York, 2353
Sanyo Audio Manufacturing (U.S.A.)
   Corp., 2354
Sanyo Fisher Service Corp., 2354
Sanyo Fisher U.S.A. Corp., 2354
Sanyo Manufacturing Corp., 2354
Sapirstein-Stone-Weiss Foundation, 2354
Sara Lee Corp., 2355
Sara Lee Foundation, 2355
Sara Lee Hosiery, 2356
Sargent Electric Co., 2357
Sargent Foundation, Newell B., 2357
Sarkeys Foundation, 2357
Sarofim Foundation, 2358
Saroyan Foundation, William, 2358
Sasco Foundation, 2358
Sattler Beneficial Trust, Daniel A. and
   Edna J., 2359
Saturno Foundation, 2359
Saul Foundation, Joseph E. & Norma G.,
   2359
Saunders Charitable Foundation, Helen
   M., 2360
Saunders Foundation, 2360
Savannah Electric & Power Co., 2360
Savin Corp., 2361

Sawyer Charitable Foundation, 2361

Scaife Family Foundation, 2361

Scaife Foundation, Sarah, 2362

Scaler Foundation, 2363

SCANA Corp., 2363

Schadt Foundation, 2363

Schaffer Foundation, H., 2364

Schaffer Foundation, Michael & Helen, 2364

Schamach Foundation, Milton, 2364

Schapiro Fund, M. A., 2365

Schautz Foundation, Walter L., 2365

Schecter Private Foundation, Aaron and Martha, 2365

Scheirich Co. Foundation, H.J., 2366

Scheirich Co., H.J., 2366

Schenck Fund, L. P., 2366

Schepp Foundation, Leopold, 2366

Scherer Foundation, Karla, 2367

Schering Laboratories, 2367

Schering Trust for Arthritis Research, Margaret Harvey, 2368

Schering-Plough Corp., 2367

Schering-Plough Foundation, 2367

Scherman Foundation, 2368

Schermer Charitable Trust, Frances, 2369

Scheuer Family Foundation, S. H. and Helen R., 2369

Schey Foundation, 2370

Schieffelin & Somerset Co., 2370

Schieffelin Residuary Trust, Sarah I., 2370

Schiff Foundation, 2371

Schiff Foundation, Dorothy, 2371

Schiff Foundation, John J. and Mary R., 2372

Schiff, Hardin & Waite, 2372

Schiff, Hardin & Waite Foundation, 2372

Schillig Trust, Ottilie, 2373

Schilling Foundation, 2373

Schilling Motors, 2373

Schimmel Foundation, 2373

Schindler Elevator Corp., 2373

Schiro Fund, 2373

Schlegel Corp., 2374

Schlegel Foundation, Oscar C. and Augusta, 2374

Schlessman Foundation, 1112

Schlieder Educational Foundation, Edward G., 2374

Schlinger Foundation, 2374

Schlink Foundation, Albert G. and Olive H., 2375

Schloss & Co., Marcus, 2375

Schlumberger Foundation, 2375

Schlumberger Ltd., 2375

Schmidlapp Trust No. 1, Jacob G., 2376

Schmidlapp Trust No. 2, Jacob G., 2377

Schmidt & Sons, C., 2377

Schmidt Charitable Foundation, William E., 2377

Schmidt Foundation, Christian, 2377

Schmitt Foundation, Arthur J., 2378

Schneider Foundation Corp., Al J., 2378

Schneider Foundation, Robert E., 2378

Schneiderman Foundation, Roberta and Irwin, 2379

Schnuck Markets, 2379

Schoenbaum Family Foundation, 2379

Schoenleber Foundation, 2379

Scholastic Inc., 2380

Scholl Foundation, Dr., 2380

Scholler Foundation, 2381

Schoonmaker J-Sewkly Valley Hospital Trust, 2381

Schott Foundation, 2381

Schottenstein Foundation, Jerome & Saul, 2382

Schottenstein Stores Corp., 2382

Schowalter Foundation, 2382

Schrafft and Bertha E. Schrafft Charitable Trust, William E., 2383

Schramm Foundation, 2383

Schreiber Foods, Inc., 2383

Schroeder Foundation, Walter, 2384

Schulman Inc., A., 2384

Schulman Management Corp., 2384

Schultz Foundation, 23842385

Schumann Foundation, Florence and John, 2385

Schumann Fund for New Jersey, 2386

Schurz Communications Foundation, Inc., 2506

Schust Foundation, Clarence L. and Edith B., 2387

Schwab & Co., Charles, 2387

Schwab Foundation, Charles and Helen, 2388

Schwan's Sales Enterprises, 2388

Schwartz and Robert Schwartz Foundation, Bernard, 2388

Schwartz Foundation, Arnold A., 2388

Schwartz Foundation, Bernard Lee, 2389

Schwartz Foundation, David, 2389

Schwartz Fund for Education and Health Research, Arnold and Marie, 2389

Schwob Foundation, Simon, 2390

SCI Systems, Inc., 2390

Science Applications International Corp., 2390

Scientific Brake & Equipment Co., 2391

Scientific-Atlanta, 2390

SCM Chemicals Inc., 2391

Scott and Fetzer Co., 2391

Scott and Fetzer Foundation, 2391

Scott Foundation, Virginia Steele, 2392

Scott Foundation, Walter, 2392

Scott Foundation, William E., 2392

Scott Foundation, William R., John G., and Emma, 2393

Scott Fund, Olin, 2393

Scott Paper Co., 2394

Scott Paper Co. Foundation, 2394

Scott, Foresman & Co., 2391

Scott, Jr. Charitable Foundation, Walter, 2394

Scotty's, Inc., 2395

Scoular Co., 2395

Scoular Foundation, 2395

Scripps Co., E.W., 2395

Scripps Foundation, Ellen Browning, 2396

Scripps Howard Foundation, 2395

Scrivner of North Carolina Inc., 2397

Scrivner, Inc., 2397

Scroggins Foundation, Arthur E. and Cornelia C., 2397

SCT Foundation, 2398

SCT Yarns, 2398

Scurlock Foundation, 2398

Scurry Foundation, D. L., 2399

SDB Foundation, 2399

Sea-Land Service, 2399

Seaboard Corp., 2399

Seabury Foundation, 2399

Seafirst Corp., 2400

Seafirst Foundation, 2400

Seagate Technology, 2401

Seagram & Sons, Joseph E., 2401

Sealaska Corp., 2402

Sealaska Heritage Foundation, 2402

Sealed Air Corp., 2402

Sealed Power Foundation, 2527

Sealright Co., Inc., 2402

Sealright Foundation, Inc., 2402

Sealy, Inc., 2402

Searle & Co., G.D., 2402

Searle Charitable Trust, 2402

Sears Family Foundation, 2403

Sears, Roebuck and Co., 2404

Sears-Roebuck Foundation, 2404

Seascape Senior Housing, Inc., 2405

Seasongood Good Government Foundation, Murray and Agnes, 2405

Seattle Times Co., 2405

Seaver Charitable Trust, Richard C., 2405

Seaver Institute, 2406

Seaway Food Town, 2406

Seay Charitable Trust, Sarah M. and Charles E., 2407

Seay Memorial Trust, George and Effie, 2407

Sebastian Foundation, 2408

SECO, 2408

Second Foundation, 2408

Security Benefit Life Insurance Co., 2408

Security Benefit Life Insurance Co. Charitable Trust, 2408

Security Capital Corp., 2409

Security Life Insurance Co. of America, 2409

Security Life of Denver, 2409

Security State Bank, 2410

Security State Bank Charitable Trust, 2410

Sedco Inc., 2410

Sedgwick James Inc., 2410

See Foundation, Charles, 2410

Seebee Trust, Frances, 2411

Seeley Foundation, 2411

Seevak Family Foundation, 2411

Sefton Foundation, J. W., 2412

Sega of America, 2412

Sega Youth Education & Health Foundation, 2412

Segal Charitable Trust, Barnet, 2413

Segerstrom Foundation, 2413

Sehn Foundation, 2413

Seibel Foundation, Abe and Annie, 2414

Seid Foundation, Barre, 2414

Seidman Family Foundation, 2414

Seiler Corp., 2415

Selby and Marie Selby Foundation, William G., 2415

Self Foundation, 2416

Semmes Foundation, 2416

Semple Foundation, Louise Taft, 2417

Seneca Foods Corp., 2417

Seneca Foods Foundation, 2417

Senior Citizens Foundation, 2418

Senior Services of Stamford, 2418

Sentinel Communications Co., 2418

Sentry Insurance Co., 2419

Sentry Life Group Foundation, 2419

Sequa Corp., 2419

Sequa Foundation of Delaware, 2419

Sequoia Foundation, 2419

Servco Foundation, 2420

Servco Pacific, 2420

Service Corp. International, 2421

ServiceMaster Co. L.P., 2421

ServiceMaster Foundation, 2421

Servico, Inc., 2421

Servistar Corp., 2421

Servistar Foundation, 2421

Seton Co., 2421

Setzer Foundation, 2422

Seven Springs Foundation, 2422

Seventh Generation, 2422

Sewall Foundation, Elmina, 2422

Sewell Foundation, Warren P. and Ava F., 2423

Sexton Foundation, 2423

Seybert Institution, 2423

Seybert Institution for Poor Boys and Girls, Adam and Maria Sarah, 2423

Seymour and Troester Foundation, 2424

Seymour Foundation, W. L. and Louise E., 2424

SGS-Thomson Microelectronics Inc., 2424

Shafer Foundation, Richard H. and Ann, 2424

Shaffer Family Charitable Trust, 2425

Shaklee Corp., 2425

Shapell Foundation, 2426

Shapell Foundation, Nathan and Lilly, 2425

Shapell Industries, Inc., 2426

Shapero Foundation, Nate S. and Ruth B., 2426

Shapiro Charitable Trust, J. B. & Maurice C., 2426

Shapiro Charity Fund, Abraham, 2427

Shapiro Family Foundation, Soretta and Henry, 2427

Shapiro Foundation, Carl and Ruth, 2427

Shapiro Foundation, Charles and M. R., 2427

Shapiro Fund, Albert, 2428

Shapiro, Inc., 2426

Share Foundation, 2428

Share Trust, Charles Morton, 2429

Shared Medical Systems Corp., 2429

Sharon Steel Corp., 2429

SharonSteel Foundation, 2429

Sharp Electronics Corp., 2429

Sharp Foundation, 2430

Sharp Foundation, Charles S. and Ruth C., 2430

Sharp Foundation, Evelyn, 2430

Shatford Memorial Trust, J. D., 2431

Shattuck Charitable Trust, S. F., 2431

Shaw Charitable Trust, Mary Elizabeth Dee, 2431

Shaw Foundation, Arch W., 2431

Shaw Foundation, Gardiner Howland, 2432

Shaw Foundation, Walden W. and Jean Young, 2432

Shaw Fund for Mariner's Children, 2432

Shaw Industries, 2433

Shaw's Market Trust, 2434

Shaw's Supermarkets, 2434

Shawmut Bank of Franklin County, 2433

Shawmut Charitable Foundation, 2433

Shawmut National Corp., 2433

Shawmut Needham Bank, N.A., 2434

Shawmut Worcester County Bank Charitable Foundation, 2434

Shawmut Worcester County Bank, N.A., 2434

Shea Co. Foundation, J. F., 2435

Shea Co., John F., 2435

Shea Foundation, 2435

Shea Foundation, Edmund and Mary, 2435

Shea Foundation, John and Dorothy, 2436

Sheadle Trust, Jasper H., 2436

Sheafer Charitable Trust, Emma A., 2436

Sheaffer Inc., 2436

Shearson, Lehman & Hutton, 2437

Sheily Co., J.L., 2437

Sheinberg Foundation, Eric P., 2437

Sheldahl Inc., 2437

Shelden Fund, Elizabeth, Allan and Warren, 2438

Sheldon Foundation, Ralph C., 2438

Shell Oil Co., 2438

Shell Oil Co. Foundation, 2438

Sheller-Globe Foundation, 2734

Shelter Insurance Foundation, 2440

Shelter Mutual Insurance Co., 2440

Shelton Cos., 2440

Shelton Foundation, 2440

Shemanski Testamentary Trust, Tillie and Alfred, 2440

Shenandoah Foundation, 2441

Shenandoah Life Insurance Co., 2441

Shepherd Foundation, 2442

Sheppard Foundation, Lawrence B., 2442

Sheridan Foundation, Thomas B. and Elizabeth M., 2442

Sherman Educational Fund, 2443

Sherman Educational Fund, Mabel E., 2443

Sherman Family Charitable Trust, George and Beatrice, 2443

Sherman-Standard Register Foundation, 2533

Sherwin-Williams Co., 2443

Sherwin-Williams Foundation, 2443

Sherwood Medical Co., 2444

Shiffman Foundation, 2444

Shinnick Educational Fund, William M., 2445

Shirk Foundation, Russell and Betty, 2445

Shoemaker Co., R.M., 2445

Shoemaker Fund, Thomas H. and Mary Williams, 2445

Shoemaker Trust for Shoemaker Scholarship Fund, Ray S., 2446

Shoenberg Foundation, 2446

Shoney's Inc., 2446

Shook Foundation, Barbara Ingalls, 2447

Shoong Foundation, Milton, 2447

Shore Fund, 2447

Shorenstein Foundation, Walter H. and Phyllis J., 2448

Shott, Jr. Foundation, Hugh I., 2448

Shreveport Publishing Corp., 2448

Shubert Foundation, 2448

Shughart, Thomson & Kilroy Charitable Foundation Trust, 2449

Shughart, Thomson & Kilroy, P.C., 2449

Shuster Memorial Trust, Herman, 2450

Shuwa Investments Corp., 2450

Shwayder Foundation, Fay, 2450

SICO Foundation, 2451

Siebe North Inc., 2451

Siebert Lutheran Foundation, 2451

Siemens Medical Systems Inc., 2452

Sierra Health Foundation, 2452

Sierra Pacific Foundation, 2453

Sierra Pacific Industries, 2453

Sierra Pacific Resources, 2453

Sierra Pacific Resources Charitable Foundation, 2453

Sifco Foundation, 2454

Sifco Industries Inc., 2454

Sigma-Aldrich Corp., 2454

Signet Bank/Maryland, 2454

Signet Bank/Maryland Charitable Trust, 2454

Sigourney Award Trust, Mary S., 2455

Silicon Systems Inc., 2455

Silver Spring Foundation, 2455

Silverburgh Foundation, Grace, George & Judith, 2456

Silverman Fluxus Collection Foundation, Gilbert and Lila, 2456

Silverman Foundation, Marty and Dorothy, 2456

Silverweed Foundation, 2456

Silvestri Corp., 2457

Simkins Industries, Inc., 2457

Simmons Family Foundation, R. P., 2457

Simmons Foundation, Harold, 596

Simon & Schuster Inc., 2460

Simon Charitable Trust, Esther, 2457

Simon Foundation, Jennifer Jones, 2458

Simon Foundation, Robert Ellis, 2458

Simon Foundation, Sidney, Milton and Leoma, 2459

Simon Foundation, William E. and Carol G., 2459

Simone Foundation, 2460

Simplex Time Recorder Co., 2461

Simplot Co., J.R., 2461

Simplot Foundation, J.R., 2461

Simpson Foundation, 2461

Simpson Foundation, John M., 2462

Simpson Industries, 2462

Simpson Industries Fund, 2462

Simpson Investment Co., 2462

Simpson Paper Co., 2463

Simpson PSB Foundation, 2463

Singer Company, 2464

Sinsheimer Fund, Alexandrine and Alexander L., 2464

Sioux Steel Co., 2464

Sioux Steel Co. Foundation, 2464

Siragusa Foundation, 2464

SIT Investment Associates Foundation, 2465

SIT Investment Associates, Inc., 2465

Six Flags Theme Parks Inc., 2465

Sizzler International, 2465

Sizzler International Foundation, 2465

Sjostrom & Sons, 2466

Sjostrom & Sons Foundation, 2466

Skadden, Arps, Slate, Meagher and Flom Fellowship Foundation, 2466

Skaggs Alpha Beta Co., 2466

Skaggs Foundation, L. J. and Mary C., 2466

Skandia America Reinsurance Corp., 2467

SKF USA, Inc., 2467

Skidmore, Owings & Merrill, 2468

Skidmore, Owings & Merrill Foundation, 2468

Skillman Foundation, 2468

Skinner Corp., 2470

Skinner Foundation, 2470

Skirball Foundation, 2470

Sky Chefs, Inc., 2471

Skyline Corp., 2471

Slant/Fin Corp., 2471

Slant/Fin Foundation, 2471

Slaughter Foundation, Charles, 2472

Slaughter, Jr. Foundation, William E., 2472

Slemp Foundation, 2472

Slifka Foundation, Alan B., 2473

Slifka Foundation, Joseph and Sylvia, 2473

Sloan Foundation, Alfred P., 2473

Slusher Charitable Foundation, Roy W., 2475

Small Educational and Charitable Trust, Rita H., 2475

Smart Family Foundation, 2476

Smeal Foundation, Mary Jean & Frank P., 2476

Smith 1963 Charitable Trust, Don McQueen, 2487

Smith 1980 Charitable Trust, Kelvin, 2487

Smith and W. Aubrey Smith Charitable Foundation, Clara Blackford, 2476

Smith Barney, Harris Upham & Co., 2477

Smith Benevolent Association, Buckingham, 2477

Smith Charitable Foundation, Lou and Lutza, 2477

Smith Charitable Fund, Eleanor Armstrong, 2478

Smith Charitable Trust, 2478

Smith Charitable Trust, W. W., 2478

Smith Charities, John, 2479

Smith Corona Corp., 2479

Smith Corp., A.O., 2480

Smith Family Foundation, Charles E., 2481

Smith Family Foundation, Theda Clark, 2481

Smith Food & Drug, 2481

Smith Foundation, 2481

Smith Foundation, A.O., 2480

Smith Foundation, Bob and Vivian, 2482

Smith Foundation, Gordon V. and Helen C., 2482

Smith Foundation, Julia and Albert, 2482

Smith Foundation, Kelvin and Eleanor, 2483

Smith Foundation, Kenneth L. and Eva S., 2483

Smith Foundation, Lon V., 2484

Smith Foundation, Richard and Susan, 2484

Smith Fund, George D., 2484

Smith Fund, Horace, 2485

Smith Golden Rule Trust Fund, Fred G., 2485

Smith Horticultural Trust, Stanley, 2485

Smith International, 2485

Smith Memorial Fund, Ethel Sergeant Clark, 2486

Smith Oil Corp., 2487

Smith Trust, May and Stanley, 2487

Smith, Jr. Charitable Trust, Jack J., 2486

Smith, Jr. Foundation, M. W., 2486

Smithers Foundation, Christopher D., 2488

SmithKline Beecham, 2488

SmithKline Beecham Foundation, 2488

Smitty's Super Valu, Inc., 2489

Smock Foundation, Frank and Laura, 2489

Smoot Charitable Foundation, 2489

Smucker Co., J.M., 2490

Smucker Foundation, Willard E., 2490

Smysor Memorial Fund, Harry L. and John L., 2491

Smyth Trust, Marion C., 2491

Snap-on Tools Corp., 2491

Snayberger Memorial Foundation, Harry E. and Florence W., 2491

SNC Foundation, 2491

SNC Manufacturing Co., 2491

Snee-Reinhardt Charitable Foundation, 2492

SNET, 2492

Snider Foundation, 2493

Snite Foundation, Fred B., 2493

Snow Foundation, John Ben, 2493

Snow Memorial Trust, John Ben, 2494

Snyder Charitable Fund, W. P., 2494

Snyder Foundation, Frost and Margaret, 2495

Snyder Foundation, Harold B. and Dorothy A., 2495

Snyder Fund, Valentine Perry, 2495

Snyder General Corp., 2496

Society Corp., 2496

Society for Savings, 2496

Society for the Increase of the Ministry, 2496

Sofia American Schools, 2497

Soft Sheen Products Co., 2497

Software Toolworks, 2497

Sogem Holding Ltd., 2497

Solheim Foundation, 2497

Soling Family Foundation, 2498

Solo Cup Co., 2498

Solo Cup Foundation, 2498

Solomon Foundation, Sarah M., 2499

Solow Foundation, 2499

Solow Foundation, Sheldon H., 2499

Somers Corp. (Mersman/Waldron), 2499

Somers Foundation, Byron H., 2500

Sonat, 2500

Sonat Exploration, 2501

Sonat Foundation, 2500

Sonat Offshore Drilling, 2501

Sonesta Charitable Foundation, 2501

Sonesta International Hotels Corp., 2501

Sonoco Products Co., 2501

Sonoco Products Foundation, 2501

Sony Corp. of America, 2502

Sony Corp. of America Foundation, 2502

Sony USA Foundation, 2502

Sooner Pipe & Supply Corp., 2503

Sooner Pipe & Supply Corp. Foundation, 2503

Sordoni Enterprises, 2503

Sordoni Foundation, 2503

Soref Foundation, Samuel M. Soref and Helene K., 2504

Soros Foundation-Hungary, 2504

Sosland Foundation, 2505

Sotheby's, 2505

Souers Charitable Trust, Sidney W. and Sylvia N., 2505

Soundesign Corp., 2506

South Bend Tribune, 2506

South Branch Foundation, 2506

South Carolina Electric & Gas Co., 2506

South Coast Foundation, 2507

South Jersey Industries, 2507

South Plains Foundation, 2507

South Texas Charitable Foundation, 2508

South Waite Foundation, 2508

South-Western Publishing Co., 2509

Southdown, Inc., 2509

Southern Bell, 2509

Southern California Edison Co., 2509

Southern California Gas Co., 2510

Southern Co. Services, 2510

Southern Connecticut Gas Co., 2511

Southern Furniture Co., 2511

Southern Indiana Gas & Electric Co., 2511

Southern Pacific Transportation Co., 2511

Southland Corp., 2511

Southmark Corp., 2512

Southmark Foundation on Gerontology, 2512

Southtrust Corp., 2512

Southways Foundation, 2512

Southwest Airlines Co., 2513

Southwest Gas Corp., 2513

Southwest Gas Corp. Foundation, 2513

Southwestern Bell Corp., 2513

Southwestern Bell Foundation, 2513

Southwestern Electric Power Co., 2514

Southwestern Life Insurance Co., 2514

Southwestern Public Service Co., 2515

Southwire Co., 2515

Sovereign Bank Foundation, 2089

Spahn & Rose Lumber Co., 2515

Spahn & Rose Lumber Co. Charitable Foundation, 2515

Spalding Health Care Trust, 2515

Spang & Co., 2515

Spang & Co. Charitable Trust, 2515

Sparton Corp., 2516

Spartus Corp., 2516

Speas Foundation, Victor E., 2516

Speas Memorial Trust, John W. and Effie E., 2517

Special People In Need, 2517

Specialty Restaurants Corp., 2518

Spectra-Physics Analytical, 2518

Speer Foundation, Roy M., 2518

Spencer Foundation, 2518

Sperry Fund, 2519

Speyer Foundation, Alexander C. and Tillie S., 2520

Spiegel, 2520

Spiegel Family Foundation, Jerry and Emily, 2520

Spingold Foundation, Nate B. and Frances, 2521

Spiritus Gladius Foundation, 2521

Spiro Foundation, Donald W., 2521

Sprague Educational and Charitable Foundation, Seth, 2522

Sprague Memorial Institute, Otho S. A., 2523

Sprague, Jr. Foundation, Caryll M. and Norman F., 2523

Spring Arbor Distributors, 2524

Springs Foundation, 2524

Springs Industries, 2524

Sprint, 2525

Sprint Foundation, 2525

Sprint United Telephone, 2526

SPS Foundation, 2526

SPS Technologies, 2526

Spunk Fund, 2526

SPX Corp., 2527

SPX Foundation, 2527

Square D Co., 2527

Square D Foundation, 2527

St. Faith's House Foundation, 2341

St. Giles Foundation, 2342

St. Joe Paper Co., 2342

St. Mary's Catholic Foundation, 2343

St. Paul Federal Bank for Savings, 2344

Stabler Cos., Inc., 2528

Stabler Foundation, Donald B. and Dorothy L., 2528

Stackner Family Foundation, 2529

Stackpole-Hall Foundation, 2529

Stacy Foundation, Festus, 2530

Staley Company Foundation, 2531

Staley Foundation, Thomas F., 2530

Staley Manufacturing Co., A.E., 2531

Staley, Jr. Foundation, A. E., 2530

Stamps Foundation, James L., 2531

Standard Brands Paint Co., 2532

Standard Chartered Bank New York, 2532

Standard Federal Bank, 2532

Standard Motor Products, Inc., 2532

Standard Pacific Corp., 2532

Standard Products Co., 2532

Standard Products Co. Foundation, 2532

Standard Register Co., 2533

Standard Steel Speciality Co., 2533

Standard Steel Speciality Co. Foundation, 2533

Standard Textile Co., Inc., 2534

Standex International Corp., 2534

Standex International Foundation, 2534

Stanford Theater Foundation, 2534

Stanhome Inc., 2534

Stanley Charitable Foundation, A. W., 2534

Stanley Consultants, 2535

Stanley Consultants Charitable Foundation, 2535

Stanley Works, 2535

Stanley Works Foundation, 2535

Stans Foundation, 2536

Stanton Fund, Ruth and Frank, 2536

Star Bank, N.A., 2536

Star Bank, N.A., Cincinnati Foundation, 2536

Star Enterprise, 2537

Star Markets Co., 2537

Stare Fund, 2537

Stark Foundation, Nelda C. and H. J. Lutcher, 2538

Stride Rite Corp., 2585

Stroehmann Bakeries, 2586

Stroh Brewery Co., 2586

Strong Foundation, Hattie M., 2586

Strosacker Foundation, Charles J., 2587

Stroud Foundation, 2588

Strouse, Greenberg & Co., 2588

Strouse, Greenberg & Co. Charitable Fund, 2588

Stry Foundation, Paul E., 2588

Stuart Center Charitable Trust, Hugh, 2588

Stuart Foundation, 2589

Stuart Foundation, Edward C., 2589

Stuart Foundation, Elbridge and Evelyn, 2589

Stuart Foundations, 2590

Stubblefield, Estate of Joseph L., 2590

Student Loan Marketing Association, 2591

Stulsaft Foundation, Morris, 2591

Stupp Brothers Bridge & Iron Co., 2592

Stupp Brothers Bridge & Iron Co. Foundation, 2592

Stupp Foundation, Norman J., 2592

Sturgis Charitable and Educational Trust, Roy and Christine, 2593

Subaru of America Foundation, 2594

Subaru of America Inc., 2594

Subaru-Isuzu Automotive Inc., 2593

Suburban Propane, 2594

Sudbury Inc., 2595

Sudix Foundation, 2595

Sullivan Foundation, Algernon Sydney, 2595

Sullivan Foundation, Ray H. and Pauline, 2596

Sullivan Musical Foundation, William Matheus, 2596

Sulzberger Foundation, 2596

Sulzer Brothers Inc., 2597

Sulzer Family Foundation, 2597

Sumitomo Bank of California, 2597

Sumitomo Corp. of America, 2598

Sumitomo Trust & Banking Co., Ltd., 2598

Summa Development Corp., 2598

Summer Foundation, 2506

Summerfield Foundation, Solon E., 2598

Summerlee Foundation, 2599

Summit Bancorporation, 2599

Sumners Foundation, Hatton W., 2599

Sun Bank Foundation, 2600

Sun Banks Inc., 2600

Sun Chemical Corp., 2600

Sun Co., 2600

Sun Electric Corp., 2601

Sun Life Assurance Co. of Canada (U.S.), 2601

Sun Microsystems, 2601

Sun Microsystems Foundation, 2601

Sun-Diamond Growers of California, 2601

Sunbeam-Oster, 2602

Sunburst Foundation, 2602

Sunderland Foundation, Lester T., 2602

Sundet Foundation, 2603

Sundstrand Corp., 2603

Sundstrand Corp. Foundation, 2603

Sunkist Growers, 2604

Sunmark Capital Corp., 2604

Sunmark Foundation, 2604

Sunnen Foundation, 2604

Sunshine Biscuits, 2605

Sunshine Biscuits Foundation Trust, 2605

Sunwest Bank of Albuquerque, N.A., 2605

Super Food Services, 2605

Super Valu Stores, 2605

Superior Tube Co., 2606

Superior's Brand Meats, 2606

Superior-Pacific Fund, 2606

Support Systems International, 2606

Surdna Foundation, 2606

Surgical Science Foundation for Research and Development, 2607

Surrena Memorial Fund, Harry and Thelma, 2607

Susquehanna Corp., 2608

Susquehanna Investment Group, 2608

Susquehanna-Pfaltzgraff Co., 2608

Susquehanna-Pfaltzgraff Foundation, 2608

Sussman Fund, Edna Bailey, 2608

Sussman Trust, Otto, 2609

Sutcliffe Foundation, Walter and Louise, 2609

Sutherland Foundation, 2609

Sutton Family Foundation, Abraham, David and Solomon, 166

Sutton Foundation, 2609

Suzuki Automotive Foundation for Life, 80

Swalm Foundation, 2609

Swank, Inc., 2610

Swanson Family Foundation, Dr. W.C., 2610

Swanson Foundation, 2611

Swasey Fund for Relief of Public School Teachers of Newburyport, 2611

Sweatt Foundation, Harold W., 2611

Sweet Life Foods, 2611

Sweet Life Foundation, 2611

Swensrud Charitable Trust, Sidney A., 2612

Swift Co. Inc. Charitable Trust, John S., 2612

Swift Co. Inc., John S., 2612

Swift Memorial Health Care Foundation, 2612

Swift-Eckrich Inc., 2612

Swig Charity Foundation, Mae and Benjamin, 2613

Swig Foundation, 2613

Swim Foundation, Arthur L., 2613

Swinerton & Walberg Co., 2614

Swisher Foundation, Carl S., 2614

Swiss American Securities, Inc., 2614

Swiss Bank Corp., 2615

Switzer Foundation, 2615

Sylvester Foundation, Harcourt M. and Virginia W., 2615

Symmes Foundation, F. W., 2616

Synovus Charitable Trust, 2616

Synovus Financial Corp., 2616

Syntex Corp., 2617

Sysco Corp., 2617

T

T & T United Truck Lines, 2617

T.T.X. Co., 2617

Taconic Foundation, 2618

Tai and Co. Foundation, J. T., 2618

Tai and Co., J. T., 2618

Tait Foundation, Frank M., 2619

Talley Foundation, 2619

Talley Industries, Inc., 2619

Tamaki Foundation, 2619

Tamarkin Co., 2620

Tamarkin Foundation, 2620

Tambrands Inc., 2620

Tamko Asphalt Products, 2620

Tampa Electric, 2621

Tandem Computers, 2621

Tandon Corp., 2622

Tandy Corp., 2622

Tandy Foundation, Anne Burnett and Charles, 2622

Tandy Foundation, David L., 2623

Tang Foundation, 2623

Tanner Cos., 2623

Tanner Foundation, 2623

Taper Foundation, Mark, 2624

Taper Foundation, S. Mark, 2624

Tara and Richard Colburn Fund, 550

Target Stores, 2624

Tarmac America Inc., 2625

Tartt Scholarship Fund, Hope Pierce, 2625

Tasty Baking Co., 2626

Tasty Baking Foundation, 2626

Tate & Lyle Inc., 2626

Taub Foundation, 2626

Taub Foundation, Henry and Marilyn, 2627

Taub Foundation, Joseph and Arlene, 2627

Taube Family Foundation, 2627

Tauber Foundation, 2628

Tippens Foundation, 2671

Tippit Charitable Trust, C. Carlisle and Margaret M., 2671

Tisch Foundation, 2671

Tiscornia Foundation, 2672

Titan Industrial Co., 2672

Titan Industrial Foundation, 2672

Titmus Foundation, 2673

Titus Foundation, C. W., 2673

TJX Cos., 2673

TJX Foundation, 2673

TMZ Corp., 2674

Tobin Foundation, 2674

Todd Co. Foundation, A.M., 2674

Todd Co., A.M., 2674

Tokai Bank, Ltd., 2675

Tokheim Corp., 2675

Tokheim Foundation, 2675

Toledo Edison Co., 2675

Tom's of Maine, 2677

Tombstone Pizza Corp., 2676

Tombstone Pizza Foundation, 2676

Tomen America, Inc., 2676

Tomkins Corporation Foundation, 2676

Tomkins Industries, Inc., 2676

Tomlinson Family Foundation, 2676

Tomlinson Foundation, Kate and Elwyn, 2677

Toms Foundation, 2677

Tonkin Foundation, Tom and Helen, 2677

Tonya Memorial Foundation, 2678

Tootsie Roll Industries, Inc., 2678

Topps Company, 2678

Tops Markets, Inc., 2678

Torchmark Corp., 2678

Toro Co., 2679

Torrington Co., 2679

Tortuga Foundation, 2679

Tosco Corp. Refining Division, 2680

Toshiba America Foundation, 2680

Toshiba America, Inc., 2680

Totsy Foundation, 2681

Totsy Manufacturing Co., 2681

Towers Perrin, 2682

Towle Manufacturing Co., 2682

Town & Country Corp., 2682

Town Creek Foundation, 2682

Towsley Foundation, Harry A. and Margaret D., 2683

Toyota Motor Sales, U.S.A., 2683

Toyota U.S.A. Foundation, 2683

Toys "R" Us, Inc., 2684

Tozer Foundation, 2684

Tracor, Inc., 2685

Tractor & Equipment Co., 2685

Tractor & Equipment Company Foundation, 2685

Tracy Fund, Emmet and Frances, 51

Trans World Airlines, 2686

Trans-Apex, 2686

Transamerica Corp., 2686

Transamerica Fdn., 2686

Transamerica Occidental Life Insurance Co., 2687

Transco Energy Company, 2687

TransOhio Savings Bank, 2688

Transtar Inc., 2688

Tranzonic Cos., 2688

Tranzonic Foundation, 2688

Travelers Cos., 2689

Travelers Cos. Foundation, 2689

Travelers Express Co., 2690

Travelli Fund, Charles Irwin, 2690

Treadwell Foundation, Nora Eccles, 2690

Treakle Foundation, J. Edwin, 2691

Treasure Chest Advertising Co., 2691

Tredegar Industries, 2692

Trees Charitable Trust, Edith L., 2692

Tremco Foundation, 2692

Tremco Inc., 2692

Treuhaft Foundation, 2692

Trexler Foundation, 2693

Trexler Trust, Harry C., 2693

Triangle Foundation, 2694

Triangle Industries, 2694

Trico Foundation, 2694

Triford Foundation, 2694

Trimble Family Foundation, Robert Mize and Isa White, 2694

Trinity Foundation, 2695

Trinity Industries, Inc., 2695

TRINOVA Corp., 2695

TRINOVA Foundation, 2695

Trion, 2696

Trion Charitable Foundation, 2696

Tripifoods, 2696

Tripifoods Foundation, 2696

Triskelion Ltd., 2697

Tropicana Products, Inc., 2697

True Foundation, 2698

True North Foundation, 2697

True Oil Co., 2698

True Trust, Henry A., 2698

Truland Foundation, 2698

Truland Systems Corp., 2699

Trull Foundation, 2699

Truman Foundation, Mildred Faulkner, 2699

Trump Group, 2700

Trusler Foundation, 2700

Trust Co. Bank, 2700

Trust Co. of Georgia Foundation, 2700

Trust for Mutual Understanding, 2701

Trust Funds, 2702

Trustcorp Foundation, 2702

Trustcorp, Inc., 2702

Trustmark National Bank, 2702

TRW Corp., 2702

TRW Foundation, 2702

Tsai Foundation, Gerald, 2703

TSC Stores, Inc., 2703

TU Electric Co., 2704

Tuch Foundation, Michael, 2704

Tucker Anthony, Inc., 2704

Tucker Charitable Trust, Rose E., 2704

Tucker Foundation, Marcia Brady, 2705

Tucson Electric Power Co., 2705

Tucson Osteopathic Medical Foundation, 2706

Tull Charitable Foundation, 2706

Tultex Corp., 2707

Tuohy Foundation, Alice Tweed, 2707

Tupancy-Harris Foundation of 1986, 2707

Turner Broadcasting System, 2708

Turner Charitable Foundation, 2708

Turner Charitable Foundation, Harry and Violet, 2708

Turner Charitable Trust, Courtney S., 2708

Turner Construction Co., 2709

Turner Construction Co. Foundation, 2709

Turner Corp., 2709

Turner Foundation, 2709

Turner Fund, Ruth, 2709

Turrell Fund, 2710

Twentieth Century Insurance Co., 2710

Tyco Laboratories, Inc., 2711

Tyler Corp., 2712

Tyler Foundation, 2712

Tyndale House Foundation, 2712

Tyson Foods, Inc., 2712

Tyson Foundation, 2712

Tyson Fund, 2713

U

U.S. Bank of Washington, 2729

U.S. Healthcare, Inc., 2729

U.S. Leasing International, 2731

U.S. News & World Report, 2731

U.S. Oil/Schmidt Family Foundation, Inc., 2731

U.S. Silica Co., 2732

Uarco Inc., 2713

Ucross Foundation, 2713

UDC-Universal Development LP, 2713

UGI Corp., 2714

UIS, Inc., 2714

UJB Financial Corp., 2714

Ukrop Foundation, 2714

Ukrop's Super Markets, Inc., 2714

Ulrich Chemical, Inc., 2715

UNC, Inc., 2715

Unger Foundation, Aber D., 2715

Unifi, Inc., 2715
Uniform Tubes, Inc., 2715
Unigard Security Insurance Co., 2715
UniGroup Inc., 2716
Unilever United States, 2716
Unilever United States Foundation, 2716
Union Bank, 2716
Union Bank Foundation, 2716
Union Bank of Switzerland Los Angeles Branch, 2717
Union Bank of Switzerland New York Branch, 2717
Union Camp Charitable Trust, 2718
Union Camp Corp., 2718
Union Carbide Corp., 2719
Union Carbide Foundation, 2719
Union Central Charitable Contribution Trust, 2719
Union Central Life Insurance Co., 2719
Union City Body Co., 2719
Union City Body Co. Foundation, 2719
Union Electric Co., 2720
Union Electric Co. Charitable Trust, 2720
Union Equity Division of Farmland Industries, 2720
Union Foundation, 2721
Union Manufacturing Co., 2721
Union Mutual Fire Insurance Co., 2721
Union Pacific Corp., 2722
Union Pacific Foundation, 2722
Union Planters Corp., 2722
Union Texas Petroleum, 2723
Union Trust, 2723
Uniroyal Chemical Co. Inc., 2723
Unisys Corp., 2723
United Airlines, 2724
United Airlines Foundation, 2724
United Artists Theatre Circuits, 2724
United Asset Management Corp., 2724
United Brands Foundation, 506
United Co., 2725
United Coal Co. Charitable Foundation, 2725
United Conveyor Corp., 2725
United Conveyor Foundation, 2725
United Dominion Industries, 2725
United Fire & Casualty Co., 2726
United Gas Pipe Line Co., 2726
United Grocers, Inc., 2726
United Industrial Corp., 2726
United Inns, Inc., 2726
United Iron & Metal Co., 2726
United Merchants & Manufacturers, 2726
United Merchants Foundation, 2726
United Missouri Bancshares, Inc., 2727
United Parcel Service of America, 2727
United Refining Co, 2728
United Savings Association of Texas, 2728

United Service Foundation, 2728
United Services Automobile Association, 2729
United States Borax & Chemical Corp., 2729
United States Sugar Corp., 2732
United States Sugar Corporate Charitable Trust, 2732
United States Surgical Corp., 2733
United States Trust Co. of New York, 2733
United States Trust Co. of New York Foundation, 2733
United States-Japan Foundation, 2729
United Stationers Foundation, 2734
United Stationers Inc., 2734
United Technologies Corp., 2734
United Technologies, Automotive, 2734
United Telecommunications Fdn, 2525
United Telephone Co. of Florida, 2735
United Telephone System (Eastern Group), 2735
United Togs Foundation, 2735
United Togs Inc., 2735
United Van Lines, Inc., 2736
Unitrode Corp., 2736
Univar Corp., 2736
Univar Foundation, 2736
Universal Foods Corp., 2736
Universal Foods Foundation, 2736
Universal Health Services, Inc., 2737
Universal Leaf Foundation, 2737
Universal Leaf Tobacco Co., 2737
UNO-VEN Co., 2738
Unocal Corp., 2738
Unocal Foundation, 2738
Unocal-Union Oil of California, 2739
UNUM Charitable Foundation, 2739
UNUM Corp., 2739
Upjohn California Fund, 2740
Upjohn Co., 2740
Upjohn Co. Foundation, 2740
Upjohn Foundation, Harold and Grace, 2741
UPS Foundation, 2727
Upton Charitable Foundation, Lucy and Eleanor S., 2742
Upton Foundation, Frederick S., 2742
Urann Foundation, 2742
Uris Brothers Foundation, 2743
US Bancorp, 2743
US Shoe Corp., 2744
US WEST, 2744
US WEST Foundation, 2744
USAA Trust, 2729
USF&G Co., 2745
USF&G Foundation, 2745
USG Corp., 2745
USG Foundation, 2745

Ushkow Foundation, 2746
Uslico Corp., 2746
Uslico Foundation, 2746
USLIFE Corp., 2747
UST, 2747
USX Corp., 2748
USX Foundation, 2748
Utah Power & Light Co., 2749
Utica National Group Foundation, 2749
Utica National Insurance Group, 2749
Utilicorp United, 2749
Utilicorp United Charitable Foundation, 2749
Uvas Foundation, 2749

V

V and V Foundation, 2750
Valdese Manufacturing Co. Foundation, 2750
Valdese Manufacturing Co., Inc., 2750
Vale Foundation, Ruby R., 2751
Vale-Asche Foundation, 2750
Valencia Charitable Trust, 2751
Valentine Foundation, Lawson, 2751
Valero Energy Corp., 2751
Valley Bancorp, 2752
Valley Bank Charitable Contributions Distributions Trust, 2752
Valley Bank Charitable Foundation, 2754
Valley Foundation, 2752
Valley Foundation, Wayne and Gladys, 2753
Valley Line Co., 2753
Valley Line Co. Charitable Trust, 2753
Valley National Bancorp, 2754
Valley National Bank of Arizona, 2754
Valmont Foundation, 2755
Valmont Industries, 2755
Valspar Corp., 2755
Valspar Foundation, 2755
Value City Furniture, 2756
Valvoline Inc., 2756
van Ameringen Foundation, 2756
Van Andel Foundation, Jay and Betty, 2757
Van Beuren Charitable Foundation, 2757
Van Buren Foundation, 2757
Van Camp Foundation, 2758
Van Evera Foundation, Dewitt Caroline, 2758
Van Every Foundation, Philip L., 2758
Van Houten Charitable Trust, 2759
Van Huffel Foundation, I. J., 2759
van Loben Sels - Eleanor Slate van Lobel Sels Charitable Foundation, Ernst D., 2760
Van Nuys Charities, J. B. and Emily, 2760

Westport Fund, 2851
WestStar Bank N.A., 2852
Westvaco Corp., 2852
Westvaco Foundation Trust, 2852
Westwood Endowment, 2853
Wetterau, 2853
Wexner Foundation, 2854
Weyerhaeuser Co., 2854
Weyerhaeuser Co. Foundation, 2854
Weyerhaeuser Family Foundation, 2856
Weyerhaeuser Foundation, 2856
Weyerhaeuser Foundation, Frederick and Margaret L., 2857
Weyerhaeuser Memorial Foundation, Charles A., 2857
Whalley Charitable Trust, 2857
Wharton Foundation, 2858
Wharton Trust, William P., 2858
Wheat First Securites, 2858
Wheat Foundation, 2858
Wheaton Industries, 2859
Wheelabrator MPB Corporate Fund, 1897
Wheeler Foundation, 2859
Wheeler Foundation, Wilmot, 2860
Wheeler Trust, Clara, 2860
Wheeling-Pittsburgh Corp., 2860
Wheelwright Scientific School, 2860
Wheless Foundation, 2860
Whirlpool Corp., 2861
Whirlpool Foundation, 2861
Whitaker Charitable Foundation, Lyndon C., 2861
Whitaker Foundation, 2862
Whitaker Fund, Helen F., 2863
White Castle System, 2863
White Coffee Pot Family Inns, 2863
White Coffee Pot Restaurants Foundation, 2863
White Companies Charitable Trust, 2864
White Consolidated Industries, 2864
White Consolidated Industries Foundation, 2864
White Construction Co., 2864
White Foundation, Erle and Emma, 2865
White Foundation, W. P. and H. B., 2865
White Trust, G. R., 2865
Whitehall Foundation, 2865
Whitehead Charitable Foundation, 2867
Whitehead Foundation, 2867
Whitehead Foundation, Joseph B., 2867
Whitehead Foundation, Lettie Pate, 2868
Whiteley Foundation, John and Elizabeth, 2869
Whiteman Foundation, Edna Rider, 2869
Whitener Foundation, 2869
Whiteside Scholarship Fund, Robert B. and Sophia, 2870
Whiting Foundation, 2870

Whiting Foundation, Macauley and Helen Dow, 2870
Whiting Foundation, Mrs. Giles, 2871
Whiting Memorial Foundation, Henry and Harriet, 2871
Whitman Corp., 2871
Whitman Corp. Foundation, 2871
Whitney Benefits, 2872
Whitney Foundation, Helen Hay, 2872
Whitney Fund, David M., 2873
Whitney National Bank, 2874
Whittaker Corp., 2874
Whittell Trust for Disabled Veterans of Foreign Wars, Elia, 2874
Whittenberger Foundation, Claude R. and Ethel B., 2874
Whittier Foundation, L. K., 2875
Wickes Cos. Wickes Foundation, 556
Wickes Foundation, Harvey Randall, 2875
Wickson-Link Memorial Foundation, 2876
WICOR Foundation, 2876
WICOR, Inc., 2876
Widgeon Foundation, 2877
Widow's Society, 2877
Wieboldt Foundation, 2877
Wiegand Foundation, E. L., 2878
Wien Foundation, Lawrence A., 2879
Wiener Foundation, Malcolm Hewitt, 2880
Wiggins Memorial Trust, J. J., 2880
Wigwam Mills, 2881
Wigwam Mills Fund, 2881
Wilber National Bank, 2881
Wilbur Foundation, Brayton, 2881
Wilbur Foundation, Marguerite Eyer, 2881
Wilbur-Ellis Co., 2881
Wilcox General Trust, George N., 2882
Wilcox Trust, S. W., 2882
Wilder Foundation, 2882
Wildermuth Foundation, E. F., 2883
Wiley & Sons, Inc., John, 2883
Wilf Family Foundation, 2883
Wilkof Foundation, Edward and Ruth, 2884
Willamette Industries, Inc., 2884
Willard Foundation, Helen Parker, 2884
Willard Helping Fund, Cecilia Young, 2885
William Bingham II Trust for Charity, 284
William R. Hayden Foundation, 1208
Williams Charitable Trust, John C., 2885
Williams Charitable Trust, Mary Jo, 2885
Williams Cos., 2885
Williams Cos. Foundation, 2885
Williams Family Foundation, 2886
Williams Family Foundation of Georgia, 2887
Williams Foundation, Arthur Ashley, 2887

Williams Foundation, C. K., 2887
Williams Foundation, Edna Sproull, 2888
Williams Foundation, Kemper and Leila, 2888
Williams, Jr. Family Foundation, A. L., 2888
Williamson Co., 2889
Williamson Co. Foundation, 2889
Willits Foundation, 2889
Willmott Foundation, Fred & Floy, 2889
Willmott Foundation, Peter S., 2889
Wills Foundation, 2890
Wilmington Trust Co., 2890
Wilmington Trust Co. Foundation, 2890
Wilsey Bennet Co., 2890
Wilsey Foundation, 2890
Wilson Foundation, Elaine P. and Richard U., 2891
Wilson Foundation, Frances Wood, 2891
Wilson Foundation, H. W., 2892
Wilson Foundation, Hugh and Mary, 2892
Wilson Foundation, John and Nevils, 2893
Wilson Foundation, Marie C. and Joseph C., 2893
Wilson Fund, Matilda R., 2893
Wilson Public Trust, Ralph, 2894
Wilson Sanitarium for Children of Baltimore City, Thomas, 2894
Wilson Trust, Lula C., 2894
Wimpey Charitable Trust, George, 2895
Wimpey Inc., George, 2895
Winchell's Donut Houses Operating Company, 2895
Winchester Foundation, 2895
Windway Foundation, Inc., 2775
Winkler Foundation, Mark and Catherine, 2895
Winn Educational Trust, Fanny Edith, 2896
Winn-Dixie Stores, 2896
Winn-Dixie Stores Foundation, 2896
Winnebago Industries Foundation, 2896
Winnebago Industries, Inc., 2896
Winona Corporation, 2897
Winship Memorial Scholarship Foundation, 2897
Winslow Foundation, 2897
Winston Foundation, Norman and Rosita, 2898
Winston Research Foundation, Harry, 2898
Winter Construction Co., 2898
Winthrop Trust, Clara B., 2899
Wiremold Co., 2899
Wiremold Foundation, 2899
Wisconsin Bell, Inc., 2899
Wisconsin Centrifugal, 2900
Wisconsin Centrifugal Charitable Foundation, 2900

Zimmerman Foundation, Mary and
George Herbert, 2944
Zimmermann Fund, Marie and John, 2944
Zink Foundation, John Steele, 2944
Zions Bancorp., 2945

Zippo Manufacturing Co., 2945
Zlinkoff Fund for Medical Research and
Education, Sergei S., 2945
Zock Endowment Trust, 2945
Zollner Foundation, 2946

Zonas Trust, Steven K., 2946
Zuckerberg Foundation, Roy J., 2946
Zurn Industries, 2946